Weights and Measures

Imperial, with Metric Equivalents

Linear Measure
1 inch (in)	= 25.4 millimetres
1 foot (ft) = 12 inches	= 0.3048 metre
1 yard (yd) = 3 feet	= 0.9144 metre
1 (statute) mile = 1,760 yards	= 1.609 kilometres

Square Measure
1 square inch (in^2 or sq in)	= 6.45 sq centimetres
1 square foot (ft^2) = 144 sq in	= 9.29 sq decimetres
1 square yard (yd^2) = 9 sq ft	= 0.836 sq metre
1 acre = 4,840 sq yd	= 0.405 hectare
1 square mile (mile^2) = 640 acres	= 259 hectares

Cubic Measure
1 cubic inch (in^3 or cu in)	= 16.4 cu centimetres
1 cubic foot (ft^3) = 1,728 cu in	= 0.0283 cu metre
1 cubic yard (yd^3) = 27 cu ft	= 0.765 cu metre

Capacity Measure
British
1 pint (pt) = 20 fluid oz	
= 34.68 cu in	= 0.568 litre
1 quart = 2 pints	= 1.136 litres
1 gallon (gal) = 4 quarts	= 4.546 litres
1 peck = 2 gallons	= 9.092 litres
1 bushel = 4 pecks	= 36.4 litres
1 quarter = 8 bushels	= 2.91 hectolitres

American dry
1 pint = 33.60 cu in	= 0.550 litre
1 quart = 2 pints	= 1.101 litres
1 peck = 8 quarts	= 8.81 litres
1 bushel = 4 pecks	= 35.3 litres

American liquid
1 pint = 16 fluid oz	
= 28.88 cu in	= 0.473 litre
1 quart = 2 pints	= 0.946 litre
1 gallon = 4 quarts	= 3.785 litres

Avoirdupois Weight
1 grain	= 0.065 gram
1 dram	= 1.772 grams
1 ounce (oz) = 16 drams	= 28.35 grams
1 pound (lb) = 16 ounces	
= 7,000 grains	= 0.4536 kilogram
1 stone (st) = 14 pounds	= 6.35 kilograms
1 quarter = 2 stones	= 12.70 kilograms
1 hundredweight (cwt) = 4 quarters	= 50.80 kilograms
1 (long) ton = 20 hundredweight	= 1.016 tonnes
1 short ton = 2,000 pounds	= 0.907 tonne

Metric, with Imperial (British) Equivalents

Linear Measure
1 millimetre (mm)	= 0.039 inch
1 centimetre (cm) = 10 mm	= 0.394 inch
1 decimetre (dm) = 10 cm	= 3.94 inches
1 metre (m) = 10 dm	= 1.094 yards
1 decametre (dam) = 10 m	= 10.94 yards
1 hectometre (hm) = 100 m	= 109.4 yards
1 kilometre (km) = 1,000 m	= 0.6214 mile

Square Measure
1 square centimetre (cm^2 or sq cm)	= 0.155 sq in
1 square metre (m^2)	= 1.196 sq yards
1 are = 100 sq metres	= 119.6 sq yards
1 hectare (ha) = 100 ares	= 2.471 acres
1 square kilometre (km^2)	= 0.386 sq mile

Cubic Measure
1 cubic centimetre (cm^3 or cu cm)	= 0.061 cu inch
1 cubic metre (m^3)	= 1.308 cu yards

Capacity Measure
1 millilitre (ml)	= 0.002 pint (British)
1 centilitre (cl) = 10 ml	= 0.018 pint
1 decilitre (dl) = 10 cl	= 0.176 pint
1 litre (l) = 10 dl	= 1.76 pints
1 decalitre (dal) = 10 l	= 2.20 gallons
1 hectolitre (hl) = 100 l	= 2.75 bushels
1 kilolitre (kl) = 1,000 l	= 3.44 quarters

Weight
1 milligram (mg)	= 0.015 grain
1 centigram (cg) = 10 mg	= 0.154 grain
1 decigram (dg) = 10 cg	= 1.543 grain
1 gram (g) = 10 dg	= 15.43 grain
1 decagram (dag) = 10 g	= 5.64 drams
1 hectogram (hg) = 100 g	= 3.527 ounces
1 kilogram (kg) = 1,000g	= 2.205 pounds
1 tonne (metric ton) = 1,000 kg	= 0.984 (long) ton

Temperature

Fahrenheit: water boils (under standard conditions) at 212° and freezes at 32°.

Celsius or Centigrade: water boils at 100° and freezes at 0°.

Kelvin: water boils at 373.15 and freezes at 273.15.

$$C° = \tfrac{5}{9} (°F - 32)$$
$$F° = (\tfrac{9}{5}°C) + 32$$
$$K = C° + 273.15$$

The Hutchinson Encyclopedia

The
Hutchinson Encyclopedia

Hutchinson

London · Melbourne · Sydney · Auckland · Johannesburg

First published (as *Hutchinson's Twentieth Century Encyclopedia*) 1948
Second edition 1951
Third edition 1956
Fourth edition (as *Hutchinson's New 20th Century Encyclopedia*) 1964
Fifth edition 1970
Sixth edition (as *The New Hutchinson 20th Century Encyclopedia*) 1977
Seventh edition 1981
Revised impressions 1978 (twice), 1982, 1984, 1986, 1987
Eighth edition (*The Hutchinson Encyclopedia*) 1988
Revised and updated 1989
Ninth edition 1990

Random Century Ltd
20 Vauxhall Bridge Road
London SW1V 2SA

Random Century Australia (Pty) Ltd
20 Alfred Street
Milsons Point
Sydney 2061, Australia

Random Century New Zealand Ltd
PO Box 40-086, Glenfield
Auckland 10, New Zealand

Random Century South Africa (Pty) Ltd
PO Box 337, Bergvlei 2012
South Africa

set in Century Old Style

Data prepared on Telos
Pagination and typesetting by Falcon Typographic Art Ltd, Elvingston, East Lothian
Printed and bound in Singapore by Toppan Printing Co Ltd

ISBN 0 09 174552 7

Introduction

The true measure of an encyclopedia's worth must be how useful it is to the general reader at whom it is aimed, not to the expert. Any prospective reader consulting the Hutchinson Encyclopedia is therefore asked to look, not only a subject they are familiar with, but also at a topic about which they know little or nothing. Does the entry inform? Does it include up-to-date facts and figures? Is it accurate? Does it provide a useful introduction to the subject? Is it easy to understand? If relevant, is there a helpful illustration? If the answer to all these questions is yes, then the encyclopedia can be judged a success. The extensive modifications made to this 9th edition of the Hutchinson Encyclopedia, which have involved extensive rewriting of existing material as well as the addition of some 2,500 new entries, have all been made with these aims in mind. How far these aims have been achieved it is for the reader to judge.

Arrangement of entries
Entries are ordered alphabetically, as if there were no spaces between words. Thus entries for words beginning 'federal' follow the order:

> Federal Bureau of Investigation
> Federalism
> Federal Reserve System

However, we have avoided a purely mechanical alphabetization in cases where a different order corresponds more with human logic. For example, sovereigns with the same name are grouped according to country and then by number, so that King George II of England is placed before George III of England, and not next to King George II of Greece. Words beginning 'Mc' and 'Mac' are treated as if they begin 'Mac'; and 'St' and 'Saint' are both treated as if they were spelt 'Saint'.

Cross-references
These are shown by a ◊ symbol immediately preceding the reference. Cross-referencing is selective; a cross-reference is shown when another entry contains material directly relevant to the subject matter of an entry, and where the reader may not otherwise think of looking. We do not believe that the existence of a cross-reference alone is sufficient for the reader; the encyclopedia should be an aid, not an obstacle course. We have therefore avoided as far as possible entries that consist only of a cross-reference; even the shortest cross-reference gives some indication of the subject involved.

Foreign names and titles
Names of foreign sovereigns and places are usually shown in their English form, except where the foreign name is more familiar; thus, there are entries for Charles V of Spain, but Juan Carlos (not John Charles), and for Florence, not Firenze. Entries for titled people are under the name by which they are best known to the general reader: thus Anthony Eden, not Lord Avon. Cross-references have been provided in cases where confusion is possible.

Units
SI (metric) units are used throughout for scientific entries. Measurements of distances, temperatures, sizes, and so on, usually include an approximate imperial equivalent. Entries are also included for many weights and measures no longer in common use.

Science and technology
It would be needlessly pedantic to insist on formally correct terminology for every scientific entry in cases where another name is at present far more familiar. Technical terms and current terminology must of course be included. However, many of these terms are not in common use. Entries are therefore generally placed under the name by which they are better known, with the technical term given as a cross-reference. To make it easier for the non-specialist to understand, technical terms are frequently explained when used within the text of an entry, even though they may have their own entry elsewhere.

Systems of government
Individual countries are identified as one of the following systems: liberal democracy, emergent democracy, communism, nationalistic socialism, authoritarian nationalism, military authoritarianism, and absolutism.

Chinese names
Pinyin, the preferred system for transcribing Chinese names of people and places, is generally used: thus there is an entry at Mao Zedong, not Mao Tse-tung. An exception is made for a few names that are more familiar in their former (Wade-Giles) form, such as Sun Yat-sen and Chiang Kai-Shek. Where confusion is likely, Wade-Giles forms are given as cross-references.

Pronunciations
Pronunciations are given using the International Phonetic Alphabet (IPA). In general, only one pronunciation is given for each word. The pronunciation given for foreign words is the generally agreed English form; if there is no generally agreed English pronunciation, an approximation using English sounds is given.

Comments and suggestions
The continuing success of the Hutchinson Encyclopedia has been due in no small part to the many hundreds of readers, ranging as far apart as Hungary, Singapore, and Greenland, who have taken the trouble to provide invaluable supplementary information, or who have pointed out errors in the text.

The letters at the beginning of each new letter are from a typeface designed in 1660 by Johann Neudorffer.

Editors

Editor
Michael Upshall

Project Editor
Jane Dickins

Pronunciation Editor
J C Wells MA, PhD

Database Editors
Claire Debenham
Gian Douglas Home
Claire Jenkins
Bill Kitcher
Pamela Sharpe

Text Editors
Jane Anson
Genevieve Clarke
Ingrid von Essen
Jane Farron
Liz Heron
Frances Lass
Robin Maconie
Louise McConnell
Richard Shaw

Update Editors
Peter Lafferty
Barbara Taylor

Office Administration
Anne von Broen

Art Editor
Penny Hext

Design Management
Edna A Moore, Tek Art

Illustrators commissioned by Tek Art
Jane Abbott
Paul Allingham
Linda Arnold
Wendy Harris
Andrew Pagram
Cedric Robson
Charles Rush
Malcolm Ward

Cartography
Swanston Graphics
Cedric Robson
Malcolm Ward

Database Software
BRS Europe

Computer system
Radstone Technology

Page Make-Up
Marie Banidol
Rosalia Pardina Seśe
Alex N Watson (advisor)

Picture Research
Michael Nicholson
Anna Smith

Contributors

David Armstrong PhD
Christine Avery MA, PhS
John Ayto MA
Lionel Bender BSc, ChBiol, MIBiol
David Benest
Malcolm Bradbury BA, MA, PhD, Hon D Litt, FRSL
Brendan Bradley MA, MSc, PhD
Roy Brigden BA, FMA
John O E Clark BSc
Mike Corbishley BA, FSA, MIFA
Barbara Taylor Cork
David Cotton BA, PhD
Nigel Davis MSc
Ian D Derbyshire MA, PhD
J Denis Derbyshire BSc, PhD, FBIM
Peter Dews PhD
Dougal Dixon BSc, MSc
Professor George du Boulay FRCR, FRCP, Hon FACR
Robin Dunbar BA, PhD
Suzanne Duke
Jane Farron BA
Peter Fleming BA, PhD
Linda Gamlin BSc, MSc
Derek Gjertsen BA
Andrew Gleeson
Lawrence Garner BA
Michael Hitchcock PhD
Jane Insley MSc
H G Jerrard PhD
Brian Jones
Roz Kaveney BA
Robin Kerrod FRAS
Charles Kidd
Stephen Kite B Arch, RIBA
Peter Lafferty
Chris Lawn BA, MA
Judith Lewis LLB
Mike Lewis MBCS
Graham Ley BA, MPhil
Carol Lister BSc, PhD
Graham Littler BSC, MSc, FSS
Robin Maconie MA
Roslin Mair MA
Morven MacKilop
Tom McArthur PhD
Karin Mogg BSc, MSc, PhD
Bob Moore BA, PhD
Ian Morrison
David Munro BSc, PhD
Daniel O' Brien MA
Robert Paisley PhD
Carol Place BSc, PhD
Michael Pudlo MSc, PhD
Ian Ridpath FRAS
Adrian Room MA
John Rowlinson BSc, MSc, CChem, FRSC
Jack Schofield BA, MA
Mark Slade MA
Angela Smith BA
Imogen Stoke Wheeler, Director of Choreography
Glyn Stone
Ingrid von Essen
Stephen Webster BSc, MPhil
Liz Whitelegg BSc
John Woodruff

with special thanks to E M Horsley

A the first letter in nearly all the alphabets. The English *a* is derived from the Etruscan *a* through the Latin alphabet, which is the parent of the West-European alphabets. The Greeks called the first letter *alpha*; the Semites *aleph* or *alph* which meant 'ox', probably because the word began with this letter—a simple mnemonic device.

A in physics, abbreviation for ◊*Ampère*, a unit of electrical current.

A in music, the reference pitch to which instruments of an orchestra are tuned.

A1 abbreviation for *first class* (of ships).

AA abbreviation for the British *Automobile Association*.

AAA abbreviation for *Amateur Athletics Association*, the governing body in the UK for men's athletics. It was founded 1880.

Aachen /'ɑːxən/ (French *Aix-la-Chapelle*) German cathedral city and spa in the *Land* of North Rhine–Westphalia, 72 km/45 mi SW of Cologne; population (1988) 239,000. It has thriving electronics, glass, and rubber industries, and is one of Germany's principal railway junctions.

Aachen was the Roman Aquisgranum, and from the time of Charlemagne until 1531 the German emperors were crowned there. Charlemagne was born and buried in Aachen, and founded the cathedral 796. The 14th century town hall, containing the hall of the emperors, is built on the site of Charlemagne's palace.

Aalborg /'ɔːlbɔːg/ (Danish *Ålborg*) port in Denmark 32 km/20 mi inland from the Kattegat, on the south shore of the Limfjord; population (1988) 155,000. One of Denmark's oldest towns, it has a castle and the fine Budolfi church. It is the capital of Nordjylland county in Jylland (Jutland); the port is linked to Nørresundby on the north side of the fjord by a tunnel built 1969.

Aalst /ɑːlst/ (French *Alost*) industrial town (brewing, textiles) in East Flanders, Belgium, on the

river Dender 24 km/15 mi NW of Brussels; population (1982) 78,700.

Aalto /'ɑːltəʊ/ Alvar 1898–1976. Finnish architect and designer. One of Finland's first modernists, his architectural style was unique, characterized by asymmetry, curved walls, and contrast of natural materials. Buildings include the Hall of Residence, Massachusetts Institute of Technology, Cambridge, Massachusetts 1947–49; Technical High School, Otaniemi 1962–65; Finlandia Hall, Helsinki 1972. He also invented a new form of laminated bent plywood furniture in 1932.

Aaltonen /'ɑːltənen/ Wäinö 1894–1966. Finnish sculptor and painter, best known for his monumental figures and busts portraying citizens of modern Finland, following the country's independence in 1917. He was one of the early 20th-century pioneers of direct carving, and favoured granite as his medium.

The bronze monument to the athlete Nurmi (1925, Helsinki Stadium) and the bust of the composer Sibelius (1928) are good examples of his work. He also developed a more sombre style of modern classicism, well suited to his public commissions, such as the allegorical figures in the Finnish Parliament House (1930–32).

aardvark (Afrikaans name, 'earth-pig') for the nocturnal mammal *Orycteropus afer* found in central and southern Africa. A timid, defenceless animal about the size of a pig, it has a long head, pig-like snout, and large ass-like ears. It feeds on termites which it licks up with its long sticky tongue.

aardwolf nocturnal mammal *Proteles cristatus* of the ◊hyena family. It is found in E and S Africa, usually in the burrows of the aardvark, and feeds on termites.

Aarhus /'ɔːhuːs/ (Danish *Århus*) second city of Denmark, on the east coast overlooking the Kattegat; population (1988) 258,000. It is the capital of Aarhus county in Jylland (Jutland), and a shipping and commercial centre.

Aaron /'eərən/ in the Bible, the elder brother of Moses and co-leader of the Israelites in their march from Egypt to the Promised Land of Canaan. He made the Golden Calf for the Israelites to worship when they despaired of Moses' return from Mount Sinai.

Aaron /'eərən/ Hank 1934– . US baseball player. He played for 23 years with the Milwaukee (later Atlanta) Braves (1954–74) and the Milwaukee Brewers (1975–76), hitting a major-league record 755 home runs and 2,297 runs batted in. He was elected to the Baseball Hall of Fame 1982.

Aasen /'ɔːsən/ Ivar Andreas 1813–1896. Norwegian philologist, poet and playwright. Through a study of rural dialects he evolved by 1853 a native 'country language', which he called *Landsmaal*, to take the place of literary Dano-Norwegian.

abacus method of calculating with a handful of stones on 'a flat surface' (Latin *abacus*), familiar to the Greeks and Romans, and used by earlier peoples, possibly even in ancient Babylon; it still survives in the more sophisticated beadframe form of the Russian *schoty* and the Japanese *soroban*. The abacus has now been replaced by the electronic calculator.

Abadan /ˌæbə'dɑːn/ Iranian oil port on the east side of the Shatt-al-Arab; population (1986) 294,000. Abadan is the chief refinery and shipping centre for Iran's oil industry, nationalized 1951. This measure was the beginning of the worldwide movement by oil-producing countries to assume control of profits from their own resources.

Abakan /ˌæbə'kæn/ coalmining city and capital of Khakass Autonomous Region, Krasnoyarsk Territory, in S USSR; population (1987) 181,000.

abalone snail-like marine mollusc, genus *Haliotis* (also known from its shape as the ear shell), with a bluish mother-of-pearl used in ornamental work.

abb. abbreviation for *abbreviation*.

Abbado /ə'bɑːdəʊ/ Claudio 1933– . Italian conductor, long associated with La Scala, Milan. Principal conductor of London Symphony Orchestra

abacus *The ancient counting method of the abacus shares many mathematical principles with today's electronic calculator. Still widely used in the eastern world, the abacus is used here at work in China's Logan commune.*

from 1979, he also worked with the European Community Youth Orchestra from 1977.

Abbas I /'æbəs/ *the Great* c.1557–1629. Shah of Persia from 1588. He expanded Persian territory by conquest, defeating the Uzbeks near Herat in 1597 and also the Turks. The port of Bandar-Abbas is named after him. At his death his empire reached from the river Tigris to the Indus. He was a patron of the arts.

Abbas II /'æbəs/ Hilmi 1874–1944. Last ◊khedive (viceroy) of Egypt, 1892–1914. On the outbreak of war between Britain and Turkey in 1914, he sided with Turkey and was deposed following the establishment of a British protectorate over Egypt.

Abbasid dynasty /'æbəsɪdz/ dynasty of the Islamic empire who reigned as ◊caliphs in Baghdad 750–1258. They were descended from Abbas, the prophet Muhammad's uncle, and some of them, such as Harun al-Rashid and Mamun (reigned 813–33), were outstanding patrons of cultural development. Later their power dwindled, and in 1258 Baghdad was burned by the Tatars.

From then until 1517 the Abbasids retained limited power as caliphs of Egypt.

Abbas I *Called the Great, Abbas I was Shah of Persia 1588–1629. He fought a long war against the Ottoman Turks, regaining lost territory, including Baghdad. He introduced reforms, and encouraged European trade and the flowering of Persian arts. This is an engraving from Herbett's* Travels *1638.*

Abbé (French 'abbot') a French title of respect used to address any clergyman.

Abbeville /'æbvɪl/ town in N France in the Somme *département*, 19 km/12 mi inland from the mouth of the Somme; population (1982) 26,000. During World War I it was an important base for the British armies.

abbey in the Christian church, a monastery (of monks) or a nunnery or convent (of nuns), all dedicated to a life of celibacy and religious seclusion, governed by an abbot or abbess respectively. Sometimes the word is applied to a building that was once the church of an abbey, for example Westminster Abbey, London.

The first abbeys, as established in Syria or Egypt were mere collections of huts, but later massive and extensive buildings were constructed throughout Europe.

Abbey Theatre playhouse in Dublin associated with the Irish literary revival of the early 1900s. The theatre, opened in 1904, staged the works of a number of Irish dramatists, including Lady Gregory, Yeats, J M Synge, and Sean O'Casey. Burned down in 1951, the Abbey Theatre was rebuilt 1966.

Abbotsford /'æbətsfəd/ home of Sir Walter ◊Scott from 1811, on the right bank of the Tweed, Borders region. Originally a farmhouse, it was rebuilt 1817–25 as a Gothic baronial hall, and is still in the possession of his descendants.

Abbott and Costello Stage names of William Abbot (1895–1974) and Louis Cristillo (1906–1959). US comedy duo. They moved to the cinema from vaudeville, and their films, including *Buck Privates* 1941 and *Lost in a Harem* 1944, were showcases for their routines.

Abd el-Krim /'æbd el 'krɪm/ el-Khettabi 1881–1963. Moroccan chief known as the 'Wolf of the ◊Riff'. With his brother Muhammad, he led the *Riff revolt* against the French and Spanish invaders, inflicting disastrous defeat on the Spanish at Anual in 1921, but surrendered to a large French army under Pétain in 1926. Banished to the island of Réunion, he was released in 1947 and died in voluntary exile in Cairo.

abdication renunciation of an office or dignity, usually the throne, by a ruler or sovereign.

Abdication crisis the constitutional upheaval of the period 16 Nov 1936 to 10 Dec 1936 was brought about by the English king, Edward VIII's decision to marry Mrs Wallis Simpson, an American divorcee. The marriage of the 'Supreme Governer' of the Church of England to a divorced person was considered unsuitable and the king was finally forced to abdicate on 10 Dec and left for voluntary exile in France. He married Wallis Simpson on 3 June 1937.

abdomen the part of the vertebrate body containing the digestive organs; the hind part of the body in insects. In mammals, the abdomen is separated from the chest (*thorax*) by the diaphragm, a sheet of muscular tissue; in arthropods, commonly by a narrow constriction. In insects and spiders, the abdomen is characterized by the absence of limbs.

Abdul-Hamid II /'æbdʊl 'hæmɪd/ 1842–1918. Last sultan of Turkey 1876–1909. In 1908 the ◊Young Turks under Enver Pasha forced Abdul-Hamid to restore the constitution of 1876, and in 1909 insisted on his deposition. He died in confinement. For his part in the ◊Armenian massacres suppressing the revolt of 1894–96 he was known as the Great Assassin and still motivates Armenian violence against the Turks.

Abdullah /æb'dʌlə/ ibn Hussein 1882–1951. King of Jordan from 1946. He worked with the British guerrilla leader T E ◊Lawrence in the Arab revolt of World War I. Abdullah became king of Transjordan 1946; on the incorporation of Arab Palestine (after the 1948–49 Arab-Israeli War) he renamed the country the Hashemite Kingdom of Jordan. He was assassinated.

Abdullah /æb'dʌlə/ Sheikh Muhammad 1905–1982. Indian politician, known as the 'Lion of Kashmir'. He headed the struggle for constitutional government against the Maharajah of Kashmir, and in 1948 became prime minister of Kashmir. He agreed to the accession of the state to India to halt ethnic infiltration, but was dismissed and imprisoned from 1953 (with brief intervals) until 1966, when he reaffirmed the right of the people 'to decide the future of the state' (see ◊Kashmir). He became chief minister of Jammu and Kashmir 1975, accepting the sovereignty of India.

Abel /'eɪbəl/ in the Old Testament, second son of Adam and Eve; as a shepherd, he made burnt offerings of meat to God which were more acceptable than the fruits offered by his brother Cain; he was killed by the jealous Cain.

Abel /'eɪbəl/ Frederick Augustus 1827–1902. British scientist and inventor, who developed explosives. As a chemist to the War Department, he introduced a method of making gun-cotton and was joint inventor with ◊Dewar of cordite. He also invented the Abel close-test instrument for determining the ◊flash point of petroleum.

Abel /'eɪbəl/ John Jacob 1857–1938. US biochemist, discoverer of ◊adrenaline. He studied the chemical composition of body tissues, and this led, in 1898, to the discovery of adrenaline, the first hormone to be identified, which Abel called epinephrine. He later became the first to isolate ◊amino acids from blood.

Abel Niels Henrik 1802–1829. Norwegian mathematician who demonstrated that the general quintic equation could not be solved algebraically. Despite a life of poverty and ill-health he also looked at elliptic functions, integral equations, infinite series and binomial theorem. He died of tuberculosis shortly before the arrival of an offer of a position at the University of Berlin.

Abelard /'æbəlɑːd/ Peter 1079–1142. French scholastic philosopher noted for his work on logic and theology and for his love affair with ◊Heloise. Details of his controversial life are contained in the autobiographical *Historia Calamitatum Mearum/The History of My Misfortunes*.

Born near Nantes, he became canon of Notre Dame in Paris, and master of the cathedral school 1115. When his seduction of, and secret marriage to, his pupil ◊Héloïse became known, she entered a convent and he was castrated at the instigation of her uncle, Canon Fulbert, and became a monk. Resuming teaching a year later, he was cited for heresy and became a hermit at Nogent, where he built the oratory of the Paraclete, and later abbot of a monastery in Brittany. He opposed realism in the debate over universals, and propounded 'conceptualism' whereby universal terms have only a mental existence. His love letters from Héloïse survive. He died at Châlon-sur-Saône, on his way to defend himself against a new charge of heresy. Héloïse was buried beside him at the Paraclete 1164, their remains being taken to Père Lachaise, Paris 1817.

Abeokuta /ˌæbɪəʊ'kuːtə/ agricultural trade centre in Nigeria, W Africa, on the Ogun River, 103 km/64 mi N of Lagos; population (1983) 309,000.

Aberbrothock /ˌæbə'brɒθək/ another name for ◊Arbroath, town in Scotland.

Abercrombie /'æbəkrʌmbi/ Leslie Patrick 1879–1957. Pioneer of British town planning. He is known for his work replanning British cities after damage in World War II (such as the Greater London Plan, 1944) and for the ◊new town policy. See also ◊garden city.

Abercromby /'æbəkrʌmbi/ Ralph 1734–1801. Scots soldier who in 1801 commanded an expedition to the Mediterranean, charged with the liquidation of the French forces left behind by Napoleon in Egypt. He fought a brilliant action against the French at Aboukir Bay in 1801, but was mortally wounded at the battle of Alexandria a few days later.

Aberdare /ˌæbə'deə/ town in Mid Glamorgan, Wales, formerly producing high-grade coal, and

Aberdeen George Hamilton Gordon, 4th Earl of Aberdeen, painted by John Partridge c.1847.

now electrical and light engineering industries; population (1981) 36,621.

Aberdeen /ˌæbə'diːn/ city and seaport on the E coast of Scotland, administrative headquarters of Grampian region; population (1986) 214,082. Shore-based maintenance and service depots for the North Sea oil rigs.

It is Scotland's third largest city, and is rich in historical interest and fine buildings, including the Municipal Buildings (1867); King's College (1494) and Marischal College (founded 1593; housed in one of the largest granite buildings in the world, 1836) which together form Aberdeen University; St Machar Cathedral (1378), and the Auld Brig o'Balgownie (1320). Industries include the manufacture of agricultural machinery, paper, and textiles; fishing, ship-building, granite-quarrying, and engineering. Oil discoveries in the North Sea in the 1960s–70s transformed Aberdeen into the European 'offshore capital', with an airport and heliport linking the mainland to the rigs.

Aberdeen /ˌæbə'diːn/ George Hamilton Gordon, 4th Earl of Aberdeen 1784–1860. British Tory politician, prime minister 1852–55, resigned because of the Crimean War losses. Although a Tory, he supported Catholic emancipation and followed Robert Peel in his conversion to free trade.

Born in Edinburgh, he succeeded his grandfather as earl in 1801, and was a prominent diplomat. In 1828 and again in 1841 he was foreign secretary under Wellington. In 1852 he became prime minister in a government of Peelites and Whigs (Liberals), but resigned in 1855 because of the hostile criticism aroused by the miseries and mismanagement of the Crimean War.

Aberdeenshire /ˌæbə'diːnʃə/ former county in E Scotland, merged in 1975 into Grampian region.

Aberfan /ˌæbə'væn/ mining village in Mid Glamorgan, Wales. Coal waste overwhelmed a school and houses in 1966; of 144 dead, 116 were children.

aberration of starlight the apparent displacement of a star from its true position, due to the combined effects of the speed of light and the speed of the Earth in orbit around the Sun (about 30 km/18.5 mi per sec). Aberration was discovered in 1728 by James ◊Bradley, and was the first observational proof that the Earth orbits the Sun.

aberration, optical any of a number of defects that impair the image in an optical instrument. In *chromatic aberration* the image is surrounded by coloured fringes, because light of different colours is brought to different focal points by a lens. In *spherical aberration* the image is blurred because different parts of the lens or mirror have different focal lengths. In *astigmatism* the image appears elliptical or cross-shaped. In *coma*, the images appear progressively elongated towards the edge of the field of view. Optical aberration occurs because of minute variations in the glass and because different parts of the light ◊spectrum are reflected or refracted by varying amounts.

Aberystwyth /ˌæbə'rɪstwɪθ/ resort town in Wales; population (1981) 8,500. It is the unofficial capital of the Welsh-speaking area of Wales. The University College of Wales 1872, Welsh Plant

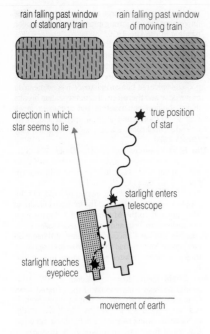

aberration of starlight

Breeding Station, and National Library of Wales are here.

abeyance doctrine whereby a peerage falls into a state of suspension between a number of co-heirs or co-heiresses; in the UK the only peerages that can fall into abeyance are baronies that have been created by writ.

Abidja'n /ˌæbiˈdʒɑːn/ port and capital of the Republic of Ivory Coast, W Africa; population (1982) 1,850,000. Products include coffee, palm oil, cocoa, and timber (mahogany). To be replaced as capital by Yamoussoukro.

Abilene /ˈæbəliːn/ town in Kansas, USA, on the Smoky Hill River; population (1980) 98,500. A western railway terminus, Abilene was a shipping point for cattle in the 1860s. Its economy includes the manufacture of aircraft and missile components and oil-field equipment.

Abingdon /ˈæbɪŋdən/ town in Oxfordshire, England, on the Thames 10 km/6 mi S of Oxford; population (1981) 22,500. The remains of the 7th-century abbey include Checker Hall, restored as an Elizabethan-type theatre. The 15th-century bridge was reconstructed 1929. There are light industries.

ab init. abbreviation for *ab initio* (Latin 'from the beginning').

Abkhazia /æbˈkɑːziə/ autonomous republic in the NW corner of the republic of ◊Georgia in SW USSR; area 8,600 sq km/3,320 sq mi. Inhabited traditionally by Abkhazis, an ethnic group converted from Christianity to Islam in the 17th century, today two thirds of the population of 526,000 are of Georgian origin. In Mar–Apr and July 1989, Abkhazis demanded secession from Georgia and reinstatement as a full Union republic; violent inter-ethnic clashes erupted in which at least 20 people died.

ablative in the grammar of certain inflected languages, such as Latin, the ablative case is the form of a noun, pronoun or adjective used to indicate the agent in passive sentences or the instrument, manner, or place of the action described by the verb.

ablution washing for a religious purpose, to purify the soul. Hindus, for example, believe that bathing in the river Ganges will purify them. Similar beliefs are found in Christianity and Shinto (for example, the mythical Izanagi purifies himself by diving to the bottom of the sea and washing himself).

ABM abbreviation for **anti-ballistic missile**; see ◊nuclear warfare.

Abo /ˈɔːbuː/ Swedish name for ◊Turku in Finland.

abolitionism in UK and US history, a movement in the late 18th and early 19th centuries, first to end the slave trade, and then to abolish the institution of ◊slavery and emancipate slaves. In the UK, the leading abolitionist was William ◊Wilberforce, who secured passage of a bill abolishing the slave trade in 1807. In the USA, slavery was officially abolished by the Emancipation Proclamation 1863 of President Abraham ◊Lincoln, but it could not be enforced until 1865 after the Union victory in the civil war.

Abomey /əˈbəumi/ town and port of ◊Benin, W Africa; population (1982) 54,500. It was once the capital of the kingdom of Dahomey, which flourished in the 17th–19th centuries, and had a mud-built defence wall 10 km/6 mi in circumference.

abominable snowman legendary creature, said to resemble a human, with long arms and a thick-set body covered with reddish-grey hair. Reports of its existence in the Himalayas, where it is known as the **yeti**, have been made since 1832, but they gained substance from a published photograph of a huge footprint in the snow in 1951. No further 'evidence' has been found.

aborigine (Latin *aborigine*, from the beginning) any indigenous inhabitant of a country. The word also refers to the original peoples of countries colonized by Europeans, and especially to ◊Australian Aborigines.

abortion the ending of a pregnancy before the fetus is developed sufficiently to survive outside the womb. Abortion may be accidental (miscarriage) or deliberate (termination of pregnancy).

Methods of deliberate abortion vary according to the gestational age of the fetus. Up to 12 weeks, the cervix is dilated and a suction curette passed into the uterus to remove its contents. Over 12 weeks, a prostoglandin pessary is introduced into the vagina, which induces labour, producing a miscarriage. In 1989 an anti-progesterone pill was introduced in France, under the name RU 486. This also leads to the expulsion of the fetus from the womb, but can be used at an earlier stage in pregnancy.

Abortion as a means of birth control has long been the subject of controversy. The argument centres largely upon whether a woman should legally be permitted to have an abortion and, that being so, under what circumstances. Another aspect is whether, and to what extent, the law should protect the fetus. Those who oppose abortion generally believe that human life begins at the moment of conception, when a sperm fertilizes an egg. This is the view held, for example, by the Roman Catholic church. Those who approve abortion may do so for specific reasons. For example, if a woman's life or health is jeopardized abortion may be recommended; equally, if there is a strong likelihood that the child will be born with severe mental or physical handicap. Other grounds for abortion include pregnancy resulting from sexual assault such as rape or incest.

In the UK an abortion must be carried out under the terms of the 1967 Abortion Act, which states that two doctors must agree that termination of the pregnancy is necessary, and the operation must be performed on approved premises.

The legal cut-off point for therapeutic abortion—in Britain 24 weeks from 1990—is largely arbitrary. It is increasingly open to question with the development of new techniques to sustain babies delivered at an earlier stage of gestation (some as young as 23 weeks). Loss of a fetus at a later gestational age is termed premature stillbirth. The failure of a private member's bill (by David Alton) to reduce the time limit on abortions from 28 weeks to 18 was defeated 1988; it was the 15th unsuccessful attempt to alter the 1967 Abortion Act. In 1988, there were 183,978 abortions performed in England and Wales, an increase of 5.5% on 1987 figures.

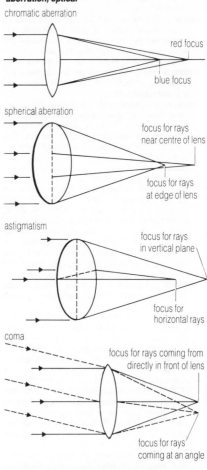

aberration, optical

chromatic aberration

red focus

blue focus

spherical aberration

focus for rays near centre of lens

focus for rays at edge of lens

astigmatism

focus for rays in vertical plane

focus for horizontal rays

coma

focus for rays coming from directly in front of lens

focus for rays coming at an angle

In the USA in 1989, a Supreme Court decision gave state legislatures the right to introduce some restrictions on abortions.

Aboukir Bay, Battle of /ˌæbuːˈkɪə/ also known as the **Battle of the Nile**: naval battle between the UK and France, in which Admiral Nelson defeated Napoleon's fleet at the Egyptian seaport of Aboukir on 1 Aug 1798.

abracadabra magic word first recorded in a Latin poem of 2nd century AD by the Gnostic poet Q Serenus Sammonicus. When written in the form of an inverted pyramid, so as to be read across the top and up the right side, it was worn as a health amulet, to ward off illnesses.

Abraham /ˈeɪbrəhæm/ *c.* 2300 BC. According to the Old Testament, founder of the Jewish nation. Jehovah promised him heirs and land for his people in Canaan, renamed him Abraham ('father of many nations') and once tested him by a command (later retracted) to sacrifice his son Isaac or, in the Koran, Ishmael.

Abraham was born in Ur, Sumeria, the son of Terah. With his father, wife Sarah, and nephew Lot, he migrated to Haran, N Mesopotamia. While in Canaan he received Jehovah's promise of land. After visiting Egypt he separated from Lot at Bethel and settled in Hebron. He was still childless at the age of 76, subsequently had a son (Ishmael) with his wife's maidservant Hagar, and then, at the age of 100, a son Isaac with his wife Sarah. Abraham was buried in Machpelah Cave, Hebron.

Abraham /ˈeɪbrəhæm/ Edward Penley 1913– . British biochemist, who isolated the antibiotic cephalosporin, capable of destroying penicillin-resistant bacteria.

Abraham, Plains of /ˈeɪbrəhæm/ plateau near Québec, Canada, where the British commander ◊Wolfe defeated the French under ◊Montcalm,

13 Sept 1759, during the French and Indian War (1754–63).

abrasive substance used for cutting and polishing or for removing small amounts of the surface of hard materials. There are two types: natural and artificial abrasives, and their hardness is measured, using the ◊Mohs scale. Natural abrasives include quartz, sandstone, pumice, diamond, and corundum; artificial abrasives include rouge, whiting, and carborundum.

abraxas a mystical word found engraved on ancient stones, used as a superstitious charm. The Greek letters of the word, when interpreted as numbers, are equivalent to 365. The title was used by Egyptian Gnostics to describe the supreme being.

Abruzzi /ə'brʊtsi/ mountainous region of S central Italy, comprising the provinces of L'Aquila, Chieti, Pescara, and Teramo; area 10,800 sq km/4,169 sq mi; population (1988) 1,258,000; capital L'Aquila. Gran Sasso d'Italia, 2,914 m/9,564 ft, is the highest point of the ◊Apennines.

Absalom /'æbsələm/ in the Old Testament, favourite son of King David; when defeated in a revolt against his father he fled on a mule, but was caught up by his hair in a tree branch and killed by Joab, one of David's officers.

abscess a collection of pus in the tissues forming in response to infection. Its presence is signalled by pain and inflammation.

abscissa in coordinate geometry, the horizontal or *x* coordinate, that is, the distance of a point from the vertical or *y*-axis. For example, a point with the coordinates (3,4) has an abscissa of 3.

abscission in botany, the controlled separation of part of a plant from the main plant body—most commonly, the falling of leaves or the dropping of fruit. In ◊deciduous plants the leaves are shed before the winter or dry season, whereas ◊evergreen plants drop their leaves continually throughout the year. Fruit-drop, the abscission of fruit while still immature, is a naturally occurring process.

Abscission occurs after the formation of an abscission zone at the point of separation. Within this a thin layer of cells, the abscission layer, becomes weakened and breaks down through the conversion of pectic acid to pectin. Consequently the leaf, fruit, or other part can easily be dislodged by wind or rain. The process is thought to be controlled by the amount of ◊auxin present. Fruit drop is particularly common in fruit trees such as apple, and orchards are often sprayed with artificial auxin as a preventive measure.

absinthe drink containing 60–80% alcohol, which was originally flavoured with oil of wormwood; the latter attacks the nervous system and is widely banned.

absolute value in mathematics, the value of a number irrespective of its sign (denoted $|n|$), and defined as the positive square root of n^2. It is often referred to as the modulus of n, written mod n.

absolute zero the lowest temperature theoretically possible, zero kelvin, equivalent to –273.16°C, at which molecules are motionless. Although the third law of ◊thermodynamics indicates the impossibility of reaching absolute zero exactly, a temperature within 3×10^{-8} kelvin of it was produced in 1984 by Finnish scientists. Near absolute zero, the physical properties of some materials change substantially; for example, some metals lose their electrical resistance (become superconductive). See ◊cryogenics.

absolutism or *absolute monarchy* a system of government in which the ruler or rulers have unlimited power. The principle of an absolute monarch, given a right to rule by God (see ◊divine right of kings), was extensively used in Europe during the 17th and 18th centuries. Absolute monarchy is contrasted with limited or constitutional monarchy, in which the sovereign's powers are defined or limited.

absorption in science, the taking up of one substance by another, such as a liquid by a solid (ink by blotting-paper) or a gas by a liquid (ammonia by water). In optics, absorption is the phenomenon by which a substance retains radiation of particular wavelengths; for example, a piece of blue glass absorbs all visible light except the wavelengths in the blue part of the spectrum. In nuclear physics, absorption is the capture by elements such as boron of neutrons produced by fission in a reactor.

abstract art non-representational art. Ornamental art without figurative representation occurs in most cultures. The modern abstract movement in sculpture and painting emerged in Europe and North America between 1910 and 1920. Two approaches produce different abstract styles: images that have been 'abstracted' from nature to the point where they no longer reflect a conventional reality; and non-objective or 'pure' art forms, supposedly without reference to reality.

Abstract art began in the avant-garde movements of the late 19th century, in Impressionism, Neo-Impressionism and Post-Impressionism. These styles of painting reduced the importance of the original subject matter and emphasized the creative process of painting itself. Then, in the first decade of the 20th century, some painters in Western Europe began to abandon the established Western convention of imitating nature and storytelling in pictures and developed a new artistic form and expression. Kandinsky is generally regarded as the first abstract artist. His highly coloured canvases influenced many younger European artists. In France, the Cubists Picasso and Braque also developed, around 1907, an abstract style; their pictures, some partly collage, were composed mainly of fragmented natural images.

Many variations of abstract art developed in Europe, as shown in the work of Mondrian, Malevich, the Italian Futurists, the Vorticists in the UK, and Dada. The sculptors, including Brancusi and Epstein, were inspired by the new freedom in form and content and Brancusi's *The Kiss* 1910 is one of the earliest abstract sculptures.

Two exhibitions of European art, one in New York in 1913 (the Armory Show), the other in San Francisco in 1917, opened the way for abstraction in US art. Many painters, including the young Georgia O'Keeffe, experimented with new styles. Morgan Russell (1886–1953) and Stanton Macdonald-Wright (1890–1973) invented their own school, Synchronism, a rival to Orphism, a similar style developed in France by Robert Delaunay.

Modern abstract art dominated Western art from 1920, and has continued to produce many variations. In the 1940s it gained renewed vigour in the works of the Abstract Expressionists. From the 1950s Minimal art provoked more outraged reactions from critics and the general public alike.

Abstract Expressionism US movement in abstract art that emphasized the act of painting, the expression inherent in paint itself, and the interaction of artist, paint, and canvas. Abstract Expressionism first emerged in New York in the early 1940s. Gorky, Kline, Pollock, and Rothko are associated with the movement.

Abstract Expressionism may have been inspired by Hans Hofmann and Arshile Gorky who were both working in the USA in the 1940s. Hofmann, who emigrated from Germany in the 1930s, had started to use dribbles and blobs of paint to create expressive abstract patterns, while Gorky, a Turkish Armenian refugee, was developing his highly coloured abstracts with wild organic forms. Abstract Expressionism was not a distinct school but rather a convergence of artistic personalities, each revolting against restricting conventions in US art. The styles of the movement's exponents varied widely: Pollock's huge dripped and splashed work, de Kooning's grotesque figures, Kline's strong calligraphic style, and Motherwell

and Rothko's calmer large abstract canvases. The movement made a strong impression on European painting in the late 1950s.

Absurd, Theatre of the avant-garde drama originating with a group of playwrights in the 1950s, including Beckett, Ionesco, Genet, and Pinter. Their work expressed the belief that in a godless universe human existence has no meaning or purpose and therefore all communication breaks down. Logical construction and argument gives way to irrational and illogical speech and to its ultimate conclusion, silence, as in Beckett's play *Breath* 1970.

Abu Bakr /ˌæbuːˈbækə/ or *Abu-Bekr* 573–634. 'Father of the virgin', name used by Abd-el-Ka'aba from about 618 when the prophet Muhammad married his daughter Aisha. He was a close adviser to Muhammad in the period 622–32. On the prophet's death, he became the first ◊caliph adding Mesopotamia to the Muslim world and instigating expansion into Iraq and Syria. Traditionally he is supposed to have encouraged some of those who had known Muhammad to memorize his teachings; these words were later written down to form the Koran.

Abu Dhabi /ˌæbuːˈdɑːbi/ sheikdom in SW Asia, on the Arabian Gulf, capital of the ◊United Arab Emirates. Formerly under British protection, it has been ruled since 1971 by Sheik Zayed Bin al-Nahayan, who is also president of the Supreme Council of Rulers of the United Arab Emirates.

Abuja /əˈbuːdʒə/ newly built city in Nigeria which is planned to replace Lagos as capital. Shaped like a crescent, it was designed by the Japanese architect Kenzo Tange.

Abu Musa /ˌæbuː ˌmuːˈsɑː/ a small island in the Persian Gulf. Formerly owned by the ruler of Sharjah, it was forcibly occupied by Iran in 1971.

Abú Nuwás /ˈæbuː ˈnuːwæs/ Hasan ibn Háni 762–c.815. Arab poet. His work was based on old forms, but the new freedom with which he used them, his eroticism, and his ironic humour, have contributed to his reputation as perhaps the greatest of Arab poets.

Abu Simbel /ˌæbuː ˈsɪmbəl/ former site of two ancient temples in S Egypt, built during the reign of Ramses II and commemorating him and his wife Nefertari; before the site was flooded by the Aswan High Dam, the temples were moved, in sections, 1966–67.

Abydos /əˈbaɪdɒs/ ancient city in Upper Egypt; the Great Temple of Seti I dates from about 1300 BC.

abyssal zone dark ocean area 2–6,000 m/6,500–19,500 ft deep; temperature 4°C/39°F. Three quarters of the area of the deep ocean floor lies in the abyssal zone. It is too far from the surface for photosynthesis to take place. Some fish and crustaceans living there are blind or have their own light sources. The region above is called the bathyal zone; the region below, the hadyal zone.

Abyssinia /ˌæbɪˈsɪniə/ former name of ◊Ethiopia.

a/c abbreviation for *account*.

AC in physics, abbreviation for ◊*alternating current*.

accelerator

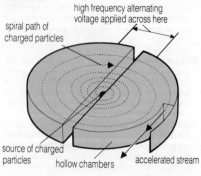

spiral path of charged particles

high frequency alternating voltage applied across here

source of charged particles

hollow chambers

accelerated stream

accelerator

acacia one of a large group of shrubs and trees of the genus *Acacia*, belonging to the pea family. Acacias include the thorn trees of the African savannah, and the *gum arabic tree Acaci, senegal* of N Africa. Acacias are found in warm regions of the Old World, particularly Australia.

Academy originally the school of philosophy founded by ◊Plato in the gardens of Academe, NW of Athens; it was closed by the Byzantine Emperor ◊Justinian, with the other pagan schools, in 529. In the modern sense a recognized society established for the promotion of one or more of the arts and sciences. The first academy was the Museum of Alexandria, founded by Ptolemy Soter in the 3rd century BC.

Academy Award annual cinema award given from 1927 onwards by the American Academy of Motion Pictures, nicknamed 'Oscar' (1931).

Academy, French or *Académie Française* literary society founded by ◊Richelieu in 1635; it is especially concerned with maintaining the purity of the French language; membership is limited to 40 'immortals' at a time.

Academy of Sciences, Soviet society founded 1725 by Catherine the Great in what is now called Leningrad; it has been responsible for such achievements as ◊Sputnik, and has branches in Ukraine (welding, cybernetics), Armenia (astrophysics), and Georgia (mechanical engineering).

Acadia /ə'keɪdɪə/ (French *Acadie*) name given to ◊Nova Scotia by French settlers 1604, from which the term ◊Cajun derives.

acanthus herbaceous plant with handsome leaves. Some 20 species are found in the Mediterranean region and the Old World tropics, including *bear's breech Acanthus mollis*, whose leaves were used as a motif in classical architecture.

a cappella (Italian 'in the style of the chapel') choral music sung without instrumental accompaniment.

Acapulco /ˌækə'pʊlkəʊ/ or *Acapulco de Juarez* port and holiday resort in Mexico; population (1985) 638,000.

ACAS abbreviation for *Advisory, Conciliation and Arbitration Service*, an independent organization set up by the UK government 1975 to advise and arbitrate in industrial disputes between staff and employers.

accelerated freeze drying see ◊AFD.

acceleration the rate of increase in the velocity of a moving body. The acceleration due to gravity is the acceleration shown by a body falling freely under the influence of gravity; it varies slightly at different latitudes and altitudes. Retardation (deceleration) is actually negative acceleration; for example, as a rising rocket slows down, it is being negatively accelerated towards the centre of the Earth. Acceleration is expressed in metres per second squared/feet per second squared.

acceleration, secular in astronomy, the continuous and non-periodic change in orbital velocity of one body around another, or the axial rotation period of a body.

An example is the axial rotation of the Earth. This is gradually slowing down owing to the gravitational effects of the Moon and the resulting production of tides which have a frictional effect on the Earth. However, the angular ◊momentum of the Earth-Moon system is maintained, because the momentum lost by the Earth is passed to the Moon. This results in an increase in the Moon's orbital period and a consequential moving away from the Earth. The overall effect is that the Earth's axial rotation period is increasing by about 15-millionths of a second a year, and the Moon is receding from the Earth at about 4 cm/1.5 a year.

accelerator device to bring charged particles (such as ◊protons) up to high speeds and energies, at which they can be of use in industry, medicine, and pure physics: when high energy particles collide with other particles, the fragments formed reveal the nature of the fundamental forces of nature. For particles to achieve the energies required, successive applications of a high voltage are

Academy Award winners (Oscars)

1971	**Best Picture:** *The French Connection* **Best Director:** William Friedkin *The French Connection* **Best Actor:** Gene Hackman *The French Connection* **Best Actress:** Jane Fonda *Klute*
1972	**Best Picture:** *The Godfather* **Best Director:** Bob Fosse *Cabaret* Best Actor: Marlon Brando *The Godfather* **Best Actress:** Liza Minnelli *Cabaret*
1973	**Best Picture:** *The Sting* **Best Director:** George Roy Hill *The Sting* **Best Actor:** Jack Lemmon *Save the Tiger* **Best Actress:** Glenda Jackson *A Touch of Class*
1974	**Best Picture:** *The Godfather II* **Best Director:** Francis Ford Coppola *The Godfather II* **Best Actor:** Art Carney *Harry and Tonto* **Best Actress:** Ellen Burstyn *Alice Doesn't Live Here Any More*
1975	**Best Picture:** *One Flew Over the Cuckoo's Nest* **Best Director:** Milos Forman *One Flew Over the Cuckoo's Nest* **Best Actor:** Jack Nicholson *One Flew Over the Cuckoo's Nest* **Best Actress:** Louise Fletcher *One Flew Over the Cuckoo's Nest*
1976	**Best Picture:** *Rocky* **Best Director:** John G Avildsen *Rocky* **Best Actor:** Peter Finch *Network* **Best Actress:** Faye Dunaway *Network*
1977	**Best Picture:** *Annie Hall* **Best Director:** Woody Allen *Annie Hall* Best Actor: Richard Dreyfuss *The Goodbye Girl* **Best Actress:** Diane Keaton *Annie Hall*
1978	**Best Picture:** *The Deerhunter* **Best Director:** Michael Cimino *The Deerhunter* **Best Actor:** John Voight *Coming Home* **Best Actress:** Jane Fonda *Coming Home*
1979	**Best Picture:** *Kramer vs Kramer* **Best Director:** Robert Beaton *Kramer vs Kramer* **Best Actor:** Dustin Hoffman *Kramer vs Kramer* **Best Actress:** Sally Field *Norma Rae*
1980	**Best Picture:** *Ordinary People* **Best Director:** Robert Redford *Ordinary People* **Best Actor:** Robert de Niro *Raging Bull* **Best Actress:** Sissy Spacek *Coalminer's Daughter*
1981	**Best Picture:** *Chariots of Fire* **Best Director:** Warren Beatty *Reds* Best Actor: Henry Fonda *On Golden Pond* **Best Actress:** Katherine Hepburn *On Golden Pond*
1982	**Best Picture:** *Gandhi* **Best Director:** Richard Attenborough *Gandhi* Best Actor: Ben Kingsley *Gandhi* Best Actress: Meryl Streep *Sophie's Choice*
1983	**Best Picture:** *Terms of Endearment* **Best Director:** James L Brooks *Terms of Endearment* **Best Actor:** Robert Duvall *Terms of Endearment* **Best Actress:** Shirley MacLaine *Terms of Endearment*
1984	**Best Picture:** *Amadeus* **Best Director:** Milos Forman *Amadeus* **Best Actor:** F Murray Abraham *Amadeus* **Best Actress:** Sally Field *Places in the Heart*
1985	**Best Picture:** *Out of Africa* **Best Director:** Sidney Pollack *Out of Africa* **Best Actor:** William Hurt *Kiss of the Spiderwoman* **Best Actress:** Geraldine Page *The Trip to Bountiful*
1986	**Best Picture:** *Platoon* **Best Director:** Oliver Stone *Platoon* **Best Actor:** Paul Newman *The Color of Money* **Best Actress:** Mariee Matlin *Children of a Lesser God*
1987	**Best Picture:** *The Last Emperor* **Best Director:** Bernardo Bertolucci *The Last Emperor* **Best Actor:** Michael Douglas *Wall Street* **Best Actress:** Cher *Moonstruck*
1988	**Best Picture:** *Rain Man* **Best Director:** Barry Levinson *Rain Man* Best Actor: Dustin Hoffman *Rain Man* **Best Actress:** Jodie Foster *The Accused*
1989	**Best Picture:** *My Left Foot* **Best Director:** Oliver Stone *Born on the 4th of July* **Best Actor:** Daniel Day-Lewis *My Left Foot* **Best Actress:** Jessica Tandy *Driving Miss Daisy*

Academy Awards

given to electrodes placed in the path of the particles. During acceleration, the particles are confined within a circular or linear track using a magnetic field.

The first circular accelerator, the *cyclotron*, was built in the early 1930s. The early cyclotrons had circumferences of about 10 cm/4 in, whereas the ◊Large Electron Positron collider (LEP) at ◊CERN near Geneva, which came into operation 1989, has a circumference of 27 km/16.8 mi, around which ◊electrons and ◊positrons are accelerated before being allowed to collide. In 1988, the USA announced plans to build the Superconducting Super collider (to be completed 1996), in Waxahachie, Texas, with a circumference of 85 km/53 mi. The world's largest *linear accelerator* is the Stanford Linear Collider, in which electrons and positrons are accelerated along a straight track, 3.2 km/2 mi long, and then steered into a head-on collision.

accelerometer apparatus for measuring ◊acceleration or deceleration that is, the rate of increase or decrease in the ◊velocity of a moving object.

Accelerometers are used to measure the efficiency of the braking systems on road and rail vehicles; those used in aircraft and spacecraft can determine accelerations in several directions simultaneously.

accent a way of speaking that identifies a person with a particular country, region, language, social class, linguistic style, or some mixture of these.

People often describe only those who belong to groups other than their own as having accents and may give them special names; for example, an Irish brogue, a Northumbrian burr. See also ◊English language.

accessory in law, accessories are criminal accomplices who may be either 'before the fact' (inciting another to commit a crime) or 'after the fact' (giving assistance after the crime). An accomplice present when the crime is committed is

an 'abettor'. In English law these distinctions no longer apply: all those involved in the commission of a crime are punishable in the same way.

acclimation or *acclimatization* the physiological changes induced in an organism by exposure to new environmental conditions. When humans move to higher altitudes, for example, the number of red blood cells rises to increase the oxygen-carrying capacity of the blood, in order to compensate for the lower levels of oxygen in the air.

accol.de symbolic blow on the shoulders with the flat of the sword, given by the sovereign, or a representative, in conferring a knighthood.

accomplice a person who is associated with another in the commission of a crime. In English law, the word is used both for persons who played a minor part in the crime and for the principal offenders. See also ◊accessory.

accordion a musical instrument of the reed organ type comprising left and right wind-chests connected by a flexible bellows. The right hand plays melody on a piano-style keyboard while the left hand has a system of push-buttons for selecting single notes or chord harmonies.

Invented by Cyrill Damien (1772–1847) in Vienna 1829, it spread throughout the world and can be heard in the popular music of France, China, Russia, and the American South.

accountancy financial management of businesses and other organizations, from balance sheets to policy decisions.

Forms of ◊inflation accounting, such as CCA (current cost accounting) and CPP (current purchasing power) are aimed at providing valid financial comparisons over a period in which money values change.

Accra /ə'krɑː/ capital and port of Ghana; population of Greater Accra region (1984) 1,420,000. The port trades in cacao, gold, and timber. Industries include engineering, brewing, and food

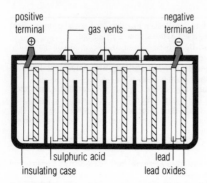

positive terminal ⊕ — gas vents — negative terminal ⊖

sulphuric acid | lead

insulating case | lead oxides

accumulator

processing. Osu (Christiansborg) Castle is the presidential residence.

Accrington /ˈåkrɪŋtən/ industrial town (textiles, engineering) in Lancashire, England; population (1981) 36,000.

accumulator in electricity, a storage battery–that is, a group of rechargeable secondary cells. An ordinary 12-volt car battery is an accumulator consisting of six lead-acid cells which are continually recharged by the car's alternator or dynamo. It has electrodes of lead and lead oxide in an electrolyte of sulphuric acid.

Another common type of accumulator is the 'nife' or Ni-Fe cell, which has electrodes of nickel and iron in a potassium hydroxide electrolyte.

accumulator a collective bet on several races, such that the winnings from one race are carried forward as the stake on the next, resulting in a potentially enormous return for a small initial stake.

accusative in the grammar of some inflected languages, such as Latin, Greek, or Russian, the accusative case is the form of a noun, pronoun, or adjective used to indicate that it is the direct object of a verb. It is also used with certain prepositions.

Acer genus of trees and shrubs of N temperate regions with over 115 species. *Acer* includes the ◊sycamores and ◊maples.

acetaldehyde common name for ◊ethanal.

acetate common name for ◊ethanoate.

acetic acid common name for ◊ethanoic acid.

acetone common name for ◊propanone.

acetylene common name for ◊ethyne.

acetylsalicylic acid chemical name for the painkilling drug ◊aspirin.

Achaea /əˈkiːə/ in ancient Greece, and also today, an area of the N Peloponnese; the *Achaeans* were the predominant society during the Mycenaean period and are said by Homer to have taken part in the siege of Troy.

Achaean League union in 275 BC of most of the cities of the N Peloponnese, which managed to defeat ◊Sparta, but was itself defeated by the Romans 146 BC.

Achaemenid dynasty /əˈkiːmənɪdz/ dynasty ruling the Persian Empire 550–330 BC, and named after Achaemenes, ancestor of Cyrus the Great, founder of the empire. His successors included Cambyses, Darius I, Xerxes, and Darius III, who, as the last Achaemenid ruler, was killed after defeat in battle against Alexander the Great in 330 BC.

Achates character in the *Aeneid*, an epic poem by the Roman poet Virgil from the 1st century BC. Achates was the friend of the hero Aeneas, hence a *fidus* (Latin 'faithful'). The name is proverbial for a faithful companion.

Achebe /əˈtʃeɪbɪ/ Chinua 1930– . Nigerian novelist, whose themes include the social and political impact of European colonialism on African people, and the problems of newly independent African nations. His first novel, *Things Fall Apart* 1958, was widely acclaimed; *Anthills of the Savannah* 1987 is also set

acid rain

As industry has expanded since the industrial revolution, the quantity of waste gases and smoke given off by factories has increased enormously. As a result more and more chemical pollutants are being added to the atmosphere. Fossil fuels, such as coal, oil, and gas, contain sulphur which is given off when they are burnt. The chemicals produced can alter the acidity of the rain and cause severe damage to plant life, lakes, and the water supply.

Sulphur dioxide (SO_2) and nitrogen oxides (NO_2) are given off with the smoke when fossil fuels burn.

A tree is damaged in a number of ways. The bark and leaves are damaged by the direct effects. The change in pH of the ground water makes the roots less effective. Fewer nutrients pass up into the tree, making it more susceptible to damage. Leaves and needles fall off and the crowns thin and die.

H_2SO_4
HNO_3
SO_2
NO_2
HNO_3

Some of the gases go directly into plants and into the ground, but most are oxidized to sulphuric acid (H_2SO_4) and nitric acid (HNO_3). These acids, dissolved in rainwater, rain down often a great distance away.

Direct effects of chemicals in the atmosphere are felt within a few kilometres of the emission. These include the deterioration of buildings and harm to human health.

Indirect effects, due to chemical changes in the ground water, can be felt thousands of kilometres away.

Sometimes lime is dropped into an acid lake to neutralize it, but this is only a temporary measure.

Acidity is measured in pH. The lower the pH value the higher the acidity. In a lake (or river) affected by acid rain, different creatures die at different pH values.

death in lakes and rivers

1. Crustaceans and snails die
2. Salmon and trout die
3. Sensitive insects die
4. Whitefish and grayling die
5. Perch and pike die
6. Eel and brook trout die

pH 7.5   7.0 (neutral) 6.5   6.0   5.5   5.0   4.5   4.0   3.5

in a fictional African country. Nobel prize 1989.

achene a dry, one-seeded ◊fruit that develops from a single ◊ovary and does not split open to disperse the seed. Achenes commonly occur in groups, for example the fruiting heads of buttercup (*Ranunculus*) and clematis. The outer surface may be smooth, spiny, ribbed, or tuberculate, depending on the species.

An achene with part of the fruit wall extended to form a membranous wing is called a **samara**; an example is the pendulous fruit of the ash (*Fraxinus*). During the development of a ◊caryopsis, the ◊carpel wall becomes fused to the seed coat; this type of fruit is typical of grasses and cereals. A cypsela is derived from an inferior ovary and is characteristic of the daisy family (Compositae). It often has a pappus of hairs attached, which aids its dispersal by the wind, as in the dandelion.

Achernar brightest star in the constellation Eridanus, and the ninth-brightest star in the sky. It is a hot, luminous blue giant with a true

luminosity 650 times that of the Sun. It is 120 light years away.

Acheson /ˈåtʃɪsən/ Dean (Gooderham) 1893–1971. US politician; as undersecretary of state 1945–47 in ◊Truman's Democratic administration, he was associated with George C ◊Marshall in preparing the Marshall Plan, and succeeded him as secretary of state 1949–53.

He helped establish NATO, and criticized Britain for having 'lost an empire and not yet found a role'.

Achilles /əˈkɪliːz/ Greek hero of Homer's ◊*Iliad*. He was the son of Peleus, king of the Myrmidons in Thessaly, and the sea nymph Thetis, who rendered him invulnerable, except for the heel by which she held him, by dipping him in the river Styx. Achilles killed Hector in the Trojan War and was himself killed by Paris who shot a poisoned arrow into Achilles' heel.

Achilles tendon the tendon pinning the calf muscle to the heelbone. It is one of the largest in the human body.

Achill Island /ˈåkɪl/ or *Eagle Island* largest of the Irish islands, off County Mayo; area 148 sq km/57 sq mi.

achromatic lens combination of lenses made from glasses of different refractive index, constructed in such a way as to minimize chromatic aberration (which in a single lens causes coloured fringes round images because the lens diffracts the different wavelengths in white light to slightly different extents).

acid a substance which, in solution in an ionizing solvent (usually water), gives rise to hydrogen ions (H+ or protons). Acids react with alkalis to form salts, and they act as solvents. Strong acids are corrosive; dilute acids have a sour or sharp taste, although in some organic acids this may be partially masked by other flavour characteristics.

Acids can be detected by using coloured indicators such as litmus and methyl orange. The strength of an acid is measured by its hydrogen ion concentration, indicated by the ◊pH value. The first known acid was vinegar (ethanoic or acetic acid). Inorganic acids include boric, carbonic, hydrochloric, hydrofluoric, nitric, phosphoric, sulphuric. Organic acids include acetic, benzoic, citric, formic, lactic, oxalic and salicylic.

acid house a type of pop ◊house music. The derivation of the term is disputed but may be from 'acid burning', Chicago slang for 'sampling', a recording technique much featured in acid house (see ◊digital sampling).

acid rain acidic rainfall thought to be caused principally by the release into the atmosphere of sulphur dioxide (SO_2) from coal-burning power stations. Acid gases, especially those of nitrogen oxides, are also contributed from other industrial activities and automobile exhaust fumes.

It is linked with damage to and death of forests and lake organisms, especially in Scandinavia, Europe, and eastern North America. In 1986 Britain emitted 1,937,000 tonnes of nitrogen oxides to the atmosphere, 40% from power stations, 40% from cars.

acid salt chemical compound formed by the partial neutralization of a dibasic or tribasic ◊acid (one that contains two or three hydrogen atoms). Although a salt, it contains replaceable hydrogen, so it may undergo the typical reactions of an acid. Examples are sodium hydrogen sulphate, $NaHSO_4$, and acid phosphates.

aclinic line the magnetic equator, an imaginary line near the equator, where the compass needle balances horizontally, where the attraction of the north and south magnetic poles is equal.

acne skin eruption caused by inflammation of the sebaceous glands which secrete an oily substance (sebum), the natural lubricant of the skin. Sometimes their openings become stopped and they swell; the contents decompose and pimples form.

Aconcagua /ˌåkənˈkågwə/ an extinct volcano in the Argentine Andes, the highest peak in the Americas. Height 6,960 m/22,834 ft. It

aclinic line

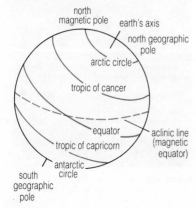

north magnetic pole
earth's axis
north geographic pole
arctic circle
tropic of cancer
equator
aclinic line (magnetic equator)
tropic of capricorn
antarctic circle
south geographic pole

was first climbed by Vines and Zeebruggen in 1897.

aconite herbaceous plant *Aconitum napellus* of the buttercup family, with hooded blue-mauve flowers, commonly known as **monkshood**. It produces aconitine, a powerful alkaloid with narcotic and analgesic properties.

There are about 100 species of the genus *Aconitum* throughout the N temperate regions, all of which contain poison. *Winter aconite Eranthus hyemalis* also belongs to the buttercup family, but has yellow buttercup-like flowers with six petals and a ruff of leaves below.

acorn fruit of the oak tree, a nut growing in a shallow cup.

acouchi any of several small South American rodents, genus *Myoprocta*. They have white-tipped tails, and are smaller relatives of the ◊agouti.

acoustic in music, a performance or instrument sounding without electrical amplification or assistance. In architecture, the sound-reflecting character of a room.

acoustic ohm c.g.s. unit of acoustic impedance (the ratio of the sound pressure on a surface to the sound flux through the surface). It is analogous to the ohm as the unit of electrical ◊impedance.

acoustics in general, the experimental and theoretical science of sound; in particular, that branch of the science that has to do with the phenomena of sound in space.

Acoustical engineering is concerned with the technical control of sound, and involves architecture and building, studying control of vibration, soundproofing, and the elimination of noise; it also includes all forms of sound recording and reinforcement, the hearing and perception of sounds, and hearing aids.

Acquaviva /ˌåkwəˈviːvə/ Claudius 1543–1615. Neapolitan general of the Jesuits from 1581 and one of their most able organizers and educators.

acquired character a feature of the body that develops during the lifetime of an individual, usually as a result of repeated use or disuse, such as the enlarged muscles of a weightlifter. ◊Lamarck's theory of evolution assumed that acquired characters were passed from parent to offspring.

Modern evolutionary theory does not recognize the inheritance of acquired characters because there is no reliable scientific evidence that it occurs, and because no mechanism is known whereby bodily changes can influence the genetic material. See also ◊central dogma.

acquired immune deficiency syndrome full name for the disease ◊AIDS.

acquittal in law, the setting free of someone charged with a crime after a trial. In English courts it follows a verdict of 'not guilty', but in Scotland the verdict may be either 'not guilty' or 'not proven'. Acquittal by the jury must be confirmed by the judge.

acre traditional English land measure (4,047 sq m/ 4,840 sq yd/0.405 ha). Originally meaning a field, it was the size that a yoke of oxen could plough in a day.

As early as Edward I's reign the acre was standardized by statute for official use, although local variations in Ireland, Scotland and some English counties continued.

Acre /ˈeɪkə/ or *'Akko* seaport in Israel; population (1983) 37,000. Taken by the Crusaders 1104, it was captured by ◊Saladin 1187 and retaken by ◊Richard I (the Lionheart) 1191. Napoleon failed in a siege 1799; Gen ◊Allenby captured it 1918; and it became part of Israel 1948.

acre-foot unit sometimes used to measure large volumes of water, such as the capacity of a reservoir (equal to its area in acres multiplied by its average depth in feet). 1 acre-foot equals 1,233.5 cu m.

acridine an organic compound which occurs in crude anthracene oil, extracted by dilute acids. It is also obtained synthetically. It is used to make many dyestuffs and some valuable drugs.

acromegaly the unsightly enlargement of prominent parts of the body, for example hands, feet, and – more conspicuously – the eyebrow ridges and lower jaw, caused by excessive output of growth hormone in adult life by the ◊pituitary gland.

acronym a word formed from the initial letters and/or syllables of other words, intended as a pronounceable abbreviation, for example *NATO* (*North Atlantic Treaty Organization*).

acrophobia a ◊phobia involving fear of heights.

acropolis citadel of an ancient Greek town. The Acropolis at Athens contains the ruins of the Parthenon, built there during the days of the Athenian empire. The term is also used for analogous structures, as in the massive granite-built ruins of Great ◊Zimbabwe.

acrostic a number of lines of writing, especially verse, whose initial letters (read downwards) form a word, phrase, or sentence. A *single acrostic* is formed by the initial letters of lines only, while a *double acrostic* is formed by both initial and final letters.

acrylic acid common name for ◊propenoic acid.

ACT abbreviation for ◊*Australian Capital Territory*.

ACTH (*adreno-cortico-tropic hormone*) a ◊hormone, secreted by the ◊pituitary gland, which controls the production of corticosteroid hormones by the ◊adrenal gland. It is commonly produced as a response to stress.

actinide chemical element with atomic numbers 89–105. All actinides are radioactive, and synthetic above uranium (atomic number 92). They are grouped because of their chemical similarities, and also by analogy with the rare-earth elements (lanthanides).

actinium rare radioactive element, atomic number 89, relative atomic mass of most stable isotope 227; the first of the ◊actinide series and a weak emitter of high-energy alpha-rays. It is made by bombarding radium with neutrons.

actinium K original name given in 1939 by its discoverer (the French scientist Marguerite Perey) to the radioactive element later (1947) called ◊francium.

action in law, one of the proceedings whereby a person enforces his or her rights in a law court. Actions fall into three principal categories, namely civil (such as the enforcement of a debt), penal (where a punishment is sought for the person sued), and criminal (where in Britain the Crown prosecutes a person accused of an offence).

action and reaction in physical mechanics, equal and opposite effects produced by a force acting on an object. For example, the pressure of expanding gases from the burning of fuel in a rocket motor (a force) produces an equal and opposite reaction which causes the rocket to move.

Action Française French extreme nationalist political movement founded 1899, first led by Charles Maurras (1868–1952); it claimed to represent the essential unity of all French people in contrast to socialist doctrines of class warfare. Its influence peaked in the 1920s.

Initially nationalist and republican, opposed to capitalism and parliamentarism, it became from 1914 predominantly nationalist. In the 1920s the movement obtained a degree of respectability through an alliance with the former prime minister Clemenceau and seats in the chamber of deputies. By the 1930s, Action Française had been superseded by more radical right-wing movements such as the Jeunesses Patriotes and the Croix de Feu.

action painting or *gesture painting* in US art, the most dynamic school of Abstract Expressionism. It emphasized the importance of the physical act of painting, sometimes expressed with both inventiveness and aggression, and on occasion performed for the camera. Jackson Pollock was the leading exponent.

Pollock was known to place his canvas on the floor, attacking it with knives and and trowels, throwing paint at it, and bicycling over it. The term 'action painting' was coined by the US art critic Harold Rosenberg in 1952.

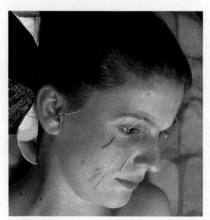

acupuncture *A woman patient being treated for persistent headaches by acupuncture.*

action potential in biology, a change in the potential difference (voltage) across the membrane of a nerve cell when an impulse passes along it. The potential change (from about −60 to +45 millivolts) accompanies the passage of sodium and potassium ions across the membrane.

Actium, Battle of naval battle in which ◊Augustus defeated the combined fleets of ◊Mark Antony and ◊Cleopatra in 31 BC. The site is at Akri, a promontory in W Greece.

activation energy in chemistry, the energy required to start a chemical reaction. Some elements and compounds will react together merely by bringing them into contact (spontaneous reaction). For others it is necessary to supply energy in order to start the reaction, even if there is ultimately a net output of energy. This initial energy is the activation energy.

act of Congress in the USA, a bill or resolution passed by both houses of Congress, the Senate and the House of Representatives, which then becomes law unless it is vetoed by the president. If vetoed, it may still become a law if it is returned to Congress again and passed by a majority of two-thirds in each house.

act of God legal term meaning some sudden and irresistible act of nature which could not reasonably have been foreseen, such as extraordinary storms, snow, frost, or sudden death.

act of indemnity in Britain, an act of Parliament relieving someone from the consequences of some action or omission which, at the time it took place, was illegal or of doubtful legality.

Adam *Inspired by Roman and Greek models, Robert Adam based his style on the principle that exterior, interior, and furnishings should blend into a harmonious whole. This portrait is attributed to G Willison and dates from 1770–75.*

Adams *US photographer Ansel Adams.*

act of Parliament in Britain, a change in the law originating in Parliament and called a statute. Such acts may be either public (of general effect), local, or private. Before an act receives the royal assent and becomes law it is a 'bill'. The body of English statute law comprises all the acts passed by Parliament: the existing list opens with the Statute of Merton, passed in 1235. An act (unless it is stated to be for a definite period and then to come to an end) remains on the statute book until it is repealed. See also ◊act of Congress.

How an act of Parliament becomes law:

1 first reading of the bill The title is read out in the House of Commons (H of C) and a minister names a day for the second reading.

2 the bill is officially printed.

3 second reading A debate on the whole bill in the H of C followed by a vote on whether or not the bill should go on to the next stage.

4 committee stage A committee of MPs considers the bill in detail and makes amendments.

5 report stage The bill is referred back to the H of C which may make further amendments.

6 third reading The H of C votes whether the bill should be sent on to the House of Lords.

7 House of Lords The bill passes through much the same stages in the Lords as in the H of C. (Bills may be introduced in the Lords, in which case the H of C considers them at this stage.)

8 last amendments The H of C considers any Lords' amendments, and may make further amendments which must usually be agreed by the Lords.

9 royal assent. The Queen gives her formal assent.

10 The bill becomes an act of Parliament at royal assent, although it may not come into force until a day appointed in the act.

Acton /'ăktən/ Eliza 1799–1859. English cookery writer and poet, whose *Modern Cookery for Private Families* 1845 influenced Mrs Beeton.

Acton /'ăktən/ John Emerich Edward Dalberg-Acton, 1st Baron Acton 1834–1902. British historian and Liberal politician. Elected to Parliament in 1859, he was a friend and adviser of Gladstone. Appointed professor of modern history at Cambridge in 1895, he planned and edited the *Cambridge Modern History*, but died after completing the first two volumes.

Actors Studio theatre workshop in New York City, established 1947 by Cheryl Crawford and Elia Kazan. Under Lee Strasberg, who became artistic director 1948, it became known for the study of Stanislavsky's ◊Method acting.

Acts of the Apostles book of the New Testament, attributed to St ◊Luke, which describes the history of the early Christian church.

actuary a mathematician who makes statistical calculations concerning human life expectancy and other risks, on which insurance premiums are based. Professional bodies are the Institute of Actuaries (England, 1848), Faculty of Actuaries (Scotland, 1856), and Society of Actuaries (US, 1949, by a merger of two earlier bodies).

acupuncture system developed in ancient China of inserting needles into the body at predetermined points to relieve pain and assist healing. The method, increasingly popular in the West, is thought to work partly by stimulating the brain's own painkillers, or endorphins.

acute in medicine, pertaining to a condition which develops and resolves quickly, for example the common cold, or meningitis. In contrast, a *chronic* condition develops over a long period.

acute angle an ◊angle between 0° and 90°.

ACV abbreviation for *air-cushion vehicle*. See ◊hovercraft.

AD abbreviation for *anno Domini* (Latin 'in the year of the Lord').

ADA computer-programming language, developed and owned by the US Department of Defense, designed for use in situations where the computer directly controls a process or machine, such as a military aircraft. The language took over five years to specify, and only became commercially available in the late 1980s. It is named after Ada ◊Lovelace, regarded as the world's first computer programmer.

Adam /'ădəm/ family of Scottish architects and designers. *William Adam* (1689–1748) was the leading Scottish architect of his day, and his son *Robert Adam* (1728–92) is considered one of the greatest British architects of the late 18th century. He transformed the prevailing Palladian fashion in architecture to a Neo-Classical style. He designed interiors for many great country houses (Harewood House, Yorkshire; Luton Hoo, Luton;). With his brother *James Adam* (1732–94), also an architect, he speculatively developed the the Adelphi near Charing Cross, London, largely rebuilt 1936.

Adam /'ădəm/ (Hebrew *adham* 'man') in the Old Testament, founder of the human race. Formed by God from the dust and given the breath of life, Adam was placed in the Garden of Eden, where ◊Eve was given to him as a companion. With her, he tasted the forbidden fruit of the Tree of Knowledge of Good

Adams *John Quincy Adams, 6th president of the USA, painted by Chapel. He travelled widely as a diplomat before a term as Monroe's secretary of state, and succeeded Monroe as president in 1825.*

adder

puff adder

and Evil, and they were expelled from the Garden.

Adam /å'dɒŋ/ Adolphe Charles 1803–1856. French composer of light operas. Some 50 of his works were staged, including the classic ballet *Giselle*.

Adam de la Halle /å'dɒm də lɑ: 'ɑ̈l/ *c.*1240–*c.*1290. French poet and composer. His *Jeu de Robin et Marion*, written in Italy about 1282, is a theatrical work with dialogue and songs set to what were apparently popular tunes of the day. It is sometimes called the forerunner of comic opera.

Adams /'ådəmz/ Ansel 1902–1984. US photographer, known for his printed images of dramatic landscapes and organic forms of the American West. He was associated with the ◊Zone System of exposure estimation.

Adams /'ådəmz/ Gerry (Gerard) 1948– . Northern Ireland politician, president of Provisional Sinn Féin (the political wing of the IRA). He was elected a member of Parliament 1983 but declined to take up his Westminster seat. He has been criticized for failing to denounce IRA violence. In the 1970s, because of his connections with the IRA, he was interned and later released.

Adams /'ådəmz/ Henry Brooks 1838–1918. US historian, the grandson of President John Quincy Adams; he wrote *Mont-Saint-Michel and Chartres* 1904, and a classic autobiography *The Education of Henry Adams* 1907.

Adams /'ådəmz/ John 1735–1826. 2nd president of the USA 1797–1801, and vice president 1789–97. Born at Quincy, Massachusetts. He was a member of the Continental Congress, 1774–78, and signed the Declaration of Independence. In 1779 he went to France and negotiated the treaties that ended the War of American Independence. In 1785 he became the first US ambassador in London.

Adams /'ådəmz/ John Coolidge 1947– . US composer and conductor, director of the New Music Ensemble 1972–81, and artistic adviser to the San Francisco Symphony Orchestra from 1978. His works include *Electric Wake* 1968, *Heavy Metal* 1971, *Bridge of Dreams* 1982, and the opera *Nixon in China* 1988.

Adams /'ådəmz/ John Couch 1819–1892. English astronomer, who deduced the existence of the planet Neptune 1845.

Adams /'ådəmz/ John Quincy 1767–1848. 6th president of the USA 1825–29. Eldest son of President John ◊Adams, he was born at Quincy, Massachusetts, and became US minister in The Hague, Berlin, St Petersburg, and London. In 1817 he became ◊Monroe's secretary of state, formulated the ◊Monroe doctrine 1823, and succeeded him in the presidency, despite receiving fewer votes than his main rival, Andrew ◊Jackson. As president, Adams was an advocate of strong federal government.

Adams /'ædəmz/ Neil 1958– . English judo champion. He won two junior and five senior European titles 1974–85, eight senior national titles, and two Olympic silver medals 1980, 1984. In 1981 he was world champion in the 78 kg class.

Adams /'ådəmz/ Richard 1920– . British novelist. A civil servant 1948–72, he wrote *Watership Down* 1972, a tale of a rabbit community, which is read by adults and children. Later novels include *The Plague Dogs* 1977 and *Girl on a Swing* 1980.

Adams /'ådəmz/ Roger 1889–1971. US organic chemist, known for his painstaking analytical work to determine the composition of naturally occuring substances such as complex vegetable oils and plant ◊alkaloids.

Addison *Kneller's portrait of the British essayist and poet Joseph Addison was done for the dining room of the Kit-Cat Club. The pictures were less than half-length because the room was so low, hence portraits to the waist are still called 'kit-cat'.*

Adams /'ådəmz/ Samuel 1722–1803. US politician, second cousin of President John Adams; he was the chief prompter of the Boston Tea Party (see War of ◊American Independence). He was also a signatory of the Declaration of Independence, and anticipated the French emperor Napoleon in calling the British a 'nation of shopkeepers'.

Adamson /'ådəmsən/ Joy 1910–1985. German-born author and painter, who worked with wildlife in Kenya, including the lioness Elsa described in *Born Free* 1960. She was murdered at her home in Kenya. She worked with her third husband, British game warden **George Adamson** (1906–1989), who was murdered by bandits.

Adamson /'ådəmsən/ Robert R 1821–1848. Scottish photographer who, with David Octavius Hill, produced 2,500 ◊calotypes (mostly portraits) in five years from 1843.xxx

Adana /'ådənə/ capital of Adana (Seyhan) province, S Turkey; population (1985) 776,000. It is a major cotton-growing centre and Turkey's fourth largest city.

adaptation in biology, any change in the structure or function of an organism that allows it to survive and reproduce more effectively in its environment. In ◊evolution, adaptation occurs as a result of random variation in the genetic make-up of organisms (produced by ◊mutation and ◊recombination) coupled with natural selection.

adaptive radiation in evolution, the production of several new species, with adaptations to different ways of life, from a single parent stock. Adaptive radiation is likely to occur whenever a species enters a new habitat that contains few, if any, similar species.

ADB abbreviation for ◊*Asian Development Bank*.

Addams /'ådəmz/ Charles 1912–1988. US cartoonist, creator of the gothically ghoulish Addams family in the *New Yorker* magazine. There was a successful television series based on the cartoon in the 1960s.

Addams /'ådəmz/ Jane 1860–1935. US sociologist and feminist, who in 1889 founded and led the social settlement of Hull House, Chicago, one of the earliest community centres. She was Vice-President of the National American Woman Suffrage Association 1911–14, and in 1915 led the Woman's Peace Party and the first Women's Peace Congress. She shared a Nobel prize 1931. Her publications include *Newer Ideals of Peace* 1907 and *Twenty Years at Hull House* 1910.

addax light-coloured ◊antelope *Addax nasomaculatus* of the Sahara desert, where it exists on the scanty vegetation without drinking. It is about 1.1 m/3.5 ft at the shoulder and both sexes have spirally twisted horns.

added value in economics, the difference between the cost of producing something and the price at which it is sold. Added value is the basis of VAT (◊value-added tax), a tax on the value added at each stage of the production process of a commodity.

addendum (Latin) something to be added.

adder venomous European snake *Vipera berus*, belonging to the viper family. Growing to about 60 cm/2 ft long, it has a thick body, triangular head, a characteristic V-shaped mark on its head, and often, zig-zag markings along the back. A shy animal, it feeds on small mammals and lizards. The *puff adder Bitis arietans* is a large yellowish thick-bodied viper up to 1.6 m/5 ft long living in Africa and Arabia. The adder is the only poisonous snake found in Britain.

addiction state of dependence on drugs, alcohol, or other substances. Symptoms include uncontrolled craving, tolerance, and withdrawal. Habitual use produces changes in chemical processes in the brain; when the substance is withheld, severe neurological manifestations, even death, may follow. These are reversed by the administration of the addictive substance, and mitigated by a gradual reduction in dosage.

Initially, only opium and its derivatives (morphine, heroin, codeine) were recognized as addictive, but many other drugs, whether therapeutic (for example, tranquillizers or ergotamine) or recreational (including cocaine and alcohol), are now known to be addictive.

Research points to a genetic predisposition to addiction; environment and psychological make-up are also important. Although physical addiction always has a psychological element, not all psychological dependence is accompanied by physical dependence. A carefully controlled withdrawal programme can reverse the chemical changes of habituation. A cure is more difficult because of the many other factors contributing to addiction.

adding machine device for adding numbers, usually operated mechanically or electro-mechanically; now largely superseded by electronic ◊calculators.

Addington /'ådɪŋtən/ Henry 1757–1844. British Tory prime minister 1801–04, later Viscount ◊Sidmouth.

Addis Ababa /'ådɪs 'åbəbə/ or *Adis Abeba* capital of Ethiopia; population (1984) 1,413,000. It was founded 1887 by Menelik, chief of Shoa, who ascended the throne of Ethiopia 1889. His former residence, Menelik Palace, is now occupied by the government; the city is the headquarters of the Organization of African Unity.

Addison /'ådɪsn/ Joseph 1672–1719. British writer. In 1704 he celebrated ◊Marlborough's victory at Blenheim in a poem, 'The Campaign', and subsequently held political appointments, including under-secretary of state and secretary to the Lord-Lieutenant of Ireland 1708. In 1709 he contributed to the *Tatler*, begun by Richard ◊Steele, with whom he was co-founder in 1711 of the *Spectator*.

Addison /'ådɪsn/ Thomas 1793–1863. British physician who first recognized the condition known as Addison's disease in 1855.

Addison's disease rare deficiency of the ◊adrenal glands which is treated with hormones.

addition reaction a chemical reaction in which the atoms of an element or compound react with a double bond or triple bond in an organic compound by opening up one of the bonds and becoming attached to it, for example $CH_2=CH_2 +HCl$ CH_3CH_2Cl. An example is the addition of hydrogen atoms to ◊unsaturated compounds in vegetable oils to produce margarine.

additive in food, a chemical added to prolong shelf life (such as salt), alter colour, or improve food value (such as vitamins or minerals). Many chemical additives are used in the manufacture of food. They are subject to regulation since individuals may be affected by constant exposure to even small concentrations of certain additives and suffer side effects such as hyperactivity. Within the European Community, approved additives are given an official ◊E number.

flavours may be natural or artificial. They are said to increase the appeal of the food. Enhancers may also be used, such as monosodium glutamate. Artificial sweeteners are widely used in beverages.

colours can be natural or artificial. They are said to increase the appeal of the food.

nutrients replace or enhance food value. Minerals and vitamins are added where the diet would otherwise be deficient, leading to diseases such as beri-beri and pellagra.

preservatives are antioxidants and antimicrobials that control natural oxidation and the action of microorganisms. See ◊food technology.

emulsifiers and *surfactants* regulate the consistency of fats in the food and the surface of the food where it is in contact with the air.

thickeners, primarily vegetable gums, regulate the consistency of the product. Pectin acts in this way on fruit products.

leavening agents lighten the texture of baked goods without the use of yeasts. Sodium bicarbonate is an example.

bleaching agents assist in the ageing of flours and so improve the quality of baked goods.

anti-caking agents prevent powdered products coagulating into solid lumps.

humectants control the humidity of the product by absorbing and retaining moisture.

clarifying agents are used in fruit juices, vinegars, and other fermented liquids. Gelatin is the most common.

firming agents restore the texture of vegetables that may be damaged during processing.

foam regulators are used in beer to provide a controlled 'head' on top of the poured product.

Addled Parliament the English Parliament that met for two months in 1614 but which failed to pass a single bill before being dissolved by James I.

address in a computer memory, a number indicating a specific location. At each address, a single piece of data can be stored. For microcomputers, this normally amounts to one ◊byte (enough to represent a single character such as a letter or number).

The maximum capacity of a computer memory depends on how many memory addresses it can have. This is normally measured in units of 1,024 bytes (known as kilobytes, or K).

Adelaide /'ådıleıd/ 1792–1849. Queen consort of ◊William IV of England. Daughter of the Duke of Saxe-Meiningen, she married William, then Duke of Clarence, in 1818. No children of the marriage survived infancy.

Adelaide /'ådıleıd/ capital and industrial city of South Australia; population (1986) 993,100. Industries include oil refining, shipbuilding, and the

Adenauer *German politician Konrad Adenauer, 1949.*

adaptation

The beaks of birds are adapted to suit their diet

toucan
long beak to pick berries from thin twigs

hummingbird
long, pointed beak to reach nectar deep inside flowers

eagle
sharp, hooked beak to tear flesh from prey

nightjar
wide gape and bristles around beak to trap flying insects

spoonbill
swings long, wide beak from side to side underwater to capture fish and aquatic insects

skimmer
scoops up fish and traps them in its scissor-like beak

oystercatcher
long, straight beak to prise open shells of bivalve molluscs, such as mussels

manufacture of electrical goods and cars. Grain, wool, fruit, and wine are exported. Founded in 1836, Adelaide was named after William IV's queen.

It is a fine example of town planning, with residential districts separated from the commercial area by the river Torrens, dammed to form a lake. Impressive streets include King William Street and North Terrace, and fine buildings include Parliament House, Government House, the Anglican cathedral of St Peter, the Roman Catholic cathedral, two universities, the State observatory, and the museum and art gallery.

Adélie Land /ə'deɪlɪ/ (French *Terre Adélie*) region of Antarctica claimed by France; mountainous, covered in snow and ice, and inhabited only by a research team. It was claimed for France 1840.

Aden /'eɪdn/ (Arabic *'Adan*) capital of South Yemen, on a rocky peninsula at the SW corner of Arabia, commanding the entrance to the Red Sea; population (1984) 318,000. It comprises the new administrative centre Madinet al-Sha'ab; the commercial and business quarters of Crater and Tawahi, and the harbour area of Ma'alla. The city's economy is based on oil refining, fishing, and shipping. A British territory from 1839, Aden became part of independent South Yemen 1967.
history After annexation by Britain, Aden and its immediately surrounding area (121 sq km/ 47 sq mi) were developed as a ship refuelling station following the opening of the Suez Canal 1869.

It was a colony 1937–63, and then, after a period of transitional violence between rival nationalist groups and British forces, was combined with the former Aden protectorate (290,000 sq km/112,000 sq mi) to create the Southern Yemen People's Republic 1967, later re-named the People's Democratic Republic of Yemen.

Adenauer /'ådənaʊə/ Konrad 1876–1967. German Christian Democrat politician, chancellor of West Germany 1949–63. With the French president de Gaulle he achieved the postwar reconciliation of France and Germany and strongly supported all measures designed to strengthen the Western bloc in Europe.

Adenauer was mayor of his native city of Cologne from 1917 until his imprisonment by Hitler in 1933 for opposition to the Nazi regime. After the war he headed the Christian Democratic Union and became chancellor; he was known as the 'Old Fox'. He supported the UK's entry into the Common Market (now the European Community).

adenoids masses of lymphoid tissue, similar to ◊tonsils, located in the upper part of the throat. They are part of a child's natural defences against the entry of germs but usually shrink and disappear by the age of ten.

Adenoids may swell and grow, particularly if infected, and block the breathing passages. If they become repeatedly infected, they may be removed surgically (adenoidectomy).

Ader /å'deə/ Clement 1841–1925. French aviation pioneer whose steam-driven aeroplane, the *Éole*, made the first powered take-off in history (1890), but it could not fly. In 1897, with his *Avion III*, he failed completely, despite false claims made later.

adhesion in medicine, the abnormal binding of two tissues as a result of inflammation. The moving surfaces of joints or internal organs may merge together if they have been inflamed.

adhesive substance that sticks two surfaces together. Natural adhesives include gelatine in its crude industrial form (made from bones, hide fragments and fish offal), and vegetable gums. Synthetic adhesives include thermoplastic and thermosetting resins, which are often stronger than the substances they join; mixtures of epoxy resin and hardener that set by chemical reaction; and elastomeric (stretching) adhesives for flexible joints.

adiabatic the expansion or contraction of a gas in which a change takes place in the pressure or volume, although no heat is allowed to enter or leave.

Adige /'ɑ:dɪdʒeɪ/ the second longest river (after the Po) in Italy, 410 km/255 mi in length. It crosses the Lombardy Plain and enters the Adriatic just north of the Po delta.

Adi Granth /'ɑ:di 'grʌ:nθ/ or *Guru Granth Sahib* the holy book of Sikhism.

ad infinitum (Latin) to infinity, endlessly.

adipose tissue a type of ◊connective tissue of vertebrates, the main energy store of the body. It is commonly called fat tissue, and consists of large spherical cells filled with fat. In mammals, major layers are in the inner layer of skin, and around the kidneys and heart.

Adirondacks /,ådə'rɒndåks/ mountainous area in NE New York State, USA; rising to 1,629 m/5,344 ft at Mount Marcy; the source of the Hudson and Ausable rivers; named after a native American people. It is noted for its scenery and sports facilities.

adit in mining, a horizontal shaft from the surface to reach the mineral seam. It was a common method of mining in hilly districts, and was also used to drain water.

adj. in grammar, abbreviation for *adjective*.

Adjani /,ɑ:dʒɔ'ni:/ Isabelle 1955– . French film actress of Algerian-German descent. She played the title role in Truffaut's *L'Histoire d'Adele H/The Story of Adele H.* 1975 and has since appeared in international productions including *La Locataire/The Tenant*; *Nosferatu Phantom der Nacht* 1979; *Ishtar* 1987.

adjective the grammatical ◊part of speech for words that describe nouns (for example, *new* and *enormous*, as in 'a new hat' and 'an enormous dog'). Adjectives generally have three degrees (grades or levels for the description of relationships): the positive degree (*new; enormous*) the comparative degree (*newer; more enormous*), and the superlative degree (*newest; most enormous*).

Some adjectives do not usually need comparative and superlative forms; one person cannot be 'more asleep' than someone else, a lone action is unlikely to be 'the most single-handed action ever seen', and many people dislike the expression 'most unique', because something unique is supposed to be the only one that there is. For purposes of emphasis or style these conventions may be set aside ('I don't know who is more unique; they are both remarkable people'). Double comparatives such as 'more bigger' are not grammatical in Standard English, but Shakespeare used a double superlative ('the most unkindest cut of all'). Some adjectives may have both of the comparative and superlative forms (*commoner* and *more common*; *commonest* and *most common*), usually shorter words take on the suffix er/est but occasionally they may be given the forms for longer words ('Which of them are the *most clear?*') for emphasis or other reasons.

When an adjective comes before a noun it is attributive; if it comes after noun and verb (for example, 'It looks *good*'), it is predicative. Some adjectives can only be used predicatively ('The child was asleep', but not 'the asleep child'). The participles of verbs are regularly used adjectivally ('a *sleeping* child', 'boiled milk') and often in compound forms ('a *quick-acting* medicine', 'a *glass-making* factory'; 'a *hard-boiled* egg', 'well-trained* teachers'). Adjectives are often formed by adding suffixes to nouns (sand: sandy; nation: nation*al*).

Adler /'ɑ:dlə/ Alfred 1870–1937. Austrian psychologist. Adler saw the 'will to power' as more influential in accounting for human behaviour than the sexual drive theory. Over this theory he parted company with ◊Freud after a ten-year collaboration.

Born in Vienna, he was a general practitioner and nerve specialist there 1897–1927, serving as an army doctor in World War I. He joined the circle of Freudian doctors in Vienna about 1900. The concepts of inferiority complex and overcompensation originated with Adler, for example in his books *Organic Inferiority and Psychic*

Compensation 1907 and *Understanding Human Nature* 1927.

Adler /'ɑ:dlə/ Larry 1914– . US musician, a virtuoso performer on the harmonica.

ad lib(itum) (Latin) 'freely' interpreted.

administrative law the law concerning the powers and control of government agencies (for example, ministers, government departments, and local authorities). These powers include making quasi-judicial decisions (such as determining planning applications) and detailed legislation by means of statutory instruments and orders. The vast increase in these powers in the 20th century in many countries has been criticised by lawyers.

In the UK powers delegated to ministers of the Crown are so wide that they sometimes enable ministers to make regulations which amend or override acts of Parliament. The courts can exercise some control over administrative action through ◊judicial review, for example a declaration that certain regulations are void because they exceed their authority (ultra vires). In the USA the Administrative Procedure Act 1946 was an attempt to cope with the problem.

admiral highest-ranking naval officer. In the UK Royal Navy and the US Navy, in descending order, the ranks of admiral are: admiral of the fleet (fleet admiral in the US), admiral, vice admiral, and rear admiral.

admiral several species of butterfly related to the tortoiseshells. The red admiral *Vanessa atalanta*, wingspan 6 cm/2.5 in, migrates each year to the Mediterranean from N Europe, where it cannot survive the winter.

Admiral's Cup sailing series first held in 1957 and held biennially. National teams consisting of four boats compete over three inshore courses (in the Solent) and two offshore courses (378 km/235 mi across the Channel from Cherbourg to the Isle of Wight and 1,045 km/650 mi from Plymouth to Fastnet lighthouse off Ireland, and back). The highlight is the Fastnet race.

Admiralty, Board of the in Britain, the controlling department of state for the Royal Navy from the reign of Henry VIII until 1964, when most of its functions–apart from that of management–passed to the Ministry of Defence. The 600-year-old office of Lord High Admiral reverted to the sovereign.

Admiralty Islands group of small islands in the SW Pacific, part of Papua New Guinea; population (1980) 25,000. The main island is Manus. The islands became a German protectorate 1884 and an Australian mandate 1920.

ad nauseam (Latin) to the point of disgust.

Adonis /ə'dəʊnɪs/ in Greek mythology, a beautiful youth beloved by the goddess ◊Aphrodite. He was killed while boar-hunting but was allowed to return from the lower world for six months every year to rejoin her. The anemone sprang from his blood.

Worshipped as a god of vegetation, he was known as *Tammuz* in Babylonia, Assyria, and Phoenicia (where it was his sister, ◊Ishtar, who brought him from the lower world). He seems also to have been identified with ◊Osiris, the Egyptian god of the underworld.

adoption the permanent legal transfer of parental rights and duties in respect of a child from one person to another. It was first legalized in England in 1926; in 1958 an adopted child was enabled to inherit if the adoptive parents died without leaving a will. The Children's Act 1975 enables an adopted child at the age of 18 to know its original name. See also ◊custody of children.

Adowa /'ådəwɑ:/ alternative form of ◊Aduwa, Ethiopia.

adrenal gland or *suprarenal gland* a gland situated on top of the kidney. The adrenals are soft and yellow, and consist of two parts. The *cortex* (outer part) secretes various steroid hormones, controls salt and water metabolism, and regulates the use of carbohydrates, proteins, and fats. The *medulla* (inner part) secretes the hormones adrenaline and noradrenaline which constrict the blood vessels of the belly and skin so that more blood is available for the heart, lungs, and voluntary muscles, an emergency preparation for the stress reaction 'fight or flight'.

adrenaline or *epinephrine* hormone secreted by the medulla of the ◊adrenal glands.

Adrian /ˈeɪdrɪən/ Edgar, 1st Baron Adrian 1889–1977. British physiologist. He received the Nobel prize for medicine in 1932 for his work with Sherrington in the field of nerve impulses.

Adrian IV /ˈeɪdrɪən/ (Nicholas Breakspear) *c.* 1100–1159. Pope 1154–59, the only British pope. He secured the execution of ◊Arnold of Brescia; crowned Frederick I Barbarossa as German emperor; refused Henry II's request that Ireland should be granted to the English crown in absolute ownership; and was at the height of a quarrel with the emperor when he died.

Adrianople /ˌeɪdrɪənˈəʊpəl/ older name of the Turkish town ◊Edirne, after the Emperor Hadrian, who rebuilt it about AD 125.

Adriatic Sea /ˌeɪdriˈætɪk/ large arm of the Mediterranean Sea, lying NW to SE between the Italian and the Balkan peninsulas. The western shore is Italian; the eastern Yugoslav and Albanian. The sea is about 805 km/500 mi long, and its area is 135,250 sq km/52,220 sq mi.

adsorption the taking up of a gas or liquid by the surface of a solid (for example, activated charcoal adsorbs gases). It involves molecular attraction at the surface, and should be distinguished from ◊absorption (in which a uniform solution results from a gas or liquid being incorporated into the bulk structure of a liquid or solid).

Adullam a biblical city with nearby caves in which David and those who had some grievance took refuge (1 Samuel 22). An Adullamite is a person who is disaffected or who secedes from a political party; the term was used to describe about 40 British Liberal MPs who voted against their leaders to defeat the 1866 Reform Bill.

adultery voluntary sexual intercourse by a married person with someone other than his or her legal partner. It is one factor which may prove 'irretrievable breakdown' of marriage in actions for judicial separation or ◊divorce in Britain. It is almost universally recognized as grounds for divorce in the USA, and is theoretically a punishable offence in some states.

Aduwa /ˈædəwɑː/ or *Adwa, Adowa* former capital of Ethiopia, about 180 km/110 mi SW of Massawa at an altitude of 1,910 m/6,270 ft; population (1982) 27,000.

Aduwa, Battle of /ˈædua/ defeat of the Italians by the Ethiopians at Aduwa in 1896 under Emperor ◊Menelik II. It marked the end of Italian ambitions in this part of Africa until Mussolini's reconquest in 1935.

adv. abbreviation for ◊*adverb*.

advanced gas-cooled reactor see ◊AGR.

Advent in the Christian calendar, the preparatory season for Christmas, including the four Sundays preceding it, beginning with the Sunday that falls nearest (before or after) St Andrew's Day (30 Nov).

Adventist a person who believes that Jesus will return to make a second appearance on the earth. Expectation of the Second Coming of Christ is found in New Testament writings generally. Adventist views are held by the Seventh-Day Adventists, Christadelphians, Jehovah's Witnesses, and the Four Square Gospel Alliance.

adverb the grammatical part of speech for words that modify or describe verbs ('She ran *quickly*'), adjectives ('a *beautifully* clear day'), and adverbs ('They did it *really* well'). Most adverbs are formed from adjectives or past participles by adding -*ly* (*quick: quickly*; or -*ally* (*automatic: automatically*).

Sometimes they are formed by adding -*wise* (*like: likewise* and *clockwise*, as in 'moving clockwise'; in 'a clockwise direction', *clockwise* is an adjective). Some adverbs have a distinct form

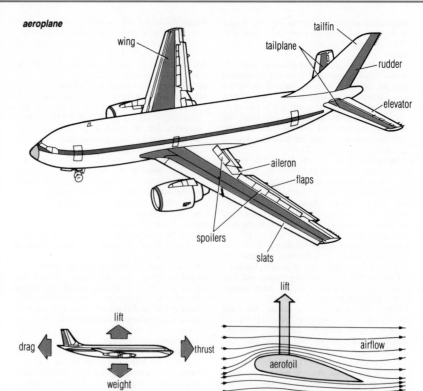

aeroplane

wing / tailplane / tailfin / rudder / elevator / aileron / flaps / spoilers / slats

lift / drag / thrust / weight

lift / airflow / aerofoil

from their partnering adjective, as with good/well ('It was *good* work; they did it *well*'). Others do not derive from adjectives (*very* in 'very nice'; *tomorrow* in 'I'll do it tomorrow'), and some are unadapted adjectives (*pretty*, as in, 'It's pretty good'). Sentence adverbs modify whole sentences or phrases: '*Generally*, it rains a lot here'; '*Usually*, the town is busy at this time of year'. Sometimes there is controversy in such matters. *Hopefully* is universally accepted in sentences like 'He looked at them hopefully' (= in a hopeful way), but some people dislike it in 'Hopefully, we'll see you again next year' (= We hope that we'll see you again next year).

advertising any of various methods used by a company to increase the sales of its products or to promote a brand name. Advertising can be seen by economists as either beneficial (since it conveys information about a product and so brings the market closer to a state of ◊perfect competition) or as a hindrance to perfect competition, since it attempts to make illusory distinction (such as greater sex appeal) between essentially similar products.

The UK's national advertising budget was £6 billion in 1988 (newspapers 40%; television 33%, magazines 20%; posters and radio taking the rest). The UK government spent over £120 million in 1988 on advertising.

Advertising Standards Authority (ASA) organization founded by the UK advertising industry 1962 to promote higher standards of advertising in the media (excluding television and radio, which have their own authority). It is financed by the advertisers, who pay 0.1% supplement on the cost of advertisements. It recommends to the media that advertisements which might breach the British Code of Advertising Practice are not published, but has no statutory power.

advocate (Latin *advocatus*, one summoned to one's aid, especially in a court of justice) a professional pleader in a court of justice. The English term is ◊barrister or counsel, but advocate is retained in Scotland and in other countries, such as France, whose legal systems are based on Roman law.

Advocate Judge manager of the prosecution in British courts martial.

Advocates, faculty of the professional organization for Scottish advocates, the equivalent of English ◊barristers. It was incorporated in 1532 under James V.

advowson the right of selecting a person to a church living or benefice; a form of ◊patronage.

Aegean civilization the cultures of Bronze Age Greece, including the ◊*Minoan civilization* of Crete and the ◊*Mycenaean civilization* of the E Peloponnese.

Aegean Islands /iːˈdʒːən/ the islands of the Aegean Sea, but more specifically a region of Greece comprising the Dodecanese islands, the Cyclades islands, Lesvos, Samos, and Chios; population (1981) 428,500; area 9,122 sq km/3,523 sq mi.

Aegean Sea /iːˈdʒiːən/ branch of the Mediterranean between Greece and Turkey; the Dardanelles connect it with the Sea of Marmara. The numerous islands in the Aegean Sea include Crete, the Cyclades, the Sporades, and the Dodecanese. There is political tension between Greece and Turkey over sea limits claimed by Greece around such islands as Lesvos, Chios, Samos, and Kos.

The Aegean Sea is named after the legendary Aegeus, who drowned himself in the belief that Theseus, his son, had been killed.

Aegina /iːˈdʒaɪnə/ (Greek *Aíyna* or *Aíyina*) Greek island in the Gulf of Aegina about 32 km/20 mi SW of Piraeus; area 83 sq km/32 sq mi; population (1981) 11,100. In 1811 remarkable sculptures were recovered from a Doric temple in the northeast (restored by Thorwaldsen) and taken to Munich.

Aegir /ˈægə/ in Scandinavian mythology, the god of the sea.

Aehrenthal /ˈeərəntɑːl/ Count Aloys von 1854–1912. Foreign minister of Austria-Hungary during the ◊Bosnian Crisis of 1908.

Aelfric /ˈælfrɪk/ *c.* 955–1020. English writer, author of two collections of homilies and the *Lives of the Saints*, written in vernacular Old English prose.

Aeneas /iːˈniːəs/ in classical legend, a Trojan prince who became the ancestral hero of the Romans. According to Homer, he was the son of Anchises and the goddess Aphrodite. During the Trojan War he owed his life several times to the intervention of the gods. Virgil's epic poem the ◊*Aeneid* is based on this legend.

Aeniad, The epic poem by Virgil, written in 12 books of hexameters and composed during the last 11 years of his life (30–19 BC). It celebrates the development of the Roman Empire through the legend of Aeneas. After the fall of Troy, Aeneas wanders for seven years and becomes shipwrecked off Africa. He is received by Dido, queen of Carthage, and they fall in love. Aeneas, however, renounces their love and sails on to Italy where he settles as founder of Latium and the Roman state.

Aeolian harp a wind-blown instrument, consisting of a shallow soundbox supporting gut strings at low tension and tuned to the same pitch. It produces an eerie harmony that rises and falls with the changing pressure of the wind. It was common in parts of central Europe during the 19th century.

Aeolian Islands /iːˈəʊliən/ another name for the ◊Lipari Islands.

Aeolus /ˈiːələs/ in Greek mythology, the god of the winds, who kept them imprisoned in a cave on the ◊Lipari Islands.

aepyornis type of huge extinct flightless bird living in Madagascar until a few thousand years ago. Some stood 3 m/10 ft high and laid eggs with a volume of 9 litres/2 gallons.

Aequi an Italian people, originating around the river Velino, who were turned back from their advance on Rome in 431 BC and were conquered in 304 BC, during the Samnite Wars. They subsequently adopted Roman customs and culture.

aerenchyma a plant tissue with numerous air-filled spaces between the cells. It occurs in the stems and roots of many aquatic plants where it aids buoyancy and facilitates transport of oxygen around the plant.

aerial or *antenna* in radio broadcasting, a conducting device that radiates or receives radio waves. The design of an aerial depends principally on the wavelength of the radio signal. Long waves (hundreds of metres) may employ long wire aerials; short waves (several centimetres wavelength) may employ rods and dipoles; microwaves may also use dipoles––often with reflectors arranged like a toast rack––or highly directional parabolic dish aerials. Because microwaves travel in straight lines, giving line-of-sight communication, microwave aerials are usually located at the tops of tall masts or towers.

aerobic (in biology, of a living organism) using molecular oxygen (usually dissolved in water) for the efficient release of energy.

Almost all living organisms are aerobic. They use oxygen to convert glucose to carbon dioxide and water, thereby releasing energy. Most aerobic organisms die in the absence of oxygen but certain organisms and cells, such as muscle cells, can function for short periods ◊anaerobically (without oxygen).

aerobics (Greek 'air' and 'life') strenuous combination of dance, stretch exercises, and running that became a health and fitness fashion in the 1980s.

aerodynamics the branch of fluid physics that studies the flow of gases, particularly the airflow around bodies (such as land vehicles, bullets, rockets, and aircraft) moving at speed through the atmosphere. For maximum efficiency, the aim is usually to design the shape of an object to produce a streamlined flow, with a minimum of turbulence in the moving air.

aeronautics the science of travel through the Earth's atmosphere, including ◊aerodynamics, aircraft structures, jet and rocket propulsion, and aerial navigation.

In **subsonic aeronautics** (below the speed of sound) aerodynamic forces increase at the rate of the square of the speed. **Transsonic aeronautics** covers the speed range from just below to just above the speed of sound, and is crucial to aircraft design. Ordinary sound waves move at about 1,225 kph/760 mph at sea level, and air in front of an aircraft moving slower than this is 'warned' by the waves so that it can move aside. However, as the flying speed approaches that of the sound waves, the warning is too late for the air to escape and the aircraft pushes the air aside, creating shock waves which absorb much power and create design problems. On the ground the shock waves give rise to a ◊sonic boom. It was once thought that the speed of sound was a speed limit to aircraft, and the term ◊sound barrier came into use. **Supersonic aeronautics** concerns speeds above that of sound and in one sense may be considered a much older study than aeronautics itself, since the study of the flight of bullets, known as ◊ballistics, was undertaken soon after the introduction of firearms. **Hypersonics** is the study of airflows and forces at speeds above five times that of sound (Mach 5), for example for guided missiles, space rockets, and advanced concepts such as ◊HOTOL. For all flight speeds streamlining is necessary to reduce the effects of air resistance.

Aeronautics is distinguished from astronautics, which is the science of travel through space. Astronavigation (navigation by reference to the stars) is used in aircraft as in ships and is a part of aeronautics.

aeroplane or *airplane* a powered heavier-than-air craft supported in flight by fixed wings. Aeroplanes are propelled by the thrust of a jet engine or airscrew (propeller). They must be designed aerodynamically, as streamlining ensures maximum flight efficiency. The shape of a plane depends on its operating speed–aircraft operating at well below the speed of sound need not be so streamlined as supersonic aircraft.

history The Wright brothers flew the first powered plane (a biplane) in Kitty Hawk, North Carolina, USA, 1903 (see also ◊flight).

design Efficient streamlining prevents the formation of shockwaves over the body surface and wings which would cause instability and power loss. The wings of an aeroplane have the cross-sectional shape of an aerofoil ('airfoil' in North America). An aerofoil is broad and curved at the front, flat underneath, curved on top, and tapers to a sharp point at the rear. It is so shaped that air passing above it is speeded up, reducing pressure below atmospheric. This follows from ◊Bernoulli's effect and results in a force acting vertically upwards, called lift, which counters the plane's weight. In level flight lift equals weight. The wings develop sufficient lift to support the plane when they move quickly through the air. The thrust which causes propulsion comes from the reaction to the air stream accelerated backwards by the propeller or the gases shooting backwards from the jet exhaust. In flight the engine thrust must overcome the air resistance, or ◊drag. Drag depends on frontal area (for example, large, airliner; small, fighter) and shape (drag coefficient); in level flight drag equals thrust. The drag is reduced by streamlining the plane, resulting in higher speed and reduced fuel consumption for a given power. Less fuel need be carried for a given distance of travel, so a larger payload (cargo or passengers) can be carried.

The shape of a plane is dictated very much by the speed at which it will operate (see ◊aeronautics). A low-speed plane operating at well below the speed of sound (about 965 kph/600 mph) need not be particularly well streamlined, and it can have its wings broad and projecting at right angles from the fuselage. An aircraft operating close to the speed of sound must be well streamlined and have swept-back wings. This prevents the formation of shock waves over the body surface and wings, which would result in instability and high power loss. Supersonic planes (faster than sound) need to be severely streamlined, and require a needle nose, highly swept-back wings, and what is often termed a 'Coke-bottle' fuselage, in order to pass through the sound barrier without suffering undue disturbance. To give great flexibility of operation at low as well as high speeds, some supersonic planes are designed with variable geometry, or ◊swing-wings. For low-speed flight the wings are outstretched; for high-speed flight they are swung close to the fuselage to form an efficient ◊delta wing configuration. Aircraft designers experiment with different designs in ◊wind tunnel tests, which indicate how their designs will behave in practice.

construction planes are constructed using light but strong aluminium alloys such as duralumin (with copper, magnesium, and so on). For supersonic planes special stainless steel and titanium may be used in areas subjected to high heat loads. The structure of the plane, or the airframe (wings, fuselage, and so on) consists of a surface skin of alloy sheets supported at intervals by struts known as ribs and stringers. The structure is bonded together by riveting or by powerful adhesives such as ◊epoxy resins. In certain critical areas, which have to withstand very high stresses (such as the wing roots), body panels are machined from solid metal for extra strength.

On the ground a plane rests on wheels, usually in a tricycle arrangement, with a nose wheel and two wheels behind, one under each wing. For all except some light planes the landing gear, or undercarriage, is retracted in flight to reduce drag. Seaplanes, which take off and land on water, are fitted with non-retractable hydrofoils.

flight control wings by themselves are unstable in flight, and a plane requires a tail to provide stability. It comprises a horizontal tailplane and vertical tailfin, called the horizontal and vertical stabilizer respectively. The tailplane has hinged flaps at the rear called elevators to control pitch (attitude). Raising the elevators depresses the tail and inclines the wings upwards (increases the angle of attack). This speeds up the airflow above the wings until lift exceeds weight and the plane climbs. However, the steeper attitude increases drag, so more power is needed to maintain speed and the engine throttle must be opened up. Moving the elevators in the opposite direction produces the reverse effect. The angle of attack is reduced, and the plane descends. Speed builds up rapidly if the engine is not throttled back. Turning (changing direction) is effected by moving the rudder hinged to the rear of the tailfin, and by backing (rolling) the plane. It is banked by moving the ailerons, interconnected flaps at the rear of the wings which move in opposite directions, one up, the other down. In planes with a delta wing, such as ◊Concorde, the ailerons and elevators are combined. Other moveable control surfaces, called flaps, are fitted at the rear of the wings closer to the fuselage. They are extended to increase the width and camber (curve) of the wings during takeoff and landing, thereby creating extra lift, while moveable sections at the front, or leading edges of the wing, called slats, are also extended at these times to improve the airflow. To land, the nose of the plane is brought up so that the angle of attack of the wings exceeds a critical point, and the airflow around them breaks down. Lift is lost (a condition known as stalling) and the plane drops to the runway. A few planes, (for example, the Harrier) have a novel method of takeoff and landing, rising and dropping vertically by swivelling nozzles to direct the exhaust of their jet engines downwards. The ◊helicopter and ◊convertiplane use rotating propellors (rotors) to obtain lift to take off vertically.

operation the control surfaces of a plane are operated by the pilot on the flight deck, by means of a control stick, or wheel, and by foot pedals (for the rudder). The controls are brought into action by hydraulic power systems. Advanced experimental high-speed craft known as control-configured vehicles (CCV) use a sophisticated computer-controlled system. The pilot instructs the computer which manoeuvre the plane must perform and the computer, informed by a series

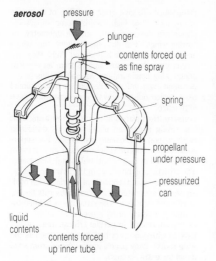

aerosol

pressure
plunger
contents forced out as fine spray
spring
propellant under pressure
pressurized can
liquid contents
contents forced up inner tube

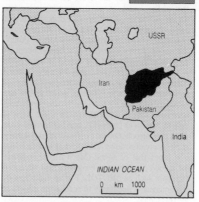

Afghanistan
Republic of
(Jamhuria Afghanistan)

USSR
Iran
Pakistan
India
INDIAN OCEAN
0 km 1000

area 652,090 sq km/251,707 sq mi
capital Kábul
towns Kandahár, Herát
physical mountainous, with rivers and desert areas
features Hindu Kush mountain range (Khyber and Salang passes and Panjshir Valley)
head of state Najibullah Ahmadzai (president) from 1986
head of government Sultan Ali Keshtmand (prime minister) from 1989
political system military emergency republic
political parties People's Democratic Party of Afghanistan (PDPA), Marxist-Leninist; Hesb-i-Islami and Jamiat-i-Islami, Islamic fundament alist mujahaddin; National Liberation Front, moderate mujahaddin

exports dried fruit, rare minerals, natural gas (piped to USSR), karakul lamb skins, Afghan coats
currency afgháni (99.25 = £1 Feb 1990)
population (1988) 10,000,000–12,000,000 (more than 5 million have become refugees since 1979); annual growth rate 0.6%
life expectancy men 37, women 37
language Pushtu
religion Muslim: 80% Sunni, 20% Shi'ite
literacy 39% male/8% female (1985 est)
GNP $3.3 bn (1985); $275 per head of population
chronology
1747 Afghanistan became an independent emirate.
1838–1919 Afghan Wars waged between Afghanistan and Britain to counter the threat to British India from expanding Russian influence in Afghanistan.
1919 Afghanistan recovered full independence following Third Afghan War.
1953 Lt-Gen Daud Khan became prime minister and introduced reform programme.
1963 Daud Khan forced to resign and constitutional monarchy established.
1973 Monarchy overthrown in coup by Daud Khan.
1978 Daud Khan ousted by Taraki and the PDPA
1979 Soviet Union entered country to prop up government; they installed Babrak Karmal in power.
1986 Replacement of Karmal as leader by Dr Najibullah Ahmadzai. Partial Soviet troop withdrawal.
1988 New non-Marxist constitution adopted.
1989 Withdrawal of Soviet troops; state of emergency imposed in response to intensification of civil war.

of sensors around the craft about the attitude, speed, and turning rate of the plane, sends signals to the control surface and throttle to enable the manoeuvre to be executed.

aerosol particles of liquid or solid suspended in a gas. Fog is a common natural example. Aerosol cans, which contain pressurized gas mixed with a propellant, are used to spray liquid in the form of tiny drops of products such as insecticides. Many commercial aerosols use chlorofluorocarbons (CFCs) as propellants, and these are now known to cause destruction of the ◊ozone layer in the Earth's atmosphere. As a consequence, the international community has agreed to phase out the use of CFCs as propellants. Unfortunately, so-called 'ozone-friendly' aerosols have the disadvantage of using flammable butane or propane as propellants.

Aeschines /ˈiːskɪniːz/ lived 4th century BC. Orator of ancient Athens, a rival of ◊Demosthenes.

Aeschylus /ˈiːskələs/ *c.*525–*c.*456 BC. Greek dramatist, widely regarded as the founder of Greek tragedy. By the introduction of a second actor he made true dialogue and dramatic action possible. Aeschylus wrote some 90 plays between 499 and 458 BC of which seven survive. These are: *The Suppliant Women* performed about 490, *The Persians* 472, *Seven against Thebes* 467, *Prometheus Bound* (about 460) and the ◊*Oresteia* trilogy 458.

Aeschylus was born at Eleusis, near Athens, of a noble family. He took part in the Persian Wars and fought at Marathon (*c.* 490). He twice visited the court of Hieron I, king of Syracuse, and died at Gela in Sicily.

Aesculapius /ˌiːskjʊˈleɪpɪəs/ in Greek and Roman mythology, the god of medicine; his emblem was a staff with a snake coiled round it, since snakes seemed to renew life by shedding their skin.

Sacred snakes were kept in the sanctuaries of Aesculapius at ◊Epidaurus and elsewhere. The customary offering to Aesculapius was a cock.

Aesir principal gods of Norse mythology – Odin, Thor, Balder, Loki, Freya, and Tyr, whose dwelling place was Asgard.

Aesop traditional writer of Greek fables. According to Herodotus he lived in the reign of Amasis of Egypt (mid-6th century BC) and was a slave of Iadmon, a Thracian. The fables, for which no evidence of his authorship exists, are anecdotal stories using animal characters to illustrate moral or satirical points.

Aesthetic movement English artistic movement of the late 19th century, dedicated to the doctrine 'art for art's sake' – that is, art as self-sufficient, not needing to justify its existence by serving any particular use. Artists associated with the movement include Beardsley and Whistler.

The idea of art for art's sake was current in Europe throughout the 19th century, but the English movement in the last two decades tended to advocate extremes of sensibility which attracted much ridicule. The writer Oscar Wilde was in his twenties an exemplary aesthete.

aesthetics the branch of philosophy which deals with the nature of beauty, especially in art. It emerged as a distinct branch of enquiry in the mid-18th century. The term was first used by the German philosopher Baumgarten (1714–62).

aestivation in zoology, a state of inactivity and reduced metabolic activity, similar to ◊hibernation, that occurs during the dry season in species such as lungfish and snails. In botany, the term is used to describe the way in which flower petals and sepals are folded in the buds. It is an important feature in ◊plant classification.

aet. abbreviation for *aetatis* (Latin 'of the age').

Aetolia /iːˈtəʊlɪə/ district of ancient Greece on the NW of the gulf of Corinth. The *Aetolian League* was a confederation of the cities of Aetolia which, following the death of Alexander the Great, became the chief rival of Macedonian power and the Achaean League.

Afars and the Issas, French Territory of the /ˈæfɑːz, ˈɪsəz/ former French territory which became the Republic of ◊Djibouti 1977.

AFD abbreviation for *accelerated freeze drying*, a common method of food preservation. See also ◊food technology.

affidavit a legal document, used in court applications and proceedings, in which a person swears that certain facts are true. In England, the oath is usually sworn before a solicitor or Commissioner for Oaths.

affiliation order in English law, formerly a court order for maintenance against the alleged father of an illegitimate child. Under the Family Law Reform Act 1987, either parent can apply for a court order for maintenance of children, no distinction being made between legitimate and illegitimate children.

In 1969 blood tests were first used to prove 'non-paternity'; they are not equally conclusive of paternity. Genetic fingerprinting was first used in 1988 in Britain to prove paternity and thereby allow immigration to the UK.

affine geometry a geometry that preserves parallelism and the ratios between intervals on any line segment.

affinity in law, relationship by marriage not blood, for example between stepparent and stepchild, which may legally preclude their marriage. It is distinguished from consanguinity or blood relationship. In Britain, the right to marry was extended to many relationships formerly prohibited, by the Marriage (Prohibited Degrees of Relationship) Act 1986.

affinity in chemistry, the force of attraction between chemical elements, which helps to keep them in combination in a molecule.

A given element may have a greater affinity for one particular element than for another (for example, hydrogen has a great affinity for chlorine, with which it easily and rapidly combines to form hydrochloric acid, but has little or no affinity for argon).

affirmation a solemn declaration made instead of taking the oath by a person who has no religious belief or objects to taking an oath on religious grounds.

affirmative action in the USA, a government-endorsed policy of positive discrimination in favour of members of minority ethnic groups and women in such areas as employment and education, designed to counter the effects of long-term discrimination against them. The policy has been controversial, and in the 1980s it was less rigorously enforced.

Africa

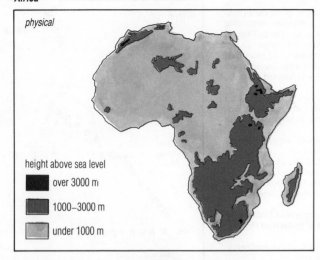

physical

height above sea level

- over 3000 m
- 1000–3000 m
- under 1000 m

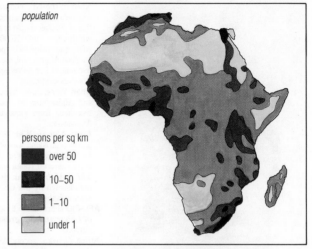

population

persons per sq km

- over 50
- 10–50
- 1–10
- under 1

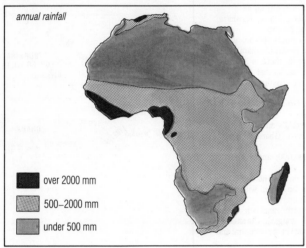

annual rainfall

- over 2000 mm
- 500–2000 mm
- under 500 mm

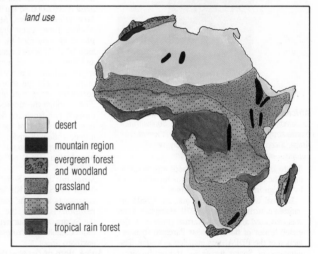

land use

- desert
- mountain region
- evergreen forest and woodland
- grassland
- savannah
- tropical rain forest

The Equal Opportunities Act 1972 set up a commission to enforce the policy in organizations receiving public funds, and many private institutions and employers adopted voluntary affirmative action programmes at the same time.

Positive discrimination in favour of ethnic-minority construction companies by local government was outlawed Jan 1989.

affluent society a society in which most people have money left over after satisfying their basic needs such as food and shelter. They are then able to decide how to spend their excess ('disposable') income, and become 'consumers'. The term was popularized by the US economist John Kenneth ◊Galbraith.

Galbraith used the term to describe the Western industrialized nations, particularly the USA, in his book *The Affluent Society* 1958, in which he advocated using more of the nation's wealth for public spending and less for private consumption.

Afghan inhabitant of Afghanistan. The dominant group, particularly in Kabul, are the Pathans. The Tadzhiks, a smaller ethnic group, are predominantly traders and farmers in the province of Herat and around Kabul; the Hazaras, another farming group, are found in the southern mountain ranges of the Hindu Kush.

The Pathans, Tadzhiks, and Hazaras are traditionally nomadic horse breeders, and speak languages belonging to the Iranian branch of the Indo-European family. The Uzbeks and Turkomen are farmers, and speak Altaic family languages. The smallest Altaic minority are the Kirghiz, who live in the Pamir. Baluchi nomads live in the south,

and Nuristani farmers live in the mountains of the NE. The majority of the population are Sunni Muslims, the most recent converts being the Nuristanis.

Afghan hound dog resembling the saluki, though less thickly coated, first introduced to Britain by army officers serving on the North-West Frontier in the late 19th century.

Afghanistan /æfˈgænɪstɑːn/ mountainous, landlocked country in S central Asia, bounded to the N by the USSR, to the W by Iran, and to the S and E by Pakistan

government the 1977 constitution was abolished after a coup 1978, and legislative and executive authority was assumed by a 57-member revolutionary council, controlled by a smaller presidium of leaders from the only political party, the communist People's Democratic Party of Afghanistan (PDPA). In Nov 1987 a grand national assembly (*Loya Jirgah*) of indirectly elected elders from various ethnic groups approved a new permanent constitution, establishing Islam as the state religion and creating a multi-party, presidential system of government. Under the terms of this constitution, the president, who is elected for a seven-year term by the *Loya Jirgah*, appoints the prime minister and is empowered to approve the laws and resolutions of the elected two-chamber national assembly (*Meli Shura*). The constitution was suspended following the withdrawal of Soviet troops in Feb 1989 and an emergency military-PDPA regime was established. At its head is President Najibullah, who chairs the Supreme Council for the Defence of the Homeland (SCDH).

history in the ancient world part of the Persian Empire, Afghanistan first became an independent emirate 1747. During the 19th century three ◊Afghan Wars were fought to secure British interests in India and counter the growing Russian influence.

During the 1950s, Lt-Gen Sardar Mohammad Daud Khan, cousin of King Mohammad Zahir Shah (ruled 1933–73), governed as prime minister and introduced a programme of social and economic modernization with Soviet aid. Opposition to his authoritarian rule forced Daud's resignation 1963; the king was made a constitutional monarch but political parties were outlawed.

After a famine 1972, Gen Daud Khan overthrew the monarchy in a Soviet-backed military coup 1973. The King fled to exile and a republic was declared. Daud introduced more moderate policies, built up support among minority ethnic groups and reduced Afghanistan's dependence on the Soviet Union by drawing closer to the nonaligned and Middle East oil states (where many Afghans were employed). A new presidential constitution was adopted 1977, although undermined by fundamentalist Muslim insurgents funded by Libya, Iran, and Pakistan.

In 1978 President Daud was assassinated in a military coup and Nur Mohammad Taraki, the imprisoned leader of the radical Khalq (masses) faction of the banned PDPA, took charge as president of a revolutionary council. A one-party constitution was adopted, a Treaty of Friendship and Mutual Defence signed with the USSR, and major reforms introduced. Conservative Muslims opposed these initiatives, thousands of refugees

African art *Bronze head of a Negro from Nigeria (undated), Museum of Mankind, London. Sophisticated bronze sculpture flourished for centuries in western Africa; it continued into the 17th century, when European traders purchased African art.*

fled to Iran and Pakistan, and there was an uprising in the Herat region. Taraki was replaced 1979 by foreign minister Hafizullah Amin.

Internal unrest continued, and the USSR organized a further coup Dec 1979. Hafizullah Amin was executed and Babrak Karmal (1929–), the exiled leader of the gradualist Parcham (banner) faction of the PDPA, was installed as leader. The numbers of Soviet forces in Afghanistan grew to over 120,000 by 1985 as Muslim guerrilla resistance by the 'mujaheddin' ('holy warriors') continued. A war of attrition developed with the USSR failing to gain control of rural areas.

Faced with high troop casualties and a drain of economic resources, the new Soviet administration of ◊Gorbachev moved towards a compromise settlement 1986. In May 1986 Karmal was replaced as PDPA leader by the Pushtun (Pathan) former secret police chief Dr Najibullah Ahmadzai (1947–), and several non-communist politicians joined the new government. In Oct 1986, 8,000 Soviet troops were withdrawn as a goodwill gesture, and in Jan 1987 the Afghan government announced a six-month unilateral ceasefire. The mujaheddin rejected this initiative, however, insisting on a full Soviet withdrawal and replacement of the communist government. The Najibullah government extended the ceasefire, and in Nov 1987 a new multi-party Islamic constitution was ratified in an attempt to promote 'national reconciliation'. In Feb 1988 the USSR announced that it would withdraw its forces in a phased manner between May 1988 and Feb 1989, and in Apr 1988 the Afghan and Pakistan governments signed an agreement providing for non-interference in each others' internal affairs and the voluntary return of refugees, with the USA and the USSR acting as guarantors.

On the completion of Soviet troop withdrawal in Feb 1989 a 'state of emergency' was imposed by the Najibullah government, which was faced with a mounting military onslaught by the mujaheddin. The guerillas, whose commanders by now controlled a number of regions outside

Kabul, including the Panjshir Valley and Hindu Kush to the NE, continued to resist the PDPA-regime's 'power-sharing' entreaties, demanding that Najibullah should first resign. The civil war, in which since 1980 15,000 Soviet troops, 70,000 Afghan security force personnel, and more than a million Afghan civilians have died, and more than five million fled as refugees to Iran and Pakistan, has thus continued.

Afghan Wars three wars waged between Britain and Afghanistan to counter the threat to British India from expanding Russian influence in Afghanistan.

First Afghan War 1838–42, when the British garrison at Kabul was wiped out.

Second Afghan War 1878–80, when Gen ◊Roberts captured Kabul and relieved Kandahar.

Third Afghan War 1919, when peace followed the dispatch by the UK of the first airplane ever seen in Kabul.

AFL-CIO abbreviation for ◊*American Federation of Labor and Congress of Industrial Organizations.*

Africa /'æfrɪkə/ second largest of the continents, three times the area of Europe.

area 30,097,000 sq km/11,620,451 sq mi

largest cities Cairo, Algiers, Lagos, Kinshasa, Abidjan, Tunis, Cape Town, Nairobi

physical dominated by a central plateau, which includes the world's largest desert (◊Sahara); Nile and Zaïre rivers, but generally there is a lack of rivers, and also of other inlets, so that Africa has proportionally the shortest coastline of all the continents; comparatively few offshore islands; 75% is within the tropics; Great Rift Valley; immensely rich fauna and flora

exports has 30% of the world's minerals; crops include coffee (Kenya), cocoa (Ghana, Nigeria), cotton (Egypt, Uganda)

population (1984) 537,000,000; annual growth rate 3%

language Hamito-Semitic in the north; Bantu below the Sahara; Khosan languages with 'click' consonants in the far south

religion Islam in the north; animism below the Sahara, which survives alongside Christianity (both Catholic and Protestant) in many central and southern areas.

Africa, Horn of /'æfrɪkə/ the projection constituted by Somalia and adjacent territories.

African inhabitant of the continent of Africa. The region is culturally heterogenous with numerous distinctive socio-linguistic groups. There are three major language families: Niger-Congo, Afro-Asiatic, and Chari-Nile.

African art the art of sub-Saharan Africa, from prehistory onwards, ranging from the art of ancient civilizations to the new styles of post-imperialist African nations. Among the best-known examples of historic African art are bronze figures from Benin and Ife (in modern Nigeria) dating from about 1500 and, also on the W coast, in the same period, bronze or brass figures for weighing gold, made by the Ashanti.

prehistoric art rock paintings are found in various regions, notably in the SW Sahara, Zimbabwe, South Africa, and, from the end of the period, East Africa. Some of the earliest pictures are of elephants. The images tend to be linear and heavily stylized, and sometimes show a geometric style. Terracotta figures from Nigeria, dating from several centuries BC, have stylized features similar to Oceanic art forms and some early South American styles.

Zimbabwe Ruins of ancient stone buildings from before AD 300 suggest a time of outstanding craft skill in the country's history; sculptures have also been found in the ruins.

Benin and Ife The bronze sculptures from the 13th–16th-century realms of Benin and Ife on the W coast of Africa (examples in the British Museum, London) are distinctive in style and demonstrate technical refinement in casting by the lost-wax method (see ◊sculpture). The Ife

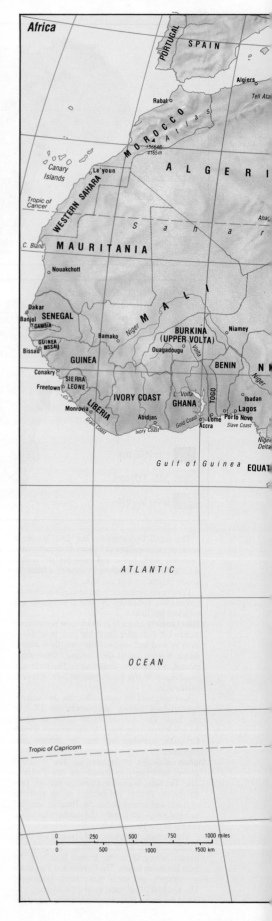

heads are naturalistic, while those of Benin are more stylized. The art of Benin includes high-relief bronze plaques with figurative scenes, and ivory carvings. Some of these appear to have been designed for the Portuguese trade.

Ashanti Metalworkers of the Ashanti people (in present-day Ghana) made weights, highly inventive forms with comically exaggerated figures.

general Over the centuries, much artistic effort was invested in religious objects and masks, with wooden sculpture playing an important role. Many everyday items, such as bowls, stools, drums, and combs, also display fine craft and a vitality of artistic invention.

Since much of Africa's history up to the late 19th century has not been researched, African art has occupied a meagre place in Western art-historical studies. In the early 20th century West African art had a profound influence on the work of many European painters and sculptors.

African National Congress (ANC) multiracial nationalist organization formed in South Africa 1912 to extend the franchise to the whole population and end all racial discrimination there. Although nonviolent, it was banned by the government 1960, and in exile in Mozambique developed a military wing, *Umkhonto we Sizwe*, which has engaged in sabotage and guerrilla training. The ANC is now based in Lusaka, Zambia, and its leader in exile is Oliver ◊Tambo; former ANC leaders include Albert Luthuli, Nelson Mandela, and Solomon Plaatje. State president F W de Klerk announced the lifting of the ban in 1990 and released from prison its deputy leader Nelson Mandela.

The ANC is supported by the Organization of African Unity as a movement aimed at introducing majority rule in South Africa.

African violet herbaceous plant *Saintpaulia ionantha* from tropical central and E Africa, with velvety green leaves and scentless purple flowers. Different colours and double varieties have been bred.

Afrikaans language along with English, an official language of the Republic of South Africa. Spoken mainly by the Afrikaners, descendants of Dutch and other 17th century colonists, it is a variety of the Dutch language, modified by circumstance and the influence of German, French, and other immigrant and local languages. It became a standardized written language about 1875.

Afrika Korps the German army in the western desert of N Africa 1941–43 in World War II, commanded by Field Marshal Rommel. They were driven out of N Africa by May 1943.

Afrikaner (formerly known as *Boer*) inhabitant of South Africa descended from the original Dutch and ◊Huguenot settlers of the 17th century. Comprising approximately 60% of the white population in the Republic, they were originally farmers but have now become mainly urbanized. Their language is Afrikaans.

Afro-Caribbean person of African descent from the West Indies. Afro-Caribbeans are the descendants of W Africans kidnapped by European slave traders, and shipped to the West Indies. Since World War II many Afro-Caribbeans have migrated to Europe, especially Britain and the Netherlands, and also to North America.

after-burning method of increasing the thrust of a gas turbine (jet) aero engine by spraying additional fuel between the turbojet and the tail pipe. Used for short-term increase of power during take-off, or combat in military aircraft.

African violet

Africa early history

BC
4–5m years	First hominids in world.
2–5m years	First 'people' *homo habilis*. First stone tools
100,000	First evidence of modern peoples *homo sapiens sapiens* in E and S Africa.
8.500	Sahara rock painting.
7,500	First pottery manufacture in Sahara.
6,500	Domestication of cattle in N Africa
6.000	First plant (native millet) domestication in N Africa. Introduction of barley, wheat and sheep from W Asia into Egypt.
4,000	Use of sail in Egypt.
3,400	Walled Egyptian towns.
3,000	Egyptian hieroglyphic writing.
2,700	Beginning of Old Kingdom Egypt.
2,650	First stepped pyramid at Saqqara, Egypt.
2,600	First 'true' pyramid at Maidum.
2.040	Egyptian Middle Kingdom.
1,800	Horse introduced into Egypt.
1500	Rock-cut tombs in Valley of the kings, new Kingdom, Egypt.
1337	Tutankhamun buried.
1166	Rameses III, last great pharaoh, dies.
500	Copper smelting in Mali and Niger.
500	Iron production in Nigeria.
331	Alexandria founded.
146	Carthage destroyed by Romans.
AD	
500	Bantu arrive in S Africa, Iron working and domesticated cattle.
600	Kingdom of Ghana. First W African state.
641	Arabs conquer Egypt.
900	Arab merchants settle in E Africa.
1250	Stone settlements in SE Africa, Great Zimbabwe. Benin Empire of Nigeria emerges.
1415	Portuguese capture Ceuta and establish empire.
1492	Conquest of N African coast by Spanish.

after-image persistence of an image on the retina of the eye after the object producing it has been removed. This leads to persistence of vision, a necessary phenomenon for the illusion of continuous movement in films and television.

after-ripening the process undergone by the seeds of some plants before germination can occur. The length of the after-ripening period in different species may vary from a few weeks to many months. It helps seeds to germinate at a time when conditions are most favourable for growth. In some cases the embryo is not fully mature at the time of dispersal and must develop further before germination can take place. Other seeds do not germinate even when the embryo is mature, probably owing to growth-inhibitors within the seed which must be leached out or broken down before germination can begin.

AG abbreviation for *Aktiengesellschaft* (German 'limited company').

Aga (Turkish 'lord') title of nobility, applied by the Turks to military commanders and, in general, to men of high station.

Agadir /ˌægəˈdɪə/ resort and seaport in S Morocco, near the mouth of the river Sus. Population (1984) 110,500. It was rebuilt after being destroyed by an earthquake in 1960.

Agadir Incident international crisis provoked by Kaiser Wilhelm II of Germany. By sending the gunboat *Panther* to demand territorial concessions from the French, he hoped to drive a wedge into the Anglo-French entente. In fact, German aggression during the second Moroccan crisis merely served to reinforce Anglo-French fears of Germany's intentions. The crisis gave rise to the term 'gunboat diplomacy'.

Aga Khan IV /ˈaːgə ˈkaːn/ 1936– . Spiritual head (*imam*) of the **Ismaili** Muslim sect (see ◊Islam). He succeeded his grandfather in 1957.

agama type of lizard, found throughout the warmer regions of the Old World. Many of the 280 species are brilliantly coloured and all are capable of changing the colour of their skin.

Agamemnon /ˌægəˈmemnən/ in Greek mythology, a Greek hero, son of Atreus, king of Mycenae. He married Clytemnestra, and their children included ◊Electra, ◊Iphigenia, and ◊Orestes. He led the capture of Troy, received Priam's daughter Cassandra as a prize, and was murdered by Clytemnestra and her lover, Aegisthus, on his return home. His children Orestes and Electra later killed the guilty couple.

Agaña /əˈgɑːnjə/ capital of Guam, in the W Pacific; population (1981) 110,000. It is a US naval base.

agar jelly-like substance obtained from seaweed and used mainly as a culture medium in biology and medicine for growing bacteria and other microorganisms.

agaric type of fungus, of typical mushroom shape. Agarics include the **field mushroom** *Agaricus campestris* and the **horse mushroom** *Agaricus arvensis*. Closely related is the ◊*Amanita* genus, including the fly agaric *Amanita puscaria*.

Agassiz /ˈægəsi/ Jean Louis 1807–1873. Swiss naturalist who emigrated to the US and became one of the foremost scientists of the 19th century. He established his name through work on the classification of the fossil fishes. Although he is credited with the discovery of the ice ages he did not believe that species themselves changed, and thus opposed Darwin.

He is now criticized for holding racist views concerning the position of blacks in American society.

agate a banded or cloudy type of ◊chalcedony, a silica, SiO_2, that forms in rock cavities. Agates are used as ornamental stones and for art objects.

Agate stones, being hard, are also used to burnish and polish gold applied to glass and ceramics.

Agate /ˈeɪgət/ James Evershed 1877–1947. British writer, known for *Ego*, a diary in nine volumes 1935–49.

agave plant with stiff sword-shaped spiny leaves arranged in a rosette. All species of the genus *Agave* come from the warmer parts of the New World. They include *Agave sisalina*, and the Mexican **century plant** *Agave americana*. Alcoholic drinks such as ◊tequila and pulque are made from agave sap.

ageing in common usage, the period of deterioration of the physical condition of a living organism that leads to death; in biological terms, the entire life-process.

Three current theories attempt to account for ageing. The first suggests that the process is genetically determined, to remove individuals that can no longer reproduce by causing their death. The second suggests that it is due to the accumulation of mistakes during the replication of ◊DNA at cell division. The third suggests that it is actively induced by pieces of DNA which move between cells, or cancer-causing viruses; these may become abundant in old cells and induce them to produce unwanted ◊proteins or interfere with the control functions of their DNA.

ageism discrimination against older people in employment, pensions, and health care. To combat it the American Association of Retired Persons (AARP) has 30 million members, and in 1988 a similar organization was founded in the UK. In the USA the association has been responsible for legislation forbidding employers to discriminate; for example, it is illegal in the USA to fail to employ, to dismiss, or to reduce working conditions or wages of people aged 40–69.

Agent Orange a selective ◊weedkiller, subsequently discovered to contain highly poisonous ◊dioxin. It became notorious after its use in the 1960s during the Vietnam War by US forces to eliminate ground cover which could protect Communists. Thousands of US troops who had handled it later developed cancer or fathered deformed babies.

Agent Orange, named after the distinctive orange stripe on its packaging, combines equal parts of 2,4-D (2,4-trichlorophenoxyacetic acid) and 2,4,5-T (2,4,5-trichlorophenoxyacetic acid), both now banned in the USA. Companies that had manufactured the chemicals faced an increasing number of lawsuits in the 1970s. All the suits were settled out of court in a single ◊class action, resulting in the largest ever payment of its kind ($180 million) to claimants.

agglutination in medicine, the clumping together of ◊antigens, such as blood cells or bacteria, to form larger, visible masses, under the influence of ◊antibodies. As each antigen clumps only in response to its particular antibody, agglutination provides a way of determining ◊blood groups and the identity of unknown bacteria.

aggression in biology, behaviour used to intimidate or injure another organism (of the same or of a different species), usually for the purposes of gaining a territory, a mate, or food. Aggression often involves an escalating series of threats aimed at intimidating an opponent without having to engage in potentially dangerous physical contact. Aggressive signals include roaring in red deer, snarling by dogs, fluffing up the feathers in birds, and raising the fins in some species of fish.

Agincourt, Battle of /ˈædʒɪnkɔː/ battle in which Henry V of England defeated the French on 24 Oct 1415, St Crispin's Day. The village of Agincourt (modern *Azincourt*) is south of Calais, in N France.

Agnew /ˈægnjuː/ Spiro 1918– . US vice president 1969–73. A Republican, he was governor of Maryland 1966–69, and vice president under ◊Nixon. He resigned in 1973, shortly before pleading 'no contest' to a charge of income-tax evasion.

Agnon /ˈægnɒn/ Shmuel Yosef 1888–1970. Israeli novelist. Born in Buczacz, Galicia (now in the USSR), the setting of his most famous book, *A Guest for the Night*. He shared a Nobel prize 1966.

agnostic a person believing that in the nature of things we cannot know anything of what lies behind or beyond the world of natural phenomena. Thus, the existence of God cannot be proven. The word was coined by T H ◊Huxley in 1869.

An atheist (see ◊atheism) denies the existence of gods or God; an agnostic asserts that God or a First Cause is one of those concepts–others include the Absolute, infinity, eternity, and immortality–that lie beyond the reach of human intelligence.

agnosticism the belief that the existence of God cannot be proven; that the human mind cannot know anything beyond material phenomena. The term was coined 1869 by T H ◊Huxley.

agoraphobia a ◊phobia involving fear of open spaces and crowded places.

Agostini /ˌægɒˈstiːni/ Giacomo 1943–. Italian motorcyclist. He won a record 122 grands prix and 15 world titles. His world titles were at 350cc and 500cc and he was five times a dual champion. In addition he won 10 races at the Isle of Man TT races; a figure bettered only by Mike ◊Hailwood and Joey Dunlop.

CAREER HIGHLIGHTS

World titles:
350cc: 1968–73 (MV Agusta), 1974 (Yamaha)
500cc: 1966–72 (MV Agusta), 1975 (Yamaha) Isle of Man
TT wins:
Junior TT: 1966, 1968–70, 1972 (all MV Augusta)
Senior TT: 1968–72 (all MV Agusta)

agouti type of small rodent, genus *Dasyprocta*, found in the forests of Central and South America. They are herbivorous, swift-running, and about the size of a rabbit.

AGR abbreviation for *advanced gas-cooled reactor*, a type of ◊nuclear reactor widely used in Britain. The AGR uses a fuel of enriched uranium dioxide in stainless steel cladding and a moderator of graphite. Carbon dioxide gas is pumped through the reactor core to extract the heat produced by the ◊fission of the uranium. The heat is transferred to water in a steam generator, and the steam drives a turbogenerator to produce electricity.

Agra /ˈɑːɡrə/ city of Uttar Pradesh, India, on the river Jumna, 160 km/100 mi SE of Delhi; population (1981) 747,318. A commercial and university centre, it was the capital of the Mogul empire 1527–1628, from which period dates the Taj Mahal.

history ◊Zahir ud-din Mohammed (known as 'Babur'), the first great Mogul ruler, made Agra his capital in 1527. His grandson Akbar rebuilt the Red Fort of Salim Shah (1566), and is buried outside the city in the splendid tomb at Sikandra. In the 17th century the buildings of ◊Shah-Jehan made Agra one of the most beautiful cities in the world. The Taj Mahal, erected as a tomb for the emperor's wife Mumtaz Mahal, took more than 20 years to build, and was completed in 1650. Agra's political importance dwindled from 1658, when Aurangzeb moved the capital back to Delhi. It was taken from the Mahrattas by Lord Lake in 1803.

Agricola /əˈɡrɪkələ/ Gnaeus Julius AD 37–93. General and politician. Born in Provence, he became Consul of the Roman Republic AD 77, and then governor of Britain AD78-85. He extended Roman rule to the Firth of Forth in Scotland and won the battle of Mons Graupius. His fleet sailed round the N of Scotland and proved Britain an island.

agricultural revolution the sweeping changes that took place in British agriculture over the period 1750–1850 in response to the increased demand for food from a rapidly expanding population. Recent research has shown these changes to be only part of a much larger, ongoing process of development.

Changes of the latter half of the 18th century included the enclosure of open fields, the introduction of four-course rotation together with new fodder crops such as turnip, and the development of improved breeds of livestock. Pioneers of the new farming were Viscount ◊Townshend (known as 'Turnip' Townshend), Jethro ◊Tull, Robert ◊Bakewell, and enlightened landowners such as Thomas Coke of Norfolk (1752–1842).

Many of the changes were in fact underway before 1750 and other important breakthroughs, such as farm mechanisation, did not occur until after 1859. Scientific and technological advances in farming during the second half of the 20th century have further revolutionized agriculture.

agriculture the practice of farming, including the cultivation of the soil (for raising crops) and the

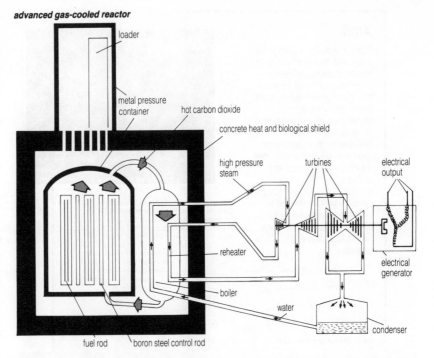

advanced gas-cooled reactor

raising of livestock. Crops are for human nourishment, animal fodder, or commodities such as cotton and sisal. Animals are raised for wool, milk, leather, dung (as fuel), or meat. The units for managing agricultural production vary from small holdings and individually owned farms to corporate-run farms and collective farms run by entire communities. Agriculture developed in Egypt and the near East at least 7,000 years ago. Soon, farming communities became the base for society in China, India, Europe, Mexico, and Peru, then spread throughout the world. Reorganization along more scientific and productive lines took place in Europe in the 18th century in response to dramatic population growth. Mechanization made considerable progress in the US and Europe during the 19th century. After World War II, there was an explosive growth in the use of agricultural chemicals: herbicides, insecticides, fungicides, and fertilizers. In the 1960s there was development of high-yielding species in the ◊*green revolution* of the Third World, and the industrialized countries began intensive farming of cattle, poultry, and pigs. In the 1980s, hybridization by genetic engineering methods and pest control by the use of chemicals plus ◊pheromones were developed.

plants For plant products, the land must be prepared (ploughing, cultivating, harrowing, and rolling). Seed must be planted and the growing plant nurtured. This may involve fertilizers, irrigation, pest control by chemicals, and monitoring of acidity or nutrients. When the crop has grown, it must be harvested and, depending on the crop, processed in a variety of ways before it is stored or sold.

Greenhouses allow cultivation of plants that would otherwise find the climate too harsh. ◊Hydroponics allows commercial cultivation of crops using nutrient-enriched solutions instead of soil. Special methods, such as terracing, may be adopted to allow cultivation in hostile terrain and to retain topsoil in mountainous areas with heavy rainfall.

livestock may be semi-domesticated, such as reindeer, or fully domesticated but nomadic (particularly where naturally growing or cultivated food supplies are sparse), or kept in one location. Animal farming involves accommodation (buildings, fencing, or pasture), feeding, breeding, gathering the produce (eggs, milk, or wool),

slaughtering, and further processing (such as butchery or tanning).

organic farming From the 1970s there has been a movement towards more sophisticated natural methods without chemical sprays and fertilizers. Nitrates have been seeping into the ground water, insecticides are found in lethal concentrations at the top of the ◊food chain, some herbicides are associated with human birth defects, and hormones fed to animals to promote fast growth have damaging effects on humans.

overproduction The greater efficiency in agriculture achieved since the 19th century, coupled with post–World War II government subsidies for domestic production in the US and the European Community (EC), have led to the development of high stocks, nicknamed 'lakes' (wine, milk) and 'mountains' (butter, beef, grain). There is no simple solution to this problem, as any large-scale dumping onto the market displaces regular merchandise. Increasing concern about the starving and the cost of storage has led the US and the EC to develop measures for limiting production, such as letting arable land lie fallow to reduce grain crops. The US has had some success at selling surplus wheat to the USSR when the Soviet crop is poor, but the overall cost of bulk transport and the potential destabilization of other economies acts against the high producers exporting their excess on a regular basis to needy countries. Intensive farming methods also contribute to soil ◊erosion and water pollution.

agate The mineral agate is characterized by fine coloured bands. These are formed by the deposition of various minerals on the walls of cavities in volcanic rocks.

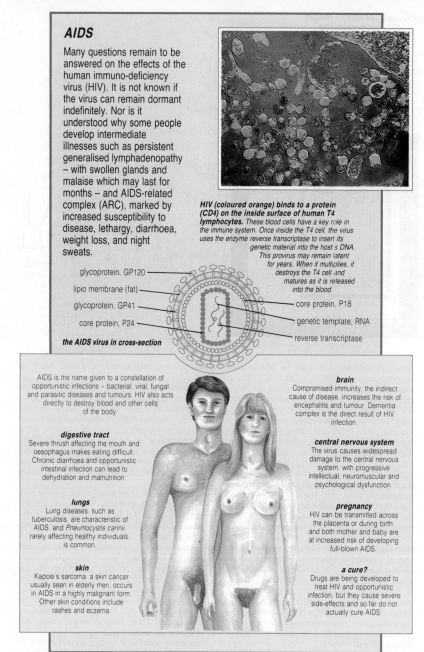

AIDS

Many questions remain to be answered on the effects of the human immuno-deficiency virus (HIV). It is not known if the virus can remain dormant indefinitely. Nor is it understood why some people develop intermediate illnesses such as persistent generalised lymphadenopathy – with swollen glands and malaise which may last for months – and AIDS-related complex (ARC), marked by increased susceptibility to disease, lethargy, diarrhoea, weight loss, and night sweats.

HIV (coloured orange) binds to a protein (CD4) on the inside surface of human T4 lymphocytes. These blood cells have a key role in the immune system. Once inside the T4 cell, the virus uses the enzyme reverse transcriptase to insert its genetic material into the host's DNA. This provirus may remain latent for years. When it multiplies, it destroys the T4 cell and matures as it is released into the blood.

glycoprotein, GP120

lipio membrane (fat)

glycoprotein, GP41

core protein, P24

core protein, P18

genetic template, RNA

reverse transcriptase

the AIDS virus in cross-section

AIDS is the name given to a constellation of opportunistic infections – bacterial, viral, fungal and parasitic diseases and tumours. HIV also acts directly to destroy blood and other cells of the body.

digestive tract
Severe thrush affecting the mouth and oesophagus makes eating difficult. Chronic diarrhoea and opportunistic intestinal infection can lead to dehydration and malnutrition.

lungs
Lung diseases, such as tuberculosis, are characteristic of AIDS. and *Pneumocystis carinii*, rarely affecting healthy individuals, is common.

skin
Kaposi's sarcoma, a skin cancer usually seen in elderly men, occurs in AIDS in a highly malignant form. Other skin conditions include rashes and eczema.

brain
Compromised immunity, the indirect cause of disease, increases the risk of encephalitis and tumour. Dementia complex is the direct result of HIV infection.

central nervous system
The virus causes widespread damage to the central nervous system, with progressive intellectual, neuromuscular and psychological dysfunction.

pregnancy
HIV can be transmitted across the placenta or during birth: and both mother and baby are at increased risk of developing full-blown AIDS.

a cure?
Drugs are being developed to treat HIV and opportunistic infection, but they cause severe side-effects and so far do not actually cure AIDS.

In the EC, a quota system for milk production coupled with price controls has reduced liquid milk and butter surpluses to manageable levels but has also driven out many uneconomic producers who, by switching to other enterprises, risk upsetting the balance elsewhere. A voluntary 'set aside' scheme of this sort was proposed in Britain (Aug 88).

Agrigento /ˌægrɪˈdʒentəʊ/ town in Sicily, noted for Greek temples; population (1981) 51,300. The Roman Agrigentum, it was long called Girgenti until renamed Agrigento 1927 under the Fascist regime.

agrimony herbaceous plant *Agrimonia eupatoria* of the rose family, with small yellow flowers on a slender spike. It grows on hedgebanks and in fields.

Agrippa /əˈgrɪpə/ Marcus Vipsanius 63–12 BC. Roman general. He commanded the victorious fleet at ◊Actium and married Julia, daughter of ◊Augustus.

agronomy study of crops and soils, a branch of agricultural science. Agronomy includes such topics as selective breeding (of plants and animals), irrigation, pest control, and soil analysis and modification.

Aguascalientes /ˌægwəskæliˈenteɪs/ city in central Mexico, and capital of a state of the same name; population (1980) 359,454. It has hot mineral springs.

Agulhas /əˈgʌləs/ southernmost cape in Africa. In 1852 the troopship *Birkenhead* sank off the cape with the loss of over 400 lives.

AH with reference to the Muslim calendar, abbreviation for *anno hegirae* (Latin 'year of the flight' of ◊Muhammad, from Mecca to Medina).

Ahab /ˈeɪhæb/ c. 875–854 BC. King of Israel. His empire included the suzerainty of Moab, and Judah was his subordinate ally, but his kingdom was weakened by constant wars with Syria. By his marriage with Jezebel, princess of Sidon, Ahab introduced into Israel the worship of the Phoenician god Baal, thus provoking the hostility of Elijah and the prophets. Ahab died in battle against the Syrians at Ramoth Gilead.

Ahaggar /əˈhægə/ or *Hoggar* mountainous plateau of the central Sahara, Algeria, whose highest point, Tahat, at 2,918 m/9,850 ft, lies between Algiers and the mouth of the Niger. It is the home of the formerly nomadic Tuaregs.

Ahasuerus /əˌhæzjuˈɪərəs/ (Latinized Hebrew form of the Persian Khshayarsha, Greek *Xerxes*). Name of several Persian kings in the Bible, notably the husband of ◊Esther. Traditionally it was also the name of the ◊Wandering Jew.

ahimsa in Hinduism, Buddhism, and especially Jainism, rule of respect for all life, and consequently nonviolence. It arises in part from the concept of reincarnation.

Ahmadiyya /ˌɑːməˈdiːə/ Islamic religious movement founded by Mirza Ghulam Ahmad (1839–1908). His followers reject the doctrine that Muhammad was the last of the prophets and accept Ahmad's claim to be the Mahdi and Promised Messiah. In 1974 the Ahmadis were denounced by their coreligionists as non-Muslims.

Ahmadnagar /ˌɑːmədˈnʌgə/ city in Maharashtra, India, 195 km/120 mi E of Bombay, on the left bank of the river Sina; population (1981) 181,000. It is a centre of cotton trade and manufacture.

Ahmad Shah /ˈɑːmæd ˈʃɑː/ 1724–1773. First ruler of Afghanistan. Elected king in 1747, he had made himself master of the Punjab by 1751. He defeated the Mahrattas at Panipat in 1761, and then the Sikhs.

Ahmedabad /ˈaməˈdɑːbɑːd/ or *Ahmadabad* capital of Gujarat, India; population (1981) 2,515,195. It is a cotton-manufacturing centre, and has many edifices of the Hindu, Muslim, and Jain faiths.

Ahmedabad was founded in the reign of Ahmad Shah 1412, and came under the control of the East India Company 1818. In 1930 ◊Gandhi marched to the sea from here to protest against the government salt monopoly.

Ahriman /ˈɑːrɪmən/ in Zoroastrianism, the supreme evil spirit, lord of the darkness and death, waging war with his counterpart Ahura Mazda (Ormuzd) until a time when human beings choose to lead good lives and Ahriman is finally destroyed.

Ahura Mazda /əˈhʊərə ˈmæzdə/ or *Ormuzd* in Zoroastrianism, the spirit of supreme good. As god of life and light, he will finally prevail over his enemy, Ahriman.

Ahváz /ɑːˈvɑːz/ industrial capital of the province of Khuzestan, W Iran; population (1986) 590,000.

Ahvenanmaa Island /ˈɑːvənənmɑː/ island in the Gulf of Bothnia, Finland; largest of the ◊Åland Islands.

AI(D) abbreviation for *artificial insemination (by donor)*. AIH is *artificial insemination by husband.*

Aidan, St /ˈeɪdn/ c. 600–651. Irish monk from Iona who converted Northumbria to Christianity and founded Lindisfarne monastery on Holy Island. His feast day is 31 Aug.

aid, development money given or lent on concessional terms to developing countries or spent on maintaining agencies for this purpose. In the late 1980s official aid from governments of richer nations amounted to $45–60 billion annually whereas voluntary organizations in the West received about $2.4 billion a year for the Third World. The ◊World Bank is the largest dispenser of aid. All industrialized United Nations member countries devote a proportion of their gross national product to aid, ranging from 0.21% (Austria) to 1.2% (Norway) (1986 figures). Each country spends more than half this contribution on direct bilateral assistance to countries with which they have historical or military links or hope to encourage trade. The rest goes to international organizations such as UN and World Bank agencies, which distribute aid multilaterally.

The UK development-aid budget in 1987 was 0.28% of GNP, with India and Kenya among the principal beneficiaries. In 1986 it spent 0.33% of GNP, or £1.75 billion, of which the European Development Fund (an arm of the European

aircraft Boeing 767 under construction at a Boeing plant in Seattle, Washington, USA

Community) received £79 million and the ◊International Development Association (an arm of the World Bank) £133.8 million. The Overseas Development Administration is the department of the Foreign Office that handles bilateral aid. The combined overseas development aid of all EC member countries is less than the sum ($20 billion) the EC spends every year on storing surplus food produced by European farmers.

In 1986, the US development-aid budget was 0.23% of GNP, or $9.784 billion, with the Philippines and Egypt among the principal beneficiaries. The United States Agency for International Development (USAID) is the State Department body responsible for bilateral aid. The USA is the largest contributor to, and thus the most powerful member of, the International Development Association.

aide-de-camp an officer who acts as private secretary to a general and would normally accompany the general on any duty.

aid, foreign another name for ◊aid, development.

Aidoo /'eɪduː/ Ama Ata 1940–. Ghanaian writer of plays, *Dilemma of a Ghost* 1965, novels, *Our Sister Killjoy* 1977, and short stories.

AIDS abbreviation for ***acquired immune deficiency syndrome***, the newest and gravest of sexually transmitted diseases (◊STDs). It is caused by the human immunodeficiency virus (HIV), now known to be a ◊retrovirus, an organism first identified 1983.

Transmission of HIV is by sexual contact where it involves transmission of sperm from one person to another, or by contaminated blood. Sexual transmission of the AIDS virus endangers heterosexual men and women as well as high-risk groups, such as homosexual and bisexual men, prostitutes, intravenous drug-users sharing needles, and haemophiliacs treated with contaminated blood products. The virus itself, however, is not selective, and there is real risk of infection spreading to the population at large. The virus has a short life outside the body, which makes transmission of the infection by methods other than sexual contact and shared syringes extremely unlikely.

Infection with HIV is not synonymous with having AIDS; many people who have the virus in their blood are not ill, and only about half of those infected will develop AIDS within ten years. Alternately, some suffer AIDS-related illnesses but not the full-blown disease. However, there is no firm evidence to suggest that the proportion of those developing AIDS from being HIV positive is less than 100%.

The effect of the virus in those who become ill is to devastate the immune system, leaving the victim susceptible to diseases that would not otherwise take hold. Diagnosis of AIDS is based on the appearance of rare tumours or opportunistic infections in unexpected candidates. Pneumocystis pneumonia, for instance, which is

aircraft carrier HMS Invincible, 1980, was used by the British in the war in the Falkland Islands in 1982. Carriers of this class, about 20,000 tonnes, have a speed of 28 knots and are designed to carry eight Sea Harrier aircraft and ten Sea King helicopters. They are armed with Sea Dart missiles.

normally only seen in the malnourished or those whose immune systems have been deliberately suppressed, is common among AIDS victims and, for them, a leading cause of death.

Some AIDS victims die within a few months, some survive for several years; roughly 50% are dead within three years. The estimated incubation period is 9.8 years. There is as yet no cure for the disease, although the new drug zidovudine (also known as ◊AZT) has had some success in curbing the virus and delaying the onset of AIDS. The search continues for an effective vaccine.

In Britain, 1,500 people had died of AIDS by Jan 1990. Between 30,000 and 50,000 people were thought to be carriers of the disease. In the USA, 90,990 cases were reported up to Apr 1989, with deaths numbering 52,435, 58% of all cases. One million Americans are thought to be infected with the virus. Worldwide cases of AIDS reached 215,500 by Jan 1990.

The total number of cases in Africa up to Oct 1988 was 19,141. In Africa, the prevalence of AIDS among high-risk groups such as prostitutes may approach 30%. Previous reports of up to 80% of certain populations being affected are thought to have been grossly exaggerated by inaccurate testing methods.

Aigun, Treaty of /'aɪguːn/ treaty between Russia and China signed in 1858 at the port of Aigun in China on the Amur River. It ceded the left bank to Russia, but has since been repudiated by China.

Aiken /'eɪkən/ Conrad (Potter) 1899–1973. US poet and novelist, whose *Collected Poems* appeared 1953.

Aiken /'eɪkən/ Howard 1900– . US mathematician. In 1939, in conjunction with engineers from IBM, he started work on the design of an automatic calculator using standard business machine components. In 1944 they completed one of the first computers, the Automatic Sequence Controlled Calculator (known as the Mark 1), a programmable computer controlled by punched paper tape and using ◊punched cards.

aikido Japanese art of self defence; one of the ◊martial arts. Two main systems of aikido are tomiki and uyeshiba.

Ailsa Craig /'eɪlsə 'kreɪg/ rocky islet in the Firth of Clyde, Scotland, about 16 km/10 mi off the coast of Strathclyde, opposite Girvan. Ailsa Craig rock is used in the manufacture of ◊curling stones. It is a breeding ground for birds.

Ain /æn/ French river giving its name to a *département* (administrative region); it is a right-bank tributary of the Rhône.

Ainsworth /'eɪnzwɜːθ/ William Harrison 1805–1882. British historical novelist. He produced in all some 40 novels and helped popularize the legends of Dick ◊Turpin in *Rookwood* 1834 and ◊Herne the Hunter in *Windsor Castle* 1834.

Aintab /aɪn'taːb/ Syrian name of ◊Gaziantep, city in Turkey.

Aintree racecourse situated on outskirts of Liverpool, Merseyside, NE England. The ◊Grand National steeplechase (established 1839) is held every spring.

The Grand National course comprises two circuits totalling 7,242 m/4 mi 880 yd, with 30 formidable jumps. The highest is The Chair at 1.56 m/5 ft 2 in.

Ainu aboriginal people of Japan, whose language is unrelated to any other. In the 4th century AD, they were driven N by ancestors of the modern Japanese; some 16,000 still inhabit the island of Hokkaido in N Japan. Others settled in Sakhalin on the Kuril islands, which were divided between Russia and Japan in the 18th century. Sakhalin was occupied by Soviet troops in 1945, and became part of the USSR two years later. The Ainu population in Sakhalin at that time numbered 1,500.

air see ◊atmosphere.

air conditioning a system that controls the state of the air inside a building or vehicle. A complete air-conditioning unit controls the temperature and humidity of the air, removes dust and odours from it and circulates it by means of a fan. US inventor W H Carrier developed the first effective air-conditioning unit in 1902 for a New York printing plant.

The air in an air conditioner is cooled by a kind of ◊refrigeration unit comprising a compressor and a condenser. It is heated by electrical wires or, in large systems, pipes carrying hot water or steam. The air is cleaned by means of filters and activated charcoal. The air may be humidified by circulating it over pans of water or through a water spray. Moisture can be extracted by condensation on cool metal plates.

A specialized air-conditioning system is installed in spacecraft as part of the life-support system. This includes the provision of oxygen to breathe and the removal of exhaled carbon dioxide.

aircraft aeronautical vehicle, which may be lighter than air (supported by buoyancy) or heavier than air (supported by the dynamic action of air on its surfaces). Balloons and airships are lighter-than-air craft. Heavier-than-air craft include the ◊aeroplane, glider, and helicopter.

aircraft carrier sea-going base for aircraft. The first purpose-designed aircraft carrier was HMS *Hermes*, completed 1913. In World War II the most famous was HMS *Ark Royal*, completed 1938. After World War II the cost and vulnerability of such large vessels was thought to have outweighed their advantages. However, by 1980 the need to have a means of destroying aircraft beyond the range of a ship's own weapons, especially on convoy duty, led to a widespread revival of aircraft carriers in the 20,000–30,000 tonne range.

Despite the cost, aircraft carriers have always remained popular with the USSR and USA. Examples include the USSR's *Komsomolec* 1979 (40,000 tonnes, 15 fixed-wing aircraft, 20 helicopters) and the USA's *Eisenhower* 1979 (81,600 tonnes, 95 aircraft). A British example is *Invincible* 1980 (19,500 tonnes). Aircraft carriers are equipped with combinations of fixed-wing aircraft, helicopters, missile launchers, and anti-aircraft guns.

air cushion vehicle (ACV) a craft that is supported by a layer, or cushion, of high-pressure

air sac

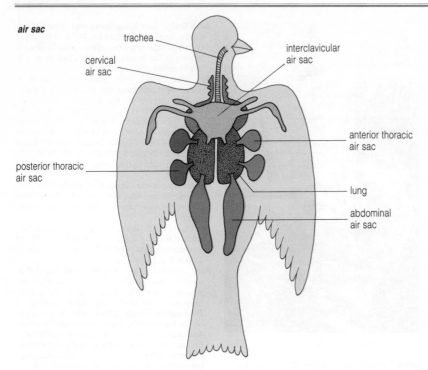

trachea

cervical
air sac

interclavicular
air sac

anterior thoracic
air sac

posterior thoracic
air sac

lung

abdominal
air sac

air. The ◊hovercraft is the best-known form of ACV.

Airedale terrier /ˈeədeɪl/ large ◊terrier dog with a rough red-brown coat. It originated about 1850 in the Aire and Wharfedale districts of Yorkshire, England, as a cross of the otter hound and Irish and Welsh terriers.

air force a nation's fighting aircraft and the organization that maintains them.

history The emergence of the aeroplane at first brought only limited recognition of its potential value as a means of waging war. Like the balloon, used since the American Civil War, it was considered a way of extending the vision of ground forces. A unified air force was established in the UK 1918, Italy 1923, France 1928, Germany 1935 (after repudiating the arms limitations of the Versailles treaty), and the USA 1947 (it began as the Aeronautical Division of the Army Signal Corps in 1907, and evolved into the Army's Air Service Division by 1918; by 1926 it was the Air Corps and in World War II the Army Air Forces). The main specialized groupings formed during World War I – such as *combat*, *bombing* (see ◊bomb), *reconnaissance*, and *transport* – were adapted and modified in World War II; activity was extended, with self-contained tactical air forces to meet the needs of ground commanders in the main theatres of land operations and for the attack on and defence of shipping over narrow seas.

In 1945–60 the piston engine was superseded by the jet engine, which propelled its craft at supersonic speeds; extremely precise electronic guidance systems lessened the difference between missile and aircraft; and flights of unlimited duration became possible with air-to-air refuelling. The US Strategic Air Command's bombers can patrol 24 hours a day armed with thermonuclear weapons. It was formerly anticipated that the pilot might become obsolete, but the continuation of conventional warfare and the evolution of tactical nuclear weapons have led in the 1970s and 1980s to the development of advanced combat aircraft able to fly supersonically beneath an enemy's radar on strike and reconnaissance missions, as well as so-called stealth aircraft that cannot be detected by radar.

airglow a faint and variable light in the Earth's atmosphere produced by chemical reactions in the ionosphere.

airlock airtight chamber that allows people to pass between areas of different pressure; also an air bubble in a pipe that impedes fluid flow. An airlock may connect an environment at ordinary pressure and an environment that has high air pressure (such as a submerged caisson used for tunnelling or building dams or bridge foundations). An airlock may also permit someone wearing breathing apparatus to pass into an airless environment (into water from a submerged submarine or into the vacuum of space from a spacecraft).

air pollution see ◊pollution.

air raid aerial attack, usually on a civilian population. In World War II (1939–45), raids were usually made by bomber aircraft, but many thousands were killed in London in 1944 by German V1 and V2 rockets. The air raids on Britain 1940–41 became known as *the Blitz*. The Allies made air raids over European cities.

air sac in birds, a thin-walled extension of the lungs. There are nine of these and they extend into the abdomen and bones, effectively increasing lung capacity. In mammals, it is another name for the alveoli in the lungs, and, in some insects, widenings of the ◊trachea.

airship a power-driven balloon. All airships have streamlined envelopes or hulls, which contain the inflation gas (originally hydrogen, now helium) and are non-rigid, semi-rigid, or rigid.

Count Ferdinand von Zeppelin pioneered the rigid airship, used for bombing raids on Britain in World War I. The destruction by fire of the British R101 in 1930 halted airship building in Britain, but the Germans continued and built the 248 m/812 ft long *Hindenburg*, which exploded at Lakehurst, New Jersey, USA, in 1937, marking the effective end of airship travel.

Early airships were vulnerable because they used highly flammable hydrogen for inflation. After World War II, interest grew in airships using the non-flammable gas helium. They cause minimum noise pollution, can lift enormous loads, and are economical on fuel. Britain's Airship Industries received large orders in 1987 from the US Navy for airships to be used for coastguard patrols.

Airy /ˈeəri/ George Biddell 1801–1892. English astronomer. At Greenwich he installed a transit telescope for accurately measuring time by the stars. The position of this instrument defines the Greenwich meridian, internationally accepted as the line of zero longitude in 1884.

Airy was made director of the Cambridge University Observatory in 1828 and became the seventh Astronomer Royal in 1835. He began the distribution of Greenwich time signals by telegraph, and ◊Greenwich Mean Time as measured by Airy's telescope was adopted as legal time in Britain in 1880.

Aisha favourite wife of ◊Muhammad.

Aisne /eɪn/ river of N France, giving its name to a *département*; length 282 km/175 mi.

Aix-en-Provence /ˈeɪks ɒm prəˈvɒns/ town in the *département* of Bouches-du-Rhône, France, 29 km/18 mi north of Marseille; population (1982) 127,000. It is the capital of Provence, and dates from Roman times, when it was known as *Aquae Sextiae*. It has a Gothic cathedral and a university 1409. The painter Cézanne was born here.

Aix-la-Chapelle /ˈeɪks læ ʃæˈpel/ French name of ◊Aachen, ancient city in Germany.

Aix-les-Bains /ˈeɪks leɪ ˈbæn/ spa with hot springs in the *département* of Savoie, France, near Lake Bourget, 13 km/8 mi north of Chambéry; population (1982) 22,534.

Ajaccio /æˈʒæksiəʊ/ capital and second largest port of Corsica; population (1982) 55,279. Founded by the Genoese in 1492, it was the birthplace of Napoleon; it has been French since 1768.

Ajanta /əˈdʒʌntə/ village in Maharashtra state, India, known for its Buddhist cave temples dating from 200 BC to the 7th century AD.

Ajax /ˈeɪdʒæks/ Greek hero in Homer's ◊Iliad. Son of Telamon, king of Salamis, he was second only to Achilles among the Greek heroes in the Trojan War. When ◊Agamemnon awarded the armour of the dead Achilles to ◊Odysseus, Ajax is said to have gone mad with jealousy, and then committed suicide in shame.

Ajman /ˈædʒmɑːn/ smallest of the seven states that make up the ◊United Arab Emirates; area 250 sq km/96 sq mi; population (1980) 36,000.

Ajmer /ɑːdʒˈmɪə/ town in Rajasthan state, India; population (1981) 376,000. Situated in a deep valley in the Aravalli mountains, it is a commercial and industrial centre, notably of cotton manufacture. It has many ancient remains, including a Jain temple. It was formerly the capital of the small state of Ajmer, which was merged with Rajasthan 1956.

ajolote Mexican reptile of the genus *Bipes*. Like other members of the amphisbaenian group it lives underground; unlike the others, which have no legs, it has a pair of front legs which are short but well developed. In line with its burrowing habits, the skull is very solid, the eyes small, and external ears absent. The scales are arranged in rings, giving the body a worm-like appearance.

AK abbreviation for ◊*Alaska*.

Akaba /ˈækəbə/ alternative transliteration of ◊Aqaba, gulf of the Red Sea.

Akbar /ˈækbɑː/ Jellaladin Muhammad 1542–1605. Mughal emperor of N India from 1556, when he succeeded his father. He gradually established his rule throughout the whole of India N of the Deccan. He is considered the greatest of the Mughal emperors, and the firmness and wisdom of his rule won him the title 'Guardian of Mankind'; he was a patron of the arts.

A Kempis Thomas see ◊Thomas à Kempis, religious writer.

Akhenaton another name for ◊Ikhnaton, pharaoh of Egypt.

Akhetaton /ˌækɪˈtɑːtɒn/ capital of ancient Egypt established by the monotheistic pharaoh ◊Ikhnaton as the centre for his cult of the Aten, the sun's disc; it is the modern Tell el Amarna 300 km/190 mi S of Cairo. His palace had formal enclosed gardens. After his death it was abandoned, and the ◊*Amarna tablets*, found in the ruins, were probably discarded by his officials.

Akhmatova /ækˈmætəvə/ Anna. Pen name of Anna Andreevna Gorenko 1889–1966. Russian poet. Among her works are the cycle *Requiem* 1963 (written in the 1930s), which deals with the

Alabama

Stalinist terror, and *Poem without a hero* 1962 (begun 1940).

In the 1920s she published several collections of poetry in the realist style of ◊Mandelshtam, but her lack of sympathy with the post-revolutionary regimes inhibited her writing, and her work was banned 1922–40 and again from 1946. From the mid-1950s her work was gradually rehabilitated in the USSR. In 1989 an Akhmatova Museum was opened in Leningrad.

Akihito /ˌæki'hiːtəʊ/ 1933– . Emperor of Japan from 1989, succeeding his father Hirohito (Showa). His reign is called the Heisei ('achievement of universal peace') era.

Unlike previous crown princes, Akihito was educated alongside commoners at the elite Gakushuin school and in 1959 he married Michiko Shoda (1934–), the daughter of a flour-company president. Their three children, the Oxford university-educated Crown Prince Hiro, Prince Aya, and Princess Nori, were raised at Akihito's home instead of being reared by tutors and chamberlains in a separate imperial dormitory.

Akins /'eɪkɪnz/ Zoe 1886–1958. US writer. Born in Missouri, she wrote poems, literary criticism, and plays, of which the best known is *The Greeks Had a Word for It* 1930.

Akkad northern Semitic people who conquered the Sumerians in 2350 BC and ruled Mesopotamia. The ancient city of Akkad in central Mesopotamia, founded by ◊Sargon I, was an imperial centre in the 3rd millennium BC; the site is unidentified, but it was on the Euphrates.

Akkaia alternative form of ◊Achaea.

Akko /'ækəʊ/ Israeli name for the port of ◊Acre.

Akola /ə'kəʊlə/ town in Maharashtra state, India, near the Purnar; population (1981) 176,000. It is an important cotton and grain centre.

Akron /'ækrən/ (Greek 'summit') city in Ohio, USA, on the Cuyahoga River, 56 km/35 mi SE of Cleveland; population (1980) 660,000. Almost half the world supply of rubber is processed here.
history Akron was first settled 1807. Dr B F Goodrich established a rubber factory 1870, and the industry grew immensely with the rising demand for car tyres from about 1910.

Akrotiri /ˌækrəʊ'tɪəri/ peninsula on the south coast of Cyprus; it has a British military base.

Aksai Chin /ˌæksaɪ/ part of Himalayan Kashmir lying to the east of the Karakoram range. Occupied by China but claimed by India.

Aksakov /æk'saːkɒv/ Sergei Timofeyevich 1791–1859. Russian writer, born at Ufa, in the Urals. Under the influence of ◊Gogol, he wrote autobiographical novels, including *Chronicles of a*

Akihito *Emperor Akihito and his wife on their wedding day, 1959.*

Russian Family 1856, and *Years of Childhood* 1858.

Aksum /'aːksʊm/ ancient Greek-influenced Semitic kingdom which flourished 1st–6th centuries AD and covered a large part of modern Ethiopia as well as the Sudan. The ruins of its capital, also called Aksum, lie NW of Aduwa, but the site has been developed as a modern city.

Aktyubinsk /æk'tjuːbɪnsk/ industrial city in the republic of Kazakh, USSR; population (1987) 248,000. Established 1869, it expanded after the opening of the Trans-Caspian railway 1905.

al- for Arabic names beginning 'al-', see rest of name; for example, for 'al-Fatah', see ◊Fatah, al-.

AL abbreviation for ◊*Alabama*.

Alabama /ˌælə'bæmə/ state of S USA; nickname Heart of Dixie/Camellia State
area 134,700 sq km/51,994 sq mi
capital Montgomery
towns Birmingham, Mobile, Huntsville, Tuscaloosa
physical the state comprises the Cumberland Plateau in the N; the Black Belt, or Canebrake, which is excellent cotton-growing country, in the centre; and S of this, the coastal plain of Piny Woods. The Alabama river is the largest in the state.
features Alabama and Tennessee rivers; Appalachian mountains; George Washington Carver Museum at the Tuskegee Institute (a college founded for blacks by Booker T Washington) and Helen Keller's birthplace at Tuscumbia
products cotton no longer prime crop, though still important; soybeans, peanuts, wood products, coal, iron, chemicals, textiles, paper
population (1987) 4,149,000
famous people Nat King Cole, Helen Keller, Joe Louis, Jesse Owens, Booker T Washington
history first settled by the French in the early 18th century, it was ceded to Britain 1763, passed to the USA 1783, and became a state 1819. It was one of the Confederate States in the American Civil War (see ◊Confederacy).

Alabama /ˌælə'bæmə/ Confederate warship cruiser (1,040 tonnes) in the American ◊Civil War. Built in the UK, it was allowed to leave port by the British, and sank 68 Union merchant ships before it was itself sunk by a Union warship off the coast of France in 1864. In 1871 the international court awarded damages of $15.5 million to the USA, a legal precedent.

The court's ruling requires a neutral country to exercise 'due diligence' to prevent the arming within its jurisdiction of a vessel intending to carry out a war against a country with which the neutral is at peace.

alabaster a naturally occurring fine-grained white or light-coloured translucent form of ◊gypsum, often streaked or mottled. It is a soft material, used for carvings, and ranks 2 on the ◊Mohs scale of hardness.

Aladdin in the ◊*Arabian Nights*, a poor boy who obtains a magic lamp: when the lamp is rubbed, a jinn (genie, or spirit) appears and fulfils its owner's wishes.

Alain-Fournier /æ'læŋ 'fʊəniel/ pen name of Henri-Alban Fournier 1886–1914. French novelist. His haunting semi-autobiographical fantasy *Le Grand Meaulnes/The Lost Domain* 1913 was a cult novel of the 1920s and 1930s. His life is intimately recorded in his correspondence with his brother-in-law Jacques Rivière.

Alamein, El, Battles of /'æləmeɪn/ in World War II, two decisive battles in the western desert, N Egypt. In the *First Battle of El Alamein* 1–27 Jul 1942 the British 8th Army under Auchinleck held the German and Italian forces under Rommel. In the *Second Battle of El Alamein* 23 Oct–4 Nov 1942 ◊Montgomery defeated Rommel.

Alamo, the /'æləməʊ/ mission fortress in San Antonio, Texas, USA; besieged 23 Feb–6 Mar 1836 by ◊Santa Anna and 4,000 Mexicans; they killed the garrison of about 180, including Davy ◊Crockett and Jim ◊Bowie.

Alamogordo /ˌæləmə'gɔːdəʊ/ town in New Mexico, USA. The first atom bomb was exploded nearby at Trinity Site 16 July 1945. It is now a test site for guided missiles.

Alanbrooke /'ælənbrʊk/ Alan Francis Brooke, 1st Viscount Alanbrooke 1883–1963. British army officer, chief of staff in World War II and largely responsible for the strategy that led to the German defeat.

He was born in Ireland. He served in the artillery in World War I, and in World War II, as commander of the 2nd Corps 1939–40, did much to aid the extrication of the British Expeditionary Force from Dunkirk. He was commander in chief of the Home Forces 1940–41 and chief of the Imperial General Staff 1941–46. He became a field marshal in 1944, was created a baron 1945 and viscount 1946.

Åland Islands /'ɔːlənd/ (Finnish Ahvenanmaa 'land of waters') group of some 6,000 islands in the Baltic Sea, at the southern extremity of the Gulf of Bothnia; area 1,481 sq km/572 sq mi; population (1983) 23,435. Only 80 are inhabited; the island of Ahvenanmaa is the largest and has a small town, Maarianhamina. When Finland became independent 1917, the Swedish-speaking islanders claimed the right of self-determination, and were granted autonomous status 1920.

Alarcón /ˌælaː'kɒn/ Pedro Antonio de 1833–1891. Spanish journalist and writer. The acclaimed *Diario/Diary* was based upon his experiences as a soldier in Morocco. His *El Sombrero de tres picos/The Three-Cornered Hat* 1874 was the basis of Manuel de Falla's ballet.

Alaric /'ælərɪk/ c. 370–410. King of the Visigoths. In 396 he invaded Greece and retired with much booty to Illyria. In 400 and 408 he invaded Italy, and in 410 captured and sacked Rome, but he died the same year on his way to invade Sicily.

The river Busento was diverted by his soldiers so that he could be buried in its course with his treasures; the labourers were killed to keep the secret.

Alaska /ə'læskə/ largest state of the USA, on the NW extremity of North America, separated from the lower 48 states by British Columbia
area 1,531,100 sq km/591,005 sq mi
capital Juneau
towns Anchorage, Fairbanks, Fort Yukon, Holy Cross, Nome
physical much of Alaska is mountainous and includes Mount McKinley, 6,194 m/20,329 ft, the highest peak in North America, surrounded by a national park. Reindeer thrive in the Arctic tundra and elsewhere there are extensive forests.
features Yukon river; Rocky Mountains, including Mount McKinley, Mount Katmai, a volcano which erupted 1912 and formed the Valley of Ten Thousand Smokes (the smoke and steam still escaping from fissures in the floor) now a national monument; Arctic Wild Life Range, with the only large herd of North American caribou; Little Diomede Island, which is only 4 km/2.5 mi from Big Diomede/Ratmanov Island in the USSR; reindeer herds on the tundra; an Act of 1980 gave environmental protection to 42 million ha/104 million acres. The chief railway line runs from Seward to Fairbanks, which is linked by motor road (via Canada) with Seattle. Air services are frequent. Near Fairbanks is the University of Alaska.
products oil, natural gas, coal, copper, iron, gold, tin, fur, salmon fisheries and canneries, lumber
population (1987) 538,000, including about 50,000 American Indians, Aleuts, and Inuits
history the first European to visit Alaska was Vitus Bering 1741. Alaska was a Russian colony from 1744 until purchased by the USA 1867 for $7,200,000; it became a state 1959. Exploited from 1968, especially in the Prudhoe Bay area to the SE of Point Barrow, are the most valuable mineral resources. An oil pipeline (1977) runs from Prudhoe Bay to the Port of Valdez, and was

Alaska

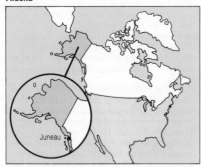

the focus of an oilspill 1989. An underground natural gas pipeline is under construction to Chicago and San Francisco.

Alaska Highway road that runs from Fort St John, British Columbia, to Fairbanks, Alaska (2,450 km/1,522 mi). It was built 1942 as a supply route for US forces in Alaska.

Alba /ˈælbə/ Celtic name for Scotland; also an alternate spelling for ◊Alva, Ferdinand Alvarez de Toledo, duke of Alva, Spanish politician and general.

Albacete /ˌælbəˈθeɪti/ market town in the province of the same name, SE Spain; population (1986) 127,000. Once famous for cutlery, it now produces clothes and footwear.

albacore name loosely applied to several sorts of fish found in warm regions of the Atlantic and Pacific oceans, in particular to a large tunny and to several species of mackerel.

Alba Iulia ˌælbəˈjuːliə (German *Karlsburg*) a city on the River Mures, W central Romania, founded by the Romans in the 2nd century AD. The Romanian kings were crowned here. Population (1985) 64,300.

Albania /ælˈbeɪniə/ country in SE Europe, bounded to the W and SW by the Mediterranean sea, to the N and E by Yugoslavia, and to the SE by Greece.
government under the 1946 constitution (amended 1950), Albania's sole and supreme legislative organ is the 250-member People's Assembly, elected every four years by universal suffrage. This assembly meets twice a year and elects a permanent 15-member presidium, with a chair who acts as state president, to take over its functions in its absence. The People's Assembly also elects a council of ministers, headed by a chair or prime minister, to act as the day-to-day executive government. The Communist Party (Albanian Party of Labour), controlled by its political bureau, is the only political party and is the leading force in the Democratic Front of Albania.
history in the ancient world the area was occupied by the Illyrians, later becoming a Roman province until the end of the 4th century AD. Albania then came under Byzantine rule, which lasted until 1347. There followed about 100 years of invasions by Bulgarians, Serbs, Venetians, and finally Turks, who arrived in 1385 and, after the death of the nationalist leader Skanderbeg (George Castriota) (1403–68), eventually made Albania part of the ◊Ottoman empire 1468.

Albania became independent 1912, and a republic 1925. In 1928 President Ahmed Beg Zogu was proclaimed King Zog. Overrun by Italy and Germany 1939–44, Albania became a republic with a communist government 1946, after a guerrilla struggle led by Enver ◊Hoxha.

At first closely allied with Yugoslavia, Albania backed ◊Stalin in his 1948 dispute with ◊Tito and developed close links with the USSR 1949–55, entering ◊Comecon 1949. Hoxha imposed a Stalinist system with rural collectivization, industrial nationalization, central planning, and one-party control. Mosques and churches were closed in an effort to create the 'first atheist state'. Hoxha remained a committed Stalinist

and, rejecting ◊Khrushchev's denunciations of the Stalin era, broke off diplomatic relations with the USSR 1961 and withdrew from Comecon. Albania also severed diplomatic relations with China 1978, after the post-Mao accommodation with the US, choosing isolation and neutrality.

The 'Hoxha experiment' left Albania with the lowest per capita income in Europe. Since his death 1985, there have been policy adjustments and a widening of external economic contacts. New economic incentives in the form of wage differentials for skilled tasks are gradually being introduced, and the number of countries with which Albania has formal diplomatic relations increased from 74 in 1978 to 111 in 1988. In Feb 1988 Albania attended the conference of Balkan states for the first time since the 1930s. Opposition to the regime began to mount during 1990, reportedly forcing the imposition of a state of emergency around the NW border town of Shkoder.

Alban, St /ˈɔːlbən/ died AD 303. First Christian martyr in England. In 793 King Offa founded a monastery on the site of Alban's martyrdom, and round this the city of St Albans grew up. According to tradition, he was born at Verulamium, served in the Roman army, became a convert to Christianity after giving shelter to a priest, and, on openly professing his belief, was beheaded.

Albany /ˈɔːlbəni/ capital of New York State, USA, situated on the river Hudson, about 225 km/140 mi north of New York City. With Schenectady and Troy it forms a metropolitan area, population (1980) 794,298.

Albany /ˈɔːlbəni/ port in Western Australia, population (1986) 14,100. It suffered from the initial development of ◊Fremantle, but has grown with the greater exploitation of the surrounding area. The Albany Doctor is a cooling breeze from the sea, rising in the afternoon.

albatross large seabird, genus *Diomedea*, with narrow wings up to 3 m/10 ft long adapted for gliding, mainly found in the S hemisphere. It belongs to the order Procellariidae (◊petrel). It is also known as the 'gooney bird', probably because of its clumsy

Alberta

way of landing. Albatrosses are becoming increasingly rare.

albedo the fraction of the incoming light reflected by a body such as a planet. A body with a high albedo, near 1, is very bright, while a body with a low albedo, near 0, is dark. The Moon has an average albedo of 0.07, Venus 0.76, Earth 0.37.

Albee /ˈælbiː/ Edward 1928– . US playwright. His internationally performed plays are associated with the theatre of the absurd and include *The Zoo Story* 1960, *The American Dream* 1961, *Who's Afraid of Virginia Woolf?* 1962 (filmed with Elizabeth Taylor and Richard Burton as the quarrelling, alcoholic, academic couple 1966), *Tiny Alice* 1965, and *A Delicate Balance* 1966.

Albéniz /ælˈbeɪnɪθ/ Isaac 1860–1909. Spanish composer and pianist, born in Catalonia. He composed the suite *Iberia* and other piano pieces, making use of traditional Spanish tunes.

Alberoni /ˌælbəˈrəʊni/ Giulio 1664–1752. Spanish-Italian priest and politician. Born in Parma, Italy. Philip V made him prime minister of Spain in 1715. In 1717 he became a cardinal. He introduced many reforms, but was forced to flee to Italy in 1719, when his foreign policies failed.

Albert /ˈælbət/ Prince Consort 1819–1861. Husband of British Queen ◊Victoria from 1840; a patron of arts and science. Albert was the second son of the Duke of Saxe-Coburg-Gotha and first

---

Albania
Socialist People's Republic of
(Republika Popullore Socialiste e Shqipërisë)

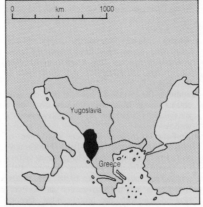

area 28,748 sq km/11,097 sq mi
capital Tirana
towns Shkodër, Vlorë, chief port Durrës
physical mainly mountainous, with rivers flowing E–W, and a small coastal plain
features Dinaric Alps, with wild boar and wolves
head of state Ramiz Alia from 1982
head of government Adil Carcani from 1982. Enver Hoxha remained premier as first secretary of Albanian Party of Labour until his death 1985

political system one-party socialist republic
political parties Party of Labour of Albania (PLA), Marxist-Leninist; Committee for the Democratic Movement in Albania (based in Yugoslavia)
exports crude oil, bitumen, chrome, iron ore, nickel, coal, copper wire, tobacco, fruit
currency lek (10.19 = £1 Feb 1990)
population (1987) 3,080,000; annual growth rate 2.1%
life expectancy men 69, women 73
language Albanian
religion Muslim 70%, although since 1967 Albania is officially a secular state
literacy 75% (1986)
GNP $2.8 bn (1986 est); $900 per head of population
chronology
1912 Albania achieved independence from Turkey.
1925 Republic proclaimed.
1928–39 Monarchy of King Zog.
1939–44 Under Italian and then German rule.
1946 Communist republic proclaimed under the leadership of Enver Hoxha.
1949 Admitted into Comecon.
1961 Break with Khrushchev's USSR.
1978 Break with 'revisionist' China.
1985 Death of Hoxha.
1987 Normal diplomatic relations restored with Canada, Greece, and West Germany.
1988 Attendance of conference of Balkan states for the first time since the 1930s.
1990 State of emergency imposed around border town of Shkoder.

cousin to Queen Victoria. He planned the Great Exhibition of 1851, which made a handsome profit (£186,000); Albert popularized the Christmas tree in England. He was regarded by the British people with groundless suspicion because of his German connections. He died of typhoid. The **Albert Memorial** 1872, designed by Sir Gilbert Scott, in Kensington Gardens, London, typifies Victorian decorative art.

Albert I /'ælbət/ 1875–1934. King of the Belgians from 1909, the younger son of Philip, Count of Flanders, and the nephew of Leopold II. In 1900 he married Duchess Elisabeth of Bavaria. In World War I he commanded the Allied army that conquered the Belgian coast in 1918, re-entering Brussels in triumph on 22 Nov. He was killed while mountaineering.

Alberta /æl'bɜːtə/ province of W Canada
area 661,200 sq km/255,223 sq mi
capital Edmonton
towns Calgary, Lethbridge, Medicine Hat, Red Deer
physical the Rocky Mountains; dry, treeless prairie in the centre and south; towards the north this merges into a zone of poplar, then mixed forest. The valley of the Peace River is the most northerly farming land in Canada (except for Inuit pastures), and there are good grazing lands in the foothills of the Rockies.
features Banff, Jasper, and Waterton Lake national parks; annual Calgary stampede, extensive dinosaur finds near Drumheller
products coal; wheat, barley, oats, sugar beet in the S; more than a million head of cattle; oil and natural gas
population (1986) 2,375,000
history in the 17th century much of its area was part of a grant to the ◊Hudson's Bay Company for the fur trade. It became a province in 1905.

Albert Canal /'ælbət/ canal designed as part of Belgium's frontier defences; it also links the industrial basin of Liège with the port of Antwerp. It was built 1930–39 and named after King Albert I.

Alberti /æl'beəti/ Leon Battista 1404–1472. Italian ◊Renaissance architect and theorist, noted for his recognition of the principles of classical architecture and their modification for Renaissance practice in *On Architecture* 1452.

Albert, Lake /'ælbət/ former name of Lake ◊Mobutu in central Africa.

Albertus Magnus, St /æl'bɜːtəs 'mægnəs/ 1206–1280. Scholar of theology, philosophy (especially Aristotle), natural science, chemistry, and physics. He was known as 'doctor universalis' because of the breadth of his knowledge. Feast day 15 Nov.

He studied at Bologna and Padua, and entered the Dominican order 1223. He taught at Cologne and lectured from 1245 at Paris University. St Thomas Aquinas was his pupil there, and followed him to Cologne 1248. He became provincial of the Dominicans in Germany 1254, and was made bishop of Ratisbon 1260. Two years later he resigned and eventually retired to his convent at Cologne. He was canonized 1932.

Albi /æl'biː/ chief town in Tarn *département*, Midi-Pyrénées, SW France, on the river Tarn, 72 km/45 mi NE of Toulouse; population (1983) 45,000. It was the centre of the Albigensian heresy (see ◊Albigenses) and the birthplace of the artist Toulouse-Lautrec. It has a 13th-century cathedral.

Albigenses /,ælbɪ'dʒensiːz/ heretical sect of Christians (associated with the ◊Cathars) who flourished in S France near Albi and Toulouse during the 11th–13th centuries. They adopted the Manichean belief in the duality of good and evil and pictured Jesus as being a rebel against the cruelty of an omnipotent God.

The Albigensians showed a consistently anti-Catholic attitude with distinctive sacraments, especially the *consolamentum*, or baptism of the spirit. An inquisition was used against the Albigensians in 1184 (although the ◊Inquisition as

alcohol

The systematic naming of simple straight-chain organic molecules

Alkane	Alcohol	Aldehyde	Ketone	Carboxylic acid	Alkene
CH_4 methane	CH_3OH methanol	HCHO methanal	–	HCO_2H methanoic acid	–
CH_3CH_3 ethane	CH_3CH_2OH ethanol	CH_3CHO ethanal	–	CH_3CO_2H ethanoic acid	CH_2CH_2 ethene
$CH_3CH_2CH_3$ propane	$CH_3CH_2CH_2OH$ propanol	CH_3CH_2CHO propanal	CH_3COCH_3 propanone	$CH_3CH_2CO_2H$ propanoic acid	CH_2CHCH_3 propene
methane	methanol	methanal	propanone	methanoic acid	ethene

we know it was not established until 1233); it was, however, ineffective, and in 1208 a crusade (1208–29) was launched against them under the elder Simon de Montfort. Thousands were killed before the movement was crushed in 1244.

albinism rare hereditary condition in which the body fails to synthesize the pigment known as melanin, normally found in the skin, hair and eyes. As a result, the hair is white, and the skin and eyes are pink. The skin and eyes are abnormally sensitive to light, and vision is often impaired.

Albinoni /,ælbɪ'nəuni/ Tomaso 1671–1751. Italian Baroque composer and violinist, whose work was studied and adapted by ◊Bach. He composed over 40 operas.

Adagio, often described as being by Albinoni, was actually composed by his biographer Remo Giazotto (1910–   ).

Albion /'ælbiən/ ancient name for Britain used by the Greeks and Romans. It was mentioned by Pytheas of Massilia (4th century BC), and is probably of Celtic origin, but the Romans, having in mind the white cliffs of Dover, assumed it to be derived from *albus* (white).

Alboin /'ælbɔɪn/ 6th century. King of the ◊Lombards about 561–573. At that time the Lombards were settled north of the Alps. Early in his reign he attacked the Gepidae, a Germanic tribe occupying Romania, killing their king and taking his daughter Rosamund to be his wife. About 568 he invaded Italy, conquering the country as far as Rome. He was murdered at the instigation of his wife, whom he had forced to drink from a wine-cup made from her father's skull.

Albone /'ɔːlbəun/ Dan 1860–1906. English inventor of one of the first commercially available farm tractors, the Ivel, in 1902. It was a three-wheeled vehicle with a midmounted twin-cylinder petrol engine that could plough an acre in 1.5 hours.

Ålborg /'ɔːlbɔːg/ alternative form of ◊Aalborg, Denmark.

Albufeira fishing village and resort on the Algarve coast of S Portugal, 43 km/27 mi W of Faro.

albumin or **albumen** sulphur-containing ◊protein substance, best known in the form of egg white. It also occurs in milk, and as a major component of serum.

The presence of albumin in the urine, termed albuminuria or proteinuria, may be a symptom of a kidney disorder.

Albuquerque /'ælbəkɜːki/ largest city of New Mexico, USA, situated east of the Rio Grande, in the Pueblo district; population (1982) 342,000. Founded 1706, it was named after Alfonso de Albuquerque. It is a resort and industrial centre, specializing in electronics.

Albuquerque /'ælbəkɜːki/ Alfonso de 1453–1515. Viceroy and founder of the Portuguese East Indies 1508–15, when the king of Portugal replaced him by his worst enemy and he died at sea

on the way home; his ship *Flor del Mar* was lost between Malaysia and India with all his treasure.

Albury-Wodonga /'ɔːbəri wə'dɒŋgə/ twin town on the New South Wales/Victoria border, Australia; population (1981) 54,214. It was planned to relieve overspill from Melbourne and Sydney, and produces car components.

Alcaeus /æl'siːəs/ *c.*611–*c.*580 BC. Greek lyric poet. Born at Mytilene in Lesvos, he was a member of the aristocratic party and went into exile when the popular party triumphed. He wrote odes, and the Alcaic stanza is named after him.

Alcatraz /'ælkətræz/ small island in San Francisco Bay, California, USA. Its fortress was a military prison 1886–1934, and then a federal penitentiary until closed 1963. The dangerous currents meant few successful escapes. Inmates included the gangster Al Capone and the 'Birdman of Alcatraz', a prisoner who used his time in solitary confinement to become an authority on cage birds. American Indian 'nationalists' took over the island 1970 as a symbol of their lost heritage.

alcázar /æl'kæθɑː/ (Arabic 'fortress') Moorish palace in Spain; one of five in Toledo was defended by the Nationalists against the Republicans for 71 days in 1936 during the Spanish ◊Civil War.

Alcazarquivir, Battle of battle on 4 Aug 1578 between the forces of Sebastian, king of Portugal (1554–1578), and those of the Berber kingdom of Fez. Sebastian's death on the field of battle paved the way for the incorporation of Portugal into the Spanish kingdom of Philip II.

alchemy (Arabic **al-Kimya**) the supposed art of transmuting base metals, such as lead and mercury, into silver and gold by the philosopher's stone, a hypothetical substance, to which was also attributed the power to give eternal life.

This aspect of alchemy constituted much of the chemistry of the Middle Ages. More broadly, however, alchemy was a system of philosophy that dealt both with the mystery of life and the formation of inanimate substances. Alchemy was a complex and indefinite conglomeration of chemistry, astrology, occultism, and magic, blended with obscure and abstruse ideas derived from various religious systems and other sources. It flourished in Europe during the Middle Ages but later fell into disrepute.

Alcibiades /,ælsɪ'baɪədiːz/ 450–404 BC. Athenian general. Handsome and dissolute, he became the archetype of capricious treachery for his military intrigues against his native state with Sparta and Persia; the Persians eventually had him assassinated. He was brought up by ◊Pericles and was a friend of ◊Socrates, whose reputation as a teacher suffered from the association.

Alcmaeonidae /,ælkmɪ'ɒnidiː/ a noble family of ancient Athens; its members included ◊Pericles and ◊Alcibiades.

Alcmene in Greek mythology, the wife of Amphitryon, and mother of Hercules (the father was Zeus, king of the gods, who visited Alcmene in the form of her husband).

Alcock /'ælkɒk/ John William 1892–1919. British aviator. On 14 June 1919 in a Vickers-Vimy biplane, he and Lt Whitten-Brown made the first nonstop transatlantic flight. Alcock died after an aeroplane accident in the same year.

Alcoforado /,ælkəʊfə'rɑ:dəʊ/ Marianna 1640–1723. Portuguese nun. The *Letters of a Portuguese Nun* 1699, supposedly written by her to a young French nobleman (who abandoned her when their relations became known), are no longer accepted as authentic.

alcohol member of a group of organic chemical compounds characterized by the presence of one or more OH (hydroxyl) groups in the molecule. The main uses of alcohols are in alcoholic drinks (ethanol), as solvents for gums and resins, in lacquers and varnishes, in the making of dyes, for essential oils in perfumery, and for medical substances in pharmacy.

Alcohols may be liquids or solids, according to the size and complexity of the molecule. The five best-known alcohols form a series in which the number of carbon and hydrogen atoms increases progressively, each one having an extra CH_2 (methylene) group in the molecule: methanol (methyl alcohol) or wood spirit (CH_3OH); ethanol (ethyl alcohol) (C_2H_5OH); propanol (propyl alcohol) (C_3H_7OH); butanol (butyl alcohol) (C_4H_9OH); and pentanol (amyl alcohol) ($C_5H_{11}OH$). The lower alcohols are liquids that mix with water; the higher alcohols, such as pentanol, are oily liquids not miscible with water, and the highest are waxy solids, for example hexadecan-1-ol (cetyl alcohol) ($C_{16}H_{33}OH$) and melissyl alcohol ($C_{30}H_{61}OH$), which occur in sperm whale oil and beeswax respectively.

alcoholic liquor an intoxicating drink. ◊Ethanol (ethyl alcohol), a colourless liquid C_2H_5OH, is the basis of all common intoxicants:

wines, ciders, and sherry contain alcohol produced by direct fermentation with yeasts of the sugar content in the relevant fruit;

malt liquors are beers and stouts, in which the starch of the grain is converted to sugar by malting, and the sugar then fermented into alcohol by yeasts. Fermented drinks contain less than 20% alcohol;

spirits are distilled from malted liquors or wines, and can contain up to 55% alcohol.

When consumed, alcohol is rapidly absorbed from the stomach and upper intestine and affects nearly every tissue, particularly the central nervous system. Tests have shown that the feeling of elation usually associated with drinking alcoholic liquors is caused by the loss of inhibitions through removal of the restraining influences of the higher cerebral centres. It also results in dilation of the blood vessels, particularly of the skin. This loss of heat from the skin actually produces a physical cooling inside the body, despite the feeling of warmth experienced. A concentration of 0.15% alcohol in the blood causes mild intoxication; 0.3% definite drunkenness and partial loss of consciousness; 0.6% endangers life. Alcohol is more rapidly absorbed at higher altitudes, as in, for example, the slightly reduced pressure of an aircraft cabin.

Alcoholics Anonymous voluntary self-help organization established 1934 in the USA to combat alcoholism; organizations now exist in many other countries.

alcoholism dependence on alcoholic liquor. It is characterized as an illness when consumption of alcohol interferes with normal physical or emotional health, and may produce physical and psychological addiction. The cost of alcoholism is high in medical and social terms, and the condition is notoriously difficult to treat.

In Britain, the cost of treating alcohol-related diseases in 1985 was estimated as at least £100 million.

alcohol strength a measure of the amount of alcohol in a drink. Wine is measured as the percentage volume of alcohol at 20°C; spirits in litres of alcohol at 20°C, although the percentage volume measure is also commonly used. A 75 cl bottle at 40% volume is equivalent to 0.3 litres of alcohol. See also ◊proof spirit.

Alcott /'ɔ:lkət/ Louisa M(ay) 1832–1888. US author of the children's classic *Little Women* 1869, which drew on her own home circumstances, the heroine Jo being a partial self-portrait. *Good Wives* 1869 was among its sequels.

Alcuin /'ælkwɪn/ 735–804. English scholar. Born in York, he went to Rome in 780, and in 782 took up residence at Charlemagne's court in Aachen. From 796 he was abbot of Tours. He disseminated Anglo-Saxon scholarship, organized education and learning in the Frankish empire, gave a strong impulse to the Carolingian Renaissance, and was a prominent member of Charlemagne's academy.

Aldabra /æl'dæbrə/ high limestone island group in the ◊Seychelles, some 400 km/260 mi NW of Madagascar; area 154 sq km/59 sq mi. A nature reserve since 1976, it has rare plants and animals, including the giant tortoise.

Aldebaran /æl'debərən/ brightest star in the constellation Taurus, and marking the eye of the 'bull'. It is a red giant 68 light years away, shining with a true luminosity of about 100 times that of the Sun. It is the 13th-brightest star in the sky.

Aldeburgh /'ɔ:ldbərə/ small town and coastal resort in Suffolk, England; site of an annual music festival founded by Benjamin ◊Britten. Also the home of the Britten-Pears School for Advanced Studies.

aldehyde group of organic chemical compounds prepared by oxidation of primary alcohols, so that the OH (hydroxyl) group loses its hydrogen to give an oxygen joined by a double bond to a carbon atom (the aldehyde group, with the formula CHO). The name is made up from *alcohol dehydr*ogenation, that is, alcohol from which hydrogen has been removed. Aldehydes are usually liquids and include methanal, ethanal, benzaldehyde, and citral.

alder tree *Alnus glutinosa* allied to the birch and found in wet habitats in Europe and N Asia. About 30 other species of alder occur in the northern hemisphere and South America.

alderman (Old English *ealdor mann* 'older man') Anglo-Saxon term for the noble governor of a shire; after the Norman Conquest the office was replaced with that of sheriff. From the 19th century aldermen were the senior members of the borough or county councils in England and Wales, elected by the other councillors, until the abolition of the office in 1974; the title is still used in the City of London, and for members of a municipal corporation in certain towns in the USA.

Aldermaston /'ɔ:ldəmɑ:stən/ site of the Atomic Weapons Establishment (AWE) in Berkshire, England. During 1958–63 the Campaign for Nuclear Disarmament (CND) made it the focus of an annual Easter protest march.

Alderney /'ɔ:ldəni/ third largest of the ◊Channel Islands, with its capital at St Anne's; area 8 sq km/3 sq mi; population (1980) 2,000. It gives its name to a breed of cattle, better known as the Guernsey.

Aldershot /'ɔ:ldəʃɒt/ town in Hampshire, England, SW of London; population (1981) 32,500. It has a military camp and barracks dating from 1854.

Aldhelm, St /'ɔ:ldhelm/ c.640–709. English prelate and scholar. He was abbot of Malmesbury from 673 and bishop of Sherborne from 705. Of his poems and treatises in Latin, some survive, notably his *Riddles* in hexameters, but his English verse has been lost. He was also known as a skilled architect.

Aldington /'ɔ:ldɪŋtən/ Richard 1892–1962. British ◊Imagist poet, novelist and critic, who was married to Hilda ◊Doolittle from 1913 to 1937. He wrote biographies of D H Lawrence and T E Lawrence. His novels include *Death of a Hero* 1929 and *All Men are Enemies* 1933.

Aldiss /'ɔ:ldɪs/ Brian 1925– . English science-fiction writer, anthologist, and critic. His novels include *Non-Stop* 1958, *The Malacia Tapestry* 1976, and the 'Helliconia' trilogy. *Trillion Year Spree* 1986 is a history of science fiction.

aleatory music (Latin *alea* 'dice') method of composition (pioneered by John ◊Cage) dating from about 1945 in which the elements are assembled by chance by using, for example, dice or computer.

Aleixandre /,æleɪk'sɑ:ndreɪ/ Vicente 1898–1984. Spanish lyric poet, born in Seville. His verse, which was influential with younger Spanish writers, had ◊Republican sympathies, and his work was for a time banned by Franco's government. Nobel Prize for Literature 1977.

Alembert /,ælɒm'beə/ Jean le Rond d' 1717–1783. French mathematician and encyclopedist. He was associated with ◊Diderot in planning the great *Encyclopédie*.

Alençon /,ælɒn'sɒŋ/ capital of the Orne *département* of France, situated in a rich agricultural plain to the SE of Caen; population (1983) 33,000. Lace, now a declining industry, was once an important product.

Alençon /,ælɒn'sɒŋ/ François, Duke of, later Duke of Anjou 1554–1584. Fourth son of Henry II of France and Catherine de' Medici. At one time he was considered as a suitor to Elizabeth I of England.

Alentejo /,ælən'teʒu:/ region of E central Portugal divided into the districts of Alto Alentejo and Baixo Alentejo. The chief towns are Evora, Neja and Portalegre.

Aleppo /ə'lepəʊ/ (Syrian *Halab*) ancient city in NW Syria; population (1981) 977,000. There has been a settlement on the site for at least 4,000 years.

Alessandria /,æli'sændriə/ town in N Italy on the river Tanaro; population (1981) 100,500. It was founded 1168 by Pope Alexander III as a defence against Frederick Barbarossa. There is an annual motorcyclists' rally at the shrine of their patroness, the Madonna of the Centaurs.

Aletsch /'ɑ:letʃ/ most extensive glacier in Europe, 23.6 km/14.7 mi long, beginning on the southern slopes of the Jungfrau in the Bernese Alps, Switzerland.

Aleutian Islands /ə'lu:ʃən/ volcanic island chain in the N Pacific, stretching 1,900 km/1,200 mi SW of Alaska, of which it forms part. Population 6,000 Inuit (Eskimo), most of whom belong to the Greek Orthodox Church, plus a large US military establishment. There are 14 large and over 100 small islands, running along the Aleutian Trench. The islands are mountainous, barren, and treeless; they are ice-free all the year round, but are often foggy.

A level or *Advanced level* in the UK, examinations taken by some students in no more than four subjects at one time, usually at the age of 18 after two years' study. Two A-level passes are normally required for entry to a university degree course.

alewife fish *Pandopus pseudoharengus* of the ◊herring group, up to 30 cm/1 ft long, found off the coast and in the Great Lakes of North America.

Alexander /,ælɪg'zɑ:ndə/ Frederick Matthias 1869–1955. Australian founder and teacher of the Alexander Technique, a psycho-physical relaxation method named after him. At one time a professional reciter, he developed throat and voice trouble, and his experiments in curing himself led him to work out the system of mental and bodily control described in his book *Use of the Self*.

Alexander /,ælɪg'zɑ:ndə/ Harold Rupert Leofric George, 1st Earl Alexander of Tunis 1891–1969. British field marshal, a commander in World War II in Burma, N Africa, and the Mediterranean. He was governor general of Canada 1946–52 and minister of defence 1952–54.

In World War II he was the last person to leave in the evacuation of Dunkirk. In Burma he fought a delaying action for five months against superior Japanese forces. In Aug 1942 he went to N Africa, and in 1943 became deputy to Eisenhower

Alexander II Despite his nickname 'the Liberator', the latter part of the reign of Alexander II of Russia was notable for conflict between the tsar and his government. Repressive measures led to several assassination attempts; he was killed by a bomb thrown into his coach in 1881.

in charge of the Allied forces in Tunisia. After the Axis forces in N Africa surrendered, Alexander became supreme Allied commander in the Mediterranean and, in 1944, field marshal.

Alexander /ˌælɪgˈzɑːndə/ Samuel 1859–1938. Australian philosopher, who originated the theory of emergent evolution: that the space-time matrix evolved matter; matter evolved life; life evolved mind; and finally God emerged from mind. His books include *Space, Time and Deity* 1920. He was professor at Manchester University 1893–1924.

Alexander /ˌælɪgˈzɑːndə/ eight popes, including:

Alexander III (Orlando Barninelli) died 1181. Pope 1159–81. His authority was opposed by ◊Frederick I Barbarossa, but Alexander eventually compelled him to render homage 1178. He supported Henry II of England in his invasion of Ireland, but imposed penance on him after the murder of Thomas ◊Becket.

Alexander VI (Rodrigo Borgia) 1431–1503. Pope 1492–1503. He was of Spanish origin, and bribed his way to the papacy, where he furthered the advancement of his illegitimate children, who included Cesare and Lucrezia ◊Borgia. When

◊Savonarola preached against his corrupt practices Alexander had him executed, and he is said to have died of poison he had prepared for his cardinals. He was a great patron of the arts.

Alexander /ˌælɪgˈzɑːndə/ three tsars of Russia:

Alexander I 1777–1825. Tsar from 1801. Defeated by Napoleon at Austerlitz 1805, he made peace at Tilsit 1807, but economic crisis led to a break with Napoleon's ◊continental system, and the opening of Russian ports to British trade; this led to Napoleon's ill-fated invasion of Russia. After the Congress of Vienna in 1815, Alexander hoped through the Holy Alliance with Austria and Prussia to establish a new Christian order in Europe. He gave a constitution to Poland.

Alexander II 1818–1881. Tsar from 1855. He embarked on reforms of the army, the government, and education, and is remembered as 'the Liberator' for his emancipation of the serfs 1861. However, the revolutionary element remained unsatisfied, and Alexander became increasingly autocratic and reactionary. He was assassinated by ◊Nihilists.

Alexander III 1845–1894. Tsar from 1881, when he succeeded his father, Alexander II. He pursued a reactionary policy, persecuting the Jews and promoting Russification. He married Dagmar (1847–1928), daughter of Christian IX of Denmark and sister of Queen Alexandra of the UK, in 1866.

Alexander /ˌælɪgˈzɑːndə/ three kings of Scotland:

Alexander I *c.*1078–1124. King of Scotland from 1107, known as the *Fierce*.

Alexander II 1198–1249. King of Scotland from 1214, when he succeeded his father William the Lion. Alexander supported the English barons in their struggle with King John after Magna Carta. By the treaty of Newcastle 1244 he acknowledged Henry III of England as his liege lord.

Alexander III 1241–1285. King of Scotland from 1249, son of Alexander II. In 1263 he extended his authority over the Western Isles, which had been dependent on Norway, and strengthened the power of the central Scottish government. He died as the result of a fall from his horse, leaving his granddaughter Margaret, the Maid of Norway, to become queen of Scotland.

Alexander I Karageorgevich 1888–1934. Regent of Serbia 1912–21 and king of Yugoslavia 1921–34, as dictator from 1929; assassinated, possibly by Italian Fascists.

Second son of ◊Peter I, king of Serbia, he was declared regent for his father in 1912, and on his father's death became king of the state of South Slavs – Yugoslavia––which had come into being in

1918. Rivalries of neighbouring powers and of the Croats, Serbs, and Slovenes within the country led Alexander to establish a personal dictatorship. He was assassinated on a state visit to France, and Mussolini's government was later declared to have instigated the crime.

Alexander Nevski, St /ˈnevski/ 1220–1263. Russian military leader, son of the grand duke of Novgorod; in 1240 he defeated the Swedes on the banks of the Neva (hence Nevski), and in 1242 defeated the Teutonic Knights on frozen Lake Peipus.

Alexander Obrenovich /əˈbrenəvits/ 1876–1903. King of Serbia from 1889 while still a minor, on the abdication of his father, King Milan. He took power into his own hands in 1893, and in 1900 married a widow, Draga Mashin. In 1903 Alexander and his queen were murdered, and ◊Peter I Karageorgevich was placed on the throne.

alexanders stong-smelling tall herbaceous plant *Smyrnium olusatrum* of the carrot family. It is found on hedgebanks and cliffs. Its yellow flowers appear in spring and early summer.

Alexander Severus /sɪˈvɪərəs/ AD 208–235. Roman emperor from 222, when he succeeded his cousin Heliogabalus. He was born in Palestine. His campaign against the Persians in 232 achieved some success, but in 235, while proceeding to defend Gaul against German invaders, he was killed in a mutiny.

Alexander the Great /ˌælɪgˈzɑːndə/ 356–323 BC. King of Macedonia and conqueror of the large Persian empire. As commander of the vast Macedonian army he conquered Greece 336. He defeated the Persian king Darius in Asia Minor 333, then moved on to Egypt, where he founded Alexandria. He defeated the Persians again in Assyria 331, then advanced further east to reach the Indus. He conquered the Punjab before diminished troops forced his retreat.

The son of King Philip of Macedonia and Queen Olympias, Alexander was educated by the philosopher Aristotle. He first saw fighting in 340, and at the battle of Chaeronea 338 contributed to the victory by a cavalry charge. At the age of 20, when his father was murdered, the Macedonian throne and army passed into his hands. He secured his northern frontier, suppressed an attempted rising in Greece by his capture of Thebes, and in 334 crossed the Dardanelles for the campaign against the vast Persian empire; at the river Granicus near the Dardanelles he won his first victory. In 333 he routed the Darius at Issus, and then set out for Egypt, where he was greeted as Pharaoh, Meanwhile, Darius assembled half a million men for a final battle, but at Arbela on the Tigris in 331 Alexander, with 47,000 men, drove the Persians into retreat.

After the victory he stayed a month in Babylon, then marched to Susa and Persepolis and in 330 to Ecbatana (now Hamadán, Iran). Soon after he learned that Darius was dead. In Afghanistan he founded colonies at Herat and Kandahar, and in 328 reached the plains of Sogdiana, where he married Roxana, daughter of King Oxyartes. India now lay before him, and he pressed on to the Indus. Near the river Hydaspes (now Jhelum) he fought one of his fiercest battles against the rajah Porus. At the river Hyphasis (now Beas) his men refused to go farther, and reluctantly he turned back down the Indus and along the coast. They reached Susa in 324, where Alexander made Darius's daughter his second wife. He died in Babylon of a malarial fever. mysticism, and ended his reign as a recluse.

Alexandra /ˌælɪgˈzɑːndrə/ 1936– . Princess of the UK. Daughter of the Duke of Kent and Princess Marina, she married Angus Ogilvy (1928–), younger son of the earl of Airlie. They have two children, James (1964–) and Marina (1966–).

Alexandra /ˌælɪgˈzɑːndrə/ 1844–1925. Queen consort of ◊Edward VII of the UK, whom

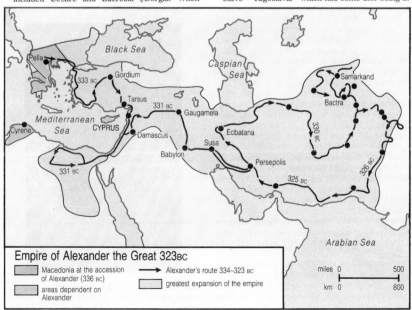

Empire of Alexander the Great 323BC

- Macedonia at the accession of Alexander (336 BC)
- areas dependent on Alexander
- → Alexander's route 334–323 BC
- greatest expansion of the empire

miles 0 — 500
km 0 — 800

she married in 1863. She was the daughter of Christian IX of Denmark. An annual Alexandra Rose Day in aid of hospitals commemorates her charitable work.

Alexandra /ˌælɪgˈzɑːndrə/ 1872–1918. Last tsarina of Russia 1894–1917. She was the former Princess Alix of Hessen, and granddaughter of Queen Victoria. She married ◊Nicholas II and, from 1907, fell under the spell of ◊Rasputin, brought to the palace to try to cure her son of haemophilia. She was shot with the rest of her family by the Bolsheviks in the Russian Revolution.

Alexandretta /ˌælɪgzɑːnˈdretə/ former name of ◊Iskenderun, a port in S Turkey.

Alexandria /ˌælɪgˈzɑːndriə/ or *El Iskandariya* city, chief port, and second largest city of Egypt, situated between the Mediterranean and Lake Maryut; population (1986) 5,000,000. It is linked by canal with the Nile and is an industrial city (oil refining, gas processing, and cotton and grain trading). Founded 331 BC by Alexander the Great, Alexandria was for over 1,000 years the capital of Egypt.

history The principal centre of Hellenistic culture, Alexandria has since the 4th century AD been the seat of a Christian patriarch. In 642 it was captured by the Muslim Arabs, and after the opening of the Cape route its trade rapidly declined. Early in the 19th century it began to recover its prosperity, and its growth was encouraged by its use as the main British naval base in the Mediterranean during both world wars. Of the large European community, most were expelled after the Suez Crisis 1956 and their property confiscated.

Few relics of antiquity remain. The Pharos, the first lighthouse and one of the seven wonders of the ancient world, has long since disappeared. The library, said to have contained 700,000 volumes, was destroyed by the caliph ◊Omar in 642. Pompey's Pillar is a column erected, as a landmark from the sea, by the emperor Diocletian. Two obelisks that once stood before the Caesarum temple are now in London (Cleopatra's Needle) and New York respectively.

Alexandria, Library of library in Alexandria, Egypt, founded 330 BC by ◊Ptolemy I Soter. It was the world's first state-funded scientific institution, and comprised a museum, teaching facilities, and a library that contained 700,000 scrolls, including much ancient Greek literature. It was destroyed 641 following the Arab conquest.

Alexandria, School of /ˌælɪgˈzɑːndriə/ the writers and scholars of Alexandria, who made the city the chief centre of culture in the Western world from about 331 BC to AD 642. They include the poets Callimachus, Apollonius Rhodius, and Theocritus; Euclid, pioneer of geometry; Eratosthenes, the geographer; Hipparchus, who developed a system of trigonometry; the astronomer Ptolemy, who gave his name to the Ptolemaic system of astronomy that endured for over 1,000 years; and the Jewish philosopher Philo. The Gnostics and Neo-Platonists also flourished in Alexandria.

alexandrite rare gemstone variety of the mineral chrysoberyl (beryllium aluminium oxide $BeAl_2O_4$), which is green in daylight but appears red in artificial light.

Alexandrovsk /ˌælɪkˈsɑːndrɒfsk/ older name of ◊Zaporozhe, city in the USSR.

Alexeev /æˈleksief/ Vasiliy 1942– . Soviet weightlifter who broke 80 world records 1970–77, a record for any sport. He was Olympic super-heavyweight champion twice, world champion seven times, and European champion on eight occasions.

At one time the most decorated man in the USSR, he was regarded as the strongest man in the world. He carried the Soviet flag at the 1980 Moscow Olympics opening ceremony, but retired shortly afterwards.

Alfred the Great *The profile of Alfred the Great featured on a coin of about 887. He defended England against the Danish invasions.*

CAREER HIGHLIGHTS

Olympic champion: 1972, 1976
World champion: 1970–71, 1973–75, 1977
European champion: 1970–78.

Alexius /əˈleksiəs/ five emperors of Byzantium, including:

Alexius I (Comnenus) /kɒmˈniːnəs/ 1048–1118. Byzantine emperor 1081–1118. The Latin (W European) Crusaders helped him repel Norman and Turkish invasions, and he devoted great skill to buttressing the threatened empire. His daughter ◊Anna Comnena chronicled his reign.

Alexius III (Angelos) died *c.* 1210. Byzantine emperor 1195–1203. He gained power by deposing and blinding his brother Isaac II, but Isaac's Venetian allies enabled him and his son Alexius IV to regain power as co-emperors.

Alexius IV /əˈleksiəs/ (Angelos) 1182–1204. Byzantine emperor from 1203, when, with the aid of the army of the Fourth Crusade, he deposed his uncle Alexius III. He soon lost the support of the Crusaders (by that time occupying Constantinople), and he was overthrown and murdered by another Alexius, Alexius Mourtzouphlus (son-in-law of Alexius III) in 1204, an act which the Crusaders used as a pretext to sack the city the same year.

alfalfa or *lucerne* perennial tall herbaceous plant *Medicago sativa* of the pea family, with spikes of small purple flowers in late summer. Native to Eurasia, it is now an important fodder crop, and is generally processed into hay, meal, or silage.

Alfa Romeo Italian car-manufacturing company, known for its racing cars. In 1985 the company was bought by Fiat.

The Alfa Romeo racing car made its debut 1919. In the 1930s it was dominant in the great long-distance races such as the *Targo Florio* and *Mille Miglia*. The Italian Giuseppe Farina drove the Alfa Romeo 158 to win the 1950 British Grand Prix, the first world championship race. He won the world title that year. Alfa left Grand Prix racing 1951 only to return for a brief spell 1978.

Alfieri /ˌælfiˈeəri/ Vittorio, Count Alfieri 1749–1803. Italian dramatist. The best of his 28 plays, most of them tragedies, are *Saul* 1782 and *Mirra* 1786.

Alfonsín Foulkes /ˌælfɒnˈsiːn ˈfuːks/ Ricardo 1927–. Argentinian politician, president 1983–89, leader of the Radical Union Party (UCR). As president from the country's return to civilian government, he set up an investigation of the army's human-rights violations. Economic problems forced him to seek help from the International Monetary Fund and introduce austerity measures.

Educated at a military academy and a university law school, Alfonsín joined the UCR at the age of 18 and eventually went on to lead it. He was active in local politics 1951–62, being imprisoned 1953 by the right-wing Perón regime, and was a member of the national congress 1963–66. With the return to civilian government in 1983 and the legalization of political activity, Alfonsín and the UCR won convincing victories and he became president. He was succeeded by the Perónist Carlos Menem.

Alfonso /ælˈfɒnsəʊ/ six kings of Portugal, including:

Alfonso I 1094–1185. King of Portugal from 1112, who made Portugal independent from León.

Alfonso 13 kings of León, Castile, and Spain, including:

Alfonso VII *c.* 1107–1157. King of León and Castile from 1126, who attempted to unite Spain. Although he protected the Moors, he was killed trying to check a Moorish rising.

Alfonso X called *el Sabio* 'the Wise' 1221–1284. King of Castile from 1252. His reign was politically unsuccessful but he contributed to learning: he made Castilian the official language of the country, and commissioned a history of Spain and an encyclopedia, as well as several translations from Arabic, concerning, among other subjects, astronomy and games.

Alfonso XI 'the Avenger' 1311–1350. King of Castile from 1312 who ruled cruelly, repressed a rebellion by his nobles, and defeated the last Moorish invasion 1340.

Alfonso XII 1857–1885. King of Spain from 1875, son of ◊Isabella II. He assumed the throne after a period of republican government following his mother's flight and effective abdication 1868.

Alfonso XIII 1886–1941. King of Spain 1886–1931. He assumed power 1906 and married Princess Ena, granddaughter of Queen Victoria of the UK, in the same year. He abdicated soon after the fall of the Primo de Rivera dictatorship (which he supported), and Spain became a republic. His assassination was attempted several times.

Alfred the Great /ˈælfrɪd/ *c.* 848–*c.* 900. King of Wessex from 871. He defended England against Danish invasion, founded the first English navy, and put into operation a legal code. He encouraged the translation of works from Latin (some of which he translated himself), and promoted the development of the ◊Anglo-Saxon Chronicle.

Alfred was born at Wantage, Berkshire, the youngest son of Ethelwulf (died 858), king of the West Saxons. In 870 Alfred and his brother Ethelred fought many battles against the Danes. He gained a victory over the Danes at Ashdown

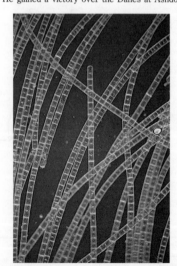

algae *Microscopic view of green filamentary algae. Algae form the basis of marine and freshwater food chains.*

871, and succeeded Ethelred as king in Apr after a series of defeats. Five years of uneasy peace followed while the Danes were occupied in other parts of England. In 876 the Danes attacked again, and in 878 Alfred was forced to retire to the stronghold of ◊Athelney, from where he finally emerged to win the victory of Edington, Wiltshire. By the Peace of Wedmore 878 the Danish leader Guthrum (died 890) agreed to withdraw from Wessex and from Mercia west of Watling Street. A new landing in Kent encouraged a revolt of the East Anglian Danes, which was suppressed 884–86, and after the final foreign invasion was defeated 892–96, Alfred strengthened the navy to prevent fresh incursions.

algae (singular **alga**) a diverse group of plants (including those commonly called seaweeds) that shows great variety of form, ranging from the lowest type of only a single cell to the higher seaweeds of considerable size and complexity of structure.

Algae were formerly included within the division Thallophyta, together with fungi and bacteria. Their classification changed with increased awareness of the important differences existing between the algae and Thallophyta, and also between the groups of algae themselves; many botanists now place each algal group in a separate class or division of its own.

They can be classified into 12 divisions, largely to be distinguished by their pigmentation, including the **green algae** Chlorophyta, freshwater or terrestrial; **stoneworts** Charophyta; **golden-brown algae** Chrysophyta; **brown algae** Phaeophyta, mainly marine and including the **kelps** Laminaria and allies, the largest of all algae; **red algae** Rhodophyta, mainly marine and often living parasitically or as epiphytes on other algae; **diatoms** Bacillariophyta; **yellow-green algae** Xanthophyta, mostly freshwater and terrestrial; and **blue-green algae** Cyanophyta, of simple cell structure and without sexual reproduction, mostly freshwater or terrestrial.

Algardi /æl'gɑːdi/ Alessandro c.1595–1654. Italian Baroque sculptor, active in Rome and at the papal court. His greatest work, on which he was intermittently occupied from 1634 to 1652, is the tomb of Pope Leo XI (Medici), in St Peter's, Rome.

Although Algardi's work is more restrained in expression than that of his contemporary and rival Bernini, it is Baroque in style, with figures often violently contorted and full of movement. His portrait busts include *St Philip Neri* 1640 (Sta Maria Vallicella, Rome).

Algarve /æl'gɑːv/ (Arabic *al-gharb* 'the west') ancient kingdom in S Portugal, the modern district of Faro, a popular holiday resort; population (1981) 323,500.

The Algarve began to be wrested from the ◊Moors in the 12th century and was united with Portugal as a kingdom in 1253. It incudes the SW extremity of Europe, Cape St Vincent, where the British fleet defeated the Spanish in 1797.

algebra system of arithmetic applying to any set of non-numerical symbols, and the axioms and rules by which they are combined or operated upon.

It is sometimes known as **generalized arithmetic**. The basics of algebra were familiar in Babylon 2000 BC, and were practised by the Arabs in the Middle Ages. In the 9th century, the Arab mathematician Muhammad ibn-Musa al-◊Khwarizmi first used the words *hisāb al-jabr* ('calculus of reduction') as part of the title of a treatise. Algebra is used in many branches of mathematics, such as matrix algebra and Boolean algebra, the method of algebraic reasoning devised in the 19th century by the British mathematician George Boole and used in working out the logic for computers.

Algeciras /ˌældʒɪ'sɪərəs/ port in S Spain, to the W of Gibraltar across the Bay of Algeciras; population (1986) 97,000. Founded by the ◊Moors 713, it was taken from them by Alfonso XI of Castile 1344. Virtually destroyed in a fresh attack by the Moors, it was re-founded 1704 by Spanish refugees from Gibraltar after that place was captured by the British.

Algeciras Conference a conference held Jan 1906 when the European powers of France, Germany, Britain, Russia, and Austria-Hungary, together with the USA, Spain, the Low Countries, Portugal, and Sweden, met to settle the question of Morocco. The conference was prompted by increased German demands in what had traditionally been seen as a French area of influence, but resulted in a reassertion of Anglo-French friendship, and the increased isolation of Germany.

Alger /'ældʒə/ Horatio 1834–1899. US writer of children's books. He wrote over 100 didactic, moral tales in which the heroes rise from poverty to riches through hard work and good deeds, including the series 'Ragged Dick' from 1867 and 'Tattered Tom' from 1871.

It is estimated that his books sold more than 20 million copies. In US usage a 'Horatio Alger tale' has now come to mean any rags-to-riches story, often an implausible one.

Algeria /æl'dʒɪəriə/ country in N Africa, bounded to the E by Tunisia and Libya, to the SE by Niger, to the SW by Mali, to the NW by Morocco, and to the N by the Mediterranean Sea.

government the 1976 constitution, amended 1979, created a socialist republic with Islam as the state religion and Arabic the official language. Algeria is a one-party state with ultimate power held by the National Liberation Front (FLN). FLN nominates the president, who is elected by universal suffrage for a five-year term. The president chooses the prime minister and the council of ministers and is the effective head of government. There is a single-chamber national people's assembly of 295 deputies, all nominees of FLN, elected for a five-year term.

history from the 9th century BC the area now known as Algeria was ruled by ◊Carthage, and subsequently by Rome (2nd century BC–5th century AD). St ◊Augustine was bishop of Hippo (now called Annaba) 396–430.

The area was invaded by the ◊Vandals after the decline of Roman rule, and was ruled by ◊Byzantium from the 6th to the 8th century, after which the ◊Arabs invaded the region, introducing ◊Islam and ◊Arabic. Islamic influence continued to dominate, despite Spain's attempts to take

Algeria
Democratic and Popular Republic of
(*al-Jumhuriya al-Jazairiya ad-Dimuqratiya ash-Shabiya*)

area 2,381,741 sq km/919,352 sq mi
capital al-Jazair (Algiers)
towns Qacentina/Constantine; ports are Ouahran/Oran, Annaba
physical coastal plains, mountain plateau, desert
features Atlas mountains, Barbary Coast
head of state Benjedid Chadli from 1979
political system one-party socialist republic
political parties National Liberation Front (FLN), nationalist socialist
exports oil, natural gas, iron, wine, olive oil
currency dinar (13.51 = £1 Mar 1989)
population (1988 est) 23,850,000 (83% Arab, 17% Berber); annual growth rate 3.0%
life expectancy men 59, women 62
language Arabic (official); Berber, French
religion Sunni Muslim
literacy 63% male/37% female (1985 est)
GDP $58.0 bn (1986); $2,645 per head of population
chronology
1954 War for independence from France led by the FLN
1963 Independence achieved. Ben Bella elected president.
1965 Ben Bella deposed by military, led by Col Houari Boumédienne.
1976 New constitution approved.
1978 Death of Boumédienne.
1979 Bendjedid Chadli elected president. Ben Bella released from house arrest. FLN adopted new party structure.
1981 Algeria helped in securing release of US prisoners in Iran.
1983 Chadli re-elected.
1988 Riots in protest at government policies; 170 killed. Reform programme introduced. Diplomatic relations with Egypt restored.
1989 Constitutional changes proposed, leading to limited political pluralism.

control in the 15th–16th centuries, and from the 16th century Algeria was under ◊Ottoman rule and flourished as a centre for the slave trade. However, the Sultan's rule was often nominal, and in the 18th century Algeria became a pirate state, preying on Mediterranean shipping. European intervention became inevitable, and in 1816 an Anglo-Dutch force bombarded Algiers. In 1830 a French army landed and seized Algiers; by 1847 the north had been brought under French control, and in 1848 was formed into the *départements* of Algiers, Oran, and Constantine. Many French colonists settled in these *départements*, which in 1881 were made part of Metropolitan France. The mountainous region inland, inhabited by the Kabyles, occupied 1850–70, and the Sahara region, subdued 1900–09, remained under military rule.

After the defeat of France 1940, Algeria came under the control of the Vichy government until the Allies landed in N Africa 1942. Post-war hopes of integrating Algeria more closely with France were frustrated by opposition in Algeria from those of both non-French and French origin. An embittered struggle for independence from France continued 1954–62, when referenda in both Algeria and France resulted in 1963 in the recognition of Algeria as an independent one-party republic with Ben Bella as its first president. In 1965 Colonel Houari Boumédienne deposed Ben Bella in a military coup, suspended the constitution and ruled through a revolutionary council.

In 1976 a new constitution confirmed Algeria as an Islamic, socialist, one-party state. Boumédienne died 1978 and power was transferred to Bendjedid Chadli, secretary-general of FLN. In 1979 Chadli released Ben Bella from the house arrest imposed on him in the 1965 coup. In the same year FLN adopted a new structure, with a central committee nominating a party leader who automatically becomes president. Chadli was re-elected under this system 1983.

During Chadli's presidency, relations with France and the USA have improved and there has been some progress in achieving greater co-operation with neighbouring states, particularly Tunisia. In 1981 Algeria acted as an intermediary in securing the release of the US hostages in ◊Iran. In 1987 a proposal by Colonel ◊Khaddhafi for political union with Libya received a cool response. Following public unrest in 1988, Chadli promised to make the government more responsive to public opinion.

Algiers /æl'dʒɪəz/ (Arabic *al-Jazair*, French *Alger*) capital of Algeria, situated on the narrow coastal plain between the Atlas mountains and the Mediterranean; population (1984) 2,442,300.

Founded by the Arabs AD 935, Algiers was taken by the Turks 1518, and by the French 1830. The old town is dominated by the Kasbah, the palace and prison of the Turkish rulers. The new town, constructed under French rule, is in European style.

Algiers, Battle of /æl'dʒɪəz/ the bitter conflict in Algiers 1954–62 between the Algerian nationalist population and the French army and French settlers. The conflict ended with Algerian independence 1962.

alginate salt of alginic acid, obtained from brown seaweeds, and used in textiles, paper, food products, and pharmaceuticals.

Algoa Bay /æl'gəʊə/ broad and shallow inlet in Cape Province, South Africa, where Diaz landed after rounding the Cape 1488.

Algol an ◊eclipsing binary, a pair of rotating stars in the constellation Perseus, one of which eclipses the other every 69 hours, causing its brightness to drop by two thirds. It is also known as Beta Persei. The brightness changes were first explained in 1782 by amateur astronomer John Goodricke.

Algol algorithmic language in computing, an early high-level programming language, developed in the 1950s and 1960s for scientific applications. A general-purpose language, Algol is best suited for mathematical work and has an algebraic style. Although no longer in common use, it has greatly influenced more recent languages such as ADA and Pascal.

Algonquin /æl'gɒŋkwɪn/ North American Indians of the eastern woodland zone to the S and E of Hudson Bay. They lived formerly along the Ottawa River and the northern tributaries of the St Lawrence, but now inhabit reserves in E Ontario and W Québec.

Algonquian languages are spoken by many other native peoples on the Atlantic coast and elsewhere, and include Cree, Blackfoot, and Cheyenne.

algorithm a procedure or series of steps by which a problem can be solved. In computer science, where the term is most often used, algorithm describes the logical sequence of operations to be performed by a program. A ◊flow chart is a visual representation of an algorithm.

Alhambra /æl'hæmbrə/ fortified palace in Granada, Spain, built by Moorish kings mainly between 1248 and 1354. The finest example of Moorish architecture, it stands on a rocky hill.

Alhazen /æl'hɑːzən/ Ibn al Haytham *c.* 965–1038. Arabian scientist, author of the *Kitab al Manazir/ Book of Optics*, translated into Latin as *Perspectiva*. For centuries it remained the most comprehensive and authoritative treatment of optics in both East and West.

Ali /'ɑːli/ *c.*600–661. 4th caliph of Islam. He was born in Mecca, the son of Abu Talib, uncle to the prophet Muhammad, who gave him his daughter Fatima in marriage. On Muhammad's death 632, Ali had a claim to succeed him, but this was not conceded until 656. After a stormy reign, he was assassinated. Around Ali's name has raged the controversy of the Sunnites and the Shi'ites (see ◊Islam), the former denying his right to the caliphate and the latter supporting it.

Ali /'ɑːli/ (Ali Pasha) 1741–1822. Turkish politician, known as *Arslan* ('the Lion'). An Albanian, he was appointed pasha (governor) of the Janina region (now Ioánnina, Greece) 1788. His court was visited by the British poet Byron. He was murdered by the sultan's order.

Ali /ɑː'liː/ Muhammad. Born Cassius Marcellus Clay 1942– . US boxer. Olympic light-heavyweight champion 1960, he went on to become world professional heavyweight champion 1964, and was the only man to regain the title twice. He was known for his quickness and extroversion.

He had his title stripped from him 1967 for refusing to be drafted into the US Army. He regained his title 1974, lost it Feb 1978 and regained it seven months later.

CAREER HIGHLIGHTS

fights: 61
wins: 56 (37 knockouts)
draws: 0
defeats: 5
first professional fight:
29 Oct 1960 v. Tunny Hunsaker *(USA)*
last professional fight:
11 Dec 1981 v. Trevor Berbick *(Canada)*

Alia /'æliə/ Ramiz 1925– . Albanian communist politician, head of state from 1982 and party leader from 1985. He has slightly modified the isolationist policies of his predecessor Enver Hoxha.

Born in Shkodër in NW Albania, the son of poor Muslim peasants, Alia joined the National Liberation Army 1944, actively opposing Nazi control. After a period in charge of agitprop work, Alia was inducted into the secretariat and Politburo of the ruling Party of Labour of Albania (APL) 1960–61. On the death of Hoxha he became party leader.

alibi (Latin 'elsewhere') the legal defence that the accused was at some other place when the crime was committed. In Britain it can usually only be used as a defence in a ◊crown court trial if the prosecution is supplied with details before the trial.

Alicante /ˌæli'kænti/ seaport and tourist resort in Valencia, SE Spain; population (1986) 266,000. The wine and fruit trade passes through the port.

Alice's Adventures in Wonderland a children's story by Lewis Carroll, published 1865. Alice dreams she follows the White Rabbit down a rabbit-hole and meets fantastic characters such as the Cheshire Cat, the Mad Hatter, and the King and Queen of Hearts.

An Alice-in-Wonderland situation has come to mean an absurd or irrational situation, because of the dreamlike logic of Alice's adventures in the book. With its companion volume *Through the Looking-Glass* 1872, it is one of the most quoted works in the English language.

alien in law, a person who is not a citizen of a particular state. In the UK, under the British Nationality Act 1981, an alien is anyone who is neither a British Overseas citizen (for example Commonwealth) nor a member of certain other categories; citizens of the Republic of Ireland are not regarded as aliens. Aliens may not vote or hold public office in the UK.

Alien and Sedition Acts laws passed by the US Congress 1798, when war with France seemed likely. The acts lengthened the period of residency required for US citizenship, gave the president the power to expel 'dangerous' aliens, and severely restricted criticism of the government. They were controversial because of the degree of power exercised by central government; they are now also seen as an early manifestation of US xenophobia (fear of foreigners).

alienation a sense of frustration, isolation, and powerlessness; a feeling of loss of control over one's life; a sense of estrangement either from society or from oneself. As a sociological concept it was developed by the German philosophers Hegel and Marx; the latter used it as a description and criticism of the condition of workers in capitalist society.

The term has also been used by non-Marxist writers to explain industrial unrest in modern factories, and to describe the sense of powerlessness felt by groups such as young people, black people, and women in Western industrial society.

Aliens Act in the UK, an act of Parliament passed by the Conservative government in 1905 to restrict the immigration of 'undesirable persons' into Britain; it was aimed at restricting Jewish immigration.

Undesirable persons were defined as people who might be a charge on the poor rates because they were without means or infirm. Since the act appeared to be stimulated by the arrival of large numbers of impoverished Europeans, many of them Jews from the Russian Empire, Prime Minister Balfour was accused of anti-Semitism.

Aligarh /ˌɑːlɪ'gɜː/ city in Uttar Pradesh, north central India; population (1981) 20,861.

alimentary canal long tube extending from the mouth to the anus, about 9 m/33 ft long in a human adult. Its function is to convey and digest food, and it consists of the oesophagus (gullet), stomach, duodenum, small and large intestines, and rectum.

alimony in the USA, and formerly in the UK, money allowance given by court order to a former wife or husband after separation or divorce; in the UK the legal term is ◊maintenance. In some legal systems the right has been extended outside marriage and is colloquially termed 'palimony'.

Ali Pasha /ˌɑːli'pɑːʃə/ Mehmed Emin 1815–1871. Grand vizier (chief minister) of the Ottoman empire 1855–56, 1858–59, 1861, and 1867–71, noted for his attempts to westernize the Ottoman Empire. After a career as ambassador to the UK, minister of foreign affairs 1846, delegate to the Congress of ◊Vienna 1855 and of Paris 1856, he was grand vizier a total of five times. While promoting friendship with Britain and France, he defended the vizier's powers against those of the sultan.

aliphatic compound any organic chemical compound that is made up of chains of carbon atoms, rather than rings (as in cyclic compounds). The chains may be linear, as in hexane C_6H_{14}, or branched, as in propan-2-ol (isopropanol) $(CH_3)_2CHOH$.

alkali (Arabic *al-qaliy* 'ashes') chemical compound classed as a base that is soluble in water. Alkalis neutralize acids and are soapy to the touch.

The hydroxides of metals are alkalis, those of sodium (caustic soda NaOH) and of potassium (caustic potash KOH) being chemically powerful; both were derived from the ashes of plants.

alkali metals group of elements in the periodic table of the elements—group I or Ia: lithium (Li), sodium (Na), potassium (K), rubidium (Rb), caesium (Cs), and francium (Fr). In general, the elements of this group are reactive, soft, low-melting-point metals.

Due to their reactivity they are only found as compounds in nature, and are used as chemical reactants rather than as structural metals.

alkaline earth elements a group of elements in the periodic table of the elements—group II or IIa: beryllium (Be), magnesium (Mg), calcium (Ca), strontium (Sr), barium (Ba), and radium (Ra). All the elements are metallic but none occurs free in nature. They and their compounds are used to make alloys, oxidizers, and drying agents.

alkaloid a physiologically active and frequently poisonous substance contained in certain plants. It is usually a base, forming salts with acids and, when soluble, giving an alkaline solution.

Substances in this group are included by custom rather than by scientific rules. Examples include morphine, cocaine, quinine, caffeine, strychnine, nicotine, and atropine.

alkane member of the family of ◊hydrocarbons having the general formula C_nH_{2n+2}, commonly known as paraffins. Lighter alkanes are colourless gases (for example, methane, ethane, propane, butane); heavier ones are liquids or solids. They are saturated compounds (containing no double or triple bonds).

alkene member of the family of ◊hydrocarbons having the general formula C_nH_{2n}, commonly known as olefins. They are unsaturated compounds, characterized by one or more double bonds between adjacent carbon atoms. Lighter alkenes are gases (for example, ethene, propene, butene); heavier ones are liquids or solids.

al-Khalil /ˌælxəˈlɪl/ Arabic name for ◊Hebron in the Israeli-occupied West Bank.

al Kūt /ælˈkuːt/ alternative term for ◊Kūlt al Imāra.

alkyne member of the family of ◊hydrocarbons with the general formula C_nH_{2n-2}, commonly known as acetylenes. They are unsaturated compounds, characterized by one or more triple bonds between adjacent carbon atoms. Lighter alkynes are gases (for example, ◊ethyne); heavier ones are liquids or solids.

Allah /ˈælə/ (Arabic al-Ilah 'the God') Islamic name for God.

Allahabad /ˌæləhəˈbaːd/ sacred city in Uttar Pradesh, India, 580 km/360 mi SE of Delhi, at the junction of the Ganges and Jumna and a 'mystic' third river, the Saraswati; population (1981) 642,000. Every 12 years a major pilgrimage and fair takes place, the participants washing away sin and sickness by bathing in the rivers. 15 million people attended the festival of the jar of nectar of immortality, Khumbha-mela Jan–Mar 1989.

Allan /ˈælən/ David 1744–1796. Scottish historical painter, director of the Academy of Arts in Edinburgh from 1786. He is noted for portrait and genre paintings such as *Scotch Wedding*.

Allan /ˈælən/ William 1782–1850. Scottish historical painter, born in Edinburgh, who spent several years in Russia and neighbouring countries, and returned to Edinburgh in 1814. He was elected president of the Royal Scottish Academy in 1838. His paintings include scenes from Walter Scott's Waverley novels.

Allbutt /ˈɔːlbʌt/ Sir Thomas Clifford 1836–1925. British physician. He invented a compact medical thermometer, proved that angina is caused by narrowing of the coronary artery, and studied hydrophobia and tetanus.

Allegheny Mountains /ˌælɪˈɡeɪni/ range over 800 km/500 mi long extending from Pennsylvania to Virginia, USA, rising to more than 1,500 m/4,900 ft and averaging 750 m/2,500 ft. The mountains are an important source of timber, coal, iron and limestone. They initially hindered western migration, the first settlement to the west being Marietta 1788.

allegory in literature, the description or illustration of one thing in terms of another; a work of poetry or prose in the form of an extended metaphor or parable that makes use of symbolic fictional characters.

An example of the use of symbolic fictional character in allegory is the romantic epic *The Faerie Queene* 1590–96 by Edmund Spenser in homage to Queen Elizabeth I. Allegory is often used for moral purposes, as in John Bunyan's *Pilgrim's Progress* 1678. Medieval allegory often used animals as characters; this tradition survives in such works as *Animal Farm* 1945 by George Orwell.

Allegri /əˈleɪɡriː/ Gregorio 1582–1652. Italian Baroque composer, born in Rome, who became a priest and entered the Sistine chapel choir 1629. His *Miserere* for nine voices was reserved for performance by the chapel choir until Mozart, at the age of 14, wrote out the music from memory.

allegro (Italian 'merry, lively') in music, a lively or quick passage, movement, or composition.

allele an alternative form of a given ◊gene, caused by a difference in the ◊DNA. Blue and brown eyes in humans are determined by different alleles of the gene for eye colour.

Organisms with two sets of chromosomes (diploids) will have two copies of each gene. If the two alleles are identical the individual is said to be ◊homozygous at that ◊locus; if different, the individual is ◊heterozygous at that locus. Some alleles show ◊dominance over others.

Allen, Lough /ˈælən/ lake in county Leitrim, Republic of Ireland, on the upper course of the river Shannon. It is 11 km/7 mi long and 5 km/3 mi broad.

Allen, Bog of /ˈælən/ morasses east of the river

Shannon in the Republic of Ireland, comprising some 96,000 ha/240,000 acres of the counties of Offaly, Leix, and Kildare, the country's main source of peat fuel.

Allen /ˈælən/ Woody. Adopted name of Allen Stewart Konigsberg 1935– . US film director and actor, known for his cynical, witty, often self-deprecating parody and off-beat humour. His films include *Sleeper 1973, Annie Hall 1977* (for which he won three Academy Awards), and *Hannah and her Sisters* 1986, all of which he directed, wrote, and appeared in. From the late 1970s, Allen has mixed his output of comedies with straight dramas in which he does not appear, such as *Interiors* 1978 and *Another Woman* 1988.

Allenby /ˈælənbi/ Sir Henry Hynman, 1st Viscount Allenby 1861–1936. British field marshal. In World War I he served in France before taking command in 1917–19 of the British forces in the Middle East. His defeat of the Turkish forces at Megiddo in Palestine in Sept 1918 was followed almost at once by the capitulation of Turkey. He was high commissioner in Egypt 1919–35.

Allende (Gossens) /aɪˈendi/ Salvador 1908–1973. Chilean left-wing politician. Elected president 1970 as the candidate of the Popular Front alliance, Allende never succeeded in keeping the electoral alliance together in government. His failure to solve the country's economic problems or to deal with political subversion allowed the army, backed by the CIA, to stage the 1973 coup which brought about the death of Allende and many of his supporters.

Allende, born in Valparaiso, became a Marxist activist in the 1930s and rose to prominence as a presidential candidate 1952, 1958, and 1964. In each election he had the support of the socialist and communist movements but was defeated by the Christian Democrats and Nationalists. As president, his socialism and nationalization of US-owned copper mines made the CIA regard him as a communist and take part in engineering the coup that replaced him by Gen Pinochet.

allergy special sensitivity of the body which makes it react, with an exaggerated response of the natural immune defence mechanism, to the introduction of an otherwise harmless foreign substance termed an *allergen*. The person subject to hay fever in summer is allergic to one or more kinds of pollen. Many asthmatics are allergic to certain kinds of dust or to microorganisms in animal fur or feathers. Others come out in nettlerash or are violently sick if they eat shellfish or eggs. Drugs may be used to reduce sensitivity.

All Fools' Day another name for ◊April Fools' Day.

Alliance, the the loose union 1981–87 formed by the British ◊Liberal Party and ◊Social Democratic Party (SDP) for electoral purposes.

The Alliance was set up soon after the formation of the SDP, and involved a joint manifesto at national elections and the apportionment of constituencies in equal numbers to Liberal and SDP candidates. The difficulties of presenting two separate parties to the electorate as if they were one proved insurmountable, and after the Alliance's poor showing in the 1987 general election the majority of the SDP voted to merge with the Liberals to form the Social and Liberal Democrats.

Alliance for Progress a programme of US assistance to Latin American countries, initiated by President Kennedy in 1961 under the auspices of the ◊Organization of American States.

Allied Mobile Force (AMF) permanent multinational military force established 1960 to move immediately to any NATO country under threat of attack. Its headquarters are in Heidelberg, West Germany.

Allier /æliˈeɪ/ river in central France, a tributary of the Loire; it is 565 km/350 mi long, and gives its name to a *département*. Vichy is the chief town on it.

Allies, the in World War I, the 23 countries allied against the Central Powers (Germany, Austria-

Hungary, Turkey and Bulgaria), including France, Italy, Russia, the UK and Commonwealth, and, in the later part of the war, the USA; and in World War II, the 49 countries allied against the ◊Axis (Germany, Italy, and Japan), including France, the UK and Commonwealth, the USA, and the USSR.

alligator reptile resembling a crocodile. There are two species: *Alligator mississipiensis* of the southern states of the USA, and *Alligator sinensis* from the swamps of the lower Chang Jiang river in China. The former grows to about 4 m/12 ft, but the latter only to 1.5 m/5 ft. Alligators swim well with lashing movements of the tail, and feed on fish and mammals but seldom attack people.

The eggs are laid in sand. The skin is of value for fancy leather, and alligator farms have been established in the USA. Closely related are the caymans of South America.

Allingham /ˈælɪŋəm/ Margery (Louise) 1904–1966. British detective novelist, creator of detective Albert Campion, as in *More Work for the Undertaker* 1949.

alliteration in poetry and prose, the use within a line or phrase of words beginning with the same sound, as in 'Two tired toads trotting to Tewkesbury'. It was a common device in Old English poetry, and its use survives in many traditional English phrases such as 'kith and kin', 'hearth and home', and so on.

Allium genus of plants belonging to the lily family. They are usually acrid in their properties, but form bulbs in which sugar is stored. Cultivated species include onion, garlic, chives, and leek.

allometry in biology, a regular relationship between a given feature (for example, the size of an organ) and the size of the body as a whole, when this relationship is not a simple proportion of body size. Thus, an organ may increase in size proportionately faster, or slower, than body size does.

allopathy the usual method of treating disease, using therapies designed to counteract the manifestations of the disease. It is sometimes incorrectly used as a name for orthodox medicine, as distinct from ◊homeopathy, which means treatment with minute doses of drugs that induce the same ailment.

allopurinol a drug prescribed for the treatment of ◊gout, which acts by reducing levels of ◊uric acid in the blood. Discovered accidentally in the early 1960s in the search for new immunosuppressives, it has no effects on acute gout attacks, and may even provoke them in the initial stages of therapy. In the long term, it prevents the deposit of urate in the joints and the formation of uric acid kidney stone.

allotment a small plot of rented land used for growing vegetables and flowers. Allotments originated in Britain during the 18th and 19th centuries, when much of the common land was enclosed (see ◊enclosure) and efforts were made to provide plots for poor people to cultivate. Later, acts of Parliament made this provision obligatory for local councils. In 1978 there were about 500,000 allotment plots in Britain.

The first Enclosure Act allowing for the provision of allotments was one of 1806 in Wiltshire; the first act of national scope was in 1819, but it was only with the Allotment Extension Act 1882 that parish authorities were required to provide allotment land. The number of allotments increased greatly following the introduction of elected county councils in 1888. Under the 1922 Act, councils are entitled to charge a rate to maintain and buy allotments. During both world wars, growing vegetables on allotments to supplement food supplies was encouraged.

allotrope different forms of the same element, for example the two forms of oxygen: 'normal' oxygen (O_2) and ozone (O_3), which have different molecular configurations.

More commonly, allotropes of an element have different crystal structures when solid, such as the white and grey forms of tin. The allotropes

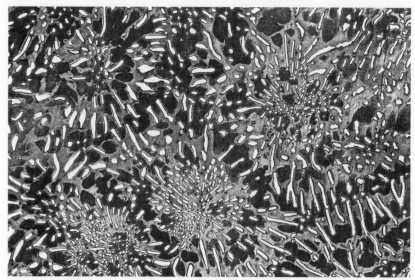

alpaca

alloy Ternary eutectic microstructure of a silver–copper–cadmium alloy, (× 600). An alloy is prepared by adding other substances to a basic metal to secure desirable properties. Eutectic alloys consist of solid solutions having the lowest melting point. They are used in fuses and safety mechanisms.

of carbon are diamond and graphite.

alloy metal blended with some other metallic or nonmetallic substance to give it special qualities, such as resistance to corrosion, or greater hardness or tensile strength. Useful alloys include bronze, brass, cupronickel, duralumin, German silver, gunmetal, pewter, solder, steel, and stainless steel. The most recent alloys include the superplastics, which may stretch 100% at specific temperatures, permitting, for example, their injection into moulds as easily as plastic.

Among the oldest alloys is bronze, whose widespread use ushered in the Bronze Age. Complex alloys are now widespread, for example in dentistry, where a cheaper alternative to gold is made of chromium, cobalt, molybdenum, and titanium.

All Saints' Day festival on 1 Nov for all Christian saints and martyrs who have no special day of their own. It is also known as All-Hallows or Hallowmas.

All Souls' Day festival in the Catholic church, held on 2 Nov (following All Saints' Day) in the conviction that the faithful by prayer and self-denial can hasten the deliverance of souls expiating their sins in purgatory.

allspice the dried fruit of the evergreen pimento or Jamaican pepper *Pimenta dioica*, used to flavour many food products. It has an aroma similar to a mixture of cloves, cinnamon, and nutmeg.

Allston /ˈɔːlstən/ Washington 1779–1843. US painter, a pioneer of the Romantic movement in the USA with his sea- and landscapes. His handling of light and colour earned him the title 'the American Titian'. He also painted classical, religious, and historical subjects.

alluvial deposit a layer of broken rocky matter, or sediment, formed from material that has been carried in suspension by a river or stream and dropped as the velocity of the current changes. River plains and deltas are made entirely of alluvial deposits, but smaller pockets can be found in the beds of upland torrents.

Alluvial deposits can consist of a whole range of particle sizes, from boulders down through cobbles, pebbles, gravel, sand, silt, and clay. The raw materials are the rocks and soils of upland areas that are loosened by erosion and washed away by mountain streams. Much of the world's richest farmland lies on alluvial deposits. These deposits can also provide an economic source of minerals. River currents produce a sorting action, with particles of heavy material deposited first while lighter materials are washed downstream. Hence heavy minerals such as gold and tin, pres-

ent in the original rocks in small amounts, can be concentrated and deposited on stream beds in commercial quantities. Such deposits are called 'placer ores'.

Allyson /ˈælɪsən/ June. Stage name of Ella Geisman 1917–. US film actress, popular in musicals and straight drama in the 1940s and 1950s. Her work includes *Music for Millions* 1945, *The Three Musketeers* 1948, and *The Glenn Miller Story* 1954.

Alma-Ata /ælˈmɑː əˈtɑː/ formerly (to 1921) *Vernyi* capital of the Republic of Kazakh, USSR; population (1987) 1,108,000. Industries include engineering, printing, tobacco processing, textile manufacturing, and leather products. Established 1854 as a military fortress and trading centre, the town was totally destroyed by an earthquake 1887.

Alma, Battle of the in the Crimean War, battle 20 Sept 1854 in which British, French, and Turkish forces defeated Russian troops, with a loss of about 9,000 men, 6,000 being Russian.

Almaden /ˌælməˈðen/ mining town in Ciudad Real province, Castilla-La Mancha, central Spain. It has the world's largest supply of mercury, worked since the 4th century BC. Population (1981) 9,700.

Almagest (Arabic *al* 'the' and Greek *majisti* 'greatest') book written by the Greek astronomer ◊Ptolemy during the 2nd century AD, which included the idea of an Earth-centred universe. It survived in an Arabic translation. Some medieval books on astronomy, astrology, and alchemy were given the same title.

Each section of the book deals with a different branch of astronomy. The introduction describes the universe as spherical and contains arguments for the Earth being stationary at the centre. From this mistaken assumption, it goes on to describe the motions of the Sun, Moon, and planets, eclipses, and the positions, brightness, and precession of the 'fixed stars'. The book drew on the work of earlier astronomers such as ◊Hipparchus.

alma mater (Latin 'bounteous mother') term applied to universities and schools, as though they are the foster-mothers of their students. It was the title given by the Romans to the goddess Ceres.

Almansa, Battle of /ælˈmænsə/ in the War of the Spanish Succession, battle 25 Apr 1707 in which British, Portuguese, and Spanish forces were defeated by the French under the Duke of Berwick at a Spanish town in Albacete, about 80 km/50 mi NW of Alicante.

Alma-Tadema /ˈælmə ˈtædɪmə/ Laurence 1836–1912. Dutch painter who settled in the UK 1870. He painted romantic, idealized scenes from Greek, Roman, and Egyptian life in a distinctive, detailed style.

Almeida /ælˈmeɪdə/ Francisco de *c.*1450–1510. First viceroy of Portuguese India 1505–08. He was killed in a skirmish with the Hottentots at Table Bay, S Africa.

Almería /ˌælmeˈriːə/ Spanish city, chief town of a province of the same name on the Mediterranean; population (1986) 157,000. The province is famous for its white grapes, and in the Sierra Nevada are rich mineral deposits.

Almohad a Berber dynasty 1130–1269 founded by the Berber prophet Muhammad ibn Tumart (*c.*1080–1130). They ruled much of Morocco and Spain, which they took by defeating the ◊Almoravids; they later took the area which today forms Algeria and Tunis. Their policy of religious 'purity' involved the forced conversion and massacre of the Jewish population of Spain. They were themselves defeated by the Christian kings of Spain in 1212, and in Morocco in 1269.

almond tree of *Prunus amygdalus*, family Rosaceae, related to the peach and apricot. Dessert almonds are the kernels of the fruit of the sweet variety *Prunus amygdalus dulcis*, which is also the source of a low-cholesterol culinary oil. Oil of bitter almonds, from the variety *Prunus amygdalus amara* is used in flavouring. Almond oil is also used for cosmetic perfumes and fine lubricants.

Almoravid a Berber dynasty 1056–1147 founded by the prophet Abdullah ibn Tashfin, ruling much of Morocco and Spain in the 11th–12th centuries. They came from the Sahara and in the 11th century began laying the foundations of an empire covering the whole of Morocco and parts of Algeria; their capital was the newly founded Marrakesh. In 1086 they defeated Alfonso VI of Castile to gain much of Spain. They were later overthrown by the ◊Almohads.

aloe genus of African plants of the family Liliaceae, distinguished by their long fleshy leaves. The drug, usually referred to as 'bitter aloes' is a powerful cathartic prepared from the juice of the leaves of several of the species.

Alost /ɑːˈlɒst/ French name for the Belgian town of ◊Aalst.

Aloysius, St /ˌæləʊˈɪsɪəs/ 1568–1591. Italian Jesuit who died while nursing plague victims. He is the patron saint of youth. Feast day 21 June.

alpaca domesticated South American member of the camel family, *Lama pacos*, found in Chile, Peru, and Bolivia, and herded at high elevations in the Andes. About 1 m/3 ft tall at the shoulder with neck and head another 60 cm/2 ft, it is mainly bred for its long, fine, silky wool, and like the llama was probably bred from the wild ◊guanaco.

alpha and omega first (Α) and last (Ω) letters of the Greek alphabet, hence the beginning and end, or sum total, of anything.

alphabet a set of conventional symbols for the pur-

alphabet

pose of writing, so called from *alpha* and *beta*, the names of the first two letters of the classical Greek alphabet.

Alphabetic writing began in W Asia during the 2nd millennium BC among the N Semitic peoples, and now takes many forms, for example the Arabic script, written from right to left, the Devanagari script of the Hindus, in which the symbols 'hang' from a line common to all the symbols, and the Greek alphabet, with the first clearly delineated vowel symbols. Each letter of the alphabets descended from Greek represents a particular sound or sounds, usually described as *vowels* (*a, e, i, o, u*, in the English version of the Roman alphabet), *consonants* (*b, p, d, t*) and *semi-vowels* (*w, y*). Letters may operate in special arrangements to produce distinct sounds (for example *a* and *e* together in words like *tale* and *take*, or *o* and *i* together to produce a 'wa' sound in the French *loi*), or may have no sound whatsoever (for example the silent letters *gh* in

'high' and 'through').

Alpha Centauri the brightest star in the constellation of Centaurus. It is actually a triple star (see ◊binary star); the two brighter stars orbit each other every 80 years, and the third, Proxima Centauri, 4.3 light years away, is the closest star to the Sun. Alpha Centauri is the third brightest star in the sky.

alpha particle positively charged particle ejected with great velocity from the nucleus of an ◊atom. It is one of the products of the spontaneous disintegration of radioactive substances such as radium and thorium, and is identical with the nucleus of a helium atom; that is, it consists of two protons and two neutrons. See ◊radioactivity.

Alphege, St /ˈælfɪdʒ/ 954–1012. Anglo-Saxon priest, bishop of Winchester from 984, archbishop of Canterbury from 1006. When the Danes attacked Canterbury he tried to protect the city, was thrown into prison, and, refusing to deliver the treasures of his cathedral, was stoned and beheaded at Greenwich on 19 Apr, his feast day.

Alps /ælps/ mountain chain, the barrier between N Italy and France, Germany and Austria.
famous peaks include **Mont Blanc** the highest at 4,807 m/15,777 ft, first climbed by Jacques Balmat and Michel Paccard 1786;
Matterhorn in the Pennine Alps 4,477 m/14,694 ft, first climbed by Edward Whymper 1865 (four of the party of seven were killed when the rope broke during their descent);
Eiger in the Bernese Alps/Oberland, 3,970 m/13,030 ft, with a near-vertical rock wall on the north face, first climbed 1858;
Jungfrau 4,166 m/13,673 ft; and
Finsteraarhorn 4,274 m/14,027 ft.
famous passes include **Brenner** the lowest, Austria/Italy;
Great St Bernard the highest, 2,472 m/8,113 ft, Italy/Switzerland (by which Napoleon marched into Italy 1800);
Little St Bernard Italy/France (which Hannibal is thought to have used); and
St Gotthard S Switzerland, which Suvorov used when ordered by the tsar to withdraw his troops from Italy. All have been superseded by all-weather road/rail tunnels. The Alps extend into Yugoslavia in the Julian and Dinaric Alps.

Alps, Australian /ælps/ highest area of the E Highlands in Victoria/New South Wales, Australia, noted for winter sports. They include the **Snowy mountains** and **Mt Kosciusko**, Australia's highest mountain, 2,229 m/7,316 ft (first noted by Polish-born Sir Paul Strzelecki 1829, and named after a Polish hero).

Alps, Lunar /ælps/ a mountain range on the Moon, NE of the Sea of Showers, cut by a valley 150 km/93 mi long.

Alps, Southern /ælps/ range of mountains running the entire length of South Island, New Zealand. They are forested to the W, with scanty scrub to the E The highest point is Mount Cook 3,764 m/12,349 ft. Scenic features include gorges, glaciers, lakes and waterfalls. Among its most famous lakes are those at the southern end of the range: Manapouri, Te Anau, and the

Alps *The French Alps, showing left to right, Aiguille du Chardonnet, Aiguil le Verte and Aiguille du Dru.*

largest, Wakatipu, 83 km/52 mi long, which lies about 300 m/1,000 ft above sea level and has a depth of 378 m/1,242 ft.

Alsace /ælˈsæs/ region of France; area 8,300 sq km/3,204 sq mi; population (1986) 1,600,000. It consists of the *départements* of Bas-Rhin and Haut-Rhin, and its capital is Strasbourg.

Alsace-Lorraine /ælˈsæs lɒˈreɪn/ area of NE France, lying west of the river Rhine. It forms the modern French regions of ◊Alsace and ◊Lorraine. The former iron and steel industries are being replaced by electronics, chemicals, and precision engineering. The German dialect spoken does not have equal rights with French, and there is autonomist sentiment. Alsace-Lorraine formed part of Celtic Gaul in Caesar's time, was invaded by the Alemanni and other Germanic tribes in the 4th century, and remained part of the German Empire until the 17th century. In 1648 part of the territory was ceded to France; in 1681 Louis XIV seized Strasbourg. The few remaining districts were seized by France after the Revolution. Conquered by Germany 1870–71 (chiefly for its iron ores), it was regained by France 1919, then again annexed by Germany 1940–44, when it was liberated by the Allies.

Alsatia /ælˈseɪʃə/ the old name for ◊Alsace, formerly part of Germany.

In 17th-century London this name was given to the district of Whitefriars between Fleet Street and the Thames. It afforded sanctuary to debtors and outlaws, a privilege derived from the convent of the Carmelite Order, established there 1241. In 1697 this privilege was withdrawn.

alsatian breed of dog known officially from 1977 as the German shepherd. It has a wolflike appearance, a thick coat with many varieties of colouring, and distinctive gait. They are used as police dogs and as guard dogs because of their intelligence. They were introduced from Germany into Britain after World War I.

Altai /ɑːˈltaɪ/ territory of the Russian Soviet Federal Socialist Republic in SW Siberia; area 261,700 sq km/101,043 sq mi; population (1985), 2,744,000. The capital is Barnaul.

Altai Mountains /ælˈtaɪ/ mountain system of W Siberia and Mongolia. It is divided into two parts, the Russian Altai, which includes the highest peak, Mount Belukha, 4,506 m/14,783 ft, and the Mongolian or Great Altai.

Altair brightest star in the constellation of Aquila. It is a white star 16 light years away and forms the so-called Summer Triangle with the stars Deneb (in Cygnus) and Vega (in Lyra). It is the 12th brightest star in the sky.

Altamira /ˌæltəˈmɪərə/ cave near the Spanish village of Santillana del Mar in Santander province where in 1879 Palaeolithic wall paintings were discovered.

Altamira /ˌæltəˈmɪərə/ an Amazonian town in the state of Pará, NE Brazil, situated at the junction of the Trans-Amazonian Highway with the Xingu river, 700 km /400 mi SW of Belém. In Feb 1989 world attention focused on the devastation of the Amazon rainforest following a protest against the building of six dams by what amounted to the largest gathering of Brazilian Indians and environmentalists in modern times.

Altdorf /ˈæltdɔːf/ capital of the Swiss canton Uri at the head of Lake Lucerne, Switzerland; population 9,000. It was the scene of the legendary exploits of William ◊Tell.

Altdorfer /ˈæltdɔːfə/ Albrecht *c.*1480–1538. German painter and printmaker, active in Regensburg, Bavaria. Altdorfer's work, influenced by the linear, classical style of the Italian Renaissance, often depicts dramatic landscapes that are out of scale with the figures in the paintings. His use of light creates tension and effects of movement. Many of his works are of religious subjects.

With Dürer and Cranach, Altdorfer is regarded as one of the leaders of the German Renaissance. *St George and the Dragon* 1510 (Alte Pinakothek,

Munich) is an example of his landscape style; *The Battle of Issus* 1529 (also Munich) is a dramatic panorama.

alternate angles in geometry, a pair of angles that lie on opposite sides of a transversal (a line cutting two other lines). If the two other lines are parallel, the alternate angles are equal.

alternating current (AC) electric current that flows for an interval of time in one direction and then in the opposite direction, that is, a current that flows in alternately reversed directions through or round a circuit. Electric energy is usually generated as alternating current in a power station, and alternating currents may be used for both power and lighting.

The advantage of alternating current over direct current (DC, from a battery) is that its voltage can be raised or lowered economically by a transformer: high voltage for generation and transmission, and low voltage for utilization and safety. Railways, factories, and domestic appliances, for example, use alternating current.

alternation of generations the typical life cycle of terrestrial plants and some seaweeds, in which there are two distinct forms occurring alternately: *diploid* (having two sets of chromosomes) and *haploid* (one set of chromosomes). The diploid generation produces haploid spores by ◊meiosis, and is called the sporophyte, while haploid generation produces gametes (sex cells), and is called the gametophyte. The gametes fuse to form a diploid ◊zygote which develops into a new sporophyte, thus the sporophyte and gametophyte alternate.

alternative energy energy sources that are renewable and ecologically safe, as opposed to sources that are expendable and often have toxic byproducts, such as coal, oil, or gas (fossil fuels), and uranium (for nuclear power). The most important alternative energy source is *hydroelectric power*, which harnesses the energy in flowing water. Other sources include *tidal power*; *windmills*; *wind turbines*; *solar power* (already successfully exploited in many parts of the world); *wave power*; and *geothermal energy* (from the heat trapped in the Earth's crust).

alternative medicine see ◊medicine, alternative.

alternator an electricity ◊generator, which produces an alternating current.

Altgeld /'ɔːltgeld/ John Peter 1847–1902. US political and social reformer. Born in Prussia, he was taken in infancy to the USA. During the Civil War he served in the Union army. He was a judge of the Supreme Court in Chicago 1886–91, and as governor of Illinois 1893–97 was a champion of the worker against the government-backed power of big business.

Althing /'ælθɪŋ/ the parliament of Iceland, established about 930 and the oldest in the world.

Althusser /ˌæltʊ'seə/ Louis 1918– . French philosopher and Marxist, born in Algeria, who from 1968 argued that the idea that economic systems determine family and political systems is too simple. He attempted to show how the ruling class ideology of a particular era is a crucial form of class control.

Althusser divides each mode of production into four key elements – the economic, political, ideological, and theoretical – all of which interact. His structuralist analysis of capitalism sees individuals and groups as agents or bearers of the structures of social relations, rather than as independent influences on history. He dismisses mainstream sociology as bourgeois and has influenced thinkers in fields as diverse as social anthropology, literature, and history. Works include *For Marx* 1965, *Lenin and Philosophy* 1969, and *Essays in Self-Criticism* 1976.

altimeter an instrument used in aircraft that measures altitude, or height above sea level. The common type is a form of aneroid ◊barometer, which works by sensing the differences in air pressure at different altitudes. This must continually be recalibrated because of the change in air pressure with changing weather conditions.

The ◊radar altimeter measures the height of the aircraft above the ground, measuring the time it takes for radio pulses emitted by the aircraft to be reflected. Radar altimeters are essential features of automatic and blind-landing systems.

Altiplano /ˌæltʊ'pla:nəʊ/ the densely populated upland plateau of the Andes of South America, stretching from Ecuador to NW Argentina. Height 3,000–4,000 m/10,000–13,000 ft.

altitude in two-dimensional geometry, the perpendicular distance from a vertex (corner) of a triangle to the base (the side opposite the vertex).

Altman /'æltmən/ Robert 1922– . US film-director. His antiwar comedy *M.A.S.H.* 1970 was a critical and commercial success; subsequent films include *McCabe and Mrs Miller* 1971, *Nashville* 1975, and *Popeye* 1980.

Altmark incident /'æltma:k/ naval skirmish in World War II. The *Altmark*, a German auxiliary cruiser, was intercepted on 15 Feb 1940 by HM destroyer *Intrepid* off the coast of Norway. It was carrying the captured crews of Allied merchant ships sunk by the German battleship *Admiral Graf Spee* in the S Atlantic, and took refuge in Jösing fjord, where it was cornered by HMS *Cossack*, under Captain Vian, and ran aground. Vian's men released 299 British sailors.

alto (Italian 'high') (1) low-register female voice, also called *contralto*; (2) high adult male voice, also known as counter tenor; (3) (French) viola.

altruism in biology, helping another individual to reproduce more effectively, as a direct result of which the altruist may leave fewer offspring itself. Female honey bees behave altruistically by rearing sisters in order to help their mother, the queen bee, reproduce, and forgo any possibility of reproducing themselves.

ALU *arithmetic and logic unit* in a computer, the part of the ◊CPU (central processing unit) that performs the basic arithmetic and logical operations on data.

alum a white crystalline powder readily soluble in water; a double sulphate of potassium and aluminium. Its chemical formula is K_2SO_4. $Al_2(SO_4)_3$. $24H_2O$, and it is the commonest member of a group of double sulphates called alums, all of which have similar formulae and the same crystalline form. They are used in papermaking and to fix dye in textiles.

alumina oxide of aluminium, AL_2O_3, sometimes called corundum, which is widely distributed in clays, slates, and shales. It is formed by the decomposition of the feldspars in granite, and used as an abrasive. Typically it is a white powder, soluble in most strong acids or caustic alkalis, but not in water. Impure alumina is called 'emery'.

aluminium the most abundant metal, symbol Al, atomic number 13, relative atomic mass 26.98. Pure aluminium is a soft white metal. It oxidizes rapidly, and is valuable for its light weight, its specific gravity being 2.70, and for this reason is widely used in shipbuilding and aircraft. In the pure state it is a weak metal, but if combined with other elements such as copper, silicon, or magnesium, it forms alloys of great strength. Aluminium sulphate is the most widely used chemical in water treatment worldwide, but accidental excess (as at Camelford, N Cornwall, England, July 1989) makes drinking water highly toxic, and discharge into rivers kills all fish.

Nearly one-twelfth of the substance of the Earth's crust is composed of aluminium compounds. Aluminium in its pure state was not readily obtained until the middle of the 19th century. Because of its rapid oxidation, much energy is needed to separate the metal from its ores. Commercially, aluminium is obtained from bauxite, a mineral composed of hydrated aluminium oxides. Aluminium is much used in steel-cored overhead cables and for canning uranium slugs for nuclear reactors. It is an essential constituent in some magnetic materials; and, as a good conductor of electricity, is used as foil in electrical capacitors. A plastic form of aluminium,

developed 1976, which moulds to any shape and extends to several times its original length, has uses in electronics, cars, building construction, and so on. In the USA the original name suggested by Humphry Davy *aluminum* is retained.

Alva /'ælvə/ or *Alba* Ferdinand Alvarez de Toledo, Duke of Alva 1508–1582. Spanish politician and general. He commanded the Spanish armies of the Holy Roman emperor Charles V and his son Philip II of Spain, and in 1567 was appointed governor of the Netherlands, where he set up a reign of terror to suppress the revolt against increased taxation, reductions in local autonomy, and the Inquisition. In 1573 he retired, and returned to Spain.

Alvarado /ˌælvə'ra:dəʊ/ Pedro de *c.* 1485–1541. Spanish conquistador. In 1519 he accompanied Hernándo Cortés in the conquest of Mexico. In 1523–24 he conquered Guatemala.

Alvarez /'ælvərez/ Luis Walter 1911–1988. US physicist who led the research team that discovered the Xi-zero atomic particle 1959. He worked on the US atomic bomb project for two years, at Chicago and Los Alamos, during World War II. Nobel prize 1968.

Alvarez was professor of physics at the University of California from 1945 and an associate director of the Lawrence Radiation Laboratory 1954–59. In 1980 he was responsible for the theory (not generally accepted) that dinosaurs disappeared because a huge meteorite crashed into Earth 70 million years ago, producing a dust cloud that blocked out the sun for several years, causing dinosaurs and plants to die.

Alvárez Quintero /'ælvərez kɪn'teərəʊ/ Serafin 1871–1938 and Joaquin 1873–1945. Spanish dramatists. The brothers, born near Seville, always worked together and from 1897 produced some 200 plays, principally dealing with Andalusia. Among them are *Papá Juan: Centenario* 1909 and *Los Mosquitos* 1928.

alveolus one of the many thousands of tiny air sacs in the ◊lung in which exchange of oxygen and carbon dioxide takes place between air and blood.

Alwar /'ʌlwɑ:/ city in Rajasthan, India, chief town of the district (formerly princely state) of the same name; population (1981) 146,000. It has fine palaces, temples, and tombs. Flour milling and trade in cotton goods and millet are important.

Alwyn /'ælwɪn/ William 1905–1985. British composer. Professor of composition at the Royal Academy of Music 1926–55, he wrote film music (*Desert Victory*, *The Way Ahead*) and composed symphonies and chamber music.

Alzheimer's disease /'æltshaɪmʒz/ a common manifestation of ◊dementia, thought to afflict one in 20 people over 65. Attacking the brain's 'grey matter', it is a disease of mental processes rather than physical function, characterized by memory loss and progressive intellectual impairment.

It was first described by Alois Alzheimer 1906. The cause is unknown, although a link with high levels of aluminium in drinking water was discovered 1989. It has also been suggested that the disease may result from a defective protein circulating in the blood. There is no treatment, but recent insights into the molecular basis of the disease may aid the search for a drug to counter its effects.

a.m. abbreviation for *ante meridiem* (Latin 'before noon').

AM in physics, abbreviation for amplitude ◊modulation, one way in which radio waves are altered for the transmission of broadcasting signals.

Amagasaki /ˌæməgə'sɑ:ki/ industrial city on the NW outskirts of Osaka, Honshu island, Japan; population (1987) 500,000.

Amal a radical Lebanese ◊Shi'ite military force, established by Musa Sadr in the 1970s; their headquarters are at Borj al-Barajneh. The movement split into extremist and moderate groups 1982, but both sides agreed on the aim of increasing Shi'ite political representation in Lebanon. Amal guerrillas were responsible for many of the attacks and kidnappings in Lebanon during the 1980s.

Amalekite /əˈmæləkaɪt/ in the Old Testament, member of an ancient Semitic people of SW Palestine and the Sinai peninsula. According to Exodus 17 they harried the rear of the Israelites after their crossing of the Red Sea, were defeated by Saul and David, and finally crushed in the reign of Hezekiah.

Amalfi /əˈmælfi/ port 39 km/24 mi SE of Naples, Italy, situated at the foot of Monte Cerrato, on the Gulf of Salerno; population 7,000. For 700 years it was an independent republic. It is an ancient archiepiscopal see (seat of archbishop) and has a Romanesque cathedral.

amalgam an alloy of mercury with other metals. Most metals will form amalgams, except iron and platinum. Amalgam is used in dentistry for filling teeth, and usually contains copper, silver, and zinc as the main alloying ingredients. The amalgam is pliable when first mixed and then sets hard.
Amalgamation, the process of forming an amalgam, is a technique sometimes used to extract gold and silver from their ores. The ores are treated with mercury, which combines with the precious metals.

Amalia /əˈmɑːliə/ Anna 1739–1807. Duchess of Saxe-Weimar-Eisenach. As widow of Duke Ernest, she reigned 1758–75 (when her son Karl August succeeded her) with prudence and skill, making the court of Weimar a literary centre of Germany. She was a friend of the writers Wieland, Goethe, and Herder.

Amanita genus of fungi, distinguished by a ring, or *volva*, round the stem, warty patches on the cap, and by the clear white colour of the gills. Many of the species are brightly coloured and highly poisonous.
The *fly agaric Amanita muscaria*, a familiar poisonous toadstool with a white-spotted red cap, that grows under birch or pine, and the deadly buff-coloured *death's cap Amanita phalloides* are both found in Britain.

Amanullah Khan /ˌæməˈnʊl ˈkɑːn/ 1892–1960. Emir (ruler) of Afghanistan 1919–29. Third son of Habibullah Khan, he seized the throne on his father's assassination and concluded a treaty with the British, but his policy of westernization led to rebellion 1928. Amanullah had to flee, abdicated 1929, and settled in Rome, Italy.

Amar Das /əˈmɑːdəs/ 1495–1574. Indian religious leader, third guru (teacher) of Sikhism 1552–74. He laid emphasis on equality and opposed the caste system. He initiated the custom of the *langar* (communal meal).

Amarillo /ˌæməˈrɪləʊ/ town in the Texan panhandle, USA; population (1980) 149,230. The centre of the world's largest cattle-producing area, it processes the live animal into frozen supermarket packets in a single continuous operation on an assembly line. It is also a centre for assembly of nuclear warheads for Western defence.

Amarna tablets /əˈmɑːnə/ collection of Egyptian clay tablets with cuneiform inscriptions, found in the ruins of the ancient ◊Akhetaton on the east bank of the Nile. The majority of the tablets, which comprise royal archives and letters of 1411–1375 BC, are in the British Museum.

Amaterasu /əˌmɑːttəˈrɑːssuː/ in Japanese mythology, the sun-goddess, grandmother of Jimmu Tenno, first ruler of Japan, from whom the emperors claimed to be descended.

Amati /əˈmɑːti/ Italian family of violin-makers, who worked in Cremona, about 1550–1700. Niccolo Amati (1596–1684) taught Andrea ◊Guarneri and Antonio ◊Stradivari.

amatol an explosive consisting of ammonium nitrate and TNT (trinitrotoluene) in almost any proportions.

Amazon /ˈæməzən/ (Indian *Amossona* 'destroyer of boats') South American river, the world's second longest, 6,570 km/4,080 mi, and the largest in volume of water. Its main headstreams, the Marañón and the Ucayali, rise in central Peru and unite to flow eastwards across Brazil for about 4,000 km/2,500 mi. It has 48,280 km/30,000 mi of navigable waterways, draining 7,000,000 sq km/2,750,000 sq mi, half the South American land mass. It reaches the Atlantic on the Equator, its estuary 80 km/50 mi wide, discharging a volume of water so immense that 64 km/40 mi out to sea fresh water remains at the surface.
The opening up of the Amazon river basin to settlers from the overpopulated E coast has resulted in a massive burning of tropical forest to create both arable and pasture land. Brazil, with one third of the world's remaining tropical rainforest, has 55,000 species of flowering plant, half of which are only found in Brazilian Amazonia. The problems of massive soil erosion, the disappearance of potentially useful plant and animal species and the possible impact of large scale forest clearance on global warming of the atmosphere have become environmental issues of international concern.

Amazon /ˈæməzən/ in Greek mythology, a member of a group of legendary female warriors living near the Black Sea, who cut off their right breasts to use the bow more easily. Their queen, Penthesilea, was killed by Achilles at the siege of Troy. The Amazons attacked Theseus and besieged him at Athens, but were defeated, and Theseus took the Amazon Hippolyta captive; she later gave birth to ◊Hippolytus. The term Amazon has come to mean a strong, fierce woman.

Amazonian Indian the indigenous inhabitants of the Amazon Basin in South America. The majority of the peoples belong to small societies whose traditional livelihood includes hunting and gathering, fishing, and shifting cultivation. A wide range of indigenous languages are spoken.

Ambala /əmˈbɑːlə/ or *Umballa* city in N India; population (1981) 121,200. It is a railway junction situated 176 km/110 mi north west of Delhi. Food processing, flour milling, and cotton ginning are among its most important industries. It is an archaeological site with prehistoric artefacts.

ambassador officer of the highest rank in the diplomatic service, who represents the head of one sovereign state at the court or capital of another.

amber fossilized gum from coniferous trees of the Middle Tertiary period. It is often washed ashore on the Baltic coast with plant and animal specimens preserved in it; many extinct species have been found preserved in this way. It ranges in colour from red to yellow, and is used to make jewellery.

ambergris fatty substance, resembling wax, found in the stomach and intestines of the sperm ◊whale, which was used in perfumery as a fixative.
Basically intestinal matter, ambergris is not the result of disease, but probably the pathological product of an otherwise normal intestine. The name derives from the French *ambre gris* (grey amber).

River Amazon

Ambler /ˈæmblə/ Eric 1909–1986. British novelist. Born in London, he used Balkan/Levant settings in the thrillers *The Mask of Dimitrios* 1939 and *Journey into Fear* 1940.

amblyopia reduced vision without apparent eye disorder.

Amboina /æmˈbɔɪnə/ or *Ambon* small island in the Moluccas, republic of Indonesia; population (1980) 209,000. The town of Amboina, formerly an historic centre of Dutch influence, has shipyards.

Ambrose, St /ˈæmbrəʊz/ *c.*340–397. One of the early Christian leaders and writers known as the Fathers of the Church. He was bishop of Milan, Italy, and wrote on theological subjects. Feast day 7 Dec.
Born at Trèves, in S Gaul, the son of a Roman prefect, Ambrose became governor of N Italy. In 374 he was chosen bishop of Milan, although he was not yet a member of the church. He was then baptized and consecrated. He wrote many hymns, and devised the arrangement of church music known as the *Ambrosian Chant*, which is still used in Milan.

ambrosia Greek 'immortal', the food of the gods, which was supposed to confer eternal life upon all who ate it.

amen Hebrew word signifying affirmation ('so be it'), commonly used at the close of a Jewish or Christian prayer or hymn. As used by Jesus in the New Testament it was traditionally translated 'verily'.

Amenhotep /ˌæmenˈhəʊte/ four Egyptian pharaohs, including:

Amenhotep III *c.*1400 BC . King of Egypt who built great monuments at Thebes, including the temples at Luxor. Two portrait statues at his tomb were known to the Greeks as the colossi of Memnon; one was cracked, and when the temperature changed at dawn it gave out an eerie sound, then thought supernatural. His son *Amenhotep IV* changed his name to ◊Ikhnaton.

America /əˈmerɪkə/ the western hemisphere of the earth, containing the continents of North America and South America, with Central America in between. This great land mass extends from the Arctic to the Antarctic, from beyond 75° N to past 55° S. The area is about 42,000,000 sq km/16,000,000 sq mi, and the estimated population is over 500,000,000.
The name America is derived from Amerigo Vespucci, the Florentine navigator who was falsely supposed to have been the first European to reach the American mainland 1497. The name is also popularly used to refer to the United States of America, a usage which many Canadians, South Americans, and other non-US Americans dislike.

American Ballet Theater founded 1939 as 'Ballet Theater' with co-directors Lucia Chase and Richard Pleasant, then from 1945 Oliver Smith. Aiming to present the best of traditional along with the best of ballets with numerous guest celebrities, they established one of the best repertoires in the world.

American Civil War 1861–65; see ◊Civil War, American.

American Federation of Labor and Congress of Industrial Organizations (AFL-CIO) federation of North American trade unions. The AFL was founded 1886, superseding the Federation of Organized Trades and Labor Unions of the USA and Canada, and was initially a union of skilled craftworkers. The CIO was known in 1935 as the Committee on Industrial Organization (it adopted its present title 1937 after expulsion from the AFL for its opposition to the AFL policy of including only skilled workers). A merger reunited them 1955, bringing most unions into the national federation, currently representing about 20% of the workforce in North America.

American Independence, War of the revolt 1775–83 of the British North American colonies that resulted in the establishment of the USA. It was caused by colonial resentment at the contemporary attitude that commercial or industrial interests of any colony should be subordinate to those of the mother country, and the unwillingness of the colonists to pay for a permanent army.

It was preceded by:

1773 A government tax on tea led Massachusetts citizens disguised as North American Indians to board the ships carrying the tea and throw it into the harbour, the *Boston Tea Party*.

1774–75 The *First Continental Congress* was held in Philadelphia to call for civil disobedience in reply to British measures.

The War:

1775 19 Apr hostilities began at Lexington and Concord, Massachusetts, the first shots being fired when British troops, sent to seize illegal military stores, were attacked by the local militia (see Paul ◊Revere). 10 May Fort Ticonderoga, New York, was captured from the British. The first battle was at ◊*Bunker Hill*, Massachusetts, 17 June, in which the colonists were defeated; George ◊Washington was appointed commander in chief of the American forces soon afterwards.

1775–76 The *Second Continental Congress* on 4 July 1776 issued the ◊*Declaration of Independence*.

1776 27 Aug at *Long Island* Washington was defeated, forced to evacuate New York and retire to Pennsylvania but recrossed the Delaware River to win successes at *Trenton* 26 Dec and *Princeton* 3 Jan 1777.

1777 A British plan, for Sir William Howe (advancing from New York) and Gen Burgoyne (from Canada) to link up, miscarried. Burgoyne surrendered at *Saratoga* in New York State 17 Oct, but Howe invaded Pennsylvania, defeating Washington at *Brandywine* 11 Sept and *Germantown* 4 Oct, and occupying Philadelphia; Washington wintered at ◊*Valley Forge* 1777–78.

1778 France, with the support of its ally Spain, entered the war on the American side (John Paul ◊Jones led a French-sponsored naval unit).

1780 12 May capture of *Charleston*, South Carolina, the most notable of a series of British victories in the south, but they alienated support by attempting to enforce conscription.

1781 19 Oct Cornwallis, besieged in *Yorktown*, Virginia (Chesapeake Bay), by Washington and the French fleet, surrendered.

1782 Peace negotiations opened.

1783 3 Sept *Treaty of Paris*: US independence recognized.

American Indian an aboriginal of the Americas. They were called Indians by Columbus because he believed he had found, not the New World, but a new route to India. They are thought to have entered North America from Asia via the former landbridge, Beringia (from Siberia to Alaska), 60,000–35,000 BC.

Some American Indians were the first cultivators of maize, potatoes, sweet potatoes, manioc, peanuts, peppers, tomatoes, pumpkins, cacao, and chicle. They used tobacco, coca (cocaine), peyote (mescalin), cinchona (quinine), and tequila.

Canada 300,000, including the Inuits; the largest group are the Six Nations (Iroquois), with a reserve near Brantford, Ontario, for 7,000. They are organized in the National Indian Brotherhood of Canada.

United States 1 million, more than half living on reservations, mainly in Arizona, where the Navajo have the largest of all reservations, Oklahoma, New Mexico, California, North Carolina, South Dakota. The population level is thought to be the same as at the time of Columbus, but now includes many people who are of mixed ancestry. There is an organized American Indian Movement (AIM).

Latin America many mestizo (mixed Indian-Spanish descent), among them half the 12 million in Bolivia and Peru. Since the 1960s there has been an increasing stress on the Indian half of their inheritance in terms of their language and culture. The few Indians formerly beyond white

contact are having their environment destroyed during the clearing of the Amazon Basin.

North America: Arctic Inuit-Aleut
sub-Arctic Algonquin, Cree, Ottawa
NE Woodlands Huron, Iroquois, Mohican, Shawnee (Tecumseh)
Great Plains Blackfoot, Cheyenne, Comanche, Pawnee, Sioux
NW Coast Chinook, Tlingit, Tsimshian
Desert West Apache, Navajo, Pueblo, Hopi, Mojave, Shoshone
SE Woodlands Cherokee, Choctaw, Creek, Hopewell, Natchez, Seminole
Central America: Maya, Toltec, Aztec, Mexican
South America: Eastern Carib, Xingu
Central Guarani, Miskito
Western Araucanian, Aymara, Chimu, Inca, Jivaro, Quechua.

American Legion community organization in the USA, originally for ex-servicemen of World War I, founded 1919.

American literature see ◊United States literature.

American Samoa see ◊Samoa, American.

American System, the in US history, a federal legislative programme following the ◊War of 1812 that was designed to promote an integrated national economy. It introduced tariffs to protect US industry from foreign competition, internal improvements to the transport network, and a national bank to facilitate economic growth.

America's Cup international yacht-racing trophy named after the US schooner *America*, owned by J L Stevens, who won a race around the Isle of Wight 1851.

Offered for a challenge 1870, it is now contested every three or four years, and is a seven-race series. The USA dominated the race, and only twice lost possession, in 1983 to Australia and in 1989 to New Zealand, but subsequently lost the cup in a lengthy legal battle. All races were held at Newport, Rhode Island, until 1987 when the Perth Yacht Club, Australia, hosted the series. Yachts are very expensive to produce and only syndicates can afford to provide a yacht capable of winning the trophy. See also ◊yachting.

americium artificial element which is a member of the ◊actinide group, atomic number 95. It is produced by bombarding plutonium with neutrons.

Its isotope of mass 243 has a ◊half-life of 7,650 years.

Amerindian an abbreviated form of American Indian used to describe the indigenous peoples of the Americas.

Amersfoort /'ɑːməzfɔːt/ town in the Netherlands, 19 km/12 mi north east of Utrecht; population (10984) 86,896. Industries include brewing, chemicals, and light engineering.

Amery /'eɪməri/ Leo(pold Stennett) 1873–1955. British Conservative politician, First Lord of the Admiralty 1922–24, secretary for the colonies 1924–29, secretary for the dominions 1925–29, and secretary of state for India and Burma 1940–45.

Ames /eɪmz/ Adelbert 1880–1955. US scientist, who studied optics and the psychology of visual perception. He concluded that much of what a

Amin Dada Idi Amin, Ugandan president from 1971 until his overthrow in 1979, surrounded by his bodyguard. He is being asked to explain to reporters how the archbishop of Uganda and two cabinet ministers met a violent death while they were in custody in 1977.

person sees depends on what he or she expects to see, based (consciously or unconsciously) on previous experience.

amethyst a variety of ◊quartz, SiO_2, coloured violet by the presence of small quantities of manganese; used as a semiprecious stone. Amethysts are found chiefly in the USSR, India, the US, Uruguay, and Brazil.

Amethyst Incident UK–China episode arising when on 20 Apr 1949 a British frigate, HMS *Amethyst*, sailing on the Chang Jiang River was fired on by communist Chinese forces. The ship was trapped for 14 weeks before breaking free and completing the journey to the sea. The temporary detention of this British vessel has been interpreted as an attempt by the Chinese to assert their sovereignty over what had been considered an international waterway.

Amhara person of Amhara culture from the central Ethiopian plateau. They comprise approximately 25% of Ethiopia's population. The Amhara language belongs to the Semitic branch of the Afro-Asiatic family.

amicus curiae (Latin 'friend of the court') in English law, a barrister advising the court in a legal case as a neutral person, not representing either side. For example, where the public interest is concerned, the Attorney General or his representative may be asked to express an opinion. Professional bodies such as the Law Society may be represented in order to give an opinion on matters affecting their members.

Amida Buddha the 'Buddha of immeasurable light'. Japanese name for *Amitābha*, the transhistorical Buddha venerated in Pure Land Buddhism, who presides over the Western Paradise where, through his infinite compassion, believers hope to be reborn.

amide an organic chemical which is derived from a fatty acid by the replacement of the hydroxyl group by an amino group ($-NH_2$). One of the simplest amides is acetamide (CH_3CONH_2), which has a strong mousey odour.

Amiel /ˈæmiˈel/ Henri Frédéric 1821–1881. Swiss philosopher and writer, who wrote *Journal Intime*

amethyst *Quartz coloured with bituminous material gives a violet colour to amethyst. The colour changes on heating.*

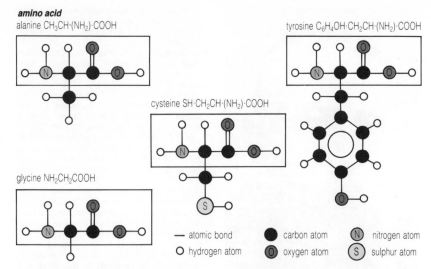

amino acid

alanine $CH_3CH \cdot (NH_2) \cdot COOH$

glycine NH_2CH_2COOH

cysteine $SH \cdot CH_2CH \cdot (NH_2) \cdot COOH$

tyrosine $C_6H_4OH \cdot CH_2CH \cdot (NH_2) \cdot COOH$

— atomic bond   ● carbon atom   Ⓝ nitrogen atom

○ hydrogen atom   Ⓞ oxygen atom   Ⓢ sulphur atom

1882–84. Born at Geneva, he became professor of philosophy at the university there.

Amiens /'æmiæn/ ancient city of NE France at the confluence of the rivers Somme and Avre; capital of Somme *département* and centre of a market gardening region irrigated by canals; population (1982) 154,500. It has a magnificent Gothic cathedral with a spire 113 m/370 ft high, and gave its name to the battles of Aug 1918, when ◊Haig launched his victorious offensive in World War I.

Amies /'eimiz/ Hardy 1909– . British couturier, one of Queen Elizabeth II's dressmakers. Noted from 1934 for his tailored clothes for women, he also designed for men from 1959.

Amin Dada /æ'mi:n 'dɑ:dɑ:/ Idi 1925– . Ugandan politician, president 1971–79. He led the coup that deposed Milton Obote 1971, expelled the Asian community 1972, and exercised a reign of terror over his people. He fled when insurgent Ugandan and Tanzanian troops invaded the country 1979.

amines class of organic chemical compounds which can be considered to be derived from ammonia, one or more of the hydrogen atoms of ammonia being replaced by other groups of atoms.

Methyl amines have unpleasant ammonia odours and occur in decomposing fish. They are all gases at ordinary temperature. The *aromatic amine compounds* include aniline, used in dyeing.

amino acid a water-soluble ◊molecule mainly composed of carbon, oxygen, hydrogen, and nitrogen. Amino acids are compounds of which the basic and acidic groups exist in the same molecule (the amine group is -NH₂). When joined in chains, amino acids form ◊peptides and ◊proteins.

The proteins of living organisms are made up of combinations of 20 kinds of amino acids, although there are others that occur infrequently in nature. Eight of these, the *essential amino acids*, cannot be synthesized by humans and must be obtained from the diet. Children need another two amino acids that are not essential for adults. Other animals also need some amino acids pre-formed in the diet, but plants can make all the amino acids they need, from simpler molecules.

Amis /'eimis/ Kingsley 1922– . English novelist and poet. His works include *Lucky Jim* 1954, a comic portrayal of life in a provincial university, and *Take a Girl Like You* 1960. He won the Booker Prize 1986 for *The Old Devils*. He is the father of Martin Amis.

Amis /'eimis/ Martin 1949– . English novelist. His works include *The Rachel Papers* 1974 and *Money* 1984.

Amman /ə'mɑːn/ capital and chief industrial centre of Jordan; population (1980) 1,232,600. It is an important communications centre, linking historic trade routes across the Middle East.

Amman is built on on the site of the Old Testament Rabbath-Ammon (Philadelphia), capital of the Ammonites. There is a fine Roman amphitheatre.

ammeter an instrument that measures electric current, usually in ◊amperes.

Ammon in Egyptian mythology, the king of the gods, the equivalent of ◊Zeus or ◊Jupiter. The name is also spelt Amen/Amun, as in the name of the pharaoh Tutankh*amen*.

In art, he is represented as a ram, as a man with a ram's head, or as a man crowned with feathers. He had temples at Siwa oasis, Libya, and Thebes, Egypt.

ammonia NH₃ a colourless pungent-smelling gas about two-thirds as dense as air. It is used mainly to produce nitrogenous fertilizers.

Ammonia is produced by the ◊Haber and cyanamide processes. It is soluble in water, forming ammonium hydroxide, NH₄OH. The solution is strongly alkaline, and forms crystalline salts on neutralization with acids. In aquatic organisms and some insects, nitrogenous waste (from breakdown of amino acids and so on) is excreted in the form of ammonia, rather than urea as in mammals.

Ammonite member of an ancient Semitic people who lived to the NW of the Dead Sea; their capital was Amman, in present-day Jordan. Worshippers of Moloch, to whom they offered human sacrifices, they were frequently at war with the Israelites.

ammonite extinct ◊cephalopod mollusc akin to the modern nautilus. The shell was curled in a plane spiral and made up of numerous gas-filled chambers, the outermost containing the body of the animal. Many species flourished between 200 million and 65 million years ago, ranging in size from that of a small coin to 2 m/6 ft across.

ammonium chloride NH₄Cl (also known as *sal ammoniac*) a volatile salt, it forms white crystals around volcanic craters, and is prepared synthetically for use in 'dry-cell' batteries.

amnesia a loss or impairment of memory. As a clinical condition it may be caused by disease or injury to the brain; in some cases it may be a symptom of an emotional disorder.

amnesty the release of political prisoners under a general pardon, or a person or group of people from liability for a particular action; for example, the occasional amnesties in Britain for those who surrender firearms that they hold illegally.

Amnesty International human-rights organization established in the UK 1961 to campaign for the release of political prisoners worldwide. It is politically unaligned. Nobel prize 1977.

amniocentesis sampling the amniotic fluid of a fetus for diagnostic purposes (the amniotic fluid surrounds the fetus in the womb). It is used to detect Down's syndrome and other abnormalities.

amnion innermost of three membranes that enclose the embryo within the egg (reptiles and birds) or within the uterus (mammals). It contains the amniotic fluid which helps to cushion the embryo.

amoeba (plural *amoebae*) one of the simplest living animals, consisting of a single cell and belonging to the group ◊Protozoa. The body consists of colourless protoplasms. Its activities are controlled by its nucleus, and it feeds by flowing round and engulfing organic debris. It reproduces by ◊binary fission. Some of its relatives are harmful parasites.

amoebiasis infection of the intestines, caused by the ◊amoeba *Entamoeba histolytica*, resulting in chronic dysentery and consequent weakness and dehydration. Endemic in the Third World, it is now occurring in Europe and North America.

Amorites ancient people of Semitic or Indo-European origin, who were among the inhabitants of ◊Canaan at the time of the Israelite invasion. They provided a number of Babylonian kings.

amortization in finance, the ending of a debt by paying it off gradually, over a period of time. The term is used to describe either the paying off of a cash debt, or the accounting procedure by which the value of an asset is progressively reduced ('depreciated') over a number of years.

Amos /'eimɒs/ book of the Old Testament or Jewish Bible written *c.* 750 BC. One of the ◊prophets,

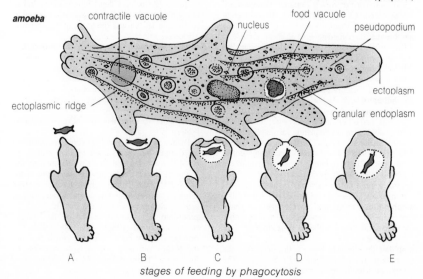

amoeba

contractile vacuole   nucleus   food vacuole   pseudopodium   ectoplasm   granular endoplasm   ectoplasmic ridge

A   B   C   D   E

stages of feeding by phagocytosis

Amos was a shepherd who foretold the destruction of Israel because of the people's abandonment of their faith.

Amoy /ə'mɔɪ/ ancient name for ◊Xiamen, a port in SE China.

amp (abbreviation for *ampere*) SI unit (symbol A) of electrical current. Electrical current is measured in a similar way to water current, in terms of an amount per unit time; one amp represents a flow of about 6×10^{18} ◊electrons per second.

The ampere is defined as the current that produces a specific magnetic force between two long, straight, parallel conductors placed 1 metre apart in a vacuum. It is named after the French scientist André Ampère.

Ampère /ɒm'peə/ André Marie 1775–1836. French physicist and mathematician who made many discoveries in electromagnetism and electrodynamics. He followed up the work of Hans ◊Oersted on the interaction between magnets and electric currents, developing a rule for determining the direction of the magnetic field associated with an electric current. The ◊ammeter and ampere are named after him.

Ampère's rule rule developed by André Ampère connecting the direction of an electic current and its associated magnetic currents. Travelling along a current-carrying wire in the direction of the current (from the positive to the negative terminal of a battery), and facing a magnetic needle, the north pole of the needle is deflected to the left-hand side.

amphetamine synthetic ◊stimulant. Used in World War II to help soldiers overcome combat fatigue, its effects made it a popular drug in the postwar years. Doctors prescribed it as an anorexic (appetite suppressant) for weight loss; as an antidepressant, to induce euphoria; as a stimulant, to increase alertness. Indications for its use today are very restricted because of severe side effects, including addiction and abuse.

amphibian (Greek 'double life') member of the class of vertebrates which generally spend their larval ('tadpole') stage in fresh water, transferring to land at maturity, although they generally return to water to breed. Like fish and reptiles, they continue to grow throughout life, and cannot maintain a temperature greatly differing from that of their environment. The class includes caecilians, worm-like in appearance; salamanders, frogs, and toads.

amphibole any one of a large group of rock-forming silicate minerals with an internal structure based on double chains of silicon and oxygen, and with a general formula $X_2Y_5Sl_8O_2 2(OH)_2$; closely related to ◊pyroxene. Amphiboles form orthorhombic, monoclinic, or triclinic ◊crystals.

Amphiboles occur in a wide range of igneous and metamorphic rocks. Common examples are ◊hornblende (X=Ca, Y=Mg, Fe, Al) and tremolite (X=Ca, Y=Mg).

amphioxus filter-feeding animal about 6 cm/2 in long with a fish-like shape and a flexible rod which forms the supporting structure of its body. It lacks organs such as heart or eyes, and lives half-buried in the sea floor, and is a primitive relative of vertebrates.

amphitheatre large oval or circular building used by the Romans for gladiatorial contests, fights of wild animals, and other similar spectacles; the arena of an amphitheatre is completely surrounded by the seats of the spectators, hence the name (Greek *amphi*, around). The Romans built many amphitheatres. The ◊Colosseum in Rome, completed AD 80, held 50,000 spectators.

amphora large pottery storage jar in the Graeco-Roman world used for wine, oil, and dry goods.

amphoteric a term used to describe the ability of some chemical compounds to behave either as an ◊acid or as a ◊base, depending on their environment.

amplifier an electronic device that magnifies the strength of a signal, such as a radio signal. The ratio of output signal strength to input signal

Amundsen *Norwegian explorer Roald Amundsen. He devoted his life to polar exploration and in 1911 became the first man to reach the South Pole.*

strength is called the gain of an amplifier. As well as achieving high gain, an amplifier should be free from distortion and able to operate over a range of frequencies. Practical amplifiers are usually complex circuits, although simple amplifiers can be built from single transistors or valves.

amplitude maximum displacement of an oscillation from the equilibrium position. For a wave motion, it is the height of a wave (or the depth of a trough). With a sound wave, for example, amplitude corresponds to the intensity (loudness) of the sound. In AM (amplitude modulation) radio broadcasting, the required audiofrequency signal is made to modulate (vary slightly) the amplitude of a continuously transmitted radio carrier wave.

ampulla small vessel with a round body and narrow neck, used for holding oil, perfumes, and so on by the ancient Greeks and Romans.

amputation loss of part or all of a limb or other body appendage through surgery or mishap.

Amritsar /æm'rɪtsə/ industrial city in the Punjab, India; population (1981) 595,000. It is the holy city of ◊Sikhism, with the Guru Nanak University (named after the first Sikh guru) and the Golden Temple from which armed demonstrators were evicted by the Indian army under Gen Dayal in 1984, 325 being killed. Subsequently, Indian prime minister Indira Gandhi was assassinated in reprisal. In 1919 it was the scene of the Amritsar Massacre.

Amritsar Massacre also called *Jallianwallah Bagh massacre* the killing of 379 Indians (and wounding of 1,200) in Amritsar in the Punjab 1919, when British troops under Gen Edward Dyer (1864–1927) opened fire without warning on an angry crowd of some 10,000, assembled to protest against the arrest of two Indian National Congress (see ◊Congress Party) leaders.

Dyer was subsequently censured and resigned his commission, but gained popular support in the UK for his action, both by mention in the House of Lords and by private subscriptions totalling £926,000. The favourable treatment Dyer received spurred Mahatma ◊Gandhi to a policy of active noncooperation with the British.

Amsterdam /'æmstədæm/ capital of the Netherlands; population (1988) 1,031,000. Canals cut through the city link it with the North Sea and the Rhine, and as a port it is second only to Rotterdam. There is shipbuilding, printing, food processing, banking, and insurance.

Art galleries include Rijksmuseum, Stedelijk, Vincent Van Gogh Museum, and Rembrandt house. Notable also are the Royal Palace (1655), and the Anne Frank house.

Amu Darya /'æ'mu: 'dɑːri'ɑː/ river formerly called Oxus in Soviet central Asia, flowing 2,540 km/1,490 mi from the ◊Pamirs to the ◊Aral Sea.

Amundsen /'æməndsən/ Roald 1872–1928. Norwegian explorer who in 1903–06, was the first person to navigate the ◊Northwest Passage. Beaten to the North Pole by ◊Peary 1910, he reached the South Pole ahead of ◊Scott 1911.

In 1918, Amundsen made an unsuccessful attempt to drift across the North Pole in the airship *Maud* and in 1925 tried unsuccessfully to fly from Spitsbergen, in the Arctic Ocean N of Norway, to the Pole by aeroplane. The following year he joined the Italian explorer Umberto Nobile in the airship *Norge*, which circled the North Pole twice and landed in Alaska. Amundsen was killed in a plane crash over the Arctic Ocean while searching for Nobile and his airship *Italia*.

Amur /ə'mʊə/ river in E Asia. Formed by the Argun and the Shilka, the Amur enters the Sea of Okhotsk. At its mouth at Nikolaevsk it is 16 km/10 mi wide. For much of its course of over 4,400 km/2,730 mi it forms, together with its tributary, the Ussuri, the boundary between the USSR and China.

Under the treaties of Aigun (1858) and Peking (1860), 984,200 sq km/380,000 sq mi of territory N and E of the two rivers were ceded by China to the tsarist government. From 1963 China raised the question of its return and there have been border clashes.

amyl alcohol common name for ◊pentanol.

amylase one of a group of ◊enzymes that break down ◊starches into their component molecules (sugars) for use in the body. It occurs widely in both plants and animals. In humans, it is found in pancreatic juices and saliva.

Anabaptist (Greek 'baptize again') a member of any of various 16th-century Protestant sects widespread in N Europe. They believed in adult rather than child baptism, and sought to establish utopian communities.

anabolic steroid ◊hormone that stimulates tissue growth. Its use in medicine is limited to the treatment of some ◊anaemias and breast cancers; it may help to break up blood clots. Side effects include aggressive behaviour, masculinization in women, and, in children, reduced height.

It is used in sports, such as weightlifting and athletics, to increase muscle bulk for greater strength and stamina, but it is widely condemned because of the side effects. In 1988 the Canadian sprinter Ben Johnson was stripped of an Olympic gold medal for taking anabolic steroids.

anabolism the process of building up body tissue, promoted by the influence of certain hormones.

anabranch (Greek *ana* 'again') stream that branches from a main river, then reunites with it. For example, the Great Anabranch in New South Wales, Australia, leaves the Darling near Menindee, and joins the Murray below the Darling-Murray confluence.

Anaconda /ˌænə'kɒndə/ town in Montana, USA, which has the world's largest copper plant; population (1980) 12,518. The city was founded as Copperopolis 1883, by the Anaconda Copper Mining Company, and was incorporated as Anaconda 1888. The town is 1,615 m/5,300 ft above sea level, and 42 km/26 mi NW of Butte.

anaconda South American snake *Eunectes murinus* allied to the boa constrictor. One of the largest snakes, growing to 9 m/30 ft or more, it is found in and near water.

anaemia a condition caused by a shortage of haemoglobin, the oxygen-carrying component of the blood. It arises either from abnormal loss or defective production of haemoglobin. Excessive loss occurs, for instance, with chronic slow bleeding or with accelerated destruction (◊haemolysis) of red blood cells. Defective production may be due to iron deficiency or malnutrition, chronic infection, kidney disease, or certain kinds of poisoning. Untreated anaemia taxes the heart and may prove fatal.

anaerobic in biology, a description of those living organisms that do not require oxygen for the release of energy food. Anaerobic organisms include many bacteria, yeasts, and internal parasites.

Obligate anaerobes such as ◊archaebacteria cannot function in the presence of oxygen, but *facultative anaerobes*, like the fermenting yeasts and some bacteria, can function with or without oxygen. Anaerobic organisms release less of the available energy from their food than ◊aerobic organisms.

anaesthetic a drug that produces loss of sensation or consciousness; the resulting state is **anaesthesia**, in which the patient is insensitive to stimuli. Anaesthesia may also happen as a result of nerve disorder.

Ever since the first successful operation in 1846 on an unconscious patient, advances have been aimed at increasing safety and control. Sedatives may be given before the anaesthetic to make the process easier. Level and duration of unconsciousness are managed precisely. Where general anaesthesia may be inappropriate (for example, in childbirth, for a small procedure, or in the elderly), many other techniques are available. A topical substance may be applied to the skin or tissue surface; a local agent may be injected into the tissues under the skin in the area to be treated; a regional block of sensation may be achieved by injection into a nerve. Spinal anaesthetic, including epidural, is injected into the tissues surrounding the spinal cord, producing loss of feeling in a larger part of the body.

Less than one in 5,000 patients aged 20–40 may become sensitized to anaesthetics as a result of previously having undergone operations. Provided this is noticed promptly by the anaesthetist, no ill effects should ensue.

Analects the most important of the four books that contain the teachings and ideas of ◊Confucianism.

analgesia relief of ◊pain. ◊Opiates alter the perception or appreciation of pain and are effective in controlling 'deep' visceral (internal) pain. Non-opiates, such as ◊aspirin, ◊paracetamol, and ◊NSAIDs relieve musculoskeletal pain and reduce inflammation in soft tissues.

Pain is the sensation that is felt when electrical stimuli travel along a nerve pathway, from peripheral nerve fibres to the brain via the spinal cord. An anaesthetic agent acts either by preventing stimuli from being sent (local), or by removing awareness of them (general). Analgesic drugs act on the brain.

Severe or chronic pain cannot be controlled by drugs. Temporary or permanent analgesia is achieved by injection of an anaesthetic agent into, or the severing of, a nerve. Implanted devices enable patients to deliver controlled electrical stimulation to block pain impulses. Production of the body's natural opiates, ◊endorphins, can be manipulated by techniques such as relaxation and biofeedback.

analogue computer computing device that performs calculations through the interaction of continuously varying physical quantities, such as voltages (as distinct from the more common ◊digital computer, which works with discrete quantities). It is said to operate in 'real time', and can therefore be used to monitor and control other events as they are happening.

Although common in engineering since the 1920s, analogue computers are not general-purpose computers and are confined to solving ◊differential equations and similar mathematical problems. The earliest analogue computing device is thought to be the flat, or planispheric, astrolabe, which originated in about the 8th century.

analysis branch of mathematics concerned with limiting processes on axiomatic number systems; ◊calculus of variations and infinitesimal calculus is now called analysis. In chemistry, analysis is the determination of the composition or properties of substances (see ◊analytical chemistry).

analytic in philosophy, a term derived from ◊Kant: the converse of ◊synthetic. In an analytic judgement, the judgement provides no new knowledge, for example: 'All bachelors are unmarried'.

analytical chemistry branch of chemistry that deals with the determination of the chemical composition of substances.

Quantitative analysis determines exact composition in terms of concentration, using such techniques as titration (volumetric analysis) and weighing (gravimetric analysis). *Qualitative analysis* determines the elements or compounds in a given sample, without necessarily finding their concentrations, using methods such as ◊chromatography and ◊spectroscopy.

analytical engine a programmable computing device, designed by Charles ◊Babbage in the 1830s. It introduced many of the concepts of the digital computer but, because of limitations in manufacturing processes, was never built.

Among the concepts introduced were input and output, an arithmetic unit, memory, sequential operation, and the ability to make decisions based on data. The design was forgotten until some of Babbage's writings were rediscovered 1937.

analytical geometry another name for ◊coordinate geometry.

Ananda /əˈnændə/ 5th century BC. Favourite disciple of the Buddha. At his plea, a separate order was established for women. He played a major part in collecting the teachings of the Buddha after his death.

Anand Marg Indian religious sect, 'the pathway to bliss'; their leader **Prabhat Ranjan Sarkar** (1921–) claims to be god incarnate. Imprisoned for alleged murder of defectors from the sect, he was released after acquittal in 1978.

anaphylaxis in medicine, a severe allergic response. Typically, the air passages become constricted, the blood pressure falls rapidly, and the victim collapses. Rare in humans, anaphylaxis can occur following wasp or bee stings, or treatment with some drugs.

anarchism (Greek *anarkhos*, 'without ruler') the political belief that society should have no government, laws, police, or other authority, but should be a free association of all its members. It does not mean 'without order'; most theories of anarchism imply an order of a very strict and symmetrical kind, but they maintain that such order can be achieved by cooperation. Anarchism must not be confused with nihilism, a purely negative and destructive activity directed against society. It is essentially a pacifist movement.

Religious anarchism, claimed by many anarchists to be exemplified in the early organization of the Christian church, has found expression in the social philosophy of the Russian writer Tolstoy and the Indian nationalist Gandhi. The growth of political anarchism may be traced through the British Romantic writers William Godwin and Shelley to the 1848 revolutionaries P J ◊Proudhon in France and the Russian ◊Bakunin, who had a strong following in Europe. The theory of anarchism is expressed in the works of the Russian revolutionary ◊Kropotkin.

From the 1960s there were outbreaks of politically motivated violence popularly identified with anarchism; in the UK, the bombing and shooting incidents carried out by the Angry Brigade 1968–71, and in the 1980s incidents directed towards peace and animal-rights issues, and to demonstrate against large financial and business corporations.

Anastasia /ˌænəˈsteɪzɪə/ 1901–1918. Russian Grand Duchess, youngest daughter of ◊Nicholas II. She was murdered with her parents but it has been alleged that Anastasia escaped. Those who claimed her identity included Anna Anderson (1902–1984). Alleged by some to be a Pole, Franziska Schanzkowski, she was rescued from a Berlin canal 1920. The German Federal Supreme Court found no proof of her claim 1970.

anastomosis in medicine, a normal or abnormal communication between two vessels (usually blood vessels) in the body. Surgical anastomosis involves the deliberate joining of two vessels or hollow parts of an organ, for example, when part of the intestine has been removed and the remaining free ends are brought together and stitched.

anathema (Greek 'set apart') something that is shunned or cursed. The word is used in the Christian church in excommunication.

Anatolia /ˌænəˈtoʊlɪə/ (Turkish **Anadolu**) alternative name for Turkey-in-Asia.

anatomy the study of the structure of the body, especially the ◊human body, as distinguished from physiology, which is the study of its functions.

Herophilus of Chalcedon (about 300 BC) is regarded as the founder of anatomy. In the 2nd century AD, the Graeco-Roman physician Galen produced an account of anatomy which was the only source of anatomical knowledge until *On the Working of the Human Body* 1543 by Andreas Vesalius. In 1628, William Harvey published his demonstration of the circulation of the blood. Following the invention of the microscope, the Italian Malpighi and the Dutch Leeuwenhoek were able to found the study of ◊histology. In 1747, Albinus (1697–1770), with the help of the artist Wandelaar (1691–1759), produced the most exact account of the bones and muscles, and in 1757–65 Albrecht von Haller gave the most complete and exact description of the organs that had yet appeared. In France the anatomy of the nervous system was advanced by Vicq d'Azyr (1748–94), and comparative anatomy by Georges Cuvier, while in England John Hunter developed an anatomical museum.

Among the anatomical writers of the early 19th century are the surgeon Charles Bell (1774–1842), Jonas Quain (1796–1865), and Henry Gray (1825–1861). Later in the century came stain techniques for microscopic examination, and the method of mechanically cutting very thin sections of stained tissues (using X-rays; see ◊radiography). Radiographic anatomy has been one of the triumphs of the 20th century, which has also been marked by immense activity in embryological investigation.

Anaximander /ˌænæksɪˈmændə/ 610–c.547 BC. Greek astronomer and philosopher. He is thought to have been the first to determine solstices and equinoxes, to have invented the sundial, and to have produced the first geographical map. He believed that the universe originated as a formless mass (*apeiron*, 'indefinite') containing within itself the contraries of hot and cold, and wet and dry, from which land, sea, and air were formed out of the union and separation of these opposites.

ANC abbreviation for ◊*African National Congress*.

ancestor worship religious attitude to deceased members of a group or family. Adherents believe that the souls of the dead remain involved in this world, and are capable of influencing events if appealed to.

Zulus used to invoke the spirits of their great warriors before engaging in battle; the Greeks deified their early heroes; and the ancient Romans held in reverential honour the *manes* or departed spirits of their forebears. Ancestor worship is a part of ◊Confucianism, and recent ancestors are venerated in the Shinto religion of Japan.

Anchorage /ˈæŋkərɪdʒ/ port and largest town of Alaska, USA, at the head of Cook Inlet; population (1984) 244,030. Established 1918, Anchorage is an important centre of administration, communication, and commerce. Industries include salmon canning, and coal and gold are mined.

anchovy small fish *Engraulis encrasicholus* of the ◊herring family. It is fished extensively, being abundant in the Mediterranean, and is also found on the Atlantic coast of Europe and in the Black Sea. It grows to 20 cm/8 in.

ancien régime the old order; the feudal, absolute monarchy in France before the French Revolution 1789.

ancient art art of prehistoric cultures and the ancient civilizations around the Mediterranean that predate the classical world of Greece and Rome, for example Sumerian and Aegean art.

Artefacts range from simple relics of the Palaeolithic period, such as pebbles carved with symbolic figures, to the sophisticated art forms of ancient Egypt and Assyria, for example mural paintings, sculpture, and jewellery.

Palaeolithic art. The earliest surviving artefacts that qualify as art are mainly from Europe, dating from approximately 30,000 to 10,000 BC. This was a period of hunter-gatherer cultures. Items that survive are small sculptures, such as the *Willendorf Venus* (Kunsthistorisches Museum, Vienna) carved from a small stone and simply painted, and symbolic sculptures carved in ivory. Later, the cave paintings of Lascaux in France and Altamira in Spain depict animals—bison, bulls, horses, and deer – and a few human figures. The animals are highly coloured and painted in profile, sometimes with lively and sinuous outlines.

Neolithic art. In Europe the period 4000–2400 BC produced great megaliths, such as Carnac in France and Stonehenge in Britain, and decorated ceramics, including pots and figurines, the pots sometimes covered in geometric ornament, heralding the later ornamental art of the Celts.

Egyptian art. The history of ancient Egypt falls into three periods, the Old, the Middle and the New Kingdoms, covering about 3,000 years between them. Within this period there is stylistic development, but also a remarkable continuity. Sculpture and painting are extremely stylized, using strict conventions and symbols based on religious beliefs. There is a strong emphasis on smooth and supple linear outlines throughout the period. Most extant Egyptian art is concerned with religion and funeral rites. During Egypt's slow decline in power, the style of art remained conservative, still subservient to the religion, but the level of technical expertise continued high, with an almost constant and prolific production of artefacts.

Egyptian Old Kingdom. The monumental sculpture of the *Sphinx* dates from about 2530 BC. The rich treasure of grave goods that survives includes the clothes, ornaments, jewellery, and weapons of the dead, as well as statues in stone and precious metals, and vivid wall paintings showing a great variety of scenes from the life of the time.

Egyptian New Kingdom. The style of painting became softer and more refined. The 18th dynasty, 1554–1305 BC, was a golden age, when the temples of Karnak and Luxor were built and the maze of tombs in the Valley of the Kings. During this period the pharaohs Ikhnaton and Tutankhamen created the most extravagant Egyptian style, exemplified by the carved images of these godlike creatures, the statues of Ikhnaton, and the golden coffins of Tutankhamen's mummified body, about 1361–1352 BC (Egyptian Museum, Cairo), and the head of Ikhnaton's queen, *Nefertiti*, about 1360 BC (Museo Archaeologico, Florence). The monumental statues of *Rameses II* in Abu Simbel date from the 13th century BC.

Sumerian art. Sculpture was highly developed, for example the remains of an inlaid harp (University Museum, Philadelphia, Pennsylvania) from the grave treasures of the royal tombs at Ur, about 2600 BC.

Assyrian art. As in ancient Egypt, this is a stylized art with figures shown in profile, and unconventional solutions to problems of perspective. This can be seen in the friezes of the palace of Nineveh, 7th century BC (examples in the British Museum, London).

Persian art. Darius I's palace in Persepolis was magnificently decorated 518–516 BC with low-relief friezes cut in stone. This period also saw a marked development in metalwork techniques.

Aegean art includes art from several cultures that developed on the islands and mainland surrounding the Aegean Sea. In the Cyclades islands, simple sculpted figures were produced; in Crete, more sophisticated art forms were developed by the Minoans about 1800–1400 BC, exemplified by the stylized wall paintings at the palace in Knossos (fragments in the Archaeological Museum, Heraklion), brilliantly inventive ceramics, and naturalistic bulls' heads in bronze and stone.

On the Greek mainland, Mycenean culture reached its peak around 1400 to 1200 BC. Surviving examples of this culture include the ruins of the palace at Mycenae, stylized gold masks, and other decorated metalwork. After the decline of Mycenae, there was little artistic activity for several centuries before the emergence of a distinctive Greek art.

Ancient Mariner, The Rime of the a poem by Samuel Taylor Coleridge, published 1798, describing the curse that falls upon a mariner and his ship when he shoots an albatross.

Ancona /æn'kəʊnə/ Italian town and naval base on the Adriatic Sea, capital of Marche region; population (1988) 104,000. It has a Romanesque cathedral and a former palace of the popes.

Andalusia /ˌændə'luːsɪə/ (Spanish *Andalucía*) fertile autonomous region of S Spain, including the provinces of Almería, Cádiz, Córdoba, Granada, Huelva, Jaén, Málaga, and Seville; area 87,300 sq km/33,698 sq mi; population (1986) 6,876,000. Málaga, Cádiz, and Algeciras are the chief ports and industrial centres. The *Costa del Sol* on the south coast is famous for its tourist resorts, including Marbella and Torremolinos.

Andalusia has Moorish architecture, having been under Muslim rule 8th–15th centuries.

Andaman and Nicobar Islands /'ændəmən ˌnɪkəbaː/ two groups of islands in the Bay of Bengal, between India and Burma, forming a Union Territory of the Republic of India; area 8,300 sq km/3,204 sq mi; population (1981) 188,000. The economy is based on fishing, timber, rubber, fruit, and rice.

The Andamans consist of five principal islands (forming the Great Andaman), the Little Andaman, and about 204 islets; area 6,340 sq km/2,447 sq mi; population (1981) 158,000. They were used as a penal settlement 1857–1942.

The Nicobars, consisting of 19 islands (7 of which are uninhabited), are 120 km/75 mi south

Andersen *Danish writer Hans Christian Andersen achieved worldwide fame with his fairy stories such as* The Snow Queen, The Ugly Duckling, *and* The Emperor's New Clothes.

of Little Andaman; area 1,953 sq km/754 sq mi; population (1981) 30,500. The main items of trade are coconut and arecanut. They were British 1869–1947.

andante (Italian 'going', 'walking') in music, a passage or movement to be performed at a walking pace; that is, at a moderately slow tempo.

Andean Group (Spanish *Grupo Andino*) South American organization aimed at economic and social cooperation between member states. It was established under the Treaty of Cartagena 1969, by Bolivia, Chile, Colombia, Ecuador, and Peru; Venezuela joined 1973, but Chile withdrew 1976. The organization is based in Lima, Peru.

Andean Indian indigenous inhabitant of the Andes Mountains in South America. The Incas extended their control over much of the Andean region 1200–1525. Pachacuti (1438–1463), the ninth Inca and first emperor, imposed the Quechua language in order to unify the different conquered groups. It is now spoken by over 10,000,000 people, and is a member of the Andean-Equatorial family.

Andersen /'ændəsən/ Hans Christian 1805–1875. Danish writer. His fairy tales such as 'The Ugly Duckling', 'The Emperor's New Clothes', and 'The Snow Queen', gained him international fame and have been translated into many languages.

Andorra
Principality of
(Principat d'Andorra)

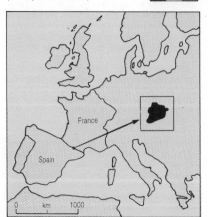

area 470 sq km/181 sq mi
capital Andorra-la-Vella
physical mountainous, with narrow valleys

features the E Pyrenees
head of state Joan Marti y Alanis (bishop of Seo de Urgel, Spain) and François Mitterrand (president of France)
head of government Josep Pintat Solens from 1984
political system feudal
political parties none
exports main industries tourism and smuggling
currency French franc (9.70 = £1 Feb 1990) and Spanish peseta (183.95 = £1 Feb 1990)
population (1988) 51,400 (25% Andorrans, 75% immigrant Spanish workers)
language Catalan (official) 30%; Spanish 59%, French 6%
religion Roman Catholic
literacy 100% (1987)
chronology
1970 Extension of franchise to third-generation women and second-generation men.
1976 First political organization (Democratic Party of Andorra) formed
1977 Franchise extended to first-generation Andorrans.
1981 First prime minister appointed by General Council.

Andrea del Sarto *Draped kneeling figure in red chalk, attributed to Andrea del Sarto.*

Andersen was born the son of a shoemaker in Odense, Fyn. His first children's stories were published 1835. Some are based on folklore; others are original. His other works include the novel *The Improvisatore* 1845, romances, and an autobiography *Mit livs eventyr/The Tale of My Life*.

Anderson /ˈændəsən/ Carl David 1905– . US physicist, who discovered the positive electron (positron) 1932; he shared a Nobel prize 1936.

Anderson /ˈændəsən/ Elizabeth Garrett 1836–1917. The first English woman to qualify in medicine. Refused entry into medical school, Anderson studied privately and was licensed by the Society of Apothecaries in London 1865. She was physician to the Marylebone Dispensary for Women and Children (later renamed the Elizabeth Garrett Anderson Hospital), now staffed by women and serving women patients.

She helped found the London School of Medicine. She was the first woman member of the British Medical Association and the first woman mayor in Britain.

Anderson /ˈændəsən/ Marian 1902– . US contralto, whose voice is remarkable for its range and richness. She toured Europe 1930, but in 1939 she was barred from singing at Constitution Hall, Washington, DC, because she was black. In 1955 she sang at the Metropolitan Opera, the first black singer to appear there. In 1958 she was appointed an alternate delegate to the United Nations.

Anderson /ˈændəsən/ Maxwell 1888–1959. US playwright, whose *What Price Glory?* 1924, written with Laurence Stallings, was a realistic portrayal of the US soldier in action during World War I.

Anderson /ˈændəsən/ Sherwood 1876–1941. US writer of sensitive, experimental, and poetic stories of small-town Midwestern life, *Winesburg, Ohio* 1919.

Andes /ˈændiːz/ the great mountain system or *cordillera* that forms the western fringe of South America, extending through some 67° of latitude and the republics of Colombia, Venezuela, Ecuador, Peru, Bolivia, Chile, and Argentina. The mountains exceed 3,600 m/12,000 ft for half their length of 6,500 km/4,000 mi. Most of the individual mountains are volcanic, with some still active.

Geologically speaking, the Andes are new mountains, having attained their present height by vertical upheaval of the entire strip of the earth's crust as recently as the latter part of the Tertiary era and the Quaternary. But they have been greatly affected by weathering. Rivers have cut profound gorges, and glaciers have produced characteristic valleys. The majority of the individual mountains are volcanic; some are still active.

The whole system may be divided into two almost parallel ranges. The southernmost extremity is Cape Horn, but the range extends into the sea and forms islands. Among the highest peaks are

Cotopaxi and Chimborazo in Ecuador, Cerro de Pasco and Misti in Peru, Illampu and Illimani in Bolivia, Aconcagua in Argentina (the highest mountain in the New World), and Ojos del Salado in Chile.

Andean mineral resources include gold, silver, tin, tungsten, bismuth, vanadium, copper, and lead. Difficult communications make mining expensive. Transport was for a long time chiefly by pack animals, but air transport has greatly reduced difficulties of communications. Three railways cross the Andes from Valparaiso to Buenos Aires, Antofagasta to Salta, and Antofagasta via Uyuni to Asunción. New roads are being built, including the ◊Pan-American Highway.

The majority of the sparse population are dependent on agriculture, the nature and products of which vary with the natural environment. Newcomers to the Andean plateau, which includes Lake ◊Titicaca, suffer from *puna*, mountain sickness, but indigenous peoples have hearts and lungs adapted to altitude.

andesite a volcanic igneous rock, intermediate in silica content between rhyolite and basalt. It is characterized by a large quantity of the feldspar ◊minerals, giving it a light colour. Andesite erupts from volcanoes at destructive plate margins (where one plate of the earth's surface moves beneath another; see ◊plate tectonics), including the Andes, from which it gets its name.

Andhra Pradesh /ˈændrə prɑːˈdeʃ/ state in E central India
area 276,800 sq km/106,845 sq mi
capital Hyderabad
towns Secunderabad
products rice, sugar cane, tobacco, groundnuts, and cotton
population (1981) 53,404,000
languages Telugu, Urdu, Tamil
history formed 1953 from the Telegu-speaking areas of Madras, and enlarged 1956 from the former Hyderabad state.

Ando /ˈændəv/ Tadao Japanese architect

Andorra /ænˈdɔːrə/ landlocked country in the E Pyrenees, bounded to the N by France and to the S by Spain.
government Andorra has no formal constitution and the government is based on its feudal origins. Although administratively independent, it has no individual international status, its joint heads of state being the bishop of Urgel, in Spain, and the president of France. They are represented by permanent delegates, the vicar general of the Urgel diocese, and the prefect of the French *département* of Pyrenées-Orientales. There is a general council of the villages, consisting of four people from each of the seven parishes, elected by Andorran citizens for a four-year term. The council submits motions and proposals to the permanent delegates for approval.

Andhra Pradesh

Hyderabad

INDIAN OCEAN

Until 1982 the general council elected the First Syndic to act as its chief executive, but there is now an executive council, headed by a prime minister. This has resulted in some separation of the legislative and executive powers and is an important step towards a more constitutional form of government. For the time being, reforms are dependent on the two co-princes, through their representatives.

history Co-princes have ruled Andorra since 1278. Until 1970 only third-generation Andorran males had the vote. Now the franchise extends to all first-generation Andorrans of foreign parentage aged 28 or over. The electorate is small in relation to the total population, up to 70% of which consists of foreign residents, who are demanding political and nationality rights. Immigration, controlled by a quota system, is restricted to French and Spanish nationals intending to work in Andorra. Since 1980 there have been signs of a fragile, but growing, democracy. There are loose political groupings but no direct party representation on the General Council. There is a technically illegal political organization, the Democratic Party of Andorra, which may well provide the basis for a future democratic system.

Andrássy /æn'drɑsɪ/ Gyula, Count Andrássy 1823–1890. Prime minister and foreign minister of the Austro-Hungarian Empire 1871–79.

André /'ɑːndreɪ/ Carl 1935– . US sculptor, a Minimalist who often uses industrial materials and basic geometrical forms. An example is the notorious *Equivalent VIII* 1976, a simple rectangle of bricks (Tate Gallery, London).

André /'ændreɪ/ John 1751–1880. British army major in the War of American Independence, who covertly negotiated the surrender of West Point with Benedict ◊Arnold, and was caught and hanged by the Americans.

Andrea del Sarto /'ændreɪə del 'sɑːtəʊ/ (Andrea d'Agnola) 1486–1531. Italian Renaissance painter active in Florence, one of the finest portraitists and religious painters of his time. His style is serene and noble, characteristic of High Renaissance art.

He trained under Piero de Cosimo and others, but was chiefly influenced by ◊Masaccio and ◊Michelangelo. In 1518 he went to work for Francis I in France, and returned to Italy in 1519 with funds to enlarge the royal French art collection; he spent it on a house for himself and never went back. His pupils included Pontormo and Vasari.

Del Sarto was the foremost painter in Florence after about 1510, along with Fra Bartolommeo, although gradually superseded by the emerging Mannerists during the 1520s. Apart from portraits, such as *A Young Man* (National Gallery, London), he painted many religious works, including the *Madonna of the Harpies* (Uffizi, Florence), an example of classical beauty reminiscent of Raphael. He painted frescoes at Sta Annunziata and the Chiostro dello Scalzo, both in Florence.

Andreas Capellanus Latin name for André le Chapelain.

André le Chapelain 12th century. French priest and author. He wrote *De Arte Honest Amandi/The Art of Honest Love*, a seminal work in ◊courtly love literature, at the request of ◊Marie de France, in whose court he was chaplain at her court in Troyes, E France.

Andress /'ændres/ Ursula 1936– . Swiss actress specializing in glamour leads. Her international career started with *Dr No* 1962. Other films include *She* 1965, *Casino Royale* 1967, *Red Sun* 1971, and *Clash of the Titans* 1981.

Andrew /'ændruː/ (full name Andrew Albert Christian Edward) 1960– . Prince of the United Kingdom, duke of York, second son of Queen Elizabeth II. He married Sarah Ferguson 1986, and their daughter, Princess Beatrice, was born 1988. Their second daughter, Eugenie, was born in 1990. He is a naval helicopter pilot.

Andrewes /'ændruːz/ Lancelot 1555–1626. Church of England bishop successively of Chichester

anechoic chamber *The anechoic room at the Building Research Centre of the UK Department of the Environment at Watford.*

(1605), Ely (1609), and Winchester (1618). He helped prepare the text of the Authorized Version of the Bible, and was known for his fine preaching.

Andrews /'ændruːz/ John 1813–1885. Irish chemist who conducted a series of experiments on the behaviour of carbon dioxide under varying temperature and pressure. In 1869 he introduced the idea of a critical temperature: 30.9°C in the case of carbon dioxide, beyond which no amount of pressure would liquefy the gas.

Andrews /'ændruːz/ Julie 1935– . British singer and actress. Formerly a child performer with her mother and father in a music-hall act, she was the original *My Fair Lady* on stage 1956. Her films include *Mary Poppins* 1964, *The Sound of Music* 1965, *'10'* 1979, and *Victor/Victoria* 1982.

Andrew, St /'ændruː/ New Testament apostle, martyred on an X-shaped cross (*St Andrew's cross*). He is the patron saint of Scotland. Feast day 30 Nov.

A native of Bethsaida, he was Simon Peter's brother. With Peter, James, and John, who worked with him as fisherfolk at Capernaum, he formed the inner circle of Jesus' 12 disciples. According to tradition he went with John to Ephesus, preached in Scythia, and was crucified at Patras.

Andreyev /æn'dreɪev/ Leonid Nicolaievich 1871–1919. Russian author. Many of his works show an obsession with death and madness including the symbolic drama *Life of Man* 1907, the melodrama *He Who Gets Slapped* 1915; and the novels *Red Laugh* 1904, and *S.O.S* 1919 published in Finland, where he fled after the Russian Revolution.

Andrić /'ændrɪtʃ/ Ivo 1892–1974. Yugoslavian novelist and nationalist. He became a diplomat, and was ambassador to Berlin 1940. *Na Drini ćuprija/The Bridge on the Drina* 1945 is an epic history of a small Bosnian town. Nobel prize 1961.

He was a member of the Young Bosnia organization, another member of which shot the heir to the Austrian throne 1914, and spent World War I in an internment camp because of his politics.

Androcles /'ændrəkliːz/ traditionally, a Roman slave who fled from a cruel master into the African desert, where he withdrew a thorn from the paw of a crippled lion. Recaptured and sentenced to combat a lion in the arena, he found his adversary was his old friend. The emperor Tiberius was said to have freed them both.

androecium the male part of a flower, comprising a number of ◊stamens.

androgen a general name for any male sex hormone, of which ◊testosterone is the most important. They are all ◊steroids and are principally

involved in the production of male ◊secondary sexual characters (such as facial hair).

Andromache /æn'drɒməki/ in Greek mythology, the faithful wife of Hector and mother of Astyanax. After the fall of Troy she was awarded to Neoptolemus, Achilles' son; she later married a Trojan seer called Helenus. Andromache is the heroine of Homer's ◊*Iliad* and the subject of a play by Euripides.

Andromache tragedy by Euripides, first produced about 426 BC. Hermione, wife of Neoptolemus, seeks revenge on Andromache, her husband's lover, whom she blames for her own childlessness, but fails in her attempt to kill Andromache and her son. Neoptolemus is murdered by Orestes, a former suitor of Hermione.

Andromeda /æn'drɒmɪdə/ in Greek mythology, an Ethiopian princess chained to a rock as a sacrifice to a sea monster. She was rescued by ◊Perseus who married her.

Andromeda /æn'drɒmɪdə/ a major constellation of the northern hemisphere, visible in autumn. Its main feature is the Andromeda galaxy. The star Alpha Andromedae forms one corner of the Square of Pegasus. It represents the princess of Greek mythology.

Andromeda Galaxy a galaxy 2.2 million light years away in the constellation of Andromeda, and the most distant object visible to the naked eye. It is the largest member of the ◊Local Group of galaxies. Like the Milky Way, it is a spiral orbited by several companion galaxies but contains about twicw as many stars. It is about 200,000 light years across.

Andropov /æn'drɒpɒf/ Yuri 1914–1984. Soviet communist politician, president 1983–84. As chief of the KGB 1967–82, he established a reputation for efficiently suppressing dissent.

Andropov was politically active from the 1930s. His part in quelling the Hungarian national rising 1956, when he was Soviet ambassador, brought him into the Communist Party secretariat 1962 as a specialist on E European affairs. He became a member of the Politburo 1973 and succeeded Brezhnev as party general secretary 1982. Elected president 1983, he introduced economic reforms, but died Feb 1984.

anechoic chamber a room that quickly absorbs all sounds created within it. All surfaces inside the chamber are covered by sound-absorbent materials such as rubber. The walls are often covered with inward-facing pyramids of rubber, to minimize reflections. It is used for experiments in ◊acoustics and for testing audio equipment.

anemone plant of the buttercup family Ranunculaceae, genus *Anemone*. The function of petals is performed by its sepals. The **Eurasian white wood anemone** *Anemone nemorosa*, or **wind-flower**, grows in shady woods, flowering in spring. The **garden anemone** *Anemone coronaria* is blue or red. The ◊pasque flower is now placed in a separate genus. *Hepatica nobilis*, once included within *Anemone*, is common in the Alps.

anemophily a type of ◊pollination in which the pollen is carried on the wind. Anemophilous flowers are usually unscented, either have very reduced petals and sepals or lack them altogether, and do not produce nectar. In some species they are borne in ◊catkins. Male and female reproductive structures are commonly found in separate flowers. The male flowers have numerous exposed stamens, often on long filaments; the female flowers have long, often branched, feathery stigmas.

Many wind-pollinated plants, such as hazel (*Corylus avellana*), bear their flowers before the leaves to facilitate the free transport of pollen. Since air movements are random, vast amounts of pollen are needed: a single birch catkin, for example, may produce over five million pollen grains.

anemometer a device for measuring wind speed and liquid flow. A **cup-type anemometer** consists of cups at the ends of arms, which rotate when

Angelou US writer Maya Angelou.

the wind blows. The speed of rotation indicates the wind speed. *Vane-type anemometers* have vanes, like a small windmill or propellor, that rotate when the wind blows. *Pressure-tube anemometers* use the pressure generated by the wind to indicate speed. The wind blowing into or across a tube develops a pressure, proportional to the wind speed, that is measured by a manometer or pressure gauge. *Hot-wire anemometers* work on the principle that the rate at which heat is transferred from a hot wire to the surrounding air is a measure of the air speed. Wind speed is determined by measuring either the electric current required to maintain a hot wire at a constant temperature, or the variation of resistance while a constant current is maintained.

aneroid a kind of ◊barometer.

Aneto, Pico /æˌnetəʊˈpiːkəʊ/ highest peak of the Pyrenees mountains, rising to 3,4040 m/11,052 ft in the Spanish province of Huesca.

aneurysm a weakening in the wall of an artery, causing it to balloon outwards, with the risk of rupture and serious blood loss. If detected in time, some aneurysms can be excised.

Angad /ˈæŋgæd/ 1504–1552. Indian religious leader, second guru (teacher) of Sikhism 1539–52, succeeding Nanak. He popularized the alphabet known as *Gurmukhi*, in which the Sikh scriptures are written.

angel (Greek *angelos*, messenger) in Christian, Jewish, and Muslim belief, supernatural being intermediate between God and humans. The Christian hierarchy has nine orders: *Seraphim*, *Cherubim*, *Thrones* (who contemplate God and reflect his glory), *Dominations*, *Virtues*, *Powers* (who regulate the stars and the Universe), *Principalities*, *Archangels*, and *Angels* (who minister to humanity). In traditional Catholic belief, every human being has a guardian angel. The existence of angels was reasserted by the Pope in 1986.

angel dust popular name for the anaesthetic ◊phencyclidine.

Angel Falls /ˈeɪndʒəl/ highest waterfalls in the New World, on the river Caroní in the tropical rainforest of Bolívar Region, Venezuela; total height 978 m/3,210 ft. Named after the aviator and prospector James Angel who flew over the falls and crash-landed nearby 1935.

angelfish name for a number of unrelated fishes. The freshwater *angelfish*, genus *Pterophyllum* of South America is a tall flattened fish with a striped body, up to 26 cm/10 in long, but usually smaller in captivity. The *angelfish* or *monkfish Squatina* is a bottom-living shark up to 1.8 m/6 ft

long with a body flattened from top to bottom. The *marine angelfish*, *Pomacanthus* and others, are long narrow-bodied fish, often brilliantly coloured, up to 65 cm/2 ft long, living around coral reefs in the tropics.

angelica type of plant, genus *Angelica*, of the umbelliferous family. *Angelica sylvestris*, the species found in Britain, is a tall perennial herb, with wedge-shaped leaves and clusters of white, pale violet, or pinkish flowers. The oil is used in perfume and liqueurs. *Angelica archangelica* is a culinary herb, the stems of which are preserved in sugar.

Angelico /ænˈdʒelɪkəʊ/ Fra (Guido di Pietro) *c.*1400–1455. Italian painter of religious scenes, active in Florence. He was a monk and painted a series of frescoes at the monastery of San Marco, Florence, begun after 1436. He also produced several altarpieces in a simple style.

Fra Angelico joined the Dominican order about 1420. After his novitiate, he resumed a career as a painter of religious images and altarpieces, many of which have small predella scenes beneath them, depicting events in the life of a saint. The central images of the paintings are highly decorated with pastel colours and gold-leaf designs, while the predella scenes are often lively and relatively unsophisticated. There is a similar simplicity to his frescoes in the cells at San Marco, which are principally devotional works.

Fra Angelico's other fresco sequences, *Scenes from the Life of Christ* (Orvieto Cathedral) and *Scenes from the Lives of SS Stephen and Lawrence* 1440s (chapel of Nicholas V, Vatican Palace), are more elaborate.

Angell /ˈeɪndʒəl/ Norman 1872–1967. British writer on politics and economics. In 1910 he acquired an international reputation with his book *The Great Illusion*, in which he maintained that any war must prove ruinous to the victors as well as to the vanquished. Nobel Peace Prize 1933.

Angelou /ˌændʒəluː/ Maya (born Marguerite Johnson) 1928– . US novelist, poet, playwright, and short-story writer. Her powerful autobiographical work, *I Know Why the Caged Bird Sings* 1970 and its sequels, tell of the struggles towards physical and spiritual liberation of a black woman growing up in the US South.

Anger /ˈæŋgə/ Kenneth 1932– . US avant-garde filmmaker, brought up in Hollywood. His films, which dispense with conventional narrative, often portray homosexual iconography and a personal form of mysticism. They include *Fireworks* 1947, *Scorpio Rising* 1964, and *Lucifer Rising* 1973.

Angers /ˌɒnˈʒeɪ/ ancient French town, capital of Maine-et-Loire *département*, on the river Maine; population (1982) 196,000. Products include electrical machinery and Cointreau liquer. It has a 12th–13th century cathedral and castle, and was formerly the capital of the duchy and province of Anjou, whose people are called Angevins–a name also applied by the English to the ◊Plantagenet kings.

Angevin relating to the reigns of the English kings Henry II, and Richard I (also known, with the later English kings up to Richard III, as the *Plantagenets*); derived from Anjou, the region in France controlled by English kings at this time. The *Angevin Empire* comprised the territories (including England) that belonged to the Anjou dynasty.

angina or *angina pectoris*. Severe pain in the chest due to impaired blood supply to the heart muscle because a coronary artery is narrowed.

angiography a technique for X-raying major blood vessels. A radio-opaque dye is injected into the bloodstream so that the suspect vessel is clearly silhouetted on the X-ray film.

angiosperm flowering plant in which the seeds are enclosed within an ovary, which ripens to a fruit. Angiosperms are divided into ◊monocotyledons (single seed-leaf in the embryo) and ◊dicotyledons (two seed-leaves in the embryo). They include

the majority of flowers, herbs, grasses, and trees except conifers.

Angkor /ˈæŋkɔː/ the ruins of the ancient capital of the Khmer Empire, NW of Cambodia. The remains date mainly from the 10th–12th century AD, and comprise temples originally dedicated to the Hindu gods, shrines associated with Theravada Buddhism, and royal palaces. Many are grouped within the great enclosure called *Angkor Thom*, but the great temple of *Angkor Wat* (early 12th century) lies outside. Angkor was abandoned in the 15th century, and the ruins were overgrown by jungle and not adequately described until 1863. Buildings on the site suffered damage during the civil war 1970–75.

Angle member of Germanic tribe that invaded Britain in the 5th century; see ◊Anglo-Saxon.

angle in geometry, an amount of turn. Angles are measured in ◊degrees or ◊radians. An angle of 90° (90 degrees) is a *right angle*. Angles of less than 90° are called *acute angles*; angles of more than 90° but less than 180° are *obtuse angles*. A *reflex angle* is an angle of more than 180° but less than 360°.

angler fish *Lophius piscatorius*, also known as the frogfish or monkfish. It lives in the N Atlantic and Mediterranean, grows to 2 m/6.5 ft, and has a flattened body and broad head and jaws.

The many species of anglerfishes form the order Lophiiformes and include deep-sea forms. Camouflaged against the sea bottom, it waits, twitching the enlarged tip of the threadlike first ray of the dorsal fin to entice prey.

Anglesey /ˈæŋgəlsi/ (Welsh *Ynys Môn*) island off the NW coast of Wales; area 720 sq km/278 sq mi; population (1981) 67,000. It is separated from the mainland by the Menai Straits, which are crossed by the Britannia tubular railway bridge and Telford's suspension bridge, built 1819–26 but since rebuilt. Nature-lovers visit Anglesey for its fauna (especially bird life) and flora, and antiquarians for its many buildings and relics of historic interest; it is also a popular holiday resort. The ancient granary of Wales, Anglesey now has industries such as toy-making, electrical goods, and bromine extraction from the sea. Holyhead is the principal town and port; but Beaumaris was the county town until the county of Anglesey was merged in Gwynedd 1974.

Anglesey /ˈæŋgəlsi/ Henry William Paget 1768–1854. British cavalry leader during the Napoleonic wars. He was twice Lord Lieutenant of Ireland, and succeeded his father as earl of Uxbridge 1812. At the Battle of Waterloo he led a charge, lost a leg, and was made a marquess.

Anglican Communion family of Christian churches including the Church of England, the US Episcopal Church, and those holding the same essential doctrines, that is the Lambeth Quadrilateral 1888 Holy Scripture as the basis of all doctrine, the Nicene and Apostles' Creeds, Holy Baptism and Holy Communion, and the historic episcopate.

In England the two archbishops head the provinces of Canterbury and York, which are subdivided into bishoprics. The Church Assembly 1919 was replaced 1970 by a General Synod with three houses (bishops, other clergy, and laity) to regulate Church matters, subject to Parliament. A decennial Lambeth Conference (so called because the first was held there 1867), attended by bishops from all parts of the Anglican Communion, is presided over by the Archbishop of Canterbury; it is not legislative but its decisions are often put into practice. In 1988 it passed a resolution seen as paving the way for the consecration of women bishops (the first was elected in the US Sept 1988).

angling fishing with rod and line. *Freshwater* and *sea-fishing* are the most common forms. Angling is the biggest participant sport in the UK. *Freshwater* coarse fishing includes members of the carp family, and pike (not usually eaten but thrown back into the water); freshwater game fish include salmon and trout. In *sea fishing* the catch includes flatfish, bass, mackerel; big-game fish (again not usually eaten) including shark, tuna or tunny, marlin, and swordfish. Competition angling exists and world championships take place for most branches of the sport. The oldest is the World Freshwater Championship, inaugurated 1957.

World Freshwater Championship

individual
1983 Rudiger Kremkus *West Germany*
1984 Bobby Smithers *England*
1985 Dave Roper *England*
1986 Lud Wever *Holland*
1987 Clive Branson *Wales*
1988 Jean-Pierre Fouquet *France*
1989 Tom Dickering *England*
team
1983 Belgium
1984 Luxembourg
1985 England
1986 Italy
1987 England
1988 England
1989 Wales

Anglo a combining language form with several related meanings. In 'Anglo-Saxon' it refers to the Angles, a Germanic people who invaded Britain in the 5th to 7th centuries. In 'Anglo-Welsh' it refers to England or the English. In 'Anglo-American' it may refer either to England and the English, or commonly but less accurately to Britain and the British; it may also refer to the English language and to the Anglo-Saxon element in US society (often in contrast to 'Hispano-American'). In many parts of the world 'an Anglo' is a person of Anglo-Saxon background or type and/or someone who speaks English.

Anglo-Irish Agreement or *Hillsborough Agreement* a concord reached 1985 between the UK and Irish premiers, Margaret Thatcher and Garret FitzGerald. One sign of the improved relations between the two countries was increased cross-border co-operation between police and security forces across the border with Northern Ireland. However, the agreement was rejected by Northern Ireland Unionists as a step towards a renunciation of British sovereignty. In Mar 1988 talks led to further strengthening of the agreement.

Anglo-Saxon one of several Germanic invaders (Angles, Saxons, and Jutes) who conquered much of Britain between the 5th and 7th centuries. The Angles settled in East Anglia, Mercia, and Northumbria; the Saxons in Essex, Sussex, and Wessex; and the Jutes in Kent and S Hampshire. After the conquest a number of kingdoms were set up, commonly referred to as the *Heptarchy*; these were united in the early 9th century under the overlordship of Wessex.

The Jutes probably came from the Rhineland and not, as was formerly believed, from Jutland. The Angles and Saxons came from Schleswig-Holstein, and may have united before the invasion. There was probably considerable intermarriage with the Romanized Celts, although the latter's language and civilization almost disappeared. The

Angola
People's Republic of
(República Popular de Angola)

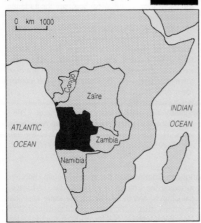

area 1,246,700 sq km/481,226 sq mi
capital and chief port Luanda
towns Lobito and Benguela, also ports
physical elevated plateau, desert in the south
features Kwanza river and Cabinda rainforest
head of state and government José Eduardo dos Santos from 1979
political system one-party socialist republic
political parties People's Movement for the Liberation of Angola-Workers' Party (MPLA-PT), Marxist-Leninist
exports oil, coffee, diamonds, palm oil, sisal, iron ore, fish
currency kwanza (50.97 = £1 Feb 1990)
population (1988 est) 9,387,000 (largest ethnic group Ovimbundu); annual growth rate 2.5%
life expectancy men 40, women 44
language Portuguese (official); Umbundu, Kimbundu
religion Roman Catholic 46%, Protestant 12%, animist 42%
literacy 59% (1985)
GDP $4.5 bn (1982); $478 per head of

population
chronology
1951 Angola became an overseas territory of Portugal.
1956 First independence movement formed, the People's Movement for the Liberation of Angola (MPLA).
1961 Unsuccessful independence rebellion.
1962 Second nationalist movement formed, the National Front for the Liberation of Angola (FNLA).
1966 Third nationalist movement formed, the National Union for the Total Independence of Angola (UNITA).
1975 Transitional government of independence formed from representatives of MPLA, FNLA, UNITA, and Portuguese government. MPLA supported by USSR and Cuba, FNLA by 'non-left' power groups of southern Africa, and UNITA by Western powers. Angola declared independent. MPLA proclaimed People's Republic under the presidency of Dr Agostinho Neto. FNLA and UNITA proclaimed People's Democratic Republic of Angola.
1976 MPLA gained control of most of the country. South African troops withdrawn but Cuban units remained.
1977 MPLA restructured to become the People's Movement for the Liberation of Angola - Workers' Party (MPLA-PT).
1979 Death of Neto, succeeded by José Eduardo dos Santos.
1980 Constitution amended to provide for an elected people's assembly. UNITA guerrillas, aided by South Africa, continued to operate South African raids on the South West Africa People's Organization's bases in Angola.
1984 The Lusaka agreement.
1985 South African forces officially withdrawn.
1986 Further South African raids into Angola. UNITA continuing to receive South African support.
1988 Peace treaty, providing for the withdrawal of all foreign troops, signed with South Africa and Cuba.
1989 Ceasefire agreed with UNITA broke down and guerrilla activity restarted.

English-speaking peoples of Britain, the Commonwealth, and the US are often referred to today as Anglo-Saxons, but the term is completely unscientific, as the Welsh, Scots, and Irish are mainly of Celtic or Norse descent, and by the 1980s fewer than 15% of Americans were of British descent.

Anglo-Saxon art the painting and sculpture of England from the 7th century to 1066. Sculpted crosses and ivories, manuscript painting, and gold and enamel jewellery survive. The relics of the Sutton Hoo ship burial, 7th century, and the *Lindisfarne Gospels* about 690 (both British Museum, London) have typical Celtic ornamental patterns, but in manuscripts of S England a different style emerged in the 9th century, with delicate, lively pen-and-ink figures and heavily decorative foliage borders.

Anglo-Saxon Chronicle a history of England from the Roman invasion to the 11th century, in the form of a series of chronicles written in Old English by monks, begun in the 9th century (during the reign of King Alfred), and continuing to the 12th century.

The Chronicle, comprising seven different manuscripts, forms a unique record of early English history and of the development of Old English prose up to its final stages in the year 1154, by which date it had been superseded by Middle English.

Anglo-Saxon language the group of dialects spoken by the Anglo-Saxon peoples who, in the 5th to 7th centuries, invaded and settled in Britain (in what became England and Lowland Scotland). Anglo-Saxon is traditionally known as Old English. See ◊English language.

Anglo-Saxon literature another name for ◊English literature.

Angola /æŋˈgəʊlə/ country in SW Africa, bounded to the W by the Atlantic ocean, to the N and NE by Zaïre, to the E by Zambia, and to the S by Namibia.

government the 1975 constitution, amended 1976 and 1980, created a one-party 'People's Republic', with political power held by the People's Movement for the Liberation of Angola - Workers' Party (MPLA-PT). The president, elected by the congress of MPLA-PT, chooses and chairs the council of ministers and is commander-in-chief of the armed forces. There is a 223-member people's assembly, 20 of whom are nominated by MPLA-PT and the rest elected by electoral colleges of 'loyal' citizens.

history Angola became a Portuguese colony in 1491 and an Overseas Territory of Portugal in 1951. In 1956 a movement for complete independence was established, the MPLA, based originally in the Congo. This was followed by the formation of two other nationalist movements, the National Front for the Liberation of Angola (FNLA) and the National Union for the Total Independence of Angola (UNITA). Civil war broke out in 1961, with MPLA supported by socialist and communist states, UNITA helped by the Western powers and FNLA backed by the 'non-left' power groups of southern Africa.

Three months of civil war followed the granting of full independence in 1975, with MPLA and UNITA the main contestants and foreign

animal

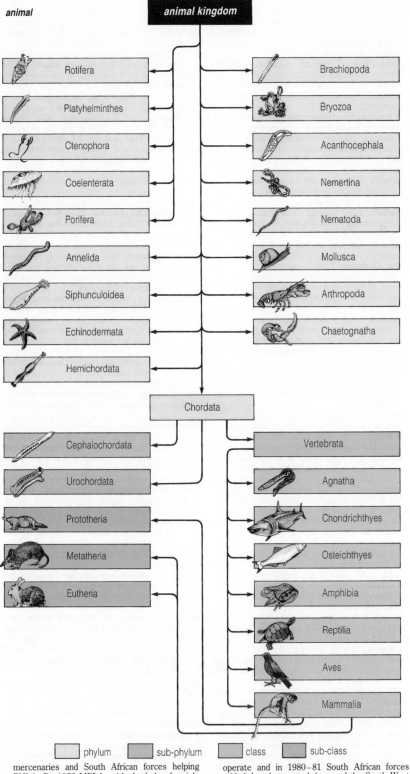

animal kingdom

Rotifera — Brachiopoda

Platyhelminthes — Bryozoa

Ctenophora — Acanthocephala

Coelenterata — Nemertina

Porifera — Nematoda

Annelida — Mollusca

Siphunculoidea — Arthropoda

Echinodermata — Chaetognatha

Hemichordata

Chordata

Cephalochordata — Vertebrata

Urochordata — Agnatha

Prototheria — Chondrichthyes

Metatheria — Osteichthyes

Eutheria — Amphibia

Reptilia

Aves

Mammalia

☐ phylum ☐ sub-phylum ☐ class ☐ sub-class

mercenaries and South African forces helping FNLA. By 1975 MPLA, with the help of mainly Cuban forces, controlled most of the country and had established the People's Republic of Angola in Luanda. Dr Agostinho Neto, the MPLA leader, became its first president. FNLA and UNITA had, in the meantime, proclaimed their own People's Democratic Republic of Angola, based in Nova Lisboa, renamed Huambo.

President Neto died in 1979 and was succeeded by José Eduardo dos Santos, who maintained Neto's links with the Soviet bloc. UNITA guerrillas, supported by South Africa, continued to

operate and in 1980–81 South African forces raided Angola to attack bases of the South West Africa People's Organization (SWAPO), who were fighting for Namibia's independence. Angola supported Namibia's claim but South Africa and the US called for the withdrawal of Cuban troops from Angola before South Africa's departure from Namibia.

In 1983 South Africa proposed a complete withdrawal of its forces if Angola could guarantee that the areas vacated would not be filled by Cuban or SWAPO units. In 1984 Angola accepted South Africa's proposals and a settlement was made,

(the Lusaka Agreement), whereby a Joint Monitoring Commission (JMC) was set up to oversee South Africa's withdrawal. In 1985 South Africa announced that this was complete and JMC was wound up. In 1986 relations between the two countries deteriorated when further South African raids into Angola occurred. UNITA also continued to receive South African support. Despite the securing of a peace treaty with South Africa and Cuba in 1988, guerrilla activity by the UNITA rebels began again in 1989.

Angora /æŋ'gɔːrə/ earlier form of ◊Ankara, Turkey, which gave its name to the Angora goat (see ◊mohair), and hence to other species of long-haired animal, such as the Angora rabbit (the source of Angora 'wool') and the Angora cat.

Angostura /ˌæŋgə'stjʊərə/ former name of ◊Ciudad Bolívar, city in Venezuela.

angostura flavouring prepared from oil distilled from the bark of *Galipea cusparia*, a tree found in Trinidad and Tobago. It is blended with herbs and other flavourings to give angostura bitters, which was first used as a stomach remedy and is now used to season food and fruit, to make a 'pink gin', and to prepare other alcoholic drinks.

Angoulême /ˌɒŋguː'leɪm/ French town, capital of the *département* of Charente, on the Charente; population (1982) 104,000. It has a cathedral, and a castle and papermills dating from the 16th century.

Angry Young Men a group of British writers who emerged about 1950 after the creative hiatus which followed World War II. They included Kingsley Amis, John Wain, John Osborne, and Colin Wilson. Also linked to the group were Iris Murdoch and Kenneth Tynan.

angst (German 'anxiety') an emotional state of anxiety without a specific cause. In ◊Existentialism, the term refers to general human anxiety at having free will, that is, of being responsible for one's actions.

ångström unit of length equal to 10^{-10} m, used for atomic measurements and the wavelengths of ◊electromagnetic radiation. It is named after the Swedish scientist A J Ångström.

Ångström /'ɒŋstrɜːm/ Anders Jonas 1814–1874. Swedish physicist, who worked in spectroscopy and solar physics.

Anguilla /æŋ'gwɪlə/ island in the E Caribbean
area 160 sq km/62 sq mi
capital The Valley
features white coral sand beaches
exports lobster, salt
currency Eastern Caribbean dollar
population (1988) 7,000
language English and Creole
government from 1982, governor, executive council, and legislative house of assembly (chief minister Emile Gumbs from 1984)
recent history a British colony from 1650, Anguilla was long associated with ◊St Christopher-Nevis, but revolted against alleged domination by the larger island, and in 1969 declared itself a republic. A small British force restored order, and Anguilla retained a special position at its own request, since 1980 a separate dependency of the UK.

angular momentum see ◊momentum.

Angus /'æŋgəs/ former county and modern district on the E coast of Scotland, merged in 1975 in Tayside region.

Anhui /ˌæn'hweɪ/ formerly **Anhwei** province of E China, watered by the Chang Jiang (Yangtze river)
area 139,900 sq km/54,000 sq mi
capital Hefei
products cereals in the north, and cotton, rice and tea in the south
population (1986) 52,170,000.

Anhwei /ˌæn'hweɪ/ former name of ◊Anhui.

anhydride a chemical compound obtained by the removal of water from another compound; usually a dehydrated acid. For example, sulphur(VI) oxide (sulphur trioxide, SO_3) is the anhydride of sulphuric acid (H_2SO_4).

anhydrite naturally occurring anhydrous calcium sulphate ($CaSO_4$). It is used commercially for the manufacture of plaster of paris and builders' plaster.

anhydrous in chemistry, the total absence of water in a chemical compound.

If the water of crystallization is removed from blue crystals of copper(II) sulphate, a white powder (anhydrous copper(II) sulphate results). Liquids from which all traces of water have been removed are also described as being anhydrous.

aniline $C_6H_5NH_2$ (**phenylamine**) the simplest aromatic chemical known. When pure, it is a colourless oily liquid; it has a characteristic odour, and turns brown in contact with air. It occurs in coal tar, and is used in the rubber industry and to make drugs and dyes. It is highly poisonous.

It was originally prepared by the dry distillation of indigo, hence its name (Portugese *anil*, indigo). It was discovered in 1826.

animal member of the kingdom Animalia, one of the major kingdoms of living things, the science of which is *zoology*. Animals are all ◊heterotrophs (they obtain their energy from organic substances produced by other organisms); they have ◊eukaryotic cells (the genetic material is contained within a distinct nucleus) bounded by a thin cell membrane rather than a thick cell wall. In the past, it was common to include the single-celled ◊protozoa with the animals, but these are now classified as protists. Thus all animals are multicellular. Most are capable of moving around but some, such as sponges and corals, are stationary.

animal behaviour the scientific study of the behaviour of animals, either by comparative psychologists (with an interest mainly in the mental processes involved in the control of behaviour) or by ethologists (with an interest in the biological context and relevance of behaviour).

animal, domestic in general, a tame animal, but in agriculture, an animal brought under human control for exploitation in respect of their labour; use of their feathers, hides, or skins; consumption of their eggs, milk, or meat. Common domestic animals include poultry, cattle, sheep, goats, buffalo, and pigs.

Almost coexistent with the emergence of humans themselves, the use of domestic animals has only since World War II led to ◊factory farming. Increasing numbers of formerly wild species have been domesticated, with stress on scientific breeding for desired characteristics.

At least 60% of the world's livestock are in developing countries but the Third World consumes only 20% of all meat and milk produced. Most domestic animals graze plants that are not edible to humans, and 40% of the world's cereal production becomes animal feed; in the USA it is 90%.

animism in psychology and physiology, the view of human personality that rejects materialistic mechanism as a valid explanation of human behaviour. In religious theory, the conception of a spiritual reality behind the material one: for example, beliefs in the soul as a shadowy duplicate of the body capable of independent activity, both in life and death.

Linked with this is the worship of natural objects such as stones and trees, thought to harbour spirits (naturism), fetishism, and ancestor worship.

anion ion carrying a negative charge. An electrolyte, such as the salt zinc chloride, is dissociated in aqueous solution or in the molten state into doubly-charged Zn^{2+} zinc ◊cations and singly-charged Cl^- anions. During electrolysis, the zinc cations flow to the cathode (to become discharged and liberate zinc metal) and the chloride anions flow to the anode (to liberate chlorine gas).

anise umbelliferous plant *Pimpinella anisum* whose fruits, aniseeds, are used to flavour foods. Aniseed oil is used in cough medicines.

Anjou /ˌɑːnˈʒuː/ an old countship and former province in northern France; capital Angers. In 1154 the count of Anjou became king of England as

Henry II, but the territory was lost by King John 1204. In 1480 the countship was annexed to the French crown. The *départements* of Maine-et-Loire and part of Indre-et-Loire, Mayenne, and Sarthe cover the area.

Ankara /ˈæŋkərə/ formerly **Angora** capital of Turkey; population (1985) 2,252,000. Industries include cement, textiles, and leather products. It replaced Istanbul (then in Allied occupation) as capital 1923.

It has the presidential palace and Grand National Assembly buildings; three universities, including a technical university to serve the whole Middle East; the Atatürk mausoleum on a nearby hilltop, and the largest mosque in Turkey at Kocatepe.

ankh ancient Egyptian symbol (derived from the simplest form of sandal), meaning 'eternal life', as in Tut*ankh*amen. It consists of a 'T' shape surmounted by an oval.

Annaba /ˈænəbə/ formerly **Bône** seaport in Algeria; population (1983) 348,000. The name means 'city of jujube trees'. There are metallurgical industries, and iron ore and phosphates are exported.

Anna Comnena /ˈænə kɒmˈniːnə/ 1083–after 1148. Byzantine historian, daughter of the emperor ◊Alexius I, who is was the historian of her father's reign. After a number of abortive attempts to alter the imperial succession in favour of her husband, Nicephorus Bryennius (*c.*1062–1137), she retired to a convent to write her major work, the *Alexiad.* It describes the Byzantine view of public office, as well as the religious and intellectual life of the period.

Anna Karenina a novel by Leo Tolstoy, published 1873–77. It describes a married woman's love affair with Vronski, a young officer, which ends with her suicide.

Annam /æˈnæm/ former country of SE Asia, incorporated in ◊Vietnam 1946 as Central Vietnam. A Bronze Age civilization was flourishing in the area when China conquered it about 214 BC. The Chinese named their conquest An-Nam, 'peaceful south'. Independent from 1428, Annam signed a treaty with France 1787, and became a French protectorate, part of Indochina 1884. During World War II Annam was occupied by Japan.

Annapolis /əˈnæpəlɪs/ seaport and capital of Maryland, USA; population (1984) 31,900. It was named after Princess (later Queen) Anne 1695. It was in session here Nov 1783–June 1784 that Congress received George Washington's resignation as commander in chief 1783, and ratified the peace treaty of the War of American Independence. The US Naval Academy is here, and John Paul ◊Jones is buried in the chapel crypt.

Annapurna /ˌænəˈpɜːnə/ mountain 8,075m/ 26,502 ft in the Himalayas, Nepál. The north face was climbed by a French expedition (Maurice Herzog) 1950 and the south by a British one 1970.

Anne /æn/ 1665–1714. Queen of Great Britain and Ireland 1702–14. Second daughter of James, Duke of York, who became James II, and Anne Hyde. She succeeded William III on the throne 1702. Events of her reign include the War of the Spanish Succession, Marlborough's victories at Blenheim, Ramillies, Oudenarde, and Malplaquet, and the union of the English and Scottish parliaments 1707. She was succeeded by George I.

She received a Protestant upbringing, and in 1683 married Prince George of Denmark. Of their many children only one survived infancy, William, Duke of Gloucester, who died at the age of 11. For the greater part of her life Anne was a close friend of Sarah Churchill, wife of John Churchill, afterwards Duke of Marlborough; the Churchills' influence helped lead her to desert her father for her brother-in-law, William of Orange, during the Revolution of 1688, and later to engage in Jacobite intrigues. Her replacement of the Tories by a Whig government 1703–04 was her own act, not due to Churchillian influence. Anne finally broke with the Marlboroughs 1710, when Mrs Masham

succeeded the duchess as her favourite, and supported the Tory government of the same year.

Anne /æn/ (full name Anne Elizabeth Alice Louise) 1950– . Princess of the UK, second child of Queen Elizabeth II, declared Princess Royal 1987. She is an excellent horsewoman, winning a gold medal at the 1976 Olympics, and is actively involved in global charity work, especially for children. In 1973 she married Captain Mark Phillips (1949–), of the Queen's Dragoon Guards; they separated in 1989. Their son Peter (1977–) was the first direct descendant of the Queen not to bear a title. They also have a daughter Zara.

annealing process of heating a material (usually glass or metal) for a given time at a given temperature, followed by slow cooling, to increase ductility and strength. It is a common form of ◊heat treatment.

Ductile metals hardened by cold working may be softened by annealing. Thus thick wire may be annealed before being drawn into fine wire. Owing to internal stresses, glass objects made at high temperature can break spontaneously as they cool unless they are annealed. Annealing releases the stresses in a controlled way and, for glass for optical purposes, also improves the optical properties of the glass.

Annecy /ænˈsiː/ capital of the *département* of Haute-Savoie, SE France, at the northern end of Lake Annecy; population (1982) 112,600 (conurbation). It has some light industry, including precision instruments, and is a tourist resort.

annelid a segmented worm of the phylum Annelida. Annelids include earthworms, leeches, and marine worms such as lugworms.

They have a distinct head and soft body, which is divided into a number of similar segments shut off from one another internally by membranous partitions, but there are no jointed appendages.

Anne of Austria /æn/ 1601–1666. Queen of France from 1615 and regent 1643–61. Daughter of Philip III of Spain, she married Louis XIII of France and on his death became regent for their son, Louis XIV, until his majority.

She was much under the influence of Cardinal Mazarin, her chief minister, to whom she was supposed to be secretly married. She is one of the main characters in Alexandre Dumas's novel *The Three Musketeers* 1844.

Anne of Cleves /æn/ 1515–1557. Fourth wife of ◊Henry VIII of England. She was the daughter of the Duke of Cleves, and was recommended to Henry as a wife by Thomas ◊Cromwell, who wanted an alliance with German Protestantism against the Holy Roman Emperor. Henry did not like her looks, had the marriage declared void after six months, and pensioned her.

Anne of Denmark /æn/ 1574–1619. Queen consort of James VI of Scotland (later James I of Great Britain 1603). She was the daughter of Frederick II of Denmark and Norway, and married James 1589. Anne was suspected of Catholic leanings, and was notably extravagant.

Annigoni /ˌænɪˈɡəʊni/ Pietro 1910–1988. Italian portrait painter. His style is influenced by Italian Renaissance portraiture. Sitters have included John F. Kennedy and Queen Elizabeth II.

annihilation in nuclear physics, a process in which a particle and its 'mirror image' particle (antiparticle) collide and disappear, with the creation of a burst of energy. The energy created is equivalent to the mass of the colliding particles in accordance with the ◊mass energy equation. For example, an electron and a positron annihilate to produce a burst of high-energy X-rays.

Annobón /ˌænəʊˈbɒn/ island in Equatorial Guinea, former name (1973–79) Pagalu. Area 17 sq km/7 sq mi; its inhabitants are descended from slaves of the Portuguese and still speak a form of that language.

anno domini (Latin 'in the year of our Lord') in the Christian chronological system, dates since the birth of Jesus, denoted by the letters AD. There is no year 0, so AD 1 follows immediately after the year 1 BC (before Christ). The system became the standard reckoning in the Western world when adopted by the English historian Bede in the 8th century. The abbreviations CE (Common Era) and BCE (before Common Era) are often used instead.

The system is based on the calculations made 525 by Dionysius Exiguus, a Scythian monk, but the birth of Jesus should more correctly be placed about 4 BC.

annual plant a plant that completes its life-cycle within one year, during which time it germinates, grows to maturity, bears flowers, produces seed and then dies. Examples include the common poppy (*Papaver rhoeas*) and groundsel (*Senecio vulgaris*). Among garden plants, some that are described as 'annuals' are actually perennials, although usually cultivated as annuals because they cannot survive winter frosts. See also ◊ephemeral, ◊biennial, ◊perennial plants.

annual rings or *growth rings* the concentric rings visible on a cut tree trunk or other woody stem. In spring and early summer, spring wood is formed which has larger and more numerous vessels than the autumn wood produced when growth is slowing down. The result is a clear boundary between the paler spring wood and the dark, dense autumn wood. The annual rings may be used to estimate the age of the plant (see ◊dendrochronology), but occasionally more than one growth ring is produced in a given year.

Annual rings represent the growth of secondary ◊xylem during the year and are caused by the seasonal size variation in the elements making up the xylem, especially the vessels.

annulus (Latin 'ring') the plane area between two concentric circles, making a flat ring.

Annunciation in the New Testament, the announcement to Mary by the angel Gabriel that she was to be the mother of Jesus; the feast of the Annunciation is 25 Mar, also known as Lady Day.

anode the electrode towards which negative particles (anions, electrons) move within a device such as the cells of a battery, electrolytic cells, and diodes.

anodizing a process that increases the resistance to ◊corrosion of a metal, such as aluminium, by building up a protective oxide layer on the surface. The natural corrosion resistance of aluminium is provided by a thin film of aluminium oxide; anodizing increases the thickness of this film and thus the corrosion protection.

It is so called because the metal becomes the ◊anode in an electrolytic bath containing a solution of, for example, sulphuric or chromic acid as the ◊electrolyte. During ◊electrolysis oxygen is produced at the anode, where it combines with the metal to form an oxide film.

anomalous expansion of water the expansion of water as it is cooled from 4 °C to 0 °C. This behaviour is unusual because most substances contract when they are cooled. It means that water has a greater density at 4 °C than at 0 °C. Hence ice floats on water, and the water at the bottom of a pool in winter is warmer than at the surface. As a result, large lakes freeze slowly in winter and aquatic life is more likely to survive.

anomie in the social sciences, a state of normlessness created by the breakdown of commonly agreed standards of behaviour and morality; the term often refers to situations where the social order appears to have collapsed. The concept was developed by the French sociologist Durkheim.

Durkheim used 'anomie' to describe societies in transition during industrialization. The term was adapted by the USA sociologist Robert Merton to explain deviance and crime in the US in terms of the disparity between high goals and limited opportunities.

anorexia lack of desire to eat, especially the pathological condition of *anorexia nervosa*, usually found in adolescent females, who may be obsessed with the desire to lose weight. It is the opposite of ◊bulimia.

In anorexia nervosa, the patient refuses to eat and finally becomes unable to do so. The result is severe emaciation and, in rare cases, death.

Anouilh /ˌænuːˈiː/ Jean 1910–1987. French playwright. His plays, influenced by the Neo-Classical tradition, include *Antigone* 1942, *L'Invitation au château/Ring Round the Moon* 1947, *Colombe* 1950, and *Becket* 1959, about Thomas à Becket and Henry II.

anoxia shortage of oxygen in the tissues. It may be due to breathing air deficient in oxygen (for instance, at high altitude or where there are noxious fumes), disease of the lungs, or some disorder where the oxygen-carrying capacity of the blood is impaired. Unless anoxia is quickly reversed, the victim collapses and dies.

Anquetil /ˌɒŋkəˈtiːl/ Jacques 1934–1988. French cyclist, the first person to win the Tour de France five times (between 1957 and 1964), a record later equalled by Eddie ◊Merckx and Bernard ◊Hinault.

CAREER HIGHLIGHTS

Tour de France: 1957, 1961–64
Tour of Italy: 1960, 1964
Tour of Spain: 1963.

Anschluss the union of Austria with Germany, accomplished by the German chancellor Hitler 12 Mar 1938.

Anselm, St /ˈænselm/ c.1033–1109. Medieval priest. Educated at the abbey of Bec in Normandy, which as an abbot (from 1078) he made a centre of scholarship in Europe, he was appointed archbishop of Canterbury by William II 1093, but was later forced into exile. He holds an important place in the development of ◊Scholasticism.

Anselm was born near Aosta in Piedmont. As archbishop of Canterbury he was recalled from exile by Henry I, with whom he bitterly disagreed on the investiture of the clergy; a final agreement gave the king the right of temporal investiture and the clergy that of spiritual investiture. Anselm was canonized 1494. In his *Proslogion* he developed the ontological proof of theism, which infers God's existence from our capacity to conceive of a perfect Being. His *Cur deus homo* deals with the Atonement.

Ansermet /ˈɑːnseəmeɪ/ Ernest 1883–1969. Swiss conductor with Diaghilev's Russian Ballet 1915–

Anson This 1744 engraving shows the English admiral George Anson who circumnavigated the world and looted £500,000 of Spanish treasure.

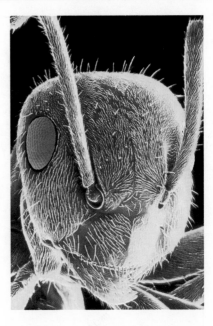

ant Electron microscope picture of the head of a black garden ant.

23. In 1918 he founded the Swiss Romande Orchestra, conducting many first performances of ◊Stravinsky.

Anshan /ˌænˈʃæn/ Chinese city in Liaoning province, 89 km/55 mi SE of Shenyang (Mukden); population (1986) 1,280,000. The iron and steel centre started here 1918, was expanded by the Japanese, dismantled by the Russians, and restored by the Communist government of China. It produces 6,000,000 tonnes of steel annually.

ANSI abbreviation for *American National Standards Institution*, the US national standards body. It sets official procedures in (amongst other areas) computing and electronics.

Anson /ˈænsən/ George, 1st Baron Anson 1697–1762. English admiral who sailed around the world 1740–44. In 1740 he commanded the squadron attacking the Spanish colonies and shipping in South America; he returned home by circumnavigating the world, with £500,000 of Spanish treasure; his chaplain's *Voyage Round the World* 1748 is a classic. He carried out reforms at the Admiralty.

ant insect belonging to the family Formicidae, and to the same order (Hymenoptera) as bees and wasps. They are characterized by a conspicuous 'waist' and elbowed antennae. About 10,000 different species are known; all are social in habit, and all construct nests of various kinds.

Ant behaviour is complex, but serves the colony rather than the individual. Ants find their way by light patterns, gravity (special sense organs are found in the joints of their legs), and chemical trails between food areas and the nest.

Communities include: *workers* sterile wingless females, often all alike although in some species large-headed 'soldiers' are differentiated; *fertile females* fewer in number and usually winged; and *males* also winged and smaller than their consorts, with whom they leave the nest on a nuptial flight at certain times of the year. After aerial mating, the males die, and the fertilized queens lose their wings when they settle, laying eggs to found their own new colonies. The eggs hatch into wormlike larvae, which then pupate in silk cocoons before emerging as adults.

Remarkable species include: *army* (New World) and *driver* (African) ants, which march nomadically in huge columns, devouring even tethered animals in their path; *leaf-cutter ants*, genus *Atta*, which use pieces of leaf to grow edible fungus in underground 'gardens'; *weaver ants*,

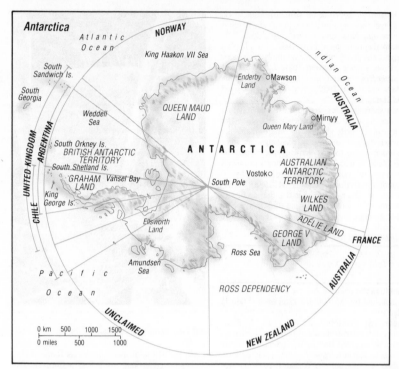

Antarctica

anteater

genus *Oecophylla*, which use their silk-producing larvae as living shuttles to bind the edges of leaves together to form the nest; ***robber ants***, *Formica sanguinea*, which raid nests of another ant *Formica fusca* for pupae, then use the adults as 'slaves' when they hatch; and ***honey ants***, in which some workers serve as distended honey stores. In some species, 'warfare' is conducted. Others are 'pastoralists', tending herds of ◊aphids and collecting a sweet secretion ('honeydew') from them.

Antabuse proprietary name for disulfiram, a drug used in the treatment of alcoholism. When taken, it produces unpleasant side effects with alcohol, such as nausea, headache, palpitations, and collapse. The 'Antabuse effect' is produced coincidentally by certain antibiotics.

antacid a substance that neutralizes stomach acid. It may be taken between meals to relieve symptoms of hyperacidity, such as pain, bloating, nausea, and 'heartburn'. Excessive or prolonged need for antacids should be investigated medically.

Antakya /æn'tɑːkjə/ or *Hatay* city in SE Turkey, site of the ancient ◊Antioch; population (1985) 109,200.

Antalya /æn'tɑːljə/ Mediterranean port on the W coast of Turkey and capital of a province of the same name; population(1985) 258,000. The port trades in agriculture and forest produce.

Antananarivo /ˌæntəˌnænəˈriːvəʊ/ formerly *Tananarive* capital of Madagascar, on the interior plateau, with a rail link to Tamatave; population (1986) 703,000.

Antarctica /ænt'ɑːktɪkə/ the Antarctic continent
area 13,727,000 sq km/5,300,000 sq mi
physical the continent, once part of ◊Gondwanaland, is a vast plateau, of which the highest point is the Vinson Massif in the Ellsworth mountains, 5,139 m/16,866 ft high. The Ross Ice Shelf is formed by several glaciers coalescing in the Ross Sea, and Mount Erebus on Ross Island is the world's southernmost active volcano. There is less than 50 mm/2 in of rainfall a year (less than the Sahara). Little more than 1% is ice-free, the temperature falling to −70°C/−100°F and below, and in places the ice is 5,000 m/16,000 ft deep, comprising over two-thirds of the world's fresh water. Each annual layer of snow preserves a record of global conditions, and where no melting at the surface of the bedrock has occurred the

ice can be a million years old. It covers extensive mineral resources, including iron, coal, and with indications of uranium and other strategic metals, as well as oil. There are only two species of flowering plants, plus a number of mosses, algae, and fungi. Animal life is restricted to visiting whales, seals, penguins, and other seabirds. Fossils of apes resembling humans have been found.
population settlement is limited to scientific research stations with changing personnel.
history in 1988, nine countries signed the Minerals Convention, laying Antarctica open to commercial exploitation; Australia refused to sign. Guidelines on environmental protection were included but regarded as inadequate by environmental pressure groups.

Antarctic Circle an imaginary line that runs around the South Pole at latitude 66° 32' S. The line encompasses the continent of Antarctica and the Antarctic Ocean.

Antarctic Ocean /ænt'ɑːktɪk/ popular name for the reaches of the Atlantic, Indian, and Pacific Oceans

Antarctic Exploration

extending south of the Antarctic Circle (66° 32' S). The term is not used by the International Hydrographic Bureau.

Antarctic Peninsula mountainous peninsula of W Antarctica extending about 1,930 km/1,200 mi N toward South America. Originally named Palmer Land after a US navigator, Captain Nathaniel Palmer, who was the first to explore the region in 1820. Claimed by Britain 1832, Chile 1942 and Argentina 1940, its name was changed to the Antarctic Peninsula in 1964.

Antarctic Treaty agreement signed 1959 between 12 nations with an interest in Antarctica (including Britain), and today with 35 countries party to it. It came into force in 1961 for a 30-year period. Its provisions (covering the area S of latitude 60°S) neither accepted nor rejected any nation's territorial claims, but barred any new ones; imposed a ban on military operations and large-scale mineral extraction, and allowed for free exchange of scientific data from bases. Since 1980 the Treaty has been extended to conserve marine resources within the larger area bordered by the Antarctic Convergence.

Antares brightest star in the constellation of Scorpius. It is a red supergiant several hundred times larger than the Sun, lies about 400 light years away, and fluctuates slightly in brightness. It is the 15th brightest star in the sky.

anteater South American animal *Myrmecophaga tridactyla* that lives almost entirely on ants and termites. It has toothless jaws, an extensile tongue, and claws for breaking into nests of its prey. It is about 50 cm/2 ft high and common in Brazil. The name is also incorrectly applied to the aardvark, the echidna and the pangolin.

antebellum (Latin *ante bellum*, 'before the war') in US usage, an adjective referring to the period just before the Civil War (1861–65). The term 'prewar' is used when describing the period before any other war.

antelope any of a number of distinct kinds of even-toed hoofed wild mammals belonging to the cow family. Most are lightly built and good runners. They are grazers or browsers, and chew the cud. They range in size from the dik-diks and duikers, only 30 cm/1 ft high, to the eland, which can be 1.8 m/6 ft at the shoulder.

Antarctic Exploration

1773–4	James Cook first sailed in Antarctic seas, but exploration was difficult before the development of iron ships able to withstand ice pressure.
1819–21	Antarctica circumnavigated by Bellingshausen.
1823	James Weddell sailed into the sea named after him.
1841–2	James Ross sighted the Great Ice Barrier named after him.
1895	Borchgrevink was one of the first landing party on the continent.
1898	Borchgrevink's British expedition first wintered in Antarctica.
1901–4	Scott first penetrated the interior of the continent.
1907–8	Shackleton came within 182 km/113 mi of the Pole.
1911	Amundsen reached the Pole, 14 Dec, overland with dogs.
1912	Scott reached the Pole, 18 Jan, initially aided by ponies.
1928–9	Byrd made the first flight to the Pole.
1935	Ellsworth first flew across Antarctica.
1957–8	Fuchs made the first overland crossing.
1959	Soviet expedition from the West Ice Shelf to the Pole.
1959	International Antarctic Treaty suspended all territorial claims, reserving an area south of 60° S latitude for peaceful purposes.
1961–2	Bentley Trench discovered, which suggested that there may be an Atlantic-Pacific link beneath the Continent.
1966–7	Specially Protected Areas established internationally for animals and plants.
1979	Fossils of apemen resembling E Africa's Proconsul found 500 km/300 mi from the Pole.
1980	International Convention on the exploitation of resources—oil, gas, fish, krill.
1982	First circumnavigation of Earth (2 Sept 1979–29 Aug 1982) via the Poles by Sir Ranulph Fiennes and Charles Burton (UK).
1988	Minerals Convention exposed Antarctica to commercial exploitation. Environmental protection clauses seen as inadequate by pressure groups.

Anthony *Early American feminist Susan Anthony. She founded the National Woman Suffrage Association in 1869*

The majority of antelopes are African, including the eland, gnu, kudu, springbok, and waterbuck, although other types live in Asia and the deserts of Arabia and the Middle East.

antenna in zoology, an appendage ('feeler') on the head. Insects, centipedes, and millipedes each have one pair of antennae but there are two pairs in crustaceans, such as shrimps. In insects, the antennae are usually involved with the senses of smell and touch. They are frequently complex structures with large surface areas that increase the ability to detect scents.

antenna in radio, another name for ◊aerial.

Antheil /'ɑːntaɪl/ George 1900–1959. US composer and pianist, the son of a Polish political exile. He is known for his *Ballet mécanique* 1926, scored for anvils, aeroplane propellers, electric bells, automobile horns, and pianos.

anthelion antisun; a kind of solar halo, sometimes appearing at the same altitude as the Sun, but opposite to it.

anthelmintic a class of drugs effective against a range of ◊parasites.

anthem in music, a short, usually elaborate, religious choral composition, sometimes accompanied by the organ; also a song of loyalty and devotion.

anther in a flower, the terminal part of a stamen in which the ◊pollen grains are produced. It is usually borne on a slender stalk or filament, and has two lobes, each containing two chambers or pollen sacs within which the pollen is formed.

antheridium an organ producing the male gametes (antherozoids) in algae, bryophytes (mosses and lichens), and pteridophytes (ferns and horsetails). It may be either single-celled, as in most algae, or multicellular, as in bryophytes and pteridophytes.

antherozoid a motile (or independently moving) male gamete produced by algae, bryophytes (mosses and liverworts), pteridophytes (ferns and horsetails), and some gymnosperms (notably the cycads). Antherozoids are formed in an ◊antheridium and, after being released, swim by means of one or more ◊flagella, to the female gametes. Higher plants have non-motile male gametes contained within ◊pollen grains.

Anthony /'ænθəni/ Susan B(rownell) 1820–1906. US pioneering feminist, who also worked for the anti-slavery and temperance movements. Her campaigns included demands for equality of pay for female teachers, the married women's property act, and women's suffrage. In 1869, with Elizabeth Cady Stanton, she founded the National Woman Suffrage Association.

She edited and published a radical women's newspaper *The Revolution* 1868–70, and worked on the *History of Woman Suffrage* 1881–86. She organized the International Council of Women and founded the International Woman Suffrage Alliance in Berlin 1904.

Anthony of Padua, St /'æntəni/ 1195–1231. Portuguese Franciscan preacher who opposed the relaxations introduced into the order. Born in Lisbon, the son of a nobleman, he became an Augustinian monk, but in 1220 joined the Franciscans. He died in Padua, Italy, and was canonized in 1232. Like St Francis, he is said to have preached to animals.

Anthony, St /'æntəni/ *c.* 251–356. Also known as Anthony of Thebes. Founder of Christian monasticism. Born in Egypt, at the age of 20 he renounced all his possessions and lived in a tomb, and at 35 sought further solitude on a mountain in the desert.

In 305 Anthony founded the first cenobitic order, or community of Christians following a rule of life under a superior. When he was about 100 he went to Alexandria and preached against the Arians. Anthony's temptations in the desert were a popular subject in art; he is also often depicted with a pig.

anthracene white glistening crystalline hydrocarbon with a faint blue fluorescence when pure. Its melting point is about 216°C and its boiling point 351°C. It occurs in the high boiling fractions of coal tar, where it was discovered in 1832 by the French chemists Auguste Laurent (1807–53) and Jean Dumas (1800–84).

anthracite (from Greek *anthrax*, 'coal') a hard, dense, glossy variety of ◊coal, containing over 90% of fixed carbon and a low percentage of ash and volatile matter, which causes it to burn without flame, smoke, or smell.

Anthracite gives intense heat, but is slow-burning and slow to light; it is therefore unsuitable for use in open fires. Its characteristic composition is thought to be due to the action of bacteria in disintegrating the coal-forming material when it was laid down during the ◊Carboniferous period.

Among the chief sources of anthracite coal are Pennsylvania in the USA; S Wales, UK; the Donbas, USSR; and Shanxi province, China.

anthrax cattle and sheep disease occasionally transmitted to humans, usually via infected hides and fleeces. It may develop as a skin lesion or as a severe pneumonia. Treatment is with antibiotics. In 1989 an outbreak of anthrax at Singret farm, in Wales, near Wrexham, killed 30 pigs, and the entire herd of 4,700 was subsequently killed.

anthropic principle in science, the idea that 'the universe is the way it is because if it were different we would not be here to observe it'. The principle arises from the observation that if the laws of science were even slightly different, it would have been impossible for intelligent life to evolve. For example, if the electric charge on the electron were only slightly different, stars would have been unable to burn hydrogen and produce the chemical elements that make up our bodies. Scientists are undecided whether the principle is an insight into the nature of the universe or a piece of circular reasoning.

anthropoid ape a synonym for ◊ape, now rarely used; see ◊primates.

anthropology (Greek *anthropos* 'man' and *logos* 'discourse') scientific study of humankind. The study was developed following 19th-century evolutionary theory to deal with the human species biologically, physically, socially, and culturally.

anthropometry science dealing with the measurement of the human body, particularly stature, body-weight, cranial capacity, and length of limb, across different living and extinct peoples.

anthropomorphism the attribution of human characteristics to animals, inanimate objects, or deities. It appears in the mythologies of many cultures and as a literary device in fables and allegories.

anthroposophy system of mystical philosophy developed by Rudolf ◊Steiner, who claimed to possess a power of intuition giving him access to knowledge not attainable by scientific means.

Antibes /ɒnˈtiːb/ resort, which includes Juan les Pins, on the French Riviera, in the *département* of Alpes Maritimes; population (1982) 63,248. There is a Picasso collection in the 17th-century castle museum.

antibiotic a drug that kills or inhibits the growth of bacteria and fungi. It is derived from living organisms such as fungi or other bacteria, which distinguishes it from other antibacterials.

The first class of antibiotics, the ◊penicillins, was quickly joined by ◊chloramphenicol, the ◊cephalosporins, erythromycins, tetracyclines, and aminoglycosides. A range of broad-spectrum antibiotics, the 4-quinolones, was developed 1989, of which ciprofloxacin was the first. Each class and individual antibiotic acts in a different way and may be effective against a broad spectrum or a specific type of disease-causing agent. Use of antibiotics has become more selective as side effects, such as toxicity, allergy, and resistance, have become better understood. Bacteria have demonstrated the ability to develop immunity following repeated or subclinical (insufficient) doses, and more advanced and synthetic antibiotics are continually required to overcome this.

antibody a protein molecule produced in the blood by ◊lymphocytes in response to the presence of invading substances, or ◊antigens, including the proteins carried on the surface of bacteria and viruses. Antibody production is just one aspect of ◊immunity in vertebrates.

Each antibody is specific for its particular antigen and combines with it to form a 'complex' that can then be disposed of by other immune cells, such as ◊macrophage, which respond to the presence of the antibodies. Large quantities of specific antibodies can now be obtained by the monoclonal technique (see ◊monoclonal antibodies).

anticholinergic drug that blocks the passage of certain nerve impulses in the ◊central nervous system.

Its wide range of effects makes it an effective component of ◊premedication; it may be put in the eyes before examination or treatment to dilate the pupil and paralyse the muscles of accommodation, or inhaled to relieve constriction of the airways in bronchitis. Tremor and rigidity can be reduced in mild ◊Parkinson's disease. Bladder muscle tone may also be improved in the treatment of urinary frequency. Its usefulness as an ◊antispasmodic is limited by side effects, such as dry mouth, visual disturbances, and urinary retention.

Antichrist in Christian theology, the opponent of Christ, by whom he is finally to be conquered. The idea of conflict between Light and Darkness is present in Persian, Babylonian, and Jewish literature, and influenced early Christian thought. The Antichrist may be a false messiah, or be connected with false teaching, or be identified with an individual, for example Nero at the time of the persecution of Christians, and the pope and Napoleon in later Christian history.

anticline in geology, a fold in the rocks of the Earth's crust in which the layers or beds bulge upwards to form an arch (seldom preserved intact).

The fold of anticline may be undulating or steeply curved. A steplike bend in otherwise gently dipping or horizontal beds is a *monocline*. The opposite of an anticline is a *syncline*.

anticoagulant a substance that suppresses the formation of ◊blood clots. Common anticoagulants are heparin, produced by the liver and lungs, and derivatives of coumarin. Anticoagulants are used medically in treating heart attacks. They are also produced by blood-feeding animals such as mosquitoes, leeches, and vampire bats, to keep the victim's blood flowing. Most anticoagulants prevent the production of thrombin, an enzyme that induces the formation from blood plasma of fibrinogen, to which blood platelets adhere and form clots.

Anti-Comintern Pact (Anti-Communist Pact) agreement signed between Germany and Japan 25 Nov 1936, opposing communism as a menace to peace and order. The pact was signed by Italy 1937 and by Hungary, Spain, and the Japanese puppet state of Manchukuo in 1939. While directed against the USSR, the agreement also had the effect of giving international recognition to Japanese rule in Manchuria.

anticonvulsant a drug used to prevent epileptic seizures (convulsions or fits). In many cases, epilepsy can be controlled completely by careful therapy with one agent. Patients should stop or change treatment only under medical supervision.

Anti-Corn Law League in UK history, an extra-parliamentary pressure group formed 1838, led by the Liberals ◊Cobden and ◊Bright, which argued for Free trade and campaigned successfully against duties on the import of foreign corn to Britain imposed by the ◊Corn Laws, which were repealed 1846.

Formed in Sept 1838 by Manchester industrialists and campaigning on a single issue, the league initiated strategies for popular mobilisation and agitation including mass meetings, lecture tours, pamphleteering, opinion polls, and parliamentary lobbying. Reaction by the conservative landed interests was organized with the establishment of the Central Agricultural Protection Society, nicknamed the Anti-League. In June 1846 political pressure, the state of the economy, and the Irish situation prompted Prime Minister ◊Peel to repeal the Corn Laws.

anticyclone an area of high atmospheric pressure caused by descending air, which becomes warm and dry. Winds radiate from a calm centre, taking a clockwise direction in the northern hemisphere and an anticlockwise direction in the southern hemisphere.

Anticyclones are characterized by clear weather and the absence of rain and violent winds. In summer they bring hot, sunny days and in winter they bring fine, frosty spells, although fog and low cloud are not uncommon. Blocking anticyclones, which prevent the normal air circulation of an area, can cause summer droughts and severe winters. For example, the summer drought in Britain in 1976, and the severe winters of 1947 and 1963 were caused by blocking anticyclones.

antidepressant a drug used to relieve symptoms in depressive illness. The two main groups are the tricyclic antidepressants (TCADs) and the monoamine oxidase inhibitors (MAOIs), which act by altering chemicals available to the central nervous system. Both may produce serious side effects.

antidiarrhoeal substance that controls diarrhoea. Choice of treatment depends on the underlying cause. One group produces constipation by slowing down motility (muscle activity of the intestine wall). These include opiates, codeine, and atropine. Bulking agents, such as vegetable fibres (for example, methylcellulose), absorb fluid. Antibiotics may be appropriate for certain systemic bacterial infections, such as typhoid, salmonella, and enteritis, caused by *Campylobacter* species. Current therapy of acute diarrhoea is based on fluid and ◊electrolyte replacement. Chronic diarrhoea, a feature of some bowel disorders (for example, Crohn's disease, colitis, coeliac disease) responds to antispasmodics, special diet, and corticosteroids.

anti-emetic a substance that counteracts nausea or vomiting.

Antietam, Battle of /æn'tiːtəm/ bloody but indecisive battle of the American Civil War 17 Sept 1862 at Antietam Creek, off the Potomac River. Gen McClellan of the Union blocked the advance of the Confederates under Robert E Lee on Maryland and Washington DC. This battle persuaded the British not to recognize the Confederacy.

antifreeze a substance added to a car's water-cooling system, for example, to prevent it freezing in cold weather. Most types of antifreeze contain the chemical ethylene ◊glycol, or (CH₂OH.CH₂OH), an organic alcohol with

Antigua and Barbuda
State of

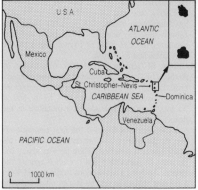

map labels: USA, Mexico, Cuba, St Christopher–Nevis, Dominica, Venezuela, ATLANTIC OCEAN, CARIBBEAN SEA, PACIFIC OCEAN, 0 1000 km

area Antigua 280 sq km/108 sq mi, Barbuda 161 sq km/62 sq mi, plus Redonda 1 sq km/0.4 sq mi
capital and chief port St John's
physical tropical island country
features Antigua is the largest of the Leeward Islands; Redonda is uninhabited
head of state Elizabeth II from 1981 represented by Wilfred Ebenezer Jacobs
head of government Vere C Bird from 1981

political system liberal democracy
political parties Antigua Labour Party (ALP), moderate, left-of-centre; Progressive Labour Movement (PLM), left-of-centre
exports sea-island cotton, rum
currency East Caribbean dollar (4.60 = £1 Feb 1990)
population (1986) 81,500; annual growth rate 1.3%
language English
religion Christian
literacy 90% (1985)
GDP $130 million (1983); $1,850 per head of population
chronology
1967 Antigua and Barbuda became an associated state within the Commonwealth, with full internal independence.
1971 PLM won the general election by defeating the ALP.
1976 PLM called for early independence but ALP urged caution. ALP won the general election.
1981 Full independence.
1983 Assisted US invasion of Grenada.
1984 ALP won a decisive victory in the general election.
1985 ALP re-elected.
1989 Another sweeping general election victory for the ALP.

a freezing point of about –15°C. The addition of this chemical depresses the freezing point of water significantly. A solution containing 33.5% by volume of ethylene glycol will not freeze until about –20°C. A 50% solution will not freeze until –35°C.

antifungal a drug that acts against fungal infection, such as ringworm and athlete's foot.

antigen any substance that causes production of ◊antibodies. Common antigens include the proteins carried on the surface of bacteria, viruses, and pollen grains. The proteins of incompatible blood groups or tissues also act as antigens, which has to be taken into account in medical procedures such as blood transfusion and organ transplants.

Antigone /æn'tɪgəni/ in Greek legend, a daughter of Jocasta, by her son ◊Oedipus. She is also the subject of a tragedy by Sophocles.

Antigone tragedy by Sophocles, written about 411 BC. Antigone buries her brother Polyneices, in defiance of the Theban king Creon, but in accordance with the wishes of the gods. Creon imprisons Antigone in a cave, but after a warning that he has defied the gods, he goes to the cave and finds that Antigone has hanged herself.

Antigonus /æn'tɪgənəs/ 382–301 BC. A general of Alexander the Great, after whose death 323 he made himself master of Asia Minor. He was defeated and slain by ◊Seleucus I at the battle of Ipsus.

Antigua and Barbuda /æn'tiːgə, bɑː'bjuːdə/ three islands (Antigua, Barbuda, and uninhabited Redonda) in the eastern Caribbean.

government Antigua and Barbuda constitute an independent sovereign nation within the Commonwealth, with the British monarch as head of state. The constitution came into effect with independence in 1981. The governor-general, representing the British monarch, is appointed on the advice of the Antiguan prime minister, who is chosen by the governor-general as the person most likely to have the support of the legislature. The parliament is similar to Britain's, with a prime minister and cabinet answerable to it. It consists of a senate and a house of representatives, each having 17 members. Senators are appointed for a five-year term by the governor-general, 11 on the advice of the prime minister, four on the advice of the leader of the opposition, one at the governor-general's own discretion, and one

on the advice of the Barbuda Council, the main instrument for local government. Members of the House of Representatives are elected by universal suffrage for a similar term. There are several political parties, the most significant being the Antigua Labour Party (ALP).

history the first European to visit Antigua was Christopher ◊Columbus 1493, although he didn't actually go ashore. He named the island after the church of Santa Maria de la Antigua at Seville. Antigua was first colonized by Britain 1632. In 1685 Charles II leased Barbuda to the Codrington family, who ran a sugar plantation on Antigua. Barbuda was a source of stock and provisions for the plantation, and was inhabited almost entirely by slaves, who used the relatively barren land co-operatively. The Codringtons finally surrendered the lease 1870. Barbuda reverted to the crown in the later nineteenth century. The Antiguan slaves were freed 1834, but remained poor, totally dependent on the sugar crop market. Between 1860 and 1959 it was administered by Britain within a federal system known as the Leeward Islands. In 1967 it was made an associated state and given full internal independence, with Britain retaining responsibility for defence and foreign affairs. Barbuda, with a population of about 1,200 people, started a separatist movement 1969, fearing that Antigua would sell Barbudan land to foreign developers. Projects approved by the central government against the wishes of Barbudans include sand mining and a plan for a toxic-waste disposal site.

In the 1971 general election, the Progressive Labour Movement (PLM) won a decisive vistory and its leader, George Walter, replaced Vere Bird, leader of the ALP, as prime minister.

The PLM fought the 1976 election on a call for early independence while the ALP urged caution until a firm economic foundation had been laid. The ALP won and in 1978 declared that the country was ready for independence. Opposition from the inhabitants of Barbuda delayed the start of constitutional talks and the territory eventually became independent as Antigua and Barbuda 1981. Despite its policy of ◊non-alignment, the ALP government actively assisted the US invasion of ◊Grenada 1983, and went on to win 16 of the 17 seats in the 1984 general election. In the 1989 general election Bird and the ALP were decisively re-elected.

antihistamine a drug which counteracts the effects of ◊histamine. H$_1$ antihistamines are used to relieve allergies, alleviating symptoms such as runny nose, itching, swelling, or asthma. H$_2$ antihistamines suppress acid production by the stomach, providing treatment for peptic ulcers that often makes surgery unnecessary.

antihypertensive therapy to control ◊hypertension. The first step is usually a change in diet to reduce salt and, if necessary, caloric intake. If further measures are required, a drug regimen may be prescribed.

The regimen may consist of one or a number of substances: a ◊diuretic; a ◊beta- or calcium-channel blocker; a vasodilator which causes blood vessel walls to expand); ACE (angiotensin-converting enzyme) inhibitor, which interrupts a biochemical cycle that increases blood pressure and has a vasodilating effect. Treatment, and regular monitoring, are continued throughout life.

anti-inflammatory a substance that reduces swelling in soft tissues. Antihistamines relieve allergic reactions; aspirin and ◊NSAIDs are effective in joint and musculoskeletal conditions; rubefacients (counter-irritant liniments) ease painful joints, tendons, and muscles; steroids, because of the severe side effects, are only prescribed if other therapy is ineffective, or if a condition is life-threatening. A ◊corticosteroid injection into the affected joint usually gives long-term relief from inflammation.

Anti-Lebanon /ˌænti'lebənən/ or *Antilibanus* mountain range on the Lebanese-Syrian border, including Mt Hermon, 2,800 m/9,200 ft. It is separated from the Lebanon mountains by the Bekaa valley.

Antilles /æn'tɪliːz/ the whole group of West Indian islands, divided north-south into the *Greater Antilles* (Cuba, Jamaica, Haiti-Dominican Republic, Puerto Rico) and *Lesser Antilles*, sub-divided into the Leeward Islands (Virgin Islands, St Kitts-Nevis, Antigua and Barbuda, Anguilla, Montserrat and Guadeloupe) and the Windward Islands (Dominica, Martinique, St Lucia, St Vincent and the Grenadines, Barbados, and Grenada).

antilogarithm the inverse of ◊logarithm. In the equation $y = b^x$, x is the logarithm of y to the base b and y is the antilogarithm of x to the base b.

antimacassar a piece of cloth protecting a seat where a person leans their head. The term is derived from Rowland's Macassar Oil, first manufactured about 1793.

antimatter in physics, a form of matter in which all the attributes of an ordinary atomic particle, such as electrical charge and spin, are reversed.

Such antiparticles can be created in particle accelerators, such as those at ◊CERN and Fermilab in the USA, and are of vital potential importance. For example, nuclear fusion of two ordinary protons would result in a fraction of their mass being converted to energy (about 1%), whereas fusion of a proton and an antiproton would result in the complete destruction of both, with all their mass being converted into energy.

antimony a metallic element, symbol Sb, atomic number 51, relative atomic mass 121.76. In the ordinary form it is a silver-white metal, brittle and readily powdered. It occurs chiefly as stibnite, and is used in a number of alloys and in photosensitive substances in colour photography and optical electronics. It has a response in the blue and blue-green areas of the spectrum.

Antioch /'æntɪɒk/ ancient capital of the Greek kingdom of Syria, founded 300 BC by Seleucus Nicator in memory of his father Antiochus, and famed for its splendour and luxury. Under the Romans it was an early centre of Christianity. The site is now occupied by the Turkish town of ◊Antakya.

Antiochus /'æntɪɒkəs/four kings of Commagene (69 BC – AD 72), affiliated to the Seleucid dynasty, including:

Antiochus I king of Commagene, who made peace with Pompey 64 BC, fought on Pompey's side

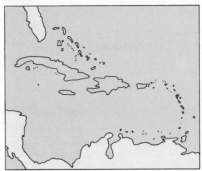

in the civil war, and repelled an attack on Samosata by Mark Antony. He was succeeded by Mithidrates I.

Antiochus II king of Commagene, who succeeded Mithidrates I, and was executed by Augustus.

Antiochus IV Epiphanes 1st century AD. King of Commagene, son of Antiochus III. He was made king in 38 by Caligula, who deposed him immediately. He was restored in 41 by Claudius, and reigned as an ally of Rome against Parthia. He was deposed on suspicion of treason in 72.

Antiochus /æn'taɪəkəs/ 13 kings of Syria of the Seleucid dynasty, including:

Antiochus I *c.* 324–*c.* 261 BC. King of Syria from 281 BC, son of Seleucus I, one of the generals of Alexander the Great. He earned the title of Antiochus Soter or Saviour by his defeat of the Gauls in Galatia 278 BC.

Antiochus II *c.* 286–*c.* 246 BC. King of Syria 261–246 BC, son of Antiochus I. He was known as Antiochus Theos, the Divine. During his reign the eastern provinces broke away from the Graeco-Macedonian rule and set up native princes. He made peace with Egypt by marrying the daughter of Ptolemy Philadelphus, but was a tyrant among his own people.

Antiochus III *the Great c.* 241–187 BC. King of Syria from 223 BC, nephew of Antiochus II. He secured a loose suzerainty over Armenia and Parthia 209, overcame Bactria, received the homage of the Indian king of the Kabul valley, and returned by way of the Persian Gulf 204. He took possession of Palestine, entering Jerusalem 198. He crossed into NW Greece, but was decisively defeated by the Romans at Thermopylae 191 and at Magnesia 190. He had to abandon his domains in Anatolia, and perished at the hands of the people of Elymais.

Antiochus IV 215–164 BC. King of Syria from 175 BC, known as Antiochus Epiphanes, the Illustrious; second son of Antiochus III. He occupied Jerusalem about 170 BC, seizing much of the Temple treasure, and instituted worship of the Greek type in the Temple in an attempt to eradicate Judaism. This produced the revolt of the Jewish people under the Maccabees, and Antiochus died before he could suppress it.

Antiochus VII Sidetes King of Syria from 138 BC. The last strong ruler of the Seleucid dynasty, he took Jerusalem 134 BC, reducing the Maccabees to subjection, and fought successfully against the Parthians.

Antiochus XIII Asiaticus 1st century BC. King of Syria 69–65 BC, the last of the Seleucid dynasty. During his reign Syria was made a Roman province by Pompey the Great.

antioxidant type of food ◊additive, used to prevent fats and oils from becoming rancid, and thus extend their shelf life. They are added to most oils.

Antioxidants are not always listed on food labels because if a food manufacturer buys an oil to make a food product, and the oil has antioxidant already added, it does not have to be listed on the label of the product. Some studies have shown that the antioxidants BHT and BHA cause behaviour disorders in animals.

antiparticle in nuclear physics, a particle that differs from another fundamental particle in having the opposite charge or magnetic moment. For example, an electron carries a negative charge whereas its antiparticle, the positron, carries a positive one. In all other respects, such as mass, the particles are identical.

Antiparticles annihilate each other, with the production of energy, when they collide. Other antiparticles include the negatively charged antiproton and the antineutron. A (hypothetical) substance consisting entirely of antiparticles is known as ◊antimatter.

antiphony in music, a form of composition using widely spaced choirs or groups of instruments to create perspectives in sound. It was developed in 17th-century Venice by Giovanni ◊Gabrieli and his pupil Heinrich ◊Schütz.

antipodes (Greek 'opposite feet') places exactly opposite on the globe. In the UK, Australia and New Zealand are called the Antipodes.

antipope a rival claimant to the elected pope for the leadership of the Roman Catholic church, for instance in the Great Schism 1378–1417 when there were rival popes in Rome and Avignon.

antipruritic skin preparation or drug administered to relieve itching.

antipsychotic a *neuroleptic* or a drug used to treat the symptoms of severe mental disorder.

antipyretic a drug, such as aspirin, used to reduce fever.

anti-racism and anti-sexism active opposition to ◊racism and ◊sexism; positive action or a set of policies designed to counteract racism and sexism, often on the part of an official body or an institution, such as a school, a business, or a government agency.

The growth of anti-racist and anti-sexist policies in the UK in the 1980s, for example in education, reflected the belief that to ensure equality of opportunity, conscious efforts must be made to counteract the effects of unconscious racism and sexism as well as the effects of previous systematic ◊discrimination against members of minority ethnic groups and women.

antirrhinum or *snapdragon* plant of genus *Antirrhinum*, belonging to the same family, Scrophulariaceae, as the foxglove and toadflax. It is native to the Mediterranean region and W North America.

anti-Semitism literally, prejudice against Semitic people (see ◊Semite), but in practice it has meant prejudice or discrimination against, and persecution of, the Jews as an ethnic group. Anti-Semitism was a tenet of Hitler's Germany, and in the Holocaust of 1933–45 about 6 million Jews died in concentration camps. It is a form of ◊racism.

The destruction of Jerusalem AD 70 led many Jews to settle in Europe. When the Roman Empire in the 4th century adopted Christianity as the official religion, this reinforced existing prejudice against a distinctive group. Anti-Semitism was increased in the Middle Ages by the Crusades, and by legislation forbidding Jews to own land or be members of a craft guild, so that to earn a living they had to become money lenders and traders (and were then resented when they prospered). From the 16th century they were forced by law in many cities to live in a separate area, or *ghetto*.

Late 18th- and early 19th-century liberal thought improved the position of Jews in European society (for example, after the French Revolution the 'rights of man' were extended to the Jews 1790) until 19th-century nationalism and the rise of unscientific theories of race. Anti-Semitism became strong in Austria, France (see ◊Dreyfus), and Germany, and from 1881 pogroms in Poland and Russia caused refugees to flee to the UK and, particularly, the USA, where freedom of religion was enshrined in the constitution. In the 20th century, fascism and the Nazi Party's application of racial theories led to organized persecution and genocide. After World War II, the creation of Israel 1948 provoked Palestinian anti-Zionism, backed by the Arab world. Anti-Semitism is still fostered by extreme right-wing groups, such as the National Front in the UK and France.

antiseptic substance killing or hindering the growth of microorganisms. The use of antiseptics was pioneered by Joseph ◊Lister.

antispasmodic drug that reduces motility, the activity of the muscular intestine walls. Anticholinergics act indirectly by way of the autonomic nervous system, which controls involuntary movement. Other drugs act directly on the smooth muscle to relieve spasm (contraction).

anti-theatre a theory advanced by Peter ◊Handke in *Insulting the Audience*, 1966.

anti-trust laws in economics, regulations preventing or restraining trusts, monopolies, or any business practice considered to be unfair or uncompetitive. In the USA, anti-trust laws prevent mergers and acquisitions which might create a monopoly situation, or one in which restrictive practices might be stimulated.

antitussive substance administered to suppress a cough. Coughing, however, is an important reflex in clearing secretions from the airways, and its suppression is usually unnecessary and possibly harmful.

antiviral a drug that acts against viruses, usually preventing them from multiplying. Most virus infections are not susceptible to antibiotics. Antivirals have been difficult drugs to develop, and do not necessarily cure the diseases.

anti-vivisection opposition to vivisection, that is, experiments on living animals, which is practised in the pharmaceutical and cosmetics industries on the grounds that it may result in discoveries of importance to medical science. Anti-vivisectionists argue that it is immoral to inflict pain on helpless creatures, and that it is unscientific, in that results achieved with animals may not be paralleled with human beings.

They also argue that it is unjust to make animals suffer in order that people may benefit, and that vivisection has not added to people's power over disease. Anti-vivisectionist groups, such as the Animal Liberation Front, sometimes take illegal action to draw attention to their cause.

antler the 'horn' of a deer, often branched, and made of bone rather than horn. Antlers are shed and regrown each year. Caribou of both sexes grow them, but in all other types of deer, only the males have antlers.

ant lion larva of one of the insects of the family Myrmeleontidae, which traps insects by waiting at the bottom of a pit it digs in sandy soil. Ant lions are mainly tropical, but also occur in some parts of Europe.

Antofagasta /ˌæntəfəˈgæstə/ port of N Chile, capital of a region of the same name. The area of the region is 125,300 sq km/48,366 sq mi, its population (1982) 341,000. The population of the town of Antofagasta is 175,000. Nitrates from the Atacama desert are exported.

Antonello da Messina /ˌæntəˈneləʊ dɑː meˈsiːnə/ c.1430– 1479. Italian painter, born in Messina, Sicily, a pioneer of the technique of oil painting, which he is said to have introduced to Italy from N Europe. Flemish influence is reflected in his technique, his use of light, and sometimes in his imagery. Surviving works include bust-length portraits and sombre religious paintings.

He visited Venice in the 1470s where his work inspired, among other Venetian painters, the young Giovanni Bellini. *St Jerome in his Study* about 1460 (National Gallery, London) and *A Young Man* 1478 (Staatliche Museen, West Berlin) are examples of his work.

Antonescu /ˌæntəˈnesku/ Ion 1882–1946. Romanian general and politician who headed a pro-German government during World War II and was executed for war crimes in 1946.

Antonine Wall /ˈæntənaɪn/ Roman line of fortification built AD 142–200. The Roman Empire's NW frontier, between the Clyde and Forth rivers, Scotland.

Antoninus Pius AD 86–161. Roman emperor who had been adopted 138 as Hadrian's heir, and succeeded him later that year. He enjoyed a prosperous reign, during which he built the ◊Antonine Wall. His daughter married ◊Marcus Aurelius Antoninus.

Antonioni /æn,təuniˈəuni/ Michelangelo 1912– . Italian film director, famous for his subtle analysis of neuroses and personal relationships of the leisured classes. His work includes *L'Avventura* 1960, *Blow Up* 1966, and *The Passenger* 1975.

Antony and Cleopatra a tragedy by William Shakespeare, written and first performed 1607–1608. Mark Antony falls in love with the Egyptian queen Cleopatra in Alexandria, but returns to Rome when his wife, Fulvia, dies. He then marries Octavia to heal the rift between her brother Augustus Caesar and himself. Antony returns to Egypt and Cleopatra, but is finally defeated by Augustus. Believing Cleopatra dead, Antony kills himself and Cleopatra takes her life rather than surrender to Augustus.

antonymy near or precise oppositeness between or among words. 'Good' and 'evil' are antonyms, 'good' and 'bad' are also antonyms, and therefore 'evil' and 'bad' are synonyms in this context. Antonymy may vary with context and situation; in discussing the weather, 'dull' and 'bright' are antonymous, but when talking about knives and blades the opposite of 'dull' is 'sharp'.

Antrim /ˈæntrɪm/ county of Northern Ireland
area 2,830 sq km/1,092 sq mi
towns Belfast (county town), port of Larne
features Giant's Causeway of natural hexagonal basalt columns, which, in legend, was built to enable the giants to cross between Ireland and Scotland; Antrim borders Lough Neagh, and is separated from Scotland by the 32 km/20 mi wide North Channel.
products potatoes, oats, linen, synthetic textiles
population (1981) 642,000.

Antwerp /ˈæntwɜːp/ (Flemish *Antwerpen*, French *Anvers*) port in Belgium on the river Scheldt, capital of the province of Antwerp; population (1988) 476,000. One of the world's busiest ports, it has shipbuilding, oil-refining, petrochemical, textile, and diamond-cutting industries. The home of Rubens is preserved, and many of his works are in the Gothic cathedral. The province of Antwerp has an area of 2,900 sq km/1,119 sq mi, and a population (1987) 1,588,000.

It was not until the 15th century that Antwerp rose to prosperity; from 1500 to 1560 it was the richest port in N Europe. After this Antwerp was beset by religious troubles and the Netherlands revolt against Spain. In 1648 the Treaty of Westphalia gave both shores of the Scheldt estuary to the United Provinces, which closed it to Antwerp trade. The Treaty of Paris 1814 opened the estuary to all nations on payment of a small toll to the Dutch, abandoned 1863. During World War I Antwerp was occupied by Germany Oct 1914–Nov 1918; during World War II May 1940–Sept 1944.

Anubis /əˈnjuːbɪs/ in Egyptian mythology, the jackal-headed god of the dead.

Anuradhapura /əˈnuərədəpuərə/ holy city in Sri Lanka; population (1981) 36,000. It is the ancient

Apartheid
☐ The South African Homelands

capital of the Sinhalese kings of Sri Lanka 5th century BC–8th century AD; rediscovered in the mid-19th century, it has a ◊Bo tree descended from the original.

Anvers /ɒŋ'veə/ French form of ◊Antwerp.

anxiety an emotional state of fear or apprehension. Normal anxiety is a response to dangerous situations. Abnormal anxiety can either be free-floating, when the person may feel anxious much of the time in a wide range of situations, or it may be phobic, when the person is excessively afraid of an object or situation.

anxiolytic drug which reduces an anxiety state.

Anyang /ˌæn'jæŋ/ city in Henan province, E China; population (1980) 430,000. It was the capital of the Shang dynasty (13th–12th centuries BC). Rich archaeological remains have been uncovered since the 1930s.

ANZAC acronym from the initials of the *Australian and New Zealand Army Corps*, applied to all troops of both countries serving in World War I and to some in World War II.

The date of their World War 1 landing in Gallipoli, Turkey, 25 Apr 1915, is marked by a public holiday, *Anzac Day*, in both Australia and New Zealand.

Anzhero-Sudzhensk /æn'ʒeərəu 'su:dʒənsk/ town in W Siberia, USSR, 80 km/50 mi N of Kemerovo in the Kuznetsk basin; population (1985) 110,000. Its chief industry is coal mining.

Anzio, Battle of in World War II, the beachhead invasion of Italy 22 Jan–23 May 1944 by Allied troops; failure to use information gained by deciphering German signals (see ◊Ultra) led to Allied troops being stranded for a period after German attacks. Anzio is a seaport and resort on the W coast of Italy, 53 km/33 mi SE of Rome; population (1984) 25,000. It is the site of the Roman town of Antium, and the birthplace of Emperor Nero.

ANZUS acronym for *Australia, New Zealand, and the United States* (Pacific Security Treaty), a military alliance established 1951. It was replaced 1954 by the ◊Southeast Asia Treaty Organization.

Aomori /'aʊməri/ port at the head of Mutsu Bay, on the N coast of Honshu Island, Japan; 40 km/25 mi NE of Hirosaki; population (1980) 288,000. The port handles a large local trade in fish and timber.

aorta the chief ◊artery, the dorsal blood vessel carrying oxygenated blood from the left ventricle of the heart in birds and mammals. It branches to form smaller arteries, which in turn supply all body organs except lungs. Loss of elasticity in the aorta provides evidence of ◊atherosclerosis, which may lead to heart disease.

Aosta /ɑ:'ɒstə/ Italian city, 79 km/49 mi NW of Turin; population (1981) 37,200. It is the capital of Valle d'Aosta (French-speaking) autonomous region, It has extensive Roman remains.

Aouita /ɑ:'wi:tə/ Said 1960– . Moroccan runner. Outstanding at middle and long distances, he won the 1984 Olympic and 1987 World Championship 5000 metres title, and has set many world records.

In 1985 he held world records at both 1500 and 5000 metres, the first man for 30 years to hold both. He has since broken the 2 miles, 3000 metres and 2000 metres world records.

Aoun /ɑ:'u:n/ Michel 1935– . Lebanese soldier and Maronite Christian politician. As commander of the Lebanese army, in 1988 he was made president without Muslim support, his appointment precipitating a civil war between Christians and Muslims. His unwillingness to accept a 1989 Arab League sponsored peace agreement increased his isolation.

Born in Beirut, he joined the Lebanese army and rose to become, in 1984, its youngest commander. When, in 1988, the Christian and Muslim communities failed to agree on a Maronite successor to the outgoing president, Amin Gemayel (as required by the constitution) Gemayel unilaterally appointed Aoun. This precipitated the creation of a rival Muslim government, and, eventually, a civil war. Aoun, dedicated to freeing his country from Syrian domination, became isolated in the presidential palace and staunchly opposed the 1989 peace plan worked out by parliamentarians under the auspices of the Arab League.

Aouzu Strip /ɑ:'u:zu:/ disputed teritory 100 km wide on the Chad–Libya frontier, occupied by Libya 1973. Lying to the N of the Tibesti masif, the area is rich in uranium and other minerals.

a.p. in physics, abbreviation for *atmospheric pressure*.

Apache /ə'pætʃɪ/ one of the North ◊American Indian peoples, related to the Navajo, who now number about 10,000. The surviving Apaches live in reservations in Arizona (the Apache state), SW Oklahoma, and New Mexico.

apartheid (Afrikaans 'apartness') the racial-segregation policy of the government of South Africa. Apartheid was legally first formulated 1948, when the Afrikaner National Party gained power. Non-whites do not share full rights of citizenship with the 4.5 million whites (for example, the 23 million black people cannot vote in parliamentary elections), and many public facilities and institutions are restricted to the use of one race only; the establishment of ◊Black National States is another manifestation of apartheid. The term 'apartheid' was coined by the South African Bureau for Racial Affairs (Sabra) in the late 1930s.

Internally, organizations opposed to apartheid have been banned, for example the African National Congress and the United Democratic Front, and leading campaigners for its abolition have been, like Steve Biko, killed, or, like Archbishop Tutu, harassed. Anger at the policy has sparked off many uprisings, from ◊Sharpeville 1960 and ◊Soweto 1976 to the Crossroads squatter camps 1986.

Abroad, there are anti-apartheid movements in many countries. In 1961 South Africa was forced to withdraw from the Commonwealth because of apartheid; during the 1960s and 1970s there were calls for international ◊sanctions, especially boycotts of sporting and cultural links; and in the 1980s advocates of sanctions have sought to extend them into trade and finance.

The South African government's reaction to internal and international pressure has been twofold: it has abolished some of the more hated apartheid laws (the ban on interracial marriages was lifted 1985 and the pass laws, which restricted the movement of non-whites, were repealed 1986); and it has sought to replace the term 'apartheid' with 'plural democracy'. Under states of emergency 1985 and 1986 it has used severe measures to quell internal opposition, and since 1986 there has been an official ban on the reporting of it in the media.

apastron the point at which an object travelling in an elliptical orbit around a star is at its furthest from the star. The term is usually applied to the position of the minor component of a ◊binary star in relation to the primary. Its opposite is ◊periastron.

apatite a common calcium phosphate mineral, $Ca_5(PO_4CO_3)_3(F, OH, Cl)$. Apatite has a hexagonal structure and occurs widely in igneous rocks, for example pegmatite, and in contact metamorphic rocks, such as marbles. It is used in the manufacture of fertilizer and as a source of phosphorus. Apatite is the chief constituent of tooth enamel, and it ranks 5 on the ◊Mohs' scale of hardness.

Apatosaurus large plant-eating dinosaur, formerly called *Brontosaurus*, which flourished about 145 million years ago. Up to 21 m/69 ft long and 30 tonnes in weight, it stood on four elephant-like legs and had a long tail, long neck, and small head. It probably snipped off low-growing vegetation with peg-like front teeth, and swallowed it whole to be ground by pebbles in the stomach.

ape any ◊primate closely related to humans, including the gibbon, orang-utan, chimpanzee, and gorilla.

Ape City Yerkes Regional Primate Center, Atlanta, Georgia, USA, where large numbers of primates are kept for physiological and psychological experiment. A major area of research at Ape City is language.

Apeldoorn /'a:pəldɔ:n/ commercial city in Gelderland province, E central Netherlands. Population (1982) 142,400. Het Loo, which is situated nearby, has been the summer residence of the Dutch royal family since the time of William of Orange.

Apelles 4th century BC. Greek painter, said to have been the greatest in antiquity. He was court painter to Philip of Macedonia and his son Alexander the Great. None of his work survives, only descriptions of his portraits and nude Venuses.

Apennines /'æpənaɪn/ chain of mountains stretching the length of the Italian peninsula. A continuation of the Maritime Alps, from Genoa it swings across the peninsula to Ancona on the E coast, and then back to the W coast and into the 'toe' of Italy. The system is continued over the Strait of Messina along the N Sicilian coast, then across the Mediterranean sea in a series of islands to the Atlas mountains of North Africa. The highest peak is Gran Sasso d'Italia at 2,914 m/9,560 ft.

Apennines a mountain range on the Moon, SE of the Sea of Showers.

aperture in photography, an opening in the camera that allows light to pass through the lens to strike the film. Controlled by shutter speed and the iris diaphragm, it can be set mechanically or electronically at various diameters.

aphasia difficulty in speaking, writing, and reading, usually caused by damage to the brain.

aphelion the point at which an object, travelling in an elliptical orbit around the Sun, is at its furthest from the Sun.

aphid small insect that lives by sucking sap from plants. There are many species, often adapted to particular plants.

In some stages, wingless females rapidly produce large numbers of live young by ◊parthenogenesis, leading to enormous infestations, and numbers can approach 2,000 million per hectare/2 acres. As well as by feeding, they can cause damage by transmitting virus diseases. Some research suggests, however, that they may help promote fertility in the soil through the waste they secrete, termed 'honeydew'. Aphids are also known as plant ice, greenfly, or blackfly.

aphrodisiac (from Aphrodite, the Greek goddess of love) anything arousing or increasing sexual desire.

Sexual activity can be stimulated in humans and animals by drugs affecting the pituitary gland. Preparations commonly sold for the purpose can be dangerous (cantharidin) or useless (rhinoceros horn), and alcohol and cannabis, popularly thought to be effective because they lessen inhibition, may have the opposite effect.

aphid Electron-microscope picture of a group of wingless aphids (green fly) feeding on a plant stem.

Apollo *Marble statue of Apollo (Pergamon Museum), Berlin. It exemplifies the idealized Greek concept of the beauty of the male form.*

Aphrodite *An 18th-century cast of the Medici Venus, Greek, 2nd century BC.*

Aphrodite /ˌæfrəˈdaɪti/ in Greek mythology, the goddess of love (Roman Venus, Phoenician Astarte, Babylonian Ishtar); said to be either a daughter of Zeus (in Homer) or sprung from the foam of the sea (in Hesiod). She was the unfaithful wife of Hephaestus, the god of fire, and the mother of Eros.

Apia /ˈɑːpiə/ capital and port of Western ◊Samoa, on the north coast of Upolu island, in the W Pacific; population (1981) 33,000. It was the home of the writer Robert Louis Stevenson.

Apis /ˈɑːpɪs/ ancient Egyptian god with a bull's head, linked with Osiris (and later merged with him into the Ptolemaic god Serapis); his cult centres were Memphis and Heliopolis, where sacred bulls were mummified.

Apocalypse in literature, a movement which developed from Surrealism 1938, and included G S Fraser, Henry Treece, J F Hendry, Nicholas Moore, and Tom Scott. Influenced by the work of Dylan Thomas, it favoured Biblical symbolism.

Apocrypha an appendix to the Old Testament of the Bible, not included in the final Hebrew canon but recognized by Roman Catholics. There are also disputed New Testament texts known as Apocrypha.

apogee the point at which an object, travelling in an elliptical orbit around the Earth, is at its furthest from the Earth.

Apollinaire /əˌpɒlɪˈneə/ Guillaume. Pen name of Guillaume Apollinaire de Kostrowitsky 1880–1918. French poet of aristocratic Polish descent. He was a leader of the *avant garde* in Parisian literary and artistic circles. His novel *Le Poète assassiné/The Poet Assassinated* 1916, followed by the experimental poems *Alcools/Alcohols* 1913 and *Calligrammes/Word Pictures* 1918, show him as a representative of the Cubist and Futurist movements.

Born in Rome and educated in Monaco, Apollinaire went to Paris in 1898. His work influenced younger French writers, such as ◊Aragon. He coined the word 'surrealism' to describe his play *Les Mamelles de Tirésias/The Breasts of Tiresias* 1917.

Apollinarius of Laodicea Christian bishop, whose views on the nature of Christ were condemned by the Council of Constantine 381, but who nonetheless laid the foundations for the later ◊Nestorian controversy. Rather than seeing the nature of Jesus as a human and divine soul somehow joined in the person of Christ, he saw Christ as a divine mind only, and not subject to a change of mind.

Apollo /əˈpɒləʊ/ in Greek and Roman mythology, the god of sun, music, poetry, prophecy, agriculture, and pastoral life, and leader of the Muses. He was the twin child (with Artemis) of Zeus and Leto. Ancient statues show Apollo as the embodiment of the Greek ideal of male beauty.

His chief cult centres were his supposed birthplace on the island of Delos, in the Cyclades, and Delphi.

Apollo asteroid a member of a group of ◊asteroids whose orbits cross that of Earth. They are named after the first of their kind, Apollo, discovered 1932, and then lost until 1973. Apollo asteroids are so small and faint that they are difficult to see except when close to Earth (Apollo is about 2 km across).

Apollo asteroids can collide with Earth from time to time. In 1937 the Apollo asteroid Hermes passed 800,000 km/500,000 mi from Earth, the closest observed approach of any asteroid. A collision with an Apollo asteroid 65 million years ago may have been responsible for the extinction of the dinosaurs. A closely related group, the Amor asteroids, come close to Earth but do not cross its orbit.

Apollonius of Perga /ˌæpəˈləʊniəs/ *c.* 260–*c.* 190 BC. Greek mathematician and geometer. In his work *Conic Sections* he showed that a plane intersecting a cone will generate an ellipse, a parabola, or a hyperbola, depending on the angle of intersection. In astronomy, he used a system of circles called epicycles and deferents to explain the motion of the planets; this system, as refined by Ptolemy, was used until the Renaissance.

Apollonius of Rhodes /ˌæpəˈləʊniəs/ *c.* 220–180 BC. Greek poet, author of the epic *Argonautica*, which tells the story of Jason and the Argonauts.

Apollonius of Tyana /ˈtaɪənə/ Greek ascetic philosopher of the Neo-Pythagorean school, who lived in the early part of the 1st century AD. He travelled in Babylonia and India, where he acquired a wide knowledge of oriental religions and philosophies, and taught at Ephesus. He was said to have had miraculous powers, but claimed that he could only see the future.

Apollo of Rhodes the Greek statue of Apollo generally known as the ◊Colossus of Rhodes.

Apollo project US space project to land a person on the Moon, achieved July 1969, when Neil Armstrong was the first to set foot there. The programme was announced 1961 by President Kennedy. The world's most powerful rocket, Saturn V, was built to launch the Apollo spacecraft, which carried three astronauts. When the spacecraft was in orbit around the Moon, two astronauts descended to the surface in a lunar module. The first Apollo mission carrying a crew, Apollo 7, Oct 1968, was a test flight in orbit around the Earth. After three other preparatory flights, Apollo 11 made the first lunar landing. Five more manned landings followed, the last 1972. The total cost of the programme was over $24 billion.

Apollo-Soyuz test project a joint US-Soviet mission begun 1972 to link a Soviet and a US spacecraft in space. The project culminated in the docking of an Apollo 18 and Soyuz 15 craft, both of which were launched 15 July 1975.

In the Apollo craft were Thomas Patten Stafford (commander), Vance DeVoe Brand, and Donald Kent Slayton, while the Soyuz vehicle carried Alexei Archipovich Leonov (commander) and Valeri Nikolayevich Kubasov. The project began with the signing of an agreement May 1972 by US president Nixon and Soviet premier Kosygin.

apologetics philosophical writings which attempt to refute attacks on the Christian faith. Famous apologists include Justin Martyr, Origen, St Augustine, Thomas Aquinas, Blaise Pascal, and Joseph Butler. The questions raised by modern scientific and historical discoveries have widened the field of apologetics.

Apo, Mount /ˈɑːpəʊ/ active volcano and highest peak in the Philippines, rising to 2,954 m/9,692 ft on the island of Mindanao.

aposematic coloration in biology, the technical name for ◊warning coloration markings that make a dangerous, poisonous, or foul-tasting animal particularly conspicuous and recognizable to a predator. Examples include the yellow and black stripes of bees and wasps, and the bright red or yellow colours of many poisonous frogs; see also ◊mimicry.

a posteriori (Latin 'from the latter') in logic, an argument which deduces causes from their effects; inductive reasoning; the converse of ◊a priori.

apostle (Greek 'messenger') in the New Testament, the 12 chief ◊disciples namely, Andrew Bartholomew, James (the Great), James (the Less), John, Jude (or Thaddeus), Matthew, Peter, Philip, Simon, Thomas, and Judas Iscariot. After the latter's death his place was taken by Matthias. In the earliest days of Christianity the term was extended to include some who had never known Jesus, notably St Paul.

Apostles discussion group founded 1820 at Cambridge University, England; members have included the poet Tennyson, the philosophers G E Moore and Bertrand Russell, the writers Lytton Strachey and Leonard Woolf, the economist Keynes, and the spies Guy Burgess and Anthony Blunt.

Apostles' Creed one of the three ancient ◊creeds of the Christian church.

Apostolic Age early period in the Christian church dominated by those personally known to Jesus or his disciples.

apostolic succession the doctrine in the Christian church that certain spiritual powers were received by the first apostles direct from Jesus, and have been handed down in the ceremony of 'laying on of hands' from generation to generation of bishops.

apostrophe a punctuation mark ('). In English it either denotes a missing letter (*mustn't* for *must not*), or indicates possession (*John's camera, the girl's dress*). Correct use of the apostrophe has caused controversy for centuries.

An apostrophe often precedes the plural *s* used with numbers and abbreviations (*the 1970's, a group of P.O.W.'s*); it is more correct, however, to omit it in such usages (*the 1970s, a group of POWs*).

For certain words ending with *s*, usage is split, as between *James's book* and *James' book*. In current English, the possessive apostrophe is often

Apollo Project *Ed Aldrin, one of the first astronauts to walk on the moon, 1969.*

omitted from such usages as *in ten months' time/in ten months time* and *Barclays Bank*. Many people otherwise competent in writing have great difficulty with the apostrophe, which has never been stable at any point in its history.

apothecaries' weights obsolete units of mass, formerly used in pharmacy. Twenty grains made one scruple; three scruples made one drachm; and eight drachms made an apothecary's ounce (oz apoth.). There are 7,000 grains in 1 lb/0.454 kg.

apothecary a person who prepares and dispenses medicines, a pharmacist. The word retains its original meaning in the USA and other countries, but in England apothecary came to mean a licensed medical practitioner. In 1815, the Society of Apothecaries was given the right to grant licences to practise medicine in England and Wales.

Appalachians /ˌæpəˈleɪtʃənz/ mountain system of E North America, stretching about 2,400 km/1,500 mi from Alabama to Québec, composed of very ancient eroded rocks. The chain includes the Allegheny, Catskill, and Blue Ridge mountains, the latter having the highest peak, Mount Mitchell, 2,045 m/6,712 ft. The eastern edge has a fall line to the coastal plain where Philadelphia, Baltimore, and Washington stand.

appeasement historically, the conciliatory policy adopted by the British government, particularly under Neville Chamberlain, towards the Nazi and Fascist dictators in Europe in the 1930s. It was strongly opposed by Winston Churchill, but the ◊Munich Agreement 1938 was almost universally hailed as its justification. Appeasement ended when Germany occupied Bohemia–Moravia Mar 1939.

Appel /ˈæpəl/ Karel 1921 Dutch painter and sculptor, founder of *Cobra* 1948, a group of European artists that developed an expressive and dynamic form of abstract painting, with thick paintwork and lurid colours.

appendicitis inflammation of the small, blind extension of the bowel in the lower right abdomen, the *appendix*. In an acute attack, the appendix may burst, causing a potentially lethal spread of infection (see ◊peritonitis). Treatment is by removal (appendectomy).

Appert /æˈpeə/ Nicolas 1750–1841. French pioneer of food preservation by ◊canning. He devised a system of sealing food in glass bottles and subjecting it to heat. His book *L'art de conserver les substances animales et végétales* appeared in 1810. Shortly after, others employed the same principles to iron or sheet steel containers plated with tin.

apple fruit of *Malus pumila*, a tree of the family Rosaceae. There are several thousand varieties of cultivated apples, which may be divided into eating, cooking, and cider apples. All are derived from the wild crab apple.

Apple trees grow best in temperate countries with a cool climate and plenty of rain during the winter. The apple has been an important food plant in Europe from earliest times.

Appleseed, Johnny character in US folk legend who wandered through the country for 40 years sowing apple seeds from which apple trees grew. The legend seems to be based on a historical figure, the US pioneer John Chapman (1774–1845).

Appleton /ˈæpəltən/ Edward Victor 1892–1965. British physicist, who worked at Cambridge under ◊Rutherford from 1920. He proved the existence of the Kennelly–Heaviside layer in the atmosphere, and the Appleton layer beyond it, and was involved in the initial work on the atomic bomb. Nobel prize 1947.

Appleton layer a band containing ionized gases in the Earth's upper atmosphere, above the ◊Kennelly–Heaviside layer. It can act as a reflector of radio signals, although its ionic composition varies with the sunspot cycle. It was named after the English physicist Edward Appleton.

application in computing, a program or job designed for the benefit of the end user, such as a payroll system or a ◊word processor. The term is used to distinguish such programs from those that control the computer itself or assist the programmer, such as a ◊compiler.

appliqué a type of embroidery used to create pictures or patterns by 'applying' pieces of material onto a background fabric. The pieces are cut into the appropriate shapes and sewn on, providing decoration for wall hangings, furnishing textiles, and clothes.

Appomattox /ˌæpəˈmætəks/ village in Virginia, USA, scene of the surrender 9 Apr 1865 of the Confederate army under Robert E Lee to the Union army under Ulysses S Grant, which ended the American Civil War.

The courthouse where the surrender was signed is now a museum, 5 km/3 mi from the modern village of Appomattox.

approx. abbreviation for *approximately*.

apricot fruit of *Prunus armeniaca*, a tree closely related to the almond, peach, plum, and cherry. It has yellow-fleshed fruit. A native of the Far East, it has long been cultivated in Armenia, from where it was introduced into Europe and the USA.

April Fools' Day the first day of April, when it is customary in W Europe and the USA to expose people to ridicule by causing them to believe some falsehood or to go on a fruitless errand.

The victim is known in England as an April Fool; in Scotland as a gowk (cuckoo or fool); and in France as a *poisson d'Avril* (April fish). There is a similar Indian custom on the last day of the Huli festival in late March.

a priori (Latin 'from what comes before') in logic, an argument that is known to be true, or false, without reference to experience; the converse of ◊a posteriori.

Apsley House /ˈæpsli/ home of the dukes of Wellington at Hyde Park Corner, London, from 1820; now the Wellington Museum.

Apuleius /ˌæpjuˈliːəs/ Lucius *c*. AD 160. Roman lawyer, philosopher and author of *Metamorphoses*, or ◊*The Golden Ass*.

Apulia /ˈpuːljə/ English form of ◊Puglia, region of Italy.

Aqaba, Gulf of /ˈækəbə/ gulf extending for 160 km/100 mi between the Negev and the Red Sea; its coastline is uninhabited except at its head, where the frontiers of Israel, Egypt, Jordan, and Saudi Arabia converge. Here are the two ports Eilat (Israeli Elath) and Aqaba, Jordan's only port.

Aquae Sulis /ˈækwaɪ ˈsuːlɪs/ Roman name of the city of ◊Bath in W England.

aqualung *s*elf-*c*ontained *u*nderwater *b*reathing *a*pparatus (scuba) worn by divers, developed in the early 1940s by the French diver Jacques Cousteau. The aqualung provides air to the diver at the same pressure as that of the surrounding water (which increases with increasing depth). Air comes from compressed-air cylinders on the diver's back, regulated by a valve system.

The vital component of an aqualung is the demand-regulator, a two-stage valve in the diver's mouthpiece. When the diver breathes in, air passes from compressed-air cylinders on the diver's back, through a valve to the inner chamber of the mouthpiece. Water entering the outer chamber pressurizes the air in the inner chamber.

aquamarine a blue variety of the mineral ◊beryl.

aquaplaning phenomenon in which the tyres of a road vehicle cease to make direct contact with the road surface, caused by the presence of a thin film of water. As a result, the vehicle can go out of control (particularly if the steered wheels are involved).

Aquaplaning can be prevented by fitting tyres with a good tread pattern at the correct pressure and by avoiding excessive speed in wet road conditions.

aquarium tank or similar container used for the study and display of living aquatic plants and animals. The same name is used for institutions that exhibit aquatic life. These have been common since Roman times, but the first modern public aquarium was opened in Regent's Park, London, England, in 1853. A recent development is the oceanarium, a large display of marine life forms.

Aquarius a zodiac constellation in the southern hemisphere near Pegasus. It is represented as a man pouring water from a jar. The Sun passes through Aquarius from late Feb to early Mar. In *astrology*, the dates for Aquarius are between about 20 Jan and 18 Feb (see ◊precession).

aquatint printmaking technique, usually combined with ◊etching to produce prints with subtle, tones as well as more precisely etched lines. Aquatint became popular in the late 18th century.

The etching plate is dusted with a fine layer of resin, which is fixed to the plate by heating. The plate is then immersed in acid, which bites through the resin, causing tiny pits on the surface of the plate. When printed, this results in a fine, grainy, tone. Areas of tone can be controlled by varnishing the plate with acid-resisting material. Denser tones are aquired by longer exposure to the acid.

Gainsborough experimented with aquatint but the first to become proficient in the technique was J B Le Prince (1733–81). Other artists attracted to it include Goya, Degas, Pissarro, Picasso, and Rouault.

Aquaviva /ˌækwəˈviːvə/ Claudius (Claudio) 1543–1615. Fifth general of the Roman Catholic monastic order of Jesuits. Born in Naples, of noble family, he entered the order in 1567 and became its head in 1581. Under his rule they greatly increased in numbers, and the revolt of the Spanish Jesuits was put down. He published a treatise on education.

aqueduct artificial channel or conduit for water, often an elevated structure of stone, wood, or iron built for conducting water across a valley.

The Greeks built a tunnel 1,280 m/4,200 ft long near Athens, 2,500 years ago. Many Roman aqueducts are still standing, for example the aqueduct at Nîmes in S France, built about AD 18 (which is 48 m/160 ft high). The largest Roman aqueduct is that at Carthage in Tunisia, which is 141 km/87 mi long and was built during the reign of Publius Aelius Hadrianus between AD 117 and 138. The longest aqueduct in Britain is the Pont Cysylltau in Clwyd, Wales, opened 1805. It is 307 m/1,007 ft long, with 19 arches up to 36 m/121 ft high. The first modern aqueduct in Britain, built 1959–72, carries the Bridgewater Canal over the Irwell at Barton. A recent aqueduct is the California State Water Project taking water from Lake Oroville in the north, through two power plants and across the Tehachapi mountains, more than 177 km/110 mi to S California.

aqueous humour watery fluid found in the space between the cornea and lens of the vertebrate eye. Similar to blood serum in composition, it is renewed every four hours.

aqueous solution a solution in which the solvent is water.

aquifer any rock formation containing water that can be extracted by a well. The rock of an aquifer must be porous and permeable (full of interconnected holes) so that it can absorb water.

An aquifer may be underlain, overlain, or sandwiched between impermeable layers, called *aquicludes*, which impede water movement. Sandstones and porous limestones make the best aquifers. They are actively sought in arid areas as sources of drinking and irrigation water.

Aquila a constellation of the equatorial region of the sky. Its brightest star is the first-magnitude ◊Altair, flanked by the stars Beta and Gamma Aquilae. It is represented by an eagle.

Aquinas /əˈkwaɪnəs/ St Thomas *c*.1226–1274. Neapolitan philosopher and theologian. His *Summa Contra Gentiles/Against the Errors of the Infidels* 1259–64 argues that reason and faith are compatible. His most significant contribution to philosophy was to synthesize the philosophy of Aristotle and Christian doctrine.

His unfinished *Summa Theologica*, begun 1265, deals with the nature of God, morality, and the work of Jesus. His works embodied the world view taught in universities up until the mid-17th century, and include scientific ideas derived from Aristotle. In 1879, they were recognized as the basis of Catholic theology by Pope Leo XIII, who had launched a modern edition of his works. He was a Dominican monk, known as the 'Angelic Doctor', and was canonized 1323.

Aquino President Corazón Aquino campaigning in Angeles City, Philippines, Jan 1987.

Aquino /ə'ki:nəʊ/ (Maria) Corazón (born Cojuangco) 1933– . President of the Philippines from 1986, when she was instrumental in the nonviolent overthrow of President Marcos. She has sought to rule in a conciliatory manner, but has encountered opposition from left (communist guerrillas) and right (army coup attempts), and her land reforms have been seen as inadequate.

The daughter of a sugar baron, she studied in the USA and married the politician Benigno Aquino 1956. The chief political opponent of the right-wing president Marcos, he was assassinated by a military guard at Manila airport 1983. Corazón Aquino was drafted by the opposition to contest the Feb 1986 presidential election and claimed victory over Marcos, accusing the government of ballot-rigging. She led a nonviolent 'people's power' campaign which overthrew Marcos 25 Feb. A devout Roman Catholic, Aquino enjoyed strong church backing in her 1986 campaign.

Aquitaine /ˌækwɪ'teɪn/ region of SW France; capital Bordeaux; area 41,300 sq km/15,942 sq mi; population (1986) 2,718,000. It comprises the *départements* of Dordogne, Gironde, Landes, Lot-et-Garonne, and Pyrénées-Atlantiques. Red wines (Margaux, St Julien) are produced in the Medoc district, bordering the Gironde. Aquitaine was an English possession 1152–1452.

history early human remains have been found in the Dordogne region. Aquitaine coincides roughly with the Roman province of Aquitania, and the ancient French province of Aquitaine. Eleanor of Aquitaine married the future Henry II of England 1152, and brought it to him as her dowry; it remained an English hands 1452.

AR abbreviation for ◊*Arkansas*.

Arab speaker of Arabic, the major Semitic language of the Afro-Asiatic family. The homeland of the Arabs comprises Saudi Arabia, Qatar, Kuwait, Bahrain, United Arab Emirates, Oman, South Yemen, and North Yemen.

Arab Emirates see ◊United Arab Emirates.

arabesque in ballet, a pose in which the dancer stands on one leg, straight or bent, with the other leg raised behind, fully extended. The arms are held in a harmonious position to give the longest possible line from fingertips to toes.

Arabia /ə'reɪbɪə/ the peninsula between the Persian Gulf and the Red Sea, in SW Asia; area 2,590,000 sq km/1,000,000 sq mi. The peninsula contains the world's richest oil and gas reserves.

Arab-Israeli Wars 22 Oct 1973. Having crossed the Suez Canal, Israeli troops entered Egypt. Part of the occupied area was within 72 km/45 mi of Cairo.

It comprises the states of Bahrain, Kuwait, North Yemen, Oman, Qatar, Saudi Arabia, the United Arab Emirates, and South Yemen.

physical A sandy coastal plain of varying width borders the Red Sea, behind which a mountain chain rises to about 2,000–2,500 m/6,600–8,200 ft. Behind this range is the plateau of the Nejd, averaging 1,000 m/3,300 ft. The interior comprises a vast desert area: part of the Hamad (Syrian) desert in the far north; Nafud in northern Saudi Arabia, and Rub'al

history the Arabian civilization was revived by Muhammad during the 7th century AD, but in the new empire created by militant Islam, Arabia became a subordinate state, and its cities were eclipsed by Damascus, Baghdad, and Cairo. Colonialism only touched the fringe of Arabia in the 19th century, and until the 20th century the interior was unknown to Europeans. Nationalism began actively to emerge at the period of World War I, and the oil discoveries from 1953 supplied sufficient resources to give the peninsula significant economic power.

Arabian Gulf /ə'reɪbɪən/ another name for the ◊Persian Gulf.

Arabian Nights tales in oral circulation among Arab storytellers from the 10th century, and probably having roots in India. They are also known as *The Thousand and One Nights* and include 'Ali Baba', 'Aladdin', 'Sinbad the Sailor', and 'The Old Man of the Sea'.

They were supposed to have been told to the sultan by his bride Scheherazade to avoid the fate of her predecessors, who were all executed following the wedding night to prevent their infidelity. She began a new tale each evening, which she would only agree to finish on the following night. Eventually the 'sentence' was rescinded.

The first European translation was by the French writer Antoine Galland (1646–1715) 1704, although the stories were known earlier. The first English translations were by E W Lane (1801–1876) 1838–40 and Richard Burton 1885–88.

Arabian sea the NW branch of the ◊Indian Ocean.

Arabic language a Hamito-Semitic language of W Asia and North Africa, originating among the Arabs of the Arabian peninsula. Arabic script is written from right to left.

The language has spread as far west as Morocco and as far east as Malaysia, Indonesia, and the Philippines. Forms of colloquial Arabic vary in the countries where it is the dominant language: Algeria, Bahrain, Egypt, Iraq, Jordan, Kuwait, Lebanon, Libya, Mali, Mauretania, Morocco, Oman, Saudi Arabia, Sudan, Syria, Tunisia, the United Arab Emirates, and the two Yemens. Arabic is also a language of religious and cultural significance in such other countries as Bangladesh, India, Iran, Pakistan, and Somalia.

A feature of the language is its consonantal roots; for example, *s-l-m* is the root for *salaam*,

a greeting that implies peace, *Islam*, the creed of submission to God and calm acceptance of His will, and *Muslim*, one who submits to that will (a believer in Islam). The *Quran*, the sacred book of Islam, is 'for reading' by a *qari* ('reader') who is engaged in *qaraat* ('reading'). The 7th-century style of the Quran is the basis of Classical Arabic.

arabic numerals the signs 0, 1, 2, 3, 4, 5, 6, 7, 8, 9, which were in use among the Arabs before being adopted by the peoples of Europe during the Middle Ages in place of Roman numerals. They appear to have originated in India, and reached Europe by way of Spain.

Arab-Israeli Wars a series of wars between Israel and various Arab states in the Middle East since the founding of the state of Israel 1948.

background Arab opposition to an Israeli state began after the Balfour Declaration 1917, which supported the idea of a Jewish national homeland. In the 1920s there were anti-Zionist riots in Palestine, then governed by the UK under a League of Nations mandate. In 1936 an Arab revolt led to a British royal commission that recommended partition (approved by the United Nations 1947, but rejected by the Arabs).

Tension in the Middle East remained high, and the conflict was sharpened and given East–West overtones by Soviet adoption of the Arab cause and US support for Israel. Several wars only increased the confusion over who had a claim to what territory. Particularly in view of the area's strategic sensitivity as an oil producer, pressure grew for a settlement, and in 1978 the ◊Camp David Agreements brought peace between Egypt and Israel, but this was denounced by other Arab countries. Israel withdrew from Sinai 1979–82, but no final agreement on Jerusalem and the establishment of a Palestinian state on the West Bank was reached. The continuing Israeli occupation of the Gaza Strip and the West Bank in the face of a determined uprising (◊intifada) by the residents of these areas has seemingly hardened attitudes on both sides.

First Arab-Israeli War 14 Oct 1948–13 Jan/24 Mar 1949. As soon as the independent state of Israel had been proclaimed by the Jews, it was invaded by combined Arab forces. The Israelis defeated them and went on to annex territory until they controlled 75% of what had been Palestine under British mandate.

Second Arab-Israeli War 29 Oct–4 Nov 1956. After Egypt had taken control of the Suez Canal and blockaded the Straits of Tiran, Israel, with British and French support, invaded and captured Sinai and the Gaza Strip, from which it withdrew under heavy US pressure after the entry of a UN force.

Third Arab-Israeli War 5–10 Jun 1967, the *Six-Day War*. It resulted in the Israeli capture of the Golan Heights from Syria; the E half of Jerusalem and the West Bank from Jordan; and, in the south, the Gaza Strip and Sinai Peninsula as far as the Suez Canal.

Fourth Arab-Israeli War 2–22/24 Oct 1973, the 'October War' or *Yom Kippur War*, so called because the Israeli forces were taken by surprise on the Day of ◊Atonement. It started with in the recrossing of the Suez Canal by Egyptian forces who made initial gains, though there was some later loss of ground by the Syrians in the north.

Fifth Arab-Israeli War From 1978 the presence of Palestinian guerrillas in Lebanon led to Arab raids on Israel and Israeli retaliatory incursions, but on 6 Jun 1982 Israel launched a full-scale invasion. By 14 Jun Beirut was encircled, and ◊Palestine Liberation Organization (PLO) and Syrian forces were evacuated (mainly to Syria) 21–31 Aug, but in Feb 1985 there was a unilateral Israeli withdrawal from the country without any gain for losses incurred. Israel maintains a 'security zone' in S Lebanon and supports the South Lebanese Army militia as a buffer against Palestinian guerrilla incursions.

Arafat *The leader of the Palestine Liberation Organization from 1969, Yasser Arafat.*

Arabistan /ˌærəbɪ'stɑːn/ former name of the Iranian province of Khuzestan, revived in the 1980s by the 2 million Sunni Arab inhabitants who demand, autonomy. Unrest and sabotage 1979–80 led to a pledge of a degree of autonomy by Ayatollah Khomeini.

Arab League an organization of Arab states established in Cairo 1945 to promote Arab unity, especially in opposition to Israel. The original members were Egypt, Syria, Iraq, Lebanon, Transjordan (Jordan 1949), Saudi Arabia, and Yemen. In 1979 Egypt was suspended and the league's headquarters transferred to Tunis in protest against the Egypt–Israeli peace, but Egypt was readmitted as a full member May 1989.

Arachne /ə'ræknɪ/ (Greek 'spider') in Greek mythology, a Lydian woman who was so skilful a weaver that she challenged the goddess Athena to a contest. Athena tore Arachne's beautiful tapestries to pieces and Arachne hanged herself. She was transformed into a spider, and her weaving became a cobweb.

Arad /'æræd/ Romanian town on the river Mures, 160 km/100 mi NE of Belgrade; population (1985) 185,900. It is an important route centre with many industries.

Arafat /'ærəfæt/ Yasser 1929– . Palestinian nationalist politician, cofounder of al-◊Fatah 1956 and president of the ◊Palestine Liberation Organization (PLO) from 1969. In the 1970s his activities in pursuit of an independent homeland for Palestinians made him a prominent figure in world politics, but in the 1980s the growth of factions within the PLO effectively reduced his power. He was forced to evacuate Lebanon 1983, but remained leader of most of the PLO.

Arafura Sea /ˌærə'fuərə/ the area of the Pacific Ocean between N Australia and Indonesia, bounded by the Timor Sea in the west and the Coral Sea in the east. It is 1,290 km/800 mi long and 560 km/350 mi wide.

Arago /ˌærə'ɡəʊ/ Dominique 1786–1853. French physicist and astronomer who made major contributions to the early study of electromagnetism. In 1820 he found out that iron enclosed in a wire coil could be magnetized by the passage of an electric current. Later in 1824 he was the first to observe the ability of a floating copper disc to deflect a magnetic needle, the phenomenon of magnetic rotation.

Aragón /'ærəɡən/ autonomous region of NE Spain including the provinces of Huesca, Teruel, and Zaragoza; area 47,700 sq km/18,412 sq mi; population (1986) 1,215,000. Its capital is Zaragoza, and products include almonds, figs, grapes, and olives. Aragón was an independent kingdom 1035–1479.
history A Roman province until taken in the 5th century by the Visigoths, who lost it to the Moors in the 8th century, it became a kingdom 1035. It was united with Castile 1479 under Ferdinand and Isabella.

Aragon /ˌærə'ɡɒn/ Louis 1897–1982. French poet and novelist. Beginning as a Dadaist, he became one of the leaders of Surrealism, published volumes of verse and in 1930 joined the Communist

Party. Taken prisoner in World War II he escaped to join the Resistance, experiences reflected in the poetry of *Le Crève-coeur* 1942 and *Les Yeux d'Elsa* 1944.

Arakan /ˌærə'kɑːn/ state of W Myanmar on the Bay of Bengal coast, some 645 km/400 mi long and strewn with islands; population (1983) 2,046,000. The chief town is Sittwe. It is bounded along its eastern side by the Arakan Yoma, a mountain range rising to 3,000 m/10,000 ft. The ancient kingdom of Arakan was conquered by Burma (now Myanmar) 1785.

Aral Sea /'ɑːrəl/ inland sea in the USSR; the world's fourth largest lake; divided between Kazakhstan and Uzbekistan; former area 62,000 sq km/24,000 sq mi, but decreasing. Water from its tributaries, the Amu Darya and Syr Darya, has been diverted for irrigation and city use, and the sea is disappearing, with long-term consequences for the climate.

Between 1960 and 1990 the water level dropped 13 m/40 ft, reducing the lake to two-thirds of its original area and increasing the area of the surrounding Aralkum salt desert. In Sept 1988 the Soviet Communist Party's Central Committee approved a plan designed to replenish the Aral Sea by securing a 25% economy by the year 2000 in the water used locally by agriculture and industry.

Aram /'ærəm/ Eugene 1704–1759. British murderer, the subject of works by the novelist Bulwer Lytton, the poet Thomas Hood, and others.

He was a schoolmaster in Knaresborough, Yorkshire, and achieved some distinction as a philologist. In 1745 he was tried and acquitted on a charge concerned with the disappearance of a local shoemaker. Several years later he was arrested in Lynn, Norfolk, following the discovery of a skeleton in a cave at Knaresborough. He was tried at York, confessed to the murder after his conviction, and was hanged.

Aramaic language a Hamito-Semitic language of W Asia, the everyday language of Palestine 2,000 years ago.

In the 13th century BC Aramaean nomads set up states in Mesopotamia, and over the next 200 years spread into N Syria, where Damascus, Aleppo, and Cemish were among their chief centres. Aramaic spread throughout Syria and Mesopotamia, becoming one of the official languages of the Persian empire under the Achæmenids and serving as a lingua franca of the day. Aramaic dialects survive among small Christian communities in various parts of W Asia.

Aran Islands /'ærən/ three rocky islands (Inishmore, Inishmaan, Inisheer) in the mouth of Galway Bay, Republic of Ireland; population approximately 4,600. The capital is Kilronan. J M ◊Synge used the language of the islands in his plays.

Aranjuez /ˌærən'xweθ/ Spanish town on the river Tagus, 40 km/25 mi SE of Madrid; population (1981) 36,000. The palace was a royal residence for centuries.

Arany /'ɒrɒni/ János 1817–1882. Hungarian writer. His comic epic *The Lost Constitution* 1846 was followed in 1847 by *Toldi*, a product of the popular nationalist school. In 1864 his epic masterpiece *The Death of King Buda* appeared. During his last years Arany produced the rest of the *Toldi* trilogy, and his most personal lyrics.

Ararat /'ærəræt/ double-peaked mountain on the Turkish-Iranian border; the higher, Great Ararat, 5,156 m/17,000 ft, was the reputed resting place of Noah's Ark after the Flood.

Ararat /'ærəræt/ wheat and wool centre in NW Victoria, Australia; population (1986) 8,000. It is a former gold-mining town.

Araucanian Indian /ˌærɔː'keɪnɪən/ any member of the original inhabitants of central Chile. An agricultural and hunting people, they were also renowned warriors, defeating the Incas and resisting the Spanish for 200 years.

araucaria coniferous tree allied to the firs. It is native to the southern hemisphere, and often attains a gigantic size. Araucarias include the **monkey-puzzle tree** *Araucaria araucana*, the **Australian bunya bunya pine** *Araucaria bidwillii*, and the **Norfolk Island pine** *Araucaria heterophylla*.

Arawak indigenous American people of the Caribbean and Amazon basin. They lived mainly by shifting cultivation in tropical forests. They were driven out of the Lesser Antilles by another American Indian people, the Caribs, shortly before the arrival of the Spanish in the 16th century.

Arbenz Guzmán /ɑː'bens ɡʊs'mæn/ Jácobo 1913–1971. Guatemalan social democratic politician and president from 1951 until his overthrow, in 1954 by rebels operating with the help of the US Central Intelligence Agency.

Guzmán brought in policies to redistribute land, much of which was owned by overseas companies, to landless peasants and encouraged labour organization. He was exiled in Mexico, Uruguay, and Cuba until his death.

Arbil /ɑː'biːl/ Kurdish town in a province of the same name in N Iraq. Occupied since Assyrian times, it was the site of a battle in 331 BC at which Alexander the Great defeated the Persians under Darius III. In 1974 Arbil became the capital of a Kurdish autonomous region set up by the Iraqi government. Population (1985) 334,000.

arbitrageur in international finance, a person who buys securities (such as currency or commodities) in one country or market for immediate resale in another market, to take advantage of different prices. Arbitrage became widespread during the 1970s and 1980s with the increasing ◊deregulation of financial markets.

arbitration submission of a dispute to a third, unbiased party for settlement. It may be personal litigation, trade-union issues, or international disputes (as the case of the warship ◊*Alabama*).

The first permanent international court was established in The Hague in the Netherlands 1900, and the League of Nations set up an additional Permanent Court of International Justice 1921 to deal with frontier disputes and the like. The latter was replaced 1945 with the International Court of Justice under the United Nations. Another arbiter is the European Court of Justice, which rules on disputes arising out of the Rome treaties regulating the European Community.

arboretum a collection of trees. An arboretum may have many species or just different varieties of one species, for example different types of pine tree.

Arbroath /ɑː'brəʊθ/ fishing town in Tayside, Scotland; population (1981) 24,100. In 1320 the Scottish Parliament asserted Scotland's independence here in a letter to the Pope.

Arbuckle /'ɑːbʌkəl/ (Roscoe Conkling) 'Fatty' 1887–1933. Big-framed US silent-film comedian, also a writer and director. His successful career in such films as *The Butcher Boy* 1917 and *The Hayseed* 1919 ended in 1921 after a sex-murder scandal. Although acquitted, he was spurned by the public and his films banned.

Arbuthnot /ɑː'bʌθnət/ John 1667–1735. Scottish physician, attendant on Queen Anne 1705–14. He was a friend of Pope, Gray, and Swift, and was the chief author of the satiric *Memoirs of Martinus Scriblerus*. He created the national character of John Bull, a prosperous farmer, in his *The History of John Bull* 1712, pamphlets advocating peace with France.

arbutus genus of evergreen shrubs, family Ericaceae. The strawberry tree *Arbutus unedo* is grown for its ornamental strawberry-like fruit.

arc in geometry, a section of a curve. A ◊circle has two kinds of arcs: an arc less than a semicircle is called a *minor arc*, and an arc greater than a semicircle is a *major arc*.

Arcadia /ɑː'keɪdɪə/ (Greek *Arkadhia*) central plateau of S Greece; area 4,419 sq km/1,706 sq mi; population (1981) 108,000. Tripolis is the capital town. Sir Philip ◊Sidney idealized the life of shepherds here in antiquity.

Arc de Triomphe /ˈɑːk də ˈtriːɒmf/ arch in the Place de l'Etoile, Paris, France, begun by Napoleon 1806 and completed 1836. It was intended to commemorate the French victories of 1805–06. Beneath it rests France's 'Unknown Soldier'.

Arc de Triomphe, Prix de L' French horse race run over 2,400 m/1.5 mi at Longchamp, near Paris. It is the most important 'open age' race in Europe, and one of the richest. It was first run 1920.

Arch /ɑːtʃ/ Joseph 1826–1919. English Radical Member of Parliament and trade unionist, founder of the National Agricultural Union (the first of its kind) 1872. He was born in Warwickshire, the son of an agricultural labourer. Entirely self-taught, he became a Methodist preacher, and was Liberal-Labour MP for NW Norfolk.

arch a curved structure consisting of several wedge-shaped stones or other hard blocks that are supported by their mutual pressure. The term is also applied to any curved structure that is an arch in form only.

Archaean or *Archaeozoic* earliest period of geological time; the first part of the Precambrian era, from the formation of Earth up to 2.5 billion years ago. Traces of life have recently been found in Archaean rocks.

archaebacteria three groups of bacteria whose DNA differs significantly from that of other bacteria (called the 'eubacteria'). All are strict anaerobes, that is, they are killed by oxygen. This is a primitive condition, and shows that the archaebacteria are related to the earliest life forms, which appeared about 4,000 million years ago, when there was little oxygen in the Earth's atmosphere.

archaeology the study of prehistory and ancient periods of history, based on the examination of physical remains.

history Interest in the physical remains of the past began in the Renaissance among dealers in and collectors of ancient art. It was further stimulated by discoveries made in Africa and Asia by Europeans during the period of imperialist colonization in the late 18th and 19th centuries, such as the antiquities discovered during Napoleon's Egyptian campaign in the 1790s. Towards the end of the 19th century archaeology became an academic study, making increasing use of scientific techniques and systematic methodologies.

methods Principal activities include preliminary field surveys, excavation (where necessary), and the classification, dating, and interpretation of finds. Related disciplines include stratigraphy (the study of geological strata), dendrochronology (the establishment of chronological sequences through the study of tree rings), palaeobotany (the study of ancient seeds and grains), epigraphy (the study of incriptions), and numismatics (the study of coins). Since 1948 radiocarbon dating has been used to establish the age of archaeological artefacts.

Archaeopteryx fossil from the limestone of Bavaria about 160 million years old, and popularly known as 'the first bird'. *Archaeopteryx* was about the size of a crow and had feathers and wings, but in many respects its skeleton is reptilian (long bony tail, teeth) and very like some small dinosaurs of the time.

Archangel /ˈɑːkeɪndʒəl/ (Russian *Arkhangelsk*) port in the northern USSR; population (1987) 416,000. It was made an open port by Boris Godunov and was of prime importance until Peter the Great built St Petersburg. It was used 1918–20 by the Allied interventionist armies in collaboration with the White Army in their effort to overthrow the newly established Soviet state. In World War II it was the receiving station for Anglo-American supplies. An open city in a closed area, it can be visited by foreigners only by air, and is a centre for ICBMs (intercontinental ballistic missiles). Although the port is blocked by ice during half the year, it is the chief timber-exporting port of the USSR.

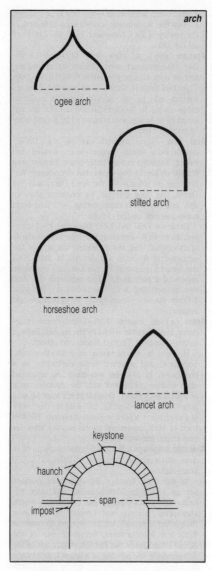

arch

ogee arch

stilted arch

horseshoe arch

lancet arch

keystone

haunch

impost

span

Plesetsk, to the south, is a launch site for crewed space flight.

archbishop in the Christian church, a bishop of superior rank, who has authority over other bishops in his jurisdiction and often over an ecclesiastical province. In the Church of England there are two archbishops––the archbishop of Canterbury ('Primate of All England') and the archbishop of York ('Primate of England').

archdeacon originally an ordained dignitary of the Christian church charged with the supervision of the deacons attached to a cathedral. Today in the Roman Catholic church the office is purely titular; in the Church of England an archdeacon still has many business duties, such as the periodic inspection of churches.

archegonium the female sex organ found in bryophytes (mosses and liverworts), pteridophytes (ferns and horsetails), and some gymnosperms. It is a multicellular, flask-shaped structure consisting of two parts: the swollen base or venter containing the egg cell, and the long, narrow neck. When the egg cell is mature the cells of the neck dissolve, allowing the passage of the male gametes, or ◊antherozoids.

Archer /ˈɑːtʃə/ Frederick 1857–1886. English jockey. He rode 2,748 winners in 8,084 races 1870–86, including 21 classic winners.

He won the Derby five times, Oaks four times, St Leger six times, the Two Thousand Guineas four times, and the One Thousand Guineas twice.

arch The Arch of Titus on Via Sacra in the Forum, Rome.

He rode 246 winners in the 1885 season, a record that stood until 1933 (see Gordon ◊Richards). Archer shot himself in a fit of depression.

CAREER HIGHLIGHTS

Derby: 1877, 1880, 1881, 1885, 1886
Oaks: 1875, 1878, 1879, 1885
St.Leger: 1877, 1878, 1881, 1882, 1885, 1886
2000 Guineas: 1874, 1879, 1883, 1885
1000 Guineas: 1875, 1879
Champion Jockey: 1874–86 (13 times)

Archer /ˈɑːtʃə/ Jeffrey 1940– . English writer and politician. A Conservative Member of Parliament 1969–74, he lost a fortune in a disastrous investment, but recouped it as a best-selling novelist. Works include *Not a Penny More, Not a Penny Less* 1975 and *First Among Equals* 1984. In 1985 he became deputy chair of the Conservative Party but resigned Nov 1986 after a scandal involving an alleged payment to a prostitute.

archerfish surface-living fish, genus *Toxotes*, living in brackish mangrove swamps of SE Asia and Australia. It grows to about 25 cm/10 in and is able to shoot down insects up to 1.5 m/5 ft above the water by spitting a water-jet from its mouth.

archery the use of the bow and arrow, originally in war and hunting; now a competitive sport.

Flint arrowheads have been found in very ancient archaeological deposits, and bowmen are depicted in the sculptures of Assyria and Egypt, and indeed all the nations of antiquity. The Japanese bow is larger and more sophisticated than the Western; its use is described in the medieval classic *Zen in the Art of Archery*. Until the introduction of gunpowder in the 14th century, bands of archers were to be found in every European army.

The English archers distinguished themselves in the French wars of the later Middle Ages; to this day the Queen's bodyguard in Scotland is known as the Royal Company of Archers. Up to the time of Charles II the practice of archery was fostered and encouraged by English rulers. Henry VIII in particular loved the sport and rewarded the scholar Roger ◊Ascham for his archery treatise *Toxophilus*. By the mid-17th century archery was no longer important in warfare and interest waned until the 1780s, although in the north of England shooting for the Scorton Arrow has been carried on, with few breaks, from 1673.

Organizations include the world governing body Fédération Internationale de Tir à l'Arc 1931; the British Grand National Archery Society 1861; and in the USA the National Archery Association 1879 and, for actual hunting with the bow, the National Field Archery Association 1940. In competitions, results are based on double FITA rounds, that is 72 arrows at each of four targets at 90, 70, 50, and 30 m (70, 60, 50, and 30 for women). The best possible score is 2,880.

Archimedes /ˌɑːkɪˈmiːdiːz/ c.287–212 BC. Greek mathematician, who made important discoveries in geometry, hydrostatics, and mechanics. He formulated a law of fluid displacement (Archimedes' principle), and is credited with the invention of the

archaeopteryx

wing structure of a flying reptile

wing structure of a bird

Archimedes screw

Archimedes screw, a cylindrical device for raising water.

He was born at Syracuse in Sicily. It is alleged that Archimedes' principle was discovered when he stepped into the public bath and saw the water overflow. He was so delighted that he rushed home naked, crying 'Eureka! Eureka!' ('I've got it! I've got it!') He used his discovery to prove that the goldsmith of the king of Syracuse had adulterated a gold crown with silver. The Archimedes screw is still used to raise water in the Nile delta. He designed engines of war for the defence of Syracuse, and was killed when the Romans besieged the town.

Archimedes' principle in physics, law stating that an object totally or partly submerged in a fluid displaces a volume of fluid that weighs the same as the apparent loss in weight of the object (which equals the upthrust on it).

If the weight of the object is less than the force exerted by the fluid, it will float partly or completely above the surface; if its weight is equal to the force, the object will come to equilibrium below the surface.

Archimedes screw one of the earliest kinds of pump, thought to have been invented by Archimedes. It consists of a spiral screw revolving inside a close-fitting cylinder. It is used, for example, to raise water for irrigation.

archipelago a group of islands, or an area of sea containing a group of islands. The islands of an archipelago are usually volcanic in origin, and they sometimes represent the tops of peaks in areas around continental margins flooded by the sea.

Volcanic islands are formed either when a hot spot within the Earth's mantle produces a chain of volcanoes on the surface, such as the Hawaiian Archipelago, or at a destructive plate margin (see ◊plate tectonics) where the subduction of one plate beneath another produces an arc-shaped island group, such as the Aleutian Archipelago. Novaya Zemlya in the Arctic Ocean, the northern extension of the Ural Mountains, resulted from continental flooding.

Archipenko /ˌɑːkɪˈpɛŋkəʊ/ Alexander 1887–1964. Russian-born abstract sculptor, who lived in France from 1908 and in the USA from 1923. He pioneered Cubist works composed of angular forms and spaces, and later experimented with clear plastic and sculptures incorporating lights.

architecture the art of building structures. The term covers the design of any structure for living or working in–houses, churches, temples, palaces, and castles – and also the style of building of any particular country at any period of history. Some theorists include under the term architecture only structures designed by a particular architect; others include so-called vernacular architecture: traditional buildings such as cottages and farms that have evolved slowly through the centuries but can claim no particular designer.

ancient architecture The earliest buildings were semi-permanent shelter structures, which began to appear during the Bronze Age: circular bases constructed of dry-stone walling, with thatched roofs. All over Europe, the same societies began to erect megaliths for religious reasons we can only guess at; Stonehenge (dating from about 2000 BC) is a fairly late example. However, it was in the Middle East 3000–1200 BC that the first civilization arose, the Babylonian, and with it the first examples of what we should call architecture. Ur was a walled city dominated by a ziggurat, a huge structure topped by a temple. The civilization of ancient Egypt provided the pyramids, massive symmetrical monuments with decorative sculptures and wall painting, and the first use of the decorated column and lintel to form colonnades. Examples include Karnak, Akhenaton, Abu Simbel, tombs of the Valley of the Kings, and the temple of Isis at Philae.

Greek and Roman Classical architecture as an art form really came into being with the Greeks, between the 16th and 2nd centuries BC. Their codification and use of the Classical orders – Doric, Ionic, and Corinthian–provided a legacy which, refined and modified by the Romans, has influenced all subsequent Western architecture. One great example of Greek architecture is the Parthenon. The Romans were the first to use bricks and cement to produce the vault, arch, and dome; they added the Tuscan and Composite orders to the Greek system. The emphasis in Roman architecture was on impressive public buildings (Colosseum), basilicas (Pantheon), triumphal arches and monuments (Trajan's Column), and aqueducts (Nîmes).

Byzantine In Byzantium a wholly Christian architecture was developed from the 4th century onwards, with churches based on the Greek cross plan (Hagia Sophia, Istanbul; St Mark's, Venice); they used formalized, symbolic painted and mosaic decoration.

archaeology

14th–16th century	The Renaissance revived interest in classical art.
1748	The Roman city of Pompeii was rediscovered.
1790	John Frere identified Old Stone Age tools and large extinct animals.
1822	Champollion deciphered Egyptian hieroglyphics.
1836	C J Thomsen devised the Stone, Bronze, and Iron Age classification.
1840s	Layard excavated the Assyrian capital Nineveh.
1868	Great Zimbabwe ruins first seen by Europeans.
1871	Schliemann began work at Troy.
1879	Stone Age paintings were first discovered at Altamira, Spain.
1880s	Pitt-Rivers developed the technique of stratification (identification of successive layers of soil with different archaeological periods).
1891	Petrie began excavating Akhetaton in Egypt.
1899–1935	A J Evans excavated Minoan Knossos in Crete.
1911	The Inca city of Machu Picchu discovered by Hiram Bingham .
1911–12	Piltdown skull 'discovered'; proved a fake 1949.
1914–18	Osbert Crawford developed the technique of aerial survey of sites.
1922	Tutankhamen's tomb in Egypt opened by Howard Carter.
1935	Dendrochronology (dating events in the distant past by counting tree rings) developed by A E Douglas.
1939	Anglo-Saxon ship-burial treasure found at Sutton Hoo, England.
1947	The first of the Dead Sea Scrolls discovered.
1948	Proconsul prehistoric ape discovered by Mary Leakey in Kenya.
1953	Ventris deciphered Minoan Linear B.
1960s	Radiocarbon dating and thermoluminescence developed.
1961	Swedish warship Wasa raised at Stockholm.
1963	W B Emery pioneered 'rescue archaeology' at Abu Simbel before flooding by the Aswan Dam.
1974	Tomb of Shi Huangdi discovered in China.
1978	Tomb of Philip II of Macedon (Alexander the Great's father) discovered in Greece.
1979	The Aztec capital Tenochtitlán excavated beneath Mexico City.
1982	The English king Henry VIII's warship Mary Rose raised.
1985	Work on wreck of the Dutch East Indiaman Amsterdam near Hastings, Sussex began. The tomb of Maya, Tutankhamen's treasurer, discovered at Saqqara, Egypt.
1988	Turin Shroud established as of medieval date by carbon dating.

Islamic In Spain, from the 7th century onwards, the Moorish occupation had a profound influence on Christian architecture, introducing the dome and the pointed arch (later incorporated into Gothic). Examples of influential Islamic buildings are the Great Mosque, Cordoba, and the Alhambra, Granada.

Romanesque The architecture of Western Christianity developed first as Romanesque, 8th to 12th centuries, is marked by rounded arches, solid volumes, and emphasis on perpendicular elements. In England, this was the period of Norman architecture (Durham Cathedral). Experiments in vaulting led into the Gothic period.

Gothic architecture developed in France in the 12th century and lasted until the 16th. It is characterized by the use of the rib vault, pointed arch, and flying buttress, particularly in religious buildings; there is an emphasis on the vertical, with galleries and arcades replacing internal walls. It is divided into Early Gothic (Sens Cathedral), High Gothic (Chartres Cathedral), and Late Gothic or Flamboyant. In England the corresponding divisions are Early English (Salisbury Cathedral), Decorated (Wells Cathedral), and Perpendicular (King's College Chapel, Cambridge).

Renaissance The 15th and 16th centuries saw the rebirth of Classical architecture in the Italian Neo-Classical movement, largely through the work of Vitruvius. Major Italian architects were Alberti, Brunelleschi, Bramante, Michelangelo, and Palladio; in England Palladianism was represented by Inigo Jones. A 16th-century offshoot was Mannerism, in which motifs were used for their manner rather than their meaning.

Baroque Architecture of the 17th and 18th centuries was exuberantly extravagant, and seen at its best in large-scale public buildings in the work of Bernini, Borromini, Vanbrugh, Hawksmoor, and Wren. Its last stage is the Rococo, characterized by still greater extravagance, a new lightness in style, and the use of naturalistic motifs such as shells, flowers, and trees.

Neo-Classical The 18th and 19th centuries returned to Classical principles, for example in the large-scale rebuilding of London and Paris by Adam, Nash, and Haussmann.

Neo-Gothic The later 19th century saw a Gothic revival, particularly evident in churches and public buildings (Houses of Parliament, London, C ◊Barry). *Art Nouveau* was a new movement arising at the end of the 19th century, characterized by sinuous, flowing shapes, informal room plans, and particular attention to interior as well as architectural design. The style is best seen in England in the work of Charles Rennie Mackintosh (Glasgow Art School) and in Spain by that of Antonio Gaudí.

Modernism An increasing emphasis on rationalism and reduction of ornament led to Modernism in the 1930s, also known as Functionalism or International Style, seeking to exclude everything that did not have a purpose, the latest technological advances in glass, steel, and concrete were used to full advantage. Major architects included Frank Lloyd Wright, Mies van der Rohe, Le Corbusier, and Alvar Aalto. *Town planning* also emerged as a discipline in its own right and whole new cities were planned, such as Le Corbusier's Chandigarh in India and Brasilia in Brazil.

Neo-Vernacular By the 1970s a reversion from the modern movement showed itself in a renewed enthusiasm for vernacular architecture (traditional local styles), to be seen in the work of, for instance, the British firm Darbourne and Darke.

Post-Modernism In the 1980s a *Post-Modernist* movement emerged, which split into two camps: *high tech*, represented in Britain by architects such as Norman Foster, Richard Rogers, and James Stirling (Hong Kong and Shanghai Bank, Lloyd's, *Staatsgalerie Stuttgart* respectively); and architects using elements from the architecture of previous times, either following

certain tenets of the Classical orders – Neo-Classicism yet again – such as Quinlan Terry, or using such elements at whim, such as Michael Graves.

archive a collection of historically valuable records, ranging from papers and documents to films, videotapes, and sound recordings.

The *National Register of Archives* (founded 1945) is in London; the *Public Record Office* (London and Kew) has documents of law and government departments from the Norman Conquest, including the ◊Domesday Book and ◊Magna Carta; the *National Portrait Gallery* has photographs, paintings, and sculptures; the *British Broadcasting Corporation Archives* have sound recordings, films, and videotapes, which form one of the world's largest collections; there is also a British National Film Archive.

archon (Greek 'ruler') in ancient Greece, title of the chief magistrate in many cities.

In Athens, there were originally three: the king archon, the eponymous archon, and the polemarch. Their numbers were later increased to nine, with the extra six keeping a record of judgements. The king archon was the elected king and religious representative of the State; the eponymous archon was the head of state and supreme judge; the polemarch was in charge of state security and commanded the army.

arc lamp an electric light that uses the illumination of an electric arc. Humphry Davy developed an arc lamp 1808, and its major use in recent years has been in cinema projectors. The lamp consists of two carbon electrodes, between which a very high voltage is maintained. Electric current arcs (jumps) between the two, creating a brilliant light.

The lamp incorporates a mechanism for automatically advancing the electrodes as they gradually burn away. Modern lamps have the electrodes enclosed in an inert gas such as xenon.

arc minute and **arc second** units for measuring small angles, used in geometry, surveying and map-making, and astronomy. An arc minute is one sixtieth of a degree, and an arc second one sixtieth of an arc minute. Small distances in the sky, as between two close stars or the apparent width of a planet's disc, are expressed in minutes and seconds of arc.

arco (Italian 'with the bow') cancels a previous instruction of a bowed string player to play *pizzicato*.

Arctic, the /ˈɑktɪk/ region north of the Arctic Circle. There is no Arctic continent, merely pack ice (which breaks into ice floes in summer) surrounding the Pole and floating on the Arctic Ocean. Pack ice is carried by the south-flowing current into the Atlantic Ocean as ◊icebergs. In winter the Sun disappears below the horizon for a time (and in summer, which only lasts up to two months, remains above it), but the cold is less severe than in parts of E Siberia or Antarctica. Land areas in the Arctic have mainly stunted tundra vegetation, with an outburst of summer flowers. Animals include reindeer, caribou, musk ox, fox, hare, lemming, wolf, polar bear, seal, and walrus. There are few birds, except in summer, when insects, especially mosquitoes, are plentiful. The aboriginal people are the ◊Inuit of the Alaskan/Canadian Arctic and Greenland. The most valuable resource is oil. The International Arctic Sciences Committee was established 1987 by the countries with Arctic coastlines to study ozone depletion and climatic change.

Arctic Circle an arbitrary line drawn around the North Pole at 66° 32 N.

Arctic Ocean ocean surrounding the North Pole; area 14,000,000 sq km/5,400,000 sq mi. Because of the Siberian and North American rivers flowing into it, it has comparatively low salinity and freezes readily. It comprises:

Beaufort Sea off Canada/Alaska coast, named after Francis ◊Beaufort; oil drilling is allowed only in winter because the sea is the breeding and migration route of the bowhead whales, staple diet of the local Inuit.

Greenland Sea between Greenland and Svalbard, and *Norwegian Sea* between Greenland and Norway. West to east along the north coast of the USSR:

Barents Sea named after Willem ◊Barents, which has oil and gas reserves and is strategically important as the meeting point of the NATO and Warsaw Pact forces. The ◊White Sea is its southernmost gulf.

Kara Sea renowned for bad weather, and known as the 'great ice cellar'.

Laptev Sea between Taimyr Peninsula and New Siberian Island.

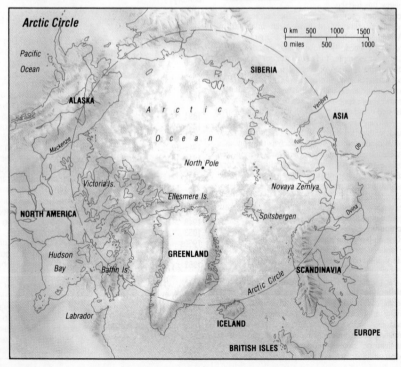

East Siberian Sea and **Chukchi Sea** between the USSR and the USA; the semi-nomadic Chukchi people of NE Siberia finally accepted Soviet rule only in the 1930s.

Arcturus brightest star in the constellation Bootes, and the fourth-brightest star in the sky. It is a red giant, 36 light years away.

Ardebil /ˌɑːdəˈbiːl/ town in NW Iran, near the Russian frontier; population (1983) 222,000. Ardebil exports dried fruits, carpets, and rugs.

Ardèche /ɑːˈdeʃ/ river in SE France, a tributary of the Rhône. Near Vallon it flows under the Pont d'Arc, a natural bridge. It gives its name to a *département*.

Arden /ˈɑːdn/ John 1930– . English playwright. His early plays *Serjeant Musgrave's Dance* 1959 and *The Workhouse Donkey* 1963 show the influence of Brecht. Subsequent works, often written in collaboration with his wife, Margaretta D'Arcy, show increasing concern with the political situation in Northern Ireland and a dissatisfaction with the professional and subsidized theatre world.

Arden, Forest of /ˈɑːdn/ former forest region of N Warwickshire, the setting for Shakespeare's *As You Like It.*

Ardennes /ɑːˈden/ wooded plateau in NE France, SE Belgium, and N Luxembourg, cut through by the river Meuse; also a *département* of ◊Champagne-Ardenne. There was heavy fighting here in World War I and World War II (see ◊Bulge, Battle of the).

are metric unit of area, equal to 100 square metres. 100 ares make one ◊hectare.

area a measure of surface. The SI unit of area is the metre squared.

areca genus of palms. The ◊betel nut comes from the species *Areca catechu.*

Arecibo /ˌærɪˈsiːbəʊ/ site in Puerto Rico of the world's largest single-dish ◊radio telescope, 305 m/1,000 ft in diameter. It is built in a natural hollow, and uses the rotation of the Earth to scan the sky. It has been used both for radar work on the planets and for conventional radio-astronomy, and is operated by Cornell University, USA.

Arequipa /ˌærɪˈkiːpə/ city in Peru at the base of the volcano El Misti; population (1988) 592,000. Founded by Pizarro 1540, it is the cultural focus of S Peru, and a busy commercial (soap, textiles) centre.

Ares /ˈeəriːz/ in Greek mythology, the god of war (Roman ◊Mars). The son of Zeus and Hera, he was worshipped chiefly in Thrace.

arête a sharp narrow ridge separating two ◊glacier valleys (a French term; in the USA often called a *combe-ridge*; in German a *grat*). The typical U-shaped cross sections of glacier valleys give arêtes very steep sides. Arêtes are common in glaciated mountain regions such as the Rockies, the Himalayas, and the Alps.

Arethusa /ˌærɪˈθjuːzə/ in Greek mythology, a nymph of the fountain and spring of Arethusa in the island of Ortygia near Syracuse, on the S coast of Sicily.

Aretino /ˌærəˈtiːnəʊ/ Pietro 1492–1556. Italian writer, born in Arezzo. He earned his living, both in Rome and Venice, by publishing satirical pamphlets while under the protection of a highly placed family. His *Letters* 1537–57 are a unique record of the cultural and political events of his time, and illustrate his vivacious, exuberant character. He also wrote poems and comedies.

Aretino began as a protégé of Pope Leo X, but left Rome after the publication of his lewd verses. He settled in Venice, and quickly became known as the 'Scourge of Princes' with his vicious satires on powerful contemporaries; he was also well paid for not taking up his pen.

Arezzo /əˈretsəʊ/ town in the Tuscan region of Italy; 80 km/50 mi SE of Florence; population (1981) 92,100. The writers Petrarch and Aretino were born here. It is a mining town and also trades in textiles, olive oil, and antiques.

architecture

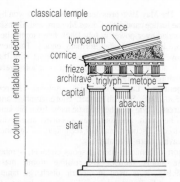

the orders of classical architecture

Gothic arch — mouldings — corbel — spandrel — spring of arch — capital — column — base

Tuscan
Doric
Ionic
Corinthian
Composite

entablature — capital — shaft — base

classical temple

entablature — pediment — cornice — tympanum — cornice — frieze — architrave — triglyph — metope — capital — abacus — column — shaft

argali wild sheep *Ovis ammon* of Central Asia. The male can grow to 1.2 m/4 ft at the shoulder, and has massive spiral horns.

Argand diagram a method for representing complex numbers by cartesian co-ordinates (x, y). The x axis represents the real numbers, and the y axis the non-real, or 'imaginary', numbers.

Argenteuil /ˌɑːʒɒnˈtɜːi/ NW suburb of Paris, France, on the Seine; population (1982) 96,045.

Argentina /ˌɑːdʒənˈtiːnə/ country in South America, bounded by Chile to the south and west, Bolivia to the northwest, and Paraguay, Brazil, Uruguay, and the Atlantic Ocean to the east.

government the return to civilian rule in 1983 brought a return to the 1853 constitution, with some changes in the electoral system. The constitution created a federal system with a president elected by popular vote through an electoral college, serving a six-year term. The president is head of both state and government, and chooses the cabinet.

Argentina is a federal union of 22 provinces, one national territory and the Federal District. The two-chamber Congress consists of a 46-member senate chosen by provincial legislatures for a nine-year term, and a directly elected chamber of 254 deputies serving a four-year term. Each province has its own elected governor and legislature, dealing with matters not assigned to the federal government. The two most significant parties are the Radical Union Party (UCR), and the Justice Party.

history originally inhabited by various South American Indian peoples, Argentina was first visited by Europeans in the early 16th century. Buenos Aires was founded first in 1536 and again in 1580 after being abandoned because of Indian attacks. Made a Spanish viceroyalty in 1776, Argentina achieved full independence in 1816, and developed as a democracy with active political parties. Since 1930 it has been subject to alternate civilian and military rule. The UCR held power from 1916 until the first military coup in 1930.

Civilian government returned in 1932 and a second military coup in 1943 paved the way for the rise of Lieutenant-General Juan Domingo Perón. Strengthened by the popularity of his wife, Eva Duarte Perón, the legendary 'Evita', Perón created the Peronista party, based on extreme nationalism and social improvement. Evita Perón died in 1952 and in 1955 her husband was overthrown and civilian rule restored. Perón continued to direct the Peronista movement from exile in Spain.

A coup in 1966 restored military rule and in 1973 the success of the Peronist party, Frente Justicialista de Liberación, brought Dr Héctor Campora to the presidency. After three months he resigned to make way for Perón, with his third wife, Maria Estela Martinez de Perón, 'Isabelita', as vice-president. Perón died in 1974 and was succeeded by his widow. Two years later, because of concern about the economy, a military coup ousted her and installed a three-man junta, led by Lieutenant-General Jorge Videla. The constitution was amended, political and trade union activity banned and several hundred people arrested.

The years 1976–83 witnessed a ferocious campaign by the junta against left-wing elements, the 'dirty war', during which it is believed that between 6,000 and 15,000 people 'disappeared'. Political activity was banned 1976–80. Although confirmed in office until 1981, in 1978 Videla retired, to be succeeded by General Roberto Viola, who promised a return to democracy. In 1981 Viola died and was replaced by General Leopoldo Galtieri.

In 1982 Galtieri, seeking popular support and wishing to distract attention from the deteriorating economy, ordered the invasion of the Islas Malvinas, the ◊Falkland Islands, over which Britain's claim to sovereignty had long been disputed. After a short war, during which 750 Argentinians were killed, the islands were reoccupied by Britain. US support for Britain pushed Argentina closer to Cuba, Nicaragua and the ◊non-aligned states.

With the failure of the Falklands invasion, Galtieri was replaced in a bloodless coup by General Reynaldo Bignone. A military inquiry reported in 1983 that Galtieri's junta was to blame for the defeat. Several officers were tried and

Argentina
Republic of
(*República Argentina*)

area 2,780,092 sq km/1,073,116 sq mi
capital Buenos Aires
towns Rosario, Córdoba, Tucumán, Mendoza, Santa Fé; ports are La Plata and Bahïa Blanca
physical mountains in the W, forest in the N and E, pampas (treeless plains) in the central area; rivers Colorado, Paraná, Uruguay, Rio de la Plata estuary
territories Tierra del Fuego; disputed claims to S Atlantic islands; part of Antarctica
features Andes, with Aconcagua the highest peak in the W hemisphere
head of state and government Carlos Menem from 1989
political system emergent democratic federal republic
political parties Radical Union Party (UCR), moderate centrist; Justice Party, right-wing Peronist
exports beef, livestock, cereals, wool, tannin, groundnuts, linseed oil, minerals (coal, copper, molybdenum, gold, silver, lead, zinc, barium, uranium), and the country has huge resources of oil, natural gas, hydroelectric power
currency austral (7,203.85 = £1 Feb 1990)
population (1986) 31,060,000 (mainly of Spanish or Italian origin, only about 30,000 American Indians surviving); annual growth rate 1.6%
life expectancy men 66, women 73
language Spanish
religion Roman Catholic (state-supported)
literacy 96% male/95% female (1985 est)
GDP $58 bn (1983); $2,350 per head of population
chronology
1816 Achieved independence from Spain, followed by civil wars.
1946 Juan Perón elected president, supported by his wife 'Evita'.
1952 'Evita' Perón died.
1955 Perón overthrown and civilian administration restored.
1966 Coup brought back military rule.
1973 The Perónist party won the presidential and congressional elections. Perón returned from exile in Spain as president, with his third wife, 'Isabelita', as vice-president.
1974 Perón died, succeeded by 'Isabelita'.
1976 Coup resulted in rule by a military junta led by Lt-Gen Jorge Videla. Congress dissolved and hundreds of people, including 'Isabelita' Perón, detained.
1976–78 Ferocious campaign against left-wing elements. The start of the 'dirty war'.
1978 Videla retired. Succeeded by Gen Roberto Viola, who promised a return to democracy.
1981 Viola died suddenly. Replaced by Gen Leopoldo Galtieri.
1982 With a deteriorating economy, Galtieri sought popular support by ordering an invasion of the British-held Falkland Islands. After losing the short war, Galtieri was removed and replaced by Gen Reynaldo Bignone.
1983 Amnesty law passed and 1853 democratic constitution revived. General elections won by Dr Raúl Alfonsín and his party. Armed forces under scrutiny.
1984 Commission on the Disappearance of Persons (CONADEP) reported on over 8,000 people who had disappeared during the 'dirty war' of 1976–83.
1985 A deteriorating economy forced Alfonsín to seek help from the IMF and introduce a harsh austerity programme.
1986 Unsuccessful attempt on Alfonsín's life.
1988 Unsuccessful army coup attempt.
1989 Carlos Menem, of the Justice Party, elected president. Pressure put on Alfonsín to hand over power before Dec 1989. 30-day state of emergency declared after rioting following price measures and dramatic inflation, 120% in June; annual rate in 1989 4,923%.
1990 Full diplomatic relations with the UK restored.

some, including Galtieri, given prison sentences. It was announced that the 1853 constitution would be revived and an amnesty was granted to all convicted of political crimes over the past ten years. The ban on political and trade union activity was lifted and general elections were held in Oct 1983. The main parties were the UCR, led by Dr Raúl Alfonsín, and the Peronist Justice Party, led by Dr Italo Luder.

Having won the election, Alfonsín announced radical reforms in the armed forces, leading to the retirement of more than half the senior officers, and the trial of the first three military juntas which had ruled Argentina since 1976. He set up the National Commission on the Disappearance of Persons (CONADEP) to investigate the 'dirty war' between 1976 and 1983. A report by CONADEP in 1984 listed over 8,000 people who had disappeared and 1,300 army officers who had been involved in the campaign of repression.

Alfonsín's government was soon faced with huge economic problems, resulting in recourse to help from the ◊IMF and an austerity programme, described by the president as an 'economy of war'.

The May 1989 presidential election was won by the Justice candidate, Carlos Menem, and Alfonsín handed over power in July 1989, five months before his term of office formally ended. The new government soon established a rapport with the UK authorities and full diplomatic relations were restored Feb 1990.

Argentina, La /ɑːˈxenˈtiːnə/ Antonia Merce 1890–1936. Spanish dancer, choreographer, and director. She took her artistic name from the land of her birth. She toured as a concert artist with Vicente Escudero and her techniques of castanet playing were revolutionary.

argon a chemically inert gaseous element, symbol Ar, atomic number 18, relative atomic mass 39.944. It is used in electric discharge lamps (see ◊discharge tube) and in argon lasers. It was discovered in air by Rayleigh and Ramsay after all oxygen and nitrogen had been removed chemically.

argonaut type of pelagic octopus, genus *Argonauta*. The 20 cm/8 in female secretes a papery shell from the web of the first pair of arms, hence the alternative name 'paper nautilus'. The male is a 1 cm/0.4 in shell-less dwarf. 'Argonaut' sometimes refers to the ◊nautilus.

Argonauts in Greek legend, the band of heroes who accompanied ◊Jason when he set sail in the *Argo* to fetch the ◊Golden Fleece.

Argonne /ɑːˈgɒn/ wooded plateau in NE France, separating Lorraine and Champagne. It was the scene of much fighting in both world wars.

Argos /ˈɑːgɒs/ city in ancient Greece, at the head of the Gulf of Nauplia, which was once a cult centre of the goddess Hera. In the Homeric age the name 'Argives' was sometimes used instead of 'Greeks'.

argument in mathematics, a specific value of the independent variable of a ◊function of x. Argument is also the name given to the angle Θ between the position vector of a ◊complex number and the limb of the real axis, usually written arg z for the complex number $z = r(cos\ \Theta + i\ sin\ \Theta)$.

argument from design a line of reasoning, argued by Bishop William Paley in 1794, that the universe is so complex that it can only have been designed by a superhuman power; and that we can learn something of that superhuman power (God) by examining how the world is. The argument from design became popular with Protestant theologians in the 18th century as a means of accommodating Newtonian science. It was attacked by David ◊Hume, among others.

Argus /ˈɑːgəs/ in Greek mythology, a giant with a hundred eyes. When he was killed by Hermes, Hera transplanted his eyes into the tail of her favourite bird, the peacock.

Argyll /ɑːˈgaɪl/ line of Scottish peers who trace their descent to the Campbells of Lochow. The earldom dates from 1457. They include:

Argyll Archibald Campbell, 5th Earl of, 1530–1573. Adherent of the Scottish presbyterian, John ◊Knox. A supporter of Mary Queen of Scots from 1561 on her return from France, he commanded her forces during the days following her escape from Lochleven Castle in 1568. He revised his position and became Lord High Chancellor of Scotland in 1572.

Argyllshire /ɑːˈgaɪlʃə/ former county on the W coast of Scotland, including many of the Western Isles, which was for the most part merged in Strathclyde region 1975, although a small area to the NW including Ballachulish, Ardgour, and Kingairloch went to the Highland region.

Århus /ˈɔːhuːs/ alternative form of ◊Aarhus, Denmark.

aria (Italian 'air') solo vocal piece in an opera or oratorio, often in three sections, the third repeating the first after a contrasting central section.

Ariadne /ˌæriˈædni/ in Greek mythology, the daughter of Minos, king of Crete. When Theseus came from Athens as one of the sacrificial victims offered to the Minotaur, she fell in love with him and gave him a ball of thread which enabled him to find his way out of the labyrinth.

Ariane /ˌæriˈæn/ a series of launch vehicles built by the European Space Agency to place satellites into Earth orbit (first flight 1979). The launch site is at Kourou in French Guiana.

Ariane is a three-stage rocket using liquid fuels, but small solid-fuel boosters can be attached to its first stage to increase carrying power. Since 1984 it has been operated commercially by Arianespace, a private company financed by European banks and aerospace industries. Future versions of Ariane may carry astronauts.

Arianism a system of Christian theology which denied the complete divinity of Jesus. It was founded about 310 by ◊Arius, and condemned as heretical at the Council of Nicaea 325.

Some 17th- and 18th-century theologians held Arian views akin to those of ◊Unitarianism (that God is a single being, and that there is no such thing as the Trinity). In 1979 the heresy again caused concern to the Vatican in the writings of such theologians as Edouard Schillebeeckx of Nijmegen University, the Netherlands.

Arias Sanchez /ˈɑːriəs ˈsæntʃes/ Oscar 1940–. Costa Rican politician, president from 1986.

Secretary-general of the left-wing National Liberation Party (PLN). He advocated a neutralist policy and in 1987 was the leading promoter of the Central American Peace Plan (see ◊Nicaragua)

Arica /ə'riːkə/ port in Chile; population (1987) 170,000. Much of Bolivia's trade passes through it, and there is contention over the use of Arica by Bolivia to allow access to the Pacific Ocean. It is Chile's most northerly city.

It is on a rainless coastline. It was several times devastated by earthquake, and was razed 1880 when captured by Chile from Peru.

arid zone infertile area with a small, infrequent rainfall that rapidly evaporates because of high temperatures. There are arid zones in Morocco, Pakistan, Australia, USA, and elsewhere.

Scarcity of water is a problem for the inhabitants of arid zones, and constant research goes into discovering cheap methods of distilling sea water and artificially recharging natural groundwater reservoirs. Another problem is the eradication of salt in irrigation supplies from underground sources or where a surface deposit forms in poorly drained areas.

Ariège /ˌæri'eɪʒ/ river in southern France, a tributary of the Garonne. It gives its name to a *département*.

Aries a zodiac constellation, in the northern hemisphere near Auriga, seen as representing the legendary ram whose golden fleece was sought by Jason and the Argonauts. Its most distinctive feature is a curve of three stars of decreasing brightness. The Sun passes through Aries from late Apr to mid-May. In *astrology*, the dates for Aries are between about 21 Mar and 19 Apr (see ◊precession).

The spring ◊equinox once lay in Aries, but has now moved into Pisces through the effect of the Earth's precession (wobble).

aril an accessory seed cover other than a ◊fruit; it may be fleshy and sometimes brightly coloured, woody, or hairy. In flowering plants (◊angiosperms) it is often derived from the stalk originally attached the ovule to the ovary wall. Examples of arils include the bright-red, fleshy layer surrounding the yew seed (yews are ◊gymnosperms, so they lack true fruits), and the network of hard filaments that partially covers the nutmeg seed; and yields the spice known as mace.

Another aril, the horny outgrowth found towards one end of the seed of the castor-oil plant (*Ricinus communis*), is called a caruncle. It is formed from the integuments (protective layers enclosing the ovule) and develops after fertilization.

Ariosto /ˌæri'ɒstəʊ/ Ludovico 1474–1533. Italian poet, born in Reggio. He wrote Latin poems and comedies on Classical lines, including, the epic poem ◊*Orlando Furioso* 1516, 1532.

Ariosto joined the household of Cardinal Ippolito d'Este 1503, and was frequently engaged in embassies and diplomacy for the Duke of Ferrara. In 1521 he became governor of a province in the Apennines, and after three years retired to Ferrara, where he died.

Aristarchus of Samos /ˌæri'staːkəs/ c.310–264 BC. Greek astronomer. The first to argue that the Earth moves round the Sun, he was ridiculed for his beliefs.

Aristides /ˌæri'staɪdiːz/ c. 530–468 BC. Athenian politician. He was one of the ten Athenian generals at the battle of ◊Marathon 490 BC and was elected chief Archon, or magistrate. Later he came into conflict with the democratic leader Themistocles, and was exiled about 483 BC. He returned to fight against the Persians at Salamis 480 BC and in the following year, commanded the Athenians at Plataea.

He was sent into political exile 482 BC because the citizens tired of hearing him praised as 'Aristides the Just', probably derived from his just assessment of the contribution to be paid by the Greek states who entered the Delian league against the Persians.

Aristippus /ˌæri'stɪpəs/ c. 435–356 BC. Greek philosopher, founder of the ◊Cyrenaic or ◊hedonist school. A pupil of Socrates, he developed the doctrine that pleasure is the only good in life. He lived at the court of ◊Dionysius of Syracuse, and then with his mistress Laïs, the courtesan, at Corinth.

Aristophanes /ˌæri'stɒfəniːz/ c.448–380 BC. Greek dramatist. Of his 11 extant plays (of a total of over 40), the early comedies are remarkable for the violent satire with which he ridiculed the democratic war leaders. He also satirized contemporary issues such as the new learning of Socrates in *The Clouds* 423, and the power of women in ◊*Lysistrata* 411. The chorus plays a prominent role, frequently giving the play its title, as in *The Wasps* 422, *The Birds* 414, and *The Frogs* 405.

Aristotle /'æristɒtl/ 384–322 BC. Greek philosopher, who advocated reason and moderation. Aristotle maintained that sense experience is our only source of knowledge, and that by reasoning we can discover the essences of things, that is, their distinguishing qualities. In his works on ethics and politics, Aristotle suggested that human happiness consists in living in conformity with nature. He derived his political theory from the recognition that mutual aid is natural to humankind, and refused to set up any one constitution as universally ideal. Of Aristotle's works some 22 treatises survive, dealing with logic, metaphysics, physics, astronomy, meteorology, biology, psychology, ethics, politics, and literary criticism.

Born in Stagira in Thrace, he studied in Athens, became tutor to ◊Alexander the Great, and in 335 opened a school in the Lyceum (grove sacred to Apollo) in Athens. It became known as the 'peripatetic school' because he walked up and down as he talked and his works are a collection of his lecture notes. When Alexander died, Aristotle was forced to flee to Chalcis, where he died.

In the Middle Ages, Aristotle's philosophy first became the foundation of Islamic philosophy, and was then incorporated into Christian theology; medieval scholars tended to accept his vast output without question. Aristotle held that all matter consisted of a single 'prime matter', which was always determined by some form. The simplest kinds of matter were the four elements: earth, water, air, and fire, which in varying proportions constituted all things. Aristotle saw nature as always striving to perfect itself, and first classified organisms into species and genera.

The principle of life he termed a soul, which he regarded as the form of the living creature, not as a substance separable from it. The intellect, he believed, can discover in sense impressions the universal, and since the soul thus transcends matter, it must be immortal. Art embodies nature, but in a more perfect fashion, its end being the purifying and ennobling of the affections. The essence of beauty is order and symmetry. He is sometimes referred to as 'the Stagirite', after his birthplace.

arithmetic branch of mathematics involving the study of numbers. The fundamental operations of arithmetic are addition, subtraction, multiplication, division, and, dependent on these four, raising to ◊powers and extraction of roots. Percentages, fractions, and ratio are developed from these operations. Fractions arise in the process of measurement.

Forms of simple arithmetic existed in prehistoric times. In China, Egypt, Babylon, and early civilizations generally, arithmetic was used for commercial purposes, for records of taxation, and for astronomy. During the Dark Ages in Europe, knowledge of arithmetic was preserved in India and later among the Arabs. European mathematics revived with the development of trade and overseas exploration. Hindu-Arabic numerals replaced Roman numerals, allowing calculations to be made on paper, instead of by the ◊abacus.

The essential feature of this number system was the introduction of zero, which allows us to

have a **place-value** system. The decimal numeral system employs ten numerals (0123456789) and therefore operates in 'base ten'. In a base-ten number, each position has a value ten times that of the position to its immediate right: for example, in the number 23 the numeral 3 represents three units (ones), and the number 2 represents two tens. The Babylonians, however, used a complex base-sixty system, residues of which are found today in the number of minutes in each hour and in angular measurement (6 × 60 degrees). The Mayas used a base-twenty system.

There have been many inventions and developments to make the manipulation of the arithmetic processes easier, such as the invention of ◊logarithms by ◊Napier in 1614 and of the slide rule in the period 1620–30. Since then there have been many forms of ready reckoners invented, mechanical and electronic calculators and computers.

Modern computers fundamentally operate in base two, using only two numerals (0,1), known as a binary system. In binary, each position has a value twice as great as the position to its immediate right, so that for example binary 111 is equal to 7 in the decimal system, and 1111 is equal to 15. Because the main operations of subtraction, multiplication, and division can be reduced mathematically to addition, digital computers carry out calculations by adding, usually in binary numbers in which the numerals 0 and 1 can be represented by off and on pulses of electric current.

Modular arithmetic, sometimes known as residue arithmetic, can only take a specific number of digits whatever the value. For example, in modular 4 system, the only values any number can take is 0,1,2,3. 7 is 3 mod 4, and 35 is 3 mod 4. Notice 3 is the residue when 7 or 35 is divided by 4. This form of arithmetic is often illustrated on a circle. It deals with events recurring in regular cycles, and is used in describing the functioning of petrol engines, electrical generators, and so on. For example, in the modulo-twelve system, the answer to a question as to what time it will be in five hours if it is now ten o'clock, can be expressed 10+5=3.

arithmetic sequence/progression/series sequence of numbers or terms that have a common difference between any one term and the next in the sequence. For example, 2, 7, 12, 17, 22, 27, ... is an arithmetic sequence with a common difference of 5. The general formula for the nth term is $a + (n - 1)d$, where a is the first term and d is the common difference. The sum s of n terms is: $s = n/2\ [2a + (n - 1)d]$.

Arius /'eəriəs/ c. 256–336. Egyptian priest whose ideas gave rise to ◊Arianism, a Christian belief which denied the complete divinity of Jesus. He was condemned at the Council of Nicaea 325.

He was born in Libya, and became a priest of Alexandria 311. In 318 he was excommunicated and fled to Palestine, but his theology spread to such an extent that the emperor Constantine called a council at Nicaea to resolve the question. Arius and his adherents were banished, though later he was allowed to return.

Arizona /ˌæri'zəʊnə/ state in SW USA; nickname Grand Canyon State
area 294,100 sq km/113,523 sq mi
capital Phoenix

towns Tucson, Scottsdale, Tempe, Mesa, Glendale, Flagstaff

physical Colorado Plateau in the north and east, desert basins and mountains in the south and west; Colorado River; Grand Canyon

features Grand Canyon National Park (the multicoloured gorge through which the Colorado flows, 6–29 km/4–18 mi wide, up to 1.5 km/1 mi deep and 350 km/217 mi long), the Painted Desert (including the Petrified Forest of fossil trees), Organ Pipe Cactus National Monument Park, Gila Desert, and Sonoran Desert; Roosevelt and Hoover dams; old London Bridge was transported 1971 to the tourist resort of Lake Havasu City

products cotton under irrigation, livestock, copper, molybdenum, silver, electronics, aircraft

population (1987) 3,469,000 including over 150,000 American Indians (Navajo, Hopi, Apache), who still own a quarter of the state

famous people Geronimo, Barry Goldwater, Zane Grey, Percival Lowell, Frank Lloyd Wright

history part of New Spain 1715; part of Mexico 1824; passed to USA after Mexican War 1848; territory 1863; state 1912.

Arizona is believed to derive its name from the Spanish *arida-zona* (dry belt). The first Spaniard to visit Arizona was the Franciscan Marcos de Niza 1539. After 1863, it developed rapidly as a result of the gold rush in neighbouring California. Irrigation has been carried out since the 1920s on a colossal scale. The Roosevelt Dam on the Salt River and the Hoover Dam on the Colorado, between Arizona and Nevada, provide the state with both hydroelectric power and irrigation water. At the end of the 19th century rich copper deposits were found in Arizona and subsequently deposits of many other minerals.

Arjan Indian religious leader, fifth guru (teacher) of Sikhism from 1581. He built the Golden Temple in ◊Amritsar and compiled the *Adi Granth*, the first volume of Sikh scriptures. He died in Muslim custody.

Arjuna Indian prince, one of the two main characters in the Hindu epic *Mahābhārata*.

Arkansas /ˈɑːkənsɔː/ state in S central USA; nickname Wonder State/Land of Opportunity

area 137,800 sq km/53,191 sq mi

capital Little Rock

towns Fort Smith, Pine Bluff, Fayetteville

physical Ozark mountains in the west; lowlands in the east; Arkansas River; many lakes

features Hot Springs National Park

products cotton, soya beans, rice, oil, natural gas, bauxite, timber, processed foods

population (1986) 2,372,000

famous people Douglas MacArthur

history explored by de Soto 1541; European settlers 1648, who traded with local Indians; part of Louisiana Purchase 1803; state 1836.

The first European settlement was Arkansas Post, founded by some of the companions of the French explorer La Salle. After seceding from the Union 1861 (see ◊Confederacy), Arizona was readmitted 1886.

Ark of the Covenant in the Old Testament or Hebrew Bible, the chest which contained the Tablets of the Law as given to Moses. It is also the cupboard in a synagogue in which the ◊Torah scrolls are kept.

Arkansas

Little Rock

Arkwright *The inventor Richard Arkwright, painted at the studio of Joseph Wright in 1790.*

Arkwright /ˈɑːkraɪt/ Richard 1732–1792. English inventor and manufacturing pioneer. He developed a machine for spinning cotton, the 'spinning frame' in Preston, Lancashire 1768. He installed steam power in his Nottingham works 1790.

Arkwright was born in Preston and experimented in machine-designing with a watchmaker, John Kay of Warrington, until, with Kay and John Smalley, he set up the 'spinning frame'. Soon afterwards he moved to Nottingham to escape the fury of the spinners, who feared that their handicraft skills would become redundant. In 1771 he went into partnership with Jedediah Strutt, a Derby man who had improved the stocking frame, and Samuel Need, and built a water-powered factory at Cromford in Derbyshire.

Arlen /ˈɑːlən/ Michael. Adopted name of Dikran Kuyumjian 1895–1956. Bulgarian novelist of Armenian descent, who became a naturalized British subject 1922. His greatest success was the cynical *The Green Hat* 1924, the story of a *femme fatale*. He died in New York.

Arles /ɑːl/ town in Bouches-du-Rhône *département*, SE France, on the left bank of the Rhône; population (1982) 50,772. It is a great fruit- and vine-growing district. Roman relics include an amphitheatre for 25,000 spectators. The cathedral of St Trophime is a notable Romanesque structure. The painters Van Gogh and Gauguin lived here 1888.

Arlington /ˈɑːlɪŋtən/ town in Virginia, USA, and suburb of Washington DC. It is the site of the National Cemetery for the dead of the United States wars. The grounds were first used as a military cemetery in 1864 during the US Civil War. By 1975, 165,142 military, naval, and civilian persons had been buried there, including the ◊Unknown Soldier of both World Wars, President J F Kennedy and his brother Robert Kennedy.

Armada fleet sent by Philip II of Spain against England 1588. See ◊Spanish Armada.

armadillo

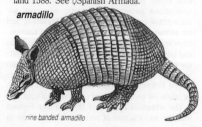

nine banded armadillo

armadillo mammal with an armour of bony plates on its back. Some 20 species live between Texas and Patagonia and range in size from the fairy armadillo at 13 cm/5 in to the giant armadillo, 1.5 m/4.5 ft long. They feed on insects, fruit, and carrion. Some can roll into an armoured ball if attacked; others rely on burrowing for protection.

They belong, with sloths and anteaters, to a group termed edentates (without teeth); nevertheless, armadillos can have up to 90 peg like teeth.

Armageddon in the New Testament (Revelation 16), the site of the final battle between the nations which will end the world; it has been identified with ◊Megiddo in Israel.

Armagh /ɑːˈmɑː/ county of Northern Ireland

area 1,250 sq km/483 sq mi

towns county town Armagh; Lurgan, Portadown, Keady

physical flat in the north, with many bogs; low hills in the south; Lough Neagh

features smallest county of Northern Ireland. There are crops in the better drained parts, especially flax. The chief rivers are the Bann and Blackwater, flowing into Lough Neagh, and the Callan tributary of the Blackwater

products chiefly agricultural: apples, potatoes, flax

population (1981) 119,000.

Armagh /ɑːˈmɑː/ county town of Armagh, Northern Ireland; population (1981) 13,000. It became the religious centre of Ireland in the 5th century when St Patrick was made archbishop. For 700 years, it was the seat of the Kings of Ulster. The Protestant Archbishop of Armagh is nominally 'Primate of All Ireland'.

Armagnac /ˈɑːmənjæk/ a deep-coloured brandy named for the former province in S France where it is produced.

armature in a motor or dynamo, the wire-wound coil which carries the current and rotates in a magnetic field. It is also the name given to the pole-piece of a permanent magnet or electromagnet. The moving, iron part of a solenoid, especially if it acts as a switch, may also be referred to as an armature.

Armenia /ɑːˈmiːniə/ constituent republic of the Soviet Union from 1936

area 29,800 sq km/11,506 sq mi

capital Yerevan

towns Leninakan

physical mainly mountainous (including Mt Ararat), wooded

products copper, molybdenum, cereals, cotton, silk

population (1987) 3,412,000; 90% Armenian, 5% Azerbaijani, Russian 2%, Kurd 2%

language Armenian

religion traditionally Armenian Christian

history an ancient kingdom formerly occupying what is now the Van region of Turkey, part of NW Iran, and what is now the Armenian republic, it became an independent republic 1918, was occupied by the Red Army 1920, and became a constituent republic of the USSR 1936. In 1988

Armenia

Yerevan

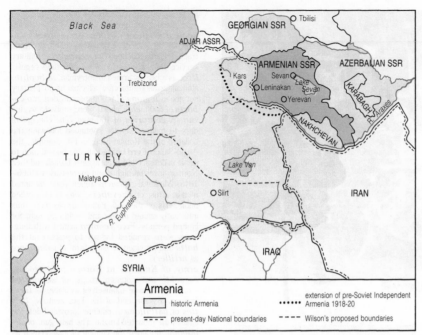

Armenia

☐ historic Armenia

‑ ‑ ‑ present-day National boundaries

•••• extension of pre-Soviet Independent Armenia 1918-20

‑ ‑ ‑ ‑ Wilson's proposed boundaries

demands for reunion with Nagorno-karabakh led to riots, strikes and, eventually during 1989-90, to a civil war that had to be quelled though the intervention of Soviet troops. The Armenian national Movement, which was formed in Nov 1989, has been at the fore of this nationalist campaign. An earthquake 1988 caused extensive loss of life and property.

Armenian church the form of Christianity adopted in Armenia in the 3rd century. The Catholicos, or exarch, is the supreme head, and Echmiadzin, near Yerevan, is his traditional seat.

About 295 Gregory the Illuminator (c. 257–332) was made exarch of the Armenian church, which has developed along national lines. The Seven Sacraments, or Mysteries, are administered, baptism being immediately followed by confirmation. Believers number about 2 million.

Armenian language one of the main divisions of the Indo-European language family. Old Armenian, the classic literary language, is still used in the liturgy of the Armenian church. Contemporary Armenian, with modified grammar and enriched with words from other languages, is used by a group of 20th-century writers.

Armenian was not written down until the 5th century AD, when an alphabet of 36 (now 38) letters was evolved. Literature flourished in the 4th–14th centuries, revived in the 18th.

Armenian massacres series of massacres of Armenians by Turkish soldiers between 1895 and 1915. Reforms promised to Armenian Christians by Turkish rulers never materialized; unrest broke out and there were massacres by Turkish troops 1895. Again in 1909 and 1915, the Turks massacred altogether more than a million Armenians, and deported others into the N Syrian desert, where they died of starvation; those who could fled to Russia or Persia, and only some 100,000 were left.

Armentières /ˌɑːmənti'eə/ town in N France on the Lys river; population (1982) 25,992. The song 'Mademoiselle from Armentières' originated during World War I, when the town was held by the British. It was flattened by German bombardment in 1918 and rebuilt.

Armidale /'ɑːmɪdeɪl/ town in New South Wales, Australia; population (1985) 21,500. The University of New England is here, and mansions of the ◊squatters survive.

Arminius /ɑː'mɪnɪəs/ 17 BC–AD 21. German chieftain. An ex-soldier of the Roman army, he annihilated a Roman force led by Varus in the Teutoburger Forest area AD 9, and saved Germany from becoming a Roman province. He thus ensured that the empire's frontier did not extend beyond the Rhine.

Arminius /ɑː'mɪnɪəs/ Jacobus. Latinized name of Jakob Harmensen 1560–1609. Dutch Protestant priest who founded Arminianism, a school of Christian theology opposed to Calvin's doctrine of predestination. His views were developed by Simon Episcopius (1583–1643). Arminianism is the basis of Wesleyan ◊Methodism in the UK.

He was born in S Holland, ordained in Amsterdam 1588, and from 1603 was professor of theology at Leyden. He asserted that forgiveness and eternal life are bestowed on all who repent of their sins and sincerely believe in Jesus. He was drawn into many controversies, and his followers were expelled from the church and persecuted.

Armistice Day anniversary of the armistice signed 11 Nov 1918, ending World War I. In the UK it is commemorated on the same day as ◊Remembrance Sunday.

armonica alternative name for the glass ◊harmonica.

Armory Show exhibition of Modern European art held in Feb 1913 in New York. It marked the arrival of abstract art in the USA, and influenced US artists. A rioting crowd threatened to destroy Marcel Duchamp's *Nude Descending a Staircase* (now in the Museum of Art, Philadelphia).

armour body protection worn in battle. Body armour is depicted in Greek and Roman art. Chain mail was developed in the Middle Ages but the craft of the armourer in Europe reached its height in design in the 15th century, when knights were completely encased in plate armour that still allowed freedom of movement. Medieval Japanese armour was articulated, made of iron, gilded metal, leather, and silk. Contemporary bulletproof vests and riot gear are forms of armour. The term is used in a modern context to refer to a mechanized armoured vehicle, such as a tank.

Since World War II armour for tanks and ships has been developed beyond an increasing thickness of steel plate, becoming an increasingly light, layered composite, including materials such as ceramics. More controversial is 'reactive' armour, consisting of 'shoeboxes' made of armour containing small, quick-acting explosive charges, which are attached at the most vulnerable points of a tank, in order to break up the force of entry of an enemy warhead. this type is used by Israel and the USSR, but the incorporation of explosive material in a tank has potential drawbacks.

The invention of gunpowder led, by degrees, to the virtual abandonment of armour until World War I, when the helmet reappeared as a defence against shrapnel. Suits of armour in the Tower of London were studied by US designers of astronaut wear. Modern armour, used by the army, police, security guards, and people at risk from assassination, uses nylon and fibreglass and is often worn beneath their clothing.

Armstrong /'ɑːmstrɒŋ/ Hank; born Henry Jackson, nicknamed 'Homicide Hank'. 1912–1988. US boxer. He was the only man to hold world titles at three different weights simultaneously. Between May and Nov 1938 he held the feather-, welter-, and lightweight titles. He retired in 1945 and became a Baptist minister.

Armstrong /'ɑːmstrɒŋ/ Edwin Howard 1890–1954. US radio engineer, who developed superheterodyne tuning for reception over a very wide spectrum of radio frequencies and frequency ◊modulation for static-free reception.

Armstrong /'ɑːmstrɒŋ/ Louis ('Satchmo') 1901–1971. US jazz trumpet player and singer, born in New Orleans. His Chicago recordings in the 1920s with the Hot Five and Hot Seven made him known for his warm and pure trumpet tone, his improvisation and gravelly voice. From the 1930s he became equally widely known as a singer and entertainer.

In 1923 Armstrong joined the Creole Jazz Band led by the cornet player Joe 'King' Oliver (1885–1938) in Chicago, but soon broke away and fronted various line-ups of his own. In 1947 he formed the Louis Armstrong All Stars and gained wide popularity. He was the first solo jazz virtuoso. He is credited with the invention of scat singing (meaningless syllables chosen for their sound).

Armstrong /'ɑːmstrɒŋ/ Neil Alden 1930– . US astronaut. In 1969, he was the first person to set foot on the Moon, and said, 'That's one

Arminius *Dutch Reformed theologian Jacobus Arminius turned against the Calvinist doctrine of predestination and formulated his ideas about conditional election, which depended on God's grace but allowed humankind free will.*

Armstrong *American jazz trumpet player and singer Louis Armstrong, or 'Satchmo', led his own Hot Five and Hot Seven bands in the 1920s. He is pictured at the front holding a slide trumpet.*

small step for a man, one giant leap for mankind'. The Moon landing was part of the ◊Apollo project.

Born in Ohio, he gained his pilot's licence at 16, and served as a naval pilot in Korea 1949–52 before joining NASA as a test pilot. He was selected to be an astronaut 1962 and landed on the Moon 20 Jul 1969.

Armstrong /ˈɑːmstrɒŋ/ Robert, Baron Armstrong of Ilminster 1927– . British civil servant, cabinet secretary in Margaret Thatcher's government. He achieved notoriety as a key witness in the 'Spycatcher' trial in Australia 1987.

After Oxford University he joined the civil service and rose rapidly to deputy-secretary rank. In 1970 he became Prime Minister Heath's principal private secretary; Thatcher later made him cabinet secretary and head of the home civil service. He achieved considerable attention as a witness

in the 'Spycatcher' trial in Australia when he admitted to having been sometimes 'economical with the truth'. He retired in 1988 and was made a life peer.

Armstrong /ˈɑːmstrɒŋ/ William George 1810–1900. English engineer, who developed a revolutionary method of making gun barrels 1855, by building a breech-loading artillery piece with a steel and wrought iron barrel (previous guns were muzzle-loaded and had cast bronze barrels). By 1880 the 150 mm/16 in Armstrong gun was the standard for all British ordnance.

army an organized military force for fighting on the ground. A national army is used to further a political policy by force either within the state or on the territory of another state. Most countries have a national army, maintained at the expense of the state, raised either by conscription (compulsory military service) or voluntarily (paid professionals). Private armies may be employed by individuals and groups.

ancient armies (–1066) Armies were common to all ancient civilizations. The Spartans trained from childhood for compulsory military service from age 21 to 26 in a full-time regular force as a heavily armed infantryman, or *hoplite*. Roman armies subjected all citizens to military service in *legions* of 6,000 men divided into *cohorts* of 600 men. Cohorts were similarly divided into six *centuries* of 100 men. The concept of duty to military service continued following the collapse of the Roman Empire. For example, the Anglo-Saxon *Fyrd* obliged all able-bodied men to serve in defence of Britain against Danish and then Norman invasion.nights and mercenaries (1066–1648) Medieval monarchs relied upon mounted men-at-arms, or *chevaliers*, who in turn called upon serfs on the land. Feudal armies were thus inherently limited in size and could only fight for limited periods. Free *yeomen* armed with longbows were required by law to practice at the *butts* and provided an early form of indirect fire as *artillery*.

army of Knights, in Europe paid troops, or soldi, and mounted troops, or *serviertes* (sergeants), made themselves available as *freelances*. By the end of the 15th century, *battles* or *battalions* or pikemen provided defence against the mounted knight. The hard gun, or *arquebus*, heralded the coming of infantrymen as known today. Those who wished to avoid military service could do so by paying *scutage*. For the majority the *conpane*, or *company*, was their home; they were placed under royal command by *ordonnances* and led by crown office holders, or *officiers*. Increased costs led to the formation of the first mercenary armies. For example, the *Great Company* of 10,000 men acted as an international racketeer, employing contractors, or *condottieri*, to serve the highest bidder. By the 16th century the long musket, pikemen, and the use of fortifications combined against the knight. *Sappers* became increasingly important in the creation and breaking of obstacles such as at Metz, the forerunner to the Maginot Line.

professional armies (1648–1792) The emergence of the nation-state saw the growth of more professional standing armies which trained in drills, used formations to maximize firepower, and introduced service discipline. The invention of the ring bayonet and the flintlock saw the demise of pikemen and the increased capability to fire from three ranks (today still the standard drill formation in the British Army). Artillery was now mobile and fully integrated into the army structure. The defects of raw levies, noble amateurs, and mercenaries led Oliver Cromwell to create the New Model Army for the larger campaigns of the English Civil War. After the Restoration, Charles II establish a small standing army, which was expanded under James II and William III. In France, a model regiment was set up under M de Martinet which set standards of uniformity for all to follow. State taxation provided for a formal system of army administration (uniforms, pay, ammunition). Nevertheless, recruits remained mainly society's misfits and delinquents. Collectively termed *other ranks*, they were divided from commissioned officers by a rigid hierarchical structure. The sheer cost of such armies forced wars to be fought by manoeuvre rather than by pitched battle, aiming to starve one's opponent into defeat while protecting one's own logistic chain.

armies of the revolution (1792–1819) Napoleon's organization of his army into autonomous *corps* of two to three *divisions*, in turn comprising two *brigades* of two *regiments* of two *battalions*, was a major step forward in allowing a rapid and flexible deployment of forces. Small-scale skirmishing by *light infantry*, coupled with the increasing devastation created by artillery or densely packed formations, saw the beginnings of

Armstrong *Seen here with fellow Apollo 11 crew-members Michael Collins and Edwin 'Buzz' Aldrin, Neil Armstrong was the first person to set foot on the Moon, on 20 July 1969.*

the *dispersed battlefield*. Victory in war was now synonymous with the complete destruction of the enemy in battle. Reservists were conscripted to allow the mass army to fight wars through to the bitter end. (Only Britain, by virtue of the English Channel and the Royal Navy, was able to avoid the need to provide such large land forces.) Officers were now required to be professionally trained; the Royal Military College was set up in Britain 1802, the St Cyr in France 1808, the Kriegsakademie in Berlin 1810, and the Russian Imperial Military Academy 1832. *Semaphore telegraph* and *observation balloons* were first steps to increasing the commander's ability to observe enemy movements. The British army, under Wellington, was very strong, but afterwards decreased in numbers and efficiency.

national armies (1815–45) The defeat of Revolutionary France saw a return to the traditions of the 18th century and a reduction in conscription. Meanwhile the railway revolutionized the deployment of forces, permitting quick mobilization, continuous resupply to the front, and rapid evacuation of casualties to the rear. By 1870, the limitation of supply inherent to the Napoleonic army had been overcome and once again armies of over 1 million could be deployed. By 1914, continental armies numbered as many as 3 million and were based on conscription. General staff were now required to manage these. *Breach-loading rifles* and *machine guns* ensured a higher casualty rate.

19th century armies The 19th century saw great development of rapidly produced missile weapons and the use of railways (the US Civil War has been called 'the railway war'). The weaknesses of the British army became apparent in the Crimean War and the Boer War.

technological armies (1918–45) The advent of the internal combustion engine allowed new advances in mobility to overcome the supremacy of the defensive over the offensive. The *tank* and the *radio* were vital to the evolution of armoured warfare or *blitzkrieg*. World War I employed enormous armies in *trench warfare*; the British army expanded from 750,000 to 5.5 million troops. Armies were able to reorganize into highly mobile formations, such as the German *Panzer Divisions*, which utilized speed, firepower, and surprise to overwhelm static defences and thereby dislocate the army's rear.

The armies of World War II were very mobile, especially the Allied forces in the Pacific, and were closely co-ordinated with the navy and air force. The requirement to fuel and maintain such huge fleets of vehicles again increased the need to maintain supplies. The complexity of the mechanized army demanded a wide range of skills not easily found through conscription.

armies of the nuclear age (1945–) The advent of tactical nuclear weapons severely compounded the problems of mass concentration and thus protected mobility assumed greater importance to allow rapid concentration and dispersal of forces in what could be a high chemical threat zone. From the 1960s there were sophisticated development in tanks and antitank weapons, mortar-locating radar, and heat-seeking missiles.

Arnauld /ɑːˈnəʊ/ French family closely associated with ◊Jansenism, a Christian church movement in the 17th century. *Antoine Arnauld* (1560–1619) was a Paris advocate and pamphleteer, strongly critical of the Jesuits. Many of his 20 children were associated with the abbey of Port Royal, which became the centre of Jansenism. His youngest child, *Antoine* (1612–94), the 'great Arnauld', was religious director of the nuns there.

With the philosopher Pascal and others, the elder Antoine produced not only Jansenist pamphlets, but works on logic, grammar, and geometry. For years he had to live in hiding, and the last 16 years of his life were spent in Brussels. Port Royal was a convent of Cistercian nuns near Versailles where his second daughter, *Angélique* (1591–1661),

became abbess through her father's influence at the age of 11. Later she served as prioress under her sister *Agnes* (1593–1671), and her niece, *La Mère Angélique* (1624–84), succeeded to both positions.

Arne /ɑːn/ Thomas Augustus 1710–1778. English composer, whose musical drama *Alfred* 1740 includes the song 'Rule Britannia!'.

Arnhem, Battle of /ˈɑːnəm/ in World War II, airborne operation by the Allies, 17–26 Sept 1944, to secure a bridgehead over the Rhine, thereby opening the way for a thrust towards the Ruhr and a possible early end to the war. It was only partly successful, with 7,600 casualties. Arnhem is a city in the Netherlands, on the Rhine SE of Utrecht; population (1988) 297,000. It produces salt, chemicals, and pharmaceuticals. The English poet Sir Philip Sidney died here 1586.

Arnhem Land /ˈɑːnəm/ plateau of the central peninsula in Northern Territory, Australia. It is named after a Dutch ship which came to port 1618. The chief town is Nhulunbuy. It is the largest of the Aboriginal reserves, and a traditional way of life is maintained, now threatened by mineral exploitation.

Arnim /ˈɑːnɪm/ Ludwig Achim von 1781–1831. German Romantic poet and novelist. Born in Berlin, he wrote short stories, a romance, *Gräfin Dolores/Countess Dolores* 1810, and plays, but left the historical novel *Die Kronenwächter* 1817 unfinished. With Clemens Brentano he collected the German folk-songs in *Des Knaben Wunderhorn/The Boy's Magic Horn* 1805–08.

Arno /ˈɑːnəʊ/ Italian river 240 km/150 mi long, rising in the Apennines, and flowing westward to the Mediterranean. Florence and Pisa stand on its banks. A flood in 1966 damaged virtually every Renaissance landmark in Florence.

Arnold /ˈɑːnld/ Benedict 1741–1801. US soldier and traitor to the American side in the War of American Independence. A merchant in New Haven, Connecticut, he joined the colonial forces but in 1780 plotted to betray the strategic post at West Point to the British. Maj André was sent by the British to discuss terms with him, but was caught and hanged as a spy. Arnold escaped to the British, who gave him an army command.

Arnold /ˈɑːnld/ Edwin 1832–1904. English scholar and poet. He wrote the *Light of Asia* 1879, a rendering of the life and teaching of the Buddha in blank verse. *The Light of the World* 1891 retells the life of Jesus.

Arnold /ˈɑːnld/ Malcolm (Henry) 1921– . English composer. His work is tonal and includes a large amount of orchestral, chamber, ballet, and vocal music. His operas include *The Dancing Master* 1951, and he has written music for more than 80 films, including *The Bridge on the*

River Kwai 1957, for which he won an Academy Award.

Arnold /ˈɑːnld/ Matthew 1822–1888. English poet and critic, son of Thomas Arnold. His poems, characterized by their elegiac mood and pastoral themes, include *The Forsaken Merman* 1849, *Thyrsis* 1867 (commemorating his friend Arthur Hugh Clough), *Dover Beach* 1867, and *The Scholar Gypsy* 1853. Arnold's critical works include *Essays in Criticism* 1865 and 1888, and *Culture and Anarchy* 1869, which attacks 19th-century philistinism.

He was educated at public schools and Oxford University. After a short spell as an assistant master at Rugby, Arnold became a school inspector 1851–86. He published two unsuccessful volumes of anonymous poetry, but two further publications under his own name 1853 and 1855 led to his appointment as professor of poetry at Oxford. Arnold first used the word 'philistine' in its present sense in his attack on the cultural values of the middle classes.

Arnold /ˈɑːnld/ Thomas 1795–1842. English schoolmaster, father of Matthew Arnold. Ordained in the Church of England 1818, he was headmaster of Rugby School 1828–42. His regime has been graphically described in Thomas Hughes's *Tom Brown's Schooldays* 1857. He emphasized training of character, and his influence on public school education was profound.

Arnold of Brescia /ˈɑːnld, ˈbreʃə/ 1100–1155. Italian Augustinian monk, who attacked the holding of property by the Catholic church; he was hanged and burned, and his ashes were thrown into the Tiber.

aromatherapy the use of aromatic essential oils to relieve tension or to induce a feeling of well-being, usually in combination with massage. It is also used to relieve minor skin complaints. Common in the Middle East for centuries, the practice was reintroduced to the West in France during the 1960s.

aromatic compounds organic chemical compounds derived from benzene. They undergo chemical substitution reactions. See also ◊cyclic compounds.

Arp /ɑːp/ Hans/Jean 1887–1966. French abstract painter and sculptor. He was one of the founders of Dada about 1917, and later associated with the Surrealists. His innovative wood sculptures use organic shapes in bright colours. In his early experimental works, such as collages, he collaborated with his wife *Sophie Taeuber-Arp* (1889–1943).

arpeggio (Italian 'like a harp') in music, a chord played as a cascade of notes.

Arran /ˈærən/ large mountainous island in the Firth of Clyde, Scotland, in Strathclyde; area

aromatic compounds

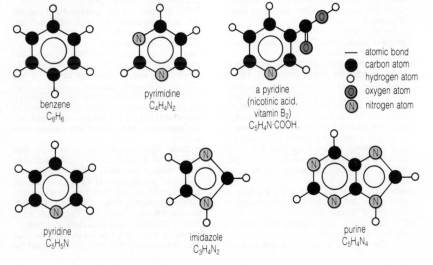

benzene
C_6H_6

pyrimidine
$C_4H_4N_2$

a pyridine
(nicotinic acid,
vitamin B_2)
$C_5H_4N\cdot COOH$.

— atomic bond
● carbon atom
○ hydrogen atom
◉ oxygen atom
◉ nitrogen atom

pyridine
C_5H_5N

imidazole
$C_3H_4N_2$

purine
$C_5H_4N_4$

427 sq km/165 sq mi; population (1981) 4,726. It is popular as a holiday resort. The chief town is Brodick.

arranger in music, a person who adapts the music of another composer. In film and musical theatre, an assistant in orchestrating a composer's piano score.

Arras /ˈærəs/ French town on the Scarpe river NE of Paris; population (1982) 80,500 (conurbation). It is the capital of Pas-de-Calais *département*, and was formerly famed for its tapestry. It was the birthplace of Robespierre.

Arras, Battle of /ˈærəs/ battle of World War I, April–May 1917. It was an effective but costly British attack on German forces in support of a French offensive, which was only partially successful, on the ◊Siegfried Line. British casualties totalled 84,000 as compared to 75,000 German casualties. In World War II the town of Arras was captured 1940 by the Germans in their advance on Dunkirk.

Arras, Congress and Treaty of a meeting in N France 1435 between representatives of Henry VI of England, Charles VII of France, and Philip the Good of Burgundy, to settle the Hundred Years' War.

The treaty and the agreement it reached was a diplomatic victory for France. Although England refused to compromise on Henry VI's claim to the French crown, France signed a peace treaty with Burgundy, England's former ally.

Arrau /əˈraʊ/ Claudio 1903– . Chilean pianist. A concert performer since the age of five, he excels in 19th-century music and is known for his thoughtful interpretation.

arrest deprivation of personal liberty with a view to detention. In Britain an arrest in civil proceedings now takes place only on a court order, usually for ◊contempt of court. In criminal proceedings an arrest may be made on a magistrate's warrant, but a police constable is empowered to arrest without warrant in all cases where he or she has reasonable ground for thinking a serious offence has been committed. Private persons may, and are indeed bound to, arrest anyone committing a serious offence or breach of the peace in their presence. In the USA police officers and private persons have similar rights and duties.

Arrhenius /əˈreɪnɪəs/ Svante August 1859–1927. Swedish scientist, the founder of physical chemistry. Born near Uppsala, he became a professor at Stockholm in 1895, and made a special study of electrolysis. He wrote *Worlds in the Making* and *Destinies of the Stars*, and in 1903 received the Nobel Prize for Chemistry.

arrhythmia a disturbance of the natural rhythm of the heart. There are various kinds of arrhythmia, some innocent, some indicative of heart disease.

arrowroot starchy substance derived from the roots and tubers of various plants. The true arrowroot *Maranta arundinacea* was used by the Indians of South America as an antidote against the effects of poisoned arrows.

The West Indian island of St Vincent is the main source of supply today. The edible starch is easily digested and is good for invalids.

arsenic a greyish-white semi-metallic crystalline element, symbol As, atomic number 33, relative atomic mass 74.91. It occurs in many ores, and is widely distributed, being present in minute quantities in the soil, the sea, and the human body. It is poisonous. The chief source of arsenic compounds is as a by-product from metallurgical processes.

As it is a cumulative poison, its presence in food and drugs is very dangerous. The symptoms of arsenic poisoning are vomiting, diarrhoea, tingling and possibly numbness in the limbs, and collapse.

arson the malicious and wilful setting fire to property, crops, possessions, in Britain covered by the Criminal Damage Act (1971).

art in the broadest sense, all the processes and products of human skill, imagination, and invention; the opposite of nature. In contemporary

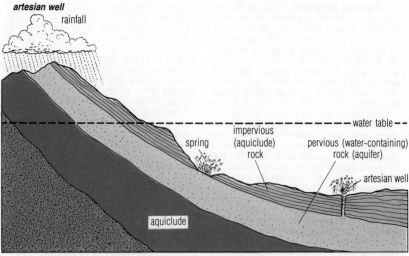

artesian well

rainfall

water table

impervious (aquiclude) rock

spring

pervious (water-containing) rock (aquifer)

artesian well

aquiclude

usage, definitions of art usually reflect aesthetic criteria, and the term may encompass literature, music, drama, painting, and sculpture. Popularly, the term is most commonly used to refer to the visual arts. In Western culture, aesthetic criteria introduced by the ancient Greeks still influence our perceptions and judgements of art.

Two currents of thought run through our ideas about art. In one, derived from Aristotle, art is concerned with *mimesis* ('imitation'), the representation of appearances, and gives pleasure through the accuracy and skill with which it depicts the real world. The other view, derived from Plato, holds that the artist is inspired by the Muses (or by God, or by the inner impulses, or by the collective unconscious) to express that which is beyond appearances – inner feelings, eternal truths, or the essence of the age. In the Middle Ages the term 'art' was used, chiefly in the plural, to signify a branch of learning which was regarded as an instrument of knowledge. The seven **liberal arts** consisted of the *trivium*, that is grammar, logic, and rhetoric, and the *quadrivium*, that is arithmetic, music, geometry, and astronomy.

In the visual arts of Western civilizations, painting and sculpture have been the dominant forms for many centuries. This has not always been the case in other cultures. Islamic art, for example, is one of ornament, for under the Muslim religion artists were forbidden to usurp the divine right of creation by portraying living creatures. In some cultures masks, tattoos, pottery, and metalwork have been the main forms of visual art. Recent technology has made new art forms possible, such as photography and cinema, and today electronic media have led to entirely new ways of creating and presenting visual images.

See also ◊ancient art, ◊medieval art, and the arts of individual countries, such as ◊French art, and individual movements, such as ◊Romanticism, ◊Cubism, ◊Impressionism.

Artaud /ɑːˈtəʊ/ Antonin 1896–1948. French theatre director. Although his play, *Les Cenci/The Cenci* 1935, was a failure, his concept of the **Theatre of Cruelty**, intended to release feelings usually repressed in the unconscious, has been an important influence on modern dramatists such as Camus and Genet and on directors and producers. Declared insane 1936, Artaud was confined in an asylum.

Art Deco style in art and architecture that emerged in Europe in the 1920s and continued through the 1930s, using rather heavy, geometric simplification of form, for example Radio City Music Hall, New York. It was a self-consciously modern style, with sharp lines, and dominated the decorative arts. The graphic artist Erté (1893–1989) was a fashionable exponent.

Artemis /ˈɑːtəmɪs/ in Greek mythology, the goddess (Roman Diana) of chastity, the Moon, and the

hunt. She is the sister of ◊Apollo. Her cult centre was at Ephesus.

arteriography a method of examining the interior of an artery by injecting into it a radio-opaque solution that is visible on an x-ray photograph. Used for the heart's coronary arteries (coronary arteriogram), for example.

arteriosclerosis hardening of the arteries, with thickening and loss of elasticity. It is associated with smoking, ageing, and a diet high in saturated fats.

artery a vessel conveys blood from the hearts of vertebrates to the body tissues. The largest of the arteries is the aorta, which in mammals leads from the left ventricle of the heart, up over the heart and down through the diaphragm into the belly. Arteries are flexible, elastic tubes consisting of three layers, the middle of which is muscular; by its rhythmic contraction this aids the pumping of blood around the body.

Not all arteries carry oxygen-rich blood; the pulmonary arteries convey oxygen-poor blood from heart to lungs. The cutting of an artery of any size is a dangerous injury. In middle and old age, the arteries normally lose their elasticity; the walls degenerate and often become impregnated with fatty deposits, resulting in arteriosclerosis.

artesian well a well in which water rises from its ◊aquifer under natural pressure. Such a well may be drilled into an aquifer that is confined by impermeable beds both above and below. If the water table (the top of the region of water saturation) in that aquifer is above the level of the well head, hydrostatic pressure will force the water to the surface.

Much use is made of artesian wells in E Australia, where aquifers filled by water in the Great Dividing Range run beneath the arid surface of the Simpson Desert. It is named after Artois, a French province, where the phenomenon was first observed.

arthritis inflammation of the joints. More common in women, **rheumatoid arthritis** usually begins in middle age in the small joints of the hands and feet, causing a greater or lesser degree of deformity and painfully restricted movement. It is alleviated by drugs, and surgery may be performed to correct deformity.

Osteoarthritis, a degenerative condition, tends to affect larger, load-bearing joints, such as the knee and hip. It appears in later life, especially in those whose joints may have been subject to earlier stress or damage; one or more joints stiffen and may give considerable pain. Joint replacement surgery is nearly always successful.

arthropod invertebrate animal with jointed legs and a segmented body with a horny or chitinous casing, the latter being shed periodically and replaced as the animal grows. This definition includes arachnids such as spiders and mites, as well as crustaceans, millipedes, centipedes, and insects.

Arthur /ˈɑːθə/ 6th century AD Legendary English king and hero in stories of ◊Camelot and the quest for the ◊Holy Grail. Arthur is said to have been born at Tintagel and be buried at Glastonbury. He may have been a Romano-British leader against pagan Saxon invaders.

The legends of Arthur and the knights of the Round Table (so shaped to avoid strife over precedence) was developed in the 12th century by Geoffrey of Monmouth and the Norman writer Wace. Later writers on the theme include the anonymous author of *Sir Gawayne and the Greene Knight* 1346, Sir Thomas Malory, Tennyson, T H White, and Mark Twain.

Arthur /ˈɑːθə/ Chester Alan 1830–1886. 21st president of the USA. He was born in Vermont, the son of a Baptist minister, and became a lawyer and Republican political appointee in New York. In 1880, Arthur was chosen as ◊Garfield's vice president, and was his successor when Garfield was assassinated the following year. Arthur held office until 1885.

Arthur /ˈɑːθə/ Duke of Brittany 1187–1203. Grandson of Henry II of England and nephew of King ◊John, who is supposed to have had him murdered, 13 Apr 1203, as a rival for the crown.

Arthur /ˈɑːθə/ Prince of Wales 1486–1502. Eldest son of Henry VII of England. He married ◊Catherine of Aragon 1501, when he was 16 and she was 15, but died the next year.

Arthur's Pass /ˈɑːθəz ˈpɑːs/ road-rail link across the Southern Alps, New Zealand, at 926 m/3,038 ft, linking Christchurch with Greymouth.

Arthur's Seat /ˈɑːθəz ˈsiːt/ hill of volcanic origin, Edinburgh, Scotland; height 251 m/823 ft; only fancifully linked with King Arthur.

artichoke two plants of the family Compositae. The **common** or **globe artichoke** *Cynara scolymus* is tall, with purplish blue flowers; the bracts of the unopened flower are eaten. The **Jerusalem artichoke** *Helianthus tuberosus* has edible tubers.

H. tuberosus is a native of North America; its common name is a corruption of the Italian for sunflower *girasole*.

article a grammatical ◊part of speech, of which there are two in English: the *definite article* 'the', which serves to specify or identify a noun (as in 'This is the book I need'), and the *indefinite article* 'a' or 'an' (before vowels), which indicates a single unidentified noun ('They gave me a piece of paper and an envelope').

artificial respiration the maintenance of breathing when the natural process is suspended.

If breathing is permanently suspended, as in paralysis, an *iron lung* is used; in cases of electric shock or apparent drowning, for example, the first choice is the expired air method, the '*kiss of life*' by mouth-to-mouth breathing until natural breathing is resumed.

artificial insemination (AI) mating achieved by mechanically injecting semen into the womb without genital contact. It is commonly used with cattle because it allows the farmer to select the type and quality of bull required for the herd, and

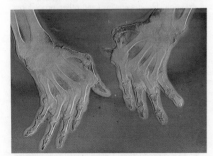

arthritis X-ray of the hands of a person suffering from extreme rheumatoid arthritis.

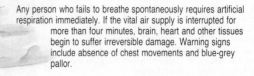

artificial respiration

This technique – mouth-to-mouth resuscitation – delivers a continuous supply of oxygen to the lungs of an unconscious person who is not breathing.

Any person who fails to breathe spontaneously requires artificial respiration immediately. If the vital air supply is interrupted for more than four minutes, brain, heart and other tissues begin to suffer irreversible damage. Warning signs include absence of chest movements and blue-grey pallor.

Often the mouth and throat are blocked by blood, stomach contents, or dentures. The victim should be turned onto one side, which may clear the airway. Any obstruction can be removed with the fingers wrapped in a clean cloth. If the person is still not breathing artificial resuscitation should be started at once.

When an unconscious person is placed in the prone position the tongue may drop into the back of the throat, filling the airway and preventing air from reaching the lungs. An open airway must be established before artificial respiration is given. The head is tilted backwards until neck and chest are in a line. Then the jaw is extended to lift the tongue. The position is maintained by keeping one hand on the forehead and the other under the chin.

An airtight seal is created by pinching the nostrils between the fingers of the hand on the forehead and placing the lips around the victim's mouth. The lungs are expanded with a steady, gentle breath, and the chest rises visibly. Exhalation occurs naturally, as the victim's mouth is uncovered. For adults, the procedure is repeated 12 times per minute.

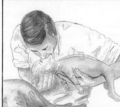

As soon as spontaneous breathing begins the victim should be placed in the recovery position. This keeps the airway clear.

The lips are placed around the nose and mouth of an infant to obtain an airtight seal. No more than little puffs are required to fill the lungs, at a rate of 20 per minute.

to control the timing and organization of the breeding programme. The practice of artificially inseminating pigs has also become widespread in recent years.

artificial intelligence (AI) a branch of cognitive science concerned with creating computer programs that can perform actions comparable with those of an intelligent human. Current AI research covers areas such as planning (for robot behaviour), language understanding, pattern recognition, and knowledge representation.

Early AI programs, developed in the 1960s, attempted simulations of human intelligence or were aimed at general problem-solving techniques. It is now thought that intelligent behaviour depends as much on the knowledge a system possesses as on its reasoning power. Present emphasis is on ◊knowledge-based systems such as ◊expert systems.

artificial limb a device to replace a limb that has been removed by surgery or one that is malformed because of genetic defects. It is one form of ◊prosthesis.

artificial selection in biology, selective breeding of individuals that exhibit particular characters which a plant or animal breeder wishes to develop. The development of particular breeds of cattle for improved meat production (such as the Aberdeen Angus) or milk production (such as Jerseys) are examples.

artillery collective term for military ◊firearms too heavy to be carried. Artillery can be mounted on ships or aeroplanes and includes cannons and missile launchers.

14th century Cannons came into general use, and were most effective in siege warfare. The term had previously been applied to catapults used for hurling heavy objects.

16th century The howitzer, halfway between a gun and a mortar (muzzle-loading cannon), was first used in sieges.

early 19th century In the Napoleonic period, field artillery became smaller and more mobile.

1914–18 In World War I, howitzers were used to demolish trench systems. Giant cannons were used in the entrenched conditions of the Western

Front and at sea against the lumbering, heavily armoured battleships, but their accuracy against small or moving targets was poor.

1970s Introduction of electronically operated target devices and remote-control firing.

1980s Howitzers became self-mobile and computer-controlled. Shells may be made to home in automatically on an unseen target, such as a tank.

Art Nouveau art style of about 1890–1910 in Europe, marked by sinuous lines and stylized flowers and foliage. Also called *Jugendstil* (Germany), *Stile Liberty* (Italy). Exponents included the illustrator Beardsley, the architect and furniture designer C R Mackintosh, and the glass and jewellery designer René Lalique.

Art Nouveau was primarily a decorative, two-dimensional style and pervaded the visual arts. The theatrical posters of Alphonse Mucha (1860–1939) exemplify the popular version.

Artois /ɑːˈtwɑː/ former province of N France, bounded by Flanders and Picardie, and almost corresponding with the modern *département* of Pas-de-Calais. Its capital was Arras. Its Latin name *Artesium* lent its name to the Artesian well first sunk at Lillers 1126.

Arts and Crafts movement an English social movement, largely anti-machine in spirit, based in design and architecture and founded by William Morris in the latter half of the 19th century. It was supported by the architect A W Pugin and by ◊John Ruskin and stressed the importance of manual processes (see also ◊Art Nouveau).

Arts Council of Great Britain UK arts organization, incorporated 1945, which aids music, drama, and visual arts with government funds.

Aruba /əˈruːbə/ island in the Caribbean, the westernmost of the Lesser Antilles; an overseas part of the Netherlands

area 193 sq km/75 sq mi

population (1985) 61,000

history Aruba obtained separate status from the other Netherlands Antilles 1986 and has full internal autonomy.

arum plant of the family Araceae. The species *Arum maculatum*, known as cuckoopint or lords-and-ladies, is a common British hedgerow plant. The arum or trumpet lily *Zantedeschia aethiopica*, an ornamental plant, is a native of South Africa.

Arunachal Pradesh /ˌɑːrəˈnɑːtʃəl prɑːˈdeʃ/ state of India, in the Himalayas on the borders of Tibet and Burma

area 83,600 sq km/32,270 sq mi

capital Itanagar

products rubber, coffee, spices, fruit, timber

population (1981) 628,000

language 50 different dialects

history formerly nominally part of Assam, and known as the North East Frontier Agency, it became a Union Territory 1972, and was renamed Arunachal Pradesh 'Hills of the Rising Sun'. It became a state 1986.

artillery On exercise in West Germany, members of the British 5th Regiment Royal Artillery and 3rd Royal Tank Regiment with an M-107 gun.

ash

Arundel /ˈærəndl/ town in Sussex, England, on the river Arun; population (1981) 2,200. It has a magnificent castle (much restored and rebuilt), the seat for centuries of the earls of Arundel and dukes of ◊Norfolk.

Arundel /ˈærəndl/ Thomas Howard, 2nd Earl of Arundel 1586–1646. English politician and patron of the arts. The Arundel Marbles, part of his collection of Italian sculptures, were given to Oxford University in 1667 by his grandson.

Arval Brethren (Latin *Fratres Arvales*, brothers of the field) body of priests in ancient Rome who offered annual sacrifices to the *lares* or divinities of the fields to ensure a good harvest. They formed a college of 12 priests, and their chief festival fell in May.

Arvand River Iranian name for the ◊Shatt al-Arab waterway.

Aryan member of an ancient people who were believed to have lived between Central Asia and E Europe, and to have reached India about 1500 BC. In the ◊Nazi period Hitler and other German theorists erroneously propagated the idea of the Aryans as a white-skinned, blue-eyed, fair-haired master-race.

Aryana /ˌeəriˈɑːnə/ ancient name of Afghanistan.

Aryan language any of the languages of the Aryan peoples of India; a 19th-century name for the ◊Indo-European languages.

Arya Samaj /ˈɑːriə səˈmɑːdʒ/ Hindu religious sect founded by Dayanand Saraswati (1825–88) about 1875. He renounced idol-worship and urged a return to the purer principles of the Rig Veda (Hindu scriptures). The movement believes that ◊caste should be determined by merit rather than birth.

ASA abbreviation for *Association of South east Asia* (1961–67), replaced by ASEAN (◊*Association of Southeast Asian Nations*).

ASA in photography, a numbering system for rating the speed of films, devised by the American Standards Association. It has now been superseded by ◊*ISO*, the International Standards Organization.

Asante (or *Ashanti*) person of Asante culture from central Ghana, west of Lake Volta. The Asante language belongs to the Kwa branch of the Niger–Congo family.

a.s.a.p. abbreviation for *as soon as possible*.

ASAT acronym for *antisatellite weapon*.

asbestos any of several related minerals of fibrous structure which offer great heat resistance because of their non-flammability and poor conductivity. Commercial asbestos is generally made from chrysolite, a ◊serpentine mineral found in Québec, the USSR, and Zimbabwe. Asbestos usage is now strictly controlled as exposure to its dust can cause cancer.

Asbestos has been used for brake linings, suits for firemen and astronauts, insulation of electric wires in furnaces, cement sheets, and pressure pipes for the building industry. Exposure to asbestos is a recognized cause of industrial cancer (mesothelioma), especially in the 'blue' form (from South Africa), rather than the more common 'white'. *Asbestosis* is a chronic lung inflammation caused by asbestos dust.

ascariasis infection by the roundworm *Ascaris lumbricoides*, an intestinal parasite in humans and other mammals.

Ascension /əˈsenʃən/ British island of volcanic origin in the S Atlantic, a dependency of ◊St Helena since 1922; population (1982) 1,625. The chief settlement is Georgetown.

A Portuguese navigator landed there on Ascension Day 1501, but it remained uninhabited, until occupied by Britain in 1815. Population (1982) 1,625. It is famous for sea turtles and sooty terns, and important for its role as a staging post to the Falkland Islands.

Ascension Day or *Holy Thursday* in the Christian calendar, the feast day commemorating Jesus's ascension into heaven. It is the fortieth day after Easter.

asceticism the renunciation of physical pleasure, for example, in eating, drinking, exercising sexual instincts; and seeking discomfort or pain, often for religious reasons.

Ascham /ˈæskəm/ Roger c.1515–1568. English scholar and royal tutor, author of *The Scholemaster* 1570 on the art of education.

After writing a treatise on archery, King Henry VIII's favourite sport, Ascham was appointed tutor to Princess Elizabeth in 1548. He retained favour under Edward VI and Queen Mary (despite his Protestant views), and returned to Elizabeth's service as her secretary after she became queen.

ASCII acronym for *American Standard Code for Information Interchange* in computing, a coding system in which numbers (between 0 and 127) are assigned to letters, digits, and punctuation symbols. For example, 45 represents a hyphen and 65 a capital A. The first 32 codes are used for control functions, such as carriage return and backspace. Strictly speaking, ASCII is a seven-bit code, although an eighth bit is often used to provide ◊parity or to allow for extra characters. The system is widely used for the storage of text and for the transmission of data between computers.

ascorbic acid (or *vitamin C*) a relatively simple organic acid found in fresh fruits and vegetables. It is soluble in water and destroyed by prolonged boiling, so soaking or overcooking of vegetables reduces their vitamin C content. Lack of ascorbic acid results in scurvy.

Ascorbic acid plays an important role in the synthesis of collagen, and lack of it causes skin sores or ulcers, tooth and gum problems, and burst capillaries (scurvy symptoms) owing to an abnormal type of collagen replacing the normal type in these tissues.

Ascot /ˈæskət/ village in Berkshire, S England 9.5 km/6 mi SW of Windsor. Queen Anne established the racecourse on Ascot Heath 1711, and the Royal Ascot meeting is a social, as well as a sporting event. Races include the Gold Cup, Ascot Stakes, Coventry Stakes, and King George VI and Queen Elizabeth Stakes.

ASEAN acronym for ◊*Association of Southeast Asian Nations*.

asepsis the practice of ensuring that bacteria are excluded from open sites during surgery, wound dressing, blood sampling, and other procedures. Aseptic technique is a first line of defence against infection.

asexual reproduction a biological term for reproductive processes that are not ◊sexual and thus do not involve fusion of ◊gametes.

Asexual processes include ◊binary fission, in which the parent organism splits into two or more 'daughter' organisms, and ◊budding, in which a new organism is formed initially as an outgrowth of the parent organism. The asexual production of spores, as in ferns and mosses, is also common, and many plants reproduce asexually by means of runners, rhizomes, bulbs, and corms; see ◊vegetative reproduction. Unlike sexual reproduction, these processes do not involve the fusion of two gametes. See also ◊parthenogenesis.

Asgard in Scandinavian mythology, the place where the gods lived. It was reached by a bridge called Bifrost, the rainbow.

ash tree of the genus *Fraxinus*, belonging to the family Oleaceae. *F. excelsior* is the European species; its timber is of importance. The mountain ash or rowan *Sorbus aucuparia* belongs to the family Rosaceae.

Ashanti /əˈʃænti/ or *Asante* region of Ghana, W Africa; area 25,100 sq km/9,700 sq mi; population (1984) 2,089,683. Kumasi is the capital. The main crop is cocoa, and the region is noted for its metalwork and textiles.

For more than 200 years forming an independent kingdom, during the 19th century the Ashanti lost their independence to the British who sent four expeditions against them, and who formally annexed their country 1901. Otomfuo Sir Osei Agyeman, nephew of the deposed king, Prempeh I, was made head of the re-established Ashanti confederation 1935 as Prempeh II, and the Golden Stool (actually a chair), symbol of the Ashanti peoples since the 17th century, was returned to Kumasi. (The rest of the Ashanti treasure is in the British Museum.) The Asantehene (King of the Ashanti) still holds ceremonies in which this stool is ceremonially paraded.

Ashbee /ˈæʃbi/ C(harles) R(obert) 1863–1942. British designer, architect, and writer, one of the major figures of the ◊Arts and Crafts movement. He founded a 'Guild and School of Handicraft' in the East End of London in 1888, but later modified his views, accepting the importance of machinery and design for industry.

He based his ideas on the social function of art from the writings of William ◊Morris and John ◊Ruskin. His Guild and School of Handicraft (later moved to Chipping Campden, Gloucestershire) aimed to achieve high standards in craftwork and quality of life, which were both threatened by the onset of mass production. At its peak, the guild employed over 100 craftworkers

Ashbery /ˈæʃbəri/ John 1927– . US poet and art critic. His collections of poetry, including *Self-Portrait in a Convex Mirror* 1975 , which won a Pulitzer Prize, are distinguished by their strong visual element and narrative power.

Ashby-de-la-Zouch /ˈæʃbi də lə ˈzuːʃ/ market town in Leicestershire, England; 26 km/16 mi NW of Leicester; population (1985) 11,906. It was named from the La Zouche family who built the castle, which was used to imprison Mary Queen of Scots 1569. The 15th-century castle features in Sir Walter Scott's novel *Ivanhoe*.

Ashcan school group of US painters active about 1908–14, whose members included Robert Henri (1865–1929), George Luks (1867–1933), William Glackens (1870–1938), Everett Shinn (1876–1953), and John Sloan (1871–1951). Their style is realist; their subjects centred on modern city life, the poor, and the outcast.

Ashcroft /ˈæʃkrɒft/ Peggy 1907– . English actress. Her many leading roles include Desdemona in *Othello* (with Paul Robeson), Juliet in *Romeo and Juliet* 1935 (with Laurence Olivier and John Gielgud), and appearances in the British TV play *Caught on a Train* 1980 (BAFTA award), the series *The Jewel in the Crown* 1984 and the film *A Passage to India* 1985.

Ashdod /ˈæʃdɒd/ deepwater port of Israel, on the Mediterranean 32 km/20 mi south of Tel-Aviv, which it superseded in 1965; population (1982) 66,000. It stands on the site of the ancient Philistine stronghold of Askalon.

Ashdown /ˈæʃdaʊn/ (Jeremy John Durham) 'Paddy' 1941– . British politician. Originally a Liberal MP, he became leader of the Social and Liberal Democrats 1988. He served in the Royal Marines as a commando, leading a Special Boat Section in Borneo, and was a member of the Diplomatic Service 1971–76.

Ashes, the cricket trophy theoretically held by the winning team in the England–Australia test series. The trophy is permanently held at ◊Lord's cricket

Ashcroft *English actress Peggy Ashcroft, photographed by Cecil Beaton in the 1930s.*

ground no matter who wins the series. It is an urn containing the ashes of stumps and bails used in a match when England toured Australia 1882–83. The urn was given to the England captain Ivo Bligh by a group of Melbourne women. The action followed the appearance of an obituary notice in the *Sporting Times* the previous summer announcing the 'death' of English cricket after defeat by the Australians in the Oval test match.

Asheville /ˈæʃvɪl/ textile town in the Blue Ridge Mountains of North Carolina, USA; population (1980) 53,583. Showplaces include the 19th-century Biltmore mansion, home of millionaire George W Vanderbilt, and the home of the writer Thomas Wolfe.

Ashford /ˈæʃfəd/ town in Kent, England, on the river Stour, SW of Canterbury; population (1985) 47,000. It has expanded in the 1980s as a new commercial and industrial centre for SE England.

Ashford /ˈæʃfəd/ Daisy 1881–1972. English author of *The Young Visiters* 1919, a classic of unconscious humour written when she was nine.

Ashanti *Bearing the king's stool in procession. An Ashanti king is always 'enstooled', not crowned.*

Ashton *British choreographer Frederick Ashton, co-founder of the Royal Ballet,*

Ashkenazi /ˌæʃkəˈnɑːzɪ/ a Jew of German or E European descent, as opposed to Sephardi, of Spanish, Portuguese, or N African descent.

Ashkenazy /ˌæʃkəˈnɑːzi/ Vladimir 1937– . Soviet-born pianist and conductor. His keyboard technique differs slightly from standard Western technique. In 1962 he was joint winner of the Tchaikovsky Competition with John Ogdon. He excels in Rachmaninov, Prokofiev, and Liszt.

After studying in Moscow, he toured the USA in 1958. He settled in England in 1963 and moved to Iceland in 1968. He was musical director of the Royal Philharmonic, London, from 1987.

Ashkhabad /ˌæʃkəˈbæd/ capital of Republic of Turkmen, USSR; population (1987) 382,000. 'Bukhara' carpets are made here.

It was established 1881 as a military fort on the Persian frontier, occupying an oasis on the edge of the Kara-Kum desert. It is the hottest place in the USSR.

Ashley /ˈæʃli/ Laura (born Mountney) 1925–1985. Welsh designer, who established and gave her name to a Neo-Victorian country style in clothes and furnishings beginning in 1953. She started an international chain of shops.

Ashmole /ˈæʃməʊl/ Elias 1617–1692. English antiquary, whose collection forms the basis of the Ashmolean Museum, Oxford.

He wrote books on alchemy and on antiquarian subjects, and amassed a fine library and a collection of curiosities, both of which he presented to Oxford University 1682. His collection was housed in the 'Old Ashmolean' (built 1679–83); the present Ashmolean Museum was erected 1897.

Ashmore and Cartier Islands /ˈæʃmɔː, ˈkɑːtieɪ/ group of islands comprising Middle, East, and West Islands (the Ashmores), and Cartier Island, in the Indian Ocean about 180 km/120 mi off the NW coast of Australia; area 5 sq km/2 sq mi. They were transferred to the authority of the Commonwealth of Australia by Britain 1931. Formerly administered as part of the Northern Territory, they became a separate Commonwealth territory 1978. They are uninhabited, and West Ashmore has an automatic weather station. Ashmore reef was declared a national nature reserve 1983.

ashram an Indian community whose members lead a simple life of discipline and self-denial and devote themselves to social service. Noted ashrams are those founded by Mahatma Gandhi at Wardha and the poet Rabindranath Tagore at Santiniketan.

Ashton /ˈæʃtən/ Frederick 1904–1988. British dancer and choreographer. He studied with Massine and Rambert before joining the Vic-Wells Ballet 1935 as chief choreographer, creating several roles for Margot Fonteyn. He was director of the Royal Ballet, London, 1963–70.

His major works include *Façade* 1931, *Cinderella* 1948, *La Fille mal gardée* 1960, *Marguerite and Armand* – for Fonteyn and Nureyev – 1963, and *A Month in the Country* 1976. He contributed much to the popularity of ballet in the mid-20th century.

Ashton under Lyne /ˈæʃtən ʌndə ˈlaɪn/ town in Greater Manchester, England; population (1981) 44,476. There are light industries, coal, and cotton.

Ash Wednesday first day of Lent, the period in the Christian calendar leading up to Easter; in the Catholic church the foreheads of the congregation are marked with a cross in ash, as a sign of penitence.

Asia /ˈeɪʃə/ largest of the continents, forming the eastern part of Eurasia to the east of the Ural mountains, one third of the total land surface of the world.

area 44,000,000 sq km/17,000,000 sq mi

largest cities (over 5 million) Tokyo, Shanghai, Osaka, Beijing, Seoul, Calcutta, Bombay, Jakarta, Bangkok, Tehran, Hong Kong

physical five main divisions: (1) Central triangular mountain mass, including the Himalayas; to the N the great Tibetan plateau, bounded by the Kunlun mountains, to the N of which lie further ranges, as well as the Gobi Desert. (2) The SW plateaux and ranges, forming Afghanistan, Baluchistan, Iran. (3) The northern lowlands, from the central mountains to the Arctic Ocean, much of which is frozen for several months each year. (4) The eastern margin and islands, where much of the population is concentrated. (5) The southern plateau and river plains, including Arabia, the Deccan, and the alluvial plains of the Euphrates, Tigris, Indus, Ganges, and Irrawaddy. The climate shows great extremes and contrasts, the heart of the continent becoming bitterly cold in winter and very hot in summer. This, with the resulting pressure and wind systems, accounts for the Asiatic monsoons, bringing heavy rain to all SE Asia, China, and Japan, between May and October.

features rivers (over 2000 miles) Ob-Irtysh, Chang Jiang, Huang He, Amur, Lena, Mekong, Yenisei, Euphrates; lakes (over 18,000 sq km/7,000 sq mi) Caspian and Aral seas, Baikal, Balkhash.

population (1984) 2,778,000,000, the most densely populated of the continents; annual growth rate 1.7%

language predominantly tonal languages (Chinese, Japanese) in the east, Indo-Iranian languages in central India and Pakistan (Hindi/Urdu), and Semitic (Arabic) in the SW

religion Hinduism, Islam, Buddhism, Christianity, Confucianism, Shintoism.

Asia Minor /ˈeɪʃə ˈmaɪnə/ historical name for *Anatolia*, the Asian part of Turkey.

Asian Development Bank (ADB) a bank founded 1966 to stimulate growth in Asia and the Far East by administering direct loans and technical assistance. Members include 30 countries within the region and 14 countries of W Europe and North America. The headquarters are in Manila, Philippines.

Japan played a leading role in the setting-up of the ADB, which was established under the aegis of the United Nations Economic and Social Council for Asia and the Pacific (ESCAP).

Asia-Pacific Economic Cooperation Conference (APEC) trade group comprising 12 Pacific Asian countries, formed Nov 1898 to promote multilateral trade and economic cooperation between member states. Its members are the USA, Canada, Japan, Australia, New Zealand, South Korea, Brunei, Indonesia, Malaysia, the Phillipines, Singapore, and Thailand.

Asia, Soviet Central see ◊Soviet Central Asia.

Asiento, Treaty of agreement between the UK and Spain 1713, whereby British traders were permitted to introduce 144,000 black slaves into the Spanish-American colonies in the course of the following 30 years. In 1750 the right was bought out by the Spanish government for $100,000.

Asimov /ˈæzɪmɒf/ Isaac 1920– . US science-fiction writer and writer on science, born in the USSR. He has published about 200 books,

and is possibly best known for his *I, Robot* 1950 and the 'Foundation' trilogy 1951–53, continued in *Foundation's Edge* 1983.

AS Level General Certificate of Education Advanced Supplementary examinations, introduced in the UK 1988 as the equivalent to 'half an ◊A Level' as a means of broadening the sixth form (age 16–18) curriculum, and including more students in the examination system.

Asmara /æsˈmɑːrə/ or *Asmera* capital of Eritrea, Ethiopia; 64 km/40 mi SW of Massawa on the Red Sea; population (1984) 275,385. Products include beer, clothes, and textiles. In 1974, unrest here precipitated the end of the Ethiopian Empire. It has a naval school.

Asnières /ˌɑːniˈeə/ NW suburb of Paris, France, on the left bank of the Seine; population (1982) 71,220. It is a boating centre and pleasure resort.

Asoka /əˈsəʊkə/ reigned 264–228 BC. Indian emperor, who was a Buddhist convert. He had edicts enjoining the adoption of his new faith carved on pillars and rock faces throughout his dominions, and many survive. In Patna there are the remains of a hall built by him.

asp any of several venomous snakes, including *Vipera aspis* of S Europe allied to the ◊adder, and the Egyptian cobra *Naja haje*, reputed to have been used by Cleopatra for her suicide.

asparagus plant of the family Liliaceae. *Asparagus officinalis* is cultivated, and the young shoots are eaten as a vegetable.

Aspasia /əˈspeɪziə/ *c.*440 BC. Greek courtesan, the mistress of the Athenian politician ◊Pericles. As a 'foreigner' from Miletus, she could not be recognized as his wife, but their son was later legitimized. The philosopher Socrates visited her salon, a meeting place for the celebrities of Athens. Her free thinking led to a charge of impiety, from which Pericles had to defend her.

aspen a variety of ◊poplar tree. *Populus tremula* is small-leaved with thin flexible branches.

Aspen Lodge /ˈæspən/ US presidential residence at the country retreat of ◊Camp David.

asphalt a type of semi-solid brown or black ◊bitumen, used in the construction industry. Considerable natural deposits of asphalt occur around the Dead Sea and in the Philippines, Cuba, Venezuela, and Trinidad. Bituminous limestone occurs at Neufchâtel, France. Asphalt is mixed with rock chips to form paving material, and the purer varieties are used for insulating material and for waterproofing masonry. Asphalt can be produced artificially by the distillation of ◊petroleum.

asphodel genus of plants belonging to the family Liliaceae. *Asphodelus albus*, the **white asphodel** or **king's spear**, is found in Italy and Greece, sometimes covering large areas, and providing grazing for sheep. *Asphodeline lutea* is the yellow asphodel.

asphyxia suffocation; a lack of oxygen which produces a build-up of carbon dioxide waste in the tissues. Asphyxia may arise from any one of a number of causes, including inhalation of smoke or poisonous gases, obstruction of the airway (by water, food, vomit, or foreign object), strangulation, or smothering. If it is not quickly relieved, brain damage or death ensues.

aspidistra Asiatic plant of the Liliaceae family. The Chinese *Aspidistra elatior* has broad, lanceolate leaves and, like all members of the genus, grows well in warm indoor conditions.

aspirin acetylsalicylic acid, a popular ◊analgesic developed in the early 20th century, for headaches and arthritis. In the long term, even moderate use may involve side effects including kidney damage and hearing defects and it is no longer considered suitable for children under 12, because of a suspected link with a rare disease, Reye's syndrome. However, recent medical research suggests that aspirin may be of value in preventing heart attack (myocardial infarction) and thrombosis.

asplenium fern of the family Aspleniaceae, generally known as *spleenwort*.

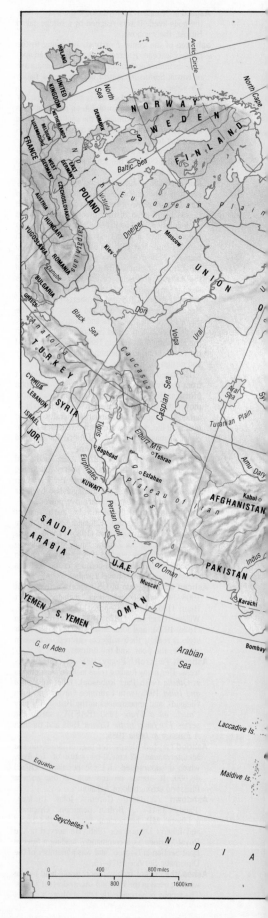

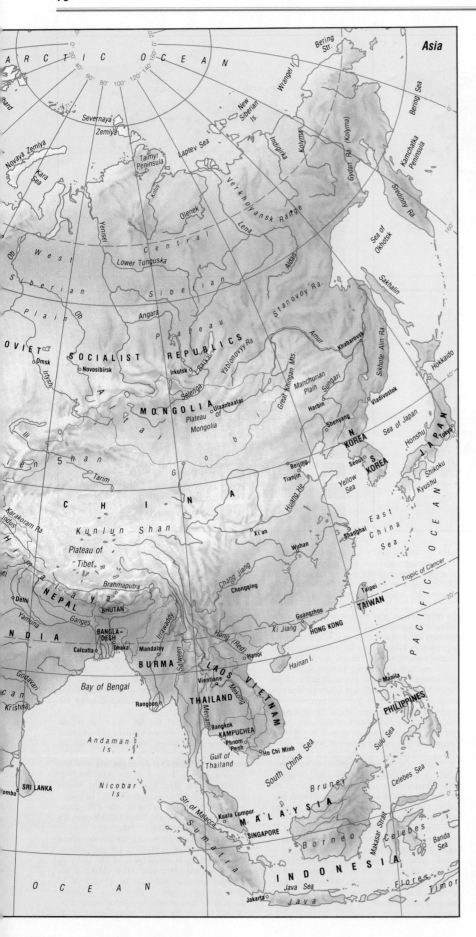

Asia

Asplund /'æsplənd/ (Erik) Gunnar 1885–1940. Swedish architect. HIs early work, for example at the Stockholm South Cemetary (1914), was in the Neo-Classical tradition. Later buildings, such as the Stockholm City Library (1924–27) and Gothenburg City Hall (1934–37), developed a refined Modern-Classical style, culminating in the Stockholm South Cemetary Crematorium (1935–40).

Asquith /'æskwɪθ/ Herbert Henry, 1st Earl of Oxford and Asquith 1852–1928. British Liberal politician, prime minister 1908–16. As chancellor of the Exchequer he introduced old-age pensions 1908. He limited the powers of the House of Lords and attempted to give Ireland Home Rule.

Asquith was born in Yorkshire. Elected Member of Parliament 1886, he was home secretary in Gladstone's 1892–95 government. He was chancellor of the Exchequer 1905–08 and succeeded Campbell-Bannerman as prime minister. Forcing through the radical budget of his chancellor (◊Lloyd George) led him into two elections 1910, which resulted in the Parliament Act 1911, limiting the right of the Lords to veto legislation. His endeavours to pass the Home Rule for Ireland Bill led to the ◊Curragh 'Mutiny' and incipient civil war. Unity was re-established by the outbreak of World War I, and a coalition government was formed May 1915. However, his attitude of 'wait and see' was not adapted to all-out war, and in Dec 1916 he was replaced by Lloyd George. In 1918 the Liberal election defeat led to the eclipse of the party.

Asquith /'æskwɪθ/ Lady Cynthia 1887–1960. British author, born Charteris. She married Herbert, second son of H H Asquith, and wrote a diary of the World War I years.

ass domesticated donkey, or the wild form from which it was derived, the African wild ass *Equus asinus*; also the Asian wild ass *Equus hemionus*. They differ from horses in their smaller size, larger ears, tufted tail, dorsal stripes, and characteristic bray.

Assad /'æsæd/ Hafez al 1930–   . Syrian Ba'athist politician. He became prime minister after the bloodless military coup 1970, and in 1971 was the first president to be elected by popular vote. He was re-elected 1978. He is a Shia (Alawite) Muslim.

Assam /æ'sæm/ state of NE India
area 78,400 sq km/30,262 sq mi
capital Dispur
towns Shilling
products half India's tea is grown here, and half its oil produced; rice, jute, sugar, cotton, coal
population (1981) 19,903,000, including
12 million Assamese (Hindus), 5 million Bengalis (chiefly Muslim immigrants from Bangladesh), and Nepális; and 2 million native people (Christian and traditional religions)
language Assamese
history a thriving region from 1000 BC; later emigrants came from China and Burma; after

Assam

Asia

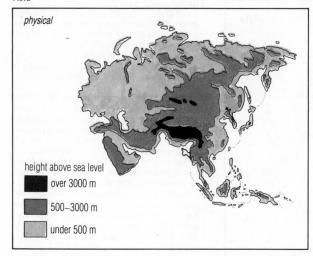

physical

height above sea level
- over 3000 m
- 500–3000 m
- under 500 m

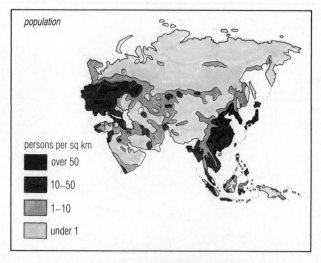

population

persons per sq km
- over 50
- 10–50
- 1–10
- under 1

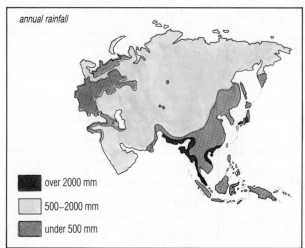

annual rainfall

- over 2000 mm
- 500–2000 mm
- under 500 mm

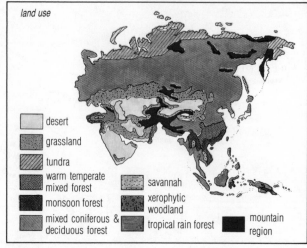

land use

- desert
- grassland
- tundra
- warm temperate mixed forest
- monsoon forest
- mixed coniferous & deciduous forest
- savannah
- xerophytic woodland
- tropical rain forest
- mountain region

Burmese invasion 1826, Britain took control; made a separate province 1874; included in the Dominion of India, except for most of the Muslim district of Silhet, which went to Pakistan 1947; the Gara, Khasi, and Jaintia tribal hill districts became the state of ◊Meghalaya 1970; the Mizo hill district became the Union Territory of Mizoram 1972; massacres of Muslim Bengalis by Hindus 1983.

assassination murder, especially of a political, royal, or public person. The term derives from a sect of Muslim fanatics in the 11th and 12th centuries known as *hashshashin* ('takers of hashish'). They were reputed either to smoke cannabis before they went out to murder, or to receive hashish as payment.

assault an act or threat of physical violence against a person without their consent. In English law it is both a crime and a ◊tort (a civil wrong). The kinds of criminal assault are: common (ordinary); aggravated (more serious, such as causing actual bodily harm); or indecent (of a sexual nature).

assault ship naval vessel designed to land and support troops and vehicles under hostile conditions.

assaying in chemistsry, the determination of the quantity of a given substance present in a sample. Usually it refers to determining the purity of precious metals.

The assay may be carried out by 'wet' methods, when the sample is wholly or partially dissolved in some reagent (often an acid), or by 'dry' or 'fire' methods, in which the compounds present in the sample are combined with other substances.

assembly code computer-programming language closely related to the internal codes of the machine

itself. It consists chiefly of a set of short mnemonics which are translated, by a program called an assembler, into ◊machine code for the computer's ◊CPU (central processing unit) to follow directly. In assembly language, for example, JMP means 'jump' and LDA is 'load accumulator'. It is used by programmers who need to write very fast or efficient programs.

assembly line a method of mass production in which a product is built up step by step by successive workers adding one part at a time.

US inventor Eli Whitney pioneered the modern concept of industrial assembly in the 1790s, when he employed unskilled labour to assemble muskets from sets of identical precision-made parts. In 1901 Ransome Olds in the USA began mass-producing motor cars on an assembly-line principle, a method further refined by the introduction of the moving conveyor belt by Henry ◊Ford 1913 and the time-and-motion studies of F W ◊Taylor. On the modern assembly line human workers now stand side by side with ◊robots.

asset a business accounting term that covers the land or property of a company or individual, payments due from bills, investments, and anything else owned that can be turned into cash. On a company's balance sheet, total assets must be equal to liabilities (money and services owed).

Assisi /ə'si:zi/ town in Umbria, Italy, 19 km/12 mi south east of Perugia; population (1981) 25,000. St Francis was born here and is buried in the Franciscan monastery, completed 1253. The churches of St Francis are adorned with frescoes by Giotto, Cimabue, and others.

Assisted Places Scheme in UK education, a scheme established 1980 by which the government assists parents with the cost of fees at ◊independent schools on a means-tested basis.

Assiut /æ'sju:t/ alternative transliteration of ◊Asyut.

assize in medieval Europe, the passing of laws, either by the king with the consent of nobles, as in the Constitutions of ◊Clarendon by Henry II, 1164, or as a complete system, such as the *Assizes of Jerusalem*, a compilation of the law of the feudal kingdom of Jerusalem in the 13th century. The term remained in use in the UK for the courts held by judges of the High Court in each county; they were abolished under the Courts Act 1971.

Associated State of the UK status of certain Commonwealth countries which have full internal government, but where Britain is responsible for external relations and defence.

Association of SouthEast Asian Nations (ASEAN) regional alliance formed in Bangkok 1967; it took over the nonmilitary role of the Southeast Asia Treaty Organization 1975. Its members are Indonesia, Malaysia, the Philippines, Singapore, Thailand, and (from 1984) Brunei; its headquarters are in Jakarta, Indonesia.

associative law in mathematics, the law that states that the result of performing certain consecutive operations is independent of the order in which they are performed. Thus addition is associative because, for example 3 + (4 + 5) gives the same sum as (3 + 4) + 5. Multiplication is also associative, for example 2 × (3 × 4) gives the same product as (2 × 3)

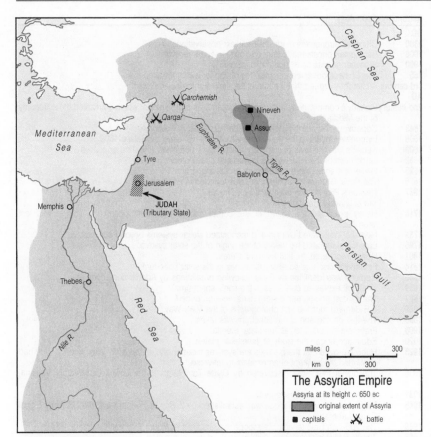

The Assyrian Empire
Assyria at its height *c.* 650 BC
original extent of Assyria
■ capitals   ✕ battle

× 4. Subtraction and division are not associative.

assortative mating in ◊population genetics, selective mating between individuals that are genetically related or have similar characteristics. If sufficiently consistent, assortative mating can theoretically eventually result in the evolution of two or more new species.

ASSR abbreviation for *Autonomous Soviet Socialist Republic.*

Assuan /æˈswɑːn/ alternative transliteration of ◊Aswan.

Assy /ˈæsi/ plateau in Haute-Savoie, E France, 1,000 m/3,280 ft above sea level. The area is noted for its numerous sanitoriums. The church of Nôtre Dame de Toute Grâce, begun 1937 and consecrated 1950, is adorned with works by Braque, Chagall, Matisse, Derain, Rouault, and other artists.

Assyria /əˈsɪriə/ empire in the Middle East *c.*2500–612 BC, in N Mesopotamia (now Iraq); capital Ninéveh. It was initially subject to Sumeria and intermittently to Babylon. The Assyrians adopted in the main the Sumerian religion and structure of society. At its greatest extent the empire included Egypt and stretched from the E Mediterranean coast to the Persian Gulf.

The land of Assyria originally consisted of a narrow strip of alluvial soil on each side of the river Tigris. The area was settled about 3500 BC and was dominated by Sumeria until about 2350 BC. For nearly 200 years Assyria was subject first to the Babylonian dynasty of Akkad and then to the Gutians, barbarians from the north. The first Assyrian kings are mentioned during the wars following the decline of the 3rd dynasty of Ur, but Assyria continued under Babylonian and subsequently Egyptian suzerainty until about 1450 BC. Under King Ashur-uballit (reigned about 1380–1340 BC) Assyria became a military power. His work was continued by Adad-nirari I, Shalmaneser I, and Tukulti-enurta I, who conquered Babylonia and assumed the title of king of Sumer and Akkad.

During the reign of Nebuchadnezzar I (1150–1110 BC), Assyria was again subject to Babylonia, but was liberated by Tiglath-pileser I. In the Aramaean invasions, most of the ground gained was lost. From the accession of Adad-nirari II 911 BC Assyria pursued a course of expansion and conquest, culminating in the mastery of Elam, Mesopotamia, Syria, Palestine, the Arabian marches, and Egypt. Of this period the Old Testament records and many 'documents' such as the Black Obelisk celebrating the conquest of Shalmaneser III in the 9th century BC survive.

The reign of Ashur-nazir-pal II (885–860 BC) was spent in unceasing warfare; he is said to have introduced 'frightfulness', evidenced by many bas-reliefs. Shalmaneser III warred against the Syrian states. At the battle of Qarqar 854 BC the Assyrian advance received a setback, and there followed a period of decline. The final period of Assyrian ascendancy began with the accession of Tiglath-pileser III (746–728 BC) and continued during the reigns of Sargon II, Sennacherib, Esarhaddon, and Ashurbanipal, culminating in the conquest of Egypt by Esarhaddon 671 BC. From this time the empire seems to have fallen into decay. Nabopolassar of Babylonia and Cyaxares of Media (see ◊Mede) united against it, Nineveh was destroyed 612 BC, and Assyria became a Median province and subsequently a principality of the Persian empire.

Much of Assyrian religion, law, social structure, and artistic achievement was derived from neighbouring sources. The Assyrians adopted the cuneiform script invented by the Sumerians, and took over the Sumerian pantheon, although the Assyrian god, Ashur (Assur), assumed the chief place in the cult. The library of Ashurbanipal excavated at Nineveh witnesses to the thoroughness with which Babylonian culture was being assimilated.

Astaire /əˈsteə/ Fred. Stage name of Frederick Austerlitz 1899–1987. US dancer, actor, singer, and choreographer, who starred in numerous films, including *Top Hat* 1935, *Easter Parade*

1948, and *Funny Face* 1957, many of which contained inventive sequences he designed himself. He made ten classic films with the most popular of his dancing partners, Ginger Rogers. He later played straight dramatic roles, in films such as *On the Beach* 1959.

Born in Omaha, Nebraska, he danced in partnership with his sister Adele (1898–1981) from 1904 until her marriage in 1932. He entered films in 1933. Among his many other films are *Roberta* 1935 and *Follow the Fleet* 1936. Astaire was a virtuoso dancer and perfectionist known for his elegant style.

Astarte /əˈstɑːti/ alternative name for the Babylonian and Assyrian goddess ◊Ishtar.

astatine a ◊halogen-like and highly radioactive element, symbol At, atomic number 85, relative atomic mass 210. It is made by bombarding bismuth in a cyclotron (particle accelerator).

aster plant of the family Compositae, belonging to the same subfamily as the daisy. The sea aster *Aster tripolium* grows wild on sea cliffs in the South of England. Other species are familiar as cultivated garden flowers, including the Michaelmas daisy *Aster nova-belgii.*

The China aster *Callistephus chinensis* belongs to a closely allied genus; it was introduced to Europe from China and Japan in the early 18th century.

asterisk a starlike punctuation mark used to link the asterisked word with a note at the bottom of a page; to mark that certain letters are missing from a word (especially a taboo word such as f**k); or to indicate that a word or usage is nonexistent, for example, 'In English we say three boys and not three *boy'.

asteroid or *minor planet* any of many thousands of small bodies, composed of rock and iron, that orbit the Sun. Most asteroids lie in a belt between the orbits of Mars and Jupiter. They are thought to be fragments left over from the formation of the ◊solar system. About 100,000 may exist, but their total mass is only a few hundredths the mass of the Moon.

They include Ceres (the largest asteroid, 1,000 km/620 mi in diameter), Vesta (which has a light-coloured surface, and is the brightest as seen from Earth), ◊Eros, and ◊Icarus. Some asteroids are on orbits that bring them close to the Earth, and some, such as the ◊Apollo asteroids, even cross the Earth's orbit. One group, the Trojans, moves along the same orbit as Jupiter, 60° ahead and behind the planet.

Astaire Stylish US dancer Fred Astaire and his partner, Ginger Rogers.

One unusual asteroid, Chiron, orbits beyond Saturn.

asthenosphere a division of the Earth's structure lying beneath the ◊lithosphere, at a depth of approximately 70 km/45 mi to 260 km/160 mi. It is thought to be the soft, partially molten layer of the ◊mantle on which the rigid plates of the Earth's surface move to produce the motions of ◊plate tectonics.

asthma difficulty in breathing due to spasm of the bronchi (air passages) in the lungs. Attacks may be provoked by allergy, infection, stress, or emotional upset. Treatment is with ◊bronchodilators to relax the bronchial muscles and thereby ease the breathing, and in severe cases by inhaled steroids which reduce inflammation of the bronchi.

Although the symptoms are similar to those of bronchial asthma, **cardiac asthma** is an unrelated condition. It is a symptom of heart deterioration.

Asti /ˈæsti/ town in Piedmont, SE of Turin, Italy; population (1983) 76,439. Asti province is famed for its sparkling wine. Other products include chemicals, textiles, and glass.

astigmatism an optical distortion, usually caused by an irregular curvature of the cornea, the transparent front 'window' of the eye.

Aston /ˈæstən/ Francis William 1877–1945. English physicist, who developed the mass spectrometer, which separates ◊isotopes by projecting their ions (charged atoms) through a magnetic field.

From 1910, he worked in the Cavendish Laboratory, Cambridge. He published *Isotopes*, and received the Nobel Prize for Chemistry 1922. His researches were of the utmost value in the development of atomic theory.

Astor /ˈæstə/ prominent US and British family. **John Jacob Astor** (1763–1848) was a US millionaire. **Waldorf Astor**, 2nd Viscount Astor (1879–1952), was Conservative Member of Parliament for Plymouth 1910–19, when he succeeded to the peerage. He was chief proprietor of the British *Observer* newspaper. His wife was Nancy Witcher Langhorne (1879–1964) **Lady Astor**, the first woman Member of Parliament to take a seat in the House of Commons 1919, when she succeeded her husband for the constituency of Plymouth. She was also a temperance fanatic and political hostess. Government policy was said to be decided at Cliveden, their country home.

Astor /ˈæstə/ Mary. Stage name of Lucille Langhanke 1906–1987. US film actress, whose

astronaut *Bruce McCandless floats free above the Earth in his manned manoeuvring unit (MMU), Feb 7 1984.*

Astronomy chronology

BC

2300	Chinese astronomers made their earliest observations.
2000	Babylonian priests made their first observational records.
1900	Stonehenge was constructed: first phase.
365	The Chinese observed the satellites of Jupiter with the naked eye.
3rd century	Aristarchus argued that the sun is the centre of the solar system.

AD

2nd century	Ptolemy's complicated earth-centred system was promulgated, which dominated the astronomy of the Middle Ages.
1543	Copernicus revived the ideas of Aristarchus in *De Revolutionibus*.
1608	Lippershey invented the telescope, which was first used by Galileo 1609.
1609	Kepler's first two laws of planetary motion were published (the third appeared 1619).
1632	Leiden established the world's first official observatory.
1633	Galileo's theories were condemned by the Inquisition.
1675	The Royal Greenwich Observatory was founded in England.
1687	Newton's *Principia* was published, including his 'law of universal gravitation'.
1718	Halley predicted the return of the comet named after him, observed 1758: it was last seen 1986.
1781	Herschel discovered Uranus and recognized stellar systems beyond our galaxy.
1796	Laplace elaborated his theory of the origin of the solar system.
1801	Piazzi discovered the first asteroid, Ceres.
1814	Fraunhofer first studied absorption lines in the solar spectrum.
1846	Neptune was identified by Galle, following predictions by Adams and Leverrier.
1859	Kirchhoff explained dark lines in the sun's spectrum.
1887	The earliest photographic star charts were produced.
1889	E E Barnard took the first photographs of the Milky Way.
1890	The first photograph of the spectrum was taken.
1908	Fragment of comet fell at Tungusta, Siberia.
1920	Eddington began the study of interstellar matter.
1923	Hubble proved that the galaxies are systems independent of the Milky Way, and by 1930 had confirmed the concept of an expanding universe.
1930	The planet Pluto was discovered by Clyde Tombaugh at the Lowell Observatory, Arizona, USA.
1931	Jansky founded radioastronomy.
1945	Radar contact with the moon was established by Z Bay of Hungary and the US Army Signal Corps Laboratory.
1948	The 200-inch Hale reflector telescope was installed at Mount Palomar, California, USA.
1955	The Jodrell Bank telescope 'dish' in England was completed.
1957	The first Sputnik satellite (USSR) opened the age of space observation.
1962	The first X-ray source was discovered in Scorpio.
1963	The first quasar was discovered.
1967	The first pulsar was discovered by Jocelyn Bell.
1969	The first manned moon landing was made by US astronauts.
1976	A 236-inch reflector telescope was installed at Mount Semirodniki (USSR).
1977	Uranus was discovered to have rings.
1977	The spacecraft Voyager 1 and 2 were launched, passing Jupiter and Saturn 1979–81.
1978	The spacecraft Pioneer Venus 1 and 2 reached Venus.
1978	A satellite of Pluto, Charon, was discovered by James Christie of the US Naval Observatory.
1979	The UK infrared telescope (UKIRT) was established on Hawaii.
1985	Halley's comet returned.
1986	Voyager 2 reached Uranus and discovered ten new moons.
1987	Bright supernova visible to the naked eye for the first time since 1604.
1989	Voyager 2 reached Neptune.

many films included *Don Juan* 1926 and *The Maltese Falcon* 1941. Her memoirs *My Story* 1959 were notorious for their frankness.

Astrakhan /ˌæstrəˈkɑːn/ city in the USSR, on the delta of the Volga, capital of Astrakhan region; population (1987) 509,000. In ancient times a Tatar capital, it became Russian 1556. It is the chief port for the Caspian fisheries.

astrolabe ancient navigational instrument, forerunner of the sextant. Astrolabes usually consisted of a flat disc with a sighting rod that could be pivoted to point at the Sun or bright stars. From the altitude of the Sun or star above the horizon, the local time could be estimated.

astrology (Greek *astron* 'star'; *legein* 'speak') study of the relative position of the planets and stars in the belief that they influence events on Earth. The astrologer casts a ◊horoscope based on the time and place of the subject's birth. Astrology has no proven scientific basis, but has been widespread since ancient times. Western astrology is based on the signs of the zodiac; Chinese astrology is based on a 60-year cycle and lunar calendar.

history A strongly held belief in ancient Babylon, astrology spread to the Mediterranean world, and was widely used by the Greeks and Romans. In Europe during the Middle Ages it had a powerful influence, since kings and other public figures had their own astrologers, and astrological beliefs are reflected in Elizabethan and Jacobean literature. Former US president Reagan reportedly scheduled events based on astrological readings.

popular prediction In the UK, the first edition of *Old Moore's Almanac*, which gives a forecast of the year ahead, appeared 1700, and there have been annual editions since. Astrological forecasts in newspapers and magazines are usually very simplistic.

astrometry the measurement of the precise positions of stars, planets, and other bodies in space. Such information is needed for practical purposes including accurate timekeeping, surveying and navigation, and calculating orbits and measuring distances in space. Astrometry is not concerned with the surface features or the physical nature of the body under study.

Before telescopes, astronomical observations were simple astrometry. Precise astrometry has shown that stars are not fixed in position, but have a proper motion caused as they and the Sun orbit the galaxy. The nearest stars also show ◊parallax (apparent change in position), from which their distances can be calculated. Above the distorting effects of the atmosphere, satellites can make even more precise measurements than ground telescopes, so refining the distance scale of space.

astronaut Western term for a person making flights into space; the Soviet term is *cosmonaut*.

astronautics the science of space travel. See ◊rocket; ◊satellite; ◊space probe.

Astronomer Royal honorary post in British astronomy. Originally it was held by the director of the Royal Greenwich Observatory; since 1972 the title of Astronomer Royal has been awarded separately. The present Astronomer Royal (since 1982) is F Graham Smith. A separate post of Astronomer Royal for Scotland is attached to the directorship of the Royal Observatory, Edinburgh.

astronomical unit the average distance of the Earth from the Sun: 149,597,870 km/92,955,800 mi. It is used to describe planetary distances.

astronomy the science of the celestial bodies: the Sun, the Moon, and the planets; the stars and galaxies; and all other objects in the universe. It is concerned with their positions, motions, distances, and physical conditions; and with their origins and evolution. Astronomy thus divides into fields such as astrophysics, celestial mechanics, and cosmology. See also ◊gamma-ray astronomy and ◊ultraviolet astronomy.

Astronomy is perhaps the oldest science; there are observational records from Babylonia, China, and Egypt. The first true astronomers, however, were the Greeks, who knew the Earth to be a sphere, and attempted to measure its size. ◊Hipparchus drew star catalogues, and estimated the sizes and distances of the Sun and Moon. Greek astronomy was summarized by ◊Ptolemy in his *Almagest*, which included the idea of an Earth-centred universe. This was still the prevailing view in 1543, when ◊Copernicus showed that the Earth and the other planets revolve around the Sun. The next century saw the laws of planetary motion expounded by ◊Kepler, who used the accurate observations made by ◊Brahe, and ◊Galileo's discoveries 1609–10 with the *refractor* telescope (invented by ◊Lippershey 1608): the moons of Jupiter, the phases of Venus, and the myriad of stars in the Milky Way. ◊Newton's *Principia* 1687 founded celestial mechanics, and firmly established the Copernican theory. About 1670 Newton built the first *reflector*, which used a mirror in place of the main lens. 100 years later, ◊Herschel began the construction of large telescopes, with which he discovered a planet, Uranus, and investigated double stars and nebulae, opening a new era in observational astronomy. In 1838 ◊Bessel made the first reasonably accurate measurement of a star's distance, and Neptune was discovered 1846 following mathematical prediction of its orbit. Photography, introduced at this time, was to have a great impact on astronomical research. Observations of the Sun's spectrum led to the introduction of spectroscopy and the development of astrophysics. Big telescopes built in the 20th century have revealed the distance and nature of the galaxies observed by Herschel. Pluto was discovered 1930. ◊Hubble found that all galaxies seem to be receding, the first evidence of an expanding, evolving universe, which forms the basis of the currently favoured ◊Big Bang theory. Advances in technology, especially electronics, have made it possible to study radiation from astronomical objects at all wavelengths, not just visible light, from gamma rays and X-rays right up to radio wavelengths. Discoveries since 1960 include ◊quasars and ◊pulsars, and a good understanding of how stars evolve. Artificial satellites, space probes, orbiting observatories, and giant optical telescopes are continually increasing knowledge of the universe.

astrophotography the use of photography in astronomical research. The first successful photograph of a celestial object was the daguerreotype plate of the Moon taken by J W Draper of the USA Mar 1840. Modern-day astrophotography uses techniques such as ◊charge coupled devices.

Before the development of photography, observations were gathered in the form of sketches made at the telescope. Several successful daguerreotypes were obtained prior to the introduction of wet plate collodion about 1850. The availability of this more convenient method meant that photography was used on a more systematic basis, including the monitoring of sunspot activity. Dry plates were introduced in the 1870s, and in 1880 Henry Draper obtained a photograph of the ◊Orion nebula. The first successful image of a comet was obtained 1882 by the Scottish astronomer David Gill, his plate displaying excellent star images. Following this, Gill and J C Kapteyn compiled the first photographic atlas of the southern sky cataloguing almost half a million stars.

Modern-day electronic innovations, notably *charge-coupled devices* (CCDs), provide a more efficient light-gathering capability than photographic paper as well as enabling information to be transferred to a computer for analysis. However, CCD images are expensive and very small in size compared to photographic plates. Photographic plates are better suited to wide-field images, whereas CCDs are used for individual objects, which may be very faint, within a narrow field of sky.

astrophysics the study of the physical nature of stars, galaxies, and the universe. It began with the development of spectroscopy in the 19th century, which allowed astronomers to analyse the composition of stars from their light.

Astrophysicists view the universe as a vast natural laboratory in which they can study matter under conditions of temperature, pressure and density that are unattainable on Earth.

Asturias /æsˈtuəriəs/ autonomous region of N Spain; area 10,600 sq km/4,092 sq mi; population (1986) 1,114,000. Half of Spain's coal is produced from the mines of Asturias. Agricultural produce includes maize, fruit, and livestock. Oviedo and Gijon are the main industrial towns.

It was once a separate kingdom and the eldest son of a king of Spain is still called Prince of Asturias.

Asturias /æsˈtuəriəs/ Miguel Ángel 1899–1974. Guatemalan author and diplomat. He published poetry, Guatemalan legends, and novels, such as *El Señor Presidente*/*The President* 1946, *Men of Corn* 1949, and *Strong Wind* 1950, attacking Latin-American dictatorships and 'Yankee imperialism'. Nobel prize 1967.

Asunción /æˌsuːnsiˈɒn/ capital and port of Paraguay, on the Paraguay river; population (1984) 729,000. It produces textiles, footwear, and food products. Founded 1537, it was the first Spanish settlement in the La Plata region.

Aswan /ˌæsˈwɑːn/ winter resort town in Upper Egypt; population (1985) 183,000. It is near the High Dam 1960–70, which keeps the level of the Nile constant throughout the year without flooding. It produces steel and textiles.

asymptote in ◊coordinate geometry, a straight line towards which a curve approaches more and more closely but never reaches. If a point on a curve approaches a straight line such that its distance from the straight line is d, then the line is an asymptote to the curve if limit d tends to zero as the point moves towards infinity. Among ◊conic sections (curves obtained by the intersection of a plane and a double cone), a ◊hyperbola has two asymptotes, which in the case of a rectangular hyperbola are at right angles to each other.

Asyut /æsˈjuːt/ commercial centre in Upper Egypt, near the Nile, 322 km/200 mi South of Cairo; population (1985) 274,400. An ancient Graeco-Egyptian city, it has many tombs of 11th and 12th dynasty nobles.

Atacama /ˌætəˈkɑːmə/ desert in N Chile; area about 80,000 sq km/31,000 sq mi. Inland are mountains, and the coastal area is rainless and barren. There are silver and copper mines, and extensive nitrate deposits.

Atahualpa /ˌætəˈwɑːlpə/ *c.*1502–1533. Last emperor of the Incas of Peru. He was taken prisoner 1532 when the Spaniards arrived, and agreed

Atatürk *The maker of modern Turkey, Kemal Atatürk, introduced many social and administrative reforms, which affected Turkish religion, justice, education, language, and the status of women.*

to pay a huge ransom, but was accused of plotting against the conquistador Pizarro and sentenced to be burned. On his consenting to Christian baptism, the sentence was commuted to strangulation.

Atalanta /ˌætəˈlæntə/ in Greek mythology, a woman hunter who challenged all her suitors to a foot race; if they lost they were killed. Aphrodite gave Milanion three golden apples to drop so that when Atalanta stopped to pick them up, she lost the race.

Atatürk /ˈætətɜːk/ Kemal. Name assumed 1934 by Mustafa Kemal Pasha 1881–1938. Turkish politician and general, first president of Turkey from 1923. After World War I he established a provisional rebel government and in 1921–22 the Turkish armies under his leadership expelled the Greeks who were occupying Turkey. He is the founder of the modern republic, which he ruled as virtual dictator, with a policy of consistent and radical westernization.

Kemal, born in Thessaloniki, was banished 1904 for joining a revolutionary society. Later he was pardoned and promotede in the army, and was largely responsible for the successful defence of the Dardanelles against the British 1915. In 1918, after Turkey had been defeated, he was sent into Anatolia to carry through the demobilization of the Turkish forces in accordance with the armistice terms, but instead established a provisional government opposed to that of Constantinople (under Allied control), and in 1921 led the Turkish armies against the Greeks, who had occupied a large part of Anatolia. He checked them at the Battle of the Sakaria, 23 Aug–13 Sept 1921, for which he was granted the title of Ghazi (the Victorious), and within a year had expelled the Greeks from Turkish soil. War with the British was averted by his diplomacy and Turkey in Europe passed under Kemal's control. On 29 Oct 1923, Turkey was proclaimed a republic with Kemal as first president. Atatürk means 'Father of the Turks'.

atavism (Latin *atavus* 'ancestor') in ◊genetics, the reappearance of a characteristic not apparent in the immediately preceding generations; in psychology, the manifestation of primitive forms of behaviour.

ataxia loss of muscular coordination due to neurological damage or disease.

Atget /ˈætdʒeɪ/ Eugène 1857–1927. French photographer. He took up photography at the age of 40, and for 30 years documented urban Paris, leaving some 10,000 photos.

Athabasca /ˌæθəˈbæskə/ lake and river in Alberta and Saskatchewan, Canada, with huge tar sand deposits (source of the hydrocarbon mixture 'heavy oil') to the SW of the lake.

Athanasian creed one of the three ancient ◊creeds of the Christian church. Mainly a definition of the Trinity and incarnation, it was written many years

Athletics

The 24th Olympics were held in Seoul, South Korea 17 Sep–2 Oct 1988.
Track and field champions:

men/women
100 metres Carl Lewis *(USA)*/Florence Griffith-Joyner *(USA)*
200 metres Joe Deloach *(USA)*/Florence Griffith-Joyner *(USA)*
400 metres Steve Lewis *(USA)*/Olga Bryzgina *(USSR)*
800 metres Paul Ereng *(Kenya)*/Sigrun Wodars *(East Germany)*
1,500 metres Peter Rono *(Kenya)*/Paula Ivan *(Romania)*
3,000 metres – /Tatyana Samolenko *(USSR)*
5,000 metres John Ngugi *(Kenya)*/ –
10,000 metres Brahim Boutaib *(Morocco)*/Olga Bondarenko *(USSR)*
Marathon Gelindo Bordin *(Italy)*/Rosa Mota *(Portugal)*
100 metres hurdles – /Jordanka Donkova *(Bulgaria)*
110 metres hurdles Roger Kingdom *(USA)*/ –
400 metres hurdles Andre Phillips *(USA)*/Debbie Flintoff-King *(Australia)*
3,000 metres steeplechase Julius Kariuki *(Kenya)*/ –
20,000 metres walk Joseph Pribilinec *(Czechoslovakia)*/ –
50,000 metres walk Viacheslav Ivanenko *(USSR)*/ –
4 × 100 metres relay USSR/USA
4 × 400 metres relay USA/USSR
high jump Gennadi Avdeyenko *(USSR)*/Louise Ritter *(USA)*
long jump Carl Lewis *(USA)*/Jackie Joyner-Kersee *(USA)*
triple jump Hristo Markov *(Bulgaria)*/ –
pole vault Sergey Bubka *(USSR)*/ –
javelin Tapio Korjus *(Finland)*/Petra Felke *(East Germany)*
hammer Sergey Litvinov *(USSR)*/ –
discus Jurgen Schult *(East Germany)*/Martina Hellmann *(East Germany)*
shot put Ulf Timmermann *(East Germany)*/Natalya Lisovaskaya *(USSR)*
decathlon Christian Schenk *(East Germany)*/ –
heptathlon/Jackie Joyner-Kersee *(USA)*

after the death of Athanasius, but was attributed to him as the chief upholder of Trinitarian doctrine.

Athanasius, St /ˌæθəˈneɪʃəs/ 298–373. Christian bishop of Alexandria, supporter of the doctrines of the Trinity and incarnation. He was a disciple of St Anthony the hermit, and an opponent of ◊Arianism in the great Arian controversy. Arianism was officially condemned at the Council of Nicaea 325, and Athanasius was appointed bishop of Alexandria 328. The Athanasian creed was not actually written by him, although it reflects his views.

Banished 335 by the emperor Constantine because of his intransigence towards the defeated Arians, in 346 he was recalled but suffered three more banishments before his final reinstatement about 366.

atheism nonbelief in, or the positive denial of, the existence of a god or gods.

Dogmatic atheism asserts that there is no God. *Sceptical atheism* maintains that the finite human mind is so constituted as to be incapable of discovering that there is or is not a God. *Critical atheism* holds that the evidence for theism is inadequate. This is akin to *philosophical atheism*, which fails to find evidence of a God manifest in the universe. *Speculative atheism* comprises the beliefs of those who, like the German philosopher Kant, find it impossible to demonstrate the existence of God. A related concept is ◊agnosticism.

Buddhism has been called an atheistic religion since it does not postulate any supreme being. The Jains are similarly atheistic, and so are those who adopt the Sankhya system of philosophy in Hinduism. Following the revolution of 1917 the USSR and later Communist states, such as Albania, adopted an atheist position.

Athelney, Isle of /ˈæθəlni/ area of firm ground in marshland near Taunton in Somerset, England, in 878 the headquarters of King ◊Alfred when he was in hiding from the Danes. The legend of his burning the cakes is set here.

Athelstan /ˈæθəlstən/ *c.*895–939. King of the Mercians and West Saxons. Son of Edward the Elder and grandson of Alfred the Great, he was crowned king 925 at Kingston-upon-Thames. He subdued parts of Cornwall and Wales, and in 937 defeated the Welsh, Scots, and Danes at Brunanburh.

Athena /əˈθiːnə/ in Greek mythology, the goddess (Roman Minerva) of war, wisdom, and the arts and crafts, who was supposed to have sprung fully grown from the head of Zeus. Her chief cult centre was Athens, where the ◊Parthenon was dedicated to her.

Athens /ˈæθɪnz/ Greek *Athinai* capital city of modern Greece and of ancient Attica; population (1981) 885,000, metropolitan area 3,027,000. Situated 8 km/5 mi NE of its port of Piraeus on the Gulf of Aegina, it is built around the rocky hills of the Acropolis 169 m/555 ft and the Areopagus 112 m/368 ft, and is overlooked from the NE by the hill of Lycabettus 277 m/909 ft. It lies in the south of the central plain of Attica, watered by the mountain streams of Cephissus and Ilissus.

The Acropolis dominates the city. Remains of ancient Greece include the Parthenon, the Erechtheum, and the temple of Athena Nike. Near the site of the ancient Agora (marketplace) stands the Theseum, and south of the Acropolis is the theatre of Dionysus. To the SE stand the gate of Hadrian and the columns of the temple of Olympian Zeus. Nearby is the marble stadium built about 330 BC and restored 1896.

The site was first inhabited about 3000 BC and Athens became the capital of a united Attica before 700 BC. Captured and sacked by the Persians 480 BC, subsequently under Pericles it was the first city of Greece in power and culture. After the death of Alexander the Great the city fell into comparative decline, but it flourished as an intellectual centre until AD 529, when the philosophical schools were closed by Justinian. In 1458 it was captured by the Turks who held it until 1833; it was chosen as the capital of modern Greece 1834. Among the modern buildings are the royal palace and several museums.

atheroma furring-up of the interior of an artery by deposits, mainly of cholesterol, within its walls.

Associated with ◊atherosclerosis, atheroma has the effect of narrowing the lumen (channel) of the artery, thus restricting bloodflow. This predisposes to a number of conditions, including thrombosis, angina, and stroke.

atherosclerosis thickening and hardening of the walls of the arteries, associated with ◊atheroma.

athletics competitive track and field events consisting of running, throwing, and jumping disciplines. *Running events* range from sprint races (100 metres) to the marathon (26 miles 385 yards). *Jumping events* are the high jump, long jump, triple jump, and pole vault (men only). *Throwing events* are javelin, discus, shot put, and hammer throw (men only).

history Among the Greeks, vase paintings show that competitive athletics were established at least by 1600 BC. Ancient athletes were well paid and sponsored. The philosopher Aristotle paid the expenses of a boxer contestant at Olympia, and chariot races were sponsored by the Greek city-states.

Today athletes are supposed to be unpaid amateurs. In aiming for the world record they may rely on development of computer selection of the best potential competitors and analysis of motion for greatest speed, and so on; specialization of equipment for maximum performance (for example, fibreglass vaulting poles, foam landing pads, aerodynamically designed javelins, composition running tracks), and the unlawful use of drugs, such as ◊anabolic steroids and growth hormones.

Athos /ˈeɪθɒs/ a mountainous peninsula on the Macedonian coast of Greece. Its peak is 2,033 m/6,672 ft high. The promontory is occupied by a community of 20 Basilian monasteries inhabited by some 3,000 monks and lay brothers.

Atkins /ˈætkɪnz/ Tommy. Popular name for the British soldier. The earliest known use of the name is in an official handbook circulated at the end of the Napoleonic War. A story that Tommy Atkins was a British soldier mortally wounded under Wellington in 1794, and that the Duke chose his name some 50 years later, seems to have first appeared in an article by Col Newnham-Davis in *Printer's Pie.*

Atlanta /ətˈlæntə/ capital and largest city of Georgia, USA; population (1980) 422,000, metropolitan area 2,010,000. There are Ford and Lockheed assembly plants, and it is the headquarters of Coca-Cola.

Originally named Terminus 1837, and renamed 1845, it was burned 1864 by General Sherman during the American Civil War. Nearby Stone Mountain Memorial shows the Confederate heroes Jefferson Davis, Robert E Lee, and Stonewall Jackson on horseback.

Atlantic, Battle of the the German campaign during World War I to prevent merchant shipping from delivering food supplies from the USA to the Allies, especially the UK. By 1917, some 875,000 tons of shipping had been lost. The odds were only turned by the belated use of naval *convoys* and *depth charges* to deter submarine attack.

Notable action included the British defeat at *Coronel* off Chile on 1 Nov 1914, the subsequent British success at the *Falkland Islands* on 8 December 1914, and the battle at *Jutland* on 31 May 1916, which effectively neutralized the German surface fleet for the rest of the war.

Atlantic, Battle of the continuous battle fought in the Atlantic Ocean throughout World War II (1939–45) by the sea and air forces of the Allies and Germany. The number of U-boats destroyed by the Allies during the war was nearly 800. At least 2,200 convoys of 75,000 merchant ships crossed the Atlantic, protected by US naval forces. Before the US entry into the war 1941, destroyers were suplied to the British under the Lend-Lease Act 1941.

The battle opened on the first night of the war, when on 4 Sept 1939 the ocean liner *Athenia*, sailing from Glasgow to New York, was torpedoed by a German submarine off the Irish coast. Germany tried U-boats, surface-raiders, indiscriminate mine-laying, and aircraft, but every method was successfully countered. The U-boats were the greatest menace, especially after the destruction of the German battleship *Bismarck* by British forces on 27 May 1941.

Atlantic Charter declaration issued during World War II by the British prime minister Churchill and the US president Roosevelt after meetings Aug 1941. It stressed their countries' good intentions and war aims and was largely a propaganda exercise to demonstrate public solidarity between the Allies.

The Atlantic Charter stated that Britain and the USA sought no territorial gains; desired no territorial changes not acceptable to the peoples concerned; respected the rights of all peoples to choose their own form of government; wished to see self-government restored to the occupied countries; would promote access by all states to trade and raw materials; desired international collaboration for the raising of economic standards; hoped to see a peace affording security to all nations, enabling them to cross the seas without hindrance; and proposed the disarmament of the aggressor states as a preliminary step to general disarmament. This charter was incorporated by reference into the Declaration of the United Nations 1941.

Atlantic City /ət'læntɪk 'sɪtɪ/ seaside resort in New Jersey, USA; population (1980) 40,000. It is noted for its 'boardwalk'; and the Miss America contest has been held here since 1921. Formerly a family resort, it has become a centre for casino gambling, which was legalized in New Jersey in the 1970s.

Atlantic College international educational experiment conceived by Kurt ◊Hahn and Air Marshall Lawrence Darvell, the first of the ◊United World Colleges. It was opened 1962 near Cardiff, Wales; there are others in Singapore and Vancouver Island, Canada.

Atlantic Ocean /ət'læntɪk/ ocean lying between Europe and Africa to the east and the Americas to the west, probably named after ◊Atlantis; area of basin 81,500,000 sq km/31,500,000 sq mi; including Arctic Ocean, and Antarctic seas, 106,200,000 sq km/41,000,000 sq mi. The average depth is 3 km/2 mi; greatest depth the Milwaukee Depth in the Puerto Rico Trench 8,650 m/28,389 ft. The Mid-Atlantic Ridge, of which the Azores, Ascension, St Helena, and Tristan da Cunha form part, divides it from north to south. Lava welling up from this central area annually increases the distance between South America and Africa. The North Atlantic is the saltiest of the main oceans, and it has the largest tidal range. In the 1960s–1980s average wave heights have increased by 25%, the largest from 12 m/40 ft to 18 m/60 ft.

Atlantis legendary island continent, said to have sunk about 9600 BC, following underwater convulsions. Although the Atlantic Ocean is probably named after it, the structure of the sea bottom rules out its ever having existed there.

One story told by the Greek philosopher Plato (derived from an account by Egyptian priests) may refer to the volcanic eruption that destroyed Santorini in the ◊Cyclades, north of Crete, about 1500 BC. The ensuing earthquakes and tidal waves brought about the collapse of the empire of Minoan Crete.

Atlas /'ætləs/ in Greek mythology, one of the ◊Titans who revolted against the gods; as a punishment, Atlas was compelled to support the heavens on his head and shoulders. Growing weary, he asked ◊Perseus to turn him into stone, and he was transformed into Mount Atlas.

atlas a book of maps. The atlas was introduced in the 16th century by ◊Mercator, who began work on it in 1585; it was completed by his son in 1594. Early atlases had a frontispiece showing Atlas supporting the globe. The first modern atlas was the *Theatrum orbis terrarum* 1570; the first English atlas has a collection of the counties of England and Wales by Christopher Saxten 1579.

Atlas Mountains /'ætləs/ mountain system of NW Africa, stretching 2,400 km/1,500 mi from the Atlantic coast of Morocco to the Gulf of Gabes, Tunisia, and lying between the Mediterranean on the north and the Sahara on the south. The highest peak is Mount Toubkal 4,165 m/13,670 ft.

Geologically the Atlas Mountains compare with the ◊Alps in age, but their structure is much less complex. They are recognized as the continuation of the great Tertiary fold mountain systems of Europe.

The Earth's atmosphere

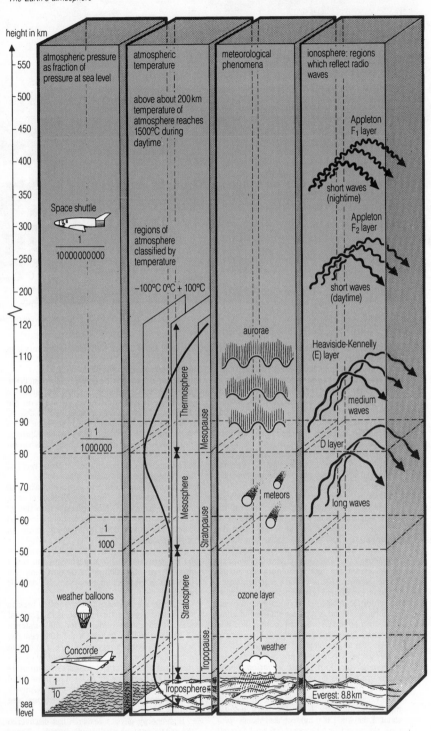

Atlas rocket US rocket, originally designed and built as an intercontinental missile, but subsequently adapted for space use. Atlas rockets launched astronauts in the Mercury series into orbit, as well as numerous other satellites and space probes.

atman in Hinduism, the individual soul or the eternal essential self.

atmosphere the mixture of gases that surrounds the Earth, prevented from escaping by the pull of the Earth's gravity. Atmospheric pressure decreases with height in the atmosphere. In its lowest layer, the atmosphere consists of nitrogen (78%) and oxygen (21%), both in molecular form (two atoms bounded together). The other 1% is largely argon, with very small quantities of other gases, including water vapour.

The lowest level, the ◊troposphere, is heated by the Earth, which is warmed by infrared and visible radiation from the Sun. Warm air cools as it rises in the troposphere, causing rain and most other weather phenomena. Infrared and visible radiations form only a part of the Sun's output of electromagnetic radiation. Almost all the shorter-wavelength ultraviolet radiation is filtered out by the upper layers of the atmosphere. The filtering process is an active one: at heights

atom bomb *Giant waterspout at Bikini Island in the W Pacific after the explosion of a US atom bomb in an underwater test. The dark streak in the column (left) was the approximate position of the battleship sunk by the blast.*

above about 50 km/31 mi ultraviolet photons collide with atoms, knocking out electrons to create a ◊plasma of electrons and positively charged ions. The resulting *ionosphere* acts as a reflector of radio waves, enabling radio transmissions to 'hop' between widely separated points on the Earth's surface. As shown on the diagram, waves of different wavelengths are reflected best at different heights. The collisions between ultraviolet photons and atoms lead to a heating of the upper atmosphere, although the temperature drops from top to bottom within the zone called the *thermosphere* as high-energy photons are progressively absorbed in collisions.

Between the thermosphere and the tropopause (at which the warming effect of the Earth starts to be felt) there is a 'warm bulge' in the temperature vs. height graph, at a level called the *stratopause*. This is due to longer-wavelength ultraviolet photons that have survived their journey through the upper layers; now they encounter molecules and split them apart into atoms. These atoms eventually bond together again, but often in different combinations. In particular, many ◊ozone molecules (oxygen-atom triplets) are formed. Ozone is a better absorber of ultraviolet than ordinary (two-atom) oxygen, and it is the *ozone layer* that prevents lethal amounts of ultraviolet from reaching the Earth's surface.

Far above the atmosphere, as so far described, lie the *Van Allen radiation belts*. These are regions in which high-energy charged particles travelling outwards from the Sun (as the so-called solar wind) have been captured by the Earth's magnetic field. The outer belt (at about 1,600 km/1,000 mi) contains mainly protons, the inner belt (at about 2,000 km/1,250 mi) contains mainly electrons. Sometimes electrons spiral down towards the Earth, noticeably at polar latitudes, where the magnetic field is strongest. When such particles collide with atoms and ions in the thermosphere, light is emitted. This is the origin of the glows visible in the sky as the *aurora borealis* (northern lights) and the *aurora australis* (southern lights). A fainter, more widespread, *airglow* is caused by a similar mechanism.

atmosphere a unit of pressure (atm) equal to 14.7 lb/in², 101,325 pascals or 760 torr. The actual pressure exerted by the atmosphere fluctuates around this value, which is the standard at sea level and 0°C used with reference to very high pressures.

atmospheric pollution see ◊pollution.

atmospheric pressure the pressure at a point in the atmosphere that is due to the weight of air above and so decreases with height. At sea level the pressure is about 101 kilopascals, 1013 millibars, 760 mmHg, or 14.7 lb/in². The exact value varies according to temperature and weather. Changes in atmospheric pressure, measured with a barometer, are used in weather forecasting.

atoll a continuous or broken circle of ◊coral reef and low coral islands surrounding a lagoon.

atom the very small, discrete particles of which all matter is composed. There are 92 kinds of atom occurring naturally, which correspond to the 92 elements. They differ in chemical behaviour and cannot be broken down by chemical means to anything simpler.

Atoms are much too small to be seen even by the microscope (the largest, caesium, has a diameter of 0.0000005 mm/0.00000002 in), and they are in constant motion. See also ◊atomic structure.

Belief in the existence of atoms dates back to the ancient Greek natural philosophers. The first scientist to gather evidence for the existence of atoms was John Dalton, in the 19th century, who believed that every atom was a complete unbreakable entity. Rutherford showed by experiment that an atom in fact consists of a *nucleus* surrounded by negatively charged particles called *electrons*. The nucleus is made up of positively charged *protons* and uncharged *neutrons*; see ◊atomic structure.

High-energy physics research has discovered the existence of other subatomic particles. These include *antiparticles* (such as the antiproton and antineutron), which are opposite in some properties but identical in others to known charged and neutral particles; *hyperons*, with masses greater than protons; and *mesons*, with masses intermediate between electrons and protons. More than 300 kinds of particle are now known. Experiments by ◊CERN and at the Fermi laboratory (Fermilab) in the USA have suggested that these particles are themselves made up of subparticles, known as *quarks*, which may be the fundamental building blocks of matter. However, some subatomic particles have been shown to change from one form to another and to behave in a way that is not always predictable (as shown by Heisenberg's ◊uncertainty principle).

Atoms as a whole are held together by the electrical forces of attraction between each negative electron and the positive protons within the nucleus. The latter *repel* one another with relatively enormous forces; a nucleus holds together only because other forces, not of a simple electrical character, attract the protons and neutrons to one another. These additional forces act only so long as the protons and neutrons are virtually in contact with one another. If, therefore, a fragment of a complex nucleus, containing some protons, becomes only slightly loosened from the main group of neutrons and protons, the strong natural repulsion between the protons will cause this fragment to fly apart from the rest of the nucleus at high speed. It is by such fragmentation of atomic nuclei (*nuclear fission*) that nuclear energy is released.

atom bomb bomb deriving its explosive force from nuclear fission (see ◊nuclear energy) as a result of a neutron chain reaction, developed in the 1940s in the USA into a usable weapon. The first atomic bombs were dropped by the USA on ◊Hiroshima and Nagasaki, Japan, 1945. The development of the hydrogen bomb in the 1950s rendered the early atom bomb obsolete. See ◊nuclear warfare.

Research began in the UK 1940 and was transferred to the USA after its entry into World War II the following year. Known as the Manhattan Project, the work was carried out under the direction of the US physicist Oppenheimer at Los Alamos, New Mexico. After one test explosion, two atom bombs were dropped on the Japanese cities of Hiroshima (6 Aug 1945) and Nagasaki (9 Aug 1945), each nominally equal to 200,000 tonnes of TNT. The USSR first detonated an atom bomb in 1949 and the UK in 1952. The test site used by the UK was in the Monte Bello Islands off Australia.

atomic clock timekeeping device regulated by various periodic processes occurring in atoms and molecules, such as atomic vibration or the frequency of absorbed or emitted radiation.

The first atomic clock was the *ammonia clock*, invented at the US National Bureau of Standards 1948. It was regulated by measuring the speed at which the nitrogen atom in an ammonia molecule vibrated back and forth. The rate of molecular vibration is not affected by temperature, pressure, or other external influences, and can be used to regulate an electronic clock.

A more accurate atomic clock is the **caesium clock**. Because of its internal structure, a caesium atom produces or absorbs radiation of a very precise frequency (9,192,631,770 Hz) that varies by less than one part in ten billion. This frequency has been used to define the second, and is the basis of atomic clocks used in international timekeeping.

Hydrogen maser clocks, based on the radiation from hydrogen atoms, are currently the most accurate. The hydrogen maser clock at the US Naval Research Laboratory, Washington, DC, is estimated to lose one second in 1,700,000 years. Cooled hydrogen maser clocks could theoretically be accurate to within one second in 300 million years.

atomic energy another name for ◊nuclear energy.

atomic force microscope (AFM) a microscope developed in the late 1980s that produces a magnified image using a diamond probe, with a tip so fine that it may consist of a single atom, dragged over the surface of a specimen to 'feel' the contours of the surface. In effect, the tip acts like the stylus of a phonograph or record player, reading the surface. The tiny up-and-down movements of the probe are converted to an image of the surface by computer, and displayed on a screen. The AFM is useful for examination of biological specimens since, unlike the ◊scanning tunnelling microscope, the specimen does not have to be electrically conducting.

atomicity the number of atoms of an ◊element that combine together to form a molecule. A molecule of oxygen (O_2) has atomicity 2; sulphur (S_8) has atomicity 8.

atomic mass unit or **dalton** (AMU) a unit of mass for measuring the relative mass of atoms and molecules. It is equal to one twelfth of the mass of a carbon-12 atom, which is equivalent to the mass of a proton or 1.66×10^{-27} kg. The ◊relative atomic mass of an atom has no units; thus oxygen-16 has an atomic mass of 16 daltons, but a relative atomic mass of 16.

atomic number the positive charge on (number of protons in) the nucleus of an atom. The 105 elements are numbered 1 (hydrogen) to 105 (hahnium) in the periodic table of elements.

atomic physics the study of the properties of the ◊atom.

atomic radiation energy given out by disintegrating atoms during ◊radioactive decay. The energy may be in the form of fast-moving particles, known as ◊alpha particles and ◊beta particles, or in the form of high-energy electromagnetic waves, known as ◊gamma radiation. Overlong exposure to atomic radiation can lead to ◊radiation sickness. Radiation biology studies the effect of radiation on living organisms.

atomic structure the internal structure of an ◊atom. The core of the atom is the **nucleus**, a particle only one ten-thousandth the diameter of the atom itself. The simplest nucleus, that of hydrogen, comprises a single positively charged particle, the **proton**. Nuclei of other elements contain more protons and additional particles of about the same mass as the proton but with no electrical charge, **neutrons**. Each **element** has its own characteristic nucleus with a unique number of protons, the **atomic number**. The number of neutrons may vary. Where atoms of a single element have different numbers of neutrons, they are called ◊isotopes. Although some isotopes tend to be unstable and exhibit ◊radioactivity, they all have identical chemical properties.

The nucleus is surrounded by a number of **electrons**, each of which has a negative charge equal to the positive charge on a proton, but which weighs only 1/1839 times as much. For a neutral atom, the nucleus is surrounded by the same number of electrons as it contains protons. The chemical properties of an element are determined by

Attenborough British director Richard Attenborough and actor Ralph Richardson working on the script of Oh! What a Lovely War in 1968. *The film won 16 international awards.*

the ease with which its atoms can gain or lose electrons. This is dependent on both the number of electrons associated with the nucleus and the force exerted on them by its positive charge.

atomic time the time as given by ◊atomic clocks, which are regulated by natural resonance frequencies of particular atoms, and display a continuous count of seconds.

In 1967 a new definition of the second was adopted in the SI system of units: the duration of 9,192,631,770 periods of the radiation corresponding to the transition between two hyperfine levels of the ground state of the caesium-133 atom. The International Atomic Time Scale is based on clock data from a number of countries; it is a continuous scale in days, hours, minutes, and seconds from the origin on 1 Jan 1958, when the Atomic Time Scale was made 0h 0 m 0s when Greenwich Mean Time was 0h 0 m 0s.

atomic weight another name for ◊relative atomic mass.

atomizer device that produces a spray of fine droplets of liquid. A vertical tube connected with a horizontal tube dips into a bottle of liquid, and at one end of the horizontal tube is a nozzle, at the other a rubber bulb. When the bulb is squeezed, air rushes over the top of the vertical tube and out through the nozzle. Following ◊Bernoulli's effect, the pressure at the top of the vertical tube is reduced, allowing the liquid to rise. The air stream picks up the liquid, breaks it up into tiny drops and carries it out of the nozzle as a spray.

Aton in ancient Egypt, the sun's disc as an emblem of the single deity whose worship was enforced by ◊Ikhnaton.

atonality music in which there is an apparent absence of ◊key; often associated with an expressionist style.

Atonality is used by film and television composers for situations of mystery or horror; it exploits **dissonance** for its power to disturb. For ◊Schoenberg, pioneer of atonal music from 1909, the intention was to liberate tonal expression and not primarily to disturb, and he rejected the term as misleading.

atonement in Christian theology, the doctrine that Jesus suffered on the cross to bring about reconciliation and forgiveness between God and humanity.

Atonement is an action that enables a person separated from God by sin to be reconciled ('at one') with him. In ancient Judaism this was achieved through the sacrificial killing of animals.

Atonement, Day of Jewish holy day (**Yom Kippur**) held on the tenth day of Tishri (Sept–Oct), the first month of the Jewish year. It is a day of fasting, penitence, and cleansing from sin, ending the Ten Days of Penitence that follow *Rosh Hashanah*, the Jewish New Year.

ATP (**adenosine triphosphate**) nucleotide molecule found in all cells. It can yield large amounts of energy, used to drive many biological processes, including muscle contraction and the synthesis of complex molecules needed by the cell. ATP is formed during photosynthesis in plants, or by the breakdown of food molecules during ◊metabolism in animals.

atrium in architecture, an inner, open courtyard.

atrophy in medicine, a diminution in size and function, or output, of a body tissue or organ. It is usually due to nutritional impairment or disease.

atropine an ◊alkaloid derived from belladonna. It acts as an ◊anticholinergic, and, as atropine sulphate, is administered as a mild antispasmodic drug.

Atropine is named after the Greek Atropos, one of the three Fates who cut people's lives short.

attainder, bill of a legislative device that allowed the English Parliament to declare guilt and impose a punishment on an individual without bringing the matter before the courts. Such bills were used intermittently from the Wars of the Roses until 1798. Some acts of attainder were also passed by US colonial legislators during the War of Independence to deal with 'loyalists' who continued to support the English crown.

Bills of attainder were used under Henry VIII and revived by James I and Charles I, whose best-known bill of attainder involved the Earl of ◊Strafford 1641. The last bill of attainder was passed against Lord Edward Fitzgerald (1763–98) for leading a rebellion in Ireland. The use of the device has generally been deplored as it did not require the accusers to prove their case and was usually employed to punish 'new' crimes of treason which were detrimental to those in power.

attar of roses perfume derived from the essential oil of roses, obtained by crushing and distilling the petals of the flowers.

attempt criminal offence in the UK under the Criminal Attempts Act 1981, which repealed the 'suspected person offence', commonly known as the 'sus' law. The offence must involve 'more than a mere preparatory act'; that is, it must include at least a partial or unsuccessful performance of the crime.

Attenborough /ˈætnbərə/ David 1926– . English traveller and zoologist, brother of Richard Attenborough. He was director of programmes for BBC television 1969–72, and commentator in the television series *Life on Earth* 1979 and *The Living Planet* 1983. He was knighted 1985.

Attenborough /ˈætnbərə/ Richard 1923– . English film actor and director. His films include *Brighton Rock* 1947 and *10 Rillington Place* 1970 (as actor), and *Oh! What a Lovely War* 1968, *Gandhi* 1982, and *Cry Freedom* 1987 (as director).

Atterbury /ˈætəbəri/ Francis 1662–1732. English bishop and Jacobite politician. In 1687 he was appointed a royal chaplain by William III. Under Queen Anne he received rapid promotion, becoming bishop of Rochester 1713. His Jacobite sympathies prevented his further rise, and in 1722 he was sent to the Tower of London and subsequently banished. He was a friend of the writers Pope and Swift.

Attica /ˈætɪkə/ (Greek *Attiki*) region of Greece comprising Athens and the district around it; area 3,381 sq km/1,305 sq mi; population (1981) 342,000. It is noted for its language, art, and philosophical thought in Classical times. It is a prefecture of modern Greece with Athens as its capital.

Attila /əˈtɪlə/ c. 406–453. King of the Huns from 434, called the 'Scourge of God'. He embarked on a career of vast conquests ranging from the Rhine to Persia. In 451 he invaded Gaul, but was defeated on the ◊Catalaunian Fields by the Roman and Visigothic armies under Aëtius (died 454) and Theodoric I. In 452 he led his Huns into Italy and only the personal intervention of Pope Leo I prevented the sacking of Rome.

He returned to Pannonia, west of the Danube, and died on the night of his marriage with Ildico, poison being suspected as the cause. He was said to have been buried with a vast treasure.

Attila Line line dividing Greek and Turkish Cyprus, so called because of a fanciful identification of the Turks with the Huns.

Attis /ˈætɪs/ in Classical mythology, a Phrygian god whose death and resurrection symbolized the end of winter and the arrival of spring. Beloved by the goddess ◊Cybele, who drove him mad as a punishment for his infidelity, he castrated himself and bled to death.

Attlee /ˈætli/ Clement (Richard), 1st Earl 1883–1967. British Labour politician. In the coalition government during World War II he was Lord Privy Seal 1940–42, dominions secretary 1942–43, and Lord President of the Council 1943–45, as well as deputy prime minister from 1942. As prime minister 1945–51 he introduced a sweeping programme of nationalization and a whole new system of social services.

Attlee was educated at Oxford and practised at the Bar 1906–09. Social work in London's East End and cooperation in poor-law reform led him to become a socialist; he joined the Fabian Society and the Independent Labour Party 1908. He became lecturer in social science at the London School of Economics 1913. After service in World War I he was mayor of Stepney, E London, 1919–20; Labour Member of Parliament for Limehouse 1922–50 and for W Walthamstow 1950–55.

In the first and second Labour governments he was undersecretary for war 1924 and chancellor of the Duchy of Lancaster and postmaster general 1929–31. In 1935 he became leader of the opposition. In July 1945 he became prime minister after a Labour landslide in the general election. The government was returned to power with a much reduced majority 1950 and was defeated 1951. In 1955 he accepted an earldom on retirement as leader of the opposition.

attorney a person who represents another in legal matters. In the USA, attorney is the formal title for a lawyer, who combines the functions performed in the UK by a barrister and a solicitor.

This use of the term is largely obsolete in Britain except in ◊Attorney General. See also ◊power of attorney.

Attorney General in England, principal law officer of the Crown and head of the English Bar; the post is one of great political importance. In the USA, it is the chief law officer of the government and head of the Department of Justice.

Attwell /ˈætwel/ Mabel Lucie 1879–1964. British artist, illustrator of many books for children, including her own stories and verse.

Atwood /ˈætwʊd/ Margaret (Eleanor) 1939– . Canadian novelist, short-story writer, and poet. Her novels, which often treat feminist themes with wit and irony, include *The Edible Woman* 1969, *Life Before Man* 1979, *Bodily Harm* 1981, *The Handmaid's Tale* 1986, and *Cat's Eye* 1989. Collections of poetry include *Power Politics* 1971, *You are Happy* 1974, and *Interlunar*.

Aube /əʊb/ river of NE France, a tributary of the Seine, length 248 km/155 mi; it gives its name to a *département*.

Auber /əʊˈbeə/ Daniel François Esprit 1782–1871. French operatic composer who studied under the Italian composer and teacher Cherubini. He wrote about 50 operas, including *La Muette de Portici/The Mute Girl of Portici* 1828 and the comic opera *Fra Diavolo* 1830.

aubergine a plant, member of the family Solanaceae. The **eggplant**, *Solanum melongena*, is native to tropical Asia. Its purple-skinned, sometimes white, fruits are eaten as a vegetable.

Aubrey /ˈɔːbri/ John 1626–1697. English antiquary. His *Brief Lives* 1898 (edited by A Clark) contains gossip and anecdotes on celebrities of his time. Aubrey was the first to claim Stonehenge as a Druid temple.

Aubrey was born in Wiltshire. He studied law but became dependent on patrons, including the antiquary Ashmole and the philosopher Hobbes. He published *Miscellanies* 1696 of folklore and ghost stories. *Lives of Eminent Men* appeared 1813 and *Remaines of Gentilisme and Judaisme* 1881. His observations on the natural history of Surrey and Wiltshire were also posthumously published.

aubrieta spring-flowering dwarf perennial plant of the family Cruciferae. It has a trailing habit and bears purple flowers. It was named in 1763 after Claude Aubriet (c.1665–1742), painter for the French Royal Garden.

Aubusson /ˌəʊbjuːˈsɒn/ town in the *département* of Creuse, France; population (1982) 6,500. Its carpet and tapestry industry dates from the 15th century.

Auchinleck /ˈɔːkɪnlek/ Sir Claude John Eyre 1884–1981. British commander in World War II. He won the First Battle of El ◊Alamein 1942 in N Egypt. In 1943 he became commander in chief India and founded the modern Indian and Pakistani armies. In 1946 he was promoted to field marshal; he retired in 1947.

Auchinleck, nicknamed 'the Auk', succeeded Wavell as commander in chief Middle East July 1941, and in the summer of 1942 was forced back to the Egyptian frontier by the German field marshal Rommel, but his victory at the First Battle of El Alamein is regarded by some as more important to the outcome of World War II than the Second Battle. From India he gave background support to the Burma campaign.

Auckland /ˈɔːklənd/ largest city in New Zealand, situated in N North Island; population (1987) 889,000. It fills the isthmus that separates its two harbours (Waitemata and Manukau), and its suburbs spread north across the Harbour Bridge. It is the country's chief port and leading industrial centre, having iron and steel plants, engineering, car assembly, textiles, food-processing, sugar-refining, and brewing.

There was a small whaling settlement on the site 1830s, and Auckland was officially founded

Attlee British Labour politician Clement Attlee.

as New Zealand's capital 1840, remaining so until 1865. The university was founded 1882.

Auckland /ˈɔːklənd/ George Eden, 1st Earl of Auckland 1784–1849. British Tory politician for whom Auckland, New Zealand, is named. He became a Member of Parliament 1810, and 1835–41 was governor general of India.

Auckland Islands /ˈɔːklənd/ six uninhabited volcanic islands 480 km/300 mi south of South Island, New Zealand; area 60 sq km/23 sq mi.

auction the sale of goods or property in public to the highest bidder. There are usually conditions of sale by which all bidders are bound.

A bid may be withdrawn at any time before the auctioneer brings down the hammer, and the seller is likewise entitled to withdraw any lot before the hammer falls. It is illegal for the seller or anyone on their behalf to make a bid for their own goods unless their right to do so has been reserved and notified before the sale. 'Rings' of dealers agreeing to keep prices down are illegal. A reserve price is kept secret, but an upset price (the minimum price fixed for the property offered) is made public before the sale. An auction where property is first offered at a high price and gradually reduced until a bid is received is known as a **Dutch auction**.

In 1988, art auctioneers (handling not only pictures, but other items of value such as furniture) were required by a British judge's ruling to recognize the possibility of the artwork being of great value, and to carry out 'proper research' on their provenance.

auction bridge card game played by two pairs of players using all 52 cards. The chief characteristic is the selection of trumps by a preliminary bid or auction. It has been succeeded in popularity by ◊contract bridge.

Aude /əʊd/ river in SE France, 210 km/130 mi long, which gives its name to a *département*. Carcassonne is the main town through which it passes.

Auden /ˈɔːdn/ W(ystan) H(ugh) 1907–1973. English poet. He wrote some of his most original poetry, such as *Look, Stranger!* 1936, in the 1930s when he led the influential left-wing literary group

Atwood Canadian novelist and poet Margaret Atwood.

that included MacNeice, Spender, and Day Lewis. He moved to the USA 1939, became a US citizen 1946, and adopted a more conservative and Christian viewpoint, such as in *The Age of Anxiety* 1947.

Born in York, Auden was associate professor of English literature at the University of Michigan from 1939, and professor of poetry at Oxford 1956–61. He also wrote verse dramas with ◊Isherwood such as *The Dog Beneath the Skin* and *The Ascent of F6* 1951 and opera librettos, notably for Stravinsky's *The Rake's Progress* 1951.

Audenarde /əʊd'nɑːd/ French form of ◊Oudenaarde, a town in Belgium.

audiometer an electrical instrument used to test hearing.

audit the official inspection of a company's accounts by a qualified accountant as required each year by British law, to ensure the company balance sheet reflects the true state of its affairs.

Audit Commission independent body in the UK established by the Local Government Finance Act 1982. It administers the District Audit Service (established 1844) and appoints auditors for the accounts of all UK local authorities. The Audit Commission consists of 15 members: its aims include finding ways of saving costs, and controlling illegal local-authority spending.

auditory canal tube leading from the outer ◊ear opening to the eardrum. It is found only in animals whose eardrums are located inside the skull, principally mammals and birds.

Audubon /'ɔːdəbɒn/ John James 1785–1851. US naturalist. In 1827, he published the first part of his *Birds of North America*, with a remarkable series of colour plates. Later, he produced a similar work on North American quadrupeds.

He was born in Santo Domingo (now Haiti) and educated in Paris. The National Audubon Society (originating 1886) has branches throughout the USA and Canada for the study and protection of birds.

Auerbach /'aʊəbæk/ Frank Helmuth 1931– . British artist, whose portraits and landscapes blend figurative and abstract work.

Augean stables one of the labours of ◊Heracles was to clean out the stables of Augeas, king of Elis in Greece. They contained 3,000 cattle and had never been cleaned before. As he was given only one day to do the labour and so diverted the river Alpheus through their yard.

Augier /,əʊʒi'eɪ/ Émile 1820–1889. French dramatist. He wrote *Le Gendre de M Poirier* 1854, in collaboration with Jules Sandeau, a realistic delineation of bourgeois society.

Augrabies Falls /əʊ'xrɑːbiːs/ falls in the Orange River, NW Cape Province, South Africa. Height 148 m/480 ft.

Augsburg /'aʊksbɑːg/ industrial city in Bavaria, West Germany; at the confluence of the Wertach and Lech rivers, 52 km/32 mi NW of Munich; population (1988) 246,000. A major industrial centre, it is named after the Roman emperor Augustus who founded it 15 BC.

Augsburg, Confession of /'aʊgzbʊəg/ statement of the Protestant faith as held by the German Reformers composed by Philip ◊Melanchthon. Presented to Charles V, Holy Roman Emperor, at the conference known as the Diet of Augsburg 1530, it is the creed of the modern Lutheran church.

Augsburg, Peace of religious settlement following the Diet of Augsburg 1555, which established the right of princes in the Holy Roman Empire (rather than the emperor himself, Ferdinand I) to impose a religion on their subjects–later summarized by the maxim *cuius regio, eius religio*. It initially applied only to Lutherans and Catholics.

augur a member of a college of Roman priests who interpreted the will of the gods from signs or 'auspices' such as the flight of birds, the condition of entrails of sacrificed animals, and the direction of thunder and lightning. Their advice was sought before battle and on other important occasions. Consuls and other high officials had

the right to consult the auspices themselves, and a campaign was said to be conducted 'under the auspices' of the general who had consulted the gods.

Augustan age the golden age of the Roman emperor ◊Augustus, during which art and literature flourished. The name is also given to later periods which used Classical ideals, such as that of Queen Anne in England.

Augustin /,əʊgu'stæn/ Eugène 1791–1861. French dramatist, the originator and exponent of the 'well-made' plays, which achieved success but were subsequently forgotten. He wrote *Une Nuit de la Garde Nationale* 1815.

Augustine of Hippo, St /ɔː'gʌstɪn/ 354–430. One of the early Christian leaders and writers known as the Fathers of the Church. He was converted to Christianity by Ambrose in Milan and became bishop of Hippo (modern Annaba, Algeria) 396. Among Augustine's many writings are his *Confessions*, a spiritual autobiography, and the influential *De Civitate Dei/The City of God* vindicating the Christian church and divine providence in 22 books.

Born in Tagaste, Numidia (Algeria), of Roman descent, he studied rhetoric in Carthage where he became the father of an illegitimate son, Adeodatus. He lectured in Tagaste and Carthage and for ten years was attached to the Manichaeist belief. In 383 he went to Rome, and on moving to Milan came under the influence of Ambrose. After prolonged study of neo-Platonism he was baptized by Ambrose together with his son. Resigning his chair in rhetoric, he returned to Africa, his mother, St Monica, dying in Ostia on the journey, and settled in Tagaste. His son died at 17. In 391, while visiting Hippo, Augustine was ordained priest. In 395 he was given the right of succession to the bishopric of Hippo and died there during its siege by the Vandals.

Many of Augustine's books resulted from his share in three great controversies: he refuted ◊Manichaeism; attacked and did much to eliminate the exclusive N African ◊Donatist sect at the conference of Carthage 411; and devoted the last 20 years of his life to refute ◊Pelagius, maintaining the doctrine of original sin and the necessity of divine grace. He estimated the number of his works at 230, and also wrote many sermons, as well as pastoral letters.

Augustine, St /ɔː'gʌstɪn/ first archbishop of Canterbury, England. He was sent from Rome to convert England to Christianity by Pope Gregory I. He landed at Ebbsfleet, Thanet, and baptized Ethelbert, King of Kent 597. He was consecrated bishop of the English at Arles in the same year, and appointed archbishop 601. Feast day 26 May.

Augustine was originally prior of the Benedictine monastery of St Andrew, Rome. In 603 he attempted unsuccessfully to unite the Roman and native Celtic churches at a conference on the Severn. He founded Christ Church, Canterbury, in 603, and the abbey of Saints Peter and Paul, now the site of Saint Augustine's Missionary College.

Augustinian member of a religious community that follows the Rule of St ◊Augustine of Hippo. It includes the Canons of St Augustine, Augustinian Friars and Hermits, Premonstratensians, Gilbertines, and Trinitarians.

Augustus /ɔː'gʌstəs/ 63 BC–AD 14. Title of Octavian (Gaius Julius Caesar Octavianus), first of the Roman emperors. He joined forces with Mark Antony and Lepidus in the Second Triumvirate. Following Mark Antony's liaison with the Egyptian Queeen Cleopatra, Augustus defeated her troops at Actium 31 BC. As emperor (from 27 BC) he reformed the government of the empire, the army, and Rome's public services, and was a patron of the arts. The period of his rule is known as the ◊Augustan Age.

Augustus *Great-nephew of Julius Caesar, the 'venerable' Augustus was the first Roman emperor. He was a ruler of great administrative ability and initative, and his reign marks the golden age of Roman literature.*

He was the son of a senator who married a niece of Julius Caesar, and he became his great-uncle's adopted son and principal heir. Following Caesar's murder, Octavian formed with Mark Antony and Lepidus the Triumvirate that divided the Roman world between them and proceeded to eliminate the opposition. Antony's victory 42 BC over Brutus and Cassius had brought the republic to an end. Antony then became enamoured of Cleopatra and spent most of his time at Alexandria, while Octavian consolidated his hold on the western part of the Roman dominion. War was declared against Cleopatra, and the naval victory at Actium left Octavian in unchallenged supremacy, since Lepidus had been forced to retire.

After his return to Rome 29 BC, Octavian was created *princeps senatus*, and in 27 BC he was given the title of Augustus ('venerable'). He then resigned his extraordinary powers and received from the Senate, in return, the proconsular command, which gave him control of the army, and the tribunician power, whereby he could initiate or veto legislation. In his programme of reforms Augustus received the support of three loyal and capable helpers, Agrippa, Maecenas, and his wife, Livia, while Virgil and Horace acted as the poets laureate of the new regime.

A firm frontier for the empire was established: to the north, the friendly Batavians held the Rhine delta, and then the line followed the course of the Rhine and Danube; to the east, the Parthians were friendly, and the Euphrates gave the next line; to the south, the African colonies were protected by the desert; to the west were Spain and Gaul. The provinces were governed either by imperial legates responsible to the *princeps* or by proconsuls appointed by the Senate. The army was made a profession, with fixed pay and length of service, and a permanent fleet was established. Finally, Rome itself received an adequate water supply, a fire brigade, a police force, and a large number of public buildings.

The years after 12 BC were marked by private and public calamities: the marriage of Augustus' daughter Julia to his stepson Tiberius proved disastrous; a serious revolt occurred in Pannonia AD 6; and in Germany three legions under Varus were annihilated in the Teutobur Forest AD 9. Augustus died a broken man, but his work remained secure.

aurora The aurora borealis showing multiple bonds near Fairbanks, Alaska.

auk any member of the family of marine diving birds that includes ◊razorbills, ◊puffins, and ◊guillemots. Confined to the northern hemisphere they feed on fish, and use their wings to 'fly' underwater in pursuit.

The smallest, at 20 cm/8 in is the little auk *Alle alle*, an arctic bird that winters as far south as Britain. The largest was the great auk *Pinguinis impennis*, 75 cm/2.5 ft and flightless, the last recorded individual being killed in 1844.

Auld Lang Syne song written by the Scottish poet Robert Burns about 1789, which is often sung at New Year's Eve gatherings; the title means 'old long since' or 'long ago'.

Auld Reekie former nickname of Edinburgh (Scottish dialect 'old smoky').

Aung San /'auŋ 'sæn/ 1914–1947. Burmese politician. As leader of the Anti-Fascist People's Freedom League he became vice president of the executive council Sept 1946. During World War II he had collaborated first with Japan and then with the UK.

Imprisoned for his nationalist activities while a student in Rangoon, Aung escaped to Japan 1940. He returned to lead the Burma Independence Army, which assisted the Japanese invasion 1942, and became defènce minister in the puppet government set up. Before long, however, he secretly contacted the Resistance movement, and from Mar 1945 openly cooperated with the British in the expulsion of the Japanese. He was assassinated by political opponents July 1947.

Aurangzeb /'ɔ:rənzeb/ or **Aurungzebe** 1618–1707. Mogul emperor of N India from 1658. Third son of Shah Jehan, he made himself master of the court by a palace revolution. His reign was the most brilliant period of the Mogul dynasty, but

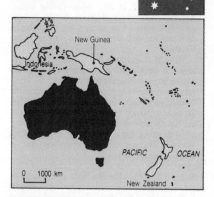

Austen Jane Austen, based on a drawing by her sister Cassandra. Her work appeared anonymously in her lifetime, and she received very little recognition or payment for it, but she has since become one of the most popular English novelists.

by despotic tendencies and Muslim fanaticism he aroused much opposition. His latter years were spent in war with the princes of Rajputana and Mahrattas.

Aurelian /ɔ:'ri:liən/ (Lucius Domitius Aurelianus) *c.* AD 214–275. Roman emperor from 270. A successful soldier, he was chosen emperor by his troops on the death of Claudius II. He defeated the Goths and Vandals, defeated and captured ◊Zenobia of Palmyra, and was planning a campaign against Parthia when he was murdered. The *Aurelian Wall*, a fortification surrounding Rome, was built by Aurelian 271. It was made of concrete, and substantial ruins exist. The *Aurelian Way* ran from Rome through Pisa and Genoa to Antipolis (Antibes) in Gaul.

Aurelius Antoninus /ɔ:'ri:liəs/ Marcus Roman emperor; see ◊Marcus Aurelius Antoninus.

Auric /ɔ:'ri:k/ Georges 1899–1983. French composer. He was one of the musical group called ◊*Les Six*. Auric composed a comic opera, several ballets, and incidental music to films of Jaques Cocteau.

auricula a plant, the *primrose Primula auricula*. It is a native of the Alps, but has been grown in English gardens for three centuries.

Auriga constellation of the northern hemisphere, represented as a man driving a chariot. Its brightest star is first-magnitude Capella; Epsilon Aurigae is an ◊eclipsing binary star, with a period of 27 years, the longest of its kind (last eclipse 1983).

The charioteer is usually identified as Erichthonius, legendary king of Athens, who invented the four-horse chariot.

Aurignacian in archaeology, an Old Stone Age culture which came between the Mousterian and the Solutrian in the Upper Palaeolithic. It is derived from a cave at Aurignac in the Pyrenees, France.

Auriol /ɔ:ri'əʊl/ Vincent 1884–1966. French socialist politician. He was president of the two Constituent Assemblies of 1946 and first president of the Fourth Republic 1947–54.

aurochs (plural *aurochs*) extinct species of wild cattle *Box primigenius* that formerly roamed Europe. It survived in Poland until 1627. Black to reddish or grey, it was up to 1.8 m/6 ft at the shoulder. It is depicted in many cave paintings.

aurora /ɔ:'rɔ:rə/ coloured light in the night sky, *aurora borealis*, 'northern lights', in the northern hemisphere, and *aurora australis* in the southern. Auroras are usually in the form of a luminous arch with its apex towards the magnetic pole followed by arcs, bands, rays, curtains, and coronas, usually green, but often showing shades of blue and red, and sometimes yellow or white. Aurorae are caused at a height of 100 km/60 mi by a fast stream of charged particles, originating in the sun. These enter the upper atmosphere and, by bombarding the gases in the atmosphere, cause them to emit visible light.

Australia
Commonwealth of

area 7,682,300 sq km/2,966,136 sq mi
capital Canberra
towns Adelaide, Alice Springs, Brisbane, Darwin, Melbourne, Perth, Sydney
physical the world's driest continent, arid in north and west Great Dividing Range in the east; NE peninsula has rainforest; rivers N–S and Darling River and Murray system E–S; Lake Eyre basin and fertile Nullarbor Plain in south
territories Norfolk Island, Christmas Island, Cocos Islands, Ashmore and Cartier Islands, Coral Sea Islands, Heard Island and McDonald Islands, Australian Antarctic Territory
features Great Australian Desert, Great Barrier Reef; unique animals include kangaroo, koala, numbat, platypus, wombat, Tasmanian devil and 'tiger'; budgerigar, cassowary, emu, kookaburra, lyre bird, black swan; and such deadly insects as the bulldog ant and funnel-web spider
head of state Elizabeth II from 1952 represented by Bill Hayden
head of government Robert Hawke from 1983
political system federal constitutional monarchy
political parties Australian Labor Party (ALP), moderate left-of-centre; Liberal Party of Australia, moderate, liberal, free-enterprise; National Party of Australia, centrist non-metropolitan

exports cereals, meat and dairy products, wool (30% of world production), fruit, wine, nuts, sugar, honey, bauxite (world's largest producer), coal, iron, copper, lead, tin, zinc, opal, mineral sands, uranium, machinery, transport equipment
currency Australian dollar (2.24 = £1 Feb 1990)
population (1988) 16,250,000; annual growth rate 1.6%
life expectancy men 72, women 79
language English
religion Anglican 36%, other Protestant 25%, Roman Catholic 33%
literacy 100% (1984)
GDP $170.2 bn (1984); $9,960 per head of population
chronology
1901 Creation of Commonwealth of Australia.
1911 Site for capital at Canberra acquired.
1944 Liberal Party founded by Robert Menzies.
1966 Menzies resigned after being Liberal prime minister for 17 years, and was succeeded by Harold Holt.
1968 John Gorton became prime minister after Holt's death.
1971 Gorton succeeded by William McMahon, heading a Liberal–Country Party coalition.
1972 Gough Whitlam became prime minister, leading a Labor government.
1975 Senate blocked the government's financial legislation; Whitlam declined to resign but was dismissed by the governor general, who invited Malcom Fraser to form a Liberal–Country Party caretaker government. The action of the governor-general, John Kerr, was severely criticized.
1977 Kerr resigned.
1983 Australian Labor Party, returned to power under Bob Hawke, sought consensus with employers and unions on economic policy to deal with growing unemployment.
1988 Labor foreign minister Bill Hayden appointed governor-general designate. Free trade agreement with New Zealand signed.
1989 Andrew Peacock returned as Liberal Party leader. National Party leader, Ian Sinclair, replaced by Charles Blunt.
1990 Hawke wins record fourth election victory, defeating Liberal Party by small majority.

Australia

physical

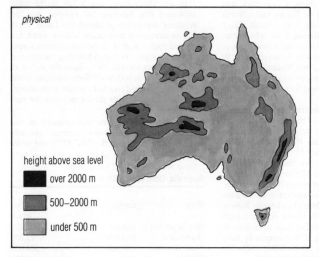

height above sea level
- over 2000 m
- 500–2000 m
- under 500 m

population

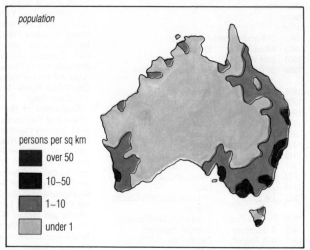

persons per sq km
- over 50
- 10–50
- 1–10
- under 1

annual rainfall

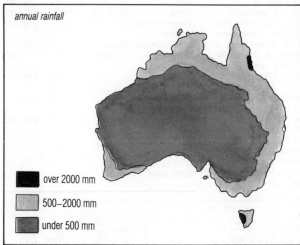

- over 2000 mm
- 500–2000 mm
- under 500 mm

land use

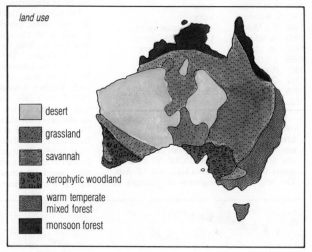

- desert
- grassland
- savannah
- xerophytic woodland
- warm temperate mixed forest
- monsoon forest

Aurora Roman goddess of the dawn. The Greek equivalent is *Eos*.

Auschwitz Polish *Oswiecim* town near Kraków in Poland, the site of a camp used by the Nazis in World War II to exterminate Jews as part of the 'final solution'. Each of the four gas chambers could hold 6,000 people.

auscultation evaluation of internal organs by listening, usually with the aid of a stethoscope.

Ausgleich the compromise between Austria and Hungary 8 Feb 1867 that established the Austro-Hungarian Dual Monarchy under Habsburg rule. It endured until the collapse of Austria-Hungary 1918.

Austen /'ɒstɪn/ Jane 1775–1817. English novelist, noted for her domestic novels of manners. All her novels are set within the confines of middle-class provincial society, and show her skill at drawing characters and situations with delicate irony. She was born at Steventon, Hampshire, where her father was rector, and began writing early; the burlesque *Love and Freindship* (sic), published 1922, was written 1790. In 1801 the family moved to Bath, and, after the death of her father 1805, to Southampton, finally settling in Chawton, Hampshire with her brother Edward.

Between 1795 and 1798 she worked on three novels. The first to be published (like its successors, anonymously) was *Sense and Sensibility* (drafted in letter form 1797–98). *Pride and Prejudice* (written 1796–97) followed, but *Northanger Abbey*, a skit on the contemporary Gothic novel (written 1798, sold to a London publisher 1803, and bought back 1816), did not appear until 1818.

The fragmentary *Watsons* and *Lady Susan* written about 1803–05 remained unfinished. The success of her published works, however, stimulated Jane Austen to write in rapid succession *Mansfield Park*, *Emma*, *Persuasion*, and the final fragment *Sanditon* written 1817. She died in Winchester, and is buried in the cathedral.

Auster /'ɔ:stə/ Paul 1947– . US novelist. His experimental use of detective story techniques to explore modern urban identity is exemplified in his *New York Trilogy*: *City of Glass* 1985, *Ghosts* 1986, and *The Locked Room* 1986.

Austerlitz, Battle of /'aʊstəlɪts/ battle on 2 Dec 1805 in which the French forces of Emperor Napoleon defeated those of Alexander I of Russia and Francis II of Austria at a small town in Czechoslovakia, formerly in Austria, 19 km/12 mi E of Brno. Its Czech name is *Slavkov*.

Austin /'ɒstɪn/ capital of Texas, USA, on the Colorado river; population (1980) 345,500. It is a centre for electronic and scientific research.

Austin /'ɒstɪn/ Alfred 1835–1913. British poet. He made his name with the satirical poem *The Season* 1861, which was followed by plays and volumes of poetry little read today; from 1896 he was Poet Laureate.

Austin /'ɒstɪn/ Herbert, 1st Baron Austin 1866–1941. English industrialist, who began manufacturing cars 1905 at Northfield, Birmingham, notably the 'Austin Seven' 1921.

Austin /'ɒstɪn/ J(ohn) L(angshaw) 1911–1960. British philosopher. Influential in later work on the philosophy of language, Austin was a pioneer in the investigation of the way words are used in everyday speech. His lectures *Sense and Sensibilia* and *How to do Things with Words* were published posthumously in 1962.

Australasia /ˌɒstrəˈleɪziə/ loosely applied geographical term, usually meaning Australia, New Zealand, and neighbouring islands.

Australia /ɒsˈtreɪliə/ the smallest continent in the world, situated south of Indonesia, between the Pacific and Indian oceans.

government Australia is an independent sovereign nation within the Commonwealth, retaining the British monarch as head of state, represented by a governor-general. The constitution came into effect 1 Jan 1901. As in the British system, the executive, in the shape of the prime minister and cabinet, is drawn from the federal parliament and is answerable to it. It consists of two chambers, an elected Senate of 76 (12 for each of the six states, two for the Australian Capital Territory and two for the Northern Territory); and a House of representatives of 148, elected by universal adult suffrage. Senators are elected for six years and members of the House for three years. Voting is compulsory, the Senate is elected by proportional representation, but the House of Representatives is elected as single-member constituencies with preferential voting.

Each state has its own constitution, governor (the monarch's representative), executive (drawn from the parliament), legislative and judicial system. Each territory has its own legislative Assembly.

The main political parties are the Liberal Party, the National Party (normally in coalition), the Australian Labor Party and the Australian Democrats.

Australian Prime Ministers

Date of taking office	Name	Party
1901	Sir Edmund Barton	Protectionist
1903	Alfred Deakin	Protectionist
1904	John Watson	Labor
1904	Sir G Reid	Free Trade/Protectionist Coalition
1905	Alfred Deakin	Protectionist
1908	Andrew Fisher	Labor
1909	Alfred Deakin	Fusion
1910	Andrew Fisher	Labor
1913	Sir J Cook	Liberal
1914	Andrew Fisher	Labor
1915	W M Hughes	Labor
1917	W M Hughes	National Labor
1923	S M Bruce	Nationalist-Country Coalition
1929	J H Scullin	Labor
1932	J A Lyons	United Australia Party-Country Coalition
1939	Sir Earle Page	Country Party-UAP Coalition
1939	R G Menzies	United Australia Party
1941	A W Fadden	Country Party-UAP Coalition
1941	John Curtin	Labor
1945	F M Forde	Labor
1945	J B Chifley	Labor
1949	R G Menzies	Liberal-Country Coalition
1966	Harold Holt	Liberal-Country Coalition
1967	John McEwen	Liberal-Country Coalition
1968	J G Gorton	Liberal-Country Coalition
1971	William McMahon	Liberal-Country Coalition
1972	Gough Whitlam	Labor
1975	Malcolm Fraser	Liberal-National Country
1983	Robert Hawke	Labor

In 1986 the last relics of the UK's legislative control over Australia were removed.

history Aborigines (Australia's native inhabitants) arrived at least 40,000 years ago. Australia was first settled 30,000–10,000 BC by immigrants from S India, Sri Lanka, and SE Asia. The first recorded sightings of Australia by Europeans were in 1606, when the Dutch ship *Duyfken* sighted the W shore of Cape York, and the Spaniard Luis Vaez de Torres sailed North of Cape York, and through Torres Strait. Later voyagers include Dirk Hartog 1616, who left an inscribed pewter plate (Australia's most famous early European relic, now in Amsterdam) in W Australia, Abel ◊Tasman, and William ◊Dampier. A second wave of immigration began 1770, when Capt James ◊Cook claimed New South Wales as a British colony.

Exploration of the interior began with the crossing of the barrier of the ◊Blue Mountains 1813. Famous explorers include Hamilton Hume (1797–1873) and William Hovell (1786–1875) who in 1824 reached Port Phillip Bay and were the first Europeans to see the river Murray; Charles ◊Sturt; Thomas Mitchell (1792–1855), surveyor-general for New South Wales 1828–55, who opened up the fertile western area of Victoria; Edward ◊Eyre, Ludwig ◊Leichhardt, Robert ◊Burke and William Wills (1834–61), and John ◊Stuart. In the 1870s the last gaps were filled in by the famous crossings of W Australia by John ◊Forrest, Ernest Giles (1835–1897) 1875–76, and Peter Warburton (1813–1889) 1873.

The gold rushes 1851–61, and sporadically to the early 1890s, contributed to the exploration as well as to the economic and constitutional growth of Australia, as did the pioneer work of the ◊overlanders. The creation of other separate colonies followed the first settlement in New South Wales at Sydney 1788: Tasmania 1825, Western Australia 1829, South Australia 1836, Victoria 1851, and Queensland 1859. The system of transportation of convicts from Britain was never introduced in South Australia and Victoria, and ended in New South Wales 1840, Queensland 1849, Tasmania 1852, and Western Australia 1868. Their contribution to the economic foundation of the country was considerable, and many would not have been convicted under a less harsh and capricious penal system than that operating in Britain at this period.

In the 1890s there was a halt in the rapid expansion that Australia had enjoyed, and the resulting depression produced the Labor Party and an increase in trade union activity, which has proved such a feature of Australian politics ever since. State powers waned following the creation of the Commonwealth 1901. Australia played an important role in both World Wars, and after World War II it embarked on a fresh period of expansion, with new mineral finds playing an important part in economic growth.

Since 1945 Australia has strengthened its ties with India and other SE Asian countries, especially since Britain's entry into the EEC 1973, and under the Labor government which came to power 1972 there was a growth of nationalism.

Australia, Commonwealth of

State	Capital	Area sq km
New South Wales	Sydney	801,600
Queensland	Brisbane	1,727,200
South Australia	Adelaide	984,000
Tasmania	Hobart	67,800
Victoria	Melbourne	227,600
Western Australia	Perth	2,525,500
Territories		
Northern Territory	Darwin	1,346,200
Capital Territory	Canberra	2,400
		7,682,300

Dependencies	Area (sq km)
Ashmore and Cartier Islands	5
Australian Antarctic Territory	6,044,000
Christmas Island	140
Cocos (Keeling) Islands	1,000,000
Heard Island and	410
McDonald Islands	410
Norfolk Island	410

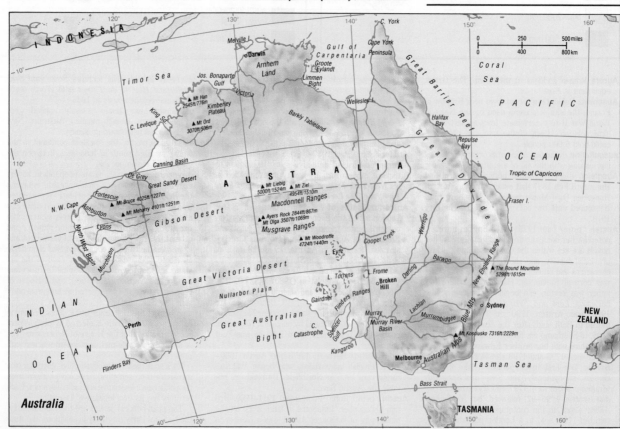

Australia

Australia *Ayers Rock in Northern Territory, Australia is the world's largest monolith. It is known by the Aborigines as Uluru.*

After heading a Liberal-Country Party government for 17 years, Robert Menzies resigned 1966 and was succeeded by Harold Holt, who died in a swimming accident 1967. In 1968 John Gorton became prime minister but lost a vote of confidence in the House and was succeeded by a Liberal-Country Party coalition under William McMahon 1971. At the end of 1972, the Australian Labor Party took office, led by Gough Whitlam.

The 1974 general election gave the Labor Party a fresh mandate to govern despite having a reduced majority in the House. In 1975 the Senate blocked the government's financial legislation and, with Whitlam unwilling to resign, the governor-general took the unprecedented step of dismissing him and his cabinet and inviting Malcolm Fraser to form a Liberal-Country party coalition caretaker administration. The wisdom of this action was widely questioned and eventually, in 1977,

governor-general John Kerr resigned. In the 1977 general election the coalition was returned with a reduced majority which became smaller 1980.

In the 1983 general election the coalition was eventually defeated and the Australian Labor Party under Bob Hawke again took office. Hawke called together employers and unions to agree a prices and incomes policy and to deal with unemployment. In 1984 he called a general election 15 months early, and was returned with a reduced majority. Hawke has placed even greater emphasis than his predecessors on links with SE Asia, and has imposed trading sanctions against South Africa as a means of influencing the dismantling of apartheid. In the 1987 general election, Labor marginally increased its majority in the House but did not have an overall majority in the Senate, where the balance was held by the Australian Democrats. The 1990 election was won by Labor, led by Bob

Hawke, with a reduced majority in the House of Representatives. The Australian Democrats maintain the balance of power in the Senate.

Australia Day public holiday in Australia, the anniversary of Captain Phillip's arrival on 26 Jan 1788 to found Port Jackson (now Sidney), the first colony.

Australian Aborigine indigenous inhabitant of the continent of Australia. They speak several hundred different languages, the most important being Aranda (Arunta), spoken in central Australia, and Murngin, spoken in Arnhem Land. In recent years there has been a movement for the recognition of Aborigine rights, campaigning against racial discrimination in housing, education, wages, and inadequate medical facilities.

Aborigines make up 1% of Australia's population of 16 million. They have an infant mortality four times the national average, and an adult life expectancy 20 years below the average 76 years of Australians generally.

Australian Antarctic Territory the islands and territories south of 60° S, between 160° E and 45° E longitude, excluding Adélie Land; area 6,044,000 sq km/2,332,984 sq mi of land, and 75,800 sq km/29,259 sq mi of ice shelf. The population on the Antarctic continent is limited to research personnel.

There are scientific bases at Mawson (1954) in MacRobertson Land, named after the explorer; at Davis (1957) on the coast of Princess Elizabeth Land, named in honour of Mawson's second-in-command; at Casey (1969) in Wilkes Land, named after Lord Casey, and at Macquarie Island (1948). It came into being 1933, when established by a British Order in Council.

Australian architecture Aboriginal settlements tended to be based around caves, or a construction of bark huts, arranged in a circular group.

Architecture of the early settlers includes Vaucluse House and the Sydney home of William Charles Wentworth. Queensland has

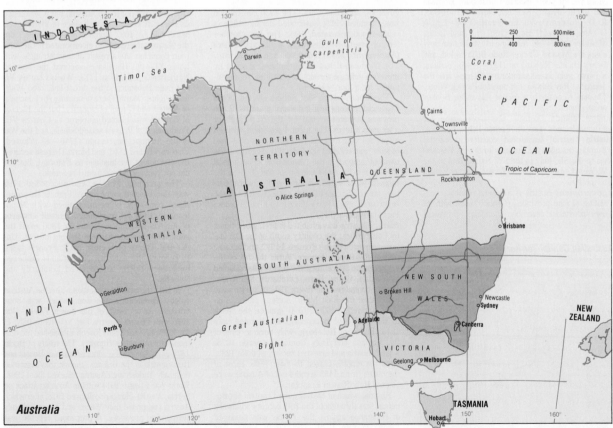

Australia

old-style homes with screened areas for coolness beneath their floors. Outstanding examples of modern architecture are the layout of the town of Canberra, by Walter Burley Griffin (1876–1937); Victoria Arts Centre, Melbourne, by Roy Grounds (1905–), who also designed the Academy of Science, Canberra; and the Sydney Opera House, by Joern Utzon (begun 1957).

Australian art art in Australia dates back to early Aboriginal works some 15,000 years ago. These are closely linked with religion and mythology, and include rock and bark paintings. True Aboriginal art is now rare. European-style art developed in the 17th century, with landscape painting predominating.

pre-colonial art Pictures and decorated objects were produced in nearly all settled areas. Subjects included humans, animals, and geometric ornament. The 'X-ray style', showing the inner organs in an animal portrait, is unique to Australian Aboriginal art.

17th–18th centuries The first European paintings were topographical scenes of and around Sydney.

late 19th–early 20th century The landscape painters of the Heidelberg School, notably Tom Roberts and later Arthur Streeton (1867–1943), became known outside Australia.

20th century The figurative painters William Dobell, Russell Drysdale, Sidney Nolan, and Albert Namatjira are among Australia's modern artists.

Australian Capital Territory territory ceded to Australia by New South Wales 1911 to provide the site of ◊Canberra, with its port at Jervis Bay, ceded 1915; area 2,400 sq km/926 sq mi; population (1987) 261,000.

Australian literature Australian literature begins with the letters, journals, and memoirs of early settlers and explorers. The first poet of note was Charles Harpur (1813–68), and idioms and rhythms typical of the country were developed by, among others, Henry Kendall (1841–82) and Andrew Barton (Banjo) Paterson (1864–1941). More recent poets include Christopher Brennan and Judith Wright, Kenneth Sleesor (1901–71), R D (Robert David) Fitzgerald (1902–), A D (Alec Derwent) Hope (1907–), and James McAuley (1917–76). Among early Australian novelists are Marcus Clarke, Rolfe Boldrewood, and Henry Handel Richardson (1870–1946). Striking a harsh vein in contemporary themes are the dramatist Ray Lawler and novelist Patrick White. Thomas Keneally is a recent Australian Booker prize winner.

Austral Islands /'ɒstrəl/ alternative name for ◊Tubuai Islands, part of ◊French Polynesia.

Austria /'ɒstrɪə/ landlocked country in central Europe, bounded by Hungary to the E, Yugoslavia to the SE, Italy to the SW, Switzerland to the W, West Germany to the NW, and Czechoslovakia to the NE.

government Austria is a federal republic, consisting of nine provinces (*Länder*), each with its own provincial assembly (*Landtag*), provincial

Austria
Republic of
(*Republik Österreich*)

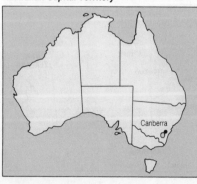

area 83,920 sq km/32,393 sq mi
capital Vienna
towns Graz, Linz, Salzburg, Innsbruck
physical mountainous, with the Danube river basin in the east
features Austrian Alps (including Zugspitze and Brenner and Semmering passes); river Danube; Hainburg, the largest primeval rainforest left in Europe, now under threat from a dam
head of state Kurt Waldheim from 1986
head of government Franz Vranitzky from 1986
political system democratic federal republic
political parties Socialist Party of Austria (SPÖ), democratic socialist; Austrian People's Party (ÖVP), progressive centrist; Freedom Party of Austria (FPÖ), moderate left-of-centre; United Green Party of Austria (VGÖ), conservative ecological; Green Alternative Party (ALV), radical ecological
exports minerals, manufactured goods
currency schilling (20.01 = £1 Feb 1990)
population (1987) 7,576,000; annual growth rate 0%
life expectancy men 70, women 77
language German
religion Roman Catholic 90%
literacy 98% (1983)
GNP $94.7 bn (1986); $12,521 per head of population
chronology
1918 Habsburg rule ended, republic proclaimed.
1938 Incorporated into German Third Reich by Hitler.
1945 1920 constitution reinstated and coalition government formed by the SPÖ and the ÖVP.
1955 Allied occupation ended and the independence of Austria formally recognized.
1966 ÖVP in power with Josef Klaus as chancellor.
1970 SPÖ formed a minority government, with Dr Bruno Kreisky as chancellor.
1983 Kreisky resigned and was replaced by Dr Fred Sinowatz, leading a coalition.
1986 Dr Kurt Waldheim elected president. Sinowatz resigned and was succeeded by Franz Vranitzky. In the Nov general election no party won an overall majority and Vranitzky formed a coalition of the SPÖ and the ÖVP, with the ÖVP leader, Dr Alois Mock, as vice-chancellor. Sinowatz denounced the coalition as a betrayal of socialist principles and resigned his SPÖ chair.
1989 Austria sought European Community membership.

governor, and councillors. The 1920 constitution was amended 1929, suspended during ◊Hitler's regime, and reinstated 1945. The two-chamber federal assembly consists of a national council (*Nationalrat*), and a federal council (*Bundesrat*). The *Nationalrat* has 183 members, elected by universal suffrage through proportional representation, for a four-year term.

The *Bundesrat* has 63 members elected by the Provincial Assemblies for varying terms. Each province provides a chair for the *Bundesrat* for a six-month term. The federal president, elected by popular vote for a six-year term, is formal head of state, and chooses the federal chancellor on the basis of support in the *Nationalrat*. The federal chancellor is head of government and chooses the cabinet. Most significant of several political parties, are the Socialist Party of Austria (SPO), the Austrian People's Party (OVP), and the Freedom Party of Austria (FPO).

history Austria was inhabited in prehistoric times by Celtic tribes; the country south of the Danube was conquered by the Romans 14 BC, and became part of the Roman Empire. After the fall of the empire in the 5th century, the region was occupied by Vandals, Goths, Huns, Lombards, and Avars. Having conquered the Avars 791, ◊Charlemagne established the East Mark, nucleus of the Austrian empire. In 973 Otto II granted the Mark to the House of Babenburg, which ruled until 1246. Rudolf of Habsburg, who became king of the Romans and Holy Roman Emperor 1273, seized Austria and invested his son as duke 1282. Until the empire ceased to exist 1806, most of the dukes (from 1453 archdukes) of Austria were elected Holy Roman Emperor.

Austria, which in 1526 acquired control of ◊Bohemia, was throughout the 16th century a bulwark of resistance against the Turks, who besieged Vienna in vain 1529. The Thirty Years' War

(1618–48) did not touch Austria, but it weakened its rulers. A second Turkish siege of Vienna 1683 failed, and by 1697 Hungary was liberated from the ◊Ottoman empire and incorporated in the Austrian dominion. As a result of their struggle with Louis XIV the Habsburgs secured the Spanish Netherlands and Milan 1713. When Charles VI, last male Habsburg in the direct line, died 1740, his daughter Maria Theresa became Archduchess of Austria and Queen of Hungary, but the Elector of Bavaria was elected emperor as Charles VII. Frederick II of Prussia seized Silesia, and the War of the Austrian Succession (1740–48) followed. Charles VII died 1745, and Maria Theresa secured the election of her husband as Francis I, but she did not recover Silesia from Frederick.

The archduke Francis who succeeded 1792 was also elected emperor as Francis II; sometimes opposing, sometimes allied with Napoleon, in 1804 he proclaimed himself emperor of Austria as Francis I, and in 1806 even the name Holy Roman Empire fell out of use. Under the Treaty of Vienna 1815, Francis failed to recover the Austrian Netherlands (annexed by France 1797), but received Lombardy and Venetia.

In 1848 the mixed nationalities within the Austrian empire flaredinto a rebellion, which was soon crushed. As a result of the Seven Weeks' War 1866 with Prussia, Austria lost Venetia to Italy. In the following year Franz Joseph established the dual monarchy of Austria–Hungary. The treaty of Berlin 1878 gave Austria the administration of Bosnia and Herzegovina in the Balkans, though they remained nominally Turkish until Austria annexed them 1908. World War I began 1914 with an Austrian attack on Serbia, Austria–Hungary collapsed 1918, after which Austria comprised only Vienna and its immediately surrounding provinces. A precarious republic was proclaimed, and in 1938 Austria was incorporated

Australian Capital Territory

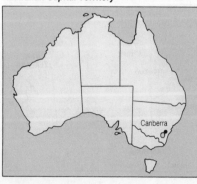

into the German Reich under Hitler. Austria returned to its 1920 constitution 1945, with a provisional government led by Dr Karl Renner. The Allies divided the country into four zones, occupied by the USSR, the USA, Britain, and France. The first post–war elections resulted in an SPO–OVP coalition government. The country was occupied until independence was formally recognized 1955. The first post–war non–coalition government was formed 1966 when the OVP came to power with Josef Klaus as chancellor. In 1970 the SPO formed a minority government under Dr Bruno Kreisky and increased its majority in the 1971 and 1975 general elections. In 1978 the government was nearly defeated over proposals to install the first nuclear power plant. The plan was abandoned, but nuclear energy remained a controversial issue. In 1983 the SPO lost its majority. Kreisky resigned, refusing to join a coalition. The SPO decline was partly attributed to the emergence of two environmentalist groups, the United Green Party (VGO), and the Austrian Alternative List (ALO). Dr Fred Sinowatz, the new SPO chairman, formed an SPO–FPO coalition government. In 1985 a controversy arose with the announcement that Dr Kurt Waldheim, former UN secretary general, was to be a presidential candidate. Despite allegations of his having been a Nazi officer in Yugoslavia, Waldheim eventually became president 1986. Later that year Sinowatz resigned as chancellor for what he described as personal reasons and was succeeded by Franz Vranitzky. The SPO–FPO coalition broke up when an extreme right–winger, Jorg Haider, became FPO leader. In the Nov elections the SPO's *Nationalrat* seats fell from 90 to 80, the OVP's from 81 to 77, while the FPO's increased from 12 to 18. For the first time the VGO was represented, winning eight seats. Vranitzky offered his resignation but was persuaded by the president to try to form a "grand coalition' of the SPO and the OVP. Agreement was reached and Vranitzky remained as chancellor with the OVP leader, Dr Alois Mock, as vice-chancellor. Sinowatz denounced the coalition as a betrayal of socialist principles and resigned as chairman of the SPO. In March 1989 Austria announced that it intended to seek membership of the European Community.

Austria provinces

Province	Capital	Area (sq km)
Burgenland	Eisenstadt	4,000
Carinthia	Klagenfurt	9,500
Lower Austria	St Pölten	19,200
Salzburg	Salzburg	7,200
Styria	Graz	16,400
Tirol	Innsbruck	12,600
Upper Austria	Linz	12,000
Vienna	Vienna	420
Vorarlberg	Bregenz	2,600

Austrian Succession, War of the war fought 1740–48 between Austria, supported by England and Holland, on the one side, and Prussia, France, and Spain on the other.
1740 The Holy Roman emperor Charles VI died and the succession of his daughter Maria Theresa was disputed by a number of European powers. Frederick the Great of Prussia seized *Silesia* from Austria.
1743 At ◊*Dettingen* an army of British, Austrians, and Hanoverians under the command of George II was victorious over the French.
1745 An Austro–English army was defeated at ◊*Fontenoy*. British naval superiority was confirmed, and there were gains in the Americas and India.
1748 The war was ended by the Treaty of Aix-la-Chapelle.
Austro-Hungarian empire /'ɒstrɪə 'hʌŋgəri/ the Dual Monarchy established by the Habsburg Franz Joseph 1867 between his empire of Austria and

his kingdom of Hungary. In 1910 it had an area of 261,239 sq km/100,838 sq mi with a population of 51 million. It collapsed autumn 1918. There were only two king-emperors: Franz Joseph 1867–1916 and Charles 1916–18.

autarchy a national economic policy which aims at achieving self-sufficiency and eliminating the need for imports (by imposing tariffs, for example). Such a goal may be difficult, if not impossible, for a small country. Countries that take protectionist measures and try to prevent free trade are sometimes described as autarchical.

authenticity in music, aiming to recreate the original style and instruments of early performances.

authoritarianism rule of a country by a dominant elite, who ruthlessly repress opponents and the press to maintain their own wealth and power. They are frequently indifferent to activities not affecting their security. An extreme form is ◊totalitarianism.

autism, infantile a rare syndrome, generally present from birth, characterized by a withdrawn state and a failure to develop normally in language or social behaviour, although the autistic child may show signs of high intelligence in other areas, such as music. Its cause is unknown.

autobiography a person's own biography, or written account of his or her life, distinguished from the journal or diary by being a connected narrative, and from memoirs by dealing less with contemporary events and personalities. *The Boke of Margery Kempe c.*1432–36 is the oldest extant autobiography in English.
A form of autobiography is the confession, which is concerned with the inner spiritual life, for example, the *Confessions* of St Augustine.

autochrome in photography, a single-plate additive colour process devised by the ◊Lumière brothers 1903. It was the first commercially available process, in use 1907–35.

autoclave pressurized vessel that uses superheated steam to sterilize materials and equipment such as surgical instruments. It is similar in principle to a pressure cooker.

auto-da-fé (Portuguese 'act of faith') religious ceremony, including a procession, solemn mass, and sermon, which accompanied the sentencing of heretics by the Spanish ◊Inquisition before they were handed over to the secular authorities for punishment, usually burning.

autogiro or *autogyro* a heavier-than-air craft that supports itself in the air with a rotary wing, or rotor. The Spanish aviator Juan de la ◊Cierva designed the first successful autogiro 1923. The autogiro's rotor provides only lift and not propulsion, unlike a helicopter in which the rotor provides both. The autogiro is propelled by an orthodox propeller.
The three- or four-bladed rotor on an autogiro spins in a horizontal plane on top of the craft, and is not driven by the engine. The blades have an aerofoil cross-section like a plane's wings do. When the autogiro moves forward, the rotor starts to rotate by itself, a state known as autorotation. When travelling fast enough, the rotor develops enough lift from its aerofoil blades to support the craft.

autoimmunity a situation where the body's immune responses are mobilized not against 'foreign' matter, such as invading germs, but against the body itself. So-called autoimmune diseases include ◊myasthenia gravis, pernicious ◊anaemia, rheumatoid ◊arthritis, and ◊lupus erythematosus.

Autolycus /ɔː'tɒlɪkəs/ in Greek mythology, an accomplished thief and trickster, son of the god ◊Hermes, who gave him the power of invisibility.

autolysis in biology, the destruction of a ◊cell after its death by the action of its own ◊enzymes, which break down its structural molecules.

automatic pilot a control device that keeps an aeroplane flying automatically on a given course at a given height and speed. Devised by US businessman Lawrence Sperry 1912, the automatic pilot contains a set of ◊gyroscopes that provide reference for the plane's course. Sensors detect when

the plane deviates from this course and send signals to the control surfaces – the ailerons, elevators, and rudder–to take the appropriate action.

automation the widespread use of self-regulating machines in industry. Automation involves the addition of control devices, using electronic sensing and computing techniques which often follow the pattern of human nervous and brain functions, to already mechanized physical processes of production and distribution, for example, steel processing, mining, chemical production, and road, rail, and air control.
The term was coined by US business consultant John Diebold, and it builds upon the process of ◊mechanization to further improve manufacturing efficiency.

automatism the performance of actions without awareness or conscious intent. It is seen in sleepwalking and in some (relatively rare) psychotic states.

automaton a mechanical figure imitating human or animal performance. Automatons are usually designed for decorative appeal as opposed to purely functional robots. The earliest recorded automaton is an Egyptian wooden pigeon of 400 BC.

autonomic nervous system in mammals, the part of the nervous system that controls the involuntary activities of the smooth muscles (of the digestive tract, blood vessels), the heart, and the glands. The **sympathetic** system responds to stress, when it speeds the heart rate, increases blood pressure and generally prepares the body for action. The **parasympathetic** system is more important when the body is at rest, since it slows the heart rate, decreases blood pressure, and stimulates the digestive system.

Autonomisti semi-clandestine amalgam of Marxist student organizations, linked with guerrilla groups and such acts as the kidnapping and murder of Italian premier Aldo Moro by the Red Brigades 1978.

autonomy in politics, term used to describe political self-government.

autopsy or *post-mortem* examination of the internal organs and tissues of a dead body, performed to try to establish the cause of death.

autosome any ◊chromosome in the cell other than a sex chromosome.

auto-suggestion conscious or unconscious acceptance of an idea as true, without demanding rational proof, but with potential subsequent effect for good or ill. Pioneered by the French psychotherapist Emile Coué (1857–1926) in healing, it is used in modern psychotherapy to conquer nervous habits, dependence on tobacco, alcohol, and so on.

autotroph any living organism that synthesizes organic substances from inorganic molecules by using light or chemical energy. All green plants and many planktonic organisms are autotrophs, using sunlight to convert carbon dioxide and water into sugars by ◊photosynthesis.
Some bacteria use the chemical energy of sulphur compounds to synthesize organic substances. Materials synthesized and stored by autotrophs provide the energy sources of all other organisms; they are the **primary producers** in all food chains. See also ◊heterotroph.

autumnal equinox see ◊equinox.

autumn crocus member of the family Liliaceae. One species, the mauve **meadow saffron** *Colchicum autumnale*, yields **colchicine**, which is used in treating gout and in plant breeding (it causes plants to double the numbers of their chromosomes).

Auvergne /əʊ'veən/ ancient province of central France and a modern region (*départements* Allier, Cantal, Haute-Loire, and Puy-de-Dôme); area 26,000 sq km/10,036 sq mi; population (1986) 1,334,000. Its capital is Clermont-Ferrand. It lies in the heart of the Central Plateau and is mountainous, composed chiefly of volcanic rocks in several masses.

It is named after the ancient Gallic Avenni tribe whose leader, Vercingetorix, was one of the greatest opponents of the Romans.

Auxerre /əʊ'seə/ capital of Yonne *département* France, 170 km/106 mi SE of Paris, on the river Yonne; population (1973) 40,000. The Gothic cathedral, founded 1215, has exceptional sculptures and stained glass.

auxin a plant ◊hormone that promotes stem and root growth in plants. Auxins influence many aspects of plant growth and development, including cell enlargement, inhibition of development of axillary buds, ◊tropisms, and the initiation of roots. *Synthetic auxins* are used in rooting powders for cuttings, and in some weedkillers, where the high concentrations cause such rapid growth that the plants die. They are also used to prevent premature fruit-drop in orchards. The most common naturally occuring auxin is known as indoleacetic acid, or IAA. It is synthesized in the shoot apex and transported to other parts of the plant.

Ava /'a:və/ former capital of Burma (now Myanmar), on the river Irrawaddy, founded by Thadomin Payä 1364. Thirty kings reigned there until 1782, when a new capital, Amarapura, was founded by Bodaw Payä. In 1823 the site of the capital was transferred back to Ava by King Baggidaw.

avalanche (from French *avaler* 'to swallow') a fall of a mass of snow and ice down a steep slope. Avalanches occur because of the unstable nature of snow masses in mountain areas. Changes of temperature, sudden sound, or earth-borne vibrations can cause a snowfield to start moving, particularly on slopes of more than 35°. The snow compacts into ice as it moves, and rocks may be carried along, adding to the damage caused.

Avalokiteśvara in Mahāyāna Buddhism, one of the most important ◊bodhisattvas, seen as embodying compassion. Known as *Guanyin* in China, *Kwannon* in Japan, he is one of the attendants of Amida Buddha.

Avalon /'ævəlɒn/ in Celtic legend, the island of the blessed or paradise; and in the Arthurian legend the land of heroes, to which the dead king was conveyed. It has been associated with Glastonbury in SW England.

avant-garde (French 'advanced guard') in the arts, those artists or works that are in the forefront of new developments in their media. The term was introduced (as was 'reactionary') after the French Revolution, when it was used to describe any socialist political movement.

Avar member of a central Asian nomadic people who in the 6th century invaded the area of Russia N of the Black Sea previously held by the Huns. They extended their dominion over the Bulgarians and Slavs in the 7th century, and were finally defeated by Charlemagne 796.

Avatar in Hindu mythology, the descent of a deity to earth in a visible form. The ten Avatars of ◊Vishnu are the best known.

Avebury /'eɪvbəri/ Europe's largest stone circle (diameter 412 m/1,352 ft), Wiltshire, England. It was probably constructed in the Neolithic period 3,500 years ago, and is linked with nearby ◊Silbury Hill. The village of Avebury was built within the circle, and many of the stones were used for building material.

Avebury /'eɪvbəri/ John Lubbock, 1st Baron Avebury 1834–1913. British banker. A Liberal (from 1886 Liberal Unionist) member of Parliament 1870–1900, he was responsible for the Bank Holidays Act 1871 introducing statutory public holidays.

Avedon /'eɪvdən/ Richard 1923– . US photographer. A fashion photographer with *Harper's Bazaar* magazine in New York in the mid-1940s, he later became one of the highest-paid commercial photographers.

Ave Maria (Latin 'Hail, Mary') Christian prayer to the Virgin Mary, which takes its name from the archangel Gabriel's salutation of the Virgin Mary (Luke 11:28) when announcing that she would be the mother of the Messiah.

avens any of several low-growing plants of the rose family. *Wood avens* or *herb bennet Geum urbanum* grows in woods and shady places on damp soils, through most of Europe, N Asia, and N Africa. It has yellow five-petalled flowers and pinnate leaves.

Water avens Geum rivale has nodding pink flowers and is found in marshes and other damp places. *Mountain avens Dryas octopetala* grows in mountain and arctic areas of Europe, Asia, and North America. A creeping perennial, it has white flowers with yellow stamens.

average number that represents the typical member of a group of numbers. The simplest averages include the arithmetic and geometric ◊means; the ◊median and the ◊root-mean-square are more complex.

Avernus /ə'vɜ:nəs/ circular lake, near Naples, Italy. Because it formerly gave off fumes that killed birds, it was thought by the Romans to be the entrance to the lower world.

Averroes /,ævə'rəʊi:z/ (Arabic **Ibn Rushd**) 1126–1198. Arabian philosopher, who argued for the eternity of matter, and denied the immortality of the individual soul. His philosophical writings, including commentaries on Aristotle and Plato's *Republic*, became known to the West through Latin translations. He influenced Christian and Jewish writers, and reconciled Islamic and Greek thought.

Born in Córdova, Spain, he was trained in medicine, and became physician to the caliph as well as judge of Seville and Córdoba. He was accused of heresy by the Islamic authorities and banished 1195. Later he was recalled, and died in Marrakesh.

'Averroism' was taught at Paris and elsewhere in the 13th century by the 'Averroists', who defended a distinction between philosophical truth and revealed religion.

Avery /'eɪvəri/ 'Tex' (Frederick Bean) 1907–1980. US cartoon-film director who used violent, sometimes surreal humour. At Warner Brothers he helped develop the characters Bugs Bunny and Daffy Duck before moving to MGM in 1942 where he created, among others, Droopy and Screwball Squirrel.

Avianus Roman fable writer, placed variously between the 1st and 6th centuries AD. He wrote 42 fables dedicated to Theodosius.

Avicenna /,ævɪ'senə/ (Arabic **Ibn Sina**) 979–1037. Arabian philosopher and physician, who studied the Koran, philosophy, and the science of his day. His *Canon Medicinae* was a standard work for centuries. His philosophical writings were influenced by al-Farabi, Aristotle, and the Neo-Platonists, and influenced the scholastics of the 13th century.

Aviemore /,ævɪ'mɔ:/ winter sports centre, in the Highlands, Scotland, SE of Inverness among the Cairngorms Mountains.

Avignon /'ævi:njɒn/ city in Provence, France, capital of Vaucluse *département*, on the river Rhône NW of Marseille; population (1982) 174,000. It was an important Gallic and Roman city, and has 14th-century walls, a 12th-century bridge (only half still standing), a 13th-century cathedral, and the palace built 1334–42 during the residence here of the popes. Avignon was papal property 1348–1791.

Avila /'ævilə/ town in Spain, 90 km/56 mi NW of Madrid; population (1986) 45,000. It is capital of the province of the same name. It has the remains of a Moorish castle, a Gothic cathedral, and the convent and church of St Teresa, who was born here. The town walls are among the best preserved medieval fortifications of those in Europe.

avocado tree of the laurel family. *Persia americana* is a native to Central America. Its dark-green pear-shaped fruit have buttery-textured flesh and are used in salads.

avocet wading bird, genus *Recurvirostra*, with characteristic long narrow upturned bill used in sifting water as it feeds in the shallows. It is about 45 cm/1.5 ft long, has long legs, partly-webbed feet, and black and white plumage. There are four species.

Avogadro /,ævə'gɑ:drəʊ/ Amedeo Conte di Quaregna 1776–1856. Italian physicist. His work on gases still has relevance for modern atomic studies.

Avogadro's hypothesis in chemistry, the law stating that equal volumes of all gases, when at the same temperature and pressure, have the same numbers of molecules. This law was first propounded by Count Amadeo Avogadro.

Avogadro's number or *Avogadro's constant* the number of carbon atoms in 12 g of the carbon-12 isotope (6.022045×10^{23}). The relative atomic mass of any element, expressed in grams, contains this number of atoms. It is named after Amadeo Avogadro.

avoirdupois system of weights based on the pound (0.45 kg), which consists of 16 ounces (each of 16 drams) or 7,000 grains (each equal to 65 mg).

Avon /'eɪvən/ county in SW England
area 1,340 sq km/517 sq mi
towns administrative headquarters Bristol; Bath, Weston-super-Mare
features River Avon
products aircraft and other engineering, tobacco, chemicals, printing, dairy products
population (1987) 951,000
famous people John Cabot, Thomas Chatterton.
history formed 1974 from the city and county of Bristol, part of S Gloucestershire, and part of N Somerset.

Avon /'eɪvən/ any of several rivers in England and Scotland. The Avon in Warwickshire is associated with Shakespeare.
the Upper, or Warwickshire, Avon, 154 km/96 mi, rises in the Northampton uplands near Naseby and joins the Severn at Tewkesbury.
the Lower, or Bristol, Avon, 121 km/75 mi, rises in the Cotswolds and flows into the Bristol Channel at Avonmouth.
the East, or Salisbury, Avon, 104 km/65 mi, rises S of the Marlborough Downs and flows into the English Channel at Christchurch.

AWACS acronym for *Airborne Warning and Control System*.

Awash /'a:wa:s/ river which rises to the S of Addis Ababa in Ethiopia and flows NE to Lake Abba on the frontier with Djibouti. Although deep inside present day Ethiopia, the Awash River is considered by Somalis to mark the eastern limit of Ethiopian sovereignty prior to the colonial division of Somaliland in the 19th century.

Awe /ɔ:/ longest (37 km/23 mi) of the Scottish freshwater lochs, in Strathclyde, SE of Oban. It is drained by the river Awe into Loch Etive.

Avon

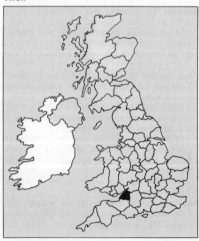

Axelrod /'æksəlrɒd/ Julius 1912– . US neuro-pharmacologist, who shared the 1970 Nobel Prize for Medicine with the biophysicists Bernard Katz and Ulf von Euler for his work on neurotransmitters (the chemical messengers of the brain).

Axelrod wanted to know why the messengers, once transmitted, ever stopped operating. Through his studies he found a number of specific ◊enzymes that rapidly degraded the neurotransmitters.

Axholme, Isle of /'ækshəum/ area of 2,000 ha/5,000 acres in Humberside, England, bounded by the Trent, Don, Idle, and Torne rivers, where 'medieval type' open field strip farming is still practised. The largest village, Epworth, is the birthplace of the Methodist John Wesley.

axil the upper angle between a leaf (or bract) and the stem from which it grows. Organs developing in the axil, such as flowers, shoots, and buds, are termed axillary, or lateral.

axiom in mathematics, a statement that is assumed to be true and upon which theorems are proved by using logical deduction. ◊Euclid used a series of axioms that he considered could not be demonstrated in terms of simpler concepts to prove his geometrical theorems.

Axis the alliance of Nazi Germany and Fascist Italy before and during World War II. The **Rome–Berlin Axis** was formed 1936, when Italy was being threatened with sanctions because of its invasion of Abyssinia. It became a full military and political alliance May 1939. A 10-year alliance between Germany, Italy, and Japan (**Rome–Berlin–Tokyo Axis**) was signed Sept 1940, and was subsequently joined by Hungary, Bulgaria, Romania, and the puppet states of Slovakia and Croatia. The Axis collapsed with the fall of Mussolini and the surrender of Italy 1943.

axis in mathematics, a line from which measurements may be taken, as in **coordinate axis**; or a line about which an object may be symmetrical, as in **axis of symmetry**; or a line about which an object or plane figure may revolve.

Axminster /'æksmɪnstə/ type of cut-pile, patterned carpet originally made in Axminster, Devon, England. It is produced by a method that permits up to 240 colours.

axolotl aquatic larval form ('tadpole') of the Mexican salamander *Ambystoma mexicanum* which may reach 30 cm/1 ft long, and normally breeds without changing to the adult form (see ◊neoteny).

axon the long thread-like extension of a ◊nerve cell that conducts electro-chemical impulses received by the cell body towards other nerve cells, or towards an effector organ such as a muscle. At the tip of the axon are ◊synapses which transmit the nerve impulse.

Axum alternative transliteration of ◊Aksum, an ancient kingdom in Ethiopia.

Ayacucho /ˌæjə'kuːtʃəu/ capital of a province of the same name in the Andean mountains of central Peru; population (1988) 94,200. The last great battle in the war of independence against Spain was fought near here in Dec 1824.

ayatollah (Arabic 'sign of God') honorific title awarded to Shi'ite Muslims in Iran by popular consent, as, for example, to Ayatollah Ruhollah ◊Khomeini.

Ayckbourn /'eɪkbɔːn/ Alan 1939– . English playwright. His prolific output, characterized by comic dialogue, includes *Absurd Person Singular* 1973, the trilogy *The Norman Conquests* 1974, *A Woman in Mind* 1986, *A Small Family Business* 1987, *Man of the Moment* 1988, and scripts for television.

Aycliffe /'eɪklɪf/ town in Durham, England, on the river Skerne; population (1981) 36,825. It developed from 1947 as a new town.

aye-aye nocturnal tree-climbing ◊lemur *Daubentonia madagascariensis* of Madagascar. It has gnawing, rodent-like teeth and a long middle finger with which it probes for insects. Just over

1 m/3 ft long, it is now very rare through loss of its forest habitat.

Ayer /eə/ A(lfred) J(ules) 1910–1989. English philosopher. He wrote *Language, Truth and Logic* 1936, an exposition of the theory of 'logical positivism', presenting a criterion by which meaningful statements (essentially truths of logic, as well as statements derived from experience) could be distinguished from meaningless metaphysical utterances (for example, claims that there is a God, or that the world external to our own minds is illusory).

He was Wykeham professor of logic at Oxford 1959–78. Later works included *Probability and Evidence* 1972 and *Philosophy in the Twentieth Century* 1982.

Ayers Rock /eəz/ vast ovate mass of pinkish rock in Northern Territory, Australia; 335 m/1,100 ft high and 9 km/6 mi round.

It is named after Sir Henry Ayers, a premier of South Australia. For the Aboriginals, whose paintings decorate its caves, it has magical significance.

Ayesha /'aɪʃə/ 611–678. Third and favourite wife of the prophet Muhammad, who married her when she was nine. Her father, Abu Bakr, became ◊caliph on Muhammad's death 632, and she bitterly opposed the later succession to the caliphate of Ali, who had once accused her of infidelity.

Aymara /ˌaɪmə'raː/ member of an ◊American Indian people of Bolivia and Peru, who were conquered first by the Incas and then by the Spaniards. Their language survives and their modern Roman Catholicism incorporates elements of their old beliefs.

Ayot St Lawrence /'eɪət sənt 'lɒrəns/ village in Hertfordshire, England, where Shaw's Corner (home of the playwright G B Shaw) is preserved.

Ayr /eə/ town in Strathclyde, Scotland, at the mouth of the river Ayr; population (1981) 49,500. 'Auld Brig' was built 15th century, the 'New Brig' 1788 (rebuilt 1879). Ayr has associations with Robert Burns.

Ayrshire /'eəʃə/ former county of SW Scotland, with a 113 km/70 mi coastline on the Firth of Clyde. In 1975 the major part was merged in the region of Strathclyde, the remaining sector, approximately south of the Water of Girvan and including Girvan itself, became part of Dumfries and Galloway.

Ayrton /'eətn/ Michael 1921–1975. British painter, sculptor, illustrator, and writer. From 1961, Ayrton developed an obsession with the ◊Daedalus myth, producing bronzes of Icarus and a fictional autobiography of Daedalus, *The Maze Maker* 1967.

Aytoun /'eɪtn/ Robert 1570–1638. Scottish poet employed and knighted by James I; he was noted for his love poems. Aytoun is the reputed author of the lines on which Robert Burns based 'Auld Lang Syne'.

Aytoun /'eɪtn/ William Edmonstoune 1813–1865. Scottish poet, born in Edinburgh, chiefly remembered for his *Lays of the Scottish Cavaliers* 1848, and for the *Bon Gaultier Ballads* 1855, which he wrote in collaboration with Sir Theodore Martin.

aye-aye

Azerbaijan

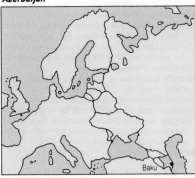

Baku

Ayurveda ancient Hindu system of medicine, the main principles of which are derived from the Vedas, that is still practised in India in Ayurvedic hospitals and dispensaries.

AZ abbreviation for ◊*Arizona*.

azalea plant of the family Ericaceae, closely related to *Rhododendron*, in which genus azaleas are now generally included. There are several species native to Asia and North America, and from these many cultivated varieties have been derived. Azaleas, particularly the Japanese varieties, make fine ornamental shrubs. Several species are highly poisonous.

Azaña /ə'θænjə/ Manuel 1880–1940. Spanish politician and first prime minister 1931–33 of the second Spanish republic. He was last president of the republic during the Civil War 1936–39, before the establishment of a dictatorship under Francisco Franco.

Azerbaijan /ˌæzəbaɪ'dʒaːn/ constituent republic (Azerbaydzhan Soviet Socialist Republic) of the USSR from 1936
area 86,600 sq km/33,436 sq mi
capital Baku
towns Kirovabad
physical Caspian Sea; the country ranges from semi-desert to the Caucasus mountains
products oil, iron, copper, fruit, vines, cotton, silk, carpets
population (1987) 6,811,000; 78% Azerbaijani, 8% Russian, 8% Armenian
language Turkic
religion traditionally Shi'ite Muslim
recent history a member of the Transcaucasian Federation 1917, it became an independent republic 1918, but was occupied by the Red Army 1920. There has been growth in Azerbaijani nationalism, spearheaded by the local 'Azerbaijani Popular front' and fanned by the dispute with neighbouring christian Armenia over Nagorno-Kovabakn and Nakhichevan. This dispute which reawakened centuries old enmities, flared up into a fullscale civil-war from Dec 1989 which prompted Azerbaijani calls for secession from the USSR and led, in Jan 1990, to the despatch of soviet troops to Baku to attempt to restore order.

Azerbaijan, Iranian /ˌæzəbaɪ'dʒaːn/ two provinces of NW Iran, Eastern Azerbaijan (capital Tabriz), population (1986) 4,114,000, and Western Azerbaijan (capital Orúmiyeh), population 1,972,000. Like the people of Soviet Azerbaijan, the people are Muslim ethnic Turks, descendants of followers of the Khans from the Mongol Empire.

There are about 5 million in Azerbaijan, and 3 million distributed in the rest of the country, where they form a strong middle class. In 1946, with Soviet backing, they briefly established their own republic. Denied autonomy under the Shah, they rose 1979–80 against the supremacy of Ayatollah Khomeini and were forcibly repressed, although a degree of autonomy was promised.

Azhar, El /ə'zaː/ Muslim university and mosque in Cairo, Egypt. Founded 970 by Jawhar, commander in chief of the army of the Fatimid caliph, it is claimed to be the oldest university in the world. It became the centre of Islamic learning, with several subsidiary foundations, and is now primarily a school of Koranic teaching.

Azilian an archaeological period following the close of the Old Stone (Palaeolithic) Age, and regarded as one of the cultures of the Mesolithic Age. It was first recognized by Piette at Mas d'Azil, a village in Ariège, France.

azimuth in astronomy, the angular distance eastwards along the horizon, measured from due north, between the astronomical ◊meridian (the vertical circle passing through the centre of the sky and the north and south points on the horizon) and the vertical circle containing the object whose position is to be measured.

Azincourt /,æzæŋ'kuə/ French form of ◊Agincourt.

azo dye a synthetic dye containing the azo group of two nitrogen atoms (N=N) connecting aromatic ring compounds. Azo dyes are usually red, brown, or yellow, and make up about half the dyes produced. They are manufactured from aromatic ◊amines.

In 1848 the mixed nationalities within the Austrian empire flared into a rebellion, which was soon crushed. As a result of the Seven Weeks' War 1866 with Prussia, Austria lost Venetia to Italy. In the following year Franz Joseph established the dual monarchy of Austria-Hungary. The treaty of Berlin 1878 gave Austria the administration of Bosnia and Herzegovina in the Balkans, though they remained nominally Turkish until Austria annexed them 1908. World War I began 1914 with an Austrian attack on Serbia, Austria-Hungary collapsed 1918, after which Austria comprised only Vienna and its immediately surrounding provinces. A precarious republic was proclaimed, and in 1938 Austria was incorporated into the German Reich under Hitler.

Austria returned to its 1920 constitution 1945, with a provisional government led by Dr Karl Renner. The Allies divided the country into four zones, occupied by the USSR, the USA, Britain, and France. The first post-war elections resulted in an SPO-OVP coalition government. The country was occupied until independence was formally recognized 1955.

The first post-war non-coalition government was formed 1966 when the OVP came to power with Josef Klaus as chancellor. In 1970 the SPO formed a minority government under Dr Bruno Kreisky and increased its majority in the 1971 and 1975 general elections. In 1978 the government was nearly defeated over proposals to install the first nuclear power plant. The plan was abandoned, but nuclear energy remained a controversial issue.

In 1983 the SPO lost its majority. Kreisky resigned, refusing to join a coalition. The SPO decline was partly attributed to the emergence of two environmentalist groups, the United Green Party (VGO), and the Austrian Alternative List (ALO). Dr Fred Sinowatz, the new SPO chairman, formed an SPO-FPO coalition government.

In 1985 a controversy arose with the announcement that Dr Kurt Waldheim, former UN secretary-general, was to be a presidential candidate. Despite allegations of his having been a Nazi officer in Yugoslavia, Waldheim eventually became president 1986. Later that year Sinowatz resigned as chancellor for what he described as personal reasons and was succeeded by Franz Vranitzky. The SPO-FPO coalition broke up when an extreme right-winger, Jorg Haider, became FPO leader. In the Nov elections the SPO's *Nationalrat* seats fell from 90 to 80, the OVP's from 81 to 77, while the FPO's increased from 12 to 18. For the first time the VGO was represented, winning eight seats. Vranitzky offered his resignation but was persuaded by the president to try to form a 'grand coalition' of the SPO and the OVP. Agreement was reached and Vranitzky remained as chancellor with the OVP leader, Dr Alois Mock, as vice-chancellor. Sinowatz denounced the coalition

The Aztec Empire in 1519
☐ area of Aztec domination

as a betrayal of socialist principles and resigned as chairman of the SPO.

In March 1989 Austria announced that it intended to seek membership of the European Community.

Austrian Succession, War of the war fought 1740–48 between Austria, supported by England and Holland, on the one side, and Prussia, France, and Spain on the other.

1740 The Holy Roman emperor Charles VI died and the succession of his daughter Maria Theresa was disputed by a number of European powers. Frederick the Great of Prussia seized *Silesia* from Austria.

1743 At ◊*Dettingen* an army of British, Austrians, and Hanoverians under the command of George II was victorious over the French.

1745 An Austro-English army was defeated at ◊*Fontenoy*. British naval superiority was confirmed, and there were gains in the Americas and India.

Azores /ə'zɔːz/ group of nine islands in the N Atlantic, an autonomous region of Portugal; area 2,247 sq km/867 sq mi; population (1987) 254,000. They are outlying peaks of the Mid-Atlantic Ridge, and are volcanic in origin. The capital is Ponta Delgada on the main island, San Miguel.

Portuguese from 1430, they were granted partial autonomy 1976, but remain a Portuguese overseas territory. The Azores command the Western shipping lanes.

Azorín /,æθɔ'riːn/ Pen name of José Martínez Ruiz 1873–1967. Spanish writer. His works include volumes of critical essays and short stories, plays and novels, such as the autobiographical *La voluntad/The Choice* 1902 and *Antonio Azorín* 1903 – the author adopted the name of the eponymous hero of the latter as his pen name.

Azov /'eizɒv/ Russian *Azovskoye More* inland sea of the USSR forming a gulf in the NE of the Black Sea; area 37,555 sq km/14,500 sq mi. Principal ports include Rostov-on-Don, Kerch, and Taganrog. Azov is an important source of freshwater fish.

AZT or *retrovir*, or *zidovudine* drug used in the treatment of ◊AIDS. Developed in the mid-1980s and approved for use by 1987, it is not a cure for AIDS, but has proved effective in suppressing the causative virus (HIV) for as long as it is being administered. Taken every four hours, night and day, it reduces the risk of opportunistic infection and relieves many neurological symptoms. Frequent blood monitoring is required to control anaemia, a potentially life-threatening side effect of AZT. Blood transfusions are often necessary, and the drug must be withdrawn if bone-marrow function is severely affected.

Aztec /'æztek/ member of a Mexican ◊American Indian people who migrated from further north in the 12th century, and in 1325 began

reclaiming lake marshland to build their capital, Tenochtitlán, on the site of modern Mexico City. Under Montezuma I (reigned from 1440), they created an empire in central and southern Mexico.

The Aztecs were renowned for their architecture, jewellery (gold, jade, and turquoise), and textiles. Their form of writing combined the hieroglyph and pictograph, and they used a complex calendar, which combined a sacred period of 260 days with the solar year of 365 days. Propitiatory rites were performed at the 'dangerous' period, once in every 52 years, when the beginning of the two coincided, and all temples were rebuilt (useful as a date mark for archaeologists). Their own god was Huitzilopochtli (Humming-bird Wizard), but they also worshipped the feathered serpent ◊Quetzalcoatl, inherited from the conquered Toltecs, and others. They practised human sacrifice on a large scale, tearing the heart from the living body or flaying people alive. War captives were obtained for this purpose, but their own people may also have been used. Pictures show that they played a type of football, in which legs rather than feet were used to propel a solid rubber ball. Some of the players were killed after the game, but it is not certain whether the losers were sacrificed for having lost, or the winners promoted to the next world for having won.

B second letter of the alphabet. It corresponds to the Greek *beta* and the Semitic *beth*; and as written in the modern W European alphabet is derived from the classical Latin.

BA in education, abbreviation for *Bachelor of Arts*.

Baabda /'bɑːbdə/ capital of the province of Jebel Lubnan in central Lebanon and site of the country's presidential palace. Situated to the SE of Beirut, it is the headquarters of the Christian military leader Michel Aoun.

Baade /'bɑːdə/ Walter 1893–1960. US astronomer, who made observations that doubled the distance scale and the age of the universe. Born in Germany, Baade worked during World War II at Mount Wilson observatory, where he discovered that stars are in two distinct populations according to their age, known as Population I (the youngest) and Population II (the oldest). Later, he found that Cepheid variable stars of Population I are brighter than had been supposed, and that distances calculated from them were wrong.

Baader /'bɑːdə/ Andreas 1943–1977. West German extreme left-wing guerrilla. A former left-wing student activist, he formed, with Ulrike ◊Meinhof, the Red Army Faction, an underground urban guerrilla organization that carried out a succession of terrorist acts in West Germany during the 1970s. Sentenced to life imprisonment in April 1977, he took his own life in Oct 1977, following the failure of the Faction's hostage-swap attempt at Mogadishu airport.

Baader–Meinhof gang /'bɑːdə 'maɪnhɒf/ popular name for the West German guerrilla group the *Rote Armee Fraktion* ('Red Army Faction'), active from 1968 against what it perceived as US imperialism. Its two leaders were Andreas Baader and Ulrike Meinhof, who died in prison under mysterious circumstances.

Baal /beɪl/ (Semitic 'lord' or 'owner') a divine title given to their chief male gods by the Phoenicians,

---

Babangida Nigeria's president since 1985, Ibrahim Babangida. The country's fifth military leader since independence, he has promised a gradual return to civilian democracy.

or Canaanites. Their worship as deities of fertility, often orgiastic and of a phallic character, was strongly denounced by the Hebrew prophets.

Baalbek /'bɑːlbek/ city of ancient Syria, in modern Lebanon, 60 km/36 mi NE of Beirut, 1,150 m/3,000 ft above sea level. Originally a centre of Baal worship. The Greeks identified Baal with Helios, the sun, and renamed Baalbek *Heliopolis*. Its ruins, including Roman temples, survive; the Temple of Bacchus, built in the 2nd century AD, is still almost intact.

Ba'ath Party socialist party aiming at the extended union of all Arab countries, active in Iraq and Syria.

Bab /bɑːb/ Mirza Ali Mohammad 1819–1850. Persian religious leader, born in Shiraz, founder of ◊Babism. In 1844 he proclaimed that he was a gateway to the Hidden Imam, a new messenger of Allah who was to come. He gained a large following whose activities caused the Persian authorities to fear a rebellion, and who were therefore persecuted. The Bab was executed for heresy.

Babangida /bɑːˈbæŋɡɪdɑː/ Ibrahim 1941– . Nigerian politician and soldier. After training in the UK and the USA, he became head of the Nigerian army in 1983 and in 1985 led a coup against President Buhari, assuming the presidency himself.

Born in Minna, Niger state, he trained at military schools in Nigeria and the UK. He became an instructor in the Nigerian Defence Academy and by 1983 had reached the rank of major-general. In 1983, after taking part in the overthrow of President Shehu Shagari, he was made army commander-in-chief.

Babbage /'bæbɪdʒ/ Charles 1792–1871. English mathematician credited with being the inventor of the computer. He designed an ◊analytical engine, a general-purpose computing device for performing different calculations according to a program input on punched cards (an idea borrowed from the Jacquard loom). This device was never built, but it embodied many of the principles on which modern digital computers are based.

As a young man Babbage assisted John Herschel with his astronomical calculations. He became involved with calculating machines when he worked on his ◊difference engine for the British Admiralty, though this was never completed.

Babbitt a satirical novel 1922 by Sinclair Lewis about a Midwestern US businessman obsessed by commerce, clubs, and material values. 'Babbittry' became the type of a Middle American cultureless innocence.

Babbitt /'bæbɪt/ Milton 1916– . US composer. After studying with ◊Sessions he developed a

---

personal style of ◊serialism influenced by jazz. He is a leading composer of electronic music using the 1960 RCA Mark II synthesizer, which he helped to design.

Babbit metal an ◊alloy of tin, copper, and antimony used to make bearings, developed by the US inventor Isaac Babbit 1839.

babbler bird of the thrush family Muscicapidae with a loud babbling cry. Babblers, subfamily Timaliinae, are found in the Old World, and there are some 250 species in the group.

Babel /'baɪbl/ Hebrew name for the city of ◊Babylon, chiefly associated with the **Tower of Babel** which, in the Genesis story in the Old Testament, was erected in the plain of Shinar by the descendants of Noah. It was a ziggurat or staged temple seven storeys high (100 m/300 ft) with a shrine of Marduk on the summit. It was built by Nabopolassar, father of Nebuchadnezzar, and was destroyed when Sennacherib sacked the city 689 BC.

Babel /'bɑːbl/ Isaak Emmanuilovich 1894–1939/40. Russian writer. Born in Odessa, he was an ardent supporter of the Revolution and fought with Budyenny's cavalry in the Polish campaign of 1921–22, an experience which inspired *Konarmiya/Red Cavalry* 1926. His other works include *Odesskie rasskazy/Stories from Odessa* 1924, which portrays the life of the Odessa Jews.

Bab-el-Mandeb /'bæb el 'mændeb/ strait that joins the Red Sea and the Gulf of Aden, and separates Arabia and Africa. The name, meaning 'gate of tears', refers to its currents.

Baber (Arabic 'lion') title given to ◊Zahir ud-din Muhammad, founder of the Mughal Empire in N India.

Babeuf /bɑːˈbɜːf/ François Noël 1760–1797. French revolutionary journalist, a pioneer of practical socialism. In 1794 he founded a newspaper in Paris, later known as the *Tribune of the People*, in which he demanded the equality of all people. He was guillotined for conspiring against the Directory (see ◊French Revolution).

Babi faith alternative name for ◊Baha'i faith.

Babington /'bæbɪŋtən/ Anthony 1561–1586. English traitor who hatched a plot to assassinate Elizabeth I and replace her by ◊Mary, Queen of Scots; its discovery led to Mary's execution and his own.

babirusa a wild pig *Babirousa babyrussa*, becoming increasingly rare, found in the moist forests and by the water of Sulawesi, Buru, and nearby Indonesian islands. The male has large upper

Babbage A prototype of the analytical engine created by English mathematician Charles Babbage.

baboon Hamadryas baboon

tusks which grow upwards through the skin of the snout and curve back towards the forehead. The babirusa is up to 80 cm/2.5 ft at the shoulder. It is nocturnal and swims well.

Babism religious movement founded by Mirza Ali Mohammad ('the Bab'). An offshoot of Islam, its main difference is the belief that Muhammad was not the last of the prophets. The movement split into two groups after the death of the Bab; Baha'ullah, the leader of one of these groups, founded the ◊Baha'i faith.

Babi Yar /'bɑːbi 'jɑː/ site of a massacre of Jews by the Germans in 1941, near Kiev, USSR.

baboon type of large monkey, genus *Papio*, with a long doglike muzzle and large canine teeth, spending much of its time on the ground in open country. Males, with head and body up to 1.1 m/3.5 ft long, are larger than females and dominant males rule the 'troops' in which baboons live. They inhabit Africa and SW Arabia.

Types include the *olive baboon Papio anubis* from W Africa to Kenya, the *chacma Papio ursinus* from S Africa, and the *sacred baboon Papio hamadryas* from NE Africa and SW Arabia. The male sacred baboon has a 'cape' of long hair.

Babrius lived about 3rd century AD. Roman writer of fables, written in Greek. He probably lived in Syria, where his stories first gained popularity. In 1842 a manuscript of his fables was discovered in a convent on Mount Athos, Greece. There were 123 fables, arranged alphabetically, but discontinued at the letter O.

Babylon /'bæbɪlən/ capital of ancient Babylonia, on the left bank of the Euphrates. The site is in modern Iraq, 88 km/55 mi S of Baghdad and 8 km/5 mi N of Hilla, which is built chiefly of bricks from the ruins of Babylon. The *hanging gardens of Babylon*, one of the ◊seven wonders of the world, were probably erected on a vaulted stone base, the only stone construction in the mud-built city. They formed a series of terraces, irrigated by a hydraulic system.

Babylonian captivity the exile of Jewish deportees to Babylon after Nebuchadnezzar II's capture of Jerusalem in 586 BC; traditionally, the captivity lasted 70 years, but Cyrus of Persia, who conquered Babylonia, actually allowed them home in 536 BC. By analogy, the name has also been applied to the papal exile to Avignon, France, 1309–77.

Bacall /bə'kɔːl/ Lauren. Stage name of Betty Joan Perske 1924– . Striking US actress who became

Babylon *A pair of the 120 lions of the processional way leading from the city wall to the Ishtar Gate, Babylon. These are made of glazed brickwork moulded in low relief.*

Bacall *Lauren Bacall made her début opposite Humphrey Bogart in* To Have and Have Not *1944.*

an overnight star when cast by Howard Hawks opposite Humphrey Bogart in *To Have and Have Not* 1944. She and Bogart married in 1945, and starred together in *The Big Sleep* 1946. Her other films include *The Cobweb* 1955 and *Harper* 1966.

Bacău /'bɑːkaʊ/ industrial city in Romania, 250 km/155 mi NNE of Bucharest, on the Bistrita; population (1985) 175,300. It is the capital of Bacău county, and is an important oil-producing region.

Baccalauréat the French examination providing the school-leaving certificate and qualification for university entrance, also available on an international basis as an alternative to English ◊A Levels.

The curriculum for the *Baccalauréat* (or '*Bac*') is much broader than the UK system, with a minimum of six compulsory subjects including a foreign language.

baccarat casino card game with two forms: *chemin de fer* and *baccarat banque*. In the former each player takes it in turn to hold the bank. In the *banque* variety, all players compete against one banker. Cards are dealt from a wooden holder known as a 'shoe'.

Bacchus /'bækəs/ in Greek and Roman mythology, the god of fertility (see ◊Dionysus) and of wine; his rites (the *Bacchanalia*) were orgiastic.

Bach /bɑːx/ Carl Philip Emmanuel 1714–1788. German composer, son of J S Bach. He introduced a new 'homophonic' style, light and easy to follow, which influenced Mozart, Haydn, and Beethoven.

In the service of Frederick the Great 1740–67, he left to become master of church music at Hamburg in 1768. He wrote over 200 pieces for keyboard instruments, and published a guide to playing the piano. Through his music and concert performances he helped to establish a leading solo role for the piano in Western music.

Bach /bɑːx/ Johann Christian 1735–1782. German composer, the 11th son of J S Bach, who became well known in Italy as a composer of operas. In 1762 he was invited to London, where he became music master to the royal family. He remained in England until his death, enjoying great popularity both as a composer and performer.

Bach /bɑːx/ Johann Sebastian 1685–1750. German composer. His appointments included positions at the courts of Weimar and Anhalt-Köthe, and from 1723 until his death, he was musical director at St Thomas's choir school in Leipzig. Bach was a master of ◊counterpoint, and his music epitomizes the Baroque polyphonic style. His orchestral music includes the six *Brandenburg Concertos*, other concertos for clavier and for violin, and four orchestral suites. Bach's keyboard music for clavier and organ, his fugues, and his choral music are of

equal importance. He also wrote chamber music and songs.

Born at Eisenach, Bach came from a distinguished musical family. At 15 he became a chorister at Lüneburg, and at 19 he was organist at Arnstadt. He married twice and had over 20 children (although several died in infancy). His second wife, Anna Magdalena Wülkens, was a soprano; she also acted as his amanuensis when his sight failed in later years.

Bach's sacred music includes 200 church cantatas, the Easter and Christmas oratorios, the two great Passions, of St Matthew and St John, and the Mass in B minor. His keyboard music includes a collection of 48 preludes and fugues known as the *Well-Tempered Clavier*; the *Goldberg Variations*; and the *Italian Concerto*. Of his organ music the most important examples are the chorale preludes. Two works written in his later years illustrate the principles and potential of his polyphonic art—the *Musical Offering* and *The Art of Fugue*.

Bach /bɑːx/ Wilhelm Friedemann 1710–1784. German composer, who was also an organist, improviser, and master of ◊counterpoint. He was the eldest son of J S Bach.

Bachelard /bæʃ'lɑː/ Gaston 1884–1962. French philosopher and scientist who argued for a creative interplay between reason and experience. He attacked both Cartesian and positivist positions, insisting that science was derived neither from first principles nor directly from experience.

bacillus member of a group of rod-like ◊bacteria that occur everywhere in the soil and air, and are responsible for diseases such as anthrax as well as causing food spoilage.

backgammon a board game for two players, often used in gambling. Its origin is ancient. The children's version is called Ludo.

The board is marked out in 24 triangular points of alternating colours, 12 to each side. Throwing two dice, the players move their 15 flat circular pieces round the board to the six points that form their own 'inner table'; the first player to move all his or her pieces off the board is the winner. Players have included Tutankhamen, Chaucer, Henry VIII, and Pepys. In the 1920s it became a casino game when a group was allowed to play a single opponent, and the US innovation of a 'doubling cube' made it more exciting by repeatedly doubling the stakes. It is now found in computerized form allowing a player to compete against the computer.

background radiation the electromagnetic radiation also known as the 3° radiation, left over from the original formation of the universe in the Big Bang around 15,000 million years ago. It corresponds to an overall background temperature of 3 K, or 3°C above absolute zero.

back to the land a movement in late Victorian England that emphasized traditional values and rural living as a reaction against industrialism and urban society.

For some, this meant moving from city to country and becoming self-supporting; for example, by growing their own food. For others, their participation was limited to encouraging a rebirth of rural crafts and traditions, such as lacemaking, quilting, and folk music.

Movements loosely associated with back to the land include ◊vegetarianism, the ◊garden city idea, and conservation societies such as the National Trust that set out to preserve 'unspoilt' features of the countryside.

Bacon /'beɪkən/ Francis 1561–1626. English politician, philosopher, and essayist. He became Lord Chancellor 1618, and the same year confessed to bribe-taking, was fined £40,000 (which was paid by the king), and spent four days in the Tower of London. Although he admitted taking the money, he claimed that he had not always given the verdict to his paymasters. His works include *Essays* 1597, notable for pith and brevity; *The Advancement of Learning* 1605, a seminal

Bacon *Sir Francis Bacon was a long-serving adviser to Elizabeth I and James I, and a writer on scientific thought and method.*

work discussing scientific method; the *Novum Organum* 1620, in which he redefined the task of natural science, seeing it as a means of empirical discovery and a method of increasing human power over nature; and *The New Atlantis* 1626, describing a Utopian state in which scientific knowledge is systematically sought and exploited.

Bacon was born in London, studied law at Cambridge from 1753, was part of the embassy in France until 1579, and became a member of Parliament 1584. He was the nephew of Queen Elizabeth's adviser Lord ◊Burghley, but turned against him when he failed to provide Bacon with patronage. He helped secure the execution of the Earl of Essex as a traitor 1601, after formerly being his follower. Bacon was accused of ingratitude, but he defended himself in *Apology* 1604. The satirist Pope called Bacon 'the wisest, brightest, and meanest of mankind'. Knighted on the accession of James I 1603, he became Baron Verulam 1618 and Viscount St Albans 1621.

His writing helped to inspire the founding of the ◊Royal Society. The **Baconian Theory**, originated by James Willmot in 1785, suggesting that the works of Shakespeare were written by Bacon, probably has no validity.

Bacon /'beɪkən/ Francis 1909– . British painter, born in Dublin. He came to London in 1925 and taught himself to paint. He practised abstract art, then developed a distorted Expressionist style, with tortured figures presented in loosely defined space. Since 1945 he has focused on studies of figures, as in his series of screaming popes based on the portrait of Innocent X by Velázquez.

Bacon began to paint about 1930 and held his first show in London in 1949. He destroyed much of his early work. *Three Studies for Figures at the Base of a Crucifixion* 1944 (Tate Gallery, London) is an early example of his mature syle. Bacon distorts and mutilates his human figures to express the complexity of their emotions.

Bacon /'beɪkən/ Roger 1214–1292. English philosopher and scientist. In 1266, at the invitation of his friend Pope Clement IV, he began his *Opus Majus*, a compendium of all branches of knowledge. In 1268 he sent this with his *Opus Minus* and other writings to the Pope. In 1277 he was condemned and imprisoned by the church for 'certain novelties' (heresy) and not released until 1292. He foresaw the magnifying properties of convex lenses, the extensive use of gunpowder, and the possibility of mechanical cars, boats, and flying machines.

Born in Somerset, and educated at Oxford and Paris, he became a Franciscan friar and was in Paris until about 1251 lecturing on Aristotle. His works include *On Mirrors, Metaphysical Questions*, and *On the Multiplication of Species*. He followed the maxim 'Cease to be ruled by dogmas and authorities; look at the world!'

bacteria (singular ***bacterium***) microscopic unicellular organisms with prokaryotic cells (see ◊prokaryote). They reproduce by ◊binary fission, and since this may occur approximately every 20 minutes, a single bacterium is potentially capable of producing 16 million copies of itself in a day.

Bacteria have a large loop of ◊DNA sometimes called a bacterial chromosome. In addition there are often small, circular pieces of DNA known as ◊plasmids that carry spare genetic information. These plasmids can readily move from one bacterium to another, even though the bacteria are of different species. In a sense they are parasites within the bacterial cell, but they survive by coding their characteristics which promote the survival of their hosts. For example, some plasmids confer antibiotic resistance on the bacteria they inhabit. The rapid and problematic spread of antibiotic resistance among bacteria is due to plasmids, but they are also useful to man in ◊genetic engineeering. Although generally considered harmful, certain types of bacteria are essential in many food and industrial processes.

bacteriology the study of ◊bacteria.

bacteriophage a ◊virus that attacks ◊bacteria.

Bactria /'bæktrɪə/ former region of central Asia (now Afghanistan, Pakistan and Soviet Central Asia) which was partly conquered by ◊Alexander the Great. During the 3rd–6th centuries BC it was a centre of E–W trade and cultural exchange.

Bactrian one of the two species of ◊camel, found in Asia.

Badajoz /ˌbædə'xəʊθ/ city in Extremadura, Spain, on the Portuguese frontier; population (1986) 126,000. It has a 13th-century cathedral and ruins of a Moorish castle. Badajoz has often been besieged, and was stormed by Wellington 1812 with the loss of 59,000 British troops.

Baden /'baːdn/ former state of SW Germany, which had Karlsruhe as its capital. Baden was captured from the Romans in 282 by the Alemanni; later it became a margravate, and in 1806 a grand duchy. A state of the German empire 1871–1918, then a republic, and under Hitler a *Gau* (province), it was divided between the *Länder* of Württemberg-Baden and Baden in 1945, and in 1952 made part of ◊Baden-Württemberg.

Baden /'baːdn/ town in Aargau canton, Switzerland, near Zurich; at an altitude of 388 m/1,273 ft; population (1981) 23,140. Its hot sulphur springs and mineral waters have been visited since Roman times.

Baden-Baden /'baːdn 'baːdn/ Black Forest spa in Baden-Württemberg, West Germany; population (1984) 49,000. Fashionable in the 19th century, it is now a conference centre.

Baden-Powell /'beɪdn 'pəʊəl/ Agnes 1854–1945. Sister of Robert Baden-Powell, she helped him found the ◊Girl Guides.

Baden-Powell /'beɪdn 'pəʊəl/ Lady Olave 1889–1977. Wife of Robert Baden-Powell from 1912, she was the first and only World Chief Guide 1918–1977.

Baden-Powell /'beɪdn 'pəʊəl/ Robert Stephenson Smyth, 1st Baron Baden-Powell 1857–1941. British general, founder of the Scout Association. He fought in defence of Mafeking (now Mafikeng) during the Second South African War. After 1907 he devoted his time to developing the Scout movement, which rapidly spread throughout the world. He was created a peer in 1929.

Baden-Württemberg /'baːdn'vʊətəmbɜːg/ administrative region (German *Land*) of West Germany
area 35,800 sq km/13,819 sq mi
capital Stuttgart
towns Mannheim, Karlsruhe, Freiburg, Heidelberg, Heilbronn, Pforzheim, Ulm
physical Black Forest; Rhine boundary south and west; source of the Danube; see also ◊Swabia
products wine, jewellery, watches, clocks, musical instruments, textiles, chemicals, iron, steel, electrical equipment, surgical instruments
population (1988) 9,390,000
history formed 1952 (following a plebiscite) by the merger of the *Länder* Baden, Württemberg-Baden, and Württemberg-Hohenzollern.

Bader /'baːdə/ Douglas 1910–1982. British fighter pilot. He lost both legs in a flying accident 1931, but had a distinguished flying career in World War II. He was knighted 1976 for his work with disabled people.

badger large mammal of the weasel family with molar teeth of a crushing type adapted to a partly vegetable diet, and short strong legs with long claws suitable for digging. The Eurasian ***common badger*** *Meles meles* is about 1 m/3 ft long, with long, coarse, greyish hair on the back, and a white face with a broad black stripe along each side. Mainly a woodland animal, it is harmless and nocturnal, and spends the day in a system of burrows called a 'sett'. It feeds on roots, a variety of fruits and nuts, insects, worms, mice, and young rabbits.

The ***American badger*** *Taxidea taxus* is a little smaller and lives in open country in North America. Various species of hog badger, ferret badger, and stink badger occur in S and E Asia, the last having the anal scent glands characteristic of the weasel family especially well developed.

Bad Godesburg /'bæd 'gəʊdəsbɜːg/ SE suburb of ◊Bonn, West Germany, formerly a spa, and the meeting place of Chamberlain and Hitler before the Munich Agreement 1938.

badlands a barren landscape cut by erosion into a maze of ravines, pinnacles, gullies and sharp-edged ridges. South Dakota and Nebraska, USA, are examples.

Badlands, which can be created by overgrazing, are so called because of their total lack of value for agriculture and their inaccessibility.

badminton indoor racket game played on a court with a feathered shuttlecock instead of a ball. Similar to lawn ◊tennis but played on a smaller court, the object is the same: to force the opponent(s) to be unable to return the shuttlecock.

Played by two or four players the court measures 6.09 m/20 ft by 13.41 m/44 ft. A 76 cm/2.5 ft deep net is stretched across the middle of the court and at a height of 1.52 m/5 ft above the ground to the top of the net. The shuttlecock must

bacteria *False colour electron microscope view of a bacteria about to divide. (× 10,000). The cell wall (in red) appears pinched at the point of division.*

badger

American badger

be volleyed. Only the server can win points. The sport is named after Badminton House, the seat of the duke of Beaufort, where the game was played in the 19th century.

Badminton: recent winners

World Championships have existed since 1977 at singles, doubles, and mixed doubles
winners (singles only):
men:
1980 Rudy Hartono *(Indonesia)*
1983 Icuk Sugiarto *(Indonesia)*
1985 Han Jian *(China)*
1987 Yang Yang *(China)*
1989 Yang Yang *(China)*
women:
1980 Wiharjo Verawaty *(Indonesia)*
1983 Li Lingwei *(China)*
1985 Han Aiping *(China)*
1987 Han Aiping *(China)*
1989 Li Lingwei *(China)*
Thomas Cup (an international team championship for men first held 1949)
recent winners:
1970 Indonesia
1973 Indonesia
1976 Indonesia
1979 Indonesia
1982 China
1984 Indonesia
1986 China
1988 China
Uber Cup (a women's international team competition, first held 1957)
recent winners:
1972 Japan
1975 Indonesia
1978 Japan
1981 Japan
1984 China
1986 China
1988 China

Badoglio /baːˈdəuljəu/ Pietro 1871–1956. Italian soldier and Fascist politician. A veteran of campaigns against the peoples of Tripoli and Cyrenaica, in 1935 he became commander in chief in Ethiopia, adopting ruthless measures to break patriot resistance; he was created viceroy of Ethiopia and duke of Addis Ababa in 1936. He succeeded Mussolini as prime minister of Italy from July 1943 to June 1944.

Baedeker /ˈbeɪdɪkə/ Karl 1801–1859. German publisher of foreign-travel guides; these are now based in Hamburg (before World War II in Leipzig).

Baedeker raids German air raids in World War II on British cities, so-called because they accurately pinpointed architectural treasures.

Baekeland /ˈbeɪklənd/ Leo Hendrik 1863–1944. US chemist, the inventor of ◊Bakelite, the first commercial plastic. He later made a photographic paper, Velox, which could be developed in artificial light.

Baer /beə/ Karl Ernst von 1792–1876. German zoologist, who was the founder of comparative ◊embryology.

Baez /baɪˈez/ Joan 1941– . US folk singer who came to prominence in the early 1960s with her versions of traditional English and American folk songs such as 'Silver Dagger'. She introduced Bob Dylan to a wide audience and has remained active as a pacifist and antiwar campaigner.

Baffin /ˈbæfɪn/ William 1584–1622. English explorer and navigator. In 1616, he and Robert Bylot explored Baffin Bay, NE Canada, and reached latitude 77° 45′ N, which for 236 years remained the 'furthest north'.

In 1612, Baffin was chief pilot of an expedition in search of the Northwest passage, and in 1613–14 commanded a whaling fleet near Spitsbergen, Norway. He piloted the *Discovery* on an expedition to Hudson Bay lead by Bylot in 1615. After 1617, Baffin worked for the ◊East India Company and

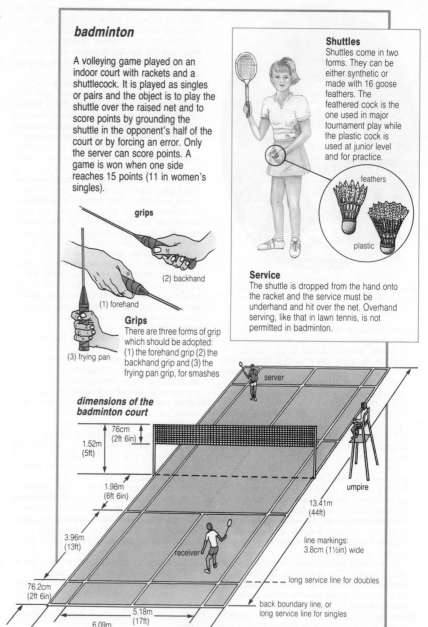

badminton

A volleying game played on an indoor court with rackets and a shuttlecock. It is played as singles or pairs and the object is to play the shuttle over the raised net and to score points by grounding the shuttle in the opponent's half of the court or by forcing an error. Only the server can score points. A game is won when one side reaches 15 points (11 in women's singles).

grips

(2) backhand
(1) forehand
(3) frying pan

Grips
There are three forms of grip which should be adopted: (1) the forehand grip (2) the backhand grip and (3) the frying pan grip, for smashes

Shuttles
Shuttles come in two forms. They can be either synthetic or made with 16 goose feathers. The feathered cock is the one used in major tournament play while the plastic cock is used at junior level and for practice.

feathers
plastic

Service
The shuttle is dropped from the hand onto the racket and the service must be underhand and hit over the net. Overhand serving, like that in lawn tennis, is not permitted in badminton.

dimensions of the badminton court

server
umpire
76cm (2ft 6in)
1.52m (5ft)
1.98m (6ft 6in)
3.96m (13ft)
76.2cm (2ft 6in)
5.18m (17ft)
6.09m (20ft)
13.41m (44ft)
line markings: 3.8cm (1½in) wide
long service line for doubles
back boundary line, or long service line for singles
receiver

made surveys of the Red Sea and Persian Gulf. In 1622 he was killed in an Anglo-Persian attack on Hormuz.

Baffin Island /ˈbæfɪn/ island in the Northwest Territories, Canada
area 507,450 sq km/195,875 sq mi
features largest island in the Canadian Arctic; mountains rise above 2,000 m/6,000 ft and there are several large lakes. The northernmost part of the strait separating Baffin Island from Greenland forms Baffin Bay; the southern end is Davis Strait.

It is named after William Baffin who carried out research here 1614 during his search for the ◊Northwest Passage.

BAFTA abbreviation for *British Academy of Film and Television Arts*.

bagatelle /ˌbægəˈtel/ (French 'trifle') in music, a short character piece, often for piano.

bagatelle a game resembling billiards but played on a board with numbered cups instead of pockets. The aim is to get the nine balls into the cups. In *ordinary bagatelle* each player delivers all the

balls in turn; in *French bagatelle* two or four players take part alternately.

Bagehot /ˈbædʒət/ Walter 1826–1877. British writer and economist, author of *The English Constitution* 1867, a classic analysis of the British political system. He was editor of *The Economist* magazine 1860–77.

Baggara /ˈbægərə/ a Bedouin people of the Nile Basin, principally in Kordofan, Sudan, W of the White Nile. They are Muslims, traditionally occupied in cattle-breeding and big-game hunting.

Baghdad /ˈbægˈdæd/ historic city and capital of Iraq, on the Tigris; population (1985) 4,649,000. Industries include oil refining, distilling, tanning, tobacco processing, and the manufacture of textiles and cement. Founded 762, it became Iraq's capital 1921.

To the SE, on the Tigris, are the ruins of *Ctesiphon*, capital of Parthia from about 250 BC–AD 226 and of the ◊Sassanian Empire about 226–641; the remains of the Great Palace include the world's largest single-span brick arch 26 m/85 ft wide and 29 m/95 ft high.

A route centre from the earliest times, it was developed by the 8th-century caliph Harun al-Rashid, though little of the Arabian Nights city remains. It was overrun 1258 by the Mongols, who destroyed the irrigation system. In 1639 it was taken by the Turks. During World War I Baghdad was captured by Gen Maude 1917.

Baghdad Pact military treaty of 1955 concluded by the UK, Iran, Iraq, Pakistan, and Turkey, with the USA cooperating; it was replaced by the ◊Central Treaty Organization (CENTO) when Iraq withdrew in 1958.

Bagnold /'bægnəʊld/ Enid 1889–1981. British author of *National Velvet* 1935, a novel about horse racing that was also successful as a film (1944).

bagpipe ancient wind instrument used outdoors and incorporating a number of reed pipes powered from a single inflated bag. Known in Roman times, it is found in various forms throughout Europe.

The bag has the advantage of being more powerful than the unaided lungs and of being able to sustain notes indefinitely. The melody pipe, bent downwards, is called a **chanter** and the accompanying harmony pipes supported on the shoulder are **drones**, which emit invariable notes to supply a ground bass.

Bagritsky /bə'grɪtski/ Eduard. Pen name of Eduard Dzyubin 1895–1934. Soviet poet. One of the Constructivist group, he published the heroic poem *Lay About Opanas* 1926, and collections of verse called *The Victors* 1932 and *The Last Night* 1932.

Baguio /bæ'gwiːəʊ/ summer resort on Luzon island in the Philippines, 200 km/125 mi N of Manila, 1,370 m/4,500 ft above sea level; population (1980) 119,000. It is the official summer residence of the Philippine president.

Bahadur Shah II /bə'haːdə 'ʃaː/ 1775–1862. Last of the Mughal emperors of India. He reigned, though in name only (including under the British), as king of Delhi 1837–57, when he was hailed by the mutineers (see ◊Indian Mutiny) as an independent emperor at Delhi. After the mutiny he was deported to Rangoon, Burma, with his family.

Baha'i religion founded in the 19th century from a Muslim splinter group, ◊Babism, by the Persian ◊Baha'ullah. The most important principle of his message was that all great religious leaders are manifestations of the unknowable God and all scriptures are sacred. There is no priesthood: all Baha'is are expected to teach, and to work towards world unification. There are about 4.5 million Baha'is worldwide.

Great stress is laid on equality regardless of religion, race, or gender. Drugs and alcohol are forbidden, as is monastic celibacy. Marriage is strongly encouraged; there is no arranged marriage, but parental approval must be given. Baha'is are expected to pray daily, but there is no set prayer. From 2 to 20 Mar, adults under 70 fast from sunrise to sunset. Administration is carried out by an elected body, the Universal House of Justice.

Bahamas /bə'haːməz/ group of islands in the Caribbean, off the SE coast of Florida.

government The Bahamas are an independent sovereign nation within the Commonwealth, with the British monarch as head of state, represented by an appointed, resident governor-general. The constitution, effective since independence in 1973, provides for a two-chamber parliament with a senate and house of assembly. The governor-general appoints a prime minister and cabinet drawn from and responsible to the legislature. The governor-general appoints 16 senate members, nine on the advice of the prime minister, four on the advice of the leader of the opposition, and three after consultation with the prime minister. The house of assembly has 49 members, elected by universal suffrage. Parliament has a maximum life of five years and may be dissolved within that period. The major political parties are the Progressive

Bahamas
Commonwealth of the

area 13,864 sq km/5,352 sq mi
capital Nassau on New Providence
physical comprises 700 tropical coral islands and about 1,000 cays
features desert islands: only 30 are inhabited; Blue Holes of Andros, the world's longest and deepest submarine caves
head of state Elizabeth II from 1973 represented by Gerald C Cash from 1979
head of government Lynden Oscar Pindling from 1967
political system constitutional monarchy
political parties Progressive Liberal Party (PLP), centrist; Free National Movement (FNM), centre-left
exports cement, pharmaceuticals, petroleum products, crawfish, rum, pulpwood; over half the islands' employment comes from tourism
currency Bahamian dollar (1.70 = £1 Feb 1990)
population (1986) 236,171; annual growth rate 1.8%
language English
religion 26% Roman Catholic, 21% Anglican, 48% other Protestants
literacy 93% (1985)
GDP $780 million (1981); $5,756 per head of population
chronology
1964 Internal self-government attained.
1967 First national assembly elections.
1972 Constitutional conference to discuss full independence.
1973 Full independence achieved.
1983 Allegations of drug trafficking by government ministers.
1984 Deputy prime minister and two cabinet ministers resigned. Pindling denied any personal involvement and was endorsed as party leader.
1987 Pindling re-elected despite claims of frauds.

Liberal Party (PLP) and the Free National Movement (FNM).

history A British colony from 1783, the Bahamas were given internal self-government in 1964 and the first elections for the national assembly on a full voting register were held in 1967. The PLP, drawing its support mainly from voters of African origin, won the same number of seats as the European-dominated United Bahamian Party (UBP). Lynden Pindling became prime minister with support from outside his party. In the 1968 elections the PLP scored a resounding victory and this was repeated in 1972, enabling Pindling to lead his country to full independence within the Commonwealth in 1973, and increase his majority in 1977.

The main contestants in the 1982 elections were the FNM, which consisted of a number of factions that had split and reunited, and the PLP. Despite allegations of government complicity in drug trafficking, the PLP was again successful and Pindling was unanimously endorsed as leader at a Party convention in 1984. The 1987 general election was won by the PLP, led by Pindling, but with a reduced majority.

Baha'ullah /,baːhaː'ʊlə/ title of Mirza Hosein Ali 1817–1892. Persian founder of the ◊Baha'i religion. Baha'ullah, 'God's Glory', proclaimed himself as the prophet the ◊Bab had foretold.

Bahawalpur /bə,haːwəl'puə/ city in the Punjab, Pakistan; population (1981) 178,000. Once the capital of a former state of Bahawalpur, it is now an industrial town producing textiles and soap. It has a university, established 1975.

Bahia /bə'iːə/ state of E Brazil
area 561,026 sq km/216,556 sq mi
capital Salvador
population (1986) 10,949,000
industry oil, chemicals, agriculture

Bahía Blanca /bə'iːə 'blæŋkə/ port in S Argentina, on the river Naposta, 5 km/3 mi from its mouth; population (1980) 233,126. It is a major distribution centre for wool and food processing. The naval base of Puerto Belgrano is here.

Bahrain /,baː'reɪn/ group of islands in the Arabian Gulf, between Saudi Arabia and Iran.
government The 1973 constitution provided for an elected national assembly of 30 members, but the assembly was dissolved in 1975 after the prime minister refused to work with it. The Emir now governs Bahrain by decree, through a cabinet chosen by him. There are no recognizable political parties.

history Traditionally an Arab monarchy, Bahrain was under Portuguese rule during the 16th century, and from 1602 was dominated by Persia. Since 1783 it has been a sheikhdom under the Khalifa dynasty. It became a British Protected State in 1816, with government shared between the ruling sheikh and a British adviser. In 1928 Iran (then Persia) claimed sovereignty but in 1970 accepted a UN report showing that the inhabitants of Bahrain preferred independence.

In 1968 Britain announced the withdrawal of its forces and Bahrain joined two other territories under British protection, Qatar and the Trucial States (now the United Arab Emirates), to form a Federation of Arab Emirates. In 1971 Qatar and the Trucial States left the Federation and Bahrain became an independent state, signing a new treaty of friendship with Britain.

In 1973 a new constitution provided for an elected national assembly but two years later the prime minister, Sheikh Khalifa, complained of obstruction by the assembly which was then dissolved. Since then the Emir and his family have ruled with virtually absolute power.

Since the Iranian revolution of 1979, relations between the two countries have been uncertain, with fears of Iranian attempts to disturb Bahrain's stability. Bahrain has now become a focal point in the Gulf, being the site of the new Gulf University and its international airport the centre of Gulf aviation. A causeway linking Bahrain with Saudi Arabia was constructed in 1986.

Baikal /baɪ'kæl/ (Russian **Baykal Ozero**) largest freshwater lake in Asia (area 31,500 sq km/12,150 sq mi) and deepest in the world (up to 1,740 m/5,710 ft), in S Siberia, USSR. Fed by more than 300 rivers, it is drained only by the Lower Angara. It has sturgeon fisheries and rich fauna.

Baikonur /,baɪkə'nuə/ the main Soviet launch site for spacecraft, at Tyuratam, near the Aral Sea. From here were launched the first satellites and all Soviet space probes and crewed Soyuz missions. It covers an area 90 km/55 mi by 140 km/85 mi, much larger than its US equivalent, the ◊Kennedy Space Center.

Bahrain
State of
(Dawlat al Bahrayn)

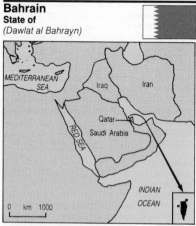

area 688 sq km/266 sq mi
capital Manama on the largest island (also called Bahrain)
towns oil port Mina Sulman
physical 33 islands, flat and hot
features a causeway 25 km/15 mi long (1985) links Bahrain to the mainland of Saudi Arabia; Sitra island is a communications centre for the lower Persian Gulf, and has a satellite-tracking station; there is a wildlife park featuring the oryx on Bahrain, and most of the south of the island is preserved for the ruling family's falconry

head of state and government Sheikh Isa biň Sulman al-Khalifa (1933–) from 1961
political system absolute emirate
political parties none
exports oil and natural gas
currency Bahrain dinar (0.64 = £1 Feb 1990)
population (1988 est) 421,000 (two thirds are nationals); annual growth rate 4.4%
life expectancy men 67, women 71
language Arabic, Farsi, English
religion Muslim (Shi'ite 60%, Sunni 40%)
literacy 79% male/64% female (1985 est)
GDP $4.1 bn (1984); $6,315 per head of population
chronology
1816 Under British protection.
1968 Britain announced its intention to withdraw its forces. Bahrain formed, with Qatar and the Trucial States, the Federation of Arab Emirates.
1971 Qatar and the Trucial States left the federation and Bahrain became an independent state.
1973 New constitution adopted, with an elected national assembly.
1975 Prime minister resigned and national assembly dissolved. Emir and his family assumed virtually absolute power.
1986 Gulf University established in Bahrain. A causeway (25 km/15 mi long) linking the island with Saudi Arabia was opened.

bail the setting at liberty of a person in legal custody on an undertaking (usually backed by some security, given either by that person or by someone else) to attend at a court at a stated time and place. If the person does not attend, the bail may be forfeited. The Bail Act of 1976 presumes that a suspect will be granted bail, unless the police can give good reasons why not, for example by showing that a further offence may take place.

Baile Atha Cliath /'blɑː ˈkliːə/ official Gaelic name of ◊Dublin, capital of the Republic of Ireland, from 1922.

Bailey /'beɪli/ Donald Coleman 1901–1985. English engineer, inventor in World War II of the portable **Bailey bridge**, made of interlocking, interchangeable, adjustable and easily transportable units.

bailiff term originating in Normandy as the name for a steward of an estate. It retained this meaning in England throughout the Middle Ages, and could also denote a sheriff's assistant. In France, the royal *bailli* or *bayle* was appointed to administer a large area of territory, the *baillage*, and was a very important local official.

Baillie /'beɪli/ Isobel 1895–1983. British soprano. Born in Hawick, Scotland, she became celebrated for her work in oratorio. She was professor of singing at Cornell University in New York 1960–61.

Bailly /bɑːˈjiː/ Jean Sylvain 1736–1793. French astronomer, who wrote about the satellites of Jupiter and the history of astronomy. Early in the French Revolution he was president of the National Assembly and mayor of Paris, but resigned in 1791 and was guillotined during the Terror.

Baily's beads bright spots of sunlight seen around the edge of the Moon for a few seconds immediately before and after a total ◊eclipse of the Sun, caused by sunlight shining between mountains at the Moon's edge. Sometimes one bead is much brighter than the others, producing the so-called **diamond ring** effect. The effect was described 1836 by the English astronomer Francis Baily (1774–1844), a wealthy stockbroker who retired in 1825 to devote himself to astronomy.

Bainbridge /'beɪnbrɪdʒ/ Beryl 1933– . English novelist, originally an actress, whose works have the drama and economy of a stage play. They include *The Dressmaker* 1973, *The Bottle Factory*

Outing 1974, and the collected short stories in *Mum and Mr Armitage* 1985.

Bainbridge /'beɪnbrɪdʒ/ Kenneth Tompkins 1904– . US physicist, who was director of the first atomic bomb test at Alamagordo, USA, in 1945. He worked at the Cavendish Laboratory, Cambridge, England, in the 1930s, and also carried out research in radar. From 1961, he was George Vasmer Everett professor of physics at Harvard University, USA.

Baird /beəd/ John Logie 1888–1946. Scottish electrical engineer, who pioneered television. In 1925 he gave the first public demonstration of television, and in 1926 pioneered fibre optics, radar (in advance of Robert ◊Watson-Watt), and 'noctovision', a system for seeing at night by using infrared rays.

Born at Helensburgh, Scotland, Baird studied electrical engineering in Glasgow at what is now the University of Strathclyde, at the same time serving several practical apprenticeships. He was working on television possibly as early as 1912, and he took out his first provisional patent 1923. He also developed video recording on both wax records and magnetic steel discs (1926–27), colour television (1925–28), three-dimensional colour television (1925–46), and transatlantic television (1928). In 1936 his mechanically scanned 240-line system competed with EMI-Marconi's 405-line, but the latter was preferred for the BBC service from 1937, partly because it used electronic scanning and partly because it handled

Baird *John Baird engaged in his pioneering work with television, 1943*

live indoor scenes with smaller, more manoeuvrable cameras. In 1944 he developed facsimile television, the forerunner of ◊Ceefax, and demonstrated the world's first all-electronic colour and three-dimensional colour receiver (500 lines).

Bairnsfather /'beənzfɑːðə/ Bruce 1888–1959. British artist, celebrated for his 'Old Bill' cartoons of World War I. In World War II he was official cartoonist to the US Army in Europe 1942–44.

Baja California /'bɑːhɑː/ the mountainous peninsula that forms the twin NW states of Lower (Spanish *baja*) California, Mexico; area 143,396 sq km/55,351 sq mi; population (1980) 1,440,600. The northern state, Baja California Norte, includes the busy towns of Mexicali and Tijuana, but the southern state, Baja California Sur, is sparsely populated.

Bakelite the first synthetic ◊plastic, discovered by Leo ◊Baekeland in 1909. Bakelite is hard, tough, and heatproof, and is used as an electrical insulator. It is made by the reaction together of phenol and formaldehyde, first producing a powdery resin which sets solid when heated. Objects are made by subjecting the resin to compression moulding (simultaneous heat and pressure in a mould).

Bakelite is one of the thermosetting plastics, which do not remelt when heated. It is often used for electrical fittings. It was discovered by Baekeland while he was working to find a substitute for shellac, a resinous substance used in lacquers and varnishes.

Baker /'beɪkə/ Benjamin 1840–1907. English engineer, who designed (with English engineer John Fowler 1817–1898) London's first underground railway (the Metropolitan and District) in 1869, the Forth Bridge, Scotland, 1890, and the original Aswan Dam on the River Nile, Egypt.

Baker III /'beɪkə/ James (Addison) 1930– . US Republican politician. Under President Reagan, he was White House Chief of Staff 1981–85 and Treasury secretary 1985–88. After managing Bush's successful presidential campaign 1988, Baker was appointed secretary of state 1989.

Baker, a lawyer from Houston, Texas, entered politics 1970 as one of the managers of his friend George Bush's unsuccessful campaign for the Senate. He served as undersecretary of commerce 1975–76 in the Ford administration and was deputy manager of the 1976 and 1980 Ford and Bush presidential campaigns. Baker was inducted into the Reagan administration 1981. He has been criticized for the unscrupulousness of the 1988 Bush campaign. The most influential member of the Bush team, he has been described as an effective 'prime minister'.

Baker /'beɪkə/ Janet 1933– . English mezzo-soprano who excels in lied, oratorio, and opera. Her performances include Dido in both *Dido and Aeneas* and *The Trojans*, and Marguerite in *Faust*. She retired from the stage in 1981 but continues to perform recitals, oratorio, and concerts.

Baker /'beɪkə/ Kenneth (Wilfrid) 1934– . British Conservative politician, education secretary 1986–89, and chair of the Conservative Party from 1989.

He was elected to the House of Commons 1968; from 1983 he represented Mole Valley. Undergoing national service in N Africa Baker was, for a time, a gunnery instructor to the Libyan army. He then read history at Oxford. Despite a reputation of being on the liberal wing of the Conservative Party, he became a minister of state in Thatcher's 1979 administration.

Baker /'beɪkə/ Richard St Barbe 1889–1982. British forestry expert, founder of the ***Men of the Trees Society***, which in 1932 became worldwide. In 1959 he settled in New Zealand.

Baker /'beɪkə/ Samuel White 1821–1893. English explorer, in 1864 the first European to sight Lake Albert Nyanza (now Lake Mobutu Sese Seko) in central Africa, and discover that the Nile flowed through it.

He founded an agricultural colony in Ceylon (now Sri Lanka), built a railway across the Dobruja, and

Baker *Chairman of Britain's Conservative Party, Kenneth Baker.*

in 1861 set out to discover the source of the Nile. His wife, Florence von Sass, accompanied him. From 1869 to 1873 he was governor-general of the Nile equatorial regions.

Bakewell /ˈbeɪkwel/ Robert 1725–1795. Pioneer improver of farm livestock. From his home in Leicestershire, England, he developed the Dishley or New Leicester breed of sheep and also worked on raising the beef-producing qualities of Longhorn cattle.

Bakewell's work was in response to a general requirement for stock that would fatten to greater weights at an earlier age and at less cost. His method was to select animals that possessed at least some of the desired characteristics, and mate those offspring which inherited the same features with near relatives in order to fix the type. Known as 'breeding in and in', the technique was widely taken up by others. Bakewell's Longhorns found less favour because they were outshone by the rapidly emerging Shorthorns, but his New Leicesters proved particularly influential as crosses to improve other native breeds of sheep.

Bakhtaran /ˌbæktəˈrɑːn/ (formerly **Kermanshah**, until 1980) capital of Bakhtaran province, NW Iran; population (1986) 561,000. The province (area 23,700 sq km/9,148 sq mi; population 1,463,000) is on the Iraqi border, and is mainly inhabited by Kurds. Industries include oil refining, carpets, and textiles.

Bakhuyzen /ˈbækhauzən/ Ludolf 1631–1708. Dutch painter of seascapes. *Stormy Sea* 1697 (Rijksmuseum, Amsterdam) is typically dramatic.

baking ◊cooking in an oven by dry heat. It is the method used for most cakes, biscuits, and pastries.

Bakke /ˈbækə/ Allan 1940– . US student who, in 1978, gave his name to a test case claiming 're-verse discrimination' when appealing against his exclusion from medical school, since less well-qualified blacks were to be admitted as part of a special programme for ethnic minorities. He won his case against quotas before the Supreme Court, although other affirmative action for minor-ity groups was still endorsed.

Bakst /bækst/ Leon. Assumed name of Leon Rosenberg 1886–1924. Russian painter and the-atrical designer. He used intense colours and fantastic images from Oriental and folk art, with an Art Nouveau tendency to graceful surface pattern. His designs for Diaghilev's touring

Ballets Russes made a deep impression in Paris 1909–14.

During 1900–09 he was scenic artist to the imperial theatres, then scenery painter and costume designer for Diaghilev's ballets. In later life, when living in Paris, he exercised worldwide influence on the decorative arts of the theatre.

Baku /bɑːˈkuː/ capital city of the Azerbaijan Republic, USSR, and industrial port (oil refining) on the Caspian Sea; population (1987) 1,741,000. Baku is a centre of the Soviet oil industry, and is linked by pipelines with Batumi on the Black Sea. The city was occupied Jan 1990 by Soviet troops, following mounting inter-ethnic conflict and Azeri demands for secession from the USSR.

Bakunin /bəˈkuːnɪn/ Mikhail 1814–1876. Russian anarchist, active in Europe. In 1848 he was ex-pelled from France as a revolutionary agitator. In Switzerland in the 1860s he became recognized as the leader of the anarchist movement. In 1869 he joined the First International (a coordinating socialist body) but, after stormy conflicts with Karl Marx, was expelled 1872.

Born of a noble family, Bakunin served in the Imperial Guard but, disgusted with tsarist methods in Poland, resigned his commission and travelled abroad. For his share in a brief revolt at Dresden 1849 he was sentenced to death. The sentence was commuted to imprisonment, and he was handed over to the tsar's government and sent to Siberia 1855. In 1861 he managed to escape to Switzerland. He had a large following, particularly in the Latin American countries. He wrote books and pamphlets, including *God and the State*.

Bala /ˈbælə/ (Welsh **Llyn Tegid**) lake in Gwynedd, N Wales, about 6.4 km/4 mi long and 1.6 km/1 mi wide. Lake Bala has a unique primitive fish, the gwyniad, protected from 1988.

Balaclava, Battle of /ˌbæləˈklɑːvə/ in the Crimean War, an engagement on 25 Oct 1854 near a town in Ukraine, 10 km/6 mi SE of Sevastopol. It was the scene of the ill-timed *Charge of the Light Brigade* of British cavalry against the Russian entrenched artillery. Of the 673 soldiers who took part, there were 272 casualties. *Balaclava helmets* were knitted hoods worn here by soldiers in the bitter weather.

Balakirev /bəˈlɑːkɪref/ Mily Alexeyevich 1837–1910. Russian composer. He wrote orchestral and piano music, songs, and a symphonic poem *Tamara*, all imbued with the Russian national character and spirit. He was leader of the group known as The Five and taught its other mem-bers, Mussorgsky, Cui, Rimsky-Korsakov, and Borodin.

Balakirev was born at Nijni-Novgorod. At St Petersburg he worked with ◊Glinka, established the Free School of Music 1862, which stressed the national element, and was director of the Imperial Chapel 1883–95.

balalaika Russian musical instrument, resembling a guitar. It has a triangular sound box, frets, and two, three, or four strings played by strumming with the fingers.

balance an apparatus for weighing or measuring mass. The various types include a *beam bal-ance*, consisting of a centrally pivoted lever with pans hanging from each end, and a *spring bal-ance*, in which the object to be weighed stretches (or compresses) a vertical coil spring fitted with a pointer that indicates the weight on a scale. Kitchen and bathroom scales are balances.

balance of nature in ecology, the idea that there is an inherent stability in most ◊ecosystems, and that human interference can disrupt this stability. Organisms in the ecosystem are adapted to each other, waste products produced by one species are used by another, resources used by some are replenished by others, and so on.

balance of payments in economics, a tabular ac-count of a country's debit and credit transactions with other countries. Items are divided into the

current account, which includes both visible trade (imports and exports) and invisible trade (such as transport, tourism, interest, and divi-dends), and the *capital account*, which includes investment in and out of the country, international grants, and loans. Deficits or surpluses on these accounts are brought into balance by buying and selling reserves of foreign currencies.

A *balance of payments crisis* arises when a country's current account deteriorates because the cost of imports exceeds income from exports. In developing countries persistent trade deficits often result in heavy government borrowing over-seas, which in turn leads to a ◊debt crisis.

balance of power in politics, the theory that the best way of ensuring international order is to have power so distributed among states that no single state is able to achieve a predominant position. The term, which may also refer more simply to the actual distribution of power, is one of the most enduring concepts in international relations. Since the development of nuclear weapons, it has been asserted that the balance of power has been replaced by a *balance of terror*.

balance of trade the balance of trade transactions of a country recorded in its current account; it forms one component of the country's ◊balance of payments.

balance sheet a statement of the financial position of a company or individual on a specific date, show-ing both ◊assets and ◊liabilities.

Balanchine /ˈbælənˌtʃiːn/ George 1904–1983. Russian-born choreographer. After leaving the USSR in 1924, he worked with Diaghilev in France. Moving to the USA in 1933, he became a major influence on modern dance, starting the New York City Ballet in 1948. His many works include *Apollon Musagète* 1928 and *The Prodigal Son* 1929 for Diaghilev, several works for music by Stravinsky such as *Agon* 1957 and *Duo Con-certante* 1972, and musicals such as *On Your Toes* 1936 and *The Boys from Syracuse* 1938.

Balaton /ˈbɒlətɒn/ lake in W Hungary; area 600 sq km/230 sq mi.

Balboa /bælˈbəʊə/ Vasco Núñez de 1475–1517. Spanish ◊conquistador, the first European to see the Pacific Ocean, on 29 Sept 1513, from the isthmus of Darien (now Panama). He was made admiral of the Pacific and governor of Panama, but was removed by Spanish court intrigue, im-prisoned, and executed.

Balcon /ˈbɔːlkən/ Michael 1896–1977. British film producer, responsible for the 'Ealing Comedies' of the 1940s and early 1950s, such as *Kind Hearts and Coronets* 1949 and *The Lavender Hill Mob* 1951.

Balder /ˈbɔːldə/ in Norse mythology, the son of ◊Odin and ◊Freya and husband of Nanna, and the best, wisest, and most loved of all the gods. He was killed, at ◊Loki's instigation, by a twig of mistletoe shot by the blind god Hodur.

baldness loss of hair from the upper scalp, espe-cially common in older men. Its onset and extent are influenced by genetic make-up and male sex ◊hormones. There is no cure, and expedients such as hair implants may have no lasting effect. Hair loss in both sexes may also occur as a result of ill-health or following radiation treatment, such as for cancer. *Alopecia*, a condition in which the hair falls out, is different from the 'male pattern baldness' described above.

Baldung Grien /ˌbældʊŋˈɡriːn/ Hans 1484/85–1545. German Renaissance painter, engraver, and designer, based in Strasbourg. He painted the theme *Death and the Maiden* in several versions.

Baldwin /ˈbɔːldwɪn/ James 1924–1987. US writer, born in Harlem, New York, who portrayed the condition of black Americans in contemporary so-ciety. His works include the novels *Go Tell It on the Mountain* 1953, *Another Country* 1962, and *Just Above My Head* 1979; the play *The Amen Corner* 1955; and the autobiographical essays *Notes of a Native Son* 1955 and *The Fire Next Time* 1963.

Baldwin *Brought up in a background of domestic strife, bigotry and religious fanaticism in Harlem, the author James Baldwin started preaching at the Fireside Pentecostal Church at the age of 14.*

Baldwin /ˈbɔːldwɪn/ Stanley, 1st Earl Baldwin of Bewdley 1867–1947. British Conservative politician, prime minister 1923–24, 1924–29, and 1935–37; he weathered the general strike 1926, secured complete adult suffrage 1928, and handled the abdication crisis of Edward VIII 1936.

Born in Bewdley, Worcestershire, the son of an iron and steel magnate, in 1908 he was elected Unionist Member of Parliament for Bewdley, and in 1916 he became parliamentary private secretary to Bonar Law. He was financial secretary to the Treasury 1917–21, and then appointed to the presidency of the Board of Trade. In 1919 he gave the Treasury £150,000 of War Loan for cancellation, representing about 20% of his fortune. He was a leader in the disruption of the Lloyd George coalition 1922, and, as chancellor under Bonar Law, achieved a settlement of war debts with the USA.

As prime minister 1923–24 and again 1924–29, Baldwin passed the Trades Disputes Act of 1927 after the general strike, granted widows' and orphans' pensions, and complete adult suffrage 1928. He joined the national government of Ramsay MacDonald 1931 as Lord President of the Council. He handled the abdication crisis during his third premiership 1935–37, but was later much criticized for his failures to resist popular desire for an accommodation with the dictators Hitler and Mussolini, and to rearm more effectively.

Baldwin I /ˈbɔːldwɪn/ 1058–1118. King of Jerusalem. A French nobleman, who joined his brother ◊Godfrey de Bouillon on the First Crusade in 1096, he established the kingdom in 1100. It was destroyed by Islamic conquest in 1187.

Bâle /bɑːl/ French form of Basle or ◊Basel, town in Switzerland.

Balearic Islands /ˌbælɪˈærɪk/ (Spanish *Baleares*) Mediterranean group of islands forming an autonomous region of Spain; including ◊Majorca, ◊Minorca, ◊Ibiza, Cabrera, and Formentera
area 5,000 sq km/1,930 sq mi
capital Palma de Mallorca
products figs, olives, oranges, wine, brandy, coal, iron, slate; tourism is important
population (1986) 755,000
history a Roman colony from 123 BC, the Balearic Islands were an independent Moorish kingdom 1009–1232; the islands were conquered by Aragon 1343.

Balewa alternative title of Nigerian politician ◊Tafawa Balewa.

Balfe /bælf/ Michael William 1808–1870. Irish composer and singer. He was a violinist and baritone at Drury Lane, London, when only 16. In 1825 he went to Italy, where he sang in Palermo and at La Scala, and in 1846 he was appointed conductor at Her Majesty's Theatre. He composed operas, including *The Bohemian Girl* 1843.

Balfour /ˈbælfə/ Arthur James, 1st Earl of Balfour 1848–1930. British Conservative politician, prime minister 1902–05 and foreign secretary 1916–19, when he issued the Balfour Declaration and was involved in peace negotiations after World War I.

Son of a Scottish landowner, he was elected a Conservative Member of Parliament in 1874. In Lord Salisbury's ministry he was secretary for Ireland 1887, and for his ruthless vigour was called 'Bloody Balfour' by Irish nationalists. In 1891 and again in 1895 he became First Lord of the Treasury and leader of the Commons, and in 1902 he succeeded Salisbury as prime minister. His cabinet was divided over Joseph Chamberlain's tariff-reform proposals, and in the 1905 elections suffered a crushing defeat.

Balfour retired from the party leadership in 1911. In 1915 he joined the Asquith coalition as First Lord of the Admiralty. As foreign secretary 1916–19 he issued the Balfour Declaration of 1917 in favour of a national home in Palestine for the Jews and signed the Treaty of Versailles. He was Lord President of the Council 1919–22 and 1925–29, and received the Order of Merit in 1916 and an earldom in 1922. He also wrote books on philosophy.

Balfour Declaration a letter, dated 2 Nov 1917, from the British foreign secretary, A J Balfour, to Lord Rothschild (chair, British Zionist Federation) stating: 'HM government view with favour the establishment in Palestine of a national home for the Jewish people' but without prejudicing non-Jewish peoples; it led to the foundation of Israel 1948.

Bali /ˈbɑːli/ island of Indonesia, E of Java, one of the Sunda Islands
area 5,800 sq km/2,240 sq mi
capital Denpasar
physical volcanic mountains
features Balinese dancing, music, drama
products gold and silver work, woodcarving, weaving, copra, salt, coffee
population (1980) 2,470,000
history Bali's Hindu culture goes back to the 7th century; the Dutch gained control of the island by 1908.

Balikesir /ˌbɑːlɪkeˈsɪə/ city in NW Turkey, capital of Aydin province; population (1985) 152,000. There are silver mines nearby.

Balikpapan /ˌbɑːlɪkˈpɑːpən/ port in Indonesia, on the E coast of S Kalimantan, Borneo; population (1980) 280,900. It is an oil-refining centre.

Baliol /ˈbeɪlɪəl/ John de *c.*1250–1314. King of Scotland 1292–96. As an heir to the Scottish throne on the death of Margaret, the Maid of Norway, his cause was supported by the English

Balearic Islands

king, Edward I, against 12 other claimants. Having paid homage to Edward, he was proclaimed king but soon rebelled and gave up the kingdom when English forces attacked Scotland.

Bali Strait /ˈbɑːli/ a narrow strait between the two islands of Bali and Java, Indonesia. It was the scene on 19–20 Feb 1942 of a naval action between Japanese and Dutch forces which served to delay slightly the Japanese invasion of Java.

Balkans /ˈbɔːlkənz/ (Turkish 'mountains') peninsula of SE Europe, stretching into the Mediterranean between the Adriatic and Aegean Seas, comprising Albania, Bulgaria, Greece, Romania, Turkey-in-Europe, and Yugoslavia. It is joined to the rest of Europe by an isthmus 1,200 km/750 mi wide between Rijeka on the W and the mouth of the Danube on the Black Sea to the E.

A byword for political dissension historically, a tendency fostered by the great ethnic diversity resulting from successive waves of invasion, the Balkans' economy developed comparatively slowly until after World War II, largely because of the predominantly mountainous terrain, apart from the plains of the Save-Danube basin in the N. Political differences have remained strong, for example the confrontation of Greece and Turkey over Cyprus, and the differing types of Communism prevailing in the rest, but in the later years of the 20th century, a tendency to regional union emerged. To *Balkanize* is to divide into small warring states.

Balkan Wars two wars 1912–13 and 1913 which resulted in the expulsion by the Balkan states of Ottoman Turkey from Europe except for a small area around Istanbul.

The *First Balkan War, 1912*, of Bulgaria, ◊Serbia, ◊Greece, and Montenegro against Turkey, forced the Turks to ask for an armistice, but the peace negotiations, in London, broke down when the Turks, while agreeing to surrender all Turkey-in-Europe W of the city of Edirne (formerly Adrianople), refused to give up the city itself. In Feb 1913 hostilities were resumed, Edirne fell on 26 Mar and on 30 May by the Treaty of London Turkey retained in Europe only a small piece of E Thrace and the Gallipoli peninsula.

The *Second Balkan War, June–July 1913*, took place when Bulgaria attacked Greece and Serbia, which were joined by Romania. Bulgaria was defeated, and Turkey secured from that country the cession of Edirne.

Balkhash /bælˈxɑːʃ/ salt lake in Kazakhstan, USSR; area 17,300 sq km/6,678 sq mi. It is 600 km/375 mi long, receives several rivers, but has no outlet. Very shallow, it is frozen throughout the winter.

Balkhash /bælˈxɑːʃ/ town on the N shore of Lake Balkhash in Kazhakstan, USSR; population (1985) 112,000. It was founded 1928. Chief industries include copper mining and salt extraction.

Ball /bɔːl/ John died 1387. English priest, one of the leaders of the ◊Peasants' Revolt 1381, known as 'the mad priest of Kent'. A follower of John Wycliffe and a believer in social equality, he was imprisoned for disagreeing with the archbishop of Canterbury, and was probably excommunicated. During the revolt, he was released from prison, and when in Blackheath, London, preached from the text 'When Adam delved and Eve span, who was then the gentleman?' When the revolt collapsed he escaped but was captured near Coventry and executed.

Ball /bɔːl/ Lucille 'Lucy' 1911–1989. US comedy actress. From 1951–57 she starred with her husband, Cuban bandleader Desi Arnaz, in *I Love Lucy*, the first US television show filmed before an audience. It was followed by *The Lucy Show* 1962–68 and *Here's Lucy* 1968–74.

She entered films as a bit player 1933, and appeared in dozens of films over the next few years, including *Room Service* 1938 (with the Marx Brothers) and *Fancy Pants* 1950 (with Bob Hope). Her TV success limited her film output after 1950; her later films include *Mame*

1974. The television series are still transmitted in many countries.

ballad (Latin *ballare* 'to dance') type of popular poem that tells a story. Of simple metrical form and dealing with some strongly emotional event, the ballad is halfway between the lyric and the epic. Most English ballads date from the 15th century. Poets of the Romantic movement both in England and in Germany were greatly influenced by the ballad revival, for example, the *Lyrical Ballads* 1798 of Wordsworth and Coleridge. Other later forms are the 'broadsheets' with a satirical or political motive, and the testamentary 'hanging' ballads of the condemned criminal.

Historically, the ballad was primarily intended for singing at the communal ring-dance, the refrains representing the chorus. In the UK collections of ballads were made in the 17th and 18th centuries, for example Bishop Percy's *Reliques of Ancient Poetry* 1765, Scott's *Minstrelsy of the Scottish Border* 1802–03, and Professor F J Child's *English and Scottish Popular Ballads* 1857–59. Opinion is divided as to whether the authorship of the ballads may be attributed to individual poets or to the community. Later ballads tend to centre round a popular folk-hero, as in the case of the *Gest of Robyn Hode* and in the US cycles concerning Jesse James and Yankee Doodle. British poets who used ballad form include Keats, Southey, Rossetti, S Dobell, Tennyson, Morris, and Kipling.

In 19th-century music the refined drawing-room ballad had a vogue, but a more robust tradition survived in the music hall. In pop music slow songs are often called 'ballads' regardless of content.

ballade in music, an instrumental piece based on a story; a form used in piano works by ◊Chopin and ◊Liszt. In literature, a poetic form developed in France in the later Middle Ages from the ◊ballad, generally consisting of one or more groups of three stanzas of seven or eight lines each, followed by a shorter stanza or envoy, the last line being repeated as a chorus.

Ballance /'bæləns/ John 1839–1893. New Zealand politician, born in N Ireland; prime minister 1891–93.

He emigrated to New Zealand, founded and edited the *Wanganui Herald*, and held many cabinet posts.

Ballantyne /'bæləntaɪn/ R(obert) M(ichael) 1825–1894. Scottish writer of children's books. Childhood visits to Canada and six years as a trapper for the Hudson's Bay company provided material for his adventure stories, which include *The Young Fur Traders* 1856, *Coral Island* 1857, and *Martin Rattler* 1858.

Ballarat /'bæləræt/ town in Victoria, Australia; population (1986) 75,200. It was founded in the 1851 gold rush, and the mining village and workings have been restored for tourists. The ◊**Eureka Stockade** miners' revolt took place here 1854.

Ballard /'bæla:d/ J(ames) G(raham) 1930– . British novelist, whose works include science fiction on the theme of disaster, such as *The Drowned World* 1962, and *High-Rise* 1975, and the partly autobiographical *Empire of the Sun* 1984, dealing with his internment in China during World War II.

Ballesteros /bælɪ'stɪərɒs/ Severiano 'Seve' 1957– . Spanish golfer who came to prominence 1976 and has been dominant in Europe, as well as winning leading tournaments in the USA. He has won the British Open three times 1979, 1984, 1988.

Born in Pedrena, N Spain, he is one of four golf-playing brothers. Seve has won more than 60 tournaments worldwide and more than £1 million on the European Tour.

CAREER HIGHLIGHTS

British Open: 1979, 1984, 1988
US Masters: 1980, 1983
World Match-play: 1981–82, 1984–85

ballet (Italian *balletto* 'a little dance') a theatrical representation in dance form in which music also

Ballesteros *Seve Ballesteros at the British Open, 1988.*

plays a major part in telling a story or conveying a mood. Some such form of entertainment existed in ancient Greece, but Western ballet as we know it today first appeared in Italy. From there it was brought by Catherine de ◊Medici to France in the form of a spectacle combining singing, dancing, and declamation. In the 20th century Russian ballet has had a vital influence on the classical tradition in the West, and modern ballet has developed in the US through the work of George ◊Balanchine and Martha ◊Graham, and in the UK through the influence of Marie ◊Rambert.

history The first important dramatic ballet, the *Ballet comique de la reine*, was produced 1581 by the Italian Balthasar de Beaujoyeux at the French court and was performed by male courtiers, with ladies of the court forming the *corps de ballet*. In 1661 Louis XIV founded *L'Académie royale de danse*, to which all subsequent ballet activities throughout the world can be traced. Long flowing court dress was worn by the dancers until the 1720s when Marie-Anne Camargo, the first great ballerina, shortened her skirt to reveal her feet, thus allowing greater movement *à terre* and the development of dancing *en l'air*.

ballet *Portrait of the 18th-century ballet dancer Marie-Anne de Cupis de Camargo, by Nicholas Lancret.*

It was not until the early 19th century that a Paris costumier, Maillot, invented tights, thus allowing complete muscular freedom. The first of the great ballet masters was J-G ◊Noverre, and great contemporary dancers were Vestris, Heinel, Dauberval, and Gardel. Carlo Blasis is regarded as the founder of Classical ballet, since he defined the standard conventional steps and accompanying gestures.

Romantic ballet The great Romantic era of ◊Taglioni, Elssler, Grisi, Grahn, and Cerrito began about 1830 but survives today only in *Giselle* 1841 and *La Sylphide* 1832. Characteristics of this era were the new calf-length Classical white dress and the introduction of dancing on the toes, *sur les pointes*. The technique of the female dancer was developed, but the role of the male dancer was reduced to that of her partner.

Russian ballet was introduced to the West by ◊Diaghilev, who set out for Paris 1909, at about the same time that Isadora ◊Duncan, a rigid opponent of Classical ballet, was touring Europe. Associated with Diaghilev were Fokine, Nijinsky, Pavlova, Massine, Balanchine, and Lifar. Ballets presented by his company, before its break-up after his death 1929, included *Les Sylphides*, *Schéhérazade*, *Petrouchka*, and *Blue Train*. Diaghilev and Fokine pioneered a new and exciting combination of the perfect technique of imperial Russian dancers and the appealing naturalism favoured by Isadora Duncan. In the USSR ballet continues to flourish, the two chief companies being the Kirov and the Bolshoi. Best-known ballerinas are Ulanova and Plisetskaya, and the best-known male dancers are Rudolf Nureyev, Mikhail Baryshnikov, and Alexander Godunov, now dancing in the West, as are the husband-and-wife team Vyacheslav Gordeyev and Nadezhda Pavlova.

American ballet was firmly established by the founding of Balanchine's School of American Ballet 1934, and by de Basil's Ballets Russes de Monte Carlo and Massine's Ballet Russe de Monte Carlo, which also carried on the Diaghilev tradition. Since 1948 the New York City Ballet with Maria Tallchief, Nora Kaye, and choreographer Jerome Robbins, under the guiding influence of Balanchine, has developed a genuine American classic style.

British ballet Marie Rambert initiated in 1926 the company that developed into the Ballet Rambert, but the modern national company, the Royal Ballet (so named 1956), grew from foundations laid by Ninette de Valois and Frederick Ashton 1928. British dancers include Margot Fonteyn, Beryl Grey, Alicia Markova, Anton Dolin, Antoinette Sibley, and Anthony Dowell; choreographers include Kenneth MacMillan.

ballet blanc /'bæleɪ 'blɒŋ/ (French 'white ballet') a ballet, such as *Giselle*, in which the female dancers wear calf-length white dresses. The costume was introduced by Marie ◊Taglioni in *La Sylphide* 1832.

ballet d'action /'bæleɪ dæk'sjɒŋ/ a ballet with a plot, developed by ◊Noverre in the 18th century.

balletomane a ballet enthusiast.

Ballinasloe /ˌbælɪnə'sləʊ/ town in Galway Bay, Republic of Ireland; population about 6,500. The annual livestock fair every Oct is the largest in Ireland.

ballistics study of the motion of projectiles. For projectiles from a gun, relevant exterior factors include temperature, barometric pressure, and wind strength; and for nuclear missiles extend to such factors as the speed at which the Earth turns.

balloon impermeable fabric bag which rises when filled with gas lighter than the surrounding air. In 1783, the first successful human ascent was in Paris, in a hot-air balloon designed by the ◊Montgolfier brothers. During the French Revolution balloons were used for observation; in World War II they were used to defend London against low-flying aircraft. They are now used for sport, and as a means of meteorological, infrared, gamma ray, and ultraviolet observation. The first transatlantic crossing by balloon was made 11–17 Aug 1978 by a US team.

ballroom dancing collective term for social dances such as the ◊foxtrot, quickstep, ◊tango, and ◊waltz.

ball valve a valve used in lavatory cisterns to cut off the water supply when it reaches the correct level. It consists of a flat rubber washer at one end of a pivoting arm and a hollow ball at the other. The ball floats on the water surface, rising as the cistern fills, and at the correct level the rubber washer is pushed against the water-inlet pipe, cutting off the flow.

balm *lemon balm*, *Melissa officinalis*, is a herb of the family Labiatae, with lemon-scented leaves. It is most widely used in herb teas.

Balmer Johann 1825–1898. Swiss physicist and mathematician who developed formulae capable of deriving the wavelengths of the hydrogen atom spectrum. The simplicity of his formula, which involves only the manipulation of integers, had a central role in the development of spectral theory.

Balmoral Castle /bælˈmɒrəl/ residence of the British royal family in Scotland on the river Dee, 10.5 km/6 mi NE of Braemar, Grampian region. The castle, built of granite in the Scottish baronial style, is dominated by a square tower and circular turret rising 30 m/100 ft. It was rebuilt 1853–55 by Prince Albert, who bought the estate in 1852.

balsam garden plants of the genus *Impatiens*, which are usually annuals with red or white flowers. In medicine and perfumery, balsam refers to plant oils and resins such as balsam of Peru from the tree *Myroxylon balsamum*.

Baltic, Battle of the /ˈbɔːltɪk/ naval battle fought off Copenhagen on 2 Apr 1801, in which a British fleet under Sir Hyde Parker, with ◊Nelson as second-in-command, annihilated the Danish navy.

Baltic Sea /ˈbɔːltɪk/ large shallow arm of the North Sea, extending NE from the narrow Skagerrak and Kattegat, between Sweden and Denmark, to the Gulf of Bothnia between Sweden and Finland. Its coastline is 8,000 km/5,000 mi long, and its area, including the gulfs of Riga, Finland, and Bothnia, is 422,300 sq km/163,000 sq mi. Its shoreline is shared by Denmark, Germany, Poland, the USSR, Finland, and Sweden.

Many large rivers flow into it, including the Oder, Vistula, Niemen, W Dvina, Narva, and Neva. Tides are hardly perceptible, salt content is low; weather is often stormy and navigation dangerous. Most ports are closed by ice from Dec until May. The Kiel canal links the Baltic and the North Sea, the Göta canal connects the two seas by way of the S Swedish lakes, and since 1975 it has been linked by the Leningrad–Belomorsk seaway with the White Sea.

Baltic States /ˈbɔːltɪk/ collective name for the former independent states of ◊Estonia, ◊Latvia, and ◊Lithuania, from 1940 republics within the USSR.

Baltic Sea

the ballet repertory

date	ballet	composer	choreographer	place
1670	Le Bourgeois Gentilhomme	Lully	Beauchamp	Chambord
1735	Les Indes Galantes	Rameau	Blondy	Paris
1761	Don Juan	Gluck	Angiolini	Vienna
1778	Les Petits Riens	Mozart	Noverre	Paris
1801	The Creatures of Prometheus	Beethoven	Viganò	Vienna
1828	La Fille Mal Gardée	Hérold	Aumer	Paris
1832	La Sylphide	Schneitzhoeffer	F. Taglioni	Paris
1841	Giselle	Adam	Coralli/Perrot	Paris
1842	Napoli	Gade/Paulli Helsted/Lumbye	Bournonville	Copenhagen
1844	La Esmeralda	Pugni	Perrot	London
1869	Don Quixote	Minkus	M. Petipa	Moscow
1870	Coppélia	Delibes	Saint-Léon	Paris
1876	Sylvia	Delibes	Mérante	Paris
1877	La Bayadère	Minkus	M. Petipa	St Petersburg
1877	Swan Lake	Tchaikovsky	Reisinger	Moscow
1882	Namouna	Lalo	L. Petipa	Paris
1890	The Sleeping Beauty	Tchaikovsky	M. Petipa	St Petersburg
1892	Nutcracker	Tchaikovsky	M. Petipa/Ivanov	St Petersburg
1898	Raymonda	Glazunov	M.Petipa	St Petersburg
1905	The Dying Swan	Saint-Saëns	Fokine	St Petersburg
1907	Les Sylphides	Chopin	Fokine	St Petersburg
1910	Carnival	Schumann	Fokine	St Petersburg
1910	The Firebird	Stravinsky	Fokine	Paris
1911	Petrushka	Stravinsky	Fokine	Paris
1911	Le Spectre de la Rose	Weber	Fokine	Monte Carlo
1912	L'Après-midi d'un Faune	Debussy	Nijinsky	Paris
1912	Daphnis and Chloë	Ravel	Fokine	Paris
1913	Jeux	Debussy	Nijinsky	Paris
1913	The Rite of Spring	Stravinsky	Nijinsky	Paris
1915	El Amor Brujo	Falla	Imperio	Madrid
1917	Parade	Satie	Massine	Paris
1919	La Boutique Fantasque	Rossini/Respighi	Massine	London
1919	The Three-Cornered Hat	Falla	Massini	London
1923	The Creation of the World	Milhaud	Börlin	Paris
1923	Les Noces	Stravinsky	Nijinska	Paris
1924	Les Biches	Poulenc	Nijinska	Monte Carlo
1927	The Red Poppy	Glière	Lashchilin/Tikhomirov	Moscow
1928	Apollon Musagète	Stravinsky	Balanchine	Paris
1928	Le Baiser de la fée	Tchaikovsky	Nijinska	Paris
1928	Bolero	Ravel	Nijinska	Paris
1929	The Prodigal Son	Prokofiev	Balanchine	Paris
1929	La Valse	Ravel	Nijinska	Monte Carlo
1931	Bacchus and Ariadne	Roussel	Lifar	Paris
1931	Façade	Walton	Ashton	London
1931	Job	Vaughan Williams	de Valois	London
1937	Checkmate	Bliss	de Valois	Paris
1937	Les Patineurs	Meyerbeer/Lambert	Ashton	London
1938	Billy the Kid	Copland	Loring	Chicago
1938	Gaîté Parisienne	Offenbach/Rosenthal	Massine	Monte Carlo
1938	Romeo and Juliet	Prokofiev	Psota	Brno, Moravia
1942	Gayaneh	Khachaturian	Anisimova	Molotov-Perm
1942	The Miraculous Mandarin	Bartók	Milloss	Milan
1942	Rodeo	Copland	de Mille	New York
1944	Appalachian Spring	Copland	Graham	Washington
1944	Fancy Free	Bernstein	Robbins	New York
1945	Cinderella	Prokofiev	Zakharov	Moscow
1949	Carmen	Bizet	Petit	London
1951	Pineapple Poll	Sullivan/Mackerras	Cranko	London
1956	Spartacus	Khachaturian	Jacobson	Leningrad
1957	Agon	Stravinsky	Balanchine	New York
1959	Episodes	Webern	Balanchine	New York
1962	A Midsummer Night's Dream	Mendelssohn	Balanchine	New York
1962	Pierrot Lunaire	Schoenberg	Tetley	New York
1964	The Dream	Mendelssohn/Lanchbery	Ashton	London
1965	The Song of the Earth	Mahler	MacMillan	Stuttgart
1967	Anastasia	Martinu	MacMillan	New York
1968	Enigma Variations	Elgar	Ashton	London
1969	The Taming of the Shrew	Stolze/Scarlatti	Cranko	Stuttgart
1972	Duo Concertante	Stravinsky	Balanchine	New York
1974	Elite Syncopations	Joplin, etc	MacMillan	London
1976	A Month in the Country	Chopin/Lanchbery	Ashton	London
1978	Mayerling	Liszt/Lanchbery	MacMillan	London
1978	Symphony of Psalms	Stravinsky	Kylian	Scheveningen, The Netherlands
1980	Gloria	Poulenc	MacMillan	London
1980	Rhapsody	Rachmaninov	Ashton	London

Balzac *French novelist Honoré de Balzac planned to depict every aspect of French life in* La Comédie Humaine, *but only managed to complete about 80 of the planned 143 volumes.*

Baltimore /ˈbɔːltɪmɔː/ industrial port and largest city in Maryland, USA, on the W shore of Chesapeake Bay, NE of Washington DC; population (1980) 2,300,000. Industries include shipbuilding, oil refining, food processing, and the manufacture of steel, chemicals, and aerospace equipment.

It was named after the founder of Maryland, Lord Baltimore (1606–1675). The city of Baltimore dates from 1729 and was incorporated 1797. At Fort McHenry Francis Scott Key wrote 'The Star Spangled Banner'. The writer Edgar Allan Poe and the baseball player Babe Ruth lived here.

Baltistan a region in the Karakoram range of NE Kashmir held by Pakistan since 1949. The home of Balti Muslims of Tibetan origin. The chief town is Skardu, but Ghyari is of greater significance to Muslims as the site of a mosque built by Sayyid Ali Hamadani, a Persian who brought the Shia Muslim religion to Baltistan in the 14th century.

Baluch inhabitant of Baluchistan, SW Asia. Their common religion is Islam, and they speak Baluchi (a member of the Iranian branch of the Indo-European language family).

Much of Baluchistan is rugged and mountainous, and in the dryer areas the Baluchs make use of tents, moving when it becomes too arid. Although the Baluch practise nomadic pastoralism, many are settled agriculturalists.

Baluchistan /bəˌluːtʃɪˈstɑːn/ mountainous desert area, comprising a province of Pakistan, part of the Iranian province of Sistán and Balúchestan, and a small area of Afghanistan. The Pakistani province has an area of 347,200 sq km/134,019 sq mi, and a population (1985) 4,908,000; its capital is Quetta. Sistán and Balúchestan has an area of 181,600 sq km/70,098 sq mi, and a population (1986) 1,197,000; its capital is Zahedan. The port of Gwadar in Pakistan is strategically important, on the Indian Ocean and the Strait of Hormuz.

Balzac /ˈbælˈzæk/ Honoré de 1799–1850. French novelist. His first success was *Les Chouans/The Chouans* and *La Physiologie du marriage/The Physiology of Marriage* 1829, inspired by Scott. This was the beginning of the long series of novels ◊*La Comédie humaine/The Human Comedy*. He also wrote Rabelaisian *Contes drôlatiques/Ribald Tales* 1833.

Born in Tours, Balzac studied law and worked as a notary's clerk in Paris, before turning to literature. His first attempts included tragedies such as *Cromwell* and novels published pseudonymously with no great success. A venture in printing and publishing 1825–28 involved him in a lifelong web of debt. His patroness, Madame de Berny, figures

in *Le Lys dans la vallée/The Lily in the Valley* 1836. Balzac planned for his major work *La Comédie Humaine/The Human Comedy* to comprise 143 volumes, depicting every aspect of society in 19th-century France, but he only managed to complete 80. The series includes *Eugénie Grandet* 1833, *Le Père Goriot* 1834, and *Cousine Bette* 1846. Balzac corresponded constantly with the Polish countess Evelina Hanska after meeting her in 1833, but they only married four months before his death in Paris. He was buried in Père Lachaise cemetery.

Bamako /ˌbæməˈkəʊ/ capital and port of Mali on the River Niger; population (1976) 404,022. It produces pharmaceuticals, chemicals, textiles, tobacco and metal products.

Bamberg /ˈbæmbɜːg/ town in Bavaria, West Germany on the river Regnitz; population (1985) 70,400. The economy is based on engineering and the production of textiles, carpets and electrical goods. It has an early 13th-century Romanesque cathedral.

bamboo plant of the group Bambuseae, belonging to the grass family Gramineae, mainly found in tropical and sub-tropical countries, and remarkable for the gigantic size which some species can attain.

The stems are hollow and jointed, and can be used in furniture, house, and boat construction. The young shoots are eaten in China; paper is made from the stem.

Banaba /ˈbɑːnəbə/ (formerly *Ocean Island*) island in the Republic of ◊Kiribati.

banana treelike tropical plants 8 m/25 ft high, of the family Musaceae, which include the edible banana, sterile hybrid forms of the genus *Musa*.

The curved yellow fruits of the commercial banana, arranged in rows of 'hands', form cylindrical masses of a hundred or more, and are exported green and ripened aboard refrigerated ships. The plant is destroyed after cropping. The *plantain*, a larger, coarser subspecies, which is used green as a cooked vegetable, is a staple of the diet in many countries. In the wild, bananas depend on bats for pollination.

Bananarama British pop group formed 1981, a vocal trio comprising, from 1988, founder members Sarah Dallin (1962–) and Keren Woodward (1963–), with Jackie O'Sullivan (1966–). They were the top-selling British female group of the 1980s.

Their many UK hits include 'Love in the First Degree' 1987 and 'I Want You Back' 1988.

Banaras /bəˈnɑːrəs/ another transliteration of Varanasi, holy Hindu city in Uttar Pradesh, India.

Banbury /ˈbænbəri/ town in Oxfordshire, England; population (1981) 35,800. The *Banbury Cross* of the nursery rhyme was destroyed by the Puritans 1602, but replaced 1858. *Banbury cakes* are criss-cross pastry cases with a mince-pie-style filling.

Banca alternative form of the Indonesian island ◊Banka.

Bancroft /ˈbænkrɒft/ George 1800–1891. US diplomat and historian. A Democrat, he was secretary of the navy 1845, when he established the US Naval Academy at Annapolis, Maryland, and as acting secretary of war (May 1846) was instrumental in bringing about the occupation of California and war with Mexico. He wrote a *History of the United States* 1834–76.

band music group, usually falling into a special category: for example, *military* comprising woodwind, brass, and percussion; *brass* solely of brass and percussion; *marching* a variant of brass; *dance*, often like a small orchestra; *jazz* and *rock and pop* generally electric guitar, bass, and drums variously augmented; and *steel* from the West Indies, in which percussion instruments made from oildrums sound like marimbas.

Banda /ˈbændə/ Hastings Kamuzu c.1902– . Malawi politican, president from 1966. He led his country's independence movement, was prime minister of Nyasaland from 1963, and became the first president of the one-party republic.

Banda studied in the US and was a medical practitioner in Britain until 1953. His rule has been authoritarian, and in 1971 he made himself life president.

Bandar Abbas /ˈbændər ˈæbəs/ port and winter resort in Iran on the Ormuz strait, Persian Gulf; population (1983) 175,000. Formerly called Gombroon, it was renamed and made prosperous by Shah Abbas I (1571–1629). It is an important naval base.

Bandaranaike /ˌbændərəˈnaɪkə/ Sirimavo (born Ratwatte) 1916– . Sri Lankan politician, who succeeded her husband Solomon Bandaranaike to become the world's first woman prime minister 1960–65 and 1970–77, but was expelled from parliament 1980 for abuse of her powers while in office. She was largely responsible for the new constitution 1972.

Bandaranaike /ˌbændərəˈnaɪkə/ Solomon West Ridgeway Dias 1899–1959. Sri Lankan nationalist politician. In 1951 he founded the Sri Lanka Freedom Party and in 1956 became prime minister, pledged to a socialist programme and a neutral foreign policy. He failed to satisfy extremists and was assassinated by a Buddhist monk.

Bandar Seri Begawan /ˈbændə ˈseri bəˈgɑːwən/ (formerly *Brunei Town*) capital of Brunei; population (1983) 57,558.

Bandar Shah /ˈbændə ˈʃɑː/ port in Iran on the Caspian Sea, and northern terminus of the Trans-Iranian railway.

bandicoot small marsupial mammal inhabiting Australia and New Guinea. There are about 11 species, family Peramelidae, rat- or rabbit-sized and living in burrows. They have long snouts, eat insects, and are nocturnal. A related group, the rabbit bandicoots or bilbys, is reduced to a single

Banda *Hastings Banda, first president of Malawi.*

Bandaranaike *Sirimavo Bandaranaike became in 1960 the world's first woman prime minister.*

bandicoot

rabbit bandicoot

species that is now endangered and protected by law.

banding in UK education, the division of school pupils into broad streams by ability. Banding is used by some local authorities to ensure that comprehensive schools receive an intake of children spread right across the ability range. It is used internally by some schools as a means of avoiding groups of widely mixed ability.

Band, the North American rock group 1961–76. They acquired their name when working as Bob Dylan's backing band, and made their solo debut 1968 with *Music from Big Pink*. Their unostentatious ensemble playing and strong original material set a new trend.

Formed in Canada as a backing group for the US rock-and-roll singer Ronnie Hawkins (1935–) and initially known as the Hawks, they took up with Dylan in 1965, touring and recording with him intermittently over the next ten years. *The Band* 1969, *Stage Fright* 1970, and *Northern Lights – Southern Cross* 1975 were all outstanding albums. In their appearance and mysterious lyrics they often evoked a bygone age, as in the song 'The Night They Drove Old Dixie Down'. Their farewell concert was filmed by Martin Scorsese as *The Last Waltz* 1978.

Bandung /'bændʊŋ/ commercial city and capital of Jawa Barat province on the island of Java, Indonesia; population (1980) 1,463,000. Bandung is the third largest city in Indonesia and was the

Bangkok *The Royal Palace, Bangkok, contains within its 1900 m perimeter walls fine temples, including the Chapel Royal of the Emerald Buddha.*

Bangladesh
People's Republic of

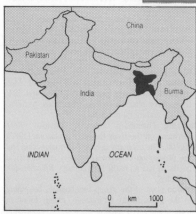

area 144,000 sq km/55,585 sq mi
capital Dhaka (formerly Dacca)
towns ports Chittagong, Khulna
physical flat delta of rivers Ganges and Brahmaputra; annual rainfall of 2,540 mm/100 in; some 75% of the land is less than 3 m/10 ft above sea level and vulnerable to flooding and cyclones
head of state Hussain Mohammad Ershad (president) from 1989
head of government Kazi Zafar Ahmad (prime minister) from 1989
political system restricted democratic republic
political parties Jatiya Dal (National Party), Islamic nationalist; Awami League, secular, moderate socialist; Bangladesh National Party,

Islamic right-of-centre
exports jute (50% of world production), tea
currency taka (54.00 = £1 Feb 1990)
population (1987) 104,100,000; annual growth rate 2.7%
life expectancy men 48, women 47
language Bangla (Bengali)
religion Sunni Muslim 85%, Hindu 14%
literacy 43% male/22% female (1985 est)
GDP $11.2 bn (1983); $119 per head of population
chronology
1947 Formed into E province of Pakistan on partition of British India.
1970 Half a million killed in flood.
1971 Independent Bangladesh emerged under leadership of Sheikh Mujibur Rahman after civil war.
1975 Mujibur Rahman assassinated. Martial law imposed.
1976–77 Maj-Gen Zia ur-Rahman assumed power.
1978–79 Elections held and civilian rule restored.
1981 Assassination of Maj-Gen Zia.
1982 Lt-Gen Ershad assumed power in army coup. Martial law imposed.
1986 Elections held but disputed. Martial law ended.
1987 State of emergency declared in response to opposition demonstrations.
1988 Assembly elections boycotted by main opposition parties. State of emergency lifted. Islam made state religion. Monsoon floods and a cyclone left 35 million homeless and thousands dead.
1989 Power devolved to Chittagong Hill Tracts to end 14-year tribal insurgency.

administrative centre when the country was the Netherlands East Indies.

Bandung Conference the first conference 1955 of the Afro-Asian nations, proclaiming anti-colonialism and neutrality between East and West.

bandy-bandy venomous Australian snake *Vermicella annulata* of the cobra family, which grows to about 75 cm/2.5 ft. It is banded in black and white. It is not aggressive toward humans.

Banff /bænf/ town and resort in Alberta, Canada; 100 km/62 mi NW of Calgary; population (1984) 4,246. It is a centre for Banff National Park (Canada's first, founded 1885) in the Rocky Mountains. Industries include brewing and ironfounding.

Banffshire /'bænfʃə/ former county of NE Scotland, now in Grampian region.

Bangalore /ˌbæŋgəˈlɔː/ capital of Karnataka state, S India; population (1981) 2,914,000. Industries include electronics, aircraft and machine tools construction, and coffee.

Bangkok /ˌbæŋˈkɒk/ capital and port of Thailand, on the river Chao Phraya; population (1987) 5,609,000. Products include paper, ceramics, cement, textiles, and aircraft. It is the headquarters of the South-East Asia Treaty Organization.

Bangkok was established as the capital by Phra Chao Tak 1769, after the Burmese had burned down the former capital Avuthia about 65 km/40 mi to the north. Features include the temple of the Emerald Buddha and the vast palace complex.

Bangladesh /ˌbæŋgləˈdɛʃ/ country in S Asia, surrounded on three sides by India, and bounded to the S by the bay of Bengal.

government Bangladesh's political system is in a transitional state. The 1972 constitution was suspended 1982 after a military coup by Lieutenant-General Ershad, who governed first

as chief martial law administrator and then, from 1983, as president with an appointed council of ministers. A move back to civilian rule began 1983–85 with local elections, and in 1986 the constitution was revived, with martial law lifted Nov.

At the head of the present system is an executive president, popularly elected for five-year terms by universal suffrage, who serves as head of state, head of the armed forces, and head of government, appointing cabinet ministers and judicial officers. There is also a single-chamber legislative parliament *Jatiya Sangsad*, composed of 300 members directly elected for five-year terms from single-member constituencies and 30 women elected by the legislature itself.

history For history before 1947 see ◊India; for history 1947–1971 see ◊Pakistan. Contemporary Bangladesh formerly comprised E Bengal province and Sylhet district of Assam in British India. Predominantly Muslim, it was formed into the E province of Pakistan when India was partitioned 1947. Substantially different in culture, language, and geography from the W provinces of Pakistan 1,000 miles away and, with a larger population, it resented the political and military dominance exerted by W Pakistan during the 1950s and 1960s. A movement for political autonomy grew after 1954 under the Awami League headed by Sheikh ◊Mujibur Rahman. This gained strength as a result of W Pakistan's indifference 1970 when cyclones killed 500,000 in floods in E Pakistan.

In Pakistan's first general elections 1970 the Awami League gained an overwhelming victory in E Pakistan and an overall majority in the all-Pakistan National Assembly. Talks on redrawing the constitution broke down, leading to E Pakistan's secession and the establishment of a Bangladesh ('Bengal Nation') government in exile in Calcutta (India) 1971. Civil war resulted in the flight of 10,000,000 E Pakistani refugees to India, administrative breakdown, famine, and cholera. The W Pakistani forces in E Pakistan surrendered 1971 after India intervened on the secessionists' side. A republic of Bangladesh was proclaimed and rapidly gained international recognition 1972.

Sheikh Mujibur Rahman became prime minister 1972 under a secular, parliamentary constitution. He introduced a socialist economic programme of nationalisation, but became intolerant of opposition, establishing a one-party presidential system Jan 1975. In Aug 1975 Sheikh Mujibur Rahman, his wife, and close relatives were assassinated in a military coup. The Awami League held power for three months under Khandakar Mushtaq Ahmed before a further military coup Nov 1975 established as president and chief martial law administrator the non-political chief justice Abu Sadat Mohammed Sayem.

In 1976, Maj Gen Zia ur-Rahman (1936–81) became chief martial law administrator. Becoming president 1977, he adopted an Islamic constitution, approved by a national referendum in May. In June he won a 4:1 majority in a direct presidential election. Maj Gen Zia's newly formed Bangladeshi Nationalist Party won a parliamentary majority. A civilian government was installed, and martial law and the state of emergency were lifted 1979. The administration was undermined, however, by charges of corruption and by a guerrilla movement in Chittagong 1980. On 30 May 1981 Maj Gen Zia was assassinated in an attempted coup, and interim power was assumed by Vice-President Justice Abdus Sattar.

With disorder increasing, the civilian administration was overthrown Mar 1982 by a coup led by Lt Gen Mohammad Hussain Ershad (1930–). Martial law was re-imposed and political activity banned. The economy improved and in 1983 a broad opposition coalition, the Movement for the Restoration of Democracy, was formed. Lt Gen Ershad promised presidential and parliamentary elections 1984, but both were cancelled after an opposition threat of a boycott and campaign of civil disobedience if martial law was not first lifted.

In Jan 1986 the ban on political activity was removed and parliamentary elections were held in May. The Awami League agreed to participate in these elections, but the Bangladesh National Party and many other opposition parties boycotted them. With a campaign marked by violence, widespread abstentions, claims of ballot-rigging, and the re-running of 37 constituency contests, Lt Gen Ershad and his Jatiya Front party gained the two-thirds majority required to pass a law granting retrospective immunity. In Oct 1986 Ershad was re-elected president in a direct election and in Nov 1986 martial law was lifted.

During 1987 the Awami League, led by Sheika Hasina Wazed (the daughter of Sheikh Mujib ur-Rahman), and the Bangladesh National Party, led by Begum Khalida Zia (the widow of Major-General Zia ur-Rahman), stepped up their campaign against the Ershad government, demanding the president's resignation and free elections. In the wake of a wave of violent strikes and demonstrations, Ershad proclaimed a state of emergency in Nov 1987, with urban curfews imposed, the two opposition leaders placed under house arrest, and antigovernment protests banned. A month later, parliament was dissolved and fresh elections called in Mar 1988. As a result of a combination of ballot-rigging and an opposition boycott, the ruling *Jatiya Dal* gained a sweeping victory. The state of emergency was lifted Apr 1988, and a bill passed by parliament June 1988 making Islam the state religion.

In Sept 1988 Bangladesh received the heaviest monsoon rains in 70 years; in the resulting floods several thousand people died and 30 million became homeless. In Mar 1989 the *Jatiya Sangsad* approved legislation devolving power to directly elected, substantially autonomous councils in three Chittagong Hill Tract districts in SE Bangladesh, which had been devastated

by a 14-year tribal insurgency led by the *Shanti Bahini* (Peace Force) organization. In June 1989, constitutional amendments were also passed restricting the President to two elected five-year terms and creating the post of elected vice-president.

In foreign affairs, Bangladesh has remained a member of the Commonwealth since 1972. It has been heavily dependent on foreign economic aid, but has pursued a broader policy of the ◊non-aligned movement. Relations with India have deteriorated since 1975 as a result of disputes over the sharing of Ganges water and the annual influx of 200,000 Bangladeshi refugees to Assam and W Bengal, which has prompted India to threaten to construct a frontier fence.

Bangor /ˈbæŋgə/ cathedral city in Gwynedd, N Wales; population (1981) 46,585. University College, of the University of Wales, is here. The cathedral was begun 1495. Industry includes chemicals and electrical goods.

Bangui /bɒŋˈgiː/ capital and port of the Central African Republic on the River Ubangi; population (1988) 597,000. Industries include beer, cigarettes, office machinery, and timber and metal products.

Banjermasin /ˌbɑːnjəˈmɑːsɪn/ river port in Indonesia, on Borneo; population (1980) 381,300. It is the capital of Kalimantan Selatan province. It exports rubber, timber and precious stones. The university was founded 1960.

banjo resonant stringed musical instrument, with a long fretted neck and circular drum-type sound box covered on the topside only by stretched skin (now usually plastic). It is played with a plectrum.

The banjo originated in the American South among black slaves (based on a similar instrument of African origin).

It was introduced to Britain in 1846.

Banjul /bænˈdʒuːl/ capital and chief port of Gambia, on an island at the mouth of the river Gambia; population (1983) 44,536. Known as Bathurst until 1973. It was established as a settlement for freed slaves in 1816.

bank a financial institution which uses funds deposited with it to lend money to companies or individuals, and which also provides financial services to its customers. A *central bank* (in the UK, the Bank of England) issues currency for the government, in order to provide cash for circulation and exchange. In terms of assets, seven of the world's top 10 banks were Japanese in 1988.

Banka /ˈbæŋkə/ or *Bang Ka* island in Indonesia off the E coast of Sumatra
area 12,000 sq km/4,600 sq mi
capital Pangkalpinang
towns port Mintok
products Banka is one of the world's largest producers of tin
population (1970) 300,000.

Bank for International Settlements (BIS) a bank established 1930 to handle German reparations settlements from World War I. The BIS (based in Basel, Switzerland) is today an important centre for economic and monetary research and assists cooperation of central banks. Its financial activities are essentially short term.

Bankhead /ˈbæŋkhed/ Tallulah 1903–1968. US actress, noted for her wit and flamboyant lifestyle. Her stage appearances include *Dark Victory* 1934, *The Little Foxes* 1939, and *The Skin of Our Teeth* 1942. Her films include Hitchcock's *Life-boat* 1943.

bank holiday in the UK, a public holiday, when banks are closed by law.

Bank holidays were instituted by the Bank Holiday Acts 1871 and 1875.

Bank of England UK central bank founded by Act of Parliament in 1694. It was entrusted with note-issue in 1844, and nationalized in 1946. It is banker to the UK government and assists in implementing financial and monetary policies

through intervention in financial and foreign exchange markets.

bank rate interest rate fixed by the Bank of England as a guide to mortgage, hire purchase rates, and so on, which was replaced in 1972 by the *minimum lending rate* (lowest rate at which the Bank acts as lender of last resort to the money market), which from 1978 was again a 'bank rate' set by the Bank.

bankruptcy the process by which the property of a person unable to pay debts is taken away under a court order and divided fairly among his or her creditors, after preferential payments such as taxes and wages. Proceedings may be instituted either by the debtor (voluntary bankruptcy), or by any creditor for a substantial sum (involuntary bankruptcy). Until 'discharged', a bankrupt is severely restricted in financial activities. When 'discharged' he or she becomes free of most debts dating from the time of bankruptcy.

Banks /bæŋks/ Joseph 1744–1820. British naturalist and explorer. He accompanied Capt ◊Cook on his voyage round the world 1768–71 and brought back 3,600 plants, 1,400 of them never before classified. A founder of the Botanical Gardens, Kew, he was President of the Royal Society from 1778–1819. The banksia genus of shrubs is named after him.

banksia genus of shrubs and trees, family Proteaceae, which are native to Australia and include the honeysuckle tree; they are named after Joseph Banks.

Bannister /ˈbænɪstə/ Roger Gilbert 1929– . English athlete, the first person to run the mile in under four minutes. He achieved this feat at Oxford, England, on 6 May 1954 in a time of 3 min 59.4 sec.

Studying at Oxford to be a doctor at the time, Bannister broke the four-minute barrier on one more occasion: at the 1954 Commonwealth Games in Vancouver, Canada, when he was involved in the 'Mile of the Century' with John Landy (Australia).

Bannockburn a town and battlefield to the S of Stirling, central Scotland. The scene of victory by King Robert the Bruce who defeated the English under Edward II in 1314.

Bannockburn, Battle of /ˈbænəkbɜːn/ battle in central Scotland, near Stirling, on 24 June 1314, when ◊Robert I (also known as Robert the Bruce) defeated the English under ◊Edward II.

bantam small variety of domestic chicken. This can either be a small version of one of the large breeds, or a separate type. Some are prolific layers, and bantam cocks have a reputation as spirited fighters.

banteng wild species of cattle *Bos banteng*, now scarce, but formerly ranging from Burma through SE Asia to Malaysia and Java, inhabiting hilly forests. Its colour varies from pale brown to blue-black, usually with white stockings and rump patch, and it is up to 1.5 m/5 ft at the shoulder.

Bannister British athlete Roger Bannister.

Banting /'bæntɪŋ/ Frederick Grant 1891–1941. Canadian physician who discovered the hormone insulin in 1921 when, experimentally, he tied off the ducts of the ◊pancreas in order to determine the function of the islets of Langerhans. He was helped by Charles ◊Best and John J R Macleod, with whom he shared the 1923 Nobel Prize for Medicine.

Bantock /'bæntək/ Granville 1868–1946. English composer and conductor; professor of music at the University of Birmingham 1908–34. His works include the oratorio *Omar Khayyám* 1906–09, *Hebridean Symphony* 1915, and *Pagan Symphony* 1928.

Bantu languages a group of related languages spoken widely over the greater part of Africa S of the Sahara, including Swahili, Xhosa, and Zulu. Meaning 'people' in Zulu, the word Bantu itself illustrates a characteristic use of prefixes: *mu-ntu* 'man', *ba-ntu* 'people'.

The Bantu-speaking peoples probably originated in N Central Africa. Until 1978, the black people of the Republic of South Africa were officially designated *Bantu(s)*.

Bantustan (or Bantu homelands) name until 1978 for the ◊Black National States in the Republic of South Africa.

banyan tropical tree *Ficus benghalensis* of the family Moraceae. It produces aerial roots which grow down from its spreading branches, forming supporting pillars which have the appearance of separate trunks.

baobab tree *Adansonia digitata*, family Bombacaceae. It has rootlike branches, hence its nickname 'upside-down tree', and edible fruit known as monkey bread.

It may live for 1,000 years and is found in Africa and Australia, a relic of the time when both were part of ◊Gondwanaland.

baptism (Greek 'to dip') immersion in or sprinkling with water as a religious rite of initiation. It was practised long before the beginning of Christianity. In the Christian baptism ceremony, sponsors or godparents make vows on behalf of the child which are renewed by the child at confirmation. It is one of the seven sacraments. The *amrit* ceremony in Sikhism is sometimes referred to as baptism.

Baptism was universal in the Christian church from the first days, being administered to adults by immersion. The baptism of infants was not practised until the 2nd century, but became general in the 6th. Baptism by sprinkling (christening) when the child is named is now general among Western Christians except for some sects, notably the ◊Baptists, where complete immersion of adults is the rule. The Eastern Orthodox Church also practises immersion.

Baptist member of any of several Protestant and evangelical Christian sects practising baptism by immersion of believers only on profession of faith. Baptists seek their authority in the Bible. Baptism originated among English Dissenters who took refuge in the Netherlands in the early 17th century, and spread by emigration and, later, missionary activity. Of the world total of approximately 31 million, some 26.5 million are in the USA and 265,000 in the UK.

The first Baptist church in America was organized in Rhode Island 1639. The Baptist Missionary Society, formed 1792, pioneered the 19th-century missionary movement which spread Baptism in Europe and to British colonies. In 1905 the Baptist World Alliance was formed.

bar c.g.s. unit of pressure (symbol bar) equal to 10 pascals or 10 dynes/cm, approximately 750 mmHg or 0.987 atm. Its diminutive, the *millibar* (one thousandth of a bar) is commonly used by meteorologists.

Barabbas /bə'ræbəs/ in the New Testament, a condemned robber released by Pilate at Passover instead of Jesus to appease a mob.

barb general name for fish of the genus *Barbus* and some related genera of the family Cyprinidae.

Barbados

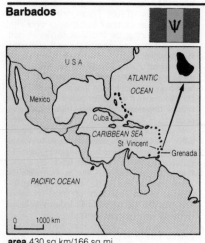

area 430 sq km/166 sq mi
capital Bridgetown
physical most easterly island of the West Indies; surrounded by coral reefs
features subject to hurricanes
head of state Elizabeth II from 1966 represented by Hugh Springer from 1984
head of government Erskine Lloyd Sandiford from 1987
political system constitutional monarchy
political parties Barbados Labour Party (BLP), moderate left-of-centre; Democratic Labour Party (DLP), moderate left-of-centre
exports sugar, rum, oil
currency Barbados dollar (3.42 = £1 Feb 1990)
population (1985) 253,000; annual growth rate 0.3%
life expectancy men 70, women 75
language English
religion Christian
literacy 99% (1984)
GDP $1 bn (1984); $3,040 per head of population
chronology
1951 Universal adult suffrage introduced. BLP won general election.
1954 Ministerial government established.
1961 Full internal self-government. DLP, led by Errol Barrow, in power.
1966 Barbados achieved full independence within the Commonwealth. Barrow became the new nation's first prime minister.
1972 Diplomatic relations with Cuba established.
1976 BLP, led by Tom Adams, returned to power.
1983 Barbados supported US invasion of Grenada.
1985 Adams died suddenly. Bernard St John became prime minister.
1986 DLP, led by Barrow, returned to power.
1987 Barrow died, succeeded by Erskine Lloyd Sandiford.

As well as the ◊barbel, barbs include many small tropical Old World species, some of which are familiar aquarium species. They are active egglaying species, usually of 'typical' fish shape and with barbels at the corner of the mouth.

Barbados /bɑː'beɪdɒs/ island in the Caribbean, one of the Lesser Antilles.

government The constitution dates from 1966 and provides for a system of parliamentary government on the British model, with a prime minister and cabinet drawn from and responsible to the legislature, consisting of a senate and a house of assembly. The senate has 21 members appointed by the governor-general, 12 on the advice of the prime minister, two on the advice of the leader of the opposition, and the rest on the basis of wider consultations. The house of assembly has 27 members elected by universal suffrage. The legislature has a maximum life of five years and may be dissolved within this period. The governor-general appoints both the prime minister (on the basis of support in the house of assembly) and the leader of the opposition. The two main political parties are the Barbados Labour Party (BLP) and the Democratic Labour Party (DLP).

history Originally inhabited by Arawak indians, who were wiped out soon after the arrival of the first Europeans, Barbados became a British colony in 1627 and remained so until independence in 1966. Universal adult suffrage was introduced in 1951 and the BLP won the first general election. Ministerial government was established in 1954 and the BLP leader, Grantley Adams, became the first prime minister. In 1955 a group broke away from the BLP and formed the DLP. Six years later full internal self-government was achieved and in the 1961 general election the DLP was victorious under its leader Errol Barrow.

When Barbados attained full independence in 1966, Barrow became its first prime minister. The DLP was re-elected in 1971 but in the 1976 general election the BLP, led now by Grantley Adams' son 'Tom', ended Barrow's 15-year rule. Both parties were committed to maintaining free enterprise and alignment with the USA although the DLP government established diplomatic relations with Cuba in 1972 and the BLP administration supported the US invasion of ◊Grenada in 1983.

In 1981 the BLP was re-elected. After Adams' sudden death in 1985 he was succeeded by his deputy Bernard St John, a former BLP leader. In the 1986 general election the DLP, led by Barrow, were returned to power with 24 of the 27 seats in the House of Assembly. Errol Barrow died in 1987, and was succeeded by Erskine Lloyd Sandiford.

Barbarossa /ˌbɑːbəˈrɒsə/ Nickname 'red beard' given to the Holy Roman emperor ◊Frederick I, and also to two brothers who were Barbary pirates. *Horuk* was killed by the Spaniards 1518; *Khair-ed-Din* took Tunis 1534 and died in Constantinople 1546.

Barbarossa, operation German code name for the plans to invade the USSR during World War II in 1941.

Barbary ape tailless yellowish-brown macaque monkey *Macaca sylvanus*, found in the mountains and wilds of Algeria and Morocco. It was introduced to Gibraltar, where legend has it that the British will leave if the colony dies out.

Barbary Coast the North African coast of the Mediterranean Sea, from which pirates operated against European shipping (taking Europeans hostage for ransom) in the 16th–19th centuries. Some of the apparently Muslim pirates were in fact European, such as the English Capt John Ward (died 1622). A famous hostage was Miguel ◊Cervantes, author of *Don Quixote*.

barbastelle insect-eating bat *Barbastella barbastellus* with 'frosted' black fur and a wingspan of about 25 cm/10 in, occasionally found in the UK but more common in Europe.

barbed wire a cheap fencing material made of strands of galvanized wire (see ◊galvanizing), with sharp barbs wound upon them at intervals. In 1873 Joseph Glidden in the USA devised a machine to mass produce barbed wire. Its use on the prairies led to range warfare between farmers and cattle ranchers, used to driving their herds cross country.

barbel freshwater fish *Barbus barbus* found in fast-flowing rivers with sand or gravel bottoms in Britain and Europe. Long-bodied, and up to 1 m/3 ft long, the barbel has four *barbels* ('little beards'—sensory fleshy filaments) near the mouth.

Barbie Klaus Barbie was the Nazi SS commander in Lyon, France, during World War II.

Barbellion /baːˈbeliən/ W N P, pseudonym of Bruce Frederick Cummings 1889–1919. English diarist, author of *The Journal of a Disappointed Man* 1919, an account of his struggle with the illness multiple sclerosis.

Barber /ˈbaːbə/ Samuel 1910–1981. US composer of works in a restrained neo-classical style, including *Adagio for Strings* 1936 and the opera *Vanessa* 1958.

barber shop in music, a style of unaccompanied close-harmony singing of sentimental ballads, revived in the US during the 19th century. Traditionally sung by four male voices, since the 1970s it has developed as a style of ◊a cappella choral singing for both male and female voices.

Barbershop originated in 17th-century European barber's shops, which offered dental and medical services. Waiting customers were provided with a cittern or guitar by managements aware of the benefits of music to those undergoing pain.

barbet small, tropical bird, often brightly coloured. There are some 78 species of barbet in the family Capitonidae, about half living in Africa. Barbets eat insects and fruits and, being distant relations of woodpeckers, drill nest holes with their beaks. The name comes from the 'little beard' of bristles at the base of the beak.

Barbican, the /ˈbaːbɪkən/ arts and residential complex in the City of London. The Barbican Arts Centre 1982 contains theatres, cinemas, exhibition and concert halls.

Barbie /ˈbaːbi/ Klaus 1913– . German Nazi, a member of the ◊SS from 1936. During World War II he was involved in the deportation of Jews from the occupied Netherlands 1940–42 and in tracking down Jews and Resistance workers in France 1942–45. He was arrested 1983 and convicted of crimes against humanity in France 1987.

His work as SS commander, based in Lyon, included the rounding-up of Jewish children from an orphanage at Izieu and the torture of the Resistance leader Jean Moulin. During this time, his ruthlessness earned him the epithet 'Butcher of Lyon'. Having escaped capture in 1945, Barbie was employed by the US intelligence services in Germany before moving to Bolivia in 1951. Expelled from there in 1983, he was returned to France where he was tried by a court in Lyon.

Barbirolli /ˌbaːbɪˈrɒli/ John 1899–1970. English conductor. He made a name as a cellist, and in 1937 succeeded Toscanini as conductor of the New York Philharmonic Orchestra. He returned to England in 1943, where he remained conductor of the Hallé Orchestra, Manchester until his death.

barbiturate a hypnosedative drug, commonly called 'sleeping pills'. Tolerance develops quickly in the user so that increasingly large doses are required to induce sleep. Its action persists for hours or days, causing confused, aggressive behaviour or disorientation. Highly addictive, most barbiturates are no longer prescribed, and are listed as controlled substances in the UK. Short-acting barbiturates are sometimes used to induce general anaesthesia.

Barbizon school /ˌbaːbɪˈzɒn/ French school of landscape painters of the mid-19th century, based at Barbizon in the forest of Fontainebleau. Members included J F Millet, Diaz de la Peña (1807–76), and Théodore Rousseau (1812–67). They aimed to paint fresh, realistic scenes, sketching and painting their subjects in the open air.

Barbour /ˈbaːbə/ John c. 1316–1395. Scottish poet whose chronicle-poem *The Brus* is among the earliest Scottish poetry.

Barbuda /baːˈbjuːdə/ one of the islands which form the state of ◊Antigua and Barbuda.

Barcelona /ˌbaːsəˈləʊnə/ capital, industrial city (textiles, engineering, chemicals), and port of Catalonia, NE Spain; population (1986) 1,694,000. As the chief centre of anarchism and Catalonian nationalism it was prominent in the overthrow of the monarchy 1931, and was the last city of the republic to surrender to Franco 1939.

history It was founded in the 3rd century BC and its importance grew until in the 14th century it had become one of the leading trading cities of the Mediterranean.

features The Ramblas, tree-lined promenades leading from the Plaza de Cataluña, the largest square in Spain; ◊Gaudí's unfinished church of the Holy Family 1883; a replica of Columbus's ship, the *Santa Maria*, in the Maritime Museum; a large collection of art by Picasso.

bar chart in statistics, a way of displaying data. The heights or lengths of the bars are proportional to the frequencies of the data they represent.

bar code a pattern of bars and spaces which can be read by a computer. They are widely used in retailing, industrial distribution, and public libraries. The code is read by a ◊scanning device, and the computer determines the code from the widths of the bars and spaces.

Bardeen /baːˈdiːn/ John 1908– . US physicist, who won a Nobel prize 1956, with Walter Brattain and William Shockley, for the development of the transistor in 1948. In 1972, he was the first double winner of a Nobel prize in the same subject (with Leon Cooper and John Schrieffer) for his work on superconductivity.

Bardot /baːˈdəʊ/ Brigitte 1934– . French film actress, whose sensual appeal did much to popularize French cinema internationally. Her films include *Et Dieu créa la Femme/And God Created Woman* 1950 and *Shalako* 1968.

Bardo Thodol also known as the *Book of the Dead* a Tibetan Buddhist text giving instructions to the

bar code

odd parity / even parity

left guard pattern / centre guard pattern / right guard pattern

0 1 2 3 4 5   6 7 8 9 0 5

number system digit / manufacturer's code / product code / check digit

newly dead about the Bardo, or state between death and rebirth.

Bardsey Island /ˈbaːdsi/ former pilgrimage centre in Gwynedd, Wales, with a 6th-century ruined abbey.

Barebones Parliament the English assembly called by Oliver ◊Cromwell to replace the 'Rump Parliament' July 1653. It consisted of 140 members nominated by the army and derived its name from one of its members, Praise-God Barbon. Although they attempted to pass sensible legislation (civil marriage; registration of births, deaths, and marriages; custody of lunatics), their attempts to abolish tithes, patronage, and the court of chancery, and to codify the law led to the resignation of the moderates and its dissolution Dec 1653.

Bareilly /bəˈreɪli/ industrial city in Uttar Pradesh, India; population (1981) 438,000. It was a Mughal capital 1657, and at the centre of the Indian Mutiny 1857.

Barenboim /ˈbærənbɔɪm/ Daniel 1942– . Israeli pianist and conductor, born in Argentina. Pianist/conductor with the English Chamber Orchestra from 1964, he became conductor of the New York Philharmonic Orchestra 1970 and musical director of the Orchestre de Paris 1975. Appointed artistic director of the Opéra Bastille, Paris, July 1987, he was fired from his post a few months before its opening in July 1989. He is a celebrated interpreter of Mozart and Beethoven.

Barents /ˈbærənts/ Willem c. 1550–1597. Dutch explorer and navigator. He made three expeditions to seek the ◊Northeast Passage; he died on the last voyage. The Barents Sea, part of the Arctic Ocean N of Norway, is named after him.

Barents Sea /ˈbærənts/ section of the E ◊Arctic Ocean. It has oil and gas reserves.

Barham /ˈbaːrəm/ Richard Harris 1788–1845. British writer and clergyman, author of verse tales of the supernatural, and *The Ingoldsby Legends*, published under his pen name Thomas Ingoldsby.

Bari /ˈbaːri/ capital of Puglia region, S Italy, and industrial port on the Adriatic; population (1988) 359,000. It is the site of Italy's first nuclear power station; the part of the town known as Tecnopolis is the Italian equivalent of ◊Silicon Valley.

Barikot /ˌbaːrɪˈɒt/ a garrison town in Konar province, E Afghanistan, near the Pakistan frontier. Besieged by mujaheddin rebels in 1985, the relief of Barikot by Soviet and Afghan troops was one of the largest military engagements of the Afghan war during Soviet occupation.

Baring-Gould /ˈbeərɪŋ ˈguːld/ Sabine 1834–1924. British writer, rector of Lew Trenchard in N Devon from 1881. He was a prolific writer of novels, books of travel, mythology and folklore, and wrote the words of 'Onward, Christian Soldiers'.

Barisal /ˌbɑrɪˈsaːl/ river port and capital city of Barisal region, S Bangladesh; population (1981) 142,000. It trades in jute, rice, fish, and oilseed.

baritone lower-range male voice between bass and tenor.

barium a metallic chemical element, symbol Ba, atomic number 56, relative atomic mass 137.36. It is silver-white in colour, oxidizes very easily, and is a little harder than lead. Barium is used in medicine, in the form of barium sulphate, which is taken in solution (a 'barium meal') and its progress followed using X-rays, to reveal abnormalities of the digestive tract.

The name comes from the Greek word for 'heavy', since barium was first discovered in barytes or heavy spar. Barium, with strontium, forms the emissive surface in cathode-ray tubes.

bark the protective outer layer on the stems and roots of woody plants, composed mainly of dead cells. To allow for expansion of the stem, the bark is continually added to from within, and the outer surface often becomes fissured or is shed as scales. The bark from the cork oak (*Quercus ruber*) is economically important and harvested commercially. The spice ◊cinnamon and the drugs cascara (used as a

barley

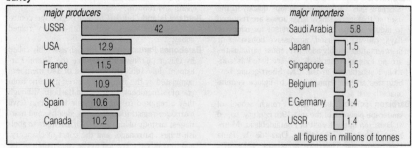

major producers		major importers	
USSR	42	Saudi Arabia	5.8
USA	12.9	Japan	1.5
France	11.5	Singapore	1.5
UK	10.9	Belgium	1.5
Spain	10.6	E Germany	1.4
Canada	10.2	USSR	1.4

all figures in millions of tonnes

laxative and stimulant) and ◊quinine all come from bark.

Bark technically includes all the tissues external to the vascular ◊cambium (the ◊phloem, cortex, and periderm), and its thickness may vary from a few millimetres to 30 cm/12 in or more, as in the giant redwood (*Sequoia*) where it forms a thick, spongy layer.

Barker /'bɑːkə/ Clive 1952– . British horror writer, whose *Books of Blood* 1984–85 are in the sensationalist tradition of horror fiction.

Barker /'bɑːkə/ George 1913– . British poet noted for his vivid imagery, as in *Calamiterror* 1937, *The True Confessions of George Barker* 1950, and *Collected Poems* 1930–50.

Barker /'bɑːkə/ Herbert 1869–1950. British manipulative surgeon, whose work established the popular standing of ◊orthopaedics, but who was never recognized by the world of orthodox medicine.

Barking and Dagenham /'bɑːkɪŋ, 'dægənəm/ borough of E Greater London

products Ford motor industry at Dagenham
population (1981) 152,600.

Barkly Tableland /'bɑːkli/ large-scale open-range cattle-raising area in Northern Territory and Queensland, Australia.

bark painting paintings on the inner side of strips of tree bark, produced by Australian Aborigines of Arnhem Land and elsewhere. In red, yellow, white, brown, and black pigments, they were often painted with the fingers as the artist lay inside a low bark-roofed shelter.

Barlach /'bɑːlæx/ Ernst 1870–1938. German Expressionist sculptor, painter, and poet. His simple, evocative figures carved in wood (for example in St Catherine's, Lübeck, 1930–32) often express melancholy.

Barletta /bɑː'letə/ industrial port on the Adriatic, Italy; population (1981) 83,800. It produces chemicals and soap; as an agriculture centre it trades in wine and fruit. There is a Romanesque cathedral, and castle.

barley cereal belonging to the family Gramineae. The cultivated barley *Hordeum vulgare* comprises three varieties—six-rowed barley, four-rowed barley or Scotch Bigg, and two-rowed barley.

barley

grain

cross
section of
a grain

Barley was one of the earliest cereals to be cultivated, and no other cereal can thrive in so wide a range of climate. Polar barley is sown and reaped well within the Arctic circle in Europe. Barley is no longer much used in bread-making, but its high protein form finds a wide use for animal feeding. Its main importance, however, is in brewing and distilling, for which low protein varieties are used.

bar mitzvah (Hebrew 'son of the commandment') in Judaism, initiation of a boy, which takes place at the age of 13, into the adult Jewish community; less common is the *bat* or *bas mitzvah* for girls at age 12. The boy reads a passage from the Torah in the synagogue on the Sabbath, and is subsequently regarded as a full member of the congregation.

barn a farm building traditionally used for the storage and processing of corn or hay. On older farmsteads, the barn is usually the largest building. It is often characterized by ventilation openings rather than windows, and has at least one set of big double doors for access. Before mechanization, corn was threshed by hand on a specially prepared floor inside these doors.

Tithe barns in England were used to store the produce paid as a tax to the parish priest by the local occupiers of the land. In the Middle Ages, monasteries often controlled the collection of tithes over a wide area, and as a result constructed some enormous tithe barns. The best surviving example is the monastic barn at Great Coxwell in Oxfordshire which was built in the middle of the 13th century and measures 46.3 m/152 ft long by 13.4 m/44 ft wide by 14.6 m/48 ft high.

Barnabas, St /'bɑːnəbəs/ in the New Testament, a 'fellow labourer' with St Paul; he went with St Mark on a missionary journey to Cyprus, his birthplace. Feast day 11 June.

barnacle marine crustacean of the subclass Cirripedia. The larval form is free-swimming, but when mature, it fixes itself by the head to rock or floating wood. The animal then remains attached, enclosed in a shell through which the cirri (modified legs) protrude to sweep food into the mouth.

Barnacles include the stalked *goose barnacle Lepas anatifera* found on ships' bottoms and the *acorn barnacles*, such as *Balanus balanoides*, common on rocks.

Barnard /'bɑːnɑːd/ Christiaan Neethling 1922– . South African surgeon who performed the first human heart transplant in 1967 in Cape Town. The patient, 54-year-old Louis Washkansky, lived for 18 days.

Barnardo /bə'nɑːdəʊ/ Thomas John 1845–1905. British philanthropist, who was known as Dr Barnardo, although not medically qualified. He opened the first of a series of homes for destitute children 1867 in Stepney, E London.

Barnard's star /'bɑːnɑːd/ second-closest star to the Sun, 6 light years away in the constellation Ophiuchus. It is a faint red dwarf of 9th magnitude, visible only through a telescope.

It is named after the US astronomer Edward E Barnard (1857–1923), who discovered in 1916 that it has the fastest proper motion of any star, crossing 1 degree of sky every 350 years. Some

observations suggest that Barnard's star may be accompanied by planets.

Barnaul /ˌbɑːnɑːˈuːl/ industrial city in S Siberia, USSR; population (1987) 596,000.

Barnes /bɑːnz/ Ernest William 1874–1953. British cleric. A lecturer in mathematics at Cambridge 1902–15, he was an ardent advocate of the significance of scientific thought on modern religion. In 1924 he became bishop of Birmingham and published the controversial work *The Rise of Christianity* 1947.

Barnes /bɑːnz/ Thomas 1785–1841. British journalist, editor of *The Times* from 1817, during which time it became known as the 'Thunderer'.

Barnes /bɑːnz/ William 1800–1886. English poet and cleric who published volumes of poems in the Dorset dialect.

Barnet /'bɑːnɪt/ borough of NW Greater London

features site of the Battle of Barnet 1470 in one of the ◊Wars of the Roses; Hadley Woods; Hampstead Garden Suburb; department for newspapers and periodicals of the British Library at Colindale; residential district of *Hendon*, which includes Metropolitan Police Detective Training and Motor Driving schools, and the Royal Air Force Battle of Britain and Bomber Command museums

population (1981) 292,500.

Barnet, Battle of in the English ◊Wars of the Roses, the defeat of Lancaster by York on 14 Apr 1471 in Barnet, Hertfordshire (now NW London).

Barnsley /'bɑːnzli/ town in S Yorkshire, England; population (1981) 128,200. It is an industrial town (iron and steel, glass, paper, carpet, and clothing) on one of Britain's richest coalfields.

Barnum /'bɑːnəm/ Phineas T(aylor) 1810–1891. US showman. In 1871, after an adventurous career, he established the 'Greatest Show on Earth' (which included the midget 'Tom Thumb') comprising circus, menagerie, and exhibition of 'freaks', conveyed in 100 rail cars. He coined the phrase 'there's a sucker born every minute'.

Barocci /bə'rɒtʃi/ Federico *c.*1535–1612. Italian artist, born and based in Urbino. He painted religious themes in a highly coloured, sensitive style that falls between Renaissance and Baroque. The *Madonna del Graffo* (National Gallery, London) shows the influence of Raphael (also from Urbino) and Correggio on his art.

Baroda /bə'rəʊdə/ former name of ◊Vadodara, in Gujarat, India.

barograph device for recording variations in atmospheric pressure.

A pen, governed by the movements of an aneroid ◊barometer, makes a continuous line on a paper strip on a cylinder which rotates over a day or week to create a *barogram*, or permanent record of variations in atmospheric pressure.

Baroja /bæ'rəʊxə/ Pio 1872–1956. Spanish novelist of Basque extraction whose works include a trilogy dealing with the Madrid underworld, *La lucha por la vida/The Struggle for Life* 1904–05, and the multi-volume *Memorias de un hombre de acción/Memoirs of a Man of Action* 1913–28.

barometer instrument that measures atmospheric pressure as an indication of weather. Most often used are the *mercury barometer* and the *aneroid barometer*.

In a mercury barometer a column of mercury in a glass tube roughly 0.75 m/2.5 ft high (closed at one end, curved upwards at the other) is balanced by the pressure of the atmosphere on the open end; any change in the height of the column reflects a change in pressure. An aneroid barometer achieves a similar result by changes in the distance between the faces of a shallow cylindrical metal box which is partly exhausted of air.

baron rank in the ◊peerage of the UK, above a baronet and below a viscount. The first English barony by patent was created in 1387, but barons by 'writ' existed earlier. Life peers, created under the Act of 1958, are always of this rank.

baronet hereditary title in the UK below the rank of baron, but above that of knight; the first creations were in 1611 by James I, who needed funds from their sale to finance an army in Ulster. A baronet does not have a seat in the House of Lords, but is entitled to the style *Sir* before his Christian name.

Barons' Wars civil wars in England:

1215–17 between King ◊John and his barons, over his failure to honour ◊Magna Carta

1264–67 between ◊Henry III (and the future ◊Edward I) and his barons (led by Simon de ◊Montfort)

1264 14 May *Battle of Lewes* at which Henry III was defeated and captured

1265 4 Aug Simon de Montfort was defeated by Edward I at Evesham and killed.

Baroque style of art and architecture characterized by extravagance in ornament, asymmetry of design, and great expressiveness. It dominated European *art* for most of the 17th century, with artists like the painter Rubens and the sculptor Bernini. In *architecture* it often involved large-scale designs, such as Bernini's piazza in Rome and the palace of Versailles in France. In *music* the Baroque era lasted from about 1600 to 1750, and its major composers included Monteverdi, Vivaldi, J S Bach, and Handel.

In painting, Caravaggio, with his bold use of light and forceful compositions, was an early exponent, but the Carracci family were more typical of the early Baroque style, producing grandiose visions in ceiling paintings that deployed illusionistic painting of florid architectural decoration. In sculpture, the greatest master was Bernini, whose *Ecstasy of St Theresa* 1645–52 (Sta Maria della Vittoria, Rome) is a fine example of overt emotionalism. Most masterpieces of the new style emerged in churches and palaces in Rome, but it soon spread through Europe. The Swiss art historian Burckhardt first used the term 'baroque'.

Barossa Valley /bə'rɒsə/ wine-growing area in the Lofty mountain ranges, South Australia.

Barotseland /bə'rɒtsɪlænd/ former kingdom in Western Province of ◊Zambia.

Barquisimeto /bɑː,kiːsɪ'meɪtəu/ capital of Lara state, NW Venezuela; population (1981) 523,000.

Barra /'bærə/ most southerly of the larger Outer Hebrides, Scotland; area 90 sq km/35 sq mi; population (1981) 1,340. It is separated from South Uist by the Sound of Barra. The main town is Castlebay.

barometer

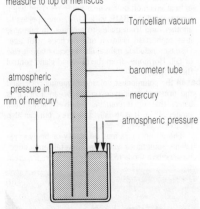

measure to top of meniscus

Torricellian vacuum

atmospheric pressure in mm of mercury

barometer tube

mercury

atmospheric pressure

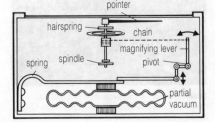

pointer

hairspring

chain

magnifying lever

spring · spindle · pivot

partial vacuum

barracuda large predatory fish *Sphyraena barracuda* found in the warmer seas of the world. It can grow over 2 m/6 ft long, and has a superficial resemblance to a pike. Young fish shoal but the older ones are solitary. The barracuda has very sharp shearing teeth, and may attack people.

Barragán /,bærə'gɑːn/ Luis 1902–1988. Mexican architect, known for his use of rough wooden beams, cobbles, lava, and adobe, his simple houses with walled gardens, and his fountains.

Barrancabermeja /bərænkɔbə'meɪxə/ a port and oil refining centre on the Magdalena River in the department of Santander, NE Colombia. A major outlet for oil from the De Mares fields which are linked by pipeline to Cartagena on the Caribbean coast.

Barranquilla /,bærən'kiːljə/ seaport in N Colombia, on the river Magdalena; population (1985) 1,120,900. Products include chemicals, tobacco, textiles, furniture and footwear.

It is Colombia's chief port on the Caribbean, and is the site of Latin America's first air terminal 1919.

Barras /bæ'rɑːs/ Paul François Jean Nicolas, Count Barras 1755–1829. French revolutionary. He was elected to the National Convention 1792, and helped to overthrow Robespierre 1794. In 1795 he became a member of the Directory (see ◊French Revolution). In 1796 he brought about the marriage of his former mistress, Joséphine de Beauharnais, with Napoleon, and assumed dictatorial powers. After Napoleon's coup d'état 19 Nov 1799, Barras fell into disgrace.

Barrault /bæ'rəu/ Jean Louis 1910– . French actor and director. His films include *La Symphonie fantastique* 1942, *Les Enfants du Paradis* 1944, and *La Ronde* 1950.

He was producer and director to the ◊Comédie Française 1940–46, and director of the Théâtre de France (formerly Odéon) from 1959 until dismissed 1968 because of statements made during the occupation of the theatre by student rebels.

barre the wooden bar running along the walls of a ballet studio at waist height, designed to help dancers keep their balance while going through the initial daily exercises.

Barre /bɑː/ Raymond 1924– . French politician, member of the centre-right Union pour la Démocratie Française; prime minister 1976–81, when he also held the Finance Ministry portfolio and gained a reputation as a tough and determined budget-cutter (nicknamed Monsieur Economy).

Barre, born on the French dependency of Réunion, was a liberal economist at the Sorbonne and vice president of the European Commission 1967–72. He served as minister of foreign trade to President Giscard d'Estaing and became prime minister on the resignation of Chirac 1976. He built up a strong political base in the Lyon region during the early 1980s.

barrel a unit of liquid capacity, the value of which depends on the liquid being measured. It is used particularly for petroleum, a barrel of which contains 159 litres/35 imperial gallons; a barrel of alcohol contains 189 litres/41.5 imperial gallons.

barrel organ portable pipe organ, played by turning a handle.

Turning the handle works a pump and drives a replaceable cylinder upon which music is recorded as a pattern of ridges controlling the passage of air to the pipes.

It was a common entertainment and parish church instrument in England during the 18th and 19th centuries.

Barren Lands/Grounds the ◊tundra region of Canada, W of Hudson Bay.

Barrie /'bæri/ J(ames) M(atthew) 1860–1937. Scottish playwright and novelist, author of *The Admirable Crichton* 1902 and the children's fantasy *Peter Pan* 1904.

He became known by his studies of Scottish rural life in plays such as *A Window in Thrums* 1889 which began the vogue of the Kailyard school. His reputation as a playwright was established with

Barrymore US actor John Barrymore was the youngest of the three talented Barrymores, whose parents were also actors.

The Professor's Love Story 1894 and *The Little Minister*. His later plays include *Quality Street* 1901 and *What Every Woman Knows* 1908.

barrier reef a ◊coral reef that lies offshore, separated from the mainland by a shallow lagoon.

barrister in the UK, a lawyer qualified by study at the ◊Inns of Court to plead for a client in court. In Scotland they are called ◊advocates. Barristers act for clients through the intermediary of ◊solicitors. In the highest courts, only barristers can represent litigants but this distinction between barristers and solicitors seems likely to change in the 1990s. In the USA an attorney (lawyer) may serve both functions. When pupil barristers complete their training they are 'called to the bar': this is the name of the ceremony in which they are admitted as members of the profession. A ◊Queen's Counsel is a senior barrister.

barrow a burial mound, usually composed of earth but sometimes of stones, examples of which are found in many parts of the world. There are two main types, *long*, dating from the New Stone Age, and *round*, from the early Bronze Age.

Long barrows may be a mere mound, but usually they contained a chamber of wood or stone slabs in which were placed the bodies of the deceased. Such are especially common in the southern counties of England from Sussex to Dorset. They seem to have been communal burial places of the long-headed Mediterranean race.

Round barrows were the work of the round-headed or Beaker people of the early Bronze Age. The commonest type is the bell barrow, consisting of a circular mound enclosed by a ditch and an outside bank of earth. Many dot the Wiltshire downs in England. In historic times certain of the Saxon and most of the Danish invaders were barrow-builders.

Barrow /'bærəu/ most northerly town in the USA, at Point Barrow, Alaska; the world's largest Inuit settlement. There is oil at nearby Prudhoe Bay.

Barrow /'bærəu/ 1900–1934. US criminal; see ◊Bonnie and Clyde.

Barrow /'bærəu/ Isaac 1630–1677. British mathematician, theologian, and classicist. His *Lectiones geometricae* 1670 contains the essence of the theory of ◊calculus, which was later expanded by ◊Newton and ◊Leibniz.

Barrow-in-Furness /'bærəu ɪn 'fɜːnɪs/ port in Cumbria, England; population (1985) 72,600. Industries include shipbuilding and nuclear submarines.

Barthes *French critic Roland Barthes caused great controversy in the academic world.*

Barry /ˈbæri/ port in S Glamorgan, Wales; population (1981) 44,000. With ***Barry Island***, it is a holiday resort.

Barry /ˈbæri/ Charles 1795–1860. English architect of the Neo-Gothic Houses of Parliament at Westminster, London, 1840–60, in collaboration with ◊Pugin.

Barry /ˈbæri/ Comtesse du see ◊Du Barry, mistress of Louis XV of France.

Barrymore /ˈbærimɔː/ US family of actors, the children of British-born Maurice Barrymore and Georgie Drew, both stage personalities.

Lionel Barrymore (1878–1954) first appeared on the stage with his grandmother, Mrs John Drew, in 1893. He played numerous film roles from 1909, including *A Free Soul* 1931, Academy Award, and *Grand Hotel* 1932, but was perhaps best known for his annual radio portrayal of Scrooge in Dickens's *A Christmas Carol*.

Ethel Barrymore (1879–1959) played with the British actor Henry Irving in London in 1898 and in 1928 opened the Ethel Barrymore Theatre in New York; she also appeared in many films from 1914, including *None but the Lonely Heart* 1944, Academy Award.

John Barrymore (1882–1942), was a flamboyant personality who often appeared on stage and screen with his brother and sister. In his early years he was a Shakespearean actor. From 1923 he acted almost entirely in films, including *Dinner at Eight* 1933, and became a screen idol, nicknamed 'the Profile'.

Barstow /ˈbɑːstəʊ/ Stan 1928– . English novelist. Born in W Yorkshire, his novels describe northern working-class life including *A Kind of Loving* 1960.

Bart /bɑː/ Jean 1651–1702. French naval hero. The son of a fisherman, he served in the French navy, and harassed the British fleet in many daring exploits.

Bart /bɑːt/ Lionel 1930– . English composer, author of both words and music for many musicals including *Fings Ain't Wot They Us'd T'Be* 1959 and *Oliver!* 1960.

barter the exchange of goods or services, without the use of money.

Barth /bɑːt/ Heinrich 1821–1865. German geographer and explorer who in explorations of North Africa beteen 1844 and 1855 established the exact course of the river Niger.

He studied the coast of North Africa from Tunis to Egypt 1844–45, travelled in the Middle East

1845–47, crossed the Sahara from Tripoli 1850, and then spent five years exploring the country between Lake Chad and Cameroon which he described in the five-volume *Travels and Discoveries in Central Africa* 1857–58.

Barth /bɑːt/ John 1930–. US novelist, born in Baltimore, influential in experimental writing in the 1960s. Chief works include *The Sot-Weed Factor* 1960, *Giles Goat-Boy* 1966, and *Lost in the Funhouse* 1968, interwoven fictions based on language games.

Barth /bɑːt/ Karl 1886–1968. Swiss Protestant theologian. Socialist in his political views, he attacked the Nazis. His *Church Dogmatics* 1932–62 makes the resurrection of Jesus the focal point of Christianity.

Barthes /bɑːt/ Roland 1915–1980. French critic. He was an influential theorist of ◊semiology, the science of signs and symbols. One of the French 'new critics', he attacked traditional literary criticism in his early works, including *Sur Racine/On Racine* 1963, and set out his own theories in *Eléments de sémiologie* 1964. He also wrote an autobiographical novel, *Roland Barthes sur Roland Barthes* 1975.

Bartholdi /bɑːˈtɒldi/ Frédéric Auguste 1834–1904. French sculptor. He designed the ***Statue of Liberty*** overlooking New York harbour, 1884.

Bartholomew, Massacre of St /bɑːˈθɒləmjuː/ see ◊St Bartholomew, Massacre of.

Bartholomew, St /bɑːˈθɒləmjuː/ in the New Testament, one of the apostles. Legends relate that after the Crucifixion he took Christianity to India, or that he was a missionary in Anatolia and Armenia, where he suffered martyrdom by being flayed alive. Feast day 24 Aug.

Bartók /ˈbɑːtɒk/ Béla 1881–1945. Hungarian composer. Regarded as a child prodigy, he studied music at the Budapest Conservatory later working with ◊Kodály in recording and and transcribing local folk music for a government project. This led him to develop a personal musical language combining folk elements with mathematical concepts of tone and rhythmic proportion. His large output includes six string quartets, a ballet *The Miraculous Mandarin* 1919, which was banned because of its subject matter, concertos, an opera, and graded teaching pieces for piano. He died in the US having fled from Hungary in 1940.

Bartolommeo /bɑːˌtɒləˈmeɪəʊ/ Fra, also called Baccio della Porta *c.*1472–*c.*1517. Italian religious painter of the High Renaissance, active in Florence. His painting of the *Last Judgment* 1499 (Museo di S Marco, Florence) influenced Raphael.

Barton /ˈbɑːtn/ Edmund 1849–1920. Australian politician. He was leader of the federation movement from 1896 and first prime minister of Australia 1901–03.

Bart's short for St Bartholomew's Hospital, in Smithfield, London, one of the great teaching

Bartók *Hungarian composer Béla Bartók.*

hospitals of England. It was founded by Henry VIII at the Reformation.

Baruch /bəˈruːk/ Bernard (Mannes) 1870–1965. US financier. He was a friend of British prime minister Churchill and a self-appointed, unpaid adviser to US presidents Wilson, F D Roosevelt, and Truman. He strongly advocated international control of nuclear energy.

baryon in nuclear physics, a type of ◊elementary particle.

Baryshnikov /bəˈrɪʃnɪkɒf/ Mikhail 1948– . Soviet dancer, now in the USA. He joined the Kirov Ballet in 1967 and soon gained fame worldwide as a soloist. After defecting 'on artistic, not political grounds' while in Canada in 1974, he danced with various companies, becoming director of the American Ballet Theatre in 1980.

He has created many roles, notably in Twyla Tharp's *Push Comes to Shove* 1976 (music by Haydn/Lamb) and in Jerome Robbins's *Opus 19* 1979 (Prokofiev). He made his film debut in *The Turning Point* 1978 and has since acted in other films, including *White Nights* 1985. He made his dramatic stage debut in *Metamorphosis* 1989.

baryte barium sulphate, $BaSO_4$, the most common mineral of barium. It is white or light-coloured, and has a comparatively high density (specific gravity 4.6); the latter property makes it useful in the production of high density drilling muds. Baryte occurs mainly in ore veins, where it is often found with calcite and with lead and zinc minerals. It crystallizes in the orthorhombic system and can form tabular crystals or radiating fibrous massses.

baryton a bowed stringed instrument producing an intense singing tone. It is based on an 18th-century viol and modified by the addition of sympathetic (freely vibrating) strings.

The baryton was a favourite instrument of Prince Nicholas Esterhazy, patron of the Austrian composer Joseph Haydn who, to please him, wrote many trios for violin, baryton, and cello.

basal metabolic rate (BMR) the amount of energy needed by an animal just to stay alive. It is measured when the animal is awake but resting, and includes the energy required to keep the heart beating, sustain breathing, repair tissues, and keep the brain and nerves functioning. Measuring the animal's consumption of oxygen gives an accurate value for BMR, because oxygen is needed to release energy from food.

A cruder measure of BMR estimates the amount of heat given off, some heat being released when food is used up. BMR varies from one species to another, and from males to females. In humans, it is highest in children and declines with age. Disease, including mental illness, can make it rise or fall. Hormones from the ◊thyroid gland control the BMR.

basalt the commonest volcanic ◊igneous rock, and the principal rock type on the ocean floor; it is basic, that is, it contains relatively little silica (under 50%). It is usually dark grey, but can also be green, brown, or black.

The groundmass may be glassy or finely crystalline, sometimes with large ◊crystals embedded. Basaltic lava tends to be runny and flows for great

basalt *The Giant's Causeway in Antrim, Ireland, consisting of several thousand hexagonal pillars of basalt set together in a honeycomb pattern.*

base

binary (base 2)	octal (base 8)	decimal (base 10)	hexadecimal (base 16)
0	0	0	0
1	1	1	1
10	2	2	2
11	3	3	3
100	4	4	4
101	5	5	5
110	6	6	6
111	7	7	7
1000	10	8	8
1001	11	9	9
1010	12	10	A
1011	13	11	B
1100	14	12	C
1101	15	13	D
1110	16	14	E
1111	17	15	F
10000	20	16	10
1111111	377	255	FF
11111010001	3721	2001	7D1

distances before solidifying. Successive eruptions of basalt have formed the great plateaux of Colorado and the Indian Deccan. In some places, such as Fingal's Cave in the Inner Hebrides of Scotland and the Giant's Causeway in Antrim, Northern Ireland, shrinkage during the solidification of the molten lava caused the formation of hexagonal columns.

bascule bridge type of movable bridge in which one or two counterweighted deck members pivot upwards to allow shipping to pass underneath. One of the best-known examples is the double bascule Tower Bridge, in London.

base in mathematics, the number of different single-digit symbols used in a particular number system. Thus our usual (decimal) counting system of numbers has the base 10 (using the symbols 0,1,2,3,4,5,6,7,8,9). In the ◊binary number system, which has only the numbers 1 and 0, the base is 2. A base is also a number which, when raised to a particular power (that is, when multiplied by itself a particular number of times as in $10 = 10 \times 10 = 100$), has a ◊logarithm equal to the power. For example, the logarithm of 100 to the base 10 is 2.

In general, any number system subscribing to a place value system with base value b may be represented by $\dots b^4 b^3 b^2 b^1 b^0 \, b^{-1} b^{-2} b^{-3} \dots$. Hence in base 10 the columns represent $\dots 10^4 10^3 10^2 10^1 10^0 10^{-1} 10^{-2} 10^{-3} \dots$, in base 2 $\dots 2^4 2^3 2^2 2^1 2^0 2^{-1} 2^{-2} 2^{-3} \dots$, and in base 8 $\dots 8^4 8^3 8^2 8^1 8^0 8^{-1} 8^{-2} 8^{-3} \dots$. For bases beyond 10, the denary numbers 10, 11, 12, and so on. must be replaced by a single digit. Thus in base 16, all numbers up to 16 must be represented by single-digit 'numbers', since 10 in hexadecimal would mean 16 in decimal. Hence decimal 10,11,12,13,14,15 are represented in hexadecimal by letters A, B, C, D, E, F.

base or ◊alkali in chemistry, a substance that reacts with an ◊acid to give a salt. Inorganic bases are usually oxides or hydroxides of metals, which react with dilute acids to form a salt and water. Many carbonates also react with dilute acids, additionally giving off carbon dioxide.

A more general definition of a base is a compound that combines with protons (hydrogen ions), such as many organic compounds that contain nitrogen.

baseball national summer game of the USA, derived in the 19th century from the English game of ◊rounders. Baseball is played between two teams, each of nine players, on a pitch ('field') marked out in the form of a diamond, with a base at each corner. The ball is struck with a cylindrical bat, and the players try to score ('make a run') by

baseball

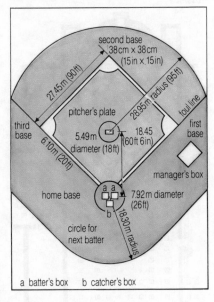

a batter's box   b catcher's box

circuiting the bases. A 'home run' is a circuit on one hit.

The game is divided into nine innings (inning is the singular form), each with two halves, with each team taking turns to bat while the other team takes the field, pitching, catching, and fielding.

The pitcher throws the ball, and the batter tries to make a 'hit'. Having the ball, the batter tries to make a run, either in stages from home base to first, second, and third base, and back to home base, or in a 'home run'.

The batter is declared out if (1) he (or she, but the professional leagues have not yet admitted women) fails to hit the ball after 3 'strikes', (2) he hits the ball into the air and it is caught by a fielder, (3) he is touched by the ball in the hand of one of his opponents while he is between bases, or (4) a fielder standing on one of the bases catches the ball before the batter reaches the base.

The first batter is followed by the other members of his team in rotation until three members of the batting side are put out: the opposing team then take their turn to bat. After nine innings, the team scoring the most runs wins the game. The game is controlled by umpires.

Cooperstown contains the Baseball Hall of Fame (1939) and the National Museum of Baseball. The National Association of Baseball Players was formed 1858 and the first professional team was the Cincinnati Red Stockings 1869. Baseball is also popular in Japan.

The *World Series* was first held as an end-of-season game between the winners of the two professional leagues, the National League and the American League, in 1903, and was established as a series of seven games in 1905.

World Series: recent winners

1978	New York Yankees
1979	Pittsburgh Pirates
1980	Philadelphia Phillies
1981	Los Angeles Dodgers
1982	St Louis Cardinals
1983	Baltimore Orioles
1984	Detroit Tigers
1985	Kansas City Royals
1986	New York Mets
1987	Minnesota Twins
1988	Los Angeles Dodgers
1989	Oakland Athletics

Basel /'bɑːzəl/ or *Basle* (French *Bâle*) financial, commercial, and industrial city in Switzerland; population (1987) 363,000. Basel was a strong

military station under the Romans. In 1501 it joined the Swiss confederation, and later developed as a centre for the Reformation.

It has the chemical firms Hoffman-La Roche, Sandoz, Ciba-Geigy (dyes, vitamins, agrochemicals, dietary products, genetic products). There are trade fairs, and it is the headquarters of the Bank for International Settlements. There is an 11th-century cathedral (rebuilt after an earthquake 1356), a 16th-century town hall, and a university dating from the 15th century.

base lending rate the rate of interest to which most bank lending is linked, the actual rate depending on the status of the borrower. A prestigious company might command a rate only 1% above base rate while an individual would be charged several points above. An alternative method of interest rates is ◊LIBOR.

basenji breed of dog originating in Central Africa, where it is used as a hunter. About 41 cm/1.3 ft tall, it has a wrinkled forehead, curled tail, and short glossy coat. It is remarkable because it has no true bark.

base pair in biochemistry, the linkage of two base (purine or pyrimidine) molecules in ◊DNA which are found in nucleotides and which form the basis of the genetic code.

One base lies on one strand of the DNA double helix, and one on the other, so the base pairs link the two strands, rather like the rungs of a ladder. In DNA, there are four bases: adenine and guanine (purines) and cytosine and thymine (pyrimidines). Adenine always pairs with thymine and cytosine with guanine.

Bashkir /bæʃˈkɪə/ autonomous republic of the USSR, with the Ural Mountains on the E
area 143,600 sq km/55, 430 sq mi
capital Ufa
products minerals, oil
population (1982) 3,876,000
history Bashkir was annexed by Russia 1557, and became the first Soviet Autonomous Republic 1919.

Bashkirtseff /bæʃˈkɪəstsef/ Marie 1860–1884. Russian diarist and painter whose journals, written in French, were cited by Simone de Beauvoir as the archetypal example of 'self-centred female narcissism', but also as the discovery by the female of her independent existence. She died of tuberculosis at 24.

Bashō /'bɑːʃəʊ/ pen name of Matsuo Munefusa, Japanese poet 1644–1694. He was master of the *haiku*, a 17-syllable poetic form with lines of 5, 7, and 5 syllables, which he infused with subtle allusiveness and made the accepted form of poetic expression in Japan. His most famous work is *Oku-no-hosomichi/The Narrow Road to the Deep North* 1694, an account of a visit to northern Japan, which consists of haikus interspersed with prose passages.

BASIC Beginner's All-purpose Symbolic Instruction Code a computer-programming language, developed in 1964, originally designed to take advantage of ◊time-sharing computers (where many people can use the computer at the same time). Most versions use an ◊interpreter program, which allows programs to be entered and run with no intermediate translation, although recent versions have been implemented as a ◊compiler. The language is relatively easy to learn, and is popular among users of microcomputers.

Basic English a simplified form of English devised and promoted by C K ◊Ogden in the 1920s and 1930s as an international auxiliary language; as a route into Standard English for foreign learners; and as a reminder to the English-speaking world of the virtues of plain language. Its name derives from the letters of *B*ritish, *A*merican, *S*cientific, *I*nternational, *C*ommercial.

Basic has a vocabulary of 850 words (plus names, technical terms, and so on), only 18 of which are verbs or 'operators'. *Get* therefore replaces 'receive', 'obtain', and 'become', while *buy* is replaced by the phrase 'give money for'.

basic-oxygen process

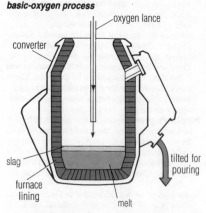

basic-oxygen process the most widely used method of steel-making, involving the blasting of oxygen at supersonic speed into molten pig iron.

Pig iron from a blast furnace, together with steel scrap, is poured into a converter, and a jet of oxygen is then projected into the mixture. The excess carbon in the mix and other impurities quickly burn out or form a slag, and the converter is emptied by tilting. It takes only about 45 minutes to refine 350 tonnes of steel. The basic-oxygen process was developed in 1948 at a steelworks near the Austrian towns of Linz and Donawitz. It is a modern version of the ◊Bessemer process.

basidiocarp the spore-bearing body, or 'fruiting body', of all basidiomycete ◊fungi, except the rusts and smuts. A well-known example is the edible mushroom. Other types include globular basidiocarps (puffballs) or flat ones that project from tree trunks (brackets). They are made up of a mass of tightly packed, intermeshed ◊hyphae.

The tips of these hyphae develop into the reproductive cells, or basidia, which form a fertile layer known as the hymenium or the **gills** of the basidiocarp. Four spores are budded off from the surface of each basidium.

basidiocarp

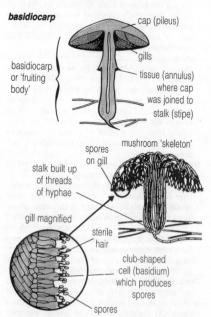

Basie /'beɪsi/ 'Count' (William) 1904–1984. US band leader, pianist, and organist who developed the big-band sound and a simplified, swinging style of music. He led impressive groups of musicians in a career spanning more than 50 years.

basil plant *Ocimum basilicum* of the family Labiatae. A native of the tropics, it is cultivated in Europe as a culinary herb.

Basil II /'bæzl/ c. 958–1025. Byzantine emperor

basilica

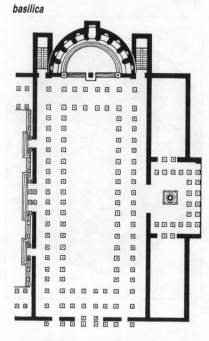

basilica Plan of the Basilica Ulpia in Rome.

from 976. His achievement as emperor was to contain, and later decisively defeat, the Bulgarians, earning for himself the title **Bulgar-Slayer** after a victory 1014. After the battle he blinded almost all 15,000 of the defeated, leaving only a few men with one eye to lead their fellows home. The Byzantine empire reached its greatest extent at the time of his death.

Basildon /'bæzldən/ industrial ◊new town in Essex, England; population (1981) 152,500. It was designated as a new town in 1949 from several townships. Industries include chemicals, clothing, printing, and engineering.

basilica type of Roman public building; a large roofed hall flanked by columns, generally with an aisle on each side, used for judicial or other public business. The earliest known basilica, at Pompeii, dates from the 2nd century BC. The type was adopted by the early Christians for their churches.

Basilicata /bə,zɪlɪ'kɑːtə/ mountainous region of S Italy, comprising the provinces of Potenza and Matera; area 10,000 sq km/3,860 sq mi; population (1988) 622,000. Its capital is Potenza. It was the Roman province of Lucania.

basilisk a South American lizard genus *Basiliscus*. It is able to run bipedally when travelling fast (about 11 kph/7 mph) and may dash a short distance across the surface of water.

basil

The male has a well-developed crest on the head, body, and tail.

Basil, St /'bæzl/ c. 330–379. Cappadocian monk, known as 'the Great', founder of the Basilian monks. Elected bishop of Caesarea 370, Basil opposed the heresy of ◊Arianism. He wrote many theological works and composed the 'Liturgy of St Basil', in use in the Eastern Orthodox Church. Feast day 2 Jan.

Born in Caesarea, Anatolia, he studied in Constantinople and Athens, visited the hermit saints of the Egyptian desert, entered a monastery in Anatolia about 358, and developed a monastic rule based on community life, work, and prayer. These ideas form the basis of monasticism in the Greek Orthodox church, and influenced the foundation of similar monasteries by St Benedict.

Basingstoke /'beɪzɪŋstəʊk/ industrial town in Hampshire, England, 72 km/45 mi WSW of London; population (1981) 67,500. It is the headquarters of the UK Civil Service Commission.

Baskerville /'bæskəvɪl/ John 1706–1775. English printer and typographer, who experimented in casting types from 1750 onwards. The Baskerville typeface is named after him.

He manufactured fine printing paper and inks, and in 1756 published a quarto edition of the Classical poet Virgil, which was followed by 54 highly crafted books.

basketball ball game between two teams of five players on an indoor enclosed court. The object is, via a series of passing moves, to throw the large inflated ball through a circular hoop and net, which is 3.05 m/10 ft above the ground and positioned at each end of the court. Basketball was invented by YMCA instructor Dr James Naismith at Springfield, Massachusetts, 1891. The most famous basketball team is the ◊Harlem Globetrotters.

World Championship first held 1950 for men, 1953 for women; held every four years

men	
1950	Argentina
1954	USA
1959	Brazil
1963	Brazil
1967	USSR
1970	Yugoslavia
1974	USSR
1978	Yugoslavia
1982	USSR
1986	USA
women	
1953	USA
1957	USA
1964	USSR
1967	USSR
1971	USSR
1975	USSR
1979	USA
1983	USSR
1987	USA

basketry an ancient craft used to make a wide range of objects, from sandals and baskets to furniture, by interweaving or plaiting rushes, cane, or other equally strong, natural fibres. **Wickerwork** is a more rigid type of basketry worked onto a sturdy frame, usually made from strips of willow.

Basle /bɑːl/ alternative form of ◊Basel, city in Switzerland.

Basov /'bɑːsɒf/ Nikolai Gennadievich 1912– . Soviet physicist who in 1953, with his compatriot Alexander Prokhorov, developed the microwave amplifier called a ◊maser. They were awarded the Nobel Prize for Physics 1964, which they shared with Charles Townes of the USA.

Basque /bæsk/ a member of a people who occupy the autonomous Basque region (created 1980) of N Spain and the French *département* of Pyrénées-Atlantiques. The Basques are a pre-Indo-European people who largely maintained their independence until the 19th century and speak their own Euskara tongue. During the

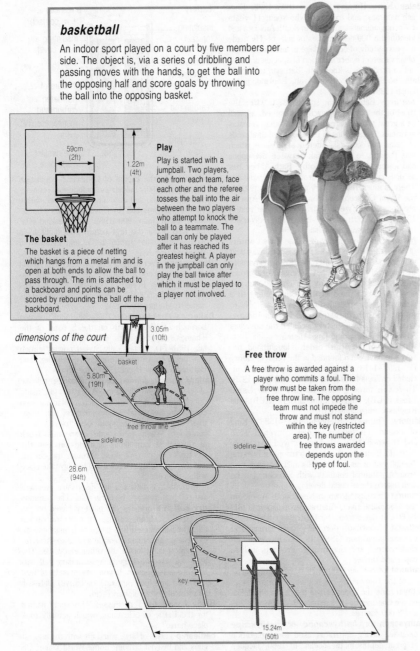

basketball

An indoor sport played on a court by five members per side. The object is, via a series of dribbling and passing moves with the hands, to get the ball into the opposing half and score goals by throwing the ball into the opposing basket.

59cm (2ft)

1.22m (4ft)

The basket

The basket is a piece of netting which hangs from a metal rim and is open at both ends to allow the ball to pass through. The rim is attached to a backboard and points can be scored by rebounding the ball off the backboard.

Play

Play is started with a jumpball. Two players, one from each team, face each other and the referee tosses the ball into the air between the two players who attempt to knock the ball to a teammate. The ball can only be played after it has reached its greatest height. A player in the jumpball can only play the ball twice after which it must be played to a player not involved.

dimensions of the court

3.05m (10ft)

basket

5.80m (19ft)

free throw line

sideline

28.6m (94ft)

sideline

15.24m (50ft)

key

Free throw

A free throw is awarded against a player who commits a foul. The throw must be taken from the free throw line. The opposing team must not impede the throw and must not stand within the key (restricted area). The number of free throws awarded depends upon the type of foul.

Spanish Civil War 1936–39, they were on the Republican side, and were defeated by Franco. The Basque separatist movement ETA (*Euskadi ta Azkatasuna*/Basque Nation and Liberty) and the French organization *Enbata*/Ocean Wind engaged in guerrilla activity from 1968 in an unsuccessful attempt to secure a united Basque state.

Basque Country /bæsk/ (French *Pays Basque*) homeland of the Basque people in the W Pyrenees. The Basque Country includes the Basque Provinces of N Spain and the French arrondissements of Bayonne and Maulaon.

Basque language a language of W Europe known to its speakers, the Basques, as *Euskara*, and apparently unrelated to any other language on earth. It is spoken by some half a million people in N Spain and SW France, around the Bay of Biscay ('the Basque bay'), as well as by emigrants in both Europe and the Americas.

Although officially discouraged in the past, Basque is now accepted as a regional language in both France and Spain, and is of central importance to the Basque nationalist movement.

Basque Provinces /bæsk/ (Spanish *Vascongadas*, Basque *Euskadi*) autonomous region of NW Spain, comprising the provinces of Vizcaya, Alava, and Guipuzcoa; area 7,300 sq km/2,818 sq mi; population (1986) 2,133,000.

Basra /'bæzrə/ (Arabic *al-Basrah*) principal port in Iraq, in the Shatt-al-Arab delta, 97 km/60 mi from the Persian Gulf; population (1985) 617,000. Exports include wool, oil, cereal, and dates.

bass /bæs/ long-bodied scaly sea fish *Morone labrax* found in the N Atlantic and Mediterranean. Other fish of the same family (Serranidae) are also called bass, as are North American freshwater fishes of the family Centrarchidae, such as black bass and small-mouthed bass.

They grow to 1 m/3 ft, and are often seen in shoals.

bass /beɪs/ (1) lowest range of male voice; (2) lower regions of musical pitch; (3) a double bass (see ◊violin family).

Bass /bæs/ George 1763–*c*.1808. English naval surgeon who with Matthew ◊Flinders explored the coast of New South Wales and the strait that

bears his name between Tasmania and Australia 1795–98.

Bassein /bɑː'seɪn/ port in Myanmar (Burma), in the Irrawaddy delta, 125 km/78 mi from the sea; population (1983) 355,588. Bassein was founded in the 13th century.

Basse-Normandie /'bæs ˌnɔːmɒn'diː/ or **Lower Normandy** coastal region of NW France lying between Haute-Normandie and Brittany (Bretagne). It includes the *départements* of Calvados, Manche, and Orne; area 17,600 sq km/6,794 sq mi; population (1986) 1,373,000. Its capital is Caen. Apart from stock farming, dairy farming and the production of textiles, the area is noted for its Calvados (apple brandy).

The invasion of Europe by Allied Forces in June 1944 began in June 1944 when troops landed on the beaches of Calvados.

basset type of dog with a long low body, wrinkled forehead, and long pendulous ears, originally bred in France for hunting hares.

Basseterre /'bæs 'teə/ capital and port of St Kitts-Nevis, in the Leeward Islands; population (1980) 14,000. Industries include data processing, rum, clothes and electrical components.

Basse-Terre /'bæs 'teə/ port on the Leeward Island Basse-Terre; population (1982) 13,600. It is capital of the French overseas *département* of Guadeloupe.

Basse-Terre /'bæs 'teə/ main island of the French West Indian island group of Guadeloupe; area 848 sq km/327 sq mi; population (1982) 141,300. It has an active volcano: Grande Soufrière rising to 1,484 m/4,870 ft.

basset horn a musical ◊woodwind instrument resembling a clarinet, pitched in F and ending in a brass bell.

bassoon a double-reed woodwind instrument, the bass of the oboe family. It doubles back on itself in a tube about 2.5 m/7.5 ft long. Its tone is rich and deep.

It is descended from the bass pommer, which was approximately 2 m/6 ft in length and perfectly straight.

Bass Rock /bæs/ islet in the Firth of Forth, Scotland, about 107 m/350 ft high, with a lighthouse.

Bass Strait /bæs/ channel between Australia and Tasmania, named after the British explorer George Bass (1760–1912); oil was discovered there in the 1960s.

bastard feudalism a late medieval development of ◊feudalism in which grants of land were replaced by money as rewards for service. Conditions of service were specified in a contract, or indenture, between lord and retainer. The system allowed large numbers of men to be raised quickly for wars or private feuds.

Bastia /'bæstiə/ port and commercial centre in NE Corsica, France; population (1983) 50,500.

Bastille /bæs'tiːl/ the castle of St Antoine, part of the fortifications of Paris, which was used for centuries as a state prison; it was singled out for the initial attack by the mob that set the French Revolution in motion 14 July 1789. Only seven prisoners were found in the castle when it was stormed; the governor and most of the garrison were killed, and the Bastille was razed.

Bastos /'bæstɒs/ August Roa 1917– . Paraguayan writer of short stories and novels, including *Son of Man* 1960 about the Chaco War between Bolivia and Paraguay, in which he fought.

Basutoland /bə'suːtəʊlænd/ former name for ◊Lesotho.

bat flying mammal in which the forelimbs are developed as wings capable of rapid and sustained flight. There are two main groups of bats: **megabats** or **flying foxes**, which eat fruit, and **microbats**, which mainly eat insects. Although by no means blind, many microbats rely largely on echolocation for navigation and finding prey, sending out pulses of high-pitched sound and listening for the echo. Bats are nocturnal, and those native to temperate countries hibernate in winter. There are about 1,000 species of bats forming the order

Chiroptera, making this the second-largest mammal order; bats make up nearly one quarter of the world's mammals. Although bats are widely distributed, bat populations around the world have declined alarmingly and many species are now endangered.

megabats The Megachiroptera live in the tropical regions of the Old World, Australia, and the Pacific and feed on fruit, nectar and pollen. Relatively large, up to 900 g/2 lb and 1.5 m/5 ft wingspan, they have large eyes and a long face earning them the name 'flying fox'. Many rainforest trees depend on bats for pollination and seed dispersal, and some 300 bat-dependent plant species yield more than 450 economically important products. Some bats are keystone species on whose survival whole ecosystems may depend.

microbats Most bats are Microchiroptera, mainly small and insect-eating, though some species eat blood (◊vampire bats), frogs, or fish. They roost in caves, crevices, and hollow trees. A single bat may eat 3,000 insects in one night.

A bat's wings consist of a thin hairless skin stretched between the four fingers of the hand and from the last finger down to the hindlimb. The thumb is free and has a sharp claw to help in climbing. The hind feet have five toes with sharp hooked claws that suspend the animal head downwards when resting. Some bats live to be over 30 years old. An adult female bat usually rears only one pup a year. The bumble bee bat, inhabiting SE Asian rainforests, is the smallest mammal in the world. In China bats are associated with good luck.

Bataan /bə'tɑːn/ peninsula in Luzon, the Philippines, which was defended against the Japanese in World War II by US and Filipino troops under Gen MacArthur 1 Jan–9 Apr 1942. MacArthur was evacuated, but some 67,000 Allied prisoners died on the *Bataan Death March* to camps in the interior.

Batak several distinct but related peoples of N Sumatra in Indonesia. Numbering approximately 2.5 million, the Batak speak languages belonging to the Austronesian family.

The most numerous and most centrally located are the Toba Batak who live to the S and W of Lake Toba. Although the Batak possess distinctive traditional beliefs, they were influenced by Hinduism between the 2nd and 15th centuries AD. The syllabic script of the Batak, which was inscribed on bamboo, horn, bone, and tree bark, is based on Indian scripts. Although the island of Sumatra has many Muslim peoples, the majority of Batak did not adopt Islam. Since 1861 German and other missionaries have been active in N Sumatra and today over 80% of the Batak profess Christianity. Many Batak are rice farmers and produce handicrafts such as dyed textiles.

Batavia /bə'teɪvɪə/ former name until 1949 for ◊Jakarta, capital of Indonesia on Java.

Batavian Republic /bə'teɪvɪən/ name given to the ◊Netherlands by the French 1795; it lasted until the establishment of the kingdom of the Netherlands 1814 at the end of the Napoleonic Wars.

batch system in computing, a system for processing data with little or no operator intervention. Batches of data are prepared in advance, and processed during regular 'runs' (for example, each night, or at weekends). This enables efficient use of the computer and is well suited to applications of a repetitive nature, such as a company payroll.

Bateman /'beɪtmən/ H(enry) M(ayo) 1887–1970. Australian cartoonist, lived in England. His cartoons were based on themes of social embarrassment and confusion, in such series as *The Man who ...* (as in *The Guardsman who dropped his rifle*).

Bates /beɪts/ Alan 1934– . English actor. A versatile male lead in over 60 plays and films, his roles include *Zorba the Greek* 1965, *Far from the Madding Crowd* 1967, *Women in Love* 1970, *The Go-Between* 1971, *The Shout* 1978, and *Duet for One* 1986.

Bates /beɪts/ H(enry) W(alter) 1825–1892. English naturalist and explorer, who spent 11 years collecting animals and plants in South America and identified 8,000 new species of insects. He made a special study of ◊camouflage in animals, and his observation of insect imitation of species unpleasant to predators is known as 'Batesian mimicry'.

Bath /bɑːθ/ historic city in Avon, England; population (1981) 75,000.

features Bath has hot springs 37°C/93°F; the ruins of the baths for which it is named, as well as a great temple, are the finest Roman remains in Britain. Excavations in 1979 revealed thousands of coins and 'curses', offered at a place which was thought to be the link between the upper and lower worlds. The Gothic Bath Abbey has an unusually decorated W front and fan vaulting. There is much 18th-century architecture, notably the Royal Crescent by John Wood. The Assembly Rooms 1771 were destroyed in an air raid in 1942 but reconstructed in 1963. The University of Technology was established 1966.

history The Roman city of Aquae Sulis ('waters of Sul'—the British goddess of wisdom) was built in the first 20 years after the Roman invasion. In medieval times the hot springs were crown property, administered by the church, but the city was transformed in the 18th century to a fashionable spa, presided over by 'Beau' ◊Nash. At his home here the astronomer Herschel discovered Uranus 1781. Visitors included the novelists Smollett, Fielding, and Jane Austen.

Bath, Order of the British order of knighthood, believed to have been founded in the reign of Henry IV (1399–1413). Formally instituted 1815, it included civilians from 1847 and women from 1970. There are three grades: Knights of the Grand Cross (GCB), Knights Commanders (KCB), and Knights Companions (CB).

Báthory /'bɑːtəri/ Stephen 1533–1586. King of Poland, elected by a diet convened 1575 and crowned 1576. Báthory proved extremely sucessful in driving the Russian troops of Ivan the Terrible out of his country. His military successes brought potential conflicts with Sweden, but he died before these could develop.

Bathurst /'bæθɜːst/ town in New South Wales, on the Macquarie river, Australia; population (1981) 19,600. It dates from the 1851 gold rush.

Bathurst /'bæθɜːst/ port in New Brunswick, Canada; population (1981) 19,500. Industries include copper and zinc mining. Products include paper and timber.

Bathurst former name (until 1973) of ◊Banjul, capital of the Gambia.

bathyal zone the upper part of the ocean which lies on the Continental shelf at a depth of between 200 and 2,000 metres.

bathyscaph or *bathyscaphe* or *bathyscape* deep-sea diving apparatus used for exploration at great depths in the ocean. In 1960, Jacques Picard and Don Walsh took the bathyscaph *Trieste* to a depth of 10,917 m/35,820 ft in the Challenger Deep in the ◊Mariana Trench off the island of Guam in the Pacific Ocean.

bathysphere a steel sphere used for observation in deep-sea diving. It is lowered into the ocean by cable.

batik Javanese technique of hand-applied colour design for fabric; areas to be left undyed in a colour are sealed with wax. Practised throughout Indonesia, the craft was introduced to the West by the Dutch.

Batista /bə'tiːstə/ Fulgencio 1901–1973. Cuban dictator 1933–44 and 1952–59, whose authoritarian methods enabled him to jail his opponents and amass a large personal fortune. He was overthrown by rebel forces led by Fidel ◊Castro 1959.

Batoni /bə'təʊni/ Pompeo 1708–1787. Italian painter, celebrated for his detailed portraits of princes and gentlemen visiting Rome on the Grand Tour.

Baton Rouge /'bætn 'ruːʒ/ port on the Mississippi

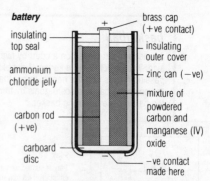

battery

river, USA, the capital of Louisiana; population (1980) 241,500. Industries include oil refining, petrochemicals, and iron. The bronze and marble state capitol was built by Governor Huey ◊Long.

Batten /'bætn/ Jean 1909–1982. New Zealand aviator, who made the first return solo flight by a woman Australia–Britain 1935, and established speed records.

Battenberg /'bætnbɜːg/ title (conferred 1851) of German noble family; its members included ◊Louis, Prince of Battenberg, and Louis Alexander, Prince of Battenberg, who changed his name to Mountbatten 1917.

Battersea /'bætəsi/ district of the Inner London borough of Wandsworth on the S bank of the Thames, noted for its park (including a funfair 1951–74), a classically styled power station now being converted into a leisure complex, and Battersea Dogs' Home (1860) for strays.

battery energy storage device allowing release of electricity on demand. A battery is made up of one or more cells, each containing two conducting ◊electrodes (one positive, one negative) immersed in a liquid ◊electrolyte, in a container. When an outside connection (such as through a light bulb) is made between the electrodes, a current flows through the circuit, and chemical reactions releasing energy take place within the cells.

Primary cell batteries are disposable, secondary cell batteries are rechargeable. The common *dry cell* is a primary cell battery based on the ◊Leclanché cell and consists of a central carbon electrode immersed in a paste of manganese dioxide and ammonium chloride as the electrolyte. The zinc casing forms the other electrode. The lead–acid *car battery* is a secondary cell battery, or accumulator. It consists of sets of lead (positive) and lead peroxide (negative) plates in an electrolyte of sulphuric acid.

Battle /'bætl/ town in Sussex, England, named for the Battle of ◊Hastings, which actually took place here.

battleship a class of large warships with the biggest guns and heavist armour. Some World War II US battleships have been returned to active duty.

Batumi /bə'tuːmi/ port and capital in the Republic of Adzhar, USSR; population (1984) 111,000. Main industries include oil refining, food canning, and engineering.

baud in engineering, a unit of electrical signalling speed equal to one pulse per second, measuring the rate at which signals are sent between electronic devices such as telegraphs and computers.

Baudelaire /ˌbəʊdə'leə/ Charles Pierre 1821–1867. French poet, whose work combined rhythmical and musical perfection with a morbid romanticism and eroticism, finding beauty in decadence and evil. His first book of verse was *Les Fleurs du mal*/◊*Flowers of Evil* 1857.

Baudouin /ˌbəʊduː'æn/ 1930– . King of the Belgians from 1951. In 1950 his father, ◊Leopold III, abdicated and Baudouin was known until his succession in July 1951 as *Le Prince Royal*. In 1960 he married Fabiola de Mora y Aragón (1928–), member of a Spanish noble family.

Bauhaus /'baʊhaʊs/ a German school of architecture and design founded 1919 by the architect

Walter ◊Gropius at Weimar in Germany, in an attempt to fuse all the arts and crafts into a unified whole. Moved to Dessau under political pressure 1925, it was closed by the Nazis 1933. Associated with the Bauhaus were the artists Klee and Kandinsky and the architect Mies van der Rohe. The international style of Modern architecture spread worldwide from there and in 1972 the *Bauhaus Archive* was installed in new premises in W Berlin.

Baul member of Bengali mystical sect that emphasizes freedom from compulsion, from doctrine, and from social caste; they avoid all outward forms of religious worship. Not ascetic, they aim for harmony between physical and spiritual needs.

An oral tradition is passed down by gurus (teachers). The Bāuls are known for their music and poetry.

Baum /bɔːm/ L(yman) Frank 1856–1919. US writer, best known for the children's fantasy *The Wonderful Wizard of Oz* 1900.

Bausch /bauʃ/ Pina 1940– . German dance choreographer and director of the unique Wuppertal Tanztheater. Her works incorporate dialogue, elements of psychoanalysis, comedy and drama. She never accepts requests to restage her creations.

bauxite the principal ore of ◊aluminium, consisting of a mixture of hydrated aluminium oxides and hydroxides, generally contaminated with compounds of iron, which give it a red colour. Chief producers of bauxite are Australia, Guinea, Jamaica, the USSR, Suriname, and Brazil.

Bavaria /bəˈveəriə/ (German *Bayern*) administrative region (German *Land*) of West Germany
area 70,600 sq km/27,252 sq mi
capital Munich
towns Nuremberg, Augsburg, Würzburg, Regensburg
features largest of the German *Länder*; forms the Danube basin; festivals at Bayreuth and Oberammergau
products beer, electronics, electrical engineering, optics, cars, aerospace, chemicals, plastics, oil-refining, textiles, glass, toys
population (1988) 11,083,000
famous people Lucas Cranach, Hitler, Franz Josef Strauss, Richard Strauss
religion 70% Roman Catholic, 26% Protestant
history the last king, Ludwig III, abdicated 1918, and Bavaria declared itself a republic.

Baudelaire Perhaps the first great poet of the modern city, celebrating its contrasts of rich and poor, beauty and ugliness, Baudelaire spent almost all his adult life in Paris.

bay

The original Bavarians were Teutonic invaders from Bohemia who occupied the country at the end of the 5th century AD. They were later ruled by dukes who recognized the supremacy of the emperor. The house of Wittelsbach ruled parts or all of Bavaria 1181–1918; Napoleon made the ruler a king 1806. In 1871 Bavaria became a state of the German Empire.

Bawa /bauə/ Geoffrey 1919– . Sri Lankan architect, formerly a barrister. His buildings are a contemporary interpretation of vernacular traditions, and include houses, hotels, and gardens. More recently he has designed public buildings such as the New Parliamentary Complex, Kotte, Colombo, Sri Lanka (1982), and Ruhuru University, Matara, Sri Lanka (1984).

Bax /bæks/ Arnold Edward Trevor 1883–1953. English composer. His works were often based on Celtic legends and include seven symphonies, *The Garden of Fand* (a symphonic poem), and *Tintagel* (an orchestral tone poem). He was Master of the King's Musick 1942–53.

Baxter /ˈbækstə/ George 1804–1867. English engraver and printmaker; inventor in 1834 of a special process for printing in oil colours, which he applied successfully in book illustrations.

Baxter /ˈbækstə/ Richard 1615–1691. English cleric. During the Civil War he was a chaplain in the Parliamentary army, and after the Restoration he became a royal chaplain. In 1662 the Act of Uniformity drove him out of the church. In 1685 he was imprisoned for nearly 18 months for alleged sedition.

bay name given to various species of laurel *Laurus* and some other plants. Its aromatic evergreen leaves are used for flavouring in cookery, and there is also a golden-leaved variety.

The victor's laurel awarded in Classical Greece and Rome was the sweet bay *Laurus nobilis*, a native of S Europe.

Bayard /ˈbeɪɑːd/ Pierre du Terrail (Chevalier) 1473–1524. French soldier. He served under Charles VIII, Louis XII, and Francis I, and was killed in action at the crossing of the Sesia in Italy. His heroic exploits in battle and in tournaments, his chivalry and magnanimity won him the name of 'knight without fear and without reproach'.

Bay City /ˈbeɪ ˈsɪti/ industrial city in Michigan, USA; population (1980) 41,600. Industries include shipbuilding and engineering.

Bayern /ˈbaɪən/ German name for ◊Bavaria, region of West Germany.

Bayes /beɪz/ Thomas 1702–1761. English mathematician, whose invetigations into probability led to what is now known as Bayes' theorem.

Bayesian statistics a form of statistics that uses the knowledge of prior probability together with the probability of actual data to determine posterior probabilities, using Bayes' theorem.

Bayes' theorem in statistics, a theorem relating the ◊probability of particular events taking place to the probability that events conditional upon them have occurred.

For example, the probability of picking an ace at random out of a pack of cards is $4/52$. If two cards are picked out, the probability of the second card being an ace is conditional on the first card: if the first card was an ace the probability will be $3/51$, if not it will be $4/51$. Bayes' theorem gives the probability that given that the second card is an ace, the first card is also.

Bayeux /baɪˈɜː/ town in N France; population (1982) 15,200. Its museum houses the Bayeux Tapestry. There is a 13th-century Gothic cathedral. Bayeux was the first town in W Europe to be liberated by the Allies in World War II, 8 June 1944.

Bayeux Tapestry a linen hanging 70 m/231 ft long and 50 cm/20 in wide, made about 1067–70, which gives a vivid pictorial record of the invasion of England by ◊William I (the Conqueror) 1066. It is an embroidery rather than a true tapestry, sewn with woollen threads in blue, green, red, and yellow, containing 72 separate scenes with descriptive wording in Latin. It is exhibited at the museum of Bayeux in Normandy, France.

Bayle /beɪl/ Pierre 1647–1706. French critic and philosopher, who was suspended for his views of ◊rationalism in 1693. Three years later his *Dictionnaire historique et critique* appeared, which had a wide influence, particularly on the French Encyclopedists.

Bayliss /ˈbeɪlɪs/ William Maddock 1860–1924. English physiologist, who discovered the hormone secretin with E H ◊Starling in 1902. Secretin plays an important part in digestion. During World War I, he introduced the use of saline (salt water) injections to help the injured recover from ◊shock.

Bay of Pigs inlet on the S coast of Cuba about 145 km/90 mi SW of Havana, the site of an unsuccessful invasion attempt by 1,500 US-sponsored Cuban exiles 17–20 Apr 1961; 1,173 were taken prisoner.

The creation of this anti-revolutionary force by the CIA had been authorized by the Eisenhower administration and the project was executed under that of J F Kennedy. In 1962 most of the Cuban prisoners were ransomed for $53 million in food and medicine.

bayonet a short sword attached to the muzzle of a firearm. The bayonet was placed inside the barrel of the muzzle-loading muskets of the late 17th century. The *sock* or ring bayonet, invented 1700, allowed a weapon to be fired without interruption, leading to the demise of the pike.

Since the 1700s, bayonets have evolved into a variety of types. During World War I, the French used a long needle bayonet, while the Germans attached a bayonet, known as the butcher's knife, to their Mauser 98s. As armies have become more mechanized, bayonets have tended to decrease in length.

Although many military leaders have advocated the use of the bayonet, in practice it has been rarely used. For example, at Inkerman during the Crimean War 1854, only 6% of casualties were attributed to the bayonet. However, the morale effects associated with the fixing of bayonets has generally been considered to outweigh their disadvantages, which include restriction of movement and lack of real utility.

The new British Army rifle, the SA-80, is fitted with a bayonetard; its predecessor, the SLR, was similarly equipped and used, though rarely, during the 1982 Falklands conflict.

Bayonne /baɪˈɒn/ river port in SW France; population (1983) 127,000. It trades in timber, steel, fertilizer, and brandy. It is a centre of ◊Basque life. The bayonet was invented here.

bayou (corruption of French *boyau* 'gut') in the Gulf States, USA, an ◊oxbow lake or marshy offshoot of a river. Bayous may be formed, as in the lower Mississippi, by a river flowing in wide curves or meanders in flat country, and then cutting a straight course across them in times of flood, leaving loops of isolated water behind.

Bay Psalm Book, the Puritan translation of the

psalms into metre, printed in 1639 and considered the first work of American literature.

Bayreuth /baɪˈrɔɪt/ town in Bavaria, West Germany; population (1983) 71,000. It was the home of composer Richard ◊Wagner. The Wagner theatre was established 1876, and opera festivals are held every summer.

Bazaine /bæˈzeɪn/ Achille François 1811–1888. Marshal of France. From being a private soldier in 1831 he rose to command the French troops in Mexico 1862–67, and was made a marshal in 1864. In the Franco-Prussian War Bazaine commanded the Third Corps of the Army of the Rhine, allowed himself to be taken in the fortress of Metz, and surrendered on 27 Oct 1870 with nearly 180,000 men. For this he was court-martialled 1873 and imprisoned, but in 1874 escaped to Spain.

Bazalgette /ˈbæzldʒet/ Joseph 1819–1890. British civil engineer who, as Chief Engineer to the London Board of Works, designed London's sewer system, a total of 155 km/83 mi of sewers, covering an area of 256 sq km/100 sq mi. It was completed 1865. He also designed the Victoria Embankment 1864–70, which was built over the river Thames and combined a main sewer, a water frontage, an underground railway, and a road.

BBC abbreviation for ◊*British Broadcasting Corporation*.

BBC English see ◊English language.

BC abbreviation for *before Christ*.

B cell or B ◊lymphocyte a type of immune cell that is responsible for producing ◊antibodies. Each B cell produces just one type of antibody, specific for a single ◊antigen.

BCG abbreviation for *bacillus of ◊Calmette and Guérin*, used as a vaccine to confer active immunity to ◊tuberculosis (TB). It was developed in France after World War I from live bovine TB bacilli. These bacteria were bred in the laboratory over many generations until they became attenuated (weakened). Each inoculation contains enough live, attenuated bacilli to provoke an immune response: the formation of specific ◊antibodies. The recipient then has lifelong protection against TB.

beach strip of land bordering the sea, normally consisting of boulders and pebbles on exposed coasts or sand on sheltered coasts. It is usually defined by the high- and low-water marks.

The material of the beach consists of a rocky debris eroded from exposed rocks and headlands. The material is transported to the beach, and along the beach, by waves that hit the coastline at an angle, resulting in a net movement of the material in one particular direction. This movement is known as *longshore drift*. Attempts are often made to halt longshore drift by erecting barriers, or jetties, at right angles to the movement. Pebbles are worn into round shapes by being battered against one another by wave action and the result is called shingle. The finer material, the sand, may be subsequently moved about by the wind and form sand dunes. Apart from the natural process of longshore drift, a beach may be threatened by the commercial use of sand and aggregate, by the mineral industry – since particles of metal ore are often concentrated into workable deposits by the wave action—and by pollution.

Concern for the conditions of bathing beaches led in the 1980s to a directive from the European Economic Community on water quality. In Britain, beaches free of industrial pollution, litter, and sewage, and with water of the highest quality, have the right (since 1988) to fly a blue flag.

Beach Boys, the US pop group formed 1961. They began as exponents of vocal-harmony surf music with Chuck Berry guitar riffs (hits included 'Surfin' USA' 1963, 'Help Me, Rhonda' 1965) but the compositions, arrangements, and production by Brian Wilson (1942–) became highly complex under the influence of psychedelic rock, peaking with 'Good Vibrations' 1966.

Beachy Head /ˈbiːtʃi/ (French *Béveziers*) the loftiest headland 162 m/532 ft on the S coast of England, between Seaford and Eastbourne in Sussex, the E termination of the South Downs. The lighthouse off the shore is 38 m/125 ft high.

Beaconsfield /ˈbekənzfiːld/ town in Buckinghamshire, England; 37 km/23 mi WNW of London; population (1981) 10,900. It has associations with Benjamin Disraeli (whose title was Earl of Beaconsfield), political theorist Edmund Burke, and the poet Edmund Waller.

Beaconsfield /ˈbikənzfiːld/ title taken by Benjamin ◊Disraeli, prime minister of Britain 1868 and 1874–80.

Beadle /ˈbiːdl/ George Wells 1903–1989. US biologist. Born in Wahoo, Nebraska, he was professor of biology at the California Institute of Technology 1946–61, and in 1958 shared a Nobel prize with Edward L Tatum for his work in biochemical genetics.

beagle short-haired hound with pendant ears, sickle tail, and bell-like voice for hunting hares on foot ('beagling').

Beagle Channel /ˈbiːgl/ channel to the south of Tierra del Fuego, South America, named after the ship of ◊Darwin's voyage. Three islands at its E end, with krill and oil reserves within their 322 km/200 mi territorial waters, and the dependent sector of the Antarctic with its resources, were disputed between Argentina and Chile, and were awarded to Chile 1985.

beak the horn-covered projecting jaws of a bird, or other horny jaws such as those of the tortoise or octopus. The beaks of birds are adapted by shape and size to specific diets.

Beaker people people thought to be of Iberian origin who spread out over Europe in the 2nd millennium BC, and who began Stonehenge in England. They were skilled in metal-working, and their remains include earthenware beakers, hence the name.

Beale /biːl/ Dorothea 1831–1906. British pioneer in women's education, who was influential in raising the standard of women's education and the status of women teachers. She was headmistress of the Ladies' College at Cheltenham from 1858, and founder of St Hilda's Hall, Oxford, 1892.

beam weapon a weapon capable of destroying a target by means of a high-energy beam. Beam weapons similar to the 'death ray' of science fiction have been explored, particularly during Ronald Reagan's presidential term in the USA.

The *high-energy laser* (HEL) produces a beam of high accuracy that burns through the surface of its target. The USSR is thought to have an HEL able to put orbiting spacecraft out of action. The *charged particle beam* (CPB) uses either electrons or protons, which have been accelerated almost to the speed of light, to slice through its target.

bean any seed of numerous leguminous plants. Beans are rich in nitrogenous or protein matter and are grown both for human consumption and as food for cattle and horses. Varieties of bean are grown throughout Europe, the USA, South America, China, Japan, and SE Asia.

The broad bean *Vicia faba* has been cultivated in Europe since prehistoric times. The French bean, kidney bean, or haricot *Phaseolus vulgaris* is probably of South American origin; the runner bean *Phaseolus coccineus* is closely allied to it, but differs in its climbing habit. Among beans of warmer countries are the Lima or butter bean *Phaseolus lunatus* of South America; the soya *Glycine max*, much used in China and Japan, and the wing bean *Psophocarpus tetragonolobus* of SE Asia. The tuberous roots of the latter have potential as a main crop in tropical areas where protein deficiency is common. The Asiatic mung bean *Phaseolus mungo* forms the bean sprouts of China. Canned baked beans are a variety of *Phaseolus vulgaris*, which grows well in the USA.

bear large mammal with a heavily built body, short

bear

powerful limbs, and very short tail. Bears breed once a year, producing one to four cubs. In northern regions they hibernate, and the young are born in the winter den. They are found mainly in North America and N Asia. The skin of the polar bear is black to conserve 80–90% of the solar energy trapped and channelled down the hollow hairs of its fur.

Bears walk on the soles of the feet and have long, non-retractable claws. There are seven species of bear, including the *brown bear Ursus arctos*, formerly ranging across most of Europe, N Asia, and North America, but now reduced in number. It varies in size from under 2 m/7 ft long in parts of the Old World to 2.8 m/9 ft long and 780 kg/1,700 lb in Alaska. The grizzly bear is a North American variety of this species. The white *polar bear Thalarctos maritimus* is up to 2.5 m/8 ft long, has furry undersides to the feet, and feeds mainly on seals. It is found in the North polar region. The North American *black bear Euarctos americanus* and the *Asiatic black bear Selenarctos thibetanus* are smaller, only about 1.6 m/5 ft long. The latter has a white V-mark on its chest. The *spectacled bear Tremarctos ornatus* of the Andes is similarly sized, as is the *sloth bear Melursus ursinus* of India and Sri Lanka, which has a shaggy coat and uses its claws and protrusible lips to obtain termites, one of its favourite foods. The smallest bear is the Malaysian *sun bear Helarctos malayanus*, rarely more than 1.2 m/4 ft long, a good climber, whose favourite food is honey. The bear family, Ursidae, is related to carnivores such as dogs and weasels, and all are capable of killing prey. The panda is probably related to both bears and raccoons.

bear a speculator who sells stocks or shares on the stock exchange expecting a fall in the price in order to buy them back at a profit, the opposite of a ◊bull. In a bear market, prices fall and bears prosper.

bearbaiting baiting by dogs of a chained bear. Popular in Britain and Europe in the 16th century, it was outlawed in Britain 1835. The Master of Bears was a one-time Crown appointment.

bearberry evergreen prostrate-growing shrub, genus *Arctostaphylos*, of the heather family found on moorland and rocky places. Most bearberries are American but *Arctostaphylos uva-ursi* is also found in Asia and Europe in northern mountainous regions. It bears small pink flowers in spring, followed by red berries that are edible but dry.

Beardsley /ˈbɪədzli/ Aubrey (Vincent) 1872–1898. British illustrator, whose meticulously executed black-and-white work displays the sinuous line and decorative mannerisms of Art Nouveau and was often charged with being grotesque and decadent. He became known through the *Yellow Book* magazine and his drawings for Oscar Wilde's *Salome* 1893.

Bear, Great and Little common names of the constellations ◊Ursa Major and ◊Ursa Minor.

bearing a device used in a machine to allow free movement between two parts, typically the rotation of a shaft in a housing. The sleeve or journal bearing is used for the big-end and main bearings on a car ◊crankshaft. Ball-bearings are widely used to support shafts, as in the spindle in the hub of a bicycle wheel.

Beardsley Isolde *by Aubrey Beardsley (private collection).*

bearing

roller bearing

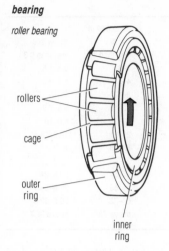

rollers

cage

outer ring

inner ring

journal bearing

journal

ball bearing

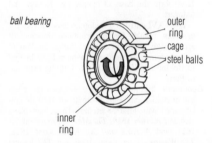

outer ring

cage

steel balls

inner ring

Beatles, the *(Left to right) John Lennon, Ringo Starr, George Harrison, and Paul McCartney in 1963, at the start of their career.*

The **sleeve** or **journal bearing** is the simplest bearing. It is a hollow cylinder, split into two halves. **Ball-bearings** consist of two rings, one fixed to a housing, one to the rotating shaft. Between them is a set, or race, of steel balls. In other machinery the balls are replaced by cylindrical rollers or thinner, **needle bearings**. In precision equipment such as watches and aircraft instruments, bearings may be made from material such as ruby. They are known as **jewel bearings**. For some applications bearings made from nylon and other plastics are used. They need no lubrication because their surface is naturally waxy.

bearing angle that a fixed, distant point makes with true or magnetic north at the point of observation, or the angle of the path of a moving object with respect to the north lines. Bearings are measured in degrees and given as three-digit numbers increasing clockwise. For instance, NW would be denoted as 045M or 045T, depending whether the reference line were magnetic (M) or true (T) north.

Beas /'biːəs/ river in Himachal Pradesh, India, an upper tributary of the Sutlej, which in turn joins the Indus. It is one of the five rivers that give the Punjab its name. The ancient Hyphasis, it marked the limit of the invasion of India by Alexander the Great.

Beat Generation the beatniks of the 1950s and 1960s, characterized by dropping out of conventional life styles and opting for life on the road, drugs, and anti-materialist values; and the associated literary movement whose members included William S Burroughs, Allen Ginsberg, and Jack Kerouac (who is credited with coining the term).

beatification in the Catholic church, the first step towards ◊canonization. Persons who have been beatified can be prayed to, and the title 'Blessed' can be put before their names.

Beatitudes in the New Testament, the sayings of Jesus reported in Matthew 6: 1–12 and Luke 6: 20–38, depicting the spiritual qualities that characterize members of the Kingdom of God.

Beatles, the /'biːtlz/ English pop group 1960–70. The members, all born in Liverpool, were John Lennon (1940–80, rhythm guitar, vocals), Paul McCartney (1942– , bass, vocals), George Harrison (1943– , lead guitar, vocals), and Ringo Starr (formerly Richard Starkey, 1940– , drums). Using songs written by Lennon and

McCartney, they brought the Mersey beat to prominence with worldwide hits including 'She Loves You' 1963, 'I Want To Hold Your Hand' 1963, and 'Can't Buy Me Love' 1964.

The Beatles gained early experience in Liverpool and Hamburg, West Germany. They had a top-30 hit with their first record, 'Love Me Do', 1962, and every subsequent single and album released until 1967 reached number one in the UK charts. At the peak of Beatlemania they starred in two films, *A Hard Day's Night* 1964 and *Help!* 1965. Their song 'Yesterday' 1965 was covered by 1,186 different performers in the first ten years. The album *Sgt Pepper's Lonely Hearts Club Band* 1967, recorded on two four-track machines, anticipated subsequent technological developments.

The Beatles were the first UK group to challenge the US dominance of rock and roll, and remained influential until their break-up 1971. They subsequently pursued separate careers as performers with varying success. **John Lennon** collaborated intermittently with his wife Yoko Ono (1933–) from 1968 and his solo work includes *Imagine* 1971; he was shot dead 1980. **Paul McCartney** formed the group Wings 1971–80 and also recorded solo.

beat music style of pop music that evolved in the UK in the early 1960s, known in its purest form as ◊Mersey beat, and as British Invasion in the USA. The beat groups characteristically had a simple, guitar-dominated line-up, vocal harmonies, and catchy tunes. They included the Beatles (1960–70), the Hollies (1962–), and the Zombies (1962–67).

Beaton /'biːtn/ Cecil 1904–1980. English portrait and fashion photographer, designer, illustrator, diarist, and conversationalist. He produced portrait studies and also designed scenery and costumes for ballets, and sets for plays and films.

Beaton /'biːtn/ David 1494–1546. Scottish nationalist cardinal and politician, adviser to James V. Under Mary, Queen of Scots, he was opposed to the alliance with England and persecuted reformers such as George Wishart, who was condemned to the stake; he was killed by Wishart's friends.

Beatrix /'bɪətrɪks/ 1936– . Queen of the Netherlands. The eldest daughter of Queen ◊Juliana, she succeeded to the throne on her mother's abdication 1980. In 1966, she married W German diplomat Claus von Amsberg (1926–), who was created Prince of the Netherlands. Her heir is Prince Willem Alexander (1967–).

beats regular variations in the loudness of the sound when two notes of nearly equal pitch or ◊frequency are heard together. The beats result from the ◊interference between the sound waves of the notes. The frequency of the beats equals the difference in frequency of the notes.

Musicians use the effect when tuning their instruments. A similar effect can occur in electrical circuits when two alternating currents are present, producing regular variations in the overall current.

Beaton *British photographer and designer Cecil Beaton in 1951.*

Beaufort scale

Number and description	Features	Air speed mi per hr	m per sec
0 calm	smoke rises vertically; water smooth	less than 1	less than 0.3
1 light air	smoke shows wind direction; water ruffled	1–3	0.3–1.5
2 slight breeze	leaves rustle; wind felt on face	4–7	1.6–3.3
3 gentle breeze	loose paper blows around	8–12	3.4–5.4
4 moderate	branches sway	13–18	5.5–7.9
5 fresh breeze	small trees sway, leaves blown off	19–24	8.0–10.7
6 strong breeze	whistling in telephone wires; sea spray	25–31	10.8–13.8
7 moderate gale	large trees sway	32–38	13.9–17.1
8 fresh gale	twigs break from trees	39–46	17.2–20.7
9 strong gale	branches break from trees	47–54	20.8–24.4
10 whole gale	trees uprooted, weak buildings collapse	55–63	24.5–28.4
11 storm	widespread damage	64–72	28.5–32.6
12 hurricane	widespread structural damage	above 73	above 32.7

Beatty /'bi:ti/ David, 1st Earl Beatty 1871–1936. British admiral in World War I. He commanded the cruiser squadron 1912–16 and bore the brunt of the Battle of Jutland. In 1916 he became commander of the fleet, and in 1918 received the surrender of the German fleet.

Beatty /'beiti/ Warren. Stage name of Warren Beaty 1937– . US film actor and director, popular for such films as *Bonnie and Clyde* 1967 and *Heaven Can Wait* 1978. His more recent productions include *Reds* 1981 and *Ishtar* 1987.

Beauclerk family name of the Dukes of St Albans; descended from King Charles II by his mistress Eleanor Gwyn.

Beaufort /'bəufət/ Francis 1774–1857. British admiral, hydrographer to the Royal Navy from 1829; the Beaufort scale and the Beaufort Sea in the Arctic Ocean are named after him.

Beaufort /'bəufət/ Henry 1375–1447. English priest, bishop of Lincoln from 1398, Winchester from 1405. As chancellor of England, he supported his half-brother Henry IV, and made enormous personal loans to Henry V to finance war against France. As a guardian of Henry VI from 1421, he was in effective control of the country until 1426. In the same year he was created a cardinal. In 1431 he crowned Henry VI as king of France in Paris.

Beaufort scale system of recording wind velocity, devised in 1806 by Francis Beaufort. It is a numerical scale ranging from 0 to 17, calm being indicated by 0 and a hurricane by 12; 13–17 indicate degrees of hurricane force. In 1874, the scale received international recognition; it was modified in 1926. Measurements are made at 10 m/33 ft above ground level.

Beaufort Sea /'bəufət/ section of the Arctic Ocean off Alaska and Canada, named after Francis Beaufort. Oil drilling is allowed only in the winter months because the sea is the breeding and migration route of bowhead whales, the staple diet of local Inuit.

Beauharnais /,bəua:'nei/ Alexandre, Vicomte de Beauharnais 1760–1794. French liberal aristocrat. He served in the American War of Independence, and became a member of the National Convention in the early days of the French Revolution. He was the first husband of Josephine, consort of Napoleon I. Their daughter Hortense (1783–1837) married Louis, a younger brother of Napoleon, and their son became ◊Napoleon III. Beauharnais was guillotined during the Terror.

Beaujolais /'bəuʒəlei/ red wine produced in the area S of Burgundy in E France. Beaujolais is best drunk while young; the broaching date is the third Thursday in Nov, when the new vintage is taken to London in the Beaujolais *nouveau* (new Beaujolais) race.

Beaulieu /'bju:li/ village in Hampshire, England, 9 km/6 mi SW of Southampton; population (1985) 1,200. The former abbey is the home of Lord Montagu of Beaulieu and has the Montagu Museum of vintage cars.

Beauly Firth /'bju:li/ arm of the North Sea cutting into Scotland N of Inverness, spanned by Kessock Bridge 1982.

Beaumarchais /,bəuma:'ʃei/ Pierre Augustin Caron de 1732–1799. French dramatist. His great comedies *Le Barbier de Seville/The Barber of Seville* 1775 and *Le Mariage de Figaro/The Marriage of Figaro* (1778, but prohibited until 1784) form the basis of operas by ◊Rossini and ◊Mozart.

Louis XVI entrusted Beaumarchais with secret missions, notably for the profitable shipment of arms to the American colonies during the War of Independence. Accused of treason in 1792, he fled to Holland and England, but in 1799 he returned to Paris.

Beaumont /'bəumont/ Francis 1584–1616. English dramatist and poet. From about 1608 he collaborated with John ◊Fletcher. Their joint plays include *Philaster* 1610, *The Maid's Tragedy* about 1611, and *A King and No King* about 1611. *The Woman Hater* about 1606 and *The Knight of the Burning Pestle* about 1607 are ascribed to Beaumont alone.

Beaumont /'bəumont/ William 1785–1853. US surgeon who conducted pioneering experiments on the digestive system. In 1882 he saved the life of a Canadian trapper wounded in the side by a gun blast; the wound only partially healed and through an opening in the stomach wall, Beaumont was able to observe the workings of the stomach. His *Experiments and Observations on the Gastric Juice and the Physiology of Digestion* was published in 1833.

Beaune /bəun/ town SW of Dijon, France; population (1982) 21,100. It is the centre of the Burgundian wine trade, and has a wine museum. Other products include agricultural equipment and mustard.

Beauregard /,bəurə'ga:/ Pierre 1818–1893. US Confederate general whose opening fire on ◊Fort Sumter, South Carolina, started the American Civil War 1861.

Beauvais /bəu'vei/ town 76 km/47 mi NW of Paris, France; population (1982) 54,150. It is a market town trading in fruit, dairy produce, and agricultural machinery. It has a Gothic cathedral, the tallest in France: 68 m/223 ft, and is famous for tapestries (◊Gobelin), now made in Paris.

Beauvoir /bəu'vwa:/ Simone de 1908–1986. French socialist, feminist, and writer, who taught philosophy at the Sorbonne university in Paris 1931–43. Her book *Le Deuxième sexe/The Second Sex* 1949 is a classic text that became a seminal work for many feminists. Her novel of postwar Paris, *Les Mandarins/The Mandarins* 1954, has characters resembling the writers Camus, Koestler, and ◊Sartre. She also published autobiographical volumes.

beaver aquatic rodent *Castor fiber* with webbed hind feet, broad flat scaly tail, and thick waterproof fur. It has very large incisor teeth and fells trees to feed on the bark and to use the logs to construct the 'lodge', in which the young are reared, food is stored, and where much of the winter is spent.

Beavers can construct dams on streams, and thus modify the environment considerably. They once ranged across Europe, N Asia, and North America, but in Europe now only survive where they are protected, and are reduced elsewhere, partly through trapping for the fur.

Beaverbrook /'bi:vəbruk/ William Maxwell Aitken, 1st Baron Beaverbrook 1879–1964. British newspaper proprietor and politician, born in Canada. Between World War I and II he used his newspapers, especially the *Daily Express*, to campaign for Empire free trade and against Prime Minister Baldwin.

Bebel /'beibəl/ August 1840–1913. German socialist and founding member of the *Verband deutsche Arbeitervereine* (League of Workers' Clubs), together with Wilhelm Liebknecht. Also known as the Eisenach Party, it was based in Saxony and SW Germany before being incorporated into the SPD (*Sozialdemokratische Partei Deutschlands*) 1875.

Bebington /'bebiŋtən/ town on Merseyside, England; population (1981) 64,150. Industries include oil and chemicals. There is a model housing estate originally built 1888 for Unilever workers, Port Sunlight.

bebop or *bop* a rhythmically complex, highly improvisational, 'hot' jazz style which was developed in the USA in the 1940s by Charlie Parker, Dizzy Gillespie, Thelonius Monk, and other musicians.

Beaumarchais French comic dramatist Pierre Augustin Caron de Beaumarchais. He was forced to flee France during the Revolution.

Beauvoir Simone de Beauvoir, the distinguished French literary figure and philosopher of the feminist movement.

Becket *Thomas à Becket unexpectedly turned to oppose King Henry II when he was made archbishop of Canterbury. In this scene from a French manuscript published about 70 years after his murder, Thomas excommunicates his enemies and argues with Henry and Louis VII of France.*

Beccaria /ˌbekəˈriːə/ Cesare, Marese di Beccaria 1738–1794. Italian philanthropist, born in Milan. He opposed capital punishment and torture; advocated education as a crime preventative; influenced ◊Bentham; and coined the phrase 'the greatest happiness of the greatest number', the tenet of ◊utilitarianism.

Bechet /ˈbeʃeɪ/ Sidney (Joseph) 1897–1959. US jazz musician, born in New Orleans. He played clarinet and was the first to forge an individual style on soprano saxophone. He was based in Paris in the late 1920s and the 1950s.

Bechuanaland /ˌbetʃuˈɑːnələænd/ former name until 1966 of ◊Botswana.

Becker /ˈbekə/ Boris 1967– . West German lawn-tennis player. In 1985 he became the youngest winner of a singles title at Wimbledon at the age of 17. He has won the title three times and helped West Germany to win the Davis Cup 1988.

Becker /ˈbekə/ Lydia 1827–1890. English botanist and campaigner for women's rights. In 1865 she established the Manchester Ladies Literary Society as a forum for women to study scientific subjects. In 1867 she co-founded and became secretary of the National Society for Women's Suffrage. In 1870 she founded a monthly newsletter, *The Women's Suffrage Journal*.

Becket /ˈbekɪt/ St Thomas à 1118–1170. English priest and politician. A friend of ◊Henry II, Becket was his chancellor from 1155, but on becoming archbishop of Canterbury 1162 transferred his allegiance to the church. In 1164 he opposed Henry's attempt to regulate the relations between church and state, and had to flee the country; he returned in 1170, but the reconciliation soon broke down. Encouraged by a hasty outburst of the king's, four knights murdered Becket before the altar of Canterbury cathedral. He was declared a saint in 1172, and his shrine became the busiest centre of pilgrimage in England until the Reformation.

Beckett /ˈbekɪt/ Samuel 1906–1989. Irish novelist and dramatist, who wrote in French and English. *En attendant Godot/Waiting for Godot* 1952 is possibly the best-known example of Theatre of the ◊Absurd. This genre is taken to further extremes in *Fin de Partie/Endgame* 1957 and *Happy Days* 1961. Nobel Prize for Literature 1969.

Beckford /ˈbekfəd/ William 1760–1844. British author and eccentric. Forced out of England by scandals about his private life, he published *Vathek* 1787 in Paris, a fantastic Arabian Nights tale, and on returning to England in 1796 rebuilt his home, Fonthill Abbey in Wiltshire, as a Gothic fantasy.

Beckmann /ˈbekmən/ Max 1884–1950. German Expressionist painter, who fled the Nazi regime in 1933 for the USA. After World War I his art was devoted to themes of cruelty in human society, portraying sadists and their victims with a harsh style of realism.

Beckmann was born in Leipzig. He fought in World War I, and was discharged following a breakdown, reflected in the agony of his work; pictures include *Carnival* and *The Titanic*. He

bee

later painted huge triptychs, full of symbolic detail. He died in New York.

becquerel SI unit (symbol Bq) of ◊radioactivity, equal to one radioactive disintegration (change in the nucleus of an atom when a particle or ray is given off) per second. The becquerel is much smaller than the previous standard unit, the ◊curie, and so can be used for measuring smaller quantities of radioactivity. It is named after Antoine Becquerel.

Becquerel /ˌbekəˈrel/ Antoine Henri 1852–1908. French physicist, who discovered penetrating, invisible radiation coming from uranium salts, the first indication of ◊radioactivity, and shared a Nobel prize with the ◊Curies in 1903.

bed in geology, a single ◊sedimentary rock unit with a distinct set of physical characteristics or contained fossils, readily distinguishable from those of beds above and below. Well-defined partings called ***bedding planes*** separate successive beds or strata.

The depth of a bed can vary from a fraction of a centimetre to several metres or feet, and can extend over any area. The term is also used to indicate the floor beneath a body of water (lake bed) and a layer formed by a fall of particles (lava bed).

bedbug flattened wingless red-brown insect *Cimex lectularius* with piercing mouthparts. It hides by day in crevices or bedclothes and emerges at night to suck human blood.

Beddoes /ˈbedəʊz/ Thomas Lovell 1803–1849.

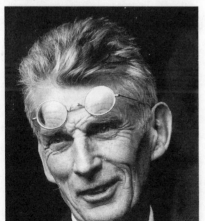

Beckett *Irish novelist and dramatist Samuel Beckett, winner of the Nobel Prize for Literature in 1969.*

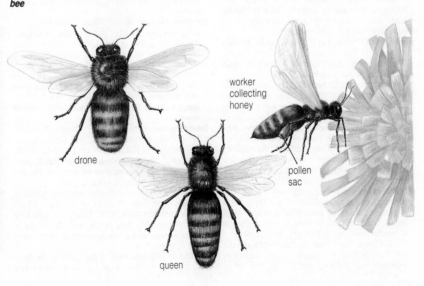

drone

worker collecting honey

pollen sac

queen

bee *The head of a honey worker bee.*

British poet and dramatist. His play *Death's Jest Book* was begun in 1825, but it was not published until 1850, much revised.

Bede /biːd/ *c.* 673–735. English theologian and historian, known as **the Venerable Bede**, active in Durham and Northumbria. He wrote many scientific, theological, and historical works. His *Historia Ecclesiastica Gentis Anglorum/Ecclesiastical History of the English People* 731 is an important source for early English history.

Born at Monkwearmouth, Durham, he entered the local monastery at the age of seven, later transferring to Jarrow, where he became a priest in about 703. He devoted his life to writing and teaching; among his pupils was Egbert, archbishop of York.

Bedford /ˈbedfəd/ town in Bedfordshire, England; population (1983) 89,200. Industries include agricultural machinery and airships. It is the administrative headquarters of Bedfordshire. John Bunyan wrote *The Pilgrim's Progress* 1678 while imprisoned here.

Bedfordshire /ˈbedfədʃə/ county in central S England
area 1,240 sq km/479 sq mi
towns administrative headquarters Bedford; Luton, Dunstable
features Whipsnade Zoo 1931, near Dunstable, a zoological park belonging to the London Zoological Society (2 sq km/500 acres); Woburn Abbey, seat of the duke of Bedford
products cereals, vegetables, agricultural machinery, electrical goods
population (1987) 526,000
famous people John Bunyan.

Bedlam /ˈbedləm/ abbreviation of **Bethlehem**, the earliest mental hospital in Europe. The hospital was opened in the 14th century in London and is now in Surrey.

Bedlington breed of ◊terrier with short body, long legs, and curly hair, usually grey, named after a district of Northumberland, England.

Bedouin (Arabic 'desert-dweller') member of a nomadic people of Arabia and N Africa, now becoming increasingly settled. Their traditional trade was the rearing of horses and camels.

Beds abbreviation for ◊*Bedfordshire*.

bee four-winged insect of the super-family Apoidea in the order Hymenoptera, usually with a sting. There are over 12,000 species, of which less than 1 in 20 are social in habit.

Most familiar is the **bumblebee** genus *Bombus*, which is larger and stronger than the hive bee and so is adapted to fertilize plants in which the pollen and nectar lie deep, as in red clover; it can work in colder weather than the hive bee. The **hive** or **honey bee** *Apis mellifera* establishes perennial colonies of about 80,000, the majority being infertile females (workers), with a few larger fertile males (drones), and a single very large fertile female (the queen).

Solitary bees include species useful in pollinating orchards in spring, and may make their nests in tunnels under the ground or in hollow plant stems; 'cuckoo' bees lay their eggs in the nests of bumblebees, which they closely resemble.

Social bees, apart from the bumblebee and the hive bee, include the stingless South American *vulture bee Trigona hypogea*, discovered in

beech

1982, which is solely carnivorous.

Bees transmit information to each other about food sources by a 'dance', each movement giving rise to sound impulses which are picked up by tiny hairs on the back of the bee's head, the orientation of the dance also having significance. They use the sun in navigation (see also under ◊migration). Besides their use in crop pollination and production of honey and wax, bees (by a measure of contaminants brought back to their hives) can provide an inexpensive and effective monitor of industrial and other pollution of the atmosphere and soil.

Most bees are pacific unless disturbed, but some South American species are aggressive. Bee stings may be fatal to people who are allergic to them, but this is comparatively rare. A vaccine treatment against bee stings, which uses concentrated venom, has been developed; see ◊melitin.

Beebe /ˈbiːbiː/ Charles 1877–1962. US naturalist, explorer, and writer. His interest in deep-sea exploration led to a collaboration with the engineer Otis Barton and the development of a spherical diving vessel, the bathysphere. On 24 August 1934 the two men made a record-breaking dive to 923 m/3028 ft. Beebe's expeditions are described in a series of memoirs.

beech genus of trees *Fagus*, of the family Fagaceae. The **common beech** *Fagus sylvaticus*, found in European forests, has a smooth grey trunk and edible nuts or 'mast' which are used as animal feed or processed for oil. The timber is used in furniture.

Beecham /ˈbiːtʃəm/ Thomas 1879–1961. British conductor and impresario. He established the Royal Philharmonic Orchestra in 1946 and fostered the works of composers such as Delius, Sibelius, and Stravinsky.

Beecher /ˈbiːtʃə/ Harriet unmarried name of Harriet Beecher ◊Stowe, author of *Uncle Tom's Cabin*.

Beecher /ˈbiːtʃə/ Henry Ward 1813–1887. US Congregational minister and opponent of slavery, son of the pulpit orator Lyman ◊Beecher and brother of the writer Harriet Beecher ◊Stowe.

Beecher /ˈbiːtʃə/ Lyman 1775–1863. US Presbyterian minister, the father of Harriet Beecher ◊Stowe and Henry Ward Beecher. As pastor from 1847 of Plymouth church, Brooklyn, New York, he was a leader in the movement for the abolition of slavery.

Beeching /ˈbiːtʃɪŋ/ Richard, Baron Beeching 1913–1985. British scientist and administrator. He was chair of British Railways Board 1963–65, producing the controversial **Beeching Report** 1963 planning concentration on intercity passenger traffic and a freight system.

bee-eater bird *Merops apiaster* found in Africa, S Europe, and Asia. It feeds on a variety of insects, including bees, which it catches in its long narrow bill. Chestnut, yellow, and blue-green, it is gregarious, and generally nests in river banks and sandpits.

Beelzebub (Hebrew 'lord of the flies') in the New Testament, the leader of the devils, sometimes

identified with Satan and sometimes with his chief assistant (see ◊devil). In the Old Testament Beelzebub was a god worshipped by the Philistines.

beer alcoholic drink made from malt (fermented barley or other grain), flavoured with hops. Beer contains between 1% and 6% alcohol. One of the oldest alcoholic drinks, it was brewed in ancient Egypt and Babylon.

The medieval distinction between beer (containing hops) and **ale** (without hops) has now fallen into disuse and in modern terminology beer is strictly a generic term including ale, stout, and lager. **Stout** is top fermented, but is sweet and strongly flavoured with roasted grain; **lager** is a light beer, bottom fermented and matured over a longer period (German *Lager* 'store').

Beerbohm /ˈbɪəbəʊm/ Max 1872–1956. British caricaturist and author, the half-brother of the actor and manager Herbert Beerbohm Tree (1853–1917). A perfectionist in style, he contributed to *The Yellow Book*; wrote the novel of Oxford undergraduate life *Zuleika Dobson* 1911; and published volumes of caricature, including *Rossetti and his Circle* 1922.

Beersheba /bɪəˈʃiːbə/ industrial town in Israel; population (1987) 115,000. It is the chief centre of the Negev desert, and has been a settlement from the Stone Age.

beet plant of the genus *Beta*, family Chenapodiaceae, which includes the **common beet** *Beta vulgaris*. One variety of *Beta vulgaris* is used to produce sugar, and another, the mangelwurzel, is grown as cattle fodder; the **beetroot** or **red beet** *Beta rubra* is a salad plant.

The family also includes the Asian **spinach** *Spinacia oleracea* of which the leaves are used as a vegetable; **spinach beet**, used as a spinach substitute, is *Beta vulgaris cicle*, commonly known as ◊goosefoot.

Beethoven /ˈbeɪthəʊvən/ Ludwig van 1770–1827. German composer and pianist, whose mastery of musical expression in every genre made him the dominant influence on 19th-century music. Beethoven's repertoire includes concert overtures; the opera *Fidelio*; five piano concertos and two for violin (one unfinished); 32 piano sonatas, including the *Moonlight Appassionata*; 17 string quartets; the *Mass in D (Missa solemnis)*; and nine symphonies as well many youthful works. He usually played his own piano pieces and conducted his orchestral works until he was hampered by deafness 1801; nevertheless he continued to compose.

Born in Bonn, the son and grandson of musicians, Beethoven became deputy organist at the court of the Elector of Cologne at Bonn before he was 12; later he studied under ◊Haydn and possibly ◊Mozart, whose influence dominated his early work. Beginning in 1809 he received a small allowance from aristocratic patrons.

beetle common name of insects in the order

Beeton, Mrs *Isabella Beeton, who became a byword for household management as 'Mrs Beeton'.*

Begin *Israeli politician Menachem Begin.*

Coleoptera (Greek 'sheath-winged') with leathery forewings folding down in a protective sheath over the membranous hindwings, which are those used for flight. They pass through a complete metamorphosis. They include some of the largest and smallest of all insects; the largest is the **Hercules beetle** *Dynastes hercules* of the South American rainforests, 15 cm/6 in long, the smallest only 0.05 cm/0.02 in. The largest order in the animal kingdom, beetles number some 370,000 named species, with many not yet described.

Beetles are found in virtually every land and freshwater habitat, and feed on virtually anything edible. Examples include: **click beetle** or **skipjack** species of the family Elateridae, so called because if they fall on their backs they right themselves with a jump and a loud click; the larvae, known as **wireworms**, feed on the roots of crops. In some tropical species of Elateridae the beetles have luminous organs between the head and abdomen and are known as **fireflies**. The potato pest *Colorado beetle Leptinotarsa decemlineata* is striped in black and yellow. The **blister beetle** *Lytta vesicatoria*, a shiny green species from S Europe, was once sold pulverized as an aphrodisiac and contains the toxin cantharidin. The **furniture beetle** *Anobium punctatum* and its relatives are serious pests of timber buildings and furniture through their 'woodworm' larvae.

Beeton, Mrs /'biːtn/ (Isabella Mary Mayson) 1836–1865. British writer on cookery and domestic management. Wife of a publisher, she produced *Beeton's Household Management* 1859, the first comprehensive work on domestic science.

begging soliciting, usually for money and food. It is prohibited in many Western countries, and stringent measures are taken against begging in the USSR. In the Middle East and Asia almsgiving is often considered a religious obligation.

Begging is illegal in Britain; legislation began in the 14th century, and it is an offence to solicit alms on the public highway, to expose any sore or malformation to attract alms, to cause a child to beg, or to send begging letters containing false statements. The 1824 Vagrancy Act was introduced to push destitute veterans of the Napoleonic wars of the streets of London. In the 1980s it became increasingly used against young homeless people. By 1990 there were at least 60 convictions a week under the act and lawyers had begun to campaign for its repeal.

Begin /'beigin/ Menachem 1913– . Israeli politician, born in Poland. He was a leader of the extremist Irgun Zvai Leumi organization in Palestine from 1942; prime minister of Israel 1977–83, as head of the right-wing Likud party; and in 1978 shared a Nobel Peace Prize with President Sadat of Egypt for work on the ◊Camp David Agreements for a Middle East peace settlement.

begonia plant of the genus *Begonia*, of the tropical and subtropical plant family Begoniaceae. Begonias have fleshy and succulent leaves, and some have large brilliant flowers. There are numerous species native to the tropics, in particular South America and India.

Behan /'biːən/ Brendan 1923–1964. Irish dramatist. His early experience of prison and knowledge of the workings of the ◊IRA (recounted in his autobiography *Borstal Boy* 1958) provided him with two recurrent themes in his plays. *The Quare Fellow* 1954 was followed by the tragicomedy *The Hostage* 1958, first written in Gaelic.

behaviourism school of psychology originating in the USA, of which the leading exponent was John Broadus ◊Watson. Behaviourists maintain that all human activity can ultimately be explained in terms of conditioned reactions or reflexes and habits formed in consequence. Leading behaviourists include ◊Pavlov.

behaviour therapy in psychology, the application of behavioural principles, derived from learning theories, to the treatment of clinical conditions such as ◊phobias, ◊obsessions, sexual and interpersonal problems. For example, in treating a phobia the person is taken into the situation that he or she is afraid of, in gradual steps. Over time, the fear typically reduces, and the problem becomes less acute.

behemoth (Hebrew 'beasts') in the Old Testament (Job 40), an animal cited by God as evidence of his power; usually thought to refer to the hippopotamus. It is used proverbially to mean any huge creature.

Behn /ben/ Aphra 1640–1689. English novelist and playwright, the first professional English writer. She was often criticized for her sexual explicitness, and tended to present her novels and plays from a woman's point of view. In 1688 her novel *Oronooko*, an attack on slavery, was published. Between 1670 and 1687 fifteen of her plays were produced including *The Rover*, which attacked forced and mercenary marriages. She had the patronage of James I and was employed as a government spy in Holland in 1666.

Behrens /'bɛərənz/ Peter 1868–1940. German architect. He pioneered the adaptation of architecture to industry, and designed the AEG turbine factory in Berlin 1909, a landmark in industrial design. He influenced ◊Le Corbusier and ◊Gropius.

Behring /'beəriŋ/ Emil von 1854–1917. German physician who discovered that the body produces antitoxins, substances able to counteract poisons released by bacteria. Using this knowledge, he developed new treatments for diseases such as ◊diptheria.

Educated in Berlin, Behring was Robert ◊Koch's assistant before becoming professor of hygiene at Halle and Marburg. He won the 1901 Nobel Prize for Medicine.

Beiderbecke /'baɪdəbek/ Bix (Leon Bismarck) 1903–1931. US jazz cornetist, composer, and pianist. A romantic soloist with Paul Whiteman's orchestra, he was inspired by the classical composers Debussy, Ravel, and Stravinsky.

Beijing /'beidʒiŋ/ or **Peking** capital of China; part of its NE border is formed by the Great Wall of China; population (1986) 5,860,000. The municipality of Beijing has an area of 17,800 sq km/6,871 sq mi, and a population (1986) of 9,750,000. Industries include textiles, petrochemicals, steel, and engineering. The Forbidden City, built 1406–20 as Gu Gong (Imperial Palace) of the Ming emperors, and the Summer Palace are here. Beijing, founded 3,000 years ago, was the 13th-century capital of the Mongol emperor Kublai Khan. Later replaced by Nanking, it was again capital from 1421, except 1928–49, when it was renamed Peiping.

Features include Tiananmen Gate (Gate of Heavenly Peace) and Tiananmen Square, where, in 1989, Chinese troops massacred over 1,000 students and civilians demonstrating for greater freedoms and democracy; the Forbidden City, where there were 9,000 ladies in waiting and 10,000 eunuchs in service (it is now the seat of the government); the Great Hall of the People 1959 (used for official banquets); museums of Chinese history and of the Chinese revolution; Chairman Mao Memorial Hall 1977 (shared from 1983 with Zhou Enlai, Zhu De, and Liu Shaoqi); the Summer Palace built by the dowager empress Zi Xi (damaged by the European powers 1900, but restored 1903); Temple of Heaven (Tiantan); and Ming tombs 50 km/30 mi to the NW. Beijing was held by Japan 1937–45.

Beira /'baɪrə/ port at the mouth of the river Pungwe, Mozambique; population (1986) 270,000. It is a major port, and exports minerals, cotton, and food products. A railway through the **Beira Corridor** links the port with Zimbabwe.

Beirut /ˌbeɪˈruːt/ or **Beyrouth** capital and port of Lebanon, devastated by civil war in the 1970s and 1980s and occupied by armies of neighbouring countries; population (1980) 702,000. The city is divided into a Christian eastern and a Muslim western sector by the Green Line.

history Until the civil war 1975–76, Beirut was an international financial and educational centre, with four universities (Lebanese, Arab, French, and US); it was also a centre of espionage. It was besieged and virtually destroyed by the Israeli army July–Sept 1982 to enforce the withdrawal of the forces of the Palestinian Liberation Organization. After the ceasefire, 500 Palestinians were massacred in the Sabra–Chatila camps 16–18 Sept 1982 by dissident ◊Phalangist and ◊Maronite troops, with alleged Israeli complicity. Civil disturbances continued, characterized by sporadic street fighting and hostage taking. In 1987 Syrian troops were sent in.

Bejaia /bɪˈdʒaɪə/ formerly **Bougie** port in Algeria, 193 km/120 mi E of Algiers; population (1982) 145,000. It is linked by pipeline with oil wells at Hassi Messaoud. It exports wood and hides.

Bekka, the /'beˈkɑː/ or **El Beqa'a** a governorate of E Lebanon separated from Syria by the Anti-Lebanon mountains. The Bekka Valley has been of strategic importance in the Syrian struggle for control of N Lebanon. In the early 1980s the valley was penetrated by Shia Muslims who established an extremist Hezbollah stronghold with the support of Iranian Revolutionary Guards. Zahlé and the ancient city of Baalbek are the chief towns.

bel unit of sound measurement equal to ten ◊decibels.

Belasco /bəˈlæskəʊ/ David 1859–1931. US playwright. His works include *Madame Butterfly* 1900 and *The Girl of the Golden West* 1905, both of which Puccini used as libretti for operas.

Belaúnde Terry /'belɑːˈʊndeɪ 'teri/ Fernando 1913– . President of Peru 1963–68 and 1980–85. He championed land reform and the construction of roads to open up the Amazon valley. He fled to the USA in 1968 after being deposed by a military junta. After his return, his second term in office was marked by rampant inflation, huge foreign debts, terrorism, mass killings, and human-rights violations by the armed forces.

Belau, Republic of /bəˈlaʊ/ formerly **Palau** self-governing island group in Micronesia; area 500 sq km/193 sq mi; population (1988) 14,000. It is part of the US Trust Territory, and became internally self-governing 1980.

There are 26 larger islands (8 inhabited) and about 300 islets. Three referendums have shown that Belau wishes to remain 'non-nuclear', although the USA is exerting strong pressure to secure nuclear facilities for itself.

Spain held the islands from about 1600, and sold them to Germany 1899. Japan seized them in World War I, administered them by League of Nations mandate, and used them as a naval base during World War II. They were captured by the USA 1944, and became part of their Trust Territory 1947.

bel canto /'bel 'kæntəʊ/ (Italian 'beautiful song') in music, an 18th-century Italian style of singing with emphasis on perfect technique and beautiful

tone. The style reached its peak in the operas of
Rossini, Donizetti, and Bellini.

Belém /bə'lem/ port and naval base in N Brazil;
population (1980) 758,000. The chief trade centre
of the Amazon Basin, it is also known as Pará, the
name of the state of which it is capital. It was
founded about 1615 as Santa Maria de Belém do
Grás Pará.

belemnite extinct relative of the squid, with rows of
little hooks rather than suckers on the arms. The
parts of belemnites most frequently found as fossils are the bullet-shaped shells that were within
the body. Like squid, these animals had an ink sac
which could be used to produce a smokescreen
when attacked.

Belfast /,bel'fɑ:st/ industrial port (shipbuilding,
engineering, electronics, textiles, tobacco) and
capital of Northern Ireland since 1920; population
(1985) 300,000. From 1968 it has been heavily
damaged by guerrilla activities.

history Belfast grew up around a castle built in
1177 by John de Courcy. With the settlement
of English and Scots, Belfast became a centre
of Irish Protestantism in the 17th century. An
influx of Huguenots after 1685 extended the
linen industry and the 1800 Act of Union with
England resulted with the promotion of Belfast
as an industrial centre. It was created a city in
1888, with a lord mayor from 1892. The former
parliament buildings are to the S at Stormont.

Belfort /bel'fɔ:/ town in NE France; population
(1983) 54,500. It is in the strategic **Belfort
Gap** between the Vosges and Jura mountains.
The capital of the *département* of Territoire de
Belfort, industries include chemicals, engineering,
plastics, and textiles.

Belgae a people who lived in Gaul in Roman times,
N of the Seine and Marne rivers. They were
defeated by Caesar in 57 BC. Many of the Belgae
settled in SE England during the 2nd century BC.

Belgic remains in Britain include coins, minted
in Gaul, pottery made on a wheel, and much of
the finest Iron Age Celtic art.

Belgaum /bel'gɔ:m/ city in Karnataka, S India;
population (1981) 300,000. The main industry is
cotton manufacture. It is also known for its Jain
temples.

Belgian Congo former name 1908–60 of ◊Zaïre.

Belgian literature writers in French have included
Georges Eekhoud (1854–1927), who wrote
of Flemish peasant life; Emile Verhaeren
(1855–1916); and Maurice Maeterlinck. For
writers in Flemish, see ◊Flemish literature.

Belgium /'beldʒəm/ country in N Europe,
bounded to the NW by the North Sea, to the
SW by France, to the E by Luxembourg and West
Germany, and to the NE by the Netherlands.

government the constitution dates from 1831 and
was most recently revised 1971. The prime minister and cabinet are drawn from and answerable
to the legislature, which exercises considerable
control over the executive. The legislature consists of a senate and a chamber of representatives. The senate has 182 members, 106 nationally elected, 50 representing the provinces, 25
co-opted and, by right, the heir to the throne.
It has a life of four years. The chamber of
representatives has 212 members elected by
universal suffrage, through a system of proportional representation, for a four-year term. On
the basis of parliamentary support, the monarch
appoints the prime minister, who chooses the
cabinet.

The multiplicity of political parties reflects the
linguistic and social divisions. The main parties
are the Dutch-speaking Social Christian Party
(CVP), the French-speaking Social Christian
Party (PSC), the Dutch-speaking Socialist Party
(SP), the French-speaking Socialist Party (PS),
the Dutch-speaking Liberal Party (PVV), the French-
speaking Liberal Party (PRL), and the Flemish
People's Party (VU).

history known from 15 BC as the Roman province of Belgica, the area was overrun by the

Belgium
Kingdom of
(French *Royaume de Belgique*,
Flemish *Koninkrijk België*)

area 30,600 sq km/11,815 sq mi
capital Brussels
towns Ghent, Liège, Charleroi, Bruges, Mons,
Namur, Leuven; ports are Antwerp, Ostend,
Zeebrugge
physical mostly flat, with hills and forest in SE
features Ardennes; rivers Scheldt and Meuse
head of state King Baudouin from 1951
head of government Wilfried Martens from
1981
political system liberal democracy
political parties Flemish Social Christian
Party (CVP), centre-left; French Social Christian
Party (PSC), centre-left; Flemish Socialist Party
(SP), left-of-centre; French Socialist Party (PS),
left-of-centre; Flemish Liberal Party (PVV),
moderate centrist; French Liberal Reform Party
(P RL), moderate centrist; Flemish People's
Party (VU), federalist
exports iron, steel, textiles, manufactured
goods, petrochemicals
currency Belgian franc (59.60 = £1 Feb 1990)
population (1987) 9,880,000 (comprising
Flemings and Walloons); annual growth
rate 0.1%

life expectancy men 70, women 77
language in the north (Flanders) Flemish (a
Dutch dialect, known as *Vlaams*) 55%; in the
south (Wallonia) Walloon (a French dialect
which is almost a separate language) 44%;
11% bilingual; German (E border) 0.6%; all are
official
religion Roman Catholic
literacy 98% (1984)
GDP $111 bn (1986); $9,230 per head of
population
chronology
1830 Belgium became an independent
kingdom.
1914 Invaded by Germany.
1940 Again invaded by Germany.
1948 Belgium became founder member of
Benelux Customs Union.
1949 Belgium became founder member of
Council of Europe and North Atlantic Treaty
Organization.
1951 Leopold III abdicated in favour of his son
Baudouin.
1952 Belgium became founder member of
European Coal and Steel Community (ECSC).
1957 Belgium became founder member of the
European Community (EEC).
1971 Steps towards regional autonomy taken.
1972 German-speaking members of the cabinet
included for the first time.
1973 Linguistic parity achieved in government
appointments.
1974 Separate regional councils and ministerial
committees established.
1978 Wilfried Martens succeeds Leo
Tindemans as prime minister.
1980 Open violence over language divisions.
Regional assemblies for Flanders and Wallonia
and a three-member executive for Brussels
created.
1981 Short-lived coalition led by Mark Eyskens
was followed by the return of Martens.
1987 Martens head of caretaker government
after breakup of coalition.
1988 Following a general election,
Martens formed a new CVP–PS–SP–PSC–VU
coalition.

Franks from the 3rd century AD onwards. Under ◊Charlemagne Belgium became the centre of
the Carolingian dynasty, and the peace and order
during this period fostered the growth of such
towns as Ghent, Bruges, and Brussels; following
the division of his empire 843 the area became part
of Lotharingia. By the 11th century seven feudal
states had emerged: the counties of Flanders,
Hainault, and Namur, the duchies of Brabant,
Limburg, and Luxembourg, and the bishopric of
Liège, all nominally subject to the French kings or
the German emperor, but in practice independent.
From the 12th century the economy flourished;
Bruges, Ghent, and Ypres became centres of
the cloth industry, while the artisans of Dinant
and Liège exploited the copper and tin of the
Meuse valley. During the 15th century the states
came one by one under the rule of the dukes of
Burgundy, and in 1477, by the marriage of Mary,
heir of Charles the Bold, duke of Burgundy, to
Maximilian, Archduke of Austria, passed into the
◊Habsburg dominions.

Other dynastic marriages brought all the Low
Countries under Spain, and in the 16th century
the religious and secular tyranny of Philip II led
to revolt in the Netherlands; the independence of
the Netherlands as the Dutch Republic was recognized 1648; the south, reconquered by Spain,
remained Spanish until the Treaty of ◊Utrecht
1713 transferred it to Austria. In 1719 the Austrian Netherlands was annexed by revolutionary
France. The Congress of Vienna reunited North
and South Netherlands as one kingdom under

William, King of Orange-Nassau; but historical
differences, and the fact that the language of
the wealthy and influential in the south was (as
it remains) French, made the union uneasy. A
rising 1830 of the largely French-speaking people in the south, and continuing disturbances,
led in 1839 to the Great Powers' recognition of
the South Netherlands as the independent and
permanently neutral kingdom of Belgium, with
Leopold of Saxe-Coburg (widower of Charlotte,
daughter of George IV of England) as king, and
a parliamentary constitution.

Although Prussia had been a party to the treaty
1839 recognizing Belgium's permanent neutrality,
Germany invaded Belgium 1914 and occupied a
large part of it until 1918. Again in 1940 Belgium
was overrun by Germany, to whom Leopold III
surrendered. His government escaped to London,
and Belgium had a strong resistance movement.
After Belgium's liberation by the Allies 1944–45
the king's surrender caused acute controversy,
ended only by his abdication 1951 in favour of his
son Baudouin.

Since 1945 Belgium has been a major force
for international cooperation in Europe, being a
founder member of the ◊Benelux Economic Union, the Council of Europe, and the EC.

Belgium's main problems stem from the division
between French- and Dutch-speaking members of
the population, aggravated by the polarization between the predominantly Conservative Flanders
in the north, and the mainly Socialist French-
speaking Wallonia in the south. About 55% of

Belgium

North Sea

THE NETHERLANDS

Ostend (Oostende)
Bruges (Brugge)
Antwerp
Ghent (Gand)

WEST GERMANY

Scheldt (Schelde)

Leuven (Louvain)
Brussels (Bruxelles)

B E L G I U M

Meuse

Liège (Luik)

Namur (Namen)

Sambre

FRANCE

LUXEMBOURG

0 km   20
0 miles   20

the population speak Dutch, 44% French, and the remainder German.

Belgium has a hereditary monarchy. In 1951 King Leopold III, who had reigned since 1934, abdicated in favour of his son, Baudouin. From 1971–73, attempts to close the linguistic and social divisions included the transfer of greater power to the regions, the inclusion of German-speaking members in the cabinet, and linguistic parity in the government. In 1974 separate regional councils and ministerial committees were established.

In 1977 a coalition government, headed by Leo Tindemans (CVP) proposed the creation of a federal Belgium, based on Flanders, Wallonia, and Brussels, but the proposals were not adopted and in 1978 Tindemans resigned. He was succeeded by Wilfried Martens, heading another coalition.

In 1980 the language conflict developed into open violence and it was eventually agreed that Flanders and Wallonia should be administered by separate regional assemblies, with powers to spend up to 10% of the national budget on cultural facilities, health, roads, and urban projects. Brussels was to be governed by a three-member executive. Such was the political instability that by 1980 Martens had formed no less than four coalition governments. In 1981 a new coalition, led by Mark Eyskens (CVP), lasted less than a year and Martens again returned to power.

In 1981–82 economic difficulties resulted in a series of public sector strikes and in 1983 linguistic divisions again threatened the government. Between 1983 and 1985 there was much debate about the siting of US cruise missiles in Belgium before a majority vote in parliament allowed their installation. The 1985 elections led to Martens forming another coalition. The 1987 general election produced no decisive result and Martens formed a new five-party coalition government that broke up Mar 1989, when the king asked Martens to form a new caretaker government pending a general election and the adoption of a new constitution, devolving more power to the regions.

Belgrade /ˌbelˈgreɪd/ (Serbo-Croat *Beograd*) capital of Yugoslavia and Serbia, and Danube river port linked with the port of Bar on the Adriatic; population (1981) 1,470,000. Industries include light engineering, food processing, textiles, pharmaceuticals, and electrical goods.

Belgrano /belˈgrɑːnəʊ/ Manuel 1770–1820. Argentinian revolutionist. He was a member of the military group that led the 1810 revolt against Spain. Later, he commanded the revolutionary army until he was replaced by José de ◊San Martín in 1814.

Belgravia /belˈgreɪvɪə/ district of London, laid out in squares by Thomas Cubitt (1788–1855) from 1825–30, and bounded to the N by Knightsbridge.

Belisarius /ˌbelɪˈsɑːrɪəs/ *c.*505–565. Roman general under Emperor ◊Justinian I.

Belitung /bɪˈliːtʊŋ/ alternative name for the Indonesian island of ◊Billiton.

Belize /bəˈliːz/ country in Central America, bounded to the north by Mexico, to the west and south by Guatemala, and to the east by the Caribbean Sea.

government the 1981 constitution provides for a parliamentary government on the British model with a prime minister and cabinet drawn from the legislature and accountable to it. The national assembly consists of a senate and a house of representatives. The senate has eight members appointed by the governor general for a five-year term, five on the advice of the prime minister, two on the advice of the leader of the opposition, and one after wider consultations. The house of representatives has 28 members elected by universal suffrage. The governor general appoints both the prime minister and the leader of the opposition.

history once part of the ◊Maya civilization, and colonized in the 17th century, British Honduras, as it was called until 1973, became a recognized British colony in 1862. A 1954 constitution provided for internal self-government, with Britain responsible for defence, external affairs, and internal security.

The first general election under the the the new constitution, and all subsequent elections until 1984, were won by the People's United Party (PUP), led by George Price. In 1964 full internal self-government was granted and Price became prime minister. In 1970 the capital was moved from Belize City to the new town of Belmopan. In 1975 British troops were sent to defend the long-disputed frontier with Guatemala. Negotiations begun in 1977 were inconclusive.

In 1980 the United Nations called for full independence for Belize. A constitutional conference in 1981 broke up over Guatemala's demand for territory rather than just access to the Caribbean. In 1981, full independence was achieved with George Price as the first prime minister. Britain agreed to protect the frontier and to assist in the training of Belizean forces. In 1984 the PUP's uninterrupted 30-year rule ended when the United Democratic Party (UDP) leader, Manuel Esquivel, became prime minister. Britain reaffirmed its undertaking to protect Belize's disputed frontier. The PUP, still led by George Price, unexpectedly won the Sept 1989 general election by a margin of 15 to 13 seats in the House of Representatives.

Belize City /bɪˈliːz/ chief port of Belize, and capital until 1970; population (1980) 40,000. It was destroyed by a hurricane 1961 and it was decided to move the capital inland, to Belmopan.

bell ancient musical instrument in all sizes comprising a suspended hollow metal container with a beater attached, which rings when shaken. Church bells are massive instruments, cast in bronze, and mounted in towers from where their sound can be heard over a wide area. Their shape is a flared bowl with a thickened rim engineered to produce a clangorous mixture of tones. Orchestral *tubular bells*, made of brass or steel, offer a chromatic scale of pitches of reduced power, and are played by striking with a wooden mallet.

The world's largest bell is the 'Tsar Kolokol' or 'King of Bells', 220 tonnes, cast in 1734, stands on the ground of the Kremlin, Moscow, where it fell when being hung. The 'Peace Bell' at the United Nations headquarters, New York, was cast in 1952 from coins presented by 64 countries.

Bell /bel/ Alexander Graham 1847–1922. British scientist, and inventor of the telephone. He patented his invention in 1876, and later experimented with a type of phonograph and in aeronautics invented the tricycle undercarriage.

Born in Edinburgh, he was educated at the universities of Edinburgh and London, and in 1870 went first to Canada and then to the USA where he opened a school for teachers of the deaf in Boston in 1872, and in 1873 became professor of vocal physiology at the university.

Bell /bel/ Patrick c. 1800–1869. Scottish inventor of a reaping machine, developed around 1828. It was pushed by two horses and used a rotating cylinder of horizontal bars to bend the standing

Bell Pioneer Scots scientist and inventor of the telephone, Alexander Graham Bell.

Belize

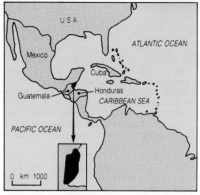

area 22,963 sq km/8,864 sq mi
capital Belmopan
towns port Belize City
physical half the country is forested, much of it high rainforest
head of state Elizabeth II from 1981 represented by Elmira Minita Gordon
head of government Manuel Esquivel from 1984
political system constitutional monarchy
political parties People's United Party (PUP), left-of-centre; United Democratic Party (UDP), moderate conservative

exports sugar, citrus, rice, lobster
currency Belize dollar (3.40 = £1 Feb 1990)
population (1987) 176,000 (including Maya minority in the interior); annual growth rate 2.5%
language English (official), but Spanish is widely spoken
religion Roman Catholic 60%, Protestant 35%, Hindu and Muslim minorities
literacy 80% (1985)
GDP $176 million (1983); $1,000 per head of population
chronology
1862 Belize became a British colony.
1954 Constitution adopted, providing for limited internal self-government. General election won by George Price.
1964 Full internal self-government granted.
1965 Two-chamber national assembly introduced, with Price as prime minister.
1970 Capital moved from Belize City to Belmopan.
1975 British troops sent to defend the frontier with Guatemala.
1977 Negotiations undertaken with Guatemala but no agreement reached.
1980 United Nations called for full independence.
1981 Full independence achieved. Price became prime minister.
1984 Price defeated in general election. Manuel Esquivel formed the government. Britain reaffirmed its undertaking to defend the frontier.
1989 Price and the PUP won the general election.

corn on to a reciprocating cutter that was driven off the machine's wheels (in much the same way as on a combine harvester).

belladonna plant of the genus *Atropa*. The dried powdered leaves of *Atropa bella-donna* or **deadly nightshade** contain ◊alkaloids. Belladonna acts as an ◊anticholinergic, and is highly toxic in large doses.

Bellarmine /'belɑːmɪn/ Roberto Francesco Romolo 1542–1621. Italian Christian theologian, cardinal, and controversialist. He taught at the Jesuit College in Rome, and became archbishop of Capua 1602. His *Disputationes de controversersiis fidei christianae* 1581–93 was an important defence of Catholicism in the 16th century. He was canonized in 1930.

Bellini *The Doge Leonardo Loredan painted by Venetian artist Giovanni Bellini (c.1501) National Gallery, London.*

Bellay /be'leɪ/ Joachim du *c.*1522–1560. French poet and prose-writer, who published the great manifesto of the new school of French poetry, the Pléiade: *Défense et illustration de la langue française* 1549.

Bell Burnell /'bel bɜː'nel/ Jocelyn 1943– . British astronomer. In 1967 he discovered the first ◊pulsar (rapidly flashing star) with Antony ◊Hewish and colleagues at Cambridge University, England.

belles lettres (French 'fine letters') literature that is appreciated more for its aesthetic qualities than for its content.

bellflower general name for many plants of the family Campanulaceae, especially those of the genus *Campanula*. The **Canterbury bell** *Campanula medium* is the garden variety, originally from S Europe. The ◊harebell is also a *Campanula*.

The ***clustered bellflower*** *Campanula glomerata* is characteristic of chalk grassland, and found in Europe and N Asia. Erect and downy, it has tight clusters of violet bell-shaped flowers in late summer.

Bellingshausen /'belɪŋzhauzən/ Fabian Gottlieb von 1779–1852. Russian Antarctic explorer, the first to sight and circumnavigate the Antarctic continent 1819–21, although he did not realize what it was.

Bellingshausen Sea /'belɪŋzhauzən/ the section of the S Pacific off the Antarctic coast. It is named after the Russian explorer Fabian Gottlieb von Bellingshausen.

Bellini /be'liːni/ family of Italian painters, founders of the Venetian school. *Giovanni Bellini* (*c.*1430–1516), produced portraits, and various religious subjects. He introduced softness in tone, harmony in composition, and a use of luminous colour that influenced the next generation of painters (including his pupils Giorgione and Titian). He worked in oil rather than tempera.

Jacopo Bellini (*c.*1400–70) was father to Gentile and Giovanni. Little of Jacopo's work has survived, but two of his sketchbooks (exhibited in the British Museum and the Louvre) contain his ideas and designs.

His younger brother, Giovanni, studied under his father. Giovanni Bellini's early works show the influence of his brother-in-law, Mantegna. His style developed from the static manner of mid-15th century Venetian work towards a High Renaissance harmony and grandeur, as in the altarpiece 1505 in Sta Zaccaria, Venice. The technique of oil painting was adopted from Antonello da Messina.

Bellini /be'liːni/ Vincenzo 1801–1835. Italian composer, born in Catania, Sicily. His operas include *La Sonnambula* 1831, *Norma* 1831, and *I Puritani* 1835.

Bellinzona /,belɪnt'səunə/ town in Switzerland, on the river Ticino, 16 km/10 mi from Lake Maggiore; population (1980) 17,000. It is the capital of Ticino canton and a traffic centre for the St Gotthard Pass. It is a tourist centre.

Belloc /'belɒk/ (Joseph) Hilaire Pierre 1870–1953. British author of nonsense verse for children, including *The Bad Child's Book of Beasts* 1896 and *Cautionary Tales* 1907. With G K ◊Chesterton, he advocated a return to the ◊guild system of the late Middle Ages in place of capitalism or socialism.

Bellot /be'ləu/ Joseph René 1826–1853. French Arctic explorer, who reached the Bellot Strait in 1852, and lost his life while searching for ◊Franklin.

Bellow /'beləu/ Saul 1915– . US novelist of Russian descent, born in Canada, who settled in Chicago with his family in 1924. His works include the picaresque *The Adventures of Augie March* 1953, the philosophically speculative *Herzog* 1964, *Humboldt's Gift* 1975, *The Dean's December* 1982, and *More Die of Heartbreak* 1987. Nobel prize 1976.

bell ringing or **campanology** the art of ringing church bells by hand, by means of a rope fastened to a wheel rotating the entire bell mechanism. **Change ringing** is an English art of ringing all the possible sequences of a number of bells in strict order, using one player to each bell. Fixed permutations of 5–12 bells are rung.

In Europe and the USA, the **carillon** performs arrangements of well-known music for up to 70 static bells. It is played by a single operator using a keyboard system of levers and pulleys acting on the striking mechanisms only. **Handbell** ringing is played solo or by a team of ringers selecting from a range of lightweight bells of pure tone resting on a table.

bells nautical term applied to half-hours of watch. A day is divided into seven watches, five of four hours each and two of two hours. Each half-hour of each watch is indicated by the striking of a bell, eight bells signalling the end of the watch.

Belmondo /bel'mɒndəu/ Jean Paul 1933– . French film actor who played the leading role in Godard's *A Bout de Souffle/Breathless* 1959. Despite appearances in some international films, he remains best known in France.

Bellow *US novelist Saul Bellow.*

Belmopan /ˌbelmə'pæn/ capital of Belize from 1970; population (1980) 3,000. It replaced Belize City as administrative centre of the country.

Beloff /'belɒf/ Max 1913– . British historian. From 1974 to 1979 he was principal of the University College at Buckingham, Britain's first independent institution at university level. He was created a life peer 1981.

Belo Horizonte /'beləʊ 'ɒrɪ'zɒnteɪ/ industrial city (steel, engineering, textiles) in SE Brazil, capital of the fast-developing state of Minas Gerais; population (1985) 3,060,000. Built in the 1890s, it was Brazil's first planned modern city.

Belorussia alternate spelling for ◊Byelorussia.

Belsen /'belsən/ site of a Nazi ◊concentration camp in Lower Saxony, West Germany.

Belshazzar in the Old Testament, the last king of Babylon, son of Nebuchadnezzar. During a feast (known as **Belshazzar's Feast**) the king saw a message, interpreted by ◊Daniel as prophesying the fall of Babylon and death of Belshazzar.

All of this is said to have happened that same night when the city was invaded by the Medes and Persians (539 BC).

Beltane Celtic name for the 1st day of May, formerly one of the Scottish quarter days. The ancient feasts held on this day were marked by the kindling of Beltane fires on the hillsides.

Bemba people of Bemba origin. Their homeland is the northern province of Zambia, although many reside in urban areas such as Lusaka and Copperbelt. The Bemba language belongs to the Bantu branch of the Niger-Congo family.

Benali /ben'æli/ Zine el Abidine 1936– . Tunisian politician, president from 1987. He was prime minister under the ageing president for life Habib ◊Bourguiba, until he forced him to retire and assumed the presidency, promising greater democracy through constitutional reform.

After training in France and the USA, Benali returned to Tunisia and became director-general of national security. He was made minister of the interior and then prime minister by Bourguiba and in 1987 staged a bloodless coup with the aid of ministerial colleagues.

Benares /bɪ'nɑːrɪz/ transliteration of Varanasi, holy city in India.

Ben Barka /ben 'bɑːkə/ Mehdi 1920–1965. Moroccan politician. He became president of the National Consultative Assembly in 1956 on the country's independence from France. He was assassinated in France.

Ben Barka had been tutor to King Hassan. As a major opposition leader after independence he was increasingly leftist in his views, and was twice sentenced to death in his absence during 1963 (for alleged involvement in an attempt on the king's life and for supporting Algeria in Algerian-Moroccan border disputes). Lured to Paris to discuss an anti-colonial film, he was kidnapped and shot by Moroccan agents with the aid of French secret-service men. His body was not found. The case disturbed Franco-Moroccan relations, and led to de Gaulle's reorganization of the French secret service.

Ben Bella /ben 'belə/ Ahmed 1916– . Algerian leader of the National Liberation Front (FLN) from 1952; prime minister of independent Algeria 1962–65, when he was overthrown by ◊Boumédienne and detained until 1980. He founded a new party, Mouvement pour la Démocratie en Algérie, in 1985.

Benbow /'benbəʊ/ John 1653–1702. English admiral, hero of several battles with France. He ran away to sea as a boy, and from 1689 served in the navy. He fought at Beachy Head 1690 and La Hogue 1692, and died of wounds received in a long fight with the French off Jamaica.

Benchley /'bentʃli/ Robert 1889–1945. US humorist and actor, born in Massachusetts. He was

Ben Bella *Algerian leader Ahmed Ben Bella worked for independence and was imprisoned in France before becoming prime minister of independent Algeria in 1962.*

associated with the writer Dorothy Parker, the *New Yorker*, and the circle of wits at the Algonquin Round Table in New York.

His books include *Of All Things* 1921 and *Benchley Beside Himself* 1943, and his film skit *How to Sleep* illustrates his ability to extract humour from daily living.

benchmark in computing, a measure of the performance of a piece of equipment or software. Benchmarks usually describe how well the product performs by comparison with similar products, rather than in absolute terms.

Benda /bæn'dɑː/ Julien 1867–1956. French writer and philosopher. He was an outspoken opponent of the philosophy of Bergson, and in 1927 published a manifesto on the necessity of devotion to the absolute truth which he felt his contemporaries had betrayed, *La Trahison des clercs/The Treason of the Intellectuals*.

Bendigo /'bendɪgəʊ/ city in Victoria, Australia, about 120 km/75 mi NNW of Melbourne; population (1986) 62,400. Founded 1851 at the start of a gold rush, the town takes its name from the pugilist William Thompson (1811–89), known as 'Bendigo'.

bends popular name for paralytic affliction of divers, arising from too rapid release of nitrogen after solution in the blood under pressure. Immediate treatment is compression and slow decompression in a special chamber.

Benedict XV /'benɪdɪkt/ 1854–1922. Pope from 1914. During World War I he endeavoured to remain neutral, and his papacy is noted for the renewal of British official relations with the Vatican, suspended since the 17th century.

Benedictine order religious order of monks and nuns in the Roman Catholic church, founded by St ◊Benedict at Subiaco, Italy, in the 6th century. St Augustine brought the order to England. At the beginning of the 14th century it was at the height of its prosperity, and had a strong influence on medieval learning.

A number of Oxford and Cambridge colleges have a Benedictine origin. At the Reformation there were nearly 300 Benedictine monasteries and nunneries in England, all of which were suppressed. The English novice house survived in France, and in the 19th century monks expelled from France moved to England and built abbeys at Downside, Ampleforth, and Woolhampton. The monks from Pierre-qui-vive, who went over in

1882, rebuilt Buckfast Abbey in Devon on the ruins of a Cistercian monastery.

benediction blessing recited at the end of a Christian service, particularly the Mass.

Benedict, St /'benɪdɪkt/ *c.* 480–*c.* 547. Founder of Christian monasticism in the West, and of the ◊Benedictine order. He founded the monastery of Monte Cassino, Italy. Here he wrote out his rule for monastic life, and was visited shortly before his death by the Ostrogothic king Totila, whom he converted to the Christian faith. Feast day 11 July.

benefice in the early Middle Ages, a donation of land or money to the Christian church as an act of devotion, but from the 12th century, the income enjoyed by clergy.

Under the Carolingian dynasty, 'benefice' was used to mean a gift of land from a lord to a ◊vassal, in which sense it is often indistinguishable from a ◊fief.

Benelux /'benɪlʌks/ customs union of **Be**lgium, **Ne**therlands and **Lux**embourg (agreed 1944, fully effective 1960); precursor of the European Economic Community.

Beneš /'beneʃ/ Eduard 1884–1948. Czechoslovak politician. He was president of the republic from 1935 until forced to resign by the Germans, and headed a government in exile in London during World War II. He returned home as president 1945, but resigned again after the communist coup 1948.

Benét /bə'neɪ/ Stephen Vincent 1898–1943. US poet who wrote the narrative poem of the Civil War *John Brown's Body* 1928.

Benevento /ˌbenɪ'ventəʊ/ historic town in Campania, S Italy; population (1981) 62,500. It is noted for the production of Strega liquer.

Bengal /ˌben'gɔːl/ former province of British India, divided 1947 into ◊West Bengal, a state of India, and East Bengal, from 1972 ◊Bangladesh. The famine in 1943, caused by a slump in demand for jute and a bad harvest, resulted in over 3 million deaths.

Bengali language a member of the Indo-Iranian branch of the Indo-European language family, the official language of Bangladesh and of the state of Bengal in India.

Benghazi /ben'gɑːzi/ or **Banghazi** historic city and industrial port in N Libya on the Gulf of Sirte; population (1982) 650,000. It was controlled by Turkey between the 16th century and 1911, and by Italy 1911–1942; an important naval supply base during World War II.

history Colonized by the Greeks in the 7th century BC (**Euhesperides**), Benghazi was taken by Rome in the 1st century BC (**Berenice**) and by

Benedict, St *Italian St Benedict, the founder of Western monasticism.*

Benin
People's Republic of
(République Populaire du Bénin)

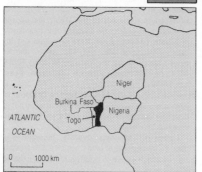

area 112,622 sq km/43,472 sq mi
capital Porto Novo
towns Abomey, Natitingou; chief port Cotonou
physical flat, humid, with dense vegetation
features coastal fishing villages on stilts
head of state and government Mathieu Kerekou from 1972
political system one-party socialist republic
political parties Party of the People's Revolution of Benin (PRPB), Marxist-Leninist

exports cocoa, groundnuts, cotton, palm oil
currency CFA franc (485.00 = £1 Feb 1990)
population (1988 est) 4,444,000; annual growth rate 3%
life expectancy men 42, women 46
language French (official); Fan 47%
religion animist 65%, Christian 17%, Muslim 13%
literacy 37% male/16% female (1985 est)
GDP $1.1 bn (1983); $290 per head of population
chronology
1851 Under French control.
1958 Became self-governing dominion within the French Community.
1960–72 Acute political instability, with switches from civilian to military rule.
1972 Military regime established by Gen Mathieu Kerekou.
1974 Kerekou announced that the country would follow a path of 'scientific socialism'.
1975 Name of country changed from Dahomey to Benin.
1977 Return to civilian rule under a new constitution.
1980 Kerekou formally elected president by the National Revolutionary Assembly.
1989 Kerekou re-elected. Marxist-Leninism dropped as official ideology.

the Vandals in the 5th century AD. It became Arab in the 7th century. With Tripoli, it was co-capital of Libya 1951–72.
Benguela /ben'gweɪlə/ port in Angola, SW Africa; population (1970) 41,000. It was founded 1617. Its railway runs inland to the copper mines of Zaïre and Zambia.
Benguela current the cold ocean current in the S Atlantic Ocean, moving northwards along the west coast of Southern Africa and merging with the south equatorial current at a latitude of 15° S. Its rich plankton supports large, commercially exploited fish populations.
Ben-Gurion /ben 'gʊəriən/ David. Adopted name of David Gruen 1886–1973. Israeli socialist politician, the country's first prime minister 1948–53, and again 1955–63. He was born in Poland.
Benin /be'niːn/ country in W Africa, sandwiched between Nigeria on the E and Togo on the W, with Burkina Faso to the NW, Niger to the NE, and the Atlantic Ocean to the S.
government The constitution is based on a Fundamental Law (*Loi Fondamentale*) of 1977, which established a national revolutionary assembly with 196 members, representing socioprofessional classes rather than geographical constituencies, elected for a five-year term by universal suffrage. The assembly elects the president, as head of state, to serve a similar five-year term. Since 1975 Benin has been a one-party state, committed to 'scientific socialism'. The party is the Party of the People's Revolution of Benin (PRPB) and is chaired by the president.
history Known until 1975 as Dahomey, in the 12th–13th centuries the country was settled by the Aja, whose kingdom reached its peak in the 16th century. Later known as the Dahomey, in the 17th–19th centuries they captured and sold their neighbours as slaves to Europeans.
Under French influence from the 1850s, Benin formed part of French West Africa from 1899, and in 1958 became a self-governing dominion within the French Community. In 1960 it became fully independent.
Benin went through a period of political instability 1960–72, with swings from civilian to military rule and disputes between regions. In 1972 the deputy chief of the army, Mathieu Kerekou, established a military regime pledged to give fair representation to each region. His initial instrument of government was the National Council of the Revolution (CNR). In 1974 Kerekou announced that the country would follow

'scientific socialism', based on Marxist-Leninist principles.
In 1977 CNR was dissolved and a civilian government formed. A fundamental law established a national revolutionary assembly which in 1980 elected Kerekou as president and head of state. He was re-elected in 1984 and after initial economic and social difficulties, his government grew more stable and relations with France, Benin's biggest trading partner, improved considerably. In 1983 President Mitterrand became the first French head of state to visit Benin. In Aug 1989 President Kerekou was re-elected for another five-year term. It was announced Dec 1989 that Marxist-Leninism was no longer the official ideology and that further constitutional reforms, allowing for more private enterprise, would be agreed.
Benin /be'niːn/ former African kingdom 1200–1897, now part of Nigeria. It reached the height of its power in the 14th–17th centuries when it ruled the area between the Niger Delta and Lagos. The kingdom traded in spices, ivory, palm oil, and slaves until its decline and eventual incorporation into Nigeria.
Benjamin /'bendʒəmɪn/ Arthur 1893–1960. Australian pianist and composer who taught composition at the Royal College of Music in London from 1925, where ◊Britten was one of his pupils. His works include *Jamaican Rumba*, inspired by a visit to the West Indies in 1937.
Benn /ben/ Tony (Anthony Wedgwood) 1925– . British Labour politician, one of the most influential figure on the party's left wing. He was minister of technology 1966–70 and of industry 1974–75, but his campaign against entry to the European Community led to his transfer to the Department of Energy 1975–79. He unsuccessfully contested Neil Kinnock for the leadership 1988.
Son of Lord Stansgate, a Labour peer, he succeeded his father 1960, though he never used his title and in 1963 was the first person to disclaim it under the Peerage Act. In 1981 he challenged Denis Healey for the deputy leadership of the party and was so narrowly defeated that he established himself as the acknowledged leader of the left.
Bennett /'benɪt/ (Enoch) Arnold 1867–1931. English novelist. Coming from one of the 'five towns' of the Potteries which formed the setting of his major books, he became a London journalist 1893 and editor of *Woman* 1896. His books include *Anna of the Five Towns* 1904, *The Old Wives' Tale*

1908, and the trilogy *Clayhanger, Hilda Lessways*, and *These Twain* 1910–15.
Bennett /'benɪt/ Alan 1934– . English playwright. His works (set in his native north of England) treat subjects such as senility, illness, and death with macabre comedy. They include TV films, for example *An Englishman Abroad* 1982; the cinema film *A Private Function* 1984; and plays like *Forty Years On* 1968 and *Getting On* 1971.
Bennett /'benɪt/ Richard Rodney 1936– . English composer of jazz, film music, symphonies, and operas. His film scores for *Far from the Madding Crowd* 1967, *Nicholas and Alexandra* 1971, and *Murder on the Orient Express* 1974 all received Oscar nominations. His operas include *The Mines of Sulphur* 1963 and *Victory* 1970.
Ben Nevis /ben 'nevɪs/ highest mountain in the British Isles (1,342 m/4,406 ft), in the Grampians, Scotland.
Benny /'beni/ Jack. Stage name of Benjamin Kubelsky 1894–1974. US comedian, active mainly in radio and television. His film appearances, mostly in the 1930s and 1940s, included a starring role in *To Be or Not To Be* 1942. He also played in *Charley's Aunt* 1941, *It's In the Bag* 1945, and *A Guide for the Married Man* 1967.
Benoni /bɪ'nəʊni/ city in the Transvaal, South Africa, 27 km/17 mi E of Johannesburg; population (1980) 207,000. It was founded 1903 as a gold-mining centre.
Benson /'bensən/ E(dward) F(rederic) 1867–1940. British writer. He specialized in novels gently satirizing the foibles of upper-middle-class society, and wrote a series of books featuring the formidable female antagonists Mapp and Lucia, including *Queen Lucia* 1920. He was the son of Edward White Benson.
Benson /'bensən/ Edward White 1829–1896. British cleric, first headmaster of Wellington College 1859–68, and, as archbishop of Canterbury from 1883, responsible for the 'Lincoln Judgment' on questions of ritual in 1887.
bent name for grasses of the genus *Agrostris*. *A. stolonifera*, commonly known as **creeping bent** or **fiorin**, is common in lowland Britain, Europe, N Asia, and North America. It spreads by stolons and bears large attractive panicles of yellow or purple flowers on thin stalks.
Bentham /'benθəm/ Jeremy 1748–1832. English philosopher, legal and social reformer, founder of ◊utilitarianism. The essence of his moral philosophy is found in the pronouncement of his *Principles of Morals and Legislation* (written 1780, published 1789), that the object of all legislation should be 'the greatest happiness for the greatest number'.
He declared that the 'utility' of any law is to be measured by the extent to which it promotes the pleasure, good, and happiness of the people concerned. In 1776, he published *Fragments on Government*. He made suggestions for the reform of the poor law 1798, which formed the basis of the reforms enacted in 1834, and in his *Catechism of Parliamentary Reform* 1817, he proposed annual elections, the secret ballot, and universal

Bentham *English philosopher Jeremy Bentham, founder of utilitarianism.*

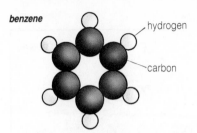

benzene — hydrogen, carbon

male suffrage. He was also a pioneer of prison reform. In economics Bentham was an apostle of *laissez-faire*, and in his *Defence of Usury* 1787 and *Manual of Political Economy* 1798 he contended that his principle of 'utility' was best served by allowing every man (sic) to pursue his own interests unhindered by restrictive legislation. He was made a citizen of the French Republic in 1792.

Bentinck /'bentɪŋk/ Lord William Cavendish 1774–1839. British colonial administrator, first governor general of India 1828–35. He acted against the ancient Indian rituals of thuggee and suttee, and established English as the medium of instruction.

Bentiu an oil-rich region to the W of the White Nile, in the Upper Nile province of S Sudan.

Bentley /'bentli/ Edmund Clerihew 1875–1956. British author. He invented the four-line humorous verse form known as the ◊clerihew, first used in *Biography for Beginners* 1905 and in *Baseless Biography* 1939. He was also the author of the classic detective story *Trent's Last Case* 1912.

Bentley /'bentli/ John Francis 1839–1902. British architect, a convert to Catholicism, who designed the vast and moving Westminster Cathedral, London (1895–1903). It is outwardly Byzantine but inwardly shaped by shadowy vaults of bare brickwork. The campanile is the tallest church tower in London.

Bentley /'bentli/ Richard 1662–1742. British classical scholar, whose textual criticism includes *Dissertation upon the Epistles of Phalaris* 1699. He was Master of Trinity College, Cambridge University, from 1700.

bentonite type of clay, consisting mainly of montmorillonite and resembling ◊fuller's earth, which swells when wet. It is used in papermaking, moulding sands, drilling muds for oil wells, and as a decolorant in food processing.

bentwood originally a country style of wooden furniture, mainly chairs, made by steam-heating and then bending rods of wood to form the back, legs, and seat frame. Recently, designers such as Marcel ◊Breuer and Alvar ◊Aalto have developed a different form by bending sheets of plywood.

Benue /'benuei/ river in Nigeria, largest affluent of the Niger; it is navigable for most of its length of 1,400 km/870 mi.

Benz /bents/ Karl 1844–1929. German automobile engineer, who produced the world's first petrol-driven motorcar. He built his first model engine 1878 and the petrol-driven car 1885.

benzaldehyde C_6H_5CHO in chemistry, a clear colourless liquid with the characteristic odour of almonds. It is used as a solvent, and to make perfumes and dyes. It occurs in certain leaves, such as the cherry, laurel, and peach, and in a combined form in certain nuts and kernels. It can be extracted from such natural sources, but is usually made from toluene.

Benzedrine a trade name for ◊amphetamine, a stimulant drug.

benzene C_6H_6 in chemistry, a clear liquid hydrocarbon of characteristic odour, occurring in coal tar. It is used as a solvent in the synthesis of many chemicals.

The benzene molecule consists of a ring of six carbon atoms, all of which are in a single plane, and it is one of the simplest ◊cyclic compounds. Benzene is the simplest of a class of compounds collectively known as ***aromatic compounds***. Some are considered carcinogenic (cancer-inducing).

benzodiazepine mood-altering drug (tranquillizer), for example Librium or Valium. It interferes with the process by which information is transmitted from one brain cell to another, and various ill effects arise from continued use. It was originally developed as a muscle relaxant.

benzoic acid $C_6H_5CO_2H$ in chemistry, a white crystalline solid, sparingly soluble in water, and used as a preservative for certain foods. It is obtained chemically by the direct oxidation of benzaldehyde, and occurs in certain natural resins, some essential oils, and as hippuric acid.

benzoin or ***gum*** a resin obtained by making incisions in the bark of *Styrax benzoin*, a tree native to the East Indies. Benzoin is used in the preparation of cosmetics, perfumes, and incense.

Ben Zvi /ben 'zvi:/ Izhak 1884–1963. Israeli politician, president 1952–63. He was born in Atpoltava, Russia, and became active in the Zionist movement in Ukraine. In 1907 he went to Palestine but was deported 1915 with ◊Ben-Gurion. They served in the Jewish Legion under Gen Allenby, who commanded the British forces in the Middle East.

Beograd /'beɪougræd/ the Serbo-Croatian form of ◊Belgrade, capital of Yugoslavia.

Beowulf /'beɪəwulf/ Anglo-Saxon poem (composed *c.*700), the only complete surviving example of Germanic folk-epic. It exists in a single manuscript copied about 1000 in the Cottonian collection of the British Museum.

Béranger /,beirɒn'ʒeɪ/ Pierre Jean de 1780–1857. French poet, famous for his light satirical lyrics, dealing with love, wine, popular philosophy, and politics.

Berber a people of N Africa, who since prehistoric times have inhabited Barbary, the Mediterranean coastlands from Egypt to the Atlantic. Their language is Berber, spoken by about one-third of Algerians and nearly two-thirds of Moroccans.

Berbera /'bɜːbərə/ seaport in Somalia, with the only sheltered harbour on the S side of the Gulf of Aden; population (1982) 55,000. It is in a strategic position on the oil route, and has a new deep sea port completed 1969. It was under British control 1884–1960.

Berchtesgaden /,beəxtɪs'gɑːdn/ village in SE Bavaria, West Germany, site of Hitler's country residence, the Berghof, which was captured by US troops 4 May 1945 and destroyed.

Berchtold /'beəxtəult/ Count Leopold von 1863–1942. Prime minister and foreign minister of Austria-Hungary 1912–15, and a crucial figure in the events that led to World War I.

Berdichev /bɪə'diːtʃef/ town in Ukraine, USSR, 48 km/30 mi S of Zhitomir; population (1980) 60,000. Industries include engineering and food processing.

Berdyaev /bɪə'djaɪef/ Nikolai Alexandrovich 1874–1948. Russian philosopher, who often challenged official viewpoints. Although appointed professor of philosophy in 1919 at the university

of Moscow, his defence of Orthodox Christian religion caused his exile in 1922. His books include *The Meaning of History* 1923 and *The Destiny of Man* 1935.

Berdyansk /bɪə'djænsk/ city and port on the Berdyansk Gulf of the Sea of Azov, in SE Ukraine, USSR; population (1985) 130,000.

Berengaria of Navarre the only English queen never to set foot in England. Daughter of King Sancho VI of Navarre, she married Richard I of England in Cyprus 1191, and accompanied him on his crusade to the Holy Land.

Berenson /'berənsən/ Bernard 1865–1959. US art expert, born in Lithuania, once revered as a leading scholar of the Italian Renaissance. He amassed a great fortune, and many of his attributions of previously anonymous Italian paintings were later disproved.

Berezniki /bɪ'reznɪ'kiː/ city in the USSR, on the Kama river N of Perm; population (1987) 200,000. It was formed 1932 by the amalgamation of several older towns. Industry includes chemicals and paper.

Berg /beəg/ Alban 1885–1935. Austrian composer. He studied under ◊Schoenberg and was associated with him as one of the leaders of the serial, or 12-tone, school of composition. His output includes orchestral, chamber and vocal music, and two operas *Wozzeck* 1925, a grim story of working-class life and the unfinished *Lulu* 1929–35.

His music is emotionally expressive, and sometimes anguished, but can also be lyrical, as in the *Violin Concerto* 1935.

Berg /bɜːg/ Paul 1926– . US molecular biologist. In 1972, using gene-splicing techniques developed by others, Berg spliced and combined into a single hybrid ◊DNA from an animal tumour virus (SV40) and DNA from a bacterial virus. His work aroused fears in other workers and excited continuing controversy. For his work on recombinant DNA, Berg shared the 1980 Nobel Prize for Chemistry with Walter ◊Gilbert and Frederick ◊Sanger.

Bergama /'beəgəmə/ modern form of ◊Pergamum, ancient city in Turkey.

Bergamo /'beəgəməu/ city in Lombardy, Italy; 48 km/30 mi NE of Milan; population (1988) 119,000. Industries include silk and metal. The Academia Carrara holds a noted collection of paintings.

bergamot tree *Citrus bergamia*; from the rind of its fruit a fragrant orange-scented essence used as a perfume is obtained. The sole source of supply is S Calabria, but the name comes from the town of Bergamo, in Lombardy.

Bergen /'beəgən/ industrial port (shipbuilding, engineering, fishing) in SW Norway; population

Berg *Austrian composer Alban Berg.*

Bergius *German chemist and Nobel prizewinner for chemistry in 1931.*

(1988) 210,000. Founded 1070, Bergen was a member of the Hanseatic League.

Bergen-op-Zoom /'beəxən ɒ 'zəʊm/ fishing port in SW Netherlands; population (1982) 45,100. It produces chemicals, cigarettes and precision goods.

Bergisch Gladbach /'beəgɪʃ 'glædbæx/ industrial city in North Rhine–Westphalia, West Germany; population (1988) 102,000.

Bergius /'beəgiəs/ Friedrich Karl Rudolph 1884–1949. German research chemist who invented processes for converting coal into oil, and wood into sugar. Nobel Prize 1931.

Bergman /'beəgmən/ Ingmar 1918– . Swedish film producer and director. His work deals with complex moral, psychological, and metaphysical problems and is often heavily tinged with pessimism. His films include *Wild Strawberries* 1957, *Persona* 1966, and *Fanny and Alexander* 1982.

Bergman /'beəgmən/ Ingrid 1917–1982. Swedish actress, whose early films include *Casablanca* and *For Whom the Bell Tolls* both 1943. By leaving her husband for film producer Roberto Rossellini, she broke an unofficial moral code of Hollywood 'star' behaviour and was ostracized for many years. During her 'exile', she made films in Europe such as *Stromboli* 1949 (directed by Rossellini). Later films include *Anastasia* 1956, for which she won an Academy Award.

Bergson /'beək'sɒn/ Henri 1859–1941. French philosopher, who believed that time, change, and development were the essence of reality. He thought that time was not a succession of distinct and separate instants, but a continuous process in which one period merged imperceptibly into the next.

In *Creative Evolution* 1907 he expressed his dissatisfaction with the materialist account of evolution popularized by such thinkers as Herbert ◊Spencer, and attempted to prove that all evolution and progress are due to the working of the *élan vital*, or life-force. He was professor of philosophy at the Collège de France (1900–21). Nobel Prize for Literature 1928.

Bergman *Swedish actress Ingrid Bergman.*

Beria /'beəriə/ Lavrenti 1899–1953. Soviet politician, who became head of the Soviet police force and minister of the interior in 1938. On Stalin's death in 1953, he was shot after a secret trial.

beri-beri endemic polyneuritis, an inflammation of the nerve endings, mostly occurring in the tropics and resulting from deficiency of vitamin B.

Bering /'beərɪŋ/ Vitus 1681–1741. Danish explorer, the first European to sight Alaska. He died on Bering Island in the Bering Sea, both named after him, as are Bering Strait, which separates Asia (USSR) from North America (Alaska), and Beringia.

Beringia /bə'rɪndʒiə/ former land bridge 1,600 km/1,000 mi wide between Asia and North America; it existed during the ice ages that occurred before 35,000 BC and during the period 2400–9000 BC. It is now covered by Bering Strait and Chukchi Sea.

Bering Sea /'beərɪŋ/ section of the N Pacific

between Alaska and Siberia, from the Aleutian Islands N to Bering Strait.

Bering Strait /'beərɪŋ/ strait between Alaska and Siberia, linking the N Pacific and Arctic oceans.

Berio /'beəriəu/ Luciano 1925– . Italian composer. His style has been described as graceful ◊serialism, and he has frequently experimented with electronic music and taped sound. His works include nine *Sequenzas/Sequences* 1957–75 for various solo instruments or voice, *Sinfonia* 1969 for voices and orchestra, *Points on the curve to find...* 1974, and a number of dramatic works, including the opera *Un re in ascolto/A King Listens* 1984, loosely based on Shakespeare's *The Tempest*.

After studying in Milan and the US, he came into contact with members of the European avant garde such as Stockhausen, Boulez, and Bruno Maderna; with Maderna he founded an electronic studio in Milan 1955. Although Berio's compositional techniques are severe, the effect is softened by a pervasive wit and theatricality.

He was married 1950–65 to the soprano Cathy Berberian (1925–83), who gave the first performances of many of his works. He lived in the US 1963–72.

Beriosova /ˌberi'ɒsəvə/ Svetlana 1932– . British ballerina. Born in Lithuania and brought up partly in the USA, she danced with the Royal Ballet from 1952. Her style had a lyrical dignity and she excelled in *The Lady and the Fool*, *Ondine*, and *Giselle*.

Berkeley /'bɜːkli/ town on San Francisco Bay in California, USA; population (1980) 103,500. It is the headquarters of the University of California, noted for its nuclear research.

Berkeley /'bɜːkli/ Busby 1895–1976. US film choreographer and director, famous for his ingeniously extravagant sets and his use of female dancers to create large-scale pattern effects through movement and costume, as in *Gold Diggers of 1933* 1933.

Berkeley /'bɑːkli/ George 1685–1753. Irish philosopher, who believed that nothing exists apart from perception, and that a thing which is not perceived cannot be known and therefore cannot exist. For Berkeley, everyday objects are collections of ideas or sensations, hence the dictum *esse est percipi* ('to exist is to be perceived'). He became Bishop of Cloyne 1734.

Berkeley /'bɑːkli/ Lennox (Randal Francis) 1903–1989. English composer. His works for the voice include *The Hill of the Graces* 1975, verses from Spenser's *Fairie Queene* set for eight-part unaccompanied chorus; and his operas *Nelson* 1953 and *Ruth* 1956.

berkelium an artificially-made radioactive element, symbol Bk, atomic number 97. It was discovered at Berkeley, USA, in 1949 by Glenn Seaborg and others.

Berks abbreviation for *Berkshire*.

Berkshire

Berlin

Berkshire /'bɑːkʃə/ or *Royal Berkshire* county in S central England
area 1,260 sq km/486 sq mi
towns administrative headquarters Reading; Eton, Slough, Maidenhead, Ascot, Bracknell, Newbury, Windsor
features rivers Thames and Kennet; Inkpen Beacon 297 m/975 ft; Bagshot Heath; Ridgeway Path, walkers' path (partly prehistoric) running from Wiltshire across the Berkshire Downs into Hertfordshire; Windsor Forest and Windsor Castle; Eton College; Royal Military Academy at Sandhurst; atomic-weapons research establishment at Aldermaston, and the former main UK base for US cruise missiles at Greenham Common, Newbury
products general agricultural and horticultural, electronics, plastics, pharmaceuticals
population (1987) 741,000
famous people King Alfred, Stanley Spencer.

Berlin /bɜː'lɪn/ industrial city (machine tools, electrical goods, paper and printing) within East Germany, with a Western sector; population (1988) East Berlin 1,223,000; West Berlin 1,879,000. East Berlin is the capital of East Germany, and of the county (*Bezirk*) of East Berlin; area 400 sq km/154 sq mi. West Berlin is an administrative region (*Land*) of West Germany; area 480 sq km/185 sq mi. The ◊Berlin Wall dividing the city was built 1961 and demolished 1989.

Unter den Linden, the tree-lined avenue once the whole city's focal point, has been restored in the East. West Berlin includes the fashionable Kurfürstendamm and the residential Hansa quarter. Prominent buildings include the Reichstag (former parliament building); Schloss Bellevue (Berlin residence of the president); Schloss Charlottenburg (housing several museums); Congress Hall; restored 18th-century State Opera, Dahlem picture gallery. The environs of Berlin include the Grünewald forest and Wannsee lake.

First mentioned about 1230, the city grew out of a fishing village, joined the Hanseatic League in the 15th century, became the permanent seat of the Hohenzollerns, and was capital of the Brandenburg electorate 1486–1701, of the kingdom of Prussia 1701–1871, and of united Germany 1871–1945. From the middle of the 18th century it developed into an important commercial and cultural centre. In World War II air raids and conquest by the Soviet army 23 Apr–2 May 1945 destroyed much of the city. After the war, Berlin was divided into four sectors – British, US, French, and Soviet – and until 1948 was under quadripartite government by the Allies; in that year the USSR withdrew from the combined board, blockaded the city for 327 days (supplies were brought in by air by the Allies), and created

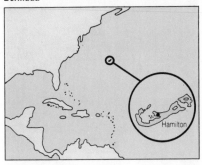

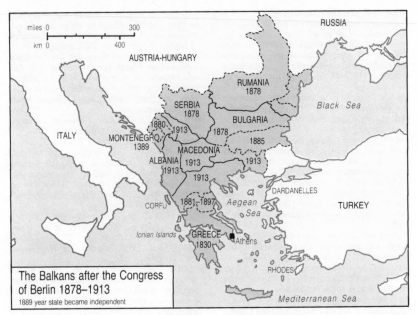

The Balkans after the Congress of Berlin 1878–1913
1889 year state became independent

a separate municipal government in their sector. The other three sectors (West Berlin) were made a *Land* of the Federal Republic May 1949, and in Oct 1949 East Berlin was proclaimed capital of East Germany.

Berlin /bɜːˈlɪn/ Irving. Adopted name of Israel Baline 1888–1989. Russian-born US composer, whose hits include 'Alexander's Ragtime Band', 'Always', 'God Bless America', and 'White Christmas', and the musicals *Top Hat* 1935, *Annie Get Your Gun* 1950, and *Call Me Madam* 1953. He also wrote film scores such as *Blue Skies* and *Easter Parade*.

Berlin /bɜːˈlɪn/ Isaiah 1909– . British philosopher. The son of a refugee from the Russian Revolution, he was professor of social and political theory at Oxford 1957–67. His books include *Historical Inevitability* 1954 and *Four Essays on Liberty* 1969. He was awarded the Order of Merit in 1971.

Berlin blockade in June 1948, the closing of entry to Berlin from the west by Soviet forces. It was an attempt to prevent the other Allies (USA, France, and Britain) unifying the western part of Germany. The British and US forces responded by sending supplies to the city by air for over a year (the **Berlin airlift**). In May 1949 the blockade was lifted; the airlift continued until Sept. The blockade marked the formal division of the city into Eastern and Western sectors.

Berlin, Conference of a conference 1884–85 of the major European powers, called by Chancellor Otto von Bismarck to decide on the colonial partition of Africa.

Berlin, Congress of congress of the European powers (Russia, Turkey, Austria-Hungary, Britain, France, Italy, and Germany) held at Berlin in 1878 to determine the boundaries of the Balkan states after the Russo-Turkish war. Prime Minister Disraeli attended as Britain's chief envoy, and declared on his return to England that he had brought back 'peace with honour'.

Berlinguer /ˌbeəlɪŋˈgweə/ Enrico 1922–1984. Italian Communist who freed the party from Soviet influence. By 1976 he was near to the premiership, but the ◊Red Brigade murder of Aldo Moro, the prime minister, revived the socialist vote.

Berlin Wall the dividing line between East and West Berlin 1961–89. Beginning 13 Aug 1961, it was reinforced by the Russians with armed guards and barbed wire to prevent the escape of unwilling inhabitants of East Berlin to the rival political and economic system of West Berlin. The interconnecting link between East and West Berlin was **Checkpoint Charlie**, where both

sides exchanged captured spies. Escapers from East to West were shot on sight. On 9 Nov 1989 the East German government opened its borders to try to halt the mass exodus of its citizens to the West via other Eastern bloc countries, thus making the Wall obsolete.

Berlioz /ˈbeəlɪəʊz/ (Louis) Hector 1803–1869. French romantic composer and the founder of modern orchestration. Much of his music was inspired by drama and literature and has a theatrical quality. He wrote symphonic works, such as *Symphonie fantastique* and *Roméo et Juliette*; dramatic cantatas including *La Damnation de Faust* and *L'Enfance du Christ*; sacred music; and three operas, *Béatrice et Bénédict*, *Benvenuto Cellini*, and *Les Troyens*.

Berlioz studied music at the Paris Conservatoire. He won the Prix de Rome 1830, and spent two years in Italy. In 1833 he married Harriet Smithson, an Irish actress playing Shakespearean parts in Paris, but they separated in 1842. After some years of poverty and public neglect, he went to Germany in 1842 and conducted his own works. He subsequently visited Russia and England. In 1854 he married Marie Recio, a singer.

Bermuda /bəˈmjuːdə/ British colony in the NW Atlantic
area 54 sq km/21 sq mi
capital and chief port Hamilton
features consists of about 150 small islands, of which 20 are inhabited, linked by bridges and causeways; Britain's oldest colony; the USA has a naval air base and there is a NASA tracking station
products Easter lilies, pharmaceutical; tourism and banking are important

Berlin Wall *The day after the breaching of the Berlin Wall on Nov 9 1989, un armed soldiers of the German Democratic Republic took up positions at the Brandenberg Gate.*

Bermuda

currency Bermuda dollar
population (1988) 58,100
language English
religion Christian
government under the constitution of 1968, Bermuda is a fully self-governing British colony, with a Governor, Senate and elected House of Assembly (premier from 1982 John Swan, United Bermuda Party).
recent history the islands were named after Juan de Bermudez, who visited them in 1515, and were settled by British colonists in 1609. Racial violence in 1977 led to intervention, at the request of the government, by British troops.

Bermuda Triangle the sea area bounded by Bermuda, Florida and Puerto Rico, which gained the nickname Deadly Bermuda Triangle in 1964 when it was suggested that unexplained disappearances of ships and aircraft were exceptionally frequent there; analysis of the data did not eventually confirm the idea.

Bern /beən/ (French **Berne**) capital of Switzerland and of Bern canton, in W Switzerland on the Aar; population (1987) 300,000. It joined the Swiss confederation 1353 and became the capital 1848. Industries include textiles, chocolate, pharmaceuticals, light metal, and electrical goods.

Bern was founded 1191, and made a free imperial city by Frederick II 1218. Its name is derived from the bear in its coat of arms, and there has been a bear pit in the city since the 16th century. The minster was begun 1421, the town hall 1406, and the university 1834. It is the seat of the Universal Postal Union.

Bernadette, St /ˌbɜːnəˈdet/ 1844–1879. French saint, born in Lourdes in the French Pyrenees. In Feb 1858 she had a vision of the Virgin Mary in a grotto, and it became a centre of pilgrimage. Many sick people who were dipped in the water of a spring there were said to have been cured. Feast day 16 Apr.

The grotto of Massabielle was opened to the public by command of Napoleon III, and a church built on the rock above became a shrine. At the age of 20 Bernadette became a nun at Nevers, and nursed the wounded of the Franco-Prussian War.

Bernadotte /ˌbɜːnəˈdɒt/ Count Folke 1895–1948. Swedish diplomat and president of the Swedish Red Cross. In 1945 he conveyed the Nazi commander Himmler's offer of capitulation to the British and US governments, and in 1948 was United Nations mediator in Palestine, where he was assassinated by Stern Gang guerrillas. He was a nephew of Gustaf VI of Sweden.

Bernadotte /ˌbɜːnəˈdɒt/ Jean-Baptiste Jules 1764–1844. Marshal in Napoleon's army, who in 1818 became ◊Charles XIV of Sweden. Hence, Bernadotte is the family name of the present royal house of Sweden.

Bernanos /ˌbeənəˈnəʊs/ Georges 1888–1948. French author. Born in Paris, he achieved fame in 1926 with *Sous le soleil de Satan/The Star of Satan*. His strongly Catholic viewpoint emerged equally in his *Journal d'un curé de campagne/The Diary of a Country Priest* 1936.

Bernard /beəˈnɑː/ Claude 1813–1878. French physiologist and founder of experimental medi-

Bernhardt French actress Sarah Bernhardt.

cine. Bernard first demonstrated that digestion is not restricted to the stomach, but takes place throughout the small intestine. He discovered the digestive input of the pancreas, several functions of the liver, and the vasomotor nerves which dilate and contract the blood vessels and thus regulate body temperature. This led him to the important concept of the *milieu intérieur* ('internal environment') whose stability is essential to good health. Bernard was a member of the French Academy and served in the Senate.

Bernard of Clairvaux, St /kleə'vəʊ/ 1090–1153. Christian founder in 1115 of Clairvaux monastery in Champagne, France. He reinvigorated the ◊Cistercian order, preached the Second Crusade in 1146, and had the scholastic philosopher Abelard condemned for heresy. He is often depicted with a beehive. Feast day 20 Aug.

Bernard of Menthon, St /mɒn'tɒn/ (or **Bernard of Montjoux**) 923–1008. Christian priest, founder of the hospices for travellers on the Alpine passes that bear his name. The large, heavily built **St Bernard dogs** formerly used to find travellers lost in the snow were also called after him. He is the patron saint of mountaineers. Feast day 28 May.

Bernese Oberland /'bɜːniːz 'əʊbələænd/ or **Bernese Alps** the mountainous area in the S of Berne canton which includes some of the most famous peaks, such as the Jungfrau, Eiger, and Finsteraarhorn. Interlaken is the chief town.

Bernhard /'beənɑːt/ Prince of the Netherlands 1911– . Formerly Prince Bernhard of Lippe-Biesterfeld, he married Princess ◊Juliana in 1937. When Germany invaded the Netherlands in 1940, he escaped to England and became liaison officer for the Dutch and British forces, playing a part in the organization of the Dutch Resistance. In 1976 he was widely censured for his involvement in the purchase of Lockheed aircraft by the Netherlands.

Bernhardt /'bɜːnhɑːt/ Sarah. Stage name of Rosine Bernard 1845–1923. French actress who dominated the stage of her day, frequently performing at the Comédie-Française in Paris. She excelled in tragic roles, including Cordelia in Shakespeare's *King Lear*, the title role in Racine's *Phèdre*, and the male roles of Hamlet and of Napoleon's son in ◊Rostand's *L'Aiglon*.

Bernini /beə'niːni/ Giovanni Lorenzo 1598–1680. Italian sculptor, architect, and painter, a leading figure in the development of the Baroque style. His work in Rome includes the colonnaded piazza in front of St Peter's Basilica, Rome (1656), fountains (as in the Piazza Navona), and papal monuments. His sculpture includes *The Ecstasy of St Theresa* 1645–52 (Sta Maria della Vittoria,

Rome), and numerous portrait busts.

Bernini's sculptural style is full of movement and drama, making great play with billowing drapery and facial expressions. His subjects were religious and mythological. A fine example is the marble *Apollo and Daphne* for the Cardinal Borghese, 1622–25 (Borghese Palace, Rome), with the figures shown in full flight. Inside St Peter's, he created several marble monuments and the elaborate canopy over the high altar. He also produced many fine portrait busts, one of Louis XIV of France.

Bernoulli /bɜː'nuːli/ Swiss family of mathematicians. *Jakob* (1654–1705) discovered Bernoulli numbers, a series of complex fractions used in higher mathematics. *Johann* (1667–1748), brother of Jakob, found the equation to the ◊catenary (1690) and developed exponential ◊calculus (1691). Johann's son *Daniel* (1700–1782) made important contributions in hydrodynamics (the study of fluids).

Jakob Bernoulli's best-known work was on transcendental curves (1696), the so-called **Bernoulli numbers**, and probability theory (published posthumously in *Ars Conjectandi* 1713). Johann Bernoulli concentrated more on applied mathematics. Daniel, Johann's son, was a mathematical physicist who made important contributions to ◊trigonometry and differential equations (◊differentiation), and in physics proposed **Bernoulli's principle**, which states that the pressure of a moving fluid decreases the faster it flows (which explains the origin of lift on the aerofoil of an aircraft's wing). This and other work on hydrodynamics was published in *Hydrodynamica* 1738.

Bernoulli effect a drop in hydraulic pressure, such as that in a fluid flowing through a constriction in a pipe. It is also responsible for the pressure differences on each surface of an aerofoil, which gives lift to the wing of an aircraft. The effect was named after the Swiss physicist Daniel Bernoulli.

Bernstein /'bɜːnstaɪn/ Edouard 1850–1932. German socialist thinker, proponent of reformist rather than revolutionary socialism, whereby a socialist society could be achieved within an existing parliamentary structure merely by workers' parties obtaining a majority.

Bernstein /'bɜːnstaɪn/ Leonard 1918– . US composer, conductor, and pianist. He has conducted major orchestras throughout the world. His works, which established a vogue for realistic, contemporary themes, include symphonies such as *The Age of Anxiety* 1949; ballets such as *Fancy Free* 1944; scores for musicals including *Wonderful Town* 1953 and *West Side Story* 1957; and *Mass* 1971 in memory of President J F Kennedy.

Born in Lawrence, Massachussetts, he was educated at Harvard University and the Curtis Institute of Music. From 1958 to 1970 he was musical director of the New York Philharmonic. Among his other works are *Jeremiah* 1944, *Facsimile* 1946, *Candide* 1956, and the *Chichester Psalms* 1965.

Berri /'beri/ Nabih 1939– . Lebanese politician and soldier, leader of Amal ('Hope'), the Syrian-backed Shi'ite nationalist movement. He was minister of justice in government of President ◊Gemayel from 1984. In 1988 Amal was disbanded after defeat by the Iranian-backed Hezbollah ('Children of God') during the Lebanese civil wars.

Berrigan /'berɪgən/ Daniel 1921– and Philip 1924– . US Roman Catholic priests. The brothers, opponents of the Vietnam War, broke into the draft-records offices at Catonsville, Maryland, to burn the files with napalm, and were sentenced in 1968 to three and six years' imprisonment, but went underground. Subsequently Philip Berrigan was tried with others in 1972 for allegedly conspiring to kidnap President Nixon's adviser Henry Kissinger and blow up government offices in Washington, DC, and sentenced to two years' imprisonment.

berry a fleshy, many-seeded ◊fruit that does not split open to release the seeds. The outer layer

of tissue, the exocarp, forms an outer skin which is often brightly coloured to attract birds to eat the fruit and thus disperse the seeds. Examples of berries are the tomato and the grape.

A *pepo* is a type of berry that has developed a hard exterior, such as the cucumber fruit. Another type is the *hesperidium*, which has a thick, leathery outer layer, such as that found in citrus fruits, and fluid-containing vesicles within, which form the segments.

Berry /'beri/ Family name of Viscount Camrose, Viscount Kemsley and Lord Hartwell.

Berry /'beri/ Chuck (Charles Edward) 1926– . US rock-and-roll singer, prolific songwriter, and guitarist. His characteristic guitar riffs became staples of rock music, and his humorous storytelling lyrics were also influential. He had a string of hits in the 1950s beginning with 'Maybellene' 1955.

Berryman /'berimən/ John 1914–1972. US poet, whose complex and personal works include *Homage to Mistress Bradstreet* 1956, *77 Dream Songs* 1964 (Pulitzer Prize), and *His Toy, His Dream, His Rest* 1968.

berserker legendary Scandinavian warrior whose frenzy in battle transformed him into a wolf or bear howling and foaming at the mouth (hence 'to go berserk'), and rendered him immune to sword and flame.

Berthelot /,beətə'ləʊ/ Pierre Eugène Marcellin 1827–1907. French chemist and politician, who carried out research into dyes and explosives, and proved that hydrocarbons and other organic compounds can be synthesized from inorganic materials.

Bertholet /,beətə'leɪ/ Claude Louis 1748–1822. French chemist, who carried out research on dyes and bleaches (introducing the use of ◊chlorine as a bleach) and determined the composition of ◊ammonia.

Modern chemical nomenclature is based on a system worked out by Bertholet and Antoine ◊Lavoisier.

Bertolucci /,beətəʊ'luːtʃi/ Bernardo 1940– . Italian director, whose work combines political and historical satire with an elegant visual appeal. His films include *The Spider's Stratagem* 1970, *Last Tango in Paris* 1972, and *The Last Emperor* 1987, for which he received an Academy Award.

Bertrand de Born /beə'trɒn də 'bɔːn/ *c.*1140–*c.*1215. Provençal ◊troubadour. He was viscount of Hautefort in Périgord, accompanied Richard Lionheart to Palestine, and died a monk.

Berwick /'berɪk/ James Fitzjames, Duke of Berwick 1670–1734. French marshal, illegitimate son of the Duke of York (afterwards James II of England) and Arabella Churchill (1648–1730), sister of the great duke of Marlborough, his enemy in battle. He was made duke of Berwick in 1687. After the revolution of 1688 he served under his

Berry US rock-and-roll singer Chuck Berry.

Berzelius *Swedish chemist Jöns Jakob Berzelius.*

father in Ireland, joined the French army, fought against William III and Marlborough, and in 1707 defeated the English at Almansa in Spain. He was killed at the siege of Philippsburg.

Berwickshire /'berɪkʃə/ former county of SE Scotland, a district of Borders region from 1975.

Berwick-upon-Tweed /'berɪk əpɒn 'twiːd/ port in NE England, at the mouth of the Tweed, Northumberland, 5 km/3 mi SE of the Scottish border; population (1981) 26,230. It is a fishing port. Other industries include iron foundries and shipbuilding.

features three bridges cross the Tweed: the Old Bridge 1611–34 with 15 arches, the Royal Border railway bridge 1850 constructed by Robert Stephenson, and the Royal Tweed Bridge 1928.

history held alternately by England and Scotland for centuries, Berwick was in 1551 made a neutral town; it was attached to Northumberland in 1885.

beryl a mineral, beryllium aluminium silicate, $Be_3Al_2Si_6O_{18}$, which forms crystals chiefly in granite. It is the chief ore of beryllium. Two of its gem forms are aquamarine (light-blue crystals) and emerald (dark-green crystals).

beryllium a light, silvery, hard, metallic element, symbol Be, atomic number 4, relative atomic mass 9.013. It is used as a source of neutrons

Besant *British socialist and feminist activist Annie Besant.*

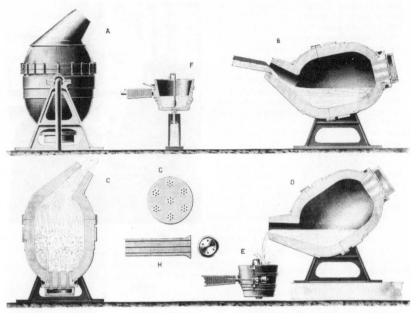

Bessemer *The British metallurgist Henry Bessemer patented an economical process by which pig iron blasted by a current of air is turned directly into steel. This is a diagram of the first movable form of his converter and ladle, taken from his autobiography.*

when bombarded, to make windows for X-ray tubes, to toughen copper for high-grade gearwheels and spark-free tools, and as a neutron reflector, ◊moderator, and uranium sheathing in nuclear reactors.

Berzelius /bə'ziːlɪəs/ Jöns Jakob 1779–1848. Swedish chemist, whose accurate determination of atomic and molecular weights helped to establish the laws of combination and the atomic theory. He invented (1813–14) the system of chemical symbols now in use and did valuable work on ◊catalysts.

Besançon /bə'zɒnsɒn/ town on the river Doubs, France; population (1983) 120,000. It is the capital of Franche-Comté. The first factory to produce artificial fibres was established here 1890. Industries include textiles and clock-making. It has fortifications by ◊Vauban, Roman remains and a Gothic cathedral. The writer Victor Hugo and the Lumière brothers, inventors of cinematography, were born here.

Besant /'besənt/ Annie 1847–1933. British socialist and feminist activist. Separated from her clerical husband in 1873 because of her freethinking views, she was associated with the radical atheist Charles Bradlaugh and the ◊Fabians. She and Bradlaugh published a treatise advocating birth control and were prosecuted; as a result she lost custody of her daughter. In 1889 she became a disciple of Mme ◊Blavatsky. She thereafter preached theosophy and, as a supporter of Indian independence, became president of the Hindu National Congress in 1917.

Besant /'besənt/ Walter 1836–1901. British writer. He wrote novels in partnership with James Rice (1844–82), and produced an attack on the social evils of the East End of London, *All Sorts and Conditions of Men* 1882, and an unfinished *Survey of London* 1902–12.

Bessarabia /ˌbesə'reɪbɪə/ territory in SE Europe, annexed by Russia 1812, which broke away at the Russian Revolution to join Romania. The cession was confirmed by the Allies, but not by Russia, in a Paris treaty of 1920; Russia reoccupied it 1940 and divided it between the Moldavian and Ukrainian republics. Romania recognized the position in the 1947 peace treaty.

Bessel /'besl/ Friedrich Wilhelm 1784–1846. German astronomer and mathematician, the first person to find the approximate distance to a

star by direct methods when he measured the ◊parallax of 61 Cygni in 1838. In mathematics, he introduced the series of functions now known as Bessel functions.

Bessemer /'besɪmə/ Henry 1813–1898. British civil engineer, who invented a method of converting molten pig-iron into steel (the Bessemer process).

Bessemer process the first cheap method of making ◊steel, invented by Henry Bessemer in England in 1856. It has since been superseded by more efficient steelmaking processes, particularly the ◊basic-oxygen process. In the Bessemer process compressed air is blown into the bottom of a converter, a furnace shaped rather like a cement mixer, containing molten pig iron. The excess carbon in the iron burns out, other impurities form a slag, and the furnace is emptied by tilting.

Best /best/ Charles Herbert 1899–1978. Canadian physiologist, one of the team of Canadian scientists including Frederick ◊Banting whose researches resulted in 1922 in the discovery of insulin as a treatment for diabetes.

A Banting–Best Department of Medical Research was founded in Toronto, and Best was its director from 1941 to 1967.

Best /best/ George 1946– . Irish footballer. He won two League championship medals and was a member of the Manchester United side that won the European Cup in 1968.

Born in Belfast, he joined Manchester United as a youth and made his debut at 17; seven months later he made his international debut for Northern Ireland. He also played for Stockport County, Fulham, Bournemouth, Hibernian, and in the US. Trouble with managers, fellow players, and the media led to his early retirement.

CAREER HIGHLIGHTS

Football League
appearances: 411
goals: 147
League championship: 1965, 1967
Footballer of the Year: 1968
internationals
appearances: 37
goals: 9
European Cup: 1968
European Footballer of the Year: 1968

bestiary in medieval times, a book with stories and

illustrations which depicted real and mythical animals or plants to illustrate a (usually Christian) moral. The stories were initially derived from the Greek *Physiologus* (*c.* 2nd century AD), a collection of 48 such stories, written in Alexandria.

Translations of the *Physiologus* into vernacular languages (French, Italian, and English) date from the 13th century; illustrated versions are known from the 9th century. Much of modern folklore about animals derives from the bestiary, such as the myth of the phoenix burning itself to be born again.

bestseller any book that sells more copies than most other books in a short period of time. The first modern bestseller is often said to have been Margaret Mitchell's novel *Gone with the Wind* 1936. The Bible has sold more copies than any other book over time. Book sales were generally far higher in the 19th century. Many newspapers print bestseller charts, and potential bestsellers are often heavily promoted by publishers. In the UK the paperback with the highest sales in the 1980s was *The Secret Diary of Adrian Mole Aged 13 3/4* by the humourist Sue Townsend (over 3 million copies sold).

beta-blocker a drug that blocks impulses that stimulate certain nerve endings (beta receptors) serving the heart muscles. This reduces the heart rate and the force of contraction, which in turn reduces the amount of oxygen (and therefore the blood supply) required by the heart. Beta-blockers are banned from use in competitive sport. They may be useful in the treatment of angine, arrhythmia, and raised blood pressure, and following myocardial infarctions. They must be withdrawn from use gradually.

beta decay the disintegration of the nucleus of an atom to produce a ◊beta particle, or high-speed electron. During beta decay, a proton in the nucleus changes into a neutron. The mass lost in this change is converted into kinetic (movement) energy of the beta particle. The weak nuclear force, one of the fundamental ◊forces of nature that operate inside the nucleus, causes beta decay.

beta particle an electron emitted from a radioactive substance that is undergoing spontaneous disintegration. Beta particles do not exist in the nucleus, but are created on disintegration when a neutron converts to a proton to emit an electron.

Betelgeuse /ˈbiːtldʒɜːz/ a red supergiant star in the constellation of Orion, over 300 times the diameter of the Sun, about the same size as the orbit of Mars. It lies 650 light years away and is the tenth brightest star in the sky, although its brightness varies.

betel nut fruit of the areca palm (*Areca catechu*), used as a masticatory by peoples of the East: chewing it results in blackened teeth and a mouth stained deep red.

bête noire (French 'black beast') something particularly disliked.

Bethe /ˈbeɪtə/ Hans Albrecht 1906– . German-born US physicist. He worked on the first atomic bomb, and was in 1967 awarded a Nobel prize for his discoveries concerning energy production in stars.

Bethe left Germany for England in 1933, working at Manchester and Bristol universities. In 1935 he moved to the USA where he became professor of theoretical physics at Cornell University; his research was interrupted by the war and by his appointment as head of the theoretical division of the Los Alamos atomic bomb project. He has since become a leading peace campaigner, and opposed the US government's Strategic Defence Initiative or 'Star Wars' programme.

Bethlehem /ˈbeθlɪhem/ city in E Pennsylvania, USA; population (1980) 70,400. The former steel industry has been replaced by high technology.

Bethlehem /ˈbeθlɪhem/ (Hebrew *Beit-Lahm*) town on the W bank of the river Jordan, S of Jerusalem. Occupied by Israel in 1967; population (1980) 14,000. In the New Testament it was the birthplace of Jesus and associated with King

Betjeman *The poet John Betjeman was regarded with much affection for his ability to capture the popular mood, and for his care for England's architectural heritage.*

David.

Bethmann Hollweg /ˈbeɪtmæn ˈhɒlveg/ Theobald von 1856–1921. German politician, imperial chancellor 1909–17, largely responsible for engineering popular support for World War I in Germany, but his power was gradually superseded by a military dictatorship under ◊Ludendorff.

Béthune /beɪˈtjuːn/ city in N France, W of Lille; population (1982) 258,400. Industries include textiles, machinery, and tyres.

Betjeman /ˈbetʃɪmən/ John 1906–1984. English poet and essayist, originator of a peculiarly English light verse, nostalgic and delighting in Victorian and Edwardian architecture. His *Collected Poems* appeared in 1968 and a verse autobiography *Summoned by Bells* in 1960. He was knighted in 1969 and became Poet Laureate in 1972.

betony plant of the family Labiatae, *Betonica officinalis* is a hedgerow weed in Britain. It has a hairy stem and leaves, and reddish-purple flowers.

Betterton /ˈbetətən/ Thomas *c.* 1635–1710. British actor. A member of the Duke of York's company after the Restoration, he attracted the attention of Charles II. He was greatly admired in many Shakespearean parts, including Hamlet and Othello.

Betti /ˈbeti/ Ugo 1892–1953. Italian poet and dramatist. His best-known plays are *Delitto all'isola delle capre/Crime on Goat Island* 1948 and *La Regina e gli insorte/The Queen and the Rebels* 1949.

betting wagering money on the outcome of a game, race, or other event, not necessarily sporting.

In the UK, on-course betting on **horses** and **dogs** may be through individual bookmakers at given odds, or on the tote (totalizator), when the total amount (with fixed deductions) staked is divided among those making the correct forecast. Off-course betting is mainly through betting 'shops' (legalized 1960) which, like bookmakers, must have a licence. **Football** betting is in the hands of 'pools' promoters who must be registered with a local authority to which annual accounts are submitted. The size of the money prizes is determined by the number of successful forecasts of the results of matches received; the maximum first dividend on football pools is fixed at £1 million.

In France, there are no individual bookmakers; all betting is through the *Pari-mutuel*, the equivalent of the British totalizator.

Betty /ˈbeti/ William Henry West 1791–1874. British boy actor, called the 'Young Roscius' after the greatest comic actor of ancient Rome. He was

Bevan *Aneurin Bevan at his desk when minister of health, 1945.*

famous, particularly in Shakespearean roles, from the ages of 11 to 17.

Betws-y-coed /ˈbetʊs ə ˈkɔɪd/ village in Gwynedd, Wales; population (1981) 750. It is a tourist centre, noted for its waterfalls.

Beuys /bɔɪs/ Joseph 1921–1986. German sculptor and performance artist. By the 1970s he had gained an international reputation. His sculpture makes use of unusual materials such as felt and fat. He was strongly influenced by his wartime experiences.

Bevan /ˈbevən/ Aneurin 1897–1960. British Labour politician. Son of a Welsh miner, and himself a miner at 13, he became member of Parliament for Ebbw Vale 1929–60. As minister of health 1945–51, he inaugurated the National Health Service (NHS); he was minister of labour Jan–Apr 1951, when he resigned (with Harold Wilson) on the introduction of NHS charges and led a Bevanite faction against the government. He was noted as an orator.

Beveridge /ˈbevərɪdʒ/ William Henry, 1st Baron Beveridge 1879–1963. British economist. A civil servant, he acted as Lloyd George's lieutenant in the social legislation of the Liberal government before World War I. The *Beveridge Report* 1942 formed the basis of the welfare state in Britain.

Beverly Hills /ˈbevəli/ residential part of greater Los Angeles, California, USA, known as the home of Hollywood film stars. Population (1980) 32,400.

Bevin /ˈbevɪn/ Ernest 1881–1951. British Labour politician. Chief creator of the Transport and General Workers' Union, he was its general secretary 1921–40, when he entered the war cabinet as minister of labour and National Service. He organized the 'Bevin boys', chosen by ballot to work in the coal mines as war service, and was foreign secretary in the Labour government 1945–51.

Bewick /ˈbjuːɪk/ Thomas 1753–1828. British wood engraver, excelling in animal subjects. His illustrated *General History of Quadrupeds* 1790 and *History of British Birds* 1797, 1804 display his skill.

Bexhill-on-Sea /ˌbeksˈhɪl/ seaside resort in E Sussex, England; population (1981) 35,500.

Beza /beɪˈzɑː/ Théodore (properly De Bèsze) 1519–1605. French church reformer. He settled in Geneva, Switzerland, where he worked with the Protestant leader Calvin and succeeded him in 1564–1600 as head of the reformed church there. He wrote in defence of the burning of ◊Servetus (1554) and translated the New Testament into Latin.

Bezier curve a curved line that connects a series of points (or 'nodes') in the smoothest possible way. The shape of the curve is governed by a series of complex mathematical formulae. They are used in ◊computer graphics and ◊CAD.

Béziers /bezˈjeɪ/ city in Languedoc-Roussillon, S France; population (1983) 84,000. It is a centre of the wine trade. It was once a Roman station, and was the site of a massacre 1209 in the Albigensian Crusade.

bézique (French *bésigue*) card game believed to have originated in Spain. Brought to England 1861 it became very popular and in 1887 the Portland Club drew up a standardized set of rules for the popular variety **Rubicon bézique**. Each player has a pack of cards but all cards with a face value of 2–6 are taken out.

BFI abbreviation for **British Film Institute**. Founded in 1933, the organization was created to promote the cinema as a 'means of entertainment and instruction'.

The BFI comprises the National Film Archive (1935) which acts as a distributor and a library, and the National Film Theatre (1951).

BFPO abbreviation for **British Forces Post Office**.

Bhagalpur /'bɑ:glpʊə/ town in N India, on the river Ganges; population (1981) 225,000. It manufactures silk and textiles. Several Jain temples are here.

Bhagavad-Gītā /'bʌɡəvəd 'gi:tə/ (Hindu 'the Song of the Blessed') religious and philosophical Sanskrit poem, dating from around 300 BC, forming an episode in the sixth book of the *Mahābhārata*, one of the two great Hindu epics. It is the supreme religious work of Hinduism.

bhakti (Sanskrit 'devotion') in Hinduism, a tradition of worship that emphasizes love and devotion rather than ritual, sacrifice, or study.

Bhamo /bə'məʊ/ town in Burma, near the Chinese frontier, on the Irrawaddy river. It is the inland limit of steam navigation and is mainly a trading centre.

bhang another name for ◊cannabis.

bhangra a type of pop music evolved in the UK in the late 1970s from traditional Punjabi music, combining electronic instruments and ethnic drums.

Bharat /'bʌrət/ Hindi name for ◊India.

Bharat Natyam /'bʌrət 'nɑ:tjəm/ type of Indian classical dancing.

Bhatgaon /bɑ:t'gɑ:ɒn/ Bhadgaon or Bhaktapur town in Nepál, 11 km/7 mi SE of Katmandu; population (1981) 48,500. A religious centre from the 9th century, it has a palace.

Bhavnagar /baʊ'nʌgə/ port in Gujarat, NW India, in the Kathiawar peninsula; population (1981) 308,000. It is a centre for textile industry. It was capital of the former Rajput princely state of Bhavnagar.

bhikku a Buddhist monk who is totally dependent on alms and the monastic community (*sangha*) for support.

Bhindranwale /'bɪndrəwɒlə/ Sant Jarnail Singh 1947–1984. Indian Sikh fundamentalist leader, who campaigned for the creation of a separate state of Khalistan during the early 1980s, precipitating a bloody Hindu-Sikh conflict in the Punjab. He was killed in the siege of the Golden Temple in ◊Amritsar.

Born into a poor Punjabi Jat farming family, he trained at the orthodox Damdani Taksal Sikh missionary school, becoming its head priest 1971 and assuming the name Bhindranwale. Initially encouraged by the politician Sanjay Gandhi in the hope of dividing the Akali Dal (a Punjabi political party), the fundamentalist Bhindranwale violently campaigned against the heretical activities of Nirankari Sikhs during the later 1970s. His campaign broadened into the separatist demand.

Having taken refuge in the Golden Temple complex in Amritsar and built up an arms cache for guerrilla activities, Bhindranwale, along with around 500 followers, died at the hands of Indian security forces who stormed the temple in 'Operation Blue Star' June 1984.

Bhopal /bəʊ'pɑ:l/ industrial city (textiles, chemicals, electrical goods, jewellery); capital of Madhya Pradesh, central India; population (1981) 672,000. Nearby Bhimbetka Caves, discovered 1973, have the world's largest collection of prehistoric paintings which are about 10,000 years old. In 1984 some 2,000 people died after an escape of poisonous gas from a factory owned by the US company

Bhutto Benazir Bhutto at a press conference in Islamabad, Dec 31 1988.

Union Carbide; the long-term effects are yet to be discovered.

history the city was capital of the former princely state of Bhopal, founded 1723, which became allied to Britain in 1817. It was merged with Madhya Pradesh in 1956.

bhp abbreviation for **brake horsepower**.

Bhubaneswar /,bʊvə'neɪʃwə/ city in NE India; population (1981) 219,200. It is the capital of Orissa. Utkal University was founded 1843. A place of pilgrimage and centre of Siva worship, it has temples of the 6th–12th centuries; it was capital of the Kesaris (Lion) dynasty of Orissa 474–950.

Bhumibol Adulyadej /'pu:mɪpəʊn ə'dʊnlədeɪt/ 1927– . King of Thailand from 1946. Educated in Bangkok and Switzerland, he succeeded on the assassination of his brother, formally taking the throne 1950. In 1973 he was active, with popular support, in overthrowing the military government of Field Marshal Kittikachorn and ending a sequence of army-dominated regimes in power from 1932.

Bhutan /bu:'tɑ:n/ mountainous, landlocked country in SE Asia, bordered to the north by China and to the south by India.

government Bhutan is a hereditary monarchy, and although since 1953 there has been an elected national assembly (*Tshogdu*) and since 1965 a partly elected royal advisory council with whom the monarch shares power, in the absence of a written constitution, it is in effect an absolute monarchy. There are, however, certain written rules governing the methods of electing members of the Royal Advisory Council and *Tshogdu*. There are no political parties, though there is a gradual trend towards greater democracy.

history Ruled by Tibet from the 16th century and by China from 1720, Bhutan was invaded by Britain in 1865 and a trade agreement signed, under which an annual subsidy was paid to Bhutan. In 1907 the first hereditary monarch was installed and three years later, under the Anglo-Bhutanese Treaty, foreign relations were placed under the control of the British government in India.

When India became independent in 1945, an Indo-Bhutan treaty of friendship was signed, under which Bhutan agreed to seek Indian advice on foreign relations but not necessarily to accept it. There is no formal defence treaty, but India would regard an attack on Bhutan as an act of aggression against itself. In 1952 King Jigme Dorji Wangchuk came to power and in 1953 a national assembly was established.

In 1959, after the Chinese annexation of Tibet, Bhutan gave asylum to some 4,000 Tibetan refugees who in 1979 were given the choice of taking up Bhutanese citizenship or returning to Tibet. Most became citizens and the rest went to India.

the Bible

The Books of the Old Testament

Name of book	Chapters	Date written
the Pentateuch or Five Books of Moses:		
Genesis	50	mid 8th century BC
Exodus	40	950–586 BC
Leviticus	27	mid 7th century BC
Numbers	36	850–650 BC
Deuteronomy	34	mid 7th century BC
Joshua	24	*c.*550 BC
Judges	21	*c.*550 BC
Ruth	4	end 3rd century BC
1 Samuel	31	*c.*900 BC
2 Samuel	24	*c.*900 BC
1 Kings	22	550–600 BC
2 Kings	25	550–600 BC
1 Chronicles	29	*c.*300 BC
2 Chronicles	36	*c.*300 BC
Ezra	10	*c.*450 BC
Nehemiah	13	*c.*450 BC
Esther	10	*c.*200 BC
Job	42	600–400 BC
Psalms	150	6th–2nd century BC
Proverbs	31	350–150 BC
Ecclesiastes	12	*c.*200 BC
Song of solomon	8	3rd century BC
Isaiah	66	end 3rd century BC
Jeremiah	52	604 BC
Lamentations	5	586–536 BC
Ezekiel	48	6th century BC
Daniel	12	*c.*166 BC
Hosea	14	*c.*732 BC
Joel	3	*c.*500 BC
Amos	9	775–750 BC
Obadiah	1	6th–3rd century BC
Jonah	4	600–200 BC
Micah	7	end 3rd century BC
Nahum	3	*c.*626 BC
Habakkuk	3	*c.*600 BC
Zephaniah	3	3rd century BC
Haggai	2	*c.*520 BC
Zechariah	14	*c.*520 BC
Malachi	4	*c.*430 BC

The Books of the New Testament

Name of book	Chapters	Date written
the four Gospels:		
Matthew	28	before AD 70
Mark	16	before AD 70
Luke	24	AD 70–80
John	21	AD 90–100
The Acts of the Apostles	28	AD 70–80
Romans	16	AD 120
1 Corinthians	16	AD 57
2 Corinthians	13	AD 57
Galatians	6	AD 53
Ephesians	6	AD 140
Philippians	4	AD 63
Colossians	4	AD 140
1 Thessa-lonians	5	AD 50–54
2 Thessa-lonians	3	AD 50–54
1 Timothy	6	before AD 64
2 Timothy	4	before AD 64
Titus	3	before AD 64
Philemon	1	AD 60–62
Hebrews	13	AD 80–90
James	5	before AD 52
1 Peter	5	before AD 64
2 Peter	3	before AD 64
1 John	5	AD 90–100
2 John	1	AD 90–100
3 John	1	AD 90–100
Jude	1	AD 75–80
Revelation	22	AD 81–96

Bible Two plates from the Bible Pauperum c. 1470. The left-hand page shows Joseph in the pit, the burial of Jesus, and Jonah. The right-hand plate shows David slaying Goliath, the resurrection of Christ, and Samson and the lion.

In 1968, as part of a move towards greater democracy, the king appointed his first cabinet. He died in 1972 and was succeeded by his Western-educated son Jigme Singye Wangchuk.

In 1983 Bhutan became a founder member of the South Asia Regional Co-operation organization (SARC) and in 1985 the first meeting of SARC foreign ministers was held in Bhutan.

Bhutan
Kingdom of
(Druk-yul)

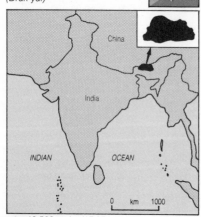

area 46,500 sq km/17,954 sq mi
capital Thimbu
physical occupies S slopes of the Himalayas, and is cut by valleys of tributaries of the Brahmaputra
head of state and government Jigme Singye Wangchuk from 1972
political system absolute monarchy

political parties none
exports timber, minerals
currency ngultrum (28.50 = £1 Feb 1990); also Indian currency
population (1988) 1,400,000; annual growth rate 2%
life expectancy men 47, women 45
language Dzongkha (a Tibetan dialect), Nepáli, and English (all official)
religion Mahayana Buddhist, 35% Hindu
literacy 10%
GDP $150 million (1983); $120 per head of population
chronology
1865 Trade treaty with Britain signed.
1907 First hereditary monarch installed.
1910 Anglo-Bhutanese Treaty signed.
1945 Indo-Bhutan Treaty of Friendship signed.
1952 King Jigme Dorji Wangchuk installed.
1953 National assembly established.
1959 4,000 Tibetan refugees given asylum.
1968 King established first cabinet.
1972 King died and was succeeded by his son Jigme Singye Wangchuk.
1979 Tibetan refugees told to take up Bhutanese citizenship or leave; most stayed.
1983 Bhutan became a founder member of the South Asian Regional Cooperation organization (SARC).

Bhutto /ˈbuːtəʊ/ Benazir 1953– . Pakistani politician, leader of the Pakistan People's Party (PPP) from 1984 (in exile until 1986), and prime minister of Pakistan from 1988. She is the first female leader of a Muslim state.

Benazir Bhutto was educated at Harvard and Oxford universities. She returned to Pakistan 1977 but was placed under house arrest after Gen ◊Zia ul Haq seized power from her father, Prime Minister Zulfiqar Ali Bhutto. On her release she moved to the UK and became, with her mother Nusrat (1934–), the joint leader in exile of the opposition PPP. When martial law had been lifted, she returned to Pakistan Apr 1986 to launch a campaign for open elections. In her first year in office she struck an uneasy balance with the military establishment and improved Pakistan's relations with India. She led her country back into the Commonwealth 1989 and became in 1990 the first head of government to bear a child while in office.

Bhutto /ˈbuːtəʊ/ Zulfiqar Ali 1928–1979. Pakistani politician, president 1971–73 and then prime minister until the 1977 military coup led by Gen ◊Zia ul Haq. In 1978 he was sentenced to death for conspiracy to murder a political opponent, and was hanged.

Biafra, Bight of /biˈæfrə/ name until 1975 of the Bight of ◊Bonny, W Africa.

Biafra, Republic of /biˈæfrə/ African state proclaimed in 1967 when fears that Nigerian central government was increasingly in the hands of the rival Hausa tribe led the predominantly Ibo Eastern Region of Nigeria to secede under Lt-Col Odumegwu Ojukwu, an Oxford-educated Ibo. On the proclamation of Biafra, civil war ensued with the rest of the federation. In a bitterly fought campaign federal forces had confined the Biafrans to a shrinking area of the interior by 1968, and by 1970 Biafra ceased to exist.

Bialystok /bjæˈwɪstɒk/ city in E Poland; population (1985) 245,000. It is the capital city of Bialystok region. Industries include textiles, chemicals and tools. Founded 1310, the city belonged to Prussia 1795–1807 and to Russia 1807–1919.

Biarritz /biəˈrɪts/ town on the Bay of Biscay, France; near the Spanish border; population (1982) 28,000. A seaside resort and spa town, it was popularized by Queen Victoria and Edward VII.

biathlon cross-country race on skis. It also involves accurate shooting with rifles at prepared targets at set intervals, and is used as a military training exercise in some countries.

Biber /'bi:bə/ Heinrich von 1644–1704. Bohemian composer, Kapellmeister at the Archbishop of Salzburg's court. A virtuoso violinist, he composed a wide variety of musical pieces including the *Nightwatchman Serenade*.

Bible (Greek *ta biblia* 'the books') the sacred book of the Jewish and Christian religions. The Hebrew Bible, recognized by both Jews and Christians, is called the ◊*Old Testament* by Christians. The ◊*New Testament* comprises books recognized by the Christian church from the 4th century as canonical. The Roman Catholic Bible also includes the ◊*Apocrypha.*

The first English translation of the entire Bible was by a priest, Miles Coverdale, 1535; the Authorized Version or *King James Bible* 1611 was long influential in the clarity and beauty of its language. A revision of the Authorized Version carried out 1959 by the British and Foreign Bible Society produced the widely-used Revised Standard Version. A conference of British churches 1946 recommended a completely new translation into English from the original Hebrew and Greek texts; work on this was carried out over the following two decades, resulting in the publication of the New English Bible (New Testament 1961, Old Testament and Apocrypha 1970).

Missionary activity led to the translation of the Bible into the languages of people they were trying to convert, and by 1975 parts of the Bible had been translated into over 1,500 different languages, with 261 complete translations.

Bible society society founded for the promotion of translation and distribution of the Scriptures. The largest is the British and Foreign Bible Society, founded in 1804.

Biblical criticism study of the content and origin of the Bible. *Lower* or *textual criticism* is directed to the recovery of the original text; *higher* or *documentary criticism* is concerned with questions of authorship, date, and literary sources; *historical criticism* seeks to ascertain the actual historic content of the Bible, aided by archaeological discoveries and the ancient history of neighbouring peoples.

bicarbonate the familiar name for a salt derived from carbonic acid (solution of carbon dioxide in water) in which only one of the hydrogen atoms has been replaced by a ◊cation (negative ion). Because carbonic acid is a weak acid, bicarbonates (hydrogen carbonates) behave more as bases than acids (see ◊acid salt). The presence of calcium and magnesium hydrogen carbonates in water causes 'temporary hardness'.

bicarbonate of soda a white crystalline solid ($NaHCO_3$) more properly called sodium hydrogen carbonate. It neutralizes acids and is used in medicine to treat acid indigestion. It is also used in baking powders and effervescent drinks.

Bichat /bi:'ʃɑ:/ Marie François Xavier 1771–1802. French physician and founder of ◊histology. He studied the organs of the body, their structure, and the ways in which they are affected by disease. This led to his discovery and naming of 'tissues', a basic medical concept. He argued that disease does not affect the whole organ but only certain of its constituent tissues.

He was physician at the Hôtel-Dieu hospital in Paris, and here, in a single year, he carried out 600 ◊autopsies. He identified 21 types of tissue.

bichir African fish, genus *Polypterus*, found in tropical swamps and rivers. Cylindrical in shape, some species grow to 70 cm/2.3 ft or more. They show many 'primitive' features, such as breathing air by using the swimbladder, having a spiral valve in the intestine, having heavy bony scales, and having a larva with external gills. These, and the fleshy fins, lead some scientists to think they are related to lungfish and coelacanths.

bicycle a pedal-driven two-wheeled vehicle used in ◊cycling.

Bidault /bi:'dəʊ/ Georges 1899–1983. French politician. As a leader of the *Movement Républicaine Populaire*, he held office as prime minister and foreign minister in a number of unstable administrations of 1944–54. As head of the ◊*Organisation de l'Armée Secrète* from 1962, he left the country, but was allowed to return in 1968.

Biedermeier early 19th-century Germanic style of art and furniture, derogatively named after Gottlieb Biedermaier, a fictional character embodying bourgeois taste.

Biel /bi:l/ (French *Bienne*) town in NW Switzerland; population (1987) 83,000. Its main industries include engineering, scientific instruments, and watchmaking.

Bielefeld /'bi:ləfeld/ city in North Rhine-Westphalia, West Germany, 55 km/34 mi E of Münster; population (1988) 299,000. Industries include textiles, drinks, chemicals, machinery, and motorcycles.

Bielostok /bjelə'stɒk/ Russian form of ◊Bialystok, city in Poland.

Bienne /bjen/ French form of ◊Biel, town in Switzerland.

biennial plant a plant that completes its life cycle in two years. During the first year it grows vegetatively and the surplus food produced is stored in its ◊perennating organ, usually the root. In the following year these food reserves are used for the production of leaves, flowers and seeds, after which the plant dies. Many root vegetables are biennials, including the carrot *Daucus carota* and parsnip *Pastinaca sativa*. Some garden plants which are grown as biennials are actually perennials, for example the wallflower *Cheiranthus cheiri*.

Bierce /bɪəs/ Ambrose (Gwinett) 1842–1914. US author. He established his reputation as a master of supernatural and psychological horror with his *Tales of Soldiers and Civilians* 1891 and *Can Such Things Be?* 1893. He also wrote *The Devil's Dictionary* 1906, a collection of ironic definitions. He disappeared on a secret mission to Mexico.

Bierstadt /'bɪəstæt/ Albert 1830–1902. US landscape painter. His spectacular panoramas fell out of favour after the American Civil War. A classic work is *Thunderstorm in the Rocky Mountains* 1859 (Museum of Fine Arts, Boston).

Biffen /'bɪfɪn/ (William) John 1930– . British Conservative politician. In 1971 Biffen was elected to Parliament for a Shropshire seat. Despite being to the left of Margaret Thatcher, he held key positions in government from 1979, including leader of the House of Commons from 1982, but was dropped after the general election of 1987.

bigamy in law, the offence of marrying a person while already lawfully married. In some countries marriage to more than one wife or husband is lawful; see also ◊polygamy.

big band jazz sound – ◊swing music created in the late 1930s and 1940s by bands of 15 or more players, such as those of Duke ◊Ellington and Benny ◊Goodman.

Big Bang in economics, popular term for the major changes instituted in late 1986 to the organization and practices of the City of London as Britain's financial centre, with the aim of ensuring that London retained its place as one of the leading world financial centres. Facilitated in part by computerization and on-line communications, the changes included the liberalization of the London ◊Stock Exchange. This involved merging the functions of jobber (dealer in stocks and shares) and broker (who mediates between the jobber and the public), introducing negotiated commission rates, and allowing foreign banks and financial companies to own British brokers/jobbers, or themselves to join the London Stock Exchange.

In the year before and after the Big Bang the City of London was marked by hyperactivity: there were many takeovers, mergers and acquisitions as companies sought to improve their

Bihar

competitiveness. Salaries reached unprecedented levels and there was a great deal of job mobility as British and foreign financial companies sought out the skills they needed. Share prices rose sharply and trading was helped by the introduction of computerized systems. The level of activity could not be sustained, and in Oct 1987 the frenzied trading halted abruptly and share prices fell sharply around the world on what became known as ◊Black Monday.

Big Bang in astronomy, the hypothetical 'explosive' event that marked the origin of the universe as we know it. At the time of the Big Bang, the entire universe was squeezed into a hot, super-dense state. The Big Bang explosion threw this material outwards, producing the expanding universe (see ◊red shift). The cause of the Big Bang is unknown; observations of the current rate of expansion of the universe suggest that it took place between 10 billion and 20 billion years ago. See also ◊cosmology.

Big Ben popular name for the bell in the clock tower of the Houses of Parliament in London, cast at the Whitechapel Bell Foundry in 1858, and known as 'Big Ben' after Benjamin Hall, First Commissioner of Works at the time. It weighs 13,700 kg (13.5 tons).

Big Bertha any of three large German howitzer guns that were mounted on railway wagons during World War I.

Big Dipper North American nickname for the Plough, the seven brightest and most prominent stars in the constellation ◊Ursa Major.

Biggin Hill /'bɪgɪn/ airport in the SE London borough of Bromley. It was the most famous of the Royal Air Force stations in the Battle of Britain in World War II.

bight a coastal indentation, such as the Bight of ◊Bonny, W Africa, and the Great Australian Bight.

Bihar /bɪ'hɑ:/ or *Behar* state of NE India
area 173,900 sq km/67,125 sq mi
capital Patna
features river Ganges in the north, Rajmahal Hills in the south
products copper, iron, coal, rice, jute, sugarcane, grain, oilseed
population (1981) 69,823,000
language Hindi, Bihari
famous people Chandragupta, Asoka
history the ancient kingdom of Magadha roughly corresponded to central and S Bihar.

Bijapur /'bɪdʒə'pʊə/ ancient city in Karnataka, Republic of India. It was founded around AD 1489 by Yusuf Adil Shah (died 1511), the son of Murad II, as the capital of the Muslim kingdom of Biafra. The city and kingdom was annexed by the Mughal emperor Aurangzeb in 1686.

Bikaner /bɪkə'nɪə/ city in Rajasthan, N India; population (1981) 280,000. Once capital of the Rajput state of Bikaner, it is now noted for carpets.

Bikini /bɪˈkiːni/ atoll in the ◊Marshall Islands, W Pacific, where the USA carried out atom-bomb tests 1946–63. Radioactivity will last there for 100 years. Its name was given to a two-piece swimsuit said to have an explosive effect.

Biko /ˈbiːkəʊ/ Steve (Stephen) 1946–1977. South African civil rights leader. An active opponent of ◊apartheid, he was arrested in Sept 1977 and died in detention six days later.

He founded the South African Students Organization (SASO) in 1968 and was co-founder in 1972 of the Black People's Convention, also called the Black Consciousness movement, a radical association of South African students that aimed to develop black pride. Since his death in the custody of South African police he has been a symbol of the anti-apartheid movement.

bilateralism in economics, a trade agreement between two countries or groups of countries in which they give each other preferential treatment. Usually the terms agreed result in balanced trade and are favoured by countries with limited foreign exchange reserves. Bilateralism is incompatible with free trade.

Bilateral agreements are common among the USSR and Eastern bloc countries, both between themselves and with the rest of the world. This is partly because their currencies are as yet inconvertible and partly because bilateralism enables them to make estimates of international trade in their economic plans.

Bilbao /bɪlˈbaʊ/ industrial port (iron and steel, chemicals, cement, food) in N Spain, capital of Biscay province; population (1986) 378,000.

bilberry plant *Vaccinium myrtillus* of the family Ericaceae, closely resembling the cranberry, but distinguished by its bluish berries.

bilby a rabbit-eared bandicoot *Macrotis lagotis*, a lightly-built marsupial with big ears and long nose. This burrowing animal is mainly carnivorous, and its pouch opens backwards.

Bildungsroman (German 'education novel') novel that deals with the cultural and emotional development of its central character, tracing his or her life from inexperienced youth to maturity. The first example of the type is generally considered to be ◊Wieland's *Agathon* 1765–66, but it was ◊Goethe's *Wilhelm Meisters Lehrjahr/Wilhelm Meister's Apprenticeship* 1795–96 that established the genre. Although taken up by writers in other languages, it remained chiefly a German form, and later notable examples have included ◊Mann's *Der Zauberberg/The Magic Mountain* 1924.

bile a brownish fluid produced by the liver. In most vertebrates, it is stored in the gall bladder and emptied into the small intestine as food passes through. *Bile salts* assist the digestion of fats; *bile pigments* are the breakdown products of old red blood cells which are passed into the gut to be eliminated with the faeces.

bilharzia or *schistosomiasis* disease causing anaemia, inflammation, formation of scar tissue, diarrhoea, dysentery, enlargement of the spleen and liver, and cirrhosis of the liver. It is contracted by bathing in water contaminated with human sewage. Some 300 million people are thought to suffer from this disease in the tropics.

Freshwater snails that live in this water act as host to the first larval stage of flukes of the genus *Schistosoma*; when these larvae leave the snail in their second stage of development, they are able to pass through human skin, become sexually mature, and produce quantities of eggs which pass to the intestine or bladder. The human host eventually dies, but before then numerous eggs have passed from the body in urine or faeces to continue the cycle. Treatment is by means of drugs usually containing antimony, to kill the parasites. In 1987 a vaccine was under development.

billabong (Australian *billa bung* 'dead river') a stagnant pond.

billet doux (French 'sweet note') a letter to or from one's lover.

billiards indoor game played, normally by two players, with tapered poles called cues and composition balls (one red, two white) on a rectangular table covered with a green baize cloth with six pockets, one at each corner and in each of the long sides at the middle. Scoring strokes are made by potting the red ball, potting the opponent's ball, potting another ball off one of these two, or hitting the two other balls on the table with the cue ball.

Billiards is played in many different forms. The most popular is the three-ball game played on a standard English billiards table, which is approximately 3.66 m/12 ft by 1.83 m/6 ft in size. *Carom*, played on a table without pockets, is popular in Europe. Another form is ◊pool, popular in the US and Britain.

World Professional Championship

instituted in 1870, organized on a challenge basis; restored as an annual tournament in 1980

1980	Fred Davis (England)
1981	not held
1982	Rex Williams (England)
1983	Rex Williams (England)
1984	Mark Wildman (England)
1985	Ray Edmonds (England)
1986	Robert Foldvari (Australia)
1987	Norman Dagley (England)
1988	Norman Dagley (England)
1989	Mike Russell (England)

Billingsgate /ˈbɪlɪŋzɡeɪt/ chief London wholesale fish market, formerly (from the 9th century) near London Bridge. It re-opened in 1982 at the new Billingsgate market, West India Dock, Isle of Dogs.

billion a thousand million (1,000,000,000). In Britain, this number was formerly known as a milliard, and a million million (1,000,000,000,000) as a billion, but the first definition is now more prevalent.

Billiton /ˈbɪlɪtɒn/ Indonesian island in the Java Sea, between Borneo and Sumatra, one of the Sunda Islands; area 4,830 sq km/1,860 sq mi. The chief port is Tanjungpandan. Tin mining is the chief industry.

Bill of Exchange a form of commercial credit instrument, or IOU, used in international trade. In Britain, a Bill of Exchange is defined by the Bills of Exchange Act 1882 as an unconditional order in writing addressed by one person to another, signed by the person giving it, requiring the person to whom it is addressed to pay on demand or at a fixed or determinable future time a certain sum in money to or to the order of a specified person, or to the bearer. US practice is governed by the Uniform Negotiable Instruments Law, drafted on the same lines as the British, and accepted by all states by 1927.

Bill of Rights in Britain, Act of 1689 embodying the Declaration of Rights presented by the House of Commons to William and Mary before they replaced James II on the throne. It made illegal the suspension of laws by royal authority without Parliament's consent; the power to dispense with laws; the establishment of special courts of law; levying money by royal prerogative without Parliament's consent; and the maintainance of a standing army in peacetime without Parliament's consent. It also asserted a right to petition the sovereign, freedom of parliamentary elections, freedom of speech in parliamentary debates, and the necessity of frequent parliaments. See also ◊constitution. In the USA, the first ten amendments (1791) to the US constitution are:

1 giving freedom of worship, of speech, of the press, of assembly, and to petition the government;

2 asserting the right to keep and bear arms (which has hindered modern attempts to control illicit use of arms);

3 prohibiting billeting of soldiers in private homes in peacetime;

4 forbidding unreasonable search and seizure;

Billy the Kid. *The US outlaw William Bonney, Billy the Kid, who was shot by Sheriff Pat Garrett in 1881.*

5 asserting that none are to be 'deprived of life, liberty or property without due process of law' or be compelled in any criminal case to be a witness against himself or herself (frequently quoted in the McCarthy era);

6 giving the right to speedy trial, to call witnesses, and have defence counsel;

7 giving the right to trial by jury;

8 outlawing excessive bail or fines, or 'cruel and unusual punishment', not to be inflicted (used in recent times to oppose the death penalty);

9 and 10 safeguarding to the states and people all rights not specifically delegated to the central government.

Billy Bunter a fat, bespectacled schoolboy who featured in stories by Frank ◊Richards, set at Greyfriars School. His adventures, in which he attempts to raise enough money to fund his passion for eating, appeared in the children's paper *Magnet* between 1908 and 1940, and subsequently in books in the 1940s and on television 1952–62.

Billy the Kid /ˈbɪli/ Nickname of William H Bonney 1859–1881. US outlaw, a leader in the Lincoln County cattle war in New Mexico, who allegedly killed his first man at 12 and 22 people in total. He was sentenced to death for murdering a sheriff, but escaped (killing two guards), and was finally shot by Sheriff Pat Garrett while trying to avoid recapture.

Biloxi /bɪˈlɒksi/ port in Mississippi, USA; population (1980) 49,300. Chief occupations include tourism and seafood canning. It is named after a local Indian people.

bimah in Judaism, raised platform in a synagogue from which the ◊Torah scroll is read.

bimetallic strip strip made from two metals each having a different coefficient of thermal expansion, which therefore bends when subjected to a change in temperature. It is used widely for temperature measurement and control.

bimetallism monetary system in which two metals, traditionally gold and silver, both circulate at a ratio fixed by the state, are coined by the ◊mint on equal terms, and are legal tender to any amount. The system was in use in the 19th century.

Advocates of bimetallism have argued that the 'compensatory action of the double standard' makes for a currency more stable than one based only on gold, since the changes in the value of the two metals taken together may be expected to be less than the changes in one of them. One of the many arguments against the system is that the ratio of the prices of the metals is frozen regardless of the supply and demand.

bimodal in statistics, a frequency distribution of data that has two distinct peaks.

binary in music, a form in two matching sections.

binary fission in biology, a form of ◊asexual reproduction, whereby a single-celled organism divides into two smaller 'daughter' cells. It can also occur in a few simple multicellular organisms, such as sea anemones, producing two smaller sea anemones of equal size.

binary number system or **binary number code** a system of numbers to ◊base 2 using combinations of the two digits 1 and 0. Binary numbers play a key role in digital computers, where they form the basis of the internal coding of information, the values of ◊bits (short for 'binary digits') being represented as on/off (1 and 0) states of switches and high/low voltages in circuits.

The value of any position in a binary number increases by powers of 2 (doubles) with each move from right to left (1, 2, 4, 8, 16, and so on). For example, 1011 in the binary number system means $(1 \times 8) + (0 \times 4) + (1 \times 2) + (1 \times 1)$, which adds up to 11 in the everyday, ◊decimal system.

binary star a pair of stars moving in orbit around their common centre of mass. Observations show that most stars are binary, or even multiple, for example the nearest star system to the Sun, ◊Alpha Centauri.

A **spectroscopic binary** is a binary in which two stars are so close together that they cannot be seen separately, but their separate light spectra can be distinguished by a spectroscope. Another type is the ◊eclipsing binary.

binary weapon in chemical warfare, weapon consisting of two substances that in isolation are harmless but when mixed together form a poisonous nerve gas. They are loaded into the delivery system separately and combine after launch.

binding energy in physics, the amount of energy needed to break the nucleus of an atom into the neutrons and protons that make it up.

Bingham /'bɪŋəm/ Hiram 1875–1919. US explorer and politician, who from 1907 visited Latin America, discovering ◊Machu Picchu, Vitcos, and other Inca settlements in Peru. He later entered politics, becoming a senator.

bingo or **lotto** game of chance played with numbered balls and cards each divided into 27 squares, 15 of them containing random numbers between 1 and 90. As the numbers are called out, also at random, the corresponding numbers are marked off

binoculars

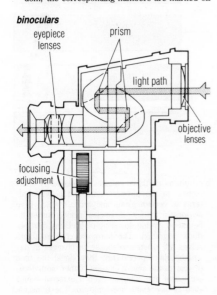

the players' card(s). The first person to complete a line across or full card (known as a 'full house', hence the alternative name 'housey-housey') wins a prize.

binoculars an optical instrument for viewing an object in magnification with both eyes, for example, field-glasses and opera-glasses. Binoculars consist of two telescopes containing lenses and prisms, which produce a stereoscopic effect as well as magnifying the image. Use of prisms has the effect of 'folding' the light path, allowing for a compact design.

The first binocular telescope was constructed by a Dutchman, H Lippershey (c.1570–c.1619), in 1608. Later development was largely due to Ernst Abbé (1840–1905) of Jena, who at the end of the 19th century designed prism binoculars that foreshadowed the instruments of today, in which not only magnification but also stereoscopic effect is obtained.

binomial in algebra, an expression consisting of two terms, such as $a + b$, $a - b$. The **binomial theorem**, discovered by Isaac ◊Newton and first published in 1676, is a formula whereby any power of a binomial quantity may be found.

binomial system of nomenclature in biology, the system in which all organisms are identified by a two-part Latinized name. Devised by the biologist ◊Linnaeus, it is also known as the Linnean system. The first name identifies the ◊genus, the second the ◊species within that genus.

binturong shaggy-coated mammal *Arctitis binturong*, the largest member of the mongoose family, nearly 1 m/3 ft long excluding a long muscular tail with a prehensile tip. Mainly nocturnal and tree-dwelling, the binturong is found in the forests of SE Asia, feeding on fruit, eggs, and small animals.

Binyon /'bɪnjən/ Laurence 1869–1943. British poet. His verse volumes include *Lyric Poems* 1894 and *London Visions*, but he is best remembered for his ode *For the Fallen* 1914.

Bío-Bío /'biːəʊ 'biːəʊ/ longest river in Chile; length 370 km/230 mi from its source in the Andes to its mouth on the Pacific. The name is an Araucanian-language term 'much water'.

biochemistry science concerned with the chemistry of living organisms: the structure and reactions of proteins (especially enzymes), nucleic acids, carbohydrates, and lipids.

The study of biochemistry has increased our knowledge of how animals and plants react with their environment, for example, in creating and storing energy by photosynthesis, taking in food and releasing waste products, and passing on their characteristics through their genes. It is important in many areas of research, including medicine and agriculture.

biodegradable capable of being broken down by living organisms, principally bacteria and fungi. Biodegradable substances, for example fruit, vegetables, and sewage, can be rendered harmless by natural processes. Nonbiodegradable substances, such as most plastics and heavy metals, accumulate in the environment and may cause serious problems of ◊pollution.

bioeconomics theory put forward in 1979 by Chicago economist Gary Becker that the concepts of sociobiology apply also in economics. The competitiveness and self-interest built into human genes are said to make capitalism an effective economic system, whereas the selflessness and collectivism proclaimed as the socialist ideal are held to be contrary to human genetic make-up and to produce an ineffective system.

bioengineering the application of engineering to biology and medicine. Common applications include the design and use of artificial limbs, joints and organs, including hip joints and heart valves.

biofeedback modification or control of a biological system by its results or effects. For example, a change in the position or ◊trophic level of one species affects all levels above it.

Many biological systems are controlled by negative feedback. When enough of the hormone thyroxine has been released into the blood, the hormone adjusts its own level by 'switching off' the gland that produces it. In ecology, as the numbers in a species rise, the food supply available to each individual is reduced. This acts to reduce the population to a sustainable level.

biog. abbreviation for *biography*.

biogenesis biological term coined 1870 by T H Huxley to express the hypothesis that living matter always arises out of other similar forms of living matter. It superseded the opposite idea of ◊spontaneous generation or abiogenesis (that is, that living things may arise out of non-living matter).

biogeography the study of how and why plants and animals are distributed around the world; more specifically, a theory describing the geographical distribution of ◊species developed by Robert MacArthur and E O ◊Wilson. The theory argues that for many species, ecological specializations mean that suitable habitats are patchy in their occurrence. Thus for a dragonfly, ponds in which to breed are separated by large tracts of land, and for edelweiss adapted to alpine peaks the deep valleys between cannot be colonized.

biography an account of a person's life. When it is written by that person, it is an ◊autobiography. Biography can be simply a factual narrative, but it was also established as a literary form in the 18th and 19th centuries. Among ancient biographers are Xenophon, Plutarch, Tacitus, Suetonius, and the authors of the Gospels of the New Testament. In the English language Lytton Strachey's *Eminent Victorians* opened the modern era of frankness; 20th-century biographers include Richard Ellmann (James Joyce and Oscar Wilde), Michael Holroyd (1935–) (Lytton Strachey and George Bernard Shaw) and Elizabeth Longford (Queen Victoria and Wellington).

Medieval biography was mostly devoted to religious edification and produced chronicles of saints and martyrs; among the biographies of laymen are Einhard's *Charlemagne* and Asser's *Alfred*. In England modern biography begins with the early Tudor period and such works as *Sir Thomas More* 1626, written by his son-in-law William Roper (1498–1578). By the 18th century it became a literary form in its own right through Johnson's *Lives of the Most Eminent English Poets* 1779–81 and Boswell's biography of Johnson 1791. 19th-century biographers include Southey, Elizabeth Gaskell, G H Lewes, J Morley, and Carlyle. The general tendency was to provide irrelevant detail and suppress the more personal facts.

The earliest *biographical dictionary* in the modern sense was that of Pierre Bayle 1696, followed during the 19th century by the development of national biographies in Europe, and the foundation of the *English Dictionary of National Biography* in 1882 and the *Dictionary of American Biography* in 1928.

Bioko /bi'əʊkəʊ/ island in the Bight of Bonny, W Africa, part of Equatorial Guinea; area 2,017 sq km/786 sq mi; produces coffee, cacao and copra; population (1983) 57,190. Formerly a Spanish possession, as Fernando Po, it was known 1973–79 as Macías Nguema Bijogo.

biological clock a regular internal rhythm of activity, produced by unknown mechanisms, and not dependent on external time-signals. Such clocks are known to exist in almost all animals, and also in many plants, fungi, and unicellular organisms. In higher organisms, there appears to be a series of clocks of graded importance. For example, although body temperature and activity cycles in human beings are normally 'set' to 24 hours, the two cycles may vary independently, showing that two clock mechanisms are involved. Exposing humans to bright light can change the biological clock and help, for example, people suffering from jet-lag.

Caption for binoculars diagram:
eyepiece lenses
prism
light path
objective lenses
focusing adjustment

biological computer proposed technology for computing devices based on growing complex organic molecules (biomolecules) as components. Its theoretical basis is that cells, the building blocks of all living things, have chemical systems that can store and exchange electrons and therefore function as electrical components. It is currently the subject of long-term research.

biological control the control of pests such as insects and fungi through biological means, rather than the use of chemicals. This can include breeding resistant crop strains, inducing infertility in the pest, breeding viruses that attack the pest species, or introducing the pest's natural predator. Biological control tends to be naturally self-regulating, but as living systems are so complex it is difficult to predict all the consequences of introducing a biological controlling agent.

biological oxygen demand (BOD) the amount of dissolved oxygen taken up by microorganisms in a sample of water. Since these microorganisms live by decomposing organic matter, and the amount of oxygen used is proportional to their number and metabolic rate, BOD can be used as a measure of the extent to which the water is polluted with organic compounds.

biological shield a shield around a nuclear reactor that protects personnel from the effects of ◊radiation. It usually consists of a thick wall of steel and concrete.

biological warfare use of living organisms, or of infectious material derived from them, to bring about death or disease in humans, animals, or plants. It was condemned by the Geneva Convention 1925, to which the United Nations has urged all states to adhere. Nevertheless research in this area continues. See also ◊chemical warfare.

biology the science of life. Strictly speaking, biology includes all the life sciences, for example anatomy and physiology, cytology, zoology and botany, ecology, genetics, biochemistry and biophysics, animal behaviour, embryology, and plant breeding.

bioluminescence the production of light by living organisms. It is a feature of many fish, crustaceans, and other marine animals, especially deep-sea organisms. On land, bioluminescence is seen in some nocturnal insects such as glowworms and fireflies, and in certain bacteria and fungi. Light is usually produced by the oxidation of luciferin, a reaction catalysed by the ◊enzyme luciferase. This reaction is unique, being the only known biological oxidation that does not produce heat. Animal luminescence is involved in communication, camouflage, or luring prey, but its function in other organisms is unclear.

biomass the gross weight of organisms present in a given area. It may be specified for one particular species (such as earthworm biomass), for a category of species (for example herbivore biomass) or for all species (total biomass).

biome a large-scale natural assemblage of plants and animals living in a particular type of environment. Examples include the tundra biome and the desert biome.

biometry literally, the measurement of living things, but generally used to mean the application of mathematics to biology. The term is now obsolete, since mathematical or statistical work is an integral part of most biological disciplines.

bionics a word coined from 'biological electronics', referring to the design and development of electronic or mechanical artificial systems that imitate those of living things. The artificial bionic arm, for example, uses electronics to amplify minute electrical signals generated in body muscles to work electric motors, which operate the joints of artificial fingers and wrist.

The first person to receive two bionic ears was Peter Stewart, an Australian journalist, in 1989. His left ear was fitted with an array of 22 electrodes, replacing the hairs that naturally convert sounds into electrical impulses. Five years previously he had been fitted with a similar device in his right ear. See ◊prosthesis.

biophysics the application of physical laws to the properties of living organisms. Examples include using the principles of ◊mechanics to calculate the strength of bones and muscles, and ◊thermodynamics to study plant and animal energetics.

biopsy removal of a tissue sample from the body for diagnostic examination.

biorhythms rhythmic changes, mediated by ◊hormones, in the physical state and activity patterns of certain plants and animals which have seasonal activities. Examples include winter hibernation, spring flowering or breeding, and periodic migration. The hormonal changes themselves are often a response to changes in day length (◊photoperiodism); they signal the time of year to the animal or plant. Other biorhythms are innate and continue even if external stimuli such as day length are removed. These include

bird

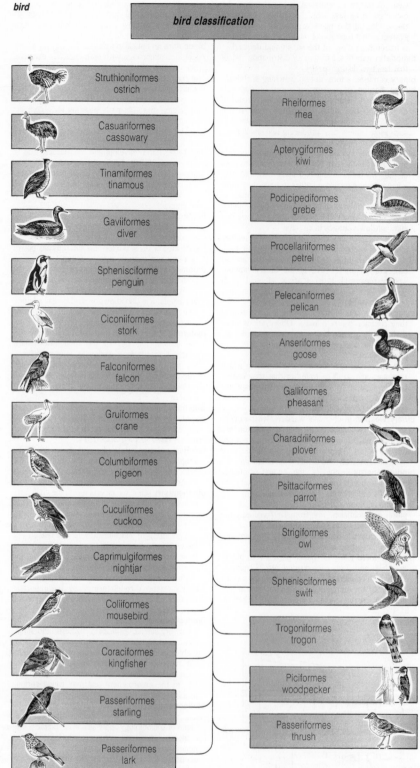

bird classification

Struthioniformes ostrich

Casuariformes cassowary

Tinamiformes tinamous

Gaviiformes diver

Sphenisciforme penguin

Ciconiiformes stork

Falconiformes falcon

Gruiformes crane

Columbiformes pigeon

Cuculiformes cuckoo

Caprimulgiformes nightjar

Coliiformes mousebird

Coraciformes kingfisher

Passeriformes starling

Passeriformes lark

Rheiformes rhea

Apterygiformes kiwi

Podicipediformes grebe

Procellariiformes petrel

Pelecaniformes pelican

Anseriformes goose

Galliformes pheasant

Charadriiformes plover

Psittaciformes parrot

Strigiformes owl

Sphenisciformes swift

Trogoniformes trogon

Piciformes woodpecker

Passeriformes thrush

a 24-hour or ◊circadian rhythm, a 28-day or circalunar rhythm (corresponding to the phases of the moon), and even a year-long rhythm in some organisms. Such innate biorhythms are linked to an internal or ◊biological clock, whose mechanism is still poorly understood. Often both types of rhythm operate; thus many birds have a circalunar rhythm that prepares them for the breeding season, and a photoperiodic response. There is also a theory that human activity is governed by three biorhythms: the **intellectual** (33 days), the **emotional** (28 days), and the **physical** (23 days). Certain days in each cycle are regarded as 'critical', especially if one coincides with that of another cycle.

biosensor a device based on microelectronic circuits that can directly measure medically important variables for the purpose of diagnosis or monitoring treatment. One such device measures the blood sugar level of diabetics by using a single drop of blood, and shows the result on a liquid crystal display within a few minutes.

biosphere or **ecosphere** that region of the Earth's surface (land and water), and the atmosphere above it, that can be occupied by living organisms.

biosynthesis the synthesis of organic chemicals from simple inorganic ones by living cells. One important biosynthetic reaction is the conversion of carbon dioxide and water to glucose by plants during ◊photosynthesis. Other biosynthetic reactions produce cell constituents including proteins and fats.

Biosynthesis requires energy; in photosynthesis this is obtained from sunlight, but more often it is supplied by the ◊ATP molecule. The term is also used in connection with biotechnology processes.

Biot /bi'əu/ Jean 1774–1862. French physicist who studied the polarization of light. In 1804 he made a balloon ascent to a height of three miles, in an early investigation of the Earth's atmosphere.

biotechnology the industrial use of living organisms, to manufacture food, drugs, or other products. Historically biotechnology has largely been restricted to the brewing and and baking industries, using ◊fermentation by yeast, but the most recent advances involve ◊genetic engineering, in which single-celled organisms with modified ◊DNA are used to produce substances such as insulin.

biotin a vitamin of the B-complex; it is found in many different kinds of food, with egg-yolk, liver and yeast containing large amounts.

birth rate

birch tree of the genus *Betula*, including about 40 species found in cool temperate parts of the northern hemisphere. The white or silver birch *Betula pendula* is of industrial importance to man, as its timber is quick-growing and durable. The bark is used for tanning and dyeing leather, and an oil is obtained from it.

Birch /bɜːtʃ/ John M 1918–1945. US Baptist missionary, commissioned by the US Air Force to carry out intelligence work behind the Chinese lines, where he was killed by the communists; the US extreme right-wing nationalist **John Birch Society** 1958 is named after him.

bird backboned animal of the class Aves, the biggest group of land vertebrates, characterized by warm blood, feathers, wings, breathing through lungs, and egg-laying by the female.

Birds are bipedal, with the front limb modified to form a wing and retaining only three digits. The heart has four chambers, and the body is maintained at a high temperature (about 41°C 106°F). Most birds fly, but some groups (such as ostriches) are flightless, and others include flightless members. Many communicate by sounds, or by visual displays, in connection with which many species are brightly coloured, particularly the males. Birds have highly developed patterns of instinctive behaviour. Hearing and, especially, eyesight are well developed, but the sense of smell is usually poor. Typically the eggs are brooded in a nest, and, on hatching, the young receive a period of parental care. There are nearly 8,500 species of birds.

Bird /bɜːd/ Isabella 1832–1904. British traveller and writer, who wrote extensively of her journeys in the USA, Persia, Tibet, Kurdistan, China, Japan, and Korea. Her published works include *The Englishwoman in America* 1856, *A Lady's Life in the Rocky Mountains* 1874, *Unbeaten Tracks in Japan* 1880, *Among the Tibetans* 1894, and *Pictures from China* 1900. Her last great journey was made in 1901 when she travelled over 1,609 km/1,000 mi in Morocco.

bird of paradise one of 40 species of crow-like birds, family Paradiseidae, native to New Guinea and neighbouring islands. Females are drably coloured, but the males have bright and elaborate plumage used in courtship display. Hunted almost to extinction for their plumage, they are now being conserved.

Birdseye /'bɜːdzaɪ/ Clarence 1886–1956. US inventor who pioneered food refrigeration processes. While working as a fur trader in Labrador in 1912–16 he was struck by the ease with which food could be preserved in an Arctic climate.

Back in the US he found that the same effect could be obtained by rapidly freezing prepared food between two refrigerated metal plates.

birdwatching the observation and study of wild birds in their natural habitat. In the UK the Royal Society for the Protection of Birds, founded 1889, has a network of reserves in all types of habitat (180,000 acres), and is the largest voluntary wildlife-conservation body in Europe, with a membership (1989) of 560,000.

Birkenhead /'bɜːkənhed/ seaport in Merseyside, England, on the Mersey estuary opposite Liverpool; population (1981) 123,884. Chief industries include shipbuilding and engineering. The rail Mersey Tunnel 1886 and road Queensway Tunnel 1934 link Birkenhead with Liverpool.

history the first settlement grew up round a Benedictine priory, and Birkenhead was still a small village when William Laird established a small shipbuilding yard, the forerunner of the huge Cammell Laird yards. In 1829 the first iron vessel in Britain was built at Birkenhead. Wallasey dock, first of the series, was opened in 1847.

Birkenhead /'bɜːkənhed/ Frederick Edwin Smith, 1st Earl of Birkenhead 1872–1930. British Conservative politician. A flamboyant character, known as 'FE', he joined with Baron Carson in organizing armed resistance in Ulster to Irish Home Rule; he was Lord Chancellor 1919–22, and a much criticized secretary for India 1924–28.

Birmingham /'bɜːmɪŋəm/ industrial city in the West Midlands, second largest city of the UK; population (1986) 1,006,527, metropolitan area 2,632,000. Industries include motor vehicles, machine tools, aerospace control systems, plastics, chemicals, and food. It is the site of the National Exhibition Centre. As mayor, Joseph ◊Chamberlain carried out reforms in the 1870s.

features Aston University is linked to a ◊science park; a school of music and symphony orchestra; the art gallery has a Pre-Raphaelite collection; the repertory theatre was founded 1913 by Sir Barry Jackson (1897–1961). Lawn tennis was invented here. Sutton Park, in the residential suburb of Sutton Coldfield, has been a public country recreational area since the 16th century.

Birmingham /'bɜːmɪŋhæm/ industrial city (iron, steel, chemicals, building materials, computers, cotton textiles) and commercial centre in Alabama, USA; population (1980) 847,500.

Birmingham Six six men convicted 1975 of planting bombs in two Birmingham pubs in 1974, killing 21 people. Four of the six signed confessions while in custody. Doubts about the legality of their convictions grew after investigations by journalists in 1985 and 1986; in 1990 a television programme named four other people who it alleged carried out the attacks.

Biro /'bɪrəu/ Lazlo 1900–1985. Hungarian-born Argentinian who invented a ballpoint pen in 1944. His name became generic for ballpoint pens in the UK.

Birobijan /'bɪrəbɪ'dʒɑːn/ town in Kharabovsk Territory, E USSR, near the Chinese border; population (1981) 72,000. Industries include sawmills and clothing. It was capital of the Jewish Autonomous Region 1928–51 (sometimes also called Birobijan).

birth the act of producing young individuals from within the body of female animals. Both viviparous and ovoviviparous animals give birth to young. In viviparous animals, embryos obtain nourishment from the mother via a ◊placenta or other means. In ovoviviparous animals, fertilized eggs develop and hatch in the oviduct of the mother and gain little or no nourishment from maternal tissues. See also ◊pregnancy.

Birth of a Nation, The epic silent film about the Reconstruction and the Ku Klux Klan in the US South, directed 1915 by D W Griffith and considered by many to be the first film masterpiece.

birth rate the number of births per year per thousand of the population. In the UK in the 20th century this has fallen from 28 to less than 10

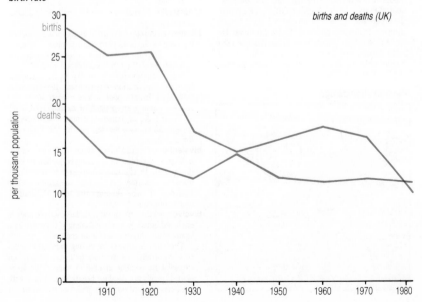

births and deaths (UK)

births

deaths

per thousand population

owing to increased use of contraception, better living standards, and falling infant mortality. The average household now contains 1.8 children. The population growth rate remains high in developing countries. While it is now below replacement level in the UK, in Bangladesh it stands at 28, in Nigeria at 34, and in Brazil at 23 per thousand people per year.

Birmingham Six six men convicted 1975 of planting bombs in two Birmingham pubs in 1974, killing 21 people. Four of the six signed confessions while in custody. Doubts about the legality of their convictions grew after investigations by journalists in 1985 and 1986; in 1990 a television programme named four other people who it alleged carried out the attacks.

Biro /'bɪrəʊ/ Lazlo 1900–1985. Hungarian-born Argentinian who invented a ballpoint pen in 1944. His name became generic for ballpoint pens in the UK.

Birobijan /'bɪrəbɪ'dʒɑ:n/ town in Kharabovsk Territory, E USSR, near the Chinese border; population (1981) 72,000. Industries include sawmills and clothing. It was capital of the Jewish Autonomous Region 1928–51 (sometimes also called Birobijan).

birth the act of producing young individuals from within the body of female animals. Both viviparous and ovoviviparous animals give birth to young. In viviparous animals, embryos obtain nourishment from the mother via a ◊placenta or other means. In ovoviviparous animals, fertilized eggs develop and hatch in the oviduct of the mother and gain little or no nourishment from maternal tissues. See also ◊pregnancy.

Birth of a Nation, The epic silent film about the Reconstruction and the Ku Klux Klan in the US South, directed 1915 by D W Griffith and considered by many to be the first film masterpiece.

birth rate the number of births per year per thousand of the population. In the UK in the 20th century this has fallen from 28 to less than 10 owing to increased use of contraception, better living standards, and falling infant mortality. The average household now contains 1.8 children. The population growth rate remains high in developing countries. While it is now below replacement level in the UK, in Bangladesh it stands at 28, in Nigeria at 34, and in Brazil at 23 per thousand people per year.

Birtwistle /'bɜ:twɪsl/ Harrison 1934– . English avant-garde composer. He has specialized in chamber music: for example, his chamber opera *Punch and Judy* 1967 and *Down by the Greenwood Side* 1969.

Birtwistle's early music was influenced by ◊Stravinsky and by the medieval and renaissance masters, and for many years he worked alongside Maxwell ◊Davies. Orchestral works include *The Triumph of Time* 1972 and *Silbury Air* 1977; he has also written one large-scale opera *The Mask of Orpheus* 1986 and has experimented with electronic music. His *Chronometer* 1972 is based on clock sounds.

Biscay, Bay of /'bɪskeɪ/ bay of the Atlantic Ocean between N Spain and W France, known for rough seas and exceptionally high tides.

bise a cold dry northerly wind experienced in southern France and Switzerland.

bishop (Greek 'overseer') priest next in rank to an archbishop in the Roman Catholic, Eastern Orthodox, and Anglican churches. A bishop has charge of a district called a *diocese*.

Originally bishops were chosen by the congregation, but in the Roman Catholic church they are appointed by the Pope, although in some countries, such as Spain, the political authority nominates appointees. In the Eastern Orthodox church bishops are always monks. In the Church of England the prime minister selects bishops on the advice of the archbishop of Canterbury; when a diocese is very large, assistant (suffragan) bishops are appointed. Bishops are responsible for meeting to settle matters of belief or discipline;

Bismarck *Prusso-German politician Prince Otto von Bismarck in army uniform.*

they ordain priests and administer confirmation (as well as baptism in the Orthodox church). In nonconformist churches the bishop's role is mostly that of a supervisory official.

Bishop /'bɪʃəp/ Isabella married name of the travel writer Isabella ◊Bird.

Bishop /'bɪʃəp/ Ronald Eric 1903–1989. British aircraft designer. He joined the de Havilland Aircraft Company 1931 as an apprentice, and designed the Mosquito bomber, the Vampire fighter, and the Comet jet airliner.

Bishop /'bɪʃəp/ William Avery 1894–1956. Canadian air ace, who won the Victoria Cross in 1917.

Biskra /'bɪskrɑ:/ oasis town in Algeria on the edge of the Sahara; population (1968) 60,000.

Bismarck /'bɪzmɑ:k/ Otto Eduard Leopold, Prince von Bismarck 1815–1898. German politician, prime minister of Prussia 1862–90 and chancellor of the German Empire 1871–90. He pursued an aggressively expansionist policy, with wars against Denmark 1863–64, Austria 1866, and France 1870–71, which brought about the unification of Germany.

Bismarck was ambitious to establish Prussia's hegemony inside Germany and eliminate the influence of Austria. He secured Austria's support for his successful war against Denmark, then in 1866 went to war against Austria and its allies (the ◊Seven Weeks' War), his victory forcing Austria out of the German Bund and unifying the N German states in the North German Confederation under his own chancellorship 1867. He then defeated France, under Napoleon III, in the Franco-Prussian War 1870–71, proclaimed the German Empire 1871, and annexed Alsace-Lorraine. He tried to secure his work by a ◊Triple Alliance 1881 with Austria and Italy, but ran into difficulties at home with the Roman Catholic church and the

Bismarck Archipelago

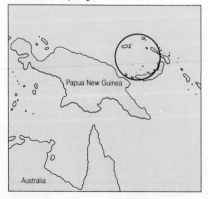

socialist movement, and was forced to resign by William II 18 Mar 1870.

Bismarck Archipelago /'bɪzmɑ:k/ group of over 200 islands in SW Pacific Ocean, part of ◊Papua New Guinea; area 49,660 sq km/19,200 sq mi. Largest island New Britain.

bismuth a pinkish-white metallic element, symbol Bi, atomic number 83, relative atomic mass 208.98. It is a poor conductor of heat and electricity, and is used in alloys of low melting point, and in medical compounds to soothe gastric ulcers.

bison large, hoofed mammal of the bovine family. There are two species, both brown. The **European bison** or **wisent**, *Bison bonasus*, of which only a few protected herds survive, is about 2 m/7 ft high and weighs a tonne. The **North American bison** (often known as 'buffalo') *Bison bison* is slightly smaller, with a heavier mane and more sloping hindquarters. Formerly roaming the prairies in vast numbers, it was almost exterminated in the 19th century, but survives in protected areas.

Crossed with domestic cattle, the latter has produced a hardy modern hybrid, the 'beefalo', producing a lean carcass on an economical grass diet.

Bissau /bɪˈsaʊ/ capital and chief port of Guinea-Bissau, on an island at the mouth of the Geba river; population (1988) 125,000. Originally a fortified slave-trading centre, Bissau became a free port 1869.

bit in computing, the smallest unit of information; a binary digit or place in a binary number. A ◊byte is eight bits.

bit in building and construction, a tool used for drilling or boring, as in a carpenter's brace and bit. It also refers to the cutting part of any tool, for example the blade of a plane.

Bithynia /bɪˈθɪnɪə/ district of NW Asia which became a Roman province 74 BC.

Bitolj /'bi:tɒl/ or **Bitola** town in Yugoslavia, 32 km/20 mi north of the Greek border; population (1981) 137,800.

history Held by the Turks (under whom it was known as Monastir) from 1382, it was taken by the Serbs in 1912 during the First ◊Balkan War. Retaken by Bulgaria in 1915, it was again taken by the Allies in Nov 1916.

bit pad a computer input device; see ◊graphics tablet.

bittern any of several small herons, in particular the common bittern *Botaurus stellaris* of Europe and Asia. It is shy, stoutly built, has a streaked camouflage pattern and a loud booming call. An inhabitant of marshy country, it is now quite rare in Britain.

bittersweet alternative name for the woody ◊nightshade plant.

bitumen an impure mixture of hydrocarbons, including such deposits as petroleum, asphalt, and natural gas, although sometimes the term is restricted to a soft kind of pitch resembling asphalt.

Solid bitumen may have arisen as a residue from the evaporation of petroleum. If evaporation took place from a pool or lake of petroleum, the residue might form a pitch or asphalt lake, such as Pitch Lake in Trinidad. Bitumen was used in ancient times as a mortar, and by the Egyptians for embalming.

bivalent in biology, a name given to the pair of homologous chromosomes during reduction division (◊meiosis). In chemistry the term is sometimes used to describe an element or group with a ◊valency of two, although the term 'divalent' is more common.

bivalve marine or freshwater mollusc whose body is enclosed between two shells hinged together by a ligament on the dorsal side of the body.

The shell is closed by strong 'adductor' muscles. Ventrally, a retractile 'foot' can be put out to assist movement in mud or sand. Two large plate-like gills are used for breathing and also, with the ◊cilia present on them, make a mechanism for collecting the small particles of food on which bi-valves depend. The bivalves form one of the five classes of molluscs, the Lamellibranchiata, other-wise known as Bivalvia or Pelycypoda, containing about 8,000 species.

Bizerta /bɪˈzɜːtə/ or *Bizerte* port in Tunisia, N Africa; population (1984) 94,500. Chief industries include fishing, oil refining and metal works.

Bizet /ˈbiːzeɪ/ Georges (Alexandre César Léopold) 1838–1875. French composer of operas, among them *Les Pêcheurs de perles*/*The Pearl Fish-ers* 1863, and *La jolie Fille de Perth*/*The Fair Maid of Perth* 1866. He also wrote the concert overture *Patrie* and incidental music to Daudet's *L'Arlésienne*. His operatic masterpiece *Carmen* was produced a few months before his death in 1875.

Bjelke-Patterson /ˈbjelkə ˈpætəsən/ Joh(annes) 1911– . Australian right-wing politician, leader of the Queensland National Party (QNP) and premier of Queensland 1968–87.

Bjelke-Patterson, the son of a Danish Lutheran pastor, had a consistently right-wing political stance throughout his long career, which was not without blemish: he was accused more than once of electoral gerrymandering. In 1987 he broke the coalition of the QNP with the Australian Liberal Party to run for prime minister, but his action, by splitting the opposition, merely strengthened the hand of the Labor prime minister Bob Hawke. He was voted out of office in 1987.

Björneborg /ˌbjɜːnəˈbɔːri/ Swedish name of the town of ◊Pori, Finland.

Björnson /ˈbjɜːnsɒn/ Björnstjerne 1832–1910. Norwegian novelist, playwright, poet, and journal-ist. His plays included *The Newly Married Couple* 1865 and *Beyond Human Power* 1883, dealing with politics and sexual morality. Among his novels is *In God's Way* 1889. Nobel prize 1903.

black English term first used in 1625 to describe West Africans, now used to refer to Africans S of the Sahara and to people of African descent living outside Africa. In the UK and some other countries (but not North America) the term is sometimes also used for people originally from the Indian subcontinent.

The term 'black', at one time considered offen-sive by many people, was first adopted by mili-tants in the USA in the mid-1960s to emphasize ethnic pride; they rejected the terms 'coloured' and 'Negro' as euphemistic. It has since become the preferred term in the USA and largely in the UK.

history Black people were first brought to the West Indies from Africa in large numbers as slaves by Spaniards in the early 16th century, and to the North American mainland (also to S America by the Portuguese) in the early 17th century as in-dentured servants and subsequently as slaves to work on southern plantations. African blacks were also taken to Europe to work as servants. Some coastal societies in W Africa were heavily involved in the slave trade and became wealthy on its pro-ceeds. Black seafarers settled in European ports on the Atlantic seaboard, especially in Liverpool and Bristol, England. Although blacks fought be-side whites in the war of American Independence, the US Constitution ratified 1788 protected the slave trade, and slaves had no ◊civil rights. Slav-ery was gradually abolished in the northern US states during the early 19th century, but as the foundation of the southern economy it was one of the issues that led to the secession of the southern states, which provoked the American Civil War 1861–65. During the Civil War about 200,000 blacks fought in the Union (Northern) Army, but in segregated units led by white officers.

The Emancipation Proclamation 1863 of Presi-dent Abraham Lincoln officially freed the slaves (about 4 million); it could not be enforced until the Union victory 1865 and the period after the war known as ◊Reconstruction. Freed slaves were often resented by poor whites as eco-nomic competitors, particularly in the South,

Bizet *French composer Georges Bizet's best known work is the opera Carmen 1875.*

and vigilante groups such as the ◊Ku Klux Klan were formed to intimidate them. In addition, although freed slaves had full US citizenship under the 14th Amendment in the Constitution and were thus entitled to vote, they were often disenfranchised in practice by literacy tests and poll taxes. A 'separate but equal' policy was established when the US Supreme Court ruled 1896 that segregation was legal if equal facilities were provided for blacks and whites. The ruling was overturned 1954, with the Supreme Court decision outlawing segregation in state schools. This led to a historic confrontation in Little Rock, Arkansas, 1957 when Governor Orval Faubus attempted to prevent black pupils from entering Central High School, and President Eisenhower sent federal troops to enforce their right to attend.

Another landmark in the struggle for civil rights was the ◊Montgomery bus boycott in Alabama 1955; it also first brought Martin Luther ◊King to national attention. In the early 1960s the civil-rights movement had gained impetus, largely under the leadership of King, who in 1957 had founded the ◊Southern Christian Lead-ership Conference, a coalition group advocating non-violence. Moderate groups such as the Na-tional Association for the Advancement of Col-ored people had been active since early in the century; for the first time they were joined in large numbers by whites, particularly students, as in the historic march converging on Washington DC 1963 from all over the USA. At about this time, impatient with the lack of results gained through moderation, the militant ◊Black Power movement began to emerge, as in the Black Panther Party founded 1966, and black separa-tist groups such as the ◊Black Muslims gained support.

Increasing pressure led to the passage of civil-rights acts 1964 and 1968, and the voting-rights act 1965 under President Johnson, which guaran-teed equal rights under the law and prohibited discrimination in public facilities, schools, em-ployment, and voting. However, in the 1980s, despite legislation and affirmative action (positive discrimination), in practice blacks, who make up some 12% of the US population, continued to suffer discrimination and inequality of opportu-nities, particularly in education, employment, and housing. Nevertheless, the positive contributions of blacks in most fields, including the arts, the

Black *Scottish chemist and physicist Joseph Black by Tassie in 1788.*

sciences and politics, have played an important part in US history.

Unlike the USA, England did not have a history of slavery at home; Britain outlawed the slave trade 1807 and abolished slavery in the British Empire 1833. In the UK only a tiny proportion of the population was black until late after World War II, when immigration from Commonwealth countries increased. Legislation such as the Race Relations Act 1976 specifically outlawed discrimination on grounds of race and emphasized the official policy of equality of opportunity in all areas, and the Commission for Racial Equality was established 1977 to work towards eliminating discrimination; nevertheless, there is still considerable evidence of ◊racism in British society as a whole. The Swann Report on education 1985 emphasized that Britain was a multicultural society, and suggested various ways in which teachers could ensure that black children were able to reach their full po-tential. Black people are now beginning to take their place in public life in the UK; the election of Diane Abbott (1953–) as Britain's first black woman member of Parliament 1987 was a notable example.

Black /blæk/ Davidson 1884–1934. Canadian anatomist. In 1927, when professor of anatomy at the Union Medical College, Peking, he un-earthed the remains of ◊Peking man, a very early human.

Black /blæk/ James 1924– . British physiologist, director of therapeutic research at Wellcome La-boratories (near London) from 1978. He was active in the development of ◊beta-blockers and anti-ulcer drugs. Nobel prize 1988.

Black /blæk/ Joseph 1728–1799. Scottish physi-cist and chemist, who in 1754 discovered carbon dioxide (which he called 'fixed air'). By his inves-tigations in 1761 of latent heat and specific heat, he laid the foundation for the work of his pupil James Watt.

Born in Bordeaux, France, he qualified as a doctor in Edinburgh. In chemistry, he prepared the way for the scientists Cavendish, Priestley, and Lavoisier.

Black and Tans nickname of a specially raised force of military police employed by the British in 1920–21 to combat the Sinn Feiners (Irish na-tionalists) in Ireland; the name was derived from the colours of the uniforms.

Black Beauty the story of a horse's life, by Anna ◊Sewell, published in 1877. The book, which de-scribes the experiences of Black Beauty under many different owners, revived the genre of 'ani-mal autobiography' popular in the late 18th and early 19th centuries.

black beetle another name for ◊cockroach, although cockroaches belong to an entirely different order of insects (Dictyoptera) from the beetles (Coleoptera).

blackberry fruit of the bramble *Rubus fruticosus*, a prickly shrub, closely allied to the raspberry, that is native to northern parts of Europe. It produces pink or white blossoms and edible, black, compound fruits. There are 400 or so types of bramble found in Britain. In the past some have been regarded as distinct species.

blackbird bird *Turdus merula* of the thrush family. The male is black with yellow bill and eyelids, the female dark brown with a dark beak. About 25 cm/10 in long, it lays three to five blue-green eggs with brown spots. Its song is rich and flute-like.

Found across Europe and Asia, the blackbird adapts well to human presence and gardens, and is one of the commonest British birds. North American 'blackbirds' belong to a different family of birds, the Icteridae.

black body in physics, a hypothetical object that completely absorbs all thermal (heat) radiation falling on it. It is also a perfect emitter of thermal radiation.

Although a black body is hypothetical, a practical approximation can be made by using a small hole in the wall of a constant-temperature enclosure. The radiation emitted by a black body is of all wavelengths, but with maximum radiation at a particular wavelength that depends on the body's temperature. As the temperature increases, the wavelength of maximum intensity becomes shorter (see ◊Wien's law). The total energy emitted at all wavelengths is proportional to the fourth power of the temperature (see ◊Stefan's law). Attempts to explain these facts failed until the development of ◊quantum theory in 1900.

black box popular name for the robust box, usually orange-painted for easy recovery, containing an aeroplane's flight and voice recorders. It monitors the plane's behaviour and the crew's conversation, thus providing valuable clues to the cause of a disaster.

The maritime equivalent is the **voyage recorder**, installed in ships from 1989. It has 350 sensors to record the performance of engines, pumps, navigation lights, alarms, radar, and hull stress.

Black Boy autobiography of the US left-wing writer Richard Wright, published 1945, and considered to sum up the experience of growing up black in the USA.

blackbuck antelope *Antilope cervicapra* found in central and NW India. It is related to the gazelle, from which it differs in having the horns spirally twisted. The male is black above and white beneath, whereas the female and young are fawn-coloured above. It is about 76 cm/2.5 ft in height.

Blackburn /ˈblækbɜːn/ industrial town (engineering) in Lancashire, England, 32 km/20 mi NW of Manchester; population (1981) 88,000. It was pre-eminently a cotton-weaving town until World War II.

blackcap ◊warbler *Sylvia atricapilla*. The male has a black cap, the female a reddish-brown one. About 14 cm/5.5 in long, the blackcap likes wooded areas, and is a summer visitor to N Europe.

blackcock large grouse *Lyrurus tetrix* found on moors and in open woods in N Europe and Asia. The male is mainly black with a lyre-shaped tail, and up to 54 cm/1.7 ft in height. The female is speckled brown and only 40 cm/1.3 ft high.

Black Country central area of England, around and to the north of Birmingham. Heavily industrialized, it gained its name in the 19th century from its belching chimneys, but pollution laws have given it a changed aspect.

blackcurrant a variety of ◊currant.

Black Death modern name (first used in England in the early 19th century) for the great epidemic of bubonic ◊plague that ravaged Europe in the 14th century, killing between one third and one half of the population. The cause of the Black Death was the bacterium *Pasteurella pestis*, transmitted by rat fleas.

It gives rise both to bubonic and pneumonic forms (the latter being invariably fatal if untreated). Outbreaks of both forms still occur, mostly in hot countries, but the plague has never happened to the extent seen in the late Middle Ages. It remained endemic for the next three centuries, the most notable outbreak being the Great Plague of London in 1665, when about 100,000 of the 400,000 inhabitants died.

black earth the exceedingly fertile soil, a kind of ◊loess, that covers a belt of land in NE North America, Europe, and Asia.

In Europe and Asia it extends from Bohemia through Hungary, Romania, S Russia, and Siberia, as far as Manchuria, and was deposited when the great inland ice sheets melted at the close of the last ◊ice age.

black economy the unofficial economy of a country, which includes undeclared earnings from a second job ('moonlighting'), and enjoyment of undervalued goods and services (such as company 'perks'), designed for tax evasion purposes. In industrialized countries, it has been estimated to equal about 10% of ◊gross domestic product.

Blackett /ˈblækɪt/ Patrick Maynard Stuart, Baron Blackett 1897–1974. British physicist. He was awarded a Nobel prize in 1948 for work in cosmic radiation and his perfection of the Wilson cloud chamber.

blackfly plant-sucking insect, a type of ◊aphid.

Blackfoot /ˈblækfʊt/ member of a ◊Plains Indian people who now live predominantly in Saskatchewan, Canada. Their name is derived from their black moccasins, and their language belongs to the Algonquian family.

Black Forest /blæk/ (German *Schwarzwald*) mountainous region of coniferous forest in Baden-Württemberg, West Germany. Bounded west and south by the Rhine, which separates it from the Vosges, it has an area of 4,660 sq km/1,800 sq mi and rises to 1,493 m/4,905 ft in the Feldberg. Parts of the forest have recently been affected by ◊acid rain.

Blackheath /ˌblæk'hiːθ/ English common which gives its name to a residential suburb of London partly in Greenwich, partly in Lewisham. Wat Tyler encamped on Blackheath in the 1381 Peasants' Revolt.

Black Hills mountains in the Dakotas and Wyoming, USA.

black hole an object whose gravity is so great that nothing can escape from it, not even light. They are thought to form when massive stars shrink at the ends of their lives. A black hole can grow by sucking in more matter, including other stars, from the space around it. Matter that falls into a black hole is squeezed to infinite density at the centre of the hole. Black holes can be detected because gas falling towards them becomes so hot that it emits X-rays.

Satellites above the Earth's atmosphere have detected X-rays from a number of objects in our galaxy that might be black holes. Massive black holes containing the mass of millions of stars are thought to lie at the centres of ◊quasars. Microscopic black holes may have been formed in the chaotic conditions of the ◊Big Bang. The English physicist Stephen Hawking has shown that such tiny black holes could 'evaporate' and explode in a flash of energy.

Black Hole of Calcutta incident in Anglo-Indian history: according to tradition Suraj-ud-Dowlah, the nawab of Bengal, confined 146 British prisoners on the night of 20 June 1756 in one small room, of whom only 23 allegedly survived. Later research reduced the deaths to 43, a result of negligence rather than intention.

blackmail the criminal offence of the unwarranted demanding of money with menaces of violence, or threats of detrimental action such as exposure of some misconduct on the part of the victim.

black market illegal trade in food or other rationed goods, for example petrol and clothing, during World War II and after.

Black Monday a worldwide stockmarket crash that began 19 Oct 1987, prompted by the announcement of worse-than-expected US trade figures and the response by US Secretary of the Treasury Baker who indicated that the sliding dollar needed to decline further. This caused a world panic as fears of the likely impact of a US recession were voiced by the major industrialized countries. Between 19 and 23 Oct the New York Stock Exchange fell by 33%, the London Stock Exchange Financial Times 100 Index by 25%, the European index by 17%, and Tokyo by 12%. The total paper loss on the London Stock Exchange and other City of London institutions was £94 billion. The expected world recession did not occur; by the end of 1988 it was clear that the main effect had been a steadying in stock market activity and only a slight slowdown in world economic growth.

Blackmore /ˈblækmɔː/ R(ichard) D(oddridge) 1825–1900. English novelist, author of *Lorna Doone* 1869, a romance set on Exmoor, SW England, in the late 17th century.

Black Mountain poets group of experimental US poets of the 1950s who were linked with the Black Mountain liberal arts college, North Carolina. They rejected the formalistic constraints of rhyme and metre. Leading members included Charles Olsen (1910–70) and Robert Creeley (1926–   ).

Black Mountains group of hills in S Powys, Wales, overlooking the Wye Valley and honeycombed with caves discovered 1966.

Black Muslim member of a religious group founded 1929 in the USA and led from 1934 by Elijah Muhammad (1897–1975) (then Elijah Poole) after a vision of Allah. Its growth from 1946 as a black separatist organization was due to Malcolm X (1926–65), son of a Baptist minister, who in 1964 broke away and founded his own Organization for Afro-American Unity, preaching 'active self-defence'.

Black National State an area in the Republic of South Africa set aside for development to self-government by black Africans in accordance with ◊apartheid. Before 1980 these areas were known as black homelands or **bantustans**. They make up less than 14% of the country; tend to be in arid areas, though some have mineral wealth; and may be in scattered blocks. Those that have so far reached nominal independence are Transkei 1976, Bophuthatswana 1977, Venda 1979, and Ciskei 1981. They are not recognized outside South Africa because of their racial basis, and 11 million blacks live permanently in the country's white-designated areas.

blackout temporary loss of consciousness, or of electrical power; in wartime, the policy of keeping cities in darkness to conceal them from enemy aircraft at night.

Blackpool /ˈblækpuːl/ seaside resort in Lancashire, England, 45 km/28 mi N of Liverpool; population (1981) 148,000. Amusement facilities include 11 km/7 mi of promenades, known for their 'illuminations' of coloured lights, fun fairs, and a tower 152 m/500 ft high. Political party conferences are often held here.

Black Power a movement towards black separatism in the USA during the 1960s, embodied in the **Black Panther Party** founded 1966 by Huey Newton and Bobby Seale. Its ultimate aim was the establishment of a separate black state in the USA established by a black plebiscite under the aegis of the UN. Following a National Black Political Convention in 1972, a National Black Assembly was established to exercise pressure on the Democratic and Republican parties.

The Black Power concept arose when existing ◊civil-rights organizations such as the National Association for Advancement of Colored People and the Southern Christian Leadership Conference were perceived to be ineffective in producing major change in the status of black people. Stokely Carmichael then advocated the exploitation of political and economic power and abandonment of nonviolence, with a move towards the type of separatism first developed by the ◊Black Muslims. Leaders such as Martin Luther King rejected this approach, but the Black Panther Party (so named because the panther, though not generally aggressive, will fight to the death under attack) adopted it fully and achieved nationwide influence.

Black Prince name given to ◊Edward, Prince of Wales, eldest son of Edward III of England.

Black Sea (Russian **Chernoye More**) inland sea in SE Europe, linked with the seas of Azov and Marmara, and via the Dardanelles with the Mediterranean. Uranium deposits beneath it are among the world's largest.

Black September a guerrilla splinter group of the ◊Palestine Liberation Organization formed in 1970. Operating from bases in Syria and the Lebanon, it was responsible for the kidnap attempts at the Munich Olympics 1972 which led to the deaths of 11 Israelis, and more recent hijack and bomb attempts carried out by individuals such as Leila Khaled.

Blackshirts term widely used to describe fascist paramilitary organisations. Originating with Mussolini's fascist Squadristi in the 1920s, it was also applied to the Nazi SS (*Schutzstaffel*) and to the followers of Oswald Mosley's British Union of Fascists.

blacksnake several species of snake. *Pseudechis porphyriacus* is a venomous snake of the cobra family found in damp forests and swamps in E Australia. *Coluber constrictor* from the E USA is a relative of the grass snake about 1.2 m/4 ft long, and without venom.

Black Stone in Islam, sacred stone built into the east corner of the ◊Kaaba which is a focal point of the *hajj*, or pilgrimage, to Mecca. There are a number of stories concerning its origin, one of which states that it was sent to Earth at the time of the first man, Adam; Muhammad declared that it was given to Abraham by Gabriel. It has been suggested that it is of meteoric origin.

Blackstone /'blækstəʊn/ William 1723–1780. English jurist, who published his *Commentaries on the Laws of England* 1765–70. Called to the Bar in 1746, he became professor of law at Oxford 1758, and a Justice of the Court of Common Pleas 1770.

Black Stump, the in Australia, an imaginary boundary between civilization and the outback, as in the phrase *this side of the black stump*.

blackthorn densely branched spiny bush *Prunus spinosa*, family Rosaceae. It produces white blossom on black, leafless branches in early spring; its sour blue-black fruit, sloes, may be used to flavour gin.

Black Thursday the day of the Wall Street stock market crash 29 Oct 1929, which was followed by the worst economic depression in US history.

Blackwell /'blækwel/ Elizabeth 1821–1910. First British woman to qualify in medicine, in 1849.

Black Sea

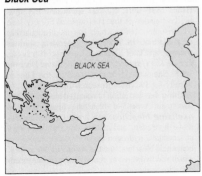

Blake English poet and artist William Blake was a mystic and visionary. His paintings and engravings include illustrations for Dante's Divine Comedy and Milton's Paradise Lost: in this example from Book One of Paradise Lost, Satan arouses the rebel angels after the fall.

Blackwell studied medicine at the University of Geneva in New York State. On her return to Britain, she became the first woman to appear in the Medical Register. Her example inspired Elizabeth Garrett ◊Anderson and many other aspiring female doctors.

black widow North American spider *Latrodectus mactans*. The male is small and harmless, but the female is 1.3 cm/0.5 in long with a red patch below the abdomen and a powerful venomous bite. The bite causes pain and fever in human victims, but they usually recover.

bladder hollow elastic-walled organ in the ◊urinary systems of amphibians, mammals, and some reptiles. Urine enters the bladder through two ureters, one leading from each kidney, and leaves it through the urethra.

bladderwort carnivorous aquatic plant, genus *Utricularia*, of the family Lentibulariaceae, which feeds on small crustacea.

Blagonravov /,blægɒnrə'vɒf/ Anatoly Arkadievich 1894–1975. Russian engineer, a specialist in rocketry and instrumentation. He directed the earth satellite programme leading to the launching of Sputniks 1 and 2.

Blake /bleɪk/ Robert 1599–1657. British admiral of the Parliamentary forces during the English Civil War. Appointed 'general-at-sea' 1649, he destroyed Prince Rupert's privateering fleet off Cartagena, Spain, in the following year. In 1652 he won several engagements against the Dutch. In 1654 he bombarded Tunis, the stronghold of the Barbary corsairs, and in 1657 captured the Spanish treasure fleet in Santa Cruz.

He represented his native Bridgwater, Somerset, in the Short Parliament of 1640, and distinguished himself in defending Bristol 1643 and Taunton 1644–45 in the Civil War. In the naval war with the Netherlands (1652–54) he was eventually defeated by ◊Tromp off Dungeness, and revenged himself in 1653 by defeating the Dutch admiral off Portsmouth and the northern Foreland.

Blake /bleɪk/ William 1757–1827. English painter, engraver, poet, and mystic, a leading figure in the Romantic period. His visionary, symbolic poems include *Songs of Innocence* 1789 and *Songs of Experience* 1794. He engraved the text and illustrations for his works and hand-coloured them, mostly in watercolour. He also illustrated works by others, including the poet Milton, and created a highly personal style.

He was born in Soho, London, and apprenticed to an engraver 1771–78. Blake illustrated the Bible, works by Dante and Shakespeare, and his own poems. His figures are heavily muscled with elongated proportions. In his later years he attracted a group of followers including Samuel Palmer, who called themselves the Ancients. Henry Fuseli was another admirer. Blake's poem *Jerusalem* 1820 was set to music by Charles Parry (1848–1918).

Blakey /'bleɪki/ Art (Muslim name Abdullah Ibn Buhaina) 1919– . US jazz drummer, known for his dynamic style with rolls and explosions. He formed and led the Jazz Messengers from 1955, and widely expanded percussion possibilities, including the assimilation of African rhythms.

Blamey /'bleɪmi/ Thomas Albert 1884–1951. The first Australian field marshal. Born in New South Wales, he served at Gallipoli, Turkey, and on the Western Front in World War I. In World War II he was commander in chief of the Allied Land Forces in the SW Pacific 1942–45.

Blanc /blɒŋ/ Louis 1811–1882. French socialist and journalist. In 1839 he founded the *Revue du progrès*, in which he published his *Organisation du travail*, advocating the establishment of cooperative workshops and other socialist schemes. He was a member of the provisional government of 1848 (see ◊revolutions of 1848) and from its fall lived in the UK until 1871.

Blanchard /blɒnˈʃɑː/ Jean Pierre 1753–1809. French balloonist, who made the first balloon flight across the Channel with John Jeffries in 1785. He made the first balloon flight in the USA in 1793.

Blanche of Castile /blɑnʃ, kæˈstiːl/ 1188–1252. Queen of France, wife of ◊Louis VIII of France, and regent for her son Louis IX (St Louis of France) from the death of her husband in 1226 until Louis IX's majority in 1234, and again from 1247 while he was away on a Crusade. She effectively quelled a series of revolts by the barons, and in 1229 negotiated the Treaty of Paris, by which Toulouse came under control of the monarchy.

blank verse in literature, the unrhymed iambic pentameter or ten-syllable line of five stresses. Originated by the Italian Gian Giorgio Trissino in his tragedy *Sofonisba* 1514–15, it was introduced to England about 1540 by the Earl of Surrey, and developed by Marlowe. More recent exponents of blank verse in English include Thomas Hardy, T S Eliot, and Robert Frost.

After its introduction from Italy, blank verse was used with increasing freedom by Shakespeare, Fletcher, Webster, and Middleton. It was remodelled by Milton, who was imitated in the 18th century by Thomson, Young, and Cowper, and revived in the early 19th century by Wordsworth, Shelley, and Keats, and later by Tennyson, Browning, and Swinburne.

Blavatsky *Russian 19th-century theosophist Helena Blavatsky convinced a large following that she had intuitive insight into the divine nature.*

Blériot *The pilot's licence of French aviator Louis Blériot. He made the first flight across the English Channel from Baraques to Dover.*

Blanqui /blɒŋˈkiː/ Louis Auguste 1805–1881. French revolutionary politician. He formulated the theory of the 'dictatorship of the proletariat', used by Karl Marx, and spent a total of 33 years in prison for insurrection. He became a martyr figure for the French workers' movement.

Blantyre-Limbe /'blæntaɪə 'lɪmbeɪ/ the chief industrial and commercial centre of Malawi, in the Shire highlands; population (1985) 355,000. It produces tea, coffee, rubber, tobacco, and textiles.

It was formed by the union of the towns of Blantyre (named after the explorer Livingstone's birthplace) and Limbe in 1959.

Blarney /'blɑːni/ small town in County Cork, Republic of Ireland, possessing, inset in the wall of the 15th-century castle, the **Blarney Stone**, reputed to give persuasive speech to those kissing it.

Blashford-Snell /'blæʃfəd 'snel/ John 1936– . British explorer and soldier. His expeditions have included the first descent and exploration of the Blue Nile 1968; the journey N to S from Alaska to Cape Horn, crossing the Darien Gap between Panama and Colombia for the first time 1971–72; and the first complete navigation of the Zaïre river, Africa 1974–75.

From 1963 he organized adventure training at Sandhurst military academy. He was director of Operation Drake 1977–81 and Operation Raleigh 1978–82. Publications include *A Taste for Adventure* 1978.

Blasis /blæˈsiː/ Carlo 1797–1878. Italian ballet teacher of French extraction. He was successful as a dancer in Paris and in Milan, where he established a dancing school in 1837. His celebrated treatise on the art of dancing, *Traité élémentaire, théoretique et pratique de l'art de la danse* 1820, forms the basis of classical dance training.

blasphemy (Greek 'evil-speaking') written or spoken insult directed against religious belief or sacred things with deliberate intent to outrage believers. Blasphemy against the Christian church is still an offence in English common law, despite several recommendations (for example by the Law Commission 1985) that it should be abolished or widened to apply to all religious faiths. In 1977 the magazine *Gay News* and its editor were successfully prosecuted for publishing a poem that suggested Jesus was a homosexual. In 1989 Salman Rushdie was accused by orthodox Muslims of blasphemy against the Islamic faith in his book *The Satanic Verses*.

Blasphemy was originally defined as 'publishing any matter which contradicts the teaching of the Church of England'; since 1883 it is redefined as a 'vilification' attack on Christianity, likely to 'outrage the feelings of believers'. Following *The Satanic Verses*, demands have been made to extend blasphemy laws to cover Islam, or abolish blasphemy laws entirely.

blast furnace furnace in which temperature is raised by the injection of an air blast. It is employed in the extraction of metals from their ores, particularly pig-iron from iron ore. The principle has been known for thousands of years, but the modern blast furnace is a heavy engineering development combining a number of special techniques. The blast furnace was introduced to England from France about 1500.

blastocyst in mammals, a stage in the development of the ◊embryo that is roughly equivalent to the ◊blastula of other animal groups.

blastomere in biology, a cell formed in the early stages as a fertilized ovum splits.

blastula an early stage in the development of a fertilized egg, when the egg changes from a solid mass of cells to a hollow ball of cells (the blastula), containing a fluid-filled cavity (the blastocoel). See also ◊embryology.

Blaue Reiter, der /'blauə 'raɪtə/ (German 'the Blue Rider') a group of German Expressionist painters based in Munich, some of whom had left *die* ◊*Brücke*. They were interested in the value of colours, in folk art, and in the necessity of painting 'the inner, spiritual side of nature', but styles were highly varied. Wassily Kandinsky and Franz Marc published a book of their views in 1912 and there were two exhibitions (1911, 1912).

Blavatsky /blɑˈvætski/ Helena Petrovna (born Hahn) 1831–1891. Russian spiritualist and mystic, co-founder of the Theosophical Society (see ◊Theosophy) 1875, which has its headquarters near Madras. In Tibet she underwent spiritual training, and later became a Buddhist. Her books include *Isis Unveiled* 1877 and *The Secret Doctrine* 1888. She was declared a fraud by the London Society for Psychical Research 1885.

bleaching decolorization of coloured materials. The two main types of bleaching agent are the **oxidizing bleaches**, which add oxygen and remove hydrogen, and include the ultraviolet rays in sunshine, hydrogen peroxide, and chlorine in household bleaches, and the **reducing bleaches**, which add hydrogen or remove oxygen, for example sulphur dioxide.

Bligh The British sailor William Bligh, 1792.

Bleaching processes have been known from antiquity, especially those acting through sunlight. Both natural and synthetic pigments usually possess highly complex molecules, the colour property often being due only to a part of the molecule. Bleaches usually attack only that small part, giving another substance similar in chemical structure but colourless.

bleak freshwater fish *Alburnus alburnus* of the carp family. It is up to to 20 cm/8 in long, and lives in still or slow-running clear water in Britain and Europe. In E Europe its scales are used in the preparation of artificial pearls.

bleeding loss of blood from the circulation; see ◊haemorrhage.

Blenheim /ˈblɛnɪm/ centre of a sheep-grazing area in the NE of South Island, New Zealand; population (1986) 18,300.

Blenheim, Battle of battle on 13 Aug 1704 in which English troops under ◊Marlborough defeated the French and Bavarian armies near the Bavarian village of Blenheim (now in West Germany) on the left bank of the Danube.

blenny any fish of the family Blenniidae, mostly small fishes found near rocky shores, with elongated bodies tapering from head to tail, no scales, and long pelvic fins set far forward. The most common British species is the *shanny Blennius pholis*.

Blériot /ˈblɛrɪəʊ/ Louis 1872–1936. French aviator who, in a 24-horsepower monoplane of his own construction, made the first flight across the English Channel on 25 July 1909.

blesbok African antelope *Damaliscus albifrons* about 1 m/3 ft high, with curved horns, brownish body, and a white blaze on the face. It was seriously depleted in the wild at the end of the 19th century. A few protected herds survive in South Africa. It is farmed for meat.

Blessington /ˈblɛsɪŋtən/ Marguerite, Countess of Blessington 1789–1849. Irish writer. A doyenne of literary society, she published *Conversations with Lord Byron* 1834, travel sketches, and novels.

Bligh /blaɪ/ William 1754–1817. British admiral. Bligh accompanied Captain ◊Cook on his second voyage 1772–74, and in 1787 commanded HMS *Bounty* on an expedition to the Pacific. On the return voyage the crew mutinied 1789, and Bligh was cast adrift in a boat with 18 men. He was appointed governor of New South Wales in 1805, where his discipline again provoked a mutiny 1808. He returned to Britain, and was made an admiral in 1811.

He went to Tahiti with the *Bounty* to collect breadfruit shortly before the mutiny, and gained the nickname 'Breadfruit Bligh'. In protest against

harsh treatment, he and those who supported him were put in a small craft with no map and few provisions. They survived after drifting 5,822 km/3,618 mi.

blight number of plant diseases caused mainly by parasitic species of ◊fungus, which produce a whitish appearance on leaf and stem surfaces, for instance *potato blight Phytophthora infestans*. General damage caused by aphids or pollution is sometimes known as blight.

Blighty popular name for England among British troops in World War I.

blimp an airship: any self-propelled, lighter-than-air craft that can be steered. A blimp with a soft frame is also called a *dirigible*; a ◊zeppelin is rigid-framed.

British lighter-than-air aircraft were divided in World War I into A-rigid and B-limp (that is, without rigid internal framework), a barrage balloon therefore becoming known as a blimp. The cartoonist David Low adopted the name for his stuffy character *Colonel Blimp*.

blindness complete absence or impairment of sight. It may be caused by heredity, accident, disease, or deterioration with age.

Education of the blind was begun by Valentin Haüy, who published a book with raised lettering 1784, and founded a school. Aids to the blind include the use of the ◊Braille and ◊Moon alphabets in reading and writing, and of electronic devices now under development which convert print to recognizable mechanical speech; guide dogs; and sonic torches.

blind spot the area where the optic nerve and blood vessels pass through the retina of the ◊eye. No visual image can be formed as there are no light-sensitive cells in this part of the retina.

Bliss /blɪs/ Arthur (Drummond) 1891–1975. English composer, who became Master of the Queen's Musick in 1953. Works include *A Colour Symphony* 1922, music for ballets *Checkmate* 1937, *Miracle in the Gorbals* 1944, and *Adam Zero* 1946; an opera *The Olympians* 1949; and dramatic film music, including *Things to Come* 1935.

Blitzkrieg (German 'lightning war') a swift military campaign, as used by Germany at the beginning of World War II 1939–41. The abbreviation *Blitz* was applied to the German air raids on London 1940–41.

Blitzstein /ˈblɪtstiːn/ Marc 1905–1964. US composer. Born in Philadelphia, he was a child prodigy as a pianist at the age of six. He served with the US Army 8th Air Force 1942–45, for which he wrote *The Airborne* 1946, a choral symphony. His operas include *The Cradle Will Rock* 1937.

Blixen /ˈblɪksən/ Karen, born Karen Dinesen 1885–1962. Danish writer. Her autobiography *Out of Africa* 1937 is based on her experience of running a coffee plantation in Kenya. She wrote fiction, mainly in English, under the pen name Isak Dinesen.

BL Lacertae object a starlike object which forms the centre of a distant galaxy, with a prodigious energy output. BL Lac objects, as they are called, seem to be intermediate between ◊quasars and ◊Seyfert galaxies. They are so named because the first to be discovered lies in the small constellation Lacerta.

bloc (French) a group, generally used of politically allied countries, as in 'the Soviet bloc'.

Bloch /blɒk/ Ernest 1880–1959. US composer, born in Geneva, Switzerland. He went to the USA in 1916 and became founder-director of the Cleveland Institute of Music 1920–25. Among his works are the lyrical drama *Macbeth* 1910, *Schelomo* for cello and orchestra 1916, five string quartets, and *Suite Hébraïque*, for viola and orchestra 1953. He often used themes based on Jewish liturgical music and folk song.

Bloch /blɒk/ Felix 1905–1983. Swiss–US physicist. He shared a Nobel prize with E M Purcell in 1952 for his work on nuclear magnetic resonance (NMR) spectroscopy.

Blondin The French tightrope walker Charles Blondin.

He was born in Zürich, and was professor of physics at Stanford University, USA, 1934–71.

Bloch /blɒk/ Konrad 1912– . US chemist whose research, lasting more than a decade, concerned cholesterol. Making use of the ◊radioisotope carbon-14, Bloch was able to follow the complex steps by which the body chemically transforms acetic acid into cholesterol. For his ability in this field Bloch shared the 1964 Nobel Prize in Physiology or Medicine with Feodor Lynen (1911–).

block and tackle a type of ◊pulley.

Bloemfontein /ˈbluːmfɒnteɪn/ capital of the Orange Free State and judicial capital of the Republic of South Africa; population (1985) 204,000. Founded 1846, the city produces canned fruit, glassware, furniture, and plastics.

Blois /blwɑː/ town on the river Loire in central France; population (1983) 49,500. It has a château partly dating from the 13th century.

Blok /blɒk/ Alexander Alexandrovich 1880–1921. Russian poet who, as a follower of the French Symbolist movement, used words for their symbolic rather than actual meaning. He backed the 1917 Revolution, as in his most famous poems *The Twelve* 1918, and *The Scythians* 1918, the latter appealing to the West to join in the revolution.

Blomberg /ˈblɒmbeək/ Werner von 1878–1946. German soldier and Nazi politician, minister of defence 1933–35 and minister of war and head of the *Wehrmacht* (army) 1935–38 under Hitler's chancellorship. He was discredited by his marriage to a prostitute and dismissed in Jan 1938, enabling Hitler to exercise more direct control over the armed forces. In spite of his removal from office, Blomberg was put on trial for war crimes in 1946 at Nuremberg.

Blomdahl /ˈblɒmdɑːl/ Karl-Birger 1916–1968. Swedish composer of ballets and symphonies in expressionist style. His opera *Aniara* 1959 incorporates electronic music and is set in a spaceship.

Blondin /ˈblɒmdɪn/ Charles. Assumed name of Jean François Gravelet 1824–1897. French tightrope walker, who walked across a rope suspended above Niagara Falls, USA. He first crossed the falls 1859 at a height of 48.75 m/160 ft. He repeated the feat blindfolded and then pushing a wheelbarrow.

blood liquid circulating in the arteries, veins, and capillaries of vertebrate animals. In humans it makes up 5% of the body weight, occupying a volume of 5.5 l/10 pt. It consists of a colourless, transparent liquid called *plasma*, containing microscopic cells of three main varieties. *Red cells* form nearly half the volume of the blood, with 5,000 billion cells per litre. Their red colour is caused by ◊haemoglobin. Some *white*

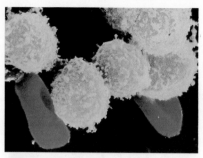

blood False-colour electron microscope view of human blood showing a number of lymphocytes and two red blood cells (× 880).

cells ($\lozenge$leucocytes) ingest invading bacteria and so protect the body from disease; these also help to repair injured tissues. Others ($\lozenge$lymphocytes) produce antibodies, which help provide immunity. Blood *platelets* assist in the clotting of blood.

Blood cells constantly wear out and die, and are replaced from the bone marrow. Dissolved in the plasma are salts, proteins, sugars, fats, hormones, and fibrinogen, which are transported around the body, the last having a role in clotting. The term 'blood' also refers to the corresponding fluid in those invertebrates which possess a closed $\lozenge$circulatory system.

Blood /blʌd/ Thomas 1618–1680. Irish adventurer, known as Colonel Blood, who attempted to steal the crown jewels from the Tower of London, England, 1671.

Blood and Iron (German: *Blut und Eisen*) the methods used by German chancellor, $\lozenge$Bismarck to unify Germany 1862–1871. The phrase came from Bismarck's speech in which he declared that 'the great questions of the day will be decided, not by speeches and majority votes … but by iron and blood.'

blood-brain barrier a theoretical term for the mechanism which prevents many substances circulating in the bloodstream (including some germs) from invading the brain.

The blood-brain barrier is not a single entity, but a defensive complex comprising various physical features and chemical reactions having to do with the permeability of cells. It ensures that 'foreign' proteins, carried in the blood vessels supplying the brain, do not breach the vessel walls, thereby entering the actual brain tissue. Many drugs are unable to cross the blood-brain barrier.

blood group the classification of blood types according to antigenic activity. Red blood cells of one individual may carry molecules on their surface which act as $\lozenge$antigens in another individual whose red blood cells lack these molecules. The two main antigens are designated A and B. These give rise to four blood groups: having A only (A), having B only (B), having both (AB), and having neither (O). Each of these groups may or may not contain the $\lozenge$rhesus factor. Correct typing of blood groups is vital in transfusion since incompatible types of donor and recipient blood will result in blood clotting, with possible death of the recipient.

These ABO blood groups were first described by Karl $\lozenge$Landsteiner in 1902. Subsequent research revealed at least 14 main types of blood groupings, 11 of which are involved with induced $\lozenge$antibody production. Blood typing is also of importance in forensic science, cases of disputed paternity, and in anthropological studies.

bloodhound ancient breed of dog. Black and tan in colour, it has long, pendulous ears, and distinctive wrinkles on the head. Its excellent powers of scent have been employed in tracking and criminal work from very early times.

blood poisoning infection caused by bacteria or bacterial toxins present in the blood (septicaemia); treatment is by antibiotics.

blood pressure the pressure, or tension, of the blood in the arteries and veins of the $\lozenge$circulatory system, due to the muscular activity of the heart.

In mammals, the left ventricle of the $\lozenge$heart pumps blood into the arterial system. This pumping is assisted by waves of muscular contraction by the $\lozenge$arteries themselves, but resisted by the elasticity of the inner and outer walls of the same arteries. Pressure is greatest when the heart ventricle contracts (**systolic pressure**) and least when the ventricle is filling up with blood and pressure is solely maintained by the elasticity of the arteries (**diastolic pressure**). Blood pressure is measured in millimetres of mercury, with an instrument called a sphygmomanometer. Normal human blood pressure is around 120/80 mm Hg; the first number represents the systolic pressure and the second the diastolic. Large deviations from this figure usually indicate ill health.

blood test a laboratory evaluation of a blood sample. There are numerous blood tests, from simple typing to establish its group (in case a $\lozenge$transfusion is needed) to sophisticated biochemical assays of substances, such as hormones, present in the blood only in minute quantities.

The majority of tests fall into one of three categories: haematology (testing the state of the blood itself), microbiology (identifying infection), and blood chemistry (reflecting chemical events elsewhere in the body). Before operations, a common test is haemoglobin estimation to determine how well a patient might tolerate blood loss during surgery.

bloom whitish powdery or wax-like coating over the surface of certain fruits that easily rubs off when handled. It often contains $\lozenge$yeasts that live on the sugars in the fruit. The term bloom is also used to describe a rapid increase in number of certain species of algae found in lakes and ponds.

Bloom /bluːm/ Claire 1931– . British actress. Born in London, she first made her reputation on the stage in Shakespearean roles. Her films include *Richard III* 1956 and *The Brothers Karamazov* 1958, and television appearances include *Brideshead Revisited* 1980.

Bloomer /ˈbluːmə/ Amelia Jenks 1818–1894. US campaigner for women's rights. She introduced in 1849, when unwieldy crinolines were the fashion, a knee-length skirt combined with loose trousers gathered at the ankles, which became known as *bloomers* (also called 'rational dress'). She published the magazine *The Lily* 1849–54, which campaigned for women's rights and dress reform, and lectured with Susan B $\lozenge$Anthony in New York, USA.

Bloomsbury /ˈbluːmzbəri/ area in Camden, London, England, between Gower Street and High Holborn. It contains London University headquarters, the British Museum and the Royal Acadamy of Dramatic Arts. Between world wars it was the home of the Bloomsbury Group.

Bloomsbury Group a group of writers and artists based in Bloomsbury, London. The group included the artists $\lozenge$Duncan Grant and Vanessa Bell, and the writers Lytton $\lozenge$Strachey and Leonard and Virginia $\lozenge$Woolf.

Blow /bləʊ/ John 1648–1708. British composer. He taught $\lozenge$Purcell, and wrote church music, for example the anthem 'I Was Glad when They Said unto Me' 1697. His masque *Venus and Adonis* 1685 is sometimes called the first English opera.

blowfly fly, genus *Calliphora*, also known as *bluebottle*, or one of the related genus *Lucilia*, *greenbottle*. It lays its eggs in dead flesh, on which the maggots feed.

Bloy /blwɑː/ Léon-Marie 1846–1917. French author. He achieved a considerable reputation with his literary lampoons in the 1880s.

blubber the thick layer of $\lozenge$fat under the skin of marine mammals, which provides an energy store and an effective insulating layer, preventing the loss of body heat to the sea. Blubber has been used (when boiled down) in engineering, food

bluebell

processing, cosmetics and printing, but all of these products can now be produced synthetically, thus saving the lives of animals.

Blücher /ˈbluːkə/ Gebhard Leberecht von 1742–1819. Prussian general and field marshal, popular as 'Marshal Forward'. He took an active part in the patriotic movement, and in the War of German Liberation defeated the French as commander in chief at Leipzig 1813, crossed the Rhine to Paris 1814, and was made prince of Wahlstadt (Silesia). In 1815 he was defeated by Napoleon at Ligny, but played a crucial role in the British commander Wellington's triumph at Waterloo, near Brussels.

blue a sporting term used in the UK to describe a student of Oxford or Cambridge who represents their university at any game or sporting activity. The actual award is a ribbon, either light-blue (Cambridge) or dark-blue (Oxford), depending on which university is represented. The first blues are believed to have been awarded after the 1836 $\lozenge$Boat Race.

Blue Arrow UK company whose attempted purchase of the US company Manpower Inc in 1987 prompted an investigation by the Serious Fraud Squad.

County Nat-West, the investment banking company of the National Westminster Bank, failed to disclose that only 38% of a rights issue (sale of shares) by Blue Arrow, intended to finance the purchase, had been taken up, and concealed the ownership of some of the shares. Two National Westminster investment bankers, one securities company, and 11 individuals were charged with fraud and conspiracy in Nov 1989.

Bluebeard /ˈbluːbɪəd/ folktale character, popularized by the writer Charles Perrault in France about 1697, and historically identified with Gilles de $\lozenge$Rais. He murdered six wives for disobeying his command not to enter a locked room, but was himself killed before he could murder the seventh.

bluebell name given in Scotland to the harebell *Campanula rotundifolia*, and in England to the wild hyacinth *Endymion nonscriptus*, belonging to the family Liliaceae.

bluebird North American bird, genus *Sialia*, belonging to the thrush family. The *eastern bluebird Sialia sialis* is regarded as the herald of spring. Slightly larger than a robin, it has a similar reddish breast, the upper plumage being sky-blue, and a distinctive song.

bluebuck several antelopes, including the *blue $\lozenge$duiker Cephalophus monticola* of South Africa, about 33 cm/13 in high. The male of the Indian $\lozenge$nilgai antelope is also known as the bluebuck.

The bluebuck or *blaubok Hippotragus leucophaeus* was a large blue-grey South African antelope. Once abundant, it was hunted to extinction, the last being shot in 1800.

blue chip in business and finance, a stock which is considered strong and reliable in terms of the dividend yield and capital value. Blue chip companies are favoured by stock market investors more interested in security than risk taking.

Blue Division the Spanish volunteers who fought with the German army against the USSR during World War II.

Bluefields one of three major port facilities on the E coast of Nicaragua, situated on an inlet of the Caribbean Sea.

bluegrass dense, spreading grass, *Poa compressa*, which is blue-tinted and grows in clumps. It provides pasture for horses and is abundant in Kentucky, USA, which is known as the bluegrass state.

blue-green algae single-celled, primitive organisms that resemble bacteria in their internal cell organization, sometimes joined together in colonies or filaments. Blue-green algae are among the oldest known living organisms; remains have been found in rocks up to 3,500 million years old. They are widely distributed in aquatic habitats, on the damp surfaces of rocks and trees, and in the soil.

Blue-green algae and bacteria are ◊prokaryotic organisms. Some can fix nitrogen so are important in the nitrogren cycle, while others follow a symbiotic existence, for example living with fungi in lichens.

blue gum Australian tree *Eucalyptus globulus* with bluish bark, a chief source of eucalyptus oil.

Blue Mountains part of the ◊Great Divide, New South Wales, Australia, ranging 600–1,100 m/2,000–3,600 ft and blocking Sydney from the interior until the crossing 1813 by surveyor William Lawson, Gregory Blaxland, and William Wentworth.

Blue Nile (Arabic *Bahr el Azraq*) river rising in the mountains of Ethiopia. Flowing W then N for 2,000 km/1,250 mi it eventually meets the White Nile at Khartoum. The river is dammed at Roseires where a hydroelectric scheme produces 70% of Sudan's electricity.

blueprint process used for copying engineering drawings and architectural plans, so called because it produces a white copy of the original against a blue background.

The plan to be copied is made on transparent tracing paper, which is placed in contact with paper sensitized with a mixture of iron ammonium citrate and potassium hexacyanoferrate. The paper is exposed to ◊ultraviolet light, and then washed in water. Where the light reaches the paper, it turns blue (Prussian blue). The paper underneath the lines of the drawing is unaffected, so remains white.

blue riband or *blue ribbon* the highest distinction in any sphere; for example, the blue riband of horse racing in the UK is held by the winner of the Derby.

The term derives from the blue riband of the Order of the Garter (see under ◊knighthood). The term *cordon bleu* in French has the same meaning. The *Blue Riband of the Atlantic* is held by the vessel making the fastest crossing without refuelling. The trophy was first presented 1935. The *Queen Mary* won it 1938 and held the record until the *United States* created a new record of 3 dy 10 hr 31 min 1952. Richard Branson's time of 3 dy 8hr 31 min in *Virgin Atlantic Challenger* 1985 was a new record time but failed to wrest the trophy from its home at the US Maritime Museum on Long Island because he refuelled three times, which is against the conditions that must be met to win the trophy. On 27 July 1989, Tom Gentry of the USA in his craft *Gentry Eagle* broke the record with a time of 67 hr 7 min. He was presented with the Blue Riband Trophy by Richard Branson.

Blue Ridge Mountains range extending from West Virginia to Georgia, USA, and including Mount Mitchell 2,045 m/6,712 ft; part of the ◊Appalachians.

blues 12-bar folk song in which, typically, the second line of the three-line verse is a repetition of the first, with variations, so giving the singer time to improvise the third line. It originated in the USA among blacks in the rural South in the late 19th century, and the words are often melancholy. Blues guitar and vocal styles have influenced jazz and, particularly, pop music.

1920s–30s The *rural* or *delta blues* was usually performed solo with guitar or harmonica, for example by Robert Johnson (1911–38) and Bukka White (1906–77), but the earliest recorded style, *classic blues*, by musicians such as W C Handy (1873–1958) and Bessie Smith (1894–1937), was sung with a small band.

1940s–50s Urban blues, using electric amplification, emerged in the cities of the North, especially Chicago. As exemplified by Howlin' Wolf (real name Chester Burnett, 1910–76), Muddy Waters (real name McKinley Morganfield, 1915–83), and John Lee Hooker (1917–), urban blues became *rhythm and blues*.

1960s The jazz-influenced guitar style of B B King (1925–) inspired many musicians of the *British blues boom*, including Eric Clapton (1945–).

1980s The 'blues *noir*' of Robert Cray (1953–) found a wide audience.

blue shift in astronomy, a manifestation of the ◊Doppler effect in which an object appears bluer when it is moving towards the observer or the observer is moving towards it (blue light is of a higher frequency than other colours in the spectrum). The blue shift is the opposite of the ◊red shift.

bluestocking term, often disparaging, for a learned woman. It originated in 1750 in England with the literary gatherings of Elizabeth Vesey (1715–91), the wife of an Irish MP, in Bath, and Elizabeth Montagu, a writer and patron, in London. According to the novelist, Fanny Burney, the term arose when the poet Benjamin Stillingfleet protested that he had nothing formal to wear. She told him to come in his 'blue stockings' – that is, ordinary clothes. The regulars at these gatherings became known as the Blue Stocking Circle. The writer Hannah ◊More (1745–1833) described it in the poem *Bas Bleu, or Conversation* 1786.

Blum /bluːm/ Léon 1872–1950. French politician. He was converted to socialism by the ◊Dreyfus affair 1899, and in 1936 became the first socialist prime minister of France. He was again premier for a few weeks 1938. Imprisoned under the Vichy government 1942 as a danger to French security, he was released by the Allies 1945. He again became premier for a few weeks 1946.

Blunden /ˈblʌndən/ Edmund 1896–1974. English poet. He served in World War I, and published the prose work *Undertones of War* 1928. His poetry is mainly about rural life. Among his scholarly contributions was the discovery and publication of some poems by the 19th-century poet John Clare.

Blunt /blʌnt/ Anthony 1907–1983. British art historian and double agent. As a Cambridge lecturer, he recruited for the Soviet secret service, and, as a member of the British Secret Service 1940–45, passed information to the Russians. In 1951 he assisted the defection to the USSR of the British agents Guy ◊Burgess and Donald Maclean (1913–83). He was author of many respected works on French and Italian art.

Unmasked in 1964, he was given immunity after his confession, but was stripped of his knighthood in 1979 when the affair became public. He was director of the Courtauld Institute of Art 1947–74 and Surveyor of the Queen's Pictures 1945–1972.

Blunt /blʌnt/ Wilfrid Scawen 1840–1922. British poet. He married Lady Anne Noel, Byron's granddaughter, and travelled with her in the Middle East, becoming a supporter of Arab nationalism. He also supported Irish Home Rule (imprisoned 1887–88), and wrote anti-imperialist books, poetry and diaries.

Blyth /blaɪð/ Charles 'Chay' 1940– . British sailing adventurer who rowed across the Atlantic with Captain John Ridgeway in 1966 and sailed solo around the world in a westerly direction during 1970–71. In 1973–74 he sailed around the world with a crew in the opposite direction, and in 1977 he made a record-breaking transatlantic crossing from Cape Verde to Antigua.

Blyton /ˈblaɪtn/ Enid 1897–1968. British writer of children's books. She created the character Noddy and the adventures of the 'Famous Five' and 'Secret Seven', but has been criticized by educationalists for social, racial, and sexual stereotyping.

BMA abbreviation for *British Medical Association*.

BMR abbreviation for ◊*basal metabolic rate*.

BNF abbreviation for *British Nuclear Fuels*.

boa type of non-venomous snake that kills its prey by constriction. The *boa constrictor Constrictor constrictor*, can be up to 5.5 m/18.5 ft long, but is rarely more than 4 m/12 ft. It feeds mainly on small mammals and birds. Other boas include the ◊anaconda and the *emerald tree boa Boa canina*, about 2 m/6 ft long and bright green.

Some small burrowing boas live in N Africa and W Asia, and other species live on Madagascar and some Pacific islands, but the majority of boas live in S and Central America. The name boa is sometimes used loosely to include the pythons of the Old World, also of the family Boidae, which share with boas vestiges of hind limbs and constricting habits.

Boadicea /ˌbəʊədɪˈsiːə/ alternative spelling of British queen ◊Boudicca.

boar wild member of the pig family, such as the Eurasian *wild boar Sus scrofa*, from which domestic breeds derive. The wild boar is sturdily built, being 1.5 m/4.5 ft long and 1 m/3 ft high, and possesses formidable tusks. Of gregarious nature and mainly woodland-dwelling, it feeds on roots, nuts, and some carrion and insects.

The dark coat of the adult boar is made up of coarse bristles with varying amounts of underfur, but the young are striped. The male domestic pig is also known as a boar, the female as a sow.

boarding school school offering board and lodging as well as tuition.

Most boarding education in the UK is provided in the private, fee-paying sector, but there are a number of state schools with boarding facilities.

boardsailing another name for ◊Windsurfing, a watersport combining elements of surfing and sailing, also called sailboarding.

Boateng /ˈbwɑːteŋ/ Paul 1951– . British Labour politician. He became Member of Parliament for Brent South 1987. He has served on numerous committees on crime and race relations.

boat people those Vietnamese who left their country following the takeover of South Vietnam 1975 by North Vietnam. 160,000 Vietnamese fled to Hong Kong, many being attacked at sea by Thai pirates, and in 1989 50,000 remained there in cramped, squalid refugee camps. Only 10% of those who have arrived since the policy of 'screening' (questioning about reasons for leaving Vietnam) began in 1988 have been given refugee status; the others are classified as 'economic migrants'. The UK government began forced repatriation in 1990, when the total number of boat people in SE Asia was about 90,000, an increase of 30,000 from 1988.

Boat Race annual UK rowing race between the crews of Oxford and Cambridge universities. It is held during the Easter vacation over a 6.8 km/4.25 mi course on the river Thames between Putney and Mortlae, SW London.

The Boat Race was first held in 1829 from Hambledon Lock to Henley Bridge. Up to and including the 1990 race it had been staged 136 times; Cambridge had 69 wins, Oxford 66 and there had been one dead heat, in 1877. The reserve crews also have their own races. The Cambridge reserve crew is called Goldie, Oxford's is called Isis.

bobcat cat *Felis rufa* living in a variety of habitats from S Canada through to S Mexico. It is similar to the lynx, but only 75 cm/2.5 ft long, with reddish fur and less well-developed ear-tufts.

bobolink North American songbird *Dolichonyx oryzivorus*, named from its call.

Bobruisk /bəˈbruːɪsk/ town in Byelorussia, USSR, on the Beresina river; population (1987) 232,000. Industries include timber, machinery, tyres, and chemicals.

bobsleighing or *bobsledding* the sport of racing steel-bodied, steerable toboggans, crewed by two or four people, down mountain ice-chutes at speeds of up to 130 kmph/80 mph. It was introduced as an Olympic event in 1924 and world championships have been held every year since 1931.

Recent Winners

Olympic Champions four-person event introduced at the 1924 Winter Olympics, two-person in 1932

two-person/four-person
1964 Great Britain/Canada
1968 Italy/Italy
1972 West Germany/Switzerland
1980 Switzerland/East Germany
1984 East Germany/East Germany
1988 USSR/Switzerland

World Champions four-person championship introduced 1924, two-person 1931; in Olympic years winners automatically become world champions

two-person/four-person
1980 Switzerland/East Germany
1981 East Germany/East Germany
1982 Switzerland/Switzerland
1983 Switzerland/Switzerland
1984 East Germany/East Germany
1985 East Germany/East Germany
1986 East Germany/Switzerland
1987 Switzerland/East Germany
1988 USSR/Switzerland
1989 East Germany/Switzerland

Boccaccio /bɒˈkɑːtʃiəʊ/ Giovanni 1313–1375. Italian poet, author of a collection of tales called the ◊*Decameron* 1348–53.

Son of a Florentine merchant, he lived in Naples 1328–41, where he fell in love with the unfaithful 'Fiametta', who inspired his early poetry. Before returning to Florence in 1341 he had written *Filostrato* and *Teseide* (used by Chaucer in his *Troilus and Criseyde* and *Knight's Tale*).

Boccherini /ˌbɒkəˈriːni/ (Ridolfo) Luigi 1743–1805. Italian composer and cellist. He studied in Rome, made his mark in Paris in 1768, and was court composer in Prussia and Spain. Boccherini composed some 350 instrumental works, an opera, and oratorios.

Boccioni /bɒtʃiˈəʊni/ Umberto 1882–1916. Italian painter and sculptor. One of the founders of the ◊*Futurist* movement, he was a pioneer of abstract art.

Bochum /ˈbɒxʊm/ town in the Ruhr district, West Germany; population (1988) 381,000. Industry includes metallurgy, vehicles, and chemicals.

Böcklin /ˈbɒklɪn/ Arnold 1827–1901. Swiss Romantic painter. His mainly imaginary landscapes have a dreamlike atmosphere, for example *Island of the Dead* 1880 (Metropolitan Museum of Art, New York).

He was strongly attracted to Italy, and lived for years in Rome. Many of his paintings are peo-

Bodichon *English feminist Barbara Bodichon, probably the model for the heroine of George Eliot's novel* Romola.

pled with mythical beings such as nymphs and naiads.

Bode /ˈbəʊdə/ Johann Elert 1747–1826. German astronomer, director of the Berlin observatory. He published the first atlas of all stars visible to the naked eye, *Uranographia* 1801.

Bode's law is a numerical sequence that gives the approximate distances, in astronomical units (distance between Earth and Sun = one astronomical unit) of the planets from the Sun by adding 4 to each term of the series 0, 3, 6, 12, 24, etc, and then dividing by 10. Bode's law predicted the existence of a planet between Mars and Jupiter, which led to the discovery of the asteroids. The 'law' breaks down for Neptune and Pluto. The relationship was first noted by the German mathematician Johann Titius in 1772 (it is also known as the *Titius–Bode law*).

Bodensee /ˈbəʊdnzeɪ/ German name for Lake ◊Constance, north of the Alps.

Bodhidharma /ˌbəʊdɪˈdɜːmə/ 6th century AD. Indian Buddhist. He entered China from S India *c.*520, and was the founder of *Zen*, the school of Mahāyāna Buddhism in which intuitive meditation, prompted by contemplation, leads to enlightenment.

According to one legend, Bodhidharma sat in uninterrupted meditation until after nine years his legs withered and fell off.

bodhisattva in Mahāyāna Buddhism, someone who seeks ◊enlightenment in order to help other living beings. A bodhisattva is free to enter ◊nirvana but voluntarily chooses to be reborn until all other beings have attained it.

Bodichon /ˈbəʊdɪʃɒn/ Barbara (born Leigh-Smith) 1827–1891. English feminist and campaigner for women's education and suffrage. She wrote *Women and Work* 1857, and was a founder of the magazine *The Englishwoman's Journal* in 1858.

Born into a radical family that believed in female equality, she attended Bedford College, London. She was a founder of the college for women that became Girton College, Cambridge.

Bodin /bəʊˈdæn/ Jean 1530–1596. French political philosopher, whose six-volume *De la République* 1576 is considered the first work on political economy.

An attorney in Paris, in 1574 he published a tract explaining that prevalent high prices were due to the influx of precious metals from the New World. His theory of an ideal government emphasized obedience to a sovereign ruler.

Bodley /ˈbɒdli/ Thomas 1545–1613. English scholar and diplomat after whom the Bodleian Library in Oxford is named. After retiring from Queen Elizabeth I's service in 1597, he restored the library, which was opened as the Bodleian Library 1602. He was knighted in 1604.

The library had originally been founded in the 15th century by Humphrey, Duke of Gloucester (1391–1447).

Bodmin /ˈbɒdmɪn/ administrative headquarters of Cornwall, England, 48 km/30 m from Plymouth; population (1984) 15,000.

Bodmin Moor to the NE is a granite upland, culminating in Brown Willy 419 m/1,375 ft.

Bodoni /bəˈdəʊni/ Giambattista 1740–1813. Italian printer who managed the printing-press of the Duke of Parma and produced high-quality editions of the classics. He designed several typefaces, including one bearing his name, which is in use today.

Boehme /ˈbɜːmə/ Jakob 1575–1624. German mystic. He claimed divine revelation of the unity of everything and nothing, and found in God's eternal nature a principle to reconcile good and evil. He was the author of the treatise *Aurora* 1612. By trade he was a shoemaker.

Boeing /ˈbəʊɪŋ/ William Edward 1881–1956. US industrialist, and founder of the Boeing Airplane Company 1917. Its military aircraft include the flying fortress bombers used in World War II, and the Chinook helicopter; its

Bogart *US film actor Humphrey Bogart.*

commercial craft include the ◊jetfoil, and the Boeing 747 and 707 jets.

Boeotia /biˈəʊʃə/ ancient district of central Greece, of which ◊Thebes was the chief city; the *Boeotian League* (formed by 10 city states in the 6th century BC) superseded ◊Sparta in the leadership of Greece in the 4th century BC.

Boer a Dutch settler or descendant of Dutch and Huguenot settlers in South Africa; see also ◊Afrikaner.

Boer War war between the Dutch settlers in South Africa and the British; see ◊South African Wars.

Boethius /bəʊˈθiəs/ Anicius Manilus Severinus 480–524. Roman philosopher. While imprisoned on suspicion of treason by ◊Theodoric, he wrote treatises on music and mathematics and *De Consolatione Philosophiae/The Consolation of Philosophy*, a dialogue in prose. It was translated into European languages during the Middle Ages and into English by Alfred the Great, Geoffrey Chaucer, and Queen Elizabeth I.

bog an area of soft, wet, spongy ground consisting of decaying vegetable matter or ◊peat. Bogs occur on the uplands of cold or temperate areas where drainage is poor.

The typical bog plant is sphagnum moss; rushes, cranberry, cotton grass, and sundew also grow under these conditions. Unlike marshes, bogs usually have little open water, and the water is acidic and low in oxygen.

Bogarde /ˈbəʊɡɑːd/ Dirk. Stage-name of Derek van den Bogaerde 1921– . British film actor, who appeared in comedies and adventure films such as *Doctor in the House* 1954 and *Campbell's Kingdom* 1957, before acquiring international recognition for complex roles in films such as *The Servant* 1963. He distinguished himself in films made with director Joseph Losey, such as *Accident* 1967, and with Luchino Visconti in *Death in Venice* 1971.

He has also written autobiographical books and novels, for example *A Postillion Struck by Lightning* 1977, *Snakes and Ladders* 1978, *Orderly Man* 1983, and *Backcloth* 1986.

Bogart /ˈbəʊɡɑːt/ Humphrey 1899–1957. US film actor, who achieved fame with his portrayal of a gangster in *The Petrified Forest* 1936. He became a cult figure as the romantic, tough 'loner' in such films as *The Maltese Falcon* 1941 and *Casablanca* 1943. He won an Academy Award for his role in *The African Queen* 1952.

Boğazköy /bɔːˈɑːzkɔɪ/ village in Turkey 145 km/90 mi E of Ankara. It is on the site of *Hattusas*, the ancient ◊Hittite capital established about 1640 BC. Thousands of tablets discovered here over a number of years by the German Oriental Society revealed, when their cuneiform writing was deciphered by Bedrich Hrozny (1879–1952), a great deal about the customs, religion, and history of the Hittite people.

bogbean aquatic or bog plant *Menyanthes trifoliata*, with a creeping rhizome and leaves and flower held above water. The leaves have three lobes, and the flowers are pink with white hairs, ten to twenty on a spike. Flowering in midsummer, it is found over much of the northern hemisphere.

Bogdanovich /bɒgˈdænəvɪʃ/ Peter 1939– . US film director, screenwriter, and producer, formerly a critic. *The Last Picture Show* 1971 was followed by two films that attempted to capture the style of old Hollywood, *What's Up Doc?* 1972 and *Paper Moon* 1973. Both made money but neither was a critical success.

Bognor Regis /ˈbɒgnə ˈriːdʒɪs/ seaside resort in West Sussex, England, 105 km/66 mi SW of London; population (1981) 53,200. It owes the Regis in its name to the convalescent visit by King George V 1929.

Bogomils heretics who originated in 10th-century Bulgaria and spread throughout the Byzantine empire. They take their name from Bogomilus, or Theophilus, who taught in Bulgaria 927–950. Despite persecution, they were only expunged by the Ottomans after the fall of Constantinople 1453.

Bogotá /ˌbɒgəˈtɑː/ capital of Colombia, South America; 2,640 m/8,660 ft above sea level on the edge of the plateau of the E Cordillera; population (1985) 4,185,000. It was founded 1538.

Bohemia /bəʊˈhiːmiə/ kingdom of central Europe from the 9th century, under Habsburg rule 1526–1918, when it was included in Czechoslovakia. The name Bohemia derives from the Celtic Boii, its earliest known inhabitants.

It became part of the Holy Roman Empire as the result of Charlemagne's establishment of a protectorate over the Celtic, Germanic, and Slav tribes settled in this area. Christianity was introduced 9th century, the See of Prague being established 975, and feudalism was introduced by King Ottaker I of Bohemia (1197–1230). Mining became increasingly important from the 12th century, and attracted large numbers of German settlers, leading to a strong Germanic influence in culture and society. In 1310, John of Luxemburg (died 1346) founded a German-Czech royal dynasty which lasted until 1437. His son, Charles IV, became Holy Roman Emperor 1355 and, during his reign, the See of Prague was elevated to an archbishopric and a university was founded there. During the 15th century, divisions within the nobility and religious conflicts

Bokassa *Marshal Jean Bokassa changed his country's name to the Central African Empire, and crowned himself emperor in 1977.*

culminating in the Hussite Wars (1420–36) led to decline.

Bohlen /ˈbəʊlən/ Charles 'Chip' 1904–1974. US diplomat. Educated at Harvard, he entered the foreign service in 1929. Interpreter and adviser to presidents Roosevelt at Tehran and Yalta, and Truman at Potsdam, he served as ambassador to the USSR 1953–57.

Böhm /bɜːm/ Karl 1894–1981. Austrian conductor known for his interpretation of Beethoven, and of the Mozart and Strauss operas.

Bohr /bɔː/ Aage 1922– . Danish physicist who produced a new model of the nucleus in 1952, known as the collective model. For this work, he shared the 1975 Nobel Prize for Physics.

Bohr /bɔː/ Niels Henrik David 1885–1962. Danish physicist. He founded the Institute of Theoretical Physics in Copenhagen, of which he became director in 1920. Nobel prize 1922. In 1952, he helped to set up ◊CERN in Geneva.

After work with ◊Rutherford at Manchester, he became professor at Copenhagen in 1916. He fled from the Nazis in World War II and took part in work on the atomic bomb in the USA.

Boiardo /bɔɪˈɑːdəʊ/ Matteo Maria, Count 1434–1494. Italian poet, famed for his *Orlando Innamorato/Roland in Love* 1486.

boil small abscess originating around a hair root or in a sweat gland.

Boileau /bwæˈləʊ/ Nicolas 1636–1711. French poet and critic. After a series of contemporary satires, his *Epîtres/Epistles* 1669–77 led to his joint appointment with Racine as royal historiographer in 1677. Later works include *L'Art poétique/The Art of Poetry* 1674 and the mock-heroic *Le Lutrin/The Lectern* 1674–83.

boiler a vessel that converts water into steam. Boilers are used in conventional power stations to generate steam to feed steam ◊turbines, which drive the electricity generators. They are also used in steam ships, which are propelled by steam turbines, and steam locomotives. Every boiler has a furnace in which fuel (coal, oil, or gas) is burned to produce hot gases, and a system of tubes in which heat is transferred from the gases to the water.

The common kind of boiler used in ships and power stations is the ***water-tube*** type, in which the water circulates in tubes surrounded by the hot furnace gases. The water-tube boilers at power stations produce steam at a pressure of up to 300 atmospheres and at a temperature of up to 600°C to feed the steam turbines. It is more efficient than the ***fire-tube*** type that is used in steam locomotives. In this boiler the hot furnace gases are drawn through tubes surrounded by water.

boiling point for any given liquid, the temperature at which the application of heat raises the temperature of the liquid no further, but converts it to vapour.

The boiling point of water under normal pressure is 100°C/212°F. The lower the pressure, the lower the boiling point and vice versa.

Bois-le-Duc /ˈbwɑː lə ˈdjuːk/ French form of ◊'s-Hertogenbosch, a town in North Brabant, Netherlands.

Bokassa /bɒˈkæsə/ Jean-Bédel 1921– . President and later self-proclaimed emperor of the Central African Republic 1966–79. Commander in chief from 1963, in Dec 1965 he led a military coup which gave him the presidency, and on 4 Dec 1977 he proclaimed the Central African Empire with himself as emperor for life. His regime was characterized by arbitrary state violence and cruelty. In exile 1979–86, he was tried and imprisoned.

Bokassa, born at Bobangui, joined the French army 1939 and was awarded the Croix de Guerre for his service with the French colonial forces in Indochina. When the Central African Republic achieved independence 1960, he was invited to establish an army. After seizing power, he annulled the constitution and made himself president for life 1972, and marshal of the republic 1974. In

Boleyn *Portrait of Anne Boleyn by an unknown artist (1530s) National Portrait Gallery, London.*

1976 he called in the former president Dacko, whom he had overthrown, as his adviser. Backed by France, Dacko deposed him in a coup while Bokassa was visiting Libya. In exile until 1986, he then returned to the Central African Republic to face the charges against him and received a death sentence, commuted to life imprisonment 1988.

Bokhara /bɒˈkɑːrə/ another form of ◊Bukhara, city in Asian USSR.

Bol /bɒl/ Ferdinand 1610–1680. Dutch painter, a pupil and for many years an imitator of ◊Rembrandt. There is uncertainty in attributing some works between them. After the 1660s he developed a more independent style and prospered as a portraitist.

Boldrewood /ˈbəʊldəwʊd/ Rolf. Pen name of Thomas Alexander Browne 1826–1915. Australian writer, born in London, he was taken to Australia as a child in 1830. He became a pioneer squatter, and a police magistrate in the goldfields. His books include *Robbery Under Arms* 1888.

bolero /bɒˈleərəʊ/ a Spanish dance in triple time for a solo dancer or a couple, usually with castanet accompaniment. It was used as the title of a one-act ballet score by Ravel, choreographed by Nijinsky for Ida Rubinstein in 1928.

boletus European fungus, resembling the mushroom, and belonging to the class Basidiomycetes. *Boletus eulis* is edible, but some species are poisonous.

Boleyn /bəˈlɪn/ Anne 1507–1536. Queen of England. Second wife of King Henry VIII, she was married to him in 1533 and gave birth to the future Queen Elizabeth I in the same year. Accused of adultery and incest with her half-brother (a charge invented by Thomas Cromwell), she was beheaded.

Bolingbroke /ˈbʊlɪŋbrʊk/ Henry John, Viscount Bolingbroke 1678–1751. British Tory politician and philosopher. He was foreign secretary 1710–14 and a Jacobite conspirator.

He was secretary of war 1704–08, became foreign secretary in Harley's ministry in 1710, and in 1713 negotiated the Treaty of Utrecht. His plans to restore the 'Old Pretender' James Francis Edward Stuart were ruined by Queen Anne's death only five days after he had secured the dismissal of Harley in 1714. He fled abroad, returning in 1723, when he worked to overthrow Robert Walpole. His books, such as *Idea of a Patriot King* 1738, influenced the 19th-century prime minister Disraeli.

Bolingbroke /ˈbʊlɪŋbrʊk/ Henry of Bolingbroke title of ◊Henry IV of England.

Bolívar /bɒˈliːvɑː/ Simón 1783–1830. South American nationalist, leader of revolutionary armies, known as **the Liberator**. He fought the Spanish colonial forces in several uprisings and eventually liberated his native Venezuela 1821, Colombia and Ecuador 1822, Peru 1824, and Bolivia (a new state named after him, formerly Upper Peru) 1825.

Born in Venezuela, Bolívar joined the nationalists working for Venezuelan independence, and was sent to Britain in 1810 as the representative

Bolívar *A portrait of Simón Bolívar, the Liberator, by an unknown artist.*

of their government. Forced to flee to Colombia in 1812, he joined the revolutionaries there, and invaded Venezuela in 1811. A bloody civil war followed and in 1814 Bolívar had to withdraw to Colombia, and eventually to the West Indies, from where he raided the Spanish-American coasts. In 1817 he returned to Venezuela to set up a provisional government, crossed into Colombia 1819, where he defeated the Spaniards, and returning to Angostura proclaimed the republic of Colombia, comprising Venezuela, New Granada (present-day Colombia), and Quito (Ecuador), with himself as president. The independence of Venezuela was finally secured in 1821, and 1822 Bolívar (along with Antonio ◊Sucre) liberated Ecuador. He was invited to lead the Peruvian struggle in 1823; and, final victory having been won by Sucre at Ayacucho in 1824, he turned his attention to framing a constitution. In 1825 the independence of Upper Peru was proclaimed, and the country adopted the name Bolivia in Bolívar's honour.

Bolivia /bə'lɪvɪə/ landlocked country in South America, bordered to the north and east by Brazil, to the southeast by Paraguay, to the south by Argentina, and to the west by Chile and Peru.

government Becoming independent in 1825 after nearly 300 years of Spanish rule, Bolivia adopted its first constitution in 1826 and since then a number of variations have been produced. The present one provides for a congress consisting of a 27-member senate and a 130-member chamber of deputies, both elected for four years by universal suffrage. The president, directly elected for a four-year term, is head of both state and government, and chooses the cabinet. For administrative purposes, the country is divided into nine departments, each governed by a prefect appointed by the president. Most significant among the many political parties are the National Revolutionary Movement (MNR), and the Nationalist Democratic Action Party (ADN).

history Once part of the ◊Inca civilization, and conquered by Spain in 1538, Bolivia took its name from Simón Bolívar, who liberated it in 1825. Between 1836–39 Bolivia formed a Peruvian-Bolivian Confederation under Bolivian President Andrés Santa Cruz, a former president of Peru. Chile declared war on the confederation, Santa Cruz was defeated, and the confederation was dissolved. Bolivia was again at war with Chile 1879–84, when it lost its coastal territory and land containing valuable mineral deposits, and with Paraguay (the Chaco War) 1932–35, again losing valuable territory.

In the 1951 election, Dr Victor Paz Estenssoro, the MNR candidate exiled in Argentina since

Bolivia
Republic of
(República de Bolivia)

area 1,098,581 sq km/424,052 sq mi
capital La Paz (seat of government), Sucre (legal capital and seat of judiciary)
towns Santa Cruz, Cochabamba
physical high plateau between mountain ridges; forest and lowlands in the E
features Andes, and lakes Titicaca and Poopó
head of state and government Víctor Paz Estenssoro from 1985
political system emergent democratic republic
political parties National Revolutionary Movement (MNR), centre-right; Nationalist Democratic Action Party (ADN), extreme right-wing; Movement of the Revolutionary Left (MIR), left-of-centre
exports tin (second largest world producer), other non-ferrous metals, oil, gas (piped to Argentina), agricultural products
currency boliviano (5.16 = £1 Feb 1990)
population (1988 est) 7,000,000; (Quechua 25%, Aymara 17%, Mestizo 30%, European 14%); annual growth rate 2.7%
language Spanish (official); Aymara, Quechua
religion Roman Catholic (state-recognized)
literacy 84% male/65% female (1985 est)
GDP $3 bn (1983); $570 per head of population

chronology
1825 Independence achieved (formerly known as Upper Peru).
1952 Dr Víctor Paz Estenssoro elected president.
1956 Dr Hernan Siles Zuazo became president.
1960 Estenssoro returned to power.
1964 Army coup led by vice-president.
1966 Gen René Barrientos became president.
1967 Uprising, led by 'Che' Guevara, put down with US help.
1969 Barrientos killed in air crash, replaced by vice-president Siles Salinas. Army coup deposed him.
1970 Army coup put Gen Juan Torres Gonzalez in power.
1971 Torres replaced by Col Hugo Banzer Suarez.
1973 Banzer promised a return to democratic government.
1974 An attempted coup prompted Banzer to postpone elections, and ban political and trade-union activity.
1978 Elections declared invalid after allegations of fraud.
1980 More inconclusive elections followed by another coup, led by Gen Garcia. Allegations of corruption and drug trafficking led to cancellation of US and EEC aid.
1981 Garcia forced to resign. Replaced by Gen Celso Torrelio Villa.
1982 Torrelio resigned. Replaced by military junta led by Gen Vildoso. Because of worsening economy, Vildoso asked congress to install a civilian administration. Dr Siles Zuazo chosen as president.
1983 Economic aid from USA and Europe resumed.
1984 New coalition government formed by Siles. Attempted abduction of president by right-wing officers. The president undertook a five-day hunger strike as an example to the nation.
1985 President Siles resigned. Election result inconclusive. Dr Paz Estenssoro, at the age of 77, chosen by congress.
1989 Jaime Paz Zamora (MIR) elected president.

1946, failed to win an absolute majority and an army junta took over. A popular uprising, supported by MNR and a section of the army, demanded the return of Paz, who became president and began a programme of social reform. He lost the 1956 election, but returned to power in 1960. In 1964 a coup, led by Vice-President General René Barrientos, overthrew Paz and installed a military junta. Two years later Barrientos won the presidency. He was opposed by left-wing groups and in 1967 a guerrilla uprising led by Dr Ernesto 'Che' ◊Guevara was only put down with US help.

In 1969 President Barrientos died in an air crash and was replaced by the vice-president. He was later replaced by General Alfredo Ovando, who was ousted by General Juan Torres, who in turn was ousted by Colonel Hugo Banzer in 1971. Banzer announced a return to constitutional government but another attempted coup in 1974 prompted him to postpone elections, ban all trade union and political activity and proclaim that military government would last until at least 1980. Banzer agreed to elections in 1978 but there were allegations of fraud and, in that year, two more military coups.

In the 1979 elections Dr Siles and Dr Paz received virtually equal votes and an interim administration was installed. An election in 1980 proved equally inconclusive and was followed by the 189th military coup in Bolivia's 154 years of independence. General Luis García became president but resigned the following year after

allegations of drug trafficking. He was replaced by General Celso Torrelio who promised to fight corruption and return the country to democracy within three years. In 1982 a mainly civilian cabinet was appointed but rumours of an impending coup resulted in Torrelio's resignation. A military junta led by the hard-line General Guido Vildoso was installed.

With the economy deteriorating, the junta asked congress to elect a president and Dr Siles Zuazo was chosen to head a coalition cabinet. Economic aid from Europe and the USA, cut off in 1980, was resumed but the economy continued to deteriorate. The government's austerity measures proved unpopular and in June the president was temporarily abducted by a group of right-wing army officers. In an attempt to secure national unity, President Siles embarked on a five-day hunger strike.

Siles resigned in 1985 and an election was held. No candidate won an absolute majority and Dr Victor Paz Estenssoro, aged 77, was chosen by congress. Despite austerity measures, including a wage freeze, inflation continues and the currency has weakened.

In the 1989 congressional elections the MNR won marginally more votes in the Chamber of Deputies than the ADN, but did not obtain a clear majority. After an indecisive presidential contest Jaime Paz Zamora, of the Movement of the Revolutionary Left (MIR) was eventually declared president.

Böll West German writer Heinrich Böll speaking at a peace rally in Bonn in 1983.

Bolkiah /'ɒlkiɑ:/ Hassanal 1946– . Sultan of Brunei from 1967, following the abdication of his father, Omar Ali Saifuddin (1916–86). On independence, in 1984, Bolkiah also assumed the posts of prime minister and defence minister.

As head of an oil- and gas-rich micro-state, the sultan is reputedly the world's richest individual, with an estimated total wealth of $2 billion, which includes the Dorchester and Beverly Hills hotels in London and Los Angeles, and, at a cost of $40 million, the world's largest palace. He was educated at a British military academy.

Böll /bɜ:l/ Heinrich 1917–1985. West German novelist. A radical Catholic and anti-Nazi, he attacked Germany's political past and the materialism of its contemporary society. His many publications include poems, short stories, and novels which satirize German society, for example *Billard um Halbzehn/Billiards at Half-Past Nine* 1959 and *Gruppenbild mit Dame/Group Portrait with Lady* 1971. Nobel Prize for Literature 1972.

Bollandist member of a group of Belgian Jesuits who edit and publish the *Acta Sanctorum*, the standard collection of saints' lives and other scholarly publications. They are named after John Bolland (1596–1665), who published the first two volumes in 1643.

boll-weevil small American beetle *Anthonomus grandis* of the weevil family. The female lays eggs in the unripe pods or 'bolls' of the cotton plant, and on these the larva feeds, causing great destruction.

Bologna /bə'lɒnjə/ industrial city and capital of Emilia-Romagna, Italy, 80 km/50 mi north of Florence; population (1988) 427,000. It was the site of an Etruscan town, later of a Roman colony, and became a republic in the 12th century. It came under papal rule 1506, and was united with Italy 1860.

The city has a cathedral and medieval towers, and the university, which dates from the 11th century, laid the foundations of the study of anatomy and was attended by the poets Dante, Petrarch, and Tasso, and the astronomer Copernicus.

bolometer sensitive ◊thermometer which measures the energy of radiation by registering the change in electrical resistance of a fine wire when it is exposed to heat or light. The US astronomer Samuel Langley devised it in 1880 for measuring radiation from stars.

Bolshevik (from Russian *bolshinstvo* 'a majority') member of the majority of the Russian Social Democratic Party, who split from the ◊Mensheviks 1903. The Bolsheviks advocated the

destruction of capitalist political and economic institutions, and the setting-up of a socialist state with power in the hands of the workers. The Bolsheviks effected the ◊Russian Revolution 1917.

Bolt /bəʊlt/ Robert (Oxton) 1924– . British dramatist, noted for his historical plays, especially *A Man for All Seasons* 1960, about Thomas More (filmed 1967), and for his screenplays, including *Lawrence of Arabia* 1962 and *Dr Zhivago* 1965.

Bolton /'bəʊltən/ city in Greater Manchester, England, 18 km/11 mi NW of Manchester; population (1985) 261,000. Industries include chemicals and textiles.

Boltzmann /'bɒltsmæn/ Ludwig 1844–1906. Austrian physicist who studied the kinetic theory of gases, which explains the properties of gases by reference to the motion of their constituent atoms and molecules. He derived a formula, the *Boltzmann distribution*, which gives the number of atoms or molecules with a given energy at a specific temperature. This involves a constant, called the Boltzmann constant.

Boltzmann's constant in physics, the constant that relates the kinetic energy (energy of motion) of a gas atom or molecule to temperature. Its symbol is k and its value is 1.380662×10^{-23} joules per Kelvin. It is equal to the gas constant, R, divided by ◊Avogadro's number.

Bolzano /bɒlt'sɑːnəʊ/ (German *Bozen*) town in Italy, in Trentino-Alto Adige region on the Isarco in the Alps; population (1988) 101,000. Bolzano belonged to Austria until 1919. The people are mostly German speaking.

Boma /'bəʊmə/ port in Zaïre, on the estuary of the river Zaïre 88 km/55 mi from the Atlantic; population (1976) 93,965. The oldest European settlement in Zaïre, it was a centre of the slave trade, and capital of the Belgian Congo until 1927.

bomb a container filled with explosive or chemical material and generally used in warfare. There are also ◊incendiary bombs, and nuclear bombs and missiles (see ◊nuclear warfare). Any object designed to cause damage by explosion can be called a bomb (car bombs, letter bombs). Initially dropped from aeroplanes (from World War I), bombs were in World War II also launched by rocket (◊V1, V2). The 1960s saw the development of missiles that could be launched from aircraft, land sites, or submarines. In the 1970s laser guidance systems were developed to hit small targets with accuracy.

Aerial bombing started in World War I (1914–18) when the German air force carried out 103 raids on Britain, dropping 269 tonnes of bombs. In World War II (1939–45) nearly twice this tonnage was dropped on London in a single night, and at the peak of the Allied air offensive against Germany, more than ten times this tonnage was regularly dropped in successive nights on one target. Raids in which nearly 1,000 heavy bombers participated were frequent. They were delivered either in 'precision' or 'area' attacks and advances were made in *blind bombing*, in which the target is located solely by instruments and is not visible through a bombsight. In 1939 bombs were commonly about 115 kg/250 lb and

bomb Fireball resulting from the test detonation of a hydrogen bomb at Bikini Atoll on 21 May 1956.

230 kg/500 lb, but by the end of the war the ten-tonner was being produced.

The fission or ◊*atom bomb* was developed in the 1940s and the USA exploded three during World War II: first a test explosion on 16 Jul 1945, at Alamogordo, New Mexico, USA, then on 6 Aug the first to be used in actual warfare was dropped over ◊Hiroshima, and three days later another over Nagasaki, Japan.

The fusion or ◊hydrogen bomb was developed in the 1950s, and by the 1960s intercontinental 100-megatonne nuclear warheads could be produced (5,000 times more powerful than those of World War II). The USA and the USSR between them possess a stockpile sufficient to destroy all humankind, directly or by radioactive *fallout* released into the atmosphere (see also ◊nuclear winter). More recent bombs produce less fallout, a 'dirty' bomb being one that produces large quantities of radioactive debris from a U-238 (uranium isotope) casing.

The danger of nuclear weapons increases with the number of nations possessing the ability to produce them (USA 1945, USSR 1949, UK 1952, France 1960, China 1964), and nuclear arms verification has been complicated by the ban on above-ground testing. Testing grounds include Lop Nor (China); Mururoa Atoll in the S Pacific (France); Nevada Desert, Amchitka Islands in the Aleutians (USA); Semipalatinsk in central Asia, Novaya Zemlya Islands in the Arctic (USSR).

Under the Outer Space Treaty 1966 nuclear warheads may not be sent into orbit, but this measure has been circumvented by more sophisticated weapons. The Fractional Orbital Bombardment System (FOBS) sends a warhead into a low partial orbit, followed by a rapid descent to Earth. This both renders it less vulnerable to ballistic missile defence systems and cuts the warning time to three minutes.

The rapid development of *laser guidance systems* in the 1970s meant that precise destruction of small but vital targets could be more effectively achieved with standard 450 kg/1,000 lb high-explosive bombs. The laser beam may be directed at the target by the army from the ground, but additional flexibility is gained by coupling ground-directed beams with those of guidance carried in high-performance aircraft accompanying the bombers, for example, the Laser Ranging Marker Target System (LRMTS).

Bombay /,bɒm'beɪ/ former province of British India. Together with a number of interspersed princely states, it was included in the domain of India in 1947, and the major part became in 1960 the two new states of ◊Gujarat and ◊Maharashtra. The capital was the city of Bombay.

Bombay /,bɒm'beɪ/ industrial port (textiles, engineering, pharmaceuticals, diamonds), commercial centre, and capital of Maharashtra, W India; population (1981) 8,227,000. It is the centre of the Hindi film industry.

features World Trade Centre 1975, National Centre for the Performing Arts 1969.

history Bombay was founded 13th century, came under Mogul rule, was occupied by Portugal 1530, and passed to Britain 1662 as part of Catherine of Bragança's dowry. It was headquarters of the East India Company 1685–1708. The city expanded rapidly with the development of the cotton trade and the railway in the 1860s.

bombay duck small fish *Harpodon nehereus*, found off the Bombay coast and in other Eastern waters. Salted and dried, it is eaten with dishes such as curry.

bona fide (Latin 'in good faith') legal phrase which signifies that a contract is undertaken without intentional misrepresentation.

Bonampak /bɒnəm'pæk/ site of classic ◊Mayan city, on the river Usumacinta near the Mexico and Guatemala border, with extensive remains of wall paintings depicting battles, torture, and sacrifices. Rediscovered 1948, the paintings shed

bone

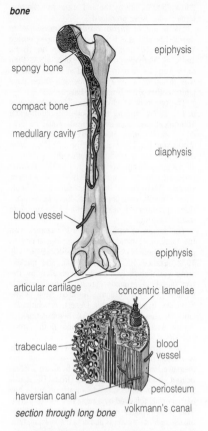

epiphysis

spongy bone

compact bone

medullary cavity

diaphysis

blood vessel

epiphysis

articular cartilage

concentric lamellae

trabeculae

blood vessel

haversian canal

periosteum

volkmann's canal

section through long bone

new light on Mayan society, which to that date had been considered peaceful.

Bonaparte /'bəʊnəpɑːt/ Corsican family of Italian origin, which gave rise to the Napoleonic dynasty: see ◊Napoleon I, ◊Napoleon II, and ◊Napoleon III. Other well-known members were the brothers and sister of Napoleon I:

Joseph 1768–1844, whom Napoleon made king of Naples 1806 and Spain 1808;

Lucien 1775–1840, whose handling of the Council of Five Hundred on 10 Nov 1799 ensured Napoleon's future;

Louis 1778–1846, made king of Holland 1806–10, who was the father of Napoleon III;

Caroline 1782—1839, who married Joachim ◊Murat in 1800;

Jerome 1784–1860, made king of Westphalia in 1807.

Bonar Law British Conservative politician. See ◊Law, Andrew Bonar.

Bonaventura, St /ˌbɒnəven'tʊərə/ (John of Fidanza) 1221–1274. Italian Roman Catholic theologian. He entered the Franciscan order in 1243, became professor of theology at Paris, France, and in 1256 general of his order. In 1273 he was created cardinal and bishop of Albano. His eloquent writings earned him the title of the 'Seraphic Doctor'. Feast day 15 July.

bond in chemistry, the result of the forces of attraction that hold together atoms of an element or elements to form a molecule.

The type of bond formed depends on the elements concerned and their electronic structure. In an *ionic* or *electrovalent bond*, common among inorganic compounds, the combining atoms gain or lose electrons to become ions; for example, sodium (Na) loses an electron to form a sodium ion (Na^+) while chlorine (Cl) gains an electron to form a chloride ion (Cl^-) in the ionic bond of sodium chloride (NaCl). In a *covalent bond*, the atomic orbitals of two atoms overlap to form a molecular orbital containing two electrons, which are thus effectively shared between the two atoms. Covalent bonds are common in organic

compounds, such as the four carbon–hydrogen bonds in methane (CH_4). In a *dative covalent* or *coordinate bond*, one of the combining atoms supplies both of the valence electrons in the bond.

bond in commerce, a security issued by a government, local authority, company, bank, or other institution on fixed interest. Usually a long-term security, a bond may be irredeemable, secured or unsecured. Property bonds are non-fixed securities with the yield fixed to property investment. See also ◊Eurobond.

Bond /bɒnd/ Edward 1935– . British dramatist, whose work has aroused controversy because of the savagery of some of his themes, for example the brutal killing of a baby, symbol of a society producing unwanted children, in *Saved* 1965. His later works include *Black Mass* 1970 about apartheid, *Bingo* 1973, and *The Sea* 1973.

Bondfield /'bɒndfiːld/ Margaret Grace 1873–1953. British socialist who became a trade-union organizer to improve working conditions for women. She was a Labour member of Parliament 1923–24 and 1926–31, and was the first woman to enter the cabinet—as minister of labour, 1929–31.

Bondi /'bɒndi/ Hermann 1919– . British cosmologist, born in Austria. In 1948 he joined with Fred ◊Hoyle and Thomas Gold (1920–) in developing the steady-state theory of cosmology, which suggested that matter is continuously created in the universe.

bondservant another term for a slave or serf used in the Caribbean in the 18th and 19th centuries; a person who was offered a few acres of land in return for some years of compulsory service. The system was a means of obtaining labour from Europe.

bone hard connective tissue of most vertebrate animals consisting of a network of collagen fibres impregnated with calcium phospate. In strength, the toughest bone is comparable with reinforced concrete. Bones develop initially from ◊cartilage. Humans have about 206 distinct bones in the ◊skeleton. The interior of long bones comprises a spongy matrix filled with soft marrow, which produces blood cells.

Bône /bəʊn/ (or Bohn) former name of ◊Annaba, Algerian port.

bone china (softpaste) semi-porcelain made of 5% bone ash added to 95% kaolin, first made in the West in imitation of Chinese porcelain.

bongo Central African antelope *Boocercus euryceus*, living in dense humid forests. Up to 1.4 m/4.5 ft at the shoulder, it has spiral-shaped horns which may be 80 cm/2.6 ft or more in length. The body is rich chestnut, with narrow white stripes running vertically down the sides, and a black belly.

Bonham-Carter /'bɒnəm 'kɑːtə/ Violet, Lady Asquith of Yarnbury 1887–1969. British peeress, president of the Liberal party 1945–47.

Bonheur /bɒ'nɜː/ Rosa (Marie Rosalie) 1822–1899. French painter, noted for her realistic animal portraits, such as *Horse Fair* 1853 (Metropolitan Museum of Art, New York).

Bonhoeffer /'bɒnhɜːfə/ Dietrich 1906–1945. German Lutheran theologian and opponent of Nazism. Involved in an anti-Hitler plot, he was executed by the Nazis in Flossenburg concentration camp. His *Letters and Papers from Prison* 1953 advocate the idea of 'religionless' Christianity.

Boniface /'bɒnifeɪs/ name of nine popes, including:

Boniface VIII Benedict Caetani *c.* 1228–1303. Pope from 1294. He clashed unsuccessfully with Philip IV of France over his taxation of the clergy, and also with Henry III of England.

Boniface exempted the clergy from taxation by the secular government in a bull (edict) in 1296, but was forced to give way when the clergy were excluded from certain lay privileges. His bull of 1302 *Unam Sanctam*, asserting the complete temporal and spiritual power of the papacy, was equally ineffective.

Boniface, St /'bɒnifeɪs/ 680–754. English Benedictine monk, known as the 'Apostle of Germany'; originally named Wynfrith. After a missionary journey to Frisia in 716, he was given the task of bringing Christianity to Germany by Pope Gregory II in 718, and was appointed archbishop of Mainz in 746. He returned to Frisia in 754 and was martyred near Dockum. Feast day 5 June.

Bonin and Volcano islands /'bəʊnɪn/ Japanese islands in the Pacific, N of the Marianas and 1,300 km/800 mi E of the Ryukyu islands. They were under US control 1945–68.

The *Bonin Islands* (Japanese *Ogasawara Gunto*) number 27 (in three groups), the largest being Chichijima: area 104 sq km/40 sq mi, population (1970) 300.

The *Volcano Islands* (Japanese *Kazan Retto*) number three, including Iwo Jima, scene of some of the fiercest fighting of World War II; total area 28 sq km/11 sq mi.

Bonington /'bɒnɪŋtən/ Chris(tian) 1934– . British mountaineer. He took part in the first ascent of Annapurna II 1960, Nuptse 1961, and the first British ascent of the N face of the Eiger 1962, climbed the central Tower of Paine in Patagonia 1963, and was the leader of an Everest expedition 1975 and again in 1985, reaching the summit.

Bonington /'bɒnɪŋtən/ Richard Parkes 1801–1828. British painter, noted for fresh, atmospheric seascapes and landscapes in oil and watercolour. He was much admired by Delacroix.

bonito various species of small tuna, predatory fish of the mackerel family. The ocean bonito *Katsuwonus pelamis* grows to 1 m/3 ft and is common in tropical seas. The bonito *Sarda sarda* is found in the Mediterranean and tropical Atlantic and grows to the same length but has a narrow body.

bon marché (French) cheap.

bon mot (French) a witty remark.

Bonn /bɒn/ industrial city (chemicals, textiles, plastics, aluminium), capital of West Germany, 18 km/11 mi SSE of Cologne, on the left bank of the Rhine; population (1988) 292,000.

Bonn was an important Roman outpost. It was captured by the French 1794, annexed 1801, and was allotted to Prussia 1815. Beethoven was born here. It became the West German capital 1949.

Bonnard /bɒ'nɑː/ Pierre 1867–1947. French Post-Impressionist painter. With other members of *les* ◊Nabis, he explored the decorative arts (posters, stained glass, furniture). He painted domestic interiors and nudes.

Bonner /'bɒnə/ Yelena 1923– . Soviet human-rights campaigner. Disillusioned by the Soviet invasion of Czechoslovakia 1968, she resigned from the Communist Party (CPSU) after marrying her second husband Dr Andrei ◊Sakharov in 1971, and became active in the dissident movement.

Bonner was brought up in Leningrad by her grandmother after the arrest and subsequent imprisonment and execution of her parents in Stalin's 'great purge' of 1937. She suffered serious eye injuries while fighting for the Red Army during World War II and afterwards worked as a doctor. She joined the CPSU in 1965. Following hunger strikes by Sakharov, she was granted permission to travel to Italy for specialist eye treatment in 1981 and 1984, but was later banished to internal exile in Gorky.

Bonneville Salt Flats /'bɒnəvɪl/ bed of a prehistoric lake in Utah, USA, of which the Great Salt Lake is the surviving remnant. It has been used for motor speed records.

Bonnie and Clyde *Bonnie Parker* (1911–34) and *Clyde Barrow* (1900–34). Infamous US criminals who carried out a series of small-scale robberies in Texas, Oklahoma, New Mexico, and Missouri between Aug 1932 and May 1934. They were eventually betrayed and then killed in a police ambush.

booby

Abbott's booby

Much of their fame emanated from encounters with the police and their coverage by the press. Their story was filmed as *Bonnie and Clyde* 1967 by the US director Arthur Penn.

Bonny, Bight of /'bɒnɪ/ name since 1975 of the former Bight of Biafra, an area of sea off the coasts of Nigeria and Cameroon.

bonsai (Japanese 'bowl cultivation') the art of producing miniature trees by selective pruning. It originated in China many centuries ago and later spread to Japan. Some specimens in the imperial Japanese collection are over 300 years old.

bon ton (French 'good tone') fashionable manners.

Bonus Expeditionary Force in US history, a march on Washington DC by unemployed ex-servicemen during the great ◊Depression to lobby Congress for immediate cash payment of a promised war veterans's bonus.

During the spring of 1932, some 15,000 veterans camped by the river Potomac or squatted in disused government buildings. They were eventually dispersed by troops.

bon voyage (French) have a good journey.

boobook owl *Ninox novaeseelandiae* found in Australia, so named because of its call.

booby tropical seabird, genus *Sula*, closely related to the northern ◊gannet. There are six species, including the circumtropical brown booby *Sula leucogaster*. Their name was given to them by sailors who saw their tameness as stupidity.

One species, Abbott's booby, breeds only on Christmas Island, in the western Indian Ocean. Unlike most boobies and gannets it nests high up in trees. Large parts of its breeding ground have been destroyed by phosphate mining, but conservation measures now protect the site.

boogie-woogie a form of jazz played on the piano, using a repeated motif in the left hand. It was common in the USA from around 1900 to the 1940s. Boogie-woogie players included Pinetop Smith (1904–29), Meade 'Lux' Lewis (1905–64), and Jimmy Yancey (1898–1951).

book a portable written record. Early substances used to make books include leaves, bark, linen, silk, clay, leather, and papyrus. About AD 100–150, the codex or paged book, as against the roll, began to be adopted. Vellum was generally used for book production by the beginning of the 4th century, and its use lasted until the 15th, when it was superseded by paper. Books only became widely available after the invention of the ◊printing press in the 17th century. Printed text is also reproduced in ◊microform.

bookbinding the securing of the pages of a book between protective covers by sewing and/or gluing. Cloth binding was first introduced in 1822, but since World War II synthetic bindings have been increasingly employed, and most hardback books are bound by machine.

Bookbinding did not emerge as a distinct craft until ◊printing was introduced to Europe in the 15th century. Until that time scrolls, not books, were usual. Gold tooling, the principal ornament

of leather bookbinding, was probably introduced to Europe from the East by the Venetian Aldus Manutius (1450–1515).

Booker Prize British literary prize of £20,000 awarded annually (from 1969) by the Booker company (formerly Booker McConnell) to a novel published in the UK during the previous year.

Booker Prize for fiction

1969	P H Newby *Something to Answer For*
1970	Bernice Rubens *The Elected Member*
1971	V S Naipaul *In a Free State*
1972	John Berger *G*
1973	J G Farrell *The Siege of Krishnapur*
1974	Nadine Gordimer *The Conservationist;* Stanley Middleton *Holiday* (joint winners)
1975	Ruth Prawer Jhabvala *Heat and Dust*
1976	David Storey *Saville*
1977	Paul Scott *Staying On*
1977	Iris Murdoch *The Sea, The Sea*
1979	Penelope Fitzgerald *Offshore*
1980	William Golding *Rites of Passage*
1981	Salman Rushdie *Midnight's Children*
1982	Thomas Keneally *Schindler's Ark*
1983	J M Coetzee *Life and Times of Michael K*
1984	Anita Brookner *Hotel du Lac*
1985	Keri Hulme *The Bone People*
1986	Kingsley Amis *The Old Devils*
1987	Penelope Lively *Moon Tiger*
1988	Peter Carey *Oscar and Lucinda*
1989	Kazuo Ishiguro *The Remains of the Day*.

book-keeping process of recording commercial transactions in a systematic and established procedure. These records provide the basis for the preparation of accounts.

The earliest-known work on double-entry book-keeping, a system in which each item of a business transaction is entered twice—as debit and as credit—was by Luca Pacioli, published in Venice in 1494. The method he advocated had, however, been practised by Italian merchants for several hundred years before that date. The first English work on the subject, by the schoolmaster Hugh Oldcastle, appeared in 1543.

booklouse tiny wingless insect *Atropus pulsatoria* that lives in books and papers, feeding on starches and moulds. There are many species of 'booklice' in the order Psocoptera, but most live in bark, leaves, and lichens. They thrive in dark, damp conditions.

Book of the Dead ancient Egyptian book, known as the *Book of Coming Forth by Day*, and buried with the dead as a guide to reaching the kingdom of Osiris, the god of the underworld.

Books of Hours see ◊Hours, Books of

Book Trust British association of authors, publishers, booksellers, librarians, and readers, to encourage the reading and production of better books. Founded as the National Book Council in 1925, it was renamed the National Book League in 1944 and renamed Book Trust in 1986.

Boole /buːl/ George 1814–1864. English mathematician, whose work *The Mathematical Analysis of Logic* 1847 established the basis of modern mathematical logic, and whose *Boolean algebra* can be used in designing computers.

boomerang hand-thrown wooden missile shaped in a curved angle, developed by the Australian aborigines. It is used to kill game, as a weapon, or as recreation, and can return to the thrower if the target is missed.

boomslang venomous African snake *Dispholidus typus*, often green but sometimes brown or blackish. It lives in trees, has fangs at the back of its mouth, and feeds on tree-dwelling lizards such as chameleons. Their venom can be fatal; however, boomslangs rarely attack people.

Boone /buːn/ Daniel 1734–1820. US pioneer, who explored the Wilderness Road (East Virginia/Kentucky) 1775 and paved the way for the first westward migration of settlers.

Boorman /'bɔːmən/ John 1933– . British film director who, after working in television, subsequently directed successful films both in

Booth *William Booth was a British evangelist and itinerant preacher who established a mission among the poor in Whitechapel, London. The churches were reluctant to accept his converts, and in 1878 he founded the Salvation Army and became its first general.*

Hollywood (*Deliverance* 1972, *Point Blank* 1967) and in Britain (*Excalibur* 1981, *Hope and Glory* 1987).

booster the first-stage rockets of a space-launching vehicle, or additional rockets strapped on to the main rocket to assist take-off.

The US *Delta* rocket, for example, has a cluster of nine strap-on boosters that fire on lift-off. Europe's *Ariane 3* rocket uses twin strap-on boosters, as does the US space shuttle.

Boot /buːt/ Jesse 1850–1931. British entrepreneur and founder of pharmacy chain. In 1863 Boot took over his father's small Nottingham shop trading in medicinal herbs. Recognizing that the future lay with patent medicines, he concentrated on selling cheaply, advertising widely, and offering a wide range of medicines. In 1892, Boot also began to manufacture drugs. He had 126 shops by 1900 and more than 1,000 by his death.

boot or *bootstrap* in computing, the process of starting up the computer. Most computers have a small, built-in program whose only job is to load a slightly larger program, usually from a disc, which in turn loads the main ◊operating system.

The term is derived from mountaineering, where a bootlace might be used to pull a rope through a difficult opening.

Boötes constellation of the northern hemisphere representing a herdsman driving a bear (Ursa Major) around the pole. Its brightest star is ◊Arcturus.

Booth /buːð/ Charles 1840–1916. British sociologist, author of the study *Life and Labour of the People in London* 1891–1903, and pioneer of an old-age pension scheme.

Booth /buːθ/ John Wilkes 1839–1865. US actor and fanatical Confederate who assassinated President ◊Lincoln 14 Apr 1865; he escaped with a broken leg and was later shot in a barn in Virginia when he refused to surrender.

Booth /buːð/ William 1829–1912. British founder of the ◊Salvation Army in 1878, and its first 'general'.

Born in Nottingham, the son of a builder, he experienced religious conversion at the age of 15. In 1865 he founded the Christian Mission, in Whitechapel, E London, which in 1878 became the Salvation Army. *In Darkest England, and the Way Out* 1890 contained proposals for

borage

flower

the physical and spiritual redemption of the many down-and-outs.

His wife Catherine (1829–90, born Mumford), whom he married in 1855, became a public preacher in about 1860, initiating the ministry of women. Their eldest son, **William Bramwell Booth** (1856–1929), became chief of staff of the Salvation Army in 1880 and was general from 1912 until his deposition 1929. **Evangeline Booth** (1865–1950), 7th child of Gen William Booth, was a prominent Salvation Army officer, and 1934–39 was general. She became a US citizen. **Catherine Bramwell Booth** (1884–1987), a granddaughter of William Booth, was a commissioner in the Salvation Army.

Boothby /'buːðbi/ Robert John Graham, Baron Boothby 1900–1986. Scottish politician. He became a Unionist member of Parliament 1924 and was parliamentary private secretary to Churchill 1926–29. He advocated Britain's entry into the European Community, and was a noted speaker.

Boothe Luce /buːθ/ Clare 1903–1987. US journalist, playwright, and politician. She was managing editor of the magazine *Vanity Fair* 1933–34, and wrote several successful plays, including *The Women* 1936 and *Margin for Error* 1939.

She was born in New York, was a Republican member of Congress 1943–47 and ambassador to Italy 1953–57. She was married to the magazine publisher Henry Robinson Luce.

Bootle /'buːtl/ port in Merseyside, England, adjoining Liverpool; population (1981) 62,463. The National Girobank headquarters is here.

bootlegging the illegal manufacture, distribution, or sale of a product. The term originated in the USA, when the sale of alcohol to American Indians was illegal and bottles were hidden for sale in the legs of the jackboots of unscrupulous traders. It was later used for all illegal liquor sales in the period of ◊Prohibition in the USA 1920–33, and is often applied to unauthorized commercial tape recordings and copying of computer software.

bop short for ◊bebop, a style of jazz.

Bophuthatswana /bəʊˌpuːtətˈswɑːnə/ Republic of

area 40,330 sq km/15,571 sq mi

capital Mmabatho or Sun City, a casino resort frequented by many white South Africans

features divided into six 'blocks'

exports platinum, chrome, vanadium, asbestos, manganese

currency South African rand

population (1985) 1,622,000

language Setswana, English

religion Christian

government executive president elected by the Assembly: Chief Lucas Mangope

recent history first 'independent' Black National State from 1977, but not recognized by any country other than South Africa.

Bora-Bora /ˌbɔːrəˈbɔːrə/ one of the 14 Society Islands of French Polynesia. Situated 225 km/140 mi NW of Tahiti. Area 39 sq km/15 sq mi. Exports include mother-of-pearl, fruit and tobacco.

borage salad plant *Borago officinalis* cultivated in Britain and occasionally naturalized. It has small blue flowers and hairy leaves.

Borah /'bɔːrə/ William Edgar 1865–1940. US Republican politician. Born in Illinois, he was a senator for Idaho from 1906. An arch-isolationist, he was one of those chiefly responsible for the USA's repudiation of the League of Nations.

Borås /buˈrɔːs/ town in SW Sweden; population (1982) 211,197. Chief industries include textiles and engineering.

borax hydrous sodium borate, $Na_2B_4O_7.10H_2O$, found as soft, whitish crystals or encrustations on the shores of hot springs and in the dry beds of salt lakes in arid regions, where it occurs with other borates, halite, and ◊gypsum. It is used in bleaches and washing powders.

A large industrial source is Borax Lake, California. Borax is also used in glazing pottery, in soldering, as a mild antiseptic, and as a metallurgical flux.

Borchert /'bɔːʃət/ Wolfgang 1921–1947. German playwright and prose writer. Borchert was sent home wounded during World War II while serving on the Russian front, for alleged anti-Nazi comments. *Draussen vor der Tür/The Outsider* 1947 is a surreal play about the chaotic conditions that a German soldier finds when he returns to Germany after walking home from the Russian front.

Bordeaux /bɔːˈdəʊ/ port on the Garonne, capital of Aquitaine, SW France, a centre for the wine trade, oil refining, aeronautics and space industries; population (1982) 640,000. Bordeaux was under the English crown for three centuries until 1453. In 1870, 1914, and 1940 the French government was moved here because of German invasion.

Border /'bɔːdə/ Allan 1955– . Australian cricketer, captain of the Australian team from 1985. He has played for New South Wales and Queensland, and in England for Gloucestershire and Essex. He made his test debut for Australia 1978–79.

CAREER HIGHLIGHTS

Test Cricket:
Appearances (up to 1989): 102
Runs: 7,831
Average: 52.55
Best: 205 v. New Zealand 1987–88
Wickets: 27
Average: 32.14
Best: 7–46 v. West Indies 1988–89

Border *Allan Border playing for the Ashes in the second test at Lords, London, 1989.*

Borders /'bɔːdəz/ region of Scotland

area 4,700 sq km/1,815 sq mi

towns administrative headquarters Newtown St Boswells; Hawick, Jedburgh

features river Tweed; Lammermuir, Moorfoot, and Pentland hills; home of the novelist Walter Scott at Abbotsford; Dryburgh Abbey, burial place of Field Marshal Haig and Scott; ruins of 12th-century Melrose Abbey

products knitted goods, tweed, electronics, timber

population (1987) 102,000

famous people Duns Scotus, Mungo Park.

Bordet /bɒˈdeɪ/ Jules 1870–1961. Belgian bacteriologist and immunologist who researched the role of blood serum in the human immune response. He was the first to isolate, in 1906, the whooping cough bacillus.

bore a surge of tidal water up an estuary or a river, caused by the funnelling of the rising tide by a narrowing river mouth. A very high tide, possibly fanned by wind, may build up when it is held back by a river current in the river mouth. The result is a broken wave, a metre or a few feet high, that rushes upstream.

Famous bores are found in the rivers Severn (England), Seine (France), Hooghly (India),

Borges *The Argentinian author and former university professor Jorge Luis Borges is seen here after receiving an honorary degree at the University of Oxford in 1970.*

and Chiang Jiang (China), where bores of over 4 m/13 ft have been reported.

Borelli /bəˈreli/ Giovanni Alfonso 1608–1679. Italian scientist who explored the links between physics and medicine, and showed how mechanical principles could be applied to animal ◊physiology. This approach, known as *iatrophysics*, has proved basic to understanding how the mammalian body works.

Borg /bɒːg/ Bjorn 1956– . Swedish lawn-tennis player who won the men's singles title at Wimbledon five times 1976–80, a record since the abolition of the challenge system 1922.

CAREER HIGHLIGHTS

Wimbledon (singles): 1976–80
French Open (singles): 1974–75, 1978–81
Davis Cup: 1975 (member of winning Swedish team)
Grand Prix Masters: 1980–81
WCT Champion: 1976
ITF World Champion: 1978–80

Borges /ˈbɔːxes/ Jorge Luis 1899–1986. Argentinian poet and short-story writer. In 1961 he became director of the National Library, Buenos Aires, and was professor of English literature at the university there. He is known for his fantastic and paradoxical work *Ficciones/Fictions* 1944.

Borgia /ˈbɔːdʒə/ Cesare 1476–1507. Italian general, illegitimate son of Pope ◊Alexander VI. Made a cardinal at 17 by his father, he resigned to become captain-general of the papacy, campaigning successfully against the city republics of Italy. Ruthless and treacherous in war, he was an able ruler (the model of Machiavelli's *The Prince*), but his power crumbled on the death of his father. He was a patron of artists, including Leonardo da Vinci.

Borgia /ˈbɔːdʒə/ Lucrezia 1480–1519. Duchess of Ferrara from 1501. She was the illegitimate daughter of Pope ◊Alexander VI and sister of Cesare Borgia. She was married at 12 and again at 13 to further her father's ambitions, both marriages being annulled by him. At 18 she was again married, but her husband was murdered in 1500 on the order of her brother, with whom (as well as with her father) she was said to have committed incest. Her final marriage was to the son and heir of the Duke of Ferrara. She made the court a centre of culture and was a patron of authors and artists such as Ariosto and Titian.

Borglum /ˈbɔːgləm/ Gutzon 1871–1941. US sculptor. He created a six-tonne marble head of Lincoln in Washington DC and a series of giant heads of

Born *German physicist Max Born seated surrounded by his colleagues at Göttingen in 1922; left to right: William Osler, Niels Bohr, James Franck, and Oscar Klein.*

presidents Washington, Jefferson, Lincoln, and Theodore Roosevelt carved on *Mount Rushmore*, South Dakota (begun 1930).

boric acid or *boracic acid* H_3BO_3, an acid formed by the combination of hydrogen and oxygen with non-metallic boron. It is a weak antiseptic.

Boris III /ˈbɒris/ 1894–1943. Tsar of Bulgaria from 1918, when he succeeded his father, Ferdinand I. From 1934 he was virtual dictator until his sudden and mysterious death following a visit to Hitler. His son Simeon II was tsar until deposed in 1946.

Boris Godunov see ◊Godunov, Boris, tsar of Russia from 1598.

Borlaug /ˈbɔːlɔːg/ Norman Ernest 1914– . US microbiologist and agronomist. He developed high-yielding varieties of wheat and other grain crops to be grown in Third World countries, and was the first to use the term ◊Green Revolution. Nobel Peace Prize 1970.

Bormann /ˈbɔːmæn/ Martin 1900–1945. German Nazi leader. He took part in the abortive Munich ◊putsch of 1923, and rose to high positions in the National Socialist Party, becoming party chancellor in May 1941. He was believed to have escaped the fall of Berlin in May 1945, and was tried in his absence and sentenced to death at Nuremberg 1945–46, but a skeleton uncovered by a mechanical excavator in Berlin in 1972 was officially recognized as his by forensic experts in 1973.

Born /bɔːn/ Max 1882–1970. German physicist, who received a Nobel prize in 1954 for fundamental work on the ◊quantum theory. He left Germany for Britain during the Nazi era.

Borneo /ˈbɔːniəʊ/ third largest island in the world, one of the Sunda Islands in the W Pacific; area 754,000 sq km/290,000 sq mi. It comprises the Malaysian territories of ◊*Sabah* and ◊*Sarawak*; ◊*Brunei*; and, occupying by far the largest part, the Indonesian territory of ◊*Kalimantan*. It is mountainous and densely forested. In coastal areas the people of Borneo are mainly of Malaysian origin, with a few Chinese, and the interior is inhabited by the indigenous Dayaks. It was formerly under both Dutch and British colonial influence until Sarawak was formed in 1841.

Bornholm /ˈbɔːnˈhəʊm/ Danish island in the Baltic Sea, 35 km/22 mi SE of the nearest point of the Swedish coast. It constitutes a county of the same name
area 587 sq km/227 sq mi
capital Rönne
population (1985) 47,164.

Bornu /bɔːˈnuː/ kingdom of the 9th–19th centuries to the west and south of Lake Chad, W central Africa. Converted to Islam in the 11th century, it reached its greatest strength in the 15th–18th centuries. From 1901 it was absorbed in the British, French, and German colonies in this area, which now form the states of Niger, Cameroon, and Nigeria. The largest section of ancient Bornu falls in the modern state of Bornu in Nigeria, of which the capital is Maiduguri.

Borobudur /ˌbɒrəʊˈbuːdə/ site of Buddhist shrine near ◊Yogyakarta, Indonesia.

Borodin /ˈbɒrədɪn/ Alexander Porfir'yevich 1833–1887. Russian composer. Born in St Petersburg the illegitimate son of a Russian prince, he became by profession an expert in medical chemistry, but in his spare time devoted himself to music. His principal work is the opera *Prince Igor*; left unfinished, it was completed by Rimsky-Korsakov and Glazunov and includes the Polovtsian Dances.

Borodino, Battle of /ˌbɒrəˈdiːnəʊ/ battle NW of Moscow in which French troops under Napoleon defeated the Russians under Kutusov 7 Sept 1812.

boron a chemical element, symbol B, atomic number 5, relative atomic mass 10.81. It is used to harden steel and, because it absorbs slow neutrons, to make control rods for nuclear reactors. It is found in two forms, brown (non-metallic) and black (metallic).

borough unit of local government in the UK from the 8th century until 1974, when it continued as an honorary status granted by royal charter to a district council, entitling its leader to the title of mayor.

Borromeo /ˌbɒrəʊˈmeɪəʊ/ Carlo 1538–1584. Italian Roman Catholic saint and cardinal. He wound up the affairs of the Council of Trent, and largely drew up the catechism that contained its findings. Feast day 4 Nov.

Born at Arona of a noble Italian family, Borromeo was created a cardinal and archbishop of Milan by his uncle Pope Pius IV in 1560. He lived the life of an ascetic, and in 1578 founded the community later called the Oblate Fathers of St Charles. He was canonized 1610.

Borromini /ˌbɒrəʊˈmiːni/ Francesco 1599–1667. Italian ◊Baroque architect. He worked under Bernini, later his rival, on St Peter's Basilica, Rome, and created the oval-shaped church of San Carlo alle Quattro Fontane, Rome.

Borrow /ˈbɒrəʊ/ George Henry 1803–1881. British author and traveller. He travelled on foot through Europe and the East. His books, incorporating his knowledge of languages and Romany lore, include *Zincali* 1840, *The Bible in Spain* 1843, *Lavengro* 1851, *The Romany Rye* 1857, and *Wild Wales* 1862.

Borrowers, The a story for children by Mary Norton (1903–), published in the UK 1952. It describes a family of tiny people who live secretly under the floor in a large country house and subsist by 'borrowing' things from the 'human beans' who live above. Their survival and way of life come under threat in several sequels.

borstal institutions in the UK, formerly places of detention for offenders aged 15–21. The name was taken from Borstal prison near Rochester, Kent, where the system was first introduced in 1908. From 1983 they were officially known as youth custody centres, and have now been replaced by young offender institutions.

borzoi (Russian 'swift') large breed of dog originating in Russia, 75 cm/2.5 ft or more at the shoulder. It is of the greyhound type, white with darker markings, with a thick silky coat.

Boscawen /bɒsˈkəʊən/ Edward 1711–1761. English admiral who served against the French in the mid-18th century wars. To his men he was known as 'Old Dreadnought'.

Bosch /bɒs/ Hieronymus (Jerome) 1460–1516. Early Netherlandish painter. His fantastic visions of weird and hellish creatures, as shown in *The Garden of Earthly Delights* about 1505–10 (Prado, Madrid), show astonishing imagination and a complex imagery. His religious subjects focused not on the holy figures but on the mass of ordinary witnesses, placing the religious event in a contemporary Netherlandish context and creating cruel caricatures of human sinfulness.

Bosch is named from his birthplace, 's Hertogenbosch, in Brabant (now in Belgium). His work foreshadowed Surrealism and was probably inspired by a local religious brotherhood. However, he was an orthodox Catholic and a prosperous painter, not a heretic, as was once believed. After his death, his work was collected by Philip II of Spain.

Bosch /bɒʃ/ Juan 1909– . President of the Dominican Republic 1963. His left-wing Partido Revolucionario Dominicano won a landslide victory in the 1962 elections. In office, he attempted agrarian reform and labour legislation. Opposed by the USA, he was overthrown by the army. His achievement was to establish a democratic political party after three decades of dictatorship.

Boscovich /ˈbɒskəvɪtʃ/ Ruggiero 1711–1787. Italian scientist. An early supporter of Newton, he developed a theory of the atom as a single point with surrounding fields of repulsive and attractive forces that was popular in the 19th century.

Bose /bəʊs/ Jagadis Chunder 1858–1937. Indian physicist and plant physiologist. Born near Dacca, he was professor of physical science at Calcutta

1885–1915, and studied plant life, especially the growth and minute movements of plants, and their reaction to electrical stimuli. He founded the Bose Research Institute, Calcutta.

Bose /bəʊs/ Satyendra Nath 1894–1974. Indian physicist. With ◊Einstein, he formulated the Bose–Einstein law of quantum mechanics, and was professor of physics at the University of Calcutta 1945–58.

Bosnia and Herzegovina /'bɒznɪə, 'hɜːtsɪgə'vi :nə/ (Serbo-Croat *Bosna-Hercegovina*) constituent republic of Yugoslavia
area 51,100 sq km/19,725 sq mi
capital Sarajevo
features barren, mountainous country
population (1986) 4,360,000, including 1,630,000 Muslims, 1,320,000 Serbs, and 760,000 Croats
language Serbian variant of Serbo-Croat
religion Sunni Muslim, Serbian Orthodox, and Roman Catholic
history once the Roman province of ◊Illyria, it enjoyed brief periods of independence in medieval times, then was ruled by the Ottoman Empire 1463–1878 and Austria 1878–1918, when it was incorporated in the future Yugoslavia.

Bosnian Crisis period of international tension 1908 when Austria attempted to capitalize on Turkish weakness after the ◊Young Turk revolt by annexing provinces of Bosnia and Herzegovina. Austria obtained Russian approval in exchange for conceding Russian access to the Bosporus straits (see ◊straits question).

The speed of Austrian action took Russia by surprise, and domestic opposition led to the resignation of Russian foreign minister Izvolsky. Russia also failed to obtain necessary French and British agreements on the straits.

Bosporus /'bɒspərəs/ (Turkish *Karadeniz Boğazi*) strait 27 km/17 mi long joining the Black Sea with the Sea of Marmara and forming part of the water division between Europe and Asia. Istanbul stands on its W side. The *Bosporus Bridge* 1973 links Istanbul and Turkey-in-Asia (1,621 m/5,320 ft). In 1988 a second bridge across the straits was opened, linking Asia and Europe.

Bossuet /,bɒsju'eɪ/ Jacques Bénigne 1627–1704. French Roman Catholic priest and theologian. Appointed to the Chapel Royal in 1662, he became known for his funeral orations. He was bishop of Meaux from 1681.

Bossuet was tutor to the young dauphin (crown prince). He became involved in a controversy between Louis XIV and the Pope and did his best to effect a compromise. He wrote an *Exposition de la foi catholique* 1670 and *Histoire des variations des églises protestantes* 1688.

Boston /'bɒstən/ seaport in Lincolnshire, England, on the Witham river; population (1981) 26,500. St Botolph's is England's largest parish church, and its tower 'Boston stump' is a landmark for sailors.

Boston /'bɒstən/ industrial and commercial centre, capital of Massachusetts, USA; population (1980) 563,000; metropolitan area 2,800,000. It is a publishing centre, and Harvard University and Massachusetts Institute of Technology are nearby. A centre of opposition to British trade restrictions, it was the scene of the Boston Tea Party 1773.

Boston Tea Party US colonists' protest 1773 against the British tea tax before the War of ◊American Independence. A consignment of tea (valued at £15,000 and belonging to the East India Company), intended for sale in the American colonies, was thrown overboard by a group of Bostonians disguised as Indians during the night of 16 Dec 1773 from the three ships that had brought it from England. The British government, angered by this and other colonial protests against British policy, took retaliatory measures 1774, including the closing of the port of Boston.

Boswell /'bɒzwəl/ James 1740–1795. Scottish lawyer, biographer, and diarist. He was a member

Boswell *Scottish diarist James Boswell met Dr Johnson in 1763 and travelled with him in England and in Europe, meeting many of the notable people of their day, and writing down their conversations. The sketch is by George Dance 1793.*

of Samuel ◊Johnson's London Literary Club, and in 1773 the two men travelled to Scotland together, as recorded in Boswell's *Journal of the Tour to the Hebrides* 1785. His *Life of Samuel Johnson* was published 1791.

Born in Edinburgh, Boswell studied law but centred his ambitions on literature and politics. He first met Johnson 1763, before setting out on a European tour during which he met the French thinkers Rousseau and Voltaire, and the Corsican nationalist general Paoli (1726–1807), whom he commemorated in his popular *Account of Corsica* 1768. In 1766 he became a lawyer, and in 1772 renewed his acquaintance with Johnson in London. Establishing a place in his intimate circle, he became a member of the Literary Club 1773, and in the same year accompanied Johnson on the journey later recorded in the *Journal of the Tour to the Hebrides* 1785. On his succession to his father's estate 1782, he made further attempts to enter Parliament, was called to the English bar 1786, and was recorder of Carlisle 1788–90. In 1789 he settled in London, and in 1791 produced the classic English biography, the *Life of Samuel Johnson*. His long-lost personal papers were acquired for publication by Yale University 1949, and the *Journals* are of exceptional interest.

Bosworth, Battle of /'bɒzwəθ/ last battle of the ◊Wars of the Roses, fought on 22 Aug 1485 near the village of Market Bosworth, 19 km/12 mi W of Leicester, England. Richard III, the Yorkist king, was defeated and slain by Henry of Richmond, who became Henry VII.

BOT abbreviation for Board of Trade, former UK government organization, merged in the Department of Trade and Industry from 1970.

botanic garden a place where a wide range of plants is grown, providing the opportunity to see a botanical diversity not likely to be encountered elsewhere. Among the earliest forms of botanic garden was the *physic garden*, devoted to the study and growth of medicinal plants (for example, the Chelsea Physic Garden in London, established in 1673 and still in existence). Following increased botanical exploration, botanic gardens were used as testing grounds for potentially important new economic plants being sent back from all parts of the world.

A modern botanic garden serves many purposes: education, science, and conservation. Many are associated with universities and also maintain large collections of preserved specimens (see ◊herbarium), libraries, research laboratories, and gene banks.

botany the study of plants. It is subdivided into a number of specialized studies, such as the identification and classification of plants (taxonomy), their external formation (plant morphology), their internal arrangement (plant anatomy), their microscopic examination (histology), their life history (plant physiology), and their distribution over the Earth's surface in relation to their surroundings (plant ecology). Palaeobotany concerns the study of fossil plants, while economic botany deals with the utility of plants. Horticulture, agriculture, and forestry are specialized branches of botany.

history The most ancient botanical record is carved on the walls of the temple at Karnak, Egypt, about 1500 BC. The Greeks in the 5th and 4th centuries BC used many plants for medicinal purposes, the first Greek *Herbal* being drawn up about 350 BC by Diocles of Carystus. Botanical information was collected into the works of Theophrastus of Eresus (380–287 BC), a pupil of Aristotle, who founded the technical plant nomenclature. Cesalpino in the 16th century sketched out a system of classification based on flowers, fruits, and seeds, while Jung (1587–1658) used flowers only as his criterion. John Ray (1627–1705) arranged plants systematically, based on his findings on fruit, leaf, and flower, and described about 18,600 plants.

The Swedish botanist Carl von Linné, or ◊Linnaeus, who founded systematics in the 18th century, included in his classification all known plants and animals, giving each a ◊binomial descriptive label. His work greatly aided the future study of plants, as botanists found that all plants could be fitted into a systematic classification based on Linnaeus' work. Linnaeus was also the first to recognize the sexual nature of flowers. This was followed up later by Charles ◊Darwin and others.

Later work revealed the detailed cellular structure of plant tissues, and the exact nature of ◊photosynthesis. Julius von Sachs (1832–97) defined the function of ◊chlorophyll and the significance of plant ◊stomata. In the second half of the 20th century much has been learned about cell function, repair, and growth by the hybridization of plant cells (the combination of the nucleus of one cell with the protoplasm of another).

Botany Bay /'bɒtənɪ/ inlet on the E coast of Australia, 8 km/5 mi S of Sydney, New South Wales. Chosen in 1787 as the site for a penal colony, it proved unsuitable. Sydney now stands on the site

Botha *South African politician and former president P W Botha, who held office from 1978 to 1989.*

Botham *English cricketer Ian Botham batting for England at the Benson and Hedges challenge at Perth, Australia, 1986.*

of the former settlement. The name Botany Bay continued to be popularly used for any convict settlement in Australia.

Botero /bɒˈteərəʊ/ Fernando 1932– . Colombian painter. He studied in Spain and gained an international reputation for his paintings of fat, vulgar figures, often of women, parodies of conventional sensuality.

botfly type of fly, family Oestridae. The larvae are parasites which feed on the skin (warblefly of cattle) or in the nasal cavity (nostril-flies of sheep, deer). The horse botfly, family Gasterophilidae, has a parasitic larva which feeds in the horse's stomach.

Botha /ˈbəʊtə/ Louis 1862–1919. South African soldier and politician, a commander in the Second South African War. In 1907 Botha became premier of the Transvaal and in 1910 of the first Union government. On the outbreak of World War I in 1914 he rallied South Africa to the Commonwealth, suppressed a Boer revolt under Gen de Wet, and conquered German South West Africa.

Botha was born in Natal. Elected a member of the Volksraad in 1897, he supported the more moderate Joubert against Kruger. On the outbreak of the Second South African War he commanded the Boers besieging Ladysmith, and in 1900 succeeded Joubert in command of the Transvaal forces. When the Union of South Africa was formed 1910, Botha became prime minister, and at the Versailles peace conference in 1919 he represented South Africa.

Botha /ˈbəʊtə/ P(ieter) W(illem) 1916– . South African politician. Prime minister from 1978, he initiated a modification of ◊apartheid, which later slowed in the face of Afrikaner (Boer) opposition. In 1984 he became the first executive state president. In 1989 he unwillingly resigned both party leadership and presidency after suffering a stroke, and was succeeded by F W de Klerk.

Botham /ˈbəʊθəm/ Ian (Terrence) 1955– . English cricketer, a prolific all-rounder. His 373 test wickets, 109 catches, and 5,057 runs in 94 appearances by the end of the 1988 English season were a record until surpassed by Richard Hadlee (New Zealand) in 1989. He has played county cricket for Somerset and Worcestershire as well as playing in Australia.

Botham made his Somerset debut 1974 and first played for England against Australia at Trent Bridge 1977; he took five wickets for 74 runs in Australia's first innings. In 1987 he moved from Somerset to Worcestershire and helped them to

win the Refuge Assurance League in his first season.

Botham also played Football League soccer for Scunthorpe United. He raised money for leukemia research with much-publicized walks from John o'Groats to Land's End in the UK, and Hannibal-style across the Alps.

CAREER HIGHLIGHTS

all first-class matches
runs: 16,841
average: 34.02
best: 228 (Somerset v. Gloucestershire 1980)
wickets: 1061
average: 26.76
best: 8–34 (England v. Pakistan 1978)
test cricket
runs: 5,119
average: 34.13
best: 208 (England v. India, 1982)
wickets: 376
average: 28.28
best: 8–34 (England v. Pakistan 1978)

Bothe /ˈbəʊtə/ Walther 1891–1957. German physicist, who showed in 1929 that the cosmic rays bombarding the Earth are composed not of photons but of more massive particles. Nobel Prize for Physics 1954.

Bothwell /ˈbɒθwəl/ James Hepburn, 4th Earl of Bothwell c.1536–1578. Scottish nobleman, husband of ◊Mary, Queen of Scots, 1567–70, alleged to have arranged the explosion that killed Darnley, her previous husband, in 1567.

Tried and acquitted a few weeks after the assassination, he abducted Mary, and (having divorced his wife) married her on 15 May. A revolt ensued, and Bothwell was forced to flee to Norway and on to Sweden. In 1570 Mary obtained a divorce on the ground that she had been ravished by Bothwell before marriage. Later, Bothwell was confined in a castle in Zeeland, the Netherlands, where he died insane.

bo tree another name for the ◊peepul or wild ◊fig.

Botswana /bɒtˈswɑːnə/ landlocked country in central southern Africa, bounded to the S and E by South Africa, to the W and N by Namibia, and to the NE by Zimbabwe.

Botswana

area 582,000 sq km/225,000 sq mi
capital Gaborone
physical desert in SW, plains in E, fertile lands and swamp in N
features larger part of Kalahari Desert, including Okavango Swamp, remarkable for its wildlife; diamonds are mined at Orapa and Jwaneng in partnership with De Beers of South Africa
head of state and government Quett Ketamile Joni Masire from 1980

government The 1966 constitution blends the British system of parliamentary accountability with representation for each of Botswana's major ethnic groups. It provides for a national assembly of 40 members, 34 elected by universal suffrage, four by the assembly itself, plus the speaker and the attorney-general, and has a life of five years. The president is elected by the assembly for its duration and is an ex-officio member of it and answerable to it. There is also a 15-member house of chiefs, consisting of the chiefs of Botswana's eight principal ethnic groups, plus four members elected by the chiefs themselves and three elected by the house in general. The president may delay a bill for up to six months and then either sign it or dissolve the assembly and call a general election. The house of chiefs is consulted by the president and the assembly in matters affecting them. The president appoints a cabinet which is answerable to the assembly. Most significant of the seven political groupings are the Botswana Democratic Party (BDP), and the Botswana National Front (BNF).

history Inhabited by the Tswana from the 18th century, Botswana occupies a delicate position geographically and politically. It was originally Bechuanaland which, at the request of local rulers, became a British protectorate in 1885. On passing the Union of South Africa Act in 1910, making South Africa independent, the British Parliament provided for the possibility of Bechuanaland becoming part of South Africa, but said that this would not happen without popular consent. Successive South African governments requested the transfer but Botswana preferred full independence.

The 1960 constitution provided for a legislative council, though remaining under British High Commission control. In 1963 High Commission rule ended and in the legislative assembly elections the newly formed Bechuanaland Democratic Party (BDP) won a majority. Its leader, Seretse Khama, had been deposed as chief of the Bangangwato Tribe in 1950, and had since lived in exile, after marrying an Englishwoman two years before.

political system democratic republic
political parties Botswana Democratic Party (BDP), moderate centrist; Botswana National Front (BNF), moderate left-of-centre
exports diamonds, copper-nickel, meat
currency pula (3.14 = £1 Feb 1990)
population (1988) 1,210,000 (80% Bamangwato, 20% Bangwaketse); annual growth rate 3.8%
life expectancy men 53, women 56
language English (official); Setswana (national)
religion Christian (majority)
literacy 73% male/69% female (1985 est)
GDP $810 million (1984); $544 per head of population
chronology
1885 Became a British protectorate.
1960 New constitution created a legislative council.
1963 End of high-commission rule.
1965 Capital transferred from Mafeking to Gaborone. Internal self-government granted. Seretse Khama elected head of government.
1966 Full independence achieved. New constitution came into effect. Name changed from Bechuanaland to Botswana. Seretse Khama elected president.
1980 Seretse Khama died and was succeeded by vice-president Quett Masire.
1984 Masire re-elected.
1985 South African raid on Gaborone.
1987 Joint permanent commission with Mozambique established, to improve relations.
1989 The BDP and Masire re-elected.

Botticelli The Mystic Nativity (1500) National Gallery, London.

In 1966 the country, renamed Botswana, became an independent state within the Commonwealth with Sir Seretse Khama, as he had now become, as president. He continued to be re-elected until his death in 1980 when he was succeeded by the vice-president, Dr Quett Masire, who was re-elected in 1984. In the Oct 1989 elections the BDP won 31 of the 34 National Assembly seats and Quett Masire was again re-elected.

Since independence Botswana has earned a reputation for stability. It is a member of the ◊non-aligned movement. South Africa has accused it of providing bases for the African National Congress (ANC). This has always been denied by both Botswana and the ANC itself. South Africa has persistently pressed Botswana to sign a non-aggression pact, similar to the ◊Nkomati Accord between South Africa and Mozambique.

Botticelli /ˌbɒtɪˈtʃeli/ Sandro 1445–1510. Florentine painter of religious and mythological subjects. He was patronized by the ruling Medici family, for whom he painted *Primavera* 1478 and *The Birth of Venus* about 1482–84 (both in the Uffizi, Florence). From the 1490s he was influenced by the religious fanatic Savonarola and developed a harshly expressive and emotional style.

His real name was Filipepi, but his elder brother's nickname Botticelli 'little barrel' was passed on to him. His work for the Medicis was designed to cater to the educated classical tastes of the day. As well as his sentimental, beautiful young Madonnas, he produced a series of inventive compositions, including *tondi*, circular paintings. He broke with the Medicis after their execution of Savonarola.

bottlebrush trees and shrubs common in Australia, belonging to the genera *Melaleuca* and *Callistemon*, with characteristic cylindrical, composite flowerheads, often brightly coloured.

Bottrop /ˈbɒtrɒp/ city in North Rhine-Westphalia, West Germany; population (1988) 112,000.

botulism a rare but often fatal type of food poisoning. It is caused by the bacterium *Clostridium botulinum*, sometimes found in canned food.

Boucher /buːˈʃeɪ/ François 1703–1770. French Rococo painter, court painter from 1765. He was much patronized for his light-hearted, decorative scenes, for example *Diana Bathing* 1742 (Louvre, Paris). He also painted portraits and decorative chinoiserie for Parisian palaces. He became director of the Gobelin tapestry works, Paris, in 1755.

Boucher de Crèvecoeur de Perthes /buːˈʃeɪ də krevˈkɜː də ˈpeət/ Jacques 1788–1868. French

geologist, whose discovery of Palaeolithic hand-axes in 1837 challenged the acccepted view of human history dating only from 4004 BC, as proclaimed by the calculations of Bishop James ◊Usher.

Boudicca /ˈbuːdɪkə/ died AD 60. Queen of the Iceni (native Britons), often referred to by the Latin form ***Boadicea***. Her husband, King Prasutagus, had been a tributary of the Romans, but on his death AD 60 the territory of the Iceni was violently annexed, Boudicca was scourged and her daughters raped. Boudicca raised the whole of SE England in revolt, and before the main Roman armies could return from campaigning in Wales she burned London and Colchester. Later the British were virtually annihilated somewhere between London and Chester, and Boudicca poisoned herself.

Boudin /buːˈdæŋ/ Eugène 1824–1898. French painter, a forerunner of Impressionism, noted for his fresh seaside scenes painted in the open air.

Bougainville /ˈbuːɡənvɪl/ island province of Papua New Guinea; largest of the Solomon Islands archipelago

area 10,620 sq km/4,100 sq mi

capital Kieta

products copper, gold and silver

population (1989) 128,000

history named after the French navigator ◊Bougainville who arrived in 1768. In 1976 Bougainville became a province (with substantial autonomy) of Papua New Guinea. A state of emergency was declared 1989 after secessionist violence.

Bougainville /ˈbuːɡənvɪl/ Louis Antoine de 1729–1811. French navigator who made the first French circumnavigation of the world in 1766–69 and the first systematic observations of longitude. He served with the French in Canada during the Seven Years' War. Several Pacific islands are named after him, as is the climbing plant bougainvillea.

bougainvillea genus of South American climbing plants, family Nyctaginaceae, now cultivated in warm countries throughout the world for the red and purple bracts that cover the flowers. They are named after the French navigator Louis Bougainville.

Bougie /buːˈʒiː/ name until 1962 of ◊Bejaia, port in Algeria.

Bouguer anomaly in geophysics, an increase in the Earth's gravity observed near a mountain or dense rock mass. This is due to the gravitational force exerted by the rock mass of the rocks. It is named after its discoverer, the French mathematician Pierre Bouguer (1698–1758), who first observed it in 1735.

Bouguereau /buːɡəˈrəʊ/ Adolphe William 1825–1905. French academic painter of historical and mythological subjects. He was respected in his day but his style is now thought to be insipid.

Bou Kraa /ˈbuːkraː/ the principal phosphate mining centre of Western Sahara, linked by conveyor belt to the Atlantic coast near La'youn.

Boulanger /ˌbuːlɒnˈʒeɪ/ George Ernest Jean Marie 1837–1891. French general. He became minister of war 1886, and his anti-German speeches nearly provoked a war with Germany 1887. In 1889 he was suspected of aspiring to dictatorship by a coup d'état. Accused of treason, he fled into exile and committed suicide.

Boulanger /buːlɒnˈʒeɪ/ Lili (Juliette Marie Olga) 1893–1918. French composer, the younger sister of Nadia Boulanger. At the age of 19, she won the Prix de Rome with the cantata *Faust et Halkne* for voices and orchestra.

Boulanger /ˌbuːlɒnˈʒeɪ/ Nadia (Juliette) 1887–1979. French music teacher and conductor. A pupil of Fauré and admirer of Stravinsky, she included among her composition pupils at the American Conservatory in Fontainebleau (from 1921) Aaron Copland, Roy Harris, Walter Piston, and Philip Glass.

boules (French 'balls') a French game (also called *boccie* and *pétanque*) between two players or teams; it is similar to bowls.

Boules is derived from the ancient French game *jeu Provençal*. The object is to deliver a boule (or boules) from a standing position to land as near the jack (target) as possible. The boule is approximately 8 cm/3 in in diameter and weighs 620–800 g/22–28 oz. The standard length of the pitch, normally with a sand base, is 27.5 m/90 ft.

Boulestin /ˌbuːleˈstæn/ Marcel 1878–1943. French cookery writer and restaurateur. He was influential in spreading the principles of simple but high-quality French cooking in Britain in the first half of the 20th century, with a succession of popular books such as *What Shall We Have Today?* 1931.

Boulez /ˈbuːlez/ Pierre 1925– . French composer and conductor. He studied with ◊Messiaen and has promoted contemporary muic with a series of innovative *Domaine Musical* concerts and recordings in the 1950s, as conductor of the BBC Symphony and New York Philharmonic orchestras during the 1970s, and as founder-director of IRCAM, a music research studio in Paris opened in 1976. His music, strictly serial and expressionistic in style, includes the cantatas *Le Visage nuptial* 1946–52 and *Le Marteau sans maître* 1955, both to texts by René Char; and *Pli selon pli* 1962 for soprano and orchestra; and *Répons* 1981 for soloists, orchestra, tapes, and computer-generated sounds.

boulle or **buhl** a type of ◊marquetry, in brass and tortoise shell. Originally Italian, it has acquired the name of its most skilful exponent, the French artisan André-Charles Boulle (1642–1732).

Boulogne-sur-Mer /buːˈlɔɪn sjʊə ˈmeə/ town on the English Channel, Pas-de-Calais *département*, France; population (1983) 99,000. Industries include oil refining, food processing, and fishing. It is also a ferry port and seaside resort. Boulogne was a medieval countship, but became part of France 1477.

Boult /bəʊlt/ Adrian (Cedric) 1889–1983. British conductor of the BBC Symphony Orchestra 1930–50 and the London Philharmonic 1950–57. He promoted the work of Holst and Vaughan Williams, and was a noted interpreter of Elgar.

Boulting /ˈbəʊltɪŋ/ John 1913–1985 and Roy 1913– . British director–producer team that was particularly influential in the years following World War II. Their films include *Brighton Rock* 1947, *Lucky Jim* 1957, and *I'm All Right Jack* 1959. They were twins.

Boulton /ˈbəʊltən/ Matthew 1728–1809. British factory-owner, who helped to finance James ◊Watt's development of the steam engine. Boulton had an engineering works at Soho near Birmingham, and in 1775 he went into partnership with Watt to develop engines to power factory machines that had previously been driven by water.

Boumédienne /ˌbuːmeɪdˈjen/ Houari. Adopted name of Mohammed Boukharouba 1925–1978. Algerian politician who brought the nationalist leader Ben Bella to power by a revolt 1962, and superseded him as president 1965–78 by a further coup.

Boundary Peak highest mountain in Nevada state, USA, rising to 4,006 m/13,143 ft on the Nevada–California frontier.

Bounty, Mutiny on the naval mutiny in the Pacific 1789 against British captain William ◊Bligh.

Bourbon /ˈbʊəbən/ name 1649–1815 of the French island of Réunion in the Indian Ocean.

Bourbon /ˈbʊəbən/ Charles, Duke of Bourbon 1490–1527. Constable of France, honoured for his courage at the Battle of Marignano 1515. Later he served the Holy Roman emperor Charles V, and helped to drive the French from Italy. In 1526 he was made duke of Milan, and in 1527 allowed his troops to sack Rome. He was killed by a shot the artist Cellini claimed to have fired.

Bourbon, duchy of originally a seigneury (feudal domain) created in the 10th century in the county of Bourges, central France, held by the Bourbon family. It became a duchy 1327.

The lands passed to the Capetian dynasty (see ♢Capet) as a result of the marriage of the Bourbon heiress Beatrix to Robert of Clermont, son of Louis IX. Their son Pierre became the first duke of Bourbon 1327. The direct line ended with the death of Charles, Duke of Bourbon, in 1527.

Bourbon /'buəbən/ French royal house (succeeding that of ♢Valois) beginning with Henry IV, and ending with Louis XVI, with a brief revival under Louis XVIII, Charles X, and Louis Philippe. The Bourbons ruled Spain almost uninterruptedly from Philip V to Alfonso XIII, and were restored in 1975 (♢Juan Carlos); they also ruled Naples and several Italian duchies. The Grand Duke of Luxembourg is also a Bourbon by male descent.

Bourdon /buə'dɒŋ/ Eugène 1808–1884. French engineer and instrument maker, who invented the pressure gauge that bears his name. The key to a Bourdon gauge is a tapering, C-shaped tube closed at its narrow end which changes circumference slightly when a gas or liquid under pressure flows into it. Levers and gears make the movement of the end of the tube work a pointer, which indicates pressure on a circular scale.

bourgeois (French) a member of the middle class; adjective implying that a person is unimaginative, conservative, and materialistic.

Bourgeois /buə'ʒwɑ:/ Léon Victor Auguste 1851–1925. French politician. Entering politics as a Radical, he was prime minister in 1895, and later served in many cabinets. He was one of the pioneer advocates of the League of Nations. Nobel peace prize 1920.

bourgeoisie (French) the middle classes. The French word originally meant the freemen of a borough. Hence it came to mean the whole class above the workers and peasants, and below the nobility. Bourgeoisie (and *bourgeois*) has also acquired a contemptuous sense, as implying commonplace, philistine respectability. By socialists it is applied to the whole propertied class, as distinct from the proletariat.

Bourges /buəʒ/ city in central France, 200 km/125 mi south of Paris; population (1982) 92,000. Industries include aircraft, engineering, and tires. It has a 13th-century Gothic cathedral and notable art collections.

Bourgogne /buə'gɒŋ/ region of France, which includes the *départements* of Côte-d'Or, Nièvre, Sâone-et-Loire, and Yonne; area 31,600 sq km/12,198 sq mi; population (1986) 1,607,000. Its capital is Dijon. It is famous for its wines, such as Chablis and Nuits-Saint-Georges, and for its cattle (the Charolais herdbook is maintained at Nevers). A former independent kingdom and duchy (see ♢Burgundy), it was incorporated into France 1477.

Bourguiba /buə'gi:bə/ Habib ben Ali 1903– . Tunisian politician, first president of Tunisia 1957–87. Educated at the University of Paris, he became a journalist and was frequently imprisoned by the French for his nationalist aims as leader of the Néo-Destour party. He became prime minister 1956, president (for life from 1974) and prime minister of the Tunisian republic 1957, and was overthrown in a coup 1987.

Bournemouth /'bɔ:nməθ/ seaside resort in Dorset, England; population (1981) 145,000.

Bournonville /,buənɒŋ'vi:l/ August 1805–1879. Danish dancer and choreographer. He worked with the Royal Danish Ballet for most of his life, giving Danish ballet a worldwide importance. His ballets, many of which have been revived in the last 50 years, include *La Sylphide* 1836 (music by Lövenskjöld) and *Napoli* 1842.

Bouts /bauts/ Dierick c. 1420–1475. Early Netherlandish painter. Born in Haarlem, he settled in Louvain some time before 1448, painting portraits and religious scenes influenced by Rogier van der Weyden. *The Last Supper* 1464–68 (St Pierre, Louvain) is considered one of his finest works. His figures tend to be stiff and elongated and his spatial effects sometimes awkward; his background landscapes are beautiful.

Bouvet Island /'bu:veɪ/ uninhabited island in the S Atlantic Ocean, area 48 sq km/19 sq mi, a dependency of Norway since 1930. Discovered by the Frenchman Jacques Bouvet in 1738, it was made the subject of a claim by Britain in 1825, but this was waived in Norway's favour in 1928.

Bouvines, Battle of a victory for Philip II (Philip Augustus) of France in 1214, near the village of Bouvines in Flanders, over the Holy Roman emperor Otto IV and his allies. The battle, one of the most decisive in medieval Europe, ensured the succession of Frederick II as emperor, and confirmed Philip as ruler of the whole of N France and Flanders; it led to the renunciation of all English claims to the region.

Bovet /bɒ'veɪ/ Daniel 1907– . Swiss physiologist. He pioneered research into antihistamine drugs used in the treatment of nettle rash and hay fever, and was awarded a Nobel prize 1957 for his production of a synthetic form of curare, used as a muscle relaxant in anaesthesia.

bovine somatotropin (BST) a hormone that increases an injected cow's milk yield by 10–40%. It is a protein naturally occurring in milk, and breaks down within the human digestive tract into harmless amino acids. However, following trials in the UK 1988, doubts have arisen whether such a degree of protein addition could in the long term be guaranteed 'harmless' either to cattle or to humans.

Although no evidence had been found by 1990 of adverse side effects, there were calls for the drug to be banned because of potential consumer resistance to this method of increasing output of a commodity, milk, that currently has a production surplus.

bovine spongiform encephalopathy (BSE) disease of cattle, allied to ♢scrapie, which renders the brain spongy and may drive an animal mad. It has been identified only in the UK, but with more than 13,400 cases confirmed between the first diagnosis Nov 1986 and Feb 1990, it already poses a threat to the valuable export trade in livestock. The disease has also killed two wildlife-park animals.

Bow /bəu/ Clara 1905–1965. US silent-film actress, known as the 'It' girl after her vivacious performance in *It* 1927. Her other films included *Wings* 1927 and *The Wild Party* 1929. Scandals about her romances and her mental and physical fragility led to the end of her career, and she spent many of her later years in sanatoriums.

Bow Bells the bells of St Mary-le-Bow church, Cheapside, London; a person born within the sound of Bow Bells is traditionally considered a true Cockney. The bells also feature in the legend of Dick ♢Whittington.

The church was nearly destroyed by bombs in 1941. The bells, recast from the old metal, were restored in 1961.

Bowdler /'baudlə/ Thomas 1754–1825. British editor, whose prudishly expurgated versions of Shakespeare and other authors gave rise to the verb 'bowdlerize'.

Bowen /'bəuɪn/ Elizabeth 1899–1973. Irish novelist. She published her first volume of short stories, *Encounters* in 1923. Her novels include *The Death of the Heart* 1938, *The Heat of the Day* 1949, and *The Little Girls* 1964.

bower-bird Australian bird related to the ♢birds of paradise. The males are dully-coloured, and build elaborate bowers of sticks and grass, decorated with shells, feathers, or flowers to attract the females. There are 17 species in the family Ptilonorhynchidae.

bowfin North American fish *Amia calva* with a swimbladder highly developed as an air sac, enabling it to breathe air.

bowhead Arctic whale *Balaena mysticetus* with huge curving upper jaw bones supporting the plates of baleen which it uses to sift the water for planktonic crustaceans. Averaging 15 m/50 ft long and 90 tonnes in weight, these slow-moving, placid whales were once extremely common, but by the 17th century were already becoming scarce through hunting. Only an estimated 3,000 remain and continued hunting by the Inuit may result in extinction.

Bowie /'bəuɪ/ David. Stage name of David Jones 1947– . British pop singer and songwriter, born in Brixton, London. He became a glitter-rock star with the album *The Rise and Fall of Ziggy Stardust and the Spiders from Mars* 1972, and collaborated in the mid-1970s with the electronic virtuoso Brian Eno (1948–) and Iggy Pop. He has also acted in plays and films, including Nicolas Roeg's *The Man Who Fell to Earth* 1976.

Bowie /'bəuɪ/ 'Jim' (James) 1796–1836. US frontiersman and folk hero. A colonel in the Texan forces during the Mexican War, he is said to have invented the single-edge, guarded hunting and throwing knife known as a *Bowie knife*. He was killed in the battle of the ♢Alamo.

Bowles /bəulz/ Paul 1910– . US novelist and composer. Born in New York, he settled in Morocco, the setting of novels like *Let It Come Down* 1952 and the stories of *The Delicate Prey* 1950.

bowls outdoor and indoor game popular in England and Commonwealth countries. It has been played in Britain since the 13th century and was popularized by Francis Drake, who is reputed to have played bowls on Plymouth Hoe as the Spanish Armada arrived 1588.

The outdoor game is played on a finely cut grassed area called a rink. It is played at either singles, pairs, triples, or fours. The object is to get your bowl (or bowls) nearer the jack (target) than your opponent(s). Bowls are called 'woods': most are made of lignum vitae. There are two popular forms: *lawn bowls*, played on a flat surface, and *crown green bowls*, played on a rink with undulations and a crown at the centre of the green. This latter version is more popular in the Midlands and N England.

Bowie British pop singer and songwriter David Bowie has also acted in films, notably The Man Who Fell to Earth 1976.

Bowls: recent winners

World Championship first held 1966 for men, 1969 for women
men: singles/pairs
1972 Malwyn Evans *(Wales)*/Hong Kong
1976 Doug Watson *(South Africa)*/South Africa
1980 David Bryant *(England)*/Australia

box   160

1984 Peter Bellis *(New Zealand)*/USA
1988 Peter Bryant *(England)*/New Zealand
triples/fours
1972 USA/England
1976 South Africa/South Africa
1980 England/Hong Kong
1984 Ireland/England
1988 New Zealand/Ireland
women: singles/pairs
1973 Elsie Wilke *(New Zealand)*/Australia
1977 Elsie Wilke *(New Zealand)*/Hong Kong
1981 Norma Shaw *(England)*/Ireland
1985 Merle Richardson *(Australia)*/Australia
1988 Janet Ackland *(Wales)*/Ireland
triples/fours
1973 New Zealand/New Zealand
1977 Wales/Australia
1981 Hong Kong/England
1985 Australia/Scotland
1988 Australia/Australia

CROWN GREEN BOWLS

the *Waterloo Handicap*, first held 1907 at The Waterloo Hotel, Blackpool, is crown green bowling's principal tournament
1980 Vernon Lee
1981 Roy Nicholson
1982 Dennis Mercer
1983 Stan Frith
1984 Steve Ellis
1985 Tommy Johnstone
1986 Brian Duncan
1987 Brian Duncan
1988 Ingham Gregory
1989 Brian Duncan

box small evergreen trees and shrubs, genus *Buxus*, of the family Buxaceae. The **common box** B. *sempervirens* is slow growing, and ideal for hedging.

boxer breed of dog, about 60 cm/2 ft tall, with a smooth coat and a set-back nose; it is generally given a docked tail. It is usually brown but may be brindled or white.

Boxer member of the *I Ho Ch'üan* ('Society of Harmonious Fists'), Chinese nationalists who in 1900 at the instigation of the empress dowager besieged the foreign legations in Beijing and murdered European missionaries and thousands of Chinese Christian converts (the **Boxer Rebellion**). An international punitive force was dispatched, Beijing was captured 14 Aug 1900, and China agreed to pay a large indemnity.

boxfish type of fish of which the scales are hexagonal bony plates fused to form a box covering the body, only the mouth and fins being free of the armour.

Boxfishes, also known as **trunkfishes**, family Ostraciodontidae, swim slowly. The **cowfish**, genus *Lactophrys*, with two 'horns' above the eyes, is a member of this group.

boxing fighting with fists. The modern sport dates from the 18th century, when fights were with bare knuckles and with untimed rounds. Each round ended with a knockdown. Fighting with gloves became the accepted form in the latter part of the 19th century after the formulation of the Queensberry Rules 1867. The last bare-knuckle fight was between John L Sullivan and Jake Kilrain 1899.

Jack Broughton (1704–89) was one of the early champions and in 1743 drew up the first set of boxing rules. All modern-day boxing follows the original Queensberry Rules, but with modifications. Contests take place in a square roped ring 4.3–6.1 m/14–20 ft square. All rounds last for 3 min. Amateur bouts last for three rounds and professional bouts 12 rounds. Boxers are classified according to weight and can fight opponents from the same weight division or a heavier division. The weight divisions in professional boxing range from **straw-weight** (also known as paper-weight and mini-flyweight), under 49 kg/108 lb, to **heavyweight**, over 88 kg/195 lb.

boxing

world champions (WBC, World Boxing Council; WBA, World Boxing Association; IBF, International Boxing Federation; WBO, World Boxing Organization)
heavyweight
1979 John Tate *USA* (WBA)
1980 Mike Weaver *USA* (WBA)
1982 Mike Dokes *USA* (WBA)
1983 Gerry Coetzee *South Africa* (WBA)
1984 Larry Holmes *USA* (IBF)
1984 Tim Witherspoon *USA* (WBC)
1984 Pinklon Thomas *USA* (WBC)
1984 Greg Page *USA* (WBA)
1985 Michael Spinks *USA* (IBF)
1985 Tony Tubbs *USA* (WBA)
1986 Tim Witherspoon *USA* (WBA)
1986 Trevor Berbick *Canada* (WBC)
1986 Mike Tyson *USA* (WBC/WBA)
1986 James Smith *USA* (WBA)
1987 Mike Tyson *USA* (WBC)
1987 Tony Tucker *USA* (IBF)
1987 Mike Tyson *USA* (Undisputed)
1990 James Douglas *USA* (Undisputed)
Great heavyweight champions include:
John L Sullivan (bare-knuckle champion) 1882–92
Jim Corbett (first Marquess of Queensberry champion) 1892–97
Jack Dempsey 1919–26
Joe Louis 1937–49
Rocky Marciano 1952–56
Muhammad Ali 1964–67, 1974–78, 1978–79
Larry Holmes 1978–85
Mike Tyson 1986–1990

boyar a landowner in the Russian aristocracy. During the 16th century boyars formed a powerful interest group threatening the tsar's power, until their influence was decisively broken by Ivan the Terrible in 1565 when he confiscated much of their land.

Boycott /'bɔɪkɒt/ Charles Cunningham 1832–1897. English land agent in County Mayo, Ireland, who strongly opposed the demands for agrarian reform by the Irish Land League 1879–81, with the result that the peasants refused to work for him; hence the word 'boycott'.

Boycott /'bɔɪkɒt/ Geoffrey 1940– . England cricketer born in Yorkshire, England's most prolific run-maker with 8,114 runs in test cricket. He was banned as a test player in 1982 for taking part in matches against South Africa.

He played in 108 test matches and in 1981 overtook Gary Sober's world record test runs. Twice, in 1971 and 1979, his average was over 100 runs in an English season. He was released by Yorkshire after a dispute in 1986.

Boyle *The fourteenth child of the Earl of Cork, Robert Boyle enunciated the law of the compressibility of gases (Boyle's law) in 1662.*

Boyd-Orr /'bɔɪd 'ɔː/ John 1880–1971. British nutritionist and health campaigner. He was awarded the Nobel Peace Prize in 1949 in recognition of his work towards alleviating world hunger.

Boyer /bwɑː'jeɪ/ Charles 1899–1978. French film actor, who made his name in Hollywood in the 1930s as a screen 'lover' in films such as *Mayerling* 1937 and *The Garden of Allah* 1936.

Boyle /bɔɪl/ Charles, 4th Earl of Orrery 1676–1731. Irish soldier and diplomat. The orrery, a mechanical model of the solar system in which the planets move at relative velocities, is named after him.

Boyle /bɔɪl/ Robert 1627–1691. Irish physicist and chemist, who published the seminal *The Skeptical Chymist* 1661. He was the first chemist to collect a gas, enunciated *Boyle's law* in 1662, was one of the founders of the Royal Society, and endowed the Boyle Lectures for the defence of Christianity.

Boyle's law in physics, law stating that the volume of a given mass of gas at a constant temperature is inversely proportional to its pressure. It was discovered in 1662 by Robert Boyle.

Boyne /bɔɪn/ a river in the Irish Republic. Rising in the Bog of Allen in County Kildare, it flows 110 km/69 mi NE to the Irish Sea near Drogheda. The Battle of the Boyne was fought at Oldbridge near the mouth of the river in 1690.

Boyne, Battle of the battle fought 1 Jul 1690 in E Ireland, in which James II was defeated by William III and fled to France. It was the decisive battle of the War of English Succession, confirming a Protestant monarch. It took its name from the river Boyne.

Boyoma Falls /bɔɪ'əʊmə/ series of seven cataracts in under 100 km/60 mi in the Lualaba (upper Zaïre river) above Kisangani, central Africa. They have a total drop of over 60 m/200 ft.

Boy Scout a member of the ◊Scout organization.

Bozen /'bəʊtsən/ German form of ◊Bolzano, town in Italy.

Bo Zhu Yi /'bəʊ 'dʒu: 'ji:/ 772–846. Chinese poet (formerly known as *Po Chü-i*). President from 841 of the imperial war department, he criticized government policy. He is said to have checked his work with an old peasant woman for clarity of expression.

BP abbreviation for *British Pharmacopoeia*; also *British Petroleum*.

BR abbreviation for *British Rail*.

Brabançonne, La /ˌbræbən'sɒn/ national anthem of Belgium, written and composed during the revolution of 1830.

Brabant /brə'bænt/ (Flemish *Braband*) former duchy of W Europe, comprising the Dutch province of ◊North Brabant and the Belgian provinces of Brabant and Antwerp. They were divided when Belgium became independent 1830. The present-day Belgian province of Brabant has an area of 3,400 sq km/1,312 sq mi, and a population (1987) of 2,222,000.

During the Middle Ages it was an independent duchy, and after passing to Burgundy, and thence to the Spanish crown, was divided during the Dutch War of Independence. The southern portion was Spanish until 1713, then Austrian until 1815, when the whole area was included in the Netherlands. In 1830 the influential French-speaking part of the population in the S Netherlands rebelled and when Belgium was recognized 1839, S Brabant was included in it.

Brabham Grand Prix racing team started 1962 by the top Australian driver, Jack Brabham. Their first car, designed by Ron Tauranac, gained its first win 1964, and in 1966 Brabham won the world title in his own Repco-powered car. It was the first time anyone had won the world title in a car bearing their own name. Denny Hulme won the title for the company the following year. Brabham retired in 1970 and the company lost some of its impetus. It returned to Grand Prix racing in 1989.

Bracegirdle /'breɪsgɜːdl/ Anne *c.* 1663–1748. British actress, the mistress of ◊Congreve, and possibly his wife; she played Millamant in his *The Way of the World*.

Brachiopoda phylum of marine clamlike creatures with about 300 species. They are suspension feeders, ingesting minute food particles from water. A single internal organ, the iophophore, handles feeding, aspiration, and excretion.

bracken species of fern *Pteridium aquilinum*, abundant in most parts of Europe. It has a perennial root-stock that throws up large fronds.

bracket fungus ◊fungus of the class Basidiomycetes, with bracket-shaped fruiting body, often seen on tree trunks.

Bracknell /'bræknəl/ ◊new town in Berkshire, England, founded 1949; population (1981) 49,000. The headquarters of the Meterological Office is here, and (with Washington DC) is one of the only two global area forecasting centres (of upper-level winds and temperatures) for the world's airlines.

bract a leaflike structure, in whose ◊axil a flower or inflorescence develops. Bracts are generally green and smaller than the true leaves. However, in some plants they may be brightly coloured and conspicuous, taking over the role of attracting pollinating insects to the flowers, whose own petals are small; examples include poinsettia (*Euphorbia pulcherrima*) and bougainvillea.

A whorl of bracts surrounding an ◊inflorescence is termed an *involucre*. A *bracteole* is a leaflike organ that arises on an individual flower stalk, between the true bract and the ◊calyx.

Bracton /'bræktən/ Henry de died 1268. English judge, writer on English law, and chancellor of Exeter cathedral from 1264. He compiled an account of the laws and customs of the English, *De Legibus et Consuetudinibus Anglie*, the first of its kind.

Bradbury /'brædbəri/ Malcolm 1932– . British novelist and critic, noted for his comic and satiric portrayals of academic life. His best-known work is *The History Man* 1975, set in a provincial English university. Other works include *Rates of Exchange* 1983.

Bradbury /'brædbəri/ Ray 1920– . US writer, born in Illinois. He was one of the first science-fiction writers to make the genre 'respectable' to a wider readership. His work shows nostalgia for small-town Midwestern life, and includes *The Martian Chronicles* 1950, *Something Wicked This Way Comes* 1962, and *Fahrenheit 451* 1953.

Bradford /'brædfəd/ industrial city (engineering, machine tools, electronics, printing) in West Yorkshire, England, 14 km/9 mi W of Leeds; population (1981) 281,000. From the 13th century, Bradford developed as a great wool-manufacturing and, later, cloth-manufacturing centre, but the industry declined from the 1970s with Third World and Common Market competition. The city has received a succession of immigrants, Irish in the 1840s, German merchants in the mid-19th century, then Poles and Ukrainians, and more recently West Indians and Asians.

features A 15th-century cathedral; Cartwright Hall art gallery; the National Museum of Photography, Film, and Television 1983 (with Britain's largest cinema screen, 14 × 20 m); and the Alhambra, built as a music hall and restored for ballet, plays, and pantomime.

Bradlaugh /'brædlɔː/ Charles 1833–1891. British freethinker and radical politician. In 1880 he was elected Liberal member of Parliament for Northampton, but was not allowed to take his seat until 1886 because, as an atheist, he (unsuccessfully) claimed the right to affirm instead of taking the oath. He was associated with the feminist Annie Besant.

He served in the army, was a lawyer's clerk, became well known as a speaker and journalist under the name of Iconoclast, and from 1860 ran the *National Reformer*. He advocated the freedom of the press, contraception, and other social reforms.

Bradley /'brædli/ Francis Herbert 1846–1924. British philosopher. In *Ethical Studies* 1876 and *Principles of Logic* 1883 he attacked the utilitarianism of J S Mill, and in *Appearance and Reality* 1893 and *Truth and Reality* 1914 he outlined his Neo-Hegelian doctrine of the universe as a single ultimate reality.

Bradley /'brædli/ James 1693–1762. English astronomer, who in 1728 discovered the aberration (apparent change in position) of starlight. From the amount of aberration in star positions, he was able to calculate the speed of light. In 1748 he announced the discovery of ◊nutation (variation in the Earth's axial tilt). He became Astronomer Royal 1742.

Bradley /'brædli/ Omar Nelson 1893–1981. US general in World War II. In 1943 he commanded the 2nd US Corps in Tunisia and Sicily, and in 1944 led the US troops in the invasion of France. He was chief of staff of the US Army 1948–49 and chair of the joint chiefs of staff 1949–53. He was appointed general of the army 1950.

Bradman /'brædmən/ Donald George 1908– . Australian test cricketer with the highest average in test history. From 52 test matches he averaged 99.94 runs per innings. He only needed four runs from his final test innings to average 100 but was dismissed at second ball.

Bradman was born in New South Wales, came to prominence at an early age, and made his test debut in 1928. He played for Australia for 20 years and was captain 1936–48. He twice scored triple centuries against England and in 1930 scored 452 not out for New South Wales against Queensland, the highest first-class innings until 1959.

CAREER HIGHLIGHTS

all first-class matches
runs: 28,067
average: 95.14
best: 452 not out (New South Wales v. Queensland, 1930)
test cricket
runs: 6,996
average: 99.94
best: 334 (Australia v. England, 1930)

Bradshaw /'brædʃɔː/ George 1801–1853. British publisher who brought out the first railway timetable in 1839. Thereafter *Bradshaw's Railway Companion* appeared at regular intervals. He was apprenticed to an engraver on leaving school, and set up his own printing and engraving business in the 1820s, beginning in 1827 with an engraved map of Lancashire.

Braemar village in Grampian, Scotland, where the most famous of the ◊Highland Games, the *Braemar Gathering*, takes place every August.

Braga /'brɑːgə/ city in N Portugal 48 km/30 mi NNE of Oporto; population (1981) 63,800. Industries include textiles, electrical goods and vehicle manufacture. It has a 12th-century cathedral, and the archbishop is primate of the Iberian peninsula. As *Bracara Augusta* it was capital of the Roman province Lusitania.

Bragança /brə'gænsə/ name of the royal house of Portugal whose members reigned 1640–1853; another branch were emperors of Brazil 1822–89.

Bragança /brə'gænsə/ capital of a province of the same name in NE Portugal, 176 km/110 mi NE of Oporto; population (1981) 13,900. It was the original family seat of the House of Bragança, which ruled Portugal 1640–1910.

Brahms The composer in his study.

Bragg /bræg/ William Henry 1862–1942. British physicist. In 1915 he shared with his son *(William) Lawrence Bragg* (1890–1971) the Nobel Prize for physics for their research work on X-rays and crystals.

Brahe /'brɑːhə/ Tycho 1546–1601. Danish astronomer, who made accurate observations of the planets from which the German astronomer and mathematician Johan ◊Kepler proved that planets orbit the Sun in ellipses. His discovery and report of the 1572 supernova made him famous, and his observations of the comet of 1577 proved that it moved on an orbit among the planets, thus disproving the Greek view that comets were in the Earth's atmosphere.

Brahe was a colourful figure who had to wear a metal nose after his own was cut off in a duel, and who took an interest in alchemy. In 1576 Frederick II of Denmark gave him the island of Hven, where he set up an observatory. Brahe was the greatest observer in the days before telescopes, making the most accurate measurements of the positions of stars and planets. He moved to Prague as imperial mathematician in 1599, where he was joined by Kepler, who inherited his observations when he died.

Brahma /'brɑːmə/ in Hinduism, the creator of the cosmos, who forms with Vishnu and Siva the Trimurti, or three aspects of the absolute spirit. Also an alternative form of Brahman.

Brahman in Hinduism, the supreme being, an impersonal spirit into whom the atman, or soul, will eventually be absorbed when its cycle of rebirth is ended.

Brahmanism the earliest stage in the development of ◊Hinduism. Its sacred scriptures are the ◊Vedas, with their accompanying literature of comment and explanation known as Brahmanas, Aranyakas, and Upanishads.

Brahmaputra /ˌbrɑːmə'puːtrə/ river in Asia 2,900 km/1,800 mi long, a tributary of the Ganges.

It rises in the Himalayan glaciers as Zangbo and runs E through Tibet, to the mountain mass of Namcha Barwa. Turning S, as the Dihang, it enters India and flows into the Assam valley near Sadiya. Now known as the Brahmaputra, it flows generally W until, shortly after reaching Bangladesh, it turns S and divides into the Brahmaputra proper, without much water, and the main stream, the Jamuna, which joins the Padma arm of the Ganges. The river is navigable for 1,285 km/800 mi from the sea.

Brahma Samaj /'brɑːmə sə'mɑːdʒ/ Indian monotheistic religious movement, founded in 1830 in Calcutta by Ram Mohun Roy, who attempted to recover the simple worship of the Vedas and purify Hinduism. The movement had split into a number of sects by the end of the 19th century and is now almost defunct.

brain

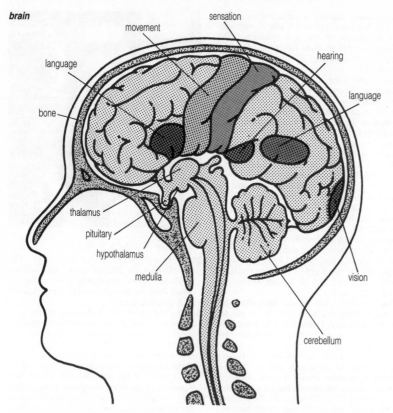

Brahms /brɑːmz/ Johannes 1833–1897. German composer, pianist, and conductor. Considered one of the greatest composers of symphonic music and of songs, his works include four symphonies; ◊lied; concertos for piano and for violin; chamber music; sonatas; and the choral *A German Requiem* 1868. He performed and conducted his own works.

In 1853 the violinist Joachim introduced him to Liszt and Schumann. From 1868 Brahms made his home in Vienna. Although his music has romantic qualities, it is essentially a sophistication of the classical tradition from the point to which Beethoven had brought it.

Brăila /brə'iːlə/ port in Romania on the river Danube, 170 km/106 mi from its mouth; population (1983) 226,000. It is a naval base. Industries include the manufacture of artificial fibres, iron and steel, machinery, and paper. It was controlled by the Ottoman Empire 1544–1828.

Braille /breɪl/ a system of writing for the blind. Letters are represented by a combination of raised dots on paper or other materials, which are then read by touch. It was invented in 1829 by *Louis Braille* (1809–52), who was blind from the age of three.

brain in higher animals, a mass of interconnected ◊nerve cells, forming the anterior part of the ◊central nervous system, whose activities it coordinates and controls. In ◊vertebrates, the brain is contained in the skull. An enlarged portion of the upper spinal cord, the *medulla oblongata*, contains centres for the control of respiration, heartbeat rate and strength, and blood pressure. Overlying this is the *cerebellum*, which is concerned with coordinating complex muscular processes such as maintaining posture and moving limbs. The cerebral hemispheres (*cerebrum*) are paired outgrowths of the front end of the forebrain, in early vertebrates mainly concerned with the senses, but in higher vertebrates greatly developed and involved in intelligent behaviour.

In humans, the nerve fibres from the two sides of the body cross over as they enter the brain, so that the left cerebral hemisphere is associated with the right side of the body and vice versa. In right-handed people, the left hemisphere seems to be more important in controlling verbal and some mathematical skills whereas the right hemisphere is more important in spatial perception. In general, however, skills and abilities are not closely localized. In the brain, nerve impulses are passed across ◊synapses by neurotransmitters, in the same way as in other parts of the nervous system.

In mammals the cerebrum is the largest part of the brain, carrying the *cerebral cortex*. This consists of a thick surface layer of cell bodies (grey matter) below which fibre tracts (white matter) connect various parts of the cortex to each other and to other points in the central nervous system. As cerebral complexity grows, the surface of the brain becomes convoluted into deep folds. In higher mammals, there are large unassigned areas of the brain which seem to be connected with intelligence, personality, and higher mental faculties. Language is controlled in two special regions usually in the left side of the brain; *Broca's area* governs the ability to talk, and *Wernicke's area* is responsible for the comprehension of spoken and written words.

brain damage impairment of the brain, which can be caused by trauma (for example, accidents) or disease (such as encephalitis), or which may be present at birth. Depending on the area of the brain affected, language, movement, sensation, judgement, or other abilities may be impaired.

Braine /breɪn/ John 1922–1986. English novelist. His novel *Room at the Top* 1957 created the character of Joe Lampton, one of the first of the northern working-class anti-heroes.

brainstem the central core of the brain, where the top of the spinal cord merges with the undersurface of the brain.

The oldest part of the brain in evolutionary terms, the brainstem is the body's own life-support centre, containing regulatory mechanisms for vital functions such as breathing, heart rate, and blood pressure. It is also involved in controlling the level of consciousness by acting as a relay station for nerve connections to and from the higher centres of the brain.

In many countries, death of the brainstem is now formally recognized as death of the person as a whole. Such cases are the principal donors of organs for transplantation. So-called 'beating-heart donors' can be maintained for a limited period by modern life-support equipment.

Brains Trust nickname applied to a group of experts who advised US president F D Roosevelt on his *New Deal* policy.

Braithwaite /'breɪθweɪt/ Eustace Adolph 1912– . Guyanese author. His experiences as a teacher in London prompted *To Sir With Love* 1959. His *Reluctant Neighbours* 1972 deals with black/white relations.

Braithwaite /'breɪθweɪt/ Richard Bevan 1900– . British philosopher, who experimented in the provision of a rational basis for religion and moral choice. Originally a physicist and mathematician, he was Knightbridge professor of moral philosophy at Cambridge 1953–67.

brake a device used to slow down or stop the movement of a moving body or vehicle. The mechanically applied caliper brake used on bicycles uses a scissor action to press hard rubber blocks against the wheel rim. The main braking system of a car works hydraulically, or by means of liquid pressure. When the driver depresses the brake pedal, liquid pressure forces pistons to apply brakes on each wheel.

Two types of car brakes are used. *Disc brakes* are used on the front wheels of most cars. Braking pressure forces brake pads against both sides of a steel disc that rotates with the wheel. *Drum brakes* are fitted on rear wheels of most cars. Braking pressure forces brake shoes to expand outwards into contact with a drum rotating with the wheels. The brake pads and shoes have a tough ◊friction lining that grips well and withstands wear. Disc brakes are the more efficient and less prone to fading (losing their braking power) when they get hot.

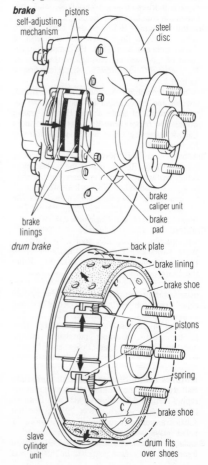

Brando Marlon Brando as the rebellious biker Johnny in The Wild One 1954.

Many trucks and trains have **air brakes**, which work by compressed air. On landing, jet planes reverse the thrust of their engines to reduce their speed quickly. Space vehicles use retrorockets for braking in space. They use the air resistance, or drag of the atmosphere, to slow down when they return to Earth.

Bramah /'brɑːmə/ Ernest. Pen name of Ernest Bramah Smith 1868–1948. British short-story writer, creator of Kai Lung, and of Max Carrados, a blind detective.

Bramah /'brɑːmə/ Joseph 1748–1814. British inventor of a flushing water closet (1778), an 'unpickable' lock (1784), and the hydraulic press (1795). The press made use of ◊Pascal's principle (that pressure in fluid contained in a vessel is evenly distributed) and employed water as the hydraulic fluid; it enabled the 19th-century bridge-builders to lift massive girders.

Bramante /brə'mænti/ Donato *c.* 1444–1514. Italian Renaissance architect and artist. Inspired by Classical designs, he was employed by Pope Julius II in rebuilding part of the Vatican and St Peter's in Rome.

bramble bush that produces the ◊blackberry.

brambling bird *Fringilla montifringilla* belonging to the finch family, about 15 cm/6 in long. It breeds in N Europe and Asia.

Branagh /'brænə/ Kenneth 1960– . British actor and director. He launched his Renaissance Theatre Company in 1987, was a notable Hamlet and Touchstone in 1988, and in 1989 directed and starred in a film of Shakespeare's *Henry V*.

Brancusi /bræɲ'kuːzi/ Constantin 1876–1957. Romanian sculptor, active in Paris from 1904, a pioneer of abstract forms and conceptual art. He was one of the first sculptors in the 20th century to carve directly from his material, working with marble, granite, wood, and other materials. He developed increasingly simplified natural or organic forms, such as the sculpted head that gradually came to resemble an egg (*Sleeping Muse* 1910, Musée National d'Art Moderne, Paris).

In 1904 he walked from Romania to Paris, where he worked briefly in Rodin's studio. He began to explore direct carving in marble (producing many versions of Rodin's *The Kiss*). By the 1930s he had achieved monumental simplicity with structures of simple repeated forms (*Endless Column* and other works in Tirgu Jiu public park, Romania). Brancusi was revered by his contemporaries, and remains a seminal figure in 20th-century sculpture.

Brand /brænd/ 'Dollar' (Adolf Johannes) 1934– . Former name of the South African musician Abdullah ◊Ibrahim.

Brandenburg /'brændənbɜːg/ former Prussian and German province, capital Potsdam. It was divided 1945 between Poland and East Germany.

The area, then inhabited by Slavonic tribes, was conquered in the 12th century by Albert the Bear. Frederick of Hohenzollern became margrave 1415, and an elector of the Holy Roman Empire; the elector Frederick III became Frederick I of Prussia 1701. When Germany was united 1871, Brandenburg became one of its provinces. That part of it east of the river Oder came under Polish administration, as agreed at the Potsdam Conference 1945; the remainder became a *Land* (region) of East Germany, abolished 1952 when its boundaries were obliterated in the newly created administrative counties of Neubrandenburg, Potsdam, Frankfurt-an-der-Oder, and Cottbus.

Brandenburg /'brændənbɜːg/ town in E Germany, on the river Havel, 60 km/36 mi W of Berlin; population (1981) 94,700. Industries include textiles, cars, and aircraft. It has a 12th-century cathedral.

Brando /'brændəʊ/ Marlon 1924– . US actor, whose casual, mumbling speech and use of ◊Method acting earned him a place as one of the most distinctive screen actors. His films include *A Streetcar Named Desire* 1951, *On the Waterfront* 1954 (Academy Award), *The Godfather* and *Last Tango in Paris* both 1972.

Brandt /brænt/ Bill 1905–1983. British photographer who produced a large body of richly printed and romantic black-and-white studies of people, London life, and social behaviour.

Brandt /brænt/ Willy. Adopted name of Karl Herbert Frahm 1913– . West German socialist politician, federal chancellor (premier) 1969–74. He played a key role in the remoulding of the Social Democratic Party (SPD) as a moderate socialist force (chair 1964–87). As mayor of West Berlin 1957–66, Brandt became internationally known during the Berlin Wall crisis 1961. Nobel Peace Prize 1971.

Brandt, born in Lübeck, changed his name when he fled to Norway 1933 and became active in the anti-Nazi resistance. He returned 1945 and entered the Bundestag (federal parliament) 1949. In the 'grand coalition' 1966–69 he served as foreign minister and introduced *Ostpolitik*, a policy of reconciliation between East and West Europe, which was continued when he became federal chancellor 1969, and culminated in the 1972 signing of the Basic Treaty with East Germany. He resigned from the chancellorship 1974 following the discovery that a close aide, Günther Guillaume, had been an East German spy. Brandt continued to wield considerable influence in the SPD, especially over the party's new radical left wing. He chaired the Brandt Commission 1977–83, and was a member of the European Parliament 1979–83.

Brandt Commission officially the Independent Commission on International Development Issues, established in 1977 and chaired by the former West German chancellor Willy Brandt.

Branson British entrepreneur Richard Branson, 1986.

Consisting of 18 eminent persons acting independently of governments, the commission examined the problems of developing countries and sought to identify corrective measures that would command international support. It was disbanded in 1983.

Its main report, published in 1980 under the title *North–South: A Programme for Survival*, made detailed recommendations for accelerating the development of poorer countries (involving the transfer of resources to the latter from the rich countries).

brandy (Dutch *brandewijn* 'burnt wine') spirit distilled from fermented grape juice (notably that of France, for example Armagnac and Cognac), or that of other fruits such as calvados (from apples) and Kirschwasser (from cherries). Brandy contains up to 55% alcohol.

Brangwyn /'bræŋgwɪn/ Frank 1867–1956. British artist. Of Welsh extraction, he was born in Bruges, Belgium. He initially worked for William Morris as a textile designer. He produced furniture, pottery, carpets, schemes for interior decoration, and architectural designs, as well as book illustrations, lithographs, and etchings.

Branson /'brænsən/ Richard 1950– . British entrepreneur, whose Virgin company developed quickly, diversifying from retailing records to the airline business.

He was born in Surrey, England, and the 1968 launch of *Student* magazine proved to be the first of his many successful business ventures. There are plans for Virgin to begin transmissions from a direct satellite link in 1990.

Braque /brɑːk/ Georges 1882–1963. French painter, who, with Picasso, founded the Cubist movement around 1907–10. They worked together at L'Estaque in the south of France and in Paris. Braque soon began to experiment in collages, and invented a technique of gluing paper, wood, and other materials to canvas. His later work became more decorative.

Brasília /brə'zɪliə/ capital of Brazil from 1960, some 1,000 m/3,000 ft above sea level; population (1980) 411,500. It was designed by Lucio Costa (1902–63), with Oscar Niemeyer as chief architect, as a completely new city to bring life to the interior.

brass

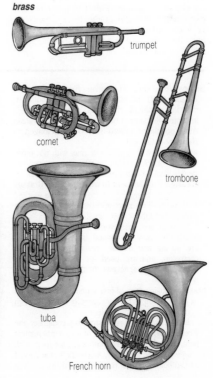

trumpet

cornet

trombone

tuba

French horn

Brazil
Federative Republic of
(*República Federativa do Brasil*)

area 8,511,965 sq km/3,285,618 sq mi
capital Brasília
towns São Paulo, Belo Horizonte, Curitiba, Fortaleza; ports are Rio de Janeiro, Recife, Porto Alegre, Salvador
physical the densely forested Amazon basin covers the N half of the country with a network of rivers; the S is fertile; enormous energy resources, both hydroelectric (Itaipú dam on the Paraná, and Tucuruí on the Tocantins) and nuclear (uranium ores)
features Mount Roraima, Xingu National Park. Brazil is the world's sixth largest arms exporter, and sells training planes to the RAF. In 1988, the annual inflation rate was 600%.
head of state and government Fernando Collor from 1989
political system emergent democratic federal republic
political parties Social Democratic Party (PDS), moderate left-of-centre; Brazilian Democratic Movement Party (PMDB), centre-left; Liberal Front Party (PFL), moderate left-of-centre; Workers' Party, left-of-centre; National Reconstruction Party (PRN), centre-right
exports coffee, sugar, cotton, textiles, motor vehicles, iron, chrome, manganese, tungsten and other ores, as well as quartz crystals, industrial diamonds

currency cruzado (introduced 1986; value = 100 cruzeiros, the former unit) (44.13 = £1 Feb 1990)
population (1988) 144,262,000 (including 200,000 Indians, survivors of 5 million, especially in Rondonia and Mato Grosso, mostly living on reserves); annual growth rate 2.2%
life expectancy men 61, women 66
language Portuguese; 120 Indian languages
religion Roman Catholic 89%, Indian faiths
literacy 79% male/76% female (1985 est)
GDP $218 bn (1984); $1,523 per head of population
chronology
1822 Brazil became an independent empire, ruled by Dom Pedro, son of the refugee King John VI of Portugal.
1889 Monarchy abolished and republic established.
1891 Constitution for a federal state adopted.
1930 Dr Getulio Vargas became president.
1945 Vargas deposed by the military.
1946 New constitution adopted.
1950 Vargas returned to office.
1954 Vargas committed suicide.
1956 Juscelino Kubitschek became president.
1960 Capital moved to Brasília.
1961 João Goulart became president.
1964 Bloodless coup made Gen Castelo Branco president. He assumed dictatorial powers, abolishing free political parties.
1967 New constitution adopted. Branco succeeded by Marshal da Costa e Silva.
1969 Da Costa e Silva resigned and a military junta took over.
1974 Gen Ernesto Geisel became president.
1978 Gen Baptista de Figueiredo became president.
1979 Political parties legalized again.
1984 Mass calls for a return to fully democratic government.
1985 Tancredo Neves became first civilian president for 21 years. Neves died and was succeeded by the vice-president, José Sarney.
1988 New constitution approved, transferring power from the president to the congress. Measures announced to halt large-scale burning of Amazonian rainforest for cattle grazing.
1989 Forest Protection Service and Ministry for Land Reform abolished. International concern over how much of the Amazon has been burned. Fernando Color (PRN) elected president.

Braşov /brɑːˈʃɒv/ (Hungarian **Brassó**, German **Krondstadt**) industrial city (machine tools, industrial equipment, chemicals, cement, woollens) in central Romania at the foot of the Transylvanian Alps; population (1985) 347,000. It belonged to Hungary until 1920.

brass an ◊alloy of copper and zinc, with not more than 5% or 6% of other metals. The zinc content ranges from 20% to 45%, and the colour varies accordingly from coppery to whitish yellow. Brasses are usually classed into those that can be worked cold (up to 25% zinc) and those that are better worked hot (about 40% zinc).

Brasses are characterized by the ease with which they may be shaped and machined; they are strong and ductile, resist many forms of corrosion, and are used for electrical fittings, ammunition cases, screws, household fittings, and ornaments.

brass in music, class of instruments made of brass or other metal, which are directly blown through a 'cup' or 'funnel' mouthpiece.

In the symphony orchestra they comprise: the **French horn**, a descendant of the natural hunting horn, valved, and curved into a circular loop, with a wide bell; the **trumpet**, a cylindrical tube curved into an oblong, with a narrow bell and three valves

(the state **fanfare trumpet** has no valves); the **trombone**, an instrument with a 'slide' to vary the effective length of the tube (the **sackbut**, common from the 14th century, was its forerunner); and the **tuba**, normally the lowest-toned instrument of the orchestra; valved and with a very wide bore to give sonority, it has a bell that points upward.

In the brass band (in descending order of pitch) they comprise: the **cornet**, a three-valved instrument, looking like a shorter, broader trumpet, and with a wider bore; the **flugelhorn**, a valved instrument, rather similar in range to the cornet; the **tenor horn**; **B-flat baritone**; **euphonium**; **trombone**; and **bombardon** (bass tuba). A brass band normally also includes bass and side drums, triangle, and cymbals.

Brassaï /ˌbræsɑːˈiː/ Adopted name of Gyula Halesz 1899–1986. French photographer of Hungarian origin. From the early 1930s on he documented, mainly by flash, the nightlife of Paris, before turning to more abstract work.

Brassica genus of plants of the family Cruciferae. The best-known species is the common cabbage *Brassica oleracea* with its varieties broccoli, cauliflower, kale, and brussels sprouts.

Bratby /ˈbrætbi/ John 1928– . British artist, one of the leaders of the 'kitchen-sink' school of

the 1950s (so called because of a preoccupation in early work with working-class domestic interiors.)

Bratislava /ˈbrætɪslɑːvə/ (German **Pressburg**, Hungarian **Pozsony**) industrial port (engineering, chemicals, oil refining) in Czechoslovakia, on the Danube; population (1986) 417,000. It was the capital of Hungary 1526–1784, and is now capital of the Slovak Socialist Republic and second largest city in Czechoslovakia.

Brattain /ˈbrætn/ Walter Houser 1902–1987. US physicist. In 1956, he was awarded a Nobel prize jointly with William Shockley and John Bardeen for their work on the development of the transistor, which replaced the comparatively costly and clumsy vacuum tube in electronics.

He was born in Amoy, China, the son of a teacher. During 1929–67 he was on the staff of Bell Telephone Laboratories.

Brauchitsch /ˈbrauxɪtʃ/ Walther von 1881–1948. German field marshal. A staff officer in World War I, he became in 1938 commander in chief of the army and a member of Hitler's secret cabinet council. He was dismissed after his failure to invade Moscow 1941. Captured in 1945, he died before being tried.

Braun /braun/ Eva 1910–1945. German Nazi. Secretary to Hitler's photographer and personal friend, Heinrich Hoffmann, she was Hitler's mistress for years, and married him in the air-raid shelter of the Chancellery in Berlin on 29 Apr 1945. They then committed suicide together.

Braunschweig /ˈbraunʃvaɪk/ German form of ◊Brunswick.

Brautigan /ˈbrɔːtɪgən/ Richard 1935–1984. US novelist, author of playful fictions of modern California such as *Trout Fishing in America* 1967, and Gothic works like *The Hawkline Monster* 1974.

Brazil /brəˈzɪl/ country in South America, bounded to the SW by Uruguay, Argentina, Paraguay and Bolivia, to the W by Peru and Colombia, to the N by Venezuela, Guyana, Suriname and French Guiana, and to the E by the Atlantic Ocean.

government Brazil is a federal republic of 23 states, three territories and a federal district (Brasilia). There is a two-chamber national congress consisting of a senate of 69 members, on the basis of one senator per state, elected for an eight-year term, and a chamber of deputies, whose numbers vary, elected for a four-year term. The number of deputies is determined by the population of each state and each territory is represented by one deputy. Elections to both chambers are by universal suffrage. The cabinet is chosen by the president, who is elected by universal adult suffrage for a five-year term and is not eligible for re-election. The states and the federal district each have an elected governor. The two main political parties are the Social Democratic Party (PDS) and the Brazilian Democratic Movement Party (PMDB).

history Inhabited from about 5000 BC by American Indians, Brazil was a Portuguese colony from AD 1500. In 1808, after ◊Napoleon invaded Portugal, King John VI moved his capital from Lisbon to Brazil. In 1821 he returned to Lisbon and his son, Crown Prince Pedro, remained as regent. In 1822 Pedro declared Brazil an independent kingdom and took the title Emperor Pedro I His son, Pedro II, persuaded large numbers of Portuguese to emigrate and the centre of Brazil developed quickly, largely on the basis of slavery, which was abolished in 1888, despite right-wing opposition. In 1889 a republic was founded and in 1891 a constitution for a federal state adopted.

After social unrest in the 1920s, the world economic crisis of 1930 produced a revolt which brought Dr Getúlio Vargas to the presidency. He held office, as a benevolent dictator, until the army forced him to resign in 1945 and Gen Eurico Dutra became president. In 1950 Vargas returned to power but committed suicide in 1954 and was succeeded by Dr Juscelino Kubitschek.

In 1961 Dr Jânio Quadros became president but resigned after seven months, to be succeeded by Vice-President João Goulart. Suspecting him of having left-wing leanings, the army forced a restriction of presidential powers and created the office of prime minister. A referendum in 1963 brought back the presidential system, with Goulart choosing his own cabinet.

In a bloodless coup in 1964, Gen Castelo Branco assumed dictatorial powers and banned all political groupings except for two artificially created parties, the pro-government National Renewal Alliance (ARENA) and the opposition PMBD. In 1967 Branco named Marshal da Costa e Silva as his successor and a new constitution was adopted. In 1969 da Costa e Silva resigned because of ill health and a military junta took over. In 1974 Gen Ernesto Geisel became president until succeeded by Gen Baptista de Figueiredo in 1978. In 1979 the ban on opposition parties was lifted.

President Figueiredo held office until 1985; his last few years as president witnessing economic decline, strikes, and calls for the return of democracy. In 1985 Tancredo Neves became the first civilian president for 21 years, but died within months of taking office. He was succeeded by Vice-President José Sarney, who continued to work with Neves' cabinet and policies. The constitution was again amended to allow direct presidental elections. In Mar 1989 the moderate members of PMDB and PDS, the Liberal Party Front (PFL), pulled out of their coalition with PMDB, forcing President Sarney to reconstruct the government. In the Dec 1989 presidential election Fernando Collor of the National Reconstruction Party (PRN) narrowly defeated Luis Inacio da Silva of the Workers' Party.

Brazil nut seed, rich in oil and highly nutritious, of the South American tree *Bertholletia excelsa.* The seeds are enclosed in a hard outer casing, each fruit containing 10–20 arranged like the segments of an orange. The timber of the tree is also valuable.

brazing a method of joining two metals by melting an ◊alloy into the joint. It is similar to soldering but takes place at a much higher temperature. Copper and silver alloys are widely used for brazing, at temperatures up to about 900°C.

Brazzaville /'bræzəvɪl/ capital of the Congo, industrial port (foundries, railway repairs, shipbuilding, shoes, soap, furniture, bricks) on the river Zaïre, opposite Kinshasa; population (1984) 595,000. It was the African headquarters of the Free (later Fighting) French during World War II. There is a cathedral 1892 and the Pasteur Institute 1908. It stands on Pool Malebo (Stanley Pool).

Brazzaville was founded by the Italian Count Pierre Savorgnan de Brazza (1852–1905), employed in African expeditions by the French government.

breast

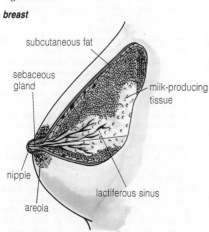

subcutaneous fat
sebaceous gland
milk-producing tissue
nipple
lactiferous sinus
areola

Brecht German dramatist and poet Bertolt Brecht.

bread food made with ground cereals, usually wheat, and water, though with many other variants of the contents. The dough may be unleavened or raised (usually with yeast) and then baked.

Bread has been a staple of human diet in many civilizations as long as agriculture has been practised, and some hunter-gatherer peoples made it from crushed acorns or beech nuts. Potatoes, banana, and cassava bread are among some local specialities, but most breads are made from fermented cereals which form glutens when mixed with water. The earliest bread was unleavened and was made from a mixture of flour and water and dried in the sun on flat stones. The Egyptians first used ovens and made leavened bread. The yeast creates gas making the dough rise.

Traditionally, bread has been made from whole grains: wheat, barley, rye, or oats, ground into a meal which varied in quality. Modern manufacturing processes have changed this to optimize profit and shorten manufacturing time. Fermentation is speeded up by using ascorbic acid and potassium bromide with fast-acting flour improvers. White bread was developed by the end of the 19th-century by roller-milling, which removed the wheat germ to satisfy fashionable consumer demand.

breadfruit fruit of a tree *Artocarpus communis* of the mulberry family Moraceae. It is highly nutritious, and when toasted is said to taste like bread. It is native to the South Sea Islands.

Breakspear /'breɪkspɪə/ Nicholas. Original name of ◊Adrian IV, the only English pope.

bream deep-bodied, flattened fish *Abramis brama* of the carp family, growing to about 50 cm/1.6 ft, typically found in lowland rivers across Europe. The sea breams are also deep-bodied flattened fish, but unrelated, belonging to the family Sparidae. The **red sea bream** *Pagellus bogaraveo*, up to 45 cm/1.5 ft, is heavily exploited as a food fish in the Mediterranean.

Bream /briːm/ Julian (Alexander) 1933– . British virtuoso of the guitar and lute. He has revived much Elizabethan lute music and encouraged composition by contemporaries for both instruments. Britten and Henze have written for him.

breast organ on upper front of the human female, also known as a ◊mammary gland. Each of the two breasts contains milk-producing cells, and a network of tubes or ducts which lead to an opening in the nipple.

Milk-producing cells in the breast do not become active until a woman has given birth to a baby. Breast milk is made from substances extracted from the mother's blood as it passes through the breasts. It contains all the nourishment a baby needs, including antibodies to help fight infection.

Breathalyzer instrument for on-the-spot checking by the police of the amount of alcohol in the blood of a suspect driver, who breathes into a plastic bag connected to a tube containing a chemical (such as a diluted solution of potassium dichromate in 50% sulphuric acid) that changes colour. Another method is to use a gas chromatograph, again from a breath sample.

breathing in terrestrial animals, the process of taking air into the lungs for ◊gas exchange. It is sometimes referred to as external respiration, for true respiration is a cellular (internal) process.

breccia a coarse clastic ◊sedimentary rock, made up of broken fragments (clasts) of pre-existing rocks. It is similar to ◊conglomerate but the fragments in breccia are large and jagged.

Brecht /brext/ Bertolt 1898–1955. German dramatist and poet, who aimed to destroy the 'suspension of disbelief' usual in the theatre and to express Marxist ideas. He adapted John Gay's *Beggar's Opera* as *Die Dreigroschenoper/The Threepenny Opera* 1928, set to music by Kurt Weill. Later plays include *Mutter Courage/Mother Courage* 1941, set in the Thirty Years' War, and *Der kaukasische Kreidekreis/The Caucasian Chalk Circle* 1949.

As an anti-Nazi, he left Germany in 1933 for Scandinavia and the USA. He became an Austrian citizen after World War II, and in 1949 established the Berliner Ensemble theatre group in East Germany.

Brecknockshire /'breknɒkʃə/ former county of Wales, merged in ◊Powys in 1974.

Breda /breɪˈdɑː/ town in North Brabant, Netherlands; population (1988) 156,000. It was here that Charles II of England made the declaration that paved the way for his restoration 1660.

Breda, Treaty of /breɪˈdɑː/ 1667 treaty that ended the Second Anglo-Dutch War (1664–67). By the terms of the treaty, England gained New Amsterdam, which was renamed New York.

breed a recognizable group of domestic animals, within a species, with distinctive characteristics that have been produced by ◊artificial selection.

Breeders' Cup end-of-season racehorse meeting in the USA. Leading horses from the USA and Europe compete for $10 million prize money, with the top prize going to the winner of the Breeders' Cup Turf. It was first held 1984.

breeding in biology, the crossing and selection of animals and plants to change the characteristics of an existing ◊breed or ◊cultivar (variety), or to produce a new one.

breeding in nuclear physics, process in a reactor in which more fissionable material is produced than is consumed in running the reactor. For example, plutonium-239 can be made from the relatively plentiful (but non-fissile) uranium-238, or uranium-233 can be produced from thorium. The Pu-239 or U-233 can then be used to fuel other reactors. The French breeder reactor *Phénix*, one of the most successful, generates 250 megawatts of electrical power.

Breizh /breiz/ Celtic name for ◊Bretagne, region of France.

Bremen /'breɪmən/ industrial port (iron, steel, oil refining, chemicals, aircraft, shipbuilding, cars) in West Germany, on the Weser 69 km/43 mi from the open sea; population (1988) 522,000.

Bremen was a member of the ◊Hanseatic League, and a free imperial city from 1646. It became a member of the North German Confederation 1867, and of the German Empire 1871.

Bremen /'breɪmən/ administrative region (German *Land*) of West Germany, consisting of the cities of Bremen and Bremerhaven; area 400 sq km/154 sq mi; population (1988) 652,000.

Bremerhaven /ˌbreɪməˈhɑːfən/ formerly (until 1947) *Wesermünde* port at the mouth of the Weser, Germany; population (1988) 132,000. Industries include fishing and shipbuilding. It serves as an outport for Bremen.

Brennan /'brenən/ Christopher (John) 1870–1932. Australian Symbolist poet, influenced by Baudelaire and Mallarmé. Although one of Australia's greatest poets, he is virtually unknown outside his native country. His complex, idiosyncratic verse includes *Poems* 1914 and *A Chant of Doom and Other Verses* 1918.

Brennan /'brenən/ Walter 1894–1974. US actor, often seen in Westerns as the hero's sidekick. His work includes *The Westerner* 1940, *Bad Day at Black Rock* 1955, and *Rio Bravo* 1959.

Brenner /'brenə/ Sidney 1927– . South African scientist, one of the pioneers of genetic engineering. Brenner discovered messenger ◊RNA (a link between ◊DNA and ◊ribosomes, where proteins are synthesized) 1960.

Brenner studied medicine at university, but then moved into molecular biology at Oxford. He worked for many years with Francis Crick, doing much research on the nematode worm.

Brenner Pass /'brenə/ lowest of the Alpine passes, 1,370 m/4,495 ft; it leads from Trentino–Alto Adige, Italy, to the Austrian Tirol, and is 19 km/12 mi long.

Brentano /bren'tɑːnəʊ/ Franz 1838–1916. German-Austrian philosopher, whose *Psychology from the Empirical Standpoint* 1874 developed the concept of 'intentionality', the directing of the mind to an object, for example in perception.

Brentano /bren'tɑːnəʊ/ Klemens 1778–1842. German writer, leader of the Young ◊Romantics. He published a seminal collection of folktale and song with Ludwig von ◊Arnim (*Des Knaben Wunderhorn*) 1805–08, and popularized the legend of the Lorelei (a rock in the ◊Rhine). He also wrote mystic religious verse *Romanzen vom Rosenkranz* 1852.

Brenton /'brentən/ Howard 1942– . British dramatist, noted for *The Romans in Britain* 1980 and a translation of Brecht's *The Life of Galileo*.

Brescia /'breʃə/ ancient *Brixia* historic and industrial city (textiles, engineering, firearms, metal products) in N Italy, 84 km/52 mi E of Milan; population (1988) 199,000. It has medieval walls and two cathedrals (12th and 17th centuries).

Breslau /'breslaʊ/ German name of ◊Wroclaw, town in Poland.

Brest /brest/ naval base and industrial port (electronics, engineering, chemicals) on *Rade de Brest* (Brest Roads), a great bay at the western extremity of Bretagne, France; population (1983) 201,000. Occupied as a U-boat base by the Germans 1940–44, the town was destroyed by Allied bombing and rebuilt.

Brest /brest/ town in Byelorussia, USSR, on the river Bug and the Polish frontier; population (1987) 238,000. It was in Poland (*Brześć nad Bugiem*) until 1795 and 1921–39. The *Treaty of ◊Brest-Litovsk* (an older Russian name of the town) was signed here.

Brest-Litovsk, Treaty of treaty signed 3 Mar 1918 between Russia and Germany, Austria-Hungary, and their allies. Under it, Russia agreed to recognize the independence of the Baltic states, Georgia, Ukraine, and Poland, and pay heavy compensation. Under the Nov 1918 Armistice that ended World War I, it was annulled.

Bretagne /bre'tən/ (English *Brittany*) region of NW France in the Breton peninsula between the Bay of Biscay and the English Channel; area 27,200 sq km/10,499 sq mi; population (1986) 2,764,000. Its capital is Rennes, and includes the *départements* of Côte-du-Nord, Finistère, Ille-et-Vilaine, and Morbihan. It is a farming region.

history Bretagne was established by the Celts in the 5th century and was the Gallo-Roman province of Armorica after being conquered by Julius Caesar 56 BC. It was devastated by Norsemen after the Roman withdrawal. During the Anglo-Saxon invasion of Britain so many Celts migrated across the Channel that it gained the name of Brittany. It became a strong, expansionist state which maintained its cultural and political independence, despite pressure from the Carolingians, Normans, and Capetians. In 1171, the duchy of Brittany was inherited by Geoffrey, son of Henry II of England, and remained in the Angevin dynasty's possession until 1203, when Geoffrey's son Arthur was murdered by King ◊John, and the title passed to the Capetian Peter of Dreux. Under the Angevins,

Brezhnev *Soviet leader Leonid Brezhnev. Appointed secretary-general of the Communist Party in 1964 and president in 1977, he held both offices until his death.*

feudalism was introduced, and French influence greatly increased under the Capetians. By 1547 it had been formally annexed by France, and the ◊Breton language was banned in education. A separatist movement developed after World War II, and there has been guerrilla activity.

Brétigny, Treaty of /ˌbretɪn'jiː/ treaty made between Edward III of England and John II of France in 1360 at the end of the first phase of the Hundred Years' War, under which Edward received Aquitaine and its dependencies in exchange for renunciation of his claim to the French throne.

Breton /'bretɒn/ André 1896–1966. French author, among the leaders of ◊Dada. *Les Champs magnétiques/Magnetic Fields* 1921, an experiment in automatic writing, was one of the products of the movement. He was also a founder of ◊Surrealism, publishing *Le Manifeste de surréalisme/Surrealist Manifesto* 1924. Other works include *Najda* 1928, the story of his love affair with a medium.

Breton language a member of the Celtic branch of the Indo-European language family; the language of Brittany in France, related to Welsh and Cornish, and descended from the speech of Celts who left Britain as a consequence of the Anglo-Saxon invasions of the 5th and 6th centuries. Officially neglected for centuries, Breton is now a recognized language of France.

Bretton Woods /'bretn/ township in New Hampshire, USA, where the United Nations Monetary and Financial Conference was held in 1944 to discuss post-war international payments problems. The agreements reached on financial assistance and measures to stabilize exchange rates led to the creation of the International Bank for Reconstruction and Development in 1945 and the International Monetary Fund.

Breuer /'brɔɪə/ Josef 1842–1925. Viennese physician, one of the pioneers of psychoanalysis. He applied it successfully to cases of hysteria, and collaborated with Freud in *Studien über Hysterie/Studies in Hysteria* 1895.

Breuer /'brɔɪə/ Marcel 1902– . Hungarian-born architect and designer, who studied and taught at the ◊Bauhaus. His tubular steel chair 1925 was the first of its kind. He moved to England, then to the USA, where he was in partnership with Gropius 1937–40. His buildings show an affinity with natural materials; the best known is the Bijenkorf, Rotterdam (with Elzas) 1953.

Breuil /'brɔɪ/ Henri 1877–1961. French prehistorian, professor of historic ethnography and director of research at the Institute of Human Palaeontology, Paris, from 1910. He established the genuine antiquity of Palaeolithic cave art and stressed the anthropological approach to the early human history.

breviary (Latin 'a summary or abridgement') in the Roman Catholic church, the book of instructions for reciting the daily services. It is usually in four volumes, one for each season.

brewing the making of ◊beer, ale, or other alcoholic beverage from ◊malt and ◊barley by steeping (mashing), boiling, and fermenting.

brewster unit (symbol B) for measuring the reaction of optical materials to stress, defined in terms of the slowing-down of light passing through the material when it is stretched or compressed.

Brewster /'bruːstə/ David 1781–1868. Scottish physicist, who made discoveries regarding the diffraction and polarization of light, and invented the kaleidoscope.

Brezhnev /'breʒnef/ Leonid Ilyich 1906–1982. Soviet leader. A protégé of Stalin and Khrushchev, he came into power as general secretary of the Soviet Communist Party (CPSU) 1964–82 and was president 1977–82. Domestically he was conservative; abroad, the USSR established itself as a military and political superpower during the Brezhnev era, extending its influence in Africa and Asia.

Brezhnev, born in Ukraine, joined the CPSU in the 1920s. In 1938 he was made head of propaganda by the new Ukrainian party chief Khrushchev, and ascended in the local party hierarchy. After World War II he caught the attention of the CPSU leader Stalin, who inducted Brezhnev into the secretariat and Politburo 1952. Brezhnev was removed from these posts after Stalin's death 1953, but returned 1956 with Khrushchev's patronage. In 1960, as criticism of Khrushchev mounted, he was moved to the ceremonial post of state president and began to criticize Khrushchev's policies.

Brezhnev stepped down as president 1963 and returned to the Politburo and secretariat. He was elected CPSU general secretary 1964, when Khrushchev was ousted, and gradually came to dominate the conservative and consensual coalition. In 1977 he regained the additional title of state president under the new constitution. He suffered an illness (thought to have been a stroke or heart attack) Mar–Apr 1976 which was believed to have affected his thought and speech so severely that he was not able to make decisions. These were made by his entourage, for example committing troops to Afghanistan to prop up the government there. Within the USSR, economic difficulties mounted; the Brezhnev era was a period of caution and stagnation, although outwardly imperialist.

Brezhnev Doctrine Soviet doctrine 1968 designed to justify the invasion of Czechoslovakia. It laid down for the USSR as a duty the direct maintenance of 'correct' socialism in countries within the Soviet sphere of influence. In 1979 it was extended, by the invasion of Afghanistan, to the direct establishment of 'correct' socialism in countries not already within its sphere. The doctrine was renounced by Mikhail ◊Gorbachev in 1989. Soviet troops were withdrawn from Afghanistan and the satellite states of E Europe were allowed to decide their own forms of government, with non-communist and 'reform communist' governments being established from Sept 1989.

Brian /'braɪən/ Havergal 1876–1972. English composer of 32 symphonies in visionary romantic style, including the *Gothic* 1919–27 for large choral and orchestral forces.

Brian /'braɪən, bə'ruː/ known as *Brian Boru* ('Brian of the Tribute') 926–1014. King of Ireland from 976, who took Munster, Leinster, and Connacht to become ruler of all Ireland. He defeated the Norse at Clontarf, thus ending

bridge

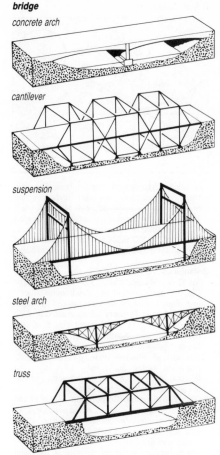

concrete arch

cantilever

suspension

steel arch

truss

Norse control of Dublin, although he was himself killed. His exploits were celebrated in several chronicles.

Briand /bri'ɒn/ Aristide 1862–1932. French radical socialist politician. He was prime minister 1909–11, 1913, 1915–17, 1921–22, 1925–26, and 1929, and foreign minister 1925–32. In 1925 he concluded the ◊Locarno Pact and in 1928 the ◊Kellogg–Briand Pact; in 1930 he outlined a scheme for a United States of Europe.

bric-à-brac (French) odds and ends, usually old, ornamental, less valuable than antiques.

brick a common building material, rectangular in shape, made of clay that has been fired in a kiln. Bricks are made by kneading a mixture of crushed clay and other materials into a stiff mud and extruding it into a ribbon. The ribbon is cut into individual bricks which are fired at a temperature up to about 1,000°C. Bricks may alternatively be pressed into shape in moulds.

Refractory bricks used to line furnaces are made from heat-resistant materials such as silica and dolomite. They must withstand operating temperatures of 1,500°C or more. Sun-dried bricks of mud reinforced with straw were first used in Mesopotamia some 8,000 years ago. Similar mud bricks, called adobe, are still used today in Mexico and other countries where the climate is warm and dry.

bridewealth or **brideprice** the goods or property presented by a man and his family to the family of his wife as part of their marriage agreement. It is the usual practice among peoples in parts of Africa, Asia, and the Pacific. In most S Asian countries the alternative custom is ◊dowry.

Bridewealth is regarded as compensation to the woman's family for giving her away in marriage, and it usually means that the children she bears will belong to her husband's family group rather than her own. It may require a large amount

of valuables such as livestock, shell items, and cash. People whose own customs do not include bridewealth, particularly Europeans, have often criticized it as 'buying' a wife, on the assumption that it subjugates women to men more than other kinds of marriage.

bridge a construction that provides a continuous path or road over water, valleys, ravines, or above other roads. Bridges may be classified into four main groups: **arch**, for example Sydney Harbour bridge (steel arch) with a span of 503 m/1,650 ft; **beam or girder**, for example Rio–Niteroi, Guanabara Bay, Brazil, centre span 300 m/984 ft, length 13,900 m/8 mi 3,380 ft; ◊**cantilever**, for example Forth rail bridge, Scotland, which is 1,658 m/5,440 ft long with two main spans, two cantilevers each, one from each tower; **suspension**, for example Humber bridge, England, with a centre span of 1,410 m/4,628 ft.

The world's longest suspension bridge is the Minami Bisan-seto Bridge in Japan: 1,723 m/5,655 ft. It is part of the Seto Ohashi, or Great Bridge of Seto, a system of six bridges linking the islands of Honshu and Shikoku, opened 1988. Steel is pre-eminent in the construction of long-span bridges because of its high strength-to-weight ratio, but in other circumstances reinforced concrete has the advantage of lower maintenance costs. The Newport Transporter Bridge (built 1906) is a high-level suspension bridge which carries a car suspended a few feet above the water. It was used in preference to a conventional bridge where expensive high approach roads would have to be built.

bridge card game derived from whist. First played among members of the Indian Civil Service about 1900, bridge was brought to England in 1903 and played at the Portland Club in 1908. It is played in two forms: ◊auction bridge and ◊contract bridge.

Bridge /brɪdʒ/ Frank 1879–1941. English composer, the teacher of Benjamin Britten. His works include the orchestral *The Sea* 1912, and *Oration* 1930 for cello and orchestra.

Bridgeport /'brɪdʒpɔːt/ city in Connecticut, USA, on Long Island Sound; population (1980) 142,500. Industries include metal goods, electrical appliances and aircraft. The university was established 1927. The nearby town of Stratford has the American Shakespeare Festival Theater.

Bridges /'brɪdʒɪz/ Robert (Seymour) 1844–1930. British poet, Poet Laureate from 1913, author of *The Testament of Beauty* 1929, a long philosophical poem. In 1918 he edited and published posthumously the poems of Gerard Manley ◊Hopkins.

Bridgetown /'brɪdʒtaʊn/ port and capital of Barbados, founded 1628; population (1987) 8,000. Sugar is exported through the nearby deep-water port.

Bridget, St /'brɪdʒɪt/ 453–523. A patron saint of Ireland, also known as St Brigit or *St Bride*. She founded a church and monastery at Kildare, and is said to have been the daughter of a prince of Ulster. Feast day 1 Feb.

Bridgewater /'brɪdʒwɔːtə/ Francis Egerton, 3rd Duke of Bridgewater 1736–1803. Pioneer of British inland navigation. With James ◊Brindley as his engineer, he constructed 1762–72 the Bridgewater canal from Worsley to Manchester, and thence to the Mersey, a distance of 67.5 km/42 mi.

Bridgman /'brɪdʒmən/ Percy Williams 1882–1961. US physicist. His research into machinery producing high pressure led in 1955 to the creation of synthetic diamonds by General Electric.

Born in Cambridge, Massachusetts, he was educated at Harvard, where he was Hollis professor of mathematics and natural philosophy 1926–50 and Higgins university professor 1950–54.

Bridgwater /'brɪdʒwɔːtə/ port in Somerset, England, on the river Parret; population (1981) 26,000. Industries include plastics and electrical goods. The site of the Battle of ◊Sedgemoor is 5 km/3 mi SE.

Bridie /'braɪdi/ James. Pen name of Osborne Henry Mavor 1888–1951. Dramatist and professor of medicine, and a founder of Glasgow

Citizens' Theatre. His plays include *Tobias and the Angel* 1930, and *The Anatomist* 1931.

Brieux /bri'ɜː/ Eugène 1858–1932. French dramatist, an exponent of the naturalistic problem play attacking social evils. His most powerful plays are *Les trois filles de M Dupont* 1897; *Les Avariés/Damaged Goods* 1901, long banned for its outspoken treatment of syphilis; and *Maternité*.

Briggs /brɪgz/ Barry 1934– . New Zealand motorcyclist who won four individual world speedway titles 1957–66 and took part in a record 87 world championship races. In the British League he rode for Wimbledon, New Cross, Southampton, Swindon, and Hull.

CAREER HIGHLIGHTS

World Champion:
individual: 1957–58, 1964, 1966
team: 1968, 1971
British League Riders Champion: 1965–70

Brighouse /'brɪghaʊs/ Harold 1882–1958. British playwright. Born and bred in Lancashire, in his most famous play, *Hobson's Choice* 1916, he dealt with a Salford bootmaker's courtship, using the local idiom.

Bright /braɪt/ John 1811–1889. British Liberal politician, a campaigner for free trade, peace, and social reform. A Quaker millowner, he was among the founders of the Anti-Corn Law League in 1839, and was largely instrumental in securing the passage of the Reform Bill of 1867.

After entering Parliament in 1843 Bright led the struggle there for free trade, together with Richard ◊Cobden, which achieved success in 1846. His *laissez-faire* principles also made him a prominent opponent of factory reform. His influence was constantly exerted on behalf of peace, as when he opposed the Crimean War, Palmerston's aggressive policy in China, Disraeli's anti-Russian policy, and the bombardment of Alexandria. During the American Civil War he was outspoken in support of the North. He sat in Gladstone's cabinets as president of the Board of Trade 1868–70 and chancellor of the Duchy of Lancaster 1873–74 and 1880–82, but broke with him over the Irish Home Rule Bill. Bright owed much of his influence to his skill as a speaker.

Bright /braɪt/ Richard 1789–1858. British physician. He was for many years on the staff of Guy's Hospital, London; *Bright's disease*, an inflammation of the kidneys, is named after him.

Brighton /'braɪtn/ resort on the E Sussex coast, England; population (1981) 146,000. It has Regency architecture and Brighton Pavilion 1782 in oriental style. There are two piers and an aquarium. The University of Sussex was founded 1963.

history Originally a fishing village called Brighthelmstone, it became known as Brighton at the beginning of the 19th century, when it was already a fashionable health resort patronized by the Prince Regent, afterwards George IV.

brill flatfish *Scophthalmus laevis*, which lives in shallow water over sandy bottoms in the NE Atlantic and Mediterranean. It is a freckled sandy brown, and grows to 60 cm/2 ft.

Brillat-Savarin /'bri'jɑː ˌsævə'ræ̃/ Jean Anthelme 1755–1826. French gastronome, author of *La Physiologie du Goût* 1825, a compilation of observations on food and drink regarded as the first great classic of gastronomic literature. Most of his professional life was spent as a politician.

Brindisi /'brɪndɪzi/ (ancient *Brundisium*) port and naval base on the Adriatic, in Puglia, on the heel of Italy; population (1981) 90,000. Industries include food processing and petrochemicals. It is one of the oldest Mediterranean ports, at the end of the Appian Way from Rome. The poet Virgil died here 19 BC.

Brindley /'brɪndli/ James 1716–1772. British canal builder, the first to employ tunnels and aqueducts extensively, in order to reduce the number of locks on a direct-route canal. His 580 km/360 mi of canals included the Bridgewater (Manchester–Liverpool) and Grand Union (Manchester–Potteries) canals.

brine common name for a solution of sodium chloride (NaCl) in water. Brines are used extensively in the food manufacturing industry for canning of vegetables, pickling vegetables (sauerkraut manufacture), and curing of meat.

Brinell /brɪˈnel/ Johann Auguste 1849–1925. Swedish engineer, who devised the Brinell hardness test in 1900.

Brinell hardness test test for the hardness of a substance according to the area of indentation made by a 10-mm/0.4-in hardened steel or sintered tungsten carbide ball under standard loading conditions in a test machine. It is equal to the load (kg) divided by the surface area (mm²), and is named after its inventor Johann Brinell.

Brisbane /ˈbrɪzbən/ industrial port (brewing, engineering, tanning, tobacco, shoes; oil pipeline from Moonie), capital of Queensland, E Australia, near the mouth of Brisbane river, dredged to carry ocean-going ships; population (1986) 1,171,300

Brisbane /ˈbrɪzbən/ Thomas Makdougall 1773–1860. Scottish soldier, colonial administrator, and astronomer. After serving in the Napoleonic Wars under Wellington, he was governor of New South Wales 1821–25, and Brisbane in Queensland is named after him. He catalogued over 7,000 stars.

brisling the processed form of sprat *Sprattus sprattus* fished in Norwegian fjords, then seasoned and canned.

Brissot /briːˈsəʊ/ Jacques Pierre 1754–1793. French revolutionary leader, born in Chartres. He became a member of the legislative assembly and the National Convention, but his party of moderate republicans, the ◊Girondins, or Brissotins, fell foul of Robespierre and Brissot was guillotined.

bristlecone pine see ◊pine.

bristletail primitive wingless insect, order Thysanura. Up to 2 cm/0.8 in long, bristletails have a body tapering from front to back, two long antennae and three 'tails' at the rear end. They include the *silverfish Lepisma saccharina* and the *firebrat Thermobia domestica.*

Two-tailed bristletails, order Diplura, live under stones and fallen branches, feeding on decaying material.

Bristol /ˈbrɪstəl/ industrial port (aircraft engines, engineering, microelectronics, tobacco, chemicals, paper, printing), administrative headquarters of Avon, SW England; population (1986) 391,000. The old docks have been redeveloped for housing, industry, yachting facilities, and the National Lifeboat Museum.

features 12th-century cathedral; 14th-century St Mary Redcliffe; 16th-century Acton Court, built by Sir Nicholas Poynz, a courtier of Henry VIII;

Brindley A portrait of James Brindley, the first canal builder to use tunnels and aqueducts extensively.

the Georgian residential area of Clifton; the Clifton Suspension Bridge designed by Brunel and his SS *Great Britain*, which is being restored in dry dock.

history John Cabot sailed from here 1497 to Newfoundland, and there was a great trade with the American colonies and the West Indies in the 17th–18th centuries, including slaves. The poet Chatterton was born here.

Bristow Eric 1957– . English darts player nicknamed 'the Crafty Cockney'. He has won all the game's major titles, including the world professional title a record five times between 1980 and 1986.

CAREER HIGHLIGHTS

World professional champion: 1980–81, 1984–86
World Masters: 1977, 1979, 1981, 1983–84
World Cup (team): 1979, 1981, 1983, 1985, 1987
World Cup (individual): 1983, 1985
British Open: 1978, 1981, 1983, 1985–86
News of the World: 1983–84
World Pairs: 1987 (with Peter Locke)

Britain or *Great Britain* island off the NW coast of Europe, one of the British Isles. It consists of ◊England, ◊Scotland, and ◊Wales, and is part of the ◊United Kingdom. The name is derived from the Roman name Britannia, which is in turn derived from ancient Celtic.

Britain, ancient /ˈbrɪtn/ the period in the British Isles excluding Ireland from pre-history to the Roman occupation. Britain was inhabited for thousands of years by people who kept livestock and grew corn; traces of human occupation in the *Old Stone Age* have been found at Cheddar Caves, Somerset. In the *New Stone Age* they buried their chiefs in long ◊barrows; remains of flint mining can be found at Grimes Graves, Norfolk. In the *Bronze Age* they used round barrows. About 1800 BC, the ◊Beaker people invaded, and left traces of their occupation at Avebury and Stonehenge (stone circles). About 450 BC the *Iron Age* began. Around 400 BC Britain was conquered by the ◊Celts, who built hillforts and left burial sites containing chariots. The Celts were a tall, fair-haired people who migrated in two waves from Europe. First came the Goidelic Celts, of whom traces may still be seen in the Gaels of Ireland and the Highlands; there followed the Brythonic Celts or Bretons, who were closely allied in descent and culture to the Gauls of France. The early Britons were highly skilled in pottery and metalwork. Tin mines in Cornwall attracted merchant seamen from Carthage. In 55–54 BC Julius Caesar raided England. AD 43 was the beginning of the Roman conquest; surviving remains can be seen at Bath, Fishbourne (near Chichester), Hadrian's Wall, Watling Street, London (Temple of Mithras), Dover, St Alban's, and Dorchester. In 407 the Romans withdrew, but partially reoccupied the country about 417–27 and about 450. For later history, see ◊England, history; ◊Scotland, history; ◊Wales, history, and ◊United Kingdom.

Britain, Battle of /ˈbrɪtn/ World War II air battle between German and UK air forces over Britain lasting from 10 July to 12 Oct 1940.

At the outset the Germans had the advantage because they had seized airfields in the Netherlands, Belgium, and France, which were basically safe from attack and from which SE England was within easy range. On 1 Aug 1940 the Luftwaffe had about 4,500 aircraft of all kinds, compared to about 3,000 for the RAF. The Battle of Britain had been intended as a preliminary to the German invasion plan *Seelöwe* (Sea Lion), which Hitler indefinitely postponed 17 Sept and abandoned 10 Oct, choosing instead to invade the USSR.

The Battle of Britain has been divided into five phases: 10 July–7 Aug, the preliminary phase; 8–23 Aug, attack on coastal targets; 24 Aug–6 Sept, attack on Fighter Command airfields; 7–30 Sept, daylight attack on London, chiefly by heavy bombers; and 1–31 Oct, daylight attack

British Columbia

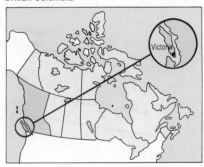

on London, chiefly by fighter-bombers. The main battle was between some 600 Hurricanes and Spitfires and the Luftwaffe's 800 Messerschmidt 109s and 1,000 bombers (Dornier 17s, Heinkel 111s, and Junkers 88s). Losses Aug–Sept were, for the RAF: 832 fighters totally destroyed; for the Luftwaffe: 668 fighters and some 700 bombers and other aircraft.

Britannicus /brɪˈtænɪkəs/ Tiberius Claudius *c.* AD 41–55. Roman prince, son of the Emperor Claudius and Messalina; so-called from his father's expedition to Britain. He was poisoned by Nero.

British Antarctic Territory colony created in 1962 and comprising all British territories S of latitude 60°S: the South Orkney Islands, the South Shetland Islands, the Antarctic Peninsula and all adjacent lands, and Coats Land, extending to the South Pole; total land area 660,000 sq km/170,874 sq mi. Scientific personnel are the only population: about 300.

British Broadcasting Corporation (BBC) in the UK, the state-owned broadcasting network, converted from a private company (established 1922) to a public body under royal charter 1927. It operates television, national and local radio stations, and is financed solely by the sale of television viewing licences. It is not allowed to carry advertisements, but overseas radio broadcasts (World Service) have a government subsidy.

British Columbia /kəˈlʌmbɪə/ province of Canada on the Pacific
area 947,800 sq km/365,851 sq mi
capital Victoria
towns Vancouver, Prince George, Kamloops, Kelowna
physical Rocky Mountains and Coast Range; the coast is deeply indented; rivers include the Fraser and Columbia; there are over 80 lakes; more than half the land is forested
products fruit and vegetables; timber and wood products; fish; coal, copper, iron, lead; oil and natural gas, and hydroelectricity
population (1986) 2,889,000
history Captain Cook explored the coast in 1778; a British colony was founded on Vancouver Island in 1849, and the gold rush of 1858 extended settlement to the mainland; it became a province in 1871. In 1885 the Canadian Pacific Railroad linking British Columbia to the E coast was completed.

British Commonwealth of Nations former official name of the ◊Commonwealth.

British Council semi-official organization set up 1935 (royal charter 1940) to promote a wider knowledge of the UK, excluding politics and commerce, and to develop cultural relations with other countries.

British Empire, Order of the British order of chivalry, instituted by George V in 1917. There are military and civil divisions, and the ranks are GBE, Knight Grand Cross or Dame Grand Cross; KBE, Knight Commander; DBE, Dame Commander; CBE, Commander; OBE, Officer; MBE, Member. In 1974 awards for civilian gallantry previously made within the order were replaced by the Queen's Gallantry Medal (QGM), which ranks after the George Cross and George Medal.

British Empire

Current name	Colonial names and history	Colonized	Independent
India	British E India Co. 18th cent.–1858	18th cent.	1947
Pakistan	British E India Co. 18th cent.–1858	18th cent.	1947
Sri Lanka	Portuguese, Dutch 1602–1796; Ceylon 1802–1972	16th cent.	1948
Ghana	Gold Coast	1618	1957
Nigeria		1861	1960
Cyprus	Turkish to 1878, then British rule	1878	1960
Sierra Leone	British protectorate	1788	1961
Tanzania	German E Africa to 1921; British mandate from League of Nations/UN as Tanganyika	19th cent.	1961
Jamaica	Spanish to 1655	16th cent.	1962
Trinidad & Tobago	Spanish 1532–1797; British 1797–1962	1532	1962
Uganda	British protectorate	1894	1962
Kenya	British colony from 1920	1895	1963
Malaysia	British interests from 1786; Federation of Malaya 1957–63	1874	1963
Malawi	British protectorate of Nyasaland 1907–53; Federation of Rhodesia & Nyasaland 1953–64	1891	1964
Malta	French 1798–1814	1798	1964
Zambia	N Rhodesia—British protectorate; Federation of Rhodesia and Nyasaland 1953–64	1924	1964
The Gambia		1888	1965
Singapore	Federation of Malaya 1963–65	1858	1965
Guyana	Dutch to 1796; British Guiana 1796–1966	1620	1966
Botswana	Bechuanaland—British protectorate	1885	1966
Lesotho	Basutoland	1868	1966
Bangladesh	British E India Co. 18th cent.–1858; British India 1858–1947; E Pakistan 1947–71	18th cent.	1971
Zimbabwe	S Rhodesia from 1923; UDI under Ian Smith 1965–79	1895	1980

British Empire the various territories all over the world conquered or colonized by Britain from about 1600, most now independent or lost to other powers; the British Empire was at its largest at the end of World War I, with over 25% of the world's population and area. The ◊Commonwealth is composed of former and remaining territories of the British Empire.

The first successful British colony was Jamestown, Virginia, founded 1607. British settlement spread up and down the east coast of North America and by 1664, when the British secured New Amsterdam (New York) from the Dutch, there was a continuous fringe of colonies from the present South Carolina in the south to what is now New Hampshire in the north. These colonies, and others formed later, had their own democratic institutions, but the attempt of George III and his minister Lord North to coerce the colonists into paying taxes to Britain roused them to resistance, which came to a head in the War of ◊American Independence 1775–81 and led to the creation of the United States of America from the 13 English colonies then lost.

Colonies and trading posts were set up in many parts of the world by the British, who also captured them from other European empire builders. Settlements were made in Gambia and on the Gold Coast 1618; in Bermuda 1609 and others of the West Indian islands; Jamaica was taken from Spain 1655; Acadia (Nova Scotia) was secured from France by the Treaty of Utrecht 1713, which recognized Newfoundland and Hudson Bay (as well as Gibraltar in Europe) as British. New France (Québec), Cape Breton Island, and Prince Edward Island became British as a result of the Seven Years' War 1756–63.

In the Far East, the East India Company, chartered 1600, set up factories, as their trading posts were called, on the W coast of India at Surat, 1612; on the E coast at Madras, 1639; and on the Hooghli, one of the mouths of the Ganges, 1640. Bombay came to the British crown 1662, and was granted to the East India Company for £10 a year. A struggle in the following century between the French and British East India companies ended 1763 in the triumph of the British. The company, subsequently involved in more than one war with Indian princes, steadily increased its possessions and the territories over which it held treaty rights up to the eve of the Indian Mutiny 1857. Although

this rising was put down, it resulted in the taking over of the government of British India by the crown 1858; Queen Victoria was proclaimed Empress of India 1 Jan 1877. Ceylon (now Sri Lanka) had also been annexed to the East India Company 1796, and Burma (now Myanmar), after a series of Anglo-Burmese Wars from 1824, became a province of British India 1886.

Constitutional development in Canada started with an act 1791 which set up Lower Canada (Québec), mainly French-speaking, and Upper Canada (Ontario), mainly English-speaking. In the War of 1812, the USA wrongly assumed that Canada would join the union. But there was sufficient discontent there to lead to rebellion 1837 in both Canadas. After the suppression of these risings, Lord Durham was sent out to advise on the affairs of British North America; his report, published 1839, became the basis for the future structure of the Empire. In accordance with its recommendations, the two Canadas were united 1840 and given a representative legislative council: the beginning of colonial self-government. With the British North America Act 1867, the self-governing dominion of Canada came into existence; to the original union of Ontario, Québec, New Brunswick, and Nova Scotia were later added further territories until the federal government of Canada controlled all the northern part of the continent except Alaska.

In the antipodes, colonization began with the desire to find a place for penal settlement after the loss of the original American colonies. The first shipload of convicts landed in Australia 1788 on the site of the future city of Sydney. New South Wales was opened to free settlers 1819, and in 1853 transportation of convicts was abolished. Before the end of the century five Australian colonies—New South Wales, Western Australia, South Australia, Victoria, Queensland—and the island colony of Tasmania had each achieved self-government; an act of the Imperial Parliament at Westminster created the federal commonwealth of Australia, an independent dominion, 1901. New Zealand, annexed 1840, was at first a dependency of New South Wales. It became a separate colony 1853 and a dominion 1907.

The Cape of Good Hope in South Africa was occupied by two English captains 1620, but neither the home government nor the East India Company was interested. The Dutch occupied it

1650, and Cape Town remained a port of call for their East India Company until 1795 when, French revolutionary armies having occupied the Dutch Republic, the British seized it to keep it from the French, and under the Treaty of Paris 1814 bought it from the new kingdom of the Netherlands for $6 million. British settlement began 1824 on the coast of Natal, proclaimed a British colony 1843.

The need to find new farmland and establish independence from British rule led a body of Boers (Dutch 'farmers') from the Cape to make the Great Trek northeast 1836, to found Transvaal and Orange Free State. Conflict between the British government, which claimed sovereignty over those areas (since the settlers were legally British subjects), and the Boers culminated, after the discovery of gold in the Boer territories, in the South African War 1899–1902, which brought Transvaal and Orange Free State definitely under British sovereignty. Given self-government 1907, they were formed, with Cape Colony (self-governing 1872) and Natal (self-governing 1893), into the Union of South Africa 1910, fourth dominion of the Empire. The British South Africa Company, chartered 1889, extended British influence over Southern Rhodesia (a colony 1923) and Northern Rhodesia (a protectorate 1924); with Nyasaland, taken under British protection 1891, the Rhodesias were formed into a federation 1953–63 with representative government. Uganda was made a British protectorate 1894. Kenya, formerly a protectorate, became a colony 1920, certain districts on the coast forming part of the sultan of Zanzibar's dominions remaining a protectorate.

In W Africa, British control was extended from time to time in Gambia and the Gold Coast. Sierra Leone colony was founded 1788 with the cession of a strip of land to provide a home for liberated slaves; a protectorate was established over the hinterland 1896. British influence in Nigeria began through the activities of the National Africa Company (the Royal Niger Company from 1886) which bought Lagos from an African chief 1861, and steadily extended its hold over the Niger Valley until it surrendered its charter 1899; in 1900 the two protectorates of N and S Nigeria were proclaimed. World War I ousted Germany from the African continent, and in 1921–22, under League of Nations mandate, Tanganyika was transferred to British administration, SW Africa to South Africa; Cameroons and Togoland, in West Africa, were divided between Britain and France.

The establishment of the greater part of Ireland as the Irish Free State, with dominion status, occurred 1922. A new constitution adopted by the Free State 1937 dropped the name and declared Ireland (Eire) to be a 'sovereign independent state'; 12 years later Southern Ireland became a republic outside the Commonwealth, though remaining in a special relationship with Britain.

British India became independent 1947 as the two dominions of India (predominantly Hindu in religion) and Pakistan (predominantly Muslim). India decided to become a republic 1950 but, with the full consent of the other members, to remain within the Commonwealth. This made it simple for other members to adopt a similar status on becoming independent, since it entails recognition of the Queen as head of the Commonwealth, but not as ruler of the individual state.

British Expeditionary Force (BEF) a British army serving in France in World War I 1914–18; also the 1939–40 army in Europe in World War II, which was evacuated from Dunkirk, France. The BEF commanders in World War I were first J French and then D Haig; in World War II Gen Gort.

British Honduras former name of ◊Belize, a country in Central America.

British Indian Ocean Territory British colony in the Indian Ocean directly administered by the Foreign and Commonwealth Office. It consists of the

Chagos Archipelago, some 1,900 km/1,200 mi NE of Mauritius
area 60 sq km/23 sq mi
features lagoons; US naval and air base on Diego Garcia
products copra, salt fish, tortoiseshell
population (1982) 3,000
history purchased in 1965 for $3 million by Britain from Mauritius to provide a joint US/UK base.

The island of Aldabra, Farquhar, and Desroches, some 485 km/300 mi N of Madagascar, originally formed part of the British Indian Ocean Territory, but were returned to the administration of the Seychelles in 1976.

British Isles group of islands off the NW coast of Europe, consisting of Great Britain (England, Wales, and Scotland), Ireland, the Channel Islands, Orkney and Shetland, the Isle of Man, and many others which are included in various counties, such as the Isle of Wight, Scilly Isles, Lundy Island, and the Inner and Outer Hebrides. The islands are divided from Europe by the North Sea, Strait of Dover, and the English Channel, and face the Atlantic to the west.

British Legion organization to promote the welfare of British veterans of war service and their dependants. Established under the leadership of D Haig in 1921 (royal charter 1925) it became the **Royal British Legion** 1971; it is nonpolitical. The sale on Remembrance Sunday of Flanders poppies made by disabled members raises much of its funds.

British Library the national library of the UK. Created 1973, it comprises the **reference division** (the former library departments of the British Museum, being rehoused at the Euston Road, London, site); **lending division** at Boston Spa, Yorkshire, from which full text documents and graphics can be sent, using a satellite link, to other countries; and **bibliographic services division** (incorporating the British National Bibliography).

British Museum largest museum of the UK. Founded in 1753 with the purchase of Hans Sloane's library and art collection, and the subsequent acquisition of the Cottonian, Harleian, and other libraries, the British Museum was opened at Montagu House, Bloomsbury, London, in 1759.

Rapid additions led to the construction of the present buildings (designed by Robert Smirke) by 1852, with later extensions in the circular reading room (1857), and the N wing or Edward VII galleries (1914). In 1881 the Natural History Museum was transferred to S Kensington.

British Somaliland /sə'mɑ:lilænd/ British protectorate over 176,000 sq km/67,980 sq mi of territory on the Somali coast of Africa from 1884 until the independence of Somalia in 1960. British authorities were harassed by a self-proclaimed messiah known as the 'Mad Mullah' from 1901 until 1910.

British Standards Institute (BSI) the UK national standards body. Although government funded, the institute is independent. The BSI interprets international technical standards for the UK, and also sets its own. For consumer goods, it sets standards which products should reach (the BS standard), as well as testing products to see that they conform to that standard (as a result of which the product may be given the BSI 'kite' mark).

British Telecom a British company that formed part of the Post Office until 1980, and was privatized in 1984. It is responsible for ◊telecommunications, including the telephone network, and radio and television broadcasting. Previously a monopoly, it now faces commercial competition for some of its services. It operates Britain's ◊viewdata network called ◊Prestel.

British thermal unit imperial unit (symbol Btu) of heat, now replaced in the SI system by the ◊joule (1 Btu is approximately 1,055 joules). Burning 1 cubic foot of natural gas releases about 1,000 Btus of heat.

One Btu is defined as the amount of heat required to raise the temperature of 0.45 kg/1 lb of

Britten *English composer Benjamin Britten.*

water by 1°F. The exact value depends on the original temperature of the water.

British Virgin Islands part of the ◊Virgin Islands group in the West Indies.

British Volunteer Programme name embracing the various schemes under which volunteers from the UK have been sent to work in overseas developing countries since 1966. Voluntary Service Overseas (VSO), (1958) is the best known of these organizations, which inspired the US ◊Peace Corps.

Brittain /'brɪtn/ Vera 1894–1970. English socialist writer, a nurse to the troops overseas 1915–19, as told in her *Testament of Youth* 1933; *Testament of Friendship* 1950 commemorated Winifred ◊Holtby. She married political scientist Sir George Catlin (1896–1979); their daughter is Shirley ◊Williams.

Brittan /'brɪtn/ Leon 1939– . British Conservative politician and lawyer. Chief secretary to the Treasury 1981–83, home secretary 1983–85, secretary for trade and industry 1985–86 (resigned over his part in the ◊Westland affair) and senior European Commissioner from 1988.

Brittany /brə'tænj/ English name for ◊Bretagne, region of W France.

Britten /'brɪtn/ (Edward) Benjamin, 1913–1976. English composer. He often wrote for the individual voice; for example the title role in the opera *Peter Grimes* 1945, based on verses by Crabbe, was created for Peter ◊Pears. Among his many works are the *Young Person's Guide to the Orchestra* 1946; the chamber opera *The Rape of Lucretia* 1946; *Billy Budd* 1951; *A Midsummer Night's Dream* 1960; and *Death in Venice* 1973.

Britten studied at the Royal College of Music. From 1939 to 1942 he worked in the USA, then returned to England and devoted himself to composing at his home in ◊Aldeburgh, Suffolk, where he established an annual music festival. His oratorio *War Requiem* 1962 was written for the re-dedication of Coventry Cathedral.

brittle-star type of ◊starfish, with a small, central, rounded body and long, flexible, spiny arms used for walking. The **small brittle-star** *Amphipholis squamata* is greyish, about 4.5 cm/2 in across, and found on the seabed almost worldwide. It broods its young, and its arms can be luminous.

About 2,000 species of brittle-star and basket-star are known, composing the ◊echinoderm class Ophiuroidea.

BRM (British Racing Motors) racing-car manufacturer founded 1949 by Raymond Mays. Their early days in Grand Prix racing were a disaster and it was not until 1956 that they started having moderate success. Their first Grand Prix win was 1959, and in the next thirty years they won 17

Grand Prix races. Their world champions include Graham Hill.

Brno /'bɜːnəʊ/ industrial city in central Czechoslovakia (chemicals, arms, textiles, machinery), population (1984) 380,800. Now third largest city in Czechoslovakia, Brno was formerly capital of the Austrian crownland of Moravia.

Broad /brɔːd/ Charles Dunbar 1887–1971. British philosopher. His books include *Perception, Physics and Reality* 1914, and *Lectures on Psychic Research* 1962, discussing modern scientific evidence for survival after death.

Born in London, he was educated at Trinity College, Cambridge, and was Knightbridge professor of moral philosophy at the university 1933–53.

broad arrow the mark resembling an arrowhead on British government stores. Of doubtful origin, the broad arrow came into general use in the 17th century and is still used to mark government property, such as military supplies. It has long been abolished on prison dress.

broadbill bird of the family Eurylaimidae found in Africa and S Asia. Broadbills are forest birds and are often found near water. They have brilliant coloration and wide bills, and feed largely on insects.

broadcasting the transmission of sound and vision programmes by radio and television. Broadcasting may be organized under complete state control, as in the USSR, or private enterprise, as in the USA, or may operate under a compromise system, as in Britain, where there is a television and radio service controlled by the state-regulated ◊British Broadcasting Corporation (the BBC), and also commercial ◊Independent Television (formerly the Independent Broadcasting Authority).

In the USA, broadcasting is only limited by the issue of licences from the Federal Communications Commission to competing commercial companies; in Britain, the BBC is a centralized body appointed by the state and responsible to Parliament, but with policy and programme content not controlled by the state; in Japan, which ranks next to the USA in the number of television sets owned, there is a semi-governmental radio and television broadcasting corporation (NHK) and numerous private television companies.

broad-leaved tree another name for a tree belonging to the ◊angiosperms, such as ash, beech, oak, maple, or birch. Their leaves are generally broad and flat, in contrast to the needle-like leaves of most ◊conifers. See also ◊deciduous tree.

Broadmoor /'brɔːdmɔː/ special hospital (established 1863) in Crowthorne, Berkshire, England, for those formerly described as 'criminally insane'.

Broads, Norfolk /brɔːdz/ area of some twelve interlinked freshwater lakes in E England, created about 600 years ago by the digging out of peat deposits; they are noted for wildlife and boating facilities.

Broadway /'brɔːdweɪ/ major avenue in New York running from the tip of Manhattan NW and crossing Times Square at 42nd Street, at the heart of the theatre district, where Broadway is knwn as 'the Great White Way'. New York theatres situated outside this area are described as **off-Broadway**; those even smaller and farther away are **off-off-Broadway**.

broccoli a variety of ◊cabbage.

Broch /brɒx/ Hermann 1886–1951. Austrian novelist, who used experimental techniques in *Die Schlafwandler/The Sleepwalkers* 1932, *Der Tod des Vergil/The Death of Virgil* 1945, and *Die Schuldlosen/The Guiltless*, a novel in 11 stories. He went to the USA 1938 after being persecuted by the Nazis.

Brocken /'brɒkən/ highest peak of the Harz Mountains (1,142 m/3,746 ft) in East Germany. On 1 May (Walpurgis night) witches were said to gather here.

The **Brocken Spectre** is a phenomenon of mountainous areas, so named because first scientifically observed at Brocken in 1780. The greatly enlarged shadow of the observer, accompanied by coloured rings, is cast by a low sun upon a cloud bank.

brocket name for a deer stag in its second year, when it has short straight pointed antlers. *Brocket deer* genus *Mazama* include a number of species of small, shy, solitary deer found in Central and South America. They are up to 1.3 m/4 ft in body length and 65 cm/2 ft at the shoulder, and have similar small straight antlers even when adult.

broderie anglaise (French 'English embroidery') a type of embroidered fabric, usually white cotton, in which holes are cut in patterns and oversewn, often to decorate lingerie, shirts, and skirts.

Brodsky /'brɒdski/ Joseph 1940– . Russian poet, who emigrated to the USA in 1972. His work, often dealing with themes of exile, is admired for its wit and economy of language, particularly in its use of understatement. Many of his poems, written in Russian, have been translated into English (*A Part of Speech* 1980). More recently he has also written in English. Nobel prize 1987.

Broglie, de see ◊de Broglie.

Broken Hill /'brəʊkən/ mining town in New South Wales, Australia; population (1981) 27,000. It is the base of the Royal Flying Doctor Service.

Broken Hill /'brəʊkən/ town in Zambia, formerly called ◊Kabwe, until 1967.

brolga Australian crane *Grus rubicunda*, about 1.5 m/5 ft tall, mainly grey with a red patch on the head.

Bromberg /'brɒmbɜ:g/ German name of ◊Bydgoszcz, port in Poland.

brome general name for annual grasses of the genus *Bromus* and some related grasses.

bromeliad plant of the family Bromeliaceae, to which the pineapple belongs. Bromeliads originate in tropical America, where there are some 1,400 species. Some are terrestrial, growing in habitats ranging from scrub desert to tropical forest floor. Many, however, are epiphytes and grow on trees. The epiphytes are supported by the tree but do not take nourishment from it, instead using rain and decayed plant and animal remains for sustenance. Some species, such as *Spanish moss Tillandsia usneoides*, can even grow on telegraph wires.

In many bromeliads the leaves are arranged in rosettes, and in some the leaf bases trap water to form little pools, in which organisms ranging from microscopic to frog may pass the whole life cycle. Many bromeliads have attractive flowers; often, too, the leaves are coloured and patterned. They are therefore popular greenhouse plants.

Bromfield /'brɒmfi:ld/ Louis 1896–1956. US novelist. His most notable books are *The Strange Case of Miss Annie Spragg* 1928, and *Mrs Parkington* 1943, dealing with the golden age of New York society.

bromide a chemical compound derived from ◊bromine in which bromine is the more ◊electronegative element. Bromides may be ionic compounds containing a bromide ion (Br⁻) or non-ionic compounds containing covalent bonds (usually bromine joined to a non-metal).

bromine an element that exists as a red, volatile liquid at room temperature; symbol Br, atomic number 35, relative atomic mass 79.909. Bromine is poisonous and a member of the halogen series of elements.

It is found in small quantities in sea water and is used as an anti-knock petrol additive. Its compounds are used in photography and in the chemical and pharmaceutical industries. Salts of bromine are known as bromides.

bromocriptine a drug that mimics the actions of the naturally occurring substance dopamine. It acts on the pituitary gland to inhibit the release of prolactin, the hormone that regulates lactation, and thus reduces or suppresses milk production. It is also used in the treatment of Parkinson's disease.

Bromocriptine may also be given to control excessive prolactin secretion, and to treat prolactinoma (a hormone-producing tumour). Recent research has established its effectiveness in reversing some cases of infertility.

bronchitis inflammation of the bronchi (air passages) of the lungs, usually caused initially by a viral infection, such as a cold or flu. It is aggravated by environmental pollutants.

bronchodilator a drug that relieves obstruction of the airways by causing the bronchi and bronchioles to relax and widen. It is useful in the treatment of asthma.

Bronson Charles. Stage name of Charles Bunchinsky 1922– . US film actor. His films are mainly violent thrillers such as *Death Wish* 1974. He was one of *The Magnificent Seven* 1960.

Brontë /'brɒnti/ family of English writers, including the three sisters *Charlotte* (1816–55), *Emily Jane* (1818–48), and *Anne* (1820–49), and their brother *Patrick Branwell* (1817–48). Their best-known works are Charlotte Brontë's *Jane Eyre* 1847 and Emily Brontë's *Wuthering Heights* 1847. Later works include Anne's *The Tenant of Wildfell Hall* 1848 and Charlotte's *Shirley* 1849 and *Villette* 1853.

The Brontë's were brought up by an aunt at Haworth rectory (now a museum) in Yorkshire. In 1846 the sisters published a volume of poems under the pen names Currer (Charlotte), Ellis (Emily), and Acton (Anne) Bell. In 1847 (using the same names) they published the novels *Jane Eyre, Wuthering Heights*, and *Agnes Grey*, Anne's much weaker work. During 1848–49 Branwell, Emily, and Anne all died of tuberculosis, aided in Branwell's case by alcohol and opium addiction; he is remembered for his portrait of the sisters. Charlotte married her father's curate, A B Nicholls, in 1854, and died during pregnancy.

Bronx, the /'brɒŋks/ borough of New York City, USA, NE of Harlem river; area 109 sq km/ 42 sq mi; population (1980) 1,169,000. Largely residential, it is named after an early Dutch settler, James Bronck.

bronze ◊alloy of copper and tin, yellow or brown in colour. It is harder than pure copper, more suitable for ◊casting, and also resists ◊corrosion. Bronze may contain as much as 25% tin, together with small amounts of other metals, particularly lead. Bronze is one of the first metallic alloys known and used widely by early peoples during the period of history known as the Bronze Age.

Bell-metal, the bronze used for casting bells, contains 15% or more tin. *Phosphor bronze* is hardened by the addition of a small percentage of phosphorus. *Silicon bronze* (for telegraph wires) and *aluminium bronze* are similar alloys of copper with silicon or aluminium and small amounts of iron, nickel, or manganese, but usually no tin.

Bronze Age period of early history and prehistory when bronze was the chief material used for tools and weapons. It lies between the Stone Age and the Iron Age and may be dated 5000–1200 BC in the Middle East and about 2000–500 BC in Europe. Recent discoveries in Thailand suggest that the Far East, rather than the Middle East, was the cradle of the Bronze Age.

Mining and metalworking were the first specialized industries, and the invention of the wheel revolutionized transport. Agricultural productivity, and hence the size of the population that could be supported, was transformed by the ox-drawn plough.

Bronzino /brɒnd'zi:nəʊ/ Agnolo 1503–1572. Italian painter active in Florence, court painter to Cosimo I, Duke of Tuscany. He painted in an elegant, Mannerist style, and is best known for portraits and the allegory *Venus, Cupid, Folly and Time* about 1545 (National Gallery, London).

Brook /brʊk/ Peter 1925– . British theatrical producer and director. Known for his experimental productions with the Royal Shakespeare Company in England, he began working with the

Brontë Emily, Anne, and Charlotte Brontë painted by their brother, Patrick Branwell, c. 1835.

Paris-based Le Centre International de Créations Théâtrales in 1970. Films he has directed include *Lord of the Flies* 1962 and *Meetings with Remarkable Men* 1979.

Brooke /brʊk/ James 1803–1868. British administrator who became rajah of Sarawak, on Borneo, 1841.

Born near Benares, he served in the army of the East India Company. In 1838 he headed a private expedition to Borneo, where he helped to suppress a revolt, and when the sultan gave him the title of rajah of Sarawak Brooke became known as the 'the white rajah'. He was succeeded as rajah by his nephew, Sir Charles Johnson (1829–1917), whose son Sir Charles Vyner (1874–1963) in 1946 arranged for the transfer of Sarawak to the British crown.

Brooke /brʊk/ Peter Leonard 1934– . British Conservative politician. The son of a former home secretary, Lord Brooke of Cumnor, he entered the House of Commons in 1977. He was appointed chairman of the Conservative Party by Margaret Thatcher in 1987. He was made Northern Ireland secretary in 1989.

Educated at Marlborough and Balliol College, Oxford, Brooke worked as a management consultant in New York and Brussels. He became an MP in 1977 and entered Thatcher's government in 1979. Following a number of junior appointments, he succeeded Norman Tebbit as chair of the Conservative Party in 1987. After an undistinguished two years in that office, he succeeded Tom King as Northern Ireland secretary. He aroused criticism for observing that at some future time negotiations with the IRA might take place.

Brooke /brʊk/ Rupert Chawner 1887–1915. English poet, symbol of the World War I 'lost generation'. His poems, the best-known being the five war sonnets (including 'Grantchester' and 'The Great Lover'), were published posthumously.

Born in Rugby, where he was educated, Brooke travelled abroad after a nervous breakdown in 1911, but in 1913 won a fellowship at King's College, Cambridge. Later that year he toured America (*Letters from America* 1916), New Zealand, and the South Seas, and in 1914 became an officer in the Royal Naval Division. After fighting at Antwerp, he sailed for the Dardanelles, but died of blood-poisoning on the Greek island of Skyros, where he is buried.

Brookeborough /'brʊkbərə/ Basil Brooke, Viscount Brookeborough 1888–1973. Unionist politician of Northern Ireland. He entered Parliament in 1929, held ministerial posts 1933–45, and was prime minister of Northern Ireland 1943–63. He was a staunch advocate of strong links with Britain.

Brook Farm farm in W Roxbury, near Boston, Massachusetts, USA, which in 1841–47 was the scene of an idealistic experiment in communal living, led by George Ripley (1802–80), a former Unitarian minister. Financial difficulties and a fire led to the community's dissolution.

Brooklands former UK motor racing track near Weybridge, Surrey. One of the world's first

Brooks *Louise Brooks as Lulu in* Pandora's Box *1928.*

purpose-built circuits, it was opened 1907 as a testing ground for early motorcars. It was the venue for the first British Grand Prix (then known as the RAC Grand Prix) 1926. It was sold to aircraft builders Vickers 1946.

Brooklyn /'brʊklɪn/ borough of New York City, USA, occupying the SW end of Long Island. It is linked to Manhattan Island by Brooklyn Bridge 1883 and others, and by the Verrazano-Narrows Bridge (see ◊bridge) 1964 to Staten Island. Brooklyn US Navy Yard is here. Of the more than 60 parks, Prospect is the most important. There is also a botanic garden, and a beach and funfair at Coney Island.

Brookner /'brʊknə/ Anita 1928– . British novelist and art historian, whose novels include *Hotel du Lac* 1984, winner of the Booker prize, *A Misalliance* 1986, and *Latecomers* 1988.

Brooks /brʊks/ Louise 1906–1985. US actress, known for her roles in silent films such as *Die Büchse der Pandora/Pandora's Box* and *Das Tagebuch einer Verlorenen/Diary of a Lost Girl* both 1929, and directed by G W ◊Pabst. She retired from the screen 1938.

Brooks /brʊks/ Mel. Assumed name of Melvin Kaminsky 1926– . US film director, whose comic films include *Blazing Saddles* 1974 and *History of the World Part I* 1981.

broom shrub of the family Leguminosae, especially species of *Cytisus*, such as the yellow-flowered **common broom** *Cytisus scoparius* of Britain.

Broome David 1940– . British show jumper. He won the 1970 world title on a horse named Beethoven. His sister (Liz Edgar) is also a top-class show jumper.

CAREER HIGHLIGHTS

World Championship:
individual: bronze 1960, gold 1970
team: gold 1978; bronze 1982
Olympic Games:
individual: bronze 1960, 1968

Brothers Karamazov, The a novel by Dostoievsky, published 1879–80. It describes the reactions and emotions of four brothers after their father's murder. One of them is falsely convicted of the crime, although his illegitimate brother is guilty.

Brougham /brʊm/ Henry Peter, 1st Baron Brougham and Vaux 1778–1868. British Whig politician and lawyer. From 1811 he was chief adviser to the Princess of Wales (afterwards Queen Caroline), and in 1820 he defeated the attempt of George IV to divorce her. He was lord chancellor 1830–34, supporting the Reform Bill.

Born in Edinburgh, he was a founder of the *Edinburgh Review* 1802. He sat in Parliament 1810–12 and from 1816, and supported the causes of public education and law reform. He was one of the founders of University College, London, 1828. When the Whigs returned to power 1830, Brougham accepted the chancellorship and a peerage a few weeks later. His allegedly dictatorial and eccentric ways led to his exclusion from office when the Whigs next assumed power 1835. After 1837 he was active in the House of Lords.

Brouwer /'braʊə/ Adriaen 1605–1638. Flemish painter who studied with Frans Hals. He excelled in scenes of peasant revelry.

Brown /braʊn/ 'Capability' (Lancelot) 1715–1783. English landscape gardener. He acquired his nickname because of his continual enthusiam for the 'capabilities' of natural landscapes. He advised on gardens of stately homes including Blenheim, Stowe, and Petworth, sometimes also contributing to the architectural designs.

Brown /braʊn/ (James) Gordon 1951– . British Labour politician. He entered Parliament in 1983, rising quickly to the opposition front bench, with a reputation as an outstanding debater.

Brown, the son of a Church of Scotland minister, won a first in history at Edinburgh University before he was 20. After four years as a college lecturer and three as a television journalist, he entered the House of Commons, for Dunfermline East in 1983. He topped the Labour Party shadow-cabinet poll in 1989.

Brown /braʊn/ Charles Brockden 1771–1810. US novelist and magazine editor. He is called the 'father of the American novel' for his *Wieland* 1798, *Ormond* 1799, *Edgar Huntly* 1799, and *Arthur Mervyn* 1800. His works also pioneered the Gothic and fantastic tradition of US fiction.

Brown /braʊn/ Earle 1926– . US composer who pioneered ◊graphic notation and mobile form during the 1950s. He was an associate of ◊Cage.

Brown /braʊn/ Ford Madox 1821–1893. British painter, associated with the ◊Pre-Raphaelite Brotherhood. His pictures include *The Last of England* 1855 (Birmingham Art Gallery) and *Work* 1852–65 (City Art Gallery, Manchester), packed with realistic detail and symbolic incident.

Brown /braʊn/ George, Baron George-Brown 1914–1985. British Labour politician. He entered Parliament 1945, was briefly minister of works 1951, and contested the leadership of the party on the death of Gaitskell, but was defeated by Harold Wilson. He was secretary for economic affairs 1964–66 and foreign secretary 1966–68. He was created a life peer 1970.

Brown /braʊn/ John 1800–1859. US slavery abolitionist. With 18 men, he seized, on the night of 16 Oct 1859, the government arsenal at Harper's Ferry in W Virginia, apparently intending to distribute weapons to runaway slaves who would then defend the mountain stronghold, which Brown hoped would become a republic of former slaves. On 18 Oct the arsenal was stormed by US Marines under Col Robert E ◊Lee. Brown was tried and hanged on 2 Dec, becoming a martyr and the hero of the popular song 'John Brown's Body' about 1860.

Born in Connecticut, he settled as a farmer in Kansas in 1855. In 1856 he was responsible for the 'Pottawatomie massacre' when five pro-slavery farmers were killed. In 1858 he formed the plan for a refuge for runaway slaves in the mountains of Virginia.

Brown /braʊn/ Robert 1773–1858. Scottish botanist, a pioneer of plant classification and the first to describe and name the cell nucleus.

On an expedition to Australia in 1801 he collected 4,000 species of plant and later classified them according to the 'natural' system of Bernard de Jussieu (1699–1777) rather than relying upon the system of ◊Linnaeus. The agitated movement of small particles suspended in water, now explained by kinetic theory, was described by Brown in 1827 and later became known as ***Brownian motion***.

Browne /braʊn/ Hablot Knight 1815–1882. British illustrator, pseudonym Phiz, known for his illustrations of Dickens's works.

Browne /braʊn/ Robert 1550–1633. English Puritan religious leader, founder of the Brownists. He was imprisoned several times in 1581–82 for attacking Episcopalianism. He founded a community in Norwich, East Anglia and in the Netherlands which continued on ◊Nonconformist lines, developing into modern ◊Congregationalism.

Browne, born in Stamford, Lincolnshire preached in Norwich and then retired to Middelburg in the Netherlands, but returned after making his peace with the church and became master of Stamford Grammar School. From 1591 he was a rector in Northamptonshire. In a work published in 1582 Browne advocated Congregationalist doctrine.

Browne /braʊn/ Thomas 1605–1682. English author and physician. Born in London, he travelled widely in Europe before settling in Norwich in 1637. He is noted for his personal richness of style in *Religio Medici/The Religion of a Doctor* 1643, a justification of his profession; *Vulgar Errors* 1646, an examination of popular legend and superstition; *Urn Burial* and *The Garden of Cyrus* 1658; and *Christian Morals* 1717. He was knighted in 1671.

Brownian movement continuous random motion of particles in a fluid medium (gas or liquid) as they are subject to impact from the molecules of the medium. This was observed in 1827 by the Scottish botanist Robert Brown (1773–1858), but not convincingly explained until ◊Einstein in 1905.

Browning /'braʊnɪŋ/ Elizabeth Barrett 1806–1861. English poet. In 1844 she published *Poems* (including 'The Cry of the Children'), which led to her friendship and secret marriage with Robert Browning in 1846. The *Sonnets from the Portuguese* 1847 were written during their courtship. Later works include *Casa Guidi Windows* 1851 and the poetic novel *Aurora Leigh* 1857.

Browning was born near Durham. As a child she fell from her pony and injured her spine, and was subsequently treated by her father as a confirmed invalid. Freed from her father's oppressive influence, her health improved, she wrote strong verse about social injustice and oppression in Victorian England.

Browning /'braʊnɪŋ/ Robert 1812–1889. English poet, married to Elizabeth Barrett Browning. His work is characterized by the use of dramatic monologue and an interest in obscure literary and historical figures. It includes the play *Pippa Passes* 1841, and the poems 'The Pied Piper of Hamelin' 1842, 'My Last Duchess' 1842, 'Home Thoughts from Abroad' 1845, and 'Rabbi Ben Ezra' 1864.

Browning, born in Camberwell, London, wrote his first poem 'Pauline' 1833 under the influence of Shelley; it was followed by 'Paracelsus' 1835

Browning *Lyric poet Elizabeth Barrett Browning was one of 12 children of a tyrannical father. Robert Browning admired her work; they married in 1846.*

Browning *Admired for his innovative works incorporating psychological analysis and obscure historical characters, Robert Browning was one of the most popular Victorian poets.*

and 'Sordello' 1840. In 1837 he achieved moderate success with his play *Strafford*, and in the pamphlet series of *Bells and Pomegranates* 1841–46, which contained *Pippa Passes*, *Dramatic Lyrics* 1842 and *Dramatic Romances* 1845, he included the dramas *King Victor and King Charles*, *Return of the Druses*, and *Colombe's Birthday*.

In 1846 he met Elizabeth Barrett; they married the same year and went to Italy. There he wrote *Christmas Eve and Easter Day* 1850 and *Men and Women* 1855, the latter containing some of his finest love-poems and dramatic monologues, which were followed by *Dramatis Personae* 1864, and *The Ring and the Book* 1868–69, based on an Italian murder story. After his wife's death in 1861 Browning settled in England and enjoyed an established reputation, although his late works, such as *Red-Cotton Night-Cap Country* 1873, *Dramatic Idylls* 1879–80, and *Asolando* 1889, still prompted opposition by their rugged obscurity of style.

brown ring test an analytical chemistry test for the detection of ◊nitrates.

Browns Ferry /ˌbraʊnz ˈferi/ site of a nuclear power station on the Alabama River, central Alabama. A nuclear accident in 1975 resulted in the closure of the plant for 18 months. This incident marked the beginning of widespread disenchantment with nuclear power in the USA.

Brownshirts the SA (*Sturm-Abteilung*), or Storm Troops, the private army of the German Nazi party; so called from the colour of their uniform.

Brubeck /ˈbruːbek/ Dave (David Warren) 1920– . US jazz pianist, a student of the French composer Milhaud. The Dave Brubeck Quartet (formed 1951) combined improvisation with modern classical discipline.

Bruce one of the most important Scottish noble houses. Robert I and his son, David II were both kings of Scotland descended from Robert de Bruis (died 1094), a Norman knight who came to England with William the Conqueror 1066.

Bruce /bruːs/ James 1730–1794. Scottish explorer, the first European to reach the source of the Blue Nile 1770, and to follow the river downstream to Cairo 1773.

Bruce /bruːs/ Robert de, 5th Lord of Annandale 1210–1295. Scottish noble, one of the unsuccessful claimants to the throne at the death of Alexander II 1290. His grandson was ◊Robert I (the Bruce).

Bruce /bruːs/ Robert the king of Scotland; see ◊Robert I.

Bruce /bruːs/ Stanley Melbourne, 1st Viscount Bruce of Melbourne 1883–1967. Australian

National Party politician, prime minister 1923–29. He was elected to parliament in 1918. As prime minister he introduced a number of social welfare measures.

brucellosis disease of cattle, goats, and pigs, also known when transmitted to humans as **undulant fever** since it remains in the body and recurs. It was named after Australian doctor David Bruce (1855–1931) and is caused by bacteria present in the milk of infected cattle. It has largely been eradicated in Britain through vaccination of the animals and pasteurization of milk.

Bruch /brʊx/ Max 1838–1920. German composer, professor at the Berlin Academy 1891. He wrote three operas including *Hermoine* 1872, *Kol Nidrei* for cello and orchestra, violin concertos, and many choral works.

Brücke, die /ˈbrʊkə/ (German 'the bridge') German Expressionist art movement 1905–13, formed in Dresden. Ernst Ludwig Kirchner was one of its founders and Emil Nolde a member 1906–07. Influenced by African art, they strove for spiritual significance, using raw colours to express different emotions. In 1911 the ◊Blaue Reiter took over as the leading group in German art.

Bruckner /ˈbrʊknə/ (Joseph) Anton 1824–1896. Austrian Romantic composer. He was cathedral organist at Linz 1856–68, and from 1868 he was professor at the Vienna Conservatoire. His works include many choral pieces and ten symphonies, the last unfinished. His compositions were influenced by ◊Wagner and Beethoven.

Bruderhof (German 'Society of Brothers') Christian Protestant sect with beliefs similar to the Mennonites. They live in groups of families (single persons are assigned to a family), marry only within the sect (divorce is not allowed), and retain a 'modest' dress for women (cap or headscarf, and long skirts).

Originally established in Germany, there are Bruderhof communities in the USA, and in Robertsbridge, E Sussex, UK; they support themselves by making children's toys.

Brueghel /ˈbrɜːxəl/ family of Flemish painters, the eldest of whom, *Pieter Brueghel* (c.1525–69), was one of the greatest artists of his time. He painted satirical and humorous pictures of peasant life, many of which include symbolic details illustrating folly and inhumanity, and a series of Months (five survive), including *Hunters in the Snow* (Kunsthistorisches Museum, Vienna).

Bruckner *Austrian composer Anton Bruckner. He was often persuaded to abridge and modify the orchestration of his lengthy works, so there are problems in establishing authentic versions.*

The elder Pieter was nicknamed 'Peasant' Brueghel. Two of his sons were painters. *Pieter Brueghel the Younger* (1564–1638), called 'Hell' Brueghel, specialized in religious subjects, and another son, *Jan Brueghel* (1568–1625), called 'Velvet' Brueghel, painted flowers and land- and seascapes.

Bruges /bruːʒ/ (Flemish *Brugge*) historic city in NW Belgium; capital of W Flanders province, 16 km/10 mi from the North Sea, with which it is connected by canal; population (1985) 117,700. Bruges was the capital of medieval ◊Flanders, and was the chief European wool manufacturing town as well as its chief market.

features Among many notable buildings are the 14th-century cathedral, the church of Nôtre Dame with a Michelangelo statue of the Virgin and Child, the Gothic town hall and market hall; there are remarkable art collections. It was named for its many bridges. The College of Europe is the oldest centre of European studies. The modern port handles coal, iron ore, oil and fish. Local manufacturers include lace, textiles, paint, steel, beer, furniture and motors.

Brugge /ˈbrʊxə/ Flemish form of ◊Bruges, town in Belgium.

Brulé French adventurer and explorer. He travelled with ◊Champlain to the New World in 1608 and settled in Québec, where he lived with the Algonquin Indians. He explored the great lakes and travelled as far south as Chesapeake Bay. Returning north, he was killed and eaten by Huron Indians.

Brummell /ˈbrʌməl/ George Bryan 'Beau' 1778–1840. British dandy and leader of fashion. A friend of the Prince of Wales, the future George IV, he later quarrelled with him, and was driven by gambling losses to exile in France in 1816.

Brundtland /ˈbrʊntlænd/ Gro Harlem 1939– . Norwegian Labour politician, prime minister 1981 and from 1986, environment minister 1974–76.

The *Brundtland Report* 1987, produced by the World Commission on Environment and Development, was chaired by her.

Brunei /ˈbruːnaɪ/ country on the N coast of Borneo, surrounded to the landward side by Sarawak, and bounded to the N by the South China Sea.

government The 1959 constitution gives supreme authority to the sultan, advised by various councils. Since the constitution was suspended after a revolution in 1962, the sultan rules by decree. One political party, the Brunei National United Party (BNUP), a multi-ethnic splinter group formed by former members of the Brunei National Democratic Party (BNDP), is allowed. While loyal to the sultan, it favours the establishment of an elected prime ministerial system. Other parties have been banned or have closed down.

history An Islamic monarchy from the 15th century, Brunei became a British protected state in 1888. Under an agreement of 1906, a British Resident was appointed as adviser to the sultan, Sir Muda Omar Ali Saiffuddin Saadul Khairi Waddien, known as Sir Omar(1916–86). Japan occupied Brunei 1941–45.

In 1959 Britain was made responsible for defence and external affairs until independence, and a proposal that Brunei should join the Federation of Malaysia was opposed by a revolution which was put down with British help. As a result the sultan decided to rule by decree. In 1967 he abdicated in favour of his son, Hassanal Bolkiah, but continued to be his chief adviser. Four years later Brunei was given full internal self-government. In 1984 full independence was achieved, the sultan becoming prime minister, minister of finance and home affairs, and presiding over a cabinet of six, three of whom were close relatives. Britain agreed to maintain a small force to protect the oil and gas fields that make Brunei the wealthiest nation, per head of population, in Asia.

Brunei
(Negara Brunei Darussalam)

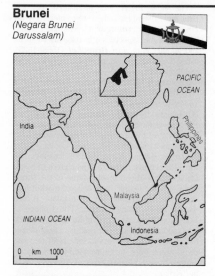

area 5,765 sq km/2,225 sq mi
capital and chief port Bandar Seri Begawan
physical 75% of the area is forested; the Limbang valley splits Brunei in two, and its cession to Sarawak 1890 is disputed by Brunei
head of state and of government Muda Hassanal Bolkiah Mu'izzaddin Waddaulah from 1968
political system absolute monarchy
political parties Brunei National United Party (BNUP)

exports liquefied natural gas (world's largest producer) and oil, both expected to be exhausted by 2000
currency Brunei dollar (3.17 = £1 Feb 1990)
population (1986) 226,300 (65% Malay, 25% Chinese; few Chinese granted citizenship); annual growth rate 12%
language 50% Malay (official), 26% Chinese (Hokkien), English
religion Muslim
literacy 75% male/50% female (1971)
GDP $3.8 bn (1983); $20,000 per head of population
chronology
1888 Brunei became a British protectorate.
1941–45 Occupied by Japan.
1959 Written constitution made Britain responsible for defence and external affairs.
1962 Sultan began rule by decree.
1963 Proposal to join Malaysia abandoned.
1967 Sultan abdicated in favour of his son Hassanal Bolkiah.
1971 Brunei given internal self-government.
1975 UN resolution called for independence for Brunei.
1984 Full independence achieved, with Britain maintaining a small force to protect the oil and gas fields.
1985 A 'loyal and reliable' political party, the Brunei National Democratic Party (BNDP), legalized.
1986 Death of former sultan, Sir Omar. Formation of multi-ethnic Brunei National United Party (BNUP).
1988 BNDP disbanded.

In 1985 the sultan cautiously allowed the formation of the loyal and reliable Brunei National Democratic Party (BNDP), an organization dominated by businessmen. A year later, ethnic Chinese and government employees, who were debarred from joining the BNDP, formed, with breakaway members of the other party, the Brunei National United Party (BNUP), the country's only political party after the dissolution of the BNDP 1988. Since the death of the sultan's father, Sir Omar, 1986 the pace of political reform has quickened, with key cabinet portfolios being assigned to non-members of the royal family. A more nationalist socio-economic policy has also begun, with preferential treatment given to native Malays in the commercial sphere rather than the traditional Chinese, and an Islamic state is being constructed.

Brunei Town former name (until 1970) of ◊Bandar Seri Begawan, Brunei.

Brunel /bruːˈnel/ Isambard Kingdom 1806–1859. British engineer and inventor. In 1833 he became engineer to the Great Western Railway, which adopted the 2.1 m/7 ft gauge on his advice. He built the Clifton Suspension Bridge over the river Avon at Bristol and the Saltash Bridge over the river Tamar near Plymouth. His ship-building designs include the *Great Western* 1838, the first steamship to cross the Atlantic regularly; the

Brunel *Isambard Kingdom Brunel, engineer of the Great Western Railway.*

Great Britain 1845, the first large iron ship to have a screw propeller; and the *Great Eastern* 1858, which laid the first transatlantic telegraph cable.

The son of Marc Brunel, he made major contributions to ship-building and bridge construction, and assisted his father in the Thames tunnel project. Brunel University in Uxbridge, London, is named after both father and son.

Brunel /bruːˈnel/ Marc Isambard 1769–1849. British engineer and inventor, and father of Isambard Kingdom Brunel, who constructed the Rotherhithe tunnel under the river Thames in London from Wapping to Rotherhithe 1825–43.

Born in France, he came to England in 1799, did engineering work for the Admiralty, and improved the port of Liverpool.

Brunelleschi /ˌbruːnəˈleski/ Filippo 1377–1446. Italian Renaissance architect. One of the earliest and greatest Renaissance architects, he pioneered the scientific use of perspective. He was responsible for the construction of the dome of Florence Cathedral (completed 1438), a feat deemed impossible by many of his contemporaries.

Bruning /ˈbruːnɪŋ/ Heinrich 1885–1970. German politician. Elected to the Reichstag (parliament) 1924, he led the Catholic Centre Party from 1929 and was federal chancellor (premier) 1930–32, when political and economic crisis forced his resignation.

Brünn /brʊn/ German form of ◊Brno, a town in Czechoslovakia.

Bruno /ˈbruːnəʊ/ Giordano 1548–1600. Italian philosopher. He entered the ◊Dominican order 1563, but his sceptical attitude to Catholic doctrines forced him to flee Italy 1577. After visiting Geneva and Paris, he lived in England 1583–85, where he wrote some of his finest works. After returning to Europe, he was arrested by the ◊Inquisition 1593 in Venice, and burned at the stake for his adoption of Copernican astronomy and his heretical religious views.

Bruno, St /ˈbruːnəʊ/ 1030–1101. German founder of the monastic Catholic ◊Carthusian order. He was born in Cologne, became a priest, and controlled the cathedral school of Rheims 1057–76. Withdrawing to the mountains near Grenoble after

an ecclesiastical controversy, he founded the monastery at Chartreuse in 1084. Feast day 6 Oct.

Brunswick /ˈbrʌnzwɪk/ (German *Braunschweig*) former independent duchy, a republic from 1918, which is now part of ◊Lower Saxony, West Germany.

Brunswick /ˈbrʌnzwɪk/ (German *Braunschweig*) industrial city (chemical engineering, precision engineering, food processing) in Lower Saxony, West Germany; population (1988) 248,000. It was one of the chief cities of N Germany in the Middle Ages, and a member of the ◊Hanseatic League. It was capital of the duchy of Brunswick from 1671.

Brusa /ˈbruːsə/ alternative form of ◊Bursa, a town in Turkey.

Brussels /ˈbrʌsəlz/ (Flemish *Brussel*, French *Bruxelles*) capital of Belgium, industrial city (lace, textiles, machinery, chemicals); population (1987) 974,000 (80% French-speaking, the suburbs Flemish-speaking). It is the headquarters of the European Economic Community and since 1967 of the international secretariat of NATO. First settled in the 6th century AD, and a city from 1321, Brussels became the capital of the Spanish Netherlands 1530 and of Belgium 1830.

features The 13th-century church of Sainte Gudule; the Hôtel de Ville, Maison du Roi, and others in the Grand Place; and the royal palace; the Musées Royaux des Beaux-Arts de Belgique hold a large art collection. its most famous statue is the bronze fountain Manneken Pis (1388), of a tiny naked boy urinating.

Brussels sprout one of the small edible buds along the stem of a variety of ◊cabbage.

Brussels, Treaty of /ˈbrʌsəlz/ pact of economic, political, cultural, and military alliance established 17 Mar 1948 for 50 years by the UK, France, and the Benelux countries, joined by West Germany and Italy 1955. It was the forerunner of the North Atlantic Treaty Organization and the European Community.

Brussilov /bruːˈsiːlɒf/ Aleksei Alekseevich 1853–1926. Russian general, military leader in World War I, who achieved major sucesses against the Austro-Hungarian forces in 1916. Later he was commander of the Red Army 1920 which drove the Poles to within a few miles of Warsaw before being repulsed.

Brutus /ˈbruːtəs/ Marcus Junius *c.*78–42 BC. Roman soldier, a supporter of ◊Pompey (against Caesar) in the civil war. Pardoned by ◊Caesar and raised to high office by him, he nevertheless plotted Caesar's assassination to restore the purity of the Republic. Brutus committed suicide when he was defeated (with ◊Cassius) by ◊Mark Antony, Caesar's lieutenant, at Philippi 42 BC.

Bruxelles /bruːˈsel/ French form of ◊Brussels, capital of Belgium.

Bryan William Jennings 1860–1925. US politician who campaigned unsuccessfully for the presidency three times: as the Populist and Democratic nominee 1896, as an anti-imperialist Democrat 1900, and as a Democratic tariff reformer 1908. He served as President Wilson's secretary of state 1913–15. In the early 1920s he was a leading fundamentalist and opponent of Clarence Darrow in the ◊Scopes monkey trial.

Bryansk /briˈænsk/ city in W central USSR, SW of Moscow on the Desna; population (1987) 445,000. Industries include sawmilling, textiles, and steel.

Bryant /ˈbraɪənt/ Arthur 1899–1985. British historian, noted for his studies of Restoration figures such as Pepys and Charles II, and a series covering the Napoleonic Wars including *The Age of Elegance* 1950. He was knighted in 1954.

Bryant /ˈbraɪənt/ David 1931– . English flat-green (lawn) bowls player. He has won every honour the game has offered, including four outdoor world titles (three singles and one triples) 1966–88 and three indoor titles 1979–81.

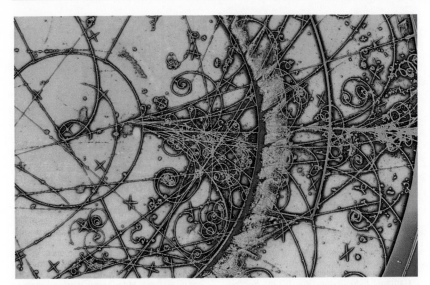

bubble-chamber Artificially coloured bubble chamber at CERN, the European particle-physics laboratory outside Geneva.

CAREER HIGHLIGHTS

World outdoor champion:
singles: 1966, 1980 (singles and triples), 1988
World indoor champion:
1979–81
Commonwealth Games:
singles: 1962, 1970, 1974, 1978
fours: 1962
English Bowling Association titles:
singles: 1960, 1966, 1971–73, 1975
pairs: 1965, 1969, 1974
triples: 1966, 1977
fours: 1957, 1968–69, 1971

Bryce /braɪs/ James, 1st Viscount Bryce 1838–1922. British Liberal politician, and professor of civil law at Oxford University 1870–93. He entered Parliament 1880, holding office under Gladstone and Rosebery. He was author of *The American Commonwealth* 1888, ambassador to Washington 1907–13, and improved US-Canadian relations.

Brynner /'brɪnə/ Yul. Stage name of Youl Bryner 1915–1985. US actor who made baldness his trademark. He played the king in *The King and I* both on stage 1951 and on film 1956; he is also memorable as the leader of *The Magnificent Seven* 1960.

bryony two hedgerow climbing plants found in Britain: *white bryony Bryonia cretica* belonging to the gourd family Cucurbitaceae, and *black bryony Tamus communis* of the yam family Dioscoreaceae.

bryophyte a member of the Bryophyta, a division of the plant kingdom containing three classes, the Hepaticae (◊liverwort), Musci (◊moss), and Anthocerotae (◊hornwort). Bryophytes are generally small, low-growing, terrestrial plants with no vascular (water-conducting) system as in higher plants. Their lifecycle shows a marked ◊alternation of generations. Bryophytes chiefly occur in damp habitats and require water for the dispersal of the male gametes (◊antherozoids).

The sporophyte, consisting only of a spore-bearing capsule on a slender stalk, is wholly or partially dependent on the gametophyte (the familiar moss or liverwort 'plant') for water and nutrients. In some liverworts the plant body is a simple ◊thallus, but in the majority of bryophytes it is differentiated into stem, leaves, and rhizoids.

Bryusov /bri'u:spf/ Valery 1873–1924. Russian Symbolist poet and critic.

Brześćnad Bugiem /'bʒeʃtʃnad 'bu:gjem/ Polish name of ◊Brest, a town in the USSR.

Brzezinski /brə'ʒɪnski/ Zbigniew 1928– . US Democrat politician, born in Poland; he taught at Harvard University, USA, and became a US citizen 1949. He was national-security adviser to President Carter 1977–81 and chief architect of Carter's human-rights policy.

BSc abbreviation for *Bachelor of Science*.

BSI abbreviation for ◊*British Standards Institute*.

BST abbreviation for *British Summer Time*; ◊*bovine somatotropin*.

BT abbreviation for *British Telecom*.

Btu abbreviation for ◊*British thermal unit*.

bubble-chamber in physics a device for observing the nature and movement of atomic particles, and their interaction with radiations. It is a vessel filled with a highly superheated liquid; this boils violently, creating a string of bubbles along the trail of the ionizing particles which can be photographed and studied. By using a pressurized liquid medium instead of a gas, it overcomes drawbacks inherent in the earlier ◊cloud chamber. It was invented by Donald ◊Glaser in 1952.

bubble memory in computing, a memory device based on the creation of small 'bubbles' on a magnetic surface. Bubble memories typically store up to four megabits (4 million ◊bits) of information. They are not sensitive to shock and vibration, unlike other memory devices such as disc drives, yet, like magnetic discs, they do not lose their information when the computer is switched off.

Buber /'bu:bə/ Martin 1878–1965. Israeli philosopher, a Zionist and advocate of the reappraisal of ancient Jewish thought in modern terms. Born in Vienna, he was forced to abandon a professorship in comparative religion at Frankfurt by the Nazis, and taught social philosophy at the Hebrew University, Jerusalem, 1937–51.

Bubiyan /,bu:bɪ'jɑ:n/ an island of Kuwait claimed by Iraq.

Bucaramanga /bu'kɑ:rə'mæŋgə/ industrial (coffee, tobacco, cacao, cotton) and commercial city in N central Colombia; population (1985) 493,929. Founded by the Spanish in 1622.

buccaneer a member of various groups of seafarers off the Spanish American coast in the 17th century, who plundered Spanish ships and colonies. Unlike true pirates, they were acting on (sometimes spurious) commission.

Bucer /'butsə/ Martin 1491–1551. German Protestant reformer, regius professor of divinity at Cambridge University from 1549, who tried to reconcile the views of his fellow Protestants Luther and Zwingli and the significance of the eucharist.

Buchan /'bʌxən/ John, Baron Tweedsmuir 1875–1940. Scottish politician and author. Called to the Bar in 1901, he was Conservative Member of Parliament for the Scottish universities 1927–35, and governor general of Canada 1934–40. His adventure stories include *The Thirty-Nine Steps* 1915, *Greenmantle* 1916, and *The Three Hostages* 1924.

Buchanan /bə'kænən/ George 1506–1582. Scottish humanist. Forced to flee to France in 1539 owing to some satirical verses on the Franciscans, he returned to Scotland about 1562 as tutor to Mary Queen of Scots. He became principal of St Leonard's College, St Andrews, in 1566, and wrote *Rerum Scoticarum Historia/A History of Scotland* 1582, which was biased against ◊Mary Queen of Scots.

Buchanan /bə'kænən/ Jack 1891–1957. British musical-comedy actor. His songs such as 'Good-Night Vienna' epitomized the period between World Wars I and II.

Bucharest /,bu:kə'rest/ (Romanian *Bucureşti*) capital and largest city of Romania; population (1985) 1,976,000, the conurbation of Bucharest district having an area of 1,520 sq km/587 sq mi and a population of 2,273,000. Originally a citadel built by Vlad the Impaler (see ◊Dracula) to stop the advance of the Ottoman invasion in the 14th century. It became the capital of the princes of Wallachia 1698 and of Romania 1861.

Buchenwald /'bu:xənvælt/ site of a Nazi concentration camp 1937–45 at a village NE of Weimar, East Germany.

Buchman /'bʊkmən/ Frank N D 1878–1961. US right-wing Christian evangelist. In 1938 he launched in London the anticommunist campaign, the *Moral Re-Armament* movement.

Buchner /'bʊxnə/ Eduard 1860–1917. German chemist who researched the process of fermentation. In 1897 Buchner observed that fermentation could be produced mechanically, by cell-free extracts. Buchner argued that it was not the whole yeast cell which produced fermentation, only the presence of the enzyme he named zymase. Nobel prize 1907.

Buck /bʌk/ Pearl S 1892–1973. US novelist. Daughter of missionaries to China, she wrote novels about Chinese life, such as *East Wind–West Wind* 1930 and *The Good Earth* 1931. Nobel Prize for Literature 1938.

Buckingham /'bʌkɪŋəm/ market town in Buckinghamshire, England; on the river Ouse. University College was established 1974, and was given a royal charter as the University of Buckingham 1983.

Buckingham /'bʌkɪŋəm/ George Villiers, 1st Duke of Buckingham 1592–1628. English courtier, adviser to James I and later Charles I. After Charles's accession, Buckingham attempted to form a Protestant coalition in Europe which led to war with France, but he failed to relieve the Protestants besieged in La Rochelle 1627.

Introduced to the court of James I in 1614, he soon became his favourite and was made Earl of Buckingham in 1617 and a duke in 1623. He failed to arrange the marriage of Prince Charles and the Infanta of Spain 1623, but on returning to England negotiated Charles's alliance with Henrietta Maria, sister to the French king. His policy on the French Protestants was attacked in Parliament, and when about to sail again for La Rochelle he was assassinated in Portsmouth.

Buckingham /'bʌkɪŋəm/ George Villiers, 2nd Duke of Buckingham 1628–1687. English politician, a member of the ◊Cabal under Charles II. A dissolute son of the 1st duke, he was brought up with the royal children. His play *The Rehearsal* satirized the style of the poet Dryden, who portrayed him as Zimri in *Absalom and Achitophel*.

Buckingham Palace London home of the British sovereign, built 1703 for the duke of Buckingham, but bought by George III in 1762 and reconstructed by ◊Nash 1821–36; a new front was added in 1913.

Buckinghamshire /'bʌkɪŋəmʃə/ county in SE central England
area 1,880 sq km/726 sq mi

Buckingham *Four times imprisoned in the Tower of London, dissolute courtier George Villiers, 2nd Duke of Buckingham, was satirically portrayed as Zimri in Dryden's* Absalom and Achitophel.

towns administrative headquarters Aylesbury; Buckingham, High Wycombe, Beaconsfield, Olney
features ◊Chequers (country seat of the prime minister); Burnham Beeches and the church of the poet Gray's 'Elegy' at Stoke Poges; Cliveden, a country house designed by Charles Barry (now a hotel, it was used by the newspaper-owning Astors for house parties); Bletchley Park, home of World War II code-breaking activities, now used as a training post for GCHQ (Britain's electronic surveillance centre); homes of the poets William Cowper at Olney and John Milton at Chalfont St Giles, and of the Tory prime minister Disraeli at Hughenden
products furniture, especially beech; agricultural
population (1987) 621,000.
Buckley /'bʌkli/ William 1780–1856. Australian convict, who escaped from Port Phillip and lived 1803–35 among the Aborigines before giving himself up, hence ***Buckley's chance*** meaning an 'outside chance'.
Buckley /'bʌkli/ William F(rank) 1925– . US conservative political writer, novelist, and founder-editor of the *National Review* 1955. In such books as *Up from Liberalism* 1959, and in a weekly television debate 'Firing Line', he represented the 'intellectual' right-wing, anti-liberal stance in US political thought.
Bucks abbreviation for ◊*Buckinghamshire*.
buckthorn thorny shrubs of the family Rhamnaceae, of which two species, the buckthorn *Rhamnus catharticus* and the alder buckthorn *Frangula alnus*, are native to Britain.
buckwheat high nutritive value grain plant *Fagopyrum esculentum*, of the family Polygonaceae. The plant grows to about 1 m/3 ft, and the seeds are either eaten whole or ground into flour. It is eaten both by humans and animals. Buckwheat can grow on poor soil in a short summer.
bud an undeveloped shoot usually enclosed by protective scales; inside is a very short stem and numerous undeveloped leaves, or flower parts, or both. Terminal buds are found at the tips of shoots, while axillary buds develop in the ◊axils of the leaves, often remaining dormant unless the

terminal bud is removed or damaged. Adventitious buds may be produced anywhere on the plant, their formation sometimes stimulated by an injury, such as that caused by pruning.
Budaeus /bu:'di:əs/ Latin form of the name of Guillaume Budé 1467–1540. French scholar. He persuaded Francis I to found the Collège de France, and also the library that formed the nucleus of the French national library, the Bibliothèque Nationale.
Budapest /,bju:də'pest/ capital of Hungary, industrial city (chemicals, textiles) on the Danube; population (1985) 2,089,000. Buda, on the right bank of the Danube, became the Hungarian capital 1867 and was joined with Pest, on the left bank, 1872.

Budapest saw fighting between German and Soviet troops in World War II 1944–45, and between the Hungarians and Soviet troops in the rising of 1956.
Buddenbrooks a novel by the German writer Thomas Mann, published 1901. Set in N Germany during the 19th century, it describes the decline of a family.
Buddha /'budə/ 'enlightened one', title of Prince *Gautama Siddhārtha* c.563–483 BC. Religious leader, founder of Buddhism, born at Lumbini in Nepál. At the age of 29, he left a life of luxury, and his wife and son, to escape from the burdens of existence. After six years of austerity he realized that asceticism, like overindulgence, was futile, and chose the middle way of meditation. He became enlightened under a bo tree near Buddh Gaya in Bihar, India. He began teaching at Varanasi, and founded the Sangha, or order of monks. He spent the rest of his life moving around N India and died at Kusinagara in Uttar Pradesh.

Buddha acquired the ***Four Noble Truths***: the fact of frustration or suffering; that suffering has a cause; that it can be ended; and that it can be ended by following the ***Noble Eightfold Path*** – right views, right intention, right speech, right action, right livelihood, right effort, right mindfulness, and right concentration – and so arriving at nirvana, the extinction of all craving for things of the senses.
Buddh Gaya /'bud gə'jɑ:/ village in Bihar, India, where Gautama became ◊Buddha while sitting beneath a bo (*bodhi*, wisdom) tree; a descendant of the original bo tree (*Ficus religiosa*, peepul tree) is preserved.
Buddhism one of the great world religions, which originated in India about 500 BC. It derives from the teaching of Buddha, who is regarded as one of a series of such enlightened beings; there are no gods. The chief doctrine is that of ***karma***, good or evil deeds meeting an appropriate reward or punishment either in this life or (through reincarnation) a long succession of lives. The main divisions are ***Theravāda*** (or Hīnayāna) in SE

Buckinghamshire

Budapest *The Parliament building on the eastern side of the river Danube.*

Asia and ***Mahāyāna*** in N Asia; ***Lamaism*** in Tibet and ***Zen*** in Japan are among the many Mahāyāna sects. Its symbol is the lotus. There are over 247.5 million Buddhists worldwide.
scriptures The only complete canon of the Buddhist scriptures is that of the Sinhalese (Sri Lanka) Buddhists, in Páli, but other schools have essentially the same canon in Sanskrit. The scriptures, known as *pitaka*s (baskets), date from the 2nd to 6th centuries AD. There are three divisions: ***vinaya*** (discipline), listing offences and rules of life; the ***sūtras*** (discourse), or ***dharma*** (doctrine), the exposition of Buddhism by Buddha and his disciples; ***abhidharma*** (further doctrine), later discussions on doctrine.
beliefs The self is not regarded as permanent, and the aim of the ***Noble Eightfold Way*** is to break the chain of karma and achieve dissociation from the body by attaining ***nirvana*** ('blowing out'), the eradication of all desires, either in annihilation or by absorption of the self in the infinite. Great reverence is accorded to the historic Buddha (Śākyamuni) and other such advanced incarnations, the next Buddha (Maitreya) being due c. AD 3000.
divisions Theravāda Buddhism, the School of the Elders, also known as ***Hīnayāna*** or Lesser Vehicle, prevails in SE Asia (Sri Lanka, Thailand, and Burma), and emphasizes the mendicant, meditative life as the way to break the cycle of ***samsāra***, or death and rebirth. Its scriptures are written in ***Páli***, an Indo-Aryan language with its roots in N India. In India itself Buddhism was replaced by Hinduism, but still has 5 million devotees and is growing.

Mahāyāna, or Greater Vehicle, which arose at the beginning of the Christian era, exhorts the individual not merely to attain nirvana as an individual, but to become a trainee Buddha, or ***bodhisattva***, and so save others; this meant

Buddha *13th-century Thai bronze Buddha.*

Buenos Aires *The Congress National, Plaza Congress in Buenos Aires, Argentina.*

the faithful could be brought to enlightenment by a bodhisattva without following the austerities of Theravāda, and the cults of various Buddhas and bodhisattvas arose. Mahāyāna Buddhism prevails in N Asia (China, Korea, Japan, and Tibet). ◊*Zen* originated *c.* AD 520 in China, and from the 12th century was adopted in Japan; Japan also has the lay organization *Sōka Gakkai* (Value Creation Society), founded 1937, which equates absolute faith with immediate material benefit, and by the 1980s was followed by more than 7 million households.

budding a type of ◊asexual reproduction in which an outgrowth develops from a cell to form a new individual. The majority of yeasts reproduce in this way. In horticulture, the term is used for a technique of plant propagation whereby a bud (or scion) and a sliver of bark from one plant are transferred to an incision made in the bark of another plant (the stock). This method of ◊grafting is often used for roses.

In a suitable environment yeasts grow rapidly, forming long chains of cells as the buds themselves produce further buds before being separated from the parent. Simple invertebrates, such as hydra, can also reproduce by budding.

buddleia genus of shrubs and trees, family Buddleiaceae, of which the best-known is the *butterfly bush Buddleia davidii.* Its purple or white flowerheads are attractive to insects.

Budge Donald 1915– . US tennis player, the first person to perform the Grand Slam when he won Wimbledon, French, US, and Australian championships 1938.

Altogether he won 14 Grand Slam events at singles and doubles, including Wimbledon singles twice. Budge turned professional 1938.

CAREER HIGHLIGHTS

Wimbledon
singles: 1937–38
doubles: 1937–38
mixed: 1937–38
US Open
singles: 1937–38
doubles: 1936, 1938
mixed: 1937–38
French Open
singles: 1938
Australian Open
singles: 1938

budgerigar small Australian parakeet *Melopsittacus undulatus* which feeds mainly on grass seeds. Normally it is bright green, but yellow, white, blue, and mauve varieties have been produced. It breeds freely in captivity.

budget an estimate of income and expenditure for some future period, used in the financial planning of a business or country. National budgets set out estimates of government income and expenditure and generally include changes in taxation. Interim budgets are not uncommon, particularly when dramatic changes in economic conditions occur.

Budějovice see ◊České Budějovice, town in Czechoslovakia.

Budweis /ˈbʊdvaɪs/ German form of České Budějovice, a town in Czechoslovakia.

Buenos Aires /ˈbweɪnɒs ˈaɪrɪz/ capital and industrial city of Argentina, on the south bank of the River Plate; population (1980) 9,927,000. It was founded 1536, and became the capital 1853.

features Palace of Congress; on the Plaza de Mayo, the cathedral and presidential palace (known as the Pink House); university 1821.

Buffalo /ˈbʌfələʊ/ industrial port in New York State, USA, at the E end of Lake Erie; population (1980) 1,200,000. It is linked with New York City by the New York State Barge Canal.

buffalo two species of wild cattle. The Asiatic *water buffalo Bubalis bubalis* is found domesticated throughout S Asia and wild in parts of India and Nepál. It likes moist conditions. Usually grey or black, up to 1.8 m/6 ft high, both sexes carry large horns. The *African buffalo Syncerus caffer* is found in Africa south of the Sahara where there is grass, water, and cover in which to retreat. There are various types, the biggest up to 1.6 m/5 ft high, black, and with massive horns set close together over the head.

buffer in computing, part of the memory used to hold data while it is waiting to be used. For example, a program might store data in a printer buffer until the printer is ready to print it.

buffer a mixture of chemical compounds chosen to maintain a steady ◊pH.

The commonest buffers consist of a mixture of a weak organic acid and one of its salts or a mixture of ◊acid salts of phosphoric acid. The addition of either an acid or a base causes a shift in the ◊chemical equilibrium, thus keeping the pH constant.

Buffer State country that keeps two antagonistic powers apart by removing their common border. For example, Poland between Germany and Russia.

Buffet /buːˈfeɪ/ Bernard 1928– . French figurative painter who created distinctive thin, spiky forms with bold, dark outlines. He was a precocious talent in the late 1940s.

Buffon /buːˈfɒn/ Comte de 1707–1778. French naturalist and author of the 18th century's most significant work of natural history, the 44 volume *Histoire naturelle* (1749–1804), 36 of which he completed before his death. In *The Epochs of Nature*, one of the volumes, he questioned for the first time the received biblical chronology and raised the Earth's age from the traditional figure of 6,000 years to the seemingly colossal estimate of 75,000 years.

Bug /buːg/ two rivers in E Europe: the *West Bug* rises in SW Ukraine and flows to the Vistula, and the *South Bug* rises in W Ukraine and flows to the Black Sea.

bug in computing, an error in a program. It can be an error in the logical structure of a program or a syntactic error, such as a spelling mistake. Some bugs cause a program to fail immediately; others remain dormant, causing problems only when a particular combination of events occurs. Debugging is the process of finding bugs and eliminating them from a program.

bug in entomology, insects belonging to the order Hemiptera. All these have piercing mouthparts adapted for sucking the juices of plants or animals, the 'beak' being tucked under the body when not in use.

They include: the ◊*bedbug*, which sucks human blood; the *shieldbug*, or stinkbug, which has a strong odour and feeds on plants; the ◊*pondskater*, ◊*water boatman* and other water bugs, ◊*aphids*, and ◊*cicadas*.

Buganda /buːˈgændə/ two provinces (North and South Buganda) of Uganda, home of the Baganda people, and formerly a kingdom from the 17th century. The *kabaka* or king, Sir Edward Mutesa II (1924–69), was the first president of independent Uganda 1962–66, and his son Ronald Mutebi (1955–) is *sabataka* (head of the Baganda clans).

Bugatti racing and sports-car company, founded by the Italian Ettore Bugatti (1881–1947). The first car was produced 1908, and one of the great Bugattis was the Type 35, produced 1924. Bugatti cars are credited with more race wins than any other.

The Type 35 is credited with 2,000 race wins and dominated motor racing 1924–26. Bugatti also built classic road cars, including the Royale. All Bugatti's cars bore a distinctive horseshoe-shaped radiator. In 1986, a second-hand Bugatti exchanged hands for a world record $8.1 million.

bugle in music, a valveless brass instrument with a shorter tube and less expanded bell than the trumpet. Constructed of copper plated with brass, it has long been used as a military instrument for giving a range of signals based on the tones of a harmonic series.

bugle low-growing perennial plant *Ajuga reptans*, family Labiatae, with two-lipped blue flowers in a purplish spike. The leaves may be smooth edged or faintly toothed, the lower ones with a long stalk. Bugle is found across Europe and N Africa, usually in damp woods or pastures.

bugloss several plants of the family Boraginaceae, distinguished by their rough bristly leaves and small blue flowers.

buhl alternative spelling for ◊boulle, a type of marquetry.

building society in the UK, financial institution that attracts investment in order to lend money, repayable at interest, for the purchase or building of a house on security of a ◊mortgage. Since the 1970s building societies have considerably expanded their services and in many ways now compete with clearing banks.

Building societies originated 1781 from the ◊friendly societies in England. In Britain the Building Societies Act 1986 enabled societies to raise up to 20% of their funds on the international capital market. Among other changes, the act provided that building societies could grant unsecured loans of up to £5,000; they were also able to offer interest-bearing cheque accounts, a challenge to the clearing banks' traditional role in this area. From 1988 societies were able to operate in other EC countries. In the USA the equivalent institution is called a *savings and loan association*; the first was founded in 1831.

Bujumbura /ˌbuːdʒʊmˈbʊərə/ capital of Burundi; population (1986) 272,600. Formerly called Usumbura (until 1962), the town was founded in 1899 by German colonists. The university was established 1960.

Bukavu /buːˈkɑːvuː/ port in E Zaïre, on Lake Kivu; population (1982) 209,050. Mining is the chief industry. Called Costermansville until 1966, it is capital of Itivu region.

Bukhara /bʊˈxɑːrə/ city in Uzbekistan, USSR; population (1987) 220,000. It is capital of Bukhara region which has given its name to carpets (made in Ashkhabad). It is an Islamic centre, with a Muslim theological training centre. An ancient city in central Asia, it was formerly the capital of the independent emirate of Bukhara, annexed to Russia 1868. It was included in Bukhara region 1924.

Bukharest /ˌbuːkəˈrest/ alternative form of ◊Bucharest, capital of Romania.

Bukharin /bʊˈxɑːrɪn/ Nikolai Ivanovich 1888–1938. Russian politician and theorist. A moderate, he was the most influential Bolshevik thinker after Lenin. Executed on Stalin's orders for treason in 1938, he was posthumously rehabilitated in 1988.

He wrote the major defence of war communism in his *Economics of the Transition Period* 1920, and was one of the chief supporters of the ◊New Economic Policy, which in turn led to the doctrine of ◊Socialism in One Country. He drafted the Soviet constitution of 1936, but in 1938 was imprisoned and tried for treason in one of Stalin's 'show trials'. He pleaded guilty to treason, but defended his moderate policies and denied criminal charges. He was nonetheless executed, as were all other former members of Lenin's Politburo

Bulgaria
People's Republic of
(Narodna Republika Bulgaria)

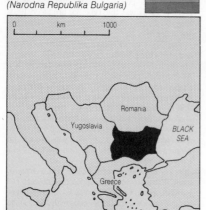

area 110,912 sq km/42,812 sq mi
capital Sofia
towns Plovdiv, Rusé; Burgas and Varna are Black Sea ports
physical Balkan and Rhodope mountains; river Danube in the north
features Black Sea coast
head of state Petar Mladenov from 1989
head of government Andrey Loukanov from 1990
political system socialist pluralist republic
political parties Bulgarian Communist Party (BCP), socialist ; Bulgarian Agrarian People's Union (BZNS), peasants' organization loyal (to 1989) to BCP; Union of Democratic Forces (UDF), pro-democracy opposition movement
exports textiles, chemicals, non-ferrous metals, timber, minerals, machinery

currency lev (1.34 = £1 Feb 1990)
population (1988) 8,970,000 (including 9,000,000–1,500,000 ethnic Turks, concentrated in the S and NE); annual growth rate 0.5%
life expectancy men 69, women 74
language Bulgarian, Turkish
religion Eastern Orthodox Christian 90%, Sunni Muslim 10%
literacy 96% male/93% female (1980 est)
GNP $26 bn (1983); $2,625 per head of population
chronology
1908 Bulgaria became a kingdom independent of Turkish rule.
1944 Soviet invasion of German-occupied Bulgaria.
1946 Monarchy abolished and communist-dominated people's republic proclaimed.
1947 Soviet-style constitution adopted.
1949 Death of Georgi Dimitrov.
1954 Election of Todor Zhivkov as Communist Party general secretary.
1971 Constitution modified. Zhivkov elected president.
1985–88 Large-scale administrative and personnel changes made haphazardly under Soviet stimulus.
1987 New electoral law introduced multi-candidate elections.
1989 310,000 ethnic Turks fled in opposition to the 'Bulgarianization' campaign of forced assimilation. Zhivkov ousted by Petar Mladenov in Nov and expelled from BCP. Sweeping pluralist reforms instituted, and opposition parties allowed to form; Bulgarianization abandoned.
1990 BCP monopoly of power ends (Jan); Alexander Lilov elected new BCP leader and Andrey Loukanov prime minister (Feb).

7th century by the Bulgars from Asia, eventually absorbed the invaders. In 865 Khan Boris adopted Easern Orthodox Christianity, and under his son Simeon (893–927), who assumed the title Tsar, Bulgaria became a leading power. It was ruled by ◊Byzantium from the 11th century, and although a second Bulgarian empire was founded after the 14th century Bulgaria formed part of the ◊Ottoman empire for almost 500 years, becoming an independent kingdom in 1908.

Bulgaria allied itself with Germany during World War I. From 1919 a government of the leftist Agrarian party introduced land reforms, but was overthrown in 1923 by a facist coup. A monarchical-facist dictatorship was established 1934 under King ◊Boris III. During World War II Bulgaria again allied itself with Germany, being occupied in 1944 by the USSR. In 1946 the monarchy was abolished and a republic was proclaimed under a communist-leaning alliance, the Fatherland Front, led by Georgi ◊Dimitrov (1882–1949). Bulgaria reverted largely to its 1919 frontiers.

The new republic adopted a Soviet-style constitution in 1947. Vulko Chervenkov, Dimitrov's brother-in-law, became the dominant political figure 1950–54, introducing a Stalinist regime. He was succeeded by the more moderate Todor ◊Zhivkov, under whom Bulgaria became one of the Soviet Union's most loyal satellites.

During the 1980s the country faced mounting economic problems, chiefly caused by the rising cost of energy imports. During 1985–89, under the promptings of the Soviet leader ◊Gorbachev, a haphazard series of administrative and economic reforms was instituted. This proved insufficient, however, to placate reformists both inside and outside the BCP. In Nov 1989, influenced by the democratization movements sweeping other E European countries and backed by the Army and the USSR, the foreign secretary, Petar ◊Mladenov, ousted Zhivkov and other members of the 'old guard' in a skilful committee coup. Mladenov became leader of the BCP and president of the State Council, and quickly promoted genuine political pluralism. In Dec 1989 legislation was passed to end the BCP's 'leading role' in the state and allow the formation of free opposition parties and trade unions; political prisoners were freed; the secret police wing responsible for dissident surveillance was abolished; and free elections were promised for 1990. In Feb 1990 Alexander Lilov, a reformer, was elected party chief, and Andrey Loukanov became prime minister. A special commission was established to investigate allegations of nepotism and high-level embezzlement of state funds. Zhivkov was placed under house arrest, and later imprisoned, pending trial on charges of corruption and abuse of power.

Bulgaria's relations with neighbouring Turkey deteriorated during 1989, following the flight of 310,000 ethnic Turks from Bulgaria to Turkey after the Bulgarian government's violent supression of their protests at the programme of 'Bulgarianization' (forcing them to adopt Slavic names and resettle elsewhere). The new Mladenov government announced Dec 1989 that the forced assimilation programme would be abandoned; this provoked demonstrations by anti-Turk nationalists, abetted by BCP conservatives, but encouraged more than 100,000 refugees to return from Turkey.

Bulge, Battle of the or *Ardennes offensive* in World War II, Hitler's plan, codenamed 'Watch on the Rhine', for a breakthrough by his field marshal ◊Rundstedt aimed at the US line in Ardennes 16 Dec 1944–28 Jan 1945. There were 77,000 Allied casualties and 130,000 German, including Hitler's last powerful reserve, his Panzer elite.

bulimia (Greek 'ox hunger') counteraction of stress or depression by uncontrollable overeating, compensated for by forced vomiting or an overdose of laxatives.

bull a speculator who buys stocks or shares on the stock exchange expecting a rise in the price in

except Trotsky, who was murdered, and Stalin himself.

Bukovina /ˌbukəˈviːnə/ region in SE Europe, divided between the USSR and Romania. It covers 10,500 sq km/4,050 sq mi.

history Part of Moldavia during the Turkish regime, it was ceded by the Ottoman Empire to Austria 1777, becoming a duchy of the Dual Monarchy 1867–1918; then it was included in Romania. N Bukovina was ceded to the USSR 1940 and included in Ukraine as the region of Chernovty; the cession was confirmed by the peace treaty 1947, but the question of its return has been raised by Romania. The part of Bukovina remaining in Romania became the district of Suceava.

Bulawayo /ˌbuləˈweɪəʊ/ industrial city and railway junction in Zimbabwe; population (1982) 415,000. It lies at an altitude of 1,355 m/4,450 ft on the river Matsheumlope, a tributary of the Zambezi, and was founded on the site of the kraal (enclosed village), burned down 1893, of the Matabele chief Lobenguela. It produces agricultural and electrical equipment. The former capital of Matabeleland, Bulawayo developed with the exploitation of goldmines in the neighbourhood.

bulb instrument of vegetative reproduction consisting of a modified leaf bud with fleshy leaves containing a reserve food supply; roots form from its base. It is a characteristic of many monocotyledenous plants such as the daffodil, snowdrop, and onion. Bulbs are grown on a commercial scale in temperate countries, such as England and Holland.

bulbil a small bulb that develops above ground from a bud. Bulbils may be formed on the stem from axillary buds, as in *Saxifraga hypnoides*, or in the place of flowers, as seen in many species of onion (*Allium*). They drop off the parent plant and develop into new individuals, providing a means of ◊vegetative reproduction and dispersal.

bulbul small fruit-eating bird of the family Pycnonotidae. There are about 120 species, mainly in the forests of the Old World tropics.

Bulgakov /bʊlˈgɑːkɒf/ Mikhail Afanasyevich 1891–1940. Russian novelist and playwright. His novel *The White Guard* 1924, dramatized as *The Days of the Turbins* 1926, deals with the Revolution and the civil war.

His satiric approach made him unpopular with the Stalin regime, and he was unpublished from the 1930s. *The Master and Margarita*, a fantasy about the devil in Moscow, was not published until 1967.

Bulganin /bʊlˈgɑːnɪn/ Nikolai 1895–1975. Russian military leader and politician. He helped to organize Moscow's defence in World War II, became a marshal of the USSR 1947, and was minister of defence 1947–49 and 1953–55. On the fall of Malenkov he became prime minister (chair of Council of Ministers) 1955–58 until ousted by Khrushchev.

Bulgaria /bʌlˈgɛərɪə/ country in SE Europe, bounded to the N by Romania, to the W by Yugoslavia, to the S by Greece, to the SW by Turkey, and to the E by the Black Sea.

government Under the 1971 constitution the supreme legislative and executive organ of power in Bulgaria is the 400-member national assembly, elected every five years by universal adult suffrage. It meets at least three times a year, but elects a permanent 28-member state council, headed by a president who acts as head of state, to take over its functions in its absence. The national assembly also elects a council of ministers, headed by a prime minister, which forms the executive government. The controlling force has traditionally been the Bulgarian Communist Party (BCP).

history In the ancient world Bulgaria comprised ◊Thrace and Moesia, and was the Roman province of Moesia Inferior. It was later occupied by the Slavs who, conquered in the

order to sell them later at a profit, the opposite of a ◊bear. In a bull market, prices rise and bulls profit.

Bull /bʊl/ John. Typical Englishman, especially as represented in cartoons. The name came into use after the publication of Dr John Arbuthnot's *History of John Bull* 1712 advocating the Tory policy of peace with France.

Bull /bʊl/ John *c.* 1562–1628. British composer, organist, and virginalist. Most of his output is for keyboard, and includes ◊'God Save the King'. He also wrote sacred vocal music.

Bull /bʊl/ Olaf 1883–1933. Norwegian lyric poet, son of humourist and fiction writer Jacob Breda Bull (1853–1930), who often celebrated his birthplace Christiania (now Oslo) in his poetry.

bull papal document or edict issued by the pope; so called from the circular seals (medieval Latin *bulla*) attached to them. Famous papal bulls include Leo X's condemnation of Luther in 1520 and Pius IX's proclamation of papal infallibility in 1870.

bull-baiting the setting of dogs to attack a chained bull, one-time 'sport' popular in the UK and Europe. It became illegal in Britain in 1835.

bulldog British dog of ancient but uncertain origin. The head is broad and square, with a deeply wrinkled skull, small folded ears, and nose laid back between the eyes.

Coming into prominence in the days of bull-baiting, it developed the characteristic lower jaw which left the nostrils free for breathing while the dog retained its grip on the bull's throat. The peculiar alignment of the lower jaw made it extremely difficult for the dog to release its grip.

bulldozer an earth-moving machine widely used in construction work for clearing rocks and tree stumps and levelling a site. The bulldozer is a kind of ◊tractor with a powerful engine and a curved blade at the front, which can be lifted and forced down by hydraulic rams. It usually has crawler or ◊caterpillar tracks so that it can move easily over rough ground.

Buller /'bʊlə/ Redvers Henry 1839–1908. British commander against the Boers in the South African War 1899–1902. He was defeated at Colenso and Spion Kop, but relieved Ladysmith; he was superseded by Lord Roberts.

Bulletin, The weekly Sydney magazine established in 1880 which, until the 1920s, was the chief Australian periodical. It has done much to foster Australian literature and cinema.

bullfighting the national 'sport' of Spain, which involves the ritualized taunting of a bull in a circular ring, until its eventual death at the hands of the matador. Originally popular in Greece and Rome, it was introduced into Spain by the Moors in the 11th century.

Picadores on horseback first taunt the bull and wound it with lances before the *banderillos* pierce the bull's neck with darts. The final act, the kill, is performed by the *matador*, who has a red cape and sword. He teases the bull further with the cape and then plunges the sword between the bull's left shoulder and shoulder blade. The bull eventually bleeds to death.

bullfinch bird *Pyrrhula pyrrhula* of the finch family, with a thick head and neck, and short heavy bill. It is small, blue-grey or black, the males being reddish and the females brown on the breast. Bullfinches are 14.5 cm/6 in long, and usually seen in pairs. Bullfinches feed on tree buds as well as seeds and berries, and are usually seen in woodland. They are found across N Europe and Asia.

bullhead or *miller's thumb* small fish *Cottus gobio* found in fresh water in the N hemisphere, often under stones. It has a large head, a spine on the gill cover, and grows to 10 cm/4 in.

Related bullheads, such as the *father lasher Myxocephalus scorpius*, live in coastal waters. They are up to 30 cm/1 ft long. The male guards the eggs and fans them with his tail.

Bullock Report the report of a committee of inquiry

headed by Lord Bullock, published in 1975, on the teaching of English in the UK. The report, *A Language for Life*, recommended improvements in the teaching of reading, writing, and spoken English in both primary and secondary schools.

bullroarer musical instrument consisting of a piece of wood fastened by one of its pointed ends to a cord. It is twirled round the head to make a whirring noise, and is used by Australian Aborigines during religious rites.

Bull Run, Battles of /'bʊl rʌn/ in the American Civil War, two victories for the Confederate army under Gen Robert E Lee at Manassas Junction, NE Virginia: **1st Battle of Bull Run** 21 July 1861; **2nd Battle of Bull Run** 29–30 Aug 1862.

bull terrier heavily built, smooth-coated breed of dog, usually white, originating as a cross between terrier and bulldog. It was formerly used in bull-baiting, and *pit-bull terriers* are used in illegal dog fights.

Bülow /'bju:ləʊ/ Hans (Guido) Frieherr von 1830–1894. German conductor and pianist. He studied with ◊Wagner and ◊Liszt, and in 1857 married Cosima, daughter of Liszt. From 1864 he served Ludwig II of Bavaria, conducting first performances of Wagner's *Tristan und Isolde* and *Die Meistersinger*. His wife left him and married Wagner in 1870.

Bülow /'bju:ləʊ/ Prince Bernhard von 1849–1929. German diplomat and politician. He was chancellor of the German Empire 1900–09 under Kaiser Wilhelm II and, holding that self-interest was the only rule for any state, adopted attitudes to France and Russia which unintentionally reinforced the trend towards opposing European power groups: the ◊Triple Entente (Britain, France, Russia) and ◊Triple Alliance (Germany, Austria-Hungary, Italy).

bulrush two plants: the *great reed-mace* or *cat's tail Typha latifolia* with chocolate-brown tight-packed flower spikes reaching up to 15 cm/6 in long, and a type of sedge *Scirpus lacustris* with tufts of reddish-brown flowers at the top of a rounded, rush-like stem. *T. latifolia* grows in large patches in reed swamps, while *S. lacustris* is found beside water. Both are widely distributed and used for basket-weaving and thatching.

Bulwer-Lytton /'bʊlwə 'lɪtn/ Edward George Earle Lytton, 1st Baron Lytton 1803–1873. See ◊Lytton.

bumblebee large ◊bee, usually dark-coloured but banded with yellow, orange or white, belonging to the genus *Bombus*. Most species live in small colonies, usually underground, often in an old mousehole. The queen lays her eggs in a hollow nest of moss or grass at the beginning of the season. The larvae are fed on pollen and honey, and develop into workers. All the bees die at the end of the season except fertilized females, which hibernate and produce fresh colonies in the spring. Bumblebees are found naturally all over the world, with the exception of Australia, where they have been introduced to facilitate the pollination of some cultivated varieties of clover.

Bunche /bʌntʃ/ Ralph 1904–1971. US diplomat. Grandson of a slave, he was principal director of the UN Department of Trusteeship 1947–54, and UN undersecretary acting as mediator in Palestine 1948–49 and as special representative in the Congo 1960. Nobel peace prize 1950.

Bundelas Rajput clan, prominent in the 14th century, which gave its name to the Bundelkhand in N central India. The clan had replaced the ◊Chandelā in the 11th century and continued to resist the attacks of other Indian rulers until coming under British control after 1812.

Bunin /'bu:nɪn/ Ivan Alexeyevich 1870–1953. Russian writer, author of *Derevnya/The Village* 1910, which tells of the passing of peasant life; and *Gospodin iz San Frantsisko/The Gentleman from San Francisco* 1916, about the death of a millionaire on Capri, which won him a Nobel prize in 1933. He was also a poet and translated Byron into Russian.

Bunyan *Portrait of John Bunyan by Thomas Sadler (1684–85) National Portrait Gallery, London.*

Bunker Hill, Battle of the first considerable engagement in the War of ◊American Independence, 17 June 1775, near a small hill in Charlestown (now part of Boston), Massachusetts, USA; although the colonists were defeated they were able to retreat to Boston and suffered fewer casualties than the British.

Bunsen /'bʊnzən/ Robert Wilhelm von 1811–1899. German chemist, credited with the invention of the **Bunsen burner**. His name is also given to the carbon–zinc electric cell, which he invented in 1841 for use in arc lamps. In 1859 he discovered two new elements, caesium and rubidium.

bunting a number of sturdy, finch-like birds with short thick bills, of the family Emberizidae. Most live in the Americas. Some live in the Old World, such as the ◊ortolan, the ◊yellowhammer, and the *snow bunting* of the far north, which is largely white-plumaged, and migrates to temperate Europe in the winter.

Buñel /'bu:njuel/ Luis 1900–1983. Spanish ◊Surrealist film director. He collaborated with Salvador Dali in *Un Chien Andalou* 1928, and established his solo career with *Los Olvidados/The Young and the Damned* 1950. His works are often controversial and anticlerical, with black humour and erotic imagery. Later films include *Le Charme discret de la Bourgeoisie/The Discreet Charm of the Bourgeoisie* 1972 and *Cet Obscur Objet du Désir/That Obscure Object of Desire* 1977.

Bunyan /'bʌnjən/ John 1628–1688. English author. A Baptist, he was imprisoned in Bedford 1660–72 for preaching. During a second jail sentence in 1675 he started to write *Pilgrim's Progress*, the first part of which was published in 1678.

At 16, during the Civil War, he was conscripted into the Parliamentary army. Released in 1646, he passed through a period of religious doubt before joining the ◊Baptists in 1653. In 1660 he was committed to Bedford county jail for preaching, where he remained for 12 years, refusing all offers of release conditional on his not preaching again. During his confinement he wrote *Grace Abounding* describing his early spiritual struggles. Set free in 1672, he was elected pastor of the Bedford congregation, but in 1675 was again arrested and imprisoned for six months in the jail on Bedford Bridge, where he began *The Pilgrim's Progress*. The book was an instant success, and a second part followed in 1684. Other works include *The Life and Death of Mr Badman* 1680 and *The Holy War* 1682.

bunyip mythical animal of the Australian Aborigines; it is a river creature, rather like a slender, long-necked hippopotamus. The word has been adopted in Australian English to mean 'fake' or 'impostor'.

buoy a floating object used to mark channels for shipping or warn of hazards to navigation. Buoys come in different shapes, such as a pole (spar buoy), cylinder (car buoy), and cone (nun buoy). Light buoys carry a small tower surmounted by a flashing lantern, and bell buoys house a bell, which rings as the buoy moves up and down with the waves.

buoyancy the lifting effect of a fluid on a body wholly or partly immersed in it. This was studied by ◊Archimedes in the 3rd century BC.

bur or **burr** in botany, a type of 'false fruit' or ◊pseudocarp, surrounded by numerous hooks; for instance, that of burdock (*Arctium*). The term is also used to include any type of fruit or seed bearing hooks, such as that of goosegrass (*Galium aparine*) and wood avens (*Geum urbanum*). Burs catch in the feathers or fur of passing animals, and thus may be dispersed over considerable distances.

Burbage /'bɜːbɪdʒ/ Richard *c.* 1567–1619. English actor, thought to have been ◊Shakespeare's original Hamlet, Othello, and Lear. He also appeared in first productions of works by Ben Jonson, Thomas Kyd, and John Webster. His father *James Burbage* (*c.* 1530–97) built the first English playhouse, known as 'the Theatre'; his brother *Cuthbert Burbage* (*c.* 1566–1636) built the original ◊Globe Theatre 1599 in London.

burbot long, rounded fish *Lota lota* of the cod family, the only one living entirely in fresh water. Up to 1 m/3 ft long, it lives on the bottom of clear lakes and rivers, often in holes or under rocks. It is found in Europe, Asia, and North America.

Burckhardt /'bʊəkhɑːt/ Jacob 1818–1897. Swiss art historian, professor of history at Basel University 1858–93. His *The Civilization of the Renaissance in Italy* 1860, intended as part of a study of world cultural history, has been highly influential.

Burckhardt /'bʊəkhɑːt/ Johann Ludwig 1784–1817. Swiss traveller whose knowledge of Arabic enabled him to travel throughout the Middle East, visiting Mecca disguised as a Muslim pilgrim in 1814. In 1817 he discovered the ruins of Petra.

burden of proof in court proceedings, the duty of a party to produce sufficient evidence to prove that his or her case is true. In English law a higher standard of proof is required in criminal cases (beyond all reasonable doubt), than in civil cases (on the balance of probabilities).

burdock plant *Arctium lappa* of the family Compositae. A bushy herb, it has hairy leaves, and its ripe fruit are enclosed in ◊burs with strong hooks. It is a common roadside weed in Britain.

bureaucracy an organization whose structure and operations are governed to a high degree by written rules and a hierarchy of offices: in its broadest sense, all forms of administration; in its narrowest, rule by officials.

The earliest bureaucracy was probably in China. The German sociologist Max Weber saw the growth of bureaucracy in industrial societies as an inevitable reflection of the underlying shift from traditional authority to a rational and legal system of organization and control. Contemporary writers have highlighted the problems of bureaucracy, such as its inflexibility and rigid adherence to rules, and the term today is often used critically rather than in its original neutral sense.

burette in chemistry, a piece of apparatus, used in ◊titrations, for the controlled delivery of measured variable quantities of a liquid. It consists of a long, narrow, calibrated glass tube, with a tap at the bottom, leading to a narrow-bore exit.

Burgas /'bʊəgəs/ Black Sea port and resort in Bulgaria; population (1987) 198,000.

Burgenland /'bʊəgənlænd/ federal state of SE Austria, extending from the Danube south along the west border of the Hungarian plain; area 4,000 sq km/1,544 sq mi; population (1987) 267,000. It is a largely agricultural region adjoining the Neusiedler See, and produces timber, fruit, sugar, wine, lignite, antimony, and limestone. Its capital is Eisenstadt.

Bürger /'bjʊəgə/ Gottfried 1747–1794. German Romantic poet, remembered for his ballad 'Lenore' 1773.

Burges /'bɜːdʒɪz/ William 1827–1881. British Gothic revivalist architect. His chief works are Cork Cathedral 1862–76, additions to and remodelling of Cardiff Castle 1865, and Castle Coch near Cardiff 1875. His style is

Burgess /'bɜːdʒɪs/ Anthony. Pen name of Anthony John Burgess Wilson 1917– . British novelist, critic, and composer. His prolific work includes *A Clockwork Orange* 1962, set in a future London terrorized by teenage gangs, and the panoramic *Earthly Powers* 1980. His vision has been described as bleak and pessimistic, but his work is also comic and satiric, as in his novels featuring the poet Enderby.

Burgess /'bɜːdʒɪs/ Guy (Francis de Moncy) 1910–1963. British spy, a diplomat recruited by the USSR as agent; linked with Kim ◊Philby, Donald Maclean (1913–83), and Anthony ◊Blunt.

Burgess Shale Site the site of unique fossil-bearing rock formations in Yoho National Park, British Colombia, Canada. The shales in this corner of the Rocky Mountains contain more than 120 species of marine invertebrate fossils. Although discovered in 1909 by Charles Walcott, the Burgess Shales have only recently been used as evidence in the debate concerning the evolution of life.

burgh former unit of Scottish local government, abolished in 1975; the terms **burgh** and **royal burgh** once gave mercantile privilege but are now only an honorary distinction.

burgh or **burh** or **borough** a term originating in Germanic lands 9th–10th centuries, referring to a fortified settlement, usually surrounding a monastery or castle. Later, it was used to mean new towns, or towns which enjoyed particular privileges relating to government and taxation, and whose citizens were called **burghers**.

Burgh /də 'bɜːg/ Hubert de died 1243. English ◊justiciar and regent of England. He began his career in the administration of Richard I, and was promoted to the justiciarship by King John and remained in that position under Henry III from 1216 until his dismissal. He was a supporter of King John against the barons, and ended French intervention in England by his defeat of the French fleet in the Strait of Dover in 1217. He reorganized royal administration and the Common Law.

burgher a term used from the 11th century to describe citizens of ◊burghs who were freemen of the burgh, and had the right to participate in its government. They usually had to possess a house within the burgh.

Burghley /'bɜːli/ William Cecil, Baron Burghley 1520–1598. English politician, chief adviser to Elizabeth I as secretary of state from 1558 and Lord High Treasurer from 1572. He was largely responsible for the religious settlement of 1559, and took a leading role in the events preceding the execution of Mary, Queen of Scots, in 1587.

One of Edward VI's secretaries, he lost office under Queen Mary, but on Queen Elizabeth's succession became one of her most trusted ministers. He carefully avoided a premature breach with Spain in the difficult period leading up to the attack by the Spanish Armada in 1588, did a great deal towards abolishing monopolies and opening up trade, and was created Baron Burghley 1571.

burglary in UK law, the offence of entering a building as a trespasser with the intent to commit theft or other serious crime; the maximum sentence is 14 years, though aggravated burglary (involving the use of firearms or other weapons) can mean life imprisonment.

Burgos /'bʊəgɒs/ city in Castilla-León, Spain, 217 km/135 mi north of Madrid; population (1986) 164,000. It produces textiles, motor parts, and chemicals. It was capital of the old kingdom of Castile and the national hero El Cid is buried in the Gothic cathedral, built 1221–1567.

Burgoyne /'bɜːgɔɪn/ John 1722–1792. British general and dramatist. He served in the American War of Independence and surrendered 1777 to the colonists at Saratoga, New York State, in one of the pivotal battles of the war. He wrote comedies, among them *The Maid of the Oaks* 1775 and *The Heiress* 1786. He figures in George Bernard Shaw's play *The Devil's Disciple*.

Burke Born in Dublin, the British Whig politician and theorist Edmund Burke was a friend of many prominent literary figures, including Dr Johnson and Oliver Goldsmith. The picture is after the Irish painter James Barry.

Burgundy /'bɜːgəndi/ ancient kingdom and duchy in the valleys of the rivers Saône and Rhône, France. The Burgundi were a Teutonic tribe and overran the country about 400. From the 9th century to the death of Duke ◊Charles the Bold in 1477, Burgundy was the nucleus of a powerful principality. On Charles's death the duchy was incorporated into France. The capital of Burgundy was Dijon. The modern region to which it corresponds is ◊Bourgogne.

Burke /bɜːk/ Edmund 1729–1797. British Whig politician and political theorist, born in Dublin, Ireland. In Parliament from 1765, he opposed the government's attempts to coerce the American colonists, for example in *Thoughts on the Present Discontents* 1770, and supported the emancipation of Ireland, but denounced the French Revolution, for example in *Reflections on the Revolution in France* 1790.

Burke wrote *Philosophical Inquiry into the Origin of our Ideas on the Sublime and Beautiful* 1756, on aesthetics. He was paymaster of the forces in Rockingham's government 1782 and in the Fox–North coalition 1783, and after the collapse of the latter spent the rest of his career in opposition. He attacked Warren Hastings's misgovernment in India and promoted his impeachment. Burke defended his inconsistency in supporting the American but not the French Revolution in his *Appeal from the New to the Old Whigs* 1791 and *Letter to a Noble Lord* 1796, and attacked the suggestion of peace with France in *Letters on a Regicide Peace* 1795–97. He retired 1794. He was a noted orator and is regarded by modern Conservatives as the greatest of their political theorists.

Burke /bɜːk/ John 1787–1848. First publisher, in 1826, of ◊*Burke's Peerage*.

Burke /bɜːk/ Martha Jane *c.* 1852–1903. Real name of US heroine ◊Calamity Jane.

Burke /bɜːk/ Robert O'Hara 1820–1861. Australian explorer who made the first south-to-north crossing of Australia (from Victoria to the Gulf of Carpentaria), with William Wills (1834–61). Both died on the return journey, and only one of their party survived.

Burke was born in Galway, Ireland, and became a police inspector in the goldfields of Victoria.

Burke /bɜːk/ William 1792–1829. Irish murderer. He and his partner *William Hare*, living in Edinburgh, dug up the dead to sell for dissection. They increased their supplies by murdering at least 15 people. Burke was

Burkina Faso
'Land of Upright Men'

area 274,122 sq km/105,811 sq mi
capital Ouagadougou
towns Bobo-Dioulasso
physical landlocked plateau, savannah country; headwaters of the river Volta
head of state and government Blaise Compaore from 1987
political system one-party military republic
political parties Organization for Popular Democracy – Workers' Movement (ODP-MT), nationalist left-wing
exports cotton, groundnuts, livestock, hides, skins
currency CFA franc (485.00 = £1 Feb 1990)
population (1988) 8,530,000; annual growth rate 2.4%
life expectancy men 44, women 47
language French (official); about 50 native languages
religion animist 53%, Sunni Muslim 36%, Roman Catholic 11%
literacy 21% male/6% female (1985 est)
GDP $1.2 bn (1983); $180 per head of population
chronology
1958 Became a self-governing republic within the French Community.
1960 Full independence achieved, with Maurice Yameogo as the first president.
1966 Military coup led by Col Lamizana. Constitution suspended, political activities banned, and a supreme council of the armed forces established.
1969 Ban on political activities lifted.
1970 Referendum approved a new constitution leading to a return to civilian rule.
1974 After experimenting with a mixture of military and civilian rule, Lamizana reassumed full power.
1977 Ban on political activities removed. Referendum approved a new constitution based on civilian rule.
1978 Lamizana elected president.
1980 Lamizana overthrown in a bloodless coup led by Col Zerbo.
1982 Zerbo ousted in a coup by junior officers. Maj Ouédraogo became president and Thomas Sankara prime minister.
1983 Sankara seized complete power.
1984 Upper Volta renamed Burkina Faso.
1987 Sankara killed in coup led by Blaise Compaore.
1989 New government party ODP-MT formed by merger of other pro-government parties. Coup against Compaore foiled.

hanged on the evidence of Hare. Hare is said to have died a beggar in London in the 1860s.

Burke's Peerage popular name of the *Genealogical and Heraldic History of the Peerage, Baronetage, and Knightage of the United Kingdom*, first issued by John Burke in 1826. The most recent edition was in 1970.

Burkina Faso /bɜːˈkiːnə ˈfæsuː/ landlocked country in W Africa, bounded to the E by Niger, to the NW and W by Mali, and to the S by Ivory Coast, Ghana, Togo and Benin.

government A military coup in 1980 suspended the 1977 constitution and after two further coups in 1982 and 1983, power was taken by a national revolutionary council, comprising the only political factions: the Patriotic League for Development (LIPAD), the Union of the Communist Struggle (ULC) and the Communist Officers' Regrouping (ROC).

history The area now known as Burkina Faso was conquered in the 12th century by the Mossi, whose powerful warrior kingdoms lasted for over 500 years. In the 1890s it became a province of French West Africa, known as Upper Volta.

In 1958 it became a self-governing republic and in 1960 achieved full independence with Maurice Yameogo as president. A military coup in 1966 removed Yameogo and installed Col Sangoulé Lamizana as president and prime minister. He suspended the constitution, dissolved the national assembly, banned political activity and set up a supreme council of the armed forces as the instrument of government.

In 1969 the ban on political activity was lifted and in 1970 a referendum approved a new constitution, based on civilian rule, which was to come into effect after four years of combined military and civilian government. After disagreements between military and civilian members of the government, Gen Lamizana announced in 1974 a return to army rule and dissolved the national assembly.

In 1977 political activity was allowed again and a referendum approved a constitution which would create a civilian goverment. In the 1978 elections the Volta Democratic Union (UI in the national assembly and Lami dent, but a deteriorating econom ... w strikes and a bloodless coup led by Col Zerbo overthrew him in 1980. Zerbo formed a government of national recovery, suspended the constitution and dissolved the national assembly.

In 1982 Zerbo was ousted and Maj Jean-Baptiste Ouédraogo emerged as leader of a military regime, with Capt Thomas Sankara as prime minister. In 1983 Sankara seized power in another coup, becoming president and ruling through a council of ministers. Opposition members were arrested, the national assembly was dissolved, and a National Revolutionary Council (CNR) set up. In 1984 Sankara announced that the country would be known as Burkina Faso ('land of the incorruptible'), symbolizing a break with its colonial past; his government strengthened ties with Ghana and established links with Benin and Libya. Sankara was killed in Oct 1987 in a military coup led by a former close colleague, Capt Blaise Compaore (1951–). In April 1989 a restructuring of the ruling political groupings took place, and Sept 1989 a plot to oust Compaore was discovered and foiled.

burlesque in the 17th and 18th centuries, a form of satirical comedy parodying a particular play or dramatic genre. For example, ◊Gay's *The Beggar's Opera* 1728 is a burlesque of 18th-century opera, and ◊Sheridan's *The Critic* 1777 satirizes the sentimentality in contemporary drama.

In the USA from the mid-19th century, burlesque referred to a sex and comedy show invented by Michael Bennett Leavitt in 1866 with acts including acrobats, singers, and comedians. During the 1920s striptease was introduced to counteract the growing popularity of the movies; Gypsy Rose Lee was the most famous stripper. Burlesque was frequently banned in the USA.

Burlington /ˈbɜːlɪŋtən/ Richard Boyle, 3rd Earl of 1694–1753. British architectural patron and architect; one of the premier exponents of Palladianism in Britain. His buildings, such as Chiswick House in London (1725–29), are characterized by absolute adherence to the Classical rules. His major protégé was William Kent.

Burma former name (to 1989) of ◊Myanmar.

Burmese inhabitant of Burma (now Myanmar), a state with over 20 ethnic groups, all of whom have the right to Burmese nationality. The largest group are the Burmans, speakers of a Sino-Tibetan language, who migrated from the hills E of Tibet, settling in the area around Mandalay by the 11th century AD.

From the Mons, speakers of a Mon-Khmer language, the Burmans acquired Hīnyāna Buddhism and a written script based on Indian syllables. The Burmans are mainly settled in the valleys where they cultivate rice in irrigated fields. The highland people often use shifting cultivation methods and, although there are many minorities, the major groupings are Karen, Kachin, Chin, Naga, Palaung, and Wa.

burn destruction of body tissue by extremes of temperature or corrosive substances. Superficial burns cause blistering and irritation but usually heal spontaneously. Deep burns are disfiguring, and may be life-threatening.

Burns cause plasma, the fluid component of the blood, to leak from the blood vessels, and it is this loss of circulating fluid that engenders ◊shock. Emergency treatment is directed at replacing the fluid volume, preventing infection (a dire threat to the severely burned), and the management of pain. Plastic, or reconstructive, surgery, including skin grafting, may be required to compensate for damaged tissue and minimize disfigurement.

Burnaby Frederick 1842–1885. English soldier, traveller, and founder of the weekly critical journal *Vanity Fair*. He travelled to Spain, Sudan, and Russian Asia during his leave from the Horse Guards. His books include *A Ride to Khiva* 1876 and *On Horseback through Asia Minor* 1877. Burnaby joined the British Nile expedition to relieve Gen Gordon, under seige in Khartoum, Sudan, and was killed in action at the battle of Abu Klea.

Burne-Jones /ˈbɜːn ˈdʒəʊnz/ Edward Coley 1833–1898. British painter. Influenced by William Morris and the Pre-Raphaelite Rossetti, he was inspired by legend and myth, as in *King Cophetua and the Beggar Maid* 1880–84 (Tate Gallery, London), but moved towards Symbolism. He also designed tapestries and stained glass.

Burnes /bɜːnz/ Alexander 1805–1841. Scottish soldier, linguist, diplomat, and traveller in Central Asia. As a lieutenant in the Indian army he acted as assistant to the political agent at Kutch, carrying out surveys in the North West Frontier region. Following journeys to Rajputana and Lajhore he led an expedition across the Hindu Kush to Bokhara described in his *Travels into Bokhara* 1834. In 1836–37 he led a diplomatic mission to the Afghan leader Dost Mohammed, described in his book *Kabul* 1842. He was killed in Kabul during a rising that sparked off the first Afghan War.

burnet herb *Sanguisorba minor* of the rose family, also known as **salad burnet**. It smells of cucumber and can be used in salads.

Burlington Based on Palladio's Villa Rotonda, Italy, Chiswick House, London was designed by Lord Burlington 1725–29, and set in a garden designed by William Kent.

Burne-Jones *The Burne-Jones and Morris families, photographed by Frederick Hollyer in 1874. Burne-Jones (rear, left) and William Morris (standing) became close friends at Oxford.*

Burnet /'bɜːnɪt/ Gilbert 1643–1715. British historian and bishop, author of *History of His Own Time* 1723–24. His Whig views having brought him into disfavour, he retired to The Hague on the accession of James II, and became the confidential adviser of William of Orange, with whom he sailed to England in 1688. He was appointed bishop of Salisbury in 1689.

Burnet /'bɜːnɪt/ Macfarlane 1899–1985. Australian physician, authority on immunology and viral diseases. He was awarded the Order of Merit in 1958 in recognition of his work on such diseases as influenza, polio and cholera.

Burnett /bə'net/ Frances Eliza Hodgson 1849–1924. English writer, living in the USA from 1865, whose novels for children include the rags-to-riches tale *Little Lord Fauntleroy* 1886 and the sentimental *The Secret Garden* 1909.

Burney /'bɜːni/ Fanny (Frances) 1752–1840. English novelist and diarist, daughter of the musician Dr Charles Burney (1726–1814). She achieved success with *Evelina*, published anonymously 1778, became a member of Dr ◊Johnson's circle, received a post at court from Queen Charlotte, and in 1793 married the émigré Gen D'Arblay. She published two further novels, *Cecilia* 1782 and *Camilla* 1796, and her diaries and letters appeared in 1842.

Burnham /'bɜːnəm/ Forbes 1923–1985. Guyanese Marxist-Leninist politician. He was prime minister 1964–80, leading the country to independence 1966 and declaring it the world's first cooperative republic 1970. He was executive president 1980–85. Resistance to the US landing in Grenada 1983 was said to be due to his forewarning the Grenadans of the attack.

Burnham /'bɜːnəm/ James 1905–1987. US philosopher, who argued in *The Managerial Revolution* 1941 that world control is passing from politicians and capitalists to the new class of business executives, the managers.

Burnley /'bɜːnli/ town in Lancashire, England, 19 km/12 mi NE of Blackburn; population (1983) 92,000. Formerly a cotton-manufacturing town.

Burns /bɜːnz/ John 1858–1943. British labour leader, sentenced to six weeks' imprisonment for his part in the Trafalgar Square demonstration on 'Bloody Sunday' 13 Nov 1887, and leader of the strike in 1889 securing the dockers' tanner (wage of 6d per hour). An Independent Labour member of parliament 1892–1918, he was the first person from the labouring classes to be a member of the

Cabinet, as president of the Local Government Board 1906–14.

Burns /bɜːnz/ Robert 1759–1796. Scottish poet, notable for his use of the Scots dialect at a time when it was not considered suitably 'elevated' for literature. Burns's first volume, *Poems, Chiefly in the Scottish Dialect*, appeared in 1786. In addition to his poetry Burns wrote or adapted many songs, including 'Auld Lang Syne'.

Born at Alloway near Ayr, he became joint tenant with his brother of his late father's farm at Mossgiel in 1784, but was unsuccessful. Following the success of his first volume of poems in 1786 he farmed at Ellisland, near Dumfries. He became district excise officer, on the failure of his farm in 1791. His fame rests equally on his poems (such as 'Holy Willie's Prayer', 'Tam o'Shanter', 'The Jolly Beggars', and 'To a Mouse') and his songs—sometimes wholly original, sometimes adaptations—of which he contributed some 300 to Johnson's *Scots Musical Museum* 1787–1803 and Thomson's *Scottish Airs with Poetry* 1793–1811.

Burns /bɜːnz/ Terence 1944– . British economist. A monetarist, he was director of the London Business School for Economic Forecasting 1976–79, and became chief economic adviser to the Thatcher government 1980.

burr alternative name for ◊bur.

Burr /bɜː/ Aaron 1756–1836. US politician, on George Washington's staff during the War of Independence. He tied with Thomas Jefferson in the presidential election of 1800, but Alexander ◊Hamilton influenced the House of Representatives to vote Jefferson in, Burr becoming vice president. He killed Hamilton in a duel in 1804, became a social outcast, and had to leave the USA for some years following the 'Burr conspiracy', which implicated him variously in a scheme to conquer Mexico, or part of Florida, or to rule over a seceded Louisiana.

Burr /bɜː/ Raymond 1917– . Canadian character actor who played Perry Mason in the television series of the same name and in several films. He played the murderer in Alfred Hitchcock's *Rear Window* 1954, and his other films include *The Adventures of Don Juan* 1948 and *Godzilla* (English-language version) 1956.

Burra /'bʌrə/ Edward 1905–1976. British painter devoted to themes of city life, its hustle, humour, and grimy squalor. His watercolour scenes of Harlem, New York, 1933–34, are characteristic. Postwar works include religious paintings and landscapes.

Burroughs /'bʌrəuz/ Edgar Rice 1875–1950. US novelist, born in Chicago. He wrote *Tarzan of the Apes* 1914, the story of an aristocratic child lost in the jungle and reared by apes, and many other thrillers.

Burroughs /'bʌrəuz/ William S 1914– . US novelist, born in St Louis, Missouri. He dropped out and, as part of the ◊Beat Generation, wrote *Junkie* 1953, *The Naked Lunch* 1959, *The Soft Machine* 1961, and *Dead Fingers Talk* 1963. Later novels include *Queer* 1986.

Burroughs /'bʌrəuz/ William Steward 1857–1898. US industrialist, who invented the first hand-operated adding machine to give printed results.

Bursa /'bɜːsə/ city in NW Turkey, with a port at Mudania; population (1985) 614,000. It was the capital of the Ottoman Empire 1326–1423.

Burt /bɜːt/ Cyril Lodowic 1883–1971. British psychologist. A specialist in child and mental development, he argued in *The Young Delinquent* 1925 the importance of social and environmental factors in delinquency. After his death it was discovered that he falsified some of his experimental results in an attempt to prove his theory that intelligence is largely inherited.

Burton /'bɜːtn/ Richard Francis 1821–1890. British traveller, master of 35 oriental languages, and translator of the *Arabian Nights* 1885–88, the *Kama Sutra*, and *The Perfumed Garden* 1886. In 1853 he made the pilgrimage to Mecca in disguise; in 1856 he was commissioned by the Foreign Office to explore the sources of the Nile, and (with Speke) reached Lake Tanganyika 1858. His wife burned his other manuscripts after his death.

Burton /'bɜːtn/ Richard. Stage name of Richard Jenkins 1925–1984. Welsh actor. He was remarkable for his voice, as in the radio adaptation of Dylan Thomas's *Under Milk Wood*, and for his marital and acting partnership with Elizabeth Taylor, with whom he appeared in the films *Cleopatra* 1962 and *Who's Afraid of Virginia Woolf?* 1966. His later works include *Equus* 1977 and *1984* 1984.

Burton /'bɜːtn/ Robert 1577–1640. English philosopher, who wrote an analysis of depression, *Anatomy of Melancholy* 1621, a compendium of information on the medical and religious opinions of the time, much used by later authors. Born in Leicester, he was educated at Oxford, and remained there for the rest of his life as a fellow of Christ Church.

Burton-upon-Trent /'bɜːtn əpɒn 'trent/ town in Staffordshire, England, NE of Birmingham; population (1983) 57,725. Industries include brewing, tyres, and engineering.

Burundi /bu'rundi/ country in east-central Africa, bounded to the N by Rwanda, to the W by Zaïre, to the S by Lake Tanganyika, and to the SE and E by Tanzania.

government Under its 1981 constitution, Burundi's only political party is the Union for National Progress (UPRONA). The president is elected by universal suffrage for a five-year term and a 65-member national assembly has the same period of tenure, 52 of its members being elected by suffrage and 13 appointed by the president. Ultimate power lies with UPRONA.

history Originally inhabited by the Twa, but taken over by the Hutu in the 13th century, Burundi was overrun in the 15th century by the Tutsi. In 1890, ruled by a Tutsi king and known as Urundi, it became part of German East Africa and during World War I was occupied by Belgium. Later, as part of Ruanda-Urundi, it was administered by Belgium as a League of Nations, and then United Nations, trust territory.

The 1961 elections, supervised by the UN, were won by UPRONA, a party formed by Louis, one of the sons of the reigning king, Mwambutsa IV. Louis was assassinated after only two weeks as prime minister, and was succeeded by his brother-in-law, André Muhirwa. In 1962 Urundi separated from Ruanda, and, as Burundi, was given internal self-government and then full independence.

Burundi
Republic of
(Republika y'Uburundi)

area 27,834 sq km/10,744 sq mi
capital Bujumbura
towns Kitega
physical grassy highland
features Lake Tanganyika, Great Rift Valley; source of the White Nile
head of state and government Pierre Buyoya from 1987
political system one-party military republic
political parties Union for National Progress (UPRONA), nationalist socialist
exports coffee, cotton, tea, nickel, hides, livestock; there are also 500 million tonnes of peat reserves in the basin of the Akanyaru river
currency Burundi franc (295.25 = £1 Feb 1990)
population (1988) 5,130,000 (of whom 15%

are the Nilotic Tutsi, still holding most of the land and political power, and the remainder the Bantu Hutu); annual growth rate 2.8%
life expectancy men 45, women 48
language Kirundi (a Bantu language) and French (official); Kiswahili
religion Roman Catholic over 50%, with a Sunni Muslim minority
literacy 43% male/26% female (1985)
GDP $1 bn (1983); $273 per head of population
chronology
1962 Separated from Ruanda-Urundi, as Burundi, and given independence as a monarchy under King Mwambutsa IV.
1966 King deposed by his son Charles, who became Ntare V and was in turn deposed by his prime minister, Capt Michel Micombero, who declared Burundi a republic.
1972 Ntare V killed, allegedly by the Hutu ethnic group. Massacres of 150,000 Hutus by the rival Tutsi ethnic group, of which Micombero was a member.
1973 Micombero made president and prime minister.
1974 UPRONA declared the only legal political party, with the president as its secretary general.
1976 Army coup deposed Micombero. Col Jean-Baptiste Bagaza appointed president by Supreme Revolutionary Council.
1981 New constitution adopted, providing for a national assembly.
1984 Bagaza elected president as sole candidate.
1987 Bagaza deposed in coup in Sept. Maj Pierre Buyoya headed new Military Council for National Redemption.
1988 Some 24,000 majority Hutus killed by Tutsis. First Hutu prime minister appointed.

In 1966 King Mwambutsa IV, after a 50-year reign, was deposed by another son, Charles, with army help, and the constitution was suspended. Later that year Charles, now Ntare V, was deposed by his prime minister, Capt Michel Micombero, who declared Burundi a republic. Micombero was a Tutsi, whose main rivals were the numerically superior Hutu. In 1972 the deposed Ntare V was killed, allegedly by the Hutu, giving the Tutsi an excuse to massacre large numbers of Hutu.

In 1973 amendments to the constitution made Micombero president and prime minister and in the following year UPRONA was declared the only political party. In 1976 Micombero was deposed in an army coup led by Col Jean-Baptiste Bagaza, who became president, with a prime minister and a new council of ministers. In 1977 the prime minister announced a return to civilian rule and a five-year plan to eliminate corruption and secure social justice, including promoting some Hutu to government positions.

In 1978 the post of prime minister was abolished and in 1981 a new constitution, providing for a national assembly, was adopted after a referendum. Bagaza was re-elected 1984 (he was the only presidential candidate) but was deposed in a military coup Sept 1987, his government being replaced by a 'Military Council for National Redemption' headed by Maj Pierre Buyoya, believed to be a Tutsi.

Bury /'beri/ town in Greater Manchester, England, on the river Irwell, 16 km/10 mi N of central Manchester; population (1986) 173,650. Industries include cotton, chemicals, and engineering.

Buryat /,buri'ɑːt/ republic of the USSR, in Soviet central Asia
area 351,300 sq km/135,600 sq mi
capital Ulan-Udé
physical bounded on the S by Mongolia, on the W by Lake Baikal; mountainous and forested
products coal, timber, building materials, fish, sheep, cattle

population (1986) 1,014,000
history settled by Russians 17th century; annexed from China by treaties 1689 and 1727.

Bury St Edmunds /'beri/ market town in Suffolk, England, on the river Lark; population (1985) 29,500. It was named after St Edmund, and there are remains of a Benedictine abbey founded in 1020.

bus a vehicle that carries fare-paying passengers on a fixed route, with frequent stops where passengers can get on and off.

An omnibus appeared briefly on the streets of Paris in the 1660s, when the mathematician Blaise Pascal introduced the first horse-drawn vehicles for public use. But a successful service, again in Paris, was not established until 1827. Two years later George Shillibeer introduced a horse-drawn bus in London. Many bus companies sprang up, the most successful being the London General Omnibus Company, which operated from 1856 until 1911, by which time petrol-driven buses had taken over. Following deregulation in the 1980s, private bus operators in Britain were allowed to set up fare-paying routes.

Busby /'bʌzbi/ Richard 1606–1695. English headmaster of Westminster school from 1640, renowned for his use of flogging. Among his pupils were Dryden, Locke, Atterbury, and Prior.

Bush /buʃ/ Alan (Dudley) 1900– . British composer. A student of ◊Ireland, he later adopted a didactic simplicity in his compositions in line with his Marxist beliefs. He has written a large number of works for orchestra, voice, and chamber groups. His operas include *Wat Tyler* 1952, and *Men of Blackmoor* 1956.

Bush /buʃ/ George 1924– . US Republican president from 1989. He was director of the Central Intelligence Agency (CIA) 1976–81 and US vice president 1981–89. Evidence came to light in 1987 linking him with the ◊Irangate scandal. His responses as president to the Soviet leader Gorbachev's diplomatic initiatives were criticized as inadequate but sending US troops to depose

his former ally, Gen Noriega of Panama, proved a popular move at home.

Bush, son of a Connecticut senator, moved to Texas in 1948 to build up an oil-drilling company. A congressman 1967–70, he was appointed US ambassador to the United Nations (1971–73) and Republican national chair(1973–74) by President Nixon. During the Ford administration, Bush was a special envoy to China 1974–75. During his time as head of the CIA he is alleged to have supported the cocaine-trafficking Noriega of Panama as a US ally. Panama was also used as a channel for the secret supply of arms to Iran and the Nicaraguan Contra guerrillas, of which Bush, then vice president, claimed to have been unaware. In the trial of Oliver ◊North evidence emerged that Bush had visited the president of Honduras in 1985 and offered him extra US aid in exchange for help to the Contras. When, in Dec 1989, Noriega proved uncontrollable, Bush sent an invasion force to Panama and set up a puppet government; Noriega was sent to the USA to stand trial.

bushbuck antelope *Tragelaphus scriptus* found over most of Africa S of the Sahara. Up to 1 m/3 ft high, the males have keeled horns twisted into spirals, and are brown to blackish. The females are generally hornless, lighter and redder. All have white markings, including stripes or vertical rows of dots down the sides. Rarely far from water, bushbuck live in woods and thick brush.

bushel dry or liquid measure equal to 8 gallons/36.37 l (2219.36 cu in) in Britain; some US states have different standards according to the goods measured.

bushido chivalric code of honour of the Japanese military caste, the ◊samurai; the term dates only from the 17th century, and became a nationalist, militarist slogan in the years before World War II.

Bushman former term for a member of the Kung, an aboriginal people of southern Africa, still living to some extent nomadically, especially in the Kalahari Desert. Formerly numerous, only some 26,000 remain. They are traditionally hunters and gatherers, and speak a Khoisan language. Their early art survives in cave paintings.

bushmaster large snake *Lachesis muta* related to the rattlesnakes. Up to 4 m/12 ft long, found in wooded areas of South and Central America, it has a powerful venomous bite. When alarmed, it produces a noise by vibrating its tail amongst dry leaves.

bushranger Australian armed robber of the 19th century. The first bushrangers were escaped convicts. The last gang was led by Ned ◊Kelly and his brother Dan in 1878–80. They form the subject of many Australian ballads.

business plan a key management tool, which focuses on business objectives, the products or services involved, estimated market potential, expertise in the firm, projected financial results, the money required from investors, and the likely investment return. Although a business plan is necessary for management to focus on a firm's future growth and plan for change, it is also vital when there is a need to raise capital. Potential investors will want to see a business plan before making any assessment of the firm's viability.

business school institution for training in management and marketing, such as the London Business School (LBS), Harvard in the USA, and Insead in France.

Busoni /buːˈsɔːni/ Ferruccio (Dante Benvenuto) 1866–1924. Italian pianist, composer, and music critic. Much of his music was for the piano, but he also composed several operas including *Doktor Faust*, completed by a pupil after his death.

Buss /bʌs/ Frances Mary 1827–1894. British pioneer in education for women. She first taught in a school run by her mother, and at 18, she founded her own school for girls in London, which became the North London Collegiate School in 1850. She founded the Camden School for Girls in 1871, and was influential in raising the status of women teachers and the academic standard of women's education in the UK. She is often associated with Dorothea ◊Beale, a fellow pioneer.

bust in finance, a failure or bankruptcy.

Bustamante /ˌbʌstəˈmænti/ (William) Alexander (born Clarke) 1884–1977. Jamaican socialist politician. As leader of the Labour Party, he was the first prime minister of independent Jamaica 1962–67.

bustard type of bird, family Otididae, related to cranes but with rounder bodies, thicker necks, and relatively short beaks, found on the ground on open plains and fields.

The **great bustard** Otis tarda is one of the heaviest flying birds at 18 kg/40 lb, and the larger males may have a length of 1 m/3 ft and wingspan of 2.3 m/7.5 ft. It is found in Europe and N Asia, but is extinct in Britain, although attempts are being made by the Great Bustard Trust (1970) to naturalize it again on Salisbury Plain. The **little bustard** Otis tetrax is less than half the size of the great bustard, and is also found in continental Europe. The **great Indian bustard** is endangered because of hunting and loss of its habitat to agriculture; there are less than 1,000 individuals left.

butadiene CH_2:CHCH:CH_2 (modern name **buta-1,3-diene**) an inflammable gas derived from petroleum, and used in making synthetic rubber.

butane C_4H_{10} an alkane (paraffin hydrocarbon) gas, a by-product of petroleum manufacture or from natural gas. Liquefied under pressure, it is used as a fuel for industrial and domestic purposes, for example in portable cookers.

Bute /bjuːt/ island and resort in the Firth of Clyde, Scotland; area 120 sq km/46 sq mi. The chief town is Rothesay. It is separated from the mainland in the north by a winding channel, the **Kyles of Bute**. With Arran and the adjacent islands it made up the former county of Bute, merged 1975 in the region of Strathclyde.

Bute /bjuːt/ John Stuart, 3rd Earl of Bute 1713–1792. British Tory politician, prime minister 1762–63. On the accession of George III in 1760, he became the chief instrument in the king's policy for breaking the power of the Whigs and establishing the personal rule of the monarch through Parliament.

Bute succeeded his father 1723, and in 1737 was elected a representative peer for Scotland. His position as the king's favourite and the supplanter of the popular prime minister Pitt the Elder made him hated in the country. He resigned 1763 after the Seven Years' War.

Buthelezi /ˌbuːtəˈleɪzi/ Chief Gatsha 1928– . Zulu leader and politician, chief minister of KwaZulu, a black 'homeland' in the Republic of South Africa from 1970. He is founder and president of ◊**Inkatha** 1975, a paramilitary organization for attaining a nonracial democratic political system.

Great-grandson of King ◊Cetewayo, Buthelezi is strongly opposed to KwaZulu becoming a ◊Black National State, but envisages a confederation of the black areas, with eventual majority rule over all South Africa under a one-party socialist system. Inkatha gets its name from the grass coil worn by Zulu women for carrying head loads: its many strands give it strength.

Butler /ˈbʌtlə/ Joseph 1692–1752. British priest, who became dean of St Paul's in 1740 and bishop of Durham in 1750; his *Analogy of Religion* 1736 argued that it is no more rational to accept ◊deism, arguing for God as the first cause, than revealed religion (not arrived at by reasoning).

Butler /ˈbʌtlə/ Josephine (born Gray) 1828–1906. British social reformer. She promoted women's education and the Married Women's Property Act, and campaigned against the Contagious Diseases Acts of 1862–70, which made women in garrison towns liable to compulsory examination for venereal disease. As a result of her campaigns the acts were repealed in 1883.

Butler /ˈbʌtlə/ Reg(inald) 1913–1981. British sculptor, once an architect and a blacksmith, best known for cast or forged iron works, abstract and figurative. In 1953 he won the international competition for a monument to The Unknown Political Prisoner (a model is in the Tate Gallery, London).

Butler /ˈbʌtlə/ Richard Austen, Baron Butler 1902–1982. British Conservative politician, known from his initials as Rab. As minister of education 1941–45, he was responsible for the Education Act 1944; he was chancellor of the Exchequer 1951–55, Lord Privy Seal 1955–59, and foreign minister 1963–64. As a candidate for the premiership, he was defeated by Harold Macmillan in 1957 (under whom he was home secretary 1957–62), and by Douglas-Home in 1963. He was master of Trinity College, Cambridge, 1965–78.

Butler /ˈbʌtlə/ Samuel 1612–1680. English satirist. His poem *Hudibras*, published in three parts in 1663, 1664, and 1678, became immediately popular for its biting satire against the Puritans.

Butler /ˈbʌtlə/ Samuel 1835–1902. English author, who made his name in 1872 with his satiric attack on contemporary utopianism, *Erewhon* ('nowhere' reversed), but is now remembered for his autobiographical *The Way of All Flesh* written 1872–85 and published 1903.

The Fair Haven examined the miraculous element in Christianity. *Life and Habit* 1877 and other works were devoted to a criticism of the theory of natural selection. In *The Authoress of the Odyssey* he maintained that the *Odyssey* was the work of a woman.

Butlin /ˈbʌtlɪn/ 'Billy' (William) 1899–1980. British holiday-camp entrepreneur. Born in South Africa, he went in early life to Canada, but later entered the fair business in the UK. He originated a chain of camps that provide accommodation, meals, and amusements at an inclusive price.

Butor /bjuːˈtɔː/ Michel 1926– . French writer, a practitioner of the 'anti-novel'. His works include *Passage de Milan/Passage from Milan* 1954, *Degrès/Degrees* 1960, and *L'Emploi du temps/Passing Time* 1963. *Mobile* 1962 is a volume of essays.

Butskellism UK term for political policies tending towards the middle ground in an effort to gain popular support, named after R A ◊Butler (moderate Conservative) and Hugh ◊Gaitskell (moderate Labour politician).

butte /bjuːt/ a steep-sided flat-topped hill, formed in horizontally layered sedimentary rocks, largely in arid areas. A large butte with a pronounced tablelike profile is a ◊mesa. Buttes and mesas are characteristic of semi-arid areas where remnants of resistant rock layers protect softer rock underneath, as in the plateau regions of Colorado, Utah, and Arizona, USA.

Butte /bjuːt/ mining town in Montana, USA, in the Rocky Mountains; population (1980) 37,200. Butte was founded in 1864 during a rush for gold, soon exhausted; copper was found some 20 years later.

butter foodstuff made from the fatty portion of milk. Making butter by hand, which is done by skimming off the cream and churning it, was traditionally a convenient means of preserving milk.

The transfer of buttermaking from a farm-based to a factory-based process began in the last quarter of the 19th century with the introduction of centrifugal separators for the instant separation of cream from milk. It could then be conveyed into large steam-powered churns. Today, most butter is made on a continuous system that was devised in Germany during World War II. Inside a single machine, the cream is churned, the buttermilk drawn off, and the butter washed, salted, and worked, to achieve an even consistency. A continuous stream of finished butter is extruded from the machine ready for wrapping.

buttercup plant of the genus *Ranunculus* with divided leaves and yellow flowers. Species include the **common buttercup** Ranunculus acris and the **creeping buttercup** Ranunculus repens.

Butterfield William 1814–1900. English architect. His work is Gothic Revival characterized by vigorous, aggressive forms and multicoloured striped and patterned brickwork, as in the church of All Saints, Margaret Street, London, and Keble College, Oxford.

His schools, parsonages, and cottages develop an appealing functional secular style that anticipates the work of Philip ◊Webb and other ◊Arts and Crafts architects. At Baldersby, Yorkshire, UK, a whole village of church, rectory, almshouse, school, and cottages shows his work in all its aspects.

butterfly insect belonging, like moths, to the order Lepidoptera, in which the wings are covered with tiny scales, often brightly coloured. There are some 15,000 species of butterfly, many of which are under threat throughout the world because of the destruction of habitat.

Butterflies have a tubular proboscis through which they suck up nectar, or, in some species, carrion, dung, or urine. ◊Metamorphosis is complete; the pupa, or chrysalis, is usually without the protection of a cocoon. Adult lifespan may be only a few weeks, but some species hibernate and lay eggs in the spring.

The largest family, Nymphalidae, has some 6,000 species; it includes the peacock, tortoiseshells, and fritillaries. The family Pieridae includes the **cabbage white**, one of the few butterflies injurious to crops. The Lycaenidae are chiefly small, often with metallic coloration, for example the blues, coppers, and hairstreaks. The **large blue** Lycaena arion (extinct in Britain from 1979, but re-established 1984) has a complex life history: it lays its eggs on wild thyme, and the caterpillars are then taken by Myrmica ants to their nests. The ants milk their honey glands, while the caterpillars feed on the ant larvae. In the spring, the caterpillars finally pupate and emerge as butterflies. The mainly tropical Papilionidae, or swallowtails, are large and very beautiful, especially the South American species. The world's largest butterfly is **Queen Alexandra's birdwing** Ornithoptera alexandrae of Papua New Guinea, with a body 7.5 cm/3 in long and a wingspan of 25 cm/10 in. The most spectacular migrant is the orange and black **monarch butterfly** Danaus plexippus, which may fly from N Canada to Mexico in the autumn.

Butterflies usually differ from moths in having the antennae club-shaped rather than plumed or feathery, no 'lock' between the fore and hindwing, and resting with the wings in the vertical position rather than flat or sloping.

butterfly fish several fishes, not all related. The **freshwater butterfly fish** Pantodon buchholzi of W Africa can leap from the water and glide for a short distance on its large wing-like pectoral fins. Up to 10 cm/4 in long, it lives in stagnant water. The **tropical marine butterfly fishes**, family Chaetodontidae, are brightly coloured with laterally flattened bodies, often with long snouts which they poke into crevices in rocks and coral when feeding.

butterwort insectivorous plant, genus *Pinguicula*, with purplish flowers and a rosette of leaves covered with a sticky secretion that traps insects.

Buxtehude /ˌbʊkstəˈhuːdə/ Diderik 1637–1707. Danish composer and organist at Lübeck, Germany, who influenced ◊Bach and ◊Handel. He is remembered for his organ works and cantatas, written for his evening concerts or *Abendmusiken*.

Buxton /ˈbʌkstən/ spa town in Derbyshire, England; population (1981) 21,000. It has been known from Roman times for its hot springs. It has a restored Edwardian opera house.

butterfly

An adult female cabbage white lays her eggs on the underside of a cabbage leaf. The caterpillars that emerge are "feeding and growing machines". They look quite unlike the winged adults. In autumn, the caterpillars cease feeding, rest on a tree or post, and form a cocoon around themselves. The following spring, the young adults emerge, mate, then die.

As the adult emerges from the cocoon its wings fill with blood and harden.

forewing
hindwing
compound eye
antenna
proboscis
6. adult
eye
antenna
position of legs and proboscis
5. chrysalis
wing
silk girdle
4. pupa
spiracle
abdomen
3. full-size caterpillar

eggs laid
1. egg
2.5mm
2. caterpillar
thoracic segments
spiracles
clasper
true legs
false legs

silk girdles

life cycle stages

development timescale					sheds skin		earliest emergence			
stage	1	2			3 & 4		5	can remain pupating for up to 6 months ►		6
weeks	1	2	3	4	5	6	7	8		34

Caterpillars have biting mouthparts and simple eyes. They bite off pieces of leaves with their jaws. Adult butterflies have sucking mouthparts, with which they feed on nectar, and large, compound eyes.

eyes
antenna
jaws
caterpillar

antenna
eye
tube-like mouthparts
butterfly

buyer's market a market having an excess of goods and services on offer and where prices are likely to be declining. The buyer benefits from the wide choice and competition available.

buzzard any of a number of species of medium-sized hawks with broad wings, often seen soaring. The **common buzzard** *Buteo buteo* of Europe and Asia is about 55 cm/1.8 ft long with a wingspan of over 1.2 m/4 ft. It preys on a variety of small animals up to the size of a rabbit. The **rough-legged buzzard** *Buzzard lagopus* lives in the northern tundra and eats lemmings. The **honey buzzard** *Pernis apivora* feeds largely, as its name suggests, on honey and insect larvae. It summers in Europe and W Asia and winters in Africa.

Byblos /'bɪblɒs/ ancient Phoenician city (modern Jebeil), 32 km/20 mi N of Beirut, Lebanon. Known to the Assyrians and Babylonians as Gubla, it had a thriving export of cedar and pinewood to Egypt as early as 1500 BC. In Roman times called Byblos, it boasted an amphitheatre, baths, and a temple dedicated to an unknown male god, and was noted for its celebration of the resurrection of Adonis, worshipped as a god of vegetation.

Bydgoszcz /'bɪdgɒʃtʃ/ industrial river port in N Poland, 105 km/65 mi NE of Poznan on the river **Byelorussia**

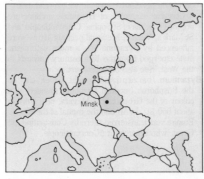

Minsk

Byrd *US explorer Richard Byrd was the first man to fly to both the North (1926) and South (1929) Poles.*

Warta; population (1985) 361,000. As **Bromberg** it was under Prussian control 1772–1919.

Byelorussia /bɪˌeləʊˈrʌʃə/ (Russian **Belaruskaya** or 'White Russia') constituent republic of western USSR since 1919
area 207,600 sq km/80,154 sq mi
capital Minsk
features more than 25% forested; rivers W Dvina, Dnieper and its tributaries, including the Pripet and Beresina; the Pripet Marshes in the east. The climate is mild and damp
products peat, agricultural machinery, fertilizers, glass, textiles, leather, salt, electrical goods, meat, dairy produce
population (1987) 10,078,000; 79% Byelorussian, 12% Russian, 4% Polish, 2% Ukrainian, 1% Jewish.

Byng /bɪŋ/ George, Viscount Torrington 1663–1733. British admiral. He captured Gibraltar 1704, commanded the fleet that prevented an invasion of England by the 'Old Pretender' James Francis Edward Stuart 1708, and destroyed the Spanish fleet at Messina 1718. John ◊Byng was his fourth son.

Byng /bɪŋ/ John 1704–1757. British admiral. Byng failed in the attempt to relieve Fort St Philip when in 1756 the island of Minorca was invaded by France. He was court-martialled and shot. As the French writer Voltaire commented, it was done 'to encourage the others'.

Byng /bɪŋ/ Julian, 1st Viscount of Vimy 1862–1935. British general in World War I, commanding troops in Turkey and France, where, after a victory at Vimy Ridge, he took command of the Third Army. On Nov 20–Dec 7 1917 he led a successful tank attack on Cambrai. He was governor general of Canada 1921–26, and was made a viscount in 1926 and a field marshal in 1932.

Byrd /bɜːd/ Richard Evelyn 1888–1957. US aviator and explorer. The first to fly over the North Pole (1926), he also flew over the South Pole

Byrd *British composer William Byrd, often regarded as the greatest Tudor composer. He was a firm Catholic, and was several times prosecuted as a recusant, but wrote for both Catholic and Anglican churches.*

Byron *A portrait of Lord Byron by Thomas Phillips (signed 1835) National Portrait Gallery, London.*

(1929), and led five overland expeditions in Antarctica. See ◊Arctic and ◊Antarctic tables.

Byrd /bɜːd/ William 1543–1623. British composer. His church choral music (set to Latin words, as he was a firm Catholic) represents his most important work. He also composed secular vocal and instrumental music.

He became organist at Lincoln cathedral in 1563. He shared with ◊Tallis the honorary post of organist in Queen Elizabeth's Chapel Royal, and in 1575 he and Tallis were granted a monopoly in the printing and selling of music.

Byrds, the /bɜːdz/ US pioneering folk-rock group 1964–73. Remembered for their 12-string guitar sound and the hits 'Mr Tambourine Man' 1965 (a version of Bob Dylan's song) and 'Eight Miles High' 1966, they moved towards country rock in the late 1960s.

The Byrds formed in Los Angeles at the time of the Beatles' greatest influence, and initially comprised Roger McGuinn (1942–), David Crosby (1941–), Gene Clark (1941–), Chris Hillman (1942–), and Michael Clarke (1944–), most of whom had a folk-music background. Before long they went free-form psychedelic, then country and western, and dissolved 1973 after many changes of line-up that left only the guitarist McGuinn of the original members.

Byron /ˈbaɪrən/ George Gordon, 6th Baron Byron 1788–1824. English poet, who became the symbol of Romanticism and political liberalism throughout Europe in the 19th century. His reputation was established with the first two cantos of *Childe Harold* 1812. Later works include *The Prisoner of Chillon* 1816, *Beppo* 1818, *Mazeppa* 1819, and, most notably, *Don Juan* 1819–24. He left England in 1816, spending most of his later life in Italy.

Born in London, Byron succeeded his great-uncle to the title in 1798. Educated at Harrow and Cambridge, he published his first volume *Hours of Idleness* 1807, and attacked its harsh critics in *English Bards and Scotch Reviewers* 1809. Overnight fame came with the first two cantos of *Childe Harold*, romantically describing his tours in Portugal, Spain, and the Balkans (third canto 1816, fourth 1818). In 1815 he married the mathematician Anne Milbanke (by whom he had a daughter, Augusta Ada Byron), separating from her a year later amid much scandal. He then went to Europe where he became friendly with Percy and Mary ◊Shelley. He engaged in Italian revolutionary politics, and sailed for Greece in 1823 to further the Greek struggle for independence, but died of fever at Missolonghi. He is remembered for his lyrics, his colloquially easy *Letters*, and, particularly in Europe, as the 'patron saint' of romantic liberalism. His friend Thomas ◊Moore wrote one of the first biographies of Byron.

Byron /ˈbaɪrən/ Robert 1904–1941. British writer on travel and architecture, including *The Byzantine Achievement* 1929 and *The Road to Oxiana* 1937, an account of a journey Iran–Afghanistan in 1933–34.

byte in computing, a basic unit of storage of information. A byte is eight ◊bits and can hold either a single character (letter, digit, or punctuation symbol) or a number between 0 and 255. Not all computers use bytes, although the unit is widely used in microcomputers.

Byte also now refers to a single memory location; large computer memory size is measured in thousands of bytes (kilobytes or KB) or millions of bytes (megabytes or MB).

Byzantine Empire the *Eastern Roman Empire* 395–1453, with its capital at Constantinople (Byzantium).

330 Emperor Constantine removed his capital to Constantinople.

395 The Roman Empire was divided into eastern and western halves.

476 The Western Empire was overrun by barbarian invaders.

527–565 Justinian I temporarily recovered Italy, N Africa, and parts of Spain.

7th–8th century Syria, Egypt, and N Africa were lost to the Arabs, who twice besieged Constantinople (673–77, 718), but the Byzantines maintained their hold on Anatolia.

8th–9th century The ◊Iconoclastic controversy brought the emperors into conflict with the papacy, and in 867 the Greek Orthodox church broke with the Roman.

867–1056 Under the Macedonian dynasty the Byzantine Empire reached the height of its prosperity; the Bulgars proved a formidable danger, but after a long struggle were finally crushed in 1018 by ◊Basil II ('the Bulgar-Slayer'). After Basil's death the Byzantine Empire declined because of internal factions.

1071–73 The Seljuk Turks conquered most of Anatolia.

1204 The Fourth Crusade sacked Constantinople and set Baldwin of Flanders (1171–1205) on the throne.

1261 The Latin (W European) Empire was overthrown; the Byzantine Empire maintained a precarious existence.

1453 The Turks captured Constantinople.

Byzantine literature written mainly in the Greek *koinē*, a form of Greek accepted as the literary language of the 1st century AD and increasingly separate from the spoken tongue of the people, it is chiefly concerned with theology, history, and commentaries on the Greek classics. Its chief authors are the theologians St Basil, Gregory of Nyssa, Gregory of Nazianzus, Chrysostom (4th century AD), and John of Damascus (8th century); the historians Zosimus (about 500), Procopius (6th century), Bryennius and his wife ◊Anna Comnena (about 1100), and Georgius Acropolita (1220–82); and the encyclopedist Suidas (about 975). Drama was non-existent, and poetry, save for the hymns of the 6th–8th centuries, scanty and stilted, but there were many popular saints' lives.

Byzantine style a style in the visual arts and architecture, which originated in Byzantium (4th–5th centuries) and spread to Italy, throughout the Balkans, and to Russia, where it survived for many centuries. It is characterized by heavy stylization, strong linear emphasis, the use of rigid artistic stereotypes, and rich colours, particularly gold. Byzantine artists excelled in mosaic work and manuscript painting. In architecture the dome supported on pendentives was in widespread use.

Classical examples of Byzantine architecture are the churches of St Sophia, Constantinople, and St Mark's, Venice. Medieval painting styles were influenced by Byzantine art; a more naturalistic style emerged from the 13th century onwards in the West. See also ◊medieval art.

Byzantium /baɪˈzæntɪəm/ ancient Greek city on the Bosphorus (modern Istanbul), founded as a colony of the Greek city of Megara, near Corinth about 660 BC. In AD 330 the capital of the Roman Empire was transferred there by Constantine the Great, who renamed it ◊Constantinople.

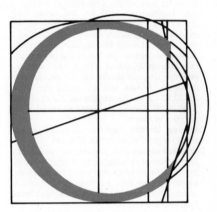

C third letter of the alphabet. It corresponds to Hebrew *gimel* and Greek *gamma*, both derived from the Semitic word for 'camel'. Originally representing a hard *g*, it was also used by the Romans for *k*. In the Roman numeral system the C stands for a hundred.

C a general-purpose computer-programming language popular on minicomputers and microcomputers. Developed in the early 1970s from an earlier language called BCPL, C is closely associated with the operating system ◊Unix. It is good for writing fast and efficient systems programs, such as operating systems (which control the operations of the computer).

c. abbreviation for *circa* (Latin 'about').

C abbreviation for *centum* (Latin 'hundred'); *century*; *centigrade*; ◊*Celsius*.

CA abbreviation for ◊*California*.

Cabal, the (from *kabbala*) a group of politicians, the English king Charles II's ministers 1667–73, whose initials made up the word by coincidence – Clifford (Thomas Clifford 1630–1673), Ashley (Anthony Ashley Cooper, 1st Earl of ◊Shaftesbury), ◊Buckingham (George Villiers, 2nd Duke of Buckingham), Arlington (Henry Bennett, 1st Earl of Arlington 1618–1685), and ◊Lauderdale (John Maitland, Duke of Lauderdale).

cabbage plant *Brassica oleracea* of the family Cruciferae, allied to the turnip and wild charlock. It is an important table vegetable, and the numerous cultivated varieties – all probably descended from the wild cabbage—include kale, Brussels sprouts, common cabbage, savoy, cauliflower, sprouting broccoli, and kohlrabi.

cabbala alternative spelling of ◊kabbala.

caber, tossing the (Gaelic *cabar* 'pole') Scottish athletic sport, a ◊Highland Games event. The caber (a tapered tree-trunk about 6 m/20 ft long, weighing about 100 kg/220 lb) is held in the palms of the cupped hands and rests on the shoulder. The thrower runs forward and tosses the caber,

rotating it through 180 degrees so that it lands on its opposite end and falls forward. The best competitors toss the caber about 12 m/40 ft.

Cabinda /kə'bɪndə/ or Kabinda African coastal enclave, a province of ◊Angola; area 7,770 sq km/3,000 sq mi; population (1980) 81,300. The capital is also called Cabinda. There are oil reserves. Cabinda, which was attached to Angola in 1886, has made claims to separate independence.

cabinet (a small room, implying secrecy) the group of ministers holding a country's most important executive offices who decide government policy. In Britain the cabinet system originated under the Stuarts; under William III it became customary for the king to select his ministers from the party with a parliamentary majority. The US cabinet, unlike the British, does not initiate legislation, and its members, appointed by the president, may not be members of Congress.

The first British 'cabinet councils' or subcommittees of the ◊Privy Council undertook special tasks. When George I ceased to attend cabinet meetings, the office of prime minister, not officially recognized until 1905, came into existence to provide a chair (Robert Walpole was the first). Cabinet members are chosen by the prime minister; policy is collective and the meetings are secret, minutes being taken by the secretary of the cabinet, a high civil servant; secrecy has been infringed in recent years by 'leaks' or unauthorized disclosures to the press.

The UK Cabinet

Prime Minister
Lord President of the Council and Leader of the House of Lords
Lord Chancellor
Secretary of State for Foreign and Commonwealth Affairs
Chancellor of the Exchequer
Home Secretary
Secretary of State for Trade and Industry
Secretary of State for Defence
Secretary of State for Wales
Lord Privy Seal and Leader of the House of Commons
Secretary of State for Social Services
Secretary of State for Northern Ireland
Minister of Agriculture, Fisheries and Food
Secretary of State for the Environment
Secretary of State for Employment
Secretary of State for Education and Science
Chief Secretary to the Treasury
Secretary of State for Scotland
Secretary of State for Energy
Chancellor of the Duchy of Lancaster
Secretary of State for Transport

cable unit of length, used on ships, originally the length of a ship's anchor cable (120 fathoms: 216 m/720 ft), but now taken as one tenth of a ◊nautical mile (182.4 m/608 ft).

cable car a method of transporting passengers up steep slopes by cable. In the *cable railway*, passenger cars are hauled along rails by a cable wound by a powerful winch. A pair of cars usually operates together on the funicular principle, one going up as the other goes down. The other main type is the *aerial cable car* (French *téléphérique*), where the passenger car is suspended from a trolley that runs along an aerial cableway.

A unique form of cable-car system operates in San Francisco, where it has been working since 1873. The street cars travel along rails and are hauled by moving cables under the ground.

cable television distribution of broadcast signals through cable relay systems. Narrowband systems were originally used to deliver services to areas with poor 'off-air' reception; modern systems with wider bandwith coaxial and fibre optic cable are increasingly used for distribution and development of home-based interactive services.

Cabot /'kæbət/ Sebastian 1474–1557. Italian navigator and cartographer, the second son of Giovanni ◊Caboto. He explored the Brazilian coast and the River Plate for Charles V 1526–30.

He was also employed by Henry VIII, Edward VI, and Ferdinand of Spain. He planned a voyage to China by way of the Northeast Passage, the sea route along the N Eurasian coast, encouraged the formation of the Company of Merchant Adventurers of London 1551, and in 1553 and 1556 directed the Company's expeditions to Russia, where he opened British trade.

Caboto /kæ'bəʊtəʊ/ Giovanni or *John Cabot* 1450–1498. Italian navigator. Commissioned with his three sons by Henry VII of England to discover unknown lands, he arrived at Cape Breton Island on 24 June 1497, thus becoming the first European to reach the North American mainland (he thought he was in NE Asia). In 1498 he sailed again, touching Greenland, and probably died on the voyage.

Cabral /kə'brɑːl/ Pedro Alvarez 1460–1526. Portuguese explorer. He set sail from Lisbon for the East Indies Mar 1500, and accidentally reached Brazil by taking a course too far W. He claimed the country for Portugal 25 Apr, as Spain had not followed up Vicente Pinzón's landing there earlier in the year. Continuing around Africa, he lost seven of his fleet of 13 ships (◊Diaz being one of those drowned), and landed in Mozambique. Proceeding to India, he negotiated the first Indo-Portuguese treaties for trade, and returned to Lisbon July 1501.

Cabrini /kə'briːni/ Frances or Francesca 1850–1917. First Roman Catholic saint in the USA. Born in Lombardy, Italy, she founded the Missionary Sisters of the Sacred Heart, and established many schools and hospitals in the care of her nuns. She was canonized 1946.

cacao evergreen tree, *Theobroma cacao*, growing in tropical America, West Africa, the West Indies and Sri Lanka, whose seeds are cocoa beans from which ◊cocoa and chocolate are prepared.

The trees mature at five to eight years, and produce two crops a year of the fruit. This is 17–25 cm long, hard, and ridged, with the beans inside. The seeds are called *cocoa nibs*; when left to ferment, then roasted and separated from the husks, they contain about 50% fat, part of which is removed to make chocolate and cocoa. The Aztecs made a restorative from cocoa beans and chillis, which they called chocolatl.

cachalot name for the sperm whale; see ◊whale.

cactus (plural *cacti*) plant of the family Cactaceae, although the term is commonly applied to many different succulent and prickly plants. True cacti have a woody axis (central core) overlaid with an enlarged fleshy stem, which assumes various forms and is usually covered with spines.

Cactus flowers are often large and brightly coloured; the fruit is fleshy and often edible, as in the case of the prickly pear. The Cactaceae are a New World family, although some species have been introduced to the Old World, for example, in the Mediterranean area. They grow in dry, rocky situations.

cactus

CAD abbreviation for *computer-aided design* the use of computers for creating and editing design drawings. CAD also allows such things as automatic testing of designs and multiple or animated three-dimensional views of designs. CAD systems are widely used in architecture, electronics, and engineering, for example in the motor vehicle industry where cars designed with the assistance of computers are now commonplace. A related development is ◊CAM (computer-assisted manufacture).

caddis fly insect of the order Trichoptera. Adults are generally dull brown, moth-like, with wings covered in tiny hairs. Mouthparts are poorly developed, and many do not feed as adults. They are usually found near water.

The larvae are aquatic, and many live in cases, open at both ends which they make out of sand or plant remains. Some species make silk nets among aquatic vegetation to help trap food.

Cade /keɪd/ Jack d. 1450. English rebel. He was a prosperous landowner, but led a revolt in Kent against the misgovernment of Henry VI 1450, defeated the royal forces at Sevenoaks, and occupied London. After being promised reforms and pardon, the rebels dispersed, but Cade was hunted down and killed.

cadenza /kəˈdenzə/ in music, an unaccompanied bravura passage in the style of an improvisation for the soloist during a concerto.

Cádiz /kəˈdɪz/ Spanish city and naval base, capital and seaport of the province of Cádiz, standing on Cádiz Bay, an inlet of the Atlantic, 103 km/64 mi south of Seville; population (1986) 154,000. After the discovery of the Americas 1492, Cádiz became one of the most important ports in Europe. Francis Drake burned a Spanish fleet here 1587 to prevent the sailing of the ◊Armada.

Probably founded by the Phoenicians about 1100 BC, it was a centre for the tin trade with Cornwall, England. It was recaptured from the ◊Moors by the king of Castile 1262. Modern development was restricted by its peninsular location until a bridge to the further shore of Cádiz Bay was completed 1969.

cadmium a metallic element, symbol Cd, atomic number 48, relative atomic mass 112.41. Cadmium is a soft, silver-white, highly toxic metal. It is used in electroplating, as a constituent of one of the lowest-melting alloys, and in bearing alloys with low coefficients of friction. Cadmium is also used in control rods in nuclear reactors owing to its high absorption of neutrons. The industrial importance of cadmium has greatly increased in recent years. Cadmium sulphide is used in photovoltaic cells.

Cadwalader /kædˈwɒlədə/ 7th century. Welsh hero. The son of Cadwallon, king of Gwynedd, N Wales, he defeated and killed Eadwine of Northumbria in 633. About a year later he was killed in battle.

caecilian tropical amphibian of rather worm-like appearance. There are about 170 species known, forming the amphibian order Apoda (also known as Caecilia or Gymnophiona). Caecilians have a grooved skin that gives a 'segmented' appearance, have no trace of limbs, and mostly live below ground. Some species bear live young, others lay eggs.

Caedmon /ˈkædmən/ 7th century. Earliest-known English poet. According to the Northumbrian historian Bede, when Caedmon was a cowherd at the Christian monastery of Whitby, he was commanded to sing by a stranger in a dream, and on waking produced a hymn on the Creation. The original poem is preserved in some manuscripts. Caedmon became a monk and may have composed other religious poems.

Caen /kɑːn/ capital of Calvados *département*, France, on the river Orne; population (1982) 183,526. It is a business centre, with ironworks, and electric and electronic industries. Caen building stone is famous. The town is linked by canal with the English Channel 14.5 km/9 mi to the north east. The church of St Étienne was founded by William the Conqueror, and the university by Henry VI of England in 1432. Caen was captured by the British in World War II, after five weeks' fighting, on 9 July 1944, during which the town was badly damaged.

Caerleon /kɑːˈliːən/ small town in Gwent, Wales, on the Usk, 5 km/3 mi NE of Newport; population (1981) 6,711. It stands on the site of the Roman fortress of Isca. There is a Legionary Museum and remains of an amphitheatre.

Caernarvon /kəˈnɑːvən/ or *Caernarfon* administrative headquarters of Gwynedd, N Wales, situated on the SW shore of the Menai Strait; population (1981) 10,000. Formerly a Roman station, it is now a market town and port. The first Prince of Wales (later ◊Edward II) was born in Caernarvon Castle; Edward VIII was invested here 1911 and Prince Charles 1969. The Earl of Snowdon became Constable of the castle 1963.

Caernarvonshire /kəˈnɑːvənʃə/ former county of N Wales, merged in ◊Gwynedd 1974.

Caerphilly /kəˈfɪli/ market town in Mid Glamorgan, Wales, 11 km/7 mi N of Cardiff; population (1981) 42,736. The castle was built by Edward I. The town is noted for its mild Caerphilly cheese.

Caesar /ˈsiːzə/ powerful family of ancient Rome, which included Gaius Julius ◊Caesar, whose grandnephew and adopted son ◊Augustus assumed the name of Caesar and passed it on to his adopted son ◊Tiberius. Henceforth, it was used by the successive emperors, becoming a title of the Roman rulers. The titles 'tsar' in Russia and 'kaiser' in Germany were both derived from the name Caesar.

Caesar /ˈsiːzə/ Gaius Julius *c*. 102–44 BC. Roman statesman and general. He formed with Pompey and Crassus the First Triumvirate in 60 BC. He conquered Gaul 58–50 and invaded Britain 55 and 54. He fought against Pompey 49–48 defeating him at Pharsalus. After a period in Egypt Caesar returned to Rome as dictator from 46. He was assassinated by conspirators on the ◊Ides of March 44.

A patrician, Caesar allied himself with the popular party, and when elected Aedile 65 nearly ruined himself with lavish amusements for the Roman populace. Although a free thinker, he was elected chief pontiff 63 and appointed governor of Spain 61. Returning to Rome 60, he formed with Pompey and Crassus the First Triumvirate. As governor of Gaul, he was engaged in its subjugation 58–50, defeating the Germans under Ariovistus and selling thousands of the Belgic tribes into slavery. In 55 he crossed into Britain, returning for a further campaigning visit 54. A revolt by the Gauls under Vercingetorix 52 was crushed 51. His own commentaries on the campaigns show a mastery worthy of fiction, as does his account of the ensuing Civil War. His governorship of Spain was to end 49, and, Crassus being dead, Pompey became his rival. Declaring

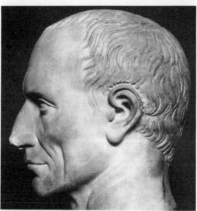

Caesar Roman statesman and military commander, Gaius Julius Caesar.

'the die is cast', Caesar crossed the Rubicon (the small river separating Gaul from Italy) to meet the army raised against him by Pompey. In the ensuing civil war, he followed Pompey to Epirus 48, defeated him at Pharsalus, and chased him to Egypt, where he was murdered. Caesar stayed some months in Egypt, where Cleopatra, queen of Egypt, gave birth to his son, Caesarion. He executed a lightning campaign 47 against King Pharnaces II (ruled 63–47 BC) in Asia Minor, which he summarized: *Veni vidi vici* 'I came, I saw, I conquered'. With his final victory over the sons of Pompey at Munda in Spain 45, he established his position, having been awarded a ten-year dictatorship 46. On 15 Mar 44 he was stabbed to death at the foot of Pompey's statue (see ◊Brutus, ◊Cassius) in the Senate house.

Caesarea /ˌsiːzəˈrɪə/ ancient city in Palestine (now ◊Qisarya). It was built by Herod the Great 22–12 BC, who also constructed a port (*portus Augusti*). It was the administrative capital of the province of Judaea.

Caesarea Mazaca /ˌsiːzəˈrə məˈzaːkə/ ancient name for the Turkish city of ◊Kayseri.

Caesarean section a surgical operation to deliver a baby by way of an incision in the mother's abdominal wall. It may be recommended for almost any obstetric complication implying a threat to mother or baby. In the USA in 1987, 24% of all births were by Caesarian section.

caesium a chemical element, symbol Cs, atomic number 55, relative atomic mass 132.91. It is used in the manufacture of photoelectric cells.

A highly radioactive isotope, caesium 137 (◊half-life 30 years) is a waste product from nuclear power stations and is used for mass radiation and sterilization of foodstuffs, medically for irradiation of surface tumours, and as the basis of atomic clocks.

Caetano /kaɪˈtɑːnəʊ/ Marcello 1906–1980. Portuguese right-wing politician. Professor of administrative law at Lisbon from 1940, he succeeded the dictator Salazar as prime minister from 1968 until his exile after the revolution of 1974. He was granted political asylum in Brazil.

cafeteria self-service restaurant, originating in New York in the 1880s. The term was first used in the UK about 1923.

caffeine one of a group of organic substances called ◊alkaloids. Caffeine is found in tea and coffee, and is partly responsible for their stimulant effect.

Too much caffeine can be detrimental to health (more than six average cups of tea or coffee a day).

Cage /keɪdʒ/ John 1912– . US composer. A pupil of ◊Schoenberg and ◊Cowell, he joined others in reacting against the European art music tradition in favour of a more realistic idiom open to non-Western attitudes. Working in films during the 1930s, he asssembled and toured a percussion orchestra incorporating ethnic instruments and noise-makers, for which the *First Constrution in Metal* 1930 was composed. He also invented the ◊prepared piano to tour as accompanist with the dancer Merce Cunningham, a lifelong collaborator. His effect on contemporary musical thinking is summed up by the piano piece *4 minutes 33 seconds* 1952, in which a performer holds an audience in expectation without playing a note.

Cagliari /kælˈjɑːri/ capital and port of Sardinia, Italy, on the Gulf of Cagliari; population (1988) 222,000.

Cagnes-sur-Mer /ˈkæn sjʊə ˈmeə/ capital of the *département* of Alpes-Maritimes; SW of Nice, France; population (1986) 35,214. The château (13th–17th century) contains mementoes of Renoir, who lived and died here 1900–19.

Cagney /ˈkægni/ James 1899–1986. US actor who moved to films from Broadway. Usually associated with gangster roles in films such as *The Public Enemy* 1931, he was an actor of great versatility, playing Bottom in *A Midsummer Night's Dream* 1935 and singing and dancing in *Yankee Doodle Dandy* 1942.

Caine British film actor Michael Caine is known for his dry Cockney wit.

cahier (French 'notebook') usually the working notes or drawings of a writer or artist.

Cahora Bassa /kə·bɔːrə ˈbæsə/ the largest hydro-electric scheme in Africa, created as a result of the damming of the Zambezi river to form a 230 km/144 mi-long reservoir in W Mozambique.

Cain /keɪn/ in the Old Testament, the first-born son of Adam and Eve. He murdered his brother Abel from motives of jealousy, as Abel's sacrifice was more acceptable to God than his own.

Cain /keɪn/ James M(allahan) 1892–1977. US novelist. He was the author of thrillers, including *The Postman Always Rings Twice* 1934, *Mildred Pierce* 1941, and *Double Indemnity* 1943.

Caine /keɪn/ Michael. Stage-name of Maurice Micklewhite 1933– . British actor, noted for his dry, laconic Cockney style. His long cinematic career includes the films *Alfie* 1966, *California Suite* 1978, *Educating Rita* 1983, and *Hannah and her Sisters* 1986.

Ça Ira /ˈsɑ ˈiːə'rɑː/ song of the French Revolution, written by a street singer, Ladré, and set to an existing tune by Bécourt, a drummer of the Paris opera.

cairn Scottish breed of ◊terrier. Shaggy, short-legged, and compact, it can be sandy, greyish brindle, or red. It was formerly used for flushing out foxes and badgers.

Cairngorms /ˈkeəŋɡɔːmz/ mountain group in Scotland, north part of the ◊Grampians, the highest peak being Ben Macdhui 1,309 m/4,296 ft. Aviemore (Britain's first complete holiday and sports centre) was opened in 1966, and 11 km/7 mi to the south is the Highland Wildlife Park at Kincraig.

Cairns /keənz/ seaport of Queensland, Australia; population (1984) 38,700. Its chief industry is sugar exporting.

Cairo /ˈkaɪrəʊ/ Arabic *El Qahira* capital of Egypt, on the east bank of the Nile 13 km/8 mi above the apex of the Delta and 160 km/100 mi from the Mediterranean; the largest city in Africa and in the Middle East; population (1985) 6,205,000, Greater Cairo (1987) 13,300,000. El Fustat (Old Cairo) was founded by Arabs about AD 64, Cairo itself about 1000 by the ◊Fatimid ruler Gowhar. The Great Pyramids and Sphinx are at nearby Giza.

It is the site of the mosque which houses the El Azhar university AD 972. The city is 32 km/20 mi north of the site of the ancient Egyptian centre of ◊Memphis.

The modern government and business quarters reflect Cairo's importance as an administrative and commercial centre, and the semi-official newspaper *al Ahram* is an influential voice in the Arab world. At Helwan, 24 km/15 mi to the south, an industrial centre is developing, with iron and steel works powered by electricity from the Aswan High Dam. There are two secular universities: Cairo University (1908) and Ein Shams (1950).

history The Mosque of Amr dates from AD 643; the Citadel, built by Sultan Saladin in the 12th century, contains the impressive 19th-century Mohammed Ali mosque.

caisson a hollow cylindrical or boxlike structure, usually of reinforced ◊concrete, that is sunk into a river bed to form the foundations of a bridge.

An *open caisson* is open at the top and at the bottom, where there is a wedge-shaped cutting edge. Material is excavated from inside, allowing the caisson to sink. A *pneumatic caisson* has a pressurized chamber at the bottom, in which workers carry out the excavation. The air pressure prevents the surrounding water entering and the workers enter and leave the chamber through an air lock, allowing for a suitable decompression period to prevent ◊decompression sickness, or the bends.

Cajun member of a French-speaking community of Louisiana, USA, descended from French-Canadians who in the 18th century were driven there from Nova Scotia (then known as Acadia, from which the name Cajun comes). *Cajun music* has a lively beat and features steel guitar, fiddle, and accordion.

cal abbreviation for ◊calorie.

CAL *computer-assisted learning* the use of computers in education and training, where the computer displays instructional material to a student and asks questions about the information given. The student's answers determine the sequence of the lessons.

Calabar /ˈkæləbɑː/ port and capital of Cross River State, SE Nigeria, on the Cross River, 64 km/40 mi from the Atlantic; population (1983) 126,000. Rubber, timber, and vegetable oils are exported. It was a centre of the 18th–19th-century slave trade.

calabash evergreen tree, *Crescentia cujete*, family Bignoniaceae. They are found in South America, India, and Africa, and produce gourds, 50 cm/1.64 ft across, which are used as water containers.

Calabria /kəˈlæbriə/ mountainous earthquake region occupying the 'toe' of Italy, comprising the provinces of Catanzaro, Cosenza and Reggio; capital Catanzaro; area 15,100 sq km/5,829 sq mi; population (1988) 2,146,000. Reggio is the industrial centre.

Calamity Jane Martha Jane Burke, known as 'Calamity Jane'. She made her name as a sharpshooter in the mining camps of South Dakota.

Calais /ˈkæleɪ/ port in N France; population (1982) 101,000. Taken by Edward III in 1347, it was saved from destruction by the personal surrender of the Burghers of Calais commemorated in Rodin's sculpture; the French retook it 1558. Following German occupation May 1940–Oct 1944, it surrendered to the Canadians.

Calais, Pas de /ˈpɑ də ˈkæleɪ/ French name for the Strait of ◊Dover.

calamine a zinc mineral. When referring to skin-soothing lotions and ointments, calamine means a pink powder of zinc oxide and 0.5% iron (II) oxide, used in treating eczema, measles rash, and insect bites or stings.

In UK terminology it refers to zinc carbonate ($ZnCO_3$), in the USA to zinc silicate ($Zn_4Si_2O_7(OH)_2$).

Calamity Jane nickname of Martha Jane Burke *c.* 1852–1903. US heroine of Deadwood, South Dakota. She worked as a teamster, transporting supplies to the mining camps, adopted male dress and, as an excellent shot, promised 'calamity' to any aggressor. Many fictional accounts of the 'wild west' featured her exploits.

calceolaria genus of plants, family Scrophulariaceae, with brilliantly coloured slipper-shaped flowers. Native to South America, they were introduced to Europe in the 1830s.

calcination the ◊oxidation of metals by burning in air.

calcite a common, colourless, white, or light-coloured rock-forming mineral, calcium carbonate, $CaCO_3$. It is the main constituent of ◊limestone and marble, and forms many types of invertebrate shell.

Calcite often forms ◊stalactites and ◊stalagmites in caves and is also found deposited in veins through many rocks because of the ease with which it is dissolved and transported by groundwater; ◊oolite is its spheroidal form. It rates 3 on the ◊Mohs' scale of hardness. Large crystals up to 1 m/3 ft have been found in Oklahoma and Missouri, USA. ◊Iceland spar is a transparent form of calcite used in the optical industry; as limestone it is used in the building industry.

calcium a silvery-white metallic element, one of the alkaline earth metals; symbol Ca, atomic number 20, relative atomic mass 40.07. It is widely distributed, mainly in the form of its carbonate $CaCO_3$ which occurs in a fairly pure condition as calcite in chalk and limestone. Calcium is an essential component of bones, teeth, shells, milk, and leaves, and it forms 1.5% of the human body. Calcium ions in animal cells are involved in regulating muscle contraction, hormone secretion, digestion, and glycogen metabolism in the liver. Calcium compounds are important to the chemical industry.

Calcium was discovered by Sir Humphry Davy in 1808. Its compounds include slaked lime (calcium hydroxide $Ca(OH)_2$), plaster of Paris (calcium sulphate $CaSO_4 2H_2O$), calcium hypochlorite ($CaOCl_2$) a bleaching agent, calcium nitrate ($Ca(NO_3)_2 4H_2O$) a nitrogenous fertilizer, calcium carbide (CaC_2) which reacts with water to give acetylene, calcium cyanamide ($CaCN_2$) the basis of pharmaceuticals, fertilizers, and plastics including melamine, calcium cyanide ($Ca(CN)_2$) used in the extraction of gold and silver and in electroplating, and others used in baking powders, and fillers for paints.

calculator a pocket-sized electronic computing device for performing numerical calculations. It can add, subtract, multiply, and divide; many also have squares, roots, and advanced trigonometric and statistical functions. Input is by a small keyboard and results are shown on a one-line screen which is typically a ◊liquid crystal display (LCD). The first electronic calculator was manufactured by the Bell Punch Company, USA, in 1963.

calculus (Latin 'pebble') branch of mathematics that permits the manipulation of continuously varying quantities, used in practical problems involving such matters as changing speeds, problems of flight, varying stresses in the framework of a bridge, and alternating current theory. **Integral calculus** deals with the method of summation or adding together the effects of continuously varying quantities. **Differential calculus** deals in a similar way with rates of change. Many of its applications arose from the study of the gradients of the tangents to curves.

There are several other branches of calculus, including calculus of errors and calculus of variation. Differential and integral calculus, each of which deals with small quantities which during manipulation are made smaller and smaller, compose the **infinitesimal calculus**. **Differential equations** relate to the derivatives of a set of variables and may include the variables. Many give the mathematical models for physical phenomena such as ◊simple harmonic motion. Differential equations are solved generally through integrative means, depending on their degree. If no known mathematical processes are available, integration can be performed graphically or by a machine, increasingly by computers.

history Calculus originated with Archimedes in the 3rd century BC as a method for finding the areas of curved shapes and for drawing tangents to curves. These ideas were not developed until the 17th century, when the French philosopher Descartes introduced ◊coordinate geometry, showing how geometrical curves can be described and manipulated by means of algebraic expressions. Then the French mathematician Fermat used these algebraic forms in the early stages of the development of differentiation. Later the German philosopher Leibniz and the British scientist Newton immensely advanced the study.

Calcutta /kæl'kʌtə/ largest city of India, on the Hooghly, the most westerly mouth of the Ganges, some 130 km/80 mi N of the Bay of Bengal. It is the capital of West Bengal; population (1981) 9,166,000. Chiefly a commercial and industrial centre (engineering, shipbuilding, jute, and other textiles). Calcutta was the seat of government of British India 1773–1912.

history Calcutta was founded 1686–90 by Job Charnock, head of Hooghli factory of the East India Company. Captured by Suraj-ud-Dowlah in 1756, during the Anglo-French wars in India, in 1757 it was retaken by Robert Clive. Buildings include a magnificent Jain temple, the palaces of former Indian princes; and the Law Courts and Government House, survivals of the British Raj. Across the river is ◊Howrah, and between Calcutta and the sea there is a new bulk cargo port, Haldia, which is the focus of oil refineries, petrochemical plants, and fertilizer factories.

Educational institutions include the University of Calcutta (1857), oldest of several universities; the Visva Bharati at Santiniketan, founded by Rabindranath Tagore; the Bose Research Institute; and a fine museum.

Caldecott /'kɔːldɪkət/ Randolph 1846–1886. British artist and illustrator of books for children, for example *John Gilpin* 1848.

Calder /'kɔːldə/ Alexander 1898–1976. US abstract sculptor, the inventor of **mobiles**, suspended shapes that move in the lightest current of air. In the 1920s he began making wire sculptures with movable parts; in the 1960s he created **stabiles**, large coloured sculptures of sheet metal.

caldera in geology, a very large basin-shaped ◊crater. Calderas are found at the tops of volcanoes, where the original peak has collapsed into an empty chamber beneath. The basin, many times larger than the original volcanic vent, may be flooded, producing a crater lake, or the flat floor may contain a number of small volcanic cones, produced by volcanic activity after the collapse.

Typical calderas are Kilauea, Hawaii; Crater Lake, Oregon, USA; and the summit of Olympus Mons, on Mars. Some calderas are wrongly referred to as craters, such as Ngorongoro, Tanzania.

caldera Huge caldera of Las Cañadas, S Tenerife, Canary Islands. Lava is flowing from the summit in the foreground.

Calderón de la Barca /ˌkældə'rɒn de lɑː bɑːkə/ Pedro 1600–1681. Spanish dramatist and poet. After the death of Lope de Vega, he was considered to be the leading Spanish dramatist. Most famous of some 118 plays is the philosophical *La Vida es sueño/Life is a Dream* 1635.

Born in Madrid, Calderón studied law at Salamanca (1613–19). In 1620 and 1622 he was successful in poetical contests at Madrid, and while still writing dramas served in the army in Milan and the Netherlands (1625–35). By 1636 his first volume of plays was published and he had been made master of the revels at the court of Philip IV, receiving a knighthood in 1637. In 1640 he assisted in the suppression of the Catalan rebellion. After the death of his mistress he became a Franciscan in 1650, was ordained in 1651, and appointed to a prebend of Toledo in 1653. As honorary chaplain to the king in 1663, he produced outdoor religious plays for the festival of the Holy Eucharist. His works include the tragedies *El pintor de su deshonra/The Painter of his own Dishonour* 1645, *El Alcalde de Zalamea/The Mayor of Zalamea* 1640, and *El Médico de su honra/The Surgeon of his Honour*

Calderón de la Barca Don Pedro Claderón de la Barca produced his first play at the age of 13. A prolific poet and dramatist, he combined raw emotion with detailed examination of intellectual themes in over 100 plays.

1635; the historical *El Príncipe constante/The Constant Prince* 1629; and the dashing intrigue *La Dama duende/The Phantom Lady* 1629.

Caldey Island /'kɔːldi/ island off the coast of ◊Dyfed, Wales, near Tenby.

Caldwell /'kɔːldwel/ Erskine (Preston) 1903–1987. US novelist, whose *Tobacco Road* 1932 and *God's Little Acre* 1933 are earthy and vivid presentations of poverty-stricken Southern sharecroppers.

Caledonian Canal /ˌkælɪ'dəʊniən/ a waterway in north west Scotland, 98 km/61 mi long, linking the Atlantic and the North Sea. Of its 98 km/61 mi length only a 37 km/23 mi stretch is artificial, the rest being composed of lochs Lochy, Oich, and Ness. The canal was built by Thomas ◊Telford, 1803–23.

calendar the division of the ◊year into months, weeks, and days and the method of ordering the years. From year one, an assumed date of the birth of Jesus, dates are calculated backwards (BC 'before Christ', or BCE 'before common era') and forwards (AD, Latin, *anno domini* 'in the year of the Lord' or CE 'common era'). The **lunar month** (period between one new moon and the next) averages naturally 29.5 days, but the Western calendar uses for convenience a **calendar month** with a complete number of days, 30 or 31 (Feb has 28). For adjustments, since there are slightly fewer than six extra hours a year left over, they are added to Feb as a 29th day every 4th year (**leap year**).

The **month names** in most European languages were probably derived as follows: January from Janus, Roman god; February from *Februar*, Roman festival of purification; March from Mars, Roman god; April from Latin *aperire*, to open; May from Maia, Roman goddess; June from Juno, Roman goddess; July from Julius Caesar, Roman general; August from Augustus, Roman emperor; September, October, November, December (originally the 7th–10th months) from the Latin words meaning 7th, 8th, 9th, and 10th, respectively.

The **days of the week** are Monday named after the Moon; Tuesday from Tiu or Tyr, Anglo-Saxon and Norse god; Wednesday from Woden or Odin, Norse god; Thursday from Thor, Norse god; Friday from Freya, Norse goddess; Saturday from Saturn, Roman god; and Sunday named after the Sun.

All early calendars except the ancient Egyptian were lunar. The word calendar comes from the Latin *Kalendae* or *calendae*, the first day of each month, on which in ancient Rome solemn proclamation was made of the appearance of the new moon.

California

The *Western* or *Gregorian calendar* derives from the *Julian Calendar* instituted by Julius Caesar 46 BC and adjusted by Pope Gregory XIII 1582, who eliminated the accumulated error and avoided its recurrence by restricting century leap years (those with an extra day) to those divisible by 400. Other states only gradually changed from ◊Old Style to New Style; Britain adopted the Gregorian calendar 1752, when the error amounted to 11 days, and 3 Sept 1752 became 14 Sept (at the same time the beginning of the year was put back from 25 Mar to 1 Jan). Russia did not adopt it until the Oct Revolution of 1917, so that the event (25 Oct) is currently celebrated 7 Nov.

The *Jewish calendar* is a complex combination of lunar and solar cycles, varied by considerations of religious observance. A year may have 12 or 13 months, which normally alternate between 29 and 30 days; New Year (Rosh Hashonah) falls between 5 Sept and 5 Oct. The calendar dates from the hypothetical creation of the world (taken as 7 Oct 3761 BC).

The *Chinese calendar* is lunar, with a cycle of 60 years. Both the traditional and, from 1911, the Western calendar are in use in China.

The *Muslim calendar* is lunar, with 12 months of alternately 30 and 29 days, and a year of 354 days. This results in the calendar rotating around the seasons in a 30-year cycle, so that when the 9th month of Ramadan (when Muslims fast during the day) occurs in summer, hardship is incurred. The era is counted as beginning on the day Muhammad fled from Mecca AD 622.

Calgary /ˈkælgəri/ city in Alberta, Canada, on the Bow river, in the foothills of the Rockies; at 1,048 m/3,440 ft it is one of the highest Canadian towns; population (1986) 671,000. It is the centre of a large agricultural region, and the oil and financial centre of Alberta and W Canada. Founded as Fort Calgary by the North West Mounted Police 1875, it was reached by the Canadian Pacific Railway 1885, and developed rapidly after the discovery of oil 1914.

It has oil-linked and agricultural industries, such as fertilizer factories and flour mills, and is also a tourist centre; the annual Calgary Exhibition and Stampede is held in July. The University of Calgary became independent of the University of Alberta 1966.

Calhoun /kælˈhuːn/ John Caldwell 1782–1850. US politician, born in South Carolina. He was vice president 1825–29 under John Quincy Adams and 1829–33 under Andrew Jackson. Throughout he was a defender of the *states' rights* against the federal government, and of the institution of black slavery.

Cali /ˈkæli/ city in SW Colombia, in the Cauca Valley 975 m/3,200 ft above sea level, founded in 1536. Cali has textile, sugar and engineering industries. Population (1985) 1,398,276.

calibration preparing the scale of a measuring instrument for use. A mercury ◊thermometer, for example, can be calibrated with a Celsius scale by noting the heights of the mercury column at two standard temperatures—the freezing point (0°C) and boiling point of water (100°C) – and dividing up the distance between them into 100 equal parts and continuing these divisions above and below.

calico a cotton frabric. In the USA, a printed cotton; in the UK, a plain woven cotton material.

The name derives from Calicut, India, an original source of calico.

California /ˌkælɪˈfɔːniə/ Pacific state of the USA; nickname the Golden State, originally because of its gold mines, but more recently because of its sunshine
area 411,100 sq km/158,685 sq mi
capital Sacramento
towns Los Angeles, San Diego, San Francisco, San José, Fresno
physical Sierra Nevada (including Yosemite and Sequoia National Parks, Lake Tahoe and Mount Whitney, 4,418 m/14,500 ft, the highest mountain in the lower 48 states); and the Coast Range; Death Valley 86 m/282 ft below sea level; Colorado and Mojave deserts (Edwards Air Force base is in the latter); Monterey Peninsula; Salton Sea; offshore in the Pacific there are huge underwater volcanoes with tops 8 km/5 mi across
features California Institute of Technology (Caltech); Lawrence Livermore Laboratory (named after Ernest Lawrence), which shares nuclear weapons research with Los Alamos; Stanford University, which has the Hoover Institute and is the powerhouse of ◊Silicon Valley; Paul Getty art museum at Malibu, built in the style of a Roman villa
products leading agricultural state with fruit (peaches, citrus, grapes in the valley of the San Joaquin and Sacramento rivers), nuts, wheat, vegetables, cotton, rice, all mostly grown by irrigation, the water being carried by immense concrete-lined canals to the Central Valley and Imperial Valley; beef cattle, timber, fish, oil, natural gas, aerospace, electronics (Silicon Valley), food-processing, films and television programmes. There are also great reserves of energy (geothermal) in the hot water which lies beneath much of the state
population (1987) 27,663,000, most populous state of the USA, 66% non-Hispanic white; 20% Hispanic; 7.5% Black; 7% Asian (including many Vietnamese)
famous people Bret Harte, W R Hearst, Jack London, Marilyn Monroe, Richard Nixon, William Saroyan, John Steinbeck
history colonized by Spain 1769, it was ceded to the USA after the Mexican War 1848, and became a state 1850. Gold had been discovered in the Sierra Nevada Jan 1848, and was followed by the gold rush 1849–56.

California current the cold ocean ◊current in the East Pacific Ocean flowing southwards down the west coast of North America. It is part of the North Pacific ◊gyre (a vast, circular movement of ocean water).

California, Lower English name for ◊Baja California.

californium a transuranic element, symbol Cf, atomic number 98. It is a radioactive metal produced in very small quantities and used in nuclear reactors as a neutron source.

Caligula /kəˈlɪgjʊlə/ Gaius Caesar AD 12-41. Roman emperor, son of Germanicus and successor to Tiberius in AD 37. Caligula was a cruel tyrant and was assassinated by an officer of his guard. Believed to have been mentally unstable, he is remembered for giving a consulship to his horse Incitatus.

calima (Spanish 'haze') dust cloud in Europe, coming from the Sahara Desert, which sometimes causes heatwaves and eye irritation.

caliph title of civic and religious heads of the world of Islam. The first caliph was ◊Abu Bakr. Nominally elective, the office became hereditary, held by the Ummayyad dynasty 661–750 and then by the ◊Abbasids. During the 10th century the political and military power passed to the leader of the caliph's Turkish bodyguard; about the same time an independent ◊Fatimid caliphate sprang up in Egypt. After the death of the last Abbasid (1258) the title was claimed by a number of Muslim chieftains in Egypt, Turkey, and India. The most powerful of these were the Turkish sultans of the Ottoman Empire.

The title was adopted by the prophet Muhammad's successors. The last of the Turkish caliphs was deposed by Kemal Atatürk in 1924.

calla another name for ◊arum lily.

Callaghan /ˈkæləhæn/ (Leonard) James 1912– . British Labour politician. As chancellor of the Exchequer 1964–67, he introduced corporation and capital-gains tax, and resigned following devaluation. He was home secretary 1967–70 and prime minister 1976–79 in a period of increasing economic stress.

As foreign secretary 1974 Callaghan renegotiated Britain's membership of the European Community. In 1976 he succeeded Harold Wilson as prime minister and in 1977 entered into a pact with the Liberals to maintain his government in office. Strikes in the winter of 1978–79 led to his being the first prime minister since Ramsay MacDonald 1924 to be forced into an election by the will of the Commons, and he was defeated at the polls May 1979. In 1980 he resigned the party leadership under left-wing pressure, and in 1985 announced that he would not stand for Parliament in the next election. He was made a life peer 1987 and a Knight Companion of the Garter in June of that year.

Callaghan Morley 1903– . Canadian novelist and short story writer, whose realistic novels include *Such Is My Beloved* 1934, *More Joy In Heaven* 1937, and *Close To The Sun Again* 1977.

Callao /kaɪˈaʊ/ chief commercial and fishing port of Peru, 12 km/7 mi SW of Lima; population (1988) 318,000. Founded 1537, it was destroyed by an earthquake 1746. It is Peru's main naval base, and produces fertilizers.

Callas /ˈkæləs/ Maria. Adopted name of Maria Kalogeropoulos 1923–1977. US lyric soprano, born in New York of Greek parents. With a voice of fine range and a gift for dramatic expression, she excelled in operas including *Norma, Madame Butterfly, Aïda, Lucia di Lammermoor,* and *Medea.*

Callicrates /kəˈlɪkrəti:z/ 5th century BC. Athenian architect (with Ictinus) of the ◊Parthenon.

calligraphy the art of handwriting, regarded in China and Japan as the greatest of the visual arts, and playing a large part in Islamic art because the depiction of the human and animal form is forbidden. The present letter forms have gradually evolved from originals shaped by the tools used to make them—the flat brush on paper, the chisel on stone, the stylus on wax and clay, and the reed and quill on papyrus and skin.

In Europe during the 4th and 5th centuries books were written in square capitals ('majuscules') derived from classical Roman inscriptions (Trajan's Column in Rome is the outstanding example). The rustic capitals of the same period were written more freely, and the uncial capitals, more rounded, were used from the 4th to the 8th centuries. During this period the cursive hand was also developing, and the interplay of this with the formal hands, coupled with the need for speedier writing, led to the small letter forms ('minuscules'). During the 7th century the half-uncial was developed with ascending and descending strokes and was adopted by all countries under Roman rule. The cursive forms developed differently in different countries. In Italy the italic script was evolved and became the model for italic typefaces. Printing and the typewriter undermined the need for calligraphy in the West until the 20th-century revival inspired by Edward Johnston (1872–1944).

Callimachus /kəˈlɪməkəs/ 310–240 BC. Greek poet and critic known for his epigrams. Born in Cyrene, he taught in Alexandria where he is reputed to have been head of the great library.

Calliope /kəˈlaɪəpi/ in Greek mythology, the ◊Muse of epic poetry, and chief of the Muses.

callipers a measuring instrument used, for example, to measure the internal and external diameter of pipes. Some callipers are made like a pair of compasses, having two legs, often curved, pivoting about a screw at one end. The ends of the

legs are placed in contact with the object to be measured, and the gap between the ends is then measured against a rule. The slide calliper looks like an adjustable spanner, and carries a scale for direct measuring, usually with a ◊vernier scale for accuracy.

Callisto /kə'lɪstəʊ/ in Greek mythology, ◊nymph beloved by Zeus (Jupiter).

Callisto /kə'lɪstəʊ/ second-largest moon of Jupiter, 4,800 km/3,000 miles in diameter, orbiting every 16.7 days at a distance of 1.9 million km/1.2 million mi from the planet. Its surface is covered with large craters.

Callot /kæ'ləʊ/ Jacques 1592/93–1635. French engraver and painter. His series of etchings *Great Miseries of War* 1632–33, prompted by his own experience of the Thirty Years' War, are brilliantly composed and full of horrific detail.

callus in botany, a tissue that forms at a damaged plant surface. Composed of large, thin-walled ◊parenchyma cells, it grows over and around the wound, eventually covering the exposed area.

Calmette /kæl'met/ Albert 1863–1933. French bacteriologist. A student of Pasteur, he developed (with Camille Guérin 1872–1961) the ◊BCG vaccine against tuberculosis in 1921.

calomel mercury (I) (mercurous) chloride, Hg_2Cl_2, a white, heavy powder formerly used as a laxative, now used as a pesticide and fungicide.

calorie c.g.s. unit of heat, now replaced by the ◊joule (1 calorie is approximately 4.2 joules). It is the heat required to raise the temperature of 1 gram of water by 1°C. In dietetics, the Calorie or kilocalorie is equal to 1,000 calories.

The kilocalorie measures the energy value of food in terms of its heat output. Twenty-eight grams/1 oz of protein yields 120 kilocalories, carbohydrate 110, fat 270, and alcohol 200.

calorific value the amount of heat generated by a given mass of fuel when it is completely burned. It is measured in joules per kilogram. Calorific values are measured experimentally with a bomb calorimeter.

calorimeter an instrument used in physics to measure heat. A simple calorimeter consists of a heavy copper vessel which is polished (to reduce heat losses by radiation) and lagged with insulating material (to reduce losses by convection and conduction).

In a typical experiment, such as to measure the heat capacity of a piece of metal, the calorimeter is filled with water, whose temperature rise is measured using a thermometer when a known mass of the heated metal is immersed in it. Chemists use a bomb calorimeter to measure the heat produced by burning a fuel completely in oxygen.

calotype a paper-based photograph using a wax paper negative, the first example of the ◊negative/positive process invented by Talbot around 1834.

Calpe /'kælpi/ former name of ◊Gibraltar.

Caltanissetta /,kæltənɪ'setə/ town in Sicily, Italy, 96 km/60 mi south east of Palermo; population (1981) 61,146. It is the chief centre of the island's sulphur industry. It has a baroque cathedral.

Calvados /,kælva'dɒs/ *département* in Basse-Normandie region of France, which has given its name to an apple brandy distilled from cider.

Calvary /'kælvəri/ (Aramaic *Golgotha* 'skull') in the New Testament, the site of Jesus's crucifixion at Jerusalem. Two chief sites are suggested: one is where the Church of the Sepulchre now stands; the other is the hill beyond the Damascus gate.

Calvin /'kælvɪn/ John 1509–1564. French-born Swiss Protestant church reformer and theologian. He was a leader of the Reformation in Geneva and set up a strict religious community there. His theological system is known as Calvinism, and his church government as ◊Presbyterianism. Calvin wrote (in Latin) *Institutes of the Christian Religion* 1536 and commentaries on the New Testament and much of the Old Testament.

Calvin *The founder of Presbyterianism, John Calvin.*

Calvin, born in Noyon, Picardie, studied theology and then law, and about 1533 became prominent in Paris as an evangelical preacher. In 1534 he was obliged to leave Paris and retired to Basel, where he studied Hebrew. In 1536 he accepted an invitation to go to Geneva, Switzerland, and assist in the Reformation, but was expelled 1538 because of public resentment at the many and too drastic changes he introduced. He returned to Geneva 1541 and established in the face of strong opposition a rigorous theocracy (government by priests). In 1553 he had the Spanish theologian Servetus burned for heresy. He supported the Huguenots in their struggle in France and the English Protestants persecuted by Queen Mary I.

Calvin /'kælvɪn/ Melvin 1911– . US chemist who, using radioactive carbon-14 as a tracer, determined the biochemical processes of ◊photosynthesis, in which green plants use ◊chlorophyll to convert carbon dioxide and water into sugar and oxygen. Nobel Prize 1961.

Calvinism Christian doctrine as interpreted by John Calvin and adopted in Scotland, parts of Switzerland, and the Netherlands. Its central doctrine is predestination, under which certain souls (the elect) are predestined by God through the sacrifice of Jesus to salvation, and the rest to damnation. Although Calvinism is rarely accepted today in its strictest interpretation, the 20th century has seen a Neo-Calvinist revival through the work of Karl ◊Barth.

Calypso /kə'lɪpsəʊ/ in Greek mythology, a sea ◊nymph who waylaid the homeward-bound Odysseus for seven years.

calypso /kə'lɪpsəʊ/ in music, a type of West Indian satirical ballad with a syncopated beat.

calyptra in mosses and liverworts, a layer of cells that encloses and protects the young sporophyte (spore capsule), forming a sheathlike hood around the capsule. Also used to describe the root cap, a layer of ◊parenchyma cells covering the end of a root that gives protection to the root tip as it grows through the soil. This is constantly being worn away and replaced by new cells from a special ◊meristem, the calyptrogen.

calyx the collective term for the ◊sepals of a flower, forming the outermost whorl of the ◊perianth. It surrounds the other flower parts, and protects them while in bud. In some flowers, for example, the campions (*Silene*), the sepals are fused along their sides, forming a calyx-tube.

cam a part of a machine that transmits a regular movement to another part when it rotates. The most common type of cam, often called an *edge cam*, is in a car engine, in the form of a rounded projection on a shaft, the camshaft. When the camshaft turns, the cams press against linkages (followers) that open the valves in the cylinders. A *face cam* is a disc with a groove in its face, in which the follower travels. A *cylindrical cam*

carries angled parallel grooves which impart a to-and-fro motion to the follower when it rotates.

CAM *computer-aided manufacture* the use of computers to control production processes; in particular, the control of machine tools and ◊robots in factories. In some factories, the whole design and production system has been automated by linking ◊CAD (computer-aided design) to CAM.

Very flexible manufacturing with CAD/CAM can be utilized by computer-based sales and distribution methods to mass-produce semi-customized products.

Camagüey /,kæmə'gweɪ/ city in Cuba; population (1986) 260,800. It is capital of Camagüey province in the centre of the island. Founded about 1514, it was capital of the Spanish West Indies during the 19th century. It has a 17th century cathedral.

Camargo /,kæmɑ:'gəʊ/ Marie-Anne de Cupis de 1710–1770. French ballet dancer of Spanish descent. Born in Brussels, she became a ballet star in Paris in 1726. She was the first ballerina to wear a shortened skirt, which allowed freedom of movement and increased visibility, and the first to attain the ◊entrechat quatre.

Camargue /kæ'mɑ:g/ the marshy area of the ◊Rhône delta, S of Arles, France: area about 780 sq km/300 sq mi. Bulls and horses are bred there, and the nature reserve, which is known for its bird life, forms the southern part.

cambium a layer of actively dividing cells (lateral ◊meristem), found within stems and roots, which gives rise to ◊secondary growth in perennial plants, causing an increase in girth. There are two main types of cambium: vascular cambium, which gives rise to secondary xylem and phloem tissues, and cork cambium or phellogen, which gives rise to secondary cortex and cork tissues (see ◊bark).

Cambodia country in SE Asia, bordered to the N and NW by Thailand, N by Laos, E and SE by Vietnam, and SW by the South China Sea.

government under the 1981 constitution, the sole and supreme legislative body in Cambodia is the national assembly, whose 117 members are elected for five-year terms by universal suffrage. The assembly elects from within its ranks a smaller, permanent council of state, headed by the state president. In addition, it appoints a council of ministers, headed by a prime minister, to carry out day-to-day government. The dominating force in Cambodia is the Communist Party (Kampuchean People's Revolutionary Party) supported by the mass organization, the Kampuchean United Front for National Construction and Defence.

history the area now known as Cambodia was once occupied by the Khmer empire, an ancient civilization which flourished during the 6th–15th centuries. After this the region was ruled by Siam (Thailand), and in 1863 became a French protectorate. During World War II it was occupied by Japan. France regained control of the country in 1946, but granted it semi-autonomy within the French Union in 1949 and full independence in 1953. Prince Norodom Sihanouk (1922–), who had been elected king in 1941, abdicated in favour of his parents and became prime minister as leader of the Popular Socialist Community in 1955. In 1960, when his father died, he became head of state.

Sihanouk remained neutral during the ◊Vietnam War and was overthrown by a right-wing revolt led by pro-US Lt-Gen Lon Nol in 1970. Lon Nol first became prime minister (1971–72) and then president (1972–75) of what was termed the new Khmer Republic. His regime was opposed by the exiled Sihanouk and by the Communist Khmer Rouge (backed by N Vietnam and China) who merged to form the National United Front of Cambodia. A civil war developed and despite substantial military aid from the USA during its early stages, Lon Nol's government fell in 1975. The country was renamed Kampuchea, with Prince Sihanouk as head of state.

Cambodia
State of
*(Former name to 1989 **Kampuchea**)*

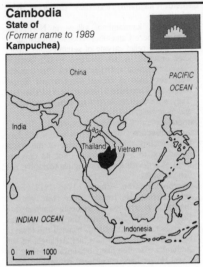

area 181,035 sq km/69,880 sq mi
capital Phnom Penh
towns Battambang, and the seaport Kompong Som
physical mostly forested; flat, with mountains in S; Mekong River runs N–S
features ruins of ancient capital Angkor
head of state Heng Samrin from 1979
head of government Hun Sen from 1985

political system communism
political parties Kampuchean People's Revolutionary Party (K PRP), Marxist-Leninist; Party of Democratic Kampuchea (Khmer Rouge), exiled ultra-nationalist communist; Khmer People's National Liberation Front (KPNLF), exiled anti-communist; Sihanoukists, exiled pro-democracy forces allied to Prince Sihanouk
exports rubber, rice
currency Cambodian riel (371.14 = £1 Feb 1990)
population (1985 est) 7,280,000; annual growth rate 2.6%
life expectancy men 42, women 45
language Khmer (official), French
religion Theravada Buddhist
literacy 78% male/39% female (1980 est)
GDP $100 per head of population (1984)
chronology
1863–1941 French protectorate.
1941–45 Occupied by Japan.
1946 Recaptured by France.
1953 Granted full independence.
1970 Prince Sihanouk overthrown by US-backed Lon Nol.
1975 Lon Nol overthrown by Khmer Rouge.
1978–79 Vietnamese invasion and installation of Heng Samrin government.
1987 Partial withdrawal of Vietnamese troops.
1988 Vietnamese troop withdrawal continued.
1989 Name of State of Cambodia re-adopted and Buddhism declared state religion. Vietnamese forces fully withdrawn (Sept). Civil war intensified.

The Khmer Rouge proceeded ruthlessly to introduce an extreme Communist programme, forcing urban groups into rural areas, which led to over 2,500,000 deaths from famine, disease and maltreatment. In 1976 a new constitution removed Prince Sihanouk from power, appointed Khieu Samphan (the former deputy prime minister) president and placed the Communist Party of Kampuchea, led by ◊Pol Pot, in control. The Khmer Rouge developed close links with China and fell out with its former sponsors Vietnam and the Soviet Union.

In a Vietnamese invasion of Kampuchea launched in 1978, Pol Pot was overthrown and a pro-Vietnamese puppet government was set up under Heng Samrin, head of the newly formed Kampuchean National United Front for National Salvation. The defeated regime kept up guerrilla resistance under Pol Pot, causing over 300,000 Kampuchean refugees to flee to Thailand in 1979.

In 1982 the resistance movement broadened with the formation in Kuala Lumpur (Malaysia) of an anti-Vietnamese coalition and Democratic Kampuchea government-in-exile with Prince Sihanouk (then living in N Korea) as president, Khieu Samphan (political leader of the now less extreme Khmer Rouge) as vice-president, and Son Sann (an ex-premier and contemporary leader of the non-communist Khmer People's National Liberation Front) as prime minister. The coalition received sympathetic support from ◊ASEAN countries and China. However, its 60,000 troops were outnumbered by the 170,000 Vietnamese who supported the Heng Samrin government. With the resistance coalition's base-camps being overrun in 1985, a military victory appeared unlikely.

Hopes of a political settlement were improved by the retirement of the reviled Pol Pot as Khmer Rouge military leader in 1985 and by the appointment of the reformist Hun Sen as prime minister. A mixed-economy domestic approach was adopted and indigenous Khmers promoted to key government posts; at the same time, prompted by the new Soviet leader Gorbachev, the Vietnamese began a phased withdrawal. In

spring 1989, following talks with the resistance coalition, the Phnom Penh government agreed to a package of constitutional reforms, including the adoption of Buddhism as the state religion and a change of name to the ideologically neutral State of Cambodia. Despite the breakdown of further talks over possible future power-sharing agreements, withdrawal of the Vietnamese army was completed Sept 1989. However, the United Nations continued not to recognize the Hun Sen government and the civil war intensified, with the Khmers Rouge making advances in the W provinces, capturing the border town of Pailin Oct 1989. The Phnom Penh government was left with an army of 40,000, backed by a 100,000-strong militia, against the resistance coalition's 45,000 guerrillas, half of whom belonged to the Khmer Rouge.

Cambon /kæmˈbɒn/ Paul 1843–1924. French diplomat who was ambassador to London during the years leading to the outbreak of World War I, and a major figure in the creation of the Anglo-French entente during 1903–04.

Camborne-Redruth /ˈkæmbɔːn, redˈruːθ/ town in Cornwall, 16 km/10 mi SW of Truro, England; population (1985) 18,500. It has tin mines and there is a School of Metalliferous Mining.

Cambrai /kɒmˈbreɪ/ chief town of Nord *département*, France; on the river Escaut (Scheldt); population (1982) 36,600. Industries include light textiles (cambric is named after the town), and confectionery. The Peace of Cambrai or Ladies' Peace (1529) was concluded on behalf of Francis I of France by his mother Louise of Savoy and on behalf of Charles V by his aunt Margaret of Austria. Cambrai was severely damaged during World War I.

Cambrai, Battles of /kɒmˈbreɪ/ two battles in World War I at Cambrai in NE France; in the *First Battle*, Nov–Dec 1917, the town was almost captured by the British when large numbers of tanks were used for the first time; in the *Second Battle*, 26 Aug–5 Oct 1918, the town was taken during the final British offensive.

Cambrian period of geological time 590–505 million years ago; the first period of the Palaeozoic era.

All invertebrate animal life appeared, and marine algae was widespread. The earliest fossils with hard shells, such as trilobites, date from this period.

The name comes from Cambria, an old name for Wales, where Cambrian rocks are typically exposed and were first described.

Cambridge /ˈkeɪmbrɪdʒ/ city in England, on the river Cam (a river sometimes called by its earlier name, Granta), 80 km/50 mi north of London; population (1989) 101,000. It is the administrative headquarters of Cambridgeshire. The city is centred on Cambridge University (founded 12th century).

history As early as 100 BC, a Roman settlement grew up on a slight rise in the low-lying plain, commanding a ford over the river. Apart from those of Cambridge University, notable buildings include St Benet's church, the oldest building in Cambridge; the round church of the Holy Sepulchre; and the Guildhall 1939.

The Cambridge science park was started by Trinity College 1973. Industries include the manufacture of scientific instruments, radio, electronics, paper, flour milling, and fertilizers.

Cambridge /ˈkeɪmbrɪdʒ/ city in Massachusetts, USA; population (1980) 95,322. Industries include paper and publishing. Harvard University 1636 (the oldest educational institution in the USA, named after John Harvard 1607–38, who bequeathed it his library and half his estate), Massachusetts Institute of Technology 1861, and the John F Kennedy School of Government and Memorial Library are here, as well as a park named after him.

Cambridgeshire /ˈkeɪmbrɪdʒʃə/ county in E England
area 3,410 sq km/1,316 sq mi
towns administrative headquarters Cambridge; Ely, Huntingdon, Peterborough
features rivers Ouse, Cam, and Nene; Isle of Ely; Cambridge University; RAF Molesworth, near Huntingdon, Britain's second ◊cruise missile base was de-activated Jan 1989
products mainly agricultural
population (1987) 642,000.

Cambridge University English university, founded probably in the 12th century, though the earliest of the existing colleges, Peterhouse, was not founded until about 1284. Among its highly reputed departments is the Cavendish Laboratory, founded 1873, for experimental physics. The Cambridge Science Park was started by Trinity College 1973. The Royal Greenwich Observatory moved there in 1990.

The chancellor is the titular head, and the vice-chancellor the active head. The Regent House is the legislative and executive body, with the Senate as the court of appeal. Each college has its own corporation, and is largely independent. The head

Cambridgeshire

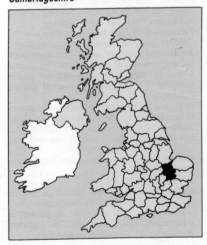

of each college assisted by a council of fellows, manages its affairs.

Famous students of the university include Rupert Brooke, S T Coleridge, Thomas Gray, Christopher Marlowe, John Milton, Samuel Pepys, and William Wordsworth. In 1990, there were 10,000 undergraduate and 3,000 postgraduate students.

Cambridge Colleges

1280–84 Peterhouse
1326 Clare
1347 Pembroke
1348 Gonville and Caius
1350 Trinity Hall
1352 Corpus Christi
1441 King's
1448 Queens'
1473 St Catherine's
1496 Jesus
1505 Christ's
1511 St John's
1542 Magdalene
1546 Trinity
1584 Emmanuel
1596 Sidney Sussex
1800 Downing
1869 Girton
1871 Newnham
1882 Selwyn
1885 Hughes Hall
1896 St Edmund's House
1954 New Hall
1960 Churchill
1964 Darwin
1965 Wolfson College
1966 Lucy Cavendish College
1966 Clare Hall
1966 Fitzwilliam
1978 Robinson College

Cambs abbreviation for ◊*Cambridgeshire.*

Cambyses /kæm'baɪsiːz/ 6th century BC. Emperor of Persia 529–522 BC. Succeeding his father Cyrus, he assassinated his brother Smerdis and conquered Egypt in 525. Here he outraged many of the local religious customs, and was said to have become mad. He died in Syria on his journey home, probably by suicide.

Camden /'kæmdən/ industrial city of New Jersey, USA, on the Delaware River; population (1980) 84,900. The city is linked with Philadelphia, Pennsylvania, by the Benjamin Franklin suspension bridge (1926). The Walt ◊Whitman House, where the poet lived 1884–92, is now a museum.

Camden /'kæmdən/ inner borough of NW Greater London

features the Camden Town Group of artists; includes the districts of
Bloomsbury with London University, Royal Academy of Dramatic Art (RADA), and the British Museum; and home between World War I and II of 'intellectual' writers and artists including Leonard and Virginia Woolf, and Lytton Strachey;
Fitzrovia W of Tottenham Court Road with the Telecom Tower and Fitzroy Square as its focus;
Hampstead, with Primrose Hill, Hampstead Heath, and nearby Kenwood House; Keats's home, now a museum; the churchyard where the painter Constable is buried; and Hampstead Garden Suburb;
Highgate, with a cemetery which has the graves of George Eliot, Michael Faraday, and Karl Marx;
Holborn, with the Inns of Court (Lincoln's Inn and Gray's Inn); Hatton Garden (diamond dealers), the London Silver Vaults;
Somers Town between Euston and King's Cross railway stations;
population (1981) 171,563.

Camden /'kæmdən/ William 1551–1623. English antiquary. He published his topographical survey *Britannia* 1586, and was headmaster of Westminster School from 1593. The *Camden Society* (1838) commemorates his work.

Camden Town Group school of British painters 1911–13, based in Camden Town, London, in part inspired by W R ◊Sickert. The work of Spencer Gore (1878–1914) and Harold Gilman (1876–1919) is typical of the group, rendering everyday town scenes in Post-Impressionist style.

camel large cud-chewing mammal of the even-toed hoofed order Artiodactyla. Unlike typical ruminants, it has a three-chambered stomach. It has two toes which have broad soft soles for walking on sand, and hoofs resembling nails. There are two species, the single-humped *Arabian camel* (*Camelus dromedarius*), and the twin-humped *Bactrian camel* (*Camelus bactrianus*) from Asia. They carry a food reserve of fatty tissue in the hump, can go without drinking for long periods, can feed on salty vegetation, and can withstand extremes of heat and cold, thus being well adapted to desert conditions.

The Arabian camel has long been domesticated, so that its original range is not known. It is used throughout Arabia and N Africa, and has been taken to other places such as North America and Australia, in the latter country playing an important part in the development of the interior. The dromedary is, strictly speaking, a lightly-built, fast, riding variety of the Arabian camel, but often the name is applied to all one-humped camels. Arabian camels can be used as pack animals, for riding, racing, milk production, and for meat.

The Bactrian camel is native to the central Asian deserts, where a small number still live wild, but most are domestic animals. With a head and body length of 3 m/10 ft and shoulder height of about 2 m/6 ft, the Bactrian camel is a large animal, but not so long in the leg as the Arabian. It has a shaggy winter coat.

camellia oriental evergreen shrub of the family Theaceae, closely allied to the tea plant. Numerous species, including *Camellia japonica* and *Camellia reticulata*, have been introduced into Europe.

Camelot /'kæmələt/ legendary capital of King ◊Arthur.

Camembert /'kæməmbeə/ village in Normandy, France, where Camembert cheese originated.

cameo small relief carving of semiprecious stone, shell or glass. A pale-coloured surface layer is carved to reveal a darker ground. Fine cameos were produced in ancient Greece and Rome, during the Renaissance, and in the Victorian era. They were used for decorating goblets and vases, and as jewellery.

camera apparatus used in ◊photography.

camera obscura a darkened box with a tiny hole for projecting the inverted image of the scene outside on to a screen inside. For its development as a device for producing photographs, see ◊photography.

Cameron /'kæmərən/ Charles 1746–1812. Scottish architect. He trained under Isaac Ware in the Palladian tradition before being summoned to Russia in 1779. He created the palace complex at Tsarskoe Selo (Pushkin), planned the town of Sofia, and from 1803 as Chief Architect of the Admiralty executed many buildings, including the Naval Hospital and barracks at Kronstadt.

Cameron Julia Margaret 1815–1879. British photographer. She made lively, revealing portraits of the Victorian intelligentsia using a large camera, five-minute exposures, and wet plates. Her subjects included Darwin and Tennyson.

Cameroon /ˌkæmə'ruːn/ country in W Africa, bounded NW by Nigeria, NE by Chad, E by the Central African Republic, S by Congo, Gabon, and Equatorial Guinea, and W by the Atlantic.

government Cameroon was a federal state until 1972 when a new constitution, revised 1975, made it unitary. The constitution provides for a president and a single-chamber national assembly of 180, each elected for a five-year term. The president has the power to choose the cabinet, to lengthen or shorten the life of the assembly, and may stand for re-election. The only political party is the Democratic Assembly of the

Cameroon
United Republic of
(République du Cameroun)

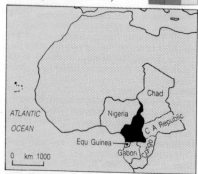

area 465,054 sq km/179,511 sq mi
capital Yaoundé
towns chief port Douala
physical desert in the far N in the Lake Chad basin, dry savanna plateau in the intermediate area, and in the S dense tropical rainforest
features Mount Cameroon 4,070 m/13,358 ft, an active volcano on the coast, W of the Adamawa Mountains
head of state and of government Paul Biya from 1982
political system authoritarian nationalism
political parties Democratic Assembly of the Cameroon People (RDPC), nationalist left-of-centre
exports cocoa, coffee, bananas, cotton, timber, rubber, groundnuts, gold, aluminium
currency CFA franc (485.00 = £1 Feb 1990)
population (1988 est) 11,082,000; annual growth rate 2.7%

life expectancy men 49, women 53
language French and English in pidgin variations (official), but there has been discontent with the emphasis on French; there are 163 indigenous peoples with many African languages
religion Roman Catholic 35%, animist 25%, Muslim 22%, Protestant 18%
literacy 68% male/45% female (1985 est)
GDP $7.3 bn (1984); $802 per head of population
chronology
1884 Under German rule.
1916 Captured by Allied forces in World War I.
1922 Divided between Britain and France.
1946 French and British Cameroons made UN trust territories.
1960 French Cameroon became the independent Republic of Cameroon. Ahmadou Ahidjo elected president.
1961 N part of British Cameroon merged with Nigeria and S part joined the Republic of Cameroon to become the Federal Republic of Cameroon.
1966 A one-party regime introduced.
1972 New constitution made Cameroon a unitary state, the United Republic of Cameroon.
1973 New national assembly elected.
1982 Ahidjo resigned and was succeeded by Paul Biya.
1983 Biya began to remove his predecessor's supporters and was accused by Ahidjo of trying to create a police state. Ahidjo went into exile in France.
1984 Biya re-elected and defeated a plot to overthrow him. Country's name changed to Republic of Cameroon.
1988 Biya re-elected.

camouflage *A well camouflaged giant bush cricket or katydid from Aguas Calientes, Peru.*

Cameroon People (RDPC), formed 1966 by a merger of the governing party of each state of the original federation and the four opposition parties. The state president is also president of the party.

history First visited by Europeans 1472, when the Portuguese began slave-trading in the area, in 1884 Cameroon became a German Protectorate. After World War I, France governed about 80% of the area under a League of Nations mandate, with Britain administering the remainder. In 1946 both became UN trust territories.

In 1957 French Cameroons became a state within the French Community and three years later achieved full independence as the Republic of Cameroon. After a plebiscite 1961, the northern part of British Cameroons merged with Nigeria, and the southern part joined the Republic of Cameroon to form the Federal Republic of Cameroon. The French zone became East Cameroon and the British part West Cameroon.

Ahmadou Ahidjo, who had been the first president of the republic 1960, became president of the federal republic and was re-elected 1965. In 1966 Cameroon was made a one-party state when the two government parties and most of the opposition parties merged into the Cameroon National Union (UNC). Extreme left-wing opposition to the UNC was crushed 1971. In 1972 the federal system was abolished and a new national assembly was elected 1973.

In 1982 Ahidjo resigned, nominating Paul Biya as his successor. In 1983 Biya began to remove Ahidjo's supporters and in protest Ahidjo resigned the presidency of UNC. Biya was re-elected 1984 while Ahidjo went into exile in France. Biya strengthened his position by abolishing the post of prime minister and reshuffling his cabinet. He also changed the nation's name from the United Republic of Cameroon to the Republic of Cameroon. Many of Ahidjo's supporters were executed after a failed attempt to overthrow Biya. In 1985 UNC changed its name to RPDC and Biya tightened his control by more cabinet changes.

In Aug 1986 a volcanic vent under Lake Nyos released a vast quantity of carbon dioxide and hydrogen sulphide, which suffocated large numbers of people and animals. In Apr 1988 Biya was re-elected president with 98.75% of the vote.

Camoens /ˈkæməuenz/ or **Camões**, Luís Vaz de 1524–1580. Portuguese poet and soldier. He went on various military expeditions, and was shipwrecked in 1558. His poem, *Os Lusiades*/*The Lusiads*, published 1572, tells the story of the explorer Vasco da Gama and incorporates much Portuguese history; it has become the country's national epic. His posthumously published lyric poetry is also now valued.

Camoens lost an eye fighting in North Africa, and, having wounded an equerry of the king in 1552, was banished to India. He received a small pension, but died in poverty of plague.

Camorra Italian secret society formed about 1820 by criminals in the dungeons of Naples, and continued once they were outside. It dominated politics from 1848, was suppressed in 1911, but many members eventually surfaced in the US ◊Mafia. The Camorra still operates in the Naples area.

camouflage colours or structures that allow an animal to blend with its surroundings, to avoid detection by other animals. Camouflage can take the form of matching the background colour, of counter-shading (darker on top, lighter below, to counteract natural shadows) or of irregular patterns that break up the outline of the animal's body. More elaborate camouflage involves closely resembling a feature of the natural environment; it is akin to ◊mimicry.

Campagna Romana /kæmˈpænjə rəumɑːnə/ lowland stretch of the Italian peninsula, including and surrounding the city of Rome. Lying between the Tyrrhenian Sea and the Sabine Hills to the NE, and the Alban Hills to the SE, it is drained by the lower course of the Tiber and a number of small streams, most of which dry up in the summer. Prosperous in Roman times, it later became virtually derelict through over-grazing, lack of water, and the arrival in the area of the malaria-carrying Anopheles mosquito. Extensive land reclamation and drainage in the 19th and 20th centuries restored its usefulness.

Campania /kæmˈpeɪniə/ agricultural region (wheat, citrus, wine, vegetables, tobacco) of S Italy, including the volcano ◊Vesuvius; capital Naples; industrial centres Benevento, Caserta, and Salerno; area 13,600 sq km/5,250 sq mi; population (1988) 5,732,000. There are ancient sites at Pompeii, Herculaneum, and Paestum.

campanile bell-tower erected near, or attached to, churches or town halls in Italy. The leaning tower of Pisa is a famous example; another is the great campanile of Florence, 90 m/275 ft high.

Campbell family name of the Dukes of Argyll; seated at Inveraray Castle, Argyll.

Campbell /ˈkæmbəl/ Colin, 1st Baron Clyde 1792–1863. British field marshal. He commanded the Highland Brigade at ◊Balaclava in the Crimean War, and as commander in chief during the Indian Mutiny raised the siege of Lucknow and captured Cawnpore.

Campbell /ˈkæmbəl/ Donald Malcolm 1921–1967. British car and speedboat enthusiast, son of Malcolm Campbell, who simultaneously held the land-speed and water-speed records. In 1964 he set the world water-speed record of 444.57 kph/276.3 mph on Lake Dumbleyung, Australia, with the turbo-jet hydroplane *Bluebird*, and achieved the land-speed record of 648.7 kph/403.1 mph at Lake Eyre salt flats, Australia. He was killed in an attempt to raise his water-speed record on Coniston Water, England.

Campbell /ˈkæmbəl/ Gordon 1886–1953. British admiral in World War I. He commanded Q-ships, which were armed vessels that masqueraded as merchant ships to decoy German U-boats to destruction.

Campbell /ˈkæmbəl/ Malcolm 1885–1948. British racing driver who at one time held both land- and water-speed records. His car and boat were both called *Bluebird*.

He nine times set the land-speed record, pushing it up to 484.5 kph/301.1 mph at Bonneville, USA, in 1935, and three times broke the water-speed record, the best being 228.1 kph/141.74 mph on Coniston Water, England, in 1939. His son Donald Campbell emulated his feats.

Campbell /ˈkæmbəl/ Mrs Patrick (born Beatrice Stella Tanner) 1865–1940. British actress, whose roles included Paula in Pinero's *The Second Mrs Tanqueray* 1893 and Eliza in *Pygmalion*, written for her by G B Shaw, with whom she had an amusing correspondence.

Campbell /ˈkæmbəl/ Roy 1901–1957. South African poet, who established his reputation with the *The Flaming Terrapin* 1924. Born in Durban, he became a professional jouster and bull-fighter in Spain and Provence, France. He fought for Franco in the Spanish Civil War, and was with the Commonwealth forces in World War II.

Campbell /ˈkæmbəl/ Thomas 1777–1844. Scottish poet. Following the successful publication of his *Pleasures of Hope* in 1799, he travelled in Europe, and there wrote his war poems *Hohenlinden* and *Ye Mariners of England*.

Campbell-Bannerman /ˈkæmbəl ˈbænəmən/ Henry 1836–1908. British Liberal politician, prime minister 1905–08. He granted self-government to the South African colonies, and passed the Trades Disputes Act 1906.

Campbell-Bannerman, born in Glasgow, was chief secretary for Ireland 1884–85, war minister 1886 and again 1892–95, and leader of the Liberals in the House of Commons from 1899. In 1905 he became prime minister, and led the Liberals to an overwhelming electoral victory 1906. He began the conflict between Commons and Lords that led to the Parliament Act of 1911. He resigned 1908.

Camp David /ˈkæm ˈdeɪvɪd/ official country home of US presidents in the Appalachian mountains, Maryland; it was originally named Shangri-la by F D Roosevelt, but was renamed Camp David by Eisenhower (after his grandson).

Camp David Agreements two framework agreements signed at Camp David, USA, in 1978 by the Israeli prime minister Begin and president Sadat of Eygpt, at the instance of US president Carter, covering an Egypt–Israel peace treaty and phased withdrawal of Egypt from Sinai, which was completed in 1982, and an overall Middle East settlement including the election by the Palestinians of the West Bank and Gaza Strip of a 'self-governing authority'.

Campeche /kæmˈpetʃi/ port on the Bay of ◊Campeche, Mexico; population (1984) 120,000. It is the capital of Campeche state. Timber and fish are exported, and there is a university, established 1756.

Campbell *Donald Campbell in his jet boat Bluebird just before his fatal attempt at the water-speed record on 5 Jan 1967.*

Campin A Woman *National Gallery, London.*

Campeche, Bay of south west area of the Gulf of Mexico, site of a major oil pollution disaster from the field off Yucatan peninsula in 1979.

Camperdown /ˈkæmpədaʊn/ Dutch *Kamperduin* village on the NW Netherlands coast, off which a British fleet defeated the Dutch 11 Oct 1797 in the Revolutionary Wars.

camphor a volatile, aromatic ◊ketone substance ($C_{10}H_{16}O$) obtained from the camphor tree. It is distilled from chips of the wood of the root, trunk, and branches. It is used in insect repellents and in the manufacture of celluloid.

The camphor tree (*Cinnamomum camphora*), a member of the Lauraceae, is native to South China, Taiwan, and Japan.

Campi /ˈkæmpi/ family of Italian painters practising in Cremona, N Italy, in the 16th century, the best known being *Giulio Campi* (*c*.1502–72).

Campin /kɒmˈpæn/ Robert active 1406–1444. Netherlandish painter of the early Renaissance, active in Tournai, one of the first northern masters to use oil. He has been identified as the *Master of Flémalle*, and several altarpieces are attributed to him. Rogier van der Weyden was his pupil.

His outstanding work is *Mérode altarpiece*, about 1425 (Metropolitan Museum of Art, New York), which shows a distinctly naturalistic style, with a new subtlety in modelling and a grasp of pictorial space.

Campinas /kæmˈpiːnəs/ city of Sa Paulo state, Brazil, situated on the central plateau; population (1980) 566,700. It is a coffee-trading centre, there are also metallurgical and food industries.

campion /ˈkæmpiən/ several plants of the genera *Lychnis* and *Silene*, belonging to the family Caryophyllaceae, which include the garden campion *Lychnis coronaria*, the wild white and red campions *Silene alba* and *Silene dioica*, and the bladder campion *Silene vulgaris*.

Campion /ˈkæmpiən/ Edmund 1540–1581. English Jesuit and Roman Catholic martyr. He took deacon's orders in the English church, but fled to Douai, France, where in 1571 he recanted Protestantism. In 1573 he became a Jesuit in Rome, and in 1580 was sent to England as a missionary. He was betrayed as a spy in 1581, imprisoned in the Tower of London, and hanged, drawn, and quartered as a traitor.

Campion /ˈkæmpiən/ Thomas 1567–1620. English poet and musician. He was the author of the critical *Art of English Poesie* 1602, and four *Bookes of Ayres*, for which he composed both words and music.

Canada
Dominion of

area 9,971,000 sq km/3,849,803 sq mi

capital Ottawa

towns Toronto, Montréal, Vancouver, Edmonton, Calgary, Winnipeg, Québec, Hamilton

physical St Lawrence Seaway, Mackenzie river; Great Lakes; Arctic Archipelago; Rocky Mountains; Great Plains or Prairies; Canadian Shield

head of state Elizabeth II from 1952 represented by Governor-General Jeanne Sauvé

head of government Brian Mulroney from 1984

political system federal constitutional monarchy

political parties Progressive Conservative Party, free-enterprise centrist; Liberal Party, nationalist left-of-centre; New Democratic Party, moderate left-of-centre

exports wheat, timber, pulp, newsprint, fish (especially salmon), furs (ranched fox and mink exceed the value of wild furs), oil, natural gas, aluminium, asbestos, coal, copper, iron, nickel, motor vehicles and parts, industrial and agricultural machinery, fertilizers

currency Canadian dollar (2.04 = £1 Feb 1990)

population (1987) 25,600,000 (including 300,000 North American Indians, of whom 75% live on over 2,000 reserves in Ontario and the four western provinces; some 300,000 Métis (of mixed descent) and 19,000 Inuit (or Eskimo), of whom 75% live in the Northwest Terri-tories). Over half Canada's population lives in Ontario and Québec. Annual growth rate 1.1%

life expectancy men 72, women 79

language English, French (both official) (about 70% speak English, 20% French, and the rest are bilingual); there are also North American Indian languages and the Inuit Inuktitut

religion Roman Catholic 40%, Protestant 35%

literacy 99%

GDP $317 bn (1984); $13,000 per head of population

chronology

1957 Progressive Conservatives returned to power after 22 years in opposition.

1961 New Democratic Party (NDP) formed.

1963 Liberals elected under Lester Pearson.

1968 Pearson succeeded by Pierre Trudeau.

1979 Joe Clark, leader of the Progressive Conservatives, formed a minority government.

1980 Clark defeated on budget proposals. Liberals under Trudeau returned with a large majority.

1982 Canada Act removed Britain's last legal control over Canadian affairs.

1983 Clark replaced as leader of the Progressive Conservatives by Brian Mulroney.

1984 Trudeau retired and was succeeded as Liberal leader and prime minister by John Turner. Progressive Conservatives won the federal election with a large majority, and Mulroney became prime minister.

1988 Conservatives re-elected with reduced majority on platform of free trade with the USA.

1989 Free trade agreement signed. Turner resigned as Liberal Party leader, and Ed Broadbent as New Democratic Party leader.

Campobasso /ˌkæmpəʊˈbæsəʊ/ capital of Molise region, Italy, about 190 km/120 mi south east of Rome; population (1981) 48,300. It is noted for cutlery.

Campo-Formio, Treaty of /ˈkæmpəʊ ˈfɔːmiəʊ/ peace settlement during the Revolutionary Wars in 1797 between Napoleon and Austria, by which France gained the region of modern Belgium and Austria was compensated with Venice and part of modern Yugoslavia.

Cam Ranh /ˈkæm ˈræn/ port in South Vietnam. In the Vietnam War it was a US base, and is now a major staging complex for the Soviet Pacific fleet.

Camus /kæˈmjuː/ Albert 1913–1960. Algerian-born French writer. A journalist in France, he

Camus French novelist and dramatist Albert Camus.

was active in the Resistance during World War II. His novels, which owe much to ◊existentialism, include *L'Etranger*/*The Outsider* 1942, *La Peste*/*The Plague* 1948, and *L'Homme Révolté*/*The Rebel* 1952. Nobel prize 1957.

Canaan /ˈkeɪnən/ an ancient region between the Mediterranean and the Dead Sea, in the Bible the 'Promised Land' of the Israelites. Occupied as early as the 3rd millennium BC by the Canaanites, a Semitic-speaking people who were known to the Greeks of the 1st millennium BC as Phoenicians. The capital was Ebla (now Tell Mardikh, Syria).

The Canaanite Empire included Syria, Palestine, and part of Mesopotamia. It was conquered by the Israelites during the 13th to 10th century BC. Ebla was excavated 1976–77 where an archive of inscribed tablets dating to the 3rd millennium BC includes place names such as Gaza and Jerusalem (no excavations at the latter had suggested occupation at so early a date).

Canada /ˈkænədə/ country occupying the N part of the North American continent, bounded to the S by the USA, to the N by the Arctic Ocean, to the NW by Alaska, to the E by the Atlantic Ocean, and to the West by the Pacific Ocean.

government The Canada Act of 1982 gave Canada power to amend its constitution and added a charter of rights and freeedoms. This represented Canada's complete independence, though it remains a member of the Commonwealth.

Canada is a federation of ten provinces, Alberta, British Columbia, Manitoba, New Brunswick, Newfoundland, Nova Scotia, Ontario, Prince

Canada: history

c.35,000 BC	People arrived to North America from Asia by way of Beringia.
c. AD1000	Vikings, including Leif Ericsson, landed in N E Canada, and started settlements which did not survive.
1497	John Cabot landed on Cape Breton Island.
1534	Jacques Cartier discovered the Gulf of St Lawrence.
1603	Champlain began his exploration of Canada.
1608	Champlain founded Québec.
1759	Wolfe captured Québec.
1763	France ceded Canada to Britain under the Treaty of Paris.
1775–83	War of American Independence involved Loyalist influx to New Brunswick and Ontario.
1791	Canada divided into English-speaking Upper Canada (Ontario) and French-speaking Lower Canada (Québec).
1793	Alexander Mackenzie reached Pacific by land.
1812–14	War of 1812 between Britain and USA fought mainly in Upper Canada; US invasions repelled by both provinces.
1837	Rebellions led by William Lyon Mackenzie in Upper Canada and Louis Joseph Papineau in Lower Canada.
1840	Responsible government granted, and Upper and Lower Canada united.
1866	British Columbia created, entered confederation 1871.
1867	British North America Act created the Dominion of Canada (Ontario, Québec, Nova Scotia, and New Brunswick).
1869	Northwest Territories created and entered confederation; rising by Louis Riel.
1870	Manitoba created (from Northwest Territories) and joined confederation.
1873	Prince Edward Island entered confederation.
1885	Northwest Rebellion crushed and leader Louis Riel hanged. Canadian Pacific Railway completed.
1901–02	South African War – Canadian contingent sent.
1905	Alberta and Saskatchewan formed from the Northwest Territories and entered confederation.
1914–18	World War I – Canadian troops at 2nd Battle of Ypres, Vimy Ridge, Passchendaele, the Somme, and Cambrai.
1931	Canada became a self-governing Dominion. Norway renounced its claim to the Sverdrup Islands, confirming Canadian sovereignty in the entire Arctic Archipelago north of the Canadian mainland.
1939–45	World War II – Canadian participation in all theatres.
1949	Newfoundland joined the confederation.
1950–53	Korean War – Canada participated in United Nations force, and subsequently participated in almost all United Nations peacekeeping operations. For subsequent history see Canada box.

Canada: Provinces

Province (Capital)	Area sq km
Alberta (*Edmonton*)	661,187
British Columbia (*Victoria*)	948,599
Manitoba (*Winnipeg*)	650,088
New Brunswick (*Fredericton*)	73,437
Newfoundland (*St John's*)	404,517
Nova Scotia (*Halifax*)	54,558
Ontario (*Toronto*)	1,068,587
Prince Edward Island (*Charlottetown*)	5,657
Québec (*Québec*)	1,540,676
Saskatchewan (*Regina*)	651,901
Territories	
Northwest Territories (*Yellowknife*)	3,379,689
Yukon Territory (*Whitehorse*)	536,327
	9,975,223

Edward Island, Québec, and Saskatchewan, and two territories, Northwest Territories and Yukon. Each province has a single-chamber assembly, popularly elected; the premier (the leader of the party with the most seats in the legislature) chooses the cabinet. The two-chamber federal parliament consists of the Senate, whose 104 members are appointed by the government for life or until the age of 75, who must be resident in the provinces they represent, and the House of Commons, which has 295 members, elected by universal suffrage in single-member constituencies.

The federal prime minister is the leader of the best-supported party in the House of Commons and is accountable, with the cabinet, to it. Parliament has a maximum life of five years. Legislation must be passed by both chambers and then signed by the governor-general.

history Canada was reached by an English expedition led by John Cabot 1497 and a French expedition under Jacques Cartier 1534. Both countries developed colonies from the 17th century, with hostility between them culminating in the French and Indian Wars (1689–1763), in which France was defeated. Antagonism continued and in 1791 Canada was divided into English-speaking Upper Canada and French-speaking Lower Canada (Ontario and Québec). The two were united as Canada Province 1841–67, when the self-governing Dominion of Canada was founded.

The Progressive Conservatives returned to power 1957, after 22 years of Liberal Party rule. In 1963 the Liberals were reinstated in office under Lester Pearson, until he was succeeded by Pierre Trudeau 1968. Trudeau maintained Canada's defensive alliance with the USA but sought to widen its world influence. Faced with the problem of Québec's separatist movement he set about creating the 'Just Society'. He won both the 1972 and 1974 elections.

In 1979, with no party having an overall majority in the Commons, the Progressive Conservatives formed a government under Joe Clark. Later that year Trudeau announced his retirement from politics but when, in Dec 1979, Clark was defeated on his budget proposals, Trudeau reconsidered his decision and won the 1980 general election with a large majority.

Trudeau's third administration was concerned with 'patriation', or the extent to which the British parliament should determine Canada's constitution. The position was resolved with the passing of the Canada Act 1982, the last piece of UK legislation to have force in Canada.

In 1983 Clark was replaced as leader of the Progressive Conservatives by Brian Mulroney, a corporate lawyer who had never run for public office, and in 1984 Trudeau retired to be replaced as Liberal leader and prime minister by John Turner, a former minister of finance. Within nine days of taking office, Turner called a general election and the Progressive Conservatives, under Mulroney, won 211 seats, the largest majority in Canadian history, with the Liberal Party and the New Democratic Party (NDP) winning 40 and 30 seats respectively.

Soon after taking office, Mulroney began an international realignment, placing less emphasis on links established by Trudeau with Asia, Africa, and Latin America, and more on cooperation with Europe and a closer relationship with the USA. The election of 1988 was fought on the issue of free trade with the USA, and the Conservatives won with a reduced majority. Despite the majority of voters opting for the Liberals or NDP, who both opposed free trade, an agreement was signed with the USA 1989. Turner and Ed Broadbent, leader of the NDP, both resigned 1989.

Canadian art painting and sculpture of Canada after colonization.

Early painters of Canadian life include Cornelius Krieghoff (1815–72), who recorded Indian and pioneer life, and Paul Kane (1810–71), painter of the Plains Indians. In the late 19th century a Canadian style developed with the landscapes of Tom Thomson (1877–1917) and the 'Group of Seven', formed in 1913, who developed an expressive landscape style. Maurice Cullen (1866–1934), an Impressionist, and J W Morrice (1865–1924), a Fauve, introduced new European trends.

Before World War II Emily Carr (1871–1945) was one of the most original talents, developing expressive studies of nature. Canadian artists have since joined the international arena. The Automatistes, led by the Surrealist Paul-Emile Borduas (1905–60), rebelled against the Canadian establishment, and Jean-Paul Riopelle (1923–) has made a significant contribution to Abstract Expressionism.

Canadian literature Canadian literature in English began early in the 19th century in the Maritime Provinces with the humorous tales of T C Haliburton (1796–1865); Charles Heavysege (1816–76), a poet of note, belonged to Kingston, Ontario. The later 19th century brought the lyrical output of Charles G D Roberts (1860–1943), Bliss Carman (1861–1929), Archibald Lampman (1861–99), and Duncan Campbell Scott (1862–1944).

Realism in fiction developed with Frederick P Grove (1871–1948), Mazo de la Roche (1885–1961), creator of the 'Jalna' series, and Hugh MacLennan (1907–). Humour of worldwide appeal emerged in Stephen Leacock (1869–1944), Brian Moore (1921–), author of *The Luck of Ginger Coffey* (1960), and Mordecai ◊Richler. Also popular outside Canada was Lucy Montgomery (1874–1942), whose *Anne of Green Gables* 1908, became a children's classic. Saul Bellow and Marshall McLuhan were both Canadian-born, and contemporary novelists invlude Robertson ◊Davies and Margaret ◊Atwood. See also ◊French Canadian literature.

canaille (French) the mob, rabble.

canal artificial waterway constructed for drainage, irrigation, or navigation. *Irrigation canals* carry water for irrigation from rivers, reservoirs, or

Canadian Prime Ministers

1867	John A Macdonald (*Conservative*)
1873	Alexander Mackenzie (*Liberal*)
1878	John A Macdonald (*Conservative*)
1891	John J Abbott (*Conservative*)
1892	John S D Thompson (*Conservative*)
1894	Mackenzie Bowell (*Conservative*)
1896	Charles Tupper (*Conservative*)
1896	Wilfred Laurier (*Liberal*)
1911	Robert L Bordern (*Conservative*)
1920	Arthur Meighen (*Conservative*)
1921	William Lyon Mackenzie King (*Liberal*)
1926	Arthur Meighen (*Conservative*)
1926	William Lyon Mackenzie King (*Liberal*)
1930	Richard Bedford Bennett (*Conservative*)
1935	William Lyon Mackenzie King (*Liberal*)
1948	Louis Stephen St Laurent (*Liberal*)
1957	John G Diefenbaker (*Conservative*)
1963	Lester Bowles Pearson (*Liberal*)
1968	Pierre Elliot Trudeau (*Liberal*)
1979	Joseph Clark (*Progressive Conservative*)
1980	Pierre Elliot Trudeau (*Liberal*)
1984	John Turner (*Liberal*)
1984	Brian Mulroney (*Progressive Conservative*)

wells, and are carefully designed to maintain an even flow of water over the whole length. *Navigation and ship canals* are constructed at one level between ◊locks, and frequently link with other forms of waterway—rivers and sea links—to form a waterway system. The world's two major international ship canals are the Suez canal and the Panama canal which provide invaluable short cuts for shipping between Europe and the East and between the east and west coasts of the Americas.

Irrigation canals fed from the Nile have maintained life in Egypt since the earliest times; the division of the waters of the Upper Indus and its tributaries for the extensive system in Pakistan and Punjab, India, was for more than ten years a major cause of dispute between India and Pakistan, settled by a treaty in 1960; the Murray basin, Victoria, Australia, and of the Great Valley of California, USA, are examples of 19th and 20th century irrigation canal development.

Probably the oldest ship canal to be still in use is the Grand Canal waterway in China, which links Tianjin and Hangzhou, and interconnects the Huang He (Yellow River) and Chang Jiang. It was originally built in three stages 485 BC–AD 283, reaching a total length of 1,780 km/1,107 mi. Large sections silted up in later years, but the entire system was dredged, widened and rebuilt 1958–72 in conjunction with work on flood protection, irrigation and hydroelectric schemes.

The first major British canal was the Manchester-Bridgewater Canal 1761–76, constructed for the 3rd Duke of Bridgewater to carry coal from his collieries to Manchester. The engineer, ◊Brindley, overcame great difficulties in the route. Today many of Britain's canals form part of an inter-connecting system of waterways some 4,000 km/2,500 mi long. Many which have become disused commercially have been restored for recreation and the use of pleasure craft.

Where speed is not a prime factor, the cost-effectiveness of transporting goods by canal has encouraged a modern revival and Belgium, France, Germany, and the USSR are among countries which have extended and modernized their canal facilities. The Baltic–Volga Waterway begun in the USSR in 1964 will link the northern port of Klaipeda with Kahovka, at the mouth of the Dnieper on the Black Sea, a distance of 2,430 km/1,510 mi. A further canal cuts across the north Crimea, thus shortening the voyage of ships from the Dnieper through the Black Sea to the Sea of Azov. The Panama Canal 1904–14 links the Atlantic and Pacific Oceans (64 km/40 mi). In North America, the St Lawrence Seaway 1954–59 extends from Montreal to Lake Ontario (290 km/180 mi) and, with the deepening of the Welland Canal and some of the river channels, provides a waterway that enables ocean-going vessels to travel during the ice-free months between the Atlantic and Duluth, Minnesota,

canals and waterways

Name	Country	Opened	Length km	mi
Amsterdam	Netherlands	1876	26.6	16.5
Baltic-Volga	USSR	1964	2,430	1,510
Baltic-White Sea	USSR	1933	235	146
Corinth	Greece	1893	6.4	4
Elbe and Trave	Germany	1900	66	41
Göta	Sweden	1832	185	115
Grand Canal	China	485 BC–AD1972	1,050	650
Kiel	West Germany	1895	98	61
Manchester	England	1894	57	35.5
Panama	Panama	1914	81	50.5
Princess Juliana	Netherlands	1935	32	20
St Lawrence	Canada	1959	3,770	2,342
Saulte Ste Marie	USA	1855	2.6	1.6
Saulte Ste Marie	Canada	1895	1.8	1.1
Welland	Canada	1929	45	28
Suez	Egypt	1869	166	103

USA, at the western end of Lake Superior, some 3,770 km/2,342 mi.

Canaletto /ˌkænəˈletəʊ/ Antonio (Giovanni Antoni Canal) 1697–1768. Italian painter celebrated for his paintings of views (*vedute*) of Venice (where he lived for some years) and of the Thames and London 1746–56.

Much of his work is very detailed and precise, with a warm light and a sparkling of tiny highlights on the green waters of canals and rivers. His later style became clumsier and more static.

Canaries current the cold ocean current in the North Atlantic Ocean flowing SW from Spain along the NW coast of Africa. It meets the northern equatorial current at a latitude of 20° N.

canary bird *Serinus canaria* of the finch family, found wild in the Canary Islands and Madeira. It is greenish with a yellow underside. Canaries have been bred as cage-birds in Europe since the 15th century, and many domestic varieties are yellow or orange.

Some canaries are used in mines as detectors of bad air.

Canary Islands /kəˈneəri/ (Spanish **Canarias**) group of volcanic islands 100 km/60 mi off the NW coast of Africa, forming the Spanish provinces of Las Palmas and Santa Cruz de Tenerife; area 7,300 sq km/2,818 sq mi; population (1986) 1,615,000.

features The chief centres are Santa Cruz on Tenerife (which also has the highest peak in extra-continental Spain, Pico de Teide 3,713 m/12,186 ft), and Las Palmas on Gran Canaria. The province of Santa Cruz comprises Tenerife, Palma, Gomera, and Hierro, and the province of Las Palmas comprises Gran Canaria, Lanzarote, and Fuerteventura. There are also six uninhabited islets. The Northern Hemisphere Observatory (1981) is on the island of Las Palma, the

first in the world to be remotely controlled. Observation conditions are among the best in the world, since there is no moisture, no artificial light pollution, and little natural ◊airglow. The Organization of African Unity (OAU) supports an independent Guanch Republic (so-called from the indigenous islanders, a branch of the N African Berbers) and revival of the Guanch language.

Canberra /ˈkænbərə/ capital of Australia (since 1908), situated in the Australian Capital Territory enclosed within New South Wales, on a tributary of the Murrumbidgee; area (Australian Capital Territory including the port at Jervis Bay) 2,432 sq km/939 sq mi; population (1986) 285,800.

It contains the Parliament House, first used by the Commonwealth Parliament in 1927, the Australian National University (1946), the Canberra School of Music (1965), and the National War Memorial.

cancan /ˈkænkæn/ high-kicking stage dance for women (solo or line of dancers) originating in Paris about 1830. The music usually associated with the cancan is the *galop* from Offenbach's *Orpheus in the Underworld.*

cancer a group of diseases characterized by abnormal proliferation of cells. Regardless of where the cancer arises, its cells are usually degenerate, capable only of reproducing themselves (tumour formation) so as to outnumber the surrounding healthy cells. Malignant cells tend to spread from their site of origin by travelling through the bloodstream or lymphatic system.

There are more than 100 types of cancer. Some, like lung or bowel cancer, are common; others are exceedingly rare. The full causation remains unexplained. Triggering agents (◊carcinogens) include chemicals such as those found in

Canaries Island

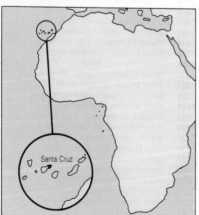

Canaletto The Bacino di S. Marco on Ascension Day *(c.1740) Royal Collection, London.*

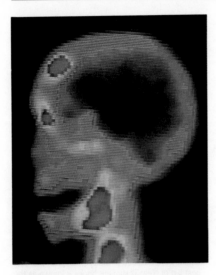

cancer *Skull of a person suffering from bone cancer, showing the areas of cancerous bone in red.*

cigarette smoke, other forms of smoke, asbestos dust, exhaust fumes and many industrial chemicals. Some viruses can also trigger the cancerous growth of cells (see ◊carcinogens) as can X-rays and radioactivity. Dietary factors are important in some cancers, for example, lack of fibre in the diet may predispose people to bowel cancer and a diet high in animal fats and low in fresh vegetables and fruit increases the risk of breast cancer. Psychological ◊stress may increase the risk of cancer, especially if the person concerned is not able to control the source of the stress. In some families there is a genetic tendency towards a particular type of cancer.

While cancer is undoubtedly one of the leading causes of death in the developed world, it is by no means incurable. Cures are sometimes achieved with highly specialized treatments, such as surgery, chemotherapy with ◊cytotoxic drugs, and irradiation, or a combination of all three. ◊Monoclonal antibodies have been used therapeutically against some cancers, with limited success. Combining a monoclonal antibody with a drug that will kill the cancer cell, to produce a highly specific ◊magic bullet drug, may be more promising. At present public health programmes place most emphasis on prevention and early detection giving a better chance of cure.

Cancer the faintest zodiac constellation (its brightest stars are fourth magnitude), through which the Sun passes during late Jul and early Aug. It is represented as a crab, and its main feature is the star cluster Praesepe, popularly known as the Beehive. It is in the northern hemisphere, near Ursa Major. In **astrology**, the dates for Cancer are between about 22 June and 22 July (see ◊precession).

Cancún /kæn'kuːn/ Caribbean resort in Mexico, site in 1981 of a north-south summit to discuss the widening gap between the developed countries and the Third World.

candela SI unit (symbol cd) of luminous intensity, which replaced the old units of candle and standard candle. It measures the brightness of a light itself, rather than the amount of light falling on an object, which is called *illuminance* and measured in ◊lux.

One candela is defined as the luminous intensity in a given direction of a source that emits monochromatic radiation of frequency 540×10^{-12} Hz and whose radiant energy in that direction is 1/683 watt per steradian.

Candela /kæn'deɪlə/ Felix 1910– . Spanish-born Mexican architect, originator of the hypar (hyperbolic paraboloid) from 1951, in which doubly curved surfaces are built up on a framework of planks sprayed with cement. Professor at the National School of Architecture, University of Mexico, from 1953.

Candia /'kændiə/ Italian name for the Greek island of ◊Crete, also formerly the name of the largest city, ◊Iráklion, founded about AD 824.

Candida albicans a yeast-like fungus that is present in the human digestive tract, and in the vagina, and causes no harm in most healthy people. However it can cause problems if it multiplies excessively, as in vaginal candidiasis or ◊thrush, whose main symptom is intense itching. The most common form of thrush is oral, which occurs commonly in those taking steroids or prolonged courses of antibiotics.

Newborn babies may pick up the yeast during birth and suffer an infection of the mouth and throat. There is also some evidence that overgrowth of Candida may occur in the intestines, causing diarrhoea, bloating and other symptoms, such as headache and fatigue, but this is not yet proven. Occasionally, Candida can infect ◊immunocompromised patients, such as those with AIDS. Treatment for candidiasis is based on anti-fungal drugs.

Candide a satire by Voltaire, published 1759 , which describes the misfortunes of Candide. The story's happy conclusion endorses the belief of Candide's mentor, Pangloss, that 'all is for the best in the best of all possible worlds', which itself satirizes the philosophies of Leibniz and Jean-Jacques Rousseau.

candle means of producing light consisting typically of a vertical cylinder of wax (such as tallow or paraffin wax) with a central wick of string. A flame applied to the end of the wick melts the wax, and the burning wax produces a luminous flame. The wick is treated with a substance such as alum so that it carbonizes but does not rapidly burn out.

Formerly candles and oil lamps were the chief form of artificial lighting. Accurately made candles – which burned at a steady rate – were calibrated along their length and used as a type of clock. The candle was also the name of a unit of luminous intensity, now replaced by the candela (cd), equal to 1/60 of the luminance of 1 cm^2 of a black body radiator at a temperature of 2,042K.

Candlemas in the Christian church, the Feast of the Purification of the Blessed Virgin Mary and the Presentation of the Infant Christ in the Temple, celebrated on 2 Feb; church candles are blessed on this day.

cane the reedlike stem of various plants, such as the sugar cane and bamboo, and particularly of the group of palms called rattans, consisting of the genus *Calamus* and its allies. Their slender stems are dried and used for making walking sticks, baskets, and furniture.

Canea /'kɑːniə/ (Greek *Khania*) principal port of Crete, midway along the north coast; population (1981) 47,338. It was founded in 1252 by the Venetians, and is still surrounded by a wall. Vegetable oils, soap, and leather are exported. Heavy fighting took place here during World War II, after the landing of German parachutists in May 1941. In 1971 it was replaced by Iráklion as administrative capital of Crete.

Canes Venatici constellation of the northern hemisphere near Ursa Major, representing the hunting dogs of ◊Boötes, the herdsman. Its stars are faint, and it contains the Whirlpool galaxy (M51), the first spiral galaxy to be recognized.

Canetti /kə'neti/ Elias 1905– . Bulgarian-born writer. He was exiled from Austria as a Jew 1938, and settled in England 1939. His books, written in German, include the novel *Die Blendung/Auto da Fé*; and an autobiography *The Tongue Set Free* (translated 1988). He was concerned with crowd behaviour and the psychology of power. Nobel prize 1981.

Canis Major brilliant constellation of the southern hemisphere, representing one of the two dogs following at the heel of Orion. Its main star is Sirius, the 'dog star', and the brightest star in the sky.

Canis Minor small constellation of the equatorial region, representing the second of the two dogs

Canetti *The first Bulgarian to win the Nobel Prize for Literature was Elias Canetti in 1981.*

of Orion (the other dog is represented by Canis Major). Its brightest star is Procyon.

cannabis the dried leaf and female flowers (marijuana) and resin (hashish) of certain varieties of ◊hemp *Cannabis sativa* which are smoked or eaten and have an intoxicating and stimulating effect.

Cannabis is a soft drug in that any dependence is psychological rather than physical. It has medicinal use in countering depression and the side effects of cancer therapy (pain and nausea). Cultivation of cannabis is illegal in the UK and USA except under licence.

Cannae /'kæniː/ village in Puglia, Italy, site of ◊Hannibal's defeat of the Romans 216 BC.

Cannes /kæn/ resort in Alpes-Maritimes *département*, S France; population (1982) 73,000, conurbation 296,000. An important film festival is held here annually. Formerly only a small seaport, in 1834 it attracted the patronage of Lord ◊Brougham (who died here) and other distinguished visitors, and became a fashionable and popular holiday resort. A new town (La Bocca) grew up facing the Mediterranean.

cannibalism the practice of eating human flesh, also called **anthropophagy**. The name is derived from the Caribs, a South American and West Indian people, alleged by the conquering Spaniards to eat their captives.

canning /'kænɪŋ/ food preservation in hermetically sealed containers by the application of heat. Originated by Nicolas Appert in France 1809 with glass containers, it was developed by Peter Durand in England 1810 with cans made of sheet steel thinly coated with tin to delay corrosion.

Canneries were established in the USA before 1820, but the US canning industry began to grow considerably in the 1870s when the manufacture of cans was mechanized and factory methods of processing were used. The quality and taste of early canned food was frequently dubious but by the end of the 19th century, scientific research made greater understanding possible of the food preserving process, and standards improved. Cans for beer and soft drinks are generally made of aluminium. More than half the aluminium cans used in the USA are now recycled.

In Britain, imports of canned fruit, beef, vegetables, and condensed milk rose substantially after World War I. A British canning industry was slow to develop compared to the USA or Australia, but it began to grow during the 1920s, and by 1932, the Metal Box Company was producing over 100 million cans a year.

Canning *A bust in the National Portrait Gallery, London, of British politician George Canning. His advancement came through his writing ability, much appreciated by the then prime minister William Pitt. Canning was himself twice foreign secretary, and prime minister for a short time. He died in office.*

Canning /'kænɪŋ/ Charles John, 1st Earl 1812–1862. British administrator, first viceroy of India from 1858. As governor-general of India from 1856, he suppressed the Indian Mutiny with an unvindictive firmness that earned him the nickname 'Clemency Canning'. He was the son of George Canning.

Canning /'kænɪŋ/ George 1770–1827. British Tory politician, foreign secretary 1807–10 and 1822–27, and prime minister 1827 in coalition with the Whigs. He was largely responsible during the Napoleonic Wars for the seizure of the Danish fleet and British intervention in the Spanish peninsula.

Canning entered Parliament 1793. His verse, satires, and parodies for the *Anti-Jacobin* 1797–98 led to his advancement by Pitt the Younger. His disapproval of the ◊Walcheren expedition 1809 involved him in a duel with Castlereagh and led to his resignation as foreign secretary. He was president of the Board of Control 1816–20. On Castlereagh's death 1822, he again became foreign secretary, supported the national movements in Greece and South America, and was made prime minister 1827. When Wellington, Peel, and other Tories refused to serve under him, he formed a coalition with the Whigs. He died in office.

Cannizzaro /ˌkæniˈzɑːrəʊ/ Stanislao 1826–1910. Italian chemist who revived interest in the work of Avogadro 1811, which had revealed the difference between ◊atoms and ◊molecules, and so established atomic and molecular weights as the basis of chemical calculations.

Cannizzaro also worked in aromatic organic chemistry, and reactions of the type he discovered in 1853 for making benzyl alcohol and benzoic acid from benzaldehyde are named after him.

Cannon /'kænən/ Annie Jump 1863–1941. US astronomer who, from 1896, worked at Harvard College Observatory and carried out revolutionary work with the classification of stars by examining their spectra. Her system, still used today, has spectra arranged according to temperature and runs from O through B, A, F, G, K, and M. O-type stars are the hottest, with surface temperatures of 35,000K. She also discovered over 300 ◊variable stars and five ◊novae.

Cano /'kɑːnəʊ/ Alonso 1601–1667. Spanish sculptor, painter, and architect, an exponent of the Baroque style in Spain. He was active in Seville, Madrid, and Granada, and designed the façade of Granada Cathedral 1667.

From 1637 he was employed by Philip IV to restore the royal collection at the Prado in Madrid. Many of his religious paintings show the influence of the Venetian masters. He also created monumental carved screens, such as the reredos (altar screen) in Lebrija, near Seville, and graceful free-standing polychrome carved figures.

Cano /'kɑːnəʊ/ Juan Sebastian del *c.*1476–1526. Spanish voyager. It is claimed that he was the first sea captain to sail around the world. He sailed with Magellan in 1519 and, after the latter's death in the Philippines, brought the *Victoria* safely home to Spain.

canoeing sport of propelling a lightweight, shallow boat, pointed at both ends, by paddles or sails. Modern-day canoes are made from fibre-glass, but original boats were of wooden construction covered in bark or skin. Canoeing was popularized as a sport in the 19th century and the Royal Canoe Club in Britain was founded 1866.

Two types of canoe are used. The *kayak,* derived from the Eskimo model, has a keel and the canoeist sits. The *Canadian style canoe* has no keel and the canoeist kneels. In addition to straightforward racing, there are slalom courses, with up to 30 'gates' to be negotiated through rapids and round artificial rock formations. Penalty seconds are added to course time for touching suspended gate poles or missing a gate. One to four canoeists are carried.

It was introduced into the *Olympic Games* 1936. Recent winners in all current classes:

men: kayak singles
500 metres
1980 Vladimir Parfenovich *(USSR)*
1984 Ian Ferguson *(New Zealand)*
1988 Zsolt Gyulay *(Hungary)*
1,000 metres
1980 Rudiger Helm *(East Germany)*
1984 Alan Thompson *(New Zealand)*
1988 Greg Barton *(USA)*
kayak pairs
500 metres
1980 USSR
1984 New Zealand
1988 New Zealand
1,000 metres
1980 USSR
1984 Canada
1988 USA
kayak fours
1,000 metres
1980 East Germany
1984 New Zealand
1988 Hungary
Canadian singles
500 metres
1980 Sergey Postrekhin *(USSR)*
1984 Larry Cain *(Canada)*
1988 Olaf Heukrodt *(East Germany)*
1,000 metres
1980 Lubomir Lubenov *(Bulgaria)*
1984 Ulrich Eicke *(West Germany)*
1988 Ivan Klementiev *(USSR)*
Canadian pairs
500 metres
1980 Hungary
1984 Yugoslavia
1988 USSR
1,000 metres
1980 Romania
1984 Romania
1988 USSR
women: kayak singles
500 metres
1980 Birgit Fischer *(East Germany)*
1984 Agneta Anderson *(Sweden)*
1988 Vania Guecheva *(Bulgaria)*
kayak pairs
500 metres
1980 East Germany
1984 Sweden
1988 East Germany

canon a type of priest in the Roman Catholic and Anglican churches. Canons, headed by the dean, are attached to a cathedral and constitute the *chapter*.

Originally, in the Catholic church, a canon was a priest in a cathedral or collegiate church. Canons lived within its precinct, and their lives were ordered by ecclesiastical rules (termed ◊canon law). About the 11th century a distinction was drawn between **regular** or Augustinian canons who observed the rules, and **secular** canons who lived outside the precinct, and were in effect the administrative officers of a cathedral, but in holy orders. After the Reformation, all canons in England became secular canons.

canon in theology, the collection of writings that is accepted as authoritative in a given religion, such as the *Tripitaka* in Theravāda Buddhism. In the Christian church, it comprises the books of the ◊Bible.

The canon of the Old Testament was drawn up at the assembly of rabbis held at Jamnia in Palestine between AD 90 and 100; certain excluded books were included in the ◊Apocrypha. The earliest list of New Testament books is known as the Muratorian Canon (*c.*160–70). Bishop Athanasius promulgated about 365 a list which corresponds with that in modern Bibles.

canon in music, an echo form for two or more parts repeating and following a leading melody at regular time-intervals to achieve a harmonious effect. It is often found in Classical music, for example ◊Vivaldi and JS ◊Bach.

canonical hours in the Catholic church, seven set periods of devotion: **matins** and **lauds**, **prime**, **terce**, **sext**, **nones**, **evensong** or **vespers**, **compline**. In the Anglican church, the period 8 am–6 pm within which marriage can be legally performed in a parish church without a special licence.

canonization in the Catholic church, the admission of one of its members to the Calendar of ◊Saints. The evidence of the candidate's exceptional piety is contested before the Congregation for the Causes of Saints by the Promotor Fidei, popularly known as the **devil's advocate**. Papal ratification of a favourable verdict results in ◊beatification, and full sainthood (conferred in St Peter's basilica, the Vatican) follows after further proof.

Under a system laid down mainly in the 17th century, the process of investigation was seldom completed in under 50 years, although in the case of a martyr it took less time. Since 1969 the gathering of the proof of the candidate's virtues has been left to the bishop of the birthplace, and, miracles being difficult to substantiate, stress is placed on extraordinary 'favours' or 'graces' that can be proved or attested by serious investigation. Many modern saints have come from the Third World where the expansion of the Catholic church is most rapid, for example the American Mohawk Indian Kateri Tekakwitha (died 1680), beatified in 1980.

canon law the rules and regulations of the Christian church, especially the Greek Orthodox, Roman Catholic, and Anglican churches. Its origin is sought in the declarations of Jesus and the apostles. In 1983 Pope John Paul II issued a new canon-law code reducing offences carrying automatic excommunication, extending the grounds for annulment of marriage, removing the ban on marriage with non-Catholics, and banning trade-union and political activity by priests.

The earliest compilations were in the East, and the canon law of the Eastern Orthodox Church is comparatively small. Through the centuries, a great mass of canon law was accumulated in the Western church, which in 1918 was condensed in the *Corpus juris canonici* under Benedict XV. Even so, however, this is supplemented by many papal decrees.

The canon law of the Church of England remained almost unchanged from 1603 until it was completely revised 1969, and is kept under constant review by the Canon Law Commission of the General Synod.

Canopus second-brightest star in the sky, magnitude −0.7, lying in the constellation Carina. It is a yellow-white supergiant about 200 light years away. It is thousands of times more luminous than the Sun.

Canossa /kə'nɒsə/ ruined castle 19 km/12 mi SW of Reggio, Italy. The Holy Roman emperor Henry IV did penance here before Pope ◊Gregory VII in 1077 for having opposed him in the question of investitures.

Canova /kə'nəʊvə/ Antonio 1757–1822. Italian Neo-Classical sculptor, based in Rome from 1781. He received commissions from popes, kings, and emperors for his highly finished marble portrait busts and groups. He made several portraits of Napoleon.

Canova was born near Treviso. His reclining marble *Pauline Borghese* 1805–07 (Borghese Gallery, Rome) is a fine example of cool, polished classicism. He executed the tombs of popes Clement XIII, Pius VII, and Clement XIV, and his marble sculptures include *Cupid and Psyche* (Louvre, Paris) and *The Three Graces* (Hermitage, Leningrad).

Cánovas del Castillo /'kænəvæs del kæ'stɪljəʊ/ Antonio 1828–1897. Spanish politician and chief architect of the political system known as the *turno político* through which his own conservative party, and that of the liberals under Práxedes Sagasta, alternated in power. Elections were rigged to ensure the appropriate majorities. Cánovas was assassinated in 1897 in an attack carried out by anarchists.

Cantab abbreviation for *Cantabrigiensis* (Latin 'of Cambridge').

Cantabria /kæn'tæbriə/ autonomous region of N Spain; area 5,300 sq km/2,046 sq mi; population (1986) 525,000; capital Santander.

Cantabrian Mountains /kæn'tæbriən/ (Spanish *Cordillera Cantabrica*) mountains running along the north coast of Spain, reaching 2,648 m/8,688 ft in the Picos de Europa massif. The mountains have coal and iron deposits.

Cantal /kɒn'tɑːl/ volcanic mountain range in central France, which gives its name to Cantal *département*. The highest point is the Plomb du Cantal, 1,858 m/6,096 ft.

cantaloupe several small varieties of melon, *Cucumis melo*, distinguished by their small, round, ribbed fruits.

cantata in music, an extended work for voices, from the Italian, meaning 'sung', as opposed to ◊sonata 'sounded' for instruments. A cantata can be sacred or secular, sometimes uses solo voices, and usually has orchestral accompaniment. The first printed collection of sacred cantata texts dates from 1670.

Canterbury /'kæntəbəri/ city in Kent, England, on the Stour, 100 km/62 m SE of London; population (1984) 39,000.

The Roman Durovernum, Canterbury was the Saxon capital of Kent. The modern name derives from *Cantwarabyrig* (Old English 'fortress of the men of Kent'). In 597 King Ethelbert welcomed Augustine's mission to England here, and the city has since been the metropolis of the Anglican Communion and seat of the Archbishop of Canterbury.

Canterbury, Archbishop of /'kæntəbəri/ primate of all England, archbishop of the Church of England, and first peer of the realm, ranking next to royalty. He crowns the sovereign, has a seat in the House of Lords, and is a member of the Privy Council. He is appointed by the prime minister. His official residence is at Lambeth Palace, London, and second residence at the Old Palace, Canterbury. Robert ◊Runcie was appointed 1980.

Formerly selected by political consultation, since 1980 the new archbishops have been selected by a church group, the Crown Appointments Commission (formed 1977). The first holder of the office was St Augustine 601–04; his 20th-century successors have been: Randal T Davidson 1903, C G Lang 1928, William Temple 1942, G F Fisher 1945, A Michael Ramsey 1961, D Coggan 1974, and Robert A K Runcie 1980.

Canterbury Plains /'kæntəbəri/ area of rich grassland between the mountains and the sea on the east coast of South Island, New Zealand, source of Canterbury lamb. Area 10,000 sq km/4,000 sq mi.

Canterbury Tales an unfinished collection of stories in prose and verse (*c.*1387) by Geoffrey Chaucer, told by a group of pilgrims on their way to Thomas à Becket's tomb at Canterbury. The tales and preludes are notable for their vivid character portrayal and colloquial language. Each pilgrim has to tell two stories on the way to Canterbury, and two on the way back, but only 24 tales were written.

cantilever a beam or structure that is fixed at one end only, though it may be supported at some point along its length, for example a diving board. The cantilever principle, widely used in construction engineering, eliminates the need for a second main support at the free end of the beam, allowing for more elegant structures and reducing the amount of materials required. Many large-span ◊bridges have been built on the cantilever principle.

A typical cantilever bridge consists of two beams cantilevered out from either bank, each supported part way along, with their free ends meeting in the middle. The multiple-cantilever Forth Rail Bridge (completed 1890) across the Firth of Forth in Scotland has twin main spans of 521 m/1,710 ft.

canton in France, an administrative district, a subdivision of the *arrondissement*; in Switzerland, one of the 23 subdivisions forming the Confederation.

Canton /,kæn'tɒn/ former name of Kwangchow or ◊Guangzhou in China.

Canton and Enderbury /'kæntən, 'endəbəri/ two atolls in the Phoenix group, which forms part of the Republic of ◊Kiribati. They were a UK–USA condominium 1939–80, and there are US aviation, radar and tracking stations.

cantor in Judaism, the prayer leader in a synagogue; the cantor is not a rabbi, and the position can be taken by any lay person.

Cantor /'kæntɔː/ Georg 1845–1918. German mathematician who defined real numbers and produced a treatment of irrational numbers using a series of transfinite numbers. Cantor's set theory has been used in the development of topology and real function theory.

Canute /kə'njuːt/ *c.* 995–1035. King of England from 1016, Denmark from 1018, and Norway from 1028. Having invaded England 1013 with his father, Sweyn, king of Denmark, he was acclaimed king on his father's death 1014 by his ◊Viking army. Canute defeated ◊Edmund Ironside at Assandun, Essex, 1016, and became king of all England on Edmund's death. He succeeded his brother Harold as king of Denmark 1018, compelled King Malcolm to pay homage by invading Scotland about 1027, and conquered Norway 1028. He was succeeded by his illegitimate son Harold I.

The legend of Canute disenchanting his flattering courtiers by showing that the sea would not retreat at his command was first told by Henry of Huntingdon in 1130.

Canute /kə'njuːt/ (Cnut VI) 1163–1202. King of Denmark from 1182, son and successor of Waldemar Knudsson. With the aid of his brother and successor, Waldemar II, and Absalon, archbishop of Lund, he resisted Frederick Barbarossa's northward expansion, and established Denmark as the dominant power in the Baltic.

cantus firmus (Latin 'fixed voice-part') in music, any familiar melody sung by an early composer as the basis for musical invention.

canyon (Spanish *can*, 'tube') a deep narrow valley or gorge running through mountains. Canyons are formed by stream down-cutting, usually in areas of low rainfall, where the stream or river receives water from outside the area.

There are many canyons in the western USA and in Mexico, for example the Grand Canyon of the Colorado River in Arizona, the canyon in Yellowstone National Park, and the Black Canyon in Colorado.

Cao Chan /'tsaʊ 'tʃæn/ or *Ts'ao Chan* 1719–1763. Chinese novelist whose tragic love story *Hung Lou Meng/ The Dream of the Red Chamber* published 1792, which involves the downfall of a Manchu family, is semi-autobiographical.

cap. abbreviation for *capital*.

CAP abbreviation for ◊*Common Agricultural Policy*.

capacitance, electrical ratio of the electric charge on a body to the resultant change of potential.

capacitor device for storing electric charge, used in electronic circuits; it consists of two metal plates separated by an insulating layer called a dielectric.

Its *capacitance* is the ratio of the charge stored on either plate to the potential difference between the plates. The SI unit of capacitance is the ◊farad, but most capacitors have much smaller capacitances, and the microfarad (a millionth of a farad) is the commonly used practical unit.

Cape Breton /'bretn/ island forming the northern part of the province of Nova Scotia, Canada; area 10,282 sq km/3,970 sq mi; population (1988) 170,000. Bisected by a waterway, it has road and rail links with the mainland across the Strait of Canso. It has coal resources and steelworks, and there has been substantial development in the strait area, with docks, oil refineries, and newsprint production from local timber. In the north the surface rises to 550 m/1,800 ft at North Cape, and the coast has many fine harbours. There are cod fisheries. The climate is mild and very moist. The chief towns are Sydney and Glace Bay.

history The first British colony was established in 1629, but was driven out by the French. In 1763 Cape Breton was ceded to Britain and attached to Nova Scotia 1763–84 and from 1820.

Cape Byron /'baɪrən/ the eastern extremity of Australia, in New South Wales, just south of the border with Queensland.

Cape Canaveral /kə'nævərəl/ promontory on the Atlantic coast of Florida, USA, 367 km/228 mi N of Miami, used as a rocket launch site by ◊NASA.

First mentioned in 1513, it was known 1963–73 as Cape Kennedy. The ◊Kennedy Space Center is nearby.

Cape Coast /'keɪp 'kəʊst/ port of Ghana, West Africa, 130 km/80 mi west of Accra; population (1982) 73,000. It was superseded as the main port since 1962 by Tema. The town, first established by the Portuguese in the 16th century, is built on a natural breakwater, adjoining the castle.

Cape Cod /'keɪp 'kɒd/ hook-shaped peninsula in SE Massachusetts, USA; 100 km/60 mi long and 1.6–32 km/1–20 mi wide; population (1980) 150,000. Its beaches and woods make it a popular tourist area. It is separated from the rest of the state by the Cape Cod Canal. The islands of Martha's Vineyard and Nantucket are just south of the cape. Basque and Norse fishermen are believed to have visited Cape Cod many years before the English Pilgrims landed at Provincetown 1620. It was named after the cod that were caught in the dangerous shoals of the cape. The ◊Kennedy family home is at the resort of Hyannis Port.

Cape Coloured South African term for people of mixed African and European descent, mainly living in Cape Province.

Cape gooseberry plant *Physalis peruviana* of the potato family. Originating in South America, it is grown elsewhere, including South Africa from where it takes its name. It is cultivated for its fruit, a yellow berry surrounded by a papery ◊calyx.

Cape Horn /'keɪp hɔ:n/ most southerly point of South America, in the Chilean part of the archipelago of ◊Tierra del Fuego; notorious for gales and heavy seas. It was named in 1616 by its Dutch discoverer Willem Schouten (1580–1625) after his birthplace (Hoorn).

Čapek /'tʃæpek/ Karel (Matelj) 1890–1938. Czech writer whose works often deal with social injustice in an imaginative, satirical way. *R.U.R.* 1921 is a play in which robots (a term he coined) rebel against their controllers; the novel *Valka s Mloky/War With the Newts* 1936 is a science-fiction classic.

Capella brightest star in the constellation Auriga, and the sixth brightest star in the sky. It consists of a pair of yellow giant stars 45 light years away orbiting each other every 104 days.

Cape of Good Hope /'keɪp əv gʊd 'həʊp/ South African headland forming a peninsula between Table Bay and False Bay, Cape Town. The first European to sail round it was Bartholomew Diaz in 1488. Formerly named Cape of Storms, it was given its present name by King John II of Portugal.

Cape Province /'keɪp 'prɒvɪns/ (Afrikaans **Kaapprovinsie**) largest province of the Republic of South Africa, named after the Cape of Good Hope

area 641,379 sq km/247,638 sq mi, excluding Walvis Bay

capital Cape Town

towns Port Elizabeth, East London, Kimberley, Grahamstown, Stellenbosch

physical Orange river, Drakensberg, Table Mountain (highest point Maclear's Beacon 1087 m/3567 ft); Great Karoo Plateau, Walvis Bay

products fruit, vegetables, wine; meat, ostrich feathers; diamonds, copper, asbestos, manganese

population (1985) 5,041,000, officially including 2,226,200 Coloured; 1,569,000 Black; 1,264,000 White; 32,120 Asian

history the Dutch occupied the Cape in 1652, but it was taken by the British in 1795 after the French Revolutionary armies had occupied the Netherlands, and was sold to Britain for £6 million in 1814. The Cape achieved self-government in 1872. It was an original province of the Union in 1910.

The Orange river was proclaimed the northern boundary in 1825. Griqualand West (1880) and the southern part of Bechuanaland (1895) were later incorporated; and Walvis Bay, although administered with SW Africa, is legally an integral part of Cape Province.

caper shrub *Capparis spinosa*, native to the Mediterranean and belonging to the family Capparidaceae. Its flower buds are preserved in vinegar as a condiment.

capercaillie large bird *Tetrao urogallus* of the grouse type found in coniferous woodland in Europe and N Asia. At nearly 1 m/3 ft long, the male is the biggest gamebird in Europe, with a largely black plumage and rounded tail which is fanned out in courtship. The female is speckled brown and about 60 cm/2 ft long.

Hunted to extinction in Britain in the 18th century, the capercaillie was reintroduced from Sweden in the 1830s and has re-established itself in Scotland.

Capet /'kæ'pet/ Hugh 938–996. King of France from 987, when he claimed the throne on the death of Louis V. He founded the **Capetian dynasty**, of which various branches continued to reign until the French Revolution, for example, ◊Valois and ◊Bourbon.

Cape Town /'keɪptaʊn/ (Afrikaans **Kaapstad**) port and oldest town in South Africa, situated in the SW on Table Bay; population (1985) 776,617. Industries include horticulture and trade in wool, wine, fruit, grain, and oil. It is the legislative capital of the Republic of South Africa, and capital of Cape Province, and was founded in 1652.

Cape Verde
Republic of
(República de Cabo Verde)

area 4,033 sq km/1,557 sq mi
capital Praia
physical archipelago of ten islands 565 km/350 mi W of Senegal
features strategically important because it dominates the western shipping lanes
head of state and government Aristides Pereira from 1975
political system one-party socialist state
political parties African Party for the Independence of Cape Verde (PAICV), African-nationalist
exports bananas, coffee
currency Cape Verde escudo (123.10 = £1 Feb 1990)
population (1988) 359,000 (including 100,000 Angolan refugees); annual growth rate 1.9%
life expectancy men 57, women 61
language Creole dialect of Portuguese
religion Roman Catholic 80%
literacy 61% male/39% female (1985)
GDP $110 million (1983); $300 per head of population
chronology
1974 Moved towards independence through a transitional Portuguese-Cape Verde government.
1975 Full independence achieved. National people's assembly elected. Aristides Pereira became the first president.
1980 Constitution adopted providing for eventual union with Guinea-Bissau.
1981 Union with Guinea-Bissau abandoned and the constitution amended; became one-party state.

It includes the Houses of Parliament, City Hall, Cape Town Castle (1666), and Groote Schuur, 'great barn', the estate of Cecil Rhodes (he designated the house as the home of the premier, and a university and the National Botanical Gardens occupy part of the grounds). The naval base of **Simonstown** is to the SE; in 1975 Britain's use of its facilities was ended by the Labour government in disapproval of South Africa's racial policies.

Cape Verde /vɜ:d/ group of islands in the Atlantic, off the coast of Senegal.

government The 1980 constitution provides for a national people's assembly of 83, elected by universal suffrage for a five-year term, and a president, elected for a similar term by the assembly. The constitution had also provided for union with Guinea-Bissau but this was deleted in 1981 and an amendment inserted replacing the African Party for the Independence of Portuguese Guinea and Cape Verde (PAIGC) with the African Party for the Independence of Cape Verde (PAICV) as the only political party. As well as combining the roles of head of state and head of government, the president is secretary-general of PAICV. There is an opposition party, the Independent Democratic Union of Cape Verde (UCID), but it operates from Lisbon.

history The Cape Verde islands were first settled in the 15th century by Portugal, the first black inhabitants being slaves imported from W Africa.

A liberation movement developed in the 1950s. The mainland territory to which Cape Verde is linked, Guinea, now Guinea-Bissau, was granted independence in 1974, and a process began for their eventual union. A transitional government was set up, composed of Portuguese and PAIGC members. In 1975 a national people's assembly was elected and Aristides Pereira, PAIGC secretary-general, became president of Cape Verde. The 1980 constitution provided for the union of the two states but in 1981 this aspect was deleted because of insufficient support and the PAIGC became the PAICV. Pereira was re-elected and relations with Guinea-Bissau improved. Under President Pereira, Cape Verde has adopted a policy of non-alignment and achieved considerable respect within the region.

Cape Wrath /rɑ:θ/ headland at the NW extremity of Scotland.

Cape York /jɔ:k/ peninsula, the most northerly point (10° 41'S) of the Australian mainland, so named by Captain James ◊Cook in 1770. The peninsula is about 800 km/500 mi long and 640 km/400 mi wide at its junction with the mainland. Its barrenness deterred early Dutch explorers, although the south is being developed for cattle (Brahmin type) and in the north there are large bauxite deposits.

capillarity the spontaneous movement of liquids up or down narrow tubes, or capillaries. The movement is due to unbalanced molecular attraction at the boundary between the liquid and the tube. If liquid molecules near the boundary are more strongly attracted to molecules in the material of the tube than to other nearby liquid molecules, the liquid will rise in the tube. If liquid molecules are less attracted to the material of the tube than to other liquid molecules, the liquid will fall.

capillary in anatomy, a fine blood vessel, between 8 and 20 thousandths of a millimetre in diameter, that connects the ◊arteries and ◊veins of vertebrates. Water, proteins, soluble food substances, gases, and white blood cells pass through the capillary wall (consisting of a single layer of cells) between the fluid (lymph) bathing the body tissue outside the capillary and the ◊blood within the capillary.

capillary in physics, a very narrow, thick-walled tube, usually made of glass, such as in a thermometer. Properties of fluids, such as surface tension and viscosity, can be studied using capillary tubes.

capital in architecture, a stone placed on the top of a column, pier, or pilaster, and usually wider on the upper surface than the diameter of the supporting shaft. It consists of three parts: the top member called the **abacus**, a block that acts as the supporting surface to the superstructure; the middle portion known as the bell or **echinus**; and the lower part called the necking or **astragal**. See also ◊order.

capital in economics, accumulated or inherited wealth held in the form of assets (such as stocks and shares, property, and bank deposits). In stricter terms, capital is defined as the stock of goods used in the production of other goods, and may be **fixed capital** (such as buildings, plant, and machinery) that is durable, or **circulating capital** (raw materials and components) that is used up quickly.

capital bond an investment bond, which is purchased by a single payment, set up for a fixed period, and offered for sale by a life insurance company. The emphasis is on capital growth of the lump sum invested rather than on income.

capital expenditure spending on fixed assets such as plant and equipment, trade investments or the purchase of other businesses.

capital gains tax an income tax levied on the change of value of a person's assets, often property.

capitalism economic system in which the principal means of production, distribution, and exchange are in private (individual or corporate) hands and competitively operated for profit. A *mixed economy* combines the private enterprise of capitalism and a degree of state monopoly, as in nationalized industries.

capital punishment punishment by death. It was abolished in the UK 1965 for all crimes except treason. It is retained in many other countries, including the USA (37 states), France, and the USSR.

In Britain, the number of capital offences was reduced from over 200 at the end of the 18th century, until capital punishment was abolished 1866 for all crimes except murder, treason, piracy, and certain arson attacks. Its use was subject to the royal prerogative of mercy. The punishment was carried out by hanging (in public until 1866). In the USA, the Supreme Court declared it unconstitutional 1972 (as a cruel and unusual punishment) but decided 1976 that this was not so in all circumstances. It was therefore reintroduced in some states. Many countries use it for crimes other than murder, including corruption and theft (USSR) and drug offences (Malaysia and elsewhere). Methods of execution include electrocution, lethal gas, hanging and shooting (USA), shooting (USSR), garrotting (Spain), and the guillotine (France). In South Africa over 1,500 death sentences were passed 1978–1987. There were 1,500 executions in China 1983–89, and 64 in the USSR 1985–88, although the true figure may be higher in both cases. In 1989 the number of capital offences in the USSR was reduced to six. The International Covenant on Civil and Political Rights 1977 ruled out imposition of the death penalty on those under the age of 18. The covenant was signed by President Carter on behalf of the USA, but in 1989 the US Supreme Court decided that it could be imposed from the age of 16 for murder, and that the mentally retarded could also face the death penalty.

capitulum in botany, a flattened or rounded head (inflorescence) of numerous, small, stalkless flowers. The capitulum is surrounded by a circlet of petal-like bracts and has the appearance of a large, single flower. It is characteristic of plants belonging to the daisy family Compositae such as the daisy *Bellis perennis* and the garden marigold *Calendula officinalis*; but is also seen in parts of other families, such as scabious *Knautia* and teasels *Dipsacus*. The individual flowers are known as ◊florets.

Capodimonte /'kæpəudi'mɒnteɪ/ village, N of Naples, Italy, where porcelain known by the same name was first produced under King Charles III of Naples about 1740. The porcelain is usually white, painted with colourful folk figures, landscapes, or flowers.

Capone /kə'pəʊn/ Al(phonse) 1898–1947. US gangster, born in Brooklyn, New York, the son of an Italian barber. During the ◊Prohibition period Capone built up a criminal organization in the city of Chicago. He was imprisoned 1931–39 for income-tax evasion, the only charge that could be sustained against him. His nickname was *Scarface*.

Caporetto /,kæpə'retəʊ/ former name of ◊Kobarid, Yugoslavia.

Capote /kə'pəʊti/ Truman. Pen name of Truman Streckfuss Persons 1924–1984. US novelist. He wrote *Breakfast at Tiffany's* 1958; set a trend with *In Cold Blood* 1966, reconstructing a Kansas killing; and mingled recollection and fiction in *Music for Chameleons* 1980.

Cappadocia ancient region of Asia Minor, in E central Turkey. It was conquered by the Persians in 584 BC but in the 3rd century BC became an independent kingdom. The region was annexed as a province of the Roman Empire in AD 17.

The area includes over 600 Byzantine cave churches cut into volcanic rock, dating mainly from the 10th and 11th centuries.

Capone Alphonse 'Al' Capone (centre), notorious gangster in Chicago during the Prohibition era. This photograph was taken whilst he was under indictment in the Chicago Federal Court, 1931. He was imprisoned 1931–39 for tax evasion.

Capra /'kæprə/ Frank 1897– . US film director. His films, which often have idealistic heroes, include *It Happened One Night* 1934, *Mr Deeds Goes to Town* 1936, and *You Can't Take It With You* 1938.

Capri /kə'pri:/ Italian island at the south entrance of the Bay of Naples; 32 km/20 mi S of Naples; area 13 sq km/5 sq mi. It has two towns, Capri and Anacapri, and is famous for its flowers, beautiful scenery, and ideal climate.

capriccio /kə'prɪtʃɪəʊ/ (Italian 'caprice') in music, a short instrumental piece, often humorous or whimsical in character.

Capricorn another term for Capricornus.

Capricornus zodiac constellation in the southern hemisphere near Sagittarius containing the ◊globular cluster M30. It is represented as a fish-tailed goat, and its brightest stars are third magnitude. The Sun passes through it late Jan to mid-Feb. In *astrology*, the dates for Capricornus are between about 22 Dec and 19 Jan (see ◊precession).

Caprivi /kə'pri:vi/ Georg Leo, Count von Caprivi 1831–1899. German imperial chancellor 1890–94.

Caprivi Strip /kə'pri:vi/ NE access strip for ◊Namibia to the Zambezi river.

capsicum plant of the nightshade family Solanaceae, native to Central and South America. The differing species produce green-to-red fruits that vary in size. The small ones are used whole to give the hot flavour of chilli, or ground to produce cayenne pepper; the large pointed or squarish pods, known

as sweet peppers, are mild-flavoured and used as a vegetable.

capsule in botany, a dry, usually many-seeded ◊fruit formed from an ovary composed of two or more fused ◊carpels, which splits open to release the seeds. The same term is used for the spore-containing structure of mosses and liverworts; this is borne at the top of a long stalk or seta.

Capsules burst open (dehisce) in various ways, including lengthwise, by a transverse lid, for example scarlet pimpernel (*Anagallis arvensis*), or by a number of pores, either towards the top of the capsule, for example poppy (*Papaver*), or near the base, as in certain species of *Campanula*.

Captain Marvel US comic-book character created 1940 by C(larence) C(harles) Beale (1910–1989). Captain Marvel is a 15-year-old schoolboy, Billy Batson, who transforms himself into a superhuman hero.

Capua /'kæpjuə/ Italian town in Caserta province on the Volturno, in a fertile plain N of Naples; population (1981) 18,000. There was heavy fighting here in 1943 during World War II, and the Romanesque cathedral was almost destroyed.

Capuchin a member of the ◊Franciscan order of monks in the Roman Catholic church, instituted by Matteo di Bassi (died 1552), an Italian monk who wished to return to the literal observance of the rule of St Francis; their rule was drawn up in 1529. The brown habit with the pointed hood (French *capuche*) that he adopted gave his followers the name. The order was recognized by the pope in 1619, and has been involved in missionary activity.

capuchin type of monkey, genus *Cebus* found in Central and South America, so called because the hairs on the head resemble the cowl of a capuchin monk. Capuchins live in small groups, feed on fruit and insects, and have a tail that is semi-prehensile and can give support when climbing through the trees.

capybara largest rodent *Hydrochoerus hydrochaeris*, up to 1.3 m/4 ft long and 50 kg/110 lb in weight. It is found in South America, and belongs to the guinea-pig family. The capybara inhabits marshes and dense vegetation around water. It has thin yellowish hair, swims well, and can rest underwater with just eyes, ears, and nose above the surface.

car a self-propelled vehicle with a petrol or diesel engine, for use on roads. Usually four wheeled,

Capote US novelist and journalist Truman Capote.

most cars have an engine at the front although an exception is the German Volkswagen 'Beetle', one of the first economy cars. Racing cars have the engine situated in the middle for balance.

Although it is recorded that in 1479 Gilles de Dom was paid 25 livres by the treasurer of Antwerp in the Low Countries for supplying a self-propelled vehicle, the ancestor of the automobile is generally agreed to be N Cugnot's cumbersome steam carriage 1769, still preserved in Paris.

Steam was an attractive form of power to the English pioneers, and in the 19th century practical steam coaches by Hancock and Goldsworthy Gurney were used for public transport, until stifled out of existence by punitive road tolls and legislation. Another Parisian, Jean Etienne Lenoir, made the first gas engine 1860, and in 1885 ◊Benz built and ran the first petrol-driven motorcar; and Panhard 1890 (front radiator, engine under bonnet, sliding-pinion gearbox, wooden ladder-chassis) and Mercédès 1901 (honeycomb radiator, in-line four-cylinder engine, gate-change gearbox, pressed-steel chassis) set the pattern for the modern car. Emerging with Haynes and Duryea in the early 1890s, US demand was so fervent that 300 makers existed by 1895: many so ephemeral that there were only 109 left by 1900.

In England cars were still considered to be light locomotives in the eyes of the law, and since the notorious Red Flag Act 1831 had theoretically required someone to walk in front with a red flag. Despite these obstacles, which put UK development another ten years behind all others, in 1896 F W Lanchester produced an advanced and reliable vehicle, later much copied. The period 1905–06 inaugurated a world motorcar boom continuing to the present day.

Among the legendary cars of this century are: De Dion Bouton, with the first practical high-speed engines; Mors, notable first for racing and later as a silent tourer (silentium mortis); Napier, the 24-hour record-holder at Brooklands in 1907, unbeaten for 17 years; the incomparable Silver Ghost Rolls-Royce; the enduring Model T ◊Ford (known to rivals as the car that popularized walking); and the many types of Bugatti and Delage, from record-breakers to luxury tourers.

After World War I popular motoring began with the era of cheap, light (baby) cars made by Citroën, Peugeot, and Renault (France); Austin 7, Morris, Clyno, and Swift (England); Fiat (Italy); and the cheap though bigger Ford, Chevrolet, and Dodge in the USA. During the inter-war years a great deal of racing took place, and experience thus gained benefited the everyday motorist in improved efficiency, reliability, and safety. There was a divergence between the lighter, economical European car, with good handling; and the heavier US car, cheap, rugged, and well adapted to long distances at speed. By this time motoring had become a universal pursuit.

After World War II small European cars tended to fall into three categories: front engine and rear drive, the classic arrangement; front engine and drive; rear engine and drive; in about equal numbers. From the 1950s a creative resurgence produced in practical form automatic transmission for small cars, rubber suspension, and transverse engine mounting, self-levelling ride, disc brakes, and safer wet-weather tyres. The drive against pollution from the 1960s and the fuel crisis from the 1970s led to experiments with steam cars (cumbersome), diesel engines (slow and heavy, although economical), and, a more promising development, a hybrid car using both electricity and petrol. Of more immediate application was the stratified-charge petrol engine, using a fuel injector to achieve 20% improvement in petrol consumption; weight reduction in the body by the use of aluminium and plastics; and 'slippery' body designs with low air resistance, or drag. Microprocessors were also developed to measure temperature, engine speed, pressure, and oxygen content

car: chronology

1769	Nicholas-Joseph Cugnot in France built a steam tractor.
1801	Richard Trevithick built a steam coach.
1860	Jean Etienne Lenoir built a gas-fuelled internal combustion engine.
1861	The British government passed the 'Red Flag' Act, requiring a man to precede a 'horseless carriage' with a red flag.
1876	Nikolaus August Otto improved the gas engine, making it a practical power source.
1885	Gottlieb Daimler developed a lightweight petrol engine and fitted it to a bicycle to create the prototype of the modern motorbike; Karl Benz fitted his lightweight petrol engine to a three-wheeled carriage to pioneer the motor car.
1886	Gottlieb Daimler fitted his engine to a four-wheeled carriage to produce a four-wheeled motor car.
1891	René Panhard and Emile Levassor established the modern design of cars by putting the engine in front.
1896	Frederick Lancaster introduced epicyclic gearing, which foreshadowed automatic transmission.
1901	The first Mercedes took to the roads. It was the direct ancestor of the modern car; Ransome Olds in the USA introduced mass production on an assembly line.
1906	Rolls-Royce introduced the legendary Silver Ghost, which established their reputation for superlatively engineered cars.
1908	Henry Ford also used assembly-line production to manufacture his famous Model T, nicknamed the Tin Lizzie because it used lightweight steel sheet for the body, which looked 'tinny'.
1911	Cadillac introduced the electric starter and dynamo lighting.
1913	Ford introduced the moving conveyor belt to the assembly line, further accelerating production of the Model T.
1920	Duesenberg began fitting four-wheel hydraulic brakes.
1922	The Lancia Lambda featured unitary (all-in-one) construction and independent front suspension.
1928	Cadillac introduced the synchromesh gearbox, facilitating gear changing.
1934	Citroën pioneered front-wheel drive in their 7CV model.
1936	Fiat introduced their baby car, the Topolino, 500 cc.
1938	Germany produced their 'people's car, the Volkswagen 'beetle'.
1948	Jaguar launched the XK120 sports car; Michelin introduced the radial-ply tyre; Goodrich produced the tubeless tyre.
1950	Dunlop announced the disc brake.
1951	Buick and Chrysler introduced power steering.
1952	Rover's gas-turbine car set a speed record of 243 kph/152 mph.
1954	Bosch introduced fuel-injection for cars.
1955	Citroën produced the advanced DS-19 'shark-front' car with hydropneumatic suspension.
1957	Felix Wankel built his first rotary petrol engine.
1959	BMC (now Rover) introduced the Issigonis-designed Mini, with front-wheel drive, transverse engine and independent rubber suspension.
1966	California introduced legislation to reduce air pollution by cars.
1972	Dunlop introduced safety tyres, which sealed themselves after a burst.
1980s	Lean-burn engines were introduced to improve fuel consumption; electronic ignition and engine controls became widely available; on-board computers were introduced to monitor engine performance, speech synthesizers to issue audible warnings.

of exhaust gases, and readjust the engine accordingly.

A typical modern European medium-sized saloon car has a semi-monocoque construction in which the body panels, suitably reinforced, support the road loads through independent front and rear sprung suspension, with seats located within the wheelbase for comfort. It is usually powered by a ◊petrol engine using a carburettor to mix petrol and air for feeding to the engine cylinders (typically four or six), and the engine is usually water cooled. In the 1980s high performance diesel engines are being developed for use in private cars, and it is anticipated that this trend will continue for reasons of economy. From the engine, power is transmitted through a clutch to a 4- or 5-speed gearbox and thence, in a front-engine rear-drive car, through a drive (propeller) shaft to a ◊differential gear, which drives the rear wheels. In a front-engine, front-wheel drive car, clutch, gearbox, and final drive are incorporated with the engine unit. An increasing number of high-performance cars are being offered with four-wheel drive. This gives superior roadholding in wet and icy conditions.

In Britain, the Ministry of Transport was established 1919, roads were improved, and various laws and safety precautions imposed to govern the use of cars. A driver must possess a licence, and a vehicle must be registered with the local licensing authority, displaying the number assigned to it. A road tax is imposed, and the law also insists on insurance for third-party risks. Motoring organizations include the Automobile Association (AA) and the Royal Automobile Club (RAC).

Caracalla *Marcus Aurelius Antoninus Caracalla, Roman emperor AD 211–17.*

caracal cat *Felis caracal* related to the ◊lynx. It has long black ear-tufts, a short tail, and short reddish-fawn fur. It lives in bush and desert country in Africa, Arabia, and India, hunting birds and small mammals at night. Head and body length is about 75 cm/2.5 ft.

Caracalla /ˌkærəˈkælə/ Marcus Aurelius Antoninus AD 186–217. Roman emperor, so-called from the celtic cloak (caracalla) that he wore. He succeeded his father Septimus Severus in 211, ruled with cruelty and extravagance, and was assassinated.

With the support of the army he murdered his brother Geta and thousands of his followers to secure sole possession of the throne. During his reign Roman citizenship was given to all subjects of the Empire, and he built on a grandiose scale, for example the Baths of Caracalla in Rome.

Caracas /kəˈrækəs/ chief city and capital of Venezuela; situated on the Andean slopes, 13 km/8 mi south of its port La Guaira on the Caribbean coast; population of metropolitan area (1981) 1,817,000. Founded 1567, it is now a major industrial and commercial centre, notably for oil companies.

It is the birthplace of Simón ◊Bolívar and has many fine buildings, including Venezuela University, which forms a city within a city, and has gates guarded by university police. As in most Latin American countries, the university is independent and self-governing, and no state police or soldiers are allowed to enter. The city has suffered several severe earthquakes.

Caractacus /kəˈræktəkəs/ died *c.* AD 54. British chieftain, who headed resistance to the Romans in SE England AD 43–51, but was defeated on the Welsh border. Shown in Claudius's triumphal procession, he was released in tribute to his courage and died in Rome.

Caradon /ˈkærədən/ Baron title of Hugh ◊Foot, British Labour politician.

caramel a complex mixture of substances produced by heating sugars, without charring, until they turn brown. Caramel is used as colouring and flavouring in foods. Its production in the manufacture of sugar confection gives rise to a toffee-like sweet of the same name.

caramelization the process for the production of caramel from sugar by heating. Complex chemical reactions are involved, resulting in a number of compounds that contribute to the colour and flavour of caramel. Commercially, the process is speeded up by the addition of selected ◊amino acids.

carat unit for measuring the mass of precious stones, derived from the Arabic word *quirrat*, meaning seed. Originally, 1 carat was the weight of a coral seed; it is now taken as 0.2 g/0.00705 oz. It is also the unit of purity in gold (US karat). Pure gold is 24-carat; 22-carat (the purest used in jewellery) is 22 parts gold and two parts alloy (to give greater strength).

Caravaggio /ˌkærəˈvædʒɪəʊ/ Michelangelo Merisi da 1573–1610. Italian early Baroque painter, active in Rome 1592–1606, then in Naples and finally Malta. His life was as dramatic as his art (he had to leave Rome after killing a man). He created a forceful style, using contrasts of light and shade and focusing closely on the subject figures, sometimes using dramatic foreshortening.

He was born in Caravaggio, near Milan. His compositions were unusual, with little extraneous setting, making strong designs in the two-dimensional plane. He painted from models, making portraits of real Roman people as saints and Madonnas, which caused outrage. An example is *The Conversion of St Paul* (Sta Maria del Popolo, Rome).

He had a number of direct imitators (Caravaggisti), and a group of Dutch and Flemish artists who visted Rome, including Honthorst and Terbrugghen were inspired by him.

caraway plant *Carum carvi* of the family Umbelliferae. It is grown for its aromatic seed, which is used in cookery, medicine, and perfumery.

carbide compound of carbon and one other chemical element, usually a metal, silicon, or boron.

Calcium carbide (CaC_2) can be used as the starting material for many basic organic chemical syntheses, by the addition of water and generation of ethyne (acetylene). Some metallic carbides are used in engineering because of their extreme hardness and strength. Tungsten carbide is an essential ingredient of carbide tools and 'high-speed' tools. The 'carbide process' was used during World War II to make organic chemicals from coal rather than from oil.

carbohydrate a chemical compound composed of carbon, hydrogen, and oxygen, all with the basic formula $Cm(H_2O)n$, and related compounds with the same basic structure but modified ◊functional groups.

The simplest carbohydrates are sugars (**monosaccharides**, such as glucose and fructose, and **disaccharides**, such as sucrose), which are soluble compounds, some with a sweet taste. When these basic sugar units are joined together in long chains they form **polysaccharides**, such as starch and glycogen, which often serve as food stores in living organisms. As such they form a

caraway

fruit

seed heads

major energy-providing part of the human diet. Even more complex carbohydrates are known, including ◊chitin, which is found in the cell walls of fungi and the hard outer skeletons of insects, and ◊cellulose, which makes up the cell walls of plants. Carbohydrates form the chief foodstuffs of herbivorous animals.

carbolic acid common name for the aromatic compound ◊phenol.

carbon one of the most widely distributed non-metallic elements; symbol C, atomic number 6, relative atomic mass 12.011. It occurs on its own as diamonds and graphite (crystalline forms), in carbonaceous rocks such as chalk and limestone, as carbon dioxide in the atmosphere, as hydrocarbons in petroleum, coal, and natural gas, and as a constituent of all organic substances.

In its amorphous form, it is familiar as coal, charcoal, and soot. Of the inorganic carbon compounds, the most important is **carbon dioxide**, a colourless gas formed when carbon is burned in an adequate supply of air, and **carbon monoxide** (CO), formed when carbon is oxidized in a limited supply of air. **Carbon disulphide** (CS_2) is a dense liquid with a sweetish odour. Another group of compounds is the **carbon halides**, inlcuding carbon tetrachloride (CCl_4). Being non-inflammable, it is used in certain fire appliances, but as it reacts with oxygen at high temperatures to produce phosgene ($COCl_2$), the fumes are dangerous.

When added to steel, carbon forms a wide range of alloys with useful properties. In pure form, it is used as a moderator in nuclear reactors; as colloidal graphite (Dag, Aquadag), it is a good lubricant and, when deposited on a surface in a vacuum, obviates photoelectric and secondary emission of electrons. Carbon is used as a fuel in the form of coal or coke. The radioactive isotope carbon-14 is used as a tracer in biological research.

Carbonari /ˌkɑːbəˈnɑːri/ a secret political revolutionary society in S Italy in the first half of the 19th century. They later played a part in ◊Mazzini's nationalist 'Young Italy' movement.

carbohydrate

polysaccharide

glucose molecules linked to form polysaccharide glycogen (animal starch)

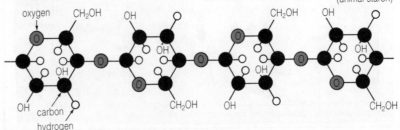

oxygen   CH₂OH   OH   CH₂OH   OH

OH

OH   carbon

hydrogen

carbon

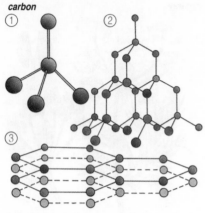

1. the basic unit of the diamond structure
2. *diamond* a giant three dimensional structure
3. *graphite* a two dimensional structure

carbonate a chemical compound formed by the combination of a carbonate group (CO_3) with another element, usually a metal.

The carbon dioxide (CO_2) dissolved by rain falling through the air, and liberated by decomposing animals and plants in the soil, forms with water carbonic acid (H_2CO_3), which unites with various basic substances to form carbonates. Calcium carbonate ($CaCO_3$) (chalk, limestone, and marble) is one of the most abundant carbonates known, being a constituent of mollusc shells and the hard outer skeletons of crabs and similar creatures.

carbon cycle the sequence by which carbon circulates and is recycled through the natural world. The carbon element from carbon dioxide in the atmosphere is taken up during the process of ◊photosynthesis, and the oxygen component is released back into the atmosphere. Today, the carbon cycle is being altered by the increased consumption of fossil fuels, and burning of large tracts of tropical forests, as a result of which levels of carbon dioxide are building up in the atmosphere and probably contributing to the ◊greenhouse effect.

A 1989 meeting of 68 nations at Noordwijk, Netherlands agreed to 'stabilize' emmissions of carbon dioxide by the year 2000, but could not agree on what the level should be because of opposition by the USA and Japan.

carbon dating another name for ◊radiocarbon dating.

carbon dioxide a colourless gas (CO_2) formed by the oxidation of carbon. It is produced during the process of respiration by living things.

carbon fibre a fine, black silky filament of pure carbon produced by heat treatment from a special grade of Courtelle acrylic fibre, used for reinforcing plastics. The resulting ◊composite is very stiff and weight-for-weight has four times the strength of high-tensile steel. It is used in aerospace, cars, electrical and sports equipment.

Carboniferous period of geological time 360–286 million years ago, the fifth period of the Palaeozoic era. In the USA it is regarded as two periods: the Mississippian (lower) and the Pennsylvanian (upper). Typical of the lower-Carboniferous rocks are shallow-water ◊limestones, while upper-Carboniferous rocks have ◊delta deposits with ◊coal (hence the name). Amphibians were abundant, and reptiles evolved.

carbon monoxide a colourless, odourless gas (CO) formed when carbon is oxidized in a limited supply of air. It is a poisonous constituent of car exhaust fumes, forming a stable compound with haemoglobin in the blood, thus preventing the haemoglobin from transporting oxygen to the body tissues.

carborundum silicon carbide (SiC), an artificial compound of carbon and silicon. It is a hard, black substance, used as an abrasive.

Discovered in 1891 by E G Acheson, it is harder than ◊corundum but not as hard as ◊diamond.

carbuncle a bacterial infection of the skin, similar to a ◊boil, but deeper and more widespread. It may only be cleared with antibiotics.

carbuncle in gemology, a garnet cut to resemble a rounded knob.

carburation regular combustion, usually in a closed space, of carbon compounds such as petrol, kerosene, or fuel oil. Regulated combustion is distinct from more rapid burning such as explosion or detonation, and applies to combustion in the cylinders of reciprocating petrol engines of the types used in aircraft, road vehicles, or marine vessels. The device by which the liquid fuel is atomized and mixed with air is called a *carburettor*.

Carcassonne /ˌkɑːkəˈsɒn/ city in SW France, capital of Aude *département*, on the river Aude, which divides it into the ancient and modern town;

population (1982) 42,450. Its medieval fortifications (restored) are the finest in France.

Carchemish /ˈkɑːkəmɪʃ/ (now Karkamis, Turkey) centre of the ◊Hittite New Empire (c. 1400–1200 BC) on the Euphrates, 80 km/50 mi NE of Aleppo, and taken by Sargon II of Assyria 717 BC. Nebuchadnezzar II of Babylon defeated the Egyptians here 605 BC.

carcinogen any agent that increases the chance of a cell becoming cancerous (see ◊cancer), including various chemical compounds, some viruses, X-rays and other forms of ionizing radiation. The term is often used more narrowly to mean chemical carcinogens only.

carcinoma a type of malignant ◊tumour arising from the skin, the glandular tissues, or the mucous membranes that line the gut and lungs.

Cardano /kɑːˈdɑːnəʊ/ Girolamo 1501–1576. Italian physician, mathematician, philosopher, astrologer, and gambler. He is remembered for his theory of chance, his use of algebra, and many medical publications, notably the first clinical description of typhus fever.

Born at Pavia, he became professor of medicine there in 1543, and wrote two works on physics and natural science, *De Subtilitate rerum* 1551 and *De Varietate rerum* 1557.

Cárdenas /ˈkɑːdɪnæs/ Lázaro 1895–1970. Mexican centre-left politician and general, president 1934–40. In early life a civil servant, Cárdenas took part in the revolutionary campaigns 1915–29 that followed the fall of President Díaz (1830–1915). As president of the republic, he attempted to achieve the goals of the revolution by building schools, distributing land to the peasants, and developing transport and industry. He was minister of defence 1943–45.

cardiac pertaining to the ◊heart.

Cardiff /ˈkɑːdɪf/ capital of Wales (from 1955), and administrative headquarters of South and Mid Glamorgan, at the mouth of the Taff, Rhymney, and Ely rivers; population (1983) 279,800. Besides steelworks, there are automotive component, flour milling, paper, cigar, and other industries.

The city dates from Roman times, the later town being built around a Norman castle. The castle was the residence of the Earls and Marquesses of Bute from the 18th century and was given to the city 1947 by the fifth marquess. Coal was exported until the 1920s. As coal declined, iron and steel exports continued to grow, and an import trade in timber, grain and flour, tobacco, meat, and citrus fruit developed.

The docks on the Bristol Channel were opened 1839 and greatly extended by the second Marquess of Bute (1793–1848). The derelict docks have now been redeveloped for industry.

In Cathays Park is a group of public buildings including the Law Courts, City Hall, the National Museum of Wales, the Welsh Office (established 1964), a major part of the University of Wales (Institute of Science and Technology, National School of Medicine, and University College of S Wales), and the Temple of Peace and Health. Llandaff, on the right bank of the Taff, seat of an archbishop from the 6th century, was included in Cardiff 1922; its cathedral, virtually rebuilt in the 19th century and restored 1948–57 after air raid damage in World War II, has Jacob Epstein's sculpture *Christ in Majesty*. At St Fagan's is the Welsh National Folk Museum, containing small rebuilt historical buildings from rural Wales in which crafts are demonstrated. The city is the headquarters of the Welsh National Opera.

Cardiff /ˈkɑːdɪf/ Jack 1914– . British director of photography. He is regarded as one of cinema's finest colour cameramen for *A matter of life and death* 1946; *The African Queen* 1951; *Conan the Destroyer* 1984. He also directed the film *Sons and Lovers* 1960.

Cardiff Arms Park Welsh rugby ground officially known as the National Stadium, situated in Cardiff. The stadium became the permanent home of the

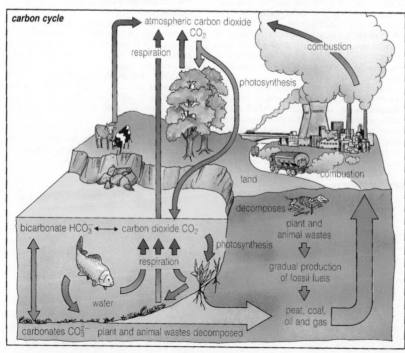

carbon cycle

cardioid

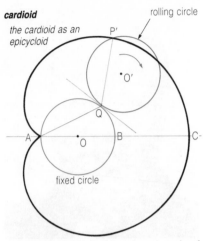

the cardioid as an epicycloid

Welsh national team in 1964 and has a capacity of 64,000.

Cardiff rugby club joined forces with the cricket club in 1876 to lay out their first pitch. The complex underwent a major overhaul in 1960 when the Glamorgan cricket club moved out.

Cardiganshire /ˈkɑːdɪgənʃə/ former county of Wales, which was in 1974 merged, together with Pembroke and Carmarthen, into Dyfed.

Cardin /ˈkɑːdæn/ Pierre 1922– . French fashion designer; the first women's designer to show a collection for men, in 1960.

cardinal in the Roman Catholic church, the highest rank next to the pope. Cardinals act as an advisory body to the pope and elect him. Their red hat is the badge of office. The number of cardinals has varied; there were 151 in 1989.

Originally a cardinal was any priest in charge of a major parish, but in 1567 the term was confined to the members of the Sacred College, from whom, since 1973, 120 (below the age of 80) elect the pope and are themselves elected by him. They advise on all matters of doctrine, canonizations, convocation of councils, liturgy, and temporal business.

cardinal number in mathematics, one of the series of numbers 0,1,2,3,4... Cardinal numbers relate to quantity, whereas ordinal numbers (first, second, third, fourth ...) relate to order.

cardioid heart-shaped curve traced out by a point on the circumference of a circle that rolls around the edge of another circle of the same diameter. The polar equation of the cardioid is of the form $r = a(1 + cos \Theta)$. It is also the pattern of response of an undirectional microphone.

cards common name for ◊playing cards.

Carducci /kɑːˈduːtʃi/ Giosuè 1835–1907. Italian poet. Born in Tuscany, he was appointed in 1860 professor of Italian literature in Bologna, and won a distinguished place by his lecturing, critical work, and poetry. His revolutionary *Inno a Satana/Hymn to Satan* 1865 was followed by several other volumes of verse, in which his nationalist sympathies are apparent. Nobel Prize 1906.

Cardwell /ˈkɑːdwel/ Edward, Viscount Cardwell 1813–1886. British Liberal politician. He entered Parliament as a supporter of the Conservative prime minister ◊Peel in 1842, and 1868–74 was secretary for war under Gladstone, when he carried out many reforms, including the abolition of the purchase of military commissions and promotions.

Carême /kəˈreɪm/ Antonin 1784–1833. French chef who is regarded as the founder of classical French *haute cuisine*. At various times he was chief cook to the Prince Regent in England and Tsar Alexander I in Russia.

care order a court order that places a child in the care of a local authority.

Carew /kəˈruː/ Thomas c. 1595–c. 1640. English poet. He was a gentleman of the privy chamber to Charles I in 1628, and a lyricist as well as craftsman of the school of ◊Cavalier poets.

Carey /ˈkeəri/ Henry 1690–1743. British poet and musician, remembered for the song 'Sally in Our Alley'. 'God Save the King' (both words and music) has also been attributed to him.

Carey /ˈkeəri/ Peter 1943– . Australian novelist. He has combined work in advertising with a writing career since 1962, and his novels include *Bliss* 1981, *Illywhacker* (Australian slang for 'con man') 1985, and *Oscar and Lucinda* 1988, which won the Booker prize.

cargo cult Melanesian religious movement, dating from the 19th century. Adherents believe the arrival of cargo is through the agency of a messianic spirit figure, and heralds a new paradise.

Carib /ˈkærɪb/ a member of a group of ◊American Indian aboriginal people of South America and the islands of the West Indies in the Caribbean Sea. In 1796 the English in the West Indies deported most of them to Roatan Island off Honduras. They have since spread extensively in Honduras and Nicaragua.

Caribbean Community (CARICOM) organization for economic and foreign policy coordination in the Caribbean region, established by the Treaty of Chaguaramas 1973. The leading member is Trinidad and Tobago; headquarters Georgetown, Guyana; others are Antigua, Barbados, Belize, Dominica, Grenada, Guyana, Jamaica, Montserrat, St Christopher (St kitts) Nevis, Anguilla, St Lucia, and St Vincent. From 1979 a left-wing Grenadan coup led to a progressive regional subgroup including St Lucia and Dominica.

Caribbean Sea /ˌkærɪˈbiːən/ part of the Atlantic Ocean between the N coasts of South and Central America and the West Indies, about 2,740 km/1,700 mi long and between 650 km/400 mi–1,500 km/900 mi wide. It is here that the Gulf Stream turns towards Europe.

caribou the ◊reindeer of North America.

caricature exaggerated portrayal of individuals or types, aiming to ridicule or otherwise expose the subject. Classical and medieval examples survive. Artists of the 18th, 19th, and 20th centuries have often used caricature as a scourge on society and politics. Notable exponents include Rowlandson, Daumier, and Grosz.

Grotesque drawings have been discovered in Pompeii and Herculaneum, and Pliny refers to

caricature George Rowlandson's Catching an Elephant 1812, Guildhall Library, London. Rowlandson's caricatures usually focused on the most hideous aspects of the lowest and highest levels of society in Georgian England.

a grotesque portrait of the poet Hipponax. Humorous drawings were executed by the ◊Carracci family and their Bolognese followers (the Italian 'eclectic' school of the 16th century). Charles Philipon (1800–62) founded in Paris in 1830 *La Caricature*, probably the first periodical to specialize in caricature.

British caricaturists include Gillray, Hogarth, Rowlandson, Cruikshank, Lear, Doyle, Du Maurier, Beerbohm, Low, 'Vicky', 'Giles', Cummings, Ronald Searle, Lancaster, Calman, Herb Block, Gerald Scarfe, Ralph Steadman (the last two producing grotesque, distorted figures), and Peter Fluck and Roger Law (three-dimensional puppets for the television series *Spitting Image*).

CARICOM abbreviation for Caribbean Community and Common Market, an organization for economic and foreign policy coordination in the region, established 1973 to replace the former Caribbean Free Trade Association. Its members are Antigua and Barbuda, the Bahamas, Barbados, Belize, Dominica, Grenada, Guyana, Jamaica, Monserrat, St Christopher and Nevis, St Lucia, St Vincent and the Grenadines, and Trinidad and Tobago.

caries decay and disintegration usually of the substance of teeth or bone.

Carina constellation of the southern hemisphere, representing a ship's keel. Its brightest star is Canopus; it also contains Eta Carinae, a massive and highly luminous star embedded in a gas cloud. It has varied unpredictably in the past; some astronomers think it is likely to explode as a supernova within 10,000 years.

Carinthia /kəˈrɪnθiə/ (German *Kärnten*) alpine federal province of SE Austria, bordering Italy and Yugoslavia in the south; capital Klagenfurt; area 9,500 sq km/3,667 sq mi; population (1987) 542,000. It was an independent duchy from 976, and a possession of the Habsburg dynasty 1276–1918.

Carisbrooke /ˈkærɪzbrʊk/ village SW of Newport, Isle of Wight. Charles I was imprisoned in its castle 1647–48.

Carissimi /kəˈrɪsɪmi/ Giacomo 1605–1674. Italian composer, a pioneer of the oratorio.

Carl XVI Gustaf /kɑːl/ 1946– . King of Sweden from 1973. He succeeded his grandfather Gustaf VI, his father having been killed in an air crash in 1947. Under the new Swedish constitution which became effective on his grandfather's death, the monarchy was effectively stripped of all power at his accession.

Carlisle /kɑːˈlaɪl/ city in Cumbria, England; situated on the river Eden at the W end of Hadrian's Wall; population (1981) 71,000. It is the administrative headquarters of Cumbria, England, the county town of the former county of Cumberland, situated on the Eden at the W end of Hadrian's Wall. It is an important railway centre; textiles, engineering, and biscuit making are the chief industries. There is a Norman cathedral and a castle. The bishopric dates from 1133. Population (1981) 70,706.

Carlist a supporter of the claims of the Spanish pretender Don Carlos de Bourbon (1788–1855), and his descendants, to the Spanish crown. The Carlist revolt continued, especially in the Basque provinces, until 1839. In 1977 the Carlist political party was legalized and Carlos Hugo de Bourbon Parma (1930–) renounced his claim as pretender and became reconciled with King Juan Carlos. See also ◊Bourbon.

Carlos four kings of Spain. See ◊Charles.

Carlos I /ˈkɑːlɒs/ 1863–1908. King of Portugal, of the Braganza-Coburg line, from 1889 until he was assassinated in Lisbon with his elder son Luis. He was succeeded by his younger son Manoel.

Carlos /ˈkɑːlɒs/ Don 1545–1568. Spanish prince. Son of Philip II, he was recognized as heir to the thrones of Castile and Aragon, but became mentally unstable and had to be placed under restraint following a plot to assassinate his father. His story was the subject of plays by Schiller, Alfieri, Otway, and others.

Carlow /ˈkɑːləʊ/ county in the Republic of Ireland, in the province of Leinster; county town Carlow; area 900 sq km/347 sq mi; population (1986) 41,000. Mostly flat except for mountains in the south, the land is fertile, and dairy farming is important.

Carlsbad /ˈkɑːlzbæd/ German name of ◊Karlovy Vary, a spa town in W Bohemia, Czechoslovakia.

Carlson /ˈkɑːlsən/ Chester 1906–1968. US scientist, who invented ◊xerography. A research worker with Bell Telephone, he was sacked from his post in 1930 during the Depression, and set to work on his own to develop an efficient copying machine. By 1938 he had invented the Xerox photocopier.

Carlsson /ˈkɑːlsən/ Ingvar (Gösta) 1934– . Swedish socialist politician, leader of the Social Democratic Party, deputy prime minister 1982–86 and prime minister from 1986.

After studying in Sweden and the USA, Carlsson became president of the Swedish Social-Democratic Youth League in 1961. He was elected to the Riksdag (parliament) in 1964 and became a minister in 1969. With the return to power of the Social Democrats in 1982, Carlsson became deputy to Prime Minister Palme and on his assassination in 1986 succeeded him.

Carlucci /kɑːˈluːtʃi/ Frank (Charles) 1930. US politician, a pragmatic moderate. A former diplomat and deputy director of the CIA, he was national security adviser 1986–87 and defence secretary from Nov 1987 under Reagan, supporting Soviet-US arms reduction.

Educated at Princeton and Harvard, Carlucci, after fighting in the Korean War, was a career diplomat during the later 1950s and 1960s. He returned to the USA in 1969 to work under presidents Nixon, Ford and Carter, his posts including US ambassador to Portugal and deputy director of the CIA. An apolitical Atlanticist, Carlucci found himself out of step with the hawks in the Reagan administration, and left to work in industry after barely a year as deputy secretary of defence. In Dec 1986, after the ◊Irangate scandal, he replaced John ◊Poindexter as national security adviser.

Carlyle /kɑːˈlaɪl/ Thomas 1795–1881. Scottish essayist and social historian. His work included *Sartor Resartus* 1836, describing his loss of Christian belief, *French Revolution* 1837, *Chartism* 1839, and *Past and Present* 1843. He was a friend of J S ◊Mill and Ralph Waldo ◊Emerson.

Carlyle was born at Ecclefechan in Dumfriesshire. In 1821 he passed through the spiritual crisis described in *Sartor Resartus*. He married Jane Baillie Welsh (1801–66) in 1826 and they moved to her farm at Craigenputtock, where *Sartor Resartus* was written. His reputation was established with the *French Revolution*. The series of lectures he gave 1837–40 included *On Heroes, Hero-Worship*, and *The Heroic in History* 1841. He also wrote several pamphlets, including *Chartism* 1839, attacking the doctrine of ◊laissez-faire; the notable *Letters and Speeches of Cromwell* 1845; and the miniature life of his friend *John Sterling* 1851. Carlyle then began his *History of Frederick the Great* 1858–65, and after the death of his wife in 1866 edited her letters 1883 and prepared his *Reminiscences* 1881, which shed an unfavourable light on his character and his neglect of her, for which he could not forgive himself. His house in Cheyne Row, Chelsea, London, is a museum.

Carmarthenshire /kəˈmɑːðənʃə/ former county of S Wales, and formerly also the largest Welsh county. It bordered on the Bristol Channel, and was merged in 1974, together with Cardigan and Pembroke, into Dyfed. The county town was Carmarthen, population (1981) 12,302.

Carmelite order mendicant order of friars in the Roman Catholic church. The order was founded on Mount Carmel in Palestine by Berthold, a crusader from Calabria, about 1155, and spread to Europe in the 13th century. The Carmelites have devoted themselves largely to missionary work and mystical theology. They are known from their white overmantle (over a brown habit) as **White Friars**.

Traditionally Carmelites originated in the days of Elijah, who according to the Old Testament is supposed to have lived on Mount Carmel. Following the rule which the patriarch of Jerusalem drew up for them about 1210, they lived as hermits in separate huts. About 1240 the Muslim conquests compelled them to move from Palestine, and they took root in the west, particularly in France and England, where the order began to live communally, by begging. The most important reform movement was initiated by St ◊Teresa. In 1562 she founded a convent in Avila and with the cooperation of St John of the Cross and others she established a stricter order of barefoot friars and nuns (the **Discalced Carmelites**).

Carmichael /kɑːˈmaɪkəl/ 'Hoagy' (Hoagland Howard) 1899–1981. US jazz composer, pianist, singer, and actor. His songs include 'Stardust' 1927, 'Rockin' Chair' 1930, 'Lazy River' 1931, and 'In the Cool, Cool, Cool of the Evening' 1951 (Academy Award).

Carmina Burana medieval lyric miscellany compiled from the work of wandering 13th-century scholars and including secular (love songs and drinking songs) as well as religious verse. A cantata (1937) by Carl ◊Orff is based on the material.

Carnac /ˈkɑːnæk/ village in Brittany, France; population (1982) 4,000. It has megalithic remains of tombs and stone alignments of the period 2000–1500 BC. The largest of the latter has 1,000 stones up to 4 m/13 ft high arranged in 11 rows, with a circle at the western end.

Carnap /ˈkɑːnæp/ Rudolf 1891–1970. German philosopher, and exponent of logical ◊empiricism. He was a member of the Vienna Circle who adopted Ernst ◊Mach as their guide. His books include *The Logical Syntax of Language* 1934, and *Meaning and Necessity* 1956. He was born in Wuppertal, Germany, and went to the USA 1935, where he was professor of philosophy at the University of California 1954–62.

Carnarvon alternate spelling of ◊Caernarvon.

Carnarvon Range /kəˈnɑːvən/ section of the Great Divide, Queensland, Australia, about 900 m/1,000 ft high. There are many Aboriginal paintings in the sandstone caves along its 160 km/100 mi length.

Carnatic /kɑːˈnætɪk/ region of SE India, in Madras state. It is situated between the Eastern Ghats and the Coromandel Coast, and was formerly an important trading centre.

carnation numerous double-flowered cultivated varieties of the clove-pink *Dianthus caryophyllus*. They are divided into flake, bizarre, and picotees, according to whether the petals exhibit one or more colours on their white ground, have the colour dispersed in strips, or have a coloured border to the petals.

carnauba palm, *Copernicia cerifera*, which is native to South America and produces fine wax and timber.

Carné /kɑːˈneɪ/ Marcel 1906– . French director of the films *Le Jour se lève* 1939 and *Les Enfants du Paradis* 1944.

Carnegie family name of the earls of Northesk and Southesk and of the Duke of Fife, who is descended from Queen Victoria.

Carnegie /kɑːˈneɪgi/ Andrew 1835–1919. US industrialist and philanthropist, who developed the Pittsburgh iron and steel industries. He endowed public libraries, education, and various research trusts.

Born in Dunfermline, Scotland, he was taken by his parents to the USA in 1848, and at 14 became a telegraph boy in Pittsburgh. Subsequently he became a railway employee, rose to be superintendent, introduced sleeping-cars and invested successfully in oil. He developed the Pittsburgh iron and steel industries, and built up a vast empire which he disposed of to the United

Carnegie *On his retirement, the industrialist Andrew Carnegie devoted his life to the philanthropic distribution of his huge fortune.*

States Steel Trust in 1901. Then he moved to Skibo castle in Sutherland, Scotland, and devoted his wealth to endowing libraries and universities, the Carnegie Hero Fund, and other good causes. On his death the Carnegie Trusts continued his benevolent activities. *Carnegie Hall* in New York, opened in 1891 as The Music Hall, was renamed in 1898 because of his large contribution to its construction.

Carnegie /kɑːˈneɪgi/ Dale 1888–1955. US author and teacher, a former YMCA public-speaking instructor, who wrote *How to Win Friends and Influence People* 1938.

carnelian semi-precious gemstone variety of ◊chalcedony consisting of quartz (silica) with iron impurities, which give it a translucent red colour. It is found mainly in Brazil, India, and Japan.

Carniola /ˌkɑːniˈəʊlə/ a former crownland and duchy of Austria, most of which was included in Slovenia, part of the kingdom of the Serbs, Croats, and Slovenes (later Yugoslavia) in 1919. The westerly districts of Idrija and Postojna, then allocated to Italy, were transferred to Yugoslavia in 1947.

carnivore an animal which eats other animals. Sometimes confined to animals that eat the flesh of ◊vertebrate prey, it is often used more broadly, to include animals that eat any other animals, even microscopic ones. Carrion-eaters may or may not be included. The mammalian order *Carnivora* includes cats, dogs, bears, badgers, and weasels.

Carnot /ˈkɑːnəʊ/ Lazare 1753–1823. French general and politician. A member of the National Convention in the French Revolution, he organized the armies of the republic. He was war minister 1800–01 and minister of the interior 1815 under Napoleon. His work on fortification, *De la défense de places fortes* 1810, became a military textbook.

Carnot joined the army as an engineer, and his transformation of French military technique in the revolutionary period earned him the title of 'Organizer of Victory'. After the coup d'état of 1797 he went abroad, but returned in 1799 when Napoleon seized power. In 1814 as governor of Antwerp he put up a brilliantly successful defence. Minister of the interior during the Hundred Days, he was proscribed at the restoration of the monarchy and retired to Germany.

Carnot /ˈkɑːnəʊ/ Marie François Sadi 1837–1894. French president from 1887, grandson of Lazare Carnot. He successfully countered the Boulangist anti-German movement (see ◊Boulanger) and in 1892 the scandals arising out of French financial activities in Panama. He was assassinated by an Italian anarchist at Lyons.

Carnot /ˈkɑːnəʊ/ Nicolas Leonard Sadi 1796–1832. French scientist and military engineer, son of Lazare Carnot, who founded ◊thermodynamics;

Carnot *It is as the founder of thermodynamics that the distinguished military engineer and scientist Sadi Carnot is remembered. He died at the age of 36, victim of a cholera epidemic.*

his pioneering work was *Réflexions sur la puissance motrice du feu/On the Motive Power of Fire*.

Carnot cycle changes in the physical condition of a gas in a reversible heat engine, necessarily in the following order: (1) isothermal expansion (without change of temperature), (2) adiabatic expansion (without change of heat content), (3) isothermal compression, and (4) adiabatic compression.

The principles derived from a study of this cycle are important in the fundamentals of heat and ◊thermodynamics.

carnotite potassium uranium vanadate, $K_2(UO_2)_2$ $(VO_4)_2.3H_2O$, an important radioactive ore of vanadium and uranium with traces of radium. A yellow powdery mineral, it is mined chiefly in the Colorado Plateau, USA; Radium Hill, Australia; and Shaba, Zaïre.

Caro /'kɑːrəʊ/ Anthony 1924– . British sculptor, noted for bold, large abstracts, using ready-made angular metal shapes, often without bases. Works include *Fathom* (outside the Economist Building, London).

carob small tree of the Mediterranean region, *Ceratonia siliqua*, also known as the *locust* tree. Its 20 cm/8 in pods are used as animal fodder; they are also the source of a chocolate substitute.

carol song that in medieval times was associated with a round dance; now those that are sung at annual festivals, such as Easter, and Christmas.

Christmas carols were common as early as the 15th century. The custom of singing carols from house to house, collecting gifts, was called wassailing. Many carols such as 'God Rest You Merry, Gentlemen' and 'The First Noel', date back at least as far as the 16th century.

Carol two kings of Romania:

Carol I /'kærəl/ 1839–1914. First king of Romania, 1881–1914. A prince of the house of Hohenzollern-Sigmaringen, he was invited to become prince of Romania, then under Turkish suzerainty, 1866. In 1877, in alliance with Russia, he declared war on Turkey, and the Congress of Berlin 1878 recognized Romanian independence.

Carol II /'kærəl/ 1893–1953. King of Romania 1930–40. Son of King Ferdinand, he married Princess Helen of Greece and they had a son, Michael. In 1925 he renounced the succession and settled in Paris with his mistress, Mme Lupescu. Michael succeeded to the throne in 1927, but in 1930 Carol returned to Romania and was proclaimed king. In 1938 he introduced a new constitution under which he became practically absolute. He was forced to abdicate by the pro-Nazi ◊Iron Guard Sept 1940, and went to Mexico and married his mistress 1947.

Caroline of Brunswick *The wife of George IV of England, Caroline of Brunswick was paid to renounce the title of queen on her husband's accession. This portrait was painted by J Lonsdale around 1820.*

Carolina /ˌkærəˈlaɪnə/ two separate states of the USA; see ◊North Carolina and ◊South Carolina.

Caroline of Anspach /'kærəlaɪn, 'ænspæx/ 1683–1737. Queen of George II of Great Britain. The daughter of the Margrave of Brandenburg-Anspach, she married George, Electoral Prince of Hanover, in 1705, and followed him to England in 1714 when his father became King George I. She was the patron of many leading writers and politicians.

Caroline of Brunswick /'kærəlaɪn, 'brʌnzwɪk/ 1768–1821. Queen of George IV of Great Britain, who unsuccessfully attempted to divorce her on his accession to the throne 1820.

Second daughter of Karl Wilhelm, duke of Brunswick, and Augusta, sister of George III, she married her first cousin the Prince of Wales in 1795, but after the birth of Princess ◊Charlotte Augusta a separation was arranged. When her husband ascended the throne in 1820 she was offered an annuity of £50,000 provided she agreed to renounce the title of queen and to continue to live abroad. She returned forthwith to London, where she assumed royal state. In July 1820 the government brought in a bill to dissolve the marriage, but Lord ◊Brougham's splendid defence led to the bill's abandonment. On 19 July 1821 Caroline was prevented by royal order from entering Westminster Abbey for the coronation. She died on 7 Aug, and her funeral was the occasion of popular riots.

Carolines /'kærəlaɪnz/ scattered archipelago in Micronesia, Pacific Ocean, consisting of over 500 coral islets; area 1,200 sq km/463 sq mi. The chief islands are Ponape, Kusai, and Truk in the eastern group, and Yap and Belau in the western.

They are well watered and productive. Occupied by Germany 1899, Japan 1914, and mandated by the League of Nations to that country 1919, they were fortified, contrary to the terms of the mandate. Under Allied air attack in World War II, they were not conquered. In 1947 they became part of the US Trust Territory of the ◊Pacific Islands.

Carolingian dynasty Frankish dynasty descending from ◊Pepin the Short (died 768) and named after his son Charlemagne; its last ruler was Louis V of France (reigned 966–87), who was followed by Hugh Capet.

carotenoids a group of yellow, orange, red, or brown pigments found in many living organisms, particularly in the ◊chloroplasts of plants. There are two main types, the *carotenes* and the *xanthophylls*. Both types are long-chain lipids (fats).

Some carotenoids act as accessory pigments in ◊photosynthesis, and in certain algae they are the principal light-absorbing pigments functioning more efficiently than ◊chlorophyll in low-intensity light. *Carotenes* can also occur in organs such as petals, roots and fruits, giving them their characteristic colour, as in the yellow and orange petals of wallflowers. They are also responsible for the autumn colours of leaves, persisting longer than the green chlorophyll, which masks them during the summer.

Carothers /kəˈrʌðəz/ Wallace 1896–1937. US chemist, who carried out research into polymerization. By 1930 he had discovered that some polymers were fibre-forming, and in 1937 produced nylon.

carotid artery a major blood vessel supplying blood to the head. There are two carotid arteries, one on each side of the neck.

carp fish *Cyprinus carpio* found all over the world. It commonly grows to 50 cm/1.8 ft and 3 kg/7 lb, but may be even larger. It lives in lakes, ponds and slow rivers. The wild form is drab, but cultivated forms may be golden, or may have few large scales (mirror carp) or be scaleless (leather carp).

A large proportion of European freshwater fishes belong to the carp family, Cyprinidae, and related fishes are found in Asia, Africa, and North America. Its fast growth, large size, and ability to live in still water with little oxygen have made it a good fish to farm, and it has been cultivated for hundreds of years and spread by human agency. Members of this family have a single non-spiny dorsal fin, pelvic fins well back on the body, and toothless jaws, although teeth in the throat form an efficient grinding apparatus. Minnows, roach, rudd, and many others including goldfish belong to this family. Chinese *grass carp Ctenopharyngodon idella* have been introduced (one sex only) to European rivers for weed control.

Carpaccio /kɑːˈpætʃiəʊ/ Vittorio 1450/60–1525/26. Italian painter, known for scenes of his native Venice. His series *The Legend of St Ursula* 1490–98 (Accademia, Venice) is full of detail of contemporary Venetian life. His other great series is the lives of saints George and Jerome 1502–07 (S Giorgio degli Schiavone, Venice).

Carpathian Mountains /kɑːˈpeɪθiənz/ Central European mountain system, forming a semi-circle through Czechoslovakia-Poland-USSR-Romania, 1450 km/900 mi long. The central *Tatra mountains* on the Czech-Polish frontier include the highest peak, Gerlachovka, 2663 m/8737 ft.

Carpeaux /kɑːˈpəʊ/ Jean-Baptiste 1827–1875. French sculptor, whose lively naturalistic subjects include *La Danse* 1865–69 for the Opéra, Paris.

Another example is the *Neapolitan Fisherboy* 1858 (Louvre, Paris). Their Romantic charm belies his admiration of Michelangelo. He studied in Italy 1856–62 and won the Prix de Rome 1854.

carpe diem (Latin 'seize the day') live for the present.

carpel a female reproductive unit in flowering plants (◊angiosperms). It usually comprises an ◊ovary containing one or more ovules, the stalk or style, and a ◊stigma at its top which receives the pollen. A flower may have one or more carpels, and they may be separate or fused together. Collectively the carpels of a flower are known as the ◊gynoecium.

Carpentaria, Gulf of /ˌkɑːpənˈteəriə/ A shallow gulf opening out of the Arafura Sea on the N of Australia. It was discovered by Tasman in 1606 and named in 1623 in honour of Pieter Carpentier, Governor-General of the Dutch East Indies.

Carpenter /'kɑːpəntə/ Edward 1844–1929. English socialist and writer. Inspired by reading ◊Thoreau, he resigned his post as tutor at Cambridge University 1874 to write poems and books, such as *Civilization: Its Cause and Cure* 1889 and *Love's Coming of Age* 1896, a plea for toleration of homosexuality.

Carroll *Charles Lutwidge Dodgson—Lewis Carroll—who, as well as a mathematician and author of the Alice books, was a pioneer of portrait photography, pictured here by Rejlander polishing a lens.*

Carpenter /'kɑːpəntə/ John 1948– . US director of horror and science fiction films. His career began with *Dark Star* 1974 and *Halloween* 1978, and continued with such films as *The Thing* 1981 and *They Live* 1988.

carpetbagger in US history, derogatory name for the entrepreneurs and politicians from the North who moved to the Southern states during ◊Reconstruction after the Civil War of 1861–65.

Carpini /kɑːˈpiːni/ Johannes de Plano 1182–1252. Franciscan friar and traveller. Sent by Pope Innocent IV on a mission to the Great Khan, he visited Mongolia 1245–47 and wrote a history of the Mongols.

Carracci /kəˈrɑːtʃi/ Italian family of painters in Bologna, noted for murals and ceilings. The foremost of them, ***Annibale Carracci*** (1560–1609), decorated the Farnese Palace, Rome, with a series of mythological paintings united by simulated architectural ornamental surrounds (completed 1604).

Ludovico Carracci (1555–1619) with his cousin ***Agostino Carracci*** (1557–1602) founded Bologna's Academy of Art. Agostino collaborated with his brother Annibale on the Farnese Palace decorative scheme, which paved the way for a host of elaborate murals in Rome's palaces and churches, ever more inventive illusions of pictorial depth and architectural ornament. Annibale also painted early landscapes like *Flight into Egypt* 1603 (Doria Gallery, Rome).

Carradine /'kærədiːn/ Richmond Reed ('John') 1906–1988. US film actor who often played sinister roles. He appeared in many major Hollywood films, such as *Stagecoach* 1939 and *The Grapes of Wrath* 1940, but was later seen mostly in 'B' horror films, including *House of Frankenstein* 1944.

carragheen species of deep reddish branched seaweed, *Chondrus crispus*. Named after Carragheen in Ireland, it is found elsewhere in N Europe. It is exploited commercially in food and medicinal preparations, and as cattle feed.

Carrara /kəˈrɑːrə/ town in Tuscany, Italy, 60 km/37 mi NW of Livorno; population (1981) 66,000. Known for its quarries of fine white marble. These were worked by the Romans, abandoned in the 5th century AD, and came into use again with the revival of sculpture and architecture in the 12th century.

Carrel /kəˈrel/ Alexis 1873–1944. US surgeon born in France, whose experiments paved the way for organ transplantation. Working at the Rockefeller Institute, Carrel devised a way of joining blood vessels end to end (anastomosing). This was important in the development of transplant surgery, as was his work on keeping organs viable outside the body. He was awarded the Nobel Prize for Medicine in 1912.

Carreras /kəˈreərəs/ José 1947 . Spanish tenor, whose roles include Handel's Samson, and whose recordings include *West Side Story* 1984. In 1987, he became seriously ill with leukaemia, but returned to work 1988.

Carrhae, Battle of /'kæri:/ battle in which the invading Roman general Crassus was defeated and killed by the Parthians in 53 BC. The ancient town of Carrhae is near Haran, Turkey.

carriage driving sport in which two or four-wheeled carriages are pulled by two or four horses. Events include ◊dressage, obstacle driving and the marathon. Prince Philip of Britain is one of the sport's leading exponents.

Carrickfergus /ˌkærɪkˈfɜːgəs/ seaport on Belfast Lough, County Antrim, N Ireland; population (1985) 30,000.

carrier /'kæriə/ anyone who harbours an infectious organism without ill effects, but who can, however, pass the infection to others. It can also apply to those who carry a recessive gene for a disease without ill effect.

Carrington /'kærɪŋtən/ Peter Alexander Rupert, 6th Baron Carrington 1919– . British Conservative politician. He was defence secretary 1970–74, and led the opposition in the House of Lords 1964–70 and 1974–79. While foreign secretary 1979–82, he negotiated independence for Zimbabwe, but resigned after failing to anticipate the Falklands crisis. He was secretary-general of NATO 1984–88.

Carroll /'kærəl/ Lewis. Pen name of Charles Lutwidge Dodgson 1832–1898. English mathematician and writer of children's books. He wrote the children's classics *Alice's Adventures in Wonderland* 1865, and its sequel *Through the Looking Glass* 1872, published under the pen name Lewis Carroll. He also published mathematics books under his own name.

Born in Daresbury, Cheshire, Dodgson was a mathematics lecturer at Oxford 1855–1881. *Alice's Adventures in Wonderland* grew out of a story told by Dodgson to amuse three little girls, including the original 'Alice', the daughter of Dean Liddell, Dean of Christ Church. During his lifetime Dodgson refused to acknowledge any connection with any books not published under his own name. Among later works was the mock-heroic nonsense poem 'The Hunting of the Snark' 1876. He was among the pioneers of portrait photography.

carrot hardy European biennial *Daucus carota* of the family Umbelliferae. Grown since the 16th century for its edible root, it has a high sugar content and also contains carotene, which can be converted by the human liver to vitamin A.

carrying capacity in ecology, the maximum number of animals of a given species that a particular area can support. When the carrying capacity is exceeded, there is insufficient food (or other resources) for all members of the population. The population may then be reduced by emigration, reproductive failure, or death through starvation.

Carry on films a series of low budget British comedies with an emphasis on unsubtle double entendre. Probably the most successful film run in post-war Britain, the first was *Carry on Sergeant* 1958 and the series continued for 20 years with titles like *Carry on Nurse*, *Carry on Spying*, *Carry on Screaming* and *Carry on Doctor*.

All were produced by Peter Rogers and directed by Gerald Thomas. Most were written by either Norman Hudis or Talbot Rothwell. Regular stars included Kenneth Williams, Charles Hawtrey, Sid James and Joan Sims.

Carse of Gowrie /'kɑːs əv 'gauri/ fertile lowland plain bordering the Firth of Tay. It is 24 km/15 mi long, and is one of Scotland's most productive agricultural areas. William III landed here before the Battle of the Boyne, 1690.

Carson /'kɑːsən/ Christopher 'Kit' 1809–68. US frontiersman, guide, and Indian agent, who later fought for the Federal side in the Civil War. Carson City was named after him.

Carson /'kɑːsən/ Edward Henry, Baron Carson 1854–1935. Irish politician and lawyer, who played a decisive part in the trial of the writer Oscar Wilde. In the years before World War I he led the movement in Ulster to resist Irish ◊Home Rule by force of arms if need be.

Carson was a well-known barrister both in England and Ireland. On the outbreak of war he campaigned in Ulster in support of the government, and took office under both Asquith and Lloyd George (attorney general 1915, First Lord of the Admiralty 1916, member of the war cabinet 1917–18). He was a Lord of Appeal in Ordinary 1921–29.

Carson /'kɑːsən/ Rachel 1907–1964. US naturalist. An aquatic biologist with the US Fish and Wildlife Service 1936–49, she then became its editor-in-chief until 1952. In 1951, she published *The Sea Around Us*, and in 1963 *Silent Spring*, attacking the indiscriminate use of pesticides.

Carson /'kɑːsən/ William (Willie) 1942– . British jockey, born in Scotland, who has ridden three Epsom Derby winners as well as the winners of most major races in England and abroad.

The top flat race jockey on five occasions, he has ridden over 2,500 winners in Britain. For many years he has ridden for the Royal trainer, Major Dick Hern.

Carson City /'kɑːsən 'sɪti/ capital of Nevada, USA; population (1980) 30,810. Smallest of the state capitals, it is named after Kit ◊Carson.

Cartagena /ˌkɑːtəˈdʒiːnə/ city in the province of Murcia, Spain; on the Mediterranean; population (1986) 169,000. It is a seaport and naval base. It was founded as ***Carthago Nova*** about 225 BC by the Carthaginian Hasdrubal, son-in-law of Hamilcar Barca. It continued to flourish under the Romans and the Moors, and was conquered by the Spanish 1269. It has a 13th-century cathedral and Roman remains.

Cartagena /ˌkɑːtəˈdʒiːnə/ or ***Cartagena de los Indes*** port, industrial centre, and capital of the department of Bolívar, NW Colombia; population (1985) 531,000. Plastics and chemicals are produced here.

It was founded 1533, and taken by Drake 1586. A pipeline brings petroleum to the city from the De Manes oilfields.

carte blanche (French 'white paper') no instructions, complete freedom to do as one wishes.

cartel (German ***Kartell***, a group) firms that remain independent but which enter into agreement to set mutually acceptable prices for their products. A cartel may restrict output or raise prices in order to prevent entrants to the market and increase member profits. They therefore represent a form of ◊oligopoly.

National laws concerning cartels differ widely and international agreement is difficult to achieve.

Carson *US frontiersman 'Kit' Carson.*

Carter *39th President of the USA Jimmy Carter, who sponsored the Camp David Agreements but failed to achieve the release of US hostages in Iran.*

Both the Treaty of Rome and Stockholm Convention governing European Community (EC) and European Free Trade Association (EFTA), respectively contain provisions for control. In Germany, cartels are the most common form of monopolistic organisation.

Carter /'kɑːtə/ Angela 1940– . English writer of the ◊magic realist school. Her novels include *The Magic Toyshop* (filmed by David Wheatley 1987) and *Nights at the Circus* 1984. She co-wrote the script for the film *The Company of Wolves* 1984, based on one of her stories.

Carter /'kɑːtə/ Elliott (Cook) 1908– . US composer. His early music shows the influence of ◊Stravinsky, but after 1950 it became increasingly intricate and densely written in a manner resembling ◊Ives. He invented 'metrical modulation', which allows different instruments or groups to stay in touch while playing at different speeds. He has written four string quartets, the *Symphony for Three Orchestras* 1967, and the song cycle *A Mirror on Which to Dwell* 1975.

Carter /'kɑːtə/ Jimmy (James Earl) 1924– . 39th president of the USA 1977–81, a Democrat. In 1976 he narrowly wrested the presidency from Ford. Features of his presidency were the return of the Panama Canal Zone to Panama, the Camp David Agreements for peace in the Middle East, and the Iranian seizure of US embassy hostages. He was defeated by Reagan 1980.

Carter Doctrine assertion in 1980 by President Carter of a vital US interest in the Persian Gulf region (prompted by Soviet invasion of Afghanistan): any outside attempt at control would be met by force if necessary.

Carteret /'kɑːtəret/ Philip. English navigator who discovered the Pitcairn Islands in 1767 during a round-the-world expedition 1766–69. He retired in 1794 with the rank of rear-admiral.

Cartesian coordinates in ◊coordinate geometry, a system used to represent vectors or to denote the position of a point on a plane (two dimensions) or in space (three dimensions) with reference to a set of two or more axes. The Cartesian coordinate system can be extended to any finite number of dimensions (axes), and is used thus in theoretical mathematics. It is named after Descartes.

For a plane defined by two axes at right angles (a horizontal x-axis and a vertical y-axis), the coordinates of a point are given by its perpendicular

distances from the y-axis and x-axis, written in the form (x,y). For example, a point P 3 units from the y-axis and 4 units from the x-axis has Cartesian coordinates $(3,4)$. In three-dimensional coordinate geometry, points are located with reference to a third, z-axis. The system is used to create technical drawings of machines or buildings, and in computer-aided design (◊CAD).

Carthage /'kɑːθɪdʒ/ ancient Phoenician port in N Africa, 16 km/10 mi N of modern Tunis, Tunisia. An important trading centre, from the 6th century BC it was in conflict with Greece, and then with Rome, and was destroyed 146 BC at the end of the ◊*Punic Wars*. About 45 BC Roman colonists settled in Carthage, and it rose to be the wealthy and important capital of the province of Africa. After its capture by the Vandals in AD 439 it was little more than a pirate stronghold. From 533 it formed part of the Byzantine Empire until its final destruction by the Arabs in 698.

Carthage is said to have been founded in 814 BC by Phoenician emigrants from Tyre, led by the princess Dido. It developed an extensive commerce throughout the Mediterranean, and traded with the Tin Islands, whose location is believed to have been either Cornwall or SW Spain. After the capture of Tyre by the Babylonians in the 6th century BC it became the natural leader of the Phoenician colonies in N Africa and Spain, and there soon began a prolonged struggle with the Greeks which centred mainly in Sicily, the E of which was dominated by Greek colonies, while the W was held by Carthaginian trading stations. About 540 BC the Carthaginians defeated a Greek attempt to land in Corsica, and in 480 a Carthaginian attempt to conquer the whole of Sicily was defeated by the Greeks at Himera.

The population of Carthage before its destruction by the Romans is said to have numbered over 700,000. The constitution was an aristocratic republic with two chief magistrates elected annually and a senate of 300 life members. The religion was Phoenician, including the worship of the Moon-goddess Tanit, the great Sun god Baal-Hammon, and the Tyrian Meklarth: human sacrifices were not unknown. The real strength of Carthage lay in its commerce and its powerful navy; its armies were for the most part mercenaries.

Carthusian order Roman Catholic order of monks and, later, nuns, founded by St Bruno in 1084 at Chartreuse, near Grenoble, France. Living chiefly in unbroken silence, they ate one vegetarian meal a day and supported themselves by their own labours; the rule is still one of severe austerity.

The first rule was drawn up by Guigo, the fifth prior. The order was introduced into England about 1178, when the first Charterhouse was founded at Witham in Essex. They were suppressed at the Reformation, but there is a Charterhouse at Parkminster, Sussex, established in 1833.

Cartier /ˌkɑːti'eɪ/ Georges Étienne 1814–1873. French-Canadian politician. He fought against the British in the rebellion 1837, was elected to the Canadian parliament 1848, and was joint prime minister with John A Macdonald 1858–62. He brought Québec into the Canadian federation 1867.

Cartier /ˌkɑːti'eɪ/ Jacques 1491–1557. French navigator who was the first European to sail up the St Lawrence river in 1534. He named the site of Montreal.

Cartier-Bresson /ˌkɑːti'eɪ breˈsɒn/ Henri 1908– . French photographer, one of the greatest photographic artists. His documentary work was achieved in black and white, using a small format camera. He was noted for his ability to structure the image and to capture the decisive moment.

cartilage flexible bluish-white connective ◊tissue made up of the protein collagen. In cartilaginous fish, it forms the skeleton; in other vertebrates, it forms the embryonic skeleton which is replaced by ◊bone in the adult, except in areas of wear

such as bone endings, and the discs between the backbones. It also supports the larynx, nose, and external ear of mammals.

Cartland /'kɑːtlənd/ Barbara 1904– . English romantic novelist. She published her first book *Jigsaw* in 1921, and since then has produced a prolific stream of stories of chastely romantic love, usually in idealized or exotic settings, for a mainly female audience (such as *Love Climbs In* 1978 and *Moments of Love* 1981).

cartography the art and practice of drawing ◊maps.

cartomancy the practice of telling fortunes by cards, often ◊tarot cards.

cartoon a humorous or satirical drawing or ◊caricature; a strip cartoon or ◊comic strip; traditionally, the base design for a large fresco, mosaic, or tapestry, transferred to wall or canvas by tracing or picking out (pouncing). Surviving examples include Leonardo da Vinci's *Virgin and St Anne* (National Gallery, London).

Cartwright /'kɑːtraɪt/ Edmund 1743–1823. British inventor. He patented the power loom 1785, built a weaving mill 1787, and patented a wool-combing machine 1789.

Born in Nottinghamshire, he went to Oxford and became a country rector (and also a farmer). He went bankrupt in 1793.

Caruso /kəˈruːsəʊ/ Enrico 1873–1921. Italian operatic tenor. In 1902 he starred in Monte Carlo, in Puccini's *La Bohème*. He is chiefly remembered for performances as Canio in Leoncavallo's *Pagliacci*, and the Duke in Verdi's *Rigoletto*.

Carver /'kɑːvə/ George Washington 1864–1943. US agricultural chemist. Born a slave in Missouri, he devoted his life to improving the economy of the US South and the condition of blacks. He advocated the diversification of crops, promoted peanut production, and was a pioneer in the field of plastics.

Carver /'kɑːvə/ Raymond 1939–1988. US story writer and poet, author of vivid stories of contemporary US life. *Cathedral* 1983 collects many of his stories; *Fires* 1985 also has essays and poems.

Cary /'keəri/ (Arthur) Joyce (Lunel) 1888–1957. British novelist. In 1918 he entered the Colonial Service, and Nigeria, where he had served, gave a background to such novels as *Mister Johnson* 1939. Other books include *The Horse's Mouth* 1944.

caryatid building support or pillar in the shape of a woman, the name deriving from the Karyatides, who were the priestesses at the temple of Artemis at Karyai; a male figure is a *telamon* or *atlas*.

caryopsis a dry, one-seeded ◊fruit in which the wall of the seed becomes fused to the carpel wall during its development. It is a type of ◊achene, and therefore develops from one ovary and does not split open to release the seed. The caryopsis is typical of members of the grass family Gramineae, including the cereals.

Casablanca /ˌkæsəˈblæŋkə/ (Arabic *Dar el-Beida*) port, commercial and industrial centre on the Atlantic coast of Morocco; population (1981) 2,409,000. It trades in fish, phosphates,

caryatid *The Erectheon, Porch of the Caryatids at the Parthenon, Athens.*

Cassatt *The Paris Basin, Musée du Petit Palais, Paris, by US artist Mary Cassatt. Cassatt settled in France in her early thirties, where she worked closely with the Impressionists.*

and manganese. The Great Hassan II Mosque, completed 1989, is the world's largest; it is built on a platform (40,000 sq m/430,000 sq ft) jutting out over the Atlantic, with walls 60 m/200 ft high, topped by a hydraulic sliding roof, and a minaret 175 m/574 ft high. Casablanca was occupied by the French from 1907 until Morocco became independent 1956.

Casablanca Conference World War II meeting of the US and UK leaders Roosevelt and Churchill, 14–24 Jan 1943, at which the Allied demand for the unconditional surrender of Germany, Italy, and Japan was issued.

Casals /kə'saːlz/ Pablo 1876–1973. Catalan cellist, composer, and conductor. As a cellist, he is renowned for his interpretations of JS Bach's unaccompanied suites. He left Spain in 1939 to live in Prades, in the French Pyrenees, where he founded an annual music festival. He wrote instrumental and choral works, including the Christmas oratorio *The Manger.*

In 1919 Casals founded the Barcelona orchestra, which he conducted until leaving Spain at the outbreak of the Spanish Civil War in 1936. He was an outspoken critic of fascism, and a tireless crusader for peace. In 1956 he moved to Puerto Rico where he launched the Casals Festival 1957 and toured extensively in the USA. He married three times; his first wife was the Portuguese cellist Guilhermina Suggia.

Casanova de Seingalt /ˌkæsə'nəʊvə də sæŋ'gælt/ Giovanni Jacopo 1725–1798. Italian adventurer, spy, violinist, librarian, and, according to his *Memoirs,* one of the world's great lovers. From 1774 he was a spy in the Venetian police service. In 1782 a libel got him into trouble, and after more wanderings he was in 1785 appointed Count Waldstein's librarian at his castle of Dûx in Bohemia, where he wrote his *Memoirs* (published 1826–38, although the complete text did not appear until 1960–61).

Cascade Range /kæ'skeɪd/ volcanic mountains in western USA and Canada, extending 1,120 km/700 mi from N California through Oregon and Washington to the Fraser river. They include Mount St Helens and Mount Rainier (the highest peak, 4,392 m/14,408 ft), which is noted for its glaciers. The mountains are the most active in the USA, excluding Alaska and Hawaii.

Cascais /kə'ʃaɪʃ/ fishing port and resort town on the Costa do Sol, 25 km/16 mi W of Lisbon, Portugal.

case grammar a theory of language structure which proposes that the underlying structure of language should contain some sort of functional information about the roles of its components; thus in the sentence, 'The girl opened the door,' the phrase 'the girl' would have the role of agent, not merely that of grammatical subject.

casein main protein of milk, from which it can be separated by the action of acid, rennin, or bacterial action (souring); also the main component of cheese. It is used commercially in cosmetics, glues, and as a sizing for coating paper.

Casement /'keɪsmənt/ Roger David 1864–1916. Irish nationalist. While in the British consular service he exposed the ruthless exploitation of the people of the Belgian Congo and in Peru, for which he was knighted in 1911 (degraded 1916). He was hanged for treason by the British for his part in the Irish republican Easter Rising.

In 1914 Casement went to Germany and attempted to induce Irish prisoners of war to form an Irish brigade to take part in a republican insurrection. He returned to Ireland in a submarine in 1916 (actually to postpone, not start, the Easter Rising), was arrested, tried for treason, and hanged.

Caserta /kə'zɜːtə/ town in S Italy 33 km/21 mi NE of Naples; population (1981) 66,318. It trades in chemicals, olive oil, wine and grain. The base for Garibaldi's campaigns in the 19th century, it was the Allied headquarters in Italy 1943–45, and the German forces surrendered to Field Marshal Alexander here in 1945.

Cash /kæʃ/ Johnny 1932– . US country singer, songwriter, and guitarist. His early hits, recorded for Sun Records in Memphis, Tennessee, include the million-selling 'I Walk the Line' 1956. Many of his songs have become classics.

cash crop crop grown solely for sale rather than for the farmer's own use, for example, coffee, cotton, or sugar beet. Many Third World countries grow cash crops to meet their debt repayments rather than grow food for their people. The price for these crops depends on financial interests, such as those of the multinational companies and the International Monetary Fund. In Britain, the most widespread cash crop is the potato.

cashew tree of tropical America *Anacardium occidentale,* family Anacardiaceae. Extensively cultivated in India and Africa, it produces edible kidney-shaped nuts.

cashmere a natural fibre originating from the wool of the goats of Kashmir, India. Used for shawls, scarves, sweaters, and coats, it can also be made artificially.

Caslavska Vera 1943– . Czechoslovak gymnast, the first of the great modern-day stylists. She won a record 21 world, Olympic and European gold medals 1959–68; she also won eight silver and three bronze medals.

Caspian Sea /'kæspiən/ world's largest inland sea, divided between Iran and the USSR. Area about 400,000 sq km/155,000 sq mi, with a maximum depth of 1,000 m/3,250 ft. The chief ports are Astrakhan and Baku. It is now approximately 28 m/90 ft below sea level due to drainage in the north, and the damming of the Volga and Ural rivers for hydroelectric power.

An underwater ridge divides it into two halves, of which the shallow north is almost salt-free. There are no tides. The damming has led to shrinkage over the last 50 years, and the growth of industry along its shores has caused pollution and damaged the Russian and Iranian caviar industries.

Cassandra /kə'sændrə/ in Greek mythology, the daughter of ◊Priam, king of Troy. Her prophecies (for example of the fall of Troy) were never believed, because she had rejected the love of Apollo. She was murdered with Agamemnon by Clytemnestra.

Cassatt /kə'sæt/ Mary 1845–1926. US Impressionist painter and printmaker. In 1868 she settled in Paris. Her colourful pictures of mothers and children show the influence of Japanese prints, for example *The Bath* 1892 (Art Institute, Chicago).

cassava plant *Manihot utilissima,* also known as **manioc,** belonging to the family Euphorbiaceae. Native to South America, it is now widely grown in the tropics for its starch-containing roots. The bitter cassava yields a flower called Brazilian arrowroot, from which tapioca and bread are made.

Cassavetes /ˌkæsə'veɪtiːz/ John 1929–1989. US film director and actor, who directed experimental, apparently improvised films, including *Shadows* 1960, and *The Killing of a Chinese Bookie* 1980. His acting appearances included *The Dirty Dozen* 1967, and *Rosemary's Baby* 1968.

Cassel /'kæsəl/ alternative spelling of ◊Kassel, an industrial town in West Germany.

cassia bark of a plant, *Cinnamomum cassia,* of the family Lauraceae. It is aromatic, and closely resembles the true cinnamon, for which it is a widely used substitute. *Cassia* is also a genus of plants of the family Leguminosae, many of which have strong purgative properties; *Cassia senna* is the source of the laxative senna.

Cassini /kæ'siːni/ Giovanni Domenico 1625–1712. Italian-French astronomer, who discovered four moons of Saturn and the gap in the rings of Saturn now called the ***Cassini division.***

Born in Italy, he became director of the Paris Observatory in 1671. His son, grandson, and great-grandson in turn became directors of the Paris Observatory.

Cassino /kæ'siːnəʊ/ town in S Italy, 80 km/50 mi NW of Naples; at the foot of Monte Cassino; population (1981) 31,139. It was the scene of heavy fighting during World War II in 1944, when most of the town was destroyed. It was rebuilt 1.5 km/1 mi to the north. The famous abbey on the summit of Monte Cassino, founded by St Benedict in 529, was rebuilt in 1956.

Cassiopeia in Greek mythology, the mother of ◊Andromeda.

Cassiopeia prominent constellation of the northern hemisphere, representing the mother of Andromeda. It has a distinctive W-shape, and contains one of the most powerful radio sources in the sky, Cassiopeia A, the remains of a ◊supernova (star explosion), as well as open and globular clusters.

cassiterite or ***tinstone*** chief ore of tin, consisting of reddish-brown to black stannic oxide (SnO_2), usually found in granite rocks. When fresh it has

cassowary

a bright ('adamantine') lustre. It was formerly extensively mined in Cornwall; today Malaysia is the world's major supplier. Other sources of cassiterite are in Africa, Indonesia, and South America.

Cassius /'kæsiəs/ Gaius died 42 BC. Roman soldier, one of the conspirators who killed Julius ◊Caesar in 44. He fought at Carrhae 53,, and with the republicans against Caesar at Pharsalus 48, was pardoned and appointed praetor, but became a leader in the conspiracy of 44, and after Caesar's death joined Brutus. He committed suicide after his defeat at ◊Philippi 42 BC.

Cassivelaunus /,kæsɪvə'laʊnəs/ chieftain of the British tribe, the Catuvellauni, who led the British resistance to Caesar in 54 BC.

Casson /'kæsən/ Hugh 1910– . British architect, professor at the Royal College of Art 1953–75, and president of the Royal Academy 1976–84. His books include *Victorian Architecture* 1948. He was director of architecture for the Festival of Britain 1948–51.

cassowary large flightless bird, genus *Casuarius*, found in New Guinea and N Australia, usually in forests. Cassowaries are related to emus, but have a bare head with a horny casque, or helmet, on top, and brightly coloured skin on the neck. The loose plumage is black and the wings are tiny, but cassowaries can run and leap well, and defend themselves by kicking. They stand up to 1.5 m/5 ft tall.

Castagno /kæ'stænjəʊ/ Andrea del *c.* 1421–1457. Italian Renaissance painter, active in Florence. In his frescoes in Sta Apollonia, Florence, he adapted the pictorial space to the architectural framework and followed ◊Masaccio's lead in perspective.

Castagno's work is sculptural and strongly expressive, anticipating the Florentine late-15th-century style, as in his *David* about 1450–57 (National Gallery, Washington DC).

castanets Spanish percussion instrument made of two hollowed wooden shells, held in the hand to produce a rhythmic accompaniment to dance.

caste (Portuguese *casta* 'race') grouping of Hindu society from ancient times into four main classes from which some 3,000 subsequent divisions derive: *Brahmans* (priests), *Kshatriyas* (nobles and warriors), *Vaisyas* (traders and farmers), and *Sudras* (servants); plus a fifth class, *Harijan* (untouchables).

The four main classes are said to have originated from the head, arms, thighs, and feet respectively of Brahma, the creator; the fifth was probably the aboriginal inhabitants of the country, known variously as Scheduled Castes, Depressed Classes, Untouchables, Harijan (name coined by Gandhi, 'children of God'), and were considered to be polluting by touch, or even by sight, to others. Discrimination against them was made illegal in 1947, but persists.

Castel Gandolfo /kæs'tel gæn'dɒlfəʊ/ village in Italy 24 km/15 mi SE of Rome. The castle, built by Pope Urban VIII in the 17th century, is still used by the Pope as a summer residence.

Castellón de la Plana /,kæstel'jɒn de lɑ: 'plɑ:nə/ port in Spain, facing the Mediterranean to the east; population (1981) 124,500. It is the capital of Castellón province, and is the centre of an orange-growing district.

Castelo Branco /kəʃ'telu: 'bræŋku:/ Camilo 1825–1890. Portuguese novelist. His work fluctuates between mysticism and Bohemianism, and includes *Amor de perdição/Love of Perdition* 1862, written during his imprisonment for adultery, and *Novelas do Minho* 1875, stories of the rural north.

Illegitimate and then orphaned, he led a dramatic life. Other works include *Onde está a felicidade?/Where is Happiness?* 1856 and *A brazileira de Prazins/The Brazilian girl from Prazins* 1882. Created a viscount in 1885, he committed suicide when overtaken by blindness.

Castiglione /kæs,ti:li'əʊni/ Baldassare, Count Castiglione 1478–1529. Italian author and diplomat, who described the perfect Renaissance gentleman in *Il Cortegiano/The Courtier* 1528.

Born near Mantua, Castiglione served the Duke of Milan, and in 1506 was engaged by the Duke of Albino on a mission to Henry VII of England. While in Spain in 1524 he was created bishop of Avila.

Castile /kæs'ti:l/ kingdom founded in the 10th century, occupying the central plateau of Spain. Its union with Aragon in 1479 was the foundation of the Spanish state. It comprised the two great basins separated by the Sierra de Gredos and the Sierra de Guadarrama, known traditionally as Old and New Castile. The area now forms the modern regions of ◊Castilla-León and ◊Castilla-La Mancha.

The kingdom of Castile grew from a small area in the north. In the 11th century Old Castile was united with León; in 1085 the kingdom of Toledo was captured from the Moors and became New Castile, with Toledo the capital of the whole. Castile was united with ◊Aragon in 1479 under ◊Ferdinand and Isabella.

Castilian language a member of the Romance branch of the Indo-European language family originating in NW Spain, in the provinces of Old and New Castile. It is the basis of present-day standard Spanish (see ◊Spanish language) and is often seen as the same language, the terms *castellano* and *español* being used interchangeably

Castiglione *perhaps the best expression of the Renaissance spirit has come from the Italian author and diplomat, Count Baldassare Castiglione, in his celebrated dialogue on courtly life* Il Cortegiano.

in both Spain and the Spanish-speaking countries of the Americas.

Castilla /kæs'ti:lja/ Ramón 1797–1867. President of Peru 1841–51 and 1855–62. He dominated Peruvian politics for over two decades, bringing political stability. Income from guano exports was used to reduce the national debt and improve transport and educational facilities. He abolished black slavery and the head tax on Indians.

Castilla-La Mancha /kæ'sti:ljə lɑ: 'mæntʃə/ autonomous region of central Spain; area 79,200 sq km/30,571 sq mi; population (1986) 1,665,000. It includes the provinces of Albacete, Ciudad Real, Cuenca, Guadalajara, and Toledo. Irrigated land produces grain and chickpeas, and merino sheep graze here.

Castilla-León /kæ'sti:ljə leɪ'ɒn/ autonomous region of central Spain; area 94,100 sq km/36,323 sq mi; population (1986) 2,600,000. It includes the provinces of Ávila, Burgos, León, Palencia, Salamanca, Segovia, Soria, Valladolid, and Zamora. Irrigated land produces wheat and rye. Cattle, sheep, and fighting bulls are bred in the uplands.

casting the process of producing solid objects by pouring molten material into a shaped mould and allowing it to cool. Casting is used to shape such materials as glass, plastics, and especially metals and alloys.

The casting of metals has been practised for more than 6,000 years, using first copper, bronze, then iron. The traditional method of casting metal is *sand casting*. Using a model of the object to be produced, a hollow mould is made in a damp sand and clay mix. Molten metal is then poured into the mould, taking its shape when it cools and solidifies. The sand mould is broken up to release the casting. Permanent metal moulds called *dies* are also used for casting, particularly of small items in mass-production processes where molten metal is injected under pressure into cooled dies. *Continuous casting* is a method of shaping bars and slabs, which involves pouring molten metal into a hollow, water-cooled mould of the desired cross section.

cast iron a cheap but invaluable constructional material, most commonly used for car engine blocks. Cast iron is partly refined pig (crude) ◊iron, which is very fluid when molten and highly suitable for shaping by ◊casting, as it contains too many impurities, especially carbon, to be readily shaped in any other way. Solid cast iron is heavy and can absorb great shock, but is very brittle.

castle /'kɑ:səl/ the private fortress of a king or noble. The earliest castles in Britain were built following the Norman Conquest, and the art of castle building reached a peak in the 13th century. By the 15th century, the need for castles for domestic defence had largely disappeared, and the advent of gunpowder made them largely useless against attack. See also ◊château.

structure The main parts of a typical castle are: the *keep*, a large central tower containing store rooms, soldiers's quarters, and a hall for the lord and his family; the *inner bailey* or walled courtyard surrounding the keep; the *outer bailey* or second courtyard, separated from the inner bailey by a wall; crenellated *embattlements* through which missiles were discharged against an attacking enemy; rectangular or round *towers* projecting from the walls; the *portcullis*, a heavy grating which could be let down to close the main gate; and the *drawbridge* crossing the ditch or moat surrounding the castle. Sometimes a tower called a *barbican* was constructed over a gateway as an additional defensive measure.

history

11th century The *motte and bailey* castle (the motte was a mound of earth, and the bailey a courtyard enclosed by a wall); the earliest example is on the Loire river in France, dated 1010. The first *rectangular keep* dates from this time; the best known is the White Tower in the Tower of London.

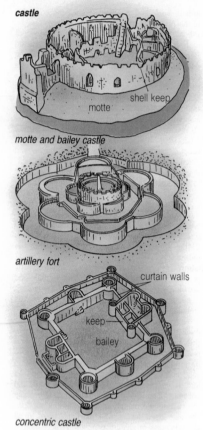

castle

shell keep

motte

motte and bailey castle

artillery fort

curtain walls

keep

bailey

concentric castle

castle (Top) Stokesay Castle in Shropshire, England, built between the 12th and 13th centuries. (Bottom) Bodiam Castle, built by Sir Edward Dalyngrigge in the 14th century.

12th century Development of more substantial defensive systems, based in part on the Crusaders' experiences of sieges during the First Crusade 1096; the first **curtain walls** with projecting towers were built (as at Framlingham, Suffolk).

13th century Introduction of the **round tower**, both for curtain walls (Pembroke, Wales) and for keeps (Conisborough, Yorkshire); **concentric planning** (particularly in the castles of Wales, such as Beaumaris and Harlech); **fortified town walls**.

14th century First use of gunpowder; inclusion of gunports in curtain walls (Bodiam, Sussex).

15th century Fortified manor houses now adequate for private dwelling.

16th century End of the castle as a practical means of defence; fortified coastal defences, however, continued to be built (Falmouth, Cornwall).

Castle /'kɑːsəl/ Barbara, Baroness Castle (born Betts) 1911– . British Labour politician, a cabinet minister in the Labour governments of the 1960s and 1970s. She led the Labour group in the European Parliament 1979–89.

She was minister of overseas development 1964–65, transport 1965–68, employment 1968–70 (when her White Paper 'In Place of Strife', on trade-union reform, was abandoned as too controversial), and social services 1974–76, when she was dropped from the cabinet by prime minister James Callaghan. She criticized Callaghan in her *Diaries* 1980.

Castleford /'kɑːsəlfəd/ town in W Yorkshire, England; population (1981) 36,000.

Castle Hill rising Irish convict revolt in New South Wales, Australia, 4 Mar 1804; a number were killed while parleying with the military under a flag of truce.

Castlemaine /'kɑːsəlmeɪn/ Lady (born Barbara Villiers) 1641–1709. Mistress of Charles II of England and mother of his son the Duke of Grafton (1663–90).

She was the wife from 1659 of Roger Palmer (1634–1705), created Earl of Castlemaine in 1661. She was the chief mistress of Charles 1660–70,

when she was created Duchess of Cleveland. Among her descendants through the Duke of Grafton is Diana, Princess of Wales.

Castlemaine /'kɑːsəlmeɪn/ town in Victoria, Australia, about 105 km/65 mi NW of Melbourne, on the Loddon. Site of the earliest gold strikes in 1851, its population rose to 30,000 at that period. It survives as an agricultural marketing centre.

Castlereagh /'kɑːsəlreɪ/ Robert Stewart, Viscount Castlereagh 1769–1822. British Tory politician. As chief secretary for Ireland 1797–1801, he suppressed the rebellion of 1798, and helped the younger Pitt secure the union of England, Scotland, and Ireland in 1801. As foreign secretary 1812–22 he coordinated European opposition to Napoleon and represented Britain at the Congress of Vienna 1814–15.

When his father, an Ulster landowner, was made an earl in 1796, he took the courtesy title of Viscount Castlereagh. In 1821 he succeeded his father as Marquess of Londonderry. He sat in the Irish House of Commons from 1790.

In Parliament at Westminster he was war secretary 1805–06 and 1807–09, when he had to resign after a duel with foreign secretary George ◊Canning. Castlereagh was foreign secretary from 1812, when he devoted himself to the overthrow of Napoleon and subsequently to the Congress of Vienna and the congress system. Abroad his policy favoured the development of material liberalism, but at home he repressed the Reform movement, and popular opinion held him responsible for the Peterloo massacre of peaceful demonstrators in 1819.

Castor second brightest star in the constellation Gemini, and the 23rd brightest star in the sky. Along with ◊Pollux, it forms a prominent pair at the eastern end of Gemini.

Castor is 45 light years away, and is one of the finest ◊binary stars in the sky for small telescopes. The two main components orbit each other over a period of 400–500 years. A third, much fainter, star orbits the main pair over a period probably exceeding 10,000 years. Each of the three visible components is a spectroscopic binary, making Castor a sextuple star system.

Castor and Pollux/Polydeuces /'kɑːstə, ˌpɒlʌks, pɒlɪ'djuːsiːz/ in Greek mythology, twin sons of Leda (by ◊Zeus), brothers of ◊Helen and

◊Clytemnestra. Protectors of mariners, they were transformed at death into the constellation Gemini.

castoreum the preputial follicles of the beaver, abbreviated as 'castor', and used in perfumery.

castor oil plant tall tropical and subtropical shrub *Ricinus communis*, also known as **Palma Christi**, family Euphorbiaceae. The seeds yield the purgative castor oil, and also ricin, one of the most powerful poisons known, which can be targeted to destroy cancer cells, while leaving normal cells untouched.

castration removal of the male testicles. It prevents reproduction, and also much modifies the secondary sexual characteristics: for instance, the voice may remain high as in childhood, and growth of hair on the face and body may become weak or cease, owing to the removal of the hormones normally secreted by the testes.

Castration was formerly used to preserve the treble voice of boy singers or, by Muslims, to provide trustworthy harem guards called eunuchs.

Male domestic animals, especially stallions and bulls, are castrated to prevent undesirable sires from reproducing, to moderate their aggressive and savage disposition and, for bulls, to improve their value as beef cattle. Cockerels are castrated (capons) to improve their flavour and increase their size. The effects of castration can also be achieved by chemical means, by administration of hormones, in humans and animals.

castrato in music, a high male voice of unusual brilliance and power achieved by castration before puberty. The practice was outlawed in the mid-19th century.

Castries /kæ'striːz/ port and capital of St Lucia, on the NW coast of the island; population (1988) 53,000. It produces textiles, chemicals, wood products, tobacco, and rubber products. The town was rebuilt after destruction by fire 1948.

Castro /'kæstrəʊ/ Cipriano 1858–1924. Venezuelan dictator 1899–1908, known as 'the Lion of the Andes'. When he refused to pay off foreign debts in 1902, British, German, and Italian ships blockaded the country. He presided over a corrupt government. There were frequent rebellions during his rule, and opponents of his regime were exiled or murdered.

Castro (Ruz) /'kæstrəʊ 'ruːs/ Fidel 1927– . Cuban Communist politician, prime minister 1959–76 and president from 1976. He led two unsuccessful coups against the right-wing Batista regime and led the revolution that overthrew the dictator 1959. From 1979 he was also president of the nonaligned movement, although promoting the line of the USSR, which subsidized his regime.

Of wealthy parentage, Castro was educated at Jesuit schools and, after studying law at the University of Havana, he gained a reputation through his work for poor clients. He opposed the Batista dictatorship, and took part in an unsuccessful attack on the army barracks at Santiago de Cuba in 1953. After some time in exile in the USA and Mexico, Castro attempted a secret landing in Cuba in 1956 in

Castro (Ruz) Cuban revolutionary and premier Fidel Castro, in Czechoslovakia, 1972.

which all but 11 of his supporters were killed. He eventually gathered an army of over 5,000 which overthrew Batista in 1959 and he became prime minister a few months later. His brother Raúl was appointed minister of armed forces.

The Castro regime introduced a centrally planned economy based on the production for export of sugar, tobacco, and nickel. Aid for developmemt has been provided by the USSR while Cuba joined ◊COMECON in 1972. By nationalizing US-owned businesses in 1960 Castro gained the enmity of the USA, which came to a head in the ◊Cuban missile crisis of 1962. His regime became socialist and he epoused Marxism-Leninism until in 1974 he rejected Marx's formula 'from each according to his ability and to each according to his need' and decreed that each Cuban should 'receive according to his work'.

casuarina genus of trees and shrubs with many species native to Australia and New Guinea, but also found in Africa and Asia. The river she-oak, *Casuarina cunninghamiana*, has fronded branches resembling cassowary feathers, hence the latin name.

casus belli (Latin) a justification for war, grounds for a dispute.

cat small domesticated carnivorous mammal *Felis catus* often kept as a pet and for catching small pests such as rodents. Found in many colour variants, it may have short, long, or no hair, but the general shape and size is constant. All cats walk on the pads of their toes, and have retractile claws. They have strong limbs, large eyes, and acute hearing. The canine teeth are long and well-developed, as are the shearing teeth in the side of the mouth.

Domestic cats have a common ancestor, the **African wild cat** *Felis libyca*, found across Africa and Arabia. This is similar to the **European wild cat** *Felis silvestris*. Domestic cats can interbreed with either of these wild relatives. Various other species of small wild cat live in all continents except Antarctica and Australia. Large cats such as the lion and tiger also belong to the cat family Felidae.

catabolism the breakdown of body tissues that occurs in many disease processes, such as fever, and in starvation.

catacomb underground cemetery such as the catacombs of the early Christians, including those beneath the basilica of St Sebastian in Rome, where bodies were buried in niches in the walls of the tunnels.

Catalan language a member of the Romance branch of the Indo-European language family, an Iberian language closely related to Provençal in France. It is spoken in Catalonia in NE Spain, the Balearic Isles, Andorra, and a corner of SW France.

Since the end of the Franco regime in Spain in 1975, Catalan nationalists have vigorously promoted their regional language as co-equal in Catalonia with Castilian Spanish.

Catalaunian Fields /ˌkætəˈlɔːniən/ plain near Troyes, France, scene of the defeat of Attila the Hun by the Romans and Goths under the Roman general Aëtius (died 454) in 451.

catalepsy in medicine, an abnormal state in which the patient is apparently or actually unconscious.

There is no response to stimuli, and the rate of heartbeat and breathing is slow. A similar condition can be drug induced, or produced by hypnosis, but catalepsy as ordinarily understood occurs spontaneously. It is essentially an extreme form of resistive stupor, generally considered to be a defence against the environment or reality.

Catal Hüyük /tʃæˈtɑːl huːˈjuːk/ Neolithic site (6000 BC) discovered by James Mellaart 1961 in Anatolia, SE of Konya. It was a fortified city, and had temples with wall paintings, and there were rich finds including jewellery, obsidian, and mirrors. Together with finds at Jericho, it demonstrated much earlier development of

cat

Manx

Persian
White Longhair

European wild cat

Siamese

Japanese bob tail

Egyptian mau

Sphynx

Balinese
blue point

Turkish angora

urban life in the ancient world than previously imagined.

Catalonia /ˌkætəˈləʊniə/ (Spanish *Cataluña*) autonomous region of NE Spain; area 31,900 sq km/12,313 sq mi; population (1986) 5,977,000. It includes Barcelona (the capital), Gerona, Lérida, and Tarragona. Industries include wool and cotton textiles, and hydroelectric power is produced.

The north is mountainous, and the Ebro basin breaks through the Castellón mountains in the south. The soil is fertile, but the climate in the interior is arid. Catalonia leads Spain in industrial development. Tourist resorts have developed along the Costa Brava.

history The region has a long tradition of independence, enjoying autonomy 1932–39, but lost its privileges for supporting the Republican cause in the ◊Spanish Civil War. Autonomy and official use of the Catalan language were restored 1980.

French Catalonia is the adjacent *département* of Pyrénées-Orientales.

catalpa tree belonging to the Bignoniaceae family, found in North America, China, and the West Indies. The Indian bean tree, *Catalpa bignoniodes*, has been introduced into Europe. It has large, heart-shaped leaves, and white, yellow, and purple streaked bell-shaped flowers.

catalyst a substance that alters the speed of a chemical or biochemical reaction but which remains unchanged at the end of the reaction. Enzymes are biochemical catalysts. In practice most catalysts are used to speed up reactions.

catalytic converter device for reducing toxic emissions from the internal combustion engine. It converts harmful exhaust products to relatively harmless ones by passing exhaust gases over a mixture of catalysts. *Oxidation catalysts* convert hydrocarbons into carbon dioxide and water; *three-way catalysts* convert oxides of nitrogen back into nitrogen. Catalytic converters are standard in the USA, where a 90% reduction in pollution from cars was achieved without loss of engine performance or fuel economy.

catamaran (Tamil 'tied log') a twin-hulled sailing vessel, based on the aboriginal craft of South America and the Indies, made of logs lashed together, with an outrigger. A similar vessel with three hulls is known as a trimaran.

Cat and Mouse Act popular name for the *Prisoners, Temporary Discharge for Health, Act* 1913; an attempt by the UK Liberal government under ◊Asquith to reduce embarrassment caused by the incarceration of ◊suffragettes accused of violent offences against property.

When they embarked on hunger strikes, prison authorities introduced forced feeding, which proved humiliating and sometimes dangerous to the women. Following a public outcry the hunger strikers were released on a licence that could be revoked without further trial. The government was accused of playing cat to suffragette mice by its adoption of powers of release and re-arrest.

Catania /kə'tɑːniə/ industrial port in Sicily; population (1988) 372,000. It exports local sulphur.

cataract opacity of the lens of the eye. Fluid accumulates between the fibres of the lens and gives place to deposits of ◊albumin; these coalesce into rounded bodies; the lens fibres break down; and areas of the lens become filled with opaque products of degeneration.

The condition nearly always affects both eyes, usually one more than the other. In most cases the treatment is replacement of the lens with an artificial implant. Most common are senile cataracts, although the condition is seen in infancy.

catarrh inflammation of the mucous membrane of the nose, with excessive production of mucus.

catastrophe theory mathematical theory developed by René Thom in 1972, in which he showed that the growth of an organism proceeds by a series of gradual changes, which are triggered by, and in turn trigger, large-scale changes or 'catastrophic' jumps. It also has applications in engineering; for example, the gradual strain on the structure of a bridge that eventually results in a sudden collapse, and has been extended to economic and psychological events.

catastrophism theory that the geological features of the Earth were formed by a series of sudden, violent 'catastrophes' beyond the ordinary workings of nature. The theory was largely the work of Georges ◊Cuvier. It was later replaced by the concepts of ◊uniformitarianism and ◊evolution.

Catch-22 black-humour novel by Joseph Heller, published 1961, about a US squadron flying absurd bombing missions in Italy in World War II; the crazed military justifications involved made the phrase 'catch-22' represent all false authoritarian logic.

catch crop crop that is inserted between two principal crops in a rotation to provide some quick livestock grazing at a time when the land would otherwise be lying idle.

In the gap between harvesting a crop of winter-sown wheat and sowing a spring variety of barley,

catchment area

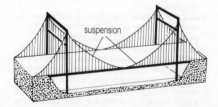

for example, an additional catch crop of stubble turnips or ryegrass can be produced for stock to graze in the late winter period when other green fodder is scarce. This practice is only suited to lighter soils, which are likely to be accessible to stock in winter without damage.

Catcher in the Rye, The 1951 novel of a young man's growing up and his fight to maintain his integrity in a 'phoney' adult world; written by J D Salinger, it became an international student classic.

catchment area area from which water is collected by a river and its tributaries.

Cateau-Cambrésis, Treaty of treaty that ended the dynastic wars between the Valois of France and the Habsburg Empire, 2–3 Apr 1559.

catechism teaching by question and answer on the Socratic method, but especially as a means of instructing children in the basics of the Christian creed. A person being instructed in this way in preparation for baptism or confirmation is called a *catechumen*.

A form of catechism was used for the catechumens in the early Christian church. Little books of catechism became numerous at the Reformation. Luther published simple catechisms for children and uneducated people, and a larger catechism for the use of teachers. The popular Roman Catholic catechism was that of Peter Canisius 1555; that with the widest circulation now is the Explanatory Catechism of Christian Doctrine. Protestant catechisms include Calvin's Geneva Catechism 1537; that composed by Cranmer and Ridley with additions by Overall 1549–1661, incorporated in the Book of Common Prayer; the Presbyterian Catechism 1647–48; and the Evangelical Free Church Catechism 1898.

catecholamine a type of chemical that functions as a ◊neurotransmitter or a ◊hormone. They include dopamine, epinephrine (adrenaline), and norepinephrine (noradrenaline).

catechu an extract of the leaves and shoots of *Uncaria gambier*, an East Indian acacia. It is rich in tannic acid, which is released slowly, a property that makes it a useful intestinal astringent in diarrhoea.

categorical imperative a technical term in Kant's moral philosophy designating the supreme principle of morality for rational beings. The imperative orders us to act only in such a way that we

catenary

A suspension bridge takes up a catenary curve

can will a maxim, or subjective principle, of our action to be a universal law.

category in philosophy, a fundamental concept applied to being, which cannot be reduced to anything more elementary. Aristotle listed ten categories: substance, quantity, quality, relation, place, time, position, state, action, passion.

catenary a curve taken up by a flexible cable suspended between two points, under gravity; for example, the curve of overhead suspension cables that hold the conductor wire of an electric railway or tramway.

caterpillar larval stage of a ◊butterfly or ◊moth. Worm-like in form, the body is segmented, may be hairy, and often has scent glands. The head has strong biting mandibles, silk glands, and a spinneret.

Many caterpillars resemble the plant on which they feed, dry twigs, or rolled leaves. Others are highly coloured and rely for their protection on their irritant hairs, disagreeable smell, or on their power to eject a corrosive fluid. Yet others take up a 'threat attitude' when attacked.

Caterpillars emerge from eggs that have been laid by the female insect on the food plant and feed greedily, increasing greatly in size and casting their skins several times, until the pupal stage is reached. The abdominal segments bear a varying number of 'pro-legs' as well as the six true legs on the thoracic segments.

caterpillar track a track on which track-laying vehicles such as tanks and bulldozers run, which takes the place of ordinary tyred wheels. It consists of an endless flexible belt of metal plates. A track-laying vehicle has a track each side, and its engine drives small cog wheels that run along the top of the track in contact with the ground. The advantage of such tracks over wheels is that they distribute the vehicle's weight over a wider area, and are thus ideal for use in soft and waterlogged ground conditions.

catfish fish belonging to the order Siluriformes, in which barbels (feelers) on the head are well-developed, so giving a resemblance to the whiskers of a cat. Catfishes are found worldwide, mainly but not exclusively in fresh water, and are plentiful in South America.

The E European *giant catfish* or *wels Silurus glanis* grows to 1.5 m/5 ft long or more. It has been introduced to several places in Britain.

The unrelated marine *wolf-fish Anarhicas lupus*, a deep-sea relative of the blenny, growing 1.2 m/4 ft long, is sometimes called a catfish.

Cathar (medieval Latin 'the pure') member of a sect in medieval Europe usually numbered among the Christian heretics. They started about the 10th century in the Balkans where they were called Bogomils, spread to SW Europe where they were often identified with the ◊Albigenses, and by the middle of the 14th century had been destroyed or driven underground by the Inquisition. They believed in reincarnation for everyone except their members.

The Cathars believed that this world is under the domination of Satan, and men and women are the terrestrial embodiment of spirits who were inspired by him to revolt and were driven out of heaven. At death the soul will become again imprisoned in flesh, whether of human or animal, unless it has been united in this life with Christ. If a human has become one of the Cathars, death brings release, the Beatific Vision, and immortality in Christ's presence. Baptism with the spirit – the *consolamentum* – was the central rite, which was held to remedy the disaster of the Fall. The spirit received was the Paraclete, the Comforter, and it was imparted by imposition of hands. The Believers, or *Credentes*, could approach God only through the Perfect (the ordained priesthood), who were implicitly obeyed in everything, and lived lives of the strictest self-denial and chastity.

cathedral (Latin *cathedra*, a seat or throne) Christian church containing the throne of a bishop or

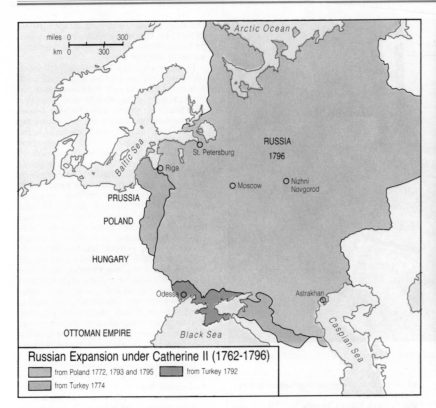

Russian Expansion under Catherine II (1762-1796)

from Poland 1772, 1793 and 1795   from Turkey 1792
from Turkey 1774

Catherine II *An intelligent ruler and patron of the arts, Catherine the Great of Russia is remembered as a benevolent despot who significantly increased Russia's territory, into Turkey, Sweden, and Poland.*

archbishop, which is usually situated on the south side of the choir. A cathedral is governed by a dean and chapter.

Formerly, cathedrals were distinguished as either monastic or secular, the clergy of the latter not being members of a regular monastic order. Some cathedrals, such as Lincoln and York, are referred to as 'minsters', the term originating in the name given to the bishop and cathedral clergy who were often referred to as a *monasterium*. After the dissolution of the monasteries by Henry VIII, most of the monastic churches were re-founded and are called Cathedrals of the New Foundation. Cathedrals of dioceses founded since 1836 include St Albans, Southwark, Truro, Birmingham, and Liverpool. There are cathedrals in most of the important cities of Europe; UK cathedrals include Canterbury cathedral (spanning the Norman to Perpendicular periods), Exeter cathedral (13th-century Gothic), and Coventry (rebuilt after World War II, consecrated 1962).

Cather /'kæðə/ Willa (Sibert) 1876–1947. US novelist. Born in Virginia, she moved as a child to Nebraska. Her novels and short stories frequently explore life in the pioneer West, for example in *Death Comes for the Archbishop* 1927, set in New Mexico. Other chief works are *My Antonia* 1918 and *A Lost Lady* 1923.

Catherine I /'kæθrɪn/ 1683–1727. Empress of Russia from 1724. A Lithuanian peasant girl, born Martha Skavronsky, she married a Swedish dragoon and eventually became the mistress of Peter the Great. In 1703 she was rechristened as Katarina Alexeievna, and in 1711 the tsar divorced his wife and married Catherine. She accompanied him in his campaigns, and showed tact and shrewdness. In 1724 she was proclaimed empress, and after Peter's death 1725 she ruled capably with the help of her ministers. She allied Russia with Austria and Spain in an anti-English bloc.

Catherine II /'kæθrɪn/ *the Great* 1729–1796. Empress of Russia from 1762, and daughter of the German prince of Anhalt-Zerbst. In 1745, she married the Russian grand duke Peter. Catherine was able to dominate him, and six months after he became tsar 1762 she ruled alone. During her

reign Russia extended its boundaries to include territory from Turkey 1774, and profited also by the partitions of Poland.

Catherine's private life was notorious throughout Europe, but she did not permit her lovers to influence her policy. She admired and aided the French ◊Encyclopédistes, including d'Alembert, and corresponded with the radical writer Voltaire.

Catherine de' Medici /deɪ 'medɪtʃi/ 1519–1589. French queen consort of Henry II, whom she married 1533, and mother of Francis II, Charles IX, and Henry III. At first outshone by Henry's mistress Diane de Poitiers (1490–1566), she became regent 1560–63 for Charles IX, and was politically powerful until his death 1574.

At first scheming with the ◊Huguenots, she later opposed them, instigating the Massacre of ◊St Bartholomew 1572.

Catherine of Alexandria, St Christian martyr. According to legend she disputed with 50 scholars, refusing to give up her faith and marry Emperor Maxentius. Her emblem is a wheel, on which her persecutors tried to kill her (the wheel broke and she was beheaded). Feast day 25 Nov.

Catherine of Aragon /'ærəgən/ 1485–1536. First queen of Henry VIII of England, 1509–33, and mother of Mary I; Henry divorced her without papal approval.

She married Henry's elder brother Prince Arthur 1501 (the marriage was allegedly unconsummated), and on his death 1502 was betrothed to Henry, marrying him on his accession 1509. Of their six children, only a daughter lived. Wanting a male heir, Henry sought an annulment 1526 on the grounds that the union with his brother's widow was invalid despite a papal dispensation. When the Pope demanded that the case be referred to him, Henry married Anne Boleyn, afterwards receiving the desired decree of nullity from Cranmer, the archbishop of Canterbury, in 1533. The Reformation in England followed, and Catherine went into retirement until her death.

Catherine of Braganza /brə'gænzə/ 1638–1705. Queen of Charles II of England 1662–85. The daughter of John IV of Portugal (1604–56), she brought the Portuguese possessions of Bombay and Tangier as her dowry. Her childlessness and

practice of her Catholic faith were unpopular, but Charles resisted pressure for divorce. She returned to Lisbon 1692.

Catherine of Genoa, St /'dʒenəʊə/ 1447–1510. Italian mystic, who devoted herself to the sick and to meditation. Her feast day is 15 Sept.

Catherine of Siena /si'enə/ 1347–1380. Catholic mystic, born in Siena, Italy. She attempted to reconcile the Florentines with the Pope, and persuaded Gregory XI to return to Rome from Avignon 1376. In 1375 she is said to have received on her body the stigmata, the impression of Jesus' wounds. Her *Dialogue* is a classic mystical work. Feast day 29 Apr.

Catherine of Valois /væl'wɑː/ 1401–1437. Queen of Henry V of England, whom she married 1420, and the mother of Henry VI. After the death of Henry V, she secretly married Owen Tudor (*c*.1400–61) about 1425, and their son became the father of Henry VII.

Catherwood /'kæθəwʊd/ Frederick 1799–1854. British topographical artist and archaeological illustrator who accompanied John Lloyd ◊Stephens in his exploration of central America 1839–40 and the Yucatan 1841–42. His engravings, published 1844, were the first accurate representation of Mayan civilization in the West.

Catherine de' Medici *During her regency Catherine de' Medici virtually ruled France.*

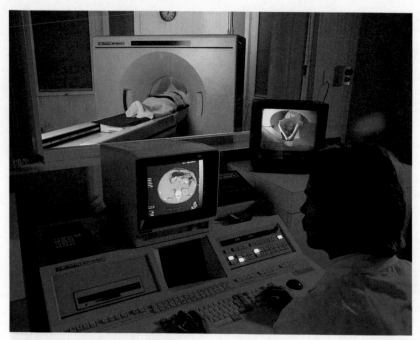

CAT scan *CAT scan in progress, showing the scanner and patient in the background and the radiographer working at the scanner's computer terminal.*

catheter a fine tube inserted into the body to introduce or remove fluids. The original catheter was the urinary one, passed by way of the urethra (which ducts urine away from the bladder). In modern practice, catheters can be inserted into blood vessels, either in the limbs or trunk, to provide blood samples and local pressure measurements, and to deliver drugs and/or nutrients directly into the bloodstream.

cathode the electrode towards which positive particles (cations) move within a device such as the cells of a battery, electrolytic cells, and diodes.

cathode-ray tube a form of vacuum tube in which a beam of electrons is produced and focused on to a fluorescent screen. It is an essential component of television receivers, computer visual display units, and oscilloscopes.

Catholic church the whole body of the Christian church, though usually applied to Roman Catholicism.

Catholic Emancipation acts passed in Britain 1780–1829 to relieve Catholics of restrictions imposed from the time of Henry VIII.

Catiline /ˈkætɪlaɪn/ (Lucius Sergius Catilina) c.108–62 BC. Roman politician. Twice failing to be elected to the consulship in 64/63 BC, he planned a military coup, but ◊Cicero exposed his conspiracy. He died at the head of the insurgents.

cation an ion carrying a positive charge. During electrolysis, cations in the electrolyte move to the cathode (negative electrode).

catkin in flowering plants (angiosperms), a pendulous inflorescence, bearing numerous small, usually unisexual flowers. The tiny flowers are stalkless and the petals and sepals are usually absent or much reduced in size. Many types of trees bear catkins, including willows, poplars, and birches. Most plants with catkins are wind-pollinated, so the male catkins produce large quantities of pollen. Some ◊gymnosperms also have catkin-like structives that produce pollen, for example, the swamp cypress *Taxodium*.

Catlin /ˈkætlɪn/ George 1796–1872. US painter and explorer. From the 1830s he made a series of visits to the Great Plains, painting landscapes and scenes of American Indian life.

He produced an exhibition of over 500 paintings with which he toured America and Europe. His style is factual, with close attention to detail. Many of his pictures are in the Smithsonian Institute, Washington DC.

Cato /ˈkeɪtəʊ/ Marcus Porcius 234–149 BC. Roman politician. Appointed censor (senior magistrate) in 184, he excluded from the Senate those who did not meet his high standards. He was so impressed by the power of ◊Carthage, on a visit in 157, that he ended every speech by saying 'Carthage must be destroyed.' His farming manual is the earliest surviving work in Latin prose.

Cato Street Conspiracy unsuccessful plot hatched in Cato Street, Edgware Road, London, to murder the Tory foreign secretary Castlereagh and his ministers on 20 Feb 1820. The leader, the Radical Arthur Thistlewood (1770–1820), who intended to set up a provisional government, was hanged with four others.

CAT scan or **CT scan** (computerized *a*xial *t*omography) a sophisticated method of diagnostic imaging. Quick and non-invasive, CAT scanning is an important aid to diagnosis, pinpointing disease without the need for exploratory surgery.

The CAT scanner passes a narrow fan of X-rays through successive slices of the suspect body part. These slices are picked up by crystal detectors in a scintillator, and converted electronically into cross-sectional images displayed on a viewing screen. Gradually, using views taken from any angle, a complete picture of the organ or tissue can be built up.

cats' cradle worldwide game played on the fingers with looped string, and linked with magic, illusion, and folk-tale.

cat's-eyes reflective studs used to mark the limits of traffic lanes, invented by the Englishman Percy Shaw as a road safety device in 1934.

A cat's-eye stud has two pairs of reflective prisms (the eyes) set in a rubber pad, which reflect the light of a vehicle's head-lamps back to the driver. When a vehicle goes over a stud, it moves down inside an outer rubber case; the surfaces of the prisms brush against the rubber and are thereby cleaned.

Catskills /ˈkætskɪlz/ US mountain range, mainly in SE New York state; the highest point is Slide Mt, 1,281 m/4,204 ft.

Catterick /ˈkætərɪk/ village near Richmond in N Yorkshire, England, where there is an important military camp.

cattle large, ruminant, even-toed, hoofed mammals of the family Bovidae, including wild species such as buffalo, bison, yak, gaur, gayal, and banteng, as well as domestic breeds.

Fermentation in the four-chambered stomach allows them to make good use of the grass which is normally the main part of the diet. There are two main types of domesticated cattle. The European breeds are variants of *Bos taurus* descended from the ◊aurochs, and the *zebu Bos indicus*, the humped cattle of India, which are useful in the tropics for their ability to withstand the heat and diseases to which European breeds succumb.

The old established beef breeds are mostly British in origin. The Hereford, for example, is the premier English breed ideally suited to rich lowland pastures, but will also thrive on poorer land such as that found in the US Midwest and the Argentine pampas. Of the Scottish beef breeds, the Aberdeen Angus, a black and hornless variety, produces high-quality meet through intensive feeding methods. Other breeds include the Devon, a hardy early-maturing type, and the Beef Shorthorn, now less important than it once was but still valued for an ability to produce good calves when crossed with less promising cattle. In recent years, more interest has been shown in other European breeds, their tendency to have less fat being more suited to modern tastes. Examples include the Charolais and the Limousin from central France, and the Simmental, originally from Switzerland.

For dairying purposes, a breed is found in many countries of the world is that variously known as the Friesian, Holstein, or Black and White. It can give enormous milk yields, up to 13,000 litres in a single lactation, and will produce calves ideally suited for intensive beef production. Other dairying types include the Jersey and Guernsey, whose milk has a high butterfat content, and the Ayrshire, a smaller breed capable of staying outside all the year round.

Catullus /kəˈtʌləs/ Gaius Valerius c.84–54 BC. Roman lyric poet, born in Verona of a well-to-do family. He moved in the literary and political society of Rome and wrote lyrics describing his unhappy love affair with Clodia, probably the wife of the consul Metellus, calling her Lesbia. His longer poems include two wedding-songs. Many of his poems are short verses to his friends.

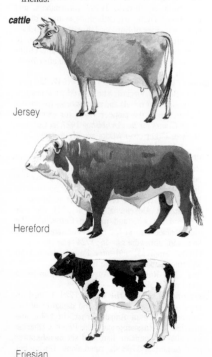

cattle

Jersey

Hereford

Friesian

Caucasoid or *Caucasian* former racial classification used for any of the light-skinned peoples; so named because the German anthropologist J F Blumenbach (1752–1840) theorized that they originated in the Caucasus.

Caucasus /'kɔːkəsəs/ series of mountain ranges between the Caspian and Black Seas, USSR; 1200 km/750 mi long. The highest is Elbruz, 5633 m/18,480 ft. Arabian thoroughbreds are raised at Tersk farm in the northern foothills.

Cauchy /'kəʊʃi/ Augustin Louis 1789–1857. French mathematician, noted for his rigorous methods of analysis. His prolific output included work on complex funtions, determinants and probability, and on the convergence of infinite series. In calculus he refined the concepts of the limit and the definite integral.

In 1843 he published a defence of academic freedom of thought which was instrumental in the abolition of the oath of allegiance soon after the fall of Louis Philippe in 1848.

caucus in the USA a closed meeting of regular party members, for example to choose a candidate for office. The term was originally used in Boston, Massachusetts, in the 18th century. In the UK it was first applied to the organization introduced by the Liberal politician Joseph Chamberlain in 1878 and is generally used to mean a local party committee.

cauda tail, or tail-like appendage; part of the *cauda equina*, a bundle of nerves at the bottom of the spinal cord in vertebrates.

cauliflower variety of cabbage *Brassica oleracea*, distinguished by its large flattened head of fleshy, aborted flowers. It is similar to broccoli but less hardy.

causality in philosophy, a consideration of the connection between cause and effect, usually referred to as the 'causal relationship'. If an event in the world is assumed to have a cause, two important questions arise: what is the relationship between cause and effect, and must it follow that every event is caused? The Scottish philosopher David Hume considered these questions to be in principle unanswerable.

Causley /'kɔːzli/ Charles Stanley 1917– . British poet, born in Launceston, Cornwall. He published his first volume *Hands to Dance* in 1951; his ballad 'Samuel Sweet' is particularly noteworthy.

caustic soda former name for *sodium hydroxide*, NaOH.

cauterization the use of special instruments to burn or fuse small areas of body tissue with a minimum bleeding. Tiny blood vessels are cauterized to minimize blood loss during surgery.

Cauthen /'kɔːθən/ Steve 1960– . US jockey. He has ridden in England since 1979 and has twice won the Derby, on Slip Anchor in 1985 and on Reference Point in 1987. He rode Affirmed to the US Triple Crown in 1978 at the age of 18 and won 487 races in 1977. He was UK champion jockey in 1984, 1985, and 1987.

Cauvery /'kɔːvəri/ or *Kaveri* river of S India, rising in the W Ghats and flowing 765 km/475 mi SE to meet the Bay of Bengal in a wide delta. A major source of hydroelectric power since 1902 when India's first hydropower plant was built on the river.

Cavaco Silva /kə'vækəʊ 'sɪlvə/ Anibal 1939– . Portuguese politician, finance minister 1980–81, and prime minister and Social Democratic Party (PSD) leader from 1985. Under his leadership Portugal joined the European Community (EC) 1985 and the Western European Union (WEU) 1988.

Born at Loule, he studied economics in Britain and the US, and was a university teacher and research director in the Bank of Portugal. In 1978, with the return of constitutional government, he was persuaded to enter politics. His government fell in 1987, but an election later that year gave him Portugal's first absolute majority since democracy was restored.

Cavafy /kə'vɑːfi/ Constantinos. Pen name of Konstantínos Pétrou 1863–1933. Greek poet. An Alexandrian, he threw light on the Greek past, recreating the classical period with zest. He published only one book of poetry, and remained almost unknown until translations appeared in 1952.

Cavalier horseman of noble birth, but in particular a supporter of Charles I in the English Civil War, typically with courtly dress and long hair (as distinct from a Roundhead); also a supporter of Charles II after the Restoration.

Cavalier poets poets of Charles II's court, including Thomas Carew, Robert Herrick, Richard Lovelace, and Sir John Suckling. They wrote witty, light-hearted love lyrics.

Cavalli /kə'væli/ (Pietro) Francesco 1602–1676. Italian composer, organist at St Mark's, Venice, and the first to make opera a popular entertainment with such works as *Xerxes* 1654, later performed in honour of Louis XIV's wedding in Paris. Twenty-seven of his operas survive.

Cavan /'kævən/ agricultural inland county of the Republic of Ireland, in the province of Ulster; area 1,890 sq km/730 sq mi; population (1986) 54,000.

The river Erne divides it into a narrow, mostly low-lying peninsula, 30 km/20 mi long, between Leitrim and Fermanagh, and an eastern section of wild and bare hill country. The soil is generally poor, and the climate moist and cold. The chief towns are Cavan, the capital, population about 3,000; Kilmore, seat of Roman Catholic and Protestant bishoprics; and Virginia.

cave a roofed-over cavity in the Earth's crust usually produced by the action of underground water or by waves on a seacoast. Caves of the former type commonly occur in areas underlain by limestone, such as Kentucky and many Balkan regions, but not in chalk country where the rocks are soluble in water. A *pothole* is a vertical hole in rock caused by water descending a crack and is thus open to the sky.

Cave animals often show loss of pigmentation or sight, and under isolation specialized species may develop. The scientific study of caves is called speleology. Notable caves include the Mammoth Cave in Kentucky, 6.4 km/4 mi long and 38 m/125 ft high; the Caverns of Adelsberg (Postumia) near Trieste, which extend for many miles; Carlsbad Cave, New Mexico, the largest in the USA; the Cheddar caves, England; Fingal's Cave, Scotland, renowned for its range of basalt columns; and Peak Cavern, England.

Cave /keɪv/ Edward 1691–1754. British printer, founder under the pseudonym Sylvanus Urban of *The Gentleman's Magazine* 1731–1914, the first periodical to be called a magazine. Dr Samuel ◊Johnson was an influential contributor 1738–44.

caveat emptor (Latin 'let the buyer beware') the buyer is responsible for checking the quality of goods purchased.

Cavendish, Spencer see ◊Hartington, Spencer Compton Cavendish.

cave canem (Latin) beware of the dog.

cavefish cave-dwelling fish, which may belong to one of several quite unrelated groups, independently adapted to life in underground waters. They have in common a tendency to blindness and atrophy of the eye, enhanced touch-sensitive organs in the skin, and loss of pigment.

The *Kentucky blind-fish Amblyopsis spelaea*, which lives underground in limestone caves, has eyes which are vestigial and beneath the skin, and a colourless body. The Mexican *cave characin* is a blind, colourless form of *Astyanax fasciatus* found in surface rivers of Mexico.

Cavell /'kævəl/ Edith Louisa 1865–1915. British matron of a Red Cross hospital in Brussels, Belgium, in World War I, who helped Allied soldiers escape to the Dutch frontier. She was court-martialled by the Germans and condemned to death. Her last words were: 'Patriotism is not enough. I must have no hatred or bitterness towards anyone.'

Cavendish family name of dukes of Devonshire; the family seat is at Chatsworth, Derbyshire.

Cavendish /'kævəndɪʃ/ Frederick Charles, Lord Cavendish 1836–1882. British administrator, second son of the 7th duke of Devonshire. He was appointed chief secretary to the lord-lieutenant of Ireland in 1882. On the evening of his arrival in Dublin he was murdered in Phoenix Park with Burke, the permanent Irish undersecretary, by members of the Irish Invincibles, a group of Irish Fenian extremists founded 1881.

Cavendish /'kævəndɪʃ/ Henry 1731–1810. British physicist. He discovered hydrogen, which he called 'inflammable air' 1766, and determined the compositions of water and of nitric acid.

A grandson of the 2nd Duke of Devonshire, he devoted his life to scientific pursuits, living in rigorous seclusion at Clapham Common, London. The ◊Cavendish experiment was a device of his to discover the mass and density of the Earth.

Cavendish /'kævəndɪʃ/ Thomas 1555–1592. English navigator, and commander of the third circumnavigation of the world. He sailed in July 1586, touched Brazil, sailed down the coast to Patagonia, passed through the Straits of Magellan, and returned to Britain via the Philippines, the Cape of Good Hope, and St Helena, reaching Plymouth after two years and 50 days.

Cavendish experiment measurement of the gravitational attraction between lead and gold spheres, which enabled Henry ◊Cavendish to calculate a mean value for the mass and density of Earth, using Newton's Law of Universal Gravitation.

Cavendish-Bentinck family name of Dukes of Portland.

cave temple example of rock architecture, such as Ajanta in western India; Alamira, near Santander, Spain.

caviar the salted roes of the sturgeon. Caviar is prepared by beating and straining the fish ovaries until the eggs are free from fats and then adding salt. The USSR and Iran are the main exporters of caviar.

cavitation the formation of cavities in fluids with loss of pressure at high velocities, in accordance with the ◊Bernoulli effect. This can result in vibration, noise, and damage to, for instance, propellers or other machine parts of hydraulic engines.

Cavite /kə'viːti/ town and port of the Philippine Republic; 13 km/8 mi S of Manila; population (1980) 88,000. It is the capital of Cavite province, Luzon. It was in Japanese hands Dec 1941–Feb 1945. After the Philippines achieved independence in 1946, the US Seventh Fleet continued to use the naval base.

Cavour As prime minister of Piedmont, Cavour was largely responsible for achieving the unification of Italy in 1861.

Cavour /kə'vuə/ Camillo Benso, Count 1810–1861. Italian nationalist politician. Editor of *Il ◊Risorgimento* from 1847. Prime minister of Piedmont 1852–59 and 1860–61, he enlisted the support of Britain and France for the concept of a united Italy achieved in 1861, having expelled the Austrians 1859 and assisted Garibaldi in liberating S Italy 1860.

Cavour was born in Turin, and served in the army in early life; he entered politics in 1847. From 1848 he sat in the Piedmontese parliament, and held cabinet posts 1850–52. As prime minister, he sought to secure French and British sympathy for the cause of Italian unity by sending Piedmontese troops to fight in the Crimean War. In 1858 he had a secret meeting with Napoleon III at Plombières, where they planned the war of 1859 against Austria, which resulted in the union of Lombardy with Piedmont. The central Italian states also joined the kingdom of Italy, although Savoy and Nice were to be ceded to France. With Cavour's approval Garibaldi overthrew the Neapolitan monarchy, but to prevent him from marching on Rome Cavour occupied part of the Papal States, which with Naples and Sicily were annexed to Italy.

cavy a type of short-tailed South American rodent, family Caviidae, of which the *guinea-pig Cavia porcellus* is an example. Wild cavies are greyish or brownish with rather coarse hair. They live in small groups in burrows, and have been kept for food since ancient times.

Cawnpore /,kɔ:n'pɔ:/ former spelling of ◊Kanpur, Indian city.

Caxton /'kækstən/ William *c.*1422–1491. First English printer. He learned the art of printing in Cologne, Germany 1471 and set up a press in Belgium, where he produced the first book printed in English, his own version of a French romance, *Recuyell of the Historyes of Troye* 1474. Returning to England in 1476 he established himself in London, where he produced the first book printed in England, *Dictes or Sayengis of the Philosophres* 1477.

Born in Kent, Caxton was apprenticed to a London cloth dealer 1438, and set up his own business in Bruges 1441–70; he became governor of the English merchants there, negotiating on their behalf with the dukes of Burgundy. In 1471 he went to Cologne, where he learned the art of printing, and then set up his own press in Bruges in partnership with Colard Mansion, a calligrapher. The books from Caxton's press in Westminster included editions of the poets Chaucer, Gower, and John Lydgate (*c.*1370–1449). He translated many texts from French and Latin and revised some English ones, such as Malory's *Morte d'Arthur*. Altogether he printed about 100 books.

Cayenne /keɪ'en/ capital and chief port of French Guiana, on Cayenne island at the mouth of the river Cayenne; population (1982) 38,135. It was founded in 1634, and used as a penal settlement from 1854 to 1946.

cayenne pepper condiment derived from the dried fruits of ◊*Capsicum*, a genus of plants of the family Solanaceae. It is wholly distinct in its origin from black or white pepper, which is derived from a different plant (*Piper nigrum*).

Cayley /'keɪli/ Arthur 1821–1895. British mathematician, who developed matrix algebra, used by ◊Heisenberg in his elucidation of quantum mechanics.

Cayley /'keɪli/ George 1773–1857. British aviation pioneer, inventor of the first piloted glider in 1853, and the caterpillar tractor.

Cayman Islands /'keɪmən/ British island group in the West Indies
area 260 sq km/100 sq mi
features comprises three low-lying islands, Grand Cayman, Cayman Brac, and Little Cayman
exports seawhip coral, shrimps; honey; jewellery
currency CI dollar
population (1988) 22,000

Cayman Islands

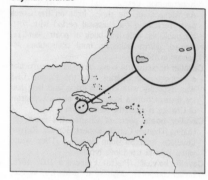

language English
government governor, executive council, and legislative assembly
GNP $10,900 per head of population.
history settled by military deserters in the 17th century, the islands became a pirate lair in the 18th century. Administered with Jamaica until 1962, when they became a separate colony, they are now a tourist resort, international financial centre, and tax haven.

CB abbreviation for *citizens' band* (radio).

CBI abbreviation for ◊*Confederation of British Industry*.

CC abbreviation for ◊*county council*; *cricket club*.

cc abbreviation for *cubic centimetre*; *carbon copy/copies*.

CD abbreviation for *Corps Diplomatique* (French 'Diplomatic Corps'); *compact disc*.

CD-ROM in computing, a storage device, consisting of a metal disc with a plastic coating, on which information is etched in the form of microscopic pits. A CD-ROM typically holds about 550 ◊megabytes of data. CD-ROMs cannot have information written on to them by the computer, but must be manufactured from a master.

They are used for distributing large quantities of text, such as dictionaries, encyclopedias, and technical manuals. The technology is similar to that of the audio compact disc.

CDU abbreviation for the centre-right Christian Democratic Union in the Federal Republic of Germany.

CE abbreviation for ◊*Church of England* (often *C of E*); Common Era (see under ◊calendar).

céad míle fáilte (Irish 'a hundred thousand welcomes') a conventional form of greeting.

Ceauşescu /tʃau'ʃesku/ Nicolae 1918–1989. Romanian politician, leader of Romanian Communist Party (RCP), in power 1965–89. He pursued a policy line independent of and critical of the USSR. He appointed family members, including his wife, to senior state and party posts, and governed in a personalized and increasingly repressive manner, zealously implementing schemes that impoverished the nation. He was overthrown in a bloody revolutionary coup Dec 1989 and executed, along with his wife Elena, on Christmas Day 1989.

Ceauşescu joined the underground RCP in 1933 and was imprisoned for antifascist activities 1936–38 and 1940–44. After World War II he was elected to the Grand National Assembly and was soon given ministerial posts. He was inducted into the party secretariat and Politburo in 1954–55. In 1965 Ceauşescu became leader of the RCP and from 1967 chair of the state council. He was elected president in 1974. Following his execution, the full extent of his repressive rule and personal extravagance became public.

Cebu /seɪ'bu:/ chief city and port of the island of Cebu in the Philippines; population (1980) 490,000; area 5,086 sq km/1,964 sq mi.

The oldest city of the Philippines, founded as San Miguel in 1565, it became the capital of the Spanish Philippines.

Ceauşescu Former Romanian communist leader, Nicolae Ceausescu. A neo-Stalinist, he held sway over the country from 1965 until his popular overthrow and execution in December 1989.

Cecil /'sesəl/ Henry Richard Amherst 1943– . Scottish-born racehorse trainer with stables at Warren Place, Newmarket. The most successful English trainer of all time in terms of prize money, he has been the top trainer eight times.

He was the first trainer to win over £1 million in a season (1985). He trained Slip Anchor and Reference Point to win the Epsom Derby.

Cecil /'sɪsəl/ Robert, 1st Earl of Salisbury 1563–1612. Secretary of state to Elizabeth I of England, succeeding his father, Lord Burghley; he was afterwards chief minister to James I, who created him earl of Salisbury 1605.

Cecilia /sə'si:liə/ Christian patron saint of music, martyred in Rome in the 2nd or 3rd century, who is said to have sung hymns while undergoing torture. Feast day 22 Nov.

CEDA (*Confederación Española de Derechas Autonomas*) a federation of right-wing parties under the leadership of José Maria Gil Robles founded during the Second Spanish Republic 1933 to provide a right-wing coalition in the Spanish Cortes. Supporting the Catholic and Monarchist causes, the federation was uncommitted as to the form of government.

cedar type of coniferous tree. The cedar of Lebanon *Cedrus libani* grows to a great height and age in the mountains of Syria and Asia Minor. Of the historic forests on Mount Lebanon itself, only a few groups of trees remain. Together with the Himalayan cedar *Cedrus deodara* and the Atlas cedar *Cedrus atlantica*, it has been introduced into England.

cedar

Cedar Rapids /'si:də 'ræpɪdz/ town in E Iowa, USA; population (1980) 110,243. Communications equipment is manufactured here.

Ceefax one of Britain's two ◊teletext systems (the other is Oracle), or 'magazines of the air', developed by the BBC and first broadcast in 1973. 'Ceefax' is a corruption of 'see facts'.

CEGB abbreviation for the former *Central Electricity Generating Board*.

celandine two plants belonging to different families, and resembling each other only in their bright yellow flowers. The greater celandine *Chelidonium majus* belongs to the Papaveraceae family, and is common in hedgerows. The lesser celandine *Ranunculus ficaria* is a member of the buttercup family, and is a familiar wayside and meadow plant.

Celebes /sə'li:bɪz/ English name for ◊Sulawesi, an island of Indonesia.

celeriac variety of garden celery with a turnip-like root. The root is the edible part, as the stems are small and bitter. It is a member of the family Umbelliferae.

celery plant *Apium graveolens* of the family Umbelliferae. It grows wild in ditches and salt-marshes, and has a coarse texture and acrid taste. Cultivated celery is grown under cover to make it less bitter.

celesta a keyboard glockenspiel producing sounds of disembodied purity. It was invented by Auguste Mustel 1886 and first used to effect by Tchaikovsky in *The Nutcracker* ballet music.

celestial mechanics the branch of astronomy that deals with the calculation of the orbits of celestial bodies, their gravitational attractions (such as those that produce Earth's tides), and also the orbits of artificial satellites and space probes. It is based on the laws of motion and gravity laid down by ◊Newton.

Celestial Police a group of astronomers in Germany 1800–15, who set out to discover a supposed missing planet thought to be orbiting the Sun between Mars and Jupiter, a region now known to be occupied by types of ◊asteroid. Although they

did not discover the first asteroid (found 1801), they discovered the second, Pallas (1802), third, Juno (1804), and fourth, Vesta(1807). The first asteroid was actually discovered by the Italian Giuseppe Piazzi at the Palmermo Observatory, Sicily, 1 Jan 1801.

celestial sphere the imaginary sphere surrounding the Earth, on which the celestial bodies seem to lie. The positions of bodies such as stars, planets and galaxies are specified by their coordinates on the celestial sphere. The equivalents of latitude and longitude on the celestial sphere are called ◊declination and ◊right ascension (which is measured in hours from 0 to 24). The *celestial poles* lie directly above the Earth's poles, and the *celestial equator* lies over the Earth's equator. The celestial sphere appears to rotate once around the Earth each day, actually a result of the rotation of the Earth on its axis.

celestine or *celestite* mineral consisting of strontium sulphate, SrSO$_4$, occurring as white or light blue crystals. It is the principal source of strontium.

Celestine is found in small quantities in Germany, Italy, and the US. In the UK it is found in Somerset.

celibacy a way of life involving voluntary abstinence from sexual intercourse. In some religions, such as Christianity and Buddhism, celibacy is a requirement for certain religious roles, such as the priesthood or a monastic life. Other religions, including Judaism, strongly discourage celibacy.

Céline /se'li:n/ Louis Ferdinand. Pen name of Louis Destouches 1884–1961. French novelist, whose writings (the first of which was *Voyage au bout de la nuit/Journey to the End of the Night* 1932) were controversial for their cynicism and misanthropy.

cell in biology, a discrete, membrane-bound portion of living matter, the smallest unit capable of an independent existence. All living organisms consist of one or more cells, with the exception of ◊viruses. Bacteria, protozoa and many other microorganisms consist of single cells, whereas

a human is made up of billions of cells. Essential features of a cell are the membrane, which encloses it and restricts the flow of substances in and out; the jellylike material within, often known as ◊protoplasm, the ◊ribosomes, which carry out protein synthesis, and the ◊DNA, which forms the hereditary material.

cell, electric in physics, apparatus in which chemical energy is converted into electrical energy; the popular name is 'battery', but this is actually a collection of cells in one unit. A *primary* electric cell cannot be replenished, whereas in a *secondary* cell, or accumulator, the action is reversible and the original condition can be restored by an electric current.

The first battery was made by Volta in 1800. Types of primary cells include the Daniell, Lalande, Leclanché, and so-called 'dry' cells; secondary cells include Planté, Faure, and Edison. Newer types include the Mallory (mercury depolarizer), which has a very stable discharge curve and can be made in very small units, for example for hearing aids, and the Venner accumulator, which can be made substantially solid for some purposes.

Cellini /tʃe'li:ni/ Benvenuto 1500–1571. Italian sculptor and goldsmith working in the Mannerist style; author of an arrogant autobiography (begun 1558). Among his works are a graceful bronze *Perseus* 1545–54 (Loggia dei Lanzi, Florence) and a magnificent gold salt cellar made for Francis I of France 1540–43 (Kunsthistorisches Museum, Vienna), topped by nude reclining figures.

Cellini was born in Florence and apprenticed to a goldsmith. In 1519 he went to Rome, and later worked for the papal mint, once being imprisoned on a charge of having embezzled pontifical jewels. He worked for a time in France at the court of Francis I, but finally returned to Florence in 1545.

cello short for *violoncello*, a member of the violin family, and fourth member of a string quartet. Much in demand as a solo instrument because of its exeptional range and brilliance of tone, its repertoire extends from Bach to Beethoven, Dvorak, and Elgar.

cellophane a transparent wrapping film made from wood ◊cellulose, widely used for packaging, first produced by Swiss chemist Jacques Edwin Brandenberger in 1908.

It is made from woodpulp, in much the same way that the artificial fibre ◊rayon is made: the pulp is dissolved in chemicals to form a viscose solution, which is then pumped through a long narrow slit into an acid bath where the emergent viscose stream turns into a film of pure cellulose, known as cellophane.

cellphone a telephone based on a cellular radio network.

cellular radio a system of radiotelephony for vehicles, also called the cellphone system, that uses an interconnected network of low-powered transmitters, with each transmitter serving a limited area, or cell, about 5 km/3 mi across. The transmitters are linked to the telephone system via a central computer, which switches a telephone call to the receiver vehicle's cell. The cellular system allows the use of the same set of frequencies with the minimum risk of interference. Nevertheless, in crowded city areas, cells can become overloaded. This has led to a move away from analogue transmissions to digital methods that allow more calls to be made within a limited frequency range.

cellulite fatty compound alleged by some dietitians to be produced in the body by liver disorder and to cause lumpy obesity. Medical opinion generally denies its existence.

cellulitis inflammation of body tissue, accompanied by swelling, redness, and pain.

celluloid transparent or translucent highly inflammable plastic material once used in photographic film, now replaced by non-inflammable cellulose acetate.

celestial sphere

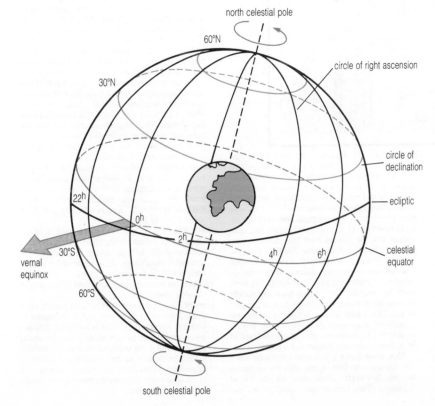

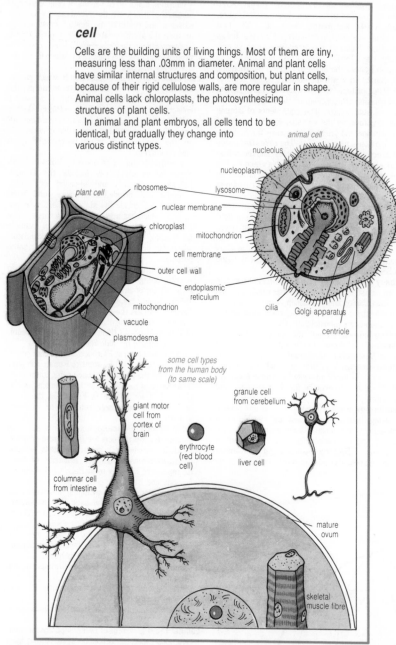

cell

Cells are the building units of living things. Most of them are tiny, measuring less than .03mm in diameter. Animal and plant cells have similar internal structures and composition, but plant cells, because of their rigid cellulose walls, are more regular in shape. Animal cells lack chloroplasts, the photosynthesizing structures of plant cells.

In animal and plant embryos, all cells tend to be identical, but gradually they change into various distinct types.

animal cell

nucleolus
nucleoplasm
lysosome
ribosomes
plant cell
nuclear membrane
chloroplast
mitochondrion
cell membrane
outer cell wall
endoplasmic reticulum
cilia
Golgi apparatus
mitochondrion
vacuole
centriole
plasmodesma

some cell types from the human body (to same scale)

granule cell from cerebellum
giant motor cell from cortex of brain
erythrocyte (red blood cell)
liver cell
columnar cell from intestine
mature ovum
skeletal muscle fibre

cell Drawing based on an electron microscope view of a lymphocyte, a type of white blood cell, about 0.01 mm across. These cells help defend the body against viruses and some bacteria.

were pioneers of iron working, reaching their peak in the period from the 5th century to the Roman conquest (the *La Tène* culture). They were known for their warring, feasting, and gold, bead, and enamel ornaments. Classical authors named the fair, tall people of N Europe Celts and only gradually distinguished them from Germanic peoples.

Celtic art a style of art that originated in about 500 BC, probably on the Rhine, and spread westwards to Gaul and the British Isles, and southwards to Italy and Turkey. Metalwork using curving incised lines and inlays of coloured enamel and coral survived at La Tène, a site at Lake Neuchâtel, Switzerland. Celtic manuscript illumination and sculpture from Ireland and Anglo-Saxon Britain of the 6th–8th centuries has intricate spiral and geometric ornament, as in *The Book of Kells* (Trinity College, Dublin) and the *Lindisfarne Gospels* (British Museum, London). Celtic burial goods from Vix, Burgundy, include a huge bronze krater, or vase-shaped bowl (Châtillon-sur-Seine, France).

Celtic languages a branch of the Indo-European family, divided into two groups: the *Brythonic* or *P-Celtic* (Welsh, Cornish, Breton, and Gaulish) and the *Goidelic* or *Q-Celtic* (Irish, Scottish, and Manx Gaelic). Celtic languages once stretched from the Black Sea to Britain, but have been in decline for centuries, limited to the so-called 'Celtic Fringe' of W Europe.

As their names suggest, a major distinction between the two groups is that where Brythonic has 'p' (as in Old Welsh *map*, 'son') Goidelic has a 'q' sound (as in Gaelic *mac*, 'son'). Gaulish is the long-extinct language of ancient Gaul, Cornish died out as a natural language in the late 18th century and Manx in 1974. All surviving Celtic languages have experienced official neglect in recent centuries and have suffered from emigration; currently, however, governments are more inclined than in the past to encourage their use.

Celtic League nationalist organization based in Ireland, aiming at an independent Celtic federation. It was founded 1975 with representatives from Alba (Scotland), Breizh (Brittany), Eire, Kernow (Cornwall), Cymru (Wales) and Ellan Vannin (Isle of Man).

Celtic Sea /'keltɪk/ name commonly used by workers in the oil industry in the 1970s for the sea area between Wales, Ireland, and SW England, to avoid nationalist significance. It is separated from the Irish Sea by St George's Channel.

cembalo an accompanying keyboard instrument in classical music.

cement a bonding agent used to unite particles in a single mass or to cause one surface to adhere to another. *Portland cement* is a powder obtained from burning together a mixture of lime (or chalk) and clay, and is the universal medium for building in brick or stone or for the production of concrete. In geology, a chemically precipitated material such as carbonate that occupies the interstices of clastic rocks is called cement.

cellulose a complex ◊carbohydrate composed of long chains of glucose units. It is the principal constituent of the cell wall of higher plants. Molecules of cellulose are organized into long, unbranched microfibrils which give support to the cell wall. Cellulose is the most abundant substance found in the plant kingdom.

cellulose nitrate an ◊ester made by the action of nitric acid and sulphuric acid on cellulose, and used to make lacquers and explosives ('gun cotton'). Celluloid is a form of cellulose nitrate.

Celsius /'selsɪəs/ a temperature scale in which one division or degree is taken as one hundredth part of the interval between the freezing point (0°C) and the boiling point (100°C) of water at standard atmospheric pressure.

The degree centigrade (°C) was officially renamed Celsius in 1948 to avoid confusion with the angular measure known as the centigrade (a hundredth of a grade). Named after the Swedish astronomer Anders Celsius (1701–44), who devised it in 1742, but in reverse (freezing point was 100°; boiling point 0°).

Celt /kelt/ (Greek *Keltoi*, term used for people of alpine Europe and Iberia) a people whose first known territory was in central Europe about 1200 BC, in the basin of the upper Danube, the Alps, and parts of France and S Germany. In the 6th century they spread into Spain and Portugal where they intermarried with Iberians and were known as Celtiberi. Over the next 300 years, they also spread into the British Isles (see ◊Britain, ancient), N Italy (sacking Rome 390 BC), Greece, and the Balkans, though they never established a united empire, probably because they were divided into numerous tribes. Their conquests were made by emigrant bands which made permanent settlements in these areas, as well as in the part of Asia Minor later known as Galatia. In the 1st century BC they were defeated by the Roman empire and by Germanic tribes, and confined to W Europe, especially Britain and Ireland.

They developed a transitional culture between the Bronze and Iron Ages, 9th–5th centuries BC (the *Hallstatt* culture, from its site SW of Salzburg). They farmed and raised cattle, and

The term cement covers a variety of materials, such as fluxes and pastes, and also bituminous products obtained from tar. In 1824 Joseph Aspdin, an English bricklayer, created and patented the first Portland cement, so named because its colour in the hardened state resembled that of Portland stone, a limestone used in building.

cenotaph (Greek 'empty tomb') monument to commemorate a person or persons not actually buried at the site, as in the Whitehall Cenotaph, London, designed by Edwin Lutyens to commemorate the dead of both World Wars.

Cenozoic or *Caenozoic* era of geological time that began 65 million years ago and is still in process. It is divided into the Tertiary and Quaternary periods. The Cenozoic marks the emergence of mammals as a dominant group, including humans, and the formation of the mountain chains of the Himalayas and the Alps.

censor in ancient Rome, either of two senior magistrates, high officials elected every five years to hold office for 18 months. Their responsibilities included public morality, a census of the citizens, and a revision of the Senatorial list.

censor in Freudian psychology, the psychic function that prevents unacceptable unconscious impulses from reaching the conscious mind, that is, so-called ◊repression.

censorship the suppression by authority of material considered immoral, heretical, subversive, libellous, damaging to state security, or otherwise offensive. It is generally more stringent under totalitarian or strongly religious regimes and in wartime.

The British government uses the ◊D-notice and the ◊Official Secrets Act to protect itself. Laws relating to obscenity, libel, and blasphemy act as a form of censorship. The media exercise a degree of self-censorship, for example in the film industry.

censorship, film control of the content and presentation of films. Film censorship dates back almost as far as the cinema. In Britain, the British Board of Film Censors (now the British Board of Film Classification), established 1912, gave each film a rating. Censorship did not begin in the USA until 1922, with the founding of the Motion Picture Producers and Distributors of America (see ◊Hays Office). In some countries, self-regulation of the industry has not been regarded as sufficient; in the Soviet Union, for example, state censorship has forbidden the treatment of certain issues.

In Britain, children were not prevented from seeing certain films until 1933, when the 'H' (for 'horrific') certificate was introduced.

census official count of the population of a country, originally for military call-up, later for assessment of social trends as other information regarding age, sex, and occupation of each individual was included. The first US census was taken 1790 and the first in Britain 1801. They may become unnecessary as databanks are built up on computers, and ceased in Denmark 1982.

centaur in Greek mythology, a creature half man and half horse. Centaurs were supposed to live in Thessaly, and be wild and lawless; the mentor of Hercules, Chiron, was an exception.

The earliest representation of centaurs (about 1800–1000 BC) were excavated near Famagusta in 1962, and are two-headed. Some female representations are also known.

Centaurus large bright constellation of the southern hemisphere, represented as a centaur. It contains the closest star to the Sun, Proxima Centauri. Omega Centauri, the largest and brightest globular cluster of stars in the sky, is 16,000 light years away. Centaurus A, a peculiar galaxy 15 million light years away, is a strong source of radio waves and X-rays.

CentCom abbreviation for US ◊*Central Command*, a military strike force.

centigrade common name for the ◊Celsius temperature scale.

Central African Republic
(République centrafricaine)

area 622,436 sq km/240,260 sq mi
capital Bangui
physical most of the country is on a plateau, with rivers flowing N and S. The N is dry and there is rainforest in the SW
head of state and government André Kolingba from 1981
political system one-party military republic
political parties Central African Democratic Assembly (RDC), nationalist
exports diamonds, uranium, coffee, cotton, timber
currency CFA franc (485.00 = £1 Feb 1990)
population (1988) 2,860,000; annual growth rate 2.3%

centipede jointed-legged animal of the group Chilopoda, members of which have a distinct head and a single pair of long antennae. Their bodies are composed of segments (which may number nearly 200), each of similar form and bearing a single pair of legs. Most are small, but the tropical *Scolopendra gigantea* may reach 30 cm/1 ft in length. **Millipedes**, class Diplopoda, have a lesser number of segments (up to 100), but have two pairs of legs on each.

Nocturnal, frequently blind, and all carnivorous, they eat animal food usually when rotten, live in moist, dark places, and protect themselves by a poisonous secretion. They have a pair of poison claws, and strong jaws with poison fangs. The bite of some tropical species is dangerous to humans. Several species live in Britain, *Lithobius forficatus* being the most common.

CENTO abbreviation for ◊*Central Treaty Organization*.

Central African Republic /'sentrəl 'æfrɪkən rɪ'pʌblɪk/ landlocked country in Central Africa, bordered NE and E by the Sudan, S by Zaïre and the Congo, W by Cameroon, and NW by Chad.

government After a coup in Sept 1981, the constitution of Feb the same year was suspended and all executive and legislative powers placed in the hands of a Military Commitee for National Recovery (CMRN). Four years later CMRN was dissolved and a new 22-member council of ministers, composed of both military and civilian members, was established. The president is head of both state and government and presides over the council of ministers. All political activity has been banned since the coup but the main opposition groups, although passive, still exist. They are the Patriotic Front Ubangi Workers' Party (FPO-PT), the Central African Movement for National Liberation (MCLN), and the Movement for the Liberation of the Central African People (MPLC). A new constitution was approved by referendum 1986, providing for a 52-member national assembly elected for a five-year term at the summons of the president. Despite this manifesto, however, the country remains under military rule.

life expectancy men 41, women 45
language Sangho, French (both official)
religion animist over 50%; Christian 35%, both Catholic and Protestant; Muslim 10%
literacy 53% male/29% female (1985 est)
GNP $690 million (1983); $310 per head of population
chronology
1960 Central African Republic achieved independence from France with David Dacko elected president.
1962 The republic made a one-party state.
1965 Dacko ousted in a military coup led by Col Bokassa.
1966 Constitution rescinded and national assembly dissolved.
1972 Bokassa declared himself president for life.
1976 Bokassa made himself emperor of the Central African Empire.
1979 Bokassa deposed by Dacko following violent repressive measures by the self-styled emperor, who went into exile.
1981 Dacko deposed in a bloodless coup, led by Gen André Kolingba, and a military government established.
1983 Clandestine opposition movement formed.
1984 Amnesty for all political party leaders announced.
1985 New constitution introduced, with some civilians in the government.
1986 Formal trial of Bokassa started. Kolingba re-elected.
1988 Bokassa found guilty and received death sentence, later commuted to life imprisonment.

history A French colony from the late 19th century, the territory of Ubangi-Shari became self-governing within French Equatorial Africa in 1958 and two years later achieved full independence. Barthélémy Boganda, who had founded the Movement for the Social Evolution of Black Africa (MESAN), had been a leading figure in the campaign for independence and became the country's first prime minister. A year before full independence he was killed in an air crash and was succeeded by his nephew, David Dacko, who became president in 1960, and in 1962 established a one-party state, with MESAN as the only political organization. Dacko was overthrown in a military coup in Dec 1965 and the commander-in-chief of the army, Colonel Jean-Bédel Bokassa, assumed power.

Bokassa annulled the constitution and made himself president-for-life in 1972, and marshal of the Republic in 1974. An authoritarian regime was established and in 1976 ex-president Dacko was recalled to be the president's personal adviser. At the end of that year the republic was restyled the Central African Empire (CAE) and in 1977 Bokassa was crowned emperor at a lavish ceremony his country could ill afford. His rule became increasingly dictatorial and idiosyncratic, leading to revolts by students and, in Apr 1979, by school children who objected to the compulsory wearing of school uniforms, made by a company owned by the Bokassa family. Many of the children were imprisoned and it is estimated that at least 100 were killed, with the emperor allegedly personally involved.

In Sept 1979, while Bokassa was in Libya, Dacko ousted him in a bloodless coup, backed by France. The country became a republic again, with Dacko as president. He initially retained a number of Bokassa's former ministers but, following student unrest, they were dropped and in Feb 1981 a new constitution was adopted, with an elected national assembly. Dacko was elected president for a six-year term in Mar but opposition to him grew and in Sept 1981 he was deposed in another bloodless coup, led by the armed forces' chief-of-staff, General André Kolingba.

The constitution and all political organizations were suspended, and a military government installed. Undercover opposition to the Kolingba regime continued, with some French support, but relations with France were improved by an unofficial visit by President Mitterrand in Oct 1982.

By 1984 there was evidence of a gradual return to constitutional government. The leaders of the banned political parties were granted an amnesty and at the end of the year the French president paid a state visit. In Jan 1985 proposals for a new constitution were announced and in Sept civilians were included into Kolingba's administration.

Central America /'sentrəl ə'merɪkə/ the part of the Americas that links Mexico with the isthmus of Panama, comprising Belize, Costa Rica, El Salvador, Guatemala, Honduras, Nicaragua, and Panama.

It is also an isthmus, crossed by mountains that form part of the *Cordilleras*. Much of Central America formed part of the Maya civilization. Spanish settlers married indigenous women, and the area remained out of the mainstream of Spanish Empire history. When the Spanish Empire collapsed in the early 1800s, the area formed the Central American Federation, with a constitution based on that of the USA. Demand for cash crops (bananas, coffee, cotton), especially from the USA, created a strong landowning class controlling a serflike peasantry by military means. There has been US military intervention in the area, for example in Nicaragua, where the dynasty of Gen Anastasio Somoza was founded. US president Carter reversed support for such regimes, but in the 1980s, the Reagan and Bush administrations again favoured military and financial aid to right-wing political groups, including the ◊Contras in Nicaragua.

Central American Common Market ODECA (*Organización de Estados Centro-americanos*), established in 1960 by El Salvador, Guatemala, Honduras (seceded 1970), and Nicaragua; Costa Rica joined in 1962.

Central Command, US a military strike force consisting of units from the US army, navy, and air force, which operates in the Middle East and North Africa. Headquarters in Fort McDill, Florida. It was established 1979, following the Iranian hostage crisis and the Soviet invasion of Afghanistan, and was known as the Rapid Deployment Force until 1983.

Central Criminal Court in the UK, Crown Court in the City of London, able to try all treasons and serious offences committed in the City or Greater London. First established 1834, it is popularly known as the Old Bailey after part of the medieval defences of London; the present building is on the site of Newgate Prison.

central dogma in genetics and evolution, the fundamental belief that ◊genes can affect the nature of the physical body, but that changes in the body (for example, through use or accident) cannot be translated into changes in the genes.

central heating a system of heating from a central source, typically of a house, as opposed to heating each room individually with a separate fire. The most common type of central heating used in British houses is the hot-water system. Water is heated in a furnace burning oil, gas or solid fuel, and is then pumped through radiators in each room. The level of temperature can be selected by adjusting a ◊thermostat.

Central heating has its origins in the ◊hypocaust heating system introduced by the Romans nearly 2,000 years ago. Central heating systems are usually switched on and off by a time switch. Another kind of central heating system uses hot air, which is pumped through ducts to grills in the rooms. Underfloor heating is used in some houses, the heat coming from electric elements buried in the floor. It uses cheaper 'off-peak' electricity, as does the heating system using night-storage radiators.

Central Intelligence Agency (CIA) US intelligence organization established 1947 by President

central nervous system

Truman. It has actively intervened overseas, generally to undermine left-wing regimes or to protect US financial interests, for example in Zaïre (when it was still the Congo) and Nicaragua. William Webster became director 1987. From 1980 all covert activity by the CIA has by law to be reported to Congress, preferably beforehand, and must be authorized by the president.

Developed from the wartime Office of Strategic Services and set up on the lines of the British Secret Service, the CIA was intended solely for use overseas in the Cold War. It was involved in the restoration of the Shah of Iran 1953; South Vietnam (during the Vietnam War); Chile (the coup against President Allende); Cuba (the ◊Bay of Pigs). On the domestic front, it was illegally involved in the ◊Watergate political scandal and in the 1970s lost public confidence when US influence collapsed in Iran, Afghanistan, Nicaragua, Yemen, and elsewhere. Past directors include William Casey, Richard ◊Helms, and George ◊Bush. Its domestic counterpart is the Federal Bureau of Investigation.

Central Mount Stuart /'stjuːət/ flat-topped mountain 844 m/2,770 ft high, at approximately the central point of Australia. It was originally named in 1860 by explorer J McDouall Stuart after another explorer, Charles Sturt – Central Mount Sturt—but later became known by his own name.

central nervous system the part of the nervous system with a concentration of ◊nerve cells which coordinates various body functions. In ◊vertebrates, the central nervous system consists of a brain and a dorsal nerve cord (the spinal cord) within the spinal column. In worms, insects, and crustaceans, it consists of two central nerve cords with concentrations of nerve cells, known as ◊ganglia in each segment, and a small brain in the head.

Some simple invertebrates, such as sponges and jellyfish, have no central nervous system but a simple network of nerve cells, called a *nerve net*.

Central Powers originally the signatories of the ◊Triple Alliance 1882; Germany, Austria and Hungary. During the first world

war, Italy remained neutral before joining the ◊Allies.

Central Provinces and Berar former British province of India, now part of ◊Madhya Pradesh.

Central Region region of Scotland, formed 1975 from the counties of Stirling, S Perth, and W Lothian
area 2,600 sq km/1,004 sq mi
towns administrative headquarters Stirling; Falkirk, Alloa, Grangemouth
features Stirling Castle; field of Bannockburn; Loch Lomond; the Trossachs
products agriculture; industries including brewing and distilling, engineering, electronics
population (1987) 272,000
famous people Rob Roy Macgregor.

Central Treaty Organization (CENTO) military alliance which replaced the ◊Baghdad Pact 1959; it collapsed when the withdrawal of Iran, Pakistan, and Turkey 1979 left the UK as the only member.

Centre /sɒntr/ region of N central France; area 39,200 sq km/15,131 sq mi; population (1986) 2,324,000. It includes the departments of Cher, Eure-et-Loire, Indre, Indre-et-Loire, Loire-et-Cher, and Loiret. Its capital is Orléans.

Centre, the /'sentə/ region of central Australia, including the tourist area between the Musgrave and MacDonnell ranges which contains Ayers Rock and Lake Amadeus.

centre of gravity the point in an object about which its weight is evenly balanced. In a uniform gravitational field, this is the same as the ◊centre of mass.

centre of mass or *centre of gravity* the point in or near an object from which its total weight appears to originate and can be assumed to act. A symmetrical homogeneous object such as a sphere or cube has its centre of mass at its physical centre; a hollow shape (such as a cup) may have its centre of mass in space inside the hollow.

For an object to be in stable equilibrium, a perpendicular line down through its centre of mass runs within the boundaries of its base; if tilted until this line falls outside the base, the object becomes unstable and topples over.

Centre Party (German *Zentrumspartei*) German political party established 1871 to protect Catholic interests. Although alienated by Chancellor Bismarck's ◊*Kulturkampf* 1873–78, in the following years the *Zentrum* became an essential component in the government of imperial Germany. The party continued to play an important part in the politics of Weimar Germany before being barred by Hitler in the summer of 1933.

centrifugal force a useful (but unreal) concept in physics. It may be regarded as a force that acts radially outwards from a spinning or orbiting object, thus balancing the ◊centripetal force. For an object of mass m moving with a velocity v in a

Central Scotland

circle of radius *r*, the centrifugal force *F* equals mv/r (outwards).

centrifuge apparatus for rotating containers at high speeds. One use is for separating mixtures of substances of different densities.

The mixtures are placed in the containers and the rotation sets up centrifugal forces, causing them to separate according to their densities. A common example is the separation of the lighter cream from the heavier milk in this way. The ultracentrifuge is a very high-speed centrifuge, used for separating ◊colloids, and in biochemistry, and may operate at several million revolutions per minute. Large centrifuges are used for physiological research, for example, in astronaut training where bodily response is tested to many times the normal gravitational force.

centriole a structure found in the ◊cells of animals that plays an important role in the processes of ◊meiosis and ◊mitosis (cell division).

centripetal force force that acts radially inwards on an object moving in a curved path. For example, with a weight whirled in a circle at the end of a length of string, the centripetal force is the tension in the string. For an object of mass *m* moving with a velocity *v* in a circle of radius *r*, the centripetal force *F* equals mv/r (inwards). The reaction to this force is the ◊centrifugal force.

centromere part of the ◊chromosome where there are no ◊genes. Under the microscope, it usually appears as a constriction in the strand of the chromosome, and is the point at which the spindle fibres are attached during ◊meiosis and ◊mitosis (cell division).

Cephalonia /ˌsefəˈləʊniə/ former name of ◊Kefallinia, largest of the Ionian islands, off the W coast of Greece.

cephalopod type of predatory marine mollusc with the mouth and head surrounded by tentacles. They are the most intelligent, the fastest-moving, and the largest of all animals without backbones, and there are remarkable luminescent forms which swim or drift at great depths. Cephalopods have the most highly developed nervous and sensory systems of all invertebrates, the eye in some paralleling closely that found in vertebrates. Examples include octopus, squid, and cuttlefish. Shells are rudimentary or absent in most cephalopods.

Typically they move by swimming with the mantle (fold of outer skin) aided by the arms, but can squirt water out of the siphon (funnel) to propel themselves backwards by jet propulsion. They grow very rapidly and may be mature in a year. The female common octopus lays 150,000 eggs after copulation, and stays to brood them for as long as six weeks. After they hatch the female dies, and, although reproductive habits of many cephalopods are not known, it is thought that dying after spawning may be typical.

cephalosporin class of broad-spectrum antibiotics. The first one was extracted from sewage-contaminated water, and other naturally-occurring ones have been isolated from moulds taken from soil samples. Synthetic cephalosporins can be designed to be effective against a particular ◊pathogen.

Cepheid variable a yellow supergiant star that varies regularly in brightness every few days or weeks as a result of pulsations. The time that a Cepheid variable takes to pulsate is directly related to its average brightness; the longer the pulsation period, the brighter the star.

This relationship, the *period luminosity law* (discovered by ◊Leavitt), allows astronomers to use Cepheid variables as 'standard candles' to measure distances in our galaxy and to nearby galaxies. They are named after their prototype, Delta Cephei, whose light variations were noted 1784 by English astronomer John Goodricke.

Cepheus constellation of the north polar region, representing King Cepheus of Greek mythology, husband of Cassiopeia and father of Andromeda. It contains the Garnet Star, Mu Cephei, a red

supergiant of variable brightness that is one of the reddest-coloured stars known, and Delta Cephei, prototype of the ◊Cepheid variables.

Ceram /sɔˈræm/ or *Seram* Indonesian island, in the Moluccas; area 17,142 sq km/6,621 sq mi. Chief town is Ambon.

ceramic non-metallic mineral (clay) used to form articles that are then fired at high temperatures. Ceramics are divided into heavy clay products (bricks, roof tiles, drainpipes, sanitary ware), refractories or high-temperature materials (linings for furnaces used to manufacture steel, fuel elements in nuclear reactors), and ◊pottery, which uses china clay, ball clay, china stone, and flint. Super-ceramics, such as silicon carbide, are lighter, stronger, and more heat-resistant than steel for use in motor and aircraft engines and have to be cast to shape since they are too hard to machine.

Cerberus /ˈsɜːbərəs/ in Greek mythology, the three-headed dog guarding the entrance to ◊Hades, the underworld.

cereal grass grown for its edible starch seeds. The term refers primarily to barley and wheat, but may also refer to oats, maize, rye, millet, and rice. They store easily, and contain about 75% carbohydrate and 10% protein. In 1984, world production exceeded 1.8 billion tonnes. Between 1975–85, cereal yields in Britain doubled, and now commonly exceed six tonnes per hectare. If all the world's cereal crop was consumed directly by humans, everyone could obtain adequate protein and carbohydrate; however, a large proportion of cereal production, especially in affluent nations, is used as animal feed to boost the production of meat, milk, butter, and eggs.

cerebellum part of the brain of ◊vertebrate animals which controls muscular movements, balance, and coordination. It is relatively small in lower animals such as newts and lizards, but large in birds since flight demands precise coordination. The human cerebellum is also well developed, because of the need for balance when walking or running, and for coordinated hand movements.

cerebral pertaining to that part of the brain known as the cerebral hemispheres, concerned with higher brain functions.

cerebral haemorrhage or *apoplectic fit* a form of stroke in which a blood vessel bursts in the brain, caused by factors such as high blood pressure combined with hardening of the arteries, or chronic poisoning with lead or alcohol. It may cause death, or damage parts of the brain and lead to paralysis or mental impairment. The effects are usually long-term. It is one form of stroke.

cerebral hemisphere one of the two halves of the ◊cerebrum.

cerebral palsy abnormality of the brain caused by oxygen deprivation before birth, injury during birth, haemorrhage, meningitis, viral infection, or faulty development. It is characterized by muscle spasm, weakness, lack of coordination, and impaired movement.

cerebrum part of the vertebrate ◊brain, formed from two paired cerebral hemispheres. In birds and mammals, it is the largest part of the brain. It is covered with an infolded layer of grey matter, the cerebral cortex, which integrates brain function. The cerebrum coordinates the senses, and is responsible for learning and other higher mental faculties.

Ceres /ˈsɪəriːz/ the largest asteroid, 1,020 km/634 mi in diameter, and the first to be discovered (by Giuseppe Piazzi 1801). Ceres is a rock that orbits the Sun every 4.6 years at an average distance of 420 million km/260 million mi. Its mass is about one-sixtieth that of the Moon.

Ceres /ˈsɪəriːz/ in Roman mythology, the goddess of agriculture; see ◊Demeter.

cerium chemical element, symbol Ce, atomic number 58. It is a metal in the ◊lanthanide series, and is used as a sparking component in lighter flints.

cermet a heat-resistant material containing ceramics and metal, widely used in jet engines. Cermets behave much like metals but have the great heat resistance of ceramics. Tungsten carbide, molybdenum boride, and aluminium oxide are among the ceramics used; iron, cobalt, nickel, and chromium are among the metals.

CERN nuclear research organization founded 1954 as a cooperative enterprise among European governments. It has laboratories at Meyrin, near Geneva, Switzerland. It was originally known as the *Conseil Européen pour la Recherche Nucléaire*, but subsequently renamed *Organisation Européene pour la Recherche Nucléaire*, although still familiarly known as CERN.

In 1965, the original laboratory was doubled in size by extension across the border from Switzerland into France. The world's largest particle ◊accelerator, the ◊Large Electron Positron Collider (LEP) is at CERN.

Cernăuţi /ˌtʃeənəˈuts/ Romanian form of ◊Chernovtsy.

Cervantes /sɜːˈvæntiːz/ Saavedra, Miguel de 1547–1616. Spanish novelist, playwright, and poet, whose masterpiece, ◊Don Quixote (in full *El ingenioso hidalgo Don Quixote de la Mancha*) was published 1605. In 1613, his *Novelas Exemplares/Exemplary Novels* appeared, followed by *Viaje del Parnaso/The Voyage to Parnassus* 1614. A spurious second part of *Don Quixote* prompted Cervantes to bring out his own authentic second part in 1615, often considered superior to the first in construction and characterization.

Born at Alcalá de Henares, he entered the army in Italy, and was wounded in the battle of Lepanto 1571. While on his way back to Spain 1575, he was captured by Barbary pirates and was taken to Algiers, where he became a slave until ransomed 1580. Returning to Spain, he wrote several plays, and in 1585 his pastoral romance *Galatea* was printed. He was employed in Seville 1587 provisioning the Armada. While working as a tax collector, he was imprisoned more than once for deficiencies in his accounts. He sank into poverty, and little is known of him until 1605 when he published *Don Quixote*. It immediately achieved great success and was soon translated into English and French.

cervical cancer ◊cancer of the cervix (the neck of the womb).

cervical smear removal of a small sample of tissue from the cervix to screen for changes implying a likelihood of cancer. The procedure is also known as the 'Pap' test after its originator, George Papanicolau.

cervix literally the neck, but commonly used as an abbreviation for *cervix uteri*: the neck of the womb.

César /seˈzɑː/ adopted name of César Baldaccini 1921–. French sculptor who uses iron and scrap metal and, in the 1960s, crushed car bodies. His subjects are imaginary insects and animals.

České Budějovice /ˈtʃeskeɪ ˈbuːdʒɪəʊˌviːtseɪ/ (German *Budweis*) town in Czechoslovakia, on the river Vltava; population (1984) 92,800. It is a commercial and industrial centre for S Bohemia, producing beer, timber and metal products.

c'est la vie (French) that's life.

CET abbreviation for *Central European Time*.

Cetewayo /ketʃˈwaɪəʊ/ (Cetshwayo) c. 1829–1884. King of Zululand, S Africa 1873–83, whose rule was threatened by British annexation of the Transvaal 1877. Although he defeated the British at Isandhlwana 1879, he was later that year defeated by them at Ulundi. Restored to his throne 1883, he was then expelled by his subjects.

Cetinje /ˈtsetiːnjeɪ/ town in Montenegro, Yugoslavia, 19 km/12 mi SE of Kotor; population (1981) 20,213. Founded 1484 by Ivan the Black, it was capital of Montenegro until 1918. It has a palace built by Nicholas, the last king of Montenegro.

Cetus (latin 'whole') constellation straddling the celestial equator (see ◊celestial sphere), representing the whale. Its brightest star is Diphda (Beta

Cézanne Mountains in Provence *(c.*1886) *National Gallery, London.*

Ceti). Cetus contains the long-period variable star ♢Mira and ♢Tau Ceti, one of the nearest stars visible with the naked eye.

Ceuta /'sju:tə/ Spanish seaport and military base in Morocco, Spanish N Africa; 27 km/17 mi S of Gibraltar and overlooking the Mediterranean approaches to the Straits of Gibraltar; area 18 sq km/7 sq mi; population (1986) 71,000. It trades in tobacco and petrol products.

Cevennes /se'ven/ collective name given to a series of mountain ranges on the southern, south eastern and eastern borders of the Central Plateau of France. The highest peak is Mt Mézenc 1,754 m/5,755 ft.

Ceylon /sɪ'lɒn/ former name of ♢Sri Lanka.

Cézanne /seɪ'zæn/ Paul 1839–1906. French Post-Impressionist painter, a leading figure in the development of modern art. He broke away from the Impressionists' spontaneous vision to develop a style that captured not only light and life, but the structure of natural forms, in landscapes, still lifes, portraits, and his series of bathers.

He was born in Aix-en-Provence, where he studied, and was a friend of the novelist Emile Zola. In 1872 Cézanne met Pissarro and settled near him in Pontoise, outside Paris, but soon abandoned Impressionism. His series of paintings of Mont Sainte-Victoire in Provence from the 1880s into the 1900s show an increasing fragmentation of the painting's surface and a movement towards abstraction, with layers of colour and square brushstrokes achieving monumental solidity. He was greatly revered by early abstract painters, notably Picasso and Braque.

cf. abbreviation for *confer* (Latin 'compare').

CFC abbreviation for ♢*chlorofluorocarbon.*

CFE abbreviation for ***Conventional Forces in Europe.*** Talks began in Vienna in Mar 1989 designed to reduce these non-nuclear forces (American, Soviet, French, British, and German) in Europe.

c. g. s. system system of units based on the centimetre, gram, and second, as units of length, mass, and time. It has been replaced for scientific work by the ♢SI system to avoid inconsistencies in definition of the thermal calorie and electrical quantities.

Chablis/'ʃæbli:/ town in the Yonne département of central France, famous for white burgundy wine of the same name.

Chabrier /'ʃæbrieɪ/ (Alexis) Emmanuel 1841–1894. French composer who wrote *España* 1883, an orchestral rhapsody, and the light opera *Le Roi malgré lui/King Against His Will* 1887. His orchestration inspired Debussy and Ravel.

Chabrol /ʃæ'brɒl/ Claude 1930– . French film director. Originally a critic, he was one of the French 'new wave' directors. His works of murder and suspense, which owe much to Hitchcock, include *Les Biches/The Girlfriends* 1968; *Le Boucher/The Butcher* 1970; *Cop au Vin* 1984.

chacma a type of ♢baboon.

Chaco /'tʃɑ:kəʊ/ province of Argentina; area 99,633 sq km/38,458 sq mi; population (1980) 701,400. Its capital is Resistencia, in the SE. The chief crop is cotton, and there is forestry.

Chad
Republic of *(République du Tchad)*

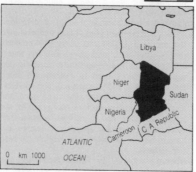

area 1,284,000 sq km/495,624 sq mi
capital N'djamena
physical savanna and part of Sahara Desert in the N; rivers in the S flow N to Lake Chad in the marshy E
head of state and government Hissène Habré from 1982
political system authoritarian nationalism
political parties National Union for Independence (UNIR), nationalist
exports cotton, meat, livestock, hides, skins, bauxite, uranium, gold, oil
currency CFA franc (485.00 = £1 Feb 1990)
population (1987) 5,241,000; annual growth rate 2.3%
life expectancy men 41, women 45
language French (official), Arabic
religion Muslim (north); Christian, animist (south)
literacy 40% male/11% female (1985 est)

GDP $360 million (1984); $88 per head of population
chronology
1960 Independence from France achieved, with François Tombalbaye as president.
1963 Violent opposition in the Muslim north, led by the Chadian National Liberation Front (Frolinat), backed by Libya.
1968 Revolt quelled with French help.
1975 Tombalbaye killed in military coup led by Felix Malloum. Frolinat continued its resistance.
1978 Malloum brought former Frolinat leader Hissène Habré into his government but they were unable to work together.
1979 Malloum forced to leave the country. An interim government was set up under Gen Goukouni. Habré continued his opposition with his Army of the North (FAN).
1981 Habré now in control of half the country, forcing Goukouni to flee to Cameroon and then Algeria, where, with Libyan support, he set up a government in exile.
1983 Habré's regime recognized by the Organization for African Unity (OAU) but in the north Goukouni's supporters, with Libyan help, fought on. A ceasefire was agreed, dividing the country into two halves either side of latitude 16° N.
1984 Libya and France agreed a withdrawal of forces.
1985 Fighting between Libyan-backed and French-backed forces intensified.
1987 Chad, France, and Libya agree on ceasefire proposed by OAU.
1988 Full diplomatic relations with Libya restored.
1989 Libyan troop movements reported on border. Habré met Col Khaddhafi. In Dec Habré re-elected and a new constitution announced.

It includes many lakes, swamps, and forests, producing timber and quebracho (a type of wood used in tanning). Until 1951, it was a territory, part of Gran Chaco, a great zone, mostly level, stretching into Paraguay and Bolivia. The north of Gran Chaco was the scene of the Bolivia-Paraguay border dispute 1932–35, settled by arbitration 1938.

Chaco War /'tʃɑ:kəʊ/ war between Bolivia and Paraguay 1932–35 over boundaries in the N Gran Chaco, settled by arbitration 1938.

chacun à son goût (French) each to their own taste.

Chad /tʃæd/ landlocked country in central N Africa, bounded to the north by Libya, to the east by Sudan, to the south by the Central African Republic, and to the west by Cameroon, Nigeria, and Niger.

government The 1982 provisional constitution provides for a president who appoints and leads a council of ministers which exercises executive and legislative power. In 1984 a new regrouping, the National Union for Independence (UNIR), was undertaken in an attempt to consolidate the president's position, but a number of opposition groups exist.

history Called Kanem when settled by Arabs in the 7th–13th centuries, the area later became known as Bornu and in the 19th century was conquered by Sudan. From 1913 a province of French Equatorial Africa, Chad became an autonomous state within the French Community in 1958, with François Tombalbaye as prime minister.

Full independence was achieved in 1960 and Tombalbaye became president. He soon faced disagreements between the Arabs of the north, who saw Libya as an ally, and the black African Christians of the south, who felt more sympathy for Nigeria. In the north the Chadian National Liberation Front (Frolinat) revolted against the government. In 1975 Tombalbaye was killed in

a coup led by former army chief-of-staff, Félix Malloum, who became president of a supreme military council and appealed for national unity, but Frolinat continued its opposition, supported by Libya, which held a strip of land in the north, believed to contain uranium.

By 1978 Frolinat, led by Gen Goukouni Oueddi, had expanded its territory but was halted with French aid. Malloum tried to reach a settlement by making former Frolinat leader, Hissène Habré, prime minister, but disagreements developed between them.

In 1979 fighting broke out again between government and Frolinat forces and Malloum fled the country. Talks resulted in the formation of a provisional government (GUNT), with Goukouni holding the presidency with Libyan support. A proposed merger with Libya was rejected and Libya withdrew most of its forces.

The Organization for African Unity (OAU) set up a peacekeeping force but civil war broke out and by 1981 Hissène Habré's Armed Forces of the North (FAN) controlled half the country. Goukouni fled and set up a 'government in exile'. In 1983 a majority of OAU members agreed to recognize Habré's regime but Goukouni, with Libyan support, fought on.

After Libyan bombing, Habré appealed to France for help. 3,000 troops were sent as instructors, with orders to retaliate if attacked. Following a Franco-African summit in 1983, a ceasefire was agreed, with latitude 16° N dividing the opposing forces. Libyan president Col Khaddhafi's proposal of a simultaneous withdrawal of French and Libyan troops was accepted. By Dec all French troops had left but Libya's withdrawal was doubtful.

Habré dissolved the military arm of Frolinat and formed a new party, the National Union for Independence (UNIR), but opposition to his regime grew. In 1987 Goukouni was reported to be under house arrest in Tripoli. Meanwhile

Chadwick *The discoverer of the neutron in 1932 (for which he was awarded a Nobel prize in 1935). James Chadwick was working with Hans Geiger in Germany when World War I broke out; he was interned for its duration.*

Libya intensified its military operations in northern Chad, Habré's government retaliated, and France renewed, if reluctantly, its support. It was announced in Mar 1989 that France, Chad, and Libya had agreed to observe a ceasefire proposed by the Organization of African Unity (OAU). A meeting in July 1989 between Habré and Khaddhaffi reflected the improvement in relations between Chad and Libya. Habré was endorsed as president Dec 1989 for another seven-year term, under a revised constitution.

Chad, Lake /tʃæd/ lake on the NE boundary of Nigeria. It once varied in extent between rainy and dry seasons from 50,000 sq km/20,000 sq mi to 20,000 sq km/7,000 sq mi, but a series of droughts 1979–89 reduced its area by 80%. The Lake Chad basin is being jointly developed for oil by Cameroon, Chad, Niger, and Nigeria. It was first seen by European explorers 1823.

Chadli /ʃæd'li:/ Benjedid 1929– . Algerian socialist politician, president from 1979. An army colonel, he supported Boumédienne in the overthrow of Ben Bella 1965, and succeeded Boumédienne 1979, pursuing more moderate policies.

chador (Hindi 'square of cloth') all-enveloping black garment for women worn by some Muslims and Hindus. It dates from the 6th century BC and was revived by Ayatollah Khomeini in Iran in response to the Koran request for 'modesty' in dress.

The chador originated in the period of Cyrus the Great and the Achaemenian empire in Persia. Together with the ◊purdah (Persian 'veil') and the idea of female seclusion, it persisted under Alexander the Great and the Byzantine Empire, and was adopted by the Arab conquerors of the Byzantines.

Chadwick /'tʃædwɪk/ Edwin 1800–1890. English social reformer. Author of the Poor Law Report of 1834. He played a prominent part in the campaign which resulted in the ◊Public Health Act 1848. He was commissioner of the first Board of Health 1848–54.

Self-educated protégé of Jeremy ◊Bentham and advocate of ◊utilitarianism, he used his influence to implement measures to eradicate cholera, improve sanitation in urban areas, and clear slums in British cities.

Chadwick /'tʃædwɪk/ James 1891–1974. British physicist. In 1932, he discovered the particle in an atomic nucleus which became known as the neutron because it has no electric charge. He was awarded a Nobel prize 1935, and in 1940 was one

Chagall *The Blue Circus (1950) Tate Gallery, London.*

of the British scientists reporting on the atomic bomb.

Chadwick studied at Cambridge under ◊Rutherford. He was Lyon Jones professor of physics at Liverpool 1935–48, and master of Gonville and Caius College, Cambridge, 1948–59.

Chadwick /'tʃædwɪk/ Lynn 1914– . British abstract sculptor, known for mobiles (influenced by Calder) in the 1940s and welded ironwork from the 1950s.

chafer type of beetle, family Scarabaeidae. The adults eat foliage or flowers, and the underground larvae feed on roots, especially of grasses and cereals, and can be very destructive. Examples include the ◊*cockchafer* and the *rose chafer Cetonia aurata*, about 2 cm/0.8 in long and bright green.

chaffinch bird *Fringilla coelebs* of the finch family, common throughout much of Europe and W Asia. About 15 cm/6 in long, the male is olive-brown above, with a bright chestnut breast, a bluish-grey cap, and two white bands on the upper part of the wing; the female is duller.

Chagall /ʃæ'gæl/ Marc 1887–1985. French painter and designer, born in Russia; much of his highly coloured, fantastic imagery was inspired by the village life of his boyhood. He also designed stained glass, mosaics (for Israel's Knesset in the 1960s), tapestries, and stage sets.

Chagall is an original figure, often seen as a precursor of Surrealism, as in *The Dream* (Metropolitan Museum of Art, New York). He lived mainly in France from 1922. His stained glass can be found notably in a chapel in Vence, in the south of France, 1950s, and in a synagogue near Jerusalem. He also produced illustrated books.

Chagas' Disease /'ʃɑːɡəs/ named after Brazilian doctor Carlos Chagas (1879–1934), a disease caused by a trypanosome parasite transmitted by insects, which results in incurable damage to the heart and brain.

Chagos Archipelago /'tʃɑːɡəs ,ɑːkɪ'peləɡəʊ/ island group in the Indian Ocean; area 60 sq km/23 sq mi. Formerly a dependency of ◊Mauritius, it now forms the ◊British Indian Ocean Territory. The chief island is Diego Garcia, now a UK/USA strategic base.

Chaillu /ʃaɪ'uː/ Paul Belloni du 1835–1903. French-born US explorer. In 1855 he began a four year journey of exploration in West Africa. His *Explorations and Adventures in Equatorial Africa* 1861 describes his discovery of the gorilla in Gabon.

Chain /tʃeɪn/ Ernst Boris 1906–1979. German biochemist who worked on the development of penicillin. Chain was born in Germany but fled to Britain 1933. After the discovery of ◊penicillin

by Alexander Fleming, Chain worked to isolate and purify it. For this work, he shared the 1945 Nobel Prize for Medicine with Fleming and Howard Florey. He also discovered penicillinase, an enzyme which destroys penicillin.

chain reaction in nuclear physics, a fission reaction which is maintained because neutrons released by the splitting of some atomic nuclei themselves go on to split others, releasing even more neutrons. Such a reaction can be controlled (as in a nuclear reactor) by using moderators to absorb excess neutrons. Uncontrolled, a chain reaction produces a nuclear explosion (as in an atomic bomb).

Chaka /'ʃɑːɡə/ alternative spelling of ◊Shaka, Zulu chief.

Chalatenango /tʃəlæti'nænɡəʊ/ a department on the N frontier of El Salvador; area 2507 sq km/968 sq mi; population (1981) 235,700; capital Chalatenango. It is largely controlled by FMLN guerrilla insurgents.

Chalcedon, Council of an ecumenical council of the early Christian church, convoked 451 by the Roman emperor Marcian, and held at Chalcedon (modern Kadiköy, Turkey). The council, attended by over 500 bishops, resulted in the *Definition of Chalcedon*, an agreed doctrine for both the E and W churches.

The council was assembled to repudiate the ideas of Eutyches (378–454) on Christ's divine nature subsuming the human; it also rejected the ◊Monophysite doctrine that Christ had only one nature, and repudiated ◊Nestorianism. It reached a compromise definition of Christ's nature which it was hoped would satisfy all factions: Christ was one person in two natures, united 'unconfusedly, unchangeably, indivisibly, inseparably'.

chalcedony a form of quartz, SiO_2, in which the crystals are so fine-grained that they are impossible to distinguish with a microscope (cryptocrystalline). Agate, onyx, tiger's eye, and carnelian are ◊gem varieties of chalcedony.

Chaldaea an ancient region of Babylonia.

Chaliapin /ˌʃæli'æpɪn/ Fyodor Ivanovich 1873–1938. Russian bass singer, born in Kazan of peasant parentage. His greatest role was that of Boris Godunov in Mussorgsky's opera of the same name. Chaliapin left the USSR in 1921 to live and sing in the world's capitals.

chalice cup, usually of precious metal, used in celebrating the ◊Eucharist in the Christian church.

chalk a soft, fine-grained, whitish rock composed of calcium carbonate $CaCO_3$, extensively quarried for use in cement, lime, and mortar, and in the manufacture of cosmetics and toothpaste. Blackboard chalk consists of ◊gypsum and not chalk.

Chalk was once thought to derive from the remains of microscopic animals or foraminifera. In 1953, however, it was seen under the electron microscope to be composed chiefly of coccoliths, unicellular lime-secreting algae, and hence primarily of plant origin. It is formed from deposits of deep-sea sediments called oozes.

Chalk was laid down in the later ◊Cretaceous period and covers a wide area in Europe. In England it stretches in a belt from Wiltshire and Dorset continuously across Buckinghamshire and Cambridgeshire to Lincolnshire and Yorkshire,

chalk *cliffs near Lulworth, Dorset, provide some of the finest coastal scenery in England.*

Chamberlain *Neville Chamberlain waving the Munich Agreement that he negotiated with Hitler 1938.*

and also forms the North and South Downs, and the cliffs of S and SE England.

Chalmers /'tʃɑːməz/ Thomas 1780–1847. Scottish theologian. At the Disruption of the ◊Church of Scotland 1843, Chalmers withdrew from the church along with a large body of other priests, and became principal of the Free Church college, thus founding the ◊Free Church of Scotland.

As minister of Tron Church, Glasgow, from 1815, Chalmers became noted for his eloquence and for his proposals for social reform. In 1823 he became professor of moral philosophy at St Andrews, and in 1828 of theology at Edinburgh.

Châlons-sur-Marne /ʃɑːˈlɒn sjʊə ˈmɑːn/ capital of the *département* of Marne, NE France; population (1982) 54,400. It is a market town and trades mainly in champagne. Tradition has it that Attila was defeated in his attempt to invade France, at the **Battle of Châlons** (451), by the Roman general Aëtius and the Visigoth Theodoric.

Chalon-sur-Saône /ʃɑːˈlɒn sjʊə ˈsəʊn/ town in the *département* of Saône-et-Loire, France, on the river Saône and the Canal du Centre; population (1982) 58,000. It has mechanical and electrical engineering, and chemical industries.

Chamberlain /'tʃeɪmbəlɪn/ (Arthur) Neville 1869–1940. British Conservative politician, son of Joseph Chamberlain. He was prime minister 1937–40; his policy of appeasement towards the fascist dictators Mussolini and Hitler (with whom he concluded the ◊Munich Agreement 1938) failed to prevent the outbreak of World War II. He resigned 1940 following the defeat of the British forces in Norway.

Younger son of Joseph Chamberlain and half-brother of Austen Chamberlain, he was born in Birmingham, of which he was lord mayor in 1915. He was minister of health in 1923 and 1924–29 and worked at slum clearance. In 1931 he was chancellor of the Exchequer in the national government, and in 1937 succeeded Baldwin as prime minister. Trying to close the old Anglo-Irish feud, he agreed to return to Eire those ports that had been occupied by the navy. He also attempted to appease the demands of the European dictators, particularly Mussolini. In 1938 he went to Munich and negotiated with Hitler the settlement of the Czechoslovak question. He was ecstatically received on his return, and claimed that the Munich Agreement brought 'peace in our time'. Within a year, however, Britain was at war with Germany.

Chamberlain /'tʃeɪmbəlɪn/ (Joseph) Austen 1863–1937. British Conservative politician, elder son of Joseph Chamberlain; as foreign secretary 1924–29 he negotiated the Pact of ◊Locarno, for which he won the Nobel Peace Prize 1925, and signed the ◊Kellogg-Briand pact 1928.

He was elected to Parliament 1892 as a Liberal-Unionist, and after holding several minor posts was chancellor of the Exchequer 1903–06. During World War I he was secretary of state for India 1915–17 and member of the war cabinet 1918. He was chancellor of the Exchequer 1919–21 and Lord Privy Seal 1921–22, but failed to secure the leadership of the party 1922, as many Conservatives resented the part he had taken in the Irish

settlement of 1921. He was foreign secretary in the Baldwin government 1924–29, and negotiated and signed the Locarno Pact 1925 to fix the boundaries of Germany, and the Kellogg-Briand pact 1928 to ban war and provide for peaceful settlement of disputes.

Chamberlain /'tʃeɪmbəlɪn/ Joseph 1836–1914. British politician, reformist mayor of and member of Parliament for Birmingham; in 1886, resigned from the cabinet over Gladstone's policy of home rule for Ireland, and led the revolt of the Liberal-Unionists.

By 1874 Chamberlain had made a sufficient fortune in the Birmingham screw-manufacturing business to devote himself entirely to politics. He adopted radical views, and took an active part in local affairs. Three times mayor of Birmingham, he carried through many schemes of municipal development. In 1876 he was elected to Parliament and joined the republican group led by Charles Dilke, the extreme left wing of the Liberal Party. In 1880 he entered Gladstone's cabinet as president of the Board of Trade. The climax of his radical period was reached with the unauthorized programme, advocating, among other things, free education, graduated taxation, and small holdings of 'three acres and a cow'.

As colonial secretary in Salisbury's Conservative government, Chamberlain was responsible for relations with the Boer republics up to the outbreak of war in 1899. In 1903 he resigned to campaign for imperial preference or tariff reform as a means of consolidating the empire. From 1906 he was incapacitated by a stroke. Chamberlain was one of the most colourful figures of British politics, and his monocle and orchid made him a favourite subject for political cartoonists.

Chamberlain /'tʃeɪmbəlɪn/ Owen 1920– . US physicist whose graduate studies were interrupted by wartime work on the Manhattan project at Los Alamos. After World War II, working with Italian physicist Emilio Segre, he discovered the existence of the anti-proton. Both men were awarded the Nobel Prize for physics in 1959.

Chamberlain /'tʃeɪmbəlɪn/ Wilton Norman 'Wilt' 1936– . US basketball player, who set a record by averaging 50.4 points a game during the 1962 season, and was the only man to score 100 points in a game. He was known as 'Wilt the Stilt' because of his height 2.16 m/7 ft 1 1/8 in.

CAREER HIGHLIGHTS

Total games 1,045
Points: 31,419 (average 30.1 per game)
Most points in a game 100 v New York Knickerbockers (1962)
Most points in a season 4,029 (1962) (average 50.4 per game)
Most seasons as NBA top scorer 7 (1960–66)

Chamberlain, Lord /'tʃeɪmbəlɪn/ in the UK, chief officer of the royal household, who engages staff and appoints retail suppliers. Until 1968 the Lord Chamberlain licensed and censored plays before their public performance. The office is temporary, and appointments are made by the government.

Chamberlain, Lord Great /'tʃeɪmbəlɪn/ in the UK, the only officer of state whose position survives from Norman times; responsibilities include the arrangements for the opening of Parliament, assisting with the regalia at coronations, and organizing the ceremony when bishops and peers are created.

chamber music music suitable for performance in a small room or chamber, rather than in the concert hall, and usually written for instrumental combinations, played with one instrument to a part, as in the string quartet.

It came into use as a reaction to earlier music for voices such as the madrigal, which allowed accompanying instruments little freedom for technical display. At first a purely instrumental style, it developed through Haydn and Beethoven into a private and often experimental medium making unusual demands on players and audiences

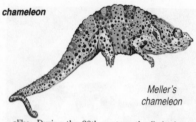

Meller's chameleon

alike. During the 20th century the limitations of recording and radio have encouraged many composers to scale down their orchestras to chamber proportions, as in Berg's *Chamber Concerto* and Stravinsky's *Agon*.

Chambers /'tʃeɪmbəz/ William 1726–1796. British architect, popularizer of Chinese influence (as in the pagoda in Kew Gardens, London) and designer of Somerset House, London.

Chambéry /ˌʃɒmbeˈriː/ former capital of Savoy, now capital of Savoie *département*, France; population (1982) 96,000. It is the seat of an archbishopric, and has some industry; it is also a holiday and health resort. The town gives its name to a French vermouth.

chambré (French) (of wine) at room temperature, as opposed to chilled.

chameleon type of lizard, some 80 or so species of family Chameleontidae. Some species have highly developed colour-changing abilities, which are caused by changes in the intensity of light, of temperature, and of emotion, which affect the dispersal of pigment granules in the layers of cells beneath the outer skin.

The tail is long and highly prehensile, assisting the animal when climbing. Most chameleons live in trees and move very slowly. The tongue is very long, protusile, and covered with a viscous secretion; it can be shot out with great rapidity to 20 cm/8 in for the capture of insects. The eyes are on 'turrets', move independently, and can swivel forward to give stereoscopic vision for 'shooting'. Most live in Africa and Madagascar, but the *common chameleon Chameleo chameleon* is found in Mediterranean countries; two species live in SW Arabia, and one species in India and Sri Lanka.

Chamisso /ʃæˈmɪsəʊ/ Adelbert von. Pen name of Louis-Charles-Adélaide Chamisso de Boncourt 1781–1831. German writer, author of the story 'Peter Schlemihl', the man who sold his shadow. The son of a French family who left France because of the French Revolution, he was subsequently a botanist with Otto von Kotzebue's trip around the world 1815–18, recounted in *Reise um de Welt* 1821. His verse includes the cycle of lyrics *Frauenliebe und Frauenleben* 1831, set to music by Schumann.

chamois goat-like mammal *Rupicapra rupicapra* found in mountain ranges of S Europe and Asia Minor. It is brown, with dark patches running through the eyes, and can be up to 80 cm/2.6 ft high. Chamois are very sure footed, and live in herds of up to 30 members.

Both sexes have horns which may be 20 cm/8 in long. These are set close together and go up vertically, forming a hook at the top. Chamois skin is very soft, and excellent for cleaning glass, but the chamois is now comparatively rare and 'chamois leather' is often made from the skin of sheep and goats.

Chamonix /ˈʃæməni/ holiday resort at the foot of Mont Blanc, in the French Alps; population (1982) 9,255. Site of the first Winter Olympics in 1924.

champagne /ˌʃæmˈpeɪn/ French sparkling wine, produced from fine grapes and blended wines, the former grown in a strictly defined area of the Marne region around Reims and Epernay in Champagne. Fermentation takes place after the bottle has been sealed, which causes the effervescence.

Production in 1844 was 7,000,000 bottles; in 1987, it was 217,800,000 bottles, of which the UK was the world's largest consumer with 15,351,000 bottles.

Champagne-Ardenne /ʃæm,peɪn ɑːˈden/ region of NE France; area 25,600 sq km/9,882 sq mi; population (1986) 1,353,000. Its capital is Reims, and it comprises the *départements* of Ardennes, Aube, Marne, and Haute-Marne. It has sheep and dairy farming, and vineyards.

It forms the plains east of the Paris basin. Its chief towns are Epernay, Troyes, and Chaumont. The capital of the ancient province of Champagne was Troyes.

Champaigne /,ʃæm'peɪn/ Philippe de 1602–1674. French artist, the leading portrait painter of the court of Louis XIII. Of Flemish origin, he went to Paris 1621, and gained the patronage of Cardinal Richelieu. His style is elegant, cool, and restrained.

champignon fungus *Marasmius oreades*, family Agaricaceae, which is edible, and a popular food in France. It is known as the fairy-ring champignon because mushrooms occur in rings around the outer edge of the underground mass of fungus.

Champlain /ʃæm'pleɪn/ lake situated in northeast USA, named after Samuel de Champlain, who saw it in 1609. It is linked to the St Lawrence and Hudson rivers.

Champlain /ʃæm'pleɪn/ Samuel de 1567–1635. French pioneer, soldier, and explorer in Canada. Having served in the army of Henry IV and on an expedition to the West Indies, he began his exploration of Canada 1603. In a third expedition 1608 he founded and named Québec, and was appointed lieutenant-governor of French Canada 1612.

Champollion /,ʃɒmpɒl'jɒn/ Jean François, le Jeune 1790–1832. French Egyptologist who in 1822 deciphered Egyptian hieroglyphics with the aid of the ◊Rosetta Stone.

chance the theory of ◊probability. As a science, it originated when the Chevalier de Méré consulted ◊Pascal about how to reduce his gambling losses. In correspondence with another mathematician, ◊Fermat, Pascal worked out the foundations of the theory of chance. This underlies the science of statistics.

chancel the part of a Christian church where the choir and clergy sit, formerly kept separate from the nave.

The term originated in the early Middle Ages, when chancels were raised above the level of the nave, from which they were separated by a rood screen, a pierced partition bearing the image of the Crucifixion. The chancel has usually been regarded as the preserve and responsibility of the clergy, while the upkeep and repair of the nave was left to the parishioners.

Chancellor, Lord UK state official, originally the royal secretary, today a member of the cabinet, whose office ends with a change of government. The Lord Chancellor acts as speaker of the House of Lords, may preside over the court of appeal, and is head of the judiciary.

Until the 14th century he was always an ecclesiastic, who also acted as royal chaplain and Keeper of the Great Seal. Under Edward III the Lord Chancellor became head of a permanent court to consider petitions to the king: the *court of chancery*. In order of precedence the Lord Chancellor comes after the archbishop of Canterbury.

chancellor of the Duchy of Lancaster in the UK, honorary post held by a cabinet minister who has other nondepartmental responsibilities. The chancellor of the Duchy of Lancaster was originally the monarch's representative controlling the royal lands and courts within the duchy.

chancellor of the Exchequer in the UK, senior cabinet minister responsible for the national economy. The office, established under Henry III, originally entailed keeping the Exchequer seal.

Chancery in the UK, a division of the high court that deals with such matters as the administration of the estates of deceased persons, the execution of trusts, the enforcement of sales of land, and ◊foreclosure of mortgages. Before reorganization of the court system in 1875, it administered the rules of ◊equity as distinct from ◊common law.

Chan Chan /'tʃæn 'tʃæn/ capital of the pre-Inca ◊Chimu kingdom in Peru.

Chandelā or *Candella* a Rajput dynasty which ruled the Bundelkhand region of central India from the 9th to the 11th century. They fought against Muslim invaders, until they were replaced by the Bundelās.

Chandernagore /,tʃʌndənə'gɔː/ ('city of sandalwood') city, on the river Hooghly, India; in the state of W Bengal; population (1981) 102,000. Formerly a French settlement, it was ceded to India by treaty in 1952.

Chandigarh /,tʃʌndɪ'gɑː/city of N India, in the foothills of the Himalayas; population (1981) 421,000. It is also a Union Territory; area 114 sq km/44 sq mi; population (1981) 450,000.

It was inaugurated 1953 to replace Lahore (capital of British Punjab), which went to Pakistan under partition 1947. Planned by the architect Le Corbusier, since 1966, when it became a Union Territory, it has been the capital city of both Haryana and Punjab, until a new capital is built for the former.

Chandler /'tʃɑːndlə/ Raymond 1888–1959. US crime writer, who created the 'private eye' hero Philip Marlowe, a hard-boiled detective, in books which include *The Big Sleep* 1939, *Farewell, My Lovely* 1940, and *The Long Goodbye* 1954.

Born in Chicago, he was educated at Dulwich College public school in London, England.

Chandragupta Maurya /'tʃʌndrə,guptə 'maʊriə/ ruler of N India *c.*321–*c.*297 BC, founder of the Maurya dynasty (in modern Bihar, India). He overthrew the Nanda dynasty 325, and then conquered the Punjab 322 after the death of ◊Alexander, expanding his empire to the borders of Persia. He is credited as having united most of India under one administration.

Chandrasekhar /,tʃændrə'seɪkə/ Subrahmanyan 1910– . Indian-born US astrophysicist, who made pioneering studies of the structure and evolution of stars. The *Chandrasekhar limit* of 1.4 Suns is the maximum mass of a ◊white dwarf before it turns into a ◊neutron star. Born in Lahore, he studied in Madras, India, and Cambridge, England, before emigrating to the USA. He was awarded the 1983 Nobel Prize for physics.

Chanel /ʃæ'nel/ Coco (Gabrielle) 1883–1971. French fashion designer, creator of the 'little black dress', informal cardigan suit, costume jewellery, and perfumes.

Chaney /'tʃeɪni/ Alonso ('Lon') 1883–1930. US star of silent films, often in grotesque or monstrous roles such as *The Phantom of the Opera* 1925. A master of make-up, he sometimes employed extremely painful devices for added effectiveness, as in the title role in *The Hunchback of Notre Dame* 1923.

Chaney /'tʃeɪni/ Creighton ('Lon Jr') 1906–1973. US actor, son of Lon Chaney, who gave an acclaimed performance as Lennie in *Of Mice and Men* 1940. He went on to star in many 1940s horror films, including the title role in *The Wolfman* 1941. His other work includes *My Favorite Brunette* 1947 and *The Haunted Palace* 1963.

Chang /tʃæŋ/ Michael 1972– . US tennis player who, at the age of 17 years 3 months, became the youngest ever winner of a Grand Slam event when he beat Stefan Edberg to win the French Open in 1989. He beat the top seed Ivan Lendl on his way to the title.

Changchiakow /'tʃæŋ ,tʃɪə 'kaʊ/ former name for ◊Zhangjiakou, trading centre in Hesei province, China.

Chang Ch'ien lived 2nd century BC. Chinese explorer who pioneered the ◊Silk Road.

Changchun /,tʃæŋ'tʃʊn/ industrial city and capital of Jilin province, China; population (1986) 1,860,000. Machinery and motor vehicles are manufactured. It is also the centre of an agricultural district.

As Hsingking ('new capital'), it was the capital of Manchukuo 1932–45 during Japanese occupation.

change of state in physics, when a gas condenses to a liquid or a liquid freezes to a solid. Similar changes take place when a solid melts to form a liquid or a liquid vaporizes (evaporates) to produce gas. The first set of changes are brought about by cooling, the second set by heating. In the unusual change of state called *sublimation*, a solid changes directly to a gas without passing through the liquid state. For example, solid carbon dioxide (dry ice) sublimes to carbon dioxide gas.

Chang Jiang /'tʃæŋ dʒi'æŋ/ longest river (formerly Yangtze Kiang) of China, flowing about 6,300 km/3,900 mi from Tibet to the Yellow Sea. It is a major commercial waterway.

It has 204 km/127 mi of gorges, below which is Gezhou Ba, the first dam to harness the river. The entire length of the river was first navigated 1986.

Changsha /,tʃæŋ'ʃɑː/ river port, on the Chang Jiang, capital of Hunan province, China; population (1986) 1,160,000. It trades in rice, tea, timber, and non-ferrous metals; works antimony, lead, and silver; and produces chemicals, electronics, porcelain, and embroideries. Mao Zedong was a student here 1912–18.

Channel, English stretch of water between England and France, leading in the west to the Atlantic Ocean, and in the east via the Strait of Dover to the North Sea; also known as La Manche (French 'the sleeve') from its shape.

The English Channel is 450 km/280 mi long W–E; 27 km/17 mi wide at its narrowest (Cap

Chanel The French couturier 'Coco' Chanel in 1929.

Chang Tennis player Michael Chang playing to win the French Open 1989.

Channel Islands

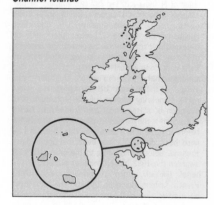

Gris Nez–Dover) and 117 km/110 mi wide at its widest (Ushant–Land's End).

Channel Country /'tʃænl/ area of SW Queensland, Australia, in which channels such as Cooper's Creek (where explorers Burke and Wills died in 1861) are cut by intermittent rivers. Summer rains supply rich grass for cattle, and there are the 'beef roads', down which herds are taken in linked trucks for slaughter.

Channel Islands /'tʃænl/ comprising the islands of Jersey, Guernsey, Alderney, Great and Little Sark, with the lesser Herm, Brechou, Jethou, and Lihou
area 194 sq km/75 sq mi
features the climate is very mild, and the soil productive. Financially the islands are a 'tax haven'
exports flowers, early potatoes, tomatoes, butterflies
currency English pound, also local coinage
population (1981) 128,878
language official language French (◊Norman French) but English more widely used
religion chiefly Anglican
famous people Lily Langtry
history originally under the duchy of Normandy, they are the only part still held by Britain. The islands came under the same rule as England 1066, and are dependent territories of the English Crown
government the main islands have their own parliaments and laws. Unless specially signified, the Channel Islands are not bound by British acts of parliament, though the British government is responsible for defence and external relations.

Channel swimming popular test of endurance since Capt Matthew Webb (1848–1883) first swam from Dover to Calais in 1875. His time was 21 hr 45 min for the 34 km/21 mi journey.

The current record is 7 hr 40 min by Penny Dean of the USA 1978. The first to swim nonstop in both directions was the Argentinian Antonio Abertondo in 1961. The Channel Swimming Association was formed 1927, and records exist for various feats; double crossing, most crossings, and youngest and oldest to complete a crossing.

Channel tunnel a tunnel being built beneath the English Channel, linking Britain with mainland Europe. It will comprise twin rail tunnels 50 km/31 mi long and 7.3 m/24 ft in diameter located 40 m/130 ft beneath the seabed. Specially designed shuttle trains carrying cars and lorries will run every few minutes between terminals at Folkestone, Kent, and Sangatte W of Calais, France. The latest estimated cost is £6 billion. It is scheduled to be operational 1993.

chanson a type of song common in France and Italy, often based on a folk tune that originated with the ◊troubadours. Josquin ◊Desprez was a chanson composer.

chanson de geste the epic poetry of the High Middle Ages. It probably developed from oral

Channel tunnel

The rail link between the UK and France has the potential to reduce the travel time between London and Paris to about three hours, matching the total time of a journey by air. An Anglo-French consortium raised money for work to begin at both ends of the projected route in 1987, with a deadline for completion of 1993.

The machines used to bore the Channel tunnel each weigh 500 tonnes/492 tons. They have rotating heads with tungsten-carbide "picks", and special trains travel behind them to deliver equipment and remove spoil. 700,000 concrete segments will form the tunnel lining, and trackwork, mechanical and electrical equipment and signals will be installed.▶

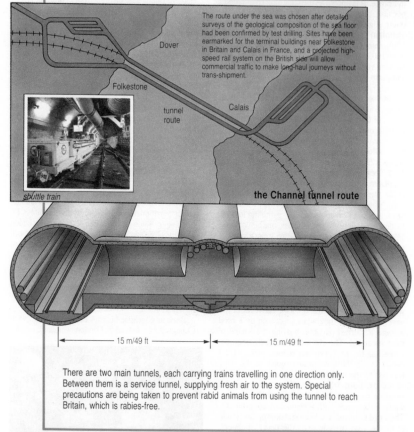

The route under the sea was chosen after detailed surveys of the geological composition of the sea floor had been confirmed by test drilling. Sites have been earmarked for the terminal buildings near Folkestone in Britain and Calais in France, and a projected high-speed rail system on the British side will allow commercial traffic to make long-haul journeys without trans-shipment.

shuttle train

the Channel tunnel route

— 15 m/49 ft —   — 15 m/49 ft —

There are two main tunnels, each carrying trains travelling in one direction only. Between them is a service tunnel, supplying fresh air to the system. Special precautions are being taken to prevent rabid animals from using the tunnel to reach Britain, which is rabies-free.

poetry recited in royal or princely courts, and it deals with the exploits of heroes, especially those associated with Charlemagne and the Crusades.

Chanson de Roland an early 12th-century epic poem which describes the Romantic legend based on the life of Roland, one of the 12 Paladins or peers of Charlemagne, killed by the Basques at Roncesvalles.

chant word used in common speech to denote any vocal melody or song, especially of a slow and solemn character; in music, a type of simple melody used in services of the Christian Church, for singing psalms and canticles, and in some forms of Buddhism. The Ambrosian and ◊Gregorian chants are forms of ◊plainsong melody.

chanterelle edible fungus *Cantharellus cibarius* which is bright yellow and funnel shaped. It grows in deciduous woodland.

Chantilly /ʃæn'tɪli/ town in Oise département, France, NE of Paris; population (1982) 10,208. It is the centre of French horseracing, and was

the headquarters of the French military chief Joffre 1914–17. Formerly renowned for its lace and porcelaine.

Chantrey /'tʃɑːntri/ Francis Legatt 1781–1841. British sculptor, known for portrait busts and monuments. His unaffected studies of children were much loved in his day, notably *Sleeping Children* 1817 (in Lichfield cathedral).

chantry in medieval Europe, a religious ceremony in which, in return for an endowment of land, the souls of the donor, his family, and his friends would be prayed for. A chantry could be held at an existing altar, or in a specially-constructed chantry chapel, in which the donor's body was usually buried.

Chantries became widespread in the later Middle Ages, reflecting the acceptance of the doctrine of ◊Purgatory, together with the growth of individualistic piety (as in the ◊devotio moderna) and the decline in the popularity of monasteries, to which they were seen as an alternative. Their foundation required the consent of the local bishop, and a licence from the king for the alienation of land in

Chaplin *Comic film actor Charlie Chaplin, seen here with Jackie Coogan in* The Kid *1920.*

◊mortmain. They were suppressed in Protestant countries during the Reformation.

Chao Phraya /ˈtʃau prəˈjaː/ chief river (formerly Menam) of Thailand, flowing 1,200 km/750 mi into the Bight of Bangkok, an inlet of the Gulf of Thailand.

chaos theory branch of mathematics used to deal with chaotic systems, for example, an engineered structure, such as an oil platform, which is subjected to irregular, unpredictable wave stress.

chaparral thick scrub country of south west USA. Thorny bushes have replaced what was largely evergreen oak trees.

chapel a place of worship used by some Protestant Christian denominations, and also a part of a building used for Christian worship. A large church or cathedral may have several chapels.

Chapel Royal in the UK, the royal retinue of priests, singers, and musicians (including Tallis, Byrd, and Purcell) of the English court from 1135.

There are chapels royal, in the sense of chapel buildings, at the former royal palaces of St James's, Hampton Court, the Tower of London (St John the Evangelist, and St Peter AD Vincula), and Windsor Castle (with a royal chapel also in Windsor Great Park), and a royal church at Sandringham, Norfolk.

Chaplin /ˈtʃæplɪn/ Charles Spencer ('Charlie') 1889–1977. English actor-director. He made his reputation as a tramp with smudge moustache, bowler hat, and cane, in silent films from the mid-1910s, including *The Rink* 1916, *The Kid* 1921, and *The Gold Rush* 1925. His works often contrast buffoonery with pathos, and later films combine dialogue with mime and music, such as *The Great Dictator* 1940, and *Limelight* 1952.

Born in south London, he first appeared on the stage at the age of five. His other films include *City Lights* 1931, *Modern Times* 1936, and *Monsieur Verdoux* (in which he spoke for the first time) 1947. *Limelight* 1952 was awarded an Oscar for Chaplin's musical theme. He left the USA in 1952 when accused of Communist sympathies in the McCarthy era, and moved to Switzerland. He was four times married, his third wife being Paulette Goddard, and the fourth, Oona, daughter of Eugene O'Neill. He received special Oscars 1928 and 1972, and was knighted 1975.

Chapman /ˈtʃæpmən/ Frederick Spencer 1907–1971. British explorer, mountaineer, and writer, who explored Greenland, the Himalayas, and Malaya. He accompanied Gino Watkins on the British Arctic Air Routes Expedition 1930–31, recalled in *Northern Lights* 1932, and in 1935 he joined a climbing expedition to the Himalayas. For two years he participated in a government mission to Tibet described in *Lhasa, the Holy City* 1938, before setting out to climb the 7,315 m/24,000 ft peak, Chomollari.

Chapman /ˈtʃæpmən/ George 1559–1634. English poet and dramatist. His translations of Homer (completed 1616) were celebrated; his plays include the comedy *Eastward Ho!* (with Jonson and Marston) 1605, and the tragedy *Bussy d'Amboise* 1607.

chapter the collective assembly of canons (priests) who together administer a cathedral.

char or **charr** fish *Salvelinus alpinus* related to the trout, living in the Arctic coastal waters, and also in Europe and North America in some freshwaters, especially upland lakes.

Numerous variants have been described, but they probably all belong to the same species.

characin freshwater fish belonging to the family Characidae. There are over 1,300 species, mostly in South and Central America, but also in Africa. Most are carnivores. In typical characins, unlike the somewhat similar carp family, the mouth is toothed, and there is a small dorsal adipose fin just in front of the tail.

Most characins are small fishes, often colourful, and they include ◊tetras and ◊piranhas.

characteristic in mathematics, the integral part of any ◊logarithm. For example, in base 10, 10 = 1, 10 = 10, 10 = 100, and so on; the powers to which 10 is raised are the characteristics.

To determine the power to which 10 must be raised to obtain a number between 10 and 100, say 20, the logarithm for 2 is found (0.3010), and the characteristic 1 added to make 1.3010.

charcoal black, porous form of ◊carbon, produced by heating wood or other organic materials in the absence of air (a process called destructive distillation). It is used as a fuel, for smelting metals such as copper and zinc; in the form of **activated charcoal**, for purifying and filtration of drinking water and other liquids and gases; and by artists for making black line drawings.

production Charcoal was traditionally produced by burning dried wood in a kiln, a process lasting several days. The kiln was either a simple hole in the ground, or an earth-covered mound. Modern kilns are of brick or iron, both of which allow the waste gases to be collected and used.

history Charcoal had many uses in earlier centuries. Because of the high temperature at which it burns (1100°C), it was used in furnaces and blast furnaces before the development of coke. It was also used in an industrial process for obtaining acetic acid in producing wood tar and ◊wood pitch, and (when produced from alder or willow trees) as a component of gunpowder.

Charcot /ˈʃaːkəu/ Jean-Martin 1825–1893. French neurologist who studied diseases of the nervous system. He became known for his work on hysteria, sclerosis, locomotor ataxia, and senile diseases.

Charcot worked at a hospital in Paris where he studied the way certain mental illnesses cause physical changes in the brain. He exhibited hysterical women at weekly public lectures, which became highly fashionable events. Among his pupils was Sigmund ◊Freud.

Chardin /ʃaˈdæn/ Jean-Baptiste-Siméon 1699–1779. French painter of naturalistic still lifes and quiet domestic scenes that recall the Dutch tradition. His work is a complete contrast to that of contemporary Rococo painters. He developed his own technique using succesive layers of paint to achieve depth of tone and is generally considered one of the finest exponents of the genre.

Chardonnet /ˌʃaːdɒˈneɪ/ Hilaire Bernigaud 1839–1924. French chemist who developed artificial silk in 1883, the first artificial fibre.

Charente /ʃæˈrɒnt/ French river, rising in Haute-Vienne *département* and flowing past Angoulême and Cognac into the Bay of Biscay below Rochefort. Length 360 km/225 mi. Its wide estuary is much silted up. It gives its name to two *départements*, Charente and Charente-Maritime (formerly Charente-Inférieure).

charge see ◊electric charge.

charge couple device (CCD) device used by astronomers to detect solid photons of light which usually consist of alternate layers of metal, silicon dioxide, and silicon. They contain large numbers of light-sensitive electric circuits known as picture elements (or pixels). Each pixel stores an electronic charge proportional to the amount of light reaching it from the telescopic image focused on to the CCD. Following each exposure, additional circuits are used to control the transfer of the acquired data to computers for analysis. An image can then be built up on photographic film.

charged particle beam high-energy beam of electrons or protons, which does not burn through the surface of its target like a ◊laser, but cuts through it. Such beams are being developed as weapons.

Charge of the Light Brigade disastrous charge of British Light Brigade of cavalry against the Russian entrenched artillery on 25 Oct 1854 during the Crimean War at ◊Balaclava.

Charing Cross /ˈtʃɛərɪŋ ˈkrɒs/ district in Westminster, London, around Charing Cross mainline railway station, deriving its name from the site of the last of twelve stone crosses erected by Edward I in 1290 at the resting-places of the coffin of his queen, Eleanor. The present cross is modern.

chariot a horse-drawn carriage with two wheels, used in ancient Egypt, Greece, and Rome, for fighting, processions, and races; it is thought to have originated in Asia. Typically, the fighting chariot contained a driver and a warrior, who would fight on foot, with the chariot providing rapid mobility.

Julius Caesar and Tacitus both write of chariots being used by the British against Roman armies in the 1st century AD. The most complete remains of a chariot found in Britain were at Llyn Cerrig Bach in Anglesey, Wales, but many parts of chariots, such as axle-caps and harness mounts, have been found.

charismatic a recent movement within the Christian church that emphasizes the role of the Holy Spirit in the life of the individual believer, and in the life of the Church. See ◊Pentecostal movement.

Charlemagne /ˌʃaːləˈmeɪn/ Charles I, *the Great* 742–814. King of the Franks from 768 and Holy Roman emperor from 800. By inheritance (his father was ◊Pepin the Short) and extensive campaigns of conquest, he united most of W Europe by 804, when after 30 years of war the Saxons came under his control. He reformed the legal, judicial, and military systems, established schools, promoted Christianity, commerce, agriculture, arts, and literature. In his capital Aachen, scholars gathered from all over Europe.

Pepin was mayor of the palace in Merovingian Neustria until he was crowned king by Pope Stephen II (died 757) in 754, and his sons Carl (Charlemagne) and Carloman were crowned as joint heirs. When Pepin died 768, Charlemagne inherited the northern part of the Frankish kingdom, and when Carloman died 771, he also took possession of his countries. In 770 he married the daughter of the king of the Lombards, whom he divorced a year later.

He was engaged in his first Saxon campaign when the Pope's call for help against the Lombards reached him; he crossed the Alps, captured Pavia, and took the title of king of the Lombards.

The pacification and christianizing of the Saxon peoples occupied the greater part of Charlemagne's reign. The Westphalian leader Widukind did not submit until 785, when he received baptism. From 792 N Saxony was subdued, and in 804 the country was finally pacified. In 777 the emir of Zaragoza asked for Charlemagne's help against the emir of Córdoba. Charlemagne crossed the Pyrenees 778, and reached the Ebro,

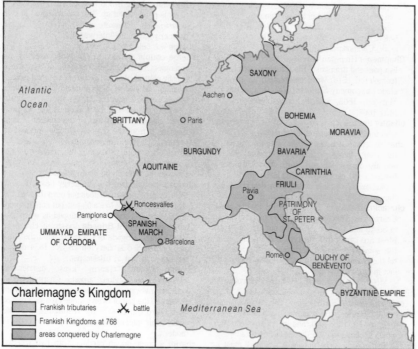

Charlemagne's Kingdom

- Frankish tributaries ✕ battle
- Frankish Kingdoms at 768
- areas conquered by Charlemagne

but had to turn back from Zaragoza. The rearguard action of Roncesvalles, in which ◊Roland, warden of the Breton March, and other Frankish nobles were ambushed and killed by Basques, was later glorified in the *Chanson de Roland*. In 801 the district between the Pyrenees and the Llobregat was organized as the Spanish March. The independent duchy of Bavaria was incorporated in the kingdom 788, and the ◊Avar people were subdued 791–96, and accepted Christianity. Charlemagne's last campaign was against a Danish attack on his northern frontier 810.

The supremacy of the Frankish king in the western world found outward expression in the bestowal of the imperial title: in Rome, during Mass on Christmas Day 800, Pope Leo III crowned Charlemagne emperor. He enjoyed diplomatic relations with Byzantium, Baghdad, Mercia, Northumbria, and other countries. Jury courts were introduced, the laws of the Franks revised, and other peoples' laws written down. A new coinage was introduced, weights and measures were reformed, and communications were improved. Charlemagne also took a lively interest in theology, organized the church in his dominions, and furthered missionary enterprises and monastic reform.

The **Carolingian Renaissance** of learning began when he persuaded the Northumbrian scholar Alcuin to enter his service 781. Charlemagne gathered a kind of academy around him. Although he never learned to read, he collected the old heroic sagas, began a Frankish grammar, and promoted religious instruction in the vernacular. He died 28 Jan 814 in Aachen, where he was buried. Soon a cycle of heroic legends and romances developed around him, including epics by Ariosto, Boiardo, and Tasso.

Charleroi /ˌʃɑːləˈrwɑː/ town in Belgium on the river Sambre, Hainault province; population (1985) 212,000. Its coal industry declined in the 1970s.

Charles /tʃɑːlz/ (Mary) Eugenia 1919– . Dominican politician, prime minister from 1980.

Born at Pointe Michel, she qualified as a barrister in England and returned to practise in the Windward and Leeward Islands in the West Indies. She was co-founder and first leader of the centrist Dominica Freedom Party (DFP). Two years after Dominica's independence the DFP won the 1980 general election and she

became the Caribbean's first female prime minister.

Charles /ʃɑːl/ Jacques Alexandre César 1746–1823. French physicist, who studied gases and made the first ascent in a hydrogen-filled balloon 1783. His work on the expansion of gases led to the formulation of ◊Charles' law.

Charles /tʃɑːlz/ Ray 1930– . US singer, songwriter, and pianist, whose first hits were 'I've Got A Woman' 1955, 'What'd I Say' 1959, and 'Georgia on My Mind' 1960. He has recorded gospel, blues, rock, soul, country, and rhythm and blues.

Charles /tʃɑːlz/ two kings of Britain:

Charles I 1600–1649. King of Great Britain and Ireland from 1625, son of James I of England (James VI of Scotland). He accepted the ◊Petition of Right 1628, but then dissolved Parliament and ruled without one 1629–40. His advisers were ◊Strafford and ◊Laud, who persecuted the Puritans and provoked the Scots to revolt. The ◊Short Parliament, summoned 1640, refused funds, and the ◊Long Parliament later that year rebelled. Charles declared war on Parliament 1642 but surrendered 1646 and was beheaded 1649. He was the father of Charles II.

Charles was born at Dunfermline, and became heir to the throne on the death of his brother Henry 1612. He married Henrietta Maria, daughter of Henry IV of France. When he succeeded his father, friction with Parliament began at once. The parliaments of 1625 and 1626 were dissolved, and that of 1628 refused supplies until Charles had accepted the Petition of Right. In 1629 it

Charles I *A portrait by Daniel Mytens (1631), National Portrait Gallery, London.*

attacked Charles' illegal taxation and support of the Arminians (see Jacobus ◊Arminius) in the church, whereupon he dissolved Parliament and imprisoned its leaders.

For 11 years he ruled without a parliament, the Eleven Years' Tyranny, raising money by expedients, such as ◊ship money, that alienated the nation, while the ◊Star Chamber suppressed opposition by persecuting the Puritans. When Charles attempted in 1637 to force a prayer book on the English model on Presbyterian Scotland he found himself confronted with a nation in arms. The Short Parliament, which met Apr 1640, refused to grant money until grievances were redressed, and was speedily dissolved. The Scots then advanced into England and forced their own terms on Charles. The Long Parliament met 3 Nov 1640 and declared extra-parliamentary taxation illegal, abolished the Star Chamber and other prerogative courts, and voted that Parliament could not be dissolved without its own consent. Laud and other ministers were imprisoned, and Strafford condemned to death. After the failure of his attempt to arrest the parliamentary leaders 4 Jan 1642, Charles, confident that he had substantial support among those who felt that Parliament was becoming too radical and zealous, withdrew from London, and on 22 Aug declared war on Parliament by raising his standard at Nottingham (see English ◊Civil War).

Charles's defeat at Naseby June 1645 ended all hopes of victory; in May 1646 he surrendered at Newark to the Scots, who handed him over to Parliament Jan 1647. In June the army seized him and carried him off to Hampton Court. While the army leaders strove to find a settlement, Charles secretly intrigued for a Scottish invasion. In Nov he escaped, but was recaptured and held at Carisbrooke Castle; a Scottish invasion followed 1648, and was shattered by ◊Cromwell at Preston. In Jan 1649 the House of Commons set up a high court of justice, which tried Charles and condemned him to death. He was beheaded 30 Jan before the Banqueting Hall in Whitehall.

Charles II 1630–1685. King of Great Britain and Ireland from 1660, when Parliament accepted the restoration of the monarchy; son of Charles I. His chief minister Clarendon arranged his marriage 1662 with Catherine of Braganza, but was replaced 1667 with the ◊Cabal of advisers. His plans to restore Catholicism in Britain led to war with the Netherlands 1672–74 and a break with Parliament, which he dissolved 1681. He was succeeded by James II.

Charles was born in St James's Palace, London; during the Civil War he lived with his father at Oxford 1642–45, and after the victory of Cromwell's Parliamentary forces withdrew to the Continent. Accepting the ◊Covenanters' offer to make him king, he landed in Scotland 1650, and was crowned at Scone 1 Jan 1651. An attempt to invade England was ended 3 Sept by Cromwell's victory at Worcester. Charles escaped, and for nine years he wandered through France, Germany, Flanders, Spain, and Holland until the opening of negotiations by George Monk 1660. In Apr Charles issued the Declaration of ◊Breda, promising a general amnesty and freedom of conscience. Parliament accepted the Declaration and he was proclaimed king 8 May 1660, landed at Dover on the 26th, and entered London three days later.

Charles wanted to make himself absolute, and favoured Catholicism for his subjects as most consistent with absolute monarchy. The disasters of the Dutch war furnished an excuse for banishing Clarendon 1667, and he was replaced by the Cabal of Clifford and Arlington, both secret Catholics, and ◊Buckingham, Ashley (Lord ◊Shaftesbury), and ◊Lauderdale, who had links with the ◊Dissenters. In 1670 Charles signed the Secret Treaty of Dover, the full details of which were known only to Clifford and Arlington, whereby he promised Louis XIV of France he would declare himself a Catholic, re-establish

Charles II The Restoration of the monarchy in 1660 was greeted with joy in England and Charles II showed himself to be an exceptionally affable and energetic king. He had many mistresses, including Nell Gwynn. The portrait by Peter Lely shows the face of the bon viveur.

Charles V The Holy Roman Emperor and King of Spain, Charles V aimed to preserve the medieval idea of the Empire, and persecuted any separatist political or religious movements in order to achieve this essentially unrealistic end.

Catholicism in England, and support Louis's projected war against the Dutch; in return Louis was to finance Charles and in the event of resistance to supply him with troops. War with the Netherlands followed 1672, and at the same time Charles issued the Declaration of Indulgence, suspending all penal laws against Catholics and Dissenters.

Charles The Prince of Wales pictured with Princess Diana and their two sons Prince William and Prince Henry. Prince Charles is noted for his keen interest in environmental and inner-city issues.

In 1673, Parliament forced Charles to withdraw the Indulgence and accept a Test Act exluding all Catholics from office, and in 1674 to end the Dutch war. The Test Act broke up the Cabal, while Shaftesbury, who had learned the truth about the treaty, assumed the leadership of the opposition. ◊Danby, the new chief minister, built up a court party in the Commons by bribery, while subsidies from Louis relieved Charles from dependence on Parliament. In 1678 ◊Oates's announcement of a 'popish plot' released a general panic, which Shaftesbury exploited to introduce his Exclusion Bill, excluding James, Duke of York, from the succession as a Catholic; instead he hoped to substitute Charles' illegitimate son ◊Monmouth.

In 1681 Parliament was summoned at Oxford, which had been the Royalist headquarters during the Civil War. The Whigs attended armed, but when Shaftesbury rejected a last compromise, Charles dissolved Parliament and the Whigs fled in terror. Charles now ruled without a Parliament, financed by Louis XIV. When the Whigs plotted a revolt their leaders were executed, while Shaftesbury and Monmouth fled to the Netherlands.

Charles was a patron of the arts and science. His mistresses included Lady ◊Castlemaine, Nell ◊Gwyn, Lady ◊Portsmouth, and Lucy ◊Walter.

Charles (full name Charles Philip Arthur George) 1948– . Prince of the United Kingdom, heir to the British throne, and Prince of Wales since 1958 (invested 1969). He is the first-born child of Queen Elizabeth II and the Duke of Edinburgh. He studied at Trinity College, Cambridge, 1967–70, before serving in the RAF and Royal Navy. He is the first royal heir since 1659 to have an English wife, Lady Diana Spencer, daughter of the 8th Earl Spencer. They have two sons: Prince William, born 1982, and Prince Henry, born 1984.

Prince Charles's concern for social and environmental issues has led to many self-help projects for the young and underprivileged, and he is a leading critic of unsympathetic features of contemporary architecture.

Charles /tʃɑːlz/ ten kings of France, including:

Charles I better known as the emperor ◊Charlemagne.

Charles II *the Bald* ; see ◊Charles II, Holy Roman emperor.

Charles III *the Simple* 879–929. King of France 893–922, son of Louis the Stammerer. He was crowned at Reims. In 911 he ceded what later became the duchy of Normandy to the Norman chief Rollo.

Charles IV *the Fair* 1294–1328. King of France from 1322, when he succeeded Philip V as the last of the direct Capetian line.

Charles V *the Wise* 1337–1380. King of France from 1364. He was regent during the captivity of his father, John II, in England 1356–60, and became king on John's death. He reconquered nearly all France from England 1369–80.

Charles VI *the Mad* or *the Well-Beloved* 1368–1422. King of France from 1380, succeeding his father Charles V, he was under the regency of his uncles until 1388. He became mentally unstable 1392, and civil war broke out between the dukes of Orleans and Burgundy. Henry V of England invaded France 1415, conquering Normandy, and in 1420 forcing Charles to sign the Treaty of Troyes, recognizing Henry as his successor.

Charles VII 1403–1461. King of France from 1429. Son of Charles VI, he was excluded from the succession by the Treaty of Troyes, but recognized by the South of France. In 1429 Joan of Arc raised the siege of Orléans and had him crowned at Reims. He organized France's first standing army and by 1453 he had expelled the English from all of France except Calais.

Charles VIII 1470–1498. King of France from 1483, when he succeeded his father, Louis XI. In 1494 he unsuccessfully tried to claim the Neapolitan crown, and when he entered Naples 1495 was forced to withdraw by a coalition of Milan, Venice, Spain, and the Holy Roman Empire. He defeated them at Fornovo, but lost Naples. He died while preparing a second expedition.

Charles IX 1550–1574. King of France from 1560. Second son of Henry II and Catherine de' Medici, he succeeded his brother Francis II at the age of ten, but remained under the domination of his mother for ten years while France was torn by religious wars. In 1570 he fell under the influence of the ◊Huguenot leader Admiral Coligny (1517–72); alarmed by this, Catherine instigated his order for the Massacre of ◊St Bartholomew, which led to a new religious war.

Charles X 1757–1836. King of France from 1824. Grandson of Louis XV and brother of Louis XVI and Louis XVIII, he was known as the Count of Artois before his accession. He fled to England at the beginning of the French Revolution, and when he came to the throne on the death of Louis XVIII, he attempted to reverse the achievements of the Revolution. A revolt ensued 1830, and he again fled to England.

Charles /tʃɑːlz/ seven rulers of the Holy Roman Empire:

Charles I better known as ◊Charlemagne.

Charles II *the Bald* 823–877. Holy Roman emperor from 875 and (as Charles II) king of France from 843. Younger son of Louis I (the Pious), he warred against his eldest brother, Emperor Lothair I. The Treaty of Verdun 843 made him king of the West Frankish Kingdom (modern France and the Spanish Marches).

Charles III *the Fat* 839–888. Holy Roman emperor 881–87; he became king of the West Franks 885, thus uniting for the last time the whole of Charlemagne's dominions, but was deposed.

Charles IV 1316–1378. Holy Roman emperor from 1355 and king of Bohemia from 1346. Son of John of Luxembourg, king of Bohemia, he was elected king of Germany 1346 and ruled all Germany from 1347. He was the founder of the first German university in Prague 1348.

Charles V 1500–1558. Holy Roman emperor 1519–56. Son of Philip of Burgundy and Joanna of Castile, he inherited vast possessions which led to rivalry from Francis I of France, whose alliance with the Ottoman Empire brought Vienna under siege 1529 and 1532. Charles was also in conflict with the Protestants in Germany until the Treaty of Passau 1552, which allowed the Lutherans religious liberty.

Charles was born in Ghent and received the Netherlands from his father 1506; Spain, Naples, Sicily, Sardinia, and the Spanish dominions in N Africa and America on the death of his maternal grandfather, Ferdinand V of Castile (1452–1516); and from his paternal grandfather, Maximilian I, the Habsburg dominions 1519, when he was elected emperor. He was crowned in Aachen 1520. From 1517 the empire was split by the rise of Lutheranism, Charles making unsuccessful attempts to reach a settlement at Augsburg 1530 (see Confession of ◊Augsburg), and being forced by the Treaty of Passau to yield most of the Protestant demands. Worn out, he abdicated in favour of his son Philip II in the Netherlands 1555 and Spain 1556. He yielded the imperial crown to his brother Ferdinand I, and retired to the monastery of Yuste, Spain.

Charles VI 1685–1740. Holy Roman emperor from 1711, father of ◊Maria Theresa, whose succession to his Austrian dominions he tried to ensure, himself claimant to the Spanish throne 1700, thus causing the War of the ◊Spanish Succession.

Charles VII 1697–1745. Holy Roman emperor from 1742, opponent of ◊Maria Theresa's claim to the Austrian dominions of Charles VI.

Charles (Karl Franz Josef) 1887–1922. Emperor of Austria and king of Hungary from 1916, the last of the Habsburg emperors. He succeeded his great-uncle, Franz Josef, in 1916, but was forced to withdraw to Switzerland 1918, although he refused to abdicate. In 1921 he attempted unsuccessfully to regain the crown of Hungary and was deported to Madeira, where he died.

Charles /tʃɑːlz/ (Spanish *Carlos*) four kings of Spain:

Charles I 1500–1558; see ◊Charles V, Holy Roman emperor.

Charles II 1661–1700. King of Spain from 1665; second son of Philip IV, he was the last of the Spanish Habsburg kings. Mentally handicapped from birth, he bequeathed his dominions to Philip of Anjou, grandson of Louis XIV, which led to the War of the ◊Spanish Succession.

Charles III 1716–1788. King of Spain from 1759. Son of Philip V, he became duke of Parma in 1732, and in 1734 conquered Naples and Sicily. On the death of his half-brother Ferdinand VI (1713–1759), he became king of Spain, handing over Naples and Sicily to his son Ferdinand (1751–1825). During his reign Spain was twice at war with Britain: during the Seven Years' War, when he sided with France and lost Florida; and when he backed the Americans in the War of Independence and regained it. At home he carried out a programme of reforms and expelled the Jesuits.

Charles IV 1748–1819. King of Spain from 1788, when he succeeded his father, Charles III, but left the government in the hands of his wife and her lover, the minister Manuel de Godoy (1767–1851). In 1808 Charles was induced to abdicate by Napoleon's machinations in favour of his son Ferdinand VII (1784–1833), who was subsequently deposed by Napoleon's brother Joseph. Charles was awarded a pension by Napoleon, and died in Rome.

Charles (Swedish *Carl*) 15 kings of Sweden. The first six were local chieftains:

Charles VII King of Sweden from about 1161, who helped to establish Christianity in Sweden.

Charles VIII King of Sweden from 1448. He was elected regent of Sweden 1438, when Sweden broke away from Denmark and Norway. He stepped down 1441 when Christopher III of Bavaria (1418–48) was elected king, but after his death became king. He was twice expelled by the Danes and twice restored.

Charles IX 1550–1611. King of Sweden from 1604, the youngest son of Gustavus Vasa. In 1568 he and his brother John led the rebellion against Eric XIV (1533–77); John became king as John III, and attempted to Catholicize Sweden, and Charles led the opposition. John's son Sigismund, king of Poland and a Catholic, succeeded to the Swedish throne 1592, and Charles led the Protestants. He was made regent 1595, and deposed Sigismund 1599. Charles was elected king of Sweden 1604. He was involved in unsuccessful wars with Russia, Poland, and Denmark. He was the father of Gustavus Adolphus.

Charles X 1622–1660. King of Sweden from 1654, when he succeeded his cousin Christina. He waged war with Poland and Denmark, and in 1657 invaded Denmark by leading his army over the frozen sea.

Charles XI 1655–1697. King of Sweden from 1660, when he succeeded his father Charles X. His mother acted as regent until 1672 when Charles took over the government. He was a remarkable general, and reformed the administration.

Charles XII 1682–1718. King of Sweden from 1697, when he succeeded his father, Charles XI. From 1700 he was involved in wars with Denmark, Poland, and Russia. He won a succession of victories, until in 1709 while invading Russia, he was defeated at Poltava in Ukraine, and forced to take refuge in Turkey until 1714. He was killed while besieging Fredrikshall.

Charles XIII 1748–1818. King of Sweden from 1809, when he was elected; he became the first king of Sweden and Norway 1814.

Charles XIV (Jean Baptiste Jules ◊Bernadotte) 1763–1844. King of Sweden and Norway from 1818. A former marshal in the French army, in 1810 he was elected crown prince of Sweden, under the name of Charles John (*Carl Johan*). Loyal to his adopted country, he brought Sweden into the alliance against Napoleon 1813, as a reward

Charles Edward Stuart *Prince Charles Edward Stuart, painted c. 1729, was known to the English as the Young Pretender and to the Scots as Bonnie Prince Charlie. His story inspired the well-known 'Skye Boat Song'.*

for which Sweden received Norway. He was the founder of the present dynasty.

Charles XV 1826–1872. King of Sweden and Norway from 1859, when he succeeded his father Oscar I. A popular and liberal monarch, his main achievement was the reform of the constitution.

Charles Albert 1798–1849. King of Sardinia from 1831. He showed liberal sympathies in early life, and after his accession introduced some reforms. On the outbreak of the 1848 revolution he granted a constitution and declared war on Austria. His troops were defeated at Custozza and Novara. In 1849 he abdicated in favour of his son Victor Emmanuel and retired to a monastery, where he died.

Charles Augustus /tʃɑːlz ɔːˈɡʌstəs/ 1757–1828. Grand Duke of Saxe-Weimar in Germany. He succeeded his father in infancy, fought against the French in 1792–94 and 1806, and was the patron and friend of the writer Goethe.

Charles Edward Stuart /tʃɑːlz ˈedwəd ˈstjuːət/ 1720–1788. British prince, known as the Young Pretender or Bonnie Prince Charlie, grandson of James II. In the Jacobite rebellion 1745 Charles won the support of the Scottish Highlanders and his army invaded England, but was beaten back by the Duke of ◊Cumberland and routed at ◊Culloden 1746.

He was born in Rome, the son of James, the Old Pretender, and created Prince of Wales at birth. In July 1745 he sailed for Scotland, and landed in Invernessshire with seven companions. On 19 Aug he raised his father's standard, and within a week had rallied an army of 2,000 Highlanders. He entered Edinburgh almost without resistance, won an easy victory at Prestonpans, invaded England, and by 4 Dec had reached Derby, where his officers insisted on a retreat. The army returned to Scotland and won a victory at Falkirk, but was forced to retire to the Highlands before Cumberland's advance. On 16 Apr at Culloden Charles's army was routed by Cumberland, and he fled. For five months he wandered through the Highlands with a price of £30,000 on his head before escaping to France. He visited England secretly in 1750, and may have made other visits. In later life he degenerated into a friendless drunkard. He settled in Italy 1766.

Charles's law law stated by Jacques Charles in 1787, and independently by Joseph Gay-Lussac (1778–1850) in 1802, which states that the volume of a given mass of gas at constant pressure increases by 1/273 of its volume at 0°C for each

°C rise of temperature, that is, the coefficient of expansion of all gases is the same. The law is only approximately true and the coefficient of expansion is generally taken as 0.003663 per °C.

Charles Martel /'tʃɑːlz mɑːˈtel/ *c.*688–741. Frankish ruler (◊Mayor of the Palace) of the east of the Frankish kingdom from 717 and the whole kingdom from 731. His victory against the Moors 732 between Poitiers and Tours earned him his nickname of Martel, 'the Hammer', and halted the Islamic advance into Europe. An illegitimate son of Pepin of Heristal (Pepin II, Mayor of the Palace *c.*640–714), he was grandfather of Charlemagne.

Charles the Bold /'tʃɑːlz/ Duke of Burgundy 1433–1477. Son of Philip the Good, he inherited Burgundy and the Low Countries from him 1465. He waged wars attempting to free the duchy from dependence on France and restore it as a kingdom. He was killed in battle.

Charles' ambition was to create a kingdom stretching from the mouth of the Rhine to the mouth of the Rhône. He formed the League of the Public Weal against Louis XI of France, invaded France 1471, and conquered the country as far as Rouen. The Holy Roman emperor, Lorraine, and the Swiss united against him; he captured Nancy, but was defeated at Granson, and again at Morat 1476. Nancy was lost and he was killed while attempting to recapture it. His possessions in the Netherlands passed to the Habsburgs by the marriage of his daughter Mary to Maximilian I of Austria.

Charleston /'tʃɑːlstən/ a back-kicking dance of the 1920s that originated in Charleston, South Carolina, and became an American craze.

Charleston /'tʃɑːlstən/ chief city of West Virginia, USA, on the Kanawha river; population (1980) 64,000. It is the centre of a district producing coal, natural gas, salt, clay, timber and oil. Home of the pioneer Daniel ◊Boone.

Charleston /'tʃɑːlstən/ main port and city of South Carolina, USA; population (1980) 486,000. Industries include textiles, clothing, and paper products. The city dates from 1670. Fort Sumter, in the sheltered harbour of Charleston, was bombarded by Confederate batteries 12–13 April 1861, thus beginning the Civil War. There are many historic houses and fine gardens.

charlock annual plant *Sinapis arvensis* of the family Cruciferae, also known as **wild mustard**. It is a common weed in Britain, reaching a height of 60 cm/2 ft, with yellow flowers.

Charlotte /'tʃɑːlət/ city in North Carolina, USA, on the border with South Carolina; population (1980) 314,500. Industries include data processing, textiles, chemicals, machinery, and food products. It was the gold-mining centre of the country until 1849. The Mint Museum of Arts has paintings, sculpture, and ceramics. Birthplace of James K Polk, 11th president of the USA.

Charlotte Amalie /'tʃɑːlət əˈmɑːljə/ capital and tourist resort of the US Virgin Islands; population (1980) 11,756.

Charlotte Augusta /'tʃɑːlət ɔːˈɡʌstə/ Princess 1796–1817. Only child of George IV and Caroline of Brunswick, and heir to the British throne. In 1816 she married Prince Leopold of Saxe-Coburg (later Leopold I of the Belgians), but died in childbirth 18 months later.

Charlotte Sophia /'tʃɑːlət səˈfaɪə/ 1744–1818. British queen consort. The daughter of the German duke of Mecklenburg-Strelitz, she married George III of Great Britain and Ireland 1761, and bore him nine sons and six daughters.

Charlottetown /'tʃɑːləttaʊn/ capital of Prince Edward Island, Canada; population (1986) 16,000. The city trades in textiles, fish, timber, vegetables, and dairy produce. It was founded by the French in the 1720s.

Charlton /'tʃɑːltən/ Jack 1935– . English footballer, older brother of Robert (Bobby) and nephew of Jackie Milburn. He spent all his playing career with Leeds United and played more than 750 games for them.

He and his brother both appeared in the England team that won the World Cup 1966. After retiring, Charlton managed Middlesborough to the 2nd division title. Appointed manager of the Republic of Ireland national squad in 1986, he took the team to the 1988 European Championship finals after which he was made an 'Honorary Irishman'. He led Ireland to the World Cup finals for the first time in 1990.

CAREER HIGHLIGHTS

World Cup 1966
Football League 1969
FA Cup 1972
Football League Cup 1968
Fairs Cup 1968, 1971
Footballer of the Year 1967

Charlton /'tʃɑːltən/ Robert 'Bobby' 1937– . English footballer, younger brother of Jack Charlton, who scored a record 49 goals in 106 appearances. He spent most of his playing career with Manchester United.

With Manchester United he won two League championship medals, one FA Cup winner's medal and a European Cup winner's medal. He was Footballer of the Year and European Footballer of the Year. On retiring he had an unsuccessful spell as manager of Preston North End. He later became a director of Manchester United.

CAREER HIGHLIGHTS

Football League appearances 644, goals 206
International appearances 106, goals 49
World Cup 1966
Football League championship 1965, 1967
FA Cup 1963
European Cup 1968
Footballer of the Year 1966
European Footballer of the Year 1966

charm in physics, property possessed by one type of ◊quark (very small particles found inside protons and neutrons), called the charm quark. The effects of charm are only seen in experiments with particle ◊accelerators. See ◊elementary particles.

Charon /'keərən/ in Greek mythology, the boatman who ferried the dead over the river Styx to the underworld.

Charpentier /ʃɑːˈpɒntieɪ/ Gustave 1860–1956. French composer who wrote an opera about Paris working-class life, *Louise* 1900.

Charpentier /ʃɑːˈpɒntieɪ/ Marc-Antoine 1645–1704. French composer. He wrote sacred music including a number of masses; other works include instrumental theatre music and the opera *Médée* 1693.

Charrière /ˌʃæriˈeə/ Isabelle Van Zuylen de 1740–1805. Dutch aristocrat, who settled in Colombier, Switzerland, in 1761. Her works include plays, tracts, and novels, including *Caliste* 1786. She had many early feminist ideas.

Charter 88 British political campaign begun 1988, calling for a written constitution to prevent what it termed the development of 'an elective dictatorship'. Those who signed the Charter, including many figures from the arts, objected to what they saw as the autocratic premiership of Prime Minister Margaret Thatcher.

Charteris /'tʃɑːtəris/ Leslie 1907– . British novelist. Born in Singapore, his varied career in many exotic occupations gave authentic background to some 40 novels about Simon Templar, the 'Saint', a gentleman-adventurer on the wrong side of the law, which have been adapted for films, radio and television. The first was *The Saint Meets the Tiger* 1928. He became a US citizen 1946.

Chartism radical British democratic movement, mainly of the working classes, which flourished around 1838–50. It derived its name from the People's Charter, a programme comprising six points: universal male suffrage, equal electoral districts, vote by ballot, annual parliaments, abolition of the property qualification for, and payment of, members of Parliament.

château *The château of Azay le Rideau, France.*

Chartres /'ʃɑːtrə/ capital of the *département* of Eure-et-Loir, NW France, 96 km/59 mi SW of Paris, on the river Eure; population (1982) 39,243. The city is an important agricultural centre for the fertile Plaine de la Beauce. Its cathedral of Nôtre Dame, completed about 1240, is a masterpiece of Gothic architecture.

chartreuse /ʃɑːˈtrɜːz/ green or yellow liqueur distilled since 1607 by the Carthusian monks at La Grande Chartreuse monastery, France, and also in Tarragona, Spain.

Chartreuse, La Grande /ʃɑːˈtrɜːz/ the original home of the Carthusian order of Roman Catholic monks, established by St Bruno around 1084, in a remote valley 23 km/14 mi NNE of Grenoble (in the modern *département* of Isère), France. The present buildings date from the 17th century.

Charybdis /kəˈrɪbdɪs/ in Greek mythology, a whirlpool formed by a monster of the same name on one side of the narrow straits of Messina, Sicily, opposite the monster Scylla.

Chase /tʃeɪs/ James Hadley. Pen name of René Raymond 1906–1985. He served in the Royal Air Force during World War II, and wrote *No Orchids for Miss Blandish* 1939, and other popular novels.

chasing indentation of a design on metal by small chisels and hammers. This method of decoration was familiar in ancient Egypt, Assyria, and Greece; it is used today on fine silverware.

chasuble the outer garment worn by the priest in the celebration of the Christian Mass. The colour of the chasuble depends on which feast is being celebrated.

château term originally applied to a French medieval castle, but now used to describe a country house or important residence in France. The château was first used as a domestic building in the late 15th century; by the reign of Louis XIII (1610–43) fortifications such as moats and keeps were no longer used for defensive purposes, but merely as decorative features. The Loire valley contains some particularly fine examples of châteaux.

Chateaubriand /ˈʃætəʊbriˈɒn/ François René, vicomte de 1768–1848. French author. In exile from the French Revolution 1794–99, he wrote *Atala* 1801 (written after his encounters with North American Indians); and the autobiographical *René*, which formed part of *Le Génie de Christianisme/The Genius of Christianity* 1802.

He visited the USA 1791 and, on his return to France, fought for the royalist side which was defeated at Thionville 1792. He lived in exile in England until 1800. When he returned to France, he held diplomatic appointments under Louis XVIII. He later wrote *Mémoires d'outre tombe/Memoirs from Beyond the Tomb* 1849–50.

Châtelet /ˌʃɑːtəˈleɪ/ Emilie de Breteuil, Marquise du 1706–1749. French scientific writer, mistress of ◊Voltaire, and translator into French of Newton's *Principia*.

Her marriage to the Marquis du Châtelet in 1725 gave her the leisure to study physics and mathematics. She met Voltaire in 1733, and settled with him at her husband's estate at Cirey, in the Duchy of Lorraine. Her study of Newton, with whom she collaborated on various scientific works, influenced Voltaire's work. She independently produced the first (and only) French translation of Newton's *Principia Mathematica* (published posthumously in 1759).

Chatham /'tʃætəm/ town in Kent, England; population (1983) 146,000. The Royal Dockyard 1588–1984 was from 1985 converted to a 'new town' including an industrial area, marina, and museum as a focus of revival for the whole Medway area.

Chatham Islands /'tʃætəm/ two Pacific islands (Chatham and Pitt), forming a county of South Island, New Zealand; area 960 sq km/371 sq mi; population (1981) 750. The chief settlement is ◊Waitangi.

Chattanooga /,tʃætə'nuːgə/ city in Tennessee, USA on the Tennessee River; population (1986) 426,000. It is the focus of the Tennessee Valley Authority area. Developed as a salt-trading centre after 1835, it now produces chemicals, textiles, and metal products.

Chatterji /'tʃætədʒiː/ Bankim Chandra 1838–1894. Indian novelist. Born in Bengal, where he established his reputation with his first book, *Durges-Nandini* 1864, he became a favourite of the nationalists. *Ananda Math* 1882 contains the Indian national song 'Bande-Mataram'.

Chatterton /'tʃætətən/ Thomas 1752–1770. English poet, whose medieval-style poems and brief life were to inspire English Romanticism. Born in Bristol, he studied ancient documents he found in the Church of St Mary Redcliffe, and composed poems he ascribed to a 15th-century monk, 'Thomas Rowley', which were accepted as genuine. He committed suicide in London, after becoming destitute.

He sent examples to Horace Walpole who was advised that they were forgeries. He then began contributing to periodicals in many styles, including Junius.

Chatwin /'tʃætwɪn/ Bruce 1940–1989. English writer. His works include *The Songlines* 1987, written after living with Aborigines, and *Utz* 1988, about a manic porcelain collector in Prague.

Chaucer /'tʃɔːsə/ Geoffrey c.1340–1400. English poet, author of *The Canterbury Tales* about 1387, a collection of tales told by pilgrims on their way to the Thomas à Becket shrine. He was the most influential English poet of the Middle Ages. The popularity of his work assured the dominance of southern English in literature. Chaucer's other work includes the French-influenced *Romance of the Rose* and an adaptation of Boccaccio's *Troilus and Criseyde*.

Chaucer was born in London. Taken prisoner in the French wars, he had to be ransomed by Edward III 1360. He married Philippa Roet 1366, becoming in later life the brother-in-law of ◊John of Gaunt. He achieved various appointments, for example, controller of London customs, and was sent on missions to Italy (where he may have met ◊Boccaccio and ◊Petrarch), France, and Flanders. His early work showed formal French influence, as in his adaptation of the French allegorical poem on courtly love *Romance of the Rose*; more mature works reflected the influence of Italian realism, as in his long narrative poem *Troilus and Criseyde*, adapted from Boccaccio. In *The Canterbury Tales* he showed his own genius for metre and characterization.

chauvinism a warlike patriotism, as exhibited by Nicholas Chauvin, one of Napoleon I's veterans and his fanatical admirer. In the mid-20th century the expression **male chauvinism** was coined to mean the belief in superiority of the male sex over the female.

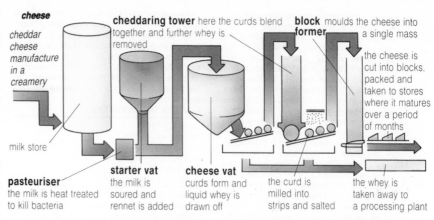

cheese

cheddar cheese manufacture in a creamery

milk store

pasteuriser the milk is heat treated to kill bacteria

starter vat the milk is soured and rennet is added

cheese vat curds form and liquid whey is drawn off

cheddaring tower here the curds blend together and further whey is removed

the curd is milled into strips and salted

block former moulds the cheese into a single mass

the cheese is cut into blocks, packed and taken to stores where it matures over a period of months

the whey is taken away to a processing plant

Chávez /'tʃɑːves/ Carlos 1899–1978. Mexican composer. A student of the piano and of the complex rhythms of his country's folk music, he founded the Mexico Symphony Orchestra. His composed a number of ballets, seven symphonies, and concertos for both violin and piano.

Chayefsky /'tʃeɪˈefski/ (Sidney) 'Paddy' 1923–1981. US writer. He established his reputation with the television plays *Marty* 1955 (for which he won an Oscar when he turned it into a film), and *Bachelor Party* 1957. He also won Oscars for *The Hospital* 1971 and *Network* 1976.

Cheapside /'tʃiːpsaɪd/ a street running from St Paul's Cathedral to Poultry, in the City of London, England. The scene of the 13th century 'Cheap', a permanent fair and general market. Christopher Wren's church of St Mary-le-Bow in Cheapside has the famous Bow Bells.

Checheno-Ingush /tʃɪˈʃenəu ɪŋˈguːʃ/ autonomous republic in the W USSR; area 19,300/7,350 sq mi; population (1986) 1,230,000. It was conquered in the 1850s, and is a major oilfield. The capital is Grozny. The population includes Chechens (53%) and Ingushes (12%).

check digit in computing, a digit added to important codes for ◊error detection.

Cheddar /'tʃedə/ village in Somerset, England; population (1983) 3,994. It is famous for cheese, its limestone gorge, and caves with stalactites and stalagmites. In 1962 excavation revealed the site of a Saxon palace.

cheese Food made by clotting milk from cows, sheep, or goats with ◊rennet or lactic acid, to produce solid **curds** and liquid **whey**. The whey is drained off and the curds are salted, put into moulds, and pressed into firm blocks. Cheese is ripened with bacteria or surface fungi, and kept for a time to mature before eating.

There are six main types of cheese. **Soft cheeses** may be ripe or unripe, and include cottage cheese and high-fat soft cheeses such as Bel Paese, Camembert, and Neufchatel. **Semi-hard cheeses**

are ripened by bacteria (Munster) or by bacteria and surface fungi (Port Salut, Gouda, St Paulin); they may also have penicillin moulds injected into them (Roquefort, Gorgonzola, Blue Stilton, Wensleydale). **Hard cheeses** are ripened by bacteria, and include Cheddar, Cheshire, and Cucciocavallo; some have large cavities within them, such as Swiss Emmental and Gruyère. **Very hard cheeses**, such as Parmesan and Spalen, are made with skimmed milk. **Processed cheese** is made with dried skim milk powder and additives, and **whey cheese** is made by heat coagulation of the proteins from whey; examples are Mysost and Primost.

In France (from 1980) cheese has the same *appellation controlée* status as wine if made only in a special defined area, for example Cantal and Roquefort, but not Camembert and Brie, which are also made elsewhere.

cheesecloth fine muslin or cotton fabric of very loose weave, originally used to press curds during the cheesemaking process.

cheetah large wild cat *Acinonyx jubatus* native to Africa, Arabia, and SW Asia, but now rare in

Chaucer Posthumous portrait of the English poet Geoffrey Chaucer by an unknown artist, National Portrait Gallery, London.

Chekhov Russian writer Anton Chekhov, author of The Cherry Orchard.

some areas. Yellowish with black spots, it has a slim lithe build. It is up to 1 m/3 ft tall at the shoulder, and up to 1.5 m/5 ft long. It can reach 110 kph/70 mph, but tires after about 400 metres. Cheetahs live in open country where they hunt small antelopes, hares, and birds.

A cheetah's claws do not retract as fully as in most cats.

Cheever /'tʃiːvə/ John 1912–1982. US writer. His short stories and novels include *The Wapshot Chronicle* 1937, *Bullet Park* 1969, *World of Apples* 1973, and *Falconer* 1977.

chef d'oeuvre (French) a masterpiece.

Chefoo /,tʃiː'fuː/ former name of part of ◊Yantai in China.

Cheka secret police operating in the USSR 1918–23. It originated from the tsarist Okhrana and became successively the OGPU (GPU) 1923–34, NKVD 1934–46, and MVD 1946–53, before its present form, the ◊KGB.

The name is formed from the initials *che* and *ka* of the two Russian words meaning 'extraordinary commission', formed for 'the repression of counter-revolutionary activities and of speculation', and extended to cover such matters as espionage and smuggling.

Chekhov /'tʃekɒf/ Anton (Pavlovich) 1860–1904. Russian dramatist and writer. He began to write short stories and comic sketches as a medical student. His plays concentrate on the creation of atmosphere and delineation of internal development, rather than external action. His first play *Ivanov* 1887 was a failure, as was *The Seagull* 1896 until revived by Stanislavsky 1898 at the Moscow Arts Theatre, for which Chekhov went on to write his major plays *Uncle Vanya* 1899, *The Three Sisters* 1901 and *The Cherry Orchard* 1904.

Born at Taganrog, he qualified as a doctor 1884, but devoted himself to writing short stories rather than medical practice. A collection *Particoloured Stories* 1886 consolidated his reputation, and gave him leisure to develop his style: *My Life* 1895, *The Lady with the Dog* 1898 and *In the Ravine* 1900.

Chekiang /,tʃeki'æŋ/ former name for ◊Zhejiang province of SE China.

chela in Hinduism, a follower or pupil of a guru (teacher).

chelate type of chemical compound whose molecules consist of one or more metal atoms or charged ions joined to chains of organic residues by coordinate (or dative covalent) chemical ◊bonds.

The parent organic compound is known as a *chelating agent* (for example EDTA, ethylenediaminetetraacetic acid, used in chemical analysis).

Chelmsford /'tʃelmzfəd/ town in Essex, England, 48 km/30 mi NE of London; population (1981) 58,000. It is the administrative headquarters of the county, and a market town with radio, electrical, engineering, and agricultural machinery industries.

Chelsea /'tʃelsi/ historic area of the Royal Borough of Kensington and Chelsea, London, immediately north of the Thames, where it is crossed by the Albert and Chelsea bridges. The Royal Hospital was founded in 1682 by Charles II for old and disabled soldiers, 'Chelsea Pensioners', and the National Army Museum 1960 covers campaigns 1485–1914. The Physic Garden for botanical research was established in the 17th century; and the home of Thomas Carlyle in Cheyne Row is a museum. The Chelsea Flower Show is held annually by the Royal Horticultural Society in the grounds of Royal Hospital. Ranelagh Gardens 1742–1804 and Cremorne Gardens 1845–77 were celebrated places of entertainment.

Chelsea porcelain factory thought to be the first porcelain factory in England. Based in SW London, it dated from the 1740s and produced softpaste porcelain in imitation of Chinese high-fired porcelain. Later items are distinguishable by the anchor mark on the base. Chelsea porcelain includes plates and other items decorated with botanical, bird, and insect paintings. The factory was taken over by William Duesbury of Derby 1769 (after which the so-called 'Chelsea-Derby' was produced), and pulled down 1784.

Cheltenham /'tʃeltənəm/ spa at the foot of the Cotswolds, Gloucestershire, England; population (1981) 73,000. There are annual literary and music festivals, a racecourse (the Cheltenham Gold Cup is held annually), and Cheltenham College (founded 1854). The home of the composer Gustav Holst is now a museum, and to the SW is Prinknash Abbey, a Benedictine house that produces pottery. Cheltenham is also the centre of the British government's electronic surveillance operations (◊GCHQ). The Universities' Central Council on Admissions (UCCA) 1963 and the Polytechnics and Colleges Admissions System (PCAS) 1985 are here.

Chelyabinsk /,tʃeli'æbɪnsk/ industrial town and capital of Chelyabinsk region, W Siberia, USSR; population (1987) 1,119,000. It has iron and engineering works, and makes chemicals, motor vehicles, and aircraft.

It lies east of the Ural Mountains, 240 km/150 mi SE of Sverdlovsk. It was founded 1736 as a Russian frontier post.

chemical change the change that occurs when two or more substances (reactants) interact with each other resulting in the production of different substances (products) with different chemical compositions.

chemical element another name for ◊element.

chemical equation method of indicating the reactants and products of a chemical reaction by using chemical symbols and formulae. These may indicate atoms, ions, radicals, or molecules.

The equation should balance, that is, the total number of atoms of a particular element among the reactants (on the left-hand side of the equation) must be the same as the number of atoms of that element among the products (on the right-hand side). For example, the equation $2H_2 + O_2 \rightarrow 2H_2O$ denotes that two molecules of hydrogen combine with one molecule of oxygen to form two molecules of water; there are four atoms of hydrogen and two atoms of oxygen represented on each side of the equation, so it balances.

Substituting the molecular weights of the participating substances indicates the proportions of masses involved. In this case $2 \times 2 = 4$ grams of hydrogen $+ 2 \times 16 = 32$ grams of oxygen $\equiv 2 \times 18 = 36$ grams of water. The double arrows in the equation $3H_2 + N_2 \rightleftharpoons 2NH_3$ indicate that the formation of ammonia from hydrogen and nitrogen is a reversible reaction (in this example depending on the temperature and pressure of the reactants).

chemical equilibrium a condition in which the products of a reversible chemical reaction are formed at the same rate at which they decompose back into the reactants, so that the concentration of each reactant and product remains constant.

chemical warfare use in war of gaseous, liquid, or solid substances intended to have a toxic effect on humans, animals, or plants. Together with biological warfare, it was banned 1925 by the Geneva Convention, although this has not always been observed. In 1989, when the 149-nation Conference on Chemical Weapons unanimously voted to outlaw chemical weapons, the total US stockpile was estimated at 30,000 tonnes and the Soviet stockpile at 300,000 tonnes.

In a deal with the USA, the USSR offered to eliminate its stocks; the USA is destroying its current stocks and replacing them with new 'binary' nerve-gas weapons. Some 20 nations currently hold chemical weapons, including Iraq, Iran, Israel, Syria, Libya, South Africa, and China.

There are several types of chemical weapons. *Irritant gases* may cause permanent injury or death. Examples include chlorine, phosgene (Cl_2CO), and mustard gas ($C_4H_8Cl_2S$), used in World War I (1914–18) and allegedly used by Soviet forces in Afghanistan, by Vietnamese forces in Laos, and by Iraq against Iran during their 1980–88 war. *Tear gases*, such as CS gas, used in riot control, affect the lungs and eyes, causing temporary blindness. *Nerve gases* are organophosphorus compounds similar to insecticides, which are taken into the body through the skin and lungs and break down the action of the nervous system. Developed by the Germans for World War II, they were not used.

Incapacitants are drugs designed to put an enemy temporarily out of action by, for example, impairing vision or inducing hallucinations. They have not so far been used. *Toxins* are poisons to be eaten, drunk, or injected; for example, ricin (derived from the castor-oil plant) and the botulism toxin. Ricin has been used in individual cases, and other toxins have allegedly been used by Soviet forces in Afghanistan and Vietnamese forces in Cambodia. *Herbicides* are defoliants used to destroy vegetation sheltering troops and the crops of hostile populations. They were used in Vietnam by the USA and in Malaya by the UK. ◊Agent Orange became notorious because it caused cancer and birth abnormalities among Vietnam War veterans and US factory staff. *Binary weapons* are two chemical components that become toxic in combination, after the shell containing them is fired.

chemiluminescence alternative term for ◊bioluminescence.

chemisorption in chemistry, the attachment, by chemical means, of a single layer of molecules, atoms, or ions of gas to the surface of a solid or, less frequently, a liquid. It is the basis of catalysis and of great industrial importance.

chemistry the science concerned with the composition of matter, and of the changes which take place in it under certain conditions.

All matter can exist in three states: gas, liquid, or solid. It is composed of minute particles termed *molecules*, which are constantly moving, and may be further divided into ◊atoms. Molecules which contain atoms of one kind only are known as *elements*; those that contain atoms of different kinds are called *compounds*.

Examination and possible breakdown of compounds to determine their components is *analysis*, and the building up of compounds from their components is *synthesis*. When substances are brought together without changing their molecular structure they are said to be *mixtures*. Chemical compounds are produced by a chemical action that alters the arrangement of the atoms in the molecule. Heat, light, vibration, catalytic action, radiation or pressure, as well as moisture (for ionization), may be necessary to produce a chemical change.

Organic chemistry is the branch of chemistry that deals with carbon compounds. *Inorganic chemistry* deals with the description, properties, reactions, and preparation of the elements and their compounds, with the exception of carbon compounds.

Physical chemistry is concerned with the quantitative explanation of chemical phenomena and reactions, and the measurement of data required for such explanations. This branch studies in particular the movement of molecules, and the effects of temperature and pressure, often with regard to gases and liquids.

Symbols are used to denote the elements. The symbol is usually the first letter or letters of the English or Latinized name of the element, for example C, carbon; Ca, calcium; Fe, iron (ferrum). These symbols represent one atom of the element; molecules containing more than one atom are denoted by a subscript figure, for example, water, H_2O. In some substances a group of atoms acts as a single entity, and these are enclosed in brackets in the symbol, for example $(NH_4)_2SO_4$, ammonium sulphate. The symbolic representation of a molecule is known as a *formula*. A figure placed before a formula represents the number of molecules of one substance present in another, for example $2H_2O$, two molecules of water. Chemical

chemistry chronology

1 AD	Gold, silver, copper, lead, iron, tin, and mercury were known.
1100	Alcohol was first distilled.
1242	Gunpowder was introduced to Europe from the Far East.
1540	Date of first known scientific observation and experiment.
1604	Italian mathematician, astronomer and physicist Galileo invented the thermometer.
1620	Scientific method of reasoning was expounded by English philosopher Francis Bacon in his *Novum Organum*.
1649	Carbon, sulphur, antimony, and arsenic were known.
1650	Leyden University in the Netherlands set up the first chemistry laboratory.
1660	Law concerning effect of pressure on gas (*Boyle's Law*) was established by English chemist Robert Boyle; definition of the element.
1662	The Royal Society was formed.
1742	Invention of the Centigrade scale.
1746	Lead chamber process developed for manufacturing sulphuric acid; German chemist Andreas Marggraf discovered zinc.
1750	Swedish chemist Axel Cronstedt discovered cobalt and nickel.
1756	Scottish chemist and physicist Joseph Black discovered carbon dioxide.
1772	German chemist Karl Scheele discovered oxygen, two years before Priestley.
1774	Scheele discovered chlorine; Swedish chemist Johan Gahn discovered manganese; Lavoisier demonstrated his *law of conservation of mass*.
1777	Lavoisier explained burning; sulphur was known to be an element.
1779	Dutch scientist Jan Ingenhousz demonstrated photosynthesis.
1781	English scientist Henry Cavendish showed water to be a compound.
1792	Italian physicist Alessandro Volta demonstrated the electrochemical series.
1793	German chemist Hieronymus Richter demonstrated the *law of equivalent proportions*.
1799	Twenty-seven elements were known.
1800	Volta designed his electric battery.
1801	Dalton demonstrated his *law of partial pressures*.
1803	Dalton expounded his atomic theory.
1807	Sodium and potassium were first prepared by Davy.
1808	Gay-Lussac announced his *law of volumes*.
1811	Publication of Italian physicist Amedeo Avogadro's hypothesis on the relationship of volumes of gases and

	numbers of molecules to temperature and pressure.
1813	French chemist Bernard Courtois discovered iodine.
1818	Berzelius's atomic symbols were elaborated.
1819	French scientists Henri Dulong and Alexis-Thérèse Petit's *law of atomic heats* was demonstrated.
1825	French chemist Antoine-Jerôme Balard prepared bromine. Matches were invented.
1828	The first organic compounds, alcohol and urea, were synthesized.
1834	Faraday expounded the *laws of electrolysis*.
1836	Acetylene was discovered.
1840	Liebig expounded the carbon and nitrogen cycles.
1846	Scottish chemist Thomas Graham's *law of diffusion* (*Graham's Law*) was expounded.
1850	Ammonia was first made from coal-gas.
1853	German chemist Robert Bunsen invented his burner.
1858	Cannizzaro's method of atomic weights was expounded.
1866	Nobel invented dynamite.
1868	The first plastic substance – celluloid – was made.
1869	Mendeleyev expounded his Periodic Table.
1879	Saccharin was discovered.
1886	French chemist Ferdinand Moissan isolated fluorine.
1894	Ramsay and Rayleigh discovered inert gases.
1897	The electron was discovered by English physicist Sir Joseph Thomson.
1898	The Curies discovered radium.
1912	Vitamins were discovered by British biochemist Gowland Hopkins; British physicist Lawrence Bragg demonstrated that crystals have a regular arrangement of atoms.
1919	Artificial disintegration of atoms by Rutherford.
1920	Rutherford discovered the proton.
1927	British chemist Neil Sidgwick's *theory of valency* was announced.
1928	Vitamin C was crystallized.
1932	Deuterium (heavy water) was discovered; Chadwick discovered the neutron.
1933	British chemist Norman Haworth synthesized Vitamin C.
1942	Plutonium was first synthesized.
1945	The atomic bomb was exploded.
1953	Hydrogen was converted to helium.
1954	Einsteinium and fermium were synthesized.

reactions are expressed by means of equations, as in: NaCl + H_2SO_4 → $NaHSO_4$ + HCl. This equation states the fact that sodium chloride (NaCl) on being treated with sulphuric acid (H_2SO_4) is converted into sodium bisulphate (sodium hydrogen sulphate, $NaHSO_4$) and hydrogen chloride (HCl).

Elements are divided into **metals**, which have lustre and conduct heat and electricity, and non-metals, which usually lack these properties. The **periodic system**, developed by Newlands in 1863 and established by Mendeleev in 1869, classified elements according to their relative atomic masses, that is, the least weight of the element present in a molecular weight of any of its compounds. Those elements which resemble each other in general properties were found to bear a relation to one another by weight, and these were placed in groups or families. Certain anomalies in this system were removed by classifying the elements according to their atomic number. The

latter is equivalent to the positive charge on the nucleus of the atom.

history Ancient civilizations were familiar with certain chemical processes, for example, extracting metals from their ores, and making alloys. The alchemists endeavored to turn base metals into gold, and modern chemistry may be said to have evolved from alchemy towards the end of the 17th century. Robert Boyle defined elements as the simplest substances into which matter could be resolved. The alchemical doctrine of the four elements (earth, air, fire, and water) gradually lost its hold, and the theory that all combustible bodies contained a substance called phlogiston (a weightless 'fire element' generated during combustion) was discredited in the 18th century by the experimental work of Black, Lavoisier, and Priestley (who discovered the presence of oxygen in the air). Cavendish discovered the composition of water, and Dalton put forward the atomic theory, which ascribed a precise relative weight to the 'simple atom' characteristic of each element. Much research then took place leading to the development in modern times of ◊biochemistry, ◊chemotherapy, and ◊plastics.

Chemnitz /ˈkemnɪts/ former name for ◊Karl-Marx-Stadt, industrial city in East Germany.

chemosynthesis method of making ◊protoplasm (contents of a cell) using the energy from chemical reactions, in contrast to the use of light energy employed for the same purpose in ◊photosynthesis. The process is used by certain bacteria, which can synthesize organic compounds from carbon dioxide and water using the energy from special methods of ◊respiration.

An important group of chemosynthetic organisms are the nitrifying bacteria which change free nitrogen into a form that can be taken up by plants, for example, nitrobacteria which oxidize nitrites to nitrates. This is a vital part of the ◊nitrogen cycle. As chemosynthetic bacteria can survive without light energy, they can live in dark and inhospitable regions, including the hydrothermal vents of the Pacific ocean. Around these vents, where temperatures reach up to 350°C/662°F, the chemosythetic bacteria are the basis of a food web supporting fishes and other marine life.

chemotherapy medical treatment with chemicals. It usually refers to treatment of cancer or mental illness with drugs.

Chemulpo /ˌtʃemʊlˈpəʊ/ former name for ◊Inchon, port and summer resort on the W coast of South Korea.

Chenab /tʃɪˈnæb/ a tributary of the river ◊Indus.

Chengchow /ˌtʃeŋˈtʃaʊ/ former name of ◊Zhengzhou, capital of Henan province of China.

Chengde /ˌtʃeŋˈdeɪ/ town, formerly **Chengteh** in Hebei province, China, NE of Beijing; population (1984) 325,800. It is a market town for agricultural and forestry products. It was the summer residence of the Manchu rulers and has an 18th-century palace and temples.

Chengdu /ˌtʃeŋˈduː/ formerly **Chengtu** ancient city capital of Sichuan province, China; population (1986) 2,580,000. It is an important rail junction and has railway workshops, textile, electronics, and engineering industries. It has well-preserved temples.

Chengteh former name for ◊Chengde.

Chengtu former name for ◊Chengdu.

Chénier /ˌʃeɪniˈeɪ/ André de 1762–1794. French poet, born in Constantinople. His lyrical poetry was later to inspire the Romantic movement, but he was known in his own time for his uncompromising support of the constitutional royalists after the Revolution. In 1793 he went into hiding, but finally he was arrested, and on 25 July 1794, guillotined. While in prison he wrote *Jeune Captive*/*Captive Girl* and the political *Iambes*, published after his death.

Chepstow /ˈtʃepstəʊ/ market town in Gwent, Wales, on the Wye; population (1984) 12,500. The high tides, sometimes 15 m/50 ft above low level, are the highest in Britain. There is

Chernobyl *The damage caused to the nuclear reactor in the 1986 accident at the Chernobyl power station near Kiev, USSR.*

a Norman castle, and the ruins of Tintern Abbey are 6.5 km/4 mi to the N.

cheque (US *check*) an order written by the drawer to a commercial or central bank to pay a specific sum on demand.

Usually the cheque should bear the date on which it is payable, a definite sum of money to be paid, written in words and figures, to a named person or body, or to the bearer, and be signed by the drawer. It is then payable on presentation at the bank on which it is drawn. If the cheque is 'crossed', as is usual British practice, it is not negotiable and can be paid only through a bank; in the US a cheque is always negotiable.

cheque card card issued from 1968 by savings and clearings banks in Europe, which guarantees payment by the issuing bank when it is presented with a cheque for payment of goods or service.

It bears the customer's signature and account number, for comparison with those on the cheque, and payment to the vendor by the issuing bank is immediate, no commission being charged. It is also known as a banker's card. Unlike the ◊credit card, it cannot be used by itself for the purchase of goods.

Chequers /ˈtʃekəz/ country home of the prime minister of the UK. It is an Elizabethan mansion in the Chiltern hills near Princes Risborough, Buckinghamshire, and was given to the nation by Lord Lee of Fareham under the Chequers Estate Act 1917, which came into effect Jan 1921.

Cher /ʃeə/ French river which rises in Creuse *département* and flows into the Loire below Tours. Length 355 km/220 mi. It gives its name to a *département*.

Cherbourg /ˈʃeəbʊəg/ French port and naval station at the northern end of the Cotentin peninsula, in Manche *département*; population (1982) 85,500 (conurbation). There is an institute for studies in nuclear warfare, and Cherbourg has large shipbuilding yards. During World War II, Cherbourg was captured June 1944 by the Allies, who thus gained their first large port of entry into France. Cherbourg was severely damaged; restoration of the harbour was completed 1952. There is a nuclear processing plant at nearby Cap la Hague. There are ferry links to Southampton, Weymouth, and Rosslare.

Cherenkov /tʃɪˈreŋkɒf/ Pavel 1904– . Soviet physicist. In 1934, he discovered **Cherenkov radiation**; this occurs as a bluish light when charged atomic particles pass through water or other media at a speed in excess of that of light. He shared a Nobel prize 1958 with his colleagues Ilya ◊Frank and Igor Tamm.

Cherenkov discovered that this effect was independent of any medium and depended for its production on the passage of high velocity electrons.

Cherepovets /ˌtʃerɪpəˈvets/ iron and steel city in W USSR, on the Volga-Baltic waterway; population (1985) 299,000.

Chéret /ʃeˈreɪ/ Jules 1836–1932. One of the first French ◊poster artists.

Chernenko /tʃəˈneŋkəʊ/ Konstantin 1911–1985. Soviet politician, leader of the Soviet Communist Party (CPSU) and president 1984–85. He was a protégé of Brezhnev and from 1978 a member of the Politburo.

Chernenko, born in central Siberia, joined the Komsomol (Communist Youth League) 1929 and the CPSU 1931. The future CPSU leader Brezhnev brought him to Moscow to work in the central apparatus 1956 and later sought to establish Chernenko as his successor, but he was passed over in favour of the KGB chief Andropov. When Andropov died Feb 1984 Chernenko was selected as the CPSU's stop-gap leader by cautious party colleagues, and was also elected president. From July 1984 he gradually retired from public life because of failing health.

Chernigov /tʃəˈnɪgɒf/ town and port on the river Desna in N Ukraine; population (1987) 291,000. It has an 11th-century cathedral. Lumbering, textiles, chemicals, distilling, and food-canning are among its industries.

Chernobyl /tʃəˈnəʊbəl/ town in Ukraine, USSR. In Apr 1986, a leak, caused by overheating, occurred in a non-pressurized boiling-water nuclear reactor. The resulting clouds of radioactive isotopes were traced as far away as Sweden; over 250 people were killed, and thousands of square kilometres contaminated.

Chernovtsy /tʃəˈnɒftsiː/ city in Ukraine, USSR; population (1987) 254,000. Industries include textiles, clothing, and machinery. Former names: Czernowitz (before 1918), Cernăuţi (1918–1940, when it was part of Romania), Chrenovitsy (1940–44).

Cherokee /ˈtʃerəkiː/ North ◊American Indian people, formerly living in the mountain country of Alabama, the Carolinas, Georgia, and Tennessee. Sequoyah (*c.*1770–1843), devised the syllabary used for writing down the Indian languages. They now live mainly in North Carolina and Oklahoma, where they established their capital at Tahlequah. Their language belongs to the Iroquoian family.

cherry tree of the genus *Prunus*, distinguished from plums and apricots by its fruit, which is spherical and smooth and not covered with a bloom.

Cultivated cherries are derived from two species, the sour cherry *Prunus cerasus*, and the gean *Prunus avium*, which grow wild in Britain. The former is the ancestor of morello, duke, and Kentish cherries; the latter of the sweet cherries—hearts, mazzards, and bigarreaus. Besides

chervil

those varieties that are grown for their fruit, others are well-known ornamental trees.

Cherry Orchard, The a play by Anton Chekhov, first produced 1904. Its theme, the demise of the way of life of a landowning family, is symbolized by the felling of a cherry orchard after it has been sold to an entrepreneur.

cherub (Hebrew *kerubh*) (plural **cherubim**) a type of angel in Christian belief, usually depicted as a young child with wings. Cherubim form the second order of ◊angels.

Cherubini /ˌkeruˈbiːni/ Luigi (Carlo Zanobi Salvadore Maria) 1760–1842. Italian composer. His first opera *Quinto Fabio* 1779 was produced at Alessandria. In 1784 he went to London and became composer to King George III, but from 1788 he lived in Paris, where he produced a number of dramatic works including *Médée* 1797, *Les Deux Journées* 1800, and the ballet *Anacréon* 1803. After 1809 he devoted himself largely to church music.

chervil plants, genus *Chaerophyllum*, of the family Umbelliferae. The garden chervil *Chaerophyllum cerefolium* has leaves with a sweetish odour, resembling parsley. It is used as a garnish, and as a pot-herb.

Cherwell /ˈtʃɑːwəl/ Frederick Alexander Lindemann 1886–1957. British physicist. He was director of the Physical Laboratory of the RAF at Farnborough in World War I, and personal adviser to ◊Churchill on scientific and statistical matters during World War II. He was professor of experimental philosophy at the Clarendon Laboratory, Oxford 1919–56.

Ches. abbreviation for ◊*Cheshire*.

Chesapeake Bay /ˈtʃesəpiːk/ largest of the inlets on the Atlantic coast of the USA, bordered by Maryland and Virginia. Its wildlife is threatened by urban and industrial development.

Cheshire /ˈtʃeʃə/ county in NW England
area 2,320 sq km/896 sq mi
towns administrative headquarters Chester; Warrington, Crewe, Widnes, Macclesfield, Congleton
physical chiefly a fertile plain; Mersey, Dee, and Weaver rivers
features salt mines and geologically rich former copper workings at Alderley Edge (in use from Roman times until the 1920s); Little Moreton Hall; discovery of Lindow Man, the first 'bogman', dating from around 500 BC, to be found in mainland Britain; Quarry Bank Mill at Styal is a cotton industry museum
products textiles, chemicals, dairy products
population (1987) 952,000
famous people Mrs Gaskell lived at Knutsford (the locale of *Cranford*), John Speed.

Cheshire /ˈtʃeʃə/ (Geoffrey) Leonard 1917– . British pilot. Commissioned with the Royal Air Force on the outbreak of the World War II, he won the Victoria Cross, Distinguished Service Order

Cheshire

chess

the way each piece can move

arrangement of the chessmen

(with 2 bars), and Distinguished Flying Cross. A devout Roman Catholic, he founded the first Cheshire Foundation Home for the Incurably Sick 1948. In 1959 he married Susan Ryder (1923–) who established a foundation for the sick and disabled of all ages and became a life peeress 1978.

Chesil bank /'tʃezəl/ shingle bank extending 19 km/11 mi along the coast of Dorset, England, from Abbotsbury to the Isle of Portland.

chess board game originating as early as the 2nd century AD. Two players use 16 pieces each, on a board of 64 squares of alternating colour, to try and force the opponent into a position where the main piece (the king) is threatened, and cannot move to another position without remaining threatened.

The Fédération Internationale des Echecs (FIDE) was established 1924. Leading players are rated according to the Elo System and Bobby Fischer (USA) is one of the greatest Grand Masters of all time with a rating of 2,785. A world championship was established 1851.

Chess World Champions

first official world champion recognized 1886.
Recent champions:
men
1957 Vassiliy Smyslov *(USSR)*
1958 Mikhail Botvinnik *(USSR)*
1960 Mikhail Tal *(USSR)*
1961 Mikhail Botvinnik *(USSR)*
1963 Tigran Petrosian *(USSR)*
1969 Boris Spassky *(USSR)*
1972 Bobby Fischer *(USA)*
1975 Anatoliy Karpov *(USSR)*
1985 Gary Kasparov *(USSR)*
women
1950 Lyudmila Rudenko *(USSR)*
1953 Elizaveta Bykova *(USSR)*
1955 Olga Runtsova *(USSR)*
1958 Elizaveta Bykova *(USSR)*
1962 Nona Gaprindashvili *(USSR)*
1978 Maya Chiburdanidze *(USSR)*

Chester /'tʃestə/ city in Cheshire, Englan, on the river Dee 26 km/16 mi S of Liverpool; population (1984) 117,000. It is the administrative headquarters of Cheshire. Industries include engineering and the manufacture of car components. Its name derives from the Roman *Castra Devana*, 'the camp on the Dee', and there are many Roman and later remains. It is the only English city to retain its city walls (two miles long) intact. The cathedral dates from the 11th century but was restored in 1876. The church of St John the Baptist

chestnut

is a well-known example of early Norman architecture. The 'Rows' are covered arcades dating from the Middle Ages. From 1070 to the reign of Henry III, Chester was the seat of a ◊county palatine (a county whose lord exercised some of the roles usually reserved for the monarch). The town hall dates from 1869. Although the silting up of the Dee destroyed Chester's importance as a port, navigation has been greatly improved by dredging.

Chesterfield /'tʃestəfiːld/ market town of Derbyshire, England; 40 km/25 mi N of Derby, on the Rother river; population (1981) 78,200. Industries include coal-mining engineering, and glass. Burial place of the engineer George ◊Stephenson. All Saints' Church is renowned for its crooked spire.

Chesterfield /'tʃestəfiːld/ Philip Dormer Stanhope, 4th Earl of Chesterfield 1694–1773. English politician and writer, author of *Letters to his Son* 1774 – his illegitimate son, Philip Stanhope (1732–68).

Born in London, he was ambassador to Holland 1728–32 and 1744. In Ireland, he established schools, helped to reconcile Protestants and Catholics, and encouraged manufacturing. An opponent of Walpole, he was a Whig MP 1715–26, Lord-Lieutenant of Ireland 1745–46, and Secretary of State 1746–48. A member of the literary circle of Swift, Pope, and Bolingbroke, he incurred the wrath of Dr Samuel ◊Johnson by failing to carry out an offer of patronage.

Chesterton /'tʃestətən/ G(ilbert) K(eith) 1874–1936. English novelist, essayist, and satirical poet, author of a series of novels featuring the naive priest-detective 'Father Brown'. Other novels include *The Napoleon of Notting Hill* 1904 and *The Man Who Knew Too Much* 1922.

Born in London, he studied art but quickly turned to journalism. Like Hilaire Belloc he was initially a Socialist sympathizer and joined the Catholic Church 1922.

chestnut tree, genus *Castanea*, belonging to the same family, Fagaceae, as the oak and beech. The Spanish or sweet chestnut, *Castanea sativa*, produces a fruit that is a common article of diet in Europe and the USA; its timber is also valuable. The horse chestnut or conker tree, *Aesculus hippocastanum*, is quite distinct, belonging to a different family.

It is native to the Balkans and Italy; it was introduced to Britain in Roman times, but is not common elsewhere in northern Europe.

Chetnik member of a Serbian nationalist group that operated underground during the German occupation of Yugoslavia during World War II. Led by Col Draza ◊Mihailovič, the Chetniks initially received aid from the Allies, but this was later transferred to the communist partisans led by Tito.

Chevalier /ʃə'vælieɪ/ Maurice 1888–1972. French singer and actor. He began as dancing partner to the revue artiste ◊Mistinguett at the ◊Folies-Bergère, and made numerous films including *Innocents of Paris* 1929, which revived his song 'Louise', *The Merry Widow* 1934, and *Gigi* 1958.

Chiang Kai-shek *Chinese nationalist leader Chiang Kai-shek helped to unite China in the 1920s and fought a bitter war with the communist Mao Zedong before being driven out of mainland China to Taiwan in 1949.*

Chevening /'tʃiːvnɪŋ/ residence near Sevenoaks, Kent, bequeathed to the nation by the 7th Earl of Stanhope for royal or ministerial use. Prince Charles lived there 1974–80.

Cheviots /'tʃiːviəts/ range of hills 56 km/35 mi long, mainly in Northumberland, forming the border between England and Scotland for some 48 km/30 mi. The highest point is the Cheviot 816 m/2,676 ft. For centuries the area was a battleground between the English and the Scots. It gives its name to a breed of sheep.

Chevreul /ʃə'vrɜːl/ Michel-Eugene 1786–1889. French chemist who studied the composition of fats and identified a number of fatty acids, including 'margaric acid', which became the basis of margarine.

Chevreul was Director of the Natural History Museum and Director of Dyeing at the Gobelin tapestry factory.

chewing gum confectionery mainly composed of chicle (juice of the sapodilla tree *Achras zapota* of Central America), flavoured, especially with mint, and usually sweetened. The first patent was taken out in the USA 1871.

Chiang Ching former name of the Chinese actress ◊Jiang Qing, third wife of Mao.

Chiang Ching-kuo /tʃiˈæŋ ˌtʃɪŋˈkwəʊ/ 1910–1988. Taiwanese politician, son of Chiang Kai-shek. Prime minister from 1971, he became president 1978.

Chiang Kai-shek /'tʃæŋ kaɪ 'ʃek/ Pinyin *Jiang Jie Shi* 1887–1975. Chinese ◊Guomindang (Kuomintang) general and politician, president of China 1928–31 and 1943–49, and of Taiwan from 1949, where he set up a breakaway right-wing government on his expulsion from the mainland by the communist forces. He was a commander in the civil war that lasted from the end of imperial rule 1911 to the Second ◊Sino-Japanese War and beyond, having split with the communist leader Mao Zedong 1927.

Chiang took part in the revolution of 1911 that overthrew the Manchu Ch'ing dynasty, and on the death of the Guomindang leader Sun Yat-sen was made commander in chief of the nationalist armies in S China 1925. Collaboration with the communists, broken 1927, was resumed after the ◊Xian incident 1936, and Chiang nominally headed the struggle against the Japanese invaders, receiving the Japanese surrender 1945. In Dec 1949 he took refuge on the island of Taiwan, maintaining a large

Chichen Itzá *The main pyramid of Chichen Itzá, Mexico.*

army in the hope of reclaiming the mainland. His authoritarian regime enjoyed US support until his death. He was succeeded as president by his son Chiang Ching-kuo.

Chiba /'tʃiːbə/ industrial city (paper, steel, textiles) in Kanton region, E Honshu island, Japan, 40 km/25 mi west of Tokyo; population (1987) 793,000.

Chibchas /'tʃɪbtʃɑːz/ South American Indians of Colombia, whose civilization was overthrown by the Spaniards in 1538. Their practice of covering their chief with gold dust, after applying an underlay of gum, fostered the legend of El Dorado, the city of gold.

Chicago /ʃɪ'kɑːgəʊ/ financial and industrial (iron, steel, chemicals, textiles) city in Illinois, USA, on Lake Michigan; population (1980) 3,005,000, metropolitan area 7,581,000. The famous stockyards are now closed.

It contains the world's first skyscraper (built 1887–88), and some of the world's tallest modern skyscrapers, including the Sears Tower, 443 m/1,454 ft. The Museum of Science and Industry, opened 1893, has 'hands on' exhibits including a coal-mine, a World War II U-boat, an Apollo spacecraft and lunar module; and exhibits by industrial firms. 50 km/30 mi to the west is the Fermilab, the US centre for particle physics. The Chicago river cuts the city into three 'sides'. Chicago is known as the Windy City, possibly from the breezes of Lake Michigan, and its citizens' (and, allegedly, politicians') voluble talk; the lake shore ('the Gold Coast') is occupied by luxury apartment blocks. It has a renowned symphony orchestra, an art institute, the University of Chicago, and five professional sports teams.

history The site of Chicago was visited by Jesuit missionaries 1673, and Fort Dearborn, then a frontier fort, was built here 1803. The original layout of Chicago was a rectangular grid, but many outer boulevards have been constructed on less rigid lines. As late as 1831 Chicago was still an insignificant village, but railways connected it with the east coast by 1852, and by 1871, when it suffered a disastrous fire, it was a city of more than 300,000 inhabitants. Rapid development began again in the 1920s, and during the years of Prohibition 1919–33, the city became notorious for the activities of its gangsters. The opening of the St Lawrence Seaway 1959 brought Atlantic shipping to its docks.

Chicago School of Sociology the first university department of sociology, founded in Chicago 1892 under Albion Small. He was succeeded by Robert E Park, who with W I Thomas, Ernest Burgess, Louis Wirth, and R McKenzie created an important centre for the social sciences in the 1920s and 1930s, studying urban life including crime and deviance in Chicago.

A Neo-Chicagoan school emerged in the 1940s under Erving Goffman and Howard Becker.

Chicano /tʃɪ'kɑːnəʊ/ a Spanish-speaking American of Mexican descent in the SW USA. The term was originally used for those who became US citizens because of the ◊Mexican War. The word probably derives from the Spanish word *Mexicanos*.

Chichen Itzá /tʃɪ'tʃen ɪt'sɑː/ Mayan city in Yucatán, Mexico, which flourished 11th–13th centuries. Excavated 1924–40 by Sylvanus Griswold Morley, the remains include temples

with sculptures and colour reliefs, an observatory, and a sacred well into which sacrifices, including human beings, were cast.

Probably founded about 500 by the Itzá, it displays Classic and Post-Classic architecture, and has a strong ◊Toltec influence.

Chichester /'tʃɪtʃɪstə/ city and market town in Sussex; 111 km/69 mi SW of London, near Chichester Harbour; population (1981) 24,000 It is the administrative headquarters of West Sussex. It was a Roman township, and the remains of the Roman palace built around AD 80 at nearby Fishbourne are unique outside Italy. There is a cathedral consecrated 1108, later much rebuilt and restored, and the Chichester Festival Theatre (1962).

Chichester /'tʃɪtʃɪstə/ Francis 1901–1972. English sailor and navigator. In 1931, he made the first E-W crossing of the Tasman Sea in *Gipsy Moth*, and in 1966–67 circumnavigated the world in his yacht *Gipsy Moth IV*.

chicken domestic fowl; see under ◊poultry.

chicken pox a common but mild disease, also known as varicella, caused by a virus of the ◊herpes group, and transmitted by airborne droplets. Chicken pox chiefly attacks children under ten. The incubation period is two to three weeks.

The temperature rises, and spots (later inflamed blisters) develop on the torso, then on the face and limbs. The sufferer recovers in a few days, but remains infectious until the last scab disappears.

chickpea seeds of the annual *Cicer arietinum*, family Leguminosae, which is grown for food in India and the Middle East.

chickweed weed *Stellaria media*, family Caryophyllaceae, with small white star-like flowers.

Chiclayo /tʃɪ'klaɪəʊ/ capital of Lambayeque department, NW Peru; population (1988) 395,000.

chicle juice from the sapodilla tree *Achras zapota* of Central America, which forms the basis of chewing gum.

chicory plant *Cichorium intybus*, family Compositae. It grows wild in Britain, mainly on chalky soils, and has large, usually blue, flowers. Its long taproot is used dried and roasted as a coffee substitute. As a garden vegetable, grown under cover, its blanched leaves are used in salads.

Chiengmai /dʒi'eŋ 'maɪ/ or **Chiang Mai** town in N Thailand; population (1982) 104,910. There is a trade in teak and lac (as shellac, a resin used in varnishes and polishes), and many handicraft industries. It is the former capital of the Lan Na Thai kingdom.

chiffchaff bird *Phylloscopus collybita* of the warbler family, found in woodlands and thickets in Europe and N Asia during the summer, migrating S for winter. About 11 cm/4.3 in long, olive above, greyish below, with an eyestripe and usually dark legs, it looks similar to a willow-warbler but has a distinctive song.

Chifley /'tʃɪflɪ/ Joseph Benedict 'Ben' 1885–1951. Australian Labor prime minister 1945–49. He united the party in fulfilling a welfare and nationalization programme 1945–49 (although he failed in an attempt to nationalize the banks 1947) and initiated an immigration programme and the Snowy Mountains hydroelectric project.

Chifley was minister of postwar reconstruction 1942–45 under Curtin, when he succeeded him as prime minister. He crushed a coal miners' strike 1949 by using troops as mine labour. He was leader of the Opposition from 1949 until his death.

Chihuahua /tʃɪ'wɑːwə/ capital of Chihuahua state, Mexico, 1,285 km/800 mi NW of Mexico City; population (1984) 375,000. Founded in 1707, it is the centre of a mining district.

chihuahua smallest breed of dog, developed in the USA from Mexican origins. It may weigh only 1 kg/2.2 lb. The domed head and wide set ears are characteristic, and the skull is large compared to the body. It can be almost any colour, and occurs in both smooth (or even hairless) and long-coated varieties.

chilblain painful inflammation of the skin of the feet or hands, due to cold. The parts turn red, swell, itch violently, and are very tender. In bad cases, the skin cracks, blisters, or ulcerates.

child abuse the molesting of children by parents and other adults. In the UK, it can give rise to various criminal charges, such as gross indecency with children. A local authority can take abused children away from their parents by obtaining a care order from a juvenile court under the Children's and Young Persons Act 1969 (replaced by the Children's Act 1989). Controversial methods of diagnosing sexual abuse led to a public inquiry in Cleveland, England 1988, which severely criticised the handling of such cases.

childbirth the expulsion of a baby from its mother's body following ◊pregnancy. In a broader sense, it is the period of time involving labour and delivery of the baby, plus the effort and pain involved.

Childe /tʃaɪld/ Gordon 1892–1957. Australian archaeologist, director of the London Institute of Archaeology 1946–57. He discovered the prehistoric village of Skara Brae in the Orkneys, and published *The Dawn of European Civilization* 1939.

Childers /'tʃɪldəz/ (Robert) Erskine 1870–1922. Irish Sinn Féin politician, author of the spy novel *The Riddle of the Sands* 1903. He was executed as a Republican guerrilla.

Before turning to Irish politics, Childers was a clerk in the House of Commons in London. In 1921 he was elected to the Irish Parliament as a supporter of the Sinn Féin leader de Valera, and took up arms against the Irish Free State 1922. Shortly afterwards he was captured, court-martialled, and shot by the Irish Free State government of William T Cosgrave.

Children's Crusade a ◊Crusade by some 10,000 children from France, the Low Countries, and Germany, in 1212, to recapture Jerusalem. Motivated by religious piety, many of them were sold into slavery or died of disease.

children's literature works specifically written for children. The earliest known illustrated children's book in English is *Goody Two Shoes* 1765, possibly written by Oliver Goldsmith. *Fairy tales* were originally part of a vast range of oral literature, credited only to the writer who first recorded them, such as Charles Perrault. During the 19th century several writers, including Hans Christian Andersen, wrote original stories in the fairytale genre; others, such as the Grimm brothers, collected (and sometimes adapted) existing stories.

Early children's stories were always written with a moral purpose; this was particularly true in the 19th century, apart from the unique case of Lewis Carroll's *Alice* books. The late 19th century was the great era of children's literature in the UK, with Lewis Carroll, Beatrix Potter, Charles Kingsley, and J M Barrie. It was also the golden age of illustrated children's books, with such artists as Kate Greenaway and Randolph Caldecott. Among 20th-century children's writers in English have been Kenneth Grahame (*The Wind in the Willows* 1908) and A A Milne (*Winnie the Pooh* 1926). *Adventure stories* have often appealed to children even when written for adults; examples include *Robinson Crusoe* by Daniel Defoe, and the satirical *Gulliver's Travels* by Jonathan Swift.

Chile /'tʃɪli/ South American country, bounded to the north by Peru and Bolivia, to the east by Argentina, and to the south and west by the Pacific Ocean.

government Since 1973 Chile has been ruled by a military junta. A new constitution announced 1981 took effect 1989. It provides for the election of a president for an eight-year, non-renewable, term and a legislature consisting of a senate with 26 elected and 9 appointed members and a chamber of deputies with 120 elected members, all serving four-year terms. Marxist and 'totalitarian' groups and political activity were all banned until 1989. Strikes in the public services are not allowed and the economy is based on 'free market principles'.

Chile
Republic of
(República de Chile)

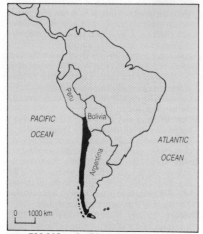

0   1000 km

area 736,905 sq km/284,445 sq mi
capital Santiago
towns Concepción, Viña del Mar, Temuco; ports are Valparaíso, Antofagasta, Arica, Iquique
physical Andes mountains along E border, Atacama Desert in N, arable land and forest in the S
territories Easter Island, Juan Fernández Island, half of Tierra del Fuego, and part of Antarctica
head of state and government Patricio Aylwin Azodar from 1990
political system emergent democratic republic

political parties Christian Democratic Party (PDC), moderate centrist; National Renewal Party (RN), right-wing
exports copper, iron, nitrate (Chile is the chief mining country of South America), pulp and paper
currency peso (491.48 = £1 Feb 1990)
population (1988) 12,680,000 (the majority mestizo, of mixed American Indian and Spanish descent); annual growth rate 1.6%
life expectancy men 67, women 73
language Spanish
religion Roman Catholic
literacy 95.4% (1985)
GNP $21.8 bn (1983); $1,950 per head of population
chronology
1818 Achieved independence from Spain.
1964 PDC formed government under Eduardo Frei.
1970 Dr Salvador Allende became the first democratically elected Marxist president. He embarked on an extensive programme of nationalization and social reform.
1973 Government overthrown by the CIA-backed military, led by Gen Augusto Pinochet. Allende killed. Policy of repression began during which all opposition was put down and political activity banned.
1983 Growing opposition to the regime from all sides, with outbreaks of violence.
1988 Plebiscite asking whether Pinochet should serve a further term resulted in a clear 'No' vote.
1989 President Pinochet agreed to constitutional changes to allow pluralist politics. Patricio Aylwin (PDC) elected president.
1990 (Jan) Aylwin reaches accord on end to military junta government.

Pinochet demanded the retention of his post as army commander-in-chief after his relinquishment of the presidency.

In 1985, the richest 20% of the population consumed 30% more than in 1970, and the poorest 40% of the population consumed 50% less than in 1970.

Chilean Revolution in Chile, the presidency of Salvador ◊Allende 1970–73, the Western hemisphere's first democratically elected Marxist-oriented president of an independent state.

chiliasm another word for millenarianism; see ◊millennium.

chilli (North American *chili*) the pod, or powder made from the pod, of a variety of ◊Capsicum, *Capsicum frutescens*. It is widely used in cooking.

Chillon /ʃɪ'lɒn/ a fortress on an island rock at the E end of Lake Geneva, Switzerland, dating from the 8th century. The 16th-century Genovese republican and patriot, François Bonward (Bonnivard) (1496–c.1570), commemorated by the English poet Byron, was imprisoned here 1530–36.

Chiltern Hundreds, *stewardship of* in the UK, a nominal office of profit under the crown. British members of Parliament may not resign; therefore, if they wish to leave office during a Parliament they may apply for this office, a formality which disqualifies them from being an MP.

Chilterns /'tʃɪltənz/ range of chalk hills extending for some 72 km/45 mi in a curve from a point N of Reading to the Suffolk border. Coombe Hill, near Wendover, 260 m/852 ft high, is the highest point.

chimaera fish of the group Holocephali. They have thick bodies that taper to a long thin tail, large fins, smooth skin, and a cartilaginous skeleton. They can grow to 1.5 m/4.5 ft. Most chimaeras are deep-water fish, and even *Chimaera monstrosa*, a relatively shallow-living form caught commonly round European coasts, lives at a depth of 300–500 m/1000–1600 ft.

Chimbote /tʃɪm'bəʊti/ largest fishing port in Peru; population (1981) 216,000.

chimera in biology, an organism composed of tissues that are genetically different. Chimeras can develop naturally if a ◊mutation occurs in a cell of a developing embryo, but are more commonly produced artificially by implanting cells from one organism into the embryo of another.

chimera or *chimaera* in Greek mythology, a fire-breathing animal with a lion's head, a goat's body, and tail in the form of a snake; hence any apparent hybrid of two or more creatures. The chimera was

history The area now known as Chile was originally occupied by the Araucanian Indians, and invaded by the ◊Incas 15th century. The first European to see it was ◊Magellan, who in 1520 sailed through the strait now named after him. A Spanish expedition under Pedro de Valdivia founded Santiago 1541, and Chile was subsequently colonized by Spanish settlers who established an agricultural society, though the Indians continued to rebel until the late 19th century. Becoming independent from Spain 1818, Chile went to war with Peru and Bolivia 1879, and gained considerable territory from them.

Most of the 20th century has been characterized by left- versus right-wing struggles. The Christian Democrats under Eduardo Frei held power 1964–70, followed by a left-wing coalition led by Dr Salvador ◊Allende, the first democratically elected Marxist head of state. He promised social justice by constitutional means and began nationalizing industries, including US-owned copper mines.

The ◊CIA saw Allende as a pro-Cuban communist and encouraged opposition to him. In 1973 the army, led by Gen Augusto Pinochet, overthrew the government. Allende was killed or, as the new regime claimed, committed suicide. Pinochet became president and his opponents were tortured, imprisoned, or just 'disappeared'. More than 700 people have disappeared after being arrested by the military. In 1976 Pinochet proclaimed an 'authoritarian democracy' and in 1977 banned all political parties. His policies were 'endorsed' by a referendum 1978.

In 1980 a 'transition to democracy' by 1989 was announced, but imprisonment and torture continued. By 1983 opposition to Pinochet had increased, with demands for a return to democratic government. He attempted to placate opposition by initiating public works. In 1984 an anti-government bombing campaign began, aimed

mainly at electricity installations, resulting in a 90-day state of emergency, followed by a 90-day state of siege. In 1985, as opposition grew in the Catholic Church and the army as well as among the public, another state of emergency was declared, but the bombings and killings continued.

In Oct 1988 Pinochet's proposal to remain in office for another eight-year term was rejected in a plebiscite. Another plebiscite in Aug 1989 approved constitutional changes leading to a return to pluralist politics and in Dec the PDC candidate, Patricio Aylwin Azocar, was elected president, his term of office beginning Mar 1990.

China 'People's Power' thwarted. Students confront troops in peaceful demonstrations in Tiananmen Square. In the brutal military reprisals of June 1989 more than 2,000 unarmed protesters were shot dead.

killed by the hero Bellerophon on the winged horse Pegasus.

chimpanzee highly intelligent African ape *Pan troglodytes* that lives mainly in rain forests but sometimes in wooded savannah. They are covered in thin but long black body hair, except for the face, hands, and feet, which may have pink or black skin. Chimpanzees normally walk on all fours, supporting the front of the body on the knuckles of the fingers, but can stand or walk upright for a short distance. They can grow to 1.4 m/4.5 ft tall, and weigh up to 50 kg/110 lb. They are strong, and climb well, but spend time on the ground. They live in loose social groups. The bulk of the diet is fruit, with some leaves, insects, and occasional meat. Chimpanzees can use 'tools', fashioning twigs to extract termites from their nests.

Chimpanzees are found in an area from W Africa to W Uganda and Tanzania in the east. Studies of chromosomes suggest that chimpanzees are the closest apes to humans, perhaps sharing 99% of the same genes. They can communicate with humans with the aid of machines or sign language, but are probably precluded from human speech by the position of the voicebox.

Chimu /'tʃiːmuː/ South American civilization that flourished in Peru about 1250–1470, when they were conquered by the Incas. They produced fine work in gold, realistic portrait pottery, savage fanged images in clay, and possibly a system of writing or recording by painting beans in particular patterns. They built aqueducts carrying water many miles, and the maze-like city of Chan Chan, 36 sq km/14 sq mi, on the coast near Trujillo.

The Chimu people built enormous adobe brick mounds or *huacas* as the base of temples and palaces. Chan Chan consists of nine complexes, probably built by successive kings and forming their eventual tombs, where they were buried. Their agricultural system depended on remarkable irrigation schemes; defaulting peasants seem to have been ritually mutilated. The invading Incas ensured victory by cutting the Chimu aqueducts.

China /'tʃaɪnə/ country in SE Asia, bounded N by Mongolia, NW and NE by the USSR, SW by India and Nepál, S by Bhutan, Burma, Laos, and Vietnam, SE by the South China Sea, and E by the East China Sea, North Korea, and the USSR.

government China is divided into 21 provinces, five autonomous regions, and three municipalities (Beijing, Shanghai, and Tianjin), each having an elected local people's government with policy-making power in defined areas.

Ultimate authority resides in the single-chamber *National People's Congress* (NPC), composed of 2,970 deputies indirectly elected every five years through local people's congresses. Deputies to local people's congresses are directly

China
People's Republic of
(Zhonghua Renmin Gonghe Guo)

area 9,139,300 sq km/3,528,684 sq mi
capital Beijing (Peking)
towns Chongqing (Chungking), Shenyang (Mukden), Wuhan, Nanjing (Nanking), Harbin; ports Tianjin (Tientsin), Shanghai, Qingdao (Tsingtao), Lüda (Lü-ta), Guangzhou (Canton)
physical two-thirds of China is mountains (in the N and SW) or desert; the east is irrigated by rivers Huang He (Yellow River), Chang Jiang (Yangtze-Kiang), Xi Jiang (Si Kiang)
features Great Wall of China; Kongur Shan mountain
head of state Yang Shangkun from 1988
head of government Li Peng from 1987
political system communis republic
political parties Chinese Communist Party (CCP), Marxist-Leninist-Maoist
exports tea, livestock and animal products, silk, cotton, oil, minerals (China is the world's largest producer of tungsten), chemicals, light industrial goods
currency yuan (8.03 = £2 Feb 1990)
population (1989) 1,112,000,000 (of whom the majority are Han or ethnic Chinese; the 67 million of other ethnic groups, including Tibetan, Uigur, and Zhuang, live in border areas). The number of people of Chinese origin outside China, Taiwan, and Hong Kong is estimated at 15–24 million. Annual growth rate 1.2%
life expectancy men 67, women 69
language Chinese
religion officially atheist, but traditionally Taoist, Confucianist, and Buddhist; Muslim 13

million; Catholic 3–6 million (divided between the 'patriotic' church established 1958 and the 'loyal' church subject to Rome); Protestant 3 million
literacy 82% male/66% female (1985 est)
GDP $313 bn (1983); $566 per head of population
chronology
1949 People's Republic of China proclaimed by Mao Zedong.
1954 Soviet-style constitution adopted.
1956–57 Hundred Flowers Movement encouraged criticism of the government.
1958–60 Great Leap Forward commune experiment to achieve 'true communism'.
1960 Withdrawal of Soviet technical advisers.
1962 Sino-Indian border war.
1962–65 Economic recovery programme under Liu Shaoqi; Maoist 'socialist education movement' rectification campaign.
1966–68 Great Proletarian Cultural Revolution and overthrow of Liu Shaoqi.
1969 Ussuri river border clashes with USSR.
1970–76 Reconstruction under Mao and Zhou Enlai; purge of extreme left.
1971 Entry into United Nations.
1972 US president Nixon visited Beijing.
1975 New state constitution. Unveiling of Zhou's Four Modernizations programme.
1976 Death of Zhou Enlai and Mao Zedong; appointment of Hua Guofeng as prime minister and Communist Party chairman. Deng in hiding. Gang of Four arrested.
1977 Rehabilitation of Deng Xiaoping.
1979 Economic reforms introduced. Diplomatic relations opened with USA. Punitive invasion of Vietnam.
1980 Zhao Ziyang appointed prime minister.
1981 Hu Yaobang succeeded Hua as party chairman. Imprisonment of Gang of Four.
1982 New state constitution adopted.
1984 'Enterprise management' reforms for industrial sector.
1986 Student demonstrations for democracy.
1987 Hu was replaced as party leader by Zhao, with Li Peng as prime minister. Deng left the Politburo but remained influential.
1988 Yang Shankun became state president. Economic reforms encountered increasing problems; inflation rocketing.
1989 Following the death of Hu Yaobang pro-democracy student demonstrations in Tiananmen Square, Beijing, were crushed by the army, who killed over 2000 demonstrators. Zhao Ziyang replaced as party leader by Jiang Zemin in a swing towards conservatism.

Chimu A bottle in the form of a musician, and high on the neck a monkey. Animals were often used to ornament Chimu pottery.

elected through universal suffrage in constituency contests. The NPC, the 'highest organ of state power', meets annually and elects a permanent, 133-member committee to assume its functions between sittings. The committee has an inner body comprising a chairman (presently Peng Zhen) and 19 vice-chairmen. The NPC also elects for a five-year term a State Central Military Commission (SCMC), leading members of the judiciary, the vice-president, and the state president, who must be at least 45 years of age. The president is restricted to two terms in office, and performs primarily ceremonial functions. Executive administration is effected by a prime minister and a cabinet (state council) which includes three vice-premiers, 31 departmental ministers, eight commission chiefs, an auditor-general, and a secretary-general, and is appointed by the NPC.

China's controlling force is the *Chinese Communist Party* (CCP). It has a parallel hierarchy comprising elected congresses and committees functioning from village level upwards and taking orders from above. A national party congress

every five years elects a 285-member central committee (175 of whom have full voting powers) which meets twice a year and elects an 18-member politburo and 5-member secretariat to exercise day-to-day control over the party and to frame state and party policy goals. The Politburo meets weekly and is China's most significant political body.

history For early history see ◊China, history. Imperial rule ended in 1911 with the formation of a republic in 1912. After several years of civil war the nationaliist ◊Guomindang, led by ◊Chiang Kai-shek, was firmly installed in power in 1926, with Communist aid. In 1927 Chiang Kai-shek began a purge of the Communists, who began the 'Long March' (1934–36) to Shaanxi, which became their base.

In 1931 Japan began its penetration of Manchuria, and in 1937 began the second ◊Sino-Japanese War, during which both Communists and Nationalists fought Japan. Civil war resumed after the Japanese surrender in 1945, until in 1949, following their elimination of Nationalist resistance on the mainland, the Communists inaugurated the People's

Republic of China, the Nationalists having retired to Taiwan.

To begin with, the communist regime concentrated on economic reconstruction. A centralized Soviet-style constitution was adopted in 1954, industries were nationalized and central planning and moderate land reform introduced. The USSR provided economic aid, while China successfully intervened in the ◊Korean War. Development during this period was based on material incentives and industrialization.

From 1958, under state president and CCP chairman ◊Mao Zedong, China embarked on a major new policy, the Great Leap Forward. This created large self-sufficient agricultural and industrial communes in an effort to achieve classless 'true communism'. The experiment proved unpopular and impossible to co-ordinate, and over 20,000,000 people died in the floods and famines of 1959–62. A breach in Sino-Soviet relations brought a withdrawal of Soviet technical advisers in 1960.

The failure of the 'Great Leap' reduced Mao's influence 1962–65, and a successful 'recovery programme' was begun under President Liu Shaoqi. Private farming plots and markets were re-introduced, communes reduced in size, and income differentials and material incentives restored.

Mao struck back against what he saw as a return to capitalism by launching the Great Proletarian Cultural Revolution (1966–69), a 'rectification campaign' directed against 'rightists' in the CCP which sought to re-establish the supremacy of (Maoist) ideology over economics. During the campaign, Mao, supported by People's Liberation Army (PLA) chief ◊Lin Biao and the Shanghai-based 'Gang of Four' (comprising Mao's wife Jiang Qing, radical intellectuals Zhang Chunqiao and Yao Wenyuan and former millworker Wang Hongwen), encouraged student (Red Guard) demonstrations against party and government leaders.

The chief targets were Liu Shaoqi, ◊Deng Xiaoping (head of the CCP secretariat) and Peng Zhen (Mayor of Beijing). All were forced out of office. The campaign grew anarchic during 1967, necessitating PLA intervention and the dispersal of Red Guards into the countryside to 'learn from the peasants'. Government institutions fell into abeyance during the Cultural Revolution and new 'Three Part Revolutionary Committees', comprising Maoist party officials, trade unionists and PLA commanders, took over administration.

By 1970, Mao sided with pragmatic Prime Minister ◊Zhou Enlai and began restoring order and a more balanced system. A number of 'ultra-leftists' were ousted in 1970 and in 1971 Lin Biao died en route to Mongolia after a failed coup. In 1972–73 Deng Xiaoping, finance minister Li Xiannian, and others, were rehabilitated, and a policy of détente towards the USA began. This reconstruction movement was climaxed by the summoning of the NPC in 1975 for the first time in 11 years to ratify a new constitution and approve an economic plan termed the 'Four Modernizations' - agriculture, industry, defence, and science and technology—which aimed at placing China on a par with the West by the year 2000.

The deaths of Zhou Enlai and Mao Zedong in 1976 unleashed a violent succession struggle between the leftist 'Gang of Four', led by Jiang Qing, and moderate 'rightists', grouped around vice-premier Deng Xiaoping. Deng was forced into hiding by the 'Gang'; and Mao's moderate protegé ◊Hua Guofeng became CCP chairman and head of government in 1976. Hua arrested the 'Gang' on charges of treason and held power 1976–78 as a stop-gap leader, continuing Zhou Enlai's modernization programme.

His authority was progressively challenged, however, by Deng Xiaoping, who returned to office in 1977 after campaigns in Beijing. By 1979, after further popular campaigns, Deng had gained effective charge of the government, controlling a majority in the Politburo. State and judicial bodies began to meet again, Liu Shaoqi was rehabilitated as a party hero and economic reforms were introduced. These involved the dismantling of the commune system, the introduction of direct farm incentives under a new 'responsibility system' and the encouragement of foreign investment in 'Special Economic Zones' in coastal enclaves. By June 1981 Deng's supremacy was assured when his protegés ◊Hu Yaobang and ◊Zhao Ziyang became party chairman and prime minister and the 'Gang of Four' were sentenced to life imprisonment (Yao Wenyuan received 20 years).

In 1982, Hua Guofeng and a number of senior colleagues were ousted from the Politburo, and the NPC adopted a definitive constitution, restoring the post of state president (abolished since 1975) and establishing a new civil rights code. The new administration was a collective leadership, with Hu Yaobang in control of party affairs, Zhao Ziyang overseeing state administration and Deng Xiaoping (a party vice-chairman and SCMC chairman) formulating long-term strategy and supervizing the PLA.

The triumvirate pursued a three-pronged policy aimed firstly at streamlining the party and state bureaucracies and promoting to power new, younger, and better-educated technocrats. By 1986 half the CCP's provincial-level officers had been replaced. Secondly, they sought to curb PLA influence by retiring senior commanders and reducing numbers from 4.2 to 3 million. Thirdly, they gave priority to economic modernization by extending market incentives and local autonomy, and by introducing a new 'open door' policy to encourage foreign trade and investment.

These economic reforms met with substantial success in the agricultural sector (output more than doubled 1978–85), but had adverse side effects, widening regional and social income differentials and fuelling a wave of 'mass consumerism' which created balance of payments problems. Contact with the West brought demands for full-scale democratization in China. These calls led in 1986 to widespread student demonstrations, and party chief Hu Yaobang was dismissed in 1987 for failing to check the disturbances. Hu's departure imperilled the post-Dengist reform programme, as conservative forces, grouped around the veteran Politburo members Chen Yun and Peng Zhen, sought to halt the changes and re-establish central party control, evidenced during 1987 by the launching of a campaign against 'borgeois liberalization' (Western ideas).

Chen Yun, Peng Zhen, and Deng Xiaoping all retired from the Politburo in Oct 1987, and soon after ◊Li Peng, the adopted son of Zhou Enlai, took over as prime minister, Zhao Ziyang having become CCP chair. With inflation spiralling, economic reform was halted in autumn 1988 and an austerity budget introduced in 1989. This provoked urban unrest and, following Hu Yaobang's death Apr 1989, a student-led pro-democracy movement was launched in Beijing that rapidly spread to provincial cities. There were mass demonstrations during the Soviet leader Mikhail Gorbachev's visit to China in May. However, soon after Gorbachev's departure a brutal crackdown was launched against the demonstrators by Li Peng and President Yang Shangkun, with Deng Xiaoping's support. Martial law was proclaimed and in June 1989 more than 2,000 unarmed protesters were massacred in the capital's Tiananmen Square. A month later Zhao Ziyang, who had sought compromise with the demonstrators, was ousted as CCP chief and replaced by Jiang Zemin, the Shanghai party chief and new protegé of Deng Xiaoping. A crackdown on dissidents was launched, as the pendulum swung sharply away from reform towards conservatism.

In foreign affairs, China's 1960 rift with ◊Khrushchev's Soviet Union over policy differences became irrevocable in 1962 when Russia sided with India during a brief Sino-Indian border war. Relations with the Soviet Union deteriorated further in 1969 after border clashes in the disputed Ussuri river region. China pursued a nonaligned strategy, projecting itself as the voice of Third World nations, although it achieved nuclear capability by 1964. During the early 1970s, concern with Soviet expansionism brought rapprochement with the US, bringing China's entry to the UN (at ◊Taiwan's expense) in 1971 and culminating in the establishment of full Sino-American diplomatic relations in 1979. In recent years there has been a partial rapprochement with the USSR, culminating in Gorbachev's visit in May 1989. However, a new rift became evident in 1990, with the Chinese government denouncing the Soviet leader's 'revisionism'.

In recent years there has been political decentralization and a diminishing of direct party control over government organs. Competition has been introduced into party and state elections and non-party bodies, such as the broad-front Chinese People's Political Consultative Conference, have been revived and inducted into the policy-making process. Until the Tiananmen Square massacre in June 1989, relations with the West were warm during the Deng administration, with economic contacts broadening.

china clay a clay mineral formed by the decomposition of ◊feldspars. The alteration of aluminium silicates results in the formation of **kaolinite**, $Al_2Si_2O_5(OH)_2$, from which **kaolin**, or white china clay, is derived.

Kaolinite is economically important in the ceramic and paper industries. It is mined in the UK, the US, France, and Czechoslovakia.

China, history *500,000 BC* The earliest human remains found in China are those of 'Peking man' (*Sinanthropus pekingensis*).
18,000 BC Humans of the modern type are first known to have inhabited the region.
5000 BC A simple agricultural society was established.
c.2800–c.2200 BC The **Sage kings**, a period of agricultural development, known only from legend.
c.2000–c.1500 BC The **Xia dynasty**, a bronze age with further agricultural developments, including irrigation, and the first known use of writing.
c.1500–c.1066 BC The **Shang dynasty** is the first of which we have documentary evidence; bronze vases survive of its art. The first Chinese calendar was made.
c.1066–221 BC During the **Zhou dynasty**, the feudal structure of society broke down in a period of political upheaval, though iron, money, and written laws were all in use, and philosophy flourished (see ◊Confucius). The dynasty ended in the 'Warring States' period (403–221 BC), with the country divided into small kingdoms.
221–206 BC The shortest and most remarkable of the dynasties, the **Qin**, corresponds to the reign of Shih Huang Ti, who curbed the feudal nobility and introduced orderly government; he built roads and canals, and began the ◊Great Wall of China to keep out invaders from the north.
206 BC–AD 220 The **Han dynasty** was a long period of peace, during which territory was expanded, the keeping of historical records was systematized, and an organized civil service set up. Art and literature flourished, and ◊Buddhism was introduced.
220–439 The country was divided under **Three Kingdoms**: the Wei, Chu, and Wu. Confucianism was superseded by Buddhism and Taoism. After prolonged fighting, the Wei became the most powerful, eventually founding the **Jin dynasty** (265–439), which expanded to take over from the barbarian invaders who ruled much of China at that time, but lost the territory they had gained to the Tatar invaders from the north.
581–618 Reunification came with the **Sui dynasty** when the government was reinstated, the barbarian invasions stopped, and the Great Wall refortified.

618–907 During the *Tang dynasty* the system of government became more highly developed and centralized, and the empire covered most of SE and much of central Asia. Sculpture, painting, and literature (especially poetry) flourished again.

907–960 The period known as the *Five Dynasties and Ten Kingdoms* held war, economic depression, and loss of territory in N China, central Asia, and Korea. Printing was developed, including the first use of paper money.

960–1279 The *Song dynasty* was a period of calm and creativity. Central government was restored, and movable type was invented. At the end of the dynasty, the northern and western frontiers were neglected, and Mongol invasions.

1279–1368 The *Yuan dynasty* saw the beginning of Mongol rule in China, including Kublai Khan, who was reputedly visited by Marco Polo. There were widespread revolts, centred in Mongolia.

1368–1644 The Mongols were expelled by the first of the native Chinese *Ming dynasty*, who expanded the empire. Mongolia was captured by the second Ming emperor. It was a period of architectural development, and Beijing flourished as the new capital. Portuguese explorers reached Canton 1517, and other Europeans followed.

1644–1912 The last of the dynasties was the *Manchu*, who were non-Chinese nomads from Manchuria. They gave several great rulers to China, up to the empress dowager Tz'e Hsi (died 1908). Initially trade and culture flourished, but during the 19th century it seemed likely that China would be partitioned among the European powers, all trade being conducted through treaty ports in their control. Conservatism led to a decline, including the ◊*Boxer Rebellion* 1900 against Western influence, suppressed by European troops.

1911–12 Revolution broke out, and the infant emperor Henry ◊P'u-i was deposed. For history 1911–present, see ◊Chinese Revolution and ◊China.

China Sea /'tʃaɪnə/ area of the Pacific Ocean bordered by China, Vietnam, Borneo, the Philippines, and Japan. Various groups of small islands and shoals, including the Paracels, 500 km/300 mi east of Vietnam, have been disputed by China and other powers because they lie in oil-rich areas. North of Taiwan it is known as the *East China Sea* and to the south as the *South China Sea*.

chincherinchee plant *Ornithogalum thyrsoides*, family Liliaceae. Native to South Africa, it has spikes of long-lasting, white or yellow wax-like flowers.

chinchilla South American rodent *Chinchilla laniger* found in high, rather barren areas of the Andes in Bolivia and Chile. About the size of a small rabbit, it has long ears and a long bushy tail, and shelters in rock crevices. These gregarious animals have thick soft silver-grey fur, and were hunted almost to extinction for it. They are now farmed and protected in the wild.

Chindits /'tʃɪndɪts/ an Indian army division in World War II that carried out guerrilla operations against the Japanese in Burma under the command of the British Brig Orde Wingate (1903–44) The name derived from the mythical Chinthay–half lion, half eagle–at the entrance of Burmese pagodas to scare evil spirits.

Chinese inhabitant of China or a person of Chinese descent. They comprise approximately 25% of the world's population, and the Chinese language is the largest member of the Sino-Tibetan family. Although dialects vary, there is a common written language.

Chinese traditions embrace a range of philosophies and religions, including Confucianism, Taoism, and Buddhism. The veneration of ancestors remains an enduring feature of Chinese culture and there are lineage villages. The extended family is the traditional unit, the five-generation family

being the ideal. Recent attempts by the government to restrain population growth have included restricting married couples to one child.

The majority of Chinese are engaged in agriculture, cultivating irrigated rice fields in the south, and growing millet and wheat in the north. Many other Chinese work in commerce, industry, and government. Descendents of Chinese migrants are found throughout SE Asia, and further afield in Australia, North America, and Europe.

Within China there are many minorities who speak non-Chinese languages belonging to the Sino-Tibetan family (for example Tibetan, Miao, and Zhuang). There are also peoples who speak languages belonging to the Altaic (such as Uigur, Mongol, and Manchu) and Indo-European (such as Russian) families, while in the NE there are Koreans. The Chinese have endured long periods of domination under the Mongols (AD 1271–1368) and the Manchus (AD 1644–1911).

Chinese architecture Traditionally of timber construction there are few existing buildings predating the Ming dynasty (1368–1644) but records such as the *Ying Tsao Fa Shih/Method of Architecture* (1103) show that Chinese architecture has changed little throughout the ages. Curved roofs are a characteristic feature; typical also is the pagoda with a number of tiled roofs one above the other. The Chinese are renowned for their wallbuilding. The Great Wall of China was built about 228–210 BC as a northern frontier defence, and Beijing's fine city walls date from the Ming period.

Chinese buildings usually face south, a convention which can be traced back to the 'Hall of Brightness', a building from the Zhou dynasty (1050–221 BC), and is still retained in the functionally Western style modern Chinese architecture. Although some sections of Beijing have been destroyed by modernisation it still contains fine examples of buildings from the Ming dynasty, such as the Altar of Heaven, the ancestral temple of the Ming tombs, and the Five Pagoda Temple. The introduction of Buddhism from India is believed to have exerted considerable influence on Chinese architecture.

Chinese art the painting and sculpture of China. From the Bronze Age to the Cultural Revolution, Chinese art shows a stylistic unity unparalleled in any other culture. From about the 1st century AD Buddhism inspired much sculpture and painting. The *Han dynasty* (206 BC–AD 220) produced outstanding metalwork, ceramics, and sculpture. The *Song dynasty* (960–1278) established standards of idyllic landscape and nature painting in a delicate calligraphic style.

Neolithic art accomplished pottery dates back to about 2500 BC, already showing a distinctive Chinese approach to form

Bronze Age art rich burial goods, with bronzes and jade carvings, survive from the second millennium BC, decorated with hieroglyphs and simple stylized animal forms. Astonishing life-size terracotta figures from the Qin period (about 221–206 BC) guard the tomb of Emperor Shi Huangdi in the old capital of Xian. Bronze horses, naturalistic but displaying the soft curving lines of the Chinese style, are a feature of the Han dynasty

early Buddhist art once Buddhism was established in China it inspired a new monumental art, with huge rock-cut Buddhas and graceful linear relief sculptures at the monasteries of Yungang, about 460–535, and Longmen. Bronze images show the same curving lines and rounded forms.

Tang dynasty (618–907) art shows increasing sophistication in idealized images and naturalistic portraits too, like the carved figures of Buddhist monks (Luohan). This period also produced brilliant metalwork and ceramics of great delicacy. It is known that the aims and, broadly speaking, the style of Chinese painting were already well established, but little survives, with the notable exception of some Tang scrolls and silk paintings.

Chinese art *Part of the Sacred Way to the Ming Tombs (50 km/30 mi from Peking) is lined with statues of courtiers, soldiers, politicians, and animals.*

Song dynasty the golden age of painting was the Song dynasty (960–1278). The imperial court created its own workshop, fostering a fine calligraphic art, mainly devoted to natural subjects – landscape, mountains, trees, flowers, birds, and horses—though genre scenes, particularly of court beauties, were also very popular. Scrolls, albums, and fans of silk or paper were painted with watercolours and ink, using soft brushes that produced many different textures. Painting was strongly associated with literature, and painters added poems or quotations to their work to intensify the effect. Ma Yuan (c.1190–1224) and Xia Gui (active c.1180–1230) are among the painters, and Muqi (1180–1270?), a monk known for exquisite brushwork. The Song dynasty also produced the first true porcelain, achieving a classic simplicity and delicacy in colouring and form.

Ming dynasty (1368–1644) painters continued the landscape tradition, setting new standards in idealized visions. The painter Dong Qichang wrote a history and theory of Chinese painting. The Song style of porcelain gradually gave way to increasingly elaborate decorative work, and pale shades were superseded by rich colour, including Ming blue-and-white patterned ware.

Qing dynasty (1644–1911) the so-called Individualist Spirits emerged, painters who developed bolder, personal styles of brushwork. But the strong spirit that supported traditional art began to fade in the 19th and 20th centuries.

influence Chinese art had great impact on surrounding countries. The art of Korea was almost wholly inspired by Chinese example for many centuries. Along with Buddhism, Chinese styles of art were established in Japan in the 6th–7th centuries BC, and continued to exert a profound influence, though Japanese culture soon developed an independent style.

Chinese language a language or group of languages of the Sino-Tibetan family, spoken in China, Taiwan, Hongkong, Singapore, and Chinese communities throughout the world. Varieties of spoken Chinese differ greatly, but share a written form using thousands of ideographic symbols which have changed little in 2,000 years. Nowadays, *putonghua* ('common speech'), based on the educated Beijing dialect known as 'Mandarin' Chinese, is promoted throughout China as the national spoken and written language.

Because the writing system has a symbolic form (rather like numbers and road signs) it can be read and interpreted regardless of the reader's own dialect. The Chinese dialects are tonal, that is, they depend upon the tone of a syllable to indicate its meaning: *ma* with one tone means 'mother', with another means 'horse'. The characters of Chinese script are traditionally written vertically and read right-left but are now commonly written horizontally and read left-right, using 2,000 simplified characters. A variant of the Roman alphabet has been introduced and is used in schools to help with pronunciation. This, *Pinyin*, is prescribed for international use by the People's Republic of China, for personal and place names; as in Beijing rather than Peking. Pinyin spellings are generally used in this volume, but are not accepted by the government of Taiwan.

Chinese literature *Poetry* written in the ancient literary language understood throughout China, Chinese poems, often only four lines long, consist of rhymed lines of a fixed number of syllables, ornamented by parallel phrasing and tonal pattern. The oldest poems are contained in the *Book of Songs* (800–600 BC). Among Chinese poets are the nature poet T'ao Ch'ien (372–427), the master of technique Li Po (701–62), the autobiographical Po Chüi (772–846), and the wide-ranging Su Tung-p'o (1036–1101); and among the moderns using the colloquial language under European influence and experimenting in free verse are Hsu Chih-mo (1895–1931), and Pien Chih-lin (1910–).

Prose typical Chinese history is less literary than an editing of assembled documents with moral comment, but the essay has long been cultivated under strict rules of form and style. An example is the essay of Han Yü (768–824) *Upon the Original Way*, recalling the nation to Confucianism. Until the 16th century the short story was confined to the anecdote, startling by its strangeness, related in the literary language, for example, those of the poetic Tuan Ch'eng-shih (died 863), but after that time the more novelistic type in the colloquial tongue developed by its side. The Chinese novel evolved from the street storyteller's art, and has consequently always used the popular language. The early romances *Three Kingdoms*, *All Men are Brothers*, and *Golden Lotus* are anonymous, the earliest known author being Wu Che'ng-en (*c*.1505–80); the most realistic of the great novelists is Ts'ao Chan (died 1763).

20th-century Chinese novels have largely adopted European form, and have been influenced by Russia, as have the realistic stories of Lu Hsün. In typical Chinese drama, the stage presentation far surpasses the text in importance (the dialogue was not even preserved in early plays), but the present century has seen experiments in the European manner.

Chinese Revolution a series of major political upheavals in China 1911–49. A nationalist revolt overthrew the imperial dynasty 1912. Led by Sun Yat-sen 1923–25, and by Chiang Kai-shek 1925–49, the nationalists, or Guomindang, came under increasing pressure from the growing communist movement. The 10,000 km/6,000 mi **Long March** of the communists 1934–35 to escape from the nationalist forces saw Mao Zedong emerge as leader. After World War II, the conflict expanded into open civil war 1946–49, until the Guomindang were defeated at Nanking. This effectively established communist rule in China under the leadership of Mao.

The Chinese revolution came about with the collapse of the Manchu Ch'ing dynasty, a result of increasing internal disorders, pressure from foreign governments, and the weakness of central government. A nationalist revolt led to a provisional republican constitution being proclaimed and a government established in Beijing (Peking). Led by Sun Yat Sen and Chiang Kai-shek, the nationalists were faced with the problems of restoring the authority of central government and meeting the challenges from militaristic factions and the growing communist movement. After 1930, Chiang launched a series of attacks on the communists in SE China whose encirclement led to an attempt by communist army commander Chu

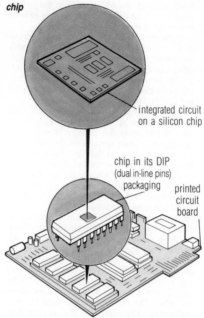

chip

integrated circuit on a silicon chip

chip in its DIP (dual in-line pins) packaging

printed circuit board

Teh to break out. The resulting Long March to NW China from Oct 1934–Oct 1935 reduced the communists' army from over 100,000 to little more than 8,000, mainly as a result of skirmishes with Chiang's forces, and the severity of the conditions. During the march, a power struggle developed between Mao Zedong and Chang Kuo T'ao which eventually split the force. Mao's group finally based itself in Yen'an where it remained throughout the war with the Japanese, forming an uneasy alliance with the nationalist Guomindang to expel the invaders. Mao's troops formed the basis of the Red Army which renewed the civil war against the nationalists 1946 and emerged victorious after defeating the Guomindang at Nanking 1949, thereby effectively establishing communist rule in China under Mao's leadership.

Chinghai /ˌtʃɪŋˈhaɪ/ former name of ◊Qinghai, NW province of China.

chinook (American Indian 'snow-eater') a warm dry wind that blows downhill on the eastern side of the Rocky Mountains. It often occurs in winter and spring when it produces a rapid thaw, and so is important to the agriculture of the area.

chip a complete electronic circuit on a slice of silicon (or other ◊semiconductor) crystal only a few millimetres square. It is also called ◊silicon chip and ◊integrated circuit.

chipmunk several species of small ground squirrel with characteristic stripes along its side. Chipmunks live in North America and E Asia, in a variety of habitats, usually wooded, and take shelter in burrows. They have pouches in their cheeks for carrying food. They climb well but spend most of their time on or near the ground. The *Siberian chipmunk Eutamias sibiricus*, about 13 cm/5 in body length, is found in N Russia, N China, and Japan.

Chippendale /ˈtʃɪpəndeɪl/ Thomas *c*. 1718–1779. English furniture designer. He set up his workshop in St Martin's Lane, London 1753. His book *The Gentleman and Cabinet Maker's Director* 1754, was a significant contribution to furniture design. He favoured Louis XVI, Chinese, Gothic, and Neo-Classical styles, and worked mainly in mahogany.

Chirac /ˈʃɪəræk/ Jacques 1932– . French conservative politician, prime minister 1974–76 and 1986–88. He established the neo-Gaullist Rassemblement pour la République (RPR) 1976, and became mayor of Paris 1977.

Chirac held ministerial posts during the Pompidou presidency and gained the nickname 'the Bulldozer'. In 1974 he became prime minister to

President Giscard d'Estaing, but the relationship was uneasy. Chirac contested the 1981 presidential election and emerged as the National Assembly leader for the parties of the right during the socialist administration of 1981–86. Following the rightist coalition's victory 1986, Chirac was appointed prime minister by President Mitterrand in a 'cohabitation' experiment. The term was marked by economic decline, nationality reforms, and student unrest. Student demonstrations in autumn 1986 forced him to scrap controversial plans for educational reform. He was defeated in the May 1988 elections, and replaced by the moderate Socialist Michel Rocard.

Chirico /ˈkɪərɪkəʊ/ Giorgio de 1888–1978. Italian painter born in Greece, the founder of Metaphysical painting, a style that presaged Surrealism in its use of enigmatic imagery and dreamlike settings. Early examples date from 1910.

Chiron /ˈkaɪrən/ in Greek mythology, the son of Cronos by a sea nymph. A ◊centaur, he was the wise tutor of Jason and Achilles among others.

Chiron /ˈkaɪrən/ an outer asteroid discovered by Charles Kowal 1977, orbiting between Saturn and Uranus. It appears to have a dark surface resembling that of asteroids in the inner solar system, probably consists of a mixture of ice and dark stony material, and may have a diameter of about 200 km/120 mi.

chiropody the care and treatment of feet.

chiropractic manipulation of the spine and other parts to relieve apparently non-related conditions, claimed to be caused by pressure on the nerves. It is not fully recognized by orthodox medicine.

Chissano Joaquim 1939– . Mozambique politician, president from 1986. He was secretary to Samora ◊Machel, who led the National Front for the Liberation of Mozambique (Frelimo) during the campaign for independence in the early 1960s. When Mozambique was given internal self-government in 1974 Chissano was appointed prime minister. After independence he served under Machel as foreign minister and on his death in 1986 succeeded him as president.

Chita /tʃiːˈtɑː/ town in E Siberia, USSR, on the Chita river; population (1987) 349,000. It is on the Trans-Siberian railway, and has chemical works, engineering works, and coal mines.

chitin a complex long-chain compound, or ◊polymer; a nitrogenous derivative of glucose. Chitin is found principally in the ◊exoskeleton of insects and other arthropods. It combines with protein to form a covering that can be hard and tough, as in scorpions, or soft and flexible, as in caterpillars. In crustaceans such as crabs, it is impregnated with calcium carbonate for extra strength.

Chirac French politician Jacques Chirac, 1986.

chives   *flower*

root

Chitin also occurs in some ◊protozoans and coelenterates, such as certain jellyfish, in the jaws of annelid worms, and as the cell-wall polymer of fungi.

Chittagong /'tʃɪtəgɒŋ/ city and port in Bangladesh, 16 km/10 mi from the mouth of the Karnaphuli river, on the Bay of Bengal; population (1981) 1,388,476. Industries include steel, engineering, chemicals, and textiles.

chivalry the code of gallantry and honour that medieval knights were supposed to observe. The word originally meant the knightly class of the feudal Middle Ages.

chive bulbous plant *Allium schoenoprasum* with long, tubular leaves, and dense, round flowerheads in blue or lilac. It is used as a garnish for salads.

Chkalov /'xkɑ:lɒv/ name 1938–57 of ◊Orenburg, town in the USSR.

Chladni /'klædni/ Ernest Florens Friedrich 1756–1827. German physicist, a pioneer in the field of ◊acoustics.

chlamydia single-celled organism that can only live parasitically in animal cells. They are thought to be descendants of bacteria that have lost certain metabolic processes. In humans, chlamydias cause ◊trachoma, a disease found mainly in the tropics (a leading cause of blindness), and psittacosis, which is contracted from birds by inhaling particles of dried droppings.

chloracne eruption of the skin, symptomatic of contact with chlorinated organic chemicals and a contaminated environment.

chloral or *trichloroethanal* an oily colourless liquid with a characteristic pungent smell. It is soluble in water, and its compound, chloral hydrate, is a powerful sleep-inducing agent.

chloramphenicol first of the broad-spectrum antibiotics to be used commercially. It was discovered in a Peruvian soil sample. Because of its toxicity, its use is limited to treatment of life-threatening infection, such as meningitis and typhoid fever.

chlorates in chemistry, salts whose acid contains both chlorine and oxygen (ClO, ClO_2, ClO_3, and ClO_4). Common chlorates are those of sodium, potassium, and barium. Certain chlorates are used in weedkillers.

chlorella single-cell, freshwater alga, 3–10 micrometres in diameter, which obtains its growth energy from light and can increase its weight by four times in 12 hours. Nutritive content: 50% protein, 20% fat, 20% carbohydrate, 10% phosphate, calcium, and other inorganic substances.

chlorides salts of hydrochloric acid (HCl), commonly formed by its action on various metals or by the direct combination of the metal and chlorine. Sodium chloride (NaCl) is common table salt.

chlorine a chemical element, a greenish-yellow gas with an irritating, suffocating smell; symbol Cl, atomic number 17, relative atomic mass 35.457. It is an important bleaching agent and is used as a germicide for drinking and swimming-pool water. It is also an oxidizing agent and has many applications in organic chemistry.
It is never found uncombined in nature, but is widely distributed in combination with the alkali metals, as ◊chlorides or ◊chlorates. Chlorine was discovered 1774 by Scheele, but Humphrey Davy first proved it to be an element 1810. During World War I, it was used as a weapon. It rapidly attacks the membranes of the nose, throat, and lungs, producing bronchitis or pneumonia.

chlorofluorocarbon (CFC) synthetic chemical, which is odourless, nontoxic, nonflammable, and chemically inert. CFCs are used as propellants in ◊aerosol cans, refrigerants in refrigerators and air conditioners, in the manufacture of foam boxes for take-away food cartons, and as cleaning substances in the electronics industry. They are partly responsible for the destruction of the ◊ozone layer. In Feb 1989, EEC members agreed to ban all CFC production in member countries by 2000.
When CFCs are released into the atmosphere, they drift up slowly into the stratosphere, where, under the influence of ultraviolet radiation from the Sun, they break down into chlorine atoms which destroy the ozone layer and allow harmful radiation from the Sun to reach the Earth's surface. CFCs can remain in the atmosphere for more than 100 years. Replacements for CFCs are being developed, and research into safe methods of destroying existing CFCs is being carried out.

chloroform or *trichloromethane* $CHCl_3$ a clear, colourless, toxic liquid with a characteristic, pungent, sickly-sweet smell and taste, formerly used as an anaesthetic (now superseded by less harmful substances). It is used as a solvent and in the synthesis of organic chemical compounds.

chlorophyll green pigment present in the majority of plants, which is responsible for the absorption of light energy during the light reaction of ◊photosynthesis. It absorbs the red and blue-violet parts of sunlight but reflects the green, thus giving the characteristic colour to most plants.
Chlorophyll is found within chloroplasts, present in large numbers in the leaves. Cyanobacteria and other photosynthetic bacteria also have chlorophyll, though of a slightly different type. Chlorophyll is similar in structure to ◊haemoglobin, but with magnesium instead of iron as the reactive part of the molecule.

chloroplast a structure (organelle) within a plant cell containing the green pigment chlorophyll. Chloroplasts occur in most cells of the green plant which are exposed to light, often in large numbers. Typically, they are flattened and disc-like, with a double membrane enclosing the stroma, a gel-like matrix. Within the stroma are stacks of fluid-containing cavities, or vesicles, where ◊photosynthesis occurs.
It is thought that the chloroplasts were originally free-living cyanobacteria, which invaded larger, non-photosynthetic cells and developed a symbiotic relationship with them. Like ◊mitochondria, they contain a small amount of ◊DNA and divide by fission. Chloroplasts are a type of ◊plastid.

chlorosis an abnormal condition of green plants in which the stems and leaves turn pale green or yellow. The yellowing is due to a reduction in the levels of the green chlorophyll pigments. It may be caused by a deficiency in essential elements (such as magnesium, iron, or manganese), a lack of light, genetic factors, or virus infection.

chocolate a drink or confectionery derived from ◊cocoa.

Chodowiecki /·kɒdəv'jetski/ Daniel Nicolas 1726–1801. German painter and engraver. His works include engravings of scenes from the Seven Years' War and the life of Christ, and the portrait *Jean Calas and his family.*

choir a body of singers, normally divided into two or more parts, and commonly four (soprano, alto, tenor, bass). The words *choir* and *chorus* are frequently interchangeable, although all church groups use the former, while larger groups, which may have several hundred members, invariably use the latter.

Choiseul /ʃwæ'zɜ:l/ Etienne François, duc de Choiseul 1719–1785. French politician. Originally a protégé of Mme de Pompadour, the mistress of Louis XV, he became minister for foreign affairs 1758, and held this and other offices until 1770. He banished the Jesuits, and was a supporter of the Enlightenment philosophers Diderot and Voltaire.

choke in physics, a coil employed as an electrical ◊inductance, particularly the type used as a 'starter' in the circuit of fluorescent lighting.

cholecystectomy surgical removal of the gall bladder.

cholera intestinal infection caused by a bacterium (*Vibrio cholerae*), and characterized by violent diarrhoea. Transmitted in contaminated water or food, it is still prevalent in many tropical areas.
The formerly high death rate has been much reduced by treatments to prevent dehydration and loss of body salts. There is an effective vaccine that must be repeated at frequent intervals for people exposed to continuous risk of infection.

cholesterol a waxy, fatty, ◊steroid substance that is ubiquitous and vital in the body. It is made by the liver, and also provided in the diet by foods such as eggs, butter, and meat. A high level of cholesterol in the blood is thought to contribute to atherosclerosis (hardening of the arteries).
Cholesterol is the starting point for steroid hormones, including the sex hormones; it is an integral part of all cell membranes; it is broken down by the liver into bile salts, which are involved in fat absorption by the digestive system; and it is an essential component of *lipoproteins*, which transport fats and fatty acids in the blood. **Low-density lipoprotein cholesterol** (LDL-cholesterol), when present in excess, can enter the tissues and deposit on the surface of the arteries as atherosclerosis. **High-density lipoprotein cholesterol** acts as a scavenger, transporting fat and cholesterol from the tissues to the liver for breakdown. Blood cholesterol levels can be altered by reducing the amount of fat in the diet and by changing some of the saturated fat to polyunsaturated fat, which gives a reduction in LDL-cholesterol. HDL-cholesterol can be increased by exercise.

Chomsky /'tʃɒmski/ Noam 1928– . US professor of linguistics. He proposed a theory of transformational generative grammar, which attracted widespread interest because of the claims it made about the relationship between language and the mind, and the universality of an underlying language structure. He is also a leading spokesman against imperialist tendencies of the US government.

Chongjin /·tʃʊŋ'dʒɪn/ capital of North Hamgyong province on the NE coast of North Korea; population (1984) 754,000.

Chongqing /·tʃʊŋ'tʃɪŋ/ or *Chungking*, also known as *Pahsien* city in Sichuan province, China, which stands at the confluence of the ◊Chang Jiang and the Jialing Jiang; population (1984) 2,733,700. Industries include iron, steel, chemicals, synthetic rubber, and textiles.
For over 4,000 years it has been an important commercial centre in one of the most remote and economically deprived regions of China. It was opened to foreign trade in 1891, and it remains a focal point of road, river, and rail transport. When both Beijing and Nanjing were occupied by the Japanese, it was the capital of China 1938–46.

Choong /tʃʊŋ/ Ewe Beng 'Eddy' 1930– . Malayan badminton player. Only 157.48 cm/5 ft 2in tall he was a dynamic player and won most major honours in a career between 1950–1957, including the All-England singles title four times 1953–1957.

CAREER HIGHLIGHTS

All England Championships:
singles 1953–54, 1956–57
doubles 1951–53 (with brother David)
mixed 1953
Thomas Cup
1955 (with Malaya).

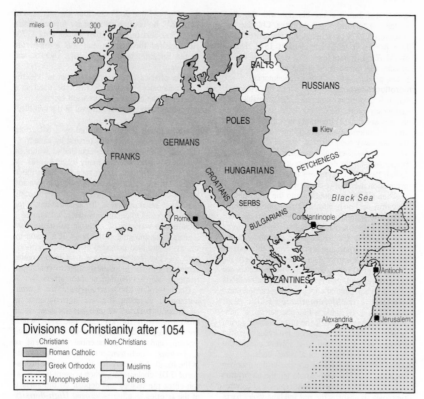

miles 0   300
km 0   300

BALTS

RUSSIANS

POLES

GERMANS

Kiev

FRANKS

PETCHENEGS

CROATIANS

HUNGARIANS

SERBS

Rome

BULGARIANS

Black Sea

Constantinople

BYZANTINES

Antioch

Alexandria

Jerusalem

Divisions of Christianity after 1054

Christians   Non-Christians

▨ Roman Catholic

▨ Greek Orthodox   ▨ Muslims

⠿ Monophysites   ☐ others

Choonhavan Major-General Chatichai 1922– .
Thai politician, prime minister of Thailand from
1988. He has promoted a peace settlement in
neighbouring Cambodia as part of a broader vision
of transforming Indochina into a thriving, open-
trading zone.

A field marshal's son, he fought in World War II
and the ◊Korean War. After a successful career
as a diplomat and businessman, he moved into
politics and became leader of the conservative
Chat Thai party and, in 1988, prime minister.

Chopin /'ʃɒpæn/ Frédéric (François) 1810–1849.
Polish composer and pianist. He made his debut
as a pianist at the age of eight. As a performer,
Chopin revolutionized the technique of pianoforte-
playing, and concentrated on solo piano pieces.
His compositions for piano are characterized by
their lyrical and poetic quality.

Born the son of a French father and a Polish
mother. From 1831 he made his home in Paris,
where he became known in the fashionable salons,
although he rarely performed in public. In 1836 Liszt
introduced him to Mme Dudevant (George ◊Sand),
with whom he had a close relationship 1838–46.
During this time she nursed him in Majorca for
tuberculosis, while he composed intensively and for
a time regained his health. He died 17 Oct 1849 and
was buried in Père Lachaise cemetery in Paris.

Chopin A daguerreotype of the composer.

Chopin /'ʃəʊpæn/ Kate 1851–1904. US novelist
and story writer. Her novel *The Awakening*
1899 is now regarded as a classic of feminist
sensibility.

chorale /kɒ'rɑːl/ a traditional hymn tune of the
German Protestant Church, harmonized in four
parts for singing by a congregation.

chord in geometry, a straight line joining any two
points on a curve. The chord that passes through
the centre of a circle (the longest chord) is the
diameter. The longest and shortest chords of an
ellipse (a regular oval) are called the major and
minor axes.

chord in music, a group of three or more notes
sounded together. The resulting combination of
tones may be either harmonious or dissonant.

chordate animal belonging to the phylum Chordata,
which includes vertebrates, sea squirts, amphioxus, and others. All these animals, at some stage
of their lives, have a supporting rod of tissue (notochord or backbone) running down their bodies.

chorea a disease of the nervous system marked by
involuntary movements of the face muscles and
limbs, formerly called St Vitus' dance. See also
◊Huntington's chorea.

choreography the art of creating and arranging ballet and dance for performance; originally, in the
18th century, the art of dance notation.

chorion outermost of the three membranes
enclosing the embryo of reptiles, birds, and
mammals; see also ◊amnion.

chorus a group of singers. See ◊choir.

Chou En-lai /'tʃəʊ en'laɪ/ former name for Chinese politician ◊Zhou Enlai.

chough bird *Pyrrhocorax pyrrhocorax* of the crow
family, about 38 cm/15 in long, black-feathered,
and with red bill and legs. It lives on sea-cliffs
and mountains from Europe to E Asia, but is
now rare.

The *alpine chough Pyrrhocorax graculus* is
similar, but has a yellow bill and is found up to
the snowline in mountains from the Pyrenees to
Central Asia.

chow chow breed of dog originating in China in
ancient times. About 45 cm/1.5 ft tall, it has a
broad neck and head, round cat-like feet, soft
woolly undercoat with a coarse outer coat, and

a mane. Its coat should be of one colour, and it
has an unusual blue-black tongue.

Chrétien de Troyes /'kreti'æn də 'trwɑː/ medieval
French poet, born in Champagne about the middle
of the 12th century. His epics, which include *Le
Chevalier de la Charrette*; *Perceval*, written for
Philip, Count of Flanders; *Erec*; *Yvain*; and other
Arthurian romances, introduced the concept of the
Holy Grail.

Christ (Greek *khristos* 'anointed one') the ◊Messiah
as prophesied in the Hebrew Bible, or Old Testament. See ◊Jesus.

Christchurch /'kraɪstʃɜːtʃ/ town in Dorset, England, adjoining Bournemouth at the junction of the
Stour and Avon rivers, population (1983) 40,300.
Light industry includes the manufacture of plastics
and electronics. There is a Norman and Early English priory church.

Christchurch /'kraɪstʃɜːtʃ/ city on South Island,
New Zealand, 11 km/7 mi from the mouth of
the Avon river; population (1986) 299,300. Principal city of the Canterbury plains, it is the
seat of the University of Canterbury. Industries include fertilizers and chemicals, canning
and meat-processing, rail workshops, and shoes.
Christchurch uses as its port a bay in the sheltered
Lyttelton Harbour on the N shore of the Banks
Peninsula, which forms a denuded volcanic mass.
Land has been reclaimed for service facilities, and
rail and road tunnels (1867 and 1964 respectively)
link Christchurch with Lyttelton.

christening Christian ceremony of ◊baptism of infants, including giving a name.

Christian /'krɪstjən/ follower of ◊Christianity, the
religion derived from the teachings of Jesus. In the
New Testament (Acts 11:26) it is stated that the
first to be called Christians were the disciples in
Antioch (now Antakya, Turkey).

Christian /'krɪstjən/ ten kings of Denmark and
Norway, including:

Christian I 1426–1481. king of Denmark from 1448,
and founder of the Oldenburg dynasty. In 1450 he
established the union of Denmark and Norway that
lasted until 1814.

Christian III 1503–1559. king of Denmark and Norway from 1535. Under his reign the Reformation
was introduced.

Christian IV 1577–1648. king of Denmark and Norway from 1588. He sided with the Protestants in
the Thirty Years' War (1618–48), and founded
Christiania (now Oslo, capital of Norway). He was
succeeded by Frederick II 1648.

Christian VIII 1786–1848. king of Denmark
1839–48. He was unpopular because of his
opposition to reform. His attempt to encourage
the Danish language and culture in Schleswig and
Holstein led to an insurrection there shortly after
his death. He was succeeded by Frederick VII.

Christian IX 1818–1906. King of Denmark from
1863. His daughter Alexandra married Edward
VII of the UK and another, Dagmar, married
Tsar Alexander III of Russia; his second son,
George, became king of Greece. In 1864 he lost
the duchies of Schleswig and Holstein after a war
with Austria and Prussia.

Christian X 1870–1947. king of Denmark and
Iceland from 1912, when he succeeded his father
Frederick VIII. He married Alexandrine, Duchess
of Mecklenburg-Schwerin, and was popular for his
democratic attitude. During World War II he was
held prisoner by the Germans in Copenhagen. He
was succeeded by Frederick IX.

Christiania /'krɪsti'ɑːniə/ former name of Norwegian capital of ◊Oslo (1624–1924), after King
Christian IV who replanned it after a fire in 1624.

Christianity world religion derived from the teaching of Jesus Christ in the first third of the 1st
century, with a present-day membership of about
1 billion. Its main divisions are the ◊Roman Catholic, ◊Orthodox, and ◊Protestant churches.

beliefs An omnipotent God the Father is the
fundamental concept, together with the doctrine
of the Trinity, that is, the union of the three persons of the Father, Son, and Holy Spirit in one

Christianity: history

1st century	The Christian church is traditionally said to have originated on the first Whitsun Day, but was separated from the parent Jewish church by the declaration of Saints Barnabas and Paul that the distinctive rites of Judaism were not necessary for entry into the Christian church.
3rd century	Christians were persecuted under the Roman emperors Severus, Decius, and Diocletian.
312	Emperor Constantine established Christianity as the religion of the Roman Empire.
4th century	A settled doctrine of Christian belief evolved, with deviating beliefs condemned as heresies. Questions of discipline threatened disruption within the church; to settle these, Constantine called the Council of Arles 314, followed by the councils of Nicaea 325, and Constantinople 381.
5th century	Councils of Ephesus 431 and Chalcedon 451. Christianity was carried northwards by figures such as Saints Columba and Augustine in England.
800	Holy Roman Emperor Charlemagne crowned by the Pope. The church assisted the growth of the feudal system of which it formed the apex.
1054	The Orthodox Church split from the Roman Catholic Church.
11th–12th centuries	Secular and ecclesiastical jurisdiction were often in conflict, for example, Emperor Henry IV and Pope Gregory VII, Henry II of England and his archbishop Becket.
1096–1291	The church supported a series of wars in the Middle East, the Crusades.
1233	The Inquisition was established to suppress heresy.
14th century	Increasing worldliness (against which the foundation of the Dominican and Franciscan monastic orders was a protest) and ecclesiastical abuses led to dissatisfaction in the 14th century and the appearance of the reformers Wycliffe and Huss.
15th–17th centuries	Thousands of women were accused of witchcraft and executed.
early 16th century	The Renaissance brought a re-examination of Christianity in N Europe by the humanists Erasmus, More, and Colet.
1517	The German priest Martin Luther started the Reformation, an attempt to return to primitive Christianity, and became leader of the Protestant movement.
1519–64	In Switzerland the Reformation was carried out by Calvin and Zwingli.
1529	Henry VIII renounced papal supremacy and proclaimed himself head of the Church of England.
1545–63	The Counter-Reformation was initiated by the Catholic church at the Council of Trent.
1560	The Church of Scotland was established according to Calvin's Presbyterian system.
16th–18th centuries	Missionaries in the Third World suppressed indigenous religions.
18th century	During the Age of Reason, Christianity was questioned, and the Bible examined on the same basis as secular literature. In England the Church of England suffered the loss of large numbers of Nonconformists.
19th century	The evolutionary theories of Darwin and others challenged orthodox belief.
1948	The World Council of Churches was founded as part of the ecumenical movement to reunite various Protestant sects and, to some extent, the Protestant churches and the Catholic church.
1950s–80s	Christian fundamentalism spread by television in USA.
1969	A liberation theology of freeing the poor from oppression emerged in South America, and attracted papal disapproval.
1972	The United Reformed Church was formed by the union of the Presbyterian Church in England and the Congregational Church.
1989	Barbara Harris, first female bishop, ordained in the USA.

Godhead. Christians believe that Jesus died for the sins of the people, and his divinity is based on the belief of his resurrection after death, and his ascension into Heaven. The main commandments are to love God and to love one's neighbour as oneself.

Christian Science a sect, the Church of Christ, Scientist, established in the USA by Mary Baker Eddy 1879. Christian Scientists believe that since God is good and is spirit, matter and evil are not truly real. Consequently they refuse all medical treatment. It has its own daily newspaper, the *Christian Science Monitor*.

Christian Science is regarded by its adherents as the restatement of primitive Christianity with its full gospel of salvation from all evil, including sickness and disease as well as sin. According to its adherents, Christian Science healing is brought about by the operation of truth in human conscience. There is no ordained priesthood, but there are public practitioners of Christian Science healing who are officially authorized.

The headquarters of the First Church of Christ, Scientist is in Boston, Massachusetts, USA, with branches in most parts of the world. The textbook of Christian Science is Eddy's *Science and Health with Key to the Scriptures* 1875.

Christians of St Thomas sect of Indian Christians on the Malabar Coast, named after the apostle who is supposed to have carried his mission to India. In fact the Christians of St Thomas were established in the 5th century by Nestorians from Persia. They now form part of the Assyrian Church (see under ◊Nestorianism) and have their own patriarch.

Christie /ˈkrɪsti/ Agatha 1890–1976. English detective novelist who created the characters Hercule Poirot and Miss Jane Marple. Her prolific output included the novels *The Murder of Roger Ackroyd* 1926 and *Ten Little Indians* 1939, and the play *The Mousetrap* 1952.

Born in Torquay as Agatha Miller, she married Colonel Archibald Christie 1914 and served during World War I as a nurse. Her first crime novel, *The Mysterious Affair at Styles* 1920, introduced Hercule Poirot. She often broke 'purist' rules, as in *The Murder of Roger Ackroyd* 1926 in which the narrator is the murderer. She caused a nationwide sensation 1926 by disappearing for ten days (possibly because of amnesia) when her husband fell in love with another woman. After a divorce 1928, she married the archaeologist Max Mallowan (1904–78) 1930.

Christie /ˈkrɪsti/ Julie 1940– . British film actress, who became a star in the 1960s following her award-winning performance in *Darling* 1965. She also appeared in *Doctor Zhivago* 1965; *The Go-Between* 1971; *Don't Look Now* 1973; *Memoirs of a Survivor* 1982; and *Power* 1986.

Christina /krɪsˈtiːnə/ 1626–1689. Queen of Sweden 1632–54. Succeeding her father Gustavus Adolphus at the age of six, she assumed power 1644, but disagreed with the former regent ◊Oxenstjerna. Refusing to marry, she eventually nominated her cousin Charles Gustavus (Charles X) as her successor. As a secret convert to Roman Catholicism, which was then illegal in Sweden, she had to abdicate 1654, and went to live in Rome, twice returning to Sweden unsuccessfully to claim the throne.

Christine de Pisan /ˈkrɪstiːn də ˈpiːzɒn/ 1364–1430. French poet and historian. Her works include love lyrics, philosophical poems, a poem in praise of Joan of Arc, a history of Charles V, and various defences of women, including *La cité des dames/The City of Ladies*.

Born in Venice, she was brought to France as a child when her father entered the service of Charles V. In 1389, after the death of her husband, the Picardian nobleman Etienne Castel, she began writing to support herself and her family,

Christmas 25 Dec, a religious holiday, traditionally marked by feasting and gift-giving. In the Christian church, it is the day on which the birth of Jesus is celebrated, although the actual birth date is unknown. Many of its customs have a non-Christian origin and were adapted from celebrations of the winter ◊solstice.

The choice of a date near the winter solstice owed much to missionary desire to facilitate conversion of members of older religions, which held festivals at that time of year.

Christmas Island /ˈkrɪsməs/ island in the Indian Ocean, 360 km/224 mi S of Java; area 140 sq km/54 sq mi; population (1986) 2,000. It has phosphate deposits. Found to be uninhabited when reached by Captain W Mynars on Christmas Day 1643, it was annexed by Britain 1888; occupied by Japan 1942–45, and transferred to Australia 1958. After a referendum 1984, it was included in Northern Territory.

Christmas rose see ◊hellebore.

Christmas tree type of tree brought indoors and decorated for Christmas, usually the Norway spruce *Picea abies*. The custom was a medieval German tradition and is now practised in many Western countries. Christmas trees were introduced to Britain in the 19th century by Albert, the Prince Consort.

Christo Adopted name of Christo Javacheff 1935– . US sculptor, born in Bulgaria, active in Paris in the 1950s and in New York from 1964. He is known for his wrapped works: structures such as bridges and buildings, and even areas of coastline, are temporarily wrapped in synthetic fabric tied down with rope. The *Running Fence* 1976 across California was another temporary work.

Christoff /ˈkrɪstɒf/ Boris 1918– . Bulgarian bass who made his operatic debut in 1946. His roles included Boris Godunov, Ivan the Terrible, and Mephistopheles.

Christophe /kriːˈstɒf/ Henri 1767–1820. West Indian slave, one of the leaders of the revolt against the French 1791, who was proclaimed king of Haiti 1811. His government distributed plantations to military leaders. He shot himself when his troops deserted him because of his alleged cruelty.

Christopher, St /ˈkrɪstəfə/ the patron saint of travellers. His feast day on 25 July was dropped from the Roman Catholic liturgical calendar 1969.

Traditionally he was a martyr in Syria in the 3rd century, and legend describes his carrying the Christ child over the stream; despite his great strength he found the burden increasingly heavy, and was told that the child was Christ bearing the sins of all the world.

Christ's Hospital /ˈkraɪsts ˈhɒspɪtl/ English independent school for boys, known as the Blue Coat school after the blue gown which forms part of the boys' dress. Founded in 1552, it moved from Newgate Street, London, to Horsham, Sussex, in 1902. There is a girls' school in Hertford which belongs to the same foundation. The English writers Coleridge and Lamb were educated at Christ's Hospital.

chromatic scale a musical scale proceeding by

semitones. All 12 notes in the octave are used rather than the 7 notes of the diatonic scale.

chromatography a technique for separating a mixture, usually in solution, into its constituent components. This is done by passing the mixture (the 'mobile phase' through another substance (the 'stationary phase'), usually a liquid or solid. The different components of the mixture are absorbed or impeded to different extents, and hence separate.

Analytical chromatography uses very small quantities, often millionths of a gram or less, to identify and quantify components of a mixture. Examples are the determination of the identities and amounts of amino acids in a protein, and the determination of the alcohol content of blood and urine samples. *Preparative chromatography* is used on a large scale for the purification and collection of one or more of the constituents, for example the recovery of protein from abattoir and other effluent wastes.

chromium a chemical element, symbol Cr, atomic number 24, relative atomic mass 52.01. It is a bluish-white metal capable of taking a high polish, and with a high melting-point. It is used decoratively and, alloyed with nickel, for electrical heating wires. Resistant to abrasion and corrosion, it is used to harden steel, and is a constituent of stainless steel and many other useful alloys. It is used extensively in chromium plating and as a ◊catalyst.

Compounds include sodium and potassium chromates and dichromates (for tanning leather), and potassium and ammonium chrome alums. It occurs chiefly as chrome-iron ore. The USSR, Zimbabwe, and Brazil are important sources.

chromosome a structure in a cell nucleus that carries the ◊genes. Each chromosome consists of one very long strand of DNA, coiled and folded to produce a compact chromosome. The point on a chromosome where a particular gene occurs is known as its locus. Most higher organisms have two copies of each chromosome (they are ◊diploid) but some have only one (they are ◊haploid). See also ◊mitosis and ◊meiosis.

chromosphere (Greek 'colour' and 'sphere') a layer of mostly hydrogen gas about 10,000 km/6,000 mi deep above the visible surface of the Sun (the photosphere). It appears pinkish-red during ◊eclipses of the Sun.

chronic in medicine, description of a condition which is of slow onset, and which then runs a prolonged course, such as rheumatoid arthritis or chronic bronchitis. In contrast, an *acute* condition develops quickly and may be of relatively short duration.

Chronicles two books of the Old Testament or Hebrew Bible containing genealogy and history.

chronicles, medieval books modelled on the Old Testament Books of Chronicles. Until the later Middle Ages, they were usually written in Latin by clerics, who borrowed extensively from each other.

Two influential early examples were written by Gregory of Tours in the 6th century and ◊Bede. In the later Middle Ages, vernacular chronicles appear, written by laymen, but by then the chronicle tradition was in decline, soon to be supplanted by Renaissance histories.

chronometer instrument for measuring time, especially used at sea. It is designed to remain accurate through all conditions of temperature and pressure. The first accurate marine chronometer, capable of an accuracy of half a minute a year, was made 1761 by John Harrison in England.

chrysanthemum plant of the family Compositae, with about 200 species. There are many cultivated varieties but some uncertainty as to the wild species from which they have been evolved. In the Far East the common chrysanthemum has been cultivated for more than 2,000 years, and is the national emblem of Japan.

The *ox-eye daisy Leucanthemum vulgare*, now placed in a closely related genus to the

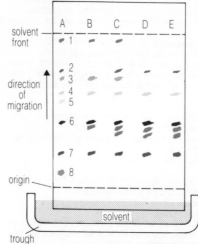

chromatography

chrysanthemum, and the *corn marigold Chrysanthemum segetum* are common weeds in Britain. Chrysanthemums may be grown from seed, but are more usually reproduced by cutting or division. They were introduced to England 1789.

chrysolite an alternative name for the mineral ◊olivine.

chub freshwater fish *Leuciscus cephalus* of the carp family. Rather thickset and cylindrical, it grows up to 60 cm/2 ft, is dark greenish or grey on the back, silvery yellow below, with metallic flashes on the flanks. It lives generally in clean rivers, from Britain to the USSR.

Chubu /'tʃuːbuː/ mountainous coastal region of central Honshu island, Japan; population (1986) 20,694,000; area 66,774 sq/km/25,791 sq mi. Chief city is Nagoya.

Chufu /'tʃuːfuː/ former name for ◊Qufu, town in Shandong province, China.

Chugoku /tʃuː'gəʊku:/ southwestern region of Honshu island, Japan; population (1986) 7,764,000; area 31,881 sq km/12,314 sq mi. Chief city is Hiroshima.

Chukchi a people of NE Siberia who speak a language belonging to the Paleo-Asiatic family. Numbering approximately 14,000, the Chukchi are now citizens of the USSR.

They are primarily reindeer herders. Individual Chukchi stalk seals, while larger groups hunt whales from boats. Historically the Chukchi are known to have raided neighbouring groups and were the predominant people of NE Siberia.

Chukchi Sea /'tʃʊktʃiː/ part of the Arctic Ocean, situated to the north of Bering Strait between Asia and North America.

Chukovsky /tʃuː'kɒfski/ Kornei Ivanovitch 1882–1969. Russian critic and poet. The leading authority on the 19th century Russian poet Nekrasov, he was also an expert on the Russian language, for example *Zhivoi kak zhizn/A Life as Life* 1963, and beloved as 'Grandpa' Kornei Chukovsky for his nonsense poems which owe much to the English nursery rhymes and nonsense verse that he admired.

Chun Doo-hwan /'tʃʌn ˌduː'hwɑːn/ 1931– . South Korean military ruler who seized power 1979; president 1981–88 as head of the newly formed Democratic Justice Party.

Chun, trained in Korea and the USA, served as an army commander from 1967 and was in charge of military intelligence 1979 when President Park was assassinated by the chief of the Korean Central Intelligence Agency (KCIA). Gen Chun took charge of the KCIA and, in a coup, assumed control of the army and the South Korean government. In 1981 Chun was appointed president, and oversaw a period of rapid economic growth, governing in an authoritarian manner.

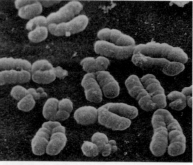

chromosome *False-colour electron microscope view of a group of human chromosomes. Each group consists of two strands joined at their centre, and can produce an exact copy of itself.*

Chungking /ˌtʃʊŋ'kɪŋ/ former name for ◊Chongqing, city in Sichuan province, China.

church a building designed as a Christian place of worship.

Church /tʃɜːtʃ/ Frederic Edwin 1826–1900. US painter, a follower of the Hudson River school's style of grand landscape. During the 1850s he visited South America and the Arctic.

Church Army religious organization within the Church of England founded 1882 by Wilson Carlile (1847–1942), an industrialist converted after the failure of his textile firm, who took orders 1880. Originally intended for evangelical and social work in the London slums, it developed along Salvation Army lines, and has done much work among ex-prisoners and for the soldiers of both World Wars.

Churchill /'tʃɜːtʃɪl/ town in province of Manitoba, Canada, situated on Hudson Bay.

Churchill /'tʃɜːtʃɪl/ Caryl 1938– . British playwright, whose predominantly radical and feminist works include *Cloud Nine* 1979, *Top Girls* 1982, and *Serious Money* 1987.

Churchill /'tʃɜːtʃɪl/ Charles 1731–1764. British satiric poet. Once a priest in the Church of England, he wrote coarse and highly personal satires dealing with political issues.

Churchill /'tʃɜːtʃɪl/ Randolph (Henry Spencer) 1849–1895. British Conservative politician, chancellor of the Exchequer and leader of the House of Commons 1886, father of Winston Churchill.

Born at Blenheim Palace, son of the 7th duke of Marlborough, he entered Parliament 1874. In 1880 he formed a Conservative group known as the Fourth Party with Drummond Wolff (1830–1908), J E Gorst (1835–1916), and Arthur Balfour, and in 1885 his policy of Tory democracy was widely accepted by the party. In 1886 he became chancellor of the Exchequer, but resigned within six months because he did not agree with the demands made on the Treasury by the War Office and the Admiralty. In 1874, he married Jennie Jerome (1854–1921), daughter of a wealthy New Yorker.

Churchill /'tʃɜːtʃɪl/ Winston (Leonard Spencer) 1874–1965. British Conservative politician. In Parliament from 1900, as a Liberal until 1923, he held a number of ministerial offices, including 1st Lord of the Admiralty 1911–15 and chancellor of the Exchequer 1924–29. Absent from the cabinet in the 1930s, he returned Sept 1939 to lead a coalition government 1940–45, negotiating with Allied leaders in World War II; he was again prime minister 1951–55. Nobel Prize for Literature 1953.

He was born at Blenheim Palace, the elder son of Lord Randolph Churchill. During the Boer War he was a war correspondent and made a dramatic escape from imprisonment in Pretoria. In 1900 he was elected Conservative Member of Parliament for Oldham, but he disagreed with Chamberlain's tariff-reform policy, and joined the Liberals. Asquith made him president of the Board of Trade 1908, where he introduced legislation for the establishment of labour exchanges. He became home secretary 1910.

In 1911 Asquith appointed him First Lord of the Admiralty. In 1915–16 he served in the trenches in France, but then resumed his parliamentary duties and was minister of munitions under Lloyd George 1917, when he was concerned with the development of the tank. After the armistice he was secretary for war 1918–21, and then as colonial secretary played a leading part in the establishment of the Irish Free State. During the post-war years he was active in support of the Whites (anti-Bolsheviks) in Russia.

In 1922–24 Churchill was out of Parliament. He left the Liberals 1923, and was returned for Epping as a Constitutionalist 1924. Baldwin made him chancellor of the Exchequer, and he brought about Britain's return to the gold standard and was prominent in the defeat of the General Strike of 1926. In 1929–39 he was out of office as he disagreed with the Conservatives on India, rearmament, and Chamberlain's policy of appeasement.

On the first day of World War II he went back to his old post at the Admiralty. In May 1940 he was called to the premiership as head of an all-party administration and made a much quoted 'blood, tears, toil, and sweat' speech to the House of Commons. He had a close relationship with US president Roosevelt, and in Aug 1941 concluded the ◊Atlantic Charter with him. He travelled to Washington, Casablanca, Cairo, Moscow, and Tehran, meeting the other leaders of the Allied war effort. In Feb 1945 he met Stalin and Roosevelt in the Crimea and agreed on the final plans for victory. On 8 May he announced the unconditional surrender of Germany.

On 23 May 1945 the coalition was dissolved, and Churchill formed a caretaker government drawn mainly from the Conservatives. Defeated in the general election in July, he became leader of the opposition until the election Oct 1951, in which he again became prime minister. In Apr 1955 he resigned. His home from 1922, Chartwell in Kent, is a museum.

His books include a six-volume history of World War II (1948–54) and a four-volume *History of the English-Speaking Peoples* (1956–58).

Church in Wales the Welsh Anglican church; see ◊Wales, Church in.

Church of England the established form of Christianity in England, a member of the Anglican Communion. It was dissociated from the Roman Catholic Church 1534. There were approximately 1,100,000 regular worshippers 1988.

structure In England the two archbishops head the provinces of Canterbury and York, which are subdivided into bishoprics. The Church Assembly 1919 was replaced 1970 by a *General Synod* with three houses (bishops, other clergy, and laity) to regulate church matters, subject to Parliament and the royal assent. A *Lambeth Conference* (first held 1867), attended by bishops from all parts of the Anglican Communion, is held every ten years and presided over in London by the archbishop of Canterbury. It is not legislative but its decisions are often put into practice. The *Church Commissioners* for England 1948 manage the assets of the church (in 1989 valued at £2.64 billion) and endowment of livings.

The main parties, all products of the 19th century, are: the *Evangelical* or *Low Church*, which maintains the church's Protestant character; the *Anglo-Catholic* or *High Church*, which stresses continuity with the pre-Reformation church and is marked by ritualistic practices, the use of confession, and maintenance of religious communities of both sexes; and the *Liberal* or *Modernist*, concerned with the reconciliation of the Church with modern thought. There is also the *Pentecostal Charismatic* movement, emphasizing spontaneity and speaking in tongues.

history

2nd century Christianity arrived in England during the Roman occupation.

597 St Augustine became first archbishop of Canterbury.

1529–34 At the **Reformation** the chief change was political: the sovereign (Henry VIII) replaced the pope as head of the church and assumed the right to appoint archbishops and bishops.

1536–40 The monasteries were closed down.

1549 First publication of the **Book of Common Prayer**, the basis of worship throughout the Anglican Church.

1563–1604 The **Thirty-Nine Articles**, the Church's doctrinal basis, were drawn up, enforced by Parliament, and revised.

17th–18th centuries Colonizers took the Church of England to North America (where three US bishops were consecrated after the War of Independence, whose successors still lead the Episcopal Church in the USA), Australia, New Zealand, and India.

19th century Missionaries were active in Africa. The **Oxford Movement**, led by the academic priests Newman, Keble, and Pusey, eventually developed into Anglo-Catholicism.

20th century There were moves towards reunion with the Methodist and Roman Catholic churches. Modernism, a liberal movement, attracted attention 1963 through a book by a bishop, J A T Robinson. The **ordination of women** was accepted by some overseas Anglican churches, for example the US Episcopal Church 1976; the Lambeth conference 1978 stated that there was no theological objection to women priests.

Church of Scotland the established form of Christianity in Scotland, first recognized by the state 1560. It is based on the Protestant doctrines of the reformer Calvin and governed on Presbyterian lines. The Church went through several periods of episcopacy in the 17th century, and those who adhered to episcopacy after 1690 formed the Episcopal Church of Scotland, an autonomous church in communion with the Church of England. In 1843, there was a split in the Church of Scotland (the Disruption), in which almost a third of its ministers and members left and formed the Free Church of Scotland. Its membership 1988 was about 850,000.

Chuvash /'tʃuːvæʃ/ autonomous Soviet Socialist Republic of the USSR, it lies W of the Volga, 560 km/350 mi E of Moscow; area 18,300 sq km /7,100 sq mi; population (1986) 1,320,000. The capital is Cheboksary, population (1985) 389,000. Lumbering and grain-growing are important and there are phosphate and limestone deposits, and electrical and engineering industries.

CIA abbreviation for ◊**Central Intelligence Agency**.

Ciano /'tʃɑːnəʊ/ Galeazzo 1903–1944. Italian

Churchill *Winston Churchill, March 1944.*

Fascist politician. Son-in-law of Mussolini, he was foreign minister 1936–43, when his loyalty became suspect. He voted against Mussolini at the meeting of the Grand Council 25 July 1943 that overthrew the dictator, but was later tried for treason and shot by the Fascists.

Cibachrome in photography, a process of printing directly from transparencies. Distinguished by rich, saturated colours, it can be home-processed and the colours are highly resistant to fading. It was introduced 1963. It is marketed by Ilford UK Ltd.

cicada insect of the family Cicadidae. Most species are tropical, but a few occur in Europe and North America. Young cicadas live underground, for up to 17 years in some species. The adults live on trees, whose juices they suck. The males produce a loud, almost continuous, chirping by vibrating membranes in resonating cavities in the abdomen. The rare *Cicadetta montana*, about 2 cm/0.8 in long, lives in the New Forest, England.

Cicero /'sɪsərəʊ/ 106–43 BC. Roman orator, writer, and statesman. His speeches, and philosophical and rhetorical works are models of Latin prose, and his letters provide a picture of contemporary Roman life. As consul 63 BC he exposed Catiline's conspiracy in four major orations.

Born in Arpinium, Cicero became an advocate in Rome, spent three years in Greece studying oratory, and after the dictator Sulla's death distinguished himself in Rome on the side of

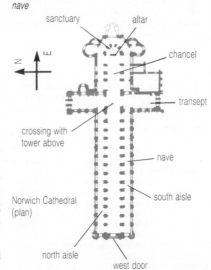

nave

sanctuary   altar

chancel

transept

crossing with
tower above

nave

Norwich Cathedral
(plan)

south aisle

north aisle

west door

Cicero *Sculpture of Roman statesman and writer Cicero. His informal letters, with their references to his wives – both of whom he divorced – and to his beloved daughter, Tulia, who died while still a young woman, show the human side of the public figure.*

the popular party. When the First Triumvirate was formed 59, Cicero was exiled and devoted himself to literature. He sided with Pompey during the civil war (49–48 BC) but was pardoned by Caesar and returned to Rome. After Caesar's assassination 44 he supported Octavian (the future Emperor Augustus) and violently attacked Antony in speeches known as the Philippics. On the reconciliation of Antony and Octavian he was executed by Antony's agents.

cichlid freshwater fish of the family Cichlidae. Cichlids are somewhat perch-like, but have a single nostril on each side instead of two. They are mostly predatory, and have deep, colourful bodies, flattened from side to side so that some are almost disc shaped. Many are territorial in the breeding season and may show care of the young. There are more than 1,000 species found in South and Central America, Africa, and India.

The *discus fish Symphysodon* produces a skin secretion on which the young feed. Other cichlids, such as those of the genus *Tilapia*, brood their young in the mouth.

cicisbeo (Italian) 18th century term for an aristocratic married woman's lover, similar to *cavaliere servente.*

CID abbreviation for ◊*Criminal Investigation Department.*

Cid /sɪd/ Rodrigo Diaz de Bivar 1040–1099. Spanish soldier, nicknamed *El Cid* ('the lord') by the Moors. Born in Castile of a noble family, he fought against the king of Navarre, and won his nickname *el Campeador* (the Champion) by killing the Navarrese champion in single combat. Essentially a mercenary, fighting both with and against the Moors, he died while defending Valencia against them, and in subsequent romances became Spain's national hero.

cider in the UK, a fermented drink made from the juice of the apple; in the USA the term cider usually refers to unfermented (non-alcoholic) apple juice. Cider has been known for more than 2,000 years, and for many centuries has been a popular drink in France and England, which are now its main centres of production.

The French output is by far the greater, mainly from Normandy and Brittany. In a good year about 30 million gallons are produced in Britain, mainly in W England from Hereford to Devon, and in Kent and Norfolk.

Cienfuegos /ˌsiːenˈfweɪɡɒs/ port and naval base in Cuba; population (1985) 124,600. It trades in sugar, fruit and tobacco.

Cierva /θiˈeəvə/ Juan de la 1895–1936. Spanish engineer. In trying to produce an aircraft that would not stall and could fly slowly, he invented the ◊autogiro, the forerunner of the helicopter, but differing from it in having unpowered rotors that revolve freely.

cif in economics, abbreviation for *cost, insurance, and freight* or *charged in full*. Many countries value their imports on this basis, whereas exports are usually valued ◊fob. For balance of payments purposes, figures are usually adjusted to include the freight and insurance costs.

cigar a compact roll of tobacco leaves for smoking. It was originally a sheath of palm leaves filled with tobacco, smoked by the Indians of Central and North America. Cigar smoking was introduced into Spain soon after 1492, and spread all over Europe in the next few centuries. From about 1890 cigar smoking was gradually supplanted in popularity in Britain by cigarette smoking.

The first cigar factory was opened in Hamburg 1788, and about that time cigar smoking became popular in Britain. The first cigars were made by hand—as is still the case with the more expensive cigars, including most of those made in Cuba—but in the USA from about the 1850s various machine methods were employed.

cigarette (French 'little cigar') a thin paper tube stuffed with shredded tobacco for smoking, usually plugged with a filter. The first cigarettes were the *papelitos* smoked in South America

about 1750. The habit spread to Spain, and then throughout the world, and is today the most general form of tobacco smoking.

In some countries, through the tax on tobacco, smokers contribute a large part of the national revenue. Greater awareness of the links between smoking and health problems since the 1960s have led to bans on television advertising and health warnings on cigarette packets in countries such as the UK and the USA. Greece, where cigarettes are cheap, has the largest number of smokers in Europe, and cigarette smoking is still very common in the Third World, where there are fewer restrictions on advertising.

cigarette cards card included in packets of cigarettes, bearing a printed view, drawing, portrait, etc. Cigarette cards originated in the USA in the 1870s and continued to be issued up until World War II. They are now popular collectors' items.

cilia (singular *cilium*) small thread-like organs on the surface of some cells, composed of contractile fibres which produce rhythmic waving movements. Some single-celled organisms move by means of cilia. In multicellular animals, they keep lubricated surfaces clear of debris. They also move food in the digestive tracts of some invertebrates.

Cimabue /ˌtʃiːməˈbuːeɪ/ Giovanni (Cenni de Peppi) *c.*1240–1302. Italian painter, active in Florence, traditionally styled the 'father of Italian painting'. Among the works attributed to him are *Madonna and Child* (Uffizi, Florence), a huge Gothic image of the Virgin which nevertheless has a new softness and solidity that leads forwards to Giotto.

Cimarosa /ˌtʃiːpməˈrəʊzə/ Domenico 1749–1801. Italian composer of operas that include *Il Matrimonio segreto/The Secret Marriage* 1792.

cimbalom in music, a type of ◊dulcimer.

Cimino /tʃɪˈmiːnəʊ/ Michael 1943– . US film director, who established his reputation with *The Deer Hunter* 1978 (which won five Academy Awards). His other films include *Heaven's Gate* 1981, and *The Year of the Dragon* 1986.

cinchona shrub or tree of the family Rubiaceae, found growing wild in the Andes. ◊Quinine is produced from the bark of some species and its culture has been introduced into India, Sri Lanka, the Philippines, and Indonesia.

Cincinnati /ˌsɪnsɪˈnæti/ city and port in Ohio, USA, on the Ohio river; population (1980) 1,400,000. Chief industries include machinery, clothing, furniture making, wine, chemicals, and meat-packing. Founded 1788, it became a city 1819. It attracted large numbers of European immigrants, particularly Germans, during the 19th century. It has two universities, and a major symphony orchestra.

Cincinnatus /ˌsɪnsɪˈnɑːtəs/ Lucius Quintus lived 5th century BC. Early Roman general. Appointed dictator in 458 BC he defeated the Aequi (an Italian people) in a brief campaign, then resumed life as a yeoman farmer.

Cinderella traditional European fairy tale, of which about 700 versions exist, including one by Charles ◊Perrault. Cinderella is an ill-treated youngest daughter who is enabled by a fairy godmother to attend the royal ball. She captivates Prince Charming but must flee at midnight, losing a tiny glass slipper by which the prince later identifies her.

ciné camera a camera which takes a rapid sequence of still photographs – 24 frames (pictures) each second. When the pictures are projected one after the other at the same speed on to a screen, they appear to show movement, because our eyes hold on to the image of one picture before the next one appears.

The ciné camera differs from an ordinary still camera in having a motor that winds on the film continuously, but the film is held still by a claw mechanism while each frame is exposed. When the film is moved between frames, a semicircular disc slides between the lens and the film and prevents exposure.

cinema a modern form of art and entertainment,

consisting of 'moving pictures' projected on to a screen. Cinema borrows from the other arts, such as music, drama, and literature, but is entirely dependent for its origins on technological developments, including the technology of film.

film history The first moving pictures were shown in the 1890s. Edison persuaded James J Corbett (1866–1933), the world boxing champion 1892–97, to act a boxing match for a film. Lumière in France, R W Paul in England, Latham in the USA, and others were making moving pictures of actual events (for example, *The Derby* 1896, shown in London on the evening of the race), and of simple scenes such as a train coming into a station. In 1902 Georges Méliès of France made a fantastic story film, *A Trip to the Moon*, which ran in London for nine months; and in 1903 Edwin S Porter directed *The Great Train Robbery* for Edison. It was a story in a contemporary setting, and cost about $100. The film was shown all over the world, and earned more than $20,000.

film technique For a number of years, films of 'indoor' happenings were 'shot' out of doors by daylight in Hollywood, USA. The sunny climate was the basis of its outstanding success as a centre of film production, though the first film studio was Edison's at Fort Lee, New Jersey. In England, the pioneer company of Cricks and Martin set up a studio at Mitcham (where a romantic domestic drama, *For Baby's Sake*, was made 1908).

D W Griffith, the US director, revolutionized film technique, introducing the close-up, the flashback, the fade-out, and the fade-in. His first epic was *The Birth of a Nation* 1915, and his second, *Intolerance*, with spectacular scenes in the Babylonian section, followed 1916.

film personalities At first, players' names were considered of no importance, though one who appeared nameless in *The Great Train Robbery*, G M Anderson, afterwards became famous as 'Bronco Billy' in a series of cowboy films, the first Westerns. The first movie performer to become a name was Mary Pickford; cinemagoers found her so attractive that they insisted on knowing who she was. World War I virtually stopped film production in Europe, but Hollywood continued to flourish in the 1920s, creating such stars as Rudolph Valentino, Douglas Fairbanks Sr, Lillian Gish, Gloria Swanson, Richard Barthelmess, and Greta Garbo outstanding among dramatic actors; Charles Chaplin, Harry Langdon, Buster Keaton, Harold Lloyd among comedians.

The introduction of sound from the late 1920s banished silent stars who turned out to have unsuitable voices, and changed the style of acting to a slightly less flamboyant approach. British stage stars who made the transition to film include Edith Evans, Alec Guinness, Laurence Olivier, and Ralph Richardson. US stars of the golden Hollywood era include Clark Gable, the Marx Brothers, Judy Garland, and Joan Crawford.

artistic development Concern for artistry began with Griffith, but developed in Europe, particularly in the USSR and Germany, where directors exploited film's artistic possibilities, during both the silent and the sound era. Silent films were never completely silent; there was always a musical background, integral to the film, whether played by a solo pianist in a suburban cinema, or a 100-piece orchestra in a big city theatre. The arrival of sound films (*The Jazz Singer* 1927), seen at first as having only novelty value, soon brought about a wider perspective and greater artistic possibilities through the combination of sight and sound. Successful directors included Jean Renoir in France, Lang and Murnau in Germany, Hitchcock in Britain and the USA, and Pudovkin and Eisenstein in the USSR. After World War II Japanese films were first seen in the West (although the industry dates back to the silent days), and India developed a thriving cinema industry.

Apart from story films, the industry produced news films, or 'documentaries', depicting factual life, of which the pioneers were the US film-makers Robert Flaherty (*Nanook of the North* 1920, *Man of Aran* 1932–34) and the Scottish John Grierson (*Drifters* 1929, *Night Mail* 1936); and cartoon films, which achieved their first success with Patrick Sullivan's *Felix the Cat* 1917, later surpassed in popularity by Walt Disney's *Mickey Mouse*.

the influence of television By the 1960s, increasing competition from television, perceived at the time as a threat to the existence of cinema, led the film industry both to make films for the new medium, and to concentrate on the wide-screen spectaculars dealing with historical and biblical themes, for example, *Cleopatra* 1963. Also exploited were areas of sexuality and violence considered unsuitable for family television viewing, such as *Last Tango in Paris* 1973. A distinction was usually made by critics between 'art' films and 'popular' films; the latter included such genres as the Chinese Western or kung-fu film, which had a vogue in the 1970s, and films controversial for the potential glorification of violence, epitomized by the character Rambo, a loner who takes the law into his own hands, as played by Sylvester Stallone.

Another popular genre was science fiction, such as *Star Wars* 1977, *Close Encounters of the Third Kind* 1977, and *ET* 1982, with expensive special effects. By the late 1980s cinema both as art and as pure entertainment seemed to be undergoing a revival, partly aided by the growth over the preceding decade of the video industry, which made major films widely available for viewing at home.

CinemaScope trade name for a wide-screen process using anamorphic lenses, in which images are compressed during filming and then extended during projection over a wider-than-average screen. The first film to be made in CinemaScope was *The Robe* 1953.

cinema vérité a style of film-making that aims to capture truth on film by observing, recording, and presenting real events and situations as they occur without exercising any directorial, editorial, or technical control.

Cinerama a wide-screen process devised in 1937 by Fred Waller of Paramount's special-effects department. Originally three 35-mm cameras and three projectors were used to record and project a single image. Three aspects of the image were recorded and then projected on a large curved screen with the result that the images blended together to produce an illusion of vastness. The first Cinerama film was *How the West Was Won* 1962. It was eventually abandoned in favour of a single-lens 70-mm process.

cinnabar mercuric sulphide, HgS, the only important ore of mercury. It is deposited in veins and impregnations near recent volcanic rocks and hot springs. The mineral itself is used as a red pigment, commonly known as **vermilion**. Cinnabar is found in the USA (California), Spain (Almadén), Peru, Italy, and Yugoslavia.

cinnamon bark of a tree *Cinnamomum zeylanicum*, grown in India and Sri Lanka. The bark is ground to make the spice used in curries and confectionery. Oil of cinnamon is obtained from waste bark, and is used as flavouring in food and medicine.

cinquefoil plant, genus *Potentilla*, of the rose family, usually with five-lobed leaves and brightly coloured flowers. It is widespread in northern temperate regions.

Cinque Ports /sɪŋk/ group of ports in S England, originally five, Sandwich, Dover, Hythe, Romney, and Hastings, later including Rye, Winchelsea, and others. Probably founded in Roman times, they rose to importance after the Norman conquest, and until the end of the 15th century were bound to supply the ships and men necessary against invasion.

The office of Lord Warden of the Cinque Ports survives as an honorary distinction (Winston Churchill 1941–65, Robert Menzies 1965–78, the

cinema chronology

1826–34	Various machines were invented to show moving images: the stroboscope, zoetrope, and thaumatrope.
1872	Eadweard Muybridge demonstrated movement of horses' legs using 24 cameras.
1877	Invention of Praxinoscope; developed as a projector of successive images on screen in 1879 in France.
1878–95	Marey, a French physiologist, developed various forms of camera for recording human and animal movements.
1887	Augustin le Prince produced the first series of images on a perforated film; Thomas Edison, having developed the phonograph, took the first steps in developing a motion-picture recording and reproducing device to accompany recorded sound.
1888	William Friese-Green showed the first celluloid film and patented a movie camera.
1889	Edison invented 35mm film.
1890–94	Edison, using perforated film, perfected his Kinetograph camera and Kinetoscope individual viewer; developed commercially in New York, London, and Paris.
1895	The Lumière brothers, Auguste (1862–1954) and Louis (1864–1948), projected, to a paying audience, a film of a train arriving at a station. Some of the audience fled in terror.
1896	Pathe introduced the Berliner gramophone, using discs in synchronization with film. Lack of amplification, however, made the performances ineffective.
1899	Edison tried to improve amplification by using banks of phonographs.
1900	Attempts to synchronize film and disc were made by Gaumont in France and Goldschmidt in Germany, leading later to the
	American Vitaphone system.
1902	Georges Méliès (1861–1938) made *Le Voyage dans la lune/A Trip to the Moon*.
1903	The first 'western' was made in the USA: *The Great Train Robbery* by Edwin S Porter.
1906	The earliest colour film (Kinemacolor) was patented in Britain by George Albert Smith.
1908–1911	In France, Emile Cohl experimented with film animation.
1910	With the dominating influence of the Hollywood Studios, film actors and actresses began to be recognized as international stars.
1912	In Britain, Eugene Lauste designed experimental 'sound on film' systems.
1914–18	Full newsreel coverage of World War I.
1915	*The Birth of a Nation*, D W Griffith's epic on the American civil war, was released in the USA.
1918–19	A sound system called Tri-Ergon was developed in Germany which led to sound being recorded on film photographically. The photography of sound was also developed by Lee De Forest in his Phonofilm system.
1923	The first sound film (as Phonofilm) was demonstrated.
1927	Release of the first major sound film, *The Jazz Singer*, Warners in New York. The first Academy Awards (Oscars) were given.
1928	Walt Disney released his first Mickey Mouse cartoon, *Steamboat Willie*.
1932	Technicolor (three-colour) process was used for a Walt Disney cartoon film.
1952	Cinerama (wide-screen presentation) was introduced in New York.
1953	Commercial 3-D (three-dimensional cinema) and wide screen Cinemascope were launched in the USA.
1976–77	Major films became widely available on video for viewing at home.

Queen Mother from 1979). The official residence is Walmer Castle.

circadian rhythm the metabolic rhythm found in most organisms, which generally coincides with the 24-hour day. Its most obvious manifestation is the regular cycle of sleeping and waking, but body temperature and the concentration of ◊hormones which influence mood and behaviour also vary over the day. In humans, alteration of habits (such as rapid air travel round the world) may result in the circadian rhythm being out of phase with actual activity patterns, causing malaise until it has had time to adjust.

Circassia /sə'kæsiə/ former name of an area of the N Caucasus, ceded to Russia by Turkey in 1829 and now part of the Karachai-Cherkess region of the USSR.

Circe /'sɜːsi/ in Greek mythology, an enchantress. In the *Odyssey* of Homer she turned the followers of Odysseus into pigs when she held their leader captive.

circle path followed by a point that moves so as to keep a constant distance, the **radius**, from a fixed point, the **centre**. The longest distance in a straight line from one side of a circle to the other, passing through the centre, is called the **diameter**. It is twice the radius. The ratio of the distance all the way round the circle (the **circumference**) to the diameter is an ◊irrational number called π (**pi**), roughly equal to 3.14159. A circle of radius r and diameter d has a circumference C equal to πd, or $C = 2\pi r$, and an area $A = \pi r^2$.

The area of a circle (πr^2) can be shown by dividing it into very thin sectors and reassembling them to make an approximate rectangle. The proof of $A = \pi r^2$ can only be done by using ◊integral calculus.

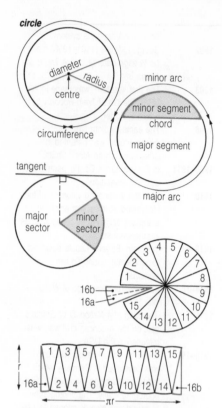

circle

diameter
radius
centre
circumference
tangent

minor arc
minor segment
chord
major segment
major arc

major sector
minor sector

16b
16a

16a
16b

πr

circuit in physics or electrical engineering, an arrangement of electrical components through which a current can flow. There are two basic circuits, series and parallel. In a series circuit, the components are connected end-to-end so that the current flows through all components one after the other. In a parallel circuit, components are connected side-by-side so that part of the current passes through each component. A circuit diagram shows in graphical form how components are connected together, using standard symbols for the components.

circuit breaker a switching device designed to protect an electric circuit from excessive current. It has the same action as a ◊fuse, and many houses now have a circuit-breaker between the incoming mains supply and the domestic circuits. They usually work by means of ◊solenoids. The circuit-breakers at electricity generating stations have to be specially designed to prevent dangerous arcing (the release of luminous discharge) when the high voltage supply is switched off. They may use an air blast or oil immersion to quench the arc.

circuits in England and Wales, the six different centres to which High Court and Circuit Judges travel to try civil and criminal cases: Midland and Oxford, N Eastern, Northern, S Eastern, Wales and Chester, and Western). In the USA the Court of Appeals sits in ten judicial circuits—hence circuit courts—and Washington DC.

circulatory system the system of vessels in an animal's body that transports essential substances (blood or other circulatory fluid) to and from the different parts of the body. Except for simple animals such as sponges and coelenterates (jellyfish, sea anemones, corals), all animals have a circulatory system.

The blood of fish passes once around the body before returning to a two-chambered heart (single circulation). The blood of birds and mammals passes to the lungs and back to the heart before circulating around the remainder of the body (double circulation). In all vertebrates, blood flows in one direction. Valves in the heart, large arteries, and veins prevent back-flow, and the muscular walls of the arteries assist in pushing the

blood around the body. Although most animals have a heart or hearts to pump the blood, normal body movements circulate the fluid in some small invertebrates. In the *open system*, as in snails and slugs, the blood (more correctly called ◊haemolymph) passes from the arteries into a body cavity (haemocoel), and from here is gradually returned to the heart, via the gills, by other blood vessels. In the *closed system* of earthworms, blood flows directly from the main artery to the main vein, via smaller lateral vessels in each body segment. Vertebrates, too, have a closed system with a network of tiny ◊capillaries carrying the blood from arteries to veins.

circumcision surgical removal of part of the foreskin (prepuce) of the penis, usually performed in the newborn.

It is usually requested for cultural reasons rather than as a medical necessity. There is some evidence that it protects against the development of cancer of the penis later in life, and that women with circumcised partners are less at risk from cancer of the cervix, although these theories have not been proved beyond doubt.

Circumcision, Feast of Roman Catholic and Anglican religious festival, celebrated annually on 1 Jan in commemoration of Jesus's circumcision.

circumference in geometry, the curved line that encloses a plane figure, for example, a ◊circle or an ellipse.

circumlocution a roundabout, verbose way of speaking or writing when someone tries to appear impressive or to evade clarity and action.

Charles Dickens in the novel *Little Dorrit* invented the Circumlocution Office as a satirical representation of a typical government department.

circumnavigation sailing around the world. The first ship to sail around the world was the *Victoria*, one of the Spanish squadron of five vessels that sailed from Seville in Aug 1519 under the Portuguese navigator Ferdinand Magellan.

Four vessels were lost on the way, but the *Victoria* arrived back in Spain in Sept 1522 under Cano. Magellan himself did not complete the voyage, as he died in the Philippines in 1521. The first English circumnavigator was Drake in 1577–80 in the Golden Hind.

circus (Latin 'circle') an entertainment, often held in a large tent ('big top'), involving performing animals, acrobats, and clowns. In 1871 P T ◊Barnum created the 'Greatest Show on Earth' in the USA. The popularity of animal acts decreased in the 1980s. Originally, in Roman times, a circus was an arena for chariot races and gladiatorial combats.

Cirencester /ˈsaɪrənˌsestə/ market town in Gloucestershire, England; population (1981) 15,620. It is the 'capital' of the Cotswolds. Light industry is based on engineering and the manufacture of electrical goods. It was the second largest town in Roman Britain, and has an amphitheatre which seated 8,000, and the Corinium Museum. The Royal Agricultural College is based here.

cirrhosis a liver disorder characterized by partial degeneration and scarring. It may be caused by an infection such as viral hepatitis, by chronic alcoholism, blood disorder, or malnutrition. If cirrhosis is diagnosed early enough, it can be arrested by treating the cause; otherwise it will progress and may prove fatal.

Cisalpine Gaul region of the Roman province of Gallia (N Italy) S of the Alps; *Transalpine Gaul*, the region N of the Alps, comprised Belgium, France, the Netherlands, and Switzerland.

The *Cisalpine Republic* was the creation of Napoleon in N Italy 1797, known as the Italian Republic 1802–04 and the Kingdom of Italy 1804–15.

Ciskei, Republic of /ˌsɪsˈkaɪ/ a Bantu homeland in South Africa, which became independent 1981, although this is not recognized by any other country.
area 7,700 sq km/2,974 sq mi
capital Bisho

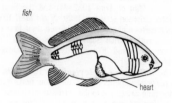

circulatory system

fish
heart

bird
heart

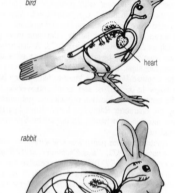

rabbit
heart

features one of the two homelands of the Xhosa people created by South Africa (the other is Transkei).
products pineapples, timber, metal products, leather, textiles
population (1984) 903,681
language Xhosa
government president, with legislative and executive councils.

Cistercian order Roman Catholic monastic order established at Cîteaux 1098 by St Robert de Champagne, abbot of Molesme, as a stricter form of the Benedictine order. Living mainly by agricultural labour, the Cistercians made many advances in farming methods in the Middle Ages. The *Trappists*, so called from the original house at La Trappe in Normandy (founded by Dominique de Rancé in 1664), follow a particularly strict version of the rule (including the maintenance of silence, manual labour, and a vegetarian diet).

cistron in genetics, the segment of ◊DNA that is required to synthesize a complete polypeptide chain. It is the molecular equivalent of a ◊gene.

CITES abbreviation for *Convention on International Trade in Endangered Species*, an international agreement signed by 81 countries under the auspices of the ◊IUCN to regulate the trade in ◊endangered species of animals and plants.

cithara ancient musical instrument, resembling a lyre but with a flat back. It was strung with wire and plucked with a plectrum or (after the 16th century) with the fingers. The bandurria and laud, still popular in Spain, are instruments of the same type.

Citizens Advice Bureau (CAB) UK organization established 1939 to provide information and advice to the public on any subject, such as personal problems, financial, house purchase, or consumer rights. If required, the bureau will act on behalf of citizens, drawing on its own sources of legal and other experts. There are more than 600 bureaux located all over the UK.

citizens' band (CB) short-range radio communication (around 27 MHz) facility used by members of the public in the USA and many European countries to chat or call for assistance in emergency.

Use of a form of citizens' band called Open Channel (above 928 MHz) was legalized in the UK in 1980.

citizenship status as a member of a state. In most countries citizenship may be acquired either by birth or by naturalization. The UK has five different categories of citizenship, with varying rights.

Under the British Nationality Act 1981, amended by the British Nationality (Falkland Islands) Act 1983 and the Hong Kong Act 1985, only a person designated as a *British citizen* has a right of abode in the UK; basically, anyone born in the UK to a parent who is a British citizen, or to a parent who is lawfully settled in the UK. Four other categories of citizenship are defined: *British Dependent Territories citizenship*, *British Overseas citizenship*, *British subject*, and *Commonwealth citizen*. Rights of abode in the UK differ widely for each.

Citlaltépetl /ˌsɪtlæl'tepek/ (Aztec 'star mountain') a dormant volcano, the highest mountain in Mexico, height 5,700 m/18,700 ft, north of the city of Orizaba (after which it is sometimes named). It last erupted in 1687.

citric acid an organic acid widely distributed in the plant kingdom, especially in citrus fruits. It is a white powder with a sharp acid taste. At one time it was commercially prepared from concentrated lemon juice, but now the main source is the fermentation of sugar with certain moulds.

citronella lemon-scented oil used in cosmetics and insect-repellants, obtained from the S Asian grass *Cymbopogon nardus*.

citrus genus of trees and shrubs, family Rutaceae, found in the warmer parts of the world, particularly Asia. They are evergreen and aromatic, and several species—the orange, lemon, lime, citron, and grapefruit—are cultivated for fruit.

city generally, a large and and important town; in the UK one awarded the title by the crown, and traditionally a cathedral town. In ancient Europe cities were states in themselves. In the early Middle Ages, cities were usually those towns that were episcopal sees (seats of bishops).

City, The the financial centre of London, England.

city technology college in the UK, a planned network of some 20 schools, financed jointly by government and industry, designed to teach technological subjects in inner-city areas to students aged 11–18. By 1990 few schools had been built.

The scheme is a controversial one, (a) because of government plans to operate the schools independently of local education authorities; (b) because of selection procedures; and (c) because of its vocational training at a time when there is also a drive towards a broader curriculum. The first college opened in Sept 1987 at Solihull, West Midlands.

Ciudad Bolívar /sju:'ða:ð bɒ'li:va:/ city in SE Venezuela, on the river Orinoco, 400 km/250 mi from its mouth; population (1981) 183,000. Gold is mined in the vicinity. The city is linked with Soledad across the river by the Angostura bridge (1967), the first to span the Orinoco. Capital of Bolívar state, it was called Angostura 1824–49.

Ciudad Guayana /sju:'ða:ð gwaɪ'ɑ:nə/ city in Venezuela, on the S bank of the river Orinoco, population (1981) 314,500. Main industries include iron and steel. The city was formed by the union of Puerto Ordaz and San Felix, and has been opened to ocean-going ships by dredging.

Ciudad Juárez /sju:'ða:ð 'xwa:res/ city on the Rio Grande, in Chihuahua state, N Mexico, on the border with the USA; population (1986) 596,000. It is a centre for cotton.

Ciudad Real /sju:'ða:ð reɪ'æl/ city of central Spain; 170 km/105 mi S of Madrid; population (1981) 50,150. It is capital of Ciudad Real province. It trades in livestock and produces textiles and pharmaceuticals. Its chief feature is its huge Gothic cathedral.

Ciudad Trujillo /sju:'ða:ð tru:'xi:əʊ/ name 1936–1961 of ◊Santo Domingo, capital city and seaport of the Dominican Republic.

civet small to medium-sized carnivorous mammal found in Africa and Asia, belonging to the family Viverridae, which also includes ◊*mongooses* and ◊*genets*. Distant relations of cats, they generally have longer jaws and more teeth. All have a scent gland in the inguinal (groin) region.

Extracts from this gland are taken from the *African civet Civettictis civetta* and used in perfumery. This civet is 70 cm/2.3 ft long, darkly spotted, and hunts small animals at night. As well as eating animal matter, many species, especially *palm civets* such as the SE Asian *Arctogalidia trivirgata*, are fond of fruit.

Civic Forum (Czech *Občanské Forum*) Czech democratic movement, formed Nov 89, led by Vaclav ◊Havel. In Dec 1989 it participated in forming a coalition government after the collapse of communist rule (see ◊Czechoslovakia). Its Slovak counterpart is ◊Public Against Violence.

civil aviation the operation of passenger and freight transport by air. With increasing traffic, control of air space is a major problem, and in 1963 Eurocontrol was established by Belgium, France, West Germany, Luxembourg, the Netherlands, and the UK to supervise both military and civil movement in the air space over member countries. There is also a tendency to coordinate services and other facilities between national airlines, for example, the establishment of Air Union by France (Air France), West Germany (Lufthansa), Italy (Alitalia) and Belgium (Sabena) 1963.

In the UK there are about 170 airports, those for London (Heathrow, City, and Gatwick), Prestwick, and Edinburgh being managed by the British Airports Authority (1965). The British Airways Board supervises British Airways, formerly British European Airways (BEA) and British Overseas Airways Corporation (BOAC); there are also independent companies.

Close cooperation is maintained with authorities in other countries, including the Federal Aviation Agency, which is responsible for development of aircraft, air navigation, traffic control, and communications in the USA. The Civil Aeronautics Board is the US authority prescribing safety regulations and investigating accidents. There are no state airlines in the USA, although many of the private airlines are large. The world's largest airline is the Soviet Union's government-owned Aeroflot, which operates some 1,300 aircraft over 1 million km/620,000 mi of routes and carries some 110 million passengers a year.

civil defence organized activities by the civilian population of a state to mitigate the effects of enemy attack on them.

During World War II (1939–45) civil-defence efforts were centred on providing adequate warning of air raids to permit the civilian population to reach shelter; then firefighting, food, rescue, communications, and ambulance services were needed. Since then, the threat of nuclear weapons has led to the building of fallout shelters in the USA, the USSR, and elsewhere. China has networks of tunnels in the cities that are meant to enable the population to escape nuclear fallout and reach the countryside, but which do not protect against the actual blast.

In Britain the Ministry of Home Security was constituted 1939 to direct air-raid precautions in World War II. The country was divided into 12 regions, each under a commissioner to act on behalf of the central government in the event of national communications systems being destroyed. Associated with the air-raid wardens were ambulance and rescue parties, gas officers, breakdown gangs, and so on. The National Fire Service was based on existing local services, and about five million people enrolled as firewatchers and firefighters. The Civil Defence Corps and Auxiliary Fire Service were disbanded in 1968.

A new structure of 'Home Defence' is now being created in Britain, in which the voluntary services, local authorities, the ◊Home Service Force, and the Territorial Army would cooperate. Regulations that came into force in 1983 compel local authorities to take part in civil defence exercises. Councils have to provide blast-proof bunkers and communication links, train staff and take part in the exercises.

civil disobedience the deliberate breaking of laws considered unjust, a form of nonviolent direct action; the term was coined by the US writer Thoreau in an essay of that name 1849. It was advocated by Mahatma Gandhi to prompt peaceful withdrawal of British power from India. Civil disobedience has since been employed by, for instance, the US civil rights movement in the 1960s and the peace movement in the 1980s.

civil engineering the branch of engineering that is concerned with the construction of roads, bridges, aqueducts, water-works, tunnels, canals, irrigation works, and harbours.

The term is thought to have been used for the first time by British engineer John Smeaton in about 1750, to distinguish civilian from military engineering projects. The professional organization in Britain is the Institution of Civil Engineers, which was founded in 1828 and is the oldest engineering institution in the world.

Civil Engineers, Institution of the first national body concerned with the engineering profession in England, founded in 1828. The celebrated builder of roads, bridges and canals, Thomas Telford, became its first president.

civil law the legal system based on Roman law. It is one of the two main European legal systems, English (common) law being the other.

During the Middle Ages Roman law was adopted, with local modifications, all over Europe, mainly through the Church's influence; its later diffusion was largely due to the influence of the French *Code Napoléon*, based on Roman law, which was adopted in the 19th century by several states of E Europe and Asia, and in Egypt. Inside the Commonwealth, Roman law forms the basis of the legal systems of Scotland and Québec, and is also the basis of that of South Africa. A second meaning of civil law is the law relating to matters other than criminal law, such as ◊contract and ◊tort.

civil list in the UK, the annual sum provided from public funds to meet the official expenses of the sovereign and immediate dependants; private expenses are met by the ◊privy purse.

Three-quarters of the civil list goes on wages for the royal household; the dependants it covers are the consort of a sovereign, children of a sovereign (except the Prince of Wales, who has the revenues from the Duchy of Cornwall), and widows of those children. Payments to other individual members of the royal family are covered by a contribution from the Queen.

civil list pension in the UK, a pension originally paid out of the sovereign's civil list, but granted separately since the accession of Queen Victoria. These are paid to persons in need, who have just claims on the royal beneficence, who have rendered personal service to the crown, or who have rendered service to the public by their discoveries in science and attainments in literature, art, or the like. The recipients are nominated by the prime minister, and the list is approved by Parliament.

civil rights the rights of the individual citizen. In many countries they are specified (as in the Bill of Rights of the US constitution) and guaranteed by law to ensure equal treatment for all citizens. In the USA, the struggle to obtain civil rights for former slaves and their descendants, both through legislation and in practice, has been a major theme since the Civil War.

civil service the body of administrative staff appointed to carry out the policy of a government. Members of the UK civil service may not take an active part in politics, and do not change with the government.

In Britain, civil servants were originally in the personal service of the sovereign. They were recruited by patronage, and many of them had only nominal duties. The great increase in public expenditure during the Napoleonic Wars led to a move in Parliament for reform of the civil service, but it was not until 1854 that two civil servants, Charles Trevelyan and Stafford Northcote, issued a report as a result of which recruitment by competitive examination, carried out under the Civil Service Commission 1855, came into force. Its recommendations only began to be effective when nomination to the competitive examination was abolished in 1870.

The two main divisions of the British civil service are the **Home** and **Diplomatic** services, the latter created in 1965 by amalgamation of the Foreign, Commonwealth, and Trade Commission services. All employees are paid out of funds voted annually for the purpose by Parliament.

Since 1968 the Civil Service Department has been controlled by the prime minister (as minister for the civil service), but everyday supervision is exercised by the Lord Privy Seal. The head of the Home Civil Service is also permanent secretary to the Civil Service Department. The present emphasis is on the professional specialist, and the *Civil Service College* (Sunningdale Park, Ascot, Berkshire) was established in 1970 to develop training. Their permanence gives civil servants in the upper echelons an advantage over ministers, who are in office for a comparatively brief time, and in the 1970s and 1980s it was alleged that ministerial policies in conflict with civil-service views tended to be blocked from being put into practice.

civil society the part of a society or culture outside the government and state-run institutions. For Marx and Hegel, civil society was that part of society where self-interest and materialism were rampant, although Adam ◊Smith believed that enlightened self-interest would promote the general good. Classical writers and earlier political theorists such as John ◊Locke used the term to describe the whole of a civilized society.

civil war war between rival groups within the same country.

Civil War, American also called *War Between the States* war 1861–65 between the Southern or Confederate States of America and the Northern or Union states. The former wished to maintain their 'states' rights', in particular the institution of slavery, and claimed the right to secede from the Union; the latter fought initially to maintain the Union, and later (1863) to emancipate the slaves.

The war, and in particular its aftermath, when the South was occupied by Northern troops in the period known as ◊Reconstruction, left behind lasting bitterness. Industry prospered in the North while the economy of the South, which had been based on slavery, continued to decline.

1861 Seven Southern states set up the Confederate States of America (president Jefferson Davis) 8 Feb; ◊*Fort Sumter*, Charleston, captured 12–14 Apr; Robert E Lee (Confederate) was victorious at the *1st Battle of Bull Run* 21 July.

1862 Battle of *Shiloh* 6–7 Apr was indecisive. Gen Grant (Unionist) captured New Orleans in May, but the Confederates were again victorious at the *2nd Battle of Bull Run* 29–30 Aug. Lee's advance was then checked by Gen McClellan at ◊*Antietam* 17 Sept.

1863 The *Emancipation Proclamation* was issued by President Lincoln 1 Jan, freeing the slaves; *Battle of Gettysburg* (Union victory) 1–4 July marked the turning point of the war; Grant overran the Mississippi states, capturing *Vicksburg* 4 July.

1864 In the *Battle of Cold Harbor* near Richmond, Virginia, 1–12 June, Lee delayed Grant in his advance on Richmond. The Union Gen Sherman marched through Georgia to the sea, taking *Atlanta* 1 Sept and Savannah 22 Dec.

1865 Lee surrendered to Grant at *Appomattox* courthouse 9 Apr; Lincoln was assassinated 14

Apr; last Confederate troops surrendered 26 May. There were 359,528 Union dead and 258,000 Confederate dead.

Civil War, English in British history, the struggle in the middle years of the 17th century between the king and the Royalists (Cavaliers) on one side, and the Parliamentarians (also called Roundheads) on the other.

1642 On 22 Aug ◊Charles I raised his standard at Nottingham. The Battle of ◊Edgehill on 23 Oct was indecisive.

1644 The Battle of ◊Marston Moor on 2 July was a victory for the Parliamentarians under ◊Cromwell.

1645 The Battle of ◊Naseby on 14 June was a decisive victory for Cromwell.

1646 On 5 May 1646 Charles surrendered to the Scottish army.

1648 A Royalist and Presbyterian rising in Mar to Aug was soon crushed by Cromwell and his New Model Army.

1649–50 Cromwell's invasion of Ireland.

1650 Cromwell defeated the Royalists under the future ◊Charles II at Dunbar, Scotland.

1651 The Battle of Worcester was another victory for Cromwell.

Civil War, Spanish war 1936–39 precipitated by a military revolt led by Gen Franco against the Republican government. Inferior military capability led to the gradual defeat of the Republicans by 1939.

Franco's insurgents (Nationalists, who were supported by Fascist Italy and Nazi Germany) seized power in the south and northwest, but were suppressed in areas such as Madrid and Barcelona by the workers' militia. The loyalists (Republicans) were aided by the USSR and the volunteers of the International Brigade, which included several writers, among them George Orwell.

1937 Bilbao and the Basque country were bombed into submission by the Nationalists.

1938 Catalonia was cut off from the main Republican territory.

1939 Barcelona fell in Jan and Madrid in Apr, and Franco established a dictatorship.

Civitavecchia /ˌtʃiːvɪtəˈvekjə/ ancient port on the W coast of Italy, in Lazio region; 64 km/40 mi NW of Rome; population (1971) 42,300. Industries include fishing, and the manufacture of cement and calcium carbide.

Clackmannanshire /klækˈmænənʃə/ former county (the smallest) in Scotland, bordering the Firth of Forth. It was merged with Central Region in 1975. The county town was Alloa.

Clacton-on-Sea /ˈklæktən ɒn ˈsiː/ seaside resort in Essex, England; 19 km/12 mi SE of Colchester; population (1981) 43,600. The 16th-century St Osyth's priory is nearby.

cladistics a method of biological ◊classification (taxonomy) that uses a formal step-by-step procedure for objectively assessing the extent to which organisms share particular characters, and for assigning them to taxonomic groups. These taxonomic groups (◊species, ◊genus, family) are termed *clades*.

cladode a flattened stem that is leaf-like in appearance and function. It is an adaptation to dry conditions because a stem contains fewer ◊stomata than a leaf, and water loss is thus minimized. The true leaves are usually reduced to spines or small scales. Examples of plants with cladodes are butcher's broom *Ruscus aculeatus, Asparagus,* and certain cacti. Cladodes may bear flowers or fruit on their surface and this distinguishes them from leaves.

Clair /kleə/ René, pseudonym of René-Lucien Chomette 1898–1981. French film-maker, originally a poet, novelist, and journalist. His *Sous les Toits de Paris/Under the Roofs of Paris* 1930 was one of the first sound films.

clam common name for a ◊bivalve mollusc. The *giant clam Tridacna gigas* of the Indopacific can

clam

giant clam

grow to 1 m/3 ft across in 50 years and weigh, with the shell, 500 kg/1,000 lb.

The term is used particularly of edible species, such as the North American **hard clam** *Venus mercenaria,* used in clam chowder, and whose shells were formerly used as money by North American Indians.

clan (Gaelic *clann* 'children') social grouping based on ◊kinship, familiar in the Highland clans of Scotland. Theoretically each clan is descended from a single ancestor from whom the name is derived, for example, clan MacGregor ('son of Gregor'). Rivalry between clans was often bitter, and they played a large role in the Jacobite revolts of 1715 and 1745, after which their individual tartan Highland dress was banned 1746–82.

Clapperton /ˈklæpətən/ Hugh 1788–1827. English explorer who crossed the Sahara from Tripli with Dixon Denham and discovered Lake Chad 1823. With his servant, Richard Lander, he attempted to reach the Niger, but died at Sokoto. Lander eventually reached the mouth of the Niger in 1830.

Clapton /ˈklæptən/ Eric 1945– . English blues and rock guitarist, singer, and composer, member of the groups Yardbirds and Cream in the 1960s. One of the pioneers of heavy rock and an influence on younger musicians, he later adopted a more subdued style.

Clare /kleə/ county on the west coast of the Republic of Ireland, in the province of Munster; area 3,190 sq km/1,231 sq mi; population (1986) 91,000. Shannon airport is here.

The coastline is rocky and dangerous, and inland Clare is an undulating plain, with mountains on the E, W, and NW, the chief range being the Slieve Bernagh mountains in the SE rising to over 518 m/1,700 ft. The principal rivers are the Shannon and its tributary, the Fergus. There are over 100 lakes in the county, Lough Derg is on the E border. The county town is Ennis. At Ardnachusha, 5 km/3 mi N of Limerick, is the main power station of the Shannon hydroelectric installations. The county is said to be named after Thomas de Clare, an Anglo-Norman settler to whom this area was granted 1276.

Clare /kleə/ John 1793–1864. English poet. His work includes *Poems Descriptive of Rural Life* 1820, *The Village Minstrel* 1821, and *Shepherd's Calendar* 1827. Clare's work was largely rediscovered in the 20th century.

Born at Helpstone, near Peterborough, the son of a farm labourer, Clare spent most of his life in poverty. He was given an annuity from the Duke of Exeter and other patrons, but had to turn to work on the land. He spent his last 20 years in

Clapton *Eric Clapton (right) with George Harrison (left) at the Live Aid concert, 1985.*

Clare The poet John Clare, by William Hilton in 1820. He spent his last years in a mental institution, where he wrote some of his most poignant poetry.

Northampton asylum. His early life is described in his autobiography, first published 1931.

Clarence /'klærəns/ English ducal title, which has been conferred on a number of princes. The last was Albert Victor 1864–92, eldest son of Edward VII.

Clarendon /'klærəndən/ Edward Hyde, 1st Earl of Clarendon 1609–1674. English politician and historian, chief adviser to Charles II 1651–67. A Member of Parliament 1640, he joined the Royalist side 1641. The *Clarendon Code* (1661–65) was designed to secure the supremacy of the Church of England.

In the ◊Short and ◊Long parliaments he attacked Charles I's unconstitutional actions and supported the impeachment of Charles's minister Strafford. In 1641 he broke with the revolutionary party and became one of the royal advisers. When civil war began he followed Charles to Oxford, and was knighted and made chancellor of the Exchequer. On the king's defeat in 1646 he followed Prince Charles to Jersey, where he began his *History of the Rebellion*, published 1702–04, which provides memorable portraits of his contemporaries.

In 1651 he became chief adviser to the exiled Charles II. At the Restoration he was created earl of Clarendon, while his influence was further increased by the marriage of his daughter Anne to James, Duke of York. His moderation earned the hatred of the extremists, however, and he lost Charles's support by openly expressing disapproval of the king's private life. After the disasters of the Dutch war 1667, he went into exile.

Clarendon /'klærəndən/ George William Frederick Villiers, 4th Earl of Clarendon 1800–1870. British Liberal diplomat, Lord Lieutenant of Ireland 1847–52, foreign secretary 1853–58, 1865–66, and 1868–70.

He was posted to Ireland at the time of the potato famine. His diplomatic skill was shown at the Congress of Paris 1856 and in the settlement of the dispute between Britain and the USA over the ◊*Alabama* cruiser.

Clarendon, Constitutions of in English history, a series of resolutions agreed by a council summoned by Henry II at Clarendon in Wiltshire 1164. The Constitutions aimed at limiting the secular power of the clergy, and were abandoned after the murder of Thomas Becket. They form an important early English legal document.

Clare, St /kleə/ *c.* 1194–1253. Christian saint. Born in Assisi, Italy, she became at 18 a follower of St Francis, who founded for her the convent of San Damiano. Here she gathered the first members of the *Order of Poor Clares*. In 1958 she was proclaimed by Pius XII the patron saint of television, since in 1252 she saw from her convent sickbed the services celebrating Christmas

in the basilica of St Francis in Assisi. Feast day 12 Aug.

claret English term for the red wines of Bordeaux, since the 17th century.

clarinet a musical ◊woodwind instrument with a single reed and a cylindrical tube, broadening at the end, developed in Germany in the 18th century. At the lower end of its range it has a rich 'woody' tone, which becomes increasingly brilliant towards the upper register. Its ability both to blend and to contrast with other instruments make it popular for chamber music and as a solo instrument. It is also heard in military and concert bands and as a jazz instrument.

Equally effective both in fast virtuoso passages and as an expressive melodic instrument, the clarinet's potential was quickly exploited, and it found a place in the orchestra by the late 18th century. Music for the instrument is written in one key, for simplicity, but is played in a different key. There are different types of clarinet, varying in range, including the bass clarinet, which has become a regular member of the orchestra.

Clark /klɑːk/ James 'Jim' 1936–1968. Scottish-born motor racing driver, one of the finest in the post-war era. He was twice world champion in 1963 and 1965. He spent all his Formula One career with Lotus.

His partnership with Lotus boss Colin Chapman was one of the closest in the sport. He won 25 Formula One Grand Prix races, a record at the time, before losing his life at Hockenheim, West Germany, in April 1968 during a Formula Two race.

Clark /klɑːk/ Joe (Joseph) Charles 1939– . Canadian Progressive Conservative politician, born in Alberta. He became party leader 1976, and in May 1979 defeated ◊Trudeau at the polls to become the youngest prime minister in Canada's history. Following the rejection of his government's budget, he was defeated in a second election Feb 1980. He became Secretary of State for External Affairs (foreign minister) in the ◊Mulroney government (1984–).

Clark /klɑːk/ Kenneth, Lord Clark 1903–1983. British art historian, director of the National Gallery, London, 1934–45. He popularized the history of art through his television series *Civilization* 1969. His books include *Leonardo da Vinci* 1939 and *The Nude* 1956.

Clark /klɑːk/ Mark (Wayne) 1896–1984. US general in World War II. In 1942 he became chief of staff for ground forces, led a successful secret mission by submarine to get information in N Africa preparatory to the Allied invasion, and commanded the 5th Army in the invasion of Italy.

Clark, born in New York, fought in France in World War I and between the wars held various military appointments in the USA. He was commander in chief of the United Nations forces in the Korean War 1952–53.

Clarke /klɑːk/ Arthur C(harles) 1917– . English science fiction and non-fiction writer, who originated the plan for the modern system of communications satellites 1945. His works include *Childhood's End* 1953 and the screenplay of *2001: A Space Odyssey* 1968.

Clarke /klɑːk/ Jeremiah 1659–1707. English composer. Organist at St Paul's, he composed 'The Prince of Denmark's March', a harpsichord piece that was arranged by Sir Henry ◊Wood as a 'Trumpet Voluntary' and wrongly attributed to Purcell.

Clarke /klɑːk/ Kenneth (Harry) 1940– . British Conservative politician, member of Parliament from 1970, a cabinet minister from 1985, and minister of health from 1988.

Clarke was politically active as a law student at Cambridge. He was elected to Parliament for Rushcliffe, Nottinghamshire, in 1970. In 1982 he became a minister of state, in 1985 paymaster general, with special responsibility for employment, in 1987 chancellor of the Duchy of Lancaster, and in 1988 was given the newly

independent Department of Health. Clarke was once secretary of the left-of-centre Bow Group.

Clarke /klɑːk/ Marcus Andrew Hislop 1846–1881. Australian writer. Born in London, he went to Australia when he was 18, and worked as a journalist in Victoria. He wrote *For the Term of his Natural Life* in 1874, a novel dealing with life in the early Australian prison settlements.

Clarke /klɑːk/ Ronald William 1937– . Australian middle- and long-distance runner. A prolific record breaker, he broke 17 world records ranging from 2 miles to the one-hour run.

The first man to break 13 min for the 3 miles (1966), he was also the first to better 28 min for the 10,000 metres. Despite his record-breaking achievements, he never won a gold medal at a major championship.

Clarke orbit an alternative name for ◊*geostationary orbit*, an orbit 35,900 km/22,300 mi high, in which satellites circle at the same speed as the Earth turns. This orbit was first suggested by space writer Arthur C Clarke in 1945.

Clarkson /'klɑːksən/ Thomas 1760–1846. British philanthropist. From 1785 he devoted himself to a campaign against slavery. He was one of the founders of the Anti-Slavery Society 1823 and was largely responsible for the abolition of slavery in British colonies 1833.

class in sociology, the main form of social stratification in industrial societies, based primarily on economic and occupational factors, but also referring to people's style of living or sense of group identity.

Within the social sciences, class has been used both as a descriptive category and as the basis of theories about industrial society. The most widely used descriptive classification in the UK divides the population into five main classes, with the main division between manual and non-manual occupations. Such classifications have been widely criticized, however, on several grounds: that they reflect a middle-class bias that brain is superior to brawn; that they classify women according to their husband's occupation rather than their own; that they ignore the upper class, the owners of land and industry. Theories of class may see such social divisions either as a source of social stability (see ◊Durkheim) or social conflict (as did ◊Marx).

class in biological classification, a group of related ◊orders. For example, all mammals belong to the class Mammalia and all birds to the class Aves. Among plants, all class names end in 'idae' (such as Asteridae) and among fungi in 'mycetes'; there are no equivalent conventions among animals. Related classes are grouped together in a ◊phylum.

class action in law, a court procedure where one or more claimants represent a larger group of people who are all making the same kind of claim against the same defendant. The court's decision is binding on all the members of the group.

This procedure is used particularly in the USA. The same effect is sometimes achieved in out-of-court settlements in Britain, for example the Opren case in 1987, when a large number of people claimed damages as a result of harmful side-effects of the drug Opren. It was settled on the basis that the members of the Opren Action Group would receive a global sum out of which the individual claims would be met, all members of the group then being bound not to take any further action.

classical music written in the late 17th–18th century; Western music of any period that does not belong to the folk or popular traditions.

classical economics school of economic thought that dominated 19th-century thinking. It originated with Adam Smith's *The Wealth of Nations* 1776, which embodied many of the basic concepts and principles of the classical school. Smith's theories were further developed in the writings of John Stuart Mill and David Ricardo. Central to the theory were economic freedom, competition and *laissez faire* government. The idea that economic growth could be promoted by free trade, unassisted by government, was in conflict with ◊mercantilism.

The belief that agriculture was the most important determinant of economic health was also rejected in favour of manufacturing development and the importance of labour productivity was stressed. The theories put forward by the classical economists are still an important influence on economists today.

Classicism in literature, music, and art, a style that emphasizes the qualities traditionally considered characteristic of ancient Greek and Roman art, that is, reason, balance, objectivity, restraint, and strict adherence to form. The term Classicism is often used to characterize the culture of 18th-century Europe, and contrasted with 19th-century Romanticism.

classification in biology, the arrangement of organisms into a hierarchy of groups, on the basis of their similarities in biochemical, anatomical or physiological characters. The basic grouping is a ◊species, several of which may constitute a ◊genus, which in turn are grouped into families, and so on up through orders, classes, phyla (or, in plants, divisions) to kingdoms.

class interval in statistics, the range of each class of data, used when dealing with large amounts of data. To obtain an idea of the distribution, the data are broken down into convenient classes, which must be mutually exclusive and are usually equal. The class interval defines the range of each class; for example if the class interval is 5 and the data begin at zero, the classes are 0–4, 5–9, 10–14, and so on.

clathrates compounds formed by small molecules filling in the holes in the structural lattice of another compound, for example, sulphur dioxide molecules in ice crystals. Clathrates are therefore intermediate between mixtures and compounds.

Claude /'kləʊd/ Georges 1870–1960. French industrial chemist responsible for inventing neon signs. He discovered in 1896 that acetylene, normally explosive, could be safely transported when dissolved in acetone. He later demonstrated that neon gas could be used to provide a bright red light in signs. These were displayed publicly for the first time at the Paris Motor Show 1910. As an old man, Claude spent the period 1945–49 in prison as a collaborator.

Claudel /kləʊ'del/ Paul 1868–1955. French poet and dramatist. A fervent Catholic, he was influenced by the Symbolists and achieved an effect of mystic allegory in such plays as *L'Annonce faite à Marie/Tidings Brought to Mary* 1912 and *Le Soulier de satin/The Satin Slipper* 1929, set in 16th-century Spain. His verse includes *Cinq Grandes Odes/Five Great Odes* 1910.

Claude Lorrain /'kləʊd lɒ'ræn/ (Claude Gellée) 1600–1682. French landscape painter, active in Rome from 1627. His distinctive, luminous, Classical style had great influence on late 17th- and 18th-century taste. His subjects are mostly mythological and historical, with insignificant figures lost in great expanses of poetic scenery, as in *The Enchanted Castle* 1664 (National Gallery, London).

Born in Lorraine, he established himself in Rome, where his many patrons included Pope Urban VIII. His *Liber Veritatis*, which contains some 200 drawings after his finished works, was made to prevent forgeries of his work by contemporaries.

Claudian /'klɔ:dɪən/ or *Claudius Claudianus* c.370–404. Last of the great Latin poets of the Roman empire. He was probably born at Alexandria, and wrote official panegyrics, epigrams, and the epic *The Rape of Proserpine*.

Claudius /'klɔ:dɪəs/ Tiberius Claudius Nero 10 BC–AD 54. Nephew of ◊Tiberius, made Roman emperor by his troops AD 41, after the murder of his nephew Caligula. Claudius was a scholar, historian, and able administrator. During his reign the Roman Empire was considerably extended, and in 43 he took part in the invasion of Britain.

Claudius *One of the most intriguing of the Roman emperors, Claudius wrote historical works and an autobiography, none of which survives. This statue of the deified Claudius is from the Lateran Museum, Rome.*

Lame and suffering from a speech impediment, he was frequently the object of ridicule. He was dominated by his third wife, ◊Messalina, whom he ultimately had executed, and is thought to have been poisoned by his fourth wife, Agrippina the Younger. His life is described by the novelist Robert Graves in his books *I Claudius* 1934 and *Claudius the God* 1934.

Clause 28 in British law, a controversial clause in the Local Government Bill 1988 (now section 28 of the Local Government Act 1988) that prohibits local authorities promoting homosexuality by publishing material, or by promoting the teaching in state schools of the acceptability of homosexuality as a 'pretended family relationship'. It became law despite widespread opposition.

Clausewitz /'klaʊzəvɪts/ Karl von 1780–1831. Prussian officer and writer on war, born near Magdeburg. He is known mainly for his book *Vom Kriege/On War* 1833. Translated into English 1873, the book gave a new philosophical foundation to the science of war, and put forward a concept of strategy that was influential until World War I.

clausius in engineering, a unit of ◊entropy (the loss of energy as heat in any physical process). It is defined as the ratio of energy to temperature above absolute zero.

Clausius /'klaʊzɪəs/ Rudolf Julius Emaneul 1822–1888. German physicist, one of the founders of the science of thermodynamics. In 1850, he enunciated its second law: heat cannot of itself pass from a colder to a hotter body.

claustrophobia a ◊phobia involving fear of enclosed spaces.

Claverhouse /'kleɪvəhaʊs/ John Graham, Viscount Dundee 1649–1689. Scottish soldier. Appointed by Charles II to suppress the ◊Covenanters from 1677, he was routed at Drumclog 1679, but three weeks later won the battle of Bothwell Bridge, by which the rebellion was crushed. Until 1688 he was engaged in continued persecution and became known as 'Bloody Clavers', regarded by the Scottish people as a figure of evil. Then his army joined the first Jacobite rebellion and defeated the loyalist forces in the pass of Killiecrankie, where he was mortally wounded.

claves musical percussion instrument of Latin American origin, consisting of small hardwood batons struck together.

clavichord stringed keyboard instrument, common in Renaissance Europe and in 18th-century Germany. Notes are sounded by a metal blade striking the string. The clavichord was a forerunner of the pianoforte.

clavier in music, general term for an early keyboard instrument.

Clausewitz *The Prussian army officer Karl von Clausewitz, famous for describing war as a continuation of politics by other means.*

claw a hard, hooked pointed outgrowth of the digits of mammals, birds, and some reptiles. Claws are composed of the protein keratin, and grow continuously from a bundle of cells in the lower skin layer. Hooves and nails are modified structures with the same origin as claws.

clay a very fine-grained ◊sedimentary deposit that has undergone a greater or lesser degree of consolidation. When moistened it is plastic, and it hardens on heating, which renders it impermeable. It may be white, grey, red, yellow, blue, or black, depending on its composition. Clay minerals consist largely of hydrous silicates of aluminium and magnesium together with iron, potassium, sodium, and organic substances. The crystals of clay minerals have a layered structure, capable of holding water, and are responsible for its plastic properties. According to international classification, in mechanical analysis of soil, clay has a grain size of less than 0.002 mm/0.00008 in.

Types of clay include adobe, alluvial clay, building clay, brick, cement, china clay, ferruginous clay, fireclay, fusible clay, puddle clay, refractory clay, and vitrifiable clay. Clays have a variety of uses, some of which, such as pottery and bricks, date back to prehistoric times.

Clay Cassius Marcellus original name of boxer Muhammad ◊Ali.

Clay /kleɪ/ Frederic 1838–1889. British composer. Born in Paris, he wrote light operas and the cantata *Lalla Rookh* 1877, based on the poem by Thomas Moore.

Clay /kleɪ/ Henry 1777–1852. US politician. He stood three times unsuccessfully for the presidency, as a Democratic-Republican 1824, as a National Republican 1832, and as a Whig 1844. He supported the War of 1812 against Britain, and tried to hold the Union together on the slavery issue by the Missouri Compromise of 1820, and again in the compromise of 1850. He was secretary of state 1825–29, and is also remembered for his 'American system', which favoured the national bank, internal improvements to facilitate commercial and industrial development, and the raising of protective tariffs.

Clay /kleɪ/ Lucius DuBignon 1897–1978. US commander-in chief of the US occupation forces in Germany 1947–49. He broke the Soviet blockade of Berlin 1948 after 327 days, with an *airlift*—a term he brought into general use—which involved bringing all supplies into West Berlin by air.

Clayton /'kleɪtn/ Jack 1921– . British film director, originally a producer. His first feature, *Room at*

Cleese *English actor John Cleese in* A Fish Called Wanda *1988*

the Top 1958, heralded a new maturity in British cinema. Other works include *The Great Gatsby* 1974; *The Lonely Passion of Judith Hearne* 1987.

cleanliness unit unit for measuring air pollution: the number of particles greater than 0.5 micrometres in diameter per cubic foot of air. A more usual measure is the weight of contaminants per cubic metre of air.

Cleese /kliːz/ John 1939– . English actor and comedian. For television he has written for the satirical *That Was The Week That Was* and *The Frost Report*, and the comic *Monty Python's Flying Circus* and *Fawlty Towers*. His films include *A Fish Called Wanda* 1988.

Cleethorpes /ˈkliːθɔːps/ seaside resort in Humberside, NE England; on the Humber estuary; population (1981) 35,500.

clef in music, the symbol used to indicate the pitch of the lines of the staff in musical notation.

cleft palate fissure of the roof of the mouth, often accompanied by a hare lip, the result of a genetic defect.

Cleisthenes /ˈklaɪsθəniːz/ ruler of Athens. Inspired by Solon, he is credited with the establishment of democracy in Athens 507 BC.

cleistogamy the production of flowers that never fully open and which are automatically self-fertilized. Cleistogamous flowers are often formed late in the year, after the production of normal flowers, or during a period of cold weather, as seen in several species of *Viola*.

Cleland /ˈklelənd/ John 1709–1789. English author. He wrote *Fanny Hill, the Memoirs of a Woman of Pleasure* 1748–49 to try to extract himself from the grip of his London creditors. The book was considered immoral, and Cleland was called before the Privy Council, but was granted a pension to prevent further misdemeanours.

clematis genus of temperate woody climbers with showy flowers, family Ranunculaceae. The wild *traveller's joy* or *old man's beard*, *Clematis vitalba*, is the only British species, although many have been introduced, and garden hybrids bred.

Clemenceau /ˌklemɒnˈsəʊ/ Georges 1841–1929. French politician and journalist (prominent in defence of ◊Dreyfus). He was prime minister 1906–09 and 1917–20. After World War I he presided over the Peace Conference in Paris that drew up the Treaty of ◊Versailles, but failed to secure for France the Rhine as a frontier.

Clemenceau was mayor of Montmartre, Paris, in the war of 1870, and in 1871 was elected a member of the National Assembly at Bordeaux. He was elected a deputy in 1876 after the formation of the Third Republic. An extreme radical, he soon earned the nickname of 'the Tiger' on account of his ferocious attacks on politicians whom he disliked. In 1893 he lost his seat and spent the next ten years in journalism. In 1902 he was elected senator for the Var, and was soon one of the most powerful politicians in France. He became prime minister for the second

time in 1917, and made the decisive appointment of Marshal ◊Foch as supreme commander.

Clemens /ˈklemənz/ Samuel Langhorne. Real name of the US writer Mark ◊Twain.

Clement VII /ˈklemənt/ 1478–1534. Pope 1523–34. He refused to allow the divorce of Henry VIII of England and Catherine of Aragon. Illegitimate son of a brother of Lorenzo di Medici, the ruler of Florence, he commissioned monuments for the Medici chapel in Florence from the Renaissance artist Michelangelo.

Clemente /kləˈmenti/ Roberto (Walker) 1934–1972. Puerto Rican baseball player, born in Carolina, who played for the Pittsburgh Pirates 1955–72. He had a career batting average of 0.317, was the 11th player in history to reach 3,000 hits, and was a right fielder with an outstanding arm. He died in a plane crash while flying to aid Nicaraguan earthquake victims.

Clementi /kleˈmenti/ Muzio 1752–1832. Italian pianist and composer. He settled in London in 1782 as a teacher and then as proprietor of a successful pianoforte and music business. He was the founder of the new technique of piano playing, and his series of studies, *Gradus ad Parnassum* 1817 is still in use.

clementine small orange, originally thought to be an accidental hybrid of a tangerine and an orange. It has a flowery taste and scent, a loosely fitting skin, and is in season in winter. It is commonly grown in N Africa and Spain.

Clement of Alexandria /ˈklemənt/ *c.* AD 150–215. Greek theologian who applied Greek philosophical ideas to Christian doctrine, and was the teacher of the theologian Origen.

Clement of Rome, St /ˈklemənt/ late 1st century AD. One of the early Christian leaders and writers known as the Fathers of the Church. According to tradition he was the third or fourth bishop of Rome, and a disciple of St Peter. He wrote a letter addressed to the church at Corinth (First Epistle of Clement), and many other writings have been attributed to him.

Clements /ˈklemənts/ John 1910– . British actor and director, whose productions included revivals of Restoration comedies and the plays of G B Shaw.

Cleon /ˈkliːən/ Athenian demagogue and military leader in the Peloponnesian War (431–404 BC). After the death of Pericles, to whom he was opposed, he won power as representative of the commercial classes and leader of the party, advocating a vigorous war policy. He was killed fighting the Spartans at Amphipolis.

Cleopatra /ˌkliːəˈpætrə/ *c.* 68–30 BC. Queen of Egypt 51–48 BC and 47–30 BC. When Julius Caesar arrived in Egypt, he restored her to the throne from which she had been ousted in favour of her brother, Ptolemy XIII, and Ptolemy was killed. Cleopatra became Caesar's mistress, returned with him to Rome, and gave birth to a son, Caesarion. After Caesar's assassination 44 BC she returned to Alexandria and resumed her position as queen of Egypt. In 41 BC she met Mark Antony, and subsequently bore him three sons. In 32 BC Rome declared war on Egypt and scored a decisive victory in the naval Battle of Actium off the W coast of Greece 31 BC. Cleopatra fled with her 60 ships to Egypt; Antony abandoned the struggle and followed her. Both he and Cleopatra committed suicide.

Cleopatra was Macedonian, and the last ruler of the Macedonian dynasty, which ruled Egypt from 323 BC until annexation by Rome 31 BC. She succeeded her father jointly with her younger brother Ptolemy XIII, whom she married according to Pharaonic custom. Shakespeare's play *Antony and Cleopatra* recounts how Cleopatra killed herself with an asp (poisonous snake) after Antony's suicide.

Cleopatra's Needle either of two ancient Egyptian granite obelisks erected at Heliopolis in the 15th century BC by Thothmes III, and removed to Alexandria by the Roman emperor Augustus about

14 BC. They have no connection with Cleopatra's reign. One of the pair was taken to London 1878 and erected on the Victoria Embankment; it is 21 m/68.5 ft high. The other was given by the khedive of Egypt to the USA, and erected in Central Park, New York, in 1881.

clerihew humorous verse form invented by Edmund Clerihew ◊Bentley, characterized by a first line consisting of a person's name.

The four lines rhyme AABB, but the metre is often distorted for comic effect. An example, from Bentley's *Biography for Beginners* 1905, is: *Sir Christopher Wren/ Said, 'I am going to dine with some men./ If anybody calls/ Say I am designing St Paul's'*.

Clermont-Ferrand /ˈklɛəmɒnfeˈrɒn/ city, capital of Puy-de-Dôme *département*, in the Auvergne region of France; population (1983) 256,000. It is a centre for agriculture, and its rubber industry is the largest in France.

Car tires are manufactured here; other products include chemicals, preserves, foodstuffs, and clothing. The Gothic cathedral is 13th-century. Urban II ordered the First Crusade at a council here 1095. The 17th-century writer Blaise Pascal was born here.

Cleveland /ˈkliːvlənd/ county in NE England
area 580 sq km/224 sq mi
towns administrative headquarters Middlesbrough; Stockton on Tees, Billingham, Hartlepool
features river Tees, with Seal Sands wildfowl refuge at its mouth; North Yorkshire Moors National Park
population (1987) 555,000
products steel, chemicals; Teesside, the industrial area at the mouth of the Tees, has Europe's largest steel complex (at Redcar) and chemical site (ICI, using gas and local potash), as well as an oil fuel terminal at Seal Sands and natural gas terminal at St Fergus, 19 km/12 mi south of Fraserburgh in the Grampians.

Cleveland /ˈkliːvlənd/ largest city of Ohio, USA, on Lake Erie at the mouth of the river Cuyahoga; population (1981) 574,000, metropolitan area 1,899,000. Its chief industries are iron and steel, and petroleum refining.

Iron ore from the Lake Superior region and coal from Ohio and Pennsylvania mines are brought here.

Cleveland /ˈkliːvlənd/ (Stephen) Grover 1837–1908. 22nd and 24th president of the USA, 1885–89 and 1893–97; the first Democratic president elected after the Civil War, and the only president to hold office for two nonconsecutive terms. He attempted to check corruption in public life, and in 1895 initiated arbitration proceedings that eventually settled a territorial dispute with Britain concerning the Venezuelan boundary.

click-beetle type of ◊beetle that can regain its feet from lying on its back by jumping into the air and turning over, clicking as it does so.

Cliff /klɪf/ Clarice 1899–1972. English pottery designer. Her Bizarre ware, characterized by brightly coloured floral and geometric decoration on often geometrically shaped china, became increasingly popular in the 1930s.

Born in the Potteries, Staffordshire, she started as a factory apprentice at the age of 13, trained at evening classes and worked for many years at the Wilkinson factory, where she married the managing director, Colley Shorter. In 1963 Clarice Cliff became art director of the factory, which was part of the Royal Staffordshire Pottery in Burslem.

Clift /klɪft/ (Edward) Montgomery 1920–1966. US film and theatre actor. A star of the late 1940s and 1950s in films such as *Red River* 1948 and *A Place in the Sun* 1951, he was disfigured in a car accident in 1957 but continued to make films. He played the title role in *Freud* 1962.

climacteric synonym for ◊menopause, or change of life.

climate weather conditions at a particular place over a period of time. Climate encompasses

Cleveland

all the meteorological elements and the factors that influence them. The primary factors that determine the variations of climate over the surface of the Earth are: (a) the effect of latitude and the tilt of the Earth's axis to the plane of the orbit about the Sun (66.5°); (b) the large-scale movements of different wind belts over the Earth's surface; (c) the temperature difference between land and sea; (d) contours of the ground; and (e) location of the area in relation to ocean currents. Catastrophic variations to climate may be caused by the impact of another planetary body, or by clouds resulting from volcanic activity.

How much heat the Earth receives from the Sun varies in different latitudes and at different times of the year. In the equatorial region the mean daily temperature of the air near the ground has no large seasonal variation. In the polar regions the temperature in the long winter, when there is no incoming solar radiation, falls far below the summer value. Climate types were first classified by Vladimir Köppen in 1918.

The temperature of the sea, and of the air above it, varies little in the course of day or night, whereas the surface of the land is rapidly cooled by lack of solar radiation. In the same way the annual change of temperature is relatively small over the sea and great over the land. Continental areas are thus colder than the sea in winter and warmer in summer. Winds that blow from the sea are warm in winter and cool in summer, while winds from the central parts of continents are hot in summer and cold in winter.

On average, air temperature drops with increasing land height at a rate of 1°C/1.8°F per 90 m/300 ft. Thus places situated above mean sea level usually have lower temperatures than places at or near sea level. Even in equatorial regions, high mountains are snow-covered during the whole year.

The complexity of the distribution of land and sea, and the consequent complexity of the general circulation of the atmosphere, have a direct effect on the distribution of the climate. Centred on the equator is a belt of tropical rainforest, which may be either constantly wet or monsoonal (seasonal with wet and dry seasons in each year). On each side of this is a belt of savannah, with lighter rainfall and less dense vegetation. Usually there is then a transition through ◊steppe (semi-arid) to desert (arid), with a further transition through steppe to ◊Mediterranean climate with dry summer, followed by the moist temperate climate of middle latitudes. Next comes a zone of cold climate with moist winter. Where the desert extends into middle latitudes, however, the zones of Mediterranean and moist temperate climates are missing, and the transition is from desert to a cold climate with moist winter. In the extreme east of Asia a cold climate with dry

winters extends from about 70° N to 35° N. The polar caps have ◊tundra and glacial climates, with little or no ◊precipitation (rain or snow).

climatology the study of climate, its global variations and causes.

climax community an assemblage of plants and animals that is relatively stable in its environment (for example, oak woods in Britain). It is brought about by ecological ◊succession, and represents the point at which succession ceases to occur.

climax vegetation the state of equilibrium that is reached after a series of changes have occurred in the vegetation of a particular habitat. It is the final stage in a ◊succession, where the structure and species of a habitat do not develop further, providing conditions remain unaltered.

clinical psychology discipline dealing with the understanding and treatment of health problems, particularly mental disorders. The main problems dealt with include anxiety, phobias, depression, obsessions, sexual and marital problems, drug and alcohol dependence, childhood behavioural problems, psychoses (such as schizophrenia), mental handicap, and brain damage (such as dementia).

Other areas of work include forensic psychology (concerned with criminal behaviour) and health psychology. *Assessment procedures* assess intelligence and cognition (for example, in detecting the effects of brain damage) by using psychometric tests. *Behavioural approaches* are methods of treatment that apply learning theories to clinical problems. *Behaviour therapy* helps clients change unwanted behaviours (such as phobias, obsessions, sexual problems) and to develop new skills (such as improving social interactions). *Behaviour modification* relies on operant conditioning, making selective use of rewards (such as praise) to change behaviour. This is particularly useful for children, the mentally handicapped and for patients in institutions, such as mental hospitals. *Cognitive therapy* is a new approach to treating emotional problems, such as anxiety and depression, by teaching clients to change negative thoughts and attitudes. *Counselling*, developed by Rogers, is widely used to help clients solve their own problems. *Psychoanalysis*, as developed by Freud and Jung, is little used by clinical psychologists today. It emphasizes childhood conflicts leading to adult problems.

clinometer hand-held surveying instrument for measuring angles of slope.

Clio in Greek mythology, the inventor of epic poetry and history. One of the nine ◊Muses.

Clive /klaɪv/ Robert, Baron Clive of Plassey 1725–1774. British general and administrator, who established British rule in India by victories over the French at Arcot in the Carnatic (a region in SE India) 1751 and over the nawab of Bengal, Suraj-ud-Dowlah, at Calcutta and Plassey 1757. On his return to Britain his wealth led to allegations that he had abused his power.

clo unit of thermal insulation of clothing. Standard clothes have an insulation of about 1 clo; the warmest clothing is about 4 clo per 2.5 cm/1 in of thickness. See also ◊tog.

cloaca the common opening of the digestive, urinary and reproductive tracts; a cloaca is found in most vertebrates; placental mammals, however have a separate anus and urinogenital opening instead of one posterior opening to the body, the cloacal aperture. The cloaca forms a chamber in which products can be stored before being voided from the body via a muscular opening.

clock any device that measures the passage of time, though customarily a timepiece consisting of a train of wheels driven by a spring or weight controlled by a balance wheel or pendulum. The watch is a portable clock.

history In ancient Egypt the time during the day was measured by a shadow-clock, a primitive form of ◊sundial, and at night the water-clock was used. Up to the late 16th century the only clock available

Clive *Known as the legendary 'Clive of India', Robert Clive has been called the founder of the British empire in India.*

for use at sea was the sand-clock, of which the most familiar form is the hour-glass. The Royal Navy kept time by half-hour sand-glasses until 1820. During the Middle Ages various types of sundials were widely used, and portable sundials were in use from the 16th to the 18th century. Watches were invented in the 16th century—the first were made in Nuremberg shortly after 1500 – but it was not until the 19th century that they became cheap enough to be widely available.

The first known public clock was set up at Milan in 1353; the first in England was the Salisbury cathedral clock of 1386, which is still working. The time-keeping of both clocks and watches was revolutionized in the 17th century by the application of pendulums to clocks and of balance-springs to watches.

types of clock The *marine chronometer* is a precision timepiece of special design and of the finest workmanship, used at sea for giving Greenwich mean time (GMT). Electric timepieces were made possible by the discovery early in the last century of the magnetic effects of electric currents. One of the earliest and most satisfactory methods of electrical control of a clock was invented by Matthaeus Hipp in 1842. In the modern mains electric clock, the place of the pendulum or spring-controlled balance-wheel is taken by a small synchronous electric motor which counts up the alternations (frequency) of the mains electric supply, and then by a suitable train of wheels records the time by means of hands on a dial. The *quartz crystal clock* (made possible by the ◊piezoelectric effect of certain crystals) has great precision, with a short-term accuracy of about one-thousandth of a second per day. More accurate still is the *atomic clock*. This utilizes the natural resonance of certain atoms, for example, caesium, as a regulator controlling the frequency of a quartz crystal ◊oscillator. It is accurate to within one millionth of a second per day.

cloisonné ornamental technique in which thin metal strips are soldered in a pattern onto a metal surface, and the resulting compartments (cloisons) filled with coloured ◊enamels and fired. Cloisonné vases and brooches were made in medieval Europe, but the technique was perfected in Japan and China during the 17th, 18th, and 19th centuries.

cloister a convent or monastery, and more particularly a covered walk within these, often opening onto a courtyard.

Cloisters The branch of the Metropolitan Museum of Art in Fort Tryon Park, New York. A number of medieval buildings transported to the USA from Europe have been carefully reassembled and medieval tapestries, pictures, and books are among the exhibits.

clone group of cells or organisms arising by asexual reproduction from a single 'parent' individual. Clones therefore have exactly the same genetic make-up. The term has been adopted by computer technology, in which it describes a (non-existent) device that mimics an actual one to enable certain software programs to run correctly.

closed in mathematics, a set of data *S* is closed if an operation (such as addition or multiplication) done on any members of the set gives a result that is also a member of the set.

For example, the set of even numbers is closed with respect to multiplication, because two even numbers multiplied by each other always give another even number.

closed-circuit TV (CCTV) a localized television system in which programmes are sent over relatively short distances, the camera, receiver and controls being linked by cable. Closed-circuit TV systems are used in department stores and large offices as a means of internal security, monitoring people's movements.

closed shop a company or firm, public corporation, or other body that requires its employees to be members of the appropriate trade union. The practice became legally enforceable in the UK 1976, but was rendered largely inoperable by the Employment Acts 1980 and 1982. Usually demanded by unions, the closed shop may be preferred by employers as simplifying negotiation, but it was condemned by the European Court of Human Rights in 1981. The Europeand Community's Social Charter, for which the UK Labour Party announced its support Dec 1989, calls for an end to the closed Shop. In the USA the closed shop was made illegal by the Taft-Hartley Act 1947, passed by Congress over Truman's veto.

clothes moth type of moth whose larvae feed on clothes, upholstery, and carpets. The adults are small golden or silvery moths. The natural habitat of the larvae is in the nests of animals, feeding on remains of hair and feathers, but they have adapted to human households and can cause considerable damage, especially the common clothes-moth *Tineola bisselliella*.

cloud water vapour condensed into minute water particles that float in masses in the atmosphere. Clouds, like fogs or mists, which occur at lower levels, are formed by the cooling of air charged with water vapour, which generally condenses around tiny dust particles.

Clouds are classified according to the height at which they occur and their shape. *Cirrus* and *cirrostratus* clouds occur at 10,000 m/33,000 ft. The former, sometimes called mares'-tails, consist of minute specks of ice and appear as feathery white wisps, while cirrostratus clouds stretch across the sky as a thin white sheet. Three types of cloud are found at 3,000–7,500 m/10,000–24,000 ft: cirrocumulus, altocumulus, and altostratus. *Cirrocumulus* clouds occur in small or large rounded tufts, sometimes arranged in the familiar pattern called mackerel sky. *Altocumulus* clouds are similar, but larger, white clouds, also arranged in lines. *Altostratus* clouds are like heavy cirrostratus clouds and may stretch across the sky as a grey sheet.

The lower clouds, occurring at heights of up to 1,800 m/6,000 ft, may be of two types. *Stratocumulus* clouds are the dull grey clouds that give rise to a leaden sky which may not yield rain. *Nimbus* clouds are dark-grey, shapeless rain clouds.

Two types of clouds, *cumulus* and *cumulonimbus*, are placed in a special category because they are produced by daily ascending air currents, which take moisture into the cooler regions of the atmosphere. Cumulus clouds have

cloud

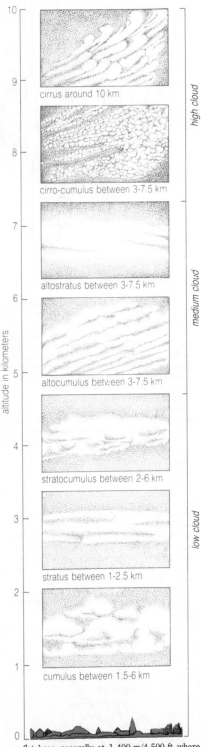

cirrus around 10 km

cirro-cumulus between 3-7.5 km

altostratus between 3-7.5 km

altocumulus between 3-7.5 km

stratocumulus between 2-6 km

stratus between 1-2.5 km

cumulus between 1.5-6 km

high cloud

medium cloud

low cloud

altitude in kilometers

a flat base generally at 1,400 m/4,500 ft where condensation begins, while the upper part is dome-shaped and extends to about 1,800 m/6,000 ft. Cumulonimbus clouds have their base at much the same level, but extend much higher, often up to over 6,000 m/20,000 ft. Short heavy showers and sometimes thunder may accompany them. *Stratus* clouds, occurring below 1,000 m/3,500 ft, have the appearance of sheets parallel to the horizon and are like high fogs.

cloud chamber apparatus for tracking ionized particles. It consists of a vessel filled with air or other gas, saturated with water vapour. When suddenly expanded, the vapour cools and a cloud of tiny droplets forms on any nuclei, dust, or ions present. If single fast-moving ionizing particles collide with the air or gas molecules, they show as visible tracks.

Much information about interactions between such particles and radiations has been obtained from photographs of these tracks. This system has been developed in recent years by the use of liquid hydrogen or helium instead of air or gas. The cloud chamber was devised in 1897 by C T R Wilson at Cambridge University, UK.

Clouet /ˈkluːeɪ/ François *c.*1515–1572. French portrait painter, who succeeded his father Jean Clouet as court painter. He worked in the Italian style of Mannerism. His half-nude portrait of Diane de Poitiers, *The Lady in her Bath* 1499–1566 (National Gallery, Washington), is also thought to to be a likeness of Marie Touchet, mistress of Charles IX (1550–74).

Clouet /ˈkluːeɪ/ Jean (known as *Janet*) 1486–1541. French artist, court painter to Francis I. His portraits, often compared to Holbein's, show an outstanding naturalism, particularly his drawings.

Clough /klʌf/ Arthur Hugh 1819–1861. British poet. Many of his lyrics are marked by a melancholy scepticism that reflects his struggle with his religious doubt.

clove the unopened flower bud of the clover tree *Eugenia caryophyllus*. A member of the family Myrtaceae, the clover tree is a native of the Moluccas. Cloves are used for flavouring in cookery and confectionery. Oil of cloves, which has tonic and carminative qualities, is employed in medicine. The aromatic quality of cloves is shared to a large degree by the leaves, bark, and fruit of the tree.

clover leguminous plant, of which there are many species, mostly belonging to the genus *Trifolium*. Found mainly in temperate regions, clover plants have trifoliate leaves and roundish flowerheads or a spike of small flowers. Many species are cultivated as fodder plants for cattle.

The most important source of fodder is the red clover *Trifolium pratense*. White or Dutch clover *Trifolium repens* is common in pastures. Eighteen species are native to Britain.

Clovis /ˈkləʊvɪs/ 465–511. Merovingian king of the Franks from 481. He succeeded his father Childeric as king of the Salian (northern) Franks, defeated the Gallo-Romans (Romanized Gauls) near Soissons 486, ending their rule in France, and defeated the Alemanni, a confederation of Germanic tribes, near Cologne 496. He embraced Christianity and subsequently proved a powerful defender of orthodoxy against the Arian ◊Visigoths, whom he defeated at Poitiers 507. He made Paris his capital.

club an association of persons for social purposes, indulgence in sport or hobbies, or discussion of matters of common interest. The London men's clubs of today developed from the taverns and coffee-houses of the 17th and 18th centuries. The oldest is White's, evolved from a chocolate-house of the same name in 1693.

Other historic London clubs include Boodles, 1762; Brooks's, 1764; the Portland (cards), 1816; the Athenaeum, 1824; the Garrick (dramatic and literary), 1831; the Carlton (Conservative), 1832; the Reform (Liberal), 1836; the Savage (literary and art), 1857; the Press Club, 1882; the Royal Automobile, 1897. The Working Men's Club and Institute Union was founded in 1862, thus extending the range of social membership. Women's clubs include the Alexandra, 1883 and University Women's, 1887.

club moss flowerless plant of the order Lycopodiales belonging to the Pteridophyta family and allied to the ferns and horsetails.

These plants have a wide distribution, but were far more numerous in Palaeozoic times,

clutch

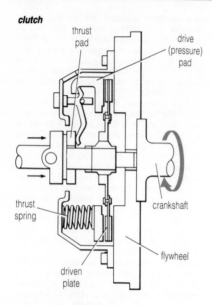

thrust pad

drive (pressure) pad

thrust spring

crankshaft

driven plate

flywheel

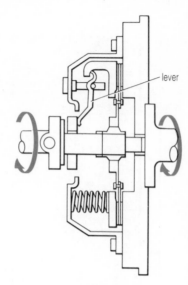

lever

disengaged (pedal pressed down)

engaged (pedal up)

the Lepidodendroids of the coal measures being large trees. The living species are all of small size. The common club moss or stag's horn moss *Lycopodium clavatum* is found on upland heaths.

Club of Rome informal international organization, set up after a meeting at the Accademia dei Lincei, Rome, in 1968, which aims to promote greater understanding of the interdependence of global economic, political, natural, and social systems.

The organization seeks to initiate new policy directives and take action to overcome some of the major global problems facing humanity which traditional national organizations and short-term policies are unable to tackle effectively. Members include industrialists, economists, and research scientists: Membership is limited to 100 people.

clubroot a disease affecting cabbages, turnips, and allied plants of the Cruciferae family. It is caused by a ◊slime mould *Plasmodiophora brassicae*. This attacks the roots of the plant, which send out knotty outgrowths, hence the popular name of finger-and-toe disease; eventually the whole plant decays.

Cluj /kluːʒ/ (German **Klausenberg**) city in Transylvania, Romania, located on the river Somes; population (1985) 310,000. It is a communications centre for Romania and the Hungarian plain. Industries include machine tools, furniture, and knitwear.

There is a 14th-century cathedral, and Romanian (1872) and Hungarian (1945) universities.

Clunies-Ross /ˈkluːniz ˈrɒs/ family that established a benevolently paternal rule in the ◊Cocos Islands. John Clunies-Ross settled on Home Island in 1827: the family's rule ended in 1978 with the purchase of the Cocos by the Australian government.

Cluny /ˈkluːni/ town in Saône-et-Loire *département*, France; on the river Grosne; population (1982) 4,500. Its abbey, now in ruins, was the foundation house 910–1790 of the Cluniac order, originally a reformed branch of the Benedictines. Cluny, once a lace-making centre, has an important cattle market.

clusec unit for measuring the power of a vacuum pump.

cluster in music, the effect of playing simultaneously and without emphasis all the notes within a chosen interval. Invented by ◊Cowell for the piano, it was adopted by ◊Penderecki for string orchestra; in radio and film an organ cluster is the traditional sound of reverie.

clutch a device for disconnecting rotating shafts, particularly in a car's transmission system. In a car with a manual gearbox, the driver depresses

the clutch when changing gear, thus disconnecting the engine from the gearbox.

The clutch consists of two main plates, a pressure plate and a driven plate, which is mounted on a shaft leading to the gearbox. When the clutch is engaged, the pressure plate presses the driven plate against the engine ◊flywheel and drive goes to the gearbox. Depressing the clutch springs the pressure plate away, freeing the driven plate. Cars with **automatic transmission** have no clutch. Drive is transmitted from the flywheel to the automatic gearbox by a liquid coupling or ◊torque converter.

Clutha /ˈkluːθə/ longest river in South Island, New Zealand, 322 km/201 mi long. It rises in the Southern Alps, has hydroelectric installations and flows to meet the sea near Kaitangata.

Clwyd /ˈkluːɪd/ county in N Wales
area 2,420 sq km/934 sq mi
towns administrative headquarters Mold; Flint, Denbigh, Wrexham; seaside resorts Colwyn Bay, Rhyl, Prestatyn
physical rivers Dee and Clwyd; Clwydian Range with Offa's Dyke along the main ridge
features Chirk, Denbigh, Flint, and Rhuddlan castles; Greenfield Valley, NW of Flint, was in the forefront of the industrial revolution before the advent of steam, and now has a museum of industrial archaeology.
products dairy and meat products, optical glass, chemicals, limestone, microprocessors, plastics

Clwyd

population (1987) 403,000
language 19% Welsh, English.

Clyde /klaɪd/ river in Strathclyde, Scotland; 170 km/103 mi long. The Firth of Clyde and Firth of Forth are linked by the Forth and Clyde canal, 56 km/35 mi long. The shipbuilding yards have declined in recent years.

The nuclear submarine bases of Faslane (Polaris) and Holy Loch (USA Poseidon) are here.

Clydebank /ˈklaɪdbæŋk/ town on the Clyde, Strathclyde, Scotland; 10 km/6 mi NW of Glasgow; population (1981) 51,700. At the John Brown yard famous liners such as the *Queen Elizabeth II* were built.

Clytemnestra /ˌklaɪtəmˈniːstrə/ in Greek mythology, the wife of ◊Agamemnon.

cm abbreviation for *centimetre*.

CND abbreviation for *Campaign for Nuclear Disarmament*.

Cnossus alternative form of ◊Knossos.

Cnut alternative spelling of ◊Canute.

c/o abbreviation for *care of*.

co. abbreviation for *company*.

CO abbreviation for *Commanding Officer*.

coaching conveyance by coach–a horse-drawn passenger carriage on four wheels, sprung and roofed in. Public *stagecoaches* made their appearance in the middle of the 17th century; the first British mail coach began in 1784, and they continued until 1840 when railways began to take over the traffic.

The main roads were kept in good repair by turnpike trusts, and large numbers of inns – many of which still exist – catered for stagecoach passengers and horses. In the UK, coaches still in use on ceremonial occasions include those of the Lord Mayor of London 1757 and the state coach built in 1761 for George III. The influence of coach design may be seen in the railway carriage.

coal a black or blackish mineral substance of fossil origin, the result of the transformation of ancient plant matter under progressive compression. It is used as a fuel and in the chemical industry. Coal is classified according to the proportion of carbon and volatiles it contains. The main types are ◊anthracite (shiny, with more than 90% carbon), *bituminous coal* (shiny and dull patches, more than 80% carbon), and ◊lignite (woody, grading into ◊peat, 70% carbon).

In England, coal was mined on a small scale from Roman times until the Industrial Revolution. From about 1800, coal was carbonized commercially to produce ◊coalgas for gas lighting and ◊coke for smelting iron ore. By the second half of the 19th century, study of the byproducts (◊coaltar, pitch, and ammonia) formed the basis of organic chemistry, which eventually led to the development of the plastics industry in the 20th century. The York, Derby, and Notts coalfield is Britain's chief reserve, extending N of Selby. Under the Coal Industry Nationalization Act 1946 Britain's mines were administered by the National Coal Board, now known as British Coal.

coal gas gas produced when coal is destructively distilled or heated out of contact with the air. Its main constituents are methane, hydrogen, and carbon monoxide. Coal gas has been superseded by ◊natural gas for domestic purposes.

coalition an association of political groups, usually for some limited or short-term purpose, such as fighting an election or forming a government when one party has failed to secure a majority in a legislature.

coaltar black oily material resulting from the destructive distillation of coal.

Further distillation of coal tar yields a number of fractions: light oil, middle oil, heavy oil, and anthracene oil; the residue is called **pitch**. On further fractionation a large number of substances are obtained, about 200 of which have been isolated. They are used as dyes and in medicines.

Coastal Command combined British naval and Royal Air Force system of defence organized during World War II 1939–45.

coastal erosion the sea eroding the land by the constant battering of waves. This produces two effects. The first is a hydraulic effect, in which the force of the wave compresses air pockets in coastal rocks and cliffs, and the air then expands explosively. The second is the effect of abrasion, in which rocks and pebbles are flung against the cliffs, wearing them away.

In areas where there are beaches, the waves cause longshore drift, in which sand and stone fragments are carried parallel to the shore, causing buildups in some areas and beach erosion in others.

coastguard governmental organization whose members patrol a nation's seacoast to prevent smuggling, assist distressed vessels, watch for oil slicks, and so on.

The US Coast Guard 1915 has wide duties, including enforcing law and order on the high seas and navigable waters. During peacetime, it is administered under the Department of Transportation; in time of war, the Department of the Navy. In the UK the HM Coastguard was formed to prevent smuggling after the Napoleonic Wars, and is now administered by the Department of Trade.

Coatbridge /ˈkəʊtbrɪdʒ/ town in Strathclyde, Scotland; 13 km/8 mi E of Glasgow; population (1981) 51,000. Coal and iron are mined nearby. Industries include iron, ore, steel, and engineering.

Coates /kəʊts/ Eric 1886–1957. English composer. He is remembered for the orchestral suites *London* 1933, including the 'Knightsbridge' march; 'By the Sleepy Lagoon' 1939; 'The Dam Busters March' 1942; and the songs 'Bird Songs at Eventide' and 'The Green Hills of Somerset'.

coati climbing mammal related to the ◊raccoon, with a long flexible pig-like snout used for digging, a good sense of smell, and long claws and long tail. Coatis live in packs in the forests of South and Central America. The **common coati** *Nasua nasua* of South America is about 60 cm/2 ft long, with a tail about the same length. Coatis are sometimes called **coatimundis**.

co-axial cable an electric cable that consists of a central conductor surrounded by a conducting tube or sheath. It can transmit the high-frequency signals used in television, telephone, and other telecommunications transmissions.

cobalt metallic element, closely resembling nickel in appearance, symbol Co, atomic number 27, relative atomic mass 58.94. It occurs in a number of ores and is used as a pigment and in alloys.

Cobalt is used to cement carbides in tools in the high-speed machining of metals because it maintains its hardness at great heat. Radioactive cobalt-60 (◊half-life 5.3 years) is produced by neutron radiation in heavy-water reactors, and is used in large quantities as a source of gamma rays in cancer therapy, substituting for the more costly radium. Cobalt alloys are used to make magnets (in electronic equipment) and (alloyed with other metals) in jet engines because of their heat resistance.

cobalt ore cobalt is extracted from a number of minerals, the main ones being **smaltite**, $(Co,Ni)As_3$; **linnaeite**, Co_3S_4; **cobaltite**, CoAsS; and **glaucodot**, $(Co, Fe)AsS$.

All commercial cobalt is obtained as a byproduct of other metals. Zaïre is the largest producer of cobalt, and it is obtained there as a byproduct of the copper industry. Other producers include Canada and Morocco. Cobalt is also found in the manganese nodules that occur on the ocean floor, and was successfully refined in 1988 from the Pacific Ocean nodules, although this process has yet to prove economic.

Cobb /kɒb/ Ty(rus Raymond), nicknamed 'the Georgia Peach' 1886–1961. US baseball player, one of the greatest batters and base runners of all time. He played for Detroit and Philadelphia 1905–28, and won the American League batting

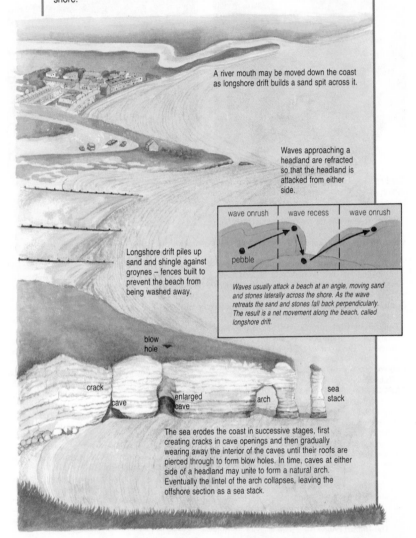

coastal erosion

The sea erodes the land by the constant battering of waves. The force of the waves creates a hydraulic effect, compressing air to form explosive pockets in the rocks and cliffs. The waves also have an abrasive effect, flinging rocks and pebbles against the cliff faces and wearing them away.

In areas where there are beaches, the waves cause longshore drift, in which sand and stone fragments are carried in a particular direction parallel to the shore.

A river mouth may be moved down the coast as longshore drift builds a sand spit across it.

Waves approaching a headland are refracted so that the headland is attacked from either side.

Longshore drift piles up sand and shingle against groynes – fences built to prevent the beach from being washed away.

wave onrush   wave recess   wave onrush

pebble

Waves usually attack a beach at an angle, moving sand and stones laterally across the shore. As the wave retreats the sand and stones fall back perpendicularly. The result is a net movement along the beach, called longshore drift.

blow hole

crack   cave   enlarged cave   arch   sea stack

The sea erodes the coast in successive stages, first creating cracks in cave openings and then gradually wearing away the interior of the caves until their roofs are pierced through to form blow holes. In time, caves at either side of a headland may unite to form a natural arch. Eventually the lintel of the arch collapses, leaving the offshore section as a sea stack.

average championship 12 times. He holds the all-time record for runs scored, 2,254, and batting average, 367. He had 4,191 hits in his career, a record that stood for almost 60 years.

Cobbett /ˈkɒbɪt/ William 1763–1835. British Radical politician and journalist, who published the weekly *Political Register* 1802–35. He spent much time in North America. His crusading essays on farmers's conditions were collected as *Rural Rides* 1830.

Born in Surrey, the self-taught son of a farmer, Cobbett enlisted in the army 1784 and serviced in Canada. He subsequently lived in the USA as a teacher of English, and became a vigorous pamphleteer, at this time supporting the Tories. In 1800 he returned to England. With increasing knowledge of the sufferings of the farm labourers, he became a Radical and leader of the working-class movement. He was imprisoned 1809–11 for criticizing the flogging of British troops by German mercenaries. He visited the USA again 1817–19. He became a strong advocate of parliamentary reform,

and represented Oldham in the Reformed Parliament after 1832.

Cobden /ˈkɒbdən/ Richard 1804–1865. British Liberal politician and economist, co-founder with John Bright of the Anti-Corn Law League 1839. A member of Parliament from 1841, he opposed class and religious privileges and believed in disarmament and free trade.

Born in Sussex, the son of a farmer, Cobden became a calico manufacturer in Manchester. With other businessmen he founded the Anti-Corn Law League and began his lifelong association with John Bright, until 1845 devoting himself to the repeal of the ◊Corn Laws. A typical early Victorian radical, he believed in the abolition of privileges, a minimum of government interference, and the securing of international peace through free trade and by disarmament and arbitration. He opposed trade unionism and most of the factory legislation of his time, because he regarded them as opposed to liberty of contract. His opposition to the Crimean War made him unpopular. He was

Cobbett *An unknown artist's impression of the bucolic William Cobbett, the British journalist and politician.*

Cobden *The British Liberal politician Richard Cobden, captured here in 1869 in a portrait by L Dickinson.*

cobra

Indian cobra

largely responsible for the commercial treaty with France in 1860.

Cobden-Sanderson /'kɒbdən 'saːndəsən/ Thomas James 1840–1922. British bookbinder and painter. Influenced by William ◊Morris and ◊Burne-Jones, he opened his own workshop in Maiden Lane, Strand, London, 1884; he founded the Doves Press 1900–16.

Cobh /kəuv/ seaport and market town on Great Island, Republic of Ireland; in the estuary of the Lee, county Cork; population (1981) 8,400. Formerly an important port of call for Transatlantic steamers. The town was known as Cove of Cork until 1849 and Queenstown until 1922.

Coblenz alternative spelling of the German city ◊Koblenz.

COBOL (*CO*mmon *B*usiness-*O*riented *L*anguage) a computer-programming language, designed in the late 1950s for business use. COBOL facilitates the writing of programs that deal with large computer files and handle business arithmetic. It has become the major language for commercial data processing.

cobra type of venomous, smooth-scaled snake found in Africa and S Asia, species of which can grow from 1 m/3 ft to over 4.3 m/14 ft. The neck stretches into a 'hood' when the snake is alarmed. Its venom contains nerve toxins that are powerful enough to kill humans.

The *Indian cobra Naja naja* is about 1.5 m/5 ft long, and found over most of S Asia. Some individuals have 'spectacle' markings on the hood. The *hamadryad Naja hannah* of S and SE Asia can be 4.3 m/14 ft or more, and eats snakes. The *ringhals Hemachatus hemachatus* of S Africa, and the *black-necked cobra Naja nigricollis*, found on the African savannah, both about 1 m/3 ft long, are able to spray venom towards the eyes of an attacker.

Cobra a group of European abstract painters formed by Karel ◊Appel.

Coburg /'kəubɜːg/ town in Bavaria, West Germany, on the river Itz; 80 km/50 mi SE of Gotha; population (1984) 44,500. Industries include machinery, toys and porcelain. Formerly the capital of the duchy of Coburg, it was part of Saxe-Coburg-Gotha 1826–1918, and a residence of its dukes.

Coburn /'kəubɜːn/ James 1928– . US film actor, popular in the 1960s and 1970s. His films include *The Magnificent Seven* 1960, *Our Man Flint* 1966, and *Cross of Iron* 1977.

coca South American shrub *Erythroxylon coca*, family Erythroxylaceae, whose dried leaves are

the source of cocaine. It was used as a holy drug by the Andean Indians.

Coca-Cola a sweetened, fizzy drink, originally flavoured by coca and cola nuts, containing caramel and caffeine. Invented 1886, Coca-Cola was sold in every state of the USA by 1895 and in 155 countries by 1987.

cocaine an alkaloid extracted from the leaves of the coca tree. It has limited medical application, mainly as a local anaesthetic agent that is readily absorbed by mucous membranes (lining tissues) of the nose and throat. It is both toxic and addictive. Its use as a stimulant is illegal. ◊Crack is a derivative of cocaine.

Cocaine was first extracted from the coca plant in Germany in the 19th century. Most of the world's cocaine is produced from coca grown in Peru, Bolivia, Columbia, and Ecuador. Estimated annual production totals 215,000 tonnes, with most of the processing done in Columbia.

Cochabamba /ˌkɒtʃəˈbæmbə/ city in central Bolivia, SE of La Paz; population (1985) 317,000. Its altitude is 2,550 m/8,370 ft; it is important for agricultural trading and oil refining.

Its refinery is linked by pipeline with the Camiri oilfields. It is the third largest city in Bolivia.

Cochin /'kəutʃɪn/ former princely state lying west of the Anamalai hills in S India. It was part of Travancore-Cochin from 1949 until merged into Kerala in 1956.

Cochin /'kəutʃɪn/ seaport in Kerala state, India, on the Malabar coast; population (1983) 686,000. It is a fishing port and naval training base. An industrial centre with oil refineries, ropes and clothing are also manufactured here. It exports coir, copra, tea, and spices. Vasco da Gama established a Portuguese factory at Cochin 1502, and St Francis Xavier made it a missionary centre 1530. The Dutch held Cochin from 1663–1795 when it was taken by the English.

Cochin-China /'kɒtʃɪn 'tʃaɪnə/ region of SE Asia. With Cambodia it formed part of the ancient Khmer empire. In the 17th–18th centuries it was conquered by Annam. Together with Cambodia it became, 1863–67, the first part of the Indochinese peninsula to be occupied by France. Since 1949 it has been part of Vietnam.

cochineal red dye, obtained from the cactus-eating Mexican ◊scale insect *Dactylopius coccus*, used in food and fabrics.

cochlea part of the inner ◊ear. It is equipped with approximately 10,000 hair cells, which move in response to sound waves and thus stimulate

nerve cells to send messages to the brain. In this way they turn vibrations of the air into electrical signals.

Cochran /'kɒkrən/ C(harles) B(lake) 1872–1951. British impresario who promoted entertainment ranging from wrestling and roller-skating to Diaghilev's *Ballets Russes*.

Cockaigne, Land of in medieval English folklore, a mythical country of leisure and idleness, where fine food and drink were plentiful and to be had for the asking.

cockatiel Australian parrot *Nymphicus hollandicus*, about 20 cm/8 in long, with greyish plumage, yellow cheeks, a long tail, and a crest like a cockatoo. They are popular as pets and aviary birds.

cockatoo type of parrot, usually white with tinges of red, yellow, or orange, and an erectile crest on the head. They are native to Australia, New Guinea, and nearby islands.

There are about 17 species, one of the most familiar being the Australian **sulphur-crested cockatoo** *Cacatua sulphurea*, about 30 cm/1 ft long, pure white with a yellow crest.

cockchafer or **maybug** beetle *Melolontha melolontha*, up to 3 cm/1.2 in long, with clumsy, buzzing flight, seen on early summer evenings. They damage trees by feeding on the foliage and flowers. The larvae, sometimes called **rookworms**, live underground, feeding on grass and cereal roots.

Cockcroft /'kɒkrɒft/ John Douglas 1897–1967. British physicist. In 1932, he and E T S Walton succeeded in splitting the nucleus of the atom for the first time. In 1951 they were jointly awarded a Nobel prize.

Born in Todmorden, W Yorkshire, Cockcroft held an engineering appointment with Metropolitan-Vickers, and took up research work under ◊Rutherford at the Cavendish Laboratory, Cambridge. He succeeded ◊Appleton as Jacksonian professor of natural philosophy, Cambridge (1939–46), and worked on the atomic bomb during World War II. He was director at Harwell atomic research establishment 1946–58.

Cockerell /'kɒkərəl/ Charles 1788–1863. English architect who built mainly in a Neo-Classical style derived from antiquity and from the work of Christopher Wren. His buildings include the Ashmolean Museum and Taylorian Institute in Oxford 1841–45.

Cockerell /'kɒkərəl/ Christopher 1910– . British engineer, who invented the ◊hovercraft 1959.

From a first interest in radio, he switched to electronics, working with the Marconi Company from 1935 to 1950. In 1953 he began work on the hovercraft, carrying out his early experiments on Oulton Broad, Norfolk.

cock-fighting the pitting of game-cocks against one another to make sport for onlookers and gamblers. In most countries it is illegal because of its cruelty.

Fighting cocks have steel spurs attached to their legs. They are between one and two years old when matched. The sport was very popular in feudal England. A royal cockpit was built in Whitehall by Henry VIII, and royal patronage continued in the next century. During the Cromwellian period it was banned, but at the Restoration it received a new lease of life until it was banned in 1849. Cock-fighting is still legal in some countries and continues surreptitiously in others.

cockle bivalve mollusc with ribbed, heart-shaped shell. The **common cockle** *Cerastoderma edule*

coconut

is up to 5 cm/2 in across, and is found in sand or mud on shores and in estuaries around N European and Mediterranean coasts. It is gathered in large numbers for food.

cockney a native of the City of London. According to tradition cockneys must be born within sound of ◊Bow Bells in Cheapside. The term cockney is also applied to the dialect of the Londoner, of which a striking feature is rhyming slang.

cock-of-the-rock South American bird genus *Rupicola* of the family Cotingidae which also includes the cotingas and umbrella birds. The male cock-of-the-rock has brilliant orange plumage including the head crest, the female is a duller brown. Males clear an area of ground and use it as a communal display ground, spreading wings, tail, and crest to attract mates.

cockroach insect of the family Blattidae, distantly related to the mantises. There are 3,500 species, mainly in the tropics. They have long, antennae, biting mouthparts, and can fly, but rarely do so.

The *common cockroach*, or *black-beetle Blatta orientalis*, is common in dirty houses, is nocturnal, omnivorous, and contaminates food. The *German cockroach Blattella germanica* and *American cockroach Periplaneta americana* are pests in kitchens, bakeries, and warehouses. In Britain only two innocuous species are native, but several have been introduced with imported food and have become severe pests. They are very difficult to eradicate.

cocktail effect the effect of two toxic, or potentially toxic, chemicals when taken together rather than separately. Such effects are known to occur with some mixtures of chemicals, with one ingredient making the body more sensitive to another ingredient. This sometimes occurs because both chemicals require the same ◊enzyme to break them down. Chemicals such as pesticides and food additives are only ever tested singly, not in combination with other chemicals that may be consumed at the same time, so no allowance is made for cocktail effects.

cocoa and chocolate

product	description
plain chocolate	partly defatted cocoa mass, 30–52%, mixed with a little sugar
coating chocolate	a higher proportion of cocoa butter and less cocoa solids
milk chocolate	sweetened chocolate with powdered or condensed milk added. In the UK it must contain 20% cocoa solids. Often flavoured or filled
white chocolate	cocoa butter flavoured with sugar and vanilla
cooking chocolate	cocoa mass and vegetable fat
cocoa powder	cocoa mass with 18% cocoa butter, sweetened
Dutch cocoa	cocoa treated with weak alkali to improve colour, flavour, and solubility
drinking chocolate	pre-cooked cocoa powder with added sugar and flavourings

cocoa and chocolate (Aztec *xocolatl*) food products made from the ◊cacao (or cocoa) bean, fruit of a tropical tree *Theobroma cacao* . Chocolate was introduced to Europe as a drink in the 16th century; eating chocolate was first produced in the late 18th century. Cocoa and chocolate are widely used in confectionary, drinks, and some savoury dishes.

Preparation consists chiefly of roasting, winnowing, and grinding the nib (the edible portion of the bean). If drinking *cocoa* is required, a proportion of the cocoa butter is removed by hydraulic pressure and the remaining cocoa is reduced by further grinding and sieving to a fine powder. In *chocolate* all the original cocoa butter remains. Sugar and usually milk are added; in the UK cheaper vegetable fats are widely substituted.

history Cacao is believed to be indigenous to the forests of the Amazon and Orinoco, and the use of the beans was introduced into Europe after the conquest of Mexico by Cortez. A 'cocoa-house' was opened in London in 1657; others followed and became fashionable meeting places. In 1828 a press was invented that removed two thirds of the cocoa butter from the beans, leaving a cake-like mass that when mixed with sugar and spices made a palatable drink. Joseph Fry combined the cocoa mass with sugar and cocoa butter to obtain a solid chocolate bar, which was turned into milk chocolate by a Swiss, Daniel Pieter, who added condensed milk developed by Henri Nestlé (1814–1890). In Mexico cacao was mixed with hot spices, whisked to a froth and drunk cold. Cocoa powder was a later development. The Ivory Coast is the world's top cocoa exporter (32% of the world total in 1986).

coconut fruit of the coconut palm *Cocos nucifera*, which grows throughout the lowland tropics. The fruit has a large outer husk of fibres, which is split off and used for coconut matting and ropes. Inside this is the nut exported to temperate countries. Its hard shell contains white flesh and coconut milk, which makes a nourishing drink.

The white meat can be eaten or dried prior to the extraction of its oil, which makes up nearly two thirds of it. The oil is used in the making of soap and margarine and in cooking; the residue is used in cattlefeed.

Cocos Islands /ˈkəʊkɒs/ or *Keeling Islands* group of 27 small coral islands in the Indian Ocean, about 2,770 km/1,720 mi NW of Perth, Australia; area 14 sq km/5.5 sq mi; population (1986) 616. They are owned by Australia.

Discovered by William Keeling 1609, they were uninhabited until 1826, annexed by Britain 1857, and transferred to Australia as the Territory of Cocos (Keeling) Islands 1955. The Australian government purchased them from John ◊Clunies-Ross 1978. In 1984 the islanders voted to become part of Australia.

Cocteau /ˈkɒktəʊ/ Jean 1889–1963. French poet, dramatist, and film director. A leading figure in European modernism, he worked with Picasso, Diaghilev, and Stravinsky. He produced many volumes of poetry, ballets such as *Le Boeuf sur le toit/The Nothing Doing Bar* 1920, plays, for example, *Orphée/Orpheus* 1926, and a mature novel of bourgeois French life, *Les Enfants terribles/Children of the Game* 1929, which he made into a film 1950.

cod sea fish *Gadus morhua* found in the N Atlantic and Baltic. Brown to grey with spots, white below, it can grow to 1.5 m/5 ft.

The most important cod fisheries are in the North Sea, and off the coasts of Iceland and Newfoundland, Canada. Much of the catch is salted and dried. Formerly one of the cheapest fish, decline in numbers from overfishing has made it one of the most expensive.

COD abbreviation for *cash on delivery*.

coda (Italian 'tail') in music, a concluding section of a movement added to indicate finality.

code in law, the body of a country's civil or criminal law. The *Code Napoléon* in France 1804–10 was

Cocteau French playwright, novelist, poet, and film director Jean Cocteau in 1929.

widely copied in European countries with civil law systems.

codeine an opium derivative, that provides ◊analgesia in mild to moderate pain. It is also effective in suppressing coughs.

codex plural *codices* a register written on folded sheets, later bound together to form a book. During the 2nd century AD codices began to replace the earlier rolls. They were widely used by the medieval Church to keep records, from about 1200 onwards.

cod liver oil oil obtained by subjecting fresh cod livers to pressure at a temperature of about 85°C. It is is highly nutritious, being a valuable source of the vitamins A and D. Overdose can be harmful.

codon in genetics, a triplet of bases (see ◊base pair) in a molecule of DNA or RNA that codes for a particular amino acid during the process of protein synthesis. There are 64 codons in the ◊genetic code.

Cody /ˈkəʊdi/ Samuel Franklin 1862–1913. US aviation pioneer. He made his first powered flight on 16 Oct 1908 at Farnborough, England, in a machine of his own design. He was killed in a flying accident.

Born in Texas, USA, he took British nationality in 1909. He spent his early days with a cowboy stage and circus act, and made kites capable of lifting people.

Cody /ˈkəʊdi/ William Frederick 1846–1917. US scout and performer, known as *Buffalo Bill* from his contract to supply buffalo carcasses to railway labourers (over 4,000 in 18 months). From 1883 he toured USA and Europe with a Wild West show.

Coe /kəʊ/ Sebastian 1956– . English middle-distance runner. He was Olympic 1,500 metre

Cody US showman 'Buffalo Bill' Cody. His nickname stemmed from his earlier career supplying buffalo meat to railway construction gangs.

champion 1980 and 1984. Between 1979 and 1981 he broke eight individual world records at 800 m, 1,000 m, 1,500 m, and one mile.

CAREER HIGHLIGHTS

Olympic Games
1980: 1500 m gold, 800 m silver
1984: 1500 m gold, 800 m silver
world records
800 m: 1979, 1981
1,000 m: 1980, 1981
one mile: 1979, 1981 (twice)
1,500 m: 1979
4 × 800 m relay: 1982

co-education the education of boys and girls together in one institution.

There has been a marked switch away from single-sex education and in favour of co-education over the last 20 years in the UK, although there is some evidence to suggest that girls perform better in a single sex institution, particularly in maths and science. In 1954, the USSR returned to its earlier co-educational system, partly abolished in 1944. In the USA, 90% of schools and colleges are co-educational. In Islamic countries, co-education is discouraged beyond the infant stage.

coefficient the number part in front of an algebraic term, signifying multiplication. For example, in the expression $4x^2 + 2xy - x$, the coefficient of x^2 is 4 (because $4x^2$ means $4 \times x^2$), that of xy is 2, and that of x is –1 (because $–1 \times x = -x$).

In general algebraic expressions, coefficients are represented by letters that may stand for numbers; for example, in the equation $ax^2 + bx + c = 0$, a, b, and c are coefficients, which can take any number.

coefficient of relationship the probability that any two individuals share a given gene by virtue of being descended from a common ancestor. In sexual reproduction of diploid species, an individual shares half its genes with each parent, with its offspring, and (on average) with each sibling, but only a quarter (on average) with its grandchildren or its siblings's offspring, an eighth with its great-grandchildren, and so on.

coelacanth lobe-finned fish *Latimeria chalumnae* up to 2 m/6 ft long. They have bone and muscle at the base of the fins and are distantly related to the lobefins, which were the ancestors of all land animals with backbones. They live in deep water surrounding the Comoros Islands, off the coast of Madagascar. Believed to be extinct, they were rediscovered 1938.

coeliac disease a disorder of the absorptive surface of the small intestine. It is mainly associated with an intolerance to gluten, a constituent of wheat.

coelom in all but the simplest animals, the fluid-filled cavity that separates the body wall from the gut and associated organs, and allows the gut muscles to contract independently of the rest of the body.

Coetzee /ˌkuːˈtsɪə/ J(ohn) M 1940– . South African author whose novel *In the Heart of the Country* 1975 dealt with the rape of a white woman by a black man. In 1983 he won the ◊Booker Prize for *Life and Times of Michael K.*

coffee a drink made from the roasted and ground seeds or berries of any of several species of the Coffea shrub, cultivated in the tropics. It contains a stimulant, ◊caffeine. Coffee drinking began in Arab countries in the 14th century but did not become common in Europe until 300 years later. In the 17th century the first coffee houses were opened in London.

cultivation Naturally about 5 m/17 ft tall, the shrub is pruned to about 2 m/7 ft, is fully fruit-bearing in five or six years, and lasts for 30 years. Coffee grows best on frost-free hillsides with moderate rainfall. The world's largest producers are Brazil, Colombia, and the Ivory Coast; others include Indonesia, Ethiopia, India, the Philippines, and Cameroon.

cogito, ergo sum (Latin) 'I think, therefore I am'; quotation from French philosopher René Descartes.

Coe *Britain's Sebastian Coe, seen winning his first Olympic title, the 1,500 metres at the Moscow Games in 1980. Jürgen Straub (GDR, No. 338) and Steve Ovett (GB 279) won the silver and bronze medals.*

Cognac /ˈkɒnjæk/ town in Charente *département*, France, 40 km/25 mi W of Angoulême; population (1982) 21,000. Situated in a vine-growing district, Cognac has given its name to a brandy. Bottles, corks, barrels, and crates are manufactured here.

cognition in psychology, a general term covering the functions involved in dealing with information, for example, perception (seeing, hearing, and so on), attention, memory, and reasoning.

cognitive therapy a treatment for emotional disorders, particularly ◊depression and ◊anxiety, developed by Professor Aaron T Beck in the USA. This approach encourages the client to challenge the distorted and unhelpful thinking that is characteristic of these problems. The treatment includes ◊behaviour therapy and has been particularly helpful for people suffering from depression.

coherence in physics, property of two or more waves of a beam of light or other ◊electromagnetic radiation having the same frequency and the same ◊phase or a constant phase difference.

cohesion in physics, a phenomenon in which interaction between two surfaces of the same material in contact makes them cling together (with two different materials the similar phenomenon is called adhesion). According to kinetic theory, cohesion is caused by attraction between particles at the atomic or molecular level. ◊Surface tension, which causes liquids to form spherical droplets, is caused by cohesion.

COI abbreviation for *Central Office of Information*.

coil in medicine, another name for an ◊intrauterine device.

Coimbatore /kəʊˌɪmbəˈtɔː/ city in Tamil Nadu, S India, on the Noyil river; population (1981) 917,000. It has textile industries and the Indian Air Force Administrative College.

Coimbra /kəʊˈɪmbrə/ city in Portugal, on the Mondego river, 32 km/19 mi from the sea; population (1981) 71,800. It produces fabrics, paper, pottery and biscuits. There is a 12th-century Romanesque cathedral incorporating part of an older mosque, and a university, founded in Lisbon 1290 and transferred to Coimbra 1537. Coimbra was the capital of Portugal 1139–1385.

coin a form of money. In modern times the right to make and issue coins is a state monopoly and the great majority are tokens, in that their face value is greater than that of the metal of which they consist. A milled edge, originally used on gold and silver coins to avoid fraudulent 'clipping'

of the edges of precious-metal coins, is retained in some modern token coinage.

The invention of coinage is attributed to the Chinese in the 2nd millennium BC, the earliest types being small-scale bronze reproductions of barter objects such as knives and spades. In the western world, coinage of stamped, guaranteed weight originated with the Lydians of Asia Minor (early 7th century BC) who used electrum, a local natural mixture of gold and silver; the first to issue gold and silver coins was Croesus of Lydia in the 6th century BC.

coke /kəʊk/ a clean, light fuel produced by the carbonization of certain types of coal. When this coal is strongly heated in airtight ovens, in order to release all volatile constituents, the brittle, silver-grey coke is left. It comprises 90% carbon together with very small quantities of water, hydrogen, and oxygen, and makes a useful industrial and domestic fuel. The process was patented in England 1622, but it was only in 1709 that Abraham Darby devised a commercial method of producing coke.

Coke /kəʊk/ Edward 1552–1634. Lord Chief Justice of England 1613–17. Against Charles I he drew up the ◊Petition of Right 1628. His *Institutes* are a legal classic, and he ranks as the supreme common lawyer.

Coke was called to the Bar in 1578, and in 1592 became speaker of the House of Commons and solicitor-general. As attorney-general from 1594 he conducted the prosecution of Elizabeth I's former favourites Essex and Raleigh, and of the Gunpowder Plot conspirators. In 1606 he became Chief Justice of the Common Pleas, and began his struggle, as champion of the common law, against James I's attempts to exalt the royal prerogative. An attempt to silence him by promoting him to the dignity of Lord Chief Justice proved unsuccessful, and from 1620 he led the parliamentary opposition and the attack on Charles I's adviser Buckingham.

Coke /kəʊk/ Thomas William 1754–1842. English pioneer and promoter of the improvements associated with the Agricultural Revolution. His innovations included regular manuring of the soil, the cultivation of fodder crops in association with corn, and the drilling of wheat and turnips.

He also developed a fine flock of Southdown sheep at Holkham, Norfolk, which were superior to the native Norfolks, and encouraged his farm tenants to do likewise. These ideas attracted attention at the annual sheep shearings, an early form of agricultural show, which Coke held on his home farm from 1776. By the end of the century these had become major events, with many visitors coming to see and discuss new stock, crops, and equipment.

cola or **kola** genus of tropical trees, family Sterculiaceae. Their nuts are chewed in W Africa for their high caffeine content, and in the West are used to flavour soft drinks.

Colbert /kɒl'beə/ Claudette. Stage name of Claudette Lily Cauchoin 1905– . French-born film actress, who lived in Hollywood from childhood. She was ideally cast in sophisticated, romantic roles, but had a natural instinct for comedy and appeared in several of Hollywood's finest, including *It Happened One Night* 1934 and *The Palm Beach Story* 1942.

Colbert /kɒl'beə/ Jean-Baptiste 1619–1683. French politician, chief minister to Louis XIV, and controller-general (finance minister) from 1665. He reformed the Treasury, promoted French industry and commerce by protectionist measures, and tried to make France a naval power equal to England or the Netherlands, while favouring a peaceful foreign policy.

Colbert, born in Reims, entered the service of Cardinal Mazarin and succeeded him as chief minister to Louis XIV. In 1661 he set to work to reform the Treasury. The national debt was largely repaid, and the system of tax collection was drastically reformed. Industry was brought under state control, shipbuilding was encouraged by bounties, companies were established to trade with India and America, and colonies were founded in Louisiana, Guiana, and Madagascar. In his later years Colbert was supplanted in Louis's favour by the war minister Louvois (1641–91), who supported a policy of conquests.

Colchester /'kəʊltʃɪstə/ town and river port in England, on the river Colne, Essex; 80 km/50 mi NE of London; population (1981) 82,000. In an agricultural area, it is a market centre with clothing manufacture and engineering and printing works. The University of Essex (1961) is to the SE at Wivenhoe.

history Claiming to be the oldest town in England (Latin *Camulodunum*), Colchester dates from the time of ◊Cymbeline (AD *c.*10–43). It became a colony of Roman ex-soldiers in AD 50, and one of the most prosperous towns in Roman Britain despite its burning by Boudicca (Boadicea) in 61. Most of the Roman walls remain, as well as ruins of the Norman castle, and St Botolph's priory. Holly Tree Mansion (1718) is a museum of 18th–19th century social life.

cold, common minor disease caused by a variety of viruses. Symptoms are headache, chill, nasal discharge, sore throat, and occasionally cough. Research indicates that the virulence of a cold depends on psychological factors and either reduction or increase of social or work activity as a result of stress in the previous six months.

There is little immediate hope of an effective cure since the viruses transform themselves so rapidly. Colds remain a major cause of industrial absenteeism.

cold-blooded common name for ◊**poikilothermy**.

Cold Harbor, Battle of /'kəʊld 'hɑːbə/ in the American Civil War, engagement near Richmond, Virginia, 1–12 June 1864, in which the Confederate Army under Lee repulsed Union attacks under Grant.

Colditz /'kəʊldɪts/ town in East Germany, near Leipzig, site of a castle used as a high-security prisoner-of-war camp (Oflag IVC) in World War II. Among daring escapes was that of British Capt Patrick Reid and others Oct 1942. It became a museum 1989.

Cold War the tensions from about 1945 between the USSR and Eastern Europe on the one hand, and the USA and Western Europe on the other. The Cold War was been exacerbated by propaganda, covert activity by intelligence agencies, and economic sanctions, and intensified at times of conflict. Arms reduction agreements between the USA and USSR in the late 1980s, and a diminution of Soviet influence in Eastern Europe, symbolized by the opening of the Berlin Wall 1989, led to a reassessment of positions.

origins Mistrust between the USSR and the West dates from the Russian Revolution 1917, and contributed to the disagreements during World War II over the future structure of Eastern Europe. The ◊Atlantic Charter signed 1941 by the USA and Britain favoured self-determination, whereas Stalin insisted that the USSR should be allowed to keep the territory obtained as a result of the Hitler–Stalin pact of August 1939.

After the war the USA was keen to have all of Europe open to Western economic interests, while the USSR, afraid of being encircled and attacked by its former allies, saw Eastern Europe as its own sphere of influence and, in the case of Germany, was looking to extract reparations. As the USSR increased its hold on the countries of Eastern Europe, the USA pursued a policy of 'containment' which involved offering material aid to Western Europe (the ◊Marshall Plan) and also to Mediterranean countries such as Greece and Turkey. Berlin became the focal point of E–W tension, culminating in the Soviet blockade of the British, US, and French zones of the city 1948, which was relieved by a sustained airlift of supplies.

The increasing divisions between the capitalist and the communist world were reinforced by the creation of military alliances, the ◊North Atlantic Treaty Organization (NATO) 1949 in the West, and the ◊Warsaw Pact 1955 in the East.

1950–53 The Korean War.
1956 The USSR intervened in Hungary.
1962 The Cuban missile crisis.
1964–75 The USA participated in the Vietnam War.
1968 The USSR intervened in Czechoslovakia.
1972 SALT I accord on arms limitation signed by USA and USSR, beginning a thaw, or détente, in E–W relations.
1979 The USSR invaded Afghanistan.
1980–81 US support for the Solidarity movement in Poland. US president Reagan called the USSR an 'evil empire'.
1982 US military intervention in Central America increased.
1983 US president Reagan proposed to militarize space (Star Wars).
1986 Soviet leader Gorbachev made a proposal for nuclear disarmament which was turned down by Reagan.
1989 Widespread reform took place in Eastern European countries, including the opening of the Berlin Wall. USA planned reduction in conventional forces in Europe.

cold-working method of shaping metal at or near atmospheric temperature.

Cole /kəʊl/ Thomas 1801–1848. US painter, founder of the ***Hudson River school*** of landscape artists.

Cole wrote *Essay on American Scenery* in 1835. Apart from panoramic views such as *The Oxbow* 1836 (Metropolitan Museum of Art, New York), he painted a dramatic historical series, *The Course of the Empire* 1830s, influenced by Claude, Turner, and John Martin.

Coleman /'kəʊlmən/ Ornette 1930– . US alto saxophonist and jazz composer. In the late 1950s he rejected the established structural principles of jazz for free avant-garde improvisation.

Colenso /kə'lenzəʊ/ John William 1814–1883. Bishop of Natal, South Africa, from 1853. He was the first to write down the Zulu language. He championed the Zulu way of life (including polygamy) in relation to Christianity, and applied Christian morality to race relations in South Africa.

Cole, Old King legendary British king, supposed to be the father of St Helena, who married the Roman emperor Constantius, father of Constantine; he is also supposed to have founded Colchester.

Coleridge English poet and critic Samuel Taylor Coleridge.

The historical Cole was possibly a North British chieftan named Coel, of the 5th century, who successfully defended his land against the Picts and Scots. The nursery rhyme is only recorded from 1709.

coleoptile the protective sheath that surrounds the young shoot tip of a grass during its passage through the soil to the surface. Although of relatively simple structure, most coleoptiles are very sensitive to light, ensuring that seedlings grow upwards.

Coleridge /'kəʊlərɪdʒ/ Samuel Taylor 1772–1834. English poet, one of the founders of the Romantic movement. A friend of Southey and Wordsworth, he collaborated with the latter on *Lyrical Ballads* 1798. His poems include 'The Ancient Mariner', 'Christabel', and 'Kubla Khan'; critical works include *Biographia Literaria* 1817.

While at Cambridge, Coleridge was driven by debt to enlist in the Dragoons, and then in 1795, as part of an abortive plan to found a communist colony in the USA with Robert Southey, married Sarah Fricker, from whom he afterwards separated. He became addicted to opium and from 1816 lived at Highgate under medical care. As a philosopher, he argued inferentially that even in registering sense-perceptions the mind was performing acts of creative imagination, rather than being a passive arena in which ideas interacted mechanistically. As a critic, he used psychological insight to brilliant effect in his *Biographia Literaria* and Shakespearean criticism.

Coleridge-Taylor /'kəʊlərɪdʒ 'teɪlə/ Samuel 1875–1912. English composer, the son of a West African doctor and an English mother. He wrote the cantata *Hiawatha's Wedding Feast* 1898, a setting in three parts of Longfellow's poem. He was a student and champion of traditional black music.

Colet /'kɒlɪt/ John c. 1467–1519. English humanist, influenced by the Italian reformer Savonarola and the Dutch scholar Erasmus. He reacted against the scholastic tradition in his interpretation of the Bible, and founded modern biblical exegesis. In 1505 he became dean of St Paul's Cathedral, London.

Colette /kɒ'let/ Sidonie-Gabrielle 1873–1954. French writer. At 20 she married Henri Gauthier-Villars, a journalist known as 'Willy'. Her four 'Claudine' novels, based on her own early life, were written under her husband's direction and signed by him. Divorced in 1906, she was a striptease and mime artist for a while, but continued to write, for example, *Chéri* 1920, *La Fin de Chéri/The End of Chéri* 1926, and *Gigi* 1944.

colic a spasmodic attack of pain in the abdomen. Colicky pains are usually caused by the blockage, and subsequent distension, of a hollow organ, for example the bowel, gall bladder (biliary colic) or ureter (renal colic). Characteristically the pain is severe during contraction of the muscular wall of the organ, then recedes temporarily as the muscle tires.

Coligny /ˌkɒlɪn'jiː/ Gaspard de 1517–1572. French admiral and soldier, and prominent

◊Huguenot. About 1557 he joined the Protestant party, helping to lead the Huguenot forces during the Wars of Religion. After the Treaty of St Germain 1570, he became a favourite of the young king Charles IX, but was killed on the first night of the massacre of St ◊Bartholomew.

colitis inflammation of the colon (large intestine). Sulphonamides are among the drugs used in its treatment. It may be caused by food poisoning or some types of dysentery.

collage (French 'gluing' or 'pasting') a technique of pasting paper to create a picture. Several artists in the early 20th century used collage: Arp, Braque, Ernst, and Schwitters, among others.

Many artists also experimented with *photomontage*, creating compositions from pieces of photographs rearranged with often disturbing effects.

collagen a strong, rubbery ◊protein that plays an important structural role in the bodies of ◊vertebrates. Collagen supports the ear flaps and the tip of the nose in humans, as well as being the main constituent of tendons and ligaments. Bones are made up of collagen, with the mineral calcium phosphate providing increased rigidity.

collateral security available in return for a loan. Usually stocks, shares, property, or life assurance policies will be accepted as collateral.

collective farm (Russian *kolkhoz*) a farm in which a group of farmers pool their land, domestic animals, and agricultural implements, retaining as private property enough only for the members's own requirements. The profits of the farm are divided among its members.

The system was first developed in the USSR in 1917, where it became general after 1930. Stalin's collectivization drive 1929–33 wrecked a flourishing agricultural system and alienated the Soviet peasants from the land: 15 million people were left homeless, 1 million of whom were sent to labour camps and some 12 million deported to Siberia. In subsequent years, millions of those peasants forced into collectives died. Collective farming is practised in other countries; it was adopted from 1953 in China, and Israel has a large number of collective farms including the ◊kibbutzes.

collective security a system for achieving international stability by an agreement among all states to unite against any aggressor. Such a commitment was embodied in the post-World War I League of Nations and also in the United Nations Organization, although neither body was able to live up to the ideals of its founders.

collective unconscious in psychology, the term used for the shared pool of memories inherited from ancestors that Carl Jung suggested coexisted with individual ◊unconscious recollections, and which might be active both for evil in precipitating mental disturbance or for good in prompting achievements (for example, in the arts).

collectivization the policy pursued by Stalin in the USSR after 1928 to reorganize agriculture by taking land into state or collective ownership. Much of this was achieved during the first two ◊Five Year Plans but only with much coercion and loss of life among the peasantry.

College of Arms or *Heralds' College* an English heraldic body formed in 1484 by Richard III incorporating the heralds attached to the Royal Household; reincorporated by Royal Charter of Philip and Mary in 1555. There are three Kings of Arms, six Heralds, and four Pursuivants, who specialize in genealogical and heraldic work. The College establishes the right to bear Arms, and the Kings of Arms grant Arms by letters patent. In Ireland the office of Ulster King of Arms was transferred in 1943 to the College of Arms in London and placed with that of Norroy King of Arms, who now has jurisdiction in Northern Ireland as well as in the north of England.

college of higher education in the UK, a college controlled by the local education authorities in

Collins English rock star Phil Collins.

which a large proportion of the work undertaken is at degree level or above.

collenchyma a plant tissue composed of somewhat elongated cells with thickened cell walls, especially at the corners where adjacent cells meet. It is a supporting and strengthening tissue found in non-woody plants, particularly in the stems and leaves.

collie type of sheepdog originally bred in Britain. The *rough* and *smooth collies* are about 60 cm/2 ft tall, and have long narrow heads and muzzles. The *border collie* is a working dog, often black and white, about 45 cm/1.5 ft tall, with a dense coat. The *bearded collie* is a little smaller, and rather like an Old English sheepdog in appearance.

Collier /'kɒlɪə/ Jeremy 1650–1726. British Anglican cleric, a ◊Nonjuror, who was outlawed 1696 for granting absolution on the scaffold to two men who had tried to assassinate William III. His *Short View of the Immorality and Profaneness of the English Stage* 1698 was aimed at the dramatists Congreve and Vanbrugh.

Collier /'kɒlɪə/ Lesley 1947– . British ballerina, a principal dancer of the Royal Ballet from 1972.

She had major roles in MacMillan's *Anastasia* 1971, and *Four Seasons* 1975, van Manen's *Four Schumann Pieces* 1975, Ashton's *Rhapsody* and Tetley's *Dance of Albiar* both 1980.

collimator (a) a small telescope attached to a larger optical instrument to fix its line of sight; (b) an optical device for producing a nondivergent beam of light; (c) any device for limiting the size and angle of spread of a beam of radiation or particles.

collinear in mathematics, lying on the same straight line.

Collingwood /'kɒlɪŋwʊd/ Cuthbert, Baron Collingwood 1748–1810. British admiral, who served with Horatio Nelson in the West Indies against France and blockaded French ports 1803–05; after Nelson's death he took command at the Battle of Trafalgar.

Collingwood /'kɒlɪŋwʊd/ Robin George 1889–1943. English philosopher, who believed that any philosophical theory or position could only be properly understood within its own historical context and not from the point of view of the present. His aesthetic theory is outlined in *Principles of Art* 1938.

Collins /'kɒlɪnz/ (William) Wilkie 1824–1889. English novelist, author of mystery and suspense novels, including *The Woman in White* 1860 (with its fat villain Count Fosco), often called the first English detective novel, and *The Moonstone* 1868 (with Sergeant Cuff, one of the first detectives in English literature).

Collins /'kɒlɪnz/ Michael 1890–1922. Irish Sinn Féin leader, a founder and director of intelligence of the Irish Republican Army 1919, minister for finance in the Provisional government of the Irish Free State 1922, commander of the Free State

forces and for ten days head of state; killed in the civil war.

Born in County Cork, Collins became an active member of the Irish Republican Brotherhood, and in 1916 fought in the Easter Rising. In 1918 he was elected a Sinn Féin member to the Dáil, and became a minister in the Republican Provisional government. In 1921 he and Arthur Griffith (1872–1922) were mainly responsible for the treaty that established the Irish Free State. During the ensuing civil war, Collins took command and crushed the opposition in Dublin and the large towns within a few weeks. When Griffith died on 12 Aug Collins became head of the state and the army, but he was ambushed near Cork by fellow Irishmen on 22 Aug and killed.

Collins /'kɒlɪnz/ Phil 1951– . English pop singer, drummer, and actor. A member of the group Genesis from 1970, he has also pursued a successful solo career from 1981, with hits (often new versions of old songs) including 'In the Air Tonight' 1981 and 'Groovy Kind of Love' 1988.

Collins /'kɒlɪnz/ William 1721–1759. British poet. His *Persian Eclogues* 1742 were followed in 1746 by his series 'Odes', the best-known being 'To Evening'.

Collodi /kɒ'ləʊdi/ Carlo. Pen name of Carlo Lorenzini 1826–1890. Italian journalist and writer, who in 1881–83 wrote *The Adventure of Pinocchio*, the children's story of a wooden puppet who became a human boy.

colloid a substance composed of extremely small particles whose size is between those in suspension and those in true solution (between 1 and 1,000 microns across). The two components are the *continuous phase* and the *dispersed phase*; the latter is distributed in the former. There are various types of colloids: those involving gases include an aerosol (a dispersion of a liquid or solid in a gas, as in fog or smoke) and a foam (a dispersion of a gas in a liquid). Liquids form both the dispersed and continuous phases in an *emulsion*.

Milk is a natural emulsion of liquid fat in a watery liquid; synthetic emulsions such as some paints and cosmetic lotions have chemical emulsifying agents to stabilize the colloid and stop the two phases from separating out. Colloidal solutions (a solid dispersed in a liquid) are called *sols*. A sol in which both phases contribute to the molecular three-dimensional network of the colloid take on a jelly-like form and are known as *gels*; gelatine, starch 'solution' and silica gel are common examples. Colloids were first studied thoroughly by the British chemist Thomas ◊Graham who defined them as substances which (in solution) will not diffuse through a semi-permeable membrane (as opposed to crystalloids, solutions of inorganic salts, which will diffuse through).

Colman /'kəʊlmən/ Ronald 1891–1958. British actor. Born in Richmond, Surrey, he went to the USA in 1920 where his charm, good looks and speaking voice soon brought success in romantic Hollywood roles. His films include *Beau Geste* 1924, *The Prisoner of Zenda* 1937, *Lost Horizon* 1937, and *A Double Life* 1947, for which he received an Academy Award.

Colmar /'kɒlmɑ:/ capital of Haut-Rhin *département*, France, between the river Rhine and the Vosges mountains; population (1983) 82,500. It is the centre of a wine growing and market gardening area. Industries include engineering, food processing, and textiles. The church of St Martin is 13th–14th century, and the former Dominican monastery, now the Unterlinden Museum, contains a famed Grünewald altarpiece.

Cologne /kə'ləʊn/ (German *Köln*) industrial and commercial port in North Rhine-Westphalia, West Germany, on the left bank of the Rhine, 35 km/22 mi from Düsseldorf; population (1988) 914,000. To the north is the Ruhr coalfield, on which many of Cologne's industries are based. They include motor vehicles, railway wagons, chemicals, and machine tools. Cologne can be reached by ocean-going vessels and has developed into a great trans shipment centre, and is also the headquarters of Lufthansa, the state airline.

Founded by the Romans 38 BC and made a colony AD 50 under the name Colonia Claudia Arae Agrippinensis (hence the name Cologne), it became an important Frankish city and during the Middle Ages was ruled by its archbishops. It was a free imperial city from 1288 until the Napoleonic age. In 1815 it passed to Prussia. The great Gothic cathedral was begun in the 13th century but its towers were not built until the 19th century (completed 1880). Its university (1388–1797) was refounded 1919. Cologne suffered severely from aerial bombardment during World War II; 85% of the city and its three Rhine bridges were destroyed.

Colombes /kɒ'lɒmb/ suburb of Paris, France; population (1983) 83,260. It is capital of Hauts-de-Seine *département*. Tyres, electronic equipment, and chemicals are manufactured.

Colombey-les-Deux-Eglises /,kɒlɒm'beɪ leɪ 'dɜːz eɪ'gliːz/ village (the name means Colombey with the two churches) in Haute-Marne, France; population (1981) 700. General ◊de Gaulle lived and was buried here.

Colombia /kə'lɒmbiə/ country in South America, bounded N and W by the Caribbean and the Pacific, and having borders with Panama to the NW, Venezuela to the E and NE, Brazil to the SE, and Peru and Ecuador to the SW.

government The 1886 constitution provides for a president, a two-chamber congress of senate of 114 members, and a house of representatives of 199 members, all elected by universal suffrage for a four-year term. The president appoints the cabinet. Although it does not have a fully federal system, Colombia is divided into 32 regions, enjoying considerable autonomy, with governors appointed by the president and locally elected legislatures. Most significant among many political parties are the Liberal Party and the Conservative Party.

history Until it was conquered by Spain in the 16th century, the area was inhabited by the Chibcha. From 1538 Colombia formed part of a colony known as New Granada, comprising Colombia, Panama, and most of Venezuela. In 1819 the area included Ecuador, and became independent as Gran Colombia, a state set up by Simón Bolívar. Colombia became entirely independent in 1886.

Cologne *The twin towers of the majestic cathedral dominate the city from every angle. The present building was begun in 1248 but only completed in the 19th century.*

Colombia
Republic of
(República de Colombia)

area 1,141,748 sq km/440,715 sq mi
capital Bogotá
towns Medellin, Cali, Bucaramanga; ports Barranquilla, Cartagena
physical the Andes mountains run N–S; plains in the E; Magdalena River runs N to the Caribbean
head of state and government Virgilio Barco Vargas from 1986
political system emergent democratic republic
political parties Liberal Party, centrist; Conservative Party, right-of-centre
exports emeralds (world's largest producer), coffee (second largest world producer), bananas, cotton, meat; sugar, oil, skins, hides
currency peso (769.83 = £1 Feb 1990)
population (1985) 29,482,000 (68% mestizo,

life expectancy men 61, women 66
language Spanish
religion Roman Catholic
literacy 89% male/87% female (1985 est)
GNP $42.5 bn (1983); $1,112 per head of population
chronology
1886 Full independence achieved. Conservatives in power.
1930 Liberals in power.
1946 Conservatives in power.
1948 Left-wing mayor of Bogotá assassinated. Widespread outcry.
1949 Start of civil war, La Violencia, during which 280,000 people died.
1957 Hoping to halt the violence, Conservatives and Liberals agreed to form a National Front, sharing the presidency.
1970 National Popular Alliance (ANAPO) formed as a left-wing opposition to the National Front.
1974 National Front accord temporarily ended.
1975 Civil unrest because of disillusionment with the government.
1978 Liberals, under Julio Turbay, revived the accord and began an intensive fight against drug dealers.
1982 Liberals maintained their control of Congress but lost the presidency. The Conservative president, Belisario Betancur, attempted to end the violence by granting left-wing guerrillas an amnesty, freeing political prisoners, and embarking on a public works programme.
1984 Minister of justice assassinated, allegedly by drug dealers. Campaign against them stepped up.
1986 Virgilio Barco Vargas, Liberal, elected president by a record margin.
1989 Campaign against drug traffickers intensified.

In 1948 the left-wing mayor of Bogotá was assassinated and there followed a decade of near civil war, 'La Violencia', during which it is thought that over 250,000 people died. Left-wing guerrilla activity continued into the 1980s. In 1957, in an effort to halt the violence, the Conservatives and Liberals formed a National Front, alternating the presidency between them. They were challenged in 1970 by the National Popular Alliance (ANAPO), with a special appeal to the working classes, but the Conservative-Liberal coalition continued and when in 1978 the Liberals won majorities in both chambers of congress and the presidency, they kept the National Front accord.

In 1982 the Liberals kept their majorities in congress but Dr Belisario Bentacur won the presidency for the Conservatives. He sought a truce with the left-wing guerrillas by granting them an amnesty and freeing political prisoners. He also embarked on a radical programme of public works. His plans suffered a major blow in 1984 when his minister of justice, who had been using harsh measures to curb drug dealing, was assassinated. Betancur reacted by strengthening his anti-drug campaign. In the 1986 elections Liberal Virgilio Barco Vargas won the presidency by a record margin. Three months after taking office, he announced the end of the National Front accord, despite a provision in the constitution that the opposition party always has the opportunity to participate in government if it wishes to. In 1989, with strong support from US President Bush, Barco stepped up his war on Columbia's drug barons.

Colombo /kə'lʌmbəʊ/ capital and principal seaport of Sri Lanka, on the west coast near the mouth of the Kelani; population (1981) 588,000, Greater Colombo about 1,000,000. It trades in tea, rubber, and cacao. It has iron and steel works, and an oil refinery.

Colombo was mentioned as Kalambu about 1340, but the Portuguese renamed it in honour of the explorer Christopher Columbus. The Dutch seized it 1656 and surrendered it to Britain 1796. Since 1983, the chief government offices have been located at nearby Sri-Jayawardenapura east of the city.

Colombo /kə'lɒmbəʊ/ Matteo Realdo *c.* 1516–1559. Italian anatomist who discovered pulmonary circulation, the process of blood circulating from the heart to the lungs and back.

This showed that ◊Galen's teachings were wrong, and was of help to ◊Harvey in his work on the heart and cirulation. Colombo was a pupil of ◊Vesalius, and became his successor at Padua.

Colombo Plan plan for cooperative economic development in S and SE Asia, established 1951. The member countries meet annually to discuss economic and development plans such as irrigation, hydroelectric schemes, and technical training.

The plan has no central fund but technical assistance and financing of development projects is arranged through individual governments or the International Bank for Reconstruction and Development.

colon in anatomy, the part of the large intestine between the caecum and rectum, where water and mineral salts are absorbed from digested food, and the residue formed into faeces or faecal pellets.

colon in punctuation, a mark (:) intended to direct the reader's attention forward, usually because what follows explains or develops what has just been written (for example, the farmer owned a variety of dogs: a spaniel, a pointer, a terrier, a border collie, and three mongrels).

Colón /kɒ'lɒn/ second largest city in Panama, at the Caribbean end of the Panama Canal; population (1980) 60,000. Founded in 1850, and named Aspinwall in 1852, it was renamed Colón in 1890 in honour of the explorer Christopher Columbus.

Colón, Archipiélago de /kɒ'lɒn/ official name of the ◊Galápagos Islands.

colonialism another name for ◊*imperialism*.

Colorado

Colonna /kɒˈlɒnə/ Vittoria *c*.1492–1547. Roman poet. Many of her Petrarchan poems idealize her husband, killed at the battle of Paria 1525. She was a friend of Michelangelo, who addressed sonnets to her.

colophon originally an inscription on the last page of a book giving the writer or printer's name, and place and year of publication. In modern practice it is a decorative device on the title page or spine of a book, the 'trade-mark' of the individual publisher.

Colorado /ˌkɒləˈrɑːdəʊ/ river in North America, rising in the Rocky Mountains and flowing 2,333 km/1,450 mi to the Gulf of California through Colorado, Utah, Arizona, and N Mexico. The many dams along its course, including Hoover and Glen Canyon, provide power and irrigation water, but have destroyed wildlife and scenery, and very little water now reaches the sea. To the west of the river in SE California is the **Colorado Desert**, an arid area of 5,000 sq km/2,000 sq mi.

Colorado /ˌkɒləˈrɑːdəʊ/ state in the central W USA; nickname Centennial State
area 269,700 sq km/104,104 sq mi
capital Denver
towns Colorado Springs, Aurora, Lakewood, Fort Collins, Greeley, Pueblo
physical Great Plains in the east; the main ranges of the Rocky Mountains; high plateaus of the Colorado Basin in the west
features Rocky Mountain National Park; Pike's Peak; prehistoric cliff dwellings of the Mesa Verde National Park; Garden of the Gods (natural sandstone sculptures); Dinosaur and Great Sand Dunes national monuments; 'ghost' mining towns
products cereals, meat and dairy products, oil, coal, molybdenum, uranium, iron, steel, machinery
population (1986) 3,267,000
famous people Jack Dempsey, Douglas Fairbanks
history it first attracted fur traders, and Denver was founded following the discovery of gold 1858. Colorado became a state 1876.

Colorado Springs /ˈkɒlərɑːdəʊ ˈsprɪŋz/ health resort in Colorado, USA, 120 km/75 mi SE of Denver; population (1986) 380,000. At an altitude of about 1,800 m/6,000 ft, and surrounded by magnificent scenery, it is also a local trade centre.

coloratura in music, a rapid ornamental vocal passage with runs and trills. A *coloratura soprano* is a light, high voice suited to such music.

Colosseum /ˌkɒləˈsiːəm/ amphitheatre in ancient Rome, begun by the emperor Vespasian to replace the one destroyed by fire during the reign of Nero, and Completed by his son Titus AD 80. It was 187 m/615 ft long and 49 m/160 ft high, and seated 50,000 people. Early Christians were martyred there by lions and gladiators. It could be flooded for mock sea battles.

Colossians epistle in the New Testament to the church at Colossae; attributed to St Paul.

Colossus of Rhodes /kəˈlɒsəs əv ˈrəʊdz/ bronze statue of Apollo erected at the entrance to the harbour at Rhodes 292–280 BC. Said to have been about 30 m/100 ft high, it was counted as one of the Seven Wonders of the World, but in 224 BC fell as a result of an earthquake.

colour blindness an incurable defect of vision that reduces the ability to discriminate one colour from another. Between 2% and 6% of men

Colosseum *The Colosseum in Rome, Italy.*

and less than 1% of women have colour blindness.

In the most common types there is confusion among the red–yellow–green range of colours; for example, many colour-blind observers are unable to distinguish red from yellow or yellow from green. The cause of congenital colour blindness is not known, although it probably arises from some defect in the retinal receptors. Lead poisoning and toxic conditions caused by excessive smoking can lead to colour blindness.

colourings food ◊additives used to alter or improve the colour of processed foods. They include artificial colours, such as tartrazine and amaranth, which are made from petrochemicals, and the 'natural' colours such as chlorophyll, caramel, and carotene. Some of the natural colours are actually synthetic copies of the naturally occurring substances, and some of these, notably the synthetically produced caramels, may be injurious to health.

colours, military flags or standards carried by military regiments, so-called because of the various combinations of colours employed to distinguish one country or one regiment from another.

In the UK each battalion carries the sovereign's colour and the regimental colour, which bears the title, crest, and motto of the regiment with the names of battle honours.

Colt /kəʊlt/ Samuel 1814–1862. US gunsmith who invented the revolver 1835 that bears his name.

He built up an immense arms-manufacturing business at Hartford, Connecticut, his birthplace, and later in England.

Coltrane /kɒlˈtreɪn/ John (William) 1926–1967. US jazz saxophonist, a member of the Miles ◊Davis quintet. His performances were noted for experimentation, and his quartet was highly regarded for its innovations in melody and harmony.

coltsfoot plant *Tussilago farfara*, family Compositae. The solitary yellow flowerheads have many narrow rays and the stems have large purplish scales. The large leaf, up to 22 cm/9 in across, is shaped like a horse's foot and gives the plant its common name. Coltsfoot grows in Europe, N Asia and N Africa, often on bare ground and in waste places.

colugo SE Asian climbing mammal of the order Dermoptera, about 60 cm/2 ft long including tail. It glides between forest trees using a flap of skin which extends from head to forelimb to hindlimb to tail. It may glide 130 m/427 ft or more, losing little height. It feeds largely on buds and leaves, and rests hanging upside down under branches. There are two species, *Cynocephalus variegatus* of Indochina and Indonesia, and *Cynocephalus volans* of the Philippines.

Colum /ˈkɒləm/ Padraic 1881–1972. Irish poet and playwright. He was associated with the foundation of the Abbey Theatre, Dublin, where his plays *Land* 1905, and *Thomas Muskerry* 1910, were performed. His *Collected Poems* 1932 show his gift for lyrical expression.

Columba, St /kəˈlʌmbə/ 521–597. Irish Christian abbot, missionary to Scotland. He was born in County Donegal of royal descent, and founded monasteries and churches in Ireland. In 563 he sailed with 12 companions to Iona, and built a monastery there that was to play an important part in the conversion of Britain. Feast day 9 June.

From his base on Iona St Columba made missionary journeys to the mainland. Legend has it that he drove a monster from the river Ness, and he crowned Aidan, an Irish king of Argyll.

Columban, St /kəˈlʌmbən/ 543–615. Irish Christian abbot. He was born in Leinster, studied at Bangor, and about 585 went to the Vosges, France, with 12 other monks and founded the monastery of Luxeuil. He preached in Switzerland, then went to Italy, where he built the abbey of Bobbio in the Apennines. Feast day 23 Nov.

Columbia /kəˈlʌmbiə/ river in W North America, over 1,950 km/1218 mi; it rises in British Columbia, Canada, and flows through Washington state, USA, to the Pacific below Astoria. It is harnessed for irrigation and power by the Grand Coulee and other great dams. It is famous for salmon fishing.

Columbia /kəˈlʌmbiə/ capital of South Carolina, USA, on the Congaree River; population (1980) 445,000. Manufacturing includes textiles, plastics, electrical goods, fertilizers, and hosiery.

Columbia, District of /kəˈlʌmbiə/ seat of the federal government of the USA, bordering the capital, Washington; area 178 sq km/69 sq mi. Situated on the Potomac River, it was ceded by Maryland as the national capital site 1790.

Columbia Pictures US film production and distribution company founded 1924. It grew out of a smaller company founded 1920 by Harry and Jack Cohn and Joe Brandt. Under Harry Cohn's guidance, Columbia became a major studio by the 1940s, producing such commercial hits as *Gilda* 1946. After Cohn's death in 1958 the studio remained successful, producing international films such as *Lawrence of Arabia* 1962.

columbine plant *Aquilegia vulgaris*, family Ranunculaceae. It is a perennial herb, with deeply divided leaves, and purple flowers with spurred petals. It grows wild in woods and is a familiar garden plant.

columbium former name for the chemical element ◊niobium.

Columbus /kəˈlʌmbəs/ capital city of Ohio, USA, on the rivers Scioto and Olentangy; population (1980) 1,093,000. It has coal and natural gas resources nearby; its industries include the manufacture of cars, planes, missiles, electrical goods, mining machinery, refrigerators, and telephones.

Columbus /kəˈlʌmbəs/ Christopher (Spanish *Cristobal Colon*) 1451–1506. Italian navigator and explorer who made four voyages to the New World: 1492 to San Salvador Island, Cuba, and Haiti; 1493–96 to Guadaloupe, Montserrat, Antigua, Puerto Rico, and Jamaica; 1498 to Trinidad and the mainland of South America; 1502–04 to Honduras and Nicaragua.

Born in Genoa, Columbus went to sea at an early age, and settled in Portugal 1478. Believing that Asia could be reached by sailing westward, he eventually won the support of King Ferdinand and Queen Isabella of Spain and on 3 Aug 1492 sailed from Palos with three small ships, the *Niña*, the *Pinta*, and his flagship the *Santa Maria*. On 12 Oct land was sighted, probably Watling Island (now San Salvador Island), and within a few weeks he reached Cuba and Haiti, returning to Spain in Mar 1493. After his third voyage in 1498, he became involved in quarrels among the colonists sent to Haiti, and in 1500 the governor sent him back to Spain in chains. Released and compensated by the king, he made his last voyage 1502–04, during which he hoped to find a strait leading to India. He died in poverty in Valladolid and is buried in Seville cathedral.

In 1968 the site of the wreck of the *Santa Maria*, sunk off Hispaniola 25 Dec 1492, was located.

Columbus *An engraving of the portrait by Sebastiano del Piombo; the original is in the Uffizi, Florence.*

column in architecture, a structure, round or polygonal in plan, erected vertically as a support for some part of a building. Cretan paintings reveal the existence of wooden columns in Aegean architecture, about 1500 BC. The Hittites, Assyrians, and Egyptians also used wooden columns, and in modern times they are a feature of the monumental architecture of China and Japan. In classical architecture there are five principal types of column; see ◊order.

Colwyn Bay /'kɒlwɪn 'beɪ/ seaside town in Clwyd, North Wales, known as the 'garden resort of Wales'. Population (1981) 26,300.

coma in medicine, a state of deep unconsciousness from which the subject cannot be roused. There are many possible causes, including head injury, cerebral haemorrhage, and drug overdose.

coma in optics, one of the geometrical aberrations of a lens, whereby skew rays from a point object make a comet-shaped spot on the image plane instead of meeting at a point.

coma in astronomy, the hazy cloud of gas and dust that surrounds the nucleus of a ◊comet.

Comaneci /,kɒmə'netʃ/ Nadia 1961– . Romanian gymnast. She won three gold medals at the 1976 Olympics at the age of 14, and was the first gymnast to record a perfect score of 10 in international competition.

combination in mathematics, a selection of a number of objects from some larger number of objects when no account is taken of order within any one arrangement. For example, 123, 213, and 312 are regarded as the same combination of three digits from 1234. Combinatorial analysis is important in the study of ◊probability.

The number of ways of selecting r objects from a group of n is given by the formula $n!/[r!(n-r)!]$, where $n!$ (factorial n) is $n \times (n-1) \times (n-2) \times (n-3)... \times 2 \times 1$.

Combination Laws laws passed in Britain 1799 and 1800 making trade unionism illegal, introduced after the French Revolution for fear that the unions would become centres of political agitation. The unions continued to exist, but claimed to be friendly societies or went underground, until the acts were repealed 1824, largely owing to the radical Francis Place.

combine harvester or **combine** a machine used for harvesting cereals and other crops, so-called because it combines the actions of reaping (cutting the crop) and threshing (beating the ears so that the grain separates).

Combines, drawn by horses, were used in the Californian cornfields in the 1850s. Today's mechanical combine harvesters are capable of cutting a swathe of up to 9 m/30 ft or more.

combustion burning, defined in chemical terms as rapid combination of a substance with oxygen accompanied by the evolution of heat and usually light. A slow-burning candle flame and the

combine harvester
crop flow through self-propelled combine harvester

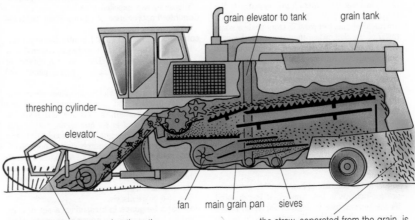

the pentagonal pick-up reel gathers the crop, for cutting and transfer by elevator to the threshing cylinder

the straw, separated from the grain, is carried to the back of the harvester and discarded

explosion of a mixture of petrol vapour and air are extreme examples of combustion.

Comecon (*Co*uncil for *M*utual *E*conomic *Co*operation, or CMEA) economic organization established 1949 and prompted by the ◊Marshall Plan, linking the USSR with Bulgaria, Czechoslovakia, Hungary, Poland, Romania, East Germany (from 1950), Mongolia (from 1962), Cuba (from 1972), and Vietnam (from 1978), with Yugoslavia as an associated member. Albania also belonged 1949–61.

The secretariat is based in Moscow and regular annual meetings are held in the member countries. Trade between comet countries is hampered by the lack of a convertible currency, the transferable rupee being merely an accounting device. It was agreed in 1987 that official relations should be established with the European Community.

Comédie Française /,kɒmeɪ'di: ffrɒn'seɪz/ the French national theatre (for both comedy and tragedy) in Paris, founded 1680 by Louis XIV. Its base is the Salle Richelieu on the right bank of the Seine, and the Théatre de Odéon, on the left bank, is a testing ground for avant-garde ideas.

comedy a drama that aims to make its audience laugh, usually with a happy or amusing ending, as opposed to tragedy. The comic tradition has enjoyed many changes since its Greek roots; the earliest comic tradition developed in ancient Greece, in the farcical satires of Aristophanes. Great comic playwrights include Shakespeare, Molière, Goldoni, Marivaux, G B Shaw, and Oscar Wilde. Genres of comedy include pantomime, satire, farce, black comedy, and ◊commedia dell'arte.

The comic tradition was established by the Greek dramatists Aristophanes and Menander, and the Roman writers Terence and Plautus. In medieval times, the Vices and Devil of the Morality plays developed into the stock comic characters of the Renaissance *Comedy of Humours* with such notable villains as Jonson's Mosca in *Volpone*. The timeless comedies of Shakespeare and Molière were followed in England during the 17th century by the witty *comedy of manners* of Restoration writers such as Etherege, Wycherley, and Congreve. Their often coarse but always vital comedies were toned down in the later Restoration dramas of Sheridan and Goldsmith. Sentimental comedy dominated most of the 19th century, though little is remembered in the late 20th century, which prefers the realistic tradition of Shaw and the elegant social comedies of Wilde. The polished comedies of Coward and Rattigan from the 1920s to 1940s were eclipsed during the late 1950s and 1960s by a trend towards satire and cynicism as seen in the works of Joe Orton and Peter Nichols, alongside absurdist comedies by Samuel Beckett and Jean Genet. From the 1970s the 'black comedies' of Alan Ayckbourn have dominated the English stage.

comet a small, icy body orbiting the Sun on a usually highly elliptical path. A comet consists of a central nucleus a few kilometres across, often likened to a dirty snowball because it consists mostly of ice mixed with dust. As the comet approaches the Sun the nucleus heats up, releasing gas and dust which form a tenuous ◊coma, up to 100,000 km/60,000 mi wide, around the nucleus. Gas and dust stream away from the coma to form

major comets

Name	First recorded sighting	Orbital period (years)	Notes
Halley's Comet	240 BC	76	parent of Aquarid and Orionid meteor showers
Comet Tempel-Tuttle	AD 1366	33	parent of Leonid meteors
Biela's Comet	1772	6.6	broke in half 1846; not seen since 1852
Encke's Comet	1786	3.3	parent of Taurid meteors
Comet Swift-Tuttle	1862	120 approx	parent of Perseid meteors; believed lost
Comet Ikeya-Seki	1965	880	so-called 'sun-grazing' comet, passed 500,000 km/300,000 mi above surface of Sun on Oct 21 1965
Comet Kohoutek	1973		observed from space by Skylab astronauts; period too long to calculate accurately
Comet West	1975	500,000	nucleus broke into four parts
Comet Bowell	1980		ejected from solar system after close encounter with Jupiter
Comet IRAS–Araki–Alcock	1983	•	passed only 4 million km/2.8 million mi from Earth on May 11, 1983; period too long to calculate accurately

one or more tails, which may extend for millions of kilometres.

Comets are believed to have been formed at the birth of the solar system. Billions of them may reside in a halo (the **Oort cloud**, named after the Dutch astronomer Jan ◊Oort) beyond Pluto. The gravitational effect of passing stars pushes some towards the Sun, when they eventually become visible from Earth. Most comets swing around the Sun and return to distant space, never to be seen again for thousands or millions of years, although some, called **periodic comets**, have their orbits altered by the gravitational pull of the planets so that they reappear every 200 years or less. Of the 800 or so comets whose orbits have been calculated, about 160 are periodic. The brightest is ◊Halley's Comet. The one with the shortest known period is Encke's comet, which orbits the Sun every 3.3 years. A dozen or more comets are discovered every year, some by amateur astronomers.

comfort index estimate of how tolerable conditions are for humans in hot climates. It is calculated as the temperature in degrees Farenheit plus a quarter of the relative ◊humidity, expressed as a percentage. If the sum is less than 95, conditions are tolerable for those unacclimatized to the tropics.

comfrey tall perennial *Symphytum officinale*, family Boraginaceae. Up to 1.2 m/4 ft tall, it has hairy, winged stems, lanceolate (tapering) leaves, and white, yellowish, purple, or pink bell-shaped flowers in drooping clusters.

Comfrey was once an important medicinal plant for treating wounds and various ailments, and is still sometimes used as a poultice. It is found throughout Europe and in W Asia.

comic book publication in strip-cartoon form. Most comics are aimed at children, although artistically sophisticated adult comics are produced in Japan and several European countries, notably France, and developed in the 1980s into the **graphic novel**.

Comic books grew from comic strips in newspapers or, like those of Walt ◊Disney, as spinoffs from animated cartoon films. The first superhero, Superman, created 1938 by Jerome Siegel and Joseph Shuster, soon had his own periodical, and others followed; the Marvel Comics group, formed 1961, was selling 50 million copies a year worldwide by the end of the 1960s and found a cult readership among college students for titles like *Spiderman* and *The Incredible Hulk*. In Japan 1.9 billion comics were sold in 1987 – a third of all publications there.

British children's comics such as the *Beano* and *Dandy* are unsophisticated in style and content; for teenagers, *Viz* follows a similar slapstick formula, while *Crisis* promotes political awareness.

comic strip or **strip cartoon** a sequence of several frames of drawings in ◊cartoon style. Strips may work independently or form instalments of a serial, and are usually humorous or satirical in content. Longer stories in comic-strip form are published separately as comic books. The first modern comic strip was 'The Yellow Kid' by Richard Felton Outcault, which appeared in the Sunday newspaper *New York World* 1896; it was immediately successful and others soon followed. One of the most admired comic strips has been the US 'Krazy Kat', which began 1910 and ended with the death of its creator, Richard Herriman, in 1944. Current strip cartoons include the US 'Peanuts' by Charles M Schulz (1922–), which began 1950 and was read daily by 60 million people by the end of the 1960s, and the political 'Doonesbury' by Gary Trudeau; the British 'Andy Capp' by Reginald Smythe (1917–); and the French 'Asterix' by Albert Uderzo and René Goscinny, which began in the early 1960s.

Comines /kɒˈmiːn/ Philippe de *c.*1445–1509. French diplomat in the service of Charles the Bold, Louis XI, and Charles VIII; author of *Mémoires* 1489–98.

Cominform *Com*munist *Inform*ation Bureau 1947–56, established by the Soviet politician Andrei Zhdanov (1896–1948) to exchange information between European communist parties. Yugoslavia was expelled 1948.

Comintern abbreviation of ◊*Com*munist *Intern*ational.

comma a punctuation mark (,), intended to provide breaks or pauses inside a sentence; commas may come at the end of a clause, after a phrase, or in lists (for example, apples, pears, plums, and pineapples).

Many occasional writers, uncertain where sentences properly end, use a comma instead of a period (or full stop), writing *We saw John last night, it was good to see him again*, rather than *We saw John last night. It was good to see him again*. The meaning is entirely clear in both cases. One solution in such situations is to use a **semicolon** (;), which combines period and comma and bridges the gap between the close association of the comma and the sharp separation of the period. See also ◊parenthesis.

command language in computing, a set of commands and the rules governing their use by which users control a program. For example, an ◊operating system may have commands such as SAVE and DELETE, or a payroll program may have commands for adding and amending staff records.

commando member of a specially trained, highly mobile military unit. The term originated in South Africa, where it referred to Boer military reprisal raids against Africans in the nineteenth century and, in the South African Wars, against the British. Commando units have often carried out operations behind enemy lines.

In Britain, the first commando units were the British Combined Operations Command who raided enemy-occupied territory in World War II after the evacuation of Dunkirk 1940. Among the Commando raids were those on the Lofoten Islands (3–4 Mar 1941), Vaagsö, Norway (27 Dec 1941), St Nazaire (28 Mar 1942), and Dieppe (19 Aug 1942). In 1940 Commandos were sent to the Middle East. One of their most daring exploits was the raid Nov 1941 on Rommel's HQ in the desert. At the end of the war the army Commandos were disbanded, but the role was carried on by the Royal Marines.

commedia dell'arte popular form of Italian improvised drama in the 16th and 17th centuries, performed by trained troupes of actors and involving stock characters and situations. It exerted considerable influence on writers such as Molière and Goldoni, and on the genres of ◊pantomime, harlequinade, and the ◊Punch and Judy show. It laid the foundation for a tradition of mime, particularly in France, that has continued with the contemporary mime of Jean-Louis Barrault and Marcel Marceau.

comme il faut (French 'as it should be') socially correct and acceptable.

commensalism a relationship between two ◊species whereby one (the commensal) benefits from the association, whereas the other neither benefits nor suffers. For example, certain species of millipede and silverfish inhabit the nests of army ants and live by scavenging on the refuse of their hosts, but without affecting the ants.

Commissioner for Oaths in England, a person appointed by the Lord Chancellor with power to administer oaths or take affidavits. All practising solicitors have these powers.

committal proceedings in the UK, a preliminary hearing in a magistrate's court to decide whether there is a case to answer before a higher court. From 1967 the proceedings were unreported unless a defendant, or one of them, wished the restriction lifted.

Committee of Imperial Defence an informal group established 1902 to coordinate planning of the British Empire's defence forces. Initially meeting on a temporary basis, it was established permanently in 1904. Members were usually cabinet ministers

concerned with defence, military leaders, and key civil servants. The committee was influential but had no executive power. It was taken over by the War Council in wartime.

commodity something produced for sale. Commodities may be **consumer goods**, such as radios, or **producer goods**, such as copper bars. **Commodity markets** deal in raw or semi-raw materials that are amenable to grading and that can be stored for considerable periods without deterioration.

Commodity markets developed to their present form in the 19th century, when industrial growth facilitated trading in large, standardized quantities of raw materials. Most markets encompass trading in 'commodity futures', that is trading for delivery several months ahead. Major commodity markets exist in Chicago, Tokyo, London, and elsewhere. Though specialized markets exist, such as that for silkworm cocoons in Tokyo, most trade relates to cereals and metals. 'Softs' is a term used for most materials other than metals.

Commodus /ˈkɒmədəs/ Lucius Aelius Aurelius AD 161–192. Roman emperor from 180, son of Marcus Aurelius Antoninus. He was a tyrant, spending lavishly on gladiatorial combats, confiscating the property of the wealthy, persecuting the Senate, and renaming Rome 'Colonia Commodia'. There were many attempts against his life, and he was finally strangled at the instigation of his mistress and advisors, who had discovered themselves on the emperor's death list.

common in the UK, unenclosed wasteland and pasture used in common by the inhabitants of a parish or district or the community at large. Commons originated in the Middle Ages, when every manor had a large area of unenclosed, uncultivated land over which freeholders had rights to take the natural produce. All common land (such as village greens) must now be registered under the Commons Registration Act 1965; otherwise the rights of common are lost.

Common Agricultural Policy (CAP) system that allows the member countries of the European Community (EC) jointly to organize and control agricultural production within their boundaries.

The objectives of the CAP were outlined in the Treaty of Rome: to increase agricultural productivity, to provide a fair standard of living for farmers and their employees, to stabilize markets, and to assure the availability of supply at a price that was reasonable to the consumer. The policy, applied to most types of agricultural product, was evolved and introduced between 1962 and 1967, and has since been amended to take account of changing conditions and the entry of additional member states. At the heart of the CAP is a price support system based on setting a target price for a commodity, imposing a levy on cheaper imports, and intervening to buy produce at a predetermined level to maintain the stability of the internal market. When the CAP was devised, the six member states were net importers of most essential agricultural products, and the intervention mechanism was aimed at smoothing out occasional surpluses caused by an unusually productive season. Over the last decade since agricultural yields within the EC have increased greatly, so that huge surpluses of cereals and livestock have put the CAP under intense financial and political strain, and led to mounting pressure for reform.

common law that part of the English law not embodied in legislation. It consists of rules of law based on common custom and usage and on judicial decisions. English common law became the basis of law in the USA and many other English-speaking countries.

Common law developed after the Norman Conquest (1066) as the law common to the whole of England, rather than local law. As the court system became established (under Henry II), and judges' decisions became recorded in law reports, the doctrine of **precedent** developed. This means that, in deciding a particular case, the court must have regard to the principles of law laid down in earlier reported cases on the same, or similar points, though the law may be extended or varied if the facts of the particular case are sufficiently different. Hence, the common law (sometimes also called 'case law' or 'judge-made law') is important in keeping the law in harmony with the needs of the community, where no legislation is applicable or where the legislation requires interpretation.

A narrower meaning of common law is law embodied in decisions of the common law courts, as opposed to ◊equity, which was originally established by the judges of the Court of Chancery.

common logarithms another name for ◊logarithms to the base 10.

Common Market popular name for the ◊European Community (EC).

Common Prayer, Book of the service book of the Church of England, based largely on the Roman breviary. The first Book of Common Prayer in English was known as the First Prayer Book of Edward VI, published in 1549, and is the basis of the Book of Common Prayer still, although not exclusively, in use.

The Second Prayer Book of Edward VI appeared in 1552, but was withdrawn in 1553 on Mary's accession. In 1559 the Revised Prayer Book was issued, closely resembling that of 1549. This was suppressed by Parliament in 1645, but its use was restored in 1660 and a number of revisions were made. This is the officially authorized Book of Common Prayer, but an act of 1968 legalized alternative services, and the Worship and Doctrine Measure 1974 gave the church control of its worship and teaching. The church's Alternative Service Book 1980, in modern language, is also in use.

Commons, House of the lower but more powerful of the two parts of the British and Canadian ◊parliaments.

Commonwealth body politic founded on law for the common 'weal' or good. 17th-century political philosophers such as Thomas Hobbes and John Locke used the term to mean an organized political community. Specifically, it was applied to the Cromwellian regime 1649–1660.

Commonwealth conference any consultation between the prime ministers (or defence, finance, foreign, or other ministers) of the sovereign independent members of the Commonwealth. These are informal discussion meetings, and the implementation of policies is decided by individual governments.

Recent Commonwealth conferences have been Singapore 1971, the first outside the UK; Sydney 1978, the first regional meeting; Lusaka 1979, the first regular session in Africa; and Vancouver 1987. Colonial conferences were instituted 1887, also meeting 1894, 1897, and 1902. The 1907 conference resolved that imperial conferences be held every four years, and these met regularly until 1937 (the most notable being 1926, which defined the relationship of the self-governing members of the Commonwealth).

Commonwealth Day a public holiday in parts of the Commonwealth, celebrated on the second Monday in Mar (the official birthday of Elizabeth II). It was called *Empire Day* until 1958 and celebrated on 24 May (Queen Victoria's birthday) until 1966.

Commonwealth Development Corporation organization founded as the Colonial Development Corporation 1948 to aid the development of dependent Commonwealth territories; the change of name and extension of its activities to include those now independent were announced 1962.

Commonwealth Games multi-sport gathering of competitors from Commonwealth countries. Held every four years, the first meeting (known as the British Empire Games) was at Hamilton, Canada, Aug 1930.

Commonwealth, British

Country	Capital	(Area in 1,000 sq km)
IN AFRICA		
Botswana	Gaborone	(575)
British Indian Ocean Terr.	Victoria	(0.2)
Gambia	Banjul	(11)
Ghana	Accra	(239)
Kenya	Nairobi	(583)
Lesotho	Maseru	(30)
Malawi	Zomba	(117)
Mauritius	Port Louis	(2)
Nigeria	Lagos	(924)
St Helena	Jamestown	(0.1)
Seychelles	Victoria	(65)
Sierra Leone	Freetown	(73)
Swaziland	Mbabane	(17)
Tanzania	Dodoma	(943)
Uganda	Kampala	(236)
Zambia	Lusaka	(752)
Zimbabwe	Salisbury	(391)
IN THE AMERICAS		
Anguilla	The Valley	(0.09)
Antigua	St John's	(0.4)
Bahamas	Nassau	(14)
Barbados	Bridgetown	(0.4)
Belize	Belmopan	(23)
Bermuda	Hamilton	(0.05)
Brit. Virgin Is.	Road Town	(0.2)
Canada	Ottawa	(9,976)
Cayman Islands	Georgetown	(0.3)
Dominica	Roseau	(0.7)
Falkland Is.	Stanley	(12)
Grenada	St George's	(0.3)
Guyana	Georgetown	(210)
Jamaica	Kingston	(12)
Montserrat	Plymouth	(0.1)
St Christopher-Nevis	Basseterre Charlestown	(0.4)
St Lucia	Castries	(0.6)
St Vincent and the Grenadines	Kingstown	(0.2)
Trinidad and Tobago	Port of Spain	(0.5)
Turks and Caicos Is.	Grand Turk	(0.4)
IN THE ANTARCTIC		
Australian Antarctic Terr.		(5,403)
Brit. Antarctic Terr.		(390)
Falklands Is. Dependencies		(1.6)
(N.Z.) Ross Dependency		(453)

Country	Capital	(Area in 1,000 sq km)
IN ASIA		
Bangladesh	Dacca	(143)
Brunei	Bandar Seri Begawan	(6)
Cyprus	Nicosia	(9)
Hong Kong	Victoria	(1.2)
India	Delhi	(3,215)
Malaysia, Rep. of	Kuala Lumpur	(332)
Maldives	Malé	(0.3)
Singapore	Singapore	(0.6)
Sri Lanka	Colombo	(66)
IN AUSTRALASIA AND THE PACIFIC		
Australia	Canberra	(7,704)
Norfolk Island		(0.03)
Fiji	Suva	(18)
Kiribati	Tarawa	(0.7)
*Nauru		(0.02)
New Zealand	Wellington	(269)
Cook Islands		(0.2)
Niue Island		(0.3)
Tokelau Islands		(0.01)
Papua New Guinea	Port Moresby	(475)
Pitcairn		(0.005)
Solomon Islands	Honiara	(30)
Tonga	Nuku'alofa	(0.7)
*Tuvalu	Funafuti	(0.02)
Vanuatu	Vila	(15)
Western Samoa	Apia	(3)
IN EUROPE		
*United Kingdom		
England	London	(131)
Wales	Cardiff	(21)
Scotland	Edinburgh	(79)
N. Ireland	Belfast	(14)
Isle of Man	Douglas	(0.5)
Channel Islands		(0.2)
Gibraltar	Gibraltar	(0.006)
Malta	Valletta	(0.3)
TOTAL		(33,932)

*Special members

Commonwealth Games: venues

1930 Hamilton, Canada
1934 London, England
1938 Sydney, Australia
1950 Auckland, New Zealand
1954 Vancouver, Canada
1958 Cardiff, Wales
1962 Perth, Australia
1966 Kingston, Jamaica
1970 Edinburgh, Scotland
1974 Christchurch, New Zealand
1978 Edmonton, Canada
1982 Brisbane, Australia
1986 Edinburgh, Scotland
1990 Auckland, New Zealand

Commonwealth, the (British) voluntary association of 48 states that have been or still are ruled by Britain (see ◊British Empire). Independent states are full 'members of the Commonwealth', while dependent territories, such as colonies and protectorates, rank as 'Commonwealth countries'. Small self-governing countries, such as Nauru, may have special status. The Commonwealth is founded more on tradition and sentiment than political or economic factors. Queen Elizabeth II is the formal head, and its secretariat, headed from Oct 1989 by Nigerian Emeka Anyaoko as secretary-general, is based in London.

On 15 May 1917 Jan Smuts, representing South Africa in the imperial war cabinet of World War I, suggested that 'British commonwealth of nations' was the right title for the British Empire. The name was recognized in the Statute of Westminster 1931, but after World War II a growing sense of independent nationhood led to the simplification of the title to the Commonwealth.

commune a group of people or families living together, sharing resources and responsibilities.

Communes developed from early 17th-century religious communities such as the Rosicrucians and Muggletonians, to more radical groups such as the ◊Diggers 1649 and the ◊Quakers. Many groups moved to America to found communes, such as the Philadelphia Society (1680s) and the Shakers, which by 1800 had ten groups in North America. The Industrial Revolution saw a new wave of utopian communities associated with the ideas of Robert ◊Owen and François Fourier. Communes had a revival during the 1960s, when many small groups were founded. In 1970 it was estimated there were 2,000 communes in the USA, many of them based on a religious affiliation, but only 100 in England.

The term can also refer to the 11th-century to 12th-century association of ◊burghers in north and central Italy. The communes of many cities asserted their independence from the overlordship of either the holy roman emperor or the pope, only to fall under the domination of oligarchies or despots during the 13th and 14th centuries.

Commune, Paris two periods of government in France; see ◊Paris Commune.

communication in biology, the signalling of information by one organism to another, usually with the intention of altering the recipient's behaviour. Signals used in communication may be *visual* (such as a smile), *auditory* (for example, the whines or barks of a dog), *olfactory* (such as

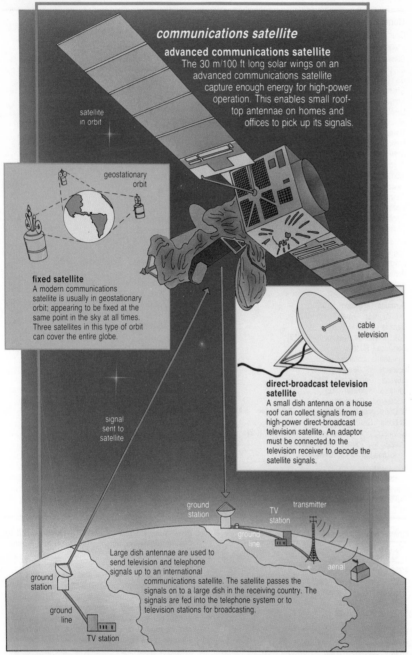

communications satellite

advanced communications satellite
The 30 m/100 ft long solar wings on an advanced communications satellite capture enough energy for high-power operation. This enables small rooftop antennae on homes and offices to pick up its signals.

satellite in orbit

geostationary orbit

fixed satellite
A modern communications satellite is usually in geostationary orbit; appearing to be fixed at the same point in the sky at all times. Three satellites in this type of orbit can cover the entire globe.

cable television

direct-broadcast television satellite
A small dish antenna on a house roof can collect signals from a high-power direct-broadcast television satellite. An adaptor must be connected to the television receiver to decode the satellite signals.

signal sent to satellite

ground station
TV station
transmitter
ground line
aerial

Large dish antennae are used to send television and telephone signals up to an international communications satellite. The satellite passes the signals on to a large dish in the receiving country. The signals are fed into the telephone system or to television stations for broadcasting.

ground station
ground line
TV station

the odours released by the scent glands of a deer), *electrical* (as in the pulses emitted by electric fish), or *tactile* (for example, the nuzzling of male and female elephants).

communications satellite a relay station in space for sending telephone, television, telex, and other messages around the world. Messages are sent to and from the satellites via ground stations. Most communications satellites are in ◊geostationary orbit, appearing to hang fixed over one point on the Earth's surface.

The first satellite to carry TV signals across the Atlantic Ocean was Telstar in July 1962. The world is now linked by a system of communications satellites called Intelsat. Other satellites are used by individual countries for internal communications, or for business or military use. A new generation of satellites, called *direct broadcast satellites*, are powerful enough to transmit direct to small domestic aerials. The power for such satellites is produced by solar panels made up of semiconductor material, usually silicon, which generate electricity when illuminated with sunlight. The

total energy requirement of a satellite is small; a typical communications satellite needs about 1.5 kw of power, the same as an electric fire.

Communion, Holy in the Christian church, another name for the ◊Eucharist.

communism (French *commun* 'common, general') revolutionary socialism based on the theories of the political philosophers Marx and Engels, emphasizing common ownership of the means of production and a planned economy. The first communist state was the USSR after the revolution of 1917. Revolutionary socialist parties and groups united to form communist parties in other countries (in the UK 1920). After World War II, communism was enforced in those countries that came under Soviet occupation. China emerged after 1961 as a rival to the USSR in world communist leadership, and other countries have adapted communism to their own needs. The late 1980s saw a movement for more individual freedoms in many communist countries, culminating in the abolition or overthrow of communist rule in some E European

countries, and further state repression in China.

Marx and Engels in the *Communist Manifesto* 1848 put forward the theory that human society, having passed through successive stages of slavery, feudalism, and capitalism, must advance to communism. This combines with a belief in economic determinism to form the central communist concept of *dialectical materialism*. Marx believed that capitalism had become a barrier to progress and needed to be replaced by a *dictatorship of the proletariat* (working class), which would build a socialist society.

The Social Democratic parties formed in Europe in the second half of the 19th century professed to be Marxist, but gradually began to aim at reforms of capitalist society rather than at the radical social change envisaged by Marx. The Russian Social Democratic Labour Party, led by Lenin, remained Marxist, and changed its name to Communist Party after the Nov 1917 Revolution to emphasize its difference from Social Democratic parties elsewhere. The communal basis of feudalism was still strong in Russia, and Lenin and Stalin were able to impose the communist system.

China's communist revolution was completed 1949 under Mao Zedong. Both China and the USSR took strong measures to maintain or establish their own types of 'orthodox' communism in countries on their borders (USSR in Hungary and Czechoslovakia, and China in North Korea and Vietnam), and in more remote areas (USSR in the Arab world and Cuba, and China in Albania), and (both of them) in the newly emergent African countries, as the fount of doctrine and source of technological aid.

In 1956 the Soviet premier Khrushchev denounced *Stalinism*, and there were uprisings in Hungary and Poland. During the late 1960s and the 1970s it was debated whether the state requires to be maintained as 'the dictatorship of the proletariat' once revolution on the economic front has been achieved, or whether it may then become the state of the entire people: Engels, Lenin, Khrushchev, and ◊Liu Shaoqi held the latter view; Stalin and Mao the former.

Many communist parties in capitalist countries, for example, Japan and the *Eurocommunism* of France, Italy, and the major part of the British Communist Party, have rejected Soviet dominance since the 1960s or later. In the 1980s there was an expansion of political and economic freedom in E Europe: the USSR remained a single-party state, but with a relaxation of strict party orthodoxy and a policy of *perestroika* ('restructuring'), while the other Warsaw Pact countries moved towards an end to communist rule and its replacement by free elections and an increasingly democratic political system.

In the Third World, Libya has attempted to combine revolutionary socialism with Islam; the extreme communist Khmer Rouge devastated Kampuchea 1975–78; Latin America suffers from the US fear of communism in what it regards as its back yard, with the democratically elected Marxist regime in Chile violently overthrown 1973, and the socialist government of Nicaragua (until it fell 1990) involved in a prolonged civil war against US-backed guerrillas.

Communism Peak (Russian *Pik Kommunizma*) highest mountain in the USSR, in the Pamir range in Tadzhikistan; 7,495 m/24,599 ft. It was known as Mount Garmo until 1933, and Mount Stalin 1933–62.

community in the social sciences, the sense of identity, purpose, and companionship that comes from belonging to a particular place, organization, or social group. The concept dominated sociological thinking in the first half of the 20th century, and inspired the academic discipline of *community studies*.

community in ecology, an assemblage of plants, animals and other organisms living within a circumscribed area. Communities are usually named by reference to a dominant feature such as a characteristic plant species (for example, beech wood community), or prominent physical feature (for example, a freshwater pond community).

community architecture movement enabling people to work directly with architects in the design and building of their own homes and neighbourhoods. It is an approach strongly encouraged by the Prince of Wales.

Community charge official name for the ◊poll tax.

community council in Wales, name for a ◊parish council.

community school/education the philosophy asserting that educational institutions are more effective if they involve all members of the surrounding community. It was pioneered by Henry Morris during his time as chief education officer for Cambridgeshire 1922–54.

community service scheme introduced in Britain by the Criminal Justice Act 1972, under which minor offenders are sentenced to spare-time work in the service of the community (aiding children, the elderly, or the handicapped), instead of prison. The offender must consent, be 16 or over, and have committed no violence.

commutative in mathematics, adjective any operation $*$ for which $a * b = b * a$. For example, addition is commutative $(4 + 2 = 2 + 4)$, but subtraction is not $(4 - 2 = 2,$ but $2 - 4 = -2)$.

commutator a device in a DC (direct current) electric motor that reverses the current flowing in the armature coils as the armature rotates. A DC generator, or ◊dynamo, uses a commutator to convert the AC (alternating current) generated in the armature coils into DC. A commutator consists of opposite pairs of conductors insulated from one another, and contact to an external circuit is provided by carbon or metal brushes.

Como /'kəʊməʊ/ city in Lombardy, Italy; on Lake Como at the foot of the Alps; population (1981) 95,500. Motor cycles, glass, silk, and furniture are produced here. The river Adda flows N–S through the lake, and the shores are famous for their beauty. Como has a marble cathedral, built 1396–1732, and is a tourist resort.

Comodoro Rivadavia /ˌkɒmə'dɔːˌriːvə 'dɑ:viə/ port in, Patagonia, SE Argentina; population (1984) 120,000. Argentina's main oilfields and natural gas are nearby.

Comorin /'kɒmərɪn/ the most southerly cape of the Indian sub-continent, in Tamil Nadu, where the Indian Ocean, Bay of Bengal and Arabian Sea meet.

Comoros /'kɒmərəʊz/ group of islands comprising Njazidja, Nzwani, and Mwali, situated in the Indian Ocean between Madagascar and the E coast of Africa. The fourth island in the group, Mayotte, is a French dependency.

government Under the 1978 constitution there is a president, elected by universal adult suffrage for a six-year term, with an appointed council of ministers and a single-chamber federal assembly of 42 members elected for five years. Although each of the four main islands has a degree of autonomy, with its own governor and council, the system is a limited form of federalism, since the president appoints the governors and the federal government is responsible for the islands' resources. The Comoros is officially Muslim, and since 1979 has been a one-party state although unofficial opposition groups exist.

history Originally inhabited by Asians, Africans, and Indonesians, The Comoros became a French colony in 1912 and were attached to Madagascar 1914–47, when they were made a French Overseas Territory. Internal self-government was obtained in 1961 but full independence was not achieved until 1975, because of Mayotte's reluctance to sever links with France. Although the Comoros joined the United Nations in 1975, with Ahmed Abdallah as president, Mayotte remained under French administration. Relations with France deteriorated as Ali Soilih, who had overthrown Abdallah, became more powerful as president

Comoros
Federal Islamic Republic of
(République fédérale islamique des Comores)

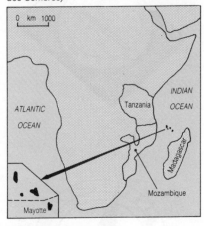

area 1,862 sq km/719 sq mi
capital Moroni
physical comprises the islands of Njazidja, Nzwani, and Mwali (formerly Grand Comoro, Anjouan, Maheli); poor soil
features active volcano on Njazidja
head of state and government vacant; interim military administration
political system authoritarian nationalism
political parties Comoran Union for Progress (Udzima), nationalist Islamic
exports copra, vanilla, cocoa, sisal, coffee, cloves, essential oils
currency CFA franc (485.00 = £1 Feb 1990)
population (1987) 423,000; annual growth rate 3.1%
life expectancy men 48, women 52
language Comorian (Swahili and Arabic dialect), Makua, French, Arabic (official)
religion Muslim (official)
literacy 15%
GNP $154 million (1982); $339 per head of population
chronology
1975 Independence achieved, but Mayotte remained part of France. Ahmed Abdallah elected president. The Comoros joined United Nations.
1976 Abdallah overthrown by Ali Soilih.
1978 Soilih killed by mercenaries working for Abdallah. Islamic republic proclaimed and Abdallah elected president.
1979 The Comoros became a one-party state. Powers of the federal government increased.
1985 Constitution amended to make Abdallah head of government as well as head of state.
1989 Abdallah killed by French mercenaries. Interim military government installed.

under a new constitution. In 1978 he was killed by French mercenaries working for Abdallah.

A federal Islamic republic was proclaimed, a new constitution adopted and Abdallah elected president. Diplomatic relations with France were restored. In 1979 the Comoros became a one-party state and government powers were increased. In the same year a plot to overthrow Abdallah was foiled. In 1984 he was re-elected president and in the following year the constitution was amended, abolishing the post of prime minister and making Abdallah head of government as well as head of state. Mayotte remains an uneasy member of the federation, with its future uncertain. In Nov 1989 Abdallah was killed during an attack on the presidential palace led by a French mercenary, Col Bob Denard. Denard was subsequently arrested by French army units and returned to France. A provisional military administration was set up.

compact disc a record disc, some 12 cm/4.5 in across, with up to an hour's playing time on one side. Entirely different from a conventional LP (gramophone) record, the compact disc is silvery in colour with a transparent plastic coating; the metal disc underneath is etched by a ◊laser beam with microscopic pits which carry a digital code representing the music. During playback, a laser beam reads the code and produces signals that are changed into near-exact replicas of the original sounds.

CD-ROM, or compact disc read-only memory, is used to store written text or pictures rather than music. The discs are ideal for large works, such as catalogues and encyclopedias. CD-I, or

compact disc

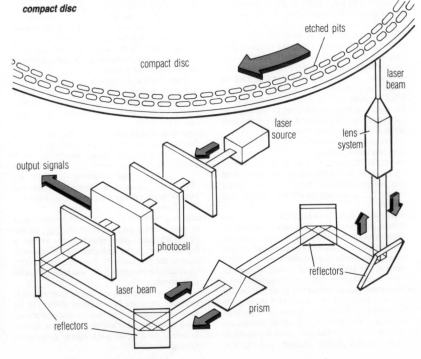

compact disc interactive, is a form of CD-ROM used with a computerized reader, which responds intelligently to the user's instructions. These discs are used, for example with audio-visual material, for training. Recordable CDs, called WORMs or 'write once read many times', are used as computer discs, but are as yet too expensive for home use. Erasable CDs, which can be erased and recorded many times, are also used by the computer industry. These are coated with a compound of cobalt and gadolinium, which alters the polarization of light falling on it. In the reader, the light reflected from the disc is passed through polarizing filters and the changes in polarization are converted into electrical signals.

Companion of Honour British order of chivalry, founded by George V 1917. It is of one class only, and carries no title, but Companions append 'CH' to their names. The number is limited to 65 and the award is made to both men and women.

company a number of people grouped together as a business enterprise. Types of company include public limited companies, partnerships, joint ventures, sole proprietorships, and branches of foreign companies. Most companies are private and, unlike public companies, cannot offer their shares to the general public.

For most companies in Britain the liability of the members is limited to the amount of their subscription, under an act of 1855 promoted by Judge Lord Bramwell. This brought British law into line with European practice, which had already been adopted in the USA. This *limitation of liability* is essential to commercial expansion when large capital sums must be raised by the contributions of many individuals. The affairs of companies are managed by directors, a public company having at least two, and their accounts must be audited.

The development of ◊multinational corporations, enterprises that operate in a number of countries, has been the cause of controversy in recent years because of the conflict of interest that occurs. This is particularly true of developing countries, where the presence of multinationals may cause distortions in the marketplace.

comparative advantage law of international trade first elaborated by David Ricardo showing that trade becomes advantageous if the cost of production of particular items differs between one country and another.

At a simple level, if wine is cheaper to produce in country A than in country B, and the reverse is true of cheese, A can specialize in wine and B in cheese and they can trade to mutual benefit.

compass an instrument for finding direction. The most commonly used is a magnetic compass, consisting of a thin piece of magnetic material with the north-seeking pole indicated, free to rotate on a pivot and mounted on a compass card on which the points of the compass are marked. When the compass is properly adjusted and used, the north-seeking pole will point to the magnetic north, from which true north can be found from tables of magnetic corrections.

Compasses not dependent on the magnet are gyrocompasses, dependent on the ◊gyroscope, and radiocompasses, dependent on the use of radio. These are unaffected by the presence of iron and by magnetic anomalies of the earth's magnetic field, and are widely used in ships and aircraft.

compensation point in biology, the point at which there is just enough light for a plant to survive. At this point all the food produced by ◊photosynthesis is used up by ◊respiration. For aquatic plants, the compensation point is the depth of water at which there is just enough light to sustain life (deeper water = less light = less photosynthesis).

competence and performance in linguistics, the potential and actual utterances of a speaker. As formulated by the linguist ◊Chomsky, a person's linguistic competence is the set of internalized rules in his or her brain that make it possible to understand and produce language–that stipulate,

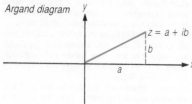
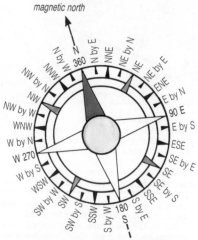

magnetic north

for example, in what order words can be put to form a sentence. A person's performance consists of the actual phrases and sentences he or she produces on the basis of these rules.

competition in ecology, the interaction between two or more organisms, or groups of organisms (for example, species), that use a common resource which is in short supply. Competition invariably results in a reduction in the numbers of one or both competitors, and has played an important role in ◊evolution, contributing both to the decline of certain species, and to the evolution of ◊adaptations.

competition, perfect in economics, a market situation in which there are many potential and actual buyers and sellers, each being too small to be an individual influence on the price; the market is open to all and the products being traded are homogeneous. At the same time, the producers are seeking the maximum profit and consumers the best value for money.

There are many economic, social, and political barriers to perfect competition, not least because the underlying assumptions are unrealistic and in conflict. Nevertheless some elements are important in free trade.

Compiègne /ˌkɒmpiˈeɪn/ town in Oise *département*, France, on the river Oise near its confluence with the river Aisne; population (1983) 37,250. It has an enormous chateau, built by Louis XV. The armistices of 1918 and 1940 were signed (the latter by Hitler and Pétain) in a railway coach in the forest of Compiègne.

compiler a computer program that translates other programs into a form in which they can be run by the computer. Most programs are written in high-level languages, designed for the convenience of the programmer. The compiler converts these into the ◊machine code, which the computer understands.

Different compilers are needed for different computer languages (and different dialects of the same language). In contrast to an ◊interpreter, using a compiler adds slightly to the time needed to develop the program but results in the program running faster.

complement in mathematical set theory, all the members of a 'universal set' that are not members of a particular set. A set and its complement add up to the whole.

complementary angle two angles are complimentary if they add up to 90°.

complementary numbers in number theory, the numbers obtained by subtracting a number from its base. For example, the complement of 7 in numbers to base ten is 3. Complementary numbers are important in computers, the only mathematical operation of which digital computers (including pocket calculators) are directly capable is addition. Two numbers can be subtracted by adding one number to its complement; two numbers can be divided by using successive subtraction (which, using complements, becomes successive addition); and multiplication can be performed by using successive addition.

complementation in genetics, the interaction that can occur between two different mutant forms of a gene in a ◊diploid organism, to make up for each other's deficiencies and allow the organism to function normally.

complex in psychology, a group of ideas and feelings which have become repressed because they are distasteful to the person in whose mind they arose but which are still active in the depths of the person's unconscious mind, continuing to affect his or her life and actions, even though he or she is no longer fully aware of their existence. Typical examples include the ◊Oedipus complex and the inferiority complex.

complex number in mathematics, a number written in the form $a + ib$, where a and b are ◊real numbers and i is the square root of –1 (that is, $i^2 = -1$); i used to be known as the imaginary part of the complex number. Some equations in algebra, such as those of the form $x^2 + 5 = 0$, cannot be solved without recourse to complex numbers, because the real numbers do not include square roots of negative numbers.

The sum of two or more complex numbers is obtained by adding separately their real and imaginary parts, for example,

$$(a + bi) + (c + di) = (a + c) + (b + d)i.$$

Complex numbers can be represented graphically on an Argand diagram, which uses rectangular ◊Cartesian coordinates in which the x-axis represents the real part of the number and the y-axis the imaginary part. Thus the number $z = a + bi$ is plotted as the point (a, b). Complex numbers have important applications in various areas of science, such as the theory of alternating currents in electricity.

compliance in the UK, abiding by the terms of the Financial Services Act 1986. Companies undertaking any form of investment business are regulated by the Act and must fulfil their obligations to investors under it, under four main headings: efficiency, competitiveness, confidence, and flexibility.

componential analysis in linguistics, the analysis of the elements of a word's meaning. The word *boy*, for example, might be said to have three basic meaning elements (or semantic properties): 'human', 'young,' and 'male'; and so might the word *murder*: 'kill', 'intentional', and 'illegal'.

components in mathematics, the vectors produced when a single vector is resolved into two or more parts. The components add up to the original vector.

Compositae the daisy family; dicotyledonous flowering plants characterized by flowers borne in composite heads. It is the largest family of flowering plants, the majority being herbaceous. Birds seem to favour the family for use in nest 'decoration', possibly because many species either repel or kill insects (see ◊pyrethrum). Species include the daisy and dandelion; food plants such as the artichoke, lettuce, and safflower; and the garden chrysanthemum, dahlia, daisybush, and zinnia.

composite in industry, a purpose-designed engineering material created by combining single materials with complementary properties into a composite form. Most composites have a structure in which one component consists of discrete elements such as fibres (for example, asbestos, glass or carbon steel in continuous or short lengths, or 'whiskers', specially grown crystals a few millimetres long, such as silicon carbide) dispersed in a continuous matrix, such as plastics, concrete or steel.

Composite in classical architecture, one of the five types of ◊column. See ◊order.

composite function in mathematics, a function made up of two or more other functions carried out in sequence, usually denoted by * or ○. (*f* * *g*) *x* = *f* [*g*(*x*)].

Usually, composition is not ◊commutative; (*f* * *g*) is not the same as (*g* * *f*).

compos mentis (Latin) of sound mind.

compost a mixture of ◊biodegradable vegetation, such as leaves, fruit, and manure, which breaks down as a result of the action of bacteria and fungi. Compost is used for agricultural purposes.

As the ◊decomposers feed, they raise the temperature in the centre of the compost as high as 66°C/150°F. Compost is used as a fertilizer or spread on the soil surface to prevent evaporation and ◊erosion and protect against frost. A compost heap provides food and shelter for a variety of animals.

compound chemical substance made up of two or more ◊elements bonded together, so that they cannot be separated by physical means. They may be made up of electrovalent or covalent bonds.

compound interest interest calculated by increasing the original capital by the amount of interest each time the interest becomes due. When simple interest is calculated, only the interest on the original capital is added.

comprehensive school in the UK, a secondary school which admits pupils of all abilities, and therefore without any academic selection procedure.

Most secondary education in the USA and the USSR has always been comprehensive, but most W European countries, including France and the UK, have switched to a selective to a comprehensive system within the last 20 years. In England, the 1960s and 1970s saw a slow but major reform of secondary education, in which the most state-funded local authorities replaced selective grammar schools (taking only the most academic 20% of children) and secondary modern schools (for the remainder), with comprehensive schools capable of providing suitable courses for children of all abilities. By 1985, only 3.2% of secondary pupils were still in grammar schools. Scotland and Wales have switched completely to comprehensive education, while Northern Ireland retains a largely selective system.

compressor a machine that compresses a gas, usually air, commonly used to power pneumatic tools, such as road drills, paint sprayers, and dentists', drills.

Reciprocating compressors use pistons moving in cylinders to compress the air. Rotary compressors use a varied rotor moving eccentrically inside a casing. The air compressor in jet and ◊gas turbine engines consists of a many-varied rotor rotating at high speed within a fixed casing, where the rotor blades slot between fixed, or stator blades on the casing.

computer

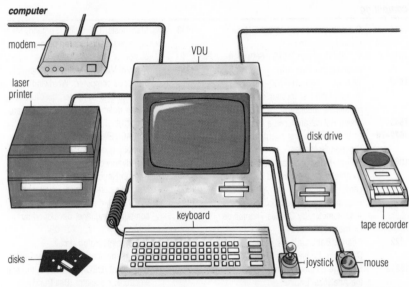

modem
laser printer
disks
VDU
disk drive
tape recorder
keyboard
joystick
mouse

Compromise of 1850 in US history, legislative proposals designed to resolve sectional conflict between north and south over the admission of California to the Union in 1850. Slavery was prohibited in California, but a new fugitive slave law was passed to pacify the slave states. The Senate debate on the compromise lasted nine months: acceptance temporarily revitalized the union.

Compton /'kɒmptən/ Arthur Holly 1892–1962. US physicist known for his work on X-rays. Working at Chicago 1923 he found that X-rays scattered by such light elements as carbon increased their wave lengths. Compton concluded from this unexpected result that the x-rays were displaying both wave-like and particle-like properties, since named the Compton effect. He shared the 1927 Nobel Physics prize with Charles ◊Wilson.

Compton originally studied at Princeton University, USA, but worked for a year with the physicists J J Thomson and Ernest Rutherford at Cambridge University, UK. His interests included philosophy and the relationship between science and religion.

Compton-Burnett /'kʌmptən 'bɜːnɪt/ Ivy 1892–1969. English novelist. She used dialogue to show reactions of small groups of characters dominated by the tyranny of family relationships. Her novels, set at the turn of the century, include *Pastors and Masters* 1925, *More Women than Men* 1933, *Mother and Son* 1955.

compulsory purchase in the UK the right of the state and authorized bodies to buy land required for public purposes even against the wishes of the owner. Under the Land Compensation Act 1973, fair recompense is payable.

computer a programmable electronic device that processes data and performs calculations and other symbol manipulation tasks. There are three types: the ◊*digital computer*, which manipulates information coded as ◊binary numbers, the ◊*analogue computer*, which works with continuously varying quantities, and the *hybrid computer*, which has characteristics of both analogue and digital computers.

There are four sizes of digital computer, corresponding roughly to their memory capacity and processing speed. *Microcomputers* are the smallest and most common, used in small businesses, at home, and in schools. They are usually single-user machines. *Minicomputers* are found in medium-sized businesses and university departments. They may support from a dozen to 30 or so users at once. *Mainframes*, which can often service several hundreds of users simultaneously, are found in large organizations such as national companies and government departments. *Supercomputers* are mostly used for highly complex scientific tasks, such as analysing the results of nuclear physics experiments and weather forecasting.

history Computers are only one of the many kinds of ◊computing device. The first mechanical computer was conceived by Charles ◊Babbage in 1835, but it never went beyond the design stage. In 1943, more than a century later, Thomas Flowers built Colossus, the first electronic computer. Working with him at the time was Alan Turing, a mathematician who seven years earlier had published a paper on the theory of computing machines that had a major impact on subsequent developments. John von Neumann's computer, EDVAC, built in 1949, was the first to use binary arithmetic and to store its operating instructions internally. This design still forms the basis of today's computers.

basic components At the heart of a computer is the ◊CPU (central processing unit), which performs all the computations. This is supported by memory, which holds the current program and data, and 'logic arrays', which help move information around the system. A main power supply is needed and, for a mini or mainframe computer, a cooling system. The computer's 'device driver' circuits control the ◊peripheral devices that can be attached. These will normally be keyboards and ◊VDU screens for user input and output, disc-drive units for mass memory storage, and printers for printed output.

computer game or *video game* a computer-controlled game in which the computer (usually) opposes the human player. They typically employ fast, animated graphics on a ◊VDU (screen) and synthesized sound.

Commercial computer games became possible with the advent of the ◊microprocessor in the mid-1970s and rapidly became popular as arcade games.

computer generations the classification of computers into five broad groups: first generation (the earliest computers, developed in the 1940s and 1950s, made from valves and wire circuits); second generation (from the early 1960s, based on transistors and printed circuits); third generation (from the late 1960s, using integrated circuits, and often sold as families of computers, such as the IBM 360 series); fourth generation (using ◊microprocessors and large-scale integration, still in current use); and fifth generation (based on parallel processors and very large-scale integration, currently under development).

computing

1614	Scottish mathematician John Napier invented logarithms.	**1948**	Manchester University (England) Mark I completed: first stored-program computer.
1615	William Oughtred (1575–1660) invented the slide rule.	**1951**	Ferranti Mark I: the first commercially produced computer; 'Whirlwind', the first real-time computer, built for the US air-defence system; investigation of transistor.
1623	Wilhelm Schickard (1592–1635) invented the first mechanical calculating machine.		
1645	Blaise Pascal produced a calculator.		
1672–74	Leibniz built his first calculator, the Stepped Reckoner.	**1952**	EDVAC (Electronic Discrete Variable Computer) completed at the Institute for Advanced Study, Princeton, USA (by von Neumann and others).
1801	Joseph-Marie Jacquard developed an automatic loom controlled by punched cards.		
		1953	Magnetic core memory developed.
1820	First mass-produced calculator (the Arithmometer, by Charles Thomas de Colmar 1785–1870).	**1957**	FORTRAN, the first high-level computer language, developed by IBM.
1822	Charles Babbage's first model for the Difference Engine.	**1958**	The first integrated circuit.
1830s	Babbage created the first design for the Analytical Engine.	**1963**	The first minicomputer built by Digital Equipment (DEC); the PDP-8; the first electronic calculator (Bell Punch Company).
1890	Herman Hollerith developed the punched card ruler for the US census.		
1936	Alan Turing published the mathematical theory of computing.	**1964**	IBM System/360: the first compatible family of computers.
1938	Konrad Zuse constructed the first binary calculator, using Boolean algebra.	**1965**	The first supercomputer: the Control Data CD6600.
		1970	The first microprocessor: the Intel 4004.
1943	'Colossus' electronic code-breaker developed at Bletchley Park, England; Harvard University Mark I or Automatic Sequence-Controlled Calculator (partly financed by IBM): the first program-controlled calculator.	**1974**	CLIP–4, the first computer with a parallel architecture.
		1975	The first personal computer: Altair 8800.
		1981	The Xerox Start system, the first WIMP system (Windows, Icons, Menus and Pointing devices).
1945	ENIAC (Electronic Numerator, Integrator, Analyser, and Computer) completed at the University of Pennsylvania.	**1985**	The Inmos T414 Transputer, the first 'off the shelf' RISC microprocessor for building parallel computers.

computer graphics the techniques involved in creating images by computer. These are widely used in the film and television industries for producing animated charts and diagrams.

computer literacy the ability to understand and make use of computer technology in an everyday context.

computer numerical control the control of machine tools, most often milling machines, by a computer. The pattern of work for the machine to follow, which often involves performing repeated sequences of actions, is described using a special-purpose programming language.

computer simulation representation of a real-life situation in a computer program. For example, the program might simulate the flow of customers arriving at a bank. the user can alter variables, such as the number of cashiers on duty, and see the effect.

computer terminal see ◊terminal.

computer memory

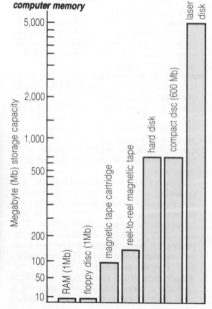

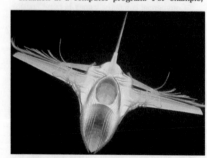

computer graphics A computer graphics image of air flow over an F-16 jet fighter aircraft produced on a Cray supercomputer.

computing device any device built to perform or help perform computations, such as the ◊abacus, ◊slide rule, or ◊computer.

Probably the earliest known example is the abacus. Mechanical devices with sliding scales (similar to the slide rule) date back to ancient Greece. In 1642, the French mathematician Pascal built a mechanical adding machine, and in 1671 the German philosopher Leibniz produced a machine to perform multiplication. The first mechanical computer, the ◊analytical engine, was designed by Charles Babbage in 1835. For the subsequent history of computing see ◊computer.

Comte /kɒmt/ Auguste 1798–1857. French philosopher, regarded as the founder of sociology, a term he coined 1830. He sought to establish sociology as an intellectual and 'scientific' discipline, using ◊positivism as the basis of a new science of social order and social development.

Comte, born in Montpellier, was expelled from the Paris Ecole Polytechnique for leading a student revolt in 1816. In 1818 he became secretary to the socialist Saint-Simon and was much influenced by him. He began lecturing on the 'Positive Philosophy' in 1826, but almost immediately succumbed to a nervous disorder and once tried to commit suicide in the Seine. On his recovery he resumed his lectures and mathematical teaching.

In his six-volume *Cours de philosophie positive* 1830–42 he argued that human thought and social development evolve through three stages: the theological, the metaphysical, and the positive or scientific. He divided human knowledge into a hierarchy, with sociology at the top of the academic pyramid. Positivism offered a method of logical analysis and provided an ethical and moral basis for predicting and evaluating social progress. Though he originally sought to proclaim society's evolution to a new golden age of science, industry, and rational morality, his radical ideas were increasingly tempered by the political and social upheavals of his time.

Conakry /ˌkɒnəˈkriː/ capital and chief port of the Republic of Guinea; population (1980) 763,000. It is on the island of Tumbo, linked with the mainland by a causeway and by rail with Kankan, 480 km/300 mi NE. Bauxite and iron ore are mined nearby.

concave lens a converging ◊lens – that is, a parallel beam of light gets wider as it passes through such a lens. A concave lens is thinner at its centre than at the edges.

Common forms include *biconcave* (with both surfaces curved inwards) and *plano-concave* (with one flat surface and one concave). The whole lens may be further curved overall (making a *convexo-concave* or diverging meniscus lens, as in some spectacle lenses).

concentration in chemistry, how much of a substance (◊solute) is present in a specified amount of a solution. Either amount may be specified as a mass or a volume (liquids only). Common units used are ◊moles per cubic decimetre, grams per cubic decimetre, grams per 100 cubic centimetres, or grams per 100 grams. It also refers to the process of increasing the concentration of a solution by removal of some of the substance in which the solute is dissolved (◊solvent).

concentration camp a prison camp devised by the British during the Boer War in South Africa 1899 for the detention of Afrikaner women and children. The system of concentration camps was developed by the Nazis in Germany and occupied Europe to imprison political and ideological opponents after Hitler became chancellor Jan 1933. Several hundred camps were established in Germany and occupied Europe, the most infamous being the extermination camps of Auschwitz, Belsen, Maidanek, Sobibor, and Treblinka. The total number of people murdered at the camps may have exceeded four million, and some inmates were subjected to medical experimentation before being killed.

At Oswiecim (Auschwitz), a vast camp complex was created for imprisonment and slave labour as

concentration camp Auschwitz: the most infamous Nazi concentration camp, liberated by the American 7th Army, 3 May 1945.

well as extermination. At Maidanek, about 1.5 million people were exterminated, cremated, and their ashes used as fertilizer. Many camp officials and others responsible were tried after 1945 for war crimes, and executed or imprisoned. Foremost was Adolf ◊Eichmann, the architect of the extermination system, who was tried and executed by the state of Israel in 1961.

concentric circles two or more circles that share the same centre.

Concepción /ˌkɒnseps'jɒn/ city in Chile, near the mouth of the river Bió-Bió; population (1987) 294,000. It is capital of the province of Concepción. It is in a rich agricultural district, and is also an industrial centre for coal, steel, paper, and textiles.

conceptacle flask-shaped cavities found in the swollen tips of certain brown seaweeds, notably the wracks, *Fucus*. The gametes are formed within them and released into the water via a small pore in the conceptacle, known as an ostiole.

concertina a portable reed organ related to the ◊accordion but smaller in size and rounder in shape, with buttons for keys. It was invented in England in the 19th century.

concert master in music, the leader of an orchestra, usually the principal violinist.

concerto composition, usually in three movements, for solo instrument (or instruments) and orchestra. It developed during the 18th century from the *concerto grosso* form for string orchestra, in which a group of solo instruments is contrasted with a full orchestra.

Corelli and Torelli were early concerto composers, followed by Vivaldi, Handel, and Bach (*Brandenburg concertos*). Mozart wrote about 40 concertos, mostly for piano. Recent concerto composers include Gershwin, Korngold, Schoenberg, Berg, and Bartók, who have developed the form along new lines.

Conchobar in Celtic mythology, king of Ulster whose intended bride, Deirdre, eloped with Noísi. She died of sorrow when Conchobar killed her husband and his brothers.

concilliar movement the 15th-century attempt to urge the supremacy of church councils over the popes, particularly with regard to the ◊Great Schism, and the reformation of the church.

Councils were held in Pisa 1409, Constance 1414–18, Pavia-Siena 1423–24, Basle 1431–49, and Ferrara-Florence-Rome 1438–47. After ending the Schism in 1417 with the removal of John XXIII (1410–15), Gregory XII (1406–15), and Benedict XIII (1394–1423), and the election of Martin V (1417–31), the movement fell into disunity over questions of reform, allowing Eugenius IV (1431–47) to use Ferrara-Florence-Rome to reasssert papal supremacy.

conclave (Latin 'a room locked with a key') A secret meeting, in particular the gathering of cardinals in Rome to elect a new pope. They are locked away in the Vatican Palace until they have reached a decision. The result of each ballot is announced by a smoke signal–black for

an indecisive vote and white when the choice is made.

Wooden cells are erected near the Sistine Chapel, one for each cardinal, accompanied by his secretary and a servant, and all are sworn to secrecy. This section of the palace is then locked and no communication with the outside world is allowed until a new pope is elected.

Concord /'kɒŋkəd/ town in Massachusetts, USA; population (1980) 16,300. Site of the first battle of the War of American Independence, 19 Apr 1775. The writers Ralph Emerson, Henry Thoreau, Nathaniel Hawthorne, and Louisa Alcott lived here.

concordance book containing an alphabetical list of the words in some important work with references to the places in which they occur. The first concordance was one prepared to the Vulgate by a Dominican in the 13th century.

The most famous is A Cruden's concordance of the Bible 1737, of which many editions have appeared. There are also concordances to Shakespeare, Milton, and other writers.

concordat agreement regulating relations between the papacy and a secular government, for example, that for France between Pius VII and the emperor Napoleon, which lasted 1801–1905; Mussolini's concordat, which lasted 1929–78 and safeguarded the position of the church in Italy; and one of 1984 in Italy in which Roman Catholicism ceased to be the Italian state religion.

Concorde the only successful ◊supersonic airliner, which cruises at Mach 2, or twice the speed of sound, about 2,170 kph/1,350 mph. Concorde, the result of Anglo-French cooperation, made its first flight 1969, and entered commercial service seven years later. It is 62 m/202 ft long and has a wing span of nearly 26 m/84 ft.

concrete a building material composed of cement, stone, sand, and water. It has been used since Roman and Egyptian times. During the 20th century, it has been increasingly employed as an economic alternative to more traditional materials.

c.5600 BC Earliest discovered use of concrete at Lepenski Vir, Yugoslavia (hut floors in Stone Age village).

2500 BC Concrete used in Great Pyramid at Giza by Egyptians.

2nd century BC Romans accidentally discovered the use of lime and silican/alumina to produce 'pozzolanic' cement.

AD127 Lightweight concrete (using crushed pumice as aggregate) used for walls of Pantheon, Rome.

medieval times Concrete used for castles (infill in walls) and cathedrals (largely foundation work).

1756 John Smeaton produced the first high quality cement since Roman times (for rebuilding of Eddystone lighthouse).

1824 Joseph Aspdin of Wakefield patented Portland cement (so called because of its resemblance to Portland stone in colour).

1854 William Wilkinson patented reinforced concrete—first successful use in a building.

1880s First continuous-process rotary cement kiln installed (reducing costs of manufacturing cement).

Concorde The British-built Concorde 002 takes off for the first time, from Filton, near Bristol, Apr 1969.

1898 François Hennébique: first multi-storey reinforced concrete building in Britain (factory in Swansea).

1926 Eugène Freysinnet began experiments on pre-stressed concrete in France.

1960s Widespread use of concrete in Britain as an economical house-building material instead of traditional materials.

1980s Move away from concrete as a substitute for brick or stone in house-building due to its comparatively short lifespan.

concrete music (French *musique concrète*) music created by reworking natural sounds recorded on disc or tape, developed in 1948 by Pierre Schaeffer and Pierre Henry in the drama studios of Paris Radio. *Concrete sound* is pre-recorded natural sound used in electronic music, as distinct from purely synthesized tones or noises.

concurrent two or more lines passing through a single point, for example the diameters of a circle are all concurrent at the centre of the circle.

concussion temporary unconsciousness resulting from a blow to the head.

Condé /kɒn'deɪ/ Louis de Bourbon, Prince of Condé 1530–1569. A prominent French ◊Huguenot leader, founder of the house of Condé and uncle of Henry IV of France. He distinguished himself in the wars between Henry II and the Holy Roman emperor Charles V, particularly in the defence of Metz.

Condé /kɒn'deɪ/ Louis II 1621–1686. Prince of Condé called the *Great Condé*. French commander, who won brilliant victories during the Thirty Years' War at Rocroi 1643 and Lens 1648, but rebelled 1651 and entered the Spanish service. Pardoned 1660, he commanded Louis XIV's armies against the Spanish and the Dutch.

condensation the conversion of a vapour to a liquid as it loses heat. This is frequently achieved by letting the vapour come into contact with a cold surface.

condensation in chemistry, a reaction in which two organic compounds combine to form a larger molecule, accompanied by the removal of a smaller molecule (usually water).

condensation number in physics, the ratio of the number of molecules condensing on a surface to the total number of molecules touching that surface.

condenser in optics, a short focal-length convex ◊lens or combination of lenses used for concentrating a light source on to a small area, as used in a slide projector or microscope sub-stage lighting unit. A condenser can also be made using a concave mirror.

Conder /'kɒndə/ Charles 1868–1909. English artist, who painted in watercolour and oil, and executed a number of lithographs including the *Balzac* 1899 and the *Carnival* sets 1905.

Condillac /ˌkɒndi:'æk/ Étienne Bonnot de 1715–1780. French philosopher. He mainly followed ◊Locke, but his *Traité de sensations* 1754 claims that all mental activity stems from the transformation of sensations. He was a collaborator in the French ◊Encyclopédie. Born in Grenoble of noble parentage, he entered the Church and was appointed tutor to Louis XV's grandson, the Duke of Parma.

conditioning in psychology, two major principles of behaviour modification. In *classical conditioning*, described by Pavlov, a new stimulus can evoke an automatic response by being repeatedly associated with a stimulus that naturally provokes a response. For example, a bell repeatedly associated with food will eventually trigger salivation, even if presented without food. In *operant conditioning*, described by Thorndike and Skinner, the frequency of a voluntary response can be increased by following it with a reinforcer or reward.

condom or *sheath*, is a barrier contraceptive, made of rubber, which fits over an erect penis and holds in the sperm produced by ejaculation. It is an effective means of preventing pregnancy

California condor

if used carefully, preferably with a ◊spermicide. A condom with spermicide is 97% effective, one without spermicide is 85% effective.

condominium the joint rule of a territory by two or more states, for example, Canton and Enderbury islands, in the South Pacific Phoenix group (under the joint control of Britain and the USA for 50 years from 1939). The term has also come into use in North America to describe a type of joint property ownership of, for example, a block of flats.

condor a large flying bird *Vultur gryphus*, a South American ◊vulture, with wingspan up to 3 m/10 ft, weight up to 13 kg/28 lb, and length up to 1.2 m/3.8 ft. It is black, with some white on the wings and a white frill at the base of the neck. It lives in the Andes and along the South American coast, and feeds on carrion.

The *Californian condor Gymnogyps californianus* is a similar bird, and on the verge of extinction. It only lays one egg at a time and may not breed every year. It is the subject of a special conservation effort.

Condorcet /ˌkɒndɔːˈseɪ/ Marie Jean Antoine Nicolas Caritat, Marquis de Condorcet 1743–1794. French philosopher and politician, associated with the ◊Encyclopédistes. One of the ◊Girondins, he opposed the execution of Louis XVI, and was imprisoned and poisoned himself. His *Esquisse d'un tableau des progrès de l'esprit humain/Historical Survey of the Progress of Human Understanding* 1795 envisaged inevitable future progress, though not the perfectibility of human nature.

conductance the ability of a material to carry an electrical current, usually given the symbol G. For a direct current, it is the reciprocal of resistance: a conductor of resistance R has a conductance of $1/R$. For an alternating current, conductance is the resistance (R) divided by the impedence Z: $G = R/Z$. Conductance was formerly expressed in reciprocal ohms (or mhos); the modern SI unit is the Siemens.

conductor in physics, a material that conducts heat or electricity (as opposed to a non-conductor or insulator). A good conductor has a high electrical or thermal conductivity, generally a substance rich in free electrons such as a metal. A poor conductor (such as the non-metals glass and porcelain) has few free electrons. Carbon is exceptional in being non-metallic and yet (in some of its forms) a relatively good conductor of heat and electricity. Substances such as silicon and germanium, with intermediate conductivities, are known as *semiconductors*.

conductor in music, the member of an orchestra who beats time and controls the overall expression and balance of sound.

cone in geometry, a solid or surface generated by rotating an isosceles triangle or framework about its line of symmetry. It can also be formed by the set of all straight lines passing through a fixed point and the points of a circle or ellipse whose plane does not contain the point.

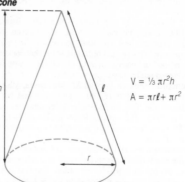

cone

$$V = \tfrac{1}{3}\pi r^2 h$$
$$A = \pi r \ell + \pi r^2$$

A circular cone of perpendicular height h and base of radius r has a volume $v = \tfrac{1}{3}\pi r^2 h$. The distance from the edge of the base of a cone to the vertex is called the slant height. In a right circular cone of slant height l, the curved surface area is $\pi r l$, and the area of the base is πr^2. Therefore the total surface area $A = \pi r l + \pi r^2 = \pi r(l + r)$.

cone in botany, the reproductive structure of the conifers, and cycads, also known as a ◊strobilus. It consists of a central axis surrounded by numerous, overlapping, scale-like sporophylls, modified leaves which bear the reproductive organs. Usually there are separate male and female cones, the former bearing pollen sacs containing pollen grains, and the larger female cones bearing the ovules which contain the ova or egg cells. The pollen is carried from male to female cones by wind (◊anemophily). The seeds develop within the female cone, and are released as the scales open in dry atmospheric conditions, which favour seed dispersal.

In some groups (for example, the pines) the cones take two or even three years to reach this stage. The cones of ◊junipers have fleshy cone scales that fuse to form a berry-like structure. One group of ◊angiosperms, the alders, also bear cone-like structures; these are the woody remains of the short female catkins, and they contain the alder ◊fruits.

Coney Island /ˈkəʊni/ seaside resort on a peninsula in the south west of Long Island, New York, USA. It has been popular for its amusement parks since the 1840s.

Confederacy in US history, popular name for the *Confederate States of America*, the government established by the Southern US states Feb 1861 when they seceded from the Union, precipitating the ◊Civil War. Richmond, Virginia, was the capital, and Jefferson Davis the president. The Confederacy fell after its army was defeated 1865 and Gen Robert E Lee surrendered.

Confederation, Articles of in US history, the means by which the 13 former British colonies created a form of national government. Ratified in 1781, the Articles established a unicameral legislature, Congress, with limited powers of raising revenue, regulating currency, and conducting foreign affairs, but the individual states retained significant autonomy. Superseded by the US Constitution in 1788.

Confederation of British Industry (CBI) UK organization of employers, established 1965, combining the former Federation of British Industries (founded 1916), British Employers' Confederation, and National Association of British Manufacturers.

conference system a system of international conferences in the 19th century promoted principally by the German chancellor Bismarck to ease the integration of a new powerful German state into the 'concert of Europe'.

The conferences were intended to settle great power disputes, mainly related to the Balkans, the Middle East, and the designation of colonies in Africa and Asia. Most important of these was the Congress of ◊Berlin 1878. The system fell into disuse with the retirement of Bismarck and the pressures of new European alliance blocks.

confession a religious practice, the confession of sins, practised in Roman Catholic, Orthodox, and most Oriental Christian churches and since the early 19th century revived in Anglican and Lutheran churches. The Lateran Council of 1215 made auricular confession (self-accusation by the penitent to a priest, who in Catholic doctrine is divinely invested with authority to give absolution) obligatory once a year.

Both John the Baptist's converts and the early Christian church practised public confession. The Roman Catholic penitent in modern times has always confessed alone to the priest in a confessional box, but from 1977 such individual confession might be preceded by group discussion, or the confession itself might be made openly by members of the group.

Confindustria a General Confederation of Industry established in Italy 1920 with the aim of countering working-class agitation. It contributed large funds to the fascist movement which, in turn, used its *squadristi* against the workers. After Mussolini's takeover of power in 1922, Confindustria became one of the major groups of the fascist corporative state.

confirmation rite practised by a number of Christian denominations, including Roman Catholic, Anglican, and Orthodox, in which a previously baptized person is admitted to full membership of the church. In Reform Judaism there is often a confirmation service several years after the bar or bat mitzvah (initiation into the congregation).

Christian confirmation is believed to give the participant the gift of the Holy Spirit. In the Anglican church it consists in the laying on of hands by a bishop, while in the Roman Catholic and Orthodox churches the participant is anointed with oil. Except in the Orthodox churches, where infant confirmation is usual, the rite takes place around early adolescence. Until recently a child preparing for confirmation was required to learn by heart a series of questions and answers known as a catechism.

Confucianism the body of beliefs and practices that are based on the Chinese classics and supported by the authority of the philosopher Confucius (Kong Zi). For about 2,500 years most of the Chinese people have derived from Confucianism their ideas of cosmology, political government, social organization, and individual conduct. Human relationships follow the patriarchal pattern. The origin of things is seen in the union of *yin* and *yang*, the passive and active principles.

The writings on which Confucianism is based include the ideas of a group of traditional books edited by Confucius, as well as his own works, such as the *Analects*, and those of some of his pupils. The ◊*I Ching* is included among the Confucianist texts.

Confederacy 1861–65

doctrine Until 1912 the emperor of China was regarded as the father of his people, appointed by heaven to rule. The Superior Man was the ideal human and filial piety was the chief virtue. Accompanying a high morality was a kind of ancestor worship.

practices Under the emperor, sacrifices were offered to heaven and earth, the heavenly bodies, the imperial ancestors, various nature gods, and Confucius himself. These were abolished at the Revolution in 1912, but ancestor worship (better expressed as reverence and remembrance) remained a regular practice in the home.

Under communism Confucianism continued. The defence minister Lin Biao was associated with the religion, and although the communist leader Mao Zedong undertook an anti-Confucius campaign 1974–76, this was not pursued by the succeeding regime.

Confucius /kən'fjuːʃəs/ Latinized form of **Kong Zi**, 'Kong the master' 551–479 BC. Chinese philosopher whose name is given to Confucianism. He devoted his life to relieving suffering of the poor through governmental and administrative reform. His emphasis on tradition and ethics attracted a growing number of pupils during his lifetime; *The Analects of Confucius*, a compilation of his teachings, was published after his death.

Confucius was born in Lu, in what is now the province of Shangdong, and his early years were spent in poverty. Married at 19, he worked as a minor official, then as a teacher. In 517 there was an uprising in Lu, and Confucius spent the next year or two in the adjoining state of Ch'i. As a teacher he was able to place many of his pupils in government posts but a powerful position eluded him. Only in his fifties was he given an office but soon resigned at the lack of power it conveyed. Then for 14 years he wandered from state to state looking for a ruler who could give him a post where he could put his reforms into practice. At the age of 67 he returned to Lu and devoted himself to teaching. At his death five years later he was buried with great pomp, and his grave outside Qufu has remained a centre of pilgrimage.

conga a popular Latin American dance, originally from Cuba, in which the participants form a winding line, take three steps forwards or backwards, and then kick.

congenital disease in medicine, a disease that is present at birth. It is not necessarily genetic in origin; for example, congenital herpes may be acquired by the baby as it passes through the mother's birth canal.

conger a large eel *Conger conger* found in the N Atlantic and Mediterranean. It is often 1.8 m/6 ft long, and sometimes as much as 2.7 m/9 ft. It lives in shallow water, hiding in crevices during the day and active by night, feeding on fish and other animals. It is valued for food and angling.

conglomerate a coarse clastic ◊sedimentary rock, composed of rounded fragments (clasts) of preexisting rocks cemented in a finer matrix, usually sand.

The fragments in conglomerates are pebble- to boulder-sized, and the rock can be regarded as the lithified equivalent of gravel. A ◊bed of conglomerate is often associated with a break in a sequence of rock beds (an unconformity), where it marks the advance of the sea over an old eroded landscape. An *oligomict conglomerate* contains one type of pebble; a *polymict conglomerate* has a mixture of pebble types. If the rock fragments are angular, it is called a ◊breccia.

Congo /'kɒŋɡəʊ/ former name 1960–71 of ◊Zaïre.

Congo /'kɒŋɡəʊ/ country in W central Africa, bounded to the north by Cameroon and the Central African Republic, to the east and south by Zaïre, to the west by the Atlantic Ocean, and to the northwest by Gabon.

government the Congo is a one-party state based on the Marxist-Leninist Congolese Labour Party (PTC). The president of the central committee of PTC is automatically elected state president for a

---

Congo
People's Republic of the
(République Populaire du Congo)

area 342,000 sq km/132,012 sq mi
capital Brazzaville
towns chief port Pointe Noire
physical Zaïre (Congo) river on the border; half the country is rainforest
head of state and government Denis Sassau-Nguesso from 1979
political system one-party socialist republic
political parties Congolese Labour Party (PCT), Marxist-Leninist
exports timber, potash, petroleum
currency CFA franc (485.00 = £1 Feb 1990)
population (1987) 2,270,000 (chiefly Bantu); annual growth rate 2.6%
life expectancy men 45, women 48
language French (official)
religion animist 50%, Christian 48%
literacy 79% male/55% female (1985 est)
GDP $2.1 bn (1983); $500 per head of population
chronology
1960 Achieved full independence from France, with Abbe Youlou as the first president.
1963 Youlou forced to resign. New constitution approved, with Alphonse Massamba-Débat as president.
1964 The Congo became a one-party state.
1968 Military coup, led by Capt Marien Ngouabi, ousted Massamba-Débat.
1970 A Marxist state, the People's Republic of the Congo, was announced, with the PCT as the only legal party.
1977 Ngouabi assassinated. Col Yhombi-Opango became president.
1979 Yhombi-Opango handed over the presidency to PCT, who chose Col Denis Sassou-Ngessou as his successor.
1984 Sassou-Ngessou elected for another five-year term.

---

five-year term and chairs the council of ministers. The single-chamber legislature is the 153-member people's national assembly, elected by universal suffrage from a list prepared by PTC.

history occupied from the 15th century by the Bakongo, Bateke, and Sanga, the area was exploited by Portuguese slave traders. From 1889 it came under French administration, becoming part of French Equatorial Africa in 1910.

The Congo became an autonomous republic within the French Community in 1958 and Abbé Fulbert Youlou, a Roman Catholic priest who involved himself in politics and was suspended by the Church, became prime minister and then president when full independence was achieved in 1960. Two years later plans were announced for a one-party state but in 1963, after industrial unrest, Youlou was forced to resign.

A new constitution was approved and Alphonse Massamba-Débat, a former finance minister, became president, adopting a policy of 'scientific socialism'. The National Revolutionary Movement (MNR) was declared the only political party. In 1968 Captain Marien Ngouabi overthrew Massamba-Débat in a military coup and the national assembly was replaced by a national council of the revolution. Ngouabi proclaimed a Marxist state but kept economic links with France.

In 1970 the nation became the People's Republic of the Congo, with the PTC as the only party and in 1973 a new constitution provided for an assembly chosen from a single party list. In 1977 Ngouabi was assassinated and Colonel Joachim Yhombi-Opango took over. He resigned in 1979, after discovering a plot to overthrow him, and was succeeded by Denis Sassou-Nguessou, who has moved away from Soviet influence, strengthening links with France, the US, and China.

In 1982 President Mitterrand of France paid an official visit to the Congo. In 1984 Sassou-Nguessou was elected for another five-year term. He increased his control by combining the posts of head of state, head of government and president of the central committee of PTC.

Congregationalism form of church government adopted by those Protestant Christians known as Congregationalists, who let each congregation manage its own affairs. The first Congregationalists were the Brownists, named after Robert Browne, who defined the congregational principle 1580.

In the 17th-century they were known as Independents, for example, the Puritan leader Cromwell and many of his Ironsides, and in 1662 hundreds of their ministers were driven from their churches and established separate congregations. The Congregational Church in England and Wales and the Presbyterian Church in England merged in 1972 to form the United Reformed Church. The latter, like its counterpart the Congregational Union of Scotland, has no control over individual churches but is simply consultative. Similar unions have been carried out in Canada (United Church of Canada, 1925) and USA (United Church of Christ, 1957).

Congress national legislature of the USA, consisting of the House of Representatives (435 members, apportioned to the states of the Union on the basis of population, and elected for two-year terms) and the Senate (100 senators, two for each state, elected for six years, one-third elected every two years). Both representatives and senators are elected by direct popular vote. Congress meets in Washington DC, in the Capitol. An ◊act of Congress is a bill passed by both houses.

Congress of Industrial Organizations (CIO) a branch of the ◊American Federation of Labor and Congress of Industrial Organizations, the federation of US trade unions.

Congress of Racial Equality (CORE) US nonviolent civil-rights organization, founded in Chicago 1942.

Congress Party Indian political party, founded 1885 as a nationalist movement. It played an important part in throwing off British rule and was the governing party from independence 1947 until 1977, when Indira Gandhi lost the leadership she had held since 1966. Heading a splinter group, known as *Congress (I)*, she achieved an overwhelming victory in the elections of 1980, and reduced the main Congress Party in turn to a minority.

The *Indian National Congress*, founded by the British A O Hume in 1885, was a moderate body until World War I when, under the leadership of Mahatma Gandhi, it began a campaign of non-violent non-cooperation with the British colonizers. It was declared illegal 1932–34, but was recognized as the paramount power in India at the granting of independence in 1947. Dominated in the early years of Indian independence by Nehru (1889–1964) the party won the elections of 1952, 1957, 1962,

1967, and 1971. In 1977 it was defeated for the first time.

congress system developed from the Congress of Vienna 1814–15, a series of international meetings in Aachen, Germany 1818, Troppali, Austria 1820, and Verona, Italy 1822. British opposition to the use of congresses by ◊Metternich as a weapon against liberal and national movements inside Europe brought them to an end as a system of international arbitration, although congresses continued to meet into the 1830s.

Congreve /ˈkɒŋgriːv/ William 1670–1729. English dramatist and poet. His first success was the comedy *The Old Bachelor* 1693, followed by *The Double Dealer* 1694, *Love for Love* 1695, the tragedy *The Mourning Bride* 1697, and *The Way of the World* 1700. His plays, which satirize the social affectations of the time, are noted for their elegant wit and wordplay.

congruent in geometry, having the same shape and size, as applied to two-dimensional or solid figures. With plane congruent figures, one figure will fit on top of the other exactly though this may first require rotation and/or reflection (making a mirror image) of one of the figures.

conic section curve obtained when a conical surface is intersected by a plane. If the intersecting plane cuts both extensions of the cone it yields a ◊hyperbola; if it is parallel to the side of the cone it produces a ◊parabola. Other intersecting planes produce a ◊circle or an ◊ellipse.

The Greek philosopher Apollonius (*c.*262–190 BC) wrote eight books with the title *Conic Sections*, which superseded previous work on the subject by Aristacus and Euclid.

conidium (plural *conidia*) an asexual spore formed by some fungi at the tip of a specialized ◊hypha or conidiophore. The conidiophores grow erect, and cells from their ends round off and separate into conidia, often forming long chains. Conidia easily become detached and are dispersed by air movements.

conifer trees and shrubs of the class Coniferales, in the gymnosperm group, which are often pyramidal in form, with leaves that are either scaled or made up of needles. Conifers include pines, firs, yews, monkey-puzzles and larches. Most are evergreen.

The flowers are the male and female cones, and pollen is distributed by the wind. The seeds develop in the female cones. The processes of maturation, fertilization, and seed ripening may extend over several years.

conjugate in mathematics, a term indicating that two elements are connected in some way. (*a* + *ib*) and (*a* − *ib*) are conjugate complex numbers. Two angles are conjugate if they add up to 360°.

conjugation in biology, the bacterial equivalent of sexual reproduction. A fragment of the ◊DNA from one bacterium is passed along a thin tube, the pilus, into the cell of another bacterium.

conjunction a grammatical ◊part of speech that serves to connect words, phrases and clauses; for example *and* in 'apples and pears' and *but* in 'we're going but they aren't'.

conjunction in astronomy, the alignment of two celestial bodies so that they have the same position as seen from Earth. *Inferior conjunction* occurs when an ◊inferior planet (or other object) passes between the Earth and Sun, and has an identical right ascension to the Sun. *Superior conjunction* occurs when a ◊superior planet (or other object) passes behind, or on the far side of, the Sun, and has the same right ascension as the Sun. *Planetary conjunction* takes place when a planet is closely aligned with another celestial object, such as the Moon, a star, or another planet, as seen from Earth.

Because the orbital planes of the inferior planets are tilted with respect to the Earth, an inferior planet usually passes either above or below the Sun as seen from Earth. If they line up exactly, a ◊transit will occur.

Connecticut

conjunctivitis inflammation of the conjunctiva, the delicate membrane which lines the inside of the eyelids and covers the front of the eye. It may be caused by infection, allergy, or other irritant.

Connacht /ˈkɒnɔːt/ province of the Republic of Ireland, comprising the counties of Galway, Leitrim, Mayo, Roscommon, and Sligo; area 17,130 sq km/6,612 sq mi; population (1986) 431,000. The chief towns are Galway, Roscommon, Castlebar, Sligo, and Carrick-on-Shannon. Mainly lowland, it is agricultural and stock-raising country, with poor land in the west.

The chief rivers are the Shannon, Moy, and Suck, and there are a number of lakes. The Connacht dialect is the national standard.

Connecticut /kəˈnetɪkət/ state in New England, USA; nickname Constitution State/Nutmeg State
area 13,000 sq km/5,018 sq mi
capital Hartford
towns Bridgeport, New Haven, Waterbury
physical highlands in the NW; Connecticut River
features Yale University; Mystic Seaport (reconstruction of 19th-century village, with restored ships)
products dairy, poultry, and market garden products; tobacco, watches, clocks, silverware, helicopters, jet engines, nuclear submarines
population (1983) 3,138,000
famous people Phineas T Barnum, George Bush, Katharine Hepburn, Harriet Beecher Stowe, Mark Twain
history settled by Puritan colonists from Massachusetts 1635, it was one of the Thirteen Colonies, and became a state 1788.

connectionist machine a computing device built from a large number of interconnected simple processors, which are able both to communicate with each other and process information separately. The underlying model is that of the human brain.

These 'massively parallel' computers, as they are sometimes known, are still at the development stage.

connective tissue in animals, tissue made up of a noncellular substance, the ◊extracellular matrix, in which some cells are embedded. The skin, bones, tendons, cartilage, and adipose tissue (fat) are the main connective tissues. There are also small amounts of connective tissue in organs such as the brain and liver, where they maintain shape and structure.

Connell /ˈkɒnl/ James Irish socialist who wrote the British Labour Party anthem 'The Red Flag' during the 1889 London strike.

Connemara /ˌkɒnɪˈmɑːrə/ the western part of county Galway, Republic of Ireland, noted for its rocky coastline and mountainous scenery.

Connery /ˈkɒnəri/ Sean 1930–. Scottish film actor, the most famous interpreter of James Bond in several films based on the novels of Ian Fleming. His films include *Dr No* 1962, *From Russia with Love* 1963, *Marnie* 1964, *Goldfinger* 1964, *Diamonds are Forever* 1971, *A Bridge too Far* 1977, and *The Untouchables* 1987.

Connery *Actor Sean Connery shot to fame as the first James Bond in* Dr No *1962.*

Connolly /ˈkɒnəli/ Cyril 1903–1974. English writer. As founder-editor of the literary magazine *Horizon* 1930–50, he had considerable critical influence. His books include *The Rock Pool* 1935, a novel of artists on the Riviera, and *The Unquiet Grave* 1945.

Connolly /ˈkɒnəli/ Maureen 1934–1969. US lawn tennis player, nicknamed 'Little Mo' because she stood only 91 cm/5 ft 2 in tall. In 1953 she became the first woman to complete the Grand Slam by winning all four major tournaments.

All her singles titles (won at nine major championships) and her Grand Slam titles were won between 1951 and 1954. She also represented the USA in the Wightman Cup. After a riding accident 1954 her career was ended. She died of cancer 1969.

CAREER HIGHLIGHTS

Wimbledon
singles: 1952–54
US Open
singles: 1951–53
French Open
singles: 1953–54
doubles: 1954
mixed: 1954
Australian Open
singles: 1953
doubles: 1953.

Connors /ˈkɒnəz/ Jimmy 1952– . US lawn tennis player. A popular and entertaining player, he became well known for his 'grunting' during play. He won the Wimbledon title 1974, and has since won ten Grand Slam events. He was one of the first players to popularize the two-handed backhand.

CAREER HIGHLIGHTS

Wimbledon
singles: 1974, 1982
doubles: 1973
US Open
singles: 1974, 1976, 1978, 1982–83
doubles: 1975
Australian Open
singles: 1974

conquistador Spanish word for 'conqueror', applied to such explorers and adventurers in the Americas as Cortés (Mexico) and Pizarro (Peru).

Conrad /ˈkɒnræd/ Joseph 1857–1924. British novelist, of Polish parentage, born Teodor Jozef Konrad Korzeniowski in the Ukraine. His novels include *Almayer's Folly* 1895, *Lord Jim* 1900, *Heart of Darkness* 1902, *Nostromo* 1904, *The Secret Agent* 1907, and *Under Western Eyes* 1911. His works vividly evoked for English readers the mysteries of sea life and exotic foreign settings, and explored the psychological isolation of the 'outsider'.

Conrad /'kɒnræd/ several kings of the Germans and Holy Roman Emperors, including:

Conrad I King of the Germans from 911, when he succeeded Louis the Child, the last of the German Carolingians. During his reign the realm was harassed by Magyar invaders.

Conrad II King of the Germans from 1024, Holy Roman emperor from 1027. He ceded the march Sleswick (Schleswig), south of the Jutland peninsula, to King Canute, but extended his rule into Lombardy and Burgundy.

Conrad III 1093–1152. Holy Roman emperor from 1138, the first king of the Hohenstaufen dynasty. Throughout his reign there was a fierce struggle between his followers, the *Ghibellines*, and the *Guelphs*, the followers of Henry the Proud, duke of Saxony and Bavaria (1108–1139), and later of his son Henry the Lion (1129–1195).

Conrad IV 1228–1254. Elected king of the Germans 1237. Son of the Holy Roman emperor Frederick II, he had to defend his right of succession against Henry Raspe of Thuringia (died 1247) and William of Holland (1227–1256).

Conrad V (Conradin) 1252–1268. Son of Conrad IV, recognized as king of the Germans, Sicily, and Jerusalem by German supporters of the ◊Hohenstaufens 1254. He led Ghibelline forces against Charles of Anjou at the battle of Tagliacozzo, N Italy 1266, and was captured and executed.

Conran /'kɒnrən/ Terence 1931– . British designer and retailer of furnishings, fashion, and household goods. He is a director of the Habitat and Conran companies, with retail outlets in the UK, USA, and elsewhere.

In 1964 he started the Habitat company, then developed Mothercare. His Storehouse group of companies gained control of British Home Stores 1986.

consanguinity relationship by blood, whether lineal, by direct descent, or collateral, by virtue of a common ancestor. The degree of consanguinity is important in laws relating to the inheritance of property and also in relation to marriage, which is forbidden in many cultures between parties closely related by blood. See also ◊affinity.

conscientious objector person refusing compulsory service, usually military, on moral, religious, or political grounds.

consciousness the state of being aware of oneself and one's surroundings.

conscription legislation for all able-bodied male citizens (and female in some countries, such as Israel) to serve with the armed forces. It originated in France 1792, and in the 19th and 20th centuries became the established practice in almost all European states. Modern conscription systems often permit alternative national service for conscientious objectors.

Conscription remains the norm for most NATO and Warsaw Pact countries as well as neutral states. It is also practised by governments in the Third World. In South Africa, the penalty for evading conscription is up to six years' imprisonment.

In Britain conscription was introduced for single men between 18 and 41 in Mar 1916 and for married men two months later, but was abolished after World War I. It was introduced for the first time in peace Apr 1939, when all men aged 20 became liable to six months' military training. The National Service Act, passed Sept 1939, made all men between 18 and 41 liable to military service, and in 1941 women also became liable to be called up for the women's services as an alternative to industrial service. Men reaching the age of 18 continued to be called up until 1960.

consent, age of the age at which consent may legally be given to sexual intercourse by a girl or boy. In the UK it is 16 (21 for male homosexual intercourse).

The Criminal Law Amendment Act raised the age of consent from 13 to 16, and that of abduction from 16 to 18, after a campaign by W T

Constable Salisbury Cathedral and Archdeacon Fisher's House from the River *(1820)* National Gallery, London.

Stead, editor of the *Pall Mall Gazette*, exposed the white slave trade from England to Paris and Brussels. Stead's purchase of a girl to demonstrate the existence of the trade led to his prosecution, conviction, and imprisonment for three months.

conservation in the life sciences, care for, and protection of, the ◊biosphere. Since the 1950s it has been increasingly realized that the Earth, together with its atmosphere, animal and plant life, mineral and agricultural resources, form an interdependent whole which is in danger of irreversible depletion and eventual destruction unless positive measures are taken to conserve a balance.

conservation, architectural attempts to maintain the character of buildings and historical areas. In England this is subject to a growing body of legislation that has designated more ◊listed buildings. There are now over 6,000 conservation areas throughout England alone.

conservation of energy in chemistry, the principle that states that in a chemical reaction, the total amount of energy in the system remains unchanged.

For each component there may be changes in energy due to change of physical state, changes in the nature of chemical bonds, and either an input or output of energy. However, there is no net gain or loss of energy.

conservatism an approach to government and economic management identified with a number of Western political parties, such as the British Conservative, West German Christian Democratic, and Australian Liberal parties. It tends to be explicitly nondoctrinaire and pragmatic but generally emphasizes free-enterprise capitalism, minimal government intervention in the economy, rigid law and order, and the importance of national traditions.

Conservative Party UK political party, one of the two historic British parties; the name replaced *Tory* in general use from 1830 onwards. Traditionally the party of landed interests, it broadened its political base under Disraeli's leadership in the 19th century. The modern Conservative Party's free-market capitalism is supported by the world of finance and the management of industry;

Opposed to the *laissez-faire* of the Liberal manufacturers, the Conservative Party supported, to some extent, the struggle of the working class against the harsh conditions arising from the Industrial Revolution. The split of 1846 over Peel's Corn Law policy led to 20 years out of office, or in office without power, until Disraeli 'educated' his party into accepting parliamentary and social change, extended the franchise to the artisan (winning

considerable working-class support), launched imperial expansion, and established an alliance with industry and finance.

The Irish Home Rule issue of 1886 drove Radical Imperialists and old-fashioned Whigs into alliance with the Conservatives, so that the party had nearly 20 years of office, but fear that Joseph Chamberlain's protectionism would mean higher prices led to a Liberal landslide in 1906. The Conservative Party fought a rearguard action against the sweeping reforms that followed and only the outbreak of World War I averted a major crisis. During 1915–45, except briefly in 1924 and 1929–31, the Conservatives were continually in office, whether alone or as part of a coalition, largely thanks to the break-up of the traditional two- party system by the rise of Labour.

Labour swept to power after World War II, but the Conservative Party formulated a new policy in their Industrial Charter of 1947, visualizing an economic and social system in which employers and employed, private enterprise and the state, work to mutual advantage. Antagonism to further nationalization returned the Conservatives to power in 1951 with a small majority, and prosperity kept them in office throughout the 1950s.

Narrowly defeated in 1964 under Douglas Home, the Conservative Party from 1965 elected its leaders, beginning with Edward Heath, who became prime minister 1970. The imposition of wage controls led to confrontation with the unions and, when Heath sought a mandate Feb 1974, a narrow defeat, repeated in a further election in Oct 1974. Margaret Thatcher replaced Heath, and under her leadership the Conservative Party returned to power in May 1979, and was re-elected for a third term in 1987. Its economic policies increased the spending power of the majority, but also the gap between rich and poor; nationalized industries were sold off (see ◊privatization); military spending and close alliance with the USA was favoured and the ratings system was overhauled with the introduction of the unpopular poll tax.

conspicuous consumption selection and purchase of goods for their social rather than their inherent value. These might include items with an obviously expensive brand-name tag. The name was coined by US economist Thorsten Veblen.

constable (Latin *comes stabuli* 'count of the stable') a low-ranking police officer. In medieval Europe, a constable was an officer of the king, originally responsible for army stores and stabling, and later responsible for the army in the king's absence. In England the constable subsequently became an official at a sheriff's court of law, leading to its modern meaning.

Constable /'kʌnstəbəl/ John 1776–1837. English landscape painter. The scenes of his native Suffolk are well loved and include *The Haywain* 1821 (National Gallery, London), but he travelled widely in Britain, depicting castles, cathedrals, landscapes, and coastal scenes. His many sketches are often considered among his best work. The paintings are remarkable for their freshness and were influential in France as well as the UK.

Constable first worked in his father's mills in East Bergholt, Suffolk, but in 1795 was sent to study art in London. He inherited the Dutch tradition of sombre realism, particularly the style of Jacob ◊Ruysdael, but he aimed to capture the momentary changes of nature as well as to create monumental images of British scenery, such as *The White Horse* 1819 (Frick Collection, New York) and *Flatford Mill* 1825. He was finally elected to the Royal Academy in 1829 but his greatest impact was in France, where his admirers included Delacroix.

Constance /'kɒnstəns/ (German *Konstanz*) town in Baden-Württemberg, Germany, on the section of the Rhine joining Lake Constance and the Untersee; population (1983) 69,100. Suburbs stretch across the frontier into Switzerland. Constance has clothing, machinery, and chemical factories and printing works.

Constance, Council of /'kɒnstəns/ council held by the Roman Catholic church 1414–17 in Constance, Germany. It elected Pope Martin V, which ended the Great Schism 1378–1417 when there were rival popes in Rome and Avignon.

Constance, Lake /'kɒnstəns/ (German *Bodensee*) lake between Germany, Austria, and Switzerland, through which the river Rhine flows; area 540 sq km/200 sq mi.

constant in mathematics, a fixed quantity or one that does not change its value in relation to ◊variables. For example, in the algebraic expression $y = 5x - 3$, the number 3 is a constant. In physics, certain quantities are regarded as universal constants, such as the speed of light in a vacuum.

Constanța /kɒn'stæntsə/ chief Romanian port on the Black Sea, capital of Constanța region, and third largest city of Romania; population (1985) 323,000. It has refineries, shipbuilding yards, and food factories.

It is the exporting centre for the Romanian oilfields, to which it is connected by pipeline. It was founded as a Greek colony in the 7th century BC, it was later named after the Roman emperor Constantine I (4th century AD). Ovid, the Roman poet, lived in exile here.

constantan a high-resistance alloy of approximately 40% nickel and 60% copper with a very low temperature coefficient. It is used in electrical resistors.

constant composition, law of in chemistry, the law that states that the proportions of the amounts of the elements in a pure compound are always the same and are independent of the method used to produce it.

Constant de Rebecque /kɒn'stɒn də rə'bek/ (Henri) Benjamin 1767–1830. French writer and politician. An advocate of the Revolution, he opposed Napoleon and in 1803 went into exile. Returning to Paris after the fall of Napoleon in 1814 he proposed a constitutional monarchy. He published the autobiographical novel *Adolphe* 1816, which reflects his affair with Madame de ◊Staël, and later wrote the monumental study *De la Religion* 1825–31.

Constantine /,kɒnstən'tiːn/ city in Algeria; population (1983) 449,000. It produces carpets and leather goods. It was one of the important towns in the Roman province of Numidia, but declined and was ruined, but restored 313 by Constantine the Great, whose name it bears. It was subsequently ruled by Arabs, Turks, and Salah Bey 1770–92, who built many of the Muslim buildings. It was captured by the French 1837.

Constantine II /'kɒnstəntaɪn/ 1940– . King of the Hellenes (Greece). In 1964 he succeeded his father Paul I, went into exile 1967, and was formally deposed 1973.

Constantine the Great /'kɒ nstəntɪn/ AD 274–337. First Christian emperor of Rome and founder of Constantinople. He defeated Maxentius, joint-emperor of Rome 321, and in 313 formally recognized Christianity.

Born at Naissus (Nish, Yugoslavia), Constantine was the son of Constantius. He was already well known as a soldier when his father died at York in 306 and he was acclaimed by the troops there as joint-emperor in his father's place. A few years later Maxentius, the joint-emperor in Rome (whose sister had married Constantine), challenged his authority and mobilized his armies to invade Gaul. Constantine won a crushing victory outside Rome in 312. During this campaign he was said to have seen a vision of the cross of Jesus superimposed upon the sun, accompanied by the words, 'In this sign conquer'. By the Edict of Milan 313 he formally recognized Christianity as one of the religions legally permitted within the Roman Empire, and in 314 summoned the bishops of the Western world to the Council of Arles. Sole emperor of the West since 321, by defeating Licinius, the emperor in the East, Constantine became sole Roman emperor 324. He increased the autocratic power of the emperor, issued legislation to tie the farmers and workers to their crafts in a sort of caste system, and enlisted the support of the Christian Church. He summoned, and presided over, the first general council of the Church at Nicaea 325. Constantine moved his capital to Byzantium on the Bosporus 330 and renamed it Constantinople (now Istanbul).

Constantinople /,kɒnstæntɪ'nəʊpəl/ former name of Istanbul, Turkey, 330–1453. It was founded by the Roman emperor Constantine the Great by the enlargement of the Greek city of Byzantium in 328, and became capital of the Byzantine Empire 330. Its elaborate fortifications enabled it to resist a succession of sieges, but it was captured by crusaders 1204, and was the seat of a Latin (W European) kingdom until recaptured by the Greeks 1261. An attack by the Turks 1422 proved unsuccessful, but it was taken by another Turkish army 29 May 1453 after nearly a year's siege, and became the capital of the Ottoman Empire.

constant prices a series of prices adjusted to reflect real purchasing power. If wages were to rise by 15% from £100 per week (to £115) and the rate of inflation was 10% (requiring £110 to maintain spending power), the real wage would have risen by 5%. Also an index used to create a constant price series, unlike ◊current prices.

constellation one of the 88 areas into which the sky is divided for the purposes of identifying and naming celestial objects. The first constellations were simple patterns of stars in which early civilizations visualized gods, sacred beasts, and mythical heroes.

The constellations in use today are derived from a list of 48 known to the ancient Greeks, who inherited some from the Babylonians. The modern list of 88 constellations was adopted by the International Astronomical Union, astronomy's governing body, in 1930.

constitution the fundamental laws of a state, laying down the system of government and defining the relations of the legislature, executive, and judiciary to each other and to the citizens. Since the French Revolution almost all countries (the UK is one exception) have adopted written constitutions; that of the USA (1787) is the oldest.

The constitution of the UK does not exist as a single document but as an accumulation of customs and precedents, together with laws defining certain of its aspects. Among the most important of the latter are Magna Carta 1215, the Petition of Right 1628, and the Habeas Corpus Act 1679, limiting the royal powers of taxation and of imprisonment; the Bill of Rights 1689 and the Act of

Settlement 1701, establishing the supremacy of ◊Parliament and the independence of the judiciary; and the Parliament Acts 1911 and 1949, limiting the powers of the Lords. The Triennial Act 1694, the Septennial Act 1716, and the Parliament Act 1911 limited the duration of Parliament, while the Reform Acts of 1832, 1867, 1884, 1918, and 1928 extended the electorate.

The proliferation of legislation during the 1970s, often carried on the basis of a small majority in the Commons and by governments elected by an overall minority of votes, led to demands such as those by the organization ◊Charter 88 for the introduction of a written constitution as a safeguard for the liberty of the individual.

Constructivism revolutionary art movement founded in Moscow 1917 by the Russians Naum Gabo, Antoine Pevsner (1886–1962), and Vladimir Tatlin (1885–1953). Tatlin's abstract sculptures, using wood, metal, and clear plastic, were hung on walls or suspended from ceilings. The brothers Gabo and Pevsner soon left the USSR and joined the European avant-garde.

consul the chief magistrate of ancient Rome following the expulsion of the last king in 510 BC. The consuls were two annually elected magistrates, both of equal power; they jointly held full civil power in Rome and the chief military command in the field. After the establishment of the Roman Empire the office became purely honorary.

Today, a 'consul' is a state official, with political and commercial responsibilities, who looks after the nation's citizens in major foreign cities.

consumer durable a good that is required to satisfy personal requirements and which has a long life, such as furniture and electrical goods, as opposed to food and drink which are *perishables* and have to be replaced frequently.

consumer protection laws and measures designed to ensure fair trading for buyers. Responsibility for checking goods and services for quality, safety and suitability has in the past few years moved increasingly away from the consumer to the producer.

In earlier days it was assumed that consumers could safeguard themselves by common sense, testing before purchase, and confronting the seller personally if they were dissatisfied. Today the technical complexities of products, the remoteness of outlets from the original producer, and pressures from advertising, require protection for the consumer.

In Britain, an early organization for consumer protection was the British Standards Institution, set up in 1901, which certifies with a 'kitemark' goods reaching certain standards. Statutory protection is now given by Acts such as the Trade Descriptions Act 1968 (making false descriptions of goods and services illegal), the Fair Trading Act 1973, the Unfair Contract Terms Act 1977 and the Consumer Safety Acts 1978 and 1987. In 1974 the government Department of Prices and Consumer Protection was set up.

In the USA both federal and state governments make special provisions for consumer protection. In 1962 President Kennedy set out the four basic rights of the consumer: to safety, to be informed, to choose and to be heard. There are many private consumer associations, and among the most influential of crusaders for greater protection has been Ralph ◊Nader.

consumers' association a group formed to protect consumer interests usually where the quality and price of goods or services is concerned.

In the UK, the Consumers' Association regularly surveys and tests products and services, and publishes details of its findings in its monthly magazine *Which?*.

consumption the purchasing and using of goods and services. In economics, it means a country's total expenditure over a given period (usually a year) on goods and services (including expenditure on raw materials and defence).

consumption (Latin *consumptio* 'wasting') former name for the disease ◊tuberculosis.

Conti British stage and film actor Tom Conti specializes in character roles, as in Shirley Valentine 1989.

contact lens a lens made of hard or soft plastic, which is worn beneath the eyelid in contact with the cornea and conjunctiva of the eye, to correct defective vision. In special circumstances, contact lenses may be used as protective shells, or for cosmetic purposes such as changing eye colour.

The earliest use of contact lenses in the late 19th century was protective, or in the correction of corneal malformation. It was not until the 1930s that simplification of fitting technique by taking eye impressions made their general use possible. A recent development has been the 'soft' plastic lens, which avoids the discomfort suffered by prolonged use of earlier types, and in some cases enables the contact lenses to be worn for lengthy periods without removal.

contact process the main method of manufacturing sulphuric acid, an important industrial chemical. A mixture of sulphur dioxide and air is passed over a hot (450°C) catalyst of vanadium/vanadium oxide. The sulphur trioxide produced is then absorbed by a spray of dilute acid.

contado in northern and central Italy from the 9th to 13th centuries, the territory under a count's jurisdiction. During the 13th century, this jurisdiction passed to the cities, and it came to refer to the rural area over which a city exerted political and economic control.

Contadora /ˌkɒntəˈdɔːrə/ Panamanian island of the Pearl Island group in the Gulf of Panama. It was the first meeting place 1983 of the foreign ministers of Colombia, Mexico, Panama, and Venezuela (now known as the ***Contadora Group***) who came together to discuss the problems of Central America.

Contadora Group an alliance formed between Colombia, Mexico, Panama, and Venezuela Jan 1983 to establish a general peace treaty for Central America.

The process was designed to include the formation of a Central American parliament (similar to the European parliament). Support for Contadora has come from Argentina, Brazil, Peru, and Uruguay, as well as from the Central American states.

Containment US policy dating from 1947 designed to prevent the spread of communism beyond the borders of the USSR.

contempt of court behaviour that shows contempt for the authority of a court, such as: disobeying a court order; behaviour that disrupts, prejudices, or interferes with court proceedings; and abuse of judges, inside or outside a court. The court may punish contempt with a fine or imprisonment.

Many British trade unions (such as the National Union of Seamen in 1988) have lost substantial parts of their funds through fines for contempt for disobeying court orders prohibiting illegal picketing.

Conti /ˈkɒnti/ Tom 1945– . British stage and film actor specializing in character roles. His films include; *The Duellists* 1976; *Merry Christmas Mr Lawrence* 1983; *Reuben, Reuben* 1983; *Beyond Therapy* 1987; *Shirley Valentine* 1989.

continent any one of the large land masses of Earth, as distinct from ocean. They are Asia, Africa, North America, South America, Europe, Australia, and Antarctica. Continents are constantly moving and evolving (see ◊plate tectonics). A continent does not end at the coastline; its boundary is the edge of the shallow continental shelf (part of the continental ◊crust, made of ◊sial), which may extend several hundred miles or kilometres out to sea.

At the centre of each continental mass lies a shield or ◊craton, a deformed mass of old ◊metamorphic rocks dating from Precambrian times. The shield is thick, compact, and solid (the Canadian Shield is an example), having undergone all the mountain-building activity it is ever likely to, and is usually worn flat. Around the shield is a concentric pattern of fold mountains, with older ranges, such as the Rockies, closest to the shield, and younger ranges, such as the coastal ranges of North America, farther away. This general concentric pattern is modified when two continental masses have drifted together and they become welded with a great mountain range along the join, the way Europe and N Asia are joined along the Urals. If a continent is torn apart, the new continental edges have no fold mountains, for instance South America has fold mountains (the Andes) along its western flank, but none along the east where it tore away from Africa 200 million years ago.

Continental Congress in US history, the federal legislature of the original 13 states, acting as a provisional revolutionary government during the War of ◊American Independence. It was convened in Philadelphia 1774–89, when the constitution was adopted. The second Continental Congress, convened May 1775, was responsible for drawing up the Declaration of Independence.

continental drift in geology, theory proposed by the German meteorologist Alfred Wegener in 1915 that, about 200 million years ago, Earth consisted of a single large continent (Pangaea) that subsequently broke apart to form the continents known today. Such vast continental movements could not be satisfactorily explained until the study of ◊plate tectonics in the 1960s.

Continental System the system of economic preference and protection within Europe created by the French emperor Napoleon in order to exclude British trade. Apart from its function as economic warfare, the system also reinforced the French

continental drift

Upper Carboniferous period

Eocene

Lower Quaternary

economy at the expense of other European states. It lasted 1806–13 but failed due to British naval superiority.

continuity in mathematics, functions of a real variable that have an absence of 'breaks'. A function f is said to be continuous at a point a if $\lim f(x) = f(a)$.

continuity in cinema, the coordination of sequences in the production of a film.

continuo abbreviation for *basso continuo*; in music, the bass line on which a keyboard player, often accompanied by a bass stringed instrument, built up a harmonic accompaniment in 17th-century Baroque music.

continuum in mathematics, a ◊set that is infinite and and everywhere continuous, for example, the set of points on a line.

Contra member of a Central American right-wing guerrilla force attempting to overthrow the democratically elected Nicaraguan Sandinista government from 1979. The Contras, many of them mercenaries or former members of the deposed Somoza's guard (see ◊Nicaraguan Revolution), have operated mainly from bases outside Nicaragua, especially in Honduras, with covert US funding as revealed by the ◊Irangate hearings 1986–87. In 1989 US president Bush announced an agreement with Congress to provide $41 million in aid to the Contras until Feb 1990. The Sandinista government was defeated by the National Opposition Union, a US-backed coalition, in the Feb 1990 elections.

contrabassoon a larger version of the ◊bassoon, sounding an octave lower.

contraceptive drug or device that prevents pregnancy. The contraceptive pill (the ◊Pill) contains female hormones that interfere with egg

continent

Sierra Nevada (new marginal mountains)   Rockies (old marginal mountains)   Ozark Plateau (shield)   Appalachians (old impact mountains)

Pacific   Atlantic

section across USA

production or the first stage of pregnancy. The 'morning-after' pill can be taken after unprotected intercourse. Barrier contraceptives include ◊condoms (sheaths) and ◊caps, also called Dutch caps or diaphragms; they prevent the sperm entering the cervix (neck of the womb). ◊Intrauterine devices, also known as IUDs or coils, cause a slight inflammation of the lining of the womb; this prevents the fertilized egg from becoming implanted.

Other contraceptive methods include ◊sterilization (women) and ◊vasectomy (men), but these are usually non-reversible. 'Natural' methods include withdrawal of the penis before ejaculation (coitus interruptus), and avoidance of intercourse at the time of ovulation (◊rhythm method). These methods are unreliable and normally only used on religious grounds. A new development is a sponge impregnated with spermicide that is inserted into the vagina.

The effectiveness of a contraceptive method is often given as a percentage. To say that a method has 95% effectiveness means that, on average, out of 100 healthy couples using that method for a year, 95 will not conceive.

contract agreement between two or more parties that will be enforced by law according to the intention of the parties. It always consists of an offer and an acceptance of that offer.

In English law a contract must either be made under seal (in a ◊deed) or there must be consideration to support it, that is, there must be some benefit to one party to the contract or some detriment to the other. Even a contract made in the proper form may be unenforceable if it is made under a mistake, misrepresentation, duress, or undue influence, or if one of the parties does not have the capacity to make it (for example, ◊minors and people who are psychologically disturbed). Illegal contracts are void, including those to commit a crime or civil wrong, to trade with the enemy, immoral contracts, and contracts in restraint of trade, such as contracts binding a servant indefinitely not to compete with his or her master after the service is over. Contracts by way of gaming and wagering are also void.

contract bridge card game first played 1925. From 1930 it quickly outgrew ◊auction bridge in popularity.

The game originated in 1925 on a steamer en route from Los Angeles to Havana, and was introduced by H S Vanderbilt, one of the players.

contractile root in botany, a thickened root at the base of a corm, bulb, or other organ that helps position it at an appropriate level in the ground. Contractile roots are found, for example, on the corms of *Crocus*. After they have become anchored in the soil the upper portion contracts, pulling the plant deeper into the ground.

contralto in music, a low-registered female voice; also called an ◊alto.

contrapuntal in music, a work employing ◊counterpoint.

control experiment an essential part of a scientifically valid experiment, designed to show that the factor being tested is actually responsible for the effect observed. In the control experiment all factors, apart from the one under test, are exactly the same as in the test experiments, and all the same measurements are carried out. In drug trials, a placebo (a harmless substance) is given alongside the substance being tested in order to compare effects.

convection a type of heat energy transfer that involves the movement of a fluid (gas or liquid). According to kinetic theory, molecules of fluid in contact with the source of heat expand and tend to rise within the bulk of the fluid. Less energetic, cooler molecules sink to take their place, setting up convection currents. This is the principle of natural convection in many domestic hot-water systems and room space-heating.

convent religious house for ◊nuns.

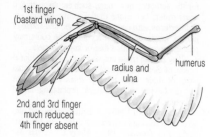

convergent evolution
bird wing

1st finger
(bastard wing)

radius and
ulna

humerus

2nd and 3rd finger
much reduced
4th finger absent

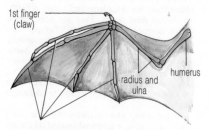

bat wing

1st finger
(claw)

radius and
ulna

humerus

conventionalism the view that *a priori* truths, logical axioms, or scientific laws have no absolute validity, but are disguised conventions representing one of a number of possible alternatives. The French philosopher and mathematician Jules Henri Poincaré introduced this position into philosophy of science.

convergence in mathematics, property of a series of numbers in which the difference between consecutive terms gradually decreases. The sum of a converging series approaches a limit as the number of terms tends to ◊infinity.

convergent evolution the independent evolution of similar structures in species (or other taxonomic groups) that are not closely related, as a result of living in a similar way. Thus, birds and bats have wings, not because they are descended from a common winged ancestor, but because their respective ancestors independently evolved flight.

converse in mathematics, the opposite way round; the converse of the statement 'if a, then b' is 'if b, then a'. The converse does not always hold true; for example, the converse of 'if $x = 3$, then $x^2 = 9$' is 'if $x^2 = 9$, then $x = 3$', which is not true, as x could also be -3.

convertiplane type of ◊vertical take-off aircraft with rotors on its wings that spin horizontally for take-off, but which tilt to spin in a vertical plane for forward flight.

At take-off it looks like a two-rotor helicopter, with both rotors facing skywards. As forward speed is gained, the rotors tilt slowly forward until they are facing directly ahead. There are several different forms of convertiplane. The LTV-Hillier-Ryan XC-142, designed in the US, had wings, carrying the four engines and propellors, which rotated. The German VC-400 had two rotors on each of its wing tips. Neither of these designs went into production. A recent Boeing and Bell design, the Osprey, uses a pair of tilting engines, with propellors 11.5 m/38 ft across, mounted at the end of the wings. It is eventually intended to carry about 50 passengers direct to city centres. The design should also be useful for search and rescue operations and for transport to offshore oil rigs.

convex lens a converging ◊lens – that is, a parallel beam of light passing through it converges and is eventually brought to a focus; it can therefore produce a real image on a screen. Such a lens is wider at its centre than at the edges.

Common forms include *biconvex* (with both surfaces curved towards) and *plano-convex* (with

one flat surface and one convex). The whole lens may be further curved overall, making a *concavo-convex* or converging meniscus lens, as in some spectacle or lenses.

conveyancing the administrative process involved in transferring title to land, usually on its sale or purchase. In England and Wales, conveyancing is usually by solicitors, but, since 1985, can also be done by licensed conveyancers. Conveyancing has been simplified by the registration of land with the ◊Land Registry.

The English system has been criticised for the delays in its procedure, particularly before binding contracts are exchanged, which can lead to gazumping (the vendor accepting a higher offer). In Scotland, this is avoided because a formal offer is legally binding.

conveyor a device used for transporting materials. Widely used throughout industry is the *conveyor belt*, usually a rubber or fabric belt running on rollers. Trough-shaped belts are used, for example in mines, for transporting ores and coal. *Chain conveyors* are also used in coal mines to remove coal from the cutting machines. Overhead endless chain conveyors are used to carry components and bodies in car assembly works. Other types include *bucket conveyors* and *screw conveyors*, powered versions of ◊Archimedes screw.

convocation in the Church of England, the synods (councils) of the clergy of the provinces of Canterbury and York. The General Synod established 1970 took over the functions and authority of the Convocation of Canterbury and York which continued to exist only in a restricted form.

convolvulus or *bindweed* genus of plants of the family Convolvulaceae. They are characterized by their twining stems, and by their petals, which are united into a tube.

The field bindweed *Convolvulus arvensis*, a trailing plant with handsome white or pink-and-white-streaked flowers, is a common weed in Britain.

convoy system grouping of ships to sail together under naval escort in wartime. In World War I (1914–18) navy escort vessels were at first used only to accompany troopships, but the convoy system was adopted for merchant shipping when the unrestricted German submarine campaign began 1917. In World War II (1939–45) it was widely used by the Allies to keep the Atlantic sea lanes open.

convulsion a series of violent contractions of the muscles over which the patient has no control. It may be associated with loss of consciousness.

Convulsions may arise from any one of a number of causes, including brain disease (such as ◊epilepsy), injury, poisoning, and electrocution.

Conwy /'kɒnwi/ port in Wales on the river Conwy, Gwynedd; population (1981) 12,950. Known until 1972 by the anglicized form *Conway*. Still surrounded by walls, Conwy has the ruins of a castle rebuilt by Edward I in 1284.

Coober Pedy /'kuːbə 'piːdi/ (native Australian 'white man in a hole') town in the Great Central Desert, Australia; 700 km/437 mi NW of Adelaide, S Australia; population (1976) 1,900. Opals were discovered in 1915, and are mined amid a moonscape of diggings in temperatures up to 60°C/140°F.

Cooch Behar /'kuːtʃ bɪ'hɑː/ former princely state in India, it was merged in West Bengal in 1950.

Cook, Mount /kʊk/ highest point, 3,764 m/12,353 ft, of Southern Alps, range of mountains running through New Zealand.

Cook /kʊk/ James 1728–1779. English naval explorer. After surveying the St Lawrence 1759, he made three voyages: 1769–71 to Tahiti, New Zealand, and Australia; 1772–75 to the South Pacific; and 1776–79 to the South and North Pacific, attempting to find the Northwest Passage and charting the Siberian coast. He was killed in Hawaii.

In 1768 Cook was given command of an expedition to the South Pacific to witness Venus

Cook *English navigator and explorer Captain James Cook.*

eclipsing the sun. He sailed in the *Endeavour* with Joseph ◊Banks and other scientists, reaching Tahiti Apr 1769. He then sailed around New Zealand and made a detailed survey of the E coast of Australia, naming New South Wales and Botany Bay. He returned to England 12 June 1771. Now a commander, Cook set out 1772 with the *Resolution* and *Adventure* to search for the Southern Continent. The location of Easter Island was determined, and the Marquesas and Tonga Islands plotted. He also went to New Caledonia and Norfolk Island. Cook returned 25 July 1775, having sailed 60,000 mi in three years. On 25 June 1776, he began his third and last voyage with the *Resolution* and *Discovery*. On the way to New Zealand, he visited several of the Cook or Hervey Islands and revisited the Hawaiian or Sandwich Islands. The ships sighted the North American coast at latitude 45° N and sailed N hoping to discover the Northwest Passage. He made a continuous survey as far as the Bering Strait, where the way was blocked by ice. Cook then surveyed the opposite coast of the strait (Siberia), and returned to Hawaii early 1779, where he was killed in a scuffle with islanders.

Cook /kʊk/ Peter 1937–. English comic actor and writer best known for his partnership with Dudley Moore. Together they appeared in revue (*Beyond the Fringe* 1959–64) and opened London's first satirical nightclub, the Establishment, in 1960. His films include *The Wrong Box* 1966; *Bedazzled* 1968; *The Bed Sitting Room* 1969; a parody of *The Hound of the Baskervilles* 1977; and *Supergirl* 1984.

Cook /kʊk/ Robin Finlayson 1946–. English Labour politician. A member of the moderate-left Tribune Group, he entered Parliament in 1974 and became a leading member of Labour's shadow cabinet.

The son of a headmaster, he graduated in English literature at Edinburgh University and worked for the Workers' Educational Association (WEA) before entering politics.

Cook /kʊk/ Thomas 1808–1892. Pioneer British travel agent and founder of Thomas Cook & Son. He introduced traveller's cheques (then called 'circular notes'), in the early 1870s.

Cooke /kʊk/ Alistair 1908– . US journalist. Born in the UK, he was *Guardian* correspondent in the USA 1948–72, and contributes a weekly *Letter from America* to BBC radio.

Cooke /kʊk/ Sam 1931–1964. US soul singer and songwriter, who began his career as a gospel singer and turned to pop music in 1956. His hits include 'You Send Me' 1957 and 'Wonderful World' 1960 (re-released 1986).

Cookham-on-Thames /'kʊkəm ɒn 'temz/ village in Berkshire, England. The artist Stanley ◊Spencer lived here for many years and a memorial gallery of his work was opened in 1962.

cooking the heat treatment of food to make it palatable, digestible, and safe. It breaks down connective tissue in meat, making it tender, and softens the cellulose in plant tissue. Some nutrients may be lost in the process, but this does not affect the overall nutritional value of a balanced diet.

cooking

cooking method moist heat	
broiling	direct heat over flame
pan broiling	heat through hot dry metal
sautéing	pan broiling with fat
deep frying	food is immersed in hot fat
shallow frying	fat is used to stop sticking
simmering	in pan with water below boiling point
stewing	prolonged simmering
fricasée	sauté and stewing
devilling	grilled or fried after coating food
steaming	cooking by steam
pressure cooking	by steam at above 100°C under pressure
dry heat	
baking	cooked in an oven, often with raising agent added
roasting	cooked in an oven
grilling	direct heat onto food
microwave	
microwave	microwaves cause oscillation of food molecules, which produces heat

NUTRIENT LOSS DURING COOKING	
cooking method	nutrients lost
boiling	40–70% vitamin C, some
steaming/	vitamin B
pressure cooking	and phosphorus
toasting	10–30% thiamin
baking	a little vitamin B and C
microwave	some vitamin B and C
dry heat	20–30% vitamin B

Cook Islands /kʊk/ group of six large and a number of smaller Polynesian islands 2,600 km/1,600 mi NE of Auckland, New Zealand; area 290 sq km/112 sq mi; population (1986) 17,000. Their main products include fruit, copra, and crafts. They became a self-governing overseas territory of New Zealand 1965.

The chief island, Rarotonga, is the site of Avarua, the seat of government. Niue, geographically part of the group, is separately administered. The Cook Islands were visited by Capt Cook 1773, annexed by Britain 1888, and transferred to New Zealand 1901. They have common citizenship with New Zealand.

Cook Strait /kʊk/ strait dividing North and South Island, New Zealand. A submarine cable carries electricity from South to North Island.

coolabah Australian riverside tree *Eucalyptus microtheca*.

Coolidge /'kuːlɪdʒ/ (John) Calvin 1872–1933. 30th president of the USA 1923–29, a Republican. As governor of Massachusetts 1919, he was responsible for crushing a Boston police strike. He became vice president 1921 and president on the death of Warren Harding. He was re-elected 1924, and his period of office was marked by economic prosperity.

Cooney /'kuːni/ Ray (Raymond) 1932– . British actor, director, and playwright, known for his farces *Two into One* 1981 and *Run for Your Wife* 1983.

Cooper Grand prix motor racing team formed by John Cooper. They built Formula Two and Formula Three cars before building their revolutionary rear-engined Cooper T45 in 1958.

Jack Brabham won the 1959 world title in a Cooper and the team won the Constructor's Championship. Both Brabham and Cooper retained their titles the following year. However, other rear-engined cars subsequently proved more successful and in 1968 Cooper left Formula One racing.

Cooper /'kuːpə/ (Alfred) Duff 1890–1954. British Conservative diplomat. Entering Parliament as a Unionist in 1924, he held ministerial posts 1935–38, when he resigned over the Munich Agreement, and 1940–41; he was ambassador to France 1944–47. Knighted in 1948, he was created Viscount Norwich in 1952.

Cooper /'kuːpə/ Gary 1901–1962. US film actor. He epitomized the lean, true-hearted Yankee, slow of speech but capable of outdoing the 'bad-men' in *Lives of a Bengal Lancer* 1935, *Mr Deeds Goes to Town* 1936, *Sergeant York* 1940 (Academy Award 1941), and *High Noon* 1952.

Cooper /'kuːpə/ Henry 1934 . English heavyweight boxer, the only man to win three Lonsdale Belts outright, 1961, 1965, and 1970. He fought for the world heavyweight title but lost in 6th round to Muhammad Ali 1966.

A former greengrocer, Cooper was famed for his left-hook known as 'Henry's hammer', and for an eye that bled easily. He held the British heavyweight title between 1959–71 and lost it to Joe Bugner in a controversial fight.

CAREER HIGHLIGHTS

Professional fights:	55
wins:	40
knockouts:	27
draws:	1
defeats:	14
1st professional fight: 14 Sept 1954 v. Harry Painter (GB)	
last professional fight: 16 Mar 1971 v. Joe Bugner (GB)	

Cooper /'kuːpə/ James Fenimore 1789–1851. US writer of 50 novels, becoming popular with *The Spy* 1821. He wrote volumes of *Leatherstocking Tales* about the frontier hero Leatherstocking and American Indians before and after the American Revolution, including *The Last of the Mohicans* 1826.

Cooper was born in New Jersey, grew up on the family frontier settlement of Cooperstown, New York State, and sailed as an apprentice seaman to Europe. After success as a writer, he lived in Paris for seven years before returning to Cooperstown.

Cooper Leon 1930– . UK physicist who in 1955 began work on the puzzling phenomena of ◊superconductivity. He proposed that at low temperatures electrons would be bound in pairs (since known as Cooper pairs) and in this state electrical resistance to their flow through solids would disappear. He shared the 1972 Nobel physics prize with ◊Bardeen and Schriefer.

Cooper /'kuːpə/ Samuel 1609–1672. English miniaturist. His subjects included Milton, members of Charles II's court, Samuel Pepys's wife, and Oliver Cromwell.

Cooper /'kuːpə/ Susie. Married name Susan Vera Barker 1902– . English pottery designer. Her style has varied from colourful Art Deco to softer, pastel decoration on more classical shapes. She started her own company 1929. It became part of the Wedgwood factory, where she was senior designer from 1966.

co-operative movement the banding together of groups of people for mutual assistance in trade, manufacture, the supply of credit, or other services. The original principles of co-operative movement were laid down 1844 by the Rochdale Pioneers, under the influence of Robert Owen, and by Charles Fourier in France.

Producers' co-operative societies, formed on a basis of co-partnership among the employees, exist on a large scale in France, Italy, Spain, and the USSR. Agricultural co-operative societies have been formed in many countries for the collective purchase of seeds, fertilizers, and other commodities, while societies for co-operative marketing of agricultural produce are prominent in the USA, Ireland, Denmark, the USSR, and Eastern Europe. Agricultural credit societies are strong in rural economies of Europe and Asia, including parts of India. The USA also has a co-operative farm credit system. Soviet economic co-operatives were in 1988 given legal and financial independence, the right to appear in foreign markets and to set up joint ventures with foreign companies.

In the UK the 1970s and 1980s have seen a growth in the number of workers' co-operatives, set up in factories otherwise threatened by closure due to economic depression.

Co-operative Party political party founded in Britain 1917 by the co-operative movement, to maintain its principles in parliamentary and local government. A written constitution was adopted 1938. The party had strong links with the Labour Party; from 1946 Co-operative Party candidates stood in elections as Co-operative and Labour Candidates and, after the 1959 general election, agreement was reached to limit the party's candidates to 30.

Co-operative Wholesale Society (CWS) a British concern, the largest co-operative organization in the world, owned and controlled by the numerous co-operative retail societies, which are also its customers. Founded 1863, it acts as wholesaler, manufacturer, and banker, and owns factories, farms, and estates, in addition to offices and warehouses.

Cooper's Creek /'ku:pə/ river, often dry, in ◊Channel Country, SW Queensland, Australia.

coordinate in geometry, a number that defines the position of a point relative to a point or axis. Cartesian coordinates define a point by its perpendicular distances from two or more axes drawn through a fixed point at right angles to each other; ◊polar coordinates define a point in a plane by its distance from a fixed point and direction from a fixed line.

coordinate geometry or *analytical geometry* a system of geometry in which points, lines, shapes, and surfaces are represented by algebraic expressions. In plane (two-dimensional) coordinate geometry, the plane is usually defined by two axes at right angles to each other, the horizontal x-axis and the vertical y-axis, meeting at O, the origin. A point on the plane can be represented by a pair of ◊Cartesian coordinates, which define its position in terms of its distance along the x-axis and along the y-axis from O. These distances are respectively the x and y coordinates of the point.

Lines are represented as equations; for example, $y = 2x + 1$ gives a straight line, and $y = 3x + 2x$ gives a ◊parabola (a curve). The graphs of varying equations can be drawn by plotting the coordinates of points that satisfy their equations, and joining up the points. One of the advantages of coordinate geometry is that geometrical solutions can be obtained without drawing but by manipulating algebraic expressions. For example, the coordinates of the point of intersection of two straight lines can be determined by finding the unique values of x and y that satisfy both of the equations for the lines, that is, by solving them as a pair of ◊simultaneous equations. The curves studied in simple coordinate geometry are the ◊conic sections (circle, ellipse, parabola, and hyperbola), each of which has a characteristic equation.

Coorg /kʊəg/ or *Kurg* mountainous district of the state of Karnataka, in the Western Ghats of India. Formerly the princely state of Coorg, it was merged in Karnataka in 1956.

coot water bird *Fulica atra* belonging to the rail family. About 38 cm/1.2 ft long, and mainly black, it has a stark white forehead and big feet with lobed toes. They are found on inland waters in Europe, Asia, N Africa, and Australia, feeding on plants, insects, and small fish. Eight other species are distributed around the world, mostly in the Americas.

Coote /ku:t/ Eyre 1726–1783. Irish general in British India. His victory 1760 at Wandiwash, followed by the capture of Pondicherry, ended French hopes of supremacy. He returned to India as commander in chief 1779, and several times defeated ◊Hyder Ali, sultan of Mysore.

Copán /kəʊ'pæn/ town in W Honduras; population (1983) 19,000. The nearby site of a Maya city, including a temple and pyramids, was bought by John Stephens of the USA in the 1830s for $50.

cope semicircular cape, without sleeves, worn by priests of the Western Christian church in processions and on some other formal occasions, but not when officiating at Mass.

Copenhagen /ˌkəʊpən'heɪgən/ (Danish *København*) capital of Denmark, on the islands of Zealand and Amager; population (1988) 1,344,000 (including suburbs).

To the NE is the royal palace at Amalienborg; the 17th-century Charlottenburg Palace houses the Academy of Arts, and parliament meets in the Christiansborg Palace. The statue of Hans Andersen's 'Little Mermaid' (by Edvard Eriksen) is at the harbour entrance. The Tivoli amusement park is on the shore of the Øresund.

Copenhagen was a fishing village until 1167, when the bishop of Roskilde built the castle on the site of the present Christiansborg palace. A settlement grew up, and it became the Danish capital 1443. The university was founded 1479. The city was under German occupation Apr 1940–May 1945.

Copenhagen, Battle of /ˌkəʊpən'heɪgən/ naval victory 2 Apr 1801 by a British fleet under Sir Hyde Parker (1739–1807) and ◊Nelson over the Danish fleet. Nelson put his telescope to his blind eye and refused to see Parker's signal for withdrawal.

Copepoda subclass of ◊crustaceans, mainly microscopic, found in plankton.

Coper /'kəʊpə/ Hans 1920–1981. German potter, originally an engineer. His work resembles Cycladic Greek pots in its monumental quality.

Coperario /ˌkəʊpə'rɑ:rɪəʊ/ John c.1570–1626.. English composer of songs with lute or viol accompaniment. Born John Cooper, he changed his name after studying in Italy. His works include several masques, such as *The Masque of Flowers* 1614, and sets of fantasies for organ and solo viol.

Copernicus /kə'pɜ:nɪkəs/ Nicolaus 1473–1543. Polish astronomer, who believed that the Sun, not Earth, is at the centre of the solar system, thus defying established doctrine. For 30 years he worked on the hypothesis that the rotation and the orbital motion of Earth were responsible for the apparent movement of the heavenly bodies. His great work *De Revolutionibus Orbium Coelestium* was not published until the year of his death.

Born at Torun on the Vistula, then under the Polish king, he studied at Krakow and in Italy, and lectured on astronomy at Rome. On his return to Pomerania 1505 he became physician to his uncle, the bishop of Ermland, and was made canon at Frauenburg, although he did not take holy orders. Living there until his death, he interspersed astronomical work with the duties of various civil offices.

coplanar in geometry, lines or points that all lie in the same plane.

Copland /'kəʊplənd/ Aaron 1900– . US composer. Copland's early works, such as the piano concerto of 1926, were in the jazz idiom but he gradually developed a gentler style with a regional flavour drawn from American folk music.

Born in New York, he studied in France with Nadia Boulanger, and in 1940 became instructor in composition at the Berkshire Music Center. After 1945 he was the assistant director. Among his later works are the ballets *Billy the Kid* 1939; *Rodeo* 1942; and *Appalachian Spring* 1944, based on a poem by Hart Crane; and *Inscape for Orchestra* 1967.

Copley /'kɒplɪ/ John Singleton 1738–1815. American painter. He was the leading portraitist of the colonial period, but from 1775 he lived mainly in London, where he painted lively historical scenes such as *The Death of Major Pierson* 1783 (Tate Gallery, London).

Coppola US film director and screenwriter Francis Ford Coppola, 1979.

Copley was born in Boston, Massachussetts. Some of his history paintings are unusual in portraying recent dramatic events, such as *Brook Watson and the Shark* 1778 (National Gallery, Washington).

copper a chemical element, and one of the earliest metals used by humans; symbol Cu, atomic number 29, relative atomic mass 63.54. It is orange-pink in colour, very malleable and ductile, and used principally on account of its toughness, softness, pliability, high thermal and electrical conductivity, and resistance to corrosion.

When alloyed with tin, copper forms bronze, a relatively hard metal, the discovery of which opened a new age in human pre-history. Brass is an alloy of copper and zinc.

copper ore any mineral from which copper is extracted, including native copper, Cu; chalcocite, Cu_2S; chalcopyrite, $CuFeS_2$; bornite, Cu_5FeS_4; azurite, $Cu_3(CO_3)_2(OH)_2$; malachite, $Cu_2CO_3(OH)_2$; and chrysocolla, $CuSiO_3.nH_2O$.

Native copper and the copper sulphides are usually found in veins associated with igneous intrusions. Chrysocolla and the carbonates are products of the weathering of copper-bearing rocks. Copper was one of the first metals to be worked, because it occurred in native form and needed little refining. Today the main producers are the US, the USSR, Zambia, Chile, Peru, Canada, and Zaïre.

coppicing a severe type of pruning where trees are cut down to near ground level at regular intervals, typically every 3–20 years, to promote the growth of numerous shoots from the base.

This form of woodland management used to be commonly practised, especially on hazel and chestnut, to produce large quantities of thin branches for firewood, fencing, and so on; alder, eucalyptus, maple, poplar, and willow were also coppiced. The resulting thicket was known as a coppice or copse. See also ◊pollarding.

Coppola /'kɒpələ/ Francis Ford 1939– . US film director and screenwriter. He directed *The Godfather* 1972, which became one of the biggest money-makers of all time. Other successes include *Apocalypse Now* 1979, and *The Cotton Club* 1984.

copra dried kernel of the ◊coconut.

Copt a descendant of those ancient Egyptians who accepted Christianity in the 1st century and refused to adopt Islam after the Arab conquest. They now form a small minority (about 5%) of Egypt's population. The head of the Coptic Church is the Patriarch of Alexandria, currently Shenonda III (1923–), 117th pope of Alexandria. Imprisoned by President Sadat 1981, he is opposed by Muslim fundamentalists.

Before the Arab conquest a majority of Christian Egyptians had adopted Monophysite views (that Christ had 'one nature' rather than being human and divine). When this was condemned by the Council of Chalcedon 451, they became schismatic and were persecuted by the orthodox party, to which they were opposed on nationalistic as well as religious grounds. They readily

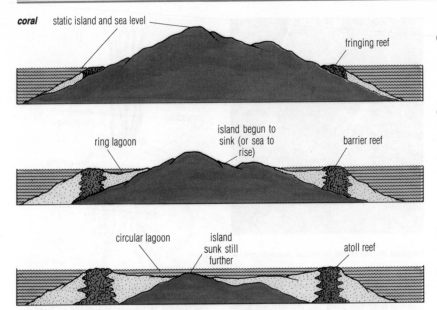

coral static island and sea level — fringing reef

ring lagoon   island begun to sink (or sea to rise)   barrier reef

circular lagoon   island sunk still further   atoll reef

accepted Arab rule, but were later subjected to persecution by their new masters. They are mainly town-dwellers, distinguishable in dress and customs from their Muslim compatriots. They rarely marry outside their own sect.

Coptic language a member of the Hamito-Semitic language family and a minority language of Egypt. It is descended from the language of the ancient Egyptians and is the ritual language of the Coptic Christian Church. It is written in the Greek alphabet with some additional characters derived from Demotic script.

copulation the act of mating in animals with internal ◊fertilization. Male mammals have a ◊penis or other organ, which is used to introduce spermatozoa into the reproductive tract of the female. Most birds transfer sperm by pressing their cloacas (the openings of their reproductive tracts) together.

copyhold a kind of land tenure common from medieval times. The term derives from the copy of the record written by the landowner stating the tenant's rights and dues. The document thus showed legal entitlement to the land.

copyright law applying to literary, musical, and artistic works (including plays, recordings, films, radio and television broadcasts, and, in the USA and Britain, computer programs), which prevents the reproduction of the work, in whole or in part, without the author's consent.

Copyright applies to a work, not an idea. For example, the basic plots of two novels might be identical, but copyright would only be infringed if it was clear that one author had copied from another. Translations are protected in their own right. The copyright holder may assign the copyright to another, or license others to reproduce or adapt the work. In the USA (since 1978) and Britain, copyright lasts for 50 years after publication of the work or the death of the author, whichever is the later. Copyright is internationally enforceable under the Berne Convention 1886 (ratified by Britain, among others), and the Universal Copyright Convention 1952 (more widely ratified, including the USA, the USSR and Britain). Both conventions have been revised, most recently in Paris in 1971. Under the Universal Copyright Convention works must be marked with the copyright symbol accompanied by the name of the copyright owner and the year of its first publication. The Berne Convention gives a longer minimum period of protection of copyright.

coral marine organism related to sea anemones, and belonging to the class Anthozoa of the phylum Cnidaria. It has a skeleton of lime (calcium carbonate) extracted from the surrounding water. Corals

exist in warm, salt seas, at moderate depths with sufficient light.

Corals live in a symbiotic relationship with microscopic ◊algae (zooxanthellae), which are incorporated into the structure. The algae receive carbon dioxide from the ◊polyps, and the polyps receive nutrients from the algae. Corals also have a relationship with the fish that rest or take refuge within their branches, and which excrete nutrients that make the corals grow faster.

The majority of corals are omnivorous and form large colonies. Their accumulated skeletons make up large coral reefs and atolls. The Great Barrier Reef, to the NE of Australia, is about 1,600 km/1,000 mi long. *Barrier reefs* are separated from the shore by a saltwater lagoon, which may be as much as 30 km/20 mi wide; there are usually navigable passes through the barrier into the lagoon. *Atolls* resemble a ring surrounding a lagoon, and do not enclose an island. They are usually formed by the gradual subsidence of an extinct volcano, the coral growing up from where the edge of the island once lay. *Fringing reefs* are so called because they build up on the shores of continents or islands, the living animals mainly occupying the outer edges of the reef. Some coral is valued for decoration or jewellery,

for example Mediterranean *red coral Corallum rubrum.*

Coralli /ˌkɒrəˈliː/ Jean 1779–1854. French dancer and choreographer of Italian descent. He made his debut as a dancer in 1802. He choreographed *Le Diable boîteux* 1836 for the Austrian ballerina Fanny Elssler, *Giselle* 1841 and *La Péri* 1843 for the Italian ballerina Grisi; and many other well-known ballets.

Coral Sea /ˈkɒrəl/ or *Solomon Sea* part of the Pacific Ocean lying between NE Australia, New Guinea, the Solomon Islands, Vanuatu, and New Caledonia. It contains numerous coral islands and reefs. The Coral Sea Islands are a Territory of Australia; they comprise scattered reefs and islands over an area of about 1,000,000 sq km. They are uninhabited except for a meteorological station on Willis Island.

The Great Barrier Reef lies along its western edge.

coral tree several tropical trees of the genus *Erythrina*, family Leguminosae, with bright red or orange flowers, and producing a very lightweight wood.

Coram /ˈkɔːrəm/ Thomas 1668–1751. English philanthropist, who established the Foundling Hospital for orphaned and abandoned children in Holborn, London, 1741. The site, now Coram's Fields, is still a children's foundation.

cor anglais or *English horn* alto member of the ◊oboe family, of distinctive melancholy tone, used by Prokofiev in *Peter and the Wolf* to represent a duck.

Corbière /ˌkɔːbiˈeə/ Tristan 1845–1875. French poet. His *Les Amours jaunes/Yellow Loves* 1873 went unrecognized until Verlaine called attention to it in 1884. Many of his poems, such as *La Rhapsodie Foraine/Wandering Rhapsody*, deal with life in his native Brittany.

Corby /ˈkɔːbi/ town in Northamptonshire, England; population (1981) 52,500. Formerly a major steel centre, it is now an enterprise zone producing plastics.

cord unit for measuring the volume of timber. One cord = 3.456 cubic metres/128 cubic feet.

Corday /kɔːˈdeɪ/ Charlotte 1768–1793. French Girondin (right-wing republican during the French Revolution). After the overthrow of the Girondins by the more extreme Jacobins May 1793, she stabbed to death the Jacobin leader, Marat, with a bread knife as he sat in his bath in July of the same year. She was guillotined.

cordillera a group of mountain ranges and their valleys, all running in a specific direction, formed by

Córdoba Córdoba's vast horizontal Mezquita was originally a mosque transformed into a cathedral in 1236.

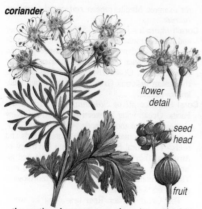

coriander

flower detail

seed head

fruit

Copland The American composer Aaron Copland.

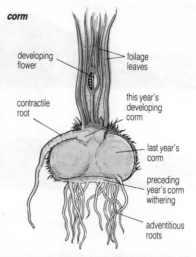

corm

developing flower

foilage leaves

contractile root

this year's developing corm

last year's corm

preceding year's corm withering

adventitious roots

the continued convergence of two ◊tectonic plates along a line.

Cordilleras, the /ˌkɔːdɪlˈjeərəz/ the mountainous western section of North America, with the Rocky Mountains and the coastal ranges parallel to the contact between the North American and the Pacific plates.

Córdoba /ˈkɔːdəbə/ city in central Argentina, on the Rio Primero; population (1980) 982,000. It is capital of Córdoba province. Main industries include cement, glass, textiles and vehicles. Founded in 1573, it has a university 1613, a military aviation college, an observatory, and a cathedral.

Córdoba /ˈkɔːdəbə/ capital of Córdoba province, Spain, on the river Guadalquivir; population (1986) 305,000. Paper, textiles, and copper products are manufactured here. It has many Moorish remains, including the mosque, now a cathedral, founded by 'Abd-ar-Rahman I in 785; it is one of the largest Christian churches in the world. Córdoba was probably founded by the Carthaginians, and held by the Moors 711–1236.

core the innermost part of the structure of Earth. It is divided into an inner core, the upper boundary of which is 1,700 km/1,060 mi from the centre, and an outer core, 1,820 km/1,130 mi thick. Both parts are thought to consist of iron-nickel alloy, with the inner core being solid and the outer core being liquid. The temperature may be 3,000°C/5,400°F.

These hypotheses are based on seismology (the observation of the paths of earthquake waves through the Earth), and calculations of the Earth's density.

Corelli /kəˈreli/ Arcangelo 1653–1713. Italian composer and violinist. He was one of the first virtuoso violinists and his music, marked by graceful melody, includes a set of *concerti grossi* and five sets of chamber sonatas.

Born near Milan, he studied in Bologna and in about 1685 settled in Rome, under the patronage of Cardinal Pietro Ottoboni, where he published his first violin sonatas.

Corelli /kəˈreli/ Marie. Pseudonym of British novelist Mary Mackay 1855–1924. Trained for a musical career, she turned instead to writing (she was said to be Queen Victoria's favourite novelist) and published *The Romance of Two Worlds* 1886. Her works were later ridiculed for their pretentious style.

Corfe Castle /kɔːf/ village in the Isle of Purbeck, Dorset, England, built around the ruins of a Norman castle destroyed in the Civil War.

Corfu /kɔːˈfuː/ (Greek *Kérkira*) most northerly, second largest of the Ionian islands, off the coast of Epirus in the Ionian Sea; area 1,072 sq km/414 sq mi; population (1981) 96,500. Its businesses include tourism, fruit, olive oil, and textiles. Its largest town is the port of Corfu (Kérkira), population (1981) 33,560. Corfu was colonized by Corinthians about 700 BC, Venice held it 1386–1797, Britain from 1815–64.

Cori /ˈkɔːri/ Carl (1896–) and Gerty 1896–1957. Husband and wife team of US biochemists, both

born in Prague who, together with Bernardo Houssay, received a Nobel prize 1947 for their discovery of how glycogen—a derivative of ◊glucose – is broken down and resynthsized in the body, for use as a store and source of energy.

coriander a pungent spice, the dried ripe fruit of the plant *Coriandoam sativum*, a member of the parsley family. It is used commercially as a flavouring in meat products, bakery goods, tobacco, gin, and curry powder. Coriander is much used in cooking in the Middle East, India, Mexico, and China.

Corinna /kəˈrɪnə/ Greek lyric poet of 6th century BC, said to have instructed Pindar. Only fragments of her poetry survive.

Corinth /ˈkɒrɪnθ/ (Greek *Kórinthos*) port in Greece, on the isthmus connecting the Peloponnese with the mainland; population (1981) 22,650. The rocky isthmus is dissected by the 6.5 km/4 mi Corinth canal, opened 1893. The site of the ancient city-state of Corinth lies 7 km/4.5 mi SW.

Corinth was already a place of some commercial importance in the 9th century BC. At the end of the 6th century BC it joined the Peloponnesian League, and took a prominent part in the ◊Persian and the ◊Peloponnesian wars. In 146 BC it was conquered by the Romans. The emperor Augustus (63 BC–AD 14) made it capital of the Roman province of Achaea. St Paul visited Corinth AD 51 and addressed two epistles to its churches. After many changes of ownership it became part of independent Greece in 1822. Corinth's ancient monuments include the ruined temple of Apollo (6th century BC).

Corinthian in classical architecture, one of the five types of ◊column.

Corinthians two ◊epistles (Corinthians I, Corinthians II) in the New Testament to the church at Corinth; attributed to ◊Paul.

Coriolis effect a result of the deflective force of the Earth's W to E rotation. Winds, ocean currents, and aircraft are deflected to the right of their direction of travel in the Northern hemisphere and to the left in the Southern hemisphere.

The effect has to be allowed for in launching guided missiles, but despite popular belief it has negligible effect on the clockwise or anti-clockwise direction of water running out of a bath. Named after its discoverer, French mathematician Gaspard Coriolis (1792–1843).

Cork /kɔːk/ largest county of the Republic of Ireland, in the province of Munster; county town Cork; area 7,460 sq km/2,880 sq mi; population (1986) 413,000. It is agricultural but there is also some copper and manganese mining, marble quarrying, and river and sea fishing. Natural gas and oil fields are found off the S coast at Kinsale.

It includes Bantry Bay and the village of Blarney. There is a series of ridges and vales running NE-SW across the county. The Nagles and Boggeraph mountains run across the centre,

separating the two main rivers, the Blackwater and the Lee. Towns are Cobh, Bantry, Youghal, Fermoy, and Mallow. Natural gas, found off the S coast at Kinsale, is supplied to Northern Ireland.

Cork /kɔːk/ city and seaport of county Cork, on the river Lee, at the head of the long inlet of Cork Harbour; population (1986) 174,000. Cork is the second port of the Republic of Ireland. The lower section of the harbour can berth liners, and the town has distilleries, shipyards, and iron foundries. St Finbarr's seventh-century monastery was the original foundation of Cork. It was eventually settled by Danes who were dispossessed by the English 1172. University College (1845) became the University of Cork 1968. The city hall was opened 1937. There is a Protestant cathedral dedicated to the city's patron saint: St Finbarr, and a Roman Catholic cathedral of St Mary and St Finbarr.

cork /kɔːk/ the light, waterproof, outer layers of the bark of the stems and roots of almost all trees and shrubs. The cork oak *Quercus suber*, a native of S Europe and N Africa, is cultivated in Spain and Portugal; the outer layers of its bark provide the cork that is used commercially.

corm a short, swollen, underground plant stem, surrounded by protective scale-leaves, as seen in *Crocus*. It stores food, provides a means of ◊vegetative reproduction, and acts as a ◊perennating organ.

During the year the corm gradually withers as the food reserves are used for the production of leafy, flowering shoots formed from axillary buds. Several new corms are formed at the base of these shoots, above the old corm.

Corman /ˈkɔːmən/ Roger 1926– . US film director and producer. He directed a stylish series of Edgar Allan Poe films starring Vincent Price that began with *House of Usher* 1960. After 1970 Corman confined himself to production and distribution.

cormorant seabird *Phalacrocorax carbo*, about 90 cm/3 ft long, with webbed feet, long neck and beak, and glossy black plumage. There are some 30 species of cormorant worldwide including a flightless form *Nannopterum harrisi* in the Galápagos Islands. It generally feeds on bottom-living fish in shallow water. In W Europe it is found mainly in coastal areas, but in some places it is common by lakes and rivers.

corn the main ◊cereal crop of a region, for example, wheat in the UK, oats in Scotland and Ireland, maize in the USA.

corncrake bird *Crex crex* of the rail family. About 25 cm/10 in long, it is drably coloured, shy, and has a persistent rasping call. It lives in meadows and crops in temperate regions, but has become rare where mechanical methods of cutting corn are used.

Cornwall

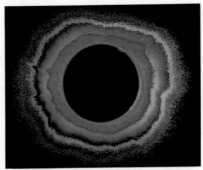

corona The corona, the Sun's outer atmosphere, which can only be seen during a total solar eclipse.

Corneille /kɔːˈneɪ/ Pierre 1606–1684. French dramatist. His many tragedies, such as *Oedipe* 1659, glorify the strength of will governed by reason, and established the French classical dramatic tradition for the next two centuries. His first play, *Mélite*, was performed 1629, followed by others that gained him a brief period of favour with Cardinal Richelieu. *Le Cid* 1636 was attacked by the Academicians although it achieved huge public success. Later plays were based on Aristotle's unities.

Although Corneille enjoyed public popularity, periodic disfavour with Richelieu marred his career, and it was not until 1639 that Corneille (again in favour) produced plays such as *Horace* 1639, *Polyeucte* 1643, *Le Menteur* 1643, and *Rodogune* 1645, leading to his election to the Académie 1647. His later plays were approved by Louis XIV.

cornet brass band instrument. It is like a shorter, broader trumpet, with a wider bore and mellower tone, and without fixed notes. Notes of different pitch are obtained by over-blowing and by means of three pistons.

cornett a 17th-century woodwind instrument. It has a cup mouthpiece and produces a trumpet-like tone.

cornflour in the UK, the purified starch content of maize (Indian corn), used as a thickener in cooking; in the USA it is called cornstarch.

cornflower plant *Centaurea cyanus* of the family Compositae. It is distinguished from the knapweeds by its deep azure-blue flowers. Formerly a common weed in cornfields, it is now commonly grown in gardens as a herbaceous plant.

Cornforth /ˈkɔːnfɔːθ/ John 1917– . Australian chemist who settled in England 1941. In 1975 he shared a Nobel prize with Vladimir Prelog for work utilizing ◊radioisotopes as 'markers' to find out how enzymes synthesize chemicals that are mirror images of one another (stereo isomers).

Corniche /kɔːˈniːʃ/ (French 'mountain ledge') *la Grande* (Great) *Corniche*, a road with superb alpine and coastal scenery, was built between Nice and Menton, S France, by Napoleon; it rises to 520 m/1,700 ft. *La Moyenne* (Middle) and *la Petite* (Little) *Corniche*, are supplementary parallel roads, the latter being nearest the coast.

Cornish language an extinct member of the Celtic language, branch of the Indo-European language family, spoken in Cornwall until 1777. Written Cornish first appeared in 10th century documents, some religious plays were written in Cornish in the 15th and 16th centuries, but later literature is scanty, mainly folk-tales and verses.

Corn Laws in Britain until 1846, laws used to regulate the export or import of cereals, to maintain an adequate supply for consumers and a secure price for producers.

For centuries the Corn Laws formed an integral part of the mercantile system in England; they were repealed because they became an unwarranted tax on food and a hindrance to British exports.

After the Napoleonic wars, with mounting pressure from a growing urban population, the Corn Laws aroused strong opposition because of their tendency to drive up the price. They were modified 1828 and 1842 and, partly as a result of the Irish famine, repealed by Robert Peel 1846.

cornucopia (Latin 'horn of plenty') In Greek mythology, one of the horns of the goat Amaltheia, which was caused by Zeus to refill itself indefinitely with food and drink. In paintings, the cornucopia is depicted as a horn-shaped container spilling over with fruit and flowers.

Cornwall /ˈkɔːnwɔːl/ county in SW England including Scilly Islands (Scillies)
area (excluding Scillies) 3,550 sq km/1,370 sq mi
towns administrative headquarters Truro; Camborne, Launceston; resorts of Bude, Falmouth, Newquay, Penzance, St Ives
physical Bodmin Moor (including Brown Willy 419 m/1,375 ft), Land's End peninsula, St Michael's Mount, rivers Tamar, Fowey, Fal, and Camel
features Poldhu, site of first transatlantic radio signal 1901. The Stannary has six members from each of the four Stannary towns: Losthwithiel, Launceston, Helston, and Truro. The flag of St Piran, a white St George's cross on a black ground, is used by separatists.
products electronics; spring flowers; tin (mined since Bronze Age, some workings renewed in 1960s, though the industry has all but disappeared), kaolin (St Austell); fish
population (1987) 453,000
famous people John Betjeman, Humphry Davy, Daphne Du Maurier, William Golding
history the Stannary or Tinners' Parliament, established in the 11th century, ceased to meet 1752 but its powers were never rescinded at Westminster, and it was revived 1974 as a separatist movement.

Cornwallis /kɔːnˈwɒlɪs/ Charles, 1st Marquess Cornwallis 1738–1805. British soldier, eldest son of the 1st Earl Cornwallis. He led the British forces in the War of ◊American Independence until 1781, when his surrender at Yorktown ended the war. Subsequently he was twice governor general of India, and viceroy of Ireland, and was made a marquess 1793.

corolla a collective name for the petals of a flower. In some plants the petal margins are partially or completely fused to form a *corolla-tube*, for example in bindweed *Convolvulus arevensis*.

Coromandel /ˌkɒrəˈmændl/ the east coast of Tamil Nadu, India.

Coromandel Peninsula /ˌkɒrəˈmændl/ peninsula on North Island, New Zealand, east of Auckland.

corona a faint halo of hot (about 2,000,000 K) and tenuous gas around the Sun, which boils from the surface. It is visible at solar ◊eclipses or through a *coronagraph*, an instrument that blocks light from the Sun's brilliant disc. The

gas flows away from the corona to form the ◊solar wind.

Corona Australis (Latin 'Southern Crown') constellation of the southern hemisphere, located to the south of the constellation Sagittarius.

Corona Borealis (Latin 'Northern Crown') constellation of the northern hemisphere, representing the headband of Ariadne that was cast into the sky by Bacchus. Its brightest star is Gemma, which is 75 light years away.

Coronado Francisco de *c*.1500–1554. Spanish explorer who sailed to the New World in 1535 in search of gold. In 1540 he set out with several hundred men from the Gulf of California on an exploration of what are today the Southern states. Although he failed to discover any gold, his expedition came across the impressive Grand Canyon of the Colorado and introduced the use of the horse to the indigenous Indians.

coronary artery disease (Latin *corona* 'crown', from their encircling of the heart) condition in which the fatty deposits of ◊atherosclerosis form in, and therefore narrow, the coronary arteries that supply the heart muscle.

These arteries may already be hardened (arteriosclerosis). If the heart's oxygen requirements are increased, as during exercise, the blood supply through the narrowed arteries may be inadequate, and the pain of ◊angina results. A *heart attack* occurs if the blood supply to an area of the heart is cut off, for example because a blood clot (thrombus) has blocked one of the coronary arteries. The subsequent lack of oxygen damages the heart muscle (infarct), and if a large area of the heart is affected, the attack may be fatal. Coronary artery disease tends to run in families, and is linked to smoking, lack of exercise, and a diet high in saturated (mostly animal) fats, which increases the level of blood ◊cholesterol. It is a common cause of death in many developed countries, especially among older men.

coronation the ceremony of investing a sovereign with the emblems of royalty, as a symbol of inauguration in office. Since the coronation of Harold 1066, English sovereigns have been crowned in Westminster Abbey, London. The kings of Scotland were traditionally crowned at Scone; French kings in Rheims.

The British coronation ceremony combines the Hebrew rite of anointing with customs of Germanic origin, for example, the actual crowning and the presentation of the monarch to his or her subjects to receive homage. It comprises the presentation to the people; the administration of the oath; the presentation of the Bible; the anointing of the sovereign with holy oil on hands, breast, and head; the presentation of the spurs and the sword of state, the emblems of knighthood; the presentation of the armils (a kind of bracelet), robe royal, the orb, the ring, the sceptre with the cross, and the rod with the dove; the coronation with St Edward's Crown; the benediction; the enthroning; and the homage of the princes of the blood and the peerage.

A *consort* (the spouse of a sovereign) is anointed on the head, presented with a ring, crowned, and presented with the sceptre and the ivory rod.

coroner in England, an official who investigates the deaths of persons who have died suddenly by acts of violence, or under suspicious circumstances, by holding an inquest or ordering a post-mortem examination. They may also inquire into instances of ◊treasure trove. The coroner's court aims not to establish liability but to find out how and why the death occurred.

A coroner must be a barrister, solicitor, or medical practitioner with at least five years' professional service. At an inquest, a coroner is assisted by a jury of between seven and eleven people. Evidence is on oath, and medical and other witnesses may be summoned. If the jury returns a verdict of murder or manslaughter, the coroner can commit the accused for trial. In Scotland similar duties are performed by the procurator-fiscal. In the USA coroners are usually elected by the voters of the county. Coroner's courts have been criticised as autocratic since the coroner alone decides which witnesses should be called and legal aid is not available for representation in a coroner's court. Nor may any of the parties make a closing speech to the jury.

coronet a small crown worn by a peer at Coronations. A duke's coronet consists of a golden circlet, above which are eight strawberry leaves; a marquess's has four strawberry leaves with four points surmounted by pearls between them, an earl's eight strawberry leaves with eight tall points surmounted by pearls between them, a viscount's sixteen small pearls, and a baron's six large pearls.

Corot /'kɒrəʊ/ Jean-Baptiste-Camille 1796–1875. French painter, creator of a distinctive landscape style with cool colours and soft focus. His early work, particularly Italian scenes in the 1820s, influenced the Barbizon school of painters. Like them, Corot worked out of doors, but he also continued a conventional academic tradition with more romanticized paintings.

corporal punishment physical punishment of wrongdoers, for example by whipping. It was abolished as a punishment for criminals in Britain 1967 but only became illegal for punishing schoolchildren in state schools 1986. It is still used as a punishment for criminals in many countries, especially under Islamic law.

corporation an organisation that has its own legal identity, distinct from that of its members, for example a ◊company. The term is more commonly used in the USA than in Britain. In English law corporations can be either: a corporation aggregate, consisting of a number of members who may vary from time to time, as in a company; or a corporation sole, consisting of one person and his successors, for example a monarch or a bishop.

corporation tax a tax levied on a company's profits by public authorities. It is a form of income tax, and rates vary according to country, but there is usually a flat rate. It is an important source of revenue for governments.

corporatism the belief that the state in capitalist democracies should intervene to a large extent in the economy to ensure social harmony.

corporative state state in which the members are organized and represented not on a local basis as citizens, but as producers working in a particular trade, industry, or profession. Originating with the syndicalist workers' movement, the idea was superficially adopted by the fascists during the 1920s and 1930s. Catholic social theory, as expounded in some papal encyclicals, also favours the corporative state as a means of eliminating class conflict.

The concept arose in the political theories of the syndicalist movement of the early 20th century, which proposed that all industries should be taken over and run by the trade unions, a federation of whom should replace the state. Similar views were put forward in Britain by the guild socialists about 1906–25. Certain features of syndicalist theory were adopted and given a right-wing tendency by the fascist regime in Italy, under which employers' and workers' organizations were represented in the National Council of Corporations, but this was completely dominated by the Fascist Party and had no real powers.

Corporative institutions were set up by the Franco and Salazar regimes in Spain and Portugal, under the influence of fascist and Catholic theories. In Spain representatives of the national syndicates were included in the Cortes (parliament), and in Portugal a corporative chamber existed alongside the National Assembly.

corps de ballet the dancers in a ballet company who usually dance in groups, in support of the soloists.

At the Paris Opéra this is the name given to the whole company.

Corpus Christi feast celebrated in the Roman Catholic and Orthodox churches, and to some extent in the Anglican Church, on the Thursday after Trinity Sunday. It was instituted in the 13th century through the devotion of St Juliana, prioress of Mount Cornillon, near Liège, in honour of the Real Presence of Christ in the Eucharist.

corpuscular theory hypothesis about the nature of light championed by Isaac Newton, who postulated that it consists of a stream of particles or corpuscles. The theory was superseded at the beginning of the 19th century by Thomas ◊Young's wave theory. ◊Quantum theory and wave mechanics embody both concepts.

Correggio /kɒˈredʒɪəʊ/ Antonio Allegri da *c.* 1494–1534. Italian painter of the High Renaissance, whose style followed the classical grandeur of Leonardo and Titian but anticipated the Baroque in its emphasis on movement, softer forms, and contrasts of light and shade.

Based in Parma, he painted splendid illusionistic visions in the cathedral there. His religious paintings, including the night scene *Adoration of the Shepherds* about 1527–30 (Gemäldegalerie, Dresden), and mythological scenes, such as *The Loves of Jupiter* (Wallace Collection, London), were much admired in the 18th century.

Corregidor /kəˈregɪdɔː/ an island at the mouth of Manila Bay, Luzon, the Philippines, where survivors of the ◊Bataan campaign were defeated by the Japanese, 9 Apr–6 May 1942; the USA recaptured it 15 Feb 1945.

correlation a relationship or form of interdependence between two sets of data. In ◊statistics, such relationships are measured by the calculation of ◊coefficients. These generally measure correlation on a scale with 1 indicating perfect positive correlation, 0 no correlation at all, and –1 perfect inverse correlation.

Correlation coefficients for assumed linear relationships include the Pearson product moment correlation coefficient (known simply as correlation coefficient), Kendall's tau correlation coefficient, or Spearman's rho correlation coefficient, which is used in non-parametric statistics (where the data are measured on ordinal rather than interval scales). A high correlation does not always indicate dependence between two variables; it may be that there is a third (unstated) variable upon which both depend.

correspondence in mathematics, the relation between two sets where an operation on the members of one set maps some or all of them onto one or more members of the other. For example, if *A* is the set of members of a family and *B* is the set of months in the year, *A* and *B* are in correspondence if the operation is: '...has a birthday in the month of...'.

Corrèze /kɒˈreɪz/ river of central France flowing 89 km/55 mi from the Plateau des Millevaches, past Tulle, capital of Corrèze *département* (to which it gives its name), to join the Vézère. It is used for generating electricity at Bar, 9.5 km/6 mi NW of Tulle.

corrie (Welsh *cwm*; French, American *cirque*) Scottish term for a steep-walled hollow in the mountainside of a glaciated area representing the

corrie A perfect corrie overlooking Loch Broom, in the Scottish Highlands.

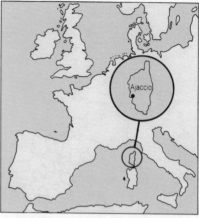

Corsica

source of a melted glacier. The weight of the ice has ground out the bottom and worn back the sides. It is open at the front, and its sides and back are formed of ◊arêtes. There may be a lake in the bottom.

Corrientes /ˌkɒriˈentes/ city of Argentina, on the Paraná river; population (1980) 180,000. Capital of Corrientes province, it is an important river port in a stock-raising district. Industries include tanning, sawmilling and textiles.

corrigendum (Latin) something to be corrected.

corroboree Australian Aboriginal dance. Some corroborees record events in history; others have a religious significance, connected with fertility and rejuvenation; some are theatrical entertainment.

corrosion the eating away and eventual destruction of metals and alloys by chemical attack. The rusting of ordinary iron and steel is the commonest form of corrosion. Rusting takes place in moist air, the iron combines with oxygen and water to form a brown-orange deposit of ◊rust, hydrated iron oxide. The rate of corrosion is increased where the atmosphere is polluted with sulphur dioxide. Salty roads or atmospheres accelerate the rusting of car bodies.

Corrosion is largely an electrochemical process, and acidic and salty conditions favour the establishment of electrolytic cells on the metal which cause it to be eaten away. Other examples of corrosion include the green deposit that forms on copper and bronze, called verdigris, a basic copper carbonate. The tarnish on silver is a corrosion product, a film of silver sulphide.

corsair a pirate based on the N African Barbary Coast. From the 16th century onward the corsairs plundered shipping in the Mediterranean and Atlantic, holding hostages for ransom or selling them as slaves. Although many punitive expeditions were sent against them, they were not suppressed until France occupied Algiers 1830.

Most pirates were Turkish or N African, but there were also many Europeans, such as the Englishman Sir Francis Verney, half-brother of Edmund Verney.

Corse /kɔːs/ French name for ◊Corsica.

Corsica /'kɔːsɪkə/ (French *Corse*) island region of France, in the Mediterranean off the W coast of Italy, north of Sardinia; it comprises the *départements* of Haute Corse and Corse du Sud
area 8,700 sq km/3,358 sq mi
capital and port Ajaccio
features ◊maquis vegetation; its mountain bandits were eradicated 1931, but the tradition of the vendetta or blood feud lingers; it is the main base of the ◊Foreign Legion
exports wine, olive oil
population (1986) 249,000, of whom just under 50% are native Corsicans; there are about 400,000 *émigrés*, mostly in Mexico and Central America, who return to retire
language French (official); the majority speak Corsican, an Italian dialect

Ferdinand Cortez A Spaniard.

Cortés *A Spanish soldier and the conqueror of Mexico, Ferdinand Cortés destroyed the powerful Aztec civilization before becoming Mexico's governor.*

famous people Napoleon
government its special status involves a 61-member regional parliament with the power to scrutinize French National Assembly bills applicable to the island and propose amendments.
history the Phocaeans of Ionia founded Alalia about 570 BC, and were succeeded in turn by the Etruscans, the Carthaginians, the Romans, the Vandals, and the Arabs. In the 14th century, Corsica fell to the Genoese, and in the second half of the 18th century a Corsican nationalist, Pasquale Paoli (1725–1807), led an independence movement. Genoa sold Corsica to France 1768. In World War II Corsica was occupied by Italy 1942–43. From 1962, French *pieds noir* (refugees from Algeria), especially vine growers, were settled in Corsica, and their prosperity helped to fan nationalist feeling, which demands an independent Corsica. This fuelled a 'national liberation front' (FNLC), banned 1983.

Cort /kɔːt/ Henry 1740–1800. British iron manufacturer. For the manufacture of ◊wrought iron, he invented the puddling process and developed the rolling mill, both of which were significant in the Industrial Revolution.

Cortázar /kɔːˈtɑːzə/ Julio 1914– . Argentine writer, born in Brussels, whose novels include *The Winners* 1960, *Hopscotch* 1963, and *62. A Model Kit* 1968. His several volumes of short stories include 'Blow-up', adapted for a film by the Italian director Antonioni.

Cortés /ˈkɔːtez/ Hernándo (Ferdinand) 1485–1547. Spanish conquistador. He overthrew the Aztec empire 1519–21, and secured Mexico for Spain.

He went to the West Indies as a young man, and in 1518 was given command of an expedition to Mexico. Landing with only 600 men, he was at first received as a god by the Aztec emperor ◊Montezuma II, but was finally expelled from Tenochtitlán (Mexico City) by a revolt. With the aid of Indian allies he recaptured the city 1521, and overthrew the Aztec empire. His conquests eventually included most of Mexico and N Central America.

corticosteroid any of several hormones secreted by the adrenal cortex; also synthetic forms with similar properties. Corticosteroids have anti-inflammatory and ◊immunosuppressive effects and may be used to treat a number of conditions including rheumatoid arthritis, severe allergies, asthma, some skin diseases, and some cancers. Side-effects can be serious, and therapy must be withdrawn very gradually.

cortisone a corticosteroid with anti-inflammatory qualities. It is commonly used in the treatment of rheumatoid arthritis.

Cortisone was discovered by T Reichstein of Basle, Switzerland, and put to practical clinical use for rheumatoid arthritis by P S Hench and E C Kendall in the USA (all three shared a Nobel prize 1950). A product of the adrenal gland, it was first synthesized from a constituent of ox-bile, and is now produced commercially from a Mexican yam and from a byproduct of the sisal plant. It is used for treating allergies and certain cancers, as well as rheumatoid arthritis. The side-effects of cortisone steroids include muscle wasting, fat redistribution, diabetes, bone thinning, and high blood pressure.

Cortona /kɔːˈtəʊnə/ town in Tuscany, N Italy, 22 km/13 mi SE of Arezzo; population (1981) 22,000. One of Europe's oldest cities. It is encircled by walls built by the Etruscans, and has a medieval castle and an 11th-century cathedral.

Cortona Pietro da. Alternative name for Italian Baroque painter ◊Pietro da Cortona.

corundum aluminium oxide, Al_2O_3, the hardest naturally occurring mineral known apart from diamond (corundum rates 9 on the Mohs' scale); lack of ◊cleavage also increases its durability. Gem quality corundum is ruby (red) or sapphire (any other colour including blue). Material of lesser quality is economically important as an abrasive and for other industrial purposes; synthetic corundum is also used in industry.

Corundum forms in silica-poor igneous and metamorphic rocks. It is a constituent of emery, which is metamorphosed bauxite. Crystals are barrel-shaped prisms of the trigonal system.

Corunna /kɒˈrʌnə/ (Spanish *La Coruña*) city in the extreme NW of Spain; population (1986) 242,000. It is the capital of Corunna province. Industry is centred upon the fisheries; tobacco, sugar refining, and textiles are also important. The ◊Armada sailed from Corunna 1588, and the town was sacked by Francis Drake 1589.

Corunna, Battle of /kɒˈrʌnə/ battle held Jan 16 1809, during the ◊Peninsular War, to cover embarkation of British troops after their retreat to Corunna; their commander, Sir John Moore, was killed after ensuring a victory over the French.

corvette term, now obsolete, revived from sailing days for small-armed vessels, such as those escorting convoys in World War II.

Corvo /ˈkɔːvəʊ/ Baron 1860–1913. Assumed name of British writer Frederick ◊Rolfe.

Cos alternative spelling of ◊Kos, a Greek island.

cosecant in trigonometry, a ◊function of an angle in a right-angled triangle found by dividing the length of the hypotenuse (the longest side) by the length of the side opposite the angle. Thus the cosecant of an angle *A*, usually shortened to cosec *A*, is always greater than 1. It is the reciprocal of the sine of the angle, that is, cosec $A = 1/\sin A$.

Cosenza /kəʊˈzentsə/ town in Calabria, S Italy; at the junction of the river Crati and the river Busento; population (1988) 106,000. It is the capital of Cosenza province and is an archiepiscopal see. ◊Alaric, king of the Visigoths, is buried here.

Cosgrave /ˈkɒzgreɪv/ Liam 1920– . Irish Fine Gael politician, prime minister of the Republic of Ireland 1973–77. As party leader 1965–77, he headed a Fine Gael–Labour coalition government from 1973. Relations between the Irish and UK governments improved under his premiership.

Cosgrave /ˈkɒzgreɪv/ William Thomas 1880–1965. Irish politician. He took part in the Easter Rising 1916, and sat in the Sinn Féin cabinet of 1919–21. Head of the Free State government 1922–33, he founded and led the Fine Gael opposition 1933–44. His eldest son is Liam Cosgrave.

cosine in trigonometry, a function of an angle in a right-angled triangle found by dividing the length of the side adjacent to the angle by the length of the hypotenuse (the longest side). It is usually shortened to cos.

cosmic radiation radiation caused by space-originating high-energy particles, consisting of protons and light nuclei, which collide with atomic nuclei in the earth's atmosphere.

Those of low energy seem to be galactic in origin, and detectors (the water-Cherenkov detector near Leeds has an area of 12 sq km/4.5 sq mi) are in use to detect extra-galactic sources (possibly the rotating discs of infalling matter round black holes) of high-energy rays.

cosmogony (Greek 'universe' + 'creation') the study of the origin and evolution of cosmic objects, especially the solar system.

cosmology the study of the structure of the universe. Modern cosmology began in the 1920s with the discovery that the universe is expanding, which suggested that it began in an explosion, the ◊Big Bang. An alternative view, the ◊*steady-state theory*, claimed that the universe has no origin, but is expanding because new matter is being continually created.

cosmonaut Soviet term for a person who travels in space.

cosmonaut *The Soviet pioneers of human space flight for scientific research, photographed in 1965. Left to right, seated: Yuri Gagarin, Pavel Belyayev, Valentina Tereshkova, Alexei Leonov, and Vladimir Komarov, standing: Pavel Popovich, Gherman Titov, Konstantin Feoktistov, Boris Yegorov, Andrian Nikolayev, and Valeri Bykovsky.*

Costa Rica
Republic of
(República de Costa Rica)

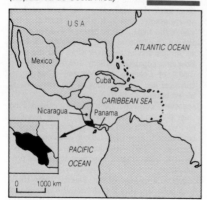

area 51,100 sq km/19,725 sq mi
capital San José
towns ports Limón, Puntarenas
physical high central plateau and tropical coast
head of state and government Oscar Arias Sánchez from 1986
political system liberal democracy
political parties National Liberation Party (PLN), left-of-centre; Christian Socialist Unity Party (PUSC), centrist
exports coffee, bananas, cocoa, sugar
currency colón (144.88 = £1 Feb 1990)
population (1988) 2,810,000 (including 1,200 Guaymí Indians); annual growth rate 2.6%
life expectancy men 71, women 76
language Spanish
religion Roman Catholic
literacy 94% male/93% female (1985 est)
GDP $2 bn (1982); $2,238 per head of population
chronology
1821 Independence achieved.
1949 New constitution adopted. National army abolished. José Figueres, co-founder of the PLN, elected president. He embarked on an ambitious socialist programme.
1958–73 Mainly Conservative administrations returned.
1974 PLN regained the presidency and returned to socialist policies.
1978 Rodrigo Carazo, Conservative, elected president. Sharp deterioration in the state of the economy.
1982 Luis Alberto Monge of the PLN elected president. Harsh austerity programme introduced to rebuild the economy. Pressure from the USA to abandon neutral stance and condemn the Sandinista regime in Nicaragua.
1983 Policy of neutrality reaffirmed.
1985 Following border clashes with Sandinista forces, a US-trained anti-guerrilla guard was formed.
1986 Oscar Arias Sánchez won the presidency on a neutralist platform.
1987 Oscar Arias Sánchez awarded Nobel Peace Prize.
1990 Rafael Calderón (PUSC) elected president.

Cosmos name used since the early 1960s for nearly all Soviet artificial satellites. Nearly 2,000 Cosmos satellites have been launched.

Cossack /'kɒsæk/ people of Russia, predominantly of Russian or Ukrainian origin, who held land in return for military service to the Czar. Before 1917 a Cossack household had a larger allotment of land than that of the ordinary peasant, and in return all the men were bound to serve in the army for 20 years.

Cossyra /kɒ'saɪrə/ ancient name for ◊Pantelleria, Italian island in the Mediterranean.

Costa Rica /'kɒstə 'riːkə/ country in Central America, bounded to the N by Nicaragua, to the S by Panama, to the E by the Caribbean, and to the W by the Pacific Ocean.

government the 1949 constitution provides for a president elected for a four-year term by compulsory adult suffrage, two elected vice-presidents, and an appointed cabinet. There is a single-chamber legislature, the 57-member assembly, also serving a four-year term. Most significant among several parties are the National Liberation Party (PLN), and the Christian Socialist Unity Party (PUSC).

history originally occupied by Guaymi Indians, the area was visited by Christopher ◊Columbus, and was colonized by Spanish settlers from the 16th century, becoming independent 1821. First part of the ◊Mexican empire, then, with El Salvador, Guatemala, Honduras, and Nicaragua, part of the ◊Central American Federation from 1824, Costa Rica became a republic 1838. Apart from a military dictatorship 1870–82, and a brief civil war 1948 after a disputed presidential election, it has been one of the most democratically governed states in Latin America.

In 1949 a new constitution abolished the army, defence resting on the Civil Guard. José Figueres, leader of the anti-government forces in the previous year, became president. He co-founded the PLN, nationalized the banks, and introduced a social security system. He was re-elected 1953.

There followed 16 years of mostly conservative rule, with the reversal of some PLN policies. In 1974 Daniel Oduber won the presidency for the PLN. He returned to socialist policies, extended the welfare state, and established friendly relations with communist states. Communist and left-wing parties were legalized.

In 1978 Rodrigo Carazo of the conservative Unity Coalition (CU) became president. His presidency was marked by economic collapse and allegations of his involvement in illegal arms trafficking between Cuba and El Salvador.

In 1982 Luis Alberto Monge, a former trade union official and co-founder of PLN, won a convincing victory in the presidential election. To reverse the damage done by the Carazo government, he introduced a 100-day emergency economic programme.

The Monge government came under pressure from the USA to abandon its neutral stance and condemn the left-wing Sandinista regime in Nicaragua. It was also urged to re-establish its army. Monge resisted the pressure and in 1983 reaffirmed his country's neutrality, but relations with Nicaragua deteriorated after border clashes between Sandinista forces and the Costa Rican Civil Guard. In 1985 Monge agreed to create a US-trained anti-guerrilla guard, increasing doubts about Costa Rica's neutrality. In 1986 Oscar Arias Sánchez became president on a neutralist platform, defeating the pro-US candidate, Rafael Angel Calderón. However, Calderón won the 1990 presidential election.

cost benefit analysis the process whereby a project is assessed for its social and welfare benefits rather than a straightforward financial return on investment. For example, this might take into account the environmental impact of an industrial plant, or convenience for users of a new railway.

Costello /kɒ'steləʊ/ Elvis. Stage name of Declan McManus 1954– . English rock singer, songwriter, and guitarist, noted for his stylistic range and intricate lyrics. His albums with his group the Attractions include *Armed Forces* 1979, *Trust* 1981, and *Blood and Chocolate* 1986.

Coster /'kɒstə/ Laurens Janszoon 1370–1440. Dutch printer. According to some sources, he invented moveable type, but after his death an apprentice ran off to Mainz with the blocks and, taking ◊Gutenberg into his confidence, began a printing business with him.

cost of living the cost of goods and services needed for an average standard of living. In Britain the cost-of-living index was introduced 1914 and based on the expenditure of a working-class family of man, woman, and three children; the standard is 100. Known from 1947 as the Retail Price Index (RPI), it is revised to allow for inflation.

Supplementary to the RPI are the Consumer's Expenditure Deflator (formerly Consumer Price Index) and the Tax and Price Index (TPI), introduced in 1979. Comprehensive indexation has been advocated as a means of controlling inflation by linking all forms of income (such as wages and investment), contractual debts and tax scales, to the RPI. Index-linked savings schemes were introduced in the UK in 1975.

In the USA a Consumer Price Index, based on the expenditure of families in the iron, steel and related industries, was introduced in 1890. The modern index is based on the expenditure of the urban wage-earner and clerical-worker families in 46 large, medium, and small cities, the standard being 100. Increases in social security benefits are linked to it, as are many wage settlements.

cotangent in trigonometry, a ◊function of an angle in a right-angled triangle found by dividing the length of the side adjacent to the angle by the length of the side opposite it. It is usually written as cotan, or cot and it is the reciprocal of the tangent of the angle, so that cotan $A = 1/\tan A$, where A is the angle in question.

cot death death of an apparently healthy baby during sleep, formal name Sudden Infant Death Syndrome (SIDS). It is most common in the winter months, and strikes boys more than girls. The condition is still largely unexplained.

Côte d'Azur /'kəʊt dæ'zjʊə/ the Mediterranean coast from Menton to St Tropez, France, renowned for its beaches; part of ◊Provence-Côte d'Azur.

Cotman /'kɒtmən/ John Sell 1782–1842. British landscape painter, with Crome a founder of the *Norwich school*, a group of realistic landscape painters influenced by Dutch examples. Cotman is best known for his early watercolour style, bold designs in simple flat washes of colour, such as *Greta Bridge, Yorkshire* 1805 (British Museum, London).

cotoneaster genus of trees and shrubs, family Rosaceae, closely allied to the hawthorn and medlar. Its fruits, though small and unpalatable, are usually bright red and conspicuous, often persisting through the winter.

Cotonou /ˌkɒtə'nuː/ chief port and largest city of Benin, on the Bight of Benin; population (1982) 487,000. Palm products and timber are exported.

Although not the official capital, it is the seat of the president, and the main centre of commerce and politics.

Cotopaxi /ˌkɒtə'pæksi/ an active volcano, situated to the south of Quito in Ecuador. It is 5,897 m/19,347 ft high, and was first climbed 1872. Its name is Quechua for 'shining peak'.

Cotswolds /'kɒtswəʊldz/ range of hills in Avon-Gloucestershire, England, some 80 km/50 mi long, between Bristol and Chipping Camden.

cotangent

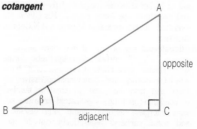

$$\text{cot(angent) } \beta = \frac{1}{\tan \beta} = \frac{\cos \beta}{\sin \beta} = \frac{\text{adjacent}}{\text{opposite}} = \frac{BC}{AC}$$

They rise to 333 m/1,086 ft at Cleeve Cloud, but average about 200 m/600 ft.

cottage industry an industry undertaken by employees in their homes and often using their own equipment. Cottage industries frequently utilize a traditional craft such as weaving or pottery, but may also use high technology.

cottar the term used in the ◊Domesday Book to describe a free smallholder and tenant of a cottage, mainly in S England.

Cottbus /'kɒtbus/ capital of Cottbus county, East Germany, on the Spree river SE of Berlin; population (1986) 126,000. Industries include textiles and carpets. Cottbus county has an area of 8,260 sq km/3,188 sq mi, and a population of 883,000.

cotton /'kɒtn/ tropical and sub-tropical herbaceous plant of the genus *Gossypium*, family Malvaceae. Fibres surround the seeds inside its ripened fruit, or boll, and these are spun into yarn for cloth.

Cotton disease (byssinosis), caused by cotton dust, affects the lungs of those working in the industry. The seeds are used to produce cooking oil and livestock feed, and the pigment gossypol has potential as a male contraceptive in a modified form. See also ◊cotton gin.

Cotton /'kɒtn/ Joseph 1905– . US actor, who was brought into films by Orson Welles. He appeared in many international productions, often in leading roles, until the early 1980s, including *Citizen Kane* 1941, *The Third Man* 1949, and *The Abominable Dr Phibes* 1971.

Cotton /'kɒtn/ Robert Bruce 1571–1631. English antiquary. At his home in Westminster he built up a fine collection of manuscripts and coins, many of which had come from the despoiled monasteries. His son, *Thomas Cotton* (1594–1662), added to the library. The collection is now in the British Museum.

cotton gin a machine that separates cotton fibres from the seed boll. The invention of the gin by Eli Whitney 1793 was a milestone in textile history.

The modern gin consists of a roller carrying a set of circular saws. These project through a metal grill in a hopper containing the seed bolls. As the roller rotates, the saws pick up the cotton fibres, leaving the seeds behind.

cottongrass type of sedge *Eriophorum angustifolium* and its related species. White down covers the fruiting heads in midsummer; these break off and are carried long distances on the wind. Cottongrass is found in wet places throughout the arctic and N temperate regions, most species being found in acid bogs.

cotton stainer type of ◊bug, family Pyrrhocoridae, that pierces and stains cotton bolls.

cottonwood name given to several species of North American poplar with fluffy seeds; also the Australian tree *Bedfordia salaoina* with downy leaves.

cotyledon a structure in the embryo of a seed plant that may form a 'leaf' after germination and is commonly known as a seed leaf. The number of cotyledons present in an embryo is an important character in the classification of flowering plants (◊angiosperms).

Monocotyledons (such as grasses, palms, and lilies) have a single cotyledon, whereas dicotyledons (the majority of species) have two. In seeds that also contain ◊endosperm (nutritive tissue) the cotyledons are thin, but where they are the primary food-storing tissue, as in peas and beans, they may be quite large. After germination the cotyledons either remain below ground (hypogeal) or, more commonly, spread out above soil level (epigeal) and become the first green leaves. In gymnosperms there may be up to a dozen cotyledons within each seed.

couch grass grass *Agropyron repens*, one of the commonest of the Gramineae. It is closely allied to wheat, but is generally regarded as a weed.

cougar alternative name for the ◊puma, a large North American cat.

coulomb /'ku:lɒm/ SI unit (symbol C) of electrical charge. One coulomb is the quantity of electricity conveyed by a current of one ◊amp in one second.

Coulomb /'ku:lɒm/ Charles Auguste de 1736–1806. French scientist, inventor of the torsion balance for measuring the force of electric and magnetic attraction. The coulomb was named after him.

council in local government in England and Wales, a popularly elected local assembly charged with the government of the area within its boundaries. Under the Local Government Act of 1972, they comprise three types: ◊county councils, ◊district councils, and ◊parish councils.

Council for Mutual Economic Assistance (CMEA) full name for ◊Comecon, organization established 1949 by Eastern bloc countries.

Council of Europe body constituted 1949 at Strasbourg, France (still its headquarters) to secure 'a greater measure of unity between the European countries'. The widest association of European states, it has a *Committee* of foreign ministers, a *Parliamentary Assembly* (with members from national parliaments), and a *European Commission* investigating violations of human rights.

The first session of the *Consultative Assembly* opened Aug 1949, the members then being the UK, France, Italy, Belgium, the Netherlands, Sweden, Denmark, Norway, the Republic of Ireland, Luxembourg, Greece, and Turkey; Iceland, West Germany, Austria, Cyprus, Switzerland, Malta, Portugal, Spain, and Liechtenstein joined subsequently.

counselling an approach to treating problems, particularly psychological ones, in which clients are encouraged to solve their own problems with support from a counsellor.

counterfeiting fraudulent imitation, especially of banknotes. It is countered by special papers, elaborate watermarks, skilled printing, and sometimes insertion of a metallic strip. See also ◊forgery.

counterpoint in music, the art of combining different forms of an original melody with apparent freedom and yet to harmonious effect. ◊Palestrina and JS ◊Bach were masters of counterpoint.

It originated in ◊plainsong, with two independent vocal lines sung simultaneously (Latin *punctus contra punctum* 'note against note').

Counter-Reformation a movement initiated by the Catholic church at the Council of Trent 1545–63 to counter the spread of the ◊Reformation. Extending into the 17th century, its dominant forces included the rise of the Jesuits as an educating and missionary group and the deployment of the Spanish ◊Inquisition in other countries.

countertenor highest natural male voice, favoured by the Elizabethans. It was revived in the UK by Alfred Deller (1912–79).

countervailing power in economics, the belief that too much power held by one group or company can be balanced or neutralized by another, creating a compatible relationship, such as trade unions in the case of strong management in a large company, or an opposition party facing an authoritarian government.

country and western the popular music of the white US South and Southwest, evolved from the folk music of the English, Irish, and Scottish settlers with a strong blues influence. Characteristic instruments are slide guitar, mandolin, and fiddle.

Lyrics typically extol family values and traditional sex roles. Country music encompasses a variety of regional styles, and ranges from mournful ballads to fast and intricate dance music.

history

1920s Jimmie Rodgers (1897–33) wrote a series of 'Blue Yodel' songs that made him the first country-music recording star.

1930s Nashville, Tennessee, became a centre for the country-music industry, with the Grand Ole Opry a showcase for performers. The Carter Family arranged and recorded hundreds of traditional songs. Hollywood invented the singing cowboy.

1940s Hank Williams (1923–53) emerged as the most influential singer and songwriter; *western swing* spread from Texas.

1950s The *honky-tonk* sound; Kentucky *bluegrass*; ballad singers included Jim Reeves (1923–64) and Patsy Cline (1932–63).

1960s The Bakersfield, California, school dominated by Buck Owens (1929–) and Merle Haggard (1937–) contrasted with lush Nashville productions of singers such as George Jones (1931–) and Tammy Wynette (1942–).

1970s Dolly Parton (1946–) and Emmylou Harris (1947–); the Austin, Texas, *outlaws* Willie Nelson (1933–) and Waylon Jennings (1937–); *country rock* pioneered by Gram Parsons (1946–73).

1980s Neotraditionalist *new country* represented by Dwight Yoakam (1957–) and Nanci Griffith (1954–).

Country Party (official name *National Country Party* from 1975) Australian political party representing the interests of the farmers and people of the smaller towns; it holds the power balance between Liberals and Labor. It developed from about 1860, gained strength after the introduction of preferential voting (see ◊vote) 1918, and has been in coalition with the Liberals from 1949.

Countryside Commission an official conservation body, created for England and Wales under the Countryside Act 1968. It replaced the National Parks Commission, and had by 1980 created over 160 Country Parks.

county administrative unit of a country or state. In the UK it is nowadays synonymous with 'shire', although historically the two had different origins. Many of the English counties can be traced back to Saxon times. In the USA a county is a subdivision of a state; the power of counties differs widely between states. The Republic of Ireland has 26 geographical and 27 administrative counties.

Under the Local Government Act of 1972, which came into effect in 1974, the existing English administrative counties were replaced by 45 new county areas of local government, and the 13 Welsh counties were reduced by amalgamation to eight. Under the Local Government (Scotland) Act of 1973 the 33 counties of Scotland were amalgamated in 1975 in nine new regions and three island areas. Northern Ireland has six geographical counties, but under the Local Government Act of 1973 administration is through 26 district councils (single-tier authorities), each based on a main town or centre.

county council in the UK, a unit of local government, whose responsibilities include broad planning policy, highways, education, personal social services, and libraries; police, fire, and traffic control; and refuse disposal.

Since the Local Government Act of 1972, the county councils in England and Wales consist of a chair and councillors (the distinction between councillors and aldermen has been abolished). Councillors are elected for four years, the franchise being the same as for parliamentary elections, and elect the chair from among their own number.

county court English court of law created by the County Courts Act 1846 and now governed by the Act of 1984. It exists to try civil cases, such as actions on ◊contract and ◊tort where the claim does not exceed £5,000, and disputes about land, such as between landlord and tenant. County courts are presided over by one or more circuit judges. An appeal on a point of law lies to the Court of Appeal.

county palatine in medieval England, a county whose lord held particularly important rights, in lieu of the king, such as pardoning treasons and murders. Under William I there were four counties palatine: Chester, Durham, Kent, and Shropshire.

courtship display

gulls courting, indulging in neck arching (left) and sky-pointing (right)

coup d'état or *coup* forcible takeover of the government of a country by elements from within that country. It differs from a revolution in typically being carried out by a small group (for example, of army officers or opposition politicians) to install their leader as head of government, rather than being a mass uprising by the people.

Early examples include the coup of 1799 in which Napoleon overthrew the Revolutionary Directory and declared himself first consul of France, and the coup of 1851 in which Louis Napoleon (then president) dissolved the French national assembly and a year later declared himself emperor. Coups of more recent times include the overthrow of the socialist government of Chile in 1973 by a right-wing junta, and the military seizure of power in Fiji by Col Rabuka in Sept 1987.

Couperin /'kuːpəræn/ François *le Grand* 1668–1733. French composer. He held various court appointments under Louis XIV and wrote vocal, chamber, and harpsichord music.

couplet in literature, a pair of lines of verse, usually of the same length and rhymed.

The **heroic couplet**, consisting of two rhymed lines in iambic pentameter, was considered particularly suitable for epic poetry, and was a convention of both serious and mock-heroic 18th-century English poetry, as in the work of Alexander Pope. An example, from Pope's *An Essay on Criticism*, is: 'A little learning is a dang'rous thing;/Drink deep, or taste not the Pierian spring'.

Courbet /'kuːəbeɪ/ Gustave 1819–1877. French artist, a portrait, genre, and landscape painter. Reacting against academic trends, both Classicist and Romantic, he sought to establish a new realism based on contemporary life. His *Burial at Ornans* 1850 (Louvre, Paris), showing ordinary working people gathered round a village grave, shocked the public and the critics with its 'vulgarity'.

His spirit of realism was to be continued by Manet. In 1871 Courbet was active in the shortlived Paris Commune and was later imprisoned for six months for his part in it.

Courrèges /kʊ'reɪʒ/ André 1923– . French couturier. Originally with Balenciaga, he founded his own firm 1961 and is credited with inventing the mini-skirt in 1964.

coursing chasing of hares by greyhounds, not by scent but by sight, as a 'sport', and as a test of the greyhound's speed. It is one of the most ancient of field sports. Since the 1880s it has been practised on enclosed or park courses.

The governing body in Great Britain is the National Coursing Club, formed in 1858. The coursing season lasts Sept–Mar: the Altcar or Waterloo meeting, which decides the championship, is held in Feb at Altcar, Lancashire. The Waterloo Cup race is known as the Courser's Derby.

court a body that hears legal actions and the building where this occurs. See ◊law court and particular kinds of court, for example ◊county court, ◊Small Claims Court, and ◊Diplock court.

Court /kɔːt/ Margaret (born Smith) 1942– . Australian tennis player. The most prolific winner in the women's game, she won a record 64 Grand Slam titles, including 24 at singles.

She was the first from her country to win the ladies title at Wimbledon (1963) and the second woman after Maureen Connolly to complete the Grand Slam (1970).

CAREER HIGHLIGHTS

Wimbledon
singles: 1963, 1965, 1970
doubles: 1964, 1969
mixed: 1963, 1965–66, 1968, 1975
US Open
singles: 1962, 1965, 1968–70, 1973
doubles: 1963, 1968–70, 1973, 1975
mixed: 1961–65, 1969–70, 1972
French Open
singles: 1962, 1964, 1969–70, 1973
doubles: 1964–66, 1973
mixed: 1963–65, 1969
Australian Open
singles: 1960–66, 1969–71, 1973
doubles: 1961–63, 1965, 1969–71, 1973
mixed: 1963–64

Courtauld /'kɔːtəʊld/ Samuel 1793–1881. British industrialist who developed the production of viscose rayon and other synthetic fibres from 1904. He founded the firm of Courtaulds in 1816 at Bocking, Essex, which at first specialized in silk and crepe manufacture.

His great-nephew, *Samuel Courtauld* (1876–1947), was chairman of the firm from 1921, and in 1931 gave his house and art collection to the University of London as the Courtauld Institute.

courtesy title in the UK, title given to the progeny of members of the peerage. For example, the eldest son of a duke, marquess, or earl may bear one of his father's lesser titles; thus the Duke of Marlborough's son is the Marquess of Blandford. They are not peers and do not sit in the House of Lords.

The younger son of a duke or marquess is entitled to bear the style of 'Lord' before his forename; the younger son of an earl, and the sons of viscounts and barons, are similarly entitled to bear the style of 'Honourable' (abbreviated to 'Hon') before their forename. The daughters of dukes, marquesses and earls are entitled to bear the style of 'Lady' before their forename, and the daughters of viscounts and barons that of 'Hon'. The sons and daughters of life peers are also entitled to this style for their lifetime. The adopted sons and daughters of peers may not use courtesy titles, nor are may they inherit a peerage from their adoptive parent. The legitimated issue of peers may bear courtesy titles, but (except sometimes in Scotland) cannot inherit the peerage.

courtly love a medieval code of amorous conduct between noble men and women. Originating in 11th-century Provence, it was popularized by troubadours under the patronage of Eleanor of Aquitaine, and codified by André le Chapelain. Essentially, it was concerned with the (usually) unconsummated love between a young bachelor knight and his lord's lady. The affair between Lancelot and Guinevere is a classic example. This theme was usually treated in an idealized form, but the relationship did reflect the social realities of noble households, in which the lady of the household might be the only noblewoman among several young unmarried knights. It influenced a great deal of medieval and 16th-century art and literature, including the 14th-century *Romance of the Rose* and Chaucer's *Troilus and Criseyde*, and was closely related to concepts of ◊chivalry.

court martial court convened for the trial of persons subject to military discipline. British courts martial are governed by the code of the service concerned —Naval Discipline, Army, or Air Force Acts—and in 1951 an appeal court was established for all three services by the Courts Martial (Appeals) Act. The procedure prescribed for the US services is similar, being based on British practice.

Courtneidge /'kɔːtnɪdʒ/ Cicely 1893–1980. British comic actress and singer, who appeared both on stage and in films. She married comedian Jack Hulbert (1892–1978), with whom she formed a successful variety partnership.

Court of Session the supreme Civil Court in Scotland, established 1532. Cases come in the first place before one of the judges of the Outer House, and from that decision an appeal lies to the Inner House which sits in two divisions called the First and Second Division. From the decisions of the Inner House an appeal lies to the House of Lords. The court sits in Edinburgh.

Court of the Lord Lyon Scottish heraldic authority composed of one King of Arms, three Heralds, and three Pursuivants who specialize in genealogical work. It embodies the High Sennachie of Scotland's Celtic kings.

Courtrai /kʊə'treɪ/ (Flemish *Kortrijk*) town in Belgium on the river Lys, in West Flanders; population (1985) 76,110. It is connected by canal with the coast, and by river and canal with Antwerp and Brussels. It has a large textile industry, especially damask, linens, and lace.

Courtrai, Battle of /kʊə'treɪ/ defeat of French knights by the Flemings of Ghent and Bruges on 11 July 1302. It is also called the 'Battle of the Spurs' because 800 gilt spurs were hung in Courtrai cathedral to commemorate the victory of billmen over unsupported cavalry.

courtship behaviour exhibited by animals as a prelude to mating. The behaviour patterns vary considerably from one species to another, but are often ◊ritualized forms of behaviour normally quite unrelated to courtship or mating (for example, courtship feeding in birds).

Cousin /kuː'zæn/ Victor 1792–1867. French philosopher, who helped to introduce German philosophical ideas into France. In 1840 he was minister of public instruction and reorganized the system of elementary education.

Cousteau /'kuːstəʊ/ Jacques-Yves 1910– . French oceanographer, celebrated for his researches in command of the *Calypso* from 1951; he pioneered the invention of the aqualung 1943 and techniques in underwater filming.

coûte que coûte (French) whatever the cost.

Coutts /kuːts/ Thomas 1735–1822. British banker. He established with his brother the firm of Coutts

Cousteau French naval officer and underwater explorer Jacques Cousteau.

& Co (one of London's oldest banking houses, founded in 1692 in the Strand), becoming sole head on the latter's death in 1778. Since the reign of George III an account has been maintained there by every succeeding sovereign; other customers have included Chatham, William Pitt, Fox, Wellington, Reynolds, and Boswell.

couvade custom of a man behaving as if he were about to give birth when his child is being born, which may include feeling or appearing to feel real pain. It has been observed since antiquity in many cultures, and may have begun either as a magic ritual or as a way of asserting paternity.

covalency in chemistry, a form of ◊valency in which two atoms unite by sharing a pair of electrons.

Covenanter in English history, one of the Presbyterian Christians who swore to uphold their forms of worship in a National Covenant, signed 28 Feb 1638, when Charles I attempted to introduce a liturgy on the English model into Scotland.

A general assembly abolished episcopacy, and in 1643 the Covenanters signed with the English Parliament the Solemn League and Covenant, promising military aid in return for the establishment of Presbyterianism in England. A Scottish army entered England and fought at Marston Moor 1644. At the Restoration Charles II revived episcopacy in Scotland, evicting resisting ministers, so that revolts followed in 1666, 1679, and 1685. However, Presbyterianism was again restored in 1688.

Covent Garden /'kɒvənt 'gɑːdn/ London square (named from the convent garden once on the site), laid out by Inigo ◊Jones in 1631. The buildings which formerly housed London's fruit and vegetable market (moved to Nine Elms, Wandsworth, in 1973) were adapted for shops and leisure. The Royal Opera House, also housing the Royal Ballet, is here, also the London Transport Museum. The Theatre Museum, opened 1987, is in the Old Flower Market.

Coventry /'kɒvəntri/ industrial city in West Midlands, England; population (1981) 313,800. Manufacturing includes cars, electronic equipment, machine tools, and agricultural machinery.

history it originated when Leofric, Earl of Mercia and husband of Lady ◊Godiva, founded a priory in 1043. Its modern industry began with bicycle manufacture in 1870. Features include the cathedral, designed by Basil Spence, and incorporating the steeple of the church built 1373–95 and destroyed in an air raid Nov 1940; St Mary's Hall,

built 1394–1414 as a guild centre; two gates of the old city walls 1356; Belgrade Theatre 1958; Art Gallery and Museum; Museum of British Road Transport, and Lanchester Polytechnic.

Coverdale /'kʌvədeɪl/ Miles 1488–1569. English Protestant priest whose translation of the Bible 1535 was the first to be printed in English. His translation of the psalms is that retained in the Book of Common Prayer.

Coverdale, born in Yorkshire, became a Catholic priest, but turned to Protestantism and in 1528 went abroad to avoid persecution. In 1539 he edited the Great Bible which was ordered to be placed in churches. After some years in Germany, he returned to England in 1548, and in 1551 was made bishop of Exeter. During the reign of Mary he left the country.

Coward /'kaʊəd/ Noël 1899–1973. English playwright, actor, producer, director, and composer, who epitomized the witty and sophisticated man of the theatre. From his first success with *The Young Idea* 1923, he wrote and appeared in plays and comedies on both sides of the Atlantic such as *Hay Fever* 1925, *Private Lives* 1930 with Gertrude Lawrence, *Design for Living* 1933, and *Blithe Spirit* 1941.

Coward also wrote for and acted in films, including the patriotic *In Which We Serve* 1942 and the sentimental *Brief Encounter* 1945. After World War II he became a nightclub and cabaret entertainer, performing songs like 'Mad Dogs and Englishmen'.

Cowell /'kaʊəl/ Henry 1897–1965. US composer and writer. He experimented with new ways of playing the piano, strumming the strings in *Aeolian Harp* 1923 and introducing clusters, using a ruler on the keys in *The Banshee* 1925.

Cowell also wrote chamber and orchestral music and was active as a critic and publisher of 20th-century music.

Cowes /kaʊz/ seaport and resort on the north coast of the Isle of Wight, England, on the Medina estuary, opposite Southampton Water; population (1981) 19,500. It is the headquarters of the Royal Yacht Squadron which holds the annual Cowes Regatta, and has maritime industries. In East Cowes is Osborne House, a favoured residence of Queen Victoria, now used as a museum.

cowfish type of ◊boxfish.

Cowley /'kaʊli/ Abraham 1618–1667. English poet. He introduced the Pindaric ode (based on the Greek poet Pindar) to English poetry, and published metaphysical verse with elaborate imagery, as well as essays.

cow parsley also known as *keck* tall perennial plant *Anthriscus sylvestris* of the carrot family. Up to 1 m/3 ft tall, its pinnate leaves, hollow furrowed stems, and heads of white flowers are a familiar sight in hedgerows and shady places. It grows in Europe, N Asia and N Africa.

Cowper /'kuːpə/ William 1731–1800. English poet. He trained as a lawyer, but suffered a mental breakdown 1763 and entered na asylum, where he underwent an evangelical conversion. He later wrote hymns (including 'God moves in a mysterious way'). His verse includes the six books of *The Task* 1785.

cowrie marine snail-like mollusc, in which the interior spiral form is concealed by a double outer lip. The shells are hard, shiny, and often coloured. Most cowries are shallow-water forms, and are found in many parts of the world, particularly the tropical Indopacific.

One species, the *European cowrie Trivia monacha* is fairly common on British shores. It is about 1.2 cm/0.5 in long, with three spots on the shell. Cowries have been used as ornaments and fertility charms, and also as currency, especially the *money cowrie Cypraea moneta*.

cowslip plant *Primula veris* of the same genus as the primrose and belonging to the family Primulaceae. The oxlip *Primula elatior* is closely allied to the cowslip.

Cox /kɒks/ David 1783–1859. British artist. Born near Birmingham, the son of a blacksmith, he studied under John ◊Varley and made a living as

a drawing master. His watercolour landscapes, many of scenes in N Wales, have attractive cloud effects, and are characterized by broad colour washes on a rough, tinted paper.

coyote wild dog *Canis latrans*, in appearance like a small wolf, living from Alaska to Central America. Its head and body are about 90 cm/3 ft long, and brown flecked with grey or black. Coyotes live in open country and can run at 65 kph/40 mph. Their main foods are rabbits and rodents.

coypu South American water rodent *Myocastor coypus*, about 60 cm/2 ft long and weighing up to 9 kg/20 lb. It has a scaly, rat-like tail, webbed hind feet, a blunt-muzzled head, and large orange incisors. The fur is reddish brown. It feeds on vegetation, and lives in burrows in river and lake banks.

Brought to Europe to farm for their fur ('nutria'), many escaped or were released. They became established in the UK in the Norfolk Broads, where they became a severe pest, but may now have been eradicated from there.

Coysevox /kwæz'vɒks/ Antoine 1640–1720. French Baroque sculptor. He was employed at the palace of Versailles, contributing a stucco relief of a triumphant Louis XIV to the Salon de la Guerre.

He also produced portrait busts, for example a terracotta of the artist Le Brun 1676 (Wallace Collection, London), and more sombre monuments, such as the *Tomb of Cardinal Mazarin* 1689–93 (Louvre, Paris).

Cozens /'kʌzənz/ John Robert 1752–1797. British landscape painter, a watercolourist whose Romantic views of Europe, painted on tours in the 1770s and 1780s, were popular in his day and influenced both Girtin and Turner.

His father, *Alexander Cozens* (c.1717–86), also a landscape painter, taught drawing at Eton public school and produced books on landscape drawing.

CPP abbreviation for *current purchasing power.*

CPU abbreviation for *central processing unit*, the part of a computer that executes individual program instructions and controls the operation of other parts.

It comprise five main elements: the ◊ALU (arithmetic and logic unit), which contains the basic operations (its 'instruction set') and applies them to data; a program counter to keep track of the program being executed; a number of ◊registers for storing intermediate results and data awaiting processing; (normally) an electronic clock, which emits regular pulses that coordinate the CPU's activities; and a control unit for organizing the processing.

CPVE *Certificate of Pre-Vocational Education* in the UK, educational qualification introduced 1986 for students over 16 in schools and colleges who want a one-year course of preparation for work or further vocational study.

crab name given to many decapod (ten-legged) crustaceans of the suborder Reptantia ('walking'), related to lobsters and crayfish. Mainly marine, some crabs live in fresh water or on land. They are alert carnivores and scavengers. They have a typical sideways walk, and strong pincers on the first pair of legs, the other four pairs being used for walking. Periodically, the outer shell is cast to allow for growth.

The true crabs (division Brachyura) have a broad, rather round, upper body shell (carapace), and a small ◊abdomen tucked beneath the body. There are many species worldwide. The European *shore crab Carcinus maenas* is common on British shores between the tidemarks, is dull green, and grows to 4 cm/1.5 in or more. The *edible crab Cancer paqurus* grows 14 cm/5.5 in long or more, lives down to 100 m/325 ft and is extensively fished. Other true crabs include: *fiddler crabs* (*Uca*), the males of which have one enlarged claw to wave at and attract females; the European *river crab Thelphusa fluviatilis*; and *spider crabs* with small bodies

CPU

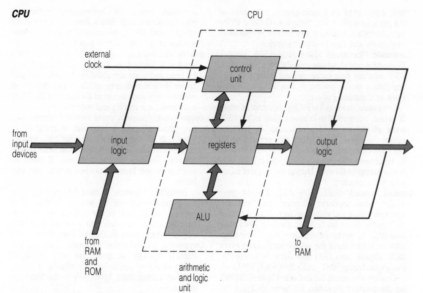

CPU

external
clock

control
unit

from
input
devices

input
logic

registers

output
logic

ALU

from
RAM
and
ROM

to
RAM

arithmetic
and logic
unit

and very long legs, including the Japanese spider crab *Macrocheira kaempferi* with a leg span of 3.4 m/11 ft.

Hermit crabs (division Anomura) have a soft, spirally twisted abdomen and make their home in empty shells of whelks and winkles for protection. The *common hermit crab Eupagurus bernhardus*, up to 10 cm/4 in long, is found off Atlantic and Mediterranean shores. Some tropical hermit crabs are found a considerable distance from the sea. The *robber crab Birgus latro* grows large enough to climb palm trees and feed on coconuts.

crab apple wild form *Malus sylvestris* from which the cultivated apple has been derived; it differs chiefly in the smaller size and bitter flavour of the fruit, used in crab-apple jelly.

The tree is common in woods and hedgerows in southern Britain and varies from a mere bush to 10 m/30 ft in height.

Crabbe /kræb/ George 1754–1832. English poet. Originally a doctor, he became a clergyman 1781, and wrote grimly realistic verse of the poor of his own time: *The Village* 1783, *The Parish Register* 1807, *The Borough* 1810 (which includes the story used in the Britten opera *Peter Grimes*), and *Tales of the Hall* 1819.

Crab Nebula cloud of gas 6,000 light years away, in the constellation of Taurus, the remains of a star that exploded as a ◊supernova (observed as a brilliant point of light on Earth 1054). At its centre is a ◊pulsar that flashes 30 times a second. The name comes from its crab-like appearance.

crack a chemical (bicarbonate) derivative of ◊cocaine in crystalline form rather than powder; it is heated and inhaled. It was first used in San Francisco in the early 1980s, and is highly addictive.

cracking method of distilling ◊petroleum products; see also ◊fractionation.

Cracow /'krækaʊ/ alternative form of ◊Kraków, Polish city.

Craig /kreɪg/ Edward Gordon 1872–1966. British director and stage designer. His innovations and theories on stage design and lighting effects, expounded in *On the Art of the Theatre* 1911, had a huge influence on stage production in Europe and the USA.

Craig /kreɪg/ James 1871–1940. Ulster Unionist politician, the first prime minister of Northern Ireland 1921–40. Craig became a member of Parliament 1906, and was a highly effective organizer of Unionist resistance to Home Rule. As prime minister he carried out systematic discrimination against the Catholic minority, abolishing proportional representation 1929 and redrawing constituency boundaries to ensure Protestant majorities.

Craigavon /ˌkreɪg'ævən/ town in Armagh, Northern Ireland; population (1981) 73,000. It was created from 1965 by the merging of Lurgan and Portadown, and named after the first prime minister of Northern Ireland.

Craik /kreɪk/ Dinah Maria (born Mulock) 1826–1887. British novelist, author *John Halifax, Gentleman* 1857, the story of the social betterment of a poor orphan through his own efforts.

Craiova /kraɪ'əʊvə/ town in S Romania, near the river Jiu; population (1985) 275,000. Industries include electrical engineering, food processing, textiles, fertilisers, and farm machinery.

crake any of several small birds related to the ◊corncrake.

Cranach /'krɑːnæx/ Lucas 1472–1553. German painter, etcher, and woodcut artist, a leading light in the German Renaissance. He painted many full-length nudes and precise and polished portraits, such as *Martin Luther* 1521 (Uffizi, Florence).

Born at Kronach in Bavaria, he settled at Wittenberg in 1504 to work for the elector of Saxony. He is associated with Dürer and Altdorfer, and was a close friend of Luther, whose portrait he painted several times. His religious paintings feature splendid landscapes. His second son **Lucas Cranach the Younger** (1515–86) had a similar style, and succeeded his father as director of the Cranach workshop.

cranberry plant *Vaccinium oxycoccos* allied to the bilberry, and belonging to the heath family Ericaceae. It is a small evergreen, growing in marshy places, and bearing small, acid, edible, crimson berries.

crane in engineering, a machine for raising, lowering or placing in position heavy loads. The three main types are the jib crane, the overhead travelling crane, and the tower crane. Most cranes have the machinery mounted on a revolving turntable. This may be mounted on trucks or be self-propelled, often being fitted with ◊caterpillar tracks.

The main features of a *jib crane* are a power winch, a rope or cable, and a moveable arm or jib. The cable, which carries a pulley block, hangs from the end of the jib and is wound up and down by the winch. The *overhead travelling crane*, chiefly used in workshops, consists of a fixed horizontal arm, along which runs a trolley carrying the pulley block. *Tower cranes*, seen on large building sites, have a long horizontal arm able to revolve on top of a tall tower. The arm carries the trolley.

crane /kreɪn/ in zoology, bird of the family Gruidae, with long legs and neck, and powerful wings. They are marsh and plain-dwelling birds, feeding on plants as well as insects and small animals. They fly well and are usually migratory. They are found in all parts of the world except South America.

The *common crane Grus grus* is still common in many parts of Europe, and winters in Africa and India. It stands over 1 m/3 ft high. The plumage of the adult bird is grey, varied with black and white, and a red patch of bare skin on the head and neck. The North American *whooping crane Grus americana* is just one of the species that are endangered, all cranes having suffered through hunting and loss of wetlands.

Crane /kreɪn/ (Harold) Hart 1899–1932. US poet. His long mystical poem *The Bridge* (1930) uses the Brooklyn Bridge as a symbol. He drowned after jumping overboard from a steamer bringing him back to the USA after a visit to Mexico.

Crane /kreɪn/ Stephen 1871–1900. US journalist and writer, who introduced grim realism into the US novel. His book *The Red Badge of Courage* 1895 deals vividly with the US Civil War.

Crane /kreɪn/ Walter 1845–1915. British artist and designer, mainly known as a book illustrator. He was influenced by William Morris and became an active socialist in the 1880s.

While apprenticed to W J Linton, a wood engraver, he came under the influence of the Pre-Raphaelites. His book illustration, both for children's and for adult books, included an edition of Spenser's *Faerie Queene* 1894–96.

crane fly or *daddy-longlegs* type of fly with long, slender, fragile legs. The larvae live in soil or water. Some soil-living larvae, *leatherjackets*, cause crop damage by eating roots, for example the common crane fly *Tipula paludosa*.

cranesbill plant of the genus *Geranium*, which contains about 400 species. The plant is named after the long, beak-like process attached to its seed vessels. When ripe, this splits into coiling spirals, which jerk the seeds out, assisting in their distribution.

The genus includes ten species native to Britain, including *herb Robert Geranium robertianum* and *bloody cranesbill Geranium sanguineum*.

craniotomy an operation to remove or turn back a small flap of skull bone to give access to the living brain.

crank a device that converts reciprocating (back-and-forwards or up-and-down) movement into rotary movement, or vice versa.

The earliest recorded use of a crank is in a water-raising machine by al-Jazari in the 17th century, 200 years before it appeared in Europe.

Cranko /'kræŋkəʊ/ John 1927–1973. British choreographer. Born in South Africa, he joined Sadler's Wells in 1946, and excelled in the creation of comedy characters, as in the *Tritsch-Tratsch Polka* 1946 and *Pineapple Poll* 1951.

crankshaft an essential component of piston engines, which converts the up-and-down (reciprocating) motion of the pistons into useful rotary motion. The familiar car crankshaft carries a number of cranks. The pistons are connected to the cranks by connecting rods and ◊bearings; when the pistons move up and down, the connecting rods force the offset crank pins to describe a circle, thereby rotating the crankshaft.

crane

whooping crane

crater *Aerial view of Meteor Crater, near Winslow, Arizona, USA. The crater, 200 m/600 ft deep and 800 m/0.5 mi across, is thought to be 25,000 years old.*

Cranmer /ˈkrænmə/ Thomas 1489–1556. English cleric, archbishop of Canterbury from 1533. A Protestant convert, under Edward VI he helped to shape the doctrines of the Church of England. He was responsible for the issue of the Prayer Books of 1549 and 1552, and supported the succession of Lady Jane Grey. He was burned at the stake as a heretic by Mary I.

Cranmer suggested in 1529 that the question of Henry VIII's marriage to Catherine of Aragon should be referred to the universities of Europe rather than to the Pope, and in 1533 he declared it null and void. Condemned for heresy under the Catholic Mary Tudor, he at first recanted, but when his life was not spared, resumed his position and was burned, first holding to the fire the hand which had signed his recantation.

craps casino game adapted from the game *hazard* by Bernard de Mandeville in the early 19th century. Played with two dice, a throw of 7 or 11 wins; a throw of 2, 3, or 12 loses.

Crashaw /ˈkræʃɔː/ Richard 1613–1649. English religious poet of the metaphysical school. He published a book of Latin sacred epigrams in 1634, then went to Paris, where he joined the Roman Catholic Church; his collection of poems *Steps to the Temple* appeared in 1646.

Crassus /ˈkræsəs/ Marcus Licinius *c.*108–53 BC. Roman general who crushed the ◊Spartacus uprising 71 BC. In 60 BC he joined with Caesar and Pompey in the First Triumvirate and obtained command in the East 55 BC. Invading Mesopotamia, he was defeated by the Parthians at the battle of Carrhae, captured, and put to death.

crater a bowl-shaped topographic feature, usually round and with steep sides. Craters are formed by explosive events such as the eruption of a volcano or by the impact of a meteorite. A ◊caldera is a much larger feature.

The Moon has more than 300,000 craters over 1 km/6 mi in diameter, formed by meteorite bombardment; similar craters on Earth have mostly been worn away by erosion. Craters are found on many other bodies in the Solar System.

Crater Lake /ˈkreɪtə ˈleɪk/ lake in the centre of ◊Chubb Crater, Oregon, USA.

craton or *shield* the core of a continent, a vast tract of highly deformed ◊metamorphic rock around which the continent has been built. Intense mountain-building periods shook these shield areas in Precambrian times before stable conditions set in. Cratons exist in the hearts of all the continents, a typical example being the Canadian Shield.

Crawford /ˈkrɔːfəd/ Joan 1908–1977. US film actress, who made her name from 1925 in dramatic films such as *Mildred Pierce* 1945, and *Whatever Happened to Baby Jane?* 1962.

Crawford /ˈkrɔːfəd/ Osbert Guy Stanhope 1886–1957. British archaeologist, who introduced aerial survey as a means of finding and interpreting remains, an idea conceived in World War I.

Crawley /ˈkrɔːli/ town in West Sussex, England, NE of Horsham; population (1981) 73,000. It was

Crawford *US movie star Joan Crawford, whose career spanned the golden age of Hollywood.*

chartered by King John 1202, and designed as a 'new town' from 1946. Industries include plastics, engineering, and printing.

crawling peg in economics, also known as *sliding-parity* or *moving-parity*, a method of achieving a desired adjustment in a currency exchange rate (up or down) by small percentages over a given period, rather than by a major one-off revaluation or devaluation.

Craxi /ˈkræksi/ Bettino 1934– . Italian socialist politician, leader of the Italian Socialist Party (PSI) from 1976, prime minister 1983–87.

Craxi, born in Milan, became a member of the Chamber of Deputies 1968 and in 1976 general secretary of the PSI. In 1983 he became Italy's first socialist prime minister, successfully leading a broad coalition until 1987.

crayfish freshwater crustacean structurally similar to, but smaller than, the lobster. They are brownish-green scavengers that are found in all parts of the world except Africa.

The *common crayfish Astacus pallipes*, up to 10 cm/4 in long, is found in rivers in chalky areas of Britain, living in burrows in the mud and emerging, chiefly at night, to feed on small animals. The *crawfish* or *spiny lobster Palinurus vulgaris*, sometimes called crayfish, is a marine lobster without pincers, growing up to 50 cm/1.8 ft. Crayfish are edible, and some species are farmed.

Crazy Horse 1849–1877. Sioux Indian chief, one of the Indian leaders at the massacre of ◊Little Bighorn. He was killed when captured.

creationism a theory concerned with the origins of matter and life, claiming, as does the Bible in Genesis, that the world and humanity were created by a supernatural Creator, not more than 6,000 years ago. It was developed in response to Darwin's theory of ◊evolution; it is not recognized by most scientists as having a factual basis.

After a trial 1981–82 a US judge ruled unconstitutional an attempt in Arkansas schools to enforce equal treatment to creationism and evolutionary theory.

creation myth legend of the origin of the world. All cultures have ancient stories of the creation of the Earth or its inhabitants. Often this involves the violent death of a primordial being from whose body everything then arises; the giant Ymir in Scandinavian mythology is an example. Marriage between heaven and earth is another common explanation, as in Greek mythology (Uranus and Gaia).

creative accounting the practice of organizing and presenting company accounts in a way that, though desirable for the company concerned,

relies on a liberal and unorthodox interpretation of general accountancy procedures.

Creative accounting has been much used by UK local authorities in recent years in an effort to avoid restrictions on expenditure imposed by central government.

Crécy, Battle of /ˈkresi/ first important battle of the Hundred Years' War, 1346. Philip VI of France was defeated by Edward III of England at the village of Crécy-en-Ponthieu, now in Somme *département*, France, 18 km/11 mi NE of Abbeville.

credit in economics, means by which goods or services are obtained without immediate payment, usually by agreeing to pay interest. The three main forms are *consumer credit* (usually extended to individuals by retailers), *bank credit* (such as overdrafts or personal loans) and *trade credit* (common in the commercial world both within countries and internationally).

credit in education, the system of evaluating courses so that a partial qualification from one institution is accepted by another on transfer to complete a course. In North America, the term also refers to the successful completion of a course.

Credit transferability is common in higher education in the USA, but is just beginning to be developed between institutions in the UK. At school level, the equivalence between an O Level pass and a Grade 1 pass at CSE, and between a BTEC diploma and A Levels is a long-standing one.

credit card card issued by an organization, such as a retail outlet or a bank, that enables the holder to obtain goods or services on credit (usually to a specified limit).

Some credit cards also act as bank cards to enable customers to obtain money more easily from branches of their bank other than their own. 'Intelligent' credit cards are now being introduced that contain coded information about the customer and the amount of credit still available. This can be 'read' by a terminal connected with the company's central computer. A number of 'intelligent' cards have been introduced in the 1980s, but not all are credit cards. Some cards require payment in advance (for example, cardphone cards) and others debit the consumer's bank account immediately on use.

credit rating measure of the willingness or ability to pay for goods, loans, or services rendered by an individual, company, or country. A country with a good credit rating will attract loans on favourable terms.

Cree an indigenous North American people whose language belongs to the Algonquian family. The Cree are distributed over a vast area in Canada from Québec to Alberta. In the USA the majority of Cree live in the Rocky Boys reservation in Montana.

creed /kriːd/ in general, any system of belief; in the Christian church the verbal confessions of faith expressing the accepted doctrines of the church. The different forms are the Apostles' Creed, the Nicene Creed, and the Athanasian Creed. The only creed recognized by the Orthodox Church is the Nicene.

The oldest is the *Apostles' Creed*, which, though not the work of the apostles, was probably first formulated in the 2nd century. The full version of the Apostles' Creed, as now used, first appeared about 750.

The use of creeds as a mode of combating heresy was established by the appearance of the *Nicene Creed*, introduced by the Council of Nicaea in 325 when ◊Arianism was widespread, and giving the orthodox doctrine of the Trinity. The Nicene Creed used today is substantially the same as the version adopted at the church council in Constantinople in 381, with a ◊filioque clause added during the 5th and 8th centuries in the Western church.

The *Athanasian Creed* is thought to be later in origin than the time of Athanasius (died 373) although it represents his views in a detailed exposition of the doctrines of the Trinity and the incarnation. Some authorities suppose it to have been composed in the 8th or 9th century but others place it as early as the 4th or 5th century.

Creed /kri:d/ Frederick George 1871–1957. Canadian inventor, who perfected the teleprinter. He perfected the Creed telegraphy system (teleprinter), first used in Fleet Street 1912 and now, usually known as Telex, in offices throughout the world.

creep in civil and mechanical engineering, property of a solid, typically a metal, under continuous stress that causes it to deform below its yield point (the point at which any elastic solid normally stretches without any increase in load or stress). Lead, tin, and zinc, for example, exhibit creep at ordinary temperatures, seen in the movement of the lead sheeting on the roofs of old buildings. Copper, iron, nickel and their alloys also show creep at high temperatures.

Creevey /'kri:vi/ Thomas 1768–1838. British Whig politician and diarist, whose lively letters and journals give information on early 19th-century society and politics. He was a member of Parliament and opposed the slave trade.

cremation disposal of the dead by burning. The custom was universal among ancient Indo-European peoples, for example, the Greeks, Romans, and Teutons. It was discontinued among Christians until the late 19th century because of their belief in the bodily resurrection of the dead. Overcrowded urban cemeteries gave rise to its revival in the West. It has remained the usual method of disposal in the East.

Cremation was revived in Italy about 1870, and shortly afterwards introduced into the UK; the first crematorium was opened 1885 in Woking, Surrey. In the UK an application for cremation must be accompanied by two medical certificates. Cremation is usually carried out in gas-fired furnaces. Ashes are scattered in gardens of remembrance or elsewhere, or deposited in urns at the crematorium or in private graves.

crème de la crème (French 'the cream of the cream') the elite, the very best.

Cremona /krɪ'məʊnə/ city in Italy, Lombardy, on the river Po, 72 km/45 mi SE of Milan; population (1981) 81,000. It is the capital of Cremona province. Once a famous violin-making centre, it now produces food products and textiles. It has a 12th-century cathedral.

Creole in the West Indies and Spanish America, originally someone of European descent born in the New World; but also someone of mixed European and African descent. In Louisiana and other states on the Gulf of Mexico, it applies either to someone of French or Spanish descent or (popularly) to someone of mixed European and African descent.

creole language ◊pidgin language which has ceased to be simply trade jargons in ports and markets and has become the mother tongue of a particular community. Many creoles have developed into distinct languages with literatures of their own, for example, Jamaican Creole, Haitian Creole, Krio in Sierra Leone, and Tok Pisin in Papua New Guinea.

The name 'creole' derives through French from Spanish and Portuguese, in which it originally referred both to children of European background born in tropical colonies and to house slaves on colonial plantations. The implication is that such groups picked up the pidgin forms of languages like Portuguese, Spanish, Dutch, French and English as used in and around the Caribbean, in parts of Africa, and in island communities in the Indian and Pacific Oceans. According to circumstance, there may in such places as Jamaica, Haiti, Mauritius and West Africa be a 'creole continuum' of usage between the strongest forms of a creole and the standard version of the language with which the creole is associated.

Crete

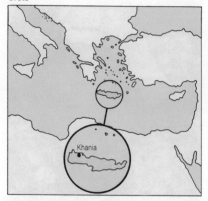

Khania

creosote name given to several of the fractions of coal tar; they are used as wood preservatives. Medicinal creosote is derived from wood tar.

crescent the curved shape of the Moon when it appears less than half illuminated. It also refers to any object or symbol resembling the crescent moon. Often associated with Islam, it was first used by the Turks on their standards after the capture of Constantinople 1453, and appears on the flags of many Muslim countries. The **Red Crescent** is the Muslim equivalent of the Red Cross.

cress a plant generally of the Cruciferae family and characterized by a pungent taste. The common garden cress *Lepidium sativum* is cultivated in Europe, N Africa, and parts of Asia.

The young plants are grown along with white mustard to be eaten while in the seed leaf stage as 'mustard and cress'.

Cretaceous (Latin 'creta' chalk) period of geological time 144–65 million years ago. It is the last period of the Mesozoic era, during which angiosperm (seed-bearing) plants evolved, and dinosaurs and other reptiles reached a peak before almost complete extinction at the end of the period. Chalk is a typical rock type of the second half of the period.

Crete /kri:t/ (Greek *Kríti*) the largest Greek island, in the E Mediterranean Sea, 100 km/62 mi SE of Greece.

area 8,378 sq km/3,234 sq mi

capital Iráklion

towns Khaniá (Canea), Rethymnon, Aghios Nikolaos

products citrus fruit, olives, wine

population (1981) 502,000

language Cretan dialect of Greek

history it has remains of the ◊Minoan civilization 3000–1400 BC, (see ◊Knossos), and was successively under Roman, Byzantine, Venetian, and Turkish rule. The island was annexed by Greece 1913.

In 1941, it was captured by German forces from Allied troops who had retreated from the mainland, and was retaken by the Allies 1944.

Creuse /krɜ:z/ river in central France flowing 255 km/158 mi generally N from the Plateau des Millevaches to the Vienne river. It traverses Creuse *département*, to which it gives its name.

Creusot, Le /krɜ:'zəʊ/ town in Saône-et-Loire *département*, France; population (1982) 32,100. It is a coal mining centre and has foundries, locomotive shops, and armaments factories.

Crewe /kru:/ town in Cheshire, England; population (1981) 59,300. It owed its growth to its position as a railway junction. At Crewe are the chief construction workshops of British Rail. Other occupations include chemical works, clothing factories and vehicles.

cribbage card game, invented in the 17th century by the English poet John Suckling, which is played with a holed board for keeping score. It can be played as singles or in pairs, the number of cards per player depending upon number of players. There is always a 'spare hand', which each player takes in turn to 'own'. Cards are discarded one at a time until the face values of discarded cards totals 31. When all players have discarded their cards the total of each players hand is calculated according to the cards held whether they be in pairs, three of a kind, four of a kind and so on.

crib death North American term for ◊cot death.

Crichton /'kraɪtn/ James c.1560–1582. Scottish scholar, known as 'the Admirable Crichton' because of his extraordinary gifts as a poet, scholar, and linguist. He was also an athlete and fencer. According to one account he was killed at Mantua in a street brawl by his pupil, a son of the Duke of Mantua, who resented Crichton's popularity.

Crick /krɪk/ Francis 1916– . British molecular biologist. From 1949 he researched into DNA's

Crick British molecular biologist Francis Crick with his colleague James Watson (left).

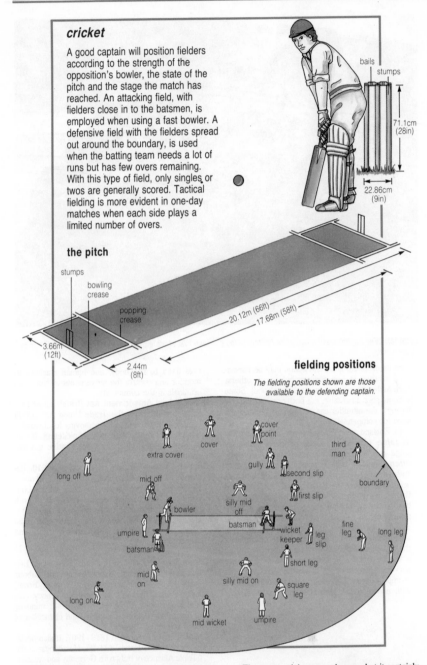

cricket

A good captain will position fielders according to the strength of the opposition's bowler, the state of the pitch and the stage the match has reached. An attacking field, with fielders close in to the batsmen, is employed when using a fast bowler. A defensive field with the fielders spread out around the boundary, is used when the batting team needs a lot of runs but has few overs remaining. With this type of field, only singles or twos are generally scored. Tactical fielding is more evident in one-day matches when each side plays a limited number of overs.

bails
stumps
71.1cm (28in)
22.86cm (9in)

the pitch

stumps
bowling crease
popping crease
20.12m (66ft)
17.68m (58ft)
3.66m (12ft)
2.44m (8ft)

fielding positions

The fielding positions shown are those available to the defending captain.

cover point
cover
extra cover
third man
gully
long off
mid off
second slip
boundary
silly mid off
first slip
bowler
batsman
umpire
wicket keeper
leg slip
fine leg
long leg
batsman
short leg
mid on
silly mid on
square leg
long on
mid wicket
umpire

molecular structure, and the means whereby characteristics are transmitted from one generation to another. For this work he was awarded a Nobel prize (with Maurice Wilkins (1916–) and James D ◊Watson).

cricket the national summer sport in England. The game is played between two sides of 11 players each on a pitch 20 m/22 yds long with a wicket at each end. The object of the game is to score more runs than the opponents. A run is normally scored by the batsman after striking the ball and exchanging ends with his partner, or by hitting the ball to the boundary line for an automatic four or six runs.

A batsman stands at each wicket and is bowled a stipulated number of balls (usually six), after which another bowler bowls from the other wicket. A batsman is usually got out by being bowled, caught, run out, stumped or l,b,w (leg before wicket) – when the ball hits his leg or her leg which is placed before the wicket. Games comprise one or two innings, or turns at batting, per team.

The exact origins are unknown, but it certainly dates back to the 16th century. It became popular in southern England in the late 18th century. Rules were drawn up in 1774 and modified following the formation of the Marylebone Cricket Club (MCC) in 1787.

Every year a series of Test Matches are played among member countries of the Commonwealth: Australia, India, New Zealand, Pakistan, England, Sri Lanka, and the West Indies. Test matches take several days, but otherwise the majority of matches last one, three or four days.

Famous grounds besides Lords, include the Oval (London), Old Trafford (Manchester), the Melbourne Ground and Sydney Oval (Australia); and the Wanderers' Ground (Johannesburg). Great cricketers have included W G Grace, Jack Hobbs, Walter Hammond, and Len Hutton; the Australian Don Bradman; the Indian K S Ranjitsinhji; the South African A D Nourse; and the West Indians Leary Constantine, Frank Worrell, and Gary Sobers.

Cricket: recent winners

County Championship first officially held 1890:
1980 Middlesex
1981 Nottinghamshire
1982 Middlesex
1983 Essex
1984 Essex
1985 Middlesex
1986 Essex
1987 Nottinghamshire
1988 Worcestershire
1989 Worcestershire
Refuge Assurance League (formerly John Player League) first held 1969:
1980 Warwickshire
1981 Essex 1982 Sussex
1983 Yorkshire
1984 Essex
1985 Essex
1986 Hampshire
1987 Worcestershire
1988 Worcestershire
1989 Lancashire
NatWest Cup (formerly called the Gillette Cup) first held 1963:
1980 Middlesex
1981 Derbyshire
1982 Surrey
1983 Somerset
1984 Middlesex
1985 Essex
1986 Sussex
1987 Nottinghamshire
1988 Middlesex
Benson and Hedges Cup first held 1972:
1980 Northamptonshire
1981 Somerset
1982 Somerset
1983 Middlesex
1984 Lancashire
1985 Leicestershire
1986 Middlesex
1987 Yorkshire
1988 Hampshire
1989 Nottinghamshire
World Cup first held 1975, contested every four years:
1975 West Indies
1979 West Indies
1983 India
1987 Australia

cricket in zoology, a type of insect belonging to the order Orthoptera and related to grasshoppers. Crickets are somewhat flattened and have long antennae. The males make a chirping noise by rubbing together special areas on the wings. The females have a long needle-like egglaying organ (ovipositor). There are 900 species known worldwide.

cri de coeur (French) a cry from the heart.

Crimea /kraɪˈmɪə/ N peninsula on the Black Sea, a region of ◊Ukraine Republic, USSR, from 1954.
area 27,000 sq km/10,425 sq mi
capital Simferopol
towns Sevastopol, Yalta
features mainly steppe, but the southern coast is a holiday resort
products iron, oil
recent history under Turkish rule 1475–1774, a subsequent brief independence was ended by Russian annexation 1783. It was the republic of Taurida 1917–20, and the Crimean Autonomous Soviet Republic from 1920 until occupied by Germany July 1942–May 1944. It was then reduced to a region, its Tatar people being deported to Uzbekistan for collaboration. Although they were exonerated 1967, and some were allowed to return, others were forcibly re-exiled 1979.

Crime and Punishment a novel by Dostoievsky, published 1866. It analyses the motives of a murderer and his reactions to the crime he has committed.

Crimean War war 1853–56 between Russia and the allied powers of England, France, Turkey, and Sardinia. The war arose from British and French mistrust of Russia's ambitions in the Balkans. It began with an allied Anglo-French expedition to the Crimea to attack the Russian Black Sea city of Sevastopol. The battles of the River Alma, Balaclava (including the charge of the Light Brigade), and Inkerman 1854 led to a siege which, due to military mismanagement, lasted for a year until Sept 1855. The war was ended by the Treaty of Paris 1856. The scandal surrounding French and British losses through disease led to the organization of proper military nursing services by Florence Nightingale.

1853 Russia invaded the Balkans (from which they were compelled to withdraw by Austrian intervention) and sank the Turkish fleet at Sinope.

1854 Britain and France declared war on Russia, invaded the Crimea and laid siege to Sevastopol (Sept 1854–Sept 1855). Battles of ◊Balaclava 25 Oct (including the Charge of the Light Brigade), ◊Inkerman 5 Nov, and the Alma.

1855 Sardinia declared war on Russia.

1856 The Treaty of Paris in Feb ended the war.

Criminal Injuries Compensation Board UK board established 1964 to administer financial compensation by the state for victims of crimes of violence. Victims can claim compensation for their injuries, but not for damage to property. The compensation awarded is similar to the amount which would be obtained for a court in ◊damages for personal injury.

Criminal Investigation Department (CID) detective branch of the London Metropolitan Police, established 1878, and comprising a force of about 4,000 men and women, recruited entirely from the uniformed police and controlled by an Assistant Commissioner. Such branches are now also found in the regional police forces.

In London, some 1,000 of the detectives are stationed at New Scotland Yard. The remaining 3,000 detectives are stationed locally in the Metropolitan Police District. Developed outside London in the later 19th century, such departments now exist in all UK forces. In practice they had been autonomous, but in 1979 new administrative arrangements were introduced so that all police officers, including CID, came under the uniformed chief superintendente of the division, so putting into practice the former theoretical position. Around the country from 1965 are Regional Crime Squads. These comprise detectives drawn from the various local forces of the region to deal with major crime, and are kept in touch by a London-based national coordinator.

The CID at New Scotland Yard

1 Central Office: deals with international crime and serious crime throughout the country. It controls the Flying Squad (a rapid deployment force for investigating serious crimes).

2 Criminal Intelligence Department: studies criminals and their methods.

3 Fingerprint Department: holds some two million prints of convicted criminals.

4 Criminal Record Office: holds information on known criminals and publishes the *Police Gazette*.

5 The Scientific Laboratory.

6 The Stolen Car Squad.

7 Special Branch: deals with crimes against the State.

8 National coordinator for the Regional Crime Squads (detectives drawn from local forces to deal with major crime).

criminal law the body of law that defines the public wrongs (crimes) which are punishable by the state and establishes methods of prosecution and punishment. It is distinct from ◊civil law, which deals with legal relationships between individuals (including organizations) such as contract law.

The laws of each country specify what actions or omissions are criminal. These include: serious moral wrongs, such as murder; wrongs which endanger the security of the state, such as treason; wrongs which disrupt an orderly society, such as evading taxes; and wrongs against the community,

Crimean War English and French allies fighting in the Crimean War share a drink together. The photograph is by Roger Fenton.

such as dropping litter. An action may be considered a crime in one country but not in others, such as homosexuality or drinking alcohol. Some actions, such as assault, are both criminal and civil wrongs; the offender can be both prosecuted and sued for compensation.

In England and Wales crimes are either: *indictable offences* serious offences triable by judge and jury in the Crown Court; *summary offences* dealt with in magistrates' courts; or *hybrid offences* tried in either kind of court according to the seriousness of the case and the wishes of the defendant. The Crown Court has power to punish those found guilty more severely than magistrates' courts. Punishments include imprisonment, fines, suspended terms of imprisonment (which only come into operation if the offender is guilty of further offences during a specified period), probation, and ◊community service. Overcrowding in prisons, and the cost of imprisonment have led to recent experiments with non-custodial sentences such as electronic

Crispi Resolutely anti-French and anti-clerical, Francesco Crispi was Italian Premier 1887–91 and 1893–96. An advocate of the Triple Alliance of Germany, Italy, and Austria, he was deposed in 1896.

tags fixed to the body, and human trackers to monitor and control the movements of convicted criminals in the community.

Criminal Law Amendment Act British act of Parliament which with the Trade Union Act (1871) legalized ◊trade unions by removing legal restrictions on union activities such as picketing. It was repealed by the incoming Conservative government in 1875.

Crippen /'krɪpən/ Hawley Harvey 1861–1910. US murderer of his wife, variety artist Belle Elmore. He buried her remains in the cellar of his London home and tried to escape to the USA with his mistress Ethel le Neve (dressed as a boy). He was arrested on board ship following a radio message, the first criminal captured 'by radio', and was hanged.

Cripps /krɪps/ (Richard) Stafford 1889–1952. British Labour politician, expelled from the Labour party 1939–45 for supporting a 'Popular Front' against Chamberlain's appeasement policy. He was ambassador to Moscow 1940–42, minister of aircraft production 1942–45, and chancellor of the Exchequer 1947–50.

Crispi /'krɪspi/ Francesco 1819–1907. Italian prime minister 1887–91 and 1893–96. He advocated the ◊Triple Alliance of Italy with Germany and Austria, but was deposed 1896.

Criterion, The English quarterly literary review 1922–39 edited by T S Eliot. His 'The Waste Land' was published in its first issue. It also published Auden, Pound, Joyce, and D H Lawrence, and introduced Proust and Valéry to UK readers.

crith unit of mass used for weighing gases. One crith is the mass of 1 litre of hydrogen gas (H_2) at standard temperature and pressure.

critical angle in optics, for a ray of light passing from a denser to a less dense medium (such as from glass to air), the smallest angle of incidence at which the emergent ray grazes the surface of the denser medium–at an angle of refraction of 90°. The ray does not pass out into the less dense medium (when the angle of incidence has to be less than the critical angle), nor is it internally reflected back into the denser medium (when the angle of incidence has to be greater than the critical angle).

critical mass in nuclear physics, the minimum mass of fissile material that can undergo a continuous ◊chain reaction. Below this mass, too many ◊neutrons escape from the surface for a chain reaction

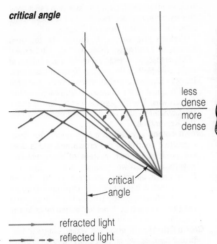

critical angle

less dense
more dense

critical angle

⎯•⎯•⎯ refracted light
⎯ ⎯ • ⎯ reflected light

crocodile

Cromwell A portrait after Samuel Cooper (1656), National Portrait Gallery, London.

to carry on; above the critical mass, the reaction may accelerate into a nuclear explosion.

critical temperature temperature above which a particular gas cannot be converted into a liquid by pressure alone. It is also the temperature at which a magnetic material loses its magnetism (the Curie point).

Crivelli /krɪ'veli/ Carlo 1435/40–1495/1500. Italian painter in the early Renaissance style, active in Venice. He painted extremely detailed, decorated religious works, sometimes festooned with garlands of fruit. His figure style is strongly N Italian, reflecting the influence of Mantegna.

CRO abbreviation for cathode ray oscilloscope, a form of ◊cathode ray tube. A common laboratory instrument, the CRO can be used to measure the voltage, frequency, and timing of an electrical signal and display its waveform, or shape.

Croatia /krəʊ'eɪʃə/ (Serbo-Croat **Hrvatska**) constituent republic of Yugoslavia
area 56,500 sq km/21,809 sq mi
capital Zagreb
physical Adriatic coastline with large islands; very mountainous, with part of the Karst region and the Julian and Styrian Alps; some marshland
population (1985) 4,660,000 including 3,500,000 Croats, 530,000 Serbs, and 25,000 Hungarians
language the Croatian variant of Serbo-Croat
history part of Pannonia in Roman times; settled by Carpathian Croats 7th century; for 800 years from 1102 an autonomous kingdom under the Hungarian Crown; Austrian crownland 1849; Hungarian crownland 1868; included in the kingdom of the Serbs, Croats, and Slovenes (called Yugoslavia from 1931) 1918; Nazi puppet state during World War II; it has remained a centre for nationalist and separatist demands from the 1970s.

Croce /'krəʊtʃi/ Benedetto 1866–1952. Italian philosopher and literary critic, an opponent of fascism. Like Hegel, he held that ideas do not represent reality but *are* reality; but unlike Hegel, he rejected every kind of transcendence.

crochet a technique similar to both knitting and lacemaking, in which one hooked needle is used to produce a loosely looped network of wool or cotton. Dating from the 19th century, crochet can be almost as fine and complex as lace. Both garments and trims are produced by crocheting.

Crockett /'krɒkɪt/ Davy 1786–1836. US folk hero, a Democrat Congressman 1827–31 and 1833–35. A series of books, of which he may have been part-author, made him into a mythical hero of the frontier, but their Whig associations cost him his office. He died in the battle of the ◊Alamo during the war for Texan independence.

Crockford /'krɒkfəd/ William 1775–1844. British gambler, founder in 1827 of Crockford's Club in St James's Street, which became the fashionable place for London society to gamble.

crocodile large aquatic carnivorous reptile, related to alligators and caimans, but distinguished from them by a more pointed snout, and a notch in the upper jaw into which the fourth tooth in the lower jaw fits. They can grow up to 6 m/20 ft long, and have long powerful tails which propel them when swimming. They can live for up to 100 years.

They are fierce hunters, the larger specimens attacking animals the size of antelopes or, occasionally, people. The female lays over 100 hardshelled eggs in holes or nestmounds of vegetation, which she guards until the eggs hatch. When in the sun, they cool themselves by opening the mouth wide, which also enables scavenging birds to pick their teeth. They can stay underwater for long periods, but surface to breathe. The nostrils can be closed underwater. They ballast themselves with stones to adjust their buoyancy. They have remained virtually unchanged for 200 million years.

About a dozen species of crocodile are found in tropical parts of Africa, Asia, Australia, and Central America. The largest is the **saltwater crocodile** *Crocodylus porosus*, which can grow to 6 m/20 ft or more, and is found in E India, Australia, and the W Pacific. The **Nile crocodile** *Crocodylus niloticus* is found in Africa and Madagascar. The **gharial** *Gavialis gangeticus* is an Indian species, which grows to 4.5 m/15 ft or more and has a very long narrow snout specialized for fish-eating.

crocus genus of plants, family Iridaceae, native to N parts of the Old World, especially S Europe and Asia Minor. It has single yellow, purple or white flowers and narrow pointed leaves.

During the dry season of the year they remain underground in the form of a corm, and produce fresh shoots and flowers in spring or autumn. At the end of the season of growth fresh corms are produced. Several species are cultivated as garden plants, the familiar mauve, white, and orange forms being varieties of *Crocus vernus*, *Crocus versicolor*, and *Crocus aureus*. To the same genus belongs the saffron *Crocus sativus*. The so-called ◊autumn crocus or meadow saffron *Colchicum* is not a true crocus, but belongs to the Liliaceae.

Croesus /'kriːsəs/ died 546 BC? Last king of Lydia, famed for his wealth. His court included ◊Solon, who warned him that no man could be called happy until his life had ended happily. When Croesus was overthrown by Cyrus the Great 546 BC and condemned to be burned to death, he called out Solon's name. Cyrus, having learned the reason, spared his life.

croft a small farm in the Highlands of Scotland, traditionally farming common land co-operatively; the 1886 Crofters Act gave security of tenure to crofters. Today, although grazing land is still shared, arable land is typically enclosed.

crocus

Crohn's disease inflammation of the bowel, also known as regional ileitis or regional enteritis. It is characterized by ulceration, abscess formation, small perforations, and the development of adhesions binding the loops of the small intestine. It tends to flare up for a few days at a time, causing diarrhoea, abdominal cramps, loss of appetite, and mild fever.

The cause of Crohn's disease is unknown, although stress may be an important factor. Mild cases respond to rest, bland diet, and drug treatment. In severe cases, surgery may be necessary to remove the diseased segment(s) of the bowel. Crohn's disease is often seen in young adults.

Croker /'krəʊkə/ Richard 1841–1922. US politician, 'boss' of Tammany Hall, the Democratic party political machine in New York 1886–1902.

Cro-magnon a type of prehistoric human, the first skeletons of which were found 1868 in the Cro-magnon cave near Les Eyzies, in the Dordogne region of France. They are thought to have superseded the Neanderthals, and lived between 40,000 and 35,000 years ago. Although biologically modern, they were larger in build than modern humans. Their culture produced flint and bone tools, jewellery, and cave paintings.

Crome /krəʊm/ John 1768–1821. British landscape painter, founder of the **Norwich school** with Cotman 1803. His works include *The Poringland Oak c.*1818 (Tate Gallery, London), showing Dutch influence.

Crompton /'krɒmptən/ Richmal, pen name of British writer R C Lamburn 1890–1969. She is remembered for her stories about the mischievous schoolboy 'William'.

Crompton /'krɒmptən/ Samuel 1753–1827. British inventor at the time of the Industrial Revolution. He invented the 'spinning mule' 1779, combining the ideas of ◊Arkwright and ◊Hargreaves. Though widely adopted, his invention brought him little financial return.

Cromwell /'krɒmwel/ Oliver 1599–1658. English general and politician, Puritan leader of the Parliamentary side in the ◊Civil War. He raised cavalry forces (later called **Ironsides**) which aided the victories at Edgehill 1642 and ◊Marston Moor 1644, and organized the New Model Army, which he led (with Gen Fairfax) to victory at Naseby 1645. As Lord Protector (ruler) from 1653, he established religious toleration, and Britain's prestige in Europe on the basis of an alliance with France against Spain.

Cromwell was born at Huntingdon, NW of Cambridge, son of a small landowner. He entered Parliament 1629 and became active in events leading to the Civil War. Failing to secure a constitutional settlement with Charles I 1646–48, he defeated the 1648 Scottish invasion at Preston. A special commission, of which Cromwell was a member, tried the king and condemned him to death, and a republic was set up.

The ◊Levellers demanded radical reforms, but he executed their leaders in 1649. He used terror to crush Irish clan resistance 1649–50; and defeated the Scots (who had acknowledged Charles II) at Dunbar 1650 and Worcester 1651. In 1653, having forcibly expelled the corrupt 'Rump' Parliament, he summoned a convention ('Barebone's Parliament'), soon dissolved as too radical, and under a constitution (Instrument of Government) drawn up by the army leaders, became Protector (king in all but name). The Parliament of l654–55 was dissolved as uncooperative, and after a period of military dictatorship, his last parliament offered him the crown; he refused because he feared the army's republicanism.

Cromwell /'krɒmwel/ Richard 1626–1712. Son of Oliver ◊Cromwell, he succeeded his father as Protector, but resigned May 1659, living in exile after the Restoration until 1680, when he returned to England.

Cromwell /'krɒmwel/ Thomas, Earl of Essex *c.* 1485–1540. English politician. Originally in Lord Chancellor Wolsey's service, he became secretary to Henry VIII 1534 and the real director of government policy. He had Henry proclaimed head of the church, suppressed the monasteries, ruthlessly crushed all opposition, and favoured Protestantism, which denied the divine right of the pope. His mistake in arranging Henry's marriage to Anne of Cleves (to cement an alliance with the German Protestant princes against France and the Holy Roman Empire) led to his being accused of treason and beheaded.

Cronkite /'krɒŋkaɪt/ Walter 1916– . US broadcast journalist, who became a household name and face throughout the USA as anchorman of the national evening news programme for CBS, a US television network, from 1962 to 1981.

Crookes /kruːks/ William 1832–1919. English scientist, whose many chemical and physical discoveries included the metal thallium 1861, the radiometer 1875, and Crooke's high vacuum tube used in X-ray techniques.

crop in birds, the thin-walled enlargement of the digestive tract between the oesophagus and stomach. It is an effective storage organ especially in seed-eating birds; a pigeon's crop can hold about 500 cereal grains. Digestion begins in the crop, by the moisturizing of food. A crop also occurs in insects and annelid worms.

crop a plant grown for human use. Over 80 crops are grown worldwide, providing people with the majority of their food, and supplying fibres, rubber, pharmaceuticals, dyes, and other materials.

There are four main groups of crops.

Food crops provide the bulk of people's food worldwide. The major types are cereals, roots, pulses, vegetables, fruits, oil crops, tree nuts, sugar, beverages, and spices. Cereals make the most important contribution to human nutrition.

Forage crops like grass, clover, and kale, are grown to feed livestock. and cover a greater area of the world than food crops. Grass, which dominates this group, is the world's most abundant crop, though much of it is still in an unimproved state.

Fibre crops produce vegetable fibres. Temperate areas produce flax and hemp, but the most important fibre crops are cotton, jute, and sisal, which are grown mostly in the tropics. Cotton dominates fibre crop production.

Miscellaneous crops include tobacco, rubber, ornamental flowers, and plants which produce perfume, pharmaceuticals, and dye. See also ◊catch crop.

crop rotation the system of regularly changing the crops grown on a piece of land. The crops are grown in a particular order to utilize and add to the nutrients in the soil and to prevent the buildup of insect and fungal pests.

In the 18th-century, a four year rotation was widely adopted with autumn-sown cereal, followed by a root crop, then spring cereal, and ending with a leguminous crop. Since then, more elaborate rotations have been devised with two, three, or four successive cereal crops, and with the root crop replaced by a cash crop such as sugar beet or potatoes, or by a legume crop such as peas or beans.

croquet outdoor game played with mallets and balls on a level hooped lawn measuring 27 m/90 ft by 18 m/60 ft. Played in France in the 16th and 17th centuries, it gained popularity in England in the 1850s, and was revived 100 years later.

Two or more players can take part and the object is to drive the balls though the hoops in rotation. A player's ball may be advanced or retarded by another ball. The headquarters of croquet is the Croquet Association (founded 1897), which is based at the Hurlingham Club, London.

Crosby /'krɒzbi/ 'Bing' (Harry Lillis) 1904–1977. US film actor and singer, who achieved world success with his distinctive style of crooning in such songs as 'Pennies from Heaven', and 'White Christmas'. He won an acting Oscar for *Going My Way* 1944, and made a series of 'road' film comedies with Dorothy Lamour and Bob Hope, the last being *Road to Hong Kong* 1962.

crossbill type of ◊finch *Loxia curvirostra* in which the hooked tips of the upper and lower beak cross one another, an adaptation for extracting the seeds from conifer cones. It is found in northern parts of Europe, Asia, and North America.

The *parrot crossbill Loxia pytopsittacus* of Europe, and the *white-winged crossbill Loxia leucoptera* of N Asia and North America feed on pine and larch respectively.

crossing over in biology, a process that occurs during ◊meiosis. While the chromosomes are lying alongside each other in pairs, each partner may break, and then link up with the segment from the other partner, so exchanging corresponding sections. It is a form of genetic ◊recombination, which increases variation and thus provides the raw material of evolution.

Crossman /'krɒsmən/ Richard (Howard Stafford) 1907–1974. British Labour politician. He was minister of housing and local government 1964–66 and of health and social security 1968–70. His posthumous *Crossman Papers* 1975 revealed confidential cabinet discussion.

crossword word puzzle comprising squares on a grid. Each square is filled by a letter, the letters forming a word that answers one of the numbered clues, which go across or down the grid. The first crossword was devised by Arthur Wynne of Liverpool, England, in the *New York World* 1913.

croup inflammation (usually viral) of a child's larynx and trachea, with croaking breathing and a cough.

crow any of 35 species of the genus *Corvus* found worldwide. They are usually 45 cm/1.5 ft long, black, with a strong bill, feathered at the base, and omnivorous with a bias towards animal food. They are considered to be very intelligent.

crowding out in economics, a situation in which an increase in government expenditure, by generating price rises and thus a reduction in the real money supply, results in a fall in private consumption and/or investment. Crowding out has been used in recent years as a justification of privatization of state-owned services and industries.

crowfoot white-flowered aquatic plants of the genus *Ranunculus*, with only a touch of yellow at the base of the petals.

Crowley /'krɔʊli/ Aleister (Edward Alexander) 1875–1947. British occultist, a member of the theosophical Order of the Golden Dawn; he claimed to practise black magic, and his books include the novel *Diary of a Drug Fiend* 1923. He designed a tarot pack that bears his name.

Crowley /'krɔʊli/ John 1942– . US writer of science fiction and fantasy, notably *Little, Big* 1980 and *Aegypt* 1987, which contain esoteric knowledge and theoretical puzzles.

crown an official head-dress worn by a king or queen. The modern crown originated with the diadem, an embroidered fillet worn by eastern rulers, for which a golden band was later substituted. A laurel crown was granted by the Greeks to a victor in the games, and by the Romans to a

triumphant general. Crowns came into use among the Byzantine emperors and the European kings after the fall of the Western Empire.

Perhaps the oldest in Europe is the Iron Crown of Lombardy, made in 591. The crown of Charlemagne, preserved in Vienna, consists of eight gold plates. Before the Norman Conquest, kings of England certainly wore crowns, and from the Conquest to the Commonwealth each king had two crowns. The old ◊regalia was broken up under the Commonwealth, and a new set was made after the Restoration.

crown colony any British colony under the direct legislative control of the crown and which does not possess its own system of representative government. Crown colonies are administered by a crown-appointed governor or by elected or nominated legislative and executive councils with an official majority. Usually the crown retains rights of veto and of direct legislation by orders in council.

Crown Courts in England and Wales, courts at particular centres, which hear more serious criminal cases referred from ◊magistrates' courts after ◊committal proceedings. They replaced ◊quarter sessions and assizes, which were abolished 1971. Appeals against conviction or sentence at magistrates' courts may be heard in Crown Courts. Appeal from a Crown Court is to the Court of Appeal.

Crown Estate title (from 1956) of land in UK formerly owned by the monarch but handed to Parliament (by George III in 1760) in exchange for an annual payment (called the civil list). It owns valuable sites in central London, and 268,400 acres in England and Scotland.

crown jewels popular name for ◊regalia.

Crown Proceedings Act UK act of Parliament which provided that the Crown (as represented by, for example, government departments) could from 1948 be sued like a private individual.

Croydon /'krɔɪdn/ borough of S London, England; it includes the suburbs of Croydon, Purley, and Coulsdon

features 11th-century Lanfranc's palace, former residence of archbishops of Canterbury; Ashcroft Theatre, founded 1962; overspill office development from central London

industries engineering, electronics, foodstuffs, pharmaceuticals

Crowley Notorius British occultist Aleister Crowley called himself 'the wickedest man alive.' He established a shrine devoted to pleasure in Sicily.

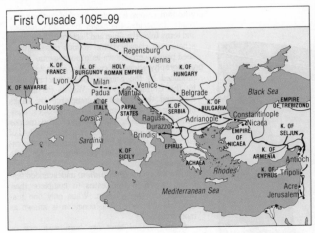

First Crusade 1095–99

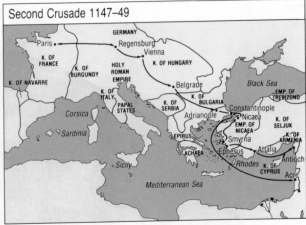

Second Crusade 1147–49

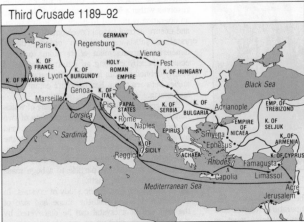

Third Crusade 1189–92

Fourth Crusade, Venice–Constantinople 1202–04

population (1981) 316,557.

crucifixion death by fastening to a cross, a form of capital punishment used by the ancient Romans, Persians, and Carthaginians, and abolished by the Roman emperor Constantine. Specifically, the Crucifixion refers to the death of ◊Jesus in this manner.

Cruden /'kruːdn/ Alexander 1701–1770. Scottish compiler of a Biblical *Concordance* 1737.

Cruelty, Theatre of a theory advanced by Antonin ◊Artaud in his book *Le Théâtre et son double* 1938 and adopted by a number of writers and directors. It aims to shock the audience into an awareness of basic, primitive human nature through the release of feelings usually repressed by conventional behaviour. In the UK Artaud's theory influenced the producer and director Peter Brook.

Cruft /krʌft/ Charles 1852–1938. British dog expert. He organized his first dog show 1886, and from that year annual shows bearing his name were held in Islington, London.

Cruikshank /'krʊkʃæŋk/ George 1792–1878. British painter and illustrator, remembered especially for his political cartoons and illustrations to Dickens's *Oliver Twist* and Defoe's *Robinson Crusoe*.

cruise missile a long-range guided missile that has a terrain-seeking radar system and flies at moderate speed and low altitude. It is descended from the German V-1 of World War II. Initial trials in the 1950s demonstrated the limitations of cruise missiles, which included high fuel consumption and relatively slow speeds (when compared to intercontinental ballistic missiles – ICBMs) as well as inaccuracy and a small warhead. Improvements to guidance systems by the use of terrain-contour matching (TERCOM) ensured pinpoint accuracy on low-level flights after launch from a mobile ground launcher (ground-launched cruise missile – GLCM), from an aircraft (air-launched cruise missile – ALCM), or from a submarine or ship (sea-launched cruise missile – SLCM).

The 1972 Strategic Arms Limitation Talks (SALT I) excluded reference to cruise missiles, and thus research into improved systems continued. During the 1970s the USSR increased its intermediate nuclear force (INF) targeted upon W Europe and at the same time improved its own air defences. NATO therefore embarked in 1979 on a 'twin-track decision' to acquire additional cruise missiles while simultaneously offering to agree to an arms control treaty to withdraw them, provided the USSR did likewise. Tomahawk GLCMs were deployed from 1983 on. The 1987 INF Treaty resulted in GLCMs being withdrawn.

crusade a war against non-Christians and heretics, sanctioned by the pope, in particular, a series of wars 1096–1291 undertaken by European rulers to recover Palestine from the Muslims. Motivated by religious zeal and the desire for more land, and by the trading ambitions of the major Italian cities, the Crusades had widely varying effects.

1st Crusade 1095–99 led by Baldwin of Boulogne, Godfrey of Bouillon, and Peter the Hermit. Motivated by occupation of Anatolia and Jerusalem by the Seljuk Turks. Crusade succeeded in recapturing Jerusalem and establishing a series of Latin kingdoms on the Syrian coast.

2nd Crusade 1147–49 led by Louis VII of France and Emperor Conrad III; a complete failure.

3rd Crusade 1189–92 led by Philip II Augustus of France and Richard I of England. Failed to recapture Jerusalem, which had been seized by Saladin 1187.

4th Crusade 1202–04 led by William of Montferrata, and Baldwin of Hainault. Directed against Egypt but diverted by the Venetians to sack and divide Constantinople.

Children's Crusade 1212 thousands of children left for the Holy Land but were sold into slavery at Marseille, or died of disease and hunger.

5th Crusade 1218–21 led by King Andrew of Hungary, Cardinal Pelagius, King John of Jerusalem, and King Hugh of Cyprus. Captured and then lost Damietta, Egypt.

6th Crusade 1228–29 led by the Holy Roman emperor Frederick II. Recovered Jerusalem by negotiation with the sultan of Egypt. City finally lost 1244.

7th and 8th Crusades 1249–54, 1270–72 both led by Louis IX of France. Acre, the last Christian fortress in Syria, was lost 1291.

crust the outermost part of the structure of Earth, consisting of two distinct parts, the oceanic crust and the continental crust. The *oceanic* crust is on average about 10 km/6.2 mi thick and consists mostly of basaltic types of rock. By contrast, the *continental* crust is primarily granitic in composition and more complex in its structure. Because of the movements of ◊plate tectonics, the oceanic crust is in no place older than about 200 million years. However, parts of the continental crust are over three billion years old.

Beneath a layer of surface sediment, the oceanic crust is made up of a layer of basalt, followed by a layer of gabbro. The composition of the oceanic crust overall shows a high proportion of *si*licon and *mag*nesium oxides, hence named *sima* by geologists. The continental crust varies in thickness between about 40 – 70 km/25 – 43 mi, being deeper beneath mountain ranges. The surface layer consists of many kinds of sedimentary and igneous rocks. Beneath lies a zone of metamorphic rocks built on a thick layer of granodiorite. *Si*licon and *al*uminium oxides dominate the composition and the name *sial* is given to continental crustal material.

crustacean one of the class of arthropods that includes crabs, lobsters, shrimps, woodlice, and barnacles. The external skeleton is made of protein and chitin hardened with lime. Each segment bears a pair of appendages, which may

crust

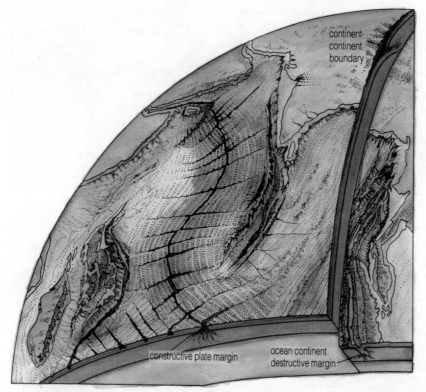

continent-continent boundary

constructive plate margin

ocean continent destructive margin

be modified for feeding, swimming, walking or grasping.

Crux constellation of the southern hemisphere, popularly known as the Southern Cross, the smallest of the 88 constellations. Its brightest star, Alpha Crucis, is a ◊double star. Near Beta Crucis lies a glittering star cluster known as the Jewel Box. The constellation also contains the Coalsack, a dark cloud of dust silhouetted against the bright starry background of the Milky Way.

cryogenics science of very low temperatures (approaching ◊absolute zero), including the production of very low temperatures and the exploitation of special properties associated with them, such as the disappearance of electrical resistance (◊superconductivity).

Low temperatures can be produced by the Joule–Thomson effect (cooling a gas by making it do work as it expands; gases such as oxygen, hydrogen, and helium may be liquified in this way, and temperatures of 0.3 kelvin can be reached. Further cooling requires magnetic methods; a magnetic material, in contact with the substance to be cooled and with liquid helium, is magnetized by a strong magnetic field. The heat generated by the process is carried away by the helium. When the material is then demagnetized, its temperature falls; temperatures of around 10^{-3} kelvin have been achieved in this way. A similar process, called **nuclear adiabatic expansion**, was used to produce the lowest temperature recorded: 3×10^{-8} kelvin, produced in 1984 by a team of Finnish scientists.

At temperatures near absolute zero, materials can display unusual properties. Some metals, such as mercury and lead, exhibit superconductivity. Liquid helium loses its viscosity and becomes a 'superfluid' when cooled to below 2 kelvin; in this state it flows up the sides of its container.

Cryogenics has several practical applications. *Cryotherapy* is a process used in eye surgery, in which a freezing probe is briefly applied to the outside of the eye to repair a break in the retina. Electronic components called ◊Josephson

junctions, which could be used in very fast computers, need low temperatures to function. Magnetic levitation (◊maglev) systems must be maintained at low temperatures. Food can be frozen for years,, and it has been suggested that space travellers could be frozen for long journeys. Freezing people with terminal illnesses, to be revived when a cure has been developed, has also been suggested.

cryolite a rare granular crystalline mineral Na_3AlF_6 used in the electrolyte reduction of ◊bauxite to aluminium. It is chiefly found in Greenland.

cryonics process of freezing at the moment of clinical death with the aim of enabling eventual resuscitation. The body, drained of blood, is indefinitely preserved in a thermos-type container filled with liquid nitrogen at $-196°C$.

The first human treated was James H Bedford, a lung cancer patient of 74, in the USA in 1967.

crystal

sodium chloride

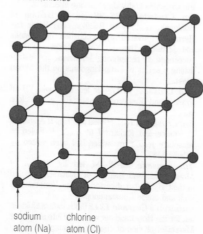

sodium atom (Na)　　chlorine atom (Cl)

cryptogam an obsolete name applied to the lower plants. It included the algae, liverworts, mosses and ferns (plus the fungi and bacteria in very early schemes of classification). In such classifications seed plants were known as phanerogams.

cryptography science of codes, for example, those produced by the Enigma coding machine used by the Germans in World War II (as in ◊Ultra), and those used in commerce by banks encoding electronic fund transfer messages, business firms sending computer-conveyed memos between headquarters, and in the growing field of electronic mail. No method of encrypting is completely unbreakable, but decoding can be made extremely complex.

cryptorchism or *cryptochidism* undescended testicles; failure of the testes to complete their descent into the scrotum. When only one testicle has descended, the condition is known as monorchism.

About 10% of boys are born with one or both testes undescended. Usually the condition resolves within a few weeks of birth. Otherwise, an operation is needed to bring the testes down and ensure normal sexual development.

crystal a substance with an orderly three-dimensional arrangement of its atoms or molecules, thereby creating an external surface of clearly defined smooth faces having characteristic angles between them. Examples are common salt and quartz.

Each geometrical figure or form, many of which may be combined in one crystal, consists of two or more faces, for example, dome, prism, and pyramid. A mineral can often be identifed by the shape of its crystals and the system of crystallization determined. A single crystal can vary in size from a sub-microscopic particle to a huge mass some 30 m/100 ft in length.

crystallography the scientific study of crystals. In 1912, it was found that the shape and size of the unit cell of a crystal can be discovered by X-rays, thus opening up an entirely new way of 'seeing' atoms. This means of determining the atomic patterns in a crystal is known as X-ray diffraction. It has been shown that even purified biomolecules, such as proteins and DNA, can form crystals, and such compounds may now be studied by the same method. Another field of application of X-ray analysis lies in the study of metals and alloys. Crystallography is also of use to the geologist studying rocks and soils. Many materials were not even suspected of being crystals until they were examined by X-ray crystallography.

By this method it has been found that many substances have unit cells or boxes which are exact cubes, for example ordinary table salt (sodium chloride).

Crystal Palace glass and iron building designed by ◊Paxton, housing the Great Exhibition of 1851 in Hyde Park, London; later rebuilt in modified form at Sydenham Hill 1854 (burned down 1936).

CSCE abbreviation for *Conference on Security and Cooperation in Europe*, popularly known as the ◊Helsinki Conference.

CSE (Certificate of Secondary Education) in the UK, the examinations taken by the majority of secondary school pupils who were not regarded as academically capable of GCE ◊O Level, until the introduction of the common secondary examination system, ◊GCSE, 1988.

CT abbreviation for ◊*Connecticut*.

Ctesiphon /ˈtɛsɪfən/ ruined royal city of the Parthians, and later capital of the Sassanian Empire, 19 km/12 mi SE of Baghdad, Iraq. A palace of the 4th century still has its throne room standing, spanned by a single vault of unreinforced brickwork some 24 m/80 ft across.

cu abbreviation for *cubic* (measure).

Cuba /ˈkjuːbə/ island in the Caribbean, the largest of the West Indies, off the south coast of Florida.

government The 1976 constitution created a socialist state with the national assembly of people's power as its supreme organ. It consists of

Cuba
Republic of
(República de Cuba)

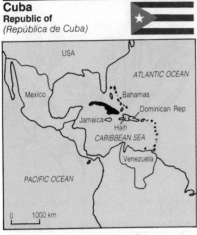

area 114,524 sq km/44,206 sq mi
capital Havana
physical comprises Cuba, the largest and westernmost of the West Indian islands, and smaller islands including Isle of Youth; low hills; Sierra Maestra mountains in E
features US base (on perpetual lease since 1934) at Guantánamo Bay (Gitmo), and Soviet base at Cienfuegos
head of state and government Fidel Castro Ruz from 1959
political system communist republic
political parties Communist Party of Cuba (PCC), Marxist-Leninist
exports sugar (largest producer after USSR), tobacco, coffee, iron, copper, nickel
currency Cuban peso (1.36 = £1 Feb 1990, official rate)
population (1987) 10,240,000 (plus 125,000 refugees from the Cuban port of Mariel – *marielitos* – in US); 66% are of Spanish descent, and a large number are of African origin; annual growth rate 0.6%
life expectancy men 72, women 75
language Spanish
religion Roman Catholic 45%
literacy 96% male/95% female (1979)
disposable national income $15.8 bn (1983);

$1,590 per head of population
chronology
1901 Cuba achieved independence.
1933 Fulgencia Batista seized power.
1944 Batista retired.
1952 Batista seized power again to begin an oppressive regime.
1953 Fidel Castro led an unsuccessful coup against Batista.
1956 Castro led a second unsuccessful coup.
1959 Batista overthrown by Castro. Constitution of 1940 replaced by a 'Fundamental Law', making Castro prime minister, his brother Raul Castro his deputy, and Ché Guevara his number three.
1960 All US businesses in Cuba appropriated without compensation. US broke off diplomatic relations.
1961 US sponsored an unsuccessful invasion, the Bay of Pigs episode. Castro announced that Cuba had become a communist state, with a Marxist-Leninist programme of economic development.
1962 Cuba expelled from the Organization of American States (OAS). Soviet nuclear missiles removed from Cuba at US insistence.
1965 Cuba's sole political party renamed Cuban Communist Party (PCC). With Soviet help, Cuba began to make considerable economic and social progress.
1972 Cuba became a full member of the Moscow-based Council for Mutual Economic Assistance (CMEA).
1976 New socialist constitution approved and Castro elected president.
1976–81 Castro became involved in extensive international commitments, assisting Third World countries, particularly in Africa.
1982 Cuba joined other Latin American countries in giving moral support to Argentina in its dispute with Britain.
1984 Castro tried to improve US-Cuban relations by discussing the exchange of US prisoners in Cuba with Cuban 'undesirables' in the US.
1988 Peace accord with South Africa signed, agreeing to withdrawal of Cuban troops from Angola.
1989 Reduction in Cuba's overseas military activities.

510 deputies elected by universal suffrage for a five-year term and elects 31 of its members to form the council of state. It also elects the head of state who is president of the council, head of government, and first secretary and chairman of the political bureau of the only party, the Cuban Communist Party (PCC). Fidel Castro thus occupies all the key positions within the state and the party.

history the first European to visit Cuba was Christopher ◊Columbus in 1492. From 1511 Cuba was a Spanish colony, its economy based on sugar plantations worked by slaves, who were first brought from Africa in 1523. Slavery was not abolished until 1886. Cuba was ceded to the USA in 1898, at the end of the ◊Spanish-American War. A republic was proclaimed in 1901, though the USA retained its naval bases and a right to intervene in internal affairs until 1934.

In 1933 an army sergeant, Fulgencio ◊Batista, seized and held power until he retired in 1944. In 1952 he regained power in a bloodless coup and began another period of rule which many Cubans found oppressive. In 1953 a young lawyer and son of a sugar planter, Dr Fidel ◊Castro, tried to overthrow him but failed. He went into exile to prepare for another coup in 1956 but was again defeated. He fled to the hills with Dr Ernesto 'Che' ◊Guevara and ten others, to form a guerrilla force.

In 1959 Castro's force of 5,000 men deposed Batista, to great popular acclaim. The 1940 constitution was suspended and replaced by a 'Fundamental Law', power being vested in a council

of ministers with Castro as prime minister, his brother Raul as his deputy and Che Guevara, reputedly, as the next in command. In 1960 the USA broke off diplomatic relations after all US businesses in Cuba were nationalized without compensation. In 1961 it went further, sponsoring a full-scale, but abortive, invasion, the ◊'Bay of Pigs' episode. In Dec of that year Castro proclaimed a communist state whose economy would develop along Marxist-Leninist lines.

In 1962 Cuba was expelled from the Organization of American States (OAS), originally formed as a regional agency of the UN, but increasingly dominated by the USA, which initiated a full political and economic blockade. Castro responded by tightening relations with the USSR which, in the same year, supplied missiles with atomic warheads for installation in Cuba. A crisis was averted when they were dismantled at the US president's insistence.

In 1965 Guevara left Cuba, ostensibly to fight causes abroad, and the country's only political party changed its name to the Cuban Communist Party (PCC). With Soviet help, Cuba made substantial economic and social progress 1965–72, in 1972 becoming a member of the Council for Mutual Economic Assistance (CMEA), a Moscow-based organization linking communist states.

In 1976 a referendum approved a socialist constitution and Fidel Castro and his brother were elected president and vice-president. During the following five years Cuba played a larger role in

world affairs, particularly in Africa, to the disquiet of the USA.

Re-elected in 1981, Castro offered to discuss foreign policy with the USA but Cuba's support for ◊Argentina, against Britain, cooled relations and drew it closer to other Latin American countries. The 1983 US invasion of ◊Grenada lowered the diplomatic temperature still further, though Cuba has since adopted a more conciliatory posture towards the USA. The advent of ◊Gorbachev and the USSR's abandonment of its policy of supporting Third World revolutions led in 1989 to a curtailment of Cuba's foreign military interventions.

Cubango /kuːˈbæŋgəʊ/ Portuguese name for the Okavango river in Africa.

Cuban missile crisis a crisis in international relations 1962 when Soviet rockets were installed in Cuba and US President Kennedy compelled Khrushchev, by an ultimatum, to remove them. The drive by the USSR to match the USA in nuclear weaponry dates from this event.

In Aug 1979 there was a lesser crisis when US President Carter discovered a Soviet combat brigade on the island, but failed to enforce its withdrawal.

cube in geometry, a solid figure whose faces are all squares. It has six equal-area faces and 12 equal-length edges. If the length of one edge is l, the volume of the cube $V = l^3$ and its surface area $A = 6l^2$.

cubic measure a measure of volume, indicated either by the prefix cubic followed by a linear measure, as in cubic foot, or the suffix cubed, as in metre cubed.

Cubism revolutionary movement in early 20th century painting, pioneering abstract art. Its founders Braque and Picasso were admirers of Cézanne and were inspired by his attempt to create a structure on the surface of the canvas. About 1907–10 the Cubists began to 'abstract' images from nature, gradually releasing themselves from the imitation of reality. Cubism announced that a work of art exists in its own right rather than as a representation of the real world, and it attracted such artists as Juan Gris, Fernand Léger, and Robert Delaunay.

cubit earliest-known unit of length, which originated between 2800 and 2300 BC. It is approximately 50.5 cm/20.6 in long, which is about the length of the human forearm.

Cubitt /ˈkjuːbɪt/ Thomas 1788–1855. English builder and property developer. One of the earliest speculators, Cubitt rebuilt much of Belgravia, London, an area of Brighton, and the east front of Buckingham Palace.

cuboid a three-dimensional object whose faces are all either rectangles or squares. One of the faces must be a rectangle. A brick is a cuboid.

Cuchulain /kʊˈhuːlɪn/ in Celtic mythology, a legendary hero, the chief figure in a cycle of Irish legends. He is associated with his uncle Conchobar, king of Ulster; his most famous exploits are described in *Táin Bó Cuailnge*/*The Cattle-Raid of Cuchullain*.

cuckoo any of about 200 species of bird of the family Cuculidae, whose name derives from its characteristic call. Somewhat hawk-like, it is about 33 cm/1.1 ft long, bluish-grey and barred beneath (females sometimes reddish), and has a long rounded tail. It is a 'brood parasite', laying its eggs singly, at intervals of about 48 hours, in the nests of small insectivorous birds. As soon as the young cuckoo hatches, it ejects all other young birds or eggs from the nest, and is tended by 'foster-parents' until fledging. Cuckoos feed on insects, particularly hairy caterpillars that are distasteful to most birds.

The roadrunner is a type of cuckoo. The cuckoo has played a great part in European folklore and literature, and has often been introduced into music and song.

cuckoo flower or *Lady's Smock* perennial plant *Cardamine pratensis*, family Cruciferae. Native to Britain, it is common in damp meadows and marsy woods. It bears pale lilac flowers, which later turn white from Apr to June.

cuckoo-pint or **lords-and-ladies** perennial plant *Arum maculatum* of the Araceae family. The large arrow-shaped leaves appear in early spring, and the flower-bearing stalks are enveloped by a bract, or spathe. In late summer the bright red, berry-like fruits, which are poisonous, make their appearance.

cuckoo spit the frothy liquid surrounding and exuded by the larva of the ◊frog-hopper.

cucumber plant *Cucumis sativus*, family Cucurbitaceae, producing long, green-skinned fruit with crisp, translucent, edible flesh. Small cucumbers, especially the fruit of *Cucumis anguria*, are pickled as gherkins.

Cúcuta /'ku:kətə/ capital of Norte de Santander department, NE Colombia; population (1985) 379,000. It is situated in a tax-free zone close to the Venezuelan border. It trades in coffee, tobacco, and cattle. It was a focal point of the independence movement, and meeting place of the first Constituent Congress 1821.

Cuenca /'kweŋkə/ city in S Ecuador; population (1980) 140,000. It is capital of Azuay province. Industries include chemicals, food processing, agricultural machinery and textiles. It was founded by the Spanish in 1557.

Cuenca /'kweŋkə/ city in Spain, at the confluence of the rivers Júcar and Huécar; 135 km/84 mi SE of Madrid; population (1981) 42,000. It is the capital of Cuenca province. It has a 13th-century cathedral.

Cugnot Nicolas 1728–1804. French engineer who produced the first high pressure steam engine. While serving in the French army, he was asked to design a steam-operated gun-carriage. After several years labour, he produced a three-wheeled, high pressure carriage capable of carrying 400 gallons of water and four passengers at a speed of 3 mph. Although he worked further on the carriage, political conditions mitigated against much progress being made and his invention was ignored.

Cui /kwi:/ Casar Antonovich 1853–1918. Russian composer of operas and chamber music. A professional soldier, he joined ◊Balakirev's Group of Five and promoted a Russian national style.

Cuiaba /ˌku:jə'ba:/ town in Brazil, on the Cuiaba river; population (1980) 168,000. It is the capital of Mato Grosso state. Gold and diamonds are worked nearby.

Cukor /'kju:kɔ:/ George 1899–1983. US film director. He moved to the cinema from the theatre, and was praised for his skilled handling of stars such as Greta ◊Garbo (in *Camille* 1937) and Katherine Hepburn (in *The Philadelphia Story* 1940). His films were usually civilized dramas or light comedies.

Culdee /'kʌldi:/ member of an ancient order of Christian monks that existed in Ireland and Scotland from before the 9th century to about the 12th century AD, when the Celtic Church, to which they belonged, was forced to conform to Roman usages. Some survived until the 14th century, while at Armagh, Northen Ireland, they remained until the dissolution of the monasteries in 1541.

cul-de-sac (French 'bottom of the bag') a street closed off at one end.

Culham /'kʌləm/ village near Oxford, England, site of a British nuclear research establishment.

Culiacán Rosales /ˌku:liə'kæn rəʊ'za:les/ capital of Sinaloa state, NW Mexico; population (1980) 560,000. It trades in vegetables and textiles.

Culloden, Battle of /kə'lɒdn/ defeat 1746 of the Jacobite rebel army of the British Prince ◊Charles Edward Stuart by the Duke of ◊Cumberland on a stretch of moorland in Inverness-shire, Scotland.

Culshaw /'kʌlʃɔ:/ John 1924–1980. British record producer, who developed recording techniques. Managing classical recordings for the Decca record company in the 1950s and 1960s, he introduced echo chambers, and the speeding and slowing of tapes, to achieve effects not possible in live performance. He produced the first complete recordings of Wagner's *Ring* cycle.

cultivar a variety of a plant developed by horticultural or agricultural techniques. The term derives from 'cultivated variety'.

Cultural Revolution a movement begun by Chinese communist party chairman Mao Zedong 1966 and directed against bureaucracy and university intellectuals. Intended to 'purify' Chinese communism, it was also an attempt by Mao to restore his political and ideological pre-eminence inside China.

The 'revolution' was characterized by the violent activities of the Red Guards and many thousands of Party officials, and intellectuals were deported to work on the land. Although the revolution was brought to an end in 1969, the resulting bureaucratic and economic chaos had many long term effects.

culture in biology, the growing of living cells and tissues in laboratory conditions.

culture in sociology and anthropology, the way of life of a particular society or group of people, including patterns of thought, beliefs, behaviour, customs, traditions, rituals, dress, and language, as well as art, music, and literature.

Cumae /'kju:mi:/ ancient city in Italy, on the coast about 16 km/10 mi W of Naples. In was the seat of the oracle of the Cumaean Sibyl.

Cuman /'kju:mən/ member of a powerful Turki federation of the Middle Ages, which dominated the steppes in the 11th and 12th centuries and built an empire reaching from the Volga to the Danube.

For a generation they held up the Mongol advance on the Volga, but in 1238 a Cuman and Russian army was crushingly defeated near Astrakhan, and 200,000 Cumans took refuge in Hungary, where they settled, and where their language died out only about 1775. The Mameluke dynasty of Egypt was founded by Cuman ex-slaves. Most of the so-called Tatars of S Russia were of Cuman origin.

Cumberland /'kʌmbələnd/ former county of NW England, merged in 1974 with ◊Cumbria.

After the Roman withdrawal, Cumberland became part of Strathclyde, a British kingdom. In 945 it passed to Scotland, in 1157 to England, and until the union of the English and Scottish crowns in 1603 Cumberland was the scene of frequent battles between the two countries.

Cumberland /'kʌmbələnd/ Ernest Augustus, Duke of Cumberland 1771–1851. King of Hanover from 1837, the fifth son of George III of Britain. A high Tory and an opponent of all reforms, his attempts to suppress the constitution met with open resistance that had to be put down by force.

Cumberland /'kʌmbələnd/ William Augustus, Duke of Cumberland 1721–1765. British general, who ended the Jacobite rising in Scotland with the Battle of Culloden 1746; his brutal repression of the Highlanders earned him the nickname of 'Butcher'. Third son of George II, he was created Duke of Cumberland 1726. He fought in the War of the Austrian Succession at ◊Dettingen 1743 and ◊Fontenoy 1745. In the Seven Years' War he surrendered with his army at Kloster-Zeven 1757.

Cumbernauld /ˌkʌmbə'nɔ:ld/ new town in Strathclyde, Scotland; 18 km/11 mi from Glasgow; population (1981) 48,000. It was founded 1955 to take in city overspill. In 1966 it won a prize as the world's best-designed community.

Cumbria /'kʌmbriə/ county in NW England
area 6,810 sq km/2,629 sq mi
towns administrative headquarters Carlisle; Barrow, Kendal, Whitehaven, Workington, Pennith
physical Lake District National Park, including Scafell Pike 978 m/3,210 ft, highest mountain in England; Helvellyn 950 m/3,118 ft; Lake Windermere, the largest lake in England, 17 km/10.5 mi long, 1.6 km/1 mi wide
features the Grizedale Forest sculpture project is nearby; other lakes including Derwentwater, Ullswater; Furness peninsula; atomic stations at Calder Hall and Sellafield (reprocessing plant),

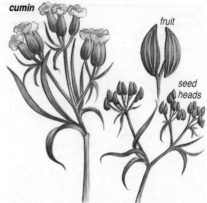

cumin

fruit

seed heads

formerly Windscale (site of a nuclear accident Oct 1957)
products the traditional coal, iron, and steel of the coast towns has been replaced by newer industries including chemicals, plastics, and electronics; in the N and E there is dairying, and West Cumberland Farmers is the country's largest agricultural cooperative
population (1987) 487,000
famous people birthplace of Wordsworth at Cockermouth, and home at Grasmere; homes of Coleridge and Southey at Keswick; Ruskin's home, Brantwood, on Coniston Water; de Quincey.

cumin seed-like fruit of the plant *Cuminum cyminum*, with a bitter flavour. It is used as a spice in cooking.

Cumming /'kʌmɪŋ/ Mansfield 1859–1923. British naval officer, first head of the British Secret Intelligence Service. The head of the service has always since been known by the initial letter 'C'.

cummings /'kʌmɪŋz/ e(dward) e(stlin) 1894–1962. US poet, whose published collections of poetry include *Tulips and Chimneys* 1923. His poems were initially notorious for their idiosyncratic punctuation and typography (he always wrote his name in lower-case letters, for example), but their lyric power has gradually been recognized.

cumulative frequency in statistics, the total frequency up to and including a certain point. It is used to draw the cumulative frequency curve, the ogive.

cuneiform an ancient writing system formed of combinations of wedge-shaped strokes, usually impressed on clay. It was probably invented by the Sumerians, and was in use in Mesopotamia as early as the middle of the 4th millennium BC.

It was adopted and modified by the Assyrians, Babylonians, Elamites, Hittites, Persians, and many other peoples with different languages. In the 5th century BC it fell into disuse, but

Cumbria

sporadically reappeared in later centuries. The decipherment of cuneiform scripts was pioneered by the German G F Grotefend 1802 and the British orientalist H C Rawlinson 1846.

Cunene /kuːˈlni/ or **Kunene** river rising near Nova Lisboa in W central Angola. It flows S to the frontier with Namibia then W to the Atlantic. Length 250 km/156 mi.

Cunha /ˈkuːnjə/ Euclydes da 1866–1909. Brazilian writer. His novel *Os Sertoes/Rebellion in the Backlands* 1902 describes the Brazilian *sertao* (backlands), and how a small group of rebels resisted government troops.

Cunningham /ˈkʌnɪŋəm/ Andrew Browne, 1st Viscount Cunningham of Hyndhope 1883–1963. British admiral in World War II, commander in chief in the Mediterranean 1939–42, maintaining British control; as commander in chief of the Allied Naval Forces in the Mediterranean Feb–Oct 1943 he received the surrender of the Italian fleet.

Cunningham /ˈkʌnɪŋəm/ John 1885–1962. British admiral in World War II. He was commander in chief in the Mediterranean 1943–46, 1st Sea Lord 1946–48, and became admiral of the fleet in 1948.

In 1940 he assisted in the evacuation of Norway and as 4th Sea Lord in charge of supplies and transport 1941–43, prepared the way for the N African invasion in 1942.

Cunningham /ˈkʌnɪŋhæm/ Merce 1919– . US dancer and choreographer. Influenced by Martha ◊Graham, with whose company he was soloist from 1939 to 1945, he formed his own dance company and school in New York in 1953. His works include *The Seasons* 1947, *Antic Meet* 1958, *Squaregame* 1976, and *Arcade* 1985.

Cunninghame-Graham /ˈkʌnɪŋəmpˈgreɪəm/ Robert Bontine 1852–1936. Scottish writer, politician, and adventurer. Author of essays and short stories such as *Success* 1902, *Faith* 1909, *Hope* 1910, and *Charity* 1912. He wrote many travel books based on his experiences as a rancher in Texas and Argentina 1869–83, and as a traveller in Spain and Morocco 1893–98. He was president of the Scottish Labour Party in 1888 and became first president of the Scottish National Party in 1928.

Cuno /ˈkuːnəʊ/ Wilhelm 1876–1933. German industrialist and politican who was briefly chancellor of the Weimar Republic 1923.

Cupid /ˈkjuːpɪd/ in Roman mythology, the god of love, identified with the Greek god ◊Eros.

cuprite Cu_2O a red oxide of copper in crystalline form.

cupro-nickel a copper alloy (75% copper and 25% nickel). In the UK in 1946, it was substituted for the 'silver' (50% silver, 40% copper, 5% nickel, and 5% zinc) previously used in coins.

Curaçao /ˌkjʊərəˈsəʊ/ island in the West Indies, one of the ◊Netherlands Antilles; area 444 sq km/171 sq mi; population (1981) 147,000. The principal industry, dating from 1918, is the refining of Venezuelan petroleum. Curaçao was colonized by Spain 1527, annexed by the Dutch West India Company 1634, and gave its name from 1924 to the group of islands renamed Netherlands Antilles in 1948. Its capital is the port of Willemstad.

curaçao /ˌkjʊərəˈsəʊ/ orange-flavoured liqueur, originally from the Caribbean island of Curaçao but now made elsewhere. The alcohol content varies between 36 and 40%.

curare poison, extracted from the bark of the South American tree *Strychnus toxifera*. It was used on arrowheads to paralyse prey by blocking nerve stimulation of the muscles. Derivatives are used in medicine as muscle relaxants during surgery.

curate in the Christian church, literally, a priest who has the cure of souls in a parish, and so used in Europe. In England, an unbeneficed clergyman who acts as assistant to a parish priest, more exactly an 'assistant curate'.

Curia Romana the judicial and administrative bodies through which the pope carries out the government

Curie *Marie Curie in her Paris laboratory.*

of the Roman Catholic Church. It includes certain tribunals; the chancellery, which issues papal bulls; various offices including that of the cardinal secretary of state; and the Congregations, or councils of cardinals, each with a particular department of work.

curie former unit (symbol Ci) of radioactivity, equal to 37×10^9 ◊becquerels. One gram of radium has a radioactivity of about 1 curie. It was named after French physicist Pierre Curie.

Curie /ˈkjʊəri/ Marie (born Sklodovska) 1867–1934. Polish scientist, who investigated radioactivity, and with her husband Pierre (1859–1906) discovered radium.

Born in Warsaw, she studied in Paris from 1891. Impressed by the publication of ◊Becquerel's experiments, Marie Curie decided to investigate the nature of uranium rays. In 1898 she reported the possible existence of some new powerful radioactive element in pitchblende ores. Her husband abandoned his own researches to assist her, and in the same year they announced the existence of polonium and radium. They isolated the pure elements in 1902.

Both scientists refused to take out a patent on their discovery, and were jointly awarded the Davy Medal (1903) and the Nobel Prize for Physics (1903; with Becquerel). In 1904 Pierre was appointed to a chair in physics at the Sorbonne, and on his death in a street accident was succeeded by his wife. She wrote a *Treatise on Radioactivity* in 1910, and was awarded the Nobel Prize for Chemistry in 1911. She died a victim of the radiation among which she had worked in her laboratory.

Curie temperature the temperature above which a magnetic material cannot be strongly magnetized. Above the Curie temperature, the energy of the atoms is too great for them to join together to form the small areas of magnetized material, or ◊domains, which combine to produce the strength of the overall magnetization.

Curitiba /ˌkʊərɪˈtiːbə/ city in Brazil, on the Curitiba river; population (1980) 844,000. The capital of Paraná state, it dates from 1654. It has a university (1912) and makes paper, furniture, textiles, and chemicals. Coffee, timber and maté are exported.

curium a metallic element, atomic number 96, relative atomic mass 247. It is radioactive and does not occur naturally, but is produced from americium. It is named after the Curies.

curlew wading bird of the genus Numenius, 55 cm/1.8 ft tall, with mottled brown plumage, long legs, and a long thin downcurved bill. Several species live in Northern Europe, Asia, and North America. The name derives from its haunting flute-like call.

One species, the Eskimo curlew, is almost extinct, never having recovered from relentless hunting in the late 19th century.

curling game played on ice with stones; sometimes described as 'bowls on ice'. One of the national games of Scotland, where it probably originated, it has spread to many countries. It can also be played on artificial (cement or tarmacadam) ponds.

Two tees are erected about 35 m/38 yd apart. There are two teams of four players. The object of the game is to deliver the stones near the tee, those nearest scoring. Each player has two stones, of equal size, fitted with a handle. The usual weight of the stone, which is shaped like a small flat cheese, is about 16–20 kg/36–42 lb. In Canada the weight is greater (about 27 kg/60 lb) and iron replaces stone. The stone is slid on one of its flat surfaces and it may be curled in one direction or another according to the twist given as it leaves the hand. The match is played for an agreed number of heads or shots, or by time.

Curnonsky /kjʊəˈnɒnski/ pseudonym of Maurice Edmond Sailland 1872–1956. French gastronome and cookery writer, who was a pioneer in the cataloguing of French regional cuisine.

Curragh, the /ˈkʌrə/ plain in County Kildare, Republic of Ireland. It is the headquarters of Irish racing and site of the national stud.

Curragh, The horse-racing course in County Kildare where all five Irish Classic races are run. At one time used for hurdle races, it is now used for flat racing only.

Racing has been held at The Curragh since the mid-1880s. The course is right-handed and in the shape of a horseshoe.

Curragh 'Mutiny' demand Mar 1914 by the British Gen Hubert Gough and his officers, stationed at Curragh, Ireland, that they should not be asked to take part in forcing Protestant Ulster to participate in Home Rule. They were subsequently allowed to return to duty, and after World War I the solution of partition was adopted.

currant berry of a small seedless variety of grape. Currants are grown on a large scale in Greece and California and used dried in cake-making. Because of the similarity of the fruit, the same name is given to several species of shrubs in the genus *Ribes*, family Grossulariaceae.

The **redcurrant** *Ribes rubrum* is a native of S Europe, Asia, and North America and occasionally grows wild in Britain. The **whitecurrant** is a cultivated, less acid variety. The **blackcurrant** *Ribes nigrum* is the most favoured for cooking. The **flowering currant** *Ribes sanguineum* is a native of North America.a

currency the particular type of money in use in a country, for example the UK pound sterling, the US dollar, the West German Deutschmark and the Japanese yen.

current the flow of a body of water or air moving in a definite direction. There are three basic types of oceanic currents: *drift currents* are broad and slow-moving; *stream currents* are narrow and swift-moving; and *upwelling currents* bring cold, nutrient-rich water from the ocean bottom.

Stream currents include the ◊Gulf Stream and the ◊Japan (or Kuroshio) Current. Upwelling currents, such as the Gulf of Guinea Current and the Peru (Humboldt) current, provide food for plankton, which in turn supports fish and sea birds. In approximate ten-year intervals, the Peru Current that runs from the Antarctic up the W coast of South America, turns warm, with heavy rain and rough seas, and has disastrous results (as in 1982–83) for the Peruvian wildlife and the anchovy industry. The phenomenon is called *El Niño* (Spanish 'the Child') because it occurs towards Christmas.

curlew

eskimo

current account in economics, that part of the balance of payments concerned with current transactions, as opposed to capital movements. It includes trade (visibles) and service transactions, such as investment, insurance, shipping, and tourism (invisibles). The state of the current account is regarded as a barometer of overall economic health.

In some countries, such as Italy, Spain, and Portugal, visibles make an extremely important contribution to the current account and may more than offset trade deficits.

current prices a series of prices that express values pertaining to a given time but which do not take account of the changes in purchasing power, unlike ◊constant prices.

curriculum in education, the range of subjects offered within an institution or course.

The only part of the school curriculum prescribed by law in the UK is religious education. Growing concern about the low proportion of 14- and 16-year-olds opting to study maths, science, and technology, with a particularly low take-up rate among girls, led to the central government in the Education Reform Act 1988 introducing a compulsory National Curriculum, which applies to all children of school age (5–16) in state schools. There are ten core subjects in the curriculum – English, maths, science, technology, history, geography, music, art, physical education, and a foreign language.

The move towards central control of the curriculum has been criticized as it removes decision-making from the local authorities and schools, and tightens control over teachers.

curriculum vitae or **CV** (Latin 'the course of life') an account of one's education and previous employment, attached to a job application.

Curtin /'kɜ:tɪn/ John 1885–1945. Australian Labor politician, prime minister and minister of defence 1941–45. He was elected leader of the Labor Party 1935. As prime minister, he organized the mobilization of Australia's resources to meet the danger of Japanese invasion during World War II.

Curtis /'kɜ:tɪs/ Tony. Stage name of Bernard Schwartz 1925– . US actor, who starred in the 1950s and 1960s in such films as *The Vikings* 1959 and *Some Like it Hot* 1959, with Jack Lemmon and Marilyn Monroe.

Curtiz /'kɜ:tɪz/ Michael (Mihaly Kersesz) 1888–1962. Hungarian-born film director who worked in Austria, Germany, and France before moving to the USA where he made several Errol Flynn films and *Casablanca* 1942.

His wide range of films includes *Doctor* 1932; *The Adventures of Robin Hood* 1938; *Mildred Pierce* 1945; and *The Commancheros* 1962.

curve in geometry, the ◊locus of a point moving according to specified conditions. The circle is the locus of all points equidistant from a given point (the centre). Other common geometrical curves are the ◊ellipse, ◊parabola, and ◊hyperbola, which are also produced when a cone is cut by a plane at different angles.

Many curves have been invented for the solution of special problems in geometry and mechanics, for example, the cissoid (the inverse of a parabola) and the ◊cycloid.

Curwen /'kɜ:wɪn/ John 1816–1880. English musician. Around 1840 he established the **tonic sol-fa** system of music notation (originated in the 11th century by Guido d'Arezzo) in which the notes of a scale are named by syllables (doh, ray, me, fah, soh, lah, te), with the ◊key indicated to simplify singing by sight.

Curzon /'kɜ:zən/ George Nathaniel, 1st Marquess Curzon of Kedleston 1859–1925. British Conservative politician. Viceroy of India from 1899, he resigned 1905 following a controversy with Kitchener. He was foreign secretary 1919–22.

Curzon /'kɜ:zən/ Robert, Lord Zouche 1810–1873. English diplomat and traveller, author of *Monasteries in the Levant* 1849.

Curzon Line Polish-Russian frontier proposed after World War I by the territorial commission of the Versailles conference 1919, based on the eastward limit of areas with a predominantly Polish population. It acquired its name after Lord Curzon suggested in 1920 that the Poles, who had invaded Russia, should retire to this line pending a Russo-Polish peace conference. The frontier established 1945 in general follows the Curzon Line.

Cusack /'kju:sæk/ Cyril 1910– . Irish actor who joined the Abbey Theatre, Dublin, 1932 and appeared in many of its productions, including Synge's *The Playboy of the Western World*. In Paris he won an award for his solo performance in Beckett's *Krapp's Last Tape*. In the UK he has played many roles as a member of the Royal Shakespeare Company and the National Theatre Company.

Cushing /'kʊʃɪŋ/ Harvey Williams 1869–1939. US neurologist who pioneered neurosurgery. He developed a range of techniques for the surgical treatment of brain tumours, and also studied the link between the ◊pituitary gland and conditions such as dwarfism.

Cushing /'kʊʃɪŋ/ Peter 1913– . British actor who specialized in horror roles in films made at Hammer studios 1957–73, including *Dracula* 1958; *Cash on Demand* 1963; *Frankenstein Must be Destroyed* 1969. Other films include *Star Wars* 1977 and *Top Secret* 1984.

Cushing's syndrome a condition in which the body chemistry is upset by excessive production of steroid hormones from the adrenal cortex.

Symptoms include weight gain in the face and trunk, raised blood pressure, excessive growth of facial and body hair (hirsutism), demineralization of bone, and sometimes diabetes-like effects. The underlying cause may be an adrenal, pituitary or lung tumour, or prolonged high-dose therapy with ◊corticosteroid drugs.

cusp a point where two branches of a curve meet, and the tangents to each branch coincide.

custard apple several tropical fruits produced by trees and shrubs of the genus *Annona*, family Annonaceae. *Annona reticulata*, **the bullock's heart**, bears a large dark-brown fruit, containing

Curzon British politician Lord Curzon with Lady Curzon in India: he became viceroy in 1899. Foreign secretary from 1919, he was disappointed in his ambitions for the premiership.

Custer US Civil War general George Armstrong Custer, remembered for his 'last stand' at the Battle of the Little Big Horn, 1876.

a sweet reddish-yellow pulp; it is a native of the West Indies.

Custer /'kʌstə/ George A(rmstrong) 1839–1876. US Civil War general. He campaigned against the Sioux from 1874, and was killed with a detachment of his troops by the forces of Sioux chief Sitting Bull in the Battle of Little Big Horn, Montana: **Custer's last stand**, 25 June 1876.

custody of children in the UK, the legal control of a minor by an adult. Parents usually have joint custody of their children, but this may be altered by a court order, which may be made in various different circumstances. In all cases, the court gives the welfare of the child paramount consideration.

In matrimonial proceedings (such as divorce), the court decides which spouse shall have custody, and provides for access by the other spouse. Custody can be transferred from parents to local authorities in care proceedings. Foster parents do not have legal custody, unless a custodianship order is made (giving a legal status between fostering and adoption). An adoption order transfers custody to the adoptive parents.

Customs and Excise government department responsible for taxes levied on certain imports, for example, tobacco, wine and spirits, perfumery, and jewellery. Excise duties are levied on certain goods produced (such as beer) and include VAT, or on licences to carry on certain trades (such as sale of wines and spirits) or other activities (theatrical entertainments, betting, and so on) within a country.

In the UK both come under the Board of Customs and Excise, which also administers VAT generally, although there are independent tax tribunals for appeal against the decisions of the commissioners. In the USA Excise duties are classed as Internal Revenue and Customs are controlled by the Customs Bureau. Membership of the ◊European Community (EC) requires the progressive abolition of all internal tariffs between member states and adoption of a common external tariff by 1992.

Cuthbert, St /'kʌθbət/ died 687. Christian saint. He travelled widely as a missionary, became prior of Lindisfarne 664, and retired 676 to Farne Island. In 684 he became bishop of Hexham and later of Lindisfarne. Feast day 20 Mar.

cuticle in zoology, the horny noncellular surface layer of many invertebrates such as insects; in botany, the waxy surface layer on those parts of plants that are exposed to the air, continuous except for the ◊stomata and ◊lenticels. All types are secreted by the cells of the ◊epidermis. A cuticle reduces water loss and, in arthropods, acts as an ◊exoskeleton.

Cuttack /kʌˈtæk/ city and river port in E India; on the Mahanadi river delta; population (1981) 327,500. It was the capital of Orissa state until 1950. The old fort (Kataka) from which the town takes its name is in ruins.

cuttle-fish small squid with an internal calcareous shell (cuttlebone). The *common cuttle Sepia officinalis* of the Atlantic and Mediterranean, is up to 30 cm/1 ft long, swims actively by means of the fins into which the sides of its oval, flattened body are expanded, and jerks itself backwards by shooting a jet of water from its 'siphon'.

It is capable of rapid changes of colour and pattern. The large head has conspicuous eyes, and the ten arms are provided with suckers. Two arms are very much elongated, and with them the cuttle seizes its prey. It has an 'ink-sac' from which a dark fluid can be discharged into the water, distracting predators from the cuttle itself. Sepia, the dark brown pigment, is obtained from the cuttle's ink-sac.

Cutty Sark British sailing ship, built 1869, one of the tea clippers that used to compete in the 19th century to bring their cargoes fastest from China to Britain.

The name, meaning 'short chemise', comes from the witch in Robert Burns's poem 'Tam O'Shanter'. The ship is preserved in dry dock at Greenwich, London. The biennial Cutty Sark International Tall Ships Race is named after it.

Cuvier /ˈkjuːvieɪ/ Georges, Baron Cuvier 1769–1832. French comparative anatomist. In 1799 he proved extinction (the phenomenon that some species have ceased to exist) by reconstructing extinct giant animals that he believed were destroyed in a series of giant deluges (see ◊catastrophism). These ideas are expressed in *Recherches sur les ossamens fossiles/Essay on the Theory of the Earth* 1817.

In 1798 Cuvier produced *Tableau élémentaire de l'histoire naturelle des animaux*, in which his scheme of classification is outlined. He was professor of natural history in the Collège de France from 1799, and at the Jardin des Plantes from 1802; and at the Restoration in 1815 he was elected chancellor of the University of Paris. Cuvier was the first to relate the structure of ◊fossil animals to that of their living relatives. His great work, *Le Règne animal/ The Animal Kingdom* 1817 is a systematic survey.

Cuxhaven /ˈkʊkshaːvən/ seaport in Germany on the S side of the Elbe estuary, at its entrance into the North Sea; population (1983) 57,800. It acts as an outpost for Hamburg.

Cuyp /kaɪp/ Aelbert 1620–1691. Dutch painter of countryside scenes, seascapes, and portraits. His

Cuvier Georges Cuvier, the founder of paleontology and comparative anatomy, believed that the Earth was periodically flooded, and explained fossils as remnants of life which had escaped the most recent deluge.

Cuzco The Inca capital of Cuzco has many Spanish buildings alongside older Inca structures.

idyllically peaceful landscapes are bathed in golden light, for example *A Herdsman with Cows by a River* (c.1650 National Gallery, London). His father was *Jacob Gerritsz Cuyp* (1594–1652), also a landscape and portrait painter.

Cuzco /ˈkʊskəʊ/ city in S Peru, capital of Cuzco department, in the Andes, over 3,350 m/11,000 ft above sea level and 560 km/350 mi SE of Lima; population (1988) 255,000. It was founded in the 11th century as the ancient capital of the ◊Inca empire, and was captured by Pizarro 1533.

The university was founded 1598. The city has a Renaissance cathedral and other relics of the early Spanish conquerors. There are many Inca remains and in the 1970s and 1980s the Inca irrigation canals and terracing nearby were being restored to increase cultivation.

CV abbreviation for ◊*curriculum vitae*.

Cwmbran /kʊmˈbrɑːn/ (Welsh 'Vale of the Crow') town in Wales, NW of Newport, on the Afon Lywel, a tributary of river Usk; population (1981) 45,000. It is the administrative headquarters of Gwent. It was established in 1949, to provide a focus for new industrial growth in a depressed area, producing scientific instruments, car components, nylon, and biscuits.

c.w.o. abbreviation for *cash with order*.

cwt abbreviation for ◊*hundredweight*, a unit of weight equal to 50.802 kg/112 lb.

cyanide in chemistry, a salt of hydrocyanic acid (or hydrogen cyanide, HCN) produced when this is neutralized by alkalis, for example potassium cyanide, KCN. The principal cyanides are potassium, sodium, calcium, mercuric, gold, and cupric. Certain cyanides are infamous as poisons.

cyanocobalamin $C_{63}H_{88}O_{14}N_{14}PCo$ chemical name for ◊vitamin B12, which is normally produced by microorganisms in the gut. The richest natural source is raw liver. The deficiency disease, pernicious anaemia, is the poor development of red blood cells with possible degeneration of the spinal chord. Sufferers develop extensive bruising and recover slowly from even minor injuries.

cyanosis bluish discoloration of the skin, usually around the mouth, due to diminished uptake of oxygen. It is most often seen in disease of the heart or lungs.

Cybele /ˈsɪbəli/ in Phrygian mythology, an earth goddess, identified by the Greeks with ◊Rhea and honoured in Rome.

cybernetics (Greek *Kubernan* 'to steer') science concerned with how systems organize, regulate, and reproduce themselves, and also how they evolve and learn. In the laboratory, inanimate objects are created that behave like living systems. Applications range from the creation of electronic artificial limbs to the running of the

fully-automated factory where decision-making machines operate up to managerial level.

Cybernetics was founded and named in 1947 by US mathematician, Norbert Wiener (1894–1964). Originally, it was the study of control systems using feedback to produce automatic processes.

cycad plant of the order Cycadales belonging to the gymnosperms. Some have a superficial resemblance to palms, others to ferns. There are ten genera and about 80–100 species, native to tropical and sub-tropical countries. The stems of many species yield an edible starchy substance resembling sago.

Cyclades /ˈsɪklədiːz/ group of about 200 Greek islands (Greek *Kikládhes*) in the Aegean Sea, lying between Greece and Turkey; area 2,579 sq km/996 sq mi; population (1981) 88,500. They include Andros, Melos, Paros, Naxos, and Siros, on which is the capital Hermoupolis.

cyclamate derivative of cyclohexysulphamic acid, formerly used as an artificial sweetener. Its use in foods was banned in the UK and the USA from 1970, when studies showed that massive doses caused cancer in rats.

cyclamen genus of perennial plants, family Primulaceae, with heart-shaped leaves and petals that are twisted at the base and bent back. The flowers are usually white or pink, and several species are cultivated.

cycle in physics, a sequence of changes that moves a system away from, and then back to, its original state. An example is a vibration that moves a particle first in one direction and then in the opposite direction, with the particle returning to its original position at the end of the vibration.

cyclic in geometry, describing a polygon of which all the vertices (corners) lie on the circumference of a circle. The term is also used in ◊group theory and ◊permutations.

cyclic compounds organic chemicals that have rings of atoms in their molecules.

They may be alicyclic (cyclopentane), aromatic (benzene), or heterocyclic (pyridine). Alicyclic compounds have localized bonding: all the electrons are confined to their own particular bond, in contrast to aromatic compounds, where certain electrons have free movement between different bonds in the ring. Aromatic compounds, because of their special structure, undergo entirely different chemical reactions. Heterocyclic compounds have a ring of carbon atoms with one or more carbons replaced by another element, usually nitrogen, oxygen, or sulphur.

Alicyclic compounds have chemical properties similar to their straight-chain (aliphatic) counterparts. Pyridine, a heterocyclic compound, is a six-membered ring with five carbons and one nitrogen (C_5H_5N). Furan is a five-membered ring containing one oxygen (C_4H_4O). Uracil contains two nitrogens in a six-membered ring ($C_4H_4N_2O_2$). These heterocyclic compounds may be aliphatic or aromatic in nature.

cycling riding a ◊bicycle for sport, pleasure, or transport. Cycle racing can take place on oval

cycling The 1988 Tour de France.

cycloid

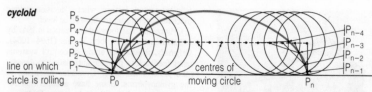

P₅, P₄, P₃, P₂, P₁
line on which circle is rolling   P₀   centres of moving circle   Pₙ
P_{n-4}, P_{n-3}, P_{n-2}, P_{n-1}

artificial tracks or on the road or across country (cyclo-cross).

Stage races are run over gruelling terrain and can last anything from three to five days up to three and a half weeks, like the ◊Tour de France, Tour of Italy, and Tour of Spain. *Criteriums* are fast, action-packed races around the closed streets of town or city centres. Each race lasts about an hour. *Road races* are run over a prescribed circuit, which the riders will lap several times. Such a race will normally cover a distance of approximately 100 miles. *Track racing* takes place on either a concrete or wooden banked circuit, either indoors or outdoors. In *time trialling* each rider races against the clock, with all the competitors starting at different intervals.

Cycling: recent winners

Tour de France first held 1903
1981 Bernard Hinault *(France)*
1982 Bernard Hinault *(France)*
1983 Laurent Fignon *(France)*
1984 Laurent Fignon *(France)*
1985 Bernard Hinault *(France)*
1986 Greg LeMond *(USA)*
1987 Stephen Roche *(Ireland)*
1988 Pedro Delgado *Spain*
1989 Greg Le Mond *USA*
Tour of Britain (Milk Race) first held 1951
1981 Sergei Krivocheyev *(USSR)*
1982 Yuri Kashirin *(USSR)*
1983 Matt Eaton *(USA)*
1984 Oleg Czougeda *(USSR)*
1985 Erik van Lancker *(Belgium)*
1986 Joey McLoughlin *(Great Britain)*
1987 Malcolm Elliott *(Great Britain)*
1988 Vasiliy Zhdanov *(USSR)*
1989 Brian Walton *(Canada)*
World Professional Road Race Champions first held at the Nuburgring *(West Germany)* 1927
1981 Freddie Maertens *(Belgium)*
1982 Giuseppe Saroni *(Italy)*
1983 Greg LeMond *(USA)*
1984 Claude Criquielon *(Belgium)*
1985 Joop Zoetemelk *(Holland)*
1986 Moreno Argentin *(Italy)*
1987 Stephen Roche *(Ireland)*
1988 Maurizio Fondriest *(Italy)*
1989 Greg Le Mond *(USA)*

cycloid in geometry, a curve resembling a series of arches traced out by a point on the circumference of a circle that rolls along a straight line. Its applications include the study of the motion of wheeled vehicles along roads and tracks.

cyclone an area of low atmospheric pressure. Cyclones are formed by the mixture of cold, dry polar air with warm, moist equatorial air. These masses of air meet in temperate latitudes; the warm air rises over the cold, resulting in rain.

Winds blow in towards the centre in an anticlockwise direction in the northern hemisphere, clockwise in the southern hemisphere; the systems are characterized by variable weather. They bring rain or snow, winds up to gale force, low cloud, and sometimes fog. Tropical cyclones are a great danger to shipping. A ◊tornado is a rapidly moving cyclone. In middle and high latitudes low-pressure systems are referred to as depressions or lows, rather than cyclones.

Cyclops /ˈsaɪˈkləʊpiːz/ in Greek mythology, one of a legendary nation of giants who lived in Sicily, had a single eye, and lived as shepherds; Odysseus encountered them in Homer's *Odyssey*.

cyclosporin an ◊immunosuppressive, derived from fungi. In use by 1978, it revolutionized transplant surgery by reducing the incidence and severity of rejection of donor organs.

cyclotron type of particle ◊accelerator.

Cygnus large prominent constellation of the northern hemisphere, representing a swan. Its brightest star is first-magnitude Deneb.

cylinder in geometry, a surface generated by a set of lines that are parallel to a fixed line and passing through a plane curve not in the plane of the fixed line; a tubular solid figure with a circular base, ordinarily understood to be a right cylinder, that is, having its curved surface at right angles to the base.

The volume of a cylinder is given by: $V = \pi r^2 h$ where V is the volume, r is the radius, and h is the height. Its total surface area A has the formula: $A = 2\pi r(h + r)$ where $2\pi rh$ is the curved surface area, and $2\pi r^2$ is the area of both circular ends.

cymbal ancient ◊percussion, instrument consisting of a shallow circular brass dish held together at the centre; either used in pairs clashed together or singly, struck with a beater. Smaller finger cymbals or *crotala*, used by Debussy and Stochausen, are more solid and have loose rivets to extend the sound.

Cymbeline play by Shakespeare, first acted about 1610 and printed 1623. It combines various sources to tell the story of Imogen (derived from Ginevra in Boccaccio's *Decameron*), the daughter of the legendary British king Cymbeline, who proves her virtue and constancy after several ordeals.

Cymbeline another name for *Cunobelin*, king of the Catuvellauni (AD 5–40), who fought unsuccessfully against the Roman invasion of Britain. His capital was at Colchester.

Cymru /ˈkʌmri/ Celtic name for ◊Wales.

Cynewulf /ˈkɪnɪwʊlf/ lived early 8th century. Anglo-Saxon poet. He is thought to have been a Northumbrian monk, and is the undoubted author of 'Juliana' and part of the 'Christ' in the Exeter Book (a collection of poems now in Exeter Cathedral), and of the 'Fates of the Apostles' and 'Elene' in the Vercelli Book (a collection of Old English manuscripts housed at Vercelli, Italy), in all of which he inserted his name in the form of runic acrostics.

Cynic a school of Greek philosophy, founded in Athens about 400 BC by Antisthenes, a disciple of Socrates, who advocated a stern and simple morality, and a complete disregard of pleasure and comfort.

His followers, led by ◊Diogenes (*c.*340 BC), not only showed a contemptuous disregard for pleasure, but despised all human affection as a source of weakness. Their 'snarling contempt' for ordinary people earned them the name of Cynic, which in Greek means 'dog-like'.

cylinder

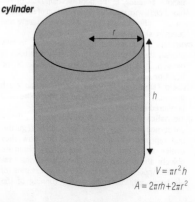

r

h

$V = \pi r^2 h$
$A = 2\pi rh + 2\pi r^2$

cypress coniferous tree or shrub of the genera *Cupressus* and *Chamaecyparis*, family Cupressaceae. There are about 20 species found mainly in the temperate regions of the northern hemisphere. They have minute scale-like leaves and small globular cones made up of woody scales and containing an aromatic resin.

Cyprian, St /ˈsɪprɪən/ *c.*210–258. Christian martyr, one of the earliest Christian writers, and bishop of Carthage about 249. He wrote a treatise on the unity of the church. Feast day 16 Sept.

Cyprus /ˈsaɪprəs/ island in the Mediterranean, off the S coast of Turkey.

government Under the 1960 constitution, power is shared between Greek and Turkish Cypriots, but in 1963 the Turks ceased participating and 1964 set up a separate community in N Cyprus, refusing to acknowledge the Greek government in the south.

The Greek Cypriot government claims to be the government of all Cyprus and is generally accepted as such, except by the Turkish community. There are, therefore, two republics, each with a president, council of ministers, legislature and judicial system. The 'Turkish Republic of Northern Cyprus' has its own representatives overseas.

Greek Cyprus has a president who appoints and heads a council of ministers, elected for five years by universal adult suffrage, and a single-chamber legislature, the 80-member house of representatives, also elected for five years. The four main political parties are the Democratic Front (DIKO), the Progressive Party of the Working People (AKEL) the Democratic Rally (DISY), and the Socialist Party (EDEK).

Under the separate constitution adopted by Turkish Cyprus 1985, there is a president, council of ministers, and legislature similar to that in the south. Turkey is the only country to have recognized this government.

history For early history, see ◊Greece, ancient. The strategic position of Cyprus has long made it a coveted territory, and from the 15th century BC it was colonized by a succession of peoples from the mainland. In the 8th century it was within the Assyrian empire, then the Babylonian, Egyptian, and Persian. As part of Ptolemaic Egypt, it was seized by Rome 58 BC. From AD 395 it was ruled by Byzantium, until taken 1191 by England during the Third ◊Crusade. In 1489 it was annexed by Venice, and became part of the Ottoman empire 1571. It came under British administration 1878, and was annexed by Britain 1914. In 1955 a guerrilla war against British rule was begun by Greek Cypriots seeking 'Enosis', or unification with Greece. The chief organization in this campaign was the National Organization of Cypriot Combatants (EOKA) and its political and military leaders were the head of the Greek Orthodox Church in Cyprus, Archbishop Makarios, and General Grivas. See also ◊Greece.

In 1956 Makarios and other Enosis leaders were deported by the British government. After years of negotiation, Makarios was allowed to return to become president of a new, independent Greek-Turkish Cyprus, retaining British military and naval bases.

In 1963 the Turks withdrew from power-sharing and fighting began. The following year a United Nations peace-keeping force was set up to keep the two sides apart. After a prolonged period of mutual hostility, relations improved and talks were resumed, with the Turks arguing for a federal state and the Greeks wanting a unitary one.

In 1971 General Grivas returned to the island and began a guerrilla campaign against the Makarios government, which he believed had failed the Greek community. Three years later he died and his supporters were purged by Makarios, who was himself deposed 1974 by Greek officers of the National Guard and an Enosis extremist, Nicos Sampson, who became president. Makarios fled to Britain.

Cyprus

divided between the southern
Republic of Cyprus (Greek
Kypriaki Dimokratia), and the Turkish
**Republic of Northern
Cyprus** (Turkish *Kibris Cumhuriyeti)*

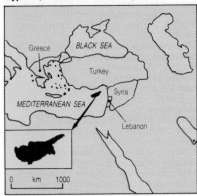

area 9,251 sq km/3,571 sq mi, 37% in Turkish
hands
capital Nicosia (divided between the Greeks
and Turks)
towns ports Paphos, Limassol, and Larnaca
(Greek); and Morphou, and ports Kyrenia and
Famagusta (Turkish)
physical central plain between two E–W
mountain ranges
features Attila Line; two British military
enclaves on the S coast at Episkopi (includes
Royal Air Force Akrotiri) and Dhekelia; there is
also an outpost of British Government Communications Headquarters in the mountains
heads of state and government Georgios
Vassiliou (Greek) from 1988, Rauf Denktaş
(Turkish) from 1976
political system democratic divided republic
political parties Democratic Front (DIKO),
centre-left; Progressive Party of the Working
People (AKEL), socialist; Democratic Rally
(DISY) , centrist; Socialist Party (EDEK),
socialist
exports citrus, grapes, Cyprus sherry,
potatoes, copper, pyrites
currency Cyprus pound (0.79 = £1 Feb 1990)
population (1987) 680,400 (Greek Cypriot
81%, Turkish Cypriot 19%); annual growth
rate 1.2%
life expectancy men 72, women 76
language Greek and Turkish (official); English
religion Greek Orthodox, Sunni Muslim
literacy 99% (1984)
GNP $2.11 bn (1983); $3,986 per head of
population
chronology
1955 Guerrilla campaign for *enosis,* or union
with Greece, started by Archbishop Makarios
and Gen Grivas.
1956 Makarios and *enosis* leaders deported.
1959 Compromise agreed and Makarios
returned to be elected president of an
independent Greek-Turkish Cyprus.
1960 Full independence achieved, with Britain
retaining its military bases.
1963 Turks set up their own government in N
Cyprus. Fighting broke out between the two
communities.
1964 UN peacekeeping force installed.
1971 Grivas returned to start a guerrilla war
against the Makarios government.
1974 Grivas died. A military coup deposed
Makarios, who fled to Britain. Nicos Sampson
appointed president. Turkish army sent to N
Cyprus to confirm the Turkish Cypriots' control.
The military regime in S Cyprus collapsed and
Makarios returned. N Cyprus declared itself the
Turkish Federated State of Cyprus (TFSC), with
Rauf Denktaş as president.
1977 Makarios died and was succeeded by
Spyros Kyprianou.
1983 An independent Turkish Republic of
Northern Cyprus (TRNC) was proclaimed but
was recognized only by Turkey.
1984 UN peace proposals rejected.
1985 Summit meeting between Kyprianou and
Denktaş failed to reach agreement.
1988 Georgios Vassiliou elected president.
Talks with Denktaş, under UN auspices, began.
1989 Vassiliou and Denktaş agreed to draft an
agreement for the future reunification of the
island, but peace talks abandoned in Sept.

At the request of the Turkish Cypriot leader,
Turkey sent troops to the island, taking control
of the north and dividing Cyprus along what
became known as the 'Attila Line', cutting off
about a third of the total territory. Later in 1975
Sampson resigned, the military regime which had
appointed him collapsed, and Makarios returned.
The Turkish Cypriots established an independent

government for what they called the 'Turkish
Federated State of Cyprus' (TFSC), with Rauf
Denktaş as president.

In 1977 Makarios died and was succeeded by
Spyros Kyprianou, who had been president of the
house of representatives. In 1980 UN-sponsored
peace talks were resumed. The Turkish Cypriots
offered to hand back about 4% of the 35% of the

territory they controlled, and to resettle 40,000 of
the 200,000 refugees who had fled to the north,
but stalemate was reached on a constitutional
settlement.

The Turks wanted equal status for the two
communities, equal representation in goverment
and firm links with Turkey. The Greeks, on the
other hand, favoured an alternating presidency,
strong central government, and representation in
the legislature on a proportional basis.

Between 1982 and 1985 several attempts by
the Greek government in Athens and the UN
to find a solution failed and the Turkish Republic
of Northern Cyprus (TRNC), with Denktaş as
president, was formally declared, but recognized
only by Turkey.

In 1985 a meeting between Denktaş and
Kyprianou failed to reach agreement and the
UN secretary-general drew up proposals for a
two-zone federal Cyprus, with a Greek president
and a Turkish vice-president, but this was not.
found acceptable. Meanwhile, both Kyprianou and
Denktaş had been re-elected.

In 1988 Georgios Vassiliou was elected president of the Greek part of Cyprus, and in Sept talks
began betwen him and Denktaşh. However, these
were abandoned in Sept 1989, reportedly because
of Denktaşh's intransigence. The dispute between
the communities remains unresolved but, because
of its strategic importance in the Mediterranean,
Cyprus is a problem that causes concern among
leading nations.

Cyrano de Bergerac /ˈsɪrənəʊ də ˈbɜːʒəræk/
Savinien de 1619–1655. French writer. He joined
a corps of guards at 19, and performed heroic feats
which made him famous. He is the hero of a classic
play by ◊Rostand, in which his notoriously long
nose is used as a counterpoint to his chivalrous
character.

Cyrenaic a school of Greek ◊hedonistic philosophy
founded about 400 BC by Aristippus of Cyrene. He
regarded pleasure as the only absolutely worthwhile thing in life, but taught that self-control and
intelligence were necessary to choose the best
pleasures.

Cyrenaica /ˌsaɪrəˈneɪɪkə/ area of E Libya, colonized by the Greeks in the 7th century BC; later
held by the Egyptians, Romans, Arabs, Turks, and
Italians. Present cities in the region are Benghazi,
Derna, and Tobruk.

The Greek colonies passed under the rule of
the Ptolemies 322 BC, and in 174 BC Cyrenaica
became a Roman province. It was conquered by
the Arabs in the 7th century, by Turkey in the
16th, and by Italy 1912, when it was developed
as a colony. It was captured by the British 1942,
and under British control until it became a province of the new kingdom of Libya from 1951. In
1963 it was split into a number of smaller divisions
under the constitutional reorganization. There are
archaeological ruins at Cyrene and Apollonia.

Cyril and Methodius two brothers, both Christian
saints: Cyril 826–869 and Methodius 815–885.
Born in Thessalonica, they were sent as missionaries to what is today Moravia. They invented a
Slavonic alphabet, and translated the Bible and the
liturgy from Greek to Slavonic.

The language (known as *Old Church Slavonic*) remained in use in churches and for
literature among Bulgars, Serbs, and Russians
up to the 17th century. The *cyrillic alphabet* is
named after Cyril and may also have been invented
by him. Feast day 14 Feb.

Cyril of Alexandria, St /ˈsɪrəl/ 376–444. Bishop
of Alexandria from 412, persecutor of Jews and
other non-Christians, and suspected of ordering
the murder of Hypatia (*c.*370–*c.*415), a philosopher
whose influence was increasing at the expense of
his. He was violently opposed to ◊Nestorianism.

Cyrus the Great /ˈsaɪrəs/ died 529 BC. Founder
of the Persian Empire. As king of Persia, originally subject to the ◊Medes, whose empire he
overthrew 550 BC. He captured ◊Croesus 546 BC,
and conquered all Asia Minor, adding Babylonia

Mediterranean Sea

miles 0   20
km 0   20

Kyrenia
Kyrenia Mountains
TURKISH-CYPRIOT HELD
Morphou
Kokkina
Lefka   Nicosia   Famagusta
DHEKELIA
GREEK-CYPRIOT HELD
Troodos
Troodos Mountains   Larnaca
Paphos
Limassol
AKROTIRI

Cyprus at beginning of 1984
United Nations buffer zone
British sovereign bases

(including Syria and Palestine) to his empire 539 BC, allowing exiled Jews to return to Jersualem. He died fighting in Afghanistan.

cystic fibrosis hereditary disease involving defects of various tissues, including the sweat glands, the mucous glands of the bronchi (air passages), and the digestive glands. The sufferer experiences repeated chest infections and digestive disorders, and generally fails to thrive.

Once universally fatal at an early age, there is no definitive cure, but treatments have raised both the quality and expectancy of life. Management is by diets and drugs, physiotherapy to keep the chest clear, and use of antibiotics to combat infection and minimize damage to the lungs. Some sufferers have benefited from heart-lung transplants. In 1989 the gene for cystic fibrositis was identified by teams of researchers in Michigan and Toronto. This discovery promises more reliable antenatal diagnosis of the disease, which is incurable.

cystitis inflammation of the bladder, usually caused by bacterial infection, and resulting in frequent and painful urination.

cytochrome a type of protein, responsible for part of the process of ◊respiration by which food molecules are broken down in ◊aerobic organisms. Cytochromes are part of the electron transport chain, which uses energized electrons to reduce molecular oxygen (O_2) to oxygen ions (O^{2-}). These combine with hydrogen ions (H^+) to form water (H_2O), the end product of aerobic respiration. As electrons are passed from one cytochrome to another energy is released and used to make ◊ATP.

cytokine chemical messengers that carry information from one cell to another, for example the ◊lymphokines.

cytokinin a type of ◊plant hormone that stimulates cell division. Cytokinins affect several different aspects of plant growth and development, but only if ◊auxin is also present. They may delay the process of senescence or ageing, break the dormancy of certain seeds and buds, and induce flowering.

cytology the study of ◊cells, especially in relation to their functions. Major advances have been made possible in this field by the development of ◊electron microscopes.

cytoplasm the part of the cell outside the ◊nucleus. Strictly speaking, this includes all the ◊organelles (mitochondria, chloroplasts, and so on) but often cytoplasm refers to the jelly-like matter in which the organelles are embedded (correctly termed the cytosol).

In many cells, the cytoplasm is made up of two parts, the *ectoplasm* (or plasmagel), a dense gelatinous outer layer concerned with cell movement, and the *endoplasm* (or plasmasol), a more fluid inner part where most of the organelles are found.

cytoskeleton in a living cell, a matrix of protein filaments and tubules that occurs within the cytosol (the liquid part of the cytoplasm). It gives the cell a definite shape, transports vital substances around the cell, and may also be involved in cell movement.

cytotoxic drug drug used to kill the cells of a malignant tumour, or as an ◊immunosuppressive following organ transplantation; it may also damage healthy cells. Side effects include nausea, vomiting, hair loss, and bone marrow damage.

czar alternative form of tsar, an emperor of Russia.

Czechoslovakia /ˌtʃekəʊsləˈvækiə/ landlocked country in E central Europe, bounded to the NE by Poland, E by the USSR, S by Hungary and Austria, W by West Germany, and NW by East Germany.

government Since 1968 Czechoslovakia has been a federation of two, Czech and Slovak, national republics. The supreme legislative body in the CSR is the federal assembly *Federalni Shromazdeni*, composed of two chambers of equal rights, the directly elected, 200-deputy chamber of the people and the 150-deputy chamber of nations. The first

Czechoslovakia
Socialist Republic of
(Československá Socialistická Republika)

area 127,903 sq km/49,371 sq mi
capital Prague
towns Brno, Bratislava, Ostrava
physical Carpathian Mountains, rivers Morava, Labe (Elbe), Vltava (Moldau); hills and plateau; Danube plain in S
features divided by valley of the Morava into the W, densely populated area with good communications, and the E, sparsely populated, comparatively little-developed Slovak area
head of state Vaclav Havel from 1989
head of government Marion Calfa from 1989
political system socialist pluralist republic
political parties Communist Party of Czechoslovakia (CCP), Marxist-Leninist; Civic Forum, Czech pluralist reform coalition; Public Against Violence, Slovak pluralist reform coalition; Agrarian Party, farmers' party supporting collectivization; Czechoslovak Socialist Party

and Czechoslovak Freedom Party, pre-1989 allies of CCP; Green Party
exports machinery, timber, ceramics, glass, textiles
currency koruna (61.11 commercial rate, 27.96 tourist rate = £1 Feb 1990)
population (1986) 15,521,000 (63% Czech, 31% Slovak, with Hungarian, Polish, German, Russian, and other minorities); annual growth rate 0.4%
life expectancy men 68, women 75
language Czech and Slovak (official)
religion 75% Roman Catholic, 15% Protestant
literacy 99% (1981)
GNP $85.8 bn (1982); $5,800 per head of population
chronology
1945 Liberation of Czechoslovakia.
1948 Communists assumed power in coup and new constitution framed.
1968 Prague Spring experiment with liberalization ended by Soviet invasion.
1969 Czechoslovakia became a federal state. Husák elected Communist Party leader.
1977 Emergence and suppression of Charter 77 human-rights movement.
1985–86 Criticism of Husák rule by new Soviet leadership.
1987 Husák resigned as Communist leader; replaced by Miloš Jakeš.
1988 Personnel overhaul of party and state bodies, including replacement of Prime Minister Štrougal by the technocrat Adamec.
1989 Communist regime of Jakeš, Husák, and Adamec overthrown in Nov-Dec bloodless 'gentle revolution' following mass pro-democracy protests in Prague and throughout the country, directed by the newly formed Civic Forum. Communist monopoly of power ended, with 'Grand Coalition' government formed. Vaclav Havel appointed president and Alexander Dubček chair of national parliament.
1990 22,000 prisoners released (Jan). Havel announced agreement with USSR for complete withdrawal of Soviet troops by May 1991 (Feb).

is elected for five-year terms and has a 2:1 Czech majority. The second is divided equally between members chosen by each of the Czech and Slovak National Councils.

The federal assembly elects, for a five-year term, the president of the CSR, who appoints a prime minister and federal government accountable to the federal assembly. Traditionally, if the president is Czech, the prime minister will be Slovak, and vice versa. The federal government has authority in defence and foreign affairs. In other areas, power is shared with the national councils elected by the national republics.

Formerly, the controlling force was the Czechoslovak Communist Party (CCP). Political pluralism began in 1989, with the emergence of Civic Forum, an intelligensia-led reform coalition embracing liberals, Christian Democrats and social democrats. Other political parties include the Agrarian Party; Czechoslovak Socialist Party and Czechoslovak Freedom Party, former allies of the CCP; and the Green Party.

history Czechoslovakia came into existence as an independent republic 1918 after the break-up of the ◊Austro-Hungarian empire at the end of World War I. It consisted originally of the Bohemian crownlands (Bohemia, ◊Moravia, and part of ◊Silesia) and ◊Slovakia, the area of Hungary inhabited by Slavonic peoples; to which was added as a trust part of Ruthenia when the Allies and Associated Powers recognized the new republic under the treaty of St Germain-en-Laye. Besides the Czech and Slovak peoples, the country included substantial minorities of German origin, long settled in the north, and of Hungarian (or Magyar) origin in the south. But despite the problems of welding into a nation such a mixed group of people,

until the troubled 1930s Czechoslovakia made considerable political and economic progress. It was the only E European state to retain a parliamentary democracy throughout the inter-war period, with five coalition governments, dominated by the Agrarian and National Socialist parties, with Thomas ◊Masaryk serving as president. It also had a highly developed industrial sector.

The rise to power of ◊Hitler in Germany brought a revival of opposition among the German-speaking population, and nationalism among the Magyar speakers. In addition, the Slovakian clerical party demanded autonomy for Slovakia. In 1938 the ◊Munich Agreement was made between Britain, France, Germany, and Italy, without consulting Czechoslovakia, and this took the Sudetenland from Czechoslovakia and gave it to Germany. Six months later Hitler occupied all Czechoslovakia. A government-in-exile was established in London under Eduard ◊Beneš until the liberation 1945 by Soviet and US troops. In the same year some 2,000,000 Sudeten Germans were expelled, and Czech Ruthenia was transferred to Ukraine, USSR. Elections 1946 gave the left a slight majority and in Feb 1948 the communists seized power, winning an electoral victory in May. Beneš, who had been president since 1945, resigned. The country was divided into 19 and then, in 1960, into ten regions plus Prague and Bratislava.

There was a Stalinist regime during the 1950s, under Presidents Klement Gottwald (1948–53), Antonin Zapotocky (1953–57), and Antonin Novotný (1957–68). Pressure from students and intellectuals brought about policy changes from 1965, and in 1968, following Novotný's replacement as CCP leader by Alexander ◊Dubček

Czechoslovakia *Czechoslovak protesters demonstrating against the Soviet invasion 1968.*

and as president by war hero Gen Ludvík Svoboda (1895–1979) and the appointment of Oldřich Černik as prime minister, a liberalization programme ('Socialist Democratic Revolution') began, promising the return of freedom of assembly, speech, and movement, and the imposition of restrictions on the secret police.

Despite assurances that Czechoslovakia would remain within the Warsaw Pact, the USSR viewed these events with suspicion and in Aug 1968 sent 600,000 troops from Warsaw Pact countries to restore the orthodox line. After the invasion a purge of liberals began in the CCP, with Dr Gustáv ◊Husák (a Slovak Brezhnevite) replacing Dubček as CCP leader 1969 and Lubomír Štrougal (a Czech) becoming prime minister 1970. Svoboda remained as president until 1975 and negotiated the Soviet withdrawal.

In 1968 a new constitution transformed unitary Czechoslovakia into a federal state. In 1973 an amnesty was extended to some of the 40,000 who had fled after the 1968 invasion, signalling a slackening of repression. In 1977, following the signature of a human rights manifesto ('Charter 77') by over 700 intellectuals and former party officials in response to the 1975 ◊Helsinki Conference, a new crackdown commenced. The arrest of dissidents continued during the events of 1981 in ◊Poland.

Czechoslovakia under Dr Husák emerged as a loyal ally of the USSR during the 1970s and early 1980s. However, following Mikhail ◊Gorbachev's accession to the Soviet leadership in 1985, pressure for economic and administrative reform mounted. In Dec Husak, while remaining president, was replaced as CCP leader by Miloš Jakeš (1923–   ), a Czech-born economist. Working with prime minister Ladislav Adamec, a reformist, he began to introduce a reform programme (*prestavba*, 'restructuring') on USSR's ◊perestroika model. However, his approach was cautious and dissident activity, which became increasingly widespread 1988–89, was suppressed. Influenced by events elswhere in E Europe, a series of initially student-led pro-democracy rallies were held in Prague's Wenceslas Square from 17 Nov 1989. Support for the protest movement rapidly increased following the security forces' brutal suppression of the early rallies; by 20 Nov there were more than 200,000 demonstrators in Prague, and a growing number in Bratislava. An umbrella opposition movement, Civic Forum, was swiftly formed under the leadership of playwright and Charter 77 activist Vaclav ◊Havel, which attracted the support of prominent members of the small political parties that were members of the CCP-dominated ruling National Front coalition.

With the protest movement continuing to grow, Jakeš resigned as CCP leader 24 Nov, being replaced by Karel Urbanek (1941–   ), a South Moravian, and the politburo was purged. This was not enough to satisfy the opposition, however, and less than a week later, following a brief general strike, the national assembly voted to amend the constitution to strip the CCP of its 'leading role' in the government, and thus of its monopoly on power. Opposition parties, beginning with Civic Forum and its Slovak counterpart, Public Against Violence, were legalized. On 7 Dec Adamec resigned as prime minister and was replaced by Marion Calfa, who formed a coalition government in which key posts, including the foreign, financial, and labour ministries, were given to former dissidents.

On 27 Dec the rehabilitated Dubček was sworn in as chairman of the federal assembly, and on 29 Dec Havel became president of Czechoslovakia. The new reform government immediately extended an amnesty to 22,000 prisoners; secured agreements from the CCP that it would voluntarily give up its existing majorities in the federal and regional assemblies and state agencies; and promised multi-party elections for June 1990. It also announced plans for reducing the size of the armed forces, called on the USSR to pull out its 75,000 troops stationed in the country by the end of 1990, and applied for membership of the International Monetary Fund and World Bank.

Czerny /'tʃeəni/ Carl 1791–1857. Austrian composer and pianist. He wrote an enormous quantity of religious and concert music, but is chiefly remembered for his books of graded studies and technical exercises used in piano teaching.

Częstochowa /ˌtʃenstə'xəuvə/ town in Poland, on the river Vistula; 193 km/120 mi SW of Warsaw; population (1985) 247,000. It produces iron goods, chemicals, paper, and cement. The basilica of Jasna Góra is a centre for Catholic pilgrims (it contains the painting known as the Black Madonna).

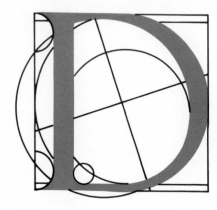

D fourth letter of the alphabet; it corresponds to the Semitic *daleth* and the Greek *delta*.

d. abbreviation for *day*; *diameter*; *died*; in the UK, d was the sign for a *penny* (Latin *denarius)* until decimalization of the currency in 1971.

D abbreviation for *500* in the Roman numeral system.

DA abbreviation for *district attorney*.

dab marine flatfish *Limanda limanda* of the plaice family found in the NE Atlantic. Light-brown or grey, with dark-brown spots and rough-scaled on the coloured side, it grows to about 25 cm/10 in.

Dacca /'dækə/ former spelling (until 1984) of ◊Dhaka, capital of Bangladesh.

dace freshwater fish *Leuciscus leuciscus* of the carp family. Common in England and mainland Europe, it is silvery and grows up to 30 cm/1 ft.

Dachau /'dæxaʊ/ site of a Nazi ◊concentration camp during World War II in Bavaria, West Germany.

dachshund (German 'badger-dog') small hound of German origin, bred originally for badger digging. It has a long body and short legs. Several varieties are bred: standard size (up to 10 kg/22 lb); miniature (5 kg/11 lb or less); long-haired; smooth-haired; and wire-haired.

Dacia /ˌdeɪsɪə/ ancient region forming much of modern Romania. The various Dacian tribes were united around 60 BC, and for many years posed a threat to the Roman empire; they were finally conquered by the Roman emperor Trajan AD 101–106, and the region became a province of the same name. It was abandoned to the invading Goths in about 275.

dacoit member of an armed gang of robbers in India or Burma.

Dada artistic and literary movement founded 1915 in Zürich, Switzerland, by the Romanian poet Tristan Tzara (1896–1963) and others in a spirit of rebellion and disillusion during World War I. Other Dadaist groups were soon formed by the artists ◊Duchamp and Man ◊Ray in New York and ◊Picabia in Barcelona. Dada had a considerable impact on early 20th-century art, questioning established artistic rules and values.

With the German writers Hugo Ball and Richard Huelsenbeck, Tzara founded the Cabaret Voltaire in Zürich 1916, where works by Hans Arp, the pioneer Surrealist Max Ernst, and others were exhibited. In New York in the same period the artist Man Ray met Duchamp and Picabia and began to apply Dadaist ideas to photography. In the 1920s Dada evolved into Surrealism.

Dadd /dæd/ Richard 1817–1887. British painter. In 1843 he murdered his father and was committed to an insane asylum, but continued to paint minutely detailed pictures of fantasies and fairy tales, such as *The Fairy Feller's Master-Stroke* 1855–64 (Tate Gallery, London).

daddy-longlegs popular name for a ◊crane fly.

Dadra and Nagar Haveli /dəˈdrɑː ˈnʌɡəˈveli/ since 1961 a Union Territory of W India; capital Silvassa; area 490 sq km/189 sq mi; population (1981) 104,000. Formerly part of Portuguese Daman. It produces rice, wheat, millet, and timber.

Daedalus /ˈdiːdələs/ in Greek mythology, an Athenian artisan supposed to have constructed the labyrinth for King Minos in which the ◊Minotaur was imprisoned. He fled from Crete with his son ◊Icarus using wings made from feathers fastened with wax.

Daedalus in space travel, a futuristic project proposed by the British Interplanetary Society to send a ◊robot probe to nearby stars. The probe, 20 times the size of the Saturn V moon rocket, would be propelled by thermonuclear fusion, in effect, a series of small hydrogen-bomb explosions. Interstellar cruise speed would be about 40,000 km/25,000 mi per second.

daffodil any of several species of the genus *Narcissus*, distinguished by their trumpet-shaped corollas. The common daffodil of N Europe *Narcissus pseudonarcissus* has large yellow flowers and grows from a large bulb. There are numerous cultivated forms.

Dafydd ap Gwilym /ˈdævɪð æ ˈɡwɪlɪm/ *c.*1340–*c.*1400. Welsh poet. His work is notable for its complex but graceful style, its concern with nature and love rather than with heroic martial deeds, and for its references to classical and Italian poetry. He was born into an influential Cardiganshire family, and is traditionally believed to have led a life packed with amorous adventures.

Dagestan /ˌdæɡɪˈstɑːn/ autonomous republic of western USSR, situated E of the ◊Caucasus, bordering the Caspian Sea. Capital Makhachkala; area 50,300 sq km/14,700 sq mi; population (1982) 1,700,000. It is mountainous, with deep valleys, and its numerous ethnic groups speak a variety of distinct languages. Annexed from Iran in 1723, which strongly resisted Russian conquest, it became an autonomous republic in 1921.

Daglish /ˈdæɡlɪʃ/ Eric Fitch 1892–1966. British artist and author. He wrote a number of natural history books, and illustrated both these and classics by Izaak Walton, Thoreau, Gilbert White, and W H Hudson with exquisite wood engravings.

Daguerre /dæˈɡeə/ Louis Jacques Mande 1789–1851. French pioneer of photography. Together

daffodil

Daguerre Frenchman Louis Daguerre discovered how to produce a single photographic image as a result of accidentally spilt iodine on some of his silvered plates.

with Niépce, he is credited with the invention of photography (though others were reaching the same point simultaneously). He invented the ◊daguerreotype in 1838, a single image process, superseded ten years later by ◊Talbot's negative/positive process.

daguerreotype in photography, a single-image process using mercury vapour and an iodine-sensitized silvered plate; discovered by Daguerre in 1838.

Dahl /dɑːl/ Johann Christian 1788–1857. Norwegian landscape painter in the Romantic style. He trained in Copenhagen but was active chiefly in Dresden from 1818. He was the first great painter of the Norwegian landscape, in a style that recalls the Dutch artist ◊Ruisdael.

Dahl /dɑːl/ Roald 1916– . British writer, celebrated for short stories with a twist, for example, *Tales of the Unexpected* 1979, and for children's books including *Charlie and the Chocolate Factory* 1964.

dahlia genus of perennial plants, family Compositae, comprising 20 species and many cultivated forms. The dahlia is a stocky plant with showy flowers that come in a wide range of colours. It is native to Mexico.

Dahomey /dəˈhəʊmi/ former name (until 1975) of the People's Republic of ◊Benin.

Dahrendorf /ˈdɑːrəndɔːf/ Ralf (Gustav) 1929– . German sociologist, director of the London School of Economics 1974–84. His works include *Life Chances* 1980, which sees the aim of society as the improvement of the range of opportunities open to the individual.

Dáil Eireann /ˈdɔɪl ˈeərən/ the lower house of the legislature of the Republic of Ireland. It consists of 148 members elected by adult suffrage on a basis of proportional representation.

Daimler /ˈdeɪmlə/ Gottlieb 1834–1900. German engineer who pioneered the modern motorcar. In 1886 he produced his first motor vehicle and a motor-bicycle. He later joined forces with Karl ◊Benz and was one of the pioneers of the high-speed 4-stroke petrol engine.

Born in Württemberg, he had engineering experience at the Whitworth works, Manchester, England, before joining N A Otto of Cologne in the production of an internal-combustion gas engine 1872.

Dairen /ˌdaɪˈren/ former name for the Chinese port of Dalian, part of ◊Lüda.

dairying the business of producing and handling ◊milk and milk products. In the US and the UK, over 70% of the milk produced is consumed in its liquid form, whereas New Zealand relies on easily transportable milk products such as butter, cheese, and condensed and dried milk. It is now usual for dairy farms to concentrate on the production of milk and for factories to take over the handling, processing, and distribution of milk as well as the manufacture of dairy products.

In Britain, the Milk Marketing Board (1933), to which all producers must sell their milk, forms a connecting link between farms and factories.

daisy genus of hardy perennials, family Compositae. The *common daisy Bellis perennis* has a single white or pink flower rising from a rosette of leaves. It is a common lawn weed.

daisy bush genus *Olearia* of Australian and New Zealand shrubs, family Compositae, with flowers like daisies and felted or holly-like leaves.

Dakar /'dækɑ:/ capital and chief port (with artificial harbour) of Senegal; population (1984) 1,000,000.

It is an industrial centre, and there is a university 1957. Founded 1862, it was formerly the seat of government of ◊French West Africa. In July 1940 an unsuccessful naval action was undertaken by British and Free French forces to seize Dakar as an Allied base.

Dakota /də'kəutə/ see ◊North Dakota and ◊South Dakota.

Daladier /,dælæd'jeɪ/ Edouard 1884–1970. French Radical politician. As prime minister Apr 1938–Mar 1940, he was largely responsible both for the ◊Munich Agreement and France's declaration of war on Germany. Arrested on the fall of France (see ◊Riom), he was a prisoner in Germany 1943–45. He was re-elected to the Chamber of Deputies 1946–58.

Dalai Lama /'dælaɪ 'lɑ:mə/ 14th incarnation 1935– . Spiritual and temporal head of the Tibetan state until 1959, when he went into exile in protest against Chinese annexation and oppression. Tibetan Buddhists believe that each Dalai Lama is a reincarnation of his predecessor and also of ◊Avalokiteśvara (see ◊Lamaism). Nobel Peace Prize 1989 in recognition of his commitment to the nonviolent liberation of his homeland.

Enthroned 1940, the Dalai Lama temporarily fled 1950–51 when the Chinese overran Tibet, and in Mar 1959 made a dramatic escape from Lhasa to India, when a local uprising against Chinese rule was suppressed. He then settled at Dharmsala in the Punjab. His people continue to demand his return, and the Chinese offered to lift the ban on his living in Tibet, providing he refrained from calling for Tibet's independence. His deputy, the ◊Panchen Lama, has cooperated with the Chinese but failed to protect the monks. When he was in Britain 1988, the British government refused to let him talk about Tibet.

Dalcroze Emile Jaques see ◊Jaques-Dalcroze, Emile.

Dale /deɪl/ Henry Hallett 1875–1968. British physiologist, who in 1936 shared a Nobel prize with Otto Loewi (1873–1961) for work on the chemical transmission of nervous effects.

D'Alembert see ◊Alembert, French mathematician.

Dalen /dɑ:'leɪn/ Nils 1869–1937. Swedish industrial engineer who invented the light-controlled valve. This allowed lighthouses to operate automatically and won him the 1912 Nobel Physics prize.

Dalgarno /dæl'gɑ:nəu/ George 1626–1687. Scottish schoolteacher and inventor of the first sign-language alphabet 1680.

Dalglish /dæl'gli:ʃ/ Kenneth 'Kenny' 1951– . Scottish footballer, the only man to play 200 League games in England and Scotland, and score 100 goals in each country.

Born in Glasgow, he made over 200 appearances for Glasgow Celtic before joining Liverpool 1977. He won all domestic honours as a player and since becoming Liverpool manager in 1985 has led the club to similar successes. He played for Scotland 102 times.

Dalí Autumnal Cannibalism *(1936) Tate Gallery, London.*

CAREER HIGHLIGHTS

as a player: Football League appearances: 352
goals: 118
international appearances: 102 goals: 30
European Cup: 1978, 1981, 1984
European Super Cup: 1977
Football League: 1979–80, 1982–84, 1986
FA Cup: 1986 Milk Cup: 1982, 1983, 1984
Scottish Premier Division: 1977
Scottish 1st Division: 1970–75
Scottish FA Cup: 1972, 1974–75, 1977
Scottish League Cup: 1975
Player of the Year (FWA): 1979, 1983
Player of the Year (PFA): 1983
as a manager: Football League: 1986, 1988
FA Cup: 1986
Manager of the Year: 1986, 1988, 1989

Dalhousie /dæl'hauzi/ James Andrew Broun Ramsay, 1st Marquess and 10th Earl of Dalhousie 1812–1860. British administrator, governor general of India 1848–56. In the second Sikh War he annexed the Punjab 1849, and, after the second Burmese War, Lower Burma 1853. He reformed the Indian army and civil service and furthered social and economic progress.

Dalí /'dɑ:li/ Salvador 1904–1989. Spanish painter. In 1928 he collaborated with Buñuel on the film *Un Chien Andalou.* In 1929 he joined the ◊Surrealists and became notorious for his flamboyant eccentricity. Influenced by the psychiatric theories of Freud, he developed a repertoire of dramatic images, such as the distorted human body, limp watches, and burning giraffes. These are painted with a meticulous, polished clarity. He also painted religious themes and many portraits of his wife Gala.

Dalí, born near Barcelona, initially came under the influence of the Italian Futurists. He is credited as co-creator of *Un Chien Andalou* but his role is thought to have been subordinate; he abandoned film after collaborating on the script for Buñuel's *L'Age d'Or* 1930. He designed ballet costumes, scenery, jewellery, and furniture. The books *Secret Life of Salvador Dalí* 1942 and *Diary of a Genius* 1966 are autobiographical. He died 23 Jan 1989, and was buried beneath a crystal dome in the museum of his work at Figueras on the Costa Brava, Spain.

Dalian /,dɑ:li'æn/ one of the two cities comprising the Chinese port of ◊Lüda.

Dallapiccola /,dælə'pɪkələ/ Luigi 1904–1975. Italian composer. In his early years he was a Neo-Classicist in the manner of Stravinsky, but he soon turned to Serialism, which he adapted to his own style. His works include the operas *Il Prigioniero/The Prisoner* 1949 and *Ulisse/Ulysses* 1968, as well as many vocal and instrumental compositions.

Dallas /'dæləs/ commercial city in Texas, USA; population (1980) 904,000, metropolitan area (with Fort Worth) 2,964,000. Industries include

banking, insurance, oil, aviation, aerospace and electronics. Dallas-Fort Worth Regional Airport (opened 1973) is one of the world's largest. John F ◊Kennedy was assassinated here 1963.

It is a cultural centre, with a symphony orchestra, opera, ballet, and theatre; there is an annual Texas State Fair. Founded as a trading post 1844, it developed as the focus of a cotton area, and then as a mineral and oil-producing centre, with banking and insurance operations. After World War II growth increased rapidly.

Dalmatia /dæl'meɪʃə/ region of Croatia, Bosnia and Herzegovina, and Montenegro in Yugoslavia. The capital is Split. It lies along the eastern shore of the Adriatic and includes a number of islands. The interior is mountainous. Important products are wine, olives, and fish. Notable towns in addition to the capital are Zadar, Sibenik, and Dubrovnik.

history Dalmatia became Austrian 1815, and by the treaty of Rapallo 1920 became part of the kingdom of the Serbs, Croats, and Slovenes (Yugoslavia from 1931), except for the town of Zadar (Zara), and the island of Lastovo (Lagosta), which, with neighbouring islets, were given to Italy until transferred to Yugoslavia 1947. Dalmatia was made a region of Croatia 1949.

dalmatian breed of dog, about 60 cm/2 ft tall, white with spots that are black or brown. It was formerly used as a coach dog.

dalmatic the outer liturgical vestment of the deacon in the Roman Catholic Church; a mantle worn at Mass and in solemn processions.

Dalton /'dɔ:ltən/ Hugh, Baron Dalton 1887–1962. British Labour politician and economist. Chancellor of the Exchequer from 1945, he oversaw nationalization of the Bank of England, but resigned 1947 after making a disclosure to a lobby correspondent before a budget speech.

His name is associated with the 2 1/2% Irredeemable Treasury Stock known as Daltons, introduced 1946 and bought by many savers, which rapidly depreciated in value. He was created a life peer 1960.

Dalton /'dɔ:ltən/ John 1776–1844. British chemist, the first to propose the existence of atoms, which he considered to be the smallest parts of matter. Extending the range of compounds, he produced the first list of relative atomic masses, *Absorption of Gases* 1805. He was also the first scientist to note and record colour-blindness.

From experiments with gases he noted that the proportions of two components combining to form another were always consistent. From this he suggested that if substances combine in simple numerical ratios then the macroscopic weight proportions represent the relative atomic masses of those substances.

Dalton Labour chancellor of the Exchequer Hugh Dalton was forced to resign in 1947.

dam

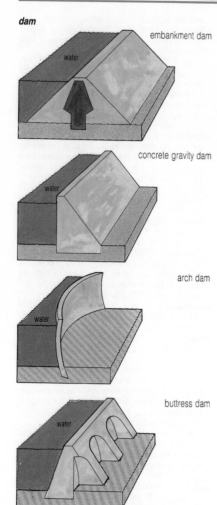

embankment dam

concrete gravity dam

arch dam

buttress dam

Daly /'deɪlɪ/ Augustin 1838–1899. US theatre manager. He began as a drama critic and playwright before building his own theatre in New York 1879 and another, Daly's, in Leicester Square, London 1893–1937.

Dalziel family /'dælziel/ British wood-engravers. George (1815–1902), Edward (1817–1905), John (1822–60), and Thomas Bolton (1823–1906) were all sons of Alexander Dalziel of Wooler, Northumberland. George went to London in 1835 and was joined by his brothers. They produced illustrations for the classics and magazines.

dam a structure built to hold back water in order to prevent flooding, provide water for irrigation and storage, and to provide hydroelectric power. The biggest dams are of the earth- and rock-fill type, also called **embankment dams**. Such dams are generally built on broad valley sites. Deep, narrow gorges dictate a **concrete dam**, where the strength of reinforced concrete can withstand the water pressures involved. A valuable development in arid regions, as in parts of Brazil, is the **underground dam**, where water is stored on a solid rock base, with a wall to ground level, so avoiding rapid evaporation.

Many concrete dams are triangular in cross-section, with their vertical face pointing upstream. Their sheer weight holds them in position, and they are called **gravity dams**. Other concrete dams are more slightly built in the shape of an arch, with the curve facing upstream: the **arch dam** derives its strength from the arch shape, just as an arch bridge does.

Major dams include: **Rogun** (USSR), the world's highest at 325 m/1,067 ft; **New Cornelia Tailings** (USA), the world's biggest in volume, 209 million m³; **Owen Falls** (Uganda), the world's largest reservoir capacity, 204.8 billion m³; and **Itaipu** (Brazil/Paraguay), the world's most powerful, 12,700 megawatts.

The earliest dam in Britain is at the Roman Dolaucothi gold mine in Dyfed, Wales, dating from the 1st century AD.

Dam /dæm/ Carl 1895–1976. Danish biochemist who discovered vitamin K. For his success in this field he shared the 1943 Nobel physiology or medicine prize with Edward Doisy.

In 1928 Dam began a series of experiments to see if chickens could live on a cholesterol-free diet. The birds, it turned out, were able to metabolize their own supply. Yet they continued to die from spontaneous haemorrhages. Dam concluded that their diet lacked an unknown essential ingredient, which he eventually found in abundance in green leaves. As it controlled coagulation, Dam named the new compound vitamin K.

damages in English law, compensation for a ◊tort (such as personal injuries caused by negligence) or for a breach of contract. In the case of breach of contract the complainant can claim all the financial loss he or she has suffered. Damages for personal injuries include compensation for loss of earnings, as well as for the injury itself. The court might reduce the damages if the claimant was partly to blame. In the majority of cases, the parties involved reach an out-of-court settlement (a compromise without going to court.)

Daman /dəˈmɑːn/ or **Dama** part of the Union Territory of Daman and ◊Diu; area 110 sq km/42 sq mi; capital Panaji; population (1981) 79,000. Daman has an area of 72 sq km/28 sq mi and a population (1981) 49,000. The town of Daman is a port on the W coast of India, 160 km/100 mi north of Bombay; population (1981) 21,000. Daman was seized by Portugal 1531 and ceded to Portugal by the Shar of Gujarat 1539. It was annexed by India 1961 and was part of the Union Territory of ◊Goa, Daman, and Diu until Goa became a separate state 1987. The economy is based on tourism and fishing.

Damaraland /dəˈmɑːrəlænd/ central region of Namibia, home of the nomadic Bantu-speaking ◊Hereros.

Damascus /dəˈmæskəs/ (Arabic **Dimashq**) capital of Syria, on the river Barada, SE of Beirut; population (1981) 1,251,000. It produces silk, wood products, and brass and copper ware. Said to be the oldest continuously inhabited city in the world, Damascus was an ancient city even in Old Testament times; most notable of the old buildings is the Great Mosque, completed as a Christian church in the 5th century.

The Assyrians destroyed it about 733 BC. In 332 BC it fell to one of the generals of Alexander the Great; in 63 BC it came under Roman rule. In AD 635 it was taken by the Arabs, and has since been captured many times, by Egyptians, Mongolians, and Turks. In 1918, during World War I, it was taken from the Turks by the British with Arab aid, and in 1920 became the capital of French-mandated Syria.

The 'street which is called straight' is associated with St Paul, who was converted while on the road to Damascus. The tomb of ◊Saladin is here. The fortress dates from 1219.

damask textile of woven linen, cotton, wool, or silk, with a reversible figured pattern. It was first made in the city of Damascus, Syria.

Dame in the UK honours system, title of a woman who has been awarded the Order of the Bath, Order of St Michael and St George, Royal Victorian Order, or Order of the British Empire. It is also the legal title of the wife or widow of a knight or baronet, placed before her name.

Damien, Father /ˌdæmiˈæn/ 1840–1889. Name adopted by Belgian missionary Joseph de ◊Veuster.

Damietta /ˌdæmiˈetə/ English name for the Egyptian port of ◊Dumyat.

damnation in Christian and Muslim belief, a state of eternal punishment which will be undergone by those who are not worthy of salvation; sometimes equated with ◊hell.

Damocles /'dæməkliːz/ lived 4th century BC. In Classical legend, a courtier of the elder Dionysius, ruler of Syracuse, Sicily. Having extolled the happiness of his sovereign, Damocles was invited by him to a feast, during which he saw above his head a sword suspended by a single hair. He recognized this as a symbol of the insecurity of the great.

Damodar /'dæmədɑː/ Indian river flowing 560 km/350 mi from Chota Nagpur plateau in Bihar, through Bihar and West Bengal states to join the ◊Hooghly River 40 km/25 mi SW of Calcutta. The Damodar Valley is an industrial centre with a hydroelectric project, combined with irrigation works.

damper incorrectly called shock absorber, a device for reducing the vibration of, for example, a spring. Dampers are used in conjunction with coil springs in most car suspension systems, and are usually of the telescopic type, consisting of a piston in an oil-filled cylinder. The resistance to movement of the piston through the oil creates the damping effect.

Dampier /'dæmpiə/ William 1652–1715. English explorer and hydrographic surveyor who circumnavigated the world three times.

He was born in Somerset, and went to sea in 1668. He led a life of buccaneering adventure, circumnavigated the globe, and published his *New Voyage Round the World* in 1697. In 1699 he was sent by the government on a voyage to Australia and New Guinea, and again circled the world. He accomplished a third circumnavigation 1703–07, and on his final voyage 1708–11 rescued Alexander ◊Selkirk (on whose life Defoe's *Robinson Crusoe* is based) from Juan Fernandez in the S Pacific. Named after him are: **Dampier**, a newly developed port on the remote N coast of Western Australia; **Dampier Archipelago** in the Indian Ocean, NW of the coast of Western Australia; and **Mount Dampier**, a peak of the Southern Alps in South Island, New Zealand (3,440 m/11,287 ft).

damselfly a predatory, winged, often colourful insect with two pairs of similar wings which are generally folded back over the body when at rest, large, prominent eyes, and long, slender body.

damson type of plum tree **Prunus damascena**, distinguished by its small, oval, edible fruit, which is dark purple or blue to black in colour.

Dana /'deɪnə/ Richard Henry 1815–1882. US author who went to sea and worked his passage round Cape Horn to California and back, writing an account in *Two Years before the Mast* 1840.

Danaë /'dæneiiː/ in Greek mythology, daughter of Acrisius, king of Argos. He shut her up in a bronze tower because of a prophecy that her son would kill his grandfather. Zeus became enamoured of her and descended in a shower of gold, and by him she became the mother of ◊Perseus.

Da Nang /dɑː ˈnæŋ/ port and second city (formerly Tourane) of South Vietnam, 80 km/50 mi SE of Hué; population (1975) 500,000. Following the reunion of North and South Vietnam, the major part of the population was dispersed 1976 to rural areas. A US base in the Vietnam War, it is now used by the USSR.

Danby /'dænbi/ Thomas Osborne, Earl of Danby 1631–1712. British Tory politician. He entered Parliament 1665, acted 1673–78 as Charles II's chief minister and in 1674 was created earl of Danby, but was imprisoned in the Tower of London 1678–84. In 1688 he signed the invitation to William of Orange to take the throne. Danby was again chief minister 1690–95, and in 1694 was created duke of Leeds.

dance rhythmic movement of the body, usually performed in time to music. Its primary purpose may be religious, magical, martial, social, or artistic—the last two being characteristic of nontraditional societies. The pre-Christian era had a strong tradition of ritual dance, and ancient Greek dance still exerts an influence on

dance chronology

1909	The first Paris season given by Diaghilev's troupe of Russian dancers, later to become known as the Ballets Russes, marked the beginning of one of the most exciting periods in Western ballet.
1913	The première of Stravinsky's *The Rite of Spring* provoked a scandal in Paris.
1914	The foxtrot was introduced in England.
1926	Martha Graham, one of the most innovative figures in modern ballet, gave her first recital in New York. In England, students from the Rambert School of Ballet, opened by Marie Rambert in 1920, gave their first public performance in *A Tragedy of Fashion*, the first ballet to be choreographed by Frederick Ashton.
1928	The first performance of George Balanchine's *Apollon Musagète* in Paris, by the Ballets Russes, marked the birth of neoclassicism in ballet.
1931	Ninette de Valois' Vic-Wells ballet gave its first performance in London. In 1956 the company became the Royal Ballet.
1933	The Hollywood musical achieved artistic independence through Busby Berkeley's kaleidoscopic choreography in *Forty-Second Street* and Dave Gould's airborne finale in *Flying down to Rio*, in which Fred Astaire and Ginger Rogers appeared together for the first time.
1940	The Dance Notation Bureau was established in New York for recording ballets and dances.
1948	The New City Ballet was founded with George Balanchine as principal choreographer. The immensely popular film *The Red Shoes* appeared, choreographed by Massine and Robert Helpman and starring Moira Shearer.
1950	The Festival Ballet, later to become the London Festival Ballet, was created by Alicia Markova and Anton Dolin who had first danced together with the Ballets Russes in 1929.
1952	Gene Kelly starred and danced in the film *Singin' in the Rain*.
1953	The American experimental choreographer Merce Cunningham, who often worked with the composer John Cage, formed his own troupe.
1954	Bill Haley's *Rock Around the Clock* heralded the age of rock and roll.
1956	The Bolshoi Ballet opened its first season in the West at Covent Garden in London, with Galina Ulanova dancing in *Romeo and Juliet*, startling

	audiences with its dramatic style.
1957	Jerome Robbins choreographed Leonard Bernstein's *West Side Story*, demonstrating his outstanding ability to work in both popular and classical forms.
1960	The progressive French choreographer Maurice Béjart became director of the Brussels-based *Ballet du XXième Siècle* company.
1961	Rudolf Nureyev defected while dancing with the Kirov Ballet in Paris. He was to have a profound influence on male dancing in the West. The South African choreographer John Cranke became director of the Stuttgart Ballet for which he was to produce several major ballets.
1962	Glen Tetley's ballet *Pierrot Lunaire*, in which he was one of the three dancers, was premiered in New York. In the same year he joined the Nederlands Dans Theater.
1965	American choreographer Twyla Tharp produced her first works.
1966	The School of Contemporary Dance was founded in London, from which Robin Howard and the choreographer Robert Cohan created the London Contemporary Dance Theatre, later to become an internationally renowned company. The choreographer Norman Morrice joined the Ballet Rambert and the company began to concentrate on contemporary works.
1968	Arthur Mitchell, the first black dancer to join the New York City Ballet, founded the Dance Theatre of Harlem.
1974	Mikhail Baryshnikov defected while dancing with a Bolshoi Ballet group in Toronto.
1978	The release of Robert Stigwood's film *Saturday Night Fever* popularized disco dancing worldwide.
1980	Natalia Makarova, who had defected in 1979, staged the first full-length revival of Petipa's *La Bayadère* in the West with the American Ballet Theatre in New York.
1981	Wayne Sleep, previously principal dancer with the Royal Ballet, starred as lead dancer in Andrew Lloyd-Webber's musical *Cats*, choreographed by Gillian Lynne.
1983	Break dancing was established as a cult with the release of the film *Flashdance*.
1984	The avant-garde group Michael Clark and Company made its debut in London.

they were representatives of a tradition stretching back to 740, the year in which Emperor Ming Huang established the Pear Garden Academy. The first comparable European institution, *L'Académie royale de danse*, was founded by Louis XIV 1661.

Social dances have always tended to rise upward through the social scale; for example, the medieval court dances derived from peasant country dances. One form of dance tends to typify a whole period, thus the galliard represents the 16th century, the minuet the 18th, the waltz the 19th, and perhaps the quickstep the 20th.

The nine dances of the modern world championships in ◊ballroom dancing are the standard four (waltz, ◊foxtrot, ◊tango, and quickstep), the Latin-American styles (samba, rumba, cha-cha-cha, and paso doble), and the Viennese waltz. A British development since the 1930s, which has spread to some extent abroad, is 'formation' dancing in which each team (usually eight couples) performs a series of ballroom steps in strict coordination.

Popular dance crazes have included the jitterbug in the 1940s, ◊jive in the 1950s, the twist in the 1960s, disco dancing in the 1970s, and break dancing in the 1980s. In general, since the 1960s popular dance in the West has moved away from any prescribed sequence of movements and physical contact between participants, the dancers performing as individuals with no distinction between the male and the female role. Dances requiring skilled athletic performance, such as the hustle and the New Yorker, have been developed.

In Classical dance, the second half of the 20th century has seen a great cross-fertilization from dances of other cultures. Troupes have visited the West, not only from the USSR and Eastern Europe, but from such places as Indonesia, Japan, South Korea, Nigeria, and Senegal. In the 1970s jazz dance, pioneered in the USA by Matt Mattox, became popular. It includes elements of ballet, modern, tap, Indian classical, Latin American, and Afro-American dance, and may be summed up as 'free-style dance'.

Dance /dɑːns/ Charles 1946– . British film and television actor who achieved fame in *The Jewel in the Crown* 1984. He has also appeared in *Plenty* 1986, *Good Morning Babylon*, *The Golden Child* 1987, *White Mischief* 1988.

dance of death (German *Totentanz*, French *danse macabre*) a popular theme in painting of the late medieval period, depicting an allegorical representation of death (usually a skeleton) leading the famous and the not-so-famous to the grave. One of the best-known representations is a series of woodcuts by Hans Holbein the Younger.

dandelion wild flower *Taraxacum officinale* belonging to the Compositae family. The stalk rises from a rosette of leaves that are deeply indented like a lion's teeth, hence the name (from French *dent de lion*). The flowerheads are bright yellow. The fruit is surmounted by the hairs of the calyx which constitute the familiar dandelion 'puff'.

The milky juice of the dandelion has laxative properties, and the young leaves are sometimes eaten in salads. In the Russian species *Taraxacum koksaghyz* the juice forms an industrially usable latex, relied upon especially during World War II.

Dandie Dinmont breed of ◊terrier that originated in the Scottish border country. It is short-legged and long-bodied, with drooping ears and a long tail, about 25 cm/10 in tall. Its hair, about 5 cm/2 in long, can be greyish or yellowish. It is named after the character Dandie Dinmont in Walter Scott's novel *Guy Mannering* 1815.

Dandolo /'dændələu/ Venetian family that produced four doges (rulers), of whom the most outstanding, **Enrico Dandolo** (*c.*1120–1205), became doge in 1193. He greatly increased the dominions of the Venetian republic and accompanied the crusading army that took Constantinople in 1203.

dance movement today. Although Western folk and social dances have a long history, the Eastern dance tradition long predates the Western. The European Classical tradition dates from the 15th century in Italy, the first printed dance text from 16th-century France, and the first dance school in Paris from the 17th century. The 18th century saw the development of European Classical ballet as we know it today, and the 19th century saw the rise of Romantic ballet. In the 20th century many divergent styles and ideas have grown from

a willingness to explore a variety of techniques and amalgamate different traditions.

history European dance is relatively young in comparison to that of the rest of the world. The first Indian book on dancing, the *Natya Sastra*, existed a thousand years before its European counterpart. The *bugaku* dances of Japan, with orchestra accompaniment, date from the 7th century and are still performed at court. When the Peking (Beijing) Opera dancers first astonished Western audiences during the 1950s,

Dance *British film and TV actor Charles Dance gained recognition in* The Jewel in the Crown *1984.*

Dane citizen of Denmark; in English history, a ◊Viking.

danegeld in English history, a tax imposed from 991 by Anglo-Saxon kings to pay tribute to the Vikings. After the Norman Conquest the tax continued to be levied until 1162, and the Normans used it to finance military operations.

Danelaw 11th-century name for the area of N and E England settled by the Vikings in the 9th century. It stretched from the river Tees to the river Thames, and occupied about half of England. Within its bounds, Danish law, customs, and language prevailed. Its linguistic influence is still apparent.

dangling participle see ◊participle.

Daniel /'dæniəl/ 6th century BC. Jewish folk hero and prophet at the court of Nebuchadnezzar; also the name of a book of the Old Testament or Jewish Bible, probably compiled in the 2nd century BC. It includes stories about Daniel and his companions Shadrach, Meshach, and Abednego, set during the Babylonian captivity of the Jews.

One of the best-known stories is that of Daniel in the den of lions, where he was thrown for refusing to compromise his beliefs, and was preserved by divine intervention. The book also contains a prophetic section dealing with the rise and fall of a number of empires.

Daniel /'dæniəl/ Glyn 1914– . British archaeologist. Prominent in the development of the subject, he was Disney professor of archaeology, Cambridge, 1974–81. His books include *Megaliths in History* 1973 and *A Short History of Archaeology* 1981.

Daniel /'dæniəl/ Samuel 1562–1619. English poet, author of the sonnet collection *Delia* 1592. He was

Danelaw extent of Danish rule in England by 886
area subject to Norsemen

Daniell cell

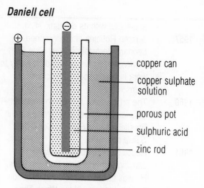

copper can
copper sulphate solution
porous pot
sulphuric acid
zinc rod

master of the revels at court from 1603, for which he wrote masques.

Daniell /'dæniəl/ John Frederic 1790–1845. British chemist and meteorologist who invented a primary electrical cell in 1836. In its original form, the *Daniell cell* consists of a central zinc anode dipping into a porous pot containing zinc sulphate solution. The porous pot is, in turn, immersed in a solution of copper sulphate contained in a copper can, which acts as the cell's cathode. The use of a porous barrier prevents polarization (the covering of the anode with small bubbles of hydrogen gas) and allows the cell to generate a continuous current of electricity.

Danish language a member of the North Germanic group of the Indo-European language family, spoken in Denmark and Greenland and related to Icelandic, Faroese, Norwegian, and Swedish. As one of the languages of the Vikings, who invaded and settled in parts of Britain during the 9th to 11th centuries, Old Danish had a strong influence on English.

They, *their*, and *them*, as well as such *sk-* words as *sky*, *skill*, *skin*, *scrape*, and *scrub*, are of Danish origin. Danish place-name endings include *by* (a farm or town), as in Derby, Grimsby, and Whitby.

Dankworth /'dæŋkwɜ:θ/ John 1927– . British jazz musician, composer, and bandleader, influential in the development of British jazz from about 1950. His film scores include *Saturday Night and Sunday Morning* 1960 and *The Servant* 1963.

D'Annunzio /dæ'nʊntsiəʊ/ Gabriele 1863–1938. Italian poet, novelist, and playwright. He wrote the play *La Gioconda* for the actress Eleonora ◊Duse in 1898. His mystic nationalism prepared the way for Fascism.

Dante Alighieri /'dænti ˌælɪ'gjeəri/ 1265–1321. Italian poet. His masterpiece is ◊*Divina Commedia/The Divine Comedy* 1300–21. Other works include the prose philosophical treatise *Convivio* 1306–08; *Monarchia* 1310–13, expounding his political theories; *De vulgari eloquentia/Concerning the Vulgar Tongue* 1304–06, an original Latin work on Italian, its dialects, and kindred languages; and *Canzoniere/Lyrics*, containing his scattered lyrics.

Dante was born in Florence. He first met Beatrice (Portinari) in 1274 and conceived a love for her that survived her marriage to another and her death in 1290, as he described in *Vita Nuova/New Life* about 1295. In 1289 Dante fought in the battle of Campaldino, won by Florence against Arezzo, and from 1295 took an active part in Florentine politics. In 1300 he was one of the six Priors of the Republic, and, since he favoured the moderate White Guelphs rather than the Black, was convicted in his absence of misapplication of public moneys in 1302 when the Black Guelphs became predominant. He spent the remainder of his life in exile, in central and northern Italy.

Danton /dɒn'tɒn/ Georges Jacques 1759–1794. French revolutionary. Originally a lawyer, during the early years of the Revolution he was one of the most influential people in Paris. He organized the rising 10 Aug 1792 that overthrew the monarchy, roused the country to expel the Prussian invaders,

Dante Alighieri *Italian poet Dante Alighieri by Andrea del Castagno.*

and in Apr 1793 formed the revolutionary tribunal and the *Committee of Public Safety*, of which he was the real leader until July. Thereafter he lost power, and when he attempted to recover it, he was arrested and guillotined.

Danube /'dænju:b/ (German *Donau*) second longest of European rivers, rising on the east slopes of the Black Forest, and flowing 2,858 km/1,776 mi across Europe to enter the Black Sea in Romania by a swampy delta.

The head of river navigation is Ulm, in Baden-Württemberg; Braila, Romania, is the limit for ocean-going ships. Cities on the Danube include Linz, Vienna, Bratislava, Budapest, Belgrade, Ruse, Braila, and Galati. A canal connects the Danube with the ◊Main, and thus with the Rhine system. Plans to dam the river for hydroelectric power at Nagymaros in Hungary, with participation by Austria and Czechoslovakia, were abandoned on environmental grounds 1989.

Danzig /'dæntsɪg/ German name for the Polish port of ◊Gdańsk.

River Danube

Danube

Danton *French revolutionary leader Georges Jacques Danton, organizer of the uprising in France 1792, who was overthrown and guillotined in the following year by Robespierre and the leaders of the Reign of Terror.*

Daphne /'dæfni/ in Greek mythology, a nymph who was changed into a laurel tree to escape from Apollo's amorous pursuit.

Daqing oilfield near ◊Harbin, China.

D'Arblay, Madame /'dɑːbleɪ/ married name of British writer Fanny ◊Burney.

Darby /'dɑːbi/ Abraham 1677–1717. English iron manufacturer who developed a process for smelting iron ore using coke instead of the more expensive charcoal.

He employed the cheaper iron to cast strong thin pots for domestic use as well as the huge cylinders required by the new steam pumping-engines. In 1779 his son (also Abraham) constructed the world's first iron bridge, over the river Severn at Coalbrookdale.

darcy c.g.s. unit (symbol D) of permeability, used mainly in geology to describe the permeability of rock (for example, to oil, gas, or water).

Dardanelles /,dɑːdə'nelz/ Turkish strait connecting the Sea of Marmara with the Aegean Sea (ancient name Hellespont, Turkish name *Canakkale Boğazi*); its shores are formed by the ◊Gallipoli peninsula on the NW and the mainland of Turkey-in-Asia on the SE. It is 75 km/47 mi long and 5–6 km/3–4 mi wide.

Dar el-Beida /'dɑːr el 'beɪdə/ Arabic name for the port of ◊Casablanca, Morocco.

Dar es Salaam /'dɑːr es sə'lɑːm/ (Arabic 'haven of peace'); chief seaport in Tanzania, on the Indian Ocean, and capital of Tanzania until its replacement by ◊Dodoma in 1974; population (1985) 1,394,000.

Dardanelles

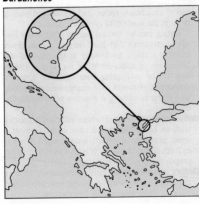

It is the Indian Ocean terminus of the TanZam Railway, and a line also runs to the lake port of Kigoma; a road links it with Ndola in the Zambian copperbelt, and oil is carried to Zambia by pipeline from Dar es Salaam's refineries. University College (1963) became the University of Dar es Salaam in 1970.

Darfur /dɑː'fʊə/ province in the west of the Republic of Sudan; area 196,555 sq km/75,920 sq mi; population (1983) 3,093,699. The capital is El Fasher (population 30,000). The area is a vast rolling plain producing gum arabic, and there is also some stock raising. Darfur was an independent sultanate until conquered by Egypt in 1874.

Darien /'deəriən/ former name for the Panama isthmus as a whole, and still the name of an eastern province of Panama; area 16,803 sq km/6,490 sq mi; population (1980) 26,500. The *Gulf of Darien*, part of the Caribbean, lies between Panama and Colombia. The *Darien Gap* is the complex of swamp, jungle and ravines, which long prevented the linking of the North and South American sections of the Pan-American Highway, stretching about 300 km/200 mi between Canitas, Panama, and Chigorodo, Colombia. At the Colombian end is the Great Atrato Swamp, 60 km/35 mi across and over 300 m/1,000 ft deep. The *Darien Expedition* was a Scottish attempt to colonize the isthmus 1698–99, which failed disastrously owing to the climate and Spanish hostility. The British Trans-Americas Expedition, led by John Blashford-Snell, made the first motorized crossing in 1972.

Darío /dæ'riːəʊ/ Rubén. Pen name of Félix Rubén García Sarmiento 1867–1916. Nicaraguan poet. His *Azul/Azure* 1888, a collection of prose and verse influenced by French Symbolism, created a sensation. He went on to establish *modernismo*, the Spanish-American modernist literary movement, and his vitality and eclecticism influenced every poet writing in Spanish after him, both in the New World and in Spain.

Darius I /də'raɪəs/ *the Great* c. 558–486 BC. King of Persia 521–486 BC. A member of a younger branch of the Achaemenid dynasty, he won the throne from the usurper Gaumata (died 522 BC), reorganized the government, and in 512 BC marched against the Scythians, a people north of the Black Sea, and subjugated Thrace and Macedonia.

An expedition in 492 BC to crush a rebellion in Greece failed, and the army sent into Attica 490 BC was defeated at ◊Marathon. Darius had an account of his reign inscribed on the mountain at Behistun, Persia.

Darjeeling /dɑː'dʒiːlɪŋ/ town and health resort in West Bengal, India; situated 2,150 m/7,000 ft above sea level, on the southern slopes of the Himalayas; population (1981) 57,600. It is connected by rail with Calcutta, 595 km/370 mi to the south. It is the centre of a tea-producing district.

Darkhan /dɑː'kɑːn/ or *Darhan* industrial town in Outer Mongolia, near the border with the USSR; population (1988) 80,000. Cement and bricks are made, and to the south is Erdenet, where copper and molybdenum are mined.

Darlan /dɑː'lɒn/ Jean François 1881–1942. French admiral and politician. He entered the navy 1899, and was appointed admiral and commander in chief 1939. He commanded the French navy 1939–40, took part in the evacuation of Dunkirk, and entered the Pétain cabinet as naval minister. In 1941 he was appointed vice-premier, and became strongly anti-British and pro-German, but in 1942 he was dropped from the cabinet by Laval and sent to N Africa, where he was assassinated.

Darling /'dɑːlɪŋ/ river in SE Australia, a tributary of the Murray, which it joins at Wentworth. It is 3,075 km/1,910 mi long and its waters are conserved in Menindee Lake 155 sq km/60 sq mi, and others nearby. The name comes from Sir Ralph Darling (1775–1858), governor of New South Wales 1825–31. The *Darling Range*, a ridge in W Australia, has a highest point of about 582 m/1,669. The *Darling Downs* in SE Queensland is an agricultural and stockraising area.

Darling /'dɑːlɪŋ/ Grace 1815–1842. British heroine. She was the daughter of a lighthouse keeper on the Farne Islands, off Northumberland. On 7 Sept 1838 the *Forfarshire* was wrecked, and Grace Darling and her father rowed through a storm to the wreck, saving nine lives. She was awarded a medal for her bravery.

Darlington /'dɑːlɪŋtən/ town in Durham, England, on the river Skerne, near its junction with the Tees; population (1981) 85,400. It has coal and ironstone mines, and produces iron and steel goods, and knitting wool. The world's first passenger railway was opened between Darlington and Stockton on 27 Sept 1825.

Darmstadt /'dɑːmstæt/ town in the *Land* of Hessen, West Germany, 29 km/18 mi south of Frankfurt-am-Main; population (1988) 134,000. Industries include iron founding, and the manufacture of chemicals, plastics, and electronics. It is a centre of the European space industry. It has a ducal palace and a technical university.

Darnley /'dɑːnli/ Henry Stewart or Stuart, Lord Darnley 1545–1567. British aristocrat, second husband of Mary Queen of Scots from 1565, and father of James I of England (James VI of Scotland). On the advice of her secretary, David ◊Rizzio, Mary refused Darnley the crown matrimonial; in revenge Darnley led a band of nobles who murdered Rizzio in Mary's presence. Darnley was assassinated 1567.

He was born in England, the son of the 4th Earl of Lennox (1516–71) and Lady Margaret Douglas (1515–78), through whom he inherited a claim to the English throne. Mary was his first cousin. Mary and Darnley were reconciled after the murder of Rizzio 1566, but soon Darnley alienated all parties and a plot to kill him was formed by ◊Bothwell. Mary's part in it remains a subject of controversy.

Darrow /'dærəʊ/ Clarence (Seward) 1857–1938. US lawyer, born in Ohio, a champion of liberal causes and defender of the underdog. He defended many trade-union leaders, including Eugene ◊Debs 1894. He was counsel for the defence in the Nathan Leopold and Richard Loeb murder trial in Chicago 1924, and in the ◊Scopes monkey trial. He was an opponent of capital punishment.

CHARLES ROBERT DARWIN, LL.D., F.R.S.

In his *Descent of Man* he brought his own Species down as low as possible—*i.e.*, to "A Hairy Quadruped furnished with a Tail and Pointed Ears, and probably *Arboreal* in its habits"—which is a reason for the very general Interest in a "Family Tree." He has lately been turning his attention to the "Politic Worm."

Darwin Cartoon of Charles Robert Darwin by Linley Sambourne.

Dart /dɑːt/ Raymond 1893–1988. Australian anthropologist. He discovered the fossil remains of the 'southern African ape' *Australopithecus africanus* 1924, near Taungs in Botswana.

Dartford /'dɑːtfəd/ industrial town in Kent, England, 27 km/17 mi SE of London; population (1981) 42,000. Cement, chemicals, and paper are manufactured. The *Dartford Tunnel* (1963) runs under the Thames to Purfleet, Essex.

Dartmoor /'dɑːtmʊə/ plateau of SW Devon, England, over 1,000 sq km/400 sq mi in extent, of which half is some 300 m/1,000 ft above sea level. Most of Dartmoor is a National Park. The moor is noted for its wild aspect, and rugged blocks of granite, or 'tors', crown its higher points, the highest being *Yes Tor* 618 m/2,028 ft and *High Willhays* 621 m/2,039 ft. Devon's chief rivers have their sources on Dartmoor. There are numerous prehistoric remains. Near Hemerdon there are tungsten reserves.

Dartmoor Prison, opened in 1809 originally to house French prisoners-of-war, is at Princetown in the centre of the moor, 11 km/7 mi east of Tavistock.

Dartmouth /'dɑːtməθ/ English seaport at the mouth of the river Dart; 43 km/27 mi east of Plymouth, on the Devon coast; population (1981) 62,298. It is a centre for yachting, and has an excellent harbour. The Britannia Royal Naval College dates from 1905.

Dartmouth /'dɑːtməθ/ port in Nova Scotia, Canada, on the NE of Halifax harbour; population (1986) 65,300. It is virtually part of the capital city itself. Industries include oil refining and shipbuilding.

darts indoor game played on a circular board. Darts (like small arrow shafts) about 13 cm/5 in long are thrown at segmented targets and score points according to their landing place.

The game is possibly derived from target practice with broken arrow-shafts in days when archery was a compulsory military excercise for all. The pilgrims are believed to have played darts aboard the *Mayflower* in 1620. The present-day numbering system was designed by Brian Gamlin of Bury, Lancashire, England, in 1896.

Darts: World Champions

1980	Eric Bristow (England)
1981	Eric Bristow (England)
1982	Jocky Wilson (Scotland)
1983	Keith Deller (England)
1984	Eric Bristow (England)
1985	Eric Bristow (England)
1986	Eric Bristow (England)
1987	John Lowe (England)
1988	Bob Anderson (England)
1989	Jocky Wilson (Scotland)

Darwin /'dɑːwɪn/ capital and port in Northern Territory, Australia, in NW Arnhem Land; population (1986) 69,000. It serves the uranium mining site at Rum Jungle to the south. Destroyed 1974 by a cyclone, the city was rebuilt on the same site.

Darwin is the north terminus of the rail line from Birdum; commercial fruit and vegetable growing is being developed in the area. Founded 1869, under the name of Palmerston, the city was renamed after Charles Darwin 1911.

Darwin /'dɑːwɪn/ Charles Robert 1809–1882. English scientist who developed the modern theory of ◊evolution and proposed the principle of ◊natural selection. After research in South America and the Galápagos Islands as naturalist on HMS *Beagle* 1831–36, Darwin published *On the Origin of Species by Means of Natural Selection or the Preservation of Favoured Races in the Struggle for Life* 1859. This explained the evolutionary process through the principles of natural and sexual selection, refuting earlier theories. It aroused bitter controversy because it disagreed with the literal interpretation of the Book of Genesis in the Bible.

Darwin /'dɑːwɪn/ Erasmus 1731–1802. British poet, physician, naturalist, and grandfather of Charles Darwin. He wrote *The Botanic Garden* 1792, which included a versification of the Linnaean system 'The Loves of the Plants', and *Zoonomia* 1794–96, which anticipated aspects of evolutionary theory, but tended to ◊Lamarck's interpretation.

Darwinism, social in US history, an influential social theory, drawing on the work of Charles Darwin and Herbert Spencer, which claimed to offer a scientific justification for late 19th-century *laissez-faire* capitalism (the principle of unrestricted freedom in commerce).

Popularized by academics and by entrepreneurs like Andrew ◊Carnegie, social Darwinism naturalized competitive individualism and a market economy unregulated by government.

Dasam Granth a collection of the writings of the tenth Sikh guru (teacher), Gobind Singh, and of poems by a number of other writers. It is written in a script called Gurmukhi, the written form of Punjabi popularized by Guru Angad. It contains a retelling of the Krishna legends, devotional verse, and diverting anecdotes.

Dasht-e-Kavir Desert /'dæʃti kæ'vɪə/ or Dasht-i-Davir Desert. Salt desert SE of Tehran, Iran; US forces landed here in 1980 in an abortive mission to rescue hostages held at the American Embassy in Tehran.

Das Kapital an exposition of Karl Marx's theories of economic production, published in three volumes 1867–95. It focuses on the exploitation of the worker and appeals for a classless society where the production process is shared equally.

dasyure type of ◊marsupial, also known as a 'native cat', found in Australia and New Guinea. Various species have body lengths from 25 cm/10 in to 75 cm/2.5 ft. They have long, bushy tails and dark coats with white spots. They are agile, nocturnal carnivores, able to move fast and climb.

data facts, figures, and symbols, especially as stored in computers. The term is often used to mean raw, unprocessed facts, as distinct from information, to which a meaning or interpretation has been applied.

database in computing, a structured collection of data. The database makes data available to the various programs that need it, without those programs needing to be aware of how the data are actually stored. There are three main types (or 'models'): hierarchical, network, and ◊relational, of which relational is the most widely used. A *free-text database* is one that holds the text of articles or books in a form that permits rapid searching.

A telephone directory stored as a database might allow all the people whose names start with the letter B to be selected by one program, and all those living in London by another. A collection of databases is known as a *databank*.

A database-management system (DBMS) program ensures that the integrity of the data is maintained by controlling the degree of access of the ◊application programs using the data. Databases are normally used by large organizations with mainframes or minicomputers.

data compression in computing, techniques for reducing the amount of storage needed for a given amount of data. They include word tokenization (where frequently used words are stored as shorter codes), variable bit lengths (where common characters are represented by fewer ◊bits than less common ones), and run-length encoding (where a repeated value is stored once along with a count).

data-flow diagram in computing, a diagram illustrating the route taken by data through the various programs in an application.

data processing (DP) the use of computers for performing clerical tasks such as stock control, payroll, and dealing with orders. DP systems are typically ◊batch systems, running on mainframe computers. DP is sometimes called EDP (electronic data processing).

A large organization usually has a special department to support its DP activities, which might include the writing and maintenance of software (programs), control and operation of the computers, and an analysis of the organization's information requirements.

data protection the safeguarding of information about individuals stored on computers, ensuring privacy. The Council of Europe adopted in 1981 a Data Protection Convention, which led in the UK to the Data Protection Act 1984. This requires computer databases containing personal information to be registered, and users to process only accurate information and to retain the information only for a necessary period and for specified purposes. Subject to certain exemptions, individuals have a right of access to their personal data and to have any errors corrected.

date palm of the genus *Phoenix*. The female tree produces the fruit, dates, in bunches weighing 9–11 kg/20–25 lb.

Dates are an important source of food in the Middle East, being rich in sugar; they are dried for export. The tree also supplies timber, and materials for baskets, rope, and animal feed. The most important species is *Phoenix dactylifera*; native to North Africa, SW Asia, and parts of India, it grows up to 25 m/80 ft high.

dating the science of determining the age of geological structures, rocks, and fossils, and placing them in the context of geological time.

Dating can be carried out by identifying fossils of creatures that lived only at certain times (marker fossils), by looking at the physical relationships of rocks to other rocks of a known age, or by measuring how much of a rock's radioactive elements have changed since the rock was formed, using the process of ◊radiometric dating.

dative in the grammar of certain inflected languages such as Latin, the dative case is the form of a noun, pronoun, or adjective used when it is the indirect object of a verb. It is also used with some prepositions.

Datura genus of plants, family Solanaceae, such as the thorn apple, with handsome trumpet-shaped blooms. They have narcotic properties.

Daudet /'dəʊdeɪ/ Alphonse 1840–1897. French novelist. He wrote about his native Provence in *Lettres de mon moulin/Letters from My Mill* 1866, and created the character Tartarin, a hero epitomizing southern temperament, in *Tartarin de Tarascon* 1872 and two sequels.

Daudet /'dəʊdeɪ/ Léon 1867–1942. French writer and journalist, who founded the militant right-wing royalist periodical *Action française* in 1899 after the ◊Dreyfus case. During World War II he was a collaborator with the Germans. He was the son of Alphonse Daudet.

Daugavpils /'daʊgəfpɪlz/ (Russian *Dvinsk*) town in Latvia, USSR, on the river Daugava (west Dvina); population (1985) 124,000. A fortress of the Livonian Knights 1278, it became the capital of Polish ◊Livonia. Industries include timber, textiles, engineering and food products.

Daulaghiri /,daʊlə'gɪərɪ/ a mountain in the ◊Himalayas, NW of Pokhara, Nepál; it rises to 8172 m/2,681 ft.

Daumier /,dəʊmi'eɪ/ Honoré 1808–1879. French artist. His sharply dramatic and satirical cartoons dissected Parisian society. His output was enormous and included 4,000 lithographs and, mainly after 1860, powerful satirical oil paintings that were little appreciated in his lifetime.

Daumier drew for *La Caricature*, *Charivari*, and other periodicals. He created several fictitious stereotypes of contemporary figures, and was once imprisoned for an attack on Louis Philippe. His paintings show a fluent technique and mainly monochrome palette. He also produced sculptures of his caricatures, such as the bronze statuette of *Ratapoil* about 1850 (Louvre, Paris).

dauphin title of the eldest son of the kings of France, derived from the personal name of a count, whose lands, the *Dauphiné* (capital Grenoble), traditionally passed to the heir to the throne from 1349 to 1830.

Dauphiné /daʊfi:'neɪ/ ancient province of France, comprising the *départements* of Isère, Drôme, and Hautes-Alpes.

After the collapse of the Roman Empire it belonged to Burgundy, then was under Frankish domination. Afterwards part of Arles, it was sold by its ruler to France in 1349, and thereafter was used as the personal fief of the heir to the throne (the dauphin) until 1560, when it was absorbed into the French kingdom. The capital was Grenoble.

Davao /'da:vaʊ/ town in the Philippine Republic, at the mouth of the Davao river on the island of Mindanao; population (1980) 611,310. It is the capital of Davao province. It is the centre of a fertile district and trades in pearls, copra, rice and corn.

Davenant /'dævənənt/ William 1606–1668. English poet and dramatist, Poet Laureate from 1638. His *Siege of Rhodes* 1656 is sometimes considered the first English opera. He was rumoured to be an illegitimate son of Shakespeare.

Daventry /'dævəntrɪ/ town in Northamptonshire, England, 19 km/12 mi W of Northampton; population (1981) 16,200. Because of its central position, it became in 1925 the site of the BBC high-power radio transmitter. Originally specializing in footwear manufacture, it received London and Birmingham overspill from the 1950s, and developed varied light industries.

David /'deɪvɪd/ *c.* 1060–970 BC. Second king of Israel. According to the Bible he played the harp for King Saul to banish his melancholy, and later slew the Philistine giant Goliath with a sling and stone. After Saul's death David was anointed king at Hebron, took Jerusalem, and made it his capital.

David probably wrote a few of the psalms and was celebrated as a secular poet. David was the youngest son of Jesse of Bethlehem. While still a shepherd boy he was anointed by Samuel, a judge who ruled Israel before Saul. Saul's son Jonathan became David's friend, but Saul, jealous of his prowess, schemed to murder him. David married

Davis US politician Jefferson Davis who became President of the American Confederacy 1861–65 during the civil war.

Michal, Saul's daughter, but after further attempts on his life went into exile until Saul and Jonathan fell in battle with the Philistines at Gilboa. Once David was king, Absalom, his favourite son, led a rebellion but was defeated and killed. David sent Uriah (a soldier in his army) to his death in the front line of battle in order that he might marry his widow, Bathsheba. Their son Solomon later became king.

In both Jewish and Christian belief, the messiah would be a descendant of David; Christians hold this prophecy to have been fulfilled by Jesus.

David /'deɪvɪd/ Elizabeth 1914– . British cookery writer. Her *Mediterranean Food* 1950 and *French Country Cooking* 1951 helped to spark an interest in foreign cuisine in Britain, and also inspired a growing school of informed, highly literate writing on food and wine.

David /dæ'vi:d/ Félicien César 1810–1876. French composer. His symphonic fantasy *Desert* 1844 was inspired by travels in Palestine. He was one of the first Western composers to introduce oriental scales and melodies into his music.

David /dæ'vi:d/ Gerard *c.*1450–1523. Netherlandish painter active chiefly in Bruges from about 1484. His style follows that of van der Weyden, but he was also influenced by the new taste in Antwerp for Italianate ornament. *The Marriage at Cana* about 1503 (Louvre, Paris) is an example of his work.

David /dæ'vi:d/ Jacques Louis 1748–1825. French painter in the Neo-Classical style. He was an active supporter of and unofficial painter to the republic during the French Revolution, for which he was imprisoned 1794–95. He was later appointed court painter to the emperor Napoleon, of whom he created well-known images such as the horseback figure of *Napoleon Crossing the Alps* 1800 (Louvre, Paris).

He won the Prix de Rome 1774 and studied in Rome 1776–80. Back in Paris, his strongly Classical themes and polished style soon earned success; a picture from this period is *The Oath of the Horatii* 1784 (Louvre, Paris). During the Revolution he was elected to the Convention and a member of the Committee of Public Safety, and narrowly escaped the guillotine. In his *Death of Marat* 1793, he turned political murder into a classical tragedy. Later he devoted himself to the empire in paintings like the enormous, pompous *Coronation of Napoleon* 1805–07 (Louvre, Paris). After Napoleon's fall, David was banished by the Bourbons and settled in Brussels.

David /'deɪvɪd/ two kings of Scotland:

David I 1084–1153. King of Scotland from 1124. The youngest son of Malcolm III Canmore and St ◊Margaret, he was brought up in the English court of Henry I, and in 1113 married Matilda,

Davis Hollywood legend Bette Davis.

widow of the 1st earl of Northampton. He invaded England 1138 in support of Queen ◊Matilda, but was defeated at Northallerton in the Battle of the Standard, and again 1141.

David II 1324–1371. King of Scotland from 1329, son of ◊Robert I (the Bruce). David was married at the age of four to Joanna, daughter of Edward II of England. In 1346 David invaded England, was captured at the battle of Neville's Cross and imprisoned for 11 years.

After the defeat of the Scots by Edward III at Halidon Hill, David and Joanna were sent to France for safety. They returned 1341. On Joanna's death 1362 David married Margaret Logie, but divorced her 1370.

David Copperfield a novel by Charles Dickens, published 1849–50. The story follows the orphan David Copperfield from his schooldays and early poverty to eventual fame as an author. Among the characters he encounters are Mr Micawber, Mr Peggotty, and Uriah Heep.

David, St /'deɪvɪd/ or *Dewi* 5th–6th century. Patron saint of Wales, Christian abbot and bishop. According to legend he was the son of a prince of Cardiganshire and uncle of King Arthur, and responsible for the adoption of the leek as the national emblem of Wales, but his own emblem is a dove. Feast day 1 Mar.

Tradition has it that David made a pilgrimage to Jerusalem, where he was consecrated bishop. He founded 12 monasteries in Wales, including one at Menevia, which he made his bishop's seat; he presided over a synod at Brefi and condemned the ideas of the British theologian Pelagius.

Davidson /'deɪvɪdsən/ John 1857–1909. Scottish poet whose modern, realistic idiom, as in 'Thirty Bob a Week', influenced T S ◊Eliot.

Davies /'deɪvɪs/ Henry Walford 1869–1941. English composer and broadcaster. From 1934 he was Master of the King's Musick, and he contributed to the musical education of Britain through his radio talks.

His compositions include the cantata *Everyman* 1904, the 'Solemn Melody' 1908 for organ and strings, chamber music, and part songs.

Davies /'deɪvɪs/ Peter Maxwell 1934– . English composer and conductor. His music combines medieval and serial codes of practice with a heightened Expressionism as in his opera *Taverner* 1962–68.

After training alongside the British composers Goehr and Birtwistle, he studied with Petrassi and later with the US composer Sessions. He has composed music-theatre works for the group the Pierrot Players, later the Fires of London. He moved to Orkney in the 1970s where he has done much to revitalize music, composing for local groups and on local themes.

Davies /'deɪvɪs/ Robertson 1913– . Canadian novelist. He gained an international reputation with *Fifth Business* 1970, the first novel of his Deptford trilogy, a panoramic work blending philosophy, humour, the occult, and ordinary life.

Davis *Steve Davis playing in the World Snooker Championships, 1981.*

Other works include *A Mixture of Frailties* 1958, *The Rebel Angels* 1981, and *What's Bred in the Bone* 1986.

Davies /'deɪvɪs/ W(illiam) H(enry) 1871–1940. Welsh poet, born in Monmouth. He went to the USA where he lived the life of a hobo, or vagrant, and lost his right foot 'riding the rods'. His first volume of poems was *Soul's Destroyer* 1906. He published his *Autobiography of a Super-Tramp* 1908.

Da Vinci see ◊Leonardo da Vinci, Italian Renaissance artist.

Davis /'deɪvɪs/ Angela 1944– . US left-wing activist for black rights, prominent in the student movement of the 1960s. In 1970 she went into hiding after being accused of supplying guns used in the murder of a judge who had been seized as a hostage in an attempt to secure the release of three black convicts (known as the **Soledad brothers** from the name of their prison). She was captured, tried, and acquitted. In 1980 she stood as the Communist vice-presidential candidate.

At the University of California she studied under Marcuse, and was assistant professor of philosophy at UCLA 1969–70.

Davis /'deɪvɪs/ Bette 1908–1989. US actress. She entered films in 1930, and established a reputation with *Of Human Bondage* 1934 as a forceful dramatic actress. Later films included *Dangerous* 1935 and *Jezebel* 1938, both winning her Academy Awards, and *Whatever Happened to Baby Jane?* 1962.

Davis /'deɪvɪs/ Colin 1927– . English conductor. He was musical director at Sadler's Wells 1961–65, chief conductor of the BBC Symphony Orchestra 1967–71, musical director of the Royal Opera 1971–86, and chief conductor of the Bavarian Radio Symphony Orchestra 1983.

Davis /'deɪvɪs/ Jefferson 1808–1889. US politician, president of the short-lived Confederate States of America 1861–65. He was a leader of the

Davis *US jazz trumpeter, composer and band leader Miles Davis was one of the originators of cool jazz.*

Davison *Militant suffragette Emily Davison, who was trampled on and killed by the King's horse at the Epsom Derby in 1913.*

Southern Democrats in the US Senate from 1857, and a defender of 'humane' slavery; in 1860 he issued a declaration in favour of secession from the USA. During the Civil War he assumed strong political leadership, but often disagreed with military policy. He was imprisoned for two years after the war, one of the few cases of judicial retribution against Confederate leaders.

Born in Kentucky, he served in the US army before becoming a cotton planter in Mississippi. He sat in the US Senate 1847–51, was secretary of war 1853–57, and returned to the Senate 1857.

Davis /'deɪvɪs/ Joe 1901–1978. British billiards and snooker player. World snooker champion a record 15 times 1927–46, he was responsible for much of the popularity of the modern game. His brother Fred was also a billiards and snooker world champion.

Davis /'deɪvɪs/ John 1550–1605. English navigator and explorer. He sailed in search of the Northwest Passage through the Canadian Arctic to the Pacific Ocean 1585, and in 1587 sailed to Baffin Bay through the straits named after him. He was the first European to see the Falkland Islands 1592.

Davis /'deɪvɪs/ Miles (Dewey Jr) 1926– . US jazz trumpeter, composer, and band leader. He recorded bebop with Charlie Parker 1945, pioneered cool jazz in the 1950s and jazz-rock fusion from the late 1960s. His influential albums include *Birth of the Cool* 1949, *Sketches of Spain* 1959, and *Bitches' Brew* 1970.

Davis /'deɪvɪs/ Steve 1957– . English snooker player, who has won every major honour in the game since turning professional 1978. He has been world champion six times, including 1989, and has won as many major titles as all the other professionals between them.

Davis won his first major title 1980 when he won the Coral UK Championship. He has also won world titles at Pairs and with the England team. His earnings regularly top £1 million through on- and off-the-table prize money and endorsements.

Davis /'deɪvɪs/ Stuart 1894–1964. US abstract painter. He used hard-edged geometric shapes in primary colours and experimented with collage. In the 1920s he produced paintings of commercial packaging, such as *Lucky Strike* 1921 (Museum

Davy *English chemist Sir Humphry Davy, inventor of the miner's safety lamp.*

of Modern Art, New York), which foreshadow Pop art.

Davis Cup annual lawn-tennis tournament for men's international teams, first held 1900 after Dwight Filley Davis (1879–1945) donated the trophy.

The Davis Cup was held on a challenge basis up to 1971. Since then it has been organized on a knockout basis, with countries divided into zonal groups with a promotion and relegation system.

Davison /'deɪvɪsən/ Emily 1872–1913. English militant suffragette, who died while trying to stop the King's horse at the Derby at Epsom (she was trampled by the horse). She joined the Women's Social and Political Union in 1906 and served several prison sentences for militant action such as stone throwing, setting fire to pillar boxes, and bombing Lloyd George's country house.

Her coffin was carried through London draped in the colours of the suffragette movement, purple, white, and green. It was escorted by 2,000 uniformed suffragettes.

Davisson /'deɪvɪsən/ Clinton 1881–1958. US physicist. He proved the French nuclear scientist de Broglie's theory that electrons, and therefore all matter, have wave structure. G P ◊Thomson carried through the same research independently, and in 1937 the two men shared a Nobel prize.

Davitt /'dævɪt/ Michael 1846–1906. Irish Fenian revolutionary. He joined the Fenians (forerunners of the Irish Republican Army) 1865, and was imprisoned for treason 1870–77. After his release, he and Charles Parnell founded the Land League 1879. Davitt was jailed several times for his share in the land-reform agitation. He was a Member of Parliament 1895–99.

Davos /dɑːˈvəʊs/ town in an Alpine valley in Grisons canton, Switzerland; at 1,559 m/5,115 ft above sea level; population (1980) 10,500. It is recogniZed as a health resort and as a winter sports centre.

Davy /'deɪvi/ Humphry 1778–1829. English chemist. As a laboratory assistant in Bristol in 1799, he discovered the respiratory effects of laughing gas (nitrous oxide). He discovered, by electrolysis, the elements sodium, potassium, calcium, magnesium, strontium, and barium. He invented the 'safety lamp' for use in mines where methane was present, enabling the miners to work in previously unsafe conditions.

In 1802 he became professor at the Royal Institution, London. He was elected President of the Royal Society in 1820.

Davy Jones personification of a malignant spirit of the sea. The phrase 'gone to Davy Jones's locker' is applied by sailors to those drowned at sea.

DDT

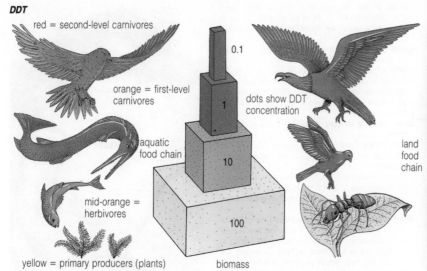

red = second-level carnivores
orange = first-level carnivores
dots show DDT concentration
0.1
1
10
100
aquatic food chain
land food chain
mid-orange = herbivores
yellow = primary producers (plants)
biomass

Deakin *Alfred Deakin was a leading figure in the negotiations to establish the Australian Commonwealth, and in drafting the constitution.*

Dawes /dɔːz/ Charles Gates 1865–1951. US Republican politician. In 1923 he was appointed by the Allied Reparations Commission president of the committee that produced the ***Dawes Plan***, a $200 million loan that enabled Germany to pay enormous war debts after World War I. It was superseded by the Young Plan (which reduced the total reparations bill) 1929. Dawes was elected vice president of the USA 1924, received the Nobel Peace Prize 1925, and was ambassador to Britain 1929–32.

Dawkins /ˈdɔːkɪnz/ Richard 1941– . British zoologist, whose book *The Selfish Gene* 1976 popularized the theories of ◊sociobiology. A second book, *The Blind Watchmaker* 1986, explains the modern theory of evolution.

dawn raid in business, sudden and unexpected buying of a significant proportion of a company's shares, usually as a prelude to a takeover bid. The aim is to prevent the target company having time to organize opposition to the takeover. In the UK the number of shares bought is often just below 5%, the figure above which the ownership of a block of shares must be disclosed under the Companies Act 1985.

Dawson /ˈdɔːsən/ Peter 1882–1961. Australian baritone, remembered for his singing of marching songs and ballads.

Dawson City /ˈdɔːsən/ town in Canada, capital until 1953 of ◊Yukon Territory, at the junction of the Yukon and Klondike rivers; population (1986) 1,700. It was founded 1896, at the time of the Klondike gold rush, when its population was 25,000.

Dawson Creek /ˈdɔːsən/ town in British Columbia, Canada; population (1981) 11,500. It is the SE terminus of the Alaska Highway.

day the time taken for the Earth to rotate once on its axis. The ***solar day*** is the time that the Earth takes to rotate once relative to the Sun. It is divided into 24 hours, and is the basis of our civil day. The ***sidereal day*** is the time that the Earth takes to rotate once relative to the stars. It is 3 minutes 56 seconds shorter than the solar day, because the Sun's position against the background of stars as seen from Earth changes as the Earth orbits it.

Day /deɪ/ Doris. Stage name of Doris von Kappelhoff 1924– . US film actress and singing star of the 1950s and early 1960s, mostly in musicals and, later, rather coy sex comedies. Her films include *Tea for Two* 1950, *Calamity Jane* 1953, and *Lover Come Back* 1962.

Day /deɪ/ Robin 1923– . British broadcasting journalist. A barrister, he pioneered the probing political interview, notably when he questioned

Harold Macmillan on the composition of his cabinet in 1958. Knighted 1981.

Dayak several indigenous peoples of Indonesian Borneo and Sarawak, including the Bahau of central and E Borneo, the Land Dayak of SW Borneo, and the Iban of Sarawak. Their language belongs to the Austronesian family.

Dayan /daɪˈæn/ Moshe 1915–1981. Israeli general and politician. As minister of defence 1967 and 1969–74, he was largely responsible for the victory in the 1967 Six-Day War (see ◊Arab-Israeli Wars), but was criticized for Israel's alleged unpreparedness in the 1973 October War, and resigned with Golda Meir. Foreign minister from 1977, he resigned in 1979 in protest over the refusal of the Begin government to negotiate with the Palestinians.

Day Lewis /ˈdeɪ ˈluːɪs/ Cecil 1904–1972. Irish poet, British poet laureate 1968–1972. With Auden and Spender, he was one of the influential left-wing poets of the 1930s. He also wrote detective novels under the pseudonym ***Nicholas Blake***.

Born at Ballintubber, Ireland, he was educated at Oxford and then taught at Cheltenham College 1930–35. His work, which includes *From Feathers to Iron* 1931, and *Overtures to Death* 1938, is marked by accomplished lyrics and sustained narrative power. Professor of poetry at Oxford 1951–56, he published critical works and translations from Latin of Virgil's *Georgics* and *Aeneid*. In 1968 he succeeded Masefield as poet laureate. His autobiography, *The Buried Day* 1960, was followed by a biography written by his eldest son Sean 1980.

Dayton /ˈdeɪtn/ city in Ohio, USA; population (1980) 830,000. It produces precision machinery, household appliances, and electrical equipment. It has an aeronautical research centre and a Roman Catholic university, and was the home of aviators Wilbur and Orville Wright.

Dayton /ˈdeɪtn/ small town in Tennessee, USA, notorious as the scene of the ◊Scopes monkey trial 1925.

Daytona Beach /deɪˈtəʊnə/ US resort on the Atlantic coast of Florida; population (1980) 54,176. It is a motor-racing centre.

Dazai /ˈdɑːzaɪ/ Osamu, pen name of Shuji Tsushima 1909–1948. Japanese novelist. The title of his novel *The Setting Sun* 1947 became in Japanese synonymous with the dead of World War II. He committed suicide.

dBASE a family of microcomputer programs for manipulating large quantities of data; also, a related ◊fourth-generation language. The first version, dBASE II, appeared in the early 1980s, since when it has become widely used.

DBE abbreviation for ***Dame Commander of the Order of the British Empire***.

DC in music, the abbreviation for ***da capo*** (Italian 'from the beginning'); in physics, the abbreviation for ***direct current*** (electricity).

DD abbreviation for ***Doctor of Divinity***.

D-day 6 June 1944, the day the Allied invasion of Europe took place during World War II. The landings took place on the Normandy coast of France and began the campaign to liberate Europe. D-day was originally fixed for 5 June, but because of unfavourable weather the invasion was postponed for 24 hours. D-day is also military jargon for any day on which a crucial operation is planned.

DDT abbreviation for ***dichloro-diphenyl-trichloroethane*** an insecticide discovered in 1939 by Swiss chemist Paul Müller. It is useful in the control of insects that spread malaria, but resistant strains develop. DDT is highly toxic, and persists in the environment and in living tissue. Its use is now banned in most countries.

DE abbreviation for ◊*Delaware*.

deacon third order of the Christian ministry; in the Anglican Communion a candidate for holy orders is ordained deacon. Male deacons become priests after a year but women do not. In the Presbyterian and Free churches a deacon is a lay assistant.

The lay order of women deaconesses was revived 1962 (legally recognized 1968); in England they may not administer the sacraments, but may conduct public worship and preach. In 1985 the General Synod voted to allow ordination of women as deacons, enabling them to perform marriages and baptisms, but not to take communion or give absolution and the blessing.

Dead Sea large lake, partly in Israel and partly in Jordan; area 1,020 sq km/394 sq mi; lying 394 m/1,293 ft below sea-level. The chief river entering it is the Jordan; it has no outlet to the sea, and the water is very salty.

Since both Israel and Jordan are using the waters of the Jordan river, the Dead Sea is now dried up in the centre and divided into two halves, but in 1980 Israel announced a plan to link it by canal with the Mediterranean. The Dead Sea Rift is part of the fault between the African and Arab plates.

Dead Sea Scrolls collection of ancient scrolls (some intact in their jars) and fragments of scrolls found 1947–56 in caves on the W side of the Jordan 12 km/7 mi S of Jericho and 2 km/1 mi from the N end of the Dead Sea, at ◊Qumran. They date mainly from about 150 BC–AD 68, when the monastic community that owned them was destroyed by the Romans because of its support for a revolt against their rule. They include copies of Old Testament books a thousand years earlier than those previously known to be extant.

deafness lack or deficiency in the sense of hearing, either inborn or caused by injury or disease of the inner ear.

Of assistance are hearing aids, lip-reading, a cochlear implant in the ear in combination with a special electronic processor, sign language (signs for concepts), and 'cued speech' (phonetic).

Deakin /'di:kɪn/ Alfred 1856–1919. Australian Liberal politician, prime minister 1903–04, 1905–08, and 1909–10. In his second administration, he enacted legislation on defence and pensions.

Deal /di:l/ port and resort on the east coast of Kent, England; population (1981) 26,000. It was one of the ◊Cinque Ports. Julius Caesar is said to have landed here in 55 BC. The castle was built by Henry VIII and houses the town museum.

deamination the removal of the amino group (–NH$_2$) from an unwanted ◊amino acid. This is the nitrogen-containing part, and it is converted into ammonia, uric acid, or urea (depending on the type of animal) to be excreted in the urine. In vertebrates, deamination occurs in the ◊liver.

dean *education* in universities and medical schools, the head of administration; in the colleges of Oxford and Cambridge, member of the teaching staff charged with the maintenance of discipline;
Anglican Communion head of the chapter of a cathedral or collegiate church; a rural dean presides over a division of an archdeaconry;
Roman Catholic senior cardinal bishop, head of the college of cardinals.

Dean /di:n/ Basil 1888–1978. British founder and director-general of ◊ENSA 1939, which provided entertainment for the Allied forces in World War II.

Dean /di:n/ James (Byron) 1931–1955. US actor. Killed in a road accident after only his first film, *East of Eden* 1955, had been shown, he posthumously became a cult hero with *Rebel Without a Cause* and *Giant*, both 1956. He became a symbol of teenage rebellion against American middle-class values.

Dearborn /'drəbɔːn/ city in Michigan, USA; on the Rouge river; 16 km/10 mi SW of Detroit; population (1980) 158,366. Settled in 1795, it was the birthplace and home of Henry ◊Ford, who built his first car factory here. Car manufacture is still the main industry. Dearborn also makes aircraft parts, steel, and bricks.

death a permanent ending of all the functions needed to keep an organism alive. Death used to be pronounced when a person's breathing and heartbeat stopped. The advent of mechanical aids has made this point difficult to determine, and a person is now pronounced dead when the brain ceases to control the vital functions.

For a donor in transplant surgery the World Health Organization definition 1968 is that there should be no brain–body connection, muscular activity, blood pressure, or ability to breathe unaided by machine. In religious belief it may be seen as the prelude to rebirth (as in Hinduism and Buddhism); under Islam and Christianity,

there is the concept of a Day of Judgement and consignment to Heaven or Hell; Judaism tends to concentrate more on survival through descendants.

death cap fungus ◊*Amanita phalloides*, the most poisonous mushroom known.

Death of a Salesman 1949 Broadway play by Arthur Miller, the story of the defeated sales representative Willy Loman, which captured the limitations and deceptions of the American dream of success.

death penalty another name for ◊capital punishment.

Death Valley /'deθ 'væli/ depression 225 km/140 mi long and 6–26 km/4–16 mi wide, in SE California, USA. At 85 mi/280 ft below sea level, it is the lowest point in North America. Bordering mountains rise to 3,000 mi/10,000 ft. It is one of the world's hottest places, with an average annual rainfall of 35 mm/1.4 in.

death-watch beetle insect *Xestobium rufovillosum* of the 'woodworm' family. The larvae live in oaks and willows, and can cause damage by boring in old furniture or structural timbers. To attract the female, the male beetle produces a ticking sound by striking his head on a wooden surface, and this is taken by the superstitious as a warning of approaching death.

Deauville /'dəʊvɪl/ holiday resort of Normandy in Calvados *département*, France, on the English Channel and at the mouth of the Touques, opposite Trouville; population (1982) 4,800.

de Bono /də 'bəʊnəʊ/ Edward 1933– . British medical doctor and psychologist, whose concept of lateral thinking, first expounded in *The Use of Lateral Thinking* 1967, involves thinking round a problem rather than tackling it head on.

Deborah in the Old Testament or Jewish Bible, a prophet and judge (leader). She helped lead an Israelite army against the Canaanite general Sisera, who was killed trying to flee; her song of triumph at his death is regarded as an excellent example of early Hebrew poetry.

Debray /də'breɪ/ Régis 1941– . French Marxist theorist. He was associated with Che Guevara in the revolutionary movement in Latin America in the 1960s, and in 1967 was sentenced to 30 years' imprisonment in Bolivia, but was released after three years. His writings on Latin American politics include *Strategy for Revolution* 1970. He became a specialist adviser to President Mitterrand of France on Latin American affairs.

Debrecen /'debrətsen/ third largest city in Hungary, 193 km/120 mi E of Budapest, in the Great Plain (*Alföld*) region; population (1988) 217,000. It produces tobacco, agricultural machinery, and pharmaceuticals. ◊Kossuth declared Hungary independent of the ◊Habsburgs here 1849. It is a commercial centre, and has a university founded 1912.

Debrett /də'bret/ John 1753–1822. English publisher of a directory of the peerage from 1802, baronetage in 1808, and knightage 1866–73/4; the books are still called by his name.

debridement the removal of dead or contaminated tissue from a wound.

de Broglie /də 'brəʊli/ Louis, 7th Duc de Broglie 1892–1987. French theoretical physicist. He established that all subatomic particles can be described either by particle equations or by wave equations, thus laying the foundations of wave mechanics. Nobel prize 1929.

death-watch

Debray *One of the influential theorists of the revolutionary liberation movements in Latin America, Debray was a friend of Che Guevara and was imprisoned in Bolivia in the 1960s.*

de Broglie /də 'brəʊli/ Maurice, 6th Duc de Broglie 1875–1960. French physicist, He worked on X-rays and gamma rays, and helped to establish the Einsteinian description of light in terms of photons. He was the brother of Louis de Broglie.

Debs /debz/ Eugene V(ictor) 1855–1926. US labour leader and socialist, who organized the Social Democratic Party 1897. He was the founder and first president of the American Railway Union in 1893, and was imprisoned for six months in 1894 for defying a federal injunction to end the Pullman strike in Chicago. He was socialist candidate for the presidency in every election from 1900 to 1920, except that of 1916.

Debs was born in Terre Haute, Indiana. He opposed US intervention in World War I and was imprisoned 1918–21 for allegedly advocating resistance to conscription. In 1920 he polled nearly one million votes, the highest socialist vote ever in US presidential elections, despite having to conduct the campaign from a federal penitentiary in Atlanta, Georgia.

debt something that is owed by a person or organization, usually money, goods, or services. Debt usually occurs as a result of borrowing **credit**.
Debt servicing is the payment of interest on a debt. The *national debt* of a country is the total

Dean *The American cult hero James Dean.*

de Broglie *The Nobel prizewinner for physics in 1929, Louis de Broglie was a prominent member of the French Academy of Science.*

money owed by the government to private individuals, banks, and so on; *international debt*, the money owed by one country to another, began on a large scale with the investment in foreign countries by newly industrialized countries in the late 19th–early 20th centuries. International debt became a global problem as a result of the oil crisis of the 1970s.

As a result of the Bretton Woods conference in 1944, the World Bank (officially called the International Bank for Reconstruction and Development) was established in 1945 as an agency of the United Nations to finance international development, by providing loans where private capital was not forthcoming. Loans were made largely at prevailing market rates ('hard loans') and therefore generally to the developed countries, who could afford them.

In 1960 the International Development Association (IDA) was set up as an offshoot of the World Bank to provide interest-free ('soft') loans over a long period to finance the economies of developing countries and assist their long-term development. The resulting cash surpluses of Middle Eastern oil-producing countries was channelled by western banks to Third World countries. However, a slump in the world economy, and rises in interest rates, resulted in the debtor countries paying an ever-increasing share of their national output in *debt servicing* (paying off the interest on a debt, rather than paying off the debt itself). As a result, many loans had to be *rescheduled* (renegotiated so that repayments were made over a longer term). In 1980–81 Poland ceased making repayments on international debts. Today, the countries most at risk include Mexico and Brazil, both of which have a *debt-servicing ratio* (proportion of export earnings which is required to pay off the debt) of more than 50%. In May 1987 the world's largest bank, Citibank of New York, announced that it was writing off $3 billion of international loans, mainly due to Brazil's repeated rescheduling of debt repayments. The dangers of the current scale of international debt (the so-called *debt crisis*) is that the debtor country can only continue to repay its existing debts by means of further loans; for the western countries, there is the possibility of a confidence crisis causing panic withdrawals of deposits and consequent collapse of the banking system.

Major debtor nations

Countries	Total long-term debt as % of GNP		Total long-term debt service as as % of GNP	
	1970	1987	1970	1987
Argentina	23.8	65.5	5.1	5.8
Brazil	12.2	33.7	1.6	3.0
Mexico	16.2	69.6	3.5	8.2
Morocco	18.6	117.9	1.7	8.2
Nigeria	4.3	111.3	0.7	3.9
Philippines	21.8	69.4	4.3	6.9

debt crisis any situation in which an individual, company, or country owes more to others than they can repay or pay interest on; more specifically, to the massive indebtedness of many Third World countries, which became acute in the 1980s, threatening the stability of the international banking system as many debtor countries became unable to service their debts.

debugging finding and removing errors from a computer program or system (see ◊bug).

Debussy /dəˈbuːsi/ (Achille-) Claude 1862–1918. French composer. He broke with the dominant tradition of German Romanticism and introduced new qualities of melody and harmony based on the whole-tone scale, evoking oriental music. His work includes *Prélude à l'après-midi d'un faune* 1894 and the opera *Pelléas et Mélisande* 1902.

Among his other works are numerous piano pieces, songs, orchestral pieces such as *La Mer* 1903–05, and the ballet *Jeux* 1910–13. Debussy also wrote with humour about the music of his day, using the fictional character Monsieur Croche 'anti-dilettante' (professional debunker).

Debye /dəˈbaɪ/ Peter 1884–1966. Dutch physicist. A pioneer of X-ray powder crystallography, he also worked on polar molecules, dipole moments, and molecular structure. Nobel prize 1936.

In 1940, he went to the USA where he was professor of chemistry at Cornell University 1940–52.

decagon ten-sided ◊polygon.

Decalogue the ten commandments that, according to the Bible, were delivered by God to ◊Moses, stated in the Old Testament books Exodus 20:1–17 and Deuteronomy 5:6–21. The Decalogue is recognized as the basis of morality by Jews and Christians.

Decameron, The a collection of tales by the Italian writer Boccaccio, brought together 1348–53. Each of ten young people, fleeing plague-stricken Florence, amuse their fellow travellers by telling a story on each of the ten days they spend together. The work had a great influence on English literature, particularly Chaucer's *Canterbury Tales*.

decathlon a two-day athletic competition for men consisting of ten events: 100 metres, long jump, shot put, high jump, 400 metres (day one); 110 metres hurdles, discus, pole vault, javelin, 1,500 metres (day two). Points are awarded for performances and the winner is the athlete with the greatest aggregate score. The decathlon is an Olympic event.

Decatur /dɪˈkeɪtə/ city in central Illinois, USA, on Lake Decatur, population (1980) 94,000. It has engineering, food processing, and plastics industries. It was founded in 1829 and named after Stephen ◊Decatur.

Decatur /dɪˈkeɪtə/ Stephen 1779–1820. US naval hero who during the war with Tripoli (1801–05), succeeded in burning the *Philadelphia*, which the enemy had captured. During the War of 1812 with Britain, he surrendered only after a desperate resistance in 1814. In 1815, he was active against Algerian pirates. He was killed in a duel. Decatur coined the phrase 'our country, right or wrong'.

decay, radioactive the process of continuous disintegration undergone by the nuclei of radioactive elements, such as radium and various isotopes of uranium and the transuranic elements. The associated radiation consists of alpha-rays, beta-rays, or gamma-rays (or a combination of these), and it takes place with a characteristic half-life, which is the time taken for half of any mass of a radioactive isotope to decay completely.

The original nucleotide is known as the parent substance, and the produce is a daughter nucleotide (which may or may not be radioactive). After a time t, the number of daughter atoms from an original number N of parent atoms is equal to $N \exp(-\lambda t)$, where λ is the decay, or disintegration, constant.

Deccan /ˈdekən/ triangular tableland in eastern India, stretching between the Vindhya Hills in the north, and the Western and Eastern Ghats in the south.

decibel unit (symbol dB), used originally to compare sound densities, and subsequently electrical or electronic power outputs; now also used to compare voltages. An increase of 10 decibels is equivalent to a 10-fold increase in intensity or power, and a 20-fold increase in voltage. A whisper has an intensity of 20 dB; 140 dB (a jet aircraft taking off nearby) is the threshold of pain.

The difference in decibels between two levels of intensity (or power) L_1 and L_2 is $10 \log_{10}(L_1/L_2)$; 1 dB thus corresponds to a change of about 25%. For two voltages V_1 and V_2, the difference in decibels is $20 \log_{10}(V_1/V_2)$; 1dB corresponding in this case to a change of about 12%. Commonly such differences are given now not as ratios but as absolute values, for example 10 dBV corresponds to the voltage level V_1 with V_2 set equal to 1 volt.

deciduous describing trees and shrubs that shed their leaves before the onset of winter or a dry season (see ◊abscission). In temperate regions there is little water available during winter, and leaf-fall is an adaptation to reduce ◊transpiration. Examples of deciduous trees are oak and beech.

Most deciduous trees belong to the ◊angiosperms, and the term 'deciduous tree' is sometimes used to mean 'angiosperm tree', despite the fact that many angiosperms are evergreen, especially in the tropics, and a few ◊gymnosperms (such as larches) are deciduous. The term **broadleaved** is now preferred to 'deciduous' for this reason.

decimal fractions the system of ◊fractions expressed by the use of the decimal point, that is, fractions in which the denominator is any higher power of 10. Thus $3/10$, $51/100$, $23/1,000$ are decimal fractions and are normally expressed as 0.3, 0.51, 0.023. The use of decimals greatly simplifies addition and multiplication of fractions, though not all fractions can be expressed exactly as decimal fractions. The regular use of the decimal point appears to have been introduced about 1585, but the occasional use of decimal fractions can be traced back as far as the 12th century.

decision table in computing, a method of describing a procedure for a program to follow, based on comparing possible decisions and their consequences. It is often used as an aid in systems design.

The top part of the table contains the conditions for making decisions (for example if a number is negative rather than positive and is less than 1), the bottom part describes the outcomes when those conditions are met (then either end or repeat the operation).

Decius /ˈdiːsiəs/ Gaius Messius Quintus Traianus AD 201–251. Roman emperor from 249. He fought a number of campaigns against the ◊Goths but was finally beaten and killed by them near Abritum. He ruthlessly persecuted the Christians.

Declaration of Independence historic US document stating the theory of government on which the USA was founded, based on the right 'to life, liberty, and the pursuit of happiness'. The statement was issued by the American Continental Congress on 4 July 1776, renouncing all allegiance to the British crown and ending the political connection with Britain.

Following a resolution moved on 7 June, 'that these United Colonies are, and of right ought to be, free and independent States', a committee including Thomas Jefferson and Benjamin Franklin was set up to draft a declaration; most of the work was done by Jefferson. The resolution was adopted by the representatives of 12 colonies, New York at first abstaining, on 2 July, and the Declaration on 4 July; the latter date has ever since been celebrated as Independence Day in the USA. The representatives of New York announced their adhesion on 15 July, and the Declaration was afterwards signed by the members of Congress on 2 Aug.

Declaration of Rights in Britain, the statement issued by the Convention Parliament Feb 1689, laying down the conditions under which the crown was to be offered to ◊William III and Mary. Its clauses were later incorporated in the ◊Bill of Rights.

declination in astronomy, the coordinate on the ◊celestial sphere (imaginary sphere surrounding the Earth) that corresponds to latitude on the Earth's surface. Declination runs from 0° at the celestial equator to 90° at the north and south celestial poles.

Decline and Fall of the Roman Empire, The History of the a historical work by Edward Gibbon, published in the UK 1776–88. Arranged in three parts, the work spans 13 centuries and covers the history of the empire from Trajan and the Antonines through to the Turkish seizure of Constantinople in 1453.

decolonization the gradual achievement of independence by former colonies of the European imperial powers which began after the World War I.

decomposer in biology, an organism that feeds on excreta, or dead plant and animal matter. Decomposers include dung-beetle larvae, earthworms, certain bacteria, and fungi. They play a vital role in ecological systems by freeing important chemical substances, such as nitrogen compounds, locked up in dead organisms or excreta.

decomposition the process whereby a chemical compound is reduced to its component substances. In biology, it is the destruction of dead organisms either by chemical reduction or by the action of decomposers.

decompression sickness an illness brought about by a sudden and substantial change in atmospheric pressure. It is caused by a too rapid release of nitrogen which has been absorbed into the bloodstream under pressure. It causes breathing difficulties, joint and muscle pain, and cramp, and is experienced mostly by deep-sea divers who surface too quickly. It is popularly known as 'the bends'. After a one-hour dive at 30 m/100 ft, 40 minutes of decompression are needed, according to US Navy tables.

decontamination factor in radiological protection, a measure of the effectiveness of a decontamination process. It is the ratio of the original contamination to the remaining radiation after decontamination: 1,000 and above is excellent; 10 and below is poor.

Decorated in architecture, the second period of English Gothic, covering the latter part of the 13th century and the 14th century. Chief characteristics include ornate window tracery, the window being divided into several lights by vertical bars called mullions; sharp spires ornamented with crockets and pinnacles; complex church vaulting; and slender arcade piers. Exeter Cathedral is a notable example.

decretal in medieval Europe, a papal ruling on a disputed point, sent to a bishop or abbot in reply to a request or appeal. The earliest dates from Siricius in 385. Later decretals were collected to form a decretum.

decretum a collection of papal decrees. The best known is that collected by Gratian (died 1159) in about 1140, comprising some 4,000 items. The decretum was used as an authoritative source of ◊canon law (the rules and regulations of the church).

Dedekind /'deɪdəkɪnd/ Richard 1831–1916. German mathematician who made contributions to number theory. In 1872, he introduced the *Dedekind cut* (which divides a line of infinite length representing all ◊real numbers) to categorize ◊irrational numbers as fractions, and thus increase their usefulness.

dedicated computer a computer built into another device for the purpose of controlling or supplying information to it. Their use has increased dramatically since the advent of the ◊microprocessor: washing machines, digital watches, cars, and video recorders all have their own processors.

A dedicated system is a general-purpose computer system confined to performing only one function for reasons of efficiency or convenience, for instance, a word processor.

deduction in philosophy, a form of argument in which the conclusion necessarily follows from the premises. It would be inconsistent to accept the premises but deny the conclusion.

Dee /diː/ river in Grampian region, Scotland; length 139 km/87 mi. From its source in the Cairngorms, it flows E into the North Sea at Aberdeen (by an artificial channel). It is noted for salmon fishing. Also a river in Wales and England; length 112 km/70 mi. Rising in Lake Bala, Gwynedd, it flows into the Irish Sea W of Chester. There is another Scottish river Dee (61 km/38 mi) in Kirkcudbright.

Dee /diː/ John 1527–1608. English alchemist, astrologer, and mathematician, who claimed to have transmuted metals into gold, although he died in poverty. He long enjoyed the favour of Elizabeth I, and was employed as a secret diplomatic agent.

Dee *The alchemist, astrologer, and mathematician John Dee.*

deed a legal document that passes an interest in property or binds a person to perform or abstain from some action. Deeds are of two kinds: indenture and deed poll. *Indentures* bind two or more parties in mutual obligations. A *deed poll* is made by one party only, such as when a person changes his or her name.

deep freezing method of preserving food by rapid freezing and storage at –18°C/0°F. Commercial freezing is usually done by one of the following methods: blast, the circulation of air at –40°C/–40°F; contact, in which a refrigerant is circulated through hollow shelves; immersion, for example, fruit in a solution of sugar and glycerol; or cryogenic means, for example, by liquid nitrogen spray.

Rapid freezing avoids structural change that would affect the taste or appearance of the food, as in the shrinkage and distortion of cells by formation of enlarged ice crystals in the extracellular spaces. Some 'quick-frozen' foods require thawing before use, and cooking must then be prompt. *Accelerated freeze drying* (AFD) involves rapid freezing followed by heat drying in a vacuum, for example, prawns for later rehydration. The product does not have to be stored in frozen condition.

Freezing was developed in the late 19th century and found early commercial application in the transportation of large quantities of meat on long sea voyages.

Deep-Sea Drilling Project a research project initiated by the USA in 1968 to sample the rocks of the ocean ◊crust. The operation became international in 1975, when Britain, France, Germany, Japan, and the USSR also became involved.

Over 800 boreholes were drilled in all the oceans using the ship *Glomar Challenger*, and knowledge of the nature and history of the ocean basins was increased dramatically. The technical difficulty of drilling the seabed to a depth of 2,000 m/6,500 ft was overcome by keeping the ship in position with side-thrusting propellers and satellite navigation, and by guiding the drill using a radiolocation system.

deep-sea trench a long and narrow, deep trough (◊ocean trench) in the seafloor, marking the line where one of the plates of the ◊lithosphere is sliding beneath another (see ◊plate tectonics). At this depth (below 6 km/3.6 mi) there is no light and very high pressure; deep-sea trenches are inhabited by crustaceans, coelenterates (for example, sea anemones), polychaetes (a type of worm), molluscs, and echinoderms.

deer ruminant, even-toed, hoofed mammal belonging to the family Cervidae. The male typically has a pair of antlers, shed and regrown each year. Most species of deer are forest-dwellers, and are distributed throughout Europe, Asia, and North America, but absent from Australia and Africa south of the Sahara.

Native to Britain are *red deer Cervus elaphus* and *roe deer Capreolus capreolus*. Red deer are found across Europe and can be 1.2 m/4 ft or more at the shoulder, plain dark brown with yellowish rump, and may have many points to the antlers. The roe deer is smaller, only about 75 cm/2.5 ft at the shoulder, with small erect antlers with three points or fewer. The *fallow deer Dama dama* came originally from the Mediterranean region, but was introduced to Britain in ancient times. It typically has a spotted coat and flattened 'palmate' antlers, and stands about 1 m/3 ft high. The little ◊*muntjac* has been introduced in more recent years from East Asia, and is spreading. Other species in the deer family include the ◊*elk*, ◊*wapiti*, ◊*reindeer*, and the *musk deer Moschus moschiferus* of Central Asia, which yields musk and has no antlers.

deer farming method of producing venison through the controlled breeding and rearing of deer on farms rather than hunting them in the wild. British deer-farming enterprises have been growing in number during the 1980s as more farmers seek to diversify into new sources of income. The meat is sold largely to the restaurant trade, and there is a market also for the antlers and skin.

deerhound large rough-coated dog, formerly used for hunting and killing deer. Slim and long-legged, it is 75 cm/2.5 ft or taller, usually with a bluish-grey coat.

de facto (Latin) in fact.

de Falla Manuel Spanish composer. See ◊Falla, Manuel de.

defamation in law, an attack on a person's reputation by ◊libel or ◊slander. In the UK legal aid is not available in defamation cases but a growing and profitable 'defamation industry' in the tabloid press in the 1980s led to a demand that it should be.

default in commerce, failure to meet an obligation, usually financial.

Defence, Ministry of British government department created 1964 from a temporary Ministry of Defence established after World War II together with the Admiralty, Air Ministry, and War Office. It is headed by the secretary of state for defence with undersecretaries for the Royal Navy, Army, and Royal Air Force. This centralization was influenced by the example of the US Department of ◊Defense.

Defender of the Faith one of the titles of the English sovereign, conferred on Henry VIII 1521 by Pope Leo X in recognition of the king's treatise against the Protestant Luther. It appears on British coins in the abbreviated form *F.D.* (Latin *Fidei Defensor*).

Defense, Department of US government department presided over by a secretary of defence with a seat in the president's cabinet; each of the three services has a civilian secretary, not of cabinet rank, at its head. It was established when the army, navy, and air force were unified by the National Security Act 1947.

defibrillation the use of electrical stimulation to restore a chaotic heart beat to a rhythmical pattern. In fibrillation, which may occur in most kinds of heart disease, the heart muscle quivers instead of beating; the heart is no longer working as a pump. Paddles are applied to the chest wall, and one or more electric shocks are delivered to normalize the beat.

deficit financing in economics, a planned excess of expenditure over income, dictated by government policy, creating a shortfall of public revenue which is met by borrowing. The decision to create a deficit is taken to stimulate an economy by increasing consumer purchasing, and at the same time create more jobs.

deflation in economics, a reduction in the level of economic activity, usually caused by an increase in interest rates and reduction in the money supply,

Defoe *English novelist Daniel Defoe in 1706.*

increased taxation, or a decline in government expenditure.

Deflation may be chosen as an economic policy to improve the balance of payments, through a reduction in demand and therefore of imports, and reducing inflation to stimulate exports. It can reduce wage increases, but may also reduce the level of employment.

Defoe /dɪˈfəʊ/ Daniel 1660–1731. English novelist and journalist, who wrote *Robinson Crusoe* 1719, which was greatly influential in the development of the novel. An active pamphleteer and political critic, he was imprisoned 1702–1704 following publication of the ironic *The Shortest Way With Dissenters*. Fictional works include *Moll Flanders* 1722 and *A Journal of the Plague Year* 1724. Altogether he produced over 500 books, pamphlets, and journals.

Born in Cripplegate, the son of a butcher, James Foe, Defoe was educated for the Nonconformist ministry, but became a hosier. He took part in Monmouth's rebellion, and joined William of Orange 1688. After his business had failed, he held a civil-service post 1695–99. He wrote numerous pamphlets, and first achieved fame with the satire *The True-Born Englishman* 1701, followed in 1702 by the ironic *The Shortest Way with Dissenters*, for which he was fined, imprisoned, and pilloried. In Newgate he wrote his 'Hymn to the Pillory' and started a paper, *The Review* 1704–13. Released in 1704, he travelled in Scotland 1706–07, working to promote the Union, and published *A History of the Union* 1709. During the next ten years he was almost constantly employed as a political controversialist and pamphleteer. His version of the contemporary short story 'True Relation of the Apparition of one Mrs Veal' 1706 had revealed a gift for realistic narrative, and *Robinson Crusoe*, based on the story of Alexander Selkirk, appeared 1719. It was followed among others by the pirate story *Captain Singleton* 1720, and the picaresque *Colonel Jack* 1722 and *Roxana* 1724.

De Forest /də ˈfɒrɪst/ Lee 1873–1961. US physicist who was able to exploit the commercial value of radio. Ambrose ◊Fleming invented the diode valve 1904. De Forest saw that if a third electrode was added, the triode valve could serve as an amplifier and radio communications could become a practical possibility. He patented his discovery 1906.

deforestation the destruction of forest for timber (see ◊forestry) and clearing for agriculture, without planting new trees to replace those lost (reafforestation). Deforestation causes fertile soil to be blown away or washed into rivers, leading to soil ◊erosion, drought, and flooding.

Degas *Woman at her Toilet (c. 1894) Tate Gallery, London.*

As a result of deforestation in the Himalayas, disastrous floods occur in lowland areas of India and Bangladesh. In 1989 Thailand banned all logging in an effort to prevent further decline in forests (which then covered only 18% of land surfaces compared to the 70% forest cover of 1945).

Degas /ˈdeɪɡɑː/ (Hilaire Germain) Edgar 1834–1917. French Impressionist painter and sculptor. He devoted himself to lively, informal studies of ballet, horse racing, and young women working, often using pastels. From the 1890s he turned increasingly to sculpture, modelling figures in wax in a fluent, naturalistic style.

Degas studied under a pupil of Ingres and worked in Italy in the 1850s, painting Classical themes. In 1861 he met Manet, and they developed Impressionism. Degas' characteristic style soon emerged, showing influence of Japanese prints and of photography in inventive compositions and unusual viewpoints. An example of his sculpture is *The Little Dancer* 1881 (Tate Gallery, London).

de Gaulle /də ˈɡəʊl/ Charles 1890–1970. French conservative politician and general. He organized the ◊Free French troops fighting the Nazis 1940–44, was head of the provisional French government 1944–46, and leader of his own Gaullist party. In 1958 the national assembly asked him to form a government during France's economic recovery, and to solve the crisis in Algeria. He was president 1959–69, having changed the constitution.

Born in Lille, he graduated from Saint-Cyr 1911 and was severely wounded and captured by the Germans 1916. In June 1940 he refused to accept the new prime minister Pétain's truce with the Germans, and became leader of the Free French in England. In 1944 he entered Paris in triumph and was briefly head of the provisional government before resigning over the new constitution of the Fourth Republic 1946. In 1947 he founded the Rassemblement du Peuple Français, a non-party constitutional reform movement, and when national bankruptcy and civil war

de Gaulle *French general and wartime leader Charles de Gaulle.*

loomed 1958, de Gaulle was called to form a government.

As premier he promulgated a constitution subordinating the legislature to the presidency, and took office as president 1959. Economic recovery and Algerian independence after a bloody war followed. A nationalist, he opposed 'Anglo-Saxon' influence in Europe. Re-elected president 1965, he violently quelled student demonstrations May 1968 when they were joined by workers. The Gaullist party, reorganized as Union des Democrats pour la Cinquième République, won an overwhelming majority in the elections of the same year. In 1969 he resigned after the defeat of the government in a referendum on constitutional reform. He retired to the village of Colombey-les-Deux-Eglises in NE France.

degaussing neutralization of the magnetic field of a body by encircling it with a conductor through which a current is maintained. Ships were degaussed in World War II to avoid their detonating magnetic mines.

degree in mathematics, a unit of measurement of an angle, written as °. A circle is divided into 360°; a degree is subdivided into 60 minutes. *Temperature* is also measured in degrees, which are divided decimally. See also ◊Celsius and ◊circle.

A quarter-turn (90°) is a right angle; a half-turn (180°) is the angle on a straight line. A degree of latitude is the length along a meridian such that the difference between its north and south ends is 1°. A degree of longitude is the length between two meridians making an angle of 1° at the centre of the Earth.

de gustibus non est disputandum (Latin) there is no accounting for taste.

de Havilland /də ˈhævɪlənd/ Geoffrey 1882–1965. British aircraft designer who designed the Moth, the Mosquito fighter-bomber of World War II, and the postwar Comet—the world's first jet-driven airliner to enter commercial service.

De Havilland /də ˈhævɪlənd/ Olivia 1916– . US actress, a star in Hollywood from the age of 19, when she appeared in *A Midsummer Night's Dream* 1935. She later successfully played more challenging dramatic roles in films such as *Gone with the Wind* 1939, *Dark Mirror* 1946, and *The Snake Pit* 1948.

Dehra Dun /ˈdeərə ˈduːn/ town in Uttar Pradesh, India; population (1981) 220,530. It is the capital of Dehra Dun district. It has a military academy, a forest research institute, and a Sikh temple built in 1699.

dehydration a process to preserve food. Moisture content is reduced to 10–20% in fresh produce, and this provides good protection against moulds. Bacteria are not inhibited by drying, so the quality of raw materials is vital.

The process developed commercially in France about 1795 to preserve sliced vegetables, using a hot-air blast. The earliest large-scale application was to starch products such as pasta, but after 1945 it was extended to milk, potato, soups, instant coffee, and prepared baby and pet foods. A major benefit to food manufacturers is reduction of weight and volume of the food products, lowering distribution cost.

Deighton /ˈdeɪtn/ Len 1929– . British author of spy fiction, including *The Ipcress File* 1963, and the trilogy *Berlin Game, Mexico Set, London Match* 1983–85, featuring the spy Bernard Samson.

Dei gratia (Latin) by the grace of God.

Deimos /ˈdaɪmɒs/ one of the two moons of Mars. It is irregularly shaped, 15 × 12 × 11 km/9 × 7.5 × 7 mi, orbits at a height of 24,000 km/15,000 mi every 1.26 days, and is not as roughly featured as the other moon, Phobos. Deimos was discovered by US astronomer Asaph Hall 1877, and is thought to be an asteroid captured by Mars' gravity.

deindustrialization a decline in the share of manufacturing industries in a country's economy. Typically, industrial plants are closed down and not replaced, and service industries increase.

De Klerk *South African state president and National Party leader F W De Klerk. Since coming to power in 1989 he has embarked on a programme of reform.*

Deirdre /'dɪədri/ in Celtic mythology, beautiful intended bride of ◊Conchobar.

deism belief in a supreme being; but the term usually refers to a movement of religious thought in Britain in the 17th–18th centuries, characterized by belief in the 'religion of nature' as opposed to the religion of Christianity.

The founder of English deism was Lord Herbert of Cherbury (1583–1648), and the chief writers were John Toland (1670–1722), Anthony Collins (1676–1729), Matthew Tindal (1657–1733), Thomas Woolston (1670–1733), and Thomas Chubb (1679–1747). Later, deism came to mean a belief in a personal deity who is distinct from the world and not very intimately interested in its concerns. See also ◊theism.

déjà vu (French 'already seen') the feeling that something encountered for the first time has in fact been seen before.

de jure (Latin) according to law.

Dekker /'dekə/ Thomas *c.* 1572–*c.*1632. English dramatist and pamphleteer, who wrote mainly in collaboration with others. His play *The Shoemaker's Holiday* 1600 was followed by collaborations with Thomas Middleton, John Webster, Philip Massinger, and others. His pamphlets include *The Gull's Hornbook* 1609, a lively satire on the fashions of the day.

Dekker's plays include *The Honest Whore* 1604–05 and *The Roaring Girl* 1611 (both with Middleton), *Sir Thomas Wyat* (with Webster), *Virgin Martyr* 1622 (with Massinger), and *The Witch of Edmonton* 1621 (with Ford and Rowley).

De Klerk /də 'kleək/ F(rederik) W(illem) 1936– . South African National Party politician, president from 1989. Trained as a lawyer, he entered the South African parliament in 1972. He served in the cabinets of B J Vorster and P W Botha 1978–89, and in Feb and Aug 1989 successively replaced Botha as National Party leader and state president. Projecting himself as a pragmatic conservative who sought gradual reform of the apartheid system, he won the Sept 1989 elections for his party, but with a reduced majority. In Feb 1990 he ended the ban on the ◊African National Congress opposition movement and released its effective leader, Nelson Mandela.

Delacroix /ˌdelə'krwɑ/ Eugène 1798–1863. French painter in the Romantic style. His prolific output included religious and historical subjects and portraits of friends, among them the musicians Paganini and Chopin. Against French academic tradition, he evolved a highly coloured, fluid style, as in *The*

Delacroix *A self-portrait by the leader of the French Romantic school.*

Death of Sardanapalus 1827 (Louvre, Paris).

The *Massacre at Chios* 1824 (Louvre, Paris) shows Greeks enslaved by wild Turkish horsemen, a contemporary atrocity (his use of a contemporary theme recalls Géricault's example). His style was influenced by the English landscape painter Constable. Delacroix also produced illustrations from Shakespeare, Dante, and Byron. His *Journal* is a fascinating record of his times.

Delafield /'deləfiːld/ E M, pen name of Edmée Elizabeth Monica de la Pasture 1890–1931. British writer, best remembered for her amusing *Diary of a Provincial Lady* 1931, skilfully exploiting the foibles of middle-class life.

de la Mare /'delə 'meə/ Walter 1873–1956. English poet, best known for his verse for children, such as *Songs of Childhood* 1902, and the novels *The Three Royal Monkeys* 1910 for children and, for adults, *The Memoirs of a Midget* 1921.

His debut, *Songs of Childhood*, appeared under the pseudonym Walter Ramal. Later works include poetry for adults (*The Listeners* 1912 and *Collected Poems* 1942), anthologies (*Come Hither* 1923 and *Behold this Dreamer* 1939), and short stories.

Delane /də'leɪn/ John Thaddeus 1817–1879. British journalist. As editor of *The Times* (1841–77), he first gave it international standing.

de la Ramée /də lɑ: 'rɑːmeɪ/ Louise British novelist who wrote under the name of ◊Ouida.

Delaware

de la Roche /ˌdelə'rɒʃ/ Mazo 1885–1961. Canadian novelist, author of the 'Whiteoaks' family saga.

Delaroche /ˌdelə'rɒʃ/ Paul 1797–1856. French historical artist. His melodramatic, often sentimental, historical paintings achieved great contemporary popularity; an example is *Lady Jane Grey* 1833 (National Gallery, London).

Delaunay /də,ləʊ'neɪ/ Robert 1885–1941. French painter, a pioneer in abstract art. With his wife Sonia ◊Delaunay-Terk he invented *Orphism*, an early variation on Cubism, focusing on the effects of pure colour.

He painted several series, notably *Circular Forms* (almost purely abstract) and *Windows* (inspired by Parisian cityscapes).

Delauney-Terk /də,ləʊ'neɪ/ Sonia 1885–1979. French painter and textile designer born in Russia, active in Paris from 1905. With her husband Robert ◊Delaunay she was a pioneer of abstract art.

De Laurentis /deɪ lɔː'rentɪs/ Dino 1919– . Italian producer. His earlier efforts, including Fellini's *La Strada/The Street* 1954, brought more acclaim than later epics such as *Waterloo* 1970. He then produced a series of Hollywood films: *Death Wish* 1974, *King Kong* (remake) 1976, *Dune* 1984.

Delaware /'deləweə/ state of NE USA; nickname The First State or Diamond State
area 5,300 sq km/2,046 sq mi
capital Dover
towns Wilmington, Newark
physical divided into two physical areas, one hilly and wooded, and the other gently undulating
features one of the most industrialized states; headquarters of the Dupont chemical firm (nylon)
population (1987) 644,000
products dairy, poultry, and market garden produce; chemicals, motor vehicles, textiles
famous people J P Marquand
history the first settlers were Dutch and Swedes about 1638, but in 1664 the area was captured by the British. Delaware was made a separate colony 1702, and organized as a state 1776. It was one of the original 13 states of the USA.

de la Warr /'deləweə/ Thomas West, Baron de la Warr 1577–1618. US colonial administrator, known as Delaware. Appointed governor of Virginia 1609, he arrived 1610 just in time to prevent the desertion of the Jamestown colonists, and by 1611 had reorganized the settlement. Both the river and state are named after him.

Delbruck /'delbrʊk/ Max 1906–1981. German-born US biologist who pioneered techniques in molecular biology, studying genetic changes occurring when viruses invade bacteria. Nobel Prize for medicine 1969.

He fled Nazi Germany in 1937. Switching his research interests from physics to biology he showed in 1943 that when viruses attack bacteria, mutations can occur in both bacteria and virus. In 1946 Delbruck found that when a number of different viruses reproduce inside a bacterium, recombination of viral genetic material can take place to produce 'new' viruses.

Delcassé /ˌdelkæ'seɪ/ Théophile 1852–1923. French politician. He became foreign minister 1898, but had to resign 1905 because of German hostility; he held that post again 1914–15. To a large extent he was responsible for the ◊*Entente Cordiale* with Britain.

delegated legislation in Britain, detailed legislation made by government ministers by means of, for example, statutory instruments and orders, under the authority of acts of Parliament. If a minister acts outside his or her authority (ultra vires), a court may declare the legislation void.

De Lesseps /dəle'seps/ Ferdinand, Vicomte 1805–1894. French engineer, who constructed the ◊Suez Canal 1859–1869. He reluctantly began the ◊Panama Canal 1881, but failed when he tried to construct it without locks.

Delphi *Tholos in the Sanctuary of Athena ('Marmaria') in Delphi, Greece.*

Delft /delft/ town in the Netherlands in the province of S Holland, 14 km/9 mi NW of Rotterdam; population (1984) 87,000. It produces pottery and porcelain. The Dutch nationalist leader William the Silent was murdered here in 1584. It is the birthplace of the artist Vermeer.

Delhi /'deli/ Union Territory of the Republic of India from 1956; capital New Delhi; area 1,500 sq km/579 sq mi; population (1981) 6,196,000. It produces grains, sugar cane, fruits, and vegetables.

Delibes /də'li:b/ (Clament Philibert) Léo 1836–1891. French composer. His works include the ballet *Coppélia* and the opera *Lakma*.

Delilah /də'laɪlə/ in the Old Testament or Jewish Bible, the Philistine mistress of ◊Samson.

deliquescence the phenomenon of a substance absorbing so much moisture from the air that it ultimately dissolves in it to form a solution.

Deliquescent substances make very good drying agents in the bottoms of ◊desiccators. Calcium chloride (CaCl$_2$) is one of the commonest.

delirium a state of confusion in which the subject is incoherent, frenzied, and out of touch with reality. It is often accompanied by delusions or hallucinations.

Delirium may occur in feverish illness, brain disease, and as a result of drug or alcohol intoxication. In chronic alcoholism, attacks of *delirium tremens* (DTs) may persist for several days.

Delius /'di:liəs/ Frederick (Theodore Albert) 1862–1934. English composer. His works include the the opera *A Village Romeo and Juliet* 1901; the choral pieces *Appalachia* 1903, *Sea Drift* 1904, *A Mass of Life* 1905; orchestral works such as *In a Summer Garden* 1908, *A Song of the High Hills* 1911; chamber music; and songs.

Born in Bradford, he tried orange-growing in Florida, before studying music in Leipzig in 1888, where he met Grieg. From 1890 Delius lived mainly in France and in 1903 married the artist Jelka Rosen. Although blind and paralysed for the last ten years of his life, he continued to compose.

Dell /del/ Ethel M(ary) 1881–1939. British writer of romantic fiction. Her commercially successful novels usually included a hero who was ugly: *Way*

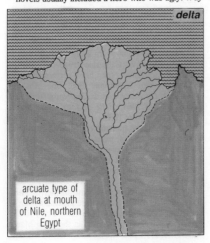

delta

arcuate type of delta at mouth of Nile, northern Egypt

of an Eagle 1912, *The Keeper of the Door* 1915, and *Storm Drift* 1930.

Deller /'delə/ Alfred 1912–1979. English ◊countertenor. He founded the Deller Consort 1950, a group that performed 16th–18th century music.

Delon /də'lɒn/ Alain 1935– . French actor, who appeared in the films *Rocco e i soui Fratelli/Rocco and his Brothers* 1960, *Il Gattopardi/The Leopard* 1963, *Texas across the River* 1966, *Scorpio* 1972, *Swann in Love* 1984.

Delors /də'lɔ:/ Jacques 1925– . French socialist politician, finance minister 1981–84. As president of the European Commission from 1984 he has overseen significant budgetary reform and the move towards a free European Community market in 1992, with increased powers residing in Brussels.

Delors, the son of a Paris banker, worked as social-affairs adviser to Prime Minister Jacques Chaban-Delmas 1969–72 before joining the Socialist Party 1973. He served as minister of economy and finance (and, later, budget) in the administration of President Mitterrand 1981–84, overseeing an austerity programme ('*rigueur*') from June 1982. Having been passed over for the post of prime minister, Delors left to become president of the European Commission.

Delos /'di:lɒs/ Greek island, smallest in the ◊Cyclades group, in the SW Aegean; area about 5 sq km/2 sq mi. The great temple of Apollo (4th century BC) is still standing.

Delphi /'delfi/ city of ancient Greece, situated in a rocky valley N of the gulf of Corinth, on the southern slopes of Mount Parnassus, site of a famous ◊oracle in the temple of Apollo. In the same temple was the *Omphalos*, a conical stone supposed to stand at the centre of the Earth. The oracle was interpreted by priests from the inspired utterances of the Pythian priestess until it was closed down by the Roman emperor Theodosius in AD 390.

A European Cultural Centre was built nearby 1966–67.

delphinium plant belonging to the Ranunculaceae family. There are some 250 species including the **great flowered larkspur** *Delphinium grandiflorum*, an Asian form and one of the ancestors of the garden delphinium. Most species have blue, purple, or white flowers in a long spike.

del Sarto /del 'sɑ:təʊ/ Andrea 1486–1531. See ◊Andrea del Sarto, Italian Renaissance painter.

delta a roughly fanlike tract of land at a river's mouth, formed by deposited silt or sediment. Familiar examples of large deltas are those of the Mississippi, Ganges and Brahmaputra, Rhône, Po, Danube, and Nile; the shape of the Nile delta is like the Greek letter Δ, and thus gave rise to the name.

The **arcuate delta** of the Nile is only one form. Others are **birdfoot deltas**, like that of the Mississippi, which is a seaward extension of the river's levee system; and **tidal deltas**, like that of the Mekong in which most of the material is swept to one side by sea currents.

Delta Force US antiguerrilla force, based at Fort Bragg, North Carolina, and modelled on the British ◊Special Air Service.

Delta rocket a US rocket used to launch many scientific and communications satellites since 1960, based on the Thor ballistic missile. Several increasingly powerful versions were produced as satellites became larger and heavier. Solid-fuel boosters were attached to the first stage to increase lifting power.

delta wing an aircraft wing shaped like the Greek letter Δ. It is a design that enables an aircraft to pass through the ◊sound barrier with little effect. The supersonic airliner Concorde and the US space shuttle have delta wings.

demand in economics, the quantity of a product or service that customers want to buy at any given price.

dementia mental deterioration as a result of physical changes in the brain. It may be due to degenerative change, circulatory disease, infection, injury, or chronic poisoning.

Demerara /,demə'reərə/ river in Guyana, 174 km/180 mi long, which gives its name to the country's chief sugar cane growing area, after which Demerara sugar is named.

demesne in the Middle Ages in Europe, land kept in the lord's possession, not leased out, but, under the system of ◊villeinage, worked by villeins to supply the lord's household.

Demeter /dɪ'mi:tə/ in Greek mythology, goddess of agriculture (identified with Roman ◊Ceres), daughter of Kronos and Rhea, and mother of Persephone by Zeus. She is identified with the Egyptian goddess Isis and had a temple dedicated to her at Eleusis where ◊mystery religions were celebrated.

Demetrius /dɪ'mitriəs/ Donskoi ('of the Don') 1350–1389. Grand prince of Moscow from 1363. He achieved the first Russian victory over the Tatars on the plain of Kulikovo, next to the Don (hence his nickname) 1380.

De Mille /də 'mɪl/ Agnes 1909– . US dancer and choreographer. One of the most significant contributors to the American Ballet Theatre with dramatic ballets like *Fall River Legend* 1948, she also led the change on Broadway to new-style musicals with her choreography of *Oklahoma!* 1943, *Carousel* 1945, and others.

De Mille studied with the modern ballet teacher Marie Rambert in the UK, dancing in ballets and musicals in Europe before making her debut as a choreographer in the USA. She has written and lectured on ballet and is a government consultant on dance.

De Mille /də 'mɪl/ Cecil B(lount) 1881–1959. US film director. He entered films with Jesse L Lasky 1913 (with whom he later established Paramount), and was one of the founders of Hollywood. He specialized in biblical epics, such as *The Sign of the Cross* 1932 and *The Ten Commandments* 1956.

Demirel /,demɪ'rel/ Suleyman 1924– . Turkish politician. Leader from 1964 of the Justice Party, he was prime minister 1965–71, 1975–77, and 1979–80. He favoured links with the West, full membership of the EEC, and foreign investment in Turkish industry.

De Mita /de'mi:tə/ Luigi Ciriaco 1928– . Italian conservative politician, leader of the Christian Democratic Party (DC) from 1982, prime minister from 1988. He entered the Chamber of Deputies in 1963 and held a number of ministerial posts in the 1970s before becoming DC secretary-general.

democracy (Greek *demos* 'the community', *kratos* 'sovereign power') government by the people, usually through elected representatives. In the modern world democracy has developed from the American and French revolutions.

Representative parliamentary government existed in Iceland from the 10th century and in England from the 13th century, but the British working classes were excluded almost entirely from the ◊vote until 1867, and women were admitted and property qualifications abolished only in 1918.

In *direct democracy* the whole people meets for the making of laws or the direction of executive officers, for example in Athens in the 5th century BC (and allegedly in modern Libya). Direct democracy today is represented mainly by the use of the ◊referendum, as in the UK, Switzerland, and certain states of the USA.

The Western concept of democracy differs from that in communist countries: the former emphasizes the control of the government by the electorate, and freedom of speech and the press; in the latter both political and economic power rest in the Communist Party.

Democratic Party one of the two main political parties of the USA. It tends to be the party of the working person, as opposed to the Republicans, the party of big business, but the divisions between the two are not clear-cut. Its stronghold has traditionally been the Southern states. In the 1960s the Northern Democrats ('Presidential wing') pressed for civil-rights reform, while Southern Democrats ('Congressional wing') voted against the president on social issues.

Originally called Democratic Republicans, the party was founded by Thomas Jefferson 1792 to defend the rights of the individual states against the centralizing policy of the Federalists. The Democratic Party held power almost continuously 1800–60, and later returned Cleveland, Wilson, F D Roosevelt, Truman, Kennedy, Johnson, and Carter. In the 20th century it has become associated with more liberal policies than the Republicans.

Democrats in UK politics, common name for the ◊Social and Liberal Democrats.

Democritus /dɪˈmɒkrɪtəs/ c.460–361 BC. Greek philosopher and speculative scientist. His most important contribution to metaphysics is his atomic theory of the universe: all things originate from a vortex of atoms, and differ according to the shape and arrangement of its atoms.

demodulation in radio, the technique of separating a transmitted audio frequency signal from its modulated radio carrier wave. At the transmitter the audio frequency signal (representing speech or music, for example) may be made to modulate the amplitude (AM broadcasting) or frequency (FM broadcasting) of a continuously transmitted radio-frequency carrier wave. At the receiver, the signal from the aerial is demodulated to extract the required speech or sound component. In early radio systems, this process was called detection.

demography the study of the size, structure, and development of human populations to establish reliable statistics on such factors as birth and death rates, marriages and divorces, life expectancy, and migration.

Demography is important in the social sciences as the basis for government planning in such areas as education, housing, welfare, transport, and taxation.

demonstration public show of support for, or opposition to, a particular political or social issue, typically by a group of people holding a rally, displaying placards, and making speeches. They usually seek some change in official policy by drawing attention to their cause.

Demonstrations can be static or take the form of elementary street theatre or processions. A specialized type of demonstration is the *picket*, in which striking or dismissed workers try to dissuade others from using or working in the premises of the employer.

In the UK, the Peasants' Revolt in 1381 began as a demonstration against the poll tax. A later instance of violent suppression of demonstrators was the ◊Peterloo massacre 1819. The ◊hunger marches organized in the 1920s–30s were a reaction to the Depression.

Official response to demonstrations was first codified by the Public Order Act 1936. This was provoked by the Cable Street riot of that year, when an anti-Jewish march through East London by Oswald Mosley and 2,500 of his Blackshirts gave rise to violent clashes. Later demonstrations include the nonstop anti-apartheid presence in front of South Africa House in London Apr 1986–Feb 1990, the women's peace camp at ◊Greenham Common, and the picketing of the News International complex in Wapping, East London, by print workers 1986.

The *Public Order Act 1986* gave police extensive new powers to restrict demonstrations and pickets. It requires those organizing a demonstration to give seven days' notice to the police and gives the police the power to say where demonstrators should stand, how long they can stay, and in what numbers, if they believe the protest could cause 'serious disruption to the life of the community' (traffic and shoppers) even though no disorder is anticipated. Penalties for disobeying

Demosthenes *Athenian orator and politician, Demosthenes.*

a police officer's instruction are three months' imprisonment for organizers and a heavy fine for followers.

Police power to ban processions that they believe might result in serious public disorder has been used with increasing frequency in recent years (11 banning orders 1970–80 and 75 in 1981–85).

de Morgan /dəˈmɔːgən/ William Frend 1839–1917. English pottery designer. He set up his own factory 1888 in Fulham, London, producing tiles and pottery painted with flora and fauna in a style typical of the Arts and Crafts Movement.

After training as a painter at the Royal Academy he worked on stained glass. Inspired by William ◊Morris and Edward ◊Burne-Jones, he started designing tiles and glass for Morris's Merton Abbey factory. Influenced by Persian and Italian styles–he spent many months in Italy in later years–he also developed lustre techniques (a way of covering pottery with an iridescent metallic surface). He then turned to writing novels, beginning with the successful *Joseph Vance* 1906.

Demosthenes /dɪˈmɒsθəniːz/ c.384–322 BC. Athenian orator and politician. From 351 BC he led the party that advocated resistance to the growing power of ◊Philip of Macedon, and in his *Philippics* incited the Athenians to war. This policy resulted in the defeat of Chaeronea 338, and the establishment of Macedonian supremacy. After the death of Alexander he organized a revolt; when it failed, he took poison to avoid capture by the Macedonians.

Demotic Greek the common or vernacular variety of the modern ◊Greek language.

demotic script a form of cursive (joined) writing derived from Egyptian hieratic script, itself a cursive form of ◊hieroglyphic. Demotic documents are known from the 6th century BC to about AD 470. It was written horizontally, from right to left.

Dempsey /ˈdempsi/ Jack ('the Manassa Mauler') 1895–1983. US heavyweight boxing champion. He beat Jess Willard 1919 to win the title and held it until losing to Gene Tunney 1926. He engaged in the 'Battle of the Long Count' with Tunney 1927.

Denbighshire /ˈdenbiʃə/ former county of Wales, largely merged in 1974, together with Flint and part of Merioneth, in Clwyd; a small area along the W border was included in Gwynedd. Denbigh, in the Clwyd valley (population about 9,000), was the county town.

Dench /dentʃ/ Judi 1934– . British actress who made her debut as Ophelia in *Hamlet* 1957 with the Old Vic Company. Her Shakespearean roles include Portia in *Twelfth Night*, Lady Macbeth, and Cleopatra. She is also a versatile comedy actress and has appeared in films, for example *A Room with a View*, and on television.

dendrite part of a ◊nerve cell or neuron. The dendrites are slender filaments projecting from

Dempsey *A fearless, aggressive fighter, 'Jack' Dempsey, known as the Manassa Mauler, was world heavyweight boxing champion from 1919–26*

the cell body. They receive incoming messages from many other nerve cells and pass them on to the cell body. If the combined effect of these messages is strong enough, the cell body will send an electrical impulse along the axon (the threadlike extension of a nerve cell). The tip of the axon passes its message to the dendrites of other nerve cells.

dendrochronology the analysis of the annual rings of trees to date past events. Samples of wood can be obtained by means of a narrow metal tube that is driven into a tree to remove a core extending from the bark to the centre. Samples taken from timbers at an archaeological site can be compared with cores from old, living trees, and the year when they were felled can be determined by locating the point where the rings of the two samples correspond.

Since annual rings are formed from the varying sizes of water-conducting cells produced by the plant in different seasons of the year, they also provide a means of determining past climatic conditions in a given area. In North America, sequences of tree rings extending back over 8,000 years have been obtained by using cores from the bristle-cone pine (*Pinus aristata*) which can live for over 4,000 years.

Dene (French *déné*) term applied to distinct but related indigenous people. In Canada, it has been used to describe the Native Americans in the Northwest Territories since the 1970s. The official body representing them is called the Dene nation.

Deneb brightest star in the constellation Cygnus, and the 19th brightest star in the sky. It is one of the greatest supergiant stars known, with a true luminosity of about 60,000 times that of the Sun. Deneb is 1,600 light years away.

Deneuve /dəˈnɜːv/ Catherine 1943– . French actress acclaimed for her performance in Polanski's film *Repulsion* 1965. She also appeared in *Les Parapluies de Cherbourg/Umbrellas of Cherbourg* 1964, *Belle de Jour* 1967, *Hustle* 1975, *The Hunger* 1983.

dengue viral fever transmitted by mosquitoes and accompanied by joint pains, a rash, and glandular swelling. A more virulent form, dengue haemorrhagic fever, thought to be caused by a second infection on top of the first, also causes internal bleeding.

Deng Xiaoping /ˈdʌŋ ˌʃaʊˈpɪŋ/ formerly *Teng Hsiao-ping* 1904– . Chinese political leader. A member of the Chinese Communist Party (CCP) from the 1920s, he took part in the Long March 1934–36. He was in the Politburo from 1955 until

Deng Xiaoping *China's 'paramount ruler' Deng Xiaoping. In effective charge of the country since 1978, he has promoted greater economic, but not political liberalization.*

ousted in the Cultural Revolution 1966–69. Reinstated in the 1970s, he gradually took power and introduced a radical economic modernization programme. He retired from the Politburo in 1987 and from his last official position (as chair of Central Military Commission) Nov 1989, but remained influential behind the scenes.

Deng, born in Sichuan province into a middle-class landlord family, joined the CCP as a student in Paris, where he adopted the name Xiaoping (Little Peace) 1925, and studied in Moscow 1926. After the Long March, he served as a political commissar to the People's Liberation Army during the civil war of 1937–49. He entered the CCP Politburo 1955 and headed the secretariat during the early 1960s, working closely with President Liu Shaoqi. During the Cultural Revolution Deng was dismissed as a 'capitalist roader' and sent to work in a tractor factory in Nanchang for 're-education'.

Deng was rehabilitated by his patron Zhou Enlai 1973 and served as acting prime minister after Zhou's heart attack 1974. On Zhou's death Jan 1976 he was forced into hiding but returned to office as vice premier July 1977. By Dec 1978, although nominally a CCP vice chair, state vice premier, and Chief of Staff to the PLA, Deng was the controlling force in China. He helped to oust ◊Hua Guofeng in favour of his protégés Hu Yaobang and Zhao Ziyang.

Despite repeated suggestions of retirement, Deng remained the dominant decisionmaker in China. His policy of 'socialism with Chinese characteristics', misinterpreted in the West as a drift to capitalism, had success in rural areas. Deng's reputation, both at home and in the West, was tarnished by his sanctioning of the army's massacre of more than 2,000 pro-democracy demonstrators in Tiananmen Square, Beijing, in June 1989.

Den Haag /den ˈhɑːx/ Dutch form of The ◊Hague.

Den Helder /den ˈheldə/ port in North Holland province, Netherlands, 65 km/40 mi N of Amsterdam, on the entrance to the North Holland Canal from the North Sea; population (1985) 63,538. It is a fishing port and naval base.

denier a unit to measure the fineness of yarns, equal to the mass in grams of 9,000 metres of yarn. Thus 9,000 metres of 15 denier nylon, used in nylon stockings, weighs 15 g/0.5 oz, and in this case the thickness of thread would be 0.00425 mm/0.0017 in. The term is derived from the French silk industry; the *denier* was an old French silver coin.

Denikin /dɪˈniːkɪn/ Anton Ivanovich 1872–1946. Russian general. He distinguished himself in the Russo-Japanese War 1904–05 and World War I.

Denmark
Kingdom of
(Kongeriget Danmark)

area 43,075 sq km/16,627 sq mi
capital Copenhagen
towns Aarhus, Odense, Aalborg, Esbjerg, all ports
physical the land is flat and cultivated; sand dunes and lagoons on the W coast and long inlets on the E
territories Faeroe Islands and Greenland
features comprises the peninsula of Jylland/Jutland, plus the main island Sjælland (Zealand), Fünen, Lolland, Bornholm, and smaller islands
head of state Margrethe II from 1972
head of government Poul Schlüter from 1982
political system liberal democracy
political parties Social Democrats (SD), left-of-centre; Conservative People's Party (KF), moderate centre-right; Liberal Party (V), centre-left; Socialist People's Party (SF), moderate left-wing; Radical Liberals (RV), radical internationalist left-of-centre; Centre Democrats (CD), moderate centrist; Progress Party (FP), radical anti-bureaucratic; Christian People's Party (KrF), interdenominational, family values
exports bacon, dairy produce, eggs, fish, mink pelts, car and aircraft parts, electrical equipment, textiles
currency krone (11.00 = £1 Feb 1990)
population (1988) 5,129,000; annual growth rate 0%
life expectancy men 72, women 78
language Danish (official)
religion Lutheran
literacy 99% (1983)
GNP $50.4 bn (1983); $12,956 per head of population
chronology
1940–45 Occupied by Germany.
1945 Iceland's independence recognized.
1947 Frederik IX succeeded Christian X.
1948 Home rule granted for Faeroe Islands.
1949 Became a founder member of NATO.
1960 Joined European Free Trade Association (EFTA).
1972 Margrethe II became Denmark's first queen for nearly 600 years.
1973 Left EFTA and joined European Community.
1979 Home rule granted for Greenland.
1985 Strong non-nuclear movement in evidence.
1987 Inconclusive general election, minority government formed.
1989 Another inconclusive election; new centre-right coalition government formed.

After the outbreak of the Bolshevik Revolution 1917 he organized a volunteer army of 60,000 Whites (counter-revolutionaries), but in 1919 was routed and escaped to France. He wrote a history of the Revolution and the Civil War.

De Niro /də ˈnɪərəʊ/ Robert 1943– . US actor. He won Oscars for *The Godfather Part II* 1974 and *Raging Bull* 1979. Other films include *Taxi Driver* 1976, *The Deer Hunter* 1978, and *The Untouchables* 1987.

Denis, St /ˈdenɪs/ first bishop of Paris and one of the patron saints of France, who was martyred by the Romans. Feast day 9 Oct.

He is often represented as carrying his head in his hands, and is often confused with Dionysius the Areopagite, who was the first bishop of Athens, and died about AD 95.

denitrification a process occurring naturally in soil, where bacteria break down ◊nitrates to give nitrogen gas, which returns to the atmosphere.

Denktash /ˈdeŋktæʃ/ Rauf R 1924– . Turkish-Cypriot politician. In 1975 the Turkish Federated State of Cyprus (TFSC) was formed in the

De Niro *US film actor Robert De Niro specializes in violent, often psychotic characters in such films as* Taxi Driver *1976.*

northern third of the island, with Denktash as its head, and in 1983 he became president of the breakaway Turkish Republic of Northern Cyprus (TRNC).

Denktash held law-officer posts under the crown before independence, in 1960. Relations between the Greek and Turkish communities progressively deteriorated, leading to the formation of the TFSC. In 1983 the TRNC, with Denktash as its president, was formally constituted, but recognized internationally only by Turkey. The accession of the independent politician Georgios Vassilou to the Cyprus presidency offered hopes of reconciliation, but meetings between him and Denktash, under UN auspices, during 1989 failed to produce an agreement.

Denmark /ˈdenmɑːk/ peninsula and islands in N Europe, bounded to the N by the Skagerrak, to the E by the Kattegat, to the S by West Germany, and to the W by the North Sea.

government Under the 1849 constitution, last revised 1953, there is an hereditary monarch with no personal political power, and a single-chamber parliament, the *Folketing*. The prime minister and cabinet are drawn from and responsible to the *Folketing*, which has 179 members elected by adult franchise, 175 representing metropolitan Denmark, two the Faroe Islands and two Greenland. Voting is by proportional representation and the *Folketing* has a life of four years, but may be dissolved within this period if the government is defeated on a vote of confidence. The government, however, need only resign on what it itself defines as a 'vital element' of policy. Most significant of the 12 political parties are the Social Democrats, the Conservative People's Party, the Liberals, the Socialist People's Party, the Radical Liberals, the Centre Democrats, the Progress Party, the Christian People's Party, and the Left Socialists.

history The original home of the Danes was Sweden, and they migrated in the 5th and 6th centuries. Ruled by local chieftains, they terrified Europe by their piratical raids during the 8th–10th centuries, until Harald Bluetooth (*c.* 940–85) unified Denmark and established Christianity. Canute (ruled 1014–35) founded an empire embracing Denmark, England, and Norway, which fell to pieces at his death. After a century of confusion Denmark again dominated the Baltic under Valdemar I, Canute VI, and Valdemar II (1157–1241). Domestic conflict then prodduced anarchy, until Valdemar IV (1340–75) restored order. Denmark, Norway, and Sweden were united under one sovereign 1397. Sweden broke away 1449 and after a long struggle had its independence recognized 1523. Christian I (1448–81) secured the duchies of Schleswig and Holstein, fiefs of the ◊Holy Roman Empire, 1460; and they were held by his descendants until 1863. Christian II (ruled 1513–23) was deposed in favour of his uncle Frederick whose son Christian III (ruled 1534–59) made Lutheranism the established religion 1536. Attempts to regain Sweden led to disastrous wars with that country 1563–70, 1643–45, 1657–60; equally disastrous was Christian V's intervention, 1625–29, on the Protestant side of the ◊Thirty Years' War.

Frederick III (ruled 1648–70) made himself absolute monarch 1665, and ruled through a burgher bureaucracy. Serfdom was abolished 1788. Denmark's adherence 1780 to the armed neutrality against Britain resulted in the naval defeat of Copenhagen 1801, and in 1807 the British bombarded Copenhagen and seized the Danish fleet to save it from ◊Napoleon. This incident drove Denmark into the arms of France, and the Allies at the Congress of Vienna took Norway from Denmark and gave it to Sweden 1815. A liberal movement then arose, which in 1848–49 compelled Frederick VII (ruled 1848–63) to grant a democratic constitution. The Germans in Schleswig-Holstein revolted with Prussian support 1848–50, and Prussia seized the provinces 1864, after a short war. North Schleswig was recovered after a plebiscite 1920.

Neutral in World War I, Denmark tried to preserve its neutrality 1939 by signing a pact with Hitler, but was occupied by Germany 1940–45. Although traditionally neutral, Denmark joined ◊NATO 1949 and the ◊European Free Trade Association (EFTA) 1960, but resigned 1973 to join the EEC.

◊Iceland was part of the Danish kingdom until 1945 and the other parts of non-metropolitan Denmark, the Faroe Islands and Greenland, were given special recognition by a constitution that has been adapted to meet changing circumstances. In 1953 provision was made for a daughter to succeed to the throne in the absence of a male heir, and a system of voting by proportional representation was introduced.

Left-wing policies have dominated Danish politics, and proportional representation, often resulting in minority or coalition governments, has encouraged this moderate approach. In the Mar 1989 general election, the centre-right coalition lost seven seats, but Prime Minister Schluter decided to continue with a minority government, holding 70 of the *Folketing* seats.

Denning /'denɪŋ/ Alfred Thompson, Baron Denning of Whitchurch 1899– . British judge, Master of the Rolls 1962–82. In 1963 he conducted the inquiry into the ◊Profumo scandal. A vigorous and highly innovative civil lawyer, he was controversial in his defence of the rights of the individual against the state, the unions, and big business.

de novo (Latin) anew.

Denpasar /den·pa:sa:/ capital town of Bali in the Lesser Sunda Islands of Indonesia. Population (1980) 88,100.

density measure of the compactness of a substance; the mass per unit volume, measured in kg per cubic metre/lb per cubic foot. *Relative density* is the ratio of the density of a substance to that of water at 4°C.

dental formula a way of showing what an animal's teeth are like. The dental formula consists of eight

Depression *A soup kitchen in Chicago during the Depression.*

numbers separated by a line into two rows. The four above the line represent the teeth in one side of the upper jaw, starting at the front. If this reads 2 1 2 3 (as for humans) it means two incisors, one canine, two premolars, and three molars (see ◊tooth). The numbers below the line represent the lower jaw. The total number of teeth can be calculated by adding up all the numbers and multiplying by two.

dentistry the care and treatment of the teeth and gums. *Orthodontics* deals with the straightening of the teeth, and *periodontology* with care of the supporting tissue.

The bacteria that start the process of dental decay are normal, non-pathogenic members of a large and varied group of microorganisms present in the mouth. They are strains of oral streptococci, but it is only in the presence of sucrose (from refined sugar) in the mouth that they become damaging to the teeth. ◊Fluoride in the water supply is one attempted solution, and in 1979 a vaccine was developed from a modified form of the bacterium *Streptococcus mutans*.

The earliest dental school was opened in Baltimore, Maryland, USA, 1839; in Britain the predecessors of the modern University College Hospital Dental School and Royal Dental Hospital and School, both within the University of London, were established 1859 and 1860. There is an International Dental Federation (1900).

dentition the type and number of teeth in a species. Different kinds of teeth have different functions, and a grass-eating animal will have well developed molars for grinding its food, whereas a meat-eater will need large canines for catching and killing its prey. The teeth that are less useful may be reduced in size or missing altogether. An animal's dentition is represented diagrammatically by a ◊dental formula.

denudation the natural loss of soil and rock debris, blown away by wind or washed away by running water, that lays bare the rock below. Over millions of years, denudation causes a general levelling of the landscape.

Denver /'denvə/ city in Colorado, USA, on the South Platte river, near the foothills of the Rocky Mountains; population (1980) 492,365, Denver-Boulder metropolitan area 1,850,000. It is a processing and distribution centre for a large agricultural area, and for natural resources (minerals, oil,

gas). It was the centre of a gold and silver boom in the 1870s and 1880s, and for oil in the 1970s.

Denver was founded 1858 with the discovery of gold, becoming a mining camp supply centre; coal is also mined nearby. There is a university, a mining school, and many medical institutions, and the US mint is sited here.

Deo (ad)juvante (Latin) with God's help.

deodar Himalayan cedar tree *Cedrus deodara*, often planted as a rapid-growing ornamental. It has valuable timber.

Deo gratias (Latin) thanks to God.

deontology an ethical theory that the rightness of an action consists in its conformity to duty, regardless of the consequences that may result from it. Deontological ethics is thus opposed to any form of utilitarianism.

Deo volente (Latin) God willing.

deoxyribonucleic acid the full name of ◊DNA.

De Palma /də'pɑ:lmə/ Brian 1941– . US film director, especially of thrillers. His technical mastery and enthusiasm for spilling blood are shown in films such as *Sisters* 1973, *Carrie* 1976, and *The Untouchables* 1987.

Depardieu /də'pɑ:djɜ:/ Gerard 1948– . Versatile French actor who has appeared in the films *Deux Hommes dans la Ville* 1973, *Le Camion* 1977, *Mon Oncle d'Amérique* 1980, *The Moon in the Gutter* 1983, and *Jean de Florette* 1985.

Department of Education and Science (DES) UK government department responsible for making education policy in England, and for the universities throughout the UK.

depilatory instrument or substance used to eradicate growing hair, usually for cosmetic reasons. Permanent eradication is by destruction of each individual hair root by an electrolytic needle or an electrocautery, but there is a danger of scarring.

deposit account in banking, an account where money is left to attract interest, sometimes for a fixed term. Unlike a current account, the deposit account does not give constant access through a chequebook.

depreciation in economics, decline of a currency's value in relation to other currencies. Depreciation also describes the fall in value of an asset (such as factory machinery) resulting from age, wear and tear, or other circumstances. It is an important factor in assessing company profit.

depression an emotional state characterized by sadness, unhappy thoughts, apathy, and dejection. Sadness is a normal response to major losses such as bereavement, and to unemployment. However, clinical depression, which is prolonged or unduly severe, often requires treatment, such as anti-depressant medication, ◊cognitive therapy, or, in very rare cases, electro-convulsive therapy (ECT), in which an electrical current is passed through the brain.

Depression is the most common reason in the UK for people consulting a general practitioner.

Depression in economics, a period of low output and investment, with high unemployment. Specifically, the term describes two periods of crisis in the world economies: 1873–96 and 1929–mid-1930s.

The term is most often used to refer to the world economic crisis precipitated by the Wall Street crash of 29 Oct 1929 when millions of dollars were wiped off US share values in a matter of hours. This forced the closure of many US banks involved in stock speculation and led to the recall of US overseas investments. This loss of US credit had serious repercussions on the European economy, especially that of Germany, and led to a steep fall in the levels of international trade as countries attempted to protect their domestic economies. Although most European countries experienced a slow recovery during the mid-1930s, the main impetus for renewed economic growth was provided by rearmament programmes later in the decade.

The Depression of 1873–96 centred on falling growth rates in the British economy but also affected industrial activity in Germany and the USA. The crisis in the British economy is now thought to have lasted longer than these dates suggest.

depression of freezing point a lowering of the ◊freezing point of a solution, below that of the pure solvent, which depends on the number of molecules of solute dissolved in it.

de profundis (Latin 'from the depths') a cry from the depths of misery. From the Bible, Psalm 130: *De profundis clamavi ad te*; 'Out of the depths have I cried to thee'.

Deptford /ˈdetfəd/ district in SE London, in the borough of Lewisham, mainly residential, with industries including engineering and chemicals. It was an important Royal naval dockyard from 1513 to 1869, on the south bank of the the river Thames.

de Quincey /də ˈkwɪnsɪ/ Thomas 1785–1859. English author, whose works include *Confessions of an English Opium-Eater* 1821 and the essays 'On the Knocking at the Gate in Macbeth' 1823 and 'On Murder Considered as One of the Fine Arts' 1827. He was a friend of the poets Wordsworth and Coleridge.

Derbyshire

Born in Manchester, de Quincey ran away from school there to wander and study in Wales. He then went to London, where he lived in extreme poverty but with the constant companionship of the young orphan Ann, of whom he writes in the *Confessions*. In 1803 he was reconciled to his guardians and was sent to university at Oxford, where his opium habit began. In 1809 he settled with the Wordsworths and Coleridge in the Lake District. He moved to Edinburgh 1828, where he eventually died. De Quincey's work had a powerful influence on ◊Baudelaire and ◊Poe among others.

Derain /dəˈræn/ André 1880–1954. French painter, who experimented with strong, almost primary colours and exhibited with the ◊Fauves, but later developed a more sombre landscape style. His work includes costumes and scenery for Diaghilev's Ballets Russes.

Derby /ˈdɑːbɪ/ industrial city in Derbyshire, England; population (1981) 216,000.

products rail locomotives, Rolls-Royce cars and aero-engines, chemicals, paper, electrical, mining and engineering equipment.

features the museum collections of Crown Derby china; the Rolls-Royce collection of aero engines; and the Derby Playhouse.

Derby the ◊blue riband of the English horse-racing season. It is run over 2.4 km/1.5 mi at Epsom, Surrey, every June. It was established 1780 and named after the 12th earl of Derby. The USA has an equivalent horse race, the **Kentucky Derby**.

Derby /ˈdɑːbɪ/ Edward Geoffrey Smith Stanley, 14th Earl of Derby 1799–1869. British politician, prime minister 1852, 1858–59, and 1866–68. Originally a Whig, he became secretary for the colonies 1830, and introduced the bill for the abolition of slavery. He joined the Tories 1834, and the split in the Tory Party over Robert Peel's free-trade policy gave Derby the leadership for 20 years.

Derby /ˈdɑːbɪ/ Edward George Villiers Stanley, 17th Earl of Derby 1865–1948. British Conservative politician, Member of Parliament from 1892. He was secretary of war 1916–18 and 1922–24, and ambassador to France 1918–20.

Derbyshire /ˈdɑːbɪʃə/ county in N central England

area 2,630 sq km/1,015 sq mi

towns administrative headquarters Matlock; Derby, Chesterfield, Ilkeston

features Peak District National Park (including Kinder Scout 636 m/2,088 ft); rivers Derwent, Dove, Rother, Trent; Chatsworth House, Bakewell (seat of Duke of Devonshire), Haddon Hall

products cereals; dairy and sheep farming. There have been pit and factory closures, but the area is being redeveloped, and there are large reserves of fluorspar.

population (1987) 919,000.

deregulation action to abolish or reduce state controls and supervision over private economic activities, as with the deregulation of the US airline industry 1978. Its purpose is to improve competitiveness. In Britain the major changes in the City of London 1986 (the ◊Big Bang) were in part deregulation.

de rigueur (French 'of strictness') demanded by the rules of etiquette.

derivative or **differential coefficient** in mathematics, the limit of the gradient of a chord between two points on a curve as the distance between the points tends to zero; for a function with a single variable, $y = f(x)$, it is denoted by $f'(x)$, $Df(x)$, or dy/dx, and is equal to the gradient of the curve.

dermatitis inflammation of the skin, usually related to allergy.

De Roburt /dəˈrɒbət/ Hammer 1923– . President of Nauru from 1968, out of office 1976–78 and briefly in 1986. During the country's occupation 1942–45, he was deported to Japan. He became head chief of Nauru in 1956 and was elected the country's first president in 1968.

derrick a simple lifting machine, consisting of a pole carrying a block and tackle. Derricks are commonly to be seen on ships such as freighters. In the oil industry the tower used for hoisting the drill pipes is known as a derrick.

derris climbing plant of SE Asia *Derris elliptica*, family Leguminosae. Its roots contain rotenone, a strong insecticide.

Derry /ˈderɪ/ county of Northern Ireland

area 2,070 sq km/799 sq mi

towns Derry (county town, formerly Londonderry), Coleraine, Portstewart

features rivers Foyle, Bann, and Roe; borders Lough Neagh

products mainly agricultural, but farming is hindered by the very heavy rainfall; flax, cattle, sheep, food processing, textiles, light engineering

population (1981) 187,000

famous people Joyce Cary.

Derry /ˈderɪ/ (Gaelic *doire*, 'a place of oaks') historic city and port on the river Foyle, County Derry, Northern Ireland; population (1981) 89,100. Known as Londonderry until 1984, Derry dates from the foundation of a monastery by St Columba in AD 546. James I of England granted the borough and surrounding land to the citizens of London and a large colony of imported Protestants founded the present city which they named Londonderry. Textiles and chemicals are produced.

dervish in Iran and Turkey, a religious mendicant, and throughout the rest of Islam a member of an Islamic religious brotherhood, not necessarily mendicant in character. The Arabic equivalent is *fakir*. There are various orders of dervishes, each with its rule and special ritual. The 'whirling dervishes' claim close communion with the deity through ecstatic dancing; the 'howling dervishes' gash themselves with knives to demonstrate the miraculous feats possible to those who trust in Allah.

Derwent /ˈdɜːwənt/ river in N Yorkshire, NE England; length 112 km/70 mi. Rising in the N Yorkshire moors it joins the river Ouse SE of Selby. Other rivers of the same name in the UK are found in Derbyshire (96 km/60 mi), Cumbria (56 km/35 mi), and Northumberland (26 km/16 mi).

DES abbreviation for *Department of Education and Science*.

Desai /deˈsaɪ/ Morarji 1896– . Indian politician. An early follower of Mahatma Gandhi, he was prime minister, as leader of the ◊Janata Party 1977–79, after toppling Indira Gandhi. Party infighting led to his resignation of both the premiership and the party leadership.

desalination the removal of salt, especially from sea water, to produce fresh water for irrigation. Distillation has usually been the method adopted, but in the 1970s a cheaper process, using certain polymer materials that filter the molecules of salt from the water by reverse osmosis, was developed.

de Savary /də ˈsævərɪ/ Peter 1944– . British entrepreneur. He acquired Land's End, Cornwall, England, in 1987 and built a theme park there. He revived Falmouth dock and the port of Hayle in N Cornwall. A yachting enthusiast, he sponsored the Blue Arrow America's Cup challenge team.

Descartes /deɪˈkɑːt/ René 1596–1650. French mathematician and philosopher. He believed that commonly accepted knowledge was doubtful because of the subjective nature of the senses, and attempted to rebuild human knowledge using as foundation '*cogito ergo sum*' ('I think, therefore I am'). He also believed that the entire material universe could be explained in terms of mathematical physics. He is regarded as the discoverer of analytical geometry and the founder of the science of optics. He was also influential in shaping contemporary theories of astronomy and animal behaviour.

Descartes was born near Tours. He served in the army of Prince Maurice of Orange, and in

Descartes *An engraving of French philosopher and mathematician René Descartes from a portrait by Frans Hals.*

1619, while travelling through Europe, decided to apply the methods of mathematics to metaphysics and science. He settled in the Netherlands in 1628, where he was more likely to be free from interference by the ecclesiastical authorities. In 1649 he visited the court of Queen Christina of Sweden, and died in Stockholm.

Descartes identified the 'thinking thing' (*res cogitans*) or mind with the human soul or consciousness; the body, though somehow interacting with the soul, was a physical machine, secondary to, and in principle separable from, the soul. He held that everything has a cause; nothing can result from nothing. He believed that, although all matter is in motion, matter does not move of its own accord; the initial impulse comes from God. He also postulated two quite distinct substances—spatial substance, or matter, and thinking substance, or mind. This is called **Cartesian dualism**, and it preserved him from serious controversy with the church.

His works include *Discourse on Method* 1637, *Meditations on the First Philosophy* 1641, and *Principles of Philosophy* 1644, and numerous books on physiology, optics, and geometry.

Coordinate geometry, as a way of defining and manipulating geometrical shapes by means of algebraic expressions, was determined by Leibniz, and only later called ◊Cartesian coordinates in honour of Descartes.

Deschamps /deɪˈʃɒm/ Eustache 1346–1406. French poet, born in Champagne. He was the author of more than 1,000 ballades, and the *Miroir de Mariage/The Mirror of Marriage*, an attack on women.

deselection in Britain, removal or withholding of a sitting Member of Parliament's official status as a candidate for a forthcoming election. The term came into use in the 1980s with the efforts of many local Labour parties to revoke the candidature of MPs viewed as too right-wing.

desert area without sufficient rainfall and, consequently, vegetation to support human life. Scientifically, this term includes the ice areas of the polar regions. Almost 33% of Earth's land surface is desert, and this proportion is increasing.

The **tropical desert** belts of latitudes from 5° to 30° are caused by the descent of air that is heated over the warm land and therefore tends to retain its moisture. Other natural desert types are the **continental deserts**, such

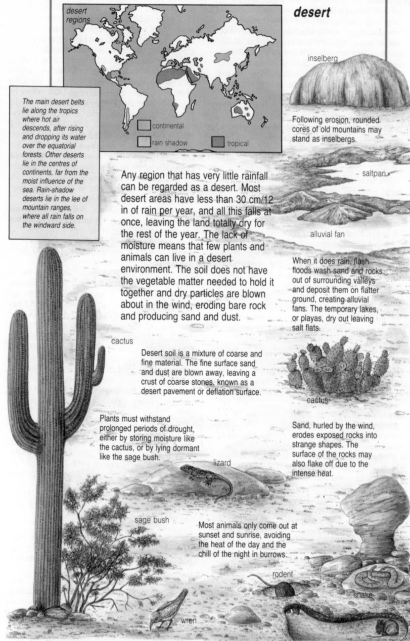

desert

The main desert belts lie along the tropics where hot air descends, after rising and dropping its water over the equatorial forests. Other deserts lie in the centres of continents, far from the moist influence of the sea. Rain-shadow deserts lie in the lee of mountain ranges, where all rain falls on the windward side.

desert regions

continental
rain shadow
tropical

inselberg

Following erosion, rounded cores of old mountains may stand as inselbergs.

saltpan

alluvial fan

When it does rain, flash floods wash sand and rocks out of surrounding valleys and deposit them on flatter ground, creating alluvial fans. The temporary lakes, or playas, dry out leaving salt flats.

Any region that has very little rainfall can be regarded as a desert. Most desert areas have less than 30 cm/12 in of rain per year, and all this falls at once, leaving the land totally dry for the rest of the year. The lack of moisture means that few plants and animals can live in a desert environment. The soil does not have the vegetable matter needed to hold it together and dry particles are blown about in the wind, eroding bare rock and producing sand and dust.

cactus

Desert soil is a mixture of coarse and fine material. The fine surface sand and dust are blown away, leaving a crust of coarse stones, known as a desert pavement or deflation surface.

cactus

Plants must withstand prolonged periods of drought, either by storing moisture like the cactus, or by lying dormant like the sage bush.

Sand, hurled by the wind, erodes exposed rocks into strange shapes. The surface of the rocks may also flake off due to the intense heat.

lizard

sage bush

Most animals only come out at sunset and sunrise, avoiding the heat of the day and the chill of the night in burrows.

rodent

snake

wren

as the Gobi, that are too far from the sea to receive any moisture; **rain-shadow deserts**, such as California's Death Valley, that lie in the lee of mountain ranges, where the ascending air drops its rain only on the windward slopes; and **coastal deserts**, such as the Namib, where cold ocean currents cause local dry air masses to descend. Desert surfaces are usually rocky or gravelly, with only a small proportion being covered with sand. Deserts can be created by changes in climate, or by the human-aided process of desertification.

desertification the creation of deserts by changes in climate, or by human-aided processes such as overgrazing, destruction of forest belts, and exhaustion of the soil by too intensive cultivation without restoration of fertility; all usually prompted by the pressures of expanding populations. The process can be reversed by special planting (marram grass, trees) and by the use of water-absorbent plastic grains (a polymer absorbent of 40 times its own weight of water), which, added to the sand, enable crops

to be grown. About 135 million people are directly affected by desertification, mainly in Africa, the Indian subcontinent, and South America.

Desert Orchid one of the most popular steeplechase horses in Britain. It has won more than 30 National Hunt races, including the King George VI Chase 1988 and Cheltenham Gold Cup 1989. It was ridden to most of its wins by Colin Brown or Simon Sherwood.

Desert Rats nickname of the British 8th Army in N Africa during World War II. Their uniforms had a shoulder insignia bearing a jerboa (N African rodent, capable of great leaps).

de Sica /deɪ ˈsiːkə/ Vittorio 1902–1974. Italian director and actor. He won his first Oscar with *Bicycle Thieves* 1948, a film of subtle realism. Later films included *Umberto D* 1952, *Two Women* 1960, and *The Garden of the Finzi-Continis* 1971.

desiccator an airtight vessel, traditionally made of glass, in which materials may be stored either to dehydrate them or to prevent them, once dried, from reabsorbing moisture.

The base of the desiccator is a chamber in which is placed a substance with a strong affinity for water, which removes water vapour from the desiccator atmosphere and from substances placed in it.

Design Centre exhibition spaces in London and Glasgow established 1956 by the Council of Industrial Design (set up by the government 1944 to improve standards in British products) to act as a showcase for goods deemed to be of a high standard of design.

desktop publishing (DTP) the use of microcomputers for small-scale typesetting and page make-up. DTP systems are capable of producing camera-ready pages (pages ready for photographing and printing), made up of text and graphics, with text set in different typefaces and sizes. The page can be previewed on the screen before final printing on a laser printer.

Des Moines /dɪ 'mɔɪn/ capital and largest town in Iowa, USA, on the Des Moines river, a tributary of the Mississippi; population (1980) 371,800. It is an important road, railway, and air centre with many manufactures.

Desmoulins /,deɪmu:'læn/ Camille 1760–1794. French revolutionary, who summoned the mob to arms on 12 July 1789, so precipitating the revolt that culminated in the storming of the Bastille. A prominent ◊Jacobin, he was elected to the National Convention 1792. His *Histoire des Brissotins* was largely responsible for the overthrow of the ◊Girondins, but shortly after he was sent to the guillotine as too moderate.

de Soto /də 'səʊtəʊ/ Hernando c.1496–1542. Spanish explorer who sailed with d'Avila (1440–1531) to Darien, Central America, 1519, explored the Yucatán Peninsula 1528, and travelled with Pizarro in Peru 1530–35. In 1538 he was made governor of Cuba and Florida. In his expedition of 1539, he explored Florida, Georgia, and the Mississippi River.

Desprez /deɪ'preɪ/ Josquin c.1440–1521. Franco-Flemish composer; see ◊Josquin Desprez.

Dessalines /,desæ'li:n/ Jean Jacques c. 1758–1806. Emperor of Haiti 1804–1806. Born in Guinea, he was taken to Haiti as a slave, where in 1802 he succeeded ◊Toussaint L'Ouverture as leader of the black revolt against the French. After defeating the French, he proclaimed Haiti's independence and made himself emperor. He was killed when trying to suppress an uprising provoked by his cruelty.

Dessau /'desaʊ/ town of Halle county, East Germany, on the river Mulde, 115 km/70 mi SW of Berlin; population (1986) 104,000. It is the former capital of Anhalt duchy and state. It manufactures chemicals, machinery, and chocolate, and was the site of the Junkers aeroplane works.

Dessau /'desaʊ/ Paul 1894–1979. German composer. He work includes incidental music to the playwright Bertolt Brecht's theatre pieces, an opera, *Der Verurteilung des Lukullus*, also to a libretto by Brecht, and numerous choral works and songs.

He studied in Berlin, becoming a theatre conductor until moving to Paris in 1933, where he studied Schoenberg's serial method with Rena Leibowitz. He collaborated with Brecht from 1942, when they met as political exiles in the USA, returning with him to East Berlin 1948.

destroyer small, fast warship designed for antisubmarine work. They played a critical role in the ◊convoy system in World War II. Modern destroyers often carry guided missiles and displace 3,700–5,650 tonnes.

detective fiction novels or short stories in which a mystery is solved mainly by the action of a professional or amateur detective. Where the mystery to be solved concerns a crime, the work may be called *crime fiction*. The earliest work of detective fiction as understood today was *Murders in the Rue Morgue* 1841 by Edgar Allan Poe, and his detective Dupin became the model for those who relied on deduction from a series

of clues. The most popular deductive sleuth was Sherlock Holmes in the stories by Arthur Conan Doyle.

The height of the genre was the period from the 1920s to the 1940s, when the leading writers were women—Agatha Christie, Margery Allingham, Dorothy L Sayers. Types of detective fiction include the *police procedural*, where the mystery is solved by detailed police work, as in the work of Swedish writers Maj Sjowall and Per Wahloo; the *inverted novel*, where the identity of the criminal is known from the beginning, only the method or the motive remaining to be discovered, as in *Malice Aforethought* by Francis Iles; the *hardboiled school* of private investigators begun by Raymond Chandler and Dashiell Hammett, which became known for its social realism and explicit violence. More recently, the form and traditions of the genre are used as a framework within which to explore other concerns, as in *Innocent Blood* and *A Taste for Death* by P D James, *The Name of the Rose* by Umberto Eco, and the works of many women writers who explore feminist ideas, for example Barbara Wilson with *Murder in the Collective*.

Like most genres, crime fiction has produced its oddities. *Murder in Pastiche* by Marion Mainwaring is written in the styles of nine famous writers. Agatha Christie, Georgette Heyer, and Ellis Peters have all written detective novels with historical settings. *Murder Off Miami* by Dennis Wheatley was a dossier containing real clues such as photographs, ticket stubs, and hairpins for the reader to solve the mystery; the solution was in a closed envelope at the back of the book.

détente (French) an easing of political tension between nations.

detention centre in Britain, an establishment for the short-term detention of young offenders (aged 14–21). In 1980 New Hall (Wakefield, Yorkshire) and Send (Woking, Surrey) were selected to give 'short, sharp shock' treatment to those sentenced to three months by the courts.

detergent a surface-active cleansing agent. The common detergents are made from fats (hydrocarbons) and sulphuric acid, and their long-chain molecules have a type of structure similar to that of soap molecules: a salt group at one end attached to a long hydrocarbon 'tail'. They have the advantage over soap in that they do not produce scum by forming insoluble salts with the calcium and magnesium ions present in hard water.

To remove dirt, which is generally attached to materials by oil or grease, the hydrocarbon 'tails' (soluble in oil or grease) penetrate the oil or grease drops, while the 'heads' (soluble in water but insoluble in grease) remain in the water and, being salts, become ionized. Consequently the oil drops become negatively charged and tend to repel one another; thus they remain in suspension and are washed away with the dirt.

Detergents were first developed from coal tar in Germany during World War I, and synthetic organic detergents came into increasing use after World War II. Domestic powder detergents for use in hot water have alkyl benzene as their main base, and may also include bleaches and fluorescers as whiteners, perborates to free stain-removing oxygen, and water softeners. Environment-friendly detergents contain no phosphates or bleaches. Liquid detergents for washing dishes are based on ethylene oxide. Cold-water detergents consist of a mixture of various alcohols, plus an ingredient for breaking down the surface tension of the water, so enabling the liquid to penetrate fibres and remove the dirt. When surface-active materials escape the normal processing of sewage, they cause troublesome foam in rivers.

determinant in mathematics, an array of elements written as a square, and denoted by two vertical lines enclosing the array. For a 2×2 matrix, the determinant is given by the difference between the products of the diagonal terms. Determinants

are used to solve sets of ◊simultaneous equations by matrix methods.

When applied to transformational geometry, the determinant of a 2×2 matrix signifies the ratio of the area of the transformed shape to the original and its sign (plus or minus) denotes whether the image is direct (the same way round) or indirect (a mirror image).

determinism in philosophy, the view that denies human freedom of action. Because everything is strictly governed by the principle of cause and effect, human action is no exception. It is the opposite of free will, and rules out moral choice and responsibility.

In antiquity, the theory of determinism was a feature of ◊Stoicism. In Christian theology, the Calvinist doctrine of predestination is deterministic. Quantum mechanics and the ◊uncertainty principle lend support to free will.

deterrence the underlying conception of the nuclear arms race: the belief that a potential aggressor will be discouraged from launching a 'first strike' nuclear attack by the knowledge that the adversary is capable of inflicting 'unacceptable damage' in a retaliatory strike. This doctrine is widely known as that of *mutual assured destruction (MAD)*. Three essential characteristics of deterrence are: the 'capability to act', 'credibility', and the 'will to act'.

Extended deterrence involves the application of deterrence to an ally geographically removed from the deterring state, a notable example being the US commitment to the defence of W Europe, requiring capabilities over and above those needed to deter attack on the USA itself. To be credible, this involves deployment of US forces within W Europe in such a manner that any threat to W Europe would also be perceived as a threat to the US. There is thus constant anxiety about the degree of commitment and fear that, in a crisis, the US (for example) would make decisions without consulting the nations that it is supposedly protecting through extended deterrence.

de Tocqueville Alexis 1805–1859. French politician, see ◊Tocqueville, Alexis de.

detonator also called *blasting cap*, a small explosive charge used to trigger off a main charge of high explosive. The relatively unstable compounds mercury fulminate and lead acid are often used in detonators, being set off by a lighted fuse or, more commonly, an electric current.

detritus in biology, the organic debris produced during the ◊decomposition of animals and plants.

Detroit /dɪ'trɔɪt/ city of Michigan, USA, situated on Detroit river; population (1980) 1,203,339, metropolitan area 4,353,000. It is an industrial centre with the headquarters of Ford, Chrysler, and General Motors, hence its nickname, Motown from 'motor town'.

It was founded 1701 and is the oldest city of any size west of the original colonies of the east coast. In 1805 it was completely destroyed by fire, but soon rebuilt. A recent major development is the waterfront Renaissance Center complex. In the 1960s and 1970s, Detroit became noted for the 'Motown Sound' of rock and soul music.

de trop (French 'of too much') not wanted, in the way.

Detsko Selo /'detskəjə sɪ'ləʊ/ former name of ◊Pushkin, near Lenigrad, which was renamed after the Russian poet in 1937.

Dettingen, Battle of /'detɪŋən/ battle in the Bavarian village of that name where on 27 June 1743, in the War of the Austrian Succession, an army of British, Hanoverians, and Austrians under George II defeated the French under Adrien-Maurice, duc de Noailles (1678–1766).

deus ex machina (Latin 'a god from a machine') a far-fetched or unlikely event that resolves an intractable difficulty. The phrase was originally used in drama to indicate a god descending from heaven to resolve the plot.

deuterium a heavy isotope of hydrogen, mass number 2 (one proton and one neutron), discovered by ◊Urey 1932. Combined with oxygen, it produces 'heavy water', used in the nuclear industry.

deuteron the ion of deuterium ('heavy hydrogen'). It consists of one proton and one neutron, and thus has a positive charge.

Deuteronomy book of the Old Testament; 5th book of the ◊Torah. It contains various laws, including the ten commandments, and gives an account of the death of Moses.

Deutschmark or **Deutsche Mark** (DM) the standard currency of West Germany.

de Valera /də vəˈlɛərə/ Eamon 1882–1975. Irish nationalist politician, prime minister of the Irish Free State/Eire/Republic of Ireland 1932–48, 1951–54, and 1957–59, and president 1959–73. Repeatedly imprisoned, he participated in the Easter Rising 1916 and was leader of ◊Sinn Féin 1917–26, when he formed the ◊Fianna Fáil party; he directed negotiations with Britain 1921 but refused to accept the partition of Ireland until 1937.

de Valera *Eamon de Valera, Irish politician, shortly before his imprisonment 1923.*

He was born in New York, the son of a Spanish father and an Irish mother, and sent to Ireland as a child, where he became a teacher of mathematics. He was sentenced to death for his part in the Easter Rising, but the sentence was commuted, and he was released under an amnesty 1917. In the same year he was elected Member of Parliament for E Clare, and president of Sinn Féin. He was rearrested May 1918, but escaped to the USA 1919. He returned to Ireland 1920 and directed the struggle against the British government from a hiding place in Dublin. He authorized the negotiations of 1921, but refused to accept the ensuing treaty which divided Ireland into the Free State and the North.

Civil war followed. De Valera was arrested by the Free State government 1923, and spent a year in prison. He formed a new party, Fianna Fáil 1926, which secured a majority 1932. De Valera became prime minister and foreign minister of the Free State, and at once abolished the oath of allegiance and suspended payment of the annuities due under the Land Purchase Acts. In 1938 he negotiated an agreement with Britain, under which all outstanding points were settled. Throughout World War II he maintained a strict neutrality, rejecting an offer by Churchill 1940 to recognize the principle of a united Ireland in return for Eire's entry into the war. He resigned after his defeat at the 1948 elections, but was again prime minister in the 1950s, and then president of the republic.

de Valois /də ˈvælwɑː/ Ninette. Stage name of Edris Stannus 1898– . Irish dancer, choreographer, and teacher. A pioneer of British national ballet, she worked with Diaghilev in Paris before opening a dance academy in London 1926. Collaborating with Lilian Baylis at the ◊Old Vic, she founded the Vic-Wells Ballet 1931, which later became the Royal Ballet and Royal Ballet School. Among her works are *Job* 1931 and *Checkmate* 1937.

devaluation in economics, lowering of the official value of a currency against other currencies, so that exports become cheaper and imports dearer. Used when a country is badly in deficit in its balance of trade, it results in the goods the country produces being cheaper abroad, so that the economy is stimulated by increased foreign demand.

The increased cost of imported food, raw materials, and manufactured goods as a consequence of devaluation may, however, stimulate an acceleration in inflation, especially when commodities are rising in price because of increased world demand. *Revaluation* is the opposite process.

Devaluations of important currencies upset the balance of the world's money markets and encourage speculation. To promote greater stability, many countries have allowed the value of their currencies to 'float', that is, to fluctuate in value.

developing in photography, the process that produces a visible image on exposed photographic film. Developing involves treating the emulsion with chemical developer, a reducing agent that changes the light-altered salts into dark metallic silver. The developed image is a negative: darkest where the strongest light hit the emulsion, lightest where the least light hit it.

development in the social sciences, the acquisition by a society of industrial techniques and technology; hence the common classification of the 'developed' nations of the First World and the poorer, 'developing' or 'underdeveloped' nations of the Third World. The assumption that development in the sense of industrialization was inherently good has been increasingly questioned since the 1960s.

Many universities today have academic departments of *development studies*, which address the theoretical questions involved in proposing practical solutions to the problems of development in the Third World.

development in music, the central process of sonata form, in which thematic material presented in the opening statement is combined and extended.

development aid see ◊aid, development.

developmental psychology the study of development of cognition and behaviour from birth to adulthood.

Deventer /ˈdeɪvəntə/ town in Overijssel province, the Netherlands, on the Ijssel, 45 km/28 mi S of the Ijssel Meer; population (1984) 64,800. It is an agricultural and transport centre, and produces carpets, precision equipment and packaging machinery.

deviance abnormal behaviour; that is, behaviour that deviates from the norms or laws of a particular society or group, and so invokes social sanctions, controls, or stigma. The term may refer to minor abnormalities (such as nail-biting) as well as to criminal acts.

Deviance is a relative concept: what is considered deviant in some societies is normal in others; and in a particular society the same act (killing someone, for example) may be either normal or deviant depending on the circumstances (in wartime or for money, for example). Some sociologists, for example Howard Becker, argue that the reaction of others, rather than the act itself, is what determines whether an act is deviant, and that deviance is merely behaviour other people so label.

devil in Christian, Jewish, and Muslim theology, the supreme spirit of evil (*Beelzebub, Lucifer, Iblis*), or an evil spirit generally. In the Middle Ages the devil in popular superstition assumed the attributes of the horned fertility gods of paganism, and was regarded as the god of witches.

In the Jewish Bible or Old Testament, the devil or Satan is mentioned only in the later books, but the later Jewish doctrine is that found in the New Testament.

The concept of the devil passed into the early Christian church from Judaism, and theology until at least the time of St Anselm represented the Atonement as primarily the deliverance, through Christ's death, of mankind from the bondage of the devil. Jesus recognized as a reality the kingdom of evil, of which Satan or Beelzebub was the prince. The belief in a personal devil continued at the Reformation, whose leader Luther regarded himself as the object of a personal Satanic persecution. With the development of liberal Protestantism in the 19th century came a strong tendency to deny the existence of a positive spirit of evil, and to explain the devil as merely a personification. However, the traditional conception was never abandoned by the Roman Catholic Church, and theologians, such as C S Lewis, have maintained the existence of a power of evil.

In Muslim theology, Iblis is one of the *jinn* (beings created by Allah from fire) who refused to prostrate himself before Adam, and who tempted Adam and his wife Hawwa (Eve) to disobey Allah, an act which led to their expulsion from Paradise. He continues to try to lead people astray, but at the Last Judgment he and his hosts will be consigned to hell.

devil ray any large ray of the genera *Manta* and *Mobula*, fish in which two 'horns' project forward from the sides of the huge mouth. These flaps of skin guide the plankton on which the fish feeds into the mouth. The largest of these rays can be 7 m/23 ft across, and weigh 1,000 kg/2,200 lb. They live in warm seas.

devil's coach horse large, black, long-bodied, omnivorous beetle *Ocypus olens*, about 3 cm/1.2 in long. It has powerful jaws and is capable of giving a painful bite. It emits an unpleasant smell when threatened.

Devil's Island /ˈdevəlz ˈaɪlənd/ (French *Ile du Diable*) smallest of the Iles du Salut, off French Guiana, 43 km/27 mi NW of Cayenne. The group of islands was collectively and popularly known by the name Devil's Island, and formed a penal colony notorious for its terrible conditions.

Alfred ◊Dreyfus was imprisoned there 1895–99. Political prisoners were held on Devil's Island, and dangerous criminals on St Joseph, where they were subdued by solitary confinement in tiny cells or subterranean cages. The largest island, Royale, now has a tracking station for the French rocket site at Kourou.

Devil's Marbles area of granite boulders, S of Tennant Creek, off the Stuart Highway in Northern Territory, Australia.

devil wind minor form of ◊tornado, usually occurring in fine weather; formed from rising thermals of warm air (as is a ◊cyclone). A fire creates a similar updraught.

A *fire devil* or *firestorm* may occur in oil-refinery fires, or in the firebombings of cities, for example Dresden, Germany, in World War II.

Devizes /dɪˈvaɪzɪz/ historic market town in Wiltshire, England; population (1982) 13,000. Formerly noted for its trade in cloth, but now a centre for brewing, engineering, and food processing. Special features include ancient earthworks and the shattered remains of a Norman castle stormed by Cromwell in 1645.

devolution the delegation of authority and duties, especially in the later 20th century the movement to decentralize governmental power, as in the UK where a bill for the setting up of Scottish and Welsh assemblies was introduced 1976 (rejected by a referendum in Scotland 1979).

The word was first widely used in this sense in connection with Ireland, with the Irish Nationalist Party leader Redmond claiming in 1898 that the Liberals wished to diminish Home Rule into 'some scheme of devolution or federalism'.

Devolution, War of war waged 1667–68 by Louis XIV of France to gain Spanish territory in the Netherlands, of which ownership had allegedly 'devolved' on his wife Maria Theresa.

It was ended by the Treaty of Aix-la-Chapelle. During the course of the war the French marshal Turenne (1611–75) conducted a remarkable series of sieges.

Devon

Devon /ˈdevən/ or **Devonshire** county in SW England
area 6,720 sq km/2,594 sq mi
towns administrative headquarters Exeter; Plymouth, and the resorts Paignton, Torquay, Teignmouth, and Ilfracombe
features rivers Dart, Exe, Tamar; Dartmoor and Exmoor National Parks
products mainly agricultural, with sheep and dairy farming; cider and clotted cream; kaolin in the south; Honiton lace; Dartington glass
population (1987) 1,010,000
famous people Francis Drake, John Hawkins, Charles Kingsley, Robert F Scott.

Devonian period of geological time 408–360 million years ago, the fourth period of the Palaeozoic era. Many desert sandstones from North America and Europe date from this time. The first land plants flourished in the Devonian period, corals were abundant in the seas, amphibians evolved from air-breathing fish, and insects developed on land.

The name comes from the county of Devon in SW England, where Devonian rocks were first studied.

Devonshire /ˈdevənʃə/ William Cavendish, 7th Duke of Devonshire 1808–1891. British aristocrat, whose development of Eastbourne, Sussex, England, was an early example of town planning.

Devonshire /ˈdevənʃə/ Spencer Compton Cavendish, 8th Duke of Devonshire 1833–1908. British Liberal politician, known as Lord Hartington 1858–91, and leader of the Liberal Party 1874–80. He broke with Gladstone over Irish Home Rule 1885, and was president of the council 1895–1903 under Salisbury and Balfour. As a free-trader, he resigned from Balfour's cabinet.

Devonshire, 8th Duke of see ◊Hartington, Spencer Compton Cavendish.

devotio moderna movement of revived religious spirituality which emerged in the Netherlands at the end of the 14th century and spread into the rest of W Europe. Its emphasis was on individual, rather than communal, devotion, including the private reading of religious works.

Its followers were drawn from the laity, including women and clergy. Lay followers formed themselves into associations known as Brethren of the Common Life. Among its followers was Thomas à Kempis (c.1380–1471), author of *Imitatio Christi*.

dew precipitation in the form of moisture that collects on the ground. It forms after the temperature of the ground has fallen below the ◊dew point of the air in contact with the ground. As the temperature falls during the night, the air and its water vapour become chilled, and condensation takes place on the cooled surfaces.

When moisture begins to form, the surrounding air is said to have reached its dew point. If the temperature falls below freezing point during the night, the dew will freeze, or if the temperature is

diabetes Diabetic child injecting herself with insulin.

low and the dew point is below freezing point, the water vapour condenses directly into ice; in both cases hoar frost is formed.

Dewar /ˈdjuːə/ James 1842–1923. Scottish chemist and physicist who invented the ◊vacuum flask (Thermos) 1872, during his research into the properties of matter at extremely low temperatures.

de Wet /də ˈvet/ Christiaan Rudolf 1854–1922. Boer general and politician. In 1907 he became minister of agriculture in the Orange River Colony; when World War I began, he headed a pro-German rising of 12,000 Afrikaners that was soon suppressed by Prime Minister Louis Botha.

Dewey /ˈdjuːi/ John 1859–1952. US philosopher, who believed that the exigencies of a modern democratic and industrial society demanded new educational techniques. He expounded his ideas in numerous writings, including *School and Society* 1899, and founded a progressive school in Chicago. A pragmatist thinker, influenced by William James, Dewey maintained that there is only the reality of experience, and made 'inquiry' the essence of logic.

Dewey /ˈdjuːi/ Melvil 1851–1931. US librarian. In 1876, he devised the *Dewey decimal system* of classification for books, now widely used in libraries.

de Wint /də ˈwɪnt/ Peter 1784–1849. English landscape artist, of Dutch descent. He was a notable watercolourist.

dew point the temperature at which the water vapour in the air is saturated. At temperatures below the dew point, water vapour condenses out of the air as droplets, which if small form a suspension as mist or fog, or if larger become deposited on objects on or near the ground as ◊dew.

Dhaka /ˈdækə/ (formerly Dacca until 1982) capital of Bangladesh from 1971, in Dhaka region, W of the river Meghna; population (1984) 3,600,000. It trades in jute, oilseed, sugar, and tea, and produces textiles, chemicals, glass, and metal products.

history A former French, Dutch, and English trading post, Dhaka became capital of East Pakistan 1947; it was handed over to Indian troops Dec 1971 to become capital of the new country of Bangladesh.

dharma (Sanskrit 'justice, order') in Hinduism, consciousness of forming part of an ordered universe, and hence the moral duty of accepting one's station in life. In Buddhism, dharma is anything that increases generosity and wisdom, and so leads towards enlightenment.

For Hindus, correct performance of dharma has a favourable effect on their ◊karma; this may enable them to be reborn to a higher caste or on a higher plane of existence, thus coming closer to the final goal of liberation from the cycle of reincarnation.

Dhaulagiri /ˌdaʊləˈɡɪəri/ mountain in the Himalayas of W central Nepál rising to 8,172 m/26,811 ft.

Dhofar /ˈdəʊfɑː/ mountainous western province of ◊Oman, on the border with South Yemen; population (1982) 40,000. South Yemen supported

guerrilla activity here in the 1970s, while Britain and Iran supported the government's military operations. The capital is Salalah, which has a port at Rasut.

dhole species of wild dog *Cuon alpinus* found in Asia from Siberia to Java. With head and body up to 1 m/3 ft long, variable in colour but often reddish above and lighter below, the dhole lives in groups of from 3 to 30 individuals.

Dholes can chase prey for long distances and are capable of pulling down deer and cattle as well as smaller prey. They are even known to have attacked tigers and leopards.

DHSS abbreviation for *Department of Health and Social Security*, UK government department until divided 1988.

diabetes a disease (*diabetes mellitus*) in which a deficiency in the islets of the pancreas prevents the body producing the hormone ◊insulin, so that it cannot use sugars properly.

Sugar, therefore, accumulates first in the blood, then in the urine. The patient experiences thirst, weight loss, and copious voiding. Without treatment, the patient may lapse into diabetic coma and die. Early-onset diabetes tends to be more severe than that developing in later years. Before the discovery of insulin by ◊Banting and ◊Best, severe diabetics did not survive. Today, treatment is by strict dietary control and oral or injected insulin. A continuous infusion of insulin can be provided via a catheter implanted under the skin, which is linked to an electric pump. This more accurately mimics the body's natural secretion of insulin, and can provide better control of diabetes. It is, however, very dangerous if the pump should malfunction.

Much rarer, *diabetes insipidus* is due to a deficiency of a hormone secreted by the ◊pituitary gland to regulate the body's water balance. It is controlled by hormone therapy. In 1989, it was estimated that 4% of the world's population had diabetes, and that there were 12 million sufferers in Canada and the USA.

diag. abbreviation for *diagram*.

diagenesis or *lithification* in geology, the physical and chemical changes by which a sediment becomes a ◊sedimentary rock. The main processes involved include compaction of the grains, and the cementing of the grains together by the growth of new minerals deposited by percolating groundwater.

Diaghilev /diˈæɡəlef/ Sergei Pavlovich 1872–1929. Russian ballet impresario, who in 1909 founded the *Ballets Russes*/Russian Ballet (headquarters in Monaco), which he directed for 20 years. Through this company he brought Russian ballet to the West, introducing and encouraging a dazzling array of dancers, choreographers, and

diagenesis

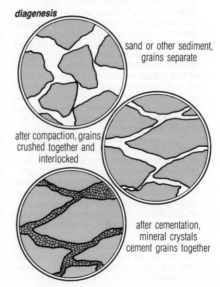

sand or other sediment, grains separate

after compaction, grains crushed together and interlocked

after cementation, mineral crystals cement grains together

composers, such as Pavlova, Nijinsky, Fokine, Massine, Balanchine, Stravinsky, and Prokofiev.

dialect a variety of a language, as spoken in a particular area ('Yorkshire dialect'), or by a particular social group ('the dialect of educated Standard English'), or both ('the black American dialects of English').

The term is used both neutrally, as above, and in a judgemental and often dismissive way ('the locals have a harsh, ugly dialect; few of them have been properly educated'). In the latter case, the standard language of a community is not seen as a dialect itself, but as the 'proper' form of that language, dialects being considered in some way corrupt. This is a matter of social attitude, not of scientific study.

dialectic a Greek term, originally associated with the philosopher Socrates' method of argument through dialogue and conversation. *Hegelian dialectic* refers to an interpretive method in which the contradiction between a thesis and its antithesis is resolved through synthesis.

dialectical materialism the political, philosophical, and economic theory of Marx and Engels, also known as ◊Marxism.

Dial, the 1840–44 US magazine of Transcendentalism, founded in Boston by several of the Transcendentalist group, including Margaret Fuller (1810–50) and Ralph W Emerson, respectively its first and second editors. Printing Thoreau and other major essayists and poets, it had great intellectual influence. Several later magazines used the same title. The *Dial* of the 1920s published modern poetry and criticism under Marianne Moore's editorship.

dialysis in medicine, a way of separating ◊colloidal particles from other, non-colloidal ones in solution using a semipermeable membrane (which allows the passage of the smaller non-colloidal particles but not the larger colloidal ones). Dialysis can thus separate, for example, salts from proteins in blood, which is the natural process in the filtration system of the kidneys, and the engineered equivalent in a dialysis (artificial kidney) machine.

diamond a generally colourless, transparent mineral, the hard crystalline form of carbon. It is regarded as a precious gemstone, and is the hardest natural substance known (10 on the ◊Mohs scale). Industrial diamonds are used for cutting, grinding, and polishing.

Diamond crystallizes in the cubic system as octahedral crystals, some with curved faces and striations. The high refractive index of 2.42 and the high dispersion of light, or 'fire', account for the spectral displays seen in cut diamonds.

Diamonds were known before 3000 BC and until their discovery in Brazil in 1725, India was the principal source of supply. Present sources are Angola, Ghana, Guyana, Sierra Leone, South Africa, Namibia, Tanzania, and Yakut (USSR); Brazil and Zaïre are noted for industrial diamonds. Diamonds may be found as alluvial diamonds on or close to the Earth's surface in riverbeds or dried watercourses; on the sea bottom (off W Africa); or, more commonly, in volcanic pipes composed of 'blue ground' or ◊kimberlite, where the original matrix has penetrated the Earth's crust from great depths. They are sorted from the residue of washed ground by X-ray. Natural diamonds may be exhausted by the year 2000 unless new deposits are found.

There are four chief varieties of diamond: well-crystallized transparent stones, colourless or only slightly tinted, valued as gems; *bort*, poorly crystallized or inferior diamonds; *balas*, an industrial variety, extremely hard and tough; and *carbonado*, or industrial diamond, also called black diamond or carbon, which is opaque, black or grey, and very tough. Industrial diamonds (20 tonnes per annum) are also produced synthetically from graphite.

Because diamonds act as perfectly transparent windows and do not absorb infrared radiation, they were used aboard NASA space probes to Venus in 1978. The tungsten-carbide tools used in steel mills are cut with industrial diamond tools.

Rough diamonds are dull or greasy before being cut, and only 20% are suitable as gems. Diamond gemstones are valued by weight (◊carat), cut (highlighting the stone's optical properties), colour, and clarity (on a six-point scale from P or 'pique', showing a flaw visible to the naked eye, to FL, or 'flawless'). They are cut by the use of diamond dust. The two most frequent forms of cut gem diamonds are the brilliant, for thicker stones, and the rose, for shallower ones. By 1980 India was on the way to replacing Antwerp and Tel Aviv as the world's chief cutting and polishing centres.

Noted diamonds include the Cullinan, or Star of Africa (3,106 carats, over 500 g/17.5 oz before cutting, South Africa, 1905); Excelsior (995.2 carats, South Africa, 1893); and Star of Sierra Leone (968.9 carats, Yengema, 1972).

Diana /daɪˈænə/ in Roman mythology, goddess of hunting and the moon (Greek ◊Artemis), daughter of Jupiter and twin of Apollo.

Diana /daɪˈænə/ Princess of Wales 1961– . The daughter of the 8th Earl Spencer, she married Prince Charles at St Paul's Cathedral 1981, the first English bride of a royal heir since 1659. She is descended from the only sovereigns from whom Prince Charles is not descended, Charles II and James II.

DIANE the collection of information suppliers or 'hosts' for the European computer network, *D*irect *I*nformation *A*ccess *N*etwork for *E*urope.

dianetics a form of psychotherapy developed by the science-fiction writer L Ron Hubbard in the US, which formed the basis for ◊scientology. Hubbard believed that all mental illness and certain forms of physical illness are caused by 'engrams', or incompletely assimilated traumatic experiences, both pre- and post-natal. These engrams can be confronted during therapy with an auditor and thus exorcised. An individual free from engrams would be a 'Clear' and perfectly healthy.

Hubbard later expanded this theory: behind each mind is a non-physical and immortal being, the Thetan, which has forgotten its true nature and is therefore trapped in a cycle of reincarnation, accumulating engrams with each lifetime. If these engrams are cleared, the individual will become an Operating Thetan, with quasi-miraculous powers.

diapause a period of suspended development that occurs in some species of insects, characterized by greatly reduced metabolism. Periods of diapause are often timed to coincide with the winter months, and improve the insect's chances of surviving adverse conditions.

diaphragm or *cap*, a barrier contraceptive that is pushed into the vagina and fits over the cervix (neck of the womb), preventing sperm from entering the womb (uterus). For a cap to be effective, a ◊spermicide must be used. This method is 97% effective if practised correctly.

diarrhoea excessive action of the bowels so that the motions are fluid or semi-fluid. It is caused by intestinal irritants (including some drugs and poisons), infection with harmful organisms (as in ◊dysentery or ◊cholera), or allergy.

Diarrhoea is the biggest killer of children in the world. The World Health Organization estimates that 4.5 million children die each year from dehydration as a result of diarrhoeal disease in less developed countries. It can be treated by giving an accurately measured solution of salt and glucose by mouth in large quantities. Since most diarrhoea is viral in orgin, antibiotics are ineffective.

diary an informal record of day-to-day events, observations, or reflections, usually not intended for a general readership. One of the earliest diaries extant is that of a Japanese noblewoman, the *Kagerō Nikki* 954–974, and the earliest diary extant in English is that of Edward VI (ruled 1547–53). Notable diaries include those of Samuel Pepys, the writer John Evelyn, the Quaker George Fox, and in the 20th century those of Anne ◊Frank and the writers André Gide and Katherine Mansfield.

diatom Diatoms form a fundamental part of the food chain of both marine and freshwater environments.

Diaspora the dispersal of the Jews, initially from Palestine after the Babylonian conquest 586 BC, and then following the Roman sack of Jerusalem AD 70 and their crushing of the Jewish revolt of 135. The term has come to refer to all the Jews living outside Israel.

diathermy the generation of heat in body tissues by the passage of high-frequency electric currents between two electrodes placed on the body, used to relieve arthritic pain.

In diathermic surgery, one electrode is very much reduced for cutting purposes and the other correspondingly enlarged and placed at a distance on the body. The high-frequency current produces, at the tip of the cutting electrode, sufficient heat to cut tissues, or to coagulate and kill tissue cells, with a minimum of bleeding.

diatom microscopic alga of the division Bacillariophyta found in all parts of the world. They consist of single cells, sometimes grouped in colonies.

The cell wall is made up of two overlapping valves known as *frustules*, which are usually impregnated with silica, and which fit together like the lid and body of a pillbox. Diatomaceous earths (diatomite) are made up of the valves of fossil diatoms, and are used in the manufacture of dynamite, and in the rubber and plastics industries.

diatonic in music, a scale consisting of the seven notes of any major or minor key.

Diaz /ˈdiːæʃ/ Bartolomeu *c.*1450–1500. Portuguese explorer, the first European to reach the Cape of Good Hope 1488, and to establish a route around Africa. He drowned during an expedition with Pedro ◊Cabral.

Díaz /ˈdiːæs/ Porfirio 1830–1915. Dictator of Mexico 1877–80 and 1884–1911. After losing the 1876 election, he overthrew the government and seized power. He was supported by conservative landowners and foreign capitalists, who invested in railways and mines. He centralized the state at the expense of the peasants and Indians, and dismantled all local and regional leadership. He faced mounting and revolutionary opposition in his final years and was forced into exile 1911.

Diaz de Solís /ˈdiːæs deɪ ˈsəʊlɪs/ Juan 1471–*c.*1516. Spanish explorer in South America, who reached the estuary of the River Plate and was killed and eaten by cannibals.

Dick /dɪk/ Philip K(endred) 1928–1982. US science-fiction writer, whose works often deal with religion and the subjectivity of reality; his novels include *The Man in the High Castle* 1962 and *Do Androids Dream of Electric Sheep?* 1968.

Dickens /ˈdɪkɪnz/ Charles 1812–1870. English novelist, popular for his memorable characters and his portrayals of the social evils of Victorian England. In 1836 he published the first number of the *Pickwick Papers*, followed by *Oliver Twist* 1838, the first of his 'reforming' novels; *Nicholas Nickleby* 1839; *Barnaby Rudge* 1840, *The Old Curiosity Shop* 1841, and *David Copperfield* 1849. Among his later books are *A Tale of Two Cities* 1859 and *Great Expectations* 1861.

Born in Portsea, Hampshire, the son of a clerk, Dickens received little formal education, although a short period spent working in a blacking factory in S London, while his father was imprisoned for

Dickens *English novelist Charles Dickens.*

debt in the Marshalsea prison during 1824, was followed by three years in a private school. In 1827 he became a lawyer's clerk, and then after four years a reporter for the *Morning Chronicle*, to which he contributed the *Sketches by Boz*. In 1836 he married Katherine Hogarth, three days after the publication of the first number of the *Pickwick Papers*. Originally intended merely as an accompaniment to a series of sporting illustrations, the adventures of Pickwick outgrew their setting and established Dickens' reputation.

In 1842 he visited the USA, where his attack on the pirating of English books by US publishers chilled his welcome; his experiences are reflected in *American Notes* and *Martin Chuzzlewit* 1843. In 1843 he published the first of his Christmas books, *A Christmas Carol*, followed in 1844 by *The Chimes*, written in Genoa during his first long sojourn abroad, and in 1845 by the even more successful *Cricket on the Hearth*. A venture as editor of the Liberal *Daily News* in 1846 was shortlived, and *Dombey and Son* 1848 was largely written abroad. *David Copperfield*, his most popular novel, appeared 1849, and contains many autobiographical incidents and characters.

Returning to journalism, Dickens inaugurated the weekly magazine *Household Words* 1850, reorganizing it 1859 as *All the Year Round*; many of his later stories were published serially in these periodicals.

In 1856 he agreed with his wife on a separation; his sister-in-law remained with him to care for his children, while Dickens formed an association with the actress Ellen Ternan. In 1858 he began making public readings from his novels, which proved such a success that he was invited to make a second US tour 1867. Among his later novels are *Bleak House* 1853, *Hard Times* 1854, *Little Dorrit* 1857, and *Our Mutual Friend* 1864. *Edwin Drood*, a mystery story influenced by the style of his friend Wilkie ◊Collins, was left incomplete on his death.

Dickens /'dɪkɪnz/ Monica (Enid) 1915– . British writer. Her first books were humorous accounts of her experiences in various jobs, beinning as a cook (*One Pair of Hands* 1939); she went on to become a novelist. She is a great-granddaughter of Charles Dickens.

Dickinson /'dɪkɪnsən/ Emily 1830–1886. US poet. Born in Amherst, Massachusetts, she lived in near seclusion there from 1862. Almost none of her many short, mystical poems were published during her lifetime. Her work became well known only in the 20th century.

Dick-Read /'dɪk 'riːd/ Grantly 1890–1959. British gynaecologist. In private practice in London 1923–48, he developed the theory of natural childbirth, that is, that by the elimination of fear and

tension, childbirth pain could be minimized and anaesthetics rendered unnecessary.

dicotyledon a subclass of the ◊angiosperms, containing the great majority of flowering plants. Dicotyledons are characterized by the presence of two seed-leaves or ◊cotyledons in the embryo, which is usually surrounded by an ◊endosperm. They generally have broad leaves with netlike veins. Dicotyledons may be small plants such as daisies and buttercups, shrubs, or trees such as oak and beech. The other subclass of the angiosperms is the ◊monocotyledons.

dictator an absolute ruler, overriding the constitution. (In ancient Rome a dictator was a magistrate invested with emergency powers for six months.) Although dictatorships were common in Latin America during the 19th century, the only European example during this period was the rule of Napoleon III. The crises following World War I produced many dictatorships, including the régimes of Atatürk and Pilsudski (nationalist), Mussolini, Hitler, Primo de Rivera, Franco, and Salazar (all right-wing) and Stalin (Communist).

dictatorship of the proletariat Marxist term for a revolutionary dictatorship established during the transition from capitalism to ◊communism after a socialist revolution.

dictionary a book that contains a selection of the words of a language, with their pronunciations and meanings, usually arranged in alphabetic order. The term 'dictionary' is also applied to any usually alphabetic work of reference containing specialized information about a particular subject, art or science; for example, a dictionary of music. Language dictionaries provide translations of one country's language into another.

The first dictionaries of English (*glossa collectae*) served to explain difficult words, generally of Latin or Greek origin, in everyday English. Samuel Johnson's dictionary of 1755 was one of the first dictionaries of standard English, and the first to give extensive coverage to phrasal verbs, to which Noah Webster in 1828 offered a US alternative. The many-volume *Oxford English Dictionary*, begun 1884 and subject to continuous revision (and now computerization), provides a detailed historical record of the vocabulary of the language.

10th century Byzantine *Lexicon* of Suidas (first A–Z).
1225 John Garland used the term 'dictionarus'.
1530 First English–English dictionary (appendix to William Temple's *Pentateuch*).
1538 Thomas Elyot's *Shorte Dictionarie for Yonge Begynners* (English–Latin).
16th century first vernacular–vernacular dictionaries: William Salesbury, Welsh–English 1547; John Florio, Italian–English 1599.
1604 Robert Cawdrey *Table Alphabeticall of hard usuall English wordes* (aimed at converting Latin to Latinate English).
1755 Samuel Johnson's dictionary of standard English.
1828 Noah Webster's US alternative to Johnson's dictionary.
1852 Peter Mark Roget's *Thesaurus of English Words*.
1884 The *Oxford English Dictionary* was begun.

Diderot /'diːdərəʊ/ Denis 1713–1784. French philosopher of the ◊Enlightenment and editor of the ◊*Encyclopédie* 1751–1780. He exerted an enormous influence on contemporary social thinking with his ◊materialism and anti-clericalism.

His materialism, most articulately expressed in *D'Alembert's Dream*, sees the natural world as nothing more than matter and motion. His account of the origin and development of life is purely mechanical.

Didion /'dɪdiən/ Joan 1934– . US novelist and journalist. Her sharp, culturally evocative writing includes the novel *The Book of Common Prayer* 1970 and the essays of *The White Album* 1979.

didjeridu musical wind instrument, made from a hollow bamboo section 1.5 m/4 ft long and blown

Diderot *A portrait, by L M Loo, of the French philosopher and encyclopedist Denis Diderot. His account of the origin and nature of life anticipated evolutionary theories.*

to produce rhythmic, booming notes. First developed and played by Australian Aborigines.

Dido /'daɪdəʊ/ Phoenician princess, legendary founder of Carthage, who committed suicide in order to avoid marrying a local prince. In the Latin epic *Aeneid*, Virgil claims that it was because ◊Aeneas deserted her.

diecasting a form of ◊casting, in which molten metal is injected into permanent metal moulds or dies.

Diefenbaker /'diːfən,beɪkə/ John George 1895–1979. Canadian Progressive Conservative politician, prime minister 1957–63, when he was defeated after criticism of the proposed manufacture of nuclear weapons in Canada.

He was born in Ontario, and moved to Saskatchewan. A brilliant defence counsel, he became known as the 'prairie lawyer'. He became leader of his party 1956 and prime minister 1957. In 1958 he achieved the greatest landslide in Canadian history. A 'radical' Tory, he was also a strong supporter of Commonwealth unity. He resigned the party leadership in 1967, repudiating a 'two nations' policy for Canada. He was known as 'the Chief'.

Diego Garcia /di'eɪgəʊ gɑː'siːə/ island in the ◊Chagos Archipelago, named after its Portuguese discoverer in 1532. See ◊British Indian Ocean Territory.

dielectric a substance (an insulator such as ceramic or glass) capable of supporting electric stress. The dielectric constant, or relative permittivity, of a substance is the ratio of the capacity of a capacitor with the medium as dielectric to that of a similar capacitor in which the dielectric is replaced by a vacuum.

Diels /diːls/ Otto 1876–1954. German chemist. In 1950 he and his former assistant, Kurt Alder, were jointly awarded the Nobel Prize for Chemistry for their research into carbon synthesis.

Diemen /'diːmən/ Anthony van 1593–1645. Dutch admiral. In 1636 he was appointed governor general of Dutch settlements in the E Indies, and wrested Ceylon and Malacca from the Portuguese. In 1636 and 1642 he supervised expeditions to Australia, on the second of which the navigator Abel Tasman discovered land not charted by Europeans, and named it **Van Diemen's Land**, now Tasmania.

different types of diet

diet	particulars
vegetarian	eat no meat
vegan	eat no food of animal origin
Hay system	do not mix protein with starches and fruits
macrobiotic	based on unrefined cereals
fruitarian	based on fruits, nuts, and seeds
Jewish	eat ◊kosher food
Muslim	eat ◊halal food
Hindus	vegetarian

NACNE (UK National Advisory Committee on Nutritional Education) guidelines for a healthy diet

component	amount
fat	should be 35% of total energy
fibres	should be 25–30 g per day
protein	should be 10–12% of total energy
cholesterol	all right if fat guidelines are followed
sugar	maximum 55 g per day
salt	maximum 9 g per day

variations in calorie intake
percentage of calorie requirement

	1961–63	1969–71	1972–74
developed countries	125	131	134
underdeveloped countries	91	92	90
world average	101	106	107

Dien Bien Phu, Battle of /'diːen 'biːen 'fuː/ decisive battle in the ◊Indo-China War at a French fortress in North Vietnam, near the Laotian border, 320 km/200 mi from Hanoi. 10,000 French troops under Général de Castries were besieged 13 Mar–7 May 1954 by the communist Vietminh. The fall of Dien Bien Phu resulted in the end of French control of Indo-China.

Dieppe /diː'ep/ channel port at the mouth of the river Arques, Seine-Maritime *département*, N France; population (1983) 39,500. There are ferry services from its harbour to Newhaven and elsewhere, and fishing, shipbuilding and pharmaceutical industries.

Diesel /'diːzəl/ Rudolf 1858–1913. German engineer who patented the diesel engine. He began his career as a refrigerator engineer and, like many engineers of the period, sought to develop a more efficient power source than the conventional steam engine. Able to operate with greater efficiency and economy, the diesel engine soon found a ready market.

diesel engine a kind of ◊internal combustion engine that burns a lightweight oil. The diesel engine operates by compressing air until it becomes sufficiently hot to ignite the fuel. They are piston-in-cylinder engines like the car ◊petrol engine, but just air (rather than an air-and-fuel mixture) is taken into the cylinder on the first piston stroke (down). The piston moves up and compresses the air until it is at a very high temperature. The fuel oil is then injected into the hot air, whereupon it burns, driving the piston down on its power stroke. For this reason the engine is called a compression-ignition engine.

The principle was first put forward in England by Herbert Akroyd (1864–1937) in 1890, and applied practically by Rudolf Diesel in Germany two years later.

diesel oil gas oil used in engines (when used in vehicle engines also known as *derv—d*iesel-engine *r*oad *v*ehicle). Like petrol, it is a petroleum product.

diet a particular selection of food, or a person's or people's regular food intake. A special diet may be recommended for medical reasons, to limit or increase certain nutrients; undertaken to lose weight, by a reduction in calorie intake; or observed on religious, moral, or emotional

Dietrich *Marlene Dietrich in* The Blue Angel *1930, the film that won her international fame.*

grounds. An adequate diet is one that fulfils the body's nutritional requirements and gives an energy intake proportional to the person's activity level (the average daily requirement is 2,400 calories). Some 450 million people in the world subsist on less than 1,500 calories, whereas in the developed countries the average daily intake is 3,300.

diet a meeting or convention of the princes and other dignitaries of the Holy Roman (German) Empire, for example, the Diet of Worms 1521 which met to consider the question of Luther's doctrines and the governance of the empire under Charles V.

dietetics a specialized branch of human nutrition, dealing with the promotion of health through good nutrition.

Therapeutic dietetics is important in the treatment of certain illnesses such as diabetes; it is sometimes used alone, but often in conjunction with drugs. See ◊food.

Dietrich /'diːtrɪk/ Marlene. Stage name of Magdalene von Losch 1904– . German actress and singer, born in Berlin, who first won fame by her appearance with Emil Jannings in the film *The Blue Angel* 1930. She went to Hollywood, becoming a US citizen in 1937. Her husky, sultry singing voice added to her appeal. Her other films include *Blonde Venus* 1932 and *Destry Rides Again* 1939.

Dieu et mon droit (French 'God and my right') motto of the royal arms of Great Britain.

difference engine a mechanical calculating machine designed, but never built, by the British mathematician Charles ◊Babbage about 1830. It was to calculate mathematical functions by solving the differences between values given to ◊variables within equations. Babbage designed the calculator so that once the initial values for the variables were set it would produce the next few thousand values without error.

differential an arrangement of gears in the final drive of a vehicle's transmission system that allows the driving wheels to turn at different speeds when cornering. The differential consists of sets of bevel gears and pinions within a cage attached

differential

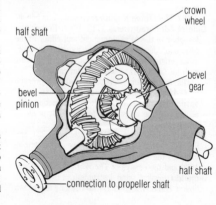

- crown wheel
- half shaft
- bevel gear
- bevel pinion
- half shaft
- connection to propeller shaft

differentiation

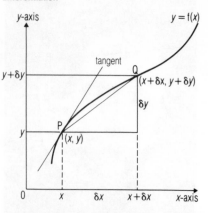

to the crown wheel. When cornering, the bevel pinions rotate to allow the outer wheel to turn faster than the inner.

differential calculus a branch of ◊analysis involving the ◊differentiation of functions and their applications such as determination of maximum and minimum points and rates of change. See also ◊calculus, ◊integral calculus.

differentiation in mathematics, a procedure for determining the gradient of the tangent to a curve $f(x)$ at any point x. The first derivative is usually expressed as dy/dx. Applications of this procedure are rates of change, maximum and minimum points. When a ◊function $f(x)$ is differentiated, the result is a derived function (or derivative) written $f'(x)$.

differentiation in embryology, the process whereby cells become increasingly different and specialized, giving rise to more complex structures which have particular functions in the adult organism. For instance, embryonic cells may develop into nerve, muscle, or bone cells.

diffraction the slight spreading of a light beam into a pattern of light and dark bands when it passes through a narrow slit or past the edge of an obstruction. The resulting patterns are known as interference phenomena. A *diffraction grating* is a device for separating a wave train such as a beam of incident light into its component frequencies (white light results in a spectrum).

The regular spacing of atoms in crystals are used to diffract X-rays, and in this way the structure of many substances has been elucidated, including recently that of proteins. Sound waves can also be diffracted by a suitable array of solid objects.

diffraction *the diffraction effect created by the use of a cross-screen filter and two polarisers*

diffusion in physical chemistry, any of at least three processes: the spontaneous mixing of gases or liquids (classed together as *fluids* in scientific usage) when brought into contact without mechanical mixing or stirring; the spontaneous passage of fluids through membranes; and the spontaneous passage of dissolved materials both through the material in which they are dissolved and also through membranes.

One important application is the separation of isotopes, particularly those of uranium. When uranium hexafluoride diffuses through a porous plate, the ratio of the 235 and 238 isotopes is changed slightly. With sufficient number of passages, the separation is nearly complete. There are large plants in the UK and the US for obtaining enriched fuel for fast nuclear reactors and the fissile uranium-235, originally required for the first atom bombs. Another application is the diffusion pump, used extensively in vacuum work, in which the gas to be evacuated diffuses into a chamber from which it is carried away by the vapour of a suitable medium, usually oil or mercury.

Digambara ('sky-clad') member of a sect of Jain monks (see ◊Jainism) who practise complete nudity.

digestion the process whereby food eaten by an animal is broken down physically, and chemically by ◊enzymes, usually in the ◊stomach and ◊intestines, to make the nutrients available for absorption and cell metabolism.

In some single-celled organisms, such as amoebae, a food particle is engulfed by the cell itself, and digested in a ◊vacuole within the cell.

digestive system the mouth, stomach, gut, and associated glands of animals, which are responsible for digesting food. The food is broken down by physical and chemical means in the ◊stomach and the soluble products absorbed in the ◊intestines. In birds, additional digestive organs are the ◊crop and ◊gizzard.

In smaller, simpler animals such as jellyfish, the digestive system is simply a cavity (coelenteron or enteric cavity) with a 'mouth' into which food is taken; the digestive portion is dissolved and absorbed in this cavity and the remains are ejected back through the mouth.

Diggers also called *true ◊Levellers*. An English 17th-century radical sect which became prominent in Apr 1649 when, headed by Gerrard Winstanley (*c.*1609–60), it set up communal colonies near Cobham, Surrey, and elsewhere. They were broken up by mobs and, being pacifists, made no resistance. Their ideas influenced the early ◊Quakers.

digit any of the numbers from 0 to 9. In computing, different numbering systems have different ranges of digits. For example, ◊hexadecimal has digits 0 to 9 and A to F, whereas binary has two digits (or ◊bits), 0 and 1.

digital in electronics and computing, a term meaning 'coded as numbers'. A digital system uses two-state, either on/off or high/low voltage pulses, to encode, receive, and transmit information. A *digital display* shows discrete values as numbers (as opposed to an analogue signal such as the continuous sweep of a pointer on a dial).

digital electronics is the technology that underlies digital techniques. Low-power, miniature, integrated circuits (chips) provide the means for the coding, storage, transmission, processing, and reconstruction of information of all kinds.

digital audio tape (DAT) tape used to record sounds in digital or numerical form. During recording, the sound is sampled more than 30,000 times a second and the values recorded as numbers on the tape in a magnetic pattern. During playback, the numbers are reconverted to sounds. The system allows high-quality reproduction because unwanted noise can be eliminated electronically during recording and playback. In addition, the DAT is a compact medium, as a cassette the size of a credit card can hold four hours of sound.

digestive system

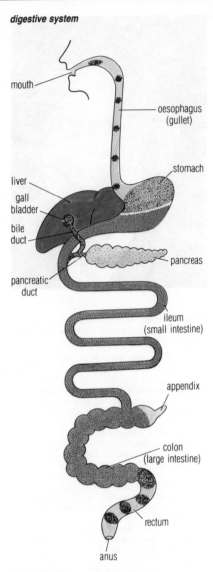

mouth
oesophagus (gullet)
stomach
liver
gall bladder
bile duct
pancreas
pancreatic duct
ileum (small intestine)
appendix
colon (large intestine)
rectum
anus

digital computer a computing device that operates on a two-state system, using symbols that are internally coded as binary numbers (numbers made up of combinations of the digits 0 and 1); see ◊computer.

digital data transmission in computing, a way of sending data by converting all signals (whether pictures, sounds, or words) into numeric (normally binary) codes before transmission and then reconverting them on receipt. This virtually eliminates any distortion or degradation of the signal during transmission, storage, or processing.

digitalis plant of the genus *Digitalis*, family Scrophulariaceae, which includes the foxgloves.

digitalis a drug that increases the efficiency of the heart by strengthening its muscle contractions and slowing its rate. Derived from the common woodland plant *Digitalis purpurea* (foxglove), it was the first cardiac drug. Digitalis therapy was pioneered in the late 1700s by William Withering, an English physician and botanist. It is extremely toxic.

digital recording a technique whereby the pressure of sound waves is sampled more than 30,000 times a second and the values recorded as numbers which, during playback, are reconverted to sound waves. This gives very high-quality reproduction.

digital sampling an electronic process used in ◊telecommunications for transforming a constantly varying (analogue) signal into one composed of discrete units, a digital signal. For example, a telephone microphone changes sound waves into

dik-dik

an analogue signal that fluctuates up and down like a wave. In the digitizing process the waveform is sampled thousands of times a second and each part of the sampled wave is given a ◊binary code number related to the height of the wave at that point, which is transmitted along the telephone line. Using digital signals, messages can be transmitted quickly, accurately and economically.

Dijon /'diːʒɒŋ/ city and capital of Bourgogne (Burgundy), France; population (1983) 216,000. As well as metallurgical, chemical, and other industries, it has a wine trade and is famed for its mustard.

dik-dik one of several species of tiny antelope, genus *Madoqua*, found in Africa south of the Sahara in dry areas with scattered brush. Dik-diks are about 60 cm/2 ft long and 35 cm/1.1 ft tall, and often seen in pairs. Males possess short, pointed horns. The name is derived from the alarm call of the animal.

dilatation and curettage (D and C) a common gynaecological procedure in which the cervix (neck of the womb) is widened, or dilated, giving access so that the lining of the womb can be scraped away (curettage). It may be carried out to terminate a pregnancy, treat an incomplete miscarriage, or discover the cause of heavy menstrual bleeding.

Dilke /dɪlk/ Charles Wentworth 1843–1911. British Liberal politician, Member of Parliament 1868–86 and 1892–1911. A Radical, he supported a minimum wage and legalization of trade unions.

dill umbelliferous herb *Anethum graveolens* used for culinary and medicinal purposes.

Dillinger /'dɪlɪndʒə/ John 1903–1934. US criminal who undertook a serious of bank robberies between June 1933 and July 1934 in several states. Although captured in Ohio and Arizona, he was able to escape on both occasions before being trapped and shot by the Federal Bureau of Investigation outside the Biograph Theater in Chicago. After the shooting, rumours circulated that he was not the man killed by the federal agents.

Dilthey /'dɪltaɪ/ Wilhelm 1833–1911. German philosopher, a major figure in the tradition of ◊hermeneutics. He argued that the 'human sciences' (*Geisteswissenschaften*) could not employ the same methods as the natural sciences, but must use the procedure of 'understanding' (*Verstehen*) to grasp

dill

flower
seed head
seed

the inner life of an alien culture or past historical period. Thus Dilthey extended the significance of hermeneutics far beyond the interpretation of texts to the whole of human history and culture.

dilution the process of reducing the ◊concentration of a solution by the addition of ◊solvent.

DiMaggio Joe 1914– . US baseball player with the New York Yankees 1936–51. In 1941 he set a record by getting hits in 56 consecutive games. He was an outstanding fielder, hit 361 home runs, and had a career average of .325. He was once married to the actress Marilyn Monroe.

Dimbleby /'dɪmbəlbi/ Richard 1913–1965. British broadcaster and provincial newspaper owner. He joined the British Broadcasting Corporation in 1936 and established himself as the foremost commentator on royal and state events and current affairs (*Panorama*) on radio and television. He is commemorated by the *Dimbleby lectures*.

dime novel yellow-backed cheap novel of a series started in the US in the 1850s by Erastus F Beadle and frequently dealing with frontier adventure. Like British 'penny dreadfuls', dime novels attained massive sales. Dime novels were especially popular with troops during the American Civil War. The 'Nick Carter' Library added detective stories to the genre.

dimension basic physical quantity such as mass (M), length (L) and time (T), which can be combined by multiplication or division to give the dimensions of derived quantities. For example, acceleration (the rate of change of velocity) has dimensions (LT^{-2}), and is expressed in such units as km sec^{-2}. A quantity that is a ratio, such as relative density or humidity, is dimensionless.

dimethyl sulphoxide by-product of the processing of wood to paper, used as an antifreeze and industrial solvent.

diminishing returns, law of in economics, the principle that additional application of one factor of production, such as an extra machine or employee, at first results in rapidly increasing output, but then eventually yields declining returns, unless other factors are modified to sustain the increase.

Dimitrov /,dɪmɪ'trɒf/ Georgi 1882–1949. Bulgarian Communist, prime minister from 1946. He was elected a deputy in 1913, and from 1919 was a member of the executive of the Comintern (see ◊International). In 1933 he was arrested in Berlin and tried with others in Leipzig for allegedly setting fire to the parliament building (see ◊Reichstag Fire). Acquitted, he went to the USSR, where he became general secretary of the Comintern until its dissolution in 1943.

DIN abbreviation for *Deutsches Institut für Normung*, the West German national standards body, which has set internationally accepted standards for (among other things) paper sizes and electrical connectors.

Dinan /di:'nɒn/ town in Côtes-du-Nord *département*, N France, on the river Rance; population (1982) 14,150. The river is harnessed for tidal hydroelectric power.

Dinant /di:'nɒn/ ancient town in Namur province, Belgium, on the river Meuse; population (1982) 12,000. It is a tourist centre for the Ardennes.

Dinaric Alps /dɪ'nærɪk/ extension of the European ◊Alps in Western Yugoslavia and NW Albania. The highest peak is Durmitor at 2,522 m/8,274 ft.

Dine /daɪn/ Jim 1935– . US Pop artist. He experimented with combinations of paintings and objects, such as a washbasin attached to a canvas.

Dine was a pioneer of happenings (art as live performance) in the 1950s and of environment art (three-dimensional works that attempt active interaction with the spectator, sometimes using sound or movement). His paintings used images of contemporary US culture: domestic objects, cars, food, and so on.

Dinesen /'dɪnɪsən/ Isak 1885–1962. Pen name of Danish writer Karen ◊Blixen, born Karen Christentze Dinesen.

Dingaan /'dɪŋgɑːn/ Zulu chief from 1828. He obtained the throne by murdering his predecessor,

Dinkins New York City mayor, David Dinkins. A moderate Democrat of humble origins, he is the first black to be elected to the position.

Shaka, and became noted for his cruelty. In warfare with the Boer immigrants into Natal he was defeated on 16 Dec 1838—'Dingaan's Day'. He escaped to Swaziland, where he was deposed by his brother Mpande and subsequently murdered.

Ding Ling /'dɪŋ 'lɪŋ/ 1904–1986. Chinese novelist. Her works include *Wei Hu* 1930 and *The Sun Shines over the Sanggan River* 1951.

She was imprisoned by the Guomindang (Chiang Kai-Shek's Nationalists) in the 1930s, wrongly labelled as rightist and expelled from the Communist Party 1957, imprisoned in the 1960s and intellectually exiled for not keeping to Maoist literary rules; she was rehabilitated 1979. Her husband was the writer Hu Yapin, executed by Chiang Kai-Shek's police 1931.

dingo wild dog of Australia. Descended from domestic animals brought from Asia by Aborigines thousands of years ago, it belongs to the same species *Canis familiaris* as other domestic dogs. It is reddish brown, with a bushy tail, and often hunts at night. It cannot bark.

Dinka person of Dinka culture from southern Sudan. The Dinka, numbering approximately 1 million, are primarily cattle herders, and inhabit the lands around the river system that flows into the White Nile. Their language belongs to the Chari-Nile family.

Dinkins /'dɪŋkɪnz/ David 1927– . Mayor of New York City from Jan 1990, a Democrat. He won a reputation as a moderate and consensual community politician and was Manhattan borough president before succeeding Ed Koch to become New York's first black mayor.

Dinorwig /dɪ'nɔːwɪg/ the location of Europe's largest pumped-storage hydroelectric scheme, completed 1984, in Gwynedd, North Wales. Six turbogenerators are involved, with a maximum output of some 1,880 megawatts. The working head of water for the station is 530 m/1,740 ft.

The main machine hall is twice as long as a football field and as high as a 16-storey building.

dinosaur (Greek *deinos* 'terrible', *sauros* 'lizard') any of a group of extinct reptiles living between 215 million and 65 million years ago. Their closest living relations are crocodiles and birds, the latter perhaps descended from the dinosaurs. Many species of dinosaur evolved during the millions of years they were the dominant large land animals. They all disappeared suddenly, perhaps because of a significant change in climate.

Brachiosaurus, a long-necked plant-eating member of the sauropod group, was about 12.6 m/40 ft to the top of its head, and weighed 80 tonnes. *Compsognathus* was only the size of a chicken, and ran on its hind legs. Not all dinosaurs had small brains. *Stegosaurus*, an armoured plant-eater 6 m/20 ft long, had a brain only about 3 cm/1.25 in long. At the other extreme, the hunting dinosaur *Stenonychosaurus*, 2 m/6 ft long, had a brain size comparable to that of a mammal or bird of today, stereoscopic vision, and grasping hands. Many dinosaurs appear equipped for a high activity level.

An almost complete fossil of a dinosaur skeleton was found in 1969 in the Andean foothills, South America; it had been a two-legged carnivore 2 m/6 ft tall and weighing more than 100 kg/220 lb. More than 230 million years old, it is the oldest known dinosaur. Eggs are known of some species. In 1982, a number of nests and eggs were found in 'colonies' in Montana, suggesting that some bred together like modern seabirds. In 1987, finds were made in China that may change much of traditional knowledge of dinosaurs, chiefly gleaned from North American specimens.

Dion Cassius /'daɪən 'kæsiəs/ AD 150–235. Roman historian. He wrote, in Greek, a Roman history in 80 books (of which 26 survive), covering the period from the founding of the city to AD 229, including the only surviving account of the invasion of Britain by Claudius in 43 BC.

Diocletian /,daɪə'kliːʃən/ Gaius Valerius Diocletianus AD 245–313. Roman emperor 284–305, when he abdicated in favour of Galerius. He reorganized and subdivided the empire, with two joint and two subordinate emperors, and in 303 initiated severe persecution of the Christians.

diode a thermionic valve (vacuum tube) with two electrodes (negative cathode and positive anode) or its semiconductor equivalent, which incorporates a *p–n* junction. Either device allows the passage of direct current in one direction only, and so is commonly used to rectify alternating current (AC), converting it to direct current (DC).

dioecious describing plants that have male and female flowers borne on separate individuals of the same species. Dioecy occurs, for example, in the willows (*Salix*). It is a way of avoiding self-fertilization.

Diogenes /daɪ'ɒdʒəniːz/ *c.*412–323 BC. Ascetic Greek philosopher of the Cynic school. He believed in freedom and self-sufficiency for the individual, and did not believe in social mores.

He was born at Sinope, captured by pirates and sold as a slave to a Corinthian named Xeniades, who appointed Diogenes tutor to his two sons. He spent the rest of his life in Corinth. He is said to have carried a lamp during the daytime, looking for one honest man. The story of his having lived in a barrel arose only from Seneca having said that was where a man so crabbed ought to have lived. His writings do not survive.

Diomede /'daɪəmiːd/ two islands off the tip of the Seward peninsula, Alaska. *Little Diomede* 6.2 sq km/2.4 sq mi, belongs to the USA, and is only 3.9 km/2.4 mi from *Big Diomede* 29.3 sq km/11.3 sq mi, owned by the USSR. They were first sighted by Vitus Bering 1728.

Dionysia /,daɪə'nɪziə/ festivals of the god ◊Dionysus (Bacchus) celebrated in ancient Greece, especially in Athens. They included the lesser Dionysia in Dec, chiefly a rural festival, and the greater Dionysia, at the end of Mar, when new plays were performed.

Dionysius /,daɪə'nɪziəs/ two tyrants of the ancient Greek city of Syracuse in Sicily. *Dionysius the Elder* (432–367 BC) seized power in 405. His first two wars with Carthage further extended the power of Syracuse, but in a third (383–378 BC) he was defeated. He was a patron of ◊Plato (see also ◊Damocles). He was succeeded by his son, *Dionysius the Younger*, who was driven out of Syracuse by Dion in 356; he was tyrant again in 353, but in 343 returned to Corinth.

dip, magnetic

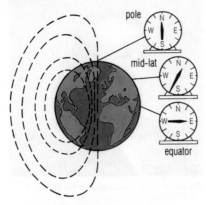

magnetic lines of force

Dionysus /ˌdaɪəˈnaɪsəs/ in Greek mythology, god of wine (son of Semele and Zeus), and also of orgiastic excess. He was identified with ◊Bacchus, whose rites were less savage. Attendant on him were ◊maenads.

Diophantus /ˌdaɪəʊˈfæntəs/ lived *c*.250. Greek mathematician in Alexandria, whose *Arithmetica* is one of the first known works on problem-solving by algebra, in which both words and symbols were used.

dioptre an optical unit in which the power of a ◊lens is expressed as the reciprocal of its focal length in metres. The usual convention is that convergent lenses are positive and divergent lenses negative. Short-sighted people need lenses of power about −0.66 dioptre; a typical value for long sight is about +1.5 dioptre.

Dior /ˈdiːɔː/ Christian 1905–1957. French couturier. He established his own Paris salon in 1947 and made an impact with the 'New Look'—long, cinch-waisted, and full-skirted—after wartime austerity.

diorite an igneous rock intermediate in composition; the coarse-grained plutonic equivalent of ◊andesite.

Diouf /diˈuːf/ Abdou 1935– . Senegalese politician, president from 1980. He became prime minister 1970 under President Leopold Senghor and, on his retirement, succeeded him, being re-elected in 1983 and 1988.

Born at Louga in NW Senegal, Diouf studied at Paris University and was a civil servant before entering politics. He was chair of the Organization of African Unity 1985–86.

dioxin common name for tetrachlorodibenzodioxin, one of a family of organic chemicals called dioxins. A highly toxic chemical, it was produced as a by-product of a defoliant used in the Vietnam War, and of the weedkiller 2,4,5-T. It causes a disfiguring skin complaint, chloracne, and has been linked with birth defects, miscarriages, and cancer.

Disasters involving release of dioxin into the environment have occurred at Seveso in Italy and Times Beach in Missouri, USA. Smaller amounts of dioxin are released from rubbish incinerators, especially if these are operated at insufficiently high temperatures, and from other fires, including garden bonfires. See also ◊hexachlorophene.

UK government figures released 1989 showed dioxin levels 100 times higher than guidelines it has set for environmental dioxin in breast milk, suggesting dioxin contamination is more widespread than previously thought.

dip, magnetic the angle between the horizontal and that taken up by a freely pivoted magnetic needle mounted vertically in the Earth's magnetic field. It is also called the angle of inclination. The dip needle parallels the lines of force of the magnetic field at any point. Thus at the north and south magnetic poles, the needle dips vertically and the angle of dip is 90°.

diphtheria infectious disease in which a membrane forms in the throat, threatening death by ◊asphyxia. Its incidence has been reduced greatly by immunization.

Diplock court in Northern Ireland, a type of court established 1972 by the British government under Lord Diplock (1907–1985) to try offences linked with guerrilla violence. The right to jury trial was suspended and the court consisted of a single judge, because allegedly potential jurors were being intimidated and were unwilling to serve. Despite widespread criticism, the Diplock courts have remained in operation.

diplodocus plant-eating dinosaur that lived about 145 million years ago, the fossils of which have been found in the western USA. Up to 27 m/88 ft long, most of this neck and tail, it weighed about 11 tonnes. It walked on four elephantine legs, had nostrils on top of the skull, and peglike teeth at the front of the mouth.

diploid having two sets of ◊chromosomes in each cell. In sexually reproducing species, one set is derived from each parent, the ◊gametes, or sex cells, of each parent being ◊haploid (having only one set of chromosomes) due to ◊meiosis (cell division).

diplomacy the process by which states attempt to settle their differences through peaceful means such as negotiation or ◊arbitration. See ◊foreign relations.

diplopia double vision occurring due to a lack of coordination of the movements of the eyes. It may arise from disorder in, or damage to, the nerve supply or muscles of the eye, or from intoxication.

dipole in chemistry, a pair of equal and opposite charges located apart, as in some ionic molecules.

The product of one charge and the distance between them is the dipole moment. In radio, a dipole is a rod aerial, usually one half-wavelength or a whole wavelength long.

dipper bird *Cinclus cinclus* found in hilly and mountainous regions across Europe and Asia, where there are clear, fast-flowing streams. It can swim, dive, or walk along the bottom using the pressure of water on its wings and tail to keep it down, while it searches for insect larvae and other small animals. It is about 18 cm/7 in long, has blackish plumage, chestnut below, with white chin and breast, and a tail shaped and cocked like a wren's.

Dirac /dɪˈræk/ Paul Adrien Maurice 1902–1984. British physicist who worked out a version of quantum mechanics consistent with special ◊relativity. The existence of the positron was one of its predictions. He shared a Nobel prize 1933.

Dire Straits UK rock group formed 1977 by the guitarist, singer, and songwriter Mark Knopfler (1949–). In the 1980s they sold a record number of compact discs, including *Brothers in Arms* 1985.

direct current an electric current that flows in one direction, and does not reverse its flow as ◊alternating current does. The electricity produced by a battery is direct current.

directed numbers ◊integers with a positive (+) or negative (–) sign attached. On a graph, a positive sign shows a movement to the right or upwards; a negative sign indicates movement downwards or to the left.

Director of Public Prosecutions (DPP) in the UK, the head of the Crown Prosecution Service (established 1985), responsible for the conduct of all criminal prosecutions in England and Wales. The DPP was formerly responsible only for the prosecution of certain serious crimes, such as murder.

Dirichlet /ˌdɪrɪˈkleɪ/ Peter Gustav Lejeune 1805–1859. German mathematician and physicist who made major contributions to number theory. *Dirichlet's theorem* states that there is an infinite series of prime numbers of the form *an* + *b*, where *a* and *b* are primes and *n* is an even integer (whole number). He analysed the convergence of the Fourier series.

This was his most important mathematical contribution, and led to his generalizing of the function concept and introduction of the modern form of representing a function in the form $y = f(x)$. Dirichlet applied his mathematical knowledge to various aspects of physics, such as an analysis of vibrating strings, and to astronomy in a critique of the ideas about the stability of the solar system as proposed by the French mathematician Laplace.

Dis /dɪs/ in Roman mythology, god of the underworld (Greek *Pluto*); ruler of Hades.

disability a limitation of a person's ability to carry out the activities of daily living, to the extent that they may need help in doing so.

Among adults the commonest disability is in walking, with almost 4.5 million adults suffering in this way in the UK in 1988. Other common disabilities are in hearing, personal care, dexterity, and continence. Most disabilities arise from debilitating illness such as arthritis or stroke, although injury is also an important cause. Other forms of disability are recognized in children: *developmental disability* is the failure to achieve a normal level of competence in some aspect of behaviour during infancy, childhood, or adolescence; a *learning disability* in a child of normal intelligence is a difficulty in acquiring one of the basic cognitive skills of speaking, reading, writing, or calculation.

disaccharide a ◊sugar made up of two monosaccharide units. Sucrose $C_{12}H_{22}O_{11}$, or table sugar, is a disaccharide.

disarmament the reduction of a country's weapons of war. Most disarmament talks since World War II have been concerned with nuclear-arms verification, but biological, chemical, and conventional weapons have also come under discussion at the United Nations and in other forums.

In the UK the Campaign for Nuclear Disarmament lobbies on this issue.

1930s League of Nations attempts to achieve disarmament failed.

1968 US president Johnson's proposals for ◊Strategic Arms Limitation Talks (SALT) were delayed by the Soviet invasion of Czechoslovakia.

1972–77 SALT I was in effect.

1979–85 SALT II, signed by the Soviet and US leaders Brezhnev and Carter, was never ratified by the US Senate, but both countries abided by it.

1986 US president Reagan revoked this pledge, against the advice of his European NATO partners.

1987 Reagan and the Soviet leader Gorbachev agreed to reduce their nuclear arsenals by 4% by scrapping intermediate-range nuclear weapons.

1990 Conventional-arms-reductions talks continued between NATO and the Warsaw Pact for force reductions in Europe.

disassociation of sensibility a divorce between intellect and emotion. T S ◊Eliot coined this phrase in 1921 in an essay on the metaphysical poets of the 17th century. He suggested that Donne, Marvell, and their contemporaries 'feel their thought as immediately as the odour of a rose' whereas later poets disengage intellect from emotion.

disc in computing, a common medium for storing large volumes of data (an alternative is ◊magnetic tape.) A magnetic disc is rotated at high speed in a disc-drive unit as a read/write (playback or record) head passes over its surfaces to record or 'read' the magnetic variations that encode the data. There are several types, including ◊floppy discs, ◊hard discs, and ◊CD-ROM.

Fixed discs provide the most storage. Up to 600 megabytes (million bytes) is quite common, though the *hard discs* of this type used with microcomputers may hold only 10 or 20 megabytes. Fixed or hard discs are built into the drive unit, occasionally stacked on top of one another.

Removable discs are common in minicomputer systems, hold about 80 megabytes of data, and are contained in a rigid plastic case which can be taken out of the drive unit. A *floppy disc* (also called diskette) is very much smaller in size and capacity. Normally holding less than one megabyte of data, it is flexible, mounted in a card envelope or rigid plastic case, and can be removed from the drive unit.

Recently, laser discs and compact discs have been used to store computer data. These have an enormous capacity (about 600 megabytes on a compact disc and billions of bytes on a laser disc) but, once written onto the disc, data cannot be erased.

Disch /dɪʃ/ Thomas M(ichael) 1940– . US writer and poet, author of science-fiction novels such as *Camp Concentration* 1968 and *334* 1972.

discharge tube usually, a glass tube from which virtually all the air has been removed (so that it 'contains' a near vacuum), with electrodes at each end. When a high-voltage current is passed between the electrodes, the few remaining gas atoms in the tube (or some deliberately introduced ones) ionize and emit coloured light as they conduct the current along the tube. The light originates as electrons change energy levels in the ionized atoms.

By coating the inside of the tube with a phosphor, invisible emitted radiation (such as ultraviolet light) can produce visible light; this is the principle of the fluorescent lamp.

disciple a follower, especially of a religious leader. The word is used in the Bible for the early followers of Jesus. The 12 main disciples of Jesus are known as the apostles.

disclaimed peerage in the UK, the Peerage Act (1963) allows a peerage to be disclaimed for life provided that it is renounced within one year of the succession, and that the peer has not applied for a writ of summons to attend the House of Lords.

Members of Parliament and Parliamentary candidates who succeed to peerages must disclaim their title within one month of succeeding; until that period expires they are not disqualified from membership of the House of Commons, provided that they do not sit or vote in the House within that time. The disclaimer of a peerage is for life and is irrevocable. The children of a disclaimed peer may use their courtesy titles, and upon the death of a disclaimed peer the heir succeeds to title. A baronetcy may not be disclaimed.

discotheque club for dancing to pop music on records (discs), originating in the 1960s. The shortened form, *disco*, was used for an international style of recorded dance music of the 1970s with a heavily emphasized beat, derived from ◊funk.

Discovery the ship in which Captain ◊Scott, commanding the National Antarctic Expedition in 1900–04, sailed to the Antarctic and back. In 1980, it became a Maritime Trust museum of exploration at St Katharine's Dock, London.

discrimination unequal distinction (social, economic, political, legal) between individuals or groups such that one has the power to treat the other unfavourably. Types of discrimination, often based on ◊stereotype, include anti-Semitism, apartheid, caste, racism, sexism, and slavery. *Positive discrimination*, or 'affirmative action', is sometimes practised in an attempt to counteract the effects of previous long-term discrimination against a minority group.

Discrimination may be on grounds of difference of colour, nationality, religion, politics, culture, class, sex, age, or a combination of such factors. Legislation has been to some degree effective in forbidding *racial discrimination*, against which there is a United Nations convention 1969 and national legislation in the UK (Race Relations Acts 1965 and 1976) and USA (Civil Rights Acts 1964 and 1968, Voting Rights Act 1965), and *sexual discrimination* (Sex Discrimination Act 1975 in the UK).

Disney Mickey Mouse, Disney's first and most famous cartoon character, made his debut in Plane Crazy 1928.

discus circular disc thrown by athletes from within a circle 2.5 m/8 ft in diameter. The men's discus weighs 2 kg/4.4 lb and the women's 1 kg/2.2 lb. Discus throwing was a competition in ancient Greece at gymnastic contests, especially at the Olympic Games. It is an event in modern Olympics and track and field meets.

disease a condition that impairs the normal state of an organism, and usually alters the functioning of one or more of its organs or systems. A disease is usually characterized by a set of ◊symptoms and signs, although these may not always be apparent to the sufferer. Diseases may be inborn (see ◊congenital disease) or acquired through infection, injury, or other cause. Many diseases have unknown causes.

disinfectant agent that kills, or prevents the growth of, bacteria and other microorganisms. Chemical disinfectants include carbolic acid (phenol), used by ◊Lister in surgery in the 1870s, ethanal, methanal, chlorine, and iodine.

disinvestment the withdrawal of investments in a country for political reasons. The term is also used in economics to describe non-replacement of stock as it wears out.

It is generally applied to the ostensive removal of funds from South Africa in recent years by such multinational companies as General Motors and Barclays Bank. Disinvestment may be motivated by fear of loss of business in the home market caused by adverse publicity, or by fear of loss of foreign resources if the local government changes.

dislocation in chemistry, a fault in the structure of a crystal.

Disney /ˈdɪzni/ Walt(er Elias) 1901–1966. US filmmaker and animator, a pioneer of family entertainment. He established his own studio in Hollywood 1923, and his first Mickey Mouse cartoon (*Plane Crazy*) appeared 1928. In addition to short cartoons the studio made feature-length animated films, including *Snow White and the Seven Dwarfs* 1938, *Pinocchio* 1940, and *Dumbo* 1941. Disney's cartoon figures, for example Donald Duck, also appeared in comic books worldwide. In 1955 Disney opened the first theme park, Disneyland, in California.

Using the new medium of sound film, Disney developed the 'Silly Symphony', a type of cartoon based on the close association of music with visual images, producing them in colour from 1932 and culminating in the feature-length *Fantasia* 1940.

Disraeli Benjamin Disraeli by John Everett Millais (1881) National Portrait Gallery, London.

The Disney studio also made nature-study films such as *The Living Desert* 1953, which have been criticized for their fictionalization of nature: wild animals would be placed in unnatural situations to create 'drama'. Feature films with human casts were made from 1946, such as *The Swiss Family Robinson* 1960 and *Mary Poppins* 1964.

dispersion in optics, dispersion describes the splitting of white light into a spectrum, for example when it passes through a prism or a diffraction grating. It occurs because the prism (or grating) bends each component wavelength to a slightly different extent. The natural dispersion of light through raindrops creates a rainbow. Dispersion also refers to the distribution of microscopic particles in a ◊colloid.

displacement activity in animal behaviour, an action that is performed out of its normal context, while the animal is in a state of stress, frustration, or uncertainty. Birds, for example, often peck at grass when uncertain whether to attack or flee from an opponent; similarly, humans scratch their heads when nervous.

displacement reaction a chemical reaction in which a less reactive element is replaced in a compound by a more reactive one.

For example, the addition of powdered zinc to a solution of copper(II) sulphate displaces copper metal, which can be detected by its characteristic colour (see ◊electrochemical series).

Disraeli /dɪzˈreɪli/ Benjamin, Earl of Beaconsfield 1804–1881. British Conservative politician and novelist. Elected to Parliament 1837, he was chancellor of the Exchequer under Lord ◊Derby 1852, 1858–59, and 1866–68, and prime minister 1868 and 1874–80. His imperialist policies brought India directly under the crown and he personally purchased control of the Suez Canal. The central Conservative Party organization is his creation. His popular, political novels reflect an interest in social reform and include *Coningsby* 1844 and *Sybil* 1845.

After a period in a solicitor's office, Disraeli wrote the novels *Vivian Grey* 1826, *Contarini Fleming* 1832, and others, and the pamphlet *Vindication of the English Constitution* 1835. Entering Parliament in 1837 after four unsuccessful attempts, he was laughed at as a dandy, but when his maiden speech was shouted down, he said: 'The time will come when you will hear me.'

Excluded from Peel's government of 1841–46, Disraeli formed his Young England group to keep a critical eye on Peel's Conservatism. Its ideas were expounded in the novel trilogy *Coningsby*, *Sybil*, and *Tancred* 1847. When Peel decided in 1846 to repeal the Corn Laws, Disraeli opposed the measure in a series of witty and effective speeches; Peel's government fell soon after, and Disraeli gradually came to be recognized as the leader of the Conservative Party in the Commons.

During the next 20 years the Conservatives formed short-lived minority governments in 1852, 1858–59, and 1866–68, with Lord Derby as prime minister and Disraeli as chancellor of the Exchequer and leader of the Commons. In 1852 Disraeli first proposed discrimination in income tax between earned and unearned income, but without success. The 1858–59 government legalized the admission of Jews to Parliament, and transferred the government of India from the East India Company to the crown. In 1866 the Conservatives took office after defeating a Liberal Reform Bill, and then attempted to secure the credit of widening the franchise by the Reform Bill of 1867. On Lord Derby's retirement in 1868 Disraeli became prime minister, but a few months later was defeated by Gladstone in a general election. During the six years of opposition that followed he published another novel, *Lothair* 1870, and established Conservative Central Office, the prototype of modern party organizations.

In 1874 Disraeli took office for the second time, with a majority of 100. Some useful reform measures were carried, such as the Artisans' Dwelling Act, which empowered local authorities to undertake slum clearance, but the outstanding feature of the government's policy was its imperialism. It was Disraeli's personal initiative that purchased from the Khedive of Egypt a controlling interest in the Suez Canal, conferred on the Queen the title of Empress of India, and sent the Prince of Wales on the first royal tour of that country. He accepted an earldom 1876. The Bulgarian revolt of 1876 and the subsequent Russo-Turkish War of 1877–78 provoked one of many political duels between Disraeli and Gladstone, the Liberal leader, and was concluded by the Congress of Berlin 1878, where Disraeli was the principal British delegate and brought home 'peace with honour' and Cyprus. The government was defeated in 1880, and a year later Disraeli died.

D'Israeli /dɪz'reɪli/ Isaac 1766–1848. British scholar, father of Benjamin ◊Disraeli and author of *Curiosities of Literature* 1791–93 and 1823.

Disruption, the split in the Church of Scotland 1843 when its Evangelical wing formed the Free Church of Scotland, hoping to recreate the spirit of John Knox and early Protestantism.

Dissenter former name for a Protestant refusing to conform to the established Christian church. For example, Baptists, Presbyterians, and Independents (now known as Congregationalists) are Dissenters.

dissident in one-party states, a person intellectually dissenting from the official line. Dissidents have been sent into exile, prison, labour camps, and mental institutions, or deprived of their jobs. In the USSR the number of imprisoned dissidents declined from more than 600 in 1986 to fewer than 100 in 1990, of whom the majority were ethnic nationalists. In China the number of prisoners of conscience increased after the 1989 Tiananmen Square massacre, and in South Africa, despite the release of Nelson Mandela in 1990, numerous political dissidents remained in jail.

In the USSR before the introduction of ◊glasnost, dissidents comprised communists who advocated a more democratic and humanitarian approach; religious proselytizers; Jews wishing to emigrate; and those who supported ethnic or national separatist movements within the USSR (among them Armenians, Lithuanians, Ukrainians, and Tatars). Their views were expressed through samizdat (clandestinely distributed writings) and sometimes published abroad. In the late 1980s Gorbachev lifted censorship, accepted a degree of political pluralism, and extended tolerance to religious believers. Almost 100,000 Jews were allowed to emigrate 1985–90. Some formerly persecuted dissidents, most prominently the physicist ◊Sakharov, emerged as supporters, albeit impatient, of the new reform programme.

dissociation the total or partial breakdown of a chemical compound into smaller constituent parts. Where dissociation is incomplete, a ◊chemical equilibrium exists between the chemical compound and its dissociation products. The extent of incomplete dissociation is defined by a numerical value (dissociation constant).

distance ratio or **velocity ratio** in a machine, the distance moved by the output force divided by the distance moved by the input force. The ratio indicates the movement magnification achieved by the machine, and also the speed or velocity magnification possible.

distemper contagious virus disease in young dogs, also found in wild animals, such as foxes. It is characterized by catarrh, cough, and general weakness, and is prevented by vaccination. In 1988 an allied virus killed over 10,000 common seals in the Baltic and North seas.

distillation process used to separate liquids from solids or from other liquids, or to purify a liquid. It works on the principle that liquids have different boiling points. The mixture is heated and vapour rises to the top of the apparatus. The liquid reforms in a condenser, and is collected.

The earliest known reference to the process is to the distillation of wine in the 12th century by Adelard of Bath. The chemical retort used for distillation was invented by Muslims, and was first seen in the West about 1570.

Distributism a campaign for land reform publicized by English writer G K Chesterton in his group the Distributist League, the journal of which he published from 1925. The movement called for a revival of smallholdings and a turn away from industrialization. Supporters included many Conservatives and traditional clergy.

distributive law in mathematics, the law that states that if there are two binary operations '×' and '+' on a set, then '×' distributes over '+' as in multiplication, so that, for example, 3 × (4 + 5) is the same as (3 × 4) + (3 × 5). See also ◊associative law and ◊commutative law.

distributor a device in a car engine's ignition system that distributes pulses of high-voltage electricity to the ◊spark plugs in the cylinders. The electricity is passed to the plug leads by the tip of a rotor arm, driven by the engine camshaft, and current is fed to the rotor arm from the ignition coil. The distributor also houses the contact-breaker, which opens and closes to interrupt the battery current to the coil, thus triggering off the high-voltage pulses. In modern cars with electronic ignition, it is absent.

district council unit of local government in England and Wales.

Under the Local Government Act 1972, 300 district councils were created to replace the former county borough, borough, and urban and rural district councils. The district councils are headed by an annually elected chair or, in an honorary borough or city, mayor or lord mayor. Councillors are elected for four years, and one-third retire at a time, so that district elections are held in three out of four years, county-council elections taking place in the fourth.

Their responsibilities cover housing, local planning and development, roads (excluding trunk and classified), bus services, environmental health (refuse collection, clean air, food safety and hygiene, and enforcement of the Offices, Shops and Railway Premises Act), rating, museums and art galleries, parks and playing fields, swimming baths, cemeteries, and so on. In metropolitan district councils education, personal social services, and libraries are also included.

District of Columbia /kə'lʌmbiə/ federal district of the USA, see ◊Washington.

Diu /'diːuː/ island off the Kathiawar peninsular, NW India, part of the Union Territory of ◊Daman and Diu; area 38 sq km/15 sq mi; population (1981) 30,000. The main town is also called Diu, population 8,020. The economy is based on tourism, coconuts, pearl millet, and salt. Diu was captured by the Portuguese 1534.

diuretic drug that rids the body of excess fluid by increasing the output of urine by the kidneys. It may be used in the treatment of heart disease, high blood pressure, kidney and liver disease, and some endocrine disorders.

diver also called **loon**, four species of bird specialized for swimming and diving, found in northern regions of the N hemisphere. The legs are set so far back that walking is almost impossible, and they come to land only to nest, but divers are powerful swimmers and good flyers. They have straight bills and long bodies, and feed on fish, crustaceans, and some water plants. Of the four species, the largest is the **white-billed diver** *Gavia adamsii*, an Arctic species 75 cm/2.5 ft long.

diverticulitis inflammation of diverticula (pockets of herniation) in the large intestine. It is usually controlled by diet and antibiotics.

divertissement (French 'entertainment') a dance, or group of dances, within a ballet or opera that has no connection with the plot, such as the character dances in the last act of *Coppélia* by Delibes.

dividend in business, amount of money that company directors decide should be taken out of profits for distribution to shareholders. It is usually declared as a percentage or fixed amount per share. Most companies pay dividends once or twice a year.

divination art of ascertaining future events or eliciting other hidden knowledge by supernatural or nonrational means. Divination played a large part in the ancient civilizations of the Egyptians, Greeks (see ◊oracle), Romans, and Chinese (see ◊I Ching), and is still practised throughout the world.

It generally involves the intuitive interpretation of the mechanical operations of chance or natural law. Forms of divination have included omens drawn from the behaviour of birds and animals; examination of the entrails of sacrificed animals; random opening of such books as the Bible; fortune-telling by cards (see ◊tarot) and palmistry; ◊dowsing; oracular trance-speaking; automatic writing; necromancy, or the supposed raising of the spirits of the dead; and dreams, often specially induced.

Divine Comedy, The a poem by the Italian Dante Alighieri 1300–21, describing a journey through Hell, Purgatory, and Paradise under the guidance of Reason and Faith. The poem makes great use of symbolism and illusion, and influenced many English writers including Milton, Byron, Shelley, and T S Eliot.

Divine Light Mission religious movement founded in 1960. It proclaims **Guru Maharaj Ji** as the present age's successor to the gods or religious leaders Krishna, Buddha, Jesus, and Muhammad, who can provide his followers with the knowledge required to attain salvation.

Divine Principle sacred writings of the ◊Unification Church. The book, which offers a reinterpretation of the Bible, is also influenced by concepts from Buddhism, Islam, and Taoism.

divine right of kings Christian political doctrine that hereditary monarchy is the system approved by God, hereditary right cannot be forfeited, monarchs are accountable to God alone for their actions, and rebellion against the lawful sovereign is therefore blasphemous.

The doctrine had its origins in the anointing of Pepin in 751 by the pope after Pepin had usurped the throne of the Franks. It was at its peak in 16th- and 17th-century Europe as a weapon against the claims of the papacy—the court of Louis XIV of France pushed this to the limit—and was in 17th-century England maintained by the supporters of the Stuarts in opposition to the democratic theories of the Puritans and Whigs.

diving the sport of entering water either from a springboard (3 m/10 ft) above the water, or from a platform (10 m/33 ft) above the water. Various differing starts are adopted, and twists and somersaults performed in midair. Points are awarded and the level of difficulty of each dive is used as a multiplying factor.

diving apparatus any apparatus used to enable a person to spend time underwater. Diving bells were in use in the 18th century, the diver breathing air trapped in a bell-shaped chamber, followed by cumbersome diving suits in the early 19th century. Complete freedom of movement came with the ◊aqualung, invented by Jacques ◊Cousteau in the early 1940s. For work at depths of several hundred metres the technique of saturation diving was developed in the 1970s, where divers live for a week or more breathing a mixture of helium and oxygen at the pressure existing on the seabed where they work.

The first diving suit, with a large metal helmet and supplied with air by pipeline, was invented by the brothers John and Charles Deane in 1828.

Saturation diving was developed particularly for working in the offshore oilfields in the North Sea and elsewhere. Working divers are ferried down to the work site by a lock-out ◊submersible. By this technique they avoid the need for lengthy periods of decompression after every dive. Slow decompression is necessary to avoid the dangerous consequences of an attack of the bends, or ◊decompression sickness.

divisions of economics economics is usually divided into the disciplines of ◊*microeconomics*, studying individual producers, consumers or markets, and ◊*macroeconomics*, studying whole economies or systems. These spheres often overlap. Straddling both spheres is the sub-discipline of *econometrics*, which analyses economic relationships using mathematical and statistical techniques. Increasingly sophisticated econometric methods are used for such topics as economic forecasting.

Economics aims to be either *positive*, presenting objective and scientific explanations of how an economy works, or *normative*, offering prescriptions and recommendations on what should be done to cure perceived ills. However objective the aim, value judgements are usually involved when economists present particular formulations.

divorce the legal dissolution of a lawful marriage. It is distinct from a decree of nullity, which is a legal declaration that the marriage was invalid. The ease with which a divorce can be obtained in different countries varies considerably, and is also affected by different religious practices.

In England, divorce could only be secured by the passing of a private act of Parliament until 1857, when the Matrimonial Causes Act set up the Divorce Court and provided limited grounds for divorce. The grounds for divorce were gradually liberalized by further acts of Parliament, culminating in the Divorce Reform Act 1969, under which the sole ground for divorce is the irretrievable breakdown of the marriage. This must be demonstrated by showing that the parties have lived apart for at least two years (or five years if one party does not consent to the divorce), or proving adultery, desertion, or unreasonable behaviour by one party. The court places great emphasis on provision for the custody and maintenance of any children. It may also order other financial arrangements, including the transfer of property.

In the USA divorce laws differ from state to state. The grounds include adultery (in all states), cruelty, desertion, alcoholism, drug addiction, and

divorce

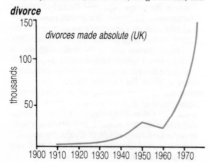

insanity. Quick divorces in states with more liberal laws have been restricted by the imposition of minimum residence periods, and the right to challenge the divorce if one party has not been notified of the proceedings. Unmarried cohabiting couples are increasingly negotiating 'pre-cohabitation agreements' which make an advance settlement of division of property and assets, including maintenance provisions. In the USSR, under laws introduced in the 1960s, divorce is easy and cheap. Maintenance for a wife after divorce is decreasing in importance, but she is likely to benefit by a more equitable division of property.

The Roman Catholic Church does not permit divorce among its members, and under Pope John Paul II conditions for annulment have been tightened. Among Muslims a wife cannot divorce her husband, but he may divorce her by repeating the formula 'I divorce you' three times: property settlements by careful parents make this a right not too frequently exercised.

Diwali ('garland of lamps') Hindu festival in Oct/Nov celebrating Lakshmi, goddess of light and wealth. It is marked by the lighting of lamps and candles, feasting, and exchange of gifts.

Dixie /ˈdɪksi/ the Southern states of the US. The word probably derives from the ◊Mason-Dixon line.

Dixieland jazz jazz style that originated in New Orleans, USA, in the early 20th century, dominated by cornet, trombone, and clarinet. The trumpeter Louis Armstrong emerged from this style. The *trad jazz* movement in the UK in the 1940s–50s was a Dixieland revival.

Diyarbakir /dɪˈjɑːbəkɪə/ town in Asiatic Turkey, on the river Tigris; population (1985) 305,000. It has a trade in gold and silver filigree work, copper, wool, and mohair, and manufactures textiles and leather goods.

Djakarta variant spelling of ◊Jakarta, capital of Indonesia.

Djibouti /dʒɪˈbuːti/ country on the E coast of Africa, at the S end of the Red Sea, bounded to the E by the Gulf of Aden, to the SE by the Somali Republic, and to the S, W, and N by Ethiopia.

government The 1981 constitution made Djibouti a one-party state, the only legal party being the People's Progress Assembly (RPP). The constitution also provides for a single-chamber legislature, the 65-member chamber of deputies, elected by universal suffrage for a five-year term, and a president, nominated by the party, who is elected for six years and may not serve more than two terms.

history First colonized by France 1862, Djibouti was part of French Somaliland 1896–1945, after which it was declared an overseas territory. In

Djibouti
Republic of
(Jumhouriyya Djibouti)

area 23,200 sq km/8,955 sq mi
capital and chief port Djibouti
physical mountains divide an inland plateau from a coastal plain; hot and arid
head of state and government Hassan Gouled Aptidon from 1977
political system authoritarian nationalism
political parties People's Progress Assembly (RPP), nationalist
exports acts mainly as a transit port for Ethiopia
currency Djibouti franc (299 = £1 Feb 1990)
population (1988) 484,000 (Issa 47%, Afar 37%, European 8%, Arab 6%); annual growth rate 3.4%
language Somali, Afar, French, Arabic
religion Sunni Muslim
literacy 17% (1985)
GNP $307 (1984); $400 per head of population
chronology
1977 Full independence achieved. Hassan Gouled elected president.
1979 All political parties combined to form the People's Progress Assembly (RPP).
1981 New constitution made RPP the only legal party. Gouled re-elected. Treaties of friendship signed with Ethiopia, Somalia, Kenya, and Sudan.
1984 Policy of neutrality reaffirmed.
1987 Gouled re-elected for a final term.

1967 it was renamed the French Territory of the Afars and the Issas. Calls for independence were frequent, sometimes violent. It was achieved 1977, with Hassan Gouled as president. In 1979 all political parties combined to form the RPP and the government embarked on the task of uniting the two main ethnic groups, the Issas, who traditionally had strong links with Somalia, and the Afars, who had been linked with Ethiopia.

In 1981 a new constitution was adopted, making RPP the only party and providing for the election of a president after nomination by RPP. President Gouled was re-elected and in 1982 a chamber of deputies was elected from a list of RPP nominees. Under Gouled, Djibouti has pursued a largely successful policy of amicable neutralism with its neighbours, concluding treaties of friendship with Ethiopia, Somalia, Kenya, and Sudan, and has tried to assist the peace process in E Africa. Although affected by the 1984–85 droughts, it managed to maintain stability with EEC aid. In 1987 Gouled was re-elected for his final term with 98.71% of the popular vote.

Djibouti /dʒɪˈbuːti/ chief port and capital of the Republic of Djibouti, on a peninsula 240 km/149 mi SW of Aden and 565 km/351 mi NE of Addis Ababa; population (1988) 290,000.

The city succeeded Obock as capital of French Somaliland 1896, and was the official port of Ethiopia from 1897.

Djilas /ˈdʒiːləs/ Milovan 1911– . Yugoslav political writer and dissident. A former close wartime colleague of Marshal Tito, in 1953 he was dismissed from high office and subsequently imprisoned because of his advocacy of greater political ◊pluralism. He was released in 1966 and formally rehabilitated in 1989.

Djilas was born in Montenegro and was a partisan during World War II. He rose to a senior position in Yugoslavia's postwar communist government before being ousted in 1953. His writings, including the books *The New Class* 1957 and *The Undivided Society* 1969, were banned until May 1989.

DM abbreviation for *Deutschmark*, the unit of currency in West Germany.

DMus abbreviation for *Doctor of Music*.

DNA abbreviation for *deoxyribonucleic acid* a complex two-stranded molecule that contains, in chemically coded form, all the information needed to build, control, and maintain a living organism. DNA is a double-stranded ◊nucleic acid that forms the basis of genetic inheritance in all organisms, except for a few viruses that depend on ◊RNA. In ◊eukaryotic organisms, it is organized into ◊chromosomes and contained in the cell nucleus.

DNA

how a cell divides

1 — original double helix

2 — forms ladder

3 — unzips

4 — new bases join onto opened zip teeth

5 — two new identical double strands

Key

S sugars
P phosphates
C cytosine
G guanine
A adenine
T thymine

Dneprodzerzhinsk /ˌnɪprədzə'ʒɪnsk/ port in Ukraine, USSR, on the river Dnieper, 48 km/30 mi NW of ◊Dnepropetrovsk; population (1987) 279,000. It produces chemicals, iron, and steel.

Dnepropetrovsk /ˌnɪprəpɪ'trɒfsk/ city in Ukraine, USSR, on the right bank of the Dnieper; population (1987) 1,182,000. It is the centre of an important industrial region, with iron, steel, chemical, and engineering industries. It is linked with the Dnieper Dam, 60 km/37 mi downstream.

Dnieper /'niːpə/ or *Dnepr* Russian river rising in the Smolensk region and flowing S past Kiev, Dnepropetrovsk, and Zaporozhe, to enter the Black Sea E of Odessa. Total length 2,250 km/1,400 mi.

D-notice in the UK, a censorship notice issued by the Department of Defence to the media to prohibit the publication of information on matters

alleged to be of national security. The system dates from 1922.

do. abbreviation for *ditto*.

Dobell /dəʊ'bel/ William 1899–1970. Australian portraitist and genre painter, born in New South Wales. In 1929–39 he studied art in the UK and the Netherlands. His portrait of *Joshua Smith* 1943 (Sir Edward Hayward, Adelaide) provoked a court case (Dobell was accused of caricaturing his subject).

Dobermann or *Dobermann Pinscher* smooth-coated dog with a docked tail, much used as a guard dog. It stands up to 70 cm/2.2 ft tall, has a long head with a flat, smooth skull, and is often black with brown markings. It takes its name from the man who bred it in 19th-century Germany.

Döblin /'dɜːbliːn/ Alfred 1878–1957. German novelist. *Berlin-Alexanderplatz* 1929 owes much to James Joyce in its minutely detailed depiction of the inner lives of a city's inhabitants, and is considered by many to be the finest 20th-century German novel. Other works include *November 1918: Eine deutsche Revolution/A German Revolution* 1939–50 (published in four parts) about the formation of the Weimar Republic.

Döblin practised as a doctor in Berlin until 1933 when his books were banned and he was exiled; he moved first to France and from 1941 lived in the USA.

Dobruja /'dɒbrʊdʒə/ district in the Balkans, bounded to the N and W by the Danube, and to the E by the Black Sea. It is low-lying, partly marshland, partly fertile steppe land. Constanta is the chief town. Dobruja was divided between Romania and Bulgaria in 1878. In 1913, after the second Balkan War, Bulgaria ceded its part to Romania, but received it back in 1940, a cession confirmed by the peace treaty of 1947.

Dobrynin /də'briːnɪn/ Anataloy Fedorovich 1919– . Soviet diplomat, ambassador to the US 1962–86, emerging during the 1970s as a warm supporter of ◊detente. Appointed 1986 to the Communist Party's Secretariat, he retired in 1988.

Dobrynin trained as an engineer before joining the Soviet diplomatic service in 1941. He served as counsellor at the Soviet embassy in Washington DC 1952–55, assistant to the minister for foreign affairs 1955–57, undersecretary at the United Nations 1957–59, and head of the USSR's American department 1959–61, before being appointed Soviet ambassador to Washington in 1962. He remained at this post for 25 years. Brought back to Moscow by the new Soviet leader, Mikhail Gorbachev, he was appointed to the Communist Party's Secretariat as head of the International Department, before retiring in 1988.

Dobzhansky /dɒb'ʒɑːnski/ Theodosius 1900–1975. US geneticist of Ukrainian origins. A pioneer of modern genetics and evolutionary theory, he showed that genetic variability between individuals of the same species is very high and that

River Dnieper

this diversity is vital to the process of evolution. His book *Genetics and the Origin of Species* was published in 1937.

dock port accommodation for commercial and naval vessels, usually simple linear quayage adaptable to ships of any size, but with specialized equipment for handling bulk cargoes, refrigerated goods, container traffic, and oil tankers. Flexible 'floating' docks are used for repairs.

In the UK, port employment was controlled until 1989 by the ◊National Dock Labour Scheme.

dock in botany, a number of plants of the genus *Rumex*, family Polygonaceae, commonly known as *sorrel*. They are annual to perennial herbs, often with lance-shaped leaves and small, greenish flowers.

Doctor Faustus, The tragical history of a drama by Christopher Marlowe, published (in two versions) 1604 and 1616, first performed in England 1594. The play, based on a medieval legend, tells how Faustus surrenders his soul to the Devil in return for 24 years of life and the services of Mephistopheles, who will grant his every wish.

Doctorow /'dɒktərəʊ/ E L 1931– . US novelist. Politically acute, artistically experimental author of the bestseller *Ragtime* 1976, set in the Jazz Age, and *World's Fair* 1985, about a Jewish New York boyhood.

dodder genus of parasitic plants, *Cuscuta*, family Convolvulaceae, without leaves or roots. The thin stem twines round the host, and penetrating suckers withdraw nourishment.

Dodds /dɒdz/ Charles 1899–1973. English biochemist. He was largely responsible for the discovery of stilboestrol, a powerful synthetic hormone used in treating prostate conditions and also for fattening cattle.

Dodds /dɒdz/ Johnny 1892–1940. US clarinetist, generally ranked among the top New Orleans jazz clarinetists. He played with the New Orleans Wanderers and was noted for his warmth of tone and improvisation.

Dodecanese /ˌdəʊdekə'niːz/ (Greek *Dhodhekánisos*, 'twelve islands') group of islands in the Aegean sea; area 1,028 sq m/2,663 sq km. Once Turkish, the islands were Italian 1912–47, when they were ceded to Greece. They include ◊Rhodes, and ◊Kos. Chief products include fruit, olives, and sponges.

dodecaphonic in music, the 12–note system of composition.

Dodge City /dɒdʒ/ city in S W Kansas, USA, on the river Arkansas; population (1980) 18,000. On the Santa Fé Trail, it was a noted frontier cattle town in the days of the Wild West.

Dodgson /'dɒdsən/ Charles Lutwidge. Real name of writer Lewis ◊Carroll.

dodo extinct bird *Raphus cucullatus* formerly found on Mauritius, but exterminated before the end of the 17th century. Related to the pigeons, it was larger than a turkey, with a bulky body and very short wings and tail. Flightless and trusting, it was easy prey to humans.

Dodecanese Islands

Dodoma /ˈdəʊdəmə/ capital (replacing Dar-es-Salaam in 1974) of Tanzania; 1,132 m/3,713 ft above sea level; population (1984) 180,000. Centre of communications, linked by rail with Dar-es-Salaam and Kigoma on Lake Tanganyika, and by road with Kenya to the N, and Zambia and Malawi to the S.

Doe /dəʊ/ Samuel Kenyon 1950– . Liberian politician and soldier. He joined the army as a private in 1969 and rose to the rank of master sergeant ten years later. In 1980 he led a coup in which President Tolbert was killed. Doe replaced him as head of state, and in 1981 made himself general and army commander in chief. In 1985 he was narrowly elected president, as leader of the newly formed National Democratic Party of Liberia.

dog mammal *Canis familiaris* descended from the wolf or jackal, domesticated by humans, and bred into many different varieties for use as working animals and pets. As well as domestic dogs there are many species of wild dog in the dog family Canidae. Wild dogs are mostly hunters, found on all continents except Antarctica.

There are over 400 different breeds of dog throughout the world, the UK Kennel Club (1873) grouping those eligible for registration (150 breeds) into sporting breeds (hound, gundog, and terrier) and non-sporting (utility, working, and toy).

Of the wild dogs, some are solitary, such as the long-legged **maned wolf** *Chrysocyon brachurus* of South America, but others hunt in groups, such as the **African hunting dog** *Lycaon pictus* and the ⟨wolf. ⟨Jackals scavenge for food, and the **raccoon dog** *Nyctereutes procyonoides* of E Asia includes plant food as well as meat in the diet. The Australian wild dog is the ⟨dingo.

doge the chief magistrate in the ancient constitutions of Venice and Genoa. The first doge of Venice was appointed 697 with absolute power (modified 1297), and from his accession dates Venice's prominence in history. The last Venetian doge, Lodovico Manin, retired 1797 and the last Genoese doge in 1804.

Dōgen /ˈdəʊgen/ 1200–1253. Japanese Buddhist monk, pupil of Eisai; founder of the Sōtō school of Zen. He did not reject study, but stressed the importance of **zazen**, seated meditation for its own sake.

dogfish small shark *Scyliorhinus caniculus* found in the NE Atlantic and Mediterranean. Bottom-living, it is sandy brown and covered with spots, and grows to about 75 cm/2.5 ft.

Various other species of small shark may also be called dogfish. It is edible, and is known in restaurants as 'rock eel' or 'rock salmon'.

Dogger Bank /ˈdɒgə/ submerged sandbank in the North Sea, about 115 km/70 mi off the coast of Yorkshire. In places the water is only 11 m/36 ft deep, but the general depth is 18–36 m/60–120 ft; it is a well-known fishing ground.

Dogon person of Dogon culture from E Mali and NW Burkina Faso. The Dogon number approximately 250,000, and their language belongs to the Voltaic (Gur) branch of the Niger-Congo family.

Dogs, Isle of /dɒgz/ district of E London, England, part of the Greater London borough of Tower Hamlets.

dog's mercury plant *Mercurialis perennis* of the family Euphorbiaceae. Dog's mercury carpets woodland floors in patches of a single sex. Male flowers are small, greenish yellow, and held on upright spike above the leaves. Female flowers droop below the upper leaves. Leaves are oval and light green. It is found across Europe. It grows to 30 cm/1 ft.

dogwood deciduous shrub *Cornus sanguinea* growing up to 4 m/12 ft high. Several of the species are notable for their coloured bark: the **Westonbirt dogwood** *Cornus alba* has brilliant red stems in winter.

dog

Foxhound

Pekinese

Pug

Cocker spaniel

working collie

Labrador retriever

Egyptian greyhound

Jack Russell terrier

Chihuahua

Dobermann pinscher

bloodhound

Old English sheepdog

Heads of small white flowers, each with four petals joined as a tube, are produced in midsummer, followed by black berries. The dogwood is characteristic of lime soils in the S of England, and is found over much of S Europe. Various other species of dogwood are planted in gardens.

Doha /ˈdəʊhɑː/ (Arabic **Ad Dawḥah**) capital and chief port of Qatar; population (1986) 217,000. Industries include oil refining, refrigeration plants, engineering, and food processing. It is the centre of vocational training for all the Gulf states.

Doi /dɔɪ/ Takako 1929– . Japanese socialist politician, leader of the Japan Socialist Party (JSP) from 1986 and responsible for much of its recent revival. She is the country's first female major party leader.

Doi was a law lecturer before being elected to Japan's House of Representatives in 1969. She assumed leadership of the JSP at a low point in the party's fortunes, and proceeded to moderate and modernize its image. With the help of 'housewife volunteers' she established herself as a charismatic political leader, and at a time when the ruling Liberal Democrats were beset by scandals, the JSP vote increased to make Doi the leader of an effective opposition.

Doi Inthanon /ˌdɔɪɪnˈθænən/ highest mountain in Thailand, rising to 2,595 m/8,513 ft SW of Chiang Mai in NW Thailand.

Doisy /ˈdɔɪzi/ Edward 1893–1986. US biochemist. In 1939 Doisy succeeded in synthesizing vitamin K, a compound earlier discovered by Carl ◊Dam, with whom he shared the 1943 Nobel Physiology or Medicine Prize.

Dolci /ˈdɒltʃi/ Carlo 1616–1686. Italian painter of the late Baroque period, active in Florence. He created intensely emotional versions of religious subjects, such as *The Last Communion of St Jerome*.

Dolci was the foremost painter in Florence in his time, and continued to be much admired in the 18th century. He was also a portraitist, and was sent to Austria in 1675 to paint the Medici wife of the emperor Leopold I.

doldrums area of low atmospheric pressure along the equator, largely applied to oceans at the convergence of the NE and SE ◊trade winds. To some extent the area affected moves N and S with seasonal changes.

The doldrums are characterized by calm or very light westerly winds, during which there may be sudden squalls and stormy weather. For this reason the areas are avoided as far as possible by sailing ships.

dolerite an igneous rock formed below the Earth's surface, a form of basalt, containing relatively little silica (basic in composition).

Dolerite is a medium-grained (hypabyssal) basalt and forms in minor intrusions, such as dykes, which cut across the rock strata, and sills, which push between beds of sedimentary rock. When exposed at the surface, dolerite weathers into spherical lumps.

Dolgellau /dɒlˈgeʃi/ (formerly Dolgelly) market town at the foot of Cader Idris in Gwynedd, Wales; on the river Wnion; population (1981) 2,400. The town is also a tourist centre. Nearby are the Gwynfynydd ('White mountain') and Clogau goldmines; a nugget from the latter has supplied gold for the wedding rings of royal brides since 1923.

Dolin /ˈdɒlɪn/ Anton. Stage name of Patrick Healey-Kay 1904–1983. British dancer and choreographer, a pioneer of UK ballet. After studying under Nijinsky, he was a leading member of Diaghilev's company 1924–27. He formed the Markova–Dolin Ballet with Alicia Markova 1935–38, and was a guest soloist with the American Ballet Theater 1940–46.

Doll /dɒl/ William Richard 1912– . British physician who proved the link between smoking and lung cancer.

Working with Professor Bradford Hill, he provided the first statistical proof of the link in 1950. In a later study of the smoking habits of doctors, they were able to show that stopping smoking immediately reduces the risk of cancer.

dollar a monetary unit containing 100 cents, adopted as the standard unit in the USA in 1785; also by Australia, Canada, Hong Kong, and a number of other countries.

Large reserves of US dollars accumulated in Asia. Singapore became from 1968 the centre of the *Asian dollar market*, working in cooperation with London.

Following the depreciation of the US dollar after the Vietnam War expenditure and the oil crisis of 1973, the European monetary system became anchored to the German mark, and in Asia the Japanese yen became important as a trading currency. See also ◊Eurodollar.

Dollfuss /ˈdɒlfuːs/ Engelbert 1892–1934. Austrian Christian Socialist politician. He was appointed chancellor in 1932, and in 1933 suppressed parliament and ruled by decree. In Feb 1934 he crushed the Social Democrats by force, and in

May Austria was declared a ◊corporative state. The Nazis attempted a coup d'état on 25 July; the Chancellery was seized and Dollfuss murdered.

Doll's House, The a play by Henrik Ibsen, first produced in Norway 1879. It describes the blackmail of Nora, sheltered wife of a successful lawyer, the subsequent revelation of her guilty secret to her husband, and marital breakdown.

dolmen prehistoric monument in the form of a chamber built of large stone slabs, roofed over by a flat stone which they support. Dolmens are grave chambers of the Neolithic period, found in Europe and Africa, and occasionally in Asia as far east as Japan. In Wales they are known as *cromlechs*.

Dolmetsch /ˈdɒlmetʃ/ Arnold 1858–1940. French-born musician and instrument-maker who settled in England in 1914 and became a leading figure in the revival of early music.

dolphin highly intelligent aquatic mammal. The river dolphins, of which there are only five species, belong to the family Platanistidae. All river dolphins are threatened by dams and pollution, and some, such as the Indus dolphin, are in danger of extinction. There are more species of marine dolphin, all belonging to the family Delphinidae. Dolphins use sound (echolocation) to navigate, to find prey, and for communication.

The *common dolphin Delphinus delphis* is found in all temperate and tropical seas. It is up to 2.5 m/8 ft long, and is dark above, white below, with bands of grey, white, and yellow on the sides, and has up to 100 teeth in its jaws, which make the 15 cm/6 in 'beak' protrude forward from the rounded head. It feeds on fish and squid.

Some species can swim at up to 56 kph/35 mph, helped by special streamlining modifications of the skin. All power themselves by beating the tail up and down, and use the flippers to steer and stabilize. The flippers betray dolphins' land-mammal ancestry with their typical five-toed limb-bone structure. The smallest dolphins are ◊porpoises.

Dolphins are popular performers in oceanaria. The usual species exhibited is the *bottle-nosed dolphin Tursiops truncatus*, found in all warm seas, mainly grey in colour and growing to a maximum 4.2 m/14 ft. The US Navy began using dolphins 1960, and in 1987 six dolphins were sent to detect mines in the Persian Gulf.

Marine dolphins are endangered by fishing nets, speedboats, and pollution. In 1990 the North Sea states agreed to introduce legislation to protect dolphins.

Also known as *dolphin* is the totally unrelated true fish *Coryphaena hippurus*, up to 1.5 m/5 ft long.

Domagk /ˈdəʊmæk/ Gerhard 1895–1964. German pathologist, discoverer of antibacterial drugs. He found that a dye substance called prontosil red contains chemicals with powerful antibacterial properties. This became the first of the sulphonamide drugs, used to treat a wide range of conditions, including pneumonia and septic wounds. Nobel prize 1939.

domain a small area in a magnetic field that behaves like a tiny magnet. Its magnetism is due to the movement of electrons in the atoms of the domain. In an unmagnetized sample, the domains point in random directions, or form closed loops, so that there is no overall magnetization of the sample. In a magnetized sample, the domains are aligned so

dolphin

that their magnetic effects combine to produce a strong overall magnetism.

Domenichino /də,menɪˈkiːnəʊ/ real name Domenico Zampieri 1582–1641. Italian Baroque painter and architect, active in Bologna, Naples, and Rome. He began as an assistant to the ◊Carracci family of painters and continued their early Baroque style in, for example, frescoes 1624–28 in the choir of S Andrea della Valle, Rome.

This style was superseded by High Baroque, and Domenichino retreated to Naples. He is considered a pioneer of landscape painting in the Baroque period.

Domenico Veneziano /dəˈmenɪkəʊvɪ,netsiˈɑːnəʊ/ c. 1400–1461. Italian painter, active in Florence. His few surviving frescoes and altarpieces show a remarkably delicate use of colour and light (which recurs in the work of Piero della Francesca, who worked with him).

He worked in Sta Egidio, Florence, on frescoes now lost. Remaining works include the *Carnesecchi Madonna and Two Saints* and the *St Lucy altarpiece*, now divided between Florence (Uffizi), Berlin, Cambridge (Fitzwilliam), and Washington (National Gallery).

Dome of the Rock building in Jerusalem dating from the 7th century AD that enshrines the rock from which, in Muslim tradition, Muhammad ascended to heaven on his ◊Night Journey. It stands on the site of the Jewish national Temple and is visited by pilgrims.

Domesday Book record of the survey of England carried out 1086 by officials of William the Conqueror, in order to assess land tax and other dues, ascertain the value of the crown lands, and enable the king to estimate the power of his vassal barons.

Northumberland and Durham were omitted, and also London, Winchester, and certain other towns. The Domesday Book is preserved in two volumes at the Public Record Office, London. The name is derived from the belief that its judgement was as final as that of Doomsday.

domestic service paid employment in the household of another person, as maid, butler, cook, gardener, and so on. It is traditionally a poorly paid occupation, reserved for those without other job skills. The social and economic conditions of the 20th century, and the introduction of labour-saving technology, have narrowed this field of employment, and work by domestic cleaners, baby-sitters, and *au pairs* in the West is mostly part-time and unregulated. In the US, undocumented foreign workers constitute a large proportion of domestic workers.

Before the Industrial Revolution it was virtually the only form of employment open to women apart from work in the fields. In 19th-century Europe the increase in prosperity created a wealthy new middle class, whose ostentatious households demanded a number of servants for their upkeep. Domestic service was seen as a more 'respectable' occupation for women than industrial employment such as work in factories, until after World War I the shortage of available men meant that more women were able to choose nondomestic employment. The mobilization of women in World War II, the increase in labour-saving devices, and the growth of alternative employment opportunities for women since the war, have meant that domestic service in Europe hardly exists today as a full-time occupation except for a tiny proportion of working people, generally in aristocratic households.

dominance in genetics, the masking of one ◊allele by another allele. For example, if a ◊heterozygous person has one allele for blue eyes and one for brown eyes, their eye colour will be brown. The allele for blue eyes is described as recessive (see ◊recessivity) and the allele for brown eyes as dominant.

dominant in music, the fifth degree of the scale, for example, G in the C major scale.

domestic service *Domestic staff on the garden steps at Erdding Park, 1912 (above), and gardeners at Polesden Lacey, 1925 (below). Senior domestic staff include the butler, housekeeper, personal maid, and head gardener.*

Domingo /dəˈmɪŋɡəʊ/ Placido 1937– . Spanish tenor who excels in romantic operatic roles. A member of a musical family, he emigrated with them to Mexico in 1950. He made his debut in 1960 as Alfredo in Verdi's *La Traviata*, then spent four years with the Israel National Opera. He sang at the New York City Opera in 1965 and has since performed diverse roles in opera houses worldwide. In 1986 he starred in the film version of *Otello*.

Dominica /ˌdɒmɪˈniːkə/ island in the West Indies, between Guadeloupe and Martinique, the largest of the Windward Islands, with the Atlantic to the E and the Caribbean to the W.

government Dominica is an independent republic within the ◊Commonwealth. The constitution dates from independence in 1978, and provides for a single-chamber, 30-member, house of assembly. 21 are representatives elected by universal suffrage, and 9 are appointed senators, 5 on the advice of the prime minister and 4 on the advice of the leader of the opposition. The assembly serves a five-year term, as does the president,

who is elected by it and acts as constitutional head of state, appointing the prime minister on the basis of assembly support. The prime minister chooses the cabinet and all are responsible to the assembly. The two main political parties are the Dominica Freedom Party (DFP) and the Labour Party of Dominica.

history Dominica was named by Christopher ◊Columbus, who visited it in 1493. It became a British possession in the 18th century, and was part of the Leeward Islands federation until 1939. In 1940 it was transferred to the Windward Islands and remained attached to that group until 1960, when it was given separate status, with a chief minister and legislative council.

In 1961 the leader of the Dominica Labour Party (DLP), Edward leBlanc, became chief minister and after 13 years in office, retired and was succeeded as prime minister by Patrick John. The DLP held office until full independence was achieved in 1978 and its leader, John, became the first prime minister under the new constitution. Opposition to John's increasingly authoritarian

style of government soon developed and in the 1980 elections the DFP won a convincing victory on a free enterprise policy programme. Its leader, Eugenia Charles, became the Caribbean's first woman prime minister.

In 1981 John was thought to be implicated in a plot against the government and a state of emergency was imposed. The next year he was tried and acquitted. He was retried in 1985, found guilty and given a 12-year prison sentence. Left-of-centre parties regrouped, making the Labour Party of Dominica (LPD) the main opposition to the DFP. In the 1985 elections Eugenia Charles was re-elected. Under her leadership, Dominica has developed links with France and the USA and in 1983 sent a small force to the US-backed invasion of ◊Grenada.

Dominican order Roman Catholic order of friars founded 1215 by St Dominic; they are also known as Friars Preachers, Black Friars, or Jacobins. The order is worldwide and there is also an order of contemplative nuns; the habit is black and white.

The first house was established in Toulouse in 1215; in 1216 the order received papal recognition, and their rule was drawn up in 1220–21. They soon spread all over Europe, the first house in England being established in Oxford in 1221. The English Dominicans were suppressed in 1559, but were restored to a corporate existence in 1622. Dominicans have included Thomas Aquinas, Savonarola, and Las Casas. In 1983 there were 7,200 friars and 4,775 nuns.

Dominican Republic /dəˈmɪnɪkən/ country in the West Indies, occupying the E of the island of Hispaniola, with Haiti to the W. The island is surrounded by the Caribbean Sea.

government Although not a federal state, the Dominican Republic has a highly devolved system of 27 provinces, each administered by an appointed governor, and a national district, which includes the capital, Santo Domingo. The 1966 constitution provides for a popularly elected president and a two-chamber congress, comprising a senate and a chamber of deputies, all elected for a four-year term. The senate has 28 members, one for each province and one for the national district, and the chamber of deputies 120 members, one per 50,000 inhabitants. The president is head of both government and state and chooses the cabinet. Most significant of a wide range of political parties are the left-wing Dominican Revolutionary Party (PRD) and the centrist Christian Social Reform Party (PRSC).

history The first European to visit the island was Christopher ◊Columbus in 1492; he named it

Domingo *Spanish opera singer Placido Domingo at the Royal Opera House, Covent Garden, London, in 1985.*

Dominica
Commonwealth of

0   1000 km

area 751 sq km/290 sq mi
capital Roseau, with a deepwater port
physical largest of the Windward Islands,
mountainous, tropical
features of great beauty, it has mountains
of volcanic origin rising to 1,620 m/5,317 ft;
Boiling Lake, an effect produced by escaping
subterranean gas
head of state Clarence Seignoret from 1983
head of government Mary Eugenia Charles
from 1980

political system liberal democracy
political parties Dominica Freedom Party
(DFP), centrist; Labour Party of Dominica (LPD),
left-of-centre
exports bananas, coconuts, citrus, lime, bay oil
currency E Caribbean dollar (4.60 = £1 Feb
1990), pound sterling, French franc
population (1987) 94,200 (mainly black African
in origin, but with a small Carib reserve of some
500); annual growth rate 1.3%
language English (official), but the Dominican
patois reflects earlier periods of French rule
religion Roman Catholic 80%
literacy 80%
GNP $79 million (1983); $460 per head of
population
chronology
1978 Dominica achieved full independence
within the Commonwealth. Patrick John, leader
of the Dominica Labour Party (DLP), elected
prime minister.
1980 DFP, led by Eugenia Charles, won a
convincing victory in the general election.
1981 Patrick John was implicated in a plot to
overthrow the government.
1982 John tried and acquitted.
1985 John retried and found guilty. Regrouping
of left-of-centre parties resulted in the new
Labour Party of Dominica (LPD). DFP, led by
Eugenia Charles, re-elected.

domino theory idea popularized by US president
Eisenhower in 1954 that if one country comes
under communist rule, adjacent countries are
likely to become communist as well. Initially
used to justify US intervention in SE Asia, the
domino theory has also been invoked in reference
to Central America.

Domitian /dəˈmɪʃən/ Titus Flavius Domitianus AD
51–96. Roman emperor from AD 81. He finalized
the conquest of Britain (see ◊Agricola), strengthened the Rhine–Danube frontier, and suppressed
immorality as well as freedom of thought (see
◊Epictetus) in philosophy and religion (Christians
were persecuted). His reign of terror led to his
assassination.

Don /dɒn/ river in Soviet Union, rising to the south
of Moscow and entering the NE extremity of the
Sea of Azov; length 1,900 km/1,180 mi. In its
lower reaches the Don is 1.5 km/1 mi wide, and
for about four months of the year it is closed by
ice. Its upper course is linked with the Volga by
a canal.

Donald /ˈdɒnld/ Ian 1910–1987. English obstetrician who introduced ◊ultrasound scanning. He pioneered its use in obstetrics as a means of scanning
the growing fetus without exposure to X-rays.
Donald's experience of using radar in World War II
suggested to him the use of ultrasound for medical
purposes.

Donaldson /ˈdɒnldsən/ Stephen 1947– . US fantasy writer, best known for two Thomas Covenant
trilogies in six volumes 1978–1983.

Donat /ˈdəʊnæt/ Robert 1905–1958. British actor
of Anglo-Polish parents. He started out in the
theatre, made one film in Hollywood (*The Count
of Monte Cristo* 1934), and his other films include
The Thirty-Nine Steps 1935, *Goodbye, Mr Chips*
1939, and *The Winslow Boy* 1948.

Donatello /ˌdɒnəˈteləʊ/ (Donato di Niccolo)
1386–1466. Italian sculptor of the early Renaissance, born in Florence. He was instrumental in reviving the Classical style, as in
his graceful bronze statue of the youthful
David (Bargello, Florence) and his equestrian statue of the general *Gattamelata* 1443
(Padua). The course of Florentine art in
the 15th century was strongly influenced by
his style.

Hispaniola ('Little Spain'). It was divided between
France and Spain in 1697, and in 1795 the Spanish
part (Santo Domingo) was ceded to France. After
a revolt it was retaken by Spain in 1808. Following
a brief independence in 1821 it was occupied by
Haiti until the establishment of the Dominican Republic in 1844.

Spain occupied the country again 1861–65, and
after independence was restored, it was in such
financial difficulties that in 1904 the USA took over
its debts and intervened militarily 1916–24.

In 1930 the elected president was overthrown
in a military coup and Gen Rafael Trujillo Molina
became dictator. He was assassinated in 1961,
and in 1963 Dr Juan Bosch, founder and leader of
the left-wing PRD, who had been in exile for over
30 years, won the country's first free elections.
Within a year he was overthrown by the military,
who set up their own three-man ruling junta.

An attempt to re-establish Bosch in 1965 was
defeated with US help, and in 1966 Joaquín
Balaguer, a protégé of Trujillo and leader of the
PRSC, won the presidency. A more democratic
constitution was adopted and Balaguer, despite his
links with Trujillo, proved a popular leader, being
re-elected in 1970 and 1974.

The 1978 election was won by the PRD candidate, Silvestre Antonio Guzmán. The PRD
was again successful in the 1982 election and
Salvador Jorge Blanco, the party's left-wing nominee, became president-designate. After allegations of fraud by his family, Guzmán committed
suicide before he had finished his term, and an
interim president was chosen before the start of
Blanco's term.

Blanco steered a restrained course in foreign
policy, maintaining good relations with the USA
and avoiding too close an association with Cuba.
The economy deteriorated, and in 1985 the Blanco
administration was forced to adopt harsh austerity
measures in return for ◊IMF help. The PRD became increasingly unpopular and the PRSC, under
Joaquín Balaguer, returned to power in 1986.
Dominic, St /ˈdɒmɪnɪk/ 1170–1221. Founder of
the Roman Catholic Dominican order of preaching
friars. Feast day 7 Aug.

Dominic, born in Old Castile, was sent by Pope
Innocent III in 1205 to preach among the Albigen-
ses in Provence. In 1208 the pope substituted the
Albigensian crusade to suppress the heretics by

force, and this was supported by Dominic. In
1215 the Dominican order was given premises
at Toulouse. Pope Honorius III, in 1218, permitted Dominic to constitute his 'holy preaching'
as an order, and by the time of his death it was
established all over W Europe.

Dominions former self-governing divisions of the
British Empire—for example Canada—that are
now members of the ◊Commonwealth.

Domino /ˈdɒmɪnəʊ/ 'Fats' (Antoine) 1928– .
US rock-and-roll pianist, singer, and songwriter,
exponent of the New Orleans style. His hits include 'Ain't That A Shame' 1955 and 'Blueberry
Hill' 1956.

Dominican Republic
(República Dominicana)

0   1000 km

area 48,446 sq km/18,700 sq mi
capital Santo Domingo
physical comprises E part of island of
Hispaniola; central mountain range; fertile
valley in N
features Pico Duarte 3,174 m/10,417 ft, highest
point in the Caribbean islands
head of state and government Joaquín
Balaguer from 1986
political system democratic republic
political parties Dominican Revolutionary Party

(PRD), moderate left-of-centre; Christian Social
Reform Party (PRSC), independent socialist;
Dominican Liberation Party (PLD), nationalist
exports sugar, gold, coffee, ferro-nickel
currency peso (14.35 = £1 Feb 1990)
population (1987) 6,708,000; annual growth
rate 2.3%
life expectancy men 61, women 65
language Spanish (official)
religion Roman Catholic
literacy 78% male/77% female (1985 est)
GNP $8.7 bn (1983); $1,221 per head of
population
chronology
1930 Military coup established the dictatorship
of Rafael Trujillo.
1961 Trujillo assassinated.
1962 First democratic elections resulted in
Juan Bosch, founder of the PRD, becoming
president.
1963 Bosch overthrown in military coup.
1966 New constitution adopted. Joaquín
Balaguer, leader of the PRSC, became
president.
1978 PRD returned to power, with Silvestre
Antonio Guzmán as president.
1982 PRD re-elected, with Jorge Blanco as
president.
1985 Blanco forced by International Monetary
Fund to adopt austerity measures to save the
economy.
1986 PRSC returned to power, with Balaguer
re-elected president.

Donatello introduced true perspective in his relief sculptures, like the panel of *St George Slaying the Dragon* about 1415–17 (Or San Michele, Florence). During a stay in Rome 1430–32 he absorbed Classical influences, and *David* is said to be the first free-standing nude since antiquity. In his later work, such as his wood-carving of the aged *Mary Magdalene* about 1456 (Baptistry, Florence), he sought dramatic expression through a distorted, emaciated figure style.

Donation of Constantine a forged 8th-century document purporting to record the Roman emperor Constantine's surrender of temporal sovereignty in W Europe to Pope Sylvester I (314–25).

In the Middle Ages, this document was used as papal propaganda in the struggle between pope and emperor, which was at its most heated during the ◊Investiture Contest. It was finally exposed by ◊Nicholas of Cusa and Lorenzo Valla in the 15th century.

Donatist a member of a puritanical Christian movement in 4th- and 5th-century N Africa, named after Donatus of Casae Nigrae, a 3rd-century bishop, later known as Donatus of Carthage.

The Donatists became for a time the major Christian movement in N Africa; following the tradition of ◊Montanism, their faith stressed the social revolutionary aspects of Christianity, the separation of church from state, and a belief in martyrdom and suffering. Their influence was ended by Bishop Augustine of Hippo; they were formally condemned 412.

Donau /ˈdaʊnaʊ/ German name for the ◊Danube.

Donbas /ˌdɒnˈbæs/ abbreviation of ◊Donets Basin, a coal-rich area in the USSR.

Doncaster /ˈdɒŋkəstə/ town in South Yorkshire, England, on the river Don; population (1981) 81,600. It has a racecourse, famous races here are the St Leger (1776) in Sept and the Lincolnshire Handicap in Mar.

history Doncaster was originally a Roman station. Conisbrough, a ruined Norman castle to the SW, features in Scott's *Ivanhoe* as Athelstan's stronghold. Coal, iron, and steel have been the dominant industries in this area for hundreds of years, though they have recently declined and are being replaced by other manufactures, such as synthetic textiles.

Donegal /ˌdɒnɪˈɡɔːl/ mountainous county in Ulster province in the NW of the Republic of Ireland, surrounded on three sides by the Atlantic; area 4,830 sq km/1,864 sq mi; population (1986) 130,000. The county town is Lifford; the market town and port of Donegal is at the head of Donegal Bay in the SW. Commercial activities include sheep and cattle raising, tweed and linen manufacture, and some deep-sea fishing. The river Erne hydroelectric project (1952) involved the building of large power stations at Ballyshannon.

Donellan 1953– . Declan British theatre director, co-founder of *Cheek by Jowl* theatre company 1981, and associate director of the National Theatre from 1989. His irreverent and audacious productions include many classics, such as Racine's *Andromaque*.

Donen /ˈdaʊnən/ Stanley 1924– . US film director, formerly a dancer, who co-directed two of Gene Kelly's best musicals, *On the Town* 1949 and *Singin' in the Rain* 1952. His other films include *Charade* 1963 and *Two for the Road* 1968.

Donets /dɒˈnets/ river of the USSR rising in Kursk region and flowing 1,080 km/670 mi through Ukraine to join the river Don 100 km/60 mi E of Rostov; see also ◊Donets Basin.

Donets Basin /dɒˈnets/ area in the bend formed by the rivers Don and Donets, which holds one of Europe's richest coalfields, together with salt, mercury, and lead, so that the *Donbas*, as the name is abbreviated, is one of the greatest industrial regions of the USSR.

Donetsk /dɒˈnets/ city in Ukraine, capital of Donetsk region, situated in the Donets Basin, a major coal mining area, 600 km/372 mi SE of Kiev, USSR; population (1987) 1,090,000. It

has blast furnaces, rolling mills, and other heavy industries.

It developed from 1871 when a Welshman, John Hughes, established a metallurgical factory, and the town was first called Yuzovka after him; renamed Stalino 1924, and Donetsk 1961.

Dongola /ˈdɒŋɡələ/ town in the Northern Province of the Sudan, above the third cataract on the river Nile. It was founded about 1812 to replace **Old Dongola**, 120 km/75 mi up river, which was destroyed by the ◊Mamelukes. The latter, a trading centre on a caravan route, was the capital of the Christian kingdom of ◊Nubia between the 6th–14th centuries.

Dongting /ˈduŋˈtɪŋ/ lake in Hunan province, China; area 10,000 sq km/4,000 sq mi.

Dönitz /ˈdɜːnɪts/ Karl 1891–1980. German admiral, originator of the wolf-pack submarine technique, which sank 15 million tonnes of Allied shipping in World War II. He succeeded Hitler in 1945, capitulated, and was imprisoned 1946–56.

Donizetti /ˌdɒnɪdˈzeti/ Gaetano 1797–1848. Italian composer who created more than 60 operas, including *Lucrezia Borgia* 1833, *Lucia di Lammermoor* 1835, *La Fille du régiment* 1840, *La Favorite* 1840, and *Don Pasquale* 1843. They show the influence of Rossini and Bellini, and are characterized by a flow of expressive melodies.

Don Juan /ˈdʒuːən/ Spanish character of Spanish legend, Don Juan Tenorio, supposed to have lived in the 14th century, and notorious for his debauchery. Tirso de Molina, Molière, Mozart, Byron, and G B Shaw have featured the legend.

donkey alternative name for ◊ass.

Donne /dʌn/ John 1571–1631. English metaphysical poet, whose work is characterized by subtle imagery and figurative language. In 1615 Donne took orders in the Church of England and as dean of St Paul's Cathedral, London, was noted for his sermons. His poetry includes the sonnets 'No man is an island' and 'Death be not proud', elegies, and satires.

Donne was brought up in the Roman Catholic faith, and matriculated early at Oxford to avoid taking the oath of supremacy. Before entering Lincoln's Inn as a law student 1592 he travelled in Europe. During his four years at the law courts he was notorious for his wit and reckless living. In 1596 he sailed as a volunteer with Essex and Raleigh, and on his return became private secretary to Sir Thomas Egerton, Keeper of the Seal. This appointment was ended by his secret marriage to Ann More (died 1617), niece of Egerton's wife, and they endured many years of poverty. The more passionate and tender of his love poems were probably written to her.

From 1621 to his death Donne was dean of St Paul's. His sermons rank him with the century's greatest orators, and his fervent poems of love and hate, violent, tender, or abusive, give him a unique position among English poets. His verse was not published in collected form until after his death, and was long out of favour, but he is now recognized as one of the greatest English poets.

Donnybrook /ˈdɒnɪbrʊk/ former village, now part of Dublin, Republic of Ireland, notorious until 1855 for its riotous fairs.

Donoghue /ˈdɒnəhjuː/ Stephen ('Steve') 1884–1945. British jockey. Between 1915 and 1925 he won the Epsom Derby six times, equalling the record of Jem Robinson (since beaten by Lester Piggott). Donoghue is the only jockey to win the race in three successive years.

Don Pacifico Affair incident in 1850 in which British foreign secretary Lord Palmerston was criticized in Parliament and elsewhere in Europe for using British naval superiority to impose his foreign policy. Palmerston sent gunboats to blockade the Greek coast in support of the claim of a Portugese merchant, David Pacifico, who was born on Gibraltar (and thus a British subject), for compensation from the Greek government after his house was burned down in anti-Semitic riots.

This action brought diplomatic protests from the governments of France and Russia, who had also guaranteed Greek independence. Palmerston successfully defended his action in Parliament, but fell from power the following year, 1851.

Don Quixote de la Mancha a satirical romance by Cervantes, published in two parts 1605 and 1615. Don Quixote, a self-styled knight, embarks on a series of chivalric adventures accompanied by Sancho Panza. Quixote's imagination leads him to see harmless objects as enemies to be fought, as in his tilting at windmills.

Doolittle /ˈduːlɪtl/ Hilda, pen name *HD* 1886–1961. US poet. She went to Europe in 1911, and was associated with Ezra Pound and the British writer Richard ◊Aldington (to whom she was married 1913–37), in founding the ◊Imagist school of poets. Her work includes the *Sea Garden* 1916 and *Helen in Egypt* 1916.

Doomsday Book a variant spelling of ◊Domesday Book, English survey of 1086.

Doone /duːn/ English family of freebooters who according to legend lived on Exmoor, Devon, until they were exterminated in the 17th century. They feature in R D ◊Blackmore's novel *Lorna Doone* 1869. The Doone Valley is near Lynton.

Doors, the US psychedelic rock group formed 1965 in Los Angeles by Jim Morrison (1943–71, vocals), Ray Manzarek (1935– , keyboards), Robby Krieger (1946– , guitar), and John Densmore (1944– , drums). Their first hit was 'Light My Fire' from their debut album *The Doors* 1967. They were noted for Morrison's poetic lyrics and flaunting performance.

doppelgänger (German 'double-goer') a ghostly apparition identical to a living person; a twin soul.

Doppler /ˈdɒplə/ Christian Johann 1803–1853. Austrian physicist. He became professor of experimental physics at Vienna, and described the Doppler effect.

Doppler effect change in observed frequency (or wavelength) of waves due to relative motion between wave source and observer. It is responsible for the perceived change in pitch of a siren as it approaches and then recedes, and for the ◊red shift of light from distant stars. It is named after the Austrian physicist Christian Doppler (1803–53).

DORA in the UK, short for the Defence of the Realm Act, passed in Nov 1914, which conferred extraordinary powers on the government for the duration of World War I.

Dorado constellation of the southern hemisphere, represented as a goldfish. It is easy to locate, since the Large ◊Magellanic Cloud marks its southern border. Its brightest star is Alpha Doradus, just under 200 light years away.

Dorati /dɒˈrɑːti/ Antal 1906–1988. US conductor, born in Hungary. He toured with ballet companies 1933–45 and went on to conduct orchestras in the USA and Europe in a career spanning more than half a century. Dorati gave many first performances of Bartók's music and recorded all Haydn's symphonies with the Philharmonia Hungarica.

Dorchester /ˈdɔːtʃɪstə/ market town in Dorset, England, on the river Frome, north of Weymouth; population (1985) 14,000. It is administrative centre for the county. *Maiden Castle* to the SW was occupied as a settlement from about 2000 BC. The novelist Thomas ◊Hardy was born nearby.

Dordogne /dɔːˈdɔɪn/ river in SW France, rising in Puy-de-Dôme *département* and flowing 490 km/300 mi to join the Garonne, 23 km/14 mi N of Bordeaux. It gives its name to a *département* and is an important source of hydroelectric power.

The valley of the Dordogne is a popular tourist area and the caves of the wooded valleys of its tributary, the Vézère, have signs of early human occupation. Famous sites include Cro-Magnon, Moustier, and the Lascaux caves, discovered in 1940, which have the earliest known examples of cave art. Images of bulls, bison, and deer were painted by the Cro-Magnon people (named from skeletons found 1868 in Cro–Magnon Cave, near Les Eyzies). The opening of the Lascaux caves to tourists led to deterioration of the paintings; the caves were closed in 1963 and a facsimile opened in 1983.

Dordrecht /'dɔːdrext/ or **Dort** river port on an island in the Maas, South Holland, Netherlands, 19 km/12 mi SE of Rotterdam; population (1988) 108,000, metropolitan area of Dordrecht-Zwijndrecht 203,000. It is an inland port with shipbuilding yards and makes heavy machinery, plastics, and chemicals.

Doré /'dɔːreɪ/ Gustave 1832–1883. French artist, chiefly known as a prolific illustrator, and also active as a painter, etcher, and sculptor. He produced closely worked engravings of scenes from, for example, Rabelais, Dante, Cervantes, the Bible, Milton, and Poe.

Doré was born in Strasbourg. His views of Victorian London 1869–71, concentrating on desperate poverty and overcrowding in the swollen city, were admired by van Gogh.

Dorian /'dɔːrɪən/ a people of ancient Greece. They entered Greece from the N and conquered most of the Peloponnese from the Achaeans and destroyed the ◊Mycenaean civilization; this invasion appears to have been completed before 1000 BC. Their chief cities were Sparta, Argos, and Corinth.

Doric in classical architecture, one of the five types of column; see ◊order.

dormancy in botany, a phase of reduced physiological activity exhibited by certain buds, seeds, and spores. Dormancy can help a plant to survive unfavourable conditions, as in annual plants that pass the cold winter season as dormant seeds, and plants that form dormant buds.

For various reasons many seeds exhibit a period of dormancy even when conditions are favourable for growth. Sometimes this can be broken by artificial methods, such as penetrating the seed coat to facilitate the uptake of water (chitting) or exposing the seed to light. See ◊after-ripening.

dormancy state of a peerage or baronetcy when it is believed that heirs to the title exist, but their whereabouts are unknown. This sometimes occurs when a senior line dies out and a cadet line has long since gone off to foreign parts.

dormouse small rodent, akin to a mouse, with a hairy tail. There are about ten species, living in Europe, Asia, and Africa. They are arboreal (live in trees), nocturnal, and hibernate during winter in cold regions.

It derives its name from French *dormir* 'to sleep' because of its hibernating habit. The *common dormouse Muscardinus avellanarius* lives all over Europe in thickets and forests with undergrowth. It is reddish fawn and 15 cm/6 in long, including tail. The *fat* or *edible dormouse Glis glis* lives in continental Europe, and is 30 cm/1 ft long including tail. It was a delicacy at Roman feasts, and was introduced to SE England.

Dorneywood /'dɔːniwʊd/ country house near Burnham Beeches, Buckinghamshire, England. Presented to the nation by Lord Courtauld-Thomson (1865–1954) as an official residence for a minister of the crown, it is used by the foreign secretary.

Dornier /,dɔːni'eɪ/ Claude 1884–1969. German aircraft designer who invented the seaplane and during World War II supplied the Luftwaffe with the 'flying pencil' bomber.

Born in Bavaria, he founded the Dornier Metallbau works at Friedrichshafen, Lake Constance, in 1922.

Dorpat /'dɔːpæt/ German name for the Estonian city of ◊Tartu.

d'Orsay /'dɔːseɪ/ Alfred Guillaume Gabriel, Count d'Orsay 1801–1857. French dandy. For 20 years he resided with Lady ◊Blessington in London at Gore House, where he became known as an arbiter of taste.

Dorset /'dɔːsɪt/ county in SW England
area 2,650 sq km/1,023 sq mi

Dorset

towns administrative headquarters Dorchester; Poole, Shaftesbury, Sherborne; resorts Bournemouth, Lyme Regis, Weymouth

features Chesil Bank (shingle bank along the coast 19 km/11 mi long); Isle of Purbeck, a peninsula where china clay and Purbeck 'marble' are quarried, and which includes Corfe Castle and the holiday resort of Swanage; Dorset Downs; Cranborne Chase; rivers Frome and Stour; Maiden Castle; Tank Museum at Royal Armoured Corps Centre, Bovington, where the cottage of T E ◊Lawrence is a museum.

products Wytch Farm is the largest onshore oil-field in the UK.

population (1987) 649,000

famous people Thomas Hardy, the novelist, born at Higher Bockhampton (Dorchester is 'Casterbridge', the heart of Hardy's Wessex).

Dorset /'dɔːsɪt/ 1st Earl of Dorset title of English poet Thomas ◊Sackville.

Dort /dɔːt/ another name for ◊Dordrecht, a port in the Netherlands.

Dortmund /'dɔːtmʊnd/ industrial centre in the ◊Ruhr, West Germany, 58 km/36 mi NE of Düsseldorf; population (1988) 568,000. It is the largest mining town of the Westphalian coalfield and the southern terminus of the Dortmund-Ems canal. Industries include iron, steel, construction machinery, engineering, and brewing.

dory /'dɔːri/ marine fish *Zeus faber* found in the Mediterranean and Atlantic. It grows up to 60 cm/2 ft, and has nine or ten long spines at the front of the dorsal fin, and four at the front of the anal fin.

It is olive brown or grey, with a conspicuous black spot ringed with yellow on each side. A stalking predator, it shoots out its mobile jaws to catch fish. It is considered to be an excellent food fish. It is also known as *John Dory*.

DOS *disc operating system* in computing, an ◊operating system specifically designed for use with disc storage; also used as an alternative name for a particular operating system, ◊MS-DOS.

Dos Passos /dəʊs 'pæsəʊs/ John 1896–1970. US author, born in Chicago. He made a reputation with the war novels *One Man's Initiation* 1919 and *Three Soldiers* 1921. His greatest work is the *USA* trilogy 1930–36, which gives a panoramic view of US life through the device of placing fictitious characters against the real setting of newspaper headlines and contemporary events.

Dos Santos /dɒs 'sæntɒs/ Jose Eduardo 1942– . Angolan left-wing politician, president from 1979, a member of the People's Movement for the Liberation of Angola (MPLA). He was in exile 1961–70 during the civil war between the MPLA and the National Union for the Total Independence of Angola (UNITA). By 1989, he had negotiated the withdrawal of South African and Cuban forces, and a ceasefire between MPLA and UNITA.

Dostoievsky *Russian novelist Fyodor Dostoievsky.*

Born in Luanda, he joined the MPLA in 1961 and went into exile during the struggle for independence and the civil war between nationalist movements backed by foreign powers. He returned to Angola in 1970 and rejoined the war, which continued after independence in 1975. He held key positions under President Agostinho Neto, and succeeded him on his death.

Dostoievsky /,dɒstɔɪ'efski/ Fyodor Mihailovich 1821–1881. Russian novelist. Remarkable for their profound psychological insight, Dostoievsky's novels have greatly influenced Russian writers, and since the beginning of the 20th century have been increasingly influential abroad. In 1849 he was sentenced to four years' hard labour in Siberia, followed by army service, for printing socialist propaganda. *The House of the Dead* 1861 recalls his prison experiences, followed by his major works ◊*Crime and Punishment* 1866, *The Idiot* 1868–69, and ◊*The Brothers Karamazov* 1880.

Born in Moscow, the son of a physician, he was for a short time an army officer. His first novel, *Poor Folk*, appeared in 1846. In 1849 Dostoievsky was arrested as a member of a free-thinking literary circle during a period of intense tsarist censorship, and after being reprieved from death at the last moment was sent to the penal settlement at Omsk for four years, where the terrible conditions increased his epileptic tendency. Finally pardoned in 1859, he published the humorous *Village of Stepanchikovo*, *The House of the Dead*, and *The Insulted and the Injured* 1862. Meanwhile he had launched two unsuccessful liberal periodicals, in the second of which his *Letters from the Underworld* 1864 appeared. Compelled to work by pressure of debt, he quickly produced *Crime and Punishment* 1866 and *The Gambler* 1867, before fleeing abroad from his creditors. He then wrote *The Idiot*, in which the hero is an epileptic like himself; *The Eternal Husband* 1870; and *The Possessed* 1871–72.

Returning to Russia in 1871, he again entered journalism and issued the personal miscellany *Journal of an Author*, in which he discussed contemporary problems. In 1875 he published *A Raw Youth*, but the great work of his last years is *The Brothers Karamazov*.

dotterel bird *Eudromias morinellus* of the plover family, nesting on high moors and tundra in Europe and Asia, migrating south for the winter. About 23 cm/9 in, it is clad in a pattern of black, brown, and white in summer, duller in winter, but always with white eyebrows and breastband. Females are larger than males, and the male incubates and rears the brood.

Dou /daʊ/ Gerard 1613–1675. Dutch genre painter, a pupil of Rembrandt. He is known for small domestic interiors, minutely observed.

He was born in Leiden, where he founded a painters' guild with Jan Steen. He had many pupils, including Metsu.

Douai /duːˈeɪ/ town in the Nord *département*, France, on the river Scarpe; population (1982)

44,515, conurbation 202,000. It has coal-mines, iron foundries, and breweries. An English Roman Catholic college was founded there 1568 by English Catholics in exile. The Douai-Reims Bible, published 1582–1610, influenced the translators of the King James' Version.

Douala /duːˈɑːlə/ or **Duala** chief port and industrial centre (aluminium, chemicals, textiles, pulp) of Cameroon, on the Wouri river estuary; population (1981) 637,000. Known as Kamerunstadt until 1907, it was capital of German Cameroon 1885–1901.

double bass a bowed string musical instrument, the bass of the ◊violin family.

double coconut treelike ◊palm plant *Lodoicea maldivica*, also known as *coco de mer*, of the Seychelles. It produces a two-lobed edible nut, one of the largest known fruits.

double decomposition a reaction between two chemical substances (usually ◊salts in solution) that results in the exchange of a constituent from each compound to create two different compounds.

For example, if silver nitrate solution is added to a solution of sodium chloride, there is an exchange of ions yielding sodium nitrate and silver chloride.

double entendre (French 'double meaning') an ambiguous word or phrase, usually one that is coarse or indelicate.

double jeopardy in law, the principle that a person cannot be prosecuted twice for the same offence. It is contained in the fifth amendment of the US constitution. In British law a defendant can plead 'autrefois convict' if he or she has already been convicted of the same offence (or 'autrefois acquit' in the case of a previous acquittal).

double star two stars that appear close together. Most double stars attract each other due to gravity, and orbit each other, forming a genuine ◊binary star, but other double stars are at different distances from Earth, and lie in the same line of sight only by chance. Through a telescope both types of double star will look the same.

Doubs /duː/ river in France and Switzerland, rising in the Jura mountains and flowing 430 km/265 mi to join the river Saône. It gives its name to a *département*.

dough a mixture consisting primarily of flour, water, and yeast, which is used in the manufacture of bread.

The preparation of dough involves thorough mixing (kneading) and standing in a warm place to 'prove' (increase in volume) so that the ◊enzymes in the dough can break down the starch from the flour into smaller sugar molecules, which are then fermented by the yeast. This releases carbon dioxide, which causes the dough to rise.

doughboy nickname for a US infantry soldier in the two world wars, especially World War I.

Doughty /ˈdaʊti/ Charles Montagu 1843–1926. English travel writer, author of the verbose *Travels in Arabia Deserta* 1888, written after two years in the Middle East searching for Biblical relics. He was a role model for T E ◊Lawrence ('Lawrence of Arabia').

Douglas /ˈdʌɡləs/ capital of the Isle of Man in the Irish Sea; population (1981) 20,000. A holiday resort and terminus of shipping routes to and from Fleetwood and Liverpool.

Douglas /ˈdʌɡləs/ Alfred (Bruce) 1870–1945. British poet who became closely associated in London with Oscar ◊Wilde. Douglas's father, the 9th Marquess of Queensberry, strongly disapproved of the relationship and called Wilde a 'posing Somdomite' (sic). Wilde's action for libel ultimately resulted in his own imprisonment.

Douglas /ˈdʌɡləs/ Gavin (or Gawain) 1475–1522. Scottish poet whose translation of Virgil's *Aeneid* 1515 into Scots was the first translation from the classics into an English-based language.

Douglas /ˈdʌɡləs/ Kirk. Stage name of Issur Danielovitch 1916– . US film actor, of Russian parents. Usually cast as a dynamic and intelligent

Douglas *Kirk Douglas accompanied by his son Michael Douglas. Both men are leading actors who portray characters of intelligence and virility.*

hero, as in *Spartacus* 1960, he was a major star of the 1950s and 1960s in such films as *Ace in the Hole/The Big Carnival* 1951, *Lust for Life* 1956, and *The War Wagon* 1967.

Douglas /ˈdʌɡləs/ Major (Clifford Hugh) 1879–1952. English social reformer, founder of the economic theory of *Social Credit*, which held that interest should be abolished, and credit should become a state monopoly. During a depression, the state should provide purchasing power by subsidizing manufacture, and paying dividends to individuals; as long as there was spare capacity in the economy, this credit would not cause inflation.

Douglas /ˈdʌɡləs/ Norman 1868–1952. British diplomat and travel writer (*Siren Land* 1911 and *Old Calabria* 1915, dealing with Italy); his novel *South Wind* 1917 is set in his adopted island of Capri.

Douglas-Hamilton family name of dukes of Hamilton: seated at Lennoxlove, East Lothian, Scotland.

Douglas-Home /ˈdʌɡləs ˈhjuːm/ William 1912– . British playwright, younger brother of Lord ◊Home of the Hirsel. His plays include *The Chiltern Hundreds* 1947, *The Secretary Bird* 1968, and *Lloyd George Knew My Father* 1972.

Douglas of Kirtleside /ˈkɜːtlsaɪd/ William Sholto Douglas, 1st Baron Douglas of Kirtleside 1893–1969. British air marshal. During World War II he was air officer commander in chief of Fighter Command 1940–42, Middle East Command 1943–44, and Coastal Command 1944–45.

Douglass /ˈdʌɡləs/ Frederick *c.*1817–1895. US anti-slavery campaigner. Born a slave in Maryland, he escaped 1838. His autobiographical *Narrative of the Life of Frederick Douglass* 1845 aroused support in northern states for the abolition of slavery. After the Civil War, he held several US government posts, including minister to Haiti.

Doukhobor member of a Christian sect of Russian origin, now mainly found in Canada, also known as 'Christians of the Universal Brotherhood'. Some of the Doukhobor teachings resemble those of the Quakers.

They were long persecuted, mainly for refusing military service—the writer Tolstoy organized a relief fund for them—but in 1898 were permitted to emigrate and settled in Canada, where they number about 13,000, mainly in British Columbia and Saskatchewan. An extremist group, 'the Sons of Freedom', staged demonstrations and guerrilla acts in the 1960s, leading to the imprisonment of about 100 of them.

Doulton /ˈdəʊltən/ Henry 1820–1897. English ceramicist. He developed special wares for the chemical, electrical, and building industries, and established the world's first stoneware drainpipe factory 1846. From 1870 he created art pottery and domestic tablewares in Lambeth, S London, and Burslem, near Stoke-on-Trent, in the ◊Potteries.

Doumer /duːˈmeə/ Paul 1857–1932. French politician. He was elected president of the Chamber in 1905, president of the Senate in 1927, and president of the republic in 1931. He was assassinated by Gorgulov, a White Russian émigré.

Doumergue /duːˈmeəɡ/ Gaston 1863–1937. French prime minister Dec 1913–June 1914 (during the time leading up to World War I); president 1924–31; and premier again Feb–Nov 1934 at head of 'national union' government.

Dounreay an experimental nuclear reactor site on the north coast of Scotland, 12 km/7 mi W of Thurso. Development started here in 1974 and continued until a decision was made in 1988 to decommission the site by 1994.

Douro /ˈdʊərəʊ/ (Spanish **Duero**) river rising in N central Spain and flowing through N Portugal to the Atlantic at Porto; length 800 km/500 mi. Navigation at the river mouth is hindered by sand bars. There are hydroelectric installations.

dove type of ◊pigeon.

Dover /ˈdəʊvə/ market town and seaport on the SE coast of Kent, England; population (1981) 33,000. It is Britain's nearest point to mainland Europe, being only 34 km/21 mi from Calais. Dover's modern development has been chiefly due to the cross-Channel traffic, which includes train, ferry, hovercraft, and other services. It was one of the ◊Cinque Ports.

history Under Roman rule, Dover (Portus Dubris) was the terminus of ◊Watling Street, and the beacon or 'lighthouse' in the grounds of the Norman castle dates from about AD 50, making it one of the oldest buildings in Britain. The Lord Warden of the Cinque Ports is Constable of Dover Castle.

Dover, Strait of /ˈdəʊvə/ (French **Pas-de-Calais**) stretch of water separating England from France, and connecting the English Channel with the North Sea. It is about 35 km/22 mi long and 34 km/21 mi wide at its narrowest part. It is one of the world's busiest sea lanes, and by 1972 increasing traffic, collisions, and shipwrecks had become so frequent that traffic-routeing schemes were enforced.

dowager the style given to the widow of a peer or baronet. She may take the style of 'Dowager Countess of Blankshire' (so as not to be confused with the wife of the current holder of the title); alternatively she may take the style of 'Mary, Countess of Blankshire' (although this is the style also used by divorced wives of peers).

Dowding /ˈdaʊdɪŋ/ Hugh Caswall Tremenheere, 1st Baron Dowding 1882–1970. British air chief marshal. He was chief of Fighter Command at the outbreak of World War II in 1939, a post he held through the Battle of Britain. He wrote works on spiritualism.

Dowell /ˈdaʊəl/ Anthony 1943– . British ballet dancer in the classical style. He was principal dancer with the Royal Ballet 1966–86, and director 1986–89.

Dowell joined the Royal Ballet in 1961. The choreographer Ashton chose him to create the role of Oberon in *The Dream* 1964 opposite Antoinette Sibley, the start of an outstanding partnership. He also created roles in *Shadowplay* (Tudor, 1967), *Manon* (MacMillan, 1974), *Four Schumann Pieces* (von Manen, 1975), and *A Month in the Country* (Ashton, 1980).

Dow Jones average a daily index of prices on New York's Wall Street stock exchange, based on 30 industrial stocks.

Dowland /ˈdaʊlənd/ John 1563–1626. English composer. He is remembered for his songs to lute accompaniment as well as music for lute alone, such as *Lachrymae* 1605.

Down /daʊn/ county in SE Northern Ireland, facing the Irish Sea on the east; area 2,470 sq km/953 sq mi; population (1981) 53,000. In the south are the Mourne mountains, in the east Strangford sea lough. The county town is Downpatrick; the main industry is dairying.

Downing Street /ˈdaʊnɪŋ/ street in Westminster, London, leading from Whitehall to St James's Park, named after Sir George Downing (died 1684), a diplomat under Cromwell and Charles II. *Number 10* is the official residence of the prime minister, *number 11* is the residence of the chancellor of the Exchequer, and *number 12* the office of the government whips.

Doyle *Creator of the popular fictional duo of Sherlock Holmes and Dr Watson, Arthur Conan Doyle.*

Downs, North and South /daʊnz/ two lines of chalk hills in SE England. They form two scarps which face each other across the Weald of Kent and Sussex, and are much used for sheep pasture. The *North Downs* run from Salisbury Plain across Hampshire, Surrey, and Kent to the cliffs of South Foreland. The *South Downs* run across Sussex to Beachy Head.

Downs, the /daʊnz/ roadstead (partly sheltered anchorage) off E Kent, England, between Deal and the Goodwin Sands. Several 17th-century naval battles took place here, including a defeat of Spain by the Dutch in 1639.

Down's syndrome chromosomal abnormality (the presence of an additional chromosome) which produces a rather flattened face, coarse, straight hair, and a fold of skin at the inner angle of the eye (hence the former name 'mongolism'). There is marked mental retardation.

dowry property or money given by the bride's family to the groom or his family as part of the marriage agreement.

dowsing ascertaining the presence of water or minerals beneath the ground with a forked twig or pendulum. Unconscious muscular action by the dowser is thought to move the twig, usually held with one fork in each hand, possibly in response to a local change in the pattern of electrical forces. The ability has been known since at least the 16th century and, though not widely recognized by science, it has been used commercially.

Dowson /ˈdaʊsən/ Ernest 1867–1900. British poet, one of the 'decadent' poets of the 1890s. He is best remembered for the lyric with the refrain 'I have been faithful to thee, Cynara! in my fashion'.

Doxiadis /ˌdɒksiˈaːdiːs/ Constantinos 1913–1975. Greek architect and town planner; designer of ◊Islamabad.

Doyle /dɔɪl/ Arthur Conan 1859–1930. British writer, creator of the detective ◊Sherlock Holmes and his assistant Dr Watson, who featured in a number of stories, including *The Hound of the Baskervilles* 1902.

Born in Edinburgh, he qualified as a doctor, and during the Second South African War was senior physician of a field hospital. He wrote *The Great Boer War* 1900, and was knighted in 1902. The first of his books, *A Study in Scarlet*, appeared in 1887 and introduced Sherlock Holmes and his ingenuous companion, Dr Watson. Other books featuring the same characters followed, including *The Sign of Four* 1889 and *The Valley of Fear* 1915, as well as several volumes of short stories, first published in the *Strand Magazine*. Conan Doyle also wrote historical romances (*Micah Clarke* 1889, and *The White Company* 1891) and the scientific romance *The Lost World* 1912 with an irascible hero Professor Challenger. In his later years he became a spiritualist.

Doyle /dɔɪl/ Richard 1824–1883. British caricaturist and book illustrator. In 1849 he designed the original cover for the humorous magazine *Punch*.

D'Oyly Carte /ˈdɔɪli ˈkaːt/ Richard 1844–1901. British producer of the Gilbert and Sullivan operas at the Savoy Theatre, London, which he built. The

Drake *Portrait of Sir Francis Drake by an unknown artist (1580–85), National Portrait Gallery, London.*

old D'Oyly Carte Opera Company founded 1876 was disbanded 1982, but a new one opened its first season 1988.

DPhil abbreviation for *Doctor of Philosophy*.

DPP abbreviation for ◊*Director of Public Prosecutions*.

Drabble /ˈdræbəl/ Margaret 1939– . British writer. Her novels include *The Millstone* 1966 (filmed as *The Touch of Love*), *The Middle Ground* 1980, and *The Radiant Way* 1987. She edited the 1985 edition of the *Oxford Companion to English Literature*.

Draco /ˈdreɪkəʊ/ 7th century BC. Athenian politician, the first to codify the laws of the Athenian city-state. These were notorious for their severity; hence *draconian*, meaning particularly harsh.

Draco /ˈdreɪkəʊ/ in astronomy, a large but faint constellation, representing a dragon coiled around the north celestial pole. The star Alpha Draconis (Thuban) was the pole star 4,800 years ago.

Dracula /ˈdrækjʊlə/ in the novel *Dracula* 1897 by Bram ◊Stoker, the caped count who, as a ◊vampire, drinks the blood of beautiful women.

draft compulsory military service; also known as ◊conscription.

drag the resistance to motion a body experiences when passing through a fluid–gas or liquid. The aerodynamic drag aircraft experience when travelling through the air represents a great waste of power, so they must be carefully shaped, or streamlined, to reduce drag to a minimum. Cars benefit from streamlining, and aerodynamic drag is used to slow down spacecraft returning from space. Boats travelling through water experience hydrodynamic drag on their hull, and the fastest vessels are ◊hydrofoils, whose hulls lift out of the water while cruising.

dragon a mythical reptilian beast, often portrayed as breathing fire.

The name is popularly given to various sorts of lizard. These include the ◊*flying dragon*; the *komodo dragon Varanus komodoensis* of Indonesia, at over 3 m/10 ft the largest living lizard; and some Australian lizards with bizarre spines or frills.

dragonfly type of insect with a long narrow body, two pairs of almost equal-sized, glassy wings with a network of veins, short, bristlelike antennae, powerful, 'toothed' mouthparts, and very large compound eyes (which may have up to 30,000 facets). They hunt other insects by sight, both as adults and as aquatic nymphs. The largest species have a wingspan of 18 cm/7 in, but fossils with wings up to 70 cm/2.3 ft across have been found.

dragoon a mounted soldier who carried an infantry weapon such as a 'dragon', or short musket, as used by the French army in the 16th century. The name was retained by some later regiments after the original meaning became obsolete.

drag racing motor sport popular in the USA. High-powered single-seater cars with large rear and small front wheels are timed over a 402.2 m/

440 yd strip. Speeds of up to 450 kph/280 mph have been attained.

Drake /dreɪk/ Francis *c.* 1545–1596. English buccaneer and explorer. Having enriched himself as a pirate against Spanish interests in the Caribbean 1567–72, he was sponsored by Elizabeth I for an expedition to the Pacific, sailing round the world 1577–80 in the *Golden Hind*, robbing Spanish ships as he went.

Drake was born in Devon and apprenticed to the master of a coasting vessel, who left him the ship at his death. He accompanied his relative, the navigator John Hawkins, in 1567 and 1572 to plunder the Caribbean, and returned to England 1573 with considerable booty. After serving in Ireland as a volunteer, he suggested to Queen Elizabeth I an expedition to the Pacific, and in Dec 1577 he sailed in the *Pelican* with four other ships and 166 men towards South America. In Aug 1578 the fleet passed through the Straits of Magellan and was then blown south to Cape Horn. The ships became separated and returned to England, all but the *Pelican*, now renamed the *Golden Hind*. Drake sailed north along the coast of Chile and Peru, robbing Spanish ships as far north as California, and then, in July 1579, SW across the Pacific. He rounded the South African Cape June 1580, and reached England Sept 1580. Thus the second voyage around the world, the first made by an English person, was completed in a little under three years. When the Spanish ambassador demanded Drake's punishment, the Queen knighted him on the deck of the *Golden Hind* at Deptford, London.

In 1581 Drake was chosen mayor of Plymouth, and in 1584–85 he represented Bossinney in Parliament. In a raid on Cádiz 1587 he burned 10,000 tons of shipping, 'singed the King of Spain's beard', and delayed the Armada for a year. He was stationed off Ushant 1588 to intercept the ◊Spanish Armada, but was driven back to England by unfavourable winds. During the fight in the Channel he served as a vice admiral in the *Revenge*. Drake sailed on his last expedition to the West Indies with Hawkins 1595, and in Jan 1596 died on his ship off Nombre de Dios.

Drakensberg /ˈdrɑːkənsbɜːg/ ('dragon's mountain') mountain range in South Africa (Sesuto name *Quathlamba*), on the boundary of Lesotho and the Orange Free State with Natal; highest point is Thaban Ntlenyana, 3,482 m/10,822 ft, near which is Natal National Park.

drama in theatre, any play performed by actors for an audience. The term is also used collectively to group plays into historical or stylistic periods–for example, Greek drama, Restoration drama–as well as referring to the whole body of work written by a dramatist for performance. Drama is distinct from literature in that it is a performing art open to infinite interpretation, the product not merely of the playwright but also of the collaboration of director, designer, actors, and technical staff. See also ◊comedy, ◊tragedy, ◊mime, and ◊pantomime.

dramatis personae (Latin) the characters in a play.

draughts board game (known as *checkers* in the USA and Canada because of the chequered board of 64 squares) with elements of a simplified form of chess. Each of the two players has 12 men (disc-shaped pieces), and attempts either to capture all the opponent's men or to block their movements.

Dravidian /drəˈvɪdiən/ a group of non-Aryan peoples of the Deccan region of India and in N Sri Lanka. The Dravidian languages include Tamil, Telugu, Malayalam, and Kannada.

Drayton /ˈdreɪtn/ Michael 1563–1631. English poet. His volume of poems *The Harmony of the Church* 1591 was destroyed by order of the archbishop of Canterbury. His greatest poetical work was the topographical survey of England, *Polyolbion* 1613–22, in 30 books.

Dreadnought class of battleships built for the British navy after 1905 and far superior in speed and amount to anything then afloat. German plans to build similar craft led to the naval race which contributed to to Anglo-German antagonism and the origins of World War II.

dream a series of events, or images, perceived during sleep. For the purposes of (allegedly) foretelling the future, dreams fell into disrepute in the scientific atmosphere of the 18th century, but were given importance by ◊Freud who saw them as wish fulfilment (nightmares being failed dreams prompted by fears of 'repressed' impulses). Dreams occur in periods of rapid eye movement (REM) by the sleeper, when the cortex of the brain is approximately as active as in waking hours, and they occupy a fifth of sleeping time.

Dreams could be a means of forgetting, a nightmare being brought to conscious attention so that the anxiety causing it can be dealt with. If a high level of acetylcholine is present (see under ◊brain) dreams occur too early in sleep, causing wakefulness, confusion, and ◊depression, which suggests that a form of memory search is involved. Prevention of dreaming, by taking sleeping tablets, for example, has similar unpleasant results.

Dred Scott Case In US history, a Supreme Court case brought by a Missouri black slave, Dred Scott (c.1800–58), seeking to obtain his freedom on the grounds that his owner had taken him to reside temporarily in the free state of Illinois. The decision of the Supreme Court against Scott in March 1857 intensified sectional discord four years before the Civil War.

Drees /dreɪs/ Willem 1886–1988. Dutch socialist politician, prime minister 1948–58. Chair of the Socialist Democratic Workers' Party from 1911 until the German invasion of 1940, he returned to politics in 1947, after being active in the resistance movement.

Drees sat in the Second Chamber of the Dutch parliament 1933–40. In 1947, as the responsible minister, he introduced a state pension scheme.

Dreikaiserbund (German 'Three Emperors' League') an informal alliance from 1872 between the emperors of Russia, Germany, and Austria-Hungary. It was effectively at an end by 1879.

Dreiser /ˈdraɪsə/ Theodore 1871–1945. US novelist, formerly a Chicago journalist. He wrote the naturalistic novels *Sister Carrie* 1900 and *An American Tragedy* 1925, based on the real-life crime of a young man who in 'making good' kills a shop assistant he has made pregnant. It was filmed as *Splendor in the Grass* 1961.

Drenthe /ˈdrentə/ low-lying northern province of the Netherlands; area 2,660 sq km/1,027 sq mi; population (1988) 437,000. Chief town is Assen. Although it is a thinly populated province of woods, fenlands and moors, stock rearing and mixed arable farming predominate on the well-drained clay and peat soils.

Dresden /ˈdrezdən/ city in East Germany, capital of Dresden county, formerly capital of Saxony; population (1986) 520,000. Industries include chemicals, machinery, glassware, and musical instruments. It was one of the most beautiful

Dresden *Following the devastating bombing of Dresden in 1945, some ruins remain among the rebuilt quarters.*

Dreyfus *French army officer Alfred Dreyfus.*

German cities prior to its devastation by Allied fire-bombing 1945. Dresden county has an area of 6,740 sq km/2,602 sq mi, and a populaton of 1,772,000.

history Under the elector Augustus II the Strong (1694–1733), it became a centre of art and culture. The manufacture of Dresden china, started at Dresden 1709, was transferred to Meissen 1710. The city was bombed by the Allies on the night 13–14 Feb 1945, 15.5 sq km/6 sq mi of the inner town being destroyed, and deaths being estimated at 35,000–135,000.

dressage (French 'the training of horses') training a horse to carry out a predetermined routine of movements. Points are awarded for discipline and style.

Dreyer /ˈdraɪə/ Carl Theodor 1889–1968. Danish director. His wide range of films include the silent classic *La Passion de Jeanne d'Arc/The Passion of Joan of Arc* 1928 and the Expressionist horror film *Vampyr* 1932, after the failure of which Dreyer made no films until *Vredens Dag/Day of Wrath* 1943.

Dreyfus /ˈdreɪfəs/ Alfred 1859–1935. French army officer, victim of miscarriage of justice, anti-Semitism, and cover-up. Employed in the War Ministry, in 1894 he was accused of betraying military secrets to Germany, court-martialled, and sent to ◊Devil's Island. When his innocence was discovered 1896 the military establishment tried to conceal it, and the implications of the Dreyfus affair were passionately discussed in the press until in 1906 he was exonerated.

Dreyfus was born in Mulhouse, E France, of a Jewish family. He had been a prisoner in the French Guiana penal colony for two years when it emerged that the real criminal was a Maj Esterhazy; the high command nevertheless attempted to suppress the facts, and used forged documents to strengthen their case. After a violent controversy, in which the future prime minister Clemenceau and the novelist ◊Zola championed Dreyfus, he was brought back for a retrial 1899, found guilty with extenuating circumstances, and received a pardon. In 1906 the court of appeal declared him innocent, and he was reinstated in his military rank.

drill large monkey *Mandrillus leucophaeus* living in forests of W Africa. Sombre-coated, black-faced, and stoutly built, with a very short tail, the male can have a head and body up to 75 cm/2.5 ft long, although females are smaller.

drilling a common woodworking and metal machinery process, which involves boring holes with a drill ◊bit. The commonest kind of drill bit is the fluted drill, which has spiral grooves around it to allow the cut material to escape. In the oil industry rotary drilling is used to bore oil wells. The drill bit usually consists of a number of toothed cutting wheels, which grind their way through the rock as the drill pipe is turned, and mud is pumped through the pipe to lubricate the bit and flush the ground-up rock to the surface.

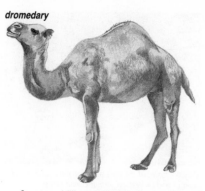

dromedary

In rotary drilling a drill bit is fixed to the end of a length of drill pipe and rotated by a turning mechanism, the rotary table. More lengths of pipe are added as the hole deepens. The long drill pipes are handled by lifting gear in a steel tower ◊derrick.

drink, soft drink that provides water, and usually sugar, in a flavoured form. Soft drinks include fruit squashes, cordials, fruit crushes, carbonated drinks, cola drinks, and ginger beer. Fruit-flavoured drinks often contain no fruit and are usually water, sugar or artificial sweetener, and synthetic flavourings. Tonic water contains no sugar, but does contain quinine.

In the UK, undiluted fruit squash must contain stipulated amounts of fruit or fruit juice. Consumption in the UK of soft drinks rose from 4,430 million litres in 1980 to 5,392 million litres in 1984. Most soft drinks in the UK are sold in non-returnable containers despite mounting pressure for recycling.

Drinkwater /ˈdrɪŋk,wɔːtə/ John 1882–1937. British poet and playwright. He was a prolific writer of lyrical and reflective verse, and also wrote many historical plays, including *Abraham Lincoln* 1918.

Drogheda /ˈdrɔɪɪdə/ seaport near the mouth of the Boyne, county Louth, Republic of Ireland. The port trades in cattle and textiles; chemicals and foodstuffs are produced. In 1649 the town was stormed by Oliver ◊Cromwell, who massacred most of the garrison, and in 1690 it surrendered to William III after the battle of the Boyne.

Drôme /drəʊm/ river in France, rising in Dauphiné Pre-Alps and flowing NW for 101 km/63 mi to join the river Rhône below Livron. It gives its name to Drôme *département*.

dromedary type of Arabian ◊camel.

drone in music, an accompanying tone or harmony that never varies. It is heard in folk music and reproduced by many instruments, including the jew's harp, bagpipe, and hurdy-gurdy.

Drosera Latin name for the plant ◊sundew.

drought period of prolonged dry weather. The area of the world subject to serious droughts, such as the Sahara, is increasing because of destruction of forests, overgrazing, and poor agricultural practices.

In the UK, drought is defined as the passing of 15 days with less than 0.2 mm of rain.

drowning suffocation by fluid. Drowning may be due to inhaling external fluid, such as water, or to the presence of body fluids in the lungs.

drug and alcohol dependence physical or psychological craving for addictive drugs such as alcohol, nicotine (in cigarettes), tranquillizers, heroin, or stimulants (for example, amphetamines). Such substances can alter mood or behaviour. When dependence is established, sudden withdrawal from the drug can cause an unpleasant reaction, which may be dangerous.

drug, generic a drug produced without a brand name that is identical to a branded product. Usually generic drugs are produced when the patent on a branded drug has expired, and are cheaper than their branded equivalents.

drug misuse the illegal use of drugs for nonmedicinal purposes.

Under the UK Misuse of Drugs Acts they comprise: (1) *most harmful* heroin, morphine, opium, and other narcotics; hallucinogens, such as mescalin and LSD, and injectable amphetamines, such as methedrine; (2) *less harmful* narcotics such as codeine and cannabis; stimulants of the amphetamine type, such as Benzedrine and barbiturates; (3) *least harmful* milder drugs of the amphetamine type. *Designer drugs*, for example ecstasy, are usually modifications of the amphetamine molecule, altered in order to evade the law as well as for different effects, and may be many times more powerful and dangerous. Crack, a smokable form of cocaine, became available to drug users in the 1980s. Sources of traditional drugs include the 'Golden Triangle' (where Myanmar, Laos, and Thailand meet), Mexico, Colombia, China, and the Middle East.

Druidism religion of the Celtic peoples of pre-Christian Britain and Gaul. The word is derived from Greek *drus* 'oak', and the Druids regarded this tree as sacred, one of their chief rites being the cutting of mistletoe from it with a golden sickle. They taught the immortality of the soul and a reincarnation doctrine, and were expert in astronomy. The Druids are thought to have offered human sacrifices.

Druidism was stamped out in Gaul after the Roman conquest. In Britain their stronghold was Anglesey, Wales, where they were extirpated by the Roman governor Agricola. They also existed in Scotland and Ireland until the coming of the Christian missionaries. What are often termed Druidic monuments—cromlechs and stone circles—are of Neolithic origin, though they may later have been used for religious purposes by the Druids. A possible example of a human sacrifice by Druids is Lindow Man, whose body was found in a bog in Cheshire 1984.

drum percussion instrument, essentially a piece of skin (parchment, plastic, or nylon) stretched over a resonator and struck with a stick or the hands. Electronic drums, first marketed in 1980, are highly touch- and force-sensitive and can also be controlled by computer.

Drummond /'drʌmənd/ William 1585–1649. Scottish poet, laird of his native Hawthornden, hence known as Drummond of Hawthornden. He was the first Scots poet of note to use southern English.

Drummond de Andrade /druːˈmɒn di ænˈdrɑːdə/ Carlos 1902–1987. Brazilian writer, generally considered the greatest modern Brazilian poet, and a prominent member of the Modernist school. His verse, often seemingly casual, continually confounds the reader's expectation of the 'poetical'.

drupe a fleshy ◊fruit containing one or more seeds which are surrounded by a hard, protective layer, for example cherry, almond and plum. The wall of the fruit (◊pericarp) is differentiated into the outer skin (exocarp), the fleshy layer of tissues (mesocarp), and the hard layer surrounding the seed (endocarp). The coconut is a drupe, but here the pericarp becomes dry and fibrous at maturity. Blackberries are an aggregate fruit composed of a cluster of small drupes.

Drury Lane Theatre /'drʊəri/ theatre first opened 1663 on the site of earlier London playhouses. It was twice burned; the present building dates from 1812.

Druse or *Druze* a religious sect in the Middle East of some 500,000 people. They are monotheists, preaching that the Fatimid caliph al-Hakim (996–1021) is God; their scriptures are drawn from the Christian gospels, the Torah (the first five books of the Old Testament), the Koran, and Sufi allegories. Druse militia groups form one of the three main factions involved in the Lebanese civil war (the others are Amal Shi'ite Muslims and Christian Maronites). The Druse military leader (from his father's assassination 1977) is Walid Jumblatt.

The Druse sect was founded in Egypt in the 11th century, and then fled to Palestine to avoid

Dryden *English poet, satirist, dramatist, and biographer John Dryden, painted in 1693 by Kneller.*

persecution; they today occupy areas of Syria, Lebanon, and Israel.

Dr Who hero of a British science-fiction television series of the same name, created 1962 by Sidney Newman and Donald Wilson; his space vehicle is the *Tardis* (*T*ime *a*nd *r*elative *d*imensions *i*n *s*pace).

dryad /'draɪæd/ in Greek mythology, a forest nymph or tree spirit.

dry-cleaning a method of cleaning textiles based on the use of volatile solvents that dissolve grease; for example, trichloroethylene. No water is used. Dry-cleaning was first developed in France in 1849.

Some solvents are known to damage the ozone layer and one, perchloroethylene, is toxic in water and gives off toxic fumes when heated.

Dryden /'draɪdn/ John 1631–1700. English poet and dramatist, noted for his satirical verse and for his use of the heroic couplet. His poetry includes the verse satire *Absalom and Achitophel* 1681, *Annus Mirabilis* 1667, and 'St Cecilia's Day' 1687. Plays include the comedy *Marriage à la Mode* 1671 and *All for Love* 1678, a reworking of Shakespeare's *Antony and Cleopatra*.

On occasion, Dryden trimmed his politics and his religion to the prevailing wind, and, as a Roman Catholic convert under James II, lost the laureateship (to which he had been appointed 1688) at the Revolution of 1688. Critical works include *Essay on Dramatic Poesy* 1668. Later ventures to support himself include a translation of Virgil 1697.

dry ice solid carbon dioxide (CO_2), used as a refrigerant. At temperatures above –79°C, it sublimes to gaseous carbon dioxide.

dry point in printmaking, a technique of engraving on copper, using a hard, sharp tool. The resulting lines tend to be fine and angular, with a strong furry edge created by the metal shavings.

dry rot infection of timber in damp conditions by fungi, such as *Merulius lacrymans*, which forms a threadlike surface. Whitish at first, the fungi later reddens as reproductive spores are formed. Fungoid tentacles also enter the fabric of the timber, rendering it dry-looking and brittle. Dry rot spreads rapidly through a building.

Drysdale /'draɪzdeɪl/ George Russell 1912–1969. Australian artist, born in England. His drawings and paintings often depict the Australian outback, its drought, desolation, and poverty, and Aboriginal life.

Dr Zhivago a novel by Boris Pasternak, published (in Italy) 1957. The novel, which describes a scientist's disillusion with the Russian revolution, was banned in the USSR as a 'hostile act' and only published there in magazine form 1988.

DSO abbreviation for *Distinguished Service Order*, British military medal.

DTI abbreviation for *Department of Trade and Industry*, UK government department.

Dual Entente an alliance between France and Russia which lasted from 1893 until the Bolshevik Revolution of 1917.

dualism in philosophy, the belief that reality is essentially dual in nature. ◊Descartes, for example, refers to thinking and material substance. These

entities interact, but are fundamentally separate and distinct. Dualism is contrasted with ◊monism.

Duarte /duːˈɑːteɪ/ José Napoleon 1925–1990. El Salvadorean politician, president 1980–82 and 1984–88. He was mayor of San Salvador 1964–70, and was elected president 1972, but exiled by the army in 1982. On becoming president again in 1984, he sought a negotiated settlement with the left-wing guerrillas 1986, but resigned following diagnosis of cancer.

Dubai /duːˈbaɪ/ one of the ◊United Arab Emirates.

Du Barry /djuːˈbæri/ Marie Jeanne Bécu, Comtesse Du Barry 1743–1793. Mistress of ◊Louis XV of France from 1768. At his death in 1774 she was banished to a convent, and at the Revolution fled to London. Returning to Paris in 1793, she was guillotined.

Dubček /'dʊbtʃek/ Alexander 1921– . Czech politician, chair of the federal assembly from 1989. As first secretary of the Communist Party 1967–69, he launched a liberalization campaign (the Prague Spring). He was arrested by invading Soviet troops, and expelled from the party 1970. In 1989 he gave speeches at pro-democracy rallies, and in Dec, after the overthrow of the hardline regime, he was elected speaker of the Czech parliament.

Dublin /'dʌblɪn/ county in Leinster province, Republic of Ireland, facing the Irish Sea; area 920 sq km/355 sq mi; population (1986) 1,021,000. It is mostly level and low-lying, but rises in the south to 753 m/2,471 ft in Kippure, part of the Wicklow mountains. The river Liffey enters Dublin Bay; Dún Laoghaire is the only other large town.

Dublin /'dʌblɪn/ (Gaelic *Baile Atha Cliath*) capital and port on the E coast of the Republic of Ireland, at the mouth of the Liffey, facing the Irish Sea; population (1981) 526,000, Greater Dublin (including Dún Laoghaire) 921,000. It is the site of one of the world's largest breweries (Guinness); other industries include textiles, pharmaceuticals, electrical goods, and machine tools. It was the centre of English rule from 1171 (exercised from Dublin Castle 1220) until 1922.

history The city was founded 840 by the invading Danes, who were finally defeated 1014 at Clontarf, now a N suburb of the city. In the Georgian period many fine squares were laid out, and the Custom House (damaged in the 1921 rising but later restored) survives. There is a Roman Catholic pro-Cathedral, St Mary's (1816), two Protestant cathedrals; and two universities: the University of Dublin and the National University of Ireland. Trinity College library contains the Book of Kells, a splendidly illuminated 8th-century gospel book produced at the monastery of Kells in county Meath, founded by St Columba. Other buildings are the City Hall (1779), the Four Courts (1796), the National Gallery, Dublin Municipal Gallery, National Museum, Leinster House (where the *Dáil Eireann* sits), and the Abbey and Gate theatres.

Dubček *Czech politician Alexander Dubček 1968.*

Dubna /dʊbˈnɑː/ town in USSR, 40 km/25 mi W of Tula; population (1985) 61,000. It is a metalworking centre, and has the Volga Nuclear Physics Centre.

Dubos /duːˈbəʊs/ René Jules 1901–1981. French-US microbiologist and forerunner of Alexander ◊Fleming. Dubos studied soil microorganisms and became interested in their antibacterial properties.

The antibacterials he discovered had limited therapeutic use since they were toxic. Nevertheless, he opened up a new field of research which eventually led to the discovery of major drugs like ◊penicillin and ◊streptomycin.

Dubrovnik /duːˈbrɒvnɪk/ (Italian *Ragusa*) port in Yugoslavia on the Adriatic sea; population (1985) 35,000. It manufactures cheese, liqueurs, silk and leather. Once a Roman station, it was for a long time an independent republic, but passed to Austrian rule 1814–1919.

Dubuffet /ˌduːbʊˈfeɪ/ Jean 1901–1985. French artist. He originated *l'art brut*, raw or brutal art, in the 1940s. He used a variety of materials in his paintings and sculptures–plaster, steel wool, straw, and so on–and was inspired by graffiti and children's drawings.

L'art brut emerged in 1945 with an exhibition of Dubuffet's own work and of paintings by psychiatric patients and naive or untrained artists. His own paintings and sculptural works have a similar quality, primitive and expressive.

Duccio di Buoninsegna /ˈduːtʃəʊ diː ˌbwɒnɪn-ˈseɪnjə/ *c.*1255–1319. Italian painter, a major figure in the Sienese school. His greatest work is his altarpiece for Siena Cathedral, the *Maestà* 1308–11; the figure of the Virgin is Byzantine in style, with much gold detail, but Duccio also created a graceful linear harmony in drapery hems, for example, and this proved a lasting characteristic of Sienese style.

Duce (Italian 'leader') title bestowed on the Fascist dictator Mussolini by his followers, and later adopted as his official title.

Duchamp /djuːˈʃɒm/ Marcel 1887–1968. US artist, born in France. He achieved notoriety with his *Nude Descending a Staircase* 1912 (Philadelphia Museum of Art), influenced by Cubism and Futurism. An active member of ◊Dada, he invented **ready-mades**, everyday items like a bicycle wheel on a kitchen stool, which he displayed as works of art.

Duchamp exhibited at the ◊Armory Show in New York 1913. A major early work which focuses on mechanical objects endowed with mysterious significance is *La Mariée mise à nu par ses célibataires, même/The Bride Stripped Bare by her Bachelors, Even* 1915–23 (Philadelphia Museum of Art). Duchamp continued to experiment with collage, mechanical imagery, and abstract sculpture throughout his career. He lived mostly in New York and became a US citizen in 1954.

duck short-legged waterbird with webbed feet and flattened bill of the family Anatidae, which also includes geese and swans. Ducks have the three front toes in a web, the hind toe free, and a

duck

pink headed duck

skin-covered bill with a horny tip provided with little plates (lamellae) through which the birds are able to strain their food from water and mud. Most species of duck live in fresh water, feeding on worms and insects as well as vegetable matter.

A typical species is the **mallard** *Anas platyrhynchos*, 58 cm/1.9 ft, found over most of the northern hemisphere. The male (drake) has a glossy green head, brown breast, grey body, and yellow bill. The female (duck) is speckled brown, with a duller bill. The male moults and resembles the female for a while just after the breeding season. There are many other species of duck including ◊teal, ◊eider, ◊merganser, ◊shelduck, and ◊shoveler. They have different-shaped bills according to their diet and habitat; for example, the shoveler has a wide spade-shaped bill for 'shovelling' insects off the surface of water.

The main threat to the survival of ducks in the wild is hunting by humans. The pink-headed duck of India and Nepál is believed to be extinct, no wild specimens having been seen since 1936.

duckweed tiny plant *Lemna minor* found floating on the surface of still water throughout most of the world, except the polar regions and tropics. Each plant consists of a flat circular leaf-like structure 0.4 cm/0.15 in or less across, with a single thin root below up to 15 cm/6 in long.

The plant buds off new individuals, and can soon cover the surface of the water. Flowers rarely appear but when they do, they are minute and sited in a pocket at the edge of the plant.

ductless gland another name for an ◊endocrine gland.

Dudintsev /duːˈdɪntsef/ Vladimir Dmitriyevich 1918– . Soviet novelist, author of the remarkably frank *Not by Bread Alone* 1956, a depiction of Soviet bureaucracy and inefficiency.

Dudley /ˈdʌdli/ town NW of Birmingham, West Midlands, England; population (1981) 187,000. Industries include light engineering and clothing manufacture.

due process of law a legal principle, dating back to the ◊Magna Carta 1215, and now enshrined in the fifth and 14th amendments of the US constitution,

that no person shall be deprived of their life, liberty, or property without due process of law (a fair legal procedure). In the USA, the provisions have been given a wide interpretation, to include, for example, the right to representation by an attorney.

Dufay /djuːˈfaɪ/ Guillaume 1400–1474. Flemmish composer. He is recognized as the foremost composer of his time, of both secular songs and sacred music (including 84 songs, eight masses, motets, and antiphons). His work marks a transition between the music of the Middle Ages and that of the Renaissance and is characterized by expressive melodies and rich harmonies.

Dufourspitze /duːˈfʊəˌʃpɪtsə/ second highest of the alpine peaks, 4,634 m/15,203 ft high. It is the highest peak in the Monte Rosa group of the Pennine alps on the Swiss–Italian frontier.

Du Fu another name for the Chinese poet ◊Tu Fu.

Dufy /ˈduːfi/ Raoul 1877–1953. French painter and designer. He originated a fluent, brightly coloured style in watercolour and oils, painting scenes of gaiety and leisure, such as horse racing, yachting, and life on the beach.

dugong marine mammal *Dugong dugong* found in the Red Sea, the Indian Ocean and W Pacific. It can grow to 3.6 m/11 ft long, and has a tapering body with a notched tail and two fore-flippers. It is herbivorous, feeding on sea grasses and seaweeds.

It may have given rise to the mermaid myth.

duiker (Afrikaans *diver*) a type of antelope common in Africa. They are shy and nocturnal, and grow to 30–70 cm/12–28 in tall. There are many species.

Duiker /ˈdaɪkə/ Johannes 1890–1935. Dutch architect of the 1920s and 1930s avant-garde period. His works demonstrate great structural vigour and transparency, and include the Zonnestraal sanatorium 1926, Open Air School, Amsterdam, 1932, and the Cineac News Cinema, Amsterdam, 1933.

Duisburg /ˈdjuːzbɜːg/ city in North Rhine-Westphalia, West Germany; population (1988) 515,000.

Duisburg river port and industrial city in North Rhine-Westphalia, West Germany, at the confluence of the Rhine and Ruhr rivers; population (1987) 515,000. It is the largest inland river port in Europe. Heavy industries include oil refining and the production of steel, copper, zinc, plastics, and machinery.

Dukakis /duːˈkɑːkɪs/ Michael 1933– . US Democrat politician, governor of Massachusetts 1974–78 and from 1982, presiding over a high-tech economic boom, the 'Massachusetts miracle'. He was a presidential candidate in 1988.

Dukakis was born in Boston, Massachusetts, the son of Greek immigrants. After studying law at Harvard and serving in Korea (1955–57), he concentrated on a political career in his home state. Elected as a Democrat to the Massachusetts legislature in 1962, he became state governor in 1974. After an unsuccessful first term, marred by his unwillingness to compromise, he was defeated in 1978. Dukakis returned as governor in 1982, committed to working in a more consensual manner. He was re-elected in 1986 and captured the Democratic Party's presidential nomination in 1988. After a poor campaign, the diligent but uncharismatic Dukakis was defeated by the incumbent vice president George Bush.

Dukas /djuːˈkɑːs/ Paul (Abraham) 1865–1935. French composer. His orchestral scherzo *L'Apprenti Sorcier/The Sorcerer's Apprentice* 1897 is full of the colour and energy that characterizes much of his work.

He was professor of composition at the Paris Conservatoire and composed the opera *Ariane et Barbe-Bleue/Ariane and Bluebeard* 1907, and the ballet *La Péri* 1912.

duke highest title in the English peerage. It originated in England in 1337, when Edward III created his son Edward duke of Cornwall. The premier

Dufy Deauville: Drying the Sails *(1933)* Tate Gallery, London.

Dumas *French dramatist and novelist Alexandre Dumas.*

Scottish duke is the duke of Hamilton (created 1643).

Dukeries /'dju:kəriz/ an area of estates in Nottinghamshire, England, with magnificent noblemen's mansions, few now surviving. Thoresby Hall, said to be the largest house in England (about 365 rooms), was sold as a hotel 1989 and the contents dispersed.

dulce et decorum est pro patria mori (Latin 'it is sweet and noble to die for one's country') quotation from Horace's *Odes*, also used by the English poet Wilfred Owen as the title for his poem denouncing World War I.

dulcimer musical instrument consisting of a shallow sound-box strung with many wires that are struck with small wooden hammers. In Hungary it is called a ◊cimbalom.

Dulles /'dʌlɪs/ Alan 1893–1969. US lawyer, director of the Central Intelligence Agency (CIA) 1953–61. He was the brother of John Foster Dulles.

Dulles /'dʌlɪs/ John Foster 1888–1959. US politician. Senior US adviser at the founding of the United Nations, he was largely responsible for drafting the Japanese peace treaty of 1951. As secretary of state 1952–59, he was critical of Britain in the Suez Crisis. He was the architect of US ◊Cold War foreign policy, securing US intervention in support of South Vietnam following the expulsion of the French in 1954.

Dulong /dju:'lɒŋ/ Pierre 1785–1838. French chemist and physicist who, along with ◊Petit, discovered in 1819 the law that an element's ◊atomic weight and ◊specific heat capacity were constant. He had earlier, in 1811, and at the cost of an eye, discovered the explosive nitrogen trichloride.

dulse edible red seaweed *Rhodymenia palmata* found on the middle and lower seashore. It may have a single broad blade up to 30 cm/1 ft long rising direct from the holdfast, or be palmate or fanshaped. The frond is tough and dark red, sometimes with additional small leaflets at the edge.

Duluth /də'lu:θ/ port in the USA on Lake Superior; by the mouth of the St Louis River, Minnesota; population (1980) 92,000. It manufactures steel, flour, timber, and dairy produce; it trades in iron ore and grain.

Dulwich /'dʌlɪdʒ/ suburb, part of the inner London borough of Southwark, England. It contains Dulwich College (founded in 1619 by Edward Alleyn, an Elizabethan actor), the Horniman Museum (1901), with a fine ethnological collection, Dulwich Picture Gallery (1814), rebuilt in 1953 after being bombed during World War II, Dulwich Park, and Dulwich Village.

Duma in Russia, before 1917, an elected assembly that met four times following the abortive 1905 revolution. With progressive demands the government could not accept, the Duma was largely powerless. After the abdication of Nicholas II, the Duma directed the formation of a provisional government.

Dumfries and Galloway

Dumas /'dju:ma:/ Alexandre 1802–1870. French author, known as Dumas *père* (the father). His play *Henri III et sa cour/Henry III and his Court* 1829 established French romantic historical drama, but today he is remembered for his romances, the reworked output of a 'fiction-factory' of collaborators. They include *Les Trois Mousquetaires/The Three Musketeers* 1844 and its sequels. Dumas *fils* was his illegitimate son.

Dumas /'dju:ma:/ Alexandre 1824–1895. French author, known as Dumas *fils* (the son), son of Dumas *père* and remembered for the play *La Dame aux camélias/The Lady of the Camellias* 1852, based on his own novel and source of Verdi's opera *La Traviata*.

Du Maurier /du: 'mɒrieɪ/ Daphne 1907–1989. British novelist, whose romantic fiction includes *Jamaica Inn* 1936, *Rebecca* 1938, and *My Cousin Rachel* 1951.

Du Maurier /du: 'mɒrieɪ/ George (Louis Palmella Busson) 1834–1896. French-born British author of the novel *Trilby* 1894—the story of a natural singer able to perform only under the hypnosis of Svengali, her tutor.

Dumbarton /dʌm'ba:tn/ town in Strathclyde, Scotland; population (1981) 23,204. Industries include marine engineering, whisky distilling and electronics.

Dumbarton Oaks an 18th-century mansion near Washington DC, USA, used as a centre for conferences and seminars. It was the scene of a conference held in 1944 that led to the foundation of the United Nations.

Dumfries /dʌm'fri:s/ administrative headquarters of Dumfries and Galloway region, Scotland; population (1981) 32,000. It has knitwear, plastics and other industries.

Dumfries and Galloway /dʌm'fri:s, 'gæləweɪ/ region of Scotland
area 6,500 sq km/2,510 sq mi
towns administrative headquarters Dumfries
features Solway Firth; Galloway Hills, setting of John Buchan's *The Thirty-Nine Steps*; Glen Trool National Park; Ruthwell Cross, a runic cross of about 800 at the village of Ruthwell; Stranraer provides the shortest sea route to Ireland
products horses and cattle (for which the Galloway area was especially famous), sheep, timber
population (1987) 147,000
famous people Robert Burns, Thomas Carlyle.

Dumfriesshire /dʌm'fri:sʃə/ former county of S Scotland, merged in 1975 in the region of Dumfries and Galloway.

Dumont D'Urville /dju:'mɒn duə'vi:l/ Jean 1780–1842. French explorer in Australasia and the Pacific. In 1838–40 he sailed round Cape Horn on a voyage to study terrestial magnetism and reached Adélie Land in Antarctica.

Dumouriez /dju:,mʊəri'eɪ/ Charles François du Périer 1739–1823. French general during the

Revolution. In 1792 he was appointed foreign minister, supported the declaration of war against Austria, and after the fall of the monarchy was given command of the army defending Paris; later he won the battle of Jemappes, but was defeated at Neerwinden (Austrian Netherlands) in 1793. After intriguing with the royalists he had to flee for his life, and from 1804 he lived in England.

dump in computing, the process of rapidly transferring data to external memory or a printer. It is usually done to help with ◊debugging or as part of an error-recovery procedure.

dumping in international trade, when one country sells goods to another at below marginal cost or at a price below that in its own country. Countries dump in order to get rid of surplus produce or to improve their competitive position in the recipient country. The practice is widely condemned by protectionists (opponents of free trade) because of the unfair competition it represents.

Dumyat /dʊm'ja:t/ (English *Damietta*) town in Egypt at the mouth of the Nile; population (1986) 121,200.

Duna /'du:nə/ Hungarian name for the ◊Danube.

Dunant /dju:'nɒn/ Jean Henri 1828–1910. Swiss philanthropist; the originator of the Red Cross. At the Battle of Solferino 1859 he helped to tend the wounded, and in *Un Souvenir de Solferino* 1862 he proposed the establishment of an international body for the aid of the wounded—an idea that was realized in the Geneva Convention 1864. He shared the Nobel Peace Prize 1901.

Dunarea Romanian name for the ◊Danube.

Dunaway /'dʌnəweɪ/ Faye 1941– . US actress whose first starring role was in *Bonnie and Clyde* 1967. Her subsequent films, including *Network* 1976 and *Mommie Dearest* 1981, received a varying critical reception.

Dunbar /dʌn'ba:/ port and resort in Lothian region, Scotland; population (1981) 6,000. Torness nuclear power station is nearby. Oliver ◊Cromwell defeated the Scots here in 1650.

Dunbar /dʌn'ba:/ William *c.*1460–*c.*1520. Scottish poet at the court of James IV. His poems include a political allegory, 'The Thrissel and the Rose' 1503, and the elegy with the refrain '*Timor mortis conturbat me*'.

Dunbartonshire /dʌn'ba:tnʃə/ former county of Scotland, bordering the N bank of the Clyde estuary, on which stand Dunbarton (the former county town), Clydebank, and Helensburgh. It was merged 1975 in the region of Strathclyde.

Duncan /'dʌŋkən/ Isadora 1878–1927. US dancer and teacher. An influential pioneer of modern dance, she adopted an expressive, free form, dancing barefoot and wearing a loose tunic, inspired by the ideal of Hellenic beauty. She toured extensively, often returning to Russia after her initial success there 1905. She died in an accident when her long scarf caught in the wheel of the car in which she was travelling.

Duncan-Sandys /'dʌŋkən 'sændz/ Duncan Edwin Sandys, Baron Duncan-Sandys 1908–1987. British Conservative politician. As minister for Commonwealth Relations 1960–64, he negotiated the independence of Malaysia 1963. He was created a life peer 1974.

Dundas /dʌn'dæs/ Henry, 1st Viscount Melville 1742–1811. British Tory politician. In 1791 he became home secretary, and with revolution raging in France, carried through the prosecution of the English and Scottish radicals. After holding other high cabinet posts, he was impeached in 1806 for corruption and, although acquitted on the main charge, held no further office.

Dundee /dʌn'di:/ city and fishing port, administrative headquarters of Tayside, Scotland, on the north side of the Firth of Tay; population (1981) 175,000. Important shipping and rail centre with marine engineering, watch and clock, and textile industries.

The city developed around the jute industry in the 19th century, and has benefited from the North Sea oil discoveries of the 1970s. There is a university (1967) derived from Queen's College (founded 1881), and other notable buildings include the Albert Institute (1867) and Caird Hall.

dune a mound or ridge of wind-drifted sand. Loose sand is blown and bounced along by the wind, up the windward side of a dune. The sand particles then fall to rest on the lee side, while more are blown up from the windward side. In this way a dune moves gradually downwind.

Dunes are features of sandy deserts and beach fronts. The typical crescent-shaped dune is called a barchan. Seif dunes are longitudinal and lie parallel to the wind direction, and star-shaped dunes are formed by irregular winds.

Dunedin /dʌnˈiːdn/ port on Otago harbour, South Island, New Zealand; population (1986) 106,864. Also a road, rail and air centre, with engineering and textile industries. The city was founded in 1848 by members of the Free Church of Scotland and the university established 1869.

Dunfermline /dʌnˈfɜːmlɪn/ industrial town near the Firth of Forth in Fife region, Scotland; population (1981) 52,000. Site of the naval base of Rosyth; industries include engineering, shipbuilding, electronics, and textiles. Many Scottish kings, including Robert the Bruce, are buried in Dunfermline Abbey. Birthplace of the industrialist Andrew Carnegie.

Dungeness /ˌdʌndʒəˈnes/ shingle headland on the south coast of Kent, England. It has nuclear power stations, a lighthouse, and a bird sanctuary.

Dunham /ˈdʌnəm/ Katherine 1912– . US dancer, born in Chicago, noted for a free, strongly emotional method. She founded her own school and company 1945.

Dunkirk /dʌnˈkɜːk/ (French *Dunkerque*) seaport on the N coast of France, in Nord *département*, on the Strait of Dover; population (1983) 83,760, conurbation 196,000. Its harbour is one of the most important in France, and it has widespread canal links with the rest of France and Belgium; ferry service to Ramsgate. Industries include oil

dune

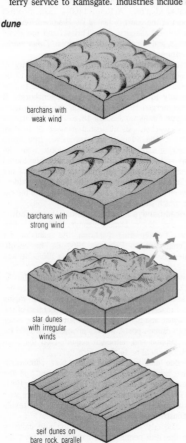

barchans with
weak wind

barchans with
strong wind

star dunes
with irregular
winds

seif dunes on
bare rock, parallel
to wind direction

refining and fishing; textiles, machinery, and soap are manufactured.

It was close to the front line during much of World War I, and in World War II, 337,131 Allied troops (including about 110,000 French) were evacuated from the beaches.

Dún Laoghaire /dʌnˈleərə/ (former name Kingstown) port and suburb of Dublin, Republic of Ireland. It is a terminal for ferries to Britain, and there are fishing industries.

dunlin small wading bird *Calidris alpina* about 18 cm/7 in long, nesting along the far northern regions on moors and marshes. Chestnut above and black below in summer, it is greyish in winter. It is the commonest small sandpiper.

Dunlop /ˈdʌnlɒp/ John Boyd 1840–1921. Scottish inventor, who founded the rubber company that bears his name. In 1887, to help his child win a tricycle race, he bound an inflated rubber hose to the wheels. The same year he developed commercially practical pneumatic tyres (first patented by R W Thomson in 1846) for bicycles and cars.

Dunmow, Little /ˈdʌnməʊ/ village in Essex, England, scene every four years of the Dunmow Flitch trial (dating from 1111), in which a side of bacon is presented to any couple who 'will swear that they have not quarrelled nor repented of their marriage within a year and a day after its celebration'; they are judged by a jury whose members are all unmarried.

dunnock European bird *Prunella modularis* similar in size and colouring to the sparrow, but with slate-grey head and breast, and more slender bill. It nests in bushes and hedges, and is often called 'hedge sparrow'.

Dunsany /dʌnˈseɪnɪ/ Edward, 15th Baron Dunsany 1878–1957. Irish writer. His works include short ironic heroic fantasies, collected in *The Gods of Pegana* 1905 and other books, but he is best known for employing the convention of a narrator sitting in a club or bar (his narrator was called Jorkens).

Duns Scotus /dʌnz ˈskəʊtəs/ John c.1265–c.1308. Franciscan monk, an important figure of medieval ◊scholasticism. On many points he turned against the orthodoxy of ◊Aquinas; for example, he rejected the idea of a necessary world, favouring a concept of God as absolute freedom capable of spontaneous activity. The church rejected his ideas, hence the word 'dunce'. In the medieval controversy over universals he advocated ◊nominalism. He was born in Scotland, and known as Doctor Subtilis.

Dunstable /ˈdʌnstəbəl/ town in SW Bedfordshire, England; at the N end of the Chiltern Hills;

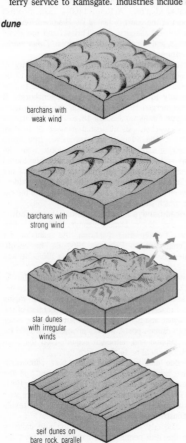

Durham John, 1st Earl of Durham, became a Whig MP in 1817. He later went to Canada as governor general and put down a revolt of the French in Lower Canada.

48 km/30 mi NW of London; population (1981) 31,000. Whipsnade Zoo is nearby. Industries include printing and engineering.

Dunstable /ˈdʌnstəbəl/ John c.1385–1453. English composer. He wrote songs and anthems, and is generally considered one of the founders of Renaissance music.

Dunstan, St /ˈdʌnstən/ c.924–988. English priest and politician, archbishop of Canterbury from 960. As abbot of Glastonbury from 945, he made it a centre of learning. Feast day 19 May.

duodecimal system system of arithmetic notation using 12 as a base, at one time considered superior to the decimal system in that 12 has more factors than 10 (2, 3, 4, 6).

It is now superseded by the universally accepted decimal system.

Duparc /djuːˈpɑːk/ (Marie Eugène) Henri Fouques 1848–1933. French composer. He studied under César ◊Franck. His songs, though only 15 in number, are memorable for their craft and for their place in the history of French songwriting.

Du Pré /duːˈpreɪ/ Jacqueline 1945–1987. English cellist. Celebrated for her proficient technique and powerful interpretations of the Classical cello repertory, particularly of ◊Elgar. She had an international concert career while still in her teens and made many recordings.

She married Daniel ◊Barenboim in 1967 and worked with him in concerts, as a duo, and in a conductor-soloist relationship until her playing career was ended by multiple sclerosis. Although confined to a wheelchair for the last 14 years of her life, she continued to work as a teacher and to campaign on behalf of other sufferers of the disease.

duralumin a lightweight aluminium ◊alloy widely used in aircraft construction, containing copper, magnesium, and manganese.

Duras /djuːˈrɑː/ Marguerite 1914– . French writer. Her works include short stories (*Des Journées entières dans les arbres*), plays (*La Musica*), film scripts (*Hiroshima Mon Amour* 1960), and novels such as *Le Vice-Consul* 1966, evoking an existentialist world from the actual setting of Calcutta. Her autobiographical novel, *La Douleur*, is set in Paris in 1945.

Durazzo /duˈrætsəʊ/ Italian form of ◊Durrës, Albanian port.

Durban /ˈdɜːbən/ principal port of Natal, South Africa, and second port of the republic; population (1985) 634,000, urban area 982,000. It exports coal, maize, and wool, imports heavy machinery and mining equipment, and is also a holiday resort.

Founded 1824 as Port Natal, it was renamed 1835 after Gen Benjamin d'Urban (1777–1849), lieutenant-governor of the east district of Cape Colony 1834–37. Natal university 1949 is divided between Durban and Pietermaritzburg.

Dürer /ˈdjʊərə/ Albrecht 1471–1528. German artist, the leading figure of the northern Renaissance. He was born in Nuremberg and travelled widely in Europe. Highly skilled in drawing and a keen student of nature, he perfected the technique of woodcut and engraving, producing woodcut series such as the *Apocalypse* 1498 and copperplate engravings such as *The Knight, Death and the Devil* 1513 and *Melancholia* 1514; he may also have invented etching. His paintings include altarpieces and meticulously observed portraits (including many self-portraits).

He was apprenticed first to his father, a goldsmith, then in 1486 to Michael Wolgemut, a painter, woodcut artist, and master of a large workshop in Nuremberg. From 1490 he travelled widely, studying Netherlandish and Italian art, then visited Colmar, Basel, and Strasbourg, and returned to Nuremberg in 1495. Other notable journeys were to Venice 1505–07, where he met Giovanni Bellini, and in 1520 to Antwerp, where he was made court painter to Charles V of

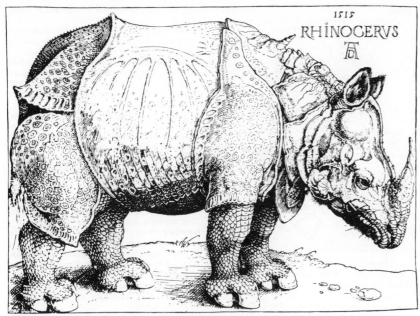

Dürer Woodcut of a rhinoceros by Albrecht Dürer. The rhinoceros was described to him by a Portuguese artist in 1515.

Spain and the Netherlands (recorded in detail in his diary).

Durga /ˈduəgə/ Hindu goddess; one of the many names for ◊*Mahadevi*.

Durham /ˈdʌrəm/ county in NE England
area 2,440 sq km/942 sq mi
towns administrative headquarters Durham; Darlington, and the new towns of Peterlee and Newton Aycliffe
features Beamish open-air industrial museum
products sheep and dairy produce; the county lies on one of Britain's richest coalfields
population (1987) 599,000.

Durham /ˈdʌrəm/ city in the county of Durham, England; population (1983) 88,600. It is administrative headquarters of the county. Founded in 995, it has a Norman cathedral dating from 1093, where the remains of ◊Bede were transferred in 1370; the castle was built by William I in 1072, and the university founded in 1832. Textiles, engineering and coal mining are the chief industries.

Durham /ˈdʌrəm/ John George Lambton, 1st Earl of Durham 1792–1840. British politician. Appointed Lord Privy Seal in 1830, he drew up the first Reform Bill of 1832, and as governor general of Canada briefly in 1837 drafted the Durham Report which led to the union of Upper and Lower Canada.

Durham

Durkheim /ˈdɜːkhaɪm/ Emile 1858–1917. French sociologist, one of the founders of modern sociology, who also influenced social anthropology.

He was the first lecturer in social science at Bordeaux University 1887–1902, professor of education at the Sorbonne in Paris from 1902 and the first professor of sociology there in 1913. He examined the bases of social order and the effects of industrialization on traditional social and moral order, and attempted to establish sociology as a respectable and scientific discipline, capable of diagnosing social ills and recommending possible cures.

His four key works are *The Division of Labour in Society* 1893, comparing social order in small-scale societies with that in industrial ones; *The Rules of Sociological Method* 1895, outlining his own brand of functionalism and proclaiming positivism as the way forward for sociology as a science; *Suicide* 1897, showing social causes of this apparently individual act; and *The Elementary Forms of Religion*, a study of the beliefs of Australian aborigines, showing the importance of religion in social solidarity.

durra or **dourra** grass of the genus *Sorghum*, also known as Indian millet, grown as cereal in parts of Asia and Africa. *Sorghum vulgare* is the chief cereal in many parts of Africa.

Durrell /ˈdʌrəl/ Gerald (Malcolm) 1925– . British naturalist. Director of Jersey Zoological Park, he is the author of travel and natural history books, and the humorous memoir *My Family and Other Animals* 1956. He is the brother of Lawrence Durrell.

Durrell /ˈdʌrəl/ Lawrence (George) 1912– . British novelist and poet. Born in India, he joined the foreign service, and has lived mainly in the E Mediterranean, the setting of his novels, including the Alexandria Quartet: *Justine, Balthazar, Mountolive,* and *Clea* 1957–60; he has also written travel books. He is the brother of Gerald Durrell.

Dürrenmatt /ˈdjʊərənmæt/ Friedrich 1921– . Swiss dramatist, author of grotesquely farcical tragicomedies, for example *The Visit* 1956 and *The Physicists* 1962.

Durrës /ˈdʊrəs/ chief port of Albania; population (1983) 72,000. It is an important commercial and communications centre, with flour mills, soap and cigarette factories, distilleries, and an electronics plant. It was the capital of Albania 1912–21.

Duse /ˈduːzeɪ/ Eleonora 1859–1924. Italian actress. She was the mistress of the poet ◊d'Annunzio from 1897, as recorded in his novel *Il Fuoco/The Flame of Life*.

Dushanbe /ˌduːʃænˈbeɪ/ formerly (1929–69) *Stalinabad* capital of Tadzhik Republic, USSR, 160 km/100 mi north of the Afghan frontier; population (1987) 582,000. It is an important road, rail, and air centre. Industries include cotton mills, tanneries, meat-packing factories, and printing works. It is the seat of Tadzhik state university.

Düsseldorf /ˈdʊsəldɔːf/ industrial city of West Germany, on the right bank of the Rhine, 26 km/16 mi NW of Cologne, capital of North Rhine-Westphalia; population (1988) 561,000. It is a river port and the commercial and financial centre of the Ruhr area, with food processing, brewing, agricultural machinery, textile, and chemical industries.

dust bowl area in the Great Plains region of North America (Texas to Kansas) that suffered extensive wind erosion as the result of drought and poor farming practice in once fertile soil. Much of the topsoil was blown away in the droughts of the 1930s.

Similar dust bowls are being formed in many areas today, noticeably across Africa, because of the same overcropping and overgrazing, resulting in ◊desert conditions.

Dutch East India Company see ◊East India Company, Dutch, a trading monopoly of the 17th and 18th centuries.

Dutch East Indies former Dutch colony which in 1945 became independent as ◊Indonesia.

Dutch elm disease a disease of elm trees (*Ulmus*), principally English elm and Dutch elm, caused by the fungus *Certocystis ulmi*. The fungus is usually spread from tree to tree by the elm-bark beetle, which lays its eggs beneath the bark. The disease has no cure and control methods involve injecting insecticide into the trees annually to prevent infection, or the destruction of all elms in a broad band around an infected area, to keep the beetles out.

It was first described in the Netherlands and by the early 1930s had spread across Britain and continental Europe, as well as occurring widely in North America. In the 1970s, a new epidemic was caused by a much more virulent form of the fungus, probably brought to Britain from Canada.

Dutch Guiana /giːˈɑːnə/ former Dutch colony which in 1948 became independent as ◊Suriname.

Dutch language a member of the Germanic branch of the Indo-European language family, often referred to by scholars as Netherlandic and taken to include the standard language and dialects of the Netherlands (excluding Frisian) and also Flemish (in Belgium and N France) and, more remotely, its offshoot Afrikaans in South Africa.

Dutilleux /ˌdjuːtɪˈjɜː/ Henri 1916– . French composer of instrumental music in elegant Neo-Romantic style. His works include *Mataboles* 1962–65 for orchestra and *Ainsi la Nuit* 1975–76 for string quartet.

Duval /djuːˈvæl/ Claude 1643–1670. English criminal. He was born in Normandy and turned highwayman after coming to England at the Restoration. His gallantry was famous. He was hanged at Tyburn, London.

Duvalier /djuːˈvæliˌeɪ/ François 1907–1971. Rightwing president of Haiti 1957–71. Known as *Papa Doc*, he ruled as a dictator, organizing the Tontons Macoutes ('bogeymen') as a private security force to intimidate and assassinate opponents of his regime. He rigged the 1961 elections in order to have his term of office extended until 1967, and in 1964 declared himself president for life. He was excommunicated by the Vatican for harassing the church, and was succeeded on his death by his son Jean-Claude Duvalier.

Duvalier /djuːˈvæliˌeɪ/ Jean-Claude 1951– . Rightwing president of Haiti 1971–86. Known as *Baby Doc*, he succeeded his father François Duvalier, becoming, at the age of 19, the youngest president in the world. He was forced by the USA to moderate his father's tyrannical regime, yet

Dvorak *Czech composer Antonin Dvořák.*

he tolerated no opposition. In 1986, with Haiti's economy stagnating and with increasing civil disorder, Duvalier fled to France.

Duve /dju:v/ Christian de 1917– . Belgian scientist, who shared a Nobel Prize for Medicine in 1974 for his work on the structural and functional organization of the cell.

Duvivier /dju:'vɪvɪeɪ/ Julien 1896–1967. French film director, whose work includes *Un Carnet de Bal* 1937 and *La Fin du Jour* 1938.

Duwez /'du:vəz/ Pol 1907– . US scientist, born in Belgium, who in 1959 developed ◊metallic glass with his team at the California Institute of Technology.

Dvořák /'dvɔ:ʒɑ:k/ Antonin (Leopold) 1841–1904. Czech composer. International recognition came with his series of Slavonic Dances 1877–86, and he was director of the National Conservatory, New York, 1892–95. Works such as his *New World Symphony* 1893 reflects his interest in American folk themes, including black and Native American. He wrote nine symphonies, tone poems, and operas, including *Rusalka* 1901; large-scale choral works; the *Carnival* and other overtures; violin and cello concertos; chamber music; piano pieces; and songs. His Romantic music extends the classical tradition of Beethoven and Brahms and displays the influence of Czech folk music.

dwarf star a ◊main-sequence star as plotted on the ◊Hertzsprung-Russell diagram. A cool dwarf star is a ◊red dwarf and a hot one is a ◊white dwarf.

dybbuk (Hebrew 'a clinging thing') in Jewish folklore, the soul of a dead sinner which has entered the body of a living person.

Dyck /'daɪk/ Anthony van 1599–1641. Flemish painter. Born in Antwerp, he was an assistant to Rubens 1618–20, then briefly worked in England at the court of James I, and moved to Italy in 1622. In 1626 he returned to Antwerp, where he continued to paint religious works and portraits. He painted his best-known portraits during his second period in England from 1632, for example, *Charles I on Horseback* about 1638 (National Gallery, London).

His characteristic portrait style emerged in the 1620s. In England he produced numerous portraits of royalty and aristocrats (some of them doomed to extinction in the Civil War), and was knighted by Charles I. His work influenced the course of British portraiture.

dye substance that, applied in solution to fabrics, imparts a colour resistant to washing. ***Direct dyes*** combine with the material of the fabric, yielding a coloured compound; ***indirect dyes*** require the presence of another substance (a mordant), with which the fabric must first be treated; ***vat dyes*** are colourless soluble substances which on exposure to air yield an insoluble coloured compound.

Naturally occurring dyes include indigo, madder (alizarin), logwood, and cochineal, but industrial dyes (introduced in the 19th century) are usually synthetic: acid green was developed 1835

and bright purple 1856. Industrial dyes include azo- dyestuffs, acridine, anthracene, and aniline.

Dyfed /'dʌvɪd/ county in SW Wales
area 5,770 sq km/2,227 sq mi
towns administrative headquarters Carmarthen; Aberystwyth, Cardigan, Lampeter
features Pembrokeshire Coast National Park, part of the Brecon Beacons National Park, including the Black Mountain, and part of the Cambrian Mountains, including Plynlimon Fawr 752 m/2,468 ft; the village of Laugharne, at the mouth of the Towey, was the home of Dylan Thomas, and features in his work as 'Milk Wood'; Museum of the Woollen Industry at Dre-fach Felindre, and of Welsh religious life at Tre'rddô l. Anthracite mines produce about 50,000 tonnes a year.
population (1987) 343,000
language 46% Welsh, English
famous people Taliesin.

Dylan /'dɪlən/ Bob. Adopted name of Robert Allen Zimmerman 1941– . US singer and songwriter, whose work in the 1960s, first in the folk-music tradition and from 1965 in an individualistic rock style, was influential on later pop music.

Dylan's early songs, on his albums *Freewheelin'* 1963 and *The Times They Are A-Changin'* 1964, were associated with the US civil-rights movement and antiwar protest. When he first used an electric rock band he was criticized by purists, but the albums *Highway 61 Revisited* 1965 and *Blonde on Blonde* 1966 are often cited as his best work. His increasingly obscure lyrics provided catchphrases for a generation and influenced innumerable songwriters.

dynamics in mechanics, the mathematical and physical study of the behaviour of bodies under the action of forces which produce changes of motion in them.

dynamics in music, symbols indicating degrees of loudness or changes in loudness.

dynamite an explosive consisting of a mixture of nitroglycerine and kieselguhr (an absorbent,

Dylan *US singer and songwriter Bob Dylan wrote hugely influential popular protest songs in the 1960s.*

chalklike material). It was first devised by Alfred Nobel.

dynamo a machine for transforming mechanical energy into electrical energy. It is also called a generator. A simple form of dynamo consists of a powerful field magnet, between the poles of which a suitable conductor, usually in the form of a coil (armature), is rotated. The mechanical energy of rotation is thus converted into an electric current in the armature.

Present-day dynamos work on the principles described by ◊Faraday in 1830, that an ◊electromotive force is developed in a conductor when it is moved in a magnetic field.

dyne c.g.s. unit (symbol dyn) of force. 10 dynes = 1 ◊newton. It is defined as the force that will accelerate a mass of 1 g by 1 cm per second per second.

dyscalculus a disability demonstrated by a poor aptitude with figures. A similar disability in reading and writing is called ◊dyslexia.

dysentery infection of the large intestine causing abdominal cramps and ◊diarrhoea.

There are two kinds of dysentery: ***amoebic*** (caused by a protozoon), which may lead to liver damage; and ***bacillary***, the kind most often seen in the temperate zones. Widely prevalent in hot countries, both forms are successfully treated with antibacterials.

dyslexia (Greek 'bad', 'pertaining to words') a malfunction in the brain's synthesis and interpretation of sensory information, popularly 'word blindness'. It results in poor ability to read and write, though the person may otherwise excel, for example, in mathematics. A similar disability with figures is called ◊dyscalculus.

dyspepsia synonym for ◊indigestion.

dysphagia difficulty in swallowing. It may be due to infection, obstruction, or spasm in the throat or oesophagus (gullet).

dyspnoea difficulty in breathing, or shortness of breath disproportionate to effort. It occurs if the supply of oxygen is inadequate or if carbon dioxide accumulates.

dysprosium an element, one of the yttrium group of rare earths (symbol Dy, atomic number 66, relative atomic mass 162.51). It was discovered in 1886 by Lecoq de Boisbaudran (1838–1912).

dystopia an imaginary society whose evil qualities are meant to serve as a moral or political warning. The term was coined in the 19th century by J S ◊Mill, and is the opposite of a ◊Utopia. George Orwell's *1984* 1949 and Aldous Huxley's *Brave New World* 1932 are influential examples. Dystopias are common in science fiction.

Dzerzhinsk /dzə'ʒɪnsk/ city in central USSR, on the Oka river, 32 km/20 mi west of Gorky; population (1987) 281,000. There are engineering, chemical, and timber industries.

Dzhambul /dʒæm'bul/ city in S Kazakhstan, USSR, in a fruit-growing area NE of Tashkent. Industries include fruit canning, sugar refining, and the manufacture of phosphate fertilizers. Population (1985) 303,000.

Dzo a river in central Portugal that flows 80 km/50 mi through a region noted for its wine.

Dzungarian Gates /dzuŋ'geəriən/ ancient route in central Asia on the border of Kazakhstan, USSR, and Xinjiang Uygur region of China, 470 km/290 mi NW of Urumqi. The route was used by the Mongol hordes on their way to Europe.

eagle

bald eagle

E the second vowel and fifth and most often used letter of the alphabet.

E abbreviation for *east*.

eagle several genera of large birds of prey of the family Accipitridae. The *golden eagle Aquila chrysaetos* has a 2 m/6 ft wingspan and is dark brown.

In Britain the golden eagle is found in the Highlands of Scotland with a few recolonizing the Lake District. The larger *spotted eagle Aquila clanga* lives in Central Europe and Asia. The *sea eagles Haliaetus* include the white-tailed sea eagle *Haliaetus albicilla* which has been renaturalized in Britain in the 1980s, having died out there 1916. Mainly a carrion-feeder, it breeds on sea cliffs. The white-headed *bald eagle Haliaetus leucocephalus* is the symbol of the USA; rendered infertile through the ingestion of agricultural chemicals, it is now very rare. Another endangered species is the Philippine eagle, sometimes called the Philippine monkey-eating eagle (although its main prey is flying lemurs). Loss of large tracts of forest, coupled with hunting by humans, have greatly reduced its numbers.

Eagling /'i:glɪŋ/ Wayne 1950– . Canadian dancer. He joined the Royal Ballet in London, appearing in *Gloria* 1980 and other productions.

Eakins /'i:kɪnz/ Thomas 1844–1916. US painter. He studied in Europe and developed a realistic style with strong contrasts between light and shade, as in *The Gross Clinic* 1875 (Jefferson Medical College, Philadelphia), a group portrait of a surgeon, his assistants and students.

Ealing /'i:lɪŋ/ borough of Greater London, England. Population (1981) 280,000. The first British sound-film studio was built here in 1931, and 'Ealing comedies' became a noted genre in British film-making. There are many engineering and chemical industries.

Ealing Studios film studios headed by Sir Michael Balcon. They produced a number of George Formby and Will Hay films in the 1940s, then a series of more genteel and occasionally satirical comedies, often written by T E B Clarke and starring Alec Guinness. Titles produced at Ealing include *Passport to Pimlico* 1948, *Kind Hearts and Coronets* 1949, *The Man in the White Suit* 1951, and *The Ladykillers* 1955.

Eanes /eɪˈɑːneʃ/ António dos Santos Ramalho 1935– . Portuguese politician, president 1976–86. He helped plan the 1974 coup which ended the Caetano regime, and as army chief of staff put down a left-wing revolt in Nov 1975.

ear the organ of hearing in animals. It responds to the vibrations that constitute sound, and these are translated into nerve signals and passed to the brain.

A mammal's ear consists of three parts. The *outer ear* is a funnel that collects sound, directing it down a tube to the ear drum (tympanic membrane), which separates the outer and *middle ear*. Sounds vibrate this membrane, the mechanical movement of which is transferred to the membrane of the *inner ear* by three small bones, the auditory ossicles. Vibrations of the inner ear membrane move fluid contained in the snail-shaped cochlea, which vibrates hair cells (stereocilia) that stimulate the auditory nerve, connected to the brain. The fluid-filled labyrinth of the inner ear detects changes of position; this, with other sensory inputs, is responsible for the sense of balance.

When a loud noise occurs, muscles behind the eardrum contract automatically, suppressing the noise to enhance perception of sound and prevent injury.

Earhart /'eəhɑːt/ Amelia 1898–1937. American aviator, born in Kansas. In 1932 she was the first woman to fly the Atlantic alone, and in 1937 disappeared without trace while making a Pacific flight. Clues found on Nikumuroro island in Kiribati in 1989 suggest that she and her male navigator might have survived a crash only to die of thirst.

earl in the British peerage, the third title in order of rank, coming between marquess and viscount; it is the oldest of British titles, being of Scandinavian origin. The premier earldom is Arundel, now united with the dukedom of ◊Norfolk. An earl's wife is a *countess.*

Earl Marshal in England, one of the Great Officers of State; the office has been hereditary since 1672 in the family of Howard, the dukes of Norfolk. The Earl Marshal is head of the College of Arms, and arranges state processions and ceremonies.

Early English in architecture, name given by Thomas Rickman (1776–1841) to the first of the three periods of the English Gothic style. It covers the period from about 1189 to about 1280, and is characterized by tall, elongated windows (lancets) without mullions (horizontal bars), often grouped in threes, fives, or sevens; the pointed arch; pillars of stone centres surrounded by shafts of black Purbeck marble; and dog-tooth (zig-zag) ornament. Salisbury Cathedral is almost entirely Early English.

major 20th-century earthquakes

date	place	magnitude (Richter scale)	number of deaths
1906	San Francisco, USA	8.3	3,000
1908	Messina, Italy	7.5	83,000
1915	Avezzano, Italy	7.5	29,980
1920	Gansu, China	8.6	100,000
1923	Tokyo, Japan	8.3	99,330
1927	Nan-Shan, China	8.3	200,000
1932	Gansu, China	7.6	70,000
1935	Quetta, India	7.5	30,000
1939	Erzincan, Turkey	7.9	30,000
1939	Chillan, Chile	8.3	28,000
1948	USSR	7.3	110,000
1970	N Peru	7.7	66,794
1976	Tangshan, China	8.2	242,000
1978	NE Iran	7.7	25,000
1988	Armenia, USSR	6.9	25,000
1989	San Francisco, USA	7.1	62

ear

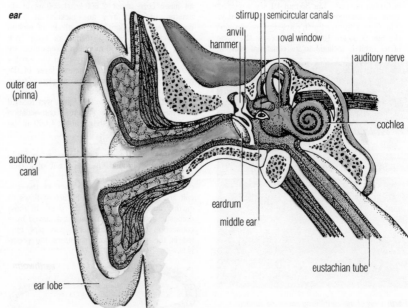

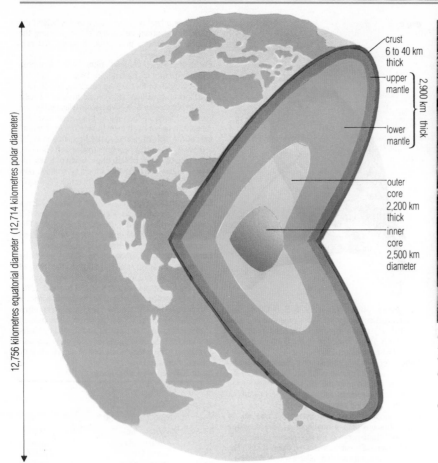

crust
6 to 40 km
thick

upper
mantle

2,900 km thick

lower
mantle

outer
core
2,200 km
thick

inner
core
2,500 km
diameter

12,756 kilometres equatorial diameter (12,714 kilometres polar diameter)

earthquake *Mexico City, 19th Sept 1985. In the space of a few minutes, 10, 000 people lost their lives and more than 200 buildings were razed.*

earthenware pottery made of porous clay and fired, whether unglazed (flowerpots, winecoolers) or glazed (most tableware).

earthquake a shaking or convulsion of the Earth's surface, the scientific study of which is called ◊seismology. Earthquakes result from a build-up of stresses within rocks until strained to fracturing point. Most occur along ◊faults (fractures or breaks) in the Earth's crust. Plate tectonic movements generate the major proportion of all earthquakes: as two plates move past each other, they can become jammed and deformed, and earthquakes occur when they spring free. Most earthquakes happen under the sea. Their force is measured on the ◊Richter scale and their intensity on the Mercalli scale.

The point at which an earthquake originates is the ***seismic focus***. The point on Earth's surface directly above this is the ***epicentre***. In 1987 a California earthquake was successfully predicted by measurement of underground pressure waves; prediction attempts have also involved the study of such phenomena as the change in gases issuing from the ◊crust, the level of water in wells, and the behaviour of animals. The possibility of earthquake prevention is remote. However, rock slippage might be slowed at movement points or promoted at stoppage points by the extraction or injection of large quantities of water underground, since water serves as a lubricant. This would ease overall pressure.

earth sciences the scientific study of the planet Earth as a whole, a synthesis of several traditional subjects such as ◊geology, ◊meteorology, oceanography, ◊geophysics, ◊geochemistry, and ◊palaeontology.

The mining and extraction of minerals and gems, the prediction of weather and earthquakes, the pollution of the atmosphere, and the forces that shape the physical world all fall within its scope of study. The emergence of the discipline reflects scientists' concern that an understanding of the global aspects of the Earth's structure and its past will hold the key to how humans affect its future, ensuring that its resources are used in a sustainable way.

earthworm annelid worm of the class Oligochaeta. Earthworms are hermaphrodite, and deposit their eggs in cocoons. They live by burrowing in the soil, feeding on the organic matter it contains. They play a most important role in the formation

Earth the third planet from the Sun. It is almost spherical, flattened slightly at the poles, and has three geological zones: the ◊core, the ◊mantle, and the ◊crust. 70% of the surface is covered with water. The Earth is surrounded by a life-supporting atmosphere and is the only planet on which life is known to exist.

mean distance from the Sun 149,500,000 km/ 92,860,000 mi

equatorial diameter 12,756 km/7,923 mi

circumference 40,070 km/24,900 mi

rotation period 23 hr 56 min 4.1 sec

year (complete orbit, or sidereal period) 365 days 5 hr 48 min 46 sec. Earth's average speed round the Sun is 30 km/18.5 mi per second; the plane of its orbit is inclined to its equatorial plane at an angle of 23.5°, the reason for the changing seasons

atmosphere nitrogen 78.09%, oxygen 20.95%, argon 0.93%, carbon dioxide 0.03%, and less than 0.0001% neon, helium, krypton, hydrogen, xenon, ozone, radon

surface land surface 150,000,000 sq km/57,500,000 sq mi (greatest height above sea level Mount Everest); water surface 361,000,000 sq km/139, 400,000 sq mi (greatest depth ◊Mariana Trench in the Pacific). The interior is thought to be an inner core about 2,600 km/1,600 mi in diameter, of solid iron and nickel; an outer core about 2,250 km/1,400 mi thick, of molten iron and nickel; and a mantle of solid rock about 2,900 km/1,800 mi thick, separated by the ◊Mohorovičić discontinuity from the Earth's crust. The crust and the topmost layer of the mantle form about 12 major moving plates, some of which carry the continents

age 4,600 million years. The Earth was formed with the rest of the ◊solar system by consolidation of interstellar dust. Life began about 4,000 million years ago

satellite the ◊Moon.

earth an electrical connection between an appliance and the ground. In the event of a fault in an electrical appliance, for example, involving connection between the live part of the circuit and the outer casing, the current flows to earth, causing no harm to the user. In most domestic installations, earthing is achieved by a connection to a metal water supply pipe buried in the ground before it enters the premises.

Earth *View of the Earth rising above the surface of the Moon, taken by the Apollo II spacecraft.*

earthworm

East Sussex

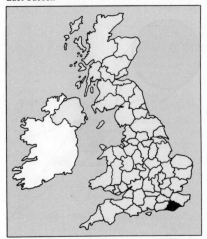

of humus, by irrigating the soil, and levelling it by transferring earth from the deeper levels to the surface as castings.

The common British earthworms belong to the genera *Lumbricus* and *Allolobophora*. These are comparitively small, but some tropical forms reach over 1 m/3 ft and *Megascolides australis*, of Queensland, Australia, over 3 m/11 ft.

earwig nocturnal insect of the order Dermaptera. The fore-wings are short and leathery, and serve to protect the hind-wings, which are large and are folded like a fan when at rest; the insects seldom fly. They are regarded as pests because they feed on flowers and fruit, but they also eat other insects, dead or alive. Eggs are laid beneath the soil, and the female cares for the young even after they have hatched. A number are found in Britain, such as the common European earwig *Forficula auricularia*.

easement in law, rights which a person may have over the land of another. The commonest example is a right of way; others are the right to bring water over another's land, and 'ancient lights', that is, the right to an uninterrupted flow of light to windows.

east one of the four cardinal points of the compass, indicating that part of the horizon where the Sun rises; when facing north, east is to the right.

The Sun, and hence the east, has held a significant place in various religions; ancient temples had their altars at the east end so that sacrifices and other rituals could be made facing the rising Sun. In the 2nd century it became customary for Christians to worship facing the east, and also to bury the dead with their feet towards the east, so that on the morning of the Resurrection they would be facing the direction from which Christ was to come in glory.

East Anglia /ˈiːst ˈæŋɡliə/ region of E England, formerly a Saxon kingdom, including Norfolk, Suffolk, and parts of Essex and Cambridgeshire. The University of East Anglia was founded at Norwich 1962, and the Sainsbury Centre for the Visual Arts, opened 1978, has a collection of ethnographic art and sculpture.

Eastbourne /ˈiːstbɔːn/ English seaside resort in East Sussex, 103 km/64 mi SE of London; population (1981) 77,500. The old town was developed in the early 19th century as a model of town planning, largely owing to the 7th duke of Devonshire. The modern town extends along the coast for 5 km/3 mi. To the E the South Downs terminate in ◊Beachy Head.

Easter spring feast of the Christian church, commemorating the Resurrection of Jesus. The English name derives from Eostre, Anglo-Saxon goddess of spring, who was honoured in Apr. Easter eggs, dyed and decorated or made of confectionery, symbolizing new life, are given as presents.

Easter Island /ˈiːstə/ or *Rapa Nui* Chilean island in the S Pacific Ocean, part of the Polynesian group, about 3,500 km/2,200 mi W of Chile; area about 166 sq km/64 sq mi; population (1985) 2,000. It was first reached by Europeans on Easter Sunday 1722. It is famous for its huge carved statues and stone houses, the work of neolithic peoples of unknown origin. The chief centre is Hanga-Roa.

Easter Rising traditionally known as the *Easter Rebellion*: in Irish history, a republican insurrection that began on Easter Monday, Apr 1916 in Dublin. It was inspired by the Irish Republican Brotherhood (IRB) in an attempt to overthrow British rule in Ireland.

Arms from Germany intended for the IRB were intercepted but the rising proceeded regardless with the seizure of the Post Office and other buildings in Dublin by 1,500 volunteers. The rebellion was crushed by the British Army within five days, both sides suffering major losses. 220 civilians, 64 rebels, and 134 members of the Crown Forces were killed during the uprising. 16 rebel leaders were subsequently executed.

East Germany /ˈiːst ˈdʒɜːməni/ see ◊Germany, East.

East India Company an English commercial company 1600–1858 that was chartered by Queen Elizabeth I and given a monopoly of trade between England and the Far East. In the 18th century it became in effect the ruler of a large part of India, and a form of dual control by the company and a committee responsible to Parliament in London was introduced by Pitt's India Act 1784. The end of the monopoly of China trade came 1834, and after the Indian Mutiny 1857 the crown took complete control of the government of British India; the India Act 1858 abolished the company.

East India Company, Dutch (*VOC*, or *Vereenigde Oost-Indische Compagnie*) a trading company chartered by the States General (parliament) of the Netherlands, and established in N Netherlands 1602. It was given a monopoly on Dutch trade in the Indonesian archipelago, and certain sovereign rights such as the creation of an army and a fleet. In the 17th century some 100 ships were regularly trading between the Netherlands and the East Indies. The company's main base was Batavia in Java (Indonesia); ships sailed there via the Cape of Good Hope, a colony founded by the company 1652 as a staging post. During the 17th and 18th centuries the company used its monopoly of East Indian trade to pay out high dividends, but wars with England and widespread corruption led to a suspension of payments 1781 and a takeover of the company by the Dutch government 1798.

East Kilbride /ˈiːst kɪlˈbraɪd/ town in Strathclyde, Scotland; population (1985) 72,000. It was an old village developed as a new town from 1947 to take overspill from Glasgow, 11 km/6 mi to the NE. It is the site of the National Engineering Laboratory. There are various light industries and some engineering, including jet engines.

East London /ˈiːst ˈlʌndən/ port and resort on the SE coast of Cape Province, South Africa. Population (1980) 160,582. Founded 1846 as Port Rex, its name was changed to East London 1848. It has a good harbour, is the terminus of a railway from the interior, and is a leading wool-exporting port.

East Lothian /ˈiːst ˈləʊðiən/ former county of SE Scotland, merged with West Lothian and Midlothian in 1975 in the new region of ◊Lothian. Haddington was the county town.

Eastman /ˈiːstmən/ George 1854–1932. US entrepreneur and inventor who founded the Kodak photographic company. From 1888 he marketed daylight-loading flexible roll films (to replace the glass plates used previously) and portable cameras. By 1900 his company was selling a pocket camera for as little as $1.

East River /iːst/ tidal strait 26 km/16 mi long, between Manhattan and the Bronx, and Long Island, in New York, USA. It links Long Island Sound with New York Bay, and is also connected, via the Harlem river, with the Hudson. There are both

Eastman Founder of the Kodak photographic company, inventor and businessman, George Eastman.

commercial and naval docks, and most famous of its many bridges is the Brooklyn.

East Siberian Sea /ˈiːst saɪˈbɪəriən/ part of the ◊Arctic Ocean, off the N coast of USSR, between the New Siberian Islands and Chukchi Sea. The world's widest continental shelf with an average width of nearly 650 km/404 mi, lies in the East Siberian Sea.

East Sussex /ˈiːst ˈsʌsɪks/ county in SE England
area 1,800 sq km/695 sq mi
towns administrative headquarters Lewes; cross-channel port of Newhaven; Brighton, Eastbourne, Hastings, Bexhill, Winchelsea, Rye
features Beachy Head, highest headland on the S coast at 180 m/590 ft, the E end of the South ◊Downs; the Weald (including Ashdown Forest); the modern Friston Forest; rivers Ouse, Cuckmere, East Rother; Romney Marsh; the 'Long Man' chalk hill figure at Wilmington, near Eastbourne; Herstmonceux, with a 15th-century castle (conference and exhibition centre) and adjacent modern buildings housing 1958–90, Greenwich Royal Observatory; other castles at Hastings, Lewes, Pevensey, and Bodiam; Battle Abbey and the site of the Battle of Hastings; Micheldam Priory; Sheffield Park garden; University of Sussex at Falmer, near Brighton, founded in 1961.
products electronics, gypsum, timber
population (1987) 698,000.
famous people former homes of Henry James at Rye, Rudyard Kipling at Burwash, Virginia Woolf at Rodmell.

East Timor /ˈtiːmɔː/ disputed territory on the island of ◊Timor in the Malay Archipelago; prior to 1975, a Portuguese colony for almost 460 years
area 14,874 sq km/5,706 sq mi
capital Dili
products coffee
population (1980) 555,000
history Following Portugal's withdrawal 1975, the left-wing Revolutionary Front of Independent East Timor (Fretilin) occupied the capital, Dili, calling for independence. In opposition, troops from neighbouring Indonesia invaded the territory, declaring East Timor (*Loro Sae*) the 17th province of Indonesia Jul 1976. This claim is not recognized by the United Nations.

The Portuguese colonizers left behind a literacy rate of under 10% and no infrastructure. A brief civil war followed their departure and, after the nationalist guerrillas' calls for independence, the invading Indonesian troops bombed villages and carried out mass executions of suspected Fretilin sympathizers. The war and its attendant famine are thought to have caused more than 100,000 deaths, but starvation had been alleviated by the mid-1980s, and the Indonesian government has built schools, roads, and hospitals. Fretilin

Eastwood *Film actor and director Clint Eastwood 1970.*

guerrillas were still active 1988, claiming to have the support of the population; the number of Indonesian troops in East Timor was estimated at 20,000.

Eastwood /ˈiːstwʊd/ Clint 1930– . US film actor and director. As the 'man with no name' caught up in Wild West lawlessness in *A Fistful of Dollars* 1964, he started the vogue for 'spaghetti westerns'. Later westerns include *The Good, the Bad, and the Ugly* 1966 and *High Plains Drifter* 1973. He also starred in the 'Dirty Harry' series, and directed *Bird* 1988.

eau de cologne a refreshing scent, weaker than perfume, whose invention is ascribed to Giovanni Maria Farina (1685–1766); he moved from Italy to Cologne in 1709 to manufacture it.

Eban /ˈebæn/ Abba 1915– . Israeli diplomat and politician, Israeli ambassador in Washington 1950–59 and foreign minister 1966–74. Born in Cape Town, and educated in England, he taught at Cambridge University before serving at Allied HQ during World War II. He subsequently settled in Israel.

Ebbw Vale /ˈebuː ˈveɪl/ town in Gwent, Wales; population (1981) 21,100. The iron and steel industries ended in the 1970s, but tin-plate manufacture and engineering continues. To the east is Blaenavon, where the Big Pit (no longer working) is a tourist attraction.

EBCDIC *E*xtended *B*inary *C*oded *D*ecimal *I*nterchange *C*ode in computing, a code used for storing and communicating alphabetic and numeric characters. It is an eight-bit code, capable of holding 256 different characters, although only 85 of these are defined in the standard version. It is still used in many mainframe computers, but almost all mini- and microcomputers now use ◊ASCII code.

ebony tropical hardwood tree, genus *Diospyros*, of the family Ebenaceae. Its very heavy, hard black timber polishes well and is used in cabinet-making, inlaying, and for piano-keys and knife-handles.

Eboracum /iːˈbɒrəkəm/ Roman name for ◊York. The archbishop of York signs himself 'Ebor'.

Ebro /ˈiːbrəʊ/ river in NE Spain, which rises in the Cantabrian Mountains and flows some 800 km/500 mi SE to meet the Mediterranean SW of Barcelona. Zaragoza is on its course, and ocean-going ships can sail as far as Tortosa, 35 km/22 mi from its mouth. It is a major source of hydro-electric power.

EC abbreviation for ◊*European Community*.

Ecce Homo (Latin 'behold the man') the words of Pontius Pilate to the accusers of Jesus; the title of paintings showing Jesus crowned with thorns, presented to the people (John 19:5).

eccentricity in geometry, a property of a ◊conic section (circle, ellipse, parabola, or hyperbola). It is the distance of any point on the curve from a fixed point (the focus) divided by the distance of that point from a fixed line (the directrix). A circle has an eccentricity of zero; for an ellipse it is less than one, for a parabola equal to one, and for a hyperbola greater than one.

Eccles /ˈeklz/ town near Manchester, England, 8 km/5 mi W of Manchester, on the river Irwell

and Manchester Ship Canal, population (1981) 37,166. Industries include cotton textiles, machinery, and pharmaceuticals. Eccles cakes, rounded pastries with a dried fruit filling, originated here.

Eccles /ˈeklz/ John Carew 1903– . Australian physiologist, who in 1963 shared a Nobel prize (with ◊Hodgkin and ◊Huxley) for work on conduction in the central nervous system. He argued that the mind has an existence independent of the brain.

Ecclesiastes also known as 'The Preacher', a book of the Old Testament or Hebrew Bible, traditionally attributed to ◊Solomon, on the theme of the vanity of human life.

ecclesiastical law church law. In England, the Church of England has special ecclesiastical courts to administer church law. Each diocese has a consistory court with a right of appeal to the Court of Arches (in the Archbishop of Canterbury's jurisdiction) or the Chancery Court of York (in the Archbishop of York's jurisdiction). They deal with the constitution of the Church of England, church property, the clergy, services, doctrine ,and practice. These courts have no influence on churches of other denominations, which are governed by the usual laws of contract and trust.

ecdysis the periodic shedding of the ◊exoskeleton by insects and other arthropods to allow growth. Prior to shedding, a new soft and expandable layer is first laid down underneath the existing one. The old layer then splits, the animal moves free of it, and the new layer expands and hardens.

Echegaray /ˌetʃiɡəˈraɪ/ José 1832–1916. Spanish dramatist. His dramas include *O locura o santidad/Madman or Saint* 1877, and *El gran Galeoto/The World and His Wife* 1881. Nobel prize 1904.

echidna or *spiny ant-eater* any of several species of toothless, egg-laying, spiny mammals, order Monotremata, found in Australia and New Guinea. They feed entirely upon ants and termites, which they dig out with their powerful claws and lick up with their prehensile tongue. When attacked, echidnas roll themselves into a ball, or try to hide by burrowing in the earth.

echinoderm marine invertebrate which has a basic body structure divided into five sectors. The phylum Echinodermata ('spiny-skinned') includes the starfish, brittlestars, sea-lilies, sea-urchins, and sea-cucumbers. The skeleton is external, made of a series of limy plates, and Echinodermata generally move by using tube-feet—small water-filled sacs which can be protruded or pulled back to the body.

echo a reflection of a sound wave, or of a ◊radar or ◊sonar signal. By accurately measuring the time taken for an echo to return to the transmitter, and by knowing the speed of a radar signal (the speed of light) or a sonar signal (the speed of sound in water), it is possible to calculate the range of the object causing the echo. A similar technique is used in echo-sounders to estimate the depth of water under a ship's keel or the depth of a shoal of fish.

Echo in Greek mythology, a nymph who pined away until only her voice remained, after being rejected by Narcissus.

echolocation method used by certain animals, notably bats and dolphins, to detect the positions of objects by using sound. The animal emits a stream of high-pitched sounds, generally at ultrasonic frequencies, and listens for the returning echoes reflected off objects ahead to determine their distance by the time difference.

Echo location is of particular value under conditions when normal vision is poor (at night in the case of bats, in murky water for dolphins). A few species of bird can also echolocate.

Eckert /ˈekət/ John Presper Jr 1919– . US mathematician who collaborated with John ◊Mauchly on the development of the ENIAC and Univac 1 computers.

Eckhart /ˈekhaːt/ Johannes, called *Meister Eckhart* c.1260–1327. German theologian and

eclipse
lunar eclipse

solar eclipse

leader of a popular mystical movement. In 1326 he was accused of heresy, and in 1329 a number of his doctrines were condemned by the pope as heretical.

eclampsia convulsions occurring due to ◊toxaemia of pregnancy.

eclipse the passage of an astronomical body through the shadow of another. The term is usually used for solar and lunar eclipses, which may be either partial or total, but also, for example, for eclipses by Jupiter of its satellites. An eclipse of a star by a body in the Solar System is called an ◊occultation.

A *solar eclipse* occurs when the Moon passes in front of the Sun as seen from Earth, and can happen only during a new Moon. During a total eclipse the Sun's ◊corona can be seen. A total solar eclipse can last just over 7.5 minutes. When the Moon is at its farthest from Earth it does not completely cover the face of the Sun, leaving a ring of sunlight visible. This is an *annular eclipse* (from the Latin word *annulus* 'ring'). Between two and five solar eclipses occur each year.

A *lunar eclipse* occurs when the Moon passes into the shadow of the Earth, becoming dim until emerging from the shadow. Lunar eclipses may be partial or total, and they can happen only at full Moon. Total lunar eclipses last for up to 100 minutes; the maximum number each year is three.

eclipsing binary a ◊binary (double) star in which the two stars periodically pass in front of each other as seen from Earth. When one star crosses in front of the other the total light received on Earth from the two stars declines. The first eclipsing binary to be noticed was ◊Algol.

ecliptic the path, against the background of stars, that the Sun appears to follow each year as the Earth orbits the Sun. It can be thought of as marking the intersection of the plane of the Earth's orbit with the ◊celestial sphere (imaginary sphere around the Earth). The ecliptic is tilted at about 23.5° with respect to the celestial equator, a result of the actual tilt of the Earth's axis with respect to the plane of its orbit around the Sun.

Eco /'ekəʊ/ Umberto 1932– . Italian cultural and literary critic (*The Role of the Reader* 1979), author of the 'philosophical thriller' *The Name of the Rose* 1983 and of *Foucault's Pendulum* 1989.

École National d'Administration (ENA) (French 'National School of administration') the most prestigious of the French *Grandes Ecoles*, higher education colleges that admit students only following a public competitive examination. The ENA was founded 1945 to train civil servants; former pupils include Laurent Fabius, Valéry Giscard d'Estaing, and Jacques Chirac.

ecology (Greek *oikos* 'house') the study of the relationship between an organism and the environment in which it lives, including other living organisms and the non-living surroundings. The term was coined by the biologist Ernst Haeckel 1866.

Ecology may be concerned with individual organisms (for example, behavioural ecology, foraging strategies), with populations or species (for example, population dynamics) or with entire communities (for example, competition between species for access to resources in an ecosystem, or predator–prey relationships). Applied ecology is concerned with the management and conservation of habitats and the consequences and control of pollution.

econometrics the use of mathematical and statistical analysis in the study of economic relationships, including testing economic theories and making quantitative predictions.

economic community or **common market** an organization of autonomous countries formed to promote trade. Examples include the Caribbean Community (Caricom) 1973, Central African Economic Community 1985, European Community (EC) 1957, and Latin American Economic System 1975.

economics (Greek 'household management') social science devoted to studying the production, distribution, and consumption of wealth. It consists of the disciplines of ◊**microeconomics**, the study of individual producers, consumers, or markets, and ◊**macroeconomics**, the study of whole economies or systems (in particular, areas such as taxation and public spending).

Economics is the study of how, in a given society, choices are made on the allocation of resources to produce goods and services for consumption, and the mechanisms and principles that govern this process. Economics seeks to apply scientific method to construct theories about the processes involved and to test them against what actually happens. Its two central concerns are the efficient allocation of available resources and the problem of reconciling finite resources with a virtually infinite desire for goods and services. Economics analyses the ingredients of economic efficiency in the production process, and the implications for practical policies, and examines conflicting demands or resources and the consequences of whatever choices are made, whether by individuals, enterprises, or governments.

Microeconomics and macroeconomics frequently overlap. They include the subdiscipline of *econometrics*, which analyses economic relationships using mathematical and statistical techniques. Increasingly sophisticated econometric methods are today being used for such topics as economic forecasting. Pioneers in this field include ◊Frisch and ◊Kantorovich.

Economics aims to be either *positive*, presenting objective and scientific explanations of how an economy works, or *normative*, offering prescriptions and recommendations on what should be done to cure perceived ills. However, almost inevitably, value judgements are involved in all economists' formulations.

Economics came of age as a separate area of study with the publication of Adam Smith's *The Wealth of Nations* 1776; the economist Alfred Marshall (1842–1924) established the orthodox position of 'Neo-Classical' economics, which, as modified by J M Keynes remains the standard today. Major economic thinkers include Ricardo, Malthus, J S Mill, Marx, Pareto, and Friedman.

economies of scale in economics, when production capacity is increased at a financial cost which is more than compensated for by the greater volume of output. In a dress factory, for example, a reduction in the unit cost may be possible only by the addition of new machinery, which would be worthwhile only if the volume of dresses produced were increased and there were sufficient market demand for them.

In business, economies of scale are usually considered in relation to specific areas of the production process which may be technical, managerial, marketing, finance, and risk. In achieving economies of scale, many factors must be considered, not least of which is the demand for a particular product.

ecosystem in ◊ecology, an integrated unit consisting of the ◊community of living organisms and the physical environment in a particular area. The relationships between species in an ecosystem can be complex and finely balanced, and removal of one species may be disastrous. The removal of a major predator, for example, can result in the destruction of the ecosystem through overgrazing by herbivores.

Energy and nutrients pass through organisms in an ecosystem in a particular sequence (see ◊food chain): energy is captured through ◊photosynthesis, and nutrients are taken up from the soil or water by plants; both are passed to herbivores that eat the plants and so to carnivores that feed on herbivores. These nutrients are returned to the soil through the ◊decomposition of excreta and dead organisms, thus completing a cycle that is crucial to the stabililty and survival of the ecosystem.

ECSC abbreviation for *European Coal and Steel Community*.

ecstasy or *MDMA* (3,4-methylenedioxymethamphetamine) illegal drug in increasing use from the 1980s. It is a modified amphetamine with mild psychedelic effects. It can be synthesized from nutmeg oil, and works by depleting serotonin in the brain.

Ecstasy was first synthesized 1914 by the Merck pharmaceutical company in Germany; it was one of eight psychedelics tested by the US army 1953, but was otherwise largely forgotten until the mid-1970s.

ECT abbreviation for ◊*electroconvulsive therapy*.

ectoparasite a ◊parasite that lives on the outer surface of its host.

ectopic term applied to an anatomical feature which is displaced or found in an abnormal position. An ectopic pregnancy is one occurring outside the womb.

ectoplasm part of a cell's ◊cytoplasm.

ectotherm a 'cold-blooded' animal (see ◊poikilothermy) such as a lizard that relies on external warmth (ultimately from the sun) to raise its body temperature so that it can become active.

ECTU abbreviation for *European Confederation of Trade Unions*.

ECU abbreviation for *European Currency Unit*, official monetary unit of the EC. It is based on the value of the different currencies used in the European Monetary System.

Ecuador /'kwədɔː/ country in South America, bounded to the N by Colombia, to the E and S by Peru, and to the W by the Pacific Ocean.

government Ecuador is not a fully federal state, but has a devolved system of 20 provinces, each administered by an appointed governor. The 1979 constitution provides for a president and a single-chamber national congress, the 72-member chamber of representatives, both popularly elected for a four-year term. The president is not eligible for re-election. Seven of the 16 political parties formed a left-wing coalition 1984.

history Conquered by the ◊Inca in the 15th century, Ecuador was invaded and colonized by Spain from 1532, becoming part of Gran Colombia 1819. After joining other South American colonies in a revolt against Spain, Ecuador was liberated 1822 by Antonio José de ◊Sucre, and became fully independent 1830. Since independence, Peru has repeatedly invaded Ecuador because of boundary disputes, which remain unresolved.

From independence onwards the political pendulum swung from the Conservatives to the Liberals, from civilian to military rule, and from democracy to dictatorship. By 1948 some stability was achieved and eight years of Liberal government ensued. In 1956, Dr Camilo Ponce became the first Conservative president for 60 years. Four years later a Liberal, Dr José Maria Velasco (president 1933–35, 1944–47, and 1952–56), was re-elected. He was deposed 1961 by the vice president, who was himself replaced by a military junta the following year. In 1968 Velasco returned from exile and took up the presidency again. Another coup 1972 put the military back in power until, in 1978, when it seemed as if Ecuador had returned permanently to its pre-1948 political pattern, a new, democratic constitution was adopted.

The 1978 constitution has survived, though economic deterioration has caused strikes, demonstrations and, in 1982, a state of emergency. In the 1984 elections there was no clear majority in the national congress, and the Conservative León Febres Cordero became president on a promise of 'bread, roofs, and jobs'. With no immediate support in congress, his policies seemed likely to be blocked but in 1985 he won a majority when five opposition members shifted their allegiance to him.

ecumenical council (Greek *oikoumenikos* 'of the whole world') a meeting of church leaders to determine Christian doctrine; their results are binding on all church members. Seven such councils are accepted as ecumenical by both Eastern and Western churches, while the Roman Catholic Church accepts a further 14 as ecumenical.

ecumenical movement movement for reunification of the various branches of the Christian church. It began in the 19th century with the extension of missionary work to the Third World, where the divisions created in Europe were incomprehensible, and gathered momentum from the need for unity in the face of growing secularism in Christian countries and of the challenge of such faiths as Islam. The *World Council of Churches* was founded 1948.

ecumenical patriarch the head of the Eastern Orthodox Church, the patriarch of Istanbul (Constantinople). The Bishop of Constantinople was recognized as having equal rights with the

Ecuador *Once an active volcano, the snow-capped peak of Mt Chimborazo rises to a height of 6,310 m/20,561 ft in the Cordillera Real of the South American Andes. It is the highest mountain in Ecuador.*

Ecuador
Republic of
(República del Ecuador)

area 270,670 sq km/104,479 sq mi
capital Quito
towns Cuenca; chief port Guayaquil
physical Andes mountains, divided by a central plateau, or Valley of the Volcanoes, including Chimborazo and Cotopaxi, which has a large share of the cultivable land and is the site of the capital
features the untouched rainforest of the Amazon basin has a wealth of wildlife; Ecuador is crossed by the equator, from which it derives its name; Galapagos Islands
head of state and government Rodrigo Borja Cevallos from 1988
political system emergent democracy
political parties Progressive Democratic Front coalition, left-of-centre (composed of six individual parties); Concentration of Popular Forces (CFP), right-of-centre; Social Christian Party (PSC), right-wing; Conservative Party (PC), right-wing; and others
exports bananas, cocoa, coffee, sugar, rice, balsa wood, fish
currency sucre (1,186.06 = £1 Feb 1990, official rate)
population (1986) 9,640,000; annual growth rate 2.9%
life expectancy men 62, women 66
language Spanish (official); Quechuan, Jivaroan
religion Roman Catholic
literacy 85% male/80% female (1985 est)
GNP $11.6 bn (1983); $1,428 per head of population
chronology
1830 Ecuador became an independent republic.
1930–48 Great political instability.
1948–55 Liberals in power.
1956 First Conservative president for 60 years.
1960 Liberals returned, with José Velasco as president.
1961 Velasco deposed and replaced by the vice-president.
1963 Military junta installed.
1968 Velasco returned as president.
1972 A coup put the military back in power.
1978 New democratic constitution adopted.
1979 Liberals in power but opposed by right- and left-wing parties.
1982 Deteriorating economy provoked strikes, demonstrations and a state of emergency.
1983 Austerity measures introduced.
1985 No party with a clear majority in the national congress. Febres Cordero narrowly won the presidency for the Conservatives.
1988 Roderigo Borja elected president for moderate left-wing coalition.
1989 Guerrilla left-wing group, *Alfaro Vive, Carajo* ('Alfaro lives, Dammit'), numbering about 1,000, lays down arms after 9 years.

Eddy *US founder of the Christian Science movement, Mary Baker Eddy. Her faith was based on the idea of divine healing.*

Bishop of Rome 451, and first termed 'patriarch' in the 6th century. The office survives today but with only limited authority, mainly confined to the Greek and Turkish Orthodox churches.

eczema an inflammatory skin condition marked by dryness, rashes, and itching, the formation of blisters, and the exudation of fluid. It may be allergic in origin, and is sometimes complicated by infection.

Edam /ˈiːdæm/ town in the Netherlands on the river Ij, North Holland province, population (1987) 24,200. It is famous for its round cheeses covered in red wax.

Edda name given to two collections of early Icelandic literature, which together constitute the chief source for Old Norse mythology. The term strictly applies to the ***Younger*** or ***Prose Edda***, compiled by Snorri Sturluson, a priest, about 1230.

The ***Elder*** or ***Poetic Edda*** is the name given to a collection of poems, discovered by Brynjólfr Sveinsson about 1643, and written by unknown Norwegian poets of the 9th to 12th centuries.

Eddery /ˈedəri/ Patrick (Pat) 1952– . Irish-born flat racing jockey who has won the jockey's championship seven times including four in succession.

He has won all the major races, including the Epsom Derby twice. He won the Prix de L'Arc de Triomphe four times, including three in succession 1985–87.

Eddington /ˈedɪŋtən/ Arthur Stanley 1882–1944. British astrophysicist, who studied the motions and equilibrium of stars, their luminosity and atomic structure, and became a leading exponent of Einstein's relativity theory. In 1919 his observation of stars during an ◊eclipse confirmed Einstein's prediction that light is bent when passing near the Sun. In *Expanding Universe* 1933 he expressed the theory that in the spherical universe the outer galaxies or spiral nebulae are receding from one another.

Eddy /ˈedi/ Mary Baker 1821–1910. US founder of the Christian Science movement. Her faith in divine healing was confirmed by her recovery from injuries caused by a fall 1866, and she based a religious sect on this belief, set out in her pamphlet *Science and Health with Key to the Scriptures* 1875.

She was born in New Hampshire and brought up as a Congregationalist. Her pamphlet *Science of Man* 1869 was followed by *Science and Health*, which she constantly revised. In 1876 she founded the Christian Science Association. In 1879 the Church of Christ, Scientist, was established, and although living in retirement after 1892 she continued to direct the activities of the movement until her death.

eddy current an electric current induced, in accordance with ◊Faraday's laws, in a conductor sited in a changing magnetic field. Eddy currents can cause much wasted energy in the cores of transformers and other electrical machines.

Eddystone Rocks /ˈedɪstən/ rocks in the English Channel, 23 km/14 mi S of Plymouth. The lighthouse, built in 1882, is the fourth on this exposed site.

Edelman /ˈedlmən/ Gerald 1929– . US biochemist. The structure of the antibody gamma globulin (IgG) was worked out by Rodney ◊Porter by 1962. Edelman tackled the related problem of working out the sequence of 1330 amino acids which composed the antibody. The task was completed by 1969 and won for Edelman a share of the 1972 Nobel Physiology or Medicine Prize with Porter.

edelweiss perennial alpine plant *Leontopodium alpinum*, family Compositae, with a white woolly star-shaped flower, found in Eurasia and the Andes.

Eden in the Old Testament book of Genesis and in the Koran, the 'garden' in which Adam and Eve were placed after their creation, and from which they were expelled for disobedience.

Eden /ˈiːdn/ river in Cumbria, NW England; length 104 km/65 mi. From its source in the Pennines, it flows NW to enter the Solway Firth NW of Carlisle.

Eden /ˈiːdn/ Anthony, 1st Earl of Avon 1897–1977. British Conservative politician, foreign secretary 1935–38, 1940–45, and 1951–55; prime minister 1955–57, when he resigned after the failure of the Anglo-French military intervention in the ◊Suez Crisis.

Upset by his prime minister's rejection of a peace plan secretly proposed by Roosevelt in Jan 1938, Eden resigned as foreign secretary in Feb 1938 in protest against Chamberlain's decision to open conversations with the Fascist dictator Mussolini, but was foreign secretary again in the wartime coalition formed Dec 1940 and in the Conservative government elected 1951. With the Soviets, he negotiated an interim peace in Vietnam 1954. In Apr 1955 he succeeded Churchill as prime minister. His use of force in the Suez Crisis led to his resignation in Jan 1957, but he continued to maintain that his action was justified.

Edgar /ˈedgə/ c.1050–c.1130. English prince, born in Hungary, known as the ***Atheling*** ('of royal blood'). Grandson of Edmund Ironside, he was supplanted as heir to Edward the Confessor by William the Conqueror. He led two rebellions against William 1068 and 1069, but made peace 1074.

Eden *British politician and prime minister, Anthony Eden.*

Edgar the Peaceful /ˈedgə/ 944–975. King of all England from 959. He was the younger son of Edmund I, and strove successfully to unite English and Danes as fellow subjects.

Edgehill, Battle of /ˌedʒˈhɪl/ the first battle of the English Civil War. It took place 1642, on a ridge in S Warwickshire, between Royalists under Charles I and Parliamentarians under the Earl of Essex. The result was indecisive.

Edgeworth /ˈedʒwɜːθ/ Maria 1767–1849. Irish novelist. Her first novel, *Castle Rackrent* 1800, dealt with Anglo-Irish country society, and was followed by the similar *The Absentee* 1812 and *Ormond* 1817.

Edinburgh /ˈedɪnbərə/ capital of Scotland and administrative centre of the region of Lothian, near the S shores of the Firth of Forth; population (1985) 440,000. A cultural centre, it is known for its annual festival of music and the arts; the university was established 1583. Industries include printing, publishing, banking, insurance, chemical manufactures, distilling, brewing, and some shipbuilding.

history In Roman times the site was occupied by Celtic peoples, and about 617 was captured by Edwin of Northumbria, from whom the town took its name. The early settlement grew up round a castle on Castle Rock, while about a mile to the east another burgh, Canongate, developed round the abbey of Holyrood, founded 1128 by David I. It remained separate from Edinburgh until 1856. Robert Bruce made Edinburgh a burgh 1329, and established its port at Leith. In 1544 the town was destroyed by the English. After the union with England 1707, Edinburgh lost its political importance, but remained culturally pre-eminent. The university has a famous medical school and the Koestler chair of parapsychology (instituted 1985), the only such professorship in the UK. The Heriot-Watt University (established 1885; university status 1966) is mainly a technical institution. *Edinburgh castle* contains the 12th-century St Margaret's chapel, the oldest building in Edinburgh. The palace of Holyrood House was built in the 15th and 16th centuries on the site of a 12th-century abbey; it is the British sovereign's official Scottish residence. ◊Rizzio was murdered here 1566, in the apartments of Mary Queen of Scots. The *Parliament House*, begun 1632, is now the seat of the supreme courts. The episcopal cathedral of St Mary, opened 1879, and St Giles parish church (mostly 15th-century) are the principal churches. The Royal Observatory has been at Blackford Hill since 1896. The two best known thoroughfares are Princes Street and the Royal Mile. Development of the area known as New Town was started 1767.

Edirne /eˈdɪəneɪ/ town in European Turkey, on the Maritza, about 225 km/140 mi NW of Istanbul; population (1985) 86,700. Founded on the site of ancient Uscadama, it was formerly known as Adrianople, named after the Emperor Hadrian c.125 AD.

Edison /ˈedɪsən/ Thomas Alva 1847–1931. US scientist and inventor. Born in Ohio, of Dutch-Scottish parentage, he became first a newsboy and then a telegraph operator. His first invention was an automatic repeater for telegraphic messages. Later came the carbon transmitter (used

Edison Pioneering scientist and inventor, Thomas Edison. His many inventions included the dictating machine with which he is photographed.

as a microphone in the production of the Bell telephone), the phonograph, the electric filament lamp, a new type of storage battery, and the kinetoscopic camera, an early film camera. He also anticipated the Fleming thermionic valve. He supported direct current (DC) transmission, but alternating current (AC) was eventually found to be more efficient and economical.

Edmonton /ˈedməntən/ locality, once a town, part of the London borough of Enfield. John Keats lived at Edmonton, and Charles Lamb lived and died here. The Bell Inn is referred to in William Cowper's poem *John Gilpin*.

Edmonton /ˈedməntən/ capital of Alberta, Canada, on the North Saskatchewan river; population (1986) 785,000. It is the centre of an oil and mining area to the north, and also an agricultural and dairying region. Petroleum pipelines link Edmonton with Superior, Wisconsin, USA, and Vancouver, British Columbia.

Edmund Ironside /ˈaɪənsaɪd/ c. 989–1016. King of England, the son of Ethelred the Unready. He led the resistance to ◊Canute's invasion 1015, and on Ethelred's death 1016 was chosen as king by the citizens of London, while the Witan (the king's council) elected Canute. Edmund was defeated by Canute at Assandun (Ashington), Essex, and they divided the kingdom between them.

Edmund, St /ˈedmənd/ c. 840–870. King of East Anglia from 855. In 870 he was defeated and captured by the Danes at Hoxne, Suffolk, and martyred on refusing to renounce Christianity. He was canonized and his shrine at Bury St Edmunds became a place of pilgrimage.

Edom /ˈiːdəm/ in the Old Testament, a mountainous area of S Palestine, which stretched from the Dead Sea to the Gulf of Aqaba. Its people, supposedly descendants of Esau, were enemies of the Israelites.

Edric the Forester /ˈedrɪtʃ/ or *Edric the Wild* (lived 11th century) an English chieftain on the Welsh border who revolted against William the Conqueror in 1067, around what is today Herefordshire, burning Shrewsbury. He was subsequently reconciled with William, and fought with him against the Scots in 1072.

education the process, beginning at birth, of developing intellectual capacity, manual skill, and social awareness, especially by giving instruction. In its more restricted sense, the term refers to the process of imparting literacy, numeracy, and a generally accepted body of knowledge.

history of education The earliest-known European educational systems are those of ancient Greece—in Sparta devoted mainly to the development of military skills and in Athens to politics, philosophy, and public speaking, but both accorded only to the privileged few.

In ancient China, formalized education received a decisive impetus from the imperial decree of 165 BC, which set up open competitive examinations for the recruitment of members of the civil service, based mainly on a detailed study of literature.

Rome adopted the Greek system of education, and spread it through western Europe. Following the disintegration of the Roman

education

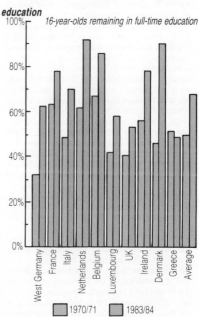

16-year-olds remaining in full-time education

(Bar chart with y-axis from 0% to 100%. Categories: West Germany, France, Italy, Netherlands, Belgium, Luxembourg, UK, Ireland, Denmark, Greece, Average. Legend: 1970/71, 1983/84)

education

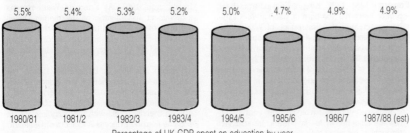

5.5%	5.4%	5.3%	5.2%	5.0%	4.7%	4.9%	4.9%
1980/81	1981/2	1982/3	1983/4	1984/5	1985/6	1986/7	1987/88 (est)

Percentage of UK GDP spent on education by year

Empire, widespread education vanished from Europe, though monks preserved both learning and the Latin tongue. Charlemagne's monastic schools which taught the 'seven liberal arts'—grammar, logic, rhetoric, arithmetic, geometry, music, and astronomy—produced the theological philosophers of the Scholastic Movement, which in the 11th–13th centuries led to the foundation of the universities of Paris (◊Sorbonne), Bologna, Padua, ◊Oxford and ◊Cambridge. The capture of Constantinople by the Turks in 1453 sent the Christian scholars who had congregated there into exile across Europe, and revived European interest in learning.

Compulsory attendance at primary schools was first established in the mid-18th century in Prussia, and has since spread almost worldwide. Compulsory schooling in industrialized countries is typically from around age 6 to around age 15; public education expenditure is typically around 5% of GNP (Spain 3.2%, Japan 4.4%, Denmark 7.7%).

UK education It was not until the 19th century in England that attempts were made to spread literacy throughout society. The Factory Act of 1802 required that during the first four years of their apprenticeship children employed by the owners of the newly arising factories were taught reading, writing, and arithmetic. The requirement was not always observed, but it embodied a new principle. The British and Foreign Schools Society (1808) and the National Society for Promoting the Education of the Poor in the Principles of the Established Church (1811) set up schools in which basic literacy and numeracy as well as religious knowledge were taught. In 1862, government grants became available for the first time for schools attended by children up to 12. The Elementary Education Act 1870 (Forster's Act) established district school boards all over the country whose duty was to provide facilities for the elementary education of all children not otherwise receiving it.

Once the principle of elementary education for all was established, the idea of widely available higher education began to be accepted. The Education Act of 1944 introduced a system of secondary education for all, and formed the foundation of much education policy today. This has been revised by two further acts in 1980, which repealed 1976 legislation enforcing ◊comprehensive reorganization, and gave new rights to parents; by the 1981 Education Act which made new provisions for the education of children with special needs, and by legislation in 1986 giving further powers to school governors as part of a move towards increased parental involvement in schools, and in 1987 on the remuneration of teachers. In 1988 a further act introduced a compulsory ◊national curriculum **in state schools**.

In the UK, the Department of Education and Science (DES), established in 1964 and headed by a Cabinet Minister, is responsible for non-military scientific research and for universities throughout Great Britain, and school education in England. In Wales, primary and secondary education is the responsibility of the Welsh Education Office. There is a Scottish Education Department, under the Secretary of State for Scotland, and until direct rule (1972), Northern Ireland had its own Ministry of Education. Local education authorities (LEAs) are education committees of county councils, responsible for providing educational services locally under the general oversight of the DES, but certain of their powers have been curtailed by the 1987 bill. In 1990 the Inner London Education Authority (ILEA) was abolished. In Northern Ireland, the responsibility for education is held by the Education and Library Boards.

US education In the USA, education is mainly the responsibility of the individual states, but the Department of Health, Education, and Welfare (1953), headed by a Secretary who is a member of the president's Cabinet, includes a

Edward the Confessor *A coin stamped with the head of the English King Edward the Confessor. His death in 1066 triggered off the events leading to the Norman conquest; William the Conqueror claimed the English throne had been bequeathed him by Edward.*

commissioner of education responsible for federal aspects. Education is normally divided into (optionally) nursery or kindergarten (to age 5), elementary or grammar school (6 to 11), junior high school (12 to 14), and high school (15 to 18). The basic school-leaving qualification is the high school diploma, normally awarded by the individual school or local school district on successful completion of a broad secondary school curriculum. There is no national school-leaving examination, although there is a national examination used to help select students for college (university) entrance, the Scholastic Aptitude Test (SAT). A large proportion of US high-school graduates goes on to higher education, either at a state-funded or private college or university.

educational psychology the work of psychologists primarily in schools, including the assessment of children with achievement problems and advising on problem behaviour in the classroom.

Edward /ˈedwəd/ the Black Prince 1330–1376. Prince of Wales, eldest son of Edward III of England. The epithet supposedly derived from his black armour. During the Hundred Years' War he fought at the Battle of Crécy 1346 and captured the French king at Poitiers 1356. In 1367 he invaded Castile and restored to the throne the deposed king, Pedro the Cruel (1334–69).

Edward /ˈedwəd/ (full name Edward Antony Richard Louis) 1964– . Prince of the UK, third son of Queen Elizabeth II. He is seventh in line to the throne after Charles, Charles' two sons, Andrew, and Andrew's two daughters.

Edward /ˈedwəd/ ten kings of England or the UK:

Edward I 1239–1307. King of England from 1272, son of Henry III. Edward led the royal forces in the ◊Barons' War 1264–67, and was on a crusade when he succeeded to the throne. He established English rule over all Wales 1282–84, and secured recognition of his overlordship from the Scottish king, though the Scots (under Wallace and Bruce) fiercely resisted actual conquest. In his reign Parliament took its approximate modern form with the ◊Model Parliament 1295. He was succeeded by his son, Edward II.

Edward II 1284–1327. King of England from 1307. Son of Edward I and born at Caernarvon Castle, he was created the first prince of Wales 1301. His invasion of Scotland 1314 to suppress revolt resulted in defeat at ◊Bannockburn. He was deposed 1327 by his wife Isabella (1292–1358), daughter of Philip IV of France, and her lover Roger de ◊Mortimer, and murdered in Berkeley Castle, Gloucestershire. He was succeeded by his son, Edward III.

Incompetent and frivolous, and entirely under the influence of his favourites, he struggled throughout his reign with discontented barons.

Edward VI *A portrait after Holbein painted about 1542 of Prince Edward. Only son of Henry VIII, he became King Edward VI at the age of ten, and died of tuberculosis before reaching adulthood.*

Edward III 1312–1377. King of England from 1327, son of Edward II. He assumed the government 1330 from his mother, through whom in 1337 he laid claim to the French throne and thus began the ◊Hundred Years' War. He was succeeded by Richard II.

Edward began his reign by attempting to force his rule on Scotland, winning a victory at Halidon Hill 1333. During the first stage of the Hundred Years' War, the English victories included the Battle of Crécy 1346 and the capture of Calais 1347. In 1360 Edward surrendered his claim to the French throne but the war resumed 1369.

Edward IV 1442–1483. King of England 1461–70 and from 1471. He was the son of Richard, Duke of York, and succeeded Henry VI in the ◊Wars of the Roses.

Edward was known as Earl of March until his accession. After his father's death he occupied London 1461, and was proclaimed king in place of Henry VI by a council of peers. His position was secured by the defeat of the Lancastrians at Towton 1461 and by the capture of Henry. He quarrelled, however, with Warwick, his strongest supporter, who in 1470–71 temporarily restored Henry, until Edward recovered the throne by his victories at Barnet and Tewkesbury. He was succeeded by his son Edward V.

Edward V 1470–1483. King of England 1483. Son of Edward IV, he was deposed three months after his accession in favour of his uncle (◊Richard III), and is traditionally believed to have been murdered (with his brother) in the Tower of London on Richard's orders.

Edward VI 1537–1553. King of England from 1547, son of Henry VIII and Jane Seymour. The government was entrusted to his uncle the Duke of Somerset (who fell 1549), and then to the Earl of Warwick, later created Duke of Northumberland. He was succeeded by his sister, Mary I.

Edward VII 1841–1910. King of Great Britain and Ireland from 1901. As Prince of Wales he was a prominent social figure, but his mother Queen Victoria considered him too frivolous to take part in political life. In 1860 he made the first tour of Canada and the USA ever undertaken by a British prince.

Edward was born at Buckingham Palace, the eldest son of Queen Victoria and Prince Albert. After his father's death 1861 he undertook many public duties, took a close interest in politics, and was on friendly terms with the party leaders. In 1863 he married Princess Alexandra of Denmark, by whom he had six children. He toured India

Edward VII *The Prince of Wales, as he was known until crowned, contemplates his prize, a wild bull shot by him during a visit to Chillingham Castle, Northumberland.*

1875–76. He succeeded to the throne 1901, and was crowned 1902. Although he overrated his political influence, he contributed to the Entente Cordiale 1904 with France and the Anglo-Russian agreement 1907.

Edward VIII 1894–1972. King of Great Britain and Northern Ireland Jan–Dec 1936, when he abdicated to marry Wallis Warfield ◊Simpson. He was created duke of Windsor and was governor of the Bahamas 1940–45, subsequently settling in France.

Eldest son of George V, he received the title of Prince of Wales 1910 and succeeded to the throne 20 Jan 1936. As king he showed concern for the problems of the Glasgow slums and the distressed areas of S Wales. In Nov 1936 a constitutional crisis arose when Edward wished to marry Mrs Simpson; it was felt that, as a divorcee, she would be unacceptable as queen. On 11 Dec Edward abdicated and left for France, where the couple were married 1937. Papers found 1987 revealed he offered to accept the presidency of a British socialist state. He was succeeded by his brother, George VI.

Edward, Lake /'edwəd/ lake in Uganda, area 2,150 sq km/830 sq mi, at about 900 m/3,000 ft above sea level in the Albertine rift valley. From 1973 to 1979 it was known as Lake Idi Amin Dada, after President Amin of Uganda.

Edward VIII *The Duke and Duchess of Windsor in a Sussex village, Sept 1939.*

Edwards /'edwədz/ Blake. Adopted name of William Blake McEdwards 1922– . US film director and writer, formerly an actor. Specializing in comedies, he directed the series of *Pink Panther* films (1963–1978), starring Peter Sellers. His other work includes *Breakfast at Tiffany's* 1961 and *Blind Date* 1986.

Edwards /'edwədz/ Gareth 1947– . Welsh rugby union player. He was appointed captain of his country when only 20 years old.

He appeared in seven championship winning teams, five Triple Crown winning teams, and two Grand Slam winning teams. In 53 international matches he scored a record 20 tries. He toured with the British Lions three times.

Edwards /'edwədz/ George 1908– . British civil and military aircraft designer, associated with the Viking, Viscount, Valiant V-bomber, VC-10, and Concorde.

Edwards /'edwədz/ Jonathan 1703–1758. US theologian, who took a Calvinist view of predestination, and initiated a religious revival, the 'Great Awakening'; author of *The Freedom of the Will* (defending determinism) 1754.

Edwards Air Force Base military USAF centre in California, situated on a dry lake bed, often used as a landing site by the Space Shuttle.

Edward the Confessor /'edwəd/ *c.*1003–1066. King of England from 1042, the son of Ethelred II. He lived in Normandy until shortly before his accession. During his reign power was held by Earl ◊Godwin and his son ◊Harold, while the king devoted himself to religion. He was buried in Westminster Abbey, which he had rebuilt. He was canonized 1161.

Edward the Elder *c.* 870–924. King of the West Saxons. He succeeded his father ◊Alfred the Great 899. He reconquered SE England and the Midlands from the Danes, uniting Wessex and ◊Mercia with the help of his sister, Athelflad. By the time Edward died, his kingdom was the most powerful in the British Isles. He was succeeded by his son ◊Athelstan.

Edward the Martyr /'edwəd/ *c.* 963–978. King of England from 975. Son of King Edgar, he was murdered at Corfe Castle, Dorset, probably at his stepmother Aelfthryth's instigation (she wished to secure the crown for her son, Ethelred). He was canonized 1001.

Edwin /'edwɪn/ *c.* 585–633. King of Northumbria from 617. He captured and fortified Edinburgh, which was named after him, and was killed in battle with Penda of Mercia, 632.

EEC abbreviation for *European Economic Community;* see ◊European Community.

eel any species of fish of the order Anguilliformes. They are snake-like, with elongated dorsal and anal fins. The males can reach 60 cm/2 ft, and the females 120 cm/4 ft.

eel-grass also known as *tape grass* or *glass wrack*. Flowering plant of tidal mud flats *Zostera marina*, family Zosteraceae. It is one of the few flowering plants to adapt to marine conditions, being completely submerged at high tide.

efficiency the output of a machine (work done by the machine) divided by the input (work put into the machine), usually expressed as a percentage. Because of losses caused by friction, efficiency is always less than 100%, although it can approach this for electrical machines with no moving parts (such as a transformer).

Since the *mechanical advantage* or force ratio is the ratio of the load (the output force) to the effort (the input force), and the *velocity ratio* is the distance moved by the effort divided by the distance moved by the load, for certain machines the efficiency can also be defined as the mechanical advantage divided by the velocity ratio.

efflorescence the loss of water of crystallization from crystals on standing in air, resulting in a dry powdery surface.

EFTA abbreviation for ◊European Free Trade Association.

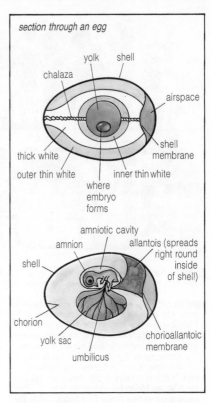

section through an egg

EFTPOS *E*lectronic *F*unds *T*ransfer at *P*oint *Of Sale* the transfer of funds from one bank account to another by electronic means. For example, a bank customer inserts a plastic card in a point-of-sale computer terminal in a supermarket, and telephone lines are used to make an automatic debit from the customer's bank account to settle the bill. See also ◊credit card.

e. g. abbreviation for *exempli gratia* (Latin 'for the sake of example').

Egbert /'egbɜ:t/ King of the West Saxons from 802, the son of Ealhmund, an under-king of Kent. By 829 he had united England for the first time under one king.

Egerton family name of Dukes of Sutherland; seated at Mertoun, Roxburghshire, Scotland.

egg in animals, the ovum, or female ◊gamete (reproductive cell). After fertilization by a sperm cell, it begins to divide to form an embryo. Eggs may be deposited by the female (◊oviparity) or they may develop within her body (◊viviparity and ◊ovoviviparity). In the oviparous reptiles and birds, the egg is protected by a shell, and well supplied with nutrients in the form of yolk. In plants, the ovum is called an egg-cell.

eggplant another name for ◊aubergine.

Egmont, Mount /'egmɒnt/ (Maori *Taranaki*) symmetrical extinct volcano in North Island, New Zealand; situated S of New Plymouth; 2,517 m/8,260 ft high.

Egmont /'egmɒnt/ Lamoral, Count of Egmont 1522–1568. Flemish nobleman, born in Hainault. As a servant of the Spanish crown, he defeated the French at St Quentin 1557 and Gravelines 1558, and became stadholder (chief magistrate) of Flanders and Artois. From 1561 he helped to lead the movement against Spanish misrule, but in 1567 the Duke of Alva was sent to crush the Resistance, and Egmont was beheaded.

ego (Latin 'I') in psychology, a general term for the processes concerned with the self and a person's conception of himself or herself, encompassing values and attitudes. In Freudian psychology, the term refers specifically to the element of the human mind that represents the conscious processes, concerned with reality, in conflict with the ◊id and the ◊superego.

Egypt The Banquet, *a fragment of wall painting, is in the British Museum, London. Dating from c. 1400 BC, it comes from the ancient Egyptian city of Thebes and shows two rows of guests waited on by serving girls.*

egret type of heron with long feathers on the head or neck. The ***great white egret*** *Egretta alba* of SE Europe and other parts of the Old World, which grows to a length of 1 m/3 ft, develops snowy-white plumes, formerly used for hat ornaments. The ***little egret*** *Egretta garzetta*, 0.6 m/2 ft, is found in Asia, Africa, S Europe and Australia.

Egypt /'iːdʒɪpt/ country in NE Africa, bounded to the N by the Mediterranean, to the E by the Suez Canal and Red Sea, to the S by Sudan, and to the W by Libya.

government The 1971 constitution provides for a single-chamber people's assembly of 458, ten nominated by the president and 448 elected for a five-year term by 48 constituencies. The president is nominated by the assembly and then elected by popular referendum for a six-year term, and is eligible for re-election. At least one vice president and a council of ministers are appointed by the president. There is also a 210-member consultative council (*Shura*), with advisory powers.

history For early history see ◊Egypt, ancient. After its conquest by ◊Augustus 30 BC Egypt passed under the rule of Roman, and later of Byzantine, governors, and Christianity superseded the ancient religion. The Arabs conquered Egypt 639–42, introducing ◊Islam and ◊Arabic to the area, and the country was ruled by successive Arab dynasties until 1250, when the ◊Mamelukes seized power. Mameluke rule lasted until 1517, when Egypt became part of the Turkish ◊Ottoman Empire.

Contact with Europe began with Napoleon's invasion and the French occupation 1798–1801. A period of anarchy followed, until in 1805 an Albanian officer, Mehemet Ali, was appointed pasha, a title which later became hereditary in his family. Under his successors Egypt met with economic difficulties over the building of the ◊Suez Canal (1859–69), to the extent that an Anglo-French commission was placed in charge of its finances. After subduing a nationalist revolt 1881–82, Britain occupied Egypt, and the government was from then on mainly in the hands of British civilian agents who directed their efforts particularly to the improvement of the Egyptian economy. On the outbreak of World War I 1914, nominal Turkish suzerainty was abolished and the country was declared a British protectorate.

Post-war agitation by the nationalist Wafd party led to the granting of nominal independence 1922, under King Fuad I. He was succeeded by King Farouk 1936, and Britain agreed to recognize Egypt's full independence, announcing a phased withdrawal of its forces, except from the Suez Canal, Alexandria, and Port Said, where it had

naval bases. The start of World War II delayed the British departure, as did the consequent campaign in Libya which ended in the defeat of the German and Italian forces which had threatened the Canal Zone.

In 1946 all British troops except the Suez Canal garrison were withdrawn. In the immediate post-war years a radical movement developed, calling for an end to the British presence and opposing Farouk for his extravagant life style and his failure to prevent the growth of ◊Israel. This led, in 1952, to a bloodless coup by a group of army officers, led by Col Gamal ◊Nasser, who replaced Farouk with a military junta. The 1923 constitution was suspended and all political parties banned. The following year Egypt declared itself a republic, with Gen Mohammed Neguib as president and prime minister. In 1954 Nasser became prime minister and an agreement was signed for the withdrawal of British troops from the Canal Zone by 1956.

After a dispute with Neguib, Nasser took over as head of state and embarked on a programme of social reform. He became a major force for the creation of Arab unity. In 1956 the presidency was strengthened by a new constitution, and Nasser was elected president, unopposed. Later that year, British forces were withdrawn, in accordance with the 1954 agreement.

When the USA and Britain cancelled their offers of financial aid for the ◊Aswan High Dam, Nasser responded by nationalizing the Suez Canal. In a contrived operation, Britain, France, and Israel invaded the Sinai Peninsula and two days later Egypt was attacked. US pressure brought a cease-fire and an Anglo-French withdrawal. The effect of the abortive Anglo-French operation was to push Egypt towards the USSR and to enhance Nasser's reputation in the Arab world.

In 1958 Egypt and Syria merged to become the United Arab Republic (UAR), with Nasser as president, but three years later Syria withdrew, though Egypt retained the title of UAR until 1971. The 1960s saw several unsuccessful attempts to federate Egypt, Syria, and Iraq. Despite these failures Nasser's prestige among his neighbours grew, while at home, in 1962, he founded the Arab Socialist Union (ASU), as Egypt's only recognized political organization.

In 1967 Egypt led an attack on Israel which developed into the 'Six Day War', in which Israel defeated all its opponents, including Egypt. One result of the conflict was the blocking of the Suez Canal, which was not reopened until 1975. After Egypt's defeat, Nasser offered to resign but was persuaded to stay on. In 1969, aged 52, he died of a heart attack and was succeeded by Vice President Col Anwar ◊Sadat.

In 1971 a new constitution was approved and the title Arab Republic of Egypt adopted. Sadat continued Nasser's policy of promoting Arab unity but proposals to create a federation of Egypt, Libya, and Syria again failed.

In 1973 an attempt was made to regain territory from Israel. After 18 days' fighting, US Secretary of State Henry ◊Kissinger arranged a cease-fire, resulting in Israel's evacuation of parts of Sinai, with a UN buffer zone separating the rival armies. This US intervention strengthened ties between the two countries while relations with the USSR cooled.

In 1977 Sadat went to Israel to address the Israeli parliament and plead for peace. Other Arab states were dismayed by this move and diplomatic relations with Syria, Libya, Algeria, and the Yemen, as well as the Palestine Liberation Organisation (PLO), were severed. Despite this opposition, Sadat pursued his peace initiative and at the ◊Camp David talks in the USA, he and the Israeli prime minister, Menachem ◊Begin, signed two agreements. The first laid a framework for peace in the Middle East and the second a framework for a treaty between the two countries. In 1979 a treaty was signed and Israel began a phased withdrawal from Sinai. Egypt was, in consequence, expelled from the Arab League.

After acceding to the presidency, Sadat had begun to introduce a more liberal regime. In 1981 he was assassinated by a group of Muslim fundamentalists who opposed him. and was succeeded by Lieut-Gen Hosni Mubarak, who had been vice-president since 1975.

Just as Sadat had continued the policies of his predecessor, so did Mubarak. In the 1984 elections the National Democratic Party, formed by Sadat 1948, won an overwhelming victory in the assembly, strengthening Mubarak's position. Although Egypt's treaty with Israel remains intact, relations between the two countries have been strained, mainly because of Israel's activities in Lebanon and Palestine. Egypt's relations with other Arab nations have improved and only Libya maintains its trade boycott; the restoration of diplomatic relations with Syria in 1989 paved the way for Egypt's resumption of its leadership of the Arab world. At home, problems with Muslim fundamentalists have increased Mubarak's dependence on military support. President Mubarak

Egypt, ancient *Egyptian mask from the Ptolemaic period, 3rd–2nd centuries BC.*

Egypt
Arab Republic of
(Jumhuriyat Misr al-Arabiya)

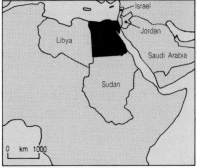

area 1,002,000 sq km/386,772 sq mi
capital Cairo
towns Gîza; ports Alexandria, Port Said
physical mostly desert; hills in E; fertile land along river Nile; the cultivated and settled area is about 35,500 sq km/13,700 sq mi
features Aswan High Dam and Lake Nasser; Sinai; remains of Ancient Egypt (Pyramids, Sphinx, Luxor, Karnak, Abu Simbel, El Faiyum)
head of state and government Hosni Mubarak from 1981
political system democratic republic
political parties National Democratic Party (NDP), moderate left-of-centre; Socialist Labour Party, right-of-centre; Socialist Liberal Party, free-enterprise; New Wafd Party, nationalist
exports cotton and textiles
currency Egyptian pound (4.45 = £1 Feb 1990)
population (1987) 49,280,000; annual growth rate 2.4%
life expectancy men 57, women 60
language Arabic (ancient Egyptian survives to some extent in Coptic)
religion Sunni Muslim 95%, Coptic Christian 5%
literacy 59% male/30% female (1985 est)
GDP $32 bn (1983); $686 per head of population

chronology
1914 Egypt became a British protectorate.
1936 Independence recognized. King Fuad succeeded by his son Farouk.
1946 Withdrawal of British troops except from Suez Canal Zone.
1952 Farouk overthrown by the army in a bloodless coup.
1953 Egypt declared a republic, with Gen Neguib as president.
1956 Neguib replaced by Col Gamal Nasser. Nasser announced nationalization of Suez Canal; Egypt attacked by Britain, France and Israel. Ceasefire agreed because of US intervention.
1958 Short-lived merger of Egypt and Syria as United Arab Republic (UAR). Subsequent attempts to federate Egypt, Syria, and Iraq failed.
1967 Six-Day War with Israel ended in Egypt's defeat and Israeli occupation of Sinai and the Gaza strip.
1970 Nasser died suddenly and was succeeded by Anwar Sadat.
1973 Attempt to regain territory lost to Israel led to fighting. Ceasefire arranged by US secretary of state Henry Kissinger.
1977 Visit by Sadat to Israel to address the Israeli parliament was criticized by Egypt's Arab neighbours.
1978–79 Camp David talks in the USA resulted in a treaty between Egypt and Israel. Egypt expelled from the Arab League.
1981 Sadat assassinated and succeeded by Hosni Mubarak.
1983 Improved relations between Egypt and the Arab world; only Libya and Syria maintained a trade boycott.
1984 Mubarak's party victorious in the people's assembly elections.
1987 Mubarak re-elected. Egypt readmitted to Arab League.
1988 Full diplomatic relations with Algeria restored.
1989 Improved relations with Libya; diplomatic relations with Syria restored.

deity of Thebes, **Ammon**, came to be regarded as supreme, a reflection of rediscovered national unity. Ikhnaton attempted, without success, to establish the monotheistic cult of **Aton**, the solar disc, as the one national god.

Egyptology the study of ancient Egypt. Interest in the subject was aroused by the discovery of the ◊Rosetta Stone 1799. Excavations continued throughout the 19th century, and gradually assumed a more scientific character, largely as a result of the work of Flinders ◊Petrie from 1880 onwards and the formation of the Egyptian Exploration Fund 1892. In 1922 the British archaeologist Howard Carter discovered the tomb of Tutankhamen, the only royal tomb with all its treasures intact.

Ehrlich /'eəlɪk/ Paul 1854–1915. German bacteriologist and immunologist, who developed the first cure for syphilis. He developed the arsenic compounds, in particular salvarsan, used in the treatment of syphilis before the discovery of antibiotics. Nobel prize 1908.

Eichendorff /'aɪkəndɔːf/ Joseph Freiherr von 1788–1857. German lyric poet and romantic novelist, born in Upper Silesia. His work was set to music by Schumann, Mendelssohn, and Wolf. He held various judicial posts.

Eichmann /'aɪkmən/ (Karl) Adolf 1906–1962. Austrian Nazi. As an ◊SS official during Hitler's regime he was responsible for atrocities against Jews and others, including the implementation of genocide. He managed to escape at the fall of Germany 1945, but was discovered in Argentina 1960, abducted by Israeli agents, tried in Israel 1961, and executed.

eider large marine duck *Somateria mollissima*, highly valued for its soft down which is used in quilts and cushions for warmth. It is found on the coasts of the Atlantic and Pacific Oceans.

Eid ul-Adha Muslim festival which takes place during the *hajj*, or pilgrimage to Mecca, and commemorates Abraham's willingness to sacrifice his son ◊Ishmael at the command of Allah.

Eid ul-Fitr Muslim festival celebrating the end of Ramadan, the month of fasting.

Eiffel /'aɪfəl/ Gustave Alexandre 1832–1923. French engineer who constructed the Eiffel Tower for the 1889 Paris exhibition. He set up his own business in Paris and quickly established his reputation with the construction of a series of ambitious railway bridges of which the 525 ft span across the Duoro at Oporto, Portugal was the longest. In 1881 he provided the iron skeleton for the Statue of Liberty.

Eiffel Tower iron tower 320 m/1,050 ft high, designed by Gustave Eiffel for the Paris Exhibition 1889. It stands in the Champ de Mars, Paris.

Eiger /'aɪgə/ mountain peak in the Swiss ◊Alps.

Eighth Route Army the Chinese **Red Army**, formed 1927 when the communists broke away from the ◊Guomindang (nationalists) and established a separate government in Jiangxi in SE China. When Japan invaded China 1937 the Red Army was recognized as a section of the national forces under the name Eighth Route Army.

Eijkman /'aɪkmən/ Christiaan 1858–1930. Dutch bacteriologist, who identified vitamin B_1 deficiency as the cause of beri-beri, and pioneered the recognition of vitamins as essential to health. Nobel prize 1929.

Eilat alternative spelling of ◊Elat, a port in Israel.

Eindhoven /'aɪndhəʊvən/ town in North Brabant province, Netherlands, on the river Dommel; population (1988) 381,000. Industries include electrical and electronic equipment.

Einstein /'aɪnstaɪn/ Albert 1879–1955. German-Swiss physicist, who formulated the theories of ◊relativity, and did important work in radiation physics and thermodynamics. In 1905 he published the special theory of relativity, and in 1915 issued his general theory of relativity. His latest conception of the basic laws governing the universe was outlined in his unified field theory, made public 1953; and of the 'relativistic theory of the

---

was re-elected, by referendum, for a second term Oct 1987.

Egypt, ancient
5000 BC Egyptian culture already well established in the Nile Valley.
3200 Menes united Lower Egypt (the delta) with his own kingdom of Upper Egypt.
2800 ◊Imhotep built the step pyramid at Sakkara.
c. 2600 Old Kingdom reached the height of its power and the kings of the 4th dynasty built the pyramids at Gîza.
c. 2200–1800 Middle Kingdom, under which the unity lost towards the end of the Old Kingdom was restored.
1730 Invading Asiatic Hyksos people established their kingdom in the Nile Delta.
c. 1580 New Kingdom established by the 18th dynasty, following the eviction of the Hyksos, with its capital at Thebes. High point of ancient Egyptian civilization under pharaohs ◊Thothmes, ◊Amenhotep, ◊Ikhnaton (who moved the capital to Akhetaton), and ◊Tutankhamen.
c. 1321 19th dynasty: Ramses I built a temple at Karnak, Ramses II one at Abu Simbel.
1191 Ramses III defeated the Indo-European Sea Peoples, but after him there was decline, and power within the country passed from the pharaohs to the priests of Ammon.
1090–663 Late New Kingdom Egypt was often divided between two or more dynasties; the nobles became virtually independent.
8th–7th centuries Brief interlude of rule by kings from ◊Nubia.

666 The Assyrians under Ashurbanipal occupied Thebes.
663–609 Psammetichus I restored Egypt's independence and unity.
525 Egypt was conquered by ◊Cambyses, and became a Persian province.
c. 405–340 A period of independence.
332 Conquest by ◊Alexander the Great. On the division of his empire, Egypt went to one of his generals, Ptolemy I, and his descendants.
30 Death of ◊Cleopatra and conquest by the Roman emperor Augustus; Egypt became a province of the Roman and Byzantine empires.
AD 641 Conquest by the Arabs; the Christianity of later Roman rule was replaced by Islam.
For modern history, see ◊Egypt.

Egyptian art see under ◊ancient art.

Egyptian religion the worship of totemic animals believed to be the ancestors of the clan. Totems later developed into gods, represented as having animal heads. The cult of ◊Osiris was important. Immortality, conferred by the magical rite of mummification, was originally the sole prerogative of the king, but was extended under the New Kingdom to all who could afford it; they were buried with the ◊Book of the Dead.

The hawk was sacred to **Ra** and **Horus**, the ibis to **Thoth**, and the jackal to **Anubis**. The story of Osiris, who was murdered, mourned by his sister and wife Isis, and then rose again, was enacted in a fertility ritual similar to that of Tammuz; by a natural development Osiris became the god of the underworld. Under the 18th Dynasty a local

Einstein *Physicist Albert Einstein, 1944.*

non-symmetric field', completed 1955. Einstein wrote that this simplified the derivations as well as the form of the field equations and made the whole theory thereby more transparent, without changing its content.

Born at Ulm, in Württemberg, West Germany, he lived with his parents in Munich and then in Italy. After teaching at the polytechnic school at Zürich, he became a Swiss citizen and was appointed an inspector of patents in Berne. In his spare time, he took his PhD at Zürich. In 1909 he was given a chairmanship of theoretical physics at the university. After holding a similar post at Prague 1911, he returned to teach at Zürich 1912, and in 1913 took up a specially created post as director of the Kaiser Wilhelm Institute for Physics, Berlin. He received the Nobel Prize for Physics 1921. After being deprived of his post at Berlin by the Nazis, he emigrated to the USA 1933, and became professor of mathematics and a permanent member of the Institute for Advanced Study at Princeton, New Jersey. During World War II he worked for the US Navy Ordnance Bureau.

Einthoven /ˈaɪnthəʊvən/ Willem 1860–1927. Dutch physiologist, inventor of the electrocardiograph. He was able to show that particular disorders of the heart alter its electrical activity in characteristic ways.

Eire /ˈeərə/ Gaelic name for the Republic of ◊Ireland.

Eisenhower *US soldier and politician Dwight D Eisenhower. After commanding Allied forces in Europe during World War II, he became 34th President of the USA in 1952.*

Eisai /ˈeɪsaɪ/ 1141–1215. Japanese Buddhist monk who introduced Zen and tea from China to Japan and founded the ◊Rinzai school.

Eisenhower, Mount /ˈaɪzən.haʊə/ Rocky Mountain peak in Alberta, Canada, included in Banff National Park, 2,862 m/9,390 ft.

Eisenhower /ˈaɪzən.haʊə/ Dwight D(avid) ('Ike') 1890–1969. 34th president of the USA 1953–60, a Republican. A general in World War II, he commanded the Allied forces in Italy 1943, then the Allied invasion of Europe, and from Oct 1944 all the Allied armies in the West. As president he promoted business interests at home and conducted the Cold War abroad. His vice president was Richard Nixon.

Eisenhower was born in Texas. He became commander in chief of the US and British forces for the invasion of N Africa Nov 1942; commanded the Allied invasion of Sicily July 1943, and announced the surrender of Italy 8 Sept 1943. In Dec he became commander of the Allied Expeditionary Force. He resigned from the army 1952 to campaign for the presidency; he was elected, and re-elected 1956. A popular politician, Eisenhower held office during a period of domestic and international tension, with the growing civil rights movement at home and the Cold War dominating international politics.

Eisenstein /ˈaɪzənstaɪn/ Sergei Mikhailovich 1898–1948. Latvian film director. He pioneered the use of montage (a technique of deliberately juxtaposing shots to create a particular meaning) as a means of propaganda, as in *The Battleship Potemkin* 1925. His *Alexander Nevsky* 1938 was the first part of an uncompleted trilogy, the second part, *Ivan the Terrible* 1944, being banned in Russia.

eisteddfod /aɪˈsteðvɒd/ (Welsh 'sitting') traditional Welsh gathering for the encouragement of the bardic arts of music, poetry, and literature.

Towns and rural communities often hold their own annual eisteddfod. The national eisteddfod traditionally dates from pre-Christian times, but it was discontinued from the late 17th century until the beginning of the 19th century. Since then it has been held annually. The meetings last three to four days, and bardic degrees are awarded. The eisteddfod ends with the ceremony of 'chairing' the bard (the best contestant in verse).

ejector seat device for propelling an aircraft pilot to safety in an emergency, invented by the British engineer James Martin (1893–1981). The first seats of 1945 were powered by a compressed spring; later seats used an explosive charge. By the early 1980s 35,000 seats had been fitted worldwide, and the lives of 5,000 pilots saved by their use.

Ekaterinburg /e.kætəriːnˈbɜːg/ pre-revolutionary name of ◊Sverdlovsk, a town in the western USSR, the site of the assassination of Tsar Nikolai II and his family in 1918.

Ekaterinodar /e.kætəriːnəʊˈdɑː/ pre-revolutionary name of ◊Krasnodar, an important industrial town in the USSR.

Ekaterinoslav /e.kætəriːnəʊˈslɑːv/ pre-revolutionary name of ◊Dnepropetrovsk, centre of an industrial region in Ukraine, USSR.

Ekman spiral effect an application of the ◊Coriolis effect to ocean currents, whereby the currents flow at an angle to the winds that drive them. It derives its name from the Swedish oceanographer Vagn Ekman (1874–1954).

In the northern hemisphere, surface currents are deflected to the right of the wind direction. The surface current then drives the subsurface layer at an angle to its original deflection. Consequent subsurface layers are similarly affected, so that the effect decreases with increasing depth. The result is that most water is transported at about right angles to the wind direction. Directions are reversed in the southern hemisphere.

El Aaiún Arabic name of ◊La'Youn.

eland largest species of antelope, *Taurotragus oryx.* Pale fawn in colour, it is about 2 m/6 ft high, and

both sexes have spiral horns about 45 cm/18 in long. It is found in central and southern Africa.

elasticity in economics, the measure of response of one variable to changes in another. If the price of butter is reduced by 10% and the demand increases by 20%, the elasticity measure is 2. Such measures are used to test the effects of changes in prices, incomes, and supply and demand. Inelasticity may exist in the demand for necessities such as water, the demand for which will remain the same even if the price changes considerably.

elasticity in physics, the ability of a solid to recover its shape once deforming forces (stresses modifying its dimensions or shape) are removed. Metals are elastic up to a certain stress (the elastic limit), beyond which greater stress gives them a permanent deformation, as demonstrated by ◊Hooke's law.

Elat /eɪˈlɑːt/ port at the head of the Gulf of Aqaba, Israel's only outlet to the Red Sea; population (1982) 19,500. Founded in 1948, on the site of the Biblical Elath, it is linked by road with Beersheba. There are copper mines and granite quarries nearby, and a major geophysical observatory opened in 1968 is 16 km/10 mi to the N.

Elba /ˈelbə/ island in the Mediterranean, 10 km/6 mi off the W coast of Italy; population (1981) 35,000; area 223 sq km/86 sq mi. Iron ore is exported from the capital, Portoferraio, to the Italian mainland, and there is a fishing industry. The small uninhabited island of ***Monte Cristo*** 40 km/25 mi to the S, supplied the title of Alexandre Dumas' hero in *The Count of Monte Cristo*. Elba was Napoleon's place of exile 1814–15.

Elbe /elb/ one of the principal rivers of Germany, 1,166 km/725 mi long, rising on the S slopes of the Riesengebirge, Czechoslovakia, and flowing NW across the German plain to the North Sea.

Elberfeld /ˈelbəfeld/ West German industrial town, merged with ◊Wuppertal in 1929.

Elbing /ˈelbɪŋ/ German name for ◊Elbląg, a Polish port.

Elbląg /ˈelblɒŋk/ Polish port 11 km/7 mi from the mouth of the river Elbląg which flows into the Vistula Lagoon, an inlet of the Baltic; population (1983) 115,900. It has shipyards, engineering works, and car and tractor factories.

Elbruz /elˈbruːs/ or ***Elbrus*** highest mountain, 5,642 m/18,517 ft, on the continent of Europe, in the Caucasus, Georgian Republic, USSR.

Elburz /elˈbʊəz/ volcanic mountain range in NW Iran, close to the S shore of the Caspian Sea, rising in Mount Damavand to 5,670 m/18,602 ft.

Eldem /elˈdem/ Sedad Hakki 1908– . Turkish architect whose work is inspired by the spatial harmony and regular rhythms of the traditional Turkish house. These qualities are reinterpreted in modern forms with great sensitivity to context, as in the Social Security Agency Complex, Zeyrek, Istanbul (1962–64), and the Ataturk Library, Istanbul (1973).

elder small tree or shrub of the genus *Sambucus,* family Caprifoliaceae. The common elder *Sambucus nigra,* found in Europe, N Africa, and W Asia, has pinnate leaves, and heavy heads of small, sweet-scented, white flowers in early summer. These are succeeded by clusters of small, black berries. The scarlet-berried *Sambucus racemosa* is found in parts of Europe, Asia, and North America.

elder in the Presbyterian church, the lay members who assist the minister (or teaching elder) in running the church.

Eldon /ˈeldən/ John Scott, 1st Earl of Eldon 1751–1838. English politician, born in Newcastle. He became a Member of Parliament 1782, solicitor-general 1788, attorney-general 1793, and Lord Chancellor 1801–05 and 1807–27. During his period the rules of the Lord Chancellor's court governing the use of the injunction and precedent in ◊equity finally became fixed.

El Dorado /ˈel dəˈrɑːdəʊ/ fabled city of gold believed by 16th-century Spaniards and other Europeans to exist somewhere in the area of the Orinoco and Amazon rivers in South America.

Eleanor of Aquitaine /ˈelɪnər əv ˌækwɪˈteɪn/ c.1122–1204. Queen of France 1137–51 and of England from 1154. She was the daughter of William X, Duke of Aquitaine, and was married 1137–52 to Louis VII of France, but the marriage was annulled. The same year she married Henry of Anjou, who became king of England 1154. Henry imprisoned her 1174–89 for supporting their sons, the future Richard I and King John, in revolt against him.

Eleanor of Castile /ˈelɪnər əv kæsˈtiːl/ c.1245–1290. Queen of Edward I of England, the daughter of Ferdinand III of Castile. She married Prince Edward 1254, and accompanied him on his crusade 1270. She died at Harby, Nottinghamshire, and Edward erected stone crosses in towns where her body rested on the funeral journey to London. Several **Eleanor Crosses** are still standing, for example at Northampton.

elector (German **Kurfürst**) any of originally seven (later ten) princes of the Holy Roman Empire who had the prerogative of electing the emperor (in effect, the king of Germany). The electors were the archbishops of Mainz, Trier, and Cologne, the court palatine of the Rhine, the Duke of Saxony, the Margrave of Brandenburg, and the king of Bohemia (in force to 1806). Their constitutional status was formalized 1356 in the document known as the **Golden Bull**, which granted them extensive powers within their own domains, acting as judges, issuing coins, and imposing tolls.

electoral college the indirect system of voting for the president and vice president of the USA. The people of each state officially vote not for the presidential candidate, but for a list of electors nominated by each party. The whole electoral-college vote of the state then goes to the winning party (and candidate).

Each state has as many electors as it has senators and representatives in Congress, so that the electoral college numbers 538, and a majority of 270 electoral votes is needed to win. The system can lead to a presidential candidate being elected with a minority of the total vote over the whole country, and it has been proposed, for example by President Carter in 1977, to substitute a direct popular vote. A constitutional amendment to this effect failed in 1979, partly because minority groups argued that this would deprive them of their politically influential block vote in key states.

electoral system see ◊vote and ◊proportional representation.

Electra in ancient Greek legend, the daughter of Clytemnestra and Agamemnon, king of Mycenae, and sister of Iphigenia and Orestes.

Electra plays by Sophocles and Euripides, produced about 418–410 BC and 417 BC respectively. Both plays explore Electra's role in the complex family tragedy which involved the deaths of her sister Chrysothemis, her parents Agamemnon and Clytemnestra, and her brother Orestes.

electrical relay an electromagnetic relay.

electric arc a continuous electric discharge of high current between two electrodes, giving out a brilliant light and heat. The phenomenon is exploited in the carbon-arc lamp, once widely used in film projectors. In the electric-arc furnace an arc struck between huge carbon electrodes and the metal charge provides the heating. In arc ◊welding an electric arc provides the heat to fuse the metal. The discharges in low-pressure gases, as in neon and sodium lights, can also be broadly considered as electric arcs.

electric bell a bell that makes use of electromagnetism. At its heart is a wire-wound coil on an iron core (an electromagnet) which, when a direct current (from a battery) flows through it, attracts an iron ◊armature. The armature acts as a switch, whose movement causes contact

---

electricity generation and supply

coal-fired power station (highly simplified)

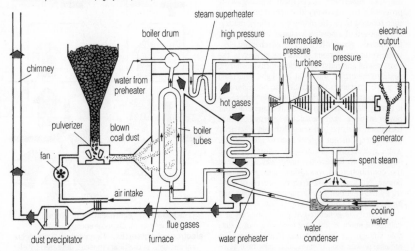

---

with an adjustable contact point to be broken, so breaking the circuit. A spring rapidly returns the armature to the contact point, once again closing the circuit, so bringing about the oscillation. The armature oscillates back and forth, and the clapper or hammer fixed to the armature strikes the bell.

electric charge property of some bodies that causes them to exert forces on each other. Two bodies both with positive or both with negative charges repel each other, whereas oppositely or 'unlike' charged bodies attract each other, since each is in the ◊**electric field** of the other. ◊Electrons possess a negative charge, and ◊protons an equal positive charge. The unit of electric charge is the **coulomb** (symbol C).

Atoms have no charge but can sometimes gain electrons to become negative **ions** or lose them to become positive ions. So-called ◊**static** electricity, seen in such phenomena as the charging of nylon shirts when they are pulled on or off, or in brushing hair, is in fact the gain or loss of electrons from the surface atoms. A flow of charge (such as electrons through a copper wire) constitutes an **electric current**; the flow of current is measured in **amperes**.

electric current rate of flow of electric charge. It is measured in amperes (coulombs per second).

electric energy in physics, the ◊energy of a body that is due to its position in an electric field (generated by an electric charge).

electric field in physics, a region in which an electric charge experiences a force owing to the presence of another electric charge. It is a type of electromagnetic field.

electric fish fish that have electricity-producing powers. The best-known example is the South American 'electric eel' *Electrophorus electricus*, in which the lateral tail muscles are modified to form electric organs capable of generating 650 volts; the current passing from tail to head is strong enough to stun another animal. Not all electric fish produce such strong discharges; most use weak electric fields to navigate and detect nearby objects.

electricity a general term used for all phenomena caused by ◊electric charge, whether static or in motion. Electric charge is caused by an excess or deficit of electrons in the charged substance, and an electric current by the movement of electrons around a circuit. Substances may be electrical **conductors**, such as metals, which allow the passage of electricity through them, or **insulators**, such as rubber, which are extremely poor conductors. Substances with intermediate conductivities are known as ◊**semiconductors**.

Electricity generated on a commercial scale was available from the early 1880s, and used

for electric motors driving all kinds of machinery; and for lighting, first by carbon arc, but later by incandescent filaments, first of carbon and then of tungsten, enclosed in glass bulbs partially filled with inert gas under vacuum. Light is also produced by passing electricity through a gas or metal vapour, or a fluorescent lamp. Other practical applications include telephone, radio, television, X-ray machines, and many other applications in ◊electronics.

The fact that amber has the power, after being rubbed, of attracting light objects, such as bits of straw and feathers, is said to have been known to Thales of Miletus and to the Roman naturalist Pliny. William Gilbert, Queen Elizabeth I's physician, found that many substances possessed this power, and he called it electric after the Greek word meaning amber.

In the early 1700s, it was recognized that there are two types of electricity; and that unlike kinds attract each other and like kinds repel. The charge on glass rubbed with silk came to be known as positive electricity, and the charge on amber rubbed with wool as negative electricity. These two charges were found to cancel each other when brought together.

In 1800, Volta found that a series of cells containing brine, in which were dipped plates of zinc and copper, gave an electric current, which later in the same year was shown to evolve hydrogen and oxygen when passed through water (◊electrolysis). Humphry Davy, in 1807, decomposed soda and potash (both thought to be elements) and isolated the metals sodium and potassium; a discovery that led the way to ◊electroplating. Other properties of electric currents discovered were the heating effect, now used in lighting and central heating, and the deflection of a magnetic needle, described by Oersted 1820 and elaborated by Ampère 1825. This work made possible the electric telegraph.

For Michael Faraday, the fact that an electric current passing through a wire caused a magnet to move suggested that moving a wire or coil of wire rapidly between the poles of a magnet would induce an electric current. He demonstrated this 1831, producing the first ◊dynamo, which became the basis of electrical engineering. The characteristics of currents were crystallized about 1827 by G S Ohm who showed that the current passing along a wire was equal to the electromotive force (emf) across the wire multiplied by a constant, which was the conductivity of the wire. The unit of resistance is named after Ohm, that of emf is named after Volta (volt), and that of current after Ampère (amp).

The work of the late 1800s indicated the wide interconnections of electricity (with magnetism, heat, and light), and about 1855 J C Maxwell formulated a single electromagnetic theory. The universal importance of electricity was decisively proved by the discovery that the atom, up until then thought to be the ultimate particle of matter, is composed of a positively charged central core, the nucleus, about which negatively charged electrons rotate in various orbits. Electricity is the most useful and most convenient form of energy, readily convertible into heat and light, and used to power machines. Electricity can be generated in one place and distributed anywhere because it readily flows through wires. It is generated at power stations where a suitable energy source is harnessed to drive ◊turbines that spin electricity generators. Current energy sources are coal, oil, water power (hydroelectricity), natural gas, and nuclear power. Research is under way to increase the contribution of wind, tidal, and geothermal power. Nuclear fuel is a cheap source of electricity but environmental considerations may limit its future development.

Electricity is generated at power stations at a voltage of about 25,000 volts, which is not a suitable voltage for long-distance transmission. For minimal power loss, transmission must take place at very high voltage (400,000 volts or more). The generated voltage is therefore increased ('stepped up') by a ◊transformer. The resulting high-voltage electricity is then fed into the main arteries of the ◊grid system, an interconnected network of power stations and distribution centres covering a large area, sometimes (as in Britain) countrywide, or even (as in Europe) from country to country. After transmission to a local substation, the line voltage is reduced by a step-down transformer and distributed to consumers.

Among specialized power units that convert energy directly to electrical energy without the intervention of any moving mechanisms, the most promising are thermionic converters. These use conventional fuels such as propane gas, as in portable military power packs, or, if refuelling is to be avoided, radioactive fuels, as in unmanned navigational aids and spacecraft.

electric light bulb ◊incandescent filament lamp, first demonstrated by Joseph Swan in the UK 1878 and Thomas Edison in the USA 1879. The modern light bulb is a thin glass bulb filled with an inert mixture of nitrogen and argon gas. It contains a filament made of fine tungsten wire. When electricity is passed through the wire, it glows white hot.

electric motor a machine that converts electrical energy into mechanical energy. There are various types, including direct-current and induction motors, most of which produce rotary motion. A linear induction motor produces linear (sideways) rather than rotary motion.

A simple *direct-current motor* consists of a horseshoe-shaped permanent ◊magnet with a wire-wound coil (◊armature) mounted so that it can rotate between the pole-pieces of the magnet. A ◊commutator reverses the current (from a battery) fed to the coil on each half-turn, which rotates because of the mechanical force exerted on a conductor carrying a current in a magnetic field. An *induction motor* employs ◊alternating current. It comprises a stationary current-carrying coil (stator) surrounding another coil (rotor), which rotates because of the current induced in it by the magnetic field created by the stator; it thus requires no commutator.

electric power the rate at which an electrical machine uses electrical ◊energy or converts it into other forms of energy, for example, light, heat, mechanical energy. Usually measured in watts (equivalent to joules per second), it is equal to the product of the voltage and the current flowing.

An electric lamp that passes 0.4 amps at 250 volts uses 100 watts of electrical power and converts it into light—in ordinary terms it is a 100-watt lamp. An electric motor that requires 6 amps at the same voltage consumes 1,500 watts

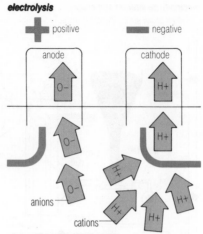

electrolysis

(1.5 kilowatts), equivalent to delivering about 2 horsepower of mechanical energy.

electrocardiogram (ECG) a recording of the electrical changes in the heart muscle, detected by electrodes attached to the chest. Electrocardiography is invaluable in the diagnosis of heart disease.

electrochemical series a list of chemical elements arranged in descending order of the ease with which they can lose electrons to form cations (positive ions). An element can be displaced (◊displacement reaction) from a compound by any element above it in the series.

electrochemistry the branch of science that studies chemical reactions involving electricity. The use of electricity to produce chemical effects, ◊electrolysis, is employed in many industrial processes, such as the manufacture of chlorine and the extraction of aluminium. The use of chemical reactions to produce electricity is the basis of batteries, such as the dry cell and the ◊Leclanché cell.

Since all chemical reactions involve changes to the electron structure of atoms, all reactions are now recognized as electrochemical in nature. Oxidation, for example, was once defined as a process in which oxygen was combined with a substance, or hydrogen was removed from a compound; it is now defined as a process in which electrons are lost.

electroconvulsive therapy (ECT) or *electroshock therapy* a treatment for ◊schizophrenia and ◊depression, given under anaesthesia and with a muscle relaxant. An electric current is passed through the brain to induce alterations in the brain's electrical activity. The treatment can cause distress, loss of concentration and memory, and so there is much controversy about its use and effectiveness.

electrocution death caused by electric current. It is used as a method of execution in some US states. The criminal is strapped in a special electric chair and an electric shock of 1,800–2,000 volts is administered.

electrode conductor by which an electric current passes in or out of a substance.

electrodynamics study of the interaction between charged particles and their emission and absorption of electromagnetic ◊radiation. *Quantum electrodynamics* (QED) combines quantum ◊mechanics and ◊relativity theory, making accurate predictions about subatomic processes involving charged particles such as electrons and protons.

electroencephalogram (EEG) a record of the electrical discharges of the brain, detected by electrodes attached to the scalp. The pattern of electrical activity revealed by electroencephalography is diagnostic in some brain disorders, especially epilepsy.

electrolysis the production of chemical changes by passing an electric current through a solution (the electrolyte), resulting in the migration of the ions

to the electrodes: positive cations to the negative electrode, or cathode, and negative anions to the positive electrode, or anode.

During electrolysis, the ions react with the electrode, either receiving or giving up electrons. The resultant atoms may be liberated as a gas, or deposited as a solid on the electrode, in amounts that are proportional to the amount of current passed, as discovered by Faraday.

One important application is *electroplating*, in which a solution of a salt, such as silver nitrate, is used and the object to be plated acts as the negative electrode, thus attracting silver ions, Ag⁺. Electrolysis is used in many industrial processes, such as coating metals for vehicles and ships, and refining bauxite into aluminium.

electrolyte a molten substance or solution in which an electric current is made to flow by the movement and discharge of ions in accordance with ◊Faraday's laws of electrolysis. The term electrolyte is frequently used to denote a substance which, when dissolved in a specified solvent, usually water, produces an electrically conducting medium.

electromagnet an iron bar with coils or wire around it, which acts as a magnet when an electric current flows through the wire. Electromagnets have many uses: in switches, electric bells, solenoids, and metal-lifting cranes.

electromagnetic field in physics, the agency by which a particle with an ◊electric charge experiences a force in a particular region of space. If it does so only when moving, it is in a pure *magnetic field*, if it does so when stationary, it is in an *electric field*. Both can be present simultaneously.

electromagnetic induction in physics, the production of an ◊electromotive force (emf) in a circuit by a change of ◊magnetic flux through the circuit. The emf so produced is known as an induced emf, and any current that may result as an induced current. The phenomenon is applied in the electric bell and induction coil.

If the change of magnetic flux is due to a variation in the current flowing in the same circuit, the phenomenon is known as self-induction; if due to a change of current flowing in another circuit, as mutual induction.

electromagnetic spectrum the complete range, over all wave lenghts, of electromagnetic waves.

electromagnetic system of units former system of absolute electromagnetic units (emu) based on the ◊c.g.s. system and having, as its primary electrical unit, the unit magnetic pole. It was replaced by ◊SI units.

electromagnetic waves oscillating electric and magnetic fields travelling together through space at a speed of nearly 300 million metres per second. The (limitless) range of possible wavelengths or ◊frequencies of electromagnetic waves, which can be thought of as making up the *electromagnetic spectrum*, includes radio waves, infrared radiation, visible light, ultraviolet radiation, X-rays, and gamma rays.

electromotive force (emf) the energy supplied by a source of electric power in driving a unit charge around an electrical circut. The unit is the ◊volt.

electron stable, negatively charged ◊elementary particle, a constituent of all ◊atoms and the basic particle of electricity. A beam of electrons will undergo ◊diffraction (scattering), and produce interference patterns, in the same way as ◊electromagnetic waves such as light; hence they may also be regarded as waves.

electronegativity the ease with which an atom can attract electrons to itself. Electronegativity gives a measure of the ability of an atom to form an ◊anion. In a covalent bond between two atoms of different electronegativities, the bonding electrons will be located close to the more electronegative atom, creating a ◊dipole.

electron gun a structure consisting of a series of ◊electrodes, including a cathode for producing an electron beam. It is an essential part of many

electromagnetic waves

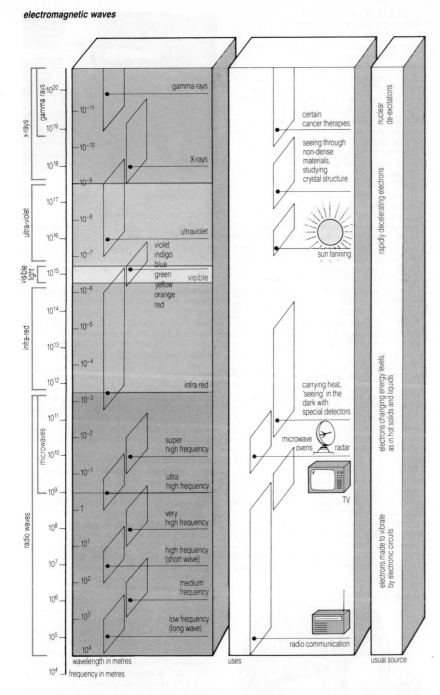

gamma-rays

X-rays

ultraviolet

violet
indigo
blue
green — visible
yellow
orange
red

infra-red

super
high frequency

ultra
high frequency

very
high frequency

high frequency
(short wave)

medium
frequency

low frequency
(long wave)

gamma rays
x-rays
ultra-violet
visible light
infra-red
microwaves
radio waves

10^{20}
10^{19}
10^{18}
10^{17}
10^{16}
10^{15}
10^{14}
10^{13}
10^{12}
10^{11}
10^{10}
10^{9}
10^{8}
10^{7}
10^{6}
10^{5}
10^{4}

10^{-11}
10^{-10}
10^{-9}
10^{-8}
10^{-7}
10^{-6}
10^{-5}
10^{-4}
10^{-3}
10^{-2}
10^{-1}
1
10^{1}
10^{2}
10^{3}
10^{4}

wavelength in metres
frequency in metres

certain
cancer therapies

seeing through
non-dense
materials,
studying
crystal structure

sun tanning

carrying heat,
'seeing' in the
dark with
special detectors

microwave
ovens — radar

TV

radio communication

uses

nuclear de-excitations

rapidly decelerating electrons

electrons changing energy levels, as in hot solids and liquids

electrons made to vibrate by electronic circuits

usual source

electron microscope

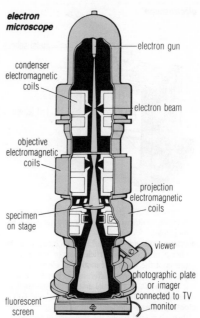

electron gun

condenser
electromagnetic
coils

electron beam

objective
electromagnetic
coils

projection
electromagnetic
coils

specimen
on stage

viewer

photographic plate
or imager
connected to TV
monitor

fluorescent
screen

electronic devices such as cathode-ray tubes (television tubes) and ◊electron microscopes.

electronic flash a discharge tube that produces a high-intensity flash of light, used for photography in dim conditions. The tube contains an inert gas such as krypton. The flash lasts only a few thousandths of a second.

electronic mail a ◊telecommunications system that sends messages to people or machines (such as computers) via computers and the telephone network rather than by letter.

Subscribers to an electronic mail system type messages in ordinary letter form on a word processor, or microcomputer, and 'drop' the letters into a central computer's memory bank by means of a computer/telephone connector (a modem). The recipient 'collects' the letter by calling up the central computer and feeding a unique password into the system.

electronic music a form of studio-based serial music composed entirely of electronically generated and modified tones, as opposed to *concrete music*, which arranges pre-recorded sounds by intuition. The term was later broadened to include pre-recorded vocal and instrumental sounds, although always implying a serial basis. ◊Maderna, ◊Stockhausen, and ◊Babbit were among the pioneers of electronic music in the 1950s.

After 1960, with the arrival of the purpose-built synthesizer developed by Robert Moog, Peter Zinovieff, and others, interest switched to computer-aided synthesis, culminating in the 4X system installed at ◊IRCAM.

electronics a branch of science that deals with the emission of ◊electrons from conductors and ◊semiconductors, with the subsequent manipulation of these electrons, and with the construction of electronic devices. The first electronic device

was the ◊thermionic valve, or vacuum tube, in which electrons moved in a vacuum, and led to such inventions as ◊radio, ◊television, ◊radar, and the digital ◊computer. Replacement of valves with the comparatively tiny and reliable transistor in 1948 revolutionized electronic development. Modern electronic devices are based on minute integrated circuits and ◊silicon chips, wafer-thin crystal slices holding tens of thousands of electronic components.

By using solid-state devices such as silicon chips and integrated circuits, extremely complex electronic circuits can be constructed, leading to ◊digital watches, pocket ◊calculators, powerful ◊microcomputers, and ◊word processors.

electronic tagging or *electronic monitoring* system for monitoring people on remand (charged with a crime but released on bail). Pioneered in the USA, electronic tagging was tested in the UK in 1989 in Nottingham. Volunteers were fitted with a tamper-proof anklet or 'tag', and their home with a special receiver-dialling unit. If the person moved out of the range of the unit, a signal would be transmitted to a central computer.

electron microscope an instrument that produces a magnified image by using a beam of ◊electrons instead of light rays, as in an optical ◊microscope. An *electron lens* is an arrangement of electromagnetic coils that controls and focuses the beam. Electrons are not visible to the eye, so instead of an eyepiece there is a fluorescent screen or a photographic plate on which the electrons form an image. The wavelength of the electron beam is much shorter than that of light, so much greater magnification and resolution (ability to distinguish detail) can be achieved.

A *high-resolution electron microscope* (HREM) can produce a magnification of seven million times. The development of the electron microscope has made possible the observation of very minute organisms, viruses, and even large molecules. A *transmission electron microscope* passes the electron beam through a very thin slice of a specimen. A *scanning electron microscope* looks at the exterior of a specimen.

electrons, delocalized ◊electrons that are not associated with individual atoms or identifiable chemical bonds, but are shared collectively by all the constituent atoms or ions of some chemical substances (such as metals, graphite, and ◊aromatic compounds).

A metallic solid consists of a three-dimensional arrangement of metal ions through which the delocalized electrons are free to travel. Aromatic

electroscope

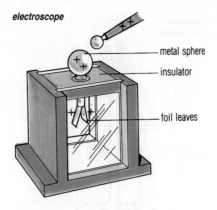

- metal sphere
- insulator
- foil leaves

compounds are characterized by the sharing of delocalized electrons by several atoms within the molecule.

electron volt unit (symbol eV) for measuring the energy of a charged particle (◊ion or ◊electron) in terms of the energy of motion an electron would gain from a potential difference of 1 volt. Because it is so small, more usual units are mega- (million) and giga- (billion) electron volts (MeV and GeV).

electrophoresis the ◊diffusion of charged particles through a fluid under the influence of an electric field. It can be used in the biological sciences to separate ◊molecules of different sizes, which diffuse at different rates. In industry electrophoresis is used in paint-dipping operations to ensure that paint reaches awkward corners.

electroplating the deposition of metals upon metallic surfaces by ◊electrolysis for decorative and/or protective purposes. It is used in the preparation of printers' blocks, 'master' audio discs, and in many other processes.

A current is passed through a bath containing a solution of a salt of the plating metal, the object to be plated being the cathode (negative electrode); the anode (positive electrode) is either an inert substance or the plating metal. Among the metals most commonly used for plating are zinc, nickel, chromium, cadmium, copper, silver, and gold.

In *electropolishing*, the object to be polished is made the anode in an electrolytic solution and by carefully controlling the conditions the high spots on the surface are dissolved away, leaving a high-quality stain-free surface. This technique is useful in polishing irregular stainless-steel articles.

electroscope an apparatus for detecting ◊electric charge. The simple gold-leaf electroscope consists of a vertical conducting (metal) rod ending in a pair of rectangular pieces of gold foil, mounted inside and insulated from an earthed metal case. An electric charge applied to the end of the metal rod makes the gold leaves diverge, because they each receive a similar charge (positive or negative) and so repel each other. The polarity of the charge can be found by bringing up another charge of known polarity and applying it to the metal rod. A like charge has no effect on the gold leaves, whereas an opposite charge neutralizes the charge on the leaves and causes them to collapse.

electrostatics study of electric charges from stationary sources (not currents).

electrovalent bond or *ionic bond* type of chemical ◊bond in which the the combining atoms lose or gain electrons to form ions.

electrum a naturally occurring alloy of gold and silver used by early civilizations to make the first coins, about the 6th century BC.

element a substance that cannot be split chemically into simpler substances. The atoms of a particular element all have the same number of protons in their nuclei. Elements are classified in the ◊periodic table. They are denoted by symbols, usually the first letter or letters of the English or Latinized name of the element: for example C, carbon; Ca, calcium; Fe, iron (ferrum). These symbols represent one atom of the element.

Of the 109 known elements, 92 occur naturally. Hydrogen and helium were produced in the ◊Big Bang. Of the rest, those up to atomic number 56 (iron) are produced by nuclear fusion within the stars, but the more massive, such as lead and uranium, are produced when an old star explodes and its gravitational energy as it collapses squashes nuclei together. The transuranium elements are artificially made by bombarding uranium or other substances with various atomic particles.

elementary particle subatomic particle that is not made up of smaller particles, and so can be considered one of the fundamental units of matter. There are three groups of elementary particles: quarks, leptons, and gauge bosons.

Quarks, of which there are six types ('up', 'down', 'charmed', 'strange', 'top', and 'bottom'), combine in groups of three to produce heavy particles called bayrons, and in groups of two to produce intermediate-mass particles called mesons. Baryons and mesons are influenced by the 'strong' nuclear force that binds the nucleus of an atom together. The ◊proton and the ◊neutron are baryons. *Leptons* are light particles. There are six types: the ◊electron, the muon, the tau, and three types of ◊neutrino. These particles are influenced by the 'weak' nuclear force. *Gauge bosons* carry forces between other particles. There are five types: the gluon, ◊photon, W particle, Z particle, and graviton. The gluon carries the strong nuclear force, the photon carries the electromagnetic force, the W and Z carry the weak nuclear force, and the graviton carries the force of gravity. See ◊force, fundamental.

elephant the two surviving species of the Proboscidea, the Asian *Elephas maximus* and African *Loxodonta africana* elephant. The elephant can grow to 4 m/13 ft and weigh up to 8 tons; it has a thick, grey, wrinkled skin, a large head, a long trunk used to obtain food and water, and upper incisors or tusks, which grow to a considerable length. The African elephant has very large ears and a flattened forehead, and the Asian species has smaller ears and a convex forehead. Elephants are herbivorous, highly intelligent, extremely social, and live in matriarchal herds. They are slaughtered needlessly for the ivory of their tusks, and this, coupled with the fact that they do not breed readily in captivity, is leading to their extinction. In Africa there were 1.3 million in 1981; fewer than 600,000 in 1990. They were placed on the list of most endangered species in 1989, and a world ban on trade in ivory was imposed.

Asiatic Elephant

African Elephant

Elgar The composer Edward Elgar.

In India, Burma, and Thailand, they are widely used for transport and logging. The period of gestation is about 19–22 months (the longest among mammals), and the lifespan is about 60–70 years. They have one of the lowest metabolic rates among placental mammals.

Elephanta /ˌelɪˈfæntə/ island in Bombay harbour, Maharashtra, India, some 8 km/5 mi from Bombay. The Temple Caves (6th century), cut out of solid rock, have sculptures of many Hindu deities executed 450–740. There was formerly a large stone elephant near the island's landing place.

elephant bird another name for the extinct ◊aepyornis.

elephantiasis in the human body, a gross local enlargement and deformity, especially of a leg, the scrotum, a labium of the vulva, or a breast. The commonest is the tropical variety caused by infestation by parasitic filarial worms; the enlargement is due to chronic blocking of the lymph channels and consequent overgrowth of the skin and tissues.

Eleusinian Mysteries ceremonies in honour of the Greek deities ◊Demeter, ◊Persephone, and ◊Dionysus, celebrated in the remains of the temple of Demeter at Eleusis, Greece. Worshippers saw visions in the darkened temple, supposedly connected with the underworld.

elevation of boiling point a raising of the boiling point of a liquid above that of the pure solvent, caused by a substance being dissolved in it. The phenomenon is observed when salt is added to boiling water; the water ceases to boil because its boiling point has been elevated.

How much the boiling point is raised depends on the number of molecules of substance dissolved. For a single solvent, such as pure water, all substances in the same molecular concentration (expressed in ◊moles) produce the same elevation of boiling point (measured using the Beckmann thermometer). The elevation e for a molar concentration C is given by the equation $e = KC$, where K is a constant for the particular solvent (called the ebullioscopic constant).

elevator mechanical device for raising or lowering goods or materials. Such a device used for lifting people in buildings is known as an elevator in the USA and as a ◊lift in Britain.

Eleven Plus examination test designed to select children for grammar school education in the UK, at the time when local authorities provided separate grammar, secondary modern, and occasionally technical schools for children over the age of 11. The examination became defunct on the introduction of ◊comprehensive schools in Scotland, Wales, and most of England during the 1960s and 1970s. although certain education authorities retain the selective system and the Eleven Plus.

El Faiyûm /el faɪˈjuːm/ city in N Egypt, 90 km/56 mi SW of Cairo; population (1985) 218,500. A centre of prehistoric culture; the crocodile god Sobek used to be worshipped nearby, and famous realistic mummy portraits of 1st–4th centuries AD were found in the area.

Eliot *Mary Ann Evans, otherwise known as the English novelist George Eliot.*

El Ferrol /el fe'rɒl/ full name *El Ferrol del Caudillo* city and port in La Coruña province, on the NW coast of Spain; population (1986) 88,000. It is a naval base, and has a deep, sheltered harbour and shipbuilding industries. It is the birthplace of Francisco Franco.

Elgar /'elgɑ:/ Edward (William) 1857–1934. English composer. His *Enigma Variations* appeared 1899, and although his celebrated choral work, the oratorio setting of Newman's *The Dream of Gerontius*, was initially a failure, it was well received at Düsseldorf in 1902. Many of his earlier works were then performed, including the *Pomp and Circumstance* marches. Among his later works are oratorios, two symphonies, a violin concerto, a cello concerto, chamber music, songs, and the tone-poem *Falstaff* 1913.

Elgin /'elgɪn/ chief town of Moray District, Grampian region, NE Scotland, on the river Lossie 8 km/5 mi S of its port of Lossiemouth on the S shore of the Moray Firth; population (1983) 20,065. There are sawmills and whisky distilleries. ◊Gordonstoun public school is nearby. Elgin Cathedral, founded 1224, was destroyed 1390.

Elgin marbles collection of ancient Greek sculptures mainly from the Parthenon at Athens, assembled by the 7th Earl of Elgin. Sent to England 1812, and bought for the nation 1816 for £35,000, they are now in the British Museum. Greece has asked for them to be returned to Athens.

Eli in the Old Testament or Jewish Bible, a priest and childhood teacher of the first prophet, Samuel.

Elijah /ɪ'laɪdʒə/ c. mid-9th century BC. in the Old Testament or Jewish Bible, a Hebrew prophet during the reigns of the Israelite kings Ahab and Ahaziah. He came from Gilead. He defeated the prophets of ◊Baal, and was said to have been carried up to heaven in a fiery chariot in a whirlwind. In Jewish belief, Elijah will return to Earth to herald the coming of the messiah.

Eliot /'eliət/ George. Pen name of Mary Ann Evans 1819–1880. English novelist, who portrayed Victorian society, particularly its intellectual hypocrisy, with realism and irony. In 1857 she published the story 'Amos Barton', the first of the *Scenes of Clerical Life*. This was followed by the novels *Adam Bede* 1859, *The Mill on the Floss* 1860, and *Silas Marner* 1861. *Middlemarch* 1872 is now considered one of the greatest novels of the 19th century. Her final book *Daniel Deronda* 1876 was concerned with anti-Semitism. She also wrote poetry.

Born at Chilvers Coton, Warwickshire, she had a strict evangelical upbringing, but on moving to Coventry with her father in 1841 was converted to free thinking (see ◊free thought). As assistant editor of the *Westminster Review* under John Chapman 1851–53, she made the acquaintance of Carlyle, Harriet Martineau, Herbert Spencer, and the philosopher and critic George Henry Lewes (1817–1878). Lewes was married but separated from his wife, and from 1854 he and Eliot lived

together in a relationship which she regarded as a true marriage and which continued until his death. In 1880 she married John Cross (1840–1924).

Eliot /'eliət/ John 1592–1632. English politician, born in Cornwall. He became a member of Parliament 1614, and with the Earl of Buckingham's patronage was made a vice admiral 1619. In 1626 he was imprisoned in the Tower of London for demanding Buckingham's impeachment. In 1628 he was a formidable supporter of the ◊Petition of Right opposing Charles II, and with other parliamentary leaders was again imprisoned in the Tower of London 1629, where he died.

Eliot /'eliət/ T(homas) S(tearns) 1888–1965. US poet, playwright, and critic, who lived in London from 1915. His first volume of poetry, *Prufrock and Other Observations* 1917 was followed by *The Waste Land* 1922 and *The Hollow Men* 1925. His plays include *Murder in the Cathedral* 1935 and *The Cocktail Party* 1949. His critical works include *The Sacred Wood* 1920. Nobel prize 1948.

Eliot was born in St Louis, Missouri, and was educated at Harvard, Paris, and Oxford. He settled in London 1915, and became a British subject 1927. He was for a time a bank clerk, later lecturing and entering publishing at Faber & Faber. As editor of *The Criterion* 1922–39, he exercised a moulding influence on the thought of his generation. In 1948 he received the Order of Merit.

Prufrock and other Observations expressed the disillusionment of the generation affected by World War I and caused a sensation by its experimental form and rhythms. His reputation was established by the desolate modernity of *The Waste Land*. *The Hollow Men* renewed the same note, but *Ash Wednesday* 1930 revealed the change in religious attitude which led him to become a Catholic. Among his other works are *Four Quartets* 1943, a religious sequence in which he seeks the eternal reality, and the poetic dramas *Murder in the Cathedral* about Thomas á Becket, *The Cocktail Party*, *The Confidential Clerk* 1953, and *The Elder Statesman* 1958. His collection *Old Possum's Book of Practical Cats* was used for the popular British composer Lloyd Webber's musical *Cats* 1981. His critical works include *Notes toward the Definition of Culture* 1949.

Elisabethville /ɪ'lɪzəbəθvɪl/ former name of ◊Lubumbashi, a town in Zaïre.

Elisha /ɪ'laɪʃə/ mid-9th century BC. In the Old Testament or Jewish Bible, a Hebrew prophet, successor to Elijah.

elite a small group in a society with power, privileges, and status above others. An elite may be cultural, educational, religious, political, or social.

Eliot *US poet T S Eliot whose reputation was made by his poem* The Waste Land, *published in 1922.*

Elizabeth I *'I have the body of a weak and feeble woman, but I have the heart and stomach of a king,' Elizabeth I told her troops.*

Sociological interest has centred on how such minorities get, use, and hold on to power, and on what distinguishes elites from ordinary members of society.

Elizabeth /ɪ'lɪzəbəθ/ city in NE New Jersey, USA; population (1980) 106,000. It was the first English settlement in New Jersey, established 1664. It has automobile, sewing machine, and tool factories, oil refineries, and chemical works.

Elizabeth /ɪ'lɪzəbəθ/ in the New Testament, mother of John the Baptist. She was a cousin of Jesus Christ's mother Mary, who came to see her shortly after the Annunciation; on this visit (called the Visitation), Mary sang the hymn of praise later to be known as the Magnificat.

Elizabeth /ɪ'lɪzəbəθ/ the Queen Mother 1900– . Wife of King George VI of England. She was born Lady Elizabeth Angela Marguerite Bowes-Lyon, and on 26 Apr 1923, she married Albert, Duke of York. Their children are Queen Elizabeth II and Princess Margaret.

She is the youngest daughter of the 14th Earl of Strathmore and Kinghorne (died 1944), through whom she is descended from Robert Bruce, king of Scotland. When her husband became King George VI 1936 she became Queen Consort, and was crowned with him 1937. She adopted the title Queen Elizabeth the Queen Mother after his death.

Elizabeth /ɪ'lɪzəbəθ/ two queens of England or the UK:

Elizabeth I 1533–1603. Queen of England 1558–1603, the daughter of Henry VIII and Anne Boleyn. Through her Religious Settlement of 1559 she enforced the Protestant religion by law and she had ◊Mary, Queen of Scots, executed 1587. Her conflict with Catholic Spain led to the defeat of the ◊Spanish Armada 1588. The Elizabethan age was expansionist in commerce and geographical exploration, and arts and literature flourished. The rulers of many European states made unsuccessful bids to marry Elizabeth, and she used these bids to strengthen her power. She was succeeded by James I.

Elizabeth was born at Greenwich, London, 7 Sept 1533. She was well educated in several languages. During her Catholic half-sister Mary's reign, Elizabeth's Protestant sympathies brought her under suspicion, and she lived in seclusion at Hatfield, Hertfordshire, until on Mary's death she became queen. Her first task was to bring about a broad religious settlement.

Many unsuccessful attempts were made by Parliament to persuade Elizabeth to marry or settle the succession. Courtship she found a useful political weapon, and she maintained friendships with, among others, the courtiers ◊Leicester, Sir Walter ◊Raleigh, and ◊Essex.

The arrival in England 1568 of Mary, Queen of Scots, and her imprisonment by Elizabeth caused a political crisis and a rebellion of the feudal nobility of the north followed 1569. Friction between English and Spanish sailors hastened the breach with Spain. When the Dutch rebelled against Spanish tyranny Elizabeth secretly encouraged them;

Elizabeth II: line of succession

Name, title, and relationship	Date of birth
Charles, Prince of Wales, eldest son of Elizabeth II	1948
Prince William, elder son of Charles	1982
Prince Henry (Harry), second son of Charles	1984
Andrew, Duke of York, second son of Elizabeth II	1960
Princess Beatrice, elder daughter of Andrew	1988
Princes Eugénie, second daughter of Andrew	1990
Prince Edward, youngest son of Elizabeth II	1964
Anne, The Princess Royal, daughter of Elizabeth II	1950
Peter Phillips, son of Anne	1977
Zara Phillips, daughter of Anne	1981
Princess Margaret, sister of Elizabeth II	1930
Viscount Linley, son of Margaret	1961
Lady Sarah Armstrong-Jones, daughter of Margaret	1964
Richard, Duke of Gloucester, nephew of George VI (father of Elizabeth II)	1944
Alexander, Earl of Ulster, son of Gloucester	1974
Lady Davina Windsor, elder daughter of Gloucester	1977
Lady Rose Windsor, younger daughter of Gloucester	1980
Edward, Duke of Kent, nephew of George VI	1935
Edward, Baron Downpatrick, grandson of Kent	1988
Lord Nicholas Windsor, son of Kent	1970
Lady Helen Windsor, daughter of Kent	1964
Lord Frederick Windsor, son of Michael (brother of Kent)	1979
Lady Gabriella Windsor, daughter of Michael	1981
Alexandra, sister of Kent	1936
James, son of Alexandra	1964

Note: George, Earl of St Andrews (son of Edward, Duke of Kent), and Prince Michael of Kent have lost their places in line to the Throne, having married Catholics.

Philip II retaliated by aiding Catholic conspiracies against her. This undeclared war continued for many years, until the landing of an English army in the Netherlands 1585, and Mary's execution 1587, brought it into the open. Philip's Armada (the fleet sent to invade England 1588) met with total disaster.

The war with Spain continued with varying fortunes to the end of the reign, while events at home foreshadowed the conflicts of the 17th century. Among the Puritans discontent was developing with Elizabeth's religious settlement, and several were imprisoned or executed. Parliament showed a new independence, and in 1601 forced Elizabeth to retreat on the monopolies question. Yet her prestige remained unabated, as was shown by the failure of Essex's rebellion 1601.

Elizabeth II /ɪˈlɪzəbəθ/ 1926– . Queen of Great Britain and Northern Ireland from 1952, the elder daughter of George VI. She married her third

Elizabeth II *Queen Elizabeth II of the United Kingdom and head of the Commonwealth. This portrait was taken during her tour of Australia in 1988.*

cousin, Philip, the Duke of Edinburgh, 1947. They have four children: Charles, Anne, Andrew, and Edward.

Princess Elizabeth Alexandra Mary was born in London 21 Apr 1926, educated privately, and assumed official duties at 16. During World War II she served in the Auxiliary Territorial Service, and by an amendment to the Regency Act she became a state counsellor on her 18th birthday. On the death of George VI she succeeded to the throne while in Kenya with her husband. She is the richest woman in the world, with an estimated wealth of £5.3 billion.

Elizabeth /ɪˈlɪzəbəθ/ 1709–1762. Empress of Russia from 1741, daughter of Peter the Great. She carried through a palace revolution and supplanted her cousin, the infant Ivan VI (1730–1764), on the throne. She continued the policy of westernization begun by Peter, and allied herself with Austria against Prussia.

Elizabethan literature literature produced during the reign of Elizabeth I of England (1558–1603). Her reign was remarkable for the development of the arts in England. The literature of her age is pre-eminent in energy, richness, and confidence. Renaissance humanism, Protestant zeal, and geographical discovery all contributed to this upsurge of creative power. Drama was the dominant form of the age, and ◊Shakespeare and ◊Marlowe were popular with all levels of society. Other writers of the period included Edmund Spenser, Philip Sidney, Frances Bacon, Thomas Lodge, Robert Greene, and John Lyly.

During this period, the resources of English were increased by the free adoption of words from Latin. This was accompanied by a growing conviction that English was capable of all the requirements of great literature. There was a balance between the university and courtly elements and the coarse gusto of popular culture. Music related closely to literature, with competence in singing and composition being seen as normal social skills. Successive editions of the the Bible were produced during these years, written with dignity, vividness, and the deliberate intention of universal understanding.

Elizavetpol /ɪˌlɪzəˈvetpɒl/ former name of ◊Kirovabad, industrial town in Azerbaijan Republic, USSR.

elk large deer *Alces alces* inhabiting N Europe, Asia, Scandinavia, and North America, where it is known as the moose. It is brown in colour, stands about 2 m/6 ft at the shoulders, has very

large palmate antlers, a fleshy muzzle, short neck, and long legs. It feeds on leaves and shoots. In North America, the ◊wapiti is called an elk.

Ellesmere /ˈelzmɪə/ second largest island of the Canadian Arctic archipelago, Northwest Territories; area 212,687 sq km/82,097 sq mi. It is for the most part barren or glacier-covered.

Ellesmere Port /ˈelzmɪə ˈpɔːt/ oil port and industrial town in Cheshire, England, on the river Mersey and the Manchester Ship Canal; population (1983) 81,900. Formerly the biggest transshipment canal port in NW England, it now has the National Waterways Museum, 1976, with old narrow boats and a blacksmith's forge.

Ellice Islands /ˈelɪs/ former name of ◊Tuvalu, a group of islands in the W Pacific Ocean.

Ellington /ˈelɪŋtən/ 'Duke' (Edward Kennedy) 1899–1974. US pianist, who had an outstanding career as a composer and arranger of jazz. He wrote numerous pieces for his own jazz orchestra, and became one of the most important figures in jazz over a 55-year span. Compositions include 'Mood Indigo', 'Sophisticated Lady', 'Solitude', and 'Black and Tan Fantasy'.

ellipse a curve joining all points around two fixed points (foci) such that the sum of the distances from those points is always constant. The diameter passing through the foci is the major axis, and the diameter bisecting this at right angles is the minor axis. An ellipse is one of a series of curves known as ◊conic sections. A slice across

Ellington *US musician, composer, and bandleader 'Duke' Ellington.*

ellipse

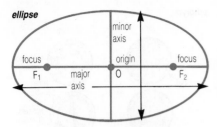

elm

a cone that is not made parallel to, or does not pass through, the base will produce an ellipse.

Ellis /'elɪs/ (Henry) Havelock 1859–1939. English psychologist and writer of many works on the psychology of sex, including *Studies in the Psychology of Sex* (seven volumes) 1898–1928.

Ellis Island /'elɪs/ island off the shore of New Jersey, USA, former reception centre for steerage-class immigrants on arrival in New York 1892–1943. No longer used, it was declared a National Historic Site 1964 by President Johnson.

Ellison /'elɪsən/ Ralph 1914– . US novelist. His *Invisible Man* 1952 portrays with humour and energy the plight of a black man whom society cannot acknowledge; it is regarded as one of the most impressive novels published in the USA in the 1950s.

Ellora /e'lɔːrə/ archaeological site in the NW Deccan, Maharashtra State, India, with 35 cave temples—Buddhist, Hindu, and Jain—varying in date from the late 6th century to the 9th century. They include Visvakarma (a hall about 26 m/86 ft long containing a huge image of the Buddha), Tin Thal (a three-storeyed Buddhist monastery cave), the Rameswara cave (with beautiful sculptures), and Siva's Paradise, the great temple of Kailasa.

elm tree of the family Ulmaceae, found in temperate regions of the N hemisphere, and in mountainous parts of the tropics. The common **English elm** *Ulmus procera* is widely distributed throughout Europe. It reaches 35 m/115 ft, with tufts of small, purplish-brown flowers which appear before the leaves.

Other species are the **wych elm** *Ulmaceae glabra*, indigenous to Britain, the North American **white elm** *Ulmaceae americana* and the **red** or **slippery elm** *Ulmaceae fulva*. Most elms (apart from the wych elm) reproduce not by seed but by suckering (new shoots arising from the root system). This non-sexual reproduction results in an enormous variety of forms.

The fungus disease *Ceratocystis ulmi*, known as **Dutch elm disease**, because of a severe outbreak in that country 1924, has reduced the numbers of elm trees in Europe and North America. It is carried from tree to tree by beetles. Elms were widespread throughout Europe to about 4,000 BC, when they suddenly disappeared and were not again common until the 12th century. This may have been the fault of an earlier epidemic of Dutch elm disease.

El Niño (Spanish 'the child') warm ocean surge of the ◊Peru (Humboldt) Current, so called because it tends to occur at Christmas, recurring about every ten years or so in the E Pacific off South America. El Niño causes the trade winds to cease, so that the cool ocean currents driven by them stops and there is an influx of warm water from the west. It can disrupt the climate of the area disastrously, and has played a part in causing famine in Indonesia 1983, bush fires in Australia because of drought, rainstorms in California and South America, and the destruction of Peru's anchovy harvest and wildlife 1982–83.

El Obeid /el əu'beɪd/ capital of Kordofan province, Sudan; population (1984) 140,025. Linked by rail with Khartoum, it is a market for cattle, gum arabic, and durra (Indian millet).

elongation in astronomy, the angular distance between either a planet or the Moon and the Sun. This angle is 0° at either inferior ◊conjunction or superior conjunction. ◊Quadrature occurs when the elongation angle is 90° and ◊opposition (opposite the Sun in the sky) when the angle is 180°.

El Paso /el 'pæsəu/ city in Texas, USA, situated at the base of the Franklin Mountains, on the Rio Grande, opposite the Mexican city of Ciudad Juárez; population (1980) 425,200. It is the centre of an agricultural and cattle-raising area, and there are electronics, food processing and packing, and leather industries, as well as oil refineries and industries based on local iron and copper mines.

El Salvador /el 'sælvədɔː/ country in Central America, bounded N and E by Honduras, S and SW by the Pacific Ocean, and NW by Guatemala.
government The 1983 constitution, amended 1985, provides for a president elected by universal suffrage for a five-year term, assisted by an appointed vice president and a council of ministers. There is a single-chamber national assembly of 60, elected by universal suffrage for a three-year term.
history Conquered by Spain 1523, El Salvador achieved independence 1829. Since then there have been frequent coups and political violence.

After a coup 1961 the conservative Party of National Conciliation (PCN) was established, winning all the seats in the national assembly. PCN stayed in power, with reports of widespread human rights violations, until challenged 1979 by a socialist guerrilla movement, the Farabundo Martí Liberation Front. A civilian-military junta deposed the president and promised to introduce democracy and free elections, though these were postponed as the violence continued.

In 1980 the archbishop of San Salvador, Oscar Romero, a well-known champion of human rights, was shot dead in his cathedral. The murder of three US nuns and a social worker prompted US president ◊Carter to suspend economic and military aid. In 1980 José Duarte, leader of a left-of-centre coalition, became president. The ◊Reagan administration supported him, as an anti-communist, and encouraged him to call elections 1982. The left-wing parties refused to participate, and the elections were held amid great violence, at least 40 people being killed on election day. The extreme right-wing ARENA party eventually won.

During 1982 some 1,600 Salvadorean troops were trained in the USA and US military advisers were said to be actively involved in the country's internal conflict. It was estimated that about 35,000 people were killed 1979–82.

Despite a new constitution 1983, guerrilla activity continued. Duarte won the 1984 presidential election and in 1985 the anti-imperialist PDC won a convincing victory in the assembly, with 33 seats. The right-wing groups ARENA and PCN won 13 and 12 seats respectively, fighting the election on a joint platform. In 1984 the president's daughter was abducted by guerrillas, forcing him to negotiate with them, in the face of criticism from opposition parties and the military. The guerrilla war continued, Duarte again attempting, in 1986, to negotiate a settlement with the rebels. In Aug 1987 they agreed to meet and discuss the Regional Peace Plan with him.

The peace initiative eventually collapsed and in the Mar 1989 elections the right-wing Alfredo Cristiani became president, taking up office in

El Salvador
Republic of
(República de El Salvador)

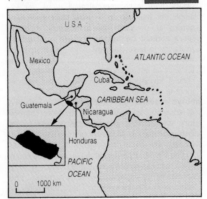

area 21,393 sq km/8,258 sq mi
capital San Salvador
physical flat in S, rising to mountains in N
features smallest and most thickly populated Central American country
head of state and government Alfredo Cristiani from 1989
political system emergent democracy
political parties Christian Democrats (PDC), anti-imperialist; National Republican Alliance (ARENA), right-wing; National Conciliation Party (PCN), right-wing
exports coffee, cotton
currency colón (10.91 = £1 Feb 1990)

population (1985) 5,480,000 (mainly of Spanish-Indian extraction, including some 500,000 illegally in the US); annual growth rate 2.9%
life expectancy men 63, women 67
language Spanish
religion Roman Catholic
literacy 75% male/69% female (1985 est)
GDP $4.3 bn (1984); $854 per head of population
chronology
1829 Achieved independence.
1961 Right-wing coup.
1972 Allegations of human-rights violations and growth of left-wing guerrilla activities. Gen Carlos Romero elected president.
1979 A coup replaced Romero with a military-civilian junta.
1980 Archbishop Oscar Romero assassinated. Country on verge of civil war. José Duarte became president.
1981 The Mexican and French governments recognized the guerrillas as a legitimate political force but the USA actively assisted the government in its battle against them.
1982 Assembly elections boycotted by left-wing parties and held amid considerable violence.
1985 Right-wing majority in the national assembly elections.
1986 Duarte sought a negotiated settlement with the guerrillas.
1988 Duarte resigned following diagnosis of terminal cancer.
1989 Alfredo Cristiani (ARENA) elected president, amid allegations of rigging; guerrillas agreed to hold peace talks.

June. In Sept the socialist guerrilla movement agreed to hold peace talks.

Elsheimer /ˈelshaɪmə/ Adam 1578–1610. German painter and etcher, active in Rome from 1600. His small paintings, nearly all on copper, depict landscapes darkened by storm or night, with figures picked out by beams of light, as in *The Rest on the Flight into Egypt* 1609 (Alte Pinakothek, Munich).

Elsinore another form of ◊Helsingør, a port on the NE coast of Denmark.

Elton /ˈeltən/ Charles 1900– . British ecologist, a pioneer of the study of animal and plant forms in their natural environments, and of animal behaviour as part of the complex pattern of life. Elton published *Animal Ecology and Evolution* 1930 and *The Pattern of Animal Communities* 1966.

Eluard /ˌeɪluːˈɑː/ Paul. Pen name of Eugène Grindel 1895–1952. French poet, born in Paris. He expressed the suffering of poverty in his verse, and was a leader of the Surrealists. He fought in World War I, the inspiration for *Poèmes pour la paix/Poems for Peace* 1918, and was a member of the Resistance in World War II. His books include *Poésie et vérité/Poetry and Truth* 1942 and *Au Rendezvous allemand/To the German Rendezvous* 1944.

Ely /ˈiːli/ city in Cambridgeshire, England, on the Great Ouse river 24 km/15 mi NE of Cambridge; population (1983) 11,030. It has sugar beet, paper, and engineering factories.

history It was the chief town of the former administrative district of the *Isle of Ely*, so called because the area was once cut off from the surrounding countryside by the fens. ◊Hereward the Wake had his stronghold here. The 11th-century cathedral is one of the largest in England. At the annual feast of St Ethelreda (Audrey), founder of a religious community at Ely in the 7th century, cheap, low-quality souvenirs were sold; the word 'tawdry', a corruption of St Audrey, derives from this practice.

Elyot /ˈeliət/ Thomas 1490–1546. English diplomat and scholar. In 1531 he published *The Governour*, the first treatise on education in English.

Elysée Palace (*Palais de l'Elysée*) building in Paris erected 1718 for Louis d'Auvergne, Count of Evreux. It was later the home of Mme de Pompadour, Napoleon I, and Napoleon III, and became the official residence of the presidents of France 1870.

Elysium /ɪˈlɪziəm/ or *Elysian Fields* in classical mythology, an afterworld or paradise (sometimes called the Islands of the Blessed) for the souls of those who found favour with the gods; it was situated near the river Oceanus.

Elzevir /ˈelzəviə/ Louis 1540–1617. Founder of the Dutch printing house of Elzevir in the the 17th century. Among the firm's publications were editions of Latin, Greek, and Hebrew works, and French and Italian classics.

Born at Louvain, Elzevir was obliged to leave Belgium in 1580 because of his Protestant and political views. He settled at Leyden as a bookseller and printer.

Emancipation Proclamation, The in US history, President Lincoln's Civil War announcement, 22 Sept 1862, stating that from the beginning of 1863 all black slaves in states still engaged in rebellion against the federal government would be emancipated. Slaves in border states still remaining loyal to the union were excluded.

Emba /ˈembə/ river 612 km/380 mi long in the Kazakh Republic, USSR, draining into the N part of the Caspian Sea.

embargo the legal prohibition by a government of trade with another country, forbidding foreign ships to leave or enter its ports. Trade embargoes may be imposed on a country seen to be violating international laws.

The US Embargo Act 1807 was passed to prevent France and the UK taking measures to stop US ships carrying war weapons to European belligerents. It proved to be a counterproductive move, as did an embargo by Middle Eastern oil producers on oil shipments to W Europe in 1974.

embezzlement in law, theft by an employee of property entrusted to him or her by an employer. In British law it is no longer a distinct offence from theft.

embolism blockage of an artery by an obstruction called an embolus (usually a blood clot, fat particle, or bubble of air).

embroidery the art of decorating cloth with a needle and thread. It includes ◊broderie anglaise, ◊gros point, and ◊petit point; all of which have been used for the adornment of costumes, gloves, book covers, curtains, and ecclesiastical vestments.

The earliest embroidery that survives in England is the stole and maniple (a decorative strip of silk worn over the arm), found in the tomb of St Cuthbert at Durham dating from 905. The ◊Bayeux 'Tapestry' is an embroidery dating from 1067–70. In Britain embroidery on canvas and linen for household purposes, together with ◊appliqué, was popular early in the 20th century. Since the 1950s there has been a revival of creative embroidery in many countries.

embryo early development stage of animals and plants following fertilization of an ovum (egg cell), or activation of an ovum by ◊parthenogenesis.

In animals the embryo exists either within an egg (where it is nourished by food contained in the yolk), or in mammals, in the ◊uterus of the mother. In mammals (except marsupials) the embryo is fed through the ◊placenta. In humans the term embryo describes the fertilized egg during its first seven weeks of existence; from the eighth week it is referred to as the fetus. The plant embryo is found within the seed in higher plants. It sometimes consists of only a few cells, but usually includes a root, a shoot (or primary bud), and one or two ◊cotyledons, which nourish the growing seedling.

embryology the study of the changes undergone by living matter from its conception as a fertilized ovum (egg) to its emergence into the world at hatching or birth. It is mainly concerned with the changes in cell organization in the embryo and the way in which these lead to the structures and organs of the adult (the process of ◊differentiation).

Applications of embryology include embryo transplants, both in commercial applications (for example, in building up a prize dairy cow herd quickly at low cost) and in obstetric medicine (as a method for helping couples with fertility problems to have children). This usually involves the surgical removal of eggs from a woman, their fertilization under laboratory conditions and, once normal development is under way, their replacement in the womb.

embryo research the study of human embryos at an early stage, in order to detect hereditary disease and genetic defects, and to investigate the problems of subfertility and infertility.

The UK Medical Research Council laid down in 1982 that experiments on human embryos were acceptable for approved research purposes, provided both donors agreed. There must also be no intent to transfer the embryo to the uterus, or to culture it beyond the stage when implantation was possible. The Warnock Report 1984 proposed to limit experiment to up to 14 days after fertilization (the point at which the embryo 'decides' to become a single individual or a multiple birth). It also recommended strict controls on AID (artificial insemination by donor); IVF (*in vitro* fertilization), fertilization outside the body ('test-tube baby') when either the sperm or the egg (or both) do not necessarily come from the couple involved as eventual parents; and condemned surrogate motherhood, or 'womb leasing', in which a woman is artificially inseminated and bears a child for another couple. In 1990, a UK act of Parliament allowed embryo research for up to 14 days after

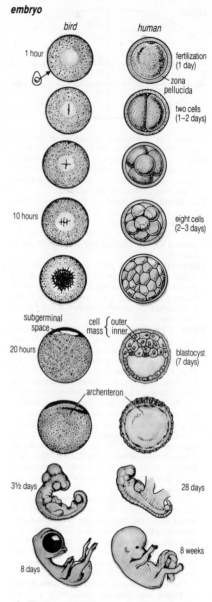

embryo

bird — human

1 hour — fertilization (1 day) — zona pellucida

two cells (1–2 days)

10 hours — eight cells (2–3 days)

subgerminal space — cell mass {outer inner

20 hours — blastocyst (7 days)

archenteron

3½ days — 28 days

8 days — 8 weeks

fertilization, under the control of an independent committee.

embryo sac a large cell within the ovule of flowering plants which represents the female ◊gametophyte when fully developed. It typically contains eight nuclei. Fertilization occurs when one of these nuclei, the egg nucleus, fuses with a male ◊gamete.

Emden /ˈemdən/ port in Lower Saxony, West Germany, at the mouth of the river Ems; population (1984) 51,000. It is an important fishing port and export outlet for the ◊Ruhr, with which it is connected by the Dortmund–Ems canal. There are oil refineries here.

emerald a clear, green gemstone variety of the mineral ◊beryl.

emergent properties features of a system that are due to the way in which its components are structured in relation to each other, rather than to the individual properties of those components. Thus the distinctive characteristics of chemical ◊compounds are emergent properties of the way in which the constituent elements are organized, and cannot be explained by the particular properties of those elements taken in isolation. In biology, ◊ecosystem stability is an emergent property of the interaction between the constituent species, and not a property of the species themselves.

Emerson *Ralph Waldo Emerson, poet and essayist. His lucid style and clarity of thought made his writings eminently quotable, although he claimed to 'hate quotations'.*

emeritus (Latin) someone who has retired from an official position but retains their title on an honorary basis, for example, a *professor emeritus*.

Emerson /'emǝsǝn/ Ralph Waldo 1803–1882. US philosopher, essayist, and poet. In 1933 he settled in Concord, Massachusetts, which he made a centre of ◊transcendentalism, and wrote *Nature* 1836, which states the movement's main principles emphasizing the value of self-reliance and the God-like nature of human souls. His two volumes of *Essays* (1841, 1844) made his reputation.

Born in Boston, Massachusetts, and educated at Harvard, Emerson became a Unitarian minister. In 1832 he resigned and travelled to Europe, meeting the British writers Carlyle, Coleridge, and Wordsworth. He made a second visit to England 1847 and incorporated his impressions in *English Traits* 1856. Much of his verse was published in the literary magazine the *Dial*. His work includes *Representative Life* 1850 and *The Conduct of Life* 1870.

emery /'emǝri/ a greyish-black opaque metamorphic rock consisting of ◊corundum and magnetite, together with other minerals such as hematite. It is used as an ◊abrasive. Emery occurs on the island of Naxos, Greece, and in Turkey.

emetic substance administered to induce vomiting.

emf in physics, abbreviation for ◊*electromotive force*.

Emi Koussi /,emɪ'ku:si/ highest point of the Tibesti massif in N Chad, rising to 3,425 m/11,204 ft.

Emilia-Romagna /e'mi:ljǝrǝʊ'mænjǝ/ region of N central Italy including much of the Po valley; area 22,100 sq km/8,531 sq mi; population (1988) 3,924,000. The capital is Bologna; other towns include Reggio, Rimini, Parma, Ferrara, and Ravenna. Agricultural produce includes fruit, wine, sugar beet, beef, and dairy products; oil and natural gas resources have been developed in the Po valley.

éminence grise /'emɪnɒns 'gri:z/ (French 'grey eminence') a power behind a throne; that is, a manipulator of power without immediate responsibility. The nickname was originally applied (because of his grey cloak) to the French monk François Leclerc du Tremblay (1577–1638), also known as Père Joseph, who in 1612 became the close friend and behind-the-scenes adviser of Cardinal Richelieu.

eminent domain in the USA, the right of federal and state government and other authorized bodies to compulsorily purchase land which is needed for public purposes. The owner is entitled to receive a fair price fo the land.

In Britain ◊compulsory purchase gives similar powers.

Eminent Persons Group group of seven Commonwealth politicians deputed by Commonwealth leaders in Dec 1985 to visit South Africa to report on the political situation there. It was chaired jointly by Malcolm Fraser of Australia and Olusegun Obasanjo, former head of the Nigerian government. Its report, *Mission to South Africa* 1986, proposed among other things the abolition of ◊apartheid.

Emin Pasha /e'mi:n/ Mehmed, born Eduard Schnitzer 1849–1892. German explorer, doctor and linguist. Appointed by Gen Gordon as chief medical officer and then governor of the Equatorial Province, he carried out extensive research in anthropology, botany, zoology, and meteorology.

Isolated by his remote location and cut off from the outside world by Arab slave traders, he was 'rescued' by an expedition led by H M Stanley in 1889. He travelled with Stanley as far as Zanzibar but returned to continue his work near Lake Victoria. Three years later he was killed by Arabs while leading an expedition to the W coast of Africa.

Emmental /'emǝntɑ:l/ district in the valley of the Emme river, Berne, Switzerland, where a hard cheese of the same name has been made since the mid 15th century.

Emmet /'emɪt/ Robert 1778–1803. Irish nationalist leader. In 1803 he led an unsuccessful revolt in Dublin against British rule, and was captured, tried, and hanged. His youth and courage made him an Irish hero.

emotivism a philosophical position in the theory of ethics. It came to prominence during the 1930s, largely under the influence of *Language, Truth and Logic* 1936 by A J ◊Ayer. Emotivists deny that moral judgments can be true or false, maintaining that they merely express an attitude or an emotional response.

Empedocles /em'pedǝkli:z/ *c.*490–430 BC. Greek philosopher and scientist. He lived at Acragas (Agrigentum) in Sicily, and is known for his analysis of the universe into the four elements—fire, air, earth, and water—which through the action of love and discord are eternally constructed, destroyed, and constructed anew. According to tradition, he committed suicide by throwing himself into the crater of Mount Etna.

emphysema an incurable condition of extreme and disabling breathlessness. It is due to the progressive loss of the thin walls dividing the air spaces in the lungs, which reduces the area available for the exchange of oxygen. Emphysema is most often seen at an advanced stage of chronic ◊bronchitis, although it may develop in other long-standing disease of the lungs.

empiricism (Greek *empeiria* 'experience' or 'experiment') in philosophy, the belief that all knowledge is ultimately derived from sense experience. It is suspicious of metaphysical schemes based on ◊*a priori* propositions, which are claimed to be true irrespective of experience. It is frequently contrasted with ◊rationalism. Empiricism developed in the 17th and early 18th centuries through the work of ◊Locke, ◊Berkeley, and ◊Hume, traditionally known as the British empiricist school.

Employers and Workmen Act UK act of Parliament 1875 which limited the penalty for a breach of contract of employer by a worker to civil damages. Previously, employees who broke their contracts faced penalties imposed under criminal law.

employers' association an organization of employers formed for purposes of collective action. In the UK there were formerly three main organizations, which in 1965 combined as the ◊Confederation of British Industry.

Employer's Liability Act UK act of Parliament 1880 which obtained for workers or their families a right to compensation from employers whose negligence resulted in industrial injury or death at work.

enamel *Enamel plate showing the Virgin and child.*

employment exchange agency for bringing together employers requiring labour and workers seeking employment. Employment exchanges may be organized by central government or a local authority (known in the UK as Job Centres); or as private business ventures (employment agencies).

employment law law covering the rights and duties of employers and employees. In the UK, in the past, relations between employer and employee were covered mainly by the ◊common law, but statute law has become increasingly important in the 20th century, particularly in giving new rights to employees.

The first major employment legislation in Britain was in the 19th century, regulating conditions in factories. Legislation in this area culminated in the Health and Safety at Work Act 1974, which set up the Health and Safety Commission. Other employees' rights include: the right to a formal contract detailing wage rates, hours of work, holidays, injury and sick pay, and length of notice to terminate employment; the right to compensation on ◊redundancy; the right not to be unfairly dismissed; and the right to maternity leave and pay. These are set out in the Employment Protection (Consolidation) Act 1978. The Equal Pay Act 1970 (in force from 1975) prevents unequal pay for men and women in the same jobs. Discrimination against employees on the ground of their sex or race are illegal under the Sex Discrimination Act 1975 and the Race Relations Act 1976. See also ◊trade union.

EMS abbreviation for ◊*European Monetary System*.

emu flightless bird *Dromaius novaehollandiae*, native to Australia. It stands about 1.8 m/6 ft high, has coarse brown plumage, small rudimentary wings, short feathers on the head and neck, and powerful legs, well adapted for running and kicking. The female has a curious bag or pouch in the windpipe that enables it to emit the characteristic loud booming note.

EMU abbreviation for *economic and monetary union*, the proposed European Community policy for a single currency and common economic policies.

emulsifier a food ◊additive used to keep oils dispersed and in suspension, in products such as mayonnaise and peanut butter. Egg yolk is a naturally occurring emulsifier, but most commercial emulsifiers are synthetic chemicals.

emulsion a type of ◊colloid, consisting of a stable dispersion of a liquid in another liquid, for example, oil and water in some cosmetic lotions.

enamel vitrified (glass-like) coating of various colours used for decorative purposes on a metallic or porcelain surface. In ◊*cloisonné* the various sections of the design are separated by thin metal wires or strips. In ***champlevé*** the enamel is poured into engraved cavities in the metal surface.

The ancient art of enamelling is believed to be of Near Eastern origin. The Egyptians, Greeks, and Romans enamelled their jewellery, and Byzantium was famed for enamels from about the 9th to 11th centuries. The enamelled altarpiece at St Mark's, Venice, which was brought from Constantinople, still survives. Byzantine work was emulated in Europe, particularly in Saxony, Brunswick, and in the Rhine valley. German enamellers were later employed in France, and during the 13th and 14th centuries the art was introduced into Italy and China. The chief centres of enamelling during the 15th and 16th centuries were the cities of Lorraine and Limoges, France.

encaustic painting an ancient technique of painting, commonly used by the Egyptians, Greeks, and Romans, in which coloured pigments were mixed with molten wax and painted on panels.

encephalin a naturally occurring chemical produced by nerve cells that has the same effect as morphine, acting as a natural painkiller. Unlike morphine, encephalins are quickly degraded by the body, so there is no build-up of tolerance to them, and hence no 'addiction'. Encephalins are a variety of ◊peptides, as are ◊endorphins, which have similar effects.

encephalitis inflammation of the brain, nearly always due to virus infection. It varies widely in severity, from short-lived, relatively slight effects to paralysis, coma, and death.

Encke's comet a comet with the shortest known orbital period, 3.3 years. It is named after German mathematician and astronomer Johann Franz Encke (1791–1865), who in 1819 calculated the orbit from earlier sightings.

It was first sighted in 1786 by the French astronomer Mechain. It was rediscovered by ◊Herschel in 1795 and independently by Pons, Huth, and Bouvard in 1805. In 1913, it became the first comet to be observed throughout its entire orbit when it was photographed near ◊aphelion (the point in its orbit furthest from the Sun) by astronomers at Mount Wilson Observatory in California, USA.

enclosure appropriation of common land as private property, or the changing of open-field systems to enclosed fields (often used for sheep). This process began in Britain in the 14th century, and became widespread in the 15th and 16th centuries. It caused poverty, homelessness, and rural depopulation, and resulted in revolts 1536, 1569, and 1607.

Numerous government measures to prevent depopulation were introduced 1489–1640, but were sabotaged by landowning magistrates at local level. A new wave of enclosures by act of Parliament 1760–1820 reduced the yeoman class of small landowning farmers to agricultural labourers, or forced them to leave the land. The Enclosure Acts applied to 4.5 million acres or a quarter of England. From 1876 the enclosure of common land in Britain was limited by statutes. Enclosures occurred throughout Europe on a large scale during the 19th century, often at the behest of governments.

encyclical a letter addressed by the pope to Roman Catholic bishops for the benefit of the laity. The first was issued by Benedict XIV in 1740, but encyclicals became common only in the 19th century. They may be doctrinal (condemning errors), exhortative (recommending devotional activities), or commemorative.

Recent encyclicals include *Pacem in terris* (Pope John XXIII, 1963), *Sacerdotalis celibatus* (on the celibacy of the clergy, Pope Paul VI, 1967), and *Humanae vitae* (Pope Paul VI, 1967, on methods of contraception).

encyclopedia a work of reference, either all fields of knowledge or one specific subject. Although most encyclopedias are alphabetic with cross-references, some are organized thematically with indexes, in order to keep related subjects together.

The earliest extant encyclopedia is the *Historia Naturalis/Natural History* AD 23–79 of ◊Pliny the Elder. The first alphabetical encyclopedia in English was the *Lexicon Technicum/Technical Lexicon*

1704, compiled by John Harris. In 1728 Ephraim Chambers published his *Cyclopaedia*, which coordinated the scattered articles by a system of cross-references, and was translated into French 1743–45. This translation formed the basis of the *Encyclopédie* edited by Diderot and d'Alembert, published 1751–72. By this time the system of engaging a body of expert compilers and editors was established, and in 1768–71 the *Encyclopaedia Britannica* first made its appearance.

Famous encyclopedias include the Chinese encyclopedia printed 1726, the German *Conversations-Lexikon/Conversation Lexicon* of Brockhaus, and the French *Grand Dictionnaire Universel du XIXme Siècle/Great Universal Dictionary of the 19th Century* of Pierre Larousse 1866–76.

Encyclopédie encyclopedia in 28 volumes written 1751–72 by a group of French scholars (*Encyclopédistes*) including D'Alembert and Diderot, inspired by the English encyclopedia produced by Ephraim Chambers 1728. Religious scepticism and ◊Enlightenment social and political views were a feature of the work.

endangered species plant or animal species whose numbers are so few that it is at risk of becoming extinct. Officially designated endangered species are listed by the International Union for the Conservation of Nature (◊IUCN).

An example of an endangered species is the Javan rhino. There are only about 50 alive today and, unless active steps are taken to promote this species' survival, it will probably be extinct within a few decades.

endemic (of a disease) more or less prevalent in a given region or country all the time. It refers most often to tropical diseases, such as ◊malaria, which are particularly hard to eradicate.

Ender /ˈendə/ Kornelia 1958– . West German swimmer. She won a record-equalling four gold medals at the 1976 Olympics at freestyle, butterfly, and relay. She won a total of eight Olympic medals 1972–76. She also won a record ten world championship medals 1973 and 1975.

CAREER HIGHLIGHTS

Olympic champion:
100 m Freestyle (1976)
200 m Freestyle (1976)
100 m Butterfly (1976) 4x100 m Medley Relay (1976)
World Champion:
100 m Freestyle (1973, 1975)
100 m Butterfly (1973, 1975)
4x100 m Freestyle Relay (1973, 1975)
4x100 m Medley Relay (1973, 1975)

Enders /ˈendəz/ John Franklin 1897–1985. US virologist. With Thomas Weller and Frederick Robbins, he discovered the ability of the polio virus to grow in cultures of different tissues, which led to the perfection of an effective vaccine. They were awarded the Nobel Prize for Medicine 1954. He also succeeded in isolating the measles virus.

endive hardy annual plant *Cichorium endivia*, family Compositae, the leaves of which are used in salads and cooking. It is related to ◊chicory.

endocrine gland a gland which secretes hormones into the bloodstream to regulate body processes. Endocrine glands are most highly developed in vertebrates, but are also found in other animals, notably insects. In humans, the main endocrine glands are the pituitary, thyroid, parathyroid, adrenal, pancreas, ovary, and testis.

endometriosis a common gynaecological complaint in which patches of endometrium (the lining of the womb) are found outside the uterus. This ◊ectopic (abnormally positioned) tissue is present most often in the ovaries, although it may invade any pelvic or abdominal site, as well as the vagina and rectum. Endometriosis may be treated with analgesics, hormone preparations, or surgery.

endoparasite a ◊parasite that lives inside its host.

endoplasm part of a cell's ◊cytoplasm.

endorphin a natural substance (a polypeptide) that modifies the action of nerve cells. Endorphins are produced by the pituitary gland and hypothalamus

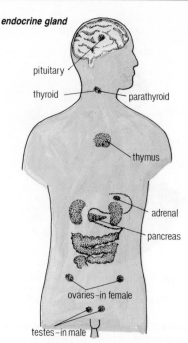

endocrine gland

pituitary
thyroid
parathyroid
thymus
adrenal
pancreas
ovaries–in female
testes–in male

of vertebrates. They lower the perception of pain by reducing the transmission of signals between nerve cells.

Endorphins not only regulate pain and hunger, but are also involved in the release of sex hormones from the pituitary gland. Opiates act in a similar way to endorphins but are not rapidly degraded by the body, as natural endorphins are, and thus have a long-lasting effect on pain perception and mood.

endoscopy the examination of internal organs or tissues by direct vision. The instrument used (an *endoscope*) is equipped with an eyepiece, lenses, and its own light source to illuminate the field of vision.

endoskeleton the internal supporting structure of vertebrates, made up of cartilage or bone. It provides support, and acts as a system of levers to which muscles are attached to provide movement. Certain parts of the skeleton (the skull and ribs) give protection to vital body organs.

Sponges are supported by a network of rigid or semi-rigid, spiky structures called spicules; a bath sponge is the proteinaceous skeleton of a sponge.

endosperm a nutritive tissue in the seeds of most flowering plants. It surrounds the embryo and is produced by an unusual process that parallels the ◊fertilization of the ovum by a male gamete. A second male gamete from the pollen grain fuses with two female nuclei within the ◊embryo sac. Thus the endosperm cells are triploid (having three sets of chromosomes). They contain food reserves such as starch, fat, and protein which are utilized by the developing seedling.

In 'non-endospermic' seeds, absorption of these food molecules by the embryo is completed early, so that the endosperm has disappeared by the time of germination.

endotherm a 'warm-blooded', or homeothermic, animal. See ◊homeothermy.

endothermic reaction a chemical reaction that requires an input of heat for it to proceed (see ◊energy of reaction).

endowment insurance a type of life insurance that may produce profits. An endowment policy will run for a fixed number of years during which it accumulates a cash value; it provides a savings plan for a retirement fund, and may be used to help with a house purchase, linked to a building society mortgage.

end user a user of a computer program, in particular someone who uses a program to perform a task (such as accounting or playing a computer game) rather than someone who writes programs (a programmer).

Endymion in Greek mythology, a beautiful young man loved by Selene, the moon goddess. He was granted eternal sleep in order to remain for ever young. The English poet Keats's poem *Endymion* 1818 is an allegory of searching for perfection.

Energiya Soviet shuttle booster, launched 15 May 1987. When fully operational, the Energiya booster will be used to launch the Soviet shuttle Buran, and will be capable, with the use of strap-on boosters, of launching payloads of up to 230 tonnes into Earth-orbit.

energy the capacity for doing ◊work. *Potential energy* (PE) is energy deriving from position; thus a stretched spring has elastic PE; an object raised to a height above the earth's surface, or the water in an elevated reservoir, has gravitational PE; a lump of coal and a tank of petrol, together with the oxygen needed for their combustion, have chemical PE (due to relative positions of atoms). Other sorts of PE include electrical and nuclear. Moving bodies possess *kinetic energy* (KE). Energy can be converted from one form to another, but the total quantity stays the same (in accordance with the conservation laws that govern many natural phenomena). For example, as an apple falls, it loses gravitational PE but gains KE.

So-called energy resources are stores of convertible energy. Non-renewable resources include the fossil fuels (coal, oil, and gas) and ◊nuclear fission 'fuels', for example uranium-235. Renewable resources, which have so far been less exploited, depend ultimately on the Sun's energy. Hydroelectric schemes are well established, and wind turbines and tidal systems are being developed.

Einstein's special theory of ◊relativity 1905 correlates any gain, E, in KE with a loss, m, in 'rest mass', by the equation $E = mc_2$, in which E is energy and c is the speed of light. The equation applies universally, not just to nuclear reactions, though it is only for these that the percentage change in rest mass is large enough to detect. Although energy is never lost, after a number of conversions it tends to finish up as KE of random motion of molecules (of the air, for example) at lowish temperatures. This is 'degraded' energy in that it is difficult to convert it back to other forms.

Burning fossil fuels causes ◊acid rain and is gradually increasing the carbon dioxide content in the atmosphere, with unknown consequences for future generations. Coal-fired power stations also release significant amounts of radioactive material, and the potential dangers of nuclear power stations are greater still.

The ultimate non-renewable but almost inexhaustible energy source would be nuclear fusion (the way in which energy is generated in the Sun), but controlled fusion is a long way off. (The hydrogen bomb is a fusion bomb.) Harnessing resources generally implies converting their energy into electrical form, because electrical energy is easy to convert to other forms and to transmit from place to place, though not to store.

energy of reaction energy released or absorbed during a chemical reaction. The energy stored in the reacting molecules is rarely the same as that stored in the product molecules. Depending on which is the greater, energy is either released or absorbed from the surroundings (see ◊conservation of energy). The amount of energy released or absorbed by the quantities of substances represented by the chemical equation is the energy of reaction.

enfant terrible (French 'terrible child') one whose rash and unconventional behaviour shocks and embarrasses others.

Enfield /'enfi:ld/ borough of NE Greater London; population (1981) 259,000. Industries include engineering—the Royal Small Arms factory was famous for its production of the Enfield rifle—textiles, furniture, and cement. Little remains of

Engels *German socialist philosopher Friedrich Engels.*

Edward VI's palace, but the royal hunting ground of Enfield Chase partly survives in the 'green belt'. The borough includes the district of Edmonton, where John Keats and Charles and Mary Lamb once lived (the Lambs are buried there); and the Bell Inn, referred to in William Cowper's poem 'John Gilpin'. From the 1970s the Lea Valley has been developed as London's first regional park.

Engadine /'engədi:n/ the upper valley of the river Inn in Switzerland, famous as a winter sports resort.

Engel Carl Ludwig 1778–1840/ German architect, who from 1815 worked in Finland., His great Neo-Classical achievement is the Senate Square in Helsinki, which is defined by his Senate House (1818–22) and University Building (1828–32) and crowned by the domed Lutheran cathedral (1830–40)

Engels /'engəlz/ Friedrich 1820–1895. German social and political philosopher, a friend of, and collaborator with, Karl ◊Marx on *The Communist Manifesto* 1848 and other key works. His later interpretations of Marxism, and his own philosophical and historical studies such as *Origins of the Family, Private Property, and the State* 1884 (which linked patriarchy with the development of private property), developed such concepts as historical materialism. His use of positivism and Darwinian ideas gave Marxism a scientific and deterministic flavour which was to influence Soviet thinking.

In 1842 Engels's father sent him to work in the cotton factory owned by his family in Manchester, England, where he became involved with ◊Chartism. In 1844 began his lifelong friendship with Karl Marx, and together they worked out the materialist interpretation of history and in 1847–48 wrote the *Communist Manifesto*. Returning to Germany during the 1848–49 revolution, Engels worked with Marx on the *Neue Rheinische Zeitung* newspaper and fought on the barricades in Baden. After the defeat of the revolution he returned to Manchester, and for the rest of his life largely supported the Marx family.

Engels's first book was *The Condition of the Working Classes in England* 1845. The lessons of 1848 he summed up in *The Peasants' War in Germany* 1850 and *Revolution and Counter-Revolution in Germany* 1851. After Marx's death Engels was largely responsible for the wider dissemination of his ideas; he edited the second and third volumes of Marx's *Capital* 1885 and 1894. Although Engels himself regarded his ideas as identical with those of Marx, discrepancies between their works are the basis of many modern Marxist debates.

engine a device for converting stored energy into useful work or movement. Most engines use a fuel as their energy store. The fuel is burnt to produce heat energy—hence the name 'heat engine'—which is then converted into movement. Heat engines can be classifed according to the fuel they use (◊petrol engine or ◊diesel engine), or according to whether the fuel is burnt inside (◊internal combustion engine) or outside (◊steam

engine) the engine, or according to whether they produce a reciprocating or rotary motion (◊turbine or ◊Wankel engine).

engineering the application of science to the design, construction and maintenance of works, machinery, roads, railways, bridges, harbour installations, engines, ships, aircraft and airports, spacecraft and space stations, and the generation, transmission and use of electrical power. The main divisions of engineering are aerospace, chemical, civil, electrical, electronic, gas, marine, materials, mechanical, mining, production, radio and structural engineering.

To practise engineering professionally a university or college training in addition to practical experience is required, but technician engineers usually receive their training through apprenticeships or similar training schemes.

engineering drawing a technical drawing that forms the plans for the design and construction of engineering components and structures. Engineering drawings show different projections, or views of objects, with the relevant dimensions, and show how all the separate parts fit together.

England /'ɪŋglənd/ largest division of the ◊United Kingdom
area 130,357 sq km/50,318 sq mi
capital London
towns Birmingham, Cambridge, Coventry, Leeds, Leicester, Manchester, Newcastle-upon-Tyne, Nottingham, Oxford, Sheffield, York; ports Bristol, Dover, Felixstowe, Harwich, Liverpool, Portsmouth, Southampton
features variability of climate and diversity of scenery; among European countries, only the Netherlands is more densely populated
exports agricultural (cereals, rape, sugar beet, potatoes); meat and meat products; electronic (especially software), and telecommunications equipment (main centres Berkshire and Cambridge); scientific instruments; textiles and fashion goods; North Sea oil and gas, petrochemicals, pharmaceuticals, fertilizers; beer; china clay, pottery, porcelain, and glass; film and television programmes, and sound recordings. Tourism is important. There are worldwide banking and insurance interests
currency pound sterling
population (1986) 47,255,000
language English, with more than 100 minority languages
religion Christian, with the Church of England as the established church, 1,600,000; and various Protestant sects, of which the largest is the Methodist 1,400,000; Roman Catholic about 4,000,000; Jewish 330,000; Muslim 1,500,000; Sikh 500,000; Hindu 300,000.

For *government* and *history*, see ◊Britain, ancient; ◊England, history; ◊United Kingdom.

England: counties

County	Administrative headquarters	Area sq km
Avon	Bristol	1,340
Bedfordshire	Bedford	1,240
Berkshire	Reading	1,260
Buckinghamshire	Aylesbury	1,880
Cambridgeshire	Cambridge	3,410
Cheshire	Chester	2,320
Cleveland	Middlesbrough	580
Cornwall	Truro	3,550
Cumbria	Carlisle	6,810
Derbyshire	Matlock	2,630
Devon	Exeter	6,720
Durham	Durham	2,440
East Sussex	Lewes	1,800
Essex	Chelmsford	3,670
Gloucestershire	Gloucester	2,640
Hampshire	Winchester	3,770
Hereford & Worcester	Worcester	3,930
Hertfordshire	Hertford	1,630
Humberside	Beverly	3,510
Isle of Wight	Newport	380

Kent	Maidstone	3,730
Lancashire	Preston	3,040
Leicestershire	Leicester	2,550
Lincolnshire	Lincoln	5,890
London, Greater		1,580
Manchester, Greater		1,290
Merseyside	Liverpool	650
Norfolk	Norwich	5,360
Northamptonshire	Northampton	2,370
Northumberland	Morpeth	5,030
North Yorkshire	Northallerton	8,320
Nottinghamshire	Nottingham	2,160
Oxfordshire	Oxford	2,610
Shropshire	Shrewsbury	3,490
Somerset	Taunton	3,460
South Yorkshire	Barnsley	1,560
Staffordshire	Stafford	2,720
Suffolk	Ipswich	3,800
Surrey	Kingston upon Thames	1,660
Tyne & Wear	Newcastle-upon-Tyne	540
Warwickshire	Warwick	1,980
West Midlands	Birmingham	960
West Sussex	Chichester	2,020
West Yorkshire	Wakefield	2,040
Wiltshire	Trowbridge	3,480

England: history for pre-Roman history, see ◊Britain, ancient.

5th–7th centuries Anglo-Saxons overran all England except Cornwall and Cumberland, forming independent kingdoms including Northumbria, Mercia, Kent, and Wessex.

c.597 England converted to Christianity by St Augustine.

829 Egbert of Wessex accepted as overlord of all England.

878 Alfred ceded N and E England to the Danish invaders but kept them out of Wessex.

1066 Norman Conquest; England passed into French hands under William the Conqueror.

1172 Henry II became King of Ireland, and established a colony there.

1215 King John forced to sign Magna Carta.

1284 Conquest of Wales, begun by the Normans, completed by Edward I.

1295 Model Parliament set up.

1338–1453 Hundred Years' War with France enabled Parliament to secure control of taxation, and, by impeachment, of the king's choice of ministers.

1348–49 Black Death killed about 30% of the population.

1381 Social upheaval led to the ◊Peasants' Revolt, which was brutally repressed.

1399 Richard II deposed by Parliament for absolutism.

1414 Lollard revolt repressed.

1455–85 Wars of the Roses.

1497 Henry VII ended the power of the feudal nobility with the suppression of the Yorkist revolts.

1529 Henry VIII became head of the English Church after breaking with Rome.

1536–43 Acts of Union united England and Wales after conquest.

1547 Edward VI adopted Protestant doctrines.

1553 Reversion to Roman Catholicism under Mary I.

1558 Elizabeth I adopted a religious compromise.

1588 Attempted invasion of England by the Spanish Armada.

1603 James I united the English and Scottish crowns; parliamentary dissidence increased.

1642–52 Civil War between Royalists and Parliamentarians, resulting in victory for Parliament.

1649 Charles I executed and the Commonwealth set up.

1653 Oliver Cromwell appointed Lord Protector.

1660 Restoration of Charles II.

1685 Monmouth rebellion.

1688 William of Orange invited to take the throne; flight of James II.

English sovereigns from 900

West Saxon Kings

Edward the Elder	901
Athelstan	925
Edmund	940
Edred	946
Edwy	955
Edgar	959
Edward the Martyr	975
Ethelred II	978
Edmund Ironside	1016

Danish Kings

Canute	1016
Hardicanute	1040
Harold I	1035

West Saxon Kings (restored)

Edward the Confessor	1042
Harold II	1066

Norman Kings

William I	1066
William II	1087
Henry I	1100
Stephen	1135

House of Plantagenet

Henry II	1154
Richard I	1189
John	1199
Henry III	1216
Edward I	1272
Edward II	1307
Edward III	1327
Richard II	1377

House of Lancaster

Henry IV	1399
Henry V	1413
Henry VI	1422

House of York

Edward IV	1461
Richard III	1483
Edward V	1483

House of Tudor

Henry VII	1485
Henry VIII	1509
Edward VI	1547
Mary I	1553
Elizabeth I	1558

House of Stuart

James I	1603
Charles I	1625

The Commonwealth

House of Stuart (restored)

Charles II	1660
James II	1685
William III and Mary	1689
Anne	1702

House of Hanover

George I	1714
George II	1727
George III	1760
George IV	1820
William IV	1830
Victoria	1837

House of Saxe-Coburg

Edward VII	1901

House of Windsor

George V	1910
Edward VIII	1936
George VI	1936
Elizabeth II	1952

1707 Act of Union between England and Scotland under Queen Anne, after which the countries became known as Great Britain.

For further history, see ◊United Kingdom.

English member of the majority population of England, part of Britain. The English have a mixed cultural heritage combining Celtic, Anglo-Saxon, Norman, and Scandinavian elements.

English architecture the main styles in English architecture are: Saxon, Norman, Early English (of which Westminster Abbey is an example), Decorated, Perpendicular (15th century), Tudor (a name chiefly applied to domestic buildings of about 1485–1558), Jacobean, Stuart (including the Renaissance and Queen Anne styles), Georgian, the Gothic revival of the 19th century, Modern, and Post-Modern. Notable architects include Christopher Wren, Inigo Jones, Vanbrugh, Hawksmoor, Charles Barry, Edwin Lutyens, Hugh Casson, Basil Spence, Frederick Gibberd, Denys Lasdun, and Richard Rogers.

Roman period (55 BC – AD 410) Notable stretches of Hadrian's Wall remain and excavations continue to reveal the forums, basilicas, baths, villas amd mosaic pavements spread across the country.

Anglo-Saxon period (449–1066) Much of the architecture of this period, being of timber, has disappeared. The stone church towers that remain, such as at Earls Barton, appear to imitate timber techniques with their 'long and short work' and triangular arches.

Norman period (1066–1189) William the Conqueror inaugurated an enormous building programme. He brought the *Romanesque style*, of round arches, massive cylindrical columns and thick walls. At Durham Cathedral, the rib vaults (1093) are an invention of European importance in the development of the Gothic style.

Gothic architecture Early English (1189–1307) This began with the very French east end of Canterbury cathedral designed in 1175 by William of Sens, and attained its English flowering in the cathedrals of Wells, Lincoln, and Salisbury. It is a simple elegant style of lancet windows, deeply carved mouldings and slender, contrasting shafts of Purbeck marble. *Decorated* (1307–77) Growing richness in carving and a fascination with line characterized this period. The double curves of the ogee arch, elaborate window tracery and vault ribs woven into star patterns may be seen in buildings such as the Lady Chapel at Ely and the Angel Choir at Lincoln. *Perpendicular* (1377–1485) The gridded and panelled cages of light of the Perpendicular style are a dramatic contrast to the Decorated period. Lacking the richness and invention of the 14th century they convey, however, an often impressive sense of unity, space and power. The chancel of Gloucester cathedral is early Perpendicular whereas Kings College chapel, Cambridge, is late Perpendicular.

Tudor and Elizabethan period (1485–1603) This period saw the Perpendicular style interwoven with growing Renaissance influence. Buildings developed a concious symmetry elaborated with continental Pattenbrook details. Hybrid and exotic works resulted such as Burghley House and Hardwick Hall (1591–97)

Jacobean (1603–25) This period showed scarcely more sophistication.

English Renaissance: Stuart period The provincial scene was revolutionized by Inigo ◊Jones with the Queens House, Greenwich 1616 and the Banqueting House, Whitehall 1619. Overnight strict Palladianism appeared among the half-timber and turrets of Jacobean London. With ◊Wren a more mannered classicism evolved, showing French Renaissance influence, for example St Paul's cathedral (1675–1710). Under Wren's pupil ◊Hawksmoor, and ◊Vanbrugh, theatrical Baroque style emerged, for example Blenheim Palace 1705–20.

Georgian architecture Lord ◊Burlington, reacting against the Baroque, inspired a revival of the pure Palladian style of Inigo Jones. William ◊Kent, also a Palladian, invented the picturesque garden as at Rousham, Oxfordshire. Alongside the great country houses, an urban architecture evolved of plain, well-proportioned houses, defining elegant streets and squares. The second half of the century mingled Antiquarian and Neo-Classical influences, exquisitely balanced in the works of Robert ◊Adam at Kedleston Hall (1757–70). John ◊Nash carrie Neo-Classicism into the new century. By the dawn of the Victorian era this had become a rather bookish Greek Revival, for example, the British Museum (1823–47).

19th century Throughout the century Classical and Gothic engaged with Victorian earnestness in the 'Battle of the Styles' Gothic for the Houses of Parliament (1840–60), Renaissance for the Foreign Office (1860–75). Meanwhile the great developments in engineering and the needs of new building types, such as railway stations, transformed the debate. ◊Paxton's prefabricated Crystal Palace (1850–51) is the most remarkable building of the era. The Arts and Crafts architects Philip ◊Webb and Norman ◊Shaw brought renewal and simplicity inspired by William Morris.

20th century The early work of ◊Lutyens and the white rendered houses of ◊Voysey such as Broadleys, Windemere (1898–99), maintained the Arts and Crafts spirit of natural materials and simplicity. Norman Shaw, however, developed an Imperial Baroque style.

After World War I classicism again dominated, grandly in the case of Lutyens's New Delhi government buildings (1912–31). There was often a clean Scandinavian influence, as in the RIBA building (1932–34), which shows growing Modernist tendencies. Modernism arrived fully with continental refugees such as Lubetkin (1901–), the founder of the Tecton architectural team who designed London Zoo (1934–38).

The strong social dimension of English 20th-century architecture is best seen in the ◊New Town movement. Welwyn Garden City was begun in 1919 and developed after World War II. The latest of the New Towns, Milton Keynes, was designated 1967. Recently English architects have again achieved international recognition, particularly Norman ◊Foster and Richard ◊Rogers for their High Tech innovation, for example the Lloyds Building (1979–84). James ◊Stirling maintains a modernist technique and planning while absorbing historicist and contextural concerns.

English art

painting

medieval English painting was chiefly religious and included wall paintings and illuminated manuscripts.

Portrait painting was taken to new levels by the German artist Hans Holbein at the court of Henry VIII. At the court of Queen Elizabeth I, Nicholas Hilliard established a tradition of miniature painting. The Flemish Anthony van Dyck, employed as a court painter by Charles I from 1632, greatly influenced English portrait painters. Joshua Reynolds, Thomas Gainsborough, and Thomas Lawrence are among the best known of the late 18th and early 19th centuries. In the 20th century, Graham Sutherland, Lucian Freud, and David Hockney have painted many portraits.

social satire In the 18th century William Hogarth and Thomas Rowlandson used art as way of criticizing the customs and behaviour of contemporary society.

animal painting An indigenous form is the sporting picture, George Stubbs being the great 18th-century exponent. Edwin Landseer became known for his animal portraits in the early 19th century.

landscape painting Among painters specializing in landscape were Richard Wilson in the 18th century and in the 19th the watercolourist Samuel Palmer, John Constable and J W M Turner. The 20th century is reflected in the war-ravaged landscapes of Paul Nash and the multifigure townscapes of L S Lowry.

The Pre-Raphaelites—Millais, Holman Hunt and Rossetti were founder members—painted literary and genre scenes in the mid-19th century.

Impressionism J M Whistler, the American who introduced the doctrine of 'art for art's sake' and settled in London, had as his disciple W R Sickert, who helped to introduce Impressionism to England. Sickert inspired the Camden Town group.

Modernism in Britain ranges from the scenes of

work and village life by Stanley Spencer to the tortured figures of Francis Bacon.

Pop art is a movement that began in the UK in the mid-1950s with the work of David Hamilton and Peter Blake.

sculpture

ancient Some early Celtic metalwork has survived.

medieval There are ecclesiastical sculptures and ivory carvings.

17th–18th centuries The woodcarvings of Grinling Gibbons, of Dutch origin, are found in stately homes and St Paul's Cathedral. One of the first widely known English sculptors was the Neo-Classicist John Flaxman.

19th century Academic portraits were produced by Francis Chantrey and Frederick Leighton.

20th century The stylized stone figures of Jacob Epstein and Eric Gill led towards the abstract forms of Henry Moore and Barbara Hepworth. Anthony Caro and Eduardo Paolozzi have used industrial metals and machine components to create their diverse and dramatic styles since the 1960s.

English horn alternative name for ◊cor anglais, musical instrument of the oboe family.

English language a member of the Germanic branch of the Indo-European language family. It developed through four major stages over about 1,500 years: *Old English* or *Anglo-Saxon* (c.500–1050), rooted in the dialects of settling invaders (Jutes, Saxons, Angles, Danes); *Middle English* (c.1050–1550), influenced by Norman French after the Conquest 1066 and by ecclesiastical Latin; *Early Modern English* (c.1550–1700), standardization of the diverse influences of Middle English, and *Late Modern English* (c. 1700 onwards), the development and spread of current Standard English. Through extensive exploration, colonization, and trade, English spread worldwide from the 17th century onwards and remains the most important international language of trade and technology. It is used in many variations, for example, British, US, Canadian, Indian, Singaporean, and Nigerian English, and many pidgins and creoles.

Historical roots The ancestral forms of English were dialects brought from the NW coastlands of Europe to Britain by Angle, Saxon, and Jutish invaders who gained footholds in the SE in the 5th century and over the next 200 years extended and consolidated their settlements from S England to the middle of Scotland. Scholars distinguish four main early dialects: of the Jutes in Kent, the Saxons in the south, the Mercians or S Angles in the Midlands, and the Northumbrians or N Angles north of the Humber. Until the Danish invasions 9th–11th centuries, Old English was a highly inflected language, but appears to have lost many of its grammatical endings in the interaction with Danish, creating a more open or analytic style of language that was further changed by the influence of Norman French after the Conquest 1066. For several centuries English was in competition with other languages: first the various Celtic languages of Britain, then Danish, then French as the language of Plantagenet England and Latin as the language of the Church. In Scotland, English was in competition with Gaelic and Welsh, as well as French and Latin. In 1362 English replaced French as the language of the law courts of England, although the records continued for some time to be kept in Latin. Geoffrey Chaucer was a court poet at this time and strongly influenced the literary style of the London dialect. When William Caxton set up his printing press in London 1477 the new hybrid language (vernacular English mixed with courtly French and learned Latin) became increasingly standardized, and by 1611, when the Authorized Version of the Bible was published, the educated English of the Home Counties and London had become the core of what is now called 'Standard English'. At the same time, however, dialect variation remained, and still remains, very great throughout Britain.

By the end of the 16th century, English was firmly established in four countries: England, Scotland, Wales, and Ireland, and with the establishment of

the colonies in North America in the early 17th century took root in what are now the USA, Canada, and the West Indies. Seafaring, exploration, commerce, and colonial expansion in due course took both the standard language and other varieties to every corner of the world. By the time of Johnson's Dictionary 1755 and the American Declaration of Independence 1776, English was international and recognizably the language we use today.

Current usage The orthography of English was more or less established by 1650, and in England in particular a form of standard educated speech (known as 'Received Pronunciation') spread out in the 19th century from the major public (private) schools. This accent was adopted in the early 20th century by the BBC for its announcers and readers, and is variously known as RP, BBC English, Oxford English, and the King's or Queen's English. It was also the socially dominant accent of the British Empire, and retains great prestige, especially as a model for foreigners acquiring the language. In the UK, however, it is no longer so assiduously sought after as it once was. Generally, Standard English today is not dependent on accent, but rather on shared educational experience, especially of the printed language. Today English is an immensely varied language, having absorbed material from many other tongues. It is spoken by more than 300 million 'native speakers', and between 400 and 800 million 'foreign users'. It is the official language of aircraft and shipping, the leading language of science, technology, computers, and commerce, and a major medium of education, publishing, and international negotiation. For this reason scholars frequently refer to its latest phase as 'World English'.

English law one of the major European legal systems, ◊Roman law being the other. English law has spread to many other countries, particularly former English colonies such as the USA, Canada, Australia, and New Zealand.

English law has a continuous history dating from the local customs of the Anglo-Saxons, traces of which survived until 1925. After the Norman Conquest there grew up, side by side with the Saxon shire courts, the feudal courts of the barons and the ecclesiastical courts. From the king's council developed the royal courts, presided over by professional judges, which gradually absorbed the jurisdictions of the baronial and ecclesiastical courts. By 1250 the royal judges had amalgamated the various local customs into the system of ◊Common Law, that is, law common to the whole country. A second system known as ◊equity developed in the Court of Chancery, in which the Lord Chancellor considered petitions.

In the 17th–18th centuries, Common Law absorbed the Law Merchant, the international code of mercantile customs. During the 19th century virtually the whole of English law was reformed by legislation, for example, the number of capital offences was greatly reduced. The Judicature Acts 1873–75 abolished a multiplicity of courts, and in their place established the Supreme Court of Judicature, organized in the Court of Appeal and the High Court of Justice; the latter has three divisions—the Queen's Bench, Chancery, and Family Divisions. All Supreme Court judges may apply both Common Law and Equity in deciding cases. From the Court of Appeal there may be a further appeal to the House of Lords.

A unique feature of English law is the doctrine of judicial ◊precedents, whereby the reported decisions of the courts form a binding source of law for future decisions. A judge is bound by decisions of courts of superior jurisdiction, but not necessarily by those of inferior courts.

English literature the earliest surviving English literature is in the form of Old English poems such as *Beowulf* and the epic fragments *Finesburh*, *Waldhere*, *Deor*, and *Widsith*—which reflect the heroic age and Germanic legends of the 4th–6th centuries, although probably not written down until the 7th century. Heroic elements survive in elegiac lyrics, for example *The Wanderer*, *The*

Seafarer, and in many poems with a specifically Christian content, such as *The Dream of the Rood*; the Saints' Lives, for example *Elene*, by the 8th-century poet Cynewulf. These poems are all written in unrhymed alliterative metre. The great prose writers of the early period were the Latin scholars Bede, Aldhelm, and Alcuin. King Alfred founded the tradition of English prose with his translations and his establishment of the Anglo-Saxon Chronicle.

With the arrival of a Norman ruling class at the end of the 11th century, the ascendancy of Norman-French in cultural life began, and it was not until the 13th century that the native literature regained its strength. Prose was concerned chiefly with popular devotional use, but verse emerged typically in the metrical chronicles, such as Layamon's *Brut*, and the numerous romances based on the stories of Charlemagne, the Arthurian legends, and the classical episodes of Troy. First of the great English poets was Chaucer, whose early work reflected the predominant French influence, but later that of Renaissance Italy. Of purely native inspiration was *The Vision of Piers Plowman* of Langland in the old alliterative verse, and the anonymous *Pearl*, *Patience*, and *Gawayne and the Grene Knight*.

Chaucer's mastery of versification was not shared by his successors, the most original of whom was Skelton. More successful were the anonymous authors of songs and carols, and of the ballads, which (for example those concerned with Robin Hood) often formed a complete cycle. Drama flowered in the form of ◊miracle and ◊morality plays, and prose, although still awkwardly handled by Wycliffe in his translation of the Bible, rose to a great height with Malory in the 15th century.

The Renaissance, which had first touched the English language through Chaucer, came to delayed fruition in the 16th century. Wyatt and Surrey used the sonnet and blank verse in typically Elizabethan forms, and prepared the way for Spenser, Sidney, Daniel, Campion, and others. With Kyd and Marlowe, drama emerged into theatrical form; it reached the highest level in Shakespeare and Jonson. Elizabethan prose is represented by Hooker, North, Ascham, Holinshed, Lyly, and others, but English prose reached full richness in the 17th century, with the Authorized Version of the Bible 1611, Bacon, Milton, Bunyan, Taylor, Browne, Walton, and Pepys. Most renowned of the 17th-century poets were Milton and Donne; others include the religious writers Herbert, Crashaw, Vaughan, and Traherne, and the Cavalier poets Herrick, Carew, Suckling, and Lovelace. In the Restoration period Butler and Dryden stand out as poets. Dramatists include Otway and Lee in tragedy. Comedy flourished with Congreve, Vanbrugh, and Farquhar.

The 18th century is known as the Augustan Age in English literature. Pope developed the poetic technique of Dryden; in prose Steele and Addison evolved the polite essay, Swift used satire, and Defoe exploited his journalistic ability. This century saw the development of the ◊novel, through the epistolary style of Richardson to the robust narrative of Fielding and Smollett, the comic genius of Sterne, and the Gothic 'horror' of Horace Walpole. The Neo-Classical standards established by the Augustans were maintained by Johnson and his circle—Goldsmith, Burke, Reynolds, Sheridan, and others—but the romantic element present in the work of poets Thomson, Gray, Young, and Collins was soon to overturn them.

The *Lyrical Ballads* 1798 of Wordsworth and Coleridge were the manifesto of the new Romantic age. Byron, Shelley, and Keats form a second generation of Romantic poets. In fiction Scott took over the Gothic tradition from Mrs Radcliffe, to create the ◊historical novel, and Jane Austen established the novel of the comedy of manners. Criticism gained new prominence in Coleridge,

Lamb, Hazlitt, and De Quincey.

During the 19th century the novel was further developed by Dickens, Thackeray, the Brontës, George Eliot, Trollope, and others. The principal poets of the reign of Victoria were Tennyson, Robert and Elizabeth Browning, Arnold, the Rossettis, Morris and Swinburne. Among the prose writers of the era are Macaulay, Newman, Mill, Carlyle, Ruskin, and Pater. The transition period at the end of the century saw the poetry and novels of Meredith and Hardy; the work of Butler and Gissing; and the plays of Pinero and Wilde.

Although a Victorian, Gerald Manley Hopkins, anticipated the 20th century with the experimentation of his verse forms. Poets of World War I include Sassoon, Brooke, Owen, and Graves. A middle-class realism developed in the novels of Wells, Bennett, Forster, and Galsworthy while the novel's break with traditional narrative and exposition came through the modernists James Joyce, D H Lawrence, Virginia Woolf, Somerset Maugham, Aldous Huxley, Christopher Isherwood, Evelyn Waugh, and Graham Greene. Writers for the stage include Shaw, Galsworthy, J B Priestley, Coward, and Rattigan and the writers of poetic drama, such as T S Eliot, Fry, Auden, Isherwood, and Dylan Thomas. The 1950s and 1960s produced the 'kitchen sink' dramatists, including Osborne and Wesker. The following decade saw the rise of Harold Pinter, John Arden, Tom Stoppard, Peter Shaffer, Joe Orton, and Alan Ayckbourn. Poets since 1945 include Thom Gunn, Roy Fuller, Philip Larkin, Ted Hughes and John Betjeman; novelists include William Golding, Iris Murdoch, Angus Wilson, Muriel Spark, Margaret Drabble, Kingsley Amis, Anthony Powell, Alan Sillitoe, Anthony Burgess, John Fowles, Ian McEwan, Angela Carter, and Doris Lessing.

English-Speaking Union society for promoting the fellowship of the English-speaking peoples of the world, founded in 1918 by Evelyn Wrench.

engraving the art of printmaking by means of blocks of metal, wood, or some other hard material. The main categories are *relief prints*, made by cutting into the block so that the raised parts of the surface make the impression, and *intaglio prints*, where the incised lines hold the ink for printing (intaglio prints are made mainly on metal, by line engraving, aquatint, dry point, etching, and mezzotint).

enhanced radiation weapon another name for the ◊neutron bomb.

enharmonic in music, a harmony capable of different interpretations, or of leading into different keys.

Eniwetok /ˌenɪˈwiːtɒk/ atoll in the ◊Marshall Islands, in the central Pacific Ocean; population (1980) 453. It was taken from Japan by the USA 1944, which made the island a naval base and conducted 43 atomic tests there from 1947. The inhabitants were re-settled at Ujelang, but insisted on returning home in 1980. Despite the clearance of nuclear debris and radioactive soil to the islet of Runit, high radiation levels persisted.

Enlightenment a European intellectual movement, reaching its high point in the 18th century. Enlightenment thinkers were believers in social progress and in the liberating possibilities of rational and scientific knowledge. They were often critical of existing society and were hostile to religion, which they saw as keeping the human mind chained down by superstition.

The American and French revolutions were justified by Enlightenment principles of human natural rights. Leading representatives of the Enlightenment were ◊Voltaire, ◊Lessing, and ◊Diderot.

enlightenment in Buddhism, the term used to translate the Sanskrit *bodhi*, awakening: perceiving the reality of the world, or the unreality of the self, and becoming liberated from suffering (Sanskrit *duhkha*). It is the gateway to nirvana.

en masse (French) as a group, in a body, all together.

Ennis /ˈenɪs/ county town of County Clare, Republic of Ireland, on the river Fergus, 32 km/20 mi NW of Limerick; population (1981) 14,600. There are distilleries, flour mills, and furniture manufacturing.

Enniskillen /ˌenɪsˈkɪlən/ county town of Fermanagh, Northern Ireland, between Upper and Lower Lough Erne; population (1981) 10,500. There is some light industry (engineering, food processing) and it has been designated for further industrial growth. A bomb exploded there at a Remembrance Day service in Nov 1987, causing many casualties.

Ennius /ˈenɪəs/ Quintus 239–169 BC. Early Roman poet. Born near Tarentum in S Italy, he wrote tragedies based on the Greek pattern. His epic poem, the *Annales*, deals with Roman history.

enosis (Greek 'union') the movement, developed from 1930, for the union of ◊Cyprus with Greece.

en plein air (French) in the open air.

en route (French) on the way.

ENSA (English National Service Association) an organization formed in 1938–39 to provide entertainment for the British and Allied forces during World War II. Directed by Basil Dean (1888–1978) from headquarters in the Drury Lane Theatre, it provided a variety of entertainment throughout the UK and also in all war zones abroad.

Enschede /ˈenskədeɪ/ textile manufacturing centre in Overijssel province, the Netherlands; population (1988) 145,000, urban area of Enschede-Hengelo 250,000.

Ensor /ˈensɔː/ James 1860–1949. Belgian painter and printmaker. His bold style uses strong colours to explore themes of human cruelty and the macabre, as in the *Entry of Christ into Brussels* 1888 (Musée Royale des Beaux-Arts, Brussels), and anticipated German Expressionism.

ENT in medicine, an abbreviation for *ear, nose, and throat*. It is usually applied to a specialist clinic or hospital department.

entail in law, the settlement of land or other property on a successive line of people, usually succeeding generations of the original owner's family. An entail can be either *general*, in which case it simply descends to the heirs, or *special*, when it descends according to a specific arrangement, for example, to children by a named wife. Entails are increasingly rare in modern times, and the power to make them has often been destroyed by legislation, for example, restrictions in certain states of the USA. In England entails can be easily terminated.

Entebbe /enˈtebi/ town in Uganda, on the NW shore of Lake Victoria, 20 km/12 mi SW of Kampala, the capital; 1,136 m/3,728 ft above sea level; population (1983) 21,000. Founded 1893, it was the administrative centre of Uganda 1894–1962.

In 1976, a French aircraft was hijacked by a Palestinian liberation group. It was flown to Entebbe airport, where the hostages on board were rescued six days later by Israeli troops.

Entente Cordiale (French 'friendly understanding') the agreement reached by Britain and France 1904 recognizing British interests in Egypt and French interests in Morocco. It formed the basis for Anglo-French cooperation before the outbreak of World War I 1914.

enteric a general term applied to infective fevers of the intestine, especially typhoid and paratyphoid.

enterprise zone special zones designated by government to encourage industrial and commercial activity, usually in economically depressed areas. Investment is attracted by means of tax reduction and other financial incentives.

In the UK, enterprise zones were introduced in 1980 to encourage regional investment, particularly in depressed inner city areas. Industrial and commercial property are exempt from rates, development land tax and from certain other restrictions. The Isle of Dogs in London's docklands was extensively developed as an enterprise zone during the 1980s.

E-numbers

a selection of food additives authorized by the European Commission

number	name	typical use
	COLOURS	
E102	tartrazine	soft drinks
E104	quinoline yellow	
E110	sunset yellow FCF	biscuits
E120	cochineal	alcoholic drinks
E122	carmoisine	jams and preserves
E123	amaranth	
E124	ponceau 4R	dessert mixes
E127	erythrosine	glacé cherries
E131	patent blue V	
E132	indigo carmine	
E142	green S	pastilles
E150	caramel	beer, soft drinks, sauces, gravy browning
E151	black PN	
E160(b)	annatto; bixin; norbixin	crisps
E180	pigment rubine (lithol rubine BK)	
	ANTIOXIDANTS	
E310	propyl gallate	vegetable oils; chewing gum
E311	octyl gallate	
E312	dodecyl gallate	
E320	butylated hydroxynisole (BHA)	beef stock cubes; cheese spread
E321	butylated hydroxytoluene (BHT)	chewing gum
	EMULSIFIERS AND STABILIZERS	
E407	carageenan	quick setting jelly mixes; milk shakes
E413	tragacanth	salad dressings; processed cheese
	PRESERVATIVES	
E210	benzoic acid	
E211	sodium benzoate	beer, jam, salad cream, soft drinks, fruit pulp
E212	potassium benzoate	fruit-based pie fillings, marinated herring and mackerel

number	name	typical use
E213	calcium benzoate	
E214	ethyl para-hydroxy-benzoate	
E215	sodium ethyl para-hydroxy-benzoate	
E216	propyl para-hydroxy-benzoate	
E217	sodium propyl para-hydroxy-benzoate	
E218	methyl para-hydroxy-benzoate	
E220	sulphur dioxide	
E221	sodium sulphate	dried fruit, dehydrated vegetables, fruit juices
E222	sodium bisulphite	and syrups, sausages, fruit-based dairy desserts, cider, beer
E223	sodium metabisulphate	and wine; also used to prevent browning of raw
E224	potassium metabisulphite	peeled potatoes and to condition biscuit doughs
E226	calcium sulphite	
E227	calcium bisulphite	
E249	potassium nitrite	
E250	sodium nitrite	bacon, ham, cured meats, corned beef and some cheeses
E251	sodium nitrate	
E252	potassium nitrate	
	OTHERS	
E450(a)	disodium dihydrogen diphosphate; trisodium diphosphate; tetrasodium diphosphate; tetrapotassium diphosphate	buffers, sequestrants, emulsifying salts, stabilizers, texturizers, raising agents, used in whipping water, fish
E450(b)	pentasodium triphosphate; pentapotassium triphosphate	and meat products, bread, processed cheese, canned vegetables
E450(c)	sodium polyphosphates; potassium polyphosphates	

entomology the study of ◊insects.

entrechat (French 'cross-caper') in ballet, criss-crossing of the legs whilst the dancer is in the air. There are two movements for each beat. Wayne ◊Sleep broke ◊Nijinsky's record of an *entrechat dix* (five beats) with an *entrechat douze* (six beats) 1973.

entrepreneur in business, a person who successfully manages and develops an enterprise through personal skill and initiative. Examples include J D ◊Rockefeller and Henry ◊Ford.

entropy in ◊thermodynamics, a parameter representing the state of disorder of a system at the atomic, ionic, or molecular level; the greater disorder, the higher the entropy. Thus the fast-moving disordered molecules of water vapour have higher entropy than those of more ordered liquid water, which in turn have more entropy than the molecules in solid crystalline ice.

At ◊absolute zero (–273°C/0 K), when all molecular motion ceases and order is assumed to be complete, entropy is zero.

enucleation surgical removal of a complete organ, or tumour; for example, the eye from its socket.

Enugu /e'nu:gu:/ town in Nigeria, capital of Anambra state; population (1983) 228,400. It is a coal-mining centre, with steel and cement works, and is linked by rail with Port Harcourt.

E number a code number for additives that have been approved for use by the European Commission. The E written before the number stands for European. E numbers do not have to be displayed on lists of ingredients, and the manufacturer may choose to list ◊additives by their name instead. E numbers cover all categories of additives apart from flavourings. Additives, other than flavourings, that are not approved by the EC, but are still used in Britain, are represented by a code number without an E.

envelope in geometry, a curve that touches all the members of a family of lines or curves. For example, a family of three equal circles all touching each other and forming a triangular pattern (like a clover leaf) has two envelopes: a small circle that fits in the space in the middle, and a large circle that encompasses all three circles.

Enver Pasha /'envə'pɑːʃə/ 1881–1922. Turkish politician and soldier. He led the military revolt 1908 that resulted in the Young Turk revolution (see ◊Turkey). He was killed fighting the Bolsheviks in Turkestan.

environment in ecology, the sum of conditions affecting a particular organism, including physical surroundings, climate and influences of other living organisms; see also ◊biosphere and ◊habitat.

In common usage, 'the environment' often means the total global environment, without reference to any particular organism. In genetics, it is the external influences that affect an organism's development, and thus its ◊phenotype.

Environmentally Sensitive Area (ESA) scheme introduced by the UK Ministry of Agriculture 1984 to protect ten of the most beautiful areas of the British countryside from the loss and damage caused by agricultural change. The areas are in the Pennine Dales, the North Peak District, the Norfolk Broads, the Breckland, the Suffolk River Valleys, the Test Valley, the South Downs, the Somerset Levels and Moors, West Penwith, Cornwall, the Shropshire Borders, the Cambrian Mountains, and the Lleyn Peninsula.

In these ESAs farmers use traditional methods to preserve the value of the land as a wildlife habitat. A farmer who joins the scheme agrees to manage the land in this way for at least five years. In return for this agreement, the Ministry of Agriculture pays the farmer a sum which reflects the financial losses incurred as a result of reconciling conservation with commercial farming. The payments help farmers to resist financial pressures to change the land in ways which would make it less valuable for wildlife, for example, by ploughing up old meadows, using more insecticides, or removing hedges.

Environmental Protection Agency US agency set up 1970 to control water and air quality, industrial and commercial wastes, pesticides, noise, and radiation. In its own words, it aims to protect 'the country from being degraded, and its health threatened, by a multitude of human activities initiated without regard to long-ranging effects upon the life-supporting properties, the economic uses, and the recreational value of air, land, and water'.

environment art large sculptural or spatial works that create environments which the spectator may enter. The US artists Jim ◊Dine and Claes ◊Oldenburg in the 1960s were early exponents.

environment-heredity controversy or *nature-nurture controversy* a long-standing dispute among philosophers, psychologists, and scientists over the relative importance of environment (upbringing, experience, and learning) and heredity (genetic inheritance) in determining the make-up of an organism, especially as related to human personality and intelligence.

Particularly controversial is the reason for differences between individuals, for example, in performing ◊intelligence tests. The environmentalist position assumes that individuals do not differ significantly in their inherited mental abilities and that subsequent differences are due to learning, or to differences in early experiences. Opponents insist that certain differences in the capacities of individuals (and hence their behaviour) can be attributed to inherited differences in their genetic make-up.

enzyme a biological ◊catalyst that converts one chemical to another, usually very swiftly, without itself being destroyed in the process. Enzymes are large, complex ◊proteins. They digest food, convert food energy into ◊ATP, help to manufacture all the molecular components of the body, produce copies of ◊DNA when the cell divides, and control the movement of substances into and out of cells.

Enzymes have many medical and industrial uses, from washing powders to drug production, and as research tools in molecular biology. They can be extracted from bacteria and moulds, and ◊genetic engineering now makes it possible to tailor the enzyme for a specific purpose, and greatly increase the rate of production.

Eocene second epoch of the Tertiary period of geological time, 55–38 million years ago. Originally considered the earliest division of the Tertiary, the name means 'early recent', referring to the early forms of mammals evolving at the time, following the extinction of the dinosaurs.

E & O E abbreviation for *errors and omissions excepted.*

EOKA (Greek *Ethnikí Organósis Kipriakóu Agónos*/National Organization of Cypriot Struggle) an underground organization formed by Gen George Grivas 1955 to fight for the independence of Cyprus from Britain and ultimately its union (*enosis*) with Greece. In 1971, 11 years after the independence of Cyprus, Grivas returned to the island to form EOKA B, to resume the fight for *enosis* which had not been achieved by the Cypriot government.

eolith a chipped stone, once thought to have been manufactured as a primitive tool during the early Stone Age, but now generally believed to be the result of natural agencies.

Eos /'i:ɒs/ in Greek mythology, the goddess of the dawn, equivalent to the Roman Aurora.

Eötvös /'ɜ:tvɜ:ʃ/ Roland von, Baron 1848–1919. Hungarian scientist, born in Budapest, who investigated problems of gravitation, and constructed the double-armed torsion balance for determining variations of gravity.

eotvos unit unit (symbol E) for measuring small changes in the intensity of the Earth's ◊gravity with horizontal distance.

Epaminondas /e·pæmɪ'nɒndæs/ *c.*420–362 BC. Theban general and politician who won a decisive victory over the Spartans at Leuctra 371. He was killed at the moment of victory at Mantinea.

Epernay /ˌepeə'neɪ/ town in Marne *département*, Champagne-Ardenne region, France; population (1986) 29,000. It is the centre of the champagne industry.

ephedrine a drug that acts like adrenaline on the sympathetic ◊nervous system (sympathomimetic). Once used to relieve bronchospasm in ◊asthma, it has been superseded by safer, more specific drugs. It is contained in some cold remedies as a decongestant. Side effects include tachycardia (rapid heartbeat), tremor, dry mouth, and anxiety.

ephemeral plant a plant with a very short life cycle, sometimes as little as six or eight weeks. It may complete several generations in one growing season. A number of common weeds are ephemerals, for example groundsel *Senecio vulgaris*, as are many desert plants. The latter take advantage of short periods of rain to germinate and reproduce, passing the dry season as dormant seeds.

Ephesians ◊epistle in the New Testament attributed to ◊Paul but possibly written after his death; the earliest versions are not addressed specifically to the church at Ephesus.

Ephesus /'efɪsəs/ ancient Greek seaport in Asia Minor, a centre of the ◊Ionian Greeks, with a temple of Artemis destroyed by the Goths AD 262. In the 2nd century AD Ephesus had a population of 300,000. It is now one of the world's largest archaeological sites. St Paul visited the city, and addressed a letter (◊epistle) to the Christians there.

epic a narrative poem or cycle of poems dealing with some great action, often the founding of a nation or the forging of national unity, and often using religious or cosmological themes. In the Western tradition, the *Iliad* and *Odyssey* attributed to Homer, were epics probably intended to be chanted in sections at feasts.

Greek and later criticism, which considered the Homeric epic the highest form of poetry, produced a genre of **secondary epic**, such as the *Aeneid* of Virgil, Tasso's *Jerusalem Delivered*, and Milton's *Paradise Lost*, which attempted to emulate Homer, often for a patron or a political cause. The term is also applied to narrative poems of other traditions: the Anglo-Saxon *Beowulf* and the Finnish *Kalevala*; in India the *Ramayana* and *Mahabharata*; the Babylonian *Gilgamesh*; all of these evolved in different societies to suit similar social needs and used similar literary techniques.

epicentre the point on the Earth's surface immediately above the seismic focus of an ◊earthquake. Most damage usually takes place at an earthquake's epicentre. The term sometimes refers to a point directly above or below a nuclear explosion ('at ground zero').

Epictetus /ˌepɪk'tiːtəs/ *c.* AD 55–135. Greek Stoic philosopher, who encouraged people to refrain from self-interest, and to promote the common good of humanity. He believed that people were in the hands of an all-wise providence, and that they should endeavour to do their duty in the position to which they were called.

Born at Hierapolis in Phrygia, he lived for many years in Rome as a slave, but eventually secured his freedom. He was banished by ◊Domitian from Rome in 89.

Epicureanism system of philosophy that claims soundly based human happiness is the highest good, so that its rational pursuit should be adopted. It was named after the Greek philosopher Epicurus. The most distinguished Roman Epicurean was ◊Lucretius.

Epicurus /ˌepɪ'kuərəs/ 341–270 BC. Greek philosopher, founder of Epicureanism, who taught at Athens from 306 BC.

epicyclic gear or **sun-and-planet gear** a gear system that consists of one or more gear wheels moving around another. Epicyclic gears are found in bicycle hub gears and in automatic gearboxes.

epicycloid in geometry, a curve resembling a series of arches traced out by a point on the circumference of a circle that rolls around another circle of a different diameter. If the two circles have the same diameter, the curve is a ◊cardioid.

If the radius of the inner circle is R and that of the rotating circle r, the epicycloid will have n cusps if $R = nr$ ($n = 1,2,3...$).

Epidaurus /ˌepɪ'dɔːrəs/ ancient Greek city and port on the E coast of Argolis, in the NE Peloponnese. The site contains a well-preserved ampitheatre of the 4th century BC; nearby are the ruins of the temple of Aesculapius, the god of healing.

epicycloid a seven cusped epicycloid

epidemic an outbreak of infectious disease affecting large numbers of people at the same time. A widespread epidemic that sweeps across many countries (such as the ◊Black Death in the late Middle Ages) is known as a *pandemic*.

epidermis the outermost layer of ◊cells on an organism's body. In plants and many invertebrates such as insects, it consists of a single layer of cells. In vertebrates, it consists of several layers of cells.

The epidermis of plants and invertebrates often has an outer ◊cuticle that protects the organism from desiccation. In vertebrates such as reptiles, birds, and mammals, the outermost layer of cells is dead, forming a tough, waterproof layer known as ◊skin.

epigeal seed germination in which the ◊cotyledons are borne above the soil.

epigram a short poem, originally a religious inscription but later a short, witty, and pithy saying.

The form was common among writers of ancient Rome, including Catullus and Martial. In English, the epigram has been employed by Ben Jonson, Herrick, Pope, Swift, and Yeats.

epigraphy (Greek *epigráphein* 'to write on') the art of writing with a sharp instrument on hard, durable materials such as stone, and also the scientific study of epigraphical writings or inscriptions.

epilepsy a medical disorder characterized by a tendency to develop fits, which are convulsions, or abnormal feelings caused by abnormal electrical discharges in the cerebral hemispheres of the ◊brain. Epilepsy can be controlled with a number of ◊anticonvulsant drugs.

Epileptic fits can be classified into four categories. The first two are generalized, where the abnormal discharges affect the whole of the cerebrum; the second two are focal in nature, involving a particular area of the cortex. In **grand mal**, a vague feeling of uneasiness leads to a phase of generalized stiffening (the tonic phase), followed by a phase of generalized jerking (the

clonic phase). A brief period of unconsciousness follows, and finally drowsiness that may last several hours. Petit mal occurs almost exclusively in school-age children; the child stops, stares, and pales slightly. The attack lasts only a few seconds. About 5% of children will have a fit at some time in their lives, but most of these are isolated instances caused by feverish illnesses. **Jacksonian** fits begin with jerking in a small area of the body, for example the angle of the mouth or the thumb. They may spread to involve the whole of one side of the body. After the fit, the affected limbs may be paralysed for several hours. **Temporal lobe** fits result in hallucinations and feelings of unreality. They may also cause disordered speech and impaired consciousness.

Most epileptics have infrequent fits that have little impact on their daily lives. Epilepsy does not imply that the sufferer has any impairment of intellect, behaviour, or personality.

Epinal /ˌeɪpɪ'nɑːl/ capital of Vosges *département*, on the Moselle, France. Population (1982) 40,954. A cotton textile centre, it dates from the 10th century.

Epiphany festival of the Christian church, held 6 Jan, celebrating the coming of the Magi (the three Wise Men) to Bethlehem with gifts for the infant Jesus, and symbolizing the manifestation of Jesus to the world. It is the 12th day after Christmas, and marks the end of the Christmas festivities.

In many countries the night before Epiphany, called **Twelfth Night**, is marked by the giving of gifts. In the Eastern Orthodox Church, the festival celebrated on this day is known as the **theophany** and commemorates the baptism of Jesus.

epiphyte plant that grows on another plant or object above the surface of the ground, and which has no roots in the soil.

An epiphyte does not parasitize the plant it grows on, but merely uses it for support. Its nutrients are obtained from rainwater, organic debris such as leaf litter, or from the air. The greatest diversity of epiphytes is found in tropical areas and includes many orchids.

Epirus /e'paɪrəs/ (Greek 'mainland') country of ancient Greece; the N part was in Albania; the remainder, in NW Greece, was divided into four provinces—Arta, Thesprotia, Yanina, and Preveza.

Epirus /ɪ'paɪrəs/ (Greek *Ipiros*) region of NW Greece; area 9,200 sq km/3,551 sq mi; population (1981) 325,000. Its capital is Yannina, and it consists of the nomes of Arta, Thesprotia, Yannina, and Preveza. There is livestock farming.

episcopacy in the Christian church, a system of government in which administrative and spiritual power over a district (diocese) is held by a bishop. The Roman Catholic, Eastern Orthodox, Anglican, and Episcopal (USA) churches are episcopalian; episcopacy also exists in some branches of the Lutheran Church, for example, in Scandinavia.

Episcopalianism US term for the ◊Anglican Communion

episiotomy an incision made in the perineum (the tissue bridging the vagina and rectum) to facilitate childbirth.

epistemology a branch of philosophy that examines the nature of knowledge and attempts to determine the limits of human understanding. Central issues include how knowledge is derived, and how it is to be validated and tested.

epistle in the New Testament, any of the 21 letters to individuals or to the members of various churches written by Christian leaders. The best known are the 13 written by St ◊Paul. In modern usage the word is applied to letters with a suggestion of pomposity and literary affectation.

The term is also used for a letter addressed to someone in the form of a poem, as in the epistles of ◊Horace and ◊Pope. The **epistolary novel**, a story told as a series of (fictitious) letters, was popularized by Samuel ◊Richardson in the 18th century.

Epidaurus The Theatre in Epidaurus, Greece, was built by the architect Polycleitos and seats 14,000.

Epstein *British sculptor who worked in stone and marble. He is photographed next to his statue Lazarus.*

EPLF abbreviation for ***Eritrean People's Liberation Front.***

EPNS abbreviation for ***electroplated nickel silver***; see ◊electroplating.

epoxy resin a synthetic ◊resin used as an ◊adhesive and as an ingredient in paints. Household epoxy resin adhesives come in component form as two separate tubes of chemical, one tube containing resin, the other a curing agent (hardener). The two chemicals are mixed just before application, and the mix soon sets hard.

Epping Forest /'epɪŋ/ a forest in ◊Essex, SE England.

EPROM (*e*rasable *p*rogrammable *r*ead-*o*nly *m*emory); a computer memory device in the form of a chip that can record data and retain it indefinitely. The data can be erased by exposure to ultraviolet light and new data added. Other kinds of memory are ◊ROM, ◊PROM, and ◊RAM.

Epsilon Aurigae an ◊eclipsing binary star in the constellation Auriga. One of the pair is an 'ordinary' star, but the other seems to be a huge, distended object whose exact nature remains unknown. The period is 27 years, the longest of its kind. The last eclipse was 1982–84.

Epsom /'epsəm/ town in Surrey, England; population (1981) 68,535. In the 17th century it was a spa producing Epsom salts. There is a racecourse, where the Derby and the Oaks are held. The site of Henry VIII's palace of Nonsuch was excavated in 1959.

Epsom salts hydrated magnesium sulphate, $MgSO_4.7H_2O$, known as a saline purgative. The name is derived from a bitter saline spring at Epsom, Surrey, England, which contains the salt in solution.

Epstein /'epstaɪn/ Jacob 1880–1959. British sculptor, born in New York. He experimented with abstract forms, but is better known for muscular nude figures such as *Genesis* 1931 (Whitworth Art Gallery, Manchester).

In 1904 he moved to the UK, where most of his major work was done. An early example showing the strong influence of ancient sculptural styles is the angel over the tomb of Oscar Wilde 1912 (Père

Lachaise, Paris), while *Rock Drill* 1913–14 (Tate Gallery, London) is Modernist and semi-abstract. Such figures outraged public sensibilities. He was better appreciated as a portraitist (bust of Einstein, 1933), and in later years executed several monumental figures, notably the huge, expressive bronze of *St Michael and the Devil* 1959 (Coventry Cathedral).

Equal Opportunities Commission commission established by the UK government 1975 to implement the Sex Discrimination Act 1975. Its aim is to prevent discrimination, particularly on sexual or marital grounds.

equation mathematical expression that represents the equality of two expressions involving constants and/or variables, and thus usually includes an equals sign (=). For example, the equation $A = \pi r^2$ equates the area A of a circle of radius r to the product πr^2. The algebraic equation $y = mx + c$ is the general one in coordinate geometry for a straight line.

The chemical equation $2H_2O = 2H_2 + O_2$ represents the decomposition of water by electrolysis into its constituent elements. A chemical equation must 'balance'; that is, a given element must have the same total number of atoms on one side of the equation as on the other (thus there are four atoms of hydrogen on each side of the above equation). Chemical equations are often written with an arrow or arrows (instead of an equals sign) to indicate the direction of the reaction; thus $2H_2O \rightarrow 2H_2 + O_2$. If the equation is true for all variables in a given domain, it is sometimes called an identity, and denoted by $\equiv$. Thus $(x + y)^2 \equiv x^2 + 2xy + y^2$ for all x, $y \in R$.

An ***indeterminate*** equation is an equation for which there is an infinite set of solutions, for example, $2x = y$. A ***diophantine*** equation is an indeterminate equation in which the solution and terms must be whole numbers (after Diophantos of Alexandria, *c*. AD 250).

equations of motion mathematical equations that give the position and velocity of a moving object at any time. Given the mass of an object, the forces acting on it, and its initial position and velocity, the equations of motion are used to calculate its position and velocity at any later time. The equations must be based on ◊Newton's laws of motion or, if speeds near that of light are involved, on the theory of ◊relativity.

equator the ***terrestrial equator*** is the ◊great circle whose plane is perpendicular to the Earth's axis (the line joining the poles). Its length is 40,092 km/24,901.8 mi, divided into 360 degrees of longitude. The ***celestial equator*** is the circle in which the plane of the Earth's equator intersects the ◊celestial sphere.

Equatorial Guinea /'ekwə·tɔːrɪəl 'gɪnɪ/ country in W central Africa, bounded N by Cameroon, E and S by Gabon, and W by the Atlantic Ocean; also several small islands off the coast and the larger island of Bioko off the coast of Cameroon

government the 1973 constitution was suspended in a military coup 1979, after which a supreme military council ruled by decree. In 1982 a new constitution was approved by referendum, providing for a president and a house of representatives of the people, elected by universal suffrage for a five-year term. The house of representatives sat for the first time 1983, its 41 members all nominated by the president and elected unopposed. The president governs with the supreme military council and a transition to civil, constitutional government is promised. All political parties have been banned.

history Reached by Portuguese explorers 1472, Bioko was ceded to Spain 1778. The mainland territory of Rio Muni (now Mbini) came under Spanish rule 1885, the whole colony being known as Spanish Guinea. From 1959 the territory was a Spanish Overseas Province, with internal autonomy from 1963.

After 190 years of Spanish rule, Equatorial Guinea became fully independent 1968, with Francisco

Macias Nguema as president with a coalition government. In 1970 he banned all political parties and replaced them with one, the United National Party (PUN). Two years later he declared himself president-for-life and established a dictatorship, controlling press and radio, and forbidding citizens to leave the country. There were many arrests and executions 1976–77. He also established close relations with the Soviet bloc.

In 1975 he was overthrown in a coup by his nephew, Col Teodoro Obiang Nguema Mbasogo, with at least the tacit approval of Spain. Macias was tried and executed. Obiang expelled the Soviet advisers and technicians, and renewed economic and political ties with Spain. He banned PUN and other political parties and ruled through a supreme military council. Coups against him 1981 and 1983 were unsuccessful. In 1982 a new constitution promised a return to civilian rule.

equestrianism skill in horse riding, especially as practised under International Equestrian Federation rules. An Olympic sport, there are three main branches of equestrianism: show jumping, three-day eventing, and dressage.

Showjumping is horse jumping over a course of fences. The winner is usually the competitor with fewest 'faults' (penalty marks given for knocking down or refusing fences), but in timed competitions it is the competitor completing the course most quickly, additional seconds being added for mistakes.

Three-Day Eventing horse trials testing the all-round abilities of a horse and rider in: dressage, testing a horse's response to control; cross-country, testing speed and endurance; and showjumping in a final modified contest.

Showjumping: recent winners

World Championship first held 1953 for men, 1965 for women; since 1978 for both concurrently
men
1953 Francisco Goyoago (Spain)
1954 Hans-Gunter Winkler (West Germany)
1955 Hans-Gunter Winkler (West Germany)
1956 Raimondo D'Inzeo (Italy)
1960 Raimondo D'Inzeo (Italy)
1966 Pierre d'Oriola (France)
1970 David Broome (UK)
1974 Hartwig Steenken (West Germany)
women
1965 Marion Coakes (UK)
1970 Janou Lefebvre (France)
1974 Janou Tissot (born Lefebvre) (France)
mixed
1978 Gerd Wiltfang (West Germany)
1982 Norbert Koof (West Germany)
1986 Gail Greenough (Canada)
European Championship first held 1957 as separate competition for men and women; since 1975 they have competed together
1977 Johan Heins (Holland)
1979 Gerd Wiltfang (West Germany)
1981 Paul Schockemohle (West Germany)
1983 Paul Schockemohle (West Germany)
1985 Paul Schockemohle (West Germany)
1987 Pierre Durand (France)
1989 John Whitaker (UK)
British Showjumping Derby first held 1961 and staged annually at Hickstead, Sussex
1980 Michael Whitaker (UK)
1981 Harvey Smith (UK)
1982 Paul Schockemohle (West Germany)
1983 John Whitaker (UK)
1984 John Ledingham (Ireland)
1985 Paul Schockemohle (West Germany)
1986 Paul Schockemohle (West Germany)
1987 Nick Skelton (UK)
1988 Nick Skelton (UK)
1989 Nick Skelton (UK)

Three-Day Eventing: recent winners

World Championship first held 1966
1970 Mary Gordon-Watson (UK)
1974 Bruce Davidson (USA)

Equatorial Guinea
Republic of
(República de Guinea Ecuatorial)

area 28,051 sq km/10,828 sq mi
capital Malabo
physical comprises mainland Rio Muni, plus
the small islands of Corisco, Elobey Grande
and Elobey Chico, and Bioko (formerly
Fernando Po) and Annobón (formerly Pagalu)
features volcanic mountains on Bioko
head of state and government Teodoro
Obiang Nguema Mbasogo from 1979
political system one-party military republic

political parties Democratic Party of Equatorial
Guinea (PDGE), militarily controlled
exports cocoa, coffee, bananas, timber
currency ekuele; CFA franc (485.00 = £1 Feb
1990)
population (1988 est) 336,000 (plus 110,000
estimated to live in exile abroad); annual growth
rate 2.2%
life expectancy men 42, women 46
language Spanish (official); pidgin English is
widely spoken, and on Pagalu (whose people
were formerly slaves of the Portuguese) a
Portuguese dialect
religion nominally Christian, mainly Catholic,
but in 1978 Roman Catholicism was banned
literacy 55% (1984)
GDP $60 million (1983); $250 per head of
population
chronology
1968 Achieved full independence from Spain.
Francisco Macias Nguema became first
president, soon assuming dictatorial powers.
1979 Macias overthrown and replaced by his
nephew, Teodoro Obiang Nguema Mbasogo,
who established a military regime. Macias tried
and executed.
1982 Obiang elected president for another
seven years. New constitution, promising a
return to civilian government, adopted.
1989 Obiang re-elected president.

1978 Bruce Davidson *(USA)*
1982 Lucinda Green (born Prior-Palmer) *(UK)*
1986 Virginia Leng (born Holgate) *(UK)*
Badminton Horse Trials first held 1949
1979 Lucinda Prior-Palmer *(UK)*
1980 Mark Todd *(New Zealand)*
1981 Captain Mark Phillips *(UK)*
1982 Richard Meade *(UK)*
1983 Lucinda Green *(UK)*
1984 Lucinda Green *(UK)*
1985 Virginia Holgate *(UK)*
1986 Ian Stark *(UK)*
1987 cancelled
1988 Ian Stark *(UK)*
1989 Virginia Leng *(UK)*

Equiano /ˌekwiˈɑːnəʊ/ Olaudah 1745–1797.
African anti-slavery campaigner and writer. He
travelled widely both as a slave and a free man.
His autobiography, *The Interesting Narrative of
the Life of Olaudah Equiano or Gustavus Vassa
the African* 1789, is one of the earliest significant
works by an African written in English.

Equiano was born near the River Niger in what
is now Nigeria, captured at the age of ten and
sold to slavers, who transported him to the West
Indies. He learned English and bought his freedom at the age of 21. He subsequently sailed to
the Mediterranean and the Arctic, before being
appointed commissary of stores for freed slaves
returning to Sierra Leone. He was an active campaigner against slavery.

equilateral of a geometrical figure, having all sides
of equal length. For example, a square and a
rhombus are both equilateral four-sided figures.
An equilateral triangle, to which the term is most
often applied, has all three sides equal and all three
angles equal (at 60°).

equilibrium in physics, an unchanging condition in
which forces on a particle or system of particles
(a body) cancel out, or in which energy is distributed among the particles of a system in the
most probable way; or the state in which a body
is at rest or moving at constant velocity. A body
is in *thermal equilibrium* if no heat enters or
leaves it, so that all its parts are at the same temperature as its surroundings. See also ◊chemical
equilibrium.

equinox the points in spring and autumn at which
the Sun's path, the ◊ecliptic, crosses the celestial
equator, so that the day and night are of approximately equal length. The *vernal equinox*

occurs about 21 Mar and the *autumnal equinox*, 23 Sept.

equity a system of law supplementing the ordinary
rules of law where the application of these would
operate harshly in a particular case; sometimes
it is regarded as an attempt to achieve 'natural
justice'. So understood, equity appears as an element in most legal systems, and in a number of
legal codes judges are instructed to apply both the
rules of strict law and the principles of equity in
reaching their decisions.

In England equity originated in decisions of
the Court of Chancery, on matters that were
referred to it because there was no adequate
remedy available in the Common Law courts.
Gradually it developed into a distinct system of
law, and until the 19th century, the two systems
of common law and equity existed side by side,
and were applied in separate law courts. The Judicature Acts 1873–75 established a single High
Court of Justice, in which judges could still apply
both common law and equity to all their decisions.
Equitable principles still exist side by side with
principles of common law in many branches of
the law.

equity a company's assets, less its liabilities, which
are the property of the owner or shareholders.
Popularly, equities are stocks and shares which,
unlike debentures and preference shares, do not
pay interest at fixed rates but pay dividends based
on the company's performance. The value of equities tend to rise over the long term, but in the
short term they are a risk investment because of
fluctuating values.

Equity common name for the British Actors' Equity
Association, the UK trade union for professional
actors in theatre, film, and television, founded
1929. In the USA its full name is the American
Actors' Equity Association and it deals only with
performers in the theatre.

Erasmus /ɪˈræzməs/ Desiderius *c.*1466–1536.
Dutch scholar and humanist. Born at Rotterdam, the illegitimate son of Rogerius Gerardus
(whose story is told in Charles Reade's novel
The Cloister and the Hearth 1861), he adopted
the Latin-Greek name which means 'beloved'.
As a youth he was a monk in an Augustinian
monastery near Gouda. After becoming a priest,
he went to study in Paris 1495 and paid the first
of a number of visits to England 1499. Here he
met Linacre, More, and Colet, and for a time he
was professor of Divinity and Greek at Cambridge

University. His pioneer edition of the Greek New
Testament was published 1516, and an edition of
the writings of St Jerome, and his own *Colloquia*
(dialogues on contemporary subjects) in 1519. He
went to Basle 1521, where he edited the writings
of the early Christian leaders.

Erastianism the belief that the church should be
subordinated to the state. The name is derived
from Thomas Erastus (1534–83), a German-
Swiss theologian and opponent of Calvinism, who
maintained in his writings that the church should
not have the power of excluding people as a punishment for sin.

Eratosthenes /ˌerəˈtɒsθəniːz/ *c.* 276–194 BC.
Greek geographer and mathematician, whose map
of the ancient world was the first to contain lines
of latitude and longitude, and who calculated the
Earth's circumference with an error of less than
322 km/200 mi. His mathematical achievements
include a method for duplicating the cube, and for
finding prime numbers (Eratosthenes' 'sieve').

erbium a metallic element, symbol Er, atomic
number 68, relative atomic mass 167.27. It is
one of the rare earths, and was discovered 1843
by Mosander.

Erebus, Mount /ˈerɪbəs/ the world's southernmost
active volcano, 3,794 m/12,452 ft high, on Ross
Island, Antarctica. It contains a lake of molten lava
which scientists are investigating in the belief that
it can provide a 'window' onto the magma beneath
the Earth's crust.

Erebus /ˈerɪbəs/ in Greek mythology, the god of
darkness and the intermediate region between upper earth and ◊Hades.

Erfurt /ˈeəfʊət/ city in East Germany on the
river Gera, capital of Erfurt county; population
(1986) 217,000. It is a rich horticultural area,
and its industries include textiles, typewriters,
and electrical goods. Erfurt county has an area
of 7,350 sq km/2,837 sq mi, and a population of
1,235,000.

erg c.g.s. unit of work, replaced in the SI system
by the ◊joule. One erg of work is done by a force
of 1 ◊dyne moving through 1 cm.

ergo (Latin) therefore.

ergonomics the study of the relationship between
people and the furniture, tools, and machinery
they use at work. The object is to improve work
performance by removing sources of muscular
stress and general fatigue, for example by presenting data and control panels in easy-to-view
form, making office furniture comfortable, and
creating a pleasant environment.

ergosterol a substance which, under the action of
the sun's ultraviolet rays on the skin, gives rise

*Erasmus An engraving by the German painter Dürer
of Desiderius Erasmus, the Renaissance Dutch scholar
and theologian.*

to the production of vitamin D—a vitamin that promotes bone-formation and deficiency of which produces ◊rickets. The sterol occurs in ergot (hence the name), in yeast, in other fungi, and in some animal fats. The principal source of commercial ergot is yeast.

ergot parasitic fungus *Claviceps purpurea*, which attacks the rye plant. Ergot poisoning is caused by eating infected bread, resulting in burning pains, gangrene, and convulsions. The large, usually dark violet grains of the fungus contains the alkaloid ergotamine.

ergotamine ◊alkaloid administered to treat migraine and to induce childbirth. Isolated from ergot, a fungus that colonizes rye, it relieves symptoms by causing the cranial arteries to constrict. Its use is limited by severe side effects, including nausea and abdominal pain; there is a slight risk of addiction.

Erhard /'eəhɑ:t/ Ludwig 1897–1977. West German Christian Democrat politician, chancellor of the Federal Republic 1963–66. The 'economic miracle' of West Germany's recovery after World War II is largely attributed to Erhard's policy of social free enterprise (German *Marktwirtschaft*).

Erica in botany, more commonly known as heather, the typical genus of the family Ericaceae. There are about 500 species, distributed mainly in South Africa and also Europe.

Ericsson /'erıksən/ John 1803–1889. Swedishborn US engineer who took out a patent to produce screw- propeller powered paddle-wheel ships in 1836. He built a number of such ships, including the *Monitor*, which was successfully deployed during the Civil War.

Ericsson /'erıksən/ Leif lived about AD 1000. Norse explorer, son of Eric 'the Red', who sailed west from Greenland about 1000 to find a country first sighted by Norsemen 986. Landing with 35 companions in North America, he called it Vinland, because he discovered grape vines growing there.

The story was confirmed 1963 when a Norwegian expedition, led by Helge Ingstad, discovered remains of a Viking settlement (dated about 1000) near the fishing village of L'Anse-aux-Meadows at the northern tip of Newfoundland.

Eric 'the Red' /'erık/ 940–1010. Allegedly the first European to find Greenland. According to a 13th-century saga, he was the son of a Norwegian chieftain, who was banished from Iceland about 982 for murder and then sailed westward and discovered a land that he called Greenland.

Eridanus the sixth-largest constellation, which meanders from the celestial equator deep into the southern hemisphere of the sky. Its brilliant star, Achernar, is the ninth-brightest star in the entire sky. It represents a river.

Eridu /'eərıdu:/ ancient city of Mesopotamia about 5000 BC, according to tradition the cradle of

Eritrea

SUDAN
Marsa Taklai
Eighena
Nakfa
Red Sea
ERITREA   At Abed   DAHLAK ISLANDS
Agordat   Keren   Massawa
Tessenai
Barentu   Asmara
ETHOPIA
AFRICA

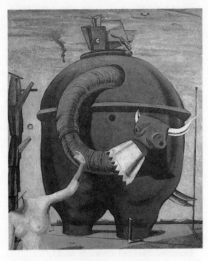

Ernst The Elephant Celébés *(1921) Tate Gallery, London.*

Sumerian civilization. On its site is now the village of Tell Abu Shahrain, Iraq.

Erie /'ıəri/ city and port on the Pennsylvania bank of Lake Erie, USA, population (1981) 120,000. It has heavy industries and a trade in iron, grain, and freshwater fish.

Erie, Lake /'ıəri/ fourth largest of the Great Lakes of North America, connected to Lake Ontario by the Niagara River, and bypassed by the Welland Canal; area 25,720 sq km/9,930 sq mi.

Erigena /ı'rıdʒınə/ Johannes Scotus 815–877. Medieval philosopher. He was probably Irish and, according to tradition, travelled in Greece and Italy. The French king Charles II (the Bald) invited him to France (before 847), where he became head of the court school. He is said to have visited Oxford, to have taught at Malmesbury, and to have been stabbed to death by his pupils. In his philosophy, he tried to combine Christianity with ◊neo-platonism.

Erin /'ıərın/ poetic name for Ireland derived from the dative case Érinn of the Gaelic name Ériu, possibly derived from Sanskrit 'western'.

Erinyes in Greek mythology, another name for the ◊Furies.

Eritrea /ˌerı'trıə/ province of N Ethiopia
area 117,600 sq km/45,394 sq mi
capital Asmara
towns ports Assab and Massawa are Ethiopia's outlets to the sea
physical coastline on the Red Sea 1,000 km/620 mi; narrow coastal plain which rises to an inland plateau
products coffee, salt, citrus fruits, grains, cotton
currency birr
population (1984) 2,615,000
language Amharic (official)
religion Islam
history part of an ancient Ethiopian kingdom until the 7th century; under Ethiopian influence until it fell to the Turks mid-16th century; Italian colony 1889–1941, where it was the base for Italian invasion of Ethiopia; under British administration 1941–52, when it became an autonomous part of Ethiopia; since 1962, when it became a region, various secessionist movements have risen; civil war 1970s, during which guerillas held most of Eritrea; Ethiopian government, backed by Soviet and Cuban forces, recaptured most towns 1978; resistance continued in the 1980s, aided by conservative Gulf states, and some cooperation with guerillas in Tigré province.

Erivan alternative transliteration of ◊Yerevan, capital of Armenian Republic, USSR.

Erlangen /'eəlæŋən/ industrial town in Bavaria, West Germany; population (1988) 100,000.

Erl-King in Germanic folklore, the king of the elves. He inhabited the Black Forest and lured children to their death. The Romantic writer J W Goethe's poem 'Erlkönig' was set to music by Franz Schubert 1816.

ermine the ◊stoat during winter, when its coat becomes white. In northern latitudes the coat becomes completely white, except for a black tip to the tail, but in warmer regions the back may remain brownish. The fur is used commercially.

ERNIE abbreviation for Electronic Random Number Indicator Equipment. In the UK, machine designed and produced by the Post Office Research Station to select a series of random 9-figure numbers to indicate prizewinners in the government's national lottery.

Ernst /eənst/ Max 1891–1976. German artist, who worked in France 1922–38 and in the USA from 1941. He was an active Dadaist, experimenting with collage, photomontage, and surreal images, and helped found the Surrealist movement 1924. His paintings are highly diverse.

Ernst first exhibited in Berlin in 1916. He produced a 'collage novel', *La Femme Cent Têtes* 1929, worked on films with Dali and Buñel, and designed sets and costumes for Diaghilev and the Ballets Russes. His pictures range from smooth Surrealist images to highly textured emotive abstracts, from 1925 making use of frottage (rubbing over textured materials). He left Paris 1938 and moved to the USA during World War II.

Eros /'ıərɒs/ in Greek mythology, boy-god of love, traditionally armed with bow and arrows. He was the son of Aphrodite, and fell in love with ◊Psyche. He is identified with the Roman Cupid.

Eros /'ıərɒs/ in astronomy, an asteroid, discovered 1898, 22 million km/14 million mi from the Earth at its nearest point. Eros was the first asteroid whose orbit comes within that of Mars to be discovered. It is elongated, measures about 36 × 12 km/22 × 7 mi, rotates around its shortest axis every 5.3 hours, and orbits the Sun every 1.8 years.

erosion the processes whereby the rocks and soil of the Earth's surface are loosened, worn away, and transported (◊weathering does not involve transportation). There are two types, chemical and physical. *Chemical erosion* involves the alteration of the mineral component of the rock, by means of rainwater or the substances dissolved in it, and its subsequent movement. *Physical erosion* involves the breakdown and transportation of exposed rocks by physical forces. In practice the two work together.

The decay of granite by the conversion of its feldspar minerals into clay by carbonic acid in rainwater, and the dissolving of limestone into caves and potholes, are examples of chemical erosion. The shattering of cliff faces in mountainous areas by the expansion of frost in the rock cracks, and the movement of boulders in an avalanche, are examples of physical erosion. Water, consisting of sea waves and currents, rivers, and rain; ice, in the form of glaciers, frost, and melting snow; and wind, hurling sand fragments against exposed rocks and moving dunes along, are the most potent forces of erosion. People also contribute to erosion by bad farming practices and the cutting down of forests, which can lead to the formation of dust bowls.

erratum (Latin) an error.

error detection in computing, the techniques whereby a program can detect incorrect data. A common method is to add a check digit to important codes, such as account numbers and product codes. The digit is chosen so that the code conforms to a rule which the program can verify. Another technique involves calculating the sum (called the ◊hash total) of each instance of a particular item of data and storing it at the end of the data.

ersatz (German) artificial, substitute, inferior.

Erse /ɜːs/ originally a Scottish form of the word 'Irish', a name applied by Lowland Scots to Scottish Gaelic and also sometimes used as a synonym for Irish Gaelic.

Ershad /ˈeəʃəd/ Hussain Mohammad 1930– . Military ruler of Bangladesh from 1982. He became chief of staff of the Bangladeshi army 1979 and assumed power in a military coup 1982. As president from 1983, Ershad introduced a successful rural-orientated economic programme. He was re-elected 1986 and lifted martial law, but faced continuing political opposition.

Erskine /ˈɜːskɪn/ Thomas, 1st Baron Erskine 1750–1823. British barrister and Lord Chancellor. He was called to the Bar in 1778 and appeared for the defence in a number of trials of parliamentary reformers for sedition. When the Whigs returned to power in 1806 he became Lord Chancellor and a baron. Among his speeches were those in defence of Lord George Gordon, Thomas Paine, and Queen Caroline.

erysipelas an acute disease of the skin due to infection by a streptococcus. Starting at some point where the skin is broken or injured, the infection spreads, producing a swollen red patch with small blisters and generalized fever. The condition is now rare.

erythrocyte another name for a ◊red blood cell.

Erzgebirge /ˈeətsɡəˌbɪəɡə/ (German 'ore mountains') mountain range on the German-Czech frontier, where the rare metals uranium, cobalt, bismuth, arsenic, and antimony are mined. Some 145 km/90 mi long, its highest summit is Mount Klinovec (Keilberg) 1,244 m/4,080 ft, in Czechoslovakia.

Erzurum /ˈeəzurum/ capital of Erzurum province, NE Turkey; population (1985) 253,000. It is a centre of agricultural trade and mining, and has a military base.

ESA abbreviation for ◊*European Space Agency.*

Esaki /ɪˈsɑːki/ Leo 1925– . Japanese physicist who in 1957 noticed that electrons could sometimes 'tunnel' through the barrier formed at the junctions of certain semiconductors. The effect is now widely used in the electronics industry. Esaki shared the 1973 Nobel physics prize with ◊Josephson and Giaver.

Esarhaddon died 669 BC. King of Assyria from 680, when he succeeded his father ◊Sennacherib. He conquered Egypt 671–74.

Esau /ˈiːsɔː/ in the Old Testament or Jewish Bible, the son of Isaac and Rebekah, and the elder twin brother of Jacob, who tricked Isaac into giving him the blessing intended for Esau by putting on goatskins. Earlier Esau had sold his birthright to Jacob for a 'mess of red pottage'. He was the ancestor of the Edomites.

Esbjerg /ˈesbjɜːɡ/ port of Ribe county, Denmark, on the west coast of Jutland; population (1988) 81,000. It is the terminus of links with Sweden and the UK, and is a base for Danish North Sea oil exploration.

escalator a moving staircase that carries people between floors or levels. The first escalator was exhibited in Paris 1900.

escape velocity minimum velocity with which an object must be projected for it to escape from the gravitational pull of a planet or moon. In the case of the Earth, the escape velocity per second is 11.2 km/6.9 mi; the Moon 2.4 km/1.5 mi; Mars 5 km/3.1 mi; and Jupiter 59.6 km/37 mi.

escheat (Old French *escheir* 'to fall') in feudal society, the reversion of lands to the lord in the event of the tenant dying without heirs or being convicted for treason. By the later Middle Ages in W Europe, tenants had insured against their lands escheating by granting them to trustees, or feoffees, who would pass them on to the grantor nominated in the will. Lands held directly by the king could not legally be disposed of in this way, and in England, royal officials, called escheators, were appointed to safeguard the king's rights.

Escher /ˈeʃə/ Maurits Cornelis 1902–1972. Dutch graphic artist. His prints are often based on mathematical concepts and contain paradoxes and illusions. The lithograph *Ascending and Descending* 1960, with interlocking staircases creating a perspective puzzle, is typical.

escrow (Old French *escroe* 'scroll') in law, a document sealed and delivered to a third party and not released or coming into effect until some condition has been fulfilled or performed; whereupon the document takes full effect.

Esenin /jeˈsenɪn/ Sergey 1895–1925. Soviet poet, born in Konstantinovo (renamed Esenino in his honour). He went to Petrograd 1915, attached himself to the Symbolists, welcomed the Russian Revolution, revived peasant traditions and folklore, and initiated the Imaginist group of poets 1919. A selection of his poetry was translated in *Confessions of a Hooligan* 1973. He was married briefly to the US dancer Isadora Duncan 1922–23.

Eskilstuna /ˈeskɪlzˌtuːnə/ town W of Stockholm, Sweden; population (1986) 88,400. It has iron foundries, steel and armament works.

Eskimo /ˈeskɪməʊ/ member (or language) of a people of the Arctic. The Eskimos of Greenland and Canada are ◊Inuit and their language Inuktitut; the Eskimos of South Alaska and Siberia are Yupik and their language Yuk.

Eskişehir /esˈkiːʃəhɪə/ city in Turkey, 200 km/125 mi west of Ankara; population (1985) 367,000. Products include meerschaum, chromium, magnesite, cotton goods, tiles, and aircraft.

espadrille (French) a type of shoe made with a canvas upper and a rope sole.

esparto grass *Stipa tenacissima*, native to S Spain, S Portugal, and the Balearics, but now widely grown in dry, sandy locations throughout the world. The plant is just over 1 m/3 ft high, producing greyish-green leaves, which are used for paper-making, ropes, baskets, mats, and cables.

Esperanto an international language devised 1887 by Dr Ludwig L Zamenhof (1859–1917) as an international auxiliary language. For its structure and vocabulary it draws on various European languages. Esperantists refer to Esperanto as a 'planned language' and to the natural languages of the world as 'ethnic languages'. Its spelling is phonetic, but the accent varies according to the regional backgrounds of its users.

espionage the practice of spying; a way to gather ◊intelligence.

Espronceda /ˌesprɒnˈθeɪðə/ José de 1808–1842. Spanish poet. Originally one of the Queen's guards, he lost his commission because of his political activity, and was involved in the Republican risings of 1835 and 1836. His lyric poetry and life style both owed much to Byron.

Esquipulas a pilgrimage town in Chiquimula department, SE Guatemala. Seat of the 'Black Christ' which is a symbol of peace throughout Central America. In May 1986 five Central American presidents met here to discuss a plan for peace in the region.

Esquivel /ˌeskɪˈvel/ Adolfo 1932– . Argentinian sculptor and architect. As leader of the Servicio de Paz y Justicia (Peace and Justice Service), a Catholic-Protestant human-rights organization, he was awarded the Nobel Peace Prize in 1980.

ESS (*Evolutionary Stable Strategy*) in ◊sociobiology, an assemblage of behavioural or physical characters (collectively termed a 'strategy') that is resistant to replacement by any forms bearing new traits, because these new traits will not be capable of successful reproduction. ESS analysis is based on ◊game theory and can be applied both to genetically determined physical characters (such as horn length) and to learned behavioural responses (for example, whether to fight or retreat from an opponent). An ESS may be conditional on the context, as in the rule 'fight if the opponent is smaller, but retreat if the opponent is larger'.

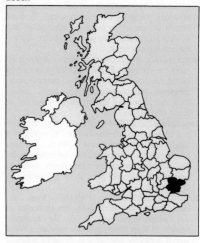

essay short piece of non-fiction, dealing often from a personal point of view with some particular subject. The essay became a recognized genre and name with the French writer Montaigne's *Essais* 1580. Francis Bacon's *Essays* 1597 are among the most famous in English. From the 19th-century the essay was increasingly used in Europe as a vehicle for literary criticism,

Abraham Cowley, whose essays appeared 1668, brought a greater ease and freedom to the genre than it had possessed before in England, but it was with the development of periodical literature in the 18th century that the essay became a widely used form. The great names are Addison and Steele, with their *Tatler* and *Spectator* papers, and later Johnson and Goldsmith. A new era was inaugurated by Lamb's *Essays of Elia* 1820; to the same period belong Leigh Hunt, Hazlitt, and De Quincey in England, Sainte Beuve in France, and Emerson and Thoreau in the USA. Hazlitt may be regarded as the originator of the modern critical essay, and his successors include Arnold and Gosse. Macaulay presents a strong contrast to Lamb in his vigorous but less personal tone. There was a revival of the form during the closing years of the 19th and beginning of the 20th centuries, in the work of R L Stevenson, Anatole France, Gautier, and Max Beerbohm. The literary journalistic tradition of the essay was continued by James Thurber, Desmond MacCarthy, and others, and the critical essay by George Orwell, Cyril Connolly, F R Leavis, T S Eliot, and others. However, its leisured approach made it a less often used form by the mid-20th century, although its spirit survived in the radio 'essays' of Alistair Cooke, and in newspapers and magazines as 'opinion pieces'.

Essen /ˈesən/ city in North Rhine-Westphalia, West Germany; population (1988) 615,000. It is the administrative centre of the Ruhr, with textile, chemical, and electrical industries.

Essene member of a Jewish religious order that existed in the area near the Dead Sea *c.* 200 BC–AD 200 whose members lived and extremaly simple life bound by strict rules; they believed the day of judgment was imminent. The ◊Dead Sea Scrolls, discovered in 1947, are believed to be the library of the community. John the Baptist may have been a member of the Essenes.

Essequibo /ˌesɪˈkwiːbəʊ/ the longest river in Guyana, South America, rising in the Guiana Highlands of S Guyana; length 1014 km/630 mi. Part of the district of Essequibo, which lies to the west of the river, is claimed by Venezuela.

Essex /ˈesɪks/ county in SE England
area 3,670 sq km/1,417 sq mi
towns administrative headquarters Chelmsford; Colchester; ports Harwich, Tilbury; resorts Southend, Clacton
features former royal hunting ground of Epping Forest (controlled from 1882 by the City of

Essex *Robert Devereux, 2nd Earl of Essex, a favourite of Elizabeth I. His career culminated in the capture of Cádiz 1596, but ended in imprisonment and execution.*

London); the marshy coastal headland of The Naze; birdlife at Maplin Sands; since 1111 at Great Dunmow the Dunmow flitch (side of cured pork) can be claimed every four years by any couple proving to a jury they have not regretted their marriage within the year (winners are few); Stansted, site of London's third airport
products dairying, cereals, fruit
population (1987) 1,522,000
famous people William Harvey.

Essex /'esɪks/ Robert Devereux, 2nd Earl of Essex 1566–1601. English soldier and politician. He fought in the Netherlands 1585–86 and distinguished himself at the Battle of Zutphen. In 1596 he jointly commanded a force that seized and sacked Cádiz. He became a favourite with Elizabeth I from 1587, but was executed because of his policies in Ireland.

In 1599 he became Lieutenant of Ireland and led an army against Irish rebels under the Earl of Tyrone in Ulster, but was unsuccessful, made an unauthorized truce with Tyrone, and returned without permission to England. He was forbidden to return to court, and when he marched into the City of London at the head of a body of supporters, he was promptly arrested, tried for treason, and beheaded on Tower Green.

Essex /'esɪks/ Robert Devereux, 3rd Earl of Essex 1591–1646. English soldier. Eldest son of the 2nd earl, he commanded the Parliamentary army at the inconclusive English Civil War Battle of Edgehill 1642. Following a disastrous campaign in Cornwall, he resigned his command 1645.

est. abbreviation for ***estimate(d)***.

estate in law, the rights which a person has in relation to any property. ***Real estate*** is an interest in any land; ***personal estate*** is an interest in any other kind of property.

estate in European history, an order of society which enjoyed a prescribed share in government. In medieval theory, there were usually three estates—the **nobility**, the **clergy**, and the **commons** — with the functions of, respectively, defending society from foreign aggression and internal disorder, attending to its spiritual

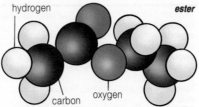

Model of the ester ethyl ethanoate, $CH_3 CO_2 CH_2 CH_3$
needs, and working to produce the wealth with which to support the other two orders.

When parliaments and representative assemblies developed from the 13th century, their organization reflected this theory, with separate houses for the nobility, the commons (usually burghers and gentry), and the clergy.

ester an organic compound formed by the reaction between an alcohol and an acid, with the elimination of water. Unlike ♦salts, esters are covalent compounds.

Esteve-Coll /ə'stevi 'kɒl/ Elizabeth Anne Loosemore 1938– . British museum administrator. Keeper of the National Art Library at the Victoria and Albert Museum 1985–88, she became director of the museum itself in 1988. Her reorganisation of it in 1989, when she split the administrative and research roles, led to widespread criticism and the resignation of several senior staff.

Esther /'estə/ in the Old Testament or Jewish Bible, the wife of the Persian king Ahasuerus, who prevented the extermination of her people by the vizier Haman, a deliverance celebrated in the Jewish festival of Purim. Her story is told in the Old Testament book Esther.

Estonia /e'stəʊnɪə/ constituent republic of the USSR from 1940
area 45,100 sq km/17,413 sq mi
capital Tallinn
features mild climate, lakes and marshes in a partly forested plain
products oil from shale, wood products, flax, dairy and pig products
population (1987) 1,556,000; 65% Estonian, 28% Russian, 3% Ukrainian, 2% Byelorussian
language Estonian, allied to Finnish
religion traditionally Lutheran
history the workers' and soldiers' soviets took control Nov 1917, were overthrown by German troops Mar 1918, and were restored Nov 1918. They were overthrown with the help of the British navy May 1919, and Estonia was a democratic republic until overthrown by a fascist coup 1934. It was incorporated into the the USSR 1940. In 1988 Estonia adopted its own constitution, with a power of veto on all Soviet legislation. In the 1989 elections many nationalists were voted in, and the parliament passed a law replacing Russian with Estonian as the main language.

As in the other Baltic republics, there has been nationalist dissent since 1980, influenced by Poland's example, and prompted by the influx of Russian workers and officials. In Nov 1988 the Estonian parliament voted for sovereign status.

Estonia

The new constitution allowed private property and placed land and natural resources under Estonian control. In the elections of Mar 1989 many party bosses lost their seats.

Estoril fashionable resort on the coast 20 km/13 mi W of Lisbon, Portugal. There is a Grand Prix motor racing circuit. Population (1981) 16,000.

estradiol a type of ♦oestrogen (female sex hormone).

estrogen alternative spelling of ♦oestrogen.

estuary a river mouth widening into the sea, where fresh water mixes with salt water and tidal effects are felt.

Esztergom /'estəgɒm/ city on the Danube, NW of Budapest, Hungary; population (1986) 31,000. It was the birthplace of St Stephen, and the former ecclesiastical capital of Hungary, with a fine cathedral.

et al. abbreviation for ***et alii*** (Latin 'and others').

Etaples /eɪ'tɑːplə/ fishing port and seaside resort on the Canche estuary, Pas de Calais *département*, France; population (1985) 11,500. During World War I it was an important British base and hospital centre.

etc. abbreviation for ***et cetera*** (Latin 'and the rest').

etching a print from a metal (usually copper or zinc) plate, which is prepared with a waxy overlayer (ground) and then drawn on with an etching needle. The exposed areas are then 'etched', or bitten into, by a corrosive agent (acid), so that they will hold ink for printing. The method was developed in Germany about 1500, the earliest dated etched print being of 1513. Among the earliest etchers were Dürer, van Dyck, Hollar, and Rembrandt. Some artists combine etching with ♦aquatint.

ethanal CH_3CHO (common name ***acetaldehyde***) in chemistry, one of the chief members of the group of organic compounds known as ♦aldehydes. It is a colourless inflammable liquid boiling at 20.8°C (69.6°F). Ethanal is used to make many other organic chemical compounds.

ethanal trimer $(CH_3CHO)_3$ (common name ***paraldehyde***) a colourless liquid formed from ethanal. It is soluble in water.

ethane C_2H_6 a colourless, odourless gas. It is the second member of the series of paraffin hydrocarbons, the first being methane.

ethane-1,2-diol modern name for ♦glycol.

ethanoate $CH_3CO_2^-$ (common name ***acetate***) in chemistry, ion of ethanoic (acetic) acid. In textiles, acetate rayon is a synthetic fabric made from modified cellulose (wood pulp) treated with acetic acid; in photography, acetate film is a nonflammable film made of cellulose acetate.

ethanoic acid CH_3CO_2H (common name ***acetic acid***) in chemistry, one of the simplest members of a series of organic acids called fatty acids. In the pure state it is a colourless liquid with an unpleasant pungent odour; it solidifies to an icelike mass of crystals at 16.7°C, and hence is often called glacial acetic acid. Vinegar is 3–6% ethanoic acid.

Cellulose (derived from wood, etc.) is treated with ethanoic acid to produce a cellulose acetate solution, which can be used to make plastic items by injection moulding, or extruded to form synthetic textile fibres.

ethanol C_2H_5OH (common name ***ethyl alcohol***) the chemical term for the alcohol found in beer, wine, cider, spirits, and other alcoholic drinks. When pure, it is a colourless liquid with a pleasant odour, miscible with water or ether, and burning in air with a pale blue flame. The vapour forms an explosive mixture with air and may be used in high-compression internal combustion engines. It is produced naturally by the fermentation of carbohydrates by yeast cells. Industrially, it can be made by absorption of ethene and subsequent reaction with water, or by the reduction of ethanal in the presence of a catalyst, and is widely used as a solvent.

Ethanol is used as a raw material in the manufacture of ether, chloral, and iodoform. It can

Ethiopia
People's Democratic Republic of
(Hebretesebawit Ityopia, formerly also known as **Abyssinia***)*

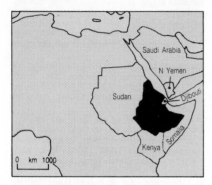

area 1,221,900 sq km/471,653 sq mi
capital Addis Ababa
towns Asmara (capital of Eritrea), Dire Dawa; ports are Massawa, Assab
physical a high plateau with mountains; plains in east; Blue Nile river
features Danakil and Ogaden deserts; ancient remains at Aksum, Gondar, Lalibela among other places; only African country to retain its independence during the colonial period
head of state and government Mengistu Haile Mariam from 1977
political system one-party socialist republic
political parties Workers' Party of Ethiopia (WPE), Marxist-Leninist; Eritrean People's Liberation Front (EPLE) a guerrilla army fighting for an independent Eritrea.
exports coffee, pulses, oilseeds, hides, skins
currency birr (3.50 = £1 Feb 1990)
population (1986) 46,000,000 (Oromo 40%, Amhara 25%, Tigré 12%, Sidama 9%); annual growth rate 2.5%
language Amharic (official); Tigré, Galla, Arabic
religion Christian (Ethiopian Orthodox church, which has had its own patriarch since 1976) 50%, Sunni Muslim 50%
literacy 18% (1985)
GNP $4.7 bn (1984); $141 per head of population
chronology
1974 Haile Selassie deposed and replaced by a military government led by Gen.Teferi Benti. Ethiopia declared a socialist state.
1977 Teferi Benti killed and replaced by Col Mengistu Haile Mariam.
1984 WPE declared the only political party.
1985 Worst famine for more than a decade. Western aid sent and internal resettlement programmes undertaken.
1987 New constitution adopted, Mengistu Mariam elected president. Provisional Military Administrative Council dissolved and elected National Assembly introduced. New famine; food aid hindered by guerrillas.
1988 Mengistu agreed to adjust his economic policies in order to secure IMF assistance. Influx of refugees from Sudan.
1989 Government forces routed from Eritrea and Tigré, rebels claimed. Coup attempt against Mengistu foiled. Another famine in north feared.
1990 Rebels capture part of Massawa.

also be added to petrol, where it improves the performance of the engine, or used as a fuel in its own right. Crops such as sugar cane may be grown to provide ethanol (by fermentation) for this purpose.

Ethelred II /ˈeθəlred/ *the Unready c.* 968–1016. King of England from 978. The son of King Edgar, he became king after the murder of his half-brother, Edward the Martyr. He tried to buy off the Danish raiders by paying Danegeld, and in 1002 ordered the massacre of the Danish settlers, provoking an invasion by Sweyn I of Denmark. War with Sweyn and Sweyn's son, Canute, occupied the rest of Ethelred's reign. He was nicknamed the 'Unready' because of his apparent lack of foresight.

ethene C_2H_4 (common name **ethylene**) a colourless, flammable gas, the first member of the alkene series of hydrocarbons. It is the most widely used synthetic organic chemical and is used to produce polyethylene (polythene), dichloroethane, and polyvinyl chloride (PVC). It also occurs naturally in plants, helping to promote growth and the ripening of fruit. It is applied to fruit that has been picked and shipped in an unripe state, to promote ripening.

ether or **diethyl ether** $C_2H_5OC_2H_5$ (modern name **ethoxyethane**) a colourless, volatile, inflammable liquid, slightly soluble in water, miscible with ethanol. It is prepared by treatment of ethanol with excess concentrated sulphuric acid at 140°C. It is used as an anaesthetic by vapour inhalation and as an external cleansing agent before surgical operations. It is also used as a solvent, and in the extraction of oils, fats, waxes, resins, and alkaloids.

ether in science, a hypothetical medium permeating all of space. The concept originated with the Greeks, and has been revived on several occasions to explain the properties and propagation of light. It was supposed that light and other electromagnetic radiation—even in outer space—needed a medium, the ether, in which to travel. The idea was abandoned with the acceptance of relativity.

Its existence was disproved in 1887 by the classic Michelson–Morley experiment, which showed that light travels at the same speed in the direction of the Earth's motion through space as it does at right angles to the motion. This later led to ♦Einstein's formulation of special relativity.

Etherege /ˈeθərɪdʒ/ George *c.*1635–*c.*1691. English Restoration dramatist whose play *Love in a Tub* 1664 was the first attempt at the **comedy of manners** (a genre further developed by Congreve and Sheridan). Later plays include *She Would if She Could* 1668 and *The Man of Mode, or Sir Fopling Flutter* 1676.

Ethical Movement movement designed to further the moral or ethical factor as the real substance and fundamental part of religion, influential in the late 19th and early 20th centuries. In the USA in 1876, Felix Adler founded an Ethical Society in New York, while in 1888 the first English Ethical Society was founded by Dr Stanton Coit.

ethics area of philosophy concerned with human values, and which studies the meanings of moral terms and theories of conduct and goodness.

The study of ethics began in ancient India and China, and began to be systematized in the Greek philosopher Socrates in the 5th century BC. Plato's *Republic* is an exposition of the nature of justice or righteousness, and ethical theory was advanced by Aristotle's *Nicomachean Ethics* and similar writings. The Cyrenaics, Epicureans, and Stoics advanced theories that have been many times revived. The 'Christian ethic' is mainly a combination of New Testament moral teaching with ideas drawn from Plato and Aristotle. Hobbes, Hume, and Butler are notable 17th–18th century British ethical philosophers. One of the greatest individual contributors to ethical theory was Kant, with his 'categorical imperative' (the obligation to obey absolute moral law). The utilitarian ethic was expounded by Bentham, J S Mill, Sidgwick, and Spencer, and opposed by F H Bradley and T H Green, who linked ethics with metaphysics, and emphasized the place of the individual in organized society. Ethicists of the 20th century include Moore, Broad, Dewey, Hartmann (1882–1950), Hare, and Stephen Toulmin (1922–), whose *Place of Reason in Ethics* 1950 first put forward the viewpoint of modern linguistic analysis.

Ethiopia /ˌiːθiˈəupiə/ country in E Africa, bounded NE by the Red Sea, E and SE by Somalia, S by Kenya, and W and NW by Sudan.

government A traditional monarchy until 1974, Ethiopia has since been ruled by a Provisional Military Administrative Council (PMAC), chaired by the head of state, who also presides over a council of ministers and is secretary-general of the only political party, the Marxist-Leninist Workers' Party of Ethiopia (WPE). Parliament was suspended 1974 when the king was deposed and Ethiopia was proclaimed a socialist state. A new constitution in 1987 created an 835-member national assembly, elected from nominees of political parties and other economic and social organizations.

history Long subject to Egypt, the area became independent about the 11th century BC. The kingdom of ♦Aksum flourished 1st–10th century AD, reaching its peak about the 4th century with the introduction of ♦Coptic Christianity from Egypt, and declining from the 7th century as ♦Islam expanded. The Arab conquests isolated Aksum from the rest of the Christian world.

During the 10th century there emerged a kingdom which formed the basis of Abyssinia, reinforced 1270 with the founding of a new dynasty. Although it remained independent throughout the period of European colonization of Africa, Abyssinia suffered civil unrest and several invasions from the 16th century, and was eventually reunited 1889 under ♦Menelik II, with Italian support. In 1896 Menelik put down an invasion by Italy, which claimed he had agreed to make the country an Italian protectorate, and annexed Ogaden in the southeast and several provinces to the west.

Ethiopia was dominated for over 50 years by ♦Haile Selassie, who became regent 1916, king 1928, and emperor 1930. The country was occupied by Italy 1935–41, and Haile Selassie went into exile in Britain. Ogaden was returned to ♦Somalia, which was also under Italian control.

Haile Selassie returned from exile 1941 and ruled until 1974, when he was deposed by the armed forces, after famine, high inflation, growing unemployment, and demands for greater democracy. His palace and estates were nationalized, parliament dissolved, and the constitution suspended.

Gen Teferi Benti, who had led the uprising and been made head of state, was killed 1977 by fellow officers and replaced by Col Mengistu Haile Mariam. The Ethiopian empire had been built up by Haile Selassie and Menelik, and annexed regions had made frequent attempts to secede. The 1975 revolution encouraged secessionist movements to increase their efforts, and the military government had to fight to keep Eritrea and Ogaden, where Somalian troops were assisting local guerrillas.

The USSR, having adopted Ethiopia as a new ally, threatened to cut off aid to Somalia, and Cuban troops assisted Mengistu in ending the fighting there. Eritrea and its neighbour, Tigré, continued their struggle for independence.

Amid this confusion there was acute famine in the north, including Eritrea, when the rains failed for three successive seasons. In addition to a massive emergency aid programme from many Western nations, the Ethiopian government tried to alleviate the problem by resettling people from the north to the more fertile south. By 1986 more than 500,000 had been resettled.

Meanwhile, the military regime had re-established normal relations with most of its neighbours, promising a return to civilian rule, and in 1986 publishing the draft of a new constitution. Tigré province was captured by the Eritrean People's Liberation Front and the Tigréan People's Liberation Front Feb 1989, the first time the government had lost control of the entire province. In Mar 1989 the new constitution was adopted, ending 12 years of military rule and electing Col Mengistu Mariam as the country's first president. A coup against him in May 1989 was put down and the military high command subsequently purged. Following a mediation offer by the former US president Jimmy ◊Carter, peace talks with the Eritrean rebels began in Aug 1989. At the same time, droughts in the north threatened another widespread famine.

ethnicity (from Greek *ethnos* 'a people') people's own sense of cultural identity, a social term that overlaps with such concepts as race, nation, class, and religion.

Social scientists use the term *ethnic group* to refer to groups or societies who feel a common sense of identity, often based on a similar culture, language, religion, and customs. It may or may not include common territory, skin colour, or common descent. The USA, for example, is often described as a *multi-ethnic society* because many members would describe themselves as members of an ethnic group (Jewish, black, or Irish, for example) as well as their national one (American).

ethnology the study of contemporary peoples, concentrating on their geography and culture, as distinct from their social systems.

ethnomethodology the study of social order and routines used by people in their daily lives, to explain how everyday reality is created and perceived. Ethnomethodologists tend to use small-scale studies and experiments to examine the details of social life and structure (such as conversations) that people normally take for granted, rather than construct large-scale theories about society.

ethology the comparative study of animal behaviour in its natural setting. Ethology is concerned with the causal mechanisms (both the stimuli that elicit behaviour and the physiological mechanisms controlling it), as well as the development of behaviour, its function, and its evolutionary history.

Ethology was pioneered during the 1930s by Konrad Lorenz and Karl von Frisch who, with Nikolaas Tinbergen, received the Nobel Prize in 1973. Ethologists believe that the significance of an animal's behaviour can be understood only in its natural context, and emphasize the importance of field studies and an evolutionary perspective. A recent development within ethology is ◊sociobiology, the study of the evolutionary function of ◊social behaviour.

ethyl alcohol common name for ◊ethanol.

ethylene common name for ◊ethene.

ethylene glycol another name for ◊glycol.

ethyne $(CH)_2$ (common name *acetylene*) in chemistry, a colourless inflammable gas. One important use is its conversion into the synthetic rubber neoprene. It is also used in oxyacetylene welding and cutting.

Ethyne was discovered by Edmund Davy 1836 by the action of water on impure by-products of the preparation of potassium. The combustion of ethyne provides more heat, relatively, than almost any other fuel known (its calorific value is five times that of hydrogen), so the gas gives an intensely hot flame, hence its use in oxyacetylene welding and cutting.

et in arcadia ego (Latin 'I also in Arcadia') death exists even in Arcadia (a fabled land).

etiolation in botany, a form of growth seen in plants receiving insufficient light. It is characterized by long, weak stems, small leaves, and a pale yellowish colour (◊chlorosis) owing to a lack of chlorophyll. The rapid increase in height enables a plant which is surrounded by others to quickly reach a source of light, when a return to normal growth usually occurs.

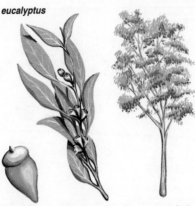

eucalyptus

Etna /'etnə/ volcano on the E coast of Sicily, 3,323 m/10,906 ft, the highest in Europe; its most recent eruptions were Dec 1985.

Eton /'i:tn/ town in Berkshire, England, on the N bank of the Thames, opposite Windsor; population (1981) 3,500.

Etruscan art sculpture, painting, and design of the first known Italian civilization. Etruscan terracotta coffins (*sarcophagi*), carved with reliefs and topped with portraits of the dead, reclining on one elbow, were to influence the later Romans and early Christians. Pottery, bronzeware, and mural paintings survive. Most examples are from excavated tombs; bright colours and a vigorous style are typical, and show influences of archaic Greece and the Middle East.

Etty /'eti/ William 1787–1849. British academic painter. He first gained success with *Telemachus Rescuing Antiope* 1811. He was a prolific painter of female nudes.

étude (French 'study') a musical exercise designed to develop technique.

etymology the study of the origin and history of words within and across languages. It has two major aspects: the study of the phonetic and written forms of words, and the semantics or meanings of those words. Etymological research has been successful in tracing the development of words and word elements within the Indo-European language family. Standard dictionaries of a language like English typically contain etymological information within square brackets at the end of each entry.

Euboea /ju:'bi:ə/ (Greek *Evvoia*) mountainous island off the E coast of Greece, in the Aegean Sea; area 3,755 sq km/1,450 sq mi; about 177 km/110 mi long; population (1981) 188,410. Mount Delphi reaches 1,743 m/5,721 ft. The chief town, Chalcis, is connected by a bridge to the mainland.

eucalyptus tree of the Myrtaceae family, native to Australia and Tasmania, where it is commonly known as a gum tree. About 90% of Australian timber belongs to the eucalyptus group, which comprises about 500 species.

Eucharist chief Christian sacrament, in which bread is eaten and wine drunk in memory of the death of Jesus. Other names for it are the Lord's Supper, Holy Communion, and (among Roman Catholics, who believe that the bread and wine are transubstantiated, that is, converted to the body and blood of Christ) the Mass. The doctrine of **transubstantiation** was rejected by Protestant churches at the Reformation.

The word comes from the Greek for 'thanksgiving', and refers to the statement in the Gospel narrative that Jesus gave thanks over the bread and the cup. In Britain, members of the Church of England are required to participate in the Eucharist at least three times a year, with Easter as one. The service is not part of the worship of Quakers or the Salvation Army.

Euclid /'ju:klɪd/ *c.* 330–*c.*260 BC. Greek mathematician, who lived at Alexandria and wrote the *Stoicheia/Elements* in 13 books, of which nine deal with plane and solid geometry, and four with

number theory. His main work lay in the systematic arrangement of previous discoveries, based on axioms, definitions, and theorems. Euclid's geometry texts have remained in common usage for over 2,000 years until recent times.

Eugène /ju:'dʒi:n/ Prince of Savoy 1663–1736. Austrian general, who had many victories against the Turkish invaders (whom he expelled from Hungary 1697 in the Battle of Zenta) and against France, especially in the War of the ◊Spanish Succession (battles of Blenheim, Oudenaarde, and Malplaquet).

The son of Prince Eugène Maurice of Savoy-Carignano, he was born in Paris. When Louis XIV refused him a commission he entered the Austrian army, and served against the Turks at the defence of Vienna 1683, and against the French on the Rhine and in Italy ten years later. In the War of the Spanish Succession 1701–14 he shared with the British commander Marlborough in his great victories against the French and won many successes as an independent commander in Italy. He again defeated the Turks 1716–18, and fought a last campaign against the French 1734–35.

Eugene Onegin a novel in verse by Aleksandr Pushkin, published 1823–31. Eugene Onegin, bored with life but sensitive, rejects the love of Tatanya, a humble country girl, but she rises in society and in turn rejects him. Onegin was the model for a number of Russian literary heroes.

eugenics (Greek 'well-born') the study of ways in which the physical and mental quality of a people can be controlled and improved by selective breeding, and the belief that this should be done. The idea was abused by the Nazi Party in Germany during the 1930s to justify the extermination of entire groups of people and the compulsory sterilization of others. Eugenics can serve the purpose of trying to control the spread of inherited genetic abnormalities by counselling prospective parents.

The term was coined by Francis ◊Galton in 1883, and the concept was originally developed in the late 19th century with a view to improving the intelligence and behaviour of humanity.

Several countries have implemented eugenic programmes; in some Chinese provinces there is compulsory sterilization of people regarded as physically or mentally defective, whereas up to Dec 1989 in Romania all abortions and contraceptives were illegal, and there was a tax on childless women aged over 24. In 1986 Singapore became the first democratic power to adopt an openly eugenic policy by guaranteeing pay rises to female university graduates when they give birth to a child, while offering grants towards house purchase for non-graduate married women on condition that they are sterilized after the first or second child.

Eugénie /,ɜ:ʒeɪ'ni:/ Marie Ignace Augustine de Montijo 1826–1920. Empress of France, daughter of the Spanish count of Montijo. In 1853 she married Louis Napoleon, who had become emperor as ◊Napoleon III. She encouraged court extravagance, Napoleon III's intervention in Mexico, and urged him to fight the Prussians. After his surrender to the Germans at Sedan, NE France, 1870 she fled to England.

eukaryote one of the two classes into which all living organisms (except bacteria and cyanobacteria) are divided. The other class is ◊prokaryote.

The cells of eukaryotes possess a clearly defined nucleus, bounded by a membrane, within which DNA is formed into distinct chromosomes. Their cells contain mitochondria, chloroplasts, and other structures (organelles) which are lacking in the cells of prokaryotes.

Euler /'ɔɪlə/ Leonhard 1707–1783. Swiss mathematician. He developed the theory of differential equations, the calculus of variations, and did important work in astronomy and optics. He was a pupil of Johann ◊Bernoulli.

He became professor of physics at the University of St Petersburg in 1730. In 1741 he was

Euripides *Marble bust of the ancient Greek dramatist Euripides, a Roman copy of a late 4th-century BC Greek original.*

invited to Berlin by Frederick the Great, where he spent 25 years before returning to Russia.

Eumenides /juːˈmenɪdiːz/ ('kindly ones') in Greek mythology, appeasing name for the ◊Furies.

eunuch a castrated man. Originally eunuchs were simply bedchamber attendants in harems in the East (*eunoukhos* is Greek for 'one in charge of a bed') but as they were usually castrated so that they should not take too great an interest in their charges, the term became applied more generally. Eunuchs often filled high offices of state in China, India, and Persia. Italian *castrati* were singers castrated as boys to preserve their high voices, a practice which ceased on the accession of Pope Leo XIII 1878.

Eupen-et-Malmédy /ɜːˈpen ˌmælmeˈdiː/ region of Belgium around the towns of Eupen and Malmédy. It was Prussian from 1814 until it became Belgian 1920 after a plebiscite; there was fierce fighting here in the German Ardennes offensive Dec 1944.

euphemism a ◊figure of speech whose name in Greek means 'speaking well (of something)'. To speak or write euphemistically is to use a milder, more polite, less direct, or even less honest expression rather than one that is considered too blunt, vulgar, direct, or revealing.

Thus 'He passed away' is preferred to *he died*; 'sleep with someone' substitutes for *have sex with someone*; and 'liquidate the opposition' softens the impact of *kill one's enemies*.

euphonium type of ◊brass instrument, like a small tuba.

Euphrates /juːˈfreɪtiːz/ (Arabic ***Furat***) river, rising in E Turkey, flowing through Syria and Iraq and joining the Tigris above Basra to form the Shatt-al-Arab, at the head of the Persian/Arabian Gulf; 3,600 km/2,240 mi in length. The ancient cities of Babylon, Eridu, and Ur were situated along its course.

Eurasian /jʊˈreɪʒən/ former term in India and the East Indies for a person born of mixed European and Asian parentage or ancestry.

Euratom /ˌjʊərˈætəm/ European Atomic Energy Commission, founded in 1957 and forming part of ◊European Community organization.

Eure /ɜː/ river rising in Orne *département*, France, and flowing SE, then N, to the Seine; length 115 km/70 mi. Chartres is on its banks. It gives its name to two *départements*, Eure and Eure-et-Loire.

Eureka (Greek 'I've got it!') exclamation made by ◊Archimedes on his discovery of fluid displacement.

eureka alternative name for the copper-nickel alloy ◊constantan, which is used in electrical equipment.

Eureka Stockade /jʊˈriːkə/ incident at Ballarat, Australia, when about 150 goldminers, or 'diggers', rebelled against authority. They took refuge behind a wooden stockade, which was taken in a few minutes by the military on 3 Dec 1854. Some 30 diggers were killed, and a few soldiers killed or wounded, but the majority of the rebels were taken prisoner. Among those

who escaped was Peter Lalor, their leader. Of the 13 tried for treason, all were acquitted, thus marking the emergence of Australian democracy.

eurhythmics practice of coordinated bodily movement as an aid to musical development. It was founded about 1900 by the Swiss musician Emil ◊Jaques-Dalcroze, professor of harmony at the Geneva conservatoire. He devised a series of

'gesture' songs, to be sung simultaneously with certain bodily actions.

Euripides /jʊˈrɪpɪdiːz/ *c.*484–407 BC. Greek dramatist whose plays deal with ordinary people and social issues rather than the more grandiose themes used by his contemporaries. He wrote more than 80 plays, of which 18 survive, including *Alcestis* 438, *Medea* 431, *Andromache* 426, *Trojan Women* 415, *Electra*

Europe

(European standards) and will be administered by CEN (European Committee for Standardization). ENs will eventually replace national codes, in Britain currently maintained by BSI (British Standards Institute), and will include parameters to reflect local requirements.

Eurocommunism policy followed by communist parties in Western Europe to seek power within the framework of national political initiative rather than by revolutionary means. In addition, Eurocommunism has enabled these parties to free themselves from total reliance on the Soviet Union.

Eurodollar US currency deposited outside the USA and held by individuals and institutions, not necessarily in Europe. They originated in the 1960s when E European countries deposited their US dollars in W European banks. Banks holding Eurodollar deposits may lend in dollars, usually to finance trade, and often redeposit with other foreign banks. The practice is a means of avoiding credit controls and exploiting interest-rate differentials.

Europa /juˈrəupə/ in astronomy, the fourth-largest moon of the planet Jupiter, diameter 3,100 km/1,900 mi, orbiting 671,000 km/417,000 mi from the planet every 3.55 days. It is covered by ice and criss-crossed by thousands of thin cracks, each some 50,000 km/30,000 mi long.

Europa /juˈrəupə/ in Greek mythology, the daughter of the king of Tyre, carried off by Zeus (in the form of a bull); she personifies the continent of Europe.

Europa Nostra international federation established 1963 by representatives of 18 organizations (including Italia Nostra, National Trust, Irish Georgian Society, Vieilles Maisons Françaises) in 11 European countries for the preservation of historic sites, buildings, and monuments.

Europe /ˈjuərəp/ second smallest continent, comprising the land west of the Ural mountains; it has 8% of the Earth's surface, with 14.5% of world population

area 10,400,000 sq km/4,000,000 sq mi

largest cities (over 1.5 million inhabitants) Athens, Barcelona, Berlin, Birmingham, Budapest, Hamburg, Istanbul, Kiev, Leningrad, London, Madrid, Manchester, Milan, Moscow, Paris, Rome, Vienna, Warsaw

features North European Plain on which stand London, Paris, Berlin, and Moscow; Central European Highlands (Sierra Nevada, Pyrenees, Alps, Apennines, Carpathians, Balkans); and Scandinavian highland, which takes in the Scottish Highlands; highest point Mount Elbruz in Caucasus mountains. Rivers (over 1,000 mi) Volga, Don, Dnieper, Danube; lakes (over 2,000 sq mi) Ladoga, Onega, Vanern. The climate ranges from the variable NW, modified by the ◊Gulf Stream, through the central zone with warm summers and cold winters, becoming bitterly cold in E Europe, to the Mediterranean zone with comparatively mild winters and hot summers. The last is the richest zone for plant life, but animal species have long been reduced everywhere by the predominance of humans

population (1985) 492,000,000 (excluding Turkey and USSR)

languages mostly of Indo-European origin, with a few exceptions, including Finno-Ugrian (Finnish and Hungarian) and Basque

religion Christianity (Protestantism, Roman Catholicism, Greek Orthodox), Islam, Judaism.

history see ◊Europe, history.

European inhabitant of the continent of Europe. The term is also sometimes applied to people of European descent living in other continents, especially in the Americas and Australia. Europe is culturally heterogeneous and although most of its languages belong to the Indo-European family, there are also speakers of Uralic (such as Hungarian) and Altaic (such as Turkish) languages, and Basque.

417, *Iphigenia in Tauris* 413, *Iphigenia in Aulis* 405, and *Bacchae* 405.

His influence on later drama was probably greater than that of the two tragedians, Aeschylus and Sophocles. A realist, he was bitterly attacked for his unorthodox 'impiety' and sympathy for the despised: slaves, beggars, and women. He went into voluntary exile from Athens to Macedonia at the end of his life.

Eurobond a bond underwritten by an international syndicate and sold in countries other than the country of the currency in which the issue is denominated. They provide longer-term financing than is possible with loans in Eurodollars.

Eurocodes a series of codes giving design rules for all types of engineering structures, except certain very specialized forms, such as nuclear reactors. The codes will be given the status of ENs

European Atomic Energy Commission (EURA-TOM) organization established by the second Treaty of Rome 1957, which seeks the co-operation of member states of the European Community in nuclear research and the rapid and large-scale development of non-military nuclear energy.

European Coal and Steel Community (ECSC) former organization established by the treaty of Paris 1951 (ratified 1952) as a single authority for the coal and steel industries of France, West Germany, Italy, Belgium, Holland, and Luxembourg, eliminating tariffs and other restrictions; in 1967 it became part of the European Community.

The ECSC arose out of the ◊Schuman plan 1950, which proposed a union of the French and German coal and steel industries so as to make future war between the two countries impossible. The ECSC was, in effect, a prototype institution for the European Community itself, under whose authority it came 1967. Subsequent members of the EC automatically became ECSC members also.

European Community (EC) political and economic alliance consisting of the European Coal and Steel Community (1952), European Economic Community (EEC, popularly called the Common Market, 1957), and the European Atomic Energy Commission (Euratom, 1957). The original six members— Belgium, France, West Germany, Italy, Luxembourg, and the Netherlands—were joined by the UK, Denmark, and the Republic of Ireland 1974, Greece 1981, Spain and Portugal 1985.

Europe: Early history

BC	
850,000	Earliest hunter-gathering peoples arrive in Europe; Palaeolithic period.
30,000	Earliest cave art.
8,300	Glaciers retreat, resulting in new animal species and flora.
6,500	Farming of cereal, sheep, and goats in Balkans and Aegean; Britain separated from Europe by rising ocean levels.
5,200	Farming spreads to Netherlands.
5,000	Gold, copper used.
4,500	Megalithic tombs.
4,000	Flint mines; farming developed in Britain.
3,500	Animals used to pull ploughs.
3,200	First wheeled vehicles; circles of megalithic stones.
2,000	Main phase of Stonehenge; fortified settlements; palaces in Minoan Crete.
1,900	Hieroglyphic Cretan writing.
1,450	Myceneans take control of Minoan Crete.
1,000	First hillforts in western Europe; iron industry in Aegean and central Europe.
753	Traditional foundation of Rome.
750	Iron working in Britain.

From 1967 the EC has the following institutions: the **Commission** of 13 members pledged to independence of national interests, who initiate Community action; the **Council of Ministers**, which makes decisions on the Commission's proposals; the ◊**European Parliament**, directly elected from 1979, which is mainly a consultative body but can dismiss the Commission; and the ◊**European Court of Justice**, to safeguard interpretation of Rome Treaties (1957) that established the Community.

European Court of Justice the court of the European Community (EC) that is responsible for interpreting Community law and ruling on breaches by member states and others of such

law. It sits in Luxembourg with judges from the member states. **The European Court of Human Rights** sits in Strasbourg to adjudicate on breaches of the European Convention of Human Rights.

European Democratic Group the group of British Conservative Party members of the European Parliament.

European Economic Community (EEC) one of the organizations of the ◊European Community (EC).

European Free Trade Association (EFTA) an organization established 1960 and as of 1988 consisting of Austria, Finland, Iceland, Norway, Sweden, and Switzerland. There are no import duties between members. Of the original members, Britain

Europe

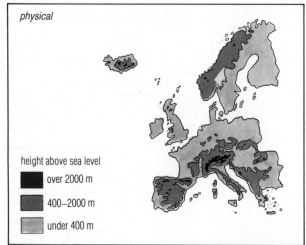

physical

height above sea level

- over 2000 m
- 400–2000 m
- under 400 m

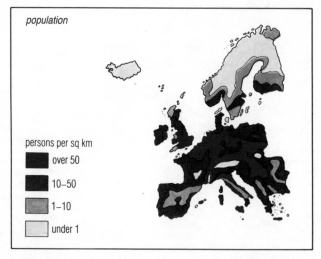

population

persons per sq km

- over 50
- 10–50
- 1–10
- under 1

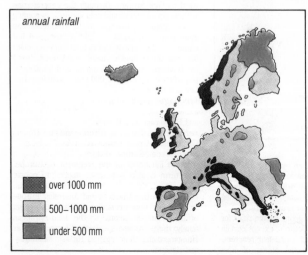

annual rainfall

- over 1000 mm
- 500–1000 mm
- under 500 mm

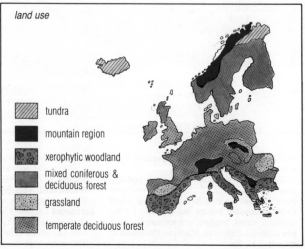

land use

- tundra
- mountain region
- xerophytic woodland
- mixed coniferous & deciduous forest
- grassland
- temperate deciduous forest

and Denmark left (1972) to join the ◊European Community, as subsequently did Portugal (1985).

In 1973 the EEC signed agreements with EFTA members setting up a free trade area of over 300 million consumers. Trade between the two groups is important and amounts for over half of total EFTA trade.

European Monetary System (EMS) an attempt by the European Community to bring financial cooperation and monetary stability to Europe. It was established 1979 in the wake of the 1974 oil crisis which brought growing economic disruption to European economies because of floating exchange rates. Central to the EMS is the **Exchange Rate Mechanism** (ERM), a voluntary system of semi-fixed exchange rates based on the European Currency Unit (ECU).

Under the ERM a central rate for each currency against the ECU is fixed. If it moves outside specified limits, the government must take action to avert the trend. The ERM has been successful in limiting fluctuations between exchange rates of participating countries: all EC members with the exception of the UK, Greece, Portugal, and Spain. The latter announced plans to join the EMS by July 1990.

European Monetary Union (EMU) the proposed European Community policy for a single currency and common economic policies. The proposal was announced by a European Community committee headed by EC Commission president Jacques Delors Apr 1989.

Three stages are envisaged for EMU. In the first stage, all controls on individual nations' capital flows would be ended, and the **European System of Central Banks** (ESCB) created. In stage two, the ESCB would begin to regulate money supply. Finally, exchange rates between member states would be fixed, and a single European currency created, and the ESCB would take over the function of all the nations' central banks.

European Parliament the parliament of the European Community, which meets in Strasbourg to comment on the legislative proposals of the Commission of the European Communities. Members are elected for a five-year term. The European Parliament has 518 seats, of which the UK, France, West Germany, and Italy have 81 each, Spain 60, the Netherlands 25, Belgium, Greece, and Portugal 24 each, Denmark 16, the Republic of Ireland 15, and Luxembourg 6.

Originally merely consultative, the European Parliament became directly elected 1979, and assumed increased powers. Though still not a true legislative body, it can dismiss the whole Commission and reject the Community budget in its entirety. Full sittings are in Strasbourg; most committees meet in Brussels, and the seat of the secretariat is in Luxembourg. After the 1989 elections the Left held 260 seats (Socialist 180, Communist 41, Green 39) and the Right 242 (Christian Democrats 123, Liberals 44, European Democratic Group 34, European Right 21, European Democratic Alliance 20).

European Space Agency (ESA) an organization of European countries (Belgium, Denmark, France, Ireland, Italy, Netherlands, Spain, Sweden, Switzerland, the UK, and West Germany) which engages in space research and technology. It was founded 1975, with headquarters in Paris.

ESA developed various scientific and communications satellites, the ◊Giotto space probe and the ◊Ariane rocket, and built ◊Spacelab. ESA plans to build its own space station, Columbus, for attachment to the US space station, and is working on its own shuttle project, Hermes.

europium a rare element, symbol Eu, atomic number 63, relative atomic mass 152. It is one of the lanthanide series of metals, used in lasers and in colour television.

Eurydice in Greek mythology, the wife of ◊Orpheus. She was a dryad, or forest nymph, and died of snake bite. Orpheus attempted unsuccessfully to fetch her back from the realm of the dead.

Evans *The poverty of the Depression and the stoical dignity of its victims is sympathetically recreated in this photograph by Walker Evans. Entitled* Depression: Bud Fields and Wife; Alabama, *1935, it is typical of Evans's social documentary pictures of the 1930s.*

Eusebio /juːˈseɪbɪəʊ/ (Eusebio Ferreira da Silva) 1942– . Portuguese footballer, born in Lourenco Marques. He made his international debut 1961 and played for his country 77 times. He spent most of his league career with Benfica, and also played in the USA.

Eusebius /juːˈsiːbɪəs/ c. 260–c. 340. Bishop of Caesarea (modern Qisarya, Israel); author of a history of the Christian church to 324.

Euskadi /ˌeɪʊˈskɑːdi/ the Basque name for the ◊Basque country.

eusociality form of social life found in insects such as honey bees and termites, in which the colony is made up of special castes (for example, workers, drones, and reproductives) whose membership is biologically determined. The worker castes do not usually reproduce. Only one mammal, the naked mole rat, has a social organization of this type. See also ◊social behaviour.

Eustachio /juːˈstɑːkɪəʊ/ Bartolommeo 1520– 1574. Italian anatomist, the discoverer of the

Eustachian tube, leading from the middle ear to the pharynx, and of the Eustachian valve in the right auricles of the heart.

Euston Road School British art school in Euston Road, London, 1937–39. William Coldstream (1908–87) and Victor Pasmore were teachers there. Despite its brief existence, the school influenced many British painters with its emphasis on careful, subdued naturalism.

Eutelsat abbreviation for **European Telecommunications Satellite Organization**.

Euterpe in Greek mythology, one of the ◊Muses (nine minor divinities) who inspired lyric poetry.

euthanasia the mercy killing of someone with an incurable disease or illness. The Netherlands legalized voluntary euthanasia 1983, but is the only country to have done so.

eutrophication the excessive enrichment of lake waters, primarily by nitrate fertilizers, washed from the soil by rain, and by phosphates from detergents in municipal sewage. These encourage the growth of algae and bacterias which use up the oxygen in the water, thereby making it uninhabitable for fishes and other animal life.

Eutyches /juːˈtaɪkiːz/ c. 384–c. 456. Christian theologian. An archimandrite (monastic head) in Constantinople, he held that Jesus had only one nature, the human nature being subsumed in the divine (a belief which became known as ◊Monophysitism). He was exiled after his ideas were condemned as heretical by the Council of ◊Chalcedon 451.

evangelicalism the beliefs of some Protestant Christian movements that stress biblical authority, faith, and personal commitment.

Evangelical Movement in Britain, a 19th-century party that stressed basic Protestant beliefs and the message of the four gospels. The movement was associated with Rev Charles Simeon (1783–1836). It aimed to raise moral enthusiasm and ethical standards among Church of England clergy.

Linked to the movement was the religious education provided by the ◊Bible Society and William ◊Wilberforce's campaign against the slave trade; it also attempted to improve the living conditions of the poor, and Evangelicals carried out missionary work in India.

Evans *A portrait study by Karsh of Ottawa of English actress Edith Evans.*

evangelist person travelling to spread the Christian gospel, and especially the authors of the four Gospels in the New Testament: Matthew, Mark, Luke, and John. See also ◊televangelist.

Evans /ˈevənz/ Arthur John 1851–1941. English archaeologist. His excavation of ◊Knossos on Crete resulted in the discovery of pre-Phoenician Minoan script and proved the existence of the legendary Minoan civilization.

Evans /ˈevənz/ Edith 1888–1976. English character actress, who performed on the London stage and on Broadway. She is particularly remembered for the film role of Lady Bracknell in Oscar Wilde's comedy*The Importance of Being Earnest* 1952.

Evans /ˈevənz/ Walker 1903–1975. US photographer, known for his documentary photographs of the people in the rural US south during the Great Depression of the 1930s. Many of his photographs appeared in James Agee's book *Let Us Now Praise Famous Men* 1941.

Evansville /ˈevənzvɪl/ industrial city (pharmaceuticals, plastics) in SW Indiana, USA, on the Ohio River; population (1980) 130,500. Abraham Lincoln spent his boyhood in nearby Spencer County.

evaporation a process in which a liquid turns to a vapour without its temperature reaching boiling point. A liquid left to stand in a saucer eventually evaporates because, at any time, a proportion of its molecules have sufficient energy to escape through the liquid surface into the atmosphere. The temperature of the liquid tends to fall because the evaporating molecules remove energy from the liquid. The rate of evaporation rises with an increase in temperature.

Eve /iːv/ in the Old Testament, the first woman, wife of ◊Adam, who was tempted by Satan in the form of a snake to eat the fruit of the Tree of Knowledge of Good and Evil, and thus brought about the expulsion from the Garden of Eden.

There are two versions of the creation myth in the Bible: in one of them, Eve was created simultaneously with Adam; in the other, she was created from his rib. In some legends, ◊Lilith was the first woman.

Evelyn /ˈiːvlɪn/ John 1620–1706. English diarist and author. He was a friend of Pepys, and like him remained in London during the Plague and the Great Fire. He wrote 300-odd books including his diary, first published 1818, which covers the period 1640–1706.

Born in Surrey, he enlisted for three years in the Royalist army 1624, but withdrew on finding his estate exposed to the enemy and lived mostly abroad until 1652. He declined all office under the Commonwealth, but after the Restoration enjoyed great favour, received court appointments, and was one of the founders of the Royal Society.

evening primrose American plant of the family Onagraceae, naturalized in Europe. It is grown as a field crop for the oil it produces, which is used in treating eczema and premenstrual tension.

eventing sport (horse trials) giving an all-round test of a horse and rider in a three-day event: dressage, testing a horse's response to control; speed and endurance across country; and finally a modified showjumping contest.

Everest, Mount /ˈevərɪst/ (Nepálese *Sagarmantha* 'head of the earth') the world's highest mountain, in the Himalayas, on the China-Nepál frontier; height 8,872 m/29,118 ft. It was first climbed by Edmund Hillary and Tenzing Norgay 1953.

The English name comes from George Everest (1790–1866), surveyor-general of India. In 1987 a US expedition obtained measurements of ◊K2, which disputed Everest's claim to be the highest mountain.

Everglades /ˈevəgleɪdz/ area of swamps and lakes in S ◊Florida, USA; area 12,950 sq km/6,000 sq mi.

evergreen plant, such as pine, spruce, or holly, that bears its leaves all year round. Most ◊conifers are evergreen. Plants that shed their leaves in winter are described as ◊deciduous.

everlasting flower flower head with coloured bracts which retains its colour when cut and dried.

Evershed /ˈevəʃed/ John 1864–1956. English astronomer who made solar observations. In 1909, he discovered the radial movements of gases in sunspots (*Evershed effect*). He also gave his name to a spectroheliograph, the Evershed spectroscope.

Evert /ˈevət/ Chris 1954– . US lawn tennis player. She won her first Wimbledon title 1974, and has since won 21 Grand Slam titles. She became the first tennis player woman to win $1 million in prize money.

CAREER HIGHLIGHTS

Wimbledon
singles: 1974, 1976, 1981
doubles: 1976
US Open
singles: 1975–78, 1980, 1982
French Open
singles: 1974–75, 1979–80, 1983, 1985–86
doubles: 1974–75
Australian Open
singles: 1982, 1984

Evesham /ˈiːvʃəm/ town in Hereford and Worcester, England, on the Avon SE of Worcester; population (1981) 15,250. Fruit and vegetables from the fertile *Vale of Evesham* are canned. In the Battle of Evesham, 4 Aug 1265, Edward, Prince of Wales, defeated Simon de Montfort, who was killed. See ◊Barons' Wars.

evidence the testimony of witnesses and production of documents and other material in court proceedings in order to prove or disprove facts at issue in the case. Witnesses must swear or affirm that their evidence is true. In English law, giving false evidence is the crime of ◊perjury.

Documentary evidence has a wide scope including maps, sound tracks, and films, in addition to documents in writing. Objects may be used as evidence, such as a weapon used in a crime. Evidence obtained illegally may be excluded from the court (such as a confession under duress).

evolution a slow process of change from one form to another, as in the evolution of the universe from its formation in the ◊Big Bang to its present state, or in the evolution of life on Earth. (For human evolution, see ◊human species, origins of.) Some Christians deny the theory of evolution as conflicting with the belief that God created all things (see ◊creationism).

With respect to the living world, the idea of continuous evolution can be traced as far back as ◊Lucretius in the 1st century BC, but it did not gain wide acceptance until the 19th century following the work of Charles ◊Lyell, J B ◊Lamarck, Charles ◊Darwin, and T H ◊Huxley. Darwin assigned the major role in evolutionary change to ◊natural selection acting on genetic variation, which is ultimately produced by spontaneous changes (◊mutations) in the genetic material of organisms. Natural selection occurs because those individuals

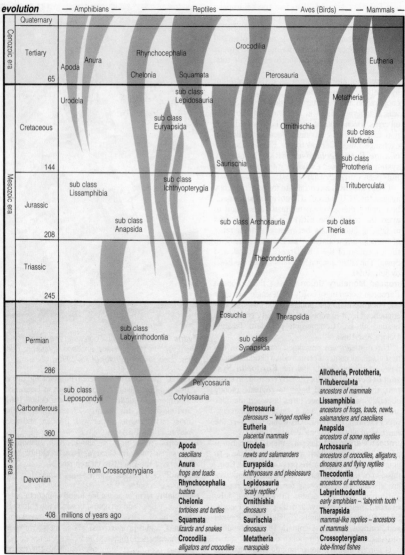

evolution

better adapted to their particular environments reproduce more effectively, thus contributing more ◊genes to future generations. The modern theory of evolution, called ◊Neo-Darwinism, combines Darwin's theory with Gregor ◊Mendel's theories on genetics. Although neither the general concept of evolution nor the importance of natural selection is doubted by biologists, there remains dispute over other possible processes involved in evolutionary change. Besides natural selection and ◊sexual selection, chance may play an important role in deciding which genes become characteristic of a population, a phenomenon called 'genetic drift'. It is now also clear that evolutionary change does not always occur at a constant rate, but that the process can have long periods of relative stability interspersed with periods of rapid change. This has led to new theories, such as the ◊punctuated equilibrium model. See also ◊adaptive radiation.

Evreux /ev'rɜ:/ capital of Eure *département* in NW France; population (1983) 46,250. It produces pharmaceuticals and rubber.

Evvoia Greek name for the island of ◊Euboea.

evzone member of a Greek infantry regiment whose soldiers wear distinctive white short-skirted uniform.

ex cathedra (Latin 'from the throne') with authority; a statement by the pope, taken to be indisputably true, and which must be accepted by Catholics.

excavator a machine designed for digging in the ground, or for earth-moving in general. Diggers using hydraulically powered digging arms are widely used on building sites. They may run on wheels or on ◊caterpillar tracks. The largest excavators are the draglines used in mining to strip away earth covering the coal or mineral deposit, so named because they cast their digging bucket away like a fishing line being cast, and then drag the bucket back along the ground, so filling it with earth. Britain's 'Big Geordie' walking dragline, which operates in the Northumberland coalfields, has a digging bucket with a capacity of 50 cu m/65 cu yd.

exchange rate the price at which one currency is bought or sold in terms of other currencies, gold, or accounting units such as the special drawing right (SDR) of the ◊International Monetary Fund. Exchange rates may be fixed by international agreement or by government policy; or they may be wholly or partly allowed to 'float' (that is, find their own level) in world currency markets, as with most major currencies since the 1970s.

excise duties levied on certain goods produced within a country; it is collected by the government's ◊Customs and Excise department.

exclamation mark or **exclamation point** a punctuation mark (!), used to indicate emphasis or strong emotion ('What a surprise!'). Usually the emphasis or emotion is built directly into the text, as part of a story, or dialogue, but the exclamation can also be placed in brackets to indicate that the writer is surprised by something, especially by something in a quotation.

Although the exclamation mark is a natural part of imaginative or emotional writing, its use is generally kept to a minimum in serious prose and technical writing.

exclusion principle in physics, a principle of atomic structure originated by Wolfgang ◊Pauli. It states that no two electrons in a single atom may have the same set of ◊quantum numbers.

excommunication exclusion of an offender from the rights and privileges of the Roman Catholic Church; famous offenders include King John, Henry VIII, and Elizabeth I.

excretion the removal of waste products from the cells of living organisms. In plants and simple animals, waste products are removed by diffusion, but in higher animals by specialized organs. In mammals, for example, carbon dioxide and water are removed via the lungs, and nitrogenous compounds and water via the liver, kidneys, and urinary system.

executor in law, a person appointed in a will to carry out the instructions of the deceased. A person so named has the right to refuse to act. The executor also has a duty to bury the deceased, prove the will, and obtain a grant of probate (that is, establish that the will is genuine and obtain official approval of his or her actions).

Exeter /'eksɪtə/ city, administrative headquarters of Devon, England, on the river Exe; population (1981) 96,000. It has medieval, Georgian and Regency architecture, including a cathedral, 1280–1369, a modern market centre, and a university, 1955. It manufactures agricultural machinery, pharmaceuticals, and textiles.

exeunt (Latin 'they go out') a stage direction.

existentialism a branch of philosophy that emphasizes the existence of the individual. It is based on the concept that the universe is absurd, although humans have free will. Existentialists argue that philosophy must begin from the concrete situation of the individual in the world, and that this situation cannot be comprehended by any purely rational system. Its origins are usually traced back to Kierkegaard, and among its proponents are Heidegger and Sartre.

exit (Latin 'he/she goes out') a stage direction.

ex lib. abbreviation for *ex libris* (Latin 'from the library of').

Exmoor /'eksmʊə/ moorland in Devon and Somerset, England, forming (with the coast from Minehead to Combe Martin) a National Park since 1954. It includes Dunkery Beacon 520 m/1,707 ft, and the ◊Doone Valley.

exobiology the study of possible life-forms that may exist elsewhere in the universe.

exocrine gland type of gland that discharges secretions, usually through a tube or a duct, on to a surface. Examples include sweat glands which release sweat on to the skin, and digestive glands which release digestive juices on to the walls of the intestine. Some animals also have ◊endocrine glands (ductless glands) that release hormones directly into the bloodstream.

Exodus in the Old Testament, the departure of the Israelites from slavery in Egypt, under the leadership of ◊Moses, for the Promised Land of Canaan. The journey included the miraculous parting of the Red Sea, Pharaoh's pursuing forces being drowned as the waters returned. Exodus is also the name of the book of the Bible that contains the story.

exorcism rite used in a number of religions for the expulsion of so-called 'evil spirits'. In Christianity it is employed, for example, in the Roman Catholic, Anglican, and Pentecostal churches.

exoskeleton the hardened external skeleton of insects, spiders, crabs, and other arthropods. It provides attachment for muscles and protection for the internal organs, as well as support. To permit growth it is periodically shed in a process called ◊ecdysis.

exosphere the uppermost layer of the ◊atmosphere. It is an ill-defined zone above the thermosphere, beginning at about 700 km/435 mi and fading off into the vacuum of space. The gases are extremely thin, with hydrogen as the main constituent.

exothermic reaction a chemical reaction during which heat is given out (see ◊energy of reaction).

expansion in physics, the increase in size of a constant mass of substance (a body) caused by, for example, increasing its temperature (thermal expansion) or its internal pressure. *Expansivity*, or coefficient of cubical (or thermal) expansion, is the expansion per unit volume per degree rise in temperature.

expectorant substance often added to cough mixture to help expel mucus from the airways. It is debatable whether it has an effect on lung secretions.

experiment in science, a practical test designed with the intention that its results will be relevant to a particular theory or set of theories. Although some experiments may be used merely for gathering more information about a topic which is already well understood, others may be of crucial importance in confirming a new theory or in undermining long-held beliefs.

Of central importance, therefore, is the manner in which experiments are performed, and the relation between the design of an experiment and its value. In general an experiment is of most value when the factors which might affect the results (variables) are carefully controlled; for this reason most experiments take place in a well-managed environment such as a laboratory or clinic.

experimental psychology the application of scientific methods to the study of mental processes and behaviour. This covers a wide range of fields of study including: **human and animal learning**, in which learning theories describe how new behaviours are acquired and modified; **cognition**, the study of a number of functions, such as perception, attention, memory, and language; and **physiological psychology**, which relates the study of cognition to different regions of the brain. **Artificial intelligence** refers to the computer simulation of cognitive processes, such as language and problem-solving.

expert system a computer program for giving advice (such as diagnosing an illness or interpreting the law) that incorporates knowledge derived from human expertise. It is a kind of ◊knowledge-based system containing rules that can be applied to find the solution to a problem. It is a form of ◊artificial intelligence.

explanation in science, an attempt to make clear the cause of any natural event, by reference to physical laws and to observations.

The extent to which any explanation can be said to be true is one of the chief concerns of philosophy, partly because observations may be wrongly interpreted, partly because explanations should help us predict how nature will behave. Although it may be reasonable to expect that a physical law will hold in the future, that expectation is problematic in that it relies on ◊induction, a much-criticized feature of human thought; in fact no explanation, however 'scientific', can be held to be true for all time, and thus the difference between a scientific and a common-sense explanation remains the subject of intense philosophical debate.

Explorer one of a series of US scientific satellites. Explorer 1, launched Jan 1958, was the first US satellite in orbit and discovered the Van Allen belts around the Earth.

explosive any material capable of a sudden release of energy and the rapid formation of a large volume of gas, leading when compressed to the development of a high-pressure wave (blast).

Combustion and explosion differ essentially only in rate of reaction, and many explosives (called **low explosives**) are capable of undergoing relatively slow combustion under suitable conditions. **High explosives** produce uncontrollable blasts. The first low explosive was ◊gunpowder; the first high explosive was nitroglycerine. In 1867, Alfred ◊Nobel produced dynamite by mixing nitroglycerine with kieselguhr, a fine, chalk-like material. Other explosives now in use include trinitrotoluene (TNT); ANFO (a mixture of ammonium nitride and fuel oil), which is widely used in blasting; and pentaerythritol tetranitrate (PETN), a sensitive explosive with high power. Military explosives are often based on cyclonite (also called RDX), which is moderately sensitive but extremely powerful. Even more powerful explosives are made by mixing RDX with TNT and aluminium. **Plastic explosives**, such as Semtex, are based on RDX mixed with oils and waxes. The explosive violence of atomic and hydrogen bombs arises from the conversion of matter to energy according to Einstein's mass–energy equation, $E = mc^2$.

exponential in mathematics, a ◊function in which the variable quantity is an exponent, that is, an

◊index or power to which another number or expression is raised.

Exponential functions and series involve the constant $e = 2.71828...$. Napier devised natural ◊logarithms in 1614 with e as the base.

Exponential functions are one of the basic functions of mathematics, written as e^x or exp x. e^x has five definitions, two of which are: (i) e^x is the solution of the differential equation $dx/dt = x$ ($x = 1$ if $t = 0$); (ii) e^x is the limiting sum of the infinite series $1 + x + (x^2!) + (x^3!) + ... + (x^n!)$.

Curves of the form $y = Ae^{-ax}$, $a > 0$ are known as decay functions; those of the form $y = Be^{-bx}$, $b < 0$ are growth functions. **Exponential growth** is not constant. It applies, for example, to population growth, where the population doubles in a short time period. A graph of population number against time produces a curve that is characteristically rather flat at first but then shoots almost directly upwards.

export goods or service produced in one country and sold to another. Exports may be visible (goods which are physically exported) or invisible (services provided in the exporting country but paid for in another country).

export credit loan, finance, or guarantee provided by a government or a financial institution enabling companies to export goods and services in situations where payment for them may be delayed or subject to risk.

exposition in music, the opening statement of sonata form in which the principal themes are clearly outlined.

exposure meter an instrument used in photography for indicating the correct exposure—the length of time the camera shutter should be open in given light conditions. Meters use substances such as cadmium sulphide and selenium as light sensors. These materials change electrically when light strikes them, the change being proportional to the intensity of the incident light. Many modern cameras have a built-in exposure meter that sets the camera controls automatically as the light conditions change.

Expressionism a style of painting, sculpture, and literature that expresses inner emotions; in particular, a movement in early-20th-century art in N and central Europe. Expressionists tended to distort or exaggerate natural appearance in order to create a reflection of an inner world, as in the Norwegian painter Munch's *Skriket/The Scream* 1893 (National Gallery, Oslo).

Other leading Expressionist artists were Ensor, Kokoschka, and Soutine. Expressionist writers include Strindberg and Wedekind. The *Blaue Reiter* group was associated with this movement, and the Expressionist trend in German art emerged even more strongly after World War I in the work of Beckmann and Grosz.

expressionism in music, atonal music that uses dissonance for disturbing effect.

extinction in biology, the complete disappearance of a species. In the past, extinctions generally occurred because species were unable to adapt quickly enough to a changing environment. Today, most extinctions are due to human activity. Some species, such as the ◊dodo of Mauritius, the ◊moas of New Zealand, and the passenger ◊pigeon of North America, have been exterminated by hunting. Others become extinct when their habitat is destroyed.

Mass extinctions are episodes during which whole groups of species have become extinct, the best known being that of the dinosaurs, other large reptiles, and various marine invertebrates about 65 million years ago. Another mass extinction occurred about 10,000 years ago when many giant species of mammal died out. This is known as the 'Pleistocene overkill' because their disappearance was probably hastened by the hunting activities of prehistoric humans. The current mass extinction is largely due to human destruction of habitats, as in the tropical forests and coral reefs; it is far more serious and damaging than mass extinctions of the past because

eye

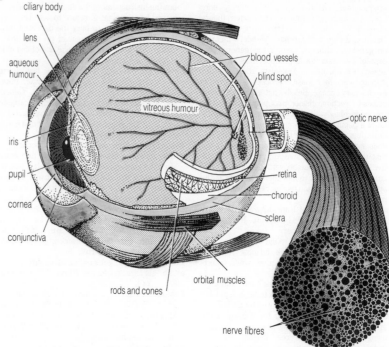

of the speed at which it occurs. Human caused climatic changes and pollution also make it less likely that the biospere can recover and evolve new species to suit a changed environment. The rate of extinction is difficult to estimate, since most losses occur in the rich environment of the tropical rainforest, where the total number of existent species is not known. Conservative estimates put the rate of loss due to deforestation alone at 4,000 to 6,000 species a year. Overall, the rate could be as high as one species an hour, with the loss of one species putting those dependent on it at risk. Australia has the worst record for extinction: 18 mammals have disappeared since Europeans settled there, and 40 more are threatened.

extinction (of a peerage or baronetcy) no longer existing, because the line of persons in remainder to the title has died out.

extracellular matrix a strong material naturally occurring in animals and plants, made up of protein and long-chain sugars (polysaccharides) in which cells are embedded. It is often called a 'biological glue', and forms an important part of ◊connective tissues such as bone and skin. The cell walls of plants and bacteria, and the ◊exoskeletons of insects and other arthropods, are also formed by types of extracellular matrix.

extradition the surrender, by one state to another, of a person accused of a criminal offence in the country to which they are extradited. It is usually governed by a treaty between the two states concerned. A state will not usually allow extradition for political offences or for an offence which it does not treat as a crime, even though it is a crime in the requesting state.

Extremadura /ˌestreɪməˈdʊərə/ autonomous region of W Spain including the provinces of Badajoz and Cáceres; area 41,600 sq km/16,058 sq mi; population (1986) 1,089,000. Irrigated land is

Expressionism Edvard Munch's The Scream 1893, National Gallery, Oslo. Munch's work is typically Expressionist in using colour, line and texture to create a reflection of an inner world.

Eyck Jan van Eyck's The Arnolfini Wedding 1434 National Gallery, London.

used for growing wheat; the remainder is either oak forest or used for pig or sheep grazing.

extroversion or **extraversion** a personality dimension described by ◊Jung and later by Eysenck. The typical extrovert is sociable, impulsive, and carefree. The opposite of extroversion is introversion; the typical introvert is quiet and inward-looking.

extrusion a common method of shaping metals, plastics, and other materials. The materials, usually hot, are forced through the hole in a metal die and take its cross-sectional shape. Rods, tubes, and sheets may be made in this way.

Eyck /aɪk/ Jan van *c.* 1380–1441. Flemish painter of the early northern Renaissance, one of the first to work in oil. His paintings are technically brilliant and sumptuously rich in detail and colour. Little is known of his brother **Hubert van Eyck** (died 1426), who is supposed to have begun the huge and complex altarpiece in St Bavo's cathedral, Ghent, *The Adoration of the Mystical Lamb*, completed by Jan 1432.

Jan van Eyck is known to have worked in The Hague 1422–24 for John of Bavaria, Count of Holland. He served as court painter to Philip the Good, Duke of Burgundy, from 1425, and worked in Bruges from 1430. Philip the Good valued him not only as a painter but also as a diplomatic representative, sending him to Spain and Portugal in 1427 and 1428, and he remained in the duke's employ after he settled in Bruges.

Oil painting allowed for much subtler effects of tone and colour and greater command of detail than the egg-tempera technique then in common use, and van Eyck took full advantage of this. In his *Arnolfini Wedding* 1434 (National Gallery, London) the bride and groom appear in a domestic interior crammed with disguised symbols, as a kind of pictorial marriage certificate. Another notable work is the *Madonna with Chancellor Rolin* probably 1435/37 (Louvre, Paris).

eye the organ of vision. The **human eye** is a roughly spherical structure contained in a bony socket. Light enters it through the **cornea**, and passes through the circular opening (**pupil**) in the *iris* (the coloured part of the eye). The light is focused by the combined action of the curved cornea, the internal fluids, and the **lens** (the rounded transparent structure behind the iris). The ciliary muscles act on the lens to change its shape, so that images of objects at different distances can be focused on the **retina**. This is at the back of the eye, and is packed with light-sensitive cells (rods and cones), connected to the brain by the optic nerve.

In contrast, the **insect eye** is compound, that is, made up of many separate facets, known as *ommatidia*, each of which collects light and directs it separately to a receptor to build up an image. Lower invertebrates, such as worms and snails, have much simpler eyes, with no lens. The mantis shrimp's eyes contain ten colour pigments to perceive colour and some flies and fishes have five, while the human eye only has three.

eyebright flower of the genus *Euphrasia*, family Scrophulariaceae. It is 2–30 cm/1–12 in high, bearing whitish flowers streaked with purple. The name indicates its traditional use as an eye-medicine. It is found in fields throughout Britain.

eyre in English history, one of the travelling courts set up by Henry II 1176 to enforce conformity to the king's will; they continued into the 13th century. *Justices in eyre* were the judges who heard pleas at these courts.

Eyre /eə/ Edward John 1815–1901. English explorer who wrote *Expeditions into Central Australia* 1845. He was Governor of Jamaica 1864–65.

Eyre /eə/ Richard (Charles Hastings) 1943– . English stage and film director. He succeeded Peter Hall as artistic director of the National Theatre, London, 1988. His films include *The Ploughman's Lunch* 1983.

Eyre, Lake /eə/ Australia's largest lake, in central South Australia, which frequently runs dry, becoming a salt marsh in dry seasons; area up to 9,000 sq km/3,500 sq mi. It is the continent's lowest point, 12 m/39 ft below sea level. It is named after E J Eyre, who reached it 1840.

Eyre Peninsula /eə/ peninsula in S Australia, which includes the iron and steel city of Whyalla. Over 50% of the iron used in Australia's steel industry is mined at Iron Knob; the only seal colony on mainland Australis is at Point Labatt.

Eysenck Hans Jurgen 1916– . English psychologist. He concentrated on personality theory and testing by developing ◊behaviour therapy. He is an outspoken critic of psychoanalysis as a therapeutic method.

Ezekiel /ɪˈziːkiəl/ lived *c.* 600 BC. In the Old Testament, a Hebrew prophet. Carried into captivity in Babylon by ◊Nebuchadnezzar 597, he preached that Jerusalem's fall was due to the sins of Israel. The book of Ezekiel begins with a description of a vision of supernatural beings.

Ezra /ˈezrə/ in the Old Testament, a Jewish scribe who was allowed by Artaxerxes, king of Persia (probably Artaxerxes I, 464–423 BC), to lead his people back to Jerusalem from Babylon 458 BC. He re-established the Mosaic law (laid down by Moses) and eradicated intermarriage.

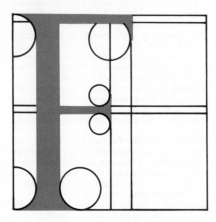

fable a story, either in verse or prose, in which animals or inanimate objects are endowed with the mentality and speech of human beings in order to point a moral. Fabulists include Aesop, Babrius, Phaedrus, Avianus, and La Fontaine.

Fabre /'fɑːbrə/ Jean Henri Casimir 1823–1915. French entomologist, noted for his vivid and intimate descriptions and paintings of the life of wasps, bees, and other insects.

Fabricius /fəˈbrɪsɪəs/ Geronimo 1537–1619. Italian anatomist and embryologist. He made a detailed study of the veins, and discovered the valves which direct the bloodflow towards the heart. He also studied the development of chick ◊embryos.

A professor of surgery and anatomy at Padua, his work greatly influenced and helped his pupil William ◊Harvey. Despite many errors, he raised anatomy and embryology to a higher scientific level.

Fabritius /fəˈbriːtsɪəs/ Carel 1622–1654. Dutch painter, a pupil of Rembrandt. His own style, lighter and with more precise detail than his master's, is evident for example in *The Goldfinch* 1654. He painted religious scenes and portraits.

facsimile transmission full name for ◊*fax* or *telefax*.

factor a number which divides into another number exactly. For example, the factors of 64 are 1, 2, 4, 8, 16, 32, and 64. In algebra, certain kinds of polynomials (expressions consisting of several or many terms) can be factorized. For example, the factors of $x^2 + 3x + 2$ are $x + 1$ and $x + 2$, since $x^2 + 3x + 2 = (x + 1)(x + 2)$.

The factors of $x^3 + 6x^2 + 11x + 6$ are $x + 1$, $x + 2$, and $x + 3$. See also ◊prime number.

factorial of a positive number, the product of all the whole numbers (integers) inclusive between 1 and the number itself. A factorial is indicated by the symbol '!'. Thus $6! = 1 \times 2 \times 3 \times 4 \times 5 \times 6 = 720$. Factorial zero, $0!$, is defined as 1.

factory act in Britain, an act of Parliament governing conditions of work, hours of labour, safety, and sanitary provision in factories and workshops. See ◊safety at work.

factory farming the intensive rearing of poultry or animals for food, usually on high-protein foodstuffs in confined quarters. Chickens for eggs and meat, and calves for veal are commonly factory farmed. Some countries restrict the use of antibiotics and growth hormones as aids to factory farming, because they can persist in the flesh of the animals after they are slaughtered. The European Commission banned steroid hormones for beef cattle at the end of 1985. Many people, particularly animal-rights activists, object to factory farming for moral as well as health reasons.

Egg-laying hens are housed in 'batteries' of cages arranged in long rows. If caged singly, they lay fewer eggs, so there are often four to a cage with a floor area of only 2,400 sq cm/370 sq in. In the course of a year, battery hens average 261 eggs each, whereas for free-range chickens the figure is 199.

factory system the basis of manufacturing in the modern world. In the factory system workers are employed at a place where they carry out specific tasks, which together result in a product. This is called the division of labour. Usually these workers will perform their tasks with the aid of machinery. Such ◊mechanization is another feature of the modern factory system, which leads to ◊mass production. Richard ◊Arkwright pioneered the system in England 1771, when he set up a cotton-spinning factory.

factotum (Latin 'do everything') someone employed to do all types of work.

Fadden /'fædn/ Arthur 'Artie' 1895–1973. Australian politician, born in Queensland. He was leader of the Country Party 1941–58 and prime minister Aug–Oct 1941.

faeces remains of food and other debris passed out of the digestive tract of animals. Faeces consist of quantities of fibrous material, bacteria and other microorganisms, rubbed-off lining of the digestive tract, bile fluids, undigested food, minerals, and water.

Faenza /faɪˈentsə/ city on the river Lamone in Ravenna province, Emilia-Romagna, Italy; population (1985) 54,900. It has many medieval remains, including the 15th-century walls. It gave its name to 'faience' pottery, a type of tin-glazed earthenware first produced there.

Faerie Queene, The a poem by Edmund Spenser, published 1590–96, dedicated to Elizabeth I. The poem, in six books, describes the adventures of six knights. Spenser used a new stanza form, later adopted by Keats, Shelley, and Byron.

Faeroe Islands or **Faeroes** alternative spelling of the ◊Faroe Islands, a group of islands in the N Atlantic.

Fagatogo /ˌfɑːgəˈtɔʌgən/ capital of American Samoa. Situated on Pago Pago Harbour, Tutuila Island.

Fahd /fɑːd/ 1921– . King of Saudi Arabia from 1982, when he succeeded his half-brother Khalid. As head of government he has been active in trying to bring about a solution to the Middle East conflicts.

Fahrenheit /'fɑːrənhaɪt/ Gabriel Daniel 1686–1736. German physicist who lived mainly in England and Holland. He devised the Fahrenheit temperature scale.

Fahrenheit scale a temperature scale invented 1714 by Gabriel Fahrenheit, no longer in scientific use. Intervals are measured in degrees (°F); °F = (°C × 9/5) + 32.

Fahrenheit took as the zero point the lowest temperature he could achieve anywhere in the laboratory, and, as the other fixed point, body temperature, which he set at 96°F. On this scale water freezes at 32°F and boils at 212°F.

fainting a sudden, temporary loss of consciousness caused by reduced blood supply to the brain. It may be due to emotional shock or physical factors such as pooling of blood in the legs from standing still for long periods.

Fairbanks /'feəbæŋks/ town in central Alaska, USA, situated on the Chena Slough, a tributary of the river Tanana; population (1983) 65,000. Founded 1902, it is a goldmining and fur-trading centre, and the terminus of the Alaska Railroad and of the Pan-American Highway.

F the sixth letter of the alphabet. Its capital form has changed little from that of the earlier Semitic alphabets.

°F abbreviation for ◊*Fahrenheit* (temperature scale).

FA abbreviation for *Football Association*.

Fabergé /'fæbəʒeɪ/ Peter Carl 1846–1920. Russian goldsmith and jeweller. His workshops in St Petersburg and Moscow were celebrated for the exquisite delicacy of their products, especially the use of gold in various shades. Among his masterpieces was a series of jewelled Easter eggs, the first of which was commissioned by Alexander III for the tsarina 1884. Fabergé died in exile in Switzerland.

Fabian Society UK socialist organization for research, discussion, and publication, founded in London 1884. Its name is derived from the Roman commander Fabius Maximus, and refers to the evolutionary methods by which it hopes to attain socialism by a succession of gradual reforms. Early members included George Bernard Shaw, and Beatrice and Sidney ◊Webb.

Fabius /'feɪbɪəs/ Laurent 1946– . French socialist politician, prime minister 1984–86. He introduced a liberal, free-market economic programme, but his career was damaged by the 1985 ◊Greenpeace sabotage scandal.

Fabius became economic adviser to the Socialist Party (PS) leader Mitterrand in 1976, entered the National Assembly 1978, and was a member of the socialist government from 1981. In 1984, at a time of economic crisis, he was appointed prime minister. He resigned after his party's electoral defeat in Mar 1986.

Fabius Maximus, Quintus /'feɪbɪəs ˈmæksɪməs/ Roman general, known as *Cunctator* or 'Delayer' because of his cautious tactics against Hannibal 217–214 BC, when he continually harassed Hannibal's armies but never risked a set battle.

Fabergé A Fabergé egg.

Fairbanks US film actor Douglas Fairbanks Jr.

Fairbanks /'feəbæŋks/ Douglas. Stage name of Douglas Elton Ulman 1883–1939. US actor. He played swashbuckling heroes in silent films such as *The Mark of Zorro* 1920, *The Three Musketeers* 1921, *Robin Hood* 1922, *The Thief of Baghdad* 1924, and *Don Quixote* 1925. He often produced and wrote his own films under a pseudonym. He was married to the film star Mary Pickford 1920–33.

Fairbanks /'feəbæŋks/ Douglas, Jr 1909– . US actor who appeared in the same type of swashbuckling film roles as his father, Douglas Fairbanks; for example in *Catherine the Great* 1934 and *The Prisoner of Zenda* 1937.

Fairfax /'feəfæks/ Thomas, 3rd Baron Fairfax of Cameron 1612–1671. English general, commander in chief of the Parliamentary army in the English Civil War. With Cromwell he formed the ◊New Model Army, defeated Charles I at Naseby, and suppressed the Royalist and Presbyterian risings 1648.

Fair Trading, Office of UK government department established 1973 to keep commercial activities under review. It covers the areas of consumer affairs and credit, ◊monopolies and mergers, and anti-competitive and ◊restrictive trade practices. The USA has a Bureau of Consumer Protection with similar scope.

fairy tale a magical story, usually a folk tale in origin. Typically in European fairy tales, a poor, brave, and resourceful hero or heroine comes through testing adventures to good fortune. The Germanic tales collected by the ◊Grimm brothers have been retold in many variants. The form may also be adapted for more individual moral and literary purposes, as was done by the Danish writer H C ◊Andersen.

Faisal /'faɪsəl/ Ibn Abdul Aziz 1905–1975. King of Saudi Arabia from 1964. The younger brother of King Saud, on whose accession 1953 he was declared crown prince. He was prime minister 1953–60 and from 1962 until his assassination by a nephew. In 1964 he emerged victorious from a lengthy conflict with his brother and adopted a policy of steady modernization of his country.

Faisalabad /'faɪsələbæd/ city in Punjab province, Pakistan; population (1981) 1,092,000. It trades in grain, cotton, and textiles.

fait accompli (French 'accomplished fact') something that has been done and cannot be undone.

Faizabad /ˌfaɪzə'bæd/ town in Uttar Pradesh, N India; population (1981) 143,167. It lies at the head of navigation of the river Ghaghara, and has sugar refineries and an agricultural trade.

fakir originally a Muslim mendicant of some religious order, but in India a general term for an ascetic.

Falaise /fə'leɪz/ town 32 km/20 mi SE of Caen, in Calvados *département* Normandy, France; population (1982) 8,820. It is a market centre, and manufactures cotton and leather goods. The castle was that of the first dukes of Normandy, and William the Conqueror was born here.

Falange Española /fæ'læŋxeɪ ˌespæn'jəʊlə/ (Spanish 'phalanx') former Spanish Fascist Party, founded 1933 by José Antonio de Rivera, son of the military ruler Miguel ◊Primo de Rivera. It was closely modelled in programme and organization on the Italian fascists and on the Nazis. In 1937, when ◊Franco assumed leadership, it was declared the only legal party, and altered its name to Traditionalist Spanish Phalanx.

Falasha a member of a small community of black Jews in Ethiopia. They suffered discrimination, and began a gradual process of resettlement in Israel after being accorded Jewish status by Israel 1975. Only about 30,000 Falashas remain in Ethiopia.

falcon genus of birds of prey *Falco*, family Falconidae, order Falconiformes. Falcons are the smallest of the hawks (15–60 cm/6–24 in). They nest in high places, and kill their prey by swooping down at high speed. They include the peregrine and kestrel.

The *peregrine falcon Falco peregrinus*, up to about 50 cm/1.8 ft long, has become re-established in North America and Britain after near extinction (by pesticides, gamekeepers, and egg collectors). When 'stooping' on its intended prey, it is the fastest creature in the world, timed at 240 kph/150 mph.

Other hawks include the *hobby Falco subbuteo*, the *merlin Falco columbarius* (called pigeon-hawk in North America), and the *kestrel Falco tinnunculus*. The hobby and the merlin are about 30 cm/1 ft in length, steel-blue above and reddish below, and nest on moors. The kestrel is just over 30 cm/1 ft long, with grey head and tail, light chestnut back with black spots, and an unmistakeable quivering hover.

Falconet /ˌfælkɒ'neɪ/ Etienne-Maurice 1716–1791. French sculptor whose works range from formal Baroque to gentle Rococo in style. He directed sculpture at the Sèvres porcelain factory 1757–66. His bronze equestrian statue of *Peter the Great* in Leningrad was commissioned 1766 by Catherine II.

falconry the use of specially trained falcons and hawks to capture birds or small mammals. Practised since ancient times in the Middle East, falconry was introduced from continental Europe to Britain in Saxon times.

The Normans, Tudors, and Stuarts were all fond of falconry, but it fell into disuse after the English Civil War. In modern times there has been some revival of interest in the West.

Falkender /'fɔːlkəndə/ Marcia, Baroness Falkender (Marcia Williams) 1932– . British political secretary to Labour prime minister Harold Wilson from 1956, she was influential in the 'kitchen cabinet' of the 1964–70 government, as described in her book *Inside No 10* 1972.

Falkirk /'fɔːlkɜːk/ town in Central Region, Scotland, 37 km/23 mi W of Edinburgh; population (1981) 37,734. An iron-founding centre, Falkirk has brewing, distilling, tanning and chemical industries.

Falkland /'fɔːklənd/ Lucius Cary, 2nd Viscount Falkland *c.*1610–1643. English soldier and politician. He was elected to the ◊Long Parliament 1640. Falkland was opposed to absolute monarchy but alienated by Puritan extremism, and tried hard to secure a compromise peace between Royalists and Parliamentarians. He was killed at the Battle of Newbury in the Civil War.

Falkland Islands /'fɔːklənd/ British Crown Colony in the S Atlantic

area 12,173 sq km/4,700 sq mi, made up of two main islands: E Falkland 6,760 sq km/2,610 sq mi, and W Falkland 5,413 sq km/2,090 sq mi

Falkland Islands

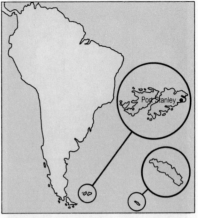

capital Stanley; new port facilities were opened 1984, and Mount Pleasant airport 1985

features in addition to the two main islands, there are about 200 small islands, all with wild scenery and rich bird life

exports wool, alginates (used as dyes and as a food additive) from seaweed beds

population (1986) 1,916

government there is a Governor (Gordon Jewkes from Oct 1985) advised by an executive council, and a mainly elected legislative council. Administered with the Falklands, but separate dependencies of the UK, are South Georgia and the South ◊Sandwich Islands; see also ◊British Antarctic Territory.

history The first European to visit the islands was Englishman John Davis 1592, and at the end of the 17th century they were named after Lord ◊Falkland, treasurer of the British navy. The first British settlers arrived 1765; Spain bought out a French settlement 1766, and the British were ejected 1770–71, but British sovereignty was never ceded, and from 1833, when a few Argentines were expelled, British settlement was continuous.

history Argentina asserts its succession to the Spanish claim to the 'Islas Malvinas', but the inhabitants oppose cession. Occupied by Argentina Apr 1982, the islands were recaptured by British military forces in May–June of the same year. The cost of the British military presence was officially £257 million for 1987.

Falkland Islands, Battle of the /'fɔːklənd/ British naval victory (under Admiral Sturdee) 8 Dec 1914 over the German admiral von Spee.

Falla /'fæljə/ Manuel de 1876–1946. Spanish composer. His opera *La vida breve/Brief Life* 1905 (performed 1913) was followed by the ballets *El amor brujo/Love the Magician* 1915 and *El sombrero de tres picos/The Three-Cornered Hat* 1919, and his most ambitious concert work, *Noches en los jardines de España/Nights in the Gardens of Spain* 1916. The folk idiom of southern Spain is an integral part of his compositions. He also wrote songs and pieces for piano and guitar.

Born in Cádiz, he lived in France, where he was influenced by the Impressionists Debussy and Ravel.

Fall of Man, the a myth that explains the existence of evil as the result of some primeval wrongdoing by humanity. It occurs independently in many cultures, but in the Bible it is recorded in the Old Testament in Genesis 3. This was the source for the epic poem of John Milton *Paradise Lost* 1667.

The Fall of Man as narrated in Genesis 3 occurred in the Garden of Eden when the Serpent tempted Eve to eat the fruit of the Tree of Knowledge. Disobeying God's will, she ate the fruit and gave some to Adam. This caused their expulsion from the Garden and in Milton's words 'brought death into the world and all our woe'.

Fallopian tube *The auricle (trumpet-shaped ending) of the female Fallopian tube, which catches the eggs released from the ovary.*

Fallopian tube or *oviduct* in mammals, one of two tubes which carry eggs from the ovary to the uterus. An egg is fertilized by sperm in the Fallopian tubes, which are lined with cells whose ◊cilia move the egg towards the ovary.

Fallopius /fəˈləʊpiəs/ Gabriel. Latinized name of Gabriello Fallopio 1523–1562. Italian anatomist who discovered the uterine tubes that are named after him. He studied the anatomy of the brain, eyes, and reproductive organs, and gave the first accurate description of the inner ear.

Fallopius studied at Padua under Andreas ◊Vesalius, and later taught there and at Ferrara and Pisa. He discovered the ◊Fallopian tubes (which he described as 'trumpets of the uterus'), and named the vagina.

fallout harmful radioactive material released into the atmosphere in the debris of a nuclear explosion and descending to the surface. Such material can enter the food chain.

fallow land ploughed and tilled, but left unsown for a season to allow it to recuperate. In Europe, it is associated with the medieval three-field system.

Fall River /fɔːl/ city and port in Massachusetts, USA; population (1980) 95,900. It stands at the mouth of the Taunton river, over the Little Fall river which gave it its name. Cotton, rubber and paper are the chief industries.

Falmouth /ˈfælməθ/ port on the S coast of Cornwall, England, on the estuary of the Fal; population (1981) 18,525. There are ship-repairing and marine engineering industries.

false-colour imagery a graphic technique that displays images in false (not true to life) colours so as to enhance certain features. It is widely used in displaying electronic images taken by spacecraft, such as earth-survey satellites like *Landsat*. Any colours can be selected by a computer processing the received data.

falsetto in music, a male voice singing in the female (soprano or alto) register.

falsificationism in philosophy of science, the belief that a scientific theory must be under constant scrutiny, and that its merit lies only in how well it stands up to rigorous testing. First expounded by the philosopher Karl ◊Popper in his *Logic of Scientific Discovery* 1934.

It is also suggested that a theory can only be held to be scientific if it makes predictions which are clearly testable. Philosophers and historians such as T S ◊Kuhn and P K ◊Feyerabend have attempted to use the history of science to show that scientific progress has resulted from a more complicated methodology than Popper suggests.

Famagusta /ˌfæməˈɡʊstə/ seaport on the E coast of Cyprus, in the Turkish Republic of Northern Cyprus; population (1985) 19,500. It was the chief port of the island prior to the Turkish invasion 1974.

family in biological classification, a group of related genera (see ◊genus). Family names are not printed in italic (unlike genus and species names), and by convention they all have the ending -idae (animals) or -aceae (plants and fungi). For example, the genera of hummingbirds are grouped in the hummingbird family, Trochilidae. Related families are grouped together in an ◊order.

family planning spacing or preventing the birth of children. Access to family-planning services (see ◊contraceptive) is an important factor in women's health as well as in limiting population growth. If all those women who wished to avoid further childbirth were able to do so, the number of births would be reduced by 27% in Africa, 33% in Asia, and 35% in Latin America; and the number of women who die during pregnancy or childbirth would be reduced by about 50%.

The average number of pregnancies per woman is two in the industrialized countries, where 71% use family planning, and six or seven in the Third World. Doubling the annual $2 billion spent there on family planning for women who want it would avert the deaths of 5.6 million infants and 250,000 mothers each year, according to a World Bank estimate.

famine a severe shortage of food affecting a large number of people. Famines arise when one group in a society loses its opportunity to exchange its labour or possessions for food. However, famine was traditionally thought to result from some inadequacy in food supplies, from natural causes such as drought or earthquake, or from some failure in food distribution. Most Western famine-relief agencies, such as the International ◊Red Cross, therefore set out to supply food or to increase its local production, rather than becoming involved in local politics.

This theory, known as the *food availability deficit* (FAD) theory, was challenged in the 1980s. Crop failures do not inevitably lead to famine; nor is it always the case that adequate food supplies are not available nearby. For example, in 1990 the Ethiopian air force bombed grain depots in a rebel-held area.

Famous Five a series of 21 stories for children by Enid ◊Blyton, published in the UK 1942–63, which describe the adventures of the 'Five' (four children and a dog) who spend their holidays together. The same author's *Secret Seven* series (1949–63) has a similar theme.

Fancy, the former popular name for ◊boxing in the days of bare-knuckle fighting.

Fangio /ˈfændʒiəʊ/ Juan Manuel 1911– . Argentinian motor-racing driver who won the world driver's title a record five times 1951–57. He drove a blue and yellow Maserati.

fan jet or *turbofan* or *turbojet* the jet engine used by most airliners, so called because of its huge front fan. The fan sends air not only into the engine itself, but also around the engine. This results in a faster and more efficient propulsive jet. See ◊jet propulsion.

Fanon /fæˈnɒn/ Frantz 1925–1961. French political writer. His experiences in Algeria during the war for liberation in the 1950s led to the writing of *Les Damnés de la terre*/*The Wretched of the Earth* 1964, which calls for violent revolution by the peasants of the Third World.

fantail type of domestic dove, often white, with a large widely fanning tail.

fantasia *fantasy* or *fancy* in music, a free-form instrumental composition of improvised character.

fantasy nonrealistic fiction. Much of the world's fictional literature could be subsumed under this term, but as a commercial and literary genre fantasy started to thrive after the success of Tolkien's *Lord of the Rings* 1954–55 in the late 1960s. Earlier works by such writers as Lord Dunsany, Hope Mirrlees, E R Eddison (1882–1945), and Mervyn Peake, not classifiable in fantasy subgenres such as ◊science fiction, ◊horror, or ghost story, could be labelled fantasy.

Much fantasy is pseudo-medieval in subject matter and tone. Modern works include Ursula LeGuin's *Earthsea Trilogy*, Stephen Donaldson's *Thomas Covenant*, and, in the more urban tradition, John Crowley's *Little Big*, Michael Moorcock's *Gloriana*, and Gene Wolfe's *Free, Live Free*. Such books overlap with the ◊magic realism of writers such as Gabriel García Márquez and Angela Carter.

Fantin-Latour /fɒnˈtæn læˈtʊə/ (Ignace) Henri (Joseph Théodore) 1836–1904. French painter, excelling in delicate still lifes, flower paintings, and portraits.

Homage à Delacroix 1864 (Musée d'Orsay, Paris) is a portrait group with many poets, authors, and painters, including Baudelaire and Whistler.

f.a.o. abbreviation for *for the attention of.*

FAO abbreviation for ◊*Food and Agriculture Organization.*

Fao /faʌ/ or Faw an oil port on a peninsula at the mouth of the Shatt al-Arab in Iraq. Iran launched a major offensive against Iraq in 1986, capturing Fao for two years.

farad SI unit (symbol F) of electrical capacitance (how much electricity a ◊capacitor can store for a given voltage). One farad is a capacitance of 1 ◊coulomb per volt. For practical purposes the microfarad (one millionth of a farad) is more commonly used.

The farad is named after the British scientist Michael Faraday, and replaced the obsolete unit the jar (so called because it represented the charge stored in a Leiden jar, the earliest electrical circuit). One farad = 9×10^8 jars.

Faraday /ˈfærədeɪ/ Michael 1791–1867. English chemist and physicist. In 1821 he began experimenting with electromagnetism, and ten years later discovered the induction of electric currents and made the first dynamo. He subsequently found that a magnetic field will rotate the plane of polarization of light. Faraday also investigated electrolysis.

In 1812 he began researches into electricity, and made his first electric battery. He became a laboratory assistant to Sir Humphry Davy at the Royal Institution 1813, and in 1833 succeeded him as professor of chemistry there. He delivered highly popular lectures at the Royal Institution, and published many treatises on scientific subjects. Deeply religious, he was a member of the Sandemanians (a small Congregationalist sect).

Faraday's laws three laws of electromagnetic induction, and two laws of electrolysis, all proposed originally by Michael Faraday.

induction (1) a changing magnetic field induces an electromagnetic force in a conductor; (2) the electromagnetic force is proportional to the rate of change of the field; (3) the direction of the induced electromagnetic force depends on the orientation of the field.

electrolysis (1) the amount of chemical change during electrolysis is proportional to the charge passing through the liquid; (2) the amount of chemical change produced in a substance by a given amount of electricity is proportional to the electrochemical equivalent of that substance.

farandole an old French dance in six-eight time, originating in Provence. The dancers join hands in a chain and follow the leader to the accompaniment of tambourine and pipe. There is a farandole in Act II of Tchaikovsky's *The Sleeping Beauty*.

farce a broad form of comedy involving stereotyped characters in complex, often improbable situations frequently revolving around extramarital relationships (hence the term 'bedroom farce').

Originating in the physical knockabout comedy of Greek satyr plays and the broad humour of

Faraday *English chemist and physicist Michael Faraday.*

medieval religious drama, the farce was developed and perfected during the 19th century by Labiche and Feydeau in France and Pinero in England.

Two notable English series in this century have been Ben ◊Travers' Aldwych farces in the 1920s and 1930s and the Whitehall farces produced by Brian Rix during the 1950s and 1960s.

Far East geographical term for all Asia east of the Indian subcontinent.

Fareham /ˈfeərəm/ town in Hampshire, England, 10 km/6 mi NW of Portsmouth; population (1981) 88,250. Bricks, ceramics, and rope are made and there is engineering and boat-building as well as varied light industries.

Fargo /ˈfɑːgəʊ/ William George 1818–1881. US transport pioneer. In 1844 he established with Henry Wells (1805–78) and Daniel Dunning the first express company to carry freight west of Buffalo. Its success led to his appointment 1850 as secretary of the newly established American Express Company, of which he was president 1868–81. He also established *Wells Fargo & Company* 1851, carrying goods express between New York and San Francisco via Panama.

Farman /ˈfɑːmən/ Henry 1874–1958. Anglo-French aviation pioneer. He designed a bi-plane 1907–08 and in 1909 flew a record 160 km/100 mi.

With his brother *Maurice Farman* (1878–1964), he founded an aircraft works at Billancourt, sup-plying the army in France and other countries. The UK also made use of Farman's inventions, for example, air-screw reduction gears, in World War II.

Farmer /ˈfɑːmə/ Frances 1913–1970. US actress who starred in such films as *Come and Get It* 1936, *The Toast of New York* 1937, and *Son of Fury* 1942, before her career was ended by alcoholism and mental illness.

Farnaby /ˈfɑːnəbi/ Giles 1563–1640. English composer. He composed pieces for the vir-ginal (an early keyboard instrument), psalms for Ravenscroft's Psalter 1621, and madrigals for voices.

Farnborough /ˈfɑːnbərə/ town in Hampshire, England, N of Aldershot; population (1981) 45,500. Experimental work is carried out at the Royal Aircraft Establishment. The mansion of Farnborough Hill was occupied by Napoleon III and the Empress Eugénie, and she, her husband and her son, are buried in a mausoleum at the Roman Catholic church she built.

Farne /fɑːn/ rocky island group in the North Sea, off Northumberland, England. A chapel stands on the site of the hermitage at St Cuthbert on Inner Farne; there are two lighthouses, the Longstone lighthouse being the scene of the rescue of shipwrecked sailors by Grace Dar-ling. The islands are a sanctuary for birds and grey seals.

Farnese /fɑːˈneɪseɪ/ an Italian family who held the duchy of Parma 1545–1731.

Farnham /ˈfɑːnəm/ town in Surrey, England on the river Wey; population (1981) 35,250. The parish church was once part of Waverley Abbey (1128), the first Cistercian house in England: Walter Scott named his first novel after the abbey. At Moor Park, the writer Jonathan ◊Swift met Stella.

Faroe Islands /ˈfeərəʊ/ or **Faroes** (Danish *Færøerne*) or **Faeroe Islands** or **Faeroes** island group (18 out of 22 inhabited) in the N Atlantic, between the Shetland Islands and Iceland, forming an outlying part of ◊Denmark.
area 1,399 sq km/540 sq mi; largest islands are Strømø, Østerø, Vagø, Suderø, Sandø, and Bordø.
capital Thorshavn on Strømø, population (1986) 15,287
features the name means 'Sheep Islands'; they do not belong to the EC
exports fish, crafted goods
population (1986) 46,000
language Færøese, Danish
government since 1948 the islands have had full self-government
history first settled by Norsemen in the 9th cen-tury, they were a Norwegian province 1380–1709. Their parliament was restored 1852. They with-drew from the EFTA 1972
currency Danish krone

Farouk /fɑˈruːk/ 1920–1965. King of Egypt 1936–52. He succeeded his father Fuad I. In 1952 he was compelled to abdicate, his son Fuad II being temporarily proclaimed in his stead.

Farquhar /ˈfɑːkə/ George 1677–1707. Irish dramatist. His plays *The Recruiting Officer* 1706 and *The Beaux' Stratagem* 1707 are in the tradition of the Restoration comedy of manners, although less robust.

Farragut /ˈfærəgʌt/ David (Glasgow) 1801–1870. US admiral, born near Knoxville, Tennessee. Dur-ing the US Civil War he took New Orleans 1862, after destroying the Confederate fleet, and in 1864 effectively put an end to blockade-running at Mo-bile. The ranks of vice-admiral (1864) and admiral (1866) were created for him by Congress.

Farrell /ˈfærəl/ J(ames) G(ordon) 1935–1979. Bri-tish historical novelist, born in Liverpool, author of *Troubles* 1970, set in Ireland, and *The Siege of Krishnapur* 1973.

Farrell /ˈfærəl/ James T(homas) 1904–1979. US novelist. His naturalistic *Studs Lonigan* trilogy 1932–35, comprising *Young Lonigan, The Young Manhood of Studs Lonigan*, and *Judgement Day*, describes the growing-up of a young Catholic man in Chicago after World War I.

Farrow /ˈfærəʊ/ Mia 1945– . US film and tele-vision actress. Popular since the late 1960s, she was associated with the director Woody Allen from 1982, both on and off screen. She starred in his films *Zelig* 1983 and *Hannah and her Sisters* 1986, as well as in Polanski's *Rosemary's Baby* 1968.

Fars /fɑːs/ province of SW Iran, comprising fertile valleys among mountain ranges running NW–SE. Population (1982) 2,035,600; area 133,300 sq km/51,487 sq mi. The capital is Shiraz, and there are imposing ruins of Cyrus the Great's city of Parargardae and of ◊Persepolis.

farthing formerly the smallest English coin, a quar-ter of a penny. It was introduced as a silver coin in Edward I's reign. The copper farthing became widespread in Charles II's reign, and the bronze 1860. It was dropped from use 1961.

fasces in ancient Rome, bundles of rods car-ried in procession by the lictors (minor offi-cials) in front of the chief magistrates, as a symbol of the latter's power over the lives and liberties of the people. An axe was in-cluded in the bundle. The fasces were revived in the 20th century as the symbol of ◊fas-cism.

Fasching /ˈfæʃɪŋ/ period preceding Lent in German-speaking towns, particularly Munich, Cologne, and Vienna, devoted to masquerades, formal balls, and street parades.

Fargo *A pioneer in mail and freight transport, American William George Fargo founded the Wells Fargo & Company, 1851.*

fascism an ideology that denies all rights to individ-uals in their relations with the state; specifically, the totalitarian nationalist movement founded in Italy 1919 by ◊Mussolini. Fascism protected the existing social order by forcible suppression of the working-class movement and by providing scape-goats for popular anger in the Jew, the foreigner, or the black person; it also provided the machinery for the economic and psychological mobilization for war. Neo-fascist groups still exist in many W European countries.

Fascism was essentially a product of the eco-nomic and political crisis of the years after World War I. The units were originally called *fasci di combattimento* (combat groups), from ◊fasces.

Fashoda /fəˈʃəʌdə/ former name (until 1905) of the town of Kodok, situated on the White Nile in SE Sudan. The capture of this town by French troops caused an international incident in 1898.

Fashoda Incident dispute 1898 in a town in Sudan, now known as Kodok, then called Fashoda, in which French forces under Colonel Marchand clashed with British forces under Lord Kitchener. Although originally a disagreement over local ter-ritorial claims, it almost led the two countries into war.

Faslane /fæzˈleɪn/ a nuclear-submarine (Polaris) base on the river Clyde in Scotland.

Fassbinder /ˈfæsbɪndə/ Rainer Werner 1946–1982. West German film director, who began his career as a fringe actor and founded his own 'anti-theatre' before moving into films. His works are mainly stylized indictments of contemporary German so-ciety. He made over 30 films, including *Die bitteren Tränen der Petra von Kant/The Bitter Tears of Petra von Kant* 1972 and *Die Ehe von Maria Braun/The Marriage of Maria Braun* 1979.

fasting the practice of going without food. It can be undertaken as a religious observance, a sign of mourning, a political protest ('hunger strike'), or for slimming purposes. Devout Muslims go without food between sunrise and sunset during the month of Ramadan.

Prolonged fasting can be dangerous. The liver breaks up its fat stores, giving the breath a smell of pear drops that indicates a condition known as ketosis, with accompanying symptoms of nausea, vomiting, fatigue, dizziness, severe depression, and irritability. Muscles and body tissues become wasted, and death eventually results.

fat in the broadest sense, another name for a ◊lipid: a substance that is soluble in alcohol but not water. More specifically used to denote a triglyceride, a chemical containing three ◊fatty acid molecules

fat

oxygen

Structure of glycerine: a typical fat

hydrogen

carbon

linked to a molecule of glycerol. The three fatty acids are often of different types. Triglycerides that are liquids at room temperature are called oils; only those that are solids are called fats.

Boiling fats in alkali forms soaps (saponification). Fats are essential constituents of food in many animals. In humans, too much fat in the diet (particularly saturated fats from animal products) is linked with heart disease.

Fatah, al- a Palestinian nationalist organization founded 1956 to bring about an independent state of Palestine. Also called the Palestine National Liberation Movement, it is the main component of the ◊Palestine Liberation Organization. Its leader is Yasser ◊Arafat.

Fata Morgana (Italian, Morgan the Fairy) a mirage, often seen in the Strait of Messina and traditionally attributed to the sorcery of ◊Morgan le Fay. She was believed to reside in Calabria, a region of S Italy.

Fates in Greek and Roman mythology, the three female figures, Atropos, Clotho, and Lachesis, envisaged as elderly spinners, who decided the length of human life, and analogous to the Roman Parcae and Norse ◊Norns.

fat-hen plant *Chenopodium album* found on waste sites and in fields, up to 1 m/3 ft tall, with lance- or diamond-shaped leaves, and compact heads of small inconspicuous flowers. Now considered a weed, fat-hen was once valued for its fatty seeds and edible leaves.

Father of the Church any of certain teachers and writers of the early Christian church, eminent for their learning and orthodoxy, experience, and sanctity of life. They lived between the end of the 1st and the end of the 7th century, a period divided by the Council of Nicaea 325 into the Ante-Nicene and Post-Nicene Fathers.

The Ante-Nicene Fathers include the Apostolic Fathers: Clement of Rome, Ignatius of Antioch, Polycarp of Smyrna, Barnabas, Justin Martyr, Clement of Alexandria, Origen, Tertullian, and Cyprian. Among the Post-Nicene Fathers are Cyril of Alexandria, Athanasius, John Chrysostom, Eusebius of Caesarea, Basil the Great, Ambrose of Milan, Augustine, Pope Leo I, Boethius, Jerome, Gregory of Tours, Pope Gregory the Great, and Bede.

Fathers and Sons a novel by Turgenev, published in Russia 1862. Its hero, Bazarov, rejects the traditional values of his landowning family in favour of nihilistic revolutionary ideas, but his love for a noblewoman destroys his beliefs.

fathom (Anglo-Saxon *faethm* 'to embrace') in mining, seafaring, and handling timber, unit of depth measurement (6 ft/1.829 m) used before metrication; it approximates to the distance between the hands when the arms are outstretched.

Fathy /ˈfæθi/ Hassan 1900–1989. Egyptian architect. In his work at the village of New Gourna in Upper Egypt he demonstrated the value of native building technology and natural materials in solving

Faulkner *US novelist William Faulkner. Spending most of his career in Mississippi, he was a pioneer of the stream-of-consciousness literary style.*

contemporary housing problems. This, together with his book *The Architecture of the Poor* 1973, influenced the growth of ◊community architecture around the world.

Fatimid dynasty of Muslim Shi'ite caliphs founded 909 by Obaidallah, who claimed to be a descendant of Fatima, the prophet Muhammad's daughter, and her husband Ali, in N Africa. In 969 the Fatimids conquered Egypt, and the dynasty continued until overthrown by Saladin 1171.

fatty acid an organic compound consisting of a hydrocarbon chain, up to 24 carbon atoms long, with a carboxyl group ($-CO_2H$) at one end.

The bonds may be single or double; where a double bond occurs the carbon atoms concerned carry one instead of two hydrogen atoms. Chains with only single bonds have all the hydrogen they can carry, so they are said to to be **saturated** with hydrogen. Chains with one or more double bonds are said to be **unsaturated** (see ◊polyunsaturates). Saturated fatty acids include palmitic and stearic acids; unsaturated fatty acids include oleic (one double bond), linoleic (two double bonds) and linolenic (three double bonds). Fatty acids are generally found combined with glycerol in tryglycerides or ◊fats.

Faulkner /ˈfɔːknə/ Brian 1921–1977. Northern Ireland Unionist politician. He was the last prime minister of Northern Ireland 1971–72 before the Stormont Parliament was suspended.

Fassbinder *German film director Rainer Werner Fassbinder.*

CONCILIVM SEPTEM NOBILIVM ANGLORVM CONIVRANTIVM IN NECEM IACOBI · I · MAGNÆ BRITANNIÆ REGIS TOTIVSQ. ANGLICI CONVOCATI PARLEMENTI ·

Fawkes *Britain's most famous subversive, Guy Fawkes, joined the Gunpowder Plot to blow up James I and both Houses of Parliament in 1605.*

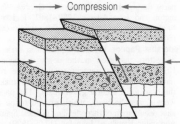

fault   ← Tension →   → Compression ←

Normal fault   Reverse fault

Faulkner /ˈfɔːknə/ William 1897–1962. US novelist who wrote in an experimental stream-of-consciousness style. His works include *The Sound and the Fury* 1929, dealing with a Southern US family in decline; *As I Lay Dying* 1930; *Light in August* 1932, a study of segregation; *The Unvanquished* 1938, stories of the Civil War; and *The Hamlet* 1940, *The Town* 1957, and *The Mansion* 1959, a trilogy covering the rise of the materialist Snopes family. Nobel prize 1949.

Faulkner served in World War I and his first novel, *Soldier's Pay* 1929, is about a war veteran. After the war he returned to Oxford, Mississippi, on which he was to model Jefferson in the county of Yoknapatawpha, the setting of his major novels.

fault in geology, a fracture in the Earth's crust along which the two sides have moved as a result of differing strains in the adjacent rock bodies. Displacement of rock masses horizontally or vertically along a fault may be microscopic, or it may be massive, causing major ◊earthquakes.

Faunus in Roman mythology, god of fertility and prophecy, with goat's ears, horns, tail and hind legs, identified with the Greek Pan.

Fauré /ˈfɔːreɪ/ Gabriel (Urbain) 1845–1924. French composer of songs, chamber music, and *Requiem* 1888. He was a pupil of Saint-Saëns, became professor of composition at the Paris Conservatoire 1896 and was director 1905–20.

Faust /faʊst/ legendary magician. The historical Georg Faust appears to have been a wandering scholar and conjurer in Germany during the opening decade of the 16th century.

Earlier figures such as Simon Magus (1st century AD, Middle Eastern practitioner of magic arts) contributed to the Faust legend. In 1587

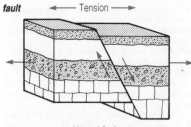

the first of a series of Faust books appeared. Marlowe's tragedy of *Dr Faustus* was acted in 1594. In the 18th century the story was a subject for pantomime in England and puppet plays in Germany. In his play *Faust* Goethe made him a symbol of humanity's striving after the infinite. Heine, Thomas Mann, and Paul Valéry also used the legend, and it inspired musical works by Schumann, Berlioz, Gounod, Boito, and Busoni.

Faust a play by Goethe, completed in two parts 1808 and 1832. Mephistopheles attempts to win over the soul of world-weary Faust but ultimately fails after helping Faust in pursuit of good.

faute de mieux (French) for want of better.

Fauvism style of painting with a bold use of vivid colours, a short-lived but influential art movement originating in Paris 1905 with the founding of the Salon d'Automne by ◊Matisse and others.

Rouault, Marquet, Derain, and Signac were early Fauves. The name originated in 1905 when the critic Louis Vauxcelles called their gallery *'une cage aux fauves'* (a cage of wild beasts).

faux pas (French 'false step') a social blunder.

Fawcett /ˈfɔːsɪt/ Millicent Garrett 1847–1929. English suffragette, younger sister of Elizabeth Garrett ◊Anderson. A non-militant, she rejected the violent acts of some of her contemporaries in the suffrage movement. She joined the first Women's Suffrage Committee 1867 and became president of the Women's Unionist Association 1889.

Fawcett /ˈfɔːsɪt/ Percy Harrison 1867–1925. British explorer. After several expeditions to delineate frontiers in South America during the rubber boom, he set off in 1925, with his eldest son John and a friend, into the Mato Grosso to find the legendary 'lost cities' of the ancient Indians, the 'cradle of Brazilian civilization'. They were never seen again.

Fawkes /fɔːks/ Guy 1570–1606. English conspirator in the Gunpowder Plot to blow up King James I and the members of both Houses of Parliament. Fawkes, a Roman Catholic convert, was arrested in the cellar underneath the House 4 Nov 1605,

tortured, and executed. The event is still commemorated in Britain every 5 Nov with bonfires, fireworks, and the burning of the 'guy', an effigy.

fax common name for *facsimile transmission* or *telefax*: the transmission of images over a ◊telecommunications link, usually the telephone network. When placed on a fax machine, the original image is scanned by a transmitting device and converted into coded signals, which travel via the telephone lines to the receiving fax machine, where an image is created that is a copy of the original. Photographs as well as printed text and drawings can be sent.

FBI abbreviation for ◊*Federal Bureau of Investigation*, agency of the Department of Justice in the USA.

feather a rigid outgrowth of the outer layer of the skin of birds, made of the protein keratin. Feathers provide insulation and facilitate flight. There are several types, including long quill feathers on the wings and tail, fluffy down feathers for retaining body heat, and contour feathers covering the body. The colouring of feathers is often important in camouflage or in courtship and other displays. Feathers are replaced at least once a year.

feather star type of marine invertebrate, or ◊echinoderm, belonging to the class Crinoidea. The arms are branched into numerous projections (hence 'feather' star), and grow from a small cup-shaped body. Below the body are appendages that can hold on to a surface, but the feather star is not permanently attached.

Antedon bifida is a species about 15 cm/6 in across, found in NW European seas. It is reddish brown and has ten arms.

February Revolution the first stage of the ◊Russian Revolution 1917.

Fécamp /ˈfeɪkɒm/ a seaport and resort of France, NE of Le Havre in the *département* of Seine Maritime; population (1982) 21,696. The main industries are shipbuilding and fishing. Benedictine liqueur was first produced here in the early 16th century.

Fechner /ˈfexnə/ Gustav 1801–1887. German psychologist. He became professor of physics at Leipzig in 1834, but in 1839 turned to the study of psychophysics (the relationship between physiology and psychology). He devised *Fechner's law*, a method for the exact measurement of sensation.

fecundity the rate at which an organism reproduces, as distinct from its ability to reproduce (◊fertility). In vertebrates, it is usually measured as the number of offspring produced by a female each year.

Fawcett An educational reformer and leader of the women's suffrage movement, Millicent Garrett Fawcett was one of the founders of Newnham College, Cambridge.

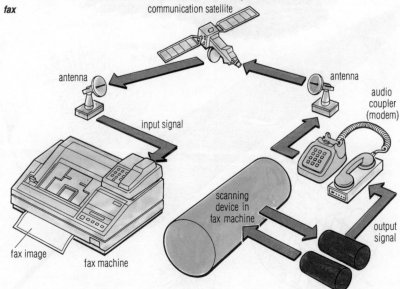

fax

communication satellite

antenna   antenna

audio coupler (modem)

input signal

scanning device in fax machine

output signal

fax image   fax machine

Federal Bureau of Investigation (FBI) agency of the Department of Justice in the USA that investigates violations of federal law not specifically assigned to other agencies, being particularly concerned with internal security. The FBI was established 1908 and built up a position of powerful autonomy during the autocratic directorship of J Edgar Hoover 1924–72.

Field divisions are maintained in more than 60 US cities. The FBI's special agents (known as **G-men**) are qualified in law, accounting, or auditing. In 1964 the agency was criticized by the Warren Commission concerning the assassination of President Kennedy, and in 1973 L Patrick Gray, the acting director, resigned when it was revealed that he had destroyed relevant material in the Watergate investigation. Through the Freedom of Information Act it became known that the FBI had kept files on many eminent citizens and that Hoover had abused his power, for example in persecuting the civil-rights leader Martin Luther King. Clarence M Kelley was director 1973–78, William Webster 1978–87, and Judge William Sessions from 1987.

Federal Deposit Insurance Corporation (FDIC) US government authority established 1933 to regulate US banks and insure them against loss.

The body was set up following the collapse of the banking sector early 1933. All members of the Federal Reserve System are required to belong to the FDIC and many other US banks that are prepared to conform to certain regulations are also members.

federalism a system of government where two or more separate states unite under a common central government while retaining a considerable degree of local autonomy. A federation should be distinguished from a **confederation**, a looser union of states for mutual assistance. Switzerland, the USSR, the USA, Canada, Australia, and Malaysia are all examples of federal government, and many supporters of the European Community see it as the forerunner of a federal Europe.

Federalist in US history, one who advocated the ratification of the US constitution 1787–1788 in place of the Articles of ◊Confederation. The Federalists became in effect the ruling political

party during the presidencies of George Washington and John Adams 1789–1801, legislating to strengthen the authority of the newly created federal government.

Federalist Papers, the in US politics, a series of 85 letters published in the newly independent USA in 1788, attempting to define the relation of the states to the nation, and making the case for a federal government. The papers were signed 'Publius', which proved to be the joint pseudonym of three leading political figures, Alexander Hamilton, John Jay (1745–1829), and James Madison.

Federal Reserve System ('Fed') US central banking system and note-issue authority, established 1913 to regulate the country's credit and monetary affairs. The Fed consists of the 12 federal reserve banks and their 25 branches and other facilities throughout the country; it is headed by a board of governors in Washington, appointed by the US president with Senate approval.

Federal Theater Project US arts employment scheme 1935–39 founded as part of Roosevelt's New Deal by the Works Progress Administration; it organized cheap popular theatre all over the USA and had long-term influence on modern US drama.

Federal Writers' Project US arts project founded 1934 by the Works Progress Administration to encourage writers during the Depression, generate compilations of regional records and folklore, and develop a series of 'American Guides' to states and regions.

Federation of British Industries former employers' association, merged with the ◊Confederation of British Industry.

feedback a principle used in self-regulating control systems, from a simple ◊thermostat and steam-engine ◊governor to automatic computer-controlled machine tools. In such systems, information about what *is* happening in a system (such as level of temperature, engine speed or size of workpiece) is fed back to a controlling device, which compares it with what *should* be happening. If the two are different, the device takes suitable action (such as switching on

a heater, allowing more steam to the engine, or resetting the tools).

feedback in biology, another term for ◊biofeedback.

feedback in music, a continuous tone, usually a high-pitched squeal, caused by the overloading of circuits between electric guitar and amplifier as the sound of the speakers is fed back through the guitar pickup. Deliberate feedback is much used in rock music.

The electric-guitar innovator Les Paul used feedback in recording ('How High the Moon' 1954) but it was generally regarded by producers as an unwanted noise until the Beatles introduced it on 'I Feel Fine' 1964. Both live and in recording, feedback was employed especially by the Who, Jimi Hendrix, and the Velvet Underground in the 1960s, and by hardcore bands in the 1980s.

Fehling's test a chemical test to determine whether an organic substance is a reducing agent (substance that donates electrons to other substances in a chemical reaction).

Feininger /ˈfaɪnɪŋə/ Lyonel 1871–1956. US abstract artist, an early Cubist. He worked at the Bauhaus, a key centre of modern design in Germany, 1919–33, and later helped to found the Bauhaus in Chicago.

Feininger was born in New York, the son of German immigrants. While in Germany, he formed the **Blaue Vier** (Blue Four) in 1924 with the painters Alexei von Jawlensky (1864–1941), Kandinsky, and Klee.

Feldman /ˈfeldmən/ Morton 1926–1988. US composer. An associate of ◊Cage and Earle ◊Brown in the 1950s, he composed large-scale set pieces using the orchestra mainly as a source of colour and texture.

feldspar one of a group of rock-forming minerals; the chief constituents of ◊igneous rock. Feldspars all contain silicon, aluminium, and oxygen, linked together to form a framework; spaces within this structure are occupied by sodium, potassium, calcium, or occasionally barium, in various proportions. Feldspars form white, grey, or pink crystals and rank 6 on the ◊Mohs scale of hardness.

The four components of feldspar are **orthoclase**, $KAlSi_3O_8$; **albite**, $NaAlSi_3O_8$; **anorthite**, $CaAl_2Si_2O_8$; and **celsian**, $BaAl_2Si_2O_8$. These are subdivided into **plagioclase feldspars**, which range from pure sodium feldspar (albite) through pure calcium feldspar (anorthite) with a negligible potassium content; and **alkali feldspars** (including orthoclase), which have a high potassium content, less sodium, and little calcium.

The type known as ◊moonstone has a pearl-like effect and is used in jewellery. Approximately 4,000 tonnes of feldspar are used in the ◊ceramics industry annually.

feldspathoid a group of silicate minerals resembling feldspars but containing less silica. Examples are nepheline ($NaAlSiO_4$) with a little potassium and leucite ($KAlSi_2)_6$. Feldspathoids occur in igneous rocks that have relatively high proportions of sodium and potassium.

felicific calculus also called **hedonic calculus** a term in ethics, attributed to Jeremy Bentham, which provides a technique for establishing the rightness and wrongness of an action. Using the calculus, one can attempt to work out the likely consequences of an action in terms of the pain or pleasure of those affected by the action.

Felixstowe /ˈfiːlɪkstəʊ/ port and resort opposite Harwich in Suffolk, England, between the Orwell and Deben estuaries; population (1981) 21,000. It is Britain's busiest container port, and also has ferry services to Gothenburg, Rotterdam, and Zeebrugge.

fellah (plural **fellahin**) in Arab countries, a peasant farmer. In Egypt, approximately 60% of the fellahin population live in rural areas, often in villages of 1,000–5,000 inhabitants.

Fellini /feˈliːni/ Federico 1920– . Italian director, whose films include *I vitelloni/The Young and the*

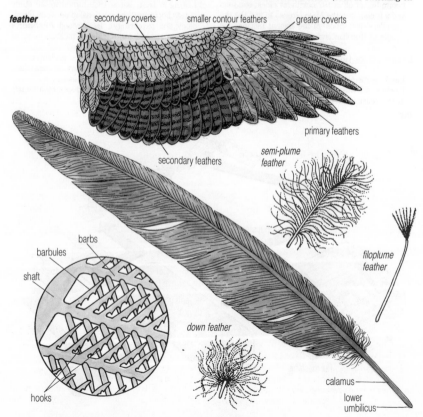

feather

secondary coverts   smaller contour feathers   greater coverts

primary feathers

secondary feathers

semi-plume feather

barbs

barbules

shaft

filoplume feather

down feather

hooks

calamus

lower umbilicus

Fellini *Italian film director Federico Fellini was a cartoonist and journalist before he began directing films in the 1950s.* La Dolce Vita *caused a scandal at the 1960 Cannes Film Festival.*

Passionate 1953, *La dolce vita* 1960, and *La città delle donne/City of Women* 1981.

felony in UK law, former term for an offence that is more serious than a ◊misdemeanour; in the USA, a felony is a crime punishable by imprisonment for a year or more. See ◊criminal law.

felt matted fabric of hair fibres and/or wool, made by joining them together using pressure, heat, or chemical action.

fem. in grammar, abbreviation for *feminine*; see ◊gender.

feminism a belief in equal rights and opportunities for women; see ◊women's movement.

fencing sport of fighting with swords including the **foil**, derived from the light weapon used in practice duels; the *épée*, a heavier weapon derived from the duelling sword proper; and the **sabre**, with a curved handle and narrow V-shaped blade. In sabre fighting, cuts count as well as thrusts. Masks and protective jackets are worn, and hits are registered electronically in competitions.

Fencing: Olympic Champions

foil—men
1968 Ion Drimba (Romania)
1972 Witold Woyda (Poland)
1976 Fabio Dal Zotto (Italy)
1980 Vladimir Smirnov (USSR)
1984 Mauro Numa (Italy)
1988 Stefano Cerioni (Italy)
foil—women
1968 Elena Novikova (USSR)
1972 Antonella Ragno-Lonzi (Italy)
1976 Ildiko Schwarczenberger (Hungary)
1980 Pascale Trinquet (France)
1984 Jujie Luan (China)
1988 Anja Fichtel (West Germany)
épée
1968 Gyozo Kulcsar (Hungary)
1972 Csaba Fenyvesi (Hungary)
1976 Alexander Pusch (West Germany)
1980 Johan Harmenberg (Sweden)
1984 Phillipe Boisse (France)
1988 Arnd Schmitt (West Germany)
sabre
1968 Jerzy Pawlowski (Poland)
1972 Viktor Sidiak (USSR)
1976 Viktor Krovopouskov (USSR)
1980 Viktor Krovopouskov (USSR)
1984 Jean-Francois Lamour (France)
1988 Jean-Francois Lamour (France)

Fender pioneering series of electric guitars and bass guitars. The first solid-body electric guitar on the market was the 1948 Fender Broadcaster (renamed the Telecaster 1950), and the first electric bass guitar was the Fender Precision 1951.

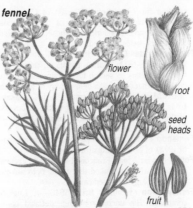

fennel

flower
root
seed heads
fruit

The Fender Stratocaster guitar dates from 1954. Their designer, Leo Fender, began manufacturing amplifiers in the USA in the 1940s.

Fénelon /ˌfɛnɪˈlɒŋ/ François de Salignac de la Mothe 1651–1715. French writer and ecclesiastic. He entered the priesthood 1675 and in 1689 was appointed tutor to the Duke of Burgundy, grandson of Louis XIV. For him he wrote his *Fables* and *Dialogues des morts/Dialogues of the Dead* 1690, *Télémaque/Telemachus* 1699, and *Plans de gouvernement/Plans of Government*.

Télémaque, with its picture of an ideal commonwealth, had the effect of a political manifesto, and Louis banished Fénelon to Cambrai, where he had been consecrated archbishop 1695. Fénelon's mystical *Maximes des Saints/Sayings of the Saints* 1697 had also led to a quarrel with the Jansenists, and condemnation by Pope Innocent XII.

Fenian a member of an Irish-American republican secret society, founded 1858 and named after the ancient Irish legendary warrior band of the Fianna. The collapse of the movement began when an attempt to establish an independent Irish republic by an uprising in Ireland 1867 failed, as did raids into Canada 1866 and 1870, and England 1867.

fennec small nocturnal desert ◊fox *Fennecus zerda* found in N Africa and Arabia. It has a head and body only 40 cm/1.3 ft long, and enormous ears which act as radiators to lose excess heat. It eats insects and small animals.

fennel perennial plant with feathery green leaves, family Umbelliferae. Fennels have an aniseed flavour. The thickened leafstalks of **sweet fennel** *Foeniculum dulce* are eaten, and the leaves and seeds of *Foeniculum vulgare* are used in seasoning.

Fens /fenz/ level, low-lying tracts of land in E England, west and south of the Wash, about 115 km/70 mi N–S and about 55 km/34 mi E–W. They fall within the counties of Lincolnshire, Cambridgeshire, and Norfolk, consisting of a huge area, formerly a bay of the North Sea, but now crossed by numerous drainage canals and forming some of the most productive agricultural land in Britain. The peat portion of the Fens is known as the *Bedford Level*.

The first drainage attempts were made by the Romans, but later attempts were unsuccessful until in 1634 the 4th earl of Bedford brought over the Dutch water-engineer Vermuyden, who introduced Dutch methods. Burwell Fen and Wicken Fen, NE of Cambridge, have been preserved undrained as nature reserves.

Fenton /ˈfɛntən/ Roger 1819–1869. English photographer. The world's first war photographer, he went to the Crimea 1855; he also founded the Royal Photographic Society in London.

Ferber /ˈfɜːbə/ Edna 1887–1968. US novelist and playwright. Her novel *Show Boat* 1926 was adapted as an operetta by Jerome Kern and Oscar Hammerstein II.

Ferdinand /ˈfɜːdɪnænd/ 1861–1948. King of Bulgaria 1908–18. Son of Prince Augustus of Saxe-Coburg-Gotha, he was elected prince of Bulgaria 1887, and in 1908 proclaimed Bulgaria's independence of Turkey and assumed the title of tsar. In 1915 he entered World War I as Germany's ally, and in 1918 abdicated.

Ferdinand /ˈfɜːdɪnænd/ five Kings of Castile, including:

Ferdinand I *the Great c.*1016–1065. King of Castile from 1035. He began the reconquest of Spain from the Moors and united all NW Spain under his and his brothers' rule.

Ferdinand V 1452–1516. King of Castile from 1474, **Ferdinand II** of Aragon from 1479, and **Ferdinand III** of Naples from 1504; first king of all Spain. In 1469 he married his cousin ◊Isabella I, who succeeded to the throne of Castile 1474; together they were known as **the Catholic Kings**. They introduced the ◊Inquisition 1480, expelled the Jews, forced the surrender of the Moors at Granada 1492, and financed Columbus' expedition to the Americas.

When Ferdinand inherited the throne of Aragon 1479, the two great Spanish kingdoms were brought under a single government for the first time. He conquered Naples 1500–03 and Navarre 1512, completing the unification of Spain and making it one of the chief powers in Europe.

Ferdinand /ˈfɜːdɪnænd/ three Holy Roman emperors:

Ferdinand I 1503–1564. Holy Roman emperor who succeeded his brother Charles V 1558; king of Bohemia and Hungary from 1526, king of the Germans from 1531. He reformed the German monetary system, and reorganized the Aulic council (*Reichshofrat*). He was the son of Philip the Handsome and grandson of Maximilian I.

Ferdinand II 1578–1637. Holy Roman emperor from 1619, when he succeeded his uncle Matthias; king of Bohemia from 1617 and Hungary from 1618. A zealous Catholic, he provoked the Bohemian revolt that led to the Thirty Years' War. He was a grandson of Ferdinand I.

Ferdinand III 1608–1657. Holy Roman emperor from 1637 when he succeeded his father Ferdinand II; king of Hungary from 1625. Although anxious to conclude the Thirty Years' War, he did not give religious liberty to Protestants.

Ferdinand /ˈfɜːdɪnænd/ 1865–1927. King of Romania from 1914, when he succeeded his uncle Charles I. In 1916 he declared war on Austria. After the Allied victory in World War I, Ferdinand acquired Transylvania and Bukovina from Austria-Hungary, and Bessarabia from Russia. In 1922 he became king of Greater Romania.

Ferghana /fəˈɡɑːnə/ town in Uzbekistan, USSR, in the fertile Ferghana valley; population (1987) 203,000. It is the capital of the important cotton and fruit-growing Ferghana region; nearby are petroleum fields.

Fergus mac Roigh in Celtic mythology, a king of Ulster, a great warrior. He was the tutor of ◊Cuchulain.

Ferguson /ˈfɜːɡəsən/ Harry 1884–1960. Irish engineer who pioneered the development of the tractor, joining forces with Henry Ford 1938 to manufacture it in the USA. He also experimented in automobile and aircraft development.

Fermanagh /fəˈmænə/ county in the southern part of Northern Ireland
area 1,680 sq km/648 sq mi
towns Enniskillen (county town), Lisnaskea, Irvinestown
physical in the centre is a broad trough of low-lying land, in which lie Upper and Lower Lough Erne
products mainly agricultural; livestock, tweeds, clothing
population (1981) 52,000.

Fermat /feəˈmɑː/ Pierre de 1601–1665. French mathematician, who with Pascal founded the theory of ◊probability and the modern theory of numbers, and made contributions to analytical geometry.

Fermat's last theorem states that equations of the form $x^n + y^n = z^n$ where x, y, z, and

Fermi *Nuclear physicist Enrico Fermi. He was awarded a Nobel prize in 1938.*

n are all ◊integers have no solutions if *n* > 2. There is no general proof of this so it constitutes a conjecture rather than a theorem.

fermentation the breakdown of sugars by bacteria and yeasts using a method of respiration without oxygen (◊anaerobic). These processes have long been utilized in baking bread, making beer and wine, and producing cheese, yoghurt, soy sauce, and many other foodstuffs.

In baking and brewing, yeasts ferment sugars to produce ◊ethanol and carbon dioxide; the latter makes bread rise and puts bubbles into beers and champagne.

Fermi /'fɜːmi/ Enrico 1901–1954. Italian physicist, who proved the existence of new radioactive elements produced by bombardment with neutrons, and discovered nuclear reactions produced by slow neutrons. Nobel prize 1938.

Born in Rome, he was professor of theoretical physics there 1926–38. He was professor at Columbia University, New York, USA, 1939–42 and from 1946 at Chicago. In 1954, the US Atomic Energy Commission made a special award to him for outstanding work in nuclear physics; these annual awards have subsequently been known as Fermi awards.

Fermilab US centre for ◊particle physics in Chicago, named after Fermi.

fermium a metallic element, symbol Fm, atomic number 100. One of the actinide series, it has been produced only in minute quantities. It is named after Enrico Fermi.

Fermor /'fɜːmɔː/ Patrick (Michael) Leigh 1915–. English travel writer who joined the Irish Guards in 1939 after four years' travel in central Europe and the Balkans. His books include *The Traveller's Tree* 1950, *Mani* 1958, *Roumeli* 1966, *A Time of Gifts* 1977, and *Between the Woods and the Water* 1986.

fern plant of the class Filicales, related to horsetails and clubmosses. Ferns are spore-bearing, not flowering, plants, and most are perennial, spreading by low-growing roots. The leaves, known as fronds, vary widely in size and shape. Some taller types, such as tree-ferns, grow in the tropics. There are over 7,000 species.

Ferns found in Britain include the polypody *Polypodium vulgare*, shield fern *Polystichum*, male fern *Dryopteris filix-mas*, hart's-tongue *Phyllitis scolopendrium*, maidenhair *Adiantum capillus-veneris*, and bracken *Pteridium aquilinum*, an agricultural weed.

Fernández /fəˈnændez/ Juan *c.* 1536–*c.* 1604. Spanish explorer and navigator. As a pilot on the Pacific coast of South America 1563, he

reached the islands off the coast of Chile that now bear his name. On one of these islands lived Alexander ◊Selkirk, on whose life Defoe's *Robinson Crusoe* is based.

Fernandez de Quirós /fəˈnændez də kɪˈrɒs/ Pedro 1565–1614. Spanish navigator, one of the first Europeans to search for the great southern continent that ◊Magellan believed lay to the south of the Magellan Strait. Despite a series of disastrous expeditions, he took part in the discovery of the Marquesas Islands and the main island of Espíritu Santo in the New Hebrides.

Fernando Po /fəˈnændəʊ ˈpəʊ/ former name (until 1973) of ◊Bioko, Equatorial Guinea.

Fernel /feəˈnel/ Jean François 1497–1558. French physician who introduced the words ◊physiology and ◊pathology into medicine.

Ferneyhough /'fɜːnihʌf/ Brian 1943– . English composer. His uncompromising, detailed compositions include *Carceri d'Invenzione*, a cycle of seven works inspired by the engravings of Piranesi, *Time and Motion Studies* 1974–77, and string quartets.

Ferranti /fəˈrænti/ Sebastian de 1864–1930. British electrical engineer who electrified central London. He made and sold his first alternator 1881. Soon after he became chief engineer with the London Electric Supply Company. He worked on the design of a large power station at Deptford but legislation permitting low-powered stations to operate killed the scheme. He resigned in 1892, moved to Oldham in Lancashire, and in 1896 opened his business to develop high-voltage systems for long-distance transmission.

Ferrar /'ferə/ Nicolas 1592–1637. English mystic and founder in 1625 of the Anglican monastic community at Little Gidding, Cambridgeshire, in 1625, which devoted itself to work and prayer. It was broken up by the Puritans in 1647.

Ferrara /fəˈrɑːrə/ industrial city and archbishopric in Emilia-Romagna region, N Italy, on a branch of

fern

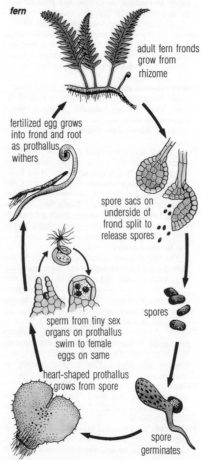

adult fern fronds grow from rhizome

fertilized egg grows into frond and root as prothallus withers

spore sacs on underside of frond split to release spores

sperm from tiny sex organs on prothallus swim to female eggs on same

heart-shaped prothallus grows from spore

spores

spore germinates

the Po delta 52 km/32 mi west of the Adriatic Sea; population (1988) 143,000. There are chemical industries and textile manufacturers.

It has the Gothic castle of its medieval rulers, the House of Este, palaces, museums, and a cathedral, consecrated 1135. The university was founded 1391. Savonarola was born here, and the poet Tasso was confined in the asylum 1579–86.

Ferrari /fəˈrɑːri/ Enzo 1898–1988. Italian founder of the Ferrari car empire, which specializes in Grand Prix racing cars and high-quality sports cars. He was a racing driver for Alfa Romeo in the 1920s, went on to become one of their designers and in 1929 took over their racing division. In 1947 the first 'true' Ferrari was seen. The Ferrari car has won more world championship Grands Prix than any other car.

Ferraro /fəˈrɑːrəʊ/ Geraldine 1935– . US Democrat politician, vice-presidential candidate in the 1984 election.

Ferraro, a lawyer, was elected to Congress in 1981 and was selected in 1984 by Walter Mondale to be the USA's first female vice-presidential candidate from one of the major parties. The Democrats were defeated by the incumbent president Reagan, and Ferraro, damaged by investigations of her husband's affairs, retired from politics.

ferret domesticated variety of ◊polecat. About 35 cm/1.2 ft long, it usually has yellowish-white fur and pink eyes, but may be the colour of a wild polecat. It is used to hunt rabbits and rats.

Ferrier /'feriə/ Kathleen (Mary) 1912–1953. English contralto who sang oratorio and opera. In Britten's *The Rape of Lucretia* 1946 she created the role of Lucretia, and she appeared in Mahler's *Das Lied von der Erde* 1947.

Ferrier /'feriə/ Susan Edmundstone 1782–1854. Scottish novelist, born in Edinburgh. Her anonymously published books include *Marriage* 1818, *Inheritance* 1824, and *Destiny* 1831, all of which give a lively picture of Scottish manners and society.

ferro-alloy an alloy of iron with a high proportion of elements such as manganese, silicon, chromium, and molybdenum. Ferro-alloys are used in the manufacture of alloy steels.

Ferrol /fe'rəʊl/ alternative name for ◊El Ferrol, a city and port in NW Spain.

Ferry /'feri/ Jules François Camille 1832–1893. French republican politician, mayor of Paris during the siege of 1870–71. As a member of the republican governments of 1879–85 (prime minister 1880–81 and 1883–85) he was responsible for the law of 1882 making primary education free, compulsory, and secular. He directed French colonial expansion in Tunisia 1881 and Indo-China (the acquisition of Tonkin in 1885).

fertility an organism's ability to reproduce, as distinct from the rate at which it reproduces (see ◊fecundity). Individuals become infertile (unable to reproduce) when they cannot generate gametes (eggs or sperm) or when their gametes cannot yield a viable ◊embryo after fertilization.

fertility drug any of a range of drugs taken to increase a female's fertility, developed in Sweden in the mid-1950s. They increase the chances of a multiple birth.

The best-known is gonadotrophin, which is made from hormone extracts (FSH and LH) taken from the human pituitary gland, and stimulates ovulation in women. As a result of a fertility drug, in 1974 the first sextuplets to survive were born to Susan Rosenkowitz of South Africa.

fertilization in ◊sexual reproduction, the union of two ◊gametes (sex cells, often called egg and sperm) to produce a ◊zygote, which combines the genetic material contributed by each parent. In self-fertilization the male and female gametes come from the same plant; in cross-fertilization they come from different plants. Self-fertilization occurs rarely in ◊hermaphrodite animals.

In terrestrial insects, mammals, reptiles and birds, fertilization occurs within the female's body; in the majority of fish and amphibians, and most aquatic invertebrates, it occurs externally, when both sexes release their gametes freely into the water. In most fungi, gametes are not released, but the hyphae of the two parents grow towards each other and fuse to achieve fertilization. In higher plants, ◊pollination precedes fertilization.

fertilizer a substance containing a range of about 20 chemical elements necessary for healthy plant growth, used to compensate the deficiencies of poor or depleted soil. Fertilizers may be *organic*, for example farmyard manure, composts, bonemeal, blood, and fishmeal; or *inorganic*, in the form of compounds, mainly of nitrogen, phosphate, and potash, which have been used on a tremendously increased scale since 1945.

Because externally applied fertilizers tend to be in excess of plant requirements and leach away to affect lakes and rivers (see ◊eutrophication), attention has turned to the modification of crop plants themselves. Plants of the pea family, including the bean, clover, and lupin, live in symbiosis with bacteria located in root nodules, which fix nitrogen from the atmosphere. Research is now directed to producing a similar relationship between such bacteria and crops such as wheat.

Fertö tó /ˈfɛatʌtʌ/ Hungarian name for the ◊Neusiedler See.

Fès /fez/ or *Fez* former capital of Morocco 808–1062, 1296–1548, and 1662–1912, in a valley north of the Great Atlas mountains, 160 km/100 mi E of Rabat; population (1982) 563,000. Textiles, carpets, and leather are manufactured, and the *fez*, a brimless hat worn in S and E Mediterranean countries, is traditionally said to have originated here.

Kairwan Islamic University dates from 859; the second university was founded 1961.

fescue widely distributed grass genus *Festuca*. Two common species in W Europe are meadow fescue, up to 80 cm/2.6 ft high, and sheep's fescue, up to 50 cm/1.6 ft high.

Fessenden /ˈfɛsəndən/ Reginald Aubrey 1866–1932. Canadian physicist who worked in the USA, first for Thomas Edison and then for Westinghouse. He patented the ◊modulation of radio waves (transmission of a signal using a carrier wave), an essential technique for voice transmission. At the time of his death, he held 500 patents.

Early radio communications relied on telegraphy by using bursts of single-frequency signals in Morse code. In 1900 Fessenden devised a method of making audio-frequency speech (or music) signals modulate the amplitude of a transmitted radio-frequency carrier wave—the basis of AM radio broadcasting.

fetal surgery operation on the fetus to correct congenital conditions such as ◊hydrocephalus. Fetal surgery was pioneered in the USA 1981. It leaves no scar tissue.

fetishism in anthropology, belief in the supernormal power of some inanimate object that is known as a fetish. Fetishism in some form is common to most cultures, and often has religio-magical significance. In psychology, the practice of associating an object with the sexual act and transferring desire to the object (such as boots).

fetus or *foetus* a stage in mammalian ◊embryo development. The human embryo is usually termed a fetus after the eighth week of development, when the limbs and external features of the head are recognizable.

In the UK, in 1989, the use of aborted fetuses for research and transplant purposes was approved provided that the mother's decision to seek an abortion is not influenced by consideration of this possible use. Each case has to be considered by an ethics committee, which may set conditions for the use of the fetal material.

feudalism the main form of social stratification in medieval Europe. A system based primarily on land, it involved a hierarchy of authority, rights, and power that extended from the monarch downwards. An intricate network of

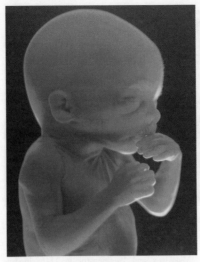

fetus *Human fetus about five months old.*

duties and obligations linked royalty, nobility, lesser gentry, free tenants, villeins, and serfs. Feudalism was reinforced by a complex legal system and supported by the Christian church. With the growth of commerce and industry from the 13th century, feudalism gradually gave way to class as the dominant form of social ranking.

In return for military service the monarch allowed powerful vassals to hold land, and often also to administer justice and levy taxes. They in turn 'sub-let' such rights. At the bottom of the system were the serfs, who worked on their lord's manor in return for being allowed to cultivate some land for themselves, and so underpinned the system. They could not be sold as if they were slaves, but they could not leave the estate. The system declined from the 13th century, partly because of the growth of a money economy, with commerce, trade, and industry, and partly because of the many peasants' revolts 1350–1550. Serfdom ended in England in the 16th century, but lasted in France until 1789 and in the rest of Western Europe until the early 19th century. In Russia it continued until 1861.

fever raised body temperature, usually due to infection.

Feyerabend /ˈfaɪərɑːbənd/ Paul K 1924– . US philosopher of science, who rejected the attempt by certain philosophers (for instance ◊Popper) to find a methodology applicable to all scientific research. His works include *Against Method* 1975.

Although his work relies on historical evidence, he argues that successive theories that apparently concern the same subject (for instance the motion of the planets) cannot in principle be subjected to any comparison that would aim at finding the truer explanation. According to this notion of incommensurability, there is no neutral or objective standpoint, and therefore no rational way in which one theory can be chosen over another. Instead, scientific progress is claimed to be the result of a range of sociological factors working to promote politically convenient notions of how nature operates.

Feynman /ˈfaɪnmən/ Richard 1918–1988. US physicist whose work provided foundations for quantum electrodynamics. For this work he was awarded the Nobel Prize for Physics. As a member of the committee investigating the *Challenger* space-shuttle disaster 1986, he demonstrated the lethal faults in the rubber seals on the shuttle's booster rocket.

Fez /fez/ alternative spelling of ◊Fès, a city in Morocco.

Fezzan /feˈzɑːn/ former province of Libya, a desert region, with many oases, and with rock paintings from about 3000 BC. It was captured

from Italy 1942, and placed under French control until 1951 when it became a province of the newly-independent United Kingdom of Libya. It was split into smaller divisions 1963.

ff abbreviation for *folios*; and *the following*.

Fianna Fàil /ˈfɪənə ˈfɔɪl/ (Gaelic 'Soldiers of Destiny') Republic of Ireland political party, founded by the Irish nationalist de Valera 1926. It has been the governing party in the Republic of Ireland 1932–48, 1951–54, 1957–73, 1977–81, 1982, and 1987– . It aims at the establishment of a united and completely independent all-Ireland republic.

Fibonacci /ˌfɪbəˈnɑːtʃi/ Leonardo *c.* 1175–*c.*1250. Italian mathematician. He published *Liber abaci* in Pisa 1202, which led to the introduction of Arabic notation into Europe. From 1960, interest increased in *Fibonacci numbers*, in their simplest form a series in which each number is the sum of its two predecessors (1, 1, 2, 3, 5, 8, 13,…). They have unusual characteristics with possible applications in botany, psychology, and astronomy (for example, a more exact correspondence than is given by ◊Bode's law to the distances between the planets and the Sun).

fibreglass glass that has been formed into fine fibres, either as long continuous filaments or as a fluffy, short-fibred glass wool. Fibreglass has applications in the field of fibre optics and as a strengthener for plastics in ◊GRP (glass-reinforced plastics).

The long filament form is made by forcing molten glass through the holes of a spinneret. Glass wool is made by blowing streams of molten glass in a jet of high-pressure steam, and is used as thermal insulation for the roof space in houses.

fibre optics transmission of light through glass or plastic fibres, known as ◊optical fibres.

fibrositis inflammation and overgrowth of fibrous tissue, especially of the sheaths of muscles; also known as muscular rheumatism.

Fichte /ˈfɪxtə/ Johann Gottlieb 1762–1814. German philosopher who developed a comprehensive form of subjective idealism, expounded in *The Science of Knowledge* 1794. He was an admirer of ◊Kant.

In 1792, Fichte published *Critique of Religious Revelation*, a critical study of Kant's doctrine of the thing-in-itself. For Fichte, the absolute ego posits both the external world (the non-ego) and finite self. Morality consists in the striving of this finite self to rejoin the absolute. In 1799 he was accused of atheism, and was forced to resign his post as professor of philosophy at Jena. He moved to Berlin, where he devoted himself to public affairs and delivered lectures, including *Reden an die deutsche Nation/Addresses to the German People* 1807–08, which influenced contemporary liberal nationalism.

Fichtelgebirge /ˈfɪxtəlɡəˌbɪəɡə/ chain of mountains in Bavaria, West Germany, on the Czechoslovak border. The highest peak is the *Schneeberg* 1,051 m/3,448 ft. There are granite quarries, uranium mining, china and glass industries, and forestry.

fiction in literature, any work or type of work whose content is completely or largely invented. In the 20th century, the term is applied to imaginative works of narrative prose (such as the novel or the short story), and contrasted with *nonfiction*, such as history, biography, or works on practical subjects, and with *poetry*.

This usage reflects the dominance in contemporary Western literature of the novel as a vehicle for imaginative literature: strictly speaking, poems can also be fictional (as opposed to factual). Genres such as the historical novel often combine a fictional plot with real events; biography may also be 'fictionalized' through the use of imagined conversations or events.

Fidei Defensor /ˈfɪdiə dɪˈfensɔː/ title of 'Defender of the Faith' (still retained by British sovereigns)

Field of the Cloth of Gold The Meeting of Henry VIII and the Emperor Maximilan I *by an unknown artist.*
Royal Collection, Hampton Court.

conferred by Pope Leo X on Henry VIII of England to reward his writing of a treatise against the Protestant Martin Luther.

fief an estate held by a ◊vassal from his lord, given after the former had sworn homage, or fealty, promising to serve the lord. As a noble tenure, it carried with it rights of jurisdiction.

In the later Middle Ages, it could also refer to a grant of money, given in return for service, as part of ◊bastard feudalism.

field in physics, an agency acting in a region of space by which an object exerts a force on another non-touching object because of certain properties they both possess. For example, there is a force of attraction between any two objects that have mass, where one is in the gravitational field of the other.

Other fields of force include ◊electric fields (caused by electric charges) and ◊magnetic fields (caused by magnetic poles), either of which can involve attractive or repulsive forces.

field enclosed area of land used for farming. Their area is traditionally measured in ◊acres; the current unit of measurement is the ◊hectare (2.47 acres).

In the Middle Ages, the farmland of a rural community was often divided into three large open fields, worked on a simple rotation basis of one year wheat, one year barley, and one year fallow (when no crop was grown). They were divided into thin strips about 20 m/66 ft wide. A farmer worked a number of strips, not necessarily adjacent to each other, in one field. These open-field communities were subsequently reorganized, the land was enclosed, and the farmers' holdings were redistributed into individual blocks, which were then divided into separate fields. This ◊enclosure process reached its peak during the 18th century.

Recent developments in agricultural science and technology have encouraged farmers to amalgamate and enlarge their fields, often to as much as 40 hectares/100 acres.

Field /fiːld/ Sally 1946– . US film and television actress. She won an Academy Award for *Norma Rae* 1979 and again for *Places in the Heart* 1984. Her other films include *Hooper* 1978, *Absence of Malice* 1981, and *Murphy's Romance* 1985.

fieldfare bird *Turdus pilaris* of the thrush family, a winter migrant in Britain, breeding in Scandinavia, N Russia, and Siberia. It has a pale-grey lower back and neck, and a dark tail.

Fielding /ˈfiːldɪŋ/ Henry 1707–1754. English novelist, whose narrative power influenced the form and technique of the novel and helped to make it the most popular form of literature in England. In 1742 he parodied Richardson's novel *Pamela* in his *Joseph Andrews*, which was followed by *Jonathan Wild the Great* 1743; his masterpiece *Tom Jones* 1749, which he described as a 'comic epic in prose'; and *Amelia* 1751.

He was appointed Justice of the Peace for Middlesex and Westminster in 1748. In failing health, he went to recuperate in Lisbon in 1754, writing on the way *A Journal of a Voyage to Lisbon.*

field marshal the highest rank in many European armies. A British field marshal is equivalent to a US ◊general.

It was introduced to Britain from Germany by George II 1736.

Field of the Cloth of Gold site between Guînes and Ardres near Calais, France, where a meeting took place between Henry VIII of England and Francis I of France June 1520, remarkable for the lavish clothes worn and tent pavilions erected. Francis hoped to gain England's support in opposing the Holy Roman emperor, Charles V, but failed.

Fields /fiːldz/ Gracie. Stage name of Grace Stansfield 1898–1979. English comedian and singer. Her humourously sentimental films include *Sally in our Alley* 1931 and *Sing as We Go* 1934.

Fields /fiːldz/ W C. Stage name of William Claude Dukenfield 1879–1946. US actor and screenwriter. His distinctive speech and professed attitudes such as hatred of children and dogs gained him enormous popularity in films such as *David Copperfield* 1935, *My Little Chickadee* (co-written with Mae West) and *The Bank Dick* both 1940, and *Never Give a Sucker an Even Break* 1941.

Fielding *Henry Fielding's concern for social justice, seen in his best-kn own novel* Tom Jones, *was also a feature of his term as a magistrate.*

field studies study of ecology, geography, geology, history, archaeology, and allied subjects, in the natural environment, with emphasis on promoting a wider knowledge and understanding of the natural environment among the public.

The Council for the Promotion of Field Studies was established in Britain in 1943, and Flatford Mill, Suffolk, was the first research centre to be opened.

Fiennes /faɪnz/ Ranulph Twisleton-Wykeham 1944– . British explorer who made the first surface journey around the world's polar axis 1979–82. Earlier expeditions included explorations of the White Nile 1969, Jostedalsbre Glacier, Norway, 1970, and the Headless Valley, Canada, 1971. Accounts of his adventures include *A Talent for Trouble* 1970, *Hell on Ice* 1979, and the autobiographical *Living Dangerously* 1987.

Fiesole /fiˈeɪzəʊleɪ/ resort town 6 km/4 mi NE of Florence, Italy, with many Etruscan and Roman relics; population (1971) 14,400. The Romanesque cathedral was completed 1028.

fife a type of small flute. Originally from Switzerland, it was known as the Swiss pipe and has long been played by military bands.

Fife /faɪf/ region of E Scotland (formerly the county of Fife), facing the North Sea and Firth of Forth
area 1,300 sq km/502 sq mi
towns administrative headquarters Glenrothes; Dunfermline, St Andrews, Kirkcaldy, Cupar
physical the only high land is the Lomond Hills, in the NW chief rivers Eden and Leven
features Rosyth naval base and dockyard (used for nuclear submarine refits) on N shore of the Firth of Forth; Tentsmuir, possibly the earliest settled site in Scotland. The ancient palace of the Stuarts was at Falkland, and eight Scottish kings are buried at Dunfermline
products potatoes, cereals, electronics, petrochemicals (Mossmorran), light engineering
population (1987) 345,000.

Fifteen, the ◊Jacobite rebellion of 1715, led by the 'Old Pretender' ◊James Francis Edward Stuart and the Earl of Mar, in order to place the former on the English throne. Mar was checked at Sheriffmuir, Scotland, and the revolt collapsed.

fifth column a group within a country secretly aiding an enemy attacking from without. The term originated 1936 during the Spanish Civil War, when Gen Mola boasted that Franco supporters were attacking Madrid with four columns and that they had a 'fifth column' inside the city.

fifth-generation computer an anticipated new type of computer based on emerging microelectronic technologies. The basis will be very fast computing machinery, with many processors working in parallel made possible by very large-scale integration (◊VLSI), which can put many more circuits onto a ◊silicon chip. Such computers will run advanced

Fife

'intelligent' programs. See also ◊computer generations.

fig fruit of the W Asian tree *Ficus carica*, family Moraceae. Produced in two or three crops a year, and eaten fresh or dried, it has a high sugar content and laxative properties. It grows extensively in S Europe.

In the wild, fig trees are dependent on the fig wasp for pollination, and the wasp in turn is parasitic on the flowers. The tropical *banyan Ficus benghalensis* has less attractive edible fruit, and roots that grow down from its branches. The *bo tree* under which Buddha became enlightened is the Indian peepul or wild fig *Ficus religiosa*.

fig. abbreviation for *figure*.

fighting fish small (6 cm/2 in long) fish *Betta splendens* and related species found in SE Asia. It can breathe air, using an accessory breathing organ above the gill, and can live in poorly oxygenated water. The male has large fins and various colours, including shining greens, reds, and blues. The female is yellowish brown with short fins.

The male builds a nest of bubbles at the water surface and displays to a female to induce her to lay. Rival males are attacked, and in a confined space, fights may occur. In Thailand, public contests are held.

figurative language usage that departs from everyday factual, plain, or literal language, and is commonly considered poetic, imaginative, or ornamental. The traditional forms of figurative language, especially in literature, are the various figures of speech.

The sentence 'Justice is blind' is doubly figurative because it suggests that justice is a person (◊personification) rather than an abstract idea, and uses 'blind' analogically to suggest unbiased (◊metaphor).

figure of speech a poetic, imaginative, or ornamental expression used for purposes of comparison, emphasis, or stylistic effect; usually one of a list of such forms dating from discussions of literary and rhetorical style in Greece in the 5th century BC. These figures include ◊euphemism, ◊hyperbole, ◊metaphor, ◊metonymy, ◊onomatopoeia, ◊oxymoron, ◊personification, the ◊pun, ◊simile, and ◊synecdoche.

figwort plant of the genus *Scrophularia*. A perennial herb, it has square stems, opposite leaves, and open two-lipped flowers in a cluster at the top of the stem.

The *common figwort Scrophularia nodosa* is found across Europe and N Asia, growing in damp woods and by hedges. It is up to 80 cm/2.6 ft long, with small reddish-brown flowers in late summer, and is pollinated by wasps.

Fiji /ˈfiːdʒiː/ group of 332 islands in the SW Pacific, about 100 of which are inhabited.

government Fiji is a constitutional monarchy within the ◊Commonwealth, with the British monarch as head of state, represented by a resident governor-general (but see below). The constitution dates from independence in 1970. The government is modelled on the British system, with a two-chamber parliament, consisting of a senate and house of representatives, and a prime minister and cabinet drawn from and responsible to the house of representatives. The senate has 22 appointed members, eight on the advice of the great council of Fijian chiefs, seven on the advice of the prime minister, six on the advice of the leader of the opposition, and one on the advice of the council of Rotuma Island, which is a Fijian dependency. It has a life of six years. The house of representatives has 52 members, elected for five years through a cross-voting system that ensures that all ethnic groups are represented.

history Originally inhabited by ◊Melanesian and ◊Polynesian peoples, Fiji's first European visitor was Abel ◊Tasman in 1643. Fiji became a British possession in 1874, and achieved full independence within the Commonwealth in 1970. Before independence there had been racial tension between Indians, descended from workers brought

Fiji

area 18,337 sq km/7,078 sq mi
capital Suva on Viti Levu
physical comprises some 800 Melanesian islands (about 100 inhabited), the largest being Viti Levu (10,386 sq km/400 sq mi) and Vanua Levu (5,535 sq km/2,137 sq mi); mountainous, with tropical forest
features Nadi airport is an international Pacific staging post
head of state Ratu Sir Penaia Ganilau from 1987
head of government Ratu Sir Kamisese Mara from 1987

to Fiji in the late 19th century, and Fijians, so the constitutution incorporated an electoral system that would ensure racial balance in the house of representatives.

The leader of the Alliance Party, Ratu Sir Kamisese Mara, became prime minister at the time of independence and has held office ever since. The Alliance Party has traditionally been supported by Fijians and the National Federation Party (NFP), led by Siddiq Koya, by Indians. The main divisions between the two have centred on land ownership, with the Fijians owning more than 80% of the land and defending their traditional rights, and the Indians claiming greater security of land tenure. The Fijian Labour Party was formed in 1985 but has so far made little impact at the polls.

An attempted coup in May 1987, led by Lt-Col Sitivina Rambuka, was abandoned after intervention by the Governor-General and the Great Council of Chiefs. Another coup by Rambuka in Sept seemed, despite indecision by its leader, more likely to succeed. On this occasion the Queen, at the instigation of the Governor-General, condemned the coup in an unprecedented fashion. Nevertheless, the coup went ahead and in Oct 1987 the Queen accepted the resignation of the Governor-General, thereby relinquishing her role as head of state and making Fiji a republic. In Aug 1989 the draft of a new constitution, embodying an electoral law that would favour indigenous Fijians, but preventing the army from taking control, was published.

filariasis collective term for several diseases, prevalent in tropical areas, caused by roundworm (nematode) parasites.

Symptoms include blocked and swollen lymph vessels leading to grotesque swellings of the legs and genitals (Bancroftian filariasis, elephantiasis); and blindness and dry, scaly skin (onchocerciasis). These diseases are spread mainly by insects, notably mosquitoes and blackflies.

Filchner /ˈfɪlʃnə/ Wilhelm 1877–1957. German explorer who travelled extensively in Central Asia, but is remembered for his expedition into the Weddell Sea of Antarctica, where his ship became ice-bound for a whole winter. He landed a party and built a hut on the floating ice shelf,

political system democratic republic
political parties Alliance Party (AP), moderate centrist; National Federation Party (NFP), moderate left-of-centre; Fijian Labour Party (FLP), left-of-centre Indian
exports sugar, coconut oil, ginger, timber, canned fish; tourism is important
currency Fiji dollar (2.57 = £1 Feb 1990)
population (1986) 714,000 (46% Fijian, holding 80% of the land communally, and 49% Indian, introduced in the 19th century to work the sugar crop); annual growth rate 1.9%
life expectancy men 67, women 71
language English (official); Fijian, Hindi
religion Hindu 50%, Methodist 44%
literacy 88% male/77% female (1980 est)
GDP $1.2 bn (1984); $1,086
chronology
1970 Full independence achieved. Ratu Sir Kamisese Mara elected as first prime minister.
1987 General election in Apr brought to power an Indian-dominated coalition led by Dr Timoci Bavadra. Military coup May by Col Sitiveni Rabuka removed new government at gunpoint. Governor General Ratu Sir Penaia Ganilau regained control within weeks. A second military coup Sept by Rabuka proclaimed Fiji a republic and suspended the constitution. In Oct Fiji ceased to be a member of the Commonwealth. In Dec a civilian government was restored with Rambuka retaining control of security as minister for home affairs.
1989 New constitution proposed.

which eventually broke up and floated northwards.

file in computing, a collection of data or a program stored in a computer's external memory, for example on disc. It might include anything from information on a firm's employees to a program for an adventure game. *Serial files* hold information as a sequence of characters, so that, to read any particular item of data, the program must read all those that precede it. *Random access files* allow the required data to be reached directly.

Files usually consist of a set of records, each having a number of fields for specific items of data. For example, the file for a class of schoolchildren might have five fields containing each child's family name (1), first name (2), house name or number (3), street name (4), and town (5). To find out which children live in the same street one would look in field 4.

file transfer in computing, the transmission of a file (data stored on disc, for example) from one machine to another. Both machines must be physically linked (for example, by a telephone line) and both must be running appropriate communications software.

filioque (Latin 'and the Son') a disputed term in the Christian creeds from the 8th century, referring to the issue of whether the Holy Spirit proceeds from God only or from God the Father and Son. Added by the Council of Frankfurt 794, the term was incorporated as Catholic doctrine in the 10th century.

Fillmore /ˈfɪlmɔː/ Millard 1800–1874. 13th president of the USA 1850–53, a Whig. He was Zachary Taylor's vice president from 1849, and succeeded him on Taylor's death. Fillmore supported a compromise on slavery 1850 to reconcile North and South, and failed to be renominated.

film, art of see ◊cinema.

film noir (French 'black film') a term originally used by French critics to describe any film characterized by pessimism, cynicism, and a dark, sombre tone. It has been used to describe Hollywood films of the 1940s and early 1950s portraying the seedy side of the criminal underworld.

Typically the *film noir* is shot with lighting that emphasizes shadow and stark contrasts, abounds in night scenes, and contains a cynical

Fingal's Cave *Great basalt columns formed by the cooling of molten lava surround the entrance to Fingal's Cave.*

antihero—an example is the character of Philip Marlowe as played by Humphrey Bogart in *The Big Sleep* 1946.

film, photographic a strip of transparent material (usually cellulose acetate) coated with a light-sensitive emulsion, used in cameras to take pictures. The emulsion contains a mixture of light-sensitive silver halide salts (for example bromide or iodide) in gelatin. Films differ in their sensitivity to light, this being indicated by their speed. When the emulsion is exposed to light, the silver salts are invisibly altered, giving a latent image, which is then made visible by the process of ◊developing. Colour film consists of several layers of emulsion, each of which records a different colour in the light falling on it.

In ***colour film*** the front emulsion records blue light, then comes a yellow filter, followed by layers that record green and red light respectively. In the developing process the various images in the layers are dyed yellow, magenta, and cyan, respectively. When they are viewed, either as a see-through transparency or as a colour print, the colours merge to produce the true colour of the original scene photographed.

film score music specially written to accompany a film on the soundtrack. Special scores were also written for some silent films and performed live as the film was shown.

filter in chemistry, a porous substance, such as blotting paper, through which a mixture can be passed to separate out its solid constituents. In optics, a filter is a piece of glass or transparent material that passes light of one colour only.

filter in electronics, a circuit that transmits a signal of some frequencies better than others. A low-pass filter transmits signals of low frequency and direct current; a high-pass filter transmits high-frequency signals; a band-pass filter transmits signals in a band of frequencies.

final solution (to the Jewish question; German *Endlosung der Judenfrage*) euphemism used by the Nazis to describe the extermination of Jews and other opponents of the regime during World War II. See ◊holocaust.

Financial Times Index (FT Index) an indicator measuring the daily movement of 30 major industrial share prices on the London Stock Exchange (1935 = 100), issued by the UK *Financial Times* newspaper. Other FT indices cover government securities, fixed-interest securities, goldmine shares, and Stock Exchange activity.

finch bird of the family Fringillidae, in the order Passeriformes. They are seed-eaters with stout conical beaks, and include chaffinches, sparrows, and canaries.

Finch /fɪntʃ/ Peter 1916–1977. British cinema actor who began his career in Australia before becoming internationally known for his roles in *A Town Like Alice* 1956; *The Trials of Oscar Wilde* 1960; *Sunday, Bloody, Sunday* 1971; *Network* 1976.

fin de siècle (French 'end of century') the art and literature of the 1890s; decadent.

Fine Gael /ˈfinə ˈɡeɪl/ (Gaelic 'United Ireland') Republic of Ireland political party founded by W J ◊Cosgrave and led by Alan Dukes from

1987. It is socially liberal but fiscally conservative.

Fingal's Cave /ˈfɪŋɡəl/ cave on the island of Staffa, Inner Hebrides, Scotland. It is lined with natural basalt columns, and is 60 m/200 ft long and 20 m/65 ft high. Fingal, based on the Irish hero Finn mac Cumhaill, was the leading character in Macpherson's Ossianic forgeries. Visited by Mendelssohn in 1829, the cave was the inspiration of his *Hebrides* overture, otherwise known as Fingal's Cave.

fingerprint the ridge pattern of the skin on a person's fingertips; this is constant through life and no two are exactly alike. Fingerprinting was first used as a means of identifying suspects in India, and was adopted by the English police 1901; it is now widely employed in police and security work.

Finistère /ˌfɪnɪsˈteə/ *département* of ◊Brittany, NW France; area 7,030 sq km/2,740 mi; population (1982) 828,500. The administrative centre is Quimper.

Finisterre /ˌfɪnɪsˈteə/ Cape promontory in the extreme NW of Spain.

Finland /ˈfɪnlənd/ country in Scandinavia, bounded N by Norway, E by the USSR, S and W by the Baltic Sea, and NW by Sweden.

government Finland is a republic which combines a parliamentary system with a strong presidency. The single-chamber parliament, the *Eduskunta*, has 200 members, elected by universal suffrage, through a system of proportional representation, for a four-year term. The president is elected for six years by a 301-member electoral college, chosen by popular vote in the same way as the parliament. The president appoints a prime minister and a cabinet, called a council of state, whose members are collectively responsible to the *Eduskunta*.

The relationship between the president, the prime minister, and the council of state is unusual, the nearest equivalent being in France. The president has supreme executive power, and can ignore even a unanimous decision reached in the council of state, but the prime minister is concerned with the day-to-day operation of the government so that to some extent they can, at times, both act as heads of government. Both the president and the *Eduskunta* can initiate legislation and the president has a right of veto, though this can be overruled by a newly appointed parliament.

Because of the system of proportional representation, there is a multiplicity of parties, and the prime minister invariably heads a coalition council of state, typically between four parties. The main parties are: the Social Democratic Party (SDP), the National Coalition Party (KOK), the Centre Party (KP), the Finnish People's Democratic League (SKDL), the Finnish Rural Party (SMP), and the Swedish People's Party (SFP).

history The Lapps, who once inhabited the area now known as Finland, were driven by Finnic nomads from Asia into the far northern region they occupy today from about the 1st century BC. The area was conquered 12th century by Sweden, and for much of the next 200 years the country was the scene of wars between Sweden and Russia. As a duchy of Sweden, Finland was allowed a measure of autonomy, becoming a grand duchy 1581. In 1809, during the Napoleonic Wars, Finland was annexed by Russia; nationalist feeling grew, and the country proclaimed its independence during the 1917 Russian revolution. The Soviet regime initially tried to regain control but acknowledged Finland's independence 1920.

In 1939 the USSR's request for military bases in Finland was rejected and the two countries were involved in the 'Winter War', which lasted for 15 weeks. Finland was defeated and forced to cede territory. In the hope of regaining it, in 1941 it joined Nazi Germany in attacking the USSR, but agreed a separate armistice 1944. It was again forced to cede territory and in 1948 signed the Finno-Soviet Pact of Friendship, Co-operation, and Mutual Assistance (the YYA Treaty). This was extended 1955, 1970, and 1983. Although the Treaty requires it to repel any attack on the USSR through Finnish territory by Germany or its allies, Finland has maintained a policy of strict neutrality. It signed a trade treaty with the EEC 1973 and a 15-year trade agreement with the USSR 1977. In 1989 it was admitted into the Council of Europe.

Finnish politics have been characterized by instability in governments, over 60 having been formed since independence, including many minority coalitions. The presidency, on the other hand, has been very stable, with only two presidents in over 30 years.

The Social Democratic and Centre parties have dominated Finland's coalition politics for many years but the 1987 general election resulted in the Social Democrats entering government in coalition

Finland
Republic of
(Suomen Tasavalta)

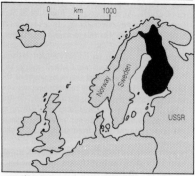

area 352,752 sq km/136,162 sq mi
capital Helsinki
towns Tampere, the port of Turku, Espoo, Vantaa
physical archipelago in south; most of the country is forest, with about 60,000 lakes; one third is within the Arctic Circle; mountains in the north
head of state Mauno Koivisto from 1982
head of government Harri Holkeri from 1987
political system democratic republic
political parties Social Democratic Party

(SDP), moderate left-of-centre; National Coalition Party (KOK), moderate right-of-centre; Centre Party (KP), radical centrist, rural-orientated; Finnish People's Democratic League (SKDL), left-wing; Swedish People's Party, independent Swedish-orientated; Finnish Rural Party (SMP), farmers and small businesses
exports metal, chemical and engineering products (icebreakers and oil rigs), paper, timber, textiles, fine ceramics, glass, furniture
currency markka (6.73 = £1 Feb 1990)
population (1987) 4,938,600; annual growth rate 0.5%
life expectancy men 70, women 78
language Finnish 94%, Swedish (official), Lapp
religion Lutheran 90%, Eastern Orthodox
literacy 99%
GNP $50.6 bn (1984); $10,477 per head of population
chronology
1917 Independence declared.
1939 Defeated by USSR in Winter War.
1941 Joined Hitler in invasion of USSR.
1944 Concluded separate armistice with Allies.
1948 Finno-Soviet Pact of Friendship, Co-operation, and Mutual Assistance signed.
1973 Trade treaty with EEC signed.
1977 Trade agreement with USSR signed.
1987 KOK–SDP coalition formed.
1988 Koivisto re-elected president.
1989 Finland joined Council of Europe.

with their arch-enemies, the Conservatives, while the Centre Party was forced into opposition.

Finland, Gulf of /'finlənd/ eastern arm of the ◊Baltic Sea, separating Finland from Estonia.

Finlandization political term signifying the limits set on the autonomy of a small state by a much more powerful neighbour, as on Finland by the USSR. Finns resent the term, feeling that it represents a false assumption that their sovereignty is under threat. It was coined by the Austrian politician Karl Gruber 1953

Finney /'fini/ Albert 1936– . English stage and film actor. He created the title roles in Keith Waterhouse's *Billy Liar* 1960 and John Osborne's *Luther* 1961, and was artistic director of the Royal Court Theatre 1972–75. His films include *Saturday Night and Sunday Morning* 1960, *Tom Jones* 1963, *Murder on the Orient Express* 1974, and *The Dresser* 1984.

Finney /'fini/ Thomas 'Tom' 1922– . English footballer, known as the 'Preston Plumber'. He played for England 76 times, and in every forward position. He was noted for his ball control and goal-scoring skills, and was the first person to win the Footballer of the Year award twice.

CAREER HIGHLIGHTS

Football League
appearances: 433
goals: 187
international
appearances: 76
goals: 30
FA Cup (runners-up medal): 1954
Footballer of the Year: 1954, 1957

Finnish language a member of the Finno-Ugric language family, the national language of Finland and closely related to neighbouring Estonian, Livonian, Karelian, and Ingrian languages. At the beginning of the 19th century Finnish had no official status, Swedish being the language of education, government, and literature in Finland. The publication of the *Kalevala*, a national epic poem, in 1835, contributed greatly to the arousal of Finnish national and linguistic feeling.

Finn Mac Cumhaill /fin mə'ku:l/ legendary Irish hero, identified with a general who organized an Irish regular army in the mid-3rd century. James Macpherson (1736–96) featured him (as Fingal) and his followers in the verse of his popular epics 1762–63, which were supposedly written by a 3rd-century bard, ◊Ossian. Although challenged by the critic Dr Johnson, the poems were influential in the Romantic movement.

Finno-Ugric a group or family of more than 20 languages spoken by some 22 million people in scattered communities from Norway in the west to Siberia in the east and to the Carpathian mountains in the south. Members of the family include Finnish, Lapp, and Hungarian.

Finsen /'finsən/ Niels Ryberg 1860–1904. Danish physician, the first to use ultraviolet light treatment for skin diseases. Nobel Prize for Medicine 1903.

finsen unit unit (symbol FU) for measuring the intensity of ultraviolet light (UV). UV of 2 FUs causes sunburn in 15 minutes.

Finsteraarhorn the highest mountain, 4,274 m/14,020 ft, in the Bernese Alps, Switzerland.

fiord /fi:'ɔ:d/ alternative spelling of ◊fjord.

fir general term applied to ◊conifers, but the correct name for only a few species, such as the **silver fir** *Abies alba*; other *Abies* species; and the **Douglas fir** *Pseudotsuga menziesii*.

Firbank /'fɜ:bæŋk/ Ronald 1886–1926. English novelist. His work, set in the Edwardian decadent period, has a malicious humour, and includes *Caprice* 1916, *Valmouth* 1918, and the posthumous *Concerning the Eccentricities of Cardinal Pirelli* 1926.

Firdausi /fiə'daʊsi/ Abdul Qasim Mansur *c.* 935–*c.*1020. Persian poet, whose epic *Shahnama/The Book of Kings* relates the history of Persia in 60,000 verses.

firearm a weapon from which projectiles are discharged by the combustion of an explosive. Firearms are generally divided into two main sections: ◊*artillery* (ordnance or cannon), with a bore greater than 2.54 cm/1 in, and ◊*small arms*, with a bore of less than 2.54 cm/1 in. Although gunpowder was known in Europe 60 years previously, the invention of guns dates from 1300–25, and is attributed to Berthold Schwartz, a German monk.

firebrat another name for the insect ◊bristletail.

fire clay a ◊clay with refractory characteristics (resistant to high temperatures), and hence suitable for lining furnaces (firebrick). Its chemical composition consists of a high percentage of silicon and aluminium oxides, and a low percentage of the oxides of sodium, potassium, iron, and calcium.

Fireclays underlie the coal seams in the UK.

firedamp a gas which occurs in coal mines and is explosive when mixed with air in certain proportions. It consists chiefly of methane CH_4 (natural gas or marsh gas), but always contains small quantities of other gases, such as nitrogen, carbon dioxide, and hydrogen, and sometimes ethane and carbon monoxide.

fire-danger rating unit index used by the UK Forestry Commission to indicate the probability of a forest fire. 0 means a fire is improbable, 100 shows a serious fire hazard.

fire extinguisher a device for putting out a fire. Many domestic extinguishers contain liquid carbon dioxide under pressure. When the handle is pressed, carbon dioxide is released as a gas which blankets the burning material and prevents oxygen reaching it. Other dry extinguishers spray powder, which then releases carbon dioxide gas. Wet extinguishers are often of the soda-acid type; when activated, sulphuric acid mixes with sodium bicarbonate, producing carbon dioxide. The gas pressure forces the solution out of a nozzle, and a foaming agent may be added to produce foam.

firefly winged nocturnal ◊beetle which emits light through the process of ◊bioluminescence.

Firenze /fi'rentsei/ Italian form of ◊Florence.

fire protection methods available for fighting fires. In the UK, a public fire-fighting service is maintained by local authorities, and similar services operate in other countries. Industrial and commercial buildings are often protected by an automatic sprinkler system: heat or smoke opens the sprinkler heads on a network of water pipes and immediately sprays the seat of the fire. In certain circumstances water is ineffective and may be dangerous; for example, for oil and petrol storage-tank fires, foam systems are used; for industrial plants containing inflammable vapours, carbon dioxide is used; where electricity is involved, vaporizing liquids create a nonflammable barrier; and for some chemicals only various dry powders can be used.

In Britain, fire protection has always depended on a combination of public service and private

enterprise. Acts of 1707 and 1774 required every parish to provide engines (horse-drawn), hoses and ladders, but insurance companies established their own, more efficient brigades for the benefit of buildings bearing their own firemarks. The latter amalgamated in the 19th century to form the basis of the present-day service, which is run by the local authorities in close cooperation.

Firestone /'faiəstəʊn/ Shulamith 1945– . Canadian feminist writer, whose book *The Dialectic of Sex: the Case for Feminist Revolution* 1970 exerted considerable influence on feminist thought. She was one of the early organizers of the women's liberation movement in the USA.

firework a pyrotechnic device, originating in China, for producing a display of coloured sparks (and sometimes noises) by burning chemicals. A firework consists of a container, usually cylindrical in shape and of rolled paper, enclosing a mixture capable of burning independently of the oxygen in the air. One of the ingredients holds a separate supply of oxygen that is readily given up to the other combustible ingredients.

Fireworks are often used in China, where they originated, and Japan. In Britain they are traditionally used on 5 Nov, Guy Fawkes Day, and in the USA on 4 July, Independence Day.

firmware a computer program held permanently in the machine in ◊ROM (read-only memory) chips, as opposed to one that is read in from external memory as it is needed.

first aid action taken immediately after some traumatic event in order to save a victim's life, to prevent further damage, or facilitate later treatment. See also ◊resuscitation.

First World War another name for ◊World War I, 1914–18.

fiscal policy that part of government policy devoted to achieving the desired level of revenue, notably through taxation, and deciding the priorities and purposes governing expenditure.

British governments after 1945 customarily made frequent adjustments to fiscal policy in order to regulate the level of economic activity. However, since 1979 the Conservative administration has placed greater emphasis on ◊monetary policy (control of the money supply).

fiscal year the financial year, which does not necessarily coincide with the calendar year.

In the UK, the fiscal year runs from 6 Apr in one year to 5 Apr in the following year. In the USA, the fiscal year runs from 1 July to 30 June.

Fischer /'fiʃə/ Emil Hermann 1852–1919. German chemist who produced synthetic sugars and from these the various enzymes. His descriptions of the chemistry of the carbohydrates and peptides laid the foundations for the science of biochemistry. Nobel prize 1902.

Fischer /'fiʃə/ Hans 1881–1945. German chemist awarded the Nobel prize 1930 for his discovery of haemoglobin in blood.

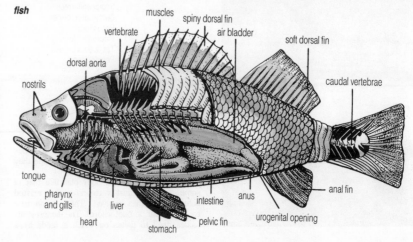

fish   muscles   spiny dorsal fin   air bladder   soft dorsal fin   vertebrate   dorsal aorta   caudal vertebrae   nostrils   tongue   pharynx and gills   heart   liver   stomach   pelvic fin   intestine   anus   urogenital opening   anal fin

Fisher John Fisher, bishop of Rochester, was beheaded in 1535 for denying the royal supremacy.

Fischer-Dieskau /ˈfɪʃə ˈdiːskaʊ/ Dietrich 1925– . German baritone, renowned for his interpretation of Schubert's songs.

fish aquatic vertebrate that breathes using gills. There are three main groups, not very closely related: the bony fishes (goldfish, cod, tuna); the cartilaginous fishes (sharks, rays); and the jawless fishes (hagfishes, lampreys).

The bony fishes are the majority of living fishes (about 20,000 species). The skeleton is bone, movement is controlled by mobile fins, and the body is usually covered with scales. The gills are covered by a single flap. Many have a swim bladder which the fish uses to adjust its buoyancy. Most lay eggs, sometimes in vast numbers. The ◊ling can produce as many as 28 million. Those species that produce small numbers of eggs very often protect them in nests, or by brooding them in their mouths. Some fishes are internally fertilized and retain eggs until hatching inside the body, then giving birth to live young. Most bony fishes are ray-finned fishes, but a few, including the lungfish and coelacanth, are fleshy-finned.

The cartilaginous fishes are efficient hunters. There are fewer than 600 known species. The skeleton is cartilage, the mouth is generally beneath the head, the nose is large and sensitive, and there is a series of gill slits along the neck

fishing and fisheries

drag net

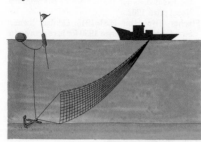

trawl net

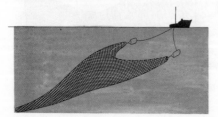

FISH CLASSIFICATION

Superclass Agnatha (jawless fishes)

Order	No of species	Examples
Petromyzoniformes	30	lampreys
Myxiniformes	15	hagfishes

Superclass Gnathostomata (jawed fishes)
Class Chondrichthyes (cartilaginous fishes)
Subclass Elasmobranchii (sharks and rays)

Order	No of species	Examples
Hexanchiformes		frilled shark, comb-toothed shark
Heterodontiformes	10	Port Jackson sharks
Lamniformes	200	'typical' sharks
Rajiformes	300	skates, rays

Subclass Holocephali (rabbitfishes)

Order	No of species	Examples
Chimaeriformes	20	chimaeras, rabbitfishes

Class Osteichthyes (bony fishes)
Subclass Sarcopterygii (fleshy finned fishes)
Coelacanths

Order	No of species	Examples
Coelacanthiformes	1	coelacanths

Lungfishes

Order	No of species	Examples
Ceratodontiformes	1	Australian lungfish
Lepidosireniformes	4	South American and African lungfish

Subclass Actinopterygii (ray-finned fishes)
Superorder Chondrostei

Order	No of species	Examples
Polypteriormes	11	bichirs and reedfish
Acipensiformes	25	paddlefish, sturgeons

Superorder Holostei

Order	No of species	Examples
Amiiformes	8	bowfin, garpikes

Superorder Teleostei

Order	No of species	Examples
Elopiformes	12	tarpons, tenpounders
Anguilliformes	300	eels
Notacanthiformes	20	spiny eels
Clupeiformes	350	herrings, anchovies
Osteoglossiformes	16	arapaima, African butterfly fish
Mormyriformes	150	elephant-trunk fishes, featherbacks
Salmoniformes	500	salmon, trout, smelt, pike
Gonorhynchiformes	15	milkfish
Cypriniformes	350	carp, barbs, characins, loaches
Siluriformes	200	catfishes
Myctophiformes	300	deep-sea lantern fishes, Bombay ducks
Percopsiformes	10	pirate perches, cave-dwelling amblyopsids
Batrachoidiformes	10	toadfishes
Gobiesociformes	100	clingfishes
Lophiiformes	150	anglerfishes
Gadiformes	450	cod, pollack, pearlfish, eelpout
Atheriniformes	600	flying fishes, toothcarps, halfbeaks
Lampridiformes	50	opah, ribbonfish
Beryciformes	150	squirrelfishes
Zeiformes	60	John Dory, boarfish
Gasterosteiforems	150	sticklebacks, pipefishes, seahorses
Channiformes	5	snakesheads
Synbranchiformes	7	cuchia
Scorpaeniformes	700	gurnards, miller's thumb, stonefish
Dactylopteriformes	6	flying gunard
Pegasiformes	4	sea-moths
Pleuronectiformes	500	flatfishes
Tetraodontiformes	250	puffer fishes, trigger fishes, sun fish
Perciformes	6500	perches, cichlids, damsel fishes, gobies, wrasses, parrotfishes, gouramis, marlin, mackerel, tunny, swordfish, spiny eels, mullets, barracudas, sea bream, croakers, ice fishes, butterfish

region. They may lay eggs ('mermaid's purses') or bear live young. Some types of cartilaginous fishes, such as the shark, retain the shape they had millions of years ago.

Jawless fishes have a body plan like that of some of the earliest vertebrates that existed before true fishes evolved. There is no true backbone but a ◊notochord. The lamprey attaches itself to fishes on which it feeds by a suckerlike rasping mouth. Hagfishes are entirely marine, very slimy, and feed on carrion and injured fishes.

Fisher /ˈfɪʃə/ Andrew 1862–1928. Australian Labor politician. Born in Scotland, he went to Australia 1885, and entered the Australian parliament 1901. He was prime minister 1908–09, 1910–13, and 1914–15, and Australian high commissioner to the UK 1916–21.

Fisher /'fɪʃə/ Geoffrey, Baron Fisher of Lambeth 1887–1972. English priest, archbishop of Canterbury 1945–61. He was the first holder of this office to visit the pope for 600 years.

Fisher /'fɪʃə/ John Arbuthnot, 1st Baron Fisher 1841–1920. British admiral, First Sea Lord 1904–10, when he carried out many radical reforms and innovations, including the introduction of the dreadnought battleship.

He served in the Crimean War 1855 and the China War 1859–60. He held various commands before becoming First Sea Lord, and returned to the post 1914, but resigned the following year, disagreeing with Churchill over sending more ships to the Dardanelles, Turkey, in World War I.

Fisher /'fɪʃə/ John, St c. 1469–1535. English bishop, created bishop of Rochester 1504. He was an enthusiastic supporter of the revival in the study of Greek, and a friend of the humanists More and Erasmus. In 1535 he was tried on a charge of denying the royal supremacy and beheaded.

Fisher /'fɪʃə/ Ronald Aylmer 1890–1962. English statistian and geneticist. He modernized Darwin's theory of evolution, thus securing the key biological concept of genetic change by natural selection. Fisher developed several new statistical techniques and, applying his methods to genetics, published *The Genetical Theory of Natural Selection* in 1930.

This classic work established that the discoveries of the geneticist Gregor Mendel could be shown to support Darwin's theory of evolution.

fish farming or **aquaculture** raising fish under controlled conditions in tanks and ponds, sometimes in offshore pens. It has been practised for centuries in the Far East, where Japan alone produces some 100,000 tonnes of fish a year. In the 1980s one-tenth of the world's consumption of fish was farmed, notably trout, Atlantic salmon, turbot, eel, mussels, and oysters.

The 300 trout farms in Britain produce over 9,000 tonnes per year, and account for 90% of home consumption.

Fishguard /'fɪʃɡɑːd/ seaport on an inlet on the S side of Fishguard Bay, Dyfed, SW Wales; population about 5,000. There is a ferry service to Rosslare in the Republic of Ireland.

fishing and fisheries fisheries can be classified by (1) type of water: freshwater (lake, river, pond); marine (inshore, midwater, deep sea); (2) catch: for example salmon fishing, (3) fishing method: diving, stunning or poisoning, harpooning, trawling, drifting.

marine fishing The greatest proportion of the world's catch comes from the oceans. The primary production area is the photic zone, the relatively thin surface layer (50 m/164 ft) of water that can be penetrated by light, allowing photosynthesis by plant ◊plankton to take place. Plankton-eating fish tend to be small in size and include herrings and sardines. Demersal fishes, such as haddock, halibut, and cod, live primarily near the ocean floor, and feed on various invertebrate marine animals. Over 20 million tonnes of them are caught each year by trawling. Pelagic fish, such as tuna, live in the open sea, near the surface, and purse seine nets are used to catch them; the annual catch is over 30 million tonnes a year.

freshwater fishing There is large demand for salmon, trout, carp, eel, bass, pike, perch, and catfish. These inhabit ponds, lakes, rivers, or swamps, and some species have been successfully cultivated (◊fish farming).

methods Lines, seine nets, and lift nets are the common commercial methods used. Purse seine nets, which close like a purse and may be as long as 30 nautical miles, have caused a crisis in the S Pacific where Japan, Taiwan, and South Korea fish illegally in other countries' fishing zones.

history Until the introduction of refrigeration, fish was too perishable to be exported, and fishing met local needs only. Between 1950 and 1970, the global fish catch increased by an average of 7% each year. On refrigerated factory ships, filleting and processing can be done at sea. Japan evolved new techniques for locating shoals (by sonar and radar) and catching them (for example, with electrical charges and chemical baits). By the 1970s, indiscriminate overfishing had led to serious depletion of stocks, and heated confrontations between countries using the same fishing grounds. A partial solution was the extension of fishing limits to 320 km/200 mi. The North Sea countries have experimented with the artificial breeding of fish eggs and release of small fry into the sea. Overfishing of the NE Atlantic led to, in 1988, hundreds of thousands of starving seals on the N coast of Norway. Marine pollution is blamed for the increasing number (up to 30%) of diseased fish in the North Sea. A United Nations resolution was passed 1989 to end drift-net fishing by June 1992.

ancillary industries These include the manufacture of nets, the processing of oil and fishmeal (nearly 25% of the fish caught annually are turned into meal for animal feed), pet food, glue, manure, and drugs such as insulin and other pharmaceutical products.

fission in physics, the splitting of the atomic nucleus (see ◊nuclear energy).

fistula an abnormal pathway developing between adjoining organs or tissues, or leading to the exterior of the body. A fistula developing between the bowel and the bladder, for instance, may give rise to urinary tract infection by organisms from the gut.

fitness in genetic theory, a measure of the success with which a genetically determined character can spread in future generations. By convention, the normal character is assigned a fitness of one, and variants (determined by other ◊alleles) are then assigned fitness values relative to this. Those with fitness greater than one will spread more rapidly and ultimately replace the normal allele; those with fitness less than one will gradually die out. See also ◊inclusive fitness.

Fitzalan-Howard family name of dukes of Norfolk; seated at Arundel Castle, Sussex.

Fitzgerald /fɪts'dʒerəld/ family name of the dukes of Leinster.

Fitzgerald /fɪts'dʒerəld/ Edward 1809–1883. English poet and translator. In 1859 he published his poetic version of the *Rubaiyat of Omar Khayyam*, which is generally considered more an original creation than a translation.

Fitzgerald /fɪts'dʒerəld/ Ella 1918– . US jazz singer, recognized as one of the greatest voices of jazz, both in solo work and with big bands. She is particularly noted for her interpretations of Gershwin and Cole Porter songs.

Fitzgerald /fɪts'dʒerəld/ F(rancis) Scott (Key) 1896–1940. US novelist. His autobiographical novel *This Side of Paradise* 1920 made him known in the postwar society of the East Coast, and *The Great Gatsby* 1925 epitomizes the Jazz Age. His wife Zelda's descent into mental illness forms the subject of *Tender is the Night* 1934.

Fitzgerald was born in Minnesota. His first book, *This Side of Paradise*, reflected his experiences at Princeton University. In *The Great Gatsby* 1925 the narrator resembles his author, and Gatsby, the self-made millionaire, is lost in the soulless society he enters. Fitzgerald's wife Zelda Sayre (1900–47), a schizophrenic, entered an asylum 1930, after which he declined into alcoholism. His other works include numerous short stories and the novels *The Beautiful and the Damned* 1922 and *The Last Tycoon*, which was unfinished at his death.

FitzGerald /fɪts'dʒerəld/ Garret 1926– . Irish politician. As *Taoiseach* (prime minister) 1981–82 and again 1982–86, he was noted for his attempts to solve the Northern Ireland dispute, ultimately by participating in the Anglo-Irish agreement 1985. He tried to remove some of the overtly

Fitzgerald US novelist F Scott Fitzgerald.

Catholic features of the constitution to make the Republic more attractive to Northern Protestants. He retired as leader of the Fine Gael Party 1987.

Fitzgerald /fɪts'dʒerəld/ George 1851–1901. Irish physicist known for his work on electromagnetics. He was professor of physics at Trinity College, Dublin. He explained the anomalous results of previous experiments by supposing that bodies moving through the ether contracted, an effect since known as the *Fitzgerald-Lorentz contraction*.

Fitzherbert /fɪts'hɜːbət/ Maria Anne 1756–1837. Wife of the Prince of Wales, later George IV. She became Mrs Fitzherbert by her second marriage 1778 and, after her husband's death 1781, entered London society. She secretly married the Prince of Wales 1785, and finally parted from him 1803.

Fitzroy family name of dukes of Grafton; descended from King Charles II by his mistress Barbara Villiers; seated at Euston Hall, Norfolk.

Fitzroy /'fɪtsrɔɪ/ Robert 1805–1865. British vice-admiral and meteorologist. In 1828 he succeeded to the command of HMS *Beagle*, then engaged on a survey of the Patagonian coast of South America, and in 1831 was accompanied by the naturalist Charles Darwin on a five-year survey. In 1843–45 he was governor of New Zealand.

five pillars of Islam the five duties required of every Muslim: repeating the **creed**, which affirms that Allah is the one God and Muhammad is his prophet; daily **prayer** or ◊salat; giving **alms**; **fasting** during the month of Ramadan; and, if not prevented by ill health or poverty, the hajj, or **pilgrimage** to Mecca, once in a lifetime.

fives a game resembling squash played by two or four players in a court enclosed on three or four sides: the ball is struck with the hand.

It dates from the 14th century, and was probably derived from the French *jeu de paume*. The name fives may refer to the five fingers, or to there originally being five players, who had to make five points to win. In Britain the game is practically confined to public schools and colleges, and there are three main forms, namely, Eton fives, Rugby fives, and Winchester fives.

Five-Year Plan a long-term strategic plan for the development of a country's economy. Five-year plans were from 1928 the basis of economic planning in the USSR, aimed particularly at developing heavy and light industry in a primarily agricultural country. They have since been adopted by many other countries.

fixed point a temperature that can be accurately reproduced and used as the basis of a temperature scale. In the Celsius scale, the fixed points are the temperature of melting ice, which is 0°C or 32°F, and the temperature of boiling water (at standard atmospheric pressure), which is 100°C or 212°F.

flamingo

fixed-point notation system of representing numbers by a single set of digits with the decimal point in its correct position (for example, 97.8, 0.978). For very large and very small numbers this requires a lot of digits, which will be limited by the capacity of a computer, in which case ◊floating-point notation is often preferred.

Fixx /fɪks/ James 1932–1984. US popularizer of jogging with his book *The Complete Book of Running* 1978. He died of a heart attack while jogging.

fjord or **fiord** narrow sea inlet enclosed by high cliffs. Fjords are found in Norway and elsewhere. *Fiordland* is the deeply indented SW coast of South Island, New Zealand; one of the most beautiful inlets is Milford Sound.

fl. abbreviation for *floruit* (Latin 'he/she flourished').

FL abbreviation for ◊*Florida*.

flag a piece of cloth used as an emblem or symbol for nationalistic, religious, or military displays, or as a means of signalling. Flags have been used since ancient times.

The *Stars and Stripes*, also called Old Glory, is the flag of the USA; the 50 stars on a field of blue represent the 50 states now in the Union, and the 13 red and white stripes represent the 13 original colonies. Each state also has its own flag. The presidential standard displays the American eagle, surrounded by 50 stars.

The British national flag, the *Union Jack*, unites the crosses of St George, St Andrew, and St Patrick, representing England, Scotland, and Ireland.

The flag of the USSR places the crossed hammer and sickle, representing the workers of town and country, on a red field, the emblem of revolution. The flags of the Scandinavian countries bear crosses; the Danish *Dannebrog* ('strength of Denmark') is the oldest national flag, used for 700 years. The Swiss flag inspired the Red Cross flag with colours reversed. Muslim states often incorporate in their flags the crescent emblem of Islam and the colour green, also associated with their faith. Similarly Israel uses the Star of David and the colour blue.

The flags of Australia and New Zealand both incorporate the Union Jack, together with symbols of the Southern Cross constellation. The Canadian flag has a maple-leaf design.

As a signal, a flag is flown upside down to indicate distress; is dipped as a salute; and is flown at half-mast to show mourning. The 'Blue Peter', blue with a white centre, announces that a vessel is about to sail; a flag half red and half white, that a pilot is on board. Many localities and public bodies, as well as shipping lines, schools, and yacht clubs, have their own distinguishing flags.

In the UK, the merchant flag places the national flag in the canton of a red flag; similarly placed on a large St George's Cross it becomes the distinguishing flag of the Royal Navy. The British royal standard combines the emblems of England, Scotland, and Ireland.

flag in botany, plant of the *Iris* genus. *Yellow flag Iris pseudacorus* grows wild in damp places throughout Europe. It has a thick rhizome, stiff, bladelike, monocotyledonous leaves, and stems up to 150 cm/5 ft high. The flowers are large and yellow. Cultivated varieties include the purple garden flag.

flag in computing, a code indicating whether or not a certain condition is true; for example, that the end of a file has been reached.

flagellant a religious fanatic who uses a whip on him- or herself as a means of penance. Flagellation is known in many religions from ancient times, and there were notable outbreaks of this type of extremist devotion in Christian Europe in the 11th–16th centuries.

flagellum a small hairlike organ on the surface of certain cells. Flagella are the motile organs of certain protozoa and single-celled algae, and of the sperm cells of higher animals. Unlike ◊cilia, flagella usually occur singly or in pairs; they are also longer and have a more complex whiplike action.

Each flagellum consists of contractile filaments producing snakelike movements which propel cells through fluids, or fluids past cells. Water movement inside sponges is also produced by flagella.

flag of convenience a flag flown by a ship registered in a country not its own in order to avoid legal or tax commitments. Applied especially to the merchant fleets of Liberia and Panama; ships registered in these countries avoid legislation governing, for example, employment of sailors and minimum rates of pay. Less than one-third of British shipping is registered in Britain today.

Flagstad /'flægstæd/ Kirsten (Malfrid) 1895–1962. Norwegian soprano who specialized in Wagnerian opera.

Flaherty /'flɑːəti/ Robert 1884–1951. US film director. He exerted great influence through his silent film of Inuit (Eskimo) life *Nanook of the North* 1920. Later films include *Man of Aran* 1934 and *Elephant Boy* 1937.

flamboyant in architecture, the late Gothic style of French architecture, contemporary with the ◊Perpendicular style in England. It is characterized by flamelike decorative work in windows, balustrades, and other projecting features.

flamen a sacrificial priest in ancient Rome. The office was held for life, but was terminated by the death of the flamen's wife (who assisted him at ceremonies) or by some misdemeanour. At first there were 3 flamens for each deity, but another 12 were later added.

flame test in chemistry, the use of a flame to identify metal ◊cations present in a solid.

A nichrome or platinum wire is moistened with acid, dipped in the test substance, and then held in a hot flame. The colour produced in the flame is characteristic of metals present; for example, sodium burns with a yellow flame, and potassium with a lilac one.

flame tree smooth-stemmed semi-deciduous tree *Sterculia acerifolia* with red or orange flowers, native to Australia, but spread throughout the tropics.

flamingo long-legged and long-necked wading bird, family Phoenicopteridae, of the stork order Ciconiiformes. Largest of the family is the *greater* or *roseate flamingo Phoenicopterus ruber*, of both Africa and South America, with delicate pink plumage, and 1.25 m/4 ft high. They sift the mud for food with their downbent bills, and build colonies of high, conelike mud nests, with a little hollow for the eggs at the top.

Flaminius /flə'mɪnɪəs/ Gaius died 217 BC. Roman consul and general. He constructed the Flaminian Way northward from Rome to Rimini 220 BC, and was killed at the battle of Lake Trasimene fighting ◊Hannibal.

Flamsteed /'flæmstiːd/ John 1646–1719. first Astronomer Royal of England, who began systematic observations of the positions of the stars, Moon, and planets at Greenwich, London, 1676. His observations were published 1725.

Flamsteed After petitioning Charles II for a national observatory, John Flamsteed, a painstaking perfectionist, was made the first Astronomer Royal in 1675.

Flanagan /'flænəgən/ Bud. Stage name of Robert Winthrop 1896–1968. British comedian, leader of the 'Crazy Gang' 1931–62. He played in variety theatre all over the world and, with his partner Chesney Allen, popularized such songs as 'Underneath the Arches'.

Flanders /'flɑːndəz/ a region of the Low Countries which in the 8th and 9th centuries extended from Calais to the Scheldt, and is now covered by the Belgian provinces of Oost Vlaanderen and West Vlaanderen (East and West Flanders), the French *département* of Nord, and part of the Dutch province of Zeeland. The language is Flemish. East Flanders, capital Ghent, has an area of 3,000 sq km/1,158 sq mi, and a population (1987) of 1,329,000. West Flanders, capital Bruges, has an area of 3,100 sq km/1,197 sq mi, and a population (1987) of 1,035,000.

flare, solar a brilliant eruption on the Sun above a ◊sunspot, thought to be caused by release of magnetic energy. Flares reach maximum brightness within a few minutes, then fade away over about an hour. They eject a burst of atomic particles into space at up to 1,000 km/600 mi per second. When these particles reach Earth they can cause radio blackouts, disruptions of the Earth's magnetic field, and ◊auroras.

flash point in physics, the temperature at which a liquid heated under standard conditions gives off sufficient vapour to ignite on the application of a small flame.

The *fire point* of the material is obtained by continuing the test and noting the temperature at

Flaubert French novelist Gustave Flaubert.

flea Electron microscope picture of a hedgehog flea infested by parasitic mites.

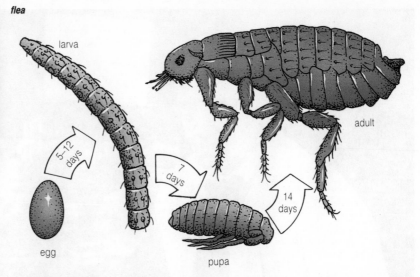

flea

larva

adult

5–12 days

7 days

14 days

egg

pupa

which full combustion occurs. For safe storage (of fuel, or oil) the flash and fire points must be high enough to reduce fire risks to a minimum, and such that no appreciable quantity of oils are driven off during exposure to the weather.

flat in music, a note or a key that is played lower in pitch than the written value, indicated by a flat sign or key signature. It can also refer to inaccurate intonation by a player.

flatfish bony fish of order Pleuronectiformes having a characteristically flat, asymmetrical body with both eyes (in adults) on the upper side. Species include turbot, halibut, plaice, sole, and flounder.

flatworm invertebrate of the phylum Platyhelminthes. Some are free-living, but many are parasitic (for example tapeworms and flukes). The body is simple and bilaterally symmetrical, with one opening to the intestine. Many are hermaphrodite (with male and female sex organs).

Four species of flatworm, introduced from New Zealand to Britain in the 1980s, have been found to be eating local earthworms after first excreting an enzyme that paralyses them.

Flaubert /ˈfləʊˈbeə/ Gustave 1821–1880. French novelist, author of *Madame Bovary* 1857. *Salammbô* 1862 earned him the Legion of Honour 1866, and was followed by *L'Education sentimentale/Sentimental Education* 1869, and *La Tentation de Saint Antoine/The Temptation of St Anthony* 1874. Flaubert also wrote the short stories *Trois contes/Three Tales* 1877.

He entered Paris literary circles 1840, but in 1846 retired to Rouen, where he remained for the rest of his life.

flax plant of the genus *Linum*, family Linaceae. The species *L. usitatissimum* is the cultivated strain; **linen** is produced from the fibre in its stems. The seeds yield **linseed oil**, used in paints and varnishes. The plant, of almost worldwide distribution, has a stem up to 60 cm/2 ft high, small leaves, and bright blue flowers.

The residue of the seeds is fed to cattle. The stems are retted (soaked) in water after harvesting, and then dried, rolled, and scutched (pounded), separating the fibre from the central core of woody tissue. The long fibres are spun into linen thread, twice as strong as cotton, yet more delicate, and especially suitable for lace; shorter fibres are used to make twine or paper.

Annual world production of flax fibre amounts to approximately 60,000 tonnes, with the USSR accounting for half of the total. Other producers are Belgium, the Netherlands, and N Ireland, where cultivation has recently been revived.

The New Zealand flax *Phormium tenax*, is unrelated to the true flax. It belongs to the Liliaceae, and is commercially grown for the fibre in its sword-shaped leaves which may be up 2 m/6 ft long.

Flaxman /ˈflæksmən/ John 1755–1826. English sculptor and illustrator in the Neo-Classical style. From 1775 he worked for the Wedgwood pottery as a designer. His public works include the monuments of Nelson 1808–10 in St Paul's Cathedral,

London, and of Burns and Kemble in Westminster Abbey.

Flaxman was born in York and studied at the Royal Academy in London. From 1787 to 1794 he was in Rome directing the Wedgwood studio there. Apart from designs for Wedgwood ware, he modelled friezes on classical subjects and produced relief portraits. In 1810 he became the first professor of sculpture at the Royal Academy.

flea black wingless insect, order Siphonaptera, with blood-sucking mouthparts. Fleas are parasitic on warm-blooded animals. Some fleas can jump 130 times their own height.

Species include *Pulex irritans*, which lives on humans; the rat flea *Xenopsylla cheopis*, the transmitter of plague and typhus; and (fostered by central heating) the cat and dog fleas *Ctenocephalides felis* and *canis*. Britain's largest flea *Histricopsylla talpae* lives on the mole and is about 8 mm/0.25 in long.

fleabane plant of the genera *Erigeron* or *Pulicaria*, family Compositae. Common fleabane *Pulicaria dysenterica* has golden-yellow flowerheads and grows in wet and marshy places.

Flecker /ˈflekə/ James Elroy 1884–1915. British poet. During a career in the consular service, he wrote several volumes of verse, including *The Bridge of Fire* 1907, *The Golden Journey to Samarkand* 1913, and *The Old Ships* 1915.

Fleet Street /ˈfliːt/ street in London, England (named after the subterranean river Fleet), traditionally the centre of British journalism. It runs

from Temple Bar eastwards to Ludgate Circus. With adjoining streets it contained the offices and printing works of many leading British newspapers until the mid-1980s, when most moved to sites farther from the centre of London.

Fleetwood /ˈfliːtwʊd/ port and seaside resort in Lancashire, England, at the mouth of the river Wyre; population (1981) 28,530. The fishing industry has declined, but the port still handles timber, petroleum, and chemicals. Ferry services operate to the Isle of Man and Belfast.

Fleming /ˈflemɪŋ/ Alexander 1881–1955. Scottish bacteriologist who discovered lysozyme (a nasal enzyme with antibacterial properties) 1922, and in 1928 the antibiotic drug ◊penicillin. With H W Florey and E B Chain, he won the Nobel Prize for Medicine 1945.

After a false start as a shipping clerk, Fleming retrained in medicine. Lysozyme was an early discovery. While studying this, he found an unusual mould growing on a neglected culture dish. He isolated and grew it in pure culture. However, its full value was not realized until Florey and Chain isolated the active ingredient, penicillin, and tested it clinically.

Fleming /ˈflemɪŋ/ Ian 1908–1964. English author of suspense novels featuring the ruthless, laconic James Bond, UK Secret Service agent No. 007.

Fleming /ˈflemɪŋ/ John Ambrose 1849–1945. English electrical physicist and engineer, who invented the thermionic valve 1904.

Fleming /ˈflemɪŋ/ Peter 1907–1971. British journalist and travel writer, remembered for his journeys up the Amazon and across the Gobi Desert recounted in *Brazilian Adventure* 1933 and *News from Tartary* 1941.

Fleming's rules memory aids for the directions of the magnetic field, current, and motion in an electric generator or motor, using one's fingers. The three directions are represented by the thumb (for motion), forefinger (for field) and second finger (current), all held at right angles to each other. The right hand is used for generators, such as a dynamo, and the left for motors. They were named after the English physicist John Fleming.

Flemish /ˈflemɪʃ/ a member of the W Germanic branch of the Indo-European language family, spoken in N Belgium and the Nord *département* of France. It is closely related to Dutch.

In opposition to the introduction of French as the official language in the Flemish provinces of Belgium after 1830 there arose a strong Flemish movement led by scholars like J F Willems (1793–1846) and writers such as H Conscience (1812–83) and, although equality of French and Flemish was not achieved until 1898, it brought about a cultural and political revival of Flemish. The Flemish movement was promoted

Fleming's rules

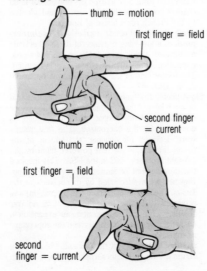

thumb = motion

first finger = field

second finger = current

thumb = motion

first finger = field

second finger = current

Fleming *Nobel-prizewinning Scottish bacteriologist Alexander Fleming discovered the antibiotic penicillin by chance in 1928, but had to wait 11 years until a method of producing the volatile drug had been perfected.*

for political reasons by the Germans in both world wars, and by the 1970s had become a threat to Belgian unity.

Flemish art the style of painting developed and practised in Flanders (a county in the Lowlands of NW Europe, largely coinciding with modern Belgium). A Flemish style emerged in the early 15th century. Paintings are distinguished by keen observation, minute attention to detail, bright colours, and superb technique—oil painting was a Flemish invention. Apart from portraits, they depict religious scenes, often placed in contemporary Flemish landscapes, townscapes, and interiors. Flemish sculpture shows German and French influence.

15th century Jan van Eyck made Bruges the first centre of Flemish art; other schools arose in Tournai, Ghent, and Louvain. The great names of the early period were Rogier van der Weyden, Dierick Bouts, Hugo van der Goes, Hans Memling, and Gerard David.

16th century Italian influences were strongly felt, and the centre shifted to Antwerp, where Quentin Massys worked. Hieronymus Bosch painted creatures of his own wild imagination, but the pictures of Pieter Brueghel are realistic reflections of Flemish life.

17th century Peter Paul Rubens and his school created a new powerful style, which was continued by van Dyck and others. Teniers and many minor artists continued the tradition of genre painting.

Flemish literature literature in Flemish, in its written form the same as Dutch (see ◊Flemish), was stimulated by the declaration, following the revolution of 1830–39, that French was the only official language in Belgium (it remained so until 1898). J F Willems (1793–1846) brought out a magazine that revived medieval Flemish works; H Conscience (1812–83) and J T van Ryswyck (1811–49) published novels in Flemish; K L Ledeganck (1805–47), Prudens van Duyse

(1804–59), and Jan de Beers (1821–88) wrote poetry. Later writers include Albrecht Rodenbach (1856–80), Pol de Mont (1857–1931), and Cyriel Buysse (1859–1932).

Flensburg /ˈflensbɜːg/ port on the E coast of Schleswig-Holstein, West Germany, with shipyards and breweries; population (1984) 86,700.

Fletcher /ˈfletʃə/ John 1579–1625. English dramatist. He collaborated with ◊Beaumont, producing, most notably, *Philaster* 1609 and *The Maid's Tragedy* 1610–11. He is alleged to have collaborated with Shakespeare on *The Two Noble Kinsmen* and *Henry VIII* in 1612.

Among plays credited to Fletcher alone are the pastoral drama *The Faithful Shepherdess* 1610 and the tragedy *Bonduca* about 1614.

fleur-de-lis (French 'flower of the lily') heraldic device in the form of a stylized iris flower, borne on coats of arms since the 12th century and adopted by the French royal house of Bourbon.

Flevoland /ˈfleɪvəʊlænd/ formerly *IJsselmeerpolders* a low-lying province of the Netherlands established 1986; area 1,410 sq km/544 sq mi; population (1988) 194,000. Chief town is Dronten. The polder land of the Ijsselmeer was reclaimed during 1950–57.

flight people first took to the air in ◊balloons and began powered flight in ◊airships, but the history of flying, both for civilian and military use, is dominated by the ◊aeroplane. The first planes were designed for ◊gliding; the advent of the petrol engine saw the first powered flight by the ◊Wright brothers 1903 in the USA. This inspired the development of aircraft throughout Europe. Biplanes were succeeded by monoplanes in the 1930s. The first jet plane (see ◊jet propulsion) was produced 1939, and after the end of World War II jetliners brought about continuous expansion in passenger air travel. In 1969 came the supersonic aircraft ◊Concorde.

history In Europe, at the beginning of the 20th century, France led in aeroplane design (Voisin

brothers) and Louis Blériot brought aviation much publicity by crossing the Channel 1909, as did the Reims air races of that year. The first powered flight in the UK was made by S F Cody 1908. In 1912 Sopwith and Bristol both built small biplanes. The first big twin-engined aeroplane was the Handley Page bomber 1917.

The stimulus of World War I (1914–18) and rapid development of the petrol engine led to increased power, and speeds rose to 320 kph/200 mph. Streamlining the body of planes became imperative: the body, wings, and exposed parts were reshaped to reduce drag. Eventually the biplane was superseded by the internally braced monoplane structure, for example, the Hawker Hurricane and Supermarine Spitfire fighters and Avro Lancaster and Boeing Flying Fortress bombers of World War II (1939–45).

jet aircraft The German Heinkel 178, built 1939, was the first jet plane, driven, not as all planes before it by a ◊propeller, but by a jet of hot gases. The first British jet aircraft, the Gloster E.28/39, flew from Cranwell, Lincolnshire, on 15 May 1941, powered by a jet engine invented by Frank Whittle. Twinjet Meteor fighters were in use by the end of the war. The rapid development of the jet plane led to enormous increases in power and speed until air-compressibility effects were felt near the speed of sound, which at first seemed to be a flight speed limit (the sound barrier). To attain ◊supersonic speed, streaming the aircraft body became insufficient: wings were swept back, engines buried in wings and tail units, and bodies were even eliminated in all-wing delta designs.

In the 1950s the first jet airliners, such as the Comet, were introduced into service. Today jet planes dominate both military and civilian aviation, although many light planes still use piston engines and propellers. The late 1960s saw the introduction of the ◊jumbo jet, and in 1976 the

Flight

1783	First human flight, by Jean F Pilâtre de Rozier and the Marquis d'Arlandes, in Paris, using a hot-air balloon made by Joseph and Etienne Montgolfier; first ascent in a hydrogen-filled balloon by Jacques Charles and M N Robert in Paris.
1785	Jean-Pierre Blanchard and John J Jeffries made the first balloon crossing of the English Channel.
1804	George Cayley flew the first true aeroplane, a model glider 1.5 m/5 ft long.
1852	Henri Giffard flew the first steam-powered airship over Paris.
1891–96	Otto Lilienthal piloted a glider in flight.
1903	First powered and controlled flight of a heavier-than-air machine by Orville Wright, at Kitty Hawk, North Carolina, USA.
1909	Louis Bleriot flew across the English Channel in 36 minutes.
1919	First flight across the Atlantic by Albert C Read, using a flying boat; first non-stop flight across the Atlantic by John William Alcock and Arthur Whitten Brown in 16 hours 27 minutes; first complete flight from Britain to Australia by Ross Smith and Keith Smith.
1923	Juan de la Cieva flew the first autogyro with a rotating wing.
1927	Charles Lindberg made the first solo, non-stop flight across the Atlantic.
1928	First trans-Pacific flight, from San Francisco to Brisbane, by Charles Kinsford Smith and C T P Ulm.
1930	Frank Whittle patented the jet engine; Amy Johnson became the first woman to fly solo from England to Australia.
1937	The first fully pressurized aircraft, the Lockheed XC-35, came into service.
1939	Erich Warsitz flew the first jet aeroplane, in Germany; Igor Sikorsky designed the first modern helicopter, with a large main rotor and a smaller tail rotor.
1947	A rocket-powered plane, the Bell X-1, was the first aircraft to fly faster than the speed of sound.
1949	The de Havilland Comet, the first jet airliner, entered service; James Gallagher made the first non-stop round-the-world flight, in a Boeing Superfortress.
1953	The first vertical take-off aircraft, the Rolls Royce 'Flying Bedstead', was tested.
1968	The world's first supersonic airliner, the Russian TU-144, flew for the first time.
1970	The Boeing 747 jumbo jet entered service, carrying 500 passengers.
1976	A Lockheed SR-17A, piloted by Eldon W Joersz and George T Morgan, set the world air speed record of 3,529.56 kmh/ 2,193.167 mph over Beale Air Force Base, California, USA.
1979	First crossing of the English Channel by a human-powered aircraft, *Gossamer Albatross*, piloted by Bryan Allen.
1981	The solar-powered Solar Challenger flew across the English Channel, from Paris to Kent, taking 5 hours for the 262 km/162.8 mi journey.
1986	Dick Rutan and Jeana Yeager made the first non-stop flight around the world without refuelling, piloting Voyager, which completed the flight in 9 days 3 minutes 44 seconds.
1987	Richard Branson made the first trans-Atlantic crossing by hot-air balloon.
1988	*Daedelus*, a human-powered craft piloted by Kanellos Kanellopoulos, flew 118 km/74 mi across the Aegean Sea.

Anglo-French Concorde, which makes a transatlantic crossing in under three hours, came into commercial service.

other developments During the 1950s and 1960s research was done on V/STOL (vertical and/or short take-off) aircraft. The British Harrier jet fighter has been the only VTOL aircraft to achieve commercial success, but STOL technology has fed into subsequent generations of aircraft. The 1960s and 1970s also saw the development of variable geometry ('swing-wing') aircraft, whose wings can be swept back in flight to achieve higher speeds. In the 1980s much progress has been made in 'fly-by-wire' aircraft with computer-aided controls.

International partnerships have developed both civilian and military aircraft. The Panavia Tornado is a joint project of British, West German, and Italian aircraft companies. It is an advanced swing-wing craft of multiple roles—interception, strike, ground support, and reconnaissance. The Airbus is a wide-bodied airliner built jointly by companies from France, West Germany, the UK, the Netherlands, and Spain.

Flinders /ˈflɪndəz/ Matthew 1774–1814. English navigator who explored the Australian coasts 1795–99 and 1801–03.

Named after him are Flinders Island, NE of Tasmania, Australia; the Flinders Range in S Australia; and Flinders River in Queensland, Australia.

Flint /flɪnt/ city in Michigan, USA, on the Flint river, 90 km/56 mi NW of Detroit. The manufacture of cars is the chief industry; population (1980) 522,000.

flint a compact, hard, brittle mineral (a variety of chert), brown, black, or grey in colour, found in nodules in limestone or shale deposits. It consists of fine-grained silica, SiO_2, in cryptocrystalline form (usually ◊quartz). Flint implements were widely used in prehistory.

When chipped, the flint nodules show a shell-like fracture and a sharp cutting edge. The earliest flint implements, belonging to Palaeolithic cultures and made by striking one flint against another, are simple, while those of the Neolithic are expertly chipped and formed, and are often ground or polished. The best flint, used for Neolithic tools, is *floorstone*, a shiny black flint that occurs deep within the chalk.

Because of their hardness (7 on the ◊Mohs' scale), flint splinters are used for abrasive purposes and, when ground into powder, added to clay during pottery manufacture. Flints have been used for making fire by striking the flint against

Flinders *English navigator and explorer Captain Matthew Flinders.*

steel, which produces a spark, and for discharging guns. Flints in cigarette lighters are made from cerium alloy.

Flints commonly occur in the ◊chalk downlands of southern England and were often used as building material.

Flint /flɪnt/ William Russell 1880–1970. Scottish artist, president of the Royal Society of Painters in Water Colours 1936–56.

Flintshire /ˈflɪntʃə/ former county of Wales, and smallest of the Welsh counties. It was merged in 1974, with Denbigh and part of Merioneth, into the new county of Clwyd; the county town of Mold became the administrative headquarters of the new region.

floating-point notation system of representing numbers as decimal fractions muliplied by ten raised to some power. For example, the number 97.8 expressed in floating-point form is 0.978×10^2 and the number 0.00978 in floating-point form is 0.978×10^{-2}. The forms 97.8 and 0.978 are known as ◊fixed-point notation.

In a computer, the numbers are represented by pairs (.978, +2) and (.978, –2) respectively. The first number of the pair is called the mantissa and the second the exponent. The definition applies equally to numbers expressed to a different base (for example, binary fractions muliplied by two raised to some power).

The advantage of floating-point notation is that very large and very small numbers can be expressed with a few digits. Thus (.978, +18) written out in full would require 18 digits (978 followed by 15 zeros).

Flodden, Battle of /ˈflɒdn/ the defeat of the Scots by the English under the Earl of Surrey 9 Sept 1513 on a site 5 km/3 mi SE of Coldstream, Northumberland, England; many Scots, including King James IV, were killed.

Flood, the in the Old Testament or Hebrew Bible and the Koran, disaster alleged to have obliterated all humanity except a chosen few (the family of ◊Noah).

The story may represent memories of a major local flood, for example, excavations at Ur in modern Iraq revealed 2.5 m/8 ft of water-laid clay dating before 4000 BC, over an area of about 645 km/400 mi by 160 km/100 mi.

floppy disc in computing, a storage device consisting of a light, flexible disc enclosed in a cardboard or plastic jacket. The disc is placed in a disc drive, where it rotates at high speed. Data are recorded magnetically on one or both surfaces.

The floppy disc was invented by IBM 1971 as a means of loading programs into the computer. They were originally 20 cm/8 in in diameter and typically held about 240 ◊kilobytes of data. Present-day floppy discs, widely used on ◊microcomputers, are usually either 13.13 cm/5.25 in or 8.8 cm/3.5 in in diameter, and generally hold between 180 kilobytes and 1.4 ◊megabytes, depending on the disc size, recording method, and whether one or both sides are used.

Flora in Roman mythology, goddess of flowers, youth, and of spring. Festivals were held in her name.

floral diagram a diagram showing the arrangement and number of parts in a flower, drawn in cross-section. An ovary is drawn in the centre, surrounded by representations of the other floral parts, indicating the position of each at its base. If any parts such as the petals or sepals are fused, this is also indicated. Floral diagrams allow the structure of different flowers to be compared, and are usually presented with the floral formula.

floral formula a symbolic representation of the structure of a flower. Each kind of floral part is represented by a letter (K for calyx, C for corolla, P for perianth, A for androecium, G for gynoecium), and a number to indicate the quantity of the part present, for example, C5 for a flower with five petals. The number is in brackets if the parts are fused. If the parts are arranged in

Florence *The cathedral of Santa Maria del Fiore 1314, Florence. The spectacular dome was constructed by Filippo Brunelleschi in the 1430s.*

distinct whorls within the flower, this is shown by two separate figures, such as A5 + 5, indicating two whorls of five stamens each.

Florence /ˈflɒrəns/ (Italian *Firenze*) capital of ◊Tuscany, N Italy, 88 km/55 mi from the mouth of the river Arno; population (1988) 421,000. It has printing, engineering, and optical industries, many crafts, including leather, gold and silver work, and embroidery, and its art and architecture attract large numbers of tourists.

The Roman town of Florentia was founded in the 1st century BC on the site of the Etruscan town of Faesulae. It was besieged by the Goths AD 405, and visited by Charlemagne 786.

In 1052, Florence passed to Countess Matilda of Tuscany (1046–1115), and from the 11th century onwards gained increasing autonomy. In 1198, it became an independent republic, with new city walls, and governed by a body of 12 citizens. In the 13th–14th centuries, the city was the centre of the struggle between the ◊Guelphs

floral diagram

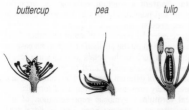

buttercup   pea   tulip

(papal supporters), and Ghibellines (supporters of the Holy Roman emperor). Despite this, Florence became immensely prosperous, and went on to reach its cultural peak during the 14th–16th centuries.

From the 15th to the 18th century, the ◊Medici family, originally bankers, were the predominant power, in spite of their having been twice expelled by revolutions. In the first of these, in 1493, a year after Lorenzo de' Medici's death, a republic was proclaimed (with ◊Machiavelli as secretary) which lasted until 1512. From 1494–98, the city was under the control of ◊Savonarola. In 1527, the Medicis again proclaimed a republic, which was to last though many years of gradual decline until 1737 when the city passed to Maria Theresa of Austria. From 1737, the city was ruled by the Habsburg imperial dynasty.

Notable Medieval and Renaissance citizens included the writers Dante and Boccaccio, and the artists Giotto, Leonardo da Vinci, and Michelangelo.

Firenze's architectural treasures include the Ponte Vecchio, 1345; the Pitti and Vecchio palaces; the churches of Santa Croce and Santa Maria Novella; the cathedral of Santa Maria del Fiore, 1314; and the Uffizi Gallery, which has one of Europe's finest art collections, based on that of the Medici. The city was badly damaged in World War II, and by floods 1966.

floret a small flower usually making up part of a larger, composite flowerhead. There are often two different types present on one flower head: disc florets in the central area, and ray florets around the edge which usually have a single petal known as the ligule. In the common daisy, for example, the disc florets are yellow, while the ligules are white.

Florey /ˈflɔːri/ Howard Walter, Baron Florey 1898–1968. Australian pathologist whose research into lysozyme, an antibacterial enzyme discovered by ◊Fleming, led him to study penicillin, which he and ◊Chain isolated and prepared for widespread use. With Fleming, they were awarded the Nobel Prize for Physiology or Medicine 1945.

Florianópolis /ˌflɔriəˈnɒpəlɪs/ seaport and resort on Santa Caterina Island, Brazil; population (1980) 153,500. It is linked to the mainland by two bridges, one of which is the largest expansion bridge in Brazil.

Florida /ˈflɒrɪdə/ most southeasterly state of the USA; mainly a peninsula jutting into the Atlantic,

which it separates from the Gulf of Mexico; nickname Sunshine State
area 152,000 sq km/58,672 sq mi
capital Tallahassee
towns Miami, Tampa, Jacksonville
physical 50% forested; lakes (including Okeechobee 1,800 sq km/695 sq mi); Everglades National Park (5,000 sq km/1,930 sq mi, with birdlife, cypresses, alligators)
features Palm Beach, an island resort between the lagoon of Lake Worth and the Atlantic; Florida Keys; John F Kennedy Space Center at Cape Canaveral; Disney World theme park
products citrus fruit, melons, vegetables, fish, shellfish, phosphates (one third of world supply), chemicals, uranium (largest US producer), space research
population (1989) 13,000,000; the fastest-growing state
history under Spanish rule from 1513 until its cession to England 1763, Florida was returned to Spain 1783, and purchased by the USA 1819, becoming a state 1845. It is a centre for drug trade in Latin America.

Florida Keys /ˈflɒrɪdə/ series of small coral islands which curve over 240 km/150 mi SW from the southern tip of Florida. The most important are Key Largo and Key West (with a US naval and air station); they depend on fishing and tourism.

florin coin; many European countries have had coins of this name. The first florin was of gold, minted in Florence in 1252. The obverse bore the image of a lily, which led to the coin being called *fiorino* (from Italian *fiore*, flower). The British florin of two shillings was first struck 1849, initially of silver, and continued in use after decimalization as the equivalent of 10p.

Florio /ˈflɔːriəʊ/ Giovanni c.1553–1625. English translator, born in London, the son of Italian refugees. He is best known for his translation of ◊Montaigne 1603.

flotation process a common method of mineral dressing (preparing ores for subsequent processing), making use of the different wetting properties of various ores. In the process the ore is finely ground and then mixed with water and a specially selected wetting agent. Air is bubbled through the mixture, forming a froth, the desired ore particles attach themselves to the bubbles and are skimmed off, while unwanted dirt or other ores remain behind.

Flotow /ˈfləʊtəʊ/ Friedrich (Adolf Ferdinand), Freiherr von 1812–1883. German composer who wrote 18 operas, including *Martha* 1847.

flotsam, jetsam, and lagan *flotsam* goods found floating at sea after a shipwreck; *jetsam* those thrown overboard to lighten a sinking vessel; *lagan* those on the sea bottom, or secured to a buoy.

flounder small flatfish *Platichthys flesus* of the NE Atlantic and Mediterranean, although it sometimes lives in estuaries. It is dully coloured, and grows to 50 cm/1.6 ft.

flow chart a diagram, often used in computing, to show the possible paths through a program. Different symbols are used to indicate processing, decision-making, input, and output. These are connected by arrows showing the flow of control through the program, that is, the paths

flowchart

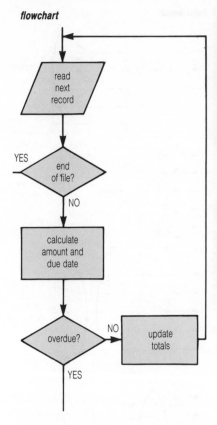

the computer can take when executing the program. It is a way of visually representing an ◊algorithm.

flower the reproductive unit of an ◊angiosperm or flowering plant, typically consisting of four whorls of modified leaves: the sepals, petals, stamens, and carpels. These are borne on a central axis or ◊receptacle. The many variations in size, colour, number and arrangement of parts are usually closely related to the method of pollination. Flowers adapted for wind-pollination typically have reduced or absent petals and sepals, and long, feathery stigmas which hang outside the flower to trap airborne pollen. In contrast, the petals of insect-pollinated flowers are usually conspicuous and brightly coloured.

The sepals and petals are collectively known as the *calyx* and *corolla* respectively and together comprise the perianth with the function of protecting the reproductive organs and attracting pollinators. The *stamens* lie within the corolla, each having a slender stalk, or filament, bearing the pollen-containing anther at the top. Collectively they are known as the *androecium*. The inner whorl of the flower comprises the *carpels*, each usually consisting of an ◊ovary in which are

flower

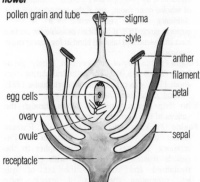

pollen grain and tube — stigma
— style
— anther
— filament
— petal
egg cells —
ovary —
ovule — — sepal
receptacle —

fluke Microscope view of adult intestinal blood flukes *Schistosoma mansoni*. The flukes (male thick and bluish, females white and threadlike) normally live in pairs in blood vessels of the intestine, causing dysentery and diarrhoea.

borne the ◊ovules, and a stigma borne at the top of a slender stalk, or style. Collectively the carpels are known as the *gynoecium*.

In size, flowers range from the tiny blooms of duckweeds scarcely visible with the naked eye to the gigantic flowers of the Malaysian *Rafflesia* which can reach over 1 m/3 ft across. Flowers may either be borne singly or grouped together in ◊inflorescences. The stalk of the whole inflorescence is termed a peduncle, and the stalk of an individual flower is termed a pedicel. A flower may contain both male and female reproductive organs, termed ◊hermaphrodite, or male and female organs may be carried in separate flowers, termed ◊monoecious if on the same plant and ◊dioecious when on separate plants.

flowering plant a term generally used for the ◊angiosperms, which bear flowers with various parts, including sepals, petals, stamens and carpels. Sometimes the term is used more broadly, to include both angiosperms and ◊gymnosperms, in which case the ◊cones of conifers and cycads may be referred to as 'flowers'. Usually, however, the angiosperms and gymnosperms are referred to collectively as ◊seed plants, or spermatophytes.

flower power a youth movement of the 1960s; see ◊hippie.

Flowers of Evil French *Les Fleurs du mal* a collection of poems by Baudelaire, published in France 1857, which deal with the conflict between good and evil. The work was condemned by the censor as endangering public morals, but paved the way for Rimbaud, Verlaine, and the Symbolist school.

Fludd /flʌd/ Robert 1574–1637. British physician who attempted to present a comprehensive account of the universe based on Hermetic principles (see ◊Hermes Trismegistus), *The History of the Macrocosm and the Microcosm* 1617.

flugelhorn an alto brass instrument, similar in appearance to the ◊cornet.

fluid a liquid or gas, in which the molecules are relatively mobile and can 'flow'.

fluid, supercritical fluid brought by a combination of heat and pressure to the point at which, as a near vapour, it combines the properties of a gas and a liquid. Supercritical fluids are used as solvents in chemical processes, such as the extraction of lubricating oil from refinery residues or the decaffeination of coffee, because they avoid the

energy-expensive need for phase changes (from liquid to gas and back again) required in conventional distillation processes.

fluke parasitic flatworm such as *Fasciola hepatica* that causes rot and dropsy of the liver in sheep, cattle, horses, dogs, and humans. Only the adult encysted stage of its life history is passed within the body, after ingestion by the host. The cyst dissolves in the stomach and the young fluke passes to the liver.

fluorescence in scientific usage, very short-lived ◊luminescence (glow not caused by high temperature). Generally, the term is often used for any luminescence regardless of the persistence. See ◊phosphorescence.

fluoride salt of hydrofluoric acid. Fluorides occur naturally in all water to a differing extent. Experiments in Britain, the USA, and elsewhere have indicated that a concentration of fluoride of 1 part per million in tap water retards the decay of teeth in children by more than 50%.

The recommended policy in Britain is to add sodium fluoride to the water to bring it up to the required amount, but implementation is up to each local authority.

fluorine chemical element, symbol F, atomic number 9, relative atomic mass 19. It occurs naturally as the minerals fluorspar (CaF_2) and cryolite (Na_3ALF_6), and is the first member of the halogen group of elements. At ordinary temperatures it is a pale yellow, highly poisonous, and reactive gas, and it unites directly with nearly all the elements. Hydrogen fluoride is used in etching glass, and the freons, which all contain fluorine, are widely used as refrigerants.

Fluorine was discovered by the Swedish chemist Carl Wilhelm Scheele (1742–86) in 1771 and isolated by the French chemist Henri Moissan (1852–1907) in 1886. Combined with uranium as UF_6, it is used in the separation of uranium isotopes.

fluorite a glassy, brittle mineral, calcium fluoride CaF_2, forming cubes and octahedra; colourless when pure, otherwise violet.

Fluorite is used as a flux in iron and steel making; colourless fluorite is used in the manufacture of microscope lenses. It is also used for the glaze on pottery, and as a source of fluorine in the manufacture of hydrofluoric acid.

Deposits of fluorite occur in the N and S Pennines; the *blue john* from Derbyshire is a banded variety used as a decorative stone.

fluorocarbon compound formed by replacing the hydrogen atoms of a hydrocarbon with fluorine. Fluorocarbons are used as inert coatings, refrigerants, synthetic resins, and as propellants in aerosols.

There is concern because their release into the atmosphere depletes the ◊ozone layer, allowing more ultraviolet light from the Sun to penetrate the Earth's atmosphere, increasing the incidence of skin cancer.

Flushing /ˈflʌʃɪŋ/ port (Dutch *Vlissingen*) on Walcheren Island, Zeeland, Netherlands; population (1987) 44,900. It stands at the entrance to the Scheldt estuary, one of the principal sea routes into Europe. Industries include fishing, shipbuilding, and petrochemicals, and there is a ferry service to Harwich. Admiral de Ruyter was born at Flushing and is commemorated in the Jacobskerk.

Flushing Meadow lawn-tennis centre in the USA, officially the national tennis centre. It is situated in the Queens district, New York, and replaced the West Side Club as the home of the US Open championships in 1978. The main court is the Stadium Court, one of the largest in the world.

flute a member of a group of ◊woodwind musical instruments (although usually made of metal), including the piccolo, the concert flute, and the bass or alto flute. Flutes are cylindrical in shape, with a narrowed end, containing a shaped aperture, across which the player blows. The air vibrations produce the note, which can be altered by placing fingers over lateral holes. Certain keys can be depressed to extend the range of the flute to three octaves.

The orchestral flute is at concert pitch—middle C to C sharp three octaves higher. The alto (sometimes known as the 'bass') flute has a range the same as that of the concert flute, but a fourth lower. The 'Bass Flute in B Flat' is usually only played in fife and drum bands.

flux in smelting, a substance that combines with the unwanted components of the ore to produce a fusible slag, which can be separated from the molten metal. For example, the mineral fluorite, CaF_2, is used as a flux in iron smelting; it has a low melting point and will form a fusible mixture with substances of higher melting point such as silicates and oxides.

flux in soldering, a substance that improves the bonding properties of solder by removing contamination form metal surfaces and preventing their oxidation, and by reducing the surface tension of the molten solder alloy. For example, with solder made of lead-tin alloys, the flux may be resin, borax, or zinc chloride.

fly any insect of the order Diptera. A fly has one pair of wings, antennae, and compound eyes; the hindwings have become modified into knoblike projections (halteres) used to maintain equilibrium in flight. There are over 90,000 species.

The mouth-parts project from the head as a proboscis used for sucking fluids, modified in some species to pierce a victim's skin and suck blood. Discs at the end of hairs on their feet secrete a fluid enabling them to walk up walls and across ceilings. Flies undergo complete metamorphosis; their larvae (maggots) are without true legs, and the pupae are rarely enclosed in a cocoon. The sexes are similar, coloration rarely vivid, though some are metallic green or blue. The fruitfly, *Drosophila*, is much used in genetic experiments as it is easy to keep, fast-breeding, and has easily visible chromosomes.

flying dragon lizard *Draco volans* of SE Asia, which can glide on flaps of skin spread and supported by its ribs. This small (7.5 cm/3 in head and body) arboreal lizard can glide between trees for 6 m/20 ft or more.

flying fish Atlantic fish *Exocoetus volitans*, family Exocoetidae, of order Beloniformes, which can glide for 100 m/325 ft over the surface of the sea on its expanded pectoral fins.

flying fox ◊bat of the order Megachiroptera.

flying lemur commonly used, but incorrect, name for ◊colugo. It cannot fly, and it is not a lemur.

flying lizard another name for ◊flying dragon.

flying squirrel any of many species of squirrel, not necessarily closely related. It is characterized by a membrane along the side of the body from forelimb to hindlimb, in some species running to neck

Flynn *Australian film actor Erroll Flynn with Olivia de Havilland in* The Charge of the Light Brigade *1936.*

and tail too, which allows it to glide through the air. Flying squirrels are found in the Old and New World, but most species are E Asian. The giant flying squirrel *Petaurista* grows up to 1.1 m/3.5 ft including tail, and can glide 65 m/210 ft.

Flynn /flɪn/ Errol 1909–1959. Australian actor. He is renowned for his portrayal of swashbuckling heroes in such films as *Captain Blood* 1935, *The Sea Hawk* 1940, and *The Master of Ballantrae* 1953.

Flynn /flɪn/ John 1880–1951. Australian missionary. Inspired by the use of aircraft to transport the wounded of World War I, he instituted in 1928 the *flying doctor* service in Australia, which can be summoned to the outback by radios in individual homesteads.

flywheel a heavy wheel in an engine that helps keep it running and smooths its motion. The ◊crankshaft in a petrol engine has a flywheel at one end, which keeps the crankshaft turning in between the intermittent power strokes of the pistons. It also comes into contact with the ◊clutch, serving as the connection between the engine and the car's transmission system.

FM in physics, the abbreviation for *frequency modulation*. Used in radio, FM is constant in amplitude and varies the frequency of the carrier wave. Its advantage over AM is its better signal-to-noise ratio.

FNLA abbreviation for *Front National de Libération de l'Angola* (French 'National Front for the Liberation of Angola').

f **number** measure of the relative aperture of a telescope or camera lens, which indicates the light-gathering power of the lens. In photography, each successive *f* number represents a halving of exposure speed.

FO abbreviation for *Foreign Office*, British government department (see ◊foreign relations).

Fo /fəʊ/ Dario 1926– . Italian playwright. His plays are predominantly political satires combining black humour with slapstick. They include *Morte accidentale di un anarchico/Accidental Death of an Anarchist* 1970, and *Non si paga non si paga/Can't Pay? Won't Pay!* 1975/1981.

fob abbreviation for *free-on-board*, used in commerce to describe a valuation of goods at point of embarkation, excluding transport and insurance costs. Export values are usually expressed fob for customs and excise purposes, while imports are usually valued ◊cif.

focal length the distance from the centre of a spherical mirror or lens to the focal point. For a concave mirror or convex lens, it is the distance at which parallel rays of light are brought to a focus to form a real image (for a mirror, this is half the radius of curvature). For a convex mirror or concave lens, it is the distance from the centre to the point at which a virtual image (an image produced by diverging rays of light) is formed.

With lenses, the greater the power (measured in dioptres) of the lens the shorter its focal length.

Foch /fɒʃ/ Ferdinand 1851–1929. Marshal of France during World War I. He was largely responsible for the first Allied victory of the ◊Marne, and commanded on the NW front Oct 1914–Sep 1916. He was appointed commander in chief of the Allied armies in the spring of 1918, and launched the Allied counter-offensive in July that brought about the negotiation of an armistice to end the war.

foetus alternativce spelling of ◊fetus, a mammalian embryo.

fog cloud that collects at the surface of the Earth, composed of water vapour that has condensed on particles of dust in the atmosphere. Cloud and fog are both caused by the air temperature falling below ◊dew point. The thickness of fog depends on the number of water particles it contains. Usually, fog is formed by the meeting of two currents of air, one cooler than the other, or by warm air flowing over a cold surface. Sea fogs commonly occur where warm

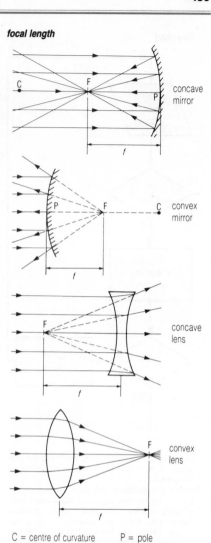

concave mirror

convex mirror

concave lens

convex lens

C = centre of curvature   P = pole
F = focus   *f* = focal length

and cold currents meet and the air above them mixes.

Fog frequently forms on calm nights as the land surface cools more rapidly than the air immediately above it. In drought areas, for example, Baja California, Canary Islands, Cape Verde islands, Namib Desert, Peru, and Chile, coastal fogs enable plant and animal life to survive without rain and are a potential source of water for human use (by means of water collectors exploiting the effect of condensation).

Officially, fog refers to a condition when visibility is reduced to 1 km/0.62 mi or less, and mist or haze to that giving a visibility of 1–2 km. A mist is produced by condensed water particles, and a haze by smoke or dust. Industrial areas uncontrolled by pollution laws have a continual haze of smoke over them, and if the temperature falls suddenly, a dense yellow smog forms. At some airports since 1975 it has been possible for certain aircraft to land and take off blind in fog, using radar navigation.

Foggia /'fɒdʒə/ city of Puglia region, S Italy; population (1988) 159,000. The cathedral, dating from about 1170, was rebuilt after an earthquake 1731. Natural gas is found nearby.

föhn /fɜːn/ warm wind that blows through the valleys of the European Alps.

Fokine /'fɔːkiːn/ Mikhail 1880–1942. Russian dancer and choreographer, born in St Petersburg. He was chief choreographer to the *Ballets Russes* 1909–14, and with ◊Diaghilev revitalized and reformed the art of ballet, promoting the idea of artistic unity

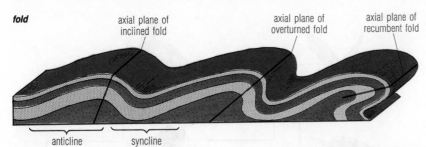

fold

axial plane of inclined fold

axial plane of overturned fold

axial plane of recumbent fold

anticline   syncline

among dramatic, musical, and stylistic elements.

His creations for Diaghilev include *Les Sylphides* 1907, *Carnival* 1910, *The Firebird* 1910, *Le Spectre de la Rose* 1911, and *Petrushka* 1911.

fold in geology, a bend in rock ◊beds. If the bend is arched up in the middle it is called an *anticline*; if it sags downwards in the middle it is called a *syncline*.

folic acid a ◊vitamin of the B-complex. It is found in liver and green leafy vegetables, and is also synthesized by the intestinal bacteria. It is essential for growth, and plays many other roles in the body. Lack of folic acid causes anaemia.

Folies-Bergère /ˈfɒli beəˈʒeə/ music hall in Paris, France, built 1869, named after its original proprietor and featuring lavish productions and striptease acts.

folk dance a dance characteristic of a particular people, nation, or region. Many European folk dances are derived from the dances accompanying the customs and ceremonies of pre-Christian times. Some later became ballroom dances (for example, the minuet and waltz). Once an important part of many rituals, folk dance has tended to die out in industrialized countries. Examples of folk dance are Morris dance, farandole, and jota.

The preservation of folk dance in England was promoted by the work of Cecil ◊Sharp.

Folkestone /ˈfəʊkstən/ port and holiday resort on the SE coast of Kent, England, 10 km/6 mi SW of Dover; population (1983) 44,200. There are ferry and hovercraft services to and from Boulogne. It is the birthplace of the physician William Henry.

folklore the oral traditions and culture of a people, expressed in riddles, songs, tales, legends, and proverbs. The term was coined 1846 by W J Thoms (1803–85), but the founder of the systematic study of the subject was Jacob ◊Grimm; see also ◊oral literature.

The approach to folklore has varied greatly: the German scholar Max Müller (1823–1900) interpreted it as evidence of nature myths; J G ◊Frazer was the exponent of the comparative study of early and popular folklore as mutually explanatory; Laurence Gomme (1853–1916) adopted a historical analysis; and Bronislaw ◊Malinowski and Alfred Radcliffe-Brown (1881–1955) examined the material as an integral element in a living culture.

folk music body of traditional music, originally transmitted orally. Many folk songs originated as a rhythmic accompaniment to manual work or to mark a specific ritual. Folk song is usually melodic, not harmonic, and the modes used are distinctive of the country of origin. See ◊roots music.

The interest in ballad poetry in the later 18th century led to the discovery of a rich body of folk song in Europe. The multiethnic background of the US has brought forth a wealth of material derived from European, African, and Latin American sources. A revival of interest in folk music began in the US in the 1950s led by the researcher Alan Lomax (1915–) and the singers Henry Belafonte (1927–), Odetta (1930–), Pete Seeger, Woody Guthrie, and Joan Baez, who wrote new material in folk-song style, dealing with contemporary topics such as nuclear weapons and racial prejudice.

In England the late 19th century saw a development in the transcribing and preserving of folk

tunes by people such as the Rev Sabine Baring-Gould and Cecil ◊Sharp. The Folk Song Society was founded 1898 and became the English Folk Dance and Song Society 1911; they censored much of the material. The folk revival of the 1980s was furthered by the virtuoso rock guitarist Richard Thompson (1949–) and groups like the Pogues (1983–), and there was growing interest in roots, or world, music, encompassing traditional as well as modern music from many cultures.

follicle in botany, a dry, usually many-seeded fruit that splits along one side only to release the seeds within. It is derived from a single ◊carpel and examples include the fruits of the *Delphinium* and columbine *Aquilegia*. It differs from a pod, which always splits open (dehisces) along both sides.

follicle in zoology, a small group of cells that surround and nourish a structure such as a hair (hair follicle) or a cell such as an egg (Graafian follicle; see ◊menstrual cycle).

follicle-stimulating hormone (FSH) a ◊hormone produced by the pituitary gland. It affects the ovaries in women, triggering off the production of an egg cell. Luteinizing hormone is needed to complete the process. In men, FSH stimulates the testes to produce sperm.

Folsom /ˈfɒlsəm/ site in New Mexico, USA, where in 1926 a flint weapon point was found embedded among the bones of an extinct type of bison, proving that human beings had existed in the Americas in the Pleistocene period.

Fomalhaut brightest star in the southern constellation Pisces Austrinus, and the 18th-brightest star in the sky; known as 'the Solitary One' because it lies in a rather barren region of sky. It is a dwarf star 23 light years away, with a true luminosity 14 times that of the Sun. Fomalhaut is one of a number of stars around which the Infra-Red Astronomy Satellite (see ◊infrared astronomy) detected excess infrared radiation, presumably from a region of solid particles around the star. This material may be a planetary system in the process of formation.

Fonda /ˈfɒndə/ Henry 1905–1982. US actor whose engaging acting style made him ideal in the role of the American pioneer and honourable man. His many films include *The Grapes of Wrath* 1940, *My Darling Clementine* 1946, and *On Golden Pond*

Fonda *US actor Henry Fonda receiving Hollywood's Life Achievement Award, photographed with his children Jane and Peter.*

1981. He was the father of the actress Jane Fonda and the actor and director *Peter Fonda* (1939–).

Fonda /ˈfɒndə/ Jane 1937– . US film actress. Her early films include *Cat Ballou* 1965 and *Barbarella* 1968, and she won Academy Awards for *Klute* 1971 and *Coming Home* 1979. She is also active in left-wing politics and in promoting physical fitness. She is the daughter of Henry Fonda.

Fontainebleau /ˈfɒntɪnbləʊ/ town to the SE of Paris, in Seine-et-Marne *département*; population (1982) 18,753. The palace was built by François I in the 16th century. Mme de Montespan lived there in the reign of Louis XIV, and Mme du Barry in that of Louis XV. Napoleon signed his abdication there in 1814. Nearby is the village of Barbizon, the haunt of several 19th-century painters (the ◊ Barbizon school).

Fontainebleau school French school of Mannerist painting and sculpture, established at the court of Francis I. He brought Italian artists to Fontainebleau near Paris to decorate his hunting lodge: *Rosso Fiorentino* (1494–1540) arrived 1530, *Francesco Primaticcio* (1504/5–1570) came 1532. They soon evolved a distinctive decorative style using a combination of stucco sculpture and painting.

Their work, with its exuberant ornament and typically Mannerist figure style, had a lasting impact on French art in the 16th century. Others associated with the school include Benvenuto ◊Cellini.

Fontana /fɒnˈtɑːnə/ Domenico 1543–1607. Italian architect. He was employed by Pope Sixtus V, and his principal works include the Vatican library and the completion of the dome of St Peter's in Rome, and the royal palace in Naples.

Fontana /fɒnˈtɑːnə/ Lucio 1899–1968. Italian painter and sculptor. He developed a unique abstract style, presenting bare canvases with straight parallel slashes.

Fontanne /fɒnˈtæn/ Lynn 1887–1983. US actress, one half of the husband-and-wife acting partnership known as the 'Lunts' with her husband Alfred ◊Lunt.

Fontenoy, Battle of /ˈfɒntənwɑː/ battle in the War of the ◊Austrian Succession 1745. Marshal Saxe and the French defeated the British, Dutch, and Hanoverians under the Duke of Cumberland at a village in Hainaut province, Belgium, SE of Tournai.

Fonteyn *One of the greatest partnerships in the history of ballet—Margot Fonteyn and Rudolf Nureyev in Giselle.*

Fonteyn /'fɒnteɪn/ Margot. Stage name of Margaret Hookham 1919– . English ballet dancer. She made her debut with the Vic-Wells Ballet in *Nutcracker* 1934 and first appeared as Giselle 1937, eventually becoming prima ballerina of the Royal Ballet, London. Renowned for her perfect physique, musicality, and interpretive powers, she created several roles in ◊Ashton's ballets and formed a successful partnership with ◊Nureyev.

Her roles included Aurora in Sergueyev's production of *The Sleeping Beauty* 1939. She was created Dame of the British Empire (DBE) 1956, and since 1954 has been president of the Royal Academy of Dancing.

Foochow /ˌfuːˈtʃaʊ/ former name of ◊Fuzhou, port and capital of Fujian province, SE China.

food anything eaten by human beings and other animals to sustain life and health. The building blocks of food are nutrients, and humans can utilize the following nutrients:

carbohydrate as starch found in bread, potatoes, and pasta; as simple sugars in sucrose and honey; as fibres in cereals, fruit, and vegetables;

protein good sources are nuts, fish, meat, eggs, milk, and some vegetables;

fat found in most animal products, fish, butter, margarine, nuts, milk, oils, and lard;

vitamins found in a wide variety of foods, except for vitamin B12 which is mainly found in animal foods;

minerals found in a wide variety of foods; a good source of calcium is milk; of iodine is seafood; of iron is liver and green vegetables;

water ubiquitous in nature;

alcohol found in alcoholic beverages, from 40% in spirits to 0.01 in low-alcohol lagers and beers.

Food is needed for both energy, measured in calories or kilojoules, and nutrients, which are converted to body tissues. Some nutrients mainly provide energy, such as fat, carbohydrate, and alcohol; other nutrients are important in other ways, such as aids to metabolism. Proteins provide energy and are necessary for cell structure.

Food and Agriculture Organization (FAO) United Nations agency that coordinates activities to improve food and timber production and levels of nutrition throughout the world. It is also concerned with investment in agriculture, and dispersal of emergency food supplies. It has headquarters in Rome and was founded 1945. The USA cut FAO funding in 1990 from $61.4 million to $18 million, because of alleged 'politicization'.

food chain or *food web* in ecology, the sequence of organisms through which energy and other nutrients are successively transferred. Since many organisms feed at several different levels (for example, omnivores feed on both fruit and meat), the relationships often form a complex web rather than a simple chain. See also ◊ecosystem and ◊heterotroph.

The sequence of the food chain comprises the ◊autotrophs, or primary producers, principally plants and photosynthetic microorganisms; the ◊herbivores that feed on them; the ◊carnivores that feed on the herbivores; and the ◊decomposers that break down the dead bodies and waste products of all these groups, ready for recycling.

food irradiation a new development in ◊food technology, whereby food is exposed to low-level radiation to kill microorganisms.

Irradiation is highly effective, and does not make the food any more radioactive than it is naturally. Some vitamins are partially destroyed, such as vitamin C, and it would be unwise to eat only irradiated fruit and vegetables. The main cause for concern is that it may be used by unscrupulous traders to 'clean up' consignments of food, particularly shellfish, with high bacterial counts. Bacterial toxins would remain in the food, so that it could still cause illness, although irradiation would have removed signs of live bacteria. Stringent regulations would be needed to prevent this happening. It has been suggested that other

food chain

hawk

tertiary consumers (carnivores)

fox

snake

frog

secondary consumers (carnivores)

grasshopper

mouse

primary consumers (herbivores)

grass

producers

beetle

worm

decomposers

damaging changes take place in the food, such as the creation of ◊free radicals, but research so far suggests that the process is relatively safe.

food poisoning an acute illness caused by harmful bacteria (for example, ◊listeriosis), poisonous food (for example, certain mushrooms, puffer fish), or poisoned food (for example, lead or arsenic introduced accidentally during manufacture). A frequent cause of food poisoning is the *salmonella* bacterium. This comes in many forms, and strains are found in some cattle, pigs, and poultry.

Deep freezing of poultry before the birds were properly cooked through has been a common cause of food poisoning. Attacks of salmonella have also come from contaminated eggs that have been eaten raw or cooked only lightly. Pork may carry the roundworm *trichinella*, and rye the parasitic fungus ergot. The most dangerous food poison is the bacillus that causes ◊botulism. This is rare but leads to muscle paralysis and, often, death. Food irradiation is intended to prevent food poisoning.

food technology the application of science to the commercial processing of foodstuffs. Food is processed to render it more palatable or digestible, or to preserve it from spoilage. Food spoils because of the action of ◊enzymes within the food that change its chemical composition, or because of the growth of bacteria, moulds, yeasts, and other microorganisms. Fatty or oily foods also suffer oxidation of the fats, giving them a rancid flavour. Traditional forms of processing include boiling, frying, flour- milling, bread-making, yoghurt- and cheese-making, brewing, and various

methods of *food preservation*, such as salting, smoking, pickling, drying, bottling, and preserving in sugar. Modern food technology still employs these traditional methods but also makes use of many novel processes and ◊additives, which allow a wider range of foodstuffs to be preserved.

Refrigeration below 5°C/41°F (or below 3°C/37°F for cooked foods) slows the processes of spoilage, but is less effective for foods with a high water content. Although a very convenient form of preservation, this process cannot kill microorganisms, nor stop their growth completely, and a failure to realize its limitations causes many cases of food poisoning. Refrigerator temperatures should be checked as the efficiency of the machinery (see ◊refrigeration) can decline with age, and higher temperatures are dangerous.

Deep freezing (−18°C/−1°F or below) stops almost all spoilage processes, although there may be some residual enzyme activity in uncooked vegetables, which is why these are blanched (dipped in hot water to destroy the enzymes) before freezing. Microorganisms cannot grow or divide, but most remain alive and can resume activity once defrosted. Some foods are damaged by freezing, notably soft fruits and salad vegetables, whose cells are punctured by ice crystals, leading to loss of crispness. Fatty foods such as cow's milk and cream tend to separate. Various processes are used for ◊deep freezing foods commercially.

Pasteurization is used mainly for milk. By holding the milk at a high temperature, but below boiling point, for a period of time, all disease-causing bacteria can be destroyed. The milk is held at

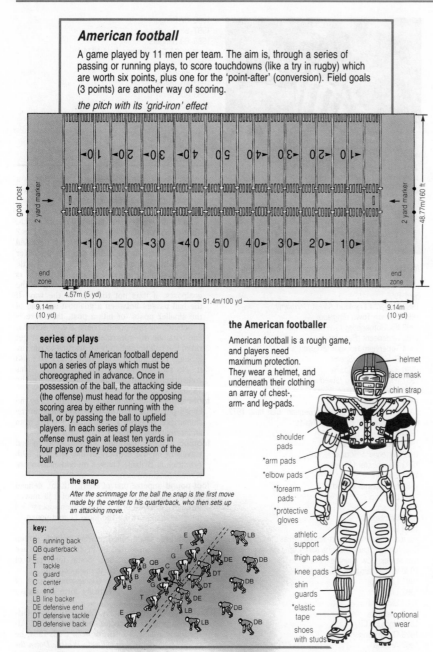

American football

A game played by 11 men per team. The aim is, through a series of passing or running plays, to score touchdowns (like a try in rugby) which are worth six points, plus one for the 'point-after' (conversion). Field goals (3 points) are another way of scoring.

the pitch with its 'grid-iron' effect

goal post

2 yard marker

2 yard marker

48.77m/160 ft

end zone

end zone

4.57m (5 yd)

91.4m/100 yd

9.14m (10 yd)

9.14m (10 yd)

series of plays

The tactics of American football depend upon a series of plays which must be choreographed in advance. Once in possession of the ball, the attacking side (the offense) must head for the opposing scoring area by either running with the ball, or by passing the ball to upfield players. In each series of plays the offense must gain at least ten yards in four plays or they lose possession of the ball.

the snap

After the scrimmage for the ball the snap is the first move made by the center to his quarterback, who then sets up an attacking move.

key:
B running back
QB quarterback
E end
T tackle
G guard
C center
E end
LB line backer
DE defensive end
DT defensive tackle
DB defensive back

the American footballer

American football is a rough game, and players need maximum protection. They wear a helmet, and underneath their clothing an array of chest-, arm- and leg-pads.

helmet

face mask

chin strap

shoulder pads

*arm pads

*elbow pads

*forearm pads

*protective gloves

athletic support

thigh pads

knee pads

shin guards

*elastic tape

shoes with studs

*optional wear

72°C for 15 seconds. Other, less harmful bacteria survive, so the milk will still go sour within a few days. Boiling the milk would destroy all bacteria, but impair the flavour.

Ultra-heat treatment is used to produce UHT milk. This process uses higher temperatures than pasteurization, and kills all bacteria present, giving the milk a long shelf life but altering the flavour.

Drying is an effective method of preservation because both microorganisms and enzymes need water to be active. Products such as dried milk and instant coffee are made by spraying the liquid into a rising column of dry, heated air.

Freeze-drying is carried out under vacuum. It is less damaging to food than straight dehydration in the sense that foods reconstitute better, and is used for quality instant coffee and dried vegetables.

Canning relies on high temperatures to destroy microorganisms and enzymes. The food is sealed into a can to prevent any recontamination by bacteria. Beverages may also be canned to preserve the carbon dioxide that makes drinks fizzy.

Pickling utilizes the effect of acetic acid, found in vinegar, in stopping the growth of moulds. In sauerkraut, lactic acid, produced by bacteria, has the same effect. Similar types of non-harmful, acid-generating bacteria are used to make yoghurt and cheese.

Curing of meat involves soaking in salt (sodium chloride) solution, with saltpetre (sodium nitrate) added to give the meat its pink colour and characteristic taste. Saltpetre (a ◊preservative was originally included by chance because it was a natural contaminant of rock salt. The nitrates in cured meats are converted to nitrites and nitrosamines by bacteria, and these are potentially carcinogenic to humans. Of all the additives in use, the time-honoured nitrates are among the most dangerous.

Irradiation is a method of preserving food by subjecting it to low-level radiation. This process does not make the food any more radioactive than it is naturally. It kills all microorganisms, apart from some viruses. However, it is highly controversial (see ◊food irradiation) and not yet widely used.

Puffing is a method of processing cereal grains. They are subjected to high pressures, then suddenly ejected into a normal atmospheric pressure, causing the grain to expand sharply. This type of process is used to make puffed wheat cereals and puffed rice cakes.

Chemical treatments are widely used, for example in margarine manufacture, where hydrogen is bubbled through vegetable oils in the presence of a ◊catalyst to produce a more solid, spreadable fat. The catalyst is later removed. Chemicals that are introduced in processing and remain in the food are known as *food additives* and include flavourings, preservatives, antioxidants, emulsifiers, and colourings.

foot imperial unit of length (symbol ft), equivalent to 0.3048 m, in use in Britain since Anglo-Saxon times. It originally represented the length of a human foot. One foot contains 12 inches and is one third of a yard.

Foot /fʊt/ Dingle 1905–1978. British lawyer and Labour politician, solicitor-general 1964–67. He was the brother of Michael Foot.

Foot /fʊt/ Hugh, Baron Caradon 1907– . British Labour politician. As governor of Cyprus 1957–60, he guided the independence negotiations, and he represented the UK at the United Nations 1964–70. He is the son of Isaac Foot and brother of Michael Foot.

Foot /fʊt/ Isaac 1880–1960. British Liberal politician. A staunch Nonconformist, he was minister of mines 1931–32. He was the father of Dingle, Hugh, and Michael Foot.

Foot /fʊt/ Michael 1913– . British Labour politician. A leader of the left-wing Tribune Group; he was secretary of state for employment 1974–76, Lord President of the Council and leader of the House 1976–79, and succeeded Callaghan as Labour Party leader 1980–83.

foot and mouth disease contagious eruptive viral fever that causes deterioration of milk yield and abortions in cattle.

In the UK, affected herds are destroyed; inoculation is practised in Europe, and in the US, a vaccine was developed in the 1980s.

football, American a contact sport similar to the English game of rugby. First match under Harvard rules was between Harvard University and McGill University, Montreal, Canada, in 1874.

The pitch is marked out with a series of parallel lines giving a gridiron effect, hence the sport's other name, 'gridiron football'. Played with an oval ball like rugby, it also uses rugby-style goalposts. Players are well padded for protection and wear protective helmets. A team consists of more than 40 players but only 11 are allowed on the field at any one time. Games are divided into four quarters of 15 minutes each.

The *Super Bowl* was first held 1967, an annual meeting between the winners of the National and American Football Conferences.

Superbowl: recent winners

1977 Oakland Raiders
1978 Dallas Cowboys
1979, 1980 Pittsburgh Steelers
1981 Oakland Raiders
1982 San Francisco 49ers
1983 Washington Redskins
1984 Los Angeles Raiders
1985 San Francisco 49ers
1986 Chicago Bears
1987 New York Giants
1988 Washington Redskins
1989 San Francisco 49ers

football, association or *soccer* a form of football originating in the UK, popular in Europe and Latin America. It is played between two teams each of 11 players, on a field 90–120 m/100–130 yds long and 45–90 m/50– 100 yds wide, with a spherical, inflated (traditionally leather) ball, circumference 0.69 m/27 in. The object of the game is to send the ball with the feet or head into the opponents' goal, an area 7.31 m/8 yds wide and 2.44 m/8 ft high.

A team is broadly divided into defence (the goalkeeper and defenders), midfield (whose players collect the ball from the defence and distribute it to the attackers), and attack (forwards or strikers). The number of players assigned to each role varies according to the tactics adopted, but a typical formation is 4–4–2 (four defenders, excluding goalkeeper, four midfield, and two forwards).

The field has a halfway line marked with a centre circle, two penalty areas, and two goal areas. Corner kicks are taken from a 1 m/1 yd segment, when the ball goes behind the goal-line off a defender; a ball kicked over the touchlines is thrown in by one of the opposing side. Only the goalkeeper is allowed to touch the ball with the hands and then only in an assigned penalty area. For major offences committed within the defenders' penalty area, a penalty kick may be awarded by the referee to the attacking team. This is taken 11 m/12 yds from the goal centre, with only the goalkeeper inside the area and standing still on the goal-line.

Played in England from the 14th century, football developed in the 19th century and the first set of rules were drawn up at Cambridge University 1848. The modern game is played in the UK according to the rules laid down by the Football Association, founded 1863. The Football League was founded 1888. Slight amendments to the rules take effect in certain competitions and overseas matches as laid down by the sport's world governing body, Fédération Internationale de Football Association (FIFA, 1904). FIFA organizes the competitions for the World Cup, held every four years from 1930.

Football

World Cup first contested 1930, held every four years
1950 Uruguay
1954 West Germany
1958 Brazil
1962 Brazil
1966 England
1970 Brazil
1974 West Germany
1978 Argentina
1982 Italy
1986 Argentina
European Championship instituted 1958, first final 1960; held every four years
1960 USSR
1964 Spain
1968 Italy
1972 West Germany
1976 Czechoslovakia
1980 West Germany
1984 France
1988 Holland
European Champions Cup first held 1955
1980 Nottingham Forest *(England)*
1981 Liverpool *(England)*
1982 Aston Villa *(England)*
1983 SV Hamburg *(West Germany)*
1984 Liverpool *(England)*
1985 Juventus *(Italy)*
1986 Steaua Bucharest *(Romania)*
1987 FC Porto *(Portugal)*
1988 PSV Eindhoven *(Holland)*
1989 AC Milan *(Italy)*
European Cup Winners' Cup first held 1960
1980 Valencia *(Spain)*
1981 Dinamo Tbilisi *(USSR)*
1982 Barcelona *(Spain)*
1983 Aberdeen *(Scotland)*
1984 Juventus *(Italy)*
1985 Everton *(England)*
1986 Dinamo Kiev *(USSR)*
1987 Ajax *(Holland)*
1988 Mechelen *(Belgium)*
1989 Barcelona *(Spain)*

football Dutch international footballer Ruud Gullit.

UEFA Cup (formerly the Inter Cities Fairs Cup) first held 1955
1980 Eintracht Frankfurt *(West Germany)*
1981 Ipswich Town *(England)*
1982 IFK Gothenburg *(Sweden)*
1983 Anderlecht *(Belgium)*
1984 Tottenham Hotspur *(England)*
1985 Real Madrid *(Spain)*
1986 Real Madrid *(Spain)*
1987 IFK Gothenburg *(Sweden)*
1988 Bayer Leverkusen *(West Germany)*
1989 Napoli *(Italy)*
FA Cup a knockout club competition, first held 1872; held annually in England and Wales
1980 West Ham United
1981 Tottenham Hotspur
1982 Tottenham Hotspur
1983 Manchester United
1984 Everton
1985 Manchester United
1986 Liverpool
1987 Coventry City
1988 Wimbledon
1989 Liverpool
Football League Cup (currently known as the Littlewoods Cup, formerly known as the Milk Cup) first final 1961 in two stages, now a single game
1980 Wolverhampton Wanderers
1981 Liverpool
1982 Liverpool
1983 Liverpool
1984 Liverpool
1985 Norwich City
1986 Oxford United
1987 Arsenal
1988 Luton Town
1989 Nottingham Forest
Division One Champions Football League founded 1888
1978–79
1979–80 Liverpool
1980–81 Aston Villa
1981–82 Liverpool
1982–83 Liverpool
1983–84 Liverpool
1984–85 Everton
1985–86 Liverpool
1986–87 Everton
1987–88 Liverpool
1988–89 Arsenal
Scottish Premier Division Champions Scottish League formed 1890–91, reformed into three divisions
1975–76
1979–80 Aberdeen
1980–81 Celtic
1981–82 Celtic
1982–83 Dundee United
1983–84 Aberdeen
1984–85 Aberdeen
1985–86 Celtic

1986–87 Rangers
1987–88 Celtic
1988–89 Rangers
Scottish FA Cup first final held 1874
1980 Celtic
1981 Rangers
1982 Aberdeen
1983 Aberdeen
1984 Aberdeen
1985 Celtic
1986 Aberdeen
1987 St Mirren
1988 Celtic
1989 Celtic

football, Australian an 18-a-side game that is a cross between Gaelic football, rugby, and soccer, and is unique to Australia, although association and rugby football are also played there.

Each side is placed in 5 lines of 3 persons each. Three players follow the ball all the time. The 2 goalposts, at each end, are 6 m/19 ft high and 6.4 m/21 ft apart. On either side are 2 smaller posts. The football is oval, and weighs a little more than a rugby ball. A goal (6 points) is scored when the ball is kicked between the goalposts, if it is not touched on the way. If the ball passes between a goalpost and one of the smaller posts, or hits a post, the score is a 'behind', or one point. There are no scrums, line-outs, or off-side rules. A player must get rid of the ball immediately on starting to run, by kicking, punching or bouncing it every 10 m/33 ft. No tackling (as in rugby) is allowed. This code originated on the Australian goldfields in the 1850s.

foot-candle unit of illuminance, now replaced by the lumen per square metre. One foot-candle is the illumination received at a distance of 1 foot from an international candle.

footpad a thief, operating on foot, who robbed travellers on the highway in the 18th and 19th centuries in Britain. Thieves on horseback were termed ◊highwaymen.

foot-pound imperial unit of energy (ft-lb), defined as the work done when a force of 1 lb moves through a distance of 1 ft. It has been superseded for scientific work by the joule (1 foot-pound = 1.356 joule).

foraminifera single-celled marine animals, often classified as an order of Protozoa, which are enclosed by a thin shell. Some form part of ◊plankton, others live on the sea bottom.

The many-chambered *Globigerina* is part of plankton. Its shells eventually form the chalky ooze of the ocean floor.

Forbes /fɔːbz/ Bryan (John Clarke) 1926– . British film producer, director, and screenwriter. After acting in films like *An Inspector Calls* 1954, he made his directorial debut with *Whistle Down the Wind* 1961; among his other films is *The L-Shaped Room* 1962.

force in physics, that influence which tends to change the state of rest or the uniform motion of a body in a straight line. It is measured by the rate of change of momentum of the body on which it acts, that is, the mass of the body multiplied by its acceleration: $F=ma$.

force ratio the magnification of a force by a machine; see ◊mechanical advantage.

forces, fundamental in physics, the four fundamental interactions believed to be at work in the physical universe. There are two long-range forces: *gravity*, which keeps the planets in orbit around the Sun, and acts between all ◊particles that have mass; and the ***electromagnetic force***, which stops solids from falling apart, and acts between all particles with ◊electric charge. There are two very short-range forces: the ***weak force***, responsible for the reactions that fuel the Sun, and for the emission of ◊beta particles from certain nuclei; and the ***strong force***, which binds together the protons and neutrons in the nuclei of atoms.

Ford *Henry Ford in his first car, a model F Ford built in 1893.*

By 1971, Steven Weinberg and Sheldon Glashow (USA), Abdus Salam (UK), and others developed a theory which suggested that the weak and electromagnetic forces were linked; experimental support came from observation at ◊CERN in the 1980s. Physicists are now working on theories to unify all four forces.

Ford /fɔːd/ Ford Madox. Adopted name of Ford Madox Hueffer 1873–1939. English writer of the novel *The Good Soldier* 1915, and editor of the *English Review* 1908, to which Thomas Hardy, D H Lawrence, and Joseph Conrad contributed. He was a grandson of the painter Ford Madox Brown.

Ford /fɔːd/ Gerald R(udolph) 1913– . 38th president of the USA 1974–77, a Republican. He was elected to the House of Representatives 1949, was nominated to the vice-presidency by Richard Nixon 1973 following the resignation of Spiro ◊Agnew, and in 1974, when Nixon resigned, Ford became president. He pardoned Nixon, and gave amnesty to those who had resisted the draft for the Vietnam War.

Ford was born in Omaha, Nebraska, was an All-American footballer at college, and graduated from Yale Law School. He was appointed vice president Dec 1973, at a time when Nixon's re-election campaign was already being investigated for 'dirty tricks', and became president the following Aug when the ◊Watergate scandal forced Nixon to resign. Ford's visit to Vladivostok 1974 resulted in agreement with the USSR on strategic arms limitation. He was defeated by Carter in the 1976 election by a narrow margin.

Ford /fɔːd/ Glenn (Gwyllym Samuel Newton) 1916– . Canadian actor, active in Hollywood during the 1940s–1960s. Usually cast as the tough but good-natured hero, he was equally at home in westerns, thrillers, and comedies. His films include *Gilda* 1946, *The Big Heat* 1953, and *Dear Heart* 1965.

Ford /fɔːd/ Henry 1863–1947. US automobile manufacturer, who built his first car 1893 and founded the Ford Motor Company 1903. His Model T (1908–27) was the first car to be constructed by purely mass-production methods, and 15 million of these cars were made.

He was a pacifist, and visited Europe 1915–16 in an attempt to end World War I. In 1936 he founded, with his son Edsel Ford (1893–1943), the philanthropic ***Ford Foundation***.

Ford /fɔːd/ John 1586–*c.* 1640. English poet and dramatist. His play *'Tis Pity She's a Whore* (performed about 1626, printed 1633) is a study of incest between brother and sister.

Among his other plays are *The Witch of Edmonton* (1621, 1658), *The Broken Heart* (about 1629, 1633), *The Chronicle History of Perkin Warbeck* 1634, and *The Lady's Trial* (about 1638, 1639).

Ford /fɔːd/ John. Assumed name of Sean O'Fearn 1895–1973. US film director. His films, especially his westerns, were of great influence, and include *Stagecoach* 1939, *The Grapes of Wrath* 1940, and *The Man who Shot Liberty Valance* 1962.

Ford made many silent films, including *The Iron Horse* 1924 and *Four Sons* 1928. After the introduction of sound, he went on to make films such as *The Informer* 1935, *She Wore a Yellow Ribbon* 1949, and *The Quiet Man* 1952. He won six directing Oscars, two of them for wartime documentaries.

foreclosure in British law, the transfer of a mortgaged property from the mortgagor to the mortgagee (for example a bank) where the mortgagor is in breach of the mortgage agreement, for example, by failing to keep up the repayments.

This is not used as frequently as another mortgagee's remedy, the power of sale, which allows the mortgagee to sell the mortgaged property, keep what is owed, and pay the balance to the mortgagor. In this case the mortgagee can also sue the mortgagor for any balance if the price obtained for the property is less than the amount owed.

Foreign Legion a volunteer corps of foreigners within a country's army. The French *Légion Etrangère*, formed 1831, is one of a number of such forces. Enlisted volunteers are of any nationality (about half are now French), but the officers are usually French. Headquarters until 1962 was in Sidi Bel Abbés, Algeria; the main base is now Corsica, with reception headquarters at Aubagne, near Marseille, France.

foreign relations a country's dealings with other countries. Specialized diplomatic bodies first appeared in Europe during the 18th century. After 1818 diplomatic agents were divided into: ***ambassadors***, papal legates, and nuncios; ***envoys*** extraordinary, ***ministers*** plenipotentiary, and other ministers accredited to the head of state; ministers resident; and ***chargés d'affaires***, who may deputize for an ambassador or minister, or

be themselves the representative accredited to a minor country. Other diplomatic staff may include counsellors and attachés (military, labour, cultural, press). ***Consuls*** are state agents with commercial and political responsibilities in foreign towns.

After World War II there was an increase in the number of countries represented by a diplomat of ambassadorial rather than lower rank, although in recent years improved communications have lessened the importance of the career diplomat as the person on the spot. Professional spies (see ◊intelligence) often inflate the number of 'diplomats' accredited to a country. In the USSR foreign relations are handled by the Foreign Ministry, in the USA by the ◊State Department.

In medieval England foreign affairs were dealt with, together with home affairs, by the king's principal secretary, an office split into two under Henry VIII. Irish and colonial affairs and relations with Mediterranean countries became the responsibility of the secretary of state for the Southern Department, the rest of Europe of the Northern Department. In 1782 the Southern Department became the Home Office and the Northern Department the Foreign Office, and colonial affairs, growing in importance, became separate departments – Colonial Office 1854, India Office 1858, Dominions Office 1925, Commonwealth Office 1947, the last of which was merged with the Foreign Office to form the Foreign and Commonwealth Office 1968.

Foreland /'fɔːlənd/ North and South headlands on the Kent coast, England. ***North Foreland***, with one lighthouse, lies 4 km/2.5 mi E of Margate; ***South Foreland***, with two, lies 4.8 km/3 mi NE of Dover.

forensic science the use of scientific techniques to solve criminal cases. A multidisciplinary field embracing chemistry, physics, botany, zoology, and medicine, forensic science includes the identification of human bodies or traces. Traditional methods such as ◊fingerprinting are still used, assisted by computers; in addition, blood analysis, forensic dentistry, voice and speech spectograms, and ◊genetic fingerprinting are increasingly applied. Ballistics (the study of projectiles, such as bullets), another traditional forensic field, today makes use of tools such as the comparison microscope and the ◊electron microscope. Chemicals, such as poisons and drugs, are analysed by ◊chromatography.

The first forensic laboratory was founded in France in 1910 by Edmond Locard, and the science developed as a systematic discipline in the 1930s. In 1932 the US Federal Bureau of Investigation established a forensic science laboratory in Washington DC, and in the UK the first such laboratory was founded in London in 1935.

Forest /'fɒrɪst/ Lee de 1873–1961. US inventor who perfected the audion tube (triode valve) and contributed to the development of radio, radar, and television.

Forester /'fɒrɪstə/ C(ecil) S(cott) 1899–1966. English novelist, born in Egypt. He wrote a series of historical novels set in the Napoleonic era which, beginning with *The Happy Return* 1937, cover the career—from midshipman to admiral—of Horatio Hornblower.

He also wrote *Payment Deferred* 1926, a subtle crime novel, and *The African Queen* 1938, later filmed with Humphrey Bogart.

forestry the science of forest management. Recommended forestry practice aims at multipurpose crops, allowing the preservation of varied plant and animal species as well as human uses (lumbering, recreation). Forestry has often been confined to the planting of a single species, such as one of the rapid-growing conifers providing softwood for paper pulp and construction timber, for which world demand is greatest. In tropical countries, logging contributes to the destruction of the ◊rainforest, causing global environmental problems.

The earliest planned forest dates from 1368 at Nuremberg, Germany; in Britain, planning

forestry *Satellite mosaic of Wales, showing the darker forested regions. These are mostly confined to mountain slopes.*

Formby *With his ukulele and the song 'Cleaning Windows', George Formby, the comedian, achieved a popular stage and screen reputation as the archetypal northern lad.*

Forster *English novelist Edward Morgan Forster photographed by Cecil Beaton.*

of forests began in the 16th century. In the UK, Japan, and other countries, forestry practices have been criticized for concentration on softwood conifers to the neglect of native hardwoods.

A tropical forest, if properly preserved, can yield medicinal plants, oils (from cedar, juniper, cinnamon, sandalwood), spices, gums, resins (used in inks, lacquers, linoleum), tanning and dyeing materials, forage for animals, beverages, poisons, green manure, rubber, and animal products (feathers, hides, honey).

Forfarshire /ˈfɔːfəʃə/ former name (from 16th century–1928) of Angus, which was absorbed in Tayside in 1975.

forgery the making of a fake document, painting, or object with deliberate intention to deceive or defraud.

Financial gain is not the only motive for forgery. Hans van Meegeren probably began painting in the style of Vermeer to make fools of the critics, but found such a ready market for his creations that he became a rich man before he was forced to confess. The archaeological ◊Piltdown Man hoax in England in 1912 also appears to have been a practical joke. In the USA, the Drake Brass Plate (supposedly set up in California by Francis Drake in 1579 and discovered 1936) and the Vinland Map (indicating that Vikings discovered America before Columbus) were both denounced as forgeries after modern scientific analysis.

The 1760s saw two literary hoaxes of considerable influence: the teenage poet Thomas Chatterton passed off his own poems as the work of a fictitious 15th-century monk, Thomas Rowley, and James Macpherson created the works of Ossian. Literary forgers proper include William Henry Ireland (1777–1835), who wrote two 'lost' Shakespearean plays, *Vortigern* and *Henry II* in the 1790s, and Thomas ◊Wise, a 20th-century book collector who concocted his own 'first editions'. Forged letters sold to *The Times* in 1886 had considerable impact on Irish politics, and the ◊Zinoviev Letter helped the Conservatives to power in the 1924 UK general election.

forget-me-not either of two plants, *Myosotis sylvatica* or *M. scorpioides*, family Boraginaceae, with bright blue flowers.

forging one of the main methods of shaping metals, which involves hammering or the more gradual application of pressure. A blacksmith hammers red-hot metal into shape on an anvil, and the traditional place of work is called a forge. The

blacksmith's mechanical equivalent is the drop forge. The metal is shaped by the blows from a falling hammer or ram, which is usually accelerated by steam or air pressure. Hydraulic presses forge by applying pressure gradually in a squeezing action.

Forlì /fɔːˈliː/ city and market centre in Emilia-Romagna region, NE Italy, south of Ravenna; population (1988) 110,000. Felt, ◊maiolica, and paper are manufactured.

formaldehyde common name for ◊methanal.

Formby /ˈfɔːmbi/ George 1904–1961. English comedian. He established a stage and screen reputation as an apparently simple Lancashire working lad, and sang such songs as 'Mr Wu' and 'Cleaning Windows', accompanying himself on the ukulele. His father was a music-hall star of the same name.

Formentor, Cape /ˌfɔːmenˈtɔː/ northern extremity of ◊Majorca, in the Balearic Islands of the West Mediterranean.

Formica trade name for a heat-proof plastic laminate, widely used for wipe-down kitchen surfaces. It is made from formaldehyde resins akin to ◊Bakelite.

formic acid common name for ◊methanoic acid.

Formosa /fɔːˈməʊsə/ former name of ◊Taiwan.

formula in chemistry, a representation of a molecule, radical, or ion, in which chemical elements are represented by their symbols. An *empirical formula* indicates the simplest ratio of the elements in a compound, without indicating how many of them there are or how they are combined. A *molecular formula* gives the number of each type of element present in one molecule. A *structural formula* shows the relative positions of the atoms and the bonds between them. Formula is also another name for a ◊chemical equation.

For ethanoic acid the empirical formula is CH_2O, the molecular formula is $C_2H_4O_2$, and the structural formula is CH_3COOH.

Forrest /ˈfɒrɪst/ John, 1st Baron Forrest 1847–1918. Australian explorer and politician. He crossed Western Australia W–E 1870, when he went along the southern coast route, and in 1874, when he crossed much further N, exploring the Musgrave Ranges. He was born in Western Australia, and was its first premier 1890–1901.

Forrestal /ˈfɒrɪstl/ James Vincent 1892–1949. US Democratic politician. As secretary of the navy from 1944, he organized its war effort, accompanying the US landings on the Japanese island Iwo Jima. He was the first secretary of the Department of National Defense 1947–49, a post created to unify the three armed services at the end of World War II.

Forssmann /ˈfɔːsmæn/ Werner 1904–1979. West German heart specialist. In 1929 he originated,

by experiment on himself, the technique of cardiac catheterization (passing a thin tube from an arm artery up into the heart itself for diagnostic purposes). Nobel Prize for Medicine 1956.

Forster /ˈfɔːstə/ E(dward) M(organ) 1879–1970. English novelist, concerned with the interplay of personality and the conflict between convention and instinct. His novels include *A Room with a View* 1908, *Howards End* 1910, and *A Passage to India* 1924. He also wrote short stories, for example 'The Eternal Omnibus' 1914; criticism, including *Aspects of the Novel* 1927, and essays, including *Abinger Harvest* 1936.

Forster published his first novel, *Where Angels Fear to Tread*, 1905. He enhances the superficial situations of his plots with unexpected insights in *The Longest Journey* 1907, *A Room with a View*, and *Howards End*. His many years spent in India and as secretary to the Maharajah of Dewas in 1921 provided him with the material for *A Passage to India*, which explores the relationship between the English and the Indians. *Maurice*, published 1971, has a homosexual theme.

Forster /ˈfɔːstə/ William Edward 1818–1886. British Liberal reformer. In Gladstone's government 1868–74 he was vice president of the council, and secured the passing of the Education Act 1870 and the Ballot Act 1872. He was chief secretary for Ireland 1880–82.

Forsyth /fɔːˈsaɪθ/ Frederick 1938– . English thriller writer. His books include *The Day of the Jackal* 1970, *The Dogs of War* 1974, and *The Fourth Protocol* 1984.

forsythia genus of temperate E Asian shrubs, family Oleaceae, which bear yellow flowers in early spring before the leaves appear.

Fortaleza /ˌfɔːtəˈleɪzə/ industrial port (also called Ceará) in NE Brazil; population (1980) 648,815. It has textile, flour-milling, and sugar-refining industries.

Fort-de-France /ˈfɔː də ˈfrɒns/ capital, chief commercial centre, and port of ◊Martinique, West Indies; population (1982) 99,844.

fortepiano an alternative name for ◊pianoforte, used to specify early pianos of the 18th and early 19th centuries.

Forth /fɔːθ/ river in SE Scotland, with its headstreams rising on the NE slopes of Ben Lomond. It flows approximately 72 km/45 mi to Kincardine where the *Firth of Forth* begins. The Firth is approximately 80 km/50 mi long, and is 26 km/16 mi wide where it joins the North Sea.

At Queensferry near Edinburgh are the Forth rail (1890) and road (1964) bridges. The *Forth and Clyde Canal* (1768–90) across the lowlands of Scotland links the Firth with the river Clyde, Grangemouth to Bowling (53 km/33 mi).

Foster *US film actress Jodie Foster won an Academy Award for her leading role in* The Accused *1988.*

A coalfield was located beneath the Firth of Forth in 1976.

Fortin /fɔːˈtæn/ Jean 1750–1831. French physicist and instrument-maker who invented a mercury barometer that bears his name. On this scale, normal atmospheric pressure is 760 mm of mercury.

It measures atmospheric pressure by means of a column of mercury, formed by filling a closed tube with mercury and upending it in a reservoir of the metal. This leaves a gap (Torricellian vacuum) at the upper end of the tube, which changes size with variations in atmospheric pressure, expressed as the height of the column of mercury in millimetres.

Fort Knox /nɒks/ US army post and gold depository in Kentucky, established 1917 as a training camp. The US Treasury gold-bullion vaults were built 1937.

Fort Lamy /læˈmiː/ former name of ◊N'djamena, capital of Chad.

FORTRAN from **for**mula **tran**slation computer-programming language suited to mathematical and scientific computations. Developed in the mid-1950s, and one of the earliest languages, it is still widely used today.

Fort Sumter /ˈsʌmtə/ fort in Charleston, South Carolina, USA, 6.5 km/4 mi SE of Charleston. The first shots of the US Civil War were fired here 12 Apr 1861, after its commander had refused the call to surrender made by the Confederate general Beauregard.

Fort Ticonderoga /ˌtaɪkɒndəˈrəʊgə/ fort in New York State, USA, on a route to Canada near Lake Champlain. It was the site 1758–59 of battles between the British and the French, and was captured from the British 10 May 1775 by Benedict Arnold and Ethan Allen (leading the ◊Green Mountain Boys).

Fortuna /fɔːˈtjuːnə/ in Roman mythology, goddess of chance and good fortune (Greek *Tyche*).

Fort Wayne /weɪn/ town in NE Indiana, USA; population (1980) 172,000. Industries include electrical goods, electronics, and farm machinery. A fort was built here against the North American Indians in 1794 by Gen Anthony Wayne (1745–96), hero of a surprise attack on a British force at Stony Point, New York, in 1779, which earned him the nickname 'Mad Anthony'.

Fort Worth /wɜːθ/ city in NE Texas, USA; population (1980) 385,164, metropolitan area (with Dallas) 2,964,000. Formerly an important cow town, it is now a grain, petroleum, aerospace, and railway centre serving the S USA.

Forty-Five the ◊Jacobite rebellion 1745, led by Prince ◊Charles Edward Stuart. With his army of Highlanders 'Bonnie Prince Charlie' occupied Edinburgh and advanced into England as far as Derby, but then turned back. The rising was crushed by the Duke of Cumberland at Culloden 1746.

Foss /fɒs/ Lukas 1922– . US composer and conductor. He wrote the cantata *The Prairie* 1942 and *Time Cycle* for soprano and orchestra 1960.

Foster *Hong Kong and Shanghai Banking Corporation Headquarters (1986) designed by British architect Norman Foster.*

Born in Germany, he studied in Europe before settling in the USA in 1937. A student of ◊Hindemith, his vocal music is composed in Neo-Classical style; in the mid-1950s he began increasingly to employ improvisation. Foss has also written chamber and orchestral music in which the players reproduce tape-recorded effects.

Fosse /fɒs/ Robert ('Bob') 1927–1987. US film director who entered films as a dancer and choreographer from Broadway, making his directorial debut with *Sweet Charity* 1968. He gained an Academy Award for his second film as director, *Cabaret* 1972. His other work includes *All That Jazz* 1979.

fossil (Latin *fossilis* 'dug up') remains of an animal or plant preserved in rocks. Fossils may be formed by refrigeration (for example, Siberian ◊mammoths); carbonization (leaves in coal); formation of a cast (dinosaur or human footprints in mud); or mineralization of bones, more generally teeth or shells. The study of fossils is called ◊palaeontology.

fossil fuel fuel, such as coal or oil, formed from the fossilized remains of plants that lived hundreds of millions of years ago. Fossil fuels are a ◊non-renewable resource and will run out eventually. Extraction of coal causes considerable environmental pollution, and burning coal contributes to problems of ◊acid rain and the ◊greenhouse effect.

Fos-sur-Mer /ˈfɒs sjuə ˈmeə/ harbour and medieval township near Marseille, France, forming the southern focus of a direct Rhône-Rhine route to the North Sea.

Foster /ˈfɒstə/ Jodie 1962– . US film actress, who began as a child in a great variety of roles. Her work includes Scorsese's *Taxi Driver* 1976, *Bugsy Malone* 1976, and *The Accused* 1988.

Foster /ˈfɒstə/ Norman 1935– . British architect of the high-tech school. His works include the Willis Faber office, Ipswich, 1978, the Sainsbury Centre for Visual Arts at the University of East Anglia 1979, and the headquarters of the Hongkong and Shanghai Bank, Hong Kong, 1986.

Foster /ˈfɒstə/ Stephen Collins 1826–1864. US songwriter. He wrote sentimental popular songs including 'My Old Kentucky Home' 1853 and

'Beautiful Dreamer' 1864, and rhythmic minstrel songs such as 'Oh! Susanna' 1848 and 'Camptown Races' 1850.

Foucault /ˈfuːkəʊ/ Jean Bernard Léon 1819–1868. French physicist who used a pendulum to demonstrate the rotation of the Earth on its axis, and invented the gyroscope.

He did investigations into heat and light, discovered ◊eddy currents induced in a copper disc moving in a magnetic field, invented a polarizer, and made improvements in the electric arc.

Foucault /ˈfuːkəʊ/ Michel 1926–1984. French philosopher, who rejected phenomenology and existentialism. His work was concerned with how forms of knowledge and forms of human subjectivity are constructed by specific institutions and practices.

Foucault was deeply influenced by ◊Nietzsche, and developed a novel analysis of the operation of power in modern society using Nietzschean concepts. His work was largely historical in character.

Fouché /ˈfuːʃeɪ/ Joseph, Duke of Otranto 1759–1820. French politician. He was elected to the National Convention (the post-Revolutionary legislature), and organized the conspiracy which overthrew the Jacobin leader Robespierre. Napoleon employed him as police minister.

fouetté (French 'whipped') in ballet, a type of ◊pirouette in which the working leg whips out to the side and then into the knee while the dancer spins on the supporting leg. Odile performs 32 *fouettés* in Act III of *Swan Lake*.

Fou-Liang /ˈfəʊ liˈæŋ/ former name of ◊Jingdezhen, a town in China.

Fountains Abbey /ˈfaʊntənz/ Cistercian abbey in North Yorkshire, England. It was founded about 1132, and suppressed 1540. The ruins were incorporated into a Romantic landscape garden 1720–40 with lake, formal water garden, temples, and a deer park.

Fouquet /ˈfuːkeɪ/ Jean *c.*1420–1481. French painter. He became court painter to Charles VIII in 1448 and to Louis XI in 1475. His *Melun diptych* about 1450 (Musées Royaux, Antwerp, and Staatliche Museen, Berlin), shows Italian Renaissance influence.

Fouquet /ˈfuːkeɪ/ Nicolas 1615–1680. French politician, a rival to Louis XIV's minister ◊Colbert. Fouquet became *procureur général* of the Paris parliament 1650 and *surintendant des finances* 1651, responsible for raising funds for the long war against Spain, a post he held until arrested and imprisoned for embezzlement (at the instigation of Colbert, who succeeded him) from 1661 until his death.

four-colour process colour ◊printing using four printing plates, based on the principle that any

Fouché *Joseph Fouché was minister of police under Napoleon. He was also instrumental in organizing the conspiracy that overthrew Robespierre in 1794.*

Fourier The French socialist François Fourier. One of his major theories was to reorganize society into self-sufficient units, living and working in cooperation.

colour is made up of differing proportions of the primary colours blue, red, and green. The first stage in preparing a colour picture for printing is to produce separate films, one each for the blue, red, and green respectively in the picture (colour separations). From these separations three printing plates are made, with a fourth plate for black. Ink colours complementary to those represented on the plates are used for printing—yellow for the blue plate, cyan for the red, and magenta for the green.

Fourdrinier machine a papermaking machine, patented by the Fourdrinier brothers Henry and Sealy in England 1803. On the machine, liquid pulp flows onto a moving wire-mesh belt, and water drains and is sucked away, leaving a damp paper web. This is passed first through a series of steam-heated rollers, which dry it, and then between heavy calender rollers, which give it a smooth finish. The machine can measure up to 90 m/300 ft in length, and is still in use.

Four Freedoms, the four kinds of liberty essential to human dignity as defined in an address to the US Congress by Franklin D Roosevelt 6 Jan 1941: freedom of speech and expression, freedom of worship, freedom from want, freedom from fear.

Fourier /'fʊrieɪ/ François Charles Marie 1772–1837. French socialist. In *Le Nouveau monde industriel/The New Industrial World* 1829–30, he advocated

that society should be organized in self-sufficient cooperative units of about 1,500 people. Conventional marriage was to be abandoned.

Fourier /'fʊrieɪ/ Jean Baptiste Joseph 1768–1830. French applied mathematician whose formulation of heat flow 1807 contains the proposal that, with certain constraints, any mathematical function can be represented by trigonometrical series. This principle forms the basis of *Fourier analysis*, used today in many different fields of physics. His idea, not immediately well received, gained currency and is embodied in his *Théorie analytique de la chaleur*/The Analytical Theory of Heat 1822.

Four Noble Truths in Buddhism, a summary of the basic concepts: life is suffering (Sanskrit *duhkha*, sour); suffering has its roots in desire (*trishna*, clinging or grasping); the cessation of desire is the end of suffering, *nirvana*; and this can be reached by the Noble Eightfold Path of *dharma* (truth).

four-stroke cycle the engine-operating cycle of most petrol and ◊diesel engines. The 'stroke' is an upward or downward movement of a piston in a cylinder. In a petrol engine the cycle begins with the induction of a fuel mixture as the piston goes down on its first stroke. On the second stroke (up) the piston compresses the mixture in the top of the cylinder. An electric spark then ignites the mixture, and the gases produced force the piston down on its third, power stroke. On the fourth stroke (up) the piston expels the burned gases from the cylinder into the exhaust.

The four-stroke cycle is also called the *Otto cycle*. The diesel engine cycle works in a slightly different way to that of the petrol engine on the first two strokes.

Fourteen Points the terms proposed by President Wilson of the USA in his address to Congress 8 Jan 1918, as a basis for the settlement of World War I that was about to reach its climax. The creation of the League of Nations was one of the points.

fourth estate the press. The term was coined by the British politician Edmund Burke in analogy with the traditional three ◊estates.

fourth-generation language in computing, a type of programming language designed for the rapid programming of ◊applications but often lacking the ability to control the individual parts of the computer. Such a language typically provides easy ways of designing screens and reports, and of using databases. Other 'generations' (the term implies a class of language rather than a chronological sequence) are ◊machine code (first generation), ◊assembly language (second), and conventional high-level languages such as ◊BASIC and ◊PASCAL (third).

Fourth of July in the USA, the anniversary of the day in 1776 when the ◊Declaration of Independence was adopted by the Continental Congress.

It is a public holiday, officially called *Independence Day*.

Fourth Republic the French constitutional regime that was established between 1944 and 1946, and lasted until 4 Oct 1958: from liberation after Nazi occupation during World War II to the introduction of a new constitution by Gen de Gaulle.

Foveaux Strait /'fɒvəʊ/ stretch of water between the extreme south of South Island, New Zealand, and Stewart Island. It is a fishing area, and produces a considerable oyster catch.

Fowey /fɔɪ/ port and resort in Cornwall, England, near the mouth of the Fowey estuary; population, with ◊St Austell (1981) 36,500. It is an outlet for the Cornish clay mining industry.

fowl a chicken or chickenlike bird. The *red jungle fowl Gallus gallus* is the ancestor of all domestic chickens. It is a forest bird of South Asia, without the size or egg-laying ability of many domestic strains. ◊*Guinea fowl* are African.

Fowler /'faʊlə/ (Peter) Norman 1938– . British Conservative politician. He was a junior minister in the Heath government, transport secretary in the first Thatcher administration 1979, social services secretary 1981, and was employment secretary 1987–89. He resigned Jan 1990.

Fowler was chair of the Cambridge University Conservative Association in 1960. He worked as correspondent for *The Times* until 1970, when he became a Member of Parliament.

Fowler /'faʊlə/ Henry Watson 1858–1933 and his brother Francis George 1870–1918. English scholars and authors of a number of English dictionaries. *Modern English Usage* 1926, the work of Henry Fowler, has become a classic reference work for advice on matters of style and disputed usage.

Fowler /'faʊlə/ William 1911– . US astrophysicist. In 1983, he and Subrahmanyan Chandrasekhar were awarded the Nobel Prize in Physics for their work on the life cycle of stars and the origin of chemical elements.

Fowles /faʊlz/ John 1926– . English writer whose novels, often concerned with illusion and reality, and with the creative process, include *The Collector* 1963, *The Magus* 1965, *The French Lieutenant's Woman 1969*, *Daniel Martin* 1977, *Mantissa* 1982, and *A Maggot* 1985.

fox member of the smaller species of wild dog of the family Canidae, which live in Europe, North America, Asia, and Africa. The fox feeds on a wide range of animals from worms to rabbits, scavenges for food, and also eats berries. It is largely nocturnal, and makes an underground den, or 'earth'. It is very adaptable, maintaining high populations in some urban areas.

The *common* or *red fox Vulpes vulpes* of Britain and Europe is about 60 cm/2 ft long plus a tail ('brush') 40 cm/1.3 ft long. The fur is reddish with black patches behind the ears and a light tip to the tail. Other foxes include the *Arctic fox Alopex lagopus*, the ◊*fennec*, the *gray foxes* genus *Urocyon* of North and Central America, and the South American genus *Dusicyon*, to which the extinct *Falkland Islands dog* belonged.

Fox /fɒks/ Charles James 1749–1806. English Whig politician. He entered Parliament 1769 as a supporter of the court, but went over to the opposition 1774. As secretary of state 1782, leader of the opposition to Pitt, and foreign secretary 1806, he welcomed the French Revolution and brought about the abolition of the slave trade.

Fox was the son of the 1st baron Holland. In 1782 he became secretary of state in Rockingham's government, but resigned when Shelburne succeeded

four-stroke cycle

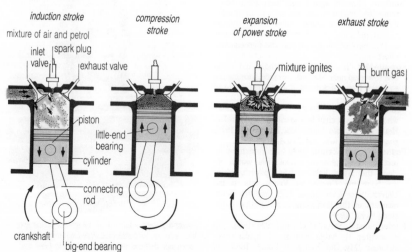

induction stroke
mixture of air and petrol
inlet valve
spark plug
exhaust valve
piston
little-end bearing
cylinder
connecting rod
crankshaft
big-end bearing

compression stroke

expansion of power stroke
mixture ignites

exhaust stroke
burnt gas

fox

Fox *Portrait of Charles James Fox by K A Hickel (c.1793) National Portrait Gallery, London.*

Rockingham. He allied with North 1783 to overthrow Shelburne, and formed a coalition ministry with himself as secretary of state. When the Lords threw out Fox's bill to reform the government of India, George III dismissed the ministry, and in their place installed Pitt.

Fox now became leader of the opposition, although cooperating with Pitt in the impeachment of Warren Hastings, the governor general of India. The 'Old Whigs' deserted to the government 1792 over the French Revolution, leaving Fox and a small group of 'New Whigs' to oppose Pitt's war of intervention and his persecution of the reformers. On Pitt's death 1806 a ministry was formed with Fox as foreign secretary, which at Fox's insistence abolished the slave trade. He opened peace negotiations with France, but died before their completion, and was buried in Westminster Abbey, London.

Fox /fɒks/ George 1624–1691. English founder of the Society of ◊Friends. He became a travelling preacher 1647, and in 1650 was imprisoned for blasphemy at Derby, where the name Quakers was first applied derogatorily to him and his followers, supposedly because he enjoined Judge Bennet to 'quake at the word of the Lord'.

Fox /fɒks/ James 1939– . British film actor, usually cast in upper-class, refined roles but renowned for his portrayal of a psychotic gangster in Nicolas Roeg's *Performance* 1970, which was followed by a ten-year break from acting.

In the 1960s Fox appeared in films like *The Servant* 1963 and *Isadora* 1968. He returned to the screen in, for example, *A Passage to India* 1984 and *Absolute Beginners* 1985.

Foxe /fɒks/ John 1516–1587. English Protestant propagandist. He became a canon of Salisbury 1563. His *Book of Martyrs* 1563 luridly described persecutions under Queen Mary, reinforcing popular hatred of Roman Catholicism.

foxglove flowering plant of the genus *Digitalis*, family Scrophulariaceae, found in Europe and the Mediterranean region. It bears showy spikes of bell-like flowers, and grows up to 1.5 m/5 ft high.

The wild species *Digitalis purpurea*, native to Britain, produces purple to reddish flowers. It was the original source of digitalis, a drug used for some heart problems.

foxhound small keen-nosed hound. It is a combination of the old southern hound and other

foxglove

breeds, and has been bred in England for 300 years.

fox-hunting the pursuit of a fox across country on horseback, aided by a pack of foxhounds, specially trained to track the fox's scent. The aim is to catch and kill the fox. In draghunting, hounds pursue a prepared trail rather than a fox.

Described by the playwright Oscar Wilde as 'the unspeakable in pursuit of the uneatable', fox-hunting has met with increasing opposition. Animal-rights activists condemn it as involving excessive cruelty, and in Britain groups such as the Hunt Saboteurs disrupt it.

Fox-hunting dates from the late 17th century, when it arose as a practical method of limiting the fox population which endangered poultry farming, but by the early 19th century it was indulged in as a sport by the British aristocracy and gentry who ceremonialized it. Fox-hunting was introduced into the USA by early settlers from England and continues in the S and middle Atlantic regions.

English 'hunts' (organized groups of hunters) include the Quorn, Pytchley, Belvoir, and Cottesmore. The recognized fox-hunting season runs from the first Monday in Nov until the following Apr.

foxtrot ballroom dance originating in the USA about 1914. It has alternating long and short steps, supposedly like the movements of the fox.

Foyle /fɔɪl/ sea-lough on the N coast of Ireland, traversed by the frontier of Northern Ireland and the Irish Republic.

f.p.s. system system of units based on the foot, pound, and second as units of length, mass, and time. It has now been replaced for scientific work by the ◊SI system.

Fracastoro /ˌfrækəˈstɔːrəʊ/ Girolamo *c.* 1478–1553. Italian physician known for his two medical books. He was born and worked mainly in Verona. His first book was written in verse, *Syphilis sive morbus gallicus/Syphilis or the French disease* 1530. It was one of the earliest texts on syphilis, a disease Fracastoro named. In a second work, *De contagione/ On contagion* 1546, he wrote, far ahead of his time, about 'seeds of contagion'.

fractal (from Latin *fractus* 'broken') an irregular shape or surface produced by a procedure of repeated subdivision. Generated on a computer screen, fractals are used in creating models for geographical or biological processes (for example, the creation of a coastline by erosion or accretion, or the growth of plants).

Sets of curves with such discordant properties were developed in Germany by Georg Cantor (1845–1918) and Karl Weierstrass (1815– 1897). The name was coined by the French mathematician Benoit Mandelbrod. Fractals are also used for computer art.

fraction (from Latin *fractus* 'broken') in mathematics, a number that indicates one or more equal parts of a whole. Usually, the number of equal parts into which the unit is divided (denominator) is written below a horizontal line, and the number of parts comprising the fraction (numerator) is written above; thus 2/3 or 3/4. Such fractions are called **vulgar** or **simple fractions**. The denominator can never be zero.

A **proper fraction** is one in which the numerator is less than the denominator. An **improper fraction** has a numerator that is larger than the denominator, for example 3/2. It can therefore be expressed as a mixed number, for example, 11/2. A combination such as 5/0 is not regarded as a fraction (an object cannot be divided into zero equal parts), and mathematically any number divided by 0 is equal to infinity. A **decimal fraction** has as its denominator a power of 10, and these are omitted by use of the decimal point and notation, for example 0.04, which is 4/100. The digits to the right of the decimal point indicate the numerators of vulgar fractions whose denominators are 10, 100, 1,000, and so on. Most fractions can be expressed exactly as decimal fractions (1/3 = 0.333...).

Fractions are also known as the **rational numbers**, that is numbers formed by a ratio. **Integers** may be expressed as fractions with a denominator of 1.

fractionation also known as **fractional distillation**, a process used to split complex mixtures (such as crude oil) into their components, usually by repeated heating, boiling, and condensation.

Fra Diavolo /ˈfrɑː diːˈævələʊ/ nickname of Michele Pezza 1771–1806. Italian brigand. He was a renegade monk, led a gang in the mountains of Calabria for many years, and was eventually executed in Naples.

Fragonard /ˌfrægəʊˈnɑː/ Jean Honoré 1732–1806. French painter, the leading exponent of the Rococo style (along with his master Boucher). His light-hearted subjects include *The Swing* about 1766 (Wallace Collection, London).

Frame /freɪm/ Janet. Pen name of Janet Paterson Frame Clutha 1924– . New Zealand novelist. After being wrongly diagnosed as schizophrenic, she reflected her experiences 1945–54 in the novel *Faces in the Water* 1961 and the autobiographical *An Angel at My Table* 1984.

Frampton /ˈfræmptən/ George James 1860–1928. British sculptor. His work includes the statue of *Peter Pan* in Kensington Gardens and the *Nurse Cavell memorial* near St Martin's, London.

franc French coin, so called from 1360 when it was a gold coin inscribed *Francorum Rex*, 'King of the Franks'. The **franc CFA** (*Communauté française d'Afrique*) is the currency of the former French territories in Africa; in France's Pacific territories the **franc CFP** (*Communauté française du pacifique*) is used. The currency units of Belgium, Luxembourg, and Switzerland are also called franc.

France /frɑːns/ country in W Europe, bounded NE by Belgium and West Germany, E by Switzerland and Italy, S by the Mediterranean, SW by Spain and Andorra, and W by the Atlantic Ocean.

government Under the 1958 Fifth Republic constitution, amended in 1962, France has a two-chamber legislature and a 'shared executive' government. The legislature comprises a national assembly, whose 577 deputies are elected for five-year terms from single-member constituencies following a two-ballot, 'run-off' majority system (proportional representation was adopted for the 1986 elections but was later rescinded), and a senate, whose 321 members are indirectly elected, a third at a time, triennially for nine-year terms from groups of local councillors.

22 national assembly and 13 senate seats are elected by overseas *départements* and territories and 12 senate seats by French nationals abroad. The national assembly is the dominant chamber, from whose ranks the prime minister is drawn and upon whose support the government rests. The senate can temporarily veto legislation. Its vetoes, however, can be overridden by the national assembly.

France's executive is functionally divided between the president and prime minister. The president, elected for a seven-year term by direct universal suffrage after gaining a majority in either a first or second 'run-off' ballot, functions as head of state, commander-in-chief of the armed forces and guardian of the constitution. The president selects the prime minister, presides over cabinet meetings, countersigns government bills, negotiates foreign treaties, and can call referenda and dissolve the national assembly. According to the constitution, however, ultimate control over policy making rests with the prime minister and council of ministers.

The president and prime minister work with ministers from political and technocratic backgrounds, assisted by a skilled and powerful civil service. A nine-member Constitutional Council (selected triennially in a staggered manner by the state president and the presidents of the senate and national assembly) and a *Conseil d'Etat*,

France

Regions and Départements

0   150 km   *Départements* are numbered by the standard French alphabetical system

staffed by senior civil servants, rule on the legality of legislation passed.

At the local level there are 21 regional councils concerned with economic planning. Below these are 96 *département* councils and almost 36,000 town and village councils. Corsica has its own directly elected 61-seat parliament with powers to propose amendments to national assembly legislation.

There are four overseas *départements* (◊French Guiana, ◊Guadeloupe, ◊Martinique, and ◊Réunion) with their own elected general and regional councils, two overseas 'collective territories' (◊Mayotte and ◊St Pierre and Miquelon) administered by appointed commissioners, and four overseas territories (◊French Polynesia, the ◊French Southern and Antarctic Territories, ◊New Caledonia, and the ◊Wallis and Futuna Islands) governed by appointed high comissioners, which form constituent parts of the French Republic, returning deputies to the national legislature.

French politics are dominated by four parties, divided into two broad right and left ideological and electoral coalitions. The 'right coalition', which was pre-eminent 1958–81, is divided between the Rassemblement (Rally) pour la République (RPR), formed in 1976 by Jacques Chirac as the successor to ◊de Gaulle's Union pour la Nouvelle République (UNR), and the Union pour la Démocratie Française (UDF), formed by President Valéry ◊Giscard d'Estaing, Prime Minister Raymond ◊Barre and Jean Lecanuet in 1978 to unite several centre-right parties. The two major parties on the left are the pro-Moscow French Communist Party (PCF), and the Socialist Party (PS). The fifth significant party is the extreme

right-wing National Front, which, although excluded from electoral coalitions, has gained ground campaigning for immigrant repatriation and the return of capital punishment.

history For history before 1945, see ◊France, history. A 'united front' provisional government headed by de Gaulle, and including communists, assumed power in the re-established republic before a new constitution was framed and adopted for a Fourth Republic in Jan 1946. This provided for a weak executive and powerful national assembly which, being elected under a generous system of proportional representation, was to be divided between numerous small party groupings. With 26 impermanent governments being formed 1946–58, real power passed to the civil service, which, by introducing a new system of 'indicative economic planning', engineered rapid economic reconstruction. Decolonization of French ◊Indochina 1954, Morocco and Tunisia 1956, and entry into the EEC 1957 were also effected.

The Fourth Republic was overthrown in 1958 by a political and military crisis over Algerian independence, which threatened to lead to a French army revolt. De Gaulle was recalled from retirement to head a government of national unity, and supervised the framing of the new Fifth Republic constitution, which strengthened the president and prime minister.

De Gaulle, who became president in 1959, restored domestic stability and presided over the decolonization of Francophone Africa, including Algerian independence in 1962. Close economic links were maintained with former colonies. De Gaulle also initiated a new foreign policy, withdrawing France from ◊NATO in

1966 and developing an autonomous nuclear deterrent force. The de Gaulle era was one of economic growth and large scale rural-urban migration. Politically, however, there was tight censorship and strong centralization, and in 1967 the public reacted against de Gaulle's paternalism by voting the 'right coalition' a reduced majority.

A year later, in 1968, the nation was paralyzed by students' and workers' demonstrations in Paris which spread to the provinces and briefly threatened the government. De Gaulle called elections and won a landslide victory. In 1969, however, he was defeated in a referendum over proposed senate and local government reforms and resigned. De Gaulle's former prime minister, Georges ◊Pompidou, was elected president and pursued Gaullist policies until his death in 1974.

Pompidou's successor as president, Valéry Giscard d'Estaing, leader of the centre-right Independent Republicans, introduced liberalizing domestic reforms and played a more active and co-operative role in the EC. Giscard faced opposition, however, from his 'right coalition' partner, Jacques ◊Chirac, who was prime minister 1974–76, and deteriorating external economic conditions. France performed better than many of its European competitors between 1974–81, with the president launching a major nuclear power programme to save on energy imports and, while Raymond ◊Barre was prime minister (1976–81), a new liberal 'freer market' economic strategy. However, with 1,700,000 unemployed, Giscard was defeated by the Socialist party leader, François ◊Mitterrand, in the 1981 presidential election.

Mitterrand's victory was the first presidential success for the 'left coalition' during the Fifth Republic and was immediately succeeded by a landslide victory for the PS and PCF in elections to the national assembly in 1981. The new administration, which included four Communist ministers, introduced a radical programme of social reform, decentralization and nationalization, and passed a series of reflationary budgets aimed at reducing unemployment.

Financial constraints, however, forced a switch towards a more conservative policy of 'rigueur' (austerity) in 1983. A U-turn in economic policy was completed in 1984 when prime minister Pierre ◊Mauroy was replaced by Laurent ◊Fabius, prompting the resignation of communist members of the cabinet. Unemployment rose to over 2,500,000 in 1985–86, increasing racial tension in urban areas. The extreme right-wing National Front, led by Jean-Marie ◊Le Pen, benefitted from this and gained seats in the Mar 1986 National Assembly elections, held under a new proportional representation system. The 'left coalition' lost its majority, the PCF having been in decline in recent years. The PS, however, had emerged as France's single most popular party.

From 1958 to 1986 tthe president and prime minister had been drawn from the same party coalition and the president had been allowed to dominate in both home and foreign afairs. In 1986, however, Mitterrand was obliged to appoint as prime minister the leader ofthe opposition, Jacques Chirac, who emerged as the dominant force in the 'shared executive'. Chirac introduced a radical 'new conservative' programme of denationalization, deregulation, and 'desocialization', using the executive's decree powers and the parliamentary 'guillotine' to steamroller measures through. His educational and economic reforms, however, encountered serious opposition from militant students and striking workers, necessitating embarrassing policy concessions. With his national standing tarnished, Chirac was comfortably defeated by Mitterrand in the May 1988 presidential election. In the national assembly elections that followed in June 1988, the socialists emerged as the largest single political party. Mitterrand duly appointed Michel ◊Rocard,

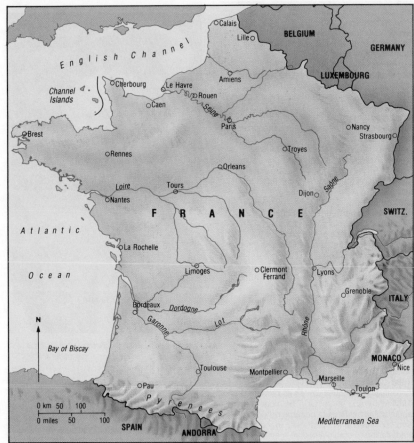

a popular, moderate, social democrat as prime minister heading a minority PS government that included several centre party representatives. Rocard implemented a progressive programme, aimed at protecting the underprivileged and improving the 'quality of life'. In June 1988 he negotiated the Matignon Accord, designed to solve the New Caledonia 'problem', which was later approved by referendum. Between 1988 and 1990 France enjoyed a strong economic upturn and attention focussed increasingly on 'quality of life', with the Green party gaining 11% of the national vote in the European Parliament elections of June 1989.

France: regions and départements

Region and Département	Capital	Area sq km
Alsace		*8,300*
Bas-Rhin	Strasbourg	
Haut-Rhin	Colmar	
Aquitaine		*41,300*
Dordogne	Périgueux	
Gironde	Bordeaux	
Landes	Mont-de-Marsan	
Lot-et-Garonne	Agen	
Pyrénées-Atlantiques	Pau	
Auvergne		*26,000*
Allier	Moulins	
Cantal	Aurillac	
Haute-Loire	Le Puy	
Puy-de-Dôme	Clermont-Ferrand	
Basse-Normandie		*17,600*
Calvados Nord	Lille	
Pas-de-Calais	Arras	
Bourgogne		*31,600*
Côte-d'Or	Dijon	
Nièvre	Nevers	
Saône-et-Loire	Mâcon	
Yonne	Auxerre	
Bretagne		*27,200*
Côtes-du-Nord	St Brieuc	
Finistère	Quimper	
Ille-et-Vilaine	Rennes	
Morbihan	Vannes	
Centre		*39,200*
Cher	Bourges	
Eure-et-Loire	Chartres	
Indre	Châteauroux	
Indre-et-Loire	Tours	
Loire-et-Cher	Blois	
Loiret	Orléans	
Champagne-Ardenne		*25,600*
Ardenne	Charleville-Mézières	
Aube	Troyes	
Marne	Châlons-sur-Marne	
Haute-Marne	Chaumont	
Corsica		*8,700*
Haute Corse	Bastia	
Corse du Sud	Ajaccio	
Franche-Comté		*16,200*
Doubs	Besançon	
Jura	Lons-le-Saunier	
Haute Saône	Vesoul	
Terre de Belfort	Belfort	
Haute-Normandie		*12,300*
Eure	Evreux	
Seine-Maritime	Rouen	
Île de France		*12,000*
Essonne	Évry	
Val-de-Marne	Créteil	
Val d'Oise	Cergy-Pontoise	
Ville de Paris		
Seine-et-Marne	Melun	
Hauts-de-Seine	Nanterre	
Seine-Saint-Denis	Bobigny	
Yvelines	Versailles	
Languedoc-Roussillon		*27,400*

France /frɒns/ Anatole. Pen name of Jacques Anatole Thibault 1844–1924. French writer, noted for the wit, urbanity, and style of his works. His earliest novel was *Le Crime de Sylvestre Bonnard/The Crime of Sylvester Bonnard* 1881; later books include the satiric *L'Île des pingouins/Penguin Island* 1908 and *Les Dieux ont soif/The Gods are Athirst* 1912. Nobel Prize 1921. He was a socialist and supporter of ◊Dreyfus.

France, history

5th century BC France, then called *Gaul*, was invaded by Celtic peoples.

57–51 Conquest by the Roman general Julius Caesar.

1st–5th century AD During Roman rule the inhabitants of France accepted Roman civilization and the Latin language. As the empire declined, Germanic tribes overran the country.

481–511 A Frankish chief, Clovis, brought the other tribes under his rule, accepted Christianity, and made Paris the capital.

511–751 Under Clovis' successors, the Merovingians, the country sank into anarchy.

741–68 Unity was restored by Pepin, founder of the Carolingian dynasty.

768–814 Charlemagne made France the centre of a great empire.

912 The province of Normandy was granted as a duchy to the Viking leader Rollo, whose invading Norsemen had settled there.

987 The first king of the House of Capet assumed the crown. Under Charlemagne's weak successors the great nobles had become semi-independent. The Capets established rule in the district around Paris, but were surrounded by vassals stronger than themselves.

11th–13th centuries The power of the Capets was gradually extended, with the support of the church and the townspeople.

1337–1453 In the Hundred Years' War Charles VII expelled the English from France, aided by Joan of Arc.

France
French Republic
(République Française)

area (including Corsica) 543,965 sq km/209,970 sq mi
capital Paris
towns Lyon, Lille, Bordeaux, Toulouse, Nantes, Strasbourg; ports Marseille, Le Havre
physical rivers Seine, Loire, Garonne, Rhône; mountain ranges Alps, Massif Central, Pyrenees, Jura, Vosges, Cévennes
territories Guadeloupe, French Guiana, Martinique, Réunion, St Pierre and Miquelon, Southern and Antarctic Territories, New Caledonia, French Polynesia, Wallis and Futuna
features Ardennes forest, Auvergne mountain region, caves of Dordogne with relics of early humans, Riviera
head of state François Mitterrand from 1981
head of government Michel Rocard from 1988
political system liberal democracy
political parties Socialist Party (PS), left-of-centre; Rally for the Republic (RPR), neo-Gaullist conservative; Union for French Democracy (UDF), centre-right; Republican Party (RP), centre-right; French Communist Party (PCF), Marxist-Leninist; National Front, far-right; Greens, environmentalist
exports fruit (especially apples), wine, cheese, cars, aircraft, chemicals, jewellery, silk, lace; tourism is important
currency franc (9.70 = £1 Feb 1990)
population (1988 est) 55,854,000 (including 4,500,000 immigrants, chiefly from Portugal, Algeria, Morocco, and Tunisia); annual growth rate 0.3%
life expectancy men 71, women 79
language French (regional languages include Breton)
religion mainly Roman Catholic; Muslim 3 million, Protestant 750,000
literacy 99% (1984)
GNP $568 bn (1983); $7,179 per head of population
chronology
1944–46 De Gaulle provisional government. Commencement of Fourth Republic.
1954 Independence of Indochina.
1956 Moroccan and Tunisian independence.
1957 Entry into EEC.
1958 Recall of de Gaulle following Algerian crisis. Commencement of Fifth Republic.
1959 De Gaulle became president.
1962 Algerian independence.
1966 France withdrew from NATO.
1968 'May events' crisis.
1969 De Gaulle resigned following referendum defeat. Pompidou became president.
1974 Giscard d'Estaing elected president.
1981 Mitterrand elected Fifth Republic's first socialist president.
1986 'Cohabitation' experiment, with the conservative Jacques Chirac as prime minister.
1988 Mitterrand re-elected. The moderate socialist Michel Rocard became prime minister and continued in this post despite the Socialist Party failing to obtain a secure majority in the National Assembly elections. Matignon Accord on future of New Caledonia approved by referendum.
1989 Greens gained 11% of vote in elections to European Parliament.

1483 Burgundy and Brittany were annexed. Through the policies of Louis XI the restoration of the royal power was achieved.
1503–1697 Charles VIII's Italian wars initiated a struggle with Spain for supremacy in W Europe which lasted for two centuries.
1592–98 Protestantism (Huguenot) was adopted by a party of the nobles for political reasons; the result was a succession of civil wars, fought under religious slogans.
1589–1610 Henry IV restored peace, established religious toleration, and made the monarchy absolute.
1634–48 The ministers Richelieu and Mazarin, by their intervention in the Thirty Years' War, secured Alsace, and made France the leading power in Europe.
1643–1763 Louis XIV embarked on an aggressive policy that united Europe against him; in his reign began the conflict with Britain that lost France its colonies in Canada and India in the War of the Spanish Succession (1701–14), War of the Austrian Succession (1756–58), and Seven Years' War (1756–63).
1789–99 The French Revolution abolished feudalism and absolute monarchy, but failed to establish democracy.
1799–1815 Napoleon's military dictatorship was facilitated by foreign wars (1792–1802, 1803–15). The Bourbon monarchy was restored 1814 with Louis XVIII.
1830 Charles X's attempt to substitute absolute for limited monarchy provoked a revolution which placed his cousin, Louis Philippe, on the throne.
1848 In the Feb revolution Louis Philippe was overthrown and the Second Republic set up.

1852–70 The president of the republic, Louis Napoleon, Napoleon I's nephew, restored the empire 1852, with the title of Napoleon III. His expansionist foreign policy ended in defeat in the Franco-Prussian War and the foundation of the Third Republic.
1863–1946 France colonized Indochina, parts of N Africa, and the S Pacific.
1914 In July France entered World War I.
1936–38 A radical-socialist-communist alliance introduced many social reforms.
1939 France declared war on Germany.
1940 The German invasion allowed the extreme right to set up a puppet dictatorship under Pétain in Vichy, but resistance was maintained by the *maquis* and the Free French under de Gaulle.
1944 Liberation from the Nazis.
For postwar history see ◊France.

Francesca /fræn'tʃeskə/ Piero della see ◊Piero della Francesca, Italian painter.
Franche-Comté /'frɒnʃ kɒn'teɪ/ region of E France; area 16,200 sq km/6,253 sq mi; population (1987) 1,086,000. Its capital is Besançon, and includes the *départements* of Doubs, Jura, Haute Saône, and Territoire de Belfort. In the mountainous Jura, there is farming and forestry, and elsewhere there is engineering and plastics industries.
Once independent and ruled by its own count, it was disputed between France, Burgundy, Austria, and Spain from the 9th century until it became a French province under the Treaty of ◊Nijmegen 1678.
franchise in business, the right given by a manufacturer to a distributor to market the manufacturer's product. Examples of franchise operations in the UK include Benetton and the Body Shop.

Francis I Unstable and vacillating as a ruler, he is remembered for the brilliance of the artists and writers of his court.

Many US companies use franchises to distribute their products. It is usual for US motor companies to give restricted franchise dealerships covering specified models, with the manufacturer fixing the quota and other stringent conditions of sale.
Francis /'frɑːnsɪs/ or *François* two kings of France:
Francis I 1494–1547. King of France from 1515. He succeeded his cousin Louis XII, and from 1519 European politics turned on the rivalry between him and the Holy Roman emperor Charles V, which led to war 1521–29, 1536–38, and 1542–44. In 1525 Francis was defeated and captured at Pavia, and released only after signing a humiliating treaty. At home, he developed absolute monarchy.
Francis II 1544–1560. King of France from 1559 when he succeeded his father, Henry II. He married Mary Queen of Scots 1558. He was completely under the influence of his mother, ◊Catherine de' Medici.
Francis II /'frɑːnsɪs/ 1768–1835. Holy Roman emperor 1792–1806. He became Francis I, Emperor of Austria 1804, and abandoned the title of Holy Roman emperor 1806. During his reign Austria was five times involved in war with France, 1792–97, 1798–1801, 1805, 1809, and 1813–14. He succeeded his father Leopold II.
Franciscan order Catholic order of friars, *Friars Minor* or *Grey Friars*, founded 1209 by Francis of Assisi. Subdivisions were the strict Observants; the Conventuals, who were allowed to own property corporately; and the ◊Capuchins, founded 1529.
The Franciscan order included such scholars as the English scientist Roger Bacon. A female order, the *Poor Clares*, was founded by St ◊Clare 1215, and lay people who adopt a Franciscan regime without abandoning the world form a third order, *Tertiaries*.
Francis Ferdinand former English name for ◊Franz Ferdinand, archduke of Austria.
Francis Joseph former English name for ◊Franz Joseph, emperor of Austria-Hungary.
Francis of Assisi, St /ə'siːzi/ 1182–1226. Italian founder of the Roman Catholic Franciscan order of friars 1209 and, with St Clare, of the Poor Clares 1212. In 1224 he is said to have undergone a mystical experience during which he received the

stigmata (five wounds of Jesus). Many stories are told of his ability to charm wild animals, and he is the patron saint of ecologists. His feast day is 4 Oct.

The son of a wealthy merchant, Francis changed his life after two dreams during an illness following spells of military service when he was in his early twenties. He resolved to follow literally the behests of the New Testament and live a life of poverty and service while preaching a simple form of the Christian gospel. In 1219 he went to Egypt to convert the sultan, and lived for a month in his camp. Returning to Italy, he resigned his leadership of the friars.

Francis of Sales, St /sæl/ 1567–1622. French bishop and theologian. He became bishop of Geneva 1602, and in 1610 founded the order of the Visitation, an order of nuns. He is the patron saint of journalists and other writers. Feast day 24 Jan.

Francis de Sales was born in Savoy. His writings include *Introduction à la vie dévote*/*Introduction to a Devout Life* 1609, written to reconcile the Christian life with living in the real world.

francium a metallic element, symbol Fr, atomic number 87, relative atomic mass 223. It is a highly radioactive metal; the most stable isotope has a half-life of only 21 minutes. Francium was discovered by Marguérite Perey (1909–   ) 1939.

Franck /fræŋk/ César Auguste 1822–1890. Belgian composer. His music, mainly religious and Romantic in style, includes the Symphony in D minor 1866–68, *Symphonic Variations* 1885 for piano and orchestra, the Violin Sonata 1886, the oratorio *Les Béatitudes*/*The Beatitudes* 1879, and many organ pieces.

Franck /fræŋk/ James 1882–1964. US physicist influential in atom technology. He was awarded the 1925 Nobel prize for his 1914 experiments on the energy transferred by colliding electrons to mercury atoms, showing that the transfer was governed by the rules of ◊quantum theory.

Born and educated in Germany, he emigrated to the USA after publicly protesting against Hitler's racial policies. Franck participated in the wartime atomic-bomb project at Los Alamos but organized the 'Franck petition' 1945, which argued that the bomb should not be used against Japanese cities. After World War II he turned his research to photosynthesis.

Franco (Bahamonde) /fræŋkəu/ Francisco (Paulino Hermenegildo Teódulo) 1892–1975. Spanish dictator from 1939. As a general, he led the insurgent Nationalists to victory in the Spanish ◊Civil War 1936–39, supported by Fascist Italy and Nazi Germany, and established a dictatorship. In 1942 Franco reinstated the Cortes (Spanish parliament), which in 1947 passed an act by which he became head of state for life.

Franco was born in Galicia, NW Spain. He entered the army 1910, served in Morocco 1920–26, and was appointed chief of staff 1935, but demoted to governor of the Canary Islands 1936. Dismissed from this post by the Popular Front (Republican) government, he plotted an uprising with German and Italian assistance, and on the outbreak of the Civil War organized the invasion of Spain by N African troops and foreign legionaries. After the death of Gen Sanjurjo, he took command of the Nationalists, proclaiming himself *Caudillo* (leader) of Spain. The defeat of the Republic with the surrender of Madrid 1939 brought all Spain under his government. On the outbreak of World War II, in spite of Spain's official attitude of 'strictest neutrality', his pro-Axis sympathies led him to send aid, later withdrawn, to the German side.

At home, he curbed the growing power of the ◊Falange (the fascist party), and in later years slightly liberalized his regime. In 1969 he nominated ◊Juan Carlos as his successor and future king of Spain. He relinquished the premiership 1973, but remained head of state until his death.

Franco-German entente resumption of friendly relations between France and Germany, designed to erase the enmities of successive wars. It was initiated by the French president de Gaulle's visit to West Germany 1962, followed by the Franco-German Treaty of Friendship and Co-operation 1963.

François /frɒn'swɑ/ French form of ◊Francis, two kings of France.

Francome /'fræŋkəm/ John 1952–   . British jockey. He holds the record for the most National Hunt winners (over hurdles or fences). Between 1970 and 1985 he rode 1,138 winners from 5,061 mounts – the second person (after Stan Mellor) to ride 1,000 winners. He took up training after retiring from riding.

CAREER HIGHLIGHTS

Cheltenham Gold Cup: 1978
Champion Hurdle: 1981
Hennessy Cognac Gold Cup: 1983–84
King George VI Chase: 1982
Champion Jockey: 1979, 1981–85 (shared title 1982)

Franco-Prussian War 1870–71. The Prussian chancellor Bismarck put forward a German candidate for the vacant Spanish throne with the deliberate, and successful, intention of provoking the French emperor Napoleon III into declaring war. The Prussians defeated the French at ◊Sedan, then besieged Paris. The Treaty of Frankfurt May 1871 gave Alsace, Lorraine, and a large French indemnity to Prussia. The war established Prussia, at the head of a unified Germany, as Europe's leading power.

frangipani tropical American tree *Plumeria rubra*, family Apocynaceae; perfume is made from its strongly scented flowers.

Franglais the French language when mixed with (usually unwelcome) elements of modern, especially American, English (for example a mineral water described as *le fast drink des Alpes*).

Frank /fræŋk/ a member of a Germanic people influential in Europe in the 3rd–8th centuries. Believed to have originated in Pomerania on the Black Sea, they had settled on the Rhine by the 3rd century, spread into the Roman Empire by the 4th century, and gradually conquered most of Gaul and Germany under the ◊Merovingian and ◊Carolingian dynasties. The kingdom of the W Franks became France, the kingdom of the E Franks became Germany.

The Salian (western) Franks conquered Roman Gaul during the 4th–5th centuries. Their ruler, Clovis, united the Salians with the Ripuarian (eastern) Franks, and they were converted to Christianity. The agriculture of the Merovingian dynasty (named after Clovis' grandfather, Merovech) was more advanced than that of the Romans, and they introduced the three-field system (see ◊field). The Merovingians conquered most of western and central Europe, and lasted until the 8th century when the Carolingian dynasty was founded under Charlemagne. The kingdom of the W Franks was fused by the 9th century into a single people with the Gallo-Romans, speaking the modified form of Latin that became modern French.

Frank /fræŋk/ Anne 1929–1945. German diarist who fled to the Netherlands with her family 1933 to escape Nazi anti-semitism. During the German occupation of Amsterdam, they remained in a sealed-off room 1942–44, when betrayal resulted in Anne's deportation and death in Belsen concentration camp. Her diary of her time in hiding was published 1947.

Previously suppressed portions of her diary were published 1989. The house in which the family took refuge is preserved as a museum. The diary has been made into a play and a film, and sold 20 million copies in more than 50 languages.

Frank /fræŋk/ Ilya 1908–   . Russian physicist known for his work on radiation. In 1934, ◊Cherenkov has noted a peculiar blue radiation sometimes emitted as electrons passed through water. It was left to Frank and his colleague at Moscow University, Igor Tamm, to realize that this form of radiation was produced by charged particles travelling faster through the medium than the speed of light in the same medium. Franck shared the 1958 Nobel physics prize with Cherenkov and Tamm.

Frankel /'fræŋkəl/ Benjamin 1906–1973. English composer. He studied the piano in Germany and continued his studies in London while playing jazz violin in nightclubs. He wrote chamber music and numerous film scores.

Frankenstein or, The Modern Prometheus a Gothic horror story by Mary Shelley, published in England 1818. Frankenstein, a scientist, discovers how to bring inanimate matter to life, and creates a man-monster. When Frankenstein fails to provide a mate to satisfy its human emotions, the monster seeks revenge by killing Frankenstein's brother and bride. Frankenstein dies in an attempt to destroy his creation.

Frankenstein law in the USA, popular name for the ruling by the Supreme Court (1980) that new forms of life created in the laboratory may be patented.

Frankenthaler /'fræŋkənθɔːlə/ Helen 1928–   . US Abstract Expressionist painter, inventor of the colour-staining technique whereby the unprimed, absorbent canvas is stained or soaked with thinned-out paint, creating deep, soft veils of translucent colour.

Frankfurt-am-Main /'fræŋkfɜːt æm 'maɪn/ city in Hessen, West Germany, 72 km/45 mi NE of Mannheim; population (1988) 592,000. It is a commercial and banking centre, with electrical and machine industries, and an inland port on the river Main. An international book fair is held annually.

history Frankfurt was a free imperial city 1372–1806, when it was incorporated into ◊Prussia. It is the birthplace of the poet Goethe. It was the headquarters of the US zone of occupation in World War II and of the Anglo-US zone 1947–49.

Frankfurt-an-der-Oder /'fræŋkfɜːt æn deə 'əudə/ city in East Germany 80 km/50 mi SE of Berlin, capital of Frankfurt county; population (1981) 81,000. It is linked by the river Oder and its canals to the Vistula and Elbe. Industries include chemicals, engineering, paper, and leather. Frankfurt county has an area of 7,190 sq km/2,775 sq mi, and a population (1986) of 708,000.

Frankfurt Parliament an assembly of liberal politicians and intellectuals that met for a few months in 1848 in the aftermath of the ◊revolutions of 1848 and the overthrow of monarchies in most of the German states. They discussed a constitution for a united Germany, but the restoration of the old order and the suppression of the revolutions ended the parliament.

Frankfurt School the members of the *Institute of Social Research*, set up at Frankfurt University, Germany, 1923 as the first Marxist research centre. With the rise of Hitler, many of its members went to the USA and set up the institute at Columbia University, New York. In 1969 the institute was dissolved.

In the 1930s, under its second director Max Horkheimer, a group that included Erich Fromm, Herbert Marcuse, and T W Adorno attempted to update Marxism and create a coherent social theory. Drawing on a variety of disciplines as well as the writings of Marx and Freud, they produced works such as *Authority and the Family* 1936 and developed a Marxist perspective known as *critical theory*. After World War II the institute returned to Frankfurt, although Marcuse and some others remained in the USA. The German and US branches diverged in the 1950s, and the institute was dissolved after Adorno's death, although Jurgen Habermas and others have since attempted to revive its theory and research programme.

frankincense resin of trees of the Old World genus *Boswellia*, burned as incense. Costly in ancient times, it is traditionally believed to be one of the three gifts brought by the Magi to the infant Jesus.

Franklin *Portrait of Benjamin Franklin after Joseph Siffred Duplessis (1783), National Portrait Gallery, London.*

Franklin /ˈfræŋklɪn/ a district of ◊Northwest Territories, Canada; area 1,422,550 sq km/549,104 sq mi.

Franklin /ˈfræŋklɪn/ Benjamin 1706–1790. US scientist and politician. He proved that lightning is a form of electricity by the experiment of flying a kite in a storm, distinguished between positive and negative electricity, and invented the lightning conductor. He helped to draft the Declaration of Independence and the US constitution, and was ambassador to France 1776–85.

Franklin, born in Boston, combined a successful printing business with scientific experiment and inventions; he published the popular *Poor Richard's Almanac* 1733–58. A member of the Pennsylvania Assembly 1751–64, he was sent to Britain to lobby Parliament about tax grievances and achieved the repeal of the ◊Stamp Act; on his return to the USA he was prominent in the deliberations leading up to independence. As ambassador in Paris, he negotiated an alliance with France and the peace settlement with Britain. As a delegate from Pennsylvania 1785–88, he helped draw up the US constitution. His autobiography appeared in 1781.

Franklin /ˈfræŋklɪn/ John 1786–1847. English naval explorer who took part in expeditions to Australia, the Arctic, and N Canada, and in 1845 commanded an expedition to look for the ◊Northwest Passage, during which he and his crew perished.

The 1845 expedition had virtually found the Passage when it became trapped in the ice. No trace of the team was discovered until 1859. In 1984, two of its members, buried on King Edward Island, were found to be perfectly preserved in the frozen ground of their graves.

Franklin /ˈfræŋklɪn/ Rosalind 1920–1958. English biophysicist whose research on X-ray diffraction of DNA crystals helped Francis Crick and James D Watson to deduce the chemical structure of DNA.

Franz Ferdinand /frænts ˈfɜːdɪnænd/ or Francis Ferdinand 1863–1914. Archduke of Austria. He became heir to his uncle, Emperor Franz Joseph, from 1884 but while visiting Sarajevo 28 June 1914, he and his wife were assassinated by Serbian nationalists. Austria used the episode to make unreasonable demands on Serbia that ultimately precipitated World War I.

Franz Josef Land /frænts ˈjəʊzef/ (Russian **Zemlya Frantsa Iosifa**) archipelago of some 85 islands in the Arctic Ocean, E of Spitsbergen and NW of Novaya Zemlya, USSR. Area 20,720 sq km/8,000 sq mi. There are scientific stations.

Franz Joseph /frænts ˈjəʊzef/ or Francis Joseph 1830–1916. Emperor of Austria-Hungary from 1848, when his uncle, Ferdinand I, abdicated. After the suppression of the 1848 revolution, Franz Joseph tried to establish an absolute monarchy, but had to grant Austria a parliamentary constitution 1861, and Hungary equality with Austria 1867. He was defeated in the Italian War 1859 and the Prussian War 1866. In 1914 he made the assassination of his nephew, Franz Ferdinand, the

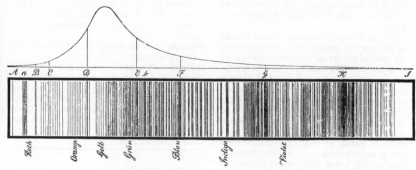

Fraunhofer *Drawing of the dark lines of the solar spectrum by the German physicist Joseph von Fraunhofer, the first accurately to map the chemical composition of the Sun's atmosphere. The curve shows the intensity of sunlight in different parts of the spectrum.*

excuse for attacking Serbia, precipitating World War I.

His only son committed suicide 1889, and the empress was assassinated 1897.

Frasch process a process used to extract underground deposits of sulphur. Superheated steam is piped to the sulphur deposit and melts it. Compressed air is then pumped down to force the molten sulphur to the surface. It was developed in the USA 1891 by German-born Herman Frasch (1851–1914).

Fraser /ˈfreɪzə/ river in British Columbia, Canada. It rises in the Yellowhead Pass of the Rockies and flows NW, then S, then W to the Strait of Georgia. It is 1,370 km/850 mi long, and famous for salmon.

Fraser /ˈfreɪzə/ (John) Malcolm 1930– . Australian Liberal politician, prime minister 1975–83; nicknamed 'the Prefect' because of a supposed disregard of subordinates.

Educated at Oxford, Fraser became a millionaire sheep farmer. In Mar 1975 he replaced Snedden as Liberal Party leader. In Nov, following the Whitlam government's economic difficulties, he blocked finance bills in the Senate, became prime minister of a caretaker government and in the consequent general election won a large majority. He lost to Hawke in the 1983 election.

Fraser /ˈfreɪzə/ Antonia 1932– . English author of biographies, including *Mary Queen of Scots* 1969; historical works, such as *The Weaker Vessel* 1984; and a series of detective novels featuring investigator Jemima Shore.

She is married to the playwright Harold Pinter, and is the daughter of Lord Longford.

Fraser /ˈfreɪzə/ Dawn 1937– . Australian swimmer, the only person to win the same swimming event at three consecutive Olympic Games: 100 metres freestyle in 1956, 1960, and 1964. The holder of 27 world records, she was the first

woman to break the one-minute barrier for the 100 metres.

CAREER HIGHLIGHTS

Olympic champion:
100 metres freestyle 1956, 1960, 1964
4 x 100 metres freestyle relay 1956
Commonwealth Games champion:
110 yards freestyle 1958, 1962
4 x 110 yards relay 1958, 1962
440 yards freestyle 1962
4 x 110 yards medley relay 1962

Fraser /ˈfreɪzə/ Peter 1884–1950. New Zealand Labour politician, born in Scotland. He held various cabinet posts 1935–40, and was prime minister 1940–49.

Fraser /ˈfreɪzə/ Simon 1776–1862. Canadian explorer and surveyor for the Hudson Bay Company who crossed the Rockies and travelled most of the way down the river that bears his name 1805–07.

fraternity and sorority student societies (fraternity for men; sorority for women) in some US and Canadian universities and colleges. Although mainly social and residential, some are purely honorary, membership being on the basis of scholastic distinction, for example Phi Beta Kappa, earliest of the fraternities, founded at William and Mary College, Virginia, 1776.

Usually named with Greek letters, they are nominally secret, with badge, passwords, motto, and initiation rites. They have a central governing body and a 'chapter' at each college.

fraud in English law, an act of deception. To establish fraud it has to be demonstrated that: (1) a false representation (for example, a factually untrue statement) has been made, with the intention that it should be acted upon; (2) the person making the representation knows it is false or does not attempt to find out whether it is true or not; and (3) the person to whom the representation is made acts upon it to their detriment.

A contract based on fraud can be declared void, and the injured party can sue for damages. In 1987 the Serious Fraud Office was set up to investigate and prosecute serious or complex criminal fraud cases.

Fraunhofer /ˈfraʊnhəʊfə/ Joseph von 1787–1826. German physicist who did important work in optics. The dark lines in the solar spectrum (**Fraunhofer lines**), which revealed the chemical composition of the sun's atmosphere, were accurately mapped by him.

Fray Bentos /fraɪ ˈbentɒs/ river port in Uruguay; population (1985) 20,000. Linked by a bridge over the Uruguay with Puerto Unzué in Argentina (1976), it is famous for its meat-packing industry, particularly corned beef.

Frazer /ˈfreɪzə/ James George 1854–1941. Scottish anthropologist, author of *The Golden Bough* 1890, a pioneer study of the origins of religion and sociology on a comparative basis. It exerted considerable influence on writers such as T S

Franz Joseph *Emperor of Austria who started World War I.*

Eliot and D H Lawrence, but by the standards of modern anthropology many of its methods and findings are unsound.

Frederick V /'fredrɪk/ known as *the Winter King* 1596–1632. Elector palatine of the Rhine 1610–23 and king of Bohemia 1619–20 (for one winter, hence the name 'winter king'), having been chosen by the Protestant Bohemians as ruler after the deposition of Catholic emperor ◊Ferdinand II. His selection was the cause of the Thirty Years' War. Frederick was defeated at the Battle of the White Mountain, near Prague, in Nov 1620 by the army of the Catholic League, and fled to Holland. He was the son-in-law of James I of England.

Frederick IX /'fredrɪk/ 1899–1972. King of Denmark from 1947. He was succeeded by his daughter who became Queen ◊Margrethe II.

Frederick /'fredrɪk/ two Holy Roman emperors:

Frederick I *c.* 1123–1190. Holy Roman emperor from 1152, known as *Barbarossa* 'red-beard'. Originally duke of Swabia, he was elected emperor 1152, and was engaged in a struggle with Pope Alexander III 1159–77, which ended in his submission; the Lombard cities, headed by Milan, took advantage of this to establish their independence of imperial control. Frederick joined the Third Crusade, and was drowned in Anatolia.

Frederick II 1194–1250. Holy Roman emperor from his election 1212, called 'the Wonder of the World'. He led a crusade 1228–29 that recovered Jerusalem by treaty without fighting. He quarrelled with the pope, who excommunicated him three times, and a feud began which lasted at intervals until the end of his reign. Frederick, who was a complete sceptic in religion, is often considered the most cultured man of his age. He was the son of Henry VI.

Frederick /'fredrɪk/ three kings of Prussia, including:

Frederick I 1657–1713. King of Prussia from 1701. He became elector of Brandenburg 1688.

Frederick II *the Great* 1712–1786. King of Prussia from 1740, when he succeeded his father Frederick William I. In that year he started the War of the ◊Austrian Succession by his attack on Austria. In the peace of 1745 he secured Silesia. The struggle was renewed in the ◊Seven Years' War 1756–63. He acquired West Prussia in the first partition of Poland 1772, and left Prussia as Germany's foremost state. He was an efficient and just ruler in the spirit of the Enlightenment, and a patron of the arts.

He received a harsh military education from his father, and in 1730 was threatened with death for attempting to run away. In the Seven Years' War, in spite of assistance from Britain, Frederick had a hard task holding his own against the Austrians and their Russian allies; the skill with which he did so proved him to be one of the great soldiers of history. In his domestic policy he was one of the 'enlightened despots' of the Age of Reason; he encouraged industry and agriculture, reformed the judicial system, fostered education, and established religious toleration. He corresponded with the French writer Voltaire, and was a talented musician.

Frederick III 1831–1888. King of Prussia and emperor of Germany 1888. The son of Wilhelm I, he married the eldest daughter (Victoria) of Queen Victoria of the UK 1858, and, as a liberal, frequently opposed Chancellor Bismarck. He died three months after his accession.

Frederick William /'fredrɪk 'wɪljəm/ 1620–1688. Elector of Brandenburg from 1640, 'the Great Elector'. By successful wars against Sweden and Poland, he prepared the way for Prussian power in the 18th century.

Frederick William /'fredrɪk 'wɪljəm/ 1882–1951. Last crown prince of Germany, eldest son of Wilhelm II. During World War I he commanded a group of armies on the western front. In 1918, he retired into private life.

Frederick William /'fredrɪk 'wɪljəm/ four kings of Prussia:

Frederick William I 1688–1740. King of Prussia from 1713, who developed Prussia's military might and commerce.

Frederick William II 1744–1797. King of Prussia from 1786. He was a nephew of Frederick II, but had little of his relative's military skill. He was unsuccessful in waging war on the French 1792–95, and lost all Prussia west of the Rhine.

Frederick William III 1770–1840. King of Prussia from 1797. He was defeated by Napoleon 1806, but contributed to his final overthrow 1813–15, and profited in territory allotted at the Congress of Vienna.

Frederick William IV 1795–1861. King of Prussia from 1840. He upheld the principle of the ◊divine right of kings, but was forced to grant a constitution 1850 after the Prussian revolution 1848. He suffered two strokes 1857, and became mentally debilitated. His brother William (later emperor) took over his duties.

Fredericton /'fredrɪktən/ capital of New Brunswick, Canada, on the St John river; population (1986) 44,000. It was formerly known as St Anne's Point, and in 1785 was named after Prince Frederick, second son of George III.

Fredrikstad /'fredrɪkstæd/ Norwegian port at the mouth of the river Glomma, dating from 1570; population (1987) 26,650. It is a centre of the timber trade, and has shipyards.

Free Church the Protestant denominations in England and Wales that are not part of the Church of England; for example, the Methodist Church, Baptist Union, and United Reformed Church (Congregational and Presbyterian). These churches joined for common action in the Free Church Federal Council 1940.

Free Church of Scotland the body of Scottish Presbyterians who seceded from the Established Church of Scotland in the Disruption of 1843. In 1900 all but a small section that retains the old name, and is known as the *Wee Frees*, combined with the United Presbyterian Church to form the United Free Church, which reunited with the Church of Scotland 1929.

A strict Free Church member, the Lord Chancellor, Mackay of Clashfern, was censured in 1988 for attending the Roman Catholic funerals of two colleagues.

freedom of the city (or borough) honour bestowed on distinguished people by a city or borough in the UK and other countries. Historically, those granted freedom of a city (called 'freemen') had the right of participating in the privileges of the city or borough.

Freedom, Presidential Medal of the highest peacetime civilian honour in the USA. Instituted by President Kennedy 1963, it is awarded to those 'who contribute significantly to the quality of American life'. A list of recipients is published each Independence Day and often includes unknown individuals as well as artists, performers, and politicians. It replaced the *Medal of Freedom*, instituted 1945, which had been conferred 24 times on an irregular basis.

free enterprise or *free market* an economic system where private capital is used in business with profits going to private companies and individuals. The term has much the same meaning as ◊capitalism.

free fall a state in which a body is falling freely under the influence of ◊gravity, as in free-fall parachuting. The term *weightless* is normally used to describe a body in free fall in space.

In orbit, astronauts and spacecraft are still held by gravity, and are in fact falling towards the Earth. Because of their speed (orbital velocity), the amount they fall towards the Earth just equals the amount the Earth's surface curves away; in effect they remain at the same height, apparently weightless.

freefalling sport also known as ◊skydiving.

Free French in World War II, movement formed by Gen ◊de Gaulle in the UK June 1940, consisting of French soldiers who continued to fight against the Axis after the Franco-German armistice. They took part in campaigns in Africa, the Middle East, Italy, France, and Germany. Their emblem was the Cross of Lorraine, a cross with two bars.

They took the name *Fighting France* 1942 and served in many campaigns, among them Gen Leclerc's advance from Chad to Tripolitania 1942, the Syrian campaigns 1941, the campaigns in the Western Desert, the Italian campaign, the liberation of France, and the invasion of Germany.

freehold in England and Wales, ownership of land which is for an indefinite period. It is contrasted with a leasehold, which is always for a fixed period. In practical effect, a freehold is absolute ownership.

freeman one who enjoys the freedom of a borough. Since the early Middle Ages, a freeman has been allowed to carry out his craft or trade within the jurisdiction of the borough, and to participate in municipal government, but since the development of modern local government, such privileges have become largely honorary.

There have generally been four ways of becoming a freeman: by apprenticeship to an existing freeman; by patrimony, or being the son of a freeman; by redemption, that is, buying the privilege; or, by gift from the borough, the usual method today, when the privilege is granted in recognition of some achievement, benefaction, or special status on the part of the recipient.

Freemasonry the beliefs and practices of a group of linked national organizations open to men over the age of 21, united by the possession of a common code of morals and certain traditional 'secrets'. Modern Freemasonry began in 18th-century Europe. Freemasons do much charitable work, but have been criticized in recent years for their secrecy, their male exclusivity, and particularly their alleged use of influence within and between organizations (for example, the police or local government) to further each other's interests. There are approximately 6 million members.

beliefs Freemasons believe in God, whom they call the 'Great Architect of the Universe'.

history Freemasonry is descended from a medieval guild of itinerant masons, which existed in the 14th century and by the 16th was admitting men unconnected with the building trade. The term 'freemason' may have meant a full member of the guild or one working in free-stone, that is, a mason of the highest class.

The present order of *Free and Accepted Masons* originated with the formation in London of the first Grand Lodge, or governing body, in 1717, and during the 18th century spread from Britain to the USA, continental Europe, and elsewhere. In France and other European countries, freemasonry assumed a political and anticlerical character; it has been condemned by the papacy, and in some countries was suppressed by the state.

free port a port where cargo may be accepted for handling, processing, and reshipment without the imposition of tariffs or taxes. Duties and tax become payable only if the products are for consumption in the country to which the free port belongs.

Free ports are established to take advantage of a location with good trade links. They facilitate the quick entry and departure of ships, unhampered by lengthy customs regulations. Important free ports include Singapore, Copenhagen, New York, and Gdańsk.

free radical in chemistry, an atom or molecule with one unpaired electron.

They tend to be highly reactive because a paired electron gives a more stable chemical group, so the free radical will readily enter reactions with other chemical compounds to achieve this pairing. Most free radicals are very short-lived as a result. If free radicals are produced in living organisms they can be very damaging.

freesia genus of South African plants, family Iridaceae, commercially grown for their scented, funnel-shaped flowers.

free thought post-Reformation movement opposed to Christian dogma, represented in Britain in the 17th and 18th century by ◊deists; in the 19th century by the radical thinker Richard Carlile (1790–1843), a pioneer of the free press, and the Liberal politicians Charles Bradlaugh and Lord Morley (1838–1923); and in the 20th century by the philosopher Bertrand Russell.

The tradition is upheld in the UK by the National Secular Society 1866, the Free Thinker 1881, the Rationalist Press Association 1899, and the British Humanist Association 1963.

Freetown /'fri:taʊn/ capital of Sierra Leone, W Africa; population (1988) 470,000. It has a naval station and a harbour. Industries include cement, plastics, footwear, and oil refining. Platinum, chromite, diamonds, and gold are traded.

It was founded as a settlement for freed slaves in the 1790s.

free trade an economic system where governments do not interfere in the movement of goods between states; there are thus no taxes on imports. In the modern economy, free trade tends to hold within economic groups such as the European Community or the Warsaw Pact, but not generally, despite such treaties as ◊GATT 1948 and subsequent agreements to reduce tariffs. The opposite of free trade is ◊protectionism.

The case for free trade, first put forward in the 17th century, received its classic statement in Adam Smith's *Wealth of Nations* 1776. The movement towards free trade began with Pitt's commercial treaty with France 1786, and triumphed with the repeal of the Corn Laws 1846. According to traditional economic theory, free trade allows nations to specialize in those commodities which can be produced most efficiently. In Britain, superiority to all rivals as a manufacturing country in the Victorian age made free trade an advantage, but when that superiority was lost the demand for protection was raised, notably by Joseph Chamberlain. The Ottawa Agreements 1932 marked the end of free trade until in 1948 GATT came into operation. A series of resultant international tariff reductions was agreed in the Kennedy Round Conference 1964–67, and the Tokyo Round 1974–79 gave substantial incentives to developing countries.

In the 1980s recession prompted by increased world oil prices and unemployment swung the pendulum back towards protectionism which discourages foreign imports by heavy duties, thus protecting home products. Within the European Community, a date of 1992 has been agreed for the abolition of all protectionist tariffs.

free verse poetry without metrical form. At the beginning of the 20th century, under the very different influences of Whitman and Mallarmé, many poets rejected regular metre in much the same spirit as Milton had rejected rhyme, preferring irregular metres which made it possible to express thought clearly and without distortion.

This was true of T S ◊Eliot and the Imagists; it was also true of poets who, like the Russians Esenin and Mayakovsky, placed emphasis on public performance.

Poets including Robert Graves and Auden have criticized free verse on the ground that it lacks the difficulty of true accomplishment, but their own metrics would have been considered loose by earlier critics. The freeness of free verse is largely relative.

free will the doctrine that human beings are free to control their own actions, and that these actions are not fixed in advance by God or fate. Some Christian theologians assert that God gave humanity free will to choose between good and evil; others that God has decided in advance the outcome of all human choices (◊predestination, as in Calvinism).

freeze-drying is a method of preserving food; see ◊food technology. The product is frozen, then put in a vacuum chamber which forces out the ice as water vapour, a process known as sublimation.

Many of the substances that give products such as coffee their typical flavour are volatile, and would be lost in a normal drying process because they would evaporate along with the water. In the freeze-drying process these volatile compounds are mostly retained.

freezing change from liquid to solid state, as when water becomes ice. For a given substance, freezing occurs at a definite temperature, known as the freezing point, that is invariable under similar conditions of pressure, and the temperature remains at this point until all the liquid is frozen. The amount of heat per unit mass that has to be removed to freeze a substance is a constant for any given substance, and is known as the latent heat of fusion.

Ice is less dense than water since water expands just before its freezing point is reached. If pressure is applied, expansion is retarded and the freezing point will be lowered. The presence of dissolved substances in a liquid also lowers the freezing point (depression of freezing point), the amount of lowering being proportional to the molecular concentration of the solution. Antifreeze mixtures for car radiators and the use of salt to melt ice on roads are common applications of this principle.

Animals in arctic conditions, for example insects or fish, cope with the extreme cold either by manufacturing natural 'antifreeze' and staying active, or by allowing themselves to freeze in a controlled fashion, that is, they manufacture proteins to act as nuclei for the formation of ice crystals in areas that will not produce cellular damage, and so enable themselves to thaw back to life again.

freezing-point depression lowering of a solution's freezing point below that of the pure solvent; it depends on the number of molecules of solute dissolved in it. Thus for a single solvent, such as pure water, all substances in the same molecular concentration produce the same lowering of freezing point. The depression d for a molar concentration C is given by the equation $d = KC$, where K is a constant for the particular solvent (called the cryoscopic constant). Measurement of freezing-point depression is a useful method of determining molecular weights of solutes.

Frege /'freigə/ Gottlob 1848–1925. German philosopher. The founder of modern mathematical logic, he published *Die Grundlagen der Arithmetik/The Foundations of Arithmetic* 1884, which was to influence ◊Russell and ◊Wittgenstein.

The *Grundgesetze* was published 1903. His work, neglected for a time, has attracted attention in recent years in Britain and the USA.

Freiburg-im-Breisgau /'fraibʊəg ɪm 'braisgau/ industrial city (pharmaceuticals, precision instruments) in Baden-Württemberg, West Germany; population (1988) 186,000. It is the seat of a university, and has a 12th-century cathedral.

Frelimo (*Fr*ont for the *Li*beration of *Mo*zambique) nationalist group aimed at gaining independence for Mozambique from the occupying Portuguese. It began operating out of S Tanzania 1963, and continued until victory 1975.

Fremantle /'fri:mæntl/ chief port of Western Australia, at the mouth of the Swan river, SW of ◊Perth; population (1981) 23,780. It has shipbuilding yards, sawmills, and iron foundries, and exports wheat, fruit, wool, and timber. It was founded as a penal settlement 1829.

Frémont /'fri:mɒnt/ John Charles 1813–1890. US explorer and politician who travelled extensively throughout the western USA. He surveyed much of the territory between the Mississippi River and the coast of California with the aim of establishing an overland route E–W across the continent. In 1842 he crossed the the Rocky Mountains, climbing a peak that is named after him.

French member of the majority population of France whose first language is French (see ◊French language). There are many socio-linguistic minorities within France and the languages spoken include Catalan, Breton, Flemish, German, Corsican, and Basque.

French /frentʃ/ Daniel Chester 1850–1931. US sculptor, designer of the seated figure of *Abraham Lincoln* 1922 for the Lincoln Memorial, Washington DC. The imposing classical style continued academic tradition.

French /frentʃ/ John Denton Pinkstone, 1st Earl of Ypres 1852–1925. British field marshal. In the second ◊South African War, he relieved Kimberley and took Bloemfontein; in World War I he was commander in chief of the British Expeditionary Force in France 1914–15; he resigned after being criticized as indecisive.

French Antarctica /'frentʃ ænt'ɑ:ktɪkə/ territory, in full *French Southern and Antarctic Territories*, created 1955; area 10,100 sq km/ 3,900 sq mi; population about 200 research scientists. It includes Adélie Land, on the antarctic continent (136–142 km long), the Kerguelen and Crozet archipelagos, and Saint Paul and Nouvelle Amsterdam islands in the southern seas. It is administered from Paris, but Port-aux-Français on Kerguelen is the chief centre, with several research stations. There are also research stations on Nouvelle Amsterdam and in Adélie Land; and a meteorological station on Possession Island in the Crozet archipelago. Saint Paul is uninhabited. In 1988, French workers, who were illegally building an airstrip, thus violating a United Nations treaty on Antarctica, attacked Greenpeace workers.

French art painting and sculpture of France. A number of influential styles have emerged in France over the centuries, from Gothic in the Middle Ages to Impressionism, Cubism, Surrealism, and others.

11th–14th century The main forms of artistic expression were manuscript painting, architecture, and sculpture. France played the leading role in creating the Gothic style.

15th century The miniatures of Jean Fouquet and the *Très riches heures* (a prayer book) of the Limbourg brothers, manuscript illuminators, show remarkable naturalism.

16th century Artists were influenced by the Italians, but the miniature tradition was kept up by the court painters such as Jean Clouet.

17th century Landscape painting became increasingly popular. Two exceptional artists in the genre were Poussin and Claude Lorrain.

18th century French painting and sculpture became dominant throughout Europe. Popular Rococo painters were Watteau, Fragonard, and Boucher. The still lifes of Chardin show Dutch influence. The Neo-Classical French school was founded by David.

early 19th century Ingres was the most widely admired painter. Delacroix was the leader of the Romantic movement. Géricault excelled as a history and animal painter.

mid-19th century Courbet and Manet were the great rebels in art, breaking with age-old conventions. The Barbizon school of landscape painting was followed by the Impressionists: Monet, Renoir, Degas, and others.

late 19th century The Pointillist Seurat took the Impressionists' ideas further. The individual styles of Cézanne and Gauguin helped prepare the way for Modernism. Rodin's powerful, realistic sculptures had great influence.

1900s Fauvism, showing the influence of Gauguin with his emphasis on pure colour, was introduced by Matisse and others. Cubism, deriving from Cézanne, was begun by Picasso and Braque.

1920s Paris was a centre of the Surrealist movement.

French Guiana

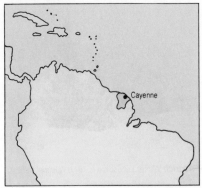

Cayenne

1930s Abstraction-création movement started in Paris to develop a form of abstract art constructed from non-figurative, usually geometrical elements.

1945–1990 After World War II the centre of the art world shifted from France to the USA.

French Canadian literature F-X Garneau's *Histoire du Canada* (1845–48) inspired a school of patriotic verse led by Octave Crémazie (1827–79) and continued by Louis Fréchette (1838–1908). A new movement began after 1900 with such poets as André Lozeau (1878–1924), Paul Morin, Robert Choquette (1862–1941), Alain Grandbois, St Denys Garneau, Eloi de Grandmont, and Pierre Trottier. Fiction reached a high point with Louis Hémon (1880–1914) whose *Maria Chapdelaine* inspired many genre works. Outstanding later novelists are Germaine Guèvremont, Gabrielle Roy, 'Ringuet' (Philippe Panneton, 1895–), Robert Elie, Roger Lemelin, and Yves Thériault.

French Community former association consisting of France and those overseas territories joined with it by the constitution of the Fifth Republic, following the 1958 referendum. Many of the constituent states withdrew during the 1960s, and it no longer formally exists, but in practice all former French colonies have close economic and cultural as well as linguistic links with France.

French Guiana /giːˈɑːnə/ (French *Guyane Française*) French overseas *département* from 1946, and administrative region from 1974, on the N coast of South America, bounded to the W by Suriname and to the E and S by Brazil
area 83,500 sq km/32,230 sq mi
capital Cayenne
towns St Laurent
features Eurospace rocket launch pad at Kourou; Îles du Salut, which include ◊Devil's Island
exports timber, shrimps, gold
population (1987) 89,000
language 90% Creole, French, Amerindian
history first settled by France 1604, the territory became a French possession 1817; penal colonies, including Devil's Island, were established from 1852; by 1945, the shipments of convicts from France ceased, and the status changed to an overseas *département* 1946, and an administrative region 1974.
currency franc
famous people Capt ◊Dreyfus.

French horn musical instrument. See ◊brass.

French India former French possessions in India: Pondicherry, Chandernagore, Karaikal, Mahé, and Yanaon (Yanam). They were all transferred to India by 1954.

French language a member of the Romance branch of the Indo-European language family, spoken in France, Belgium, Luxembourg, and Switzerland in Europe, Canada (especially the province of Québec) in North America, and various Caribbean and Pacific Islands (overseas territories such as Martinique and French Guiana), as well as certain N and W African countries (for example, Mali and Senegal).

French developed from the Latin spoken in Gaul and was established as a distinct language by the 9th century. Varieties used north of the river Loire formed the *Langue d'oil* (*oui*) while those to the south formed the *Langue d'oc*, according to their word for 'yes'. By the 13th century the dialect of the Île de France was supreme and became the official medium of the courts and administration of France 1539. Its literary form still serves as the basis of *le bon français* ('correct French'), which is officially protected by the Academie Française (founded 1635 at the behest of Cardinal Richelieu) and by occasional legislation in both France and Québec.

French literature
The Middle Ages The *Chanson de Roland* (about 1080) is one of the the greatest of the early *chansons de geste* (epic poems about deeds of chivalry), which were superseded by the Arthurian romances (seen at their finest in the work of Chrétien de Troyes in the 12th century), and by the classical themes of Alexander, Troy, and Thebes. Other aspects of French medieval literature are represented by the charming anonymous *Aucassin et Nicolette* of the early 13th century, the allegorical *Roman de la Rose/Romance of the Rose*, the first part of which was written by Guillaume de Lorris (about 1230) and the second by Jean de Meung (about 1275), and the satiric *Roman de Renart/Story of Renard* of the late 12th century. The period also produced the historians Villehardouin, Joinville, Froissart, and Comines, and the first great French poet, François Villon.

Renaissance to the 18th century A notable poet of the Renaissance was Ronsard, leader of the ◊Pléiade (a group of seven writers); others included Marot at the beginning of the 16th century and Régnier at its close. In prose the period produced the broad genius of Rabelais and the essayist Montaigne. In the 17th century came the triumph of form with the great classical dramatists Corneille, Racine, and Molière, and the graceful brilliance of La Fontaine, and the poet and critic Boileau. Masters of prose in the same period include the philosophers Pascal and Descartes; the preacher Bossuet; the critics La Bruyère, Fénelon, and Malebranche; and La Rochefoucauld, Cardinal de Retz, Mme de Sévigné, and Le Sage.

The 18th century was the age of the Enlightenment and an era of prose, with Montesquieu, Voltaire, Rousseau; the scientist Buffon; the encyclopaedist Diderot; the ethical writer Vauvenargues; the novelists Prévost and Marivaux; and the memoir writer Saint-Simon.

19th and 20th centuries In the 19th century poetry came to the fore again with the Romantics Lamartine, Hugo, Vigny, Musset, Leconte de Lisle, and Gautier; novelists of the same school were George Sand, Stendhal, and Dumas *père*, while criticism is represented by Sainte-Beuve, and history by Thiers, Michelet, and Taine. The realist novelist Balzac was followed by the school of Naturalism, whose representatives were Flaubert, Zola, the Goncourt brothers, Alphonse Daudet, Maupassant, and Huysmans. 19th-century dramatists included Hugo, Musset, and Dumas *fils*. Symbolism, a movement of experiment and revolt against classical verse and the materialist attitude, with the philosopher Bergson as one of its main exponents, found its first expression in the work of Gérard de Nerval, who was later followed by Baudelaire, Verlaine, Mallarmé, Rimbaud, Corbière, and the prose writer Villiers de l'Isle Adam; later writers in the same tradition were Henri de Régnier and Laforgue.

In the late 19th and early 20th centuries drama and poetry revived with Valéry, Claudel, and Paul Fort, who advocated 'pure poetry'; other writers were the novelists Gide and Proust, and the critics Thibaudet (1874–1936) and later St John Perse, also a poet. The Surrealist movement,

which developed from 'pure poetry' through the work of Eluard and Apollinaire, influenced writers as diverse as Giraudoux, Louis Aragon, and Cocteau. The literary reaction against the Symbolists included Charles Péguy, Rostand, de Noailles, and Romain Rolland. 20th-century novelists in the Naturalist tradition were Henri Barbusse, Jules Romains, Julian Green, François Mauriac, Francis Carco, and Georges Duhamel. Other prose writers are Maurois, Malraux, Montherlant, Anatole France, Saint-Exupéry, Alain-Fournier, Pierre Hamp, and J R Bloch, while the theatre flourished with plays by J J Bernard, Anouilh, Beckett, and Ionesco. World War II had a profound effect on French writing, and distinguished postwar writers include the Existentialist Sartre and Camus, 'Vercors' (pen name of Jean Bruller), Simone de Beauvoir, Alain Robbe-Grillet, Romain Gary, Nathalie Sarraute, and Marguerite Duras.

French Polynesia /ˌpɒlɪˈniːzɪə/ French Overseas Territory in the S Pacific, consisting of five archipelagoes: Windward Islands, Leeward Islands (the two island groups comprising the ◊Society Islands), ◊Tuamotu Archipelago (including ◊Gambier Islands), ◊Tubuai Islands, and ◊Marquesas Islands
total area 3,940 sq km/1,521 sq mi
capital Papeete on Tahiti
exports cultivated pearls, coconut oil, vanilla; tourism is important
population (1987) 185,000
languages Tahitian (official), French
government a High Commissioner (Alain Ohrel) and Council of Government; two deputies are returned to the National Assembly in France
history first visited by Europeans 1595; French Protectorate 1843; annexed to France 1880–82; became an Overseas Territory, changing its name from French Oceania 1958; self-governing 1977; following demands for independence in ◊New Caledonia 1984–85, agitation increased also in Polynesia.

French Revolution the period 1789–1795 which saw the end of the monarchy and its claim to absolute rule. On 5 May 1789, after the monarchy had attempted to increase taxation and control of affairs, the ◊States General (three 'estates' of nobles, clergy, and commons) met at Versailles to try to establish some constitutional controls. Divisions within the States General led to the formation of a National Assembly by the third (commons) estate 17 June. Repressive measures by ◊Louis XVI led to the storming of the Bastille by the Paris mob 14 July 1789.

On 20 June 1791 the royal family attempted to escape from the control of the Assembly, but Louis XVI was brought back a prisoner from Varennes and forced to accept a new constitution. War with Austria after 20 Apr 1792 threatened to undermine the revolution, but on 10 Aug the mob stormed the royal palace, and on 21 Sept the First French Republic was proclaimed.

On 21 Jan 1793 Louis XVI was executed. The moderate ◊Girondins were overthrown 2 June by the ◊Jacobins, and control of the country was passed to the infamous Committee of Public Safety, and ◊Robespierre. The mass executions of the Reign of ◊Terror began 5 Sept, and the excesses led to the overthrow of the Committee and Robespierre 27 July 1794 (9 Thermidor under the Revolutionary calendar). The Directory was established to hold a middle course between royalism and Jacobinism. It ruled until Napoleon seized power 1799.

French revolutionary calendar In the French Revolution 1789 became initially known as the 1st Year of Liberty. When monarchy was abolished on 21 Sep 1792, the 4th year became 1st Year of the Republic. This calendar was formally adopted in Oct 1793 but its usage was backdated to 22 Sep 1793 which became 1 Vendémiaire. The calendar was discarded as from 1 Jan 1806.

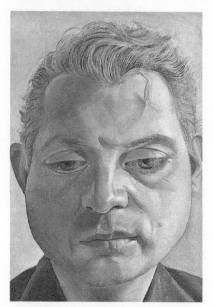

Freud *Francis Bacon (1952) Tate Gallery, London.*

French Revolutionary Calendar

Revolutionary month (date 1–30)	meaning	time period
Vendémiaire	vintage	22 Sep–21 Oct
Brumaire	fog	22 Oct–20 Nov
Frimaire	frost	21 Nov–20 Dec
Nivôse	snow	21 Dec–19 Jan
Pluviôse	rain	20 Jan–18 Feb
Ventôse	wind	19 Feb–20 Mar
Germinal	budding	21 Mar–19 Apr
Floreal	flowers	20 Apr–19 May
Prairial	meadows	20 May–18 June
Messidor	harvest	19 June–18 July
Thermidor	heat	19 July–17 Aug
Fructidor	fruit	18 Aug–16 Sep
Sansculottides	festival	17 Sep–21 Sep

French Somaliland /sə'mɑ:lilænd/ former name, until 1967, of ◊Djibouti, in E Africa.

French Sudan /su:'dɑ:n/ former name (1898–1959) of ◊Mali, NW Africa.

French West Africa group of French colonies administered from Dakar 1895–1958. They have become the modern Senegal, Mauritania, Sudan, Burkina Faso, Guinea, Niger, Ivory Coast, and Benin.

Freneau /fri'nəʊ/ Philip Morin 1752–1832. US poet whose *A Political Litany* 1775 was a mock prayer for deliverance from British tyranny.

frequency in physics, the number of cycles of a vibration occurring per unit of time. The unit of

Freud *Austrian psychiatrist and pioneer of psychoanalysis Sigmund Freud.*

frequency is the hertz (Hz); 1 Hz = 1 cycle per second. Human beings can hear sounds from objects vibrating in the range 20 Hz to 15,000 Hz.

Ultrasonic frequencies are above 15,000 Hz. 1 kHz (1 kilohertz) = 1,000 Hz, 1 MHz (1 megahertz) = 1,000,000 Hz.

Frere /frɪə/ John 1740–1807. English archaeologist, high sheriff of Suffolk and Member of Parliament for Norwich. He discovered Palaeolithic tools at Hoxne, Suffolk, in 1790 and suggested that they predated the conventional biblical timescale.

fresco mural painting technique using water-based paint on wet plaster.

Some of the earliest frescoes (about 1750–1400 BC) were found in Knossos, Crete (now preserved in the Heraklion Museum). Fresco reached its finest expression in Italy from the 13th to the 17th century. Giotto, Masaccio, Michelangelo, and many other artists worked in the medium.

Frescobaldi /ˌfreskə'bældi/ Girolamo 1583–1643. Italian composer of virtuoso pieces for the organ and harpsichord.

Fresnel /'freɪnel/ Augustin 1788–1827. French physicist who refined the theory of the ◊polarized light. In the early 19th century, physicists found it difficult to describe the manner in which light travelled. Fresnel realized in 1821 that light waves did not vibrate like sound waves longitudinally in the direction of their motion, but transversely, at right angles to the direction of the propagated wave.

Freud /frɔɪd/ Clement 1924– . British journalist, television personality, and until 1987 Liberal member of Parliament; a grandson of Sigmund Freud.

Freud /frɔɪd/ Lucian 1922– . British painter, known for realist portraits with the subject staring intently from an almost masklike face, for example *Francis Bacon* 1952 (Tate Gallery, London). He is a grandson of Sigmund Freud.

Freud /frɔɪd/ Sigmund 1865–1939. Austrian psychiatrist who pioneered study of the unconscious mind. He developed the methods of free association and interpretation of dreams that are still techniques of ◊psychoanalysis. His books include *Die Traumdeutung/The Interpretation of Dreams* 1900, *Totem and Taboo* 1913, and *Das Unbehagen in der Kultur/Civilization and its Discontents* 1930.

Freud studied medicine in Vienna and was a member of the research team that discovered the local anaesthetic effects of cocaine. From 1885–86 he studied hypnosis in Paris under the French physiologist ◊Charcot and 1889 in Nancy under two of Charcot's opponents. From 1886 to 1938 he had a private practice in Vienna, and his theories and writings drew largely on case studies of his own patients. He was also influenced by the research into hysteria of the Viennese physician ◊Breuer. In the early 1900s a group of psychoanalysts gathered around Freud. Some of these later broke away and formed their own influential schools: ◊Adler in 1911 and ◊Jung in 1913. Following the Nazi occupation of Austria in 1938, Freud left for London, where he died.

The word 'psychoanalysis' was, like much of its terminology, coined by Freud, and many terms have passed into popular usage, not without distortion. The way that unconscious forces influence people's thoughts and actions was Freud's discovery, and his theory of the repression of infantile sexuality as the root of neuroses in the adult (as in the ◊Oedipus complex) was particularly controversial. Later he also stressed the significance of aggressive drives. His work, long accepted as definitive by many, has been criticized particularly from a feminist point of view.

Freya /'frɪgə/ or *Frigga* in Scandinavian mythology, wife of Odin and mother of Thor, goddess of married love and the hearth. Friday is named after her.

Freyberg /'fraɪbɜ:g/ Bernard Cyril, Baron Freyberg 1889–1963. New Zealand soldier and administrator. He fought in World War I, and during World War II he commanded the New Zealand

Friedrich *Winter Landscape (c.1811) National Gallery, London.*

expeditionary force. He was governor-general of New Zealand 1946–52.

friar a monk of any order, but originally the title of members of the mendicant (begging) orders, the chief of which were the Franciscans or Minors (Grey Friars), the Dominicans or Preachers (Black Friars), the Carmelites (White Friars), and Augustinians (Austin Friars).

friar's balsam a mixture containing ◊benzoin, used as an inhalant for relief from colds.

Fribourg /'fri:bʊə/ city in W Switzerland, on the river Sarine, capital of the canton of Fribourg; population (1980) 37,400. It is noted for its food products, particularly the cheese of the Gruyère district.

friction in physics, the force that opposes the relative motion of two bodies in contact. The *coefficient of friction* is the ratio of the force required to achieve this relative motion to the force pressing the two bodies together.

Friction is greatly reduced by the use of lubricants such as oil, grease, and graphite, and air bearings are now used to minimize the friction in high-speed rotational machinery. In other instances friction is deliberately increased by making the surfaces rough, for example, brake linings, driving belts, soles of shoes, and tyres.

The coefficient of friction between two solid surfaces is equal to the force required to move one surface over the other, divided by the total force pressing the two surfaces together.

Friedan /fri'dæn/ Betty 1921– . US liberal feminist. Her book *The Feminine Mystique* 1963 was one of the most influential books for the women's movement in both the USA and the UK. She founded the National Organization for Women (NOW) 1966, the National Women's Political Caucus 1971, the First Women's Bank 1973, and called the First International Feminist Congress 1973.

Friedman /'fri:dmən/ Milton 1912– . US economist. The foremost exponent of ◊monetarism, he argues that a country's economy, and hence inflation, can be controlled through its money supply, although most governments lack the 'political will' to control inflation by cutting government spending and thereby increasing unemployment.

Friedrich German form of ◊Frederick.

Friedrich /'fri:drɪk/ Caspar David 1774–1840. German landscape painter in the Romantic style, active mainly in Dresden. He imbued his subjects—mountain scenes and moonlit seas—with great poetic melancholy, and was later admired by Symbolist painters.

Friendly Islands another name for ◊Tonga.

friendly society (in the USA *benefit society*) an association designed to meet the needs of sickness and old age by money payments. There are some 6,500 registered societies in the UK, with funds totalling about £385 million: among the largest are the National Deposit, Odd Fellows, Foresters, and Hearts of Oak. In the USA there are similar 'fraternal insurance' bodies, including the Modern Woodmen of America 1883 and the Fraternal Order of Eagles 1898.

In the UK the movement was the successor in this field of the great medieval guilds, but the period of its greatest expansion was in the late 18th and early 19th centuries, following the passing in 1797 of the first legislation providing for the registration of friendly societies.

Friends of the Earth (FoE or FOE environmental pressure group, established in the UK 1971, that aims to protect the environment and to promote rational and sustainable use of the Earth's resources. It campaigns on issues such as acid rain; air, sea, river, and land pollution; recycling; disposal of toxic wastes; nuclear power and renewable energy; the destruction of rainforests; pesticides; and agriculture. FoE has branches in 30 countries.

Friends, Society of Christian Protestant sect popularly known as *Quakers*, founded by George ◊Fox in England in the 17th century. They were persecuted for their nonviolent activism, and many emigrated to form communities abroad, for example in Pennsylvania and New England, USA. They now form a worldwide movement of about 200,000. Their worship stresses meditation and the freedom of all to take an active part in the service (called a meeting, held in a meeting house). They have no priests or ministers.

The name Quakers may originate in Fox's injunction to 'quake at the word of the Lord'. Originally marked out by their sober dress and use of 'thee' and 'thou' to all as a sign of equality, they incurred penalties by their pacifism and refusal to take oaths or pay tithes. In the 19th century many Friends were prominent in social reform, for example, Elizabeth ◊Fry.

Friesland /'fri:zlənd/ maritime province of the N Netherlands, which includes the Frisian Islands and land which is still being reclaimed from the former Zuyder Zee; area 3,400 sq km/1,312 sq mi; population (1988) 599,000. Its capital is Leeuwarden. Friesian cattle originated here.

The *Eleven Cities Tour* 1909 is a 210 km/124 mi skating marathon on the canals of the province held only in the rare years when the ice is hard enough. The inhabitants of the province are called ◊Frisians.

frigate warship, an escort vessel smaller than a destroyer. Before 1975 the term referred to a warship larger than a destroyer but smaller than a light cruiser. In the 18th and 19th centuries a frigate was a small, fast sailing warship.

The frigate is the most numerous type of larger surface vessel in the British Royal Navy. Britain's type-23 frigate (1988) is armoured, heavily armed (4.5 inch naval gun, 32 Sea Wolf anti-missile and anti-aircraft missiles, and a surface-to-surface missile), and, for locating submarines, has a large helicopter and a hydrophone array towed astern. Engines are diesel-electric up to 17 knots, with gas turbines for spurts of speed to 28 knots.

fringe benefit in employment, payment in kind over and above wages and salaries. These may include a pension, subsidized lunches, company car, favourable loan facilities, and private health care. Fringe benefits may, in part, be subject to income tax.

fringe theatre plays that are anti-establishment or experimental, and performed in informal venues, in contrast to mainstream commercial theatre. In the UK, the term originated in the 1960s from the activities held on the 'fringe' of the Edinburgh Festival. The US equivalent is off-off-Broadway (off-Broadway is mainstream theatre that is not on Broadway).

Less formal and expensive than conventional theatre, fringe events are held in a variety of venues: university theatres, arts centres, converted warehouses, or rooms in pubs. Notable 'fringe' writers include Howard ◊Brenton and David ◊Hare. Fringe groups that tour the country include Belt and Braces, Hull Truck, and Joint Stock.

fringing reef a ◊coral reef that is attached to the coast without an intervening lagoon.

Frink /frɪŋk/ Elisabeth 1930– . British sculptor of rugged, naturalistic bronzes, mainly based on animal forms.

Frisbee an outdoor toy, a discus-shaped object that is thrown backhand. They are used primarily for recreation, but championships are held in the USA. Frisbees (a trade name) were introduced in the USA in the late 1950s.

Frisch /frɪʃ/ Karl von 1886–1982. German zoologist, founder with Konrad Lorenz of ◊ethology, the study of animal behaviour. He specialized in bees, discovering how they communicate the location of sources of nectar by 'dances' (see ◊communication). Nobel prize 1973 shared with Lorenz and Nikolaas ◊Tinbergen.

Frisch /frɪʃ/ Max 1911– . Swiss dramatist. Influenced by ◊Brecht, his early plays such as *Als der Krieg zu Ende war/When the War Is Over* 1949 are more romantic in tone than his later symbolic dramas, such as *Andorra* 1962, dealing with questions of identity. His best-known play is *Biedermann und die Brandstifter/The Fire Raisers* 1958.

Frisch /frɪʃ/ Otto 1904–1979. Austrian physicist who coined the term 'nuclear fission'. A refugee from Nazi Germany, he worked from 1943 at ◊Los Alamos, USA, then at Cambridge, England. He was the nephew of Lise ◊Meitner.

Frisch /frɪʃ/ Ragnar 1895–1973. Norwegian economist, the inventor of ◊econometrics; he shared the first Nobel Prize for Economics in 1969 with Jan ◊Tinbergen.

Frisch–Peierls memorandum a document revealing, for the first time, how small the critical mass (the minimum quantity of substance required for a nuclear chain reaction to begin) of uranium needed to be if the isotope Uranium-235 was separated from naturally occurring uranium; the memo thus implied the feasibility of using this isotope to make an atomic bomb. It was written by Otto Frisch and Rudolf Peierls (1907–) at the University of Birmingham 1940.

Frisian a member of a Germanic people of NW Europe. In Roman times they occupied the coast of Holland, and may have taken part in the Anglo-Saxon invasions of Britain. Their language was closely akin to Anglo-Saxon, with which it formed the Anglo-Frisian branch of the West Germanic languages.

The Frisian language is almost extinct in the German districts of East Friesland, has attained some literary importance in the North Frisian Islands and Schleswig, and developed a considerable literature in the West Frisian dialect of the Dutch province of Friesland.

Frisian Islands /'fri:ziən/ chain of low-lying islands 5–32 km/3–20 mi off the NW coasts of the Netherlands and Germany, with a northerly extension off the W coast of Denmark. They were formed by the sinking of the intervening land. *Texel* is the largest and most westerly.

Frith /frɪθ/ William Powell 1819–1909. British painter, especially noted for large contemporary scenes with numerous figures and incidental detail. *Ramsgate Sands*, bought by Queen Victoria, is a fine example, and *Derby Day* 1856–58 (both Tate Gallery, London).

fritillary in botany, plant of the genus *Fritillaria*, family Liliaceae. The snake's head fritillary *Fritillaria meleagris* has bell-shaped flowers with purple-chequered markings.

fritillary butterfly of the family Nymphalidae. There are many species, most with a chequered (Latin *fritillaria*) pattern of black on orange.

Friuli-Venezia Giulia /fri'li vɪ'netsiə 'dʒu :liə/ autonomous agricultural and wine-growing region of NE Italy, bordered on the east by Yugoslavia; area 7,800 sq km/3,011 sq mi; population (1988) 1,210,000. It includes the capital Udine, Gorizia, Pordenone, and Trieste.

Formed 1947 from the province of Venetian Fruli and part of Eastern Friuli, to which Trieste was added after its cession to Italy 1954, it was granted autonomy 1963. The Slav minority

numbers about 100,000, and in Friuli there is a movement for complete independence.

Frobisher /'frəʊbɪʃə/ Martin 1535–1594. English navigator. He made his first voyage to Guinea, West Africa, 1554. In 1576 he set out in search of the Northwest Passage, and visited Labrador, and Frobisher Bay, Baffin Island. Second and third expeditions sailed 1577 and 1578.

He served as vice admiral in Drake's West Indian expedition 1585. In 1588, he was knighted for helping to defeat the Armada. He was mortally wounded 1594 fighting against the Spanish off the coast of France.

Froebel /'frəʊbəl/ Friedrich August Wilhelm 1782–1852. German educationist. He evolved a new system of education using instructive play, described in *Education of Man* 1826 and other works. In 1836 he founded the first kindergarten (German 'garden for children') in Blankenburg. He was influenced by ◊Pestalozzi.

frog amphibian of the order Anura (Greek 'tailless'). They usually have squat bodies, hind legs specialized for jumping, and webbed feet for swimming. Many frogs and ◊toads use their long, extensible tongues to capture insects. Frogs vary in size from the *Sminthillus limbatus*, 12 mm/0.5 in long, to the *giant frog Telmatobius culeus* of Lake Titicaca, 50 cm/20 in.

The males attract the females in great gatherings, usually by croaking. In some tropical species, the inflated vocal sac may exceed the rest of the body in size. Other courtship 'lures' include thumping on the ground and 'dances'. Some lay eggs in large masses (spawn) in water. Some South American frogs build little mud-pool 'nests', and African *tree frogs* make foam nests from secreted mucus. In other species, the eggs may be carried in 'pockets' on the mother's back, or brooded by the male in his vocal sac, or, as with the *midwife toad Alytes obstetricans*, carried by the male wrapped round his hind legs until hatching. Certain species of frog have powerful skin poisons (alkaloids).

The *common frog Rana temporaria* is becoming rare in Britain as small ponds disappear. The *bullfrog Rana catesbeiana*, with a far-reaching croak that carries for miles, is able to jump nine times its own length (annual jumping competitions are held at Calaveras, California, USA). The *flying frogs* of Malaysia, using webbed fore and hind feet, can achieve a 12 m/40 ft glide.

frogbit small water plant *Hydrocharis morsus-ranae* with submerged roots, floating leaves, and small green and white flowers.

frog-hopper type of leaping plant-bug, family Cercopidae, which sucks the juice from plants. The larvae are pale green, and protect themselves (from drying out and from predators) by secreting froth ('cuckoo-spit') from their anus.

frogmouth nocturnal bird, related to the nightjar, of which the commonest species, *Podargus strigoides*, is found throughout Australia, including Tasmania. Well camouflaged, it sits and awaits its prey.

Fromm /from/ Erich 1900–1980. German psychoanalyst who moved to the USA 1933 to escape the Nazis. His *The Fear of Freedom* 1941 and *The Sane Society* 1955 were source books for modern alternative lifestyles.

frond a large leaf or leaflike structure, especially of ferns where it is often pinnately divided. The term is also applied to the leaves of palms, and less

frog

Wallace's flying frog

commonly to the plant bodies of certain seaweeds, liverworts, and lichens.

Fronde French revolts 1648–53 against the administration of the chief minister ◊Mazarin during Louis XIV's minority. In 1648–49 the Paris *parlement* attempted to limit the royal power, its leaders were arrested, Paris revolted, and the rising was suppressed by the royal army under Louis II Condé. In 1650 Condé led a new revolt of the nobility, but this was suppressed by 1653.

front in meteorology, the interface between two air masses of different temperature or humidity. A *cold front* marks the line of advance of a cold air mass from below, as it displaces a warm air mass; a *warm front* marks the advance of a warm air mass pushing a cold one forward.

Warm air, being lighter, tends to rise above the cold; its moisture is carried upwards and usually falls as rain or snow, hence the changeable weather conditions at fronts. Fronts are rarely stable and move with the air mass. An *occluded front* is a composite form, where a cold front overtakes a warm front, lifting warm air above the Earth's surface. An *inversion* occurs when the normal properties get reversed; this happens when a layer of air traps another near the surface, preventing the normal rising of surface air. Warm temperatures and pollination result from inversions.

frontal lobotomy an operation on the brain. See ◊lobotomy.

Frontenac et Palluau /ˌfrɒntəˈnæk eɪ ˌpælju'əʊ/ Louis de Buade, Comte de Frontenac et Palluau 1622–1698. French colonial governor. He began his military career 1635, and was appointed governor of the French possessions in North America 1672. Although efficient, he quarrelled with the local bishop and his followers and was recalled 1682. After the Iroqois, supported by the English, won several military victories, Frontenac was reinstated 1689. He defended Québec against the English 1690 and defeated the Iroquois 1696.

frontier literature writing reflecting the US experience of frontier and pioneer life, long central to US literature. James Fenimore Cooper's *Leatherstocking Tales*, the frontier humour writing of Artemus Ward, Bret Harte, and Mark Twain, dime novels, westerns, the travel records of Francis Parkman, and the pioneer romances of Willa Cather all come into this category.

front-line states the black nations of southern Africa in the 'front line' of the struggle against the racist policies of South Africa: namely Mozambique, Tanzania, and Zambia.

frost condition of the weather when the air temperature is below freezing, 0°C/32°F. Water in the atmosphere is deposited as ice crystals on the ground or exposed objects. As cold air is heavier than warm, *ground frost* is more common than *hoar frost*, which is formed by the condensation of water particles in the same way that ◊dew collects.

Frost /frɒst/ Robert (Lee) 1874–1963. US poet whose verse, in traditional form, is written with an individual voice and penetrating vision; his best-known poems include 'Mending Wall' ('Something there is that does not love a wall'), 'The Road Not Taken', and 'Stopping by Woods on a Snowy Evening'.

frostbite the freezing of skin or flesh, with formation of ice crystals leading to tissue damage. The treatment is slow rewarming of the affected area; for example, by skin-to-skin contact or with lukewarm water. Frostbitten parts are extremely vulnerable to infection, with the risk of gangrene. Sufferers of frostbite should always receive medical attention.

Froude /fruːd/ James Anthony 1818–1894. British historian, whose *History of England from the Fall of Wolsey to the Defeat of the Spanish Armada* 1856–70 was a classic Victorian work.

FRS abbreviation for *Fellow of the ◊Royal Society*.

fructose a fruit sugar, $C_6H_{12}O_6$, which occurs naturally in honey, the nectar of flowers, and many

frog

The life cycle of frogs, and of their close relatives, the toads, comprises several distinct stages. The young, or larvae, look unlike the adults and are said to undergo a complete metamorphosis "change of form". The adult common frog mates in water. From the fertilized eggs emerge the larvae, which at first breathe solely with gills and have no legs. As they grow, they become more adult-like and eventually are able to live and breathe on land.

Adult frogs breathe using their lungs, through the moist skin, and through the lining of their mouths. They feed on worms, beetles, and flies. The aquatic tadpoles at first feed on weeds and algae, but then change to a meat diet.

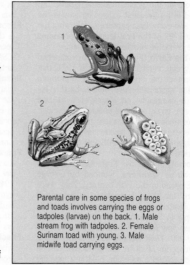

Parental care in some species of frogs and toads involves carrying the eggs or tadpoles (larvae) on the back. 1. Male stream frog with tadpoles. 2. Female Surinam toad with young. 3. Male midwife toad carrying eggs.

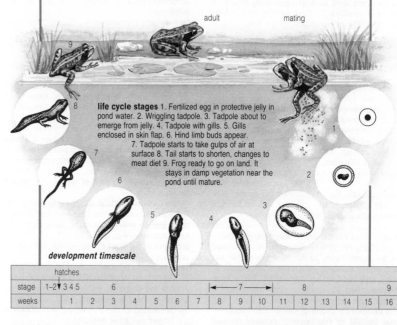

adult mating

life cycle stages 1. Fertilized egg in protective jelly in pond water. 2. Wriggling tadpole. 3. Tadpole about to emerge from jelly. 4. Tadpole with gills. 5. Gills enclosed in skin flap. 6. Hind limb buds appear. 7. Tadpole starts to take gulps of air at surface 8. Tail starts to shorten, changes to meat diet 9. Frog ready to go on land. It stays in damp vegetation near the pond until mature.

development timescale

	hatches															
stage	1–2▼3 4 5		6					←——— 7 ———→			8					9
weeks	1	2	3	4	5	6	7	8	9	10	11	12	13	14	15	16

sweet fruits, and is commercially prepared from glucose.

It is a monosaccharide, whereas the more familar cane or beet sugar is a disaccharide, made up of two monosaccharide units: fructose and glucose. It is sweeter than cane sugar.

fruit (from Latin *frui* 'to enjoy') in botany, the structure that develops from the carpel of a flower and encloses one or more seeds, except in cases of ◊parthenocarpy. Its function is to protect the seeds during their development and to aid in their dispersal. Fruits are often edible, sweet, juicy, and colourful. They provide vitamins and minerals, but little protein. Most fruits are borne by perennial plants.

Broadly, fruits are divided into three categories on the basis of the climate in which they grow. *Temperate fruits* require a cold season for satisfactory growth. In order of abundance, the principal temperate fruits are apples, pears, plums, peaches, apricots, cherries, and soft fruits like raspberries and strawberries. *Subtropical fruits* require warm conditions but can survive

light frosts; they include oranges and other citrus fruits, dates, pomegranates, and avocadoes. *Tropical fruits* succumb if temperatures drop close to freezing point; they include bananas, mangoes, pineapples, papayas, and litchis.

Fruits can also be divided into *dry* (such as the ◊capsule, ◊follicle, ◊schizocarp, ◊nut, ◊caryopsis, pod or legume, ◊lomentum and ◊achene), and those that become *fleshy* (such as the ◊drupe and ◊berry).

The fruit structure consists of the ◊pericarp or fruit wall, usually divided into a number of distinct layers. Sometimes parts other than the ovary are incorporated into the fruit structure, resulting in a false fruit or ◊pseudocarp, such as the apple and strawberry. Fruits may open to shed their seeds (dehiscent), or remain unopened and be dispersed as a single unit (indehiscent).

Simple fruits (for example, peaches) are derived from a single ovary, whereas composite or multiple fruits (for example, blackberries) are formed from the ovaries of a number of flowers. In ordinary usage, 'fruit' includes only sweet, fleshy

front

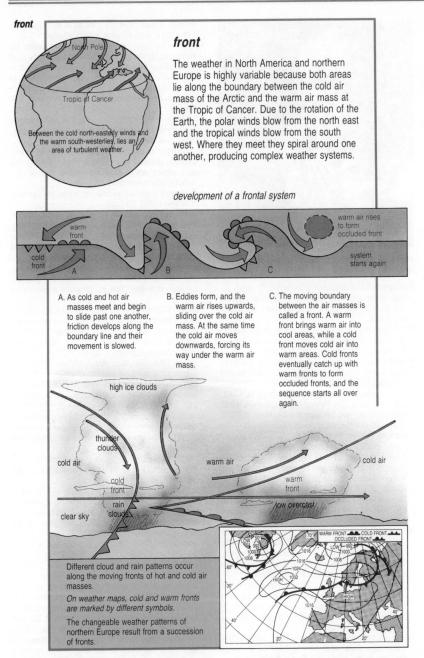

front

The weather in North America and northern Europe is highly variable because both areas lie along the boundary between the cold air mass of the Arctic and the warm air mass at the Tropic of Cancer. Due to the rotation of the Earth, the polar winds blow from the north east and the tropical winds blow from the south west. Where they meet they spiral around one another, producing complex weather systems.

development of a frontal system

A. As cold and hot air masses meet and begin to slide past one another, friction develops along the boundary line and their movement is slowed.

B. Eddies form, and the warm air rises upwards, sliding over the cold air mass. At the same time the cold air moves downwards, forcing its way under the warm air mass.

C. The moving boundary between the air masses is called a front. A warm front brings warm air into cool areas, while a cold front moves cold air into warm areas. Cold fronts eventually catch up with warm fronts to form occluded fronts, and the sequence starts all over again.

Different cloud and rain patterns occur along the moving fronts of hot and cold air masses.

On weather maps, cold and warm fronts are marked by different symbols.

The changeable weather patterns of northern Europe result from a succession of fronts.

fruit

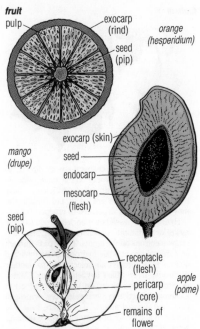

f-stop see ◊*f* number.

ft abbreviation for ◊*foot* or *feet*.

FTC abbreviation for *Federal Trade Commission*, US anti-monopoly organization; see ◊monopoly.

FT Index abbreviation for ◊*Financial Times Index*, a list of leading share prices.

Fuad /fuˈɑːd/ two kings of Egypt:

Fuad I 1868–1936. King of Egypt from 1922. Son of the Khedive Ismail, he succeeded his elder brother, Hussein Kiamil, as sultan of Egypt 1917, and when Egypt was declared independent 1922 he assumed the title of king.

Fuad II 1952– . King of Egypt 1952–53, between the abdication of his father ◊Farouk and the establishment of the republic. He was a grandson of Fuad I.

Fuchs /fʊks/ Klaus (Emil Julius) 1911–1988. German spy who worked on atom-bomb research in the UK in World War II. He was imprisoned 1950–59 for passing information to the USSR and resettled in East Germany.

Fuchs /fʊks/ Vivian 1908– . British explorer and geologist. Before World War II, he accompanied several Cambridge University expeditions to Greenland, Africa, and Antarctica. In 1957–58, he led the Commonwealth Trans-Antarctic Expedition.

fuchsia plant of the Onagraceae family, native to South and Central America and New Zealand. The genus contains a number of shrubs, small trees and herbaceous plants. The red, purple, or pink flowers hang downwards and are bell-shaped.

fuel any source of heat or energy, embracing the entire range of all combustibles and including anything that burns. *Nuclear fuel* is any material that produces atomic energy in a nuclear reactor.

frustum

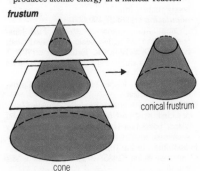

items; it excludes many botanical fruits such as acorns, bean pods, thistledown, and cucumbers (see ◊vegetable), but is often used for foodstuffs such as rhubarb that are not fruits in a botanical sense.

Recorded world fruit production in the mid-1980s was approximately 300 million tonnes per year. Technical advances in storage and transport have made tropical fruits available to consumers in temperate areas, and fresh temperate fruits available all year round.

Frunze /ˈfruːnzi/ capital (formerly Pishpek) of Kirghiz Republic, USSR; population (1987) 632,000. It produces textiles, farm machinery, metal goods, and tobacco.

frustule the cell wall of a ◊diatom. Frustules are intricately patterned on the surface with spots, ridges, and furrows, each pattern being characteristic of a particular species.

frustum in geometry, a 'slice' taken out of a solid figure by a pair of parallel planes. A conical frustum, for example, resembles a cone with the top cut off. The volume and area of a frustum are calculated

by subtracting the volume or area of the 'missing' piece from those of the whole figure.

Fry /fraɪ/ Christopher 1907– . English dramatist. He was a leader of the revival of verse drama after World War II with *The Lady's Not for Burning* 1948, *Venus Observed* 1950, and *A Sleep of Prisoners* 1951.

He has also written screenplays and made successful translations of Anouilh and Giraudoux.

Fry /fraɪ/ Elizabeth (born Gurney) 1780–1845. English Quaker philanthropist. She formed an association for the improvement of conditions for female prisoners 1817, and worked with her brother, *Joseph Gurney* (1788–1847), on an influential report 1819 on prison reform.

Fry /fraɪ/ Roger Eliot 1866–1934. British artist and art critic, a champion of Post-Impressionism and a great admirer of Cézanne. He founded the *Omega Workshops* to improve design and to encourage young artists working in modern styles.

FSH abbreviation for ◊*follicle-stimulating hormone*.

fuchsia

fuel cell cell converting chemical energy directly to electrical energy. It works on the same principle as a battery, but is continually fed with fuel, usually hydrogen. Fuel cells are silent and reliable (no moving parts), but expensive to produce.

Hydrogen is passed over an ◊electrode (usually nickel or platinum) containing a ◊catalyst, which strips electrons off the atoms. These pass through an external circuit while hydrogen ◊ions (charged atoms) pass through an ◊electrolyte to another electrode, over which oxygen is passed. Water is formed at this electrode (as a by-product) in a chemical reaction involving electrons, hydrogen ions, and oxygen atoms. If the spare heat also produced is used for hot water and space heating, some 80% efficiency in fuel is achieved.

fuel injection injecting fuel directly into the cylinders of an internal combustion engine. It is the standard method used in ◊diesel engines, and is now becoming popular for ◊petrol engines. In the diesel engine oil is injected into the hot compressed air at the top of the second piston stroke and explodes to drive the piston down on its power stroke. In the petrol engine petrol is injected into the cylinder at the start of the first induction stroke of the ◊four-stroke cycle. Such engines need no carburettor.

Fuentes /fuˈentes/ Carlos 1928– . Mexican novelist, whose first novel *La región más transparente/Where the Air is Clear* 1958 encompasses the history of the country from the Aztecs to the present day.

fugue (Latin 'flight') in music, a contrapuntal form (with two or more melodies) for a number of parts or 'voices', which enter successively in imitation of each other. It was raised to a high art by J S ◊Bach.

Führer /ˈfjʊərə/ or *Fuehrer* title adopted by Adolf ◊Hitler as leader of the ◊Nazi Party.

Fujairah /fuˈdʒaɪərə/ or *Fujayrah* one of the seven constituent member states of the ◊United Arab Emirates; area 1,150 sq km/450 sq mi; population (1985) 54,000.

Fujian /ˌfuːdʒiˈæn/ formerly *Fukien* province of SE China, bordering Taiwan Strait, opposite Taiwan
area 123,100 sq km/47,517 sq mi
capital Fuzhou
physical dramatic mountainous coastline
features it is being developed for tourists; designated as pace-setting province for modernization 1980
products sugar, rice, special aromatic teas, tobacco, timber, fruit
population (1986) 27,490,000.

Fujiyama /ˌfuːdʒiˈjɑːmə/ or *Mount Fuji* Japanese volcano and highest peak, on Honshu Island; height 3,778 m/12,400 ft. Extinct since 1707, it has a ◊Shinto shrine and a weather station on its summit.

Fukien /fuːˈkjen/ former name of ◊Fujian, a province of SE China.

Fukuoka /ˌfuːkuːˈəʊkə/ formerly *Najime* Japanese industrial port on the NW coast of Kyushu island; population (1987) 1,142,000. It produces chemicals, textiles, paper, and metal goods.

Fukushima /ˌfuːkuːˈʃiːmə/ city in N Honshu, Japan; population (1985) 271,000. It has a silk industry.

Fuller *US architect Buckminster Fuller invented the geodesic dome 1947.*

Fukuyama /ˌfuːkuːˈjɑːmə/ port in SW Honshu, Japan, at the mouth of the Ashida river; population (1985) 360,000. It has cotton, rubber and other industries.

Fula West African empire founded by people of predominantly Fulani extraction. The Fula conquered the Hausa states in the 19th century.

Fulani person of Fulani culture from the southern Sahara and Sahel. Traditionally pastoralists and traders, Fulani groups are found in Senegal, Guinea, Mali, Burkina Faso, Niger, Nigeria, Chad, and Cameroon. The Fulani language is divided into four dialects, and belongs to the West Atlantic branch of the Niger-Congo family.

Fulbright /ˈfʊlbraɪt/ William 1905– . US Democratic politician. He was responsible for the *Fulbright Act* 1946 which provided grants for thousands of Americans to study overseas and for overseas students to enter the USA; he had studied at Oxford, UK, on a Rhodes scholarship. He chaired the Senate Foreign Relations Committee 1959–74, and was a strong internationalist and supporter of the United Nations.

full employment in economics, a state in which the only unemployment is frictional (that share of the labour force which is in the process of looking for, or changing to, a new job), and when everyone wishing to work is able to find employment.

Full employment is unusual, although a few countries, including Sweden, Switzerland, and Japan, traditionally maintain low levels of unemployment. Communist countries usually claim full employment.

Fuller /ˈfʊlə/ (Richard) Buckminster 1895–1983. US architect and engineer. In 1947 he invented the lightweight *geodesic dome*, a half-sphere of triangular components independent of buttress or vault. It combined the maximum strength with the minimum structure. Within 30 years over 50,000 had been built.

Fuller /ˈfʊlə/ John Frederick Charles 1878–1966. British major general and military theorist who propounded the concept of armoured warfare, or *blitzkrieg*, as adopted by the Germans 1940.

Fuller /ˈfʊlə/ Roy 1912– . English poet and novelist. His collections of poetry include *Poems* 1939, *Epitaphs and Occasions* 1951, *Brutus's Orchard* 1957, *Collected Poems* 1962, and *The Reign of Sparrows* 1980. Novels include *My Child, My Sister* 1965 and *The Carnal Island* 1970.

Fuller /ˈfʊlə/ Thomas 1608–1661. English writer. He served as a chaplain to the Royalist army during the Civil War, and at the Restoration became the king's chaplain. He wrote *History of the Holy War* 1639, *Good Thoughts in Bad Times* 1645, its sequel *Good Thoughts in Worse Times* 1647, and the biographical *Worthies of England* 1662.

fuller's earth a soft, greenish-grey rock resembling clay, but without clay's plasticity. It is formed largely of clay minerals, rich in montmorillonite, but a great deal of silica is also present.

Its absorbent properties make it suitable for removing oil and grease, and it was formerly used for cleaning fleeces ('fulling'). It is still used in the textile industry, but its chief application is in the purification of oils. Beds of fuller's earth are found in the southern USA, Germany, Japan, and the UK.

Beds of fuller's earth in the UK are linked to contemporary volcanic activity in Mesozoic times, when fine volcanic ash settled in water.

full score in music, a complete transcript of a composition showing all parts individually, as opposed to a *short score* or *piano score* that is condensed into fewer lines of music.

full stop in punctuation another name for ◊period; it is also called full point.

fulmar several species of petrels of the family Procellariidae, which are similar in size and colour to the common gull. The northern fulmar *Fulmarus glacialis* is found in the N Atlantic and visits land only to nest, laying a single egg.

fulminate any salt of fulminic (cyanic) acid (HOCN), the chief ones being silver and mercury. The fulminates detonate, that is, they are exploded by a blow.

Fulton /ˈfʊltən/ Robert 1765–1815. US engineer and inventor who designed the first successful steamships. He produced a submarine, the *Nautilus*, in Paris, France, 1797, and experimented with steam navigation on the Seine, then returned to the USA. The first steam vessel of note, the *Clermont*, appeared on the Hudson 1807, sailing between New York and Albany. The first steam warship was the *Fulton*, of 38 tonnes, built 1814–15.

fumitory plant, genus *Fumeria*, family Fumariaceae, native to Europe and Asia. The common fumitory *F. officinalis* produces pink flowers tipped with blackish red.

Funabashi /ˌfuːnəˈbæʃi/ city in Kanto region, Honshu island, east of Tokyo; population (1987) 508,000.

Funafuti /ˌfuːnəˈfuːti/ atoll consisting of 30 islets in the West Pacific and capital of the state of ◊Tuvalu; area 2.8 sq km/1.1 sq mi; population 900.

Funchal /fʊnˈʃɑːl/ capital and chief port of the Portuguese island of Madeira, on the S coast; population (1980) 100,000. Tourism and wine are the main industries.

function in computing, a small part of a program that supplies a specific value; for example, the square root of a specified number, or the current date. Most programming languages incorporate a number of built-in functions; some allow programmers to write their own. A function may have one or more arguments (the values on which the function operates). A *function key* on a keyboard is one that, when pressed, performs a designated task, such as ending a program.

function in mathematics, a function f is a set of ordered pairs $(x, f(x))$ of which no two can have the same first element. Hence, if $f(x) = x^2$, two ordered pairs are $(-2,4)$ and $(2,4)$. In the algebraic expression $y = 4x^3 + 2$, the dependent variable y is a function of the independent variable x, generally written as $f(x)$.

Functions are commonly used in all branches of mathematics, physics, and science generally; for example, the formula $t = 2\pi\sqrt{(l/g)}$ shows that for a simple pendulum the time of swing t is a function of its length l and of no other variable quantity (π and g, the acceleration due to gravity, are ◊constants).

functional group in chemistry, a small number of atoms in an arrangement that determines the chemical properties of the group and of the molecule to which it is attached (for example the carboxylic acid group –COOH, or the amine group NH_2). Organic compounds can be considered as structural skeletons with functional groups attached.

functionalism in the social sciences, the view of society as a system made up of a number of interrelated parts, all functioning on the basis of a common value system or consensus about basic values and common goals. Every social custom and institution is seen as having a function in ensuring that society works efficiently; deviance and crime are seen as a form of social sickness.

Functionalists often describe society as an organism with a life of its own, above and beyond the sum of its members. The French sociologists Comte and ◊Durkheim and the American ◊Parsons have taken functionalist approaches.

Functionalism in architecture and design, a 20th-century school, also called Modernism or International Style, characterized by a desire to exclude everything that serves no practical purpose. It was a reaction against the 19th-century practice of imitating earlier styles, and its finest achievements are in the realm of industrial building.

Its leading exponents were the German ◊Bauhaus school and the Dutch group de ◊Stijl; prominent architects in the field were Le Corbusier and Walter ◊Gropius.

fundamental in musical acoustics, the lowest ◊harmonic of a musical tone, corresponding to the audible pitch.

fundamentalism in religion, an emphasis on basic principles or articles of faith. *Christian fundamentalism* emerged in the USA just after World War I and insists on belief in the literal truth of everything in the Bible; *Islamic fundamentalism* insists on strict observance of Muslim Shari'a law.

Christian adherents see the virgin birth, the physical resurrection of Christ, the atonement, and the Bible miracles as fundamental to their faith. They have attempted to outlaw the teaching of evolution (as in ◊Dayton, Tennessee, 1925) and replace it with ◊creationism.

fundamental particle another term for ◊elementary particle.

Fundy, Bay of /ˈfʌndi/ Canadian Atlantic inlet between New Brunswick and Nova Scotia, with a rapid tidal rise and fall of 18 m/60 ft (harnessed for electricity since 1984). In summer, fog increases the dangers to shipping.

Fünen /ˈfjuːnən/ German form of ◊Fyn, an island forming part of Denmark.

Fünfkirchen /ˈfʊnfkɪəkən/ (German 'five churches') German name for ◊Pécs, a town in SW Hungary.

fungicide a chemical used to treat fungus diseases in plants and animals. Inorganic and organic compounds containing sulphur are widely used.

fungus plural *fungi* one of the group of organisms in the kingdom Fungi, separate from green plants. Fungi lack leaves and roots; they contain no chlorophyll, and reproduce by spores. Moulds, yeasts, and mushrooms are all types of fungus.

Because fungi have no chlorophyll, they must get food from organic substances. They are either ◊parasites, existing on living plants or animals, or ◊saprophytes, living on dead matter. Some 50,000 different species have been identified, including slime moulds, mildews, rusts and smuts, mushrooms, toadstools, and puff-balls. Some are edible, but many are highly poisonous.

Before the classification Fungi came into use, they were included within the division Thallophyta, along with algae and bacteria.

funicular railway a railway with two cars connected by a wire cable wound around a drum at the top of a steep incline. In Britain, the system is used only in seaside cliff railways, but longer funicular railways of up to 1.5 km/1 mi exist in Switzerland.

funk a style of dance music of black US origin, relying on heavy percussion in polyrhythmic patterns. Leading exponents include James Brown (1928–) and George Clinton (1940–).

Funk /fʌŋk/ Casimir 1884–1967. US biochemist, born in Poland, who did pioneering research into vitamins.

---

fungus

Fungi grow from spores as fine threads, or hyphae. These have no distinct cellular structure. Mushrooms and toadstools are the fruiting bodies formed by hyphae. Gills beneath the cap of these aerial structures produce masses of spores.

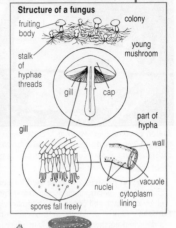

Structure of a fungus

Common British fungi (and habitat)

1. Parasol mushroom (wood) 2. Oyster fungus (birch trees) 3. Deceiver (damp woods) 4. Beefsteak fungus (deciduous trees) 5. Jew's ear fungus (elder trees) 6. Honey fungus (beneath trees) 7. Wood blewitt (woods) 8. Field mushroom (meadows) 9. Cep fungus (woods) 10. Shaggy ink cap (rich soil) 11. Common puffball (woods) 12. Fairy rings (heaths) 13. Bracket fungus (oak, beech trunks) 14. Sickener (woods) 15. Stinkhorn (rich soil, woods) 16. Blusher (woods) 17. Tinder (birch trunks) 18. Razor strop (birch trunks) 19. Fly agaric (woods) 20. Death cap (deciduous woods) 21. Devil's boletus (chalkland) 22. Yellow-staining mushroom (meadows) 23. Panther cap (deciduous woods) 24. Destroying angel (woods) 25. Red-staining mushroom (woods)

fruiting periods and edibility

months		1	2	3	4	5	6	7	8	9	10	11	12	13	14	15	16	17	18	19	20	21	22	23	24	25
	J		●	●		●								●				●	●							
	F					●												●	●							
	M					●												●	●							
	A					●												●	●							
	M					●									●	●	●									●
	J					●					●				●	●	●	●	●							●
	J	●			●	●	●	●		●	●	●	●	●	●	●	●	●	●		●					●
	A	●			●	●	●		●	●	●	●	●	●	●	●	●	●	●	●	●	●	●	●	●	●
	S	●	●		●	●	●	●	●	●	●	●	●	●	●	●	●	●	●	●	●	●	●	●	●	●
	O	●	●		●	●	●	●	●	●	●	●	●	●	●	●	●	●	●	●	●	●	●	●	●	●
	N		●	●		●	●	●		●					●	●	●	●	●							
	D		●	●		●				●								●	●							

edible   inedible   poisonous

Funk proposed that certain diseases are caused by dietary deficiencies. In 1912 he demonstrated that rice extracts cure beriberi in pigeons. As the extract contains an ◊amine, he mistakenly concluded that he had discovered a class of 'vital amines', a phrase soon reduced to 'vitamins'.

fur pelts of certain animals. Fur is used as clothing, although this is vociferously criticized by environmental groups on humane grounds, because the methods of breeding or trapping animals are often cruel. Mink, chinchilla, and sable are among the most valuable, the wild furs being finer than the farmed.

Furs have been worn since prehistoric times and have long been associated with status and luxury (ermine traditionally worn by royalty, for example), except for certain ethnic groups like the Inuit. The trade had its modern origin in the furs of North America, exploited by the Hudson's Bay Company from the late 17th century. The chief centres of the fur trade are London, New York, Leningrad, and Kastoria. It is illegal to import furs or skins of endangered species listed by ◊CITES,

for example leopard. Many synthetic fibres are more effective against cold and widely used as substitutes.

Furies in Greek mythology, the Erinyes, appeasingly called the Eumenides, ('kindly ones'). They were the daughters of Earth or of Night, represented as winged maidens with serpents twisted in their hair. They punished such crimes as filial disobedience, murder, and inhospitality.

furlong unit of measurement, originating in Anglo-Saxon England, equivalent to equal to 220 yards (201.168m).

A furlong consisted of 40 rods, poles, or perches; 8 furlongs made one statute ◊mile. Its literal meaning is 'furrow-long', and refers to the length of a furrow in the common field characteristic of medieval farming.

furnace a structure in which fuel such as coal, coke, gas, or oil is burned to produce heat for various purposes. Furnaces are used in conjunction with ◊boilers to produce hot water, for heating, and steam for driving turbines—in ships for propulsion and in power stations for generating electricity.

fusion Electrical coils, weighing 12 tonnes each, used in Europe's first large thermonuclear fusion experiment at the Joint European Torus (JET) laboratory, Culham, Oxfordshire, UK.

The largest furnaces are those used for smelting and refining metals, such as the ◊blast furnace, electric furnace and ◊open-hearth furnace.

Furness /'fɜːnɪs/ peninsula in England, formerly a detached northern portion of Lancashire, separated from the main part by Morecambe Bay. In 1974 it was included in the new county of ◊Cumbria. Barrow is its ship-building and industrial centre.

Fürth /'fjʊət/ town in Bavaria, West Germany, adjoining Nuremberg; population (1984) 98,500. It has electrical, chemical, textile, and toy industries.

further education college college in the UK for students over school-leaving age that provides courses of skills towards an occupation or trade, and general education at a level below that of a degree course.

Furtwängler /'fʊətveŋglə/ (Gustav Heinrich Ernst Martin) Wilhelm 1886–1954. German conductor; leader of the Berlin Philharmonic Orchestra 1922–54. His interpretations of the German Romantic composers, especially Wagner, were regarded as classically definitive. He remained in Germany during the Nazi regime.

furze another name for ◊gorse, a shrub.

fuse in explosives, a cord impregnated with chemicals so that it burns slowly at a predetermined rate. It is used to set off a main explosive charge, sufficient length of fuse being left to allow the person lighting it to get away to safety. In electricity, *fuse wire* is wire designed to melt when excessive current passes through. It is a safety device to prevent surges of current that could damage equipment and cause fires.

Fuseli /'fjuːzəli/ Henry 1741–1825. British artist born in Switzerland, working in the Romantic style. He painted macabre and dreamlike images such as *The Nightmare* 1781 (Detroit Institute of Arts).

fusel oil a liquid with a characteristic unpleasant smell, obtained as a by-product of the distillation of the product of any alcoholic fermentation, and used in paints, varnishes, essential oils, and plastics. Fusel oil is a mixture of fatty acids, alcohols, and esters.

Fushun /,fuː'ʃʌn/ coal-mining and oil refining centre in Liaoning province, China, 40 km/25 mi E of Shenyang; population (1984) 636,000. It has aluminium, steel, and chemical works.

fusion in physics, the fusing of the nuclei of light elements. Stars and hydrogen bombs work on the principle of nuclear fusion. So far no successful fusion reactor—one able to produce the required energy and contain the reaction—has been built.

future in business, a contract to buy or sell a specific quantity of a particular commodity or currency (or even a purely notional sum, such as the value of a particular stock index) at a particular date in the future. There is usually no physical exchange between buyer and seller. It is only the difference between the ground value and the market value that changes hands. The *futures market* trades in financial futures.

futures trading buying and selling commodities (usually cereals and metals) at an agreed price for delivery several months ahead.

Futurism a literary and artistic movement 1909–14, originating in Paris. The Italian poet ◊Marinetti published the *Futurist Manifesto* 1909 urging Italian artists to join him in Futurism. They eulogized the modern world and the 'beauty of speed and energy' in their works, trying to capture the dynamism of a speeding car or train by combining the shifting geometric planes of ◊Cubism with vibrant colours. As a movement it died out during World War I, but Futurists' exultation in war and violence was seen as an early manifestation of ◊fascism.

Gino Severini (1883–1966) painted a topsy-turvy landscape as if seen from the moving window of a *Suburban Train Arriving at Paris* 1915 (Tate Gallery), and Giacomo Balla (1871–1958) represented the abstract idea of speed by the moving object in such pictures as *Abstract Speed-wake of a Speeding Car* 1919 (Tate Gallery). Umberto Boccioni, a sculptor, froze his figures as if they were several frames of a film moving at once. ◊Vorticism was a similar movement in Britain from 1909, glorifying modern technology, speed, and violence. The work of many futurist painters, such as Carrá (1881–1966), Boccioni, and Russolo (1885–1947), is characterized by forms fragmented by penetrating shafts of light which, together with their use of colour, infuse feeling of dynamic motion into their work.

Fuzhou /,fuː'dʒəʊ/ formerly *Foochow* industrial port and capital of Fujian province, SE China; population (1986) 1,190,000. It is a centre for shipbuilding and steel production, and rice, sugar, tea, and fruit pass through the port. There are joint foreign and Chinese factories.

The Mazu (Matsu) island group, occupied by the Nationalist Chinese, is offshore.

Fyfe /faɪf/ David Maxwell, 1st Earl of Kilmuir. Scottish lawyer and Conservative politician; see ◊Kilmuir.

Fyffe /faɪf/ Will 1885–1947. Scottish music-hall comedian remembered for his vivid character sketches and for his song 'I Belong to Glasgow'.

Fylingdales /'faɪlɪŋdeɪlz/ site in the North Yorkshire Moors National Park, England, of an early-warning radar station, linked with similar stations in Greenland and Alaska, to give a four-minute warning of nuclear attack.

Fyn /fjuːn/ (German *Fünen*) island forming part of Denmark and lying between the mainland and Zealand: area 2,976 sq km/1,149 sq mi; capital Odense; population (1984) 454,000.

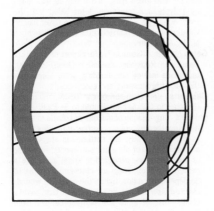

Gable *US film actor Clark Gable whose career spanned 90 films and included the role of Rhett Butler in the classic* Gone with the Wind *1939.*

G the seventh letter of the alphabet. It was formed by the Romans by adding a 'tail' to the letter C which represented the K sound.

g abbreviation for *gram*.

GA abbreviation for ◊*Georgia* (USA).

gabbro a basic (low-silica) ◊igneous rock formed deep in the Earth's crust. It contains pyroxene and calcium-rich feldspar, and may contain small amounts of olivine and amphibole. Its coarse crystals of dull minerals give it a speckled appearance.

Gabbro is the plutonic version of basalt (that is, derived from magma that has solidified below the Earth's surface), and forms in large, slow-cooling intrusions.

gabelle in French history, term used orginally for a tax on various items, but which came to be used exclusively for a tax on salt, first levied by Philip the Fair in 1286, and abolished 1790.

Gabès /'gɑːbes/ port in E Tunisia; population (1984) 92,300. Fertilizers and dates are exported. The town stands on the site of the Roman town of Tacapae.

Gable /'geɪbəl/ Clark 1901–1960. US film actor. He was a star for more than 30 years in 90 films, including *It Happened One Night* 1934, *Gone with the Wind* 1939, and *The Misfits* 1961. He was nicknamed the 'King' of Hollywood.

Gabo /'gɑːbəʊ/ Naum. Adopted name of Naum Neemia Pevsner 1890–1977. US abstract sculptor, born in Russia. One of the leading exponents of *Constructivism*, he left the USSR in 1922 for Germany and taught at the Bauhaus (a key centre of modern design). He lived in the UK in the 1930s, then in the USA from 1946. He often used transparent coloured plastics in his sculptures.

Gabon /gæˈbɒn/ country in central Africa, bounded N by Cameroon, E and S by the Congo, W by the Atlantic Ocean, and NW by Equatorial Guinea.

government The 1961 constitution, revised in 1976, 1975 and 1981, provides for a president

elected by universal suffrage for a seven-year term. As head of both state and government, the president appoints and presides over a prime minister and council of ministers, and is also founder and secretary-general of the Gabonese Democratic Party (PDG). There is a single-chamber legislature, the National Assembly, of 120 members, 111 elected and nine nominated for a five-year term. Gabon became a one-party state in 1968, the party being the PDG.

history Gabon was colonized by some of its present inhabitants (the Fang and the Omiéné) during the 16th–18th centuries. Its first European visitors were the Portuguese in the late 15th century. They began a slave trade that lasted almost 500 years. In 1889 Gabon became part of the French Congo, and was a province of French Equatorial Africa from 1908.

Gabon achieved full independence in 1960. There were then two main political parties, the Gabonese Democratic Bloc (BDG), led by Léon M'ba, and the Gabonese Democratic and Social Union (UDSG), led by Jean-Hilaire Aubame. Although the two parties were evenly matched in popular support, on independence M'ba became president and Aubame foreign minister.

In 1967 the BDG wanted the two parties to merge but the UDSG resisted, and M'ba called a general election. Before the elections M'ba

was deposed in a military coup by supporters of Aubame but was restored to office with French help. Aubame was tried and imprisoned for treason. The UDSG was outlawed and most of its members joined the BDG.

In 1967 M'ba, although in failing health, was re-elected. He died later that year and was succeeded by Albert-Bernard Bongo who, the following year, established the Gabonese Democratic Party (PDG) as the only legal party. Bongo was re-elected in 1973 and was converted to Islam, changing his first name to Omar. In 1979 Bongo, as the sole presidential candidate, was re-elected for a further seven years.

Gabon's reserves of uranium, manganese, and iron make it the richest country per head of population in Black Africa, and both M'ba and Bongo have successfully exploited these resources, gaining control of the iron-ore ventures once half-owned by the Bethlehem Steel Corporation of the USA, and concluding economic and technical agreements with China as well as maintaining ties with France. Although he has operated an authoritarian regime, Gabon's prosperity has diluted any serious opposition to President Bongo. He was again re-elected in Nov 1986, and a coup attempt against him in 1989 was defeated by loyal troops.

Gabor /'gɑːbɔː/ Dennis 1900–1979. Hungarian-British physicist. In 1947, he invented the holographic method of three-dimensional photography and in 1958 invented a type of colour TV tube of greatly reduced depth.

Gaborone /ˌgæbəˈrəʊni/ capital of Botswana from 1965, mainly an administrative centre; population (1988) 111,000. Light industry includes textiles.

Gabriel /'geɪbrɪəl/ in the New Testament, the archangel who foretold the birth of John the Baptist to Zacharias and of Jesus to the Virgin Mary. He is also mentioned in the Old Testament in the book of Daniel. In Muslim belief, Gabriel revealed the Koran to Muhammad and escorted him on his ◊Night Journey.

Gabrieli /ˌgæbrɪˈeli/ Giovanni *c.*1555–1612. Italian composer and organist. Although he composed secular music, and madrigals, he is best known for his motets, which are frequently dramatic and often use several choirs and groups of instruments. In 1585 he became organist at St Mark's, Venice,

Gadamer /'gɑːdəmə/ Hans-Georg 1900– . German ◊hermeneutic philosopher. In *Truth and Method* 1960, he argued that 'understanding' is fundamental to human existence, and that all understanding takes place within a tradition. The relation between text and interpreter can

Gabon
Gabonese Republic
(République Gabonaise)

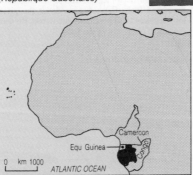

area 267,667 sq km/103,319 sq mi
capital Libreville
physical virtually the whole country is tropical rainforest; mountains alternate with lowlands; Ogooué River flows S–W
features Schweitzer hospital at Lambaréné
head of state and government Omar Bongo from 1967

political system authoritarian nationalism
political parties Gabonese Democratic Party (PDG), nationalist
exports petroleum, manganese, iron, uranium, timber
currency CFA franc (485.00 = £1 Feb 1990)
population (1988) 1,226,000; annual growth rate 1.6%
life expectancy men 47, women 51
language French (official), Bantu
religion animist 60%, Roman Catholic 35%, small Muslim minority
literacy 70% male/53% female (1985 est)
GNP $3 bn (1983); $2,613 per head of population
chronology
1960 Independence from France achieved. Léon M'ba became the first president.
1967 Attempted coup by rival party foiled with French help. M'ba died and was succeeded by his protégé, Albert-Bernard Bongo.
1968 One-party state established.
1973 Bongo re-elected; converted to Islam, he changed his first name to Omar.
1986 Bongo re-elected.
1989 Coup attempt against Bongo defeated.

be viewed as a dialogue, in which the interpreter must remain open to the truth of the text.

Gaddafi alternative form of ◊Khaddhafi, Libyan leader.

Gaddi /ˈgædi/ family of Italian painters in Florence: *Gaddo Gaddi* (c. 1250–c.1330); his son *Taddeo Gaddi* (c.1300– c.1366), who was influenced by Giotto and painted the fresco cycle *Life of the Virgin* in Santa Croce, Florence; and grandson *Agnolo Gaddi* (active 1369–96), who also painted frescoes in Santa Croce, *The Story of the Cross*, 1380s, and produced panel paintings in characteristic pale pastel colours.

Gaddis /ˈgædɪs/ William 1922– . Experimental US novelist, whose *The Recognitions* 1955, about artistic counterfeiting, is one of the best US novels of the 1950s. His other novels are *JR* 1976 and *Carpenter's Gothic* 1985.

gadfly a fly which bites cattle, such as a ◊botfly, or ◊horsefly.

gadolinium an element, symbol Gd, atomic number 64, relative atomic mass 157.25. It is a silvery-white metal, a member of the lanthanide series. It is found in the products of nuclear fission and used in electronic components, alloys, and products needing to withstand high temperatures.

Gadsden Purchase, the in US history, the purchase of approximately 77,720 sq km/30,000 sq mi in what is now New Mexico and Arizona by the USA 1853. The land was bought from Mexico for $10,000,000 in a treaty negotiated by James Gadsden (1788–1858) of South Carolina in order to construct a transcontinental railroad route, the Southern Pacific, completed in the 1880s.

Gaelic football a 15-a-side team game played mainly in Ireland. It is a kicking and catching game; goals are scored by kicking the ball into the net (as in association football) or over the crossbar (as in rugby). The game was first played 1712 and is now one of the sports under the auspices of the Gaelic Athletic Association. The leading tournament is the All-Ireland Championship culminating in the final which is played in Dublin on the third Sunday in September each year, the winners receiving the Sam Maguire Trophy.

Gaelic language a member of the Celtic branch of the Indo-European language family, spoken in Ireland, Scotland, and (until 1974) the Isle of Man.

It is, along with English, one of the national languages of the Republic of Ireland, with over half a million speakers, and is known there both as Irish and Irish Gaelic. In Scotland, speakers of Gaelic number around 90,000 and are concentrated in the Western Isles, in parts of the NW coast and in the city of Glasgow. Gaelic has been in decline for several centuries, subject until recently to neglect within the British state. There is a small Gaelic-speaking community in Nova Scotia, Canada.

Gafsa /ˈgæfsə/ oasis town in central Tunisia, centre of a phosphate-mining area; population (1984) 60,900.

Gagarin /gəˈgɑːrɪn/ Yuri (Alexeyevich) 1934–1968. Soviet cosmonaut who in 1961 became the first human in space in ◊Vostok 1.

Born in the Smolensk region, the son of a farmer, he qualified as a foundryman. He became a pilot 1957, and on 12 Apr 1961 completed one orbit of the Earth, taking 108 minutes from launch to landing. He died in a plane crash while training for the Soyuz 3 mission.

Gaia /ˈgeɪə/ or *Ge* in Greek mythology, the goddess of the Earth. She sprang from primordial Chaos and herself produced Uranus, by whom she was the mother of the Cyclopes and Titans.

Gaia hypothesis theory that the Earth's living and nonliving systems form an inseparable whole that is regulated and kept adapted for life by living organisms themselves. Since life and environment are so closely linked, there is a need for humans to understand and maintain the physical environment and living things around them. The Gaia hypothesis was elaborated by James Lovelock in the 1970s.

Gainsborough Mrs Siddons (1785) National Gallery, London.

Gainsborough /ˈgeɪnzbərə/ market town in Lincolnshire, England; population (1985) 18,715. It is an agricultural marketing centre with flour mills and the manufacture of agricultural machinery. It stands on the river Trent, which periodically rises in a tidal wave, the 'eagre'.

Gainsborough /ˈgeɪnzbərə/ Thomas 1727–1788. English landscape and portrait painter. He was born in Sudbury, Suffolk; in 1759 he settled in Bath, gaining fame as a painter of high society. In 1774 he went to London and became one of the original members of the Royal Academy. He was one of the first British artists to follow the Dutch in painting realistic landscapes rather than imaginative Italianate scenery.

Gainsborough began to paint while still at school and in 1741 went to London where he learnt etching and studied at the Academy of Arts, but remained largely self-taught. His portraits of Sir Charles Holte and the actor Garrick belong to this period. His sitters included the royal family, Mrs Siddons, Dr Johnson, Burke, and Sheridan.

Gaitskell /ˈgeɪtskəl/ Hugh Todd Naylor 1906–1963. British Labour politician. In 1950 he became minister of economic affairs, and then chancellor of the Exchequer until Oct 1951. In 1955 he defeated Aneurin Bevan for the succession to Attlee as party leader, and tried to reconcile internal differences on nationalization and disarmament. He was re-elected leader in 1960.

gal abbreviation for *gallon*.

Galahad in Arthurian legend, one of the knights of the Round Table. Galahad succeeded in the quest for the ◊Holy Grail because of his virtue. He was the son of ◊Lancelot of the Lake.

galaxy

Galápagos Islands group of 15 islands (official name *Archipeliégo de Colón*) in the Pacific, belonging to Ecuador; area 7,800 sq km/3,000 sq mi; population (1982) 6,120. The capital is San Cristóbal on the island of the same name. The islands are a nature reserve. Their unique fauna (including giant tortoises, iguanas, penguins, flightless cormorants, and Darwin's finches), are under threat from introduced species.

Galatea /ˌgæləˈtiːə/ in Greek mythology, a sea nymph who loved Acis, and when he was killed by Polyphemus transformed his blood into the river Acis. Pygmalion made a statue (later named Galatea) which he married after it was brought to life by Aphrodite.

Galaţi /gæˈlæts/ (German *Galatz*) port on the river Danube in Romania; population (1985) 293,000. Industries include ship-building, iron, steel, textiles, food processing, and cosmetics.

Galatians ◊epistle in the ◊New Testament to the churches in Galatia ; attributed to St Paul.

galaxy a congregation of millions or billions of stars, held together by gravity. *Spiral galaxies*, such as the ◊Milky Way, are flattened in shape, with a central bulge of old stars surrounded by a disc of younger stars, arranged in spiral arms like a catherine wheel. They are classified from Sa to Sc depending on how tightly the arms are wound. *Barred spirals* are spiral galaxies that have a straight bar of stars across their centre, from the ends of which the spiral arms emerge. The arms of spiral galaxies contain gas and dust from which new stars are still forming classified SBa to SBc. Elliptical galaxies contain old stars and very little gas. They include the most massive galaxies known, containing a trillion stars, classified from E0 to E7 depending on the degree of flatness. There are also irregular galaxies. Most galaxies occur in clusters, containing anything from a few to thousands of members.

Our own galaxy, the Milky Way, is about 100,000 light years in diameter, containing at least 100 billion stars. It is a member of a small cluster, the ◊Local Group. The Sun lies in one of its spiral arms, about 25,000 light years from the centre.

Galbraith /gælˈbreɪθ/ John Kenneth 1908– . Canadian economist of the Keynesian school whose major works include *The Affluent Society* 1958 and *Economics and the Public Purpose* 1974. In the former he argued that industrialized societies like the USA were suffering from private affluence accompanied by public squalor.

Galen /ˈgeɪlən/ c.130–c.AD 200. Greek physician whose ideas dominated Western medicine for almost 1,500 years. Born at Pergamum in Asia Minor, he personally attended the Roman emperor Marcus Aurelius. Central to his thinking were the theories of ◊humours and the threefold circulation of the blood.

Galen made relatively few discoveries and relied heavily on the teachings of ◊Hippocrates. He

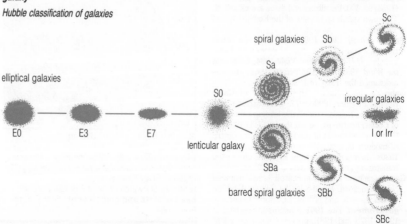

Hubble classification of galaxies

Galileo *The Galileo spacecraft about to be detached from the Earth-orbiting Space Shuttle Atlantis at the beginning of its six year journey to Jupiter.*

wrote a large number of books, over 100 of which are known.

galena chief ore of lead, consisting of lead sulphide, PbS. It is lead-grey in colour, has a high metallic lustre and breaks into cubes due to its perfect cubic cleavage. It may contain up to 1% silver, and so the ore is sometimes mined for both metals.

Galena occurs mainly among limestone deposits in Australia, Mexico, the USSR, the UK, and the USA.

Galicia /gə'lɪsɪə/ mountainous but fertile autonomous region of NW Spain, formerly an independent kingdom; area 29,400 sq km/11,348 sq mi; population (1986) 2,785,000. It includes La Coruña, Lugo, Orense, and Pontevedra. Industries include fishing and the mining of tungsten and tin. The language is similar to Portuguese.

Galicia /gə'lɪsɪə/ former province of central Europe, extending from the N slopes of the Carpathians to the Czech-Romanian border. Once part of the Austrian Empire, it was included in Poland after World War I, and divided in 1945 between Poland and the USSR.

Galilee, Sea of /'gælɪli:/ alternative name for Lake ◊Tiberias in N Israel.

galileo unit (symbol gal) of acceleration, used in geological surveying. One galileo is 10–12 metres per second per second. The Earth's gravitational field often differs by several milligals (thousandths of gals) in different places, because of the varying densities of the rocks beneath the surface.

Galileo spacecraft launched from the Space Shuttle Atlantis in Oct 1989, on a six-year journey to Jupiter.

Galileo /ˌgælɪ'leɪəʊ/ (Galileo Galilei) 1564–1642. Italian mathematician, astronomer, and physicist.

Galileo Galilei *Italian mathematician, astronomer, and physicist, Galileo Galilei.*

He developed the astronomical telescope and was the first to see sunspots, the four main satellites of Jupiter, mountains and craters on the Moon, and the appearance of going through 'phases', thus proving it was orbiting the Sun. In mechanics, Galileo discovered that freely falling bodies, heavy or light, had the same, constant acceleration (though the story of his dropping cannonballs from the Leaning Tower of Pisa is questionable), and that a body moving on a perfectly smooth horizontal surface would neither speed up nor slow down.

He discovered in 1583 that each oscillation of a pendulum takes the same amount of time despite the difference in amplitude. He invented a hydrostatic balance, and discovered that the path of a projectile was a parabola.

Galileo was born in Pisa, and in 1589 became professor of mathematics at the university there; in 1592 he became a professor at Padua; and in 1610 was appointed chief mathematician to the Grand Duke of Tuscany, Florence. Galileo's observations and arguments were an unwelcome refutation of the ideas of ◊Aristotle taught at the (Church-run) universities, especially because they made plausible for the first time the heliocentric (Sun-centred) theory of ◊Copernicus. Galileo's persuasive *Dialogues on the Two Chief Systems of the World* 1632 was banned by the Church authorities at Rome; he was made to recant by the ◊Inquisition and put under house arrest for his last years.

gall abnormal outgrowth on a plant which develops as a result of attack by insects or, less commonly, by bacteria, fungi, mites, or nematodes. The attack causes an increase in the number of cells, or an enlargement of existing cells in the plant. Gall-forming insects generally pass the early stages of their life inside the gall. A gall wasp is responsible for the conspicuous bud galls forming on oak trees, 2.5–4 cm across, popularly known as 'oak apples'.

Gall /gæl/ Franz Joseph 1758–1828. Austrian anatomist, instigator of the discredited theory of ◊phrenology.

Galla a people of E Africa, especially Ethiopia, who speak a Hamito-Semitic (Afro-Asiatic) language.

gall bladder a small muscular sac attached to the underside of the liver and connected to the small intestine by the bile duct. It stores bile from the liver.

Gallé /gæl/ Emile 1846–1904. French ◊Art Nouveau glassmaker. He produced glass in sinuous forms or rounded, solid-looking shapes

Gallipoli *Men of the British Royal Naval Division and Australian troops sharing a trench. One man is using a periscope (left) and another a 'sniperscope'.*

almost as heavy as stone, typically decorated with flowers or leaves in colour on colour.

After training in various parts of Europe, he worked at his father's glass factory and eventually took it over. A founder of the *Ecole de Nancy*, he designed furniture as well as achieving significant developments in the techniques of glassmaking.

Galle /'gælə/ Johann Gottfried 1812–1910. German astronomer who located the planet Neptune 1846, close to the position predicted by French mathematician Urbail Leverrier.

Gallegos /gæl'jeɪɡɒs/ Rómulo 1884–1969. Venezuelan politican and writer. He was Venezuela's first democratically elected president 1948 before being overthrown by a military coup the same year. He was also a professor of philosophy and literature. His novels include *La trepadora/The Climber* 1925 and *Doña Barbara* 1929.

galley ship powered by oars, and usually also with sails. Galleys typically had a crew of hundreds of oarsmen arranged in rows; they were used in warfare from antiquity until the 18th century.

Louis XIV of France maintained a fleet of some 40 galleys, crewed by over 10,000 convicts, until 1748. The maximum speed of a galley is estimated to have been only four knots, while only 20% of the oarsmen's effort was effective, and galleys could not be used in stormy weather because of their very low waterline.

Gallico /'gælɪkəʊ/ Paul (William) 1897–1976. US author. Originally a sports columnist, he began writing fiction in 1936. His books include *The Snow Goose* 1941.

Gallipoli /gə'lɪpəli/ port in European Turkey, where in World War I at the instigation of Winston Churchill, an unsuccessful attempt was made Feb 1915–Jan 1916 by Allied troops to force their way through the Dardanelles and link up with Russia. The campaign was fought mainly by Australian and New Zealand (◊ANZAC) forces, who suffered heavy losses.

gallium an element, symbol Ga, atomic number 31, relative atomic mass 69.75. It is a very scarce, grey metal which is liquid at room temperature. Gallium arsenide crystals are used in microelectronics, since electrons travel a thousand times faster through them than through silicon. It was discovered in 1875 by Lecoq de Boisbaudran.

Gällivare /'jelɪvɑːrə/ iron-mining town above the Arctic Circle in Norrbotten county, N Sweden; population (1976) 25,279.

gallon imperial liquid or dry measure, equal to 4.546 litres, and subdivided into four quarts or eight pints. The US gallon is equivalent to 3.785 litres.

Galloway /'gæləweɪ/ ancient area of SW Scotland, now part of the region of ◊Dumfries and Galloway.

gallstone a pebble-like, insoluble accretion formed in the human gall bladder from salts and other substances present in the bile. Gallstones may be symptomless or they may cause pain, indigestion, or jaundice.

Gallup /'gæləp/ George Horace 1901–1984. US journalist and statistician, founder in 1935 of the American Institute of Public Opinion and deviser of the *Gallup Polls*, in which public opinion is gauged by questioning a number of representative individuals.

Galois /gæl'wɑː/ Evariste 1811–1832. French mathematician, who originated the theory of groups. His attempts to gain recognition for his work were largely thwarted by the French mathematical establishment, who saw not his genius but his lack of formal qualifications. Galois was killed in a duel before he was 21. The night before he had hurriedly written out his unpublished discoveries on group theory, the importance of which would come to be appreciated more and more as the 19th century progressed.

Galsworthy /'gɔːlzwɜːði/ John 1867–1933. British novelist and dramatist, whose work examines the social issues of the Victorian period. He is famous for *The Forsyte Saga* 1922 and its sequel *A Modern*

Galtieri *President Leopoldo Galtieri of Argentina condemning Britain during the Falklands crisis of 1982.*

Comedy 1929. Other novels include *The Country House* 1907 and *Fraternity* 1909; plays include *The Silver Box* 1906.

Born in Kingston, Surrey, Galsworthy achieved success with *The Man of Property* 1906, the first instalment of *The Forsyte Saga* 1922, which included *In Chancery* and *To Let*. Soames Forsyte, the central character, is the embodiment of Victorian values and feeling for property, and the wife whom he also 'owns'—Irene — was based on Galsworthy's wife. Later additions to the series are *A Modern Comedy* 1929, which contained *The White Monkey, The Silver Spoon*, and *Swan Song*, and the short stories *On Forsyte Change* 1930.

Galt /gɔːlt/ John 1779–1839. Scottish novelist. He is probably best known for the *Annals of the Parish* 1821 in which he portrays the life of a Lowlands village, using the local dialect.

Born in Ayrshire, he moved to London in 1804 and lived in Canada from 1826–29. He founded the Canadian town of ◊Guelph, and Galt, on the Grand river in Ontario, was named after him.

Galtieri /ˌgælti'eəri/ Leopoldo 1926– . Argentinian general, leading member of the right-wing military junta that ordered the seizure 1982 of the Falkland Islands (Malvinas), a UK colony in the SW Atlantic claimed by Argentina. He and his fellow junta members were tried for abuse of human rights and court-martialled for their conduct of the war; he was sentenced to 12 years in prison in 1986.

Galton /gɔːltən/ Francis 1822–1911. English scientist, noted for his study of the inheritance of physical and mental attributes in humans which he called ◊eugenics.

Gama *An engraving of the Portuguese navigator Vasco da Gama. He reached Natal, now a province of South Africa, on Christmas Day 1497.*

Galvani /gæl'vɑːni/ Luigi 1737–1798. Italian physiologist. Born in Bologna, where he taught anatomy, he discovered galvanic or voltaic electricity in 1762, when investigating the contractions produced in the muscles of dead frogs by contact with pairs of different metals. His work led quickly to ◊Volta's invention of the electric battery, and later to an understanding of how nerves control muscles.

galvanizing process for rendering iron rustproof, by plunging it into molten zinc (the dipping method), or by electroplating it with zinc.

Galveston /'gælvəstən/ port in Texas, USA; population (1980) 61,902. It exports cotton, petroleum, wheat, and timber; and has chemical works and petroleum refineries. In 1900, 8,000 people died in one of the hurricanes which periodically hit the region.

Galway /'gɔːlweɪ/ county on the W coast of the Republic of Ireland, in the province of Connacht; area 5,940 sq km/2,293 sq mi; population (1986) 178,000. Towns include Galway (county town), Ballinasloe, Tuam, Clifden, and Loughrea (near which deposits of lead, zinc, and copper were found 1959).

The E is low-lying. In the S are the Slieve Aughty mountains and Galway Bay, with the Aran islands. W of Lough Corrib is Connemara, a wild area of moors, hills, lakes, and bogs. The Shannon is the principal river.

Galway /'gɔːlweɪ/ fishing port and county town of county Galway, Republic of Ireland; population (1986) 47,000. It produces textiles and chemicals. University College is part of the national university, and Galway Theatre stages Irish Gaelic plays.

Galway /'gɔːlweɪ/ James 1939– . Irish flautist, born in Belfast. He was a member of the Berlin Philharmonic Orchestra 1969–75, before taking up a solo career.

Gama /'gɑːmə/ Vasco da 1460–1524. Portuguese navigator who commanded an expedition in 1497 to discover the route to India around the Cape of Good Hope in modern South Africa. He reached land on Christmas Day 1497, which he named Natal. He then crossed the Indian Ocean, arriving at Calicut May 1498, and returning to Portugal Sept 1499.

Da Gama was born at Sines, and chosen by Portuguese King Emanuel I for his 1497 expedition. In 1502 he founded a Portuguese colony at Mozambique. In the same year he attacked and plundered Calicut in revenge for the murder of some Portuguese seamen. After 20 years of retirement, he was despatched to India again as Portuguese viceroy in 1524, but died two months after his arrival in Goa.

Gambia /'gæmbiə/ river in W Africa, which gives its name to The ◊Gambia; 1,000 km/620 mi long.

Gambia, The /'gæmbiə/ country in W Africa, surrounded to the N, E, and S by Senegal, and bordered to the W by the Atlantic Ocean.

government The Gambia is an independent republic within the ◊Commonwealth. Its constitution dates from 1970 and provides for a single-chamber legislature, the house of representatives, consisting of 49 members, 35 directly elected by universal suffrage, five elected by the chiefs, eight nonvoting, nominated members, and the attorney-general, ex-officio. It serves a five-year term, as does the president, who is elected by direct universal suffrage and appoints a vice-president, who also leads the house of representatives, and a cabinet. There are two main political parties, the Progressive People's Party (PPP) and the National Convention Party.

history The Gambia was formerly part of the ◊Mali empire, a Muslim gold-trading empire which flourished in W Africa in the 7th–15th centuries, and whose decline coincided with the arrival of the Portuguese 1455. In the late 16th century commerce was taken over from Portugal by England, and trading posts established on the Gambia River were controlled from Sierra Leone. In 1843 Gambia was made a Crown Colony, becoming an independent British colony 1888.

Political parties were formed in the 1950s, internal self-government granted 1963, and full independence within the Commonwealth achieved 1965, with Dawda K Jawara as prime minister. It declared itself a republic 1970, with Jawara as president, replacing the British monarch as head of state. He was re-elected 1972 and 1977.

With the PPP the dominant political force, there was pressure to make the Gambia a one-party state but Jawara resisted this. When an attempted coup against him 1981 was thwarted with Senegalese military aid, ties between the two countries were strengthened to the extent that plans were announced for their merger into a confederation of Senegambia. However, Senegal had doubts about the idea, and in economic terms The Gambia had more to gain. In Sept 1989 it was announced that The Gambia had formally agreed to end the confederation. In 1982 Jawara was re-elected for another five-year term, with over 60% of the popular vote and over 70% of the seats; he was again re-elected in 1987.

Gambia
Republic of The

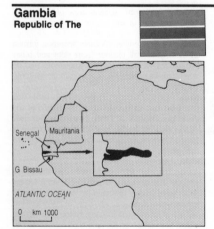

Senegal
Mauritania
G. Bissau
ATLANTIC OCEAN
0   km 1000

area 10,689 sq km/4,126 sq mi
capital Banjul
physical banks of the river Gambia
features the smallest state in black Africa
head of state and government Dawda Kairaba Jawara from 1970
political system liberal democracy

political parties Progressive People's Party (PPP), moderate centrist; National Convention Party (NCP), left-of-centre
exports groundnuts, palm oil, fish
currency dalasi (14.17 = £1 Feb 1990)
population 788,200 (1988); annual growth rate 1.9%
life expectancy men 34, women 37
language English (official)
religion Muslim 70%, with animist and Christian minorities
literacy 36% male/15% female (1985 est)
GNP $200 million (1983); $330 per head of population
chronology
1965 Achieved independence as a constitutional monarchy within the Commonwealth, with Dawda K Jawara as prime minister.
1970 Declared itself a republic, with Jawara as president.
1972 Jawara re-elected.
1981 Attempted coup foiled with the help of Senegal.
1982 Formed with Senegal the Confederation of Senegambia. Jawara re-elected.
1987 Jawara re-elected.
1989 Confederation of Senegambia dissolved.

Gandhi *Indira Gandhi, Nehru's daughter, had a controversial political career, during which she was twice prime minister of India.*

Gandhi *Mahatma ('Great Soul') Gandhi with his granddaughters.*

Gandhi *Former Indian prime minister Rajiv Gandhi in New Delhi, 1984.*

Gambier Islands /'gæmbiə/ island group, part of ◊French Polynesia, administered with the ◊Tuamotu Archipelago; area 36 sq km/14 sq mi; population (1983) 582. It includes four coral islands and many small islets. The main island is Mangareva, with its town Rikitea.

game farming protected rearing of gamebirds such as pheasants, partridges, and grouse for subsequent shooting. Game farms provide plenty of woodland and brush, which the birds require for cover, and may also plant special crops for them to feed on.

Gamelin /'gæmǝlæn/ Maurice Gustave 1872–1958. French commander in chief of the Allied armies in France 1939. Replaced by Weygand after the German breakthrough at Sedan 1940, he was tried by the ◊Vichy government as a scapegoat before the Riom 'war guilt' court 1942. He refused to defend himself and was detained in Germany until released by the Allies 1945.

gamete a cell that functions in sexual reproduction by merging with another gamete to form a ◊zygote. Examples of gametes include sperm and ova cells. In most organisms, the gametes are ◊haploid (they contain half the number of chromosomes of the parent), owing to reduction division or ◊meiosis.

In higher organisms, gametes are of two distinct types: large immobile ones known as eggs or egg-cells (see ◊ovum) and small ones known as ◊sperm. They come together at ◊fertilization. In some lower organisms the gametes are all the same, or they may belong to different mating strains but have no obvious differences in size or appearance.

game theory branch of mathematics that deals with strategic problems (such as those that arise in business, commerce, and warfare) by assuming that the people involved invariably try to win — that is, they are assumed to employ strategies that should give the greatest gain and the smallest loss. The theory was developed by Oscar Morgenstern (1902–1977) and John von ◊Neumann during World War II.

gametophyte the haploid generation in the life cycle of a plant that produces gametes; see ◊alternation of generations.

gamma radiation very high-frequency ◊electromagnetic radiation emitted by the nuclei of radioactive substances during decay. It is used to kill bacteria and other microorganisms, sterilize medical devices, and change the molecular structure of plastics to modify their properties (for example, to improve heat and abrasion resistance for insulation purposes).

Gamma rays are similar in nature to X-rays, but of shorter wavelength. Most cosmic gamma-rays cannot pass through the Earth's atmosphere; telescopes to detect them must be placed above it. Only a few of the many sources have been identified, including pulsars, radio galaxies, and quasars.

gamma-ray astronomy the study of gamma-rays produced within our galaxy, the Milky Way. They may be due to collisions between hydrogen gas and cosmic rays. Some sources have been identified, including the Crab Nebula and the Vela pulsar (the most powerful gamma-ray source detected). Gamma rays are not plentiful and only about a million gamma-ray photons have been collected. This is equivalent to the number of photons of visible light received from a star such as Sirius in about a second.

Gamma rays are difficult to detect and are generally studied by use of balloon-borne detectors and artificial satellites. The first gamma-ray satellites were SAS II (1972) and COS B (1975), although gamma-ray detectors were carried on the Apollo 15 and 16 missions. SAS II failed after only a few months, but COS B, carrying a single gamma-ray experiment, and intended to be operational for only two years, was finally switched off 1982 after a mission in which it carried out a complete survey of the galactic disc.

Gamow /'geimau/ George 1904–1968. Soviet cosmologist, nuclear physicist, and popularizer of science. His work in astrophysics included a study of the structure and evolution of stars and the creation of the elements. He also explained how the collision of nuclei in the solar interior could produce the nuclear reactions that power the Sun.

Gamow was also an early supporter of the ◊Big Bang theory of the universe and predicted that the electromagnetic radiation left over should, after having cooled down during the subsequent expansion of the universe, manifest itself as a microwave background radiation with a temperature of 10K. In 1965 Arno Allan Penzias (1933–) and Robert Woodrow Wilson (1933–) discovered the microwave background, which had a temperature of 3K, or 3° above ◊absolute zero.

Gance /gɒns/ Abel 1889–1981. French film director, whose *Napoléon* 1927 was one of the most ambitious silent epic films, including colour and triple-screen sequences, as well as multiple exposure shots.

Gandhi /'gændi/ Indira 1917–1984. Indian politician. Prime minister of India 1966–77 and 1980–84, and leader of the ◊Congress Party 1966–77 and subsequently of the Congress (I) Party. She was assassinated by members of her Sikh bodyguard, resentful of her use of troops to clear malcontents from the Sikh temple at ◊Amritsar.

Her father was India's first prime minister Jawaharlal Nehru. She married 1942 Feroze Gandhi (died 1960, not related to Mahatma Gandhi) and had two sons, Sanjay Gandhi (1946–80), who died in an air crash, and Rajiv ◊Gandhi. In 1975 the validity of her re-election to parliament was questioned and she declared a state of emergency. During this time her son Sanjay was implementing a social and economic programme (including an unpopular

family-planning policy) which led to her defeat in 1977, though he masterminded her return to power in 1980.

Gandhi /'gændi/ Mohandas Karamchand, called *Mahatma* ('Great Soul') 1869–1948. Indian nationalist leader. A pacifist, he led the struggle for Indian independence from the UK by nonviolent noncooperation (*satyagraha*, defence of and by truth) from 1915. He was several times imprisoned by the British authorities, and was influential in the nationalist ◊Congress Party and in the independence negotiations 1947. He was assassinated by a Hindu nationalist in the violence that followed the partition of India and Pakistan.

Gandhi was born in Porbandar and studied in London where he practised as a barrister. He settled in South Africa where until 1914 he led the Indian community in opposition to racial discrimination. Back in India he emerged as leader of the Indian National Congress and organized hunger strikes and civil disobedience and campaigned for social reform, including religious tolerance and an end to discrimination against the so-called untouchable ◊caste.

Gandhi /'gændi/ Rajiv 1944– . Indian politician, prime minister from 1984, following his mother Indira Gandhi's assassination, to Nov 1989. As prime minister he faced growing discontent with his party's elitism and lack of concern for social issues.

Rajiv Gandhi initially displayed little interest in politics and became an airline pilot. But after the death in a plane crash of his brother Sanjay (1946–80), he was elected to his brother's Amethi parliamentary seat 1981. In the Dec 1984 parliamentary elections he won a record majority. In 1985 he reached a temporary settlement with the moderate Sikhs which failed, however, to hold. His reputation was tarnished by a scandal concerning alleged 'kick-backs' derived by senior officials from an arms deal with the Swedish munitions firm Bofors and, following his party's defeat in the general election of Nov 1989, Gandhi was forced to resign as premier.

Ganesh /gæˈneɪsə/ Hindu god, son of Siva and Parvati; he is represented as elephant-headed and worshipped as a remover of obstacles.

Ganges /'gændʒiːz/ (Hindi *Ganga*) major river of India and Bangladesh; length 2,510 km/1,560 mi. It is the most sacred river for Hindus.

Its chief tributary is the *Yamuna* (Jumna); length 1,385 km/860 mi, which joins the Ganges near Allahabad, where there is a sacred bathing place. The Ganges is joined in its delta in Bangladesh by the ◊Brahmaputra, and its most commercially important and westernmost channel to the Bay of Bengal is the *Hooghly*. The political leaders M K Gandhi, Nehru, and Indira Gandhi were all cremated on the banks of the Yamuna at Delhi.

ganglion (plural *ganglia*) small, solid mass of nervous tissue containing many cell bodies and ◊synapses, usually enclosed in a tissue sheath; found in invertebrates and vertebrates.

Garbo *The Swedish-born actress Greta Garbo in* Anna Christie *1930, her first 'talkie'.*

In many invertebrates, the central nervous sytem consists mainly of ganglia connected by nerve cords. The ganglia in the head (cerebral ganglia) are usually well developed and are analagous to the brain in vertebrates. In vertebrates, most ganglia occur outside the central nervous system.

Gang of Four the chief members of the radical faction that tried to seize power in China after the death of Mao Zedong 1976. It included his widow, ◊Jiang Qing; the other members were Zhang Chunjao, Wang Hungwen, and Yao Wenyuan. The coup failed, and they were soon arrested.

In the UK the name was subsequently applied to four members of the Labour Party who in 1981 resigned to form the Social Democratic Party (SDP): Roy Jenkins, David Owen, Shirley Williams, and William Rodgers.

gangrene death and decay of body tissue due to bacterial action; the affected part gradually turns black.

Gangrene sets in as a result of loss of blood supply to the area. This may be due to an obstruction of a major blood vessel (as in ◊thrombosis), to injury, or to frostbite. Bacteria are able to colonize the site unopposed, and there is a notorious risk of gangrene spreading. This is why gangrenous tissue has to be removed surgically.

gangue the part of an ore deposit which is itself economically valuable; for example, calcite might occur as a gangue mineral with galena.

gannet or **solan goose** a sea-bird *Sula bassana* in the family Sulidae, found in the N Atlantic. When fully grown, it is white with black-tipped wings having a span of 1.7 m/5.6 ft. The young are speckled. It breeds on cliffs in nests made of grass and seaweed. Only one (white) egg is laid.

Gannet Peak /'gænɪt/ the highest peak in Wyoming state, USA, rising to 4,207 m/13,804 ft.

Gansu /ˌgænˈsuː/ formerly **Kansu** province of NW China
area 530,000 sq km/204,580 sq mi
capital Lanzhou
features subject to earthquakes; the 'Silk Road' (now a motor road) passed through it in the Middle Ages, carrying trade to central Asia
products coal, oil, hydroelectric power from the Huang He (Yellow) River
population (1986) 20,710,000, including many Muslims.

Ganymede /'gænɪmiːd/ in Greek mythology, a youth so beautiful he was chosen as cupbearer to Zeus.

Ganymede /'gænɪmiːd/ in astronomy, the largest moon of the planet Jupiter, and the largest moon in the solar system, 5,300 km/3,300 mi in diameter (larger than the planet Mercury). It orbits Jupiter every 7.2 days at a distance of 1.1 million km/700,000 mi. Its surface is a mixture of cratered and grooved terrain.

Gaoxiong /'gaʃiˈɒŋ/ mainland Chinese form of ◊Kaohsiung, a port in W Taiwan.

García Márquez *Colombian writer Gabriel García Márquez, whose novels have become widely known since he was awarded the Nobel Prize for Literature in 1982.*

Garbo /'gɑːbəʊ/ Greta. Stage name of Greta Lovisa Gustafsson 1905–1990. Swedish film actress. She went to the USA in 1925, and her leading role in *The Torrent* 1926 made her one of Hollywood's first stars. Her later films include *Queen Christina* 1933, *Anna Karenina* 1935, and *Ninotchka* 1939.

Garching /'gɑːkɪŋ/ town N of ◊Munich, West Germany, site of a nuclear research centre.

García Lorca /gɑːˈθiːəˈlɔːkə/ Federico See ◊Lorca, Federico García.

García Márquez /gɑːˈsiːəˈmɑːkes/ Gabriel 1928– . Colombian novelist, whose *Cien aŋ de soledad/One Hundred Years of Solitude* 1967, the story of six generations of a family, is an example of magic realism, a technique for heightening the intensity of realistic portrayal of social and political issues by introducing grotesque or fanciful material. Other books include *El amor en los tiempos del cólera/Love in the Time of Cholera* 1985. Nobel Prize for Literature 1982.

Garcia Perez /gɑːˈsiːə ˈperes/ Alan 1949– . Peruvian politician, president from 1985.

Born in Lima and educated in Peru, Guatemala, Spain and France, he joined the moderate, left-wing APRA party and in 1982 became its secretary-general. In 1985 he succeeded Fernando Belakunde as president, becoming the first civilian to do so in democratic elections. He inherited an ailing economy and has been forced to trim his socialist programme.

Garcilaso de la Vega /ˌgɑːθɪˈlɑːsəʊ/ 1539–1616. Spanish writer, called *el Inca*. Son of a Spanish conquistador and an Inca princess, he wrote an account of the conquest of Florida and *Commentarios* on the history of Peru.

Garcilaso de la Vega /ˌgɑːθɪˈlɑːsəʊ/ 1503–1536. Spanish poet. A soldier, he was a member of Charles V's expedition in 1535 to Tunis; he was killed in battle at Nice. His verse, some of the greatest of the Spanish Renaissance, includes sonnets, songs, and elegies, often on the model of Petrarch.

Gard /gɑː/ French river, 133 km/83 mi long, a tributary of the Rhône, which it joins above Beaucaire. It gives its name to Gard *département* in Languedoc-Roussillon region.

Garda, Lake /'gɑːdə/ largest lake in Italy; situated on the border between the regions of Lombardia and Veneto; area 370 sq km/143 sq mi.

garden city in the UK, a town built in a rural area and designed to combine town and country

Garfield *James Garfield, 20th president of the USA 1881.*

advantages, with its own industries, controlled developments, private and public gardens, and cultural centre. The idea was proposed by Sir Ebenezer Howard (1850–1928), who in 1899 founded the Garden City Association, which established the first garden city, Letchworth (in Hertfordshire).

A second, Welwyn, 35 km/22 mi from London, was started in 1919. Similar schemes in Europe and in the USA have not generally kept the economic structure or the industrial self-sufficiency of the rural belt which formed an integral part of Howard's original idea. The New Towns Act, 1946, provided the machinery for developing ◊new towns on some of the principles advocated by Howard (for example Stevenage, begun in 1947).

gardenia group of subtropical and tropical trees and shrubs of Africa and Asia, genus *Gardenia*, family Rubiaceae, with evergreen foliage and flattened rosettes of fragrant waxen-looking blooms, often white in colour.

garderobe a medieval lavatory. Garderobes were often built into the thickness of a castle wall, with an open drop to the moat below.

Gardiner Gerald Austin 1900–1990. British lawyer. As Lord Chancellor in the 1964–70 Labour governments, Gardiner introduced the office of ◊Ombudsman to Britain, and played a major role in the movement for abolition of capital punishment for murder (which became law in 1965).

Gardiner /'gɑːdnə/ Stephen c.1493–1555. English priest and politician. After being secretary to Cardinal Wolsey, he became bishop of Winchester in 1531. An opponent of Protestantism, he was imprisoned under Edward VI, and as Lord Chancellor 1553–55 under Queen Mary he tried to restore Roman Catholicism.

Gardner /'gɑːdnə/ Ava 1922–1990. US actress, who starred in the 1940s and 1950s in such films as *The Killers* 1946, *Pandora and the Flying Dutchman* 1951 and *The Barefoot Contessa* 1954. She remained active in films until the 1980s.

Gardner /'gɑːdnə/ Erle Stanley 1889–1970. US author of crime fiction. He created the character of the lawyer-detective Perry Mason, who later featured in film and television versions.

Gardner /'gɑːdnə/ John 1917– . English composer. Professor at the Royal Academy of Music from 1956, he has produced a symphony 1951; the opera *The Moon and Sixpence* 1957, based on the Somerset Maugham novel; and other works, including film music.

Garfield /'gɑːfiːld/ James A(bram) 1831–1881. 20th president of the USA 1881, a Republican. He was born in a log cabin in Ohio, and served in the American Civil War on the side of the Union. He was elected president but held office for only four months before being assassinated in a Washington station by a disappointed office-seeker.

garfish type of fish with a long spear-like snout. The *common garfish Belone belone*, order Beloniformes, family Belonidae, has an elongated body 75 cm/2.5 ft long.

gargoyle spout projecting from the roof-gutter of a building with the purpose of directing water away from the wall. The term is usually applied to the ornamental forms found in Gothic architecture; these were carved in stone in the form of fantastic animals, angels, or human heads. They are often found on churches and cathedrals.

Garibaldi /ˌgærɪˈbɔːldi/ Giuseppe 1807–1882. Italian soldier who played an important role in the unification of Italy by conquering Sicily and Naples 1860. From 1834 a member of the nationalist Mazzini's ◊Young Italy society, he was forced into exile until 1848 and again 1849–54. He fought against Austria 1848–49, 1859, and 1866, and led two unsuccessful expeditions to liberate Rome from papal rule in 1862 and 1867.

Born in Nice, he became a sailor, and then involved in the nationalist movement (◊***Risorgimento***). Condemned to death for treason, he escaped to South America where he became a mercenary. He returned to Italy during the 1848

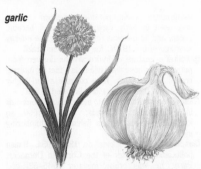
garlic

revolution, served with the Sardinian army against the Austrians, and commanded the army of the Roman republic in its defence of the city against the French. He subsequently lived in exile until 1854, when he settled on the island of Caprera. In 1860, at the head of his 1,000 **redshirts**, he won Sicily and Naples for the new kingdom of Italy. He served in the Austrian War of 1866, and fought for France in the Franco-Prussian War 1870–71.

Garland /ˈgɑːlənd/ Judy. Stage name of Frances Gumm 1922–1969. US singer and actress, whose films include *The Wizard of Oz* 1939 (including the

Garvey *Jamaican-born Marcus Garvey, at a New York parade in 1922. He was the founder of the 'Back to Africa' movement.*

song 'Over the Rainbow'), *Meet Me in St Louis* 1944, and *A Star is Born* 1954. Her unhappy personal life led to her early death from alcohol and drug addiction.

garlic perennial plant *Allium sativum*, family Liliaceae, with white flowers. The bulb, made of small segments, or cloves, is used in cookery, and its pungent essence has an active medical ingredient, allyl methyl trisulphide, which prevents blood clotting.

garnet a group of silicate minerals with the formula $X_3Y_2(SiO_4)_3$, when X is calcium, magnesium, iron, or manganese, and Y is iron, aluminium, or chromium. They are used as semiprecious gems (usually pink to deep red) and as abrasives. Garnets occur in metamorphic rocks such as gneiss and schist.

Garonne /gæˈrɒn/ river in SW France, rising on the Spanish side of the Pyrenees and flowing to the ◊Gironde estuary; length 580 km/350 mi.

Garret /gəˈret/ Almeida 1799–1854. Portuguese poet, novelist, and dramatist. As a liberal, in 1823 he was forced into 14 years of exile. His works, which he saw as a singlehanded attempt to create a national literature, include the prose *Viagens na Minha Terra/Travels in my Homeland* 1843–46, and the tragedy *Frei Luis de Sousa* 1843.

Garrick /ˈgærɪk/ David 1717–1779. British actor and theatre manager. He was a pupil of Samuel ◊Johnson. From 1747 he became joint licensee of the Drury Lane theatre with his own company, and instituted a number of significant theatrical conventions including concealed stage lighting and banishing spectators from the stage. He performed Shakespeare characters such as Richard III, King Lear, Hamlet, and Benedick, and collaborated with Colman in writing the play *The Clandestine Marriage* 1766. He retired from the stage 1766, but continued as a manager.

Garrod /ˈgærəd/ Archibald Edward 1857–1937. English physician who first recognized a class of metabolic diseases, while studying the rare disease alcaptonuria, in which the patient's urine turns black on contact with air. He calculated that the cause was a failure of the ◊metabolism to break down certain amino acids into harmless substances like water and carbon dioxide.

Garter, Order of the senior British order of knighthood, founded by Edward III in about 1347. Its distinctive badge is a garter of dark blue velvet, with the motto of the order, *Honi soit qui mal y pense* ('Shame be to him who thinks evil of it'), in gold letters, worn below the left knee. Its sash is also dark blue. Membership is limited to 25 knights, and to members of the royal family and foreign royalties; appointments are made by the sovereign alone. St George's Chapel, Windsor, is the chapel of the order. The Blue Riband is derived from the order's garter.

Garvey /ˈgɑːvi/ Marcus (Moziah) 1887–1940. Jamaican political thinker and activist, an early

Garibaldi *Italian hero of the Risorgimento, Giuseppe Garibaldi.*

advocate of black nationalism. He founded the UNIA (Universal Negro Improvement Association) in 1914, and moved to the USA in 1916, where he established branches in New York and other northern cities. Aiming to achieve human rights and dignity for black people through black pride and economic self-sufficiency, he led a **Back to Africa** movement for black Americans to establish a black-governed country in Africa. ◊Rastafarianism is based largely on his ideas.

Gary /'gærɪ/ city in NW Indiana, USA; population (1980) 151,953. It contains the steel and cement works of the United States Steel Corporation, and was named after its chair, E H Gary (1846–1927).

gas in physics, a form of matter, such as air, in which the molecules move randomly in otherwise empty space, filling any size or shape of container into which the gas is put.

A sugar-lump-sized cube of air at room temperature contains 30 million million million molecules moving at an average speed of 500 metres per second (1,800 kph/1,200 mph). Gases can be liquefied by cooling, which lowers the speed of the molecules and enables attractive forces between them to bind them together.

gas constant in physics, the constant *R* that appears in the equation $PV = nRT$, which describes how the pressure *P*, volume *V* and temperature *T* of an ideal gas are related (*n* is the amount of gas in the specimen). This equation combines ◊Boyle's law and ◊Charles' law, the best-known gas laws.

R has a value of 8.314 34 joules per kelvin per mole.

Gascony /'gæskənɪ/ ancient province of SW France. With Guienne it formed the duchy of Aquitaine in the 12th century; Henry II of England gained possession of it through his marriage to Eleanor of Aquitaine in 1152, and it was often in English hands until 1451. It was ruled by the king of France until it was united with the French royal domain in 1607 under Henry IV. The area is now divided into several *départements*, including Landes and Pyrénées-Atlantiques.

gas-cooled reactor see ◊advanced gas-cooled reactor.

gas engine type of internal combustion engine in which gas (coal gas, producer gas, natural gas, or gas from a blast furnace) is used as the fuel. The first practical gas engine was built 1860 by Jean Etienne Lenoir, and the type was subsequently developed by Nikolaus August Otto, who introduced the ◊four-stroke cycle.

gas exchange in biology, the exchange of gases between living organisms and the atmosphere; a process known in humans as ◊respiration.

In humans, and other tetrapods, gas exchange or respiration is the absorption of oxygen into the blood when air meets blood vessels in the ◊lungs, and the exhalation of carbon dioxide with water and small quantities of ammonia and waste matter. Many adult amphibia and terrestrial invertebrates can absorb oxygen directly through the skin. The bodies of insects and some spiders contain a system of air-filled tubes known as ◊tracheae. Fish and most other aquatic organisms have ◊gills as their main respiratory organ. In plants, gas exchange generally takes place via the ◊stomata.

Gaskell /'gæskəl/ 'Mrs' (Elizabeth Cleghorn) (born Stevenson) 1810–1865. British novelist. Her books include *Mary Barton* (set in industrial Manchester) 1848, *Cranford* (set in the town in which she was brought up, Knutsford, Cheshire) 1853, *North and South* 1855, *Sylvia's Lovers* 1863–64, the unfinished *Wives and Daughters* 1866, and a life of her friend Charlotte ◊Brontë.

gas laws physical laws concerning the behaviour of gases. They include ◊Boyle's law and ◊Charles' law, which are concerned with the relationships between the pressure, temperature, and volume of an ideal (hypothetical) gas.

gasohol a type of motor fuel that is 90% petrol and 10% ethanol (alcohol). The ethanol is usually obtained by fermentation, followed by distillation,

using maize, wheat, potatoes, or sugar cane. It was used in early cars before petrol became cheap, and its use was revived during the energy shortage of the 1970s, for example in Brazil.

gasoline a mixture of hydrocarbons derived from petroleum, whose main use is as a fuel for internal combustion engines. It is colourless and highly volatile. In the UK, gasoline is called petrol.

Gaspé Peninsula /gæ'speɪ/ mountainous peninsula in SE Québec, Canada; area 29,500 sq km/11,390 sq mi. It has fishing and lumbering industries.

Gasperi /'gæspərɪ/ Alcide de 1881–1954. Italian politician. A founder of the Christian Democrat Party, he was prime minister 1945–53, and worked for European unification.

Gassendi /ˌgæsɒn'diː/ Pierre 1592–1655. French physicist and philosopher who played a crucial role in the revival of atomism, and the rejection of Aristotelianism so characteristic of the period. He was a propagandist and critic of other views rather than an original thinker.

gastritis inflammation of the lining of the stomach. The term is a vague one applied to a range of conditions.

gastroenteritis inflammation of the stomach and intestines, giving rise to abdominal pain, vomiting, and diarrhoea. It may be caused by food or other poisoning, allergy, or infection.

gastro-enterology the medical speciality concerned with diseases of the ◊alimentary canal.

gastropod member of a very large class (Gastropoda) of ◊molluscs. Gastropods are single-shelled (in a spiral or modified spiral form), have eyes on stalks, and move on a flattened, muscular foot. They have well-developed heads and rough tongues. Some are marine, some freshwater, and others land creatures, but all tend to inhabit damp places. They include snails, slugs, limpets, and periwinkles.

gas turbine an engine in which burning fuel supplies hot gas to spin a ◊turbine. The most widespread application of gas turbines has been in aviation. All ◊jet engines are modified gas turbines, and some locomotives and ships also use gas turbines as a power source. They are used in industry for generating and pumping duties.

In a typical gas turbine a multi-vaned compressor draws in and compresses air. The compressed air enters a combustion chamber at high pressure, and fuel is sprayed in and ignited. The hot gases produced escape through the blades of (typically) two turbines and spin them round. One of the turbines drives the compressor, the other provides the external power which can be harnessed.

gas warfare military use of gas to produce a toxic effect on the human body. See ◊chemical warfare.

Gateshead /'geɪtshed/ port in Tyne and Wear, England; population (1981) 81,000. Industries include engineering, chemicals, and glass.

Gatling /'gætlɪŋ/ Richard Jordan 1818–1903. US inventor of a rapid-fire gun. Patented in 1862, the Gatling gun had ten barrels arranged as a cylinder rotated by a hand crank. Cartridges from an overhead hopper or drum dropped into the breech mechanism, which loaded, fired and extracted them at a rate of 320 rounds per minute.

The Gatling gun was used in the Franco-Prussian War of 1870. By 1882 rates of fire of up to 1,200 rounds per minute were achieved, but the weapon was soon superseded by Hiram Maxim's ◊machine gun in 1889.

GATT abbreviation for ◊*General Agreement on Tariffs and Trade*.

Gatwick /'gætwɪk/ site of Gatwick Airport, West Sussex, England, constructed 1956–58.

gaucho /'gautʃəu/ part Indian, part Spanish cattle herder, formerly working on the Argentine and Uruguayan pampas.

Gaudí /gau'diː/ Antonio 1852–1926. Spanish architect. His spectacular Church of the Holy

Gaudí *Spanish architect Antonio Gaudí worked exclusively in Barcelona. This is Casa Mila.*

Family, Barcelona, begun 1883, is still under construction.

Gaudier-Brzeska /'gəudieɪ 'bʒeskə/ Henri 1891–1915. French sculptor, active in London from 1911. He studied art in Bristol, Nuremberg, and Munich, and became a member of the English Vorticist movement. From 1913 his sculptures showed the influence of Brancusi and Epstein. He died in World War I.

gauge scientific measuring instrument, for example a wire-gauge or pressure-gauge. The term is also applied to the width of a railway or tramway track.

Gauguin /'gəugæn/ Paul 1848–1903. French Post-Impressionist painter. After a few years as a stockbroker, he took up full-time painting, exhibited with the Impressionists, and spent two months with van ◊Gogh in Arles 1888. On his return to Brittany he concentrated on his new style, *Synthetism*, based on the use of

Gaudier-Brzeska *A 1912 self-portrait of the French sculptor Henri Gaudier-Brzeska. He was a member of the Vorticist movement, led by Wyndham Lewis, which aimed to reflect the modern industrial world in art.*

Gauguin Te Rerioa 'The Dream' *(1897) Courtauld Collection, London.*

gazelle

powerful, expressive colours and boldly outlined areas of flat tone. He went to live in Tahiti 1891–93 and 1895–1901 and from 1901 in the Marquesas Islands. Influenced by Symbolism, he chose subjects reflecting his interest in the beliefs of other cultures.

Born in Paris, Gauguin joined a banking firm, but gave up his career 1881 in order to paint. After a visit to Martinique 1887, he went to Pont Aven in Brittany, becoming the leading artist in the Synthetic movement, and abandoning conventional perspective. In 1891 he left Paris for Tahiti, where he remained from 1895 until his death. Going beyond the Impressionists' notion of reality, he sought a more direct experience of life in the magical rites of the people and rich colours of the islands. A friend of van Gogh, he disliked theories and rules of painting, and his pictures are ◊Expressionist compositions characterized by his use of pure, unmixed colours. Among his most famous paintings is *Le Christe Jaune* 1889 (Albright-Knox Art Gallery, Buffalo, USA).

Gaul /gɔːl/ a member of the Celtic-speaking peoples who inhabited France and Belgium in Roman times.

Gauls were divided into several groups but were united by a common religion controlled by the Druid priesthood. Certain Gauls invaded Italy around 400 BC, sacked Rome, and settled between the Alps and the Apennines; this district, known as Cisalpine Gaul, was conquered by Rome in about 225 BC. The Romans conquered S Gaul between the Mediterranean and the Cevennes in about 125 BC and the remaining Gauls up to the Rhine were conquered by Julius ◊Caesar 58–51 BC.

Gaulle Charles de. See Charles ◊de Gaulle.

gaur Asiatic wild ox *Bos gaurus* which is dark grey-brown with white 'socks', and 2 m/6 ft tall at the shoulders. Its original range was from India to SE Asia and Malaysia, but its numbers and range are now diminished.

gauss c.g.s. unit (symbol Gs) of magnetic flux density, replaced by the SI unit, the ◊tesla, but still commonly used. The Earth's magnetic field is about 1/2 gauss, and changes to it over time are measured in gammas (1 gamma = 10.5 gauss).

Gauss /gaʊs/ Karl Friedrich 1777–1855. German mathematician who worked on the theory of numbers, non-Euclidian geometry, and on the mathematical development of electric and magnetic theory. In World War II, the method of countering magnetic mines was called 'degaussing'.

Gautama family name of the historical ◊Buddha.

Gautier /ˈgəʊtieɪ/ Théophile 1811–1872. French Romantic poet, whose later work emphasized the perfection of form and the 'polished' beauty of language and imagery (for example, *Emaux et Camées/Enamels and Cameos* 1852). He was also a novelist (*Mlle de Maupin* 1835) and later in his life turned to journalism.

Gavaskar /ˈgævəska:/ Sunil Manohar 1949– . Indian cricketer. Between 1971 and 1987 he scored a record 10,122 test runs in a record 125 matches (including 106 consecutive tests).

CAREER HIGHLIGHTS

all first-class matches
runs: 25,834
average: 51.46
best: 340 (Bombay v. Bengal, 1981–82)
test cricket
runs: 10,122
average: 51.12
best: 236 not out (India v. West Indies, 1983–84)

Gawain in Arthurian legend, one of the knights of the Round Table who participated in the quest for the ◊Holy Grail. He is the hero of the 14th-century epic poem *Sir Gawayne and the Greene Knight*.

Gay /geɪ/ John 1685–1732. British poet and dramatist. He was the friend of ◊Pope and Arbuthnot, and wrote *Trivia* 1716, a verse picture of 18th-century London. His *The Beggar's Opera* 1728, a 'Newgate pastoral' using traditional songs and telling of the love of Polly for highwayman Captain Macheath, was an extraordinarily popular success. Its satiric political touches led to the banning of *Polly*, a sequel.

Gaya /ˈgaɪə/ ancient city in Bihar state, NE India; population (1986) 200,000. It is a centre of pilgrimage for Buddhists and Hindus with many temples and shrines. A bo tree at ◊Buddh Gaya is said to be a direct descendant of the original tree under which Buddha sat.

Gaye /geɪ/ Marvin 1939–1984. US soul singer and songwriter, whose hits, including 'Stubborn Kinda Fellow' 1962, 'I Heard It Through the Grapevine' 1968, and 'What's Going On' 1971, exemplified the Detroit ◊Motown sound. He was killed by his father.

Gay-Lussac /ˈgeɪ lu:ˈsæk/ Joseph Louis 1778–1850. French physicist and chemist, who investigated the physical properties of gases, and discovered new methods of producing sulphuric and oxalic acids. In 1802 he discovered the law now known as ◊Charles's Law.

Gaza /ˈga:zə/ capital of the ◊Gaza Strip, once a ◊Philistine city, and scene of three World War I battles; population (1979) 120,000.

Gazankulu /ˌga:zəŋˈku:lu:/ ◊Black National State in Transvaal province, South Africa, with self-governing status from 1971; population (1985) 497,200.

Gaza Strip /ˈga:zə/ strip of Palestine under Israeli administration; capital Gaza; area 363 sq km/140 sq mi; population (1988) 564,000. Clashes between the Israeli authorities and the Palestinian people escalated to ◊intifada (uprising) 1988.

It was invaded by Israel 1956, reoccupied 1967, and retained 1973. See ◊Arab-Israeli Wars.

gazelle name given to various species of lightly built fast-running antelopes found on the open plains of Africa and S Asia, especially those of the genus *Gazella*.

Gaziantep /ˌgæziænˈtep/ Turkish city 185 km/115 mi NE of Adana; population (1985) 466,000. It has textile and tanning industries. Until 1922 it was known as Antep or Aintab.

GCC abbreviation for *Gulf Cooperation Council*.

GCE (*General Certificate of Education*) in the UK, the public examination formerly taken at the age of 16 at Ordinary Level (O Level) and at 18 at Advanced Level (A Level). The GCE O Level examination, aimed at the top 20% of the ability range, was superseded in 1988 by the General Certificate of Secondary Education (◊GCSE).

GCHQ (*Government Communications Headquarters*) the centre of the British government's electronic surveillance operations, in Cheltenham, Gloucestershire. It monitors broadcasts of various kinds from all over the world. It was established in World War I, and was successful in breaking the German Enigma code in 1940.

In addition there are six listening stations: at Bude, Cornwall; Culm Head, Somerset; Brora and Hawklaw, Scotland; Irton Moor, N Yorkshire; and Cheadle, Greater Manchester. There is an outpost in Cyprus. In 1982 Geoffrey Prime (1939–), a linguist at GCHQ, was convicted of handing the secrets of US spy satellites to the USSR.

GCSE (*General Certificate of Secondary Education*) in the UK, from 1988, the new examination for 16-year old pupils, superseding both GCE O Level and CSE, and offering qualifications for up to 60% of school leavers in any particular subject.

The GCSE includes more practical and coursework than O Level. GCSE subjects are organized as part of the ◊National Curriculum.

Gdańsk /gdænsk/ (German *Danzig*) Polish port; population (1985) 467,000. Oil is refined, and textiles, televisions, and fertilizers are produced. In the 1980s there were repeated strikes at the Lenin shipyards against the government.

Formerly a member of the ◊Hanseatic League, it was in almost continuous Prussian possession 1793–1919, when it again became a free city under the protection of the League of Nations.

gecko

Tokay gecko

Annexed by Germany 1939, it reverted to Poland 1945, when the churches and old merchant houses were restored.

GDP abbreviation for ◊*Gross Domestic Product*.

GDR abbreviation for *German Democratic Republic* (East ◊Germany).

Gdynia /ˈgdɪnjə/ port in N Poland; population (1985) 243,000. It was established in 1920 to give newly constituted Poland a sea outlet to replace lost ◊Gdańsk. It has a naval base and shipyards and is now part of the 'Tri-city' which includes Sopot and Gdańsk.

Ge /dʒiː/ in Greek mythology, an alternative name for ◊Gaia, goddess of the Earth.

gear a toothed wheel that transmits the turning movement of one shaft to another shaft. Gear wheels may be used in pairs, or in threes if both shafts are to turn in the same direction. The gear ratio, the ratio of the number of teeth on the two wheels, determines the torque ratio, the turning force on the output shaft compared with the turning shaft on the input shaft. The ratio of the angular velocities of the shafts is the inverse of the gear ratio.

The common type of gear for parallel shafts is the *spur gear*, with straight teeth parallel to the shaft axis. The *helical gear* has teeth cut along sections of a helix or corkscrew shape; the double form of the helix gear is the most efficient for energy transfer. *Bevil gears*, with tapering teeth set on the base of a cone, are used to connect intersecting shafts.

Geber /ˈdʒiːbə/ Latinized form of Jabir ibn Hayyan *c.*721–*c.*776. Arabian alchemist. His influence lasted for more than 600 years, and in the late 1300s his name was adopted by a Spanish alchemist whose writings spread the knowledge and practice of alchemy throughout Europe.

The Spanish alchemist Geber probably discovered nitric and sulphuric acids, and he propounded a theory that all metals are composed of various mixtures of mercury and sulphur.

gecko small soft-skinned lizard of the family Gekkonidae. It is common in warm climates, and has a large head and short, stout body. Its adhesive toe pads enables it to climb vertically and walk upside down on smooth surfaces in its search for flies, spiders, and other prey. The name is derived from the clicking sound which the animal makes.

Geddes /ˈgedɪs/ Patrick 1854–1932. Scottish town planner, who established the importance of surveys, research work, and properly planned 'diagnoses before treatment'. His major work is *City Development* 1904.

Geelong /dʒɪˈlɒŋ/ industrial port in S Victoria, Australia; population (1986) 148,300. In addition to oil refining and trade in grain, it produces aluminium, motor vehicles, textiles, glass, and fertilizers.

Gehenna another name for ◊hell; in the Old Testament, a valley S of Jerusalem where children were sacrificed to the Phoenician god Moloch and fires burned constantly.

Gehry /ˈgeəri/ Frank 1929– . US architect, based in Los Angeles. His architecture approaches abstract art in its use of collage and montage techniques.

His own experimental house at Santa Monica (1977), Edgemar Shopping Centre and Museum, Santa Monica (1988), and the Vitra Furniture Museum (1989)—his first building in Europe – demonstrate his vitality.

Geiger /ˈgaɪgə/ Hans 1882–1945. German physicist who produced the Geiger counter. After studying in Germany, he spent the period 1907–12 in Manchester, England, working with Ernest ◊Rutherford. In 1908 they designed an instrument to detect ◊alpha particles which was refined and made more powerful to produce the Geiger counter in the 1920s.

Geiger counter device for detecting and/or counting nuclear radiation and particles. It detects the momentary current that passes between ◊electrodes in a suitable gas when a nuclear particle or a radiation pulse causes ionization in the gas. The electrodes are connected to electronic devices which enable the intensity of radiation or the number of particles passing to be measured. It is named after Hans Geiger.

Geiger–Müller, Geiger–Klemperer, and Rutherford– Geiger counters are all devices often referred to loosely as Geiger counters.

geisha female entertainer (music, singing, dancing, and conversation) in Japanese teahouses and private parties. Geishas survive mainly as a tourist attraction. They are apprenticed from childhood and highly skilled in traditional Japanese arts and graces.

Geissler tube high-voltage ◊discharge tube in which traces of gas ionize and conduct electricity. It was developed in 1858 by the German physicist Heinrich Geissler (1814–1879).

gel a solid produced by the formation of a three-dimensional cage structure, commonly of linked large-molecular-mass polymers, in which a liquid is trapped. A gel may be a jelly-like mass (pectin, gelatine) or have a more rigid structure (silica gel).

gelatine water-soluble protein prepared from boiled hide and bone, used in cookery to set jellies, and in glues and photographic emulsions.

Gelderland /ˈgeldəlænd/ or *Guelders* province of the E Netherlands; area 5,020 sq km/1,938 sq mi; population (1988) 1,784,000. Its capital is Arnhem. In the NW is the Veluwe, a favourite holiday resort.

Geldof /ˈgeldɒf/ Bob 1954– . Irish fundraiser and rock singer, leader of the group Boomtown Rats 1975–86. He instigated the charity Band Aid, which raised large sums of money for famine relief, especially in Ethiopia, by recording a song, 'Do They Know It's Christmas?' 1984, and staging two simultaneous concerts (Live Aid) 1985, one in London and one in Philadelphia, broadcast live worldwide.

gelignite a type of ◊dynamite.

Gell-Mann /ˈgelˈmæn/ Murray 1929– . US physicist. In 1964, he formulated the theory of the ◊quark as the fundamental constituent of all matter, and smallest particle in the Universe.

He was R A Millikan professor of theoretical physics at the Californian Institute of Technology from 1967. In 1969, he was awarded a Nobel prize for his work on elementary particles and their interaction.

Gelsenkirchen /ˌgelzənˈkɪəkən/ industrial city in the ◊Ruhr, West Germany, 25 km/15 mi W of

Geldof Bob Geldof (centre) and George Michael (left) at the finale of the Live Aid concert, London 1985.

Dortmund; population (1988) 284,000. It has iron, steel, chemical, and glass industries.

gem a mineral valuable by virtue of its durability (hardness), rarity, and beauty, cut and polished for ornamental use, or engraved. Of 120 minerals known to have been used as gemstones, only about 25 are in common use in jewellery today; of these, the diamond, emerald, ruby, and sapphire are classified as precious, and all the others semiprecious, for example the topaz, amethyst, opal, and aquamarine.

Among the synthetic precious stones to have been successfully produced are rubies, sapphires, emeralds, and diamonds (first produced by General Electric in the USA 1955). Pearls are not technically gems.

Gemara in Judaism, part of the ◊Talmud, the compilation of ancient Jewish law.

Gemayel /ˌgemaɪˈel/ Amin 1942– . Lebanese politician, a Maronite Christian; president 1982–88. He succeeded his brother, president-elect *Bechir Gemayel*, on his assassination on 14 Sept 1982.

Gemeinschaft and *Gesellschaft* German terms (roughly, 'community' and 'association') coined by Ferdinand ◊Tönnies 1887 to contrast social relationships in traditional rural societies with those in modern industrial societies. He saw *Gemeinschaft* as intimate and positive, and *Gesellschaft* as impersonal and negative.

In small-scale societies where everyone knows everyone else, the social order is seen as stable and the culture homogeneous. In large urban areas life is faster and more competitive, and relationships are seen as more superficial, transitory, and anonymous.

Gemini prominent constellation of the zodiac, representing the twins Castor and Pollux. Its brightest star is ◊Pollux, and ◊Castor is a system of six stars. The Sun passes through Gemini from late June to late July. Each December, the Geminid meteors radiate from Gemini. In astrology, the dates for Gemini are between about 21 May and 21 June (see ◊precession).

Gemini project US space programme (1965–66) in which astronauts practised rendezvous and docking of spacecraft, and working outside their spacecraft, in preparation for the ◊Apollo Moon landings. Gemini spacecraft carried two astronauts and were launched by Titan rockets.

gemma (plural *gemmae*) a unit of ◊vegetative reproduction, consisting of a small group of undifferentiated green cells. Gemmae are found in certain mosses and liverworts, forming on the surface of the plant, often in cup-shaped structures, or gemmae cups. Gemmae are dispersed by splashes of rain, and can then develop into new plants. In many species gemmation is more common than reproduction by ◊spores.

gender in grammar, one of the categories into which nouns are divided in many languages, such as masculine, feminine, and neuter (as in Latin, German, and Russian), masculine and feminine (as in French, Italian, and Spanish), or animate and inanimate (as in North American Indian languages).

Grammatical gender may or may not correspond with sex: in French, *la soeur* (the sister) is feminine, but so is *la plume* (the pen). In German, *das Mädchen* (the girl) is neuter.

English nouns have only *natural gender*; that is, their grammatical gender reflects the sex of the referent of the noun rather than the form of the word itself. (For example, the name Katharine is a feminine noun because it refers to a particular girl.)

gene a unit of inherited material, encoded by a strand of nucleic acid (◊DNA or ◊RNA). In higher organisms, genes are located on the ◊chromosomes. The term 'gene', coined in 1909 by the Danish geneticist Wilhelm Johannsen (1857–1927), refers to the inherited factor that consistently affects a particular character in an individual, for example the gene for eye colour.

Also termed a Mendelian gene, after Gregor ◊Mendel, it occurs at a particular point or ◊locus on a particular chromosome and may have several variants or ◊alleles, each specifying a particular form of that character, for example the alleles for blue or brown eyes. Some alleles show ◊dominance. These mask the effect of other alleles, known as ◊recessive.

In the 1940s, it was established that a gene could be identified with a particular length of DNA, which coded for a complete protein molecule, leading to the 'one-gene-one-enzyme' principle. Later it was realized that proteins might be made up of several ◊polypeptide chains, each with a separate gene, so this principle was modified to 'one-gene-one-polypeptide'. However, the fundamental idea remains the same, that genes produce their visible effects simply by coding for proteins; they control the structure of those proteins via the genetic code, as well as the amounts produced and the timing of production. In modern genetics, the gene is identified either with the ◊cistron (a set of ◊codons that determines a complete polypeptide) or with the unit of selection (a Mendelian gene that determines a particular character in the organism on which ◊natural selection can act). Genes undergo ◊mutation and ◊recombination to produce the variation on which natural selection operates.

genealogy the study and tracing of family histories.

In the UK, the Society of Genealogists in London (established 1911) with its library, thousands of family papers, marriage index (6 million names of persons married before 1837), and collection of parish register copies, undertakes and assists research.

Genée /ʒəˈneɪ/ Adeline. Stage name of Anina Jensen 1878–1970. Danish-British dancer, president of the Royal Academy of Dancing 1920–54. Her work is commemorated by the *Adeline Genée Theatre* 1967, East Grinstead, Sussex.

gene pool the total sum of ◊alleles (variants of ◊genes) possessed by all the members of a given population or species alive at a particular time.

general senior military rank, the ascending grades being major general, lieutenant general, and general. The US rank of general of the army is equivalent to the British ◊field marshal.

General Agreement on Tariffs and Trade (GATT) an organization within the United Nations founded 1948 with the aim of encouraging ◊free trade between nations through low tariffs, abolitions of quotas, and curbs on subsidies.

General Assembly supreme court of the Church of ◊Scotland.

generator a machine that produces electrical energy from mechanical energy, as opposed to an ◊electric motor, which does the opposite.

The dynamo, for example, is a simple generator consisting of a wire-wound coil (◊armature) which is rotated between the pole-pieces of a permanent magnet. The movement (of the wire in the magnetic field) induces a current in the coil by ◊electromagnetic induction, which can be fed by means of a ◊commutator as a continuous direct current into an external circuit. Slip rings instead of a commutator produce an alternating current, when the generator is called an alternator.

Genesis first book of the Old Testament or Hebrew Bible, which includes the stories of the creation of the world, Adam and Eve, and the Flood, and the history of the Jewish patriarchs.

gene-splicing technique, invented 1973 by Stanley Cohen and Herbert Boyer, for inserting a foreign gene into bacteria to generate commercial biological products such as synthetic insulin, hepatitis-B vaccine, and interferon. It was patented in the USA 1984. See ◊genetic engineering.

genet /ʒəˈneɪ/ small, nocturnal, meat-eating mammal, genus *Genetta*, related to mongooses and civets. Most species live in Africa, but *Genetta genetta* is also found in Europe and the Middle East. It is about 50 cm/1.6 ft long with a

45 cm/1.5 ft tail, and greyish yellow with rows of black spots. It climbs well.

Genet /ʒəˈneɪ/ Jean 1910–1986. French dramatist, novelist, and poet, an exponent of the Theatre of ◊Cruelty. His turbulent life and early years spent in prison are reflected in his drama, characterized by ritual, role-play, and illusion, in which his characters come to act out their bizarre and violent fantasies. His plays include *Les Bonnes/The Maids* 1947, *Le Balcon/The Balcony* 1957, and two plays dealing with the Algerian situation: *Les Nègres/The Blacks* 1959, and *Les Paravents/The Screens* 1961.

gene therapy a proposed medical technique for curing or alleviating inherited diseases or defects. Although not yet a practical possibility for most defects, some of the basic techniques are available as a result of intensive research in ◊genetic engineering.

Gene therapy has been used for SCID (severe combined immune deficiency), with some success so far. It may also be useful for diseases such as haemoglobin irregularities, where only a relatively small group of cells—those in the bone marrow, which produce the red blood cells—need to be treated. The possibility of gene therapy for reproductive cells, to prevent genetic defects being passed on to the next generation, is more remote.

genetic code the way in which instructions for building proteins, the basic structural molecules of living matter, are 'written' in the genetic material ◊DNA. This relationship between the sequence of bases (see ◊base pair), the sub-units in a DNA molecule, and the sequence of ◊amino acids, the sub-units of a protein molecule, is the basis of heredity. The code employs ◊codons of three bases each; it is the same in almost all organisms, except for a few minor differences recently discovered in some protozoa.

genetic diseases disorders caused at least partly by defective genes or chromosomes, of which there are some 3,000, including cleft palate, cystic fibrosis, Down's syndrome, haemophilia, Huntington's chorea, some forms of anaemia, spina bifida, and Tay-Sachs disease.

genetic engineering the deliberate manipulation of genetic material by biochemical techniques. It is often achieved by the introduction of new DNA, usually by means of an infecting virus or ◊plasmid. This can be for pure research or to breed functionally specific plants, animals or bacteria. These organisms with a foreign gene added are said to to be ◊transgenic.

In genetic engineering, the transplantation of genes is used to increase our knowledge of cell function and reproduction, but it can also achieve practical ends, for example, plants grown for food could be given the ability to fix nitrogen, found in some bacteria, and so reduce the need for expensive fertilizers, or simple bacteria may be enabled to produce rare drugs. Developments in genetic engineering have led to the production of human insulin, human growth hormone and a number of other bone-marrow stimulating hormones. New strains of animals have also been produced; a new strain of mouse was patented in the USA 1989, but the application was rejected in the European patent office. A ◊vaccine against a sheep parasite (a larval tapeworm) has been developed by genetic engineering; most vaccines protect against bacteria and viruses.

There is a risk that when transplanting genes between different types of bacteria (*Escherichia coli*, which lives in the human intestine, is often used) new and harmful bacteria might be produced. For this reason strict safety precautions are observed, and the altered bacteria are disabled in some way so they are unable to exist outside the laboratory.

genetic fingerprinting technique for ascertaining the pattern of certain parts of the genetic material ◊DNA that is unique to each individual. Like skin fingerprinting, it can accurately distinguish

humans from one another, with the exception of identical twins.

Genetic fingerprinting involves isolating DNA from cells, then comparing and contrasting the sequences of component chemicals between individuals. The DNA pattern can be ascertained from a sample of skin, hair, or semen. Although differences are minimal (only 0.1% between unrelated people), certain regions of DNA, known as **hypervariable regions**, are unique to individuals. Genetic fingerprinting was discovered by Alec Jeffreys (1950–), and was first allowed as a means of legal identification at a court in Britain in 1987. It is used in paternity testing (from 1988), in forensic medicine, and in inbreeding studies.

genetics the study of inheritance and of the units of inheritance (◊genes). The founder of genetics was Gregor ◊Mendel, whose experiments with plants, such as peas, showed that inheritance takes place by means of discrete 'particles', which later came to be called genes.

Before Mendel, it had been assumed that the characteristics of the two parents were blended during inheritance, but Mendel showed that the genes remain intact although their combinations change. Since Mendel, genetics has advanced greatly, first through ◊breeding experiments and light-microscope observations (classical genetics), later by means of biochemical and electron-microscope studies (molecular genetics). An advance was the elucidation of the structure of ◊DNA by James D Watson and Francis Crick, and the subsequent cracking of the ◊genetic code. These discoveries opened up the possibility of deliberately manipulating genes, or ◊genetic engineering. See also ◊genotype, ◊phenotype or ◊monohybrid inheritance.

Geneva /dʒɪˈniːvə/ (French *Genève*) Swiss city, capital of Geneva canton, on the shore of Lake Geneva; population (1987) 385,000. It is a point of convergence of natural routes, and is a cultural and commercial centre. Industries include the manufacture of watches, scientific and optical instruments, foodstuffs, jewellery, and musical boxes.

The site on which Geneva now stands was the chief settlement of the Allobroges, a central European tribe who were annexed to Rome 121 BC; Caesar built an entrenched camp here. In the Middle Ages, Geneva was controlled by the prince-bishops of Geneva and the rulers of Savoy. Under ◊Calvin, it became a centre of the Reformation 1536–64; the Academy, which he founded 1559, became a university 1892. Geneva was annexed by France 1798; it was freed 1814 and entered the Swiss Confederation 1815. In 1864 the International Red Cross Society was established in Geneva. It was the headquarters of the ◊League of Nations, whose properties in Geneva passed 1946 into the possession of the United Nations.

Geneva Convention international agreement 1864 regulating the treatment of those wounded in war, and later extended to cover the types of weapons allowed, the treatment of prisoners and the sick, and the protection of civilians in wartime. The rules were revised at conventions held 1906, 1929, and 1949, and by the 1977 Additional Protocols.

Geneva, Lake /dʒɪˈniːvə/ (French *Lac Léman*) largest of the central European lakes, between Switzerland and France; area 580 sq km/225 sq mi.

Geneva Protocol international agreement 1925, designed to prohibit the use of poisonous gases, chemical weapons, and bacteriological methods of warfare. It came into force 1928, but was not ratified by the USA until 1974.

Genf /genf/ German form of ◊Geneva, Switzerland.

Genghis Khan /ˈdʒɛŋgɪs/ *c.*1160–1227. Mongol conqueror, ruler of all Mongol peoples from 1206. He began the conquest of N China 1213, overran the empire of the shah of Khiva 1219–25, and invaded N India, while his lieutenants advanced as far as the Crimea. When he died his empire ranged from the Yellow Sea to the Black Sea.

Temujin, as he was originally called, was the son of a chieftain. After a long struggle he established his supremacy over all the Mongols, when he assumed the title of Chingis or 'perfect warrior'. The ruins of his capital Karakorum are SW of Ulaanbaatar in Mongolia; his alleged remains are preserved at Ejin Horo, Inner Mongolia.

genitalia the reproductive organs of sexually reproducing animals, particulary the external/visible organs of mammals: in males, the penis and the scrotum, which contains the testes, and in females, the clitoris and vulva.

genitive in the grammar of certain inflected languages, the form of a word used for nouns, pronouns, or adjectives to indicate possession.

Gennesaret, Lake of /gɪˈnezərɪt/ another name for Lake ◊Tiberias (Sea of Galilee) in N Israel.

Genoa /ˈdʒenəʊə/ historic city in NW Italy, capital of Liguria; population (1988) 722,000. It is Italy's largest port; industries include oil-refining, chemicals, engineering, and textiles.

Decline followed its conquest by the Lombards 640, but from the 10th century, it established a commercial empire in the W Mediterranean, pushing back the Muslims, and founding trading posts in Corsica, Sardinia, and N Africa; during the period of the Crusades, further colonies were founded in the kingdom of Jerusalem and on the Black Sea, where Genovese merchants enjoyed the protection of the Byzantine empire. At its peak about 1300, the city had a virtual monopoly of European trade with the East. Strife between lower-class Genovese and the ruling mercantile-aristocratic oligarchy led to weakness and domination by a succession of foreign powers, including Pope John XXII (1249–1334), Robert of Anjou, king of Naples (1318–35), and Charles VI of France (1368–1422). During the 15th century, most of its trade and colonies were taken over by Venice or the Ottomans. Rebuilt after World War II, it became the busiest port on the Mediterranean, and the first to build modern container facilities. The nationalist Giuseppe Mazzini and the explorer Columbus were born here.

genocide killing or harming members of a particular national, racial, religious, or ethnic group with the intention of destroying that group. It is an international crime under the Genocide Convention 1948.

genome the full complement of ◊genes carried by a single set of ◊chromosomes for a given species.

genotype the particular set of ◊alleles (variants of genes) possessed by a given organism. The term is usually used in conjunction with ◊phenotype, which is the product of the genotype and all environmental effects. See also ◊environment–heredity controversy.

Genova /ˈdʒenəʊə/ Italian form of ◊Genoa, Italy.

genre painting (French *genre*, 'kind', 'type') painting of scenes from everyday life. Genre paintings were enormously popular in the Netherlands and Flanders in the 17th century (Vermeer, de Hooch, and Brouwer were great exponents). The term 'genre' is also used more broadly to mean a category in the arts, such as landscape painting, or literary forms such as the detective novel.

Genscher /ˈgenʃə/ Hans-Dietrich 1927– . West German politician, chairman of the Free Democratic Party (FDP) 1974–85, foreign minister from 1974.

Born in Halle, Genscher settled in West Germany 1952. He served as interior minister 1969–74 and then as foreign minister, committed to ◊Ostpolitik and European cooperation. As FDP leader, Genscher masterminded the party's switch of allegiance from the Social Democratic Party to the Christian Democratic Union which resulted in the downfall of the ◊Schmidt government 1982.

Gentile /dʒenˈtileɪ/ da Fabriano *c.* 1370–1427. Italian painter of frescoes and altarpieces in the International Gothic style. *The Adoration of the*

geological time chart

Millions of years ago	Epoch	Period	Era	Eon
0.01	Holocene	Quaternary		
1.8	Pleistocene			
5	Pliocene			
25	Miocene			
38	Oligocene	Tertiary	Cenezoic	
55	Eocene			
65	Palaeocene			
144		Cretaceous		Phanerozoic
213		Jurassic	Mesozoic	
248		Triassic		
286		Permian		
360		Carboniferous		
408		Devonian	Palaeozoic	
438		Silurian		
505		Ordovician		
590		Cambrian		
2500		Proterozioic	Precambrian	
4600		Archaean		

Magi 1423 (Uffizi, Florence) is typically rich in detail and crammed with courtly figures.

Gentile was active in Venice, Florence, Siena, Orvieto, and Rome, and collaborated with the artists Pisanello and Jacopo Bellini. His drawings after the antique suggest that he was aware of the new concerns of the Renaissance.

Gentileschi /ˌdʒentɪˈleski/ Artemisia 1593–*c.* 1652. Italian painter, born in Rome. She trained under her father Orazio Gentileschi, but her work is more melodramatic than his. She settled in Naples from about 1630, and focused on macabre and grisly subjects such as *Judith Decapitating Holofernes* (Museo di Capodimonte, Naples).

Gentileschi /ˌdʒentɪˈleski/ Orazio 1563–1637. Italian painter, born in Pisa. From 1626 he lived in London, painting for King Charles I. Like most of his contemporaries, he was influenced by Caravaggio's dramatic treatment of light and shade, as in *The Annunciation* 1623 (Turin).

Gentili /dʒenˈtiːli/ Alberico 1552–1608. Italian jurist. He practised law in Italy, but having adopted Protestantism was compelled to flee to England, where he lectured on Roman Law in Oxford. His publications, such as *De Jure Belli libri tres/On The Law Of War, Book Three* 1598, made him the first true international law writer and scholar.

Gentlemen-at-arms, Honourable Corps of in the British army, theoretically the main bodyguard of the sovereign; its functions are now ceremonial. Established 1509, the corps is, next to the Yeomen of the Guard, the oldest in the army; it was reconstituted 1862. It consists of army officers of distinction under a captain, a peer, whose appointment is political.

Gentlemen Prefer Blondes witty 1925 novel by Anita Loos, the story of the classic female gold-digger Lorelei Lee, filmed 1953 with Marilyn Monroe. Its 1928 sequel was called *But Gentlemen Marry Brunettes.*

gentry the lesser nobility, particularly in England and Wales. By the later Middle Ages, it included knights, esquires, and gentlemen, and after the 17th century, baronets. They were all of noble rank but not entitled to sit in the House of Lords.

genus (plural *genera*) group of ◊species with many characteristics in common. Thus all dog-like species (including dogs, wolves, and jackals) belong to the genus *Canis* (Latin 'dog'). Species of the same genus are thought to be descended from a common ancestor species. Related genera are grouped into ◊families.

geochemistry the science of chemistry as it applies to geology. It deals with the relative and absolute abundances of the chemical elements and their ◊isotopes in the Earth, and also with the chemical changes that accompany geologic processes.

geodesy methods of surveying the Earth for making maps and correlating geological, gravitational, and magnetic measurements. Geodesic surveys, formerly carried out by means of various measuring techniques on the surface, are now commonly made by using radio signals and laser beams from orbiting satellites.

Geoffrey of Monmouth /ˈdʒefri, ˈmɒnməθ/ *c.* 1100–1154. Welsh writer and chronicler. While a canon at Oxford, he wrote *Historia Regum Britanniae/History of the Kings of Britain c.* 1139, which included accounts of the semi-legendary kings Lear, Cymbeline, and Arthur, and *Vita Merlini*, a life of the legendary wizard. He was bishop-elect of St Asaph, N Wales 1151 and ordained a priest 1152.

geography the science of the Earth's surface; its topography, climate, and physical conditions, and how these factors affect civilization and society. It is usually divided into **physical geography**, dealing with landforms and climates; **biogeography**, dealing with the conditions that affect the distribution of animals and plants; and **human geography**, dealing with the distribution and activities of peoples on Earth.

geological time time scale embracing the history of the Earth from its physical origin to the present day. Geological time is divided into eras (Precambrian, Palaeozoic, Mesozoic, Cenozoic), which in turn are divided into periods, epochs, ages, and finally chrons.

geology the science of the Earth, its origin, composition, structure, and history. It is divided into several branches: **mineralogy** (the minerals of Earth), **petrology** (rocks), **stratigraphy** (the deposition of successive beds of sedimentary rocks), **palaeontology** (fossils), and **tectonics**

(the deformation and movement of the Earth's crust).

Geology is regarded as part of earth science, a more widely embracing subject that brings in meteorology, oceanography, geophysics, and geochemistry.

geometric mean m, of two numbers p and q is such that $m = p \times q$ and hence m, p and q are in a geometric progression.

geometric progression or **geometric series** in mathematics, a sequence of terms (progression) in which each term is a constant multiple (called the common ratio) of the one preceding it. For example, 3, 12, 48, 192, 768... is a geometric sequence with a common ratio 4, since each term is equal to the previous term multiplied by 4.

In nature, many single-celled organisms reproduce by splitting in two such that one cell gives rise to 2 then 4 then 8 cells and so on, forming a geometric sequence 1, 2, 4, 8, 16, 32 in which the common ratio is 2.

The sum of n terms of a geometric series $a + ar^2 + ar^3 + \ldots ar^n$ is given by $S_n = a(1-r^n)/(1-r)$ for all r. If $r < 1$, such a series can be summed to infinity $S_\infty = 1/(1-r)$. See ◊arithmetic sequence.

geometry branch of mathematics concerned with the properties of space, usually in terms of plane (two-dimensional) and solid (three-dimensional) figures. The subject is usually divided into **pure geometry**, which embraces roughly the plane and solid geometry dealt with in Euclid's *Elements*, and **analytical** or ◊**coordinate geometry**, in which problems are solved using algebraic methods. A third, quite distinct, type is the non-Euclidean geometries.

Geometry probably originated in ancient Egypt, in land measurements necessitated by the periodic inundations of the river Nile, and was soon extended into surveying and navigation. Early geometers were the Greek mathematicians Thales, Pythagoras, and Euclid. Analytical methods were introduced and developed by the French philosopher Descartes in the 17th century. From the 19th century various non-Euclidean geometries were devised by Gauss and Riemann in Germany, Lobachevsky in Russia, and others. These proved significant in the development of the theory of relativity and in the formulation of atomic theory.

geophysics branch of geology using physics to study the Earth's surface, interior, and atmosphere. Studies also include winds, weather, tides, earthquakes, volcanoes, and their effects.

George /dʒɔːdʒ/ Henry 1839–1897. US economist, born in Philadelphia. His *Progress and Poverty* 1879 suggested a 'single tax' on land, to replace all other taxes on earnings and savings. He hoped such a land tax would abolish poverty, by ending speculation on land values. George's ideas have never been implemented thoroughly, although they have influenced taxation policy in many countries.

George /geɪˈɔːgə/ Stefan 1868–1933. German poet. His early poetry was influenced by French ◊Symbolism, but his concept of himself as regenerating the German spirit first appears in *Des Teppich des Lebens/The Tapestry of Life* 1899, and later in *Der siebente Ring/The Seventh Ring* 1907.

Das neue Reich/The New Empire 1928 shows his realization that World War I had not had the right purifying effect on German culture. He rejected Nazi overtures and emigrated to Switzerland 1933.

George /dʒɔːdʒ/ six kings of Great Britain:

George I /dʒɔːdʒ/ 1660–1727. King of Great Britain from 1714. He was the son of the first elector of Hanover, Ernest Augustus (1629–1698), and his wife ◊Sophia, and a great-grandson of James I. He succeeded to the electorate 1698, and became king on the death of Queen Anne. He attached himself to the Whigs, and spent most of his reign in Hanover, never having learned English.

He was heir through his father to the hereditary lay bishopric of Osnabrück, and the duchy of Calenberg, which was one part of the Hanoverian possessions of the house of Brunswick. He acquired the other part by his marriage to Sophia Dorothea of Zell (1666–1726) in 1682. They were divorced 1694, and she remained in seclusion until her death. George's children were George II, and Sophia Dorothea (1687–1757), who married Frederick William (later king of Prussia) 1706, and was the mother of Frederick the Great.

George II /dʒɔːdʒ/ 1683–1760. King of Great Britain from 1727, when he succeeded his father, George I. His victory at Dettingen 1743, in the War of the Austrian Succession, was the last battle commanded by a British king. He married Caroline of Anspach 1705. He was succeeded by his grandson George III.

George III /dʒɔːdʒ/ 1738–1820. King of Great Britain from 1760, when he succeeded his grandfather George II. He supported his ministers in a hard line towards the American colonies, and opposed Catholic emancipation and other reforms. Possibly suffering from ◊porphyria, he had repeated attacks of insanity, permanent from 1811. He was succeeded by his son George IV.

He married Princess ◊Charlotte Sophia of Mecklenburg-Strelitz in 1761.

George IV /dʒɔːdʒ/ 1762–1830. King of Great Britain from 1820, when he succeeded his father George III, for whom he had been regent during the king's insanity 1811–20. Strictly educated, he reacted by entering into a life of debauchery, and in 1785 married a Catholic widow, Mrs ◊Fitzherbert, but in 1795 also married Princess ◊Caroline of Brunswick, in return for payment of his debts. He attempted to divorce her on charges of adultery, but this was dropped after Parliament passed the bill with increasingly smaller majorities. He had one child, Charlotte, who died in childbirth 1817. He was succeeded by his brother, the duke of Clarence, who became William IV.

George V /dʒɔːdʒ/ 1865–1936. King of Great Britain from 1910, when he succeeded his father Edward VII. He was the second son, and became

George IV Prince Regent of Great Britain from 1811, when his father George III was deemed unfit to rule, George IV succeeded to the throne in 1820.

George VI George VI succeeded to the throne after the unexpected abdication of his brother, Edward VIII, in 1936.

heir 1892 on the death of his elder brother Albert, Duke of Clarence. In 1893, he married Princess Victoria Mary of Teck (Queen Mary), formerly engaged to his brother. During World War I he made several visits to the front. In 1917, he abandoned all German titles for himself and his family. The name of the royal house was changed from Saxe-Coburg-Gotha (popularly known as Brunswick or Hanover) to Windsor.

His mother was Princess Alexandra of Denmark, sister of Empress Marie of Russia.

George VI /dʒɔːdʒ/ 1895–1952. King of Great Britain from 1936, when he succeeded after the abdication of his brother Edward VIII. Created Duke of York 1920, he married in 1923 Lady Elizabeth Bowes-Lyon (1900–), and their children are Elizabeth II and Princess Margaret. During World War II, he visited the Normandy and Italian battlefields.

George I 1845–1913. King of Greece 1863–1913. The son of king Christian IX of Denmark, he was nominated to the Greek throne and, in spite of early unpopularity, became a highly successful constitutional monarch. He was assassinated by a Greek, Schinas, at Salonika.

George II /dʒɔːdʒ/ 1890–1947. king of Greece 1922–23 and 1935–47. He became king on the expulsion of his father Constantine I 1922, but was himself overthrown 1923. Restored by the military 1935, he set up a dictatorship under ◊Metaxas, and went into exile during the German occupation 1941–45.

George Cross/Medal UK awards to civilians for acts of courage.

The *George Cross* is the highest civilian award in Britain for acts of courage in circumstances of extreme danger. It was instituted 1940. It consists of a silver cross with a medallion in the centre bearing a design of St George and the Dragon, and is worn on the left breast before all other medals except the Victory Cross. The George Cross was conferred on the island of Malta 1942.

The *George Medal*, also instituted 1940, is a civilian award for acts of great courage. The medal is silver and circular, bearing on one side a crowned effigy of the sovereign, and on the reverse St George and the Dragon. It is worn on the left breast.

George, St /dʒɔːdʒ/ patron saint of England. The story of St George rescuing a woman by slaying a dragon, evidently derived from the ◊Perseus legend, first appears in the 6th century. The cult of St George was introduced into W Europe by the Crusaders. His feast day is 23 Apr.

He is said to have been martyred at Lydda in Palestine 303, probably under the Roman Emperor Diocletian, but the other elements of his legend are of doubtful historical accuracy.

Georgia

Georgetown /'dʒɔːdʒtaʊn/ capital and port of Guyana; population (1983) 188,000.

Founded 1781 by the British, it was held 1784–1812 by the Dutch, who renamed it Stabroek, and ceded to Britain 1814.

Georgetown /'dʒɔːdʒtaʊn/ or *Penang* chief port of the Federation of Malaysia, and capital of Penang, on the Island of Penang; population (1980) 250,600. It produces textiles and toys. It is named after King George III.

Georgetown, Declaration of call in 1972, at a conference in Guyana of nonaligned countries, for a multipolar system to replace the two world power blocs, and for the Mediterranean Sea and Indian Ocean to be neutral.

Georgia /'dʒɔːdʒiə/ state of the S USA; nickname Empire State of the South/Peach State
area 152,600 sq km/58,904 sq mi
capital Atlanta
towns Columbus, Savannah, Macon
features Okefenokee National Wildlife Refuge (1,700 sq km/656 sq mi)
products poultry, livestock, tobacco, maize, peanuts, cotton, china clay, crushed granite, textiles, carpets, aircraft
population (1987) 6,222,000
famous people Jim Bowie, Erskine Caldwell, Jimmy Carter, Martin Luther King, Margaret Mitchell
history named after George II of England, it was founded 1733 and was one of the original ◊Thirteen States of the USA.

Georgia /'dʒɔːdʒiə/ (Georgian *Sakartvelo*, Russian *Gruzia*) constituent republic of the SW USSR from 1936
area 69,700 sq km/26,911 sq mi
capital Tbilisi
features holiday resorts and spas on the Black Sea; good climate
products tea, citrus, orchard fruits, tung oil, tobacco, vines, silk, hydroelectricity
population (1987) 5,266,000; 69% Georgian, 9% Armenian, 7% Russian, 5% Azerbaijani, 3% Ossetian, 2% Abkhazian
language Georgian
religion Georgian Church, independent of the Russian Orthodox Church since 1917
famous people Stalin
recent history independent republic 1918–21; uprising 1921 quelled by Soviet troops, who occupied Georgia; proclaimed republic 1921; linked with Armenia and Azerbaijan as the Transcaucasian

Georgia

Republic within the SW USSR 1922–36; increasing demands for autonomy in the late 1980s; nationalist demonstrators clashed with Soviet troops in Tbilisi 1989, leaving 19 demonstrators killed by poison gas.

Georgian a period of English architecture, furniture making, and decorative art between 1714 and 1830. The architecture is mainly Classical in style, although external details and interiors were often rich in Rococo carving. Furniture was frequently made of mahogany and satinwood, and mass production became increasingly common; designers included Thomas Chippendale, George Hepplewhite, and Thomas Sheraton. The silver of this period is particularly fine, and ranges from the earlier, simple forms to the more ornate, and from the Neo-Classical style of Robert Adam to the later, more decorated pre-Victorian taste.

geostationary orbit the circular path 35,900 km/22,300 mi above the Earth's equator on which a ◊satellite takes 24 hours, moving from west to east, to complete an orbit, thus appearing to hang stationary over one place on the Earth's surface. Geostationary orbits are used for weather satellites and broadcasting and communications satellites. They were first thought of by the author Arthur C Clarke.

geothermal energy energy produced by its use of natural steam, subterranean hot water, and hot dry rock for heating and electricity generation. Hot water is pumped to the surface and converted to steam or run through a heat exchanger; or dry steam is directed through turbines to produce electricity.

Gera /'geərə/ capital of Gera county and industrial city (engineering, textiles) in S East Germany; population (1986) 132,000. Gera county has an area of 4,000 sq km/1,544 sq mi and a population of 741,000.

Gerald of Wales English name of ◊Giraldus Cambrensis, medieval Welsh bishop and historian.

geranium a plant either of the family Geraniaceae, having divided leaves, and pink or purple flowers, or of the family Pelargonium, having a hairy stem, and red, pink, or white flowers.

gerbil rodent of the family Cricetidae that has elongated back legs and good hopping or jumping ability. Gerbils range from mouse- to rat-size, and have hairy tails. Many of the 13 genera live in dry, sandy, or sparsely vegetated areas of Africa and Asia. The *Mongolian jird* or *gerbil Meriones unguiculatus* is a popular pet.

gerenuk antelope *Litocranius walleri* about 1 m/3 ft at the shoulder, with a greatly elongated neck. It browses on leaves, often balancing on its hind legs to do so. Sandy brown in colour, it is well camouflaged in its E African habitat of dry scrub.

Gerhard /'dʒerɑːd/ Roberto 1896–1970. Spanish-British composer. He studied with ◊Granados and ◊Schoenberg and settled in England 1939, where he composed twelve-tone works in Spanish style. He composed the *Symphony No 1* 1952–3, followed by three more symphonies and chamber music incorporating advanced techniques.

geriatrics the branch of medicine concerned with care of the elderly sick.

Géricault /ˌʒerɪˈkəʊ/ (Jean Louis André) Théodore 1791–1824. French Romantic painter. *The Raft of the Medusa* 1819 (Louvre, Paris) was notorious for exposing a relatively recent scandal in which shipwrecked sailors had been cut adrift and left to drown.

A keen horseman himself (he was killed in a riding accident), he painted *The Derby at Epsom* 1821 (Louvre, Paris) and pictures of cavalry. He also painted portraits.

germ colloquial term for a micro organism that causes disease, such as certain ◊bacteria and ◊viruses. Formerly, it was also used to mean something capable of developing into a complete organism (such as a fertilized egg, or the ◊embryo of a seed).

Germain /ʒeəˈmæn/ Sophie 1776–1831. French mathematician, born in Paris. Although she was not allowed to study at the newly opened Ecole Polytechnique, she corresponded with ◊Lagrange and ◊Gauss. She is remembered for work she carried out in studying ◊Fermat's last theorem.

German inhabitant of Germany or person of German descent. Within East Germany the Serbs comprise a minority population who speak a Slavic language. The Austrians and Swiss Germans speak German, although they are ethnically distinct. German speaking minorities are found in France (Alsace-Lorraine), Romania (Transylvania), Czechoslovakia, USSR, Poland, and Italy (Tyrol).

German Jones /'dʒɜːmən/ Edward 1862–1936. English composer. He is remembered for his operettas *Merrie England* 1902 and *Tom Jones* 1907, and he wrote many other instrumental, orchestral and vocal works.

German art painting and sculpture in the Germanic north of Europe from the early Middle Ages to the present.
Middle Ages A revival of the arts was fostered by the emperor Charlemagne in the early 9th century. In the late 10th and early 11th centuries under the Ottonian emperors new styles emerged. German artists produced remarkable work in the Romanesque and later Gothic style. Wood carving played an important part in art.
15th century The painter Stefan Lochner, active in Cologne, excelled in the International Gothic style. Sculptors included Hans Mültscher (*c.*1400–57) and the wood carver Veit Stoss (Wit Stwosz), active in Nuremberg and Poland.
16th century The incarnation of the Renaissance in Germany was Albrecht Dürer; other painters included Hans Baldung Grien, Lucas Cranach, Albrecht Altdorfer, Grünewald, and Hans Holbein.
17th and 18th centuries Huge wall and ceiling paintings decorated new churches and princely palaces.
19th century Caspar David Friedrich was a pioneer of Romantic landscape painting in the early 19th century. At the turn of the century came Jugendstil (corresponding to French Art Nouveau).
20th century The movement known as die Brücke (the Bridge) was parallel with Fauvism. It was followed by the Munich Expressionist group Blaue Reiter (Blue Rider). After World War I, Otto Dix, George Grosz, and Max Beckmann developed satirical Expressionist styles. The Bauhaus school of design, emphasizing the dependence of form on function, was influential abroad. The painter Max Ernst moved to Paris and became a founder-member of Surrealism. Artists since 1945 include Joseph Beuys and Anselm Kiefer.

Germanic languages a branch of the Indo-European language family, divided into *East Germanic* (Gothic, now extinct), *North Germanic* (Danish, Faroese, Icelandic, Norwegian, Swedish), and *West Germanic* (Afrikaans, Dutch, English, Flemish, Frisian, German, Yiddish).

The Germanic languages differ from the other Indo-European languages most prominently in the consonant shift known as Grimm's Law. In it, the sounds *p, t, k* became either (as in English) *f, th, h,* or, as in Old High German *f, d, h*. Thus, the typical Indo-European of the Latin *pater* is *father* and *Fater* in Old High German. In addition, the Indo-European *b, d, g* moved to become *p, t, k,* or in Old High German *f, ts, kh*; compare Latin *duo*, English *two*, and German *zwei* ('tsvai').

Germanicus Caesar /dʒɜːˈmænɪkəs ˈsiːzə/ 15 BC–AD 19. Roman general. He was the adopted son of the emperor ◊Tiberius and married the emperor ◊Augustus' granddaughter Agrippina. Although he refused the suggestion of his troops that he claim the throne on the death of Augustus, his military victories in Germany made Tiberius jealous. Sent to the East, he died near Antioch, possibly murdered at the instigation of Tiberius. He was the father of ◊Caligula, and of Agrippina, mother of ◊Nero.

germanium a metallic element, symbol Ge, atomic number 32, relative atomic mass 72.6. It is a grey-white, brittle, crystalline metal in the silicon group, with chemical and physical properties between those of silicon and tin. Germanium is a semiconductor material and is used in the manufacture of transistors and integrated circuits. The oxide is transparent to infrared radiation, and is used in military applications. It was discovered 1886.

German language a member of the Germanic group of the Indo-European language family, the national language of West Germany, East Germany, and Austria, and an official language of Switzerland. There are many spoken varieties of German, the best known distinction being between High German (*Hochdeutsch*) and Low German (*Plattdeutsch*).

'High' and 'Low' refer to dialects spoken in the highlands or the lowlands rather than social status. *Hochdeutsch* originated in the central and southern highlands of Germany, Austria, and Switzerland, *Plattdeutsch* being used in the lowlands of N Germany. Standard and literary German is based on High German, in particular on the Middle German dialect used by Martin Luther for his translation of the Bible in the 16th century. Low German is closer to English in its sound system, the verb 'to make' being *machen* in High German but *maken* in Low German. Such English words as *angst, blitz, frankfurter, hamburger, poltergeist, sauerkraut* and *schadenfreude* are borrowings from High German.

German literature the fragmentary alliterative poem the *Hildebrandslied* (*c.*800), the most substantial relic of the **Old High German** period, bears no comparison with the Old English literature of the same era. In the **Middle High German** period there was a flowering of the vernacular, which had been forced into subservience to Latin after the early attempts at encouragement by Charlemagne. The court epics of Hartmann von Aue, Gottfried von Strassburg, and Wolfram von Eschenbach in the early 13th century were modelled on French style and material, but the folk-epic, the *Nibelungenlied*, revived the spirit of old heroic Germanic sagas. Adopted—in the more limited meaning—from France and Provence, the *Minnesang* reached its height in the lyric poetry of Walther von der Vogelweide.

Modern German literature begins in the 16th century with the standard of language set by Luther's Bible. In this century also came the climax of popular drama in the *Fastnachtsspiel* as handled by Hans Sachs. In the later 16th and early 17th centuries French influence was renewed and English influence, by troupes of players, was introduced: Martin Opitz's *Buch von der deutschen Poeterey* 1624, in which he advocates the imitation of foreign models, epitomizes the German Renaissance. It was followed by the Thirty Years' War, which is vividly described in Grimmelshausen's *Simplicissimus*.

In the 18th century French Classicism predominated, extolled by Gottsched but opposed by Bodmer and Breitinger, whose writings prompted the Germanic *Messias* of Klopstock. Both Lessing and Herder were admirers of Shakespeare, and Herder's enthusiasm inaugurated the *Sturm und Drang* phase which emphasized individual inspiration, and his collection of folk songs was symptomatic of the feeling which inspired Bürger's modern ballad *Lenore*. Greatest representatives of the Classical period at the end of the century were Goethe and Schiller, but their ideals were combated by the new Romantic school based on the work of the brothers Schlegel, and Tieck, which included Novalis, Arnim, Brentano, Eichendorff, Chamisso, Uhland, and Hoffmann.

With Kleist and Grillparzer in the early 19th century, stress on the poetic in drama ends, and with Hebbel the psychological aspect becomes the more important. About 1830 the 'Young German' movement, led by Heine, Gutzkow, and Laube,

Germany regions

Republic	Capital	Area sq km
West Germany	Bonn	248,710
Land (Region)		
Baden-Württemberg	Stuttgart	35,800
Bavaria	Munich	70,600
Bremen	Bremen	400
Hamburg	Hamburg	760
Hessen	Wiesbaden	21,100
Lower Saxony	Hanover	47,400
North Rhine-Westphalia	Düsseldorf	34,100
Rhineland-Palatinate	Mainz	19,800
Saarland	Saarbrücken	2,570
Schleswig-Holstein	Kiel	15,700
West Berlin	West Berlin	480
East Germany	East Berlin	108,350
Bezirk (County)		
East Berlin		400
Cottbus	Cottbus	8,260
Dresden	Dresden	6,740
Erfurt	Erfurt	7,350
Frankfurt	Frankfurt	7,190
Gera	Gera	4,000
Halle	Halle	8,770
Karl-Marx-Stadt	Karl-Marx-Stadt	6,010
Leipzig	Leipzig	4,970
Magdeburg	Magdeburg	11,530
Neubrandenburg	Neubrandenburg	10,950
Potsdam	Potsdam	12,570
Rostock	Rostock	7,080
Schwerin	Schwerin	8,670
Suhl	Suhl	3,860

was suppressed by the authorities. Other 19th-century writers include Jeremias Gotthelf, storyteller of peasant life; the psychological novelist Friedrich Spielhagen; poets and novella-writers Gottfried Keller and Theodor Storm; and the realist novelists Wilhelm Raabe and Theodor Fontane. Naturalistic drama found its chief exponents in Hauptmann and Sudermann. Influential in literature, as in politics and economics, were Marx and Nietzsche.

The lyric poets Richard Dehmel, Stefan George, and Rainer Maria Rilke stood out in the early 20th century, as did the poet and dramatist von Hofmannsthal, and the novelists Thomas and Heinrich Mann, E M Remarque, and Hermann Hesse. Just before World War I Expressionism emerged in the poetry of Georg Trakl. It dominated the novels of Franz Kafka and the plays of Ernst Toller, Franz Werfel, Georg Kaiser and Karl Sternheim, and was later to influence Bertolt Brecht. Under Nazism many major writers left the country, others were silenced or ignored. After World War II came the Swiss dramatists Max Frisch and Friedrich Dürrenmatt, the novelists Heinrich Böll, Christa Wolf, and Siegfried Lenz, the poet Paul Celan, and Günter Grass.

German measles or **rubella** a virus disease, usually caught by children, having an incubation period of two to three weeks. It is marked by a sore throat, pinkish rash, and slight fever. If a woman contracts it in the first three months of pregnancy, it may cause serious damage to the unborn child. Immunization is recommended for girls who have not contracted the disease, at about 12–14 months, or at puberty.

German Ocean German name for the ◊North Sea.

German silver or **nickel silver** a silvery alloy of nickel, copper, and zinc. It is widely used for cheap jewellery and the base metal for silver plating. The letters EPNS on silverware stand for electroplated nickel silver.

Germany /'dʒɜːmənɪ/ nation of central Europe, divided after ◊World War II into East Germany, West Germany, with land to the east of the Oder and western Neisse rivers being divided between the USSR and Poland. Reunification of the two Germanies is a major European political issue. See also ◊Germany, history.

Germany, East /'dʒɜːmənɪ/ country in E Europe, bounded to the N by the Baltic Sea, E by Poland,

S by Czechoslovakia, and SW and W by West Germany.

government East Germany is a centralized unitary state, the five *Länder* (Brandenburg, Mecklenburg, Saxony, Saxony-Anhalt and Thuringia) which existed 1945–52 having been divided into 14 counties (*Bezirke*). Under the 1968 constitution the supreme legislative and executive body in the German Democratic Republic is the people's chamber *Volkskammer*, whose 500 members (including 66 from East Berlin) are elected every five years by universal suffrage. The *Volkskammer* debates and passes laws and chooses the members and which functions as its permanent organ.

Day-to-day government executive administration is conducted by the council of ministers *Ministerrat*, headed and selected by a prime minister drawn from the largest single party within the *Volkskammer*.

history for history before 1949, see ◊Germany, history. Formerly the Soviet zone of occupation, the German Democratic Republic was established 1949, becoming a sovereign state 1954. It was recognized at first only by the Communist powers. In 1973, however, following the adoption by the Federal Republic of the new policy of ◊Ostpolitik, a Basic Treaty governing relations between East and West Germany was ratified by both states. The treaty fell short of full recognition by the Federal Republic, permanent missions rather than ambassadors being stationed in the respective nations. It led, however, to East Germany's admission to the ◊United Nations and to its full recognition by other Western states.

The years immediately after 1949 saw the rapid establishment of a Communist regime on the Soviet model, involving the creation of a one-party political system, the nationalization of industry, and the formation of agricultural collectives. Opposition to such Sovietization led, during food shortages, to demonstrations and a general strike 1953, which was suppressed by Soviet troops.

In 1961 the ◊Berlin Wall was erected to stem the growing movement of refugees to the Federal Republic. Economic reforms boosted the East German growth rate in the 1960s, significantly improving living conditions. During the following decade, with the replacement of the Stalinist Socialist Unity Party (SED) leader Walther ◊Ulbricht by the pragmatic Erich ◊Honecker, a more moderate political approach was adopted at home, while economic and diplomatic relations with the West were extended.

The German Democratic Republic was a loyal and vital member of ◊Comecon and the ◊Warsaw Pact (Soviet medium range nuclear missiles being stationed on its soil) during the ◊Brezhnev era. From 1987 Honecker was urged by the USSR to accelerate the pace of domestic economical and political reform. However, he refused to do so, and grassroots pressure for liberalization mounted. In Sept 1989, after the violent suppression of a church and civil rights activists' demonstration in Leipzig, an umbrella dissident organization, *Neue Forum* ('New Forum'), was illegally formed. The regime was further destabilized between Aug and Oct 1989 both by the exodus of more than 30,000 of its citizens to West Germany through Hungary, which had opened its borders with Austria in May, and by the illness of Honecker during the same period.

On 6 and 7 Oct the Soviet leader Mikhail ◊Gorbachev visited East Berlin, and made plain his desire to see greater reform. This catalysed the growing reform movement and a wave of demonstrations, the first since 1953, swept East Berlin, Dresden, Leipzig, and smaller towns. At first, under Honecker's orders, they were violently broken up by riot police. However, the security chief, Egon ◊Krenz, ordered a softer line and in Dresden the reformist Communist Party leader, Hans Modrow, actually marched with the protesters. Faced with the rising tide of protest and the increasing exodus to West

Germany

North Sea

Frisian Islands

Kiel
Straisund
Rostock
Lübeck
Schwerin
Bremerhaven
Hamburg
Groningen
Bremen
NETHERLANDS
Hanover
Magdeburg
Berlin
WEST GERMANY
EAST GERMANY
Dortmund
Halle
Düsseldorf
Leipzig
Kassel
Cologne
Erfurt
Dresden
BELGIUM
Kark Marx Stadt
Koblenz
Prague
LUX.
CZECHOSLOVAKIA
Mannheim
Nuremberg
FRANCE
N
Stuttgart
Regensburg
Black Forest
Danube
Munich
Salzburg
Zurich
AUSTRIA
SWITZERLAND
POLAND
Oder
Elbe
Weser
Rhine
Mosel
Spree

0 km 50 100
0 miles 50 100

Germany (between 5,000 and 10,000 people a day), which caused grave disruption to the economy, Honecker was replaced as party leader and head of state by Krenz on 18–24 Oct. In an attempt to keep up with the reform movement, Krenz sanctioned far-reaching reforms in Nov 1989 that effectively ended the SED monopoly of power and laid the foundations for a pluralist system. The Politburo was purged of conservative members; Modrow became prime minister and a new cabinet was formed; New Forum was legalized, and opposition parties allowed to form; and borders with the West were opened and free travel allowed, with the Berlin Wall being effectively dismantled. However, in early Dec, following revelations of high-level corruption during the Honecker regime, Krenz was forced to resign as SED leader and head of state, being replaced by Gregor Gysi (1948–) and Manfred Gerlach (1928–) respectively. Honecker was placed under house arrest awaiting trial on charges of treason, corruption, and abuse of power, and the Politburo was again purged.

An interim SED–opposition 'government of national responsibility' was formed Feb 1990. However, the political crisis continued to deepen, with the opposition divided over reunification with West Germany, while the popular reform movement showed signs of running out of control following the storming in Jan of the former security-police (*Stasi*) headquarters in East Berlin. The economy deteriorated further following the exodus of 344,000 people to West Germany in 1989, with a further 1,500 leaving each day, while country-wide work stoppages increased.

Elections in Mar 1990 were won by the centre-right Alliance for Germany, a three-party coalition led by the Christian Democratic Union (CDU). Talks were opened with the West German government on monetary union.

Germany, history
BC–AD 4th century The W Germanic peoples, originating in Scandinavia, overran the region between the rivers Rhine, Elbe, and Danube, where they were confined by the Roman Empire.
496 The Frankish king Clovis conquered the Alemanni.
768–814 The reign of the emperor Charlemagne, who extended his authority over Germany and imposed Christianity on the Saxons.
814–919 After Charlemagne's death Germany was separated from France under its own kings while the local officials or dukes became virtually independent.
919–1002 Central power was restored by the Saxon dynasty. Otto I, who in 962 revived the title of emperor, began the colonization of the Slav lands east of the Elbe.
1075–1250 A feud between emperors and popes enabled the princes to recover their independence.

1493–1519 A temporary revival of imperial power took place under Maximilian I.
1521 The Diet of Worms at which Charles V confronted the Protestant Martin Luther. The **Reformation** increased Germany's disunity.
1618–48 The **Thirty Years' War** reduced the empire to a mere name, and destroyed Germany's economic and cultural life.
1740–86 The rise of Brandenburg-Prussia as a military power, which had begun in the 17th century, reached its height under Frederick II.
1806 The French emperor Napoleon united W Germany in the **Confederation of the Rhine** and introduced the ideas and reforms of the French Revolution: his reforms were subsequently imitated in Prussia. The empire was abolished.
1848 Ideas of democracy and national unity inspired the unsuccessful ◊revolutions of 1848.
1867 The North German Confederation, under the leadership of Prussia, was formed.
1871 Under Chancellor Bismarck's leadership, German Empire formed after victorious wars with Austria and France. William I of Prussia became emperor.
1914–18 **World War I**. It was caused by political, industrial, and colonial rivalries with Britain, France, and Russia.
1918 A revolution overthrew the monarchy; the socialists seized power, and established the democratic **Weimar Republic**.
1922–24 Rampant inflation. In 1922 one dollar was worth 50 marks, in 1924 one dollar was worth 2.5 trillion marks.
1929–33 The economic crisis brought Germany close to revolution, until in 1933 the reaction manoeuvred the **Nazis** into power.
1933–45 At home the Nazis solved the unemployment problem by a vast rearmament programme, abolished the democratic constitution, and ruthlessly destroyed all opposition; abroad, the policy of aggression led to eventual defeat in **World War II**.
1945–52 Germany was divided, within its 1937 frontiers, into British, US, French, and Soviet occupation zones.
1949 Germany was partitioned into the communist **German Democratic Republic** (see ◊Germany, East) and the capitalist **German Federal Republic** (see ◊Germany, West).
Germany, West /'dʒɜːmənɪ/ country in W Europe, bounded to the N by the North Sea and Denmark, E by East Germany and Czechoslovakia, S by Austria and Switzerland, and W by France, Belgium, Luxembourg, and the Netherlands.
government West Germany's constitution (the Basic Law) was drafted 1948–49 by the Allied military governors and German provincial leaders in an effort to create a stable, parliamentary form of government, diffuse authority and safeguard liberties. It borrowed from British, US, and neighbouring European constitutional models. It established, firstly, a federal system of government built around ten *Länder* (states), each with its own constitution and elected parliament and government headed by a minister-president.

The *Länder* have original powers in education, police, and local government, and are responsible for the administration of federal legislation through their own civil services. They have local taxation powers and are assigned shares of federal income tax and VAT revenues, being responsible for 50% of government spending.

The constitution, secondly, created a new federal parliamentary democracy, built around a two-chamber legislature comprising a directly elected 520-member lower house *Bundestag* (federal assembly), and an indirectly elected 45-member upper house *Bundesrat* (federal council). *Bundestag* representatives are elected for four-year terms by universal suffrage under a system of 'personalized proportional representation' in which

Germany, East
German Democratic Republic
(Deutsche Demokratische Republik)

area 108,350 sq km/41,823 sq mi
capital East Berlin
towns Leipzig, Dresden, Karl-Marx-Stadt, Magdeburg; chief port Rostock
physical flat in north, mountains in south; rivers Elbe, Oder, and Neisse; many lakes, including Müritz
features Harz Mountains, Erzgebirge, Fichtelgebirge, Thüringer Wald
head of state Manfred Gerlach from 1989
head of government
political system socialist pluralist republic
political parties Socialist Unity Party (SED), Marxist-Leninist; New Forum, opposition umbrella pressure group; Social Democratic Party (SPD), left-of-centre; Liberal Democratic Party, Christan Democratic Union (CDU), National Democratic Party and Democratic Farmers Party, until 1989 allies of the SED; Free Democratic Party (FDP), liberal; Green Party, environmentalist
exports lignite, uranium, cobalt, coal, iron, steel, fertilizers, plastics
currency GDR Mark, or Ostmark (2.86 = £1 Feb 1990, not free rate)
population (1986) 16,640,000; annual growth rate –0.1%
life expectancy men 70, women 75
language German
religion Protestant 80%, Roman Catholic 11%
literacy 99% (1985)
GNP $86 bn (1983); $8,000 per head of population

chronology
1949 The German Democratic Republic established as an independent state.
1953 Riots in East Berlin suppressed by Soviet troops.
1961 The Berlin Wall erected to stem flow of refugees.
1964 Treaty of Friendship and Mutual Assistance signed with USSR.
1971 Erich Honecker elected Socialist Unity Party (SED) leader.
1973 Basic Treaty ratified, normalizing relations with Federal Republic.
1975 Friendship Treaty with USSR renewed for 25 years.
1987 Official visit of Honecker to the Federal Republic.
1989 East German visitors to Hungary permitted to enter Austria and the west; mass exodus to West Germany began (344,000 left during 1989). Oct: Honecker replaced by Egon Krenz following mass demonstrations calling for reform after Gorbachev's visit to East Berlin. Nov: New Forum opposition movement legalized; national borders, including Berlin Wall, opened. Reformist Hans Modrow appointed prime minister. Dec: Krenz replaced as party leader by Gysi and as president by Gerlach. Honecker placed under house arrest.
1990 Jan: Secret-police *(Stasi)* headquarters in East Berlin stormed by demonstrators. Feb: 'Grand Coalition' government formed; Modrow called for a neutral united Germany; Mar: multi-party electrons won by the right-wing Christian Democratic Union (CDU).

history for history before 1949, see ◊Germany, history. The Federal Republic was formed 1949 from the British, US, and French occupation zones in the west of the German Empire which were under Allied military control following Germany's surrender 1945. A policy of demilitarization, decentralization, and democratization was instituted by the Allied control powers and a new, intentionally provisional, constitution framed, which included eventual German re-unification.

West ◊Berlin was blockaded by the Soviet Union 1948–49, but survived to form a constituent *Land* in the Federal Republic, after an airlift operation by the Allied powers. Politics during the Federal Republic's first decade were dominated by the CDU, led by the popular Konrad ◊Adenauer.

Chancellor Adenauer and his economics minister, Ludwig ◊Erhard, established a successful approach to economic management, termed the 'social market economy', which combined the encouragement of free market forces with strategic state intervention on the grounds of social justice. This new approach, combined with ◊Marshall Aid and the enterprise of the labour force (many of whom were refugees from the partitioned East), brought rapid growth and reconstruction during the 1950s and 1960s, an era termed the 'miracle years'.

During this period, West Germany was also reintegrated into the international community. It gained full sovereignty 1954, entered ◊NATO 1955, emerging as a loyal supporter of the USA, and, under Adenauer's lead, joined the new ◊European Economic Community 1957. Close relations with France enabled the ◊Saarland to be transferred to German sovereignty 1957.

In 1961, East Germany's construction of the ◊Berlin Wall to prevent refugees from leaving the East created a political crisis that vaulted West Berlin's mayor, Willy ◊Brandt, to international prominence. Domestically, Brandt played a major role in shifting the SPD away from its traditional Marxist affiliation towards a more moderate position following the party's 1959 Bad Godesberg conference. Support for the SPD steadily increased after this policy switch and the party joined the CDU in a 'Grand Coalition' 1966–69, before gaining power itself, with the support of the FDP, under Brandt's leadership 1969. As chancellor, Brandt introduced the foreign policy of ◊Ostpolitik, which sought reconciliation with Eastern Europe as a means of improving contacts between East and West Germany.

Treaties 1970 normalized relations with the Soviet Union and Poland, and recognized the Oder-Neisse border line, while in 1972 a basic treaty was effected with East Germany, acknowledging the East Germany's borders and separate existence, enabling both countries to enter the UN 1973. Brandt resigned as chancellor 1974, following the revelation that his personal assistant had been an East German spy. His successor, the former finance minister, Helmut ◊Schmidt, adhered to Ostpolitik and emerged as a leading advocate of European cooperation.

The SPD–FDP coalition only narrowly defeated the CDU–CSU in the 1976 federal election, but gained a comfortable victory 1980 when the controversial Franz-Josef ◊Strauss headed the CDU–CSU ticket. Between 1980 and 1982, however, the left wing of the SPD and the liberal FDP were divided over military policy (particularly the proposed stationing of US nuclear missiles in West Germany) and economic policy, during a period of recession.

Chancellor Schmidt fought to maintain a moderate, centrist course but the FDP eventually withdrew from the federal coalition 1982 and joined forces with the CDU, led by Dr Helmut ◊Kohl, to unseat the chancellor in a 'positive vote of no confidence'. Helmut Schmidt immediately retired from politics and the SPD, led by

---

electors have one vote for an ordinary constituency seat and one for a *Land* party list, enabling adjustments in seats gained by each party to be made on a proportional basis.

Political parties must win at least 5% of the national vote to qualify for shares of 'list seats'. *Bundesrat* members are nominated and sent in blocs by *Länder* governments, each state being assigned between three and five seats depending on population size. The *Bundestag* is the dominant parliamentary chamber, electing from the ranks of its majority party or coalition a chancellor (prime minister) and cabinet to form the executive government. Once appointed, the chancellor can only be removed by a 'constructive vote of no confidence' in which a majority votes positively in favour of an alternative leader.

Legislation is effected through all-party committees. The *Bundesrat* has few powers to initiate legislation, but has considerable veto authority. All legislation relating to *Länder* responsibilities requires its approval, constitutional amendments need a two-thirds *Bundesrat* (and *Bundestag*) majority, while the *Bundesrat* can temporarily block bills or force amendments in joint *Bundestag-Bundesrat* 'conciliation committees'. *Bundestag* members also join an equal number of representatives elected by *Länder* parliaments in a special Federal Convention *Bundesversammlung* every five years to elect a federal president as head of state. The president, however, has few powers and is primarily a titular figure.

The 1949 constitution is a written document. Adherence to it is policed by an independent federal constitutional court based at Karlsruhe which is staffed by 16 judges, who serve terms of up to 12 years. All-party committees from the *Bundestag* and *Bundesrat* select eight each. The court functions as a guarantor of civil liberties and adjudicator in Federal-*Land* disputes. (Similar courts function at the *Land* level).

West German politics have been dominated since 1949 by two major parties, the Christian Democratic Union (CDU) and Social Democratic Party (SPD), and one minor party, the Free Democratic Party (FDP). The conservative CDU has gained the most support at the national level, forming the principal party of government 1949–69 and after 1982. It is represented in Bavaria by a more right-wing sister party, the Christian Social Union (CSU). The SPD is the dominant party of the left and, after adopting a more moderate policy programme, became the principal party of federal government between 1969–82. The FDP liberal party has averaged 8% of the national vote since 1949, but has regularly held the balance of power in the *Bundestag* and been a coalition partner, with a 20% share of cabinet portfolios, in all but seven years (1957–61 and 1966–69) since 1949. In recent years a fourth significant party, the ◊Green Party, has emerged, surmounting the 5% federal electoral barrier in both 1983 and 1987.

West Berlin has its own elected parliament and government and sends 22 'honorary representatives' to the federal *Bundestag* and four to the *Bundesrat*. The three Allied powers (Britain, France, and the USA) continue to exercise supreme authority over West Berlin; the *Land*'s federal parliament representatives thus possess only limited voting rights.

Germany, West
Federal Republic of Germany
(Bundesrepublik Deutschland)

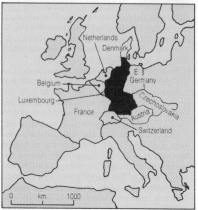

area 248,706 sq km/96,001 sq mi
capital Bonn
towns West Berlin, Cologne, Munich, Essen, Frankfurt-am-Main, Dortmund, Düsseldorf; ports Hamburg, Kiel, Cuxhaven, Bremerhaven
physical flat in N, mountainous in S with Alps; rivers Rhine, Weser, Elbe flow N, Danube flows SE
features Black Forest
head of state Richard von Weizsäcker from 1984
head of government Helmut Kohl from 1982
political system democratic republic
political parties Christian Democratic Union (CDU), right-of-centre; Social Democratic Party (SPD), left-of-centre; Free Democratic Party (FDP), liberal; Christian Social Union (CSU), Bavarian-based conservative; Greens,

environmentalist; Republicans, far-right
exports machine tools (world's leading exporter), cars, commercial vehicles, electronics, industrial goods, textiles, chemicals, iron, steel, wine
currency Deutschmark (2.89 = £1 Sept 1987)
population (1986) 61,170,000 (including 4,400,000 'guest workers', *Gastarbeiter*, of whom 1,600,000 are Turks; the rest are Yugoslavs, Italians, Greeks, Spanish, and Portuguese); annual growth rate −0.2%
life expectancy men 70, women 77
language German
religion Protestant 49%, Roman Catholic 47%
literacy 99% (1985)
GNP $655 bn (1983); $9,450 per head of population
chronology
1945 German surrender and division into four (US, French, British, Soviet) occupation zones.
1948 Berlin crisis.
1949 Establishment of Federal Republic under the 'Basic Law' Constitution with Adenauer as chancellor.
1954 Grant of full sovereignty.
1957 Entry into EEC. Recovery of Saarland.
1961 Construction of Berlin Wall.
1963 Retirement of Chancellor Adenauer.
1969 Willy Brandt became chancellor.
1972 Basic Treaty with East Germany.
1974 Resignation of Brandt. Helmut Schmidt became chancellor.
1982 Kohl became chancellor.
1988 Death of Bavarian CSU leader Franz-Josef Strauss.
1989 Rising support for far-right in local and European elections, and declining support for Kohl. Cabinet reshuffle announced. Mass influx of refugees from East Germany (May onwards). In Dec Kohl unveiled ten-point plan for reunification with East Germany.

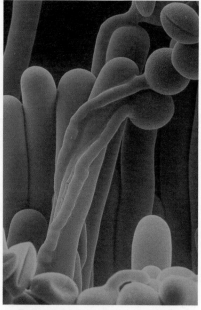

germination *False-colour electron-microscope view of pollen grains germinating on the stigma of the opium poppy.*

following free elections in East Germany, Chancellor Kohl unveiling a ten-point plan Dec 1989. The SPD were more cautious and divided over the issue.

germination in botany, the initial stages of growth in a seed, spore, or pollen grain. Seeds germinate when they are exposed to favourable external conditions of moisture, light, and temperature, and when any factors causing dormancy have been removed.

The process begins with the uptake of water by the seed. The embryonic root, or radicle,

West Germany

Hans-Jochen Vögel, was heavily defeated in the *Bundestag* elections 1983, losing votes on the left to the new environmentalist Green Party. The new Kohl administration, with the FDP's Hans-Dietrich ◊Genscher remaining as foreign minister, adhered closely to the external policy of the previous chancellorship.

At home, however, a freer market approach was introduced. With unemployment rising to 2.5 million in 1984, problems of social unrest emerged, while violent demonstrations greeted the installation of US nuclear missiles on German soil 1983–84. Internally, the Kohl administration was rocked by scandals over illegal party funding, which briefly touched the chancellor himself. However, a strong recovery in the German economy from 1985 enabled the CDU–CSU–FDP coalition to gain re-election in

the federal election 1987, with 269 *Bundestag* seats. The opposition SPD meanwhile won 186 seats, and was divided over its future and whether or not to seek alliance with the Greens, who won 42 seats.

During 1988–89, following the death of the CSU's Franz-Josef Strauss, support for the far-right Republican party began to climb, and it secured 7% of the vote in the European Parliament elections of June 1989. In 1989–90 events in East Germany and elsewhere in Eastern Europe caused half a million economic and political refugees to enter the Federal Republic, as well as re-opening the debate on reunification (*Wiedervereinigung*); this resulted in West German politics becoming more highly charged and polarized. The CDU gave strong support to swift, graduated moves towards 'confederative' reunification, if desired,

germination

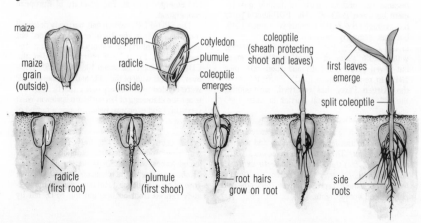

maize

maize grain (outside)

endosperm — cotyledon
radicle — plumule
(inside) — coleoptile emerges

coleoptile (sheath protecting shoot and leaves)

first leaves emerge

split coleoptile

radicle (first root)

plumule (first shoot)

root hairs grow on root

side roots

Geronimo *Apache Indian chief Geronimo who fought a rearguard action to protect tribal lands. Pictured here after his surrender. He later became a Christian farmer in Oklahoma.*

is normally the first organ to emerge, followed by the embryonic shoot, or plumule. Food reserves, either within the ◊endosperm or from the ◊cotyledons, are broken down to nourish the rapidly growing seedling. Germination is considered to have ended with the production of the first true leaves.

Germiston /'dʒɜ:mɪstən/ town in the Transvaal, South Africa; population (1980) 155,435. Industries include gold refining, chemicals, steel, textiles.

germ layer in ◊embryology, a layer of cells that can be distinguished during the development of a fertilized egg. Most animals have three such layers: the inner, middle, and outer.

The inner layer (**endoderm**) later gives rise to the gut, the middle one (**mesoderm**) develops into most of the other organs, while the outer one (**ectoderm**) gives rise to the skin and nerves. Simple animals, such as sponges, lack a mesoderm.

Gerona /xeˈrəʊnə/ town in Catalonia, NE Spain, capital of Gerona province; population (1986) 68,000. Industries include textiles and chemicals. There are ferry links with Ibiza, Barcelona, and Málaga.

Geronimo /dʒəˈrɒnɪməʊ/ 1829–1909. Chief of the Chiricahua Apache Indians and war leader. From 1875–1885, he fought US federal troops and settlers encroaching on tribal reservations in the Southwest, especially SE Arizona and New Mexico. After surrendering to Gen George Crook Mar 1886, and agreeing to go to Florida where their families were being held, Geronimo and his followers escaped. Captured again Aug 1886, they were taken to Florida, then to Alabama. The climate proved unhealthy, and they were taken to Fort Sill, Oklahoma, where Geronimo became a farmer. He dictated *Geronimo's Story of His Life* 1906.

gerrymander in politics, the rearranging of constituency boundaries to give an unfair advantage to the ruling party. It is now used more generally to describe various kinds of political trickery.

The term derives from US politician Elbridge Gerry (1744–1814), who, while governor of Massachusetts 1812, reorganized an electoral district (shaped like a salamander) in favour of the Republicans.

Gers /ʒeə/ river in France, 178 km/110 mi in length; it rises in the Lannemezan Plateau and flows north to join the Garonne 8 km/5 mi above Agen. It gives its name to a *département* in Midi-Pyrénées region.

Gershwin *Jazz pianist and composer George Gershwin. He combined popular song writing with more serious pieces, the most famous being Rhapsody in Blue 1924.*

Gershwin /'gɜ:ʃwɪn/ George 1898–1937. US composer, who wrote the tone poem *An Ameri-*

Getty *Tycoon and oil millionaire John Paul Getty who devoted much of his personal fortune to art collecting.*

can in Paris 1928, *Rhapsody in Blue* 1924, and the opera *Porgy and Bess* 1935, in which he incorporated the essentials of jazz. He also wrote popular songs with his brother, the lyricist *Ira Gershwin* (1896–1983).

Gerson /ʒɛəˈsɒn/ Jean 1363–1429. French theologian. He was leader of the ◊concilliar movement, and denounced ◊Huss at the Council of Constance 1415. His theological works greatly influenced 15th-century thought. He was chancellor of Notre Dame cathedral in Paris, and of the University of Paris from 1405.

Gertler /'gɜ:tlə/ Mark 1891–1939. English painter. He was a pacifist and a noncombatant during World War I; his *Merry-Go-Round* 1916 (Tate Gallery, London) is often seen as an expressive symbol of militarism. He suffered from depression and committed suicide.

gerund in the grammar of certain languages, such as Latin, a noun formed from a verb, and functioning as a noun to express an action or state. In English, gerunds end in *-ing*.

Gesellschaft (German 'society') a group whose concerns are of a formal and practical nature. See ◊*Gemeinschaft* and *Gesellschaft*.

gestalt the concept of a unified whole which is greater than, or different from, the sum of its parts; that is, a complete structure whose nature is not explained simply by analysing its constituent elements. A chair, for example, will generally be

Gertler *Merry-Go-Round (1916) Tate Gallery, London.*

geyser *Old Faithful, Yellowstone National Park, Wyoming, USA. Time between eruptions varies from 33 to 96 minutes and depends on the length of the previous eruption.*

recognized as a chair despite great variations between individual chairs in such attributes as size, shape, and colour. The term was first used in psychology in Germany about 1910. It has been adopted from German because there is no exact equivalent in English.

Gestalt psychology regarded all mental phenomena as being arranged in organized, structured wholes. For example, learning was seen as a reorganizing of a whole situation (often involving insight), as opposed to the behaviourists' view that it consisted of associations between stimuli and responses. Gestalt psychologists' experiments showed that the brain is not a passive receiver of information, but that it structures all its input in order to make sense of it, a belief which is now generally accepted.

Gestapo abbreviated form of *Geheime Staatspolizei*, Nazi Germany's secret police, formed 1933, and under the direction of Heinrich Himmler from 1936. The Gestapo used torture and terrorism to stamp out anti-Nazi resistance. It was declared a criminal organization at the Nuremberg Trials 1946.

gestation in all mammals except the monotremes (duck-billed platypus and spiny anteater), the period from the time of implantation of the embryo in the uterus to birth. This period varies between species; in humans it is about 266 days, in elephants 18–22 months, in cats about 60 days, and in some species of opossum as short as 12 days.

Gethsemane /geθˈseməni/ site of the garden where Judas Iscariot, according to the New Testament, betrayed Jesus. It is on the Mount of Olives, E of Jerusalem. When Jerusalem was divided between Israel and Jordan 1948, Gethsemane fell within Jordanian territory.

Getty /'geti/ J(ean) Paul 1892–1976. US oil billionaire, president of the Getty Oil Company from 1947, and founder of the *Getty Museum* (housing the world's highest-funded art gallery) in Malibu, California. In 1985 his son *John Paul Getty Jr* (1932–) established an endowment fund of £50 million for the National Gallery, London.

Gettysburg site in Pennsylvania of a decisive battle of the American ◊Civil War in 1863, won by the North. The site is now a national cemetery, at the dedication of which President Lincoln delivered the *Gettysburg Address* 19 Nov 1863, a speech in which he reiterated the principles of freedom, equality, and democracy embodied in the US constitution. It begins with 'Fourscore and seven years ago', and ends with an assertion of 'government of the people, by the people, and for the people'.

Getz /gets/ Stan(ley) 1927– . US tenor saxophonist of the 1950s 'cool jazz' school. He was the first US musician to be closely identified with the Latin American *bossa nova* sound.

geyser a natural spring that intermittently discharges an explosive column of steam and hot water into the air. One of the most remarkable geysers is Old Faithful, in Yellowstone National Park, Wyoming, USA. Geysers also occur in New Zealand and Iceland.

Gezira, El /gɪˈzɪərə/ plain in the Republic of Sudan, between the Blue and White Niles. The cultivation of cotton, sorghum, wheat, and groundnuts is made possible by irrigation.

G-forces the forces pilots and astronauts experience when their craft accelerate or decelerate rapidly. One 'G' is the ordinary pull of gravity. Early astronauts were subjected to launch and re-entry forces up to six Gs or more. Pilots and astronauts wear G-suits that prevent their blood 'pooling' too much under severe G-forces, which can lead to unconsciousness.

Ghaghara /ˈɡɑːɡərə/ or *Gogra* river in N India, a tributary of the ◊Ganges, which rises in Tibet and flows through Nepál and the state of Uttar Pradesh; length 1,000 km/620 mi.

Ghana /ˈɡɑːnə/ country in W Africa, bounded to the N by Burkina Faso, E by Togo, S by the Gulf of Guinea, and W by the Ivory Coast.

government The 1979 constitution was suspended 1981 when Flight-Lt Jerry Rawlings seized power and set up a Provisional National Defence Council (PNDC), with himself as chair. Parliament and the council of state were abolished and the government now rules by decree. All political parties were banned but opposition groups still operate from outside the country.

history The area now known as Ghana was once made up of several separate kingdoms, including those of the Fanti on the coast and the Ashanti further inland.

The first Europeans to arrive in the region were the Portuguese 1471. Their coastal trading centres, dealing in gold and slaves, flourished alongside Dutch, Danish, British, Swedish, and French traders until about 1800, when the Ashanti, having conquered much of the interior, began to invade the coast. Denmark and the Netherlands abandoned their trading centres, and the Ashanti were defeated by Britain and the Fanti 1874. The coastal region became the British colony of The Gold Coast, and after continued fighting, the inland region to the north of Ashanti 1898, and the Ashanti kingdom 1901, were made British protectorates. After 1917 the W part of Togoland, previously governed by Germany, was administered with The Gold Coast. Britain thus controlled both coastal and inland territories, and in 1957 they, together with British Togoland, became the independent Republic of Ghana.

Dr Kwame Nkrumah, a former prime minister of The Gold Coast, became president. He embarked on a policy of what he called 'African socialism' and established an authoritarian regime. In 1964 he declared Ghana a one-party state, with the Convention People's Party (CPP), which he led, as the only political organization. He then dropped his stance of nonalignment and forged links with the USSR and other communist countries. In 1966, while visiting China, he was deposed in a coup led by Gen Joseph Ankrah, whose national liberation council released many political prisoners and purged CPP supporters.

In 1969 Ankrah was replaced by Gen Akwasi Afrifa, who announced plans for a return to civilian government. A new constitution established an elected national assembly and a non-executive presidency. The Progress Party (PP) won a big majority in the assembly and its leader, Kofi Busia, became prime minister. In 1970 Edward Akufo-Addo became the civilian president.

Following economic problems, the army seized power again 1972. The constitution was suspended and all political institutions replaced by

Ghana
Republic of

area 238,305 sq km/91,986 sq mi
capital Accra
towns Kumasi, and ports Sekondi-Takoradi, Tema
physical mostly plains; bisected by river Volta
features artificial Lake Volta; relics of traditional kingdom of Ashanti
head of state and government Jerry Rawlings from 1981
political system military republic
political parties all political parties were banned 1981

exports cocoa, coffee, timber, gold, diamonds, manganese, bauxite
currency cedi (524.37 = £1 Feb 1990)
population (1988) 13,812,000; annual growth rate 3.2%
life expectancy men 50, women 54
language English (official)
religion Christian 43%, animist 38%, Muslim 12%
literacy 64% male/43% female (1985 est)
GNP $3.9 bn (1983); $420 per head of population
chronology
1957 Independence achieved, within the Commonwealth, with Kwame Nkrumah as president.
1960 Ghana became a republic and a one-party state.
1966 Nkrumah deposed and replaced by Gen Joseph Ankrah.
1969 Ankrah replaced by Gen Akwasi Afrifa, who initiated a return to civilian government.
1970 Edward Akufo-Addo elected president.
1972 Another coup placed Col Acheampong at the head of a military government.
1978 Acheampong deposed in a bloodless coup led by Frederick Akuffo. Another coup put Flight Lt Jerry Rawlings in power.
1979 Return to civilian rule under Hilla Limann.
1982 Rawlings seized power again, citing the incompetence of previous governments.
1989 Coup attempt against Rawlings foiled.

a National Redemption Council (NRC), under Col Ignatius Acheampong. In 1976 he too promised a return to civilian rule but critics doubted his sincerity and he was replaced by his deputy, Frederick Akuffo, in a bloodless coup 1978. Like his predecessors, he announced a speedy return to civilian government but before elections could be held he, in turn, was deposed by junior officers led by Flight-Lt Jerry Rawlings, claiming that previous governments had been corrupt and had mismanaged the economy.

Civilian rule was restored 1979 but two years later Rawlings led another coup, again complaining of the government's incompetence. He established a Provisional National Defence Council (PNDC), with himself as chair, again suspending the constitution, dissolving parliament and banning political parties. Although Rawlings' policies were initially supported, particularly by workers and students, his failure to revive the economy caused discontent and he has had to deal with a number of demonstrations and attempted coups, including one in Oct 1989.

Ghana, Ancient a great trading empire that flourished in NW Africa during the 5th–13th centuries. Founded by the Soninke people, the Ghana Empire was based, like the Mali Empire which superseded it, on the Saharan gold trade. At its peak in the 11th century, it occupied an area that includes parts of present-day Mali, Senegal, and Mauritania. Wars with the Berber tribes of the Sahara led to its fragmentation and collapse in the 13th century, when much of its territory was absorbed into Mali.

From its capital at Kumbi Saleh, most trade routes ran north across the Sahara and west to the coast. Trade consisted mainly of the exchange of gold from inland deposits for salt from the coast.

ghat in Hinduism, broad steps leading down to one of the sacred rivers. Some of these, known as 'burning ghats', are used for cremation.

Ghats, Eastern and Western /ɡɔːts/ twin mountain ranges in S India, to the E and W of the central plateau; a few peaks reach about 3,000 m/9,800 ft. They are connected by the Nilgiri Hills. The name is a European misnomer, the Indian word *ghat* meaning pass, not mountain.

Ghazzali, al- /ɡæˈzɑːli/ 1058–1111. Muslim philosopher and one of the most famous Sufis (Mus-

lim mystics). He was responsible for easing the conflict between the Sufi and the Ulema, a body of Muslim religious and legal scholars.

Initially, he believed that God's existence could be proved by reason, but later he became a wandering Sufi, seeking God through mystical experience; his book, *The Alchemy of Happiness*, was written on his travels.

Ghent /ɡent/ (Flemish *Gent*, French *Gand*) city and port in East Flanders, NW Belgium; population (1982) 237,500. Industries include textiles, chemicals, electronics, and metallurgy.

The cathedral of St Bavon (12th–14th centuries) has paintings by van ◊Eyck and ◊Rubens, and the university was established 1816.

Gheorgiu-Dej /ɡiɔːˈdʒuːˈdeɪ/ Gheorge 1901–1965. Romanian communist politician. A member of the Romanian Communist Party (RCP) from 1930, he played a leading part in establishing a communist regime in 1945. He was prime minister 1952–55 and state president 1961–65. Although retaining the support of Moscow, he adopted an increasingly independent line during his final years.

gherkin a young or small green ◊cucumber, used for pickling.

ghetto area of a town where Jews were compelled to live, decreed by a law enforced by papal bull 1555. Ghettos were abolished, except in E Europe, in the 19th century, but the concept was revived by the Germans and Italians 1940–45. The term now refers to any deprived area occupied by a minority group.

Ghibelline in medieval Germany and Italy, a supporter of the emperor and member of a rival party to the ◊Guelphs.

Ghiberti /ɡɪˈbeəti/ Lorenzo 1378–1455. Italian sculptor and goldsmith. In 1401 he won the commission for a pair of gilded bronze doors for Florence's baptistry. He produced a second pair (1425–52), the *Gates of Paradise*, one of the masterpieces of the Early Italian Renaissance. They show sophisticated composition and use of perspective.

He also wrote *Commentarii/Commentaries*, a mixture of art history, manual, and autobiography.

Ghirlandaio /ˌɡɪəlænˈdaɪəʊ/ Domenico *c.* 1449–1494. Italian fresco painter, head of a large and prosperous workshop in Florence. His fresco cycle 1486–90 in Sta Maria Novella, Florence, includes portraits of many Florentines and much

Gibbon *A portrait of the historian Edward Gibbon, painted c. 1773 by Henry Walton. Gibbon wrote* The History of the Decline and Fall of the Roman Empire, *a work which occupied a major part of his life; the first volume appeared in 1776, and the last in 1788.*

contemporary domestic detail. He also worked in Pisa, Rome, and San Gimignano, and painted portraits.

Ghosts a play by Henrik Ibsen, first produced 1881. Mrs Alving hides the profligacy of her late husband. The past catches up with her when her son inherits his father's syphilis and unwittingly plans to marry his half-sister.

GHQ abbreviation for *general headquarters*.

GI abbreviation for *government issue*; hence (in the USA) a common soldier.

Giacometti /ˌdʒækə'meti/ Alberto 1901–1966. Swiss sculptor and painter, who trained in Italy and Paris. In the 1930s, in his Surrealist period, he began to develop his characteristic spindly constructions, based on wire frames, emerged in the 1940s. Some are so elongated that they seem almost without volume. *Man Pointing* 1947 is one of many examples in the Tate Gallery, London.

Giambologna /ˌdʒæmbə'lɒnjə/ Giovanni da Bologna or Jean de Boulogne 1529–1608. Flemish-born sculptor active mainly in Florence and Bologna. In 1583 he completed his public commission for the Loggia dei Lanzi in Florence, *The Rape of the Sabine Women*, a dynamic group of muscular figures and a prime example of Mannerist sculpture.

He also produced the *Neptune Fountain* 1563–67 in Bologna and the equestrian statues of the Medici grand dukes Cosimo and Ferdinando. There are several versions of his figure of *Mercury* on tiptoe (1564, Bargello, Florence, for example). His workshop in Florence produced small replicas of his work in bronze.

giant in many mythologies and folklore, one of a race of outsize humanoids, often characterized as stupid and aggressive. In Greek mythology the giants grew from the spilled blood of Uranus and rebelled against the gods. During the Middle Ages in many parts of Europe, wicker effigies of giants were carried in midsummer processions and sometimes burned.

Giant's Causeway stretch of columnar basalt forming a promontory on the N coast of Antrim, Northern Ireland. It was formed by an outflow of lava in Tertiary times that has solidified in polygonal columns.

Gibberd /'gɪbəd/ Frederick 1908–1984. British architect and town planner. His works include the new towns of Harlow, England, and Santa Teresa, Venezuela; the Catholic Cathedral, Liverpool; and the Central London mosque in Regent's Park.

Gibbs *St Martin-in-the-Fields, London, by James Gibbs 1722–26.*

gibberellin plant growth substance (see also ◊auxin) that mainly promotes stem growth but may also affect the breaking of dormancy in certain buds and seeds, and the induction of flowering. Application of gibberellin can stimulate the stems of dwarf plants to additional growth, delay the ageing process in leaves, and promote the production of seedless fruit (◊parthenocarpy).

gibbon type of small ape, genus *Hylobates*, of which there are several species. The **common** or **black-handed gibbon** *Hylobates lar* is about 60 cm/2 ft tall, with a body that is hairy except for the buttocks, which distinguishes it from other types of apes. Gibbons have long arms, no tail, and are arboreal in habit, but when on the ground walk upright. They are found from Assam through the Malay peninsula to Borneo.

Gibbon /'gɪbən/ Edward 1737–1794. British historian, author of *The History of the Decline and Fall of the Roman Empire* 1776–88.

The work was a continuous narrative from the 2nd century AD to the fall of Constantinople in 1453, on which he began work while in Rome in 1764. Although immediately sucessful, he was compelled to reply to attacks on his account of the early development of Christianity by a *Vindication* 1779. From 1783 Gibbon lived in Lausanne, Switzerland, but he returned to England and died in London.

Gibbon /'gɪbən/ John Heysham 1903–1974. US surgeon who invented the heart-lung machine in 1953. It has since become indispensable in heart surgery, maintaining the circulation while the heart is temporarily inactivated.

Gibbon /'gɪbən/ Lewis Grassic, pen name of James Leslie Mitchell 1901–1935. Scottish novelist, author of the trilogy *A Scots Quair: Sunset Song, Cloud Howe* and *Grey Granite* 1932–34, set in the area S of Aberdeen, the Mearns, where he was born and brought up. Under his real name he wrote *Stained Radiance* 1930 and *Spartacus* 1933.

Gibbons /'gɪbənz/ Grinling 1648–1721. British woodcarver, born in Rotterdam. He produced carved wooden panels (especially of birds, flowers, and fruit) for St Paul's Cathedral, London, and for many aristocratic houses, including Petworth House, Sussex. He became master carver to George I in 1741.

Gibbons /'gɪbənz/ Orlando 1583–1625. English composer. A member of a family of musicians, he was appointed organist at Westminster Abbey in 1623. His finest works are his madrigals and motets.

Gibbons /'gɪbənz/ Stella Dorothea 1902–1989. English journalist. She is remembered for her

Cold Comfort Farm 1932, a classic satire on the regional novel.

Gibbs /gɪbz/ James 1682–1754. Scottish Neo-Classical architect whose works include St Martin-in-the-Fields, London 1722–26, Radcliffe Camera, Oxford 1737–49, and Bank Hall, Warrington, Cheshire 1750.

Gibbs /gɪbz/ Josiah Willard 1839–1903. US theoretical physicist and chemist who developed a mathematical approach to thermodynamics. His book *Vector Analysis* 1881 established vector methods in physics.

Gibbs' function in ◊thermodynamics, an expression representing part of the energy content of a system that is available to do external work, also known as the free energy G. In an equilibrium system at constant temperature and pressure, $G = H - TS$, where H is the enthalpy (heat constant), T the temperature, and S the ◊entropy (decrease in energy availability). The function was named after US physicist Josiah Willard Gibbs.

Gibraltar /dʒɪ'brɔːltə/ British dependency, situated on a narrow rocky promontory in S Spain

area 6.5 sq km/2.5 sq mi

features strategic naval and air base, with NATO underground headquarters and communications centre; colony of Barbary apes; the frontier zone is adjoined by the Spanish port of La Línea

exports mainly a trading centre for the import and re-export of goods

population (1988) 30,000

recent history captured from Spain 1704 by English admiral George Rooke (1650–1709), it was ceded to Britain under the Treaty of Utrecht 1713. A referendum 1967 confirmed the wish of the people to remain in association with the UK, but Spain continues to claim sovereignty, and closed the border 1969–85. In 1989, the

Gide *Parisian novelist André Gide. He also co-founded the* Nouvelle Revue Française.

Gielgud *Distinguished English stage actor and director, John Gielgud. He is noted for his many fine performances in Shakespearian productions.*

UK government announced it would reduce the military garrison by half

currency Gibraltar government notes and UK coinage

language English

religion mainly Roman Catholic

government the governor has executive authority, with the advice of the Gibraltar council, and there is an elected house of assembly (chief minister Joshua Hassan 1964–69 and from 1972).

Gibraltar, Strait of /dʒɪˈbrɔːltə/ strait between N Africa and Spain, with the Rock of Gibraltar on the north side and Jebel Musa on the south, the so-called Pillars of Hercules.

Gibson /ˈgɪbsən/ 'Mike' (Cameron Michael Henderson) 1942– . Irish rugby player. He made a world record 81 international appearances 1964–79; 69 for Ireland and 12 for the British Lions on a record five tours. Of his 69 Ireland caps, 40 were played as centre, 25 at outside-half, and 4 on the wing.

Gibson /ˈgɪbsən/ Charles Dana 1867–1944. US illustrator. He portrayed an idealized type of American young woman, known as the 'Gibson Girl'.

Gibson Desert /ˈgɪbsən/ desert in central Western Australia; area 220,000 sq km/85,000 sq mi.

Gide /ʒiːd/ André 1869–1951. French novelist, born in Paris. His work is largely autobiographical and concerned with the themes of self-fulfilment and renunciation. It includes *L'Immoraliste/The Immoralist* 1902, *La Porte étroite/Strait is the Gate* 1909, *Les Caves du Vatican/The Vatican Cellars* 1914, and *Les Faux-monnayeurs/The Counterfeiters* 1926; and an almost lifelong *Journal*. Nobel Prize for Literature 1947.

Gideon in the Old Testament, one of the Judges of Israel, who led a small band of Israelite warriors which succeeded in routing an invading Midianite army of overwhelming number in a surprise night attack.

Gigli *Italian opera singer Beniamino Gigli.*

Gilbert and George *The English artists Gilbert and George first captured the public imagination in the 1960s when they offered themselves as works of art.*

Gielgud /ˈgiːlgʊd/ John 1904– . English actor and director. He played many Shakespearean roles, including Hamlet 1929. Film roles include Clarence in *Richard III* 1955 and the butler in *Arthur* 1981 (for which he won an Oscar).

Gielgud made his debut at the Old Vic 1921. Though probably best known as a Shakespearean actor, his numerous stage appearances include performances in plays by Chekhov and Sheridan, and in works by playwrights Alan Bennett, Peter Shaffer, and David Storey. Other films include *Becket* 1964, *Oh! What a Lovely War* 1969, and *Providence* 1977.

Gierek /ˈgɪərek/ Edward 1913– . Polish Communist politician. He entered the Politburo of the ruling Polish United Workers' Party (PUWP) in 1956 and was party leader 1970–80. His industrialization programme plunged the country heavily into debt and sparked a series of ◊Solidar-

Gilbert *British humorist and dramatist W S Gilbert, best known for his collaboration with Arthur Sullivan.*

ity-led strikes.

Gierek, a miner's son, lived in France and Belgium for much of the period between 1923 and 1948, becoming a member of the Belgian Resistance. He served as party boss in Silesia during the 1960s. After replacing Gomulka as PUWP leader in Dec 1970, he embarked on an ambitious programme of industrialization. A wave of strikes in Warsaw and Gdańsk, spearheaded by the Solidarity free trade-union movement, forced Gierek to resign in Sept 1980.

Giessen /ˈgiːsən/ manufacturing town on the Lahn, Hessen, West Germany; population (1984) 71,800. Its university was established 1605.

Giffard /ʒiˈfɑː/ Henri 1825–1882. French inventor of the first passenger-carrying steerable airship, called a dirigible, built 1852. The hydrogen-filled airship was 45 m/150 ft long, had a 3 hp steam engine which drove a propeller, and was steered using a sail-like rudder. It flew at a speed of 8 kph/5 mph.

giga- prefix signifying multiplication by 10^9 (one thousand million, 1,000,000,000, or in current scientific terminology, one billion), as in **gigahertz**, a unit of frequency equivalent to 1,000,000,000 hertz.

gigabyte in computing, a measure of the capacity of ◊memory or storage, equal to 1,024 ◊megabytes. It is also used, less precisely, to mean one thousand million bytes.

Gigli /ˈdʒiːlji/ Beniamino 1890–1957. Italian lyric tenor. Following his operatic debut in 1914 he performed roles by Puccini, Gounod, and Massenet.

Gijón /xiˈxɒn/ port on the Bay of Biscay, Oviedo province, N Spain; population (1986) 259,000. It produces iron, steel, chemicals, and oil, is an outlet for the coalmines of Asturias, and is an important fishing and shipbuilding centre.

gila monster lizard *Heloderma suspectum* of SW USA and Mexico. Belonging to the only venomous genus of lizards, it has poison glands in its lower jaw, but the bite is not usually fatal to humans.

Gilbert /'gɪlbət/ Alfred 1854–1934. British sculptor, whose statue of *Eros* in Piccadilly Circus, London, was erected as a memorial to the 7th Earl of Shaftesbury.

Gilbert /'gɪlbət/ Cass 1859–1934. US architect, born in Ohio, who became known for his skyscrapers, including the Woolworth Building in New York 1913.

Gilbert /'gɪlbət/ Humphrey c.1539–1583. English soldier and navigator who claimed Newfoundland (landing at St John's) for Elizabeth I in 1583. He died when his ship sank on the return voyage.

Gilbert /'gɪlbət/ W(illiam) S(chwenk) 1836–1911. British humorist and dramatist who collaborated with Arthur ◊Sullivan, providing the libretti for their series of light comic operas from 1871; they include *HMS Pinafore* 1878, *The Pirates of Penzance* 1879, and *The Mikado* 1885.

Born in London, he was called to the Bar in 1863, but in 1869 published a collection of his humorous verse and drawings, *Bab Ballads*—'Bab' being his own early nickname—which was followed by a second volume in 1873.

Gilbert /'gɪlbət/ Walter 1932– . US molecular biologist. Gilbert worked on the problem of genetic control, seeking the mechanisms which switch genes on and off. By 1966 he had established the existence of the *lac* repressor, the molecule which suppressed lactose production. Further work on the sequencing of ◊DNA nucleotides won for Gilbert a share of the 1980 Nobel Chemistry Prize with Frederick Sanger and Paul Berg.

Gilbert /'gɪlbət/ William 1544–1603. Scientist and physician to Elizabeth I and (briefly) James I. He studied magnetism and static electricity, deducing that the Earth's magnetic field behaves as if a huge bar magnet joined the North and South poles. His book on magnets, published 1600, is the first printed scientific book based wholly on experimentation and observation. He erroneously thought that the planets were held in their orbits by magnetic forces.

Gilbert and Ellice Islands /'gɪlbət, 'elɪs/ former British colony in the Pacific, known since independence 1978 as ◊Tuvalu and ◊Kiribati.

Gilbert and George /'gɪlbət, dʒɔː.dʒ/ Gilbert Proesch 1943– and George Passmore 1942– . English painters and performance artists. They became known in the 1960s for their presentation of themselves as works of art, *living sculpture*. Their art works make much use of photography.

Gilded Age, the In US history, a derogatory term referring to the post-Civil War decades. It borrows the title of an 1873 political satire by Mark Twain and Charles Dudley Warner (1829–1900), which highlights the respectable veneer of public life covering the many scandals of graft and

Gill Self-portrait in wood (1927) by the sculptor and engraver Eric Gill.

ginkgo

corruption.

Giles /dʒaɪlz/ Carl Ronald 1916– . British cartoonist for the *Daily* and *Sunday Express* from 1943, noted for his creation of a family with a formidable 'Grandma'.

Gilgamesh /'gɪlgəmeʃ/ hero of Sumerian, Hittite, Akkadian, and Assyrian legend. The 12 verse 'books' of the *Epic of Gilgamesh* were recorded in a standard version on 12 cuneiform tablets by the Assyrian king Ashurbanipal's scholars in the 7th century BC, and the epic itself is older than Homer's *Iliad* by at least 1,500 years. One-third mortal and two-thirds divine, Gilgamesh is Lord of the Sumerian city of Uruk. The epic's incident of the Flood is similar to the Old Testament account.

Gilgit /'gɪlgɪt/ town and region on the NW frontier of Kashmir, under the rule of Pakistan.

gill in biology, the main respiratory organ of most fish and immature amphibians, and of many aquatic invertebrates. In all types, water passes over the gills, and oxygen diffuses across the gill membrane into the circulatory system while carbon dioxide passes from the system out into the water. In aquatic insects, these gases diffuse into and out of an air-filled trachea.

gill /gɪl/ imperial unit of volume for liquid measure, equal to one quarter of a pint. It is used in selling alcoholic drinks.

Gill /gɪl/ Eric 1882–1940. English sculptor and engraver. He designed the typefaces Perpetua 1925 and Gill Sans (without serifs) 1927, and created monumental stone sculptures with clean, simplified outlines, such as *Prospero and Ariel* 1929–31 (on Broadcasting House, London).

He studied lettering at the Central School of Art in London under Edward Johnston, and began his career carving inscriptions for tombstones. Gill was a leader in the revival of interest in the craft of lettering and book design.

Gillespie /gɪ'lespi/ 'Dizzy' (John Birks) 1917– . US jazz trumpeter, together with Charlie Parker the chief creator and exponent of the ◊bebop style.

Gillette /dʒɪ'let/ King Camp 1855–1932. US inventor of the Gillette safety-razor.

Gillray /'gɪlreɪ/ James 1757–1815. English caricaturist. His 1,500 cartoons, 1779–1811, satirized the French, George III, politicians, and social follies of his day.

gillyflower archaic name for the ◊carnation and related plants, used in the works of Chaucer, Shakespeare, and Spenser.

Gilpin /'gɪlpɪn/ William 1724–1804. British artist. He is remembered for his essays on the 'picturesque', which set out precise rules for the production of this effect.

gilt-edged securities stocks and shares issued and guaranteed by the British government to raise funds and traded on the Stock Exchange. A relatively risk-free investment, gilts bear fixed interest and are usually redeemable on a specified date. According to the redemption date, they are described as short (up to five years), medium, or long (15 years or more).

gin (Dutch *jenever* 'juniper') alcoholic drink made by

distilling a mash of maize, malt, or rye, with juniper flavouring. It was first produced in Holland. In Britain, the low price of corn led to a mania for gin during the 18th century, resulting in the Gin Acts of 1736 and 1751 which reduced gin consumption to a quarter of its previous level.

ginger SE Asian reed-like perennial *Zingiber officinale*, family Zingiberaceae; the hot-tasting underground root is used as a condiment and in preserves.

ginger ale and beer sweetened, carbonated drinks containing ginger flavouring, sugar, and syrup; ginger beer also contains bitters.

ginkgo tree *Ginkgo biloba*, related to the conifers and also known, from the resemblance of its leaves to those of the maidenhair fern, as the maidenhair tree. In 200 years it may reach a height of 30 m/100 ft. Unchanged in form since prehistoric times, it has been cultivated in China and Japan since ancient times, and is planted in many parts of the world, espcially the USA. The fruits have edible kernels, although the pulp is poisonous.

Ginner /'dʒɪnə/ Charles 1878–1952. British painter. He settled in London in 1910, and was one of the London Group (set up in 1913 and including followers of ◊Vorticism and the ◊Camden Town Group) from 1914. He painted street scenes and landscapes.

Ginsberg /'gɪnzbɜːg/ Allen 1926– . US poet. His *Howl* 1956 was an influential poem of the ◊Beat Generation, criticizing the materialism of contemporary US society. In the 1960s Ginsberg travelled widely in Asia, and was a key figure in introducing Eastern thought to students of that decade.

ginseng plant *Panax ginseng*, family Araliaceae, used in medicine in China.

Giolitti /dʒɔ'lɪti/ Giovanni 1842–1928. Italian liberal politician, born in Mondovi. He was prime minister 1892–93, 1903–05, 1906–09, 1911–14, and 1920–21. He opposed Italian intervention in World War I, and pursued a policy of broad coalitions, which proved ineffective in controlling Fascism after 1921.

Giono /dʒi'əunəu/ Jean 1895–1970. French novelist, whose books are chiefly set in Provence. *Que ma joie demeure*/*Joy of Man's Desiring* 1935 is an attack on life in towns and a plea for a return to country life.

Giordano /dʒɔː'dɑːnəu/ Luca 1632–1705. Italian Baroque painter, born in Naples, active in Florence in the 1680s. In 1692 he was summoned to Spain by Charles II, and painted ceilings in the Escorial palace for the next ten years.

In Florence Giordano painted a ceiling in the Palazzo Riccardi-Medici 1682–83. He also produced altarpieces and frescoes for churches. His work shows a variety of influences, including ◊Veronese, and tends to be livelier than that of earlier Baroque ceiling painters.

Giorgione /dʒɔː'dʒəuni/ del Castelfranco c. 1475–1510. Italian Renaissance painter, active in Venice, probably trained by Giovanni Bellini. His work influenced Titian and other Venetian painters. His subjects are imbued with a sense of mystery and treated with a soft technique reminiscent of Leonardo da Vinci's later works, as in *Tempest* 1504 (Accademia, Venice).

Few details of his life are certain, but Giorgione created the Renaissance poetic landscape, with rich colours and a sense of intimacy; an example is the *Madonna and Child Enthroned with Two Saints*, an altarpiece for the church of Castelfranco.

Giotto space probe built by the European Space Agency to study ◊Halley's comet. Launched by an Ariane rocket in July 1985, Giotto passed within 600 km/375 mi of the comet's nucleus on 13 Mar 1986.

Giotto /'dʒɒtəu/ di Bondone 1267–1337. Italian painter and architect. He broke away from the conventional Gothic style of the time, and had an enormous influence on subsequent Italian paint-

giraffe

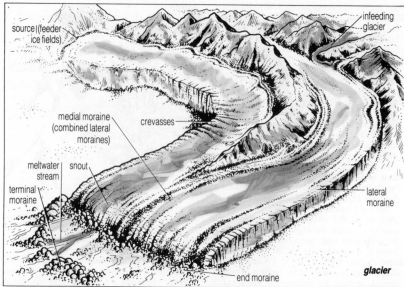

source (feeder ice fields)

infeeding glacier

medial moraine (combined lateral moraines)

crevasses

meltwater stream snout

terminal moraine

lateral moraine

end moraine

glacier

ing. The interior of the Arena Chapel, Padua, is covered in a fresco cycle (completed by 1306) illustrating the life of Mary and the life of Jesus. He is said to have designed the campanile (bell tower) in Florence.

Giotto was born in Vespignano, N of Florence. He introduced a naturalistic style, painting saints as real people. His most famous works are cycles of frescoes in churches at Assisi, Florence, and Padua. Giotto's figures occupy a definite pictorial space, and there is an unusual emotional intensity and dignity in the presentation of the story. In one of the series of frescoes he painted for the Arena Chapel, Padua, he made the Star of Bethlehem appear as a comet (◊Halley's comet had appeared 1303, just two years before). From 1334 he was official architect to Florence, and from 1335 overseer of works at the cathedral; he collaborated with Andrea ◊Pisano in decorating the cathedral facade with statues, and designing the campanile which was completed after his death.

Gippsland Lakes /ˈgɪps lænd/ series of shallow lagoons on the coast of Victoria, Australia, the main ones are Wellington, Victoria and King (broadly interconnected), and Reeve.

giraffe tallest mammal, *Giraffa camelopardalis*. It stands over 5.5 m/18 ft tall, the neck accounting for nearly half this amount. The giraffe has two small skin-covered horns on the head and a long tufted tail. The skin has a mottled appearance and is reddish brown and cream. Giraffes are now found only in Africa, S of the Sahara Desert.

Giraldus Cambrensis /dʒɪˈrældəs kæmˈbrensɪs/ c.1146–1220. Welsh historian, born in Pembroke-

Gish *US child prodigy actress Lillian Gish who starred in many of the films made by D W Griffith.*

shire. He was elected bishop of St David's in 1198. He wrote a history of the conquest of Ireland by Henry II, and *Itinerarium Cambriae* (Journey through Wales) 1191.

Girardon /ˌʒɪrɑːˈdɒn/ François 1628–1715. French academic sculptor. His *Apollo Tended by Nymphs*, commissioned 1666, is one of several marble groups sculpted for the gardens of Louis XIV's palace at Versailles.

Giraudoux /ˌʒɪrəʊˈduː/ (Hippolyte) Jean 1882–1944. French playwright and novelist, who wrote the plays *Amphitryon 38* 1929 and *La Folle de Chaillot/The Madwoman of Chaillot* 1945, and the novel *Suzanne et la Pacifique/Suzanne and the Pacific* 1921. Other plays include *La Guerre de Troie n'aura pas lieu/Tiger at the Gates* 1935

Girgenti /dʒɪəˈdʒenti/ former name (until 1927) of ◊Agrigento, a town in Sicily, Italy.

Girl Guides ◊Scout organization founded 1910 in the UK by Baden-Powell and his sister Agnes. There are three branches: Brownie Guides (age 7–11); Guides (10–16); Ranger Guides (14–20); and adult leaders—Guiders. The World Association of Girl Guides and Girl Scouts (as they are known in the US) has over 6.5 million members.

giro system of making payments by direct transfer between one bank or post-office account and another. It originated in Austria 1883, and the system was introduced in the UK 1968, the beginning of the present Girobank, set up by the Post Office.

Gironde /ʒɪˈrɒnd/ navigable estuary 80 km/50 mi long, formed by the mouths of the ◊Garonne, length 580 km/360 mi, and ◊Dordogne rivers, in SW France. The Lot, length 480 km/300 mi, is a tributary of the Garonne.

Girondin /dʒɪˈrɒndɪn/ member of the right-wing republican party in the French Revolution, so called because a number of their leaders came from the Gironde *département*. They were driven from power by the ◊Jacobins 1793.

Girtin /ˈgɜːtɪn/ Thomas 1775–1802. English painter of watercolour landscapes, a friend of J M W Turner.

Gisborne /ˈgɪzbən/ port on the E coast of North Island, New Zealand, exporting dairy products, wool and meat; population (1986) 32,200.

Giscard d'Estaing /ˈʒiːskɑː desˈtæŋ/ Valéry 1926– . French conservative politician, president 1974–81. He was finance minister to de Gaulle 1962–66 and Pompidou 1969–74. As leader of the Union pour la Démocratie Française, which he formed in 1978, Giscard has sought to project himself as leader of a 'new centre'.

Giscard was active in the wartime Resistance. After a distinguished academic career, he worked in the Ministry of Finance and entered the National

Assembly for Puy de Dôme in 1956 as an Independent Republican. After Pompidou's death he was narrowly elected president in 1974, in difficult economic circumstances; he was defeated by the socialist Mitterrand in 1981. He returned to the National Assembly in 1984. In 1989 he resigned from the National Assembly to play a leading role in the European Parliament.

Gish /gɪʃ/ Lillian. Stage name of Lillian de Guiche 1896– . US film actress, who began her career in silent films. Her most celebrated work was with the American director D W Griffith, including *Way Down East* 1920 and *Orphans of the Storm* 1922, playing virtuous heroines. She later made occasional appearances in character roles, as in *The Whales of August* 1987.

Gissing /ˈgɪsɪŋ/ George (Robert) 1857–1903. English writer, dealing with social issues. Among his books are *New Grub Street* 1891 and the autobiographical *Private Papers of Henry Ryecroft* 1903.

Giulini /dʒuːˈliːni/ Carlo Maria 1914– . Italian conductor. Principal conductor at La Scala in Milan 1953–55, and musical director of the Los Angeles Philharmonic 1978–84, he is renowned as an interpreter of Verdi.

Giulio /ˈdʒuːliəʊ/ Romano c.1499–1546. Italian painter and architect. An assistant to Raphael, he soon developed Mannerist tendencies, creating effects of exaggerated movement and using rich colours, for example in the Palazzo del Tè (1526, Mantua).

Giza, El /ˈgiːzə/ or **al-Jizah** site of the Great Pyramids and Sphinx, a suburb of ◊Cairo, Egypt; population (1983) 1,500,000. It has textile and film industries.

gizzard a muscular grinding organ of the digestive tract, below the ◊crop of birds, earthworms, and some insects, and forming part of the ◊stomach. The gizzard of birds is lined with a hardened horny layer of the protein keratin, preventing damage to the muscle layer during the grinding process. Most birds swallow sharp grit which aids maceration of food in the gizzard.

Glace Bay /gleɪs/ port on Cape Breton Island, Nova Scotia, Canada, centre of a coal-mining area; population (1986) 20,500.

glacier a body of ice, originating in mountains in snowfields above the snowline, which traverses land surfaces (glacier flow). It moves slowly down a valley or depression, and is constantly replenished from its source. The scenery produced by the erosive action of glaciers is characteristic and includes U-shaped valleys, ◊corries, ◊arêtes, and various features formed by the deposition of ◊moraine (rocky debris).

Glaciers form where annual snowfall exceeds annual melting and drainage. The snow compacts

Gladstone *19th-century British Liberal politician William Gladstone.*

to ice under the weight of the layers above. When a glacier moves over an uneven surface, deep crevasses are formed in the ice mass; if it reaches the sea or a lake, it breaks up to form icebergs. A glacier that is formed by one or several valley glaciers at the base of a mountain is called a *piedmont* glacier. A glacier that covers a large land surface or continent, for example Greenland or Antarctica, and flows outward in all directions is called an *ice sheet*.

gladiator in ancient Rome, a trained fighter, recruited mainly from slaves, criminals, and prisoners of war, who fought to the death in arenas for the entertainment of spectators. The custom, which originated in the practice of slaughtering slaves on a chieftain's grave, was introduced into Rome from Etruria in 264 BC and continued until the 5th century AD.

Gladiolus genus of S European and African cultivated perennials, family Iridaceae, with brightly coloured, funnel-shaped flowers, borne in a spike; the sword-like leaves spring from a corm.

Gladstone /ˈglædstən/ William Ewart 1809–1898. British Liberal politician. He entered Parliament as a Tory in 1833 and held ministerial office, but left the party 1846 and after 1859 identified himself with the Liberals. He was chancellor of the Exchequer 1852–55 and 1859–66, and prime minister 1868–74, 1880–85, 1886, and 1892–94. He introduced elementary education 1870 and vote by secret ballot 1872, and many reforms in Ireland, although he failed in his efforts to get a Home Rule Bill passed.

Gladstone was born in Liverpool, the son of a rich merchant. In Peel's government he was president of the Board of Trade 1843–45, and colonial secretary 1845–46. He left the Tory Party with the Peelite group in 1846. He was chancellor of the Exchequer in Aberdeen's government 1852–55, and in the Liberal governments of Palmerston and Russell 1859–66. In his first term as prime minister he carried through a series of important reforms, including the disestablishment of the Church of Ireland, the Irish Land Act, and the abolition of the purchase of army commissions and of religious tests in the universities.

During Disraeli's government of 1874–80 Gladstone strongly resisted his imperialist and pro-Turkish policy, not least because of Turkish pogroms against subject Christians, and by his Midlothian campaign of 1879 helped to overthrow Disraeli. Gladstone's second government carried the second Irish Land Act and the Reform Act 1884 but was confronted with difficult problems in

Ireland, Egypt, and South Africa, and lost prestige through its failure to relieve General ◊Gordon. Returning to office in 1886, Gladstone introduced his first Home Rule Bill, which was defeated by the secession of the Liberal Unionists, and he thereupon resigned. After six years' opposition he formed his last government; his second Home Rule Bill was rejected by the Lords, and in 1894 he resigned. He led a final crusade against the massacre of Armenian Christians in 1896.

Glamorgan /gləˈmɔːgən/ three counties of S Wales —◊Mid, ◊South, and ◊West Glamorgan – created in 1974 from the former county of Glamorganshire.

All are on the Bristol Channel, and the administrative headquarters of Mid and South Glamorgan is Cardiff; the headquarters of West Glamorgan is Swansea. *Mid Glamorgan*, which also takes in a small area of the former county of Monmouthshire to the east, contains the important coalmining towns of Aberdare and Merthyr Tydfil, and the Rhondda in the valleys. The mountains are in the northern part of the county; area 1,019 sq km/394 sq mi; population (1983) 536,400. In *South Glamorgan*, there is mixed farming in the fertile Vale of Glamorgan, and towns include Cardiff, Penarth, and Barry; area 416 sq km/161 sq mi; population (1983) 391,700. *West Glamorgan* includes Swansea, with tin-plating and copper industries, Margam, with large steel rolling mills, Port Talbot, and Neath; area 815 sq km/315 sq mi; population (1983) 366,600.

gland a specialized organ of the body that manufactures and secretes enzymes, hormones, or other chemicals. In animals, glands vary in size from small (for example, tear glands) to large (for example, the pancreas), but in plants they are always small, and may consist of a single cell. Some glands discharge their products internally (◊endocrine glands), and others externally (◊exocrine glands). Lymph nodes are sometimes wrongly called glands.

glandular fever or *infectious mononucleosis* viral disease characterized by fever and painfully swollen lymph nodes (in the neck); there may also be digestive upset, sore throat, and skin rashes. Lassitude persists and recovery is often very slow.

Glanville Ranalf died 1190. English ◊justiciar from 1180, and legal writer. His *Treatise on the Laws and Customs of England* 1188 was written to instruct practising lawyers and judges, and is now an important historical source on medieval common law.

Glaser /ˈgleɪzə/ Donald Arthur 1926– . US physicist, who invented the ◊bubble chamber in 1952, for which he received the Nobel prize in 1960.

Glasgow /ˈglæzgəʊ/ city and administrative headquarters of Strathclyde, Scotland; population (1985) 734,000. Industries include engineering, chemicals, printing, and distilling.

Buildings include the 12th-century cathedral of St Mungo, and the Cross Steeple (part of the historic Tolbooth); the universities of Glasgow, established 1451 (modern buildings by Sir Gilbert ◊Scott) and Strathclyde, established 1964; the Royal Exchange, the Stock Exchange, Kelvingrove Art Gallery (Impressionist collection); the Glasgow School of Art, designed by ◊Mackintosh; the Burrell Collection at Pollock Park, bequeathed by shipping magnate Sir William Burrell (1861–1958); Mitchell Library.

Glasgow /ˈglæzgəʊ/ Ellen 1873–1945. US novelist. Her books, set mainly in her native Virginia, often deal with the survival of tough heroines in a world of adversity. Among the best known are *Barren Ground* 1925, *The Sheltered Life* 1932, and *Vein of Iron* 1935.

Glashow /ˈglæʃəʊ/ Sheldon 1933– . US theoretical physicist. He shared the 1979 Nobel Prize for Physics with Abdus ◊Salam and Steven ◊Weinberg for their work demonstrating that weak nuclear force and the electromagnetic force are both aspects of a single force, now called *electroweak*

force. He also introduced the idea of ◊charm in particle physics.

glasnost (Russian 'openness') the Soviet leader Mikhail ◊Gorbachev's policy of liberalizing various aspects of Soviet life and opening up Soviet relations with Western countries.

Glasnost has involved the lifting of bans on many books, plays, and films, the release of political ◊dissidents, the tolerance of religious worship, a reappraisal of Soviet history (destalinization), the encouragement of investigative journalism to uncover political corruption, and the sanctioning of greater candour in the reporting of social problems and disasters (such as ◊Chernobyl).

glass a brittle, usually transparent or translucent substance which is physically neither a solid nor a liquid. Glass is made by fusing certain types of sand (silica); this fusion occurs naturally in volcanic glass (see ◊obsidian).

In the industrial production of common types of glass, the type of sand used, the particular chemicals added to it (for example lead, potassium, barium), and refinements of technique determine the type of glass produced. Types of glass include: soda glass; flint glass, used in cut-crystal ware; optical glass; stained glass; heat-resistant glass; glasses that exclude certain ranges of the light spectrum; blown glass, which is either blown individually from molten glass using a tube 1.5 m/4.5 ft long for expensive, crafted glass, or automatically blown into a mould, for example, light bulbs, and bottles; pressed glass, which is simply pressed into moulds, for jam jars, cheap vases, and light fittings; and sheet glass for windows, which is made by putting the molten glass through rollers to form a 'ribbon' or by floating molten glass on molten tin in the 'float glass' process.

Fibreglass is made from fine glass fibres. In bulk, it can be used as insulation material in construction work, woven into material, or made into glass-reinforced plastic (GRP). Fibreglass has good electrical, chemical, and weathering properties and it is also used for boat hulls, motor bodies, and aircraft components. See also ◊metallic glass.

Glass /glɑːs/ Philip 1937– . US composer. As a student of Nadia ◊Boulanger, he was strongly influenced by Indian music; his work is characterized by repeated rhythmic figures that are continually expanded and modified. His compositions include the operas *Einstein on the Beach* 1975, *Akhnaten* 1984, and *The Making of the Representative for Planet 8* 1988.

Glasse /glɑːs/ Hannah 1708–1770. British cookery writer whose *The Art of Cookery made Plain and Easy* 1747 is regarded as the first classic recipe book in Britain.

Glastonbury /ˈglæstənbəri/ market town in Somerset, England; population (1981) 6,773. Nearby are two excavated lake villages thought to have been occupied for about 150 years before the Romans came to Britain.

The first church on the site was traditionally founded in the 1st century by Joseph of Arimathea. The ruins of the Benedictine abbey built in the 10th–11th centuries by Dunstan and his followers were excavated in 1963 and the site of the grave of King Arthur and Queen Guinevere was thought to have been identified. One of Europe's largest pop festivals is held most years in June.

Glauber /ˈglaʊbə/ Johann 1604–1668. German chemist. Glauber, who made his living selling patent medicines, is remembered for his discovery of the salt known variously as 'sal mirabile' and 'Glauber's salt'.

The salt, sodium sulphate, is produced by the action of sulphuric acid on common salt, and was used by Glauber to treat almost any complaint.

Glauber's salt /ˈglaʊbəz/ in chemistry, crystalline sodium sulphate decahydrate $Na_2SO_4.10H_2O$, which melts at 31°C; the latent heat stored as it solidifies makes it a convenient thermal energy store. It is used in medicine.

glaucoma condition in which pressure inside the eye (intraocular pressure) is raised abnormally as excess fluid accumulates. It occurs when the normal flow of intraocular fluid out of the eye is interrupted. As pressure rises, the optic nerve suffers irreversible damage, leading to a reduction in the field of vision and, ultimately, loss of eyesight.

The most common type, **chronic glaucoma**, usually affects people over the age of 40, when the trabecular meshwork (the filtering tissue at the margins of the eye) becomes blocked and drainage slows down. The condition cannot be cured, but, in many cases, it is controlled by drug therapy. Laser treatment to the trabecular meshwork often improves drainage for a time; surgery to create an artificial channel for fluid to leave the eye offers more long-term relief. A tiny window may be cut in the iris during the same operation.

Acute glaucoma is a medical emergency. A sudden, precipitous rise in pressure occurs when the trabecular meshwork becomes occluded (blocked). This is treated surgically to remove the cause of the obstruction. Acute glaucoma is extremely painful. Treatment is required urgently as damage to the optic nerve begins within hours of onset.

glaze a transparent vitreous coating for pottery and porcelain.

Glencoe /glen'kəu/ glen in ◊Strathclyde region, Scotland, where members of the Macdonald clan were massacred in 1692. John Campbell, Earl of Breadalbane, was the chief instigator. It is now a winter sports area.

Glendower /glen'dauə/ Owen c.1359–1415. Welsh leader of a revolt against the English in N Wales, who defeated Henry IV in three campaigns 1400–02, although Wales was reconquered 1405–13.

Glendower, Sons of Welsh *Meibion Glyndwr* anonymous group, taking its name from Owen Glendower, active from 1979 against England's treatment of Wales as a colonial possession. Houses owned by English people in the principality and offices of estate agents dealing in them are targets for arson or bombing.

Gleneagles /glen'i:gəlz/ glen in Tayside, Scotland, famous for its golf course and for the *Gleneagles Agreement*, formulated in 1977 at the Gleneagles Hotel by Commonwealth heads of government, that 'every practical step (should be taken) to discourage contact or competition by their nationals' with South Africa, in opposition to apartheid.

Glenn /glen/ John (Herschel) 1921– . US astronaut and politician. On 20 Feb 1962, he became the first American to orbit the Earth, three times in the Mercury spacecraft Friendship 7, in a flight lasting 4 hr 55 min. After retiring from ◊NASA, he became a senator for Ohio 1974 and 1980, and unsuccessfully sought the Democratic presidential nomination 1984.

Glenrothes /glen'rɒθɪs/ town and administrative headquarters of Fife, Scotland, 10 km/6 mi N of Kirkcaldy, developed as a 'new town' from 1948; population (1981) 32,700. Industries include electronics, plastics, and paper.

gliding the art of using air currents to fly unpowered aircraft. Technically, gliding involves the gradual loss of altitude; gliders designed for soaring flight (utilizing air rising up a cliff face or hill, warm air rising as a 'thermal' above sun-heated ground, and so on) are known as sail-planes. The sport of ◊hang gliding was developed in the 1970s.

Pioneers include George ◊Cayley, Otto ◊Lilienthal, Octave Chanute (1832–1910), and the ◊Wright brothers, the latter perfecting gliding technique in 1902. The British Gliding Association dates from 1929. Launching may be by rubber catapault from a hilltop; by a winch which raises the glider like a kite; or by aircraft tow. In World War II towed troop-carrying gliders were used by the Germans in Crete and the Allies at Arnhem.

Gloucestershire

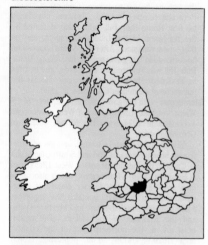

gliding tone a musical tone, continuously rising or falling in pitch between preset notes, produced by a synthesizer.

Glinka /'glɪŋkə/ Mikhail Ivanovich 1804–1857. Russian composer. He broke away from the prevailing Italian influence and turned to Russian folk music as the inspiration for his opera *A Life for the Tsar* (originally *Ivan Susanin*) 1836. His later works include another opera, *Ruslan and Lyudmila* 1842, and the orchestral *Kamarinskaya* 1848.

glissando in music, a rapid uninterrupted scale produced by sliding the finger across the keys or strings.

Glittertind /'glɪtətɪn/ the highest mountain in Norway, rising to 2,470 m/8,110 ft in the Jotunheim range.

Gliwice /glɪ'vi:tseɪ/ city in Katowice region, S Poland, formerly in German Silesia; population (1985) 213,000. It has coal-mining, iron, steel, and electrical industries. It is connected to the river Oder by the Gliwice Canal.

globefish another name for ◊puffer fish.

global warming another name for the ◊greenhouse effect, the rise in the Earth's average overall temperature resulting from the build-up of carbon dioxide, methane, and other 'greenhouse gases' in the atmosphere due to human actions.

Globe Theatre a London theatre, octagonal and open to the sky, near Bankside, Southwark, where many of Shakespeare's plays were performed by Richard Burbage and his company. Built 1599 by Cuthbert Burbage, it was burned down 1613 after a cannon, fired during a performance of Henry VIII, set light to the thatch. It was rebuilt in 1614 but pulled down in 1644. The site was rediscovered Oct 1989 near the remains of the contemporary Rose Theatre.

In 1987 planning permission was granted to the US film producer Sam Wanamaker (1919–) to build a working replica of the theatre on its original site.

globular cluster a spherical ◊star cluster of between 10,000 and a million stars. More than a hundred globular clusters are distributed in a spherical halo around our Galaxy. They consist of old stars, formed early in our Galaxy's history. Globular clusters are also found around other galaxies.

glockenspiel musical percussion instrument of light metal keys mounted on a carrying frame for use in military bands, or like a small xylophone for use in an orchestra.

Glomma /'glɒmə/ or **Glama** river in Norway, 570 km/350 mi long. The largest river in Scandinavia, it flows into the Skageak at Frederikstad.

Glos abbreviation for ◊*Gloucestershire*.

Gloucester /'glɒstə/ city, port, and administrative headquarters of Gloucestershire, England; population (1983) 92,200. Industries include the manufacture of aircraft and agricultural machinery. Its 11th–14th-century cathedral has a Norman nucleus and additions in every style of Gothic.

Gloucester /'glɒstə/ Richard Alexander Walter George, Duke of Gloucester 1944– . Prince of the UK. Grandson of ◊George V, he succeeded his father to the dukedom owing to the death of his elder brother Prince William (1941–72) in an air crash. He married in 1972 Birgitte van Deurs, daughter of a Danish lawyer. His heir is his son Alexander, Earl of Ulster (1974–).

Gloucestershire /'glɒstəʃə/ county in SW England

area 2,640 sq km/1,019 sq mi

towns administrative headquarters Gloucester; Stroud, Cheltenham, Tewkesbury, Cirencester

features Cotswold Hills; river Severn and tributaries; Berkeley Castle, where ◊Edward II was murdered; Prinknash Abbey, famous for pottery; Cotswold Farm Park, near Stow-on-the Wold, for rare and ancient breeds of farm animals

products cereals, fruit, dairy products; engineering, coal in the Forest of Dean

population (1987) 522,000

famous people Edward Jenner.

glove box a form of protection used when handling certain dangerous materials, such as radioactive substances. Gloves fixed to ports in the walls of a box allow manipulation of objects within the box. The risk that the operator might inhale fine airborne particles of poisonous materials is removed by maintaining a vacuum inside the box, so that any airflow is inwards.

glow-worm the wingless female of various luminous beetles in the family Lampyridae. The luminous organs situated under the abdomen usually serve to attract winged males for mating. There are about 2,000 species, distributed throughout the tropics, Europe, and N Asia.

Glozel /glə'zel/ archaeological site in a village near Vichy, France. A find here in 1924 was attacked as a hoax because of the disparate age of the objects. It included bones with drawings of animals 10,000 BC, axes 4000–2000 BC, inscribed clay tablets 700 BC–AD 100, and a glass kiln, possibly medieval. Thermoluminescence analysis in 1975–76 suggested the objects are genuine.

Glubb /glʌb/ John Bagot 1897–1986. British soldier, founder of the modern Arab Legion (the Jordanian army), which he commanded 1939–56.

Gluck /glʊk/ Christoph Willibald von 1714–1787. German composer who settled in Vienna as Kapellmeister to Maria Theresa in 1754. In 1762 his *Orfeo ed Euridice/Orpheus and Eurydice* revolutionized the 18th-century conception of opera by giving free scope to dramatic effect. *Orfeo* was followed by *Alceste/Alcestis* 1767 and *Paris ed Elena/Paris and Helen* 1770.

Born in Erasbach, Bavaria, he studied music at Prague, Vienna, and Milan, went to London in 1745 to compose operas for the Haymarket, but returned to Vienna in 1746 where he was knighted by the Pope. In 1762 his *Iphigénie en Aulide/Iphigenia in Aulis* 1774, produced in Paris, gave rise to controversy in which Gluck had the support of Marie Antoinette while his Italian rival Piccinni had the support of Madame Du Barry. With *Armide* 1777 and *Iphigénie en Tauride/Iphigenia in Tauris* 1779 Gluck won a complete victory over Piccinni.

glucose $C_6H_{12}O_6$ a type of sugar or carbohydrate also known as *grape-sugar* or *dextrose*. It is present in the blood, and is found in honey and fruit juices. It is a source of energy for the body, being produced from other sugars and starches to form the 'energy currency' of many biochemical reactions also involving ◊ATP.

It is usually prepared by hydrolysis from cane sugar or starch. Generally a yellowish syrup, it may be purified to a white crystalline powder. Glucose is a monosaccharide (made up of a single sugar unit).

glue a kind of ◊adhesive.

glue sniffing or *solvent abuse* the inhalation of organic solvents of the type found in paints, lighter fuel, and glue, for its hallucinatory effects. As well as being addictive, solvents are dangerous for their effects upon the user's liver, heart, and lungs. It is believed that solvents produce hallucinations by dissolving the cell membrane of brain cells, thus altering the way the cells conduct electrical impulses.

gluon type of ◊elementary particle.

glut an excess of goods in a market. A glut of agricultural produce often follows an exceptional harvest, causing prices to fall unless there is some form of intervention in the market.

glyceride an ◊ester formed between one or more acids and glycerol (propan-1,2,3-triol). A glyceride is termed mono-, di-, or triglyceride, depending on the number of hydroxyl groups from the glycerol that have reacted with the acids. Glycerides, mainly triglycerides, occur naturally as esters of ◊fatty acids in animal and plant oils and fats.

glycerine common name for glycerol, or *trihydroxypropane* $HOCH_2CH(OH)CH_2OH$ a thick, colourless, odourless, sweetish liquid. It is obtained from vegetable and animal oils and fats (by treatment with acid, alkali, superheated steam, or an enzyme), or by fermentation of glucose, and is used in the manufacture of high explosives, in antifreeze solutions, to maintain moist conditions in fruits and tobacco, and in cosmetics.

glycerol another name for ◊glycerine.

glycine $CH_2(NH_2)COOH$ the simplest amino acid, and one of the main components of proteins. When purified, it is a sweet, colourless crystalline compound.

glycogen polymer (a polysaccharide) of the sugar ◊glucose, made and retained in the liver as a carbohydrate store, for which reason it is sometimes called animal starch. It is a source of energy when needed by muscles, where it is converted back into glucose by the hormone ◊insulin and metabolized.

glycol common name for *dihydroxyethane* a thick, colourless, odourless, sweetish liquid also called ethylene glycol or ethanediol $(CH_2OH)_2$. Glycol is used in antifreeze solutions, in the preparation of ethers and esters, especially for explosives, as a solvent, and as a substitute for glycerine.

Glyndebourne /'glaɪndbɔːn/ site of an opera house in East Sussex, England, established in 1934 by John Christie (1882–1962). Operas are staged at an annual summer festival and a touring company is also based there.

GMT abbreviation for ◊Greenwich Mean Time.

gnat small fly, especially of the family Culicidae, the mosquitoes. The eggs are laid in water, where they hatch into worm-like larvae, which pass through a pupal stage to emerge as adults insects.

Species include *Culex pipiens*, abundant in England; the carrier of malaria *Anopheles maculipennis*; and the banded mosquito *Aedes aegypti*, which transmits yellow fever. Only the female is capable of drawing blood, since the male possesses no piercing mandibles.

gneiss a coarse-grained ◊metamorphic rock, formed under conditions of increasing temperature and pressure, and often occurring in association with schists and granites. It has a foliated, laminated structure, consisting of thin bands of micas and amphiboles alternating with granular bands of quartz and feldspar. Gneisses are formed during regional metamorphism; *paragneisses* are derived from sedimentary rocks and *orthogneisses* from igneous rocks. Garnets are often found in gneiss.

gnome in fairy tales, a small, mischievous spirit of the earth. The males are bearded, wear tunics and hoods, and often guard an underground treasure. The *garden gnome*, an ornamental representation of these spirits, was first was brought from Germany to England in 1850 by Sir Charles Isham for his mansion, Lamport Hall, Northamptonshire.

Gnosticism esoteric cult of divine knowledge (a synthesis of Christianity, Greek philosophy, Hinduism, Buddhism, and the mystery cults of the Mediterranean), which was a rival to, and influence, on early Christianity. The medieval French ◊Cathar and the modern *Mandean* sects (in S Iraq) descend from Gnosticism.

Gnostic 4th-century codices discovered in Egypt in the 1940s include the *Gospel of St Thomas* (unconnected with the disciple), a collection of 114 of Jesus's sayings, probably originating about AD 135. Gnosticism envisaged the world as a series of emanations from the highest of several gods, emphasized the distinction between spirit (good) and matter (evil), gave women cult-equality with men, and opposed private property.

GNP abbreviation for ◊*Gross National Product*.

gnu African antelope, also known as *wildebeest*, with a cow-like face, a beard, and mane, and heavy curved horns in both sexes. The body is up to 1.3 m/4.2 ft at the shoulder and slopes away to the hindquarters.

The *brindled gnu Connochaetes taurinus* is silver-grey with dark face, mane and tail tuft, and occurs from Kenya southwards. Vast herds move together on migration. The *white-tailed gnu Connochaetes gnou* of South Africa almost became extinct, but was saved by breeding on farms.

go game originating in China 3,000 years ago, and now the national game of Japan. It is played by placing small stones on a large grid. The object is to win territory and eventual superiority.

The board, squared off by 19 horizontal and 19 vertical lines, begins empty and gradually fills up with black and white flattish, rounded stones, as the players win territory by surrounding areas of the board with 'men' and capturing the enemy armies by surrounding them. A handicapping system enables expert and novice to play against each other. It is far more complex and subtle than chess, the mathematical possibilities being 10 to the power of 720.

Goa state of India
area 3,700 sq km/1,428 sq mi
capital Panaji
population (1981) 1,003,000
history Goa was captured by the Portuguese 1510, and the inland area was added in the 18th century. Goa was incorporated into India as a Union Territory with ◊Daman and ◊Diu 1961, and became a state 1987.

goat ruminant mammal, genus *Capra*, family Bovidae, closely related to the sheep. Both males and females have horns and beards. They are sure-footed animals, and feed on shoots and leaves more than grass.

Domestic varieties are kept for milk, or for mohair (the angora and cashmere). Wild species include the *ibex Capra ibex* of the Alps, and *markhor Capra falconeri* of the Himalayas, 1 m/3 ft high and with long twisted horns. The *Rocky mountain goat Oreamnos americanus* is a 'goat-antelope' and not closely related to true goats.

Gobbi /'gɒbi/ Tito 1913–1984. Italian baritone singer renowned for his opera characterizations of Figaro, Scarpia, and Iago.

Gobelins /'gəʊbəlæn/ French tapestry factory, originally founded as a dyeworks in Paris by Gilles and Jean Gobelin about 1450. The firm began to produce tapestries in the 16th century, and in 1662 the establishment was bought by Colbert for Louis XIV. With the support of the French government, it continues to make tapestries.

Gobi /'gəʊbi/ Asian desert divided between the Mongolian People's Republic and Inner Mongolia, China; 800 km/500 mi N–S, and 1,600 km/1,000 mi E–W. It is rich in fossil remains of extinct species.

Gobind Singh /'gəʊbɪnd 'sɪŋ/ 1666–1708. Indian religious leader, the tenth and last guru (teacher) of Sikhism, 1675–1708, and founder of the Sikh brotherhood known as the ◊Khalsa. On his death

the Sikh holy book, the *Guru Granth Sahib*, replaced the line of human gurus as the teacher and guide of the Sikh community.

God the concept of a supreme being, a unique creative entity, basic to several religions (for example Judaism, Islam, Christianity). In many cultures (for example Norse, Roman, Greek), the term 'god' refers to an abstract concept of one of several supernatural beings, the force behind an aspect of life, or a personification of that force (for example Neptune, Roman god of the sea).

Since the 17th century, advances in science and the belief that the only valid statements were those verifiable by the senses have had a complex influence on belief in God. *Monotheism* is the belief in one god; *polytheism* is the belief in more than one god; other ideas about God are ◊deism, ◊theism, and ◊pantheism.

Godalming /'gɒdlmɪŋ/ town in Surrey, England; population (1981) 18,200. Industries include engineering and textiles.

Godard /'gɒdɑː/ Jean-Luc 1930– . French film director, one of the leaders of ◊new wave cinema. His works are often characterized by experimental editing techniques and an unconventional dramatic form. His films include *A bout de souffle/Breathless* 1960, *Weekend* 1968, and *Je vous salue, Marie* 1985.

Godavari /gəʊ'dɑːvəri/ river in central India, flowing from the Western Ghats to the Bay of Bengal; length 1,450 km/900 mi. It is sacred to Hindus.

Goddard /'gɒdəd/ Robert Hutchings 1882–1945. US rocket pioneer. His first liquid-fuelled rocket was launched at Auburn, Massachusetts, USA, Mar 1926. By 1935 his rockets had gyroscopic control and carried cameras to record instrument readings. Two years later a Goddard rocket gained the world altitude record with an ascent of 3 km/1.9 mi.

Gödel /'gɜːdl/ Kurt 1906–1978. Austrian-born US mathematician and philosopher, who proved that a mathematical system always contains statements that can be neither proved nor disproved within the system; in other words, as a science, mathematics can never be totally consistent and totally complete. He worked on relativity, constructing a mathematical model of the Universe that made travel back through time theoretically possible.

Godfrey de Bouillon /'gɒdfri də buː'jɒn/ *c.*1060–1100. French crusader, second son of Count Eustace II of Boulogne. He and his brothers (◊Baldwin and Eustace) led 40,000 Germans in the First Crusade 1096. When Jerusalem was taken 1099, he was elected its ruler, but refused the title of king. After his death, Baldwin was elected king.

Godiva /gə'daɪvə/ Lady *c.*1040–1080. Wife of Leofric, earl of Mercia (died 1057). Legend has it that her husband promised to reduce the heavy taxes on the people of Coventry if she rode naked through the streets at noon. Everyone remained indoors, but 'Peeping Tom' bored a hole in his shutters, and was struck blind.

God Save the King/Queen British national anthem. The melody resembles a composition by John Bull (1563–1628) and similar words are found from the 16th century. In its present form it dates from the 1745 Rebellion, when it was used as an anti-Jacobite Party song. In the USA the song 'America', with the first line, 'My country, 'tis of thee' is sung to the same tune.

Godthaab /'gɒdhɔːb/ (Greenlandic *Nuuk*) capital and largest town of Greenland; population (1982) 9,700. It is a storage centre for oil and gas, and the chief industry is fish processing.

Godunov /'gɒdənɒv/ Boris 1552–1605. Tsar of Russia from 1598. He was assassinated by a pretender to the throne. The legend that has grown up around this forms the basis of Pushkin's play *Boris Godunov* 1831 and Mussorgsky's opera of the same name 1874.

Boris Godunov was elected after the death of Fyodor I, son of Ivan the Terrible. He died during a revolt led by one who professed to be Dmitri, a brother of Fyodor and the rightful heir. The true Dmitri, however, had died in 1591 by cutting his own throat during an epileptic fit. An apocryphal story of Boris killing the true Dmitri to gain the throne was fostered by Russian historians anxious to discredit Boris because he was not descended from the main ruling families.

Godunov's rule was marked by a strengthening of the Russian church, but was also the beginning of the Time of Troubles, a period of instability.

Godwin /'gɒdwɪn/ died 1053. Earl of Wessex from 1020. He secured the succession to the throne in 1042 of ◊Edward the Confessor, to whom he married his daughter Edith, and whose chief minister he became. King Harold II was his son.

Godwin /'gɒdwɪn/ William 1756–1836. English philosopher, novelist, and father of Mary Shelley. His *Enquiry Concerning Political Justice* 1793 advocated an anarchic society based on a faith in people's essential rationality. At first a Nonconformist minister, he later became an atheist. His first wife was Mary ◊Wollstonecraft.

Goebbels /'gɜ:bəlz/ Paul Josef 1897–1945. German Nazi leader. He was born in the Rhineland, became a journalist, joined the Nazi party in its early days, and was given control of its propaganda 1929. As minister of propaganda from 1933, he brought all cultural and educational activities under Nazi control, and built up sympathetic movements abroad to carry on the 'war of nerves' against Hitler's intended victims. On the capture of Berlin by the Allies he poisoned himself.

Goehr /gɜ:/ (Peter) Alexander 1932– . British composer, born in Berlin. A lyrical but often hard-edged serialist, he nevertheless usually remained within the forms of the symphony and traditional chamber works, and more recently turned to tonal and even Neo-Baroque models.

Goeppert-Mayer /'gɜ:upətmaɪə/ Maria 1906–1972. US physicist who worked mainly on the structure of the atomic nucleus. She shared the 1963 Nobel physics prize with ◊Wigner and Jensen.

Born in Germany, she emigrated to the USA in 1931. By 1948 she had managed to explain the stability of particular atoms. Atomic nuclei were seen as shell-like layers of protons and neutons with the most stable atoms having completely filled outermost shells.

Goering /'gɜ:rɪŋ/ Hermann 1893–1946. German field marshal from 1938 and Nazi leader. Goering was part of Hitler's 'inner circle', and with Hitler's rise to power 1933, established the Gestapo and concentration camps. Appointed successor to Hitler 1939, he built a vast economic empire in occupied Europe, but later lost favour, and was expelled from the party 1945. Tried at Nuremberg, he poisoned himself before he could be executed.

Goering was born in Bavaria. He was a renowned fighter pilot in World War I, and joined the Nazi party 1922. He was elected to the Reichstag 1928, and became its president 1932. As commissioner for aviation from 1933 he built up the ◊Luftwaffe. In 1936 he became plenipotentiary of the four-year plan for war preparations.

Goes /xu:s/ Hugo van der died 1482. Flemish painter, chiefly active in Ghent. His *Portinari altarpiece* about 1475 (Uffizi, Florence) is a huge oil painting of the Nativity, full of symbolism and naturalistic detail, and the *Death of the Virgin* about 1480 (Musée Communale des Beaux Arts, Bruges) is remarkable for the varied expressions on the faces of the apostles.

Goethe /'gɜ:tə/ Johann Wolfgang von 1749–1832. German poet, novelist, and dramatist, the founder of modern German literature, and leader of the Romantic ◊*Sturm und Drang* movement. His works include the autobiographical *Die Leiden des Jungen Werthers*/*The Sorrows of the Young Werther* 1774 and *Faust* 1808, his masterpiece. A visit to Italy 1786–88 inspired the classical dramas

Gogh Self-Portrait with Bandaged Ear *(1889) Courtauld Galleries, London*

Iphigenie auf Tauris/*Iphigenia in Tauris* 1787 and *Tasso* 1790.

Born at Frankfurt-am-Main, Goethe studied law. Inspired by Shakespeare, to whose work he was introduced by ◊Herder, he wrote the play *Götz von Berlichingen* 1773. *The Sorrows of the Young Werther* 1774 and the poetic play *Faust* 1808 made him a European figure. He was prime minister at the court of Weimar 1775–85. Other works include the *Wilhelm Meister* novels 1796–1829. He was a friend of ◊Schiller. Many of his lyrics were set to music.

Goffman /'gɒfmən/ Erving 1922–1982. Canadian social scientist. He studied the ways people try to create, present, and defend a particular self-image and the social structures surrounding, controlling, and defining human interaction. Works include *The Presentation of Self in Everyday Life* 1956 and *Gender Advertisements* 1979.

Gogh /gɒx/ Vincent van 1853–1890. Dutch painter, a Post-Impressionist. He tried various careers, including preaching, and began painting in the 1880s. He met ◊Gauguin in Paris, and when he settled in Arles, Provence, 1888, Gauguin joined him there. After a quarrel van Gogh cut off part of his own earlobe, and in 1889 he entered an asylum; the following year he committed suicide. The Arles paintings vividly testify to his intense emotional involvement in his art; among the best known are *The Yellow Chair* and several *Sunflowers* 1888 (National Gallery, London).

Born in Zundert, van Gogh worked for a time as a schoolmaster in England before he took up painting. He studied under Van Mauve at The Hague. One of the leaders of the Post-Impressionist painters, he executed still-lifes and landscapes, one of the best-known being *A Cornfield with Cypresses* 1889 (National Gallery, London).

Gogol /'gɒugɒl/ Nicolai Vasilyevich 1809–1852. Russian writer. His first success was a collection of stories, *Evenings on a Farm near Dikanka* 1831–32, followed by *Mirgorod* 1835. Later works include *Arabesques* 1835, the comedy play *The Inspector General* 1836, and the picaresque novel *Dead Souls* 1842, depicting Russian provincial society.

Born near Poltava, Gogol tried several careers before entering the St Petersburg Civil Service. From 1835 he travelled in Europe, and it was in Rome that he completed the earlier part of *Dead Souls* 1842. Other works include the short story 'The Overcoat'.

Gogra /'gɒgrə/ alternative transcription of river ◊Ghaghara in India.

goitre enlargement of the thyroid gland seen as a swelling on the neck. It is most pronounced in simple goitre, which is caused by iodine deficiency. Much more common is toxic goitre

goldcrest

(◊thyrotoxicosis), caused by over-activity of the thyroid gland.

Gokhale /gəu'ka:li/ Gopal Krishna 1866–1915. Indian political adviser and friend of Mohandas Gandhi, leader of the Moderate group in the Indian National Congress before World War I.

Golan Heights /'gəulæn/ (Arabic *Jawlan*) plateau on the Syrian border with Israel, bitterly contested in the ◊Arab-Israeli Wars, and annexed by Israel on 14 Dec 1981.

gold a heavy, precious, yellow metallic element; symbol Au, atomic number 79, atomic weight 197.0. It is unaffected by temperature changes and is highly resistant to acids. For manufacture, gold is alloyed with another strengthening metal, its purity being measured in ◊carats on a scale of 24. In 1988 the three leading gold-producing countries were: South Africa, 621 tonnes; USA, 205 tonnes; and Australia, 152 tonnes.

Gold occurs naturally in veins, but following erosion it can be transported and redeposited. It has long been valued for its durability, malleability, and ductility, and its uses include dentistry, jewellery, and electronic devices.

Gold Coast /'gəuld kəust/ the former name for ◊Ghana, but historically the W coast of Africa from Cape Three Points to the Volta river, where alluvial gold is washed down. Portuguese and French navigators visited this coast in the 14th century, and a British trading settlement developed into the colony of the Gold Coast 1618. With its dependencies of Ashanti and Northern Territories plus the trusteeship territory of Togoland, it became Ghana 1957. The name is also used for many coastal resort areas; for example, in Queensland, Australia, and Florida, USA.

Gold Coast /'gəuld kəust/ resort region on the east coast of Australia, stretching 32 km/20 mi along the coast of Queensland and New South Wales south of Brisbane; population (1986) 219,000.

goldcrest smallest British bird, *Regulus regulus*, about 9 cm/3.5 in long. It is olive green, with a bright yellow streak across the crown. This warbler builds its nest in conifers.

Golden Ass, The or ***Metamorphoses*** a ◊picaresque adventure by the Roman writer Lucius Apuleius, written about AD 160, sometimes called the world's first novel. Lucius, turned into an ass, describes his exploits with a band of robbers, weaving into the narrative several ancient legends, including that of Cupid and Psyche.

Golden Calf in the Old Testament, image made by ◊Aaron in response to the request of the Israelites for a god, when they despaired of Moses' return from Mount Sinai.

Golden Fleece in Greek mythology, fleece of the winged ram Chrysomallus, which hung on an oak tree at Colchis guarded by a dragon. It was stolen by Jason and the Argonauts.

Golden Gate /'gəuldən geɪt/ strait in California, USA, linking ◊San Francisco Bay with the Pacific, spanned by a bridge which was completed 1937. The longest span is 1,280 m/4,200 ft.

Golden Horde the invading Mongol-Tatar army that first terrorized Europe from 1237 under the leadership of Batu Khan, a grandson of Genghis Khan. Tamerlane broke their power 1395, and ◊Ivan III ended Russia's payment of tribute to them 1480.

goldenrod tall, leafy perennial *Solidago virgaurea*, family Compositae, native to North America. It produces heads of many small, yellow flowers.

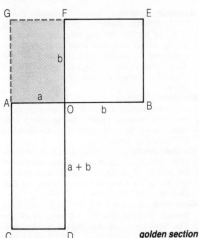

golden section

golden section visually satisfying ratio, first constructed by the Greek mathematician ◊Euclid and used in art and architecture. It is found by dividing a line AB at a point O such that the rectangle produced by the whole line and one of the segments is equal to the square drawn on the other segment. The ratio of the two segments is about 8:13 or 1:1.168, and a rectangle whose sides are in this ratio is called a **golden rectangle.**

In van Gogh's picture *Mother and Child*, for example, the Madonna's face fits perfectly into a golden rectangle.

goldfinch songbird *Carduelis carduelis* commonly found in Europe, W Asia, and N Africa. It is black, white, and red about the head, with gold and black wings.

goldfish fish of the carp family *Carassius auratus* found in E Asia. Greenish-brown in its natural state, it has for centuries been bred by the Chinese, taking on highly coloured and freakishly shaped forms.

Golding /'gəʊldɪŋ/ William 1911– . English novelist. His first book, *Lord of the Flies* 1954, was about savagery taking over among a group of English schoolboys marooned on a Pacific island. Later novels include *The Spire* 1964, *Rites of Passage* 1980, and *The Paper Men* 1984. Nobel prize 1983.

Goldoni /gɒl'dəʊni/ Carlo 1707–1793. Italian dramatist, born in Venice. He wrote popular comedies for the Sant'Angelo theatre, including *La putta onorata/The Respectable Girl* 1749, *I pettegolezzi delle donne/Women's Gossip* 1750, and *La locandiera/Mine Hostess* 1753. In 1761 he moved to Paris, where he directed the Italian theatre and wrote more plays, including *L'Eventail/The Fan* 1763.

gold rush a large-scale influx of gold prospectors to an area where gold deposits have recently been discovered. The result is a dramatic increase in population. Cities such as Johannesburg, Melbourne, and San Francisco either originated or were considerably enlarged by gold rushes.

famous gold rushes

1848 Sutter's Mill, California (the 'Fortyniners')
1851 New South Wales and Victoria, Australia
1880s Rhodesia
1886 Fortymile Creek, Yukon, Canada; Johannesburg, Transvaal; Kimberley, West Australia
1890s Klondike River, Yukon, Canada

Goldsmith /'gəʊldsmɪθ/ Jerrald ('Jerry') 1930– . US composer of film music who originally worked in radio and television. His prolific output includes *Planet of the Apes* 1968, *The Wind and the Lion* 1975, *The Omen* 1976, and *Gremlins* 1984.

Goldsmith /'gəʊldsmɪθ/ Oliver 1728–1774. Irish writer, whose works include the novel *The Vicar of Wakefield* 1766, the poem *The Deserted Village* 1770, and the play *She Stoops to Conquer* 1773. He was a member of ◊Johnson's Literary Club.

Goldwyn *US film producer Sam Goldwyn became one the most powerful people in Hollywood during its golden age.*

Goldsmith was the son of a clergyman. He was educated at Trinity College, Dublin, and Edinburgh, where he studied medicine 1752. After travelling extensively in Europe, he returned to England and became a hack writer, producing many works, including *History of England and Animated Nature* 1774. His earliest work of literary importance was *The Citizen of the World* 1762, a series of letters by an imaginary Chinese traveller. In 1761 Goldsmith met Johnson, and became a member of his 'club'. In 1764 he published the poem *The Traveller*, and followed it with collected essays 1765. *The Vicar of Wakefield* was sold (according to Johnson's account) to save him from imprisonment for debt.

gold standard system under which a country's currency is exchangeable for a fixed weight of gold on demand at the central bank. It was almost universally applied 1870–1914, but by 1937 no single country was on the full gold standard. Britain abandoned the gold standard 1931; the USA abandoned it 1971. Holdings of gold are still retained because it is an internationally recognized commodity, which cannot be legislated upon or manipulated by interested countries.

The gold standard broke down in World War I, and attempted revivals were undermined by the Great Depression. After World War II the par

Goldsmith *18th-century writer Oliver Goldsmith.*

values of the currency units of the ◊International Monetary Fund (which includes nearly all members of the United Nations not in the Soviet bloc) were fixed in terms of gold and the US and East European dollar, but by 1976 floating exchange rates (already unofficially operating from 1971) were legalized.

Goldwater /'gəʊld.wɔːtə/ Barry 1909– . US Republican politician, presidential candidate in the 1964 election, when he was heavily defeated by Lyndon Johnson. Many of Goldwater's ideas were later adopted by the Republican right and the Reagan administration.

Goldwyn /'gəʊldwɪn/ Samuel 1882–1974. US film producer. Born in Warsaw, he emigrated to the USA 1896. He founded the Goldwyn Pictures Corporation 1917, precursor of the Metro-Goldwyn-Mayer Company 1925, later allied with United Artists. He was famed for his illogical aphorisms known as 'goldwynisms', for example 'Anyone who visits a psychiatrist should have his head examined'.

golf outdoor game in which a small rubber-cored ball is hit with a club (either wooden-faced or iron-faced). The club faces have varying angles and are styled for different types of shot. The ball is hit from a tee, which elevates the ball slightly off the ground, and the object of the game is to put the ball in a hole than can be anywhere between 90 m/100 yd and 457 m/500 yd away, using the least number of strokes.

Most courses consist of 18 holes and are approximately 5,500 m/6,000 yd in length. Each hole is made up of distinct areas: the **tee**, from where plays start at each hole; the **green**, a finely manicured area in which is positioned the hole; the **fairway**, the grassed area between the tee and the green, not cut as finely as the green; and the **rough**, the perimeter of the fairway, which is left to grow naturally. Natural hazards like trees, bushes, and streams make play more difficult, and there are additional hazards in the form of sand-filled bunkers.

Golf is played in two principal forms. In **stroke play** (also known as **medal play**), the lowest aggregate score for a round determines the winner. Play may be over more than one round, in which case the aggregate score for all rounds counts. In **match play**, the object is to win holes by scoring less than your opponent(s). Equal scores on a hole is a half and neither player receives any score. Golf's handicap system allows for golfers of all levels to compete on equal terms.

The exact origin of golf is unknown, but it was certainly played in Scotland in the 15th century. The Royal & Ancient Golf Club at St Andrews dates from 1754. Major golfing events include the British and US Opens, US Masters, US Professional Golfers Association (PGA), World Match-Play Championship, and British PGA. There are golf tours in North America, Europe, and Japan.

Winners of the British Open include Tom Morris (junior and senior), James Braid, Harry Vardon, J H Taylor (all UK), Walter Hagen, Bobby Jones, Ben Hogan, Jack Nicklaus, Arnold Palmer, Tom Watson (all USA), Gary Player (South Africa), and Severiano Ballesteros (Spain).

Golf: recent winners

British Open first held 1860
1980: Tom Watson, USA
1981: Bill Rogers, USA
1982: Tom Watson, USA
1983: Tom Watson, USA
1984: Severiano Ballesteros, Spain
1985: Sandy Lyle, Great Britain
1986: Greg Norman, Australia
1987: Nick Faldo, Great Britain
1988: Severiano Ballesteros, Spain
1989: Mark Calcavecchia, USA
US Open first held 1895
1980: Jack Nicklaus, USA
1981: David Graham, Australia
1982: Tom Watson, USA

1983: Larry Nelson, USA
1984: Fuzzy Zoeller, USA
1985: Andy North, USA
1986: Ray Floyd, USA
1987: Scott Simpson, USA
1988: Curtis Strange, USA
1989 Curtis Strange, USA
Masters first held 1934
1980: Severiano Ballesteros, Spain
1981: Tom Watson, USA
1982: Craig Stadler, USA
1983: Severiano Ballesteros, Spain
1984: Ben Crenshaw, USA
1985: Bernhard Langer, West Germany
1986: Jack Nicklaus, USA
1987: Larry Mize, USA
1988: Sandy Lyle, Great Britain
1989: Nick Faldo, Great Britain
United States PGA first held 1916
1980: Jack Nicklaus, USA
1981: Larry Nelson, USA
1982: Ray Floyd, USA
1983: Hal Sutton, USA
1984: Lee Trevino, USA
1985: Hubert Green, USA
1986: Bob Tway, USA
1987: Larry Nelson, USA
1988: Jeff Sluman, USA
1989: Payne Stewart, USA

Golgi /'gɒldʒi/ Camillo 1843–1926. Italian cell biologist who with Ramon Y Cajal produced the first detailed knowledge of the fine structure of the nervous system.

Golgi's use of silver salts in staining cells proved so remarkably effective in showing up the components and fine processes of nerve cells that even the synapses—tiny gaps between the cells—were visible. The Golgi body, a series of flattened membranous cavities found in the cytoplasm of cells was first described by him in 1898.

Golgi apparatus or **Golgi body** a membranous structure found in the cells of ◊eukaryotes. It produces the membranes that surround the cell vesicles or ◊lysosomes.

Goliath /gə'laɪəθ/ in the Old Testament, champion of the ◊Philistines, who was said to have been slain with a stone from a sling by ◊David in single combat in front of the opposing armies of Israelites and Philistines.

Gollancz /gə'lænts/ Victor 1893–1967. British left-wing writer and publisher, founder in 1936 of the influential Left Book Club.

Gomez /'gəʊmɪʃ/ Diego 1440–1482. Portuguese navigator who discovered the coast of Liberia during a voyage sponsored by ◊Henry the Navigator 1458–60.

Gómez /'gəʊmes/ Juan Vicente 1864–1935. Venezuelan dictator 1908–35. The discovery of oil during his rule attracted US, British, and Dutch oil interests and made Venezuela one of the wealthiest countries in Latin America. Gómez amassed a considerable personal fortune and used his well-equipped army to dominate the civilian population.

Gompers /'gɒmpəz/ Samuel 1850–1924. US labour leader. His early career in the Cigarmakers' Union led him to found and lead the ◊American Federation of Labor 1882. Gompers advocated non-political activity within the existing capitalist system to secure improved wages and conditions for members.

Gomulka /gə'mʊlkə/ Wladyslaw 1905–1982. Polish communist politician, party leader 1943–48 and 1956–70. He introduced moderate reforms, including private farming and tolerance for Roman Catholicism.

Gomulka, born in Krosno in SE Poland, was involved in underground resistance to the Germans during World War II, taking part in the defence of Warsaw. Leader of the Communist Party in Poland from 1943, he was ousted by the Moscow-backed Boleslaw Bierut (1892–1956) in 1948, but was restored to the leadership in 1956, following riots

in Poznań. Gomulka was forced to resign in Dec 1970 after sudden food-price rises induced a new wave of strikes and riots.

gonad the part of an animal's body that produces the sperm or egg cells (ovules) required for sexual reproduction. The sperm-producing gonad is called a ◊testis, and the ovule-producing gonad is called an ◊ovary.

gonadotrophin a ◊fertility drug.

Goncharov /ˌgɒntʃə'rɒf/ Ivan Alexandrovitch 1812–1891. Russian novelist. His first novel, *A Common Story* 1847, was followed in 1858 by his humorous masterpiece *Oblomov*, which satirized the indolent Russian landed gentry.

Goncourt, de /gɒŋ'kʊə/ the brothers Edmond 1822–1896 and Jules 1830–1870. French writers. They collaborated in producing a compendium, *L'Art du XVIIIème siècle/18th-Century Art* 1859–75, historical studies, and a *Journal* 1887–96, which depicts French literary life of their day. Edmond de Goncourt founded the *Académie Goncourt*, opened 1903, which awards an annual prize, the **Prix Goncourt**, to the author of the best French novel of the year. Equivalent to the Booker Prize in prestige, it has a monetary value of only 50 francs.

Gondar /'gɒndɑː/ town in Ethiopia about 2,300 m/7,500 ft above sea level and 40 km/25 mi N of Lake Tana; population (1984) 69,000.

Gonds a non-homogenous people of Central India, about half of whom speak unwritten languages belonging to the Dravidian family. There are over 4,000,000 Gonds, most of whom live in Madhya Pradesh, E Maharashtra and N Andra Pradesh, though some are found in Orissa.

Gond beliefs embrace a range of gods and spirits, and there are a limited number of clans who coexist within a defined set of social and ritual relationships. The dynasties of one group, the Raj Gonds, rivalled those of neighbouring Hindus until the Muslim conquests of the 16th century. Traditionally, many Gonds practised shifting cultivation; agriculture and raising livestock have remained the basis of the economy.

Gondwanaland /gɒn'dwɑːnələnd/ land mass, including the continents of South America, Africa, Australia, and Antarctica, that formed the southern half of ◊Pangaea, the 'supercontinent' or world continent that existed between 250 and 200 million years ago. The northern half was ◊Laurasia. The baobab tree of Africa and Australia is a relic of Gondwandaland.

gonorrhoea a common sexually transmitted disease arising from infection with the bean-shaped bacterium *Neisseria gonorrhoeae*. After an incubation period of two to ten days, infected men experience pain while urinating, and discharge from the penis; infected women often remain symptom-free.

Untreated gonorrhea carries the threat of sterility to both sexes; there is also the risk of blindness in a baby born to an infected mother. The condition is treated with antibiotics, although ever-increasing doses may be necessary to combat resistant strains.

González Márquez /gɒn'ɑːleθ 'mɑːkeθ/ Felipe 1942– . Spanish socialist politician, leader of the Socialist Workers' Party (PSOE), prime minister from 1982.

After studying law in Spain and Belgium, in 1966 he opened the first labour-law office in his home city of Seville. In 1964 he had joined the PSOE, and he rose rapidly to the position of leader. In 1982 PSOE won a sweeping electoral victory and González became prime minister.

Good Friday (probably a corruption of God's Friday) in the Christian church, the Friday before Easter, which is kept in memory of the Crucifixion (the death of Jesus on the cross).

Good King Henry perennial plant *Chenopodium bonus-henricus* growing to 50 cm/1.6 ft, with triangular leaves which are mealy when young. Spikes of tiny greenish-yellow flowers appear above the leaves in midsummer.

Goodman /'gʊdmən/ 'Benny' (Benjamin David) 1909–1986. US clarinetist, nicknamed 'the King of Swing' for the new jazz idiom he introduced. Leader of his own band from 1934, he is remembered for numbers such as 'Blue Skies' and 'King Porter Stomp'. Bartók's *Contrasts* 1939 and Copland's *Clarinet Concerto* 1950 were written for him.

Goodman /'gʊdmən/ Paul 1911– . US writer and social critic, whose many writings (novels, plays, essays) express his anarchist, anti-authoritarian ideas. He studied youth offenders in *Growing up Absurd* 1960.

Goodwin Sands /'gʊdwɪn/ sandbanks off the coast of Kent, England, exposed at low tide, and famous for wrecks. According to legend, they are the remains of the island of Lomea, owned by Earl Godwin in the 11th century.

Goodwood racecourse NE of Chichester, West Sussex, England. Its most famous races are The Goodwood Cup and Sussex Stakes, held July/Aug.

Goodyear /'gʊdjɪə/ Charles 1800–1860. US inventor, who developed vulcanized rubber 1839, particularly important for motor-vehicle tyres.

Goody Two Shoes a children's story of unknown authorship but possibly by Oliver Goldsmith, published 1765 by John Newbery (1713–67). The heroine, Margery, is an orphan who is distraught when her brother goes to sea, but quickly recovers when she receives a gift of new shoes. She educates herself, dispenses goodness, and is eventually reunited with her brother.

Goonhilly /gʊn'hɪli/ British Telecom satellite tracking station in Cornwall, England. It is equipped with a communications satellite transmitter–receiver in permanent contact with most parts of the world.

goose name given to birds of the genera *Anser* and *Branta*. Both genders are similar in appearance: they have short, webbed feet, placed nearer the front of the body than in other members of the order Anatidae, and the beak is slightly hooked. They feed entirely on grass and plants, 'grey' geese being very destructive to young crops.

The **greylag goose** *Anser anser* is the ancestor of the tame goose. Other species include the **Canada goose** *Branta canadensis*, the **bean goose** *Anser fabalis*, the **pink-footed goose** *Anser brachyrhynchus*, and the **white-fronted goose** *Anser albifrons*. The goose builds a nest of grass and twigs on the ground, and from five to nine eggs are laid, white or cream-coloured, according to the species.

Goose Bay a settlement at the head of Lake Melville on the Labrador coast of Newfoundland, Canada. In World War II it was used as a staging post by US and Canadian troops on their way to Europe. Until 1975 it was used by the US Air Force as a low-level-flying base.

gooseberry edible fruit of *Ribes uva-crispa*, a low-growing bush related to the currant. It is straggling in its growth, bearing straight sharp spines in groups of three, and rounded, lobed leaves. The flowers are green, and hang on short stalks. The fruits are generally globular, green, and hairy, but there are reddish and white varieties.

goosefoot plants of the family Chenopodiaceae, including fat-hen or white goosefoot, *Chenopodium album*, whose seeds were used as food in Europe from Neolithic times, and also from early times in the Americas. It grows to 1 m/3 ft tall and has lance- or diamond-shaped leaves and packed heads of small inconspicuous flowers. The green part is a ◊spinach substitute.

gopher burrowing rodent of the family Geomyidae of North and Central America. It is grey or brown, grows to 30 cm/12 in, and has long teeth and claws.

Gorakhpur /'gɔːrəkpʊə/ city in Uttar Pradesh, N India, situated on the Rapti river, at the centre of an agricultural region producing cotton, rice, and grain; population (1981) 306,000.

Gorbachev *President of the Soviet Union and Communist Party leader Mikhail Gorbachev. Since coming to power in 1985, he has embarked on a programme of ambitious economic and political modernization, but has encountered mounting internal problems.*

Gorbachev /ˌgɔːˈbætʃɒf/ Mikhail Sergeyevich 1931– . Soviet president. He was a member of the Politburo from 1980 and, during the Chernenko administration 1984–85, was chair of the Foreign Affairs Commission. As general secretary of the Communist Party (CPSU) from 1985, and president of the Supreme Soviet from 1988, he introduced liberal reforms at home (see ◊perestroika, ◊glasnost) and attempted to halt the arms race abroad. In 1990 he gained significantly increased powers for the presidency.

Gorbachev, born in the N Caucasus, studied law at Moscow University and joined the CPSU 1952. In 1955–62 he worked for the Komsomol (Communist Youth League) before being appointed regional agriculture secretary. As Stavropol party leader from 1970 he impressed Andropov, and was brought into the CPSU secretariat 1978.

Gorbachev was promoted into the Politburo, and in 1983, when Andropov was general secretary, took broader charge of the Soviet economy. On Chernenko's death 1985 he was appointed party leader. He initiated reforms and introduced campaigns against alcoholism, corruption, and inefficiency, and a policy of *glasnost* ('openness'). Gorbachev radically changed the style of Soviet leadership, despite opposition to the pace of change from both conservatives and radicals.

Gordon *British army general Charles Gordon.*

Gordian knot /ˈgɔːdiən/ in Greek myth, the knot tied by King Gordius of Phrygia, only to be unravelled by the future conqueror of Asia. According to tradition, Alexander cut it with his sword in 334 BC.

gorilla

Gordimer /ˈgɔːdɪmə/ Nadine 1923– . South African novelist, an opponent of apartheid. Her first novel, *The Lying Days*, appeared in 1953, and other works include *The Conservationist* 1974, the volume of short stories *A Soldier's Embrace* 1980, and *July's People* 1981. Her books are banned in South Africa.

Gordon /ˈgɔːdn/ Charles (George) 1833–1885. British general sent to Khartoum in the Sudan 1884 to rescue English garrisons that were under attack by the ◊Mahdi; he was himself besieged by the Mahdi's army. A relief expedition under Viscount Wolseley arrived 28 Jan 1885, to find that Khartoum, after a siege of ten months, had been captured, and Gordon killed, two days before.

Gordon /ˈgɔːdn/ George 1751–1793. British organizer of the so-called **Gordon Riots** of 1778, a protest against removal of penalties imposed on Roman Catholics in the Catholic Relief Act of 1778; he was acquitted on a treason charge. Gordon and the 'No Popery' riots figure in Dickens's novel *Barnaby Rudge*.

Gordon /ˈgɔːdn/ Richard. Pen name of Gordon Ostlere 1921– . British author of a series of light-hearted novels on the career of a young doctor, beginning with *Doctor in the House* 1952. Many of them were filmed.

Gordonstoun /ˈgɔːdnztən/ ◊public school near Elgin, Grampian, Scotland, founded by Kurt Hahn in 1935, which emphasizes a spartan outdoor life. Prince Philip and Prince Charles attended this school.

Gorgon /ˈgɔːgən/ in Greek mythology, any of three sisters, Stheno, Euryale, and Medusa, who had wings, claws, enormous teeth, and snakes for hair. Medusa, the only one who was mortal, was killed by ◊Perseus, but even in death her head was still so frightful that it turned the onlooker to stone.

Gorgonzola /ˌgɔːgənˈzəʊlə/ small town NE of Milan, Italy, famous for cheese.

Goria /ˈgɔːriə/ Giovanni 1943– . Italian Christian Democrat (DC) politician, prime minister 1987–88. He entered the Chamber of Deputies 1976 and held a number of posts, including treasury minister, until he was asked to form a coalition government in 1987.

gorilla largest of the anthropoid apes, found in the dense forests of W Africa and mountains of Central Africa. The male stands about 2 m/6.5 ft, and weighs about 200 kg/450 lbs, females about half the size. The body is covered with blackish hair, silvered on the back in the male. Gorillas live in family groups of a senior male, several females, some younger males, and a number of infants. They are vegetarian, highly intelligent, and will attack only in self-defence. They are dwindling in numbers, being shot for food by some local people, or by poachers taking young for zoos, but protective measures are having some effect.

Gorillas construct stoutly built nests in trees for overnight use. The breast-beating movement, once thought to indicate rage, actually signifies only nervous excitement. There are three races of one species, *Gorilla gorilla*, these being the

Gorky *A committed, lifelong revolutionary, Maxim Gorky attracted official disapproval both before and after the 1917 Russian Revolution.*

Western lowland, Eastern lowland, and mountain gorillas.

Göring Herman Wilhelm. Nazi leader, see ◊Goering.

Gorizia /gɒˈrɪtsiə/ town in Friuli-Venezia-Giulia region, N Italy, on the Isonzo, SE of Udine; population (1981) 41,500. Industries include textiles, furniture, and paper. It has a 16th-century castle, and was a cultural centre during Habsburg rule.

Gorky /ˈgɔːki/ (Russian *Gor'kiy*) (former name Nizhny-Novgorod until 1932) city in central USSR; population (1987) 1,425,000. Cars, locomotives, and aircraft are manufactured here.

Gorky /ˈgɔːki/ Arshile 1904–1948. US painter, born in Armenia, who settled in the USA in 1920. He painted Cubist abstracts before developing a more surreal Abstract Expressionist style, using organic shapes and bold paint strokes.

Gorky /ˈgɔːki/ Maxim. Pen name of Alexei Peshkov 1868–1936. Russian writer. Born in Nizhny-Novgorod (renamed Gorky 1932 in his honour), he was exiled 1906–13 for his revolutionary principles. His works, which include the play *The Lower Depths* 1902 and the recollections *My Childhood* 1913, combine realism with optimistic faith in the potential of the industrial proletariat.

Görlitz /ˈgɜːlɪts/ manufacturing town in Dresden county, East Germany; population (1981) 81,000.

Gorlovka /ˈgɔːləvkə/ industrial town (coalmining, chemicals, engineering) on the ◊Donbas coalfield, Ukraine, USSR; population (1987) 345,000.

gorse also known as *furze* or **whin** genus of plants *Ulex*, family Leguminosae, consisting of thorny shrubs with spine-shaped leaves densely clustered along the stems, and bright yellow flowers. The gorse bush *Ulex europaeus* is an evergreen and grows on heaths and sandy areas throughout W Europe.

Gorst /gɔːst/ J(ohn) E(ldon) 1835–1916. English Conservative Party administrator. A supporter of Disraeli, Gorst was largely responsible for extending the Victorian Conservative Party electoral base to include middle- and working-class support. Appointed Conservative Party agent in 1870, he established the Conservative Central Office, and became secretary of the National Union in 1871. He was solicitor-general 1885–86.

Gort /gɔːt/ John Vereker, First Viscount Gort 1886–1946. British general, awarded a Victoria Cross after World War I, who in World War II commanded the British Expeditionary Force 1939–40, conducting a fighting retreat from Dunkirk, France.

Gorton /ˈgɔːtn/ John Grey 1911– . Australian Liberal politician. He was minister for education and science 1966–68, and prime minister 1968–71.

Goschen /ˈgəʊʃən/ George Joachim, First Viscount Goschen 1831–1907. British Liberal politician. He held several cabinet posts under Gladstone 1868–74, but broke with him in 1886 over Irish Home Rule. In Salisbury's Unionist government of 1886–92 he was chancellor of the Exchequer, and 1895–1900 was First Lord of the Admiralty.

goshawk bird *Accipiter gentilis* that is similar in appearance to the peregrine falcon, but with short wings and short legs. It is used in falconry.

Gospel (Middle English 'good news') in the New Testament generally, the message of Christian salvation; in particular the four written accounts of the life of Jesus by Matthew, Mark, Luke, and John. Although the first three give approximately the same account or synopsis (thus giving rise to the name Synoptic Gospels), their differences from John have raised problems for theologians.

The so-called fifth Gospel, or **Gospel of St Thomas** (not connected with the disciple Thomas), is a 2nd-century collection of 114 sayings of Jesus. It was found in a Coptic translation contained in a group of 13 papyrus codices, discovered in Upper Egypt 1945, which may have formed the library of a Gnostic community (see ◊Gnosticism).

gospel music a type of song developed in the 1920s in the black Baptist churches of the US South from spirituals, which were 18th-and 19th-century hymns joined to the old African pentatonic (five-note) scale. Outstanding among the early gospel singers was Mahalia Jackson (1911–72), but from the 1930s to the mid-1950s male harmony groups predominated, among them the Dixie Hummingbirds, the Swan Silvertones, and the Five Blind Boys of Mississippi.

Gosport /'gɒspɔːt/ naval port opposite ◊Portsmouth, Hampshire, England; population (1981) 77,250.

Gossaert Jan Flemish painter, known as ◊Mabuse.

Gossamer Albatross the first human-powered aircraft to fly across the English Channel, in June 1979. It was designed by Paul MacCready and piloted and pedalled by Bryan Allen. The Channel crossing took 2 hours 49 minutes. The same team was behind the first successful human-powered aircraft (*Gossamer Condor*) two years earlier.

Gosse /gɒs/ Edmund William 1849–1928. English author. Son of a marine biologist, who was a member of the ◊Plymouth Brethren, Gosse's strict Victorian upbringing is reflected in his masterpiece of autobiographical work *Father and Son* (published anonymously in 1907).

Göteborg /ˌjɜːtəˈbɔːri/ (German **Gothenburg**) port and industrial (ships, vehicles, chemicals) city on the west coast of Sweden, on the Göta Canal (built 1832), which links it with Stockholm; population (1988) 432,000. It is Sweden's second largest city.

Goth /gɒθ/ E Germanic people who settled near the Black Sea around the 2nd century AD. There are two branches, the eastern Ostrogoths, and the western Visigoths.

The **Ostrogoths** were conquered by the Huns 372. They regained their independence 454, and under ◊Theodoric the Great conquered Italy 488–93; they disappeared as a nation after the Byzantine emperor ◊Justinian I reconquered Italy 535–55.

The **Visigoths** migrated to Thrace. Under ◊Alaric they raided Greece and Italy 395–410, sacked Rome, and established a kingdom in S France. Expelled from there by the Franks, they established a Spanish kingdom which lasted until the Moorish conquest of 711.

Gotha /'gəʊtə/ town in Erfurt county, SW East Germany, former capital of the duchy of Saxe-Coburg-Gotha; population (1981) 57,600. It has a castle and two observatories; pottery, soap, textiles, precision instruments, and aircraft are manufactured here.

Gothenburg /'gɒθənbɜːg/ German form of ◊Göteborg, city in Sweden.

Gothic architecture style of architecture characterized by vertical lines of tall pillars, spires, greater

height in interior spaces, the pointed arch, rib vaulting, and the flying buttress.

Gothic architecture originated in Normandy and Burgundy in the 12th century, the term perhaps deriving from the 16th-century critic Vasari's attribution of medieval artistic styles to the Goths. It prevailed in W Europe until the 16th century when classic architecture was revived. The term Gothic was at first used disparagingly of medieval art by Renaissance architects.

In *France*, Gothic architecture may be divided into four periods. *Early Gothic*, 1130–90, saw the introduction of ogival (pointed) vaults, for example Notre Dame, Paris, begun 1160. In *lancet Gothic*, 1190–1240, pointed arches were tall and narrow, as in Chartres Cathedral, begun 1194, and Bourges Cathedral, begun 1209. *Radiating Gothic*, 1240–1350, takes its name from the series of chapels that radiate from the cathedral apse, as in Sainte Chapelle, Paris, 1226–30. *Late Gothic* or the Flamboyant style, 1350–1520, is exemplified in St Gervais, Paris.

In *Italy* Gothic had a classical basis. A notable example of Italian Gothic is Milan cathedral.

In *Germany*, the Gothic style until the end of the 13th century was at first heavily influenced by that of France; for example Cologne Cathedral, the largest in N Europe, was built after the model of Amiens.

In *England* the Gothic style is divided into ◊*Early English* 1200–75, for example Salisbury Cathedral; ◊*Decorated* 1300–75, for example York Minster; and ◊*Perpendicular* 1400–1575, for example Winchester Cathedral.

Gothic art painting and sculpture in the style that dominated European art from the late 12th century until the early Renaissance. The great Gothic church façades held hundreds of sculpted figures and profuse ornament, and manuscripts were lavishly decorated. Stained glass replaced mural painting to some extent in N European churches. The *International Gothic* style in painting emerged in the 14th century, characterized by delicate and complex ornament and increasing realism.

Gothic novel genre established by Horace Walpole's *The Castle of Otranto* 1765, and marked by mystery, violence, and horror; other exponents of the genre were Mrs Radcliffe, Matthew 'Monk' Lewis, Bram Stoker, and Edgar Allan Poe.

Gothic revival the modern resurgence of interest in Gothic architecture, especially as displayed in 19th-century Britain and the USA. Gothic revival buildings in England include the Houses of Parliament and St Pancras Station, London.

The growth of Romanticism led some writers, artists, and antiquaries to embrace a fascination with Gothic forms that emphasized the supposedly bizarre and grotesque aspects of the Middle Ages. During the Victorian period, however, a far better understanding of Gothic forms was achieved, and this resulted in some impressive Neo-Gothic architecture, as well as a good deal of desecration of genuine Gothic churches in the name of 'restoration' by such as Augustus Pugin and George Gilbert Scott.

Gotland /'gɒtlənd/ Swedish island in the Baltic Sea; area 3,140 sq km/1,212 sq mi; population (1986) 56,200. The capital is Visby. Its products are mainly agricultural (sheep and cattle), and there is tourism. It was an area of dispute between Sweden and Denmark, but became part of Sweden 1645.

Götterdämmerung (German 'twilight of the gods') in Scandinavian mythology, the end of the world.

Göttingen /'gɜːtɪŋən/ town in Lower Saxony, West Germany; population (1988) 134,000. Industries include printing, publishing, precision instruments, and chemicals. Its university was founded by George II of England 1734.

Gouda /'gaʊdə/ town in Zuid Holland, W Netherlands; population (1987) 61,500. It produces round, flat cheeses.

Gough /gɒf/ Hubert 1870–1963. British general. He was initially blamed, as commander of the Fifth Army 1916–18, for the German breakthrough on the Somme, but his force was later admitted to have been too small for the length of the front.

Goulburn /'gəʊlbɜːn/ town in New South Wales, Australia, SW of Sydney; population (1983) 22,500. It is an agricultural centre, and manufactures bricks, tiles, and pottery.

Gould /guːld/ Bryan Charles 1939– . British Labour politician, member of the shadow cabinet from 1986.

Born in New Zealand, he settled in Britain in 1964, as a civil servant and then a university lecturer. He joined the Labour Party, entering the House of Commons in 1974. He lost his seat in the 1979 general election but returned in 1983 as the member for Dagenham, having spent the intervening four years as a television journalist. His rise in the Labour Party was rapid and in 1986 he became a member of the shadow cabinet. His communication skills soon made him a nationally known figure.

Gould /guːld/ Elliott. Stage name of Elliot Goldstein 1938– . US film actor. A successful child actor, his film debut, *The Night They Raided Minsky's* 1968, led rapidly to starring roles in such films as *M.A.S.H.* 1970, *The Long Goodbye* 1972, and *Capricorn One* 1978.

Gould /guːld/ Jay 1836–1892. US financier, born in New York. He is said to have caused the financial panic on 'Black Friday', 24 Sept 1869, through his speculations in gold.

Gould /guːld/ Stephen Jay 1941– . US palaeontologist and author. In 1972 he proposed the theory of punctuated equilibrium, suggesting that the evolution of species did not occur at a steady rate but could suddenly accelerate, with rapid change occurring over a few hundred thousand years.

Gounod /'guːnəʊ/ Charles François 1818–1893. French composer. His operas include *Sappho* 1851, *Faust* 1859, *Philémon et Baucis* 1860, and *Roméo et Juliette* 1867. He also wrote sacred songs, masses, and an oratorio, *The Redemption* 1882. His music has great lyrical appeal and emotional power and it inspired many French composers of the later 19th century.

gourd name applied to various members of the family Cucurbitaceae, including the melon and pumpkin. In a narrower sense, the name applies only to the genus *Lagenaria*, of which the bottle gourd *Lagenaria siceraria* is best known.

gout disease marked by an excess of uric acid crystals in the tissues, causing pain and inflammation in one or more joints. Acute attacks are treated with ◊anti-inflammatories.

The disease, more common in men, poses a long-term threat to the blood vessels and the kidneys, so ongoing treatment may be needed to minimize the levels of uric acid in the body fluids.

government system whereby political authority is exercised. Modern systems of government distinguish between liberal (Western-style) democracies, totalitarian (one-party) states, and autocracies (authoritarian, relying on force rather than ideology). The Greek philosopher Aristotle was the first to attempt a systematic classification of governments. His main distinctions were between government by one person, by few, and by many (monarchy, oligarchy, and democracy) although the characteristics of each may vary between states and each may degenerate into tyranny (rule by an oppressive elite in the case of oligarchy or by the mob in the case of democracy).

The French philosopher Montesquieu distinguished between constitutional governments — whether monarchies or republics — which operated under various legal and other constraints, and despotism, which was not constrained in this way.

Many of the words used (dictatorship, tyranny, totalitarian, democratic) have acquired negative or

Goya A Picnic *(late 1780s) National Gallery, London.*

positive connotations that makes it difficult to use them objectively. The term *liberal democracy* was coined to distinguish Western types of democracy from the many other political systems that claimed to be democratic. Its principal characteristics are the existence of more than one political party, open processes of government and political debate, and a separation of powers.

Totalitarian has been applied to both fascist and communist states and denotes a system where all power is centralized in the state, which in turn is controlled by a single party that derives its legitimacy from an exclusive ideology.

Autocracy describes a form of government that has emerged in a number of Third World countries, where state power is in the hands either of an individual or of the army; normally ideology is not a central factor, individual freedoms tend to be suppressed where they may constitute a challenge to the authority of the ruling group, and there is a reliance upon force.

Other useful distinctions are between *federal* governments (where important powers are dispersed among various regions which in certain respects are self-governing) and *unitary* governments (where powers are concentrated in a central authority); and between *presidential* (where the head of state is also the directly elected head of government, not part of the legislature) and *parliamentary* systems (where the government is drawn from an elected legislature which can dismiss it).

Government Communications Headquarters centre of the British government's electronic surveillance operations, popularly known as ◊GCHQ.

governor in engineering, a device that controls the speed of a machine or engine.

James ◊Watt invented the steam-engine governor in 1788. It works by means of heavy balls, which rotate on the end of linkages and move in or out because of ◊centrifugal force according to the speed of rotation. The movement of the balls closes or opens the steam valve to the engine. When the engine speed increases too much, the balls fly out, and cause the steam valve to close, so the engine slows down. The opposite happens when the engine speed drops too much.

Gower /'gəʊə David 1957– . English cricketer. A left-hander, since his debut for Leicestershire 1975 he has scored over 20,000 first class runs. He made his England debut 1978, and was captain 1984 and 1989.

Grace The English cricketer W G Grace, who helped establish cricket as England's national sport.

Gower /'gaʊə/ John *c.* 1330–1408. English poet. He is remembered for his tales of love *Confessio Amantis* 1390, written in English, and other poems in French and Latin.

Gower Peninsula /'gaʊə/ peninsula in West ◊Glamorgan, S Wales.

Gowon /gəʊ'ɒn/ Yakubu 1934– . Nigerian politician, head of state 1966–75. Educated at Sandhurst, he became chief of staff, and in the military coup of 1966 seized power. After the Biafran civil war 1967–70, he reunited the country with his policy of 'no victor, no vanquished'. In 1975 he was overthrown by a military coup.

Goya /'gɔɪə/ Francisco José de Goya y Lucientes 1746–1828. Spanish painter and engraver. He painted portraits of four successive kings of Spain, and his etchings include *The Disasters of War*, depicting the French invasion of Spain 1810–14. Among his last works are the 'black paintings' (Prado, Madrid), with horrific images such as *Saturn Devouring One of his Sons* about 1822.

He was born in Aragon, and was for a time a bullfighter, the subject of some of his etchings. After studying in Italy, he returned to Spain, and was employed on a number of paintings for the royal tapestry factory. In 1789 he was court painter to Charles IV.

Goyen /'xɔɪən/ Jan van 1596–1656. Dutch landscape painter, active in Leiden, Haarlem, and from 1631 in The Hague. He was a pioneer of the realist style of landscape with ◊Ruisdael, and sketched from nature and studied clouds and light effects.

Gozzoli /'gɒtsəli/ Benozzo *c.*1421–1497. Florentine painter, a late exponent of the International Gothic style. He painted frescoes 1459 in the chapel of the Palazzo Medici-Riccardi, Florence: the walls are crammed with figures, many of them portraits of the Medici family.

GP in medicine, the abbreviation for *general practitioner*.

GP in music, abbreviation for 'general pause', a moment where all players are silent.

GPU former name (1922–23) for ◊KGB, the Soviet secret police.

Graaf /grɑːf/ Regnier de 1641–1673. Dutch physician and anatomist who discovered the ovarian follicles, which were later named Graafian follicles. He gave exact descriptions of the testicles, and named the ovaries. He was also the first to isolate and collect the secretions of the pancreas and gall bladder.

Graafian follicle during the ◊menstrual cycle, a fluid-filled capsule that surrounds and protects the developing egg cell inside the ovary. After the egg cell has been released, the follicle remains and is known as a corpus luteum.

Grable /'greɪbəl/ 'Betty' (Elizabeth Ruth) 1916–1973. US actress, singer and dancer, who starred

Graf West German top tennis player at Wimbledon 1989, where she won the Ladies Singles title.

in, *Moon over Miami* 1941, *I Wake Up Screaming* 1941, and *How to Marry a Millionaire* 1953. As a publicity stunt, her legs were insured for a million dollars.

Gracchus /'grækəs/ the brothers *Tiberius Sempronius* 163–133 BC and *Gaius Sempronius* 153–121 BC. Roman agrarian reformers. As ◊tribune 133 BC, Tiberius tried to prevent the ruin of small farmers by making large slave-labour farms illegal but was murdered. Gaius, tribune 123–122 BC, revived his brother's legislation, and introduced other reforms, but was outlawed by the Senate and committed suicide.

Grace /greɪs/ W(illiam) G(ilbert) 1848–1915. English cricketer. By profession a doctor, he became the best batsman in England. He began playing first-class cricket at the age of 16, scored 152 runs in his first Test match, and scored the first triple century 1876.

Grace scored more than 54,000 runs in his career which lasted nearly 45 years. He scored 2,739 runs in 1871, the first time any batsman had scored 2,000 runs in a season. An all-rounder, he took nearly 3,000 first class wickets. Grace played in 22 Test matches.

CAREER HIGHLIGHTS

All First Class Matches
Runs: 54,896
Average: 39.55
Best: 344 MCC v. Kent, 1876
Wickets: 2,876
Average: 17.92
Best: 10–49 MCC v. Oxford University, 1886
Test Cricket
Runs: 1,098
Average: 32.29
Best: 170 v. Australia, 1886
Wickets: 9
Average: 26.22
Best: 2–12 v. Australia, 1890.

Graces in Greek mythology, three goddesses (Aglaia, Euphrosyne, Thalia), daughters of Zeus and Hera, the personification of grace and beauty and the inspirers of the arts and the sciences.

Graf /grɑːf/ Steffi 1969– . West German lawn tennis player, who brought Martina ◊Navratilova's long reign as the world's number one female player to an end. She reached the semi-final of the US Open 1985 at the age of 16, and won five consecutive Grand Slam singles titles 1988–89.

graffiti (Italian 'scratched drawings') inscriptions or drawings carved, scratched, or drawn on public surfaces such as walls, fences, or public transport vehicles. *Tagging* is the act of writing an individual logo on surfaces with spray-paint or large felt-tip pens, common in Britain in the 1980s.

The term is derived from a traditional technique in Italian art, called *sgraffito*, of scratching a design in the thin white plaster on a wall.

grafting the operation by which a piece of living tissue is removed from one organism and transplanted into the same or a different organism where it continues growing. In horticulture, it is a technique widely used for propagating plants, especially woody species. A bud or shoot on one plant, termed the **scion**, is inserted into another, the **stock**, so that they continue growing together, the tissues combining at the point of union.

Grafting is usually only successful between species that are closely related and is most commonly practised on roses and fruit trees. Grafting of non-woody species is more difficult but it is sometimes used to propagate tomatoes and cacti. See also ◊transplant and ◊skin-grafting.

Grafton /'grɑːftən/ town in New South Wales, Australia, S of Brisbane; population (1985) 17,600. Industries include sugar, timber, and dairy products.

Grafton /'grɑːftən/ Augustus Henry, 3rd Duke of Grafton 1735–1811. British politician, grandson of the first duke, who was the son of Charles II and Barbara Villiers (1641–1709), Duchess of Cleveland. He became First Lord of the Treasury in 1766 and an unsuccessful acting prime minister 1767–70.

Graham family name of dukes of Montrose.

Graham /'greɪəm/ 'Billy' (William Franklin) 1918– . US Baptist evangelist. At 17 he was converted at an evangelistic meeting. His Evangelistic Association conducts worldwide 'crusades'.

Graham Martha 1894– . US dancer, choreographer, teacher and director. The leading exponent of modern dance in the USA, she has created over 150 works and developed a unique vocabulary of movement, the **Graham Technique** now taught worldwide.

She has had a major influence on choreographers in the contemporary dance movement such as Robert Cohan, Glen Tetley, Norman

grafting

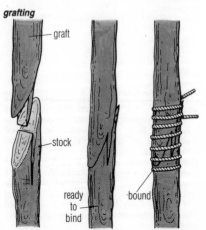

graft

stock

ready
to
bind

bound

Morrice, Paul Taylor, and Robert North. Her ballets, include *Appalachian Spring* 1944 (score by Aaron Copland) and *Clytemnestra* 1958 (music by Halim El-Dabh), the first full-length modern dance work.

Graham /'greɪəm/ Thomas 1805–1869. Scottish chemist who laid the foundations of physical chemistry (the branch of chemistry concerned with changes in energy during a chemical transformation) by his work on the diffusion of gases and liquids. *Graham's Law* states that the diffusion rate of two gases varies inversely as the square root of their densities.

His work on ◊colloids was equally fundamental; he discovered the principle of dialysis, that colloids can be separated from solutions containing smaller molecules by the differing rates at which they pass through a semi-permeable membrane (a process he termed 'osmosis'). The human kidney uses the principle of dialysis to extract nitrogenous waste.

Grahame /'greɪəm/ Kenneth 1859–1932. Scottish author. The early volumes of sketches of childhood, *The Golden Age* 1895 and *Dream Days* 1898, were followed by his masterpiece *The Wind in the Willows* 1908, an animal fantasy created for his young son, which was dramatized by A A Milne as *Toad of Toad Hall.*

Graham Land /'greɪəm/ mountainous peninsula in Antarctica, formerly a dependency of the ◊Falkland Islands, and from 1962 part of the ◊British Antarctic Territory. It was discovered by John Biscoe in 1832, and until 1934 was thought to be an archipelago.

Grahamstown /'greɪəmztaʊn/ town in SE Cape Province, South Africa; population (1985) 75,000. It is the seat of Rhodes University, established 1951, founded in 1904 as Rhodes University College.

grain the smallest unit of mass in the English system (see ◊apothecaries' weights), equal to 0.648 g. It was reputedly the weight of a grain of wheat.

Grainger /'greɪndʒə/ Percy Aldridge 1882–1961. Australian-born US composer and concert pianist. He is remembered for a number of songs and

Graham *Thomas Graham, one of the founders of physical chemistry and formulator of Graham's Law on the diffusion of gases.*

short instrumental pieces drawing on folk idioms, including *Country Gardens* 1925, and for his settings of folk songs, such as *Molly on the Shore* 1921.

He studied in Frankfurt, moved to London, then settled in the US in 1914. Grainger shared his friend ◊Busoni's vision of a free music, devising a synthesizer and composing machine far ahead of its time.

gram metric unit of mass; one thousandth of a ◊kilogram.

grammar (Greek *grammatike tekhne* 'art of letters') the principles of the correct use of language, dealing with the rules of structuring words into phrases, clauses, sentences, and paragraphs in an accepted way. Emphasis on the standardizing impact of print has meant that spoken or colloquial language is often perceived as less grammatical than written language, but all forms of a language, standard or otherwise, have ther own grammatical systems of differing complexity. People often acquire several overlapping grammatical systems within one language; for example, one formal system for writing and standard communication and one less formal system for everyday and peer-group communication.

Originally 'grammar' was an analytical approach to writing, intended to improve the understanding and the skills of scribes, philosophers, and litterateurs. When compared with Latin, English has also been widely regarded as having 'less' grammar or at least a simpler grammar; it would be truer, however, to say that English and Latin have *different* grammars, each complex in its own way. In linguistics, the contemporary study of language, grammar, or syntax is generally understood to refer to the arrangement of the elements in a language, for the purposes of acceptable communication in speech, writing, and print. All forms of a language, standard or otherwise, have their grammars or grammatical systems, which children acquire through use; a child may acquire several overlapping systems within one language (especially a non-standard form for everyday life and a standard form linked with writing, school and national life). Not even the most comprehensive grammar book (or grammar) of a language like English, French, Arabic, or Japanese completely covers or fixes the implicit grammatical system that people use in their daily lives. The rules and tendencies of natural grammar operate largely in non-conscious ways, but can, for many social and professional purposes, be studied and explicitly developed as conscious as well as inherent skills. See also ◊parts of speech.

Recent theories of the way language functions include ◊**phrase structure grammar**, ◊**transformational grammar**, and ◊**case grammar**.

Grampian Region

Grand Canyon *The silt-laden Colorado River cuts through the lowest point of the Grand Canyon, Arizona, USA.*

grammar school in the UK, a secondary school catering for children of high academic ability, usually measured by the Eleven Plus examination. Most grammar schools have now been replaced by ◊comprehensive schools.

In the USA, the term is sometimes used for a primary school (also called elementary school).

Grampian /'græmpiən/ region of Scotland
area 8,600 sq km/3,320 sq mi
towns administrative headquarters Aberdeen
features part of the Grampian Mountains (the Cairngorms); valley of the river Spey, with its whisky distilleries; Balmoral Castle (royal residence on the river Dee near Braemar, bought by Prince Albert 1852, and rebuilt in Scottish baronial style); Braemar Highland Games in Aug
products beef cattle (Aberdeen Angus and Beef Shorthorn), fishing, North Sea oil service industries, tourism (winter skiing)
population (1987) 503,000.

Grampian Mountains /'græmpiən/ a range that separates the Highlands from the Lowlands of Scotland, running NE from Strathclyde. It takes in the S Highland region (which includes **Ben Nevis**, the highest mountain in the British Isles at 1,340 m/4,406 ft), northern Tayside, and the S border of Grampian region itself (the Cairngorms, which include **Ben Macdhui** 1,309 m/4,296 ft). The region includes Aviemore, a winter holiday and sports centre.

Grampians /'græmpiənz/ western end of Australia's eastern highlands, in Victoria; the highest peak is Mount William 1,167 m/3,829 ft.

grampus another name for the killer ◊whale.

Gramsci /'græmʃi/ Antonio 1891–1937. Italian Marxist, who attempted to unify social theory and political practice. He helped to found the Italian Communist party 1921, and was elected to parliament 1924, but was imprisoned by Mussolini from 1926; his *Quaderni di carcere/Prison Notebooks* 1947 were published after his death.

Gramsci believed that politics and ideology were independent of the economic base, that no ruling class could dominate by economic factors alone, and that the working class could achieve liberation by political and intellectual struggle. His concept of **hegemony** argued that real class control in capitalist societies is ideological and cultural rather than physical, and that only the working class 'educated' by radical intellectuals could see through and overthrow such bourgeois propaganda.

His humane and gradualist approach to Marxism, particularly his emphasis on the need to overthrow bourgeois ideology, influenced European Marxists in their attempt to distance themselves from orthodox determinist Soviet communism.

Granada /grə'nɑːdə/ city in the Sierra Nevada in Andalucia, S Spain; population (1986) 281,000. It produces textiles, soap, and paper.
history founded by the ◊Moors in the 8th century, it became the capital of an independent kingdom 1236–1492, when it was the last Moorish stronghold to surrender to the Spaniards. Ferdinand and Isabella, the first sovereigns of a united Spain, are buried in the cathedral (built 1529–1703). The **Alhambra**, a fortified hilltop palace, was built in the 13th–14th centuries by the Moorish kings.

Granada /grə'nɑːdə/ Nicaraguan city on the NW shore of Lake Nicaragua; population (1985) 89,000. It has shipyards, and manufactures sugar, soap, clothing, and furniture. Founded 1523, it is the oldest city in Nicaragua.

Granados /grə'nɑːdɒs/ Enrique 1867–1916. Spanish composer-pianist. His piano-work *Goyescas* 1911, inspired by the art of ◊Goya, was converted to an opera in 1916.

Gran Chaco /'græn 'tʃɑːkəʊ/ large lowland plain in N Argentina, W Paraguay, and SE Bolivia; area 650,000 sq km/251,000 sq mi. It consists of swamps, forests (a source of quebracho timber), and grasslands, and there is cattle-raising.

Grand Banks /'grænd 'bæŋks/ continental shelf in the N Atlantic off SE Newfoundland, where the shallow waters are rich fisheries, especially for cod.

Grand Canal (Chinese **Da Yune**) the world's longest canal. It is 1,600 km/1,000 mi long, and runs north from Hangzhou to Tianjin, China. The earliest section was completed 486 BC, and the northern section was built AD 1282–92, during the reign of Kublai Khan. It is 30–61 m/100–200 ft wide, and 0.6–4.6 m/2–15 ft deep.

Grand Canyon /'grænd 'kænjən/ vast gorge containing the Colorado River, Arizona, USA. It is 350 km/217 mi long, 6–29 km/4–18 mi wide, and reaches depths of over 1.5 km/1 mi. It was made a national park in 1919.

Grand Design in the early 17th century, a plan attributed to the French minister Sully to Henry IV of France (who was assassinated before he could carry it out) for a great Protestant union against the Holy Roman Empire; the term was also applied to President de Gaulle's vision of France's place in a united Europe.

Grandes Ecoles, Les in France, selective higher education colleges which function alongside and independently of universities. Examples include the *Ecole Polytechnique* (see ◊polytechnic), the *Ecole normale superieure*, and the ◊*Ecole national d'administration*.

Grande Dixence dam /'grɒnd diːk'sɒns/ the world's highest dam, located in Switzerland, which measures 285 m/935 ft from base to crest. Completed in 1961, it contains 6 million m³/8 million cu yds of concrete.

Grand Falls /'grænd 'fɔːlz/ town in Newfoundland, Canada; population (1986) 9,100. It is the site of large paper and pulp mills.

Grand Guignol /'grɒŋ 'giːnjɒl/ genre of short horror play produced at the Grand Guignol theatre in Montmartre, Paris (named after the bloodthirsty character Guignol in late 18th-century marionette plays).

Grand National several steeplechases, the most famous being run at Aintree, England, during the Liverpool meeting in Mar or Apr over 7 km 242 m/4.5 mi, with 30 formidable jumps. It was first run 1839.

Grand Old Baby (GOB) popular name for US ◊Republican Party.

grand opera a type of opera without any spoken dialogue (unlike the *opéra-comique*), as performed at the Paris *Opéra* 1820s–1880s. Using the enormous resources of the state-subsidized opera house, grand operas were extremely long (five acts), and included incidental music and a ballet.

Composers of grand opera include Auber, Meyerbeer, and Halevy; examples include Verdi's *Don Carlos* 1867 and Meyerbeer's *Les Huguenots* 1836.

Grand Rapids /'grænd 'ræpɪdz/ city in W Michigan, USA, on the river Grand; population (1980) 602,000. It produces furniture, motor bodies, plumbing fixtures, and electrical goods.

Grand Remonstrance petition passed by the British Parliament in Nov 1641 which listed all the alleged misdeeds of Charles I and demanded Parliamentary approval for the king's ministers and the reform of the church. Charles refused to accept the Grand Remonstrance and countered it by trying to arrest five leading members of the House of Commons (Pym, Hampden, Holles, Hesilrige, and Strode). The worsening of relations between king and Parliament led to the outbreak of the English Civil War in 1642.

grand slam in tennis, the four major tournaments: the Australian Open, the French Open, Wimbledon, and the US Open. In golf, it is also the four major tournaments: the US Open, the British Open, the Masters, and the PGA. In baseball, a grand slam is a home run with runners on all the bases. A grand slam in bridge is when all 13 tricks are won by one team.

Grand Teton /'grænd 'tiːtn/ highest point of the spectacular Teton range, NW Wyoming, USA, rising to 4,197 m/13,770 ft. Grand Teton National Park was established 1929.

grand unified theory (GUT) in physics, a sought-for theory that would combine the successful theory of the strong nuclear force (called quantum chromodynamics) with the theory of the weak and electromagnetic forces. The search for the GUT is part of a larger programme seeking a ◊unified field theory, which would combine all the forces of nature (including gravity) within one framework.

Grange Movement, the in US history, a farmers' protest in the southern and midwestern states against economic hardship and exploitation. The National Grange of the Patrons of Husbandry,

granite *Hay Tor (453 m/1,490 ft), one of Dartmoor's granite tors.*

Grant *Hollywood film actor Cary Grant.*

formed 1867, was a network of local organizations, employing cooperative practices and advocating 'granger' laws. The movement petered out in the late 1870s, to be superseded by the ◊Greenbackers.

Granger /ˈgreɪndʒə/ Stewart (James) Stewart 1913– . British film actor. After several leading roles in British romantic films during World War II, he moved to Hollywood in 1950 and subsequently appeared in adventure films; for example, *Scaramouche* 1952; *The Prisoner of Zenda* 1952, *The Wild Geese* 1978.

granite a plutonic ◊igneous rock, acidic in composition (containing a high proportion of silica). The rock is coarse-grained, the characteristic minerals being quartz, feldspars (usually alkali), and micas. It may be pink or grey, depending on the composition of the feldspars. Granites are chiefly used as building materials.

Some granites are formed by melting or partial melting of existing continental crust by heat and pressure or high grade metamorphic conditions. Other granites are formed by igneous processes whereby ultrabasic mantle rock is partially melted and yields various magmas of more siliceous composition such as gabbro, diorite, and granite.

Granites often form large intrusions in the core of mountain ranges, and they are usually surrounded by zones of thermally metamorphosed rock. Granite areas have characteristic moorland scenery and may weather along joints and cracks to produce 'tors' consisting of rounded blocks that appear to have been stacked upon one another as exposed hillside.

Grant /grɑːnt/ Cary. Stage name of Archibald Leach 1904–1986. US actor, born in England. He first travelled to the USA with a troupe of acrobats. His witty, debonair screen personality made him a favourite for more than three decades. His films include *Bringing Up Baby* 1937, *The Philadelphia Story* 1940, *Arsenic and Old Lace* 1944, *Notorious* 1946, and *North by Northwest* 1959.

Grant /grɑːnt/ Duncan 1885–1978. British painter and designer, a member of the ◊Bloomsbury group and a pioneer of abstract art in the UK. He lived with Vanessa Bell from about 1914 and worked with her on decorative projects. Later works, such as *Snow Scene* 1921, showed the influence of the Post-Impressionists.

Grant /grɑːnt/ James Augustus 1827–1892. Scottish soldier and explorer who served in India and Abyssinia and, with Captain John Speke, explored the sources of the Nile 1860–63. Accounts of his travels include *A Walk across Africa* 1864 and

Grant *General Ulysses S Grant, photographed in June 1864 at City Point, near Hopewell, Virginia, his headquarters during the American Civil War.*

Botany of the Speke and Grant Expedition.

Grant /grɑːnt/ Ulysses S(impson) 1822–1885. 18th president of the USA 1869–77. He was a Union general in the American Civil War and commander in chief from 1864. As a Republican president, he carried through a liberal ◊Reconstruction policy in the South, although he failed to suppress extensive political corruption within his own party and cabinet, which tarnished the reputation of his presidency.

The son of an Ohio farmer, he had an unsuccessful career in the army 1839–54 and in business, and on the outbreak of the Civil War received a commission on the Mississippi front. He took command there in 1862, and by his capture of Vicksburg in 1863 brought the whole Mississippi front under Northern control. He slowly wore down the Confederate Gen Lee's resistance, and in 1865 received his surrender at Appomattox. He was elected president 1868 and re-elected 1872.

Grantham /ˈgrænθəm/ market town in SE Lincolnshire, England; population (1981) 30,084. It is an agricultural centre, dating from Saxon times. Margaret Thatcher was born here.

granthi in Sikhism, the man or woman who reads from the holy book, the *Guru Granth Sahib*, during the service.

grant-maintained school in the UK, a state school that has voluntarily withdrawn itself from local authority support (an action called *opting out*), and instead is maintained directly by central government. The first was Skegness Grammar School in 1989. In this way, schools have more opportunity to manage their budgets effectively.

Granville-Barker /ˈgrænvɪl ˈbɑːkə/ Harley 1877–1946. British theatre director and author. He was director and manager with J E Vedrenne at the Royal Court Theatre, London, 1904–18, producing plays by Shaw, Yeats, Ibsen, Galsworthy, and Masefield.

graph a pictorial representation of numerical data as in statistical data, or a method of showing the mathematical relationship between two or more variables by drawing a diagram.

There are often two axes or coordinates at right-angles intersecting at the origin – the zero point from which values of the variables (for example, distance and time for a moving object) are

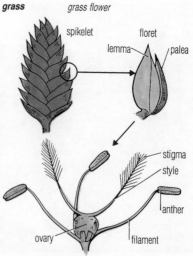

grass *grass flower*

assigned along the axes. Pairs of simultaneous values (the distance moved after a particular time) are plotted as points in the area between the axes, and the points then joined by a smooth curve to produce a graph.

graphic notation in music, a sign language referring to unorthodox sound effects, such as electronic sounds, for which classical music notation is not suitable.

graphics tablet or *bit pad* in computing, an input device in which a stylus or cursor is moved, by hand, over a flat surface. The computer can keep track of the position of the stylus, so enabling the operator to input drawings or diagrams into the computer.

A graphics tablet is often used with a form overlaid for users to tick boxes in positions that relate to specific registers in the computer, though recent development in handwriting recognition may increase its future versatility.

graphite a blackish-grey laminar crystalline form of ◊carbon. It is used as a lubricant and as the active component of pencil lead.

The carbon atoms are strongly bonded together in sheets, but the bonds between the sheets are weak so that the sheets are free to slide over one another. Graphite has a very high melting point (3,500°C/6,332°F), which gives it mechanical strength and makes it a good conductor of heat and electricity. In its pure form it is used as a moderator in nuclear reactors.

Grasmere /ˈgrɑːsmɪə/ English lake and village in the Lake District, Cumbria. William Wordsworth and his sister Dorothy lived at Dove Cottage (now a museum) 1799–1808, Thomas de Quincey later made his home in the same house, and both Samuel Coleridge and Wordsworth are buried in the churchyard of St Oswald's.

grass plant of the large family Gramineae of monocotyledons, with about 9,000 species distributed worldwide except in the Arctic regions. The majority are perennial, with long, narrow leaves and hollow stems; hermaphroditic flowers are borne in spikelets.

Grass /grɑːs/ Günter 1927– . German writer. Born in Danzig, he studied at the art academies of Düsseldorf and Berlin, worked as a writer and sculptor, first in Paris and later in Berlin, and in 1958 won the coveted 'Group 47' prize. The grotesque humour and socialist feeling of his novels *Die Blechtrommel/The Tin Drum* 1959 and *Der Butt/The Flounder* 1977 characterize many of his poems.

Grasse /grɑːs/ town near Cannes, SE France; population (1982) 38,360. It is the centre of a perfume-manufacturing region, and flowers are grown on a large scale for this purpose.

grasshopper insect of the order Orthoptera, usually with strongly developed hind legs which enables it to leap. Members of the order include

◊locusts and ◊crickets.

The **short-horned grasshoppers** Acrididae include the locust, and all members of the family feed voraciously on vegetation. The femur of each hind leg in the male usually has a row of protruding joints which produce the characteristic chirping when rubbed against the hard wing veins. Eggs are laid in a small hole in the ground, and the unwinged larvae become adult after about six moults.

There are several sober-coloured, small, and harmless species in Britain. The **long-horned grasshoppers** or **bush crickets** Tettigoniidae have a similar life-history, but differ from the Acrididae in having long antennae, and in producing their chirping by the friction of the wing covers over one another (stridulation). The **great green bush cricket** *Tettigonia viridissima* 5 cm/2 in long, is a British species of this family, which also comprises the North American katydids, notable stridulators.

grass of Parnassus plant *Parnassia palustris*, unrelated to grasses, found growing in marshes and on wet moors in Europe and Asia. It is low-growing, with a rosette of heart-shaped stalked leaves and has five-petalled, white flowers with conspicuous veins growing singly on stem tips in late summer.

grass-tree Australian plant of the genus *Xanthorrhoea*. The tall, thick stems have a grass-like tuft at the top and are surmounted by a flower-spike resembling a spear.

Grattan /'grætn/ Henry 1746–1820. Irish politician. He entered the Irish parliament in 1775. As leader of the patriot opposition he secured the abolition of all claims by the British Parliament to legislate for Ireland in 1782, but failed to prevent the Act of Union, and sat in the British Parliament from 1805.

Graubünden /grau'bundən/ (French **Grisons**) Swiss canton, the largest in Switzerland; area 7,106 sq km/2,743 sq mi; population (1986) 167,000. The inner valleys are the highest in Europe, and the main sources of the river Rhine rise here. It also includes the resort of Davos, and, in the Upper Engadine, St Moritz. The capital is Chur. Romansch is still widely spoken. Graubünden entered the Swiss Confederation 1803.

gravel a coarse ◊sediment consisting of pebbles or small fragments of rock, originating in the beds of lakes and streams or on beaches. Gravel is quarried for use in road building, railway ballast, and for an aggregate in concrete. It is obtained from quarries known as gravel pits, where it is often found mixed with sand or clay. Some gravel deposits also contain metal ores (particularly tin) or free metals (such as gold and silver).

Graves /greɪvz/ Robert (Ranke) 1895–1985. English poet and author. He was severely wounded on the Somme in World War I, and his frank autobiography *Goodbye to All That* 1929 is one of the outstanding war books. Other works include the poems *Over the Brazier* 1916; historical novels of Imperial Rome, *I Claudius* and *Claudius the God* both 1934; and books on myth, for example *The White Goddess* 1948.

Gravesend /ˌgreɪvz'end/ town on the Thames, Kent, SE England, linked by ferry with Tilbury opposite; population (1981) 52,963.

gravimetry the study of the Earth's gravitational field. Small variations in the gravitational field can be caused by varying densities of rocks and structure beneath the surface, a phenomenon called the ◊Bouguer anomaly. These variations provide information about otherwise inaccessible subsurface conditions.

gravitational lens the gravitational field from a very large body, such as a star, which deflects light. It was predicted by Einstein's General Theory of Relativity and tested successfully during the solar eclipse of 1917 when the light from stars located beyond the sun was captured on photographs.

gravity the force of attraction between two objects

gravimetry

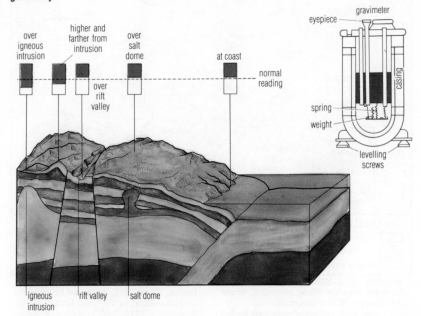

because of their masses; for instance, the force we call gravity on Earth is the force of attraction between any object in the Earth's gravitational field and the Earth itself.

According to Newton's law of gravitation, all objects fall to Earth with the same acceleration, regardless of mass. For an object of mass m at a distance d from the centre of the Earth (mass M), the force of gravity F equals GmM/d, where G is the gravitational constant. According to Newton's second law of motion, F also equals mg, where g is the acceleration due to gravity. Therefore $g = GM/d$ and is independent of the mass of the object; at the Earth's surface it equals 9.806 m s^{-2} (metres per second per second).

The general theory of relativity treats gravitation not as a force but as a curvature of space and time around a body. Relativity predicts the bending of light and the ◊red shift of light in a gravitational field; both have been observed. Another prediction of relativity is *gravitational waves*, which should be produced when massive bodies are violently disturbed. These waves are so weak that they have not yet been detected with certainty, although observations of a ◊pulsar (which emits energy at regular intervals) in orbit around another star have shown that the stars are spiralling together at the rate that would be expected if they were losing energy in the form of gravitational waves.

gravure one of the three main ◊printing methods, in which printing is done from a plate etched with a pattern of recessed cells in which the ink is held. The greater the depth of a cell, the greater the strength of the printed ink. Gravure plates are expensive to make. However, the process is economical for high-volume printing and reproduces illustrations well.

Gray /greɪ/ Eileen 1879–1976. Irish-born architect and furniture designer. She set up her own workshop and became known for her Art Deco designs which, in furniture, explored the use of tubular metal, glass, and new materials such as aluminium.

She trained as a painter at the Slade School of Art, London, then worked for a Japanese lacquer painter in Paris. She gradually concentrated on the design of furniture, woven textiles, and interiors.

Gray /greɪ/ Thomas 1716–1761. English poet, whose 'Elegy Written in a Country Churchyard' 1750 is one of the most quoted poems in English. Other poems include 'Ode on a Distant Prospect of Eton College', 'The Progress of Poesy', and

'The Bard'; these poems are now seen as the precursors of Romanticism.

A close friend of Horace ◊Walpole at Eton, Gray made a continental tour with him 1739–41, an account of which is given in his vivid letters. In 1748 his first poems appeared anonymously in Dodsley's *Miscellany*.

grayling freshwater fish *Thymallus thymallus* of the family Salmonidae. It has a long multi-rayed dorsal fin, and a coloration shading from silver to purple. It is found in northern parts of North America, Europe, and Asia.

Graz /grɑːts/ capital of Styria province, and second largest city in Austria; population (1981) 243,400. Industries include engineering, chemicals, iron, and steel. It has a 15th-century cathedral and a university founded in 1573. The famous Lippizaner horses are bred near here.

Great Artesian Basin the largest area of artesian water in the world, it underlies much of Queensland, New South Wales and South Australia, and in prehistoric times formed a sea. It has an area of 1,750,000 sq km/676,250 sq mi.

Great Australian Bight broad bay in S Australia, notorious for storms. It was discovered by a Dutch navigator, Captain Thyssen, 1627. The coast was charted by the English explorer Captain Matthew Flinders 1802.

Great Awakening, the a religious revival in the North American British colonies from the late 1730s to the 1760s, sparked off by George

Great Barrier Reef *A collection of variously formed corals and shells from the reef.*

The Great Schism 1378–1417
- allegiance to Rome
- allegiance to Avignon
- allegiance to neither

Great Wall of China *A derelict section of the Great Wall of China near Badaling, built from 214 BC to repel Turkish and Mongol invaders.*

Whitefield (1714–1770), an itinerant English Methodist preacher whose evangelical fervour and eloquence made many converts.

A second 'great awakening' occurred in the first half of the 19th century, confirming an evangelical tradition in US Protestantism.

Great Barrier Reef chain of coral reefs and islands about 2,000 km/1,250 mi long, off the E coast of Queensland, Australia at a distance of 15–45 km/10–30 mi. It forms an immense natural breakwater, and the coral rock forms a structure larger than all human-made structures on Earth combined.

The reef is in danger from large numbers of starfish, which are reported to have infested 35% of the reef. Some scientists fear the entire reef will disappear within 50 years.

Great Bear popular name for the constellation ◊Ursa Major.

Great Bear Lake lake on the Arctic Circle, in the Northwest Territories, Canada; area 31,800 sq km/12,275 sq mi.

Great Britain official name for ◊England, ◊Scotland, and ◊Wales, and the adjacent islands, from 1603 when the English and Scottish crowns were united under James I of England (James VI of Scotland). With Northern ◊Ireland it forms the ◊United Kingdom.

great circle a plane cutting through a sphere, and passing through the centre point of the sphere, cuts the surface along a great circle. Thus, on the Earth, all meridians of longitude are half great circles; among the parallels of latitude, only the equator is a great circle.

The shortest route between two points on the Earth's surface is along the arc of a great circle. These are used extensively as air routes although on maps, due to the distortion brought about by ◊projection, they do not appear as straight lines.

Great Dane large short-haired dog, usually fawn in colour, standing up to 92 cm/36 in, and weighing up to 70 kg/154 lb. It has a long head, a large nose, and small ears. It was formerly used for hunting boar and stags.

Great Divide or **Great Dividing Range** E Australian mountain range, extending 3,700 km/2,300 mi N–S from Cape York Peninsula, Queensland, to Victoria. It includes the Carnarvon Range, Queensland, which has many Aboriginal cave paintings, the Blue Mountains in New South Wales, and the Australian Alps.

Greater London Council (GLC) in the UK, local authority that governed London 1965–86. When the GLC was abolished in 1986 (see ◊local government) its powers either devolved back to the borough councils or were transferred to certain nonelected bodies.

Great Exhibition an exhibition held in Hyde Park, London, UK, in 1851, proclaimed by its originator Prince Albert as 'the Great Exhibition of the Industries of All Nations'. In practice, it glorified British manufacture: over half the 100,000 exhibits were from Britain or the British Empire. Over six million people attended the exhibition. The exhibition hall, dubbed by *Punch* magazine the ◊*Crystal Palace*, was constructed of glass with a cast-iron frame, and designed by Joseph ◊Paxton.

Great Expectations a novel by Charles Dickens, published 1860–61.

Philip Pirrip ('Pip'), brought up by his sister and her husband, the blacksmith Joe Gargery, rejects his humble background and pursues wealth, which he believes comes from the elderly Miss Havisham. Ultimately he is forced by adversity to recognize the value of his origins.

Great Lake Australia's largest freshwater lake, 1,025 m/3,380 ft above sea level, in Tasmania; area 114 sq km/44 sq mi. It is used for hydroelectric power and is a tourist attraction.

Great Lakes series of five freshwater lakes along the USA–Canada border: Lakes Superior, Michigan, Huron, Erie, and Ontario; total area 245,000 sq km/94,600 sq mi. Interconnecting canals make them navigable by large ships, and they are drained by the ◊St Lawrence River. They are said to contain 20% of the world's fresh water.

Great Leap Forward the change in Chinese economic policy introduced under the second five-year plan of 1958–62. The aim, instigated by Mao Zedong, was to convert China into an industrially based economy by transferring resources away from agriculture. This coincided with the creation of people's communes. The inefficient and poorly planned allocation of state resources led to the collapse of the strategy by 1960 and a return to more adequate support for agricultural production.

Great Leap Forward *Silos on Shashiuyu commune near Tangshan, China.*

Great Plains a semiarid region to the E of the Rocky Mountains, meridian of longitude through Oklahoma, Kansas, Nebraska and the Dakotas. The plains, which cover one-fifth of the USA, extend from Texas in the S over 2,400 km/1,500 mi N to Canada. Ranching and wheat farming have resulted in over-exploitation of the water resources to such an extent that available farmland has been reduced by erosion.

Great Powers the major European powers of the 19th century: Russia, Austria, (Austria-Hungary), France, Britain, and Prussia.

Great Red Spot a prominent feature of ◊Jupiter.

Great Rift Valley longest 'split' in the Earth's surface, 8,000 km/5,000 mi long, running south from the Dead Sea (Israel/Jordan) to Mozambique.

Great Sandy Desert desert in N Western Australia; area 415,000 sq km/160,000 sq mi. It is also the name of an arid region in S Oregon, USA.

Great Schism in European history, the period 1378–1417 in which there were rival popes in Rome and Avignon; it was ended by the election of Martin V during the Council of Constance 1414–17.

Great Slave Lake lake in the Northwest Territories, Canada; area 28,450 sq km/10,980 sq mi. It is the deepest lake (615 m/2,020 ft) in North America.

Great Trek in South African history, the movement of 12,000–14,000 Boer (Dutch) settlers from Cape Colony in 1836 and 1837 to escape British rule. They established republics in Natal (1838–43) and the Transvaal. It is seen by many white South Africans as the main event in the founding of the present republic, and also as a justification for continuing whites-only rule.

Great Wall an array of galaxies arranged almost in a perfect plane, discovered by US astronomers in Cambridge, Massachusetts, in Nov 1989. It consists of some 2,000 galaxies (about 500 million by 200 million light years) and is thought to be the largest structure ever discovered.

Great Wall of China continuous defensive wall stretching from W Gansu to the Gulf of Liaodong (2,250 km/1,450 mi). It was once even longer. It was built under the Qin dynasty from 214 BC to prevent incursions by the Turkish and Mongol peoples. Some 8 m/25 ft high, it consists of a brick-faced wall of earth and stone, has a series

grebe

great crested grebe

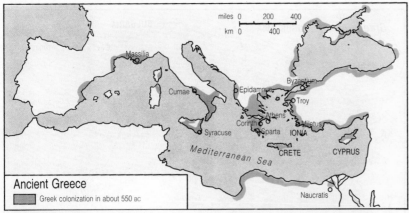

Ancient Greece

Greek colonization in about 550 BC

of square watchtowers, and has been carefully restored. It can be seen from space.

Great War another name for ◊World War I.

Great Yarmouth /'greɪt 'jɑːməθ/ alternative name for the resort and port of ◊Yarmouth in Norfolk, England.

grebe water bird of the family Podicipediae. There are 22 species, found all over the world. Recognizable by their brightly coloured head tufts and plumes, they have elaborated courtship antics. The reason that grebes pluck and eat their own feathers has not been fully explained by scientists. It may help them to digest fish.

Greco, El /'grekəʊ/ (Doménikos Theotokopoulos) 1541–1614. Spanish painter, called 'the Greek' because he was born in Crete. He studied in Italy, worked in Rome from about 1570, and by 1577 had settled in Toledo. He painted elegant portraits and intensely emotional religious scenes with increasingly distorted figures and flickering light, for example *The Burial of Count Orgaz* 1586 (Toledo).

Greece /griːs/ country in SE Europe, comprising the S Balkan peninsula, bounded N by Yugoslavia and Bulgaria, NE by Turkey, E by the Aegean Sea, S by the Mediterranean Sea, W by the Ionian Sea, NW by Albania, and numerous islands to the S and E.

government The 1975 constitution provides for a parliamentary system of government, with a president, who is head of state, a prime minister, who is head of government, and a single-chamber parliament. The president, elected by parliament for a five-year term, appoints the prime minister and cabinet. Parliament has 300 members, all elected by universal suffrage for a four-year term,

Greece
Hellenic Republic
(Elliniki Dimokratia)

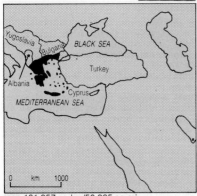

area 131,957 sq km/50,935 sq mi
capital Athens
towns ports Thessaloniki, Patras, Larisa, Iráklion
physical mountainous; a large number of islands, notably Crete, Corfu, and Rhodes
features Corinth canal; Mount Olympus; archaeological sites; US military bases at Hellenikon, Nea Makri (both near Athens), and (on Crete) at Souda Bay near Iráklion
head of state Christos Sartzetakis from 1985
head of government Xenophon Zolotas from 1989
political system democratic republic
political parties Panhellenic Socialist Movement (PASOK), democratic socialist; New Democracy Party (ND), centre-right
exports tobacco, fruit (including currants), vegetables, olives, olive oil, textiles
currency drachma (268.50 = £1 Feb 1990)
population (1987) 9,990,000; annual growth rate 0.5%
life expectancy men 72, women 76

language Greek
religion Greek Orthodox, Christian 97%
literacy 96% male/89% female (1985)
GNP $32.4 bn (1984); $3,260 per head of population
chronology
1946 Civil war between royalists and communists. Communists defeated.
1949 Monarchy re-established with Paul as king.
1964 King Paul succeeded by his son Constantine.
1967 Army coup removed the king and Col George Papadopoulos became prime minister. Martial law imposed and all political activity banned.
1973 Republic proclaimed, with Papadopoulos as president.
1974 Former premier Constantine Karamanlis recalled from exile to lead government. Martial law and ban on political parties lifted. Restoration of the monarchy rejected by a referendum.
1975 New constitution adopted, making Greece a republic.
1980 Karamanlis resigned as prime minister and was elected president.
1981 Greece became a full member of the EC. Andreas Papandreou elected Greece's first socialist prime minister.
1983 Five-year defence and economic cooperation agreement signed with the US. Ten-year economic cooperation agreement signed with USSR.
1985 Papandreou re-elected.
1988 Relations with Turkey improved. Major cabinet reshuffle following mounting criticism of Papandreou.
1989 Papandreou defeated in elections. Tzannis Tzannetakis, Conservative backbencher, became prime minister, heading first all-party government, including communists, for 15 years. This broke up and Xenophon Zolotas formed new unity government.

and the prime minister and cabinet are collectively responsible to it. Bills passed by parliament must be ratified by the president, whose veto can be overridden by an absolute majority of the total number of members. The two main political parties are the Panhellenic Socialist Movement (PASOK), and the New Democracy Party (ND).

history For ancient history, see ◊Greece, ancient. Except for the years 1686–1715, when the Morea was occupied by the Venetians, Greece remained Turkish until the outbreak of the War of Independence 1821. British, French, and Russian intervention 1827, which brought about the destruction of the Turkish fleet at Navarino, led to the establishment of Greek independence 1829. Prince Otto of Bavaria was placed on the throne 1832; his despotic rule provoked a rebellion 1843, which set up a parliamentary government, and another 1862, when he was deposed and replaced by Prince George of Denmark. Relations with Turkey were embittered by the Greeks' desire to recover Macedonia, Crete, and other Turkish territories with Greek populations. A war 1897 ended in disaster, but the ◊Balkan Wars 1912–13 won most of the disputed areas for Greece.

In a period of internal conflict from 1914, two monarchs were deposed, and there was a republic 1923–25, when a military coup restored ◊George II, who in the following year established a dictatorship under Joannis ◊Metaxas.

An Italian invasion 1940 was successfully resisted, but an intensive attack by Germany 1941 overwhelmed the Greeks. During the German occupation of Greece 1941–44, a communist-dominated resistance movement armed and trained a guerrilla army, and after World War II the National Liberation Front, as it was called, wanted to create a socialist state. If the Greek royalist army had not had massive assistance from the USA, this undoubtedly would have happened. As it was, the monarchy, in the shape of King Paul, was re-established, and he was succeeded by his son Constantine 1964.

Dissatisfaction with the government and conflicts between the king and his ministers resulted in a coup 1967, replacing the monarchy with a new regime, which, despite its democratic pretensions, was little more than a military dictatorship, with Col George Papadopoulos as its head. All political activity was banned and opponents of the government forced out of public life.

In 1973 Greece declared itself a republic and Papadopoulos became president. A civilian cabinet was appointed but before the year was out another coup brought Lieut-Gen Phaidon Ghizikis to the presidency, with Adamantios Androutsopoulos as prime minister. The government's failure to prevent the Turkish invasion of Cyprus led to its downfall and a former prime minister, Constantine Karamanlis, was recalled from exile to form a new Government of National Salvation. He immediately ended martial law, press censorship, and the ban on political parties, and in the 1974 general election his New Democracy Party (ND) won a decisive majority in parliament.

A referendum the same year rejected the return of the monarchy and in 1975 a new constitution for a democratic 'Hellenic Republic' was adopted, with Constantine Tsatsos as president. ND won the 1977 general election with a reduced majority and in 1980 Karamanlis resigned as prime minister and was elected president.

The following year Greece became a full member of the EC, having been an associate since 1962. Meanwhile, the ND was faced with a growing challenge from the Panhellenic Socialist Movement (PASOK), which won an absolute majority in parliament in the 1981 general election. Its leader, Andreas Papandreou, became Greece's first socialist prime minister.

PASOK had been elected on a radical socialist platform, which included withdrawal from the EC, the removal of US military bases, and a programme of domestic reform. Important so-

Greek art *Marble sculpture of the Venus de Milo, the Louvre, Paris.*

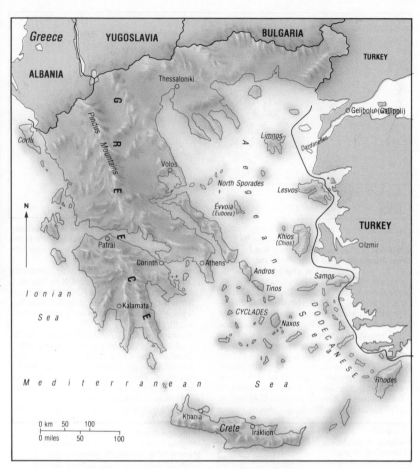

cial changes, such as lowering the voting age to 18, the legalization of civil marriage and divorce, and an overhaul of the universities and the army, were carried out, but instead of withdrawing from Europe, Papandreou was content to obtain a modification of the terms of entry, and, rather than close US bases, he signed a five-year agreement on military and economic cooperation. In 1983 he also signed a ten-year economic cooperation agreement with the USSR.

Despite introducing austerity measures to deal with rising inflation, PASOK won a comfortable majority in the 1985 elections. In 1986 the constitution was amended, limiting the powers of the president in relation to those of the prime minister. The 1989 general election proved inconclusive and eventually Tzannis Tzannatakis, an ND backbencher, formed Greece's first all-party government. However, this soon broke up and after months of negotiation Xenophon Zolotas (PASOK) put together a government of unity, comprising communists, socialists, conservatives, and non-political figures.

Greece, ancient the first Greek civilization, known as Mycenaean (*c.*1600–1200 BC) owed much to the Minoan civilization of Crete and may have been produced by the intermarriage of Greek-speaking invaders with the original inhabitants. From the 14th century BC a new wave of invasions began. The Achaeans overran Greece and Crete, destroying the Minoan and Mycenaean civilizations and penetrating Asia Minor; to this period belongs the siege of Troy (*c.*1180). The latest of the invaders were the Dorians (*c.*1100) who settled in the Peloponnese and founded Sparta; that great city-state arose during the obscure period that followed (1100–800). The mountainous geography of Greece hindered the cities from attaining any national unity, and led the Greeks to take to the sea. During the years 750–550 the Greeks not only became great traders, but founded colonies around the coasts of the Mediterranean and the Black Sea, in Asia Minor, Sicily, S Italy, S France, Spain, and N Africa. The main centres of Greek culture in the 6th century BC were the wealthy ◊Ionian ports of Asia Minor, where Greek philosophy, science, and lyric poetry originated.

Many Greek cities passed from monarchy to the rule of a landowning or merchant oligarchy and thence to democracy. Thus Athens passed through the democratic reforms of Solon (594), the enlightened 'tyranny' of Pisistratus (560–527), and the establishment of democracy

by Cleisthenes (*c.*507). Sparta remained unique, a state in which a ruling race, organized on military lines, tyrannized the original population.

After 545 BC the Ionian cities fell under the suzerainty of the Persian Empire. Aid given them by Athens in an unsuccessful revolt in 499–494 provoked Darius of Persia to invade Greece in 490 only to be defeated by the Athenians at Marathon and forced to withdraw. Another invasion by the Persian emperor Xerxes, after being delayed by the heroic defence of Thermopylae by 300 Spartans, was defeated at sea off Salamis in 480 and on land at Plataea in 479. The Ionian cities were liberated and formed a naval alliance with Athens, the Confederacy of Delos. Pericles, the real ruler of Athens 461–429, attempted to convert this into an Athenian empire and to form a land empire in Greece. Mistrust of his ambitions led to the Peloponnesian War (431–404), which destroyed the political power of Athens. In 5th-century Athens, Greek tragedy, comedy, sculpture, and architecture were at their peak, and Socrates and Plato founded moral philosophy.

After the Peloponnesian War, Sparta became the leading Greek power until it was overthrown by Thebes (378–371). The constant wars between the cities gave Philip II of Macedon (358–336) the opportunity to establish his supremacy over Greece. His son ◊Alexander the Great overthrew the decadent Persian Empire, conquered Syria and Egypt, and invaded the Punjab. After his death in 323 his empire was divided among his generals, but his conquest had nevertheless spread Greek culture to the Near East.

During the 3rd century BC the cities attempted to maintain their independence against Macedon, Egypt, and Rome by forming federations; for example, the Achaean and Aetolian Leagues. Roman intervention began in 212 and ended in

the annexation of Greece in 146. Under Roman rule Greece remained a cultural centre, until the emperor Justinian closed the university of Athens in AD 529.

Greek inhabitant of Greece or person of Greek descent.

Greek architecture the architecture of ancient Greece underpins virtually all architectural developments in Europe. The Greeks invented the entablature, which allowed roofs to be hipped (inverted V-shape), and perfected the design of columns. There were three styles, or orders of these, namely, Doric, Ionic, and Corinthian; see under ◊column and ◊order.

Of the Greek orders the *Doric* is the oldest; it is said to have evolved from a former timber prototype. The finest example of a Doric temple is the Parthenon at Athens (447–438 BC). The origin of the *Ionic* is uncertain. The earliest building in which the Ionic capital appears is the temple of Diana at Ephesus (530 BC). The famous gateway to the Acropolis at Athens (known as the Propylaea) has internal columns of the Ionic order. The most perfect example is the Erechtheum in Athens. The *Corinthian* order belongs to a later period of Greek art. The most important example of the order is the temple of Jupiter (Zeus) Olympus in Athens (174 BC), completed under Roman influence in AD 129. The Mausoleum in Halicarnassus (353 BC) was one of the Seven Wonders of the World.

Greek art sculpture, mosaic, and crafts of ancient Greece (no large-scale painting survives). It is usually divided into three periods: *Archaic* (late 8th century–480 BC), showing Egyptian influence; *Classical* (480–323 BC), characterized by dignified realism; and *Hellenistic* (323–27 BC), more exuberant or dramatic. Sculptures of human figures dominate all periods, and vase painting was a focus for artistic development for many centuries.

Archaic period Statues of naked standing men *kouroi* and draped females *korai* show an Egyptian influence in their rigid frontality. By about 500 BC the figure was allowed to relax its weight onto one leg. They were usually depicted smiling.

Classical period Expressions assumed a dignified serenity. Further movement was introduced in new poses such as in Myron's bronze *Diskobolus/The Discus Thrower* 460–50 BC, and in the rhythmic Parthenon reliefs of riders and horses supervised by Phidias. Polykleitos' sculpture *Doryphoros/The Spear Carrier* 450–440 BC was of such harmony and poise that it set a standard for beautiful proportions. Praxiteles introduced the female nude into the sculptural repertory with the graceful *Aphrodite of Knidos* about 350 BC. It was easier to express movement in bronze, hollow-cast by the lost-wax method, but relatively few bronze sculptures survive and many are known only through Roman copies in marble.

Hellenistic period Sculptures like the *Winged Victory of Samothrace* with its dramatic drapery and the tortured *Laocoon* explored the effects of movement and deeply felt emotion.

vase painting Artists worked as both potters and painters until the 5th century BC and the works they signed were exported throughout the empire. Made in several standard shapes and sizes, the pots served as functional containers for wine, water, and oil. The first decoration took the form of simple lines and circles, from which the **Geometric style** emerged near Athens in the 10th century BC. It consisted of precisely drawn patterns such as the key meander. Gradually the bands of decoration multiplied and the human figure, geometrically stylized, was added.

About 700 BC the potters of Corinth invented the **Black Figure** technique, in which the unglazed red clay was painted in black with mythological scenes and battles in a narrative frieze.

About 530 BC Athenian potters reversed the process and developed the more sophisticated **Red Figure** pottery, which allowed for more detailed and elaborate painting of the figures in red against a black background. This grew increasingly naturalistic, with lively scenes of daily life. The finest examples date from the mid-6th to the mid-5th century BC in Athens. Later painters tried to follow major art trends and represent spatial depth, dissipating the unique quality of their fine linear technique.

crafts The ancient Greeks excelled in carving gems and cameos, and in metalwork. They also invented the pictorial mosaic and from the 5th century BC onwards floors were paved with coloured pebbles depicting mythological subjects. Later, specially cut cubes of stone and glass called *tesserae* were used, and Greek artisans working for the Romans reproduced famous paintings such as *Alexander at the Battle of Issus* from Pompeii, the originals of which are lost.

Greek language a member of the Indo-European language family. **Modern Greek**, which is principally divided into the general vernacular (*Demotic Greek*) and the language of education and literature (*Katharevousa*), has a long and well-documented history: **Ancient Greek** from the 14th to the 12th centuries BC; **Archaic Greek**, including Homeric epic language, until 800 BC; **Classical Greek** until 400 BC; **Hellenistic Greek**, the common language of Greece, Asia Minor, W Asia, and Egypt to the 4th century AD; and **Byzantine Greek**, used until the 15th century and still the ecclesiastical language of the Greek Orthodox Church.

Classical Greek word-forms have greatly influenced the English language, particularly in technical vocabulary. In its earlier phases Greek was spoken mainly in Greece, the islands, the W coast of Asia Minor, and in colonies in Sicily, the Italian mainland, and S France. **Hellenistic Greek** was

Greene *English author Graham Greene converted to Catholicism in 1926.*

an important language not only in the Near East but also in the Roman Empire generally, and is the form also known as **New Testament Greek** (in which the Gospels and other books of the New Testament of the Bible were first written). **Byzantine Greek** was not only an imperial but also an ecclesiastical language, the medium of the Greek Orthodox Church, and **Modern Greek**, in both its forms, is spoken in Greece and in Cyprus, as well as wherever Greeks have settled throughout the world (especially Canada, the USA, and Australia).

Greek literature the literature of Greece.

ancient The three greatest names of early Greek literature are those of ◊Homer, reputed author of the epic *Iliad* and *Odyssey*; ◊Hesiod, whose *Works and Days* deals with agricultural life; and the lyric poet ◊Pindar. Prose came to perfection with the historians ◊Herodotus and ◊Thucydides. The 5th century saw the development of Athenian drama through the works of the tragic dramatists ◊Aeschylus, ◊Sophocles, ◊Euripides, and the comic genius of ◊Aristophanes. After the fall of Athens came a period of prose with the historian ◊Xenophon, the idealist philosopher ◊Plato, the orators ◊Isocrates and ◊Demosthenes, and the scientific teacher ◊Aristotle.

After 323 BC Athens lost its political importance, but was still a university town with teachers such as ◊Epicurus, Zeno, and Theophrastus, and the comic dramatist Menander. Meanwhile Alexandria was becoming the centre of Greek culture: the court of Philadelphus was graced by scientists such as Euclid and the poets Callimachus, Apollonius, and Theocritus. During the 2nd century BC Rome became the new centre for Greek literature, and Polybius, the historian, spent most of his life there; in the 1st century BC Rome also sheltered the poets Archias, Antipater of Sidon, Philodemus the Epicurean, and Meleager of Gadara, who compiled the first *Greek Anthology*. In the 1st century AD Latin writers overshadow the Greek, but there are still the geographer Strabo, the critic Dionysius of Halicarnassus (active around 10 BC), the Jewish writers Philo Judaeus and Josephus, the New Testament writers, and the biographer Plutarch. A revival came in the 2nd century with Lucian. To the 3rd century belong the historians Cassius Dio and Herodian, the Christian fathers Clement and Origen, and the Neo-Platonists. For medieval Greek literature, see ◊Byzantine literature.

modern After the fall of Constantinople, the Byzantine tradition was perpetuated in the classical

Greek writing of, for example, the 15th-century chronicles of Cyprus, various historical works in the 16th and 17th centuries, and educational and theological works in the 18th century. The 17th and 18th centuries saw much controversy over the various merits of the Greek vernacular ('demotic'), the classical language (*Katharevousa*), and the language of the Church, as a literary medium. Adamantios Korais (1748–1833), the first great modern, produced a compromise language, and was followed by the prose and drama writer and poet Alexandros Rhangavis ('Rangabe') (1810–92), and many others. The 10th-century epic of *Digenis Akritas* is usually considered to mark the beginnings of modern Greek vernacular literature, and the demotic was kept alive in the flourishing Cretan literature of the 16th and 17th centuries, in numerous popular songs, and in the Klephtic ballads of the 18th century. With independence in the 19th century the popular movement became prominent with the Ionian poet Dionysios Solomos (1798–1857), Andreas Kalvos (1796–1869), and others, and later with Iannis Psichari(1854–1929), short-story writer and dramatist, and the prose writer Alexandros Papadiamandis (1851–1911), who influenced many younger writers, for example Konstantinos Hatzopoulos (1868–1921), poet and essayist. After the 1920s, the novel began to emerge with Stratis Myrivilis (1892–1969) and Nikos Kazantzakis (1885–1957), author of *Zorba the Greek* 1946 and also a poet. There were also the Nobel prizewinning poets George ◊Seferis and Odysseus ◊Elytis.

Green /griːn/ Henry. Pen name of Henry Vincent Yorke 1905–1974. British novelist, whose works (for example *Loving* 1945 and *Nothing* 1950) are characterized by an experimental colloquial prose style and extensive use of dialogue.

Green /griːn/ Lucinda (born Prior-Palmer) 1953– . British three-day eventer. She has won the Badminton Horse Trials a record six times 1973–84 and was world individual champion 1982.

Green /griːn/ Thomas Hill 1836–1882. English philosopher. He attempted to show the limitations of ◊Spencer and ◊Mill, and advocated the study of ◊Kant and ◊Hegel. His chief works are *Prolegomena to Ethics* 1883 and *Principles of Political Obligation* 1895. Born in Yorkshire, he was professor of moral philosophy at Oxford from 1878.

Greenaway /ˈgriːnəweɪ/ Kate 1846–1901. British illustrator, known for her drawings of children. In 1877 she first exhibited at the Royal Academy, and began her collaboration with the colour-printer Edmund Evans, with whom she produced a number of children's books, including *Mother Goose*.

greenback paper money issued by the US government 1862–65 to help finance the Civil War. It was legal tender but could not be converted into gold.

Greenbackers, the in US history, supporters of an alliance of agrarian and industrial organizations, known as the Greenback Labor Party, which campaigned for currency inflation by increasing the paper dollars (greenbacks) in circulation. In 1880 the party's presidential nominee polled only 300,000 votes: the movement was later superseded by ◊Populism.

green belt area surrounding a large city, officially designated not to be built on but preserved as open space (for agricultural and recreational use).

The scheme was launched in the UK in 1935, and the term generally referred to the 'outer ring' proposed in the Greater London Plan by Patrick Abercrombie (1879–1957); Abercrombie envisaged a static population in this ring, with new towns beyond it.

Greene /griːn/ (Henry) Graham 1904– . English writer, whose novels of guilt, despair, and penitence include *The Man Within* 1929, *Brighton Rock* 1938, *The Power and the Glory* 1940, *The Heart of the Matter* 1948, *The Third Man* 1950,

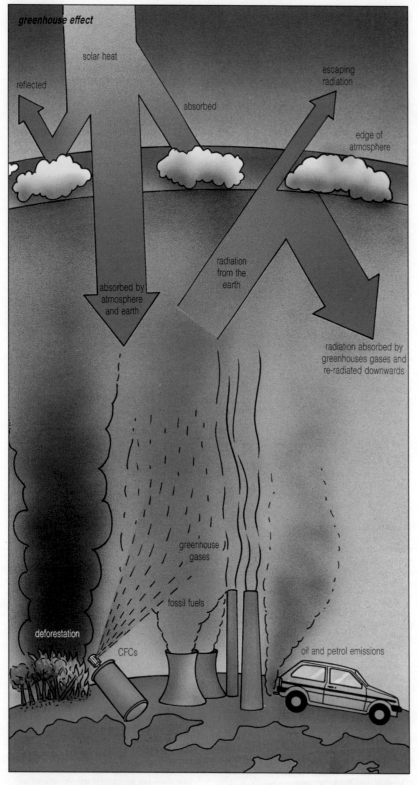

greenhouse effect

solar heat

reflected

absorbed

escaping radiation

edge of atmosphere

absorbed by atmosphere and earth

radiation from the earth

radiation absorbed by greenhouses gases and re-radiated downwards

greenhouse gases

fossil fuels

deforestation

CFCs

oil and petrol emissions

The Honorary Consul 1973, and *Monsignor Quixote* 1982.

greenfinch bird *Carduelis chloris*, common in Europe and N Africa. The male is green with a yellow breast, and the female a greenish-brown.

greenfly plant-sucking insect, a type of ◊aphid.

Greenham Common /'gri:nəm/ site of a continuous peace demonstration on common land near Newbury, Berkshire, UK, outside a US airbase. The women-only camp was established Sept 1981 in protest against the siting of US cruise missiles in the UK. The demonstrations ended 1990 with the closure of the base. Greenham Common will revert to stanby status and all missiles will be removed by 1991.

greenhouse effect a phenomenon of the Earth's atmosphere by which solar radiation, absorbed by the Earth and re-emitted from the surface, is prevented from escaping by carbon dioxide in the air. The result is a rise in the Earth's temperature; in a garden greenhouse, the glass walls have the same effect. The concentration of carbon dioxide in the atmosphere is estimated to have risen by 25% since the Industrial Revolution, and 10% since 1950; the rate of increase is now 0.5% a year. ◊Chlorofluorocarbon levels are rising by 5% a year, and nitrous oxide levels by 0.4% a year, resulting in a global warming effect of 0.5% since 1900, and a rise of about 0.1°C a year in the temperature of the world's oceans during the 1980s. Arctic ice was 6–7 m thick in 1976 and had reduced to 4–5 m by 1987. United Nations Environment Programme estimates an increase in average world temperatures of 1.5°C/2.7°F with a consequent rise of 20 cm/7.7 in in sea level by 2025.

A new computer model from the British Meteorological Office predicts a warming of 2.7° C for a doubling of carbon dioxide.

Greenland /'gri:nlənd/ (Greenlandic *Kalaalit Nunaat*) world's largest island. It lies between the North Atlantic and Arctic Oceans

area 2,175,600 sq km/840,000 sq mi

capital Godthaab (Greenlandic *Nuuk*) on the W coast

features the whole of the interior is covered by a vast ice-sheet; the island has importance in civil aviation and strategically, and military responsibilities are shared with the USA; there are lead and cryolite deposits, and offshore oil is being explored

economy fishing and fish processing

population (1983) 51,903; Inuit, Danish and other European

language Greenlandic

history Greenland was discovered about 982 by ◊Eric the Red, who founded colonies on the W coast. Christianity was introduced about 1000. In 1261 the colonies accepted Norwegian sovereignty, but early in the 15th century all communication with Europe ceased, and by the 16th century the colonies had died out. It became a Danish colony in the 18th century, and following a referendum 1979 was granted full internal self-government 1981.

Greenland Sea area of the ◊Arctic Ocean between Spitsbergen and Greenland, and north of the Norwegian Sea.

Green Mountain Boys in US history, irregular troops who fought to keep Vermont free from New York interference, and in the War of American Independence captured ◊Fort Ticonderoga. Their leader was Ethan Allen (1738–89), who was later captured by the British. Vermont is popularly called the Green Mountain State.

Greenock /'gri:nɔk/ port on the S shore of the Firth of Clyde, Strathclyde, Scotland; population (1981) 59,000. Industries include shipbuilding, engineering, and electronics. It is the birthplace of James Watt.

Green Paper a publication issued by a British government department setting out various aspects of a matter on which legislation is contemplated, and inviting public discussion and suggestions. In due course it may be followed by a ◊White Paper, giving details of proposed legislation. The first Green Paper was published in 1967.

Green Party political party aiming to 'preserve the planet and its people', based on the premise that incessant economic growth is unsustainable. The leaderless party structure reflects a general commitment to decentralization. Green parties sprang up in W Europe in the 1970s and spread in the 1980s. Parties in different countries are linked to one another but unaffiliated to any pressure group, and had a number of parliamentary seats in 1989: Austria 8, Belgium 11, Finland 4, Italy 20, Luxembourg 2, Republic of Ireland 1, Sweden 20, Switzerland 9, West Germany 42; and 24 members of the European Parliament (Belgium 3, France 9, Italy 3, Portugal 1, West Germany 8).

The British Green Party was founded 1973 as the Ecology Party (initially solely environmental). In the 1989 European elections, the British Greens polled over 2 million votes but received no seats in Parliament because Britain was the only country in Europe not to have some form of proportional representation.

Greenpeace international environmental pressure group, founded 1971, with a policy of nonviolent direct action backed by scientific research. During a protest against French atmospheric nuclear testing in the S Pacific 1985, its ship *Rainbow Warrior* was sunk by French intelligence agents, killing a crew member.

green pound the exchange rate used by the European Community for the conversion of EC agricultural prices to sterling. The prices for all EC members are set in European Currency Units (ECUs) and are then converted into green currencies for each national currency.

green revolution in agriculture, a popular term (coined by ◊Borlaug) for the change in methods of arable farming in developing countries. The intent is to provide more and better food for their populations, albeit with a heavy reliance on chemicals and machinery. It was instigated in the 1940s and 1950s, but abandoned by some countries in the 1980s.

Measures include the increased use of tractors and other machines, artificial fertilizers and pesticides, as well as the breeding of new strains of crop plants (mainly rice, wheat, and corn) and farm animals. Much of the work is coordinated by the Food and Agriculture Organization of the United Nations.

The green revolution was initially successful in SE Asia; India doubled its wheat yield in 15 years, and the rice yield in the Philippines rose by 75%. However, yields have levelled off in many areas and some countries, which cannot afford the dams, fertilizers, and machinery required, have adopted ◊intermediate technologies. High-yield varieties of cereal plants require 70–90 kg/154–198 lb of nitrogen per hectare, more than is available to small farmers in developing countries. The rich farmers therefore enjoy bigger harvests, and the gap between rich and poor in the Third World has grown.

greenshank greyish bird *Tringa nebularia* of the sandpiper group. It has long olive-green legs and a slightly upturned bill. It breeds in Scotland and N Europe.

Greenspan /'gri:nspæn/ Alan 1926– . US economist, who succeeded Paul ◊Volcker as chair of the ◊Federal Reserve Board in 1987 and successfully pumped liquidity into the market to avert a sudden 'freefall' into recession after the Wall Street share crash of Oct 1987.

Greenstreet /'gri:nstri:t/ Sidney 1879–1954. British character actor. He made an impressive film debut in *The Maltese Falcon* 1941 and became one of the cinema's best-known villains. His other films included *Casablanca* 1943 and *The Mask of Dimitrios* 1944.

Greenwich /'grenɪdʒ/ inner borough of Greater London, England; population (1981) 212,001
features the **Queen's House** 1637, designed by Inigo Jones, the first Palladian-style building in England, since 1937 housing part of the **National Maritime Museum**; the **Royal Naval College**, designed by Christopher Wren in 1694 as a naval hospital to replace a palace previously on this site (the birthplace of Henry VIII, Mary and Elizabeth I), and used as a college since 1873; the **Royal Greenwich Observatory** (founded here in 1675). The source of Greenwich Mean Time has been moved to ◊Herstmonceux, but the Greenwich meridian (0°) remains unchanged. Part of the buildings have been taken over by the National Maritime Museum, and named Flamsteed House after the first ◊Astronomer Royal. The *Cutty Sark*, most celebrated of the great tea clippers, is preserved as a museum of sail, and Francis Chichester's *Gipsy Moth IV* is also here. The borough also includes **Woolwich** with the Royal Arsenal; and Eltham Palace 1300.

Greenwich Mean Time (GMT) local time on the zero line of longitude (the **Greenwich meridian**), which passes through the Old Royal Observatory at Greenwich, London. It was replaced 1986 by Coordinated Universal Time (UTC); see ◊time.

Greenwich Village section of New York's lower Manhattan. From the 1900s it became the bohemian and artistic quarter of the city and, despite rising rentals, remains so.

More generally, the term suggests the spirit of avantgardism and political radicalism in US culture, variously associated with left-wing causes, sexual liberation, experimental art and theatre, and new magazines and movements.

Greenwood /'gri:nwʊd/ Walter 1903–1974. English novelist of the Depression, born in Salford. His own lack of a job gave authenticity to *Love on the Dole* 1933, later dramatized and filmed.

Greer /grɪə/ Germaine 1939– . Australian feminist, who became widely known on the publication of *The Female Eunuch* 1970. Later works include *The Obstacle Race* 1979, a study of contemporary women artists, and *Sex and Destiny: The Politics of Human Fertility* 1984.

Gregg /greg/ Norman 1892–1966. Australian ophthalmic surgeon, who discovered in 1941 that German measles in a pregnant woman could cause physical defects in her child.

Gregorian chant any of a body of plainsong choral chants associated with Pope Gregory the Great (540–604), which became standard in the Roman Catholic Church.

Gregory /'gregərɪ/ Isabella Augusta (born Persse) 1852–1932. Irish playwright, associated with W B Yeats in creating the ◊Abbey Theatre 1904. Her plays include the comedy *Spreading the News* 1904 and the tragedy *Gaol Gate* 1906. Her journals 1916–30 were published 1946.

Gregory /'gregəri/ 16 popes, including:

Gregory I, St, *the Great* c.540–604. Pope from 590, who asserted Rome's supremacy and exercised almost imperial powers. In 596 he sent St ◊Augustine to England. He introduced **Gregorian chant** into the liturgy. Feast day 12 Mar.

Gregory VII or *Hildebrand* c. 1023–1085. Chief minister to several popes before his election to the papacy 1073. In 1077 he forced the Holy Roman emperor Henry IV to wait in the snow at Canossa for four days, dressed as a penitent, before receiving pardon. He was driven from Rome and died in exile. Feast day 25 May.

He claimed power to depose kings, denied lay rights to make clerical appointments, and attempted to suppress simony (the buying and selling of church preferments) and to enforce clerical celibacy, making enemies with both rulers and the church.

Gregory XIII 1502–1585. Pope from 1572, who introduced the reformed **Gregorian ◊calendar**.

Gregory of Tours, St /tuə/ 538–594. French Christian bishop of Tours from 573, author of a *History of the Franks*. Feast day 17 Nov.

Grenada /grə'neɪdə/ island country in the Caribbean, the southernmost of the Windward Islands.
government The constitution, which dates from full independence in 1974, creates a system modelled on that of Britain, with a resident governor general, representing the British monarch, as the formal head of state, and a prime minister and cabinet drawn from and collectively responsible to parliament. Parliament consists of two chambers, a 15-member house of representatives, elected by universal suffrage, and a senate of 13, appointed by the governor general, seven on the advice of the prime minister, three on the advice of the leader of the opposition, and three after wider consultation.
history Prior to the arrival of Christopher ◊Columbus in 1498, Grenada was inhabited by ◊Carib Indians. The island was eventually colonized by France in 1650, and ceded to Britain in 1783. Grenada remained a British colony until 1958, when it joined the Federation of the West Indies until its dissolution in 1962. Internal self-government was achieved in 1967 and full independence within the Commonwealth in 1974. The early political life of the nation was dominated by two figures: Eric Gairy, a trade-union leader who founded the Grenada United Labour Party (GULP) in 1950, and Herbert Blaize, of the Grenada National Party (GNP).

On independence, in 1974, Gairy was elected prime minister. He was knighted in 1977 but his rule became increasingly autocratic and corrupt

Grenada

area (including the Grenadines, notably Carriacou) 310 sq km/120 sq mi
capital St George's
physical southernmost of the Windward Islands; mountainous
features smallest independent nation in the western hemisphere
head of state Elizabeth II from 1974 represented by Paul Scoon
head of government Ben Jones from 1989
political system emergent democracy
political parties New National Party (NNP), centrist; Grenada United Labour Party (GULP), nationalist left-of-centre
exports cocoa, nutmeg, bananas, mace
currency Eastern Caribbean dollar (4.56 = £1 Feb 1990)
population (1987) 92,000; annual growth rate 1.2%
language English
religion Roman Catholic
literacy 85% (1985)
GDP $116 million (1983); $500 per head of population
chronology
1974 Full independence achieved, with Eric Gairy elected prime minister.
1979 Gairy was removed in a bloodless coup led by Maurice Bishop. Constitution suspended and a people's revolutionary government established.
1982 Relations with the US and Britain deteriorated as ties with Cuba and USSR strengthened. Bishop feared impending US invasion.
1983 After Bishop's attempt to improve relations with the US, he was overthrown by left-wing opponents. A coup established the Revolutionary Military Council (RMC) and Bishop and some of his colleagues were executed. The US, accompanied by troops from some other E Caribbean countries, invaded Grenada, overthrowing the RMC. The 1974 constitution was reinstated.
1984 The newly formed NNP won 14 of the 15 seats in the house of representatives, and its leader, Herbert Blaize, became prime minister.
1989 Herbert Blaize died and was succeeded by Ben Jones.

and in 1979 he was replaced in a bloodless coup by the leader of the left-wing New Jewel Movement (NJM), Maurice Bishop. Bishop suspended the 1974 constitution, established a People's Revolutionary Government (PRG) and announced the formation of a people's consultative assembly to draft a new constitution. He promised a nonaligned foreign policy but became convinced that the USA was involved in a plot to destabilize his administration. This was strongly denied.

Grenada's relations with Britain and the USA deteriorated while links with Cuba and the USSR grew stronger. In 1983 Bishop tried to improve relations with the USA and announced the appointment of a commission to draft a new constitution. His conciliatory attitude was opposed by the more left-wing members of his regime, resulting in a military coup, during which Bishop and three of his colleagues were executed.

A Revolutionary Military Council (RMC), led by Gen Hudson Austin, took control. In response to the outcry caused by the executions, Austin promised a return to civilian rule as soon as possible but on 25 Oct about 1,900 US troops, accompanied by 300 from Jamaica and Barbados, invaded the island. It was not clear whether the invasion was in response to a request from the governor general or on the initiative of the Organization of Eastern Caribbean States (OECS). In any event, concerned that Grenada might become a Cuban base, the USA agreed to take part. Neither Britain nor other members of the Commonwealth appear to have been consulted. The RMC forces were defeated and Austin and his colleagues arrested.

In Nov the governor general appointed a nonpolitical interim council and the 1974 constitution was reinstated. Several political parties emerged from hiding, including Eric Gairy's GULP and Herbert Blaize's GNP. After considerable manoeuvring, an informal coalition of centre and left-of-centre parties resulted in the formation of the New National Party (NNP), led by Blaize. In the 1984 general election NNP won 14 of the 15 seats in the house of representatives and Blaize became prime minister. The USA withdrew most of its forces by the end of 1983 and the remainder by July 1985. In Dec 1989 Blaize died and was succeeded by a close colleague, Ben Jones.

Grenadines /'grenədi:nz/ chain of about 600 small islands in the Caribbean, part of the group known as the Windward Islands. They are divided between ◊St Vincent and ◊Grenada.

Grendel in the Old English epic poem ◊Beowulf, a monster that the hero has to kill.

Grenfell /'grenfəl/ Julian 1888–1915. British poet, eldest son of Lord Desborough, killed in World War I, author of 'Into Battle'.

Grenoble /grə'nəubəl/ alpine town in Rhône-Alpes region, SE France; population (1982) 159,500, conurbation 392,000. Industries include engineering, nuclear research, hydroelectric power, computers, technology, chemicals, plastics, and gloves. It was the birthplace of ◊Stendhal, commemorated by a museum, and the Beaux Arts gallery has a modern collection. There is a 12th–13th-century cathedral, a university 1339, and the Institut Laue-Langevin for nuclear research. The 1968 Winter Olympics were held here.

Grenville /'grenvɪl/ George 1712–1770. British Whig politician, whose introduction of the the ◊Stamp Act 1765 to raise revenue from the colonies was one of the causes of the American War of Independence. Prime minister and chancellor of the Exchequer 1763–65, Grenville took other measures to reduce the military and civil costs in North America including the Sugar Act and the Quartering Act. His inept management of the Regency Act 1765 damaged his relationship with George III. His government was also responsible for prosecuting the radical John ◊Wilkes.

Grenville Richard 1542–1591. English naval commander and adventurer, renowned for his heroic death aboard his ship *The Revenge* when attacked by Spanish warships. Grenville fought in Hungary and Ireland 1566–69, and was knighted about 1577. In 1585 he commanded the expedition that founded Virginia, USA, for his cousin, Walter ◊Raleigh. From 1586–88 he organized the defence of England against the Spanish Armada.

In 1591, as second in command of a fleet under Lord Thomas Howard that sailed to seize Spanish treasure ships returning from South America, his ship became isolated from the rest of the fleet off the Azores and was attacked by Spanish warships. After many hours hand-to-hand combat, Grenville's ship *The Revenge* succumbed; he was captured and fatally wounded. Grenville became a symbol of English nationalism and was later commemorated in the poem *The Revenge* by Tennyson (1809–92).

Grenville /'grenvɪl/ William Wyndham, Baron Grenville 1759–1834. British Whig politician, son of George Grenville. He was foreign secretary in 1791 and resigned along with Pitt in 1801 over King George III's refusal to assent to Catholic emancipation. He headed the 'All the Talents' coalition of 1806–07 which abolished the slave trade.

Grenville entered the House of Commons in 1782, held the secretaryship for Ireland, was home secretary 1791–94 and foreign secretary 1794–1801. He refused office in Pitt's government of 1804 becaus the exclusion of Charles James ◊Fox.

Gresham /'greʃəm/ Thomas c. 1519–1579. English merchant financier, who founded and paid for the Royal Exchange and propounded *Gresham's Law* that 'bad money tends to drive out good money from circulation'.

Gretna Green /'gretnə 'gri:n/ village in Dumfries and Galloway region, Scotland. It was famous for runaway marriages after they were banned in England in 1754; all that was necessary was the couple's declaration, before witnesses, of their willingness to marry. From 1856 Scottish law required at least one of the parties to be resident in Scotland for a minimum of 21 days before the marriage, and marriage by declaration was abolished in 1940.

Gretzky /'gretski/ Wayne 1961– . Canadian ice-hockey player with the Edmonton Oilers and Los Angeles Kings. He scored a record 215 points in the 1981–82 season. In 1989 he won the Hart Trophy as the National Hockey League's most valuable player of the season for a record ninth time. He broke the NHL all-time scoring record — now 1,852 points (surpassing Gordie Howe's 1,850 points).

Greuze /grɜ:z/ Jean Baptiste 1725–1805. French painter of sentimental narrative paintings, such as *The Bible Reading* 1755 (Louvre, Paris). His works were much reproduced in engravings.

Greville /'grevɪl/ Fulke, 1st Baron Brooke 1554–1628. Poet and courtier, friend and biographer of Philip Sidney. Greville's works, none of them published during his lifetime, include *Caelica*, a sequence of poems in different metres; *Mustapha* and *Alaham*, tragedies modelled on the Latin Seneca, and the *Life of Sir Philip Sidney*

Grey *Portrait of Charles Grey attributed to Thomas Phillips (c.1820), National Portrait Gallery, London.*

Grey *Portrait of Lady Jane Grey attributed to Master John (c.1545) National Portrait Gallery, London.*

1652. He has been commended for his plain style and tough political thought.

Grey /greɪ/ Beryl 1927– . British ballerina. Prima ballerina with the Sadler's Wells Company 1942–57, she then danced internationally, and was artistic director of the London Festival Ballet 1968–79.

Grey /greɪ/ Charles, 2nd Earl Grey 1764–1845. British Whig politician. He entered Parliament 1786, and in 1806 became First Lord of the Admiralty, and foreign secretary soon afterwards. As prime minister 1830–34, he carried the Great Reform Bill 1832, and the act abolishing slavery throughout the British Empire 1833.

Grey /greɪ/ Edward, 1st Viscount Grey of Fallodon 1862–1933. British Liberal politician, nephew of the 2nd Earl Grey. As foreign secretary 1905–16 he negotiated an entente with Russia in 1907, and backed France against Germany in the ◊Agadir Incident of 1911. In 1914 he said: 'The lamps are going out all over Europe; we shall not see them lit again in our lifetime.'

Grey /greɪ/ Henry, 3rd Earl Grey 1802–1894. British politician, son of Charles Grey. He served under his father as undersecretary for the colonies 1830–33, resigning because the cabinet would not back the immediate emancipation of slaves; he was secretary of war 1835–39, and colonial secretary 1846–52.

He was unique among politicians of the period in maintaining that the colonies should be governed for their own benefit, not that of Britain, and in his policy of granting self-government wherever possible. Yet he advocated convict transportation, and was opposed to Gladstone's Home Rule policy.

Grey /greɪ/ Lady Jane 1537–1554. Queen of England 9–19 July 1553, the great-granddaughter of Henry VII. She was married 1553 to Lord Guildford Dudley (died 1554), son of the Duke of ◊Northumberland. Since she was a Protestant, Edward VI was persuaded by Northumberland to set aside the claims to the throne of his sisters Mary and Elizabeth. When Edward died 6 July, Jane reluctantly accepted the crown and was proclaimed queen four days later. Mary I, however, had the support of the populace and the Lord Mayor of London announced that she was queen 19 July. Grey was executed on Tower Green.

Grey /greɪ/ Zane 1875–1939. US author of westerns, such as *Riders of the Purple Sage* 1912.

greyhound ancient breed of dog, with a long narrow muzzle, slight build, and long legs, renowned for its swiftness, it is up to 75 cm/2.5 ft tall, and can exceed 60 kph/40 mph.

greyhound racing spectator sport of watching a greyhound pursuing a mechanical dummy hare around a circular or oval track, invented in the USA 1919. It is popular in Great Britain and Australia, especially for on- and off-course betting.

The leading race in the UK is the Greyhaound Derby, first held 1927, now run at Wembley.

grid the network by which electricity is generated and distributed over a region or country. It contains many power stations and switching centres and allows, for example, high demand in one area to be met by surplus power generated in another.

Griffith *US film director D W Griffith. He pioneered many of the techniques now commonly used in film making.*

Britain has the world's largest grid system, with over 140 power stations able to supply up to 55,000 megawatts.

The term is also used for any grating system, as in a cattle grid for controlling the movement of livestock across roads, and a conductor in a storage battery or electron gun. In trigonometry, a grid is a network of uniformly spaced vertical and horizontal lines as used to locate points on a map or to construct a graph.

Grieg /griːg/ Edvard Hagerup 1843–1907. Norwegian composer. Much of his music is small scale, particularly his songs, dances, sonatas, and piano works. Among his orchestral works are the *Piano Concerto* 1869 and the incidental music for Ibsen's *Peer Gynt* 1876.

Grierson /ˈgrɪəsən/ John 1898–1972. Scottish film producer. He was a sociologist who pioneered the documentary film in Britain, viewing it as 'the creative treatment of actuality'. He directed *Drifters* 1929 and produced 1930–35 *Industrial Britain*, *Song of Ceylon*, and *Night Mail*. During World War II he created the National Film Board of Canada.

griffin mythical monster, the supposed guardian of hidden treasure, with the body, tail and hind legs of a lion, and the head, forelegs and wings of an eagle. It is often found in heraldry, for example the armorial crest of the City of London, and two griffins on the Thames Embankment guard its western boundary.

Griffith /ˈgrɪfɪθ/ D(avid) W(ark) 1875–1948. US film director. He made hundreds of 'one reel-ers' (lasting 12 minutes) 1908–13, in which he pioneered the techniques of the flash-back, cross-cut, close-up, and longshot. After much experimentation with photography and new techniques came *Birth of a Nation* 1915, followed by *Intolerance* 1916.

Griffith-Joyner /ˌgrɪfɪθˈdʒɔɪnə/ (born Griffith) Delorez Florence 1959– . US track athlete who won three gold medals at the 1988 Seoul Olympics, the 100 and 200 metres and the sprint relay. Her time in the 200 metres was a world record 21.34 seconds.

griffon small breed of dog originating in Belgium, red, black, or black and tan in colour and weighing up to 5 kg/11 lb. They are square-bodied and round-headed, and there are rough and smooth-coated varieties.

griffon vulture *Gyps fulvus*, a bird found in S Europe, W and Central Asia, and parts of Africa. It has a bald head with a neck ruff, and is 1.1 m/3.5 ft long with a wingspan of up to 2.7 m/9 ft.

Grimaldi *Joseph Grimaldi, the clown who gave the name 'Joey' to all later clowns.*

Grignard /ˈgriːnjɑː/ François Auguste-Victor 1871–1935. French chemist. The so-called ***Grignard reagents*** (compounds containing a hydrocarbon radical, magnesium, and a halogen such as chlorine) found important applications as some of the most versatile in organic synthesis. Grignard shared the 1912 Nobel Prize for Chemistry for his work on organometallic compounds.

Grillparzer /ˈgrɪlpɑːtsə/ Franz 1791–1872. Austrian poet and dramatist. His plays include the tragedy *Die Ahnfrau/The Ancestress* 1817, the classical *Sappho* 1818, and the trilogy *Das goldene Vliess/The Golden Fleece* 1821.

Born in Vienna, Grillparzer worked for the Austrian government service 1813–56. His historical tragedies *König Ottokars Glück und Ende/King Ottocar, his Rise and Fall* 1825 and *Ein treuer Diener seines Herrn/A True Servant of his Master* 1826 both involved him with the censor. Two dramas considered to be his greatest followed, *Des Meeres und der Liebe Wellen/The Waves of Sea and Love* 1831, returning to the Hellenic world, and *Der Traum, ein Leben/A Dream is Life* 1834. He wrote a bitter cycle of poems *Tristia ex Ponto* 1835 after an unhappy love-affair.

Grimaldi /grɪˈmɔːldi/ Joseph 1779–1837. British clown, born in London, the son of an Italian actor. He appeared on the stage at two years old.

He gave his name 'Joey' to all later clowns, and excelled as 'Mother Goose' performed at Covent Garden in 1806.

Grimm /grɪm/ Jakob Ludwig Karl 1785–1863. German philologist (who formulated ◊Grimm's Law) and collaborator with his brother Wilhelm Karl (1786–1859) in the *Fairy Tales* 1812–14, based on collected folk tales. Jakob's main work was his *Deutsche Grammatick/German Grammar* 1819, which gave the first historical treatment of the ◊Germanic languages.

Grimmelshausen /ˈgrɪməlzˌhauzən/ Hans Jacob Christofel von 1625–1676. German picaresque novelist whose *Der Abenteuerliche Simplicissimus/The Adventurous Simplicissimus* 1669 reflects his experiences in the Thirty Years' War.

Grimm's Law in linguistics, the rule by which certain historical sound changes have occurred in some related European languages: for example Latin 'p' became English and German 'f', as in *pater/father, Vater*.

Grimond /ˈgrɪmənd/ Jo(seph), Baron Grimond 1913– . British Liberal politician. As leader of the party 1956–67, he aimed at making it 'a new radical party to take the place of the Socialist Party as an alternative to Conservatism'.

Grimsby /ˈgrɪmzbi/ fishing port in Humberside, England; population (1985) 95,000. It declined in the 1970s when Icelandic waters were closed to British fishermen.

Gris /griːs/ Juan 1887–1927. Spanish abstract painter, one of the earliest Cubists. He developed a distinctive geometrical style, often strongly coloured. He experimented with collage and made designs for Diaghilev's ballet 1922–23.

Grisons /griːˈsɒn/ French name for the Swiss canton of ◊Graubünden.

Grivas /ˈgriːvəs/ George 1898–1974. Greek Cypriot general who led ◊EOKA's attempts to secure the union (Greek ◊enosis) of Cyprus with Greece.

Grodno /ˈgrɒdnəu/ industrial town in Byelorussia, USSR, on the Sozh river; population (1987) 263,000. Part of Lithuania from 1376, it passed to Poland 1596, Russia 1795, Poland 1920, and Russia 1939.

Gromyko /grəˈmiːkəu/ Andrei 1909–1989. President of the USSR 1985–88. As ambassador to the USA from 1943, he took part in the Tehran, Yalta, and Potsdam conferences; as United Nations representative 1946–49, he exercised the Soviet veto 26 times. He was foreign minister 1957–85. It was Gromyko who formally nominated Mikhail Gorbachev as Communist Party leader in 1985.

Groningen /ˈgrəunɪŋən/ most northerly province of the Netherlands; area 2,350 sq km/907 sq mi; population (1988) 557,000. Capital is Groningen;

Gris *Violin and Fruit Dish (1924) Tate Gallery, London.*

population (1988) 207,000. Industries include textiles, tobacco, and sugar refining.

grooming in biology, the use by an animal of teeth, tongue, feet or beak to clean fur or feathers. Grooming also helps to spread essential oils for waterproofing. In many social species, notably monkeys and apes, grooming of other individuals is used to reinforce social relationships.

Gropius /'grəʊpiəs/ Walter Adolf 1883–1969. German architect, who lived in the USA from 1937. A founder-director of the ◊Bauhaus school in Weimar 1919–28, he was an advocate of team architecture and artistic standards in industrial production. His works include the Fagus-Werke (a shoe factory in Prussia), the Model Factory at the 1914 Werkbund exhibition in Cologne, and the Harvard Graduate Center 1949–50.

grosbeak name of several thick-billed birds. The *pine grosbeak Pinicola enucleator*, also known as the *pinefinch*, breeds in Arctic forests. Its plumage is similar to that of the crossbill.

gros point a type of embroidery, using wool to fill netting (see ◊petit point). It is normally used in colourful designs on widely spaced canvas.

Gross Domestic Product (GDP) a measure (normally annual) of the total domestic output of a country, including exports, but not imports; see also ◊Gross National Product.

Grosseteste /'grəʊsteɪt/ Robert c.1169–1253. English scholar and bishop. His prolific writings include many scientific works, as well as translations of Aristotle, and commentaries on the Bible. He was a forerunner of the empirical school, being one of the earliest to suggest testing ancient Greek theories by practical experiment.

He was Bishop of Lincoln from 1235 to his death, attempting to reform morals and clerical discipline, and engaging in controversy with Innocent IV over the pope's finances.

Grossglockner /,grəʊs'glɒknə/ highest mountain in Austria, rising to 3,797 m/12,457 ft in the Hohe Tauern range of the Tirol alps.

Grossmith /'grəʊsmɪθ/ George 1847–1912. British actor and singer. Turning from journalism to the stage, in 1877 he began a long association with the Gilbert and Sullivan operas, in which he created a number of parts. He collaborated with his brother *Weedon Grossmith* (1853–1919) in the comic novel *Diary of a Nobody* 1894.

Gross National Product (GNP) the most commonly used measurement of the wealth of a country. GNP is the ◊Gross Domestic Product plus income from abroad, minus income earned during the same period by foreign investors within the country. The national income of a country is the GNP minus whatever sum of money needs to be set aside to replace ageing capital stock.

Grosz Suicide, (1916), Tate Gallery, London.

Grotius A portrait of Hugo Grotius, the 17th-century founder of international law, by A Moro.

Grosvenor family name of dukes of Westminster; seated at Eaton Hall, Cheshire, England.

Grosz /grɒs/ Georg 1893–1959. German Expressionist painter and illustrator, a founder of the Berlin group of the Dada movement 1918. Grosz excelled in savage satirical drawings criticizing the government and the military establishment. After numerous prosecutions he emigrated to the USA in 1932.

Grosz /grɒs/ Károly 1930– . Hungarian Communist politician, prime minister 1987–88. As leader of the ruling Hungarian Socialist Workers' Party (HSWP) 1988–89, he sought to establish a flexible system of 'socialist pluralism'.

Grosz, a steelworker's son, was a printer and then a newspaper editor before moving to Budapest to serve as first deputy head and then head of the HSWP agitprop department 1968–79. He was Budapest party chief 1984–87 and briefly prime minister before succeeding János Kádár as HSWP leader in May 1988. Once noted for his political orthodoxy, Grosz emerged in the late 1980s as one of the most radical reformers in the Eastern bloc. In Oct 1989 the HSWP reconstituted itself as the Hungarian Socialist Party (HSP) and Grosz was replaced as party leader by the democrat Rezso Nyers.

Grotefend /'grəʊtəfent/ George Frederick 1775–1853. German scholar. Although a student of the classical rather than the oriental languages, he nevertheless solved the riddle of the ◊cuneiform script as used in ancient Persia: decipherment of Babylonian cuneiform followed from his work.

Grotius /'grəʊtiəs/ Hugo 1583–1645. Dutch jurist and politician, born in Delft. He became a lawyer, and later received political appointments. In 1618 he was arrested as a republican and sentenced to imprisonment for life: his wife contrived his escape in 1620, and he settled in France, where he composed the *De Jure Belli et Pacis/On the Law of War and Peace* 1625, the foundation of international law. He was Swedish ambassador in Paris 1634–45.

groundnut South American annual plant, also known as the *peanut, earthnut* or *monkey nut Arachis hypogaea*, family Leguminosae. The nuts are a staple food in many tropical countries. They yield a valuable edible oil and are also used to make oilcake for cattle food.

Guangxi The limestone hills near Guilin in the Chinese province of Guangxi. In the foreground is a houseboat on the river Li.

After flowering, the flowerstalks bend and force the pods into the earth so that they can ripen in near desert conditions without desiccation.

group in mathematics, a set of elements G, finite or infinite, which can be combined by a binary operation * provided the following four conditions are satisfied: where $a, b, c, \in G$. The set is closed under *; that is, if $a * b = p$, then $p \in G$. There is an identity element $I \in G$ such that $a * I = I * a = a$. Each element a of G has an inverse a^{-1} such that $a * a^{-1} = a^{-1} * a = 1$.

grouper a number of species of sea perch (Serranidae), carniverous fish found in warm waters. Some species grow to 2 m/6.5 ft long, and can weigh 300 kg/660 lbs.

The spotted giant grouper *Promicrops itaiara* is 2–2.5 m/6–8 ft long, may weigh over 300 kg/700 lb and is sluggish in movement. Formerly game fish, they are now commercially exploited as food.

group theory in mathematics, the study of the structure and applications of sets that form groups.

grouse a fowl-like game bird of the family Tetraonidae, common in North America and N Europe. Grouse are mostly ground-living and are noted for their courtship displays, known as ◊leks.

Among the most familiar are the *red grouse Lagopus scoticus*, a native of Britain; the ◊*ptarmigans*; the *ruffed grouse Bonasia umbellus*, common in North American woods; and the *capercaillie Tetrao urogallus* and *blackcock Tetrao tetrix*, both known in Britain.

Grozny /'grɒzni/ capital of the Checheno-Ingush republic, USSR; population (1987) 404,000. It is an oil-producing centre.

GRP abbreviation for *glass-reinforced plastic*. Although usually known as ◊fibreglass, this material is only strengthened by glass fibres, the rest being plastic. GRP is now a favoured material for boat hulls and the bodies and some structural components of performance cars; it is also used in saloon car-body manufacture.

Products are usually moulded, mats of glass fibre being sandwiched between layers of a polyester plastic, which sets hard when mixed with a curing agent.

Grundy, Mrs /'grʌndi/ a symbol of rigid moral propriety, first introduced as a character in Thomas Morton's play *Speed the Plough* 1798.

Grünewald /'gru:nəvælt/ (Mathias Gothardt-Neithardt) c.1475–1528. German painter, active in Mainz, Frankfurt, and Halle. He was court painter, architect, and engineer to the prince bishop elector of Mainz 1508–14. His few surviving paintings show an intense involvement with religious subjects.

The *Isenheim altarpiece*, 1515 (Colmar Museum, France), with its horribly tortured figure of Jesus, recalls medieval traditions.

Gruyère /gru:'jeə/ district in W Switzerland, famous for pale yellow cheese with large holes.

G scale scale for measuring force by comparing it with the force due to ◊gravity, G. Astronauts in the Space Shuttle experience over 3 G on lift-off.

Guadalajara /ˌgwɑːdələˈhɑːrə/ industrial (textiles, glass, soap, pottery) capital of Jalisco state, W Mexico; population (1986) 2,587,000. It is a key communications centre.

It has a 16th–17th century cathedral, the Governor's Palace, and an orphanage with murals by the Mexican painter José Orozco.

Guadalcanal /ˌgwɑːdlkəˈnæl/ largest of the ◊Solomon Islands; area 6,500 sq km/2,510 sq mi; population (1987) 71,000. Gold, copra, and rubber are produced. During World War II it was the scene of a battle which was won by US forces after six months of fighting.

Guadeloupe /ˌgwɑːdəˈluːp/ an island group in the Leeward Islands, West Indies, an overseas *département* of France; area 1,705 sq km/658 sq mi; population (1982) 328,400. The main islands are Basse-Terre, on which is the chief town of the same name, and Grande-Terre. Sugar refining and rum distilling are the main industries.

Guam /gwɑːm/ largest of the ◊Mariana Islands in the W Pacific, an unincorporated territory of the USA
area 540 sq km/208 sq mi
capital Agaña
towns port Apra
features major US air and naval base, much used in the Vietnam War; tropical, with much rain
products sweet potatoes, fish; tourism is important
currency US dollar
population (1984) 116,000
language English, Chamorro (basically Malay-Polynesian)
religion Roman Catholic 96%
government popularly elected governor (Ricardo Bordallo from 1985) and single-chamber legislature
recent history Guam was ceded by Spain to the USA 1898, and occupied by Japan 1941–44. It was granted full US citizenship and self-government from 1950. A referendum 1982 favoured Commonwealth status.

guan type of large, pheasant-like bird which lives in the forests of South and Central America. It is olive-green or brown.

guanaco wild member of the camel family *Lama guanacoe*, found in South America on pampas and mountain plateaux. It grows to 1.2 m/4 ft at the shoulder, with head and body about 1.5 m/5 ft long. It is sandy-brown in colour, with a blackish face, and has fine wool. It lives in small herds and is the ancestor of the domestic llama.

Guanch Republic /gwɑːntʃ/ proposed name for an independent state in the ◊Canary Islands.

Guangdong /ˌgwæŋˈduŋ/ formerly *Kwantung* province of S China
area 231,400 sq km/89,320 sq mi
capital ◊Guangzhou
features tropical climate; Hainan, Leizhou peninsula, and the foreign enclaves of Hong Kong and Macao in the Pearl River delta
products rice, sugar, tobacco, minerals, fish
population (1986) 63,640,000.

Guangxi formerly *Kwangsi Chuang* autonomous region in S China
area 220,400 sq km/85,074 sq mi
capital Nanning
products rice, sugar, fruit
population (1986) 39,460,000, including the Zhuang people, allied to the Thai, who form China's largest ethnic minority.

Guangzhou /ˌgwæŋˈdʒəʊ/ formerly *Kwangchow/Canton* capital of Guangdong province, S China; population (1986) 3,290,000. Its industries include shipbuilding, engineering, chemicals, and textiles.

Sun Yat-sen Memorial Hall, a theatre, commemorates the politician, who was born nearby and founded the university. There is a rail link with Beijing and one is planned with Liuzhou.

history It was the first Chinese port opened to foreign trade, the Portuguese visiting it 1516, and

Guatemala
Republic of
(República de Guatemala)

area 108,889 sq km/42,031 sq mi
capital Guatemala City
towns Quezaltenango, Puerto Barrios (naval base)
physical mountainous, tropical
features earthquakes are frequent
head of state and government Mario Vinicio Cerezo Arevalo from 1986
political system democratic republic
political parties Guatemalan Christian Democratic Party (PDCG), Christian centre-left; Centre Party (UCN), centrist; National Democratic Co-operation Party (PDNC), centre-right; Revolutionary Party (PR), radical; Movement of National Liberation (MLN), extreme right-wing; Democratic Institutional Party (PID), moderate conservative
exports coffee, bananas, cotton
currency quetzal (6.42 = £1 Feb 1990)
population (1988) 8,990,000 (Mayaquiche Indians 54%, mestizos 42%); annual growth rate 2.8%
life expectancy men 57, women 61
language Spanish
religion Roman Catholic
literacy 63% male/47% female (1985 est)
GDP $9.9 bn (1984); $1,085 per head of population
chronology
1839 Independent republic.
1954 Col Carlos Castillo became president in a US-backed coup, halting land reform.
1963 Military coup made Col Enrique Peralta president.
1966 Cesar Méndez elected president.
1970 Carlos Araña elected president.
1974 Gen Kjell Laugerud became president. Widespread political violence.
1978 Gen Fernando Romeo became president.
1981 Growth of anti-government guerrilla movement.
1982 Gen Angel Anibal became president. An army coup installed Gen Ríos Montt as head of a junta and then as president. Political violence continued.
1983 Montt removed in a coup led by Gen Mejía Victores, who declared amnesty for the guerrillas.
1985 New constitution adopted; PDCG won congressional elections; Vincio Cerezo elected president.
1989 Coup attempt against Cerezo foiled. Over 100,000 people killed and 40,000 reported missing since 1979.

was a treaty port from 1842 until its occupation by Japan 1938.

Guantanamo /gwænˈtɑːnəməʊ/ capital of a province of the same name in SE Cuba; population (1986) 174,400; a trading centre in a fertile agricultural region producing sugar. Iron, copper, chromium and manganese are mined nearby. There is a US naval base.

Guanyin in Chinese Buddhism, the goddess of mercy. In Japan she is *Kwannon* or Kannon, an attendant of the Amida Buddha (Amitābha). Her origins were in India as the male bodhisattva Avalokiteśvara.

guarana Brazilian woody climbing plant *Paullinia cupana*, family Sapindaceae. A drink made from its roasted seeds has a high caffeine content, and it is the source of the drug known as zoom in the USA. Starch, gum, and several oils are extracted from it for commercial use.

Guaraní /ˌgwɑːrəˈniː/ a South American Indian people of modern Paraguay, S Brazil, and Bolivia.

Guardi /ˈgwɑːdi/ Francesco 1712–1793. Italian painter. He produced souvenir views of his native Venice, which were commercially less successful than Canaletto's but are now considered more atmospheric, with subtler use of reflected light.

Guareschi /gwəˈreski/ Giovanni 1909–1968. Italian author of short stories of the friendly feud between parish priest Don Camillo and the Communist village mayor.

Guarneri /ˈgwɑːrneəri/ celebrated family of stringed-instrument makers of Cremona, Italy. The one known as Giuseppe 'del Gesù' (1698–1744) produced the finest models.

Guatemala /ˌgwɑːtəˈmɑːlə/ country in Central America, bounded N and NW by Mexico, E by Belize and the Caribbean Sea, SE by Honduras and El Salvador, and SW by the Pacific Ocean.

government The 1985 constitution provides for a single-chamber national assembly of 100 deputies, 75 elected directly by universal suffrage, and the rest on the basis of proportional representation. They serve a five-year term. The president, also directly elected for a similar term, appoints a cabinet and is assisted by a vice president, and is not eligible for re-election. There is a multiplicity of political parties, the most significant being the Guatemalan Christian Democratic Party (PDCG), the Centre Party (UCN), the National Democratic Co-operation Party (PDCN), the Revolutionary Party (PR), the Movement of National Liberation (MLN), and the Democratic Institutional Party (PID).

history Formerly part of the ◊Maya empire, Guatemala became a Spanish colony 1524. Independent from Spain 1821, it then joined Mexico, becoming independent 1823. It was part of the ◊Central American Federation 1823–39, and was then ruled by a succession of dictators until the presidency of Juan José Arévalo 1944, and his successor, Col Jacobo Arbenz. Their socialist administrations both followed programmes of reform, including land appropriation, but Arbenz's nationalization of the United Fruit Company's plantations 1954 so alarmed the US government that it sponsored a revolution, led by Col Carlos Castillo Armas, who then assumed the presidency. He was assassinated 1963 and the army continued to rule until 1966. There was a brief return to constitutional government until the military returned 1970.

The next ten years saw much political violence, in which it was estimated that over 50,000 people died. In the 1982 presidential election the government candidate won but opponents complained that the election had been rigged, and before he could take office, there was a coup by a group of young right-wing officers, who installed Gen Rios Montt as head of a three-man junta. He soon dissolved the junta, assumed the presidency, and began fighting corruption and ending violence.

The anti-government guerrilla movement was, however, growing, and was countered by repressive measures by Montt, so that by 1983 opposition to him was widespread. After several unsuccessful attempts to remove him, a coup led by Gen Mejia Victores finally succeeded. Mejia Victores declared an amnesty for the guerrillas, the ending of press censorship, and the preparation of a new constitution. This was adopted 1985 and in the elections which followed, the PDCG won a majority in the congress as well as the presidency, Vinicio Cerezo becoming president. In 1989 an attempted coup against Cerezo was put down by the army.

Over 100,000 people were killed and 40,000 disappeared 1980–89. Two per cent of the population own over 70% of the land; 87% of children under the age of five suffer from malnutrition.

Guatemala City /ˌgwɑːtəˈmɑːlə/ capital of Guatemala; population (1983) 1,300,000. It produces textiles, tyres, footwear, and cement.

It was founded in 1776 when its predecessor (Antigua) was destroyed in an earthquake. It was severely damaged by another earthquake 1976.

guava tropical American tree *Psidium guajava*, family Myrtaceae; the astringent yellow pear-shaped fruit is used to make guava jelly, or it can be stewed or canned. It has a high vitamin C content.

Guayaquil /ˌgwaɪəˈkiːl/ city and chief Pacific port of Ecuador, at the mouth of the Guayas River; population (1982) 1,300,868.

Guderian /guˈdeəriən/ Heinz 1888–1954. German general in World War II. He created the Panzer armoured divisions of the German army that formed the ground spearhead of Hitler's *Blitzkrieg* strategy, and achieved an important breakthrough at Sedan in Ardennes, France 1940 and the advance to Moscow 1941.

gudgeon freshwater cyprinid fish *Gobio gobio* found in Europe and N Asia on the gravel bottoms of streams. It is olive-brown, spotted with black, up to 20 cm/8 in long, and with a distinctive barbel at each side of the mouth.

guelder rose shrub or small tree *Viburnum opulus*, native to Europe and N Africa, with white flowers and shiny red berries.

Guelders /ˈgeldəz/ another name for ◊Gelderland, a region of the Netherlands.

Guelph /gwelf/ industrial town and agricultural centre in SE Ontario, Canada, on the Speed river; population (1981) 71,250. Industries include food processing, electricals, and pharmaceuticals.

Guelph and Ghibelline rival parties in medieval Germany and Italy, which supported the papal party and the Holy Roman emperors respectively.

They originated in the 12th century as partisans of the rival German houses of Welf (hence Guelph or Guelf), dukes of Bavaria, and of the lords of ◊Hohenstaufen (whose castle at Waiblingen gave the Ghibellines their name), who struggled for the imperial crown after the death of Henry VI in 1197, until the Hohenstaufen dynasty died out in 1268. The Guelphs early became associated with the papacy because of their mutual Hohenstaufen enemy. In Italy, the terms were introduced about 1242, in Florence; the names seem to have been grafted on to pre-existing papal and imperial factions within the city-republics.

Guercino /gweəˈtʃiːnəʊ/ Adopted name of Giovanni Francesco Barbieri 1590–1666. Italian Baroque painter active chiefly in Rome. In his ceiling painting of *Aurora* 1621–23 (Villa Ludovisi, Rome), the chariot-borne figure of dawn rides across the heavens, and the architectural framework is imitated in the painting, giving the illusion that the ceiling opens into the sky.

Guercino's use of dramatic lighting recalls ◊Caravaggio, but his brighter colours are in contrasting mood. His later works, when he had retired from Rome to Bologna, are closer in style to Guido ◊Reni.

Guérin /ˈgeəræn/ Camille 1872–1961. French bacteriologist who, with ◊Calmette, developed the Bacille Calmette-Guérin (BCG) vaccine for tuberculosis.

Guernica /geəˈniːkə/ town in the ◊Basque provinces of Vizcaya, N Spain; population (1981) 18,000. It was where the Castilian kings formerly swore to respect the rights of the Basques. It was

almost completely destroyed in 1937 by German bombers aiding Franco in the Spanish Civil War, and rebuilt in 1946. The bombing inspired a painting by Picasso, and a play by Fernando Arrabal (1932–).

Guernsey /ˈgɜːnzi/ second largest of the ◊Channel Islands; area 63 sq km/24.5 sq mi; population (1986) 55,500. The capital is St Peter Port. From 1975 it has been a major financial centre. Guernsey cattle originated here.

Products include electronics, tomatoes, flowers, and more recently butterflies. Guernsey cattle are a pale fawn colour, and give rich creamy milk. Guernsey has belonged to the English Crown since 1066, but was occupied by German forces 1940–45. Guernsey has no jury system; instead, it has a Royal Court with 12 jurats (full-time unpaid jurymen appointed by an electoral college) with no legal training. This system dates from Norman times. Jurats cannot be challenged or replaced.

guerrilla irregular soldier fighting in a small unofficial unit, typically against an established or occupying power, and engaging in sabotage, ambush, and the like, rather than pitched battles against an opposing army. Guerrilla tactics have been used both by resistance armies in wartime (for example, the Vietnam War) and in peacetime by national liberation groups and militant political extremists.

The term was first applied to the Spanish and Portuguese resistance to French occupation during the Peninsular War, and guerrilla techniques were widely used in World War II, for example in Greece and the Balkans. Political activists who resort to violence, particularly **urban guerrillas**, tend to be called 'freedom fighters' by those who support their cause, 'terrorists' by those who oppose it.

Efforts by governments to put a stop to their activities have had only sporadic success. The Council of Europe has set up the European Convention on the Suppression of Terrorism, to which many governments are signatories. In the UK the Prevention of Terrorism Act 1984 is aimed particularly at the IRA. The Institute for the Study of Terrorism was founded in London 1986.

Violent activities (bombings, kidnappings, hijackings) by such groups as these have proliferated considerably in recent years; in 1984 there were 600 international incidents of politically motivated violence, a 20% increase on the average over the previous five years. Cooperation between the groups (for example in arms supply) has developed, as has state support (such as the USA's for the Contras and Libya's for many groups, including the IRA).

Groups active in recent years include:

Action Directe French group in alliance with Red Army Faction (see below); carries out bombings in Paris and elsewhere.

Amal Shi'ite Muslim militia in Lebanon.

Armed Revolutionary Nuclei (NAR) neo-fascist; 1980 bomb in Bologna railway station, Italy, killed 76.

Black September Palestinian group named from the month when PLO guerrillas active in Jordan were suppressed by the Jordanian army; killed 11 Israelis at the Munich Olympic Games 1972.

Contras right-wing guerrillas in Nicaragua who opposed the Sandinista government (see below); they received funding from the USA.

ETA Basque separatist movement in N Spain.

Hezbollah Shi'ite Muslim militia in Lebanon, the extremist wing of Amal (see above); backed by Syria and Iran.

Irish Republican Army (IRA) organization committed to the formation of a unified Irish republic.

Palestine Liberation Organization (PLO) organization committed to the creation of a separate Palestinian state.

Québec Liberation Front (FLQ) separatist organization in Canada committed to the creation of an independent French-speaking Québec; kidnapped and killed minister Pierre Laporte 1970.

Red Army Japan: killed 26 people at Lod airport in Israel 1972; attacked the US embassy in Indonesia 1986 and 1987.

Red Army Faction (RAF) opposing 'US imperialism', formerly led by Andreas Baader and Ulrike Meinhof, active in West Germany from 1968.

Red Brigades Italy: kidnap and murder of Prime Minister Aldo Moro 1978; kidnap of US Brig-Gen James Lee Dozier 1981.

Sandinista National Liberation Front (SNLF) Marxist organization which overthrew the dictatorship in Nicaragua 1978–79 to form its own government. It was defeated in Feb 1990 elections.

Symbionese Liberation Army (SLA) kidnapped Patricia Hearst, granddaughter of the newspaper tycoon, in the USA 1974.

Tamil Tigers Tamil separatist organization in Sri Lanka.

Tupamaros left-wing urban guerrillas founded by Raoul Sendic in Montevideo, Uruguay, 1960; named after the Peruvian Indian leader Tupac Amaru.

Ulster Defence Association (UDA) Protestant anti-IRA organization in Northern Ireland, formed 1971; it sometimes uses the name Ulster Freedom Fighters.

Guesdes /ged/ Jules 1845–1922. French socialist leader from the 1880s who espoused Marxism and revolutionary change. His movement, the *Partie Ouvrier Français* ('French Workers' Party'), was eventually incorporated in the foundation of the SFIO (*Section Française de l'International Ouvrière*/ 'French Section of International Labour') in 1905.

Guevara /gɪˈvɑːrə/ 'Che' (Ernesto) 1928–1967. Latin American revolutionary. He was born in Argentina and trained there as a doctor, but in 1953 left his homeland because of his opposition to the right-wing president Perón. In effecting the Cuban revolution of 1959, he was second only to Castro and Castro's brother Raúl. In 1965 he went to the Congo to fight against white mercenaries, and then to Bolivia, where he was killed in an unsuccessful attempt to lead a peasant rising. He was an orthodox Marxist, and renowned for his guerrilla techniques.

Guiana /giːˈɑːnə/ the NE part of South America, which includes ◊French Guiana, ◊Guyana, and ◊Suriname.

Guido /ˈgiːdəʊ/ Reni Italian painter, see ◊Reni.

Guienne /giːˈen/ ancient province of SW France which formed the duchy of Aquitaine with Gascony 12th century. Its capital was Bordeaux. It became English 1154 and passed to France 1453.

guild or *gild* medieval association, particularly of artisans or merchants, formed for mutual aid and protection and the pursuit of a common purpose, religious or economic. They became politically powerful in Europe. After the 16th century the position of the guilds was undermined by the growth of capitalism.

Guilds fulfilling charitable or religious functions, such as the maintenance of schools, roads, or bridges, the assistance of members in misfortune, or the provision of masses for the souls of dead members, flourished in western Europe from the 9th century, but were suppressed in Protestant countries at the Reformation.

The earliest form of economic guild, the **guild merchant**, arose in the 11th–12th centuries; this was an organization of the traders of a town, who had been granted a practical monopoly of its trade by charter. As the merchants often strove to exclude craftworkers from the guild, and to monopolize control of local government, the **craft guilds** came into existence in the 12th–13th centuries. These, which included journeymen (day workers) and apprentices as well as employers, regulated prices, wages, working conditions and apprenticeship, prevented unfair practices, and maintained high standards of craft; they also fulfilled many social, religious, and charitable functions. By the 14th century they had taken control of local government, ousting the guild merchant.

Guildford /'gɪlfəd/ city in Surrey, S England, on the river Wey; population (1981) 56,500. It has a ruined Norman castle; a cathedral designed by Edward ◊Maufe (1936–61); the University of Surrey 1966; and a theatre (1964) named after the comedy actress Yvonne Arnaud (1895–1958). There is a cattle market, and industries include flour-milling, plastics, and engineering.

Guild Socialism an early 20th-century movement in Britain whose aim was to organize and control the industrial life of the country through self-governing democratic guilds of workers. Catholic inspired, it was anti-materialistic and attempted to arrest what it saw as a spiritual decline in modern civilization. The National Guilds League was founded in 1915, and at the movement's height there were over 20 guilds, but in 1925 the League was dissolved.

Guilin /ˌgweɪ'lɪn/ (formerly **Kweilin**) principal tourist city of S China, on the Li river, Guangxi province. The dramatic limestone mountains are a major attraction.

Guillaume /'giːəʊm/ Charles 1861–1938. Swiss physicist who studied measurement and alloy development. He discovered a nickel–steel alloy, invar, which showed negligible expansion with rising temperatures. Nobel Physics Prize 1920.

As the son of a clockmaker, Guillaume came early in life to appreciate the value of precision in measurement. He spent most of his life at the International Bureau of Weights and Measures at Sèvres, which established the standards for the metre, litre, and kilogram.

guillemot diving seabird of the auk family which breeds in large numbers on the rocky N Atlantic coasts. The **common guillemot** *Uria aalge* has a sharp bill and short tail, and sooty-brown and white plumage. Guillemots build no nest, but lay one large, almost conical egg on the rock.

guillotine beheading device consisting of a metal blade that descends between two posts. It was commonly in use in the Middle Ages, but was introduced in an improved design (by physician Joseph Ignace Guillotin 1738–1814) in France in 1792 during the Revolution. It is still in use in some countries.

guillotine in politics, a device used by governments in the UK in which the time allowed for debating a bill in the House of Commons is restricted so as to ensure its speedy passage to receiving the royal assent (that is, to becoming law). The tactic of guillotining was introduced during the 1880s to overcome attempts by Irish members of Parliament to obstruct the passing of legislation.

guinea /'gɪnɪ/ English gold coin, notionally worth 21 shillings (£1.05). It has not been minted since 1817, when it was superseded by the gold sovereign, but was used until 1971 in billing professional fees.

Guinea /'gɪnɪ/ country in W Africa, bounded to the N by Senegal, NE by Mali, SE by the Ivory Coast, SW by Liberia and Sierra Leone, W by the Atlantic, and NW by Guinea-Bissau.

government The 1982 constitution, which provided for an elected national assembly, was suspended in 1984, after a military coup. A military committee for national recovery assumed power. The president is head of both state and government and leads an appointed council of ministers. The sole political party, the Democratic Party of Guinea (PDG), was dissolved after the coup and opposition groups now operate from abroad.

history Formerly part of the Muslim ◊Mali empire, which flourished in the region between the 7th and 15th centuries. Guinea's first European visitors were the Portuguese in the mid-15th century, who, together with France and Britain, established the slave trade in the area. In 1849 France proclaimed the Boké region in the E a French protectorate and expanded its territory until by the late 19th century most of W Africa was united under French rule as ◊French West Africa.

French Guinea became fully independent in 1958, under the name of Guinea, after a referendum rejected a proposal to remain a self-governing colony within the French Community. The first president was Sekou Touré, who made the PDG the only political organization and embarked upon a policy of socialist revolution. There were unsuccessful attempts to overthrow him in 1961, 1965, 1967, and 1970 and, suspicious of conspiracies by foreign powers, he put his country for a time into virtual diplomatic isolation. By 1975, however, relations with most of his neighbours had returned to normal.

Initially rigidly Marxist, crushing opposition to his policies, Touré gradually moved towards a mixed economy, private enterprise becoming legal in 1979. His regime was, nevertheless, authoritarian and harsh. He sought closer relations with Western powers, particularly France and the USA, and was re-elected unopposed in 1980. In 1984 he died while undergoing heart surgery in the USA.

Before the normal machinery for electing his successor could be put into operation, the army staged a bloodless coup, suspending the constitution and setting up a military committee for national recovery, with Col Lansana Conté at its head. He pledged to restore democracy and respect human rights, releasing hundreds of political prisoners and lifting press restrictions. Conté then made efforts to restore his country's international standing through a series of overseas visits. He succeeded in persuading some 200,000 Guineans who had fled the country during the Touré regime to return. In 1985 an attempt to overthrow him while he was out of the country was foiled by loyal troops.

Guinea-Bissau /'gɪnɪ bɪ'saʊ/ country in W Africa, bounded to the N by Senegal, E and SE by Guinea, and SW by the Atlantic.

government Guinea-Bissau is a one-party state, the 1984 constitution describing the African Party for the Independence of Portuguese Guinea and Cape Verde (PAIGC) as 'the leading force in society and in the nation'. Although Cape Verde chose independence, the title of the original party which served the two countries has been retained. The constitution also provides for a 150-member national people's assembly, all nominees of PAIGC. The assembly elects the president, who is head of both state and government. Policy is determined by PAIGC and it is there that ultimate political

power lies, the president being its secretary-general.

history Guinea-Bissau was first reached by Europeans when the Portuguese arrived in 1446, and became a slave trading centre. Until 1879 it was administered with the Cape Verde islands, but then became a separate colony under the name of Portuguese Guinea.

Nationalist groups began to form in the 1950s and PAIGC was established in 1956. Portugal refused to grant independence, fighting broke out, and by 1972 PAIGC claimed to control two-thirds of the country. The following year the 'liberated areas' were declared independent and in 1973 a national people's assembly was set up and Luiz Cabral appointed president of a state council. Some 40,000 Portuguese troops were engaged in trying to put down the uprising and were suffering heavy losses but, before a clear outcome was reached, a coup in Portugal ended the fighting and PAIGC negotiated independence with the new government in Lisbon.

In 1974 Portugal formally acknowledged Guinea-Bissau as a sovereign nation. PAIGC began to lay the foundations of a socialist state, intended to include Cape Verde, but in 1980, four days before approval of the constitution, Cape Verde withdrew, feeling that Guinea-Bissau was being given preferential treatment. A coup deposed Cabral and JoaVieira became chair of a council of revolution.

At its 1981 congress, PAIGC decided to retain its name, despite Cape Verde's withdrawal, and its position as the only party was confirmed, with Vieira as secretary-general. Normal relations between the two countries were restored in 1982. In 1984 a new constitution made Vieira head of government as well as head of state. In June 1989 he was re-elected for another five-year term.

Guinea Coast /'gɪnɪ/ the coast of W Africa between Gambia and Cape Lopez.

guinea fowl African game bird, family Numididae, especially the **helmet guinea fowl** *Numida meleagris*, which has a horny growth on the head, white-spotted feathers, and fleshy cheek wattles. It is the ancestor of the domestic fowl.

guinea pig a species of ◊cavy, a type of rodent.

Guinevere Welsh *Gwenhwyfar* in Arthurian legend, the wife of King ◊Arthur. Her adulterous love affair with the knight ◊Lancelot led ultimately to Arthur's death.

Guinea
Republic of
(République de Guinée)

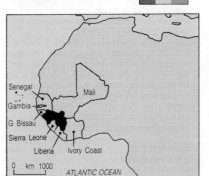

area 245,857 sq km/94,901 sq mi
capital Conakry
towns Labe, N'Zerekore, KanKan
physical mainly mountainous; sources of rivers Niger, Gambia, and Senegal; forest in SE
features Fouta Djallon, area of sandstone plateaus, cut by deep valleys
head of state and government Lansana Conté from 1984

political system military republic
political parties none since 1984
exports coffee, rice, palm kernels, alumina, bauxite, diamonds
currency syli or franc (510.75 = £1 Feb 1990)
population (1988) 6,533,000 (chief peoples are Fulani 40%, Mandingo 25%); annual growth rate 2.3%
life expectancy men 39, women 42
language French (official)
religion Muslim 62%, Christian 15%, local 35%
literacy 40% male/17% female (1985 est)
GNP $1.6 bn (1983); $305 per head of population
chronology
1958 Full independence from France achieved. Sékou Touré elected president.
1977 Strong opposition to Touré's policies of rigid Marxism forced him to accept the return of a mixed economy.
1980 Touré returned unopposed for a fourth seven-year term of office.
1984 Touré died. A bloodless coup established a military committee for national recovery, with Col Lansana Conté at its head.
1985 Attempted coup against Conté while he was out of the country was foiled by loyal troops.

Guinea-Bissau
(Republica da Guiné-Bissau)

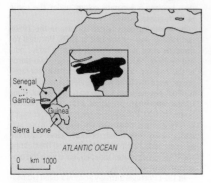

Senegal
Gambia
Guinea
Sierra Leone
ATLANTIC OCEAN
0   km 1000

area 36,125 sq km/13,944 sq mi
capital and chief port Bissau
physical flat lowlands
features the archipelago of Bijagos
head of state and government João Bernardo Vieira from 1980
political system one-party socialist republic
political parties African Party for the

Independence of Portuguese Guinea and Cape Verde (PAIGC), nationalist socialist
exports rice, coconuts, peanuts, fish, salt
currency peso (1,106.62 = £1 Feb 1990)
population (1988 est) 932,000; annual growth rate 1.9%
life expectancy men 41, women 45
language Crioulo, Cape Verdean dialect of Portuguese
religion Muslim 40%, Christian 4%
literacy 46% male/17% female (1985 est)
GDP $177 million (1982); $165 per head of population
chronology
1956 PAIGC formed to secure independence from Portugal.
1973 Two-thirds of the country declared independent, with Luiz Cabral as president of a state council.
1974 Portugal recognized independence of Guinea-Bissau.
1980 Cape Verde decided not to join a unified state. Cabral deposed and João Vieira became chair of a council of revolution.
1981 PAIGC confirmed as the only legal party, with Vieira as its secretary general.
1982 Normal relations with Cape Verde restored.
1984 New constitution adopted, making Vieira head of government as well as head of state.
1989 Vieira re-elected.

Guinness *English actor Alec Guinness.*

Guinness brewing family who produced the dark, bitter beer of the same name. In 1752 Arthur Guinness (1725–1803) inherited £100 and used it to set up a brewery in Leixlip, County Kildare. In 1759 he moved to Dublin. He was succeeded by his son, Arthur (1767–1855), who made the decision to concentrate entirely on the brewing of porter. Further advances were made by his son Benjamin (1798–1868) who decided to develop an export market in the USA and Europe. In the 1980s, the family interest in the business declined to no more than 5% as the company expanded by taking over large and established firms such as Bells in 1985 and Distillers in 1986.

Guinness /ˈgɪnɪs/ Alec 1914– . English actor. His many stage roles include Shakespeare's Hamlet 1938 and Lawrence of Arabia (in *Ross* 1960). In 1979 he gained a 'lifetime achievement' Oscar (films include *Kind Hearts and Coronets* 1949, *The Bridge on the River Kwai* 1957, and *Star Wars* 1977).

Guinness joined the Old Vic 1936. He appeared in the television adaptations of John Le Carré's *Tinker, Tailor, Soldier, Spy* 1979 and *Smiley's People* 1981.

Guinness affair a case of alleged financial fraud during the attempted takeover by the brewing company Guinness of Distillers in 1986. Those accused of acting illegally to sustain Guinness share prices include Ernest Saunders, former chief executive. The trial, which opened Feb 1990, was widely seen as the first major test of the UK government's legislation increasing control of financial dealings on London's Stock Exchange.

Guise /gwiːz/ Francis, 2nd Duke of Guise 1519–1563. French soldier and politician. He led the French victory over Germany at Metz 1552 and captured Calais from the English 1558. Along with his brother Charles (1527–74) he was powerful in the government of France during the reign of Francis II. He was assassinated attempting to crush the Huguenots.

Guise /gwiːz/ Henri, 3rd Duke of Guise 1550–1588. French nobleman who persecuted the Huguenots and was partly responsible for the Massacre of ◊St Bartholomew 1572. He was assassinated.

guitar six-stringed, flat-bodied musical instrument, plucked or strummed with the fingers. The *Hawaiian guitar*, laid across the lap, uses a metal bar to produce a distinctive gliding tone;

the solid-bodied *electric guitar*, developed in the 1950s, mixes and amplifies vibrations from microphone contacts at different points to produce a range of tone qualities.

Derived from a Moorish original, the guitar spread throughout Europe in medieval times, becoming firmly established in Italy, Spain, and the Spanish American colonies. Its 20th-century revival owes much to Andrés ◊Segovia, Julian ◊Bream, and John ◊Williams. The guitar's prominence in US popular music can be traced from the country traditions of the mid-West; it played a supporting harmony role in jazz and dance bands during the 1920s and adapted quickly to electric amplification.

Guiyang /ˈgweɪˈjæŋ/ formerly *Kweiyang* capital and industrial city of Guizhou province, S China; population (1986) 1,380,000. Industries include metals and machinery.

Guizhou /ˈgweɪˈdʒəʊ/ formerly *Kweichow* province of S China
area 174,000 sq km/67,164 sq mi
capital Guiyang
features includes many minority groups which have often been in revolt
products rice, maize, nonferrous minerals
population (1986) 30,080,000.

Guizot /giːˈzəʊ/ François Pierre Guillaume 1787–1874. French politician and historian, professor of modern history at the Sorbonne, Paris, 1812–30. He wrote a history of civilization, and became prime minister in 1847. His resistance to all reforms led to the revolution of 1848.

Gujarat /ˌgudʒəˈrɑːt/ state of W India
area 196,000 sq km/75,656 sq mi
capital Ahmedabad
features heavily industrialized; includes most of the Rann of Kutch; the Gir Forest is the last home of the wild Asian lion
products cotton, petrochemicals, oil, gas, rice, textiles
population (1984) 33,961,000
languages Gujarati, Hindi.

Gujarati inhabitant of Gujarat on the NW seaboard of India. The Gujaratis number approximately 27 million, and speak their own language, Gujarati. They are predominantly Hindu (90%), with Muslim (8%) and Jain (2%) minorities.

Gujarati language or *Gujerati* a member of the Indo-Iranian branch of the Indo-European language family, spoken in and around the state of

Gujarat in India. It is written in its own script, a variant of the Devanagari script used for Sanskrit and Hindi.

Gujranwala /ˌgudʒrənˈwɑːlə/ city in Punjab province, Pakistan; population (1981) 597,000. It is a centre of grain trading. It is a former Sikh capital, and the birthplace of Sikh leader Ranjit Singh (1780–1839).

Gulf States oil-rich countries sharing the coastline of the ◊Persian Gulf (Bahrain, Iran, Iraq, Kuwait, Oman, Qatar, Saudi Arabia, and the United Arab Emirates). Except for Iran and Iraq, the Persian Gulf States formed a Gulf Cooperation Council (GCC) 1981.

In the USA, the term refers to those states bordering the Gulf of Mexico (Alabama, Florida, Louisiana, Mississippi, and Texas).

Gulf Stream ocean ◊current branching from the warm waters of the equatorial current, which flows N from the Gulf of Mexico. It slows to a widening 'drift' off Newfoundland, splitting as it flows E across the Atlantic, and warms what would otherwise be a colder climate in the British Isles and Western Europe.

Gulf War another name for the ◊Iran–Iraq War.

gull seabird of the family Laridae. Gulls are usually 25–75 cm/10–30 in long, white with grey or black on the back and wings, and with a large beak.

The *black-headed gull Larus ridibundus*, common in Britain, is grey and white with (in summer) dark brown head and red beak; it breeds in large colonies on marshland, making a nest of dead rushes. It lays on average three eggs. The *great black-headed gull Larus ichthyaetus* is native to Asia. The larger *laughing gull* and *herring gull Larus argentatus* live in North

Gujarat

Gandhinagar

INDIAN OCEAN

Gutenberg *The earliest illustration of a printing press, as invented by Johann Gutenberg. It is from the* Danse Macabre *printed by Mathias Lyons, 1499.*

America. The latter, often known as the harbour gull, has white and pearl-grey plumage and yellow beak. The oceanic **great black-backed gull** *Larus marinus*, found in the Atlantic, is over 75 cm/2.5 ft long.

Gullit /ˈgʊlɪt/ Ruud 1962– . Dutch international footballer, who played an important role in Holland's capture of the European Championship in 1988. After playing in Holland with Haarlem, Feyenoord, and PSV Eindhoven he moved to AC Milan in 1987 for a transfer fee of £5.5 million.

CAREER HIGHLIGHTS

Dutch League 1984, 1986–7
Dutch Cup 1984
European Footballer of the Year 1987
European Championship 1988
European Cup 1989
European Super Cup 1989

Gulliver's Travels satirical novel by the Irish writer Jonathan ◊Swift published 1726. The four countries visited by the narrator Gulliver ridicule different aspects of human nature, customs, and politics.

Gulliver's travels take him to *Lilliput*, whose inhabitants are only 15 cm/6 in tall; *Brobdignag*, where they are gigantic; *Laputa*, run by mad scientists; and the land of the *Houyhnhnms*, horses who embody reason and virtue, while the human Yahoos have only the worst human qualities.

gum complex polysaccharides (carbohydrates) formed by many plants and trees, particularly by those from dry regions. Gums form five main groups: plant exudates (gum arabic); marine plant extracts (agar); seed extracts; fruit and vegetable extracts; and synthetic gums. They are used for adhesives, sizing fabrics, in confectionery, medicine, and calico printing.

Gums are tasteless and odourless, insoluble in alcohol and ether but generally soluble in water. Gum is also a common name for the ◊eucalyptus tree.

gum in mammals, the soft tissues surrounding the base of the tooth. They are liable to inflammation or to infection by microbes from food deposits (gingivitis or periodontal disease).

gum arabic substance obtained from certain species of ◊acacia, with uses in medicine, confectionery, and adhesive manufacture.

Gummer /ˈgʌmə/ John Selwyn 1939– . British Conservative politician. He was minister of state for employment 1983–84, paymaster general 1984–85, minister for agriculture 1985– ,

chair of the party 1983–85, and minister for agriculture from 1989.

gun general name for any kind of firearm; see also ◊artillery, ◊machine gun, ◊pistol, and ◊small arms.

gun metal a high-copper (88%) alloy, also containing tin and zinc, so called because it was once used to cast cannons. It is tough, hardwearing, and resists corrosion.

gunpowder or *black powder* the oldest known ◊explosive, a mixture of 75% potassium nitrate (saltpetre), 15% charcoal, and 10% sulphur. Sulphur ignites at a low temperature, charcoal burns readily, and the potassium nitrate provides oxygen for the explosion. Although progressively replaced since the late 19th century by high explosives, gunpowder is still widely used for quarry blasting, fuses, and fireworks.

Gunpowder Plot in British history, the Catholic conspiracy to blow up James I and his parliament on 5 Nov 1605. It was discovered through an anonymous letter sent to Lord Monteagle (1575–1622). Guy ◊Fawkes was found in the cellar beneath the Palace of Westminster, ready to fire a store of explosives. Several of the conspirators were killed, and Fawkes and seven others were executed.

The event is commemorated annually in England on 5 Nov by fireworks and burning 'guys' on bonfires. The searching of the vaults of Parliament before the opening of each new session, however, was not instituted until the 'Popish Plot' of 1678.

Guomindang Chinese National People's Party, founded 1894 by ◊Sun Yat-sen (Sun Zhong Shan), which overthrew the Manchu Empire 1912. By 1927 the right wing, led by ◊Chiang Kai-shek (Jiang Jie Shi), was in conflict with the left, led by Mao Zedong until the Communist victory 1949 (except for the period of the Japanese invasion 1937–45). It survives as the sole political party of Taiwan, where it is still spelled *Kuomintang*.

Gurdjieff /ˈgɜːdʒief/ George Ivanovitch 1877–1949. Russian occultist. He used stylized dance to 'free' people to develop their full capabilities, and influenced the modern human-potential movement. The mystic ◊Ouspensky was a disciple, who expanded his ideas.

gurdwara Sikh place of worship and meeting. As well as a room housing the *Guru Granth Sahib*, the holy book, the gurdwara contains a kitchen and eating area for the *langar*, or communal meal.

Gurkha /ˈgɜːkə/ soldiers of Nepálese origin, who have been recruited since 1815 for the British

army. The Brigade of Gurkhas has its headquarters in Hong Kong. In 1989 the UK government proposed to reduce the Gurkha force in Hong Kong by 50% to 4,000 men by 1992.

gurnard genus of coastal fish (*Trigla*) in the family Trigilidae, which creep along the sea bottom by means of three finger-like appendages detached from the pectoral fins. They are both tropic and temperate zone fish.

guru (Hindi *gurŭ*) a Hindu or Sikh leader, or religious teacher.

Gush Emunim /ˈgʊʃ eˈmuːnɪm/ (Hebrew 'bloc of the faithful') Israeli fundamentalist group, founded 1973, who claim divine right to the West Bank, Gaza Strip, and Golan Heights as part of Israel through settlement, sometimes extending the claim to the Euphrates.

Gustavus or Gustaf six kings of Sweden, including:

Gustavus I better known as ◊Gustavus Vasa.

Gustavus II better known as ◊Gustavus Adolphus.

Gustaf V /ˈgʊstaːf/ 1858–1950. King of Sweden from 1907, when he succeeded his father Oscar II. He married Princess Victoria, daughter of the Grand Duke of Baden, in 1881, thus uniting the reigning Bernadotte dynasty with the former royal house of Vasa.

Gustaf VI /ˈgʊstaːf/ 1882–1973. King of Sweden from 1950, when he succeeded his father Gustaf V. He was an archaeologist and expert on Chinese art. His first wife was Princess Margaret of Connacht (1882–1920), and in 1923 he married Lady Louise Mountbatten (1889–1965), sister of the Earl of Mountbatten of Burma. He was succeeded by his grandson ◊Carl XVI Gustaf.

Gustavus Adolphus /guˈstaːvəs əˈdɒlfəs/ 1594–1632. King of Sweden from 1611, when he succeeded his father Charles IX. He waged successful wars with Denmark, Russia, and Poland, and in the ◊Thirty Years' War became a champion of the Protestant cause. Landing in Germany in 1630, he defeated the German general Wallenstein at Lützen, SW of Leipzig, on 6 Nov 1632, but was killed in the battle. He was known as the 'Lion of the North'.

Gustavus Vasa /ˈvaːsə/ 1496–1560. King of Sweden from 1523, when he was elected after leading the Swedish revolt against Danish rule. He united and pacified the country and established Lutheranism as the state religion.

Gutenberg /ˈguːtnbɜːg/ Johann *c.* 1400–1468. German printer, the inventor of printing from moveable metal type (see ◊Coster, Laurens Janszoon).

Gutenberg set up a printing business in Mainz with Johann Fust (*c.*1400–66) as a partner 1440. The partnership was dissolved through monetary difficulties, but Gutenberg set up another printing press. He is believed to have printed the Mazarin and the Bamberg Bibles.

Guthrie Edwin R 1886–1959. American behaviourist, who attempted to develop a theory of learning that was independent of the traditional principles of reward or reinforcement. His ideas served as a basis for later statistical models.

Guthrie /ˈgʌθri/ Tyrone 1900–1971. British theatre director, noted for his experimental approach. Administrator of the ◊Old Vic and Sadler's Wells 1939–45, he helped found the Ontario (Stratford) Shakespeare Festival in 1953 and the Minneapolis theatre now named after him.

Guthrie /ˈgʌθri/ 'Woody' (Woodrow Wilson) 1912–1967. US folk singer and songwriter, whose left-wing protest songs, 'dustbowl ballads', and *talking blues* were an influence on, among others, Bob Dylan; they include 'Deportees', 'Hard Travelin'', and 'This Land Is Your Land'.

gutta percha juice of tropical trees, such as the Malaysian *Palaquium gutta*, which can be hardened to form a flexible, rubbery substance used for insulating electrical cables, but has now largely been replaced by synthetics.

guttation the secretion of water onto the surface of leaves through specialized pores, or ◊hydathodes.

Guyana
Cooperative Republic of

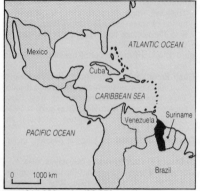

area 214,969 sq km/82,978 sq mi
capital and port Georgetown
physical mostly tropical rainforest
features Mount Roraima; Kaietur National Park including Kaietur Fall on the Potaro (tributary of Essequibo) 250 m/821 ft
head of state and government Desmond Hoyte from 1985

political system democratic republic
political parties People's National Congress (PNC), Indian nationalist socialist; People's Progressive Party (PPP), Afro-Indian Marxist-Leninist
exports sugar, rice, rum, timber, diamonds
currency Guyana dollar (50.96 = £1 Feb 1990)
population (1987) 812,000 (51% E Indians, introduced to work the sugar plantations after the abolition of slavery, 30% black, 5% Amerindian); annual growth rate 2%
life expectancy men 66, women 71
language English (official), Hindi
religion Christian 57%, Hindu 33%, Sunni Muslim 9%
literacy 97% male/95% female (1985 est)
GNP $419 million (1983); $457 per head of population
chronology
1953 Assembly elections won by left-wing party. Britain installed interim administration, claiming fear of communist takeover.
1961 Internal self-government granted.
1966 Full independence achieved.
1970 Guyana became a republic within the Commonwealth.
1980 Forbes Burnham became the first executive president under new constitution.
1985 Burnham died and was succeeded by Desmond Hoyte.

Gwyn Formerly an orange-seller outside London's Drury Lane Theatre, Nell Gwyn became the mistress of Charles II, and he was the father of her two sons. This portrait by Sir Peter Lely is in Raby Castle, County Durham.

The process occurs most frequently during conditions of high humidity when the rate of transpiration is low. Drops of water found on grass in early morning are often the result of guttation, rather than dew. Sometimes the water contains minerals in solution, such as calcium, which leaves a white crust on the leaf surface as it dries.

Guyana /gaɪˈænə/ country in South America, bounded to the N by the Atlantic Ocean, E by Suriname, S and SW by Brazil, and NW by Venezuela.

government Guyana is a sovereign republic with-in the ◊Commonwealth. The 1980 constitution provides for a single-chamber national assembly of 65 members, 53 elected by universal suffrage and 12 elected by the regions, for a five-year term. The president is the nominee of the party winning most votes in the national assembly elections and serves for the life of the assembly, appointing a cabinet which is collectively responsible to it. The main political parties are the People's National Congress (PNC), and the People's Progressive Party (PPP).

history The area now known as Guyana was a Dutch colony 1621–1796, when it was seized by Britain. In 1814 it was made a British colony under the name of British Guiana, and became part of the Commonwealth from 1831 until full independence 1966.

The move from colonial to republican status was gradual and not entirely smooth. In 1953 a constitution providing for free elections to an assembly was introduced and the left-wing PPP, led by Dr Cheddi Jagan, won the popular vote. Within months, however, the UK government suspended the constitution and put in its own interim administration, claiming that the PPP threatened to become a communist dictatorship.

In 1957 a breakaway group from the PPP founded a new party, the PNC, which was supported mainly by African-descended Guyanans, while PPP followers were mainly of Indian descent. Fresh elections, under a revised constitution, were held 1957 and PPP won again, with Jagan becoming chief minister. Internal self-government was granted 1961 and, with PPP again the successful party, Jagan became prime minister. Proportional representation was introduced 1963 and in the 1964 elections, under the new voting procedures, PPP, although winning most votes, did not have an overall majority so a PPP–PNC coalition was formed,

with PNC leader Forbes Burnham as prime minister.

This coalition took the country through to full independence 1966. PNC won the 1968 and 1973 elections and in 1970 Guyana became a republic within the Commonwealth. In 1980 a new constitution was adopted, making the president head of both state and government and as a result of the 1981 elections, which opposition parties claimed were fraudulent, Burnham became executive president. The rest of his administration was marked by economic deterioration, necessitating austerity measures, and cool relations with the Western powers, particularly the USA, whose invasion of Grenada he condemned. He died 1985 and was succeeded by Prime Minister Desmond Hoyte, who was expected to follow policies similar to those of his predecessor.

Guys /gwiːs/ Constantin 1805–1892. French artist. He was with ◊Byron at Missolonghi, and made sketches of the Crimean War for the *Illustrated London News*.

Guzmán Blanco /guːsˈmæn ˈblæŋkəʊ/ Antonio 1829–1899. Venezuelan dictator and military leader (*caudillo*). He seized power in 1870 and remained absolute ruler until 1889. He modernized Caracas to become the political capital; committed resources to education, communications, and agriculture; and encouraged foreign trade.

Gwent

Gwalior /ˈgwɑːliɔː/ city in Madhya Pradesh, India; population (1981) 543,862. It was formerly a small princely state, and has Jain and Hindu monuments.

Gwent /gwent/ county in S Wales
area 1,380 sq km/533 sq mi
towns administrative headquarters Cwmbran; Abergavenny, Newport, Tredegar
features Wye Valley; Tintern Abbey; Legionary Museum of Caerleon, and Roman amphitheatre; Chepstow and Raglan castles
products salmon and trout on the Wye and Usk; iron and steel at Llanwern
population (1987) 443,000
language 2.5% Welsh, English
famous people Aneurin Bevan and Neil Kinnock, both born in Tredegar; Alfred Russel Wallace.

Gwyn /gwɪn/ 'Nell' (Eleanor) 1651–1687. English comedy actress from 1665, formerly an orange-seller at Drury Lane Theatre, London. The poet Dryden wrote parts for her, and from 1669 she was the mistress of Charles II. The elder of her two sons by Charles II was created Duke of St Albans 1684. The king's last wish was 'Let not poor Nellie starve'.

Gwynedd /ˈgwɪnəð/ county in NW Wales
area 3,870 sq km/1,494 sq mi
towns administrative headquarters Caernarvon; Bangor, resorts Pwllheli, Barmouth
features Snowdonia National Park including Snowdon (Welsh *Yr Wyddfa*; the highest mountain in Wales, with a rack railway to the top

Gwynedd

gyroscope *High-speed photograph of a gyroscope in motion. The gyroscope is used as a stabilizing device, and in automatic pilots and gyrocompasses.*

from Llanberis) 1,085 m/3,561 ft, Cader Idris 892 m/2,928 ft, and the largest Welsh lake, Llyn Tegid (Bala) 6 km/4 mi long, 1.6 km/1 mi wide; Caernarvon Castle; ◊Anglesey is across the Menai Straits; Lleyn Peninsula and to the SW Bardsey Island, with a 6th-century ruined abbey, once a centre for pilgrimage; Welsh Slate Museum at Llanberis; Segontium Roman Fort Museum, Caernarvon; Criccieth and Harlech castles; Bodnant Garden; and the fantasy resort of Portmeirion (see ◊Williams-Ellis).

products cattle, sheep, gold (at Dolgellau), textiles, electronics, slate
population (1987) 236,000
language 61% Welsh, English

gymnastics physical exercises, originally for health and training (so-named from the way in which men of ancient Greece trained *gymnos* 'naked'). The *gymnasia* were schools for training competitors for public games.

Men's gymnastics includes high bar, parallel bars, horse vault, rings, pommel horse, and floor exercises. *Women's gymnastics* includes asymmetrical bars, side horse vault, balance beam, and floor exercises. Also popular are *sports acrobatics*, performed by gymnasts in pairs, trios, or fours to music, where the emphasis is on dance, balance, and timing, and *rhythmic gymnastics*, choreographed to music and performed by individuals or six-girl teams, with small

Gymnastics: World Championship winners

men:	individual/team
1958:	Boris Shakhlin *(USSR)*/USSR
1962:	Yuriy Titov *(USSR)*/Japan
1966:	Mikhail Voronin *(USSR)*/Japan
1970:	Eizo Kenmotsu *(Japan)*/Japan
1974:	Shigeru Kasamatsu *(Japan)*/Japan
1978:	Nikolai Adrianov *(USSR)*/Japan
1979:	Aleksandr Ditiatin *(USSR)*/USSR
1981:	Yuri Korolev *(USSR)*/USSR
1983:	Dimitri Belozertchev *(USSR)*/China
1985:	Yuri Korolev *(USSR)*/USSR
1987:	Dimitri Belozertchev *(USSR)*
women: individual/team	
1962:	Larissa Latynina *(USSR)*/USSR
1966:	Vera Caslavska *(Czechoslovakia)*/Czechoslovakia
1970:	Ludmila Tourischeva *(USSR)*/USSR
1974:	Ludmila Tourischeva *(USSR)*/USSR
1978:	Elena Mukhina *(USSR)*/USSR
1979:	Nelli Kim *(USSR)*/Romania
1981:	Olga Bitcherova *(USSR)*/USSR
1983:	Natalia Yurchenko *(USSR)*/USSR
1985:	Elena Shoushounova *(USSR)* and Oksana Omeliantchik *(USSR)*
1987:	Aurelia Dobre *(Romania)*/USSR

hand apparati such as ribbons, balls, and hoops.

Gymnastics was first revived in 19th-century Germany as an aid to military strength, and was also taken up by educationists including ◊Froebel and ◊Pestalozzi, becoming a recognized part of the school curriculum. Today it is a popular spectator sport.

gymnosperm (Greek 'naked seed') in botany, any plant whose seeds are exposed, as opposed to the structurally more advanced ◊angiosperms, where they are inside an ovary. The group includes conifers and related plants such as cycads and ginkgos, whose seeds develop in ◊cones. Fossil gymnosperms have been found in rocks about 350 million years old.

gynaecology the medical speciality concerned with diseases of the female reproductive system.

gynoecium or *gynaecium* the collective term for the female reproductive organs of a flower, con-sisting of one or more ◊carpels, either free or fused together.

Györ industrial city (steel, vehicles, textiles, foodstuffs) in NW Hungary, near the frontier with Czechoslovakia; population (1988) 131,000.

gypsum a common ◊mineral, composed of hydrous calcium sulphate, $CaSO_4.2H_2O$. It ranks 2 on the Mohs' scale of hardness. Gypsum is used for making casts and moulds, and for blackboard chalk.

A fine-grained gypsum, called *alabaster*, is used for ornamental work. Burned gypsum is known as *plaster of Paris*, because for a long time it was obtained from the gypsum quarries of the Montmartre district of Paris.

gypsy English name for a member of the ◊Romany people.

gyre the circular surface rotation of ocean water in each major sea (a type of ◊current). Gyres are large and permanent, and occupy the N and S halves of the three major oceans. Their movements are dictated by the prevailing winds and the ◊Coriolis effect. They move clockwise in the northern hemisphere and anticlockwise in the southern hemisphere.

gyroscope mechanical instrument, used as a stabilizing device and consisting, in its simplest form, of a heavy wheel mounted on an axis fixed in a ring that can be rotated about another axis, which is also fixed in a ring capable of rotation about a third axis. Important applications of the gyroscope principle include the gyrocompass, the gyropilot for automatic steering, and gyro-directed torpedoes.

The components of the gyroscope are arranged so that the three axes of rotation in any position pass through the wheel's centre of gravity. The wheel is thus capable of rotation about three mutually perpendicular axes, and its axis may take up any direction. If the axis of the spinning wheel is displaced, a restoring movement develops returning it to its initial direction.

Gysi Gregor 1948– . East German politician, elected leader of the Communist Party Dec 1989 following the resignation of Egon ◊Krenz. A lawyer, Gysi had acted as defence counsel for dissidents during the 1960s.

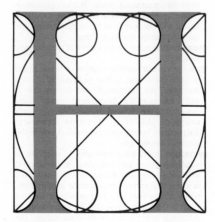

H eighth letter of the Roman alphabet, representing an aspirate in all modern alphabets derived from the Latin except in those languages, especially the Romance languages, where the aspirate is lost. It is used in several diagraphs (conventional two-letter sequences with special values), such as ch, ph, sh, th.

ha abbreviation for ◊*hectare*.

Haakon seven kings of Norway, including:

Haakon I /ˈhɔːkɒn/ (the Good) *c.* 915–961. King of Norway from about 935. The son of Harald Hárfagri ('Finehair') (*c.* 850–930), king of Norway, he was raised in England. He seized the Norwegian throne and tried unsuccessfully to introduce Christianity to Norway. His capital was at ◊Trondheim.

Haakon IV /ˈhɔːkɒn/ 1204–1263. King of Norway from 1217, the son of Haakon III. Under his rule, Norway flourished both militarily and culturally; he took control of the Faroe Islands, Greenland 1261, and Iceland 1262–64. His court was famed throughout N Europe.

Haakon VII /ˈhɔːkɒn/ 1872–1957. King of Norway from 1905. Born Prince Charles, the second son of Frederick VIII of Denmark, he was elected king of Norway on separation from Sweden, and in 1906 he took the name Haakon. In World War II he refused to surrender to Germany and, when armed resistance in Norway was no longer possible, carried on the struggle from Britain until his return in 1945.

Haarlem /ˈhɑːləm/ industrial town in the W Netherlands, 20 km/12 mi W of Amsterdam; population (1988) 214,000. At Velsea to the north a road-rail tunnel runs under the North Sea Canal, linking North and South Holland. Industries include chemicals, pharmaceuticals, textiles, and printing. Haarlem is famous for bulbs, and has a 15th–16th-century cathedral and a Frans ◊Hals Museum.

Habakkuk a prophet in, and a book of, the Old Testament or Hebrew Bible.

habanera or *havanaise* a slow dance in two-four time, originating in Havana, Cuba, which became popular when introduced into Spain during the 19th century, or the music for the dance. There is an example of this dance in Bizet's opera *Carmen*.

habeas corpus (Latin 'you have the body') in English law, a writ directed to someone who has custody of a prisoner, ordering him to bring the prisoner before the court issuing the writ, and to explain why the prisoner is detained in custody. Traditional rights to habeas corpus were embodied in law mainly owing to Lord ◊Shaftesbury, in the Habeas Corpus Act 1679; the Scottish equivalent is the Wrongous Imprisonment Act 1701. The main principles were also adopted in the US Constitution.

Haber /ˈhɑːbə/ Fritz 1868–1934. German chemist whose conversion of atmospheric nitrogen to ammonia opened the way for the synthetic fertilizer industry. His study of the combustion of hydrocarbons led to the commercial 'cracking' or fractionating of natural oil into its components, for example diesel, petrol, and paraffin. In electrochemistry he was the first to demonstrate that oxidation and reduction take place at the electrodes; from this he developed a general electrochemical theory.

In World War I he worked on poison gas and devised gas masks, hence there were protests against his Nobel prize in 1918.

habitat in ecology, the localized ◊environment in which an organism lives. Habitats are often described by the dominant plant type or physical feature, such as a grassland habitat or rocky seashore habitat.

Habsburg /ˈhæbsbɜːg/ or *Hapsburg* European royal family, former imperial house of Austria-Hungary. The name comes from the family castle in Switzerland. The Habsburgs held the title Holy Roman emperor 1273–91, 1298–1308, 1438–1740, and 1745–1806. They ruled Austria from 1278, under the title emperor 1806–1918.

hacker in popular usage, a person who attempts to gain unauthorized access to a computer, either for fun or for malicious or fraudulent purposes. Hackers generally use microcomputers and telephone lines to obtain access. In computing, the term is used in a wider sense to mean any person who works with software for enjoyment or self-education, not necessarily involving unauthorized access.

In the UK there are no specific legal remedies against hacking, although the Law Commission proposed a basis for legislation 1989.

Hackman /ˈhækmən/ Gene 1931– . US character actor. He became a star as 'Popeye' Doyle in *The French Connection* 1971 and continued to play major roles in films such as *Bonnie and Clyde* 1967, *The Conversation* 1974, and *Mississippi Burning* 1988.

Hackney /ˈhækni/ inner borough of N central Greater London; population (1984) 187,900.

features Hackney Downs and Hackney Marsh, formerly the haunt of highwaymen, now a leisure area; includes *Shoreditch*, site of England's first theatre (The Theatre) in 1576; *Hoxton*, with the Geffrye Museum of the domestic arts; *Stoke Newington*, where the writer Daniel Defoe once lived. The horse-drawn *hackney carriage* is so named because horses were bred in Hackney in the 14th century.

Haddington /ˈhædɪŋtən/ agricultural market town in Lothian, Scotland, on the river Tyne, 16 km/10 mi SW of Dunbar; population (1981) 8,117. The Protestant reformer John Knox was born here.

Haddingtonshire /ˈhædɪŋtənʃə/ name until 1921 of the Scottish county of East Lothian, since 1975 part of the region of ◊Lothian.

haddock fish *Melanogrammus aeglefinus* of the cod family found off the N Atlantic coasts. It is brown with silvery underparts, and black markings above the pectoral fins. It can grow to a length of 1 m/3 ft.

Hades /ˈheɪdiːz/ in Greek mythology, the underworld where spirits went after death, usually depicted as a cavern or pit underneath the earth. It was presided over by the god Hades or Pluto (Roman Dis).

He was the brother of Zeus, and married Persephone, daughter of Demeter and Zeus. She was allowed to return to the upper world for part of the year, bringing spring with her. The entrance to Hades was guarded by the three-headed dog Cerberus. *Tartarus* was the section where the wicked were punished, for example Tantalus.

Hadhramaut /ˌhɑːdrəˈmaʊt/ district of the People's Democratic Republic of Yemen (South Yemen), which was formerly ruled by Arab chiefs in protective relations with Britain. A remote plateau region at 1,400 m/4,500 ft, it was for a long time unknown to westerners and later attracted such travellers as Harry St John Philby and Freya Stark. Cereals, tobacco, and dates are grown by settled farmers and there are nomadic Bedouin. The chief town is Mukalla.

Hadith a collection of the teachings of ◊Muhammad and stories about his life, regarded by Muslims as a guide to living second only to the ◊Koran.

The teachings were at first transmitted orally, but this led to a large number of Hadiths whose origin was in doubt; later, scholars such as Muhammad al-Bukhari (810–870) collected together those believed to be authentic, and these collections form the Hadith accepted by Muslims today.

Hadlee /ˈhædli/ Richard John 1951– . New Zealand cricketer. In 1987 he surpassed Ian Botham's world record of 373 wickets in test cricket. He retired from international cricket in 1990.

Hadlee played first-class cricket in England for Nottinghamshire and in Australia for Tasmania. His father *Walter Arnold Hadlee* also played test cricket for New Zealand, as did his brother *Dayle Robert Hadlee*.

CAREER HIGHLIGHTS

all first-class matches
runs: 11,715; average: 31.57
best: 210 not out (Nottinghamshire v. Middlesex, 1984)
wickets: 1,447; average: 17.95
best: 9 for 52 (New Zealand v. Australia, 1985–86)
test cricket
runs: 2,884; average: 26.70
best: 151 not out (New Zealand v. Sri Lanka, 1986–87)
wickets: 396; average: 22.21
best: 9 for 52 (New Zealand v. Australia, 1985–86)

Hadrian /ˈheɪdrɪən/ AD 76–138. Roman emperor from 117. Born in Spain, he was adopted by his relative, the emperor Trajan, whom he succeeded. He abandoned Trajan's conquests in Mesopotamia and adopted a defensive policy, which included the building of Hadrian's Wall in Britain.

Hadrian's Wall Roman fortification built AD 122–126 to mark England's northern boundary and abandoned about 383; its ruins run 185 km/115 mi from Wallsend on the river Tyne to Maryport,

Hadrian's Wall A section of Hadrian's Wall leading eastwards to Housesteads Fort.

W Cumbria. At least in part, the wall was covered with a white coat of mortar.

The fort at South Shields, Arbeia, built to defend the eastern end, is being reconstructed. In 1985 Roman letters (on paper-thin sheets of wood), the earliest and largest collection of Latin writing, were discovered at Vindolanda Fort.

Haeckel /'hekəl/ Ernst Heinrich 1834–1919. German scientist and philosopher. His theory of 'recapitulation' (that embryonic stages represent past stages in the organism's evolution) has been superseded, but stimulated research in ◊embryology.

haematology the branch of medicine concerned with disorders of the blood.

haemoglobin a protein that carries oxygen. In vertebrates it occurs in red blood cells, giving them their colour. Oxygen attaches to haemoglobin in the lungs or gills where the amount dissolved in the blood is high. This process effectively increases the amount of oxygen that can dissolve in the blood. The oxygen is later released in the body tissues where it is at low concentration.

haemolymph the circulatory fluid of those molluscs and insects that have an 'open' circulatory system. Haemolymph contains water, amino acids, sugars, salts, and white cells like those of blood. Circulated by a pulsating heart, its main functions are to transport digestive and excretory products around the body. In molluscs, it also transports oxygen and carbon dioxide.

haemolysis the destruction of red blood cells. Aged cells are constantly being lysed (broken down), but increased wastage of red cells is seen in some infections and blood disorders. It may result in ◊anaemia and ◊jaundice.

haemophilia an inherited disease in which normal blood clotting is impaired. The sufferer experiences prolonged bleeding from the slightest wound, as well as painful internal bleeding without apparent cause.

Haemophilia is a familial disorder, transmitted through the female line only to male infants. Affected males are unable to synthesize Factor VIII, a protein involved in the clotting of blood. Treatment is primarily with Factor VIII (now mass-produced from donated blood), but the haemophiliac remains at risk from the slightest incident of bleeding. The disease is a painful one which causes deformities of joints. Haemophilia has afflicted a number of European royal households.

haemorrhage loss of blood from the circulation. It is 'manifest' when the blood can be seen, as when it flows from a wound, and 'occult' when the bleeding is internal, as from an ulcer or internal injury.

Rapid, profuse haemorrhage causes ◊shock, and may prove fatal if the circulating volume cannot be replaced in time. Slow, sustained bleeding may lead to ◊anaemia. Arterial bleeding is potentially more serious than blood lost from a vein. It should be stemmed by pressure above the wound.

haemorrhagic fever any of several virus diseases of the tropics, in which high temperatures over several days end in haemorrhage from nose, throat, and intestines, with up to 90% mortality. The causative organism of West African ◊Lassa fever lives in rats, but in ◊Marburg disease and Ebola fever, the host animal, which betrays no symptoms, is unknown.

haemorrhoids distended (◊varicose) veins of the anus, popularly called piles.

haemostasis the natural mechanisms by which bleeding ceases of its own accord. The damaged vessel contracts, restricting the flow, and blood ◊platelets 'plug' the opening, releasing chemicals essential to clotting.

Hâfiz /'haːfɪz/ Shams al-Din Muhammad *c.* 1326–1390. Persian lyric poet, who was born in Shiraz and taught in a Dervish college there. His *Diwan*, a collection of short odes, extolls the pleasures of life and satirizes his fellow Dervishes.

hafnium a metallic element, symbol Hf, atomic number 72, relative atomic mass 178.6. It occurs in zircon, and its properties and compounds closely resemble those of zirconium. It is highly absorbent of neutrons, and is used in control rods in nuclear reactors.

Haganah /ˌhaːgəˈnaː/ Zionist military organization in Palestine. It originated under Turkish rule before World War I to protect Jewish settlements, and many of its members served in the British forces in both world wars. After World War II it condemned guerrilla activity, opposing the British authorities only passively. It formed the basis of the Israeli army after Israel was established in 1948.

Hagen /'haːgən/ industrial city in the Ruhr, North Rhine-Westphalia, West Germany; population (1988) 206,000. It produces iron, steel, and textiles.

Hagen /'heɪgən/ Walter Charles 1892–1969. US golfer, a flamboyant and colourful character. He won 11 major championships 1914–1929. An exponent of the match-play type of game he won the US PGA championship five times, including four in succession.

CAREER HIGHLIGHTS

US Open: 1914, 1919
British Open: 1922, 1924, 1928–29
US PGA: 1921, 1924–27
Ryder Cup: 1927*, 1929*, 1931*, 1933*, 1935*, 1937**
(* playing captain; ** non-playing captain)

Hagenbeck /'haːgənbek/ Carl 1844–1913. German zoo proprietor. In 1907 he founded Hagenbeck's Zoo, near his native Hamburg. He was a pioneer in the display of animals against a natural setting.

Haggadah /həˈgaːdə/ in Judaism, the part of the Talmudic literature not concerned with religious law (the *Halakah*), but devoted to folklore and stories of heroes.

Haggai /'hægaɪ/ minor Old Testament prophet (lived *c.*520 BC), who promoted the rebuilding of the Temple in Jerusalem.

Haggard /'hægəd/ H(enry) Rider 1856–1925. English novelist. Born in Norfolk, he held colonial service posts in Natal and the Transvaal 1875–79, then returned to England to train as a barrister. He used his South African experience in his romantic adventure tales, including *King Solomon's Mines* 1885 and *She* 1887.

haggis Scottish dish made from a sheep's or calf's heart, liver, and lungs, minced up with onion, oatmeal, suet, spice, pepper, and salt, and traditionally boiled in the animal's stomach.

Hague, The /heɪg/ (Dutch *Gravenhage* or *Den Haag*) seat of the Netherlands government, linked by canal with Rotterdam and Amsterdam; population (1988) 680,000. It is also the seat of the United Nations International Court of Justice.

The seaside resort of Scheveningen (patronized by Wilhelm II and Churchill), with its Kurhaus, is virtually incorporated.

ha-ha in landscape gardening, a sunken boundary wall permitting an unobstructed view beyond a garden; a device much used by Capability ◊Brown.

Hahn /haːn/ Kurt 1886–1974. German educationist. He was the founder of Salem School in Germany. After his expulsion by Hitler, he founded ◊Gordonstoun School in Scotland and was headmaster 1934–53. He co-founded the ◊Atlantic College project in 1960, and was associated with the Outward Bound Trust.

Hahn /haːn/ Otto 1879–1968. West German physical chemist, who discovered ◊nuclear fission. Nobel Prize for Chemistry 1944.

He worked with Rutherford and Ramsay, and became director of the Kaiser Wilhelm Institute for Chemistry in 1928. With Strassmann, in 1938 he discovered that uranium nuclei split when bombarded with neutrons, which led to the development of the atomic bomb (first used in 1945).

Haig The Scottish field marshal Douglas Haig, whose Allied offensives during World War I gained little ground with huge loss of life. His poster recruitment drive, in which he appeared, urging 'Your Country Needs You', became a familiar image.

hahnium the former name for the element ◊unnilpentium.

Haifa /'haɪfə/ port in NE Israel; population (1987) 223,000. Industries include oil refining and chemicals.

Haig /heɪg/ Alexander (Meigs) 1924– . US general and Republican politician. He became President Nixon's White House chief of staff at the height of the ◊Watergate scandal, was NATO commander 1974–79, and was secretary of state to President Reagan 1981–82.

Haig /heɪg/ Douglas, 1st Earl Haig 1861–1928. British army officer, commander in chief in World War I. His Somme (France) offensive in the summer of 1916 made considerable advances only at enormous cost, and his Passchendaele (Belgium) offensive (July–Nov 1917) achieved little at huge loss. He was created field marshal 1917.

haiku 17-syllable Japanese verse form, usually divided into three lines of five, seven, and five syllables. ◊Bashō popularized the form in the 17th century. It evolved from the 31-syllable *tanka* form dominant from the 8th century.

hail precipitation in the form of pellets of ice (hailstones). It is caused by the circulation of moisture in strong convection currents, usually within cumulonimbus ◊clouds.

Water droplets freeze as they are carried upwards. As the circulation continues, layers of ice are deposited around the droplets until they become too heavy to be supported by the currents and they fall as a hailstorm.

Haile Selassie /'haɪli sɪˈlæsi/ Ras Tafari ('the Lion of Judah') 1892–1975. Emperor of Ethiopia 1930–74. He pleaded unsuccessfully to the League of Nations against Italian conquest of his country 1935–36, and lived in the UK until his restoration in 1941. He was deposed by a military coup and died in captivity. Followers of ◊Rastafarianism believe that he was the Messiah, the incarnation of God (Jah).

Hailsham /'heɪlʃəm/ Quintin Hogg, Baron Hailsham of St Marylebone 1907– . British lawyer and Conservative politician. The 2nd Viscount Hailsham, he renounced the title in 1963 to re-enter the House of Commons, and was thereby enabled to contest the Conservative Party leadership elections, but took a life peerage in 1970 on his appointment as Lord Chancellor 1970–74. He was Lord Chancellor again 1979–87.

Haile Selassie Haile Selassie was emperor of Ethiopia until he was deposed in a military coup in 1974.

Hailwood /ˈheɪlwʊd/ 'Mike' (Stanley Michael Bailey) 1940–1981. British motorcyclist. Between 1961 and 1967 he won nine world titles and 1961–79 a record 14 titles at the Isle of Man TT races.

CAREER HIGHLIGHTS

world titles
250cc: 1961, 1966–67 (all Honda)
350cc: 1966–67 (both Honda)
500cc: 1962–65 (all MV Agusta)
Isle of Man TT titles
senior TT: 1961 (Norton), 1963–65 (MV Agusta), 1966–67 (Honda), 1979 (Suzuki)
junior TT: 1962 (MV Agusta), 1967 (Honda)
250cc: 1961, 1966–67 (all Honda)
125cc: 1961 (Honda)
formula one
1978 (Ducati)

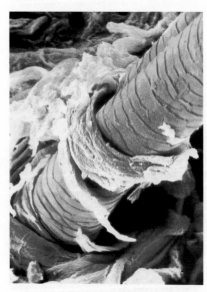

hair False colour electron microscope view of a human hair, showing the layer of highly flattened and partly overlapping cells which covers the hair surface.

Haiti
Republic of
(République d'Haiti)

area 27,750 sq km/10,712 sq mi
capital Port-au-Prince
physical mainly mountainous
features only French-speaking republic in the Americas; the island of La Tortuga off the N coast was formerly a pirate lair; US military base at Le Môle St Nicolas, the nearest point to Cuba
head of state and government Prosper Avril from 1988
political system military republic
political parties National Progressive Party (PNP), right-wing military
exports coffee, sugar, sisal, cotton, cocoa, rice
currency gourde (8.51 = £1 Feb 1990)
population (1985) 5,272,000; annual growth rate 2.5%
life expectancy men 51, women 54
language French (official, spoken by bourgeoisie), creole (spoken by 90% black majority)
religion Roman Catholic (official, but opposed to the regime)
literacy 40% male/35% female (1985 est)
GNP $1.6 bn (1983); $300 per head of population
chronology
1804 Independence from France achieved.
1915 Haiti invaded by USA, and remained under US control to 1934.
1957 Dr François Duvalier (Papa Doc) elected president.
1964 Duvalier pronounced himself president for life.
1971 Constitution amended to allow the president to nominate his successor. Duvalier died and was succeeded by his son, Jean-Claude (Baby Doc). Thousands murdered during Duvalier era.
1986 Duvalier deposed and replaced by Lt-Gen Henri Namphy, as head of a governing council.
1988 Leslie Manigat became president in Feb despite allegations of fraudulent elections. Namphy staged a military coup in June, but another coup in Sept led by Prosper Avril replaced him with a civilian government under military control.
1989 Coup attempt against Avril foiled.
1990 Opposition elements expelled.

Hainan /haɪˈnæn/ island in the South China Sea; area 34,000 sq km/13,124 sq mi; population (1986) 6,000,000. The capital is Haikou. In 1987 Hainan was designated a Special Economic Zone; in 1988 it was separated from Guangdong and made a new province. It is China's second largest island.

Hainaut /eɪˈnəʊ/ industrial province of SW Belgium; capital Mons; area 3,800 sq km/1,467 sq mi; population (1987) 1,272,000. It produces coal, iron, and steel.

Haiphong /ˌhaɪˈfɒŋ/ industrial port in N Vietnam; population (1980) 1,305,000. It has shipyards, and industries include cement, plastics, phosphates, and textiles.

hair a threadlike structure growing from mammalian skin. Each hair grows from a pit-shaped follicle embedded in the second layer of the skin, the dermis. It consists of dead cells impregnated with the protein keratin.

There are about a million hairs on the average person's head. Each grows at the rate of 5–10 mm per month, lengthening for about three years before being replaced by a new one. A coat of hair helps to insulate land mammals by trapping air next to the body. It also aids camouflage and protection, and its colouring or erection may be used for communication.

hairstreak one of a group of butterflies, belonging to the Blues (Lycaenidae), which live in both temperate and tropical regions. Most of them are brownish in their adult form, and they are nearly all tailed.

Haiti /ˈheɪti/ country in the Caribbean, occupying the W part of the island of Hispaniola; to the E is the Dominican Republic.

government The 1950 constitution was revised 1957, 1964, 1971, 1983, 1985, and 1987. Although it provides for an elected national assembly, under the Duvaliers it became a façade for their own dictatorships. In the 1984 elections about 300 government candidates contested the 59 seats, with no opposition at all. In 1985, political parties were legalized, provided they conformed to strict guidelines, but only one registered, the National Progressive Party (PNP),

which supported Duvalier's policies. The leader of the 1986 coup, Lt-Gen Henri Namphy, established a governing council, with himself as its head. The 1987 constitution provides for a 27-member senate and 77-member chamber of deputies, all popularly elected, as well as a 'dual executive' of a president and prime minister sharing power, but the future of democracy in Haiti is still under test.

history The island of Hispaniola was once inhabited by ◊Arawak Indians. They were driven out in the 14th century by ◊Caribs, 300,000 of whom were wiped out by Europeans in the 50 years following the arrival of Christopher Columbus 1492. The island was made a Spanish colony under the name of Santo Domingo, but the W part was colonized by France from the mid-16th century. In 1697 it was divided between France and Spain, and in 1795 the E of the island was ceded to France by Spain.

The period 1790–1804, when Haiti became independent, was fraught with rebellions against France, tension between blacks, whites, and mulattos, and military intervention by France and Britain. In one such rebellion the island was taken over by slaves, under ◊Toussaint L'Ouverture, and slavery was abolished, but was reinstated after he was killed by the French. After independence the instability continued, with Santo Domingo repossessed by Spain and then by Haiti, and self-proclaimed kings ruling Haiti. In 1844 Haiti and the Dominican Republic became separate states.

Friction between Haitians of African descent and mulattos, and the country's political instability, brought a period of US rule 1915–34. In the 1940s and 1950s there were several coups, the last occurring 1956, which resulted in Dr François Duvalier, a physician, being elected president. After an encouraging start, his administration degenerated into a personal dictatorship, maintained by a private army. In 1964 'Papa Doc' Duvalier made himself life-president, with the power to nominate his son as his successor.

On his father's death 1971 Jean-Claude Duvalier came to the presidency at the age of 19 and soon acquired the name of 'Baby Doc'. Although the young Duvalier repeatedly promised a return to democracy, and his rule was judged to be less despotic than his father's, there was little change. In 1985 he announced further reform of the constitution, including the legalization of political parties and the eventual appointment of a prime minister, but these were not enough to prevent his overthrow 1986. The task of establishing democratic government fell to the new military regime led by Lt-Gen Henri Namphy. The regime offered no protection to the electoral council, however, and the US government withdrew aid. Elections 30 Nov 1987 were sabotaged by armed gangs of Duvalierists who massacred voters and set fire to polling stations and to vehicles delivering ballot papers in the country.

Leslie Manigat, with army support, was made president early in 1988 but eight months later was ousted in a coup led by Gen Prosper Avril. Although Avril installed a largely civilian government, the army was still in control and a coup attempt in April 1989 was quickly put down. Early in 1990 opposition to Avril grew, but was quickly suppressed.

Haitink /'haitɪŋk/ Bernard 1929– . Dutch conductor of the Concertgebouw Orchestra, Amsterdam, from 1964, and music director of the Royal Opera House, Covent Garden, London, from 1986.

hajj the pilgrimage to ◊Mecca that should be undertaken by every Muslim at least once in a lifetime, unless he or she is prevented by financial or health difficulties. Many of the pilgrims on hajj also visit Medina, where the prophet Muhammad is buried. A Muslim who has been on hajj may take the additional name Hajji.

hake fish *Merluccius merluccius* of the cod family, found in N European, African, and American waters. Its silvery, elongated body attains 1 m/3 ft. It has two dorsal fins and one long anal fin.

Hakluyt /'hækluːt/ Richard 1553–1616. English geographer whose chief work is *The Principal Navigations, Voyages and Discoveries of the English Nation* 1598–1600. He was assisted by Sir Walter Raleigh. He lectured on cartography at Oxford, became geographical adviser to the East India Company, and was an original member of the Virginia Company.

The **Hakluyt Society**, established in 1846, published later accounts of exploration.

Hakodate /ˌhækəʊˈdɑːteɪ/ port in Hokkaido, Japan; population (1985) 319,000. It was the earliest port opened to the West, in 1854.

Halab Arabic name of ◊Aleppo, a city in Syria.

Halabja Kurdish town near the Iran border in Sulaymaniyah province, NE Iraq. In Aug 1988 international attention was focused on the town when Iraqi planes dropped poison gas, killing 5,000 of its inhabitants.

halal (Arabic 'lawful') conforming to the rules laid down by Islam. The term can be applied to all aspects of life, but is usually used for food allowed under Muslim dietary laws; this includes meat from animals that have been slaughtered in the correct ritual fashion.

Haldane /'hɔːldeɪn/ J(ohn) B(urdon) S(anderson) 1892–1964. English scientist and writer. A geneticist, Haldane was a popular science writer of such books as *The Causes of Evolution* 1933 and *New Paths in Genetics* 1941.

Haldane /'hɔːldeɪn/ Richard Burdon, Viscount Haldane 1856–1928. British Liberal politician. As secretary for war 1905–12, he sponsored the army reforms that established an expeditionary force, backed by a territorial army and under the unified control of an imperial general staff. He was Lord Chancellor 1912–15 and in the Labour government of 1924. His writings on German philosophy led to popular accusations of his being pro-German.

Hale /heɪl/ George Ellery 1868–1938. US astronomer, who made pioneer studies of the Sun and founded three major observatories. In 1889,

Haley *US pioneer of rock-and-roll music Bill Haley, remembered for his hit song 'Rock Around the Clock' 1954.*

he invented the spectroheliograph, a device for photographing the Sun at particular wavelengths.

In 1897 he founded the Yerkes Observatory in Wisconsin, with the largest refractor ever built, 102 cm/40 in. In 1917 he established on Mount Wilson, California a 2.5 m/100 in reflector, the world's largest telescope until superseded 1948 by the 5 m/200 in reflector on Mount Palomar, which Hale had had planned before he died.

Hale /heɪl/ Nathan 1755–1776. US nationalist, hanged by the British as a spy in the War of American Independence. Reputedly his final words were 'I regret that I have but one life to give for my country'.

Hale /heɪl/ Sarah Josepha Buell 1788–1879. US poet, author of 'Mary had a Little Lamb' 1830.

Hales /heɪlz/ Stephen 1677–1761. English priest and scientist who gave accurate accounts of water movement in plants. His work laid emphasis on measurement and experimentation.

Hales demonstrated that plants absorb air, and that some part of air is involved in their nutrition. He also measured plant growth and water loss, relating this to the upward movement of water from plants to leaves (transpiration).

Halévy /ˌæleɪˈviː/ Ludovic 1834–1908. French novelist and librettist. He collaborated with Hector Crémieux in the libretto for Offenbach's *Orpheus in the Underworld*; and with Henri Meilhac on librettos for Offenbach's *La Belle Hélène* and *La Vie parisienne*, and for Bizet's *Carmen*.

Haley /'heɪli/ Bill 1927–1981. US pioneer of rock and roll, originally a western-swing musician. His songs 'Rock Around the Clock' 1954 (recorded with his group the Comets and featured in the 1955 film *Blackboard Jungle*) and 'Shake, Rattle and Roll' 1955 came to symbolize the beginnings of the rock-and-roll era.

half-life during ◊radioactive decay, the time in which the strength of a radioactive source decays to half its original value. It may vary from millionths of a second to billions of years.

Radioactive substances decay exponentially; thus the time taken for the first 50% of the isotope to decay will be the same as the time taken by the next 25%, and so on. In theory, the decay process is never complete and there is always some residual radioactivity. For this reason, the half-life rather than the total decay time is measured.

halftone process a technique used in printing to reproduce the full range of tones in a photograph or other illustration. The intensity of the printed colour is varied from full strength to the lightest shades, although only one colour of ink is used. The picture to be reproduced is photographed through a screen ruled with a rectangular mesh of fine lines, which breaks up the tones of the original into dots which vary in size according to the intensity of the tone. In the darker shades

the dots are large and run together, in the lighter shades they are small and separate.

Colour pictures are broken down into a pattern of dots in the same way, the original being photographed through a number of colour filters. The process is known as *colour separation*. Plates made from the separations are then printed in sequence, yellow, magenta (blue-red), cyan (blue-green) and black, which combine to give the full colour range.

halibut fish *Hippoglossus hippoglossus* of the family Pleuronectidae found in the N Atlantic. Largest of the flatfish, it may reach over 2 m/6 ft and weigh 90–135 kg/200–300 lb. It is very dark mottled brown or green above and pure white beneath.

Halicarnassus /ˌhælɪkɑːˈnæsəs/ ancient city in Asia Minor (now Bodrum in Turkey), where the tomb of Mausolus, built about 350 BC by widowed Queen Artemisia, was one of the Seven Wonders of the World. The Greek historian Herodotus was born there.

halide the family name for a compound produced by combination of a ◊halogen, such as chlorine or iodine, with a less electronegative element (see ◊electronegativity). Halides may be formed by ◊ionic or ◊covalent bonds.

Halifax /'hælɪfæks/ capital of Nova Scotia, E Canada's main port; population (1986) 296,000. Its industries include lumber, steel, and sugar refining. It was founded 1749. It is the terminus of North America's transcontinental railway.

Halifax /'hælɪfæks/ woollen textile town in W Yorkshire, England; population (1981) 87,500.

St John's parish church is Perpendicular Gothic; All Souls' is by Gilbert ◊Scott (built for a mill owner named Ackroyd, whose home, Bankfield, is now a museum); the Town Hall is by Charles ◊Barry; and the Piece Hall of 1779 (former cloth market) has been adapted to modern use; the surviving gibbet (predecessor of the guillotine) was used to behead cloth stealers 1541–1650.

Halifax /'hælɪfæks/ Charles Montagu, Earl of Halifax 1661–1715. British financier. Appointed commissioner of the Treasury in 1692, he raised money for the French war by instituting the National Debt, and in 1694 carried out William Paterson's plan for a national bank (the Bank of England), and became chancellor of the Exchequer.

Halifax /'hælɪfæks/ Edward Frederick Lindley Wood, Earl of Halifax 1881–1959. British Conservative politician, viceroy of India 1926–31. As foreign secretary 1938–40 he was associated with Chamberlain's 'appeasement' policy. He received an earldom 1944 for services to the Allied cause while ambassador to the USA 1941–46.

Halifax *A portrait of Charles Montagu, Earl of Halifax, founder of the Bank of England, by Godfrey Kneller.*

Halifax /'hælɪfæks/ George Savile, 1st Marquess of Halifax 1633–1695. English politician. He entered Parliament in 1660, and was raised to the peerage by Charles II, by whom he was also later dismissed. He strove to steer a middle course between extremists, and became known as 'the Trimmer'. He played a prominent part in the revolution of 1688.

halitosis bad breath, which may be caused by poor oral hygiene, disease of the mouth, throat, nose, or lungs, or disturbance of the digestion.

Hall /hɔːl/ Charles 1863–1914. US chemist who developed a process for the commercial production of aluminium in 1886.

He found that when mixed with cryolite (sodium aluminium fluoride), the melting point of aluminium was lowered and electrolysis became commercially viable. It had previously been as costly as gold.

Hall /hɔːl/ Peter (Reginald Frederick) 1930– . English theatre, opera, and film director. He was director of the Royal Shakespeare Theatre in Stratford-on-Avon 1960–68 and developed the Royal Shakespeare Company as director 1968–73 until appointed director of the National Theatre 1973–88, succeeding Laurence Olivier.

His productions include *Waiting for Godot* 1955, *The Wars of the Roses* 1963, *The Homecoming* stage 1967 and film 1973, and *Amadeus* 1979. He was also appointed artistic director of opera at Glyndebourne 1984, with productions of *Carmen* 1985 and *Albert Herring* 1985–86.

Hallam /'hæləm/ Henry 1777–1859. British historian. He was called to the Bar, but a private fortune enabled him to devote himself to historical study from 1812 and his *Constitutional History of England* (1827) established his reputation.

Halle /'hælə/ capital of Halle county and industrial city in East Germany, on the river Saale, NW of Leipzig; population (1986) 235,000. Industries include mechanical engineering, the production of salt from brine springs, and lignite mining. Halle county has an area of 8,770 sq km/3,385 sq mi, and a population of 1,786,000.

Hall effect production of a voltage across a conductor or semiconductor carrying a current at right-angles to a surrounding magnetic field. It was discovered 1897 by the US physicist Edwin Hall (1855–1938). It is used in the Hall probe for measuring the strengths of magnetic fields and in magnetic switches.

Haller /'hælə/ Albrecht von 1708–1777. Swiss physician and scientist, founder of modern ◊neurology. He studied the muscles and nerves, and concluded that nerves provide the stimulus which triggers muscle contraction. He also showed that it is the nerves, not muscle or skin, that permit sensation.

Halley /'hæli/ Edmund 1656–1742. English scientist. In 1682 he observed the comet named after him, predicting that it would return 1759.

Halley's other astronomical achievements include the discovery that stars have their own ◊proper motion. He was a pioneer geophysicist and meteorologist, and worked in many other fields, including mathematics. He became the second Astronomer Royal 1720. He was a friend of ◊Newton, whose *Principia* he financed.

Halley's comet a comet that orbits the Sun about every 76 years, named after Edmund Halley. It is the brightest, most famous, and most conspicuous of the periodical comets. Recorded sightings go back over 2,000 years. It travels around the Sun in the opposite direction to the planets. Its orbit is inclined at almost 20° to the main plane of the solar system and ranges between the orbits of Venus and Neptune. It will next reappear 2061.

The comet's appearance was studied by space probes 1986, when it passed close to the Earth. The European probe, *Giotto*, showed that the nucleus of Halley's comet is a tiny and irregularly shaped chunk of ice, measuring some 15 km/10 m long by 8 km/5 m wide, coated by a layer of very

dark material, thought to be composed of carbon-rich compounds. This surface coating has a very low ◊albedo, reflecting just 4% of the light it receives from the Sun. Although the comet is one of the darkest objects known, the glowing head and tail are produced by jets of gas from fissures in the outer dust layer. These vents cover 10% of the total surface area and become active only when exposed to the Sun. The force of these jets affects the speed of the comet's travel in its orbit.

hallmark official mark on gold, silver, and (from 1913) platinum, instituted in the UK in 1327 (royal charter of London Goldsmiths) for the prevention of fraud. After 1363 personal marks of identification were added. Tests of metal content are carried out at authorized assay offices in London, Birmingham, Sheffield, and Edinburgh; each assay office has its distinguishing mark, to which is added a maker's mark, date letter, and mark guaranteeing standard.

Hallowe'en the evening of 31 Oct, immediately preceding the Christian feast of Hallowmas or All Saints' Day. Customs associated with Hallowe'en in the USA and the UK include children wearing masks or costumes, and 'trick or treating', going from house to house collecting sweets, fruit, or money.

Hallstatt /'hælʃtæt/ archaeological site in Upper Austria, SW of Salzburg. The salt workings date from prehistoric times, and in 1846 over 3,000 graves were discovered, belonging to a 9th–5th century BC Celtic civilization transitional between the Bronze and Iron ages.

hallucinogen substance that acts on the ◊central nervous system to produce hallucinations. Hallucinogens include LSD, peyote, and mescaline, and may produce panic, aggression, or even suicidal feelings, which can recur without warning several days after taking the drug. Occasionally they produce an irreversible psychotic state mimicking schizophrenia.

halogen one of a group of five elements with similar chemical bonding properties, and showing a gradation of physical properties. In order of reactivity, the elements are fluorine, F, chlorine, Cl, bromine, Br, iodine, I, and astatine, At.

Together, they form a linked group in the periodic table of elements. Salts containing a metal and a halogen are termed halides, for example table salt, NaCl.

halons in chemistry, compounds containing one or two carbon atoms, together with ◊bromine and other ◊halogens. The most commonly used are halon 1211 (bromochlorodifluoromethane) and halon 1301 (bromotrifluoromethane). The halons are gases and are widely used in fire extinguishers. As destroyers of the ◊ozone layer, they are up to ten times more effective than ◊chlorofluorocarbons, to which they are chemically related.

Levels in the atmosphere are rising by about 25% each year, mainly through the testing of fire-fighting equipment.

halophyte a plant adapted to live where there is a high concentration of salt in the soil, for example, in saltmarshes and mudflats.

Halophytes contain a high percentage of salts in their root cells, so that water can still be taken up by the process of ◊osmosis. Some species also have succulent leaves for storing water, such as **seablite** *Suaeda maritima*, and **sea rocket** *Cakile maritima*.

halothane anaesthetic agent which produces a deep level of unconsciousness when inhaled.

Hals /hæls/ Frans *c.* 1581–1666. Flemish-born painter of portraits, such as the *Laughing Cavalier* 1624 (Wallace Collection, London), and large groups of military companies, governors of charities, and others (many examples in the Frans Hals Museum, Haarlem, Holland). In the 1620s he experimented with genre scenes.

Halsey /'hɔːlsi/ William Frederick 1882–1959. US admiral, known as 'Bull'. Commander of the Third Fleet in the S Pacific from 1942 during World War

II. The Japanese signed the surrender document ending World War II on his flagship, the battleship *Missouri*.

Hamadán /ˌhæmə'dɑːn/ city in NW Iran on the site of the ancient Ecbatana, capital of the Medes; population (1986) 274,300.

Hamaguchi /ˌhæmə'guːtʃi/ Hamaguchi Osachi, also known as Hamaguchi Yuko 1870–1931. Japanese politician and prime minister 1929–30. His policies created social unrest and alienated military interests. His acceptance of the terms of the London Naval Agreement 1930 was also unpopular. Shot by an assassin Nov 1930, he died of his wounds nine months later.

Hamamatsu /ˌhæmə'mætsuː/ industrial city (textiles, chemicals, motorcycles) in Chubu region, central Honshu island, Japan; population (1987) 518,000.

Hambledon /'hæmbəldən/ village in SE Hampshire, England. The first cricket club was founded here in 1750.

Hamburg /'hæmbɜːg/ largest port of Europe, in West Germany, on the Elbe; population (1988) 1,571,000. Industries include oil, chemicals, electronics, and cosmetics.

It is capital of the *Land* of ◊Hamburg, and an archbishopric from 834. In alliance with Lübeck, it founded the ◊Hanseatic League.

Hamburg /'hæmbɜːg/ administrative region (*Land*) of West Germany
area 760 sq km/293 sq mi
capital Hamburg
features comprises the city and surrounding districts; the **hamburger**, a fried and seasoned patty of chopped beef, said to have been invented by medieval Tatar invaders of this Baltic area, was taken to the USA in the 19th century, from where it was reintroduced to Europe in the 1960s
products refined oil, chemicals, electrical goods, ships, processed food
population (1988) 1,570,000
religion Protestant 74%, Roman Catholic 8%
history in 1510 the emperor Maximilian I made Hamburg a free imperial city, and in 1871 it became a state of the German Empire. There is a university, established 1919, and the Hamburg Schauspielhaus is one of the republic's leading theatres.

Hameln /'hæməln/ (English form Hamelin) town in Lower Saxony, West Germany; population (1984) 56,300. Old buildings include the **Rattenhaus** rat-catcher's house, and the town is famous for the Pied Piper legend.

Hamersley Range /'hæməzli/ range of hills above the Hamersley Plateau, Western Australia, with coloured rocks and river gorges, as well as iron reserves.

Hamilcar Barca /hæ'mɪlkɑː 'bɑːkə/ *c.* 270–228 BC. Carthaginian general, father of ◊Hannibal. From 247 to 241 he harassed the Romans in Italy and then led an expedition to Spain, where he died in battle.

Hamilton /'hæməltən/ capital (since 1815) of Bermuda, on Bermuda Island; population (1980) 1,617. It was founded in 1612.

Hamilton /'hæməltən/ town in Strathclyde, Scotland; population (1981) 52,000. Industries include textiles, electronics, and engineering.

Hamilton /'hæməltən/ port in Ontario, Canada; population (1986) 557,000. Linked with Lake Ontario by the Burlington Canal, it has a hydroelectric plant, and steel, heavy machinery, electrical, chemical, and textile industries.

Hamilton /'hæməltən/ industrial and university town on North Island, New Zealand, on the Waikato river; population (1986) 101,800. It trades in forest, horticulture, and dairy farming products. Waikato University was established here in 1964.

Hamilton /'hæməltən/ Alexander 1757–1804. US politician, who influenced the adoption of a constitution with a strong central government, and was the first secretary of the treasury 1789–95. He led the Federalist Party, and incurred the bitter hatred of Aaron ◊Burr when he voted against

Burr and in favour of Thomas Jefferson for the presidency in 1801.

Hamilton, born in the West Indies, served during the War of Independence as captain and 1777–81 was Washington's secretary and aide-de-camp. After the war he practised as a lawyer. He was a member of the Constitutional Convention of 1787, and in the *Federalist* influenced public opinion in favour of the ratification of the constitution. As first secretary of the treasury, he proved an able controller of the national finances. Challenged to a duel with Burr, he was wounded, and died the next day.

Hamilton /ˈhæməltən/ Emma (born Amy Lyon) 1765–1815. English courtesan. In 1782 she became the mistress of Charles ◊Greville, and in 1786 of his uncle Sir William Hamilton, the British envoy at Naples, who married her 1791. After Admiral ◊Nelson's return from the Nile 1798 she became his mistress and their daughter, Horatia, was born 1801.

Hamilton /ˈhæməltən/ Iain Ellis 1922– . Scottish composer. Intensely emotional and harmonically rich, his works include striking viola and cello sonatas, the ballet *Clerk Saunders* 1951, the operas *Pharsalia* 1968 and *The Royal Hunt of the Sun* 1967–69, which renounced melody for inventive chordal formations, and symphonies.

Hamilton /ˈhæməltən/ Ian 1853–1947. Scottish general. He was chief of staff and deputy to Lord Kitchener, commander in chief in the second South African War. In 1915 he directed the land operations in Gallipoli, Turkey.

Hamilton /ˈhæməltən/ James 1st Duke of Hamilton 1606–1649. Scottish adviser to Charles I, he led an army against the ◊Covenanters 1639, and subsequently took part in the negotiations between Charles and the Scots. In the second Civil War he led the Scottish invasion of England, but was captured at Preston and executed.

Hamilton /ˈhæməltən/ Richard 1922– . English artist, a pioneer of Pop art. His collage *Just what is it that makes today's homes so different, so appealing?* 1956 (Kunsthalle, Tübingen) is often cited as the first Pop art work. Its modern 1950s interior inhabited by the bodybuilder Charles Atlas and a pin-up is typically humorous, concerned with popular culture and contemporary kitsch. His series *Swinging London 67* 1967 comments on the prosecution for drugs of his art dealer Robert Fraser and the singer Mick Jagger.

Hamilton /ˈhæməltən/ William 1730–1803. British diplomat, envoy to the court of Naples 1764–1800, whose collection of Greek vases was bought by the British Museum.

Hamilton /ˈhæməltən/ William D 1936– . New Zealand biologist. By developing the concept of ◊inclusive fitness, he was able to solve the theoretical problem of explaining ◊altruism in animal behaviour in terms of ◊Neo-Darwinism.

Hamite /ˈhæmaɪt/ member of an African people, descended, according to tradition, from Ham, son of ◊Noah in the Bible: they include the ancient Egyptians, and the Berbers and Tuareg of N Africa. Hamitic languages are related to the Semitic.

Hamito-Semitic languages a family of languages spoken throughout the world but commonly associated with North Africa and Western Asia. It has two main branches, the *Hamitic* languages of North Africa and the *Semitic* languages originating in Syria, Mesopotamia, Palestine, and Arabia, but now found from Morocco in the west to the Arabian or Persian Gulf in the east. The scripts of Arabic and Hebrew run from right to left.

The Hamitic languages include ancient Egyptian, Coptic, and Berber, while the Semitic languages include the most numerous, Arabic, and other culturally significant languages such as Hebrew, Aramaic, and Syriac.

Hamlet tragedy by William Shakespeare, first performed 1602. Hamlet, after much hesitation, avenges the murder of his father the king of

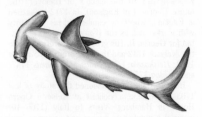

hammerhead

DEnmark, by the king's brother Claudius, who has married his mother. The play ends with the death of all three.

Hamlet's agonized indecision, real or feigned mental disorder, and awareness of role playing have been said to make him the first modern protagonist in English literature. He is haunted by his father's ghost demanding revenge, is torn between love and loathing for his mother, and becomes responsible for the deaths of his lover Ophelia, and his student companions Rosencrantz and Guildenstern. In the monologue beginning 'To be, or not to be' he contemplates suicide.

Hamm /hæm/ industrial town in Westphalia, West Germany; population (1988) 166,000. There are coal mines, and chemical and engineering industries.

Hammarskjöld /ˈhæməʃəʊld/ Dag 1905–1961. Swedish secretary-general of the United Nations 1953–61. Over the ◊Suez Crisis 1956 he opposed Britain. His attempts to solve the problem of Congo (now Zaire), where he was killed in a plane crash, were criticized by the USSR. Nobel Peace Prize 1961.

hammer in athletics, a throwing event in which only men compete. The hammer is a spherical weight attached to a chain with a handle. The competitor spins the hammer over his head to gain momentum and throws it as far as he can. The hammer weighs 7.26 kg/16 lb, and may originally have been a blacksmith's hammer.

Hammerfest /ˈhæməfest/ fishing port in NW Norway, northernmost town of Europe; population (1985) 7,500.

hammerhead several species of shark in the genus *Sphyrna*, found in tropical seas, characterized by having eyes at the ends of a double-headed 'hammer'. They can grow to 4 m/13 ft.

Hammerstein /ˈhæməstaɪn/ Oscar II 1895–1960. US lyricist and librettist, who collaborated with Jerome ◊Kern on *Show Boat* 1927, and with Richard ◊Rodgers.

Hammett /ˈhæmɪt/ Dashiell 1894–1961. US crime novelist, whose books include *The Maltese Falcon* 1930, *The Glass Key* 1931, and the *The Thin Man* 1932.

Hammett was a former Pinkerton detective agent. In 1951 he was imprisoned for contempt of court for refusing to testify during the McCarthy era of anticommunist witch-hunts. He lived with the playwright Lillian ◊Hellman.

Hammond /ˈhæmənd/ Joan 1912– . Australian soprano, known in oratorio and opera, for example, *Madame Butterfly*, *Tosca*, and *Martha*.

Hammond organ an electric organ invented in the USA by Laurens Hammond 1934 and widely used in gospel music. A precursor of the synthesizer.

Hammurabi /ˈhæmʊˈrɑːbi/ king of Babylon from *c.*1792 BC. He united his country and took it to the height of its power, although his consolidation of the legal code was bloodthirsty in its punishments.

Hampden /ˈhæmpdən/ John 1594–1643. English politician. His refusal in 1636 to pay ◊ship money made him a national figure. In the Short and Long parliaments he proved himself a skilful debater and parliamentary strategist. Charles's attempt to arrest him and four other leading MPs made the Civil War inevitable. He raised his own regiment on the outbreak of hostilities, and on 18 June 1643 was mortally wounded

Hampshire

at the skirmish of Chalgrove Field in Oxfordshire.

Hampden Park Scottish football ground, opened 1903, home of Queen's Park AFC and the national Scottish team. It plays host to the Scottish FA Cup and League Cup final each year as well as semi-final and other matches.

Its capacity is now approximately 65,000. It recorded a crowd of 149,547 for the Scotland versus England game 1937, the largest official attendance for a soccer match in Britain.

Hampshire /ˈhæmpʃə/ county of S England
area 3,770 sq km/1,455 sq mi
towns administrative headquarters Winchester; Southampton, Portsmouth, Gosport
features New Forest, area 373 sq km/144 sq mi, a Saxon royal hunting ground; Hampshire Basin, where Britain has onshore and offshore oil; Danebury, 2,500-year-old Celtic hillfort; Beaulieu (including National Motor Museum); Broadlands (home of Lord Mountbatten); Highclere (home of the Earl of Carnarvon, with gardens by Capability Brown); Hambledon, where the first cricket club was founded in 1750; site of the Roman town of Silchester, the only one in Britain known in such detail
products agricultural; oil from refineries at Fawley; chemicals, pharmaceuticals, electronics
population (1987) 1,537,000
famous people Jane Austen, Charles Dickens, Gilbert White.

Hampstead /ˈhæmpstɪd/ district of N London, part of the borough of ◊Camden.

Hampton /ˈhæmptən/ Christopher 1946– . British dramatist, resident at the Royal Court Theatre 1968–70. His plays include the comedy *The Philanthropist* 1970, *Savages* 1973, and an adaptation of *Les Liaisons Dangereuses*.

Hampton Court Palace former royal residence near Richmond, London, built 1515 by Cardinal ◊Wolsey, and presented by him to Henry VIII in 1525. Henry subsequently enlarged and improved it. In the 17th century William and Mary made it their main residence outside London, and the palace was further enlarged by Christopher Wren, although only part of his intended scheme was completed.

The last monarch to live at Hampton Court was George II, who died in 1760. During his life many of the Tudor apartments were pulled down and replaced. The palace was opened to the public, free of charge, by Queen Victoria in 1838.

hamster type of rodent of the family Cricetidae with a thickset body, short tail, and cheek pouches to carry food. A number of species are found across Asia and in SE Europe. Hamsters are often kept as pets.

Species include the *black-bellied hamster Cricetus cricetus*, about 25 cm/10 in long, which can be a crop pest and stores up to 90 kg/200 lb of seeds in its burrow. The *golden hamster*

Hampton Court Palace *Fountain Court, designed by Christopher Wren and begun in 1689. Part of the building was extensively damaged by fire in 1986.*

Mesocricetus auratus lives in W Asia and SE Europe. All hamsters now kept as pets originated from one female and 12 young captured in Syria in 1930.

Hamsun /'hæmsuːn/ Knut 1859–1952. Norwegian novelist, whose first novel *Sult/Hunger* 1890 was largely autobiographical. Other works include *Pan* 1894 and *The Growth of the Soil* 1917, which won him the Nobel prize in 1920. His hatred of capitalism made him sympathize with Nazism, and he was fined in 1946 for collaboration.

Hanbury-Tenison /'hænbəri 'tenɪsən/ (Airling) Robin 1936– . Irish adventurer, explorer, and writer, who made the first land crossing of South America at its widest point 1958. He explored the southern Sahara intermittently during 1962–66, and in South America sailed in a small boat from the Orinoco River to Buenos Aires 1964–65. After expeditions to Ecuador, Brazil, and Venezuela, he rode across France in 1984 and along the Great Wall of China in 1986. In 1969 he became chair of Survival International, an organization campaigning for the rights of threatened tribal peoples.

Hancock /'hænkɒk/ John 1737–1793. US revolutionary politician. He advocated resistance to the British as president of the Continental Congress 1775–77, and was the first to sign the Declaration of Independence in 1776. Because he signed it in a large, bold hand (in popular belief, so that it would be big enough for George III to see), his name became a colloquial term for a signature in the USA. He was governor of Massachusetts 1780–85 and 1787–93.

Hancock /'hænkɒk/ Tony (Anthony John) 1924–1968. British radio and television comedian. 'Hancock's Half Hour' from 1954 showed him always at odds with everyday life.

handball a team ball game now played indoors, popularized in Germany in the late 19th century. It is similar to association football, but played with the hands instead of the feet. The indoor game has seven players in a team; the outdoor version has 11 players.

Handel /'hændl/ Georg Friedrich 1685–1759. German composer, who became a British subject 1726. His first opera, *Almira*, was performed

Handel *Portrait by Thomas Hudson (1756) National Portrait Gallery, London.*

in Hamburg 1705. In 1710 he was appointed Kapellmeister to the elector of Hanover (the future George I of England). In 1712 he settled in England, where he established his popularity with works such as the *Water Music* 1717 (written for George I). His great choral works include the *Messiah* 1742 and the later oratorios *Samson* 1743, *Belshazzar* 1745, *Judas Maccabaeus* 1747, and *Jephtha* 1752.

Born in Halle, he abandoned the study of law 1703 to become a violinist at Keiser's Opera House in Hamburg. Visits to Italy (1706–10) inspired a number of operas and oratorios, and in 1711 his opera *Rinaldo* was performed in London. *Saul* and *Israel in Egypt* (both 1739) were unsuccessful, but his masterpiece the *Messiah* was acclaimed on its first performance in Dublin 1742. Other works include the pastoral *Acis and Galatea* 1718 and a set of variations for harpsichord that were later nicknamed 'The Harmonious Blacksmith'. In 1751 he became totally blind.

Handke /'hæntkə/ Peter 1942– . Austrian novelist and playwright, whose first play *Insulting the Audience* 1966 was an example of 'anti-theatre writing'. His novels include *Die Hornissen/The Hornets* 1966 and *The Goalie's Anxiety at the Penalty Kick* 1970. He directed and scripted the film *The Left-handed Woman* 1979.

Handley /'hændli/ Tommy 1896–1949. English radio comedian. His popular programme 'ITMA' (It's That Man Again) ran from 1939 until his death.

Hangchow /ˌhæŋ'tʃaʊ/ former name for ◊Hangzhou, port in Zhejiang province, China.

hang gliding technique of unpowered flying using air currents, perfected by a US engineer named Rogallo in the 1970s. The aeronaut is strapped into a carrier, attached to a sail wing of nylon stretched on an aluminium frame like a paper dart, and jumps into the air from a high place.

hanging execution by suspension, usually with a drop of 0.6–2 m/2–6 ft, so that the powerful jerk of the tightened rope breaks the neck. This was once a common form of ◊capital punishment in Europe and is still practised in some states in the USA. It was abolished in the UK 1965.

hanging participle see ◊participle.

Hangzhou /ˌhæŋ'dʒəʊ/ formerly **Hangchow** port and capital of Zhejiang province, China; population (1986) 1,250,000. It has jute, steel, chemical, tea, and silk industries. It has fine landscaped gardens, and was the capital of China 1127–1278 under the Sung dynasty.

Hanley /'hænli/ one of the old Staffordshire pottery towns in England, now part of ◊Stoke-on-Trent.

Hanley /'hænli/ Ellery 1961– . English rugby league player, a regular member of the Great Britain team since 1984 and the inspiration behind his club Wigan's rise to the top in the 1980s.

Hanley started his career with Bradford Northern before his transfer to Wigan in 1985 for a then world record £85,000. He has since won all the top honours of the game in Britain as well as earning a reputation in Australia, the world's top rugby league nation.

CAREER HIGHLIGHTS

Challenge Cup: 1988–89
John Player Trophy: 1986–87, 1989
Lancashire Cup: 1985–89
Man of Steel Award: 1985, 1987, 1989
Division One Player of the Year: 1987
Lance Todd Trophy: 1989

Hannibal /'hænɪbəl/ 247–182 BC. Carthaginian general from 221 BC, son of Hamilcar Barca. His siege of Saguntum (now Sagunto, near Valencia) precipitated the 2nd ◊Punic War. Following a campaign in Italy (after crossing the Alps in 218 with 57 elephants), Hannibal was the victor at Trasimene in 217 and Cannae in 216, but he failed to take Rome. In 203 he returned to Carthage to meet a Roman invasion but was defeated at Zama in 202 and exiled in 196 at Rome's insistence.

Hannibal /'hænɪbəl/ town in Missouri, USA, population (1980) 18,811. Mark Twain lived here as a boy, and made it the setting of the events of his novel *The Adventures of Huckleberry Finn*.

Hanoi /hæ'nɔɪ/ capital of Vietnam, on the Red River; population (1979) 2,571,000. Industries include textiles, paper, and engineering.

Captured by the French in 1873, it was the capital of French Indochina 1887–1946; and the capital of North Vietnam 1954–76. Hanoi University was founded 1918.

Hanover /'hænəʊvə/ industrial city, capital of Lower Saxony, West Germany; population (1988) 506,000. Industries include machinery, vehicles, electrical goods, rubber, textiles, and oil refining.

From 1386, it was a member of the ◊Hanseatic League, and from 1692 capital of the electorate of Hanover (created a kingdom 1815). ◊George I of England was also Elector of Hanover, and the two countries shared the same monarch until the accession of Victoria 1837. Since Salic Law meant a woman could not rule in Hanover, the throne passed to her uncle, Ernest, Duke of Cumberland. His son was forced by ◊Bismarck to abdicate 1866, and Hanover became a Prussian province. In 1946, Hanover was merged with Brunswick and Oldenburg to form the *Land* of Lower Saxony.

Hanover /'hænəʊvə/ German royal dynasty that ruled Great Britain and Ireland 1714–1901. Under the Act of ◊Settlement 1701, the succession passed to the ruling family of Hanover, Germany, on the death of Queen Anne. On the death of Queen Victoria the crown passed to Edward VII of the house of Saxe-Coburg.

Hansard /'hænsɑːd/ the official report of the proceedings of the British Parliament, named after Luke Hansard (1752–1828), printer of the House of Commons *Journal* from 1774. The first official reports were published from 1803 by the political journalist Cobbett, who during his imprisonment 1810–12 sold the business to his printer, Thomas Curson Hansard, son of Luke Hansard. The publication of the debates remained in the hands of the family until 1889, and is now the responsibility of the Stationery Office. The name *Hansard* was officially adopted 1943.

Hanseatic League (German *Hanse* 'group, society') a confederation of N European trading cities from the 12th century to 1669. At its height in the later 14th century the Hanseatic League included over 160 towns, among them Lübeck, Hamburg, Cologne, Breslau, and Cracow. The basis of its power was its monopoly of the Baltic trade and its relations with Flanders and England. The decline of the Hanseatic League from the 15th century was caused by the movement of trade routes and the development of national states.

The earliest association had its headquarters in Visby, Sweden; it included over 30 cities, but was gradually supplanted by that headed by Lübeck. Hamburg and Lübeck established their own trading stations in London in 1266 and 1267 respectively, which coalesced in 1282 with that of Cologne to form the so-called Steelyard. There were three other such stations: Bruges, Bergen, and Novgorod. The last general assembly 1669 marked the end of the League.

Hansel and Gretel fairy tale, collected by the Grimm brothers. Hansel and Gretel are children abandoned in the forest by their poor parents. They find a cottage made of gingerbread and are captured by the child-eating witch who lives there, but escape by wit and ingenuity. The happy ending reunites them with their parents. The story was made into a children's opera by ◊Humperdinck in 1893.

Hansom /'hænsəm/ Joseph Aloysius 1803–1882. British architect. His works include the Birmingham town hall 1831, but he is remembered as the introducer of the **hansom cab** in 1834, a two-wheel carriage with a seat for the driver on the outside.

Hants abbreviation for ◊*Hampshire*.

Hardy *English novelist and poet Thomas Hardy.*

Hanukkah eight-day festival in Judaism that takes place at the beginning of Dec. It celebrates the recapture of the Temple in Jerusalem by Judas Maccabeus in 164 BC.

During Hanukkah, candles are lit each night and placed in an eight-branched candlestick, or menorah: this commemorates the Temple lamp which stayed miraculously lit for eight days on one day's supply of oil when the Temple was freed.

Hanuman /ˈhʌnuːˈmɑːn/ in the Sanskrit epic ◊*Rāmāyana*, the Hindu monkey god and king of Hindustan (N India). He assisted Rama (an incarnation of the god Vishnu) to recover his wife Sita, abducted by Ravana of Lanka (modern Sri Lanka).

Hanway /ˈhænweɪ/ Jonas 1712–1786. British traveller in Russia and Persia, and advocate of prison reform. He is believed to have been the first Englishman to carry an umbrella.

Hanyang /ˌhænˈjæŋ/ former Chinese city, now merged in ◊Wuhan, in Hubei province.

haploid having one set of ◊chromosomes in each cell. Most higher organisms are ◊diploid, that is they have two sets, but moss, plants and many seaweeds are haploid, as are male honey bees because they develop from eggs that have not been fertilized. See also ◊meiosis.

Harlow *US film star Jean Harlow, popularly known as the 'platinum blonde'.*

Hardie *British socialist Keir Hardie, chief founder of the Independent Labour Party and the party's first candidate to stand for Parliament.*

Hapsburg /ˈhæpsbɜːg/ English form of ◊Habsburg, European royal family and former imperial house of Austria-Hungary.

Haq /hɑːk/ Fazlul 1873–1962. Leader of the Bengali Muslim peasantry. He was a member of the Viceroy's Defence Council, established 1941, and was Bengal's first Indian prime minister 1937–43.

hara-kiri ritual suicide of the Japanese samurai (military caste) from the 12th century onwards. It was carried out to avoid dishonour, either voluntarily or on the order of a feudal lord. The correct Japanese term is *seppuku*.

Harappa /həˈræpə/ ruined city of a prehistoric Indian culture, the ◊Indus Valley Civilization.

Harare /həˈrɑːri/ capital of Zimbabwe, on the Mashonaland plateau about 1,525 m/5,000 ft above sea level; population (1982) 656,000. It is the centre of a rich farming area (tobacco and maize), with metallurgical and food processing industries.

The British occupied the site in 1890, and named it Fort Salisbury in honour of Lord Salisbury, then prime minister of the UK. It was capital of the Federation of Rhodesia and Nyasaland 1953–63.

Harbin /ˌhɑːˈbɪn/ formerly ***Haerhpin*** and ***Pinkiang*** port on the Songhua river, NE China; capital of Heilongjiang province; population (1986) 2,630,000. Industries include metallurgy, machinery, paper, food processing, and sugar refining, and it is a major rail junction. Harbin was developed by Russian settlers after Russia was granted trading rights there 1896, and more Russians arrived as refugees after the October Revolution 1917.

Harcourt /ˈhɑːkət/ William Vernon 1827–1904. British Liberal politician. Under Gladstone he was home secretary 1880–85 and chancellor of the Exchequer 1886 and 1892–95. He is remembered for his remark in 1892: 'We are all Socialists now.'

hard copy output from a computer that is printed on paper rather than displayed on a screen.

hard disc in computing, a storage device consisting of a rigid magnetic disc permanently housed in a sealed case. Hard discs are the same sizes as ◊floppy discs but are much faster and have far greater memory capacities, typically between 20 and 150 ◊megabytes.

Hardenberg /ˈhɑːdnbɜːg/ Karl August von 1750–1822. Prussian politician, foreign minister to King Frederick William III of Prussia during the Napoleonic Wars. He later became chancellor. His military and civic reforms were restrained by the reactionary tendencies of the king.

Hardicanute /ˈhɑːdɪkənjuːt/ *c.*1019–1042. King of England from 1040. Son of Canute, he was king of Denmark from 1028. In England he was known as a harsh ruler.

Hardie /ˈhɑːdi/ (James) Keir 1856–1915. Scottish socialist, member of Parliament for West Ham,

London, 1892–95 and for Merthyr Tydfil, Wales, from 1900. Born in Lanarkshire, he worked in the mines as a boy, and in 1886 became secretary of the Scottish Miners' Federation. In 1888 he was the first Labour candidate to stand for Parliament; he entered Parliament independently as a Labour member in 1892 and was a chief founder of the ◊Independent Labour Party in 1893.

A pacifist, he strongly opposed the Boer War, and his idealism in his work for socialism and the unemployed made him a popular hero.

Harding /ˈhɑːdɪŋ/ (Allan Francis) John, 1st Baron Harding of Petherton 1896–1989. British field marshal. Chief of staff in Italy during World War II. As governor of Cyprus 1955–57, during the period of political agitation prior to independence (1960), he was responsible for the controversial deportation of Makarios III from Cyprus in 1955.

Harding /ˈhɑːdɪŋ/ Warren G(amaliel) 1865–1923. 29th president of the USA 1921–23, a Republican. Harding was born in Ohio, and entered the US Senate in 1914. As president he concluded the peace treaties of 1921 with Germany, Austria, and Hungary, and in the same year called the Washington Conference. He opposed US membership of the League of Nations. There were charges of corruption among members of his cabinet (the ◊Teapot Dome Scandal).

hardness a physical property of materials that governs their use. Methods of heat treatment can increase the hardness of metals. A scale of hardness was devised by Friedrich ◊Mohs in the 1800s, based upon the hardness of certain minerals from soft talc (Mohs' hardness 1) to diamond (10), the hardest of all materials. See also ◊Brinell hardness test.

The ***hardness of water*** refers to the presence of dissolved minerals in it that prevent soap lathering, particularly compounds of calcium and magnesium. Treatment with a water softener may remove them.

Hardouin-Mansart /ˈɑːdwæn mænˈsɑː/ 1646–1708. French architect, royal architect to Louis XIV from 1675. He designed the lavish Baroque extensions to the palace of Versailles (from 1678) and the Invalides Chapel in Paris 1680–91.

Hardwar /həˈdwɑː/ town in Uttar Pradesh, India, on the right bank of the Ganges; population (1981) 115,513. The name means 'door of Hari' (or Vishnu). It is one of the holy places of the Hindu religion and a pilgrimage centre. The *Kumbhmela* festival, held every 12th year in honour of the god Siva, is the most important and attracts about 1 million pilgrims.

hardware in computing, the mechanical, electrical, and electronic components of a computer system, as opposed to the various programs, which constitute ◊software.

In a microcomputer, hardware might include the circuit boards, the power supply and housing of the processor unit, the VDU (screen), external memory devices such as disc drives, a printer, the keyboard, and so on.

Hardy /ˈhɑːdi/ Oliver 1892–1957. US film comedian, member of the duo ◊Laurel and Hardy.

Hardy /ˈhɑːdi/ Thomas 1840–1928. English novelist and poet. His novels, set in rural 'Wessex' (his native West Country), portray intense human relationships played out in a harshly indifferent natural world. They include *Far From the Madding Crowd* 1874, *The Return of the Native* 1878, *The Mayor of Casterbridge* 1886, *The Woodlanders* 1887, *Tess of the D'Urbervilles* 1891, and *Jude the Obscure* 1895. His poetry includes the *Wessex Poems* 1898, the blank-verse epic *The Dynasts* 1904–08, and several volumes of lyrics.

Born in Dorset, he was trained as an architect. His first success was *Far From the Madding Crowd*. *Tess of the D'Urbervilles*, subtitled 'A Pure Woman', outraged public opinion by portraying as its heroine a woman who had been seduced. The even greater outcry that followed *Jude the Obscure* 1895 reinforced Hardy's decision to confine himself to verse.

Hare's apparatus

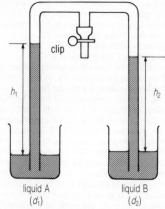

liquid A
(d_1)

liquid B
(d_2)

Hardy /'hɑːdɪ/ Thomas Masterman 1769–1839. British sailor. At Trafalgar he was Nelson's flag captain in the *Victory*, attending him during his dying moments. He became First Sea Lord in 1830.

Hardy-Weinberg equilibrium in population genetics, the relative frequency of different ◊alleles within a given population of a species, when the stable end-point of evolution in an undisturbed environment is reached.

hare mammal of the genus *Lepus*, family Leporidae, larger than the ◊rabbit, with very long black-tipped ears, long hind legs, and short upturned tail.

Throughout the long breeding season Jan–Aug, there are chases and 'boxing-matches' among males; the saying 'mad as a March hare' arises from this behaviour. They do not burrow. The young are called leverets and live in a grassy depression called a form.

Hare /heə/ David 1947– . British dramatist and director, whose plays include *Slag* 1970, *Teeth 'n' Smiles* 1975, *Pravda* 1985 (with Howard ◊Brenton), and *Wrecked Eggs* 1986.

harebell perennial plant *Campanula rotundifolia*, with bell-shaped blue flowers, found on dry grassland and heaths. Known in Scotland as the bluebell.

Hare Krishna popular name for a member of the ◊International Society for Krishna Consciousness, derived from their chant.

hare-lip facial deformity, a cleft in the upper lip and jaw, which may extend back into the palate (cleft palate). It can be remedied by surgery.

Hare's apparatus in physics, a specific kind of ◊hydrometer used to compare the relative densities of two liquids, or to find the density of one if the other is known. It was invented by US chemist Robert Hare (1781–1858).

It consists of a vertical E-shaped glass tube, with the long limbs dipping into the two liquids and a tap on the short limb. Operating the tap removes air, pushing the liquids up the tubes by atmospheric pressure. When the tap is closed, the heights of the liquids are inversely proportional to their relative densities. If a liquid of relative density d_1 rises to a height h_1, and liquid d_2 rises to h_2, $d_1/d_2 = h_2/h_1$.

Harewood /'hɑːwʊd/ George Henry Hubert Lascelles, 7th Earl of Harewood 1923– . Artistic director of the Edinburgh Festival 1961–65, director of the English National Opera 1972–85, and a governor of the BBC from 1985.

Harfleur /ɑːˈflɜː/ port in NW France; population (1985) 9,700. Important in medieval times, it was superseded by ◊Le Havre.

Hargeisa /hɑːˈɡeɪsə/ trading centre in NW Somalia; population (1988) 400,000.

Hargobind /'hɑːɡəbɪnd/ 1595–1644. Indian religious leader, sixth guru (teacher) of Sikhism 1606–44. He encouraged Sikhs to develop military skills in response to growing persecution. At the festival of ◊Diwali, Sikhs celebrate his release from prison.

Hargraves /'hɑːɡreɪvz/ Edward Hammond 1816–1891. Australian prospector, born in England. In 1851 he found gold in the Blue Mountains of New South Wales, thus beginning the first Australian gold rush.

Hargreaves /'hɑːɡriːvz/ James died 1778. English inventor, who co-invented a carding machine in 1760. About 1764 he invented his 'spinning-jenny', which enabled a number of threads to be spun simultaneously by one person.

Harijan /'hʌrɪdʒən/ (Hindi 'children of god') member of the Indian ◊caste of untouchables. The name was coined by Mahatma Gandhi.

Haringey /'hærɪŋɡeɪ/ borough of N Greater London; population (1984) 200,100. It includes the suburbs of Wood Green, Tottenham, and Hornsey. *features* Alexandra Palace, with a park; Finsbury Park (once part of Hornsey Wood); includes Tottenham with Bruce Castle, originally built in the 16th century on a site belonging to Robert Bruce's father (Rowland ◊Hill once ran a school here).

Har Krishen 1656–1664. Indian religious leader, eighth guru (teacher) of Sikhism 1661–64, who died at the age of eight.

Harlech /'hɑːlex/ town in Gwynedd, N Wales; population (1980) 1,250. The song 'March of the Men of Harlech' originated in the siege when the town was captured in 1468 by the Yorkists in the Wars of the ◊Roses.

Harlem /'hɑːləm/ commercial and residential district of Manhattan, New York City, USA. It is a centre for music, particularly jazz.

Harlem Globetrotters US touring basketball team who play exhibition matches worldwide. Comedy routines as well as their great skills are a feature of the games. They were founded by Abraham Saperstein (1903–1966) in 1927.

Harlem Renaissance a movement in US literature in the 1920s that used black life and traditional black culture as its subject matter; it was an early manifestation of black pride in the USA. The centre of the movement was the Harlem area of New York City.

Harlem was the area where black culture, including jazz, flourished among migrants to the industrial North from the Southern states and attracted a new white audience. The magazine *Crisis*, edited by W E B DuBois, was a forum for the new black consciousness; writers associated with the movement include Langston Hughes, Zora Neale Hurston, James Weldon Johnson, and Countee Cullen.

Harley /'hɑːlɪ/ Robert, 1st Earl of Oxford 1661–1724. British Tory politician, chief minister to Queen Anne 1711–14, when he negotiated the Treaty of Utrecht in 1713. Accused of treason as a Jacobite after the accession of George I, he was imprisoned 1714–17.

Harlow /'hɑːləʊ/ Jean. Stage name of Harlean Carpenter 1911–1937. US film actress, the first 'platinum blonde'. Her films include *Hell's Angels* 1930, *Dinner At Eight* 1934, and *Saratoga* 1937.

harmattan in meteorology, a dry and dusty NE wind that blows over W Africa.

harmonica or *mouth organ* a pocket-sized reed organ blown directly from the mouth; invented by Charles Wheatstone 1829.

The *glass harmonica* (or armonica) is based on the principle of playing a wine glass with a wet finger. Devised by Benjamin Franklin, it consists of a graded series of glass bowls mounted on a spindle and resting in a trough part-filled with water. Rotated by a foot-pedal, it emits pure tones of unchanging intensity when touched. Mozart, Beethoven, and Schubert all wrote pieces for it.

harmonics in music, a series of partial vibrations that combine to form a musical tone. The number and relative prominence of harmonics produced determines an instrument's tone colour (timbre). An oboe is rich in harmonics, the flute has few. Harmonics conform to successive divisions of the sounding air column or string: their pitches are harmonious.

harmonium a keyboard reed organ of the 19th century, powered by foot-operated bellows.

Widely adopted in the USA as a home and church instrument, in France and Germany the harmonium flourished as a concert solo and orchestral instrument, being written for by Karg-Elert, Schoenberg, and Saint-Saëns.

harmony in music, any simultaneous combination of sounds, as opposed to melody, which is a succession of sounds. Although the term suggests a pleasant or agreeable sound, it is applied to any combination of notes, whether consonant or dissonant. Harmony deals with the formation of chords and their interrelation and logical progression.

The founder of harmonic theory was Jean-Philippe ◊Rameau. His *Traité de l'harmonie/Treatise on Harmony* 1722 established a system of chord classification on which subsequent methods of harmony have been based.

Harold /'hærəld/ two kings of England:

Harold I died 1040. King of England from 1035. The illegitimate son of Canute, known as *Harefoot*, he claimed the throne 1035 when the legitimate heir Hardicanute was in Denmark. In 1037 he was elected king.

Harold II *c.* 1020–1066. King of England from Jan 1066. He succeeded his father Earl ◊Godwin 1053 as earl of Wessex. In 1063 William of Normandy (◊William I) tricked him into swearing to support his claim to the English throne, and when the ◊Witan elected Harold to succeed Edward the Confessor, William prepared to invade. Meanwhile, Harold's treacherous brother Tostig (died 1066) joined the king of Norway, Harald III Hardrada (1015–66), in invading Northumbria. Harold routed and killed them at Stamford Bridge 25 Sept. Three days later William landed at Pevensey, Sussex; Harold was killed at the Battle of Hastings 14 Oct 1066.

harp a plucked musical string instrument, with the strings stretched vertically within a wooden frame, normally triangular. The concert harp is now the largest musical instrument to be plucked by hand. It has up to 47 strings, and seven pedals set into the soundbox at the base to alter pitch.

The harp existed in the West as early as the 9th century, and it was common among medieval minstrels. At that time it was quite small, and was normally placed on the knees. It evolved in size owing to a need for increased volume following its introduction into the orchestra in the 19th century. The harp has also been used in folk music, as both a solo and accompanying instrument, and is associated with Wales and Ireland.

Harper's Ferry /'hɑːpəz 'ferɪ/ village in W Virginia, USA, where the Potomac meets the Shenandoah. It is famous for the incident in 1859 when antislavery leader John ◊Brown seized the government's arsenal here.

Harold II After Edward the Confessor's death, Harold, Earl of Wessex, was crowned king in Jan 1066. Harold's short but eventful rule came to an abrupt end with his death at the Battle of Hastings in Oct 1066.

Haryana

Chandigarh

INDIAN OCEAN

Harpies in early Greek mythology, wind spirits; in later legend they have horrific women's faces and the bodies of vultures.

harpsichord keyboard musical instrument, common in the 16th–18th centuries until superseded by the piano. The strings are plucked by quills. It was revived in the 20th century for the authentic performance of early music.

Har Rai 1630–1661. Indian religious leader, seventh guru (teacher) of Sikhism 1644–61.

harrier bird of prey of the genus *Circus* of the family Accipitridae. They have long wings and legs, short beaks and soft plumage. They are found throughout the world.

Three species occur in Britain: the hen harrier *Circus cyaneus*, Montagu's harrier *Circus pygargus*, and the marsh harrier *Circus aeruginosus*.

harrier breed of dog, a small hound originally used for hare-hunting.

Harrier the only truly successful vertical take-off and landing fixed-wing aircraft, often called the *jump jet*. Built in Britain, it made its first flight 1966. It has a single jet engine and a set of swivelling nozzles. These deflect the jet exhaust vertically downwards for take-off and landing, and to the rear for normal flight. Designed to fly from confined spaces with minimal ground support, it refuels in midair.

Harriman /ˈhærɪmən/ (William) Averell 1891–1986. US diplomat, administrator of ◊lend-lease in World War II, Democratic secretary of commerce in Truman's administration, 1946–1948, negotiator of the Nuclear Test Ban Treaty with the USSR in 1963, and governor of New York 1955–58.

Harris /ˈhærɪs/ southern part of ◊Lewis with Harris, in the Outer ◊Hebrides; area 500 sq km/ 193 sq mi; population (1971) 2,900. It is joined to Lewis by a narrow isthmus. Harris tweeds are produced here.

Harris /ˈhærɪs/ Arthur Travers 1892–1984. British marshal of the Royal Air Force in World War II. Known as 'Bomber Harris', he was commander in chief of Bomber Command 1942–45.

He was an autocratic and single-minded leader, and was criticized for his policy of civilian-bombing of selected cities in Germany; he authorized the fire-bombing raids on Dresden, in which more than 100,000 died.

Harris /ˈhærɪs/ Frank 1856–1931. Irish journalist, who wrote colourful biographies of the playwrights Wilde and Shaw, and an autobiography, *My Life and Loves* 1926, originally banned in the UK and the USA.

Harris /ˈhærɪs/ Joel Chandler 1848–1908. US author of the tales of 'Uncle Remus', based on black folklore, about Br'er Rabbit and the Tar Baby.

Harris /ˈhærɪs/ Paul P 1878–1947. US lawyer, who founded the first ◊*Rotary Club* in Chicago 1905.

Harris /ˈhærɪs/ Richard 1932– . Irish film actor known for playing rebel characters in such films as

This *Sporting Life* 1963; *Il Deserto rosso/The Red Desert* 1964; *Camelot* 1967; *Cromwell* 1970; *Robin and Marion* 1976; *Tarzan the Ape Man* 1981.

Harris /ˈhærɪs/ Roy 1898–1979. US composer, born in Oklahoma, who used American folk tunes. Among his works are the 10th symphony 1965 (known as 'Abraham Lincoln') and the orchestral *When Johnny Comes Marching Home* 1935.

Harrison /ˈhærɪsən/ 'Rex' (Reginald Carey) 1908–1990. British actor. His successes include *French Without Tears* 1936 and the musical *My Fair Lady* stage 1956, film 1964. Films include *Blithe Spirit* 1944 and *Cleopatra* 1962.

Harrison /ˈhærɪsən/ Benjamin 1833–1901. 23rd president of the USA 1889–93, a Republican. He called the first Pan-American Conference, which led to the establishment of the Pan American Union, to improve inter-American cooperation, and develop commercial ties. In 1948 this became the ◊Organization of American States.

Harrison /ˈhærɪsən/ William Henry 1773–1841. 9th president of the USA 1841. Elected 1840 as a Whig, he died a month after taking office. Benjamin Harrison was his grandson.

Harrisson /ˈhærɪsən/ Tom 1911–1976. British anthropologist, who set up Mass Observation with Charles Madge 1937, the earliest of the organizations for the analysis of public opinions and attitudes.

Harrogate /ˈhærəgət/ resort and spa in N Yorkshire, England; population (1981) 66,500. There is a US communications station at Menwith Hill.

harrow an agricultural implement used to break up the furrows left by the ◊plough and reduce the soil to a fine consistency or tilth, and to cover the seeds after sowing. The traditional harrow consists of spikes set in a frame; modern harrows use sets of discs.

Hart /hɑːt/ Gary 1936– . US Democrat politician, senator for Colorado from 1974. In 1980 he contested the Democratic nomination for the presidency, and stepped down from his Senate seat in 1986 to stand, again unsuccessfully, in the 1988 presidential campaign.

Hart /hɑːt/ Judith 1924– . British Labour politician and sociologist. She was minister of overseas development 1967–70 and 77–79, and minister of state 1974–75.

Harte /hɑːt/ Francis Bret 1836–1902. US writer. He became a goldminer at 18 before founding the *Overland Monthly* 1868 in which he wrote short stories of the pioneer West, for example *The Luck of Roaring Camp* and poems such as *The Heathen Chinee*. From 1885 he settled in England after five years as US consul in Glasgow.

hartebeest type of large African antelope *Alcelaphus buselaphus* with lyre-shaped horns set close on top of the head in both sexes. It may reach 1.5 m/5 ft at the rather humped shoulders, and up to 2 m/6 ft long. Clumsy-looking runners, hartebeest can still reach 65 kph/40 mph.

Hartford Convention in US history, a meeting of ◊Federalist Party delegates in Dec 1814–Jan 1815 (at the end of the War of ◊1812) in Hartford, Connecticut. The meeting considered amendments to the US constitution and the possibility of secession from the union in response to the adverse economic effects of the war on New England. The end of the war forestalled further action.

Hartington /hɑːtɪŋtən/ Spencer Compton Cavendish, 8th Duke of Devonshire, and Marquess of Hartington 1833–1908. British politician, first leader of the Liberal Unionists 1886–1903. As war minister he opposed devolution for Ireland in cabinet and later led the revolt of the Liberal Unionists that defeated Gladstone's Irish Home Rule bill in 1886. Cavendish refused the premiership three times, 1880, 1886, and 1887, and led the opposition to the Irish Home Rule bill in the House of Lords 1893.

He held the titles of Marquess of Hartington 1858–91 and 8th Duke of Devonshire 1891–1908. He entered the House of Commons 1857 and

Harvey English physician William Harvey published his theory of the circulation of the blood in 1628.

served in Earl Russell's government as secretary of state for war 1866, as postmaster general 1868–70, and as chief secretary for Ireland 1868–74. In Gladstone's second ministry he was secretary for India 1880–82 when he returned to the war ministry until the Liberal defeat in 1885.

Hartley /ˈhɑːtli/ L(eslie) P(oles) 1895–1972. English novelist, noted for his exploration of the sinister. His books include the trilogy *The Shrimp and the Anemone* 1944, *The Sixth Heaven* 1946, and *Eustace and Hilda* 1947, on the intertwined lives of a brother and sister. Later books include *The Boat* 1949, *The Go-Between* 1953, and *The Hireling* 1957.

hart's-tongue fern *Phyllitis scolopendrium*; its traplike undivided fronds, up to 60 cm/2 ft long, have prominent brown spore-bearing organs in parallel lines on the underside of the leaf. It is found on walls, shady rocky places, and in woods, especially in wet areas.

Hartz Mountains /hɑːts/ range running north to south in Tasmania, Australia, with two remarkable peaks: Hartz Mountain 1,254 m/4,113 ft, and Adamsons Peak 1,224 m/4,017 ft.

Harun al-Rashid /hæˈruːn æl ræˈʃiːd/ 763–809. Caliph of Baghdad from 786 of the Abbasid dynasty, a lavish patron of music, poetry, and letters, known from the *Arabian Nights* stories.

Harvard University /ˈhɑːvəd/ oldest educational institution in the USA, founded in 1636 at New Towne (later Cambridge), Massachusetts, and named after John Harvard (1607–38), who bequeathed half his estate and his library to it. Women were first admitted in 1969; they previously attended **Radcliffe College**, the women's college of the university.

harvestman arachnid of the order Opiliones. They are distinguished from true spiders by the absence of a waist or constriction in the oval body. They are carnivorous, and found from the Arctic to the tropics. The long-legged harvestman *Phalangium opilio*, known as daddy-long-legs, is common in Britain.

harvest-mite scarlet or rusty brown ◊mite common in summer and autumn. They are parasitic, and their bites are intensely irritating to humans.

Harvey /ˈhɑːvi/ Laurence (Lauruska Mischa Skikne) 1928–1973. British film actor of Lithuanian descent who worked both in England (*Room at the Top* 1958) and in Hollywood (*The Alamo* 1960; *The Manchurian Candidate* 1962).

Harvey /ˈhɑːvi/ William 1578–1657. English physician who discovered the circulation of blood. In 1628 he published his great book *De Motu Cordis/On the Motion of the Heart*.

After studying at Padua, Italy, under ◊Fabricius, he set out to question ◊Galen's account of the action of the heart. Later, Harvey explored the development of chick and deer ◊embryos. He was Court physician to James I and Charles I.

Harwell /'hɑːwəl/ the main research establishment of the United Kingdom Atomic Energy Authority, situated near the village of Harwell in Oxfordshire.

Harwich /'hærɪdʒ/ seaport in Essex, England; with ferry services to Scandinavia and the NW Europe; population (1981) 15,076. Reclamation of Bathside Bay mudflats is making it a rival, as a port, to Felixstowe.

Haryana /ˌhæriˈɑːnə/ state of NW India
area 44,200 sq km/17,061 sq mi
capital Chandigarh
features part of the Ganges plain, and a centre of Hinduism
products sugar, cotton, oilseed, textiles, cement, iron ore
population (1981) 12,851,000
language Hindi.

Hasdrubal Barca /'hæzdrʊbəl 'bɑːkə/ Carthaginian general, son of Hamilcar Barca and brother of Hannibal. He remained in command in Spain when Hannibal invaded Italy, and, after fighting there against the Scipios until 208, marched to Hannibal's relief. He was defeated and killed in the Metaurus valley, NE Italy.

Hašek /'hæʃek/ Jaroslav 1883–1923. Czech writer. His masterpiece is the anti-authoritarian comic satire on military life under Austro-Hungarian rule, *The Good Soldier Schweik* 1923. During World War I he deserted to the Russians, and eventually joined the Bolsheviks.

hashish resinous form of the drug ◊cannabis.

hash total in computing, an arithmetic total of a set of arbitrary numeric values, such as account numbers. Although the total itself is meaningless, it is stored along with the data to which it refers. On subsequent occasions, the program recalculates the hash total and compares it to the one stored to ensure that the original numbers are still correct.

Hassam /'hæsəm/ Childe 1859–1935. US Impressionist painter and printmaker. He was profoundly influenced by a visit to Paris in 1866. He became one of the members of **the Ten**, a group of American Impressionists who exhibited together until World War I.

Hassan II /hæ'sɑːn/ 1930– . King of Morocco from 1961; from 1976 he undertook the occupation of Western Sahara.

Hassidim or **Chasidim** a mystic sect of ultra-conservative Orthodox Jews (see ◊Judaism), founded in 18th-century Poland, which stressed intense emotion as a part of worship. Many of their ideas are based on the ◊kabbala.

Hastings /'heɪstɪŋz/ resort in East Sussex, England; population (1981) 74,803. The chief of the ◊Cinque Ports, it has ruins of a Norman castle, and the wreck of the Dutch East Indiaman, *Amsterdam* 1749, is under excavation. It is adjoined by St Leonard's, developed in the 19th century.

Hastings /'heɪstɪŋz/ Warren 1732–1818. British colonial administrator. A protégé of Lord Clive, who established British rule in India, Hastings carried out major reforms, and became governor of Bengal in 1772 and governor general of India in 1774. Impeached for corruption on his return to England in 1785, he was acquitted in 1795.

Hastings, Battle of battle 14 Oct 1066 at which William the Conqueror defeated Harold, king of England. The site is 10 km/6 mi inland of Hastings, at Senlac, Sussex; it is marked by Battle Abbey.

Having defeated an attempt by King Harald Hardreda of Norway at Stamford Bridge, Harold moved south with an army of 9,000 to counter the landing of the Duke of Normandy at Pevensey Bay, Kent. Following Harold's death after only a day's fighting, the English army disintegrated, leaving William to succeed to the throne.

Havel After several prison terms for his political ideals, playwright Vaclav Havel became president of Czechoslovakia 1989.

Hathaway /'hæθəweɪ/ Anne 1556–1623. Wife of the English dramatist ◊Shakespeare from 1582.

Hathor /'hæθɔː/ in ancient Egyptian mythology, the sky-goddess, identified with ◊Isis.

Hatshepsut /hæt'ʃepsʊt/ *c.*1540–*c.*1481 BC. Queen of Egypt during the 18th dynasty. She was the daughter of Thothmes I, with whom she ruled until the accession to the throne of her husband and half-brother Thotmes II. Throughout his reign real power lay with Hatshepsut, and she continued to rule after his death, as regent for her nephew Thotmes III.

Hatshepsut reigned as a man, and is shown dressed as a pharaoh, with a beard. Her reign was a peaceful and prosperous time in a period when Egypt was developing its armies and expanding its territories. When she died or was forced to abdicate, Thothmes III defaced her monuments. The ruins of her magnificent temple at Deir el-Bahri survive.

Hatteras /'hætərəs/ cape on the coast of N Carolina, USA, noted for shipwrecks.

Hattersley /'hætəzli/ Roy 1932– . British Labour politician. On the right wing of the Labour Party, he was prices secretary 1976–79, and in 1983 became deputy leader of the party.

Hatton /'hætn/ Derek 1948– . British left-wing politician, former deputy leader of Liverpool Council. A member of the ◊Militant Tendency, Hatton was removed from office and expelled from the Labour Party in 1987. He revealed in his autobiography (1988) how Militant acted as a subversive party-within-a-party.

Haughey /'hɔːhi/ Charles 1925– . Irish Fianna Fáil politician of Ulster descent. Dismissed in 1970 from Jack Lynch's cabinet for alleged complicity in IRA gun-running, he was afterwards acquitted. Prime minister 1979–81, Mar–Nov 1982, and 1986– .

Hausa /'haʊsə/ Muslim people of N Nigeria, whose Afro-Asiatic language is a lingua franca of W Africa.

Haussmann /əʊs'mæn/ Georges Eugène, Baron Haussmann 1809–1891. French administrator, who replanned medieval Paris 1853–70, with wide boulevards and parks. The cost of his scheme and his authoritarianism caused opposition, and he was made to resign.

haustorium plural *haustoria* a specialized organ produced by a parasitic plant or fungus that penetrates the cells of its host to absorb nutrients. It may be either an outgrowth of ◊hyphae, as in the case of parasitic fungi, or of the stems of flowering parasitic plants, as seen in dodders (*Cuscuta*). The sucker-like haustoria of a dodder penetrate the vascular tissue of the host plant without killing the cells.

Haute-Normandie /'əʊt ˌnɔːmənˈdiː/ or **Upper Normandy** coastal region of NW France lying between Basse-Normandie and Picardy and bisected by the Seine; area 12,300 sq km/4,757 sq mi; population (1986) 1,693,000. It consists of the *départements* of Eure and Seine-Maritime; its capital is Rouen. Major ports include Dieppe and Fécamp. The area is noted for its beech forests.

Havana /hə'vænə/ capital and port of Cuba; population (1986) 2,015,000. Products include cigars and tobacco. The palace of the Spanish governors, and the stronghold of La Fuerza (1583), survive. In 1898 the blowing up of the US battleship *Maine* in the harbour began the ◊Spanish-American War.

Havel /'hævel/ Vaclav 1936– . Czech playwright and politician, president from Dec 1989. His plays include *The Garden Party* 1963 and *Largo Desolato* 1985, about a dissident intellectual. Havel became widely known as a human-rights activist. He was imprisoned 1979–83 and again 1989 for support of Charter 77 (see ◊Czechoslovakia).

Havers /'heɪvəz/ Robert Michael Oldfield, Baron Havers 1923–. British lawyer, Lord Chancellor 1987–88. After a successful legal career he became Conservative MP for Wimbledon in 1970 and was solicitor-general under Edward Heath and attorney-general under Margaret Thatcher. He was made a life peer in 1987 and served briefly, and unhappily, as Lord Chancellor before retiring in 1988.

Havre, Le /'ɑːvrə/ see ◊Le Havre, port in France.

Hawaii /hə'waɪiː/ Pacific state of the USA; nickname Aloha State
area 16,800 sq km/6,485 sq mi
capital Honolulu on Oahu
towns Hilo
physical features Hawaii consists of a chain of some 20 volcanic islands, of which the chief are: *Hawaii* itself, noted for *Mauna Kea* 4,201 m/13,788 ft, the world's highest island mountain (site of a UK infrared telescope) and Mauna Loa, 4,170 m/13,686 ft, the world's largest active volcanic crater; *Maui* second largest island; *Oahu* third largest, with the greatest concentration of population and tourist attractions, for example, Waikiki beach, and site of Pearl Harbor; *Kauai*; and *Molokai*
products sugar, coffee, pineapples, bananas, flowers, offshore cobalt, nickel, and manganese deposits

Hastings Warren Hastings, governor general of India until his impeachment in 1785. His portrait is by Joshua Reynolds (c. 1766–68).

Hawaii

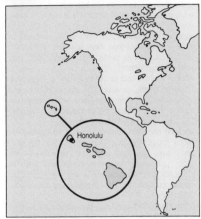

population (1987) 1,083,000 of whom about 34% are European, 25% Japanese, 14% Filipino, 12% Hawaiian, and 6% Chinese
language English
religion Christianity; minority Buddhism
famous people Father Joseph Damien
history a kingdom until 1893, Hawaii became a republic 1894, ceded itself to the USA 1898, and became a state 1959. Capt Cook, who called them the Sandwich Islands, was the first known European visitor 1778.

Hawarden /'hɑːdn/ town in Clwyd, N Wales; population 8,500. W E ◊Gladstone lived at Hawarden Castle for many years, and founded St Deiniol's theological library in Hawarden.

hawfinch European finch *Coccothraustes coccothraustes* about 18 cm/7 in long. It is rather uncommon and spends most of its time in the treetops. It feeds on berries and seeds, and can crack cherry stones with its large and powerful bill.

hawk small to medium-sized birds of prey, other than eagles and vultures, of the family Accipitridae. They have an untoothed hooked bill, short, broad wings, and keen eyesight.

The term is also applied metaphorically to people with aggressive ideas on foreign policy, in contrast to moderate *doves*; it was originally used for US advocates of continuation and escalation of the Vietnam War.

Hawke /hɔːk/ Bob (Robert) 1929– . Australian Labor politician, on the right wing of the party. He was president of the Australian Council of Trade Unions 1970–80, and became prime minister 1983.

Hawker /'hɔːkə/ Robert Stephen 1803–1875. British poet ('Song of the Western Men'), vicar of Morwenstow, Cornwall, from 1834, and originator of the harvest festival.

Hawkesbury /'hɔːksbəri/ river in New South Wales, Australia; length 480 km/300 mi. It is a major source of Sydney's water.

Hawking /'hɔːkɪŋ/ Stephen 1942– . English physicist, who has researched ◊black holes and gravitational field theory. His books include *A Brief History of Time* 1988.

Professor of gravitational physics at Cambridge from 1977, he discovered that the strong gravitational field around a black hole can radiate particles of matter. Commenting on Einstein's remark, 'God does not play dice with the Universe,' he said: 'God not only plays dice, he throws them where they can't be seen.' Confined to a wheelchair because of a muscular disease, he performs complex mathematical calculations entirely in his head.

Hawkins /'hɔːkɪnz/ Anthony Hope. Real name of British novelist Anthony ◊Hope.

Hawkins /'hɔːkɪnz/ Coleman (Randolph) 1904–1969. US virtuoso tenor saxophonist. He was until 1934 a soloist in the swing band led by Fletcher Henderson (1898–1952), and was an

Hawking *British physicist and mathematician Professor Stephen Hawking, 1988.*

influential figure in bringing the jazz saxophone to prominence as a solo instrument.

Hawkins /'hɔːkɪnz/ Jack 1910–1973. British film actor, usually cast in authoritarian roles. His films include *The Cruel Sea* 1953, *The League of Gentlemen* 1959, *Zulu* 1963, *Waterloo* 1970. After 1966 his voice had to be dubbed following an operation for throat cancer that removed his vocal chords.

Hawkins /'hɔːkɪnz/ John 1532–1595. English navigator, born in Plymouth. Treasurer to the navy 1573–89, he was knighted for his services as a commander against the Spanish Armada 1588.

Hawkins /'hɔːkɪnz/ Richard c. 1562–1622. English navigator, son of John Hawkins. He held a command against the Spanish Armada 1588, was captured in an expedition against Spanish possessions 1593–94 and not released until 1602. He was knighted 1603.

hawk moth family of moths (Sphingidae) with some 1,000 species distributed throughout the world, but mainly tropical.

The death's-head hawk moth *Acherontia atropos* is the largest of British moths. Some South American hawk moths closely resemble hummingbirds and the hummingbird hawk moth *Macroglossum stellatarum* is found in southern England.

Hawks /'hɔːks/ Howard 1896–1977. US director and producer of a wide range of films, including *Bringing Up Baby* 1936, *Ball of Fire* 1942, *The Big Sleep* 1946, and *Gentlemen Prefer Blondes* 1953.

Hawksmoor /'hɔːksmɔː/ Nicholas 1661–1736. English architect, assistant to ◊Wren in London churches and St Paul's Cathedral; joint architect with ◊Vanbrugh of Castle Howard and Blenheim Palace. The original west towers of Westminster Abbey, long attributed to Wren, were designed by Hawksmoor.

Haworth /'hauəθ/ village in W Yorkshire, home of the ◊Brontë family. It is now part of ◊Keighley.

Haworth /'hauəθ/ Norman 1883–1950. English organic chemist who was the first to synthesize a vitamin (vitamin C), in 1933. He shared a Nobel prize in 1937.

hawthorn shrubs and trees of the *Crataegus* genus, family Rosaceae. The **common hawthorn, may** or **whitethorn** *Crataegus monogyna*, a thorny shrub or small tree, bears clusters of white or pink flowers followed by groups of red berries. Native to Europe, N Africa, and W Asia, it has been naturalized in North America and Australia.

Hawthorne /'hɔːθɔːn/ Nathaniel 1804–1864. US writer of *The Scarlet Letter* 1850, a powerful novel of Puritan Boston. He wrote three other novels, including *The House of the Seven Gables* 1851, and many short stories, including *Tanglewood Tales* 1853, classic legends retold for children.

hay preserved grass used for winter livestock feed. The grass is cut and allowed to dry in the field before being removed for storage in a barn.

Hawthorne *Nathaniel Hawthorne counted fellow US novelist Melville among his early supporters.*

The optimum period for cutting is when the grass has just come into flower and contains most feed value. During the natural drying process, the moisture content is reduced from 70–80% down to a safe level of 20%. In normal weather conditions, this takes from two to five days during which time the hay is turned by machine to ensure even drying. Hay is normally baled before removal from the field. One hectare of grass can produce up to 7.5 tonnes/7.3 tons of hay.

Hay /heɪ/ Will 1888–1949. British comedy actor. Originally a music hall comedian, from the 1930s he made many films in which he usually played incompetents in positions of authority, including *Good Morning Boys* 1937; *Oh Mr Porter* 1938; *Ask a Policeman* 1939; *The Ghost of St Michaels* 1941; *My Learned Friend* 1944.

Hayden /'heɪdn/ Sterling. Stage name of John Hamilton 1916–1986. US film actor who played leading roles in Hollywood in the 1940s and early 1950s. Although later seen in some impressive character roles, his career as a whole failed to do justice to his talent. His work includes *The Asphalt Jungle* 1950, *Johnny Guitar* 1954, *Dr Strangelove* 1964, and *The Godfather* 1972.

Hayden /'heɪdn/ William (Bill) 1933– . Australian Labor politician. He was leader of the Australian Labor Party and of the opposition 1977–83, and minister of foreign affairs 1983. He became Governor-General 1989.

Haydn /'haɪdn/ Franz Joseph 1732–1809. Austrian composer. A teacher of Mozart and Beethoven, he was a major exponent of the Classical sonata form in his numerous chamber and orchestral works (he wrote over 100 symphonies). He also composed choral music, including the oratorios *The Creation* 1798 and *The Seasons* 1801. He was the first great master of the string quartet.

Born in Lower Austria, he was Kapellmeister 1761–90 to Prince Esterházy at Eisenstadt and Esterház. He visited London twice, 1791–92 and 1794–95. His work also includes operas, church music, and songs, and the 'Emperor's Hymn', adopted as the Austrian, and later the German, national anthem.

Haydon /'heɪdn/ Benjamin Robert 1786–1846. British painter artist, who became celebrated for his gigantic canvases . His attempts at 'high art' include *Christ's Entry into Jerusalem* (1820, Philadelphia). He is now more appreciated in genre pictures, for example *The Mock Election* and *Chairing the Member*, and for his lively *Autobiography and Memoirs* 1853.

Hayek /'haɪek/ Friedrich August von 1899– . Austrian economist. Born in Vienna, he taught at the London School of Economics 1931–50. His *The Road to Serfdom* 1944 was a critical study of socialist trends in Britain. He won the 1974 Nobel prize for economics.

Hazlitt *A master of invective and irony, English essayist William Hazlitt was encouraged to take up journalism by his friend Samuel Taylor Coleridge .*

Hayes /heɪz/ Rutherford B(irchard) 1822–1893. 19th president of the USA 1877–81, a Republican. Born in Ohio, he was a major-general on the Union side in the Civil War. During his presidency federal troops (see ◊Reconstruction) were withdrawn from the Southern states and the Civil Service reformed.

hay fever an allergic reaction to pollen, causing sneezing and asthmatic symptoms. In those who are specially sensitive, powerful body chemicals, related to ◊histamine, are produced at the site of entry, causing irritation. Treatment is by antihistamine drugs.

Hay-on-Wye /ˈheɪ ɒn ˈwaɪ/ town in Powys, Wales, known as the 'town of books' because of the huge secondhand bookshop started in 1961 by Richard Booth, which was followed by others.

Hays Office film-regulation body in the USA. Officially known as the Motion Picture Producers and Distributors of America, it was created 1922 by the major film companies to improve the industry's image and provide internal regulation. It terminated in 1945.

Hayworth /ˈheɪwɜːθ/ Rita. Stage name of Magarita Carmen Cansino 1918–1987. US film actress who gave vivacious performances in 1940s musicals and romantic dramas such as *Gilda* 1946 and *The Lady from Shanghai* 1948.

hazardous substances waste substances, usually generated by industry, which represent a hazard to the environment or to people living or working nearby. Examples include radioactive wastes, acidic resins, arsenic residues, residual hardening salts, lead, mercury, non-ferrous sludges, organic solvents, and pesticides. Their economic disposal or recycling is the subject of research.

Britain now imports over 200,000 tonnes of hazardous chemical waste a year. About 130,000 tonnes of the annually imported wastes are 'land-filled' (disposed of in dumps) without pretreatment.

haze factor unit of visibility in mist or fog. It is the ratio of the brightness of the mist compared with that of the object.

hazel trees of the genus *Corylus*, family Corylaceae, including **common hazel** or **cobnut** *Corylus avellana* of which the **filbert** is the cultivated variety.

Hazlitt /ˈhæzlɪt/ William 1778–1830. British essayist and critic, noted for his invective, scathing irony and gift for epigram. His critical essays include *Characters of Shakespeare's Plays* 1817–18,

Lectures on the English Poets 1818–19, *English Comic Writers* 1819, and *Dramatic Literature of the Age of Elizabeth* 1820. Other notable works are *Table Talk* 1821–22; *The Spirit of the Age* 1825, and *Liber Amoris* 1823.

H-bomb abbreviated form of ◊hydrogen bomb.

Head /hed/ Bessie 1937– . South African writer living in exile in Botswana. Her novels include *When Rain Clouds Gather* 1969, *Maru* 1971, and *A Question of Power* 1973.

Head /hed/ Edith 1900–1981. US costume designer for Hollywood films, who won eight Oscars, in such films as *The Heiress* 1949, *All About Eve* 1950, and *The Sting* 1972.

headache pain in the head, caused by minor eye strain, stress, infection, neck or jaw muscle strain, or severe physical illness, for example brain tumour. It is marked by dilation of the cerebral blood vessels and irritation of the brain linings (meninges) and of the nerves.

Headingley Leeds sports centre, home of the Yorkshire County Cricket club and Leeds Rugby League club. The two venues are separated by the large stand.

The cricket ground has been a centre for test matches since 1899 and the crowd of 158,000 for the five day England-Australia test match 1948 is an English record. The gates at the ground are in memory of Herbert Sutcliffe, one of Yorkshire's finest batsmen. Britain's first official test match against New Zealand was at Headingley 1908.

The rugby ground is one of the best in the country and has excellent turf. It was the first club to install undersoil heating. The main stand is one of the biggest in rugby league.

Heal /hiːl/ Ambrose 1872–1959. English cabinetmaker who took over the Heal's shop from his father and developed it into the renowned London store. He initially designed furniture in the Arts and Crafts style, often in oak, and in the 1930s he started using materials such as tubular steel.

Heal was a founder member of the Design and Industries Association, which aimed to improve the quality of mass-produced items. His shop provided the public with an alternative to the cheap and shoddy, or excessively expensive furniture to which they were often limited.

Healey /ˈhiːli/ Denis (Winston) 1917– . British Labour politician. While minister of defence 1964–70 he was in charge of the reduction of British forces east of Suez. He was chancellor of the Exchequer 1974–79. In 1976 he contested the party leadership, losing to James Callaghan, and again in 1980, losing to Michael Foot, to whom he was deputy leader 1980–83. In 1987 he resigned from the shadow cabinet.

health and safety in British law all employers have a statutory duty under the Health and Safety at Work Act 1974 to ensure the safety, welfare, and health of their employees at work. This duty applies to all kinds of employment. Earlier legislation dealt with conditions of work only in particular kinds of employment.

In the 19th century legislation was progressively introduced to regulate conditions of work, hours of labour, safety, and sanitary provisions in factories and workshops. The first legislation was the Health and Morals of Apprentices Act 1802. In 1833 the first factory inspectors were appointed. Legislation was extended to offices, shops, and railway premises 1963. All employees are now covered by the Health and Safety at Work Act, which is enforced by the Health and Safety Executive.

health care life expectancy is determined by overall efficiency of the body's vital organs and the rate at which these organs deteriorate. The fundamental rules of health care are concerned with:

smoking this is strongly linked to heart disease, stroke, bronchitis, lung cancer and other serious diseases.

exercise regular physical exercise improves fitness, slows down the gradual decline in efficiency of the heart and lungs, and so helps to prolong life.

alcohol recommended maximum intake is no more than 21 units of alcohol a week for men, no more than 14 for women. (Half a pint of beer, one glass of wine or single measure of spirits is equivalent to one unit.) Doctors recommend at least two alcohol-free days a week. Excessive alcohol intake can cause liver damage and may lead to dependence.

diet a healthy diet contains plenty of vegetable fibre, vitamins, protein, and carbohydrate, and substitutes polyunsaturated fats (which lower the level of blood cholesterol) for saturated (animal) fats. Too much food causes obesity.

weight obesity (defined as being 10 kg/20 lb or more above the desirable weight for the person's age, sex and height) is associated with many potentially dangerous conditions, such as coronary heart disease, diabetes, and stroke, as well as muscular and joint problems, and breathing difficulties.

health education teaching and advice on healthy living, including nutrition, sex education, and advice on drink, drugs, and other threats to health. Health education in most secondary schools in the UK is often included within a course of personal and social education, or integrated into subjects such as biology, home economics, or physical education. School governors were given specific responsibility for the content of sex education lessons in the 1986 Education Act.

health psychology a new development within ◊clinical psychology that applies psychological principles to promote physical well-being. For example, people with high blood pressure can learn methods such as relaxation, meditation, and life-style changes.

health service government provision of medical care on a national scale. From 1948 the UK has had a ***National Health Service*** (NHS) which includes hospital care, but charges are made for ordinary doctors' prescriptions, spectacles, and dental treatment, except for children and people on very low incomes. The USA has the federally subsidized schemes ***Medicare*** and ***Medicaid***. See also ◊social security.

In the USA the Medicare health-insurance scheme provides care (towards which patients pay a share) out of hospital for the elderly and disabled, and from 1985 fees for Medicare patients to join health-maintenance organizations (HMOs, covering visits to a group of doctors and hospital fees) have been paid for them. The Medicaid state scheme (to which the federal government contributes) is for people unable to afford private care.

Private health schemes such as BUPA are increasingly used in the UK as the NHS has become overstretched. US private health schemes include Blue Cross (established 1929) and Blue Shield (established 1917).

UK expenditure on public health services was £20,569 million, with an average of 317,000 beds occupied in hospitals. The number of available hospital beds in public hospitals decreased by 25% between 1971 and 1987, while the number of private hospital beds increased by 157%.

Heaney /ˈhiːni/ Seamus (Justin) 1939– . Irish poet, born in County Derry, who has written powerful verse about the political situation in Northern Ireland. Collections include *North* 1975, *Field Work* 1979, and *Station Island* 1984. In 1989, he was elected professor of poetry at Oxford University.

Heard Island and McDonald Islands /hɜːd/ group of islands forming an Australian external territory in the S Indian Ocean, about 4,000 km/2,500 mi SW of Fremantle; area 410 sq km/158 sq mi. They were discovered 1833, annexed by Britain 1910, and transferred to Australia 1947. ***Heard Island*** 42 km/26 mi by 19 km/12 mi is glacier-covered, although the volcanic mountain ***Big Ben*** 2,742 m/9,000 ft, is still active. A weather station was built 1947. Shag Island is 8 km/5 mi to the north and the craggy McDonalds are 42 km/26 mi to the west.

heart

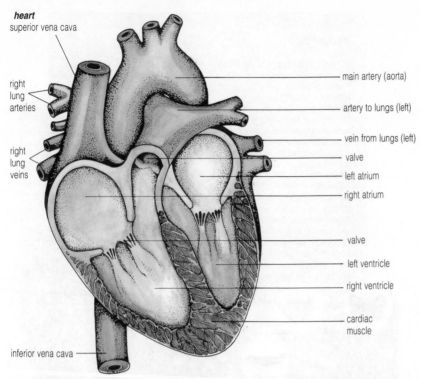

superior vena cava

right lung arteries

right lung veins

inferior vena cava

main artery (aorta)

artery to lungs (left)

vein from lungs (left)

valve

left atrium

right atrium

valve

left ventricle

right ventricle

cardiac muscle

hearing aid a device to improve the hearing of partially deaf people. Hearing aids usually consist of a battery-powered transistorized microphone/amplifier unit and earpiece. Some miniaturized aids are compact enough to fit in the ear or be concealed in the frame of spectacles.

Hearns /hɜːnz/ Thomas 1958– . US boxer, who in 1988 became the first man to win world titles at five different weight classes in five separate fights.

CAREER HIGHLIGHTS

professional fights 49; wins: 45; knockouts: 20; draws: 1; defeats: 3
(1st professional fight: 25 Nov 1977 v. Jerome Hill *(USA)*)
world titles
1980 WBA welterweight
1982 WBC super-welterweight
1987 WBC light-heavyweight
1987 WBC middleweight
1988 WBO super-middleweight

hearsay evidence second-hand evidence, by a witness giving evidence of what another person has said. It is usually not acceptable as evidence in court.

Hearst /hɜːst/ Patty (Patricia) 1955– . US socialite. A granddaughter of the newspaper tycoon William R Hearst, she was kidnapped in 1974 by an urban guerrilla outfit, the Symbionese Liberation Army. She joined her captors in a bank raid, and was imprisoned 1976–79.

Hearst /hɜːst/ William Randolph 1863–1951. US newspaper proprietor, celebrated for his introduction of banner headlines, lavish illustration, and the sensationalist approach known as 'yellow journalism'.

A campaigner in numerous controversies, and a strong isolationist, he was said to be the model for Citizen Kane in the film of that name by Orson Welles. He collected art treasures, antiques, and castles – one of which, San Simeon (Hearst Castle) in California, is a state museum.

heart a muscular organ that rhythmically contracts to force blood around the body of an animal with a circulatory system. Annelid worms and some other invertebrates have simple hearts consisting of thickened sections of main blood vessels that pulse regularly. An earthworm has

ten such hearts. Vertebrates have one heart. The fish's heart has two chambers: the thin-walled **atrium** (once called the auricle) that expands to receive blood, and the thick-walled **ventricle** which pumps it out. Amphibians and most reptiles have two atria and one ventricle; birds and mammals have two atria and two ventricles. The beating of the heart is controlled by the autonomic nervous systems, and by hormones.

heartburn irritation of the lower oesophagus (gullet) by excessively acid stomach contents, as sometimes happens during pregnancy and in cases of duodenal ulcer or obesity. It may be due to a weak valve at the entrance to the stomach that allows its contents to well up into the oesophagus.

heart-lung machine apparatus used during heart surgery to take over the functions of the heart and the lungs temporarily. It has a pump to circulate the blood around the body and is able to add oxygen to the blood and remove carbon dioxide from it. A heart-lung machine was first used for open-heart surgery in the USA 1953.

Heart of Darkness a story by Joseph Conrad, published 1902. Marlow, the narrator, tells of his journey by boat into the African interior to meet a company agent, Kurtz, who exercises great power over the indigenous people by barbaric means.

heat form of internal energy of a substance due to the kinetic energy in the motion of its molecules or atoms. It is measured by ◊temperature. Heat energy is transferred by conduction, convection, and radiation. Heat always flows from a region of higher temperature to one of lower temperature. Its effect on a substance may be simply to raise its temperature, to cause it to expand, to melt it if a solid, to vaporize it if a liquid, or to increase its pressure if a confined gas.

Quantities of heat are usually measured in units of energy, such as joules (J) or calories (C).

The *specific heat* of a substance is the ratio of the quantity of heat required to raise the temperature of a given mass of the substance through a given range of temperature to the heat required to raise the temperature of an equal mass of water through the same range. It is measured by a ◊calorimeter.

convection transmission through a fluid (liquid or gas) on currents, for example when the air in a room is warmed by a fire or radiator

conduction heat passing along a medium to neighbouring parts with no visible motion accompanying the transfer of heat, for example when the whole length of a metal rod is heated when one end is held in a fire.

radiation heat transfer by infrared rays. It can pass through a vacuum, travels at the same speed as light, can be reflected and refracted, and does not affect the medium through which it passes. For example, heat reaches the Earth from the Sun by radiation.

heat capacity in physics, the quantity of heat required to raise the temperature of a substance by one degree. The *specific heat capacity* of a substance is the heat capacity per unit of mass, measured in joules per kilogram per ◊kelvin (J kg).

Heath /hiːθ/ Edward (Richard George) 1916– . British Conservative politician, party leader 1965–75. As prime minister 1970–74 he took the UK into the European Community, but was brought down by economic and industrial-relations crises at home.

Heath entered Parliament 1950, was minister of labour 1959–60, and as Lord Privy Seal 1960–63 conducted abortive negotiations for Common Market (European Community) membership. He succeeded Home as Conservative leader 1965, the first elected leader of his party. Defeated in the general election 1966, he achieved a surprise victory 1970, but his confrontation with the striking miners as part of his campaign to control inflation led to his defeat Feb 1974 and again Oct 1974. He was replaced as party leader by Margaret Thatcher 1975, and became increasingly critical of her policies, especially in her opposition to the UK's full participation in the EC.

heather low-growing evergreen shrub, common on sandy or acid soil. The *common heather* or *ling Calluna vulgaris* is a carpet-forming shrub, growing up to 60 cm/2 ft high, bearing pale pink-purple flowers in spikes in late summer, and small leaves on a shrubby stem. It is found over much of Europe, growing up to 750 m/2,400 ft above sea level. The *bell heather Erica cinerea* is found alongside common heather.

Heathrow /ˌhiːθˈrəʊ/ site of Heathrow Airport, W of ◊London, England.

heat shield a material on the external surface of a spacecraft, which protects the astronauts and equipment inside from the heat of re-entry when

Hearst US newspaper proprietor William Randolph Hearst, a model for the central character in the film Citizen Kane.

returning to Earth. Air friction can generate temperatures of up to 1,500°C upon re-entry to the atmosphere.

heat storage means of storing heat for release later. It is usually achieved by using materials that undergo phase changes, for example, ◊Glauber's salt, and sodium pyrophosphate, which melts at 70°C. The latter is used to store off-peak heat in the home: the salt is liquefied by cheap heat during the night, and then freezes to give off heat during the day.

Other developments include the use of plastic crystals, which change their structure rather than melting when they are heated. They could be incorporated in curtains or clothing.

heat stroke or *sunstroke* illness caused by excessive exposure to heat. Mild heat stroke is experienced as lassitude and cramp, or simple fainting; recovery is prompt following rest and replenishment of salt lost in sweat. Severe heat stroke causes collapse akin to that seen in acute shock, and is potentially lethal without prompt treatment of cooling the body carefully and giving fluids to relieve dehydration.

In the case of heat stroke, the brain swells, resulting in confusion of thought; the body becomes dehydrated, blood circulation slows, and organs, such as the kidneys, fail to function. Coma may ensue, and possibly cardiac arrest.

heat treatment subjecting metals and alloys to controlled heating and cooling after fabrication to relieve internal stresses and improve their physical properties. Methods include ◊annealing, ◊quenching, and ◊tempering.

heaven in the theology of Christianity and some other religions, the destination after death of the virtuous. Many attempts have been made, particularly by Christian and Muslim writers, to describe its physical joys, but modern theologians usually describe it as a place or state in which the soul sees God as he really is.

Heaviside /'hevɪsaɪd/ Oliver 1850–1925. British physicist. In 1902, he predicted the existence of an ionized layer of air in the upper atmosphere, which was later known as the ◊Kennelly-Heaviside layer but is now called the E-layer of the ◊ionosphere. Deflection from it makes possible the transmission of radio signals round the world, which would otherwise be lost in outer space, and its presence is connected with the phenomenon of radio fading.

His theoretical work had important implications for radio transmission. His studies of electricity published in *Electrical Papers* 1892 had considerable influence on long-distance telephony.

heavy metal in music, a style of rock characterized by loudness, sex-and-violence imagery, and guitar solos. It developed out of the hard rock of the late 1960s and early 1970s (Led Zeppelin, Deep Purple) and enjoyed a resurgence in the late 1980s. Bands include Motorhead, Def Leppard, AC/DC and Guns n' Roses. The term comes from *The Naked Lunch* by US author William Burroughs.

heavy metal a metallic element of high relative atomic mass, for instance platinum, gold, and lead. Heavy metals are poisonous and tend to persist in living systems, causing, for example, gradual mercury poisoning in shellfish. Treatment of heavy metal poisoning is difficult because available drugs are not able to distinguish between heavy metals which are essential to living cells (zinc, copper), and those which are poisonous.

heavy water deuterium oxide (D_2O), water containing the isotope deuterium instead of hydrogen (relative molecular mass 20 as opposed to 18 for ordinary water).

Its chemical properties are identical with those of ordinary water, while its physical properties differ slightly. It occurs in ordinary water in the ratio of about one part by weight of deuterium to 5,000 parts by weight of hydrogen and can be concentrated by electrolysis, the ordinary water being more readily decomposed by this means

hedgerow

In Northern Europe, and especially in Britain, hedgerows are a traditional feature of the landscape. Hawthorn, blackthorn, elm and beech bushes were grown around the edges of farms and grazing land to define boundaries and to enclose cattle and sheep. With mechanized agriculture came the destruction of many hedgerows, along with the wildlife they support.

The dense growth and tough, thorny branches of hawthorn bushes are effective barriers to large mammals. But their foliage and flowers, and, those of the plants that grow around and beneath them, provide food for many caterpillars, butterflies, aphids and bees. The fruits are eaten by many birds and by voles and wood mice. Carniverous birds feed on the insects and other small animals.

Life in the hedgerow
1. Peacock butterfly 2. Blackbird's nest
3. Seven-spot ladybird 4. Hollybush
5. Comma butterfly 6. Tiger moth
7. Field mouse 8. Warbler 9. Dog rose
10. Nettle 11. Orange-tip butterfly
12. Hawthorn 13. Wren
14. Hogweed 15. Bramble bush
16. Hawfinch 17. Wood mouse
18. Hedgehog 19. Primrose
20. Chickweed

than the heavy water. It has been used in the nuclear industry.

Hebe /'hi:bi/ in Greek mythology, the goddess of youth, daughter of Zeus and Hera.

Hebei /,hʌ'beɪ/ formerly *Hopei* or *Hupei* province of N China
area 202,700 sq km/78,242 sq mi
capital Shijiazhuang
features include special municipalities of Beijing and Tianjin
products cereals, textiles, iron, steel
population (1986) 56,170,000.

Hebrew or *Israelite* a Semitic people who lived in Palestine at the time of the Old Testament, and who traced their ancestry to Abraham. The term was formerly used to describe Jews.

Hebrew Bible the sacred writings of Judaism, known to Christians as the Old Testament. It includes the Torah (the first five books, ascribed to Moses), historical and prophetic books, and psalms, all in the Hebrew language.

Hebrew language a member of the ◊Hamito-Semitic language family spoken in W Asia by the ancient Hebrews, sustained for many centuries as the liturgical language of Judaism, and revived and developed in the 20th century as modern Israeli Hebrew, the national language of the state of Israel. It is the original language of the Old Testament of the Bible.

Such English words as *cherub, Jehovah/Yahweh, kosher, rabbi, seraph,* and *shibboleth* are borrowings from Hebrew. The Hebrew alphabet is written from right to left.

Hebrews an epistle in the New Testament, probably written to the Jewish converts to Christianity. It is no longer attributed to Paul, but its authorship is unknown.

Hebrides /'hebrɪdi:z/ group of over 500 islands (fewer than 100 inhabited) off W Scotland; total area 2,900 sq km/1,120 sq mi. The Hebrides were settled by Scandinavians in the 6th–9th centuries, and passed under Norwegian rule from about 890–1266.

The *Inner Hebrides* are divided between Highland and Strathclyde regions, and include ◊Skye, ◊Mull, ◊Jura, ◊Islay, ◊Iona, ◊Rum, Raasay,

Coll, Tiree, Colonsay, Muck, and uninhabited ◊Staffa. The **Outer Hebrides** form the islands area of the ◊Western Isles administrative area, separated from the Inner Hebrides by the Little Minch. They include ◊Lewis with Harris, ◊North Uist, ◊South Uist, ◊Barra, and ◊St Kilda.

Hebron /'hebrən/ (Arabic **El Khalil**) town on the West Bank of the Jordan, occupied by Israel from 1967; population (1967) 43,000, including 4,000 Jews. It is a frontline position in the confrontation between Israelis and Arabs in the ◊Intifada. Within the mosque is the traditional site of the tombs of Abraham, Isaac, and Jacob.

Heb-Sed royal festival in ancient Egypt, apparently commemorating Menes's union of Upper and Lower Egypt.

Hecate /'hekəti/ in Greek mythology, the goddess of witchcraft and magic, sometimes identified with ◊Artemis and the moon.

Hecht /hekt/ Ben 1893–1964. US film screenwriter and occasional director, who was formerly a journalist. His play *The Front Page* was adapted several times for the cinema by other writers. His screenplays for such films as *Gunga Din* 1939, *Spellbound* 1945, and *Actors and Sin* 1952 earned him a reputation as one of Hollywood's best writers.

hectare metric unit of area equal to 100 acres or 10,000 square metres (2.47 acres).

Hector /'hektə/ in Greek mythology, a Trojan prince, son of King Priam, who, in the siege of Troy, was the foremost warrior on the Trojan side until he was killed by ◊Achilles.

Hecuba /'hekjubə/ in Greek mythology, the wife of King Priam, and mother of ◊Hector and ◊Paris. She was captured by the Greeks after the fall of Troy.

Hedda Gabler a play by Henrik Ibsen, first produced 1891. Trapped in small-town society, Hedda Gabler takes out her spiritual and sexual frustrations on everyone from her ineffectual academic husband to the reformed alcoholic writer Lövborg. When her mean-spirited revenge schemes backfire, she commits suicide.

hedgehog mammal of the genus *Erinaceus* common in Europe, W Asia, Africa, and India. The body, including the tail, is 30 cm/1 ft long. It is speckled-brown in colour, has a piglike snout, and is covered with sharp spines. When alarmed it can roll its body into a ball. Hedgehogs feed on insects, slugs, and carrion. There is concern for its survival in the wild in Europe.

hedgerow a row of closely planted shrubs or low trees. It generally acts as a land division and windbreak; it also serves as a source of food and as a refuge for wildlife. Hedgerows are an important part of the landscape in Britain, N France, Ireland, and New England, USA, but many have been destroyed to accommodate altered farming practices and larger machinery.

Between 1945 and 1985, 25% of Britain's hedgerows were destroyed: 225,000 km/140,000 mi.

hedge sparrow another name for ◊dunnock, a small bird.

Hedin /he'di:n/ Sven Anders 1865–1952. Swedish archaeologist, geographer, and explorer in central Asia and China. Between 1891 and 1908 he explored routes across the Himalayas and produced the first maps of Tibet. During 1928–33 he travelled with a Sino-Swedish expedition which crossed the Gobi Desert. His publications include *My Life as Explorer* 1925 and *Across the Gobi Desert* 1928.

hedonism the ethical theory that pleasure or happiness is, or should be, the main goal in life. Hedonist sects in ancient Greece were the Cyrenaics, who held that the pleasure of the moment is the only human good, and the Epicureans, who advocated the pursuit of pleasure under the direction of reason. Modern hedonistic philosophies, such as those of Bentham and Mill, regard the happiness of society, rather than that of the single individual, as the aim.

Hefei /,hʌ'feɪ/ or **Hofei** capital of Anhui province,

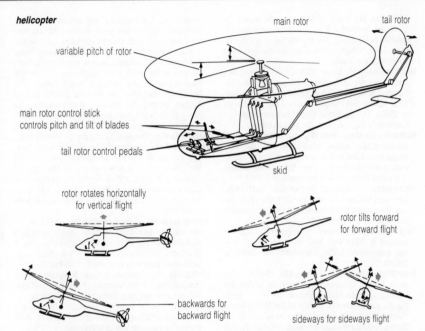

helicopter

variable pitch of rotor

main rotor

tail rotor

main rotor control stick controls pitch and tilt of blades

tail rotor control pedals

skid

rotor rotates horizontally for vertical flight

rotor tilts forward for forward flight

backwards for backward flight

sideways for sideways flight

China; population (1984) 853,000. Products include textiles, chemicals, and steel.

Hegel /'heɪgəl/ Georg Wilhelm Friedrich 1770–1831. German philosopher, who conceived of consciousness and the external object as forming a unity, in which neither factor can exist independently, mind and nature being two abstractions of one indivisible whole. Hegel believed development took place through dialectic: contradiction and the resolution of contradiction. For Hegel, the task of philosophy was to comprehend the rationality of what already exists, but leftist followers, including Marx, used Hegel's dialectic to attempt to show the inevitability of radical change, and attacked both religion and the social order.

Hegel believed the world is the unfolding and expression of one all-embracing absolute idea, an organism constantly developing by its own internal necessity so as to become the gradual embodiment of reason. Each system by its own development brings about its opposite (antithesis), and finally a higher synthesis unifies and embodies both.

He wrote *The Phenomenology of Spirit* 1807, *Encyclopaedia of the Philosophical Sciences* 1817, and *Philosophy of Right* 1821. He was professor of philosophy at Heidelberg 1817–18, and at Berlin 1818–31. As a rightist, Hegel championed religion, the Prussian state, and the existing order.

hegemony (Greek *hegemonia*, 'authority') political dominance of one power over others in a group in which all are supposedly equal. The term was first used for the dominance of Athens over the other Greek city states, later applied to Prussia within Germany, and, in modern times, to the USA and USSR throughout the world.

Hegira Arabic 'flight' see ◊Hijrah.

Heidegger /'haɪdegə/ Martin 1889–1976. German philosopher. In *Being and Time* 1927, he used the methods of ◊Husserl's phenomenology to explore the structures of human existence. His later writings meditated on the fate of a world dominated by science and technology.

He believed that Western philosophy had 'forgotten' the fundamental question of the 'meaning of Being'. Although one of his major concerns was the angst of human existence, he denied that he was an existentialist. His support for Nazism, and his unwillingness or his incapacity to defend his positions damaged his reputation.

Heidelberg /'haɪdlbɜ:g/ town on the S bank of the Neckar, 19 km/12 mi SE of Mannheim, in Baden-Württemberg, West Germany; population (1988) 136,000. Heidelberg university, the oldest

in Germany, was established 1386. The town is overlooked by the ruins of its 13th–17th century castle, 100 m/330 ft above the river.

Heidelberg /'haɪdlbɜ:g/ village near Melbourne, Australia, which gave its name to the **Heidelberg School** – a group of Impressionist artists (including Roberts, Streeton, and ◊Conder) working in teaching camps in the neighbourhood. Flourishing 1888–90, the school had its most famous exhibition 1889, the '9 by 5', from the size of the cigar-box lids used.

Heidi novel for children by the Swiss writer Johanna Spyri (1827–1901) published in 1881. Heidi, a orphan, shares a simple life with her grandfather high on a mountain, bringing happiness to those around her. Three years spent in Frankfurt as companion to a crippled girl, Clara, convince Heidi that city life is not for her and she returns to her mountain home.

Heifetz /'haɪfɪts/ Jascha 1901–1987. Russian-born US violinist, one of the great virtuosos of the 20th century. He first performed at the age of five, and before he was 17 had played in most European capitals, and in the USA, where he settled 1917. His style of playing was calm and objective.

Heike monogatari (Japanese 'tales of the Heike') Japanese chronicle, written down in the 14th century but based on oral legend describing events that took place 200 years earlier, that recounts the struggle for control of the country between the rival Genji (Minamoto) and Heike (Taira) dynasties. The conflict resulted in the end of the Heian period, and the introduction of the first **shogunate** (military dictatorship). Many subsequent Japanese dramas are based on material from the chronicle.

Heilbronn /'haɪlbrɒn/ river port in Baden-Württemberg, West Germany, on the Neckor, north of Stuttgart; population (1988) 112,000. It trades extensively in wine.

Heilongjiang /,heɪ,luŋdʒi'æŋ/ formerly **Heilungkiang** province of NE China, in ◊Manchuria
area 463,600 sq km/178,950 sq mi
capital Harbin
features China's largest oilfield, near Anda
products cereals, gold, coal, copper, zinc, lead, cobalt
population (1986) 33,320,000.

Heilungkiang /,heɪ,luŋki'æŋ/ former name of ◊Heilongjiang, a province of NE China.

Heine /'haɪnə/ Heinrich 1797–1856. German romantic poet and journalist, who wrote *Reisebilder* 1826 and *Buch der Lieder/Book of Songs* 1827. From 1831 he lived mainly in Paris, as a correspondent for German newspapers. Schubert and

Schumann set many of his songs to music. In 1835, he headed a list of writers forbidden to publish in Germany. He contracted a spinal disease 1845, which confined him to his bed from 1848 until his death.

Heinkel /'haɪŋkəl/ Ernst 1888–1958. German aircraft designer who pioneered jet aircraft. He founded his firm 1922, and built the first jet aircraft 1939 (developed independently of the Whittle jet of 1941). During World War II his company was Germany's biggest producer of warplanes.

Heinlein /'haɪnlaɪn/ Robert A(nson) 1907– . US science-fiction writer, associated with the pulp magazines of the 1940s; best known for the militaristic novel *Starship Troopers* 1959 and the utopian cult novel *Stranger in a Strange Land* 1961.

Heisenberg /'haɪzənbɜːg/ Werner Carl 1901–1976. German physicist. He was an originator of ◊quantum theory and the formulator of the ◊uncertainty principle. Nobel prize 1932.

Hejaz /hiː'dʒæz/ former independent kingdom, merged in 1932 with Nejd to form ◊Saudi Arabia; population (1970) 2,000,000; the capital is Mecca.

Hekmatyar /ˌhekmət'jɑː/ Gulbuddin 1949– . Afghani Islamic fundamentalist guerrilla leader. He became a mujaheddin guerrilla in the 1980s, leading the fundamentalist faction of the Hizb-i Islami (Islamic Party), dedicated to the overthrow of the Soviet-backed communist regime in Kabul. He has refused to countenance participation in any interim 'national unity' government which includes Afghani communists.

Hel /hel/ or *Hela* in Norse mythology, the goddess of the underworld.

Helen /'helən/ in Greek mythology, the daughter of Zeus and Leda, and the most beautiful of women. She married Menelaus, king of Sparta, but during his absence was the mistress of Paris, prince of Troy. This precipitated the Trojan War. Afterwards she returned to Sparta with her husband.

Helena, St /'helɪnə/ c. 248–328. Roman empress, mother of Constantine the Great, and a convert to Christianity. According to legend, she discovered the true cross of Jesus in Jerusalem. Her feast day is 18 Aug.

Helicon a mountain of central Greece, on which was situated a spring and a sanctuary sacred to the ◊Muses.

helicopter an aircraft which achieves both lift and propulsion by means of a rotary wing, or rotor on top of the fuselage. It can take off and land vertically, move in any direction, or remain stationary in the air.

The rotor of a helicopter has two or more blades, of aerofoil cross-section like an aeroplane's wings. Lift and propulsion are achieved by angling the blades as they rotate. Igor Sikorsky built the first practical single-rotor craft in the USA 1939. A single–rotor helicopter must also have a small tail rotor to counter the tendency of the body to spin in the opposite direction to the main rotor. Twin-rotor helicopters like the Boeing Chinook have their rotors turning in opposite directions and this prevents the body from spinning.

Helicopters are now widely used in passenger service; for life-saving in floods, earthquakes, sea and mountain rescue; and in police pursuits and

hell *Stone carving of a medieval version of hell.*

traffic control, firefighting, and agriculture. In war they carry troops and equipment in difficult terrain, and make aerial reconnaissance and attacks.

Naval carriers are increasingly being built, helicopters with depth charges and homing ◊torpedoes being guided to submarine or surface targets beyond the carrier's attack range. The helicopter may also use dunking ◊sonar to find targets beyond the carrier's radar horizon. As many as 30 helicopters may be used on large carriers, in combination with V/STOL aircraft such as the ◊Harrier. See also ◊autogiro, ◊convertiplane.

Heligoland /'helɪɡəʊlænd/ island in the North Sea, one of the North Frisian Islands; area 0.6 sq km/150 acres. It is administered by the state of Schleswig-Holstein, West Germany, having been ceded to Germany by Britain 1890 in exchange for ◊Zanzibar. It was used as a naval base in both world wars.

heliography old method of signalling, used by armies in the late 19th century, which employed sunlight reflected from a mirror to pass messages in ◊Morse code. On a clear day, a heliograph could send over distances in excess of 50 km/30 mi.

Heliopolis /ˌhiːli'ɒpəlɪs/ ancient Egyptian centre (biblical On) of the worship of the sun god Ra, NE of Cairo and near the village of Matariah.

Helios /'hiːliɒs/ in Greek mythology, the sun-god and father of ◊Phaethon, thought to make his daily journey across the sky in a chariot.

heliotrope decorative plant, genus *Heliotropium*, family Boraginaceae, with distinctive spikes of blue, lilac, or white flowers, especially the **Peruvian** or **cherry pie heliotrope** *Heliotropium peruvianum*.

helium a gaseous element, symbol He, atomic number 2, relative atomic mass 4.003. It is colourless, odourless, inert, non-inflammable, and very light. It is present in the Sun, in gases issuing from the Earth in radioactive minerals, and in small quantities in the atmosphere.

Helium is obtained by compression and fractionation of naturally occurring gases. Helium-oxygen atmospheres are used in high-pressure breathing work, as required by divers. Liquid helium is very important in cryogenics (low-temperature physics). Airships use helium because of its non-inflammability.

When ionized, by losing its two electrons in a high electric field, helium consists of just two protons and two neutrons, and is thus identical to alphaparticles ejected by many radioactive isotopes. Being less soluble than nitrogen in blood, helium does not give rise to the 'bends' when used by divers (see ◊decompression sickness).

helix in mathematics, a three-dimensional curve resembling a spring, corkscrew, or screw thread. It is generated by a line that encircles a cylinder or cone at a constant angle.

hell in various religions, a place of posthumous punishment. In Hinduism, Buddhism, and Jainism, hell is a transitory stage in the progress of the soul, but in Christianity and Islam it is eternal (◊purgatory is transitory).

In the Bible, the word 'hell' is used to translate Hebrew and Greek words all meaning 'the place of departed spirits, the abode of the dead'. In medieval Christian theology, hell is the place where unrepentant sinners suffer the torments of the damned, but the 20th-century tendency has been to regard hell as a state of damnation rather than a place.

hellebore herbaceous plant of the genus *Helleborus*, family Ranunculaceae. The poisonous **stinking hellebore** *Helleborus foetidus* has greenish flowers early in the spring; the **Christmas rose** *Helleborus niger* has white flowers from Dec onwards.

helleborine temperate orchids of the genera *Epipactis* and *Cephalanthera*, including the **marsh helleborine** *Epipactis palustris*, with pink and white flowers.

Hellenes /'heliːnz/ the Greeks, whose name for Greece is *Hellas*.

Hellenic period (from *Hellas*, Greek name for Greece) the classical period of ancient Greek civilization, from the first Olympic Games 776 BC until the death of Alexander the Great 323 BC.

Hellenistic period the period in Greek civilization from the death of Alexander 323 BC until the accession of the Roman emperor Augustus 27 BC. Alexandria in Egypt was the centre of culture and commerce during this period, and Greek culture spread throughout the Mediterranean region.

Heller /'helə/ Joseph 1923– . US novelist. He drew on his experiences in World War II to write ◊*Catch-22* 1961, satirizing war and bureaucratic methods. After the air force, he entered advertising. Other books include *Something Happened*, *Good As Gold*, and the play *We Bombed in New Haven*.

Hellespont /'helɪspɒnt/ former name of the ◊Dardanelles, the strait that separates Europe from Asia.

Hellman /'helmən/ Lillian 1907–1984. US playwright, whose work is largely concerned with contemporary political and social issues. *The Children's Hour* 1934, *The Little Foxes* 1939, and *Toys in the Attic* 1960 are all examples of the 'well-made play'.

She lived some 31 years with the writer Dashiell Hammett, and in her will founded a fund to promote Marxist doctrine. Since her death there has been controversy about the accuracy of her memoirs, for example *Pentimento* 1973.

Helmand the longest river in Afghanistan. Rising in the Hindu Kush, W of Kabul, it flows SW for 1,125 km/703 mi before entering the marshland surrounding Lake Saberi on the Iranian frontier.

Helmholtz /'helmhəʊlts/ Hermann Ludwig Ferdinand von 1821–1894. German physiologist, physicist, and inventor of the ophthalmoscope. He was the first to explain how the cochlea of the inner ear works, and the first to measure the speed of nerve impulses. In physics, he formulated the law of conservation of energy, and did important work in thermodynamics.

The ophthalmoscope made possible the examination of the inside of the eye. This was a great advance in ophthalmic medicine, as was his ophthalmometer for measuring the curvature of the eye. He also studied magnetism, electricity, and the physiology of hearing.

Helmont /'helmɒnt/ Jean Baptiste van 1577–1644. Belgian doctor. He was the first to realize that gases exist apart from the atmosphere, and claimed to have coined the word 'gas' (from the Greek *chaos*).

Helms /helmz/ Richard 1913– . US director of the Central Intelligence Agency 1966–73, when he was dismissed by Nixon. In 1977 he was convicted of lying before a congressional committee because his oath as chief of intelligence compelled

Helsingør *(English name Elsinore) Kronborg Castle about 45 km/28 mi north of Copenhagen, built by Frederick II 1574–85, the setting for Shakespeare's Hamlet.*

him to keep secrets from the public. He was originally with the Office of Strategic Services.

Héloïse /'elɔui:z/ 1101–1164. Abbess of Paraclete in Champagne, correspondent and lover of ◊Abelard. She became deeply interested in intellectual study in her youth. After her affair with Abelard, and the birth of a son, Astrolabe, she became a nun 1229, and with Abelard's assistance, founded a nunnery at Paraclete. Her letters show her strong and pious character.

helot a class of slaves in ancient Sparta who were probably the indigenous inhabitants. Their cruel treatment by the Spartans became proverbial.

Helpmann /'helpmən/ Robert 1909–1986. Australian dancer, choreographer, and actor. The leading male dancer with the Sadler's Wells Ballet, London 1933–50, he partnered Margot ◊Fonteyn in the 1940s. He was noted for his gift for mime and for his dramatic sense, also apparent in his choreographic work, for example *Miracle in the Gorbals* 1944. He was knighted 1968.

Helsingborg /'helsɪŋbɔ:g/ (Swedish *Hälsingborg*) port in SW Sweden, linked by ferry with Helsingør across the Sound; population (1986) 106,300. Industries include copper-smelting, rubber and chemical manufacture, and sugar refining.

Helsingfors /ˌhelsɪŋ'fɔ:ʃ/ Swedish name for ◊Helsinki.

Helsingør /ˌhelsɪŋ'ɜ:/ port in NE Denmark; population (1987) 57,000. It is linked by ferry with Helsingborg across the Sound; Shakespeare made it the scene of *Hamlet*.

Helsinki /'helsɪŋki/ (Swedish *Helsingfors*) capital and port of Finland; population (1988) 490,000, metropolitan area 978,000. Industries include shipbuilding, engineering, and textiles. The homes of the architect Eliel Saarinen and the composer Jean Sibelius outside the town are museums.

Helsinki Conference international conference 1975 at which 35 countries, including the USSR and the USA, attempted to reach agreement on cooperation in security, economics, science, technology, and human rights.

Some regarded the conference as marking the end of the ◊Cold War. Others felt it legitimized the division of Europe that had been a fact since the end of World War II. Human-rights groups contend that there have been many violations of the provisions of the accords. Its full title is the Helsinki Conference on Security and Cooperation in Europe (CSCE).

Helvellyn /hel'velɪn/ peak of the English Lake District in ◊Cumbria, 950 m/3,118 ft high.

Helvetia /hel'vi:ʃə/ region, corresponding to W Switzerland, occupied by the Celtic Helvetii 1st century BC–5th century AD. In 58 BC Caesar repulsed their invasion of southern Gaul at Bibracte

(near Autun) and Helvetia became subject to Rome.

Helvetius /ˌelveɪ'sju:s/ Claude Adrien 1715–1771. French philosopher. In *De l'Esprit* 1758 he argued that self-interest, however disguised, is the mainspring of all human action, and that since conceptions of good and evil vary according to period and locality there is no absolute good or evil. He also believed that intellectual differences are only a matter of education.

hematite the principal ore of iron, consisting mainly of iron (III) (ferric) oxide, Fe_2O_3. It occurs as *specular hematite* (dark, metallic lustre), *kidney ore* (reddish radiating fibres terminating in smooth, rounded surfaces), and as a red earthy deposit.

Hemel Hempstead /'heməl 'hempstɪd/ 'new' town in Hertfordshire, England; population (1981) 80,000. Industries include the manufacture of paper, electrical goods, and office equipment.

Hemingway /'hemɪŋweɪ/ Ernest 1898–1961. US writer. War, bullfighting, and fishing became prominent themes in his short stories and novels, which included *A Farewell to Arms* 1929, *For Whom the Bell Tolls* 1940, and *The Old Man and the Sea* 1952. His short, deceptively simple sentences attracted many imitators. Nobel prize 1954.

He was born in Oak Park, Illinois, and developed in his youth a passion for hunting and adventure. He became a journalist, and was wounded while serving on a volunteer ambulance crew in Italy in World War I. His style was influenced by Gertrude ◊Stein, who also introduced him to bullfighting, a theme in his first novel *The Sun Also Rises* 1926 and the memoir *Death in the Afternoon* 1932. *A Farewell to Arms* deals with wartime experiences on the Italian front, and *For Whom the Bell Tolls* has a Spanish Civil War setting. He served as war correspondent both in this conflict and in Europe during World War II. His enthusiasm for big-game hunting emerges in such stories as 'The Snows of Kilimanjaro' and 'The Short Happy Life of Francis Macomber'. Physical weakness and depression contributed to his suicide.

hemlock plant *Conium maculatum* of the family Umbelliferae, native to Europe, W Asia, and N Africa. Reaching up to 2 m/6 ft high, it bears umbels of small white flowers. The whole plant, and especially the root and fruit, is poisonous, causing paralysis of the nervous system. Hemlock is also a type of conifer, genus *Tsuga*, whose crushed leaves have a similar smell.

hemp annual plant *Cannabis sativa*, family Cannabaceae. Originally from Asia, it is cultivated in most temperate countries for its fibres, produced in the outer layer of the stem, and used in ropes, twines and, occasionally, in a type of linen or lace. ◊Cannabis is obtained from certain varieties of hemp.

The name 'hemp' is extended to similar types of fibre: sisal hemp and henequen obtained from the leaves of *Agave* species native to Yucatán and cultivated in many tropical countries, and manila hemp obtained from *Musa textilis*, a plant native to the Philippines and the Moluccas.

Henan /ˌhʌ'næn/ or *Honan* province of E central China
area 167,000 sq km/64,462 sq mi
capital Zhengzhou
features comprises river plains of the Huang He (Yellow River); in the 1980s the ruins of Xibo, the 16th-century BC capital of the Shang dynasty, were discovered here
products cereals, cotton
population (1986) 78,080,000.

henbane wild plant *Hyoscyamus niger*, found on waste ground through most of Europe and W Asia. A branching plant, up to 80 cm/2.6 ft high, it has hairy leaves and a nauseous smell. The yellow flowers are bell-shaped. Henbane is poisonous. It is sometimes grown for medicinal purposes, but its use is dangerous.

Henderson /'hendəsən/ Arthur 1863–1935. British Labour politician, born in Glasgow. He worked 20 years as an iron-moulder in Newcastle, entered Parliament 1903, and contributed to Labour's political organization. He was home secretary in the first Labour government, and was foreign secretary 1929–31, when he accorded the Soviet government full recognition. Nobel Peace Prize 1934.

Hendon /'hendən/ residential district in the borough of ◊Barnet, Greater London, England. The Metropolitan Police Detective Training and Motor Driving Schools are here, and the RAF Museum 1972 includes the Battle of Britain Museum 1980.

Hendrix /'hendrɪks/ Jimi (James Marshall) 1942–1970. US rock guitarist, songwriter, and singer, legendary for his virtuoso experimental technique and flamboyance.

He moved to the UK 1966 and formed a trio, the *Jimi Hendrix Experience*, which was successful from its first singles ('Hey Joe' and 'Purple Haze', both 1967), and attracted notice in the USA when Hendrix burned his guitar at the 1967 Monterey Pop Festival. The group disbanded early 1969 after three albums; Hendrix continued to record and occasionally perform until his death the following year. He greatly expanded the vocabulary of the electric guitar and influenced both rock and jazz musicians.

Hendry /'hendri/ Stephen 1970– . Scottish snooker player of exceptional talent. He succeeded Steve Davis at the top of the top-ranking list during the 1989–90 season.

When he won the Scottish professional title 1986, he was the youngest winner of a professional tournament. He won his first ranking event in the 1987 Rothmans Grand Prix, and became the youngest winner of the World Professional Championship in 1990.

Heng /heŋ/ Samrin 1934– . Cambodian politician. A former Khmer Rouge commander 1976–78, who had become disillusioned by its brutal tactics, he led an unsuccessful coup against ◊Pol Pot 1978 and established the Kampuchean People's Revolutionary Party (KPRP) in Vietnam, before returning, in 1979, to head the new Vietnamese-backed government.

Hengist legendary leader, with his brother Horsa, of the Jutes, who originated in Jutland and settled in Kent about 450, the first Anglo-Saxon settlers in Britain.

Henie /'heni/ Sonja 1912–1969. Norwegian skater. Norwegian champion at 11, she won ten world championships and three Olympic titles. She turned professional 1936 and made numerous films.

Henlein /'henlaɪn/ Konrad 1898–1945. Sudeten-German leader of the Sudeten Nazi Party inside Czechoslovakia, and closely allied with Hitler's German Nazis. He was partly responsible for the destabilization of the Czech state 1938 which led to the ◊Munich Agreement and secession of the Sudetenland to Germany.

Henley-on-Thames /'henli ɒn 'temz/ town in Oxfordshire, England; population (1984) 10,976. The regatta, held here annually since 1839, is in

Hemingway US author Ernest Hemingway was fascinated by bullfighting and war, themes that appear in several of his books.

Hendrix Jimi Hendrix on stage at the Isle of Wight Pop Festival, England, 1970.

July; Henley Management College, established in 1946, was the first in Europe.

Henley Royal Regatta UK rowing festival on the river Thames, inaugurated 1839. It is as much a social as a sporting occasion. The principal events are the solo Diamond Challenge Sculls, and the Grand Challenge Cup, the leading event for eights. The regatta is held in July.

Henley: recent winners

Diamond Sculls
1981 Chris Baillieu *(Great Britain)*
1982 Chris Baillieu *(Great Britain)*
1983 Steven Redgrave *(Great Britain)*
1984 Chris Baillieu *(Great Britain)*
1985 Steven Redgrave *(Great Britain)*
1986 Bjarne Eltang *(Denmark)*
1987 Peter-Michael Kolbe *(West Germany)*
1988 Hamish McGlashan *Australia)*
1989 Vaclav Chalvpa *(Czechoslovakia)*
Grand Challenge Cup
1981 Oxford University/Thames Tradesmen *(GB)*
1982 Leander/London Rowing Club *(Great Britain)*
1983 London Rowing Club/University of London *(GB)*
1984 Leander/London Rowing Club *(Great Britain)*
1985 Harvard University *(USA)*
1986 Nautilus *(Great Britain)*
1987 Soviet Army *(USSR)*
1988 Leander/University of London *(Great Britain)*
1989 RC Hansa Dortmund *West Germany*

henna small shrub *Lawsonia inermis* found in Iran, India, Egypt, and N Africa. The leaves and young twigs are ground to a powder, mixed to a paste with hot water, and applied to fingernails and hair, giving an orange-red hue. The colour may then be changed to black by applying a preparation of indigo.

Henotikon declaration published by emperor Zeno 482, aimed at reconciling warring theological factions within the early Christian Church. It refuted the Council of Chalcedon 451, and reaffirmed the heretical idea that Jesus was one person, not two. The declaration, not accepted by Rome, led to a complete split between Rome and Constantinople 484–519.

Henri /'henri/ Robert 1865–1929. US painter, a leading figure in the transition between 19th-century conventions and Modern art in America. He was a principal member of the ◊*Ashcan school*.

Henrietta Maria /ˌhenriˈetə məˈriːə/ 1609–1669. Queen of England 1625–49. The daughter of Henry IV of France, she married Charles I of England 1625. As she used her influence to encourage him to aid Roman Catholics and make himself an absolute ruler, she became highly unpopular and had to go into exile 1644–60. She returned to England at the Restoration, but retired to France 1665.

henry SI unit (symbol H) of ◊inductance (the reaction of an electric current against the magnetic field that surrounds it). One henry is the inductance of a circuit that produces an opposing voltage of 1 volt when the current changes at 1 amp per second.

Henry /'henri/ (Charles Albert David) known as *Harry* 1984– . Prince of the United Kingdom; second child of the Prince and Princess of Wales.

Henry /'henri/ Joseph 1797–1878. US physicist, inventor of the electromagnetic motor 1829, and a telegraphic apparatus. He also discovered the principle of electromagnetic induction, roughly at the same time as ◊Faraday, and the phenomenon of self-induction. A unit of inductance (henry) is named after him.

Henry /'henri/ Patrick 1736–1799. US politician, who in 1775 supported the arming of the Virginia militia against the British by a speech ending: 'Give me liberty or give me death!' He was governor of the state 1776–79 and 1784–86.

Henry /'henri/ William 1774–1836. British chemist. In 1803 he formulated *Henry's law*: when a gas is dissolved in a liquid at a given temperature, the mass that dissolves is in direct proportion to the

Henry V *Portrait by an unknown artist (c.1518–23) Royal Collection, Windsor.*

gas pressure.

Henry /'henri/ eight kings of England:

Henry I 1068–1135. King of England from 1100. Youngest son of William I, he succeeded his brother William II. He won the support of the Saxons by granting them a charter and marrying a Saxon princess. An able administrator, he established a professional bureaucracy and a system of travelling judges. He was succeeded by Stephen.

Henry II 1133–1189. King of England from 1154, when he succeeded ◊Stephen. He was the son of ◊Matilda and Geoffrey of Anjou (1113–51). He curbed the power of the barons, but his attempt to bring the church courts under control had to be abandoned after the murder of ◊Becket. During his reign the English conquest of Ireland began. He was succeeded by his son Richard I.

He was lord of Scotland, Ireland, and Wales, and count of Anjou, Brittany, Poitou, Normandy, Maine, Gascony, and Aquitaine. He was married to Eleanor of Aquitaine.

Henry III 1207–1272. King of England from 1216, when he succeeded John, but he did not assume royal power until 1227. His subservience to the papacy and his foreign favourites led to de ◊Montfort's revolt 1264. Henry was defeated at Lewes, Sussex, and imprisoned. He was restored to the throne after royalist victory at Evesham 1265. He was succeeded by his son Edward I.

Henry IV (***Bolingbroke***) 1367–1413. King of England from 1399, the son of ◊John of Gaunt. In 1398 he was banished by ◊Richard II for political

Henry VIII *Portrait by an unknown artist (c. 1542) National Portrait Gallery, London.*

activity, but returned 1399 to head a revolt and be accepted as king by Parliament. He was succeeded by his son Henry V.

He had difficulty in keeping the support of Parliament and the clergy, and had to deal with baronial unrest and ◊Glendower's rising in Wales. In order to win support he had to conciliate the church by a law for the burning of heretics, and to make many concessions to Parliament.

Henry V 1387–1422. King of England from 1413, son of Henry IV. Invading Normandy 1415, he captured Harfleur, and defeated the French at ◊Agincourt. He invaded again 1417–19, capturing Rouen. He married ◊Catherine of Valois 1420, to gain recognition as heir to the French throne by his father-in-law Charles VI. He was succeeded by his son Henry VI.

Henry VI 1421–1471. King of England from 1422, son of Henry V. He assumed royal power 1442, and identified himself with the party opposed to the continuation of the French war. After his marriage 1445, he was dominated by his wife, ◊Margaret of Anjou. The unpopularity of the government, especially after the loss of the English conquests in France, encouraged Richard, Duke of ◊York, to claim the throne, and though York was killed 1460, his son Edward IV proclaimed himself king 1461 (see ◊Wars of the Roses). Henry was captured 1465, temporarily restored 1470, but again imprisoned 1471 and then murdered.

Henry VII 1457–1509. King of England from 1485, son of Edmund Tudor, Earl of Richmond (*c.* 1430–56), and a descendant of ◊John of Gaunt. He spent his early life in Brittany until 1485, when he landed in Britain to lead the rebellion against Richard III which ended with Richard's defeat and death at ◊Bosworth. Yorkist revolts continued until 1497, but Henry restored order after the ◊Wars of the Roses by the ◊Star Chamber, and achieved independence from Parliament by amassing a private fortune through confiscations. He was succeeded by his son Henry VIII.

Henry VIII 1491–1547. King of England from 1509, when he succeeded his father Henry VII and married Catherine of Aragon, the widow of his brother. His Lord Chancellor, Cardinal Wolsey, was replaced by Thomas More 1529, for failing to persuade the pope to grant Henry a divorce. After 1532 Henry broke with the Catholic church, proclaimed himself head of the church, and dissolved the monasteries. After divorcing Catherine, his wives were Anne Boleyn, Jane Seymour, Anne of Cleves, Catherine Howard, and Catherine Parr. He was succeeded by his son Edward VI.

During the period 1513–29 Henry pursued an active foreign policy, largely under the guidance of Wolsey. With Parliament's approval Henry renounced the papal supremacy (see ◊Anglican Communion). Henry divorced Catherine 1533 and married Anne Boleyn, who was beheaded 1536, ostensibly for adultery. Henry's third wife, Jane Seymour, died 1537. He married Anne of Cleves 1540 in pursuance of Thomas Cromwell's policy of allying with the German Protestants, but rapidly abandoned this policy, divorced Anne, and beheaded Cromwell. His fifth wife, Catherine Howard, was beheaded 1542, and the following year he married Catherine Parr, who survived him.

Henry never completely lost his popularity, but wars with France and Scotland towards the end of his reign sapped the economy, and in religion he not only executed Roman Catholics, including Thomas More, for refusing to acknowledge his supremacy in the church, but also Protestants who maintained his changes had not gone far enough.

Henry /'henri/ four kings of France:

Henry I 1005–1060. King of France from 1031, who spent much of his reign in conflict with ◊William I the Conqueror, then duke of Normandy.

Henry II 1519–1559. King of France from 1547. He captured the fortresses of Metz and Verdun from the Holy Roman emperor Charles V, and Calais from the English. He was killed in a tournament.

Hepworth *British sculptor Barbara Hepworth before her 1930 exhibition with her stone* Mother and Child.

In 1526 he was sent, with his brother, to Spain as a hostage, being returned when there was peace 1530. He married Catherine de' Medici 1533, and from then was under the domination of her, Diane de Poitiers, and duke Montmorency. Three of his sons, Francis II, Charles IX, and Henry III, became kings.

Henry III 1551–1589. King of France from 1574. He fought both the ◊Huguenots (headed by his successor, Henry of Navarre) and the Catholic League (headed by the Duke of Guise). Guise expelled Henry from Paris 1588 but was assassinated. Henry allied with the Huguenots under Henry of Navarre to besiege the city, but was assassinated by a monk.

Henry IV 1553–1610. King of France from 1589. Son of Antoine de Bourbon and Jeanne, queen of Navarre, he was brought up as a Protestant, and from 1576 led the ◊Huguenots. On his accession he settled the religious question by adopting Catholicism while tolerating Protestantism. He restored peace and strong government to France, and brought back prosperity by measures for the promotion of industry and agriculture, and the improvement of communications. He was assassinated by a Catholic fanatic.

Henry /'henri/ seven Holy Roman emperors:

Henry I the Fowler *c.* 876–936. King of Germany from 919, and duke of Saxony from 912. He secured the frontiers of Saxony, ruled in harmony with its nobles, and extended German influence over the Hungarians, the Danes, and Slavonic tribes in the east. He was about to claim the imperial crown when he died.

Henry II the Saint 973–1024. King of Germany from 1002, Holy Roman emperor from 1014, when he recognized Benedict VIII as pope. He was canonized 1146.

Henry III the Black 1017–1056. King of Germany from 1028, Holy Roman emperor from 1039, who raised the empire to the height of its power, and extended its authority over Poland, Bohemia, and Hungary.

Henry IV 1050–1106. Holy Roman emperor from 1056, who was involved from 1075 in a struggle with the papacy (see ◊Gregory VII).

Henry V 1081–1125. Holy Roman emperor from 1106. He continued the struggle with the church until the settlement of the ◊investiture contest 1122.

Henry VI 1165–1197. Holy Roman emperor from 1190. As part of his plan for making the empire universal, he captured and imprisoned Richard I of England, and compelled him to do homage.

Henry VII 1269–1313. Holy Roman emperor from 1308. He attempted unsuccessfully to revive the imperial supremacy in Italy.

Henry Frederick /'henri 'fredrɪk/ Prince of Wales 1594–1612. Eldest son of James I of England and Anne of Denmark; a keen patron of Italian art.

Henry /'henri/ O. Pen name of William Sydney Porter 1862–1910. US short story writer, whose collections include *Cabbages and Kings* 1904 and *The Four Million* 1906. His stories are in a colloquial style and noted for their skilled construction with twist endings.

Henry of Blois /'henri/ died 1171. He was bishop of Winchester from 1129, Pope Innocent II's legate to England from 1139, and brother of King Stephen. He was educated at Cluny, France, before entering his brother's service. While remaining loyal to Henry II, he tried to effect a compromise between Becket and the king. He was a generous benefactor to Winchester and Cluny, and he built Glastonbury Abbey.

Henryson /'henrɪsən/ Robert 1430–1505. Scottish poet. His works include versions of Aesop and the *Testament of Cresseid*, a continuation of Chaucer.

Henry the Navigator /'henri/ 1394–1460. Portuguese prince, fourth son of John I. He set up a school for navigators 1419 and under his patronage, Portuguese seamen explored and colonized Madeira, the Cape Verde Islands, and the Azores; they sailed down the African coast almost to Sierra Leone.

Henty /'henti/ G(eorge) A(lfred) 1832–1902. British war correspondent, author of numerous historical novels for children, such as *With the Allies to Peking* 1904.

Henzada /hen'zɑ:də/ city in S central Myanmar (Burma), on the Irrawaddy river; population 284,000.

Henze /'hentsə/ Hans Werner 1926– . German composer whose large and varied output includes orchestral, vocal, and chamber music. He uses traditional symphony and concerto forms, and incorporates a wide range of styles, including jazz. In 1953 he moved to Italy where his music became more expansive, as in the opera *The Bassarids* 1966.

heparin anticoagulant drug that prevents clots from forming inside the blood vessels. It is often used after surgery, where there is risk of ◊thrombosis, or following pulmonary ◊embolism to ensure that no further clots form. Delivered by intravenous infusion, it takes effect within minutes to make blood cells less 'sticky', and may even dissolve newly formed clots.

Heparin is derived from bishydroxy coumarin, a substance found in mouldy clover. It was discovered 1934, when a farmer in Wisconsin, USA, brought a bucket of blood taken from his haemorrhaging cattle to a nearby university laboratory for tests.

hepatic pertaining to the liver.

hepatitis inflammatory disease of the liver, usually caused by a virus. Other causes include systematic lupus erythematosus or amoebic dysentery.

The viral disease known as *hepatitis A* (infectious or viral hepatitis) is spread by contaminated food, especially seafood, and via the oro-faecal route. Incubation period is about four weeks. Temporary immunity is conferred by injections of normal ◊immunoglobulin (gammaglobulin).

The virus causing *hepatitis B* (serum hepatitis) was only isolated in the 1960s. Contained in all body fluids, it is very easily transmitted. Some people become carriers. Those falling ill with the disease may be sick for weeks or months. The illness may be mild, or it may result in death from liver failure. Liver cancer is now recognized as a long-term complication of the disease. A successful vaccine was developed in the late 1970s.

Hepburn /'hepbз:n/ Audrey. Stage name of Audrey Hepburn-Rushton 1929– . British actress of Anglo-Dutch descent who tended to play innocent, child-like characters. Slender and doe-eyed, she set a different style from the pneumatic stars of the 1950s. After playing minor parts in British films in the early 1950s, she became a Hollywood star in such films as *Funny Face* 1957, *My Fair Lady* 1964, *Wait Until Dark* 1968, and *Robin and Marian* 1976.

Hepburn /'hepbз:n/ Katharine 1909– . US actress, who appeared in such films as *The African Queen* 1951, *Guess Who's Coming to Dinner* 1967, and *On Golden Pond* 1981. She won four Academy Awards.

Hephaestus /hɪ'fi:stəs/ in Greek mythology, the god of fire and metalcraft (Roman Vulcan), son of Zeus and Hera; he was lame, and married Aphrodite.

Hepplewhite /'hepəlwaɪt/ George died 1786. English furniture maker. He developed a simple, elegant style, working mainly in mahogany or satinwood, adding delicately inlaid or painted decorations of feathers, shells, or wheat-ears. His book of designs, *The Cabinetmaker and Upholsterer's Guide* 1788, was published posthumously.

heptarchy term coined by 16th-century historians to denote the seven Saxon kingdoms thought to have existed before AD 800: Northumbria, Mercia, East Anglia, Essex, Kent, Sussex, and Wessex.

heptathlon a multi-event athletics discipline for women that consists of seven events over two days. The events, in order, are: 100 metres hurdles, high jump, shot putt, 200 metres (day one); long jump, javelin, 800 metres (day two). Points are awarded for performances in each event, in the same way as the ◊decathlon. It replaced the pentathlon in international competition in 1981.

Hepworth /'hepwɜː/ Barbara 1903–1975. British sculptor. She developed a distinctive abstract style, creating hollowed forms of stone or wood with spaces bridged by wires or strings; many later works are in bronze.

Born in Wakefield, she studied at Leeds School of Art and the Royal College of Art, London. She worked in concrete, bronze, wood, and aluminium, but her preferred medium was stone. She married first the sculptor John Skeaping, and second Ben ◊Nicholson. Under Nicholson's influence she became more interested in abstract form. In 1939 she moved to St Ives, Cornwall (where her studio is now a museum). She was created Dame of the British Empire 1965.

Hera /'hɪərə/ in Greek mythology, a goddess, sister-consort of Zeus, mother of Hephaestus, Hebe, and Ares; protector of women and marriage, and identified with Roman Juno.

Heracles /'herəkliːz/ in Greek mythology, a hero (Roman **Hercules**), son of Zeus and Alcmene, famed for strength. While serving Eurystheus, king of Argos, he performed 12 labours, including the cleansing of the Augean stables.

Heraclitus /ˌhɪərə'klaɪtəs/ *c.* 544–483 BC. Greek philosopher, who believed that the cosmos is in a ceaseless state of flux and motion. Fire was the fundamental material that accounted for all change and motion in the world. Nothing in the world ever stays the same, hence the famous dictum 'one cannot step in the same river twice'.

Heraclius /ˌhɪərə'klaɪəs/ *c.* 575–641. Byzantine emperor from 610. His reign marked a turning point in the empire's fortunes. Of Armenian descent, he recaptured Armenia 622, and other provinces 622–28 from the Persians, but lost them to the Arabs 629–41.

Heraklion /hɪ'rækliən/ alternative name for ◊Iráklion.

heraldry the decoration and insignia representing a person, family, or dynasty. Heraldry originated with simple symbols used on banners and shields for recognition in battle. By the 14th century, it had become a complex pictorial language with its own regulatory bodies (courts of chivalry), used by noble families, corporations, cities, and realms.

Heralds' College another name for the ◊College of Arms, an English heraldic body.

Herapath John 1790–1868. English mathematician. His work into the behaviour of gases, though seriously flawed, was acknowledged by the physicist James Joule in his own more successful investigations.

Herat /he'ræt/ capital of Herat province, and the largest city in W Afghanistan, on the N banks of the Hari Rud; population (1980) 160,000. A principal road junction, it was a great city in ancient and medieval times.

Herault /e'rəʊ/ river in S France, 160 km/100 mi long, rising in the Cévennes and flowing into the Gulf of Lyons near Agde. It gives its name to a *département*.

herb any plant (usually a flowering plant) tasting sweet, bitter, aromatic, or pungent, used in cookery, medicine, or perfumery; technically, any plant whose aerial parts do not remain above ground at the end of the growing season.

herbarium a collection of dried, pressed plants used as an aid to identification of unknown plants and by taxonomists in the ◊classification of plants. The plant specimens are accompanied by information, such as the date and place of collection, by whom collected, details of habitat, flower colour, and local names.

Herbaria range from small collections containing plants of a particular county or region, to the large national herbaria containing millions of specimens from all parts of the world. The herbarium at the Royal Botanic Gardens, Kew, England, has over five million specimens.

Herbert /'hɜːbət/ Edward, 1st Baron Herbert

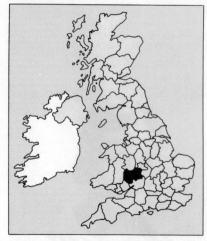

Hereford and Worcester

of Cherbury 1583–1648. English philosopher, brother of George Herbert. His *De veritate* 1624, with its theory of natural religion, founded English ◊deism.

Herbert /'hɜːbət/ Frank (Patrick) 1920–1986. US science-fiction writer, author of the *Dune* saga from 1965 onwards (filmed by David Lynch 1984), broad-scale adventure stories containing serious ideas about ecology and religion.

Herbert /'hɜːbət/ George 1593–1633. English poet. His volume of religious poems, *The Temple*, appeared in 1633, shortly before his death. His poems depict his intense religious feelings in clear, simple language.

He was the brother of Lord Edward Herbert of Cherbury. He became orator to Cambridge University 1619, and a prebendary in Huntingdonshire 1625, where his friends included the other writers Donne, Walton, and Bacon. After ordination in 1630 he became vicar of Bemerton, Wiltshire, and died of consumption.

Herbert /'hɜːbət/ Wally (Walter) 1934– . British surveyor and explorer. His first surface crossing by dog sledge of the Arctic Ocean 1968–69, from Alaska to Spitsbergen via the North Pole, was the longest sustained sledging journey (6,000 km/3,800 mi) in polar exploration.

Herbert of Lea /'hɜːbət, liː/ Sidney Herbert, 1st Baron Herbert of Lea 1810–1861. British politician. He was secretary for war in Aberdeen's Liberal–Peelite coalition of 1852–55, and during the Crimean War was responsible for sending Florence Nightingale to the front.

herbicide a type of ◊weedkiller.

herbivore an animal that feeds on green plants or their products, including seeds, fruit, and nectar, as well as ◊photosynthetic organisms in plankton. Herbivores are more numerous than other animals because their food is the most abundant. They form a vital link in the food chain between plants and carnivores.

herb Robert common wild flower *Geranium robertianum* found throughout Europe and central Asia, and naturalized in North America. About 30 cm/1 ft high, it bears hairy leaves and small pinkish to purplish flowers, and has a reddish hairy stem. When rubbed, the leaves have a strong smell.

Herculaneum /ˌhɜːkjʊ'leɪniəm/ ancient city of Italy between Naples and Pompeii. Along with Pompeii, it was buried when Vesuvius erupted AD 79. It was excavated from the 18th century onwards.

Hercules /'hɜːkjʊliːz/ Roman form of ◊Heracles.

Hercules /'hɜːkjʊliːz/ in astronomy, the fifth-largest constellation, lying in the northern hemisphere. Despite its size it contains no prominent stars. Its most important feature is a ◊globular cluster of stars 22,500 light years away, one of the best examples in the sky.

Hercules, Pillars of /'hɜːkjʊliːz/ rocks (at Gibraltar and Ceuta) that guard the entrance to the Mediterranean.

Herder /'heədə/ Johann Gottfried von 1744–1803. German poet, critic, and philosopher. Herder's critical writings indicated his intuitive rather than reasoning trend of thought. He collected folk songs of all nations 1778 and in the *Ideen zur Philosophie der Geschichte der Menschheit/Outlines of a Philosophy of the History of Man* 1784–91 he outlined the stages of human cultural development.

Born in East Prussia, he studied at Königsberg where he was influenced by Kant, became pastor at Riga, met Goethe in Strasbourg 1770, and in 1776 was called to Weimar as court preacher. He gave considerable impulse to the ◊*Sturm und Drang* ('storm and stress') movement in German literature.

heredity in biology, the transmission of traits from parent to offspring. See also ◊genetics.

Hereford /'herɪfəd/ town in the county of Hereford and Worcester, on the river Wye, England; population (1981) 630,000. The cathedral, which was begun 1079, contains the *Mappa Mundi*, a medieval map of the world. Products include cider, beer, and metal goods.

Hereford and Worcester /'herɪfəd, 'wʊstə/ county in W central England

area 3,930 sq km/1,517 sq mi

towns administrative headquarters Worcester; Hereford, Kidderminster, Evesham, Ross-on-Wye, Ledbury

features rivers Wye and Severn; Malvern Hills (high point Worcester Beacon 425 m/1,395 ft) and Black Mountains; Droitwich, once a Victorian spa, reopened its baths in 1985 (the town lies over a subterranean brine reservoir with waters buoyant enough to take a laden tea tray); fertile Vale of Evesham

products mainly agricultural, apples, pears, and cider; hops and vegetables; Hereford cattle; carpets, porcelain, some chemicals and engineering

population (1987) 665,000

famous people Edward Elgar, A E Housman, William Langland, John Masefield.

Herero /hə'reərəʊ/ nomadic Bantu-speaking people living in Namibia, SW Africa.

heresy (Greek *hairesis* 'parties' of believers) doctrine opposed to orthodox belief, especially in religion. Those holding ideas considered heretical by the Christian church have included Gnostics, Arians, Pelagians, Montanists, Albigenses, Waldenses, Lollards, and Anabaptists. Among modern dissidents in the Catholic church is Hans ◊Küng.

Hereward /'herɪwəd/ the Wake 11th century. English leader of a revolt against the Normans 1070. His stronghold in the Isle of Ely was captured by William the Conqueror 1071. Hereward escaped, but his fate is unknown.

Hergé /eə'ʒeɪ/ Assumed name of Georges Remi 1907–1983. Belgian artist, who took the name of Hergé from the pronunciation of the initial letters of his name. He was the creator of the boy reporter Tintin, who first appeared in strip-cartoon form as *Tintin in the Land of the Soviets* 1929–30.

Herman /'hɜːmən/ 'Woody' (Woodrow) 1913–1987. US band leader and clarinetist. A child prodigy, he was leader of his own orchestra at 23, and after 1945 formed his famous Thundering Herd band. Soloists in this or later versions of the band included Lester ◊Young and Stan ◊Getz.

hermaphrodite an organism that has both male and female sex organs. Hermaphroditism is the norm in species such as snails and oysters, and is standard in flowering plants. *Pseudo-hermaphrodites* have the internal sex organs of one sex but the external appearance of the other. The true sex becomes apparent at adolescence when the normal hormone activity appropriate to the internal organs begins to function.

Hermaphroditus /hɜːˌmæfrə'daɪtəs/ in Greek

mythology, the son of Hermes and Aphrodite. He was loved by a nymph who prayed for eternal union with him, so that they became one body with dual sexual characteristics, hence the term hermaphrodite.

hermeneutics a philosophical tradition concerned with the nature of understanding and interpretation of human behaviour and social traditions. From its origins in problems of biblical interpretation, hermeneutics has expanded to cover many fields of enquiry, including aesthetics, literary theory, and science. ◊Dilthey, ◊Heidegger, and ◊Gadamer are influential contributors to this tradition.

Hermes /'hɜ:mi:z/ in Greek mythology, a god, son of Zeus and ◊Maia, and messenger of the gods; he has winged sandals, a wide-rimmed hat, and a staff around which serpents coil. Identified with the Roman Mercury and ancient Egyptian Thoth, he protected thieves, travellers, and merchants.

Hermes Trismegistus /ˌtrɪsmə'gɪstəs/ supposed author of the *Hermetica* (2nd–3rd centuries AD), writings inculcating a cosmic religion, in which the sun is regarded as the visible manifestation of God. In the Renaissance these writings were thought to be by an Egyptian priest contemporary with Moses, and it is possible they contain some Egyptian material.

hermit religious ascetic living in seclusion, often practising extremes of mortification (such as the Stylites, early Christians who lived on top of pillars).

hermit crab a type of ◊crab.

Hermon /'hɜ:mən/ snow-topped mountain (Arabic Jebel esh-Sheikh), 2,814 m/9,232 ft high, on the Syria–Lebanon border. According to tradition, Jesus was transfigured here.

Herne /'heənə/ industrial city in North Rhine-Westphalia, West Germany; population (1988) 171,000.

Herne Bay /'hɜ:n/ seaside resort in Kent, SE England; population (1981) 27,528.

hernia or *rupture* protrusion of part of an internal organ through a weakness in the surrounding muscular wall, usually in the groin or navel. The appearance is that of a rounded soft lump or sweling.

Hero and Leander /'hɪərəʊ, li'ændə/ in Greek mythology, a pair of lovers. Hero was a priestess of Aphrodite at Sestos on the Hellespont, in love with Leander on the opposite shore at Abydos. When he was drowned while swimming across during a storm, she threw herself into the sea out of grief.

Herod /'herəd/ *the Great* 74–4 BC. King of the Roman province of Judaea, S Palestine, from 40 BC. With the aid of the triumvir Mark Antony he established his government in Jerusalem 37 BC. He rebuilt the Temple in Jerusalem, but his Hellenizing tendencies made him suspect to orthodox Jewry. His last years were a reign of terror, and Matthew in the New Testament alleges that he ordered the slaughter of all the infants in Bethlehem to ensure the death of Jesus, whom he foresaw as a rival. He was the father of Herod Antipas.

Herod Agrippa I /ə'grɪpə/ 10 BC–AD 44. Jewish ruler of Palestine from AD 41. His real name was Marcus Julius Agrippa, erroneously called 'Herod' in the Bible. Grandson of Herod the Great, he was made tetrarch (governor) of Palestine by the Roman emperor Caligula and king by Claudius AD 41. He put James to death and imprisoned Peter, both apostles. His son was Herod Agrippa II.

Herod Agrippa II /ə'grɪpə/ c. AD 40–93. King of Chalcis (now S Lebanon), son of Herod Agrippa I. He was appointed by Claudius about AD 50, and in AD 60 tried the apostle Paul. He helped the Roman emperor Titus take Jerusalem AD 70, then went to Rome, where he died.

Herod Antipas /'æntɪpæs/ 21 BC–AD 39. Tetrarch (governor) of the Roman province of Galilee, N Palestine, 4 BC–AD 9, son of Herod the Great. He divorced his wife to marry his niece Herodias,

who persuaded her daughter Salome to ask for John the Baptist's head when he reproved Herod's action. Jesus was brought before him on Pontius Pilate's discovery that he was a Galilean and hence of Herod's jurisdiction, but Herod returned him without giving any verdict. In AD 38 Herod Antipas went to Rome to try to get the emperor Caligula to give him the title of king, but was banished.

Herodotus /he'rɒdətəs/ *c.* 484–424 BC. Greek historian. After four years in Athens, he travelled widely in Egypt, Asia, and eastern Europe, before settling at Thurii in S Italy 443 BC. He wrote a nine-book history of the Greek-Persian struggle that culminated in the defeat of the Persian invasion attempts 490 and 480 BC. Herodotus was the first historian to apply critical evaluation to his material.

heroin or *diamorphine* a powerful ◊opiate analgesic. It is more addictive than ◊morphine but causes less nausea. It has an important place in the control of severe pain in terminal illness, severe injuries, and heart attacks, but is widely used illegally.

The major regions of opium production, for conversion to heroin, are the 'Golden Crescent' of Afghanistan, Iran, and Pakistan, and the 'Golden Triangle' across parts of Myanmar (Burma), Laos, and Thailand.

In 1971 there were 3,000 registered heroin addicts in the UK; in 1989 there were over 100,000.

heron large wading bird of the family Ardeidae, which also includes bitterns, egrets, night-herons, and boatbills. They have sharp bills, broad wings, long legs and soft plumage. They are found mostly in tropical and subtropical regions, but also in temperate zones.

The *common heron Ardea cinerea* nests in Europe, Asia, and parts of Africa in large colonies at the tops of trees. The bird is about 1 m/3 ft long, and has a long neck and long legs. The plumage is chiefly grey, but there are black patches on the sides and a black crest. The legs are olive-green, and the beak yellow, except during the breeding season when it is pink. It is a wading bird, but is rarely seen to swim or walk. It feeds on fish, frogs, and rats.

Hero of Alexandria /'hɪərəʊ/ Greek mathematician and writer, probably of the 1st century AD, who invented an automatic fountain and a kind of stationary steam-engine.

Hero of Our Time, A a novel by the Russian writer Mikhail Lermontov, published 1840. It is composed of five stories about a bitter, cynical nobleman and officer, whose attitude is contrasted with that of an older, dutiful officer.

herpes infection by viruses of the herpes group. *Herpes simplex I* is the causative agent of a common inflammation, the cold sore. *Herpes simplex II* is responsible for genital herpes, a highly contagious, sexually transmitted disease characterized by painful blisters in the genital area. It can be transmitted in the birth canal from mother to newborn. *Herpes zoster* causes chickenpox and ◊shingles.

There are a number of ◊antivirals to treat these infections, which are particularly troublesome in patients whose body immune system has been suppressed medically, for example after a transplant operation.

Herrera /e'reərə/ Francisco de **El Viejo** (the elder) 1576–1656. Spanish painter, active in Seville. He painted genre and religious scenes, with bold effects of light and shade.

Herrera /e'reərə/ Francisco de **El Mozo** (the younger) 1622–1685. Spanish still-life painter, who studied in Rome and worked in Seville and Madrid, where he was court painter and architect. His paintings reflect Murillo's influence. He was the son of the elder Herrera.

Herrick /'herɪk/ Robert 1591–1674. English poet and cleric. Born in Cheapside, London, he was a friend of Ben Jonson. In 1629 he became vicar of

Dean Prior, near Totnes. He published *Hesperides* in 1648, a collection of sacred and pastoral poetry admired for its lyric quality, including 'Gather ye rosebuds' and 'Cherry ripe'.

herring salt-water fish *Clupea harengus*, of the family Clupeidae. It swims close to the surface, and may be 25–40 cm/10–16 in long. A silvered greenish-blue, it has only one dorsal fin and one short ventral fin. The herring is found in large quantities off the shores of NE Europe, the E coast of North America, and the White Sea. Overfishing and pollution have reduced its numbers.

Herriot /ˌerɪ'əʊ/ Edouard 1872–1957. French Radical socialist politician. An opponent of Poincaré, who as prime minister carried out the French occupation of the Ruhr, Germany, he was briefly prime minister 1924–25, 1926, and 1932. As president of the chamber of deputies 1940 he opposed the policies of the right-wing Vichy government, was arrested and later taken to Germany until released 1945 by the Soviets.

Herriot /'herɪət/ James. Pen name of James Alfred Wight 1916– . English writer. A practising veterinary surgeon in Thirsk, Yorkshire from 1940, he wrote of his experiences in a popular series of books including *If Only They Could Talk* 1970, *All Creatures Great and Small* 1972, and *The Lord God Made Them All* 1981.

Herrmann /'hɜ:mən/ Bernard 1911–1975. US composer of film music. He worked for Alfred Hitchcock on several films, and wrote the chilling score for *Psycho* 1960.

Herschel /'hɜ:ʃəl/ Caroline Lucretia 1750–1848. German astronomer, sister of William Herschel, and from 1772 his assistant in England. She discovered eight comets, and was awarded the Royal Astronomical Society's gold medal for her work on her brother's catalogue of star clusters and nebulae.

Herschel /'hɜ:ʃəl/ John Fredrick William 1792–1871. English scientist and astronomer, son of William Herschel. He discovered thousands of close ◊double stars, clusters, and ◊nebulae, reported 1847. His inventions include astronomical instruments, sensitized photographic paper, and the use of sodium thiosulphite to fix it.

Herschel /'hɜ:ʃəl/ William 1738–1822. German-born British astronomer. He was a skilled telescope-maker, and pioneered the study of binary stars and nebulae. In 1781, he discovered Uranus.

Born in Hanover, Germany, he went to England 1757, and became a professional musician, while instructing himself in mathematics and astronomy, and constructing his own reflecting telescopes. While searching for double stars, he found Uranus, and later several of its satellites. This brought him instant fame and, in 1782, the post of private astronomer to George

Hertfordshire

Hertzsprung-Russell diagram

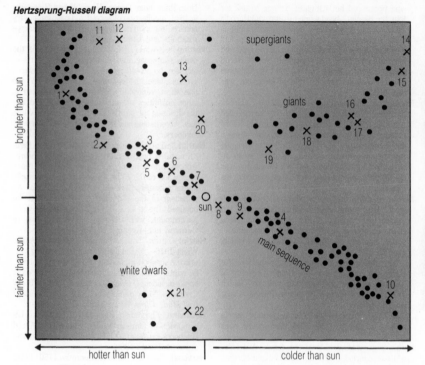

supergiants

giants

sun

main sequence

white dwarfs

brighter than sun

fainter than sun

hotter than sun

colder than sun

1	Spica	7	Procyon A	13	Polaris	18	Arcturus
2	Regulus	8	Tau Ceti	14	Betelgeuse	19	Pollux
3	Vega	9	61 Cygni A	15	Antares	20	Capella
4	61 Cygni B	10	Proxima Centauri	16	Mira	21	Sirius B
5	Sirius A	11	Rigel	17	Aldebaran	22	Procyon B
6	Altair	12	Deneb				

Heseltine *British Conservative Party politician Michael Heseltine. His resignation from the Thatcher cabinet over the Westland affair in 1986 precipitated a grave government crisis.*

III. He discovered the motion of the ◊double stars round one another, and recorded it in his *Motion of the Solar System in Space* 1783. In 1789, he built, at Slough, a 1.2 m/4 ft telescope of 12 m/40 ft focal length, but he made most use of a more satisfactory 46 cm/18 in instrument. He catalogued over 800 double stars, and found over 2,500 nebulae, catalogued by his sister Caroline Herschel; this work was continued by his son John Herschel. By studying the distribution of stars, William established the basic form of the Galaxy. He discovered infrared solar rays 1801, and was knighted 1816.

Herstmonceux /ˌhɜːstmənˈsuː/ village 11 km/ 7 mi N of Eastbourne, East Sussex, England. Since 1958 the buildings of the Royal Greenwich Observatory have been here, alongside the 15th-century castle. The Observatory is, however, to move from Herstmonceux to Cambridge, a process which is expected to take until at least 1991.

Hertford /ˈhɑːfəd/ administrative headquarters of Hertfordshire, SE England, on the river Lea; population (1981) 21,412. There are brewing, engineering, and brick industries.

Hertfordshire /ˈhɑːfədʃə/ county in SE England
area 1,630 sq km/629 sq mi
towns administrative headquarters Hertford; St Albans, Watford, Hatfield, Hemel Hempstead, Bishop's Stortford, Letchworth (the first ◊garden city, followed by Welwyn 1919, and Stevenage 1947)
features rivers Lea, Stort, Colne; part of the Chiltern Hills; Hatfield House; Knebworth House (home of Lord ◊Lytton); Brocket Hall (home of Palmerston and Melbourne); home of G B ◊Shaw at Ayot St Lawrence; Berkhamsted Castle (Norman); Rothamsted agricultural experimental station
products engineering, aircraft, electrical goods, paper and printing; general agricultural

population (1987) 987,000
famous people Graham Greene was born at Berkhamsted.

Hertling /ˈheətlɪŋ/ Count Georg von 1843–1919. German politician who was appointed imperial chancellor in Nov 1917. He maintained a degree of support in the *Reichstag* (parliament) but was powerless to control the military leadership under ◊Ludendorff.

Hertogenbosch see ◊'s-Hertogenbosch, capital of North Brabant, Netherlands.

Herts abbreviation for ◊Hertfordshire.

hertz SI unit (symbol Hz) of frequency (the number of repetitions of a regular occurrence in one second). Radio waves are often measured in megahertz (MHz), millions of hertz. It is named after Heinrich Hertz.

Hertz /heəts/ Heinrich 1857–1894. German physicist who produced and studied electromagnetic waves, showing that their behaviour resembled that of light and heat waves.

He confirmed ◊Maxwell's theory of electromagnetic waves. The unit of frequency, the hertz, is named after him.

Hertzog /ˈhɜːtsɒg/ James Barry Munnik 1866–1942. South African politician, prime minister 1924–39, founder of the Nationalist Party 1913 (the **United South African National Party** from 1933). He opposed South Africa's entry into both world wars.

Hertzog, born in Cape Colony, of Boer descent, was a general in the South African War 1899–1902, rising to assistant chief commandant of the Orange Free State Forces, and in 1910 became minister of justice in the first Union government, under Botha. In 1914 he opposed South African participation in World War I. After the 1924 elections Hertzog became prime minister, and in 1933 the Nationalist Party and Gen Smuts's South African Party were merged as the United South African National Party. In Sept 1939 his motion

against participation in World War II was rejected, and he resigned.

Hertzsprung–Russell diagram in astronomy, a graph on which the surface temperatures of stars are plotted against their luminosities. Most stars, including the Sun, fall into a narrow band called the ◊**main sequence**. When a star grows old it moves from the main sequence to the upper right part of the graph, into the area of the giants and supergiants. At the end of its life, as the star shrinks to become a white dwarf, it moves again, to the bottom left area. It is named after the Dane Ejnar Hertzsprung and the American Henry Norris Russell, who independently devised it in the years 1911–1913.

A star's position on the main sequence depends on its mass, with the least massive stars at the bottom right and the most massive at the top left.

Herzegovina /ˌheətsəɡəˈviːnə/ or **Hercegovina** part of Yugoslavia; see ◊Bosnia and Herzegovina.

Herzl /ˈheətsəl/ Theodor 1860–1904. Austrian founder of the **Zionist** movement. He was born in Budapest and became a successful playwright and journalist. The ◊Dreyfus case convinced him that the only solution to the problem of anti-Semitism was the resettlement of the Jews in a state of their own. His book *Jewish State* 1896 launched political ◊Zionism, and he was the first president of the World Zionist Organization 1897.

Herzog /ˈheətsɒg/ Werner 1942– . German film director whose highly original and visually splendid films, often shot in exotic and impractial locations, include *Aguirre der Zom Gottes*/*Aguirre Wrath of God* 1972, *Nosferatu Phantom der Nacht* 1979, and *Fitzcarraldo* 1982.

Heseltine /ˈhesəltaɪn/ Michael 1933– . English Conservative politician, member of Parliament for Henley, minister of the environment 1979–83. He succeeded John Nott as minister of defence Jan 1983 but resigned Jan 1986 over the ◊Westland affair.

Hesiod /ˈhiːsɪəd/ lived *c.* 700 BC. Greek poet. He is supposed to have lived a little later than Homer, and according to his own account he was born in Boeotia. He is the author of *Works and Days*, a poem that tells of the country life, and the *Theogony*, an account of the origin of the world and of the gods.

Hesse German novelist Hermann Hesse. The main themes of his work are self-knowledge and the opposition of emotion and intellect.

Hesperides /hes'perɪdiːz/ in Greek mythology, the Greek maidens who guarded a tree bearing golden apples in the Islands of the Blessed (also known as the Hesperides).

Hess /hes/ (Walter Richard) Rudolf 1894–1987. German Nazi leader. In 1932 he was appointed deputy Führer to Hitler. On 10 May 1941 he landed by air in the UK with compromise peace proposals, and was held a prisoner of war until 1945, when he was tried at Nuremberg as a war criminal and sentenced to life imprisonment. He died in ◊Spandau prison, Berlin.

Imprisoned with Hitler 1923–25, he became his private secretary, taking down *Mein Kampf* from his dictation. He was effectively in charge of Nazi party organizations until his flight in 1941. For the last years of his life he was the only prisoner left in Spandau.

Hess /hes/ Myra 1890–1965. British pianist. She is remembered for her morale-boosting National Gallery concerts in World War II, her transcription of the Bach chorale 'Jesu, Joy of Man's Desiring', and her interpretations of Beethoven.

Hess /hes/ Victor 1883–1964. Austrian physicist, who emigrated to the US shortly after sharing a Nobel prize in 1936 for the discovery of cosmic radiation.

Hesse /'hesə/ Hermann 1877–1962. German writer who became a Swiss citizen 1923. A conscientious objector in World War I and a pacifist opponent of Hitler, he published short stories, poetry, and novels, including *Peter Camenzind* 1904, *Siddhartha* 1922, and ◊*Steppenwolf* 1927. Later works, such as *Das Glasperlenspiel/The Glass Bead Game* 1943, tend towards the mystical. Nobel prize 1946.

Hessen /'hesən/ administrative region (German *Land*) of West Germany
area 21,100 sq km/8,145 sq mi
capital Wiesbaden
towns Frankfurt-am-Main, Kassel, Darmstadt, Offenbach am Main
physical features valleys of the Rhine and Main; Taunus mountains, rich in mineral springs, as at Homburg and Wiesbaden; see also ◊Swabia
products wine, timber, chemicals, cars, electrical engineering, optical instruments
population (1988) 5,550,000
religion Protestant 61%, Roman Catholic 33%
history until 1945, Hessen was divided in two by a strip of Prussian territory, the southern portion consisting of the valleys of the Rhine and the Main, the northern being dominated by the Vogelsberg (744 m/2,442 ft). Its capital was Darmstadt.

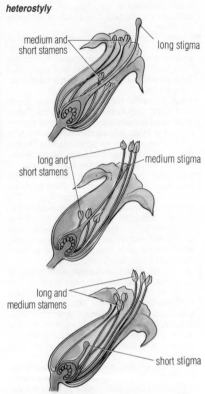

heterostyly

medium and short stamens — long stigma

long and short stamens — medium stigma

long and medium stamens — short stigma

Hestia /'hestiə/ in Greek mythology, the goddess (Roman *Vesta*) of the hearth, daughter of ◊Kronos (Roman Saturn) and Rhea.

Heston /'hestən/ Charlton. Stage name of Charles Carter 1924– . US film actor who often starred in biblical and historical epics (as Moses, for example, in *The Ten Commandments* 1956, and the title role in *Ben-Hur* 1959).

heterophony a form of choral melody singing and playing, found in folk music around the world, in which individual players have some freedom to improvise.

heterosexuality sexual preference for, or attraction mainly to, persons of the opposite sex.

heterosis or *hybrid vigour* an improvement in physical capacities that sometimes occurs in the ◊hybrid produced by mating two genetically different parents.

The parents may be of different strains or varieties within a species, or of different species, as in the mule, which is stronger and has a longer lifespan than either of its parents (donkey and horse). Heterosis is also exploited in hybrid varieties of maize, tomatoes and other crops.

heterostyly in botany, having ◊styles of different lengths. Certain flowers, such as primroses (*Primula vulgaris*), have different-sized ◊anthers and ◊styles to ensure cross-fertilization (through ◊pollination) by visiting insects.

heterotroph any living organism that obtains its energy from organic substances produced by other organisms. All animals and fungi are heterotrophs, and they include herbivores, carnivores, and saprotrophs (which feed on dead animal and plant material).

heterozygous in a living organism, having two different ◊alleles for a given trait. In ◊homozygous organisms, by contrast, both chromosomes carry the same allele. In an outbreeding population an individual organism will generally be heterozygous for some genes but homozygous for others.

heuristics in computing, a process by which a program attempts to improve its performance by learning from its own experience.

Hevesy /'hevəʃi/ Georg von 1885–1966. Swedish chemist, the discoverer of hafnium. He was the first to use radioactive isotope (lead-212) to follow

the steps of a biological process, for which he won the Nobel Prize for Chemistry 1943.

Hewish /'hjuːɪʃ/ Antony 1924– . British radio-astronomer, who was awarded, with Martin ◊Ryle, the Nobel Prize for physics 1974 for his work on ◊pulsars.

hexachlorophene a bactericide, used in minute quantities in soaps and surgical disinfectants.

Trichlorophenol is used in their preparation, and, without precise temperature control, the highly toxic TCDD, or dioxin (tetrachlorodibenzo-*p*-dioxin), may form as a byproduct.

hexadecimal number system a number system to the base 16, used in computing. In hex (as it is commonly known) the decimal numbers 0–15 are represented by the characters 0, 1, 2, 3, 4, 5, 6, 7, 8, 9, A, B, C, D, E, F. Hexadecimal numbers are easy to convert to the computer's internal ◊binary code and are more compact than binary numbers.

Each place in a number increases in value by a power of 16 going from right to left, for instance, 8F is equal to $15 + (8 \times 16) = 143$ in decimal.

Heydrich /'haɪdrɪk/ Reinhard 1904–1942. German Nazi. As head of party's security service and Heinrich ◊Himmler's deputy, he was instrumental in organizing the ◊final solution. While deputy 'protector' of Bohemia and Moravia from 1941, he was ambushed and killed by three members of the Czech forces in Britain, who had landed by parachute. Reprisals followed, including several hundred executions and the massacre of ◊Lidice.

Heyerdahl /'haɪədɑːl/ Thor 1914– . Norwegian ethnologist, who sailed on the raft *Kon Tiki* 1947 from Peru to the Tuamotu Islands along the Humboldt Current, and in 1969–70 used ancient-Egyptian-style papyrus-reed boats to cross the Atlantic. He attempted to prove that ancient civilizations could have travelled the oceans.

His voyages are described in *Kon Tiki*, translated 1950, and *The Ra Expeditions*, translated 1971. He also crossed the Persian Gulf 1977, written about in *The Tigris Expedition*, translated 1981.

Heywood /'heɪwʊd/ Thomas c. 1570–c. 1650. English actor and dramatist. He wrote or adapted over 220 plays, including the domestic tragedy *A Woman kilde with kindnesse* 1607.

Hezekiah /ˌhezɪ'kaɪə/ in the Old Testament or Jewish Bible, King of Judah from 719 BC. Against the advice of the prophet Isaiah he rebelled against Assyrian suzerainty in alliance with Egypt, but was defeated by ◊Sennacherib. He carried out religious reforms.

HF in physics, the abbreviation for *high ◊frequency*.

HGV abbreviation for *heavy goods vehicle*.

Hick Prolific batsman Graeme Hick in the Worcester v. Hampshire match, July 1988.

HI abbreviation for ◊*Hawaii*.

Hiawatha /ˌhaɪəˈwɒθə/ legendary 16th-century North American Indian teacher and Onondaga chieftain, who is said to have welded the Six Nations of the ◊Iroquois into the league of the Long House, as the confederacy was known in what is now upper New York State. He is the hero of Longfellow's epic poem *The Song of Hiawatha*.

Hiawatha, The Song of poem written by H W Longfellow 1855. It is an Indian legend told in the lilting metre of the Finnish national epic *Kalevala*. It was based on data collected by Henry R Schoolcraft (1793–1864).

hibernation a state of ◊dormancy in which certain animals spend the winter. It is associated with a dramatic reduction in body temperature, breathing, pulse rate, and other metabolic processes. It is a fallacy that animals sleep throughout the winter.

The body temperature of the arctic ground squirrel falls to below 0°C during hibernation.

hibiscus plant of the mallow family. Hibiscuses range from large herbaceous plants to trees. Popular as ornamental plants because of their brilliantly coloured red through to white bell-shaped flowers, they include *Hibiscus syriacus* and *Hibiscus rosa-sinensis*.

Some tropical species are also useful: *Hibiscus esculentus*, of which the edible fruit is okra or lady's fingers; *Hibiscus tiliaceus*, which supplies timber and fibrous bark to S Sea islanders; and *Hibiscus sabdariffa*, cultivated in the W Indies and elsewhere for its fruit.

hiccup sharp noise caused by a sudden spasm of the diaphragm with closing of the windpipe, commonly caused by digestive disorder.

hic jacet (Latin 'here lies') an epitaph.

Hick /hɪk/ Graeme 1966– . Rhodesian-born cricketer who became Zimbabwe's youngest professional cricketer at the age of 17. A prolific batsman, he joined Worcestershire, England, in 1984. He achieved the highest score in England in the 20th century in 1988 against Somerset: 405 not out.

Hickey /ˈhɪki/ William 1749–1830. British writer, whose entertaining *Memoirs* were first published 1913–1925.

Hickok /ˈhɪkɒk/ 'Wild Bill' (James Butler) 1837–1876. US pioneer and law enforcer, a legendary figure in the Wild West. In the Civil War he was a sharpshooter and scout for the Union army, and then served as marshal in Kansas, killing many outlaws. He was shot from behind while playing poker in Deadwood, South Dakota.

hickory common tree of the genus *Carya*, native to North America and Asia. It provides a valuable timber, and all species produce nuts, although some are inedible. The pecan *Carya pecan* is widely cultivated in the southern states of the USA, and the shagbark *Carya ovata* in the northern states.

Hickstead English equestrian centre built 1960 at the Sussex home of Douglas Bunn, a leading equestrian figure and administrator. The British Show Jumping Derby has been held there since 1961, as well as many other national and international events.

Hidalgo y Costilla /iːˈdælɡəʊ iː kɒˈstɪljə/ Miguel 1753–1811. Catholic priest, known as 'the Father of Mexican Independence'. A symbol of the opposition to Spain, he rang the church bell in Sept 1810 to announce to his parishioners in Dolores that the revolution against the Spanish had begun. He was captured and shot the following year.

hieroglyphic Egyptian writing system mid-4th millennium BC–3rd century AD, which combines picture signs with those indicating letters. The direction of writing is normally from right to left, the signs facing the beginning of the line. It was deciphered 1822 by the French Egyptologist Jean Champollion with the aid of the ◊Rosetta Stone, which has the same inscription carved in hieroglyphic, demotic, and Greek.

hi-fi the *high-fi*delity, or faithful, reproduction of sound from a machine that plays recorded music or speech. A typical hi-fi system includes a turntable for playing vinyl records, a cassette tape deck to play magnetic tape recordings, a tuner to pick up radio broadcasts, an amplifier to serve all the equipment, possibly a compact disc player, and two or more loudspeakers.

Modern advances in mechanical equipment and electronics, such as digital recording techniques and compact discs, have made it possible to eliminate most distortions in the sound reproduction processes.

Higashi-Osaka /hɪˈɡæʃi əʊˈsɑːkə/ industrial city (textiles, chemicals, engineering), an eastern suburb of Osaka, Kinki region, Honshu island, Japan; population (1987) 503,000.

Higgins /ˈhɪɡɪnz/ George V 1939– . US novelist, author of many detective and underworld novels, often set in Boston. The best known are *The Friends of Eddie Coyle* 1972 and *The Imposters* 1986.

Higgins Jack pseudonym of British novelist Harry ◊Patterson.

High Church a group in the ◊Church of England that emphasizes aspects of Christianity usually associated with Catholics, such as ceremony and hierarchy. The term was first used in 1703 to describe those who opposed Dissenters, and later for groups such as the 19th-century ◊Oxford Movement.

high commissioner representative of one independent Commonwealth country in the capital of another, ranking with ambassador.

Highland Region

High Country New Zealand name for the generally mountainous land above the 750–51,000 m /2,500–30,000 ft level, most of which is in South Island. The lakes, fed by melting snow, are used for hydro-electric power, and it is a skiing, mountaineering, and tourist area.

higher education in most countries, education beyond the age of 18 leading to a degree or similar qualification.

Highland Clearances the forced removal of tenants from large estates in Scotland during the early 19th century, as landowners 'improved' their estates by switching from arable to sheep farming. It led ultimately to widespread emigration to North America.

Highland Games traditional Scottish outdoor gathering which includes tossing the ◊caber, putting the shot, running, dancing, and bagpipe playing. The most famous is the Braemar Gathering.

Highland Region /ˈhaɪlənd/ administrative region of Scotland
area 26,100 sq km/10,077 sq mi
towns administrative headquarters Inverness; Thurso, Wick
features comprises almost half the country; Grampian Mountains; Ben Nevis (highest peak in the UK); Loch Ness, Caledonian Canal; Inner Hebrides; the Queen Mother's castle of Mey at Caithness; John O'Groats' House; Dounreay (with Atomic Energy Authority's prototype fast reactor, and a nuclear processing plant)
products oil services, winter sports, timber, livestock, grouse and deer hunting, salmon fishing
population (1987) 201,000.

Highlands /ˈhaɪləndz/ general name for the plateau of broken rock that covers almost all of Scotland, and extends S of the Highland region itself.

Highsmith /ˈhaɪsmɪθ/ Patricia 1921– . US crime novelist. Her first book, *Strangers on a Train* 1950, was filmed by Hitchcock, and she excels in tension and psychological exploration of character, notably in her series dealing with the amoral Tom Ripley, including *The Talented Mr Ripley* 1956, *Ripley Under Ground* 1971, and *Ripley's Game* 1974.

high tech abbreviation for **high technology** in architecture, buildings that display technical innovation of a high order and celebrate structure and services to create exciting forms and spaces. The Hong Kong and Shanghai Bank, Hong Kong, is the masterpiece of this approach. The Lloyds Building in the City of London, designed by Richard ◊Rogers, dramatically exhibits the service requirements of a large building.

highway in Britain, any road over which there is a right of way; in the USA, a term for a motorway.

highwayman in English history, a thief on horseback who robbed travellers on the highway; those who did so on foot were known as **footpads**. They continued to flourish well into the 19th century. Among the best-known highwaymen were Jonathan ◊Wild, Claude ◊Duval, John Nevison (1639–84), the original hero of the 'ride to York', Dick ◊Turpin and his partner Tom King, and Jerry Abershaw (c. 1773–95).

With the development of regular coach services in the 17th and 18th centuries, the highwaymen's activities became notorious, and the Bow Street runners (see ◊police) were organized to suppress them. Favourite haunts were Hounslow and Bagshot heaths and Epping Forest, around London.

High Wycombe /ˈwɪkəm/ market town in Buckinghamshire, on the river Wye, England; population (1981) 60,500. Products include furniture.

hijacking the illegal seizure or taking control of a vehicle and/or its passengers or goods. The term dates from 1923, and originally referred to the robbing of freight lorries. In recent times it (and its derivative **skyjacking**) has been applied to the seizure of aircraft, usually in flight, by an individual or group, often with some political aim. International treaties (Tokyo 1963, The Hague 1970, and

Hickock *Legendary frontiersman 'Wild Bill' Hickock served as a scout in the American Civil War.*

Hill Scottish photographers David Octavius Hill and Robert R Adamson produced some 2,500 calotypes between 1843 and 1848. This portrait (from about 1843) is an example of this early photography.

Montreal 1971) encourage international cooperation against hijackers and make severe penalties compulsory.

Hijrah or **Hegira** the trip from Mecca to Medina of the prophet Muhammad, which took place AD 622 as a result of the persecution of the prophet and his followers. The Muslim calendar dates from this event, and the day of the Hijrah is celebrated as the Muslim New Year.

Hilbert /'hɪlbət/ David 1862–1943. German mathematician, who founded the formalist school with the publication of *Grundlagen der Geometrie/Foundations of Geometry* in 1899, which was based on his idea of postulates. He attempted to put mathematics on a logical foundation through defining it in terms of a number of basic principles, which ◊Gödel later showed to be impossible; none the less, his attempt greatly influenced 20th-century mathematicians.

Hill British reformer Rowland Hill, who introduced the prepaid postal service, known as the penny post.

Hillary New Zealand mountaineer and explorer Edmund Hillary.

Hildebrand /'hɪldəbrænd/ Benedictine monk who became Pope ◊Gregory VII.

Hildegard of Bingen /'hɪldəgaːd, 'bɪŋən/ 1098–1179. German nun and scientific writer, abbess of the Benedictine convent of St Disibode, near the Rhine, from 1136. She wrote a mystical treatise, *Liber Scivias* 1141, and an encyclopedia of natural history, *Liber Simplicis Medicinae* 1150–60, giving both Latin and German names for the species described, as well as their medicinal uses; it is the earliest surviving scientific book by a woman.

Hildesheim /'hɪldəshaɪm/ industrial town in Lower Saxony, West Germany, linked to the Mittelland Canal; population (1988) 101,000. Products include electronics and hardware. A bishopric from the 9th century, Hildesheim became a free city of the ◊Holy Roman Empire in the 13th century. It was under Prussia 1866–1945.

Hill /hɪl/ David Octavius 1802–1870. Scottish photographer who, in collaboration with ◊Adamson, made extensive use of the ◊calotype process in their large collection of portraits taken in Edinburgh 1843–48.

Hill /hɪl/ Octavia 1838–1912. English campaigner for housing reform and public open spaces. She co-founded the ◊National Trust in 1894.

Hill /hɪl/ Rowland 1795–1879. British Post Office official who invented adhesive stamps and prompted the introduction of the penny prepaid post in 1840 (previously the addressee paid, according to distance, on receipt).

Hillary /'hɪləri/ Edmund 1919– . New Zealand mountaineer. In 1953, with Nepálese Sherpa mountaineer Tenzing Norgay, he reached the summit of Mount Everest, the world's highest peak. As a member of the Commonwealth Transantarctic Expedition 1957–58, he was the first person since Scott to reach the South Pole overland, on 3 Jan 1958.

He was in the reconnaissance party to Everest in 1951. On the way to the South Pole he laid depots for ◊Fuchs's completion of the crossing of the continent.

Hillel 1st-century Jewish teacher and member of the Pharisaic movement (see ◊Pharisee).

Hiller /'hɪlə/ Wendy 1912– . British stage and film actress. Her many roles include Catherine Sloper

Himachal Pradesh

in *The Heiress* 1947 and Eliza in the film version of Shaw's *Pygmalion* 1938.

hill figure in Britain, any of a number of ancient figures, usually of animals, cut from downland turf to show the underlying chalk. Examples include the ◊White Horses, the Long Man of Wilmington, East Sussex, and the Cerne Abbas Giant, Dorset. Their origins are variously attributed to Celts, Romans, Saxons, Druids, or Benedictine monks.

hillfort European Iron Age site with massive banks and ditches for defence, used as both a military camp and a permanent settlement. An example is Maiden Castle, Dorset, England.

Hilliard /'hɪliəd/ Nicholas *c.* 1547–1619. English miniature portraitist and goldsmith, court artist to Elizabeth I from about 1579. His sitters included Francis Drake and Walter Raleigh.

After 1600 he was gradually superseded by his pupil Isaac Oliver. A collection of his delicate portraits, set in gold cases, including *Young Man Amid Roses* about 1590, is in the Victoria and Albert Museum, London.

Hillingdon /'hɪlɪŋdən/ borough of W London; population (1984) 232,200

features London Airport at Heathrow (built on the site of a Neolithic settlement); Jacobean mansion (Swakeleys) at Ickenham; Brunel University 1966; Grand Union Canal; includes Uxbridge.

Hillsborough Agreement another name for the ◊Anglo-Irish Agreement 1985.

Hilton /'hɪltən/ James 1900–1954. English novelist. He settled in Hollywood as one of its most successful script writers, his work including *Mrs Miniver*. His books include *Lost Horizon* 1933, envisaging Shangri-la, a remote district of Tibet where time stands still; *Goodbye, Mr Chips* 1934, a portrait of an old schoolmaster; and *Random Harvest* 1941.

Hilversum /'hɪlvəsʊm/ town in North Holland province of the Netherlands, 27 km/17 mi SE of Amsterdam; population (1988) 103,000. Besides being a summer resort, Hilversum is the chief centre of Dutch broadcasting.

Himachal Pradesh /hɪˈmaːtʃəl prəˈdeʃ/ state of NW India

area 55,700 sq km/21,500 sq mi

capital Simla

features mainly agricultural state, one third forested, with softwood timber industry

products timber, grain, rice, fruit

population (1981) 4,238,000, mainly Hindu

language Pahari

history created as a Union Territory 1948, it became a full state 1971. Certain hill areas were transferred to Himachal Pradesh from the Punjab 1966.

Himalayas /ˌhɪməˈleɪəz/ vast mountain system of central Asia, extending from the Indian states of Kashmir in the W to Assam in the E, covering the S part of Tibet, Nepál, Sikkim, and Bhutan. It is the highest mountain range in the world. The two highest peaks are **Mount ◊Everest**

Hinduism Prambanan in central Java was completed about AD 900, and the three principal Hindu temples are dedicated to Brahma, Siva, and Vishnu.

and ◊*Kangchenjunga*. Other major peaks include Makalu, Annapurna, and Nanga Parbat, all over 8,000 m/26,000 ft.

Himes /haɪmz/ Chester 1909–1984. US novelist. After serving seven years in prison for armed robbery, he published his first novel *If He Hollers Let Him Go* 1945, a depiction of the drudgery and racism in a Californian shipyard. Other novels include *Blind Man with a Pistol* 1969.

Himmler /'hɪmlə/ Heinrich 1900–1945. German Nazi leader, head of the ◊SS elite corps from 1929, the police and the Gestapo secret police from 1936. During World War II he replaced Goering as Hitler's second-in-command. He was captured May 1945, and committed suicide.

Born in Munich, he joined the Nazi Party in its early days, and became chief of the Bavarian police 1933. His accumulation of offices meant he had command of all German police forces by 1936, which made him one of the most powerful people in Germany. In Apr 1945 he made a proposal to the Allies that Germany should surrender to Britain and the USA but not to the USSR, which was rejected.

Hinault /ɪ'nəʊ/ Bernard 1954– . French cyclist, one of three men to have won the ◊Tour de France five times (1978–1985), the others being Jacques ◊Anquetil and Eddie ◊Merckx.

CAREER HIGHLIGHTS

Tour de France: 1978–79, 1981–82, 1985
Tour of Italy: 1980, 1982, 1985
Tour of Spain: 1978, 1983
World Professional Road Race Champion: 1980

Hīnayāna (Sanskrit 'lesser vehicle') Mahāyāna Buddhist name for ◊Theravāda Buddhism.

Hinckley /'hɪŋkli/ market town in Leicestershire, England; population (1981) 55,250. Industries include engineering and the manufacture of footwear and hosiery.

Hindemith /'hɪndəmɪt/ Paul 1895–1963. German composer. His Neo-Classical, contrapuntal works include chamber ensemble and orchestral pieces, such as the *Symphonic Metamorphosis on Themes of Carl Maria von Weber* 1944, and the operas *Cardillac* 1926, revised 1952, and *Mathis der Maler/Mathis the Painter* 1938.

A fine viola player, he led the Frankfurt Opera Orchestra at 20, and taught at the Berlin Hochschule for music 1927–33. The modernity

of his work, such as the *Philharmonic Concerto* 1932, led to a Nazi ban. In 1939 he went to the USA, where he taught at Yale University. In 1951 he became professor of musical theory at Zürich.

Hindenburg /'hɪndənbɜːg/ German name 1915–45 of the Polish city of ◊Zabrze, in honour of General Hindenburg.

Hindenburg /'hɪndənbɜːg/ Paul Ludwig Hans von Beneckendorf und Hindenburg 1847–1934. German field marshal and right-wing politician. During World War I he was supreme commander and, together with Ludendorff, practically directed Germany's policy until the end of the war. He was president of Germany 1925–33.

Born in Posen of a Prussian Junker (aristocratic landowner) family, he was commissioned 1866, served in the Austro-Prussian and Franco-German wars, and retired 1911. Given the command in East Prussia Aug 1914, he received the credit for the defeat of the Russians at ◊Tannenberg, and was promoted to supreme commander and field marshal. Re-elected president 1932, he was compelled to invite Hitler to assume the chancellorship Jan 1933.

Hindenburg Line German western line of World War I fortifications built 1916–17.

Hindi language a member of the Indo-Iranian branch of the Indo-European language family, the official language of the Republic of India, although resisted as such by the Dravidian-speaking states of the south. Hindi proper is used by some 30% of Indians, in such N states as Uttar Pradesh and Madhya Pradesh.

Hindi has close historical and cultural links with Sanskrit, the classical language of Hinduism, and is written (from left to right) in Devanagari script. Bihari, Punjabi, and Rajasthani, the dominant language varieties in the states of Bihar, Punjab, and Rajasthan, are claimed by some to be varieties of Hindi, by others to be distinct languages.

Hinduism religion originating in N India about 4,000 years ago, which is superficially and in some of its forms polytheistic, but has a concept of the supreme spirit, ◊Brahman, above the many divine manifestations. These include the triad of chief gods (the Trimurti): Brahma, Vishnu, and Siva (creator, preserver, and destroyer). Central ideas in Hinduism include reincarnation and ◊karma; the oldest scriptures are the *Vedas*. Temple worship is almost universally performed and there are many festivals. There are over 805 million Hindus worldwide. Women are not regarded as the equals of men but should be treated with kindness and respect. Muslim influence in N India led to veiling of women and the restriction of their movements from about the end of the 12th century.

scriptures The *Veda* collection of hymns was followed by the philosophical *Upanishads*, centring on the doctrine of Brahman, and the epics *Rāmāyana* and *Mahābhārata* (which includes the *Bhagavad-Gītā*), all from before the Christian era.

beliefs The cosmos is seen as both real and an illusion (*maya*), since its reality is not lasting; the cosmos is itself personified as the goddess Maya. In addition to the various guises of the Trimurti, there are numerous lesser divinities, for example Ganesa, Hanuman, and Lakshmi, and demons, ghosts, and spirits who are also revered.

practice Hinduism has a complex of rites and ceremonies performed within the framework of the caste system under the supervision of the Brahman priests and teachers.

Hindu Kush /'hɪndu: 'kʊʃ/ mountain range in central Asia; length 800 km/500 mi; greatest height Tirich Mir 7,690 m/25,239 ft, Pakistan. The *Khyber Pass*, a narrow defile (53 km/33 mi long), separates Pakistan from Afghanistan, and was used by ◊Zahir and other invaders of India. The present road was built by the British in the Afghan Wars.

Hindustan /ˌhɪndu:'stɑːn/ ('land of the Hindus') a term loosely applied to the whole of India, but more specifically to the plain of the Ganges and

Jumna rivers, or that part of India N of the Deccan.

Hindustani /ˌhɪndu'stɑːni/ a member of the Indo-Iranian branch of the Indo-European language family, closely related to Hindi and Urdu and originating in the bazaars of Delhi. It is a lingua franca in many parts of the Republic of India.

It was the contact language during the British Raj between many of the British in India and the native Indians. It is sometimes known as Bazaar Hindi.

Hine /haɪn/ Lewis 1874–1940. US sociologist. He recorded in photographs child-labour conditions in US factories at the beginning of this century, leading to a change in the law.

Hinkler /'hɪŋklə/ Herbert John Louis 1892–1933. Australian pilot who in 1928 made the first solo flight from England to Australia. He was killed while making another attempt to fly to Australia.

Hinshelwood /'hɪnʃəlwʊd/ Cyril 1897–1967. British chemist. Hinshelwood shared the 1956 Nobel Chemistry Prize with Nikolay Semenov for his work on chemical chain reactions. He also studied the chemistry of bacterial growth.

hip-hop a style of popular music originating in New York in the early 1980s. It uses scratching (a percussive effect obtained by manually rotating a vinyl record) and heavily accented electronic drums behind a ◊rap vocal. The term 'hip-hop' also includes break dancing and graffiti.

Hipparchos acronym for the *high-precision parallax-collecting satellite* launched by the European Space Agency in Aug 1989. Named after the Greek astronomer Hipparchus, it is the world's first ◊astrometry satellite designed to provide the first measurements of the positions and apparent motions of stars from space. The accuracy of these measurements will be far greater than from ground-based telescopes. However, because of engine failure, Hipparchos is making more limited orbits than had been planned, which may restrict the data it can provide.

Hipparchus /hɪ'pɑːkəs/ *c.* 555–514 BC. Greek tyrant. Son of ◊Pisistratus, he was associated with his elder brother Hippias as ruler of Athens 527–514 BC. His affection being spurned by Harmodius, he insulted Harmodius's sister, and was assassinated by him and Aristogiton.

Hipparchus /hɪ'pɑːkəs/ *c.* 190–*c.* 120 BC. Greek astronomer, who invented trigonometry, calculated the lengths of the solar year and the lunar month, discovered the precession of the equinoxes, made a catalogue of 800 fixed stars, and advanced Eratosthenes' method of determining the situation of places on the Earth's surface by lines of latitude and longitude.

hippie a member of a youth movement of the mid-to late 1960s, which originated in San Francisco, California, and was characterized by nonviolent anarchy, concern for the environment, and rejection of Western materialism. The hippies formed an artistically prolific counterculture in North America and Europe. Their colourful psychedelic style, influenced by drugs such as ◊LSD, emerged especially in graphic art and music by bands such as Love (1965–71), the Grateful Dead (1965–), Jefferson Airplane (1965–74), and ◊Pink Floyd.

Hippocrates /hɪ'pɒkrəti:z/ *c.* 460–*c.* 370 BC. Greek physician, often called the founder of medicine. Important Hippocratic ideas include cleanliness (for patients and physicians), moderation in eating and drinking, letting nature take its course, and living where the air is good.

hippopotamus

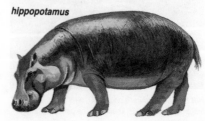

Hirohito *Emperor Hirohito of Japan in ceremonial robes.*

He was born and practised on the island of Kos and died at Larissa. He is known to have discovered aspirin in willow bark. The *Corpus Hippocraticum*, a group of some 70 works, is attributed to him, but was probably not written by him at all, although they outline the particular approach to medicine that he put forward. They include the famous *Aphorisms* and the *Hippocratic Oath*, which embodies the essence of medical ethics. He believed that health was the result of the 'humours' of the body being in balance; imbalance caused disease. These ideas were later adopted by ◊Galen.

Hippolytus /hɪ'pɒlɪtəs/ in Greek mythology, the son of Theseus, who cursed him for his supposed dishonourable advances to his stepmother Phaedra. Killed by Poseidon as he rode near the sea in his chariot, he was restored to life when his innocence was proven.

hippopotamus (Greek 'river-horse') large herbivorous hoofed mammal of the family Hippopotamidae. The *common hippopotamus Hippopotamus amphibius* is found in Africa. It is over 4 m/13 ft long, 1.5 m/5 ft high, weighs about 4,500 kg/5 tons, and has a brown or slate-grey skin. It is an endangered species.

A social and gregarious animal, the hippopotamus spends the day wallowing in rivers or waterholes only emerging at night to graze. The *pygmy hippopotamus Hippopotamus liberiensis* inhabits West Africa.

hire purchase (HP) a form of credit under which the buyer pays a deposit and makes instalment payments at fixed intervals over a certain period for a particular item. The buyer has immediate possession, but does not own the item until the final instalment has been paid.

Hire purchase of consumer durables is still common although much of the HP market has been eroded by the widespread use of credit cards, 'budget accounts' offered by shops, and bank loans. Interest rates charged on HP agreements are usually extremely high.

Hirohito /ˌhɪərəʊ'hiːtəʊ/ 1901–1989. Emperor of Japan from 1926. He succeeded his father Yoshihito. After the defeat of Japan 1945 he was made to reject belief in the divinity of the emperor and Japanese racial superiority, and accept the 1946 constitution greatly curtailing his powers. He was succeeded by his son ◊Akihito.

In 1921 Hirohito was the first Japanese crown prince to visit Europe. The imperial palace, destroyed by fire in air raids 1945, was rebuilt within the same spacious wooded compound 1969. Dis-

tinguished as a botanist and zoologist, Hirohito published several books.

Hiroshige /ˌhɪə'rəʊʃɪgeɪ/ Andō 1797–1858. Japanese artist whose landscape prints, often using snow or rain to create atmosphere, were highly popular in his time, notably *Tōkaidō gojūsantsugi/53 Stations on the Tokaido Highway* 1833.

Hiroshige was born in Edo (now Tokyo), and his last series was *Meisho Edo Hyakkei/100 Famous Views of Edo* 1856–58, uncompleted before his death. He is thought to have made over 5,000 different prints. Whistler and van Gogh were among Western painters influenced by him.

Hiroshima /hɪ'rɒʃɪmə/ industrial city (cars) and port on the S coast of Honshu, Japan, destroyed by the first wartime use of an atomic bomb 6 Aug 1945. The city has largely been rebuilt since the war; population (1987) 1,034,000.

Towards the end of World War II the city was utterly devastated by the US atom bomb. More than 10 sq km/4 sq mi was obliterated, with very heavy damage outside that area. Casualties totalled at least 137,000 out of a population of 343,000: 78,150 were found dead, others died later.

Hispanic /hɪ'spænɪk/ a Spanish-speaking person in the USA, either native-born or immigrant from Mexico, Cuba, Puerto Rico, or any other Spanish-speaking country.

Hispaniola /ˌhɪspæni'əʊlə/ (Spanish 'little Spain') West Indian island, first landing place of Columbus in the New World, 6 Dec 1492; now divided into ◊Haiti and the ◊Dominican Republic.

Hispano-Suiza /hɪ'spænəʊ 'suːɪzə/ car designed by a Swiss engineer Marc Birkigt (1878–1947), who emigrated to Barcelona, where he founded a factory that produced cars (*c.* 1900–38), legendary for their handling, elegance, and speed. During World War I the Hispano-Suiza company produced a light-alloy aero-engine for the French air force.

Hiss /hɪs/ Alger 1904– . US diplomat and liberal Democrat, a former State Department official, controversially imprisoned 1950 for allegedly having spied for the USSR.

Hiss, president of the Carnegie Endowment for International Peace and one of President Roosevelt's advisers at the 1945 ◊Yalta Conference, was accused 1948 by a former Soviet agent, Whittaker Chambers (1901–61), of having passed information to the USSR during the period 1926–37. He was convicted of perjury for swearing before the House Committee to Investigate Un-American Activities that he had not spied for the USSR (under the statute of limitations he could not be convicted of the original crime). Richard ◊Nixon was a leading member of the prosecution, which inspired the subsequent anticommunist witch-hunts of Senator Joe ◊McCarthy. There are doubts about the justice of Hiss's conviction.

histamine an inflammatory substance, released in damaged tissues, which accounts for many of the

symptoms of ◊allergy. Drugs used to neutralize its activity are known as ◊antihistamines.

histochemistry the study of plant and animal tissue by visual examination, usually with a ◊microscope. ◊Stains are often used to highlight structural characteristics, such as the presence of starch or distribution of fats.

histogram a graph with the horizontal axis having discrete units or class boundaries with contiguous end points, and the vertical axis representing the frequency. Blocks are drawn such that their area is proportional to the frequencies within a class or across several class boundaries. There are no spaces between blocks.

histology the medical speciality concerned with the laboratory study of cells and tissues.

historical novel a fictional prose narrative set in the past. Literature set in the historic rather than the immediate past has always abounded, but in the West Walter Scott began the modern tradition by setting imaginative romances of love, impersonation, and betrayal in a past based on known fact; his use of historical detail, and that of European imitators such as Manzoni, gave rise to the genre.

Some historical novels of the 19th century were overtly nationalistic, but most were merely novels set in the past to heighten melodrama while providing an informative framework; the genre was used by Victor Hugo and Charles Dickens, among many others. In the 20th century the historical novel also became concerned with exploring psychological states and the question of the difference in the mentality of the past. Examples of this are Robert Graves's novels about the Roman emperor *I, Claudius* and *Claudius the God*, and Margaret Yourcenar's *Memoirs of Hadrian*.

The less serious possibilities of the historical novel were exploited by popular writers in the early 20th century as *historical romance*, revived with some success in the late 1960s. The historical novel acquired sub-genres – the stylized *Regency novel* of Georgette Heyer (1902–74) and her imitators, and the Napoleonic War sea story of C S Forester. These forms have developed their own conventions, particularly when imitating a massively popular ancestor – this has happened in large degree to the *western*, many of which use gestures from Owen Wister's classic *The Virginian*, and to the novel of the US South in the period of the Civil War, in the wake of Margaret Mitchell's *Gone With the Wind*. In the late 20th century sequences of novels about families, often industrialists of the early 19th century, have been popular.

history the record of the events of human societies. The earliest surviving historical records are the inscriptions denoting the achievements of Egyptian and Babylonian kings. As a literary form in the Western world, historical writing or *historiography* began with the Greek Herodotus in the 4th century BC, who was first to pass beyond

Hiroshima *The total devastation caused by the atom bomb on Hiroshima towards the end of World War II.*

the limits of a purely national outlook. Contemporary historians make extensive use of statistics, population figures, and primary records to justify historical arguments.

Herodotus's contemporary Thucydides brought to history not only literary gifts but the interests of a scientific investigator and political philosopher. Later Greek history and Roman history tended towards rhetoric; Sallust preserved the scientific spirit of Thucydides, but Livy and Tacitus, in spite of their insight and literary distinction, tended to subordinate factual accuracy to patriotic or party considerations. Medieval history was dominated by a religious philosophy imposed by the church. English chroniclers of this period are Bede, William of Malmesbury, and Matthew Paris. France produced great chroniclers of contemporary events in Froissart and Comines.

The Renaissance revived historical writing and the study of history both by restoring classical models and by creating the science of textual criticism. A product of the new secular spirit was Machiavelli's *History of Florence* 1520–23. This critical approach continued into the 17th century but the 18th century ◊Enlightenment disposed of the attempt to explain history in theological terms, and produced an interpretive masterpiece by Gibbon *The Decline and Fall of the Roman Empire* 1776–88. An attempt to formulate a *historical method* and a philosophy of history, that of the Italian Vico, remained almost unknown until the 19th century. Romanticism left its mark on 19th century historical writing in the tendency to exalt the contribution of the individual ' hero', and in the introduction of a more colourful and dramatic style and treatment, variously illustrated in the works of the French historian Jules Michelet (1798–1874), and the British writers Carlyle and Macaulay.

During the 20th century the study of history has been revolutionized, partly through the contributions of other disciplines, such as the sciences and anthropology. The deciphering of the Egyptian and Babylonian inscriptions was of great importance. Researchers and archaeologists have traced the development of prehistoric human beings, and have revealed forgotten civilizations such as that of Crete. Anthropological studies of primitive society and religion, which began with Frazer's *Golden Bough* 1890, have attempted to analyse the bases of later forms of social organization and belief. The changes brought about by the Industrial Revolution and the accompanying perception of economics as a science forced historians to turn their attention to economic questions. Marx's attempt to find in economic development the most significant, although by not the only determining factor in social change, an argument partly paralleled in

Hitchcock Suspense, melodrama, and fleeting personal appearances are the hallmarks of Alfred Hitchcock's films.

History of Civilization in England 1857 by Henry Thomas Buckle (1821–62), has influenced historians since. A comparative study of civilizations is offered in A J Toynbee's *Study of History* 1934–54, and on a smaller scale by J M Roberts' *History of the World* 1976. Contemporary historians make a distinction between historical evidence or records, historical writing, and historical method or approaches to the study of history.

history of ideas the discipline that studies the history and development of ideas and theories in terms of their origins and influences. The historian of ideas seeks to understand their significance in their original contexts.

Hitachi /hɪˈtɑːtʃi/ city on Honshu, Japan; population 204,000. The chief industry is the manufacture of electrical goods.

Hitchcock /ˈhɪtʃkɒk/ Alfred 1899–1980. English director of suspense films, noted for his camera work, and for making 'walk-ons' in his own films. His films include *The Thirty-Nine Steps* 1935, *The Lady Vanishes* 1939, *Rebecca* 1940, *Strangers on a Train* 1951, *Psycho* 1960, and *The Birds* 1963.

Hitchens /ˈhɪtʃɪnz/ Ivon 1893–1979. British painter. His semi-abstract landscapes were painted initially in natural tones, later in more vibrant colours. He also painted murals, for example, *Day's Rest, Day's Work* 1963 (Sussex University).

Hitchin /ˈhɪtʃɪn/ market town in Hertfordshire, England, 48 km/30 mi NW of London; population (1985) 30,000. The cultivation and distillation of lavender, introduced from Naples in the 16th century, still continues.

Hitler /ˈhɪtlə/ Adolf 1889–1945. German Nazi dictator, born in Austria. Führer (leader) of the Nazi party from 1921, author of *Mein Kampf/My Struggle* 1925–27. Chancellor of Germany from 1933 and head of state from 1934, he created a dictatorship by playing party and state institutions against each other, and continually creating new offices and appointments. His position was not seriously challenged until the 'Bomb Plot' 20 July 1944. In foreign affairs, he reoccupied the Rhineland and formed an alliance with the Italian fascist Mussolini 1936, annexed Austria 1938, and occupied Sudetenland under the ◊Munich Agreement. The rest of Czechoslovakia was annexed Mar 1939. The ◊Hitler–Stalin pact was followed in Sept by the invasion of Poland and the declaration of war by Britain and France (see ◊World War II). He committed suicide as Berlin fell.

Born at Braunau-am-Inn, the son of a customs official, he spent his early years in poverty in Vienna and Munich. After serving as a volunteer in the German army during World War I, he was employed as a spy by the military authorities in Munich, and in 1919 joined in this capacity the German Workers' Party. By 1921 he had assumed its leadership, renamed it the National Socialist German Workers' Party, and provided it with a programme that mixed nationalism and ◊anti-Semitism. Having led an unsuccessful rising in Munich 1923, he was sentenced to nine months' imprisonment, during which he wrote his political testament, *Mein Kampf*. The party did not achieve national importance until the elections of 1930; by 1932, although Field Marshal Hindenburg defeated Hitler in the presidential elections, it formed the largest group in the Reichstag (parliament). As the result of an intrigue directed by the chancellor von Papen, Hitler became chancellor in a Nazi-Nationalist coalition 30 Jan 1933.

The opposition were rapidly suppressed, the Nationalists removed from the government, and the Nazis declared the only legal party. In 1934 Hitler succeeded Hindenburg as head of state. Meanwhile, the drive to war began; Germany left the League of Nations, conscription was reintroduced, and in 1936 the Rhineland was reoccupied. Hitler and Mussolini, who were already both involved in Spain, formed an alliance 1936. Hitler narrowly escaped death 1944 from a bomb explosion prepared by high-ranking officers.

Hitler German Nazi leader Adolf Hitler at Berchtesgaden, Bavaria.

On 29 Apr 1945, when Berlin was largely in Soviet hands, he married Eva Braun in his bunker under the chancellory building, and on the following day committed suicide with her, both bodies afterwards being burned.

Hitler–Stalin pact nonaggression treaty between Germany and the USSR signed 25 Aug 1939. It secretly allowed for the partition of Poland between the two countries and formed a sufficient security in the east for Hitler's declaration of war on Poland 1 Sept 1939. This alliance of two apparently inimical ideologies was ended only by the German invasion of the USSR 22 June 1941.

Hittite /ˈhɪtaɪt/ member of a group of peoples who inhabited Anatolia and N Syria from the 3rd to the 1st millennium BC. The city of Hattusas (now Boğazköy in central Turkey) became the capital of a strong kingdom, which overthrew the Babylonian empire. After a period of eclipse the Hittite New Empire became a great power (about 1400–1200 BC) which successfully waged war with Egypt. The Hittite language is an Indo-European language.

The original Hittites, a people of Armenian/Anatolian type, inhabited a number of city-states in E Anatolia, one of which, Hatti, gained supremacy over the others. An Indo-European people invaded the country about 2000 BC, made themselves the ruling class, and intermarried with the original inhabitants. The Hittites developed advanced military, political, and legal systems. The New Empire concluded a peace treaty with Egypt 1269 BC, but was eventually overthrown by the Sea Peoples. Small Hittite states then arose in N Syria, the most important of which was ◊Carchemish; these were conquered by the Assyrians in the 8th century BC. Carchemish was conquered 717.

The Hittites used a cuneiform script, modelled on the Babylonian, for ordinary purposes, and a hieroglyphic script for monumental inscriptions. The Hittite royal archives were discovered at Hattusas 1906–07 and deciphered 1915.

HIV abbreviation for *Human Immunodeficiency Virus*, the infectious agent that causes ◊AIDS.

HMSO abbreviation for *His/Her Majesty's Stationery Office*.

Hoare–Laval Pact plan for a peaceful settlement to the Italian invasion of Ethiopia in Oct 1935. It was devised by Samuel Hoare (1880–1959), British foreign secretary, and Pierre Laval (1883–1945), French premier, at the request of the ◊League of Nations. Realizing no European country was willing to go to war over Ethiopia, Hoare and Laval proposed official recognition of Italian claims. Public outcry in Britain against the pact's seeming approval of Italian aggression was so great that the pact had to be disowned and Hoare was forced to resign.

Hobbes *English political philosopher Thomas Hobbes believed that absolutist government was the only means of ensuring order and security.*

hoatzin tropical bird *Opisthocomus hoatzin* found only in the Amazon, resembling a small pheasant in size and appearance. Adults are olive with white markings above and red-brown below. The young are hatched naked, and have well-developed claws on the 'thumb and index fingers' of the wing, which they use to crawl reptilian-fashion about the tree – a possible reminder of their ancestry. These later fall off.

Hoban /ˈhəʊbən/ James C 1762–1831. Irish-born architect who emigrated to the USA. His best-known building is the White House, Washington DC, and he also worked on the Capitol and other public buildings.

Hobart /ˈhəʊbɑːt/ capital and port of Tasmania, Australia; population (1986) 180,000. Products include zinc, textiles, and paper. Founded 1804 as a pearl colony, it was named after Lord Hobart, then Secretary of State for the Colonies. The University of Tasmania, established 1890, is at Hobart.

Hobbema /ˈhɒbɪmə/ Meindert 1638–1709. Dutch landscape painter. He was a pupil of Ruisdael and his early work is derivative, but later works are characteristically realistic and unsentimental. He was popular with English collectors in the 18th and 19th centuries, and influenced English landscape painting.

Hobbes /hɒbz/ Thomas 1588–1679. English political philosopher, and the first thinker since Aristotle to attempt to develop a comprehensive theory of nature, including human behaviour. In *The Leviathan* 1651 he advocates absolutist government as the only means of ensuring order and security; he saw this as deriving from the ◊social contract. He was tutor to the exiled Prince Charles.

Ho Chi Minh *President Ho Chi Minh of Vietnam.*

hockey

An 11-a-side team game played either indoors or outdoors. The object is to score goals by passing a small ball (circumference about 228 mm/9 in) with the aid of a hooked stick. Goals are positioned at each end of the pitch.

the hockey stick
Hockey sticks are made of wood and must have a flat face. The rules do not restrict their length, but most are approximately 1.15 m/3 ft 9 in long.

the pitch

54.86m (180ft)
goal
penalty spot
shooting circle
91.44m (300ft)
4.57m (15ft) line
22.86m (75ft) line
14.63m (48ft)
48ft
goal line
goal

the short corner

The short corner is a free stroke awarded to the attacking team. It is taken from a position not less than 9.14 m/30 ft from the goal. The attacking team should be outside the shooting circle and no more than six defenders should be behind their own goal line.

Hobbit, The or **There and Back Again** a fantasy for children by J R R ◊Tolkien, published in the UK 1937. It describes the adventures of Bilbo Baggins, a 'hobbit' (small humanoid) in an ancient world, Middle-Earth, populated by dragons, dwarves, elves, and other mythical creatures, including the wizard Gandalf.

The Hobbit, together with Tolkien's later trilogy *The Lord of the Rings* 1954–55, achieved cult status in the 1960s.

Hobbs /hɒbz/ John Berry 'Jack' 1882–1963. England cricketer who represented his country 61 times. In all first-class cricket he scored a world record 61,237 runs, including a record 197 centuries in a career that lasted nearly 30 years.

CAREER HIGHLIGHTS

all first-class matches
runs: 61,237; average: 50.65
best: 316 not out Surrey v. Middlesex, 1926
test cricket
runs: 5,410; average: 56.94
best: 211 v. South Africa, 1924

hobby a small falcon *Falco subbuteo* found across Europe and N Asia. It is about 30 cm/1 ft long, with grey back, streaked front and chestnut thighs. It is found in open woods and heaths, and feeds on insects and small birds.

Hoboken /ˈhəʊbəʊkən/ city and port in NE New Jersey, USA, on the Hudson river; population (1980) 42,460.

Hochhuth /ˈhəʊxhuːt/ Rolf 1931– . Swiss dramatist, whose controversial play *Soldaten/Soldiers* 1968 implied that the British politician Churchill was involved in a plot to assassinate the Polish general ◊Sikorski.

Ho Chi Minh /ˌhəʊ tʃiː ˈmɪn/ adopted name of Nguyen That Tan 1890–1969. North Vietnamese Communist politician, president from 1954. He was trained in Moscow, and headed the communist Vietminh from 1941. Having campaigned against the French 1946–54, he became president and prime minister of the republic at the armistice. Aided by the communist bloc, he did much to develop industrial potential. He relinquished the premiership 1955, but continued as president.

Hockney The work of English painter David Hockney is deliberately childlike and characterized by a gentle wit. This painting, 'Peter Getting out of Nick's Pool', is typical of his Californian style: flat and shadowless, and showing his interest in depicting moving water.

Ho Chi Minh City /ˌhəʊ tʃiː ˈmɪn/ formerly *Saigon* chief port and industrial city of S Vietnam; population (1985) 3,500,000. Industries include shipbuilding, textiles, rubber, and food products. Saigon was the capital of the Republic of Vietnam (South Vietnam) 1954–76, when it was renamed.

Ho Chi Minh Trails North Vietnamese troop and supply routes to South Vietnam via Laos during the Vietnam War.

hockey a game played with hooked sticks and a ball, the object being to hit the ball into the goal. It is played between two teams, each of not more than 11 players. Hockey has been an Olympic sport since 1908 for men and since 1980 for women. In North America it is known as 'field hockey', to distinguish it from ◊ice hockey.

The ground is 91.5 m/100 yd long and 54.9 m/60 yd wide. Goals, 2.13 m/7 ft high and 3.65 m/4 yd wide, are placed within a striking circle of 14.64 m/16 yd radius, from which all shots at goal must be made. The white ball weighs about 155 g/5.5 oz, circumference about 228 mm/9 in. Most sticks are about 91 cm/3 ft long and they must not exceed 50 mm/2 in diameter. The game is started by a 'push-back'. The ball may be stopped with the hand, but not held, picked up, thrown or kicked, except by the goalkeeper in his or her own striking circle. If the ball is sent into touch, it is returned to play by a 'push-in'. The game is divided into two 35-minute periods; it is controlled by two umpires, one for each half of the field.

A game using hooked sticks was played by the ancient Greeks, and under the names of 'hurley' and 'shinty', a form of the game was played in Ireland and Scotland. Modern hockey in Britain dates from 1886 when the Men's Hockey Association rules were drafted. The women's game is governed by the All England Women's Hockey Association, founded 1895. Indoor hockey is becoming increasingly popular in the UK and Europe.

hockey: recent winners

Olympic Games	
men	
1960	Pakistan
1964	India
1968	Pakistan
1972	West Germany
1976	New Zealand
1980	India
1984	Pakistan
1988	Great Britain
women	
1980	Zimbabwe
1984	Holland
1988	Australia

Hockney /ˈhɒkni/ David 1937– . English painter, printmaker, and designer, resident in California. In the early 1960s he contributed to the Pop art movement. His portraits and views of swimming pools and modern houses reflect a preoccupation with surface pattern and effects of light. He has produced etchings, photo collages, and sets for opera.

Hockney, born in Yorkshire, studied at Bradford School of Art and the Royal College of Art, London, and exhibited at the Young Contemporaries Show of 1961. Abandoning Pop art, he developed an individual figurative style, and has prolifically experimented with technique. He was the subject of Jack Hazan's semidocumentary 1973 film *A Bigger Splash*; it is also the title of one of his paintings (1967). Hockney has designed sets for Glyndebourne, East Sussex, La Scala, Milan, and the Metropolitan Opera House, New York.

Hodeida /hɒˈdeɪdə/ or *Al Hudaydah* Red Sea port of North Yemen; population (1986) 155,000. It trades in coffee and spices.

Hodgkin /ˈhɒdʒkɪn/ Alan Lloyd 1914– . British physiologist engaged in research with Andrew Huxley on the mechanism of conduction in peripheral nerves 1946–60. In 1963 they shared

Hodgkin Nobel prizewinner in chemistry Professor Dorothy Crowfoot Hodgkin is the first woman since Florence Nightingale to be awarded the Order of Merit. She is also a campaigner for nuclear disarmament.

the Nobel Prize for Physiology and Medicine with John Eccles.

Hodgkin /ˈhɒdʒkɪn/ Dorothy Crowfoot 1910– . English biochemist who analysed the structure of penicillin, insulin, and vitamin B_{12}. Hodgkin was the first to use a computer to analyse the molecular structure of complex chemicals, and this enabled her to produce three-dimensional models. Nobel Prize for Chemistry 1964.

Hodgkin /ˈhɒdʒkɪn/ Thomas 1798–1856. British physician, who first recognized ***Hodgkin's disease*** (lymphadenoma), a cancer-like enlargement of the lymphatic glands.

Hodgkin's disease rare form of cancer (also known as *lymphadenoma*), mainly affecting the lymph nodes and spleen. It undermines the immune system, leaving the sufferer more susceptible to infection. However, it responds well to radiotherapy and ◊cytotoxic drugs, and long-term survival is usual.

Hodler /ˈhɒdlə/ Ferdinand 1853–1918. Swiss painter. His dramatic Art Nouveau paintings of allegorical, historical, and mythological subjects include large murals with dreamy Symbolist female figures such as *Day* about 1900 (Kunsthaus, Zürich).

Hodza /ˈhɒdʒə/ Milan 1878–1944. Slovak politician and prime minister of Czechoslovakia from Feb 1936. He and President Beneš were forced to agree to the secession of the Sudeten areas of Czechoslovakia to the Germans before resigning 22 Sept 1938 (see ◊Munich Agreement).

Hoess /hɜːs/ Rudolf 1900–1947. German commandant of Auschwitz concentration camp 1940–43. Under his control more than 2.5

Hoffman Dustin Hoffman at the Oscar awards ceremony, 1980.

million people were exterminated. Arrested by Allied military police in 1946, he was handed over to the Polish authorities who tried and executed him in 1947.

Hofei /ˌhəʊ'feɪ/ former name of ◊Hefei, a city in China.

Hoffa /'hɒfə/ (James Riddle) 'Jimmy' 1913–?1975. US labour leader, president of the Teamsters Union (transport workers) from 1957. He was jailed 1967–71 for attempted bribery of a federal court jury after he was charged with corruption. In 1975 he disappeared, and is generally believed to have been murdered.

Hoffman /'hɒfmən/ Abbie (Abbot) 1936–1989. US left-wing political activist, founder of the Yippies (Youth International Party), a political offshoot of the ◊hippies. He was a member of the Chicago Seven, a radical group tried for attempting to disrupt the 1968 Democratic convention.

Hoffman was arrested 52 times and was a fugitive from justice 1973–80. He specialized in imaginative political gestures to gain media attention, for example throwing dollar bills to the floor of the New York Stock Exchange 1967. His books include *Revolution for the Hell of It* 1969. He campaigned against the Vietnam War and, later, for the environment. He committed suicide.

Hoffman /'hɒfmən/ Dustin 1937– . US actor, who won Academy Awards for his performances in *Kramer vs Kramer* 1979 and *Rain Man* 1988. His other films include *The Graduate* 1967 and *Midnight Cowboy* 1969.

Hoffmann /'hɒfmən/ E(rnst) T(heodor) A(madeus) 1776–1822. German composer and writer. He composed the opera *Undine* 1816 and many fairy stories, including *Nüssknacker/Nutcracker* 1816. His stories inspired ◊Offenbach's *Tales of Hoffmann*.

Hoffmann /'hɒfmən/ Josef 1870–1956. Austrian architect, one of the founders of the Wiener Werkstätte, and a pupil of Otto ◊Wagner.

Hoffman's voltameter an apparatus for collecting gases produced by the electrolysis of a liquid.

It consists of a vertical E-shaped glass tube with taps at the upper ends of the outer limbs and a reservoir at the top of the central limb. Platinum electrodes fused into the lower ends of the outer limbs are connected to a source of direct current. At the beginning of an experiment, the outer limbs are completely filled with electrolyte by opening the taps. The taps are then closed and the current switched on. Gases evolved at the electrodes bubble up the outer limbs and collect at the top, where they can be measured.

Hofman /'həʊfmən/ August 1818–1892. German chemist who studied the extraction and exploitation of coal tar derivatives. Hofmann taught chemistry in London from 1845 until his return to Berlin in 1865.

Hofmann /'həʊfmən/ Hans 1880–1966. German-born Abstract Expressionist painter, active in Paris and Munich from 1915 until 1932, when he moved to the USA. He was influential among New York artists in the 1930s.

Apart from bold brushwork (he experimented with dribbling and dripping painting techniques in the 1940s) he used strong expressive colours. In the 1960s he moved towards a hard-edged abstract style.

Hofmeister /'həʊfmeɪstə/ Wilhelm 1824–1877. German botanist. He studied plant development and determined how a plant embryo, lying within a seed, is itself formed out of a single fertilized egg (ovule).

Hofmeister also discovered that mosses and ferns display an ◊alternation of generations, in which the plant has two forms, spore-forming and gamete-forming.

Hofstadter /'hɒfstætə/ Robert 1915– . US high-energy physicist who revealed the structure of the atomic nucleus. He demonstrated that the nucleus is composed of a high-energy core and a surrounding area of decreasing density. Nobel Prize for Physics 1961.

ET PLURIMA MORTIS IMAGO

The Company of Undertakers

Hogarth English painter and engraver William Hogarth revived the art of medieval morality pictures, often in a series, such as A Rake's Progress 1735. He published his own engravings; this one is a bitter attack on the medical men of his time.

Hofstadter helped to construct a new high-energy accelerator at Stanford University, California, with which he showed that the proton and the neutron have complex structures and cannot be considered elementary particles.

hog a member of the ◊pig family. The *river hog* *Potamochoerus porcus* lives in Africa south of the Sahara. Reddish or black, up to 1.3 m/4.2 ft long plus tail, and 90 cm/3 ft at the shoulder, these gregarious animals root for food in many types of habitat. The *giant forest hog Hylochoerus meinerzthageni* lives in thick forests of central Africa and is up to 1.9 m/6 ft long.

Hogarth /'həʊɡɑːθ/ William 1697–1764. British painter and engraver, who produced portraits and moralizing genre scenes, such as the series *A Rake's Progress* 1735.

Hogarth was born in London and apprenticed to an engraver. He published *A Harlot's Progress* 1732, a series of six engravings, in 1732. Other series followed, including *Marriage à la Mode* 1745, *Industry and Idleness* 1749, and *The Four Stages of Cruelty* 1751. His portraits are remarkably direct and characterful. In the book *The Analysis of Beauty* 1753 he proposed a double curved line as a key to successful composition.

Hogg /hɒɡ/ James 1770–1835. Scottish novelist and poet, known as the 'Ettrick Shepherd'. Born in Ettrick Forest, Selkirkshire, he worked as a shepherd at Yarrow 1790–99, and until the age of 30, he was illiterate. His novel *Confessions of a Justified Sinner* 1824 is a masterly portrayal of personified evil.

Hogg /hɒɡ/ Quintin British politician; see Lord ◊Hailsham.

Hoggar /'hɒɡə/ another form of ◊Ahaggar, a plateau in the Sahara.

Hogmanay Scottish name for New Year's Eve.

hogweed genus of plants *Heracleum*, family Umbelliferae; the *giant hogweed Heracleum mantegazzianum* grows over 3 m/9 ft high.

Hohenlinden, Battle of /ˌhəʊən'lɪndən/ in the French ◊Revolutionary Wars, a defeat of the Austrians by the French 3 Dec 1800 which, on top of the defeat at ◊Marengo, led the Austrians to make peace at the Treaty of Lunéville 1801.

Hohenlohe-Schillingsfürst /ˈhəʊənləʊəˈʃɪlɪŋsf ʊəst/ Prince Chlodwig von 1819–1901. German imperial chancellor from Oct 1894 until his replacement by Prince von Bülow Oct 1900.

Hohenstaufen /ˌhəʊənˈʃtaʊfən/ German family of princes, several members of which were Holy Roman emperors 1138–1208 and 1214–54. They were the first German emperors to make use of associations with Roman law and tradition to aggrandize their office. Conrad III, Frederick I (Barbarossa), was the first to use the title Holy Roman emperor, Henry VI, and Frederick II. The last of the line, Conradin, was executed 1268, with the approval of Pope Clement IV, while attempting to gain his Sicilian inheritance.

Hohenzollern /ˌhəʊənˈzɒlən/ German family, originating in Württemberg, the main branch of which held the titles of elector of Brandenburg from 1415, king of Prussia from 1701, and German emperor from 1871. The last emperor, Wilhelm II, was dethroned 1918. Another branch of the family were kings of Romania 1881–1947.

Hohhot /ˌhɒˈhɒt/ formerly *Huhehot* city and capital of Inner Mongolia (*Nei Mongol*) autonomous region, China; population (1984) 778,000. Industries include textiles, electronics, and dairy products. There are Lamaist monasteries and temples here.

Hokkaido /hɒˈkaɪdəʊ/ most northerly of the four main islands of Japan, separated from Honshu to the S by Tsugaru Strait and from Sakhalin to the N by Soya Strait; area 83,500 sq km/32,231 sq mi, population (1986) 5,678,000 including 16,000 ◊Ainus. The capital is Sapporo. Natural resources include coal, mercury, manganese, oil and natural gas, timber, and fisheries. Coal mining and agriculture are the main industries.

Snow-covered for half the year, Hokkaido was little developed until the Meiji Restoration 1868 when disbanded Samurai were settled here. Intensive exploitation followed World War II, including heavy and chemical industrial plants, development of electric power, and dairy farming. An artificial harbour has been constructed at Tomakomai, and an undersea rail tunnel links Hakodate with Aomori (Honshu), but remains as yet closed to public transport.

Hokusai /ˌhəʊkʊˈsaɪ/ Katsushika 1760–1849. Japanese artist, the leading printmaker of his time. He is known for *Fugaku Sanjū-rokkei/36 Views of Mount Fuji* about 1823–29, but he produced outstanding pictures of almost every kind of subject—birds, flowers, courtesans, and scenes from legend and everyday life.

Hokusai was born in Edo (now Tokyo) and studied wood engraving and book illustration. He was interested in Western painting and perspective, and introduced landscape as a wood-block-print genre. His *Manga*, a book crammed with inventive sketches, was published in 13 volumes from 1814.

Holbein /ˈhɒlbaɪn/ Hans, the Elder c. 1464–1524. German painter, active in Augsburg. His works include altarpieces, such as that of *St Sebastian*, 1516 (Alte Pinakothek, Munich). He also painted portraits and designed stained glass.

Holbein /ˈhɒlbaɪn/ Hans, the Younger 1497/98–1543. German painter and woodcut artist; the son and pupil of Hans Holbein the Elder. He travelled widely in Europe, and was active in England 1527–28 and 1532–43; he was court painter to Henry VIII from 1536. He painted outstanding portraits of Erasmus, Thomas More, and Thomas Cromwell; a notable woodcut series is *Dance of Death c.*1525.

Holbein was born in Augsburg. In 1515 he went to Basel, where he became friendly with Erasmus; in 1517 to Lucerne; he was active in Basel again 1519–26. He designed title pages for Luther's New Testament and More's *Utopia*. Pronounced Renaissance influence emerged in the *Meyer Madonna* 1526, a fine altarpiece in Darmstadt. During his time at the English court, he also painted miniature portraits, inspiring Hilliard.

Holborne /ˈhəʊlbɔːn/ Anthony 1584–1602. English composer. He wrote a book of *Pauans, Galliards, Almains and Other Short Aeirs* 1599.

Holden /ˈhəʊldən/ Edith 1871–1920. British artist and naturalist. Daughter of a Birmingham manufacturer, she made most of her observations near her native city, and her journal, illustrated with her own watercolours, was published in 1977 as *The Country Diary of an Edwardian Lady*.

Holden /ˈhəʊldən/ William. Stage name of William Franklin Beedle 1918–1981. US film actor, a star in the late 1940s and 1950s. One of his best roles was as the leader of *The Wild Bunch* 1969, and he also played leading roles in *Sunset Boulevard* 1950, *Stalag 17* 1953, and *Network* 1976.

holdfast an organ found at the base of many seaweeds, attaching them to the sea bed. It may be a flattened, sucker-like structure, or dissected and finger-like, growing into rock crevices and firmly anchoring the plant.

holding company a company with a controlling shareholding in one or more subsidiaries.

In the UK, there are many large holding companies with varying degrees of control over their subsidiaries. They frequently provide cost-saving services such as marketing or financial expertise.

Holford /ˈhɒlfəd/ William, Baron Holford 1907–1975. British architect, born in Johannesburg. The most influential architect-planner of his generation, he was responsible for much redevelopment after World War II, including St Paul's Cathedral Precinct, London.

holiday a period of allowed absence from work. The word derives from medieval *holy days*, which were saint's days when no work was done.

Holidays became a legal requirement in Britain under the Bank Holidays Acts 1871 and 1875. Under the Holidays with Pay Act 1938, paid holidays (initially one week) were made compulsory in many occupations; 11 million were entitled to a holiday in 1939. By 1955, 96% of manual labourers had two weeks' holiday.

Holiday /ˈhɒlɪdeɪ/ Billie. Stage name of Eleanor Gough McKay 1915–1959. US jazz singer, also known as 'Lady Day'. She made her debut in Harlem clubs and became known for her emotionally charged delivery and idiosyncratic phrasing; she brought a blues feel to performances with swing bands. Songs she made her own include 'Strange Fruit' and 'I Cover the Waterfront'.

holiday camp a site that provides an all-inclusive holiday, usually with entertainment, and at an inclusive price. The first holiday camp on a permanent site was opened 1894 near Douglas, Isle of Man, by Joseph Cunningham. Billy ◊Butlin's first camp (accommodating 3,000 people) opened at Skegness 1935.

Other holiday-camp proprietors included Harry Warner (1889–1964), whose camp at Hayling Island opened 1931, and Fred Pontin (born 1906). Holiday camps reached a peak of popularity in the 1950s and 1960s, but since then several have closed down. In 1985 there were 85 camps in England and Wales.

Holinshed /ˈhɒlɪnʃed/ Ralph *c.*1520–*c.*1580. English historian. He was probably born in Cheshire, went to London as assistant to a printer, and in 1578 published two volumes of the *Chronicles of England, Scotland and Ireland*, which were largely used by Shakespeare for his history plays.

holism philosophically, the concept that the whole is greater than the sum of its parts; also the idea that physical and mental wellbeing are inextricably linked, so that all aspects of a patient's life must be taken into account.

Holkeri /ˈhɒlkəri/ Harri 1937– . Finnish politician, prime minister from 1987. Joining the centrist National Coalition Party (KOK) at an early age, he eventually became its national secretary.

Holland /ˈhɒlənd/ two provinces of the ◊Netherlands; see ◊North Holland and ◊South Holland.

Holland, Parts of /ˈhɒlənd/ former separate administrative county of SE Lincolnshire, England.

Holiday Acknowledged as the supreme jazz singer of her day, Billie Holiday brought an individual blues sound to all her songs.

Holland /ˈhɒlənd/ Henry Richard Vassall Fox, 3rd Baron 1773–1840. British Whig politician. He was Lord Privy Seal 1806–07. His home at Holland House, London, was for many years the centre of Whig political and literary society.

Holland /ˈhɒlənd/ John Philip 1840–1914. Irish engineer who developed some of the first submarines. He began work in Ireland in the late 1860s and emigrated to the USA 1873. His first successful boat was launched 1881 and, after several failures, he built the *Holland* 1893, which was bought by the US Navy two years later. He continued to build submarines for various navies but died in poverty after his company failed because of financial difficulties.

Holland /ˈhɒlənd/ Sidney George 1893–1961. New Zealand politician, leader of the National Party 1940–57 and prime minister 1949–57.

Hollar /ˈhɒlə/ Wenceslaus 1607–1677. Bohemian engraver, active in England from 1637. He was the first landscape engraver to work in England and recorded views of London before the Great Fire of 1666.

Hollerith /ˈhɒlərɪθ/ Herman 1860–1929. US inventor of a mechanical tabulating machine, the first device for data processing. Hollerith's tabulator was widely publicized after being successfully used in the 1890 census. The firm he established, the Tabulating Machine Company, was later one of the founding companies of International Business Machines (IBM).

After attending the Columbia University School of Mines, Hollerith worked on the 1880 US census and witnessed the huge task of processing so much information. In 1882 he became an instructor at the Massachusetts Institute of Technology,

Holly Buddy Holly created such hits as 'Peggy Sue' and 'That'll be the Day' before his tragic death at the age of 23.

holography

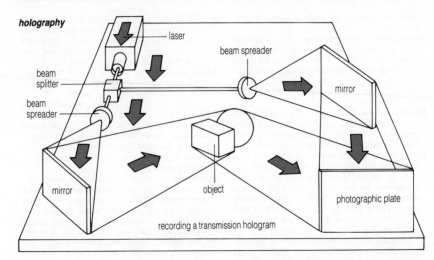

recording a transmission hologram

where he developed his machine for counting and collating census data.

Hollis /'hɒlɪs/ Roger 1905–1973. British civil servant, head of the secret intelligence service MI5 1956–65. He was alleged without confirmation to have been a double agent together with Kim Philby.

holly tree or shrub of genus *Ilex*, family Aquifoliaceae, including the **English Christmas holly** *Ilex aquifolium*, an evergreen with spiny, glossy leaves, small white flowers, and poisonous scarlet berries on the female tree, and the **Brazilian holly** *Ilex paraguayensis*, from the leaves of which the tea **yerba maté** is made.

Holly /'hɒli/ Buddy. Stage name of Charles Hardin Holley 1936–1959. US rock-and-roll singer, guitarist, and songwriter, born in Lubbock, Texas. He had a distinctive, hiccuping vocal style and was an early experimenter with recording techniques. Many of his hits with his band, the Crickets, such as 'That'll Be the Day' 1957, 'Peggy Sue' 1957, and 'Maybe Baby' 1958, have become classics. He was killed in a plane crash.

hollyhock plant of the genus *Althaea*, family Malvaceae. *Althaea rosea*, originally a native of Asia, produces spikes of large white, yellow or red flowers, 3 m/10 ft high when grown as a biennial. The hollyhock was introduced into Britain four centuries ago.

Hollywood /'hɒliwʊd/ suburb of Los Angeles, California, USA, the centre of the US film industry from 1911.

Holmes /həʊmz/ Oliver Wendell 1809–1894. US writer. In 1857 he founded the *Atlantic Monthly* with J R Lowell, in which were published the essays and verse collected in 1858 as *The Autocrat of the Breakfast-Table*.

holmium a chemical element, symbol Ho, atomic number 67, relative atomic mass 164.94, discovered 1897. One of the rare earth metals, it is used in electronic devices.

holocaust wholesale destruction; it is especially applied today to the annihilation of about 11 million people by the Hitler regime 1933–45 in the numerous concentration and extermination camps, most notably Auschwitz, Sobibor, Treblinka, and Maidanek in Poland, and Belsen, Buchenwald, and Dachau in Germany. Six million of the victims were Jews but several million Russian civilians and prisoners-of-war, gypsies, socialists, homosexuals, and others were also imprisoned and/or exterminated.

Holocene epoch of geological time that began 10,000 years ago, the second epoch of the Quaternary period. The glaciers retreated, the climate became warmer, and humans developed significantly.

holography a method of producing three-dimensional (3D) images by means of ◊laser light. Although the possibility of holography was suggested as early as 1947, it could not be demonstrated until a pure coherent light source, the laser, became available 1963. Holography uses a photographic technique to produce a picture, or hologram, which contains 3D information about the object photographed. Some holograms show meaningless patterns in ordinary light and produce a 3D image only when laser light is shone through them, but reflection holograms produce images when ordinary light is reflected from them (as found on credit cards).

The technique of holography is also applicable to sound, and it is thought possible that bats navigate by ultrasonic holography. Holographic techniques also have applications in storing dental records of people, detecting stresses and strains in construction and in retail goods, and in detecting forged paintings and documents.

Holst /həʊlst/ Gustav(us Theodore von) 1874–1934. English composer. He wrote operas, including *Savitri* 1916 and *At the Boar's Head* 1925, ballets, choral works, including *Hymns from the Rig Veda* 1911 and *The Hymn of Jesus* 1920, orchestral suites, including *The Planets* 1918, and songs. He was a lifelong friend of Ralph ◊Vaughan Williams, with whom he shared an enthusiasm for English folk music. His musical style, although tonal and drawing on folk song, tends to be severe.

Holstein /'həʊlstaɪn/ Friedrich von 1839–1909. German diplomat and foreign-affairs expert. He refused the post of foreign minister, but played a key role in German diplomacy from the 1880s until his death.

Holt /həʊlt/ Harold Edward 1908–1967. Australian Liberal politician, prime minister 1966–67.

He was minister of labour 1940–41 and 1949–58, and federal treasurer 1958–66, when he succeeded Menzies as prime minister.

Holtby /'həʊltbi/ Winifred 1898–1935. English novelist, poet, and journalist. She was an ardent advocate of women's freedom and racial equality, and wrote the novel *South Riding* 1936, set in her native Yorkshire. Her other works include an analysis of women's position in contemporary society *Women and a Changing Civilization* 1934.

Holy Alliance a 'Christian Union of Charity, Peace, and Love' initiated by Alexander I of Russia 1815 and signed by every crowned head in Europe. The alliance became associated with Russian attempts to preserve autocratic monarchies at any price, and an excuse to meddle in the internal affairs of other states. Ideas of an international army acting in the name of the alliance were rejected by Britain and Austria 1818 and 1820.

Holy Communion another name for the ◊Eucharist, a Christian sacrament.

Holy Grail in Christian legend, the dish or cup used by Jesus at the Last Supper, which, together with the spear with which he was wounded at the Crucifixion, appears as an object of quest by King

Holy Roman Emperors

Emperor	Dates of reign
Carolingian Kings and Emperors	
Charlemagne, Charles the Great	800–14
Louis I, the Pious	814–40
Lothair I	840–55
Louis II	855–75
Charles II, the Bald	875–77
Charles III, the Fat	881–87
Guido of Spoleto	891–94
Lambert of Spoleto (co-emperor)	892–98
Arnulf (rival)	896–901
Louis III of Provence	901–05
Berengar	905–24
Conrad I of Franconia (rival)	911–18
Saxon Kings and Emperors	
Henry I, the Fowler	918–36
Otto I, the Great	936–73
Otto II	973–83
Otto III	983–1002
Henry III, the Saint	1002–24
Franconian (Salian) Emperors	
Conrad II	1024–39
Henry III, the Black	1039–56
Henry IV	1056–1106
Rudolf of Swabia (rival)	1077–80
Hermann of Luxembourg (rival)	1081–93
Conrad of Franconia (rival)	1093–1101
Henry V	1106–25
Lothair II	1126–37
Hohenstaufen Kings and Emperors	
Conrad III	1138–52
Frederick I Barbarossa	1152–90
Henry VI	1190–97
Otto IV	1198–1215
Philip of Swabia (rival)	1198–1208
Frederick II	1215–50
Henry Raspe of Thuringia (rival)	1246–47
William of Holland (rival)	1246–47
Conrad IV	1250–54
The Great Interregnum	1254–73
Rulers from Noble Families	
Richard of Cornwall (rival)	1257–72
Alfonso X of Castile (rival)	1257–73
Rudolf I (Habsburg)	1273–91
Adolph I of Nassau	1292–98
Albert I (Habsburg)	1298–1303
Henry VII (Luxembourg)	1308–13
Louis IV of Bavaria	1314–47
Frederick of Habsburg (co-regent)	1314–25
Charles IV (Luxembourg)	1347–78
Wenceslas of Bohemia	1378–1400
Frederick III of Brunswick	1400
Rupert of the Palatinate	1400–10
Sigismund (Luxembourg)	1411–37
Habsburg Emperors	
Albert II	1438–39
Frederick III	1440–93
Maximillian I	1493–1519
Charles V	1519–56
Ferdinand II	1556–64
Maximillian II	1564–76
Rudolf II	1576–1612
Mathias	1612–19
Ferdinand III	1619–57
Leopold I	1658–1705
Joseph I	1705–11
Charles VI	1711–40
Charles VII of Bavaria	1742–45
Habsburg-Lorraine Emperors	
Francis I of Lorraine	1745–65
Joseph II	1765–90
Leopold II	1790–92
Francis II	1792–1806

Arthur's knights in certain stories incorporated in the Arthurian legend.

According to one story, the blood of Jesus was collected in the Holy Grail by ◊Joseph of Arimathaea at the Crucifixion, and he brought it to Britain. At least three churches in Europe possess vessels claimed to be the Holy Grail.

Holyhead /ˌhɒliˈhed/ seaport on the N coast of Holyhead Island, off Anglesey, Gwynedd, N

Wales; population (1981) 10,467. Holyhead Island is linked by road and railway bridges with Anglesey, and there are regular sailings between Holyhead and Dublin.

Holy Island /'həʊli/ or *Lindisfarne*. Island in the North Sea, area 10 sq km/4 sq mi; 3 km/2 mi off Northumberland, England, with which it is connected by a causeway. St ◊Aidan founded a monastery here in 635.

Holy Loch /'həʊli 'lɒx/ western inlet of the Firth of Clyde, W Scotland, with a US nuclear submarine base.

Holyoake /'həʊliəʊk/ Keith Jacka 1904–1983. New Zealand National Party politician, prime minister 1957 (for two months) and 1960–72.

Holy Office tribunal of the Roman Catholic church that deals with ecclesiastical discipline; see ◊Inquisition.

holy orders Christian priesthood, as conferred by the laying on of hands by a bishop. The Anglican church has three orders (bishop, priest, and deacon); the Roman Catholic Church includes also subdeacon, acolyte, exorcist, reader, and doorkeepers, and, outside the priesthood, ◊tertiary.

Holy Roman Empire the empire of ◊Charlemagne and his successors, and the German empire 962–1806, both regarded as a revival of the Roman Empire. At its height it comprised much of western and central Europe. See ◊Germany, history and ◊Habsburg.

Holyrood House /'hɒlɪruːd/ royal residence in Edinburgh, Scotland. The palace was built 1498–1503 on the site of a 12th-century abbey by James IV. It has associations with Mary Queen of Scots and Charles Edward, the Young Pretender.

Holy See the diocese of the ◊pope.

Holy Shroud Christian name for the *shroud of ◊Turin*.

Holy Spirit the third person of the Christian ◊Trinity, also known as the Holy Ghost or the Paraclete. It is usually depicted as a white dove.

Holy Week in the Christian church, the last week of ◊Lent, when Christians commemorate the events that led up to the crucifixion of Jesus. Holy Week begins on Palm Sunday and includes Maundy Thursday, which commemorates the Last Supper.

Homburg /'hɒmbɜːg/ or *Bad Homburg* town and spa at the foot of the Taunus mountains, West Germany; population (1984) 41,800. It has given its name to a soft felt hat for men, made fashionable in Homburg by Edward VII of England.

Home /hjuːm/ Alec Douglas-Home, Baron Home of the Hirsel 1903– . British Conservative politician. He was foreign secretary 1960–63, and succeeded Macmillan as prime minister 1963. He renounced his peerage (as 14th Earl of Home) to fight (and lose) the general election 1964, and resigned as party leader 1965. He was again foreign secretary 1970–74, when he received a life peerage. His brother is the playwright William Douglas-Home.

Home Counties the counties in close proximity to London, England: Hertfordshire, Essex, Kent, Surrey, and formerly Middlesex.

Home Guard unpaid force formed in Britain May 1940 to repel the expected German invasion, and known until July 1940 as the Local Defence Volunteers. It consisted of men aged 17–65 who had not been called up, formed part of the armed forces of the crown, and was subject to military law. Over 2 million strong in 1944, it was disbanded 31 Dec 1945, but revived 1951, then placed on a reserve basis 1955, and ceased activities 1957.

Home Office British government department established 1782 to deal with all the internal affairs of England except those specifically assigned to other departments. Responsibilities include the police, the prison service, immigration, race relations, and broadcasting. The home secretary, the head of the department, holds cabinet rank. There is a separate secretary of state for Scotland and for another Wales. The home secretary has certain duties in respect of the Channel Islands and the Isle of Man.

homeopathy (or *homoeopathy*) a system of medicine, introduced by the German physician Samuel Hahnemann (1755–1843), based on the treatment of a given disease by administering small quantities of a drug which produces the symptoms of that disease in a healthy person. It is contrasted with ◊allopathy.

homeostasis the maintenance of a constant state in an organism's internal environment. It includes regulation of the chemical composition of body fluids, as well as temperature and pressure.

homeothermy the maintenance of a constant body temperature in endothermic (warm-blooded) animals, by the use of chemical body processes to compensate for heat loss or gain when external temperatures change. Such processes include generation of heat by the breakdown of food and the contraction of muscles, and loss of heat by sweating, panting, and other means.

Mammals and birds are homeotherms, whereas invertebrates, fish, reptiles, and amphibians are cold-blooded poikilotherms. Homeotherms generally have a layer of insulating material to keep heat in, such as fur, feathers, or fat (see ◊blubber). Their metabolism functions more efficiently due to homeothermy, enabling them to remain active under most climatic conditions.

Homer legendary Greek epic poet of the 8th century BC; according to tradition a blind minstrel and the author of the ◊Iliad and the ◊Odyssey.

Homer /'həʊmə/ Winslow 1836–1910. US painter and lithographer, known for his seascapes, both oils and watercolours, which date from the 1880s and 1890s.

Homer, born in Boston, made his reputation as a realist painter with *Prisoners from the Front* 1866 (Metropolitan Museum, New York), recording miseries of the Civil War. After a visit to Paris he turned to lighter subjects, studies of country life, which reflect early Impressionist influence. He stayed in the UK for two years, then settled in Maine, but continued to travel to Canada, the West Indies, and elsewhere.

Home Rule the slogan of the Irish nationalist movement 1870–1914; it stood for the repeal of the Act of ◊Union 1801 and the establishment of an Irish parliament within the framework of the British Empire. The slogan was popularized after 1870 by Isaac Butt (1813–79) and ◊Parnell, his successor in the nationalist leadership. Gladstone's Home Rule bills 1886 and 1893 were both defeated; Asquith's Home Rule bill became law 1914, but was suspended during World War I. After 1918 the demand for an independent Irish republic replaced that for home rule.

home service force (HSF) force established in the UK 1982, linked to the ◊Territorial Army and recruited from volunteers of ages 18–60 with previous military (TA or Regular) experience. It was introduced to guard key points and installations likely to be the target of enemy 'special forces' and saboteurs, so releasing other units for mobile defence roles.

Homestead Act in US history, an act of Congress 1862 to encourage the settlement of land in the west by offering 65-ha/160-acre plots cheaply or even free to those willing to cultivate and improve the land. By 1900 about 32,400,000 ha/80,000,000 acres had been disposed of.

homicide in law, the killing of a human being. In British law this may be unlawful, lawful, or excusable, depending on the circumstance. Unlawful homicides are ◊murder, ◊manslaughter, ◊infanticide, and causing death by dangerous driving. Lawful homicide occurs where, for example, a police officer is justified in killing a criminal in the course of trying to arrest him. Excusable homicide occurs where a person is killed in self-defence or by accident.

homologous in biology, a term describing an organ or structure possessed by members of different taxonomic groups (for example, species, genera, families, orders) which originally derived from the same structure in a common ancestor. The wing of a bat, the arm of a monkey, and the flipper of a seal are homologous, because they all derive from the forelimb of an ancestral mammal.

homologous series various organic chemicals which form series whose consecutive members differ by a constant molecular weight.

Alkanes (paraffins), alkenes (olefins), and alkynes (acetylenes) form such series whose members differ in weight by 14, 12, and 10 atomic mass units, respectively. For example, the alkane homologous series begins with methane (CH_4), ethane (C_2H_6), propane (C_3H_8), butane (C_4H_10), and pentane (C_5H_12).

homonymy an aspect of language in which two or more words may sound and look alike (*homonymy* proper; for example, a farmer's bull and a papal bull), may sound the same but look different (*homophony*; for example, air and heir; gilt and guilt), and may look the same but sound different (*homography*; for example the wind in the trees and roads that wind).

Homonyms, homophones, and homographs seldom pose problems of comprehension, because they usually belong in different contexts. Even when brought into the same context for effect ('The heir to the throne had an air of self-satisfaction'), they are entirely clear. They may, however, be used to make puns (for example, talking about a papal bull in a china shop).

homophony in music, a melody lead and accompanying harmony, as distinct from *heterophony* and *polyphony* in which different melody lines are combined.

homosexuality sexual preference for, or attraction to, persons of one's own sex; in women it is referred to as ◊lesbianism. Men and women who are attracted to both sexes are referred to as bisexual.

homozygous in a living organism, having two identical ◊alleles for a given trait. Homozygous individuals always breed true, that is they produce offspring that resemble them in appearance when bred with a genetically similar individual; inbred varieties or species are homozygous for almost all traits. ◊Recessive alleles are only expressed in the homozygous condition. See also ◊heterozygous.

Homs /hɒms/ or *Hums* city, capital of Homs district, W Syria, near the Orontes River; population (1981) 355,000. Silk, cereals, and fruit are produced in the area, and industries include silk textiles, oil refining, and jewellery. ◊Zenobia, Queen of Palmyra, was defeated at Homs by the Roman emperor ◊Aurelian 272.

Hon. abbreviation for *Honourable*.

Honan /ˌhəʊ'næn/ former name of ◊Henan, a province of China.

Honda Japanese motor cycle and motor racing car manufacturer. They also make road cars and bikes. Their racing bikes were first seen in Europe at the 1959 Isle of Man TT races. Mike Hailwood and Tom Phillis were their first world champions 1961. They pulled out of bike racing 1967 but returned in 1979 to become one of the top teams.

They entered Formula One Grand Prix car racing in 1964 and the following season won their first race at Mexico City. They pulled out of car racing in 1968 but in the early eighties provided engines for Formula Two and Formula Three cars before supplying engines to Formula One teams in 1983. ◊Williams and ◊McLaren have both captured world titles using Honda engines.

Hondecoeter /'hɒndəkuːə/ Melchior 1636–1695. Dutch painter, noted for his large paintings of birds (both domestic fowl and exotic species) in grandiose settings.

Hondo /'hɒndəʊ/ another name for ◊Honshu, an island of Japan.

Honduras /hɒn'djʊərəs/ country in Central America, bounded to the N by the Caribbean, to the SE by Nicaragua, to the S by the Pacific, to the SW by El Salvador, and to the W and NW by Guatemala.

Honduras
Republic of
(República de Honduras)

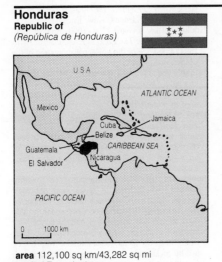

area 112,100 sq km/43,282 sq mi
capital Tegucigalpa
towns San Pedro Sula; ports Henecan (on Pacific), La Ceiba
physical mountainous; 45% forest
features areas still unexplored
head of state and government Rafael Leonardo Callejas from 1990
political system democratic republic
political parties Liberal Party of Honduras (PLH), centre-left; National Party (PN), right-wing

exports coffee, bananas, timber (including mahogany, rosewood)
currency lempira (3.41 = £1 Feb 1990)
population (1985) 4,370,000 (90% mestizo, 10% Indians and Europeans); annual growth rate 3.4%
life expectancy men 58, women 62
language Spanish
religion Roman Catholic
literacy 61% male/58% female (1985 est)
GNP $2.8 bn (1983); $590 per head of population
chronology
1838 Honduras achieved independence.
1980 After more than a century of mostly military rule, a civilian government was elected, with Dr Roberto Suazo as president. The army chief, Gen Gustavo Alvárez, retained considerable power.
1983 Close involvement with the US in providing naval and air bases and allowing Nicaraguan counter-revolutionaries to operate from Honduras.
1984 Alvárez ousted in a coup led by junior officers, resulting in a review of policy towards the US and Nicaragua.
1985 José Azeona elected president after the electoral law changed, making Suazo ineligible for presidency.
1989 Government and opposition declare support for Central American peace plan to demobilize Nicaraguan Contras based in Honduras.
1990 Rafael Callejas (PN) elected president.

government The 1982 constitution, which underwent a major revision 1985, provides for the election of a president, who is head of both state and government, by universal suffrage for a four-year term, and may not serve two terms in succession. A single-chamber national assembly of 134 members is elected in the same way for a similar term.

There is a range of political parties which sometimes unite to form broad alliances for election purposes. The most significant are the Liberal Party of Honduras (PLH) and the National Party (PN).

history Formerly inhabited by ◊Maya Indians, and reached by Christopher Columbus 1502, the area was colonized by Spain from 1526. Independent from Spain 1821, Honduras was part of the ◊United Provinces of Central America when it achieved full independence. From 1939 to 1949 it was a dictatorship under the leader of the PN.

The government changed in a series of military coups, until the return of civilian rule 1980. The army, however, controlled security and was able to veto cabinet appointments, and although the 1981 general election was won by the PLH and its leader, Dr Roberto Suazo, became president, power was in the hands of Gen Gustavo Alvarez, the commander in chief of the army. In 1982 Alvarez secured an amendment to the constitution, reducing government control over the armed forces, and was virtually in charge of foreign policy, agreeing 1983 to the establishment of US military bases in the country. The US Central Intelligence Agency was also active in assisting Nicaraguan counter-revolutionaries based in Honduras.

In 1984 Alvarez was ousted by a group of junior officers and the country's close relationship with the USA came under review. In the same year divisions arose in the PLH over selection of presidential candidates, and in 1985 the electoral law was changed. Suazo was not eligible to stand in the 1985 presidential elections and the main PLH candidate was José Azeona. Although the PN nominee won most votes, the revised constitution made Azeona the eventual winner. In the Nov 1989 presidential election, the PN candidate, Rafael Callejas, was elected.

Hone /həʊn/ William 1780–1842. British journalist and publisher. In 1817, he was unsuccessfully prosecuted for his *Political Litany*, in which he expounded the journalist's right to free expression.

Honecker /ˈhɒnekə/ Erich 1912– . East German communist politician, in power 1973–89, elected chair of the council of state (head of state) 1976. He governed in an outwardly austere and efficient manner and, while favouring East-West detente, was a loyal ally of the USSR. In Oct 1989, following a wave of pro-democracy demonstrations, he was replaced as leader of the Socialist Unity Party (SED) and head of state by Egon ◊Krenz, and in Dec expelled from the Communist Party.

Honecker, the son of a miner, joined the German Communist Party 1929 and was imprisoned for anti-fascist activity 1935–45. He was elected to the East German parliament (*Volkskammer*) 1949 and became a member of the SED Politburo during the 1950s. A security specialist, during the 1960s he served as a secretary of the National Defence Council before being appointed first secretary of the SED 1971. After Ulbricht's death 1973, Honecker became leader of East Germany. In Feb 1990, following his overthrow, he was arrested and charged with high treason, misuse of office, and corruption.

Honegger /ˈhɒnegə/ Arthur 1892–1955. Swiss composer, one of the ◊Les Six. His work was varied in form, for example, the opera *Antigone* 1927, the ballet *Skating Rink* 1922, the oratorio *Le Roi David/King David* 1921, programme music (*Pacific 231* 1923), and the *Symphonie liturgique/Liturgical Symphony* 1946.

Hōnen /ˈhəʊnen/ 1133–1212. Japanese Buddhist monk who founded the ◊Pure Land school of Buddhism.

honey a sweet syrup made by honey ◊bees from the nectar of flowers. It is made in excess of their needs as food for the winter. Honey comprises various sugars, especially laevulose and dextrose, with enzymes, colouring matter, acids, and pollen grains. It has antibacterial properties, and was widely used in ancient Egypt, Greece, and Rome as a wound salve.

honey-eater or **honey-sucker** small, brightly coloured bird of the family Meliphagidae. Honeyeaters have long, curved beaks, long tails, and

honeyeater

kauai

long tongues which they use to sip nectar from flowers. They are found in Australasia and Hawaii. Honeyeaters from Australia colonized Hawaii and and four species evolved there, of which only one, the kauai o-o, survives. It is endangered mainly owing to introduced plants and animals.

honey guides in botany, lines or spots on the petals of a flower which indicate to pollinating insects the position of the nectaries within the flower. The orange dot on the lower lip of the toadflax flower (*Linaria vulgaris*) is an example. Sometimes the markings reflect only ultraviolet light which can be seen by many insects, although it is not visible to the human eye.

honeysuckle plant of the *Lonicera* genus, Caprifoliaceae family. The **commmon honeysuckle** or **woodbine** *Lonicera periclymenum* is a climbing plant with sweet-scented flowers, reddish and yellow-tinted outside and creamy-white inside.

The North American **trumpet honeysuckle** *Lonicera sempervirens* includes scarlet and yellow varieties.

Hong Kong /ˈhɒŋ ˈkɒŋ/ British crown colony in SE Asia, comprising Hong Kong island, the Kowloon peninsula, and the mainland New Territories.
area 1,070 sq km/413 sq mi
capital Victoria (popularly Hong Kong City)
towns Kowloon, Tsuen Wan (in the New Territories)
features an enclave of Kwantung province, China, it has one of the world's finest natural harbours; Hong Kong Island is connected with Kowloon by undersea railway; a world financial centre, its stock market has four exchanges; across the border of the New Territories in China itself is the Shenzhen special economic zone
exports textiles, clothing, electronic goods, clocks, watches, cameras, plastic products; a large proportion of the exports and imports of S China are transshipped here, and the Chinese special economic zone of Shenzen is only 40 km/25 mi away; tourism is important
currency Hong Kong dollar
population (1986) 5,431,000; 57% Hong Kong Chinese, most of the remainder refugees from the mainland
languages English and Chinese
religion Confucianist, Buddhist, Taoist, with Muslim and Christian minorities

honeysuckle

Hong Kong

Victoria

government Hong Kong is a British dependency administered by a Crown-appointed governor who presides over an unelected executive council, composed of four ex-officio and 11 nominated members, and a legislative council composed of three ex-officio members, 29 appointees and 24 indirectly elected members.

history Formerly part of China, Hong Kong Island was occupied by Britain 1841, during the first of the ◊Opium Wars, and ceded by the Chinese government under the 1842 Treaty of Nanking. The Kowloon Peninsula was acquired under the 1860 Peking (Beijing) Convention and the New Territories secured on a 99-year lease from 1898.

The colony, which developed into a major *entrepôt* for Sino-British trade during the late 19th and early 20th centuries, was occupied by Japan 1941–45. The restored British administration promised, after 1946, to increase self-government. These plans were shelved, however, after the 1949 Communist revolution in China. During the 1950s almost 1,000,000 Chinese (predominantly Cantonese) refugees fled to Hong Kong. Immigration continued during the 1960s and 1970s, raising the colony's population from 1,000,000 in 1946 to 5,000,000 in 1980, and forcing the imposition of strict border controls during the 1980s. Since 1975, 160,000 Vietnamese 'boat people' have fled to Hong Kong; in 1989 50,000 remain, and the UK government proposes forced repatriation.

Hong Kong's economy expanded rapidly during the corresponding period, however, and the colony became one of Asia's major commercial, financial, and industrial centres. As the date (1997) for the termination of the New Territories' lease approached, negotiations on Hong Kong's future were opened between Britain and China 1982. These culminated in a unique agreement, signed in Beijing 1984, in which Britain agreed to transfer full sovereignty of the Islands and New Territories to China 1997 in return for Chinese assurance that Hong Kong's social and economic freedom and capitalist lifestyle would be preserved for at least 50 years.

Under this 'one country, two systems' agreement, in 1997 Hong Kong would become a special administrative region within China, with its own laws, currency, budget, and tax system, and would retain its free port status and authority to negotiate separate international trade agreements. In preparation for its withdrawal from the colony, the British government introduced indirect elections to select a portion of the new legislative council 1984, and direct elections for seats on lower tier local councils 1985. A Sino-British joint liaison group was also established to monitor the functioning of the new agreement and a 59-member basic law drafting committee (including 25 representatives from Hong Kong) formed in Beijing 1985 to draft a new constitution.

Honiara /ˌhɒniˈɑːrə/ port and capital of the Solomon Islands, on the NW coast of Guadalcanal island; population (1985) 26,000.

honi soit qui mal y pense (French 'shame on him or her who thinks evil of it') the motto of England's Order of the Garter.

Honiton /ˈhɒnɪtən/ market town in Devon, SW England, on the river Otter; population (1981) 6,627. Its hand-made pillow-lace industry is undergoing a revival.

Honolulu /ˌhɒnəˈluːluː/ (Hawaiian 'sheltered bay') capital city and port of Hawaii, USA, on the S coast of Oahu; population (1980) 365,000. It is a holiday resort, noted for its beauty and tropical vegetation, with some industry. 11 km/7 mi SW is Pearl Harbor with naval and military installations.

Honourable Company of Edinburgh Golfers the oldest golf club in the world. They were formed in 1744 as the Gentleman Golfers of Edinburgh and played over the Leith links. They drew up the first set of golf rules, which were later accepted by the ruling body of the Royal and Ancient Club of St Andrews.

They changed their name in 1759. They moved to Musselburgh in 1836 and in 1891 to their present home in Muirfield, which has staged the British Open 13 times between 1892 and 1987.

honours list military and civil awards approved by the sovereign of the UK at New Year, and on her official birthday in June. Many Commonwealth countries, for example, Australia and Canada, have their own.

Honshu /ˈhɒnʃuː/ principal island of Japan. It lies between Hokkaido to the NE and Kyushu to the SW; area 231,100 sq km/89,205 sq mi, including 382 smaller islands; population (1986) 97,283,000. A chain of volcanic mountains runs along the island, which is subject to frequent earthquakes. The main cities are Tokyo, Yokohama, Osaka, Kobe, Nagoya, and Hiroshima.

Honthorst /ˈhɒnthɔːst/ Gerrit van 1590–1656. Dutch painter who used extremes of light and shade, influenced by Caravaggio; with Terbrugghen he formed the *Utrecht school*. Around 1610–12 he was in Rome, studying Caravaggio. Later he visited England, painting *Charles I* 1628 (National Portrait Gallery, London), and became court painter in The Hague.

Hooch /hoʊx/ Pieter de 1629–1684. Dutch painter, active in Delft and, later, Amsterdam. The harmonious domestic interiors and courtyards of his Delft period were influenced by Vermeer.

Hood /hʊd/ Samuel, 1st Viscount Hood 1724–1816. British admiral. A masterly tactician, he defeated the French at Dominica in the West Indies 1783, and in the ◊Revolutionary Wars captured Toulon and Corsica.

Hooghly /ˈhuːɡli/ or *Hugli* river and town, in West Bengal, India; population (1981) 125,193. The river is the western stream of the Ganges delta. The town is on the site of a factory set up by the East India Company 1640, which was moved to Calcutta, 40 km/25 mi downstream, 1686–90.

Hooke /hʊk/ Robert 1635–1703. English scientist and inventor, originator of ◊Hooke's law. His inventions included a telegraph system, the spirit-level, marine barometer, and sea gauge. He coined the term 'cell' in biology.

He was considered the foremost mechanic of his time. He studied elasticity, furthered the sciences of mechanics and microscopy, and helped improve such scientific instruments as watches, microscopes, telescopes, and barometers. He was elected to the Royal Society 1663, and became its curator for the rest of his life. He was professor of geometry at Gresham College, London, and designed several buildings, including the College of Physicians.

Hooker /ˈhʊkə/ Joseph Dalton 1817–1911. English botanist who travelled to the Antarctic and made many botanical discoveries, documented in *Flora Antarctica* 1844–47. His works include *Genera Plantarum* 1862–63 and *Flora of British India* 1875–97. In 1865 he succeeded his father, William Jackson Hooker (1785–1865), as director of the Royal Botanic Gardens, Kew, England.

Hooker /ˈhʊkə/ Richard 1554–1600. English theologian, author of *The Laws of Ecclesiastical Polity* 1594, a defence of the episcopalian system of the Church of England.

Hooke's law in physics, law stating that the tension in a lightly stretched spring is proportional to its extension from its natural length. It was discovered by Robert Hooke.

Hook of Holland /ˈhʊk əv ˈhɒlənd/ (Dutch *Hoek van Holland*, meaning 'corner of Holland') a small peninsula and village in South Holland, the Netherlands, important as the terminus for ferry services with Harwich and Parkeston Quay, England.

hookworm parasitic roundworm (see ◊worm) *Necator*, which lives in tropic and subtropic regions, but also in humid sites in temperate climates where defecation occurs frequently. The eggs are hatched in damp soil, and the larvae bore into the human skin, usually through the feet. They make their way to the small intestine where they live by sucking blood. The eggs are expelled with faeces, and the cycle starts again.

Hooper /ˈhuːpə/ John c. 1495–1555. English Protestant reformer and martyr, born in Somerset. He adopted the views of ◊Zwingli and was appointed bishop of Gloucester 1550. He was burned to death for heresy.

hoopoe bird *Upupa epops* in the order Coraciiformes. Slightly larger than a thrush, it has a long thin bill and a bright buff-coloured crest which expands into a fan shape. The wings are black and white, and the rest of the plumage is black, white, and buff. It is found in Europe, Asia, and Africa.

Hoover /ˈhuːvə/ Herbert (Clark) 1874–1964. 31st president of the USA 1929–33, a Republican. Secretary of commerce 1921–28. He lost public confidence after the stock-market crash of 1929, when he opposed direct government aid for the unemployed in the depression that followed.

As a mining engineer, Hoover travelled widely before World War I, during which he organized relief work in occupied Europe; a talented administrator, he was subsequently associated with numerous international relief organizations, and became food administrator for the USA 1917–19. He defeated the Democratic candidate for the presidency, Al Smith (1873–1944). The shantytowns or ◊*Hoovervilles* of the homeless that sprang up around large cities were evidence of his failure to cope with the effects of the Depression. He was severely criticized for his adamant opposition to a federal dole for the unemployed, even after the funds of states, cities, and charities

Hoover US Republican Herbert Hoover was president 1929–33 during the Depression. He was criticized for his decision to aid financial institutions and for his refusal to provide federal funds for the millions of unemployed.

Hoover *As director of the FBI, J Edgar Hoover served under eight US presidents, and under his leadership the powers of the bureau were greatly extended.*

were exhausted. In 1933, he was succeeded by Roosevelt.

Hoover /ˈhuːvə/ J(ohn) Edgar 1895–1972. US director of the Federal Bureau of Investigation (FBI) from 1924. He built up a powerful network for the detection of organized crime. His drive against alleged communist activities after World War II, and his opposition to the Kennedy administration and others, brought much criticism over abuse of power.

Hoover /ˈhuːvə/ William Henry 1849–1932. US manufacturer, known for his association with the ◊vacuum cleaner. Hoover soon became a generic name for vacuum cleaner.

Hoover Dam the highest concrete dam in the USA, 221 m/726 ft, on the Colorado River at the Arizona-Nevada border, built 1931–36. Known as Boulder Dam 1933–47, its name was restored by President Truman as the reputation of the former president, Herbert Hoover, was revived. It impounds Lake Meade, and has a hydroelectric power capacity of 1,300 megawatts.

Hooverville colloquial term for any shantytown built by the unemployed and destitute in the USA during the Depression 1929–33, named after the US president Herbert Hoover, whose policies were blamed for the plight of millions.

Hope /həʊp/ Anthony. Pen name of Anthony Hope Hawkins 1863–1933. English novelist, whose romance *The Prisoner of Zenda* 1894, and its sequel *Rupert of Hentzau* 1898, introduced the imaginary Balkan state of Ruritania.

Hope /həʊp/ Bob. Stage name of Leslie Townes Hope 1904– . US comedian. His film appearances include a series of 'Road' films with Bing ◊Crosby. He entertained the troops in Vietnam during the Vietnam War, and has made many television appearances. He has received several Special ◊Academy Awards.

Hopei /ˈhəʊˈpeɪ/ former name of ◊Hebei, a province of China.

Hope's apparatus in physics, an apparatus used to demonstrate the temperature at which water has its maximum density. It is named after Thomas Charles Hope (1766–1844).

It consists of a vertical cylindrical vessel fitted with horizontal thermometers through its sides near the top and bottom, and surrounded at the centre by a ledge that holds freezing mixture (ice and salt). When the cylinder is filled with water, this gradually cools, the denser water sinking to the bottom, and eventually the upper thermometer records 0°C/32°F (the freezing point of water) and the lower one has a constant reading of 4°C/39°F (the temperature at which water is densest).

Hopewell North American Indian culture about AD 200, noted for burial mounds up to 12 m/40 ft

high, and also for Serpent Mound, Ohio; see also ◊moundbuilder.

Hopi indigenous American people, numbering approximately 6,000, who live mainly in mountain villages in the SW USA. Their language belongs to the Uto-Aztecan family. The Hopi live in the middle of the Navajo (or Dineh) reservation.

Hopkins *Welsh actor Anthony Hopkins.*

Hopkins /ˈhɒpkɪnz/ Anthony 1937– . Welsh actor. Among his stage appearances are *Equus*, *Macbeth*, *Pravda*, and the title role in *King Lear*. His films include *The Lion in Winter* 1968, *A Bridge Too Far* 1977, and *The Elephant Man*. He played television parts in *War and Peace* and *A Married Man*.

Hopkins /ˈhɒpkɪnz/ Frederick Gowland 1861–1947. English biochemist whose research into diets revealed the existence of trace substances, now known as vitamins. Hopkins shared the 1929 Nobel Prize for Medicine with Christiaan Eijkman, who had arrived at similar conclusions.

While studying diets, Hopkins noticed that, of two seemingly identical diets, only one was able

Hopkins *English poet Gerard Manley Hopkins who experienced a life-long tension between being a poet and a Jesuit priest. His poetry was written in secret, and published 30 years after his death by his friend Robert Bridges.*

to support life. He concluded that one must contain trace substances, or accessory food factors, lacking in the other. Among these were certain ◊amino acids which the body cannot produce itself. The other factors were later named vitamins.

Hopkins /ˈhɒpkɪnz/ Gerard Manley 1844–1889. English poet. His work, marked by its religious themes and use of natural imagery, includes 'The Wreck of the Deutschland' 1876 and 'The Windhover' 1877. His employment of 'sprung rhythm' greatly influenced later 20th-century poetry.

Hopkins was converted to Roman Catholicism 1866, and in 1868 began training as a Jesuit. He worked as a priest in Ireland and England, and subsequently taught. His poetry is profoundly religious and records his struggle to gain faith and peace, but also shows freshness of feeling and delight in nature. A complete edition was issued by the poet laureate Robert Bridges 1918. His *Journals and Papers* were published 1959 and three volumes of letters 1955–56.

Hopkins /ˈhɒpkɪnz/ Harry L(loyd) 1890–1946. US government official. Originally a social worker, in 1935 he became head of WPA (Works Progress Administration), which was concerned with Depression relief work. After a period as secretary of commerce 1938–40, he was appointed supervisor of the ◊lend-lease programme 1941, and undertook missions to Britain and the USSR during World War II.

hoplite in ancient Greece, a heavily armed infantry soldier.

Hopper /ˈhɒpə/ Dennis 1936– . US film actor and director who caused a sensation with *Easy Rider* 1969, the archetypal 'road' film, but whose later *The Last Movie* 1971 was poorly received by the critics. He made a comeback in the 1980s. His work as an actor includes *Rebel Without a Cause* 1955, *The American Friend/Der amerikanische Freund* 1977, and *Blue Velvet* 1986.

Hopper /ˈhɒpə/ Edward 1882–1967. US painter and etcher, whose views of New York in the 1930s and 1940s captured the loneliness and superficial glamour of city life, as in *Nighthawks* 1942 (Art Institute, Chicago). Hopper's teacher Robert Henri (1865–1929), associated with the ◊Ashcan school, was a formative influence.

Hoppner /ˈhɒpnə/ John 1758–1810. British portrait painter, fashionable in the 1780s.

hops female fruit-heads of the hop plant *Humulus lupulus*, family Cannabiaceae; these are dried and used as a tonic and in flavouring beer. In designated areas in Europe, no male hops may be grown, since seedless hops produced by the unpollinated female plant contain a greater proportion of the alpha acid that gives beer its bitter taste.

Horace /ˈhɒrɪs/ 65–8 BC. Roman lyric poet and satirist. He became a leading poet under the patronage of the emperor Augustus. His works include *Satires* 35–30 BC, the four books of *Odes* c. 24–25, *Epistles*, a series of verse letters, and a critical work *Ars Poetica*.

Born at Venusia, S Italy, the son of a freedman, Horace fought under Brutus at Philippi, lost his estate and was reduced to poverty. In about 38 Virgil introduced him to Maecenas, who gave him a farm in the Sabine hills and recommended him to the patronage of Augustus. His works are distinguished by their style, wit, and good sense.

Hordern /ˈhɔːdən/ Michael 1911– . English actor who appeared in stage roles such as Shakespeare's Lear and Prospero. His films include *The Man Who Never Was* 1956, *The Spy Who Came in From the Cold* 1965, *The Bed Sitting Room* 1969, and *Joseph Andrews* 1977.

Hore-Belisha /ˈhɔːbəˈliːʃə/ Leslie, Baron Hore-Belisha 1895–1957. British politician. A National Liberal, he was minister of transport 1934–37, introducing **Belisha beacons** to mark pedestrian crossings. As war minister from 1937, until removed by Chamberlain 1940 on grounds of temperament, he introduced peacetime conscription 1939.

horehound genus of plants *Marrubium*, family Labiatae. The *white horehound Marrubium vulgare*, found in Europe, N Africa, and W Asia and naturalized in North America, has a thick hairy stem and clusters of dull white flowers; it has medicinal uses.

horizon the limit to which one can see across the surface of the sea or a level plain, that is, about 5 km/3 mi at 1.5 m/5 ft above sea level, and about 65 km/40 mi at 300 m/1,000 ft.

hormone product of the endocrine glands, concerned with control of body functions. The main glands are the thyroid, parathyroid, pituitary, adrenal, pancreas, uterus, ovary, and testis. Hormones bring about changes in the functions of various organs according to the body's requirements. The pituitary gland, at the base of the brain, is the centre for overall coordination of hormone secretion; the thyroid hormones determine the rate of general body chemistry; the adrenal hormones prepare the organism for stressed situations such as 'fight or flight'; and the sexual hormones such as oestrogen govern reproductive functions.

hormone replacement therapy (HRT) the use of oral oestrogen to help limit the thinning of bone that occurs in women after menopause. The treatment was first used in the 1970s.

At the menopause, the ovaries cease to secrete natural oestrogen resulting in osteoporosis, or a thinning of bone, which is associated with an increased incidence of fractures, especially of the hip, in older women. Oral oestrogens, taken to replace the decline in natural hormone levels, combined with regular exercise can help to maintain bone strength in women.

Hormuz /hɔːˈmuːz/ small island, 41 sq km/16 sq mi, in the *Strait of Hormuz*, belonging to Iran. It is strategically important because oil tankers leaving the Persian Gulf for Japan and the West have to pass through the strait to reach the Arabian Sea.

horn one of a family of wind instruments, of which the French horn is the most widely used. See ◊brass instrument.

Horn /hɔːn/ Philip de Montmorency, Count of Horn 1518–1568. Flemish politician. He held high offices under the Holy Roman emperor Charles V and his son Philip II. From 1563 he was one of the leaders of the opposition to the rule of Cardinal Granvella (1517–1586) and to the introduction of the Inquisition. In 1567 he was arrested together with the Resistance leader Egmont, and both were beheaded in Brussels.

hornbeam a tree genus *Carpinus*, of the Betulaceae family. The *common hornbeam Carpinus betulus* is found in woods throughout the temperate regions of Europe and Asia. It has a twisted stem and smooth grey bark. The leaves are oval and hairy on the undersurface. It bears flowers in catkin form, followed by clusters of small nuts with distinctive winged bracts.

hornbill bird of the family of Bucerotidae, found in Africa, India, and Malaysia, and named for its powerful bill surmounted by a bony growth or casque. They are about 1 m/3 ft long, and omnivorous. During the breeding season, the female walls herself into a hole in a tree, and does not emerge until the young are hatched.

hornblende a green or black rock-forming mineral, one of the ◊amphiboles; it is a hydrous silicate of calcium, iron, magnesium, and aluminium. Hornblende is found in both igneous and metamorphic rocks.

Hornby v. Close UK court case in 1867, in which it was decided that trade unions were illegal associations. The decision, overturned two years later by a special act of Parliament, indirectly led to the full legalization of trade unions under the Trade Union Acts 1871–76.

hornet a type of ◊wasp.

hornfels a ◊metamorphic rock formed by rocks heated by contact with a hot igneous body. It is fine-grained and brittle, without foliation.

Horowitz Vladimir Horowitz enjoyed world acclaim as a virtuoso pianist, particularly with his interpretations of the Romantic repertoire.

Hornfels may contain minerals only formed under conditions of great heat, such as andalusite, Al_2SiO_5, and cordierite, $(Mg,Fe)_2Al_4Si_5O_{18}$. This rock, originating from sedimentary rock strata, is found in contact with large igneous ◊intrusions where it represents the heat-altered equivalent of the surrounding clays. Its hardness makes it suitable for road building and railway ballast.

Horniman /ˈhɔːnɪmən/ Annie Elizabeth Frederika 1860–1937. English pioneer of repertory theatre, who subsidized the Abbey Theatre, Dublin, and founded the Manchester company.

Hornung /ˈhɔːnən/ E(rnest) W(illiam) 1866–1921. English novelist, who, at the prompting of Conan ◊Doyle, created 'A J Raffles', the gentleman-burglar, and his assistant Bunny Manders in *The Amateur Cracksman* 1899.

hornwort underwater aquatic plants, family Ceratophyllaceae. They have pointed leaves and are found in slow-moving water. They may be up to 2 m/7 ft long.

horoscope in Western astrology, a chart of the position of the Sun, Moon, and planets relative to the ◊zodiac at the moment of birth, used to assess a person's character and forecast future influences.

In casting a horoscope, the astrologer draws a circular diagram divided into 12 sections, or houses, showing the 12 signs of the zodiac around the perimeter and the Sun, Moon, and planets as they were at the subject's time and place of birth. These heavenly bodies are supposed to represent different character traits and influences, and by observing their positions and interrelations the astrologer may gain insight into the subject's personality and foretell the main outlines of his

or her career. Modern astrology is not concerned with predicting specific events.

Horowitz /ˈhɒrəwɪts/ Vladimir 1904–1989. US pianist, born in Kiev, Ukraine. He made his debut in the USA 1928 with the New York Philharmonic Orchestra. Renowned for his commanding virtuoso style, he was a leading interpreter of Liszt, Schumann, and Rachmaninov.

Horrocks /ˈhɒrəks/ Brian Gwynne 1895–1985. British general. He served in World War I, and in World War II under Montgomery at Alamein and with the British Liberation Army in Europe.

horror a genre of fiction and film, devoted primarily to scaring the reader, but often also aiming at a catharsis of common fears through their exaggeration into the bizarre and grotesque. Dominant figures in the horror tradition are Mary Shelley (*Frankenstein* 1818), Bram Stoker, H P Lovecraft and, among contemporary writers, Stephen King and Clive Barker.

Horror is derived from the Gothic novel, which dealt in shock effects, as well as from folk tales and ghost stories throughout the ages. Horror writing tends to use motifs such as vampirism, the eruption of ancient evil, and monstrous transformation, which often derive from folk traditions, as well as more modern concerns such as psychopathology.

hors de combat (French) out of action.

horse hoofed odd-toed grass-eating mammal, *Equus caballus* of the family Equidae (which also includes zebras and asses). The many breeds of *domestic horse* of Euro-Asian derivation range in colour through grey, brown, and black. The yellow-brown *Mongolian wild horse* or Przewalski's horse *Equus przewalskii* (named after its Polish 'discoverer' about 1880) is the only surviving species of wild horse. It is in danger of extinction because of hunting and competition with domestic animals for food.

Breeds include the *Arab* small and agile; *thoroughbred* derived from the Arab via English mares, used in horse racing for its speed (the present stock is descended from three Arab horses introduced to Britain in the 18th century, especially the Darley Arabian); *quarter horse* used by cowboys for herding; *hackney* high-stepping harness horse; *Lippizaner* pure white horses, named after their place of origin in Yugoslavia; *shire* largest draught horse in the world at 17 hands (1 hand = 10.2 cm/4 in), descended from the medieval war horses which carried knights in armour, and marked by long hair or 'feathering' round its 'ankles'; *Suffolk punch* sturdy all-round working horse. The *pony* combines the qualities of various types of horse with a smaller build (under 14.2 hands, or 1.47 m/58 in). Pony breeds include the large *Welsh cob*, the rather smaller *New Forest*, and, smaller again, the *Exmoor* and *Dartmoor*. The smallest is the hardy *Shetland* about 70 cm/27 in high. The *mule* is the usually sterile offspring of a female horse and a male ass, and a hardy pack-animal; the *hinny* is a similarly

horse

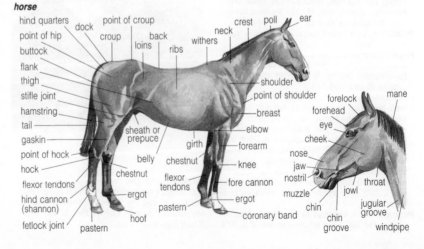

horse *Przewalski's horse, the only surviving species of wild horse.*

sterile offspring of a male horse and a female ass, but less useful as a beast of burden.

Horse, Master of the head of the department of the British royal household, responsible for the royal stables. The Earl of Westmorland became Master of the Horse 1978.

horse chestnut tree *Aesculus hippocastanatum*, originally from SE Europe but widely planted elsewhere. Its fruit contains the inedible conker. It is not related to the true chestnut.

horsefly fly of the family Tabanidae. The females suck blood from horses, cattle, and humans; males live on plants and suck nectar. The larvae are carnivorous. They are also known as clegs or gadflies. There are over 2,500 species.

Horse Guards in the UK, the Household Cavalry, or Royal Horse Guards, formed 1661. Their headquarters, in Whitehall, London, England, were erected in 1753 by Vardy from a design by Kent, on the site of the Tilt Yard of Whitehall palace.

horsepower imperial unit (symbol hp) of power, now replaced by the ◊watt. It was first used by the engineer James ◊Watt, who employed it to compare the power of steam engines with that of horses.

Watt found a horse to be capable of 366 footpounds of work per second but, in order to enable him to use the term 'horsepower' to cover the additional work done by the more efficient steam engine, he exaggerated the pulling power of the horse by 50%. Hence, one horsepower is equal to 550 foot-pounds per second/745.7 watts, which is more than any real horse could produce. The metric horsepower is 735.5 watts; the standard US horsepower is 746 watts.

horse racing the sport of racing mounted or driven horses. Two popular forms in Britain are *flat racing*, for thoroughbred horses over a flat course, and *National Hunt* racing, in which the horses have to clear obstacles.

In Britain, racing became popular in Stuart times and with its royal connections became known as the 'sport of kings'. Early racecourses include Chester, Ascot, and Newmarket. The English classics were introduced 1776 with the St Leger (run at Doncaster), followed by the Oaks 1779 and Derby 1780 (both run at Epsom), and 2,000 Guineas 1809 and 1,000 Guineas 1814 (both run at Newmarket). The governing body for the sport is the Jockey Club, founded about 1750. The National Hunt Committee was established 1866. Elsewhere, races include the Australian Melbourne Cup 1861 (at Flemington Park, Victoria) and the US Triple Crown: the Belmont Stakes 1867 (at New York), the Preakness Stakes 1873 (at Pimlico, Baltimore), and the Kentucky Derby 1875 (at Churchill Downs, Louisville). Another major race in the USA is the end-of-season Breeders' Cup 1984, with $10 million in prize money at stake.

Steeplechasing is a development of foxhunting, of which *point-to-point* is the amateur version, and *hurdling* a version with less severe, and movable, fences. Outstanding steeplechases are the Grand National 1839 (at Aintree, Liverpool) and Cheltenham Gold Cup 1924 (at Cheltenham).

horse racing: recent winners

horse/jockey (amateurs shown as Mr/Ms)

Derby
1980 Henbit/Willie Carson
1981 Shergar/Walter Swinburn
1982 Golden Fleece/Pat Eddery
1983 Teenoso/Lester Piggott
1984 Secreto/Christy Roche
1985 Slip Anchor/Steve Cauthen
1986 Shahrastani/Walter Swinburn
1987 Reference Point/Steve Cauthen
1988 Kahyasi/Ray Cochrane
1989 Nashwan/Willie Carson

Oaks
1980 Bireme/Willie Carson
1981 Blue Wind/Lester Piggott
1982 Time Charter/Billy Newnes
1983 Sun Princess/Willie Carson
1984 Circus Plume/Lester Piggott
1985 Oh So Sharp/Steve Cauthen
1986 Midway Lady/Ray Cochrane
1987 Unite/Walter Swinburn
1988 Diminuendo/Steve Cauthen
1989 Aliysa/Walter Swinburn

1,000 Guineas
1980 Quick As Lightning/Brian Rouse
1981 Fairy Footsteps/Lester Piggott
1982 On The House/John Reid
1983 Ma Biche/Freddy Head
1984 Pebbles/Philip Robinson
1985 Oh So Sharp/Steve Cauthen
1986 Midway Lady/Ray Cochrane
1987 Miesque/Freddy Head
1988 Ravinella/Gary Moore
1989 Musical Bliss/Walter Swinburn

2,000 Guineas
1980 Known Fact/Willie Carson
1981 To-Agori-Mou/Greville Starkey
1982 Zino/Freddy Head
1983 Lomond/Pat Eddery
1984 El Gran Senor/Pat Eddery
1985 Shadeed/Lester Piggott
1986 Dancing Brave/Greville Starkey
1987 Don't Forget Me/Willie Carson
1988 Doyoun/Walter Swinburn
1989 Nashwan/Walter Swinburn

St Leger
1980 Light Cavalry/Joe Mercer
1981 Cut Above/Joe Mercer
1982 Touching Wood/Paul Cook
1983 Sun Princess/Willie Carson
1984 Commanche Run/Lester Piggott
1985 Oh So Sharp/Steve Cauthen
1986 Moon Madness/Pat Eddery
1987 Reference Point/Steve Cauthen
1988 Minster Son/Willie Carson
1989 Michelozza/Steve Cauthen

Grand National
1981 Aldaniti/Bob Champion
1982 Grittar/Mr Dick Saunders
1983 Corbiere/Ben De Haan
1984 Hallo Dandy/Neale Doughty
1985 Last Suspect/Hywel Davies
1986 West Tip/Richard Dunwoody
1987 Maori Venture/Steve Knight
1988 Rhyme N'Reason/Brendan Powell
1989 Little Polveir/Jimmy Frost
1990 Mr Frisk/Marcus Armytage

Prix de L'Arc de Triomphe
1981 Gold River/Gary Moore
1982 Akiyda/Yves Saint-Martin
1983 All Along/Walter Swinburn
1984 Sagace/Yves Saint-Martin
1985 Rainbow Quest/Pat Eddery
1986 Dancing Brave/Pat Eddery
1987 Lieutenant's Lark/Robbie Davis
1988 Trempolino/Pat Eddery
1989 Tony Bin/John Reid
1990 Carroll House/Michael Kinnane

horseradish

root

The leading hurdling race is the Champion Hurdle 1927 (at Cheltenham). *Harness racing* is popular in North America. It is for standardbred horses pulling a two-wheeled 'sulky' on which the driver sits. Notable races include The Hambletonian and Little Brown Jug.

horseradish hardy perennial *Armoracia rusticana*, native to SE Europe but naturalized elsewhere, family Cruciferae. The thick, cream-coloured root is strong tasting and made into a condiment to eat with meat.

horsetail plant of the class Equisetales, related to ferns and clubmosses. There are about 35 living species, bearing their spores on cones at the stem tip. The upright stems are ribbed, and often have spaced whorls of branches. Today they are of modest size, but hundreds of millions of years ago giant tree-like forms existed.

Horsham /'hɔːʃəm/ town and market centre on the river Arun, in West Sussex, England, 26 km/16 mi SE of Guildford; population (1985) 30,000. The public school Christ's Hospital is about 3 km/2 mi to the SW. The poet Shelley was born here.

Horsley /'hɔːzli/ John Calcott 1817–1903. English artist. A skilled painter of domestic scenes, he was also responsible for frescoes in the Houses of Parliament, and is credited with designing the first Christmas card.

Horst-Wessel-Lied /.hɔːst 'vesə liːt/ song introduced by the Nazis as a second German national anthem. The text was written by Horst Wessel (1907–30), a Nazi 'martyr', to a traditional tune.

Horthy de Nagybánya /'hɔːti də 'nɒdʒbɑːnjə/ Nicholas 1868–1957. Hungarian politician and admiral. Leader of the counter-revolutionary White government, he became regent 1920 on the overthrow of the communist Bela Kun regime by Romanian intervention. He represented the conservative and military class, and retained power until World War II, trying (although allied to Hitler) to retain independence of action. In 1944 Hungary

horsetail

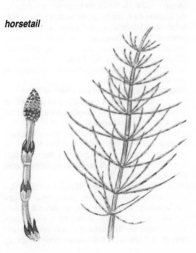

Hoskins British character actor Bob Hoskins.

was taken over by the Nazis and he was deported to Germany.

horticulture the art and science of growing flowers, fruit, and vegetables. Horticulture is practised in gardens and orchards, along with millions of acres of land devoted to vegetable farming. Some areas, like California, have specialized in horticulture because they have the mild climate and light fertile soil most suited to these crops.

In Britain, over half a million acres are devoted to professional horticulture, and vegetables account for almost three-quarters of the produce.

Horus /'hɔːrəs/ in ancient Egyptian mythology, the hawkheaded sun god, son of Isis and Osiris, of whom the pharaohs were thought to be the incarnation.

Hosea prophet in the Old Testament or Hebrew Bible. His prophecy draws parallels between his own marriage and the relationship between God and Israel.

Hoskins /'hɒskɪnz/ Bob 1942– . British character actor who progressed to fame from a series of supporting roles. Films include *The Long Good Friday* 1980, *The Cotton Club* 1984, *Mona Lisa* 1985, *A Prayer for the Dying* 1987, *Who Framed Roger Rabbit?* 1988.

hospice a residential facility specializing in the care of the terminally ill.

hospital institution for the care of the sick and injured.

In ancient times, temples of deities such as ◊Aesculapius offered facilities for treatment, and the Christian church had, by the 4th century, founded hospitals for lepers, cripples, the blind, the sick, and the poor. The oldest surviving hospital in Europe is the 7th-century Hôtel Dieu, Paris; in Britain, the most ancient are St Bartholomew's 1123 and St Thomas's 1200; and in the Americas the Hospital of Jesus of Nazareth, Mexico, 1524. Medical knowledge advanced during the Renaissance, and hospitals became increasingly secularized following the Reformation. In the 19th century, further progress was made in hospital design, administration, and staffing (Florence ◊Nightingale played a significant role in this). In the 20th century there has been an increasing trend towards specialization.

Hospitaller a member of the Order of ◊St John.

host an organism that is parasitized by another. In ◊commensalism, the partner that does not benefit may also be called the host.

hostage person taken prisoner as a means of exerting pressure on a third party, usually with threats of death or injury. Most significant internationally were 63 staff of the US embassy in Tehran taken by the Iranians 1979.

HOTOL (*Horizontal Take-Off and Landing*) British concept for a hypersonic transport and satellite launcher, which could be operational before the end of the century. It will be a single-stage vehicle with no boosters and will take off and land on a runway. It will feature a revolutionary

air-breathing rocket engine which will enable it to carry much less oxygen than a conventional space plane. HOTOL has a US rival known as the *Orient Express*.

hot spot in geology, a hypothetical region of high thermal activity in the Earth's ◊mantle. It is believed to be the origin of many chains of ocean islands, such as Polynesia and the Galapagos.

A volcano forms on the ocean crust immediately above the hot spot, is carried away by ◊plate tectonic movement, and becomes extinct. A new volcano forms beside it, above the hot spot. The result is an active volcano and a chain of increasingly old and eroded volcanic stumps stretching away along the line of plate movement.

Hottentot South African people inhabiting the SW corner of the continent when Europeans first settled there. The language resembles Bushman, and has mainly monosyllabic roots with explosive consonants which produce clicking sounds.

Houdini /huːˈdiːnɪ/ Harry. Stage name of Erich Weiss 1874–1926. US escape artist and conjurer. He attained fame by his escapes from ropes and handcuffs, from trunks under water, from straitjackets and prison cells. He also campaigned against fraudulent mindreaders and mediums.

Houdon /uːˈdɒŋ/ Jean-Antoine 1741–1828. French sculptor, a portraitist who made characterful studies of Voltaire and a Neo-Classical statue of George Washington, commissioned 1785. His other subjects included the philosophers Diderot and Rousseau, the composer Gluck, the emperor Napoleon, and the American politician Benjamin Franklin. Houdon also produced popular mythological figures, such as *Diana* and *Minerva*.

Hounsfield /'haʊnzfiːld/ Godfrey 1919– . British pioneer of ◊tomography, who shared a Nobel prize in 1979 with independent researcher Allan Cormack.

Hounslow /'haʊnzləʊ/ borough of W Greater London; population (1981) 199,782

features London Airport (established 1946 at Heathrow), Hounslow Heath, formerly famous for highwaymen; *Chiswick*, with the Palladian villa by ◊Burlington, and ◊Hogarth's home (now a museum); *Heston* site of London's first civil airport established in 1919, *Brentford*, reputed site of Caesar's crossing of the Thames in 54 BC, and the Duke of Northumberland's seat at Syon House, and *Isleworth*, Osterley, home of Thomas ◊Gresham (both with work by ◊Adam).

Houphouët-Boigny /uːˈfweɪ bwɑːnˈjiː/ Félix 1905– . Ivory Coast right-wing politician. He held posts in French ministries, and became president of the Republic of the Ivory Coast on independence 1960. He was re-elected for a sixth term 1985 representing the sole legal party.

hour a period of time comprising 60 minutes; 24 hours make 1 calendar day.

Hours, Book of in medieval Europe, a collection of liturgical prayers for the use of the faithful, especially at home. Books of Hours appeared in England in the 13th century, and contained short prayers and illustrations, with each prayer suitable for a different hour of the day, in honour of the Virgin Mary. The enormous demand for Books of Hours was a stimulus for the development of Gothic illumination. A notable example is the *Très Riches Heures du Duc de Berry*, illustrated in the early 15th century by the ◊Limbourg brothers.

housefly the commonest type of fly of the family Muscidae. Houseflies are grey, and have mouthparts adapted for drinking liquids.

Household, Royal see ◊Royal Household.

Household /'haʊshəʊld/ Geoffrey 1900–1988. British espionage and adventure novelist. His *Rogue Male* 1939 concerned an Englishman's attempt to kill Hitler, and the enemy hunt for him after his failure. Household served with British intelligence in World War II.

Houseman /'haʊsmən/ John 1902–1988. US theatre, film, and television producer and actor, born in Romania. He co-founded the Mercury Theater with Orson Welles, and collaborated with Welles

and Nicholas Ray as directors. He won an Academy Award for his acting debut in *The Paper Chase* 1973, and re-created his role in the subsequent TV series.

house music a type of dance music of the 1980s originating in the inner-city clubs of Chicago, USA, combining funk with European high-tech pop, using dub, digital sampling, and cross-fading. *Acid house* has minimal vocals and melody, instead surrounding the mechanically emphasized 4/4 beat with found noises, stripped-down synthesizer riffs, and a wandering bass line.

housing the provision of residential accommodation. All modern states have found some degree of state housing provision or subsidy essential, even in free-enterprise economies such as the USA.

Legislation in Britain began with measures passed in 1851 and the Housing of the Working Classes Act 1890. The introduction of rent control in 1915 began a long-term decline in the amount of rented accommodation, and tax relief on mortgages encourages private ownership; 14 million Britons were home-owners 1986. Flats and houses to rent (intended for people with low incomes) are also built by local authorities under the direction of the secretary of state for environment. In 1980 controversial legislation was introduced to enable council tenants to buy their homes, and nearly 1 million council houses had been sold by 1986.

Housman /'haʊsmən/ A(lfred) E(dward) 1859–1936. English poet and classical scholar. His *A Shropshire Lad* 1896, a series of deceptively simple nostalgic ballad-like poems, was popular during World War I. This was followed by *Last Poems* 1922, and *More Poems* 1936.

Houston /'hjuːstən/ port in Texas, USA; population (1981) 2,891,000; linked by canal to the Gulf of Mexico. It is an agricultural centre, and industries include petrochemicals, chemicals, plastics, synthetic rubber, and electronics.

Houston /'hjuːstən/ Sam 1793–1863. US general who won Texas' independence from Mexico 1836 and was president of the Republic of Texas 1836–45. Houston, Texas, is named after him.

Houston was governor of the state of Tennessee and later US senator and governor of the state of Texas. He took Cherokee Indian citizenship when he married a Cherokee.

Hove /həʊv/ seaside resort in East Sussex, England, adjoining Brighton; population (1981) 66,612.

Hovell /'hɒvəl/ William Hilton 1786–1875. Explorer of Australia with Hamilton ◊Hume.

hovercraft a vehicle that rides on a cushion of high-pressure air, free from all contact with the surface beneath, invented by British engineer Christopher Cockerell 1959. Hovercraft need a smooth terrain when operating overland and are best adapted to use on waterways. They are useful in places where harbours have not been established.

Large hovercraft (SR-N4) operate a swift car-ferry service across the English Channel, taking only about 35 minutes between Dover and Calais. They are fitted with a flexible 'skirt' that helps maintain the air cushion.

Howard /'haʊəd/ Alan 1937– . British actor, whose appearances with the Royal Shakespeare Company include *Henry V, Henry VI, Coriolanus,* and *Richard III*.

Howard /'haʊəd/ Catherine c. 1520–1542. Queen consort of ◊Henry VIII of England from 1540. In 1541 the archbishop of Canterbury, Thomas Cranmer, accused her of being unchaste before marriage to Henry, and she was beheaded 1542 after Cranmer made further charges of adultery.

Howard /'haʊəd/ Charles, 2nd Baron Howard of Effingham and 1st Earl of Nottingham 1536–1624. English admiral, a cousin of Queen Elizabeth I. He commanded the fleet against the Spanish Armada while Lord High Admiral 1585–1618. He cooperated with the Earl of Essex in the attack on Cádiz 1596.

hovercraft

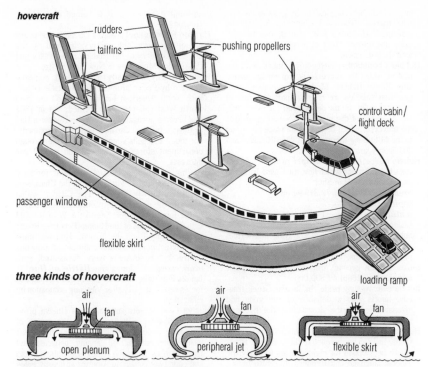

rudders
tailfins
pushing propellers
control·cabin/ flight deck
passenger windows
flexible skirt
loading ramp

three kinds of hovercraft

air | fan — open plenum

air | fan — peripheral jet

air | fan — flexible skirt

Hoyle British astronomer Professor Fred Hoyle.

Howard /ˈhaʊəd/ Constance 1919– . English embroiderer who helped to revive creative craftwork following World War II. Her work included framed pictures with fabrics outlined in bold black threads, wall hangings, and geometric studies in strong colour.

Howard /ˈhaʊəd/ Ebenezer 1850–1928. English town planner and founder of the ideal of the ◊garden city, through his book *Tomorrow* 1898 (republished as *Garden Cities of Tomorrow* 1902).

Howard /ˈhaʊəd/ John 1726–1790. English philanthropist whose work to improve prison conditions is continued today by the ***Howard League for Penal Reform.***

On his appointment as high sheriff for Bedfordshire 1773, he undertook a tour of English prisons which led to two acts of Parliament 1774, making jailers salaried officers and setting standards of cleanliness. After touring Europe 1775 he published his *State of the Prisons in England and Wales, with an account of some Foreign Prisons* 1777. He died of typhus fever while visiting Russian military hospitals at Kherson in the Crimea.

Howard /ˈhaʊəd/ Leslie. Stage name of Leslie Stainer 1893–1943. English actor, whose films include *The Scarlet Pimpernel* 1935, *Pygmalion* 1938, and *Gone with the Wind* 1939.

Howard /ˈhaʊəd/ Trevor (Wallace) 1916–1989. English actor, whose films include *Brief Encounter* 1945, *Sons and Lovers* 1960, *Mutiny on the Bounty* 1962, *Ryan's Daughter* 1970, and *Conduct Unbecoming* 1975.

Howe /haʊ/ Elias 1819–1867. US inventor, in 1846, of a ◊sewing machine using double thread.

Howe /haʊ/ Geoffrey 1926– . British Conservative politician. Under Heath he was solicitor-general 1970–72 and minister for trade 1972–74; as chancellor of the Exchequer 1979–83 under Thatcher, he put into practice the monetarist policy which reduced inflation at the cost of a rise in unemployment. In 1983 he became foreign secretary, and in 1989 he unexpectedly became deputy prime minister and leader of the House of Commons.

Howe /haʊ/ Gordie 1926– . Canadian ice-hockey player, who played for the Detroit Red Wings (National Hockey League) 1946–71 and the New England Whalers (World Hockey Association). In the NHL, he scored more goals (801), assists (1,049), and points (1,850) than any other player

in ice-hockey history. He played professional ice hockey until over 50.

Howe /haʊ/ James Wong. Adopted name of Wong Tung Jim 1899–1976. Chinese-born director of film photography, who lived in the USA from childhood. One of Hollywood's best camera operators, he is credited with introducing the use of hand-held cameras and deep focus. His work ranges from *The Alaskan* 1924 to *Funny Lady* 1975.

Howe /haʊ/ Julia Ward 1819–1910. US feminist and anti-slavery campaigner, who in 1862 wrote the 'Battle Hymn of the Republic', sung to the tune of 'John Brown's Body'.

Howe /haʊ/ Richard Earl 1726–1799. British admiral. He cooperated with his brother William against the colonists during the American War of Independence, and in the French Revolutionary Wars commanded the Channel fleets 1792–96.

Howe /haʊ/ William, 5th Viscount Howe 1729–1814. British general. During the War of American Independence he won the Battle of Bunker Hill 1775, and as commander in chief in America 1776–78 captured New York and defeated Washington at Brandywine and Germantown. He resigned in protest at lack of home government support.

Howells /ˈhaʊəlz/ William Dean 1837–1920. US novelist and editor. The 'dean' of US letters in the post-Civil War era, and editor of the *Atlantic Monthly*, he championed the realist movement in fiction and encouraged many younger authors. He wrote 35 novels, 35 plays, and many books of poetry, essays, and commentary.

His novels, filled with vivid social detail, include *A Modern Instance* 1882 and *The Rise of Silas Lapham* 1885, about the social fall and moral rise of a New England paint manufacturer, a central fable of the 'Gilded Age'.

howitzer a cannon, in use since the 16th century, with a particularly steep angle of fire. It was much developed in World War I for demolishing the fortresses of the trench system. The multinational NATO FH70 field howitzer is mobile and fires, under computer control, three 43 kg/95 lb shells at 32 km/20 mi range in 15 seconds.

Howrah /ˈhaʊrə/ or *Haora* city of West Bengal, India, on the right bank of the Hooghli, opposite Calcutta; population (1981) 742,298. The capital of Howrah district, it has jute and cotton factories, rice, flour, and saw mills, chemical factories, and

engineering works. Howrah suspension bridge, opened 1943, spans the river.

Hoxha /ˈhɒdʒə/ Enver 1908–1985. Albanian Communist politician, the country's leader from 1954. He founded the Albanian Communist Party 1941, and headed the liberation movement 1939–44. He was prime minister 1944–54, combining with foreign affairs 1946–53, and from 1954 was first secretary of the Albanian Party of Labour. In policy he was a Stalinist, and independent of both Chinese and Soviet communism.

Hoyle /hɔɪl/ Fred(erick) 1915– . English astronomer and writer. In 1948 he joined with Hermann Bondi and Thomas Gold in developing the ◊steady-state theory. In 1957, with Geoffrey and Margaret Burbidge and William Fowler, he showed that chemical elements heavier than hydrogen and helium are built up by nuclear reactions inside stars. He has created controversy by suggesting that life originates in the gas clouds of space, and is delivered to the Earth by passing comets.

His work on the evolution of stars was published in *Frontiers of Astronomy* 1955; his science fiction novels include *The Black Cloud* 1957. He was research professor at Manchester University from 1972, and at University College, Cardiff, from 1975.

hp abbreviation for ◊*horsepower*.

HQ abbreviation for *headquarters*.

HRH abbreviation for *His/Her Royal Highness*.

Hsuan Tung name adopted by Henry ◊P'u-i on becoming emperor of China 1908.

ht abbreviation for *height*.

Hua Guofeng /ˈhwɑː ˌgwəʊˈfʌŋ/ formerly *Hua Kuofeng* 1920– . Chinese politician, leader of the Chinese Communist Party (CCP) 1976–81, premier 1976–80. He dominated Chinese politics 1976–77, seeking economic modernization without major structural reform. From 1978 he was gradually eclipsed by Deng Xiaoping. Hua was ousted from the Politburo Sept 1982, but remained a member of the CCP Central Committee.

Hua, born in Shanxi into a peasant family, fought under Zhu De, the Red Army leader, during the liberation war 1937–49. He entered the CCP Central Committee 1969 and the Politburo 1973. An orthodox, loyal Maoist, Hua was selected to succeed Zhou Enlai as prime minister Jan 1976 and became party leader on Mao Zedong's death Sept 1976. He was replaced as prime minister by Zhao Ziyang Sept 1980 and as CCP chair by Hu Yaobang June 1981.

Huallaga River a tributary of the Marayon in NE Peru. The upper reaches of the river valley are renowned for the growing of coca, a major source of the drug cocaine.

Huambo /ˈwɑːmbəʊ/ town in central Angola; population (1970) 61,885. It was founded 1912, and known as Nova Lisboa 1928–78, when it

Hudson *A festival gathering of old sailing ships on the Hudson River, New York.*

was designated by the Portuguese as the future capital. It is an agricultural centre.

Huang He /ˈhwæŋ ˈhəʊ/ formerly *Hwang-ho* river in China; length 5,464 km/3,395 mi. It gains its name (meaning 'yellow river') from its muddy waters. Formerly known as 'China's sorrow' because of disastrous floods, it is now largely controlled through hydroelectric works and flood barriers. The flood barriers are ceasing to work because the silt that gives the river its name 'yellow' is continually raising the river bed.

Huangshan Mountains /ˌhwæŋˈʃɑːn/ mountain range in S Anhui province, China; the highest peak is Lotus Flower 1,873 m/5,106 ft.

Huáscar /ˈwɑːskə/ c. 1495–1532. King of the Incas. He shared the throne with his half-brother Atahualpa from 1525, but the latter overthrew and murdered him during the Spanish conquest.

Huáscaran /ˌwɑːskəˈrɑːn/ extinct volcano in the Andes, the highest mountain in Peru, 6,768 m/22,205 ft.

Hubbard /ˈhʌbəd/ L(afayette) Ron(ald) 1911–1986. US science-fiction writer of the 1930s–1940s, founder in 1954 of ◊Scientology.

Hubble /ˈhʌbəl/ Edwin Powell 1889–1953. US astronomer, who discovered the existence of other ◊galaxies outside our own, and classified them according to their shape. He proposed that the universe was expanding, a theory since confirmed.

Born in Marshfield, Missouri, Hubble originally studied law before joining ◊Yerkes Observatory 1914, subsequently moving to Mount Wilson where in 1923, he discovered ◊Cepheid variable stars outside our own galaxy. In 1925 he

introduced the classification of galaxies as spirals, barred spirals and ellipticals. In 1929 he announced *Hubble's law*, that is, that the galaxies are moving apart at a rate that increases with their distance.

Hubble's constant in astronomy, a measure of the rate at which the universe is expanding, named after Edwin Hubble. Modern observations suggest that galaxies are moving apart at a rate of 50–100 km/30–60 mi per second for every million ◊parsecs of distance. This would mean that the universe, which began at one place according to the ◊Big Bang theory, is between 10 billion and 20 billion years old.

Hubei /ˌhuːˈbeɪ/ formerly *Hupei* province of central China, through which flow the Chang Jiang and its tributary the Han Shui
area 187,500 sq km/72,375 sq mi
capital Wuhan
features in the west the land is high, the Chang breaking through from Sichuan in gorges, but elsewhere the land is low lying and fertile; many lakes
products beans, cereals, cotton, rice, vegetables, copper, gypsum, iron ore, phosphorus, salt
population (1986) 49,890,000.

hubris overweening pride. In ancient Greek tragedy, hubris was a defiance of the gods and invariably led to the downfall of the hubristic character.

Huc /uːk/ Abbé 1813–1860. French missionary in China. In 1845 he travelled to the border of Tibet, where he stopped for eight months to study the Tibetan language and Buddhist literature before moving on to the city of Lahsa.

huckleberry berry-bearing bush of the genus *Vaccinium*, including the *bilberry Vaccinium myrtillus* in Britain, and various blueberries in the USA.

Huddersfield /ˈhʌdəzfiːld/ industrial town in West Yorkshire, on the river Colne, linked by canal with Manchester and other north of England centres; population (1981) 123,888. A village in Anglo-Saxon times, it was a thriving centre of woollen manufacture by the end of the 18th century, and more recently has diversified to dyestuffs, chemicals, and electrical and mechanical engineering.

Hudson /ˈhʌdsən/ river of the NE USA; length 485 km/300 mi. First reached by European settlers 1524, it was explored 1609 by Henry Hudson, and named after him. New York stands at its mouth.

Hudson /ˈhʌdsən/ Henry c. 1565–c. 1611. English explorer. Under the auspices of the Muscovy Company 1607–08, he made two unsuccessful attempts to find the Northeast passage to China. In Sept 1609, commissioned by the Dutch East India Company, he reached New York Bay and sailed 240 km/150 mi up the river that now bears his name, establishing Dutch claims to the area. In 1610, he sailed from London in the *Discovery* and entered what is now the Hudson Strait. After an icebound winter, he was turned adrift by a mutinous crew in what is now Hudson Bay.

Hudson /ˈhʌdsən/ Rock. Stage name of Roy Scherer Jr 1925–1985. US film actor, a star from the mid-1950s to the mid-1960s, who appeared in several melodramas directed by Douglas Sirk and three comedies co-starring Doris Day (including *Pillow Talk* 1959).

Hudson /ˈhʌdsən/ W(illiam) H(enry) 1841–1922. Anglo-US author, born of US parents at Florencio near Buenos Aires, Argentina. He was inspired by recollections of early days in Argentina to write the romances *The Purple Land* 1885 and *Green Mansions* 1904, and his autobiographical *Far Away and Long Ago* 1918. He wrote several books on birds, and on the English countryside, for example, *Nature in Down-Land* 1900 and *A Shepherd's Life* 1910.

Hudson Bay /ˈhʌdsən/ inland sea of NE Canada, linked with the Atlantic by **Hudson Strait**, and with the Arctic by Foxe Channel; area 1,233,000

sq km/476,000 sq mi. It is named after Henry Hudson.

Hudson River school group of US landscape painters of the early 19th century, inspired by the dramatic scenery of the Hudson River valley and the Catskill Mountains in New York State.

Hudson's Bay Company a chartered company founded by Prince ◊Rupert 1670 to trade in furs with North American Indians. In 1783 the rival North West Company was formed, but in 1851 this became amalgamated with the Hudson's Bay Company. It is still Canada's biggest fur company, but today also sells general merchandise through department stores and has oil and natural gas interests.

Hue /huːˈeɪ/ town in Central Vietnam, formerly capital of Annam, 13 km/8 mi from the China Sea; population (1973) 209,043. The Citadel, within which is the Imperial City enclosing the palace of the former emperor, lies to the W of the Old City on the N bank of the Huong (Perfume) River; the New City is on the S bank. Hue was once an architecturally beautiful cultural and religious centre, but large areas were devastated, with many casualties, during the **Battle of Hue** 31 Jan–24 Feb 1968, when US and South Vietnamese forces retook the city after Vietcong occupation by infiltration.

Huelva /ˈwelvə/ port and capital of Huelva province, Andalusia, SW Spain, near the mouth of the Odiel; population (1986) 135,000. Industries include ship building, oil refining, fisheries, and trade in ores from Rio Tinto. Columbus began and ended his voyage to America at nearby Palos de la Frontera.

Huesca /ˈweskə/ capital of Huesca province in Aragon, northern Spain; population (1981) 41,455. Industries include engineering and food processing. Among its buildings are a fine 13th-century cathedral and the former palace of the kings of Aragon.

Huggins /ˈhʌgɪnz/ William 1824–1910. British astronomer. He built a private observatory at Tulse Hill, London, in 1856, where he embarked on research in spectrum analysis that marked the beginning of astrophysics.

Hughes /hjuːz/ David 1831–1900. US inventor who patented an early form of telex in 1855, a type-printing instrument for use with the telegraph. He brought the instrument to Europe in 1857 where it became widely used.

Hughes /hjuːz/ Howard 1905–1976. US tycoon. Inheriting wealth from his father, who had patented a successful oil-drilling bit, he created a

Hudson *US film star Rock Hudson.*

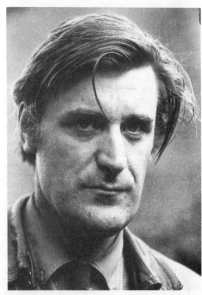

Hughes *Ted Hughes, who succeeded John Betjeman as British Poet Laureate.*

Hughes Australian prime minister William Morris Hughes (right), seen here with P G Stewart.

legendary financial empire. A skilled pilot, he manufactured and designed aircraft, and made the classic film *Hell's Angels* 1930 about aviators of World War I; later successes include *Scarface* 1932 and *The Outlaw* 1943. From his middle years he was a recluse.

Hughes /hjuːz/ Richard (Arthur Warren) 1900–1976. English writer. His study of childhood, *A High Wind in Jamaica*, was published 1929, and the trilogy *The Human Predicament* 1961–73.

Hughes /hjuːz/ Ted 1930– . English poet, Poet Laureate from 1984. His work includes *The Hawk in the Rain* 1957, *Lupercal* 1960, *Wodwo* 1967, and *River* 1983, and is characterized by its harsh portrayal of the crueller aspects of nature. He was born in Mytholmroyd, West Yorkshire. In 1956 he married the poet Sylvia Plath.

Hughes /hjuːz/ Thomas 1822–1896. English writer of the children's book *Tom Brown's Schooldays* 1857, a story of Rugby school under Thomas ◊Arnold. It had a sequel, *Tom Brown at Oxford* 1861.

Hughes /hjuːz/ William Morris 1864–1952. Australian politician, prime minister 1915–23; originally Labor, he headed a national cabinet. After resigning as prime minister 1923, he held many other cabinet posts 1934–41.

Born in London, he emigrated to Australia 1884. He represented Australia in the peace conference after World War I at Versailles.

Hugo /ˈhjuːgəʊ/ Victor (Marie) 1802–1885. French poet, novelist, and dramatist. The *Odes et poésies diverses* appeared 1822, and his verse play *Hernani* 1830 established him as the leader of French Romanticism. More volumes of verse followed between his series of dramatic novels which included *The Hunchback of Notre Dame* 1831 and ◊*Les Misérables* 1862. Originally a monarchist, he became an ardent republican, and was a senator under the Third Republic. He died a national hero.

Born at Besançon, Hugo was the son of one of Napoleon's generals. His involvement with republican ideals in the 1840s led to his banishment 1851 for opposing Louis Napoleon's coup d'état, and he lived in Guernsey until the fall of the empire 1870. He was buried in the ◊Panthéon.

Huguenot French Protestant in the 16th century; the term refered mainly to Calvinists. Severely

persecuted under Francis I and Henry II, the Huguenots survived both an attempt to exterminate them (the **Massacre of ◊St Bartholomew** 24 Aug 1572) and the religious wars of the next 30 years. In 1598 Henry IV (himself formerly a Huguenot) granted them toleration under the ◊*Edict of Nantes*. Louis XIV revoked the edict 1685, attempting their forcible conversion, and 400,000 emigrated.

Some of the nobles adopted Protestantism for political reasons, causing the civil wars 1592–98. The Huguenots lost military power after the revolt at La Rochelle 1627–29, but were still tolerated by the chief ministers Richelieu and Mazarin. Provoked by Louis XIV they left, taking their industrial skills with them; 40,000 settled in Britain, where their descendants include the actor David Garrick and the textile manufacturer Samuel Courtauld. Only in 1802 was the Huguenot church again legalized in France.

Huhehot /ˌhuːhɜːˈhəʊt/ former name of ◊Hohhot, city in Inner Mongolia.

Hull /hʌl/ Cordell 1871–1955. US Democrat politician, born in Tennessee. He was a member of Congress 1907–33, and, as Roosevelt's secretary of state 1933–44, was identified with the Good Neighbour Policy of nonintervention in Latin America, and opposed German and Japanese aggression. In his last months of office he paved the way for a system of collective security, for which

he was called 'father' of the United Nations. Nobel Peace Prize 1945.

Hull /hʌl/ officially *Kingston upon Hull* city and port, through which the river Humber flows, administrative headquarters of Humberside, England; population (1986) 258,000. It is linked with the south bank of the estuary by the Humber Bridge. Industries include fish processing, vegetable oils, flour milling, electricals, textiles, paint, pharmaceuticals, chemicals, caravans, and aircraft.

There are ferries to Rotterdam and Zeebrugge. Buildings include the 13th-century Holy Trinity Church, Guildhall, Ferens Art Gallery 1927, and the university 1954.

Hulme /hjuːm/ Keri 1947– . New Zealand novelist. She won the Booker Prize with her first novel *The Bone People* 1985.

Hulme /hjuːm/ T(homas) E(rnest) 1881–1917. British philosopher, critic and poet, killed on active service in World War I. His *Speculations* 1924 influenced T S ◊Eliot, and his few poems influenced the ◊Imagist movement.

hum, environmental a disturbing sound of frequency about 40 Hz, heard by individuals sensitive to this range, but inaudible to the rest of the population. It may be caused by industrial noise pollution or have a more exotic origin, such as the jet stream, a fast-flowing high-altitude (about 15,000 m/50,000 ft) mass of air.

human body

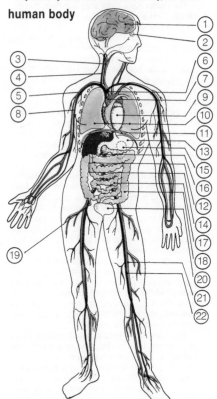

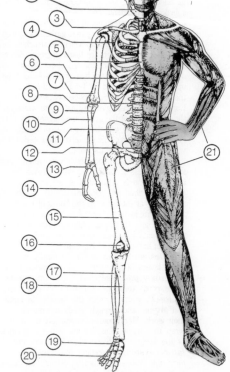

Key

1.	brain	12.	liver
2.	eye	13.	stomach
3.	carotid artery	14.	gall bladder
4.	jugular vein	15.	kidney
5.	subclavian artery	16.	pancreas
6.	superior vena cava	17.	small intestine
7.	aorta	18.	large intestine
8.	subclavian vein	19.	appendix
9.	heart	20.	bladder
10.	lungs	21.	femoral artery
11.	diaphragm	22.	femoral vein

Key

1.	cranium (skull)	12.	coccyx
2.	mandible	13.	metacarpals
3.	clavicle	14.	phalanges
4.	scapula	15.	femur
5.	sternum	16.	patella
6.	rib cage	17.	fibula
7.	humerus	18.	tibia
8.	vertebra	19.	metatarsals
9.	ulna	20.	phalanges
10.	radius	21.	superficial (upper)
11.	pelvis		layer of muscles

human body the physical structure of the human being. It develops from the single cell of the fertilized ovum, is born at 40 weeks, and usually reaches sexual maturity between 11 and 18 years of age. The bony framework (skeleton) consists of more than 200 bones, over half of which are in the hands and feet. Bones are held together by joints, some of which allow movement, produced by muscles. The circulatory system supplies muscles and organs with blood, which provides oxygen and food, and removes waste products. Body functions are controlled by the nervous system and hormones. In the upper part of the trunk is the thorax, which contains the lungs and heart. Below this is the abdomen, inside which are the digestive system (stomach and intestines), the liver, spleen, and pancreas, the urinary system (kidneys, ureters, and bladder), and, in a woman, the reproductive organs (ovaries, uterus, and vagina). In a man, the prostate gland and seminal vesicles only of the reproductive system are situated in the abdomen, the testes being in the scrotum, which, with the penis, is suspended in front of and below the abdomen. The bladder empties through a small channel (urethra); this in the female opens in the upper end of the vulval cleft, which also contains the opening of the vagina, or birth canal. In the male, the urethra is continued into the penis. In both sexes, the lower bowel terminates in the anus, a ring of strong muscle situated between the buttocks.

skeleton The skull is mounted on the spinal column, or spine, a chain of 24 vertebrae. The ribs, 12 on each side, are articulated (jointed) to the spinal column behind, and the upper seven meet the breastbone (sternum) in front. The lower end of the spine rests on the pelvic girdle, composed of the triangular sacrum, to which are attached the hip bones (ilia), which are fused in front. Below the sacrum is the tail bone (coccyx). The shoulder blades (scapulae) are held in place behind the upper ribs by muscles, and connected in front to the breast bone by the two collar bones (clavicles). Each carries a cup (glenoid cavity) into which fits the upper end of the arm bone (humerus). This articulates below with the two forearm bones, the radius and the ulna. The radius is articulated at the wrist to the bones of the hand.

The upper end of each thigh bone (femur) fits into a depression in the hip bone (acetabulum); its lower end is articulated at the knee to the shin bone (tibia) and calf bone (fibula), which are articulated at the ankle to the bones of the foot. At a moving joint, the end of each bone is formed of tough, smooth cartilage, lubricated by ◊synovial fluid. Points of special stress are reinforced by bands of fibrous tissue (ligaments).

Muscles are bundles of fibres wrapped in thin, tough layers of connective tissue (fascia); these are usually prolonged at the ends into strong, white cords (tendons, sinews) or sheets (aponeuroses), which connect the muscles to bones and organs, and through which the muscles do their work. Membranes of connective tissue also wrap the organs and line the interior cavities of the body. The blood vessels of the *circulatory system*, branching into multitudes of very fine tubes (capillaries), supply all parts of the muscles and organs with blood, which carries oxygen and food necessary for life. The food passes out of the blood to the cells in a clear fluid (lymph); this returns with waste matter through a system of lymphatic vessels to the large veins below the collar-bones and thence to the heart. Capillaries join together to form veins which return blood, depleted of oxygen, to the heart. A finely branching *nervous system* regulates the function of the muscles and organs, and makes their needs known to the controlling centres in the central nervous system, which consists of the brain and spinal cord. The inner spaces of the brain and the cord contain cerebro-spinal fluid. The body

human body: composition by weight

Class	Chemical element or substance	Bodyweight (%)
pure elements, mineral salts, etc	oxygen	65
	carbon	18
	hydrogen	10
	nitrogen	3
	calcium	2
	phosphorus	1.1
	inorganic molecules	1
	potassium	0.35
	sulphur	0.25
	sodium	0.15
	chlorine	0.15
	magnesium, iron, manganese, copper iodine, cobalt, zinc	traces
water and solid matter	water	60–80
	total solid material	20–40
organic molecules	protein	15–20
	lipid	3–20
	carbohydrate	1–15
	small organic molecules	0–1

processes are regulated both by the nervous system and by hormones secreted by the endocrine glands.

The thorax has a stout muscular floor, the diaphragm, which expands and contracts the lungs in the act of breathing.

Cavities of the body that open on to the surface are coated with mucous membrane, which secretes a lubricating fluid (mucus). The exterior suface of the body is coated with *skin*. Within the skin are the sebaceous glands, which secrete sebum, an oily fluid that makes the skin soft and pliable, and the sweat glands, which secrete water and various salts. From the skin grow hair, chiefly on the head, in the armpits, and around the sexual organs; and nails shielding the tips of the fingers and toes; both these structures are modifications of skin tissue. The skin also contains ◊nerves of touch, pain, heat, and cold.

The human *digestive system* is non-specialized, that is, it can break down a wide variety of foodstuffs. Food is mixed with saliva in the mouth by chewing and is swallowed. It enters the stomach, where it is gently churned for some time and mixed with acidic gastric juice. It then passes into the small intestine. In the first part of this, the duodenum, it is broken down further by the juice of the pancreas and duodenal glands, and mixed with bile from the liver, which splits up the fat. The jejunum and ileum continue the work of digestion and absorb most of the nutritive substances from the food. The large intestine completes the process and reabsorbs water into the body, and ejects the useless residue as faeces.

The body, to be healthy, must maintain water and various salts in the right proportions; the process is called osmoregulation. The blood is filtered in the two kidneys, which remove excess water and salts. These, with a yellow pigment derived from bile, are the urine, which passes down through two fine tubes (ureters) into the bladder, a reservoir from which the urine is emptied at intervals (micturition) through the urethra.

Heat is constantly generated by the combustion of food in the muscles and glands, and by the activity of nerve cells and fibres. It is dissipated through the skin by conduction and evaporation of sweat, through the lungs in the expired air, and in the other excreted substances. Average body temperature is about 38°C/100°F (37°C/98.4°F in the mouth).

Human Comedy, The French *La Comédie humaine* a series of novels by Balzac, published 1842–48, which were intended to depict every aspect of 19th-century French life. Of the 143 planned, only 80 were completed. They include studies of human folly and vice as in *Le Recherche de*

l'absolu/The Search for the Absolute, and analyses of professions or ranks *L'Illustre Gaudissart/The Famous Gaudissart* and *Le Curé de village/The Village Parson*.

human–computer interaction the exchange of information between a person and a computer, through the medium of a ◊user interface, studied as a branch of ergonomics.

Human Rights, Universal Declaration of charter of civil and political rights drawn up by the United Nations 1948. They include the right to life, liberty, education, and equality before the law; to freedom of movement, religion, association, and information; and to a nationality. Under the European Convention of Human Rights 1950, the Council of Europe established the *European Commission of Human Rights* (headquarters in Strasbourg, France), which investigates complaints by states or individuals, and its findings are examined by the *European Court of Human Rights* (established 1959), whose compulsory jurisdiction has been recognized by a number of states, including the UK.

Human Rights Day is 10 Dec, commemorating the adoption of the Universal Declaration of Human Rights by the UN General Assembly.

The declaration is not legally binding, and the frequent contraventions are monitored by organizations such as ◊Amnesty International. Human rights were also an issue at the ◊Helsinki Conference.

In 1988 the European Court condemned as unlawful the UK procedure of holding those suspected of terrorism for up to seven days with no judicial control.

human rights civil and political rights of the individual in relation to the state.

human species, origins of evolution of humans from ancestral ◊primates. The African apes (gorilla and chimpanzee) are shown by anatomical and molecular comparisons to be our closest living relatives. Molecular studies put the date of the split between the human and African ape lines at 5–10 million years ago. There are no ape or *hominid* (of the human group) fossils from this period; the oldest known date from 3.5 million years ago, from Ethiopia and Tanzania. These creatures are known as *Australopithecus afarensis*, and they walked upright. They were either our direct ancestors or an offshoot of the line that led to modern humans. They might have been the ancestors of *Homo habilis*, who appeared about a million years later, had slightly larger bodies and brains, and were probably the first to use stone tools. *Australopithecus robustus* and *Australopithecus gracilis* also lived in Africa at the same time, but these are not generally considered to be our ancestors.

Over 1.5 million years ago, *Homo erectus*, believed to be descended from *Homo habilis*, appeared in Africa. The *erectus* people had much larger brains, and were probably the first to use fire and the first to move out of Africa. Their remains are found as far afield as China, Spain, and S Britain. Modern humans, *Homo sapiens sapiens*, and the Neanderthals, *Homo sapiens neanderthalensis*, are probably descended from *Homo erectus*. Neanderthals were large-brained and heavily built, probably adapted to the cold conditions of the ice ages. They lived in Europe and the Middle East, and died out about 40,000 years ago, leaving *Homo sapiens sapiens* as the only remaining species of the hominid group.

Creationists believe that the origin of the human species is as written in the book of Genesis in the Old Testament of the Bible.

Humber Bridge a suspension bridge with twin towers 163 m/535 ft high, which spans the estuary of the river Humber in NE England. When completed 1980, it was the world's longest bridge with a span of 1,410 m/4,628 ft.

Humberside /ˈhʌmbəsaɪd/ county of NE England

area 3,510 sq km/1,355 sq mi

human species, origins of

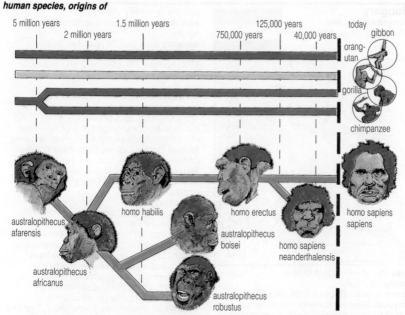

Humberside

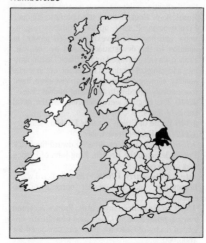

towns administrative headquarters Kingston-upon-Hull; Grimsby, Scunthorpe, Goole, Cleethorpes
features ◊Humber Bridge; fertile Holderness peninsula; Isle of Axholme, bounded by rivers Trent, Don, Idle, and Torne, where medieval open-field strip farming is still practised
products petrochemicals, refined oil, processed fish, cereals, root crops, cattle
population (1987) 847,000
famous people Amy Johnson, Andrew Marvell, John Wesley.

Humbert /'hʌmbət/ anglicized form of ◊Umberto, two kings of Italy.

Humboldt /'hʌmbəʊlt/ Friedrich Heinrich Alexander, Baron von Humboldt 1769–1859. German botanist and geologist who, with the French botanist Aimé Bonpland (1773–1858), explored the regions of the Orinoco and the Amazon rivers in South America 1800–04, and gathered 60,000 plant specimens. On his return, Humboldt devoted 21 years to writing an account of his travels.

One of the first popularizers of science, he gave a series of lectures later published as *Cosmos* 1845–62, an account of the physical sciences.

Humboldt /'hʌmbəʊlt/ Wilhelm von 1767–1835. German philologist, whose stress on the identity of thought and language influenced ◊Chomsky. He was the brother of Friedrich Humboldt.

Humboldt Current former name of the ◊Peru Current.

Hume /hju:m/ Basil 1923– . English Roman Catholic cardinal from 1976. A Benedictine monk, he was abbot of Ampleforth in Yorkshire 1963–76, and in 1976 became archbishop of Westminster, the first monk to hold the office.

Hume /hju:m/ David 1711–1776. Scottish philosopher. *A Treatise of Human Nature* 1740 is a central text of British empiricism. Hume denies the possibility of going beyond the subjective experiences of 'ideas' and 'impressions'. The effect of this position is to invalidate metaphysics.

His *History of Great Britain* 1754–62 was popular within his own lifetime but *A Treatise of Human Nature* was indifferently received. He shared many of the beliefs of the British empiricist school (see ◊empiricism), especially those of ◊Locke. *Hume's Law* in moral philosophy states that it is never possible to deduce evaluative conclusions from factual premises; this has come to be known as the is/ought problem.

Hume /hju:m/ Fergus 1859–1932. British writer. Educated in New Zealand, he returned to his native England in 1888; his *Mystery of a Hansom Cab* 1887 was one of the first popular detective stories.

Hume /hju:m/ Hamilton 1797–1873. Australian explorer. In 1824, with William Hovell, he led an expedition from Sydney to the Murray River and Port Phillip. The Melbourne–Sydney *Hume Highway* is named after him.

Hume /hju:m/ John 1937– . Northern Ireland Catholic politician, leader of the Social Democrat Party (SDLP) from 1979. Hume was a founder member of the Credit Union Party, which later became the SDLP. He is widely respected for his moderate views.

Hume /hju:m/ Joseph 1777–1855. British Radical politician. Born at Montrose, Scotland, he went out to India as an army surgeon 1797, made a fortune, and on his return bought a seat in Parliament. In 1818 he secured election as a Philosophic Radical and supported many progressive measures. His son *Allan Octavian Hume* (1829–1912) was largely responsible for the establishment of the Indian National Congress 1885.

Hume-Rothery /'hju:m 'rɒðəri/ William 1899–1968. British metallurgist who researched the constitution of alloys. He was appointed to the first chair of metallurgy 1925.

humidity the quantity of water vapour in a given volume of the atmosphere (absolute humidity), or the ratio of the amount of water vapour in the atmosphere to the saturation value at the same temperature (relative humidity); at ◊dew point the latter is 100%. Relative humidity is measured by various types of ◊*hygrometer*.

hummingbird bird of the family Trochilidae, found in the Americas. The name is derived from the sound produced by the rapid vibration of their wings, and they are the only birds able to fly backwards. They are brilliantly coloured, and have long tongues to obtain nectar from flowers and capture insects. The Cuban *bee hummingbird Mellisuga helenae* is the world's smallest bird at 5.5 cm/2 in long, and weighs 2 g/less than ¹/₁₀ oz.

humours, theory of theory prevalent in classical and medieval times that the human body was composed of four kinds of fluid: phlegm, blood, choler or yellow bile, and melancholy or black bile. Physical and mental characteristics were explained by different proportions of humours in individuals.

Humperdinck /'hʊmpədɪŋk/ Engelbert 1854–1921. German composer. He studied music in Munich and in Italy and assisted ◊Wagner at the Bayreuth Festival Theatre. He wrote the musical fairy operas *Hänsel und Gretel* 1893, and *Königskinder/King's Children* 1910.

humus component of ◊soil consisting of decomposed or partly decomposed organic matter, dark in colour and usually richer towards the surface. It has a higher carbon content than the original material and a lower nitrogen content, and is an important source of minerals in soil fertility.

Hun a member of any of a number of nomad Mongol peoples who first appeared in history in the 2nd century BC, raiding across the Great Wall into China. They entered Europe about AD 372, settled in Hungary, and imposed their supremacy on the Ostrogoths and other Germanic peoples. Under the leadership of Attila they attacked the Byzantine Empire, invaded Gaul, and threatened Rome, but after his death 453 their power was broken by a revolt of their subject peoples. The *White Huns* or Ephthalites, a kindred people, raided Persia and N India in the 5th and 6th centuries.

Hunan /ˌhuːˈnæn/ province of S central China
area 210,500 sq km/81,253 sq mi
capital Changsha
features Dongting Lake; farmhouse in Shaoshan village, where Mao Zedong was born
products rice, tea, tobacco, cotton; nonferrous minerals
population (1986) 56,960,000.

hundred a subdivision of a shire in England, Ireland, and parts of the USA. The term was originally used by Germanic peoples to denote a group of 100 warriors, also the area occupied by 100 families or equalling 100 hides (one hide being the amount of land necessary to support a peasant family). When the Germanic peoples settled in England, the hundred remained the basic military and administrative division of England until its abolition 1867.

hundred days in history, the period 20 Mar–28 June 1815, marking the French emperor Napoleon's escape from imprisonment on Elba to his departure from Paris after losing the battle of Waterloo 18 June.

hundredweight imperial unit (symbol cwt) of mass, equal to 112 lb (50.8) kg. It is sometimes called the long hundredweight, to distinguish it from the short hundredweight or *cental* (45.4 kg/100 lb).

Hundred Years' War the series of conflicts between England and France 1337–1453.

Its origins lay with the English kings' possession of Gascony (SW France), which the French kings claimed as their ◊fief, and with trade rivalries over ◊Flanders. The two kingdoms had a long history of strife before 1337, and the war has sometimes been interpreted as merely an intensification of these struggles. It was occasioned by fears of French intervention in Scotland, which the English were trying to subdue, and by the claim of ◊Edward III (through his mother Isabel, daughter of Charles IV) to the crown of France.

After the war, England kept Calais until 1558, but domestic problems, such as the War of the Roses, kept England from attempting to conquer France again. It gave up its continental aspirations, and began to develop as a sea power. In addition to the devastation caused by the war, France was also ravaged by the Black Death, famine, and gangs of bandits. The decline of the feudal nobility allowed the monarchy to establish itself more solidly, allied with the rising middle class.
1340 The English were victorious at the naval battle of Sluys.
1346 Battle of Crécy, another English victory.
1347 The English took Calais.
1356 Battle of Poitiers, where Edward the Black Prince defeated the French. King John of France was captured.
late 1350s–early 1360s France had civil wars, brigandage, and the popular uprising of the ◊Jacquerie.
1360 Treaty of Brétigny–Calais. France accepted English possession of Calais, and of a greatly enlarged duchy of Gascony. John was ransomed for £500,000.
1369–1414 The tide turned in favour of the French, and when there was another truce in 1388, only Calais, Bordeaux, and Bayonne were in English hands. A state of half-war continued for many years.
1415 Henry V invaded France and won a victory at Agincourt, followed by conquest of Normandy.
1419 In the Treaty of Troyes, Charles VI of France was forced to disinherit his son, the Dauphin, in favour of Henry V, who was to marry Catherine, Charles' daughter. Most of N France was in English hands.
1422–28 After the death of Henry V his brother Bedford was generally successful.
1429 Joan of Arc raised the siege of Orléans, and the Dauphin was crowned Charles VII at Rheims.
1430–53 Even after Joan's capture and death the French continued their successful counteroffensive, and in 1453 only Calais was left in English hands.

Hungarian or *Magyar* member of the majority population of Hungary or person of Hungarian descent. Hungarian minorities are found in Czechoslovakia, Yugoslavia, and Romania, where the Székely of Transylvania regard themselves as ethnically distinct but speak Hungarian, as do the Csángó of Moldavia.

Hungarian language a member of the Finno-Ugric language group, spoken principally in Hungary but also in parts of Czechoslovakia, Romania, and Yugoslavia. Known as *Magyar* among its speakers, Hungarian is written in a form of the Roman alphabet in which *s* corresponds to English *sh*, and *sz* to *s*.
Like the Turks, the Magyars originated in NE Asia; the term 'Hungarian' appears to derive from the Turkish *on ogur* ('ten arrows'), describing their ten tribes, which may also be the origin of the English 'ogre'.

Hungary /'hʌŋgəri/ country in central Europe, bordered to the N by Czechoslovakia, NE by the USSR, E by Romania, S by Yugoslavia, and W by Austria.
government Under the terms of the 'transitional constitution' adopted Oct 1989, Hungary is a unitary state with a one-chamber, 386-member legislature, the national assembly (*Orszaggyules*). Its members are elected for five-year terms under a mixed system of proportional and direct representation: 176 are directly elected (on a potential two-ballot run-off basis) from local constituencies; 152 are from county and metropolitan lists on a proportional basis; and 58 are elected indirectly from party-nominated national 'compensation' lists designed to favour smaller parties. Free competition is allowed in these elections. The national assembly elects a president to serve as head of state and chief executive, and a council of ministers (cabinet) headed by a prime minister.

Hungary
Hungarian Republic
(Magyar Köztársaság)

area 93,032 sq km/35,910 sq mi
capital Budapest
towns Miskolc, Debrecen, Szeged, Pécs
physical Great Hungarian Plain covers eastern half of country; Bakony Forest; rivers Danube, Tisza; Lake Balaton
head of state Matyas Szuros (acting) from 1989
head of government Károly Grosz from 1988
political system socialist pluralist republic
political parties over 50, including Hungarian Socialist Party (HSP), left-of-centre; Hungarian Democratic Forum (MDF), umbrella pro-democracy grouping; Alliance of Free Democrats (SzDSz), radical free-market opposition group heading coalition with Alliance of Young Democrats, Social Democrats, and

Smallholders Party, right-wing
exports machinery, vehicles, chemicals, textiles
currency forint (108.06 = £1 Feb 1990)
population (1988) 10,604,000 (Magyar 92%, Romany 3%, German 2.5%; there is a Hungarian minority in Romania; annual growth rate 0%
life expectancy men 67, women 74
language Hungarian (or Magyar), one of the few languages of Europe with non-Indo-European origins. It is grouped with Finnish and Estonian in the Finno-Ugrian family
religion Roman Catholic 50%, other Christian denominations 25%
literacy 99.3% male/98.5% female (1980)
GNP $18.6 bn (1983); $4,180 per head of population
chronology
1946 Republic proclaimed.
1949 Soviet-style constitution adopted.
1956 Hungarian national rising. Workers' demonstrations in Budapest, democratization reforms by Imre Nagy overturned by Soviet tanks, Kádár installed as party leader.
1968 Economic decentralization reforms.
1983 Competition introduced into elections.
1987 VAT and income tax introduced.
1988 Kádár replaced by Károly Grosz. First free trade union recognized. Rival political parties legalized.
1989 May: border with Austria opened. July: new four-man collective leadership of Hungarian Socialist Workers' Party (HSWP). Oct: new 'transitional constitution' adopted, founded on multi-party democracy and new presidentialist executive. HSWP changed name to Hungarian Socialist Party, with Nyers as new leader.
1990 HSP standing damaged by 'Danubegate' bugging scandal. March; firts round of multi-party elections.

Since 1989 opposition parties have been able to register freely and receive partial state funding. A constitutional court has also been appointed to serve as a watchdog.
history Once inhabited by Celts and Slavs, the region later became a Roman province. After the Roman era it was overrun by Germanic invaders, until the establishment of a ◊Magyar kingdom in the late 9th century, under a chief named Árpád. Hungary's first king was St Stephen (997–1038), who established a kingdom 1001 and converted the inhabitants to Christianity.
After the Árpádian line died out, Hungary was ruled 1308–86 by the ◊Angevins, and after this by other foreign princes. From 1396, successive rulers fought to keep out Turkish invaders, but were finally defeated at Mohács 1526, and the south and centre of the country came under Turkish rule for 150 years, while the east was ruled by semi-independent Hungarian princes. By the end of the 17th century the Turks had been driven out by the ◊Habsburgs, bringing Hungary under Austrian rule.
After 1815 a national renaissance began, under the leadership of Louis ◊Kossuth. The revolution of 1848–49 proclaimed a Hungarian republic and abolished serfdom, but Austria suppressed the revolt with Russian help. In 1867 the ◊Austro-Hungarian empire was established, giving Hungary self-government.
During World War I, Hungary fought on the German side, and after the collapse of the Austro-Hungarian empire, became an independent state 1918. For 133 days in 1919, Hungary was a communist republic under Béla ◊Kun, but this was brought to an end by intervention from Romania and Czechoslovakia. From 1920–44, Hungary was ruled by Admiral ◊Horthy, acting as regent for an unnamed king. After 1933, he fell more and more under German influence and, having joined

Hitler in the invasion of Russia 1941, Hungary was overrun by Communist forces 1944–45.
Horthy fled and a provisional government, including the Communist agriculture minister, Imre ◊Nagy, was formed, distributing land to the peasants. An elected assembly inaugurated a republic 1946, but it soon fell under Soviet domination, although only 70 Communists had been returned out of a total of 409 deputies.
Under Communist Party leader Matyas Rakosi (1892–1971), a Stalinist regime was imposed 1946–53, a Soviet-style constitution being adopted 1949, industry nationalized, land collectivized, and a wave of secret police terror launched.
Liberalization in the economic sphere was experienced 1953–55 when Imre Nagy, supported by Soviet premier Malenkov, replaced Rákosi as prime minister. Nagy was removed from office 1955, after the fall of Malenkov, but in 1956, in the wake of ◊Khrushchev's denunciation of Stalin in his 'secret speech', pressure for democratization mounted. Rakosi stepped down as Communist Party leader and, following student and worker demonstrations in Budapest, Nagy was recalled as prime minister and János ◊Kádár appointed general secretary of the renamed Hungarian Socialist Workers' Party (HSWP).
Nagy lifted restrictions on the formation of political parties, released the anti-communist primate Cardinal ◊Mindszenty, and announced plans for Hungary to withdraw from the ◊Warsaw Pact and become a neutral power. These changes were, however, opposed by Kádár, who set up a counter-government in E Hungary before returning to Budapest with Soviet tanks to overthrow the Nagy government 4 Nov. Some 200,000 fled to the West during the 1956 'Hungarian National Rising'.
After a period of strict repression, Kádár proceeded to introduce pragmatic liberalizing reforms

after 1960. Hungary remained, however, a loyal member of the Warsaw Pact and ◊Comecon. Its relations with Moscow significantly improved during the post-Brezhnev era, with Hungary's 'market socialism' experiment influencing Mikhail Gorbachev's ◊perestroika programme. Further reforms introduced 1987–88 included additional price deregulation, the establishment of 'enterprise councils', the introduction of value-added tax (VAT), and the creation of a stock market.

Kádár stepped down as HSWP general secretary May 1988, being replaced by the prime minister Karoly ◊Grosz, while two radical reformers, Rezso Nyers and Imre Pozsgay, were brought into the Politburo. There then began a period of far-reaching political reform in which the right to demonstrate freely, and to form rival political parties and trade unions, was ceded; the official verdict on the 1956 events was revised radically, with Nagy being posthumously rehabilitated and cleared of alleged past crimes by the Supreme Court in July 1989; and a new 'socialist pluralist' constitution was outlined.

The Hungarian Democratic Forum was formed Sept 1988 as an umbrella movement for opposition groups, and several dozen other political parties were formed 1989–90. In May 1989 the border with Austria was opened, with adverse effects for East Germany. Two months later Grosz was forced to cede power to the more radical reformist troika of Nyers (party president), Pozsgay, and Miklos Nemeth (prime minister since Nov 1988), who joined Grosz in a new four-person ruling praesidium.

In Oct 1989 a series of constitutional changes, the result of round-table talks held through the summer, were approved by the national assembly. These included the adoption of a new set of electoral rules, banning of workplace party cells, and the deletion of the word 'People's' from the country's name. Also in Oct the HSWP changed its name to the Hungarian Socialist Party (HSP), and adopted Poszgay as its presidential candidate. Conservatives, including Grosz, refused to play an active role in the new party, which had become essentially a social democratic party committed to multi-party democracy. Despite these changes, the HSP's standing was seriously damaged in the 'Danubegate' scandal of Jan 1990, when it was revealed that the secret police had bugged opposition parties and passed the information obtained to the HSP. In Feb 1990 talks were held with the USSR to discuss the withdrawal of Soviet troops stationed in Hungary.

Elections held Mar 1990 resulted in the formation of a government coalition of the Hungarian Democratic Forum (MDF), the Independent Smallholders' Party (FKgP), and the Christian Democratic People's Party (KDNP), with József Antall as prime minister. The largest opposition groups were the Alliance of Free Democrats (SZDSZ) and the HSP under Poszgay. The new government promised to introduce a social market economy and to initiate reprivatization.

hunger march a procession of the unemployed, a feature of social protest in interwar Britain. The first took place from Glasgow to London in 1922 and another in 1929. In 1932 the National Unemployed Workers' Movement organized the largest demonstration, with groups converging on London from all parts of the country, but the most emotive was probably the Jarrow Crusade of 1936, when 200 unemployed shipyard workers marched to the capital (see ◊unemployment).

Hun Sen 1950– . Cambodian political leader, prime minister from 1985. Originally a member of the Khmer Rouge army, he defected in 1977 to join Vietnam-based anti-Khmer Cambodian forces.

Born into a poor peasant family in the eastern province of Kampang-Cham, Hun Sen joined the Khmer Rouge in 1970. He rose to become a regiment commander, but, disillusioned, defected to the anti-Khmer Cambodian forces in 1977. On

THE LADY OF SHALOTT.

PART I.

I.

ON either side the river lie
Long fields of barley and of rye,
That clothe the wold and meet the sky;
And thro' the field the road runs by
 To many-tower'd Camelot;

Hunt English painter William Holman Hunt was a member of the Pre-Raphaelites who chose subjects from the Bible, Greek mythology, and English literature. Hunt illustrated Dickens and Scott and (as above) Tennyson's poem The Lady of Shalott.

his return to Cambodia, following the Vietnamese-backed communist takeover, he served as foreign minister 1979, and then as prime minister 1985, promoting economic liberalization and a thawing in relations with exiled, non-Khmer, opposition forces as a prelude to a compromise political settlement.

Hunt /hʌnt/ (James Henry) Leigh 1784–1859. English poet and essayist. Convicted for libel against the Prince Regent in his Liberal newspaper *The Examiner*, he was imprisoned 1813. The friend and, later, enemy of Byron, he also knew Keats and Shelley. His verse is little appreciated today, but he influenced the Romantics, and his book on London *The Town* 1848 and his *Autobiography* 1850 survive. The character of Harold Skimpole in Dickens' *Bleak House* was allegedly based on him.

Hunt /hʌnt/ John, Baron Hunt 1910– . British mountaineer, leader of the successful Everest expedition 1953 (with ◊Hillary and ◊Tenzing).

Hunt /hʌnt/ William Holman 1827–1910. English painter, one of the founders of the ◊Pre-Raphaelite Brotherhood 1848. Obsessed with realistic detail, he travelled to Syria and Palestine to paint biblical subjects from 1854 onwards. His works include *The Awakening Conscience* 1853 (Tate Gallery, London) and *The Light of the World* 1854 (Keble College, Oxford).

Hunter /'hʌntə/ river in New South Wales, Australia, which rises in the Mount Royal Range and flows into the Pacific near Newcastle, after a course of about 465 km/290 mi. Although the river is liable to flooding, the Hunter Valley has dairying and market gardening, and produces wines.

Hunter /'hʌntə/ John 1728–1793. Scottish surgeon, pathologist, and comparative anatomist. His main contribution to medicine was his insistence on rigorous scientific method. He was also the first to understand the nature of digestion.

Hunter did major work in comparative anatomy and dental pathology. He experimented extensively on animals, and collected a large number of specimens and preparations (Hunterian Collections), which are now housed in the Royal College of Surgeons, London.

He trained under his elder brother *William Hunter* (1718–83), anatomist and obstetrician, who became professor of anatomy in the Royal Academy 1768 and president of the Medical Society 1781. His collections are now in the Hunterian museum of Glasgow University.

Huntingdon /'hʌntɪŋdən/ town in Cambridgeshire, E England, on the river Ouse, 26 km/16 mi NW of Cambridge; population (1981) 17,467. It is a market town with a number of light industries. A bridge built in 1332 connects Huntingdon with Godmanchester on the S bank of the river, and the two towns were united in 1961. Samuel Pepys and Oliver Cromwell attended the grammar school founded 1565 in a 12th-century building, formerly part of the medieval hospital; it was opened in 1962 as a Cromwell museum.

Huntingdonshire /'hʌntɪŋdənʃə/ former English county, merged 1974 in a much enlarged Cambridgeshire.

Huntington's chorea a rare hereditary disease which begins in middle age. It is characterized by uncontrolled involuntary movements and rapid mental degeneration progressing to ◊dementia. There is no known cure.

Huntsville /'hʌntsvɪl/ town in NE Alabama, USA; population (1981) 309,000. It is an aerospace research centre.

Hunyadi /'hunjɒdi/ János Corvinus 1387–1456. Hungarian politician and general. Born in Transylvania, reputedly the son of the emperor ◊Sigismund, he won battles against the Turks from the 1440s. In 1456 he defeated them at Belgrade, but died shortly afterwards of the plague.

Hunza /'hunzə/ small state on the NW frontier of Kashmir, under the rule of Pakistan.

Hupei /,hu:'peɪ/ former name of ◊Hebei, province of China.

Hurd /hɜːd/ Douglas (Richard) 1930– . English Conservative politician, foreign secretary from 1989 and home secretary 1986–89. He entered the House of Commons 1974, representing Witney from 1983.

Hurd was in the diplomatic service 1952–66, serving in Beijing and at the United Nations in New York and Rome. He then joined the Conservative research department and became a secretary to the party leader Edward Heath. He was made a junior minister by Margaret Thatcher, and the sudden resignation of Leon Brittan projected Hurd into the home secretary's post early 1986. In 1989 he was appointed foreign secretary in the reshuffle that followed Nigel Lawson's resignation as chancellor of the exchequer.

hurdy-gurdy musical stringed instrument resembling a violin in tone but using a form of keyboard to play a melody and drone strings to provide a continuous harmony. An inbuilt wheel turned by a handle, acts as a bow.

hurling a team game played with 15 a side. It is a stick-and-ball game, popular in Ireland. First played over 3,000 years ago, at one time it was outlawed. The rules were standardized 1884, and are now under the control of the Gaelic Athletic Association.

Huron /'hjuərən/ second largest of the Great Lakes of North America, on the US-Canadian border; area 60,000 sq km/23,160 sq mi. It includes Georgian Bay, Saginaw Bay, and Manitoulin Island.

It receives Lake Superior's waters through the St Marys River, and Lake Michigan's through the Straits of Mackinac. It drains south into Lake Erie through the St Clair River, Lake St Clair, and the Detroit River.

Huron (*hure* 'head of pig') French nickname for a member of the Wyandot, nomadic North American Indian people related to the Iroquois, and living

Hurt US film actor William Hurt at the Cannes Film Festival 1985.

near lakes Huron, Erie, and Ontario in the 16th and 17th centuries. They were almost wiped out by the Iroquois but there are some decendants of survivors in Québec and Oklahoma.

hurricane a revolving storm in tropical regions, called **typhoon** in the N Pacific. It originates between 5° and 20° N or S of the equator, when the surface temperature of the ocean is above 27°C/80°F. A central calm area, called the eye, is surrounded by inwardly spiralling winds (counter-clockwise in the N hemisphere) of up to 320 kph/200 mph. A hurricane is accompanied by lightning and torrential rain, and can cause extensive damage. In meteorology, a hurricane is a wind of force 12 or more on the ◊Beaufort scale. The most intense hurricane recorded in the Caribbean/Atlantic sector was Hurricane Gilbert in 1988, with sustained winds of 280 kph/175 mph and gusts of over 320 kph/200 mph.

In Oct 1987 and Jan 1990, hurricane-force winds were experienced in S England—the strongest winds there for three centuries.

Hurstmonceux alternative spelling of ◊Herstmonceux, a village in ◊East Sussex.

Hurston /'hɜːstən/ Zora Neale 1901–1960. US novelist and short-story writer, associated with the ◊Harlem Renaissance. She collected traditional black US folk tales in *Mules and Men* 1935; her novels include *Their Eyes Were Watching God* 1937.

Hurt /hɜːt/ William 1950– . US actor whose films include *Altered States* 1980, *The Big Chill* 1983, *Kiss of the Spider Woman* 1985, and *Broadcast News* 1987.

Husák /'huːsɑːk/ Gustáv 1913– . Leader of the Communist Party of Czechoslovakia (CCP) 1969–87 and president 1975–89. After the 1968 Prague Spring of liberalization, his task was to restore control, purge the CCP, and oversee the implementation of a new, federalist constitution. He was deposed in the popular uprising of Nov-Dec 1989.

Husák, a lawyer, was active in the Resistance movement during World War II, and afterwards in the Slovak Communist Party (SCP), and was imprisoned on political grounds 1951–60. Rehabilitated, he was appointed first secretary of the SCP 1968 and CCP leader 1969–87. As titular state president he pursued a policy of cautious reform. He stepped down as party leader 1987, and was replaced as state president by Vaclav ◊Havel in Dec 1989 following the 'velvet revolution' (see ◊Czechoslovakia).

Huscarls Anglo-Danish warriors, in 10th-century Denmark and early 11th-century England. They formed the bulk of English royal armies until the Norman Conquest.

Huskisson /'hʌskɪsən/ William 1770–1830. British conservative politician, financier, and advocate of free trade. He served as secretary to the Treasury 1807–09 and colonial agent for Ceylon (now Sri Lanka). He was active in the ◊Corn Law debates and supported their relaxation in 1821.

husky sledge dog used in Arctic regions, up to 70 cm/2 ft high, and 50 kg/110 lbs, with pricked ears, thick fur, and a bushy tail.

Huss /hʌs/ John *c.* 1373–1415. Bohemian church reformer, rector of Prague University from 1402, who was excommunicated for attacks on ecclesiastical abuses. He was summoned before the Council of Constance 1414, defended the English reformer Wycliffe, rejected the pope's authority, and was burned at the stake. His followers were called Hussites.

Hussein /hʊ'seɪn/ ibn Ali *c.* 1854–1931. Leader of the Arab revolt 1916–18 against the Turks. He proclaimed himself king of the Hejaz 1916, accepted the caliphate 1924, but was unable to retain it due to internal fighting. He was deposed 1924 by Ibn Saud.

Hussein The president of Iraq, Saddam Hussein. Ruthless in his leadership, he has ruled the country with an iron fist since coming to power in 1979.

Hussein /hʊ'seɪn/ ibn Talal 1935– . King of Jordan from 1952. Great-grandson of Hussein ibn Ali, he became king after the mental incapacity of his father Talal. By 1967 he had lost all his kingdom west of the Jordan river in the ◊Arab-Israeli Wars, and in 1970 suppressed the ◊Palestine Liberation Organization acting as a guerrilla force against his rule on the remaining East Bank territories. In recent years, he has become a moderating force in Middle Eastern politics.

Hussein /hʊ'seɪn/ Saddam 1937– . Iraqi left-wing politician, in power from 1968, president from 1979. Ruthless in the pursuit of his objectives, he fought a bitter war against Iran 1980–88 and has dealt harshly with Kurdish rebels seeking a degree of independence.

Hussein joined the Arab Ba'th Socialist Party as a young man and soon became involved in revolutionary activities. In 1959 he was sentenced to death and took refuge in Egypt, but a coup in 1963 made his return possible, although in the following year he was imprisoned for plotting to overthrow the regime he had helped to instal. After his release he took a leading part in the 1968 revolution, removing the civilian government and establishing a Revolutionary Command Council (RCC). At first discreetly, and then more openly, Hussein strengthened his position and in 1979 became RCC chair and state president.

Husserl /'hʊsəl/ Edmund (Gustav Albrecht) 1859–1938. German philosopher, regarded as the founder of ◊phenomenology, a philosophy concentrating on what is consciously experienced.

He hoped phenomenology would become the science of all sciences. His main works are *Logical Investigations* 1900, *Phenomenological Philosophy* 1913, and *The Crisis of the European Sciences* 1936. He influenced ◊Heidegger, and was influential in sociology through the work of Alfred Schütz (1899–1959).

Hussite a follower of John ◊Huss. Opposed to both German and papal influence in Bohemia, the Hussites waged successful war against the Holy Roman Empire from 1419, but Roman Catholicism was finally re-established 1620.

Huston /'hjuːstən/ John 1906–1987. US film director, screenwriter, and actor. An impulsive and individualistic filmmaker, he often dealt with the themes of greed, treachery, human relationships, and the loner. His works as a director include *The Maltese Falcon* 1941 (his debut), *The Treasure of the Sierra Madre* 1947 (for which he won an Academy Award), *The African Queen* 1951, and *Prizzi's Honor* 1984.

He was the son of the actor Walter Huston and the father of the actress Anjelica Huston. His

hurricane Hurricane Elena, photographed on 2 Sept 1985, from the space shuttle Discovery.

Huxley English novelist and writer Aldous Huxley, 1936.

Huxley Biologist and humanist Thomas Henry Huxley was the foremost British exponent of Darwin's theory of evolution.

Huygens Dutch physicist Christiaan Huygens's design for an 'aerial' telescope, published 1724 in his Opera Varia. The telescope, which has no tube, works by refracting light.

other films include *Moby Dick* 1956, *The Misfits* 1961, *Fat City* 1972, and *The Dead* 1987.

Hutterian Brethren a Christian sect; see ◊Mennonite.

Hutton /'hʌtn/ Barbara 1912–1979. US heiress, granddaughter of F W ◊Woolworth, notorious in her day as the original 'poor little rich girl'. Her seven husbands included the actor Cary Grant.

Hutton /'hʌtn/ James 1726–1797. Scottish geologist, known as the 'founder of geology', who formulated the concept of ◊uniformitarianism. In 1785 he developed a theory of the igneous origin of many rocks.

His *Theory of the Earth* 1788 proposed that the Earth was indefinitely old. Uniformitarianism suggests that past events could be explained in terms of processes that work today. For example, the kind of river current that produces a certain settling pattern in a bed of sand today must have been operating many millions of years ago, if that same pattern is visible in ancient sandstones.

Hutton /'hʌtn/ 'Len' (Leonard) 1916– . English cricketer, born in Pudsey, West Yorkshire. He captained England in 23 test matches 1952–56 and was England's first professional captain. In 1938 at the Oval he scored 364 against Australia, a world record test score until beaten by Gary ◊Sobers 1958.

Huxley /'hʌksli/ Aldous (Leonard) 1894–1963. English writer. The satirical disillusion of his witty first novel, *Crome Yellow* 1921, continued throughout *Antic Hay* 1923, *Those Barren Leaves* 1925, and *Point Counter Point* 1928. *Brave New World* 1932 concerns the reproduction of the human race by mass production in the laboratory.

He was the grandson of Thomas Henry Huxley and brother of Julian Huxley. Huxley's later devotion to mysticism led to his experiments with the hallucinogenic drug mescalin, recorded in *The Doors of Perception* 1954. He also wrote the novel *Eyeless in Gaza* 1936, and two historical studies, *Grey Eminence* 1941 and *The Devils of Loudun* 1952.

Huxley /'hʌksli/ Andrew 1917– . English physiologist, awarded the Nobel Prize for Medicine 1963, with Hodgkin and Eccles, for work on nerve impulses.

Huxley /'hʌksli/ Julian 1887–1975. English biologist, first director-general of UNESCO, and a founder of the World Wildlife Fund (now the World Wide Fund for Nature).

Huxley /'hʌksli/ Thomas Henry 1825–1895. English scientist and humanist. Following the publication of Charles Darwin's *On the Origin of Species* 1859, he became known as 'Darwin's bulldog', and for many years was the most prominent and popular champion of evolution. In 1869, he coined the word 'agnostic' to express his own religious attitude.

He wrote *Man's Place in Nature* 1863, textbooks on physiology, and innumerable scientific papers. His later books, such as *Lay Sermons*

1870, *Science and Culture* 1881, and *Evolution and Ethics*, were expositions of scientific humanism. His grandsons include Aldous, Andrew, and Julian Huxley.

Hu Yaobang /'hu: ·jaʊ'bæŋ/ 1915–1989. Chinese politician, Communist Party (CCP) chair 1981–87. A protégé of the communist leader Deng Xiaoping, Hu presided over a radical overhaul of the party structure and personnel 1982–86.

Hu, born into a peasant family in Hunan province, joined the Red Army at the age of 14 and was a political commissar during the 1934–36 Long March. In 1941 he served under Deng and later worked under him in provincial and central government. Hu was purged as a 'capitalist roader' during the 1966–69 Cultural Revolution and sent into the countryside for 're-education'. He was rehabilitated 1975, but disgraced again when Deng fell from prominence 1976. In Dec 1978, with Deng established in power, Hu was inducted into the CCP Politburo and became head of the revived secretariat 1980 and CCP chair 1981. He attempted to quicken reaction against Mao. He was dismissed Jan 1987 for his relaxed handling of a wave of student unrest Dec 1986.

Huygens /'haɪɡənz/ Christiaan 1629–1695. Dutch mathematical physicist and astronomer, who propounded the wave theory of light. He developed the pendulum clock, discovered polarization, and observed Saturn's rings.

Huysmans /wi:s'mɒns/ J(oris) K(arl) 1848–1907. French novelist of Dutch ancestry. *Marthe* 1876, the story of a courtesan, was followed by other realistic novels, including *A rebours/Against Nature* 1884, a novel of self-absorbed aestheticism which symbolized the 'decadent' movement.

Hvannadalshnjukur /'vænədæls·nu:kə/ highest peak in Iceland, rising to 2,119 m/6,952 ft in SE Iceland.

Hwange /'hwæŋeɪ/ coalmining town (Wankie until 1982) in Zimbabwe; population (1982) 39,200. Hwange National Park is nearby.

Hwang-Ho /·hwæŋ'həʊ/ former name of the ◊Huang He, a river in China.

HWM abbreviation for *high water mark*.

hyacinth bulb-producing plant *Hyacinthus orientalis*, family Liliaceae, native to the E Mediterranean and Africa. The cultivated hyacinth has large, scented, cylindrical heads of pink, white, or blue flowers. The ◊water hyacinth, genus *Eichhornia*, is unrelated, a floating plant from South America.

Hyades V-shaped cluster of stars that forms the face of Taurus, the bull. It is 130 light years away and contains over 200 stars, although only about a dozen are visible to the naked eye.

hyaline membrane disease (HMD) disorder of premature babies, who are unable to produce

enough pulmonary surfactant (lung surface conditioner) to enable them to breathe properly. The lungs become hard and glassy (Latin *hyalinus* 'glassy'). A synthetic replacement for surfactant has been developed.

hybrid the offspring from a cross between individuals of two different species, or two inbred lines within a species. In most cases, hybrids between species are infertile and unable to reproduce sexually. In plants, however, doubling of the chromosomes (see ◊polyploid) can restore the fertility of such hybrids.

Hybrids between different genera are extremely rare; an example is the *leylandii* cypress which, like many hybrids, shows exceptional vigour, or ◊heterosis. In the wild, a 'hybrid zone' may occur where the ranges of two related species meet.

Hydaspes /haɪ'dæspi:z/ classical name of river ◊Jhelum, a river in Pakistan and Kashmir.

hydathode a specialized pore, or less commonly, a hair, through which water is secreted by hydrostatic pressure from the interior of a plant leaf onto the surface. Hydathodes are found on many different plants and are usually situated around the leaf margin at vein endings. Each pore is surrounded by two crescent-shaped cells and resembles an open ◊stoma, but the size of the opening cannot be varied as in a stoma. The process of water secretion through hydathodes is known as ◊guttation.

Hyde /haɪd/ Douglas 1860–1949. Irish scholar and politician. Founder-president of the Gaelic League 1893–1915, he was president of Eire 1938–45. His works include *Love Songs of Connacht* 1894.

Hyde Park /haɪd/ one of the largest open spaces in London, England. It occupies about 146 ha/350 acres in Westminster. It adjoins Kensington Gardens, and includes the Serpentine, a boating lake with a 'lido' for swimming. Rotten Row (a corruption of French *route du roi*) is a famous riding track. In 1851 the Great Exhibition was held here.

Hyderabad /'haɪdərəbæd/ capital city of the S central Indian state of Andhra Pradesh, on the Musi, population (1981) 2,528,000. Products include carpets, silks, and metal inlay work. It was formerly the capital of the state of Hyderabad. Buildings include the Jama Masjid mosque and Golconda fort.

Hyderabad /'haɪdərəbæd/ city in Sind province, SE Pakistan; population (1981) 795,000. It produces gold, pottery, glass, and furniture. The third largest city of Pakistan, it was founded 1768.

Hyder Ali /'haɪdər 'ɑːli/ *c.* 1722–1782. Indian general, sultan of Mysore from 1759. In command of the army in Mysore from 1749, he became the

hydraulics

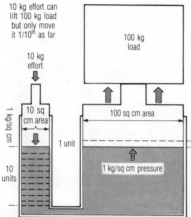

10 kg effort can lift 100 kg load but only move it 1/10th as far

10 kg effort

100 kg load

1 kg/sq cm

10 sq cm area

100 sq cm area

1 unit

10 units

1 kg/sq cm pressure

ruler of the state 1759, and rivalled British power in the area until his triple defeat by Eyre Coote 1781 during the Anglo-French wars. He was the father of Tippu Sultan.

hydra in zoology, genus of freshwater polyps, of the phylum Cnidaria (coelenterates). The body is a double-layered tube (with 6–10 hollow tentacles round the mouth), 1.25 cm/0.5 in extended, but capable of contracting to a small knob. Usually fixed to waterweed, the hydra feeds on minute animals, which are caught and paralysed by the stinging cells on the tentacles. Hydra reproduce asexually in the summer and sexually in the winter.

Hydra in astronomy, the largest constellation, winding across more than a quarter of the sky. Hydra represents the multi-headed monster slain by Heracles. Despite its huge size, it is not prominent; its brightest star is second-magnitude Alphard.

hydra in Greek mythology, a huge monster with nine heads. If one were cut off, two would grow in its place. One of the 12 labours of Heracles was to kill it.

hydrangea flowering shrub *Hydrangea macrophylla* of the Hydrangeaceae family, native to Japan. It normally produces round heads of pink flowers, but these may be blue if certain chemicals, such as alum or iron, are in the soil. It is named from the Greek for 'water vessel', after its cup-like seed capsules.

hydrate a chemical compound that has discrete water molecules combined with it. The water is known as *water of crystallization* and the number of water molecules associated with one molecule of the compound is denoted in both its name and chemical formula: for example, $CuSO_4.5H_2O$ is copper(II) sulphate pentahydrate.

hydraulics a field of study concerned with utilizing the properties of liquids, particularly the way they flow and transmit pressure. It applies the principles of ◊hydrostatics and hydrodynamics. The oldest type of hydraulic machine is the hydraulic press, invented by Joseph ◊Bramah in England 1795. The hydraulic principle of pressurised liquid increasing mechanical efficiency is commonly used on vehicle braking systems, the forging press, and the hydraulic systems of aircraft and excavators.

A hydraulic press consists of two connected pistons in cylinders, one of narrow bore, one of large bore. A force applied to the narrow piston applies a certain pressure (force per unit area) to the liquid, which is transmitted to the larger piston. Because the area of this piston is larger, the force exerted on it is larger. Thus the original force has been magnified, although the smaller piston must move a great distance to move the larger piston only a little, hence mechanical efficiency is gained in force but lost in movement.

hydride a chemical compound containing hydrogen and one other element only, in which the hydrogen is the more electronegative element (see

◊electronegativity). For the more reactive metals the hydride may be an ionic compound containing a hydride anion (H-).

hydrocarbon one of a class of chemical compounds containing only hydrogen and carbon, for example paraffin. Hydrocarbons are important in organic chemistry.

hydrocephalus a potentially serious increase in the volume of cerebrospinal fluid (CSF) within the ventricles of the brain. In infants, whose skull plates have not fused, it causes enlargement of the head, and there is a risk of brain damage from CSF pressure on the developing brain.

Hydrocephalus may be due to mechanical obstruction of the outflow of CSF from the ventricles or to faulty reabsorption. Treatment usually involves surgical placement of a shunt system to drain the fluid into the abdominal cavity. In infants, the condition is often seen in association with ◊spina bifida.

hydrochloric acid highly corrosive aqueous solution of hydrogen chloride (a colourless, corrosive gas HCl). It has many industrial uses, for example recovery of zinc from galvanized scrap iron, and the production of chlorides and chlorine. It is also produced in the stomachs of animals for digestion.

hydrocyanic acid also called *prussic acid* a solution of hydrogen cyanide gas (HCN) in water. It is a colourless, highly poisonous, volatile liquid, smelling of bitter almonds.

hydrodynamics the science of non-viscous fluids (for example water, alcohol, ether) in motion.

hydroelectric power electricity generated by moving water. In a typical hydroelectric power (HEP) scheme, water stored in a reservoir, often created by damming a river, is piped into water ◊turbines, coupled to electricity generators. In ◊pumped storage plants, water flowing through the turbines is recycled. A ◊tidal power station exploits the rise and fall of the tides. About one-fifth of the world's electricity comes from hydroelectric power.

HEP plants have prodigious generating capacities. The Grand Coulee plant in Washington State, USA, has a power output of some 10,000 megawatts. The Itaipu power station on the Paraná river (Brazil/Paraguay) has a potential capacity of 12,000 megawatts.

hydrofoil a wing that develops lift in the water in much the same way that an aeroplane wing develops lift in the air. A hydrofoil boat is one whose hull rises out of the water due to the lift. The first hydrofoil was fitted to a boat 1906. The first commercial hydrofoil went into operation 1956. One of the most advanced hydrofoil boats is the Boeing ◊jetfoil.

hydrogen a gaseous element, symbol H, atomic number 1, relative atomic mass 1.00797. The lightest element known, it occurs on Earth chiefly in combination with oxygen as water. Hydrogen is the commonest element in the universe, and the fuel of fusion reactions which take place in the Sun and stars.

It has many commercial and industrial uses, such as the hardening by hydrogenation (addition of hydrogen) of fats and oils in producing margarine, creating high-temperature flames for welding, and as a component in rocket fuel. Its isotopes, deuterium and tritium, have been used to produce the hydrogen bomb. If subjected to a pressure 500,000 times greater than that of Earth's atmosphere, hydrogen becomes a solid metal.

hydrogenation in chemistry, the process of addition of hydrogen to an unsaturated organic molecule (one that contains double bonds or triple bonds). It is widely used in the manufacture of margarine and low-fat spreads by the addition of hydrogen to vegetable oils.

hydrogen bomb ◊bomb that works on the principle of nuclear ◊fusion. Large-scale explosion results from the thermonuclear release of energy when hydrogen nuclei are condensed to helium nuclei. The first hydrogen bomb was exploded at Eniwetok Atoll by the USA 1952.

This constant release of energy is the continuing reaction in the Sun and other stars, but on Earth may result from the triggering of tritium (hydrogen isotope of atomic weight 3.0170) by an ordinary atom bomb.

hydrogen cyanide (HCN) a poisonous gas formed by the reaction of sodium cyanide with dilute sulphuric acid, used for fumigation.

The salts formed from it are cyanides, for example sodium cyanide, used in hardening steel, and extracting gold and silver from their ores. If dissolved in water, hydrogen cyanide gives hydrocyanic acid.

hydrography study and charting of the Earth's surface waters in seas, lakes, and rivers.

hydrology study of the location and movement of inland water, both frozen and liquid, above and below ground. It is applied to major civil engineering projects such as irrigation schemes, dams and hydroelectric power, and in planning water supply.

hydrolysis a chemical reaction in which the action of water or its ions breaks down a substance into smaller molecules. Hydrolysis occurs in certain inorganic salts in solution, in nearly all non-metallic chlorides, in esters, and in other organic substances. It is important in the breakdown of food by the body.

hydrometer in physics, an instrument used to measure the density of liquids compared with that of water, usually expressed in grams per cubic centimetre. It consists of a thin glass tube ending in a sphere which leads into a smaller sphere, the latter being loaded so that the hydrometer floats upright, sinking deeper into lighter liquids than heavier. It is used in brewing. The hydrometer is based on ◊Archimedes' principle.

hydrophilic (Greek 'water-loving') in chemistry, a term describing ◊functional groups with a strong affinity for water, such as the carboxylic acid group, –COOH.

hydrophily a form of ◊pollination in which the pollen is carried by water. Hydrophily is very rare but occurs in a few aquatic species. In *Canadian pondweed Elodea* and *tape grass Vallisneria*, the male flowers break off whole and rise to the water surface where they encounter the female flowers which are borne on long stalks. In *eel grasses Zostera*, which are coastal plants growing totally submerged, the filamentous pollen grains are released into the water and carried by currents to the female flowers where they become wrapped around the stigmas.

hydrophobia another name for the disease ◊rabies.

hydrophobic (Greek 'water-hating') in chemistry, a term describing ◊functional groups that repel water (compare ◊hydrophilic).

hydrophone an underwater ◊microphone and ancillary equipment capable of picking up water-borne sounds. It was originally developed to detect enemy submarines, but is now also used, for example, for listening to the sounds made by whales.

hydrophyte a plant adapted to live in water, or in waterlogged soil. Hydrophytes may have leaves with a very reduced or absent ◊cuticle and no ◊stomata (since there is no need to conserve water), a reduced root and water-conducting system, and less supporting tissue since water buoys plants up. There are often numerous spaces between the cells in their stems and roots to make gas exchange with all parts of the plant body possible. Many have highly divided leaves, which lessens resistance to flowing water, for example *spiked water milfoil Myriophyllum spicatum*.

hydroplane on a submarine, a moveable fin angled downwards or upwards when the vessel is descending or ascending. It is also a specially designed, highly manoeuvrable motorboat or ◊hydrofoil boat that skims over the surface of the water when driven at high speed.

hydroponics the cultivation of plants without soil, by using specially prepared solutions of mineral salts. Beginning in the 1930s, large crops were grown by hydroponic methods, at first in California, but since then in many other parts of the world.

J von Sachs (1832–97) 1860 and W Knop 1865 developed a system of plant culture in water whereby the relation of mineral salts to plant growth could be determined, but it was not until about 1930 that large crops could be grown. The term was first coined by W F Gericke, a US scientist.

hydrosphere the water component of the Earth, usually encompassing the oceans, seas, rivers, streams, swamps, lakes, groundwater, and atmospheric water vapour.

hydrostatics in physics, the branch of ◊statics dealing with the mechanical problems of fluids in equilibrium, that is, in a static condition. Practical applications include shipbuilding and dam design.

hydroxides inorganic compounds containing one or more hydroxyl (OH) groups and generally combined with a metal. The most important hydroxides are caustic soda (sodium hydroxide NaOH), caustic potash (potassium hydroxide KOH), and slaked lime (calcium hydroxide Ca(OH)₂).

hydroxyl group an atom of hydrogen and an atom of oxygen bonded together and covalently bonded to an organic molecule. Common compounds containing hydroxyl groups are alcohols and phenols. In chemical reactions, the hydroxyl group (–OH) frequently behaves as a single entity.

hydroxypropanoic acid modern name for ◊lactic acid.

hyena carnivorous mammal that lives in Africa and Asia. It has very strong limbs and jaws. It is a scavenger, although it will also attack and kill live prey. There are three surviving species, the **striped hyena** Hyaena hyaena found in India and N Africa; the **brown hyena** Hyaena brunnea found on the South African coasts; and the **spotted hyena** Hyaena crocuta common south of the Sahara.

The ◊aardwolf also belongs to the hyena family.

Hyères /iː'eə/ town on the Côte d'Azur in the département of Var, S France; population (1982) 41,739. It has a mild climate, and is a winter health resort. Industries include olive-oil pressing, and the export of violets, strawberries, and vegetables.

Hygieia /haɪ'dʒiːə/ in Greek mythology, the goddess of health (Roman **Salus**), daughter of Aesculapius.

hygiene the science of the preservation of health and prevention of disease. It is chiefly concerned with such external conditions as the purity of air and water, bodily cleanliness, and cleanliness in the home and workplace.

hygrometer in physics, an instrument for measuring the humidity of a gas. A **wet and dry bulb hygrometer** consists of two vertical thermometers, with one of the bulbs covered in absorbent cloth dipped into water. As the water evaporates, the bulb cools producing a temperature difference between the two thermometers. The amount of evaporation, and hence cooling of the wet bulb, depends on the relative humidity of the air.

Other hygrometers work on the basis of a length of natural fibre, such as hair or a fine strand of gut, changing with variations in humidity. In a **dew-point hygrometer**, a polished metal mirror gradually cools until a fine mist of water (dew) forms on it. This gives a measure of the ◊dew point, from which the air's relative humidity can be calculated.

hygroscopic a term used to describe a substance that can absorb moisture from the air, without becomimg wet.

Hyksos /'hɪksəʊz/ ('shepherd kings' or 'princes of the desert') a Semitic people which invaded Egypt in the 18th century BC and established their own dynasty, which lasted until 1580 BC.

Hymen /'haɪmen/ in Greek mythology, either the son of Apollo and one of the Muses, or of Dionysus and Aphrodite. He was the god of marriage, and

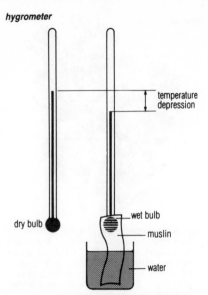

hygrometer

temperature depression

dry bulb

wet bulb

muslin

water

in art is represented as a youth carrying a bridal torch.

hymn song in praise of a deity. Examples include Ikhnaton's hymn to the Aton in ancient Egypt, the ancient Greek Orphic hymns, Old Testament psalms, extracts from the New Testament (such as Ave Maria), and hymns by the British writers John Bunyan ('Who would true valour see') and Charles Wesley ('Hark the herald angels sing'). ◊Gospel music is a form of Christian hymn-singing.

Other Christian hymn writers include Reginald Heber (1783–1826) ('From Greenland's icy mountains'), Henry Francis Lyte (1793–1847) ('Abide with me'), John S B Monsell (1811–75) ('Fight the good fight'), and Sabine Baring-Gould (1834–1924) ('Onward Christian soldiers'). William Blake's poem 'Jerusalem' ('And did those feet in ancient time') was set to music by Hubert Parry.

hyoscine a drug that acts on the autonomic nervous system, a derivative of ◊belladonna. It is frequently included in ◊premedication to dry up lung secretions and produce post-operative amnesia.

Hypatia /haɪ'peɪʃiə/ c. 370–c. 415. Greek philosopher, born at Alexandria. She studied Neo-Platonism at Athens, and succeeded her father Theon as professor of philosophy at Alexandria. She was murdered, it is thought by Christian fanatics.

hyperactivity condition of excessive activity in children, combined with inability to concentrate and difficulty in learning. Modification of the diet may help, and in the majority of cases there is improvement at puberty. The cause is not known, although some food additives have come under suspicion.

hyperbola in geometry, a curve formed by cutting a right circular cone with a plane so that the angle between the plane and the base is greater than the angle between the base and the side of the cone. All hyperbolae are bounded by two ◊asymptotes.

A member of the family of curves known as ◊conic sections, a hyperbola can also be defined as a path traced by a point that moves such that the ratio of its distance from a fixed point (focus) and a fixed straight line (directrix) is a constant and greater than 1, that is, it has an ◊eccentricity greater than 1.

hyperbole a ◊figure of speech whose Greek name suggests 'going over the top'. When people speak or write hyperbolically they exaggerate, usually to emphasize a point ('If I've told you once I've told you a thousand times not to do that').

hypercharge property of certain ◊elementary particles, analogous to electric charge, that accounts for the absence of some expected behaviour (such

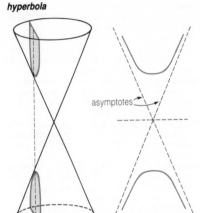

hyperbola

asymptotes

as decay) in terms of the short-range strong interaction force, which holds atomic nuclei together. ◊Protons and ◊neutrons, for example, have a hypercharge of +1 whereas a π meson has a hypercharge of zero.

hyperinflation rapid and uncontrolled ◊inflation, or increases in prices, usually associated with political and/or social instability (as in Germany in the 1920s).

hypertension abnormally high ◊blood pressure, the smooth muscle cells of the walls of the arteries being constantly contracted. It increases the risk of kidney disease, stroke, and heart attack.

hyperthyroidism or **thyrotoxicosis** overactivity of the thyroid gland due to enlargement or tumour. Symptoms include accelerated heart rate, sweating, anxiety, tremor, and weight loss. Treatment is by drugs or surgery.

hypertrophy abnormal increase in size of a body organ or tissue.

hypha (plural **hyphae**) a delicate, usually branching filament, many of which collectively form the mycelium and fruiting bodies of a ◊fungus. Food molecules and other substances are transported along hyphae by the movement of the cytoplasm, known as 'cytoplasmic streaming'.

Typically hyphae grow by increasing in length from the tips and by the formation of side-branches. Hyphae of the higher fungi (the ascomycetes and basidiomycetes) are divided by cross-walls or septa at intervals, whereas those of lower fungi (for example, bread mould) are undivided. However, even the higher fungi are not truly cellular, as each septum is pierced by a central pore, through which cytoplasm, and even nuclei, can flow. The hyphal walls contain ◊chitin, a polysaccharide.

Hyphasis /'hɪfəsɪs/ classical name of the river ◊Beas, in India.

hyphen a punctuation mark (-) with two functions: (1) to join words, parts of words, syllables, and so on, for particular purposes; and (2) to mark the break in a word continued from the end of one line to the beginning of the next line. The hyphenation of compound words in English is by no means clearcut; the same writer may in one article write, for example world view, worldview and world-view.

Broadly speaking, conventional hyphenation is a first stage in bringing two words together; if their close association is then generally agreed, the two words are written or printed as one (teapot, as opposed to tea-pot or tea pot), or are kept apart for visual and aesthetic reasons (coffee pot rather than coffee-pot or coffeepot). Practice does, however, vary greatly. There is a growing tendency in the use of certain prefixes towards omitting the hyphen (coworker rather than co-worker), often in order to economize on space.

hypnosis an artificially induced state of relaxation in which suggestibility is heightened. The subject may carry out orders after being awakened, and may be made insensitive to pain. It is sometimes used to treat addictions to tobacco or overeating, or to assist amnesia victims.

Discovered by ◊Mesmer, it was used by charlatans and entertainers until laws such as the Hypnosis Act 1952 in the UK controlled exploitation of hypnosis as entertainment.

hypnotic substance (such as ◊barbiturate, ◊benzodiazepine, alcohol) that depresses brain function, inducing sleep. Prolonged use may lead to physical or psychological addiction.

hypo in photography, a term for sodium thiosulphate, discovered 1819 by John ◊Herschel, and used as a fixative for photographic images since 1837.

hypocaust a floor raised on tile piers, heated by hot air circulating beneath it. It was first used by the Romans for baths about 100 BC, and was later introduced to private houses.

Hypocausts were a common feature of stone houses in the colder parts of the Roman Empire, but could not be used in timber-framed buildings. Typically the house of a wealthy person would have one furnace heating several rooms. In large houses there might be several such furnaces, and during the 1st century AD channels were built into walls and roofs in order to distribute heat more evenly around the building.

hypocycloid in geometry, a cusped curve traced by a point on the circumference of a circle that rolls round the inside of another larger circle (compare ◊epicycloid).

hypodermic an instrument used for injecting fluids beneath the skin. It consists of a small graduated tube with a close-fitting piston and a nozzle on to which a hollow needle can be fitted.

hypogeal a type of seed germination in which the ◊cotyledons remain below ground. The term can refer to fruits that develop underground, such as peanuts (*Arachis hypogea*).

hypoglycaemia deficiency of sugar (glucose) in the blood. It is rare in combination with other diseases, but in diabetics, low blood sugar occurs when the diabetic has taken too much insulin. A *hypoglycaemic* is a drug that lowers the level of glucose sugar in the blood. Diabetics who do not require insulin can control their blood–sugar level by diet and hypoglycaemic tablets.

hyponymy in semantics, a relationship in meaning between two words such that one (for example, *sport*) includes the other (for example, *baseball*), but not vice versa.

hyssop

hypothalamus the region of the brain below the ◊cerebrum that regulates rhythmic activity and physiological stability within the body, including water balance and temperature. It regulates the production of the pituitary gland's hormones and controls that part of the ◊nervous system regulating the involuntary muscles.

hypothermia a condition in which the deep temperature of the body drops abnormally low. If it continues untreated, coma and death ensue. Most at risk are babies (particularly if premature) and the aged.

hypothesis in science, an idea concerning an event and its possible explanation. The term is one favoured by the followers of the philosopher ◊Popper, who argue that the merit of a scientific hypothesis lies in its ability to make testable predictions.

hypothyroidism or *myxoedema* poor functioning of the thyroid gland, causing slowed mental and physical performance, sensitivity to cold and infection. This may be due to lack of iodine or a defect of the thyroid gland, both being productive of ◊goitre; or to the pituitary gland providing insufficient stimulus to the thyroid gland. Treatment of thyroid deficiency is by the hormone thyroxine (either synthetic or from animal thyroid glands).

hypsometer (Greek *hypsos* 'height') instrument for testing the accuracy of a thermometer at the boiling point of water. It was originally used for determining heights by comparing changes in the boiling point with changes in atmospheric pressure.

hyrax mammal, order Hyracoidea, that lives among rocks, in deserts, and in forests in Africa, Arabia, and Syria. It is about the size of a rabbit, with a plump body, short legs, short ears, long curved front teeth, and brownish fur. There are four toes on the front limbs, and three on the hind, each of which has a hoof. They are believed to be among the nearest living relatives of elephants.

hyssop aromatic herb *Hyssopus officinalis*, family Labiatae, found in Asia, S Europe, and around the Mediterranean. It has blue flowers, oblong leaves, and stems that are shrubby near the ground but herbaceous above.

hysterectomy surgical removal of the uterus (womb).

hysteresis phenomenon seen in the elastic and electromagnetic behaviour of materials, in which a lag occurs between the application or removal of a force or field and its effect.

If the magnetic field applied to a magnetic material is increased and then decreased back to its original value, the magnetic field inside the material does not return to its original value. The internal field 'lags' behind the external field. This behaviour results in a loss of energy, called the *hysteresis loss*, when a sample is repeatedly magnetized and demagnetized. Hence the materials used in transformer cores and electromagnets should have a low hysteresis loss.

Similar behaviour is seen in some materials when varying electric fields are applied (*electric hysteresis*). *Elastic hysteresis* occurs when a varying force repeatedly deforms an elastic material. The deformation produced does not completely disappear when the force is removed, and this results in energy loss on repeated deformations.

hysteria according to the work of ◊Freud, the conversion of a psychological conflict or anxiety feeling into a physical symptom, such as paralysis, blindness, recurrent cough, vomiting, and general malaise. The term is little used today in diagnosis.

Hythe /haɪð/ seaside resort (former ◊Cinque Port) in the Romney Marsh area of Kent, SE England; population (1981) 12,723.

ibis

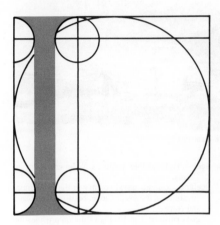

I ninth letter of the Roman alphabet, deriving, in form, from the sign for one of the several breathings of the Semitic languages. Its vocalic value was first given by the Greeks.

IA abbreviation for ◊*Iowa*.

IAEA abbreviation for ◊*International Atomic Energy Agency*.

Iaşi /'jæʃi/ (German *Jassy*) city in NE Romania, capital of Moldavia; population (1985) 314,000. It has chemical, machinery, electronic, and textile industries.

iatrogenic caused by treatment; the term 'iatrogenic disease' may be applied to any pathological condition that is caused by what the doctor says or does.

IBA abbreviation for ◊*Independent Broadcasting Authority*, UK regulatory body for commercial television and radio.

Ibadan /ɪ'bædn/ city in SW Nigeria and capital of Oyo state; population (1981) 2,100,000. Industries include chemicals, electronics, plastics, and vehicles.

Ibague /ˌiːbæ'geɪ/ capital of Tolima department, W central Colombia; population (1985) 293,000.

Iban (formerly known as *Dayak*) a people of central Borneo. Approximately 250,000 Iban live in the interior uplands of Sarawak, while another 10,000 live in the border area of W Kalimantan. The Iban speak languages belonging to the Austronesian family.

Ibáñez /iː'bɑːnjeθ/ Vincente Blasco 1867–1928. Spanish novelist and politician, born in Valencia. He was actively involved in revolutionary politics. His novels include *La barraca/The Cabin* 1898, the best of his regional works; *Sangre y arena/Blood and Sand* 1908, the story of a famous bullfighter; and *Los cuatro jinetes del Apocalipsis/The Four Horsemen of the Apocalypse* 1916, a product of the effects of World War I.

Ibarruri /iː'bæruri/ Dolores, known as **La Pasionaria** ('the passion flower') 1895–1989.

Spanish Basque politician, journalist, and orator; she was first elected to the Cortes in 1936. She helped to establish the Popular Front government, and was a Loyalist leader in the Civil War. When Franco came to power in 1939 she left Spain for the USSR, where she was active in the Communist Party. She returned to Spain in 1977 after Franco's death, and was re-elected to the Cortes (at the age of 81) in the first parliamentary elections for 40 years.

She joined the Spanish Socialist Party in 1917 and wrote for a workers' newspaper under the pen name La Pasionaria.

Iberia /aɪ'bɪəriə/ name given by ancient Greek navigators to the Spanish peninsula, derived from the river Iberus (Ebro). Anthropologists have given the name *Iberian* to a Neolithic people, traces of whom are found in the Spanish peninsula, southern France, the Canary Isles, Corsica, and part of North Africa.

ibex type of wild goat found in mountainous areas of Europe, NE Africa, and Central Asia. They grow to 100 cm/3.5 ft, and have brown or grey coats and heavy horns. They are herbivorous and live in small groups.

ibid. abbreviation for *ibidem* (Latin 'in the same place').

ibis type of wading bird, about 60 cm/2 ft tall, related to the storks and herons. It has long legs and neck, and a long curved beak. Various species occur in the warmer regions of the world.

The glossy ibis is found in all continents except South America. The sacred ibis of ancient Egypt *Threskiornis aethiopica* is still found in the Nile basin. The Japanese ibis is in danger of extinction because of loss of its habitat; fewer than 25 individual birds remain.

Ibiza /ɪ'biːθə/ one of the ◊Balearic Islands, a popular tourist resort; area 596 sq km/230 sq mi; population (1986) 45,000. The capital and port, also called Ibiza, has a cathedral.

Iblis the Muslim name for the ◊Devil.

IBM *International Business Machines* multinational company, the largest manufacturer of computers in the world. The company is a descendant of the Tabulating Machine Company, formed 1896 by Herman ◊Hollerith to exploit its punched card machines. It adopted its present name 1924. It now has an annual turnover (1988–89) of $60 billion and employs (1988) about 387,000 people.

Ibn Battuta /'ɪbən bə'tuːtə/ 1304–1368. Arab traveller born in Tangiers. In 1325, he went on an extraordinary 120,675 km/75,000 mi journey via Mecca to Egypt, E Africa, India, and China, returning some 30 years later. During this journey he also visited Spain and crossed the Sahara to Timbuktu. The narrative of his travels, *The Adventures of Ibn Battuta*, was written with an assistant, Ibn Juzayy.

Ibn Saud /'ɪbən 'saʊd/ 1880–1953. First king of Saudi Arabia from 1932. His father was the son of the sultan of Nejd, at whose capital, Riyadh, Ibn Saud was born. In 1891 a rival group seized Riyadh, and Ibn Saud went into exile with his father, who resigned his claim to the throne in his favour. In 1902 Ibn Saud recaptured Riyadh and recovered the kingdom, and by 1921 he had brought all central Arabia under his rule. In 1924 he invaded the Hejaz, of which he was proclaimed king in 1926.

Nejd and the Hejaz were united in 1932 in the kingdom of Saudi Arabia. Ibn Saud introduced programmes for modernization with revenue from oil, which was discovered in 1936.

Ibn Sina /'ɪbən 'siːnə/ Arabic name of ◊Avicenna, scholar and translator.

Ibo (or *Ebo*) person of Ibo culture from Nigeria's East-Central State. Primarily cultivators, they inhabit the richly forested tableland, bound by the River Niger to the W and the Cross River to the E. They are divided into five main divisions, and their languages belong to the Kwa branch of the Niger-Congo family.

Ibrahim Abdullah 1934– . South African pianist and composer, formerly known as 'Dollar' Brand. He first performed in the USA in 1965, and has had a great influence on the fusion of African rhythms with American jazz. His compositions range from songs to large works for orchestra.

Ibsen /'ɪbsən/ Henrik (Johan) 1828–1906. Norwegian playwright and poet, whose realistic and often controversial plays revolutionized European theatre. Driven into exile 1864–91 by opposition to the satirical *Love's Comedy* 1862, he wrote the verse dramas *Brand* 1866 and *Peer Gynt* 1867, followed by realistic plays dealing with social issues, including *Pillars of Society* 1877, ◊*The Doll's House* 1879, ◊*Ghosts* 1881, *An Enemy of the People* 1882, and ◊*Hedda Gabler* 1891. By the time of his return to Norway, he was recognized as the country's greatest living writer.

His later plays, which are more symbolic, include *The Master Builder* 1892, *Little Eyolf* 1894, *John Gabriel Borkman* 1896, and *When We Dead Awaken* 1899.

Icarus /'ɪkərəs/ in Greek mythology, the son of ◊Daedalus, who died when he flew too near the sun using wings made from feathers fastened with wax.

Icarus /'ɪkərəs/ in astronomy, an ◊Apollo asteroid 1.5 km/1 mi in diameter, discovered 1949. It orbits the Sun every 409 days at a distance of between 2.0 and 0.19 astronomical units (about 150 million km). It is the only asteroid known to approach the Sun closer than the planet Mercury. In 1968 it passed 6 million km/4 million mi from the Earth.

ICBM abbreviation for *intercontinental ballistic missile*; see ◊nuclear warfare.

ice the solid formed by water when it freezes. It is colourless and its crystals are hexagonal.

The freezing point, used as a standard for measuring temperature, is 0 for the Celsius and Réaumur scales, and 32 for the Fahrenheit. Ice expands in the act of freezing (hence burst pipes), becoming less dense than water (0.9175 at 0°C).

ice a form of methamphetamine which is smoked to give a 'high'; in use in the USA from 1989. Its

Ibsen Norwegian dramatist Henrik Ibsen.

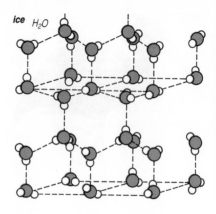

ice The crystal structrure of ice in which water molecules are held together by hydrogen bonds.

iceberg Icebergs aground in the Biscoe Islands, Antarctic Peninsula.

effect may be followed by a period of depression and psychosis.

Ice age any period of glaciation occurring in the Earth's history, but particularly that in the Pleistocene epoch, immediately preceding historic times. On the North American continent, ◊glaciers reached as far south as the Great Lakes, and an ice sheet spread over N Europe, leaving its remains as far south as Switzerland. There were several glacial advances separated by interglacial stages during which the ice melted and temperatures were higher than today.

Formerly there were thought to have been only three or four glacial advances, but recent research has shown about 20 major incidences. For example, ocean-bed cores record the absence or presence in their various layers of such cold-loving small marine animals as radiolaria, which indicate a fall in ocean temperature at regular intervals. Other ice ages have occurred throughout geological time: there were three in the Precambrian era, one in the Ordovician, and one at the end of the the Carboniferous and beginning of the Permian. The occurrence of an ice age is governed by a combination of factors (the ***Milankovitch hypothesis***): (1) the Earth's change of attitude in relation to the Sun, that is, the way it tilts in a 41,000-year cycle and at the same time wobbles on its axis in a 22,000-year cycle, making the time of its closest approach to the Sun come at different seasons; and (2) the 92,000-year cycle of eccentricity in its orbit round the Sun, changing it from an elliptical to a near circular orbit, the severest period of an ice age coinciding with the approach to circularity. There is a possibility that the ice age is not yet over. It may reach another maximum in another 60,000 years.

Major Ice Ages

Name (European/US)	date (years ago)
Pleistocene:	
Riss and Wurm/Wisconsin	80,000–10,000
Mindel/Illinoian	550,000–400,000
Gunz/Kansan	900,000–700,000
Danube/Nebraskan	1.7–1.3 million
Permo-Carboniferous	330–250 million
Ordovician	440–430 million
Verangian	615–570 million
Sturtian	820–770 million
Gnejso	940–880 million
Huronian	2,700–1,800 million

Ice Age, Little period of particularly severe winters that gripped N Europe between the 13th and 17th (or 16th and 19th) centuries. Contemporary writings and paintings show that Alpine glaciers were much more extensive than at present, and rivers such as the Thames, which do not ice over today, were so frozen that festivals could be held on them.

iceberg a floating mass of ice, about 80% of which is submerged, rising sometimes to 100 m/300 ft

above sea level. Glaciers that reach the coast become extended into a broad foot; as this enters the sea, masses break off and drift towards temperate latitudes, becoming a danger to shipping.

ice cream a frozen liquid confectionery, commercially made from the early 20th century from various milk products and sugar, and today also with 'non-milk' (animal or vegetable) fat, with usually artificial additives to give colour and flavour, and improve its keeping qualities and ease of serving. Water ices are frozen fruit juice.

history Ideally made of cream, eggs, and sugar whipped together and frozen, ice cream was made in China before 1000 BC and probably introduced to Europe by Marco Polo; water ices were known in ancient Greece and Persia. Italy and Russia were noted for ice cream even before it became a mechanized industry, first in the USA and in the 1920s in Britain. Technical developments from the 1950s made possible the mass distribution of a 'soft' ice cream resembling the original type in appearance.

ice hockey a game played on ice between two teams of six, developed in Canada from field hockey or bandy, with a puck (a rubber disc) in place of a ball. Players wear skates and protective clothing.

It is believed to have been first introduced in Canada in the 1850s, and the first game was played in Kingston, Ontario. The first rules were drawn up at McGill University, Montreal. The governing body is the International Ice Hockey Federation (IIHF) founded 1908.

Ice hockey has been included in the Olympics since 1920 when it was part of the Summer Games programme. Since 1924 it has been part of the Winter Olympics. The Stanley Cup is the game's leading playoff tournament, contested after the season-long National Hockey League, and was first held 1916.

ice hockey: recent winners

Olympic Games
1960 United States
1964 USSR
1968 USSR
1972 USSR
1976 USSR
1980 United States
1984 USSR
Stanley Cup
1980 New York Islanders
1981 New York Islanders
1982 New York Islanders
1983 New York Islanders
1984 Edmonton Oilers
1985 Edmonton Oilers
1986 Montreal Canadiens
1987 Edmonton Oilers
1988 Edmonton Oilers

Içel /i:'tʃel/ another name for ◊Mersin, a city in Turkey.

Iceland /'aɪslənd/ island country in the N Atlantic, situated S of the Arctic Circle, between Greenland and Norway.

government The 1944 constitution provides for a president, as head of state, and a legislature, the 63-member *Althing*, both elected by universal suffrage for a four-year term. Voting is by a system of proportional representation which ensures, as nearly as possible, an equality between proportions of the votes cast and seats won.

Once elected, the *Althing* divides into an upper house of 21 members and a lower house of 42. The upper-house members are chosen by the *Althing* itself and the residue of 42 automatically constitute the lower house. Members may speak in either house but only vote in the one for which they have been chosen. Legislation must

ice hockey

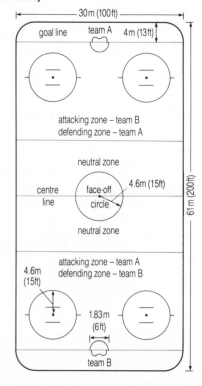

pass through three stages in each house before being submitted to the president for ratification. On some occasions the *Althing* sits as a single house. The president appoints the prime minister and cabinet on the basis of parliamentary support and they are collectively responsible to the *Althing*.

history Iceland was first occupied in 874 by Norse settlers, who founded a republic and a parliament in 930. In 1000 the inhabitants adopted Christianity, and about 1263 submitted to the authority of the king of Norway. In 1380 Norway, and with it Iceland, came under Danish rule.

Iceland remained attached to Denmark after Norway became independent in 1814. From 1918 it was independent but still recognized the Danish monarch. During World War II Iceland was occupied by British and US forces, and voted in a referendum for complete independence in 1944.

In 1949 it joined ◊NATO and the ◊Council of Europe, and in 1953 the Nordic Council. Since independence it has been governed by coalitions of the leading parties, sometimes right- and sometimes left-wing groupings, but mostly moderate.

The centre and right-of-centre parties are the Independents and Social Democrats, while those to the left are the Progressives and the People's Alliance. More recent additions have been the Social Democratic Alliance and the Women's Alliance.

Most of Iceland's external problems have been connected with overfishing of the waters around its coasts, while domestically governments have been faced with the recurring problem of inflation. The administration formed in 1983 is a coalition of Progressives and Independents, representing a fairly solid, centrist grouping. In 1985 the *Althing* unanimously declared the country a 'nuclear-free zone', banning the entry of all nuclear weapons.

The 1987 elections ended control of the *Althing* by the Independence and Progressive parties, giving more influence to the minor parties, including the Women's Alliance, which doubled its

ice cream

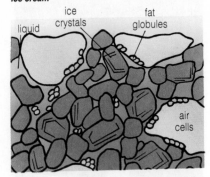

seat tally. In June 1988 Vigdis Finnbogadottir was re-elected president for a third term.

Icelandic language a member of the N Germanic branch of the Indo-European language family, spoken only in Iceland and the most conservative in form of the Scandinavian languages. Despite seven centuries of Danish rule, until 1918, Icelandic has remained virtually unchanged since the 12th century.

Since independence in 1918, Icelandic has experienced a revival, as well as governmental protection against such outside linguistic influences as English-language broadcasting. Halldor ◊Laxness, writing about Icelandic life in the style of the Sagas, was awarded a Nobel prize in 1955. Early Icelandic literature is largely anonymous and seems to have originated in Norse colonies in the British Isles (around 9th-10th centuries). The two Eddas and several Sagas date from this period.

Iceland spar a form of ◊calcite, $CaCO_3$, originally found in Iceland. In its pure form Iceland spar is transparent and exhibits the peculiar phenomenon of producing two images of anything seen through it. It is used in optical instruments. The crystals cleave into perfect rhombohedra.

Iceni /aɪˈsiːnaɪ/ an ancient people of E England,

who revolted against occupying Romans under ◊Boudicca.

Ichang /ˌiːˈtʃæŋ/ alternative form of ◊Yichang, a port in China.

I Ching or *Book of Changes* an ancient Chinese book of divination based on 64 hexagrams, or patterns of six lines. The lines may be broken or whole (yin or yang) and are generated by tossing yarrow stalks or coins. The enquirer formulates a question before throwing, and the book gives interpretations of the meaning of the hexagrams.

The *I Ching* is thought to have originated in the 2nd millennium BC, with commentaries added by Confucius and later philosophers. It is proto-Taoist in that it is not used for determining the future but for making the inquirer aware of inherent possibilities and unconscious tendencies.

ichneumon fly any parasitic wasp in the family Ichneumonidae. There are several thousand species in Europe, North America, and other regions. The eggs are laid in the eggs, larvae, or pupae of other insects, usually butterflies or moths.

icon in the Greek or Orthodox Eastern Church, a representation of Jesus, Mary, an angel or a saint, in painting, low relief, or mosaic. A *riza*, or gold and silver covering which leaves only the face and hands visible and may be adorned with jewels presented by the faithful in thanksgiving, is often added as protection.

Icons were regarded as holy objects, based on the doctrine that God became visible through Christ. Icon painting originated in the Byzantine Empire, although many were destroyed by the ◊iconoclasts, the Byzantine style remained influential in the Mediterranean region and in Russia in the middle ages until Russian, Greek, and other schools developed. Andrei Rublev was an early Russian icon painter. The *Virgin of ◊Kazan* is a famous icon.

icon in computing, a small picture on the screen representing an object or function that the user may manipulate or otherwise use. Icons make computers easier to use by allowing the user to point with the ◊mouse to pictures rather than type commands.

Iconium /aɪˈkəʊniəm/ city of ancient Turkey; see ◊Konya.

iconoclast (Greek 'image-breaker') literally, a person who attacks religious images; the Iconoclastic doctrine, rejecting the use of icons in churches, was given to the Christian party by the Byzantine emperor Leo III in 726. The same name was applied to those opposing the use of images at the Reformation, when there was much destruction in churches. Iconoclastic ideas had much in common with Islam and Judaism. Figuratively, the term is used for a person who attacks established ideals or principles.

iconography in art history, significance attached to symbols which can help to identify subject matter (for example, a saint holding keys usually represents St Peter) and place a work of art in its historical context.

id in Freudian psychology, the instinctual element of the human mind, concerned with pleasure, which demands immediate satisfaction. It is regarded as the ◊unconscious element of the human psyche, and is said to be in conflict with the ◊ego and the ◊superego.

id. abbreviation for *idem* (Latin 'the same').

ID abbreviation for ◊*Idaho*.

IDA abbreviation for ◊*International Development Association*.

Idaho /ˈaɪdəhəʊ/ state of NW USA; nickname Gem State
area 216,500 sq km/ 83,569 sq mi
capital Boise
towns Pocatello, Idaho Falls
features Rocky mountains; Snake river, which runs through Hell's Canyon, at 2,330 m/7,647 ft the deepest in North America, and has the National Reactor Testing Station on the plains of its upper reaches; Sun Valley ski and summer resort

---

Iceland
Republic of
(Lýdd–veldidd– Ísland)

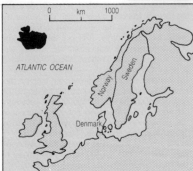

area 103,000 sq km/39,758 sq mi
capital Reykjavik
physical warmed by the Gulf Stream; glaciers and lava fields cover 75% of the country
features active volcanoes (Hekla was once thought the gateway to Hell), geysers, hot springs, and new islands being created offshore (Surtsey in 1963); subterranean hot water heats Iceland's homes
head of state Vigdís Finnbogadóttir from 1980
head of government Thorsteinn Palsson from 1987

political system democratic republic
political parties Independence Party (IP), right-of-centre; Progressive Party (PP), radical socialist; People's Alliance (PA), socialist; Social Democratic Party (SDP), moderate, left-of-centre; Citizen's Party, centrist; Women's Alliance, women and family orientated
exports cod and other fish products
currency krona (102.25 = £1 Feb 1990)
population (1987) 247,400; annual growth rate 1.2%
life expectancy men 74, women 80
language Icelandic, the most archaic Scandinavian language, in which some of the finest sagas were written
religion Evangelical Lutheran
literacy 99.9% (1984)
GDP $2.1 bn (1983); $9,000 per head of population
chronology
1944 Independence from Denmark achieved.
1949 Joined NATO and the Council of Europe.
1953 Joined the Nordic Council.
1976 'Cod War' with the UK.
1979 Iceland announced a 200-mile exclusive fishing zone.
1983 Steingrímur Hermannsson appointed to lead a coalition government.
1985 Iceland declared a nuclear-free zone.
1987 New coalition government formed by Thorsteinn Palsson after general election.
1988 Vigdís Finnbogadóttir re-elected president for a third term.

Idaho

products potatoes, wheat, livestock, timber, silver, lead, zinc, antimony
population (1984) 1,001,000
religion Christian, predominantly Mormon
history first permanently settled 1860 after the discovery of gold, Idaho became a state 1890.

idealism in philosophy, theory which states that what we ordinarily refer to as the external world is fundamentally immaterial and a dimension of mind. Objects in the world exist but, according to this theory, they lack substance.

identikit a set of drawings of different parts of the face used to compose a likeness of a person for identification. It was evolved by Hugh C McDonald (1913–) in the USA, and first used by the police in Britain 1961. It has largely been replaced by ◊photofit, based on photographs, which produces a more realistic likeness.

ideology a set of ideas, beliefs, and opinions about the nature of people and society, providing a framework for a theory about how society is or should be organized.

Ides in the Roman calendar, the 15th day of Mar, May, July, and Oct, and the 13th day of all other months (the word originally indicated the full moon); Julius Caesar was assassinated on the Ides of March 44 BC.

Idi Amin Dada, Lake /ˈɪdi æˈmiːn ˈdɑːdɑː/ former name 1973–79 of Lake ◊Edward in Uganda/Zaïre.

i.e. abbreviation for *id est* (Latin 'that is').

IEEE abbreviation for *Institute of Electrical and Electronic Engineers*, which sets technical

Iguaçu Falls The horseshoe-shaped Iguaçu Falls close to the Paraguyan border, comprising 275 separate waterfalls.

standards for electrical equipment and computer data exchange.

If /iːf/ Small French island in the Mediterranean about 3 km/2 mi off Marseille, with a castle, Château d'If, built about 1529. This was used as a state prison, and is the scene of the imprisonment of Dante in Dumas' Count of Monte Cristo.

Ifni /ˈɪfni/ a former Spanish overseas province in S W Morocco 1860–1969; area 1,920 sq km/740 sq mi. The chief town is Sidi Ifni.

Ifugao people of N Luzon in the Philippines, numbering approximately 70,000. Their language belongs to the Austronesian family.

The Ifugao live in scattered hamlets and, traditionally, recognize a class of nobles, *kadangya*, who are obliged to provide expensive feasts on particular social occasions. Although indigenous beliefs remain important, many Ifugao have adopted Christianity. In addition to cultivating highland slopes with shifting methods, they build elaborate

iguana

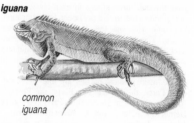

common iguana

terraced rice fields. Some Ifugao work as wage labourers outside their highland region.

Iglesias /iːˈɡleɪsiəs/ Pablo 1850–1925. Spanish politician, founder of the Spanish Socialist Party (*Partido Socialista Obrero España*, PSOE) in 1879 and in 1911 the first socialist deputy to be elected to the *Cortes* (Spanish parliament).

Igls /ˈiːɡls/ winter sports resort in the Austrian Tyrol, near Innsbruck; venue for the 1964 Winter Olympics.

Ignatius Loyola, St /ɪɡˈneɪʃəs lɔɪˈəʊlə/ 1491–1556. Spanish soldier converted 1521 to the Roman Catholic religious life after being wounded in battle, and founder of the ◊Jesuit order in 1540. Feast day 31 July.

Ignatius of Antioch, St /ɪɡˈneɪʃəs ˈæntiɒk/ 1st–2nd century AD. Christian martyr. Traditionally a disciple of St John, he was bishop of Antioch, and was thrown to the wild beasts in Rome. He wrote seven epistles, important documents of the early Christian church. Feast day 1 Feb.

igneous rock a rock formed from cooling magma or lava, and solidifying from a molten state. Igneous rocks are classified according to their crystal size, texture, chemical composition, or method of formation. They are largely composed of silica (SiO_2) and their silica content determines three main groups: acid (over 66% silica), intermediate (45–55%), and basic (45–55%). Igneous rocks that crystallize below the Earth's surface are called plutonic or intrusive, depending on the depth of formation. They have large crystals produced by slow cooling; examples include dolerite and granite. Those extruded at the surface are called extrusive or volcanic. Rapid cooling results in small crystals; basalt is an example.

ignis fatuus see ◊will-o'-the-wisp.

ignition coil a kind of ◊transformer that is an essential part of a petrol engine's ignition system. It consists of two wire coils wound around an iron core. The primary coil, which is connected to the car battery, has only a few turns. The secondary coil, connected via the ◊distributor to the ◊spark plugs, has many turns. The coil takes in a low voltage (usually 12 volts) from the battery and transforms it to a high voltage (about 20,000 volts) to ignite the engine.

When the engine is running, the battery current is periodically interrupted by means of the contact-breaker in the distributor. The collapsing current in the primary coil induces a current in the secondary coil, a phenomenon known as ◊electromagnetic induction. The induced current in the secondary coil is at very high voltage, typically about 15,000–20,000 volts. This passes to the spark plugs to create sparks.

Iguaçu Falls /ˌiːɡwæˈsuː/ or Iguassú Falls waterfall in South America, on the border between Brazil and Argentina. The falls lie 19 km/12 mi above the junction of the Iguaç with the Paraná. They are divided by forested rocky islands and form a spectacular tourist attraction. The water plunges in 275 falls, many of which have separate names. They have a height of 82 m/269 ft, and a width about 4 km/2.5 mi.

iguana lizard of the family Iguanidae, which includes about 700 species and is chiefly confined to the Americas. The common iguana *Iguana iguana* of Central and South America may reach 2 m/6 ft.

iguanodon plant-eating ◊dinosaur whose remains

ignition coil

HT lead

ignition coil

spark plug lead

condenser

contact breaker

distributor

spark plugs

car key

lead acid battery

— high-tension (20,000 volts)
— earthing
--- low-tension (12 volts = car battery voltage)

are found in strata of the Lower Cretaceous age. It varied in length from 5–10 m/16–32 ft, and when standing upright was 4 m/13 ft tall. It walked on its hind legs, balancing its body by its long tail.

IJsselmeer /ˈaɪsəlmɪə/ lake in the Netherlands, formed 1932 after the Zuider Zee was cut off by a dyke from the North Sea; freshwater since 1944. Area 1,217 sq km/470 sq mi.

ikat the Indonesian term for a textile which is produced by resist-printing the warp or weft before ◊weaving.

IKBS abbreviation for *intelligent knowledge-based system*, an alternative name for the more usual KBS (◊knowledge-based system).

ikebana the Japanese art of flower arrangement. It dates from the 6th–7th century when arrangements of flowers were placed as offerings in Buddhist temples, a practice learned from China. In the 15th century, ikebana became a favourite pastime of the nobility. Oldest of the Japanese ikebana schools is Ikenobo at Kyoto (7th century).

Ikhnaton /ɪkˈnɑːtn/ or *Akhenaton* 14th century BC. King of Egypt of the 18th dynasty (*c*.1379–62 BC), who may have ruled jointly for a time with his father Amenhotep III. He developed the cult of the sun, ◊Aton rather than the rival cult of ◊Ammon. Some historians believe that his neglect of imperial defence for religious reforms led to the loss of most of Egypt's possessions in Asia. His favourite wife was Nefertiti, and two of their six daughters were married to his successors Smenkhare and Tutankaton (later known as Tutankhamen).

IL abbreviation for ◊*Illinois*.

ILEA abbreviation for *Inner London Education Authority*. UK educational body which administered education in London. It was abolished 1990 and replaced by smaller borough-based education authorities.

Originally called the *School Board for London* 1870, it became part of London County Council (LCC) 1902. It remained when the LCC became the Greater London Council (GLC) in 1965, and survived the latter's abolition in 1986.

Île-de-France /ˈiːl də ˈfrɒns/ region of N France; area 12,000 sq km/4,632 sq mi; population (1986) 10,251,000. It includes the French capital, Paris, and the towns of Versailles, Sèvres, and St-Cloud, and is comprised of the *départements* of Essonne, Val-de-Marne, Val d'Oise, Ville de Paris, Seine-et-Marne, Hauts-de-Seine, Seine-Saint-Denis, and Yvelines. From here the early French kings extended their authority over the whole country.

Ilfracombe /ˈɪlfrəkuːm/ resort on the N coast of Devon, England; population (1981) 10,479.

Iliad Greek epic poem in 24 books, probably written before 700 BC, attributed to Homer. Its title is derived from Ilion, another name for Troy. Its subject is the wrath of Achilles, an incident during the tenth year of the Trojan War, when Achilles kills Hector to avenge the death of his friend Patroclus. The tragic battle scenes are described in graphic detail.

Ilkeston /ˈɪlkɪstən/ town in SE Derbyshire, England; population (1981) 33,031. Products include clothing and plastics.

Ilkley /ˈɪlkli/ town in W Yorkshire, England, noted for nearby *Ilkley Moor*; population (1981) 24,082.

Ille /iːl/ French river 45 km/28 mi long, which rises in Lake Boulet and enters the Vilaine at Rennes. It gives its name to the *département* of Ille-et-Vilaine in Brittany.

illegitimacy in law, the birth of a child to a mother who is not legally married; a child may be legitimated by subsequent marriage of the parents. Nationality of child is usually that of the mother. In the UK, recent acts have progressively removed many of the historic disadvantages of illegitimacy, for example, as regarding inheritance, culminating in the Family Law Reform Act 1987 under which ◊custody and ◊maintenance provisions are now the same as for legitimate children.

Illich /ˈɪlɪtʃ/ Ivan 1926– . US radical philosopher and activist, born in Austria. His works, which include *Deschooling Society* 1971, *Towards a History of Need* 1978, and *Gender* 1983, are a critique against modern economic development, especially in the Third World.

Illich was born in Vienna and has lived in the USA and Latin America. He believes that modern technology and bureaucratic institutions are destroying peasant skills and self-sufficiency and creating a new form of dependency: on experts, professionals, and material goods. True liberation can only be achieved by abolishing the institutions on which authority rests, such as schools and hospitals. His ideas have influenced development strategies in the Third World.

Illimani /ˌiːljɪˈmɑːni/ highest peak in the Bolivian Andes, rising to 6,402 m/21,004 ft E of La Paz.

Illinois /ˌɪləˈnɔɪ/ midwest state of the USA; nickname Inland Empire/Prairie State
area 146,100 sq km/56,395 sq mi
capital Springfield
towns Chicago, Rockford, Peoria, Decatur
features Lake Michigan, the Mississippi, Illinois, Ohio, and Rock rivers; Cahokia Mounds, the largest group of prehistoric earthworks in the USA; in Des Plaines, the restaurant where the first McDonald's hamburger was served 1955 became a museum 1985
products soybeans, cereals, meat and dairy products, machinery, electric and electronic equipment
population (1987) 11,582,000
famous people Walt Disney, James T Farrell, Ernest Hemingway, Edgar Lee Masters, Ronald Reagan, Frank Lloyd Wright
history originally explored by the French in the 17th century, ceded to Britain by the French 1763, Illinois passed to American control 1783, and became a state 1818.

illumination the brightness or intensity of light falling on a surface. It depends upon the brightness, distance, and angle of any nearby light sources. The SI unit is the ◊lux.

Illyria /ɪˈlɪrɪə/ ancient name for the eastern coastal region on the Adriatic, N of the Gulf of Corinth, conquered by Philip of Macedon. It became a Roman province AD 9. The Albanians are the survivors of its ancient peoples.

ilmenite an oxide of iron and titanium, iron titanate (FeTiO₃); an ore of titanium. The mineral is black, with a metallic lustre. It is found in compact masses, grains, and sand.

Ilorin /ɪˈlɔːrɪn/ capital of Kwara state, Nigeria; population (1983) 344,000. It trades in tobacco and wood products.

ILS abbreviation for *instrument landing system*, an automatic system for assisting aircraft landing at airports.

image a picture or appearance of a real object, formed by light that passes through a lens or is reflected from a mirror. If rays of light actually pass through an image, it is called a real image. Real images, such as those produced by a camera or projector lens, can be projected onto a screen. An image that cannot be projected onto a screen, such as that seen in a flat mirror, is known as a virtual image.

imaginary number term often used to describe the non-real element of a ◊complex number. For the complex number (*a* + *ib*), (*ib*) is the imaginary number where *i* = √–1, and *b* any real number.

Imagism a movement in Anglo-American poetry which flourished in London 1912–14 and affected much British and US poetry and critical thinking thereafter. A central figure was Ezra Pound, who asserted principles encouraging free verse, hard imagery, and poetic impersonality.

Pound encouraged Hilda Doolittle to sign her verse H D Imagiste and in 1914 edited the *Des Imagistes* anthology. Poets subsequently influenced include T S Eliot, W C Williams, Wallace Stevens, and Marianne Moore. Imagism established the Modern movement in English-language verse.

Illinois

imago the sexually mature stage of an ◊insect.

imam /ɪˈmɑːm/ (Arabic) in a mosque, the leader of congregational prayer, but generally any notable Islamic leader.

Imbros /ˈɪmbrɒs/ island in the Aegean (Turkish Imroz); area 280 sq km/108 sq mi. Occupied by Greece in World War I, it became Turkish under the Treaty of ◊Lausanne 1923. Population (1970) 6,786.

IMF abbreviation for ◊*International Monetary Fund*.

Imhotep /ɪmˈhəʊtep/ *c*. 2800 BC. Egyptian physician and architect, adviser to King Zoser (3rd dynasty). He is thought to have designed the step pyramid at Sakkara, and his tomb (believed to be in the N Sakkara cemetery) became a centre of healing. He was deified as the son of ◊Ptah and was identified with Aesculapius, the Greek god of medicine.

Immaculate Conception in the Roman Catholic Church, the belief that the Virgin Mary was, by a special act of grace, preserved free from ◊original sin from the moment she was conceived. This article of the Catholic faith was for centuries the subject of heated controversy, opposed by St Thomas Aquinas and other theologians, but generally accepted from about the 16th century. It became a dogma in 1854.

immigration and emigration the movement of people from one country to another. Immigration is movement to a country; emigration is movement from a country. Immigration or emigration on a large scale is often for economic reasons or because of persecution (which may create ◊refugees), and often prompts restrictive legislation by individual countries. The USA has received immigrants on a larger scale than any other country, more than 50 million during its history.

In the UK, Commonwealth Immigration Acts were passed in 1962 and 1968, and replaced by a single system of control under the Immigration Act of 1971. The British Nationality Act 1981 further restricted immigration by ruling that only a British citizen has the right to live in the United Kingdom; see ◊citizenship.

Immingham /ˈɪmɪŋəm/ town on the river Humber, Humberside, NE England; population (1981) 11,500. It is a bulk cargo handling port, with petrochemical works and oil refineries.

immiscible term describing liquids that will not mix with each other, such as oil and water. When two immiscible liquids are shaken together, a turbid mixture will be produced. This normally forms separate layers on standing.

immunity the protection that animals have against foreign microorganisms, such as bacteria and viruses, and against cancerous cells (see ◊cancer). The cells that provide this protection are called white blood cells, or leucocytes, and make up the immune system. They include neutrophils and ◊macrophages, which can engulf invading organisms and other unwanted material, and natural killer cells which destroy cells infected by viruses and cancerous cells. Some of the most important immune cells are the ◊B cells and ◊T cells. Immune cells coordinate their activities by means of chemical messengers or ◊lymphokines, including the antiviral messenger ◊interferon. The lymph

immigration

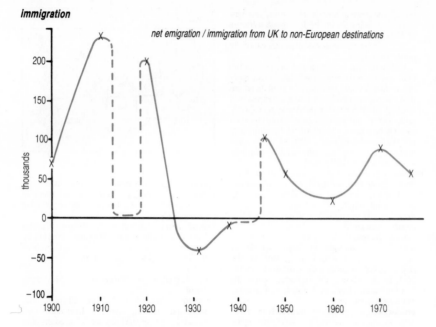

net emigration / immigration from UK to non-European destinations

nodes play a major role in organizing the immune response.

Immunity is also provided by a range of physical barriers such as the skin, tear fluid, acid in the stomach, and mucus in the airways. ◊AIDS is one of many viral diseases in which the immune system is affected.

immunization conferring immunity to infectious disease by artificial methods. The most widely used technique is ◊vaccination.

immunocompromised lacking a fully effective immune system. The term is most often used in connection with infections such as ◊AIDS where the virus interferes with the immune response (see ◊immunity).

Other factors that can impair the immune response are pregnancy, diabetes, old age, malnutrition and extreme stress, making someone susceptible to infections by microorganisms (such as listeria) that do not affect normal, healthy people. Some people are ◊immuno-deficient, others could be on ◊immunosuppressive drugs.

immuno-deficient lacking one or more elements of a working immune system. Immune deficiency is the term generally used for patients who are born with such a defect, while those who acquire such a deficiency later in life are referred to as ◊*immunocompromised* or *immunosuppressed*.

A serious impairment of the immune system is sometimes known as SCID, or Severe Combined Immune Deficiency. At one time such children would have died in infancy. They can now be kept alive in a germ-free environment, then treated with a bone-marrow transplant from a relative, to replace the missing immune cells. At present, the success rate for this type of treatment is still fairly low.

immunoglobulin or *antibody* human ◊protein which can be separated from blood, and administered to confer immediate immunity on the recipient.

Normal immunoglobulin (gammaglobulin) is obtained from plasma pooled from 1,000 donors. It is given for short-term (2–3 months) protection when a person is at risk, especially from hepatitis A (infectious hepatitis), or when a pregnant woman, not immunized against ◊German measles, is exposed to the virus.

Specific immunoglobulins react like ◊antibodies against a specific disease-causing organism. In particular, the appropriate immunoglobulin is injected when a susceptible (non-immunized) person is at risk of injection from a potentially fatal disease, such as hepatitis B (serum hepatitis), rabies, or tetanus. These immunoglobulins are prepared from blood pooled from donors convalescing from the disease.

immunosuppressive drug that suppresses the body's normal immune responses to infection or foreign tissue. It is used in the treatment of auto-immune disease, as part of chemotherapy for leukaemias, lymphomas, and other cancers, and to help prevent rejection following organ transplantation.

impala African antelope *Aepyceros melampus* found from Kenya to South Africa in savannas and open woodlands. The body is sandy brown. The males have lyre-shaped horns up to 75 cm/2.5 ft long. Impala grow up to 1.5 m/5 ft long and 90 cm/3 ft tall. They live in herds and spring high in the air when alarmed.

impeachment in the UK, a judicial procedure by which the House of Commons from 1376 brought ministers and officers of state to trial before the House of Lords, for example Bacon 1621, Strafford 1640, and Warren Hastings 1788. In the USA the House of Representatives similarly may impeach offenders to be tried before the Senate, for example President Andrew Johnson 1868. Richard ◊Nixon was forced to resign the US presidency 1974 following the threat of impeachment.

impedance the total opposition of a circuit to the passage of electric current. It has the symbol Z. For a direct current (DC) it is the total ◊resistance R of all the components in the circuit. For an ◊alternating current (AC) it includes also the reactance X (caused by ◊capacitance or ◊inductance); the impedance can be found using the equation $Z^2 = R^2 + X^2$.

Imperial College of Science and Technology institution established at South Kensington, London, in 1907, for advanced scientific training and research, applied especially to industry. Part of the University of London, it comprises three separate colleges, the City and Guilds College (engineering faculty), the Royal College of Science (pure science), and the Royal School of Mines (mining).

imperialism the attempt by one country to dominate others, either by direct rule or by less obvious means such as control of markets for goods or raw materials. The latter is often called ◊neo-colonialism. In the 19th century imperialism was synonymous with the establishment of colonies (see ◊British Empire). Many socialist thinkers believe that the role of Western (especially US) finance capital in the Third World constitutes a form of imperialism.

imperial system traditional system of units developed in the UK, based largely on the foot, pound, and second (◊f.p.s. system).

Imperial War Museum British military museum, founded 1917. It includes records of all operations fought by British forces since 1914. Its present building (formerly the Royal Bethlehem, or Bedlam, Hospital) in Lambeth Road, London, was opened 1936. It was rebuilt and enlarged 1989.

impetigo contagious bacterial infection (*Staphylococcus aureus*) of the skin which forms yellowish crusts; it is curable with antibiotics.

Imphal /ɪmˈfɑːl/ capital of Manipur state on the Manipur river, India; population (1981) 156,622, a communications and trade centre (tobacco, sugar, fruit). It was besieged Mar–June 1944, when Japan invaded Assam, but held out with the help of supplies dropped by air.

implantation in mammals, the process by which the developing ◊embryo attaches itself to the wall of the mother's uterus and stimulates the development of the ◊placenta.

In some species, such as seals and bats, implantation is delayed for several months, during which time the embryo does not grow; thus the interval between mating and birth may be a year, although the ◊gestation period is only seven or eight months.

import product or service which one country purchases from another for domestic consumption, or for processing and re-exporting (Hong Kong, for example, is heavily dependent on imports for its export business). If an importing country does not have a counterbalancing value of exports, it may experience balance-of-payments difficulties and accordingly consider restricting imports by some form of protectionism (such as an import tariff or imposing import quotas).

Importance of Being Earnest, The a romantic comedy by Oscar Wilde, first performed 1895. The courtship of two couples is comically complicated by confusions of identity and by the overpowering Lady Bracknell.

impotence a physical inability to perform sexual intercourse, although the term is not usually applied in relation to women. In men, there is a failure to achieve an erection, which may be due to illness, the effects of certain drugs, or psychological factors.

Impressionism movement in painting which originated in France in the 1860s and dominated European and North American painting in the late 19th century. The Impressionists wanted to depict real life, to paint straight from nature, and to capture the changing effects of light. The term was first used abusively to describe Monet's painting *Impression: Sunrise* 1872 (stolen from the Musée Marmottan, Paris); other Impressionists were Renoir and Sisley, soon joined by Cézanne, Manet, Degas, and others.

The starting point of Impressionism was the *Salon des Refusés*, an exhibition in 1873 of work rejected by the official Salon. This was followed by the Impressionists own exhibitions 1874–86, where their work aroused fierce opposition. Their styles were diverse, but many experimented with effects of light and movement created with distinct brushstrokes and fragments of colour juxtaposed on the canvas rather than mixed on the palette. By the 1880s, the movement's central impulse had dispersed, and a number of new styles emerged, later described as Post-Impressionism.

impressionism in music, a style of composition emphasizing instrumental colour and texture. First applied to the music of ◊Debussy.

imprinting in ◊ethology, the process whereby a young animal learns to recognize both specific individuals (for example, its mother) and its own species.

Imprinting is characteristically an automatic response to specific stimuli at a time when the animal

Impressionism Claude Monet's Impression: Sunrise *(1872), formerly Musée Marmottan, Paris. Exhibited at the first Impressionist exhibition, this was the work that inspired the movement's name. The term was originally meant to be derogatory.*

Inca Civilization

Inca Empire in 11th century

Inca Empire in 1533

is especially sensitive to those stimuli (the **sensitive period**). Thus, goslings learn to recognize their mother by following the first moving object they see after hatching; as a result, they can easily become imprinted on to other species, or even inanimate objects, if these happen to move near them at this time. In chicks, imprinting occurs only between 10 and 20 hours after hatching. In mammals, the mother's attachment to her infant may be a form of imprinting made possible by a sensitive period; this period may be as short as the first hour after giving birth.

impromptu in music, a short instrumental piece that suggests spontaneity. Composers of piano impromptus include Schubert and Chopin.

Imroz /ˈɪmrɒz/ Turkish form of ◊Imbros, an island in the Aegean.

in abbreviation for *inch*.

IN abbreviation for ◊*Indiana*.

inbreeding in ◊genetics, the mating of closely related individuals. It is considered undesirable because it increases the risk that an offspring will inherit copies of recessive alleles from both parents (see ◊recessivity) and so suffer from disabilities.

Inc. abbreviation for *Incorporated*.

Inca former ruling class of South American Indian people of Peru. The first emperor or 'Inca' (believed to be a descendant of the Sun) was Manco Capac about AD 1200. Inca rule eventually extended from Quito in Ecuador to beyond Santiago in S Chile, but the civilization was destroyed by the Spanish conquest in the 1530s. The descendants of the Incas are the ◊Quechua.

Inca art art of the Inca people of the Peruvian Andes, South America, of the 11th–16th centuries. The main sites are Cuzco, the old capital, and ◊Machu Picchu, a fortified mountain settlement. Inca artisans produced technically brilliant, highly finished masonry, with large blocks of stone fitted together with great precision. Animal and human figures are frequent sculptural subjects.

incandescence emission of light from a substance in consequence of its high temperature. The colour of the emitted light from liquids or solids depends on their temperature, and for solids generally the higher the temperature the whiter the light. Gases may become incandescent through ◊ionizing radiation, as in the glowing vacuum ◊discharge tube.

The oxides of cerium and thorium are highly incandescent and for this reason are used in gas mantles. The light from an electric filament lamp is due to the incandescence of the filament, rendered white-hot when a current passes through it.

incarnation assumption of living form (plant, animal, human) by a deity, for example the gods of Greece and Rome, Hinduism, Christianity (Jesus as the second person of the Trinity).

incendiary bomb a bomb containing inflammable matter. Usually dropped by aircraft, incendiary bombs were used in World War I, and were a major weapon in attacks on cities in World War II. To hinder firefighters, delayed-action high-explosive bombs were usually dropped with them. In the Vietnam War, the USA used ◊napalm in incendiary bombs.

incest sexual intercourse between persons thought to be too closely related to marry; the exact relationships which fall under the incest taboo vary widely between societies. A biological explanation for the incest taboo is to avoid ◊inbreeding.

Within groups in which ritual homosexuality is practised, for example in New Guinea, an incest

inbreeding

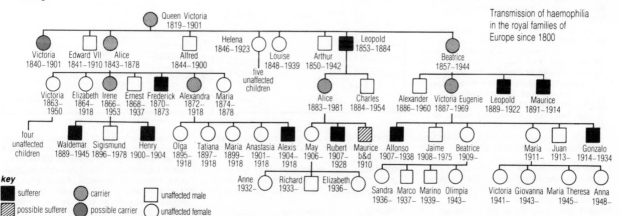

Transmission of haemophilia in the royal families of Europe since 1800

key

■ sufferer

● carrier

▨ possible sufferer

◑ possible carrier

□ unaffected male

○ unaffected female

taboo applies also to these relations, suggesting that the taboo is as much social as biological in origin.

inch imperial measure of length, a twelfth of a ◊foot. It was defined in statute by Edward II as the length of three barley grains laid end to end.

Inchon /ˌɪnˈtʃɒn/ formerly *Chemulpo* chief port of Seoul, South Korea; population (1985) 1,387,000. It produces steel and textiles.

inclination the angle between the ◊ecliptic and the plane of the orbit of a planet, asteroid, or comet. In the case of satellites orbiting a planet, it is the angle between the plane of orbit of the satellite and the equator of the planet.

inclusive fitness in ◊genetics, the success with which a given variant of a ◊gene (or allele) is passed on to future generations by a particular individual, after additional copies of the allele in the individual's relatives and their offspring have been taken into account, as well as those in its own offspring.

The concept was formulated by W D ◊Hamilton as a way of explaining the evolution of ◊altruism in terms of ◊natural selection. See also ◊fitness and ◊kin selection.

incomes policy a government-initiated exercise to curb ◊inflation by restraining rises in incomes, on either a voluntary or a compulsory basis; often linked with action to control prices, in which case it becomes a prices and incomes policy.

In Britain incomes policies have been applied at different times since the 1950s, with limited success. An alternative to incomes policy, employed by the post-1979 Conservative government in Britain, is monetary policy, which attempts to manage the economy by controlling the quantity of money in circulation (money supply).

income tax a direct tax levied on personal income, mainly wages and salaries, but which may include the value of receipts other than in cash. It is one of the main instruments for achieving a government's income redistribution objectives. In contrast, *indirect taxes* are duties payable whenever a specific product is purchased; examples include VAT and customs duties.

Most countries impose income taxes on company (corporation) profits and on individuals (personal), although the rates and systems differ widely from country to country. In the case of companies in particular, income tax returns are prepared by an accountant, who will take advantage of the various exemptions, deductions, and allowances available. Personal income taxes are usually progressive so that the poorest members of society pay little or no tax, while the rich make much larger contributions.

In the 1980s many countries have undergone tax reforms that have led to simplification and reductions in income tax rates. This has had the effect of stimulating economic activity by increasing consumer spending and in some cases discouraged tax evasion.

In the UK the rate of tax and allowances is set out yearly in the annual Finance Act, which implements the recommendations agreed to by the House of Commons in the budget presented by the chancellor of the exchequer. William Pitt introduced an income tax 1799–1801 to finance the wars with revolutionary France; it was reimposed 1803–16 for the same purpose, and was so unpopular that all records of it were destroyed when it was abolished. Peel reintroduced the tax in 1842 and it has been levied ever since, forming an important part of government finance. At its lowest, 1874–76, it was 0.83%; at its highest, 1941–46, the standard rate was 50%. In the UK, employees' tax is deducted under the ◊PAYE system.

incontinence a failure or inability to control evacuation of the bladder or bowel (or both in the case of double incontinence). It may arise as a result of injury, disease, or senility.

incubus male spirit who in the popular belief of the Middle Ages had sexual intercourse with

women in their sleep. Witches and demons were supposed to result. *Succubus* is the female equivalent.

incunabula (Latin 'swaddling clothes') the birthplace, or early stages of anything; printed books produced before 1500, when printing was in its infancy.

indemnity in law, an undertaking to compensate another for damage, loss, trouble, or expenses, or

the money paid by way of such compensation, for example under fire insurance agreements. An *act of indemnity* is passed by the UK Parliament to relieve offenders of penalties innocently incurred, as by ministers in the course of their duties.

indenture in law, a ◊deed between two or more people. Historically, an indenture was a contract between a master and apprentice. The term derives from the practice of writing the agreement

India

India
(Hindi *Bharat*)

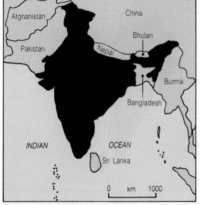

area 3,166,829 sq km/1,222,396 sq mi
capital New Delhi
towns Bangalore, Hyderabad, Ahmedabad; ports Calcutta, Bombay, Madras, Kanpur, Pune, Nagpur
physical Himalaya mountains on the N border; plains around rivers Ganges, Indus, Brahmaputra; Deccan peninsula S of the Narmada River, a plateau between the W and E Ghats mountain ranges
territories Andaman and Nicobar Islands, Lakshadweep
features the Taj Mahal monument; cave paintings (Ajanta); world's fourth-largest military: 1,362,000, behind only the USSR, China, and the US
head of state Ramaswami Iyer Venkataraman from 1987
head of government Vishwanath Pratap Singh from 1989
political system federal democratic republic
political parties Janata Dal, left-of-centre; Congress Party–Indira (Congress (I)), cross-caste and religion left-of-centre; Bharatiya Janata Party (BJP), conservative Hindu-chauvinist; Communist Party of India (CPI), pro-Moscow Marxist-Leninist; Communist Party of India–Marxist (CPI-M), West Bengal-based moderate socialist
exports tea, coffee, fish, iron ore, leather, textiles, polished diamonds
currency rupee (28.50 = £1 Feb 1990)
population (1985) 750,900,000; annual growth rate 1.9%
life expectancy men 56, women 55
language Hindi (official), English, and 14 other recognized languages: Assamese, Bengali, Gujarati, Kannada, Kashmiri, Malayalam, Marathi, Oriya, Punjabi, Sanskrit, Sindhi, Tamil, Telugu, Urdu
religion Hindu 80%, Sunni Muslim 10%, Christian 2.5%, Sikh 2%
literacy 57% male/29% female (1985 est)
GNP $190 bn (1983); $150 per head of population
chronology
1947 Independence achieved from Britain.
1950 Federal republic proclaimed.
1962 Border skirmishes with China.
1964 Death of Prime Minister Nehru. Border war with Pakistan over Kashmir.
1966 Indira Gandhi became prime minister.
1971 War with Pakistan leading to creation of Bangladesh.
1975–77 State of emergency proclaimed.
1977–79 Janata party government in power.
1980 Indira Gandhi returned in landslide victory.
1984 Assassination of Indira Gandhi. Rajiv Gandhi elected with record majority.
1987 Signing of 'Tamil' Colombo peace accord with Sri Lanka; Indian Peacekeeping Force (IPKF) sent there. Public revelation of Bofors scandal.
1988 New opposition party, Janata Dal, established by former finance minister V P Singh. Indian paratroopers foiled attempted coup in Maldives. Voting age lowered from 21 to 18.
1989 Congress (I) lost majority in general election and Janata Dal minority government formed, with V P Singh prime minister.
1990 Central rule imposed in Jammu and Kashmir following Muslim separatist violence.

twice on paper or parchment and then cutting it with a jagged edge so that both pieces fit together, proving the authenticity of each half.

Independence /ˌɪndɪˈpendəns/ city in W Missouri, USA; population (1980) 111,806. Industries include steel, Portland cement, petroleum refining, and flour milling. President Harry S Truman was raised here, and later made it his home.

Independence Day public holiday in the USA, commemorating the ◊Declaration of Independence 4 July 1776.

Independent Labour Party (ILP) British socialist party, founded in Bradford 1893 by the Scottish Member of Parliament Keir Hardie. In 1900 it joined with trades unions and Fabians in founding the Labour Representation Committee, the nucleus of the ◊Labour Party. Many members left the ILP to join the Communist Party 1921, and in 1932 all connections with the Labour Party were severed. After World War II the ILP dwindled, eventually becoming extinct. James Maxton (1885–1946) was its chair 1926–46.

independent school a school run privately without direct assistance from the state. In the UK, just over 6% of children attend private fee-paying schools. The sector includes most boarding education in the UK. Although a majority of independent secondary schools operate a highly selective admissions policy for entrants at the age of 11 or 13, some specialize in the teaching of slow learners or difficult children and a few follow particular philosophies of progressive education.

A group of old-established and prestigious independent schools are known as ◊public schools.

The Labour Party is committed to the integration of independent schools into the state system; the Conservatives have encouraged state funding of selected students within certain independent schools under the ◊Assisted Places Scheme. The near-abolition of selective education in the 1970s led to a proliferation of small independent schools at both primary and secondary levels.

Independent Television (formerly the Independent Broadcasting Authority) in the UK, the corporate body established by legislation to provide commercially funded television (ITV from 1955) and local radio (ILR from 1973) services. During the 1980s this role was expanded to include the setting up of Channel 4 (launched 1982) and the provision of services broadcast directly by satellite into homes (DBS). Government proposals in 1988 recommended replacing the IBA and the Cable Authority (body established 1984 to develop cable TV services) with an Independent Television Commission (ITC) to oversee all commercial TV services. Commercial radio, to include three new national services, would be overseen by a separate new radio authority. See also ◊satellite television.

index (also known as *power* or *exponent*; plural *indices*) in mathematics, a number that indicates the number of times a term is multiplied by itself, for example $x(2) = x \times x$, $4(3) = 4 \times 4 \times 4$.

Indices obey certain rules. Terms that contain them are multiplied together by adding the indices, for example, $x(2) \times x(5) = x(7)$; and divided by subtracting the indices, for example, $y(5) \div y(3) = y(2)$. Any number with the index 0 is equal to 1, for example, $x(0) = 1$ and $99(0) = 1$. The term is from the Latin 'sign, indicator'.

index in economics, an indicator of a general movement in wages and prices over a specified period. For example, the retail price index (RPI) records changes in the ◊cost of living. The *Financial Times* share index indicates the general movement of the London Stock Exchange market in the UK; the USA equivalent is the Dow Jones Index.

Index Librorum Prohibitorum (Latin 'Index of Prohibited Books') the list of books formerly officially forbidden to members of the Roman Catholic church. The process of condemning books and bringing the Index up to date was carried out by a congregation of cardinals, consultors, and examiners from the 16th century until its abolition in 1966.

India /ˈɪndɪə/ country in S Asia, having borders to the N with Afghanistan, China, Nepál, and Bhutan, to the E with Myanmar and to the NW with Pakistan. Situated within the NE corner of India, N of the Bay of Bengal, is ◊Bangladesh, and India is surrounded to the SE, S, and SW by the Indian Ocean.

government India is a federal republic whose 1949 constitution contains elements from both the US and British systems of government. It comprises 25 self-governing states, administered by a governor appointed by the federal president, and a council of ministers (headed by a chief minister) drawn from a legislature (legislative assembly) which is popularly elected for a five-year term. Eight of the larger states have a second chamber (legislative council). The states have primary control over education, health, police, and local government, and work in consultation with the centre in the economic sphere. In times of crisis, central rule ('president's rule') can be imposed. There are also seven union territories, administered by a lieutenant-governor appointed by the federal president. The central (federal) government has sole responsibility in military and foreign affairs and plays a key role in economic affairs.

The titular, executive head of the federal government is the president, who is elected for five-year terms by an electoral college composed of members from both the federal parliament and the state legislatures. However, real executive power is held by a prime minister and cabinet drawn from the majority party or coalition within the federal parliament.

The two-chamber federal parliament has a 545-member lower house, *Lok Sabha* (house of the people), which has final authority over financial matters and whose members are directly elected for terms of a maximum of five years from single-member constituencies by universal suffrage, and a 245-member upper house, *Rajya Sabha* (council of states), whose members are indirectly elected, a third at a time for six-year terms, by state legislatures on a regional quota basis. (Two seats in the *Lok Sabha* are reserved for Anglo-Indians, while the president nominates eight representatives of the Rajya Sabha.) Bills to become law must be approved by both chambers of parliament and receive the president's assent.

The dominant national-level party in India, which until 1989 had held power for all but three years (1977–79) since independence, is the ◊Congress Party. After splits 1969, 1978, 1981, and 1987, the main body of the party is today termed Indian National Congress (I or Indira). It is a broad, secular-based, cross-caste and religion coalition which advocates a moderate socialist approach and is based most strongly in northern and central India. The principal national-level opposition parties are the Janata (People's)

India

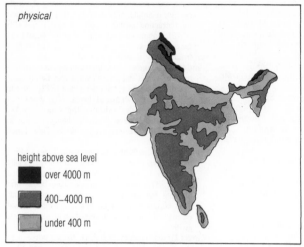

physical

height above sea level

- over 4000 m
- 400–4000 m
- under 400 m

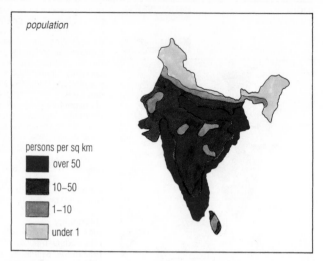

population

persons per sq km

- over 50
- 10–50
- 1–10
- under 1

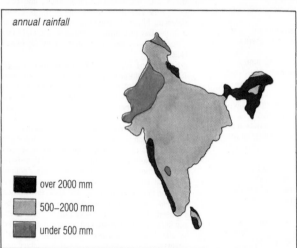

annual rainfall

- over 2000 mm
- 500–2000 mm
- under 500 mm

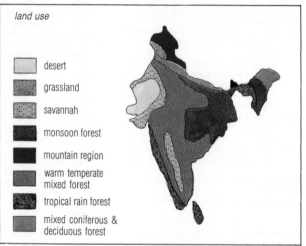

land use

- desert
- grassland
- savannah
- monsoon forest
- mountain region
- warm temperate mixed forest
- tropical rain forest
- mixed coniferous & deciduous forest

Party; the Bharatiya Janata Party (a conservative Hindu grouping); the Communist party of India (CPI); and the Communist Party of India–Marxist (CPI-M). There are also numerous regional-level parties, the most important of which are the Dravida Munnetra Kazhagam in Tamil Nadu, and the Telugu Desam in Andhra Pradesh; the Jammu and Kashmir National Conference Party; and the Shiromani Akali Dal in Punjab.

history For history before 1947, see ◊India, history. Between 1947 and 1949 India temporarily remained under the supervision of a governor-general appointed by the British monarch while a new constitution was framed and approved. Former princely states (see ◊India of the Princes; ◊Kashmir) were integrated and the old British provinces restructured into new states, and in 1950 India was proclaimed a fully independent federal republic.

During its early years the republic faced the problem of resettling refugees from Pakistan and was involved in border skirmishes over ◊Kashmir. Under the leadership of Prime Minister ◊Nehru, land reforms and a new socialist economic programme (involving protectionism), and an emphasis on heavy industries and government planning, were introduced, while sovereignty of parts of India held by France and Portugal was recovered 1950–61.

In foreign affairs, India remained within the ◊Commonwealth, was involved in border clashes with China 1962, and played a leading role in the formation of the ◊Non-Aligned Movement 1961. In 1964, Nehru died and was succeeded

as prime minister by Lal Bahadur ◊Shastri. There was a second war with Pakistan over Kashmir 1964. The new prime minister, Indira ◊Gandhi (Nehru's daughter), kept broadly to her father's policy programme, but drew closer to the Soviet Union with the signing of a 15-year economic and military assistance agreement 1973. In 1971 Indian troops invaded East Pakistan in support of separatist groups. They defeated Pakistan's troops and oversaw the creation of independent ◊Bangladesh.

In 1975, having been found guilty of electoral malpractice during the 1971 election by the Allaha-bad Court, and banned from holding elective office for six years, Indira Gandhi imposed a 'state of emergency' and imprisoned almost 1,000 political opponents. She was cleared of malpractice by the Supreme Court Nov 1975, but the 'emergency' continued for two years, during which period a harsh compulsory birth control programme was introduced under the supervision of Sanjay Gandhi (Indira's youngest son).

The 'state of emergency' was lifted Mar 1977 for elections in which the Janata opposition party was swept to power, its leader Morarji ◊Desai defeating Indira Gandhi in her home constituency. The new government was undermined by economic difficulties and internal factional strife, which led to the defection of many members to a new party, the *Lok Dal*, led by Raj Narain and Charan Singh. Desai was toppled as prime minister 1979 and a coalition, under Charan Singh, assumed power. After only 24 days in Aug 1979 Singh's government was overthrown, and in Jan

1980 Congress (I), led by Indira Gandhi and promising firmer government, was returned to power with a landslide victory.

The new Gandhi administration was economically successful, but the problems of inter-caste violence and regionalist unrest, centred in Gujerat (caste strife), Muslim Kashmir, S India, and Assam (aimed against Bangladeshi immigrants), were such that Congress (I) lost control of a number of states. The greatest unrest was in Punjab, where ◊Sikh demands for greater religious recognition and for resolution of water and land disputes with neighbouring states escalated into calls for the creation of a separate state of 'Khalistan'. In 1984, troops were sent into the Golden Temple at Amritsar to dislodge the armed Sikh extremist leader Sant Jarnail Singh Bhindranwale, resulting in the deaths of Bhindranwale and hundreds of his supporters. The ensuing Sikh backlash brought troop mutinies, culminating in the assassination of Indira Gandhi by her Sikh bodyguards Oct 1984. In Delhi, retaliating Hindus massacred 3,000 Sikhs, before the new prime minister, Rajiv ◊Gandhi (Indira's eldest son), restored order.

In the elections of Dec 1984, Congress (I), benefiting from a wave of public sympathy, gained a record victory. As prime minister, Rajiv Gandhi pledged to modernize and inject greater market efficiency into the Indian economy (vowing to 'bring India into the 21st century') and to resolve the Punjab, Assam, and Kashmir disputes. Early reforms and the spread of technology, with India launching its first space satellite, promised to give

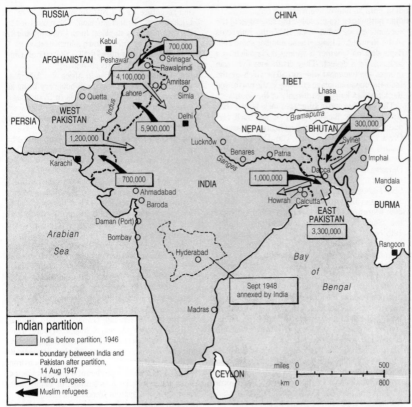

Indian partition

	India before partition, 1946
-----	boundary between India and Pakistan after partition, 14 Aug 1947
▷	Hindu refugees
◀	Muslim refugees

India: states and union territories

State	Capital	Area sq km
Andhra Pradesh	Hyderabad	276,800
Arunachal Pradesh	Itanagar	83,600
Assam	Dispur	78,400
Bihar	Patna	173,900
Goa	Panaji	3,700
Gujarat	Gandhinagar	196,000
Haryana	Chandigarh	44,200
Himachal Pradesh	Simla	55,700
Jammu and Kashmir	Srinagar	101,300
Karnataka	Bangalore	191,800
Kerala	Trivandrum	38,900
Madhya Pradesh	Bhopal	442,800
Maharashtra	Bombay	307,800
Manipur	Imphal	22,400
Meghalaya	Shillong	22,500
Mizoram	Aizawl	21,100
Nagaland	Kohima	16,500
Orissa	Bhubaneswar	155,800
Punjab	Chandigarh	50,400
Rajasthan	Jaipur	342,200
Sikkim	Gangtok	7,300
Tamil Nadu	Madras	130,100
Tripura	Agartala	10,500
Uttar Pradesh	Lucknow	294,400
West Bengal	Calcutta	87,900
Union territory		
Andaman and Nicobar Islands	Port Blair	8,300
Chandigarh	Chandigarh	114
Dadra and Nagar Haveli	Silvassa	490
Daman and Diu		110
Delhi	Delhi	1,500
Lakshadweep	Kavaratti Island	32
Pondicherry	Pondicherry	480

substance to the former vision, while progress was made towards resolving the ethnic disputes in Assam and the hill areas, with 25 years of tribal rebellion ended in Mizoram, which was made a new state of the Indian Union. However, Gandhi was unable to resolve the Punjab problem, with Sikh-Hindu ethnic conflict continuing, while in N India Hindi-Muslim relations deteriorated. Gandhi's enthusiasm for economic reform also waned from 1986 and his personal reputation was sullied by the uncovering, by finance minister V P ◊Singh, of the 'Bofors scandal', involving alleged financial kickbacks received by government-connected organizations from a $1,400 million contract for the supply of howitzers to the Indian army by the Swedish Bofors Corporation.

Gandhi's standing briefly improved in 1989 following a successful intervention by the Indian army in the Maldives in Nov 1988 to defeat a coup attempt. However, in N Sri Lanka, where an Indian Peacekeeping Force (IPKF) had been sent July 1987 as part of an ambitious peace settlement, Indian troops became bogged down in a civil war.

Despite bumper harvests 1988–89, Gandhi's popularity continued to fall. V P Singh, who was dismissed from Congress (I) in 1987, attacked his increasingly dictatorial style and became the recognized leader of the opposition forces, who united under the Janata Dal umbrella Oct 1988. In the general election of Nov 1989 a broad anti-Congress electoral pact was forged, embracing the Janata Dal, BJP, Communist Party, and Teluga Desam. This ensured that Congress (I), although emerging as the largest single party in the new parliament, failed to secure a working majority. Gandhi resigned from office and V P Singh, widely respected for his incorruptibility, took over at the head of a minority 'National Front' coalition.

Singh announced that his first objective was the lowering of racial tensions, appointed a Muslim, Mufti Mohammed Sayeed, as home affairs minister, and visited the strife-torn Sikh city of Amritsar. However, in Jan 1990 Muslim separatist violence erupted in Kashmir, forcing the imposition of direct rule and leading to a deterioration of relations with Pakistan. Relations were improved

with the neighbouring states of Bhutan, Nepál (which had been subject to a partial border blockade by India during 1989), and Sri Lanka, with whom a date (31 Mar 1990) for the withdrawal of the IPKF was agreed.

India: history

c.2500–c.1600 BC The earliest Indian civilization was that of the Indus Valley; this may have been built up by the **Dravidians**, the ancestors of the majority of the people of S India.

c.1500 BC Waves of **Aryans** began to invade from the NW, and gradually overran the north and the Deccan plateau, intermarrying with the Dravidians. From their religious beliefs developed Brahmanism (an early stage of ◊Hinduism).

c.500 BC Buddhism and Jainism arose.

321–184 BC The subcontinent, except the far south, was first unified under the **Mauryan emperors**.

c.300–500 AD The north was again united under the **Gupta dynasty**; its rule was ended by the raids of the White Huns, which plunged India into anarchy.

11th–12th centuries Raids on India were made by Muslim adventurers, Turks, Arabs, and Afghans, and in 1206 the first Muslim dynasty was set up at Delhi.

14th–16th centuries Islam was established throughout the north and the Deccan, although the south maintained its independence under the Hindu **Vijayanagar dynasty**. In the 16th century Portuguese, Dutch, French, and English traders established trading bases on the coast.

1527–1858 The **Mughal emperors** included Baber (Zahir ud-din Mohammed) and his grandson Akbar. After 1707 the Mughal Empire fell into decline.

1756–63 During the Seven Years' War the British ◊East India Company eliminated their French rivals and made themselves rulers of Bengal and the Carnatic.

1857–58 The Indian Mutiny ended the rule of the East India Company, which by then was established all over India, and transferred it to the British government.

1885 The India National Congress was founded (see ◊Congress Party) as a focus for nationalism.

1915–47 Resistance to UK rule was organized under the leadership of Mohandas ◊Gandhi.

1947 British India was divided into the independent dominions of ◊India (predominantly Hindu) and ◊Pakistan (predominantly Muslim). For subsequent history, see ◊India.

Indiana /ˌɪndiˈænə/ state of the midwest USA; nickname Hoosier State

area 93,700 sq km/36,168 sq mi

capital Indianapolis

towns Fort Wayne, Gary, Evansville, South Bend

features Wabash river; Wyandotte Cave; undulating prairies

products cereals, building stone, machinery, electrical goods, coal, steel, iron, chemicals

population (1988) 5,575,000

famous people Theodore Dreiser, Cole Porter, David Letterman

history first white settlements established 1731–35 by French traders; ceded to Britain by the French 1763; passed to American control 1783; became a state 1816.

Indianapolis /ˌɪndiəˈnæpəlɪs/ capital and largest city of Indiana, USA, on the White river; population (1986) 720,000. It is an industrial centre and venue of the 'Indianapolis 500' car race.

Indiana

Indianapolis Raceway US motor sport circuit, built 1910 following the success of Brooklands in the UK. The Indianapolis 500 is staged here at the end of May each year as part of the Memorial Day celebrations.

The circuit is 2.5 mi/4 km long and is rectangular with the four corners joined at slightly banked corners. The original circuit was made out of bricks, hence its nickname the 'Brickwall'.

Indian art the painting, sculpture, and architecture of India. Indian art dates back to the ancient Indus Valley civilization of about 3000 BC. Sophisticated artistic styles emerged from the 1st century AD. Buddhist art includes sculpture and murals. Hindu artists created sculptural schemes in caves and huge temple complexes; the Hindu style is lively, with voluptuous nude figures. The Islamic Mogul Empire of the 16th–17th centuries created an exquisite style of miniature painting, inspired by Persian examples.

Buddhist art In NW India the Gandhara kingdom produced the first known images of the Buddha in a monumental soft and rounded style which was exported, with the Buddhist religion, to China, Korea, and Japan. The Gupta kingdom, which emerged around the 4th century AD in the Ganges plain, continued to develop Buddhist art. Its sites include Sarnath and the caves of Ajanta, which have extensive remains of murals of the 5th and 6th centuries as well as sculpture.

Hindu art Hinduism advanced further in central and S India. Influenced by Buddhist art, Hindu artists created brilliant sculptural schemes in rock-cut caves at Mamallapuram, and huge temple complexes, for example in Orissa, Konarak, and Khajuraho. The Hindu style is highly sophisticated and lively, with much naturalistic detail and voluptuous nude figures. The caves at Ellora are known for their ensemble of religious art, Buddhist, Hindu, and Jain, dating from the 6th and 7th centuries.

Mogul art dates from the Muslim invasion of NW India in the Middle Ages. The invaders destroyed Buddhist and Hindu temple art and introduced their own styles (see ◊Islamic art). An early example of their work is the Q'utb mosque of about 1200 in Delhi. By the 16th century the Moguls had established an extensive empire. Court artists excelled in miniature painting, particularly in the reigns of Jehangir and Shah Jehan (from about 1566 to 1658). Their subjects ranged from portraiture and histories to birds, animals, and flowers.

Indian corn an alternative name for ◊maize.

Indian languages traditionally, the languages of the subcontinent of India; since 1947, the languages of the Republic of India. These number some 200, depending on whether a variety is classified as a language or a dialect. They divide into five main groups, the two most widespread of which are the Indo-European languages (mainly in the north) and the Dravidian languages (mainly in the south).

The Indo-European languages include two classical languages, Sanskrit and Pali, and such vernaculars as Bengali, Hindi, Gujarati, Marathi, Oriya, Punjabi, and Urdu. The Dravidian languages include Kannada, Malayalam, Tamil, and Telugu. A wide range of scripts are used, including Devanagari for Hindi, Arabic for Urdu, and distinct scripts for the various Dravidian languages. The Sino-Tibetan group of languages occurs widely in Assam and along the Himalayas.

Indian literature For the literature of ancient India see ◊Sanskrit, ◊Veda, ◊Pali, and ◊Prakrit. In the 19th century Bengali emerged as a literary language, for example in the work of philologist Ram Mohan Roy, founder of Brahma Samaj, who paved the way for such writers as Bankim Chandra Chatterji and Romesh Chunder Dutt (1848–1909). Rabindranath Tagore's Nobel prize 1913 confirmed the reputation of Bengali in world literature. Subsequent writers include the poets Buddhadeva Bose (1908–) and Amiya Chakravarty. Other literary languages are Urdu (the novelist Prem Chand and poet-philosopher Iqbal) and Gujarati (the poet Nanalal Devi and the writings of Gandhi). English is also a literary language, and writers in English—though wholly Indian in the character of their work—include the novelist Dhan Gopal Mukerji, the poet Sarojini Naidu (1879–1949), Sri Aurobindo (1872–1950), Dom Moraes (1938–), and Nehru. Tagore wrote little creatively in English, but translated many of his own works. Among overseas writers of Indian descent, the best-known is V S Naipaul.

Indian Mutiny the revolt 1857–58 of the Bengal army against the British in India. The movement was confined to the north, from Bengal to the Punjab, and central India. The majority of support came from the army and recently dethroned princes, but in some areas it developed into a peasant rising or general revolt. It included the seizure of Delhi by the rebels, and its siege and recapture by the British, and the defence of Lucknow by a British garrison. The mutiny led to the end of rule by the East India Company and its replacement by direct crown administration.

Indian National Congress (INC) the official name for the ◊Congress Party of India.

Indian Ocean ocean between Africa and Australia, with India to the N, and the S boundary being an arbitrary line from Cape Agulhas to S Tasmania; area 73,500,000 sq km/28,371,000 sq mi; average depth 3,872 m/12,708 ft. The greatest depth is the Java Trench 7,725 m/25,353 ft.

India of the Princes the 562 Indian states ruled by princes during the period of British control. They occupied an area of 715,964 sq mi (45% of the total area of pre-partition India) and had a population of over 93 million. At the partition of British India in 1947 the princes were given independence by the British government, but were advised to adhere to either India or Pakistan. Between 1947 and 1950 all except ◊Kashmir were incorporated in either country.

Most of the states were Hindu, and their rulers mainly ◊Rajputs. When India was overwhelmed by the Muslims in the 16th century, the Rajput states in the NW deserts of the outer Himalayas and in the central highlands were saved by their isolation. As the Mughal Empire disintegrated, other states were set up by mercenaries, for example Baroda, Hyderabad, Gwalior, Indore, Bhopal, Patiala, Bahawalpur, and Kolhapur. Mysore, Travancore, and Cochin were also non-Rajput states.

indicator a chemical compound that changes its structure and colour in response to its environment. The commonest chemical indicators detect changes in ◊pH, such as ◊litmus, or in the oxidation state of a system (redox indicators).

indicator species a plant or animal whose presence or absence in an area indicates certain environmental conditions. For example, some lichens are sensitive to sulphur dioxide in the air, and absence of these species indicates atmospheric pollution. Many plants show a preference for either alkaline or acid soil conditions, while certain plants, mostly trees, require aluminium, and are only found in soils where it is present.

indigenous the people, animals, or plants that are native to a country, but especially a people whose territory has been colonized by others (particularly Europeans). Examples of indigenous peoples

Indian art A party of elephant hunters travelling through a landscape *(c.1615), Victoria and Albert Museum, London.*

Indian Mutiny *An early photograph of the Indian Mutiny.*

include the Australian Aboriginals, the Maori, and American Indians. A World Council of Indigenous Peoples is based in Canada.

indigestion pain or discomfort in the abdomen, usually due to problems in the ◊digestive system.

indigo violet-blue vegetable dye obtained from plants of the genus *Indigofera*, family Leguminosae, but now replaced by a synthetic product. It was once a major export crop of India.

indium a soft, silvery, rare metallic element, symbol In, atomic number 49, relative atomic mass 114.82. It occurs in minute traces in zinc ores, and is obtained by electrolysis from solutions of complex salts. Because it captures neutrons, indium is used to monitor the neutron emission from reactors. Other uses include the manufacture of junctions in semiconductor devices, and as corrosion-resistant coatings for aircraft sleeve bearings. Discovered in 1863 by Reich and Richter, it was named indium after its indigo-blue spectrum.

Indo-Aryan languages another name for the ◊Indo-European languages.

Indochina /ˌɪndəʊˈtʃaɪnə/ French former collective name for ◊Cambodia, ◊Laos, and ◊Vietnam, which became independent after World War II.

Indochina War war 1946–1954 between France, the occupying colonial power, and nationalist forces of what was to become Vietnam.

In 1945 Vietnamese nationalist communist leader Ho Chi Minh proclaimed an independent Vietnamese republic, which soon began an armed struggle against French forces. France in turn set up a noncommunist state four years later. In 1954, after the siege of ◊Dien Bien Phu, a ceasefire was agreed between France and China that resulted in the establishment of two separate Vietnamese states, North and South Vietnam, divided by the 17th parallel. Attempts at reunification of the country led subsequently to the ◊Vietnam War.

Indo-European languages a family of languages that includes some of the world's leading classical languages (Sanskrit and Pali in India, Zend Avestan in Iran, Greek and Latin in Europe), as well as several of the most widely spoken languages (English worldwide; Spanish in Iberia, Latin America, and elsewhere; and the Hindi group of languages in N India).

When first discussed and described in the 19th century, this family was known as the Aryan and then the Indo-Germanic language family. Because of unwelcome associations with the idea of 'Aryan' racial purity and superiority and with the ideology of Nazi Germany, both titles have been abandoned by scholars in favour of the neutral 'Indo-European'.

Indo-European languages are now spoken in every inhabited continent of the world, but were once located only along a geographical band from India through Iran into NW Asia, E Europe, the northern Mediterranean lands, N and W Europe and the British Isles.

In general terms, many Indo-European languages (such as English, French and Hindi) have tended to evolve from the highly inflected to a more open or analytic grammatical style that depends less on complex grammatical endings to nouns, verbs, and adjectives. Eastern Indo-European languages are often called the *satem* group (Zend, 'a hundred') while western Indo-European languages are the *centum* group (Latin, 'a hundred'); this illustrates a split that occurred over 3,000 years ago, between those which had an *s*-sound in certain words and those which had a *k*-sound. Scholars have reconstructed a Proto-Indo-European ancestral language by comparing the sound systems and historical changes within the family, but continue to dispute the original homeland of this ancient form, some arguing for N Europe, others for Russia N of the Black Sea.

Indo-Germanic languages former name for the ◊Indo-European languages.

Indonesia /ˌɪndəʊˈniːzɪə/ country in SE Asia, made up of over 13,000 islands situated on the equator, between the Indian and Pacific Oceans.

government Under the 1945 constitution, amended 1950 and 1969, the supreme political body in Indonesia is, in theory, the 1,000-member people's consultative council (*Majelis Permusyawaratan Rakyat*). This comprises the 500 members of the legislature (house of representatives), as well as 500 appointed representatives from regional assemblies and functional groups (including 200 from the armed forces). It sits at least once every five years to elect an executive president and vice president, and determines the constitution.

The house of representatives *Dewan Perwakilan Rakyat* functions as a single-chamber legislature, comprising 400 directly elected members and 100 presidential appointees (of whom three quarters represent the armed forces). It meets at least once a year, with elections every five years. At the head of the executive, and the most powerful political figure in Indonesia, is the president, elected by the people's consultative council for five-year terms. The president works with an appointed cabinet, exercises the right of veto over house of representatives' bills and appoints governors to supervise local government in each of Indonesia's 27 provinces.

Indonesia's dominant political party is the Golkar. The Islamic Party Persatuan Pembangunan and the Christian-orientated Party Demokrasi Indonesia also operate, holding seats in the house of representatives and People's Consultative Assembly. Parties opposed to Pancasila and regionally based are debarred from functioning.

history Between 3000–500 BC, immigrants from S China displaced the original Melanesian population of Indonesia. Between 700–1450 AD, two Hindu empires developed, to be superseded by Islam from the 13th century. During the 16th century English and Portuguese traders were active in Indonesia, but in 1595 Holland took over trade in the area. In the 17th century the Dutch only managed to establish trading centres, while Indonesian kingdoms dominated the region, but by the 18th–19th centuries their control was complete, and the islands were proclaimed a Dutch colony 1816.

A nationalist movement developed during the 1920s under the pro-Communist Indonesian Nationalist Party (PNI), headed by Achmed ◊Sukarno. This was suppressed by the Dutch, but in 1942, after Japan's occupation of the islands, the PNI were installed in power as an anti-Western puppet government. When Japan surrendered to the Allies 1945, President Sukarno proclaimed Indonesia's independence. The Dutch challenged this by launching military expeditions, before agreeing to transfer sovereignty 1949. A 'special union' was established between the two countries, but was abrogated by Indonesia 1956.

The new republic was planned as a federation of 16 constituent regions, but was made unitary 1950. This led to dominance by Java (which has two-thirds of Indonesia's population), provoking revolts in Sumatra and the predominantly Christian South Moluccas. The paramount political figure in the new republic was President Sukarno, who ruled in an authoritarian manner and pursued an ambitious and expansionist foreign policy. He effected the transfer of Netherlands New Guinea (Irian Jaya) to Indonesia 1963, but failed in a confrontation with Malaysia over claims to Sabah and Sarawak.

With the economy deteriorating, in 1965 an attempted coup against Sukarno by groups connected with the Indonesian Communist Party was firmly put down by army Chief of Staff Gen ◊Suharto, who then assumed power as emergency ruler 1966. He ended hostility over Sabah and Sarawak and formally replaced Sukarno as president 1967. He proceeded to institute what was termed a 'New Order'. This involved the concentration of political power in the hands of a coterie of army and security-force officers, the propagation of a new secular state philosophy of Pancasila, which stressed unity and social justice, the pursuit of a liberal economic programme, and the fierce suppression of Communist activity.

Rising oil exports brought significant industrial and agricultural growth to Indonesia during the 1970s, self-sufficiency in rice production being attained by the 1980s. In addition, its borders were extended by the forcible annexation of the former Portuguese colony of East Timor 1976. Suharto's authoritarian approach met with opposition from left-wing groups, from radical Muslims, and from separatist groups in outlying

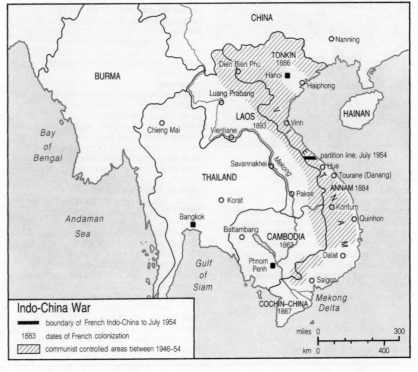

Indo-China War

━━━ boundary of French Indo-China to July 1954

1883   dates of French colonization

▨ communist controlled areas between 1946–54

islands. In Irian Jaya, following the supression of a rebellion organized by the Free Papua Movement (OPM), a 'transmigration' programme was instituted by the Suharto government, with the aim of resettling there, and on other sparsely populated 'outer islands', 65 million Javanese by 2006. This encountered strong opposition from native Melanesians, promting the emigration of more than 10,000 refugees to neighbouring Papua New Guinea. In East Timor, tens of thousands died from famine and continuing warfare; although travel restrictions were partly eased 1988, the UN refused to recognize Indonesia's sovereignty over the area.

In recent years, economic problems have mounted as a result of the fall in world prices of oil, which provides 70% of Indonesia's foreign exchange earnings. Indonesia has long pursued a ◊nonaligned foreign policy, hosting the ◊Bandung Conference of Third World nations 1955, and is a member of ◊ASEAN. Under Gen Suharto, its relations with the West have become closer.

Indore /ɪnˈdɔː/ city in Madhya Pradesh, India; population (1981) 829,327. A former capital of the princely state of Indore, it now produces cotton, chemicals, and furniture.

Indra /ˈɪndrə/ Hindu god of the sky, shown as a four-armed man on a white elephant, carrying a thunderbolt. The intoxicating drink ◊soma is associated with him.

Indre /ˈændrə/ river rising in the Auvergne mountains, France, and flowing NW for 170 km/115 mi to join the Loire below Tours. It gives its name to the *départements* of Indre and Indre-et-Loire.

indri largest living lemur *Indri indri* of Madagascar. Black and white, almost tailless, it has long arms and legs. It grows to 70 cm/2.3 ft long. It is diurnal and arboreal. Its howl is doglike or human in tone. Like all lemurs, its survival is threatened by the widespread deforestation of Madagascar.

inductance in physics, the measure of the capability of an electronic circuit or circuit component to form a magnetic field or store magnetic energy when carrying a current. Its symbol is L, and its unit of measure is the ◊henry.

induction in philosophy, the process of observing particular instances of things, in order to derive general statements and laws of nature. It is the opposite of ◊deduction, which moves from general statements and principles to the particular. Induction was criticized by ◊Hume because it relied upon belief rather than valid reasoning. In the philosophy of science, the 'problem of induction' is a crucial area of debate: however much evidence there is for a proposition, there is the possibility of a future counter-instance, which will invalidate the explanation. Therefore, it is argued, no scientific statement can be said to be true.

induction in obstetrics, deliberate intervention to initiate labour before it starts of its own accord. It involves rupture of the fetal membranes (amniotomy), and the use of the hormone oxytocin to stimulate contractions of the womb. In biology, induction is a term used for various processes, including the production of an ◊enzyme in response to a particular chemical in the cell, and the ◊differentiation of cells in an ◊embryo.

In obstetrics, induction is recommended as a medical necessity where there is risk to the mother or baby in waiting for labour to begin of its own accord. Usually, once labour has been triggered in this way, it proceeds normally.

induction coil type of electrical transformer, similar to an ◊ignition coil, that produces an intermittent high voltage from a low-voltage supply.

It has a primary coil consisting of a few turns of thick wire wound round an iron core and passing a low voltage (usually from a battery). Wound on top of this is a secondary coil made up of many turns of thin wire. An iron armature and make-and-break mechanism (similar to that in an ◊electric bell) repeatedly interrupts the current to the primary coil, producing a high, rapidly pulsing current in the secondary circuit.

inductor an element possessing the characteristic of inductance (electromagnetic property).

indulgence in the Roman Catholic church, the total or partial remission of temporal punishment for sins which remain to be expiated after penitence and confession has secured exemption from eternal punishment. The doctrine of indulgence began as the commutation of church penances in exchange for suitable works of charity or money gifts to the church, and became a great source of church revenue. This trade in indulgences roused Luther in 1517 to initiate the Reformation. The Council of Trent in 1563 recommended moderate retention of indulgences, and they continue, notably in 'Holy Years'.

Indus /ˈɪndəs/ river in Asia, rising in Tibet and flowing 3,180 km/1,975 mi to the Arabian Sea. In 1960 the use of its waters, including those of its five tributaries, was divided between India (rivers Ravi, Beas, Sutlej) and Pakistan (rivers Indus, Jhelum, Chenab).

industrialization a policy usually associated with modernization of developing countries where the process normally starts with the manufacture of simple goods that can replace imports. It is essential for economic development and largely responsible for the growth of cities.

industrial relations relationship between employers and employed, and their dealings with each other. In most industries wages and conditions are determined by *free collective bargaining* between employers and ◊trades unions. Some European countries have *worker participation* through profit-sharing and industrial democracy. Another solution is *co-ownership*, in which a company is entirely owned by its employees. The aim of good industrial relations is to achieve a motivated, capable workforce who see their work as creative and fulfilling.

When agreement cannot be reached by *free collective bargaining*, outside arbitration is often sought (in Britain the Advisory Conciliation and Arbitration Service, ACAS, was set up in 1975). Trade union powers are legally restricted in various ways, but the UK has no single legal authority that oversees them: the government proposals *In Place of Strife* 1969 favoured the setting up of a Commission on Industrial Relations, but this was shelved. Under the Industrial Relations Act 1971 an industrial court was established, with High Court status, to give judgment on matters relating to industrial disputes, but it was abolished in 1974.

Worker participation was introduced in West Germany by law in 1952, giving the works councils of a firm a right of veto in hirings and redundancies, and stipulating that at least one-third of the supervisory board be workers' representatives, the rest being 'shareholders'. A variation on this system was advocated for Britain by the Bullock Report 1977, which proposed the placing of union-nominated worker-directors on the main boards of companies. The suggestion was not taken up, nor to any extent has been the concept of co-ownership, which means that any profits not ploughed back are distributed as a bonus to the workers.

Another approach to industrial relations is that of the Japanese, who encourage in their workers a feeling of belonging amounting almost to family membership.

Industrial Revolution the sudden acceleration of technical and economic development that took place in Britain from the second half of the 18th century. The great initial invention was the steam engine, originally developed for draining mines (see ◊Newcomen) but rapidly put to use in factories and on the railways (see ◊Watt, ◊Arkwright, ◊Crompton, ◊Trevithick). This transferred the balance of political power from the landowner

Indonesia
Republic of
(Republik Indonesia)

area 1,919,443 sq km/740,905 sq mi
capital Jakarta
towns ports Surabaya, Semarang
physical comprises 13,677 tropical islands, including Islands both the Greater Sunda Islands (including Java and Madura, part of Kalimantan/Borneo, Sumatra, Sulawesi and Belitung) and the Lesser Sundas/Nusa Tenggara (including Bali, Lombok, Sumba, Timor), as well as Malaku/Moluccas and part of New Guinea (Irian Jaya)
features world's largest Islamic state; Java is one of the world's most densely populated areas
head of state and government T N J Suharto from 1967
political system authoritarian nationalist republic
political parties Golkar, military-bureaucrat-farmers ruling party; United Development Party (PPP), moderate Islamic; Indonesian Democratic Party (PDI), nationalist Christian
exports coffee, rubber, palm oil, coconuts, tin, tea, tobacco, oil, liquid natural gas
currency rupiah (3,080.43 £1 Feb 1990)
population (1987) 172,250,000 (including 300 ethnic groups); annual growth rate 2%
life expectancy men 52, women 55
language Indonesian, closely allied to Malay
religion Muslim 90%, Buddhist, Hindu, and Pancasila (a secular official ideology)
literacy 83% male/65% female (1985 est)
GNP $87 bn (1983); $560 per head of population
chronology
17th century Dutch rule established.
1942 Occupied by Japan. Nationalist government established.
1945 Japanese surrender. Nationalists declare independence under Sukarno.
1949 Formal transfer of Dutch sovereignty.
1950 Unitary constitution established.
1963 Western New Guinea (Irian Jaya) ceded by Holland.
1965–66 Attempted communist coup; Gen Suharto emergency administration.
1967 Sukarno replaced as president by Suharto.
1976 Annexation by force of the former Portuguese colony of East Timor.
1986 Institution of 'transmigration programme' to settle large numbers of Javanese on the sparsely populated outer islands, particularly Irian Jaya.
1988 Partial easing of travel restrictions to East Timor. Suharto re-elected for fifth term.
1989 Foreign debt reaches $50 billion; Western creditors offer aid on the condition that concessions are made to foreign companies, and that austerity measures are introduced.

to the industrial capitalist and created an urban working class. From 1830 to the early 20th century, the Industrial Revolution spread to Europe, its colonies, the USA, and Japan.

Industrial Workers of the World (IWW) US labour movement founded 1905, popularly known as the *Wobblies*. The IWW was dedicated to the overthrow of capitalism but divided on tactics and gradually declined in popularity after 1917. At its peak (1912–15) the organization claimed to have 100,000 members, mainly in western mining and lumber areas, and in the textile mills of New England. Demonstrations were violently suppressed by the authorities. See also ◊syndicalism.

industry the extraction and conversion of raw materials, the manufacture of goods, and the provision of services. Industry can be either low technology, unspecialized and labour intensive as in the less developed countries, or highly automated, mechanized, and specialized, using advanced technology, as in the 'industrialized' countries. Major trends in industrial activity over the last 20 years have been the growth of electronic and microelectronic technologies, the expansion of the off shore oil industry, and the prominence of Japan and the Pacific region countries in manufacturing industry, electronics, and computers.

British industry The prominent trends in industrial activity in Britain from the 1970s onwards have been the growth of the offshore oil and gas industries, the rapid growth of electronic and microelectronic technologies, and a continuous rise in the share of total employment of service industries. Recessions in 1974–75 and 1980–81, due in part to fluctuating energy costs, have been offset by increased productivity, but these gains mean that the increased output was achieved with fewer workers, and unemployment has been a persistent feature of the period.

Electronics and automated controls are now applied extensively throughout industry, particularly in steel mills, oil refineries, coal mines and chemical plants. Britain is the sixth largest user of industrial robots in the world. Another area of technological strength is ◊biotechnology, using fermentation techniques for food, beverage, and antibiotic production. The main areas of research and development expenditure are electronics, chemicals, aerospace, mechanical engineering, and motor vehicles.

The government-owned public sector includes coal, steel, British Rail, and the Post Office. Conservative government policy is to encourage economic recovery by improving performance in the face of the open market, through the ◊privatization (selling shares to the public) of public sector industry. British Telecom was sold in 1985, British Gas in 1986, British Airways in early 1987, and the water boards in 1989.

As a member of the European Community (EC), Britain has received grants from the European Regional Development Fund, which was established in 1975 to assist in the development of new or declining industrial regions.

Manufacturing, construction and the service industries account for 88% of gross domestic product, and employed 26%, 5% and 65% of the labour force respectively in 1985. The highest growth in manufacturing in the past decade has been in the chemicals, electrical and instrument engineering sectors. In 1988, the number of people employed in the manufacturing industry dropped below 5 million for the first time since the 19th century.

mineral products The British Steel Corporation accounts for 82–85% of Britain's steel output by volume, and is the world's fourth largest steel company. The private sector is strong in the manufacture of special steels, alloys and finished products for the engineering industries. Manipulation of materials by smelting, casting, rolling, extruding, and drawing is also carried out.

chemicals Accounting for about 10% of manufacturing net output, this industry produces a complete range of products including fertilizers,

plastics, pharmaceuticals, soap, toiletries, and explosives.

mechanical engineering Machine tools, industrial engines, mechanical handling equipment, construction equipment, and industrial plant are all significant products in this area. Britain is the Western world's largest producer of agricultural tractors.

motor vehicles Recent years have seen a large increase in the volume of imports in this sector, notably from Europe and Japan. However, British manufacturers still provide a major export.

aerospace In order to compete with the USA in this area, Britain resorted to European and multinational cooperative ventures, including the Airbus passenger airliner and the Ariane rocket for the launching of satellites, but in 1987 it pulled out of both Airbus and Ariane. The space industry's major strength at present is the manufacture of satellites. Aircraft (civil and military), helicopters, aero-engines, and guided weapons are major products, supported by a comprehensive range of aircraft and airfield equipment and systems.

construction Building, repair, alteration and maintenance of buildings, highways, bridges, tunnels, drainage and sewage systems, docks, harbours, and offshore structures are included, together with ancillary services such as wiring, heating, ventilation, and air conditioning.

service industries The fastest growing sectors during the 1970s (measured by employment) were financial and business services, professional and scientific services (including health and education) and leisure. In the 1980s finance continued to grow strongly, and franchising, particularly in labour-intensive areas such as hotel, catering and cleaning businesses, became a widespread new form of organization.

world industry On the global scale, the period after World War II has been marked by the development of traditional industry such as shipbuilding and motor manufacture in the low-cost countries, particularly Japan, Korea, and the Pacific region generally. This has been followed by moves into new industrial products, such as electronics and computers, in which these countries have dominated the world. In the West, the USA has been most successful partly because of the great size of its home market, while the USSR, and to a lesser extent Europe, have resorted to protectionist tariff and quota barriers, and attempts to implement economic planning as a tool for economic growth.

Indus Valley Civilization prehistoric culture existing in the NW Indian subcontinent about 2500–1600 BC. Remains include soapstone seals with engravings of elephants and snakes.

Indy /æn'di:/ (Paul Marie Théodore) Vincent d' 1851–1931. French composer. He studied under César ◊Franck, and was one of the founders of the *Schola Cantorum*. His works include operas (*Fervaal* 1897), symphonies, tone poems (*Istar* 1896), and chamber music.

inert gases or *noble gases* the group of six gaseous elements, so named because of their unreactivity: argon, helium, krypton, neon, radon, and xenon. They are used in filament bulbs, fluorescent lights, and in lasers.

inertia in physics, the tendency of an object to remain in a state of rest or uniform motion until an external force is applied, as stated by ◊Newton's first law of motion.

INF abbreviation for *intermediate nuclear forces*, as in the ◊Intermediate Nuclear Forces Treaty.

infant below full legal age; see ◊minor.

infante /ɪn'fænteɪ/ and *infanta* title given in Spain and Portugal to the sons (other than the heir apparent) and daughters respectively of the sovereign. The heir apparent in Spain bears the title of prince of Asturias.

infanticide killing of offspring, among human beings usually as a method of population control, and most frequently of girls (India and China), although

Indus Valley Civilization

boys are killed in countries where bride-prices are high.

infantile paralysis former term for poliomyelitis. See ◊polio.

infant mortality rate a measure of the number of infants dying under one year of age. Improved sanitation, nutrition, and medical care have considerably lowered figures throughout much of the world; for example in the 18th century in the UK infant mortality was 50%, compared with under 2% in 1971. In much of the Third World, however, the infant mortality rate remains high.

infarct or *infarction* death and scarring of a portion of the tissue in an organ, as a result of congestion or blockage of a vessel serving it. A myocardial infarct (MI) is a technical term for a heart attack.

infection invasion of the body by disease-causing organisms that become established, multiply, and produce symptoms.

Most pathogens (known as germs) enter or leave the body through the digestive or respiratory tracts. Polio, dysentery, and typhoid are examples of diseases contracted by ingestion of contaminated foods or fluids. Organisms present in the saliva or nasal mucus are spread by airborne or droplet infection; fine droplets or dried particles are inhaled by others when the affected individual talks, coughs, or sneezes. Diseases such as measles, mumps, tuberculosis, and the common cold are passed on in this way.

A less common route of entry is through the skin, either by contamination of an open wound (as in tetanus), or by penetration of the intact skin surface, as in a bite from a malaria-carrying mosquito. Relatively few diseases are truly contagious, that is, transmissible by direct contact. Glandular fever and herpes simplex (cold sore) may be passed on by kissing, and the group now officially bracketed as sexually transmitted diseases (◊STDs) are mostly spread by intimate contact.

inferiority complex in psychology, a ◊complex described by ◊Adler based on physical inferiority; the term is used to describe general feelings of inferiority.

inferior planet a planet (Mercury or Venus) whose orbit lies within that of the Earth, best observed when at its greatest elongation from the Sun, either at eastern elongation in the evening (setting after the Sun) or at western elongation in the morning (rising before the Sun).

inferno unit for describing the temperature inside a star. One inferno is 10^9K, or approximately 10^7 C.

infinite series in mathematics, a series of numbers consisting of a denumerably infinite sequence of terms. The sequence n, n^2, n^3, ... gives the series $n + n^2 + n^3 + ...$ For example, $1 + 2 + 3 + ...$ is a divergent infinite arithmetic series, and $8 + 4 + 2 + 1 + \frac{1}{2} + ...$ is a convergent infinite geometric series whose sum to infinity is 16.

infinity mathematical quantity that is larger than any fixed assignable quantity; symbol ∞. By convention, the result of dividing any number by zero is regarded as infinity.

inflammation a defensive reaction of the body tissues to disease or damage. Denoted by the suffix *-itis* (as in peritonitis), it may be acute or chronic, and may be accompanied by the formation of pus.

The first-century Roman writer Celsus aptly described inflammation as *rubor et tumor cum calore et dolore*: redness and swelling with heat and pain. His account is endorsed by the discovery that inflammation occurs when damaged cells release a substance (probably ◊histamine) that causes blood vessels to widen and leak into the surrounding tissues. It is this phenomenon that accounts for the redness, swelling, and heat. Pain is due partly to the pressure of swelling and also to irritation of nerve endings. Defensive white blood cells congregate within an area of inflammation to engulf and remove foreign matter and dead tissue.

inflation in economics, a rise in the general level of prices. The many causes include **cost-push inflation** that occurred in 1974 as a result of the world price increase in oil, thus increasing production costs. **Demand-pull inflation** results when overall demand exceeds supply. Suppressed inflation occurs in controlled economies and is reflected in rationing, shortages, and black market prices. Deflation, a fall in the general level of prices, is the reverse of inflation.

inflation accounting a method of accounting that allows for the changing purchasing power of money due to inflation.

inflation tax tax imposed on companies that increase wages by more than an amount fixed by law (except to take account of increased profits or because of a profit-sharing scheme).

inflection or **inflexion** in grammatical analysis, an ending or other element in a word that indicates its grammatical function (whether plural or singular, masculine or feminine).

In a highly inflected language like Latin, nouns, verbs and adjectives have many inflectional endings (for example, in the word *amabunt* the base *am* means 'love', and the complex *abunt* indicates the kind of verb, the future tense, indicative mood, active voice, third person and plurality). English only has inflections for plural and for certain forms of the verb (for example, the *s* in 'He runs' indicates the third person singular, while in 'the books' it indicates plurality).

inflorescence a flower-bearing branch, or system of branches, in plants. Inflorescences can be divided into two main types. In a **cymose inflorescence**, the terminal growing point produces a single flower and subsequent flowers arise on lower lateral branches, as in forget-me-not (*Myosotis*) and chickweed (*Stellaria*); the oldest flowers are found at the apex. A **racemose inflorescence** consists of a main axis, bearing flowers along its length, with an active growing region at the apex; as in hyacinth and lupin, the oldest flowers are found near the base or, where the inflorescence has become flattened, towards the outside.

An inflorescence is usually separated from the leaves by a stalk or peduncle and comprises two, three, or more individual flowers. The stalk of each individual flower is called a pedicel.

Types of racemose inflorescence include the **raceme** as seen in lupins, a spike which is similar but has stalkless flowers, for example, plantain (*Plantago*); and a **corymb**, which is rounded or flat-topped, as in candytuft (*Iberis*).

A **panicle** is a branched inflorescence comprising a number of racemes, as seen in many grasses, for example, oats (*Avena*). An **umbel**, as in cow parsley (*Anthriscus sylvestris*), is a special type of racemose inflorescence with all the flower stalks arising from the same point on the main stem. Other types of racemose inflorescence include the ◊catkin, ◊spadix, and ◊capitulum.

influenza a virus infection primarily affecting the air passages, but with ◊systemic effects such as fever, headache, joint pains, and lassitude.

Depending on the virus strain, influenza varies in virulence and duration, and there is always the risk of secondary (bacterial) infection of the lungs. Vaccines are effective against known strains, but will not give protection against newly evolving viruses. Treatment is with bedrest and analgesic drugs such as aspirin and paracetamol.

information technology collective term for the various technologies involved in the processing and transmission of information. They include computing, telecommunications, and microelectronics.

infrared astronomy study of infrared radiation produced by relatively cool gas and dust in space, such as in the areas around forming stars. In 1983, the Infra-Red Astronomy Satellite (IRAS) surveyed the entire sky at infrared wavelengths. It found five new comets, thousands of galaxies undergoing bursts of star formation, and the possibility of planetary systems forming around several dozen stars.

infrared radiation invisible electromagnetic radiation of wavelength between about 0.75 ◊micrometres and 1 millimetre, that is, between the limit of the red end of the visible spectrum and the shortest microwaves. All bodies above the ◊absolute zero of temperature absorb and radiate infrared radiation. Infrared radiation is used in medical photography and treatment, and in industry, astronomy, and criminology.

Infrared absorption spectra are also used in chemical analysis, particularly for organic compounds; objects which radiate infrared radiation can be photographed or made visible in the dark, or through mist or fog, on specially sensitized emulsions. This is important for military purposes and in detecting people buried under rubble. The strong absorption by many substances of infrared radiation is a useful method of applying heat, as in baking and toasting.

Ingenhousz /ˈɪŋənhuːs/ Jan 1730–1799. Dutch physician and plant physiologist who established that in the light plants absorb carbon dioxide and give off oxygen.

Ingres /ˈæŋgrə/ Jean Auguste Dominique 1780–1867. French painter, a student of David and leading exponent of the Neo-Classical style. He studied and worked in Rome about 1807–20, where he began the *Odalisque* series of sensuous female nudes, then went to Florence, and returned to France 1824. His portraits painted in the 1840s–50s are meticulously detailed and highly polished.

Ingres's style developed in opposition to the Romanticism of Delacroix. Early works include portraits of Napoleon. Later he painted huge ceilings for the Louvre and for Autun Cathedral. His portraits include *Madame Moitessier* 1856 (National Gallery, London).

Inhambane seaport on the SE coast of Mozambique, 370 km/231 mi NE of Maputo. Population (1980) 56,000.

inheritance tax in the UK, a tax imposed on large amounts of money or property passed on from one person to another, by gift, inheritance, and so on. It replaced capital transfer tax in 1986 (which in turn replaced estate duty in 1974).

inhibition, neural in biology, the process in which activity in one ◊nerve cell suppresses activity in another. Neural inhibition in networks of nerve cells leading from sensory organs, or to muscles, plays an important role in allowing an animal to

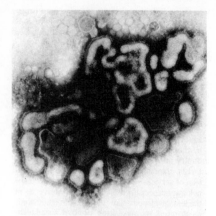

influenza An influenza virus, magnified under an electron microscope × 132,000.

make fine sensory discriminations and to exercise fine control over movements.

initiative device whereby the voters may play a direct part in making laws. A proposed law is drawn up and signed by petitioners, and submitted to the legislature. A ◊referendum may be taken on a law that has been passed by the legislature but that will not become operative unless the voters assent to it. Switzerland was the first country to make use of the device.

injunction in English law, a court order that forbids a person from doing something, or orders him or her to take certain action. It has been used, for example, to restrain unions from organizing illegal picketing. Breach of an injunction is ◊contempt of court.

ink coloured liquid used for writing, drawing, and printing. Traditional ink (blue, but later a permanent black) was produced from gallic acid and tannic acid, but inks are now based on synthetic dyes.

Inkatha South African political organization formed 1975 by Chief Gatsha ◊Buthelezi, leader of six million Zulus, the country's biggest ethnic group. Inkatha aims to create a nonracial democratic political situation. Because Inkatha has tried to work with the white regime, Buthelezi has been regarded as a collaborator by blacks and the United Democratic Front. Fighting between Inkatha and African National Congress members cost more than 1,000 lives in the first five months of 1990. The term Inkatha is from the grass coil worn by Zulu women for carrying head loads; its many strands give it strength.

infrared radiation Aerial infrared photograph of bends in the Mississippi River, USA. Healthy vegetation appears in shades of red.

Inkerman, Battle of /'ɪŋkəmən/ a battle of the Crimean War, fought on 5 Nov 1854, during which an attack by the Russians on Inkerman Ridge, occupied by the British army besieging Sebastopol, was repulsed.

INLA abbreviation for ◊Irish National Liberation Army.

Inland Sea Japanese **Seto Naikai** an arm of the Pacific Ocean , 390 km/240 mi long, almost enclosed by the Japanese islands of Honshu, Kyushu and Shikoku. It has about 300 small islands.

in loco parentis (Latin 'in place of a parent') in a parental capacity.

Inn river in S central Europe, tributary of the Danube. Rising in the Swiss Alps, it flows 507 km/317 mi NE through Austria and into Bavaria, West Germany, where it meets the Danube at Passau.

Innes-Ker family name of dukes of Roxburghe; seated at Floors Castle, Roxburghshire, Scotland.

Inness /'ɪnɪs/ George 1825–1894. US landscape painter influenced by the ◊Hudson River school. His early works such as *The Delaware Valley* 1865 (Metropolitan Museum of Art, New York) are on a grand scale and show a concern for natural effects of light. Later he moved towards Impressionism.

Innocent /'ɪnəsənt/ thirteen popes including:

Innocent III 1161–1216. Pope from 1198 who asserted papal power over secular princes, especially over the succession of Holy Roman Emperors. He also made King ◊John of England his vassal, compelling him to accept ◊Langton as archbishop of Canterbury. He promoted the fourth Crusade and crusades against the non-Christian Livonians and Letts, and Albigensian heretics.

Innocents' Day or **Childermas** festival of the Roman Catholic Church, celebrated on 28 Dec in memory of the **Massacre of the Innocents**, the children of Bethlehem who were allegedly slaughtered by King ◊Herod after the birth of Jesus.

Innsbruck /'ɪnzbrʊk/ capital of Tirol State, W Austria, population (1981) 117,000. It is a tourist and winter sports centre, and a route junction for the Brenner Pass. The 1964 and 1976 Winter Olympics were held here.

Inns of Court four private societies in London, England: Lincoln's Inn, Gray's Inn, Inner Temple, and Middle Temple. All English barristers must belong to one of these societies. They train law students and have power to call them to the English bar. Each pursues its separate existence, though joint lectures are given, and there is a common examination board. Each is under the administration of a body of Benchers (judges and senior barristers).

inoculation injection into the body of dead disease-carrying organisms, toxins, antitoxins, and so on, to produce immunity by inducing a mild form of a disease.

inorganic chemistry the branch of chemistry dealing with the elements and their compounds, excluding the more complex carbon compounds which are considered in ◊organic chemistry.

The oldest known groups of inorganic compunds are acids, bases and salts. An important group is the oxides, in which oxygen is combined with another element. Other groups are the compounds of metals with halogens (fluorine, chlorine, bromine, and iodine), which are called halides (fluorides, chlorides, and so on), and the compounds with sulphur (sulphides). The basis of the description of the elements is the ◊periodic table of elements.

Acids change blue vegetable colours (for example litmus) to red, and react with alkalis to form salts. Alkalis restore the colours of indicators changed by acids, and react with acids to form salts. All acids contain hydrogen. Acids containing one, two, or three atoms of replaceable hydrogen are called mono-, di-, or tri-basic, respectively. Salts are formed by the replacement of the acidic hydrogen by a metal or radical. If only part of the hydrogen is replaced, an acid salt is formed.

insect

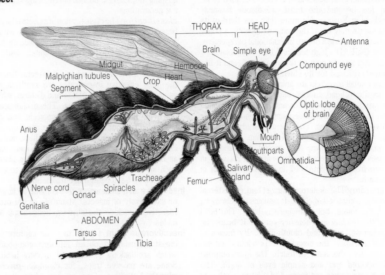

Oxides are classified into: *acidic oxides*, forming acids with water; *basic oxides*, forming bases (containing the hydroxyl group OH) with water; *neutral oxides*; and *peroxides* (containing more oxygen than the normal oxide). Acidic and basic oxides combine to form salts.

input device a device for entering information into a computer. Input devices include keyboards, joysticks, touch-sensitive screens, ◊graphics tablets, speech recognition devices, and vision systems.

inquest an inquiry held by a ◊coroner, especially into an unexplained death.

Inquisition tribunal of the Roman Catholic church established 1233 to suppress heresy (dissenting views), originally by excommunication. Sentence was pronounced during a religious ceremony, the ◊auto-da-fé. The Inquisition operated in France, Italy, Spain, and the Holy Roman Empire, and was especially active following the ◊Reformation; it was later extended to the Americas. Its trials were conducted in secret, under torture, and penalties ranged from fines, through flogging and imprisonment, to death by burning.

The Inquisition or Holy Office (renamed Sacred Congregation for the Doctrine of the Faith 1965) still deals with ecclesiastical discipline. The Roman Inquisition was established 1542, to combat the growth of Protestantism.

insanity popular and legal term for mental disorder. In medicine the corresponding term is ◊psychosis.

INSEAD abbreviation for *Institut Européen d'Administration des Affaires* business school at

insect classification

Class Insecta			
Subclass	Order	Number of species	Common names
Apterytgota	Thysanura	350	Three-pronged bristletails, silverfish
(wingless insects)	Diplura	400	Two-pronged bristletails, campodeids, japygids
	Protura	50	Minute insects living in soil
	Collembola	1500	Springtails
Pterygota (winged insects or forms secondarily wingless)			
Exopterygota	Ephemeroptera	1,000	Mayflies
(young resemble	Odonata	5,000	Dragonflies, damselflies
adults but have	Plecoptera	3,000	Stoneflies
externally	Grylloblattodea	12	Wingless soil-living insects of North America
developing wings)	Orthoptera	20,000	Crickets, grasshoppers, locusts, mantids, roaches
	Phasmida	2,000	Stick insects, leaf insects
	Dermaptera	1,000	Earwigs
	Embioptera	150	Web-spinners
	Dictyoptera	5,000	Cockroaches, praying mantises
	Isoptera	2,000	Termites
	Zoraptera	16	Tiny insects living in decaying plants
	Psocoptera	1,600	Booklice, barklice, psocids
	Mallophaga	2,500	Biting lice, mainly parasitic on birds
	Anoplura	250	Sucking lice, mainly parasitic on mammals
	Hemiptera	55,000	True bugs, including aphids, shield- and bedbugs, froghoppers, pond skaters, water boatmen
	Thysanoptera	5,000	Thrips
Endopterygota	Neuroptera	4,500	Lacewings, alder flies, snake flies, ant lions
(young unlike adults,	Mecoptera	300	Scorpion flies
undergo sudden	Lepidoptera	165,000	Butterflies, moths
metamorphosis)	Trichoptera	3,000	Caddis flies
	Diptera	70,000	True flies, including bluebeetles, mosquitoes, leather jackets, midges
	Siphonaptera	1,400	Fleas
	Hymenoptera	100,000	Bees, wasps, ants, sawflies
	Coleoptera	350,000	Beetles, including weevils, ladybirds, glow-worms, wood–worms, chafers

Fontainebleau, near Paris, France. Founded 1958, it has become the most prestigious business school in Europe. No more than one third of its students may be of the same nationality, a policy which results in a broad, international perspective, but INSEAD's high fees and lack of scholarships restrict access only to the wealthiest, and it has been criticized for its elitism.

insect small invertebrate animal whose body is divided into head, thorax, and abdomen. The head bears a pair of feelers or antennae, and attached to the thorax are three pairs of legs and usually two pairs of wings. The scientific study of insects is termed entomology. More than one million species are known, and several thousand new ones are discovered every year. Insects vary in size from 0.02 cm/0.007 in to 35 cm/13.5 in in length.

anatomy The skeleton is almost entirely external and is composed of chitin. It remains membranous at the joints, but elsewhere is hard. The head is the feeding and sensory centre. It bears the antennae, eyes, and mouth-parts. By means of the *antennae*, the insect detects odours and experiences the sense of touch. The *eyes* comprise *compound eyes* and simple eyes or *ocelli*. The compound eyes are formed of a large number of individual facets or lenses; there are about 4,000 lenses to each compound eye in the house-fly. The mouth-parts include a *labrum* or upper lip; a pair of principal jaws or *mandibles*; a pair of accessory jaws or *maxillae*; and a *labium*, or lower lip. These mouth-parts are modified in insects that feed upon a fluid diet.

The *thorax* is the locomotory centre, and is made up of three segments: the *pro-*, *meso-*, and *metathorax*. Each bears a pair of legs and, in flying insects, the second and third of these segments also bears a pair of wings.

Wings are composed of an upper and a lower membrane, and between these two layers they are strengthened by a framework of chitinous tubes known as *veins*. The hind-body or abdomen is the metabolic and reproductive centre; digestion, excretion, and the sexual functions take place. In the female, there is very commonly an egg-laying instrument or *ovipositor*, and many insects have a pair of tail feelers or *cerci*. Most insects breathe by means of fine airtubes called *tracheae* which open to the exterior by a pair of breathing pores or *spiracles*.

Growth and metamorphosis When ready to hatch from the egg, the young insect forces its way through the *chorion*, or egg-shell, and growth takes place in cycles that are interrupted by successive moults. After moulting, the new cuticle is soft and pliable, and able to adapt itself to increase in size and change of form.

Most of the lower orders of insects pass through a direct or incomplete metamorphosis. The young closely resemble the parents and are known as nymphs.

The higher groups of insects (Endopterygota) undergo indirect or complete metamorphosis. They hatch at an earlier stage of growth than nymphs and are termed *larvae*. The life of the insect is interrupted by a resting *pupal* stage when no food is taken. During this stage, the larval organs and tissues are transformed into those of the *imago* or adult. Before pupating, the insect protects itself by selecting a suitable hiding place, or making a cocoon of some material which will merge in with its surroundings. When an insect is about to emerge from the pupa, or protective sheath, it undergoes its final moult, which consists of shedding the pupal cuticle. Reproduction is by diverse means. In most insects, mating occurs once only, and death soon follows.

Many insects are pests that may be controlled by chemical insecticides (these may also kill useful insects), by importation of natural predators (that may themselves become pests), or, more recently, by the use of artificially reared sterile insects, either the males only, or in 'population

flushing' both sexes, so sharply reducing succeeding generations.

classification The classification of insects is largely based upon characters of the mouth-parts, wings, and metamorphosis. Insects are classed in two subclasses (one with two divisions), and 29 orders.

insecticide a chemical used to kill insects. Among the most effective insecticides are synthetic organic chemicals such as ◊DDT and dieldrin, which are chlorinated hydrocarbons. These chemicals, however, have proved very persistent and can also poison higher animals, and are consequently banned in many countries. Other synthetic insecticides include organic phosphorus compounds such as malathion. Insecticides prepared from plants, such as derris and pyrethrum are safer to use, but need to be applied more frequently.

insectivore an animal whose diet is made up largely or exclusively of insects. Mammals of the order Insectivora include the shrews, hedgehogs, and moles.

insectivorous plant a plant that can capture and digest animals, to obtain nitrogen compounds which are lacking in its usual marshy habitat. Some are passive traps, for example, **pitcher plants** *Nepenthes*. One pitcher plant species has container-traps holding 2 l/3.5 pt of the liquid which 'digests' its insect food, and may even trap rats. Others, for example, **sundews** *Drosera*, **butterworts** *Pinguicula* and **Venus fly trap** *Dionaea muscipula*, have an active trapping mechanism; see ◊leaf.

inselberg a prominent steep-sided hill of resistant solid rock, such as granite, rising out of a plain, usually in a tropical area. Its rounded appearance is caused by so called onion-skin ◊weathering, in which the surface is eroded in successive layers.

The Sugar Loaf in Rio de Janeiro harbour in Brazil, and Ayers Rock in Northern Territory, Australia, are famous examples. The word is German, 'island mountain'.

insemination, artificial artificial introduction of semen into the female reproductive tract to bring about fertilization. Originally used by animal breeders to improve stock by the use of high-quality males, in the 20th century it has been developed for use in humans, to help the infertile. In *in vitro* fertilization (test-tube babies), the egg is fertilized externally and then reimplanted in the womb; the first successful birth using this method was in the UK 1978.

The sperm for artificial insemination may come from the husband (AIH) or a donor (AID); an AID child is illegitimate under British law. Recent extensions of the test-tube technique have included the birth of a baby from a frozen embryo (Australia 1984) and from a frozen egg (Australia 1986). Pioneers in the field have been the British doctors Robert Edwards (1925–) and Patrick Steptoe (1913–89). As yet the success rate is relatively low; only 15–20% of in vitro fertilizations result in babies.

insider trading or **insider dealing** illegal use of privileged information in dealing on the stock exchanges, for example when a company takeover bid is imminent. Insider trading is in theory detected by the **Securities and Exchange Commission** (SEC) in the USA, and by the **Securities and Investment Board** (SIB) in the UK. Neither agency, however, has any legal powers other than public disclosure and do not bring prosecution themselves. Insider trading was made illegal by the Company Securities (Insider Dealing) Act 1985, and in 1989 it was ruled that the perpetrator was equally guilty whether the information was solicited or unsolicited.

in situ (Latin) in place, on the spot, without moving from position.

instalment credit a form of ◊hire purchase.

instinct in ◊ethology, behaviour found in all equivalent members of a given species (for example, all the males, or all the females with young) that is presumed to be genetically determined.

Examples include a male robin's tendency to attack other male robins intruding on its territory and the tendency of many female mammals to care for their offspring. Instincts differ from ◊reflexes in that they involve very much more complex actions, and learning often plays an important part in their development.

Institute for Advanced Study a department of Princeton University, USA, established 1933, to encourage gifted scientists to further their research uninterrupted by teaching duties or an imposed research scheme. Its first professor was Albert Einstein.

Instrument Landing System a landing aid for aircraft that uses ◊radio beacons on the ground and instruments on the flight deck. One beacon (localizer) sends out a vertical radio beam along the centre line of the runway. Another beacon (glide slope) transmits a beam in the plane at right-angles to the localizer beam at the ideal approach-path angle. The pilot can tell from the instruments how to manoeuvre to attain the correct approach path.

insulator poor ◊conductor of heat, sound, or electricity. Most substances lacking free (mobile) ◊electrons, such as non-metals, are electrical or thermal insulators.

insulin a ◊hormone, produced by specialized cells in the islets of Langerhans in the ◊pancreas, which regulates the ◊metabolism (rate of activity) of glucose, fats, and proteins.

Normally, insulin is secreted in response to rising blood sugar levels, after a meal for example, stimulating the body's cells to store the excess. Failure of this regulatory mechanism in ◊diabetes mellitus requires treatment with insulin injections. Types vary from pig and beef insulins to synthetic and bioengineered ones. They may be combined with other substances to make them longer- or shorter-acting. Implanted, battery-powered insulin pumps deliver the hormone at a pre-set rate, to eliminate the unnatural rises and falls that result from conventional, subcutaneous (under the skin) delivery. It is hoped that this technique may reduce some of the long-term effects of diabetes. Human insulin, produced from bacteria by ◊genetic engineering techniques, may increase the chance of sudden, unpredictable hypoglycaemia, or low blood sugar in diabetics.

insurance contract indemnifying the payer of a premium against loss by fire, death, accident, and so on, which is known as **assurance** in the case of a fixed sum (in Britain especially when the event is inevitable, for example payment of a fixed sum on death), and **insurance** where the indemnity is proportionate to the loss.

intaglio a gem or seal that has a pattern cut into one surface; an ◊engraving technique.

integer a whole number, for example 3. Integers may be positive or negative; 0 is an integer. Formally, integers are members of the set Z = (... –2, –1, 0, 1, 2, ...). Fractions, such as $1/2$ and 0.35, are known as non-integral numbers.

integral calculus branch of mathematics using the process of ◊integration. It is concerned with finding volumes and areas and summing infinitesimally small quantities.

integrated circuit a complete electronic circuit produced on a single crystal of a ◊semiconductor (intermediate between an insulator and a conductor of electricity) such as silicon. The circuit might contain more than a million transistors, resistors, and capacitors and yet measure only 8 mm/0.3 in across. See also ◊silicon chip.

The discovery in the early 1970s of the means to produce such circuits, superseding the printed circuit, began the so-called computer revolution.

integration in mathematics, a method in ◊calculus of evaluating definite or indefinite integrals. An example of a definite integral can be thought of as finding the area under a curve (as represented by an algebraic expression or function) between particular values of the function's variable. In practice, integral calculus provides scientists with a powerful tool for doing calculations that involve a continually varying quantity (such as determing the position at any given instant of a space rocket that is accelerating away from Earth). Its basic principles were discovered in the late 1660s independently by the German philosopher ◊Leibniz and the British scientist ◊Newton.

intelligence in psychology, a general concept that summarizes the abilities of an individual in reasoning and problem solving, particularly in novel situations. These consist of a wide range of verbal and non-verbal skills and therefore some psychologists dispute a unitary concept of intelligence. See ◊intelligence test.

intelligence in military and political affairs, information, usually secretly or illegally obtained, about other countries. *Counter-intelligence* is information on the activities of hostile agents. Much intelligence is gained by technical means, as at the UK electronic surveillance centre ◊GCHQ, Cheltenham.

The British secret intelligence service is M(ilitary) I(ntelligence) 6 and its agents operate abroad; the US equivalent is the Central Intelligence Agency. In the UK the counter-intelligence service MI5 has as its executive arm Scotland Yard's Special Branch. In the USA, the Federal Bureau of Investigation is responsible for counter-intelligence; in the USSR, the KGB.

Double agents increase their income, but may decrease their lifespan, by working for both sides (for example, Mata Hari); *moles* are those within the service who betray their own side, usually defecting (fleeing to the other side) when in danger of discovery (for example, Kim Philby); a *sleeper* is a spy who is inactive, sometimes for many years, until needed.

The motive for work in intelligence may be service to country (T E Lawrence, John Buchan, Graham Greene, Ian Fleming, and John Le Carré afterwards used their experiences in their books), money, or idealism, for example the German scientist Klaus Fuchs, or art historian Anthony Blunt.

MI5 has an estimated annual budget of £175 million and 2,000 full-time staff. MI6 does not officially exist in peacetime.

intelligence test test that attempts to measure innate intellectual ability, rather than acquired ability.

Workers in this field have included Francis ◊Galton, Alfred Binet (1857–1911), Cyril ◊Burt, and Hans ◊Eysenck. Binet devised the first intelligence test in 1905. The concept of intelligence quotient (IQ) was adopted by US psychologist Lewis Terman in 1915. The IQ is calculated according to the formula: $IQ = MA/CA \times 100$ in which MA is 'mental age' (the age at which an average child is able to perform given tasks) and CA is 'chronological age', hence an average person has an IQ of 100.

Intelligence tests were first used on a large scale in World War I in 1917 for two million drafted men in the USA. They were widely used in UK education as part of the Eleven Plus selection procedures, on the assumption that inborn intelligence was unalterable.

It is now generally believed that a child's ability in an intelligence test can be affected by their environment, cultural background, and teaching. There is scepticism about the accuracy of intelligence tests, but they are still widely used as a diagnostic tool when children display learning difficulties.

'Sight and sound' intelligence tests, developed by Christopher Brand in 1981, avoid cultural bias and the pitfalls of improvement by practice. Subjects are shown a series of lines being flashed on a screen at increasing speed, and are asked to identify in each case the shorter of a pair; and when two notes are relayed over headphones, they are asked to identify which is the higher. There is a close correlation between the results and other intelligence test scores.

Intelsat International Telecommunications Satellite Organization, established 1964 to operate a worldwide system of communications satellites. More than 100 countries are members of Intelsat, with headquarters in Washington, USA. Intelsat satellites are stationed in geostationary orbit (maintaining their positions relative to the Earth) over the Atlantic, Pacific, and Indian Oceans. The first Intelsat satellite was *Early Bird*, launched 1965.

intendant an official appointed by the French crown under Louis XIV to administer a territorial *département*. Their powers were extensive but counteracted to some extent by other local officials. The term was also used for certain administrators in Spain, Portugal, and Latin America.

intensity the concentration of a force or energy over a given area or time. For example, the intensity or loudness of a sound is related to the energy per unit area carried by the sound wave. Likewise, the intensity or brightness of a light source is measured by the energy per unit area carried by the light.

intentionality in philosophy, the property of consciousness whereby it is directed towards an object, even when this object does not exist in reality (such as 'the golden mountain'). Intentionality is a key concept in ◊Husserl's philosophy.

inter alia (Latin) among other things.

interdict ecclesiastical punishment that excludes an individual, community, or realm from participation in spiritual activities except for communion. It was usually employed against heretics or realms whose ruler was an excommunicant.

interest in finance, a sum of money paid by a borrower to a lender in return for the loan, usually expressed as a percentage per annum. *Simple interest* is interest calculated as a straight percentage of the amount loaned or invested. In *compound interest*, the interest earned over a period of time (for example, per annum) is added to the investment, so that at the end of the next period interest is paid on that total.

A sum of £100 invested at 10% per annum simple interest for five years earns £10 a year, giving a total of £50 interest (and at the end of the period the investor receives a total of £150). The same sum of £100 invested for five years at 10% compound interest earns a total of £61.05 interest (with £161.05 returned at the end of the period). Generally, for a sum S invested at $x\%$ simple interest for y years, the total amount returned is $S + xyS/100$. If it is invested at $x\%$ compound interest for y years, the total amount returned is $S [(100 + x)/100]^y$.

interface in computing, the point of contact between two programs or pieces of equipment. The term is most often used for the physical connection between the computer and a ◊peripheral device. For example, a printer interface is the cabling and circuitry used to transfer data from the computer to the printer and to compensate for differences in speed and coding systems.

interference in physics, the phenomenon of two or more wave motions interacting and combining to produce a resultant wave of larger or smaller amplitude (depending on whether the combining waves are in or out of ◊phase with each other).

Interference of white light (multi-wavelength) results in spectral coloured fringes, for example, the iridescent colours of oil films seen on water or soap bubbles (demonstrated by ◊Newton's rings). Interference of sound waves of similar frequency produces the phenomenon of beats, often used by musicians when tuning an instrument. With monochromatic light (of a single wavelength), interference produces patterns of light and dark bands. This is the basis of ◊holography, for example. Interferometry can also be applied to radio waves, and is a powerful tool in modern astronomy.

interferometer in physics, a device which splits a beam of light into two parts, the parts being recombined after travelling different paths to form an interference pattern of light and dark bands. Interferometers are used in many branches of science and industry where accurate measurements of distances and angles are needed.

In the Michelson interferometer, a light beam is split into two by a semi-silvered mirror. The two beams are then reflected off fully silvered mirrors and recombined. The pattern of dark and light bands is sensitive to small alterations in the placing of the mirrors, so the interferometer can detect changes in their position to within one ten-millionth of a metre. Using lasers, compact devices of this kind can be built to measure distances, for example to check the accuracy of machine tools.

In radio astronomy, interferometers consist of separate radio telescopes, each observing the same distant object, such as a galaxy, in the sky. The signal received by each telescope is fed into a computer. Because the telescopes are in different places, the distance travelled by the signal to reach each differs and the overall signal is akin to the interference pattern in the Michelson interferometer. Computer analysis of the overall signal can build up a detailed picture of the source of the radio waves.

In space technology, interferometers are used in radio and radar systems. These include space-vehicle guidance systems, in which the position of the spacecraft is determined by combining the signals received by two precisely spaced antennae mounted on it.

interferon naturally occurring protein that makes up part of the body's defences against disease. Three types (alpha, beta, and gamma) are produced to protect cells from viral infection. At present, only alpha interferon has any proven therapeutic value, and may be used to treat a rare type of ◊leukaemia.

interior decoration design, decoration, and furnishing of the inside of a building. Among early names associated with interior decoration in England are those of Inigo ◊Jones and Grinling ◊Gibbons, but the first architects to design a building as an integrated whole were the ◊Adam brothers, for example Syon House, Middlesex. In Victorian times William ◊Morris designed carpets, wallpaper, and furniture, as did Charles Rennie ◊Mackintosh and Adolph ◊Loos.

Recently the trend has been towards a less ornate and more functional style, fostered by the interaction of architects and designers working in teams, whether to remodel existing interiors, for example Misha Black and Hugh ◊Casson, or in new buildings, for example Gio Ponti's Pirelli building (Milan); Oscar ◊Niemeyer's capital city of Brasilia; and the many works of ◊Le Corbusier, Eero ◊Saarinen, and Skidmore, Owings, and Merrill (USA).

Interlaken /'ɪntəˌlɑːkən/ chief town of the Bernese Oberland, on the river Aar between lakes Brienz and Thun, Switzerland; population (1985) 13,000. The site was first occupied in 1130 by a monastery, suppressed in 1528.

Intermediate Nuclear Forces Treaty agreement signed 8 Dec 1987 between the USA and the USSR to eliminate all ground-based nuclear missiles in Europe that were capable of hitting only European targets (including European Russia). It reduced the countries's nuclear arsenals by some 2,000 (4% of the total). The treaty included provisions for each country to inspect the other's bases. A total of 1,269 weapons (945 Soviet, 234 US) was destroyed in the first year of the treaty.

intermediate technology the application of mechanics, electrical engineering, and other technologies, based on inventions and designs developed in scientifically sophisticated cultures, but utilizing materials, assembly, and maintenance methods found in technologically less advanced regions (known as the ◊Third World).

Intermediate technologies aim to allow developing countries to benefit from new techniques and inventions of the 'First World', without the burdens of costly maintenance and supply of fuels

intermediate technology
windpump

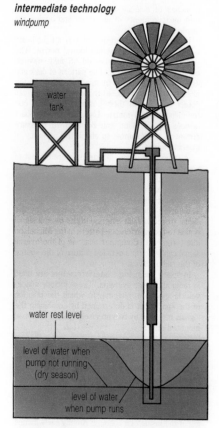

water tank

water rest level

level of water when
pump not running
(dry season)

level of water
when pump runs

and spare parts that in the Third World would represent an enormous and probably uneconomic overhead.

intermezzo in music, a short orchestral interlude often used between the acts of an opera to denote the passage of time; by extension, a short piece for an instrument to be played between other more substantial works.

internal combustion engine a heat engine in which fuel is burned inside the engine, contrasting with an external combustion engine (like the steam engine) in which fuel is burned in a separate boiler. The petrol and diesel engine are both internal combustion engines. Gas turbines, jet, and rocket engines are sometimes also considered to be internal combustion engines because they burn their fuel inside their combustion chambers.

International, the coordinating body established by labour and socialist organizations, including:

First International or *International Working Men's Association* 1864–72, formed in London under Karl ◊Marx.

Second International 1889–1940, founded in Paris.

Third (Socialist) International or *Comintern* 1919–43, formed in Moscow by the Soviet leader Lenin, advocating from 1933 a popular front (communist, socialist, liberal) against the German dictator Hitler.

Fourth International or *Trotskyist International* 1936, somewhat indeterminate, anti-Stalinist.

Revived *Socialist International* 1951, formed in Frankfurt, West Germany, a largely anti-communist association of social democrats.

International Atomic Energy Agency (IAEA) agency of the United Nations established 1957, to advise and assist member states in the development and application of nuclear power and to guard against its misuse. It has its headquarters in Vienna, and is responsible for research centres in Austria, Monaco, and the International Centre for Theoretical Physics, Trieste, established 1964.

International Bank for Reconstruction and Development official name of the ◊World Bank.

international biological standards drugs (such as penicillin and insulin) whose activity for a specific mass (called the international unit, or IU), prepared and stored under specific conditions, serves as a standard for measuring doses. For ◊penicillin, one IU is the activity of 0.0006 mg of the sodium salt of penicillin, so a dose of a million units would be 0.6 mg.

International Brigade international volunteer force on the Republican side in the Spanish ◊Civil War 1936–39.

International Civil Aviation Organization agency of the ◊United Nations, established 1947 to regulate safety and efficiency and air law; headquarters Montreal.

International Court of Justice the main judicial organ of the ◊United Nations, at The Hague, the Netherlands.

International Date Line (IDL) a modification of the 180th meridian that marks the difference in time between E and W. The date is put forward a day when crossing the line going W, and back a day when going E. The IDL was chosen at the International Meridian Conference in 1884.

International Development Association (IDA) an agency of the United Nations, established in 1960, and affiliated to the ◊World Bank.

Internationale international revolutionary socialist anthem; composed 1870 and first sung 1888. The words by Eugène Pottier (1816–1887) were written shortly after Napoleon III's surrender to Prussia; the music is by Pierre Degeyter. It was the Soviet national anthem 1917–44.

International Finance Corporation United Nations agency affiliated to the ◊World Bank. It was set up in 1956 to facilitate loans for private investment to developing countries.

International Fund for Agricultural Development agency of the ◊United Nations, established 1977, to provide funds for benefiting the poor in developing countries.

International Gothic a late Gothic style of painting prevalent in Europe in the 14th and 15th century. See ◊Gothic art.

International Labour Organization (ILO) an agency of the United Nations, first established in 1919, which formulates standards for labour and social conditions. Its headquarters are in Geneva. It was awarded the Nobel Peace Prize 1969.

international law body of rules generally accepted as governing the relations between countries, pioneered by Hugo ◊Grotius, especially in matters of human rights, territory, and war. Neither the League of Nations nor United Nations proved able to enforce it, successes being achieved only when the law coincided with the aims of a predominant major power, for example the ◊Korean War. The scope of the law is now extended to space, for example the 1967 treaty which (among other things) banned nuclear weapons from space.

International Maritime Organization a ◊United Nations agency concerned with world shipping. Established in 1958, it has its headquarters in London, England.

International Monetary Fund (IMF) specialized agency of the United Nations, headquarters Washington DC, established under the 1944 Bretton Woods agreement and operational since 1947. It seeks to promote international monetary cooperation and the growth of world trade, and to smooth multilateral payment arrangements among member states. IMF stand-by loans are available to members in balance of payments difficulties (the amount being governed by the member's quota), usually on the basis of acceptance of instruction on stipulated corrective measures.

The Fund also operates other drawing facilities, including several designed to provide preferential credit to developing countries with liquidity problems. Having previously operated in US dollars linked to gold, since 1972 the IMF has used the ◊special drawing right (SDR) as its standard unit of account, valued in terms of a weighted 'basket' of major currencies. Since the 1971

Smithsonian agreement permitting wider fluctuations from specified currency parities, IMF rules have been progressively adapted to the increasing prevalence of fully floating exchange rates.

International Settlements, Bank for (BIS) forum for European central banks, established 1930, which acts as a bank to the central banks, to prevent currency speculation. It has been superseded in some of its major functions by the ◊International Monetary Fund.

International Society for Krishna Consciousness (ISKCON) a Hindu sect based on the demonstration of intense love for Krishna (an incarnation of the god Vishnu), especially by chanting the mantra 'Hare Krishna'. Members wear distinctive yellow robes, and men often have their heads partly shaven. Their holy books are the Hindu scriptures and particularly the *Bhagavad-Gītā*, which they study daily. Their centre of worship in Britain is Bhakti-Vedanta Manor at Letchmore Heath, Hertfordshire, given to the society in 1973 by Beatle George Harrison.

The sect was introduced to the West by Swami Prabhupada (1896–1977). Members believe that by chanting the mantra and meditating on it they may achieve enlightenment and so remove themselves from the cycle of reincarnation. They are expected to live ascetic lives, avoiding meat, eggs, alcohol, tea, coffee, and other drugs, and gambling; sexual relationships should only take place within marriage and solely for procreation.

International Standards Organization international organization founded 1947 to standardize technical terms, units, and so on. Its headquarters are in Geneva.

International Telecommunication Union a body belonging to the Economic and Social Council of the ◊United Nations.

International Union for Conservation of Nature the full name of the ◊IUCN.

internment the detention of suspected criminals without trial. Common with foreign citizens during wartime, internment was introduced for the detention of people suspected of terrorist acts in Northern Ireland by the UK government in 1971. It has now been discontinued, but in 1988 there was pressure to re-introduce it following further outbreaks of violence.

interplanetary matter gas and dust thinly spread through the solar system. The gas flows outwards from the Sun as the ◊solar wind. Fine dust lies in the plane of the solar system, scattering sunlight to cause the zodiacal light. Swarms of dust shed by comets enter the Earth's atmosphere to cause ◊meteor showers.

Interpol short for *International Criminal Police Commission*, founded following the Second International Judicial Police Conference 1923 with its headquarters in Vienna, but reconstituted after World War II with its headquarters in Paris. It has an international criminal register, fingerprint file, and methods index.

interpreter a computer program that translates statements from a ◊programming language into ◊machine code and causes them to be executed. Unlike a ◊compiler, which translates the whole program at once to produce an executable machine code program, an interpreter translates the programming language each time the program is run.

intersex an individual that is intermediate between a normal male and a normal female in its appearance (for example, a genetic male that lacks external genitalia and so resembles a female).

Intersexes are usually the result of an abnormal hormone balance during development (especially during ◊gestation) or of a failure of the ◊genes controlling sex determination. The term ◊hermaphrodite is sometimes used for intersexes, but should be confined to animals that normally have both male and female organs.

Interstate Commerce Act in US history, an act of Congress in 1887 responding to public concern regarding alleged profiteering and malpractice

intrusion

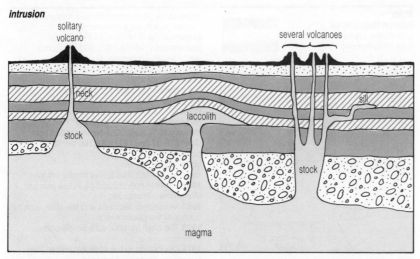

by railroad companies. It required all charges to be reasonable and fair, and established the Interstate Commerce Commission to investigate railroad management. The act proved difficult to enforce.

interstellar molecules over 50 different types of molecules existing in gas clouds in the Galaxy. Most have been detected by their radio emissions, but some have been found by the absorption lines they produce in the spectra of starlight. The most complex molecules, many of them based on ◊carbon, are found in the dense clouds where stars are forming. They may be significant for the origin of life elsewhere in space.

interval in music, the pitch difference between two notes, usually measured in terms of the diatonic scale.

intestacy the absence of a will at a person's death. In English law, special legal rules apply on intestacy for appointing administrators to deal with the deceased person's affairs, and for disposing of the deceased person's property in accordance with statutory provisions.

intestine in vertebrates, the digestive tract from the stomach outlet to the anus. The human *small intestine* is 6 m/20 ft long, 4 cm/1.5 in in diameter, and consists of the duodenum, jejunum, and ileum; the *large intestine* is 1.5 m/5 ft long, 6 cm/2.5 in in diameter, and includes the caecum, colon, and rectum. Both are muscular tubes comprising an inner lining which secretes alkaline digestive juice, a submucous coat containing fine blood vessels and nerves, a muscular coat, and a serous coat covering all, supported by a strong peritoneum, which carries the blood and lymph vessels, and the nerves. The contents are passed along slowly by ◊peristalsis. The term intestine may also be applied to the lower digestive tract of invertebrates.

Intifada (Arabic 'resurgence' or 'throwing off') Palestinian uprising; also the title of the involved *Liberation Army of Palestine*, a loosely organized group of adult and teenage Palestinians active since 1987 in attacks on Israeli troops in the occupied territories of Palestine. Their campaign for self-determination includes stone-throwing and petrol bombing. Measures taken by the Israeli government to prevent violence include fining parents of stone-throwing children up to $2,000.

The uprising began in Dec 1987 in Gaza. Rumours that a fatal traffic collision had been caused by Israeli security service agents in retaliation for the stabbing of an Israeli the previous week led to demonstrations by teenagers armed with slingshots. It subsequently spread despite attempts at repression. Some 600 Palestinians and 45 Jews were killed in the uprising to the end of 1989. Over 157 Palestinian private homes have been dynamited by military order, under a still valid British

emergency regulation promulgated 1946 to put down Jewish guerrillas. The number of soldiers on duty on the West Bank at the beginning of 1989 was said to be more than three times the number needed to conquer it during the Six-Day War.

intrauterine device IUD or coil, a contraceptive device that is inserted into the womb (uterus). It is a tiny plastic object, sometimes containing copper. By causing a mild inflammation of the lining of the uterus it prevents fertilized eggs from becoming implanted.

IUDs are not usually given to women who have not yet had children. They are generally very reliable, as long as they stay in place, with a success rate of about 98%. Some women experience heavier and more painful periods, and there is a very small risk of a pelvic infection leading to infertility.

intravenous delivery of a substance directly into a vein.

intrusion a mass of ◊igneous rock that has formed by 'injection' of molten rock into existing cracks

Invalides, Hôtel des *Established by Louis XIV, the Hôtel des Invalides was mainly designed by Jules Hardouin-Mansart. Napoleon was buried beneath the dome of its church in 1840.*

beneath the surface of the Earth, as distinct from a volcanic rock mass which has erupted from the surface.

intuition a rapid, unconscious thought process. In philosophy, intuition is that knowledge of a concept which does not derive directly from the senses. Thus, we may be said to have an intuitive idea of God, beauty, or justice. The concept of intuition is similar to Bertrand ◊Russell's theory of knowledge by acquaintance. In both cases, it is contrasted with ◊empirical knowledge.

intuitionism in mathematics, the theory that propositions can only be built up from intuitive concepts which we all recognize easily, such as unity or plurality. The concept of ◊infinity, of which we have no intuitive experience, is thus not allowed.

Inuit or *Eskimo* people inhabiting the Arctic coasts of North America, the E islands of the Canadian Arctic, and the ice-free coasts of Greenland. They were first called Eskimos ('foul eaters of raw meat') by the Algonquin Indians. Their language, Inuktitut, belongs to the Eskimo-Aleut group.

Invalides, Hôtel des building in Paris, S of the Seine, founded in 1670 as a home for disabled soldiers. The church Dôme des Invalides contains the tomb of Napoleon I. The military government of Paris has its headquarters at Les Invalides.

invar an alloy of iron containing 36% nickel, which expands or contracts very little when the temperature changes. It is used to make precision instruments (such as pendulums and tuning forks) whose dimensions must not alter.

Invercargill /ˌɪnvəˈkɑːɡəl/ city on the S coast of South Island, New Zealand; population (1986) 52,800. It has saw-mills, and meatpacking and aluminium-smelting plants.

Invergordon Mutiny incident in the British Atlantic Fleet, Cromarty Firth, Scotland, 15 Sept 1931. Ratings refused to prepare the ships for sea following the government's cuts in their pay; the cuts were consequently modified.

Inverness /ˌɪnvəˈnes/ town in Highland region, Scotland, lying in a sheltered site at the mouth of the Ness; population (1985) 58,000. A tourist centre with tweed, tanning, engineering, and distilling industries.

Inverness-shire /ˌɪnvəˈnesʃə/ largest of the former Scottish counties, it was merged in Highland region 1975.

inverse square law in physics, the statement that the magnitude of an effect (usually a force) at a point is inversely proportional to the square of the distance between that point and the point location of its cause.

◊Light, ◊sound, electrostatic force (◊Coulomb's law), gravitational force (◊Newton's law) and magnetic force (see ◊magnetism) all obey the inverse square law.

inversion in music, the mirror-image of a melody used in counterpoint; alternatively a chord whose natural order of notes is rearranged.

invertebrate an animal without a backbone. The invertebrates comprise over 95% of the million or so existing animal species and include the sponges, coelenterates, flatworms, nematodes, annelid worms, arthropods, molluscs, echinoderms, and primitive aquatic chordates such as sea-squirts and lancelets.

investiture contest the conflict between the papacy and the Holy Roman Empire 1075–1122, which centred on the right of lay rulers to appoint prelates.

It began with the decree of 1075 in which Pope Gregory VII (1021–85) forbade lay investiture, and Henry IV's excommunication the following year after he refused to accept the ruling. There was a lull in the conflict after Henry's death in 1106, but in 1111, Henry V captured Paschal II (c.1050–1118), and forced him to concede that only lay rulers could endow prelates with their temporalities (lands and other possessions). When this was overturned by the Lateran Council of 1112, the church split between pro-papal and pro-imperial factions, and fighting broke out in

Iowa

Germany and Italy. Settlement was reached in 1122 at the Diet of Worms, when it was agreed that lay rulers could not appoint prelates but could continue to invest them with their temporalities.

investment in economics, the purchase of any asset with the potential to yield future financial benefit to the purchaser (such as a house, a work of art, stocks and shares, or even a private education). More strictly, it denotes expenditure on the stock of capital goods or resources of an enterprise or project, with a view to achieving profitable production for consumption at a later date.

investment trust a public company which makes investments in other companies on behalf of its shareholders. It may issue shares to raise capital and issue fixed interest securities.

Invisible Man 1952 novel by US novelist Ralph Ellison about an unnamed hero who discovers that because of his black skin he lacks all social identity in modern US society.

in vitro fertilization (IVF) literally, fertilization 'in glass', that is, allowing eggs and sperm to fuse in a laboratory to form embryos. The embryos produced may then either be reimplanted into the womb of the otherwise infertile mother, or used for research. The first baby to be produced in the UK by this method, Louise Brown, was born in 1978.

involute (Latin 'rolled in') of a circle, a ◊spiral that can be thought of as being traced by a point at the end of a taut non-elastic thread being wound onto or unwound from a spool.

Inyangani /ˌɪnjæŋˈɡɑːni/ highest peak in Zimbabwe, rising to 2,593 m/8,507 ft near the Mozambique frontier in NE Zimbabwe.

Inyōkern /ˌɪnjəʊˈkɜːn/ village in the Mojave desert, California, USA, 72 km/45 mi NW of Mojave. It is the site of a US Naval Ordnance test station, founded in 1944, carrying out research in rocket flight and propulsion.

Io /ˈaɪəʊ/ in Greek mythology, a princess loved by ◊Zeus, who transformed her to a heifer to hide her from the jealousy of ◊Hera.

Io /ˈaɪəʊ/ in astronomy, the third largest moon of the planet Jupiter, 3,600 km/2,240 mi in diameter, orbiting in 1.77 days at a distance of 413,000 km/257,000 mi. It is the most volcanically active body in the Solar System, covered by hundreds of vents that erupt not lava but sulphur, giving Io an orange-coloured surface.

iodide a compound formed between iodine and another element in which the iodine is the more electronegative element (see ◊electronegativity, ◊halide).

iodine (Greek *iodes* 'violet') a non-metallic element, symbol I, atomic number 53, relative atomic mass 126.91. Not found in the free state, it occurs in saltpetre and as iodides in sea-water. Iodine is used in photography, in medicine as an antiseptic, and in chemicals and dyes. It collects in the thyroid gland, lack of it producing goitre. Iodine-131 (a radioactive isotope) is widely used in medical diagnosis, research and treatment.

It is a violet-black lustrous solid, changing at ordinary temperatures to a bluish-violet gas with an irritating odour, and forming a characteristic blue colour with starch. It was discovered by Bernard Courtois (1777–1838) in 1811.

Iran
Islamic Republic of
(Jomhori-e-Islami-e-Irân; until 1935 **Persia**)

area 1,648,000 sq km/636,128 sq mi
capital Tehran
towns Isfahan, Mashhad, Tabriz, Shiraz, Ahwaz; chief port Abadan
physical plateau surrounded by mountains, including Elburz and Zagros; Lake Rezayeh; Dasht-Ekavir Desert
features ruins of Persepolis
Leader of the Revolution Ali Khamenei from 1989
head of government Ali Akbar Rafsanjani from 1989
political system authoritarian Islamic republic
political parties Islamic Republican Party (IRP), fundamentalist Islamic

exports carpets, cotton textiles, metalwork, leather goods, oil, petrochemicals
currency rial (117.00 = £1 Feb 1990)
population (1988) 53,920,000 (including minorities in Azerbaijan, Baluchistan, Khuzestan/Arabistan, and Kurdistan); annual growth rate 2.9%
life expectancy men 57, women 57
language Farsi, Kurdish, Turk, Arabic, English, French
religion Shi'ite Muslim (official)
literacy 62% male/39% female (1985 est)
GDP $76.37 bn (1977); $2,160 per head of population
chronology
1946 British, US, and Soviet forces left Iran.
1951 Oilfields nationalized by Prime Minister Mohammed Mossadeq.
1953 Mossadeq deposed and the shah took full control of the government.
1975 The shah introduced a single-party system.
1978 Opposition to the shah organized from France by Ayatollah Khomeini.
1979 Shah left the country and Khomeini returned to create an Islamic state. Students seized US hostages at embassy in Tehran.
1980 Start of Gulf War against Iraq.
1981 US hostages released.
1984 Egyptian peace proposals rejected.
1985 Gulf War fighting intensified. UN secretary-general's peace moves were unsuccessful.
1988 Ceasefire in Gulf War, talks with Iraq began.
1989 Khomeini called for the murder of British writer Salman Rushdie. Khomeini died June. Ali Khamenei elected interim Leader of the Revolution. Speaker of the Iranian parliament Ali Akbar Rafsanjani elected president.

iodoform CHI_3 (modern name ***triiodomethane***) an antiseptic which crystallizes into yellow hexagonal plates. It is soluble in ether, alcohol, and chloroform, but not in water.

IOM abbreviation for ◊*Isle of Man.*

ion atom, or group of atoms, which is either positively charged (***cation***) or negatively charged (***anion***), as a result of the loss or gain of electrons.

Iona /aɪˈəʊnə/ an island in the Inner Hebrides; area 850 hectares. It is the site of a monastery founded 563 by St ◊Columba, and a centre of early Christianity. It later became a burial ground for Irish, Scottish, and Norwegian kings. It has a 13th-century abbey.

ion engine a rocket engine that uses ◊ions rather than hot gas for propulsion. Ion engines have been successfully tested in space, where they will eventually be used for gradual rather than sudden velocity changes. In an ion engine atoms of mercury, for example, are ionized—given an electric charge by an electric field, and then accelerated at high speed by a more powerful electric field.

Ionesco /ˌiːəˈneskəʊ/ Eugène 1912– . Romanian-born French dramatist, a leading exponent of the Theatre of the ◊Absurd. Most of his plays are in one act and concern the futility of language as a means of communication. These include *La Cantatrice chauve/The Bald Prima Donna* 1950 and *La Leçon/The Lesson* 1951.

Later full-length plays include *Rhinocéros* 1958 and *Le Roi se meurt/Exit the King* 1961. He has also written memoirs and a novel, *Le Solitaire/The Hermit* 1973.

Ionia /aɪˈəʊnɪə/ in Classical times the W coast of Asia Minor, settled about 1000 BC by the Ionians; it included the cities of Ephesus, Miletus, and later Smyrna.

Ionian member of a Hellenic people from beyond the Black Sea who crossed the Balkans around 1980 BC and invaded Asia Minor. Driven back by the ◊Hittites, they settled all over mainland

Greece, later being supplanted by the ◊Achaeans.

Ionian Islands /aɪˈəʊnɪən/ (Greek *Ionioi Nisoi*) island group off the W coast of Greece; area 860 sq km/332 sq mi. A British protectorate from 1815 until their cession to Greece 1864, they include: *Cephalonia* (Kefallínia); *Corfu* (Kérkyra, a Venetian possession 1386–1797); *Cythera* (Kithira); *Ithaca* (Itháki, the traditional home of ◊Odysseus); *Leukas* (Levkás); *Paxos* (Paxoí); *Zante* (Zákynthos).

Ionian Sea /aɪˈəʊnɪən/ the part of the Mediterranean which lies between Italy and Greece, to the S of the Adriatic, and containing the Ionian islands.

ionic bond another name for ◊electrovalent bond.

ionization chamber device for measuring the amount of ionizing radiation. The radiation ionizes gas in the chamber and the ions are collected and measured as an electric charge.

ionization potential a measure of the energy required to remove an ◊electron from an ◊atom. Elements with a low ionization potential readily lose electrons to form ◊cations.

ionizing radiation radiation which knocks electrons from atoms during its passage, thereby leaving ions in its path. Electrons and alpha-particles are much more ionizing than are neutrons or ◊gamma radiation.

ionosphere ionized layer of Earth's outer ◊atmosphere (60–1,000 km/38–620 mi) that contains sufficient free electrons to modify the way in which radio waves are propagated, for instance by reflecting them back to Earth. The ionosphere is thought to be produced by absorption of the Sun's ultraviolet radiation.

ion plating method of applying corrosion-resistant metal coatings. The article is placed in argon gas, together with some coating metal, which vaporizes on heating and becomes ionized (acquires charged atoms) as it diffuses through the gas to form the coating. It has important applications in the aerospace industry.

IOU short for 'I owe you'; written acknowledgment of debt, signed by the debtor; see also ◊Bill of Exchange.

IOW abbreviation for ◊*Isle of Wight*.

Iowa /'aɪəwə/ state of the midwest USA; nickname Hawkeye State
area 145,800 sq km/56,279 sq mi
capital Des Moines
towns Cedar Rapids, Davenport, Sioux City
features Grant Wood Gallery in Davenport and Herbert Hoover birthplace in West Branch
products cereals, soya beans, meat, wool, chemicals, machinery, electrical goods
population (1984) 2,837,000
famous people Buffalo Bill Cody
history part of the ◊Louisiana Purchase 1803, it remains an area of small farms; it became a state 1846.

ipecacuanha South American plant *Psychotria ipecacuanha*, family Rubiaceae, used as an emetic and in treating amoebic dysentery.

Iphigenia /ɪˌfɪdʒɪ'naɪə/ in Greek mythology, the daughter of ◊Agamemnon and Clytemnestra.

Ipoh capital of Perak state, Peninsular Malaysia; population (1980) 301,000. The economy is based on tin mining.

ipso facto (Latin) by that very fact.

Ipswich /'ɪpswɪtʃ/ river port on the Orwell estuary, administrative headquarters of Suffolk, England; population (1981) 120,500. Industries include engineering and the manufacture of textiles, plastics, and electrical goods. Home of the painter Thomas Gainsborough.

IQ intelligence quotient. It is the ratio between a subject's 'mental age' and chronological age, multiplied by 100. 100 is considered average. See ◊intelligence testing.

Iqbāl /'ɪkbæl/ Muhammad 1875–1938. Islamic poet and thinker. His literary works, in Urdu and Persian, were mostly verse in the classical style, suitable for public recitation. He sought through his writings to arouse Muslims to take their place in the modern world.

His most celebrated work, the Persian *Asrā-e khūdī/Secrets of the Self* 1915, put forward a theory of the self which was the opposite of the traditional abnegation of Islam. He was an influence on the movement which led to the creation of Pakistan.

Iquique /ɪ'kiːkeɪ/ city and seaport in N Chile, capital of the province of Tarapaca; population (1985) 120,700. It exports nitrate of soda, from its desert region.

Iquitos /ɪ'kiːtɒs/ river port on the Amazon, Peru, also a tourist centre for the rainforest; population (1988) 248,000.

i.r. in physics, abbreviation for *infrared*.

IRA abbreviation for ◊Irish Republican Army.

Iráklion /ɪ'ræklɪən/ or *Heraklion* largest city and capital (since 1971) of Crete, Greece; population (1981) 102,000.

Iran /ɪ'rɑːn/ country in SW Asia, bounded to the N by the USSR and the Caspian Sea, to the E by Afghanistan and Pakistan, to the S and SW by the Gulf of Oman, to the W by Iraq, and to the NW by Turkey.

government The constitution, which came into effect on the overthrow of the shah in 1979, provides for a president elected by universal suffrage, and a single-chamber legislature, the Islamic Consultative Assembly *Majlis*, of 270 members, similarly elected. The president and the assembly serve a four-year term. All legislation passed by the assembly must be sent to the council for the protection of the constitution, consisting of six religious and six secular lawyers, to ensure that it complies with Islamic precepts. The president is the executive head of government but, like the assembly, ultimately subject to the will of the religious leader. Although a number of political parties exist, Iran is fundamentally a one-party state, the Islamic Republican Party having been founded in 1978 to bring about the Islamic revolution.

history The name Iran is derived from the Aryan tribes, including the Medes and Persians, who overran Persia (see ◊Persia, ancient) from 1600 BC. ◊Cyrus the Great, who seized the Median throne 550, formed an empire including Babylonia, Syria, and Asia Minor, to which Egypt, Thrace, and Macedonia were later added. It was conquered by Alexander the Great 334–328, then passed to his general Seleucus (*c.*358–280) and his descendants until overrun in the 3rd century BC by the Parthians. The Parthian dynasty was overthrown AD 226 by Ardashir, founder of the ◊Sassanian Empire.

During 633–41 Persia was conquered for Islam by the Arabs, and then in 1037–55 came under the ◊Seljuk Turks. Their empire broke up 12th century and was conquered in the 13th by the ◊Mongols. After 1334 Persia was again divided until its conquest by ◊Tamerlane in the 1380s. A period of violent disorder in the later 15th century was ended by the accession of the Safavi dynasty, who ruled 1499–1736, but were deposed by the great warrior Nadir Shah (ruled 1736–47), whose death was followed by a confused period until the accession of the Qajar dynasty (1794–1925).

During the 18th century Persia was threatened by Russian expansion, culminating in the loss of Georgia 1801 and a large part of Armenia 1828. Persian claims on Herat, Afghanistan, led to war with Britain 1856–57. Revolutions in 1905 and 1909 resulted in the establishment of a parliamentary regime. During World War I the country was occupied by British and Russian forces. An officer, Col Reza Khan, seized power 1921, and a coup 1925 made him the shah, allowing him to carry out a massive programme of modernization to bring Persia, as it was then called, into the 20th century.

During World War II, Iran was occupied by British, US, and Soviet troops until 1946. Anti-British and anti-American feeling grew and in 1951 the newly elected prime minister, Dr Muhammad Mossadeq, obtained legislative approval for the nationalization of Iran's largely foreign-owned petroleum industry. With US connivance, he was deposed in a 1953 coup and the dispute over nationalization was settled the following year when oil-drilling concessions were granted to a consortium of eight companies. The shah took complete control of the government and during 1965–77 Iran enjoyed a period of political stability and economic growth, based on oil revenue.

In 1975 the shah had introduced a one-party system, based on the Iran National Resurgence Party *Rastakhis*, but opposition to his regime was growing. The most effective opposition came from the religious leader, Ayatollah Khomeini, who

Iran-Iraq War

Iran–Iraq War

area seized, then lost by Iraq (1980-82)   ■ capitals
area seized, then lost by Iran (1986-88)

campaigned from exile in France. He demanded a return to the principles of Islam and pressure on the shah became so great that in 1979 he left the country, leaving the way open for Khomeini's return. He appointed a provisional government but power was placed essentially in the hands of the 15-member Islamic Revolutionary Council, controlled by Khomeini.

Iran was declared an Islamic republic and a new constitution, based on Islamic principles, was adopted. Relations with the USA were badly affected when a group of Iranian students took 63 Americans hostage at the US embassy in Tehran, demanding that the shah return to face trial. Even the death of the shah, in Egypt 1980, did little to resolve the crisis, which ended when all the hostages were released Jan 1981.

In its early years several rifts developed within the new Islamic government and although by 1982 some stability had been attained, disputes between factions developed again in the years that followed. Externally, the war with Iraq, which broke out 1980 after a border dispute, continued with considerable loss of life on both sides. Meanwhile, Islamic law was becoming stricter, with amputation as the penalty for theft and flogging for minor sexual offences. By 1985 the failure to end the Gulf War and the harshness of the Islamic codes were increasing opposition to Khomeini's regime but his position remained secure. By 1987 both sides in the war had increased the scale of their operations, each apparently believing that outright victory was possible. A ceasefire was agreed in 1988.

Full diplomatic relations with the UK were restored Dec 1988, but the application of a death threat to the author Salman ◊Rushdie caused a severance Mar 1989. Khomeini died June 1989 and a struggle for succession began, ending with the confirmation of the former Speaker of the *Majlis*, Hoshemi Rafsanjani, as president with increased powers. Despite his reputation for moderation and pragmatism, Iran's relations with the West, and particularly the UK, were slow to improve.

Irangate or *Contragate* US political scandal involving senior members of the Reagan administration.

Arms, including Hawk missiles, were sold to Iran via Israel (at a time when the USA was publicly calling for a worldwide ban on sending arms to Iran), violating the law prohibiting the sale of US weapons for resale to a third country listed as a 'terrorist nation', as well as the law requiring sales above $14 million to be reported to Congress. The negotiator in the field was Col Oliver North, a military aide to the National Security Council, reporting in the White House to the national-security adviser (first Robert McFarlane, then John Poindexter). North and his hired help were also channelling donations to the Contras from individuals and from other countries, including $2 million from Taiwan, $10 million from the sultan of Brunei, and $32 million from Saudi Arabia.

The Congressional Joint Investigative Committee reported, in Nov 1987, that the president bore 'ultimate responsibility' for allowing a 'cabal of zealots' to seize control of the administration's policy, but found no firm evidence that President Reagan had actually been aware of the Contra diversion. North was tried and convicted in May 1989 on charges of obstructing Congress and unlawfully destroying government documents. Poindexter was found guilty on all counts in 1990.

Iranian language the main language of Iran, more commonly known as ◊Persian or Farsi.

Iran-Iraq War or *Gulf War* war between Iran and Iraq 1980–88, claimed by the former to have begun with the Iraq offensive 21 Sept 1980, and by the latter with the Iranian shelling of border posts 4 Sept 1980. Occasioned by a boundary dispute over the ◊Shatt-al-Arab waterway, it fundamentally arose because of Iran's encouragement of the

Iraq
Republic of
(al Jumhouriya al 'Iraqia)

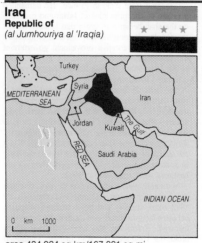

area 434,924 sq km/167,881 sq mi
capital Baghdad
towns Mosul and port of Basra
physical mountains in N, desert in W; wide valley of rivers Tigris and Euphrates NW–SE
features reed architecture of the marsh Arabs; sites of Eridu, Babylon, Nineveh, Ur, Ctesiphon
head of state and government Saddam Hussein At-Takriti from 1979
political system effective one-party socialist republic
political parties Arab Baath Socialist Party, nationalist socialist
exports dates (80% of world supply), wool, oil
currency Iraqi dinar (0.53 = £1 Feb 1990)
population (1987) 17,093,000; annual growth rate 3.6%
life expectancy men 62, women 63
language Arabic (official)
religion Shi'ite Muslim 60%, Sunni Muslim 30%, Christian 3%
literacy 68% male/32% female (1980 est)
GNP $31 bn (1981); $2,410 per head of population
chronology
1920 Iraq became a British League of Nations protectorate.
1921 Hashemite dynasty established, with Faisal I as king.
1932 Achieved full independence.
1958 Monarchy overthrown and Iraq became a republic.
1968 Military coup puts Gen al-Bakr in power.
1979 Al-Bakr replaced by Saddam Hussein.
1980 Gulf War between Iraq and Iran broke out.
1985 Gulf War fighting intensified. UN secretary-general's peace moves were unsuccessful.
1988 Ceasefire in Gulf War, talks began with Iran. Iraq accused of using chemical weapons. Harsh repression of Kurdish rebels seeking greater autonomy.
1989 Unsuccessful coup against President Hussein.

Shi'ite majority in Iraq to rise against the Sunni government of Saddam Hussein. An estimated 1 million people died in the war.

The war's course was marked by offensive and counter-offensive, interspersed with extended periods of stalemate. Chemical weapons were used, cities and the important oil installations of the area were the target for bombing raids and rocket attacks, and international shipping came under fire in the Persian Gulf (including in 1987 the US frigate *Stark*, which was attacked by the Iraqi airforce). Among Arab states, Iran was supported by Libya and Syria, the remainder supporting Iraq. Iran also benefited from secret US arms shipments, the disclosure of which in 1986 led to considerable scandal in the USA (◊Irangate). The intervention of the USA 1987, ostensibly to keep the sea lanes open, but seen by Iran as support for Iraq, heightened, rather than reduced, tension in the Gulf, and United Nations attempts to obtain a ceasefire failed. The war ended in Aug 1988 after ceasefire talks in Geneva.

Iraq /ɪˈrɑːk/ country in SW Asia, bounded to the N by Turkey, to the E by Iran, to the S by the Persian Gulf, Kuwait, and Saudi Arabia, to the SW by Jordan, and to the W by Syria.

government The 1970 constitution, amended in 1973, 1974, and 1980, provides for a president who is head of state, prime minister, and chair of a Revolutionary Command Council (RCC). Day-to-day administration is under the control of a council of ministers over which the president also presides. The president is also regional secretary of the Arab Ba'ath Socialist Party which, although not the only political party in Iraq, so dominates the country's institutions as to make it virtually a one-party state. In 1980 elections took place for the first 250-member national assembly. Elections for a second assembly were held 1984. On both occasions the Ba'ath Party dominated the results. In effect, therefore, Iraq is ruled by the Arab Ba'ath Socialist Party through its regional secretary and other leading members.

history The area now occupied by Iraq was formerly ancient Mesopotamia, and was the centre of the Sumerian, Babylonian, and Assyrian civilizations 6000 BC–AD 100. It was conquered 114 by the Romans, and was ruled 266–632 by the native Sassanids before being invaded 633 by the Arabs. In 1065 the country was taken over by the Turks, and was invaded by the Mongols 1258, Baghdad being destroyed 1401 by Tamerlane. Annexed by Suleiman the Magnificent 1533, Iraq became part of the Turkish Ottoman Empire 1638.

Occupied by Britain in World War I, Iraq was placed under British administration by the League of Nations 1920. It was the start of a long and generally amicable relationship. In 1932 Iraq became a fully independent kingdom and in 1933 the reigning king, Faisal I, died and was succeeded by his son, Ghazi. The leading figure behind the throne was the strongly pro-Western Gen Nuri-el-Said, who was prime minister 1930–58. In 1939 King Ghazi was killed in a motor accident and Faisal II became king at the age of three, his uncle Prince Abdul Ilah acting as regent until 1953 when the king assumed full powers.

In 1955 Iraq signed the Baghdad Pact, a regional collective security agreement, with the USSR seen as the main potential threat, and in 1958 joined Jordan in an Arab Federation, with King Faisal as head of state. In July of that year, a revolution overthrew the monarchy and King Faisal, Prince Abdul Ilah, and Gen Nuri were all killed. The constitution was suspended and Iraq was declared a republic, with Brig Abdul Karim Kassem as head of a left-wing military regime. He withdrew from the Baghdad Pact 1959 and, after tenuously holding power for five years, was killed 1963 in a coup led by Col Salem Aref, who established a new government, ended martial law, and within two years had introduced a civilian administration. He died in an air crash 1966 and his brother, who succeeded him, was ousted 1968 and replaced by Maj-Gen al-Bakr. He concentrated power in the hands of a Revolutionary Command Council (RCC), and made himself head of state, head of government, and chair of the RCC. In 1979 Saddam Hussain, who for several years had been the real power in Iraq, replaced al-Bakr as RCC chair and state president. In 1980 he introduced a National Charter, reaffirming a policy of ◊nonalignment and a constitution that provided for an elected national assembly. The first elections took place that year.

Iraq had, since 1970, enjoyed a fluctuating relationship with Syria, sometimes distant and sometimes close enough to contemplate a complete political and economic union. By 1980, however, the atmosphere was cool. Relations between Iraq and Iran had been tense for some years, with disagreement about the border between them, which runs down the Shatt-al-Arab waterway. The 1979 Iranian revolution made Iraq more suspicious of Iran's intentions and in 1980 a full-scale war broke out. Despite Iraq's inferior military strength, Iran gained little territory and by 1986 it seemed as if a stalemate might have been reached. The fighting intensified again in late 1986 and early 1987, by which time hundreds of thousands of lives had been lost on both sides and incalculable damage to industry and property sustained. The war came to an end 1988. In 1989 an unsuccessful coup attempt against President Hussein was reported.

IRCAM abbreviation of the French *Institut de Recherche et de Coordination Acoustique-Musique* organization in Paris for research into electronic music, using computers, synthesizers, and so on; founded 1976. Its director is Pierre ◊Boulez.

Ireland /ˈaɪələnd/ one of the British Isles, lying to the west of Great Britain, from which it is separated by the Irish Sea. It comprises the provinces of Ulster, Leinster, Munster, and Connacht, and is divided between the Republic of Ireland, which occupies the south, central, and northwest of the island, and Northern Ireland, which occupies the northeast corner and forms part of the United Kingdom.

The centre of Ireland is a lowland, about 60–120 m/200–400 ft above sea level, hills are mainly around the coasts, though there are a few peaks over 1,000 m/3,000 ft high, the highest being Carrantuohill ('the inverted reaping hook'), 1,040 m/3,415 ft, in Macgillicuddy's Reeks, County Kerry. The entire western coastline is an intricate alternation of bays and estuaries. Several of the rivers flow in sluggish courses through the central lowland, and then cut through fjord-like valleys to the sea. The ◊Shannon in particular falls 30 m/100 ft in its last 26 km/16 mi above Limerick, and is used to produce hydroelectric power.

The lowland bogs which cover parts of central Ireland are intermingled with fertile limestone country where dairy farming is the chief occupation. The bogs are an important source of fuel, in the form of ◊peat, Ireland being poorly supplied with coal.

The climate is mild, moist, and changeable. The annual rainfall on the lowlands varies from 76 cm/30 in in the east to 203 cm/80 in in some western districts, but much higher falls are recorded in the mountains.

Ireland: counties

County	Administrative headquarters	Area sq km
Ulster province		
Antrim	Belfast	2,830
Armagh	Armagh	1,250
Down	Downpatrick	2,470
Fermanagh	Enniskillen	1,680
Londonderry	Derry	2,070
Tyrone	Omagh	3,160
	NORTHERN IRELAND	13,460
Cavan	Cavan	1,890
Donegal	Lifford	4,830
Monaghan	Monaghan	1,290
Munster province		
Clare	Ennis	3,190
Cork	Cork	7,460
Kerry	Tralee	4,700
Limerick	Limerick	2,690
Tipperary (N)	Nenagh	2,000
Tipperary (S)	Clonmel	2,260
Waterford	Waterford	1,840
Leinster province		
Carlow	Carlow	900
Dublin	Dublin	920
Kildare	Naas	1,690
Kilkenny	Kilkenny	2,060
Laoighis	Portlaoise	1,720
Longford	Longford	1,040
Louth	Dundalk	820
Meath	Trim	2,340

Offaly	Tullamore	2,000
Westmeath	Mullingar	1,760
Wexford	Wexford	2,350
Wicklow	Wicklow	2,030
Connacht province		
Galway	Galway	5,940
Leitrim	Carrick-on-Shannon	1,530
Mayo	Castlebar	5,400
Roscommon	Roscommon	2,460
Sligo	Sligo	1,800
REPUBLIC OF IRELAND		68,910

Ireland: history in prehistoric times Ireland underwent a number of invasions from Europe, the most important of which was that of the Gaels in the 3rd century BC. Gaelic Ireland was divided into kingdoms, nominally subject to an *Ardri* or High King; the chiefs were elected under the tribal or Brehon law, and were usually at war with one another. Christianity was introduced by St ◊Patrick about 432, and during the 5th and 6th centuries Ireland became the home of a civilization which sent out missionaries to Britain and Europe. From about 800 the Danes began to raid Ireland, and later founded Dublin and other coastal towns, until they were defeated by Brian Boru (king from 976) at Clontarf 1014.

Anglo-Norman adventurers invaded Ireland 1167, but by the end of the medieval period English rule was still confined to the Pale, the territory around Dublin. The Tudors adopted a policy of conquest, confiscation of Irish land, and plantation by English settlers, and further imposed the ◊Reformation and English law on Ireland. The most important of the plantations was that of Ulster, carried out under James I 1610. In 1641 the Irish took advantage of the developing struggle in England between king and parliament to begin a revolt which was crushed by Oliver ◊Cromwell 1649, the estates of all 'rebels' being confiscated. Another revolt 1689–91 was also defeated, and the Roman Catholic majority held down by penal laws. In 1739–41 a famine killed one-third of the population of 1.5 million. The subordination of the Irish parliament to that of England, and of Irish economic interests to English, led to the rise of a Protestant patriot party, which in 1782 forced the British government to remove many commercial restrictions and grant the Irish parliament its independence. This did not satisfy the population, who in 1798, influenced by French revolutionary ideas, rose in rebellion, but were again defeated; and in 1800 William ◊Pitt induced the Irish parliament to vote itself out of existence by the Act of ◊Union, effective 1 Jan 1801, which gave Ireland parliamentary representation at Westminster. During another famine 1845–46, 1.5 million people emigrated, mostly to the USA. By the 1880s there was a strong movement for home rule for Ireland; Gladstone supported it but

Atlantic Ocean

Northern Ireland

Protestant majority

R. Catholic majority

Ireland, Republic of
(Irish *Éire*)

area 68,900 sq km/26,595 sq mi
capital Dublin
towns ports Cork, Dún Laoghaire, Limerick, Waterford
physical central plateau with hills; rivers Shannon, Liffey, Boyne
features Bog of Allen, source of domestic and national power; Magillicuddy's Reeks, Wicklow Mountains; Lough Corrib, lakes of Killarney; Galway Bay and Aran Islands; heavy rainfall
head of state Patrick J Hillery from 1976
head of government Charles Haughey from 1987
political system democratic republic
political parties Fianna Fáil (Soldiers of Destiny), moderate centre-right; Fine Gael (Irish Tribe), moderate centre-left; Labour Party, moderate left-of-centre; Progressive Democrats, radical free-enterprise
exports livestock, dairy products, Irish whiskey, microelectronic components and assemblies, mining and engineering products, chemicals,

tobacco, clothing; tourism is important
currency punt (1.08 = £1 Feb 1990)
population (1988) 3,540,000; annual growth rate 1.2%
life expectancy men 70, women 76
language Irish and English (both official)
religion Roman Catholic
literacy 99% (1984)
GNP $16.5 (1983); $4,750 per head of population
chronology
1916 Easter Rising: nationalists seized the Dublin general post office and proclaimed a republic. The revolt was suppressed by the British army and most of the leaders were executed.
1918–21 Guerrilla warfare against British army led to split in rebel forces.
1921 Anglo-Irish Treaty resulted in creation of the Irish Free State (Southern Ireland).
1937 Eire established as an independent state.
1949 Eire left the Commonwealth and became the Republic of Ireland.
1973 Fianna Fáil defeated after 40 years in office. Liam Cosgrave formed a coalition government.
1977 Fianna Fáil returned to power, with Jack Lynch as prime minister.
1979 Lynch resigned and was succeeded by Charles Haughey.
1981 Garret FitzGerald formed a coalition.
1983 New Ireland Forum formed, but rejected by the British government.
1985 Anglo-Irish Agreement signed.
1986 Protests by Ulster Unionists against the agreement.
1987 General election won by Charles Haughey.
1988 Relations with UK at low ebb because of disagreement over extradition decisions.
1989 Haughey failed to win a majority in the general election. Progressive Democrats (a breakaway party of Fianna Fáil) given cabinet positions in a coalition government.

was defeated by the British parliament. By 1914, home rule was conceded but World War I delayed implementation. The ***Easter Rising*** took place in Apr 1916, when nationalists seized the Dublin general post office and proclaimed a republic. After a week of fighting, the revolt was suppressed by the British army and most of the leaders executed. From 1918–21 there was guerrilla warfare against the British army, especially by the Irish Republican Army (*IRA), formed by Michael Collins 1919. This led to a split in the rebel forces, but in 1921 the Anglo-Irish Treaty resulted in partition and the creation of the Irish Free State in S Ireland. For history since that date, see ◊Ireland, Republic of; ◊Ireland, Northern.

Ireland, Northern /ˈaɪələnd/ constituent part of the UK
area 13,460 sq km/5,196 sq mi
capital Belfast
towns Londonderry, Enniskillen, Omagh, Newry, Armagh, Coleraine
features Mourne mountains, Belfast Lough and Lough Neagh; Giant's Causeway; comprises the six counties (Antrim, Armagh, Down, Fermanagh, Londonderry, and Tyrone) that form part of Ireland's northernmost province of Ulster
exports engineering, especially shipbuilding including textile machinery, aircraft components; linen and synthetic textiles; processed foods, especially dairy and poultry products—all affected by the 1980s depression and political unrest
currency as for the rest of the UK
population (1986) 1,567,000
language English
religion Protestant 54%, Roman Catholic 31%
famous people Montgomery, Alanbrooke
government because of the outbreak of violence, there has been direct rule from the UK

since 1972. Northern Ireland is entitled to send 12 members to the Westminster Parliament.

Under the Anglo-Irish Agreement 1985, the Republic of Ireland was given a consultative role (via an Anglo-Irish conference) in the government of Northern Ireland, but agreed that there should be no change in its status except by majority consent, and that there should be greater cooperation against terrorism. The agreement was approved by Parliament, but all 12 Ulster members gave up their seats, so that by-elections could be fought as a form of 'referendum' on the views of the province itself. A similar boycotting of the Northern Ireland Assembly since the Anglo-Irish agreement led to its dissolution 1986 by the UK government.

history for history pre-1921, see ◊Ireland, history. The creation of Northern Ireland dates from 1921 when the mainly Protestant counties of Ulster withdrew from the newly established Irish Free State. Spasmodic outbreaks of violence by the ◊IRA continued, but only in 1968–69 were there serious disturbances arising from Protestant political dominance and discrimination against the Roman Catholic minority in employment and housing. British troops were sent to restore peace and protect Catholics, but disturbances continued and in 1972 the parliament at Stormont was prorogued, and superseded by direct rule from Westminster.

Ireland, Republic of country occupying the main part of the island of Ireland, off the NW coast of Europe. It is bounded to the E by the Irish Sea, to the S and W by the Atlantic, and to the NE by Northern Ireland.

government The 1937 constitution provides for a president, elected by universal suffrage for a seven-year term, and a two-chamber national parliament, consisting of a senate *Seanad Eireann* and a house of representatives *Dail Eireann*, serving a five-year term. The senate has 60 members, 11 nominated by the prime minister (*Taoiseach*) and 49 elected by panels representative of most aspects of Irish life. The *Dail* consists of 166 members elected by universal suffrage through a system of proportional representation.

The president appoints a prime minister who nominated by the *Dail*, which is subject to dissolution by the president if the cabinet loses its confidence within the five-year term. Proportional representation encourages the existence of several parties, the most significant being ◊Fianna Fail, Fine Gael (United Ireland Party), the Labour Party, and the Progressive Democrats.

history For history pre-1921, see ◊Ireland, history. In 1921 a treaty gave S Ireland dominion status within the Commonwealth, while six out of the nine counties of Ulster remained part of the UK, with limited self-government. The Irish Free State, as S Ireland was formally called 1922, was accepted by IRA leader Michael Collins but not by many of his colleagues, who shifted their allegiance to Fianna Fail leader, Eamonn ◊de Valera, who eventually acknowledged the partition as well, in 1937 when a new constitution established the country as a sovereign state under the name of Eire.

The IRA continued its fight for an independent, unified Ireland through a campaign of violence, mainly in Northern Ireland but also on the British mainland and, to a lesser extent, in the Irish republic. Eire remained part of the Commonwealth until 1949, when it left, declaring itself the Republic of Ireland, while Northern Ireland remained a constituent part of the UK.

In 1973 Fianna Fail, having held office for over 40 years, was defeated and Liam Cosgrave formed a coalition of the Fine Gael and Labour parties. In 1977 Fianna Fail returned to power, with Jack Lynch as prime minister. In 1979 IRA violence intensified with the killing of Earl Mountbatten in Ireland and 18 British soldiers in Northern Ireland. Lynch resigned later the same year and was succeeded by Charles Haughey. His aim was a united Ireland, with considerable independence for the six northern counties. After the 1981 election Garrett FitzGerald, leader of Fine Gael, formed another coalition with Labour, but was defeated the following year on budget proposals and resigned. Haughey returned to office with a minority government, but he, too, had to resign later that year, resulting in the return of FitzGerald.

In 1983 all the main Irish and Northern Irish political parties initiated the New Ireland Forum as a vehicle for discussion. Its report was rejected by Margaret Thatcher's Conservative government in the UK but discussions between London and Dublin resulted in the signing of the Anglo-Irish Agreement 1985, providing for regular consultation and exchange of information on political, legal, security, and cross-border matters. The agreement also said that the status of Northern Ireland would not be changed without the consent of a majority of the people. The agreement was criticized by the Unionist parties of Northern Ireland, who asked that it be rescinded.

FitzGerald's coalition ended 1986, and the Feb 1987 election again returned Fianna Fail and Charles Haughey. In 1988 relations between the Republic of Ireland and the UK were at a low ebb because of disagreements over extradition decisions. In 1989, Haughey failed to win a majority at the election, and entered into a coalition with the Progressive Democrats (a breakaway party from Fianna Fail), putting two of their members into the cabinet.

Ireland /ˈaɪələnd/ John (Nicholson) 1879–1962. English composer. His works include the mystic orchestral prelude *The Forgotten Rite* 1917 and the piano solo *Sarnia* 1941. Benjamin ◊Britten was his pupil.

Irene /aɪˈriːni/ in Greek mythology, goddess of peace (Roman Pax).

Ireton *A supporter and son-in-law of Oliver Cromwell, English general Henry Ireton fought in several major Civil War battles.*

Irene, St /aɪˈriːni/ *c.* 752–*c.* 803. Byzantine emperor 797–802. The wife of Leo IV (750–780), she became regent for their son Constantine (771–805) on Leo's death. In 797 she deposed her son, had his eyes put out, and assumed full title of *basileus* (emperor), ruling in her own right until deposed and exiled to Lesvos by a revolt of 802. She was made a saint by the Greek Orthodox church for her attacks on iconoclasts.

Ireton /ˈaɪətən/ Henry 1611–1651. English Civil War general. He joined the Parliamentary forces and fought at ◊Edgehill 1642, Gainsborough 1643, and ◊Naseby 1645. After the Battle of Naseby, Ireton, who was opposed to the extreme republicans and ◊Levellers, strove for a compromise with Charles I, but then played a leading role in his trial and execution. He married his leader Cromwell's daughter in 1646. Lord Deputy in Ireland from 1650, he died after the capture of Limerick.

Irgun short for *Irgun Zvai Leumi* (National Military Society), a Jewish guerrilla group active against the British administration in Palestine 1946–48. Their bombing of the King David Hotel in Jerusalem 22 July 1946 cost 91 lives.

Irian Jaya /ˈɪriən ˈdʒaɪə/ the western portion of the island of New Guinea, part of Indonesia
area 420,000 sq km/162,000 sq mi
capital Jayapura
population (1980) 1,174,000
history part of the Dutch East Indies 1828 as Western New Guinea; retained by Netherlands after Indonesian independence 1949, but ceded to Indonesia 1963 by the United Nations and remained part of Indonesia by an 'Act of Free Choice' 1969; in the 1980s 283,500 hectares/700,000 acres were given over to Indonesia's controversial *transmigration programme* for the resettlement of farming families from overcrowded Java, causing destruction of rainforests and displacing indigenous people.

iridium an element, symbol Ir, atomic number 77, relative atomic mass 192.2. It is a metal of the platinum family, white, very hard and brittle, and usually alloyed with platinum or osmium. It is used for points of fountain-pen nibs, compass bearings, parts of scientific apparatus, surgical tools and electrical goods.

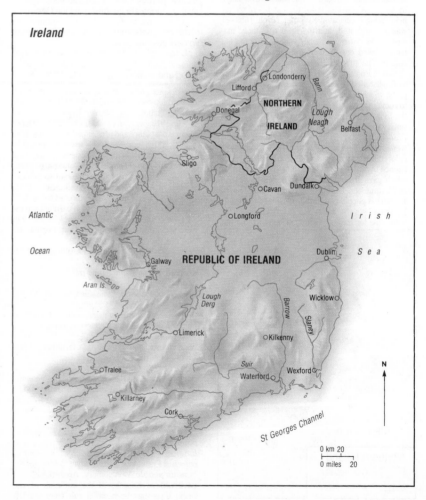

Ireland

iris

Under neutron bombardment, iridium becomes a useful source of ◊gamma radiation for industrial radiography, especially for steel up to 5 cm/2 in thick, its half-life being 74 days. Layers in the Earth's crust which are rich in iridium are thought to derive from the impact of meteorites. Iridium was first definitely identified by Smithson Tennant (1761–1815) in 1804.

iris in physiology, the coloured muscular diaphragm that controls size of the pupil in the vertebrate eye. It contains radial muscle which increases the pupil diameter and circular muscle which constricts pupil diameter. Both types of muscle respond involuntarily to light intensity.

iris in botany, perennial northern temperate flowering plants, family Iridaceae. The leaves are usually sword-shaped; the purple, white or yellow flowers have three upright inner petals and three outward- and downward-curving sepals.

The wild *yellow iris* or *flag Iris pseudoacorus* is a true water plant but adapts to border conditions. Many cultivated varieties derive from *Iris germanica*. *Orris root*, used in perfumery, is the violet scented underground stem of the S European iris *Iris florentina*. The ◊crocus also belongs to this family.

Irish Gaelic first official language of the Irish Republic, but much less widely used than the second official language, English. See ◊Gaelic language.

Irish language a common name for Irish ◊Gaelic. At one time, especially in the form 'Erse', also a name for the Gaelic of Scotland.

Irish literature early Irish literature, in Gaelic, consists of the sagas, which are mainly in prose, and a considerable body of verse. The chief cycles are that of Ulster, which deals with the mythological ◊Conchobar and his followers, and the Ossianic, which has influenced European literature through ◊MacPherson's version.

Early Irish poetry has a unique lyric quality and consists mainly of religious verse and nature poetry, for example St Patrick's hymn, Ultán's hymn to St Brigit. Much pseudo-historical verse is also extant, ascribed to such poets as Mael Mura (9th century), Mac Liac (10th century), Flann Mainistrech (11th century). Religious literature in prose includes sermons, saints' lives, for example, those in the *Book of Lismore* and in the writings of Michael O'Clery (17th century), and visions. History is represented by annals and by isolated texts like the *Cogad Gaedel re Gallaib*, an account of the Viking invasions by an eye-witness. The 'official' or 'court' verse of the 13th to 17th centuries was produced by a succession of professional poets, notably Tadhg Dall O' Huiginn (died about 1617) and Donnchadh Mór O'Dálaigh (died 1244); and Geoffrey Keating (died 1646) who wrote in both verse and prose.

The bardic schools ceased to exist by the end of the 17th century. Metre became accentual, and not as before syllabic. The greatest exponents of the new school were Egan O'Rahilly (early 18th century), and the religious poet Tadhg Gaelach O'Súilleabháin.

Irish National Liberation Army (INLA) guerrilla organization committed to the end of British rule in Northern Ireland and the incorporation of Ulster into the Irish Republic. The INLA was a 1974 offshoot of the Irish Republican Army. Among the INLA's activities was the killing of British politician Airey Neave in 1979.

Irish Republican Army (IRA) militant Irish nationalist organization, whose aim is to create a united Irish socialist republic including Ulster. The paramilitary wing of ◊Sinn Féin, it was founded 1919 by Michael ◊Collins, and fought a successful war against Britain 1919–21. It came to the fore again 1939 with a bombing campaign in Britain, and was declared illegal in Eire. Its activities intensified from 1968 onwards, as the civil-rights disorders in Northern Ireland developed. In 1970 a group in the north broke away to become the *Provisional IRA*; their commitment is to the expulsion of the British from Northern Ireland. In 1974 a further breakaway occurred, of the left-wing Irish Republican Socialist Party with its paramilitary wing, the Irish National Liberation Army.

The IRA is committed to the use of force in trying to achieve its objectives, and it regularly carries out bombings and shootings. In 1979 it murdered Lord ◊Mountbatten, and its bomb attacks in Britain have included: Birmingham, Guildford, and Woolwich pub bombs 1974; Chelsea Barracks, London, 1981; Harrods department store, London, 1983; and Brighton 1984 (an attempt to kill members of the UK cabinet during the Conservative Party conference). The IRA admitted responsibility for the Remembrance Day bomb explosion in Enniskillen 1987.

Irish Sweepstake a ◊lottery run by the Irish government, on three horse races each year, with proceeds going to the nursing services. The best known race is the Irish Derby.

Irkutsk /ɪə'kutsk/ city in S USSR; population (1987) 609,000. It produces coal, iron, steel, and machine tools. Founded 1652, it began to grow after the Trans-Siberian railway reached it 1898.

iron the most widely found metal, after aluminium; symbol Fe (Latin *ferrum*), atomic number 26, relative atomic mass 55.85. Iron is the basis of all steel, and as well as its constructional uses, when mixed with carbon and other elements, it has important chemical applications. In electrical equipment, it forms the basis of all permanent magnets and electromagnets, and the cores of transformers and magnetic amplifiers. See also ◊cast iron.

Iron is said to have first been worked into implements by the Egyptians about 3000 BC. It is extracted from four main iron ores. It is used for anodes in electronic rectifiers because it is not corroded by mercury. Traces of iron salts in glass give a sharp cut-off for ultraviolet rays. Iron is also an essential component of haemoglobin, the molecule in the blood of animals which helps absorb oxygen. A deficiency of iron in the diet causes a form of anaemia.

Iron Age the period when weapons and tools were made from iron. Iron was produced in Thailand by about 1600 BC but was considered inferior in strength to bronze until about 1000 BC when metallurgical techniques improved and steel was produced by adding carbon during the smelting process.

ironbark any species of ◊eucalyptus tree with hard tough bark.

Ironbridge Gorge /'aɪənbrɪdʒ/ site, near Telford New Town, Shropshire, England, of the Iron Bridge (1779), one of the first and most striking products of the Industrial Revolution in Britain: it is now part of an open-air museum of industrial archaeology.

ironclad a wooden warship covered with armour plate. The first to be constructed was the French *Gloire* 1858, but the first to be launched was the British HMS *Warrior* 1859. The first battle between ironclads took place during the American Civil War, when the Union *Monitor* fought the Confederate *Virginia* (formerly the *Merrimack*) 9 Mar 1862. The design was replaced by battleships of all-metal construction in the 1890s.

Iron Cross medal awarded for valour in the German armed forces. Instituted in Prussia 1813, it consists of a Maltese cross of iron, edged with silver.

Iron Curtain in Europe after World War II, the division between capitalist West and communist East. The term was first used by the UK prime minister Winston Churchill in a speech at Fulton, Missouri, USA, 1946.

Iron Gate Romanian *Porţile de Fier* narrow gorge, interrupted by rapids, in Romania. A hydroelectric scheme undertaken 1964–70 by Romania and Yugoslavia transformed this section of the river Danube into a 145 km/90 mi long lake and eliminated the rapids as a navigation hazard. Before flooding, in 1965, an archaeological survey revealed Europe's oldest urban settlement, ◊Lepenski Vir.

Iron Guard pro-fascist group controlling Romania in the 1930s. To counter its influence, King Carol II established a dictatorship 1938 but the Iron Guard forced him to abdicate 1940.

iron ore any mineral from which iron is extracted. The chief iron ores are ◊*magnetite*, a black oxide; ◊*hematite*, or kidney ore, a reddish oxide; ◊*limonite*, a black hydro-oxide; and *siderite*, a brownish carbonate.

Iron ores are found in a number of different forms, including distinct layers in igneous intrusions, as components of contact metamorphic rocks, and as sedimentary beds. Much of the world's iron is extracted in the USSR. Other important producers are the USA, Australia, France, Brazil, and Canada; over 40 countries produce significant quantities of ore.

iron pyrites FeS_2 a common iron ore. Brassy yellow, and occurring in cubic crystals, it resembles gold nuggets and is often called 'fool's gold'.

irony a literary technique that could be described as 'saying one thing and meaning another'. It can be traced through all periods of English literature, from the good-humoured and subtle irony of ◊Chaucer to the 20th-century writer's method for encountering nihilism and despair, as in Samuel Beckett's *Waiting for Godot*.

The Greek philosopher Plato used irony in his dialogues, in which Socrates elicits truth through a pretence of naivety. Sophocles' dramatic irony also has a high seriousness, as in *Oedipus Rex*, where Oedipus prays for the discovery and punishment of the city's polluter, little knowing that it is himself. Eighteenth-century scepticism provided a natural environment for irony, with ◊Swift using the device as a powerful weapon in *Gulliver's Travels* and elsewhere.

Iroquois /'ɪrəkwɔɪ/ confederation of North American Indians, the Six Nations (Cayuga, Mohawk, Oneida, Onondaga, and Seneca, with the Tuscarora from 1715), traditionally formed by Hiawatha (actually a priestly title) 1570.

irradiation in science, subjecting anything to radiation, including cancer tumours. Food can be sterilized by bombarding it with low-strength gamma rays. Although the process is now legal in several countries, uncertainty remains about possible long-term effects on consumers from irradiated food.

In the UK, irradiation treatment of food was banned 1967, but the European Commission has released a directive that will force the UK to drop its ban by 1992.

irrationalism a feature of many philosophies rather than a philosophical movement. Irrationalists deny that the world can be comprehended by conceptual thought, and often see the human mind as determined by unconscious forces.

irrational number a number that cannot be expressed as an exact ◊fraction. Irrational numbers include some square roots (for example, $\sqrt{2}$, $\sqrt{3}$ and $\sqrt{5}$ are irrational) and numbers such as π (the ratio of the circumference of a circle to its diameter, which is approximately equal to 3.14159) and e, the base of ◊natural logarithms (which is approximately 2.71828).

Irrawaddy /ˌɪrə'wɒdi/ (Burmese *Ayeryarwady*) chief river of Myanmar, flowing roughly N to S

Irving British actor-manager Henry Irving dominated the London stage for the last 30 years of Victoria's reign.

for 2,090 km/1,300 mi across the centre of the country into the Bay of Bengal. Its sources are the Mali and N'mai rivers; its chief tributaries are the Chindwin and Shweli.

irredentist a person who wishes to reclaim the lost territories of a state. The term derives from an Italian political party founded about 1878 with a view to incorporating Italian-speaking areas into the Italian state.

irrigation artificial water supply for dry agricultural areas by means of dams and channels. Irrigation has been practised for thousands of years, in Eurasia as well the Americas.

An example is the channelling of the annual Nile flood in Egypt, which has been done from earliest times to its present control by the Aswan High Dam. Drawbacks to irrigation are that it tends to concentrate salts, ultimately causing infertility, and rich river silt is retained at dams, to the impoverishment of the land and fisheries below them.

Irvine /'ɜːvɪn/ new town in Strathclyde, W Scotland; population (1984) 57,000. It overlooks the Isle of Arran, and is a holiday resort.

Irvine /'ɜːvɪn/ Andrew Robertson 1951– . British rugby union player who held the world record for the most points scored in senior international rugby with 301 (273 for Scotland, 28 for the British Lions) between 1972 and 1982.

Irving /'ɜːvɪŋ/ Henry. Stage name of John Brodribb 1838–1905. English actor. He established his reputation from 1871, chiefly at the Lyceum Theatre in London, where he became manager 1878. He staged a series of successful Shakespearean productions, including *Romeo and Juliet* 1882, with himself and Ellen ◊Terry playing the leading roles. In 1895 he was the first actor to be knighted.

Irving /'ɜːvɪŋ/ John 1942– . US novelist. His bizarre and funny novels include *The World According to Garp* 1978, a vivid comic tale about a novelist killed by a disappointed reader.

Irving /'ɜːvɪŋ/ Washington 1783–1859. US essayist and short-story writer. He published a mock-heroic *History of New York* in 1809, supposedly written by the Dutchman 'Diedrich Knickerbocker'. In 1815 he went to England where his publications include the *Sketch Book of Geoffrey Crayon, Gent.* 1820, which contained such stories as 'Rip van Winkle' and 'The Legend of Sleepy Hollow'.

Isaac /'aɪzək/ in the Old Testament, Hebrew patriarch, son of ◊Abraham and Sarah, and father of Esau and Jacob.

Isaacs /'aɪzəks/ Alick 1921–1967. Scottish virologist who with Jean Lindemann, discovered ◊interferon in 1957; a naturally occurring

substance found in cells infected with viruses. The full implications of this discovery are still being investigated.

Isaacs began his career by studying different strains of the influenza virus and the body's response to them. In 1950 he became head of the World Influenza Centre in London.

Isabella /ˌɪzə'belə/ two Spanish queens:

Isabella I *the Catholic* 1451–1504. Queen of Castile from 1474, after the death of her brother Henry IV. By her marriage with Ferdinand of Aragon 1469, the crowns of two of the Christian states in the Spanish peninsula were united. In her reign the Moors were finally driven out of Spain; she introduced the ◊Inquisition into Castile, and the persecution of the Jews, and gave financial encouragement to ◊Columbus. Her youngest daughter was Catherine of Aragon, first wife of Henry VIII of England.

Isabella II 1830–1904. Queen of Spain from 1833, when she succeeded her father Ferdinand VII (1784–1833). The Salic Law banning a female sovereign had been repealed by the Cortes (Spanish parliament), but her succession was disputed by her uncle Don Carlos de Bourbon (1788–1855). After seven years of civil war the ◊Carlists were defeated. She abdicated in favour of her son Alfonso XII in 1868.

Isabella of France daughter of King Philip IV of France, wife of King Edward II of England; a strong-willed enemy of her husband's favourites, Piers Gaveston and the Despencers, she intrigued with her lover, Roger Mortimer, to have the king deposed and murdered. She is known to history as the 'she-wolf of France'.

Isaiah /aɪ'zaɪə/ 8th century BC. In the Old Testament, the first major Hebrew prophet. The son of Amos, he was probably of high rank, and lived largely in Jerusalem.

Isaurian an 8th-century Byzantine imperial dynasty, originating in Asia Minor.

Members of the family had been employed as military leaders by the Byzantines, and they gained great influence and prestige as a result. Leo III acceded in 717 as the first Isaurian emperor, and was followed by Constantine V (718–75), Leo IV (750–80), and Leo's widow Irene, who acted as regent until her death in 802. They maintained the integrity of the empire's borders. With the exception of Irene, they attempted to suppress the use of religious icons.

Isherwood Lifelong friend of W H Auden, English novelist Christopher Isherwood was a leading intellectual of the 1930s.

ISBN abbreviation for *International Standard Book Number*.

ischaemia reduction of blood supply to any part of the body.

Ischia /'ɪskiə/ volcanic island about 26 km/16 mi SW of Naples, Italy, in the Tyrrhenian Sea; population (1985) 26,000. It has mineral springs known to the Romans, beautiful scenery, and is a holiday resort.

Ise /iː'seɪ/ city SE of Kyoto, on Honshu, Japan. It is the site of the most sacred Shinto shrine, dedicated to sun-goddess Amaterasu. It has been rebuilt every 20 years in the form of a perfect thatched house of the 7th century BC, and contains the octagonal mirror of the goddess.

Isère /ɪ'zeə/ river in SE France, 290 km/180 mi long, a tributary of the Rhône. It gives its name to the *département* of Isère.

Isfahan /ˌɪsfə'hɑːn/ or *Eşfahan* industrial (steel, textiles, carpets) city in central Iran; population (1986) 1,001,000. It was the ancient capital (1598–1722) of ◊Abbas I the Great, and its features include the Great Square, Grand Mosque, and Hall of Forty Pillars.

Isherwood /'ɪʃəwʊd/ Christopher (William Bradshaw) 1904–1986. English novelist. Educated at Cambridge, he lived in Germany 1929–33 just before Hitler's rise to power, a period which inspired *Mr Norris Changes Trains* 1935 and *Goodbye to Berlin* 1939, creating the character of Sally Bowles (the basis of the musical *Cabaret* 1968). Returning to England, he collaborated with ◊Auden in three verse plays.

Ishiguro /ˌɪʃɪ'gʊrəu/ Kazuo 1954– . Japanese-born British novelist. His novel *An Artist of the Floating World* won the 1986 Whitbread Prize, and *The Remains of the Day* won the Booker Prize 1989.

Ishmael /'ɪʃmeɪəl/ in the Old Testament, son of ◊Abraham and his wife Sarah's Egyptian maid Hagar; traditional ancestor of Muhammad and the Arab people. He and his mother were driven out by Sarah's jealousy. Muslims believe that it was Ishmael, not Isaac, whom God commanded Abraham to sacrifice, and that Ishmael helped Abraham build the ◊Kaaba in Mecca.

Ishtar /'ɪʃtɑː/ goddess of love and war worshipped by the Babylonians and Assyrians, and personified as the legendary queen Semiramis.

Isidore of Seville /'ɪzədɔː/ *c.*560–636. Writer and missionary. His *Etymologiae* was the model for later medieval encyclopedias and helped to preserve classical thought into the Middle Ages, and his *Chronica Maiora* remains an important source for the history of Visigothic Spain.

As bishop of Seville from 600, he strengthened the church in Spain and converted many Jews and Aryan Visigoths.

isinglass pure form of gelatin obtained from the cleaned and dried swim bladder of various fish, particularly the sturgeon. Isinglass is used in the clarification of wines and beer, and in cookery.

Isis /'aɪsɪs/ the upper stretches of the river Thames, England, above Oxford.

Isis /'aɪsɪs/ the principal goddess of ancient Egypt. She was the daughter of Geb and Nut (earth and sky), and as the sister-wife of Osiris searched for his body after his death at the hands of his brother Set. Her son Horus then defeated and captured Set, but cut off his mother's head because she would not allow Set to be killed. She was later identified with ◊Hathor. The cult of Isis ultimately spread to Greece and Rome.

Iskandariya Arabic name for ◊Alexandria, Egypt.

Iskenderun /ɪs'kendəruːn/ port, naval base and steel town in Turkey; population (1980) 125,000. It was founded by Alexander the Great in 333 BC and called Alexandretta until 1939.

Islam (Arabic 'submission', that is, to the will of Allah) religion founded in the Arabian peninsula in the early 7th century. It emphasizes the oneness of God, his omnipotence, benificence, and inscrutability. The sacred book is the *Koran* of the prophet ◊Muhammad, the Prophet or Messenger of Allah. There are two main Muslim sects: ◊Sunni and ◊Shi'ite. Other schools include **Sufism**, a mystical movement originating in the 8th century.

beliefs Creation, Fall of Adam, angels and ◊jinns, heaven and hell, Day of Judgment, God's predestination of good and evil, and the succession of scriptures revealed to the prophets, including Moses and Jesus, but of which the perfect, final form is the **Koran** or **Quran**, divided into 114 **suras** or chapters, said to have been divinely revealed to Muhammad, the original being preserved beside the throne of Allah in heaven.

Islamic law Islam embodies a secular law (the **Shari'a** or 'Highway'), which is clarified for Shi'ites by reference to their own version of the **sunna**, 'practice' of the Prophet as transmitted by his companions; the Sunni sect also take into account **ijma'**, the endorsement by universal consent of practices and beliefs among the faithful. A **mufti** is a legal expert who guides the courts in their interpretation. (In Turkey until the establishment of the republic 1924 the mufti had supreme spiritual authority.)

organization There is no organized church or priesthood, though Muhammad's descendants (the Hashim family) and popularly recognized holy men, mullahs, and ayatollahs are accorded respect.

observances The 'Five Pillars of the Faith' are: recitation of the creed; worship (salat) five times a day facing the holy city of ◊Mecca (the call to prayer is given by a muezzin, usually from the minaret or tower of a mosque); almsgiving; fasting sunrise to sunset through Ramadan (ninth month of the year, which varies with the calendar); and the pilgrimage to Mecca at least once in a lifetime.

history Islam has not been a missionary religion, but was seen as an enemy of Christianity by European countries in the Crusades of the Middle Ages, and Christian states united against a Muslim nation as late as the Battle of Lepanto 1571. Islam is a major force in the Arab world and is a focus for nationalism among the peoples of Soviet Central Asia. It is also a significant factor in Pakistan, Indonesia, Malaysia, and parts of Africa. It is the second largest religion in the UK. Since World War II there has been a resurgence of fundamentalist Islam, often passionately opposed to the ideas of the West, in Iran, Libya, Afghanistan, and elsewhere. In the UK 1987 the manifesto *The Muslim Voice* made demands for rights of Muslim views on education, such as single-sex teaching, and avoidance of dancing, mixed bathing, and sex education.

Islamabad /ɪz'læməbæd/ capital of Pakistan from 1967, in the Potwar district, at the foot of the Margala Hills and immediately NW of Rawalpindi; population (1981) 201,000. The city was designed

Major Islands

Name and location	sq km	sq mi
Greenland (North Atlantic)	2,175,600	840,000
New Guinea (SW Pacific)	800,000	309,000
Borneo (SW Pacific)	744,100	287,300
Madagascar (Indian Ocean)	587,000	227,000
Baffin (Canadian Arctic)	507,258	195,928
Sumatra (Indian Ocean)	473,600	182,860
Honshu (NW Pacific)	230,966	89,176
Great Britain (N Atlantic)	229,978	88,795
Victoria (Canadian Arctic)	217,206	83,896
Ellesmere (Canadian Arctic)	196,160	75,767
Sulawesi (Indian Ocean)	189,216	73,057
South Island, New Zealand (SW Pacific)	149,883	57,870
Java (Indian Ocean)	126,602	48,900
Seram (W Pacific)	118,625	45,800
North Island, New Zealand (SW Pacific)	114,669	44,274
Cuba (Caribbean Sea)	110,800	44,800
Newfoundland (NW Atlantic)	108,860	42,030
Luzon (W Pacific)	104,688	40,420
Iceland (N Atlantic)	103,000	39,800
Mindanao (W Pacific)	94,630	36,537
Ireland - N and the Republic (N Atlantic)	84,400	32,600
Hokkaido (NW Pacific)	83,515	32,245
Sakhalin (NW Pacific)	76,400	29,500
Hispaniola-Dominican Republic and Haiti (Caribbean Sea)	76,000	29,300
Banks (Canadian Arctic)	70,000	27,038
Tasmania (SW Pacific)	67,800	26,200
Sri Lanka (Indian Ocean)	64,600	24,900
Devon (Canadian Arctic)	55,247	21,331

by Constantinos Doxiadis in the 1960s. The Federal Capital Territory of Islamabad has an area of 907 sq km/350 sq mi, and a population (1985) of 379,000.

Islamic art art, architecture, and design of Muslim nations and territories. Because the Koran forbids representation in art, Islamic artistry was channelled into calligraphy and ornament. Despite this, there was naturalistic Persian painting, which inspired painters in the Mogul and Ottoman empires. Ceramic tiles decorated mosques and palaces from Spain (Alhambra, Granada) to S Russia and Mogul India (Taj Mahal, Agra). Wood, stone, and stucco sculpture ornamented buildings. Islamic artists produced excellent metalwork and, in Persia in the 16th–17th centuries, woven textiles and carpets.

Islamic art is found from NW Africa and much of Spain to NW India and Anatolia. Intricate, interlacing patterns based on geometry and stylized plant motifs (including the swirling arabesque) swarm over surfaces.

calligraphy From about the 8th century the Arabic script was increasingly elaborated. The cursive script with extended flourishes (Nashki script) was widely adopted, and calligraphy was used to ornament textiles, metalwork, tiles, and lustreware pottery.

miniature painting flourished in Persia, in cities such as Isfahan, Herat, and Shiraz, during the Safavid period 1502–1736 and after 1526 under the Mogul Empire in India.

carpets The royal Persian carpet factories produced huge and luxurious compositions featuring human and animal figures as well as calligraphic, geometrical, and floral motifs.

island an area of land surrounded entirely by water. Australia is classed as a continent rather than an island, because of its size.

Islands can be formed in many ways. **Continental islands** were once part of the mainland, but became isolated (by tectonic movement, erosion, or a rise in sea level, for example). **Volcanic islands**, such as Japan, were formed by the explosion of underwater volcanoes. **Coral islands** consist mainly of ◊coral, built up over many years. An **atoll** is a circular coral reef surrounding a lagoon; atolls were formed when a coral reef grew up around a volcanic island that subsequently sank or was submerged by a rise in sea level. **Barrier islands** are found by the shore in shallow water, and are formed by the deposition of sediment eroded from the shoreline.

Islay /'aɪleɪ/ most southerly island of the Inner Hebrides, Scotland, in Strathclyde region, separated from Jura by the Sound of Islay; area 610 sq km/235 sq mi; population (1981) 3,800. The principal towns are Bowmore and Port Ellen. It produces malt whisky, and its wildlife includes eagles and rare wintering geese.

Isle of Ely /'iːlɪ/ former county of England, in East Anglia. It was merged with Cambridgeshire in 1965.

Isle of Man /mæn/ see ◊Man, Isle of.

Isle of Wight /waɪt/ see ◊Wight, Isle of.

Islington /'ɪzlɪŋtən/ borough of N Greater London including the suburbs of Islington and Finsbury; population (1985) 167,900.

Features include 19th-century squares and terraces at Highbury, Barnsbury, Canonbury; Wesley Museum in City Road. Mineral springs (Sadler's Wells) in Clerkenwell were exploited in conjunction with a music-hall in the 17th century, and Lilian Baylis developed a later theatre as an 'Old Vic' annexe.

Ismail /,ɪzmɑːˈiːl/ 1830–1895. Khedive (governor) of Egypt 1866–79. A grandson of Mehemet Ali, he became viceroy of Egypt in 1863 and in 1866 received the title of khedive from the Ottoman sultan. In 1875 Britain, at Prime Minister Disraeli's suggestion, bought the khedive's Suez Canal shares for £3,976,582, and Anglo-French control of Egypt's finances was established. In 1879 the UK and France persuaded the sultan to appoint Tewfik, his son, khedive in his place.

Ismail I /,ɪzmɑːˈiːl/ 1486–1524. Shah of Persia from 1501, founder of the **Safavi dynasty**, who established the first national government since the Arab conquest, and Shi'ite Islam as the national religion.

Ismaili a sect of ◊Shi'ite Muslims.

Ismailia /,ɪzmaɪˈliːə/ city in NE Egypt; population (1985) 191,700. It was founded in 1863 as the headquarters for construction of the Suez Canal, and was named after the Khedive Ismail.

ISO in photography, a numbering system for rating the speed of films, devised by the International Standards Organization.

isobar a line drawn on maps and weather charts linking all places with the same atmospheric pressure (usually measured in millibars). When used in weather forecasting, the distance between the isobars is an indication of the barometric gradient.

Where the isobars are close together, cyclonic weather is indicated, bringing strong winds and

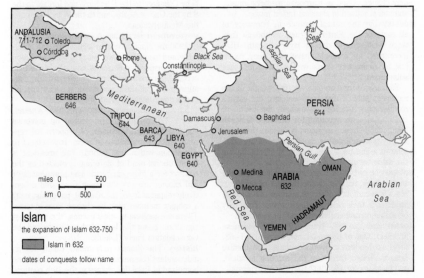

Islam
the expansion of Islam 632-750

Islam in 632

dates of conquests follow name

isobar

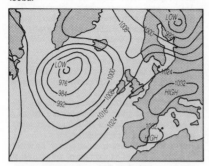

a depression, and where far apart anticyclonic, bringing calmer, settled conditions.

Isocrates /aɪˈsɒkrətiːz/ 436–338 BC. Athenian orator, a pupil of Socrates. He was a professional speechwriter and teacher of rhetoric.

isolation in medicine, the segregation of patients to prevent the spread of infection. In practice, now that many once-lethal infections have been brought under control, isolation is most often required for patients who are unusually at risk. These include patients whose immune systems have been undermined by disease or artificially suppressed by ◊cytotoxic or anti-rejection drugs. Strict isolation is also practised in the event of infection due to antibiotic-resistant microbes (see ◊nosocomial infection).

isolationism in politics, concentration on internal rather than foreign affairs. In the USA, it is usually associated with the Republican Party, especially politicians of the Midwest. Intervention in both world wars was initially resisted, and after the fruitless wars in Korea and Vietnam, there was resistance to further involvement in Europe, the Pacific, or the Middle East.

isomer a chemical compound having the same molecular composition and mass as another, but with different properties, because of the different structural arrangement of the atoms in the molecules (for example, one being a 'mirror image' of another).

isometrics system of muscular exercises without apparatus, for example by contracting particular sets of muscles. These exercises, some of which can be performed without visible movement, have been advocated as a means whereby sedentary workers can attain fitness, but can be damaging when practised by the unskilled.

isomer

butane CH₃(CH₂)₂CH₃

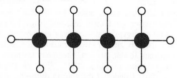

methyl propane CH₃CH(CH₃)CH₃

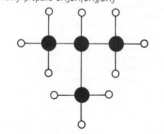

○ hydrogen atom
● carbon atom
── atomic bond

Israel
State of
(Medinat Israel)

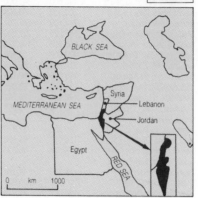

area 20,800 sq km/8,029 sq mi (as at 1949 armistice)
capital Jerusalem (not recognized by the United Nations)
towns ports Tel Aviv/Jaffa, Haifa, Eilat; Bat-Yam, Holon, Ramat Gan, Petach Tikva, Beersheba
physical coastal plain of Sharon between Haifa and Tel Aviv noted since ancient times for fertility; high arid region in south and centre; river Jordan Rift Valley along the east is below sea level
features Dead Sea, Lake Tiberias, Negev Desert, Golan Heights; historic sites: Jerusalem, Bethlehem, Nazareth; Masada, Megiddo, Jericho; caves of the Dead Sea scrolls
head of state Chaim Herzog from 1983
head of government Itzhak Shamir from 1986
political system democratic republic
political parties Israel Labour Party, moderate left-of-cent re; Consolidation Party (Likud), right-of-centre
exports citrus and other fruit, avocados, chinese leaves, fertilizers, plastics, petrochemicals, textiles, electro-optics, precision instruments, aircraft and missiles
currency shekel (3.30 = £1 Feb 1990)
population (1988) 4,442,000 (including 750,000 Arab Israeli citizens and over 1 million

Arabs in the occupied territories); under the Law of Return 1950, 'every Jew shall be entitled to come to Israel as an immigrant', those from the East and E Europe are *Ashkenazim*, and from Spain, Portugal, and Arab N Africa are *Sephardim* (over 50% of the population is now of Sephardic descent). An Israeli-born Jew is a *Sabra*; about 500,000 Israeli Jews are resident in the US. Annual growth rate 1.8%
life expectancy men 73, women 76
language Hebrew and Arabic (official); Yiddish, European and W Asian languages
religion Israel is a secular state, but the predominant faith is Judaism; also Sunni Muslim, Christian, and Druse
literacy 97% male/93% female (1985 est)
GNP $23 bn (1983); $5,609 per head of population
chronology
1948 Independent state of Israel proclaimed with Ben Gurion as prime minister.
1963 Ben Gurion resigned and was succeeded by Levi Eshkol.
1964 Palestine Liberation Organization (PLO) founded with the aim of overthrowing the state of Israel.
1967 Israel victorious in the Six-Day War.
1968 Israel Labour Party formed, led by Golda Meir.
1969 Golda Meir became prime minister.
1974 Yom Kippur War. Golda Meir succeeded by Itzhak Rabin.
1977 Menachem Begin elected prime minister. Egyptian president addressed the Knesset.
1978 Camp David talks.
1979 Egyptian-Israeli agreement signed.
1982 Israel pursued PLO fighters into Lebanon.
1983 Agreement reached for withdrawal from Lebanon.
1985 Israeli prime minister Shimon Peres had secret talks with King Hussein of Jordan.
1986 Itzhak Shamir took over from Peres under power-sharing agreement.
1988 Criticism of Israel's handling of Palestinian uprising in occupied territories. PLO acknowledges Israel's right to exist.
1989 New Likud–Labour coalition government formed under Shamir.
1990 Coalition collapses following disagreement over peace process.

isoprene CH₂CHC(CH₃)CH₂ (modern name **methylbutadiene**) a volatile fluid obtained from petroleum and coal, used to make synthetic rubber.

isorhythm in music, a form in which a given rhythm constantly repeats, although the notes may change. Used in European medieval music, and still practised in classical Indian music.

isostasy the theoretical balance in buoyancy of all parts of the Earth's ◊crust, as though they were floating on a denser layer beneath. High mountains, for example, have very deep roots, just as an iceberg floats with most of its mass submerged.

Similarly, during an ◊ice age the weight of the ice sheet pushes that continent into the earth's mantle; once the ice has melted, the continent rises again. This accounts for shoreline features being found some way inland in regions that were heavily glaciated during the Pleistocene period.

isotherm a line on a map linking all places having the same temperature at a given time.

isotope one of two or more atoms which have the same atomic number (same number of protons), but which contain a different number of neutrons, so differ in their relative atomic mass. They may be stable or radioactive, natural, or synthetic.

Isozaki /ˌɪsəʊˈzɑːki/ Arata 1931– . Japanese architect. One of Kenzo ◊Tange's team 1954–63, his Post-Modernist works include Ochanomizu Square, Tokyo (retaining the existing facades), and buildings for the 1992 Barcelona Olympics.

Israel /ˈɪzreɪəl/ ancient kingdom of N ◊Palestine, formed after the death of Solomon by Jewish peoples seceding from the rule of his son Rehoboam, and electing Jeroboam in his place.

Israel /ˈɪzreɪəl/ country in SW Asia, bounded to the N by Lebanon, to the E by Syria and Jordan, to the S by the Gulf of Aqaba, and to the W by Egypt and the Mediterranean.

government Israel has no written constitution. In 1950 the single-chamber legislature, the *Knesset*, voted to adopt a state constitution by evolution over an unspecified period of time. As in the UK, certain laws are considered to have particular constitutional significance and could, at some time, be codified into a single written document.

Supreme authority rests with the *Knesset*, whose 120 members are elected by universal suffrage, through a system of proportional representation, for a four-year term. It is subject to dissolution within that period. The president is constitutional head of state and is elected by the *Knesset* for a five-year term. The prime minister and cabinet are mostly drawn from, and collectively responsible to, the *Knesset*, but occasionally a cabinet member may be chosen from outside. There are several political parties, the two most significant being the Israel Labour Party and the Consolidation Party (Likud).

history The Zionist movement, calling for an independent community for Jews in their historic homeland of Palestine, began in the 19th century, and in 1917 Britain declared its support for the idea. In 1920 the League of Nations placed Palestine under British administration and the British government was immediately faced with the rival claims of Jews who wished to settle and the indigenous Arabs who opposed them. In 1937 Britain proposed separate Arab and Jewish communities; this was accepted by the Jews but not by the Arabs, and fighting broke out between them.

In 1947 this plan for partition was supported by the United Nations and when, in 1948, Britain ended its Palestinian mandate, an independent State of Israel was proclaimed, with David ◊Ben-Gurion as prime minister. Neigbouring Arab states sent forces to crush Israel but failed, and when a cease-fire agreement was reached, in 1949, Israel controlled more land than had been originally allocated to it. The non-Jewish-occupied remainder of Palestine, known as the West Bank, was incorporated into ◊Jordan. The creation of this state encouraged Jewish immigration on a large scale, about 2 million having arrived from all over the world by 1962. Hundreds of thousands of Arab residents fled from Israel to neigbouring countries, such as Jordan and Lebanon. In 1964 a number of exiled Palestinian Arabs founded the ◊Palestine Liberation Organization (PLO), aiming to overthrow Israel.

During the 1960s there was considerable tension between Israel and Egypt, which, under President ◊Nasser, had become a leader in the Arab world. His nationalization of the ◊Suez Canal in 1956 provided an opportunity for Israel, with Britain and France, to attack Egypt and occupy a part of Palestine it had controlled since 1949, the Gaza Strip, Israel being forced by UN and US pressure to withdraw in 1957. Ten years later, in the Six-Day War, Israel gained the whole of Jerusalem, the West Bank area of Jordan, the Sinai Peninsula in Egypt, and the Golan Heights in Syria. All were incorporated into the State of Israel.

Ben Gurion resigned in 1963 and was succeeded by Levi Eshkol, leading a coalition government, and in 1968 three of the coalition parties combined to form the Israel Labour Party. In 1969 Golda Meir became Labour Party prime minister. Towards the end of her administration another Arab-Israeli war broke out, coinciding with ◊Yom Kippur, the holiest day of the Jewish year. Israel was attacked by Egypt and Syria and after nearly three weeks of fighting, with heavy losses, a ceasefire was agreed. Golda Meir resigned in 1974 and was succeeded by Gen Itzhak Rabin, heading a Labour-led coalition.

In the 1977 elections the Consolidation (Likud) bloc, led by Menachem ◊Begin, won an unexpected victory and Begin became prime minister. Within five months relations between Egypt and Israel changed dramatically, mainly owing to initiatives by President ◊Sadat of Egypt, encouraged by US president Jimmy ◊Carter. Sadat visited Israel to address the *Knesset*, and the following year the Egyptian and Israeli leaders met at ◊Camp David, in the USA, to sign agreements for peace in the Middle East. A treaty was signed in 1979, and in 1980 Egypt and Israel exchanged ambassadors, to the dismay of most of the Arab world.

Israel withdrew from Sinai by 1982 but continued to occupy the Golan Heights. In the same year Israel, without consulting Egypt, entered Lebanon and surrounded W Beirut, in pursuit of 6,000 PLO fighters who were trapped there. A split between Egypt and Israel was avoided by the efforts of the US special negotiator, Philip Habib, who secured the evacuation from Beirut to other Arab countries of about 15,000 PLO and Syrian fighters in Aug 1982.

Israel's alleged complicity in massacres in two Palestinian refugee camps increased Arab hostility. Talks between Israel and Lebanon, between Dec 1982 and May 1983, resulted in an agreement, drawn up by US secretary of state George Shultz, calling for the withdrawal of all foreign

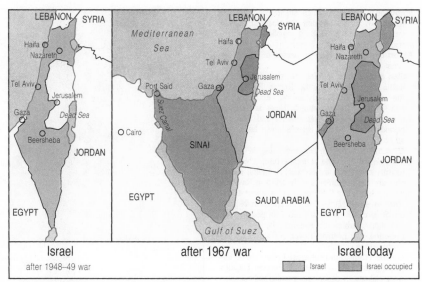

Israel
after 1948–49 war

after 1967 war

Israel today

Israel   Israel occupied

forces from Lebanon within three months. Syria refused to acknowledge the agreement and left some 30,000 troops, with about 7,000 PLO members, in the northeast; Israel retaliated by refusing to withdraw its forces from the south.

During this time Begin faced growing domestic problems, including rapidly rising inflation and opposition to his foreign policies. In 1983 he resigned and Itzhak Shamir formed a shaky coalition. Elections in July 1984 proved inconclusive, with the Labour Alignment, led by Shimon Peres, winning 44 seats in the *Knesset*, and Likud, led by Shamir, 41. Neither leader was able to form a viable coalition, so after weeks of negotiation, it was agreed that a government of national unity would be formed, with Peres as prime minister for the first 25 months, until Oct 1986, and Shamir as his deputy, and then a reversal of the positions.

Meanwhile, the problems in the Lebanon continued. In 1984, under pressure from Syria, President Gemayel of the Lebanon rejected the 1983 treaty with Israel, but the government of national unity in Tel Aviv continued to plan the withdrawal of its forces, even though it might lead to outright civil war in S Lebanon. Guerrilla groups of the Shi'ite community of S Lebanon took advantage of the situation by attacking the departing Israeli troops. Israel replied by attacking Shi'ite villages. Most of the withdrawal was complete by June 1985. Several peace initiatives by King Hussein of Jordan failed, largely because of Israeli and US suspicions about the PLO, some of whose supporters were alleged to have been involved in terrorism in the Mediterranean area. There were, however, signs of improvement in 1985. Prime Minister Peres met King Hussein secretly in the south of France and later, in a speech to the UN, Peres said he would not rule out the possibility of an international conference on the Middle East. PLO leader Yasser ◊Arafat also had talks with Hussein and later, in Cairo, denounced PLO

Istanbul *The Hagia Sophia in Istanbul, formerly a Christian place of worship, was converted to a mosque in 1453.*

guerrilla activity outside Israeli-occupied territory. Domestically, the government of national unity was having some success with its economic policies, inflation falling in 1986 to manageable levels.

The Nov 1988 general election resulted in a hung parliament; after lengthy negotiations, Shamir formed another coalition with Peres and the Labour Party. Shamir's harsh handling of Palestinian protests, and differences over dealings with the PLO, broke the partnership in Mar 1990 when the coalition fell after a vote of no confidence.

Israels /ˈɪsrɑːelz/ Jozef 1824–1894. Dutch painter. In 1870 he settled in The Hague and became a leader of the *Hague school* of landscape painters, who shared some of their ideals with the ◊Barbizon school in France. Israels's sombre and sentimental scenes of peasant life recall ◊Millet.

Issigonis /ˌɪsɪˈɡəʊnɪs/ Alec 1906–1988. British engineer who designed the Morris Minor 1948 and the Mini-Minor 1959 cars, thus creating modern economy motoring and adding the word 'mini' to the English language.

Istanbul /ˌɪstænˈbʊl/ city and chief seaport of Turkey; population (1985) 5,495,000. It produces textiles, tobacco, cement, glass, and leather. Founded as *Byzantium* about 660 BC, it was renamed *Constantinople* 330, and was the capital of the ◊Byzantine Empire until captured by the Turks 1453. As *Istamboul* it was capital of the Ottoman Empire until 1922.

features the harbour of the Golden Horn; Hagia Sophia (Emperor Justinian's church of the Holy Wisdom, 537, now a mosque); Sultan Ahmet Mosque, known as the Blue Mosque, from its tiles; Topkapi Palace of the Sultans (with a harem of 400 rooms), now a museum. The Selimye Barracks in the suburb of *Usküdar* (Scutari) was used as a hospital in the Crimean War. The rooms used by Florence Nightingale, with her personal possessions, are preserved as a museum.

isthmus a narrow strip of land joining two larger land masses. The Isthmus of Panama joins North and South America.

Itagaki /ˌiːtəˈɡɑːki/ Taisuke 1837–1919. Japanese military and political leader, the founder of Japan's first political party, the Jiyuto (Liberal Party) in 1875. Involved in the overthrow of the Tokugawa shogunate and the Meiji restoration (see ◊Mutsuhito), Itagaki became a champion of democratic principles although continuing to serve in the government for short periods.

After ennoblement in 1887 he retained the leadership of the party and cooperated with ◊Ito Hirobumi in the establishment of parliamentary government in the 1890s.

Itaipu the world's largest dam, situated on the Paraǹ River, SW Brazil. A joint Brazilian-Paraguayan venture started in 1973, it supplies hydroelectricity to a wide area.

Italian inhabitant of Italy or person of Italian descent.

Italian architecture architecture of the Italian peninsula after the fall of the Roman Empire. In the earliest styles—Byzantine, Romanesque, and Gothic—the surviving buildings are mostly churches. From the Renaissance and Baroque periods there are also palaces, town halls, and so on.

Byzantine (5th–11th centuries) Italy is rich in examples of this style of architecture, which is a mixture of oriental and classical elements; examples are the monuments of Justinian in Ravenna and the basilica of S Marco, Venice, about 1063.

Romanesque (10th–13th centuries) In N Italy buildings in this style are often striped in dark and light marble, for example the baptistery, cathedral, and Leaning Tower of Pisa; Sicily has Romanesque churches.

Gothic (13th–15th centuries) Italian Gothic differs a great deal from that of N Europe. Façades were elaborately decorated: mosaics and coloured marble were used, and sculpture placed around windows and doors. The enormous cathedral of Milan, 15th century, was built in the N European style.

Renaissance (15th–16th centuries) The style was developed by the Florentine Brunelleschi and his contemporaries, inspired by Classical models. The sculptor Michelangelo is associated with the basilica of St Peter's, Rome. In Venice the villas of Palladio continued the purity of the High Renaissance.

Baroque (17th century) The Baroque style flourished with the oval spaces of Bernini (for example, the church of S. Andrea al Quirinale, Rome) and Boronini, and the fantasies of Guarini in Turin (such as the church of S. Lorenzo).

Neo-Classicism (18th–19th centuries) In the 18th century Italian architecture was less significant, and a dry Classical revival prevailed. In the 19th century Neo-Classicism was the norm, as in much of Europe.

20th century The Futurist visions of Sant'Elia opened the century. Between World Wars I and II pure Modernism was explored (under the influence of Fascism), together with a stripped classicism. Nervi's work showed the expressive potential of structural concrete. Rationalism and a related concern with the study of the traditional types of European cities have exerted great influence, led by the work and writings of Aldo Rossi.

Italian art painting and sculpture of Italy from the early Middle Ages to the present. Schools of painting arose in many of the city states, particularly Florence and Siena and, by the 15th century, Venice. Florence was a major centre of the Renaissance, along with Venice, and Rome was the focus of the High Renaissance and Baroque styles.

13th century (Italian *Duecento*) The painter Cimabue was said by the poet Dante to be the greatest painter of his day. Already there was a strong tradition of fresco painting and monumental painted altarpieces, often reflecting Byzantine influences. A type of Gothic Classicism was developed by the sculptors Nicola and Giovanni Pisano.

14th century (*Trecento*) The Florentine Giotto broke with prevailing styles of painting. Sienese painting remained decoratively stylized but became less sombre in mood with the work of Simone Martini and the Lorenzetti brothers.

Renaissance (15th and 16th centuries) The style was seen as a 'rebirth' of the classical spirit. The earliest artists of the Renaissance were based in Florence. The sculptor Ghiberti worked on the baptistery there; Donatello set new standards in naturalistic and Classically inspired sculpture. Masaccio

and Uccello made advances in employing scientific perspective in painting. In the middle and later part of the century dozens of sculptors and painters were at work in Florence: Verrocchio, Pollaiuolo, Botticelli, Fra Angelico, Fra Filippo Lippi, and Filippino Lippi, among others.

In Venice the Bellini family of painters influenced their successors Giorgione and Titian. Tintoretto was Titian's most notable pupil.

The High Renaissance was dominated by the many-sided genius of Leonardo da Vinci, the forceful sculptures and frescoes of Michelangelo, and the harmonious paintings of Raphael.

Baroque (17th century) This dramatic style was developed by, among others, the sculptor and architect Bernini, and in painting Caravaggio, who made effective use of light and shade to create high drama.

Neo-Classicism (18th and early 19th centuries) The style was inspired by the rediscovery of Classical Roman works. The sculptor Canova was a popular exponent. Piranesi produced engravings.

20th century The Futurist movement, founded 1910, tried to portray phenomena like speed and electricity in their paintings and sculpture. The first dreamlike Metaphysical paintings of de Chirico date from the same period. Modigliani soon moved to Paris; his paintings are characterized by elongated figures. The sculptures of Marino Marini (1901–80) and Giacometti created new styles in bronze.

Italian language a member of the Romance branch of the Indo-European language family. With a strong infusion of Latin for religious, academic and educational purposes, the written standard has tended to be highly formal and divorced from the many regional dialects (often mutually unintelligible) that are still largely the everyday usage of the general population. The Italian language is also spoken in Switzerland and by people of Italian descent, especially in the US, Canada, Australia, the UK and Argentina.

Italian literature originated in the 13th century with the Sicilian school, which imitated Provençal poetry. The contemporary works of St Francis of Assisi and Jacopone da Todi reflect the religious faith of the time. Guido Guinicelli (1230–*c.* 1275) and Guido Cavalcanti (*c.* 1250–1300) developed the spiritual conception of love and influenced Dante Alighieri, whose *Divina Commedia/Divine Comedy* 1300–21 is generally recognized as the greatest work of Italian literature. Petrarch was a humanist and a poet, while Boccaccio is principally known for his tales.

The *Divina Commedia* marked the beginning of the Renaissance. Boiardo dealt with the Carolingian epics in his *Orlando Innamorato/Roland in Love* 1480–94 which was completed and transformed by Lodovico Ariosto as *Orlando Furioso/The Frenzy of Roland* 1516. Their contemporaries Niccolò Machiavelli and Francesco Guicciardini (1483–1540) are historians of note. Torquato Tasso wrote his epic *Gerusalemme Liberata/The Liberation of Jerusalem* 1575 in the spirit of the Counter-Reformation.

The 17th century was characterized by the exaggeration of the poets Giovanni Battista Marini (1569–1625) and Gabriello Chiabrera (1552–1638). In 1690 the 'Academy of Arcadia' was formed: its members included Innocenzo Frugoni (1692–1768) and Metastasio. Other writers include Salvator Rosa, the satirist.

During the 18th century Giuseppe Parini (1729–99) ridiculed the abuses of his day, while Vittorio Alfieri attacked tyranny in his

Italy: regions

Region	Capital	Area sq km
Abruzzi	Aquila	10,800
Basilicata	Potenza	10,000
Calabria	Catanzaro	15,100
Campania	Naples	13,600
Emilia-Romagna	Bologna	22,100
Friuli-Venezia Giulia*	Udine	7,800
Lazio	Rome	17,200
Liguria	Genoa	5,400
Lombardy	Milan	23,900
Marche	Ancona	9,700
Molise	Campobasso	4,400
Piedmont	Turin	25,400
Puglia	Bari	19,300
Sardinia*	Cagliari	24,100
Sicily*	Palermo	25,700
Trentino-Alto Adige*	Trento**	13,600
Tuscany	Florence	23,000
Umbria	Perugia	8,500
Valle d'Aosta*	Aosta	3,300
Veneto	Venice	18,400
		301,300

*special autonomous regions
**also Bolzano-Bozen

dramas. Carlo Goldoni wrote comedies and Ugo Foscolo (1778–1827) is chiefly remembered for his patriotic verse. Giacomo Leopardi is not only the greatest lyrical poet since Dante, but also a master of Italian prose; the Romantic, Alessandro Manzoni, is best known as a novelist, and influenced among others the novelist Antonio Fogazzaro. A later outstanding literary figure and poet, Giosuè Carducci, was followed by the verbose Gabriele d'Annunzio, writing of sensuality and violence, and Benedetto Croce, historian and philosopher, who between them dominated Italian literature at the turn of the century.

Other writers were the realist novelists Giovanni Verga and Grazia Deledda, winner of the Nobel prize 1926, the dramatist Luigi Pirandello, and the novelists Ignazio Silone and Italo Svevo. Poets of the period include Dino Campana, Giuseppe Ungaretti and among the modern school are Nobel prizewinners Eugenio Montale and Salvatore Quasimodo. Novelists of the post-Fascist period, include Alberto Moravia, Carlo Levi, Cesare Pavese (1908–50), Vasco Pratolini (1913–), Elsa Morante (1916–), Natalia Ginsburg (1916–), Giuseppe Tomasi, Prince of Lampedusa, and the writers Italo Calvino, Leonardo Sciascia, and Primo Levi.

Italian Somaliland former Italian Trust Territory on the Somali coast of Africa extending to 502,300 sq km/194,999 sq mi. Established in 1892, it was extended in 1925 with the acquisition of Jubaland from Kenya; administered from Mogadishu; under British rule 1941–50. Thereafter it reverted to Italian authority before uniting with British Somaliland in 1960 to form the independent state of Somalia.

italic style of printing in which the letters slope to the right, introduced by Aldus Manutius of Venice from 1501. It is usually used side by side with the erect Roman type, for purposes of emphasis and citation. The term is also used for the handwriting style developed in 1522 by Vatican chancery scribe Ludovico degli Arrighi for popular use (the basis for modern italic script).

Italy /'ɪtəlɪ/ country in S Europe, bounded N by Switzerland and Austria, E by Yugoslavia and the Adriatic Sea, S by the Ionian and Mediterranean Seas, and W by the Tyrrhenian Sea and France. It includes the Mediterranean islands of Sardinia and Sicily.

government The 1948 constitution provides for a two-chamber parliament consisting of a senate and a 630-member chamber of deputies. Both are elected for a five-year term by universal suffrage, through a system of proportional representation, and have equal powers. The senate's 315 elected

Italy
Republic of
(Repubblica Italiana)

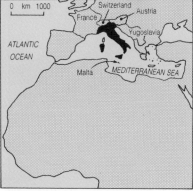

area 301,300 sq km/116,332 sq mi
capital Rome
towns Milan, Turin; ports Naples, Genoa, Palermo, Bari, Catania
physical mountainous (Maritime Alps, Dolomites, Apennines); rivers Po, Adige, Arno, Tiber; islands of Sicily, Sardinia, Elba, Capri, Ischia
features lakes Como, Maggiore, Garda; Europe's only active volcanoes: Vesuvius, Etna, Stromboli; historic towns include Venice, Florence, Siena
political parties Christian Democratic Party (DC), Catholic centrist; Italian Communist Party (PCI), pro-European socialist; Italian Socialist Party (PSI), moderate socialist; Italian Social Movement–National Right (MSI-DN), neo-fascist; Italian Republican Party (PRI), social democratic, left-of-centre; Italian Social Democratic Party (PSDI), moderate left-of-centre; Liberals (PLI), right-of-centre
exports wine, fruit, vegetables, textiles (Europe's largest silk producer), leather goods, motor vehicles, electrical goods, chemicals, marble (Carrara), sulphur, mercury, iron, steel
head of state Francesco Cossiga from 1985
head of government Giulio Andreotti from 1989
political system democratic republic
currency lira (2116.25 = £1 Feb 1990)
population (1988) 57,397,000; annual growth rate 0.1%
life expectancy men 71, women 78
language Italian, derived from Latin
religion Roman Catholic 90%
literacy 98% male/96% female (1985)
GNP $350 bn (1983); $6,914 per head of population
chronology
1946 Monarchy replaced by a republic.
1948 New constitution adopted.
1954 Trieste returned to Italy.
1976 Communists proposed the establishment of a broad-based, left–right government, the 'historic compromise'. Idea ultimately rejected by the Christian Democrats.
1978 Christian Democrat Aldo Moro, architect of the historic compromise, kidnapped and murdered by Red Brigade guerrillas.
1983 Bettino Craxi, a socialist, became leader of a broad coalition government.
1987 Craxi resigned, and the succeeding coalition fell within months.
1988 After several unsuccessful attempts to form a stable government, the leader of the Christian Democrats, Ciriaco de Mita, established a five-party coalition that included the Socialists.
1989 De Mita resigned after disagreements within his coalition government; eventually succeeded by Giulio Andreotti.

members are regionally representative and there are also seven life senators. The president is constitutional head of state and is elected for a seven-year term by an electoral college consisting of both houses of parliament and 58 regional representatives. The president appoints the prime minister and cabinet, (council of ministers), and they are collectively responsible to parliament.

Although Italy is not a federal state, each of its 20 regions enjoys a high degree of autonomy, with a regional council elected for a five-year term by universal suffrage. The voting system encourages a multiplicity of political parties, the most significant being the Christian Democrats (DC), the Communists (PCI), the Socialists (PSI), the Italian Social Movement–National Right (MSI-DN), the Republicans (PRI), the Social Democrats (PSDI), and the Liberals (PLI).

history The varying peoples inhabiting Italy – Etruscans in Tuscany, Latins and Sabines in middle Italy, Greek colonies in the south and Sicily, and Gauls in the north—were united under Roman rule during the 4th–3rd centuries BC. With the decline of the Roman Empire, and its final extinction in 476 AD, Italy became exposed to barbarian attacks, and passed in turn under the rule of the Ostrogoths and the Lombards.

The 8th century witnessed the rise of the papacy as a territorial power, the annexation of the Lombard kingdom by Charlemagne, and his coronation as emperor of the West in 800. From then until 1250 the main issue in Italian history is the relations, at first friendly and later hostile, between the papacy and the Holy Roman Empire. During this struggle the Italian cities seized the opportunity to convert themselves into self-governing republics.

By 1300 five major powers existed in Italy: the city-republics of Milan, Florence, and Venice; the papal states; and the kingdom of Naples.

Their mutual rivalries and constant wars laid Italy open 1494–1559 to invasions from France and Spain; as a result Naples and Milan passed under Spanish rule. After 1700 Austria secured Milan and replaced Spain as the dominating power, while Naples passed to a Spanish Bourbon dynasty, and Sardinia to the dukes of Savoy.

The period of French rule 1796–1814 temporarily unified Italy and introduced the principles of the French Revolution, but after Napoleon's fall Italy was again divided between Austria, the pope, the kingdoms of Sardinia and Naples, and four smaller duchies. Nationalist and democratic ideals nevertheless remained alive, and inspired attempts at revolution in 1820, 1831, and 1848–49. After this last failure the Sardinian monarchy assumed the leadership of the national movement. With the help of Napoleon III, the Austrians were expelled from Lombardy in 1859; the duchies joined the Italian kingdom; ◊Garibaldi overthrew the Neapolitan monarchy; and Victor Emmanuel II of Sardinia was proclaimed king of Italy at Turin in 1861. Venice and part of Venetia were secured by another war with Austria in 1866; in 1870 Italian forces occupied Rome, thus completing the unification of Italy, and the pope ceased to be a temporal ruler until 1929 (see ◊Vatican City State).

In 1878 Victor Emmanuel II died, and was succeeded by Humbert (Umberto) I, his son, who was assassinated in 1900. The formation of a colonial empire began in 1869 with the purchase of land on the Bay of Assab, on the Red Sea, from the local sultan. In the next 20 years the Italians occupied all ◊Eritrea, which was made a colony in 1889. An attempt to seize Ethiopia was decisively defeated at Adowa in 1896. War with Turkey 1911–12 gave Tripoli and Cyrenaica. Italy's intervention on the Allied side

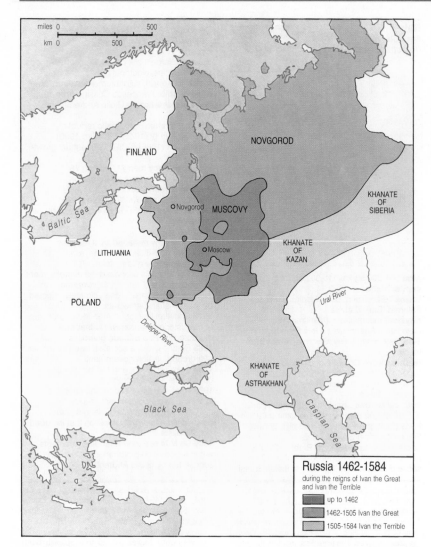

Russia 1462-1584

during the reigns of Ivan the Great and Ivan the Terrible

- up to 1462
- 1462-1505 Ivan the Great
- 1505-1584 Ivan the Terrible

Democrats, Socialists, Republicans, Social Democrats, and Liberals. Despite criticism of Craxi's strong-willed style of leadership, the coalition parties could find no acceptable alternative so continued to support him.

Under Craxi's government the state of the economy improved, although the N–S divide in productivity and prosperity persists, despite attempts to increase investment in the south. In foreign affairs Italy has demonstrated its commitment to the EEC, NATO and the UN, and in 1983 played an important part in the multinational peace-keeping force in Beirut. In 1987 the Christian Democrat Giovanni Goria formed a coalition government, which fell when the Liberal Party withdrew some three months later. He was succeeded by Ciriaco De Mita, who formed a new Christian Democrat–Socialist–Liberal coalition, but resigned a few months later after disagreements within the government. After lengthy negotiations the veteran Giulio Andreotti put together a new coalition of Christian Democrats, Socialists, and minor parties.

itch irritation of nerve endings in skin or mucous membrane. The disorder scabies, an eruption produced by the burrowing into the skin of the female of the minute parasite *Acarus scabiei*, is popularly called 'the itch'.

iteration in computing, a method of solving a problem by performing the same steps repeatedly until a certain condition is satisfied. For example, in one method of ◊sorting, adjacent items are repeatedly exchanged until the data are in the required sequence.

iteroparity in biology, the repeated production of offspring at intervals throughout the life cycle. It is usually contrasted with ◊semelparity, where each individual reproduces only once during its life. Most vertebrates are iteroparous.

Ithaca /ˈɪθəkə/ modern Greek **Ithaki** Greek island in the Ionian Sea, area 93 sq km/36 sq mi. Important in pre- classical Greece, Ithaca was (in Homer's poem) the birthplace of Odysseus.

Ito /ˈiːtəʊ/ Hirobumi 1841–1909. Japanese politician, prime minister and a key figure in the modernization of Japan, he was also involved in the Meiji restoration under ◊Mutsuhito 1866–68 and in government missions to the USA and Europe in the 1870s. As minister for home affairs, he drafted the Meiji constitution in 1889 and oversaw its implementation as prime minister the following year. While resident-general in Korea, he was assassinated by a Korean nationalist.

ITU abbreviation for *intensive therapy unit*, a high-technology facility for treating the critically ill or injured. ICU (intensive care unit) is also used.

in World War I secured it Trieste, the Trentino, and S Tirol.

The postwar period was marked by intense political and industrial unrest, culminating in 1922 in the establishment of ◊Mussolini's Fascist dictatorship. The regime embraced a policy of aggression with the conquest of Ethiopia 1935–36 and Albania 1939, and Italy entered World War II in 1940 as an ally of Germany. Defeat in Africa 1941–43 and the Allied conquest of Sicily 1943 resulted in Mussolini's downfall; the new government declared war on Germany, and until 1945 Italy was a battlefield between German occupying forces and the advancing Allies.

In 1946 Victor Emmanuel III, who had been king since 1900, abdicated in favour of his son Humbert (Umberto) II. The monarchy was abolished after a referendum in 1946 and the country became a republic, adopting a new constitution in 1948. Between 1946 and 1986 there were nine parliaments and 45 administrations.

The Christian Democrats were dominant until 1963, and after this participated in most coalition governments. In 1976 the Communists became a significant force, winning over a third of the votes for the chamber of deputies and pressing for what they called the 'historic compromise', a broad-based government with representatives from the Christian Democratic, Socialist, and Communist parties, which would, in effect, be an alliance between Communism and Roman Catholicism. The Christian Democrats rejected this. Apart from a brief period 1977–78, the other parties excluded the Communists from power-sharing,

forcing them to join the opposition. In 1980 the Socialists returned to share power with the Christian Democrats and Republicans, and participated in a number of subsequent coalitions.

In 1983, the leader of the Socialist Party, Bettino Craxi, became the republic's first Socialist prime minister, leading a coalition of Christian

Ivory Coast
Republic of
(République de la Côte d'Ivoire)

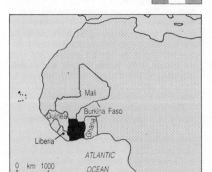

area 322,463 sq km/124,471 sq mi
capital Abidjan; capital designate Yamoussouko
towns Bouaké

physical tropical rainforest (diminishing as it is exploited) in the S: savanna and low mountains in the N
head of state and government Félix Houphouët-Boigny from 1960
political system effectively one-party republic
political parties Democratic Party of the Ivory Coast (PDCI), nationalist, free-enterprise
exports coffee, cocoa, timber, petroleum
currency CFA franc (485.00 = £1 Feb 1990)
population (1988) 11,630,000; annual growth rate 3.7%
life expectancy men 49, women 52
language French (official)
religion animist 65%, Muslim 24%, Christian 11%
literacy 53% male/31% female (1985 est)
GNP $6.7 bn (1983); $1,100 per head of population
chronology
1958 Achieved internal self-government.
1960 Achieved full independence, with Félix Houphouët-Boigny as president of a one-party state.

Iturbide /ˌɪtuəˈbiːdeɪ/ Agustín de 1783–1824. Mexican military leader (*caudillo*) who led the conservative faction in the nation's struggle for independence from Spain. In 1822 he crowned himself Emperor Agustín I. His extravagance and failure to restore order led all other parties to turn against him, and he reigned for less than a year (see ◊Mexican Empire).

IUCN (International Union for the Conservation of Nature) an organization established by the United Nations to promote the conservation of wildlife and habitats as part of the national policies of member states.

It has formulated guidelines and established research programmes (for example, International Biological Programme, IBP) and set up advisory bodies (such as Survival Services Commissions, SSC). In 1980, it launched the *World Conservation Strategy* to highlight particular problems, designating a small number of areas as *World Heritage Sites* to ensure their survival as unspoilt habitats (for example, Yosemite National Park in USA, and the Simen Mountains in Ethiopia).

Ivan /ˈaɪvən/ six rulers of Russia, including:

Ivan III *the Great* 1440–1505. Grand duke of Muscovy from 1462, who revolted against Tatar overlordship by refusing tribute to Grand Khan Ahmed 1480. He claimed the title of tsar, and used the double-headed eagle as the Russian state emblem.

Ivan IV *the Terrible* 1530–1584. Grand duke of Muscovy from 1533, he assumed power 1544, and was crowned as first tsar of Russia 1547. He conquered Kazan 1552, Astrakhan 1556, and Siberia 1581. His last years alternated between debauchery and religious austerities.

Ivanovo /iːˈvɑːnəvəʊ/ capital of Ivanovo region, USSR, 240 km/150 mi NE of Moscow; population (1987) 479,000. Industries include textiles, chemicals and engineering.

Ives /aɪvz/ Charles (Edward) 1874–1954. US composer who experimented with ◊atonality, quarter tones, clashing time signatures, and quotations from popular music of the time. He wrote five symphonies, including *Holidays Symphony* 1904–13, chamber music, including the *Concord Sonata*, and the orchestral *Three Places in New England* 1903–14 and *The Unanswered Question* 1908.

Ives /aɪvz/ Frederic Eugene 1856–1937. US inventor who developed the ◊halftone process of printing photographs in 1878. The process uses a screen to break up light and dark areas into different-sized dots. By 1886 he had evolved the halftone process now generally in use. Among his many other inventions was a three-colour printing process.

IVF abbreviation for ◊*in vitro fertilization*.

Iviza alternative spelling of ◊Ibiza, one of the ◊Balearic islands.

ivory the hard white substance of which the teeth and tusks of certain animals are composed. Most valuable are elephants' tusks, which are of unusual hardness and density. Ivory is used in carving and other decorative work, and is so valuable that poachers continue to destroy the remaining wild elephant herds in Africa to obtain it illegally. Trade in ivory was halted by Kenya 1989, but Zimbabwe continued its policy of controlled culling to enable the elephant population to thrive and to release ivory for export. China and Hong Kong have refused to obey a ban on ivory trading.

Vegetable ivory is used for buttons, toys, and cheap ivory goods. It consists of the hard albumen of the seeds of a tropical palm *Phytelephas macrocarpa*, which is imported from Colombia.

Ivory /ˈaɪvəri/ James 1928– . US film director best known for his collaboration with Indian producer Ismael ◊Merchant.

Ivory Coast (French *Côte d'Ivoire*) /ˈkəʊt dɪvˈwɑː/ country in W Africa, bounded to the N by Mali and Burkina Faso, E by Ghana, S by the Gulf of Guinea, and W by Liberia and Guinea.

government The 1960 constitution, amended in 1971, 1975, 1980 and 1985, provides for a president who is head of both state and government, elected by universal suffrage for a five-year term, and a single-chamber national assembly of 175 members, also popularly elected and serving a five-year term. The president chooses and heads a council of ministers. The only political party is the Democratic Party of the Ivory Coast (PDCI) and its chair is the state president.

history The area now known as Côte d'Ivoire was once made up of several separate kingdoms. From the 16th century the Portuguese, French, and British established trading centres along the coast, dealing in slaves and ivory. During the 19th century France acquired the region by means of treaties with local leaders, eventually incorporating it into ◊French West Africa in 1904.

It was given self-government within the French Community in 1958 and full independence in 1960, when a new constitution was adopted. Félix Houphouët-Boigny has been the country's only president. He has maintained close links with France since independence and this support, combined with a good economic growth rate, has given his country a high degree of political stability. He has been criticized by some other African leaders for maintaining links with South Africa, but has argued that a dialogue between blacks and whites is essential. He has denounced Communist intervention in African affairs, and has travelled extensively to improve relations with Western powers.

ivy tree and shrub of the genus *Hedera*, family Araliaceae. The European ivy *Hedera helix* has shiny, evergreen, triangular or oval-shaped leaves and clusters of small, yellowish-green flowers, followed by black berries.

It climbs by means of root-like suckers put out from its stem, and is injurious to trees. Ground ivy *Glechoma hederacea* is a small, creeping plant of the Labiatae family found in Britain; the North American poison ivy *Rhus toxicodendron*, also known as poison oak, belongs to the Anacardiaceae family.

Ivy League a collective term for eight long-established East Coast private universities in the USA (Harvard, Yale, Princeton, Pennsylvania, Columbia, Brown, Dartmouth, and Cornell).

Iwo Jima /ˌiːwəʊˈdʒiːmə/ largest of the Japanese Volcano Islands in the W Pacific Ocean, 1,222 km/764 mi S of Tokyo; area 21 sq km/8 sq mi. Annexed by Japan 1891, it was captured by the US 1945 after heavy fighting. It was returned to Japan 1968.

IWW abbreviation for ◊Industrial Workers of the World.

Ixion /ɪkˈsaɪən/ in Greek mythology, a king whom Zeus punished for his crimes by binding him to a fiery wheel rolling endlessly through the underworld.

Izhevsk /iːˈʒefsk/ industrial city in the E USSR, capital of Udmurt Autonomous Republic; population (1987) 631,000. Industries include steel, agricultural machinery, machine tools, and armaments. It was founded 1760.

Izmir /ɪzˈmɪə/ formerly *Smyrna* port and naval base in Turkey; population (1985) 1,490,000. Products include steel, electronics, and plastics. The largest annual trade fair in the Middle East is held here. Headquarters of ◊North Atlantic Treaty Organization SE Command.

history Originally Greek (founded about 1000 BC), it was of considerable importance in ancient times, vying with Ephesus and Pergamum as the first city of Asia. It was destroyed by ◊Tamerlane in 1402, and became Turkish in 1424. It was occupied by the Greeks in 1919 but retaken by the Turks in 1922; in the same year it was largely destroyed by fire.

Iznik /ɪzˈniːk/ modern name of ancient ◊Nicaea, a town in Turkey.

principle of the screw to magnify an applied effort; in a car jack, for example, turning the handle many times causes the lifting screw to rise slightly, and the effort is magnified to lift heavy weights. A *hydraulic jack* uses a succession of piston strokes to increase pressure in a liquid and force up a lifting ram.

jackal carnivorous member of the dog family found in S Asia, S Europe, and N Asia. It can grow to 80 cm/2.7 ft long, has greyish-brown fur, and a bushy tail.

The *golden jackal Canis aureus* of S Asia, S Europe, and N Africa is 45 cm/1.5 ft high and 60 cm/2 ft long. It is greyish-yellow, darker on the back. Nocturnal, it preys on smaller mammals and poultry, though packs will attack larger animals. It will also scavenge. The *side-striped jackal Canis adustus* is found over much of Africa, the *black-backed jackal Canis mesomelas* only in the S of Africa.

Jack and the Beanstalk English fairy tale. Jack is the lazy son of a poor widow. When he exchanges their cow for some magic beans, the beans grow into a beanstalk that Jack climbs to a realm above the clouds. There he tricks a giant out of various magical treasures before finally killing him by cutting down the beanstalk.

jackdaw bird *Corvus monedula* of the crow family, found in Europe and W Asia. It is mainly black, but greyish on sides and back of head, and about 33 cm/1.1 ft long. It nests in tree holes or on buildings.

Jackson /'dʒæksən/ largest city and capital of Mississippi, USA, on the Pearl River; population (1980) 203,000. It produces furniture, cottonseed oil, iron and steel castings, and owes its prosperity to the discovery of gasfields to the South. Named after President Andrew Jackson, it dates from 1821 and was almost destroyed in the Civil War by Gen W Sherman 1863.

Jackson /'dʒæksən/ Alexander Young 1882–1974. Canadian landscape painter, a leading member of the *Group of Seven* who aimed to create a specifically Canadian school of landscape art.

Jackson /'dʒæksən/ Andrew 1767–1845. 7th president of the USA 1829–37, a Democrat. He was born in South Carolina. He defeated a British force at New Orleans in 1815 (after the official end of the war in 1814) and was involved in the war which led to the purchase of Florida in 1819. After an unsuccessful attempt in 1824, he was elected president in 1828. Governing through a 'kitchen cabinet', he also made use of the presidential veto to oppose the renewal of the US bank charter. Re-elected in 1832, he continued his struggle against the power of finance.

Jackson /'dʒæksən/ Glenda 1936– . British actress. She has made many stage appearances, including *Marat/Sade* 1966, and her films include the Oscar-winning *Women in Love* 1971. On television she played Queen Elizabeth I in *Elizabeth R* 1971.

Jackson British actress Glenda Jackson also takes an active interest in Labour politics.

Jackson US rock singer and songwriter Michael Jackson whose success and popularity reached a peak with the Thriller *album in 1982.*

Jackson /'dʒæksən/ Jesse 1941– . US Democrat politician, campaigner for minority rights. He contested his party's 1984 and 1988 presidential nominations in an effort to increase voter registration and to put black issues on the national agenda. He is a noted public speaker.

Born in North Carolina and educated in Chicago, Jackson emerged as a powerful Baptist preacher and black activist politician, working first with the civil-rights leader Martin Luther King, then on building the political machine that gave Chicago a black mayor 1983. He sought to construct what he called a *rainbow coalition*, comprising ethnic-minority and socially deprived groups. He took the lead in successfully campaigning for US disinvestment in South Africa 1986.

Jackson /'dʒæksən/ John Hughlings 1835–1911. English neurologist and neurophysiologist. As a result of his studies of ◊epilepsy, Jackson demonstrated that particular areas of the cerebral cortex (outer mantle of the brain) control the functioning of particular organs and limbs.

Jackson went on to map these out, and his views are held to be essentially correct. In his work, he demonstrated that ◊Helmholtz's ophthalmoscope is a crucial diagnostic tool for disorders of the nervous system.

Jackson /'dʒæksən/ Lady title of British economist Barbara ◊Ward.

Jackson /'dʒæksən/ Michael 1958– . US rock singer and songwriter, known for his meticulously choreographed performances. He had his first solo hit in 1971; his worldwide popularity reached a peak with the albums *Thriller* 1982 and *Bad* 1987.

He became professional in 1969 as the youngest member of the Jackson Five, who had hits on Motown Records from their first single, 'I Want You Back'. The group left Motown in 1975 and changed their name to the Jacksons. Michael was the lead singer, but soon surpassed his brothers in popularity as a solo performer. His 1980s albums, produced by Quincy Jones (1933–), yielded an unprecedented number of hit singles, outstanding among them 'Billie Jean' 1983.

Jackson /'dʒæksən/ Thomas Jonathan, known as 'Stonewall' Jackson 1824–1863. US Confederate general. In the American Civil War he acquired his nickname and his reputation at the Battle of ◊Bull Run, from the firmness with which his brigade resisted the Northern attack. In 1862 he organized the Shenandoah valley campaign, and assisted Lee's invasion of Maryland. He helped to defeat Gen Joseph E Hooker's Union army at the battle of Chancellorsville, Virginia, but was fatally wounded by one of his own men in the confusion of battle.

J tenth letter of the modern Roman alphabet. The modern English value of *j* is that of a compound consonant, *d* followed by the sound *zh* (as in pleasure, pronounced plea*zh*'ur).

J in physics, the abbreviation for *joule*, the SI unit of energy.

Jabalpur /ˌdʒæbəl'pʊə/ industrial city on the Narbarda river in Madhya Pradesh, India; population (1981) 758,000. Products include textiles, oil, bauxite, and armaments.

jabiru species of stork *Jabiru mycteria* found in Central and South America. It is 1.5 m/5 ft high with white plumage. The head is black and red.

Jablonec /'jæblonets/ town in Czechoslovakia, on the river Neisse, NE of Prague; population (1984) 45,000. It has had a glass industry since the 14th century.

jaborandi plant *Pilocarpus microphyllus*, family Rutaceae. Native to South America, it is the source of pilocarpine, used to contract the pupil of the eye.

jacamar bird of the family Galbulidae of Central and South America. They have long sharp-pointed bills, long tails, and paired toes. The plumage is brilliantly coloured. The largest species grows to 30 cm/12 in.

jacana one of seven species of wading birds, family Jacanidae, with very long toes and claws enabling it to walk on the flat leaves of river plants, hence the name 'lily trotter'. It is found in South America, Africa, S Asia, and Australia.

The female *pheasant-tailed jacana Hydrophasianus chirurgus*, of Asia, has a 'harem' of two to four males.

jacaranda genus of tropical American ornamental trees, family Bignoniaceae, with fragrant wood and whitish blue or violet flowers.

jacinth or *hyacinth* red or yellowish-red gem, a variety of zircon.

jack a tool or machine for lifting heavy weights such as motor vehicles. A *screw jack* uses the

Jackson *Confederate general Thomas Jackson, whose tactics in resisting Union forces at the Battle of Bull Run during the American Civil War earned him the nickname 'Stonewall'.*

Jacksonian Democracy in US history, a term describing the populist, egalitarian spirit pervading the presidencies of Andrew Jackson and Martin Van Buren (1833–1841) which encouraged greater participation in the democratic process. Recent studies have questioned the professed commitment to popular control, emphasizing Jackson's alleged cult of personality.

Jacksonville /'dʒæksənvɪl/ port, resort, and commercial centre in Florida, USA; population (1980) 541,000. The port has naval installations and ship repair yards. To the N the Cross-Florida Barge Canal links the Atlantic with the Gulf of Mexico.

Jack the Ripper /dʒæk/ popular name for the unidentified mutilator and murderer of five women prostitutes in the Whitechapel area of London in 1888.

Jacob /'dʒeɪkəb/ in the Old Testament, Hebrew patriarch, son of Isaac and Rebecca, who obtained the rights of seniority from his twin brother Esau by trickery. He married his cousins Leah and Rachel, serving their father Laban seven years for each, and at the time of famine in Canaan joined his son Joseph in Egypt. His 12 sons were the traditional ancestors of the 12 tribes of Israel.

Jacob /'dʒeɪkəb/ François 1920– . French biochemist who, with Jacques ◊Monod, did pioneering research in molecular genetics and showed how the production of proteins from ◊DNA is controlled.

Jacobabad /,dʒeɪkəbə'bæd/ city in Sind province, SE Pakistan, 400 km/250 mi NE of Karachi; population (1981) 80,000. Founded by General John Jacob as a frontier post, the city now trades in wheat, rice, and millet. It has a very low annual rainfall (about 5 cm/2 in) and temperatures are among the highest in the Indian subcontinent—up to 53°C/127°F.

Jacobean /,dʒækə'biːən/ a style in the arts, particularly in architecture and furniture, during the reign of James I (1603–25) in England. Following the general lines of Elizabethan design, but using classical features more widely, it adopted many motifs from Italian ◊Renaissance design.

Jacobin /'dʒækəbɪn/ member of an extremist republican club of the French Revolution founded at Versailles 1789, which later used a former Jacobin (Dominican) friary as its headquarters in Paris. It was led by ◊Robespierre, and closed after his execution 1794. The name 'Jacobin' passed into general use for any supporter of revolutionary or leftist opinions.

Jacobite /'dʒækəbaɪt/ in Britain, a supporter of the royal house of Stuart after the deposition of James II in 1688. They included the Scottish Highlanders, who rose unsuccessfully under ◊Claverhouse in 1689; and those who rose in Scotland and N England under the leadership

Jacquard *The Jacquard loom revolutionized the art of weaving, but was originally faced with violent opposition from silk weavers. On one occasion its French inventor, Joseph Marie Jacquard, narrowly escaped with his life.*

of ◊James Edward Stuart, the Old Pretender, in 1715, and followed his son ◊Charles Edward Stuart in an invasion of England which reached Derby in 1745–46. After the defeat at ◊Culloden, Jacobitism disappeared as a political force.

Jacobs /'dʒeɪkəbz/ W(illiam) W(ymark) 1863–1943. British author, who used his childhood knowledge of London's docklands in amusing short stories such as 'Many Cargoes' 1896. He excelled in the macabre, for example 'The Monkey's Paw' 1902.

Jacquard /'dʒækɑːd/ Joseph Marie 1752–1834. French textile manufacturer, who invented a punched-card system for programming designs on a carpet-making loom. In 1804 he constructed looms that used a series of punched cards which controlled the pattern of longitudinal warp threads depressed before each sideways passage of the shuttle. On later machines the punched cards were joined to form an endless loop which represented the 'program' for the repeating pattern of a carpet.

Jacquerie /,ʒækə'riː/ French peasant uprising 1358, caused by the ravages of the English army and French nobility, which reduced the rural population to destitution. The word derives from the nickname for French peasants, Jacques Bonhomme.

Jacuzzi /dʒə'kuːzi/ Candido 1903–1986. Italian-born US inventor and engineer, who invented the Jacuzzi, a pump that enabled a whirlpool to be emulated in a domestic bath. He developed it for his 15-month-old son, a sufferer from rheumatoid arthritis.

jade a semiprecious stone consisting of either jadeite, $NaAlSi_2O_6$ (a pyroxene), or nephrite, $Ca_2(Mg,Fe)_5Si_8O_{22}(OH,F)_2$ (an amphibole), ranging from colourless through shades of green to black according to the iron content. Jade ranks 5.5–6.5 on the Mohs' scale of hardness.

The early Chinese civilization discovered jade, bringing it from E Turkestan, and carried the art of jade-carving to its peak. The Olmecs, Aztecs, Maya, and the Maoris have also used jade for ornaments, ceremony, and utensils.

Jade Emperor in Chinese religion, the supreme god, Yu Huang, of pantheistic Taoism, who watches over human actions and is the ruler of life and death.

j'adoube (French 'I adjust') used in chess to show that a player is touching a piece in order to correct its position rather than to move it.

jaguar

Jaén /xɑːˈen/ capital of Jaén province, S Spain, on the Guadalbullon river; population (1986) 103,000. It has remains of its Moorish walls and citadel.

Jaffa /'dʒæfə/ Biblical name for **Joppa** port in W Israel, part of ◊Tel Aviv-Jaffa from 1950.

It was captured by the ◊Crusaders in the 12th century, by the French emperor Napoleon in 1799, and by ◊Allenby 1917.

Jaffna capital of Jaffna district, Northern Province, Sri Lanka. The focal point of Hindu Tamil nationalism and the scene of recurring riots during the 1980s.

Jagan /'dʒeɪgən/ Cheddi 1918– . Guyanese left-wing politician. Educated in British Guyana and the USA, he led the People's Progressive Party from 1950, and in 1961 he became the first prime minister of British Guyana.

Jagan /'dʒeɪgən/ Janet 1920– . Guyanese left-wing politician, wife of Cheddi Jagan. She was general secretary of the People's Progressive Party 1950–70.

jaguar largest species of cat *Panthera onca* in the Americas. It can grow up to 2.5 m/8 ft long including the tail. The ground colour of the fur varies from creamy white to brown or black, and is covered with black spots. The jaguar is usually solitary.

Jaguar British car manufacturer, which has enjoyed a long association with motor racing. They were one of the most successful companies in the 1950s and won the Le Mans 24 Hour race five times 1951–58.

The legendary XK120 was first built 1949. In the 1960s Jaguar were unable to compete with more powerful Ferrari sports cars and they did not make a comeback until the 1980s. In 1989 the company was bought by Ford for £1.6 billion.

jaguarundi wild cat *Felis yaguoaroundi* found in forests in Central and South America. Up to 1.1 m/3.5 ft long, it is very slim, with rather short legs and short rounded ears. It is uniformly coloured dark brown or chestnut. It is a good climber, and feeds on birds and small mammals, and, unusually for a cat, has been reported to eat fruit.

Jahangir /dʒəˈhɑːngɪə/ 'Conqueror of the World', name adopted by Salim 1569–1627. Third Mughal emperor of India from 1605, when he succeeded his father ◊Akbar the Great. He designed the Shalimar Gardens in Kashmir and buildings and gardens in Lahore.

In 1622 he lost Kandahar province in Afghanistan to Persia. His rule was marked by the influence of his wife, Nur Jahan, and her conflict with Prince Khurran (later Shah Jahan). His addiction to alcohol and opium weakened his power.

Jaguar *A Jaguar prototype sports-car at the Brands Hatch circuit, Kent, 1988.*

Jamaica

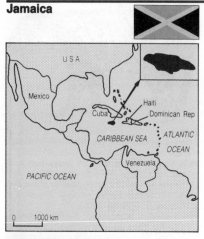

area 11,425 sq km/4,410 sq mi
capital Kingston
towns Montego Bay, Spanish Town, St Andrew
physical mountainous
features Blue Mountains (so called because of the haze over them, and renowned for their coffee); partly undersea remains of the pirate city of Port Royal, destroyed by earthquake 1692
head of state Elizabeth II from 1962 represented by Florizel Glasspole from 1973
head of government Michael Manley from 1989
political system constitutional monarchy
political parties Jamaica Labour Party (JLP), moderate, centrist; People's National Party (PNP), left-of-centre
exports sugar, bananas, bauxite, rum, coffee, coconuts, liqueurs, cigars
currency Jamaican dollar (11.65 = £1 Feb 1990)
population (1987) 2,300,000 (a mixture of several ethnic groups); annual growth rate 1.5%
life expectancy men 70, women 76
language English, Jamaican creole
religion Protestant 70%, Rastafarian
literacy 90% male/93% female (1980 est)
GNP $2.9 bn (1983); $1,340 per head of population
chronology
1959 Granted internal self-government.
1962 Achieved full independence, with Alexander Bustamente of the JLP as prime minister.
1967 JLP re-elected under Hugh Shearer.
1972 Michael Manley of the PNP became prime minister.
1980 JLP elected, with Edward Seaga as prime minister.
1983 JLP re-elected, winning all 60 seats.
1988 Island badly damaged by hurricane.
1989 PNP won a decisive victory with Michael Manley returning as prime minister.

government The 1962 constitution follows closely the unwritten British model, with a resident constitutional head of state, the governor-general, representing the British monarch and appointing a prime minister and cabinet, collectively responsible to the legislature. This consists of two chambers, an appointed, 21-member senate and a 60-member elected house of representatives. Normally 13 of the senators are appointed on the advice of the prime minister and eight on the advice of the leader of the opposition, but as the Jamaica Labour Party won all the seats in the 1983 general election there was no opposition leader, so all 21 senators were nominated by the prime minister. Members of the house are elected by universal suffrage for a five-year term, but it is subject to dissolution within that period. The main political parties are the Jamaica Labour Party (JLP), and the People's National Party (PNP).

history Before the arrival of Christopher ◊Columbus in 1494, the island was inhabited by ◊Arawak Indians. From 1509–1655 it was a Spanish colony, and after this was in British hands until 1959, when it was granted internal self-government, achieving full independence within the Commonwealth in 1962.

The two leading political figures in the early days of independence were Alexander Bustamante, leader of the JLP, and Norman Manley, leader of the PNP. The JLP won the 1962 and 1967 elections, led by Bustamante's successor, Hugh Shearer, but the PNP, under Norman Manley's son Michael, was successful in 1972. He advocated social reform and economic independence from the developed world. Despite high unemployment, Manley was returned to power in 1976 with an increased majority but by 1980 the economy had deteriorated and, rejecting the conditions attached to an IMF loan, Manley sought support for his policies of economic self-reliance.

The 1980 general election campaign was extremely violent, despite calls by Manley and the leader of the JLP, Edward Seaga, for moderation. The outcome was a decisive victory for the JLP, with 51 of the 60 seats in the house of representatives. Seaga thus received a mandate for a return to a renewal of links with the USA and an emphasis on free enterprise. He severed diplomatic links with Cuba in 1981. In 1983 Seaga called an early, snap election, with the opposition claiming they had been given insufficient time to nominate their candidates. The JLP won all 60 seats. There were violent demonstrations when the new parliament was inaugurated and the PNP said it would continue its opposition outside the parliamentary arena. In the 1989 general election Manley and the PNP won a landslide victory, after which the new prime minister pledged to pursue moderate economic policies and better relations with the USA.

Jahweh /ˈjɑːweɪ/ another spelling of ◊Jehovah, God in the Hebrew Bible or Old Testament.

jai alai another name for the ball-game ◊pelota.

Jainism Indian religion, sometimes regarded as an offshoot from Hinduism. Jains believe that non-injury to living beings is the highest religion, and their code of ethics is based on sympathy and compassion. They also believe in ◊karma. In Jainism there is no deity, and like Buddhism it is a monastic religion. Jains number about 3.3 million.

There are two main sects: the Digambaras, who originally went about naked, and the Swetambaras.

Its sacred books record the teachings of Mahavira (599–527 BC), the latest of a long series of Tirthankaras, or omniscient saints and seers. Mahavira was born in Vessali (now Bessarh), E India. He became an ascetic at the age of 30, acquired omniscience (became all-knowing) at 42, and preached for 30 years.

Jaipur /ˌdʒaɪˈpʊə/ capital of Rajasthan, India; population (1981) 1,005,000. Formerly the capital of the state of Jaipur, it was merged with Rajasthan in 1949. Products include textiles and metal products.

Jakarta /dʒəˈkɑːtə/ or **Djakarta** capital of Indonesia on the NW coast of Java; population (1980) 6,504,000. Industries include textiles, chemicals, and plastics; a canal links it with its port of Tanjung Priok where rubber, oil, tin, coffee, tea, and palm oil are among its exports; it is also a tourist centre.

Founded by the Dutch in 1619, and known as Batavia until 1949, it has the president's palace and government offices.

Jakeš /ˈjɑːkeʃ/ Miloš 1922– . Czech communist politician, a member of the Politburo from 1981 and party leader 1987–89. A conservative, he supported the Soviet invasion of Czechoslovakia in 1968. He was forced to resign in Nov 1989 following a series of pro-democracy mass rallies.

Jakeš, an electrical engineer, joined the Communist Party of Czechoslovakia (CCP) in 1945 and studied in Moscow 1955–58. As head of the CCP's central control commission, he oversaw the purge of reformist personnel after the suppression of the 1968 Prague Spring. In Dec 1987 he replaced Gustáv Husák as CCP leader. Although he enjoyed close relations with the Soviet leader Gorbachev, Jakeš was a cautious reformer who was unpopular with the people.

Jalalabad capital of Nangarhar province, E Afghanistan, on the road from Kabul to Peshawar in Pakistan. The city was besieged by mujaheddin rebels in 1989 after the withdrawal of Soviet troops from Afghanistan.

Jalgava /ˈjælɡəvə/ town in Latvian republic, USSR, called **Mitau** until 1917, 48 km/30 mi S of Riga; population about 57,000. Industries include textile and sugar-refining. The town was founded in 1265 by Teutonic knights.

Jamaica /dʒəˈmeɪkə/ island in the Caribbean, to the S of Cuba, and to the W of Haiti.

Jainism The statue of Lord Bahubali (Gomateshvera) at Sravanabelagola, Tamil Nadu, is one of the oldest and most important Jain pilgrimage centres in India.

James /dʒeɪmz/ Henry 1843–1916. US novelist, who lived in Europe from 1875 and became a naturalized British subject 1915. His novels deal with the impact of European culture on the US soul. They include *The Portrait of a Lady* 1881, *Washington Square* 1881, *The Bostonians* 1886, *The Ambassadors* 1903, and *The Golden Bowl* 1904. He also wrote more than a hundred shorter works of fiction, notably the supernatural tale *The Turn of the Screw* 1898.

His other major works include *Roderick Hudson* 1876, *The American* 1877, *The Tragic Muse* 1890, *The Spoils of Poynton* 1897, *The Awkward Age* 1899, *The Wings of the Dove* 1902.

James /dʒeɪmz/ Jesse 1847–1882. US bank and train robber, born in Missouri and a leader (with his brother Frank) of the ◊Quantrill gang. Jesse was killed by an accomplice; Frank remained unconvicted and became a farmer.

James /dʒeɪmz/ M(ontague) R(hodes) 1862–1936. British writer, theologian, linguist, and medievalist. He wrote *Ghost Stories of an Antiquary* 1904 and other supernatural tales.

James US author Henry James, who explored the effects of European culture on Americans in such novels as Daisy Miller and The Ambassadors.

James /dʒeɪmz/ P(hyllis) D(orothy) 1920– . British detective novelist, creator of the characters Superintendent Adam Dalgliesh and private investigator Cordelia Gray. She was a tax official, hospital administrator, and civil servant before turning to writing. Her books include *Death of an Expert Witness* 1977, *The Skull Beneath the Skin* 1982, and *A Taste for Death* 1986.

James /dʒeɪmz/ William 1842–1910. US psychologist and philosopher, brother of the novelist Henry James. He turned from medicine to psychology and taught at Harvard 1872–1907. His books include *Principles of Psychology* 1890, *The Will to Believe* 1897, and *Varieties of Religious Experience* 1902, one of the most important works on the psychology of religion.

James I /dʒeɪmz/ the Conqueror 1208–1276. King of Aragon from 1213, when he succeeded his father. He conquered the Balearic Islands and took Valencia from the Moors, dividing it with Alfonso X of Castile by a treaty of 1244. Both these exploits are recorded in his autobiography *Llibre deis feyts*. He largely established Aragon as the dominant power in the Mediterranean.

James /dʒeɪmz/ two kings of Britain:

James I 1566–1625. King of England from 1603 and Scotland (*James VI*) from 1567. The son of Mary, Queen of Scots, and Lord Darnley, he succeeded on his mother's abdication from the Scottish throne, assumed power 1583, established

James Notorious US bandit Jesse James, who masterminded a series of robberies before being betrayed by a member of his own gang.

James I The son of Mary, Queen of Scots, James I of England was already king of Scotland when he came to the throne in England in 1603.

a strong centralized authority, and in 1589 married Anne of Denmark (1574–1619). As successor to Elizabeth in England, he alienated the Puritans by his High Church views and Parliament by his assertion of divine right, and was generally unpopular because of his favourites, such as ◊Buckingham, and because of his schemes for an alliance with Spain. He was succeeded by his son Charles I.

James II 1633–1701. King of England and Scotland (*James VII*) from 1685, second son of Charles I. He succeeded Charles II. James married Anne Hyde 1659 (1637–71, mother of Mary II and Anne) and ◊Mary of Modena 1673 (mother of James Edward Stuart). He became a Catholic 1671, which led first to attempts to exclude him from the succession, then to the rebellions of ◊Monmouth and ◊Argyll, and finally to the Whig and Tory leaders' invitation to William of Orange to take the throne in 1688. James fled to France, led a rising in Ireland 1689, but after defeat at the Battle of the ◊Boyne 1690 remained in exile in France.

James /dʒeɪmz/ seven kings of Scotland:

James I 1394–1437. King of Scotland 1406–37, who assumed power 1424. He was a cultured and strong monarch, whose improvements in the administration of justice brought him popularity among the common people. He was assassinated by a group of conspirators led by the Earl of Atholl.

James II 1430–1460. King of Scotland from 1437, who assumed power 1449. The only surviving son of James I, he was supported by most of the nobles and parliament. He sympathized with the Lancastrians during the War of the ◊Roses, and attacked English possessions in S Scotland. He was killed while besieging Roxburgh Castle.

James III 1451–1488. King of Scotland from 1460, who assumed power 1469. His reign was marked by rebellions by the nobles, including his brother Alexander, duke of Albany. He was murdered during a rebellion.

Jammu and Kashmir

James IV 1473–1513. King of Scotland from 1488, who married Margaret (1489–1541, daughter of Henry VII) in 1503. He invaded England 1513, but was defeated and killed at ◊Flodden.

James V 1512–1542. King of Scotland from 1513, who assumed power 1528. Following an attack on Scottish territory by Henry VIII's forces, he was defeated near the border at Solway Moss 1542.

James VI of Scotland. See ◊James I of England.

James VII of Scotland. See ◊James II of England.

James Edward Stuart /dʒeɪmz/ 1688–1766. British prince, known as the Old Pretender (for ◊Jacobites James III). Son of James II, he was born at St James's Palace and after the revolution of 1688 was taken to France. He landed in Scotland in 1715 to head a Jacobite rebellion, but withdrew for lack of support. In his later years he settled in Rome.

Jameson /'dʒeɪmɪsən/ Leander Starr 1853–1917. British colonial administrator. In South Africa, early in 1896, he led the *Jameson Raid* from Mafeking into Transvaal, in support of the non-Boer colonists there, in an attempt to overthrow the government, for which he served some months in prison. Returning to South Africa, he succeeded Cecil ◊Rhodes as leader of the Progressive Party of Cape Colony, where he was prime minister 1904–08.

James, St /dʒeɪmz/ the Great died AD 44. A New Testament apostle, originally a Galilean fisherman, he was the son of Zebedee and brother of the apostle John. He was put to death by ◊Herod Agrippa. Patron saint of Spain. Feast day 25 July.

James, St /dʒeɪmz/ the Just 1st century AD. The New Testament brother of Jesus, to whom Jesus appeared after the Resurrection. Leader of the Christian church in Jerusalem, he was the author of the biblical Epistle of James.

James, St /dʒeɪmz/ the Little 1st century AD. In the New Testament, a disciple of Christ, son of Alphaeus. Feast day 3 May.

Jamestown /'dʒeɪmztaʊn/ first permanent British settlement in North America, established by Capt John Smith 1607. It was capital of Virginia 1624–99. In the nearby Jamestown Festival Park there is a replica of the original Fort James, and models of the ships (*Discovery, Godspeed,* and *Constant*) that carried the 105 pioneers.

Jammu /'dʒʌmu:/ winter capital of the state of ◊Jammu and Kashmir, India; population (1981) 206,100. It stands on the river Tavi and was linked to India's rail system in 1972.

Jammu and Kashmir /'dʒʌmu:, ˌkæʃ'mɪə/ state of N India
area 101,300 sq km/39,102 sq mi; another 78,900 sq km/30,455 is occupied by Pakistan, and 42,700 sq km/16,482 by China
capital Srinagar (winter); Jammu (summer)
towns Leh
products timber, grain, rice, fruit, silk, carpets
population (1981) 5,982,000 (Indian-occupied territory)
history in 1947 Jammu was attacked by Pakistan and chose to become part of the new state of India. Dispute over the area caused further hostilities 1971 between India and Pakistan (ended by the Simla agreement 1972).
  Part of the Mogul Empire from 1586, Jammu came under the control of Gulab Singh 1820.

Jamnagar /dʒæm'nʌgə/ city in Gujarat, India, on the Gulf of Kutch, SW of Ahmedabad; population (1981) 317,000. Its port is at Bedi.

Jamshedpur /ˌdʒʌmʃed'pʊə/ city in Bihar, India; population (1981) 439,000. It was built in 1909, and takes its name from the industrialist Jamsheedji Tata, who founded the Tata iron and steel works here and in Bombay.

Janácek /'jænətʃek/ Leoš 1854–1928. Czech composer. He became director of the Conservatoire at Brno in 1919 and professor at the Prague Conservatoire in 1920. His music, highly original and influenced by Moravian folk music, includes arrangements of folk songs, operas (*Jenufa* 1904,

Japan *A typical Japanese housing estate.*

The Cunning Little Vixen 1924), and the choral *Glagolitic Mass* 1927.

Janam Sakhis a collection of stories about the life of Nanak, the first guru (teacher) of Sikhism.

Janata alliance of political parties in India formed 1971 to oppose Indira Gandhi's Congress Party. Victory in the election brought Morarji Desai to power as prime minister but he was unable to control the various groups within the alliance and resigned 1979. His successors fared little better and the elections of 1980 overwhelmingly returned Indira Gandhi to office.

Jane Eyre a novel by Charlotte Brontë, published 1847. Jane, an orphan, is engaged as governess to Mr Rochester's ward Adèle. Rochester and Jane fall in love, but their wedding is prevented by the revelation that Rochester already has a wife. Jane flees, but later returns to find the house destroyed by fire and Rochester blinded in a vain attempt to save his wife. Jane and Rochester marry.

janissary (Turkish *yeniçeri*, 'new force') bodyguard of the sultan, the Turkish standing army 1330–1826. Until the 16th century janissaries were Christian boys forcibly converted to Islam; after this time they were allowed to marry, and recruit their own children. The bodyguard ceased to exist when it revolted against the decision of the sultan in 1826 to raise a regular force.

Jan Mayen /'jæn 'maɪən/ Norwegian volcanic island in the Arctic, between Greenland and Norway; area 380 sq km/147 sq mi. It is named after a Dutchman who visited it about 1610, and was annexed by Norway 1929.

Jannequin Clament *c.*1472–*c.*1560. French composer. He studied with Josquin ◊Desprez and is remembered for choral works that incorporate images from real life, such as birdsong and the cries of street vendors.

Jannings /'jænɪŋs/ Emil. Stage name of Theodor Emil Jarenz 1882–1950. German actor whose greatest success was in silent films of the 1920s, as in *The Last Command* 1928. In *Der blaue Engel/The Blue Angel* 1930 he played a schoolteacher who loses his head over Marlene Dietrich. He remained in Germany during the Nazi era.

Jansen /'dʒænsən/ Cornelius 1585–1638. Dutch Roman Catholic theologian, founder of Jansenism with his book *Augustinus* 1640. He became professor at Louvain, Belgium, in 1630, and bishop of Ypres, Belgium, in 1636.

Jansenism Christian teaching of Cornelius Jansen, which divided the Roman Catholic Church in France in the mid-17th century. Emphasizing the more predestinatory approach of Augustine's teaching, as opposed to that of the Jesuits, Jansenism was supported by the philosopher Pascal and Antoine Arnauld (a theologian linked with the abbey of ◊Port Royal). Jansenists were excommunicated 1719.

In 1713 a Jansenist work by Pasquier Quesnel (1634–1719), the leader of the Jansenist party, was condemned by Pope Clement XI as heretical, and after Quesnel's death Jansenism as an organized movement in France disappeared. It

Japan
(Nippon)

area 377,815 sq km/145,837 sq mi
capital Tokyo
towns Fukuoka, Kitakyushu, Kyoto, Sapporo; ports Osaka, Nagoya, Yokohama, Kobe, Kawasaki
physical mountainous, volcanic; comprises over 1,000 islands, of which the chief are Hokkaido, Honshu, Shikoku, Kyushu, Ryukyu
features Mount Fuji
head of state (figurehead) Emperor Akihito from 1989
head of government Toshiki Kaifu from 1989.
political system constitutional monarchy
political parties Liberal Democratic Party (LDP), right-of-centre; Japan Socialist Party (JSP), left-of-centre; Komeito (Clean Government Party), Buddhist-centrist; Democratic Socialist Party, centrist; Japanese Communist Party (JCP), socialist
exports televisions, cassette and video recorders, radios, cameras, computers, robots, other electronic and electrical equipment, cars and other vehicles, ships, iron, steel, chemicals, textiles
currency yen (246.25 = £1 Feb 1990)
population (1987) 122,264,000; annual growth rate 0.7%
life expectancy men 74, women 80
language Japanese
religion Shinto and Buddhist (often combined), Christian (minority). 30% of the population claim to have a personal religious faith
literacy 99% (1985)
GNP $1,200 bn (1984); $10,266 per head of population
chronology
1945 Japanese surrender. Allied control commission in power.
1946 Framing of 'Peace Constitution'.
1952 Full sovereignty regained.
1958 Joined United Nations.
1972 Ryukyu Islands regained.
1974 Resignation of Prime Minister Tanaka over Lockheed bribes scandal.
1982 Election of Yasuhiro Nakasone as prime minister.
1987 Noboru Takeshita chosen to succeed Nakasone.
1988 Recruit corporation insider-trading scandal cast shadow over government and opposition parties.
1989 Emperor Hirohito died and was succeeded by his son Akihito. Two cabinet ministers forced to resign over Recruit, and many more implicated. Takeshita eventually resigned because of the Recruit scandal, and was succeeded by Sosuke Uno in June. Uno resigned Aug over revelations that he had had affairs with geishas, and was succeeded by Toshiki Kaifu.
1990 New house of councillors' elections (Feb) won by LDP.

survived in the Netherlands, where in 1723 a regular Jansenist church was established under the bishop of Utrecht.

jansky unit of radiation received from outer space, used in radio astronomy, named after K G Jansky.

Jansky /'dʒænski/ Karl Guthe 1905–1950. US radio engineer, who discovered that the Milky Way galaxy emanates radio waves.

Born in Norman, Oklahoma, he joined Bell Telephone Laboratories, New Jersey 1928, where he investigated causes of static that created interference on radio telephone calls. Jansky found that the centre of the ◊galaxy was giving out radio waves; he did not follow up his discovery, but it marked the birth of radioastronomy.

Januarius, St /,dʒænju'eərɪəs/ or *San Gennaro* died ?305. Patron saint of Naples, Italy. Traditionally, he suffered martyrdom under the Roman emperor Diocletian. Two phials of his blood are alleged regularly to liquefy miraculously. Feast day 19 Sept.

Janus /'dʒeɪnəs/ in Roman mythology, god of doorways and passageways, the patron of the beginning of the day, month, and year, after whom January is named; he is represented as two-faced, looking both forward and back.

Japan /dʒə'pæn/ country in E Asia, occupying a group of islands of which the four main ones are Hokkaido, Honshu, Kyushu, and Shikoku. Japan is situated in the N Pacific, to the E of North and South Korea.

government Japan's 1946 constitution was framed by the occupying Allied forces with the intention of creating a consensual, parliamentary form of government and avoiding an overconcentration of executive authority. The emperor, whose functions are purely ceremonial, is head of state. The Japanese parliament is a two-chamber body composed of a 252-member house of councillors and a 512-member house of representatives. The former chamber comprises 152 representatives elected from 47 prefectural constituencies by the 'limited-vote' system and 100 elected nationally by proportional representation. Each member serves a six-year term, the chamber being elected half at a time every three years. Representatives to the lower house are elected by universal suffrage for four-year terms in multi-member constituencies. The house of representatives is the most powerful chamber, able to override (if a two-thirds majority is gained) vetoes on bills imposed by the house of councillors, and enjoying paramountcy on financial questions. Legislative business is effected through a system of standing committees. Executive administration is entrusted to a prime minister chosen by parliament, who selects a cabinet that is collectively responsible to parliament.

The major political parties are: on the right, the Liberal Democratic Party (LDP); in the centre, the Democratic Socialist Party and the Komeito (Clean Government) Party; and on the left, the Japan Socialist Party and the Japan Communist Party.

The LDP has dominated postwar Japanese politics, monopolizing government power. It is divided into five powerful, clanlike factions—the Takeshita, Abe, Miyazawa, Watanabe, and Komoto—which compete and bargain for cabinet portfolios. The ultimate prize is the position of prime minister, which each faction seeks to capture by succeeding in the biennial contests for presidency of the LDP.

history Evidence of human occupation exists on the Japanese islands from 30,000-year-old tools, but the Japanese nation probably arose from the fusion of two peoples, one from the Malay Peninsula or Polynesia, the other from Asia, who conquered the original inhabitants, the ◊Ainu. Japanese history remains legendary until the leadership of the first emperor Jimmu was recorded about 660 BC. By the 5th century AD, the art of writing had been introduced from Korea. After the introduction of Buddhism, also from Korea, in the 6th century, Chinese culture became generally accepted, but although attempts were made in the 7th century to diminish the power of the nobles and set up a strong centralized monarchy on the Chinese model, real power remained in the hands of the great feudal families until modern times.

A group of warrior families became increasingly important in organising local affairs and the 12th century saw the creation of a military government (shogunate)—a form that persisted until 1867. During the Kamakura shogunate (1192–1333), the Mongol invasions from Korea were repulsed. For the next three centuries the country remained riven by factions, and it was not until the battle of Sekigahara 1600, that Tokugawa Ieyasu defeated his rivals and established the Tokugawa shogunate (1603–1867).

Contact with Europe began 1542 when Portuguese traders arrived; they were followed by the Spanish, and in 1609 by the Dutch. Christianity was introduced by Francis ◊Xavier 1549. During the 15th–16th centuries Japan sank into a state of feudal anarchy, until order was restored 1570–1615 by three great rulers, Nobunaga, Hideyoshi, and Iyeyasu; the family of the latter, the Tokugawa, held power until the abolition of the shogunate 1867.

The fear that Roman Catholic propaganda was intended as a preparation for Spanish conquest led to the expulsion of the Spanish 1624 and the Portuguese 1639, and to the almost total extermination of Christianity by persecution; only the Dutch were allowed to trade with Japan, under irksome restrictions, while Japanese subjects were forbidden to leave the country. This isolation continued until 1853, when the USA insisted on opening trade relations; during the next few years this example was followed by the European powers. Consequently the isolationist party compelled the shogun to abdicate 1867, and executive power was restored to the emperor. During the next 30 years the privileges of the feudal nobility were abolished, a uniform code of law was introduced, and a constitution was established 1889. The army was modernized, and a powerful navy founded. Industry developed steadily and a considerable export trade was built up.

In 1894 a war with China secured Japanese control of Formosa and S Manchuria, as well as Korea, which was formally annexed 1910. A victory over Russia 1904–05 gave Japan the southern half of Sakhalin, and compelled the Russians to evacuate Manchuria. Japan formed an alliance with Britain 1902, and joined the Allies in World War I. At the peace settlement it received the German islands in the N Pacific as mandates. The 1920s saw an advance towards democracy and party government, but after 1932 the government assumed a semi-Fascist form. As a result of successful aggression against China 1931–32, a Japanese puppet monarchy under P'u-i, the last emperor of China, was established in Manchuria (see ◊Manchukuo); war with China was renewed 1937.

Japan entered World War II with the attack on Pearl Harbor 7 Dec 1941, and at first won a succession of victories in the Philippines, the Malay Peninsula, Burma, and the Netherlands Indies. Japan was finally compelled to surrender 15 Aug 1945, following the detonation of atomic bombs at ◊Hiroshima and ◊Nagasaki. An allied control commission took charge and Japan was placed under military occupation by Allied (chiefly US) troops under Gen Douglas ◊MacArthur until 1952, when the Japanese Peace Treaty came into force and full sovereignty was regained.

After Japan's defeat, Korea was made independent; Manchuria and Formosa (◊Taiwan) were returned to China; and the islands mandated to Japan after World War I were placed by the United Nations under US trusteeship. Japan regained the

◊Ryukyu Islands 1972 and the ◊Bonin and Volcano Islands 1968 from the USA, and continues to agitate for the return of the Northern Territories (the islands of the Shikotan and Habomai Group) and the southernmost ◊Kurils (Kunashiri and Etorofu).

During Allied rule, Aug 1945–Apr 1952, a major 'democratization campaign' was launched, involving radical land, social, and educational reform and the framing of a new 'Peace Constitution' 1946 in which Emperor ◊Hirohito renounced his claims to divinity and became a powerless figurehead ruler, and the nation committed itself to a pacific foreign policy. Japan concentrated during the early postwar years on economic reconstruction, tending towards neutralism in foreign affairs under the protection provided by the 1951 Security Pact.

Postwar politics in Japan were dominated by the LDP, formed 1955 from the merger of existing conservative parties and providing a regular succession of prime ministers. Real decision-making, however, centred around a broader, consensual grouping of politicians, senior civil servants, and directors of the major *zaibatsu* (finance and industrial houses). Through a paternalist, guided approach to economic development, epitomized by the operations of the Ministry for International Trade and Industry (MITI), the Japanese economy expanded dramatically during the 1950s and 1960s, with gross national product (GNP) increasing by 10% per year.

During this period, Japan was rehabilitated within the international community, entering the UN 1958 and establishing diplomatic relations with Western nations and, following the lead taken by the Nixon presidency, with Communist China 1972. Japan's internal politics were rocked 1960 and 1968–69 by violent demonstrations involving the anarchic Red Army guerrilla organization against US domination, and in 1974 by the resignation of Prime Minister Kakuei Tanaka after a bribery scandal involving the US Lockheed Corporation. This scandal tarnished the image of the LDP and led to the loss of its majority in the house of representatives 1976 and the formation of the New Liberal Club as a breakaway grouping. The LDP remained in power, however, as the largest single party in parliament.

Japanese economic growth was maintained during the 1970s, though at a reduced annual rate of 4.5%, and the country made a major impact in the markets of North America and Europe as an exporter of electrical goods, machinery, and motor vehicles. This created resentment overseas as economic recession began to grip Europe and the USA during the later 1970s, and led to calls for Japan to open up its internal market to foreign exporters and accept a greater share of the defence burden for the Asia-Pacific region. Prime ministers Miki, Fukuda, Ohira, and Suzuki resisted these pressures, and the Japanese government, in 1976, placed a rigid 1% of GNP limit on military spending.

A review of policy was instituted by Prime Minister Yasuhiro ◊Nakasone, who assumed power 1982. He favoured a strengthening of Japan's military capability, a re-evaluation of attitudes towards the country's past, and the introduction of a more liberal, open-market economic strategy at home. His policy departures were controversial and only partly implemented. However, he gained a landslide victory in the 1986 elections, and became the first prime minister since Sato (1964–72) to be re-elected by the LDP for more than one term. During 1987 his plans for tax reform, including the introduction of a 5% value-added tax (VAT), were overturned by the Diet. Despite this defeat Nakasone remained popular and was able, following factional deadlock within the LDP, to select Noboru ◊Takeshita as his successor.

Takeshita continued Nakasone's domestic and foreign policies, introducing a 3% sales tax 1988 and lowering income-tax levels to boost domestic

consumption. The new sales tax was electorally unpopular, and the government's standing during 1988–89 was further undermined by the Recruit-Cosmos insider share-dealing scandal (see ◊Recruit scandal), in which more than 40 senior LDP and opposition figures, including Takeshita, Nakasone, the deputy prime minister, and the finance and justice ministers, were implicated. The last three were forced to resign, as, eventually, was Takeshita in June 1989. This marked an inauspicious start to the new *Heisei* ('achievement of universal peace') era proclaimed on the death Jan 1989 of Hirohito (Showa) and the accession of his son ◊Akihito as emperor.

The new prime minister, Sosuke Uno, the former foreign minister, was soon dogged by a geisha sex scandal. His standing was further undermined by the LDP's unprecedented loss of its majority in the house of councillors, following elections July 1989, and after only 53 days in office he resigned Aug 1989. He was replaced by Toshiki Kaifu, a former education minister and member of the LDP's small scandal-free Komoto faction. Kaifu formed a new cabinet whose members were comparatively young and which, in an attempt to counter the growing appeal to women of the Japanese Socialist Party, led by Ms Takako Doi, included two women. Kaifu having partly repaired the damage done to the LDP by the Recruit scandal, parliament was dissolved Jan 1990 and elections called for Feb. They were won by the LDP, but with large gains for the JSP.

Japan Current or *Kuroshio* warm ocean ◊current flowing from Japan to North America.

Japanese an inhabitant of Japan.

Although Japan has a highly distinctive culture, Korean and Chinese influences were important during the early centuries AD. In addition to the art of writing, from the Chinese the Japanese learned skills in public finance, administration and animal husbandry. Confucian philosophy and Buddhism were also introduced from China, although there was some opposition to Buddhism by Shintoists. Japanese interest in China waned during the decline of the Tang Dynasty (AD 618–907).

The 12th century saw the rise of the code of warriors. Making up approximately 8% of the population, the warriors, ◊samurai, had the right to wear two swords, and were permitted to cut down a member of another class who was deemed to have offended the samurai. Merchants, although often wealthier than the samurai, belonged to a lower social order. Some highly skilled craftsmen were allowed to bear family names, a privilege usually reserved for the highest social tier. The lowest social group comprised the burakunin or eta, responsible for slaughtering animals, and engaged in such trades as tanning leather and shoemaking.

During the 19th century the privileges of the feudal nobility were abolished and Japan began to develop its industrial base. The rapid economic expansion of the post-war years has seen the decline of the extended family, in which three or more generations live under the same roof. Large corporations provide a way of life for many Japanese, although this appears to be less the case with younger generations. The descendants of Japanese migrants are found in Hawaii and North America, and there are Japanese business communities in the cities of many industrial nations.

Japanese art the painting, sculpture, and design of Japan. Japanese art was early influenced by China. Painting developed a distinct Japanese character, bolder and more angular, with the spread of Zen Buddhism in the 12th century. Ink painting and calligraphy flourished, followed by book illustration and decorative screens. Japanese prints developed in the 17th century, with multicolour prints invented around 1765. Buddhist sculpture proliferated from 580, and Japanese sculptors excelled at portraits. Japanese pottery stresses simplicity. *Jōmon* period (10,000–300 BC): Characterized by cord-marked pottery.

Yayoi period (300 BC–AD 300): Elegant pottery and *dōtaku*, bronze bells decorated with engravings.

Kofun period (300–552): Burial mounds held *haniwa*, clay figures, some of which show Chinese influence.

Asuka period (552–646): Buddhist art, introduced from Korea 552, flourished in sculpture, metalwork, and embroidered silk banners. Painters' guilds were formed.

Nara period (646–794): Religious and portrait sculptures were made of bronze, clay, or dry lacquer. A few painted scrolls, screens, and murals survive. Textiles were designed in batik, tie-dye, stencil, embroidery, and brocade.

Heian period (794–1185): Buddhist statues became formalized and were usually made of wood. Shinto images emerged. A native style of secular painting (*Yamato-e*) developed, especially in scroll painting, with a strong emphasis on surface design. Lacquerware was also decoratively stylized.

Kamakura period (1185–1392): Sculpture and painting became vigorously realistic. Portraits were important, and in painting also landscapes and religious, narrative, and humorous picture scrolls.

Ashikaga or *Muromachi* period (1392–1568): The rapid ink sketch in line and wash introduced by Zen priests from China became popular. Pottery gained in importance from the spread of the tea ceremony. Masks and costumes were made for Nō theatre.

Momoyama period (1568–1615): Artists produced beautiful screens to decorate palaces and castles. The arrival of Korean potters inspired new styles.

Tokugawa or *Edo* period (1615–1867): The print (*ukiyo-e*) originated in genre paintings of 16th- and 17th-century kabuki actors and teahouse women. It developed into the woodcut and after 1740 the true colour print, while its range of subject matter expanded. *Ukiyo-e* artists include Utamaro and Hokusai. Lacquer and textiles became more sumptuous. Tiny *netsuke* figures were mostly carved from ivory or wood.

Meiji period (1868–1912): Painting was influenced by Western art, for example Impressionism.

Shōwa period (1926–89): Attempts were made to revive the traditional Japanese painting style and to combine traditional and foreign styles.

Japanese language a traditionally isolated language of E Asia, spoken almost exclusively in the islands of Japan. Possibly related to Korean, Japanese is

Japanese art *Bando Hikozqburo (c. 1850) by Kunisada Utagawa (private collection).*

culturally and linguistically influenced by Mandarin Chinese and written in Chinese-derived ideograms as well as syllabic alphabets.

Japanese has an extensive religious and secular literature, including such terse poetic forms as the ◊haiku. English words adapted into Japanese belong in *gairaigo*, the foreign vocabulary expressed in the syllable signs of Katakana: *fairu* ('file') *ereganto* ('elegant'), and *purutoniumu* ('plutonium'). Shorter forms are common, such as *fainda* ('viewfinder') and *wapuro* ('word-processor'). Japanese has a well-defined structure of syllables, generally ending with a vowel (*dojo, judo, hiragana, samurai, Honshu, kimono, Mitsubishi, teriyaki*). Japanese is written in a triple system that has evolved from Chinese ideograms: its *Kanji* ideograms are close to their Chinese originals, while the *Hiragana* system is a syllabary for the general language, and *Katakana* a syllabary for foreign borrowings. In print, the three systems blend on the page in a manner comparable to the distinct typefaces of the Roman alphabet. Japanese is now taught in some W European countries.

Japanese literature earliest survivals include the 8th-century *Collection of a Myriad Leaves*, with poems by Hitomaro and Akahito (the principal form being the *tanka*, a five-line stanza of 5, 7, 5, 7, and 7, syllables), and the prose *Record of Ancient Matters*. The late 10th and early 11th centuries produced the writers Sei Shōnagon and Murasaki Shikibu. During the 14th century the Nō drama developed from ceremonial religious dances, combined with monologues and dialogues. The 17th century brought such scholars of Chinese studies as Fujiwara Seikwa (1560–1619) and Arai Hakuseki (1657–1725). To this period belongs the origin of *kabuki*, the popular drama of Japan, of which Chikamatsu Monzaemon (1653–1724) is the chief exponent; of *haiku* (the stanza of three lines of 5, 7, and 5 syllables), popularized by Bashō, and of the modern novel, as represented by Ibara Saikaku (1642–93). Among those reacting against Chinese influence was the poet-historian Motoori Norinaga (1730–1801). The late 19th and early 20th centuries saw the replacement of the obsolete *Tokugawa* style as a literary medium by the modern colloquial language, and the influence of Western and Russian literature produced writers such as the 'Realist' Tsubouchi Shōyo (1859–1935), followed by the 'Naturalist' and 'Idealistic' novelists, whose romantic preoccupation with self-expression gave rise to the still popular 'I-novels' of, for example, Dazai Osamu (1909–48).

A reaction against the autobiographical school came from Natsume Sōseki (1867–1916), Nagai Kafū (1879–1959), and Junichirō Tanizaki (1886–1965), who found inspiration in past traditions or in self-sublimation; later novelists include Yasunari Kawabata (1899–1972) and Yukio Mishima. Shimazaki Tōson (1872–1943) introduced Western-style poetry, for example 'Symbolism', but the traditional forms of *haiku* and *tanka* are still widely used. Western-type, modern drama (Shingeki), inspired by Ibsen and Strindberg, has been growing since the turn of the century.

Japan, Sea of /dʒəˈpæn/ sea separating Japan from the mainland of Asia.

Japji Sikh morning hymn which consists of verses from the beginning of the holy book *Guru Grath Sahib*.

Jaques-Dalcroze /ˈʒækdælˈkrəʊz/ Emile 1865–1950. Swiss composer and teacher. He is remembered for his system of physical training by rhythmical movement to music (◊eurhythmics), and founded the Institut Jaques-Dalcroze in Geneva, in 1915.

jargon language usage that irritates because it is complex and hard to understand, either because it is highly technical or occupational or because it is designed to confuse on purpose. In writing, jargon may be highly formal, while in speech it often contains ◊slang expressions.

Jargon is often used to disguise unimportant information in complicated language, to mystify certain information or to make information inaccessible to those who do not know the jargon. Jargon is often also known as *gobbledygook/gobbledegook* and *bafflegab*, and is sub-categorized as, for example, *bureaucratese* and *officialese* (the usage of bureaucrats and officials), *journalese* (the languages of newspapers), and *medicalese* (the often impenetrable usage of doctors).

Järnefelt /ˈjeənəfelt/ (Edvard) Armas 1869–1958. Finnish composer who is chiefly known for his 'Praeludium' and the lyrical 'Berceuse'.

jarrah type of ◊eucalyptus tree of W Australia, with durable timber.

Jarrett /ˈdʒærət/ Keith 1945– . US jazz pianist and composer, an eccentric innovator who performs both alone and with small groups. *The Köln Concert* 1975 is a characteristic solo live recording.

Jarrett was a member of the rock-influenced Charles Lloyd Quartet 1966–67, and played with Miles Davis 1970–71.

Jarrow /ˈdʒærəʊ/ town in Tyne and Wear, NE England, on the S bank of the Tyne, 10 km/6 mi E of Newcastle and connected with the N bank by the Tyne Tunnel (1967); population (1981) 27,075. The closure of Palmer's shipyard in Jarrow in 1933 prompted the unemployed to march to London, a landmark of the ◊Depression.

Jarry /ˈʒæri/ Alfred 1873–1907. French satiric dramatist, whose *Ubu Roi* 1896 foreshadowed the Theatre of the ◊Absurd and the French Surrealist movement.

Jaruzelski /ˌjæruːˈzelski/ Wojciech 1923– . Polish general, communist leader from 1981, president from 1985. He imposed martial law for the first year of his rule, suppressed the opposition, and banned trade union activity, but later released many political prisoners. In 1989, elections in favour of *Solidarity* forced Jaruzelski to speed up democratic reforms, overseeing a transition to a new form of 'socialist pluralist' democracy.

Jaruzelski, who served with the Soviet army 1939–43, was defence minister 1968–83 and entered the Politburo 1971. At the height of the crisis of 1980–81 he assumed power as prime minister and PUWP first secretary; in 1985 he resigned as prime minister to become president, but remained the dominant political figure in Poland. His attempts to solve Poland's economic problems were unsuccessful.

Jarvik 7 the first successful artificial heart intended for permanent implantation in a human being. Made from polyurethane plastic and aluminium, it is powered by compressed air. Dr Barney Clark became the first person to receive a Jarvik 7 in Salt Lake City in Dec 1982; it kept him alive for 112 days. In 1986 a similar heart was implanted temporarily in a British patient waiting for a human heart transplant. Recently, the US Food and Drug Administration (FDA) withdrew approval for artificial heart transplants due to evidence of adverse reactions.

jasmine genus of plants *Jasminium*, family Oleaceae, with fragrant white/yellow flowers, and yielding jasmine oil, used in perfumes. The *common jasmine Jasminium officinale* has pure white flowers; the Chinese *winter jasmine Jasminium nudiflorum* has bright yellow flowers that appear before the leaves.

Jason /ˈdʒeɪsən/ in Greek mythology, leader of the *Argonauts* who sailed in the Argo to Colchis of the ◊Golden Fleece.

jasper a hard, compact variety of ◊chalcedony SiO$_2$, usually coloured red, brown, or yellow. Jasper can be used as a gem.

Jaspers /ˈjæspəz/ Karl 1883–1969. German philosopher, whose works include *General Psychopathology* 1913, and *Philosophy* 1932. Born at Oldenburg, he studied medicine and psychology, and in 1921 became professor of philosophy at Heidelberg.

Jaurès The French socialist, politician, and journalist Jean Jaurès, assassinated in 1914, was an advocate of international peace. He was shot outside the Café du Croissant in Paris, where his admirers still meet, faithful to his memory.

Jassy /'jæsi/ German name for the Romanian city of ◊Iaşi.

Jataka collections of Buddhist legends compiled at various dates in several countries; the oldest and most complete has 547 stories. They were collected before AD 400.

They give an account of previous incarnations of the Buddha, and the verse sections of the text form part of the Buddhist canon. The Jataka stories were one of the sources of inspiration for the fables of Aesop.

jaundice yellow discoloration of the skin caused by an excess of bile pigment in the bloodstream.

Bile pigment, the final manifestation of ◊haemoglobin, is produced by the destruction of spent red blood cells (◊haemolysis). There is always some bile pigment in the blood, but normally it is disposed of by the liver, excreted into the bile and passed, by way of the bile ducts and gall bladder, into the intestine. A build-up in the blood is due to abnormal destruction of red cells (as in some cases of ◊anaemia), impaired liver function, or blockage in the excretory channels. The jaundice gradually recedes following treatment of the underlying cause. Mild jaundice is common in newborns, but a serious form occurs in ◊Rhesus disease.

Jaurès /'ʒɔures/ Jean Léon 1859–1914. French socialist politician and advocate of international peace. He was a lecturer in philosophy at Toulouse until his election in 1885 as a deputy (member of parliament). In 1893 he joined the Socialist Party, established a united party, and in 1904 founded the newspaper *L'Humanité*, becoming its editor until his assassination.

Java /'dʒɑːvə/ or **Jawa** the most important island of Indonesia, situated between Sumatra and Bali.
area (with the island of Madura) 132,000 sq km/51,000 sq mi
capital Jakarta (also capital of Indonesia)
towns ports include Surabaja and Semarang
physical about half the island is under cultivation, the rest being thickly forested. Mountains and sea breezes keep temperatures down but humidity is high, with heavy rainfall from Dec to Mar.
features a chain of mountains, some of which are volcanic, runs along the centre, rising to 2,750 m/9,000 ft. The highest mountain, Semeru 3,676 m/12,060 ft, is in the east
exports rice, coffee, cocoa, tea, sugar, rubber, quinine, teak, and petroleum

javelin British athlete Fatima Whitbread throwing the javelin.

population (with Madura) (1980) 91,270,000; including people of Javanese, Sundanese, and Madurese origin, with differing languages
religion predominantly Muslim
history occupied by Japan 1942–45 while under Dutch control, Java then became part of the republic of ◊Indonesia.

Fossilized early human remains (*Homo erectus*) were discovered 1891–92. In central Java there are ruins of magnificent Buddhist monuments and of the Sivaite temple in Prambanan. The island's last Hindu kingdom, Majapahit, was destroyed about 1520 and followed by a number of short-lived Javanese kingdoms. The Dutch East India company founded a factory in 1610. Britain took over during the Napoleonic period, 1811–16, and Java then reverted to Dutch control.

Javanese inhabitant of Java. The Javanese speak several related languages belonging to the Austronesian family.

javelin a type of spear used in athletics events. The men's javelin is about 260 cm/8.5 ft long, weighing 800 g/28 oz; the women's 230 cm/7.5 ft long, weighing 600 g/21 oz. It is thrown from a scratch line at the end of a run-up. The centre of gravity on the men's javelin was altered 1986 to reduce the vast distances (90 m/100 yd) that were being thrown.

jaws the bony structures that form the framework of the mouth in all vertebrates except lampreys and hagfish (the agnathous or jawless vertebrates). They consist of the upper jaw bone, or **maxilla**, and the lower jawbone, or **mandible**; the latter is hinged at each side to the bone of the temple by ◊ligaments.

jay genus of birds *Garrulus* of the crow family, common in Europe, Asia, and the Americas.

In the **common jay** *Garrulus glandarius*, the body is fawn with patches of white, blue and black on the wings and tail. Its own cry is a harsh screech, but it has considerable powers as a mimic. Allied is the **common blue jay** *Cyanocitta cristata*, of North America, found in pine forests.

Jayawardene /ˌdʒaɪəˈwɑːdɪnə/ Junius Richard 1906– . Sri Lankan politician. Leader of the United Nationalist Party from 1973, he became prime minister 1977, and the country's first president 1978–88.

jazz polyphonic, syncopated music characterized by improvisation, which developed in the USA at the turn of this century out of black American and other indigenous popular music.

1880–1900 Jazz originated chiefly in New Orleans from ragtime.
1920s Centre of jazz moved to Chicago (Louis Armstrong, Bix Beiderbecke) and St Louis.
1930s The **swing** bands used call-and-response arrangements with improvised solos (Paul Whiteman, Benny Goodman).
1940s Swing grew into the **big band** era (Glenn Miller, Duke Ellington); rise of **West Coast** jazz (Stan Kenton) and rhythmically complex, highly improvisational **bebop** (Charlie Parker, Dizzy Gillespie, Thelonius Monk).
1950s Jazz had ceased to be dance music; **cool jazz** (Stan Getz, Miles Davis, Modern Jazz Quartet) developed in reaction to the insistent, 'hot' bebop and **hard bop**.
1960s **Free-form** or **free jazz** (Ornette Coleman, John Coltrane).
1970s **Jazz rock** (US group Weather Report, formed 1970; British guitarist John McLaughlin, 1942–); jazz funk (US saxophonist Grover Washington Jr, 1943–); more eclectic free jazz (US pianist Keith Jarrett, 1945–).
1980s Resurgence of tradition (US trumpeter Wynton Marsalis, 1962– ; British saxophonist Courtney Pine, 1965–) and avant-garde (US chamber-music Kronos Quartet, formed 1978; anarchic British group Loose Tubes, formed 1983).

Jazz Age phrase attributed to the novelist F Scott Fitzgerald, describing the hectic excitements of the US 1920s, when hot jazz became fashionable as part of the general rage for spontaneity and generational freedom.

jazz dance dance that combines African and US techniques and rhythms and was introduced into modern dance by choreographers such as Jerome ◊Robbins and Alvin Ailey.

J-curve in economics, a graphic illustration of the likely effect of a currency devaluation on the balance of payments. Initially, there will be a deterioration as import prices increase and export prices decline, followed by a decline in import volume and upsurge of export volume.

jeans denim trousers, traditionally blue, originally cut from jean cloth ('jene fustian'), a heavy canvas made in Genoa, Italy. Levi Strauss (1830–1902), a Bavarian immigrant to the US, made sturdy trousers for goldminers in San Francisco out of jean material intended for wagon covers. Hence they became known as 'Levis'. Later a French fabric, *serge de Nîmes* (corrupted to 'denim'), was used.

Jeans /dʒiːnz/ James Hopwood 1877–1946. British mathematician and scientist. In physics, he contributed work on the kinetic theory of gases, and forms of energy radiation; and in astronomy, on giant and dwarf stars, the nature of spiral nebulae, and the origin of the cosmos. He also did much to popularize astronomy.

Jedburgh /'dʒedbərə/ small town in the Borders region, SE Scotland, on Jed Water; population (1981) 4,000. It has the remains of a 12th-century abbey.

jay

Jedda /'dʒedə/ alternative spelling for the Saudi Arabian port ◊Jiddah.

Jefferies /'dʒefrɪz/ (John) Richard 1848–1887. British naturalist and writer, whose books on the countryside included *Gamekeeper at Home* 1878, *Wood Magic* 1881, and *Story of My Heart* 1883.

Jeffers /'dʒefəz/ (John) Robinson 1887–1962. US poet. He wrote free verse, and demonstrated an antagonism to human society reflected in the isolation of his home at Carmel in California. His volumes include *Tamar and Other Poems* 1924, *The Double Axe* 1948, and *Hungerfield and Other Poems* 1954.

Jefferson /'dʒefəsən/ Thomas 1743–1826. 3rd president of the USA 1801–09, founder of the Democratic Party. Born in Virginia into a wealthy family. He published *A Summary View of the Rights of America* 1774 and as a member of the Continental Congresses of 1775–76 was largely responsible for the drafting of the Declaration of Independence. He was governor of Virginia 1779–81, ambassador to Paris 1785–89, secretary of state 1789–93, and vice president 1797–1801.

Jefferson's interests also included music, painting, architecture, and the natural sciences; he was very much a product of the 18th century enlightenment. His political philosophy of 'agrarian democracy' placed responsibility for upholding a virtuous American republic mainly upon a citizenry of independent yeoman farmers. Ironically, his two terms as president saw the adoption of some of the ideas of his political opponents, the Federalists.

Jeffrey /'dʒefri/ Francis, Lord 1773–1850. Scottish lawyer and literary critic. Born at Edinburgh, he was a founder and editor of the *Edinburgh Review* 1802–29. In 1830 he was made Lord Advocate, and in 1834 a Scottish law lord. He was hostile to the Romantic poets, and wrote of Wordsworth's *Excursion*: 'This will never do.'

Jeffreys /'dʒefrɪz/ Alec John 1950– . British geneticist, who discovered the DNA probes necessary for accurate ◊genetic fingerprinting so that a murderer or rapist could be identified by traces of blood, tissue, or semen.

Jeffreys /'dʒefrɪz/ George, 1st Baron 1648–1689. British judge. Born in Denbighshire, Scotland, he became Chief Justice of the King's Bench in 1683, and presided over many political trials, notably those of Sidney, Oates, and Baxter, becoming notorious for his brutality.

In 1685 he was made a peer and Lord Chancellor and, after ◊Monmouth's rebellion, conducted the 'bloody assizes' during which 320 rebels were executed and hundreds more flogged, imprisoned or transported. He was captured when attempting to flee the country after the revolution of 1688, and died in the Tower of London.

Jehol /,dʒʌ'hɒl/ former name for the city of Chengale in NE Hebei province, N China.

Jehosophat 4th king of Judah *c.*873–849 BC; he allied himself with Ahab, king of Israel, in the war against Syria.

Jehovah /dʒɪ'həʊvə/ also *Jahweh* in the Old Testament; in Hebrew YHVH, to which the vowels 'a o a' were later added.

Jehovah's Witness member of a religious organization originating in the USA 1872 under Charles Taze Russell (1852–1916). Jehovah's Witnesses attach great importance to Christ's second coming, which Russell predicted would occur 1914, and which Witnesses still believe is imminent. All Witnesses are expected to take part in house-to-house preaching; there are no clergy. Membership (1986) about 1 million.

Witnesses believe that after the second coming the ensuing Armageddon and Last Judgment, which entail the destruction of all except the faithful, are to give way to the Theocratic Kingdom. Earth will continue to exist as the home of humanity, apart from 144,000 chosen believers who will reign with Christ in heaven. Witnesses believe that they should not become involved in the affairs of this world, and their tenets, involving rejection

Jekyll *Using such native plants as honeysuckle and pinks, British horticulturalist Gertrude Jekyll introduced the 'wild' garden style to Britain in the early years of this century. This portrait was painted by William Nicholson in 1920.*

of obligations such as military service, have often brought them into conflict with authority. Because of a biblical injunction against eating blood, they will not give or receive blood transfusions. Adults are baptized by total immersion.

When Russell died 1916, he was succeeded by Joseph Rutherford (died 1942). The Watch Tower Bible and Tract Society and the Watch Tower Students' Association form part of the movement.

Jehu king of Israel *c.*842–815 BC. He led a successful rebellion against the family of ◊Ahab and was responsible for the death of Jezebel. He was noted for his furious chariot-driving.

Jekyll /'dʒiːkl/ Gertrude 1843–1932. English landscape gardener and writer. She created over 200 gardens, many in collaboration with the architect Edwin ◊Lutyens.

Originally a painter and embroiderer, she took up gardening at the age of 48, because of worsening eyesight. In her books, she advocated natural gardens of the cottage type, with plentiful herbaceous borders.

Jekyll and Hyde two conflicting sides of a personality, as in the novel by the Scottish writer R L Stevenson, *The Strange Case of Dr Jekyll and Mr Hyde* 1886, where the good Jekyll by means of a potion periodically transforms himself into the evil Hyde.

Jellicoe /'dʒelɪkəʊ/ John Rushworth, 1st Earl 1859–1935. British admiral, who commanded the Grand Fleet 1914–16; the only action he fought was the battle of ◊Jutland. He was 1st Sea Lord 1916–17, when he failed to push the introduction of the convoy system to combat U-boat attack.

jellyfish marine animal of the phylum Cnidaria (coelenterates) with an umbrella-shaped body composed of a semi-transparent gelatinous substance, with a fringe of stinging tentacles. Most jellyfish move freely, but some are attached by a stalk to rocks or seaweed. They feed on small animals which are paralysed by their sting.

Jena /'jeɪnə/ town SE of Weimar, Gera county, East Germany; population (1985) 107,240. Industries include the Zeiss firm of optical-instrument makers, founded 1846. Here in 1806 Napoleon defeated the Prussians, and Schiller and Hegel taught at the university which dates from 1558.

Jencks /dʒeŋks/ Charles 1939– . US architectural theorist and furniture designer. He coined the term 'post-modern architecture' and wrote the influential book *The Language of Post-Modern Architecture*.

je ne sais quoi (French 'I don't know what') a certain indescribable quality.

Jenkins /'dʒeŋkɪnz/ Roy (Harris) 1920– . British politician. He became a Labour minister 1964, was home secretary 1965–67 and 1974–76, and chancellor of the Exchequer 1967–70. He was

president of the European Commission 1977–81. In 1981 he became one of the founders of the Social Democratic Party and was elected 1982, but lost his seat 1987.

Educated at Oxford University, Jenkins was a close friend of the future Labour leader Gaitskell. A Labour MP from 1948, he was minister of aviation 1964–65, then home secretary and chancellor of the Exchequer under Harold Wilson. In 1970 he became deputy leader of the Labour Party, but resigned 1972 because of disagreement with Wilson on the issue of UK entry to the European Community. He was elected chancellor of Oxford University 1987.

Jenkins's Ear, War of war between Britain and Spain 1739 which later became part of the War of the ◊Austrian Succession 1740–48. The name derives from the claim of Robert Jenkins, a merchant captain, that his ear had been cut off by Spanish coastguards near Jamaica. The incident was seized on by opponents of Robert ◊Walpole seeking to embarrass his government's antiwar policy and to force war with Spain.

Jenner /'dʒenə/ Edward 1749–1823. English physician who pioneered vaccination. In Jenner's day, smallpox was a major killer. His discovery that inoculation with cowpox gives immunity to smallpox was a great medical breakthrough. He coined the word vaccination from the Latin word for cowpox *vaccina*.

Jenner /'dʒenə/ Henry ('Gwas Myhal') 1849–1934. English poet. He attempted to revive Cornish as a literary language, and in 1904 published a handbook of the Cornish language.

Jennings /'dʒenɪŋz/ Humphrey 1907–1950. British documentary film-maker, active in the GPO Film Unit from 1934. His wartime films provide a vivid portrayal of London in the Blitz. His films include *Post Haste* 1934, *London Can Take It* 1940, *This is England* 1941, and *Fires were Started* 1943.

Jennings /'dʒenɪŋz/ Patrick 'Pat' 1945– . Irish footballer. In his 21-year career he was an outstanding goalkeeper. He won a British record 119 international caps for Northern Ireland 1964–86, and played League football for Watford, Tottenham Hotspur, and Arsenal.

CAREER HIGHLIGHTS

Football League appearances: 757
international appearances: 119
Football League Cup: 1971, 1973
FA Cup: 1967, 1979
UEFA Cup: 1972
Footballer of the Year (FWA): 1973
Footballer of the Year (PFA): 1976

Jerablus /'dʒerəbləs/ ancient Syrian city, adjacent to Carchemish on the Euphrates.

jerboa several genera of rodents, about 15–20 cm/6–8 in long, found in Africa, Asia, and E Europe. They are mainly herbivorous and nocturnal.

Typical is the common N African jerboa *Jaculus orientalis* with a body about 15 cm/6 in long and slightly longer tail. At speed it moves in a series of long jumps with its forefeet held close to the body.

Jeremiah /,dʒerɪ'maɪə/ 7th century BC. Old Testament Hebrew prophet, whose ministry continued 626–586 BC. He was imprisoned during ◊Nebuchadnezzar's siege of Jerusalem on suspicion of intending to desert to the enemy. On the city's fall, he retired to Egypt.

Jerez de la Frontera /xe'reθ deɪ lɑ: frɒn'teərə/ city in Andalusia, SW Spain; population (1986) 180,000. It is famed for sherry, the fortified wine to which it gave its name.

Jericho /'dʒerɪkəʊ/ Israeli-administered town in Jordan, N of the Dead Sea. It was settled by 8000 BC, and by 6000 BC had become a walled city with 2,000 inhabitants. In the Old Testament it was the first Canaanite stronghold captured by the Israelites, its walls, according to the Book of ◊Joshua, falling to the blast of Joshua's trumpets.

Successive archaeological excavations since 1907 show that the walls of the city were destroyed many times.

Jeroboam first king of Israel *c.*922–901 BC after the split with Judah.

Jerome /dʒəˈrəʊm/ Jerome K(lapka) 1859–1927. English journalist and writer. His works include the humorous essays *Idle Thoughts of an Idle Fellow* 1889, the novel *Three Men in a Boat* 1889, and the play *The Passing of the Third Floor Back* 1907.

Jerome, St /dʒəˈrəʊm/ *c.* 340–420. One of the early Christian leaders and scholars known as the Fathers of the Church. His Latin versions of the Old and New Testaments form the basis of the Roman Catholic Vulgate. He is usually depicted with a lion. Feast day 30 Sept.

Born in Strido, Italy, he was baptized at Rome in 360, and subsequently travelled in Gaul, Anatolia, and Syria. Summoned to Rome as adviser to Pope Damasus, he revised the Latin translation of the New Testament and the Latin psalter. On the death of Damasus in 384 he travelled to the east, and, settling in Bethlehem, translated the Old Testament into Latin from the Hebrew.

Jersey /ˈdʒɜːzi/ largest of the ◊Channel Islands; capital St Helier; area 117 sq km/45 sq mi; population (1986) 80,000. It is governed by a lieutenant-governor representing the English Crown and an assembly. Like Guernsey, it is famous for its cattle.

Jersey City /ˈdʒɜːzi/ city of NE New Jersey, USA; population (1980) 223,500. It faces Manhattan Island, to which it is connected by tunnels. A former port, it is now an industrial centre.

Jerusalem /dʒəˈruːsələm/ ancient city of Palestine, divided 1948 between Jordan and the new republic of Israel; area (pre-1967) 37.5 sq km/14.5 sq mi, (post-1967) 108 sq km/42 sq mi, including areas of the West Bank; population (1989) 500,000, about 350,000 Israelis and 150,000 Palestinians. In 1950 the western New City was proclaimed as the Israeli capital, and, having captured from Jordan the eastern Old City 1967, Israel affirmed 1980 that the united city was the country's capital; the United Nations does not recognize the claim.

history

1400 BC Jerusalem was ruled by a king subject to Egypt.

c.1000 David made it the capital of a united Jewish kingdom.

586 The city was destroyed by Nebuchadnezzar, king of Babylonia, who deported its inhabitants.

539–529 Under Cyrus the Great of Persia the exiled Jews were allowed to return to Jerusalem and a new settlement was made.

c.445 The city walls were rebuilt.

333 Conquered by Alexander the Great.

63 Conquered by the Roman general Pompey.

AD 29 or 30 Under the Roman governor Pontius Pilate, Jesus was executed here.

70 A Jewish revolt led to the complete destruction of the city by the Roman emperor Titus.

135 On its site the emperor Hadrian founded the Roman city of Aelia Capitolina.

615 The city was pillaged by the Persian Chosroës II while under Byzantine rule.

637 It was first conquered by Islam.

1099 Jerusalem captured by the Crusaders.

1187 Recaptured by Saladin, sultan of Egypt.

1516 Became part of the Ottoman Empire.

1917 Britain occupied Palestine.

1922–1948 Jerusalem was the capital of the British mandate.

features There are seven gates into the Old City through the walls built by Selim I (1467–1520). Notable buildings include the Church of the Holy Sepulchre (built by Emperor Constantine 335) and the mosque of the Dome of the Rock. The latter stands on the site of the ◊Temple built by King Solomon in the 10th century BC, and the Western ('wailing') Wall, held sacred by Jews, is part of the walled platform on which the Temple once stood. The Hebrew University of Jerusalem

jet propulsion

turbojet — compressor, combustion chamber, turbine, air intake, driveshaft, jet exhaust

turbofan — compressor, outer driveshaft (for compressor), turbine, air intake, inner driveshaft (for fan), jet exhaust, by-pass air, fan, combustion chamber, by-pass exhaust

opened 1925. Religions are Christian, Hebrew, and Muslim, with Roman Catholic, Anglican, Eastern Orthodox, and a Coptic bishop. In 1967 Israel guaranteed freedom of access of all faiths to their holy places.

Jerusalem artichoke a type of ◊artichoke.

Jervis /ˈdʒɑːvɪs/ John, Earl of St Vincent 1735–1823. English admiral. A rigid disciplinarian, he secured the blockage of Toulon in 1795, and the defeat of the Spanish fleet off Cape St Vincent 1797, in which ◊Nelson played a key part.

Jervis Bay /ˈdʒɑːvɪs/ deep bay on the coast of New South Wales, Australia, 145 km/90 mi SW of Sydney. The Federal Government in 1915 acquired 73 sq km/28 sq mi here to create a port for ◊Canberra. It forms part of the Australian Capital Territory and is the site of the Royal Australian Naval College.

Jessop /ˈdʒesəp/ William 1745–1814. British canal engineer, who built the first canal in England entirely dependent on reservoirs for its water supply (the Grantham Canal 1793–97), and who designed (with Thomas ◊Telford) the 302 m/1,000 ft long Pontcysyllte aqueduct over the river Dee.

Born in Devon, Jessop began his career working in the office of the civil engineer John Smeaton (1724–1792). He was one of the founders of the Butterley Iron Works in 1790, and designed the forerunner of the iron rail that later became universally adopted for railways. He was chief engineer of the Grand Union Canal 1793–1805, which linked London and the Midlands over a distance of 150 km/93.5 mi.

Jesuit a member of the largest and most influential Roman Catholic religious order, also known as the *Society of Jesus*, founded by Ignatius Loyola 1534, dissolved 1773, and re-established 1814. During the 16th and 17th centuries Jesuits were successful as missionaries in Japan, China, Paraguay, and among the North American Indians. The order now has about 29,000 members (15,000 priests plus students and lay members). *history* The Society of Jesus received papal approval 1540. Its main objects were defined as educational work, the suppression of heresy, and missionary work among nonbelievers (its members

were not confined to monasteries). Loyola infused into the order a spirit of military discipline, with long and arduous training. Their political influence resulted in their expulsion during 1759–68 from Portugal, France, and Spain, and suppression by Pope Clement XIV 1773. The order was revived by Pius VII 1814, but has since been expelled from many of the countries of Europe and the Americas, and John Paul II criticized the Jesuits 1981 for their support of revolution in South America.

Their head (general) is known as the 'Black Pope' from the colour of his cassock; the general from 1983 was Pieter-Hans Kolvenbach.

Jesus /ˈdʒiːzəs/ *c.* 4 BC–AD 29 or 30. Jewish preacher on whose teachings ◊Christianity was founded. According to the accounts of his life in the four Gospels, he was born in Bethlehem, Palestine, son of God and the Virgin Mary, and brought up as a carpenter in Nazareth. After adult baptism, he gathered 12 disciples, but his preaching antagonized the authorities and he was executed. Three days after the Crucifixion there came reports of his resurrection and, later, ascension to heaven.

Through his legal father, Mary's husband Joseph, Jesus was of the tribe of Judah and family of David, the second king of Israel. In AD 26/27 his cousin John the Baptist proclaimed the coming of the promised messiah and baptized Jesus, who then made two missionary journeys through the district of Galilee. His teaching, summarized in the *Sermon on the Mount*, aroused both religious opposition from the ◊Pharisees and secular opposition from the party supporting the Roman governor, ◊Herod Antipas. When Jesus returned to Jerusalem (probably in AD 29), a week before the Passover festival, he was greeted by the people as the Messiah, and the Jewish authorities (aided by the apostle Judas) had him arrested and condemned to death, after a hurried trial, by the Sanhedrin (supreme Jewish court). They persuaded the Roman procurator, Pontius Pilate, to confirm the sentence, by stressing the threat to imperial authority of Jesus's teaching.

jet a hard, black variety of lignite, a type of coal. It is cut and polished for use in jewellery and ornaments. Articles made of jet have been found in

Bronze Age tombs. In Britain, jet occurs in quantity near Whitby and along the Yorkshire coast.

JET *Joint European Torus* ◊tokamak machine built in England to conduct experiments on nuclear fusion. It is the focus of the European effort to produce a practical fusion-power reactor.

jeté (French 'thrown') in dance, a jump from one foot to the other. A *grand jeté* is a big jump in which the dancer pushes off on one foot, holds a brief pose in mid-air, and lands lightly on the other foot.

jetfoil an advanced type of ◊hydrofoil boat built by ◊Boeing, which is propelled by water jets. It features horizontal fully submerged hydrofoils fore and aft, and has a sophisticated computerized control system to maintain its stability in all waters.

Jetfoils have been in service worldwide since 1975. A jetfoil service currently operates between Dover and Ostend, with a passage time of about 1.5 hours. Cruising speed of the jetfoil is about 80 kph/50 mph.

jet-lag effect of a sudden switch of time-zones in jet air travel, resulting in tiredness and feeling 'out of step' with day and night. In 1989 it was suggested that use of the hormone melatonin helped to lessen the effect of jetlag by re-setting the body clock. See also ◊circadian rhythm.

jet propulsion a method of propulsion in which an object is propelled in one direction by a jet, or stream of gases, moving in the other. This follows from ◊Newton's celebrated third law of motion 'to every action, there is an equal and opposite reaction'. The most widespread application of the jet principle is in the jet engine, the commonest kind of aero-engine.

The *jet engine* is a kind of ◊gas turbine. Air, after passing through a forward-facing intake, is compressed by a compressor, or fan, and fed into a combustion chamber. Fuel (usually kerosene) is sprayed in and ignited. The hot gas produced expands rapidly rearwards, spinning a turbine that drives the compressor before being finally ejected from a rearward-facing tail pipe, or nozzle, at very high speed. Reaction to the jet of gases streaming backwards produces a propulsive thrust forwards which, acts on the aircraft through its engine-mountings, not from any pushing of the hot gas stream against the static air. Thrust is proportional to the mass of the gas ejected multiplied by the acceleration imparted to it, and is stated in units of pounds force (lbf) or kilograms force (kgf), both now being superseded by the international unit, the Newton (N).

The *turbojet* is the simplest form of gas turbine, used in aircraft well into the ◊supersonic range. The *turboprop* used for moderate speeds and altitudes (up to 725 kph/450 mph and 10,000 m/30,000 ft) incorporates extra stages of turbine that absorb most of the energy from the gas stream to drive the propeller shaft via a speed reduction gear. The *turbofan* is best suited to high subsonic speeds. It is fitted with an extra compressor or fan in front, and some of the airflow bypasses the core engine, and mixes with the jet exhaust stream, to give it lower temperature and velocity. This results in greater economy, efficiency and quietness compared with the turbojet, and a higher speed than the turboprop. The *turboshaft* is used to drive the main and tail rotors of ◊helicopters, and in ◊hovercraft, ships, trains, as well as in power stations and pumping equipment. It is effectively a turboprop without its propeller, power from an extra turbine being delivered to a reduction gearbox or directly to an output shaft. Most of the gas energy drives the compressors and provides shaft power, so residual thrust is low. Turboshaft power is normally quoted as shaft horsepower (shp) or kilowatts (kW).

The *ramjet* is used for some types of missiles. At twice the speed of sound (Mach 2), pressure in the forward-facing intake of a jet engine is seven times that of the outside air, a compression ratio which rapidly mounts with increased speed (to Mach 8), with the result that no compressor or turbine is needed. The ramjet comprises merely an open-ended rather barrel-shaped tube, burning fuel in its widest section. It is cheap, light, and easily made. However, fuel consumption is high and it needs rocket-boosting to its operational speed.

Variants and additional capabilities of jets include **multi-spool engines** in which the compressors may be split into two or three parts or stages driven by independent turbines, so that each runs at its own optimum speed; **vectored thrust**, a swivelling of the jet nozzles from vertical to rearward horizontal to achieve vertical take-off followed by level flight (as in the ◊*Harrier*); **reverse thrust**, used to slow down a jet plane on landing, and achieved by blocking off the jet pipe with special doors and re-directing the gases forward through temporarily opened cascades; **reheat** (afterburning), used especially in military aircraft to obtain short-duration thrust increase of up to 70% by the controlled burning of fuel in the gas stream after it has passed through the turbine, but which increases fuel consumption.

jetsam goods deliberately sunk in the sea to lighten a vessel in a storm, or wreck. See under ◊flotsam.

jet stream a narrow band of very fast wind (velocities of over 150 kph/95 mph) found at altitudes of 10–16 km/6–10 mi in the upper troposphere or lower stratosphere. Jet streams usually occur about the latitudes of the Westerlies (35–60°).

Jevons /'dʒevənz/ William Stanley 1835–1882. British economist, who introduced the concept of *marginal utility*: the increase in total utility (satisfaction or pleasure of consumption) relative to a unit increase of the goods consumed.

Jew a follower of ◊Judaism, the Jewish religion. The term is also used to refer to members of the ethnic group, who may or may not practise the religion or identify with the cultural tradition. Prejudice against Jews is termed ◊anti-Semitism.

Jewish Agency body created by the British mandate power in Palestine 1929 to oversee the administration of the Jewish population and immigration. In 1948 it took over as the government of an independent Israel.

Jewish-American writing US writing shaped by the Jewish experience. It began out of the vast wave of Eastern European immigration at the close of the 19th century, and by the 1940s Jewish-American writing was central in US literary and intellectual life. The award of Nobel prizes to Saul Bellow and Isaac Bashevis Singer acknowledges its important role in modern letters.

The first significant Jewish-American novel was Abraham Cahan's *The Rise of David Levinsky* 1917. During the 1920s many writers, including Ludwig Lewisohn and Mary Antin, signalled the Jewish presence in US culture. In the 1930s Mike Gold's *Jews Without Money* and Henry Roth's *Call It Sleep* showed in fiction the immigrant Jewish struggle to adapt to the US experience. Novelists Bernard Malamud, Philip Roth, and Norman Mailer, poets Karl Shapiro, Delmore Schwartz, and Muriel Rukeyser, playwrights and screenwriters Arthur Miller, S N Behrman, and Woody Allen, and critics Lionel Trilling (1905–75) and Irving Howe made Jewish experience fundamental to US writing. In the 1950s the Jewish-American novel, shaped by awareness of the Holocaust, expressed themes of human responsibility. Many subsequent writers, including Stanley Elkin, Joseph Heller, Chaim Potok, Denise Levertov, Grace Paley, and Cynthia Ozick, have extended the tradition.

Jewish Autonomous Region part of the Khabarovsk Territory, USSR, on the river Amur; capital Birobidzhan; area 36,000 sq km/13,900 sq mi; population (1986) 211,000. Industries include textiles, leather, metallurgy, light engineering, agriculture, and timber. It was established as a Jewish National District 1928, and became an Autonomous Region

Jiang Jiang Zemin became China's political leader after the Tiananmen Square massacre of June 1989.

1934, but became only nominally Jewish after the Stalinist purges 1936–47 and 1948–49.

Jew's harp musical instrument consisting of a two-pronged metal frame inserted between the teeth, and a spring-like tongue plucked with the finger. The resulting drone excites resonances in the mouth that can be varied in pitch to produce a melody.

Jezebel /'dʒezəbel/ in the Old Testament, daughter of the king of Sidon. She married King Ahab of Israel, and was brought into conflict with the prophet Elijah by her introduction of the worship of Baal.

Jhansi /'dʒɑːnsi/ city in Uttar Pradesh, NE India, 286 km/178 mi SW of Lucknow; population (1981) 281,000. It is a railway and road junction, and a market centre. It was founded 1613, and was the scene of a massacre of British civilians 1857.

Jhelum /'dʒiːləm/ river rising in Kashmir and flowing into Pakistan; length about 720 km/450 mi. The Mangla Dam 1967, one of the world's largest earth-filled dams, stores flood waters for irrigation and hydroelectricity. The Jhelum is one of the five rivers which give Punjab its name, and was known in the ancient world as the Hydaspes, on whose banks Alexander the Great won a battle in 326 BC.

Jiang /dʒi'æŋ/ Zemin 1926– . Chinese political leader. The son-in-law of ◊Li Xiannian, he joined the Chinese Communist Party's politburo in 1967 after serving in the Moscow embassy and as mayor of Shanghai. He succeeded ◊Zhao Ziyang as party leader after the Tian'anmen Square massacre of 1989. A cautious proponent of economic reform coupled with unswerving adherence to the party's 'political line', he subsequently also replaced ◊Deng Xiaoping as head of the influential central military commission.

Jiang Jie Shi /dʒizæŋ ˌdʒeɪ ' ʃiː/ alternative transcription of Chinese leader ◊Chiang Kai-shek.

Jiang Qing /dʒi'æŋ 'tʃɪŋ/ formerly *Chiang Ching* 1913– . Chinese communist politician, wife of the party leader Mao Zedong. In 1960 she became minister for culture, and played a key role in the 1966–69 Cultural Revolution as the leading member of the Shanghai-based Gang of Four, who attempted to seize power 1976. Jiang was imprisoned.

Jiang was a Shanghai actress when in 1937 she met Mao Zedong at the communist headquarters in Yan'an; she became his third wife 1939. She emerged as a radical, egalitarian Maoist. Her influence waned during the early 1970s and her relationship with Mao became embittered. On Mao's death Sept 1976, the Gang of Four sought to seize power by organizing military coups in Shanghai

Jiangsu *Massed silkworm cocoons are gathered from the cut branches by a member of a commune which is striving to diversify the local economy.*

and Beijing. They were arrested for treason by Mao's successor Hua Guofeng and tried 1980–81. The Gang were blamed for the excesses of the Cultural Revolution, but Jiang asserted during her trial that she had only followed Mao's orders as an obedient wife. This was rejected and Jiang received a death sentence Jan 1981, which was subsequently commuted to life imprisonment.

Jiangsu /dʒiˌæŋˈsuː/ formerly *Kiangsu* province on the coast of E China.
area 102,200 sq km/39,449 sq mi
capital Nanjing
features includes the swampy mouth of the Chang Jiang, and the special municipality of Shanghai
products cereals, rice, tea, cotton, soya, fish, silk, ceramics, textiles, coal, iron, copper, cement
population (1986) 62,130,000.

Jiangxi /dʒiˌæŋˈʃiː/ formerly *Kiangsi* province of SE China
area 164,800 sq km/63,613 sq mi
capital Nanchang
products rice, tea, cotton, tobacco, porcelain, coal, tungsten, uranium
population (1986) 35,090,000
history the province was ◊Mao Zedong's original base in the first phase of the Communist struggle against the Nationalists.

Jibuti /dʒɪˈbuti/ variant spelling of ◊Djibouti, republic of NE Africa.

Jiddah /ˈdʒɪdə/ or *Jedda* port in Hejaz, Saudi Arabia, on the E shore of the Red Sea; population (1986) 1,000,000. Industries include cement, steel, and oil refining. Pilgrims pass through here on their way to Mecca.

jihad (Arabic 'conflict') a holy war undertaken by Muslims against non-believers. In the *Mecca Declaration* 1981, the Islamic powers pledged a jihad against Israel, though not necessarily military attack.

Jilin /ˌdʒiːˈlɪn/ formerly *Kirin* province of NE China in Central ◊Manchuria
area 187,000 sq km/72,182 sq mi
capital Changchun
population (1986) 23,150,000.

Jim Crow originally a derogatory US term for a black person. *Jim Crow laws* are laws designed to deny civil rights to blacks or to enforce the policy of segregation, which existed in parts of the USA until Supreme Court decisions and civil-

Jinnah *Muhammad Ali Jinnah, the founder of modern Pakistan.*

rights legislation of the 1950s and 1960s (Civil Rights Act 1964, Voting Rights Act 1965) denied their legality.

Jiménez /xɪˈmeɪneθ/ Juan Ramón 1881–1958. Spanish lyric poet. Born in Andalusia, he left Spain during the civil war to live in exile in Puerto Rico. Nobel prize 1956.

Jinan /ˌdʒiːˈnæn/ formerly *Tsinan* city and capital of Shandong province, China; population (1986) 1,430,000. It has food processing and textile industries.

Jindyworobaks (Aboriginal 'take-over') Australian literary group 1938–53. Founded by Reginald Ingamells (1931–55), it encouraged an individual Australian character in the country's literature.

Jingdezhen /ˌdʒɪŋdəˈdʒen/ formerly Chingtechen or Fou-liang town in Jiangxi, China. Ming blue-and-white china was produced here, the name of the clay kaolin coming from Kaoling, a hill east of Jingdezhen; some of the best Chinese porcelain is still made here.

jingoism truculent and blinkered patriotism. The term originated in 1878, when the British prime minister Disraeli's pro-Turkish policy nearly involved the UK in war with Russia. His supporters' war song included the line 'We don't want to fight, but by jingo if we do ... '.

Jinja /ˈdʒɪndʒə/ town in Busoga Province, Uganda, on the Victoria Nile E of Kampala; population (1983) 45,000. Nearby is the Owen Falls Dam 1954.

jinn in Muslim mythology, a spirit able to assume human or animal shape.

Jinnah /ˈdʒɪnə/ Muhammad Ali 1876–1948. Indian politician, Pakistan's first governor general from 1947. He became president of the Muslim League in 1916 and from 1934 he was elected annually as president. He advised the UK government on the need for a separate state of Pakistan 1942, and at the 1946 conferences in London he insisted on the partition of British India into Hindu and Muslim states.

Educated in Karachi and the UK, Jinnah was called to the British Bar in 1896. He became governor general of Pakistan on the transfer of power 15 Aug 1947.

Jinsha Jiang /ˌdʒɪnˈʃɑː dʒiˈæŋ/ river of China, which rises in SW China, and forms the Chang Jiang (Yangtze) at Yibin.

Jivaro /ˈhiːvɑːrəʊ/ American Indian peoples of E Ecuador and N Peru. They live by farming, hunting, fishing, and weaving; the Jivaro language belongs to the Andean-Equatorial family. They were formerly famous for preserving the hair and shrunken skin of the heads of their enemies as battle trophies.

jive an energetic dance popular in the 1940s and 1950s; a forerunner of rock and roll.

jnr, jr abbreviation for *junior*.

Joachim /ˈjɔʊəkɪm/ Joseph 1831–1907. Austro-Hungarian violinist and composer. He studied

under Mendelssohn and founded the Joachim Quartet (1869–1907). Joachim played and conducted the music of his friend ◊Brahms. His own compositions include pieces for violin and orchestra, chamber, and orchestral works.

Joachim of Fiore /ˈdʒəʊəkɪm ɒ fjɔːri/ *c.*1132–1202. Italian mystic, born in Calabria. In his mystical writings he interpreted history as a sequence of three ages, that of the Father, Son, and Holy Spirit, the last of which, the age of perfect spirituality, was to begin in 1260. His Messianic views were taken up enthusiastically by many followers.

Joan /dʒəʊn/ mythical Englishwoman supposed to have become pope in 855, as John VIII, and to have given birth to a child during a papal procession. The myth was exposed in the 17th century.

Joannitius /ˌdʒəʊəˈnɪtiəs/ Hunayn ibn Ishaq al Ibadi 809–873. Arabic translator, a Nestorian Christian, who translated Greek learning, including Ptolemy, Euclid, Hippocrates, Plato, and Aristotle, into Arabic or Syrian for the Abbasid court in Baghdad.

Joan of Arc, St /dʒəʊn ɑːk/ 1412–1431. French military leader. In 1429 at Chinon, NW France, she persuaded Charles VII that she had a divine mission to expel the English from France (see ◊Hundred Years' War) and secure his coronation. She raised the siege of Orléans, defeated the English at Patay, north of Orléans, and Charles was crowned in Reims. However, she failed to take Paris, and was captured May 1430 by the Burgundians, who sold her to the English. She was found guilty of witchcraft and heresy by a tribunal of French ecclesiastics who supported the English. She was burned in Rouen 30 May 1431. In 1920 she was canonized.

Job /dʒəʊb/ *c.* 5th century BC. In the Old Testament, Jewish leader who in the *Book of Job* questioned God's infliction of suffering on the righteous and endured great sufferings himself.

Although Job comes to no final conclusion, his book is one of the first attempts to explain the problem of human suffering in a world created and governed by a God who is all-powerful and all good.

jobber former name (to Oct 1986) for a dealer on the London stock exchange who negotiated with a broker who, in turn, dealt with the general public. The jobber's role is now combined with that of the broker, and is known as a ◊market-maker.

Job Centre in the UK, a state-run ◊employment exchange.

job creation schemes introduced by governments at times of high or seasonal unemployment, often involving community work or training to develop marketable skills.

Jockey Club governing body of English ◊horse racing. It was founded about 1750 at the Star and Garter, Pall Mall, London.

Jodhpur /ˌdʒɒdˈpʊə/ city in Rajasthan, India, formerly capital of Jodhpur princely state, founded in 1459 by Rao Jodha; population (1981) 493,600. It is a market centre and has the training college of the Indian Air force, an 18th-century Mughal palace, and a red sandstone fort. A style of riding breeches is named after it.

Jodl /ˈjɔʊdl/ Alfred 1892–1946. German general, born in Aachen. In World War II he drew up the Nazi government's plan for the attack on Yugoslavia, Greece, and the USSR, and in Jan 1945 became chief of staff. He headed the delegation that signed Germany's surrender in Reims 7 May 1945. He was tried for war crimes in Nuremberg 1945–46, and hanged.

Jodrell Bank /ˈdʒɒdraɪ ˈbæŋk/ site in Cheshire, England, of the Nuffield Radio Astronomy Laboratories of the University of Manchester. Its largest instrument is the 76 m/250 ft radio dish, completed 1957 and modified 1970. A 38 m × 25 m/125 ft × 82 ft elliptical radio dish was introduced 1964, capable of working at shorter wavelengths.

John Paul II *The first Polish pope, John Paul II is an accomplished linguist and author.*

These radio telescopes are used in conjunction with other smaller dishes to produce detailed maps of radio sources.

Joel prophet in the Old Testament or Hebrew Bible, of uncertain date.

Joffre /'ʒɒfrə/ Joseph Jacques Césaire 1852–1931. Marshal of France during World War I. He was chief of general staff 1911. The German invasion of Belgium 1914 took him by surprise, but his stand on the ◊Marne resulted in his appointment as supreme commander of all the French armies 1915. His failure to make adequate preparations at Verdun 1916 and the military disasters on the ◊Somme led to his replacement by Nivelle Dec 1916.

Jogjakarta /ˌjɒgjə'jɑːtə/ alternative spelling of ◊Yogyakarta, a city in Indonesia.

Johannesburg /dʒəʊ'hænɪsbɜːg/ largest city of South Africa, situated on the Witwatersrand in Transvaal; population (1985) 1,609,000. It is the centre of a large gold mining industry; other industries include engineering works, meat-chilling plants, and clothing factories.

Notable buildings include the law courts, Escom House (Electricity Supply Commission), the South African Railways Administration Building, the City Hall, Chamber of Mines and Stock Exchange, the Witwatersrand 1921 and Rand Afrikaans 1966 universities, and the Union Observatory. Johannesburg was founded after the discovery of gold 1886, and was probably named after Jan (Johannes) Meyer, the first mining commissioner.

John /dʒɒn/ Augustus (Edwin) 1878–1961. British painter of landscapes and portraits, including *The Smiling Woman* 1910 (Tate Gallery, London) of his second wife, Dorelia. He was the brother of Gwen John.

John /dʒɒn/ Elton. Stage name of Reginald Dwight 1947– . English pop singer, pianist, and composer, noted for his melodies and elaborate costumes and glasses. His lyrics are written by Bernie Taupin.

John /dʒɒn/ Gwen 1876–1939. British painter who lived in France for most of her life. Many of her paintings depict Dominican nuns (she converted to Catholicism 1913); she also painted calm, muted interiors.

John /dʒɒn/ (John Lackland) 1167–1216. King of England from 1199. He lost Normandy and almost all of the other English possessions in France to the French, and succeeded in provoking Pope Innocent III to excommunicate England 1208–13. After the revolt of the barons he was forced to seal the ◊Magna Carta 1215 at Runnymede on the Thames.

His subsequent bad reputation was only partially deserved. It resulted from his intrigues against his brother Richard I (the Lionheart), his complicity in the death of his nephew, Prince Arthur of Brittany, a rival for the English throne, and the effectiveness of his ruthless taxation policy. His attempt to limit the papacy's right of interference in episcopal elections, which traditionally were the preserve of English kings, was resented by monastic sources, and they provided

much of the evidence upon which John's reign was susequently judged.

John /dʒɒn/ two kings of France, including:

John II 1319–1364. King from 1350. He was defeated and captured by the Black Prince at Poitiers 1356. Released 1360, he failed to raise the money for his ransom and returned to England 1364, where he died.

John /dʒɒn/ 23 popes, including:

John XXII 1249–1334. Pope 1316–34. He spent his papacy in Avignon, France, engaged in a long conflict with the Holy Roman emperor, Louis of Bavaria, and the Spiritual Franciscans, a monastic order who preached the absolute poverty of the clergy.

John XXIII Angelo Giuseppe Roncalli 1881–1963. Pope from 1958. He improved relations with the USSR in line with his encyclical *Pacem in Terris/Peace on Earth* 1963, established Roman Catholic hierarchies in newly emergent states, and summoned the Second Vatican Council, which reformed church liturgy and backed the ecumenical movement.

'John XXIII' Baldassare Costa died 1419. Anti-pope 1410–15. In an attempt to end the ◊Great Schism he was elected pope by a council of cardinals in Bologna, but was deposed by the Council of Constance 1415, together with the popes of Avignon and Rome. His papacy is not recognized by the church.

John /dʒɒn/ three kings of Poland, including:

John III Sobieski 1624–1696. King of Poland from 1674. He became commander-in-chief of the army 1668 after victories over the Cossacks and Tatars. A victory over the Turks 1673 helped to get him elected to the Polish throne, and he saved Vienna from the besieging Turks 1683.

John /dʒɒn/ six kings of Portugal, including:

John I 1357–1433. King of Portugal from 1385. An illegitimate son of Pedro I, he was elected by the Cortes. His claim was supported by an English army against the rival king of Castile, thus establishing the Anglo-Portuguese Alliance 1386. He married Philippa of Lancaster, daughter of ◊John of Gaunt.

John IV 1603–1656. King of Portugal from 1640. Originally Duke of Braganza, he was elected king when the Portuguese rebelled against Spanish rule. His reign was marked by a long war against Spain, which did not end until 1668.

John VI 1769–1826. King of Portugal, and regent for his insane mother *Maria I* from 1799 until her death 1816. He fled to Brazil when the French invaded Portugal 1807, and did not return until 1822. On his return Brazil declared its independence, with John's elder son Pedro as emperor.

John Bull an imaginary figure used as a personification of England. The name was popularized by Dr ◊Arbuthnot's *History of John Bull* 1712. He is represented as a prosperous farmer of the 18th century.

John Chrysostom, St /'krɪsəstəm/ 345–407. Christian scholar, hermit, preacher, and Eastern Orthodox bishop of Constantinople 398–404. He was born in Antioch (modern Antakya, Turkey), and his feast day is 13 Sept.

John of Austria /dʒɒn/ Don 1545–1578. Spanish soldier, the illegitimate son of the Holy Roman emperor Charles V. He defeated the Turks at ◊Lepanto 1571.

John of Damascus, St /dʒɒn/ *c.* 676–*c.* 754. Eastern Orthodox theologian and hymn writer, a defender of image worship against the iconoclasts. He was born in Damascus, Syria. Feast day 4 Dec. Contained in his *The Fountain of Knowledge* is *An Accurate Exposition of the Orthodox Faith*, an important chronicle of theology from the 4th–7th centuries.

John of Gaunt /dʒɒn/ 1340–1399. English politician, born in Ghent, fourth son of Edward III, duke of Lancaster from 1362. During Edward's last years, and the years before Richard II attained the age of majority, he acted as head of government, and Parliament protested against his

Johns *Zero Through Nine (1961) Tate Gallery, London.*

corrupt rule. He supported the religious reformer Wycliffe against ecclesiastical influence at court.

John of Salisbury /dʒɒn/ *c.* 1115–1180. English philosopher and historian. His *Policraticus* portrayed the church as the guarantee of liberty against the unjust claims of secular authority.

He studied at Paris and Chartres 1130–1153, supported Thomas a Becket against Henry II, and fled to France after Becket's murder, becoming bishop of Chartres 1176.

John of the Cross, St /dʒɒn/ 1542–1591. Spanish Roman Catholic Carmelite friar from 1564, who was imprisoned several times for attempting to impose the reforms laid down by St Teresa. His verse describes spiritual ecstasy. Feast day 24 Nov.

He was persecuted and sent to the monastery of Ubeda until his death. He was beatified 1674 and canonized 1726.

John o' Groats /ə'grəʊts/ village in NE Highland region, Scotland, about 3 km/2 mi W of Duncansby Head, proverbially Britain's most northerly point. It is named after the Dutchman John de Groot who built a house there in the 16th century.

John Paul /dʒɒn pɔːl/ two popes:

John Paul I Albino Luciani 1912–1978. Pope 26 Aug–28 Sept 1978. His name was chosen as the combination of his two immediate predecessors.

John Paul II Karol Wojtyla 1920– . Pope 1978– , the first non-Italian to be elected pope since 1522. He was born near Kraków, Poland. He has been criticized for his upholding of the tradition of papal infallibility and condemnation of artificial contraception, women priests, married priests, and modern dress for monks and nuns. He has warned against involvement of priests in political activity.

In 1939, at the beginning of World War II, Wojtyla was conscripted for forced labour by the Germans, working in quarries and a chemical factory, but from 1942 studied for the priesthood at a seminary illegally open in Kraków. After the war he taught ethics and theology at the universities of Lublin and Kraków, becoming archbishop of Kraków 1964. He was made a cardinal 1967. He was shot and wounded by a Turk in an attempt on his life 1981.

Johns /dʒɒnz/ 'Captain' W(illiam) E(arl) 1893–1968. British author, from 1932, of popular novels of World War I flying ace Captain James Bigglesworth ('Biggles'), now sometimes criticized for chauvinism, racism, and sexism. Johns retired from the RAF 1930.

Johns /dʒɒnz/ Jasper 1930– . US artist. He rejected the abstract in favour of such simple

Johnson *Amy Johnson, British pilot of the 1930s.*

subjects as flags, maps, and numbers so that the viewer's concentration would be entirely directed to the craftsmanship of the artist. He uses encaustic pigments to create a rich surface, with unexpected delicacies of colour.

John, St /dʒɒn/ 1st century AD. New Testament apostle. Traditionally, he wrote the fourth Gospel and the Johannine Epistles when bishop of Ephesus, and the Book of Revelation while exiled to the Greek island of Patmos. His emblem is an eagle, his feast day 27 Dec.

St John is identified with the unnamed 'disciple whom Jesus loved'. Son of Zebedee, born in Judaea, he and his brother James were Galilean fishermen. Jesus entrusted his mother to John at the Crucifixion, where he is often shown dressed in red, with curly hair. Another of his symbols is a chalice with a little snake in it.

Johnson /'dʒɒnsən/ Amy 1904–1941. British aviator. She made a solo flight from Croydon, S London, to Australia 1930, in 19.5 days, and in 1932 made the fastest ever solo flight to Cape Town, South Africa. Her plane disappeared over the English Channel in World War II while she was serving with the Air Transport Auxiliary.

Johnson /'dʒɒnsən/ Andrew 1808–1875. 17th president of the USA 1865–69, a Democrat. He was born in Raleigh, North Carolina, and was a congressman from Tennessee 1843–53, governor of Tennessee 1853–57, senator 1857–62, and became vice-president 1864. He succeeded to the presidency on Lincoln's assassination. His conciliatory policy to the defeated South after the Civil War involved him in a feud with the radical Republicans, culminating in his impeachment be-

Johnson *Ben Johnson at the Seoul Olympics, 1988.*

Johnson *Lyndon B Johnson became president of the USA after Kennedy's assassination in 1963.*

fore the Senate 1868, which failed to convict him by one vote.

Among his achievements was the purchase of Alaska 1867. He was returned to the Senate from Tennessee 1875, but died shortly afterwards.

Johnson /'dʒɒnsən/ Ben 1961– . Jamaican-Canadian sprinter. In 1987, he broke the world record for the 100 metres, running it in 9.83 seconds. At the Olympic Games 1988, he again broke the record, but was disqualified and suspended for using anabolic steroids to enhance his performance.

Johnson /'dʒɒnsən/ Celia 1908–1982. British actress, best remembered for her starring role in the film *Brief Encounter* 1946.

Johnson /'dʒɒnsən/ Eastman 1824–1906. US painter born in Germany, trained in Düsseldorf, The Hague, and Paris. Painting in the open air, he developed a fresh and luminous landscape style.

Johnson /'dʒɒnsən/ Jack 1878–1968. US heavyweight boxer. He overcame severe racial prejudice to become the first black heavyweight champion of the world 1908 when he travelled to Australia to challenge Tommy Burns. The US authorities wanted Johnson 'dethroned' because of his color but could not find suitable challengers until 1915, when he lost the title in a dubious fight decision to the giant Jess Willard.

Johnson /'dʒɒnsən/ Lyndon (Baines) 1908–1973. 36th president of the USA 1963–69, a Democrat. He was born in Stonewall, Texas, elected to Congress 1937–49 and to the Senate 1949–60. He stood as vice president 1960, bringing crucial Southern votes to J F Kennedy, after whose

Johnson *Portrait of Samuel Johnson by James Barry (c.1777), National Portrait Gallery, London.*

assassination he succeeded as president. After the ◊Tonkin Gulf Incident, the escalation of US involvement in the ◊Vietnam War eventually dissipated the support won by his *Great Society* legislation (civil rights, education, alleviation of poverty), and he declined to stand for re-election 1968.

Johnson /'dʒɒnsən/ Pamela Hansford 1912–1981. British novelist, who in 1950 married C P ◊Snow; her novels include *Too Dear for my Possessing* 1940, and *The Honours Board* 1970.

Johnson /'dʒɒnsən/ Philip Cortelyou 1906– . US architect, who invented the term 'international style'. Originally designing in the style of ◊Mies van der Rohe, he later became an exponent of ◊Post-Modernism. His best known building is the giant AT&T building in New York 1978, a pink skyscraper with a Chippendale-style cabinet top.

He was director of architecture and design at the Museum of Modern Art, New York 1932–54, where he built the annexe and sculpture court.

Johnson /'dʒɒnsən/ Samuel, known as 'Dr Johnson' 1709–1784. English lexicographer, author, and critic, also a brilliant conversationalist and the dominant figure in 18th-century London literary society. His *Dictionary*, published 1755, remained authoritative for over a century, and is still remarkable for the vigour of its definitions. In 1764 he founded the 'Literary Club', whose members included Reynolds, Burke, Goldsmith, Garrick, and ◊Boswell, Johnson's biographer.

Born in Lichfield, Staffordshire, Johnson became first an usher and then a literary hack. In 1735 he married Elizabeth Porter and opened a private school. When this proved unsuccessful he went to London with his pupil David Garrick, becoming a regular contributor to the *Gentleman's Magazine* and publishing the poem *London* 1738. Other works include the satire imitating Juvenal, *Vanity of Human Wishes* 1749, the philosophical romance *Rasselas* 1759, an edition of Shakespeare 1765 and the classic *Lives of the Most Eminent English Poets* 1779–81. His first meeting with ◊Boswell was 1763. A visit with Boswell to Scotland and the Hebrides 1773 was recorded in *Journey to the Western Isles of Scotland* 1775. He was buried in Westminster Abbey and his house in Gough Square, London, is preserved as a museum; his wit and humanity are documented in Boswell's classic biography *Life of Samuel Johnson* 1791.

Johnson /'dʒɒnsən/ Uwe 1934– . German novelist, who left East Germany for West Berlin 1959, and wrote of the division of Germany in, for example, *Anniversaries* 1977.

John the Baptist, St /dʒɒn/ *c.*12 BC–*c.*AD 27. In the New Testament, an itinerant preacher. After preparation in the wilderness, he proclaimed the coming of Jesus, baptized him in the river Jordan, and was executed by ◊Herod Antipas at the request of Salome. His emblem is a lamb. Feast day 24 June.

John was the son of Zacharias and Elizabeth (a

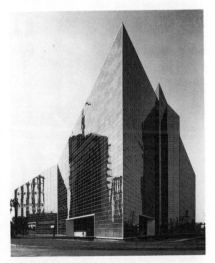

Johnson *The Crystal Cathedral, Los Angeles, by Johnson and Burgee.*

joint

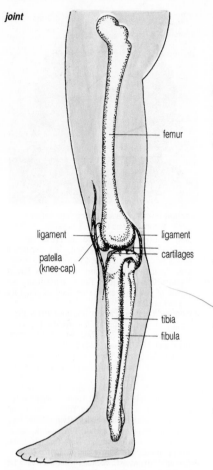

femur

ligament

ligament

patella
(knee-cap)

cartilages

tibia

fibula

cousin of Jesus' mother), and born in Nazareth, Galilee. He and Jesus are often shown together as children; as an adult, he is depicted with a shaggy beard and robes.

Johor /dʒəʊ'hɔ:/ state in S Peninsular Malaysia; capital Johor Baharu; area 19,000 sq km/7,334 sq mi; population (1980) 1,638,000. The southernmost point of mainland Asia, it is joined to Singapore by a causeway. It is mainly forested, with swamps. There is bauxite and iron.

joie de vivre (French) finding pleasure in simply being alive.

joint in any animal with a skeleton, a point of movement or articulation. In invertebrates with an ◊exoskeleton, the joints are places where the exoskeleton is replaced by a more flexible outer covering, the arthrodial membrane, which allows the limb (or other body part) to bend at that point. In vertebrates, it is the point where two bones meet. Some joints allow no motion (the sutures of the skull), others allow a very small motion (the sacro-iliac joints in the lower back), but most allow a relatively free motion. Of these, some allow a gliding motion (one vertebra of the spine on another), some have a hinge action (elbow and knee), and others allow motion in all directions (hip and shoulder joints) by means of a ball-and-socket arrangement. The ends of the bones at a moving joint are covered with cartilage for greater elasticity and smoothness, and enclosed in an envelope (capsule) of tough white fibrous tissue lined with a membrane which secretes lubricating (◊synovial) fluid. The joint is further strengthened by ligaments.

Joint European Torus an experimental nuclear fusion machine, known as ◊JET.

joint intelligence committee a weekly British cabinet meeting held to discuss international, military, and other covertly obtained information.

joint venture in business, an undertaking in which

an individual or legal entity of one country forms a company with those of another country, with risks being shared.

Joint ventures are often the result of direct investment by a company wanting to expand its markets. They frequently involve a transfer of technology in a developing country.

Joinville /ʒwæn'vi:l/ Jean, Sire de Joinville 1224–1317. French historian, born in Champagne. He accompanied Louis IX on the crusade of 1248–54, which he described in his *History of St Louis*.

Joliot-Curie /'ʒɒliəʊ 'kjʊəri/ Irène 1897–1956, and Frédéric Joliot-Curie 1900–1958. French physicists who made the discovery of artificial radioactivity for which they were jointly awarded the 1935 Nobel chemistry prize. Irene was the daughter of Marie ◊Curie and began work at her mother's Radium Institute in 1921. In 1926 she married Frédéric, a pupil of her mother and they began a long and fruitful collaboration. In 1934 they found that certain elements exposed to radiation themselves become radioactive.

Jolson /'dʒəʊlsən/ Al. Stage name of Asa Yoelson 1886–1950. Russian-born singer and entertainer, who lived in the USA from childhood. Formerly a Broadway star, he gained instant cinema immortality as the star of the first talking picture, *The Jazz Singer* 1927.

Jonah /'dʒəʊnə/ 7th century BC. Hebrew prophet whose name is given to a book in the Old Testament. According to this, he fled by ship to evade his mission to prophesy the destruction of Nineveh. The crew threw him overboard in a storm, as a bringer of ill fortune, and he spent three days and nights in the belly of a whale before coming to land.

Jonathan /'dʒɒnəθən/ Chief (Joseph) Leabua 1914–1987. Lesotho politician. As prime minister of Lesotho 1965–86, he played a pragmatic role, allying himself in turn with South Africa, then with the Organization of African Unity. His rule was ended by a coup in 1986.

Jones /dʒəʊnz/ 'Chuck' (Charles Martin) 1912– . US film animator and cartoon director who worked at Warner Brothers with characters such as Bugs Bunny, Daffy Duck, Wile E. Coyote and Elmer Fudd.

Jones /dʒəʊnz/ Gwyneth 1936– . Welsh soprano, who performed as Sieglinde in *Die Walküre* and Desdemona in *Otello*.

Jones /dʒəʊnz/ Henry Arthur 1851–1929. British playwright. Among some 60 of his melodramas, *Mrs Dane's Defence* 1900 is most notable as an early realist problem play.

Jones /dʒəʊnz/ Inigo 1573–*c.*1652. English architect. Born in London, he studied in Italy, and was influenced by the works of Palladio. He was

Jolson *Singer and film star Al Jolson. Originally a stage performer, he successfully made the transition to star in early talking films such as* The Jazz Singer.

Jones *A drawing after Robert Van Voerst of English architect Inigo Jones, National Portrait Gallery, London.*

employed by James I to design scenery for Ben Jonson's masques. In 1619 he designed his English Renaissance masterpiece, the banqueting-room at Whitehall, London.

Jones /dʒəʊnz/ John Paul 1747–1792. Scottish-born American naval officer in the War of Independence 1775. Heading a small French-sponsored squadron in the *Bonhomme Richard*, he captured the British warship *Serapis* 23 Sept 1779 in a bloody battle off Scarborough.

Jones was born in Kirkcudbright, Scotland. He was originally a trader and slaver but became a privateer 1775, and then a commodore. After the War of Independence, he joined the Russian navy as a rear admiral 1788, fighting against Turkey, but lost the Empress Catherine's favour and died in France.

Jones /dʒəʊnz/ Robert Tyre 'Bobby' 1902–1971. US golfer. He was the game's greatest amateur player, who never turned professional but won 13 major amateur and professional tournaments, including the Grand Slam of the amateur and professional opens of both the USA and Britain 1930.

Born in Atlanta, Georgia, Jones finished playing competitive golf 1930 and concentrated on his law practice. He maintained his contacts with the sport and was largely responsible for inaugurating the US Masters.

CAREER HIGHLIGHTS

British Open: 1926–27, 1930
US Open: 1923, 1926, 1929–30
British Amateur: 1930
US Amateur: 1924–25, 1927–28, 1930
US Walker Cup team: 1922, 1924, 1926, 1928*, 1930*
* indicates playing captain

Jonestown /'dʒəʊnztaʊn/ commune of the ***People's Temple Sect***, NW of Georgetown, Guyana, established 1974 by the American Jim Jones (1933–78), who originally founded the sect among San Francisco's black community. After a visiting US congressman was shot dead, Jones enforced mass suicide on his followers by instructing them to drink cyanide; 914 died, including over 240 children.

Jongkind /'jɒŋkɪnt/ Johan Bartold 1819–1891. Dutch painter active mainly in France. His studies of the Normandy coast show a keen observation of the natural effects of light. He influenced the Impressionist painter ◊Monet.

Jönköping /'jɜ:ntʃɜ:pɪŋ/ town at the S end of Lake Vättern, Sweden; population (1985) 107,362. It is an industrial centre in an agricultural and forestry region.

jonquil a species of small daffodil *Narcissus jonquilla*, family Amaryllidaceae, with yellow flowers. Native to Spain and Portugal, it is cultivated elsewhere.

Jonson /'dʒɒnsən/ Ben(jamin) 1572–1637. English dramatist, poet, and critic. *Every Man in his*

Jonson The poet and dramatist Ben Jonson, at one time a bricklayer, narrowly escaped the gallows after killing a man in a duel.

Humour 1598 established the English 'comedy of humours', in which each character embodies a 'humour', or vice, such as greed, lust, or avarice. This was followed by *Every Man out of his Humour* 1599, *Cynthia's Revels* 1600 and *Poetaster* 1601. His first extant tragedy is *Sejanus* 1603, with Burbage and Shakespeare as members of the original cast. The plays of his middle years include *Volpone, or The Fox* 1606, *The Alchemist* 1610, and *Bartholomew Fair* 1614.

Jonson was born in Westminster, London, and entered the theatre as actor and dramatist in 1597. In 1598 he narrowly escaped the gallows for killing a fellow player in a duel. He collaborated with Marston and Chapman in *Eastward Ho!* 1605, and shared their imprisonment when official exception was taken to the satirization of James I's Scottish policy.

Joplin /'dʒɒplɪn/ Janis 1943–1970. US blues and rock singer, born in Texas. She was lead singer with the San Francisco group Big Brother and the Holding Company 1966–68. Her biggest hit, Kris Kristofferson's 'Me and Bobby McGee', was released on the posthumous *Pearl* LP 1971.

Joplin /'dʒɒplɪn/ Scott 1868–1917. US ◊ragtime pianist and composer in Chicago. His 'Maple Leaf Rag' 1899 was the first instrumental sheet music to sell a million copies, and 'The Entertainer', as the theme tune of the film *The Sting* 1973, revived his popularity. He was an influence on Jelly Roll Morton and other early jazz musicians.

Joppa /'dʒɒpə/ ancient name of ◊Jaffa, a port in W Israel.

Jordaens /jɔː'dɑːns/ Jacob 1593–1678. Flemish painter, born in Antwerp. His style follows Rubens, whom he assisted in various commissions. Much of his work is exuberant and on a large scale, including scenes of peasant life, altarpieces, portraits, and mythological subjects.

Jordan /'dʒɔːdn/ river rising on Mount Hermon, Syria at 550 m/1,800 ft above sea level and flowing S for about 320 km/200 mi via the Sea of Galilee to the Dead Sea, 390 m/1,290 ft below sea level. It occupies the northern part of the Great Rift Valley; its upper course forms the boundary of Israel with Syria and the kingdom of Jordan; its lower course runs through Jordan; the West Bank has been occupied by Israel since 1967.

Jordan /'dʒɔːdn/ country in SW Asia, bordered to the N by Syria, NE by Iraq, E and SE by Saudi Arabia, S by the Gulf of Aqaba, and W by Israel.

government Jordan is not a typical constitutional monarchy on the Western model, since the king is effectively head of both state and government. The 1952 constitution, amended in 1974, 1976 and 1984, provides for a two-chamber national assem-

Jordan
Hashemite Kingdom of
(Al Mamlaka al Urduniya al Hashemiyah)

area 89,206 sq km/34,434 sq mi (West Bank, incorporated into Jordan 1950 but occupied by Israel since 1967, area 5,879 sq km/2,269 sq mi)
capital Amman
towns Zarqa, Irbid, Aqaba (the only port)
physical mostly desert
features Dead Sea, river Jordan, archaeological sites including Jerash, Roman forum
head of state and government King Hussein ibn Talai from 1952
political system absolute monarchy
political parties party activity banned 1976, and has not been fully restored
exports potash, phosphates, citrus
currency Jordanian dinar (1.13 = £1 Feb 1990)

population (1988) 2,970,000 (including Palestinian refugees); West Bank (1988) 866,000; annual growth rate 3.7%
life expectancy men 62, women 66
language Arabic
religion Sunni Muslim
literacy 87% male/63% female (1985 est)
GDP $4.2 bn (1984); $552 per head of population
chronology
1946 Achieved full independence as Transjordan.
1949 New state of Jordan declared.
1953 Hussein ibn Talai became king of Jordan.
1958 Jordan and Iraq formed Arab Federation which ended when the Iraqi monarchy was deposed.
1976 Lower house dissolved, and elections postponed until further notice.
1982 Hussein tried to mediate in Arab-Israeli conflict.
1984 Women voted for the first time.
1985 Hussein put forward a framework for a Middle East peace settlement. Secret meeting between Hussein and Israeli prime minister.
1988 Hussein announced a decision to cease administering the West Bank as part of Jordan, passing responsibility to Palestine Liberation Organization, and suspending parliament.
1989 Prime minister Zaid al-Rifai resigned and Hussein promised new parliamentary elections following criticism of economic policies. Riots over price increases up to 50% following fall in oil revenues. 80-member parliament elected and Mudar Badran appointed prime minister. Hussein abolishes martial law after 22 years.

bly comprising a senate (house of notables) of 30, appointed by the king for an eight-year term, and a 142-member house of representatives (house of deputies), elected by universal suffrage for a four-year term. The house is subject to dissolution within that period. In each chamber there is equal representation for the east and west (occupied) banks of the river Jordan. Three of Jordan's eight administrative provinces have been occupied by Israel since 1967.

The king governs with the help of a council of ministers whom he appoints and who are responsible to the assembly. Political parties were banned in 1963, partially restored in 1971, and then banned again in 1976.

history The area forming the kingdom of Jordan was occupied by the independent Nabataeans from

Joplin 'The Entertainer', Scott Joplin's ragtime masterpiece.

the 4th century BC and perhaps earlier, until AD 106 when it became part of the Roman province of Arabia. It was included in the Crusaders' kingdom of Jerusalem 1099–1187. Palestine, which included the West Bank of present-day Jordan, and Transjordan, which is the present-day East Bank, were part of the Turkish Ottoman Empire until its dissolution after World War I. Both were then placed under British administration by the League of Nations.

Transjordan acquired greater control of its own affairs, separating from Palestine in 1923 and achieving full independence when the British mandate expired in 1946. The mandate for Palestine ran out in 1948, whereupon Jewish leaders claimed it for a new state of Israel. Fighting broke out between Jews and Arabs until a cease-fire was agreed in 1949. By then Transjordan forces had occupied part of Palestine to add to what they called the new state of Jordan. The following year they annexed the W Bank. In 1953 Hussein ibn Talai came to the Jordanian throne at the age of 17. He was to rule his country for over 30 years. In 1958 Jordan and Iraq formed an Arab Federation which ended five months later when the Iraqi monarchy was overthrown.

King Hussein has survived many upheavals in his own country and neighbouring states, including attempts on his life, and has kept control of Jordan's affairs as well as playing an important role in Middle East affairs. Relations with his neighbours have fluctuated but he has generally been a moderating influence. After Israel's invasion of Lebanon in 1982, Hussein played a key role in attempts to bring peace to the area, establishing a relationship with ◊Palestine Liberation Organization (PLO) leader, Yasser ◊Arafat. By 1984 the Arab world was split into two camps, with the moderates represented by Jordan, Egypt, and Arafat's PLO, and the militant radicals by Syria, Libya, and the rebel wing of the PLO. In 1985 Hussein and Arafat put together a framework for a Middle East peace settlement. It would involve bringing together all interested parties, including

Josephine A portrait of Empress Josephine at La Malmaison, her favourite residence, which Napoleon gave her after their divorce.

the PLO, but Israel objected to the PLO representation. Further progress was hampered by the PLO's alleged complicity in a number of guerrilla operations in that year. Hussein tried to revive the search for peace by secretly meeting the Israeli prime minister in France and persuading Yasser Arafat to denounce publicly PLO violence in territories not occupied by Israel. The role of Jordan, through King Hussein, could be vital in any future peacemaking moves.

In response to mounting unrest within Jordan in 1989, Hussein promised greater democratization and in Nov elections to an 80-member parliament were held. Soon afterwards the veteran politician Mudar Badran was made prime minister.

Jordan /'dʒɔːdn/ Dorothea 1762–1816. British actress. She made her debut in 1777, and retired in 1815. She was a mistress of the Duke of Clarence (later William IV); they had ten children with the name FitzClarence.

Jörgensen /'jɜːnsən/ Jörgen 1779–1845. Danish sailor who in 1809 seized control of Iceland, announcing it was under the protection of England. His brief reign of corruption ended later the same year when he was captured by an English naval ship and taken to London, where he was imprisoned.

Joseph /'dʒəʊzɪf/ in the New Testament, the husband of the Virgin Mary, a descendant of King David, and a carpenter by trade. Although Jesus was not the son of Joseph, Joseph was his legal father. According to Roman Catholic tradition, he had a family by a previous wife, and was an elderly man when he married Mary.

Joseph /'dʒəʊzɪf/ in the Old Testament, the 11th and favourite son of ◊Jacob, sold into Egypt by his jealous half-brothers. After he had risen to power there, they and his father joined him to escape from famine.

Joseph /'dʒəʊzɪf/ Keith (Sinjohn) 1918– . British Conservative politician. A barrister, he entered parliament 1956. He held ministerial posts 1962–64, 1970–74, 1979–81, and was secretary of state for education and science 1981–86. He was made a life peer 1987.

Joseph /'dʒəʊzɪf/ Père. Religious name of Francis Le Clerc du Tremblay 1577–1638. French Catholic Capuchin friar. He was the influential secretary and agent to Louis XIII's chief minister Cardinal Richelieu, and nicknamed *Grey Eminence* in reference to his grey habit.

Joseph /'dʒəʊzɪf/two Holy Roman emperors:

Joseph I 1678–1711. Holy Roman emperor from 1705, and king of Austria, of the house of Habsburg. He spent most of his reign involved in fighting the War of Spanish Succession.

GENˡ JOUBERT ᴀɴᴅ STAFF ᴀᴛ NEWCASTLE, NATAL. Oᴄᴛ 17ᵀᴴ 1899. PHOTO ʙʏ GELL.

Joubert Boer general and politician Petrus Joubert, also known as 'Slim Piet', opposed British annexation of the Transvaal in 1877, and proclaimed its independence in 1880. He commanded the Transvaal forces in the First South African War 1880–81.

Joseph II 1741–1790. Holy Roman emperor from 1765, son of Francis I (1708–1765). The reforms he carried out after the death of his mother, ◊Maria Theresa, in 1780, provoked revolts from those who lost privileges.

Josephine /'dʒəʊzɪfiːn/ Marie Josèphe Rose Tascher de la Pagerie 1763–1814. Empress of France 1796–1809. Born on Martinique, she married in 1779 Alexandre de Beauharnais, and in 1796 Napoleon, who divorced her in 1809 because she had not produced children.

Joseph of Arimathaea, St /ˌærɪməˈθiːə/ 1st century AD . In the New Testament, a wealthy Jew, member of the Sanhedrin (supreme court), and secret supporter of Jesus. On the evening of the Crucifixion he asked the Roman procurator Pilate for Jesus's body and buried it in his own tomb. Feast day 17 Mar.

According to tradition he brought the Holy Grail to England about AD 63 and built the first Christian church in Britain, at Glastonbury.

Josephs /'dʒəʊzɪfs/ Wilfred 1927– . British composer. As well as film and television music, he has written nine symphonies, concertos, and chamber music. His works include the *Jewish Requiem* 1969 and the opera *Rebecca* 1983.

Josephson /'dʒəʊzɪfsən/ Brian 1940– . British physicist, a leading authority on superconductivity. In 1973 he shared a Nobel prize for his theoretical predictions of the properties of a supercurrent through a tunnel barrier.

Josephson junction a device used in 'superchips' (large and complex integrated circuits) to speed the passage of signals by a phenomenon called 'electron tunnelling'. Although these superchips respond a thousand times faster than the ◊silicon chip, they have the disadvantage that the components of the Josephson junctions operate only at temperatures close to ◊absolute zero. They are named after Brian Josephson.

Josephus /dʒəʊ'siːfəs/ Flavius AD 37–*c.* 100. Jewish historian and general, born in Jerusalem. He became a Pharisee, and commanded the Jewish forces in Galilee in the revolt against Rome from 66 (which ended in mass suicide at Masada). When captured, he gained the favour of Vespasian and settled in Rome as a citizen. He wrote *Antiquities of the Jews*, an early history to AD 66; *The Jewish War*, and an autobiography.

Joshua /'dʒɒʃuə/ 13th century BC. In the Old Tes-

tament, successor of Moses, who led the Jews in their conquest of the land of Canaan. The city of Jericho was the first to fall: according to the Book of Joshua, the walls crumbled to the blast of his trumpets.

Josiah /dʒəʊ'saɪə/ *c.* 647–609 BC. King of Judah. Grandson of Manasseh and son of Amon, he succeeded to the throne when eight. The discovery of a Book of Instruction (probably Deuteronomy, a book of the Old Testament) during repairs of the Temple in 621 BC stimulated thorough reform, which included the removal of all sanctuaries except that of Jerusalem. He was killed in a clash at ◊Megiddo with Pharaoh-nechoh, king of Egypt.

Josquin Desprez /ʒɒ'skæŋ deɪ'preɪ/ or *des Prés* 1440–1521. Franco-Flemish composer. His music combines a technical mastery with the feeling for words that became a hallmark of Renaissance vocal music. His works, which include 18 masses, over 100 motets, and secular vocal works, are characterized by their vitality and depth of feeling.

He spent the early part of his life in Milan, first at the cathedral and then in the service of the Sforza family. In 1484, already highly renowned, he moved to Rome and went from there to France, Ferrara, and the Netherlands.

jota a traditional northern Spanish dance in lively triple time for one or more couples who play the castanets, accompanied by guitar and singing. There is a *jota* in de ◊Falla's *The Three-Cornered Hat*.

Jotunheim /'jəʊtʊnhaɪm/ mountainous region of S Norway, containing the highest mountains in Scandinavia, Glittertind 2,453 m/8,048 ft and Galdhöpiggen 2,468 m/8,097 ft. In Norse mythology it is the home of the giants.

Joubert /ʒuː'beə/ Petrus Jacobus 1831–1900. Boer general in South Africa. He opposed British annexation of the Transvaal 1877, proclaimed its independence 1880, led the Boer Commandos in the First ◊South African War against the British 1880–81, defeated ◊Jameson 1896, and fought in the Second South African War.

joule SI unit (symbol J) of work and energy, replacing the ◊calorie (1 joule = 4.2 calories). It is defined as the work done (energy transferred) by a force of 1 newton acting over 1 metre. It can also be expressed as the work done in 1 second by a current of 1 amp at a potential difference of 1 volt. One ◊watt is equal to 1 joule per second.

Joyce Irish writer James Joyce.

Joule /dʒuːl/ James Prescott 1818–1889. British physicist whose work on the relations between electrical, mechanical, and chemical effects led to the discovery of the first law of ◊thermodynamics.

He was a brewery owner, and dedicated to precise scientific research. He determined the mechanical equivalent of heat (Joule's equivalent), and the SI unit of energy, the ◊joule, is named after him.

Joule-Thomson effect in physics, the fall in temperature of a gas as it expands adiabatically (without loss or gain of heat to the system) through a narrow jet. It can be felt when, for example, compressed air escapes through the valve of an inflated bicycle tyre. Only hydrogen does not exhibit the effect. It is the basic principle of most refrigerators.

It was named after the British scientists James Prescott ◊Joule and William Thomson (Lord Kelvin) (1824–1907).

Jounieh a port on the Mediterranean coast of Lebanon, 15 km/9 mi N of Beirut. The centre of an anti-Syrian Christian enclave.

journalism the profession of reporting, photographing, or editing news for newspapers, magazines, radio, and television. Professional bodies include the NUJ (National Union of Journalists) in the UK, and the ANG (American Newspaper Guild) in the USA.

In the UK the NCTJ (National Council for the Training of Journalists) sets standards and awards proficiency certificates. Standards are also set by awards such as those founded by J ◊Pulitzer.

Jovian /ˈdʒəʊviən/ 331–364. Roman emperor from 363. Captain of the imperial bodyguard, he was chosen as emperor by the troops after ◊Julian's death in battle with the Persians. He concluded an unpopular peace and restored Christianity as the state religion.

Jowett /ˈdʒaʊɪt/ Benjamin 1817–1893. English scholar. He promoted university reform, including the abolition of the theological test for degrees, and translated Plato, Aristotle, and Thucydides.

Jowett was ordained in 1842. He became Regius professor of Greek at Oxford University 1855, and Master of Balliol College 1870.

Joyce /dʒɔɪs/ James (Augustine Aloysius) 1882–1941. Irish writer, born in Dublin, who revolutionized the form of the English novel with his 'stream of consciousness' technique. His works include *Dubliners* 1914 (short stories), *Portrait of the Artist as a Young Man* 1916, *Ulysses* 1922, and *Finnegans Wake* 1938.

Ulysses, which records the events of a single Dublin day, experiments with language and mingles direct narrative with the unspoken and unconscious reactions of the characters. Banned at first for obscenity in England and the USA, it was enormously influential. *Finnegans Wake* 1939 continued Joyce's experiments with language, attempting a synthesis of all existence.

Joyce /dʒɔɪs/ William 1906–1946. Born in New York, son of a naturalized Irish-born American,

Juan Carlos King of Spain Juan Carlos, who succeeded General Franco in 1975 and has since supervised the country's return to democracy and membership of the European Community.

he carried on fascist activity in the UK as a 'British subject'. During World War II he made propaganda broadcasts from Germany to the UK, his upper-class accent earning him the nickname **Lord Haw Haw**. He was hanged for treason.

joystick in computing, an input device, similar to the joystick used to control the flight of an aircraft, which signals to a computer the direction and extent of displacement of a hand-held lever.

Often used to control the movement of a cursor (marker) on a computer screen, joysticks allow fast and direct input for moving predetermined specific shapes or icons (such as space-invader characters) in computer games.

JP abbreviation for ◊*justice of the peace*.

Juan Carlos /ˈhwæn ˈkɑːlɒs/ 1938– . King of Spain. The son of Don Juan, pretender to the Spanish throne, he married in 1962 Princess Sofia, eldest daughter of King Paul of Greece. In 1969 he was nominated by Franco to succeed on the restoration of the monarchy intended to follow Franco's own death; his father was excluded because of his known liberal views. He became king in 1975 and has sought to steer his country from dictatorship to democracy.

Juan Fernández Islands /ˈdʒuːən fəˈnændez/ three small volcanic Pacific islands belonging to Chile; almost uninhabited. The largest is Más-a-Tierra (sometimes called Juan Fernández Island) where Alexander Selkirk was marooned 1704–09. The islands were named after the Spanish navigator who reached them in 1563.

Juárez /ˈxwɑːreθ/ Benito 1806–1872. Mexican politician, president 1861–64 and 1867–72. In 1861 he suspended repayments of Mexico's foreign debts, which prompted a joint French, British, and Spanish expedition to exert pressure. French forces invaded and created an empire for ◊Maximilian, brother of the Austrian emperor. After their withdrawal in 1867, Maximilian was executed, and Juárez returned to the presidency.

Juba /ˈdʒuːbə/ river in E Africa, formed at Dolo, Ethiopia, by the junction of the Ganale Dorya and Dawa rivers. It flows S for about 885 km/550 mi through the Somali Republic (of which its valley is the most productive area) into the Indian Ocean.

Juba /ˈdʒuːbə/ capital of Equatoria province, Sudan Republic; situated on the left bank of the White Nile, at the head of navigation above Khartoum, 1,200 km/750 mi to the N; population (1973) 56,700.

Jubbulpore /ˌdʒʌbəlˈpʊə/ alternative name for the city of ◊Jabalpur in India.

Judaea /dʒuːˈdiːə/ southern division of ancient Palestine, see ◊Judah.

Judah /ˈdʒuːdə/ or *Judaea* district of S Palestine. After the death of King Solomon 937 BC, Judah

adhered to his son Rehoboam and the Davidic line, whereas the rest of Israel elected Jeroboam as ruler of the northern kingdom. In New Testament times, Judah was the Roman province of Judaea, and in current Israeli usage it refers to the southern area of the West Bank.

Judah Ha-Nasi 'the Prince' *c.* AD 135–*c.* 220. Jewish scholar who with a number of colleagues edited the collection of writings known as the *Mishna*, which formed the basis of the ◊Talmud, in the 2nd century AD.

Judaism the religion of the Jews, according to tradition based on a covenant between God and Abraham about 2000 BC, and the renewal of the covenant with Moses about 1200 BC. It rests on the concept of one God, whose will is revealed in the *Torah* and who has a special relationship with the Jewish people. The Torah comprises the first five books of the Bible, also known as the Pentateuch. Outside Israel, there are large Jewish populations today in the USA, USSR, and the UK, and Jewish communities throughout the world, a total of some 17 million.

scriptures The *Talmud* combines the *Mishna*, rabbinical commentary on the law handed down orally from AD 70 and put in writing about 200, and the *Gemara*, legal discussions in the schools of Palestine and Babylon from the 3rd and 4th centuries. The *Haggadah* is a part of the Talmud dealing with stories of heroes. The *Midrash* is a collection of commentaries on the scriptures written 400–1200, mainly in Palestine.

observances The *synagogue* (in US non-Orthodox usage *temple*) is the local building for worship (originally simply the place where the Torah was read and expounded); its characteristic feature is the Ark, or cupboard, where the Torah scrolls are kept. *Rabbis* are teachers skilled in the Jewish law and ritual who either act as spiritual leaders and pastors of their communities or devote themselves to study. Religious practices include: circumcision, daily services in Hebrew, observance of the *Sabbath* (sunset on Friday to sunset Saturday) as a day of rest, and, among Orthodox Jews, strict dietary laws (see ◊kosher). Holy days include *Rosh Hashanah* Jewish New Year (first new moon after the autumn equinox) and, a week later, the religious fast *Yom Kippur* (Day of Atonement).

divisions There are a number of groups within Judaism. *Orthodox Jews*, in the majority, adhere to all the traditions of Judaism, including the strict dietary laws and the segregation of women in the synagogue. *Reform Judaism* rejects the idea that Jews are the chosen people, has a liberal interpretation of the dietary laws, and takes a critical attitude to the Torah. *Conservative Judaism* comes between Orthodox and Reform in its acceptance of the traditional law, making some allowances for present conditions, though its services and ceremonies are much closer to Orthodox Judaism. *Liberal Judaism* goes further than Reform in attempting to adapt Judaism to the needs of the modern world and to interpret the Torah in the light of current scholarship. In all the groups except Orthodox, women are not segregated in the synagogue, and there are female rabbis in both Reform and Liberal Judaism. In the 20th century, particularly in the USA, many people who would call themselves Jews prefer to identify Judaism with a historical and cultural tradition rather than strict religious observance, and a contemporary debate (complicated by the history of non-Jewish attitudes towards Jews) centres on the question of how to define a Jew. As in other religions, fundamentalist movements have emerged, for example, Gush Emunim.

history
c.2000 BC Led by Abraham, the Israelites emigrated from Mesopotamia to Canaan.
18th century–1580 Some settled on the borders of Egypt and were put to forced labour.
13th century They were rescued by Moses, who aimed at their establishment in Palestine.

Moses gave the Ten Commandments to the people. The main invasion of Canaan was led by Joshua about 1274.

12th–11th centuries During the period of Judges, ascendancy was established over the Canaanites.

c.1000 Complete conquest of Palestine and the union of all Israel was achieved under David, and Jerusalem became the capital.

10th century Solomon, David's son, succeeded and enjoyed a reputation for great wealth and wisdom, but his lack of a constructive policy led, after his death, to the secession of the north (Israel) under Jeroboam, only Judah remaining under the house of David.

9th–8th centuries Assyria became the dominant power in the Middle East. Israel purchased safety by tribute, but the basis of the society was corrupt, and prophets such as Amos, Isaiah, and Micah predicted destruction. At the hands of Tiglathpileser and his successor Shalmaneser IV, the northern kingdom was organized as Assyrian provinces after the fall of Samaria 721, although Judah was spared as an ally.

586–458 Nebuchadnezzar took Jerusalem and carried off the major part of the population to Babylon. Judaism was retained during exile, and was reconstituted by Ezra on the return to Jerusalem.

520 The Temple, originally built by Solomon, was restored.

c.444 Ezra promulgated the legal code that was to govern the future of the Jewish people.

4th–3rd centuries After the conquest of the Persian Empire by Alexander the Great, the Syrian Seleucid rulers and the Egyptian Ptolemaic dynasty struggled for Palestine, which came under the government of Egypt, although with a large measure of freedom.

2nd century With the advance of Syrian power, Antiochus IV attempted intervention in Jewish internal quarrels, thus prompting a revolt 165 led by the Maccabee family.

63 Judaea's near-independence ended when internal dissension led to the Roman general Pompey's intervention and Roman suzerainty was established.

1st century AD A revolt led to the destruction of the Temple 66–70 by the Roman emperor Titus. Jewish national sentiment was encouraged by the work of Rabbi Johanan ben Zakkai (*c.*20–90), and after his day the president of the Sanhedrin (supreme court) was recognized as the patriarch of Palestinian Jewry.

2nd–3rd centuries Greatest of the Sanhedrin presidents was Rabbi Judah (*c.*135–220), who codified the traditional law in the Mishna. The Palestinian Talmud (*c.* 375) added the Gemara to the Mishna.

4th–5th centuries The intellectual leadership of Judaism passed to the descendants of the 6th-century exiles in Babylonia, who compiled the Babylonian Talmud.

8th–13th centuries Judaism enjoyed a golden era, producing the philosopher Saadiah, the poet Jehudah Ha-levi (*c.*1075–1141), the codifier Moses Maimonides, and others.

14th–17th centuries Where Christianity was the dominant religion, the Jews were increasingly segregated from mainstream life and trade by anti-Semitism, which included restrictive legislation.

18th–19th centuries Outbreaks of persecution increased with the rise of European nationalism. The Reform movement, a rejection of religious orthodoxy and an attempt to interpret Judaism for modern times, began in Germany 1810 and reached the UK 1842.

20th century Zionism (founded 1896) is a movement to create a homeland where the Jewish people would be free from persecution; this led to the establishment of the state of Israel 1948. Liberal Judaism (more radical than Reform) developed in the USA and founded its first UK synagogue 1911.

The Nazi regime 1933–45 killed six million European Jews.

Judas Iscariot /ˈdʒuːdəs Iˈskæriət/ in the New Testament, the disciple who betrayed Jesus Christ. Judas was the treasurer of the group. At the last Passover he arranged, for 30 pieces of silver, to point out Jesus to the chief priests so that they could arrest him. Afterwards Judas was overcome with remorse and committed suicide.

Jude, St lived 1st century. Supposed brother of Jesus Christ and writer of Epistle in the New Testament; patron saint of lost causes. Feast day 28 Oct.

judge a person invested with power to hear and determine legal disputes. In the UK, judges are chosen from barristers of long standing (for higher courts), and solicitors. Judges of the High Court, the crown courts, and the county courts are nominated by the Lord Chancellor, and those of the Court of Appeal and the House of Lords by the prime minister. In the USA, apart from the federal judiciary which are executive appointments, judges in most states are elected by popular vote.

Judges a book of the Old Testament, describing the history of Israel from the death of Joshua to the reign of Saul, under the command of several leaders known as Judges.

judicial review in English law, action in the High Court to review the decisions of lower courts, tribunals, and administrative bodies. Various court orders can be made: *certiorari* (which quashes the decision); *mandamus* (which commands a duty to be performed); *prohibition* (which commands that an action should not be performed because it is unauthorized); a *declaration* (which sets out the legal rights or obligations); or an ◊*injunction*.

judicial separation in the UK, an action in a magistrate's court by either husband or wife, in which it is not necessary to prove an irreconcilable breakdown of a marriage, but in which the grounds are otherwise the same as for divorce. It does not end a marriage, but a declaration may be obtained that the complainant need no longer cohabit with the defendant. The court can make similar orders to a divorce court in relation to custody of children and maintenance. A similar procedure exists in the USA.

Judith in Christian legend, a woman who saved her community from a Babylonian siege by killing the enemy general, Holofernes. The Book of Judith is part of the Apocrypha, a section of the Old Testament.

Judith, a widow, approached Holofernes on the pretext of betraying the besieged Jews. Charming him with her beauty and wit, she made him drunk and cut his head off, then incited the Jews to attack and rout the Babylonian army.

Judith of Bavaria /ˈdʒuːdɪθ bəˈveəriə/ 800–843. Empress of the French. The wife of ◊Louis the Pious (Louis I of France) from 819, she influenced her husband to the benefit of their son ◊Charles the Bold .

judo (Japanese *jū do* 'gentle way') a type of wrestling of Japanese origin. The two combatants wear loose-fitting, belted jackets and trousers to facilitate holds, and falls are broken by a square mat; when one has established a painful hold that the other cannot break, the latter signifies surrender by slapping the ground with a free hand. Degrees of proficiency are indicated by the colour of the belt: for novices white; after examination brown (three degrees); and finally black (nine degrees).

Judo is a synthesis of the most valuable methods from the many forms of jujitsu, 'the soft art', the traditional Japanese skill of self-defence and offence without weapons, which was originally practised as a secret art by the feudal Samurai. Today, judo has been adopted throughout the world in the armed forces, the police, and in many schools. It became an Olympic sport 1964.

World Championships first held 1956, now contested biennially:

open class
1981 Yasuhiro Yamashita *(Japan)*
1983 Angelo Parisi *(France)*
1985 Yoshimi Masaki *(Japan)*
1987 Noayo Ogawa *(Japan)*
1989 Noayo Ogawa *(Japan)*
over 95 kg
1981 Yasuhiro Yamashita *(Japan)*
1983 Yasuhiro Yamashita *(Japan)*
1985 Yong-Chul Cho *(South Korea)*
1987 Grigori Vertichev *(USSR)*
1989 Naoyo Ogawa *Japan*
under 95 kg
1981 Tengiz Khubuluri *(USSR)*
1983 Valeriy Divisenko *(USSR)*
1985 Hitoshi Sugai *(Japan)*
1987 Hitoshi Sugai *(Japan)*
1989 Kota Kurtanidze *(USSR)*
under 86 kg
1981 Bernard Tchoullouyan *(France)*
1983 Detlef Ultsch *(East Germany)*
1985 Peter Seisenbacher *(Austria)*
1987 Fabien Canu *(France)*
1989 Fabien Canu *(France)*
under 78 kg
1981 Neil Adams *(Great Britain)*
1983 Nobutoshi Hikage *(Japan)*
1985 Nobutoshi Hikage *(Japan)*
1987 Hirotaki Okada *(Japan)*
1989 Kim Byung-ju *(South Korea)*
under 71 kg
1981 Chon Hak Park *(South Korea)*
1983 Hidetoshi Nakanichi *(Japan)*
1985 Ahn Byeong-Keun *(South Korea)*
1987 Mike Swain *(USA)*
1989 Toshihiko Koga*(Japan)*
under 65 kg
1981 Nikolai Soludkhin *(USSR)*
1983 Nikolai Soludkhin *(USSR)*
1985 Yuri Sokolov *(USSR)*
1987 Yosuke Yamamto *(Japan)*
1989 Drago Becanovic *(Yugoslavia)*
under 60 kg
1981 Yasuhiko Mariwaki *(Japan)*
1983 Khazret Tletseri *(USSR)*
1985 Shinji Hosokawa *(Japan)*
1987 Jae Yup Kim *(South Korea)*
1989 Amiran Totikashvilli *(USSR)*.

Juggernaut /ˈdʒʌɡənɔːt/ or *Jagannath* a name for Vishnu, the Hindu god, meaning 'Lord of the World'. His temple is in Puri, Orissa, India. A statue of the god, dating from about 318, is annually taken in procession on a large vehicle (hence the word 'juggernaut'). Devotees formerly threw themselves beneath its wheels.

Jugoslavia /ˌjuːɡəʊˈslaːviə/ alternative spelling of ◊Yugoslavia.

jugular vein one of two veins in the necks of vertebrates; they return blood from the head to the superior (or anterior) vena cava and thence to the heart.

Jugurtha /dʒuːˈɡɜːθə/ died 104 BC. King of Numidia, N Africa, who, after a long resistance, was betrayed to the Romans in 107 BC and put to death.

jujitsu traditional Japanese form of self-defence; see ◊judo.

jujube tree of the *Zizyphus* genus, family Thamnaceae, with berry-like fruits. The Chinese jujube *Zizyphus jujuba*, cultivated in S Europe and frequently naturalized in the Mediterranean region, has fruit the size of small plums, known as Chinese dates when preserved in syrup.

Julian /ˈdʒuːliən/ *c.* 331–363. Roman emperor, called the 'Apostate'. Born in Constantinople, the nephew of Constantine the Great, he was brought up as a Christian but early in life became a convert to paganism. Sent by Constantius to govern Gaul in 355, he was proclaimed emperor by his troops in 360, and in 361 was marching on Constantinople when Constantius'

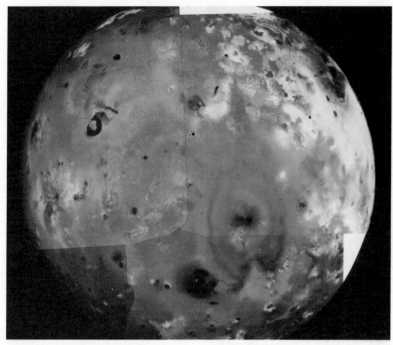

Jupiter *(Left) Jupiter, the largest planet in the solar system together with four of its moons: Io, Europa, Ganymede, and Callisto. (Right) False colour mosaic of Io, the innermost satellite of Jupiter, from the Voyager probes. A range of colours and much volcanic activity can be seen on the surface.*

death allowed a peaceful succession. He revived pagan worship and refused to persecute heretics. He was killed in battle against the Persians.

Juliana /ˌdʒuːliˈɑːnə/ 1909– . Queen of the Netherlands. The daughter of Queen Wilhelmina (1880–1962), she married Prince Bernhard of Lippe-Biesterfeld in 1937 and ruled 1948–80, when she abdicated and was succeeded by her daughter ◊Beatrix.

Julian of Norwich /ˈdʒuːliən ˈnɒrɪtʃ/ *c.*1342–1413. English mystic. She lived as a recluse, and recorded her visions in *The Revelation of Divine Love* 1403, which shows the influence of Neo-Platonism.

Julius II /ˈdʒuːliəs/ 1443–1513. Pope 1503–13, a politician who wanted to make the Papal States the leading power in Italy, and formed international alliances first against Venice and then against France. He began the building of St Peter's Church, Rome, in 1506, and was the patron of the artists Michelangelo and Raphael.

July Revolution the French revolution 27–29 July 1830 in Paris which overthrew the restored Bourbon monarchy of Charles X and substituted the constitutional monarchy of Louis Philippe, whose rule (1830–48) is sometimes referred to as the July Monarchy.

jumbo jet popular name for a generation of huge wide-bodied airliners including the *Boeing 747*, which is 71 m/232 ft long, has a wing span of 60 m/196 ft, a maximum take-off weight of nearly 380 tonnes, and can carry over 400 passengers.

Jumna /ˈdʒʌmnə/ or *Yamuna* river in India, rising in the Himalayas, in Uttar Pradesh, and joining the Ganges near Allahabad, where it forms a sacred bathing place. Agra and Delhi are also on its course. Length 1,385 km/860 mi.

jumping hare long-eared South African rodent *Pedetes capensis*, similar in appearance and habits to the ◊jerboa, but with head and body about 40 cm/1.3 ft long, and a bushy tail about the same length. It is nocturnal and herbivorous.

Juneau /ˈdʒuːnəʊ/ ice-free port and state capital of Alaska, USA, on Gastineau Channel in the remote Alaska panhandle; population (1980) 26,000. There is salmon fishing, and gold and furs are exported.

Jung /jʊŋ/ Carl Gustav 1875–1961. Swiss psychiatrist, who collaborated with ◊Freud until their disagreement in 1912 about the importance of sexuality in causing psychological problems. He studied religion and dream symbolism, and saw the unconscious as a source of spiritual insight. He also distinguished between introversion and extroversion. Works include *Modern Man in Search of a Soul* 1933.

Jungfrau /ˈjʊŋfraʊ/ (German 'maiden') mountain in the Bernese Oberland, Switzerland; 4,166 m/13,669 ft high. A railway ascends to the

plateau of the Jungfraujoch, 3,456 m/11,340 ft, where there is a winter sports centre.

jungle popular name for ◊rainforest.

Jungle Book, The a collection of short stories for children by Rudyard ◊Kipling, published in two volumes in 1894 and 1895. Set in India, the stories feature a boy, Mowgli, reared by wolves and the animals he encounters in the jungle. The stories inspired the formation by Baden Powell of the Wolf Cub division of the Boy Scout movement.

juniper aromatic evergreen tree or shrub of the genus *Juniperus*, family Cupressaceae, found throughout temperate regions. Its berries are used to flavour gin.

Junius, Letters of /ˈdʒuːniəs/ a series of letters published in the *Public Advertiser* 1769–72, under the pseudonym Junius. Written in a pungent, epigrammatic style, they attacked the 'king's friends' in the interests of the opposition Whigs. They are generally believed to be written by Philip Francis (1740–1818).

junk bond derogatory term for a security, officially rated as 'below investment grade'. It is issued in order to raise capital quickly, typically to finance a takeover to be paid for by the sale of assets once the company is acquired. Junk bonds have a high yield, but are a high-risk investment.

Junker a member of the landed aristocracy in Prussia, who were traditionally the source of most of the Prussian civil service and officer corps.

Jung *Swiss psychiatrist and pioneer psychoanalyst Carl Jung.*

Junkers /ˈjʊŋkəs/ Hugo 1859–1935. German aeroplane designer. In 1919 he founded in Dessau the aircraft works named after him. Junkers planes, including dive bombers, night fighters, and troop carriers, were used by the Germans in World War II.

Juno /ˈdʒuːnəʊ/ principal goddess in Roman mythology (identified with the Greek Hera). The wife of Jupiter, the queen of heaven, she was concerned with all aspects of women's lives.

junta (Spanish 'council') the military rulers of a country after an army takeover, as in Turkey in 1980.

Jupiter /ˈdʒuːpɪtə/ the fifth planet from the Sun, and the largest in the solar system (equatorial diameter 142,800 km/88,700 mi), with a mass more than twice that of all the other planets combined, 318 times that of the Earth's. It takes 11.86 years to orbit the Sun, at an average distance of 778 million km/484 million mi, and has at least 16 moons. It is largely composed of hydrogen and helium, liquefied by pressure in its interior, and probably with a rocky core larger than the Earth. Its main feature is the Great Red Spot, a turbulent storm of rising gas 14,000 km/8,500 mi wide and some 30,000 km/20,000 mi long.

Its visible surface consists of clouds of white ammonia crystals, drawn out into belts by the planet's high speed of rotation (9 hr 51 min at the equator, the fastest of any planet). Darker orange and brown clouds at lower levels may contain sulphur, as well as simple organic compounds. Jupiter's warm interior, a result of heat left over from its formation, drives the turbulent weather patterns of the planet. The Great Red Spot was first observed 1664. Its top is higher than the surrounding clouds; its colour is thought to be due to red phosphorus. Its strong magnetic field gives rise to a large surrounding magnetic 'shell', or magnetosphere, from which bursts of radio waves are detected. The four largest moons, Io, Europa, Ganymede, and Callisto, are the *Galilean satellites*, discovered in 1610 by Galileo (Ganymede is the largest moon in the solar system). Three small moons were discovered in 1979 by the Voyager space probes, as was a faint ring of dust around Jupiter's equator, 55,000 km/34,000 mi above the cloud tops.

Jupiter /ˈdʒuːpɪtə/ or *Jove* in mythology, chief god of the Romans, identified with the Greek ◊Zeus. He was god of the sky, associated with lightning and thunderbolt, protector in battle and bestower of victory. He was the son of Saturn, married his

Jurassic *Contorted Jurassic limestone strata in Jura, Switzerland.*

sister Juno, and reigned on Mount Olympus as lord of heaven.

Jura /'dʒʊərə/ island of the Inner Hebrides; area 380 sq km/147 sq mi; population (with Colonsay, 1971) 343. It is separated from Scotland by the Sound of Jura. The whirlpool Corryvreckan (Gaelic 'Brecan's cauldron') is off the north coast.

Jura mountains /'dʒʊərə/ series of parallel mountain ranges running SW–NE along the French-Swiss frontier between the Rhône and the Rhine, a distance of 250 km/156 mi. The highest peak is *Crête de la Neige*, 1,723 m/5,650 ft. The mountains give their name to a *département* of France; and in 1979 a Jura canton was established in Switzerland, formed from the French-speaking areas of Berne.

Jurassic period of geological time 213–144 million years ago; the middle period of the Mesozoic era. Climates worldwide were equable creating forests of conifers and ferns, dinosaurs were abundant, birds evolved, and limestones and iron ores were deposited. The name comes from the Jura mountains in France and Switzerland, where the rocks formed during this period were first studied.

Jurgens /'jʊəgəns/ Curt (Curd Jürgens) 1912–1982. German film and stage actor, who was well established in his native country before moving into French and then Hollywood films in the 1960s. His films include; *Operette/Operetta* 1940; *Et Dieu créa la Femme/And God Created Woman* 1956; *Lord Jim* 1965; *The Spy who Loved Me* 1977.

jurisprudence the science of law in the abstract; that is, not the study of any particular laws or legal system, but of the principles upon which legal systems are founded.

jury a body of lay people (usually 12) sworn to reach a verdict in a court of law. Juries are used mainly in criminal cases, but also sometimes in civil cases, such as actions for ◊defamation. Juries are used mainly in English speaking countries.

The British jury derives from Germanic custom. It was introduced into England by the Normans. Originally it was a body of neighbours who gave their opinion on the basis of being familar with the protagonists and background of a case. Under the Plantagenets it developed into an impartial panel, giving a verdict based solely on evidence heard in court. In England, jurors are selected at random from the electoral roll. Certain people are ineligible for jury service (such as lawyers and clergymen), and others can be excused (such as MPs and doctors). The jury's duty is to decide the facts of a case: the judge directs them on matters of law. If they cannot reach a unanimous verdict they can give a majority verdict (at least 10 of the 12).

The basic principles of the British system have been adopted in the USA, most Commonwealth countries and in some European countries, for example France. Grand Juries are still used in the USA at both state and federal levels. (They were abolished in England in 1933). These consist of 23 jurors who decide whether there is a case to be referred for trial.

justice of the peace (JP) in England, an unpaid magistrate appointed by the Lord Chancellor. Two or more sit to dispose of minor charges (formerly their jurisdiction was much wider), to commit more serious cases for trial by a higher court, and to grant licences for the sale of intoxicating liquor. In the USA, where they receive fees and are usually elected, their courts are the lowest in the States, and deal only with minor offences, such as traffic violations; they may also conduct marriages. See also ◊magistrates court.

justiciar the chief justice minister of Norman and early Angevin kings, second in power only to the king. By 1265, the government had been divided into various departments, such as the Exchequer and Chancery, which meant that it was no longer desirable to have one official in charge of all.

Examples include Ranalf ◊Glanville and Hubert de ◊Burgh (died 1243). The last justiciar, Hugh Despenser, was killed fighting for the baronial opposition to Henry II at the battle of Evesham 1265.

Justinian I /dʒ'stɪnɪən/ 483–562. Byzantine emperor from 527. He recovered N Africa from the Vandals, SE Spain from the Visigoths, and Italy from the Ostrogoths, largely owing to his great general Belisarius. He ordered the codification of Roman law, which has influenced European jurisprudence.

Justinian, born in Illyria, was associated with his uncle, Justin I, in the government from 518. He married the actress Theodora, and succeeded Justin in 527. Much of his reign was taken up by an indecisive struggle with the Persians. He built the church of St Sophia in Constantinople, and closed the university in Athens in 529.

Justin St /'dʒʌstɪn/ *c.* 100–*c.* 163. One of the early Christian leaders and writers known as the Fathers of the Church. Born in Palestine of a Greek family, he was converted to Christianity and wrote two *Apologies* in its defence. He spent the rest of his life as an itinerant missionary, and was martyred in Rome. Feast day 1 June.

just price traditional economic belief that everything bought and sold has a 'natural' price, which is the price unaffected by adverse conditions, or by individual or monopoly influence. The belief dates from the scholastic philosophers, and resurfaced early in the 20th century in the writings of Major ◊Douglas and his Social Credit theory.

Just So Stories a collection of stories for small children by Rudyard ◊Kipling, published in 1902. Many of the stories offer amusing explanations of how certain animals acquired their characteristic appearance, such as 'How the Leopard got his Spots', and 'How the Camel got his Hump'. They originated in stories which the author told to his children.

Jute /dʒuːt/ member of a Germanic people who originated in Jutland but later settled in Frankish territory. They occupied Kent, SE England, about 450, according to tradition under Hengist and Horsa, and conquered the Isle of Wight and the opposite coast of Hampshire in the early 6th century.

jute fibre obtained from two plants of the genus *Corchorus*: *C. capsularis* and *C. olitorius*. Jute is used for sacks and sacking, upholstery, webbing, twine, and stage canvas.

In the fabrication of bulk packaging and tufted carpet backing, it now tends to be replaced by synthetic polypropylene. The world's largest producer of jute is Bangladesh.

Jutland /'dʒʌtlənd/ (Danish *Jylland*) a peninsula of N Europe; area 29,500 sq km/11,400 sq mi. It is separated from Norway by the Skagerrak, from Sweden by the Kattegat, with the North Sea to the west. The larger northern part belongs to Denmark, and the southern part to West Germany.

Jutland, Battle of /'dʒʌtlənd/ naval battle of World War I, fought between England and Germany on 31 May 1916, off the W coast of Jutland. Its outcome was indecisive, but the German fleet remained in port for the rest of the war.

Juvenal /'dʒuːvənl/ *c.* AD 60–140. Roman satirist and poet, born probably at Aquinum. His genius for satire brought him to the unfavourable notice of the emperor Domitian. Juvenal's 16 extant satires give an explicit and sometimes brutal picture of the decadent Roman society of his time.

juvenile delinquency offences against the law that are committed by young people. The Children and Young Persons Act 1969 introduced in Britain the gradual abolition of the prosecution of children up to the age of 14, and provided three options for Juvenile Courts in respect of all care and criminal proceedings involving children up to the age of 17: binding over of parents, supervision orders, and care orders.

Community homes were to have replaced the former approved schools, remand homes and probation hostels. The Criminal Justice Act 1982 introduced new types of short-term youth custody and detention. There are similar separate systems for dealing with young offenders in most Western countries.

Jylland /'juːlæn/ Danish name for the mainland of Denmark, the N section of the Jutland peninsula. The chief towns are Aalborg, Aarhus, Esbjerg, Fredericia, Horsens, Kolding, Randers, and Vejle.

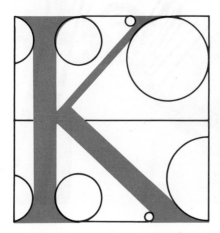

K 11th letter of the Roman alphabet, representing the voiceless velar stop. In English, it is silent before *n* at the beginning of a word (for example, in *knee*), a change accomplished, probably, in the 17th century.

K abbreviation for *kelvin*, a scale of temperature.

K abbreviation for thousand, as in a salary of £10K.

K chemical symbol for ◊potassium.

k abbreviation for *kilo-*, as in kg (kilogram) and km (kilometre).

K2 second highest mountain in the world, about 8,900 m/29,210 ft, in the Karakoram range, Kashmir, N India; it is also known as Dapsang (Hidden Peak) and formerly as Mount Godwin-Austen (after the son of a British geologist). It was first climbed 1954 by an Italian expedition.

Kaaba /'kɑ:bə/ (Arabic 'chamber') in Mecca, Saudi Arabia, the oblong building in the quadrangle of the Great Mosque, into the NE corner of which is built the Black Stone declared by the prophet Muhammad to have been given to Abraham by the archangel Gabriel, and revered by Muslims.

Kabardino-Balkar /,kæbə,di:nəʊ'bælkə/ autonomous republic (administrative unit) of the USSR, capital Nalchik; area 12,500 sq km/4,825 sq mi; population (1986) 724,000. Under Russian control from 1557, it was annexed 1827, and became an autonomous republic 1936.

kabbala /kə'bɑ:lə/ or *cabbala* (Hebrew 'tradition') ancient esoteric Jewish mystical tradition of philosophy containing strong elements of pantheism and akin to Neo-Platonism. Kabbalistic writing reached its peak period between the 13th and 16th centuries. It was largely rejected by modern rationalist Judaism as medieval superstition.

Among its earliest documents are the *Sefir Jezirah/The Book of Creation*, attributed to Rabbi Akiba (died 120). The *Zohar/Book of Light* was first written in Aramaic about the 13th century.

Kabinda part of Angola. See ◊Cabinda.

kabuki (Japanese 'music, dance, skill') drama originating in late 16th-century Japan, drawing on ◊Nō, puppet plays, and folk dance. Its colourful, lively spectacle became hugely popular in the 17th and 18th centuries. Kabuki actors specialize in particular characters, female impersonators being the biggest stars.

Kabuki was first popularized in Kyoto 1603 by the dancer Izumo Okuni who gave performances with a chiefly female troupe; from 1629 only men were allowed to act, in the interests of propriety. Unlike Nō actors, kabuki actors do not wear masks. The art was modernized and its following revived in the 1980s by Ennosuke III (1940–).

Kabul /'kɑ:bʊl/ capital of Afghanistan, 2,100 m/6,900 ft above sea level, on the river Kabul; population (1984) 1,179,300. Products include textiles, plastics, leather, and glass. It commands the strategic routes to Pakistan via the ◊Khyber Pass.

Kabwe /'kɑ:bweɪ/ town in central Zambia (formerly Broken Hill); mining industry (copper, cadmium, lead, and zinc); population (1980) 143,635.

Kabyle a Berber people of the Kabylia region of NE Algeria. As ◊Zouave they served in the French forces, although many were notable in the fight for Algerian independence.

Kádár /'kɑ:dɑ:/ János 1912–1989. Hungarian Communist leader, in power 1956–88, after suppressing the national rising. As Hungarian Socialist Workers' Party (HSWP) leader and prime minister 1956–58 and 1961–65, Kádár introduced a series of market-socialist economic reforms, while retaining cordial political relations with the USSR.

Kádár was a mechanic before joining the outlawed Communist Party and working as an underground resistance organizer in World War II. After the war he was elected to the National Assembly, served as minister for internal affairs 1948–50, and became a prominent member of the Hungarian Workers' Party (HSP). Imprisoned 1951–53 for deviation from Stalinism, Kádár was rehabilitated 1955, becoming party leader in Budapest, and in Nov 1956, at the height of the Hungarian national rising, he was appointed head of the new HSWP. With the help of Soviet troops, he suppressed the revolt. He was ousted as party general secretary May 1988, and forced into retirement May 1989.

Kaduna /kə'du:nə/ town in N Nigeria, on the Kaduna river; population (1983) 247,000. A market centre for grain and cotton; industries include textiles, cars, timber, pottery, and oil refining.

kaffir /'kæfə/ (Arabic *kāfir* 'infidel') a South African English term for a black person, often regarded as offensive. It derives from the former designation of various Bantu-speaking peoples, including the Xhosa and Pondo of Cape Province, living in much of SE Africa.

Kafka /'kæfkə/ Franz 1883–1924. Czech novelist, born in Prague, who wrote in German. His

Kafka Czech novelist Franz Kafka.

Kaifu Japanese conservative politician and prime minister Toshiki Kaifu.

three unfinished allegorical novels *Der Prozess/The Trial* 1925, *Der Schloss/The Castle* 1926, and *Amerika/America* 1927, were posthumously published despite his instructions that they should be destroyed. His short stories include 'Die Verwandlung/The Metamorphosis' 1915, in which a man turns into a beetle.

Kafue /kə'fu:eɪ/ river in central Zambia, a tributary of the Zambezi: 965 km/600 mi long. The upper reaches of the river form part of the Kafue national park 1951. *Kafue* town 44 km/27 mi S of Lusaka, population (1980) 35,000, is the centre of Zambia's heavy industry.

Kagoshima /,kægə'ʃi:mə/ industrial city (Satsumayaki porcelain) and port on Kyushu Island, SW Japan; population (1987) 525,000.

kagu crested bird *Rhynochetos jubatus* found in New Caledonia. About 50 cm/1.6 ft long, it is virtually flightless and nests on the ground. The introduction of cats and dogs has endangered its survival.

Kahlo /'kɑ:ləʊ/ Frida 1907–1954. Mexican painter, who mingled folk art with classical and modern style.

Kahn /kɑ:n/ Louis 1901–1974. US architect, born in Estonia. He developed a classically romantic style, in which functional 'servant' areas, such as stairwells and air ducts, featured prominently, often as tower-like structures surrounding the main living and working, or 'served', areas. His works are characterized by an imaginative use of concrete and brick and include the Salk Institute for Biological Studies, La Jolla, California, and the British Art Center at Yale University.

Kaieteur /,kaɪə'tʊə/ waterfall on the river Potaro, a tributary of the Essequibo, Guyana. At 250 m/822 ft it is five times as high as Niagara Falls.

Kaifeng /,kaɪ'fʌŋ/ former capital of China, 907–1127, and of Honan province; population (1984) 619,200. It has lost its importance because of the silting-up of the nearby Huang He river.

Kaifu /'kaɪfu:/ Toshiki 1932– . Japanese conservative politician, prime minister from 1989. A protégé of former premier Takeo Miki, he was selected as a compromise choice as Liberal Democratic Party president and prime minister in Aug 1989, following the resignation of Sosuke Uno. Kaifu is Japan's first premier without World War II military experience.

He entered politics 1961, was deputy chief secretary 1974–76 in the Miki cabinet, and was education minister under Nakasone. In 1987 Kaifu received what he claimed were legitimate political donations amounting to £40,000 from the Recruit company, an organization later accused of bribing a number of LDP politicians.

Kaikouras /kaɪ'kʊərəz/ double range of mountains in the NE of South Island, New Zealand, separated by the Clarence river, and reaching 2,885 m/9,465 ft.

Kaingaroa /ˌkaɪŋəˈrəʊə/ forest NE of Lake Taupo in North Island, New Zealand, one of the world's largest planted forests.

Kairouan /ˌkaɪəˈwɑːn/ Muslim holy city in Tunisia, N Africa, S of Tunis; population (1984) 72,200. It is a centre of carpet production. The city, said to have been founded AD 617, ranks after Mecca and Medina as a place of pilgrimage.

Kaiser /ˈkaɪzə/ a title formerly used by the Holy Roman emperors, Austrian emperors 1806–1918, and German emperors 1871–1918. The word, like the Russian 'tsar', is derived from the Latin *Caesar*.

Kaiser /ˈkaɪzə/ Georg 1878–1945. German playwright, the principal writer of German ◊Expressionism. His large output includes *Die Bürger von Calais/The Burghers of Calais* 1914, and *Gas* 1918–20.

Kaiser /ˈkaɪzə/ Henry J 1882–1967. US industrialist. He built up steel and motor industries, and his shipbuilding firms became known for the mass production of vessels, including the 'Liberty ships' – cheap, quickly produced, transport ships—built for the UK in World War II.

Kaiserslautern /ˌkaɪzəzˈlaʊtən/ industrial town (textiles, cars) in West Germany, in the Rhineland-Palatinate, 48 km/30 mi W of Mannheim; population (1978) 98,700. It dates from 882; the castle from which it gets its name was built by Frederick Barbarossa 1152, and destroyed by the French 1703.

Kakadu a national park E of Darwin in the Alligator Rivers Region of Arnhem Land, Northern Territory, Australia. Established in 1979, it overlies one of the richest uranium deposits in the world. As a result of this, it has become the focal point of controversy between conservationists and mining interests.

kakapo a flightless parrot *Strigops habroptilus* which lives in burrows in New Zealand. It is green, yellow, and brown, and is nocturnal. Because of the introduction of dogs and cats, it is in danger of extinction.

Kalahari Desert /ˌkæləˈhɑːri/ semi-desert area forming most of Botswana, and extending into Namibia, Zimbabwe, and South Africa; area about 900,000 sq km/347,400 sq mi. The only permanent river, the Okavango, flows into a delta in the NW forming marshes rich in wildlife. Its inhabitants are the nomadic Bushmen.

Kaldor /ˈkældɔ:/ Nicholas 1908–1986. British economist, born in Hungary, special adviser 1964–68 and 1974–76 to the UK government. He was a firm believer in the long-term capital gains tax, selective employment tax, and a fierce critic of monetarism. He advised several Third World governments on economic and tax reform.

kale a type of ◊cabbage.

kaleidoscope optical toy invented by the British physicist David Brewster 1816. It usually consists of a pair of long mirrors at an angle to each other, and arranged inside a triangular tube containing pieces of coloured glass, paper, or plastic. An axially symmetrical (hexagonal) pattern is seen by looking along the tube, which can be varied infinitely by rotating or shaking the tube.

Kalevala /ˌkɑ:ləˈvɑ:lə/ Finnish national epic poem compiled from legends and ballads by Elias Lönnrot in 1835; its hero is Väinämöinen, god of music and poetry.

Kalf /kɑ:lf/ Willem 1619–1693. Dutch painter, active in Amsterdam from 1653. He specialized in still lifes set off against a dark ground. These feature arrangements of glassware, polished metalwork, decorated porcelain, and fine carpets, with the occasional half-peeled lemon (a Dutch still-life motif).

Kalgan /ˌkɑ:lˈgɑ:n/ city in NE China, now known as ◊Zhangjiakou.

Kalgoorlie /kælˈɡʊəli/ town in Western Australia, 545 km/340 mi NE of Perth, amalgamated with

Kandinsky Battle/Cossacks *(1910) Tate Gallery, London.*

Boulder in 1966; population (1986) 25,000. Gold has been mined here since 1893.

Kali /ˈkɑ:li/ in Hindu mythology, the goddess of destruction and death. She is the wife of ◊Siva.

Kālidāsa /ˌkɑ:lɪˈdɑ:sə/ Indian epic poet and dramatist. His works, in Sanskrit, include the classic drama *Sakuntala*, the love story of King Dushyanta for the nymph Sakuntala.

Kalimantan /ˌkælɪˈmæntən/ provinces of the republic of Indonesia occupying part of the island of Borneo
area 543,900 sq km/210,000 sq mi
towns Banjermasin and Balikpapan
physical features mostly low-lying, with mountains in the N
products petroleum, rubber, coffee, copra, pepper, timber
population (1980) 6,723,086.

Kalinin /kəˈliːnɪn/ formerly (until 1933) *Tver* city of the USSR, capital of Kalinin region, a transport centre on the Volga, 160 km/100 mi NW of Moscow; population (1987) 447,000. It was renamed in honour of President Kalinin.

Kalinin /kəˈliːnɪn/ Mikhail Ivanovich 1875–1946. Soviet politician, founder of the newspaper *Pravda*. He was prominent in the October Revolution, and in 1919 became head of state (president of the Central Executive Committee of the Soviet government until 1937, then president of the Presidium of the Supreme Soviet until 1946).

Kaliningrad /kəˈliːnɪngræd/ formerly *Königsberg* Baltic naval base in USSR; population (1987) 394,000. Industries include engineering and paper. It was the capital of East Prussia until the latter was divided between the USSR and Poland 1945 under the Potsdam Agreement, when it was renamed in honour of President Kalinin.

Kali-Yuga in Hinduism, the last of the four *yugas* (ages) that make up one cycle of creation. The *Kali-Yuga*, in which Hindus believe we are now living, is characterized by wickedness and disaster, and leads up to the destruction of this world in preparation for a new creation and a new cycle of *yugas*.

Kalki in Hinduism, the last avatar (manifestation) of Vishnu, who will appear at the end of the *Kali-Yuga*, or final age of the world, to destroy it in readiness for a new creation.

Kalmar /ˈkælmɑ:/ port on the SE coast of Sweden; population (1986) 55,000. Industries include paper, matches, and the Orrefors glassworks.

Kalmyk /ˈkælmək/ or *Kalmuck* autonomous republic within the Russian SFSR, USSR, on the Caspian Sea; area 75,900 sq km/29,300 sq mi; population (1986) 325,000; capital Elista. Industry is mainly agricultural. It was settled by migrants from China in the 17th century, and abolished 1957 because of alleged collaboration of the people with the Germans during the siege of Stalingrad.

Kaltenbrunner /ˈkæltənˌbrʊnə/ Ernst 1901–1946. Austrian Nazi leader. After the annexation of Austria 1938 he joined police chief Himmler's staff, and as head of the Security Police (SD) from 1943 was responsible for the murder of millions of Jews (see ◊holocaust) and Allied soldiers in World War II. After the war, he was tried at Nuremberg and hanged.

Kaluga /kəˈluːɡə/ town in the USSR, on the river Oka, 160 km/100 mi SW of Moscow, capital of Kaluga region; population (1987) 307,000. Industries include hydroelectric installations and engineering works, telephone equipment, chemicals, and measuring devices.

Kamakura /ˌkæməˈkʊərə/ city on Honshu island, Japan; population 175,000. It was the seat of the first shogunate 1192–1333, which established the rule of the Samurai class, and the Hachimangu Shrine is dedicated to the gods of war; the 13th-century statue of Buddha (Daibutsu) is 13 m/43 ft high. From the 19th century artists and writers, for example Kawabata, settled here.

Kamara'n /ˌkæməˈrɑ:n/ island in the Red Sea, formerly belonging to South Yemen, but occupied by North Yemen 1972; area 180 sq km/70 sq mi. The former RAF station is controlled by the USSR.

Kamchatka /kæmˈtʃætkə/ mountainous peninsula separating the Bering Sea and Sea of Okhotsk, forming (together with the Chukchi and Koryak national districts) a region of the USSR. Its capital Petropavlovsk is the only town; agriculture is possible only in the South. Most of the inhabitants are fishers and hunters.

Kamenev /ˈkæmənev/ Lev Borisovich 1883–1936. Russian leader of the Bolshevik movement after 1917 who, with Stalin and Zinoviev, formed a ruling triumvirate in the USSR after Lenin's death 1924. His alignment with the Trotskyists led to his dismissal from office and from the Communist Party by Stalin 1926. Tried for plotting to murder Stalin, he was condemned and shot 1936.

Kamet /ˈkʌmeɪt/ Himalayan mountain 7,756 m/ 25,447 ft high on the Tibet–India border. The

kangaroo

Britons F S Smythe and Eric Shipton were in the group that made the first ascent in 1931.

kamikaze (Japanese 'wind' of the gods') the pilots of the Japanese air force in World War II who deliberately crash-dived their planes, loaded with bombs, usually onto ships of the US Navy.

Kampala /kæmˈpɑːlə/ capital of Uganda; population (1983) 455,000. It is linked by rail with Mombasa. Products include tea, coffee, textiles, fruit, and vegetables.

Kamperduin Dutch spelling of ◊Camperdown, village in the Netherlands.

Kampuchea former name (to 1989) of ◊Cambodia.

Kanaka /kəˈnækə/ Hawaiian word for a person; applied to the indigenous people of the South Sea islands.

Kananga /kəˈnæŋɡə/ chief city of Kasai Occidental region, W central Zaïre; situated on the Lulua river; population (1984) 291,000. It was known as Luluabourg until 1966.

Kanazawa /ˌkænəˈzɑːwə/ industrial city (textiles and porcelain) on Honshu island, in Chubu region, Japan, 160 km/100 mi NNW of Nagoya; population (1985) 430,000.

Kanchenjunga /ˌkæntʃənˈdʒʊŋɡə/ a variant spelling of ◊Kangchenjunga, a Himalayan mountain.

Kandahar /ˌkændəˈhɑː/ city in Afghanistan, 450 km/280 mi SW of Kabul, capital of Kandahar province and a trading centre, with wool and cotton factories; population (1984) 203,200. It is surrounded by a 8 m/25 ft high mud wall. It was the first capital of Afghanistan when it became independent in 1747.

Kandinsky /kænˈdɪnski/ Wassily 1866–1944. Russian painter, a pioneer of abstract art. Born in Moscow, he travelled widely, settling in Munich 1896. He was joint originator of the ◊Blaue Reiter movement 1911–12. For some years he taught at the ◊Bauhaus, then, in 1933, settled in Paris.

Kandinsky originally experimented with Post-Impressionist styles and Fauvism. From around 1910 he produced the first known examples of purely abstract work in 20th-century art. His highly coloured style had few imitators, but his theories on composition, *Concerning the Spiritual in Art* 1912, were taken up by the early abstract movement.

Kandy /ˈkændi/ city in central Sri Lanka, former capital of the kingdom of Kandy 1480–1815; population (1985) 140,000. Products include tea. One of the most sacred Buddhist shrines is situated at Kandy, and the chief campus of the University of Sri Lanka (1942) is at Peradenia, 5 km/3 mi away.

kangaroo marsupial mammal of the family Macropodidae found in Australia, Tasmania, and New Guinea. Kangaroos are plant-eaters and live in herds. They are adapted to hopping, most species having very large back legs and feet compared to the small forelimbs. The larger types can jump 9 m/30 ft at a single bound. Species vary from small rat kangaroos, only 30 cm/1 ft long, through the medium-sized wallabies, to the large red and great grey kangaroos which are the largest living marsupials. These may be 1.6 m/5.2 ft long with 1.1 m/3.5 ft tails.

Kano *A gateway into the walled city of Kano, Nigeria.*

In New Guinea and N Queensland, tree kangaroos occur. These have comparatively short hind limbs. The **great grey kangaroo** *Macropus giganteus* produces a single young ('joey') about 2 cm/1 in long after a very short gestation, usually in early summer. It remains in the pouch, with excursions as it matures, for about 280 days.

kangaroo paw bulbous plant *Anigozanthos manglesii*, family Hameodoraceae, with a row of small white flowers emerging from velvety green tubes with red bases. It is the floral emblem of Western Australia.

Kangchenjunga /ˌkæntʃənˈdʒʊŋ/ Himalayan mountain on the Nepál–Sikkim border, 8,598 m/20,208 ft high, 120 km/75 mi SE of Everest. The name means 'five treasure houses of the great snows'. Kangchenjunga was first climbed by a British expedition 1955.

Ka Ngwane /kæŋˈɡwɑːneɪ/ black homeland in Natal province, South Africa; achieved self-governing status 1971; population (1985) 392,800.

Kano /ˈkɑːnəʊ/ capital of Kano state in N Nigeria, trade centre of an irrigated area; population (1983) 487,100. Products include bicycles, glass, furniture, textiles, and chemicals. Founded about 1000 BC, Kano is a walled city, with New Kano extending beyond the walls. Goods still arrive by camel train to a market place holding 20,000 people.

Kanpur /ˈkɑːnˈpʊə/ (formerly *Cawnpore*) capital of Kanpur district, Uttar Pradesh, India, SW of Lucknow, on the river Ganges; a commercial and industrial centre (cotton, wool, jute, chemicals, plastics, iron, steel); population (1981) 1,688,000.

Kansas /ˈkænzəs/ state of central USA; nickname Sunflower State
area 213,200 sq km/82,295 sq mi
capital Topeka
towns Kansas City, Wichita, Overland Park
physical features undulating prairie; rivers Missouri, Kansas, and Arkansas
products wheat, cattle, coal, petroleum, natural gas, aircraft
population (1985) 2,450,000.

Kansas City /ˈkænzəs/ twin city in the USA at the confluence of the Missouri and Kansas rivers, partly in Kansas and partly in Missouri; a market and agricultural distribution centre and, next to Chicago, the chief livestock centre of the USA. Kansas City, Missouri, has car assembly plants and Kansas City, Kansas, has the majority of offices; population (1980) of Kansas City (Kansas) 161,087, Kansas City (Missouri)

Kansas

Kant *An 1812 engraving of the German philosopher Immanuel Kant. A moral philosopher, he believed that feelings and inclinations were not a basis for ethical decisions.*

448,159, metropolitan area 1,327,000. The city was founded as a trading post by French fur trappers about 1826.

history In the 1920s and 1930s Kansas City was run by boss Tom Pendergast, of the Ready-Mix Concrete Company, and in the nightclubs on Twelfth Street under his 'protection' jazz musicians such as Lester Young, Count Basie, and Charlie Parker performed.

Kansu alternative spelling for Chinese province ◊Gansu.

Kant /kænt/ Immanuel 1724–1804. German philosopher, who believed that knowledge is not merely an aggregate of sense impressions, but is dependent on the conceptual apparatus of the human understanding, which is itself not derived from experience. In ethics, Kant argued that right action cannot be based on feelings or inclinations, but conforms to a law given by reason, the **categorical imperative**.

Born at Königsberg (in what was then East Prussia), he attended the university there, and was appointed professor of logic and metaphysics 1770. His first book, *Gedanken von der wahren Schätzung der lebendigen Kräfte/Thoughts on the True Estimates of Living Forces*, appeared in 1747, and the *Theorie des Himmels/Theory of the Heavens* in 1755. In the latter he combined physics and theology in an argument for the existence of God. In *Kritik der reinen Vernunft/Critique of Pure Reason* 1781, he argued that God's existence could not be proved theoretically. Other works include *Prolegomena* 1783, *Metaphysik der Sitten/Metaphysic of Ethics* 1785, *Metaphysische Anfangsgründe der Naturwissenschaft/Metaphysic of Nature* 1786, *Kritik der praktischen Vernunft/Critique of Practical Reason* 1788, and *Kritik der Urteilskraft/Critique of Judgement* 1790. In 1797 ill health led to his retirement.

Kanto /ˈkæntəʊ/ flat, densely populated region of E Honshu island, Japan; population (1986) 37,156,000; area 32,377 sq km/12,505 sq mi. The chief city is Tokyo.

Kantorovich /ˌkæntəˈrəʊvɪtʃ/ Leonid 1912–1986. Russian mathematical economist, whose theory that decentralization of decisions in a planned economy could only be made with a rational price system earned him a Nobel prize in 1975.

KANU abbreviation for *Kenya African National Union* political party founded 1944 and led by Jomo ◊Kenyatta from 1947, when it was the Kenya African Union; it became KANU on independence. The party formed Kenyatta's political power base in 1963 when he became prime minister; in 1964 he became the first president of Kenya.

Kaohsiung /ˌkauʃiˈuŋ/ city and port on the west coast of Taiwan; population (1988) 1,300,000. Industries include aluminium ware, fertilizers, cement, oil refineries, iron and steel works, shipyards, and food-processing. Kaohsiung began to develop as a commercial port after 1858; its industrial development came about while it was occupied by Japan, 1895–1945.

kaoliang variety of ◊sorghum.

Kapitza /kəˈpɪtsə/ Peter 1894–1984. Soviet physicist who in 1978 shared a Nobel prize for his work on magnetism and low-temperature physics. He held important posts in Britain, for example, as assistant director of magnetic research at the Cavendish Laboratory, Cambridge, 1924–32, before returning to the USSR to work at the Russian Academy of Science.

Kaplan /ˈkæplən/ Viktor 1876–1934. Austrian engineer who invented a water turbine with adjustable rotor blades. In the machine, patented in 1920, the rotor was on a vertical shaft and could be adjusted to suit any rate of flow of water. Horizontal Kaplan turbines are used at the installation on the estuary of the river Rance in France, the world's first tidal power station.

kapok silky hairs produced round the seeds of certain trees, particularly the **kapok tree** *Bombax ceiba* of India and Malaysia, and the **silk-cotton tree** *Ceiba pentandra*, a native of tropical America. Kapok is used for stuffing cushions, mattresses, and for sound insulation; oil obtained from the seeds is used in food and soap preparation.

Kara Bogaz Gol /kəˈrɑː bəˈgæz ˈgɒl/ shallow gulf of the Caspian Sea, USSR; area 20,000 sq km/8,000 sq mi. Rich deposits of sodium chloride, sulphates, and other salts formed by evaporation.

Karachi /kəˈrɑːtʃi/ largest city and chief seaport of Pakistan, and capital of Sind province, NW of the Indus delta; industry (engineering, chemicals, plastics, textiles); population (1981) 5,208,000. It was the capital of Pakistan 1947–59.

Karafuto /ˌkɑːrəˈfuːtəu/ Japanese name for ◊Sakhalin island.

Karaganda /ˌkærəgənˈdɑː/ industrial town (coal, copper, tungsten, manganese) in Kazakh republic of USSR, linked by canal with the Irtysh River; capital of Karaganda region; population (1987) 633,000.

Karaite member of an 8th-century sect of Judaism which denied the authority of rabbinic tradition, recognizing only the authority of the scriptures.

Karajan /ˈkærəjæn/ Herbert von 1908–1989. Austrian conductor. He was conductor of the Berlin Philharmonic Orchestra 1955–89. He directed the Salzburg Festival from 1964 and became director of the Vienna State Opera in 1976. He is associated with the Classical and Romantic repertoire—Beethoven, Brahms, Mahler, and Richard Strauss.

Kara-Kalpak /kəˈrɑː kælˈpɑːk/ autonomous republic within Uzbekistan, USSR
area 158,000 sq km/61,000 sq mi
capital Nukus
towns Munyak
products cotton, rice, wheat, fish
population (1986) 1,108,000
history called after the Kara-Kalpak people, whose name means black bonnet. They live south of the Sea of Aral and were conquered by Russia 1867. An autonomous Kara-Kalpak region was formed 1926 within Kazakhstan, transferred to the Soviet republic 1930, made a republic 1932, and attached to Uzbekistan 1936.

Karakoram /ˌkærəˈkɔːrəm/ mountain range in central Asia, divided among China, Pakistan, and India. Peaks include K2, Masharbrum, Gasharbrum, and Mustagh Tower. *Ladakh* subsidiary range is in NE Kashmir on the Tibetan border.

Karakoram highway /ˌkærəˈkɔːrəm/ road constructed by China and Pakistan and completed 1978; runs 800 km/500 mi from Havelian (NW of Rawalpindi), via ◊Gilgit in Kashmir and the

karate The French International Championships 1989.

Khunjerab Pass 4,800 m/16,000 ft, to ◊Kashi in China.

Karakorum /ˌkærəˈkɔːrəm/ ruined capital of ◊Genghis Khan, SW of Ulaanbaatar in Mongolia.

Kara-Kum /kəˈrɑː ˈkuːm/ sandy desert occupying most of ◊Turkmenistan, USSR. Area about 310,800 sq km/120,000 sq mi. It is crossed by the Caspian railway.

Karamanlis /ˌkærəmænˈliːs/ Constantinos 1907– . Greek politician of the New Democracy Party. A lawyer and an anti-communist, he was prime minister Oct 1955–Mar 1958, May 1958–Sept 1961, and Nov 1961–June 1963 (when he went into self-imposed exile). He was recalled as prime minister on the fall of the regime of the 'colonels' in July 1974, and was president 1980–85.

Kara Sea /ˈkɑːrə/ (Russian *Kavaskoye More*) part of the Arctic Ocean off the N coast of the USSR, bounded to the NW by the island of Novaya Zemlya and to the NE by Severnaya Zemlya. Novy Port on the Gulf of Ob is the chief port, and the Yenisei also flows into it.

karate one of the ◊martial arts. Karate is a type of unarmed combat derived from kempo, a form of the Chinese Shaolin boxing. It became popular in the 1930s.

Karbala alternative spelling for ◊Kerbela, holy city in Iraq.

Karelia /kəˈriːliə/ autonomous republic NW of USSR
area 172,400 sq km/66,550 sq mi
capital Petrozavodsk
towns Vyborg
physical features mainly forested; Lake Ladoga
products fishing, timber, chemicals, coal
population (1986) 787,000
history constituted as an autonomous Soviet republic 1923, it was extended 1940 to include that part of Finland ceded to the USSR (North Karelia remaining Finnish territory). In 1946 the Karelo-Finnish Soviet Socialist Republic was set up but in 1956 the greater part of the republic returned to its former status as an autonomous Soviet socialist republic.

Karelian bear dog medium-sized dog, about 60 cm/2 ft high, used to protect Russian settlements from bears. Rather like a husky, the dog is a 'national treasure'. It was not exported until 1989 when some were sent to Yellowstone Park, USA, to keep bears away from tourists.

Karelian Isthmus /kəˈriːliən ˈɪsməs/ strip of land between Lake Ladoga and the Gulf of Finland, USSR, with Leningrad at the S extremity and Vyborg at the N. Finland ceded it to the USSR 1940–41 and from 1947.

Karen /kəˈren/ a people of the Far East, numbering 1.9 million in Myanmar alone, also living in Thailand, and the Irrawaddy delta. Their language belongs to the Sino-Thai family. In 1984 the Burmese government began a large-scale military campaign against the Karen National Liberation Army (KNLA), the armed wing of the Karen National Union (KNU).

Karg-Elert /kɑːˈgelət/ Sigfrid 1877–1933. German composer. After studying at Leipzig he devoted

himself to the European harmonium. His numerous concert pieces and graded studies exploit a range of impressionistic effects such as the 'endless chord'.

Kariba dam /kəˈriːbə/ concrete dam on the Zambia–Zimbabwe border, about 386 km/240 mi downstream from the Victoria Falls, constructed 1955–60 to supply power to both countries. The dam crosses Kariba Gorge, and the reservoir, Lake Kariba, has important fisheries.

Karikal /ˌkærɪˈkɑːl/ small port in India, 250 km/155 mi S of Madras, at the mouth of the right branch of the Cauvery delta. On a tract of land acquired by the French in 1739, it was transferred to India in 1954; the transfer was confirmed by treaty in 1956. See also ◊Pondicherry.

Karl-Marx-Stadt /ˈkɑːl ˈmɑːks ʃtæt/ formerly *Chemnitz* town in East Germany, capital of Karl-Marx-Stadt county, on the river Chemnitz, 65 km/40 mi SSE of Leipzig. It is an industrial centre (engineering, textiles, chemicals); population (1986) 314,000. It came within the Soviet zone of occupation after World War II, and was renamed 1954. Karl-Marx-Stadt county has an area of 6,010 sq km/2,320 sq mi, and a population of 1,870,000.

Karloff /ˈkɑːlɒf/ Boris. Stage name of William Henry Pratt 1887–1969. British actor who mostly worked in the USA. He is chiefly known for his role as the monster in *Frankenstein* 1931; most of his subsequent roles were in horror films, although he also played some conventional parts. He appeared in *Scarface* 1932, *The Lost Patrol* 1934, and *The Body Snatcher* 1945.

Karlovy Vary /ˈkɑːləvi ˈvɑːri/ (German *Karlsbad*) spa in the Bohemian Forest, W Czechoslovakia, famous from the 14th century for its alkaline thermal springs; population (1983) 59,696.

Karlsbad /ˈkɑːlzbæd/ German name of ◊Karlovy Vary, town in Czechoslovakia.

Karlsruhe /ˈkɑːlzruːə/ industrial town (nuclear research, oil refining) in Baden-Württemberg, West Germany; population (1988) 268,000.

karma (Sanskrit 'fate') in Hinduism, the sum of a human being's actions, carried forward from one life to the next to result in an improved or worsened fate. Buddhism has a similar belief, except that no permanent personality is envisaged, the karma relating only to the physical and mental elements carried on from birth to birth, until the power holding them together disperses in the attainment of Nirvana.

Karmal /ˈkɑːməl/ Babrak 1929– . Afghani communist politician. In 1965 he formed what became the banned People's Democratic Party of Afghanistan (PDPA) 1977. As president 1979–86, with Soviet backing, he sought to broaden the appeal of the PDPA but encountered wide resistance from the mujaheddin Muslim guerrillas.

Karmal was imprisoned for anti-government activity in the early 1950s. He was a member of the government 1957–62 and of the national assembly

Karloff US film actor Boris Karloff, whose many horror-movie roles included the monster in Frankenstein.

Karnataka

Bangalore

INDIAN OCEAN

1965–72. In Dec 1979 he returned from brief exile in E Europe with Soviet support to overthrow President Hafizullah Amin and was installed as the new head of state. Karmal was persuaded to step down as president and PDPA leader May 1986 as the USSR began to search for a compromise settlement with opposition groupings and to withdraw troops.

Karnak /ˈkɑːnæk/ village of modern Egypt, on the E bank of the Nile, which gives its name to the temple of Ammon (constructed by Seti I and Ramses I) around which the major part of the city of ◊Thebes was built. An avenue of rams leads to ◊Luxor.

Karnataka /kəˈnɑːtəkə/ formerly (until 1973) *Mysore* state in SW India
area 191,800 sq km/74,035 sq mi
capital Bangalore
products mainly agricultural, but its minerals include manganese, chromite, and India's only sources of gold and silver
population (1981) 37,043,000
language Kannada
famous people Hyder Ali, Tipu Sahib.

Kärnten /ˈkeəntən/ German name for ◊Carinthia, province of Austria.

Karpov /ˈkɑːpɒf/ Anatoliy 1951– . Soviet chess player. He succeeded Bobby Fischer of the USA as world champion 1975, and held the title until losing to Gary Kasparov 1985.

karri giant eucalyptus tree *Eucalyptus diversifolia*, found in the extreme SW of Australia. It may reach over 120 m/400 ft. Its exceptionally strong timber is used for girders.

Karroo /kəˈruː/ two areas of semi-desert in Cape Province, South Africa, divided into the Great Karroo and Little Karroo by the Swartberg mountains. The two Karroos together have an area of about 260,000 sq km/100,000 sq mi.

karst a landscape characterized by remarkable surface and underground forms, created as a result of the action of water on porous limestone. The feature takes its name from the Karst region on the Adriatic coast of Yugoslavia, but the name is applied to limestone landscapes throughout the world, the most dramatic of which is found near the city of Guilin in the Guangxi province of China.

karting miniature motor racing with low-framed, light-chassis cars (*karts* or *go-karts*); it originated in the USA about 1955.

In competitive racing, different formulae exist. Standard production two-stroke engines are capable of providing speeds of approximately 240 kph/150 mph.

karyotype in biology, the set of ◊chromosomes characteristic of a given species. It is described as the number, shape, and size of the chromosomes in a single cell of an organism. In humans for example, the karyotype consists of 46 chromosomes, in mice 40, crayfish 200, and in fruit flies 8. The diagrammatic representation of a complete chromosome set is called a *karyogram*.

Kasai /kɑːˈsaɪ/ river that rises in Angola and forms the frontier with Zaïre before entering Zaïre and joining the Zaïre river, of which it is the chief tributary. It is rich in alluvial diamonds. Length 2,100 km/1,300 mi.

Kashgar /ˌkæʃˈgɑː/ former name of ◊Kashi in China.

Kashi /ˌkɑːˈʃiː/ oasis town (formerly Kashgar) in Xinjiang Uyghur autonomous region, China, on the Kaxgar He, capital of Kashi district which adjoins the Kirghiz and Tadzic republics, Afganistan and Kashmir; population (1973) 180,000. It is a trading centre, the Chinese terminus of the ◊Karakoram Highway, and a focus of Muslim culture.

Kashmir /ˌkæʃˈmɪə/ former part of Jammu state in the N of British India with a largely Muslim population, ruled by a Hindu maharajah, who joined it to the republic of India 1947. There was fighting between pro-India and pro-Pakistan factions, the former being the Hindu ruling class and the latter the Muslim majority, and open war between the two countries 1965–66 and 1971. It remains divided: the NW is occupied by Pakistan, and the rest by India.

Kashmir /ˌkæʃˈmɪə/ area of Pakistan in the NW of the former state of Kashmir, now ◊Jammu and Kashmir. Azad ('free') Kashmir in the west has its own legislative assembly based in Muzaffarabad while Gilgit and Baltistan regions to the north and east are governed directly by Pakistan. The ◊Northern Areas are claimed by India and Pakistan
population 1,500,000
towns Gilgit, Skardu
features W Himalayan peak Nanga Parbat 8,126 m/26,660 ft, Karakoram Pass, Indus River, Baltoro Glacier.

Kashmiri inhabitant of the state of Jammu and Kashmir, a disputed territory divided between India and Pakistan. There are approximately 6 million Kashmiris, 4 million of whom live on the Indian side of the ceasefire line.

Kashmiri is an Indo-European language which the orthodox write using a Sarada script. Although Kashmir's ruling families are Hindu, the majority of the population are Muslims. There are Hindu Brahmins, called pandit, who perform religious services and are involved in teaching and the administration. The workers, or karkum, are often wealthier than the priestly class. In the Vale of Kashmir, the majority of Muslims are farmers,

karyotype

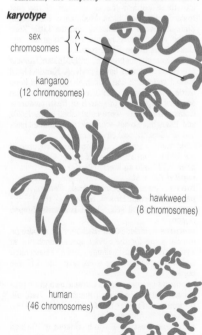

sex chromosomes { X Y }

kangaroo (12 chromosomes)

hawkweed (8 chromosomes)

human (46 chromosomes)

KASPAROV KARPOV

Kasparov Soviet chess players Anatoliy Karpov (right) and Gary Kasparov (left).

cultivating rice, wheat, and other crops. There is also a Punjabi-speaking Sikh minority, while on the borders of the Vale there are Muslim Gujars, who have an affinity with the Hindu Dogra. In Ladakh to the north, there are Buddhist peoples who have much in common with Tibetans.

Kasparov Gary 1963– . Soviet chess player. When he beat his compatriot Anatoliy Karpov to win the world title 1985, he was the youngest ever champion at 22 years 210 days.

Kassel /ˈkæsəl/ industrial town (engineering, chemicals, electronics) in Hessen, West Germany, on the river Fulda; population (1988) 185,000. There is the spectacular Wilhelmshöhe mountain park, and the ◊Grimm Museum commemorates the authors of fairy tales who lived here.

Kassem /ˈkæsem/ Abdul Karim 1914–1963. Iraqi politician, prime minister from 1958; he adopted a pro-Soviet policy. He pardoned the leaders of the pro-Egyptian party who tried to assassinate him 1959, but was executed after the 1963 coup.

Katanga /kəˈtæŋgə/ former name of the ◊Shaba region in Zaïre.

Kathiawar /ˌkætiəˈwɑː/ peninsula on the W coast of India. Formerly occupied by a number of princely states, all Kathiawar (60,723 sq km/23,445 sq mi) had been included in Bombay state by 1956, but was transferred to Gujarat in 1960. Mahatma Gandhi was born in Kathiawar at Porbandar.

Katmai /ˈkætmaɪ/ active volcano in Alaska, USA, 2,046 m/6,715 ft. Its major eruption in 1912 created the Valley of Ten Thousand Smokes.

Katmandu /ˌkætmənˈduː/ or *Kathmandu* capital of Nepál; population (1981) 235,000. Founded in the 8th century on an ancient pilgrim and trade route from India to Tibet and China, it has a royal palace, Buddhist shrines, and monasteries.

Kato /ˈkɑːtəʊ/ Kiyomasa 1562–1611. Japanese warrior and politician who was instrumental in the unification of Japan and the banning of Christianity in the country. He led the invasion of Korea 1592, and cooperated with Toyotomi Hideyoshi and Tokugawa Ieyaso in consolidating a unified Japanese state.

Katō /ˈkɑːtəʊ/ Taka-akira 1860–1926. Japanese politician and prime minister 1924–26. After a long political career with several terms as foreign minister, Katō led probably the most democratic and liberal regime of the Japanese Empire.

Katowice /ˌkætəʊˈviːtseɪ/ industrial city (anthracite, iron and coal mining, iron foundries, smelting works, machine shops) in Upper Silesia, S Poland; population (1985) 363,000.

Katsura /kætˈsʊərə/ Tarō 1847–1913. Prince of Japan, army officer, politician, and prime minister. During his first term as prime minister 1901–06, he was responsible for the Anglo-Japanese treaty of 1902, the successful prosecution of the war against Russia 1904–05, and the annexation of Korea 1910.

Having assisted in the Meiji restoration (see ◊Mutsuhito) 1866–68, Katsura became increasingly involved in politics. His support for rearmament, distaste for political parties, and oligarchic rule created unrest, and his third ministry Dec 1912–Jan 1913 lasted only seven weeks.

Kattegat /'kætɪgæt/ sea passage between Denmark and Sweden. It is about 240 km/150 mi long and 135 km/85 mi wide at its broadest point.

Katyn Forest /'kæ'tɪn/ forest near Smolensk, USSR, where 4,500 Polish officer prisoners of war (captured in the German-Soviet partition of Poland 1940) were shot; 10,000 others were killed elsewhere. In 1989 the USSR accepted responsibility for the massacre.

Katz /kæts/ Bernard 1911– . British biophysicist. In 1970 he shared a Nobel prize with Ulf von Euler of Stockholm and Julius Axelrod of Maryland for work on the biochemistry of the transmission and control of signals in the nervous system, vital in the search for remedies for nervous and mental disorders.

Kauffer /'kɔːfə/ Edward McKnight 1890–1954. US poster artist. He lived in the UK 1914–41.

Kauffmann /'kaʊfmən/ Angelica 1741–1807. Swiss Neo-Classical painter who worked extensively in England. She was a popular portraitist, and also painted mythological scenes for large country houses. Born in Grisons, she lived in Italy until 1765 and in England 1765–81.

Kaufman /'kɔːfmən/ George S(imon) 1889–1961. US playwright. Author (often in collaboration with others) of many Broadway hits, including *Of Thee I Sing* 1932, a Pulitzer Prize–winning satire on US politics, *The Man Who Came to Dinner* 1939, and *The Solid Gold Cadillac* 1952.

Kaunas /'kaʊnəs/ (Russian *Kovno* until 1917) industrial river port (textiles, chemicals, agricultural machinery) in the Lithuanian republic of the USSR, on the Niemen river; population (1987) 417,000. It was the capital of independent Lithuania 1910–40.

Kaunda /ka'ʊndə/ Kenneth (David) 1924– . Zambian politician. Imprisoned in 1958–60 as founder of the Zambia African National Congress, he became in 1964 first prime minister of North Rhodesia, then first president of Zambia. In 1973 he introduced one-party rule. He supported the nationalist movement in Southern Rhodesia, now Zimbabwe, and survived a coup attempt 1980 thought to have been promoted by South Africa. He was elected chair of the Organization of African Unity 1987.

kauri pine New Zealand timber conifer *Agathis australis*, family Araucariaceae, whose fossilized gum deposits are especially valued in varnishes; the wood is used for carving and handicrafts.

Kaunda Kenneth Kaunda was the first prime minister of Northern Rhodesia, the former name for Zambia, before becoming president when Zambia gained independence in 1964.

Kautsky /'kaʊtski/ Karl 1854–1938. German socialist theoretician, who opposed the reformist ideas of Edouard ◊Bernstein from within the Social Democratic Party. In spite of his Marxist ideas he remained in the party when its left wing broke away to form the German Communist Party (KPD).

kava narcotic, intoxicating beverage prepared from the roots or leaves of a variety of pepper plant, *Piper methysticum*, in the S Pacific islands.

Kawabata /,kaʊə'baːtə/ Yasunari 1899–1972. Japanese novelist, translator of Lady ◊Murasaki, and author of *Snow Country* 1947 and *A Thousand Cranes* 1952. His novels are characterized by melancholy and loneliness. He was the first Japanese to win the Nobel Prize for Literature 1968.

Kawasaki /,kaʊə'saːki/ industrial city (iron, steel, shipbuilding, chemicals, textiles) on Honshu island, Japan; population (1987) 1,096,000.

Kay /keɪ/ John 1704–*c*.1764. British inventor who developed the flying-shuttle, a machine to speed up the work of hand-loom weaving. In 1733 he patented his invention but was ruined by the litigation necessary for its defence. In 1753 his house at Bury was wrecked by a mob, who feared the use of machinery would cause unemployment. He is believed to have died in poverty in France.

Kayah State /'kaɪə/ division of Myanmar (formerly Burma); see ◊Karen.

kayak long light sealskin-covered boat used by Inuit fisherfolk and sealers.

Kaye /keɪ/ Danny. Stage-name of Daniel Kaminski 1913–1987. US comedian and singer. He appeared in many films, including *Wonder Man* 1944, *The Secret Life of Walter Mitty* 1946, and *Hans Christian Andersen* 1952.

kayser unit of wave number (number of waves in a unit length), used in spectroscopy. It is expressed as waves per centimetre, and is the reciprocal of the wavelength. A wavelength of 0.1 cm has a wave number of 10 kaysers.

Kayseri /'kaɪsəri/ (ancient name *Caesarea Mazaca*) capital of Kayseri province, central Turkey; population (1985) 378,000. It produces textiles, carpets, and tiles. In Roman times it was capital of the province of Cappadocia.

Kazakh a pastoral people of Kazakhstan, now part of the USSR. The Kazakhs speak a Turkic language belonging to the Altaic family.

The Kazakhs emerged during the break up of the Mongol Empire. They were originally divided into three hordes: the Great Zhuz of the east towards the Tien Shan Mountains; the Middle Zhuz of central Kazakhstan; and the Little Zhuz of the west. There is also a fourth group, the Bukey Zhuz of the Volga region.

The Kazakhs are predominantly Muslim, although pre-Islamic customs have survived. Kazakhs herd horses and make use of camels; they also keep cattle. Traditionally the Kazakhs embarked on seasonal migrations in search of fresh pastures. Collectivized herds were established in the 1920s and 1930s but Soviet economic programmes have had to adapt to local circumstances.

Kazakhstan /,kæzæk'staːn/ constituent republic of the USSR from 1936, part of Soviet Central Asia
area 2,717,300 sq km/1,049,150 sq mi
capital Alma-Ata
towns Karaganda, Semipalatinsk, Petropavlovsk
physical second largest republic in the USSR; Caspian and Aral seas, Lake Balkhash; Steppe region
features it includes the Baikonur Cosmodrome (official name for the Soviet space launch site at Tyuratam, near the coalmining town of Baikonur), and a weapons-testing area near the Chinese border
products second only to Ukraine as a grain producer; copper, lead, zinc, manganese, coal, oil
population (1987) 16,244,000; Russian 41%, Kazakh 36%, Ukrainian 6%
language Russian; Kazakh, related to Turkish
history ruled by the Mongols from the 13th century, the region came under Russian control in

the 18th century. Inhabited by the traditionally nomadic, but now largely sedentarized, Kazakh people, it joined the USSR as an autonomous republic in 1922 and became a full union republic in 1936. It was the site of ◊Khrushchev's ambitious 'Virgin Lands' agricultural extension programme during the 1950s, which led to overcropping and harvest failures during the early 1960s, but also to a large influx of Russian settlers, turning the Kazakhs into a minority in their own republic. There were riots in the capital 1986, from nationalist anti-Russian sentiment. In June 1989 four died in inter-ethnic violence in the oil town of Novy Uzen.

Kazan /kə'zæn/ capital of the Tatar Autonomous Republic in central USSR, on the river Volga; population (1987) 1,068,000. It is a transport, commercial, and industrial centre (engineering, oil refining, petrochemical, textiles, large fur trade). Formerly capital of a Tatar khanate, Kazan was captured by Ivan IV 'the Terrible' 1552.

The 'Black Virgin of Kazan', an icon so called because blackened with age, was removed to Moscow (1612–1917), where the great Kazan Cathedral was built to house it 1631; it is now in the USA. Among miracles attributed to its presence were the defeat of Poland 1612 and of Napoleon at Moscow 1812.

Kazan /kə'zæn/ Elia 1909– . US stage and film director, a founder of the ◊Actors Studio 1947. Plays he directed include *The Skin of Our Teeth* 1942, *A Streetcar Named Desire* 1947, and *Cat on a Hot Tin Roof* 1955; films include *Gentlemen's Agreement* 1948, *East of Eden* 1954, and *The Visitors* 1972.

Kazantzakis /,kæzænd'zaːkɪs/ Nikos 1885–1957. Greek writer of poems, for example, *I Odysseia/ The Odyssey* 1938, which continues Homer's *Odyssey*, and novels, for example, *Zorba the Greek* 1946.

kazoo a simple wind instrument adding a buzzing quality to the singing voice on the principle of 'comb and paper' music.

KBE abbreviation for *Knight (Commander of the Order) of the British Empire.*

KC abbreviation for *King's Counsel.*

kcal abbreviation for *kilocalorie.*

kea a hawk-like greenish parrot *Nestor notabilis* found in New Zealand, which eats insects, fruits, and sheep offal. The Maori name imitates its cry.

Kean /kiːn/ Edmund 1787–1833. British tragic actor, noted for his portrayal of villainy in the Shakespearean roles of Shylock, Richard III, and Iago.

Keane /kiːn/ 'Molly' (Mary Nesta) 1905– . Irish novelist, whose comic novels of Anglo-Irish life, include *Good Behaviour* 1981, *Time After Time* 1983, and *Loving and Giving* 1988. She also writes under the name M J Farrell.

Keaton /'kiːtn/ Buster. Stage name of Joseph Frank Keaton 1896–1966. US comedian and actor. After being a star in vaudeville, he took up a career in 'Fatty' Arbuckle comedies, and became one of the great comedians of the silent film era,

Keaton *US comedy star Buster Keaton in a scene from* The General *1927.*

with an inimitable deadpan expression masking a sophisticated acting ability. His films include *One Week* 1920, *The Navigator* 1924, *The General* 1927, and *The Cameraman* 1928.

Keats /kiːts/ John 1795–1821. English poet, a leading figure of the Romantic movement. He published his first volume of poetry 1817; this was followed by *Endymion, Isabella,* and *Hyperion* 1818, 'The Eve of St Agnes', his odes 'To Autumn', 'On a Grecian Urn', and 'To a Nightingale', and 'Lamia' 1819. His final volume of poems appeared in 1820.

Born in London, Keats studied at Guy's Hospital 1815–17, but then abandoned medicine for poetry. *Endymion* 1818 was harshly reviewed by the Tory *Blackwood's Magazine* and *Quarterly Review,* largely owing to Keats's friendship with the radical writer Leigh Hunt (1800–65). In 1819 he fell in love with Fanny Brawne. Suffering from tuberculosis, he sailed to Italy in 1820 in an attempt to regain his health, but died in Rome; the house he died in is now a museum. Valuable insight into Keats's poetic development is provided by his *Letters,* published 1848.

Keble /ˈkiːbəl/ John 1792–1866. Anglican priest and religious poet. His sermon on the decline of religious faith in Britain, preached in 1833, is taken as the beginning of the ◊Oxford Movement, a Catholic revival in the Church of England. Keble College, Oxford, was founded in 1870 in his memory.

Kebnekaise /ˈkebnəkaɪsə/ highest peak in Sweden, rising to 2,111 m/6,926 ft in the Kolen range, W of Kiruna.

Kecskemét /ˈketʃkɪmeɪt/ town in Hungary, situated on the Hungarian plain SE of Budapest; population (1988) 105,000. It is a trading centre of an agricultural region.

Kedah /ˈkedə/ state in NW Peninsular Malaysia; capital Alor Setar; area 9,400 sq km/3,628 sq mi; population (1980) 1,116,000. Products include rice, rubber, tapioca, tin, and tungsten. Kedah was transferred by Thailand to Britain 1909, and was one of the Unfederated Malay States until 1948.

Keeler /ˈkiːlə/ Christine 1942– . British model of the 1960s. She became notorious in 1963 after revelations of an affair with a Soviet attaché and the war minister John ◊Profumo, who resigned after admitting lying to the House of Commons about their relationship. Her patron, the osteopath Stephen Ward, convicted of living on immoral

earnings, committed suicide and Keeler was subsequently imprisoned for related offences.

Keeling Islands /ˈkiːlɪŋ/ another name for the ◊Cocos islands, an Australian territory.

Keelung /ˌkiːˈlʊŋ/ or *Chi-lung* industrial port (shipbuilding, chemicals, fertilizer) on the N coast of Taiwan, 24 km/15 mi NE of Taipei; population (1985) 351,904.

Keeper of the Great Seal in the Middle Ages, an officer who had charge of the Great Seal of England (the official seal authenticating state documents). During the Middle Ages the great seal was entrusted to the chancellor. Later a special Lord Keeper was appointed to take charge of it, but since 1761 the posts of chancellor and Keeper have been combined.

Keewatin /kiːˈweɪtɪn/ eastern district of Northwest Territories, Canada, including the islands in Hudson and James Bays
area 590,935 sq km/228,101 sq mi

Keats *Romantic poet John Keats. He studied at Guy's Hospital in London, but abandoned medicine for poetry.*

towns (trading posts) Chesterfield Inlet, Eskimo Point, and Coral Harbour, the last with an air base set up during World War II
physical the north is an upland plateau, the south low and level, covering the greater part of the Arctic prairies of Canada; there are a number of lakes
products trapping for furs is the main occupation
history Keewatin District was formed 1876, under the administration of Manitoba; it was transferred to Northwest Territories in 1905, and in 1912 lost land south of 60 degrees N to Manitoba and Ontario.

Kefallinia /ˌkefəliˈniːə/ English *Cephalonia* largest of the Ionian Islands off the W coast of Greece; area 935 sq km/360 sq mi; population (1981) 31,300. It was devastated by an earthquake in 1953 which destroyed the capital Argostolion.

Keflavik /ˈkepləvɪk/ fishing port in Iceland, 35 km/22 mi SW of Reykjavik; population (1986) 7,500. Its international airport was built during World War II by US forces (who called it Meeks Field). Keflavik became a NATO base in 1951.

Keighley /ˈkiːθli/ industrial (wool, engineering) town on the river Aire, NW of Bradford in W Yorkshire, England; population (1981) 57,800. Haworth, home of the Brontë family of writers, is now part of Keighley.

Keillor /ˈkiːlə/ Garrison 1942– . US writer and humorist. His hometown is Anoka, Minnesota, in the American Midwest. It inspired his Lake Wobegon stories, including *Lake Wobegon Days* 1985 and *Leaving Home* 1987, often started as radio monologues about 'the town that time forgot, that the decades cannot improve'.

Keitel /ˈkaɪtl/ Wilhelm 1882–1946. German field marshal in World War II, chief of the supreme command from 1938. He signed Germany's unconditional surrender in Berlin 8 May 1945. Tried at Nuremberg for war crimes, he was hanged.

Kekulé /ˈkekjuleɪ/ Friedrich August 1829–1896. German chemist whose theory 1858 of molecular structure revolutionized organic chemistry. He proposed two resonant forms of the ◊benzene ring.

Kelantan /keˈlæntən/ state in NE Peninsular Malaysia; capital Kota Baharu; area 14,900 sq km/5,751 sq mi; population (1980) 894,000. It produces rice, rubber, copra, tin, manganese, and gold. Kelantan was transferred by Siam to Britain 1909, and until 1948 was one of the Unfederated Malay States.

Keller /ˈkelə/ Gottfried 1819–1890. Swiss poet and novelist, whose books include *Der Grüne Heinrich/Green Henry* 1854–55. He also wrote short stories, one of which, 'Die Leute von Seldwyla/The People of Seldwyla' 1856–74, describes small-town life.

Keller /ˈkelə/ Helen (Adams) 1880–1968. US author. Born in Alabama, she became blind and deaf through an illness when 19 months old. Only the tuition of Anne Sullivan Macy enabled her to speak. She graduated with honours from Radcliffe College in 1904 and published several books, including *The Story of My Life* 1902.

Kellogg–Briand pact an agreement 1927 between the USA and France to renounce war and seek settlement of disputes by peaceful means. It took its name from the US secretary of state Frank B Kellogg (1856–1937) and the French foreign minister Aristide Briand. Other powers signed in Aug 1928, making a total of 67 signatories. The pact made no provision for measures against aggressors and became ineffective in the 1930s.

Kells, Book of /kelz/ an 8th-century illuminated manuscript of the Gospels produced at the monastery of Kells in County Meath, Ireland. It is now in Trinity College library, Dublin.

Kelly /ˈkeli/ 'Gene' (Eugene Curran) 1912– . US film actor, dancer, choreographer, and director. A major star of the 1940s and 1950s in a series of MGM musicals, including *Singin' in the Rain* 1952, his subsequent attempts at straight direction were less well received.

Kelly US film actress Grace Kelly retired from her career after her marriage to Prince Rainier of Monaco in 1956.

Kelly /'keli/ Ned (Edward) 1854–1880. Australian ◊bushranger. The son of an Irish convict, he wounded a police officer in 1878 while resisting the arrest of his brother Daniel for horse-stealing. The two brothers escaped and carried out bank robberies. Kelly wore a distinctive home-made armour. In 1880 he was captured and hanged.

Kelly /'keli/ Grace (Patricia) 1928–1982. US film actress, Princess of Monaco from 1956. She starred in *High Noon* 1952, *The Country Girl* 1954, for which she received an Academy Award, and *High Society* 1955. When she married Prince Rainier of Monaco she retired from acting.

keloid an overgrowth of fibrous tissue, usually produced at the site of a scar. Black skin is much more prone to the production of keloid, which may have a puckered appearance caused by clawlike offshoots. Surgical removal is often unsuccessful, because the keloid returns.

kelp collective name for large seaweeds, particularly of the Fucaceae and Laminariaceae families. Kelp is also a term for the powdery ash of burned seaweeds, a source of iodine.

The *brown kelp Macrocystis pyrifera*, abundant in Antarctic and sub-Antarctic waters, is one of the fastest-growing organisms known, reaching 100 m/320 ft. It is farmed for the alginate industry, its rapid surface growth allowing cropping several times a year, but it is an alien pest in European waters.

Kelvin /'kelvɪn/ William Thomson, 1st Baron Kelvin 1824–1907. Irish physicist, who pioneered the absolute scale of temperature. His work on the conservation of energy 1851 led to the second law of ◊thermodynamics.

He contributed to telegraphy by developing stranded cables and sensitive receivers, greatly improving transatlantic communications. Maritime endeavours led to a tide gauge and predictor, an improved compass, and simpler methods for fixing a ship's position at sea. He was president of the Royal Society 1890–95, and worked most of his life in Scotland.

kelvin scale temperature scale used by scientists. It begins at ◊absolute zero (−273°C) and increases in the same way as the Celsius scale, that is, 0°C is the same as 273 K and 100°C is 373 K.

Kemal Atatürk Mustafa Turkish politician; see ◊Atatürk.

Kemble /'kembəl/ 'Fanny' (Frances Anne) 1809–1893. English actress, daughter of Charles

Kemble. She first appeared as Shakespeare's Juliet in 1829.

In 1834, on a US tour, she married a Southern plantation owner and remained in the USA until 1847. Her *Journal of a Residence on a Georgian Plantation* 1835 is a valuable document in the history of slavery.

Kemble /'kembəl/ (John) Philip 1757–1823. English actor and theatre manager. He excelled in tragic roles, especially Shakespearean, including Hamlet and Coriolanus. As manager of Drury Lane 1788–1803 and Covent Garden 1803–17 in London, he introduced many innovations in theatrical management, costume, and scenery.

He was the son of the strolling player Roger Kemble (1721–1802), whose children included the actors Charles Kemble and Mrs ◊Siddons.

Kemble /'kembəl/ Charles 1775–1854. English actor and theatre manager, younger brother of Philip Kemble. His greatest successes were in romantic roles with his daughter Fanny Kemble.

Kemerovo /'kemɪrəuvəu/ coalmining town in W Siberia, USSR, centre of Kuznetz coal basin; population (1987) 520,000. It has chemical and metallurgical industries. The town, which was formed out of the villages of Kemerovo and Shcheglovisk, was known as Shcheglovisk 1918–32.

Kempe /kemp/ Margery *c.* 1373–*c.*1439. English Christian mystic. She converted to religious life after a period of mental derangement, and travelled widely as a pilgrim. Her *Boke of Margery Kempe* about 1420 describes her life and experiences, both religious and worldly. It has been called the first autobiography in English.

Kempe /'kempə/ Rudolf 1910–1976. German conductor. Renowned for the clarity and fidelity of his interpretations of the works of Richard Strauss and ◊Wagner's *Ring* cycle, he conducted Britain's Royal Philharmonic Orchestra 1961–75 and was musical director of the Munich Philharmonic from 1967.

Kempis Thomas à. Medieval German monk and religious writer; see ◊Thomas à Kempis.

Kendal /'kendl/ town in Cumbria, England, on the river Kent; population (1981) 23,411. An industrial centre (light industry; agricultural machinery and, since the 14th century, wool) and tourist centre for visitors to the ◊Lake District.

Kendall /'kendl/ Edward 1886–1972. US biochemist. Kendall isolated in 1914 the hormone thyroxin, the active compound of the thyroid gland. He went on to work on secretions from the adrenal gland, among which he discovered a compound E, which was in fact the steroid cortisone. For this Kendall shared the 1950 Nobel Prize for Medicine with Philip Hench (1896–1965) and Tadeus ◊Reichstein.

kendo Japanese armed ◊martial art in which combatants fence with bamboo replicas of samurai swords. Masks and padding are worn for protection. The earliest reference to kendo is AD 789.

Kendrew /'kendru:/ John 1917– . British biochemist. Kendrew began, in 1946, the ambitious task of determining the three-dimensional structure of the major muscle protein, myoglobin. This

Kelvin Irish physicist William Kelvin pioneered the kelvin scale of temperature.

Kennedy Thirty-fifth president of the USA, John F Kennedy was the youngest person to hold the office. He was assassinated after less than three years in power.

was completed in 1959 and won for Kendrew a share of the 1962 Nobel chemistry prize with Max Perutz.

Keneally /kɪ'ni:li/ Thomas Michael 1935– . Australian novelist, who won the ◊Booker Prize with *Schindler's Ark* 1982, a novel based on the true account of Polish Jews saved from the gas chambers in World War II by a German industrialist.

Kenilworth /'kenlwɜ:θ/ castle and small town in Warwickshire, England. The Norman castle became a royal residence and was enlarged by John of Gaunt and later by the Earl of Leicester, who entertained Elizabeth I here in 1575. It was dismantled after the Civil War; the ruins were given to the British nation by the 1st Lord Kenilworth in 1937.

Kennedy /'kenədi/ Edward (Moore) 1932– . US Democrat politician. He aided his brothers John and Robert Kennedy in the presidential campaign of 1960, and entered politics as a senator from Massachusetts 1962. He failed to gain the presidential nomination 1980, largely because of feeling about his delay in reporting a car crash at Chappaquiddick Island, near Cape Cod, Massachusetts, in 1969, in which his passenger, Mary Jo Kopechne, was drowned.

Kennedy /'kenədi/ John F(itzgerald) 1917–1963. 35th president of the USA 1961–63, a Democrat. Kennedy was the first Roman Catholic and the youngest person to be elected president. In foreign policy he carried through the unsuccessful ◊Bay of Pigs invasion of Cuba, and in 1963 secured the withdrawal of Soviet missiles from the island. His programme for reforms at home, called the *New Frontier*, was posthumously executed by Lyndon Johnson. Kennedy was assassinated while on a state visit to Dallas, Texas, on 22 Nov 1963 by Lee Harvey Oswald (1939–63), who was in turn shot dead by Jack Ruby.

Son of Joseph Kennedy, he was born in Brookline, Massachusetts, and served in the navy in the Pacific during World War II. He was elected to Congress 1946 and to the Senate 1952. In 1960 he defeated Nixon for the presidency, partly as a result of televised debates, and brought academics and intellectuals to Washington as advisers. He married the socialite *Jacqueline Lee Bouvier* (1929–) in 1953.

A number of conspiracy theories have been spun around the Kennedy assassination, which was investigated by a special commission headed by Chief Justice Earl ◊Warren. The commission determined that Oswald acted alone, although this is extremely unlikely. A later congressional committee re-examined the evidence and determined that Kennedy 'was probably assassinated as a result of a conspiracy'. Oswald was an

Kent

ex-marine who had gone to live in the USSR 1959 and returned when he could not become a Soviet citizen. Ruby was a Dallas nightclub owner, associated with the underworld and the police.

Kennedy /ˈkenədi/ Joseph (Patrick) 1888–1969. US industrialist and diplomat; ambassador to the UK 1937–40. A self-made millionaire, he groomed his four sons from an early age for careers in politics. His eldest son, Joseph Patrick Kennedy Jr (1915–44), was killed in action with the naval air force in World War II. Among his other children were John, Robert, and Edward.

Kennedy /ˈkenədi/ Robert F(rancis) 1925–1968. US Democrat politician and lawyer. He was campaign manager for his brother John F Kennedy 1961, and as attorney general 1961–64 pursued a racket-busting policy and promoted the Civil Rights Act of 1964. When Johnson preferred Hubert H Humphrey for the 1964 vice-president nomination, Kennedy resigned and was elected senator for New York. In 1968 he campaigned for the Democratic party's presidential nomination, but was assassinated by Sirhan Bissara Sirhan (1944–), a Jordanian Arab.

Kennedy /ˈkenədi/ William 1928– . US novelist, known for his *Albany Trilogy* consisting of *Legs* 1976, about the gangster 'Legs' Diamond, *Billy Phelan's Greatest Game* 1983, about a pool player, and *Ironweed* 1984, about a baseball player's return to the city of Albany, NY.

Kennedy Space Center the ◊NASA launch site on Merritt Island, near Cape Canaveral, Florida, used for Apollo and space-shuttle launches.

The Center is dominated by the Vehicle Assembly Building, 160 m/525 ft tall, used for assembly of ◊Saturn rockets and space shuttles.

Kennelly /ˈkenəli/ Arthur Edwin 1861–1939. US engineer, who gave his name to the Kennelly–Heaviside layer of the ◊ionosphere. He verified the existence of an ionized layer in the upper atmosphere in 1902, which had been predicted by ◊Heaviside.

Kennelly–Heaviside layer former term for the E-layer, the lower regions of the ◊ionosphere, which refract radio waves allowing their reception around the surface of the Earth. The Kennelly–Heaviside layer approaches the Earth by day and recedes from it at night.

Kenneth I /ˈkenɪθ/ Kenneth MacAlpin 9th century. King of Scotland. Traditionally, he is regarded as the founder of the Scottish kingdom by virtue of his final defeat of the Picts about 844. He invaded Northumbria six times, and drove the Angles and the Britons over the river Tweed.

Kenneth II died 995. King of Scotland from 971, son of Malcolm I. He invaded Northumbria several times, and his chiefs were in constant conflict with Sigurd the Norwegian over the area of Scotland north of the Spey. He is believed to have been murdered by his own subjects.

Kensington and Chelsea /ˈkenzɪŋtən, ˈtʃelsi/ borough of Greater London, England, N of the river Thames

features Kensington Gardens; museums — Victoria and Albert, Natural History, Science; Imperial College of Science and Technology 1907; Commonwealth Institute; Kensington Palace; Holland House (damaged in World War II, and partly rebuilt as a youth hostel); Leighton House

population (1986) 137,600.

Kent /kent/ county in SE England, nicknamed the 'garden of England'

area 3,730 sq km/1,440 sq mi

towns administrative headquarters Maidstone; Canterbury, Chatham, Rochester, Tunbridge Wells; resorts Folkestone, Margate, Ramsgate

features traditionally, a 'man of Kent' comes from east of the Medway and a 'Kentish man' from W Kent; New Ash Green, a new town; Romney Marsh; the Isles of Grain, Sheppey (on which is the resort of Sheerness, formerly a royal dockyard) and Thanet; Weald (agricultural area); rivers Darent, Medway, Stour; Leeds Castle (converted to a palace by Henry VIII), Hever Castle (where Henry VIII courted Anne Boleyn), Chartwell (Churchill's country home), Knole, Sissinghurst Castle and gardens

products hops, apples, soft fruit (on the Weald), coal, cement, paper

population (1987) 1,511,000

famous people Charles Dickens, Christopher Marlowe

Kent /kent/ Bruce 1929– . British peace campaigner who acted as general secretary for the Campaign for Nuclear Disarmament (CND) 1980–85. He has published numerous articles on disarmament, Christianity, and peace. He was a Catholic priest until 1987.

Kent /kent/ Edward George Alexander Edmund, 2nd Duke of Kent 1935– . British prince, grandson of George V. His father, George (1902–42), was created Duke of Kent just before his marriage in 1934 to Princess Marina of Greece and Denmark (1906–68). The second duke succeeded when his father was killed in an air crash on active service with the RAF.

He was educated at Eton public school and Sandhurst military academy, and then commissioned in the Royal Scots Greys. In 1961 he married Katharine Worsley (1933–) and his heir is George (1962–), Earl of St Andrews. His brother, Prince Michael (1942–), became an officer with the Hussars in 1962. His sister, Princess Alexandra (1936–), married in 1963 Angus Ogilvy, younger son of the 12th Earl of Airlie; they have two children, James (1964–) and Marina (1966–).

Kent and Strathearn /ˈstræθˈɜːn/ Edward, Duke of Kent and Strathearn 1767–1820. British general. The fourth son of George III, he married Victoria Mary Louisa (1786–1861), widow of the Prince of Leiningen, in 1818, and had one child, the future Queen Victoria.

Kent /kent/ William 1685–1748. British architect, landscape gardener, and interior designer. In architecture he was foremost in introducing the Palladian style into Britain from Italy. Horace Walpole called him 'the father of modern gardening'.

Kentigern, St /ˈkentɪɡən/ c.518–603. First bishop of Glasgow, born at Culross, Scotland. Anti-Christian factions forced him to flee to Wales, where he founded the monastery of St Asaph. In 573 he returned to Glasgow and founded the cathedral there. Feast day 14 Jan.

Kenton /ˈkentən/ Stan 1912–1979. US exponent of progressive jazz, who broke into West Coast jazz in 1941 with his 'wall of brass' sound. He helped introduce Afro-Cuban rhythms to US jazz, and combined jazz and classical music in his compositions, such as *Artistry in Rhythm* 1943.

Kentucky /kenˈtʌki/ state of S central USA; nickname Bluegrass State

area 104,700 sq km/40,414 sq mi

Kent *William Kent, the British landscape gardener and architect. His portrait is by B Dandridge.*

capital Frankfort

towns Louisville, Lexington-Fayette, Owensboro, Covington, Bowling Green

features horse racing at Louisville (Kentucky Derby); Mammoth Cave National Park (main cave 6.5 km/4 mi long, up to 38 m/125 ft high, where Indian councils were once held); President Lincoln's birthplace at Hodgenville; Fort Knox, US Gold Bullion Depository

products tobacco, cereals, steel goods, textiles, transport vehicles

population (1987) 3,727,000

famous people Kit Carson, Henry Clay, Jefferson Davis

history originally part of Virginia, it became a state 1792. Kentucky was first permanently settled after Daniel Boone had blazed his Wilderness Trail.

Kenya /ˈkenjə/ country in E Africa, bordered to the N by the Sudan and Ethiopia, E by Somalia, SE by the Indian Ocean, SW by Tanzania, and W by Uganda.

government The 1963 constitution, amended 1964, 1969 and 1982, provides for a president, elected by universal suffrage for a five-year term, and a single-chamber national assembly, serving a similar term. The assembly has 202 members, 188 elected by universal suffrage, 12 nominated by the president, and the attorney-general and speaker as members by virtue of their office. From 1969 to 1982 Kenya was a one-party state in fact and since then it has become one in law, the only legitimate party being the Kenya African National Union (KANU), whose leader is the state president.

history Archaeological evidence shows that the area now known as Kenya was first inhabited about 2 million years ago. In the 8th century the coast was settled by Arabs, and during

Kentucky

Kenya
Republic of
(Jamhuri ya Kenya)

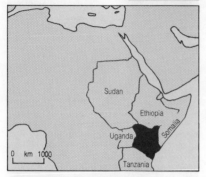

area 582,600 sq km/224,884 sq mi
capital Nairobi
towns Kisumu, port Mombasa
physical mountains and highlands in the W and centre; coastal plain in S; the N is arid
features Great Rift Valley, Mount Kenya, Lake Nakuru (flamingos), Lake Turkana (Rudolf), national parks with wildlife, Malindini Marine Reserve, Olduvai Gorge
head of state and government Daniel arap Moi from 1978
political system authoritarian nationalism
political parties Kenya African National Union (KANU), nationalist, centrist

exports coffee, tea, sisal, pineapples
currency Kenya shilling (36.70 = £1 Feb 1990)
population (1988 est) 22,800,000 (the dominant ethnic group is the Kikuyu); annual growth rate 4.1%
life expectancy men 51, women 55
language Kiswahili (official), 21% Kikuyu, 14% Luhya, English is spoken in commercial centres
religion indigenous religions with Christian and Muslim minorities
literacy 70% male/49% female (1985 est)
GDP $5.6 bn (1983); $309 per head of population
chronology
1950 Mau Mau campaign began.
1953 Nationalist leader Jomo Kenyatta imprisoned.
1956 Mau Mau campaign defeated, Kenyatta released.
1963 Granted internal self-government, with Kenyatta as prime minister.
1964 Achieved full independence as a republic, within the Commonwealth, with Kenyatta as president.
1978 Death of Kenyatta. Succeeded by Daniel arap Moi.
1982 Attempted coup against Moi foiled.
1983 Moi re-elected.
1989 Moi announced the release of all political prisoners. Confiscated ivory burned in attempt to stop elephant poaching.
1990 Foreign minister Robert Ouko found murdered (Feb).

the 15th–18th centuries the region was under Portuguese rule.

Kenya was a British colony 1895–1964, when it achieved full independence within the Commonwealth. There was near civil war during the 20 years before independence, as nationalist groups carried out a campaign of violence. The Kenya African Union (KAU) was founded in 1944 and in 1947 Jomo ◊Kenyatta, a member of Kenya's largest ethnic group, the Kikuyu, became its president. Three years later a secret society of young Kikuyu militants was formed, called Mau Mau, which had the same aims as KAU but sought to achieve them by violent means. Although Kenyatta dissociated himself from Mau Mau, the British authorities distrusted him and imprisoned him in 1953. By 1956 the guerrilla campaign had largely ended, the state of emergency was lifted and Kenyatta was released.

Kenya was granted internal self-government in 1963 and Kenyatta, who had become leader of the Kenya African National Union (KANU), became prime minister and then president after full independence in 1964. Kenyatta continued as president until his death in 1978, during which time the country achieved considerable stability. He was succeeded by Vice-President Daniel arap Moi, who built on Kenyatta's achievements, launching an impressive four-year development plan.

Kenyatta *The first president of independent Kenya, Jomo Kenyatta.*

An attempted coup by junior air force officers in 1982 was foiled and resulted in political detentions and press censorship. The air force and Nairobi University were temporarily dissolved. In the same year the national assembly declared Kenya a one-party state. President Moi was re-elected in 1983 and his position seems secure. He has had some success in tackling corruption and inefficiency in the public services and, externally, has re-established good relations with most of his E African neighbours. He was re-elected unopposed for a third successive presidential term Feb 1988. In June 1989 Moi unexpectedly announced the release of all known political detainees.

Kenya, Mount /ˈkenjə/ or **Kirinyaga** extinct volcano from which Kenya takes its name, 5200 m/17,058 ft; it was first climbed by Sir Halford Mackinder in 1899.

Kepler's second law

[figure: ellipse with Sun at one focus, points X, Y, P, O marked, shaded equal-area sectors]

ellipse

Kerala

Trivandrum
INDIAN OCEAN

Kenyatta /kenˈjætə/ Jomo. Assumed name of Kamau Ngengi *c.*1889–1978. Kenyan nationalist politician, prime minister from 1963 as well as first president of Kenya from 1964 until his death. He led the Kenya African Union from 1947 (◊*KANU* from 1963) and was active in liberating Kenya from British rule.

A member of the Kikuyu ethnic group, Kenyatta was born near Fort Hall, son of a farmer. Brought up at a Church of Scotland mission, he joined the Kikuyu Central Association (KCA), devoted to recovery of Kikuyu lands from white settlers, and became its president. He spent some years in Britain, returning to Kenya in 1946. He became president of the Kenya African Union (successor to the banned KCA 1947). In 1953 he was sentenced to seven years' imprisonment for his management of the guerrilla organization ◊Mau Mau, though some doubt has been cast on his complicity. Released to exile in N Kenya in 1958, he was allowed to return to Kikuyuland 1961 and in 1963 became prime minister (also president from 1964) of independent Kenya. His slogans were *Uhuru na moja* 'Freedom and unity' and *Harambee* 'Let's get going'.

Kenyon /ˈkenjən/ Kathleen 1906–1978. British archaeologist, whose work in ◊Jericho showed that the double walls associated with the biblical Joshua belonged to an earlier period, and that a Neolithic settlement had existed about 6800 BC.

Kepler /ˈkeplə/ Johann 1571–1630. German mathematician and astronomer. *Kepler's laws* of planetary motion are: (1) the orbit of each planet is an ellipse with the Sun at one of the foci; (2) the radius vector of each planet sweeps out equal areas in equal times; (3) the squares of the periods of the planets are proportional to the cubes of their mean distances from the Sun.

Born in Württemberg, Kepler became assistant to Tycho ◊Brahe 1600, and succeeded him as imperial mathematician 1601. His analysis of Brahe's observations of the planets led him to discover his three laws, the first two of which he published in *Astronomia Nova* 1609 and the third in *Harmonices Mundi* 1619.

Kerala /ˈkerələ/ state of SW India, formed 1956 from the former princely states of Travancore and Cochin
area 38,900 sq km/15,015 sq mi
capital Trivandrum
features most densely populated, and most literate (60%) state of India; strong religious and caste divisions make it politically unstable
products tea, coffee, rice, oilseed, rubber, textiles, chemicals, electrical goods
population (1981) 25,403,000
language Kannada, Malayalam, Tamil.

keratin fibrous protein found in the ◊skin of vertebrates and also in hair, nails, claws, hooves, feathers, and the outer coating of horns in animals such as cows and sheep.

Kew Gardens *The Temperate House, designed by Decimus Burton and completed in 1862.*

If pressure is put on some parts of the skin, more keratin is produced, forming thick calluses which protect the layers of skin beneath.

Kerbela /'kɜ:bələ/ or *Karbala* holy city of the Shi'ite Muslims, 96 km/60 m SW of Baghdad, Iraq; population (1985) 184,600. Kerbela is built on the site of the battlefield where Husein, son of Ali and Fatima, was killed in 680 while defending his succession to the khalifate; his tomb in the city is visited every year by many pilgrims.

Kerch /keətʃ/ port in the Crimea, Ukraine, USSR, at the eastern end of Kerch peninsula, an important iron-producing area; population (1987) 173,000. Kerch was built on the site of an ancient Greek settlement, and became Russian 1783.

Kerekou /,kerə'ku:/ Mathieu (Ahmed) 1933– . Benin socialist politician and soldier, president from 1980. In 1972, when deputy head of the Dahomey army, he led a coup to oust the ruling president and establish his own military government. He embarked on a programme of 'scientific socialism', changing his country's name to Benin to mark this change of direction. Re-elected president 1984, in 1987 he resigned from the army and confirmed a civilian administration.

Kerensky /'kerənski/ Alexander Feodorovich 1881–1970. Russian politician, premier of the second provisional government before its collapse Nov 1917, during the ◊Russian Revolution. He lived in the USA from 1918.

Kerguelen Islands /'kɜ:gələn/ or *Desolation Islands* volcanic archipelago in the Indian Ocean, part of the French Southern and Antarctic Territories; area 7,215 km/2,787 sq mi. It was discovered in 1772 by the Breton navigator Yves de Kerguelen, and annexed by France in 1949. Uninhabited except for scientists (centre for joint study of geomagnetism with USSR); the islands support a unique wild cabbage containing a pungent oil.

Kerkira /'keəkɪrə/ Greek form of ◊Corfu, an island in the Ionian Sea.

Kermadec Islands /'kɜ:mədek, kə'mædek/ volcanic group, a dependency of New Zealand since 1887; area 30 sq km/12 sq mi. They are uninhabited except for a meteorological station on the largest island, Raoul.

Kerman /kə'mɑ:n/ town in Kerman province, SE Iran; population (1986) 254,800. It is a centre for the mining of copper and precious metals.

Kermanshah /,kɜ:mæn'ʃɑː/ former name (until 1980) of the town of ◊Bakhtaran in NW Iran.

Kern /kɜ:n/ Jerome (David) 1885–1945. US composer. He wrote the operetta *Show Boat* 1927, which includes the song 'Ol' Man River'.

kernel the inner, softer part of a ◊nut, or of a seed within a hard shell.

Kernow /'kɜ:nəʊ/ Celtic name for ◊Cornwall, England.

kerosene a petroleum distillate, known in the UK as *paraffin*; a more highly refined form is used in jet aircraft fuel. It is a mixture of different hydrocarbons of the paraffin series.

Kerouac /'keruæk/ Jack 1923–1969. US novelist, who epitomized the ◊beat generation of the 1950s. His books include *On the Road* 1957 and *Big Sur* 1963.

Kerr /kɜ:/ Deborah 1921– . British actress, who often played genteel, ladylike roles. Her performance in British films such as *Major Barbara* 1940 *Black Narcissus* 1946 led to starring parts in Hollywood films such as *Quo Vadis* 1951, *From Here to Eternity* 1953, and *The King and I* 1956.

Kerry /'keri/ county of Munster province, Republic of Ireland, E of Cork
area 4,700 sq km/1,814 sq mi
county town Tralee
physical W coastline deeply indented, N part low-lying, but in the S are the highest mountains in Ireland including Carrantuohill 1,041 m/3,417 ft, the highest peak in Ireland; many rivers and lakes
features ◊Macgillycuddy's Reeks; Lakes of Killarney
products engineering, woollens, shoes, cutlery; tourism
population (1986) 124,000.

Kertesz /'kɜ:tes/ André 1894–1986. US photographer. A master of the 35-mm format camera, he recorded his immediate environment (Paris, New York) with wit and style.

Kesselring /'kesəlrɪŋ/ Albert 1885–1960. German field marshal in World War II, commander of the Luftwaffe (air force) 1939–40, during the invasions of Poland and the Low Countries and the early stages of the Battle of Britain. He later served under Field Marshal Rommel in N Africa, took command in Italy 1943, and was commander in chief on the western front Mar 1945. His death sentence for war crimes at the Nuremberg trials 1947 was commuted to imprisonment, and he was released 1952.

Kesteven, Parts of /kes'ti:vən/ SW area of Lincolnshire, England, formerly an administrative unit with county offices at Sleaford 1888–1974.

kestrel hawk *Falco tinnunculus* of the family Falconidae, which breeds in Europe, Asia, and Africa. About 30 cm/1 ft long, the male has a head and tail of bluish-grey, and its back is a light chestnut-brown with black spots. The female is slightly larger and reddish-brown above, with bars. The kestrel hunts mainly by hovering in mid-air while searching for prey.

Ketch /ketʃ/ Jack died 1686. English executioner, who included ◊Monmouth in 1685 among his victims; his name became a common nickname for an executioner.

ketone member of the group of organic compounds containing the carbonyl group, CO, bonded to two atoms of carbon (instead of one carbon and one hydrogen as in aldehydes). Ketones are liquids or low-melting-point solids, slightly soluble in water. An example is acetone (modern name propanone), $CH_3.CO.CH_3$, used as a solvent.

Kew Gardens /kju:/ popular name for the Royal Botanic Gardens, Kew, Surrey. They were founded 1759 by the mother of George III as a small garden and passed to the nation by Queen Victoria 1840. By then they were almost at their present size of 149 hectares and since 1841 have been open daily to the public. They contain a collection of over 25,000 living plant species and many fine buildings. Much of the collection of trees was destroyed by a gale 1987. The gardens are also a centre for botanical research.

The Herbarium is the biggest in the world, with over five million dried plant specimens. Kew also has a vast botanical library, the Jodrell Laboratory, and three museums. The buildings include the majestic Palm House 1848, designed by Decimus Burton, the Temperate House 1862, and the Chinese Pagoda, some 50 m/165 ft tall, designed by William Chambers 1761. More recently, two additions have been made to the glasshouses: the Alpine House 1981 and the Princess of Wales Conservatory, a futuristic building for plants from ten different climatic zones, 1987. Since 1964 there have been additional grounds at Wakehurst Place, Ardingly, W Sussex (the seeds of 5,000 species are preserved there in the seed physiology department, 2% of those known to exist in the world).

key in music, the ◊diatonic scale around which a piece of music is written; for example, a passage in the key of C major will mainly use the notes of the C major scale. The term is also used for the lever activated by a keyboard player, such as a piano key.

Key /ki:/ Francis Scott 1779–1843. US lawyer and poet who wrote the song 'The Star-Spangled Banner', while Fort McHenry was besieged by the British in 1814; since 1931 it has been the national anthem of the USA.

keyboard in computing, an input device resembling a typewriter keyboard, used to enter instructions and data. There are many variations on the layout and labelling of keys for different purposes. Extra numeric keys may be added, as can special-purpose function keys, such as LOAD, SAVE, PRINT, whose effect can be defined by programs in the computer.

Keynes /keɪnz/ John Maynard, 1st Baron Keynes 1883–1946. English economist, whose *The General Theory of Employment, Interest, and Money* 1936 proposed the prevention of financial crises and unemployment by adjusting demand through government control of credit and currency. He is responsible for that part of economics now known as ◊*macroeconomics*.

Keynes was Fellow of King's College, Cambridge. He held a Treasury appointment during World War I, and took part in the peace conference as chief Treasury representative, but resigned in protest against the financial terms of the treaty. He justified his action in *The Economic Consequences of the Peace* 1919. His later economic works aroused much controversy.

Keynes led the British delegation at the Bretton Woods Conference 1944, which set up the International Monetary Fund. His theories were widely accepted in the aftermath of World War II, and he was one of the most influential economists of the 20th century. His ideas are today often contrasted with those of ◊monetarism.

Keynesian economics the economic theory of J M Keynes which argues that a fall in national income, lack of demand for goods, and rising unemployment should be countered by increased government expenditure to stimulate the economy. It is opposed by monetarists (see ◊monetarism).

Key West /'ki: 'west/ town at the tip of the Florida peninsula, USA; population (1980) 24,382. As a tourist resort, it was popularized by the novelist Ernest Hemingway.

kg abbreviation for *kilogram*.

KG abbreviation for *Knight of the Order of the Garter*.

KGB the Soviet secret police, the *Komitet Gosudarstvennoye Bezhopaznosti* ('Committee of State Security'), in control of frontier and general security and the forced-labour system. KGB officers hold key appointments in all fields of daily life, reporting to administration offices in every major town.

Many KGB officers are also said to hold diplomatic posts in embassies abroad. The headquarters is in Dzerzhinsky Square, Moscow, and the Lubyanka Prison is located behind it. Earlier names for the secret police were *Okhrana* under the tsars; ◊*Cheka* 1918–23; *GPU* or OGPU (*Obedinyonnoye Gosudarstvennoye Polititcheskoye Upravleniye* 'Unified State Political Administration') 1923–34; *NKVD* (*Narodny Komisariat Vnutrennykh Del* 'People's Commissariat of Internal Affairs') 1934–46; and *MVD* ('Ministry of Internal Affairs') 1946–53. ◊Smersh was a subsection.

Khabarovsk /,kæbə'rɒfsk/ industrial city (oil refining, saw milling, meat packing) in SE Siberia, USSR; population (1987) 591,000.

Khabarovsk /,kæbə'rɒfsk/ territory of SE USSR bordering the Sea of Okhotsk and drained by the Amur; area 824,600 sq km/318,501 sq mi;

Khaddhafi *Libyan leader Colonel Moamer al Khaddhafi.*

population (1985) 1,728,000. The capital is Khabarovsk. Mineral resources include gold, coal and iron ore.

Khachaturian /ˌkætʃəˈtuəriən/ Aram Il'yich 1903–1978. Armenian composer. His use of folk themes is shown in the ballets *Gayaneh* 1942, which includes the 'Sabre Dance', and *Spartacus* 1956.

Khaddhafi /kəˈdæfi/ or ***Gaddafi*** or ***Qaddafi***, Moamer al 1942– . Libyan revolutionary leader. Overthrowing King Idris 1969, he became virtual president of a republic, although he nominally gave up all except an ideological role 1974. He favours territorial expansion in N Africa reaching as far as Zaïre, has supported rebels in Chad, and proposed mergers with a number of countries. His theories, based on those of the Chinese communist leader Mao Zedong, are contained in a *Green Book*.

Khajurāho /ˌkædʒuˈrɑːhəu/ town in Madhya Pradesh, central India, the former capital of the Candella monarchs. It has 35 sandstone temples, Jain, Buddhist, and Hindu, built in the 10th and 11th centuries. The temples are covered inside and out with erotic sculpture symbolizing mystic union with the deity.

khaki the dust-coloured uniform of British and Indian troops in India from about 1850, adopted as camouflage during the South African War 1899–1902, and later standard for military uniforms worldwide.

Khalifa /kɑːˈliːfə/ the Sudanese dervish leader ***Abdullah el Taaisha*** 1846–1899. Successor to the Mahdi as Sudanese ruler from 1885, he was defeated by the UK general ◊Kitchener at Omdurman 1898, and later killed in Kordofan.

Khalistan /ˌkɑːlɪˈstɑːn/ projected independent Sikh state. See ◊Sikhism.

Khalsa the brotherhood of the Sikhs, created by Guru Gobind Singh at the festival of Baisakhi in 1699. The Khalsa was originally founded as a militant group to defend the Sikh community from persecution.

Khama /ˈkɑːmə/ Seretse 1921–1980. Botswanan politician, prime minister of Bechuanaland 1965 and first president of Botswana from 1966 until his death.

Son of the Bamangwato chief Sekoma II (died 1925), Khama studied law in Britain and married an Englishwoman, Ruth Williams. This marriage was strongly condemned by his uncle Tshekedi Khama, regent during his minority, as contrary to tribal custom, and Seretse Khama was banished 1950. He returned 1956 on his renunciation of any claim to the chieftaincy.

khamsin a hot wind that blows from the Sahara desert over Egypt from late March to early May.

Khan /kɑːn/ Imran 1952– . Pakistani cricketer. He played county cricket for Worcestershire and Sussex in the UK, and made his test debut for Pakistan 1971, subsequently playing for his country 75 times. In first-class cricket he has scored over 16,000 runs and taken over 1,200 wickets.

CAREER HIGHLIGHTS

test cricket
appearances: 75
runs: 3,000
average: 33.70
best: 135 not out (Pakistan v. India 1986–87)
wickets: 341
average: 22.04
best: 8–58 (Pakistan v. Sri Lanka 1981–82)

Khan /kɑːn/ Jahangir 1963– . Pakistani squash player, who won the world open championship a record six times 1981–85 and 1988.

He was eight times British open champion 1982–89, and world amateur champion 1979, 1983, and 1985. After losing to Geoff Hunt (Australia) in the final of the 1981 British open he did not lose again until Nov 1986 when he lost to Ross Norman (New Zealand) in the world open final.

His father ***Roshan Khan*** was British open champion 1956.

CAREER HIGHLIGHTS

world open champion: 1981–85, 1988
world amateur champion: 1979, 1983, 1985
British open champion: 1982–89

Khan /kɑːn/ Liaquat Ali 1895–1951. Indian politician, deputy leader of the Muslim League Party 1941–47, first prime minister of Pakistan from 1947. He was assassinated by a Muslim fanatic.

Khardungla Pass road linking the Indian town of Leh with the high-altitude military outpost on the Siachen Glacier at an altitude of 5,662 m/1,744 ft in the Karakoram range, Kashmir. It is thought to be the highest road in the world.

Kharga /ˈkɑːgə/ or ***Kharijah*** oasis in the Western Desert of Egypt, known to the Romans, and from 1960 headquarters of the New Valley irrigation scheme. An area twice the size of Italy is watered from natural underground reservoirs.

Kharg Island a small island in the Persian Gulf used by Iran as a deepwater oil terminal. Between 1982 and 1988 Kharg Island came under frequent attack during the Gulf War.

Kharkov /ˈkɑːkɒf/ capital of the Kharkov region, Ukraine, USSR, 400 km/250 mi E of Kiev; population (1987) 1,587,000. It is an important railway junction and industrial city (engineering, tractors), close to the Donets Basin coalfield and Krivoy Rog iron mines. Kharkov was founded 1654 as a fortress town. Its university dates from 1805.

Khartoum /kɑːˈtuːm/ capital and trading centre of Sudan, at the junction of the Blue and White Nile; population (1983) 476,000, and of Khartoum North, across the Blue Nile, 341,000. It was founded 1830 by ◊Mehemet Ali.

General ◊Gordon was killed at Khartoum by the Mahdist rebels 1885. A new city was built after the site was recaptured by British troops under Kitchener 1898. ◊Omdurman is also a suburb of Khartoum, giving the urban area a population of over 1.3 million.

Khazar /kəˈzɑː/ people of Turkish origin from Central Asia, who formed a buffer state in the 7th–12th centuries between the Arabs and the Byzantine empire, and later between the Byzantine empire and subsequent Russian pressure from the north. Converted to Judaism about 740, they died out in the 13th century; it has been suggested they were the ancestors of the E European Jews, themselves the ancestors of the majority of modern Jewry, and hence of Aryan rather than Semitic origin.

khedive title granted by the Turkish sultan to his Egyptian viceroy 1867, retained by succeeding rulers until 1914.

Kherson /kɜːˈsɒn/ port in Ukraine, USSR, on the Dnieper river, capital of Kherson region; population (1987) 358,000. Industries include shipbuilding, soap, and tobacco manufacture. It was founded 1778 by army commander ◊Potemkin as the first Russian naval base on the Black Sea.

Khomeini *The former Iranian Shi'ite Muslim leader, the Ayatollah Khomeini.*

Khe Sanh /ˈkeɪ ˈsæn/ in the Vietnam War, US Marine outpost near the Laotian border and just south of the demilitarized zone between North and South Vietnam. Garrisoned by 4,000 Marines, it was attacked unsuccessfully by 20,000 North Vietnamese troops 21 Jan–7 Apr 1968.

Khirbet Qumran archaeological site in Jordan; see ◊Qumran.

Khmer or ***Kmer*** inhabitant of Cambodia. Khmer minorities also live in E Thailand and S Vietnam. The Khmer language belongs to the Mon Khmer family.

Cambodia came under Indian cultural influence when it was part of the SE Asian kingdom of Funan. The earliest inscriptions in the Khmer language date from the 7th century AD. The Khmer kingdom reached its zenith in the 9th–13th centuries, when the capital was at Angkor. The Khmers were eventually pushed back by the Thais into the territory they occupy today.

The Khmers practise Hinayana Buddhism and trace descent through both male and female lines. Traditionally Khmer society was divided into six groups: the royal family, the Brahmans (who officiated at royal festivals), Buddhist monks, officials, commoners, and slaves.

Khmer Republic /kmeə/ former name of ◊Cambodia, country in SE Asia.

Khmer Rouge communist movement in Cambodia (Kampuchea), which formed the largest opposition group against the US-backed regime led by Lon Nol 1970–75. By 1974 the Khmer Rouge controlled the countryside and in 1975 the capital Phnom Penh was captured and Sihanouk installed as head of state. Internal disagreements led to the creation of the Pol Pot government 1976 and mass deportations and executions of an estimated 1 million people 1975–79. From 1978, when Vietnam invaded the country, the Khmer Rouge conducted a guerrilla campaign against the Vietnamese forces. Pol Pot retired as military leader 1985 and was succeeded by the more moderate Khieu Samphan.

Khomeini /kɒˈmeɪni/ Ayatollah Ruhollah 1900–1989. Iranian Shi'ite Muslim leader, born in Khomein, central Iran. Exiled for opposition to the Shah from 1964, he returned when the Shah left the country 1979, and established a fundamentalist Islamic republic. His rule was marked by a protracted war with Iraq, and suppression of opposition within Iran.

Khorana /kɔːˈrɑːnə/ Har Gobind 1922– . Indian biochemist, who in 1976 led the team that first synthesized a biologically active gene.

Khrushchev *Soviet politician Nikita Khrushchev at the Quai d'Orsay, Paris.*

Khorramshahr /ˌkɔːrəmˈʃɑː/ former port and oil-refining centre in Iran, on the Shatt-al-Arab river and linked by bridge to the islands of Abadan. It was completely destroyed in the 1980s by enemy action in the Iran–Iraq war.

Khrushchev /krʊʃˈtʃɒf/ Nikita Sergeyevich 1894–1971. Soviet politician, secretary general of the Communist Party 1953–64, premier 1958–64. In 1956 he was the first official to denounce Stalin. A personal feud with Mao Zedong led to a breach in Soviet relations with China 1960. Khrushchev's foreign policy was one of peaceful coexistence with the West, marred by the crisis when he attempted to supply missiles to Cuba and US pressure compelled their withdrawal 1962.

Born near Kursk, the son of a miner, he fought in the post-Revolutionary civil war 1917–20, and in World War II organized the guerrilla defence of his native Ukraine. He denounced Stalinism in a secret session of the party Feb 1956. Many victims of the purges of the 1930s were either released or posthumously rehabilitated, but when Hungary revolted in Oct against Soviet domination, there was immediate Soviet intervention. In 1958 Khrushchev succeeded Bulganin as chair of the council of ministers (prime minister). His policy of competition with capitalism was successful in the space programme. Because of the Cuban crisis and the Sino-Soviet split, he was compelled to resign 1964, although by 1965 his reputation was to some extent officially restored. In Apr 1989 his Feb 1956 'secret speech' was officially published for the first time.

Khufu /ˈkuːfuː/ *c.* 3000 BC. Egyptian king of Memphis, who built the largest of the pyramids, known to the Greeks as the pyramid of Cheops (the Greek form of Khufu).

Khulna /ˈkʊlnə/ capital of Khulna region, SW Bangladesh, situated close to the Ganges delta; population (1981) 646,000. Industry includes shipbuilding and textiles; it trades in jute, rice, salt, sugar, and oilseed.

Khuzestan /ˈkuːzɪstɑːn/ SW province of Iran, which includes the chief Iranian oil resources; population (1986) 2,702,533. Towns include Ahvaz (capital), and the ports of Abadan and Khuninshahr. There have been calls for Sunni Muslim autonomy, under the name ◊Arabistan.

Khwarizmi, al- /ˈkwɑːrɪzmi/ Muhammad ibn-Musa 780–*c.*850. Arab mathematician who lived and worked in Baghdad. He introduced the ◊algorithm (a word based on his name), the word ◊algebra (*al-jabr*, in an adaptation of an earlier Indian text), the Hindu decimal system, and the concept of zero into Arab mathematics. He compiled astronomical tables, and put forward Arabic numerals.

Khyber Pass /ˈkaɪbə/ pass 53 km/33 mi long through the mountain range that separates Pakistan from Afghanistan. The Khyber Pass was used by invaders of India. The present road was constructed by the British during the Afghan Wars.

kidney

Blood enters the kidney through the renal artery. The blood is filtered through the glomeruli to extract the urine. The urine flows through the ureter to the bladder; the cleaned blood flow leaves the kidney along the renal vein.

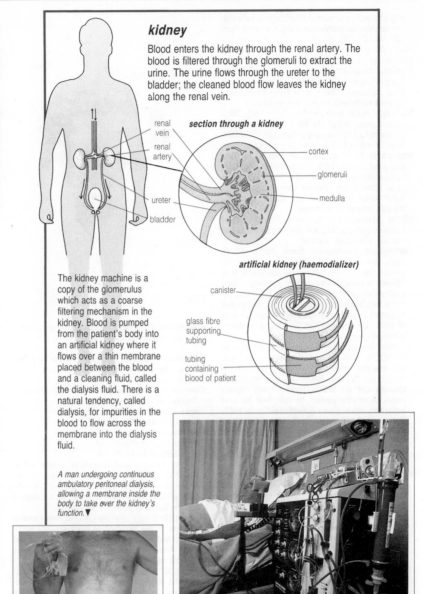

renal vein

renal artery

ureter

bladder

section through a kidney

cortex

glomeruli

medulla

artificial kidney (haemodializer)

canister

glass fibre supporting tubing

tubing containing blood of patient

The kidney machine is a copy of the glomerulus which acts as a coarse filtering mechanism in the kidney. Blood is pumped from the patient's body into an artificial kidney where it flows over a thin membrane placed between the blood and a cleaning fluid, called the dialysis fluid. There is a natural tendency, called dialysis, for impurities in the blood to flow across the membrane into the dialysis fluid.

A man undergoing continuous ambulatory peritoneal dialysis, allowing a membrane inside the body to take over the kidney's function. ▼

Elderly man undergoing renal dialysis on a kidney machine.

Kiangsi alternative spelling of ◊Jiangxi, province of China.

Kiangsu alternative spelling of ◊Jiangsu, province of China.

kibbutz Israeli communal collective settlement, with collective ownership of all property and earnings, collective organization of work, and communal housing for children; a modified version, the *Moshav Shitufi*, is similar to the ◊collective farms of the USSR. Other Israeli cooperative rural settlements include the *Moshav Ovdim* which has equal opportunity, and the similar but less strict *Moshav* settlement.

Kidd /kɪd/ 'Captain' (William) *c.*1645–1701. Scottish pirate, born in Greenock, who settled in New York. In 1696 he was commissioned by the governor of New York to suppress pirates, but he became a pirate himself. Arrested 1699, he was taken to England and hanged. His execution marked the end of some 200 years of semi-official condoning of piracy by the British government.

Kidderminster /ˈkɪdəˌmɪnstə/ market town in the West Midlands of England, on the river Stour;

population (1981) 51,300. It has had a carpet industry from about 1735.

kidnapping the abduction of a person in order to gain money for their safe release. The practice arose in the 17th century with the abduction of young people to become indentured labourers in colonial plantations, from which they could be rescued by a ransom. In English common law it is an offence which carries a maximum sentence of life imprisonment.

kidney an organ of vertebrates responsible for water regulation, excretion of waste products, and maintaining the composition of the blood. In mammals, there is a pair of kidneys situated on the rear wall of the abdomen. Each one consists of a number of long tubules; the outer parts filter the aqueous components of blood, and the inner parts selectively reabsorb vital salts, leaving waste products in the remaining fluid (urine), which is passed through the ureter to the bladder.

The action of the kidneys is vital to life, although if one is removed, the other enlarges to take over its function. A patient with two defective kidneys may continue near-normal life with the aid of a kidney machine or continuous ambulatory peritoneal ◊dialysis (CAPD).

Kiefer /'ki:fə/ Anselm 1945– . German painter. He studied under Joseph ◊Beuys, and his works include monumental landscapes on varied surfaces, often with the paint built up into relief with other substances. Much of his highly Expressionist work deals with recent German history.

Kiel /ki:l/ Baltic port (fishing, shipbuilding, electronics engineering), in West Germany, capital of Schleswig-Holstein; population (1988) 244,000. *Kiel Week* in June is a yachting meeting.

Kiel Canal /ki:l/ waterway 98.7 km/51 mi long that connects the Baltic with the North Sea. Built by Germany in the years before World War I, the canal allowed the German navy to move from Baltic bases to the open sea without travelling through international waters.

Kielce /ki'eltseɪ/ city in central Poland, NE of Kraków; population (1985) 201,000; industrial rail junction (chemicals, metals).

Kierkegaard /'kɪəkəgɑ:d/ Søren Aabye 1813–1855. Danish philosopher, considered to be the founder of ◊existentialism. He disagreed with ◊Hegel, arguing that no system of thought could explain the unique experience of the individual. He defended Christianity, suggesting that God cannot be known through reason, but only through a 'leap of faith'. He believed that God and exceptional individuals were above moral laws.

Born in Copenhagen, where he spent most of his life, he was the son of a Jewish merchant, but was converted to Christianity in 1838, although he became hostile to the established church, and his beliefs caused much controversy. A prolific author, he published his first important work *Enten-Eller/Either-Or* in 1843, and notable later works are *Begrebet Angest/Concept of Dread* 1844 and *Efterskrift/Post-script* 1846, which summed up much of his earlier writings. His many pseudonyms were sometimes used to argue with himself.

Kiev /'ki:ef/ capital of Ukraine, industrial centre (chemicals, clothing, leatherwork) and third largest city of the USSR, on the confluence of the Desna and Dnieper rivers; population (1987) 2,554,000. Founded in the 5th century, Kiev replaced ◊Novgorod as the capital of Slav-dominated Russia 882, and was the original centre of the Orthodox Christian faith 988.

The Kiev ballet and opera are renowned. The city was occupied by Germany 1941. The Slav domination of Russia began with the rise of Kiev (see also under ◊Vikings) the 'mother of Russian cities'. St Sophia cathedral (11th century) and Kiev-Pechersky Monastery (both now museums) survive, and also remains of the Golden Gate.

Kigali /kɪ'gɑ:li/ capital of Rwanda, central Africa; population (1981) 157,000. Products include coffee and minerals.

Kigoma /kɪ'gəumə/ town and port on the E shore of Lake Tanganyika, Tanzania, at the W terminal of the railway from Dar es Salaam; population (1978) 50,044.

Kikuyu person of Kikuyu culture from Kenya. They are Kenya's dominant ethnic group, and are primarily cultivators, though many are highly educated and have entered the professions. Their language belongs to the Bantu branch of the Niger-Congo family.

Kildare /kɪl'deə/ county of Leinster province, Republic of Ireland, S of Meath
area 1,690 sq km/652 sq mi
county town Naas
physical wet and boggy in the north
features includes part of the Bog of Allen; the village of Maynooth, with a training college for Roman Catholic priests; and the Curragh, a plain which is the site of the national stud and headquarters of Irish racing
products oats, barley, potatoes, cattle
population (1986) 116,000.

Kierkegaard A portrait of the philosopher sketched by his cousin, Christian Kierkegaard.

Kilimanjaro /ˌkɪlɪmæn'dʒɑ:rəʊ/ volcano in ◊Tanzania, the highest mountain in Africa, 5,900 m/19,364 ft.

Kilkenny /kɪl'keni/ county of Leinster province, Republic of Ireland, E of Tipperary
area 2,060 sq km/795 sq mi
county town Kilkenny
features river Nore
products agricultural, coal
population (1986) 73,000.

Killarney /kɪ'lɑ:ni/ market town in County Kerry, Republic of Ireland; population (1981) 7,693. A famous beauty spot in Ireland, it has ◊Macgillycuddy's Reeks (a range of mountains) and the Lakes of Killarney to the SW.

killer whale a type of whale *Orcinus orca* found in all seas of the world. It is black on top, white below, and grows up to 9 m/30 ft long. It has been observed to prey on other whales, as well as seals and sea birds.

Killy /kɪ'li:/ Jean-Claude 1943– . French skier. He won all three gold medals (slalom, giant slalom, and downhill) at the 1968 winter Olympics in Grenoble. The first World Cup winner 1967, he retained the title 1968 and also won three world titles.

CAREER HIGHLIGHTS

Olympic champion
downhill: 1968
slalom: 1968
giant slalom: 1968
world champion
combined: 1966, 1968
downhill: 1966
World Cup
overall: 1967–68
downhill: 1967
giant slalom: 1967–68
slalom: 1967

Kilmainham a jail in Dublin, Ireland, where the nationalist Charles Stuart ◊Parnell was imprisoned Oct 1881. Under the 'Kilmainham Treaty', a series of secret negotiations, he was released May 1882, since the British government realized he could quell violence more easily out of prison than in it. In return for his release, Parnell agreed to accept the Land Act of 1861.

The Kilmainham treaty marked a change in British policy in Ireland from confrontation to cooperation, with the government attempting to conciliate landowners and their tenants, who

were refusing to pay rent. This strategy was subsequently threatened by the ◊Phoenix Park murders.

Kilmarnock /kɪl'mɑ:nək/ town in Strathclyde region, Scotland, 32 km/20 mi SW of Glasgow; population (1981) 52,083. Products include carpets, agricultural machinery, and whisky; Robert Burns's first book of poems was published here 1786.

Kilmuir /kɪl'mjʊə/ David Patrick Maxwell Fyfe, 1st Earl of Kilmuir 1900–1967. British lawyer and Conservative politician. He was solicitor-general 1942–45 and attorney-general in 1945 during the Churchill governments. He was home secretary 1951–54 and lord chancellor 1954–62. In 1954 he was created viscount and in 1962 earl.

kiln high-temperature furnace used commercially for drying timber, roasting metal ores, or for making cement, bricks, and pottery. Oil- or gas-fired kilns are used to bake ceramics at up to 1,760°C/3,200°F; electric kilns do not generally reach such high temperatures.

kilo- prefix denoting multiplication by 1,000, hence *kilogram* unit of mass equal to 1,000 grams/2.2 lb; *kilometre* unit of length equal to 1,000 metres/3,280.89 ft (about 5/8 of a mile); *kiloton* unit of explosive force equivalent to 1,000 tons of TNT, used in describing nuclear bombs; and *kilowatt* unit of power equal to about 1,000 watts/1.34 horsepower.

kilobyte in computing, a unit of memory equal to 1024 ◊bytes.

kilowatt-hour commercial unit of electrical energy (symbol kWh), defined as the work done by a power of 1,000 watts in one hour. It is used to calculate the cost of electrical energy taken from the domestic supply.

Kilvert /'kɪlvət/ Francis 1840–1879. British cleric, noted for a diary recording social life on the Welsh border 1870–79 published in 1938–39.

Kimberley /'kɪmbəli/ diamond-mining town in Cape Province, South Africa, 153 km/95 mi NW of Bloemfontein; population (1980) 144,923. Its mines have been controlled by De Beers Consolidated Mines since 1887.

Kimberley /'kɪmbəli/ diamond site in Western Australia, found in 1978–79, estimated to have 5% of world's known gem-quality stones and 50% of its industrial diamonds.

kimberlite an igneous rock that is ultrabasic (containing very little silica); a type of alkaline peridotite (see ◊peridot) containing mica in addition to olivine and other minerals. Kimberlite represents the world's principal source of diamonds.

Kimberlite is found in carrot-shaped pipelike ◊intrusions called *diatremes*, where mobile material from very deep in the Earth's crust has forced itself upwards, expanding in its ascent. The material, brought upwards from near the boundary between crust and mantle, often altered and fragmented, includes diamonds. Diatremes are found principally near Kimberley, South Africa, from which the name of the rock is derived, and in the Yakut area of Siberia, USSR.

Kim Dae Jung /'kɪm ˌdeɪ 'dʒʊŋ/ 1924– . South Korean social-democratic politician. As a committed opponent of the regime of Gen Park Chung Hee, he suffered imprisonment and exile. He was a presidential candidate in 1971 and 1987.

A Roman Catholic, born in the poor SW province of Cholla, Kim was imprisoned by communist

kiln Brick kilns near Lahore in Pakistan.

troops during the Korean War. He rose to prominence as an opponent of Park and was only narrowly defeated when he challenged Park for the presidency in 1971. He was imprisoned 1976–78 and 1980–82 for alleged 'anti-government activities' and lived in the USA 1982–85. On his return to South Korea he successfully spearheaded an opposition campaign for democratization, but, being one of several opposition candidates, was defeated by the government nominee, Roh Tae Woo, in the presidential election of Dec 1987.

A political firebrand, Kim enjoys strong support among blue-collar workers and fellow Chollans, but is feared and distrusted by the country's business and military elite.

Kim Il Sung /'kɪm ˌiːl'sʊŋ/ 1912– . North Korean communist politician and marshal. He became prime minister 1948 and president 1972, retaining the presidency of the Communist Workers' Party. He likes to be known as the 'Great Leader' and has campaigned constantly for the reunification of Korea. His son *Kim Jong Il* (1942–), known as the 'Dear Leader', has been named as his successor.

kimono traditional Japanese costume. Already worn in the Han period (1,000 years ago), it is still used by women for formal wear and informally by men.

For the finest kimonos a rectangular piece of silk (about 11 m/36 ft × 0.5 m/1.5 ft) is cut into seven pieces for tailoring. The design (which must match perfectly over the seams and for which flowers are the usual motif) is then painted by hand and enhanced by embroidery or gilding. The accompanying *obi*, or sash, is also embroidered.

Kim Young Sam /'kɪm ˌjʌŋ 'sæm/ 1927– . South Korean democratic politician. A member of the National Assembly from 1954 and president of the New Democratic Party (NDP) from 1974, he lost his seat and was later placed under house arrest because of his opposition to President Park Chung Hee. In 1983 he led a pro-democracy hunger strike but in 1987 failed to defeat Roh Tae-Woo in the presidential election. In 1990 he merged the NDP with the ruling party to form the new Democratic Liberal Party (DLP).

Kincardineshire /kɪn'kɑːdɪnʃə/ former county of E Scotland, merged in 1975 in Grampian region. The county town was Stonehaven.

kinetic energy a form of ◊energy possessed by moving bodies. It is contrasted with ◊potential energy.

kinetics branch of ◊dynamics dealing with the action of forces producing or changing the motion of a body; *kinematics* deals with motion without reference to force or mass.

kinetics the branch of chemistry that investigates the rates of chemical reactions.

kinetic theory theory describing the physical properties of matter in terms of the behaviour—principally movement—of its component atoms or molecules. A gas consists of rapidly moving atoms or molecules and, according to kinetic theory, it is their continual impact on the walls of the containing vessel that accounts for the pressure of the gas.

The slowing of molecular motion as temperature falls, according to kinetic theory, accounts for the physical properties of liquids and solids, culminating in the concept of no molecular motion at ◊absolute zero (0 K/–273°C). By making various assumptions about the nature of gas molecules, it is possible to derive from the theory the various gas laws (such as ◊Avogadro's, ◊Boyle's, and ◊Charles' laws).

King /kɪŋ/ Billie Jean (born Moffitt) 1943– . US lawn tennis player. She won a record 20 Wimbledon titles 1961–79 and 39 Grand Slam titles.

Her first title was the doubles with Karen Hantze 1961, and her last, also doubles, with Martina Navratilova 1979. She won the Wimbledon singles title six times and the US Open singles title four times; French Open once; Australian Open once. Her 39 Grand Slam events at

King *Civil-rights campaigner Martin Luther King, on the march in 1965.*

singles and doubles are third only to Navratilova and Margaret Court.

CAREER HIGHLIGHTS

Wimbledon
singles: 1966–68, 1972–73, 1975
doubles: 1961–62, 1965, 1967–68, 1970–73, 1979
mixed: 1967, 1971, 1973–74
US Open
singles: 1967, 1971–72, 1974
doubles: 1964, 1967, 1974, 1978, 1980
mixed: 1967, 1971, 1973, 1976
French Open
singles: 1972
doubles: 1972
mixed: 1967, 1970
Australian Open
singles: 1968
mixed: 1968

King /kɪŋ/ Martin Luther Jr 1929–1968. US civil-rights campaigner, black leader, and Baptist minister. He first came to national attention as leader of the ◊Montgomery, Alabama, bus boycott 1955, and was one of the organizers of the massive (200,000 people) march on Washington DC 1963 to demand racial equality. An advocate of nonviolence, he was awarded the Nobel Peace Prize 1964. He was assassinated. The third Monday in Jan is celebrated as *Martin Luther King Day*, a public holiday in the USA.

Born in Atlanta, Georgia, son of a Baptist minister, King founded the ◊Southern Christian Leadership Conference 1957. A brilliant and moving speaker, he was the symbol of, and leading figure in, the campaign for integration and equal rights in the late 1950s and early 1960s. In the mid-1960s his moderate approach was criticized by black militants. Always a target of segregationists and right-wing extremists, he was shot and killed in Memphis, Tennessee. James Earl Ray was convicted of the murder, but there is little evidence to suggest that he committed the crime. Various conspiracy theories concerning the FBI, the CIA, and the Mafia have more validity.

King /kɪŋ/ Stephen 1946– . US writer of horror novels with a small-town or rural US setting. Many of his works have been filmed, including *Carrie* 1974, *The Shining* 1978, and *Christine* 1983.

King /kɪŋ/ William Lyon Mackenzie 1874–1950. Canadian Liberal prime minister 1921–26, 1926–30, and 1935–48. He maintained the unity of the English- and French-speaking populations, and was instrumental in establishing equal status for Canada with Britain.

king crab

king crab or *horseshoe crab* marine arthropod, class Arachnida, subclass Xiphosura, which lives on the Atlantic coast of North America, and the coasts of Asia. The upper side of the body is entirely covered with a rounded shell, and it has a long spine-like tail. It is up to 60 cm/2 ft long. It is unable to swim, and lays its eggs in the sand at the high-water mark.

kingcup another name for ◊marsh marigold.

kingdom the primary division in biological ◊classification. At one time only two kingdoms were recognized: animals and plants. Today most biologists prefer a five-kingdom system, even though it still involves grouping together organisms that are probably unrelated. One widely accepted scheme is: *Kingdom Animalia* (all multicellular animals); *Kingdom Plantae* (all plants, all seaweeds and other algae, including unicellular algae); *Kingdom Fungi* (all fungi, including the unicellular yeasts, but not slime moulds); *Kingdom Protista* or *Protoctista* (protozoa, diatoms, dinoflagellates, slime moulds, and various other lower organisms with eukaryotic cells) and *Kingdom Monera* (all prokaryotes—the bacteria and cyanobacteria). The first four of these kingdoms make up the eukaryotes.

When only two kingdoms were recognized, any organism with a rigid cell wall was a plant, and so bacteria and fungi were considered as plants, despite their many differences. Other organisms, such as the photosynthetic euglenoids, were claimed by both kingdoms. The unsatisfactory nature of the two-kingdom system became evident during the 19th century, and the biologist Ernst ◊Haeckel was among the first to try to reform it. High-power microscopes have revealed more about the structure of cells; it has become clear that there is a fundamental difference between cells without a nucleus (◊prokaryotes) and those with a nucleus (◊eukaryotes). However, these differences are larger than those between animals and higher plants, and are unsuitable for use as kingdoms. At present there is no agreement on how many kingdoms there are in the natural world. The five-kingdom system is widely favoured; some schemes have as many as 20.

kingfisher bird *Alcedo atthis* found in parts of Europe, Africa, and Asia. The plumage is brilliant blue-green on the back and chestnut beneath. Kingfishers feed on fish and aquatic insects. The nest is made of fishbones in a hole in a river bank.

There are about 90 species of kingfisher in the world, the largest being the Australian ◊kookaburra.

Kinglake /'kɪŋleɪk/ Alexander William 1809–1891. British historian of the Crimean War, who also wrote a Middle East travel narrative *Eothen* 1844.

King Lear tragedy by William Shakespeare, first performed 1605–06. Lear, king of Britain, favours his grasping daughters Goneril and Regan

kingfisher

with shares of his kingdom but refuses his third, honest daughter, Cordelia, a share. Rejected by Goneril and Regan, the old and unbalanced Lear is reunited with Cordelia but dies of grief when she is murdered.

Kings/Queen's Champion in English history, ceremonial office held by virtue of possessing the lordship of Scrivelsby, Lincolnshire. Sir John Dymoke established his right to champion the monarch on coronation day 1377 and it is still held by his descendant.

A document of 1332/33 described the champion as 'an armed knight on horseback to prove by his body, if necessary, against whomsoever, the King who is crowned that day is the true and right heir of the kingdom.' The last occasion upon which this office was peformed was at the coronation of King George IV in 1821 at the banquet in Westminster Hall. The gold cup from which the king drank at the banquet was his fee.

King's Council in medieval England, a court that carried out much of the monarch's daily administration. It was first established in the reign of Edward I, and became the Privy Council 1534–36.

King's Counsel in England, a ◊barrister of senior rank; the term is used when a king is on the throne, and ◊Queen's Counsel when the monarch is a queen.

King's County older name of ◊Offaly, an Irish county.

King's English see ◊English language.

king's evil another name for the skin condition ◊scrofula. In medieval England and France, it was thought that the touch of an anointed king could cure the condition. Traditionally, touching for the king's evil began in France with Clovis, and in England with Edward the Confessor, but no instances have been found before Louis IX and Edward III.

Kingsley /'kɪŋzli/ Ben (Krishna Banji) 1944– . British film actor of Indian descent, who usually plays character parts. He played the title role of *Gandhi* 1982 and also appeared in *Betrayal* 1982, *Testimony* 1987, and *Pascali's Island* 1988.

Kingsley /'kɪŋzli/ Charles 1819–1875. English author. Rector of Eversley, Hampshire, 1842–75, he was known as the 'Chartist clergyman' because of such social novels as *Alton Locke* 1850. His historical novels include *Westward Ho!* 1855 and, for children, *The Water-Babies* 1863.

He was professor of modern history at Cambridge University 1860–69 and his controversy with J H ◊Newman prompted the latter's *Apologia*.

Kingsley /'kɪŋzli/ Mary Henrietta 1862–1900. British ethnologist. She made extensive expeditions in W Africa, and published lively accounts of her findings, for example, *Travels in West Africa* 1897. She died while nursing Boer prisoners during the South African War. She was the niece of the writer Charles Kingsley.

King's Lynn /'kɪŋz 'lɪn/ port and market town at the mouth of the Great Ouse river, Norfolk, E England; population (1981) 38,000. It was an important port in medieval times. Its name was changed by Henry VIII from Lynn to King's Lynn.

King's proctor in England, the official representing the crown in certain court cases; the term is used when a king is on the throne, and ◊Queen's Proctor when the monarch is a queen.

Kingston /'kɪŋstən/ capital and principal port of Jamaica, West Indies, the cultural and commercial centre of the island; population (1983) 101,000, metropolitan area 525,000. Founded 1693, Kingston became the capital of Jamaica 1872.

Kingston /'kɪŋstən/ town in E Ontario, Canada, on Lake Ontario; population (1981) 60,313. Industries include shipbuilding yards, engineering works, and grain elevators. It grew from 1782 around the French Fort Frontenac, was captured by the English 1748, and renamed in honour of George III.

Kinnock British Labour Party leader Neil Kinnock.

Kingston-upon-Hull /'kɪŋstən əpɒn 'hʌl/ official name of ◊Hull, city in Humberside in NE England.

Kingston upon Thames /'kɪŋstən əpɒn 'temz/ borough of Greater London, England, on the S bank of the Thames, 16 km/10 mi SW of London; administrative headquarters of Surrey; population (1983) 133,600. Industries include metalworking, plastic and paint. The coronation stone of the Saxon kings is still preserved here.

Kingstown /'kɪŋztaʊn/ former name for ◊Dún Laoghaire, port near Dublin, Ireland.

Kingstown /'kɪŋztaʊn/ capital and principal port of St Vincent and the Grenadines, West Indies, in the SW of the island of St Vincent; population (1987) 29,000.

King-Te-Chen alternative spelling of ◊Jingdezhen, town in China.

kinkajou Central and South American mammal *Potos flavus* of the raccoon family. Yellowish-brown, with a rounded face and slim body, the kinkajou grows to 55 cm/1.8 ft long with a 50 cm/1.6 ft tail, and has short legs with sharp claws. It spends its time in the trees and has a prehensile tail. It feeds largely on fruit.

Kinki region of S Honshu island, Japan; population(1986) 21,932,000; area 33,070 sq km/ 12,773 sq mi. The chief city is Osaka.

Kinnock /'kɪnək/ Neil 1942– . British Labour politician, party leader from 1983. Born and educated in Wales, he was elected to represent a Welsh constituency in Parliament 1970 (Islwyn from 1983). A noted orator, he was further left than prime ministers Wilson and Callaghan, but as party leader (in succession to Michael Foot) adopted a more moderate position, initiating a major policy review 1988–89. He initiated the expulsion of the left-wing Militant Tendency members from the Labour Party 1986.

Kinross-shire /kɪn'rɒs/ former county of E central Scotland, merged in 1975 in Tayside region. Kinross was the county town.

kin selection in biology, the idea that ◊altruism shown to genetic relatives can be worthwhile, because those relatives share some genes with the individual that is behaving altruistically and may continue to reproduce; see ◊inclusive fitness.

Alarm-calling in response to predators is an example of a behaviour that may have evolved through kin selection: relatives that are warned of danger can escape and continue to breed, even if the alarm caller is caught.

Kinsey /'kɪnzi/ Alfred 1894–1956. US researcher, whose studies of male and female sexual behaviour 1948–53, based on questionnaires, were the first serious published research on this topic.

Kinshasa /kɪn'ʃɑːsə/ formerly *Léopoldville* capital of Zaïre on the river Zaïre, 400 km/250 mi

inland from Matadi; population (1984) 2,654,000. Industries include chemicals, textiles, engineering, food processing, and furniture. It was founded by the explorer Henry Stanley 1887.

kinship in anthropology, human relationship based on blood or marriage, and sanctified by law and custom. Kinship forms the basis for most human societies and for such social groupings as the family, clan, or tribe.

Kinship is universal, although its social significance varies from society to society. Most human societies have evolved strict social rules, customs, and taboos regarding kinship, particularly concerning sexual behaviour (such as the prohibition of incest).

Kinski /'kɪnski/ Klaus 1926– . German actor who has appeared in several Werner Herzog films such as *Aguirre Wrath of God* 1972, *Nosferatu* 1978, and *Venom* 1982. His other films include *For a Few Dollars More* 1965 and *Dr Zhivago* 1965.

Kipling /'kɪplɪŋ/ (Joseph) Rudyard 1865–1936. British writer, born in India. His stories for children include the *Jungle Books* 1894–1895, *Stalky and Co* 1899, and the *Just So Stories* 1902. Other works include the novel *Kim* 1901, poetry, and the unfinished autobiography *Something of Myself* 1937. In his heyday he enjoyed enormous popularity, but was subsequently denigrated for alleged 'jingoist imperialism'. Nobel prize 1907.

Born in Bombay, Kipling was educated at the United Services College at Westward Ho, England, which provided the background for *Stalky and Co*. He worked as a journalist in India 1882–89; during these years he wrote *Plain Tales from the Hills* 1888, *Soldiers Three* 1890, *Wee Willie Winkie* 1890, and others. Returning to London he published *The Light that Failed* 1890 and *Barrack-Room Ballads* 1892. He lived largely in the USA 1892–96, where he produced the two *Jungle Books* and *Captains Courageous* 1897. Settling in Sussex, SE England, he published *Kim* (set in India), the *Just So Stories*, *Puck of Pook's Hill* 1906, and *Rewards and Fairies* 1910.

Kirchhoff /'kɪəkhɒf/ Gustav Robert 1824–1887. German physicist, who with ◊Bunsen used the spectroscope to show that all elements, heated to incandescence, have their individual spectra.

Kirchner /'kɪəknə/ Ernst Ludwig 1880–1938. German Expressionist artist, a leading member of the group *Die* ◊*Brücke* in Dresden from 1905 and in Berlin from 1911. He suffered a breakdown during World War I and settled in Switzerland, where he committed suicide.

His Dresden work, which includes woodcuts, shows the influence of African art. In Berlin he turned to city scenes and portraits, using lurid colours and bold diagonal paint strokes recalling woodcut technique.

Kirghiz a pastoral people who inhabit the Central Asian region bounded by the Hindu Kush, the Himalayas, and the Tian Shan mountains. The

Kipling British short-story writer, novelist, and poet Rudyard Kipling.

Kirchner Self-Portrait with a Model *(1907),
Kunsthalle, Hamburg.*

Kirghiz are Sunni Muslims and their Turkic language belongs to the Altaic family.

There are approximately 1,500,000 Kirghiz divided between the Soviet Union (Tadzhikstan, Uzbekistan, and Kirghizia), China (Xinjiang), and Afghanistan (Wakhan corridor). The most isolated group, because of its geographical situation and international border problems, is found in Afghanistan. During the winter these people live in individual family yurts (felt-covered tents). In summer they come together in larger settlements comprising up to 20 yurts. They herd sheep, goats, and yaks, and use Bactrian camels for transporting their possessions. The highest political authority is traditionally entitled khan.

Kirghizia /kɜːˈɡɪzɪə/ constituent republic of the USSR from 1936, part of Soviet Central Asia
area 198,500 sq km/76,641 sq mi
capital Frunze
physical mountainous, an extension of the Tian Shan range
products cereals, sugar, cotton, coal, oil, sheep, yaks, horses
population (1987) 4,143,000; Kirghiz 48% (related to the Kazakhs, they are of Mongol–Tatar origin), Russian 26%, Uzbek 12%, Ukrainian 3%, Tatar 2%
language Kirghiz
religion Sunni Islam

Kirghizia

Kiribati
Republic of

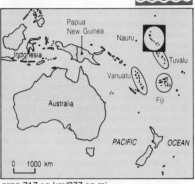

area 717 sq km/277 sq mi
capital and port Bairiki (on Tarawa Atoll)
physical comprises 33 Pacific islands: the Gilbert, Phoenix, and Line Islands, and Banaba (Ocean Island)
head of state and government Ieremia T Tabai from 1979

history annexed by Russia 1864, it was part of an independent Turkestan republic 1917–24, when it was incorporated in the USSR.
Kiribati /ˈkɪrɪbæs/ republic in the central Pacific, comprising three groups of coral atolls: the 16 Gilbert Islands, eight uninhabited Phoenix Islands, eight of the 11 Line Islands, and the volcanic island of Banaba.
government Kiribati's 1979 constitution provides for a president, the *Beretitenti*, who is head of both state and government, and is elected by universal suffrage for a four-year term, and a single-chamber legislature, the *Maneaba ni Maungatabu*. The president may not serve more than three terms. The *Maneaba* has 40 members: 38 popularly elected, one elected to represent Banaba, and the attorney-general. It also serves a four-year term. The president governs with the help of a vice president and cabinet chosen from and responsible to the *Maneaba*. There are no formal political parties, all candidates for the *Maneaba* fighting as independents, although government and opposition factions are subsequently formed within the assembly.
history The first Europeans to visit the area were the Spanish in 1606. The 16 predominantly Micronesian-peopled Gilbert Islands and nine predominantly Melanesian-peopled Ellice Islands became a British protectorate in 1892, and then the Gilbert and Ellice Islands Colony (GEIC) in 1916. The colony was occupied by Japan 1942–43 and was the scene of fierce fighting between Japanese and US forces. In preparation for self-government, a legislative council was set up in 1963, and in 1972 a governor took over from the British high commissioner. In 1974 the legislative council was replaced by an elected house of assembly and in 1975, when the Ellice Islands separated and became Tuvalu, GEIC was renamed the Gilbert Islands. The islands achieved internal self-government in 1977 and full independence within the Commonwealth in 1979, under the name of Kiribati, with Ieremia Tabai as their first president. He was re-elected 1982 and 1983.

The once phosphate-rich island of Banaba campaigned for independence or unification with Fiji in the mid-1970s. However, its environment has been ruined by overmining and its people have been forced to resettle on Rabi Island, 4,160 km/2,600 mi away in the Fiji group.
Kirin alternative name for ◊Jilin, Chinese province.
Kirk /kɜːk/ Norman 1923–1974. New Zealand Labour politician, prime minister 1972–74. Once an engine driver, he entered parliament in 1957 and led the Labour Party from 1964.

political system liberal democracy
political parties Christian Democratic Party, opposition faction within assembly; National Party, governing faction
exports copra
currency Australian dollar (2.24 = £1 Feb 1990)
population (1987) 66,250; annual growth rate 1.7%
language English and Gilbertese (official)
religion Christian, both Roman Catholic and Protestant
literacy 90% (1982)
GNP $30 million (1983) per capita.
chronology
1977 Gilbert Islands granted internal self-government.
1979 Achieved full independence, within the Commonwealth, as the Republic of Kiribati, with Ieremia Tabai as president.
1983 Tabai re-elected.
1985 Fishing agreement with Soviet state-owned company negotiated, prompting formation of Kiribati's first political party, the opposition Christian Democrats.
1987 Tabai re-elected.

Kirkcaldy /kəˈʌːdɪ/ seaport on the Firth of Forth, Fife region, Scotland; population (1981) 46,300. Manufactures include floor coverings and paper. Birthplace of the economist Adam Smith and the architect Robert Adam.
Kirkcudbright /kəˈkuːbri/ former county of S Scotland, merged 1975 in Dumfries and Galloway region. The county town was Kirkcudbright.
Kirkpatrick /kɜːkˈpætrɪk/ Jeane 1926– . US right-wing politician and professor of political science. She was an outspoken anti-Marxist permanent representative to the United Nations (as a Democrat) 1981–85, then registered as a Republican 1985.
Kirkuk /kɜːˈkuk/ town in NE Iraq; population (1985) 208,000. It is the centre of a major oilfield. Formerly it was served by several pipelines providing outlets to Lebanon, Syria, and other countries, but closures caused by the Iran–Iraq war left only the pipeline to Turkey operational.
Kirkwall /ˈkɜːkwɔːl/ administrative headquarters and port of the Orkneys, Scotland, on the N coast of the largest island, Mainland; population (1985) 6,000. The Norse cathedral of St Magnus dates from 1137.
Kirov /ˈkɪərɒf/ formerly (until 1934) *Vyatka* town NE of Gorky, on the Vyatka river, USSR; population (1987) 421,000. It is a rail and industrial centre for rolling stock, tyres, clothing, toys, and machine tools.
Kirov /ˈkɪərɒf/ Sergei Mironovich 1886–1934. Russian Bolshevik leader, who joined the party 1904 and took a prominent part in the 1917–20 civil war. His assassination 1934, possibly engineered by ◊Stalin, led to the political trials held during the next four years.
Kirovabad /ˌkɪrəvəˈbæd/ city in Azerbaijan Republic, USSR; population (1987) 270,000. Industries include cottons, woollens, and processed foods. It was known as Elizavetpol 1804–1918 and Gandzha prior to 1804 and again 1918–35.
Kirovograd /ˌkɪrəvəˈɡræd/ city in Ukrainian Republic, USSR; population (1987) 269,000. Manufacturing includes agricultural machinery and food processing. The city is on a lignite field. It was known as Yelizavetgrad until 1924 and Zinovyevsk 1924–36.
Kirriemuir /ˌkɪrɪˈmjʊə/ market town of Tayside, Scotland, called 'Thrums' in James Barrie's novels, and his birthplace.
Kisangani /ˌkɪsæŋˈɡɑːni/ formerly (until 1966) *Stanleyville* town in NE Zaïre, on the upper Zaïre river, below Stanley Falls; population (1984) 283,000. It is a communications centre.
Kishi /ˈkɪʃi/ Nobusuke 1896–1987. Japanese politician and prime minister 1957–60. A government

Kissinger *Henry Kissinger at a White House press conference, 26 Oct 1972.*

minister during World War II and imprisoned 1945, he was never put on trial and returned to politics 1953. During his premiership, Japan began a substantial rearmament programme and signed a new treaty with the USA, which gave greater equality in the relationship between the two states.

Kishinev /ˌkɪʃɪˈnjɒf/ capital of the Moldavian Republic, USSR; population (1987) 663,000. Industries include cement, food processing, tobacco, and textiles.

Founded 1436, it became Russian 1812. It was taken by Romania 1918, by the USSR 1940, and by Germany 1941, when it was totally destroyed. The USSR recaptured the site 1944, and rebuilding soon began. A series of large nationalist demonstrations were held in the city during 1989.

Kissinger /ˈkɪsɪndʒə/ Henry 1923– . German-born US diplomat. In 1969 he was appointed assistant for National Security Affairs by President Nixon, and was secretary of state 1973–77. His missions to the USSR and China improved US relations with both countries, and he took part in negotiating US withdrawal from Vietnam 1973 and in Arab-Israeli peace negotiations 1973–75. Nobel Peace Prize 1973.

Born in Bavaria, Kissinger emigrated to the USA 1938. After work in army counter-intelligence, he won a scholarship to Harvard, and subsequently became a government consultant. His secret trips to Beijing and Moscow led to Nixon's visits to both countries and a general détente. In 1973 he shared a Nobel Peace Prize with Le Duc Tho, the North Vietnamese Politburo member, for his part in the Vietnamese peace negotiations, and in 1976 he was involved in the negotiations in Africa arising from the Angola and Rhodesia crises. In 1983, President Reagan appointed him to head a bipartisan commission on Central America.

Kiswahili another name for the ◊Swahili language.

Kitaj /kɪˈtaɪ/ Ron B 1932– . US painter and printmaker, active in Britain. His work is mainly figurative, and his distinctive decorative pale palette was in part inspired by studies of the Impressionist Degas. Much of Kitaj's work is outside the predominant avant-garde trend and inspired by diverse historical styles. Some compositions are in triptych form.

Kitakyushu /ˌkiːtəˈkjuːʃuː/ industrial (coal, steel, chemicals, cotton thread, plate glass, alcohol) city and port in Japan, on the Hibiki Sea, N Kyushu, formed 1963 by the amalgamation of Moji, Kokura, Tobata, Yawata, and Wakamatsu; population (1987) 1,042,000. A tunnel 1942 links it with Honshu. Moji was opened to foreign trade 1887.

Kitasato /ˌkiːtəˈsɑːtəʊ/ Shibasaburo 1852–1931. Japanese bacteriologist who discovered the plague bacillus while investigating an outbreak of plague in Hong Kong.

Kitasato was the first to grow the tetanus bacillus in pure culture. He and the German bacteriologist Behring discovered that increasing non-lethal doses of tetanus toxin gives immunity to the disease. He founded the Tokyo Institute

for Infectious Diseases 1914, and was a friend and one-time student of Robert ◊Koch.

Kitchener /ˈkɪtʃɪnə/ city in SW Ontario, Canada; population (1986) 151,000, metropolitan area (with Waterloo) 311,000. Manufacturing includes agricultural machinery and tyres. Settled by Germans from Pennsylvania in the 1800s, it was known as Berlin until 1916.

Kitchener /ˈkɪtʃɪnə/ Horatio Herbert, Earl Kitchener of Khartoum 1850–1916. British soldier and administrator. He defeated the Sudanese dervishes at Omdurman 1898 and re-occupied Khartoum. In South Africa, he was chief of staff 1900–02 during the Boer War, and commanded the forces in India 1902–09. He was appointed war minister on the outbreak of World War I, and drowned when his ship was sunk on the way to Russia.

Kithener was born in County Kerry, Ireland. He was commissioned 1871, and transferred to the Egyptian Army 1882. Promoted to commander-in-chief 1892, he forced a French expedition to withdraw in the ◊Fashoda Incident. During the South African War he acted as Lord Roberts's chief of staff. He subsequently commanded the forces in India and acted as British agent in Egypt, and in 1914 received an earldom. As British secretary of state for war from 1914, he modernized the British forces.

kite one of several birds of prey in the family Accipitridae, found in all parts of the world except the Americas. The **red kite** *Milvus milvus*, found in Europe, has a forked tail and narrow wings, and is about 60 cm/2 ft long. There are 50 known pairs in Wales, the only place in the UK where the kite is found. The darker and slightly smaller **black kite** *Milvus migrans* is found over most of the Old World. It scavenges in addition to hunting.

Kitimat /ˈkɪtɪmæt/ port near Prince Rupert, British Columbia, Canada; population (1981) 4,300. Founded 1955, it has one of the world's largest aluminium smelters, powered by the Kemano hydro-electric scheme.

Kitwe /ˈkɪtweɪ/ commercial centre for the Zambian copperbelt; population (1987) 450,000. To the south are Zambia's emerald mines.

Kitzbühel /ˈkɪtsbjuːəl/ winter-sports resort in the Austrian Tirol, NE of Innsbruck; population (1985) 9,000.

Kivu /ˈkiːvuː/ lake in the Great Rift Valley between Zaïre and Rwanda, about 105 km/65 mi long. The chief port is Bukavu.

kiwi flightless bird *Apteryx* found only in New Zealand. Kiwis have long and hair-like brown plumage, a very long beak with nostrils at the tip, and is nocturnal and insectivorous. The egg is larger in relation to the bird's size (similar to a domestic chicken) than that of any other bird.

All kiwi species have declined since European settlement of New Zealand, and the little spotted kiwi is most at risk. It survives only on one small island reservation, which was stocked with birds from the mainland.

kiwi fruit plant *Actinidithia chinensis*, family Actinidiaceae, also known as **Chinese gooseberry**, with oval fruit of similar flavour to a gooseberry, and with a fuzzy brown skin. It

kiwi

little spotted kiwi

Klee They're Biting *(1920) Tate Gallery, London.*

is commercially grown on a large scale in New Zealand.

Klaipeda /ˈklaɪpɪdə/ formerly **Memel** port in the Lithuanian Republic of the USSR, on the Baltic coast at the mouth of the Dange river; population (1987) 201,000. Industries include shipbuilding and iron foundries. It was founded 1252 as the castle of Memelburg by the Teutonic Knights, joined the ◊Hanseatic League soon after, and has changed hands between Sweden, Russia, and Germany. Lithuania annexed Klaipeda 1923, and after German occupation 1939–45, it was restored to Lithuania.

Klammer /ˈklæmə/ Franz 1953– . Austrian skier, who won a record 35 World Cup downhill races between 1974 and 1985. Olympic gold medallist 1976. He was the combined world champion 1974, and the World Cup downhill champion 1975–78 and 1983.

Klaproth /ˈklæprəʊt/ Martin Heinrich 1743–1817. German chemist who first identified the elements uranium, zirconium, cerium, and titanium.

Klee /kleɪ/ Paul 1879–1940. Swiss painter. He settled in Munich 1906, joined the ◊Blaue Reiter group 1912, and worked at the Bauhaus school of art and design 1920–31, returning to Switzerland 1933. His style in the 1920s–30s was dominated by humorous linear fantasies.

Klee travelled with the painter August Macke to Tunisia in 1914, a trip that transformed his sense of colour. The Klee Foundation, Berne, has a large collection of his work.

Klein /klaɪn/ Melanie 1882–1960. Austrian child psychoanalyst. She pioneered child psychoanalysis and play studies, and was influenced by Sigmund ◊Freud's theories. She published *The Psychoanalysis of Children* in 1960.

Klein analysed the behaviour of children through the use of play techniques; this practice was later adopted in child guidance clinics. Her research into the origins of mental disorder psychosis, schizophrenia, and depression extended the range of patients who can usefully undergo psycholanalysis.

Klein /klaɪn/ Yves 1928–1962. French painter of bold abstracts and provocative experimental works, including imprints of nude bodies.

Kleist /klaɪst/ (Bernd) Heinrich (Wilhelm) von 1777–1811. German dramatist, whose comedy *Der zerbrochene Krug/The Broken Pitcher* 1808, and drama *Prinz Friedrich von Homburg/The Prince of Homburg* 1811, achieved success only after his suicide.

Klemperer /ˈklɛmpərə/ Otto 1885–1973. German conductor, who is celebrated for his interpretation of contemporary and classical music (especially ◊Beethoven and ◊Brahms). He conducted the Los Angeles Orchestra 1933–39 and the Philharmonia Orchestra, London, from 1959.

kleptomania (Greek *kleptēs* 'thief') a behavioural disorder characterized by an overpowering desire to possess articles for which one has no need.

Kliegl /'kliːgəl/ John H 1869–1959 and Anton T 1872–1927. German-born US brothers, who in 1911 invented the brilliant carbon-arc (klieg) lights used in television and films. They also created scenic effects for theatre and film.

Klimt /klɪmt/ Gustav 1862–1918. Austrian painter, influenced by Jugendstil ('Youth Style', a form of Art Nouveau); a founder member of the Vienna ◊*Sezession* group 1897. His works include mosaics, and his paintings have a similar jewelled effect, for example *The Kiss* 1909 (Musée des Beaux-Arts, Strasbourg). He painted many portraits.

Kline /klaɪn/ Franz 1910–1962. US Abstract Expressionist painter. He created large, graphic compositions in monochrome using angular forms, like magnified calligraphic brushstrokes.

Klondike /'klɒndaɪk/ former gold-mining area in ◊Yukon, Canada, and named after the river valley where gold was found 1896. About 30,000 people moved there during the following 15 years. Silver is still mined there.

Klopstock /'klɒpʃtɒk/ Friedrich Gottlieb 1724–1803. German poet, whose religious epic *Der Messias/The Messiah* 1748–73 and *Oden/Odes* 1771 anticipated Romanticism.

Klosters alpine skiing resort NE of Davos in E Switzerland.

km abbreviation for *kilometre*.

knapweed plant *Centaurea nigra*, also known as *hardhead*, family Compositae. The hard bract-covered buds break into purple composite heads.

Knaresborough /'neəzbərə/ market town in N Yorkshire, England; 6 km/4 mi NE of Harrogate; population (1981) 13,000. It has a castle dating from about 1070.

Kneller /'nelə/ Godfrey 1646–1723. German-born painter, who lived in London from 1674. He was court portraitist to Charles II, James II, William III, and George I.

His work includes the series *Hampton Court Beauties* (Hampton Court, Richmond, Surrey, a sequel to Lely's *Windsor Beauties*), and 48 portraits of the members of the Whig Kit Cat Club 1702–17 (National Portrait Gallery, London).

Knesset the Israeli parliament, consisting of a single chamber of 120 members elected for a period of four years.

Knickerbocker School US group of writers working in New York in the early 19th century, including Washington Irving, James Kirke Paulding (1779–1860), and Fitz-Greene Halleck.

knife fish genus *Gymnotus* and allied forms, in which the body is deep at the front, drawn to a narrow or pointed tail at the rear, the main fin being the well-developed long ventral which completes the knife-like shape. The ventral fin is rippled for forward or backward locomotion. Knife fish produce electrical fields which they use for navigation.

Knight /naɪt/ Laura 1877–1970. British painter. She focused on detailed, narrative scenes of Romany, fairground, and circus life, and ballet.

knighthood, order of fraternity carrying with it the rank of knight, admission to which is granted as a mark of royal favour or as a reward for public services. During the Middle Ages such fraternities fell into two classes, religious and secular. The first class, including the ◊Templars and the *Knights of ◊St John*, consisted of knights who had taken religious vows and devoted themselves to military service against the Saracens (Arabs) or other non-Christians. The secular orders probably arose from bands of knights engaged in the service of a prince or great noble.

These knights wore the badge of their patrons or the emblems of their patron saints. A *knight bachelor* belongs to the lowest stage of knighthood, not being a member of any specially named order. See also ◊medal.

knot

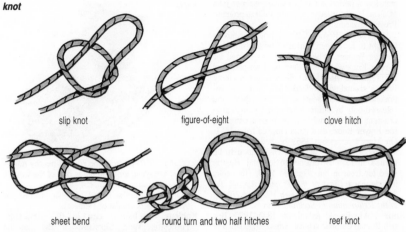

slip knot   figure-of-eight   clove hitch

sheet bend   round turn and two half hitches   reef knot

The *Order of the Garter*, founded about 1347, is the oldest in the UK; there are eight other British orders: the *Thistle* founded 1687, the *St Patrick* 1788, the *Bath* 1725, the *Star of India* 1861, the *St Michael and St George* 1818, the *Indian Empire* 1878, the *Royal Victorian Order* 1896, and the *Order of the British Empire* (OBE) 1917. The *Order of Merit*, founded 1902, comprises the sovereign and no more than 24 prominent individuals.

Most of the ancient European orders, such as the *Order of the Golden Fleece*, have disappeared as a result of political changes.

Knipper /'knɪpə/ Lev Konstantinovich 1898–1974. Soviet composer. His early work shows the influence of ◊Stravinsky, but after 1932 he wrote in a more popular idiom, as in the symphony *Poem of Komsomol Fighters* 1933–34 with its mass battle songs. He is known in the West for his song 'Cavalry of the Steppes'.

knitting method of making fabric by looping and knotting yarn with two needles. Knitting may have developed from ◊crochet, which uses a single hooked needle, or from *netting*, using a shuttle.

A mechanized process for making stockings was developed in the 16th century, but it was not until after World War II that machine knitting was revolutionized with the introduction of synthetic yarns, coloured dyes, and methods of texturing and elasticizing.

knocking in a spark-ignition petrol engine, a phenomenon that occurs when unburned fuel–air mixture explodes in the combustion chamber before being ignited by the spark. The resulting shock waves produce a metallic knocking sound. Loss of power occurs, which can be prevented by reducing the compression ratio, re-designing the geometry of the combustion chamber, or increasing the octane number of

Knossos The palace of Minos in Knossos, Crete, showing the grand staircase in the east wing (the domestic quarter).

the petrol (usually by the use of lead tetraethyl anti-knock additives).

Knossos /'knɒsɒs/ the chief city of ◊Minoan Crete, near present-day Iráklion, 6 km/4 mi SE of Candia. The archaeological site excavated by Arthur ◊Evans 1899–1935, dates from about 2000 BC, and includes the palace throne room and a labyrinth, legendary home of the ◊Minotaur.

Excavation of the palace of the legendary King Minos showed that the story of Theseus's encounter with the Minotaur in a labyrinth was possibly derived from the ritual 'bull-leaping' by youths and girls depicted in the palace frescoes and from the mazelike layout of the palace.

knot wading bird *Calidris canutus* of the sandpiper family. It is about 25 cm/10 in long. In the winter, it is grey above and white below, but in the breeding season, it is brick-red on the head and chest, and black on its wings and back. It feeds on insects and molluscs. Breeding in arctic regions, knots travel widely in winter, to be found as far south as South Africa, Australasia, and southern parts of South America.

knot unit by which a ship's speed is measured, equivalent to 1 ◊nautical mile per hour (1 knot = about 1.15 miles per hour). It is also used in aviation, not yet having been replaced by the SI unit, metres per second.

knot an intertwinement of parts of one or more ropes, cords, or strings, to bind them together or to other objects. It is constructed so that the strain on the knot will draw it tighter. Bends or hitches are knots used to fasten ropes together or to other objects; when two ropes are joined end to end, they are spliced. The craft of ◊macramé uses knots to form decorative pieces and fringes.

knotgrass annual plant *Polygonum aviculare* of the dock family, growing on bare ground including seashores. Often low-growing, but with stems up to 2 m /6 ft long, the small lance-shaped leaves have bases that sheathe the stem, giving a superficial resemblance to grass.

The small pinkish flowers grow in small clusters in the leaf axils in late summer, followed by seeds which are a favourite with birds. Knotgrass grows worldwide except in the polar regions.

knowledge-based system (KBS) a computer program that uses an encoding of human knowledge to help solve problems. It was first discovered in research into ◊artificial intelligence that adding heuristics (rules of thumb) enabled programs to tackle problems that were otherwise difficult to solve by the usual techniques of computer science.

Chess-playing programs have been strengthened by including knowledge of what makes a good position, or about overall strategies, rather than relying solely on the computer's ability to calculate variations.

Knox /nɒks/ John *c.* 1505–1572. Scottish Protestant reformer, founder of the Church of Scotland. He spent several years in exile for his beliefs, including a period in Geneva where he met John ◊Calvin. He returned to Scotland 1559 to promote Presbyterianism.

Originally a Roman Catholic priest, Knox is thought to have been converted by the reformer George Wishart. When Wishart was burned for heresy, Knox went into hiding, but later preached the reformed doctrines. He was captured by French troops in Scotland 1547, and was imprisoned in France, sentenced to the galleys, and released only by intercession of the British government 1549. In England he assisted in compiling the Prayer Book, as a royal chaplain from 1551. On Mary's accession 1553 he fled abroad and in 1557 was, in his absence, condemned to be burned. In 1559 he returned to Scotland. He was tried for treason but acquitted 1563. His books include *First Blast of the Trumpet Against the Monstrous Regiment of Women* 1558 and *History of the Reformation in Scotland* 1586.

Knox /nɒks/ Ronald Arbuthnott 1888–1957. British Roman Catholic scholar, whose translation of the Bible (1945–49) was officially approved by the Roman Catholic Church.

Knoxville /'nɒksvɪl/ city in E Tennessee, USA; population (1986) 591,000. It is the centre of a mining and agricultural region, and the administrative headquarters of the ◊Tennessee Valley Authority. The university was founded 1794.

Knutsford /'nʌtsfəd/ town in Cheshire, England; the novelist Elizabeth ◊Gaskell, who lived in Knutsford for 22 years and is buried there, wrote of it under the name Cranford; it is now a suburb of Manchester.

koala marsupial *Phascolarctos cinereus* of the family Phalangeridae, found only in E Australia. It feeds almost entirely on eucalyptus shoots. It is about 60 cm/2 ft long, and resembles a bear. It has greyish fur, which led to its almost complete extermination by hunters. Under protection from 1936, it has rapidly increased in numbers.

kōan in Zen Buddhism, a superficially nonsensical question or riddle used by a Zen master to help a pupil achieve satori (◊enlightenment). It is important in the Rinzai school of Zen.

A *kōan* supposedly cannot be understood through the processes of logic; its solution requires attainment of a higher level of insight. An often repeated example is 'What is the sound of one hand clapping?' An answer would be that the word 'clapping' by definition involves two hands, and therefore this particular *kōan* is unanswerable.

Kobarid /'kəʊbərɪd/ formerly *Caporetto* village on the Isonzo river, in Slovenia, NW Yugoslavia. Originally in Hungary, it was in Italy from 1918, and in 1947 became Kobarid. During World War I German-Austrian troops defeated Italian forces there 1917.

Kobe /'kəʊbeɪ/ deep water port in S Honshu, Japan; population (1987) 1,413,000. *Port Island*,

koala

created 1960–68 from the rock of nearby mountains, area 5 sq km/2 sq mi, is one of the world's largest construction projects.

København /kɜ:bən'haʊn/ Danish name for ◊Copenhagen, capital of Denmark.

Koblenz /'kəʊblents/ city in the Rhineland-Palatinate, West Germany, at the junction of the rivers Rhine and Mosel; population (1988) 110,000. The city dates back to Roman times. It is a centre of communications and the wine trade, with industries (shoes, cigars, paper).

Koch /kɒx/ Robert 1843–1910. German bacteriologist. Koch and his assistants devised the means to culture bacteria outside the body, and formulated the rules for showing whether or not a bacterium is the cause of a disease. Nobel Prize for Medicine 1905.

His techniques enabled him to identify the bacteria responsible for diseases like anthrax, cholera, and tuberculosis. This did not automatically lead to cures, but was crucial in their discovery. Koch was a great teacher, and many of his pupils, such as ◊Kitasato, ◊Ehrlich, and ◊Behring, became outstanding scientists.

Kodály /'kəʊdaɪ/ Zoltán 1882–1967. Hungarian composer. With ◊Bartók, he recorded and transcribed Magyar folk music, the scales and rhythm of which he incorporated in a deliberately nationalist style. His works include the cantata *Psalmus Hungaricus* 1923, a comic opera *Háry János* 1925–27, and orchestral dances and variations.

Kodiak /'kəʊdiæk/ island off the S coast of Alaska, site of a US naval base; area 9,505 sq km/3,670 sq mi. It is the home of the world's largest ◊bear. The town of Kodiak is the largest US fishing port (mainly salmon).

Koestler /'kɜ:stlə/ Arthur 1905–1983. Hungarian author. Imprisoned by the Nazis in France 1940, he escaped to England. His novel *Darkness at Noon* 1941 is a fictional account of the Stalinist purges, and draws on his experiences as a prisoner under sentence of death during the Spanish Civil War. He also wrote extensively about creativity, parapsychology, politics, and culture. A member of the Voluntary Euthanasia Society, he committed suicide, possibly as a result of

Kohl *West German chancellor Helmut Kohl at the first meeting of the European Community Emergency Summit in Brussels, Feb 1988.*

having Parkinson's disease. He endowed Britain's first chair of parapsychology at Edinburgh, established 1984.

Born in Budapest, and educated as an engineer in Vienna, he became a journalist in Palestine and the USSR. He joined the Communist party in Berlin 1931, but left it 1938. His account of being held by the Nazis are contained in *Scum of the Earth* 1941. Other novels include *Thieves in the Night* 1946, *The Lotus and the Robot* 1960, and *The Call Girls* 1972. Nonfiction includes *The Yogi and the Commissar* 1945, *The Sleepwalkers* 1959, *The Act of Creation* 1964, *The Ghost in the Machine* 1967, *The Roots of Coincidence* 1972, *The Heel of Achilles* 1974, and *The Thirteenth Tribe* 1976. Autobiographical works include *Arrow in the Blue* 1952 and *The Invisible Writing* 1954.

Koh-i-noor (Persian 'mountain of light') a fabulous diamond, originally part of the Aurangzeb treasure, seized in 1739 by the shah of Iran from the Moguls in India, taken back by Sikhs, and acquired by Britain in 1849 when the Punjab was annexed.

kohl (Arabic) powdered antimony sulphide, used in Asia and the Middle East to darken the area around the eyes.

Kohl /kəʊl/ Helmut 1930– . West German conservative politician, leader of the Christian Democratic Union (CDU) from 1976, and chancellor from 1982.

Kohl studied law and history before entering the chemical industry. Elected to the Rhineland-Palatinate *Land* (state) parliament 1959, he became state premier 1969. After the 1976 Bundestag (federal parliament) elections Kohl led the CDU in opposition. He became federal chancellor (prime minister) 1982, when the Free Democratic Party (FDP) withdrew their support from the socialist Schmidt government, and was elected at the head of the new CDU-CSU-FDP coalition. From 1984 Kohl was implicated in the Flick bribes scandal over the illegal business funding of political parties, but he was cleared of all charges by the Bonn public prosecutor May 1986, and was re-elected chancellor Jan 1987.

kohlrabi variety of kale *Brassica oleracea*. Leaves shoot from a globular swelling on the main stem; it is used for food, and resembles a turnip.

Kokand /kə'kænd/ oasis town in Uzbek Republic of USSR; population (1981) 156,000. It was the capital of Kokand khanate when annexed by Russia 1876. Industries include fertilizers, cotton, and silk.

Kokhba /'kɒxbə/ Bar. Name adopted by Simeon bar Koziba, died 135. Jewish leader of the revolt against the Hellenization campaign of the Roman emperor Hadrian 132–35, which led to the razing of Jerusalem. He was killed in battle.

Koko Nor /'kəʊkəʊ 'nɔ:/ Mongolian form of ◊Qinghai, province of China.

Kokoschka /kə'kɒʃkə/ Oskar 1886–1980. Austrian Expressionist painter and writer, who lived in the UK from 1938. Initially influenced by the

Knox *An engraving of the 16th-century Scottish Protestant reformer John Knox.*

Koestler *Hungarian-born writer Arthur Koestler was imprisoned in Spain by Franco, in France by the Nazis, and briefly in Britain, where he later settled.*

Vienna ◊**Sezession** painters, he developed a disturbingly expressive portrait style. His writings include several plays.

His early work caused a sensation in Vienna during the first decade of this century. After World War I he worked in Dresden, then in Prague, and fled from the Nazis to England, taking British citizenship 1947. To portraiture he added panoramic landscapes and townscapes in the 1920s and 1930s, and political allegories in the 1950s.

kola alternative spelling of ◊cola, genus of tropical tree.

Kola /'kəʊlə/ (Russian *Kol'skiy Poluostrov*) peninsula in N USSR, bounded by the White Sea on the S and E, and by the Barents Sea on the N; area 129,500 sq km/50,000 sq mi; coterminous with Murmansk region. Apatite and other minerals are exported. To the NW the low-lying granite plateau adjoins Norway's thinly populated county of Finnmark, and Soviet troops are heavily concentrated here.

Kolchak /kɒl'tʃæk/ Alexander Vasilievich 1875–1920. Russian admiral, commander of the White forces in Siberia during the Russian Civil War. He proclaimed himself Supreme Ruler of Russia 1918, but was later handed over to the Bolsheviks by his own men and shot.

Kolchugino /kɒl'tʃuːɡɪnəʊ/ former name (to 1925) of ◊Leninsk-Kuznetsky, town in USSR.

Kolhapur /ˌkəʊləˈpʊə/ industrial city in Maharashtra, India, noted as a film production centre; population (1981) 346,000.

kolkhoz Russian term for a ◊collective farm, as opposed to a ◊sovkhoz or state-owned farm.

Koller /'kɒlə/ Carl 1857–1944. Austrian ophthalmologist who introduced local anaesthesia 1884.

When ◊Freud discovered the pain-killing properties of ◊cocaine, Koller recognized its potential as a local anaesthetic. He carried out early experiments on animals and on himself, and the technique quickly became standard in ◊ophthalmology, dentistry, and other areas in cases where general anaesthesia is unnecessary and exposes the patient to needless risk.

Kollontai /ˌkɒlənˈtaɪ/ Alexandra 1872–1952. Russian revolutionary, politician, and writer. In 1905 she published *On the Question of the Class Struggle*, and was the only female member of the first Bolshevik government as Commissar for Public Welfare. She campaigned for domestic reforms such as acceptance of free love, simplification of divorce laws, and collective childcare.

In 1896 she saw the appalling conditions for factory workers in Russia while on a tour of a large textile factory with her husband. She was so enraged by his view that only small improvements were necessary that she left him and devoted herself to improving conditions for working women. She was harassed by the police for her views and in 1914 went into exile in Germany. On her return to Russia she joined the Bolsheviks and toured the USA to argue against its involvement in World War I. She organized the first all-Russian Congress of Working and Peasant Women 1918. Her book *The Love of Worker Bees* 1923 aroused great controversy. She was sent abroad by Stalin, first as trade minister, then as ambassador to Sweden 1943. She took part in the armistice negotiations ending the Soviet-Finnish War 1944.

Kollwitz /'kɒlvɪts/ Käthe 1867–1945. German sculptor and printmaker. Her early series of etchings of workers and their environment are realistic and harshly expressive. Later themes include war, death, and maternal love.

Köln /kɜːln/ German form of ◊Cologne, city in West Germany.

Kolwezi /kɒl'weɪzɪ/ mining town in Shaba province, SE Zaïre; population (1985) 82,000. It is important for copper and cobalt. In 1978 former police of the province invaded from Angola and massacred some 650 of the inhabitants.

Komi /'kəʊmi/ autonomous Soviet republic in the NW Urals, USSR; area 415,900 sq km/

Kollwitz *One of a series of large lithographs entitled* Death *1934–35, by German artist Käthe Kollwitz.*

DIE LEBENDEN DEM TOTEN . ERINNERUNG AN DEN 15. JANUAR 1919

160,540 sq mi; population (1986) 1,200,000. Its capital is Syktyvkar.

Komi a member of a Finnish people living mainly in Komi, USSR, in the NW Urals. Their language is Zyrian, and belongs to the Finno-Ugric family.

Komsomol Russian name for the USSR's All-Union Leninist Communist Youth League. Founded in 1918, it acts as the youth section of the Communist party.

Kong Zi Pinyin form of ◊Confucius, Chinese philosopher.

Koniev /'kɒnjef/ Ivan Stepanovich 1898–1973. Soviet marshal, who in World War II liberated Ukraine from the invading German forces 1943, and advanced from the south on Berlin to link up with the British-US forces.

Königsberg /'kɜːnɪɡzbeəɡ/ German name of ◊Kaliningrad, port in USSR.

Konoe /ˌkəʊnəʊˈjeɪ/ Fumimaro 1891–1946. Japanese politician and prime minister. Entering politics in the 1920s, Konoe was active in trying to curb the power of the army in government, and preventing an escalation of the war with China. He was prime minister for periods in the late 1930s, but finally resigned 1941 over differences with the army. He helped to engineer the fall of the ◊Tojo government 1944, but committed suicide after being suspected of war crimes.

Konstanz /'kɒnstænts/ German form of the town of ◊Constance.

Kon-Tiki /'kɒn 'tiːki/ legendary sun king who ruled the country later occupied by the ◊Incas, and was supposed to have migrated out into the Pacific. The name was used by explorer Thor Heyerdahl for his raft which sailed from Peru to the Pacific Islands 1947.

Konya /'kɒnjə/ (Roman *Iconium*) city in SW central Turkey; population (1985) 439,000. Carpets and silks are made here, and the city contains the monastery of the dancing ◊dervishes.

kookaburra or *laughing jackass* the largest of the world's kingfishers *Dacelo novaeguineae*, with an extraordinary laughing call. It feeds on insects and other small creatures. The body and tail measure 45 cm/18 in, the head is greyish with a dark eye stripe, and the back and wings are flecked brown with grey underparts. Its laugh is one of the most familiar sounds of the bush of E Australia.

kora 21-string instrument of W African origin, with a harp-like sound.

Koran (alternatively transliterated as *Quran*) the sacred book of Islam. Written in the purest Arabic, it contains 114 *suras* (chapters), and is stated

to have been divinely revealed to the prophet Muhammad about 616.

Korbut /'kɔːbʊt/ Olga 1955– . Soviet gymnast, who attracted world attention at the 1972 Olympic Games with her 'cheeky' floor routine, and won three gold medals.

Korda /'kɔːdə/ Alexander 1893–1956. Hungarian-born British film producer and director, a dominant figure during the 1930s and 1940s. His films include *The Private Life of Henry VIII* 1933, *The Third Man* 1950, and *Richard III* 1956.

Kordofan /ˌkɔːdəˈfɑːn/ province of central Sudan, known as the 'White Land'; area 146,932 sq km/56,752 sq mi; population (1983) 3,093,300. Although never an independent state, it has a character of its own. It is mainly undulating plain, with acacia scrub producing gum arabic, marketed in the chief town ◊El Obeid. Formerly a rich agricultural region, it has been overtaken by desertification.

Korea, history

2000 BC The foundation of the Korean state traditionally dates back to the **Tangun dynasty**.

1122–4th century The Chinese **Kija dynasty**.

10th century AD After centuries of internal war and invasion, Korea was united within its present boundaries.

16th century Japan invaded Korea for the first time, later withdrawing from a country it had devastated.

1905 Japan began to treat Korea as a protectorate.

1910 It was annexed by Japan. Many Japanese colonists settled in Korea, introducing both industrial and agricultural development.

1945 At the end of World War II, the Japanese in Korea surrendered, but the occupying forces at the ceasefire—the USSR north of the ◊38th parallel, and the USA south of it—resulted in a lasting division of the country as North and South Korea (see ◊Korea, North, and ◊Korea, South, for history since 1945).

Korean inhabitant of Korea. There are approximately 33 million in South Korea, 15 million in North Korea, and 3 million elsewhere, principally in Japan, China (Manchuria), and the USSR.

Korean language the language of Korea, written from the 5th century AD in Chinese characters until the invention of an alphabet by King Sejong 1443. The linguistic affiliations of Korean are unclear, but it appears to be distantly related to Japanese.

The alphabet was discouraged as 'vulgar letters' (*onmun*) and banned by the colonizing Japanese.

Korean War *US soldiers entrenched at the top of 'Old Baldy', Korea, Sept 1952.*

After World War II it was revived as 'top letters' (*hangul*).

Korea, North /kəˈrɪə/ country in E Asia, bounded N by China, E by the Sea of Japan, S by South Korea, and W by the Yellow Sea.

government Under the 1972 constitution, which replaced the 1948 Soviet-type constitution, the leading political figure is the president, who is head of the armed forces and executive head of government. The president is appointed for four-year terms by the 615-member supreme people's assembly, which is directly elected by universal suffrage. The assembly meets for brief sessions once or twice a year, its regular legislative business being carried out by a smaller permanent standing committee (Presidium). The president works with and presides over a powerful policy-making and supervisory central people's committee (which is responsible to the assembly for its activities) and an administrative and executive cabinet (Administration Council).

The controlling force in North Korea is the Communist Party (Workers' Party of Korea), headed since 1945 by Kim Il Sung. It leads the broader Democratic Front for the Reunification of the Fatherland (which includes the minor North Korean Democratic Party and the Religious Chungwoo Party) in putting forward single slates of candidates for election contests.

history For early history, see ◊Korea, history. The Democratic People's Republic of Korea was formed from the zone north of the 38th parallel of latitude, occupied by Soviet troops after Japan's

surrender in 1945. The USSR installed in power an 'Executive Committee of the Korean People', staffed by Soviet-trained Korean Communists, before North Korea was declared a People's Republic in 1948 under the leadership of the Workers' Party, with ◊Kim Il Sung as president. The remaining Soviet forces withdrew in 1949.

In 1950 North Korea, seeking unification of the Korean peninsula, launched a large-scale invasion of South Korea. This began the three-year-long ◊Korean War, which, after intervention by the USA (on the side of the South) and China (on the side of the North), ended in stalemate. The 38th parallel border between N and S was re-established by the armistice agreement of July 1953 and a United Nations–patrolled demilitarized buffer zone was created. North Korea has never accepted this agreement and remains committed to reunification.

Relations with the South have remained tense and hostile, despite the establishment in 1972 of a North–South coordinating committee to promote peaceful unification. Border incidents have been frequent and in Oct 1983 four South Korean cabinet ministers were assassinated in Rangoon (Burma) following a bombing incident organized by two North Korean army officers.

Domestically, the years since 1948 have seen economic development in a planned socialist manner. Factories were nationalized and agriculture collectivized in the 1950s, and priority in investment programmes has been given to heavy industry and rural mechanization. North Korean economic growth has, however, lagged behind that of its richer and more populous southern neighbour. In foreign affairs, North Korea adopted a neutral stance in the Sino-Soviet dispute, signing a friendship and mutual assistance treaty with China in 1961 while at the same time receiving economic and military aid from the Soviet Union. North Korea remained largely immune from the pluralist or market-socialist wave of reform that swept other communist nations in 1989–90, making only minor adjustments. Relations with the South have, however, showed signs of improving.

In recent years, North Korean politics have been dominated by the succession question, with Kim Il Sung seeking to establish his son, Kim Jong-Il (1941–), as sole heir designate. Kim Jong-Il has accompanied Kim Il Sung on diplomatic and factory tours, been designated Armed Forces Supreme Commander, begun to preside over key

party and state government meetings, and his portrait has been placed on public display across the country. Elements within the Workers' Party and armed forces appear, however, to oppose Kim's succession aims.

Korean War war 1950–53 between North Korea (supported by China) and South Korea, aided by the United Nations (including the UK, though the troops were mainly US). North Korean forces invaded the South 25 June 1950, and the Security Council of the United Nations, owing to a walkout by the USSR, voted to oppose them. After a 'concertina' campaign up and down the peninsula (initially led by US general ◊MacArthur), which ended in the restoration of the original boundary on the 38th parallel, an armistice was signed with the North, although South Korea did not participate.

Korea, South /kəˈrɪə/ country in E Asia, bordered to the N by North Korea, E by the Sea of Japan, S by the E China Sea, and W by the Yellow Sea.

government Under the 1987 constitution, executive power is held by the president, who is elected directly by popular vote. The president is restricted to one five-year term of office, and governs with a cabinet (state council) headed by a prime minister. Legislative authority resides in the single-chamber, 299-deputy national assembly *Kuk Hoe*, 224 of whose members are directly elected for four-year terms by universal suffrage in single-member constituencies, and the remainder of whom are appointed in accordance with a formula designed to reward the largest single assembly party. The assembly has the authority to impeach the president and to override presidential vetoes. There is also a nine-member constitutional court, and guarantees of freedom of speech, press, assembly, and association are written into the constitution.

The dominant party is the Democratic Liberal Party (DLP), which has strong support among the business community and the military. The main opposition party is the Party for Peace and Democracy (PPD) led by ◊Kim Dae Jung and based mainly in the underdeveloped SW region of Cholla.

history For early history, see ◊Korea, history. The Republic of Korea was formed out of the zone south of the 38th parallel of latitude which was occupied by US troops after Japan's surrender 1945. The US military government controlled the country until, following national elections, an independent republic was declared 1948. Dr Syngman ◊Rhee, leader of the right-wing Liberal Party, was the nation's first president in a constitution based on the US model. To begin with, the republic had to cope with a massive influx of refugees fleeing the Communist regime in the North; then came the 1950–53 ◊Korean War.

President Syngman Rhee, whose regime had been accused of corruption, resigned 1960 as a result of student-led disorder. A new parliamentary-style constitution gave greater power to the legislature, and the ensuing political instability precipitated a military coup led by Gen ◊Park Chung-Hee 1961. A presidential system of government was re-established, with Gen Park elected president 1963, and a major programme of industrial development began, involving government planning and financial support. This programme, utilizing the nation's plentiful supply of well-educated and industrious workers, was remarkably successful, with rapid industrial growth during the 1960s and 1970s as South Korea became a major exporter of light and heavy industrial goods.

Opposition to the repressive Park regime mounted during the 1970s. In response, martial law was imposed and in 1972 a new constitution strengthened the president's powers. A new clampdown on political dissent, launched 1975, was partially relaxed for the 1978 elections, but brought protests 1979 as economic conditions briefly deteriorated. President Park was assassinated later that year by the chief of the South

---

Korea, North
Democratic People's Republic of *(Chosun Minchu-chui Inmin Konghwa-guk)*

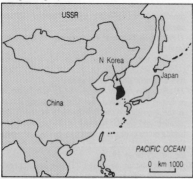

USSR

N Korea

China

Japan

PACIFIC OCEAN

0 km 1000

area 120,538 sq km/46,528 sq mi
capital Pyongyang
physical mountainous
features the richest of the two Koreas in mineral resources
head of state Kim Il Sung from 1972 (also head of Communist Party)
head of government Yon Hyong Muk from 1988

political system communism
political parties Korean Workers' Party (KWP), Marxist-Leninist-Kim Il Sungist
exports coal, iron, copper, textiles, chemicals
currency won (1.65 = £1 Feb 1990)
population (1988) 21,890,000; annual growth rate 2.5%
life expectancy men 65, women 71
language Korean
religion traditionally Buddhist and Confucian
literacy 99% (1984)
GNP $18.1 bn (1982 est); $570 per head of population
chronology
1948 Democratic People's Republic of Korea declared.
1950 North Korea invaded South Korea to begin Korean War.
1953 Armistice agreed to end Korean War.
1961 Friendship and mutual assistance treaty signed with China.
1972 New constitution, with executive president, was adopted. Talks took place with South Korea about possible reunification.
1980 Reunification talks broke down.
1983 Four South Korean cabinet ministers assassinated in Rangoon, Burma, by North Korean army officers.
1985 Increased relations with the USSR.

Korea, South
Republic of
(Daehan Minguk)

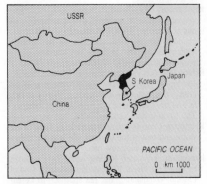

area 99,022 sq km/38,222 sq mi
capital Seoul
towns Taegu, ports Pusan, Inchon
physical mountainous
head of state Roh Tae-Woo from 1988
head of government Kang Young Hoon
from 1988
political system emergent democracy
political parties Democratic Liberal Party
(DLP), right-of-centre; Party for Peace and

Democracy (PPD), left-of-centre
exports steel, ships, chemicals, electronics,
textiles, plastics
currency won (1,172 = £1 Feb 1990)
population (1987) 42,082,000; annual growth
rate 1.6%
life expectancy men 65, women 71
language Korean
religion traditionally Buddhist and Confucian
literacy 96% male/87% female (1980 est)
GNP $78.9 bn (1984); $1,187 per head of
population
chronology
1948 Republic proclaimed.
1950–53 War with North Korea.
1960 President Syngman Rhee resigned amid
unrest.
1961 Military coup by Gen Park Chung-Hee.
Industrial growth programme.
1979 Assassination of President Park.
1980 Military coup by Gen Chun Doo-Hwan.
1987 Adoption of more democratic constitution
following student unrest. Roh Tae-Woo elected
president.
1988 Former president Chun, accused of
corruption, publicly apologized for the
misdeeds of his administration and agreed to
hand over his financial assets to the state.
1990 Two minor opposition parties united
with Democratic Justice Party to form ruling
Democratic Liberal Party.

Korean Central Intelligence Agency, and martial
law was reimposed.

An interim government, led by former prime
minister Choi Kyu-Hah, introduced liberalizing
reforms, releasing opposition leader Kim Dae
Jung 1980. However, as anti-government demonstrations developed, a new dissident clampdown
began, involving the arrest of 30 political leaders,
including Kim Dae Jung. After riots in Kim's home
city of Kwangju, President Choi resigned 1980 and
was replaced by the leader of the army, Gen Chun
Doo-Hwan. A new constitution was adopted and,
after Chun Doo-Hwan was re-elected president
1981, the new Fifth Republic was proclaimed.

Under President Chun economic growth resumed, but internal and external criticism of the
suppression of civil liberties continued. Cautious
liberalization was seen prior to the 1985 assembly
elections, with the release of many political prisoners and the return from exile of Kim Dae-Jung.
The opposition parties emerged in a strengthened
position after the 1985 election and proceeded to
launch a campaign for genuine democratization
that forced the Chun regime to frame a new,
more liberal constitution, which was adopted after
a referendum Oct 1987. The ensuing presidential
election was won by the ruling party's candidate,
Roh Tae Woo, amid opposition charges of fraud.
He took over Feb 1988, but in the national assembly elections Apr 1988 the ruling Democratic
Justice Party (DJP) fell well short of an overall
majority. Only in Feb 1990, when the DJP merged
with two minor opposition parties to form the
Democratic Liberal Party (DLP), was a stable
governing majority secured. The new coalition
declared its intention of amending the constitution
to replace the presidential executive system with
a parliamentary one, led by a powerful prime minister drawn from the majority grouping within the
national assembly, moving South Korea's political
system closer to Japan's model.

Since 1953 the constant threat of invasion from
the North has been a key factor in South Korean
politics, helping to justify stern rule. South Korea
has devoted large resources to modernizing its
armed forces, which are supported in addition by
US troops.

Korinthos /ˈkɒrɪnθɒs/ Greek form of ◊Corinth.
Kornberg /ˈkɔːnbɜːg/ Arthur 1918– . US bio-
chemist. In 1956, while working on enzymes at
Washington University, Kornberg discovered the

enzyme DNA-polymerase, which enabled molecules of ◊DNA to be synthesized for the first
time. For this work Kornberg shared the 1959
Nobel Physiology or Medicine Prize with Severo
◊Ochoa.
Korngold /ˈkɔːngəʊld/ Erich Wolfgang 1897–1957.
Austrian-born composer. He began composing operas while still in his teens and in 1934 moved
to Hollywood to become a composer for Warner
Brothers. His film scores combine a richly or-
chestrated and romantic style, reflecting the
rapid changes of mood characteristic of screen
action.
Korolev /kəˈrɒljef/ Sergei Pavlovich 1906–1966.
Soviet designer of the first Soviet intercontinental
missile, used 1957 to launch the first ◊Sputnik satellite, and 1961 to launch the ◊Vostok spacecraft
(also designed by Korolev).
Kortrijk /ˈkɔːtraɪk/ Flemish form of ◊Courtrai,
town in Belgium.
Kos /kɒs/ or **Cos** fertile Greek island, one of
the Dodecanese, in the Aegean Sea; area
287 sq km/111 sq mi. It gives its name to the
Cos lettuce.
Kosciusko /ˌkɒsiˈʌskəʊ/ highest mountain in Australia (2,229 m/7,316 ft), in New South Wales.
Paul Strzelecki, who was born in Prussian Poland, named the mountain 1839 after the Polish
revolutionary hero.
Kosciuszko /kɒsˈtʃuʃkəʊ/ Tadeusz 1746–1817.
Polish revolutionary leader, defeated by combined
Russian and Prussian forces 1794, and imprisoned
until 1796. He fought for the USA in the War of
Independence.
kosher (Hebrew 'proper') of food, conforming to
Mosaic law. Only animals that chew the cud
and have cloven hooves (cows and sheep, but
not pigs) are kosher. There are rules governing
their slaughter and preparation (such as complete
draining of blood), which also apply to fowl. Only
fish with scales and fins are kosher; shellfish are
not. Milk products may not be cooked or eaten
with meat or poultry.
There have been various explanations for the
origins of these laws, particularly hygiene: pork
and shellfish spoil quickly in a hot climate. Many
Reform Jews no longer feel obliged to observe
these laws.
Košice /ˈkɒʃitseɪ/ town in SE Czechoslovakia;
population (1986) 222,000. It has a textile industry
and is a road centre; a large part of the population

(1980) 204,700 is Magyar-speaking, and Košice
was in Hungary until 1920 and 1938–45.
Kosinski /kɒˈʃɪnski/ Jerzy 1933– . Polish-born
US novelist, author of *The Painted Bird* 1965,
about a strange boy brutally treated during World
War II, *Being There* 1971, about a retarded gardener who is thought to be a wise man because
his gardening tips are taken as metaphors for life,
and *Passion Play* 1979.
He was born in Lodz, and educated as a sociologist at the university there. He escaped from
Poland during World War II through the USSR,
eventually going to the USA 1957. He taught
himself English.
Kosovo /ˈkɒsəvəʊ/ autonomous region (since
1974) in S Serbia, Yugoslavia; capital Priština;
area 10,900 sq km/4,207 sq mi; population (1989)
1,900,000 consisting of about 200,000 Serbs and
about 1.7 million ethnic Albanians. Products include
wine, nickel, lead, and zinc. Because the region is
largely inhabited by Albanians and bordering on
Albania, there are demands for unification with
that country, while in the late 1980s Serbians
were agitating for Kosovo to be merged with the
rest of Serbia. A state of emergency was declared
Feb 1990 after fighting broke out between ethnic
Albanians, police, and the Slavonic minority.
Kossuth /ˈkɒʃuːt/ Lajos 1802–1894. Hungarian
nationalist. He proclaimed Hungarian independence of Habsburg rule 1849, and when the
Hungarians were later defeated, fled first to
Turkey, and then to Britain.
Kosygin /kɒˈsiːgɪn/ Alexei Nikolaievich 1904–
1980. Soviet politician, prime minister 1964–80.
He was elected to the Supreme Soviet 1938,
became a member of the Politburo 1946, deputy
prime minister 1960, and succeeded Khrushchev
as premier.
Kota Bharu /ˈkəʊtə ˈbɑːruː/ capital of Kelantan,
Malaysia; population (1980) 170,600.
Kota Kinabalu /ˈkəʊtəp ˌkɪnəbəˈluː/ (formerly
Jesselton) capital and port in Sabah, Malaysia;
population (1980) 59,500. Exports include rubber
and timber. It was known as Jesselton until 1968.
koto Japanese musical instrument; a long zither of
ancient Chinese origin, having 13 silk strings supported by movable bridges. It rests on the floor
and the strings are plucked with ivory plectra,
producing a brittle sound.
Kottbus /ˈkɒtbʊs/ alternative spelling of ◊Cottbus,
town in East Germany.
kouprey type of wild cattle *Bos sauveli* native to
the forest of N Cambodia. Only known to science
since 1937, it is in great danger of extinction.
Kourou /kuˈruː/ river and second-largest town of
French Guiana, NW of Cayenne, site of the Guiana
Space Centre of the European Space Agency.
Situated near the equator, it is an ideal site for
launches of satellites into ◊geostationary orbit.
Kovalevsky /ˌkɒvəˈlefski/ Sophia Vasilevna 1850–
1891. Russian mathematician; doctorate from

Kosygin Soviet politician and prime minister Alexei
Kosygin at a press conference in Denmark, 1971.

Kraków *Kraków's 14th-century Gothic cathedral.*

Göttingen University 1874 for dissertation on partial differential equations; professor of mathematics University of Stockholm 1884. In 1886 she won the *Prix Bordin* of the French Academy of Sciences for a paper on the rotation of a rigid body about a point, a problem the 18th-century mathematicians Euler and Lagrange had both failed to solve.

Kovno /'kɒvnə/ Russian form of ◊Kaunas, port in Lithuania, USSR.

Kowloon /,kaʊ'luːn/ peninsula on the Chinese coast forming part of the British crown colony of Hong Kong; the town of Kowloon is a residential area.

kph or **km/h** abbreviation for *kilometres per hour*.

Krafft-Ebing /'kræft 'eɪbɪŋ/ Baron Richard von 1840–1902. German pioneer psychiatrist, and neurologist. He published *Psychopathia Sexualis* 1886.

Kragujevac /'kræguːjeɪvæts/ garrison town and former capital (1818–39) of Serbia, Yugoslavia; population (1981) 165,000.

Krakatoa /,krækə'təʊə/ (Indonesian *Krakatau*) volcanic island in Sunda strait, Indonesia, which erupted in 1883, causing 36,000 deaths on Java and Sumatra by the tidal waves which followed. The island is now uninhabited.

Kraków /'krækaʊ/ or *Cracow* city in Poland, on the Vistula; population (1985) 716,000. It is an industrial centre producing railway wagons, paper, chemicals, and tobacco. It was capital of Poland 1300–1595.

Its university, founded in 1400, at which the astronomer ◊Copernicus was a student, is one of the oldest in central Europe. There is a 14th-century Gothic cathedral.

Kramatorsk /,kræmə'tɔːsk/ industrial town in Ukraine, USSR, in the Donbas, north of Donetsk; population (1987) 198,000. Industries include coalmining machinery, steel, ceramics, and railway repairs.

Krasnodar /,kræsnəʊ'dɑː/ industrial town at the head of navigation of the Kuban river, in SW USSR; population (1987) 623,000. It is linked by pipeline with the Caspian oilfields. The town was known as Ekaterinodar until 1920.

Krasnodar /,kræsnəʊ'dɑː/ territory of the Russian Soviet Federal Socialist Republic in the N Caucasus, adjacent to the Black Sea; area 83,600 km2/32,290; population(1985) 4,992,000. Capital is Krasnodar. In addition to stock rearing and the production of grain, rice, fruit and tobacco, oil is refined.

Krasnoyarsk /,kræsnəʊ'jɑːsk/ industrial city in central USSR; population (1987) 899,000. Industries include locomotives, paper, timber, cement, gold refining, and a large hydroelectric works. There is an early-warning and space-tracking radar phased array device at nearby Abalakova. See also ◊Novosibirsk.

Krasnoyarsk /,kræsnəʊ'jɑːsk/ territory of the Russian Soviet Federal Socialist Republic in central Siberia stretching N to the Arctic Ocean; area 2,401,600 km2/927,617 sq mi; population (1985) 3,430,000. Capital is Krasnoyarsk. It is drained by the Yenisei river. Mineral resources include gold, graphite, coal, iron ore and uranium.

Krebs /krebz/ Hans 1900–1981. German-born British biochemist. In 1953 he shared the Nobel Prize in Medicine for discovering the citric acid cycle, also known as Krebs' cycle, by which food is converted into energy in living tissues.

Krebs' cycle or *citric acid cycle* part of the chain of biochemical reactions through which organisms break down food using oxygen (aerobically) to release energy. It breaks down food molecules in a series of small steps, producing energy-rich molecules of ◊ATP.

Krefeld /'kreɪfelt/ industrial town near the river Rhine; 52 km/32 mi NW of Cologne; West Germany; population (1988) 217,000. Industries include chemicals, textiles, and machinery. The town is on the Westphalian coalfield.

Kreisler /'kraɪslə/ Fritz 1875–1962. Austrian violinist and composer, renowned as an interpreter of Brahms and Beethoven. From 1911 he was one of the earliest recording artists of classical music, some of which he composed himself.

Kremenchug /,kreɪmen'tʃuːg/ industrial town on the river Dnieper, in Ukraine Republic, USSR; population (1987) 230,000. Manufacturing includes road-building machinery, rail wagons, and processed food.

kremlin /'kremlɪn/ citadel or fortress of Russian cities. The Moscow kremlin dates from the 12th century, and the name 'the Kremlin' was once synonymous with the Soviet government.

Krenek /kə'ʒenek/ Ernst 1900– . Austrian-born composer. His jazz opera *Jonny spielt auf/Johnny plays up* 1927 received international acclaim.

He moved to the USA 1939 and explored the implications of contemporary and renaissance musical theories in a succession of works and theoretical writings.

Krenz /krents/ Egon 1937– . East German communist politician. A member of the Socialist Unity Party (SED) from 1955, he joined its politburo in 1983 and became a hardline protégé of Erich ◊Honecker, succeeding him as party leader and head of state in 1989 after widespread pro-democracy demonstrations. Pledging a 'new course', Krenz opened the country's western border and promised more open elections, but his conversion to genuine pluralism proved weak in the face of popular protest and he resigned after a few weeks in Dec 1989, as party general secretary and head of state. He was replaced by Manfred Gerlach (1928–) and Gregor Gysi (1948–) respectively.

Kreutzer /'krɔɪtsə/ Rodolphe 1766–1831. French violinist and composer of German descent to whom Beethoven dedicated his violin sonata Opus 47, known as the *Kreutzer Sonata*.

krill Antarctic crustacean, the most common species being *Euphausia superba*. Shrimp-like, it is about 6 cm/2.5 in long, with two antennae, five pairs of legs, seven pairs of light organs along the body, and is coloured orange above and green beneath.

Moving in enormous swarms, krill constitute the chief food of the baleen whales, and have been used to produce a protein concentrate for human consumption, and meal for animal feed.

Krishna /'krɪʃnə/ incarnation of the Hindu god ◊Vishnu. The devotion of the ◊bhakti movement is usually directed towards Krishna; an example of this is the ◊International Society for Krishna Consciousness. Many stories are told of Krishna's mischievous youth, and he is the charioteer of Arjuna in the *Bhagavad-Gītā*.

Krishna Consciousness Movement popular name for the ◊International Society for Krishna Consciousness.

Kristallnacht the 'night of broken glass' 9–10 Nov 1938 when the Nazi Sturmabteilung (SA) militia in Germany and Austria mounted a concerted attack on Jews, their synagogues, and their property. It followed the murder of a German embassy official in Paris by a Polish-Jewish youth. Subsequent measures included legislation against Jews owning businesses.

This *pogrom* precipitated a rush by Jews for visas to other countries, but restrictive immigration policies throughout the world, and Nazi restrictions at home, made it impossible for most of them to leave.

Kristiansen /'krɪstjənsən/ Ingrid 1956– . Norwegian athlete, an outstanding long-distance runner at 5,000 m, 10,000 m, marathon, and cross-country running. She has won all the world's leading marathons. In 1986 she knocked 45.68 seconds off the world 10,000 m record.

Krivoi Rog /krɪ'vɔɪ 'rɒg/ town in Ukraine, USSR, 130 km/80 mi SW of Dnepropetrovsk; population (1987) 698,000. The surrounding district is rich in iron ore, and there is a metallurgical industry. The name means 'crooked horn'.

Kronos or *Cronus* in Greek mythology, ruler of the world and one of the ◊Titans. He was the father of Zeus, who overthrew him.

Kronstadt /'krɒnstæt/ Russian naval base, founded by Peter the Great 1703, on Kotlin island, Gulf of Finland, commanding the sea approach to Leningrad, whose defence under siege was aided by its guns 1941–43.

Kronstadt uprising revolt in Mar 1921 by sailors of the Russian Baltic Fleet at their headquarters in Kronstadt, outside Petrograd (now Leningrad). On the orders of the leading Bolshevik Trotsky, Red Army troops, dressed in white camouflage, crossed the ice to the naval base and captured it on 18 Mar. The leaders were subsequently shot.

Following a strike by Petrograd workers in Feb 1921, the Kronstadt sailors reaffirmed their demands for the rights obtained in theory by the Revolution of 1917. The sailors were thus labelled the 'conscience of the Revolution' for demanding what had been promised, but not delivered, by the Bolsheviks. These perceived them as a threat because of their detection and resentment of the growing Bolshevik monopoly of power.

Kropotkin /krɒ'pɒtkɪn/ Peter Alexeivich, Prince Kropotkin 1842–1921. Russian anarchist. Imprisoned for revolutionary activities 1874, he escaped to the UK in 1876, and later moved to Switzerland. Expelled from Switzerland, he went to France, where he was imprisoned 1883–86. He lived in Britain until 1917, when he returned to Moscow. Among his works are *Mutual Aid* 1902 and *Modern Science and Anarchism* 1903.

Kruger /'kruːgə/ Stephanus Johannes Paulus 1825–1904. President of the Transvaal 1883–1900. He refused to remedy the grievances of the Uitlanders (English and other non-Boer white residents), and so precipitated the Second ◊South African War.

Kruger National Park /'kruːgə/ game reserve in NE Transvaal, South Africa, between the Limpopo and Crocodile rivers; it is the largest in the world (about 20,720 sq km/8,000 sq mi). The Sabie Game Reserve was established 1898 by President Kruger, and the park declared in 1926.

Krugersdorp /'kruːgəzdɔːp/ mining town in the Witwatersrand district, Transvaal, South Africa; population (1980) 103,000. Manganese, uranium, and gold are mined.

Kruger telegram message sent by Kaiser Wilhelm II of Germany to President Kruger of the Transvaal 3 Jan 1896 congratulating him on defeating the ◊Jameson raid of 1895. The text of the telegram provoked indignation, in Britain and elsewhere, and represented a worsening of Anglo-German relations, in spite of a German government retraction.

Krupp /krʊp/ German steelmaking armaments firm, founded in the early 19th century, and developed by Alfred Krupp (1812–87) by pioneering the Bessemer steelmaking process. It developed the long-distance artillery used in World War I, and supported Hitler's regime in preparation for World War II, after which the head of the firm was imprisoned.

krypton a colourless, odourless, inert gas. It is an element, symbol Kr, atomic number 36, relative atomic mass 83.8. It was discovered in 1898 by

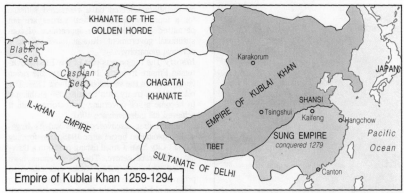

KHANATE OF THE GOLDEN HORDE

CHAGATAI KHANATE

IL-KHAN EMPIRE

Black Sea

Caspian Sea

Karakorum

EMPIRE OF KUBLAI KHAN

JAPAN

SHANSI

Tsingshui

Kaifeng

Hangchow

Pacific Ocean

TIBET

SUNG EMPIRE conquered 1279

SULTANATE OF DELHI

Canton

Empire of Kublai Khan 1259-1294

Ramsay and Travers in the residue from liquid air. It occurs in the atmosphere at about 1.5 parts per million, and is used to enhance brilliance in miners' electric lamps, and in some gas-filled electronic valves.

Kryukov /kri'u:kɒv/ Fyodor 1870–1920. Russian writer, alleged by Solzhenitsyn to be the real author of *And Quiet Flows the Don* by ◊Sholokhov.

KS abbreviation for ◊*Kansas*.

Kuala Lumpur /'kwɑ:lə 'lʊmpʊə/ capital of the Federation of Malaysia; population (1985) 1,103,000. The city developed after 1873 with the expansion of tin and rubber trading; these are now its major industries. Formerly within the state of Selangor, of which it was also the capital, it was created a federal territory 1974; area 240 sq km/93 sq mi.

Kuanyin /,kwæn'jɪn/ transliteration of ◊Guanyin, goddess of mercy in Chinese Buddhism.

Kuban /ku:'bɑ:n/ river in the USSR, rising in Georgia (see ◊Krasnodar); length 906 km/563 mi to the Sea of Azov.

Kubelik /'ku:bəlɪk/ Jan 1880–1940. Czech violinist and composer. He performed in Prague at the age of eight, and was one of the world's greatest virtuosos; he also wrote six violin concertos.

Kubelik /'ku:bəlɪk/ Rafael 1914– . Czech conductor-composer. His works include symphonies and operas, such as *Veronika* 1947. He was musical director of the Royal Opera House, Covent Garden, London 1955–58.

Kublai Khan /'ku:blaɪ 'kɑ:n/ 1216–1294. Mongol emperor of China from 1259. He completed his grandfather ◊Genghis Khan's conquest of N China from 1240, and on his brother Mungo's death 1259, established himself as emperor of China. He moved the capital to Peking and founded the Yuan dynasty, successfully expanding his empire into Indochina, but was defeated in an attempt to conquer Japan 1281.

Kubrick /'ku:brɪk/ Stanley 1928– . US director, producer, and screenwriter. His films include *Paths of Glory* 1957, *Dr Strangelove* 1964, *2001: A Space Odyssey* 1968, *A Clockwork Orange* 1971, and *The Shining* 1979.

Kuching /'ku:tʃɪŋ/ capital and port of Sarawak state, E Malaysia; on the Sarawak river; population (1980) 74,200.

kudu African antelope *Tragelaphus strepsiceros*. It is fawn-coloured with thin white vertical stripes, and stands 1.3 m/4.2 ft at the shoulder, with head and body 2.4 m/8 ft long. Males have long spiral horns. The kudu is found in bush country from Angola to Ethiopia.

The similar *lesser kudu Tragelaphus imberbis* lives in E Africa and is 1 m/3 ft at the shoulder.

kudzu Japanese creeper *Pueraria lobata*, family Leguminosae, which helps fix nitrogen (see ◊nitrogen cycle) and can be used as fodder, but became a pest in the USA when introduced to check soil erosion.

Kufra /'ku:frə/ group of oases in the Libyan Desert, N Africa, SE of Tripoli. By the 1970s the vast underground reservoirs were being used for irrigation.

Kuhn /ku:n/ Richard 1900–1967. Austrian chemist. Working at Heidelberg University in the 1930s, Kuhn succeeded in determining the structures of vitamins A, B_2, and B_6. He was awarded the 1938 Nobel Chemistry Prize, but was not able collect it until after World War II.

Kuhn /ku:n/ Thomas S 1922– . US historian and philosopher of science, who showed that social and cultural conditions affect the directions of science. *The Structure of Scientific Revolutions* 1962 argued that even scientific knowledge is relative, dependent on the ◊*paradigm* (theoretical framework) that dominates a scientific field at the time.

Such paradigms (examples being Darwinism and Newtonian theory) are so dominant that they are uncritically accepted as true, until a 'scientific revolution' creates a new orthodoxy. Kuhn's ideas have also influenced ideas in the social sciences.

Kuibyshev /'ku:ɪbɪʃev/ or **Kuybyshev** capital of Kuibyshev region, USSR, and port at the junction of the rivers Samara and Volga, situated in the centre of the fertile middle Volga plain; population (1987) 1,280,000. Its industries include aircraft, locomotives, cables, synthetic rubber, textiles, fertilizers, petroleum refining, and quarrying. It was provisional capital of the USSR 1941–43.

Founded as Samara, the name was renamed Kuibyshev 1935. *Kuibyshev Sea* is an artificial lake about 480 km/300 mi long, created in the 1950s by damming the Volga river.

Kuiper /'kaɪpə/ Gerard Peter 1905–1973. Dutch-born US astronomer, who made extensive studies of the solar system. His discoveries included the atmospheres of Mars and Titan. Kuiper was adviser to many NASA exploratory missions, and pioneered the use of telescopes on high-flying aircraft. The Kuiper Airborne Observatory, one such telescope, is named after him.

Ku Klux Klan US secret society dedicated to white supremacy, founded 1866 in the southern states of the USA to oppose ◊Reconstruction after the Civil War and to deny political rights to the black population. Members wore hooded white robes to hide their identity, and burned crosses as a rite of intimidation. It was as active in the 1960s in terrorizing civil-rights activists and organizing racist demonstrations.

Its violence led the government to pass the restrictive Ku Klux Klan Acts of 1871. The society re-emerged in 1915 in Atlanta, Georgia, and increased in strength during the 1920s as a racist, anti-semitic, anti-Catholic, and anti-Communist organization.

kulak Russian term for a peasant who could afford to hire labour, and often acted as village usurer. The kulaks resisted the Soviet government's policy of collectivization, and in 1930 they were 'liquidated as a class', with up to 5 million being either killed or deported to Siberia.

Kulturkampf German word for policy introduced by Chancellor Bismarck in Germany in 1873, which isolated the Catholic interest and attempted to reduce its power in order to create a political coalition of liberals and agrarian conservatives. The alienation of such a large section of the German population as the Catholics could not be sustained and the policy was abandoned after 1876 and replaced by an anti-Socialist policy.

Kumamoto /,ku:mə'məʊtəʊ/ city on Kyushu island, Japan, 80 km/50 mi E of Nagasaki; population (1987) 550,000. A military stronghold until the last century, the city is now a centre for fishing, food processing, and textile industries.

Kumasi /ku:'mɑ:si/ town in Ghana, W Africa, capital of Ashanti region, with trade in cocoa, rubber, and cattle; population (1984) 350,000.

history In the Fourth Ashanti War, in 1900, Sir Frederic Hodgson, governor of the Gold Coast Colony, with his wife, staff, and a small garrison were besieged in the fort at Kumasi Mar–June, when they fought their way out. Soon afterwards the kingdom of Ashanti, of which Kumasi had been the capital since the 17th century, was annexed by the British.

Kun /ku:n/ Béla 1885–1938. Hungarian politician who created a Soviet republic in Hungary Mar 1919, which was overthrown Aug 1919 by a Western blockade and Romanian military actions. The succeeding regime under Admiral Horthy effectively liquidated both socialism and liberalism in Hungary.

Kundera /'kʊndərə/ Milan 1929– . Czech writer, born in Brno. His first novel *The Joke* 1967 brought him into official disfavour in Prague, and, unable to publish further works, he moved to France. His novels include *The Book of Laughter and Forgetting* 1979 and *The Unbearable Lightness of Being* 1984.

Kung an aboriginal people of southern Africa, formerly known as **Bushman**. They still live nomadically, especially in the Kalahari Desert. Although formerly numerous, only some 26,000 now remain. They are traditionally hunters and gatherers, and speak a Khoisan language. Their early art survives in cave paintings.

Küng /kuŋ/ Hans 1928– . Swiss Roman Catholic theologian, who was barred from teaching by the Vatican 1979 'in the name of the Church' because he had cast doubt on papal infallibility, and on whether Christ was the son of God.

kung fu (Mandarin *ch'üan fa*), the Chinese art of unarmed combat, one of the ◊martial arts. It is practised in many forms, of which the most popular is *wing chun* 'beautiful springtime'. The basic principle is to use attack as a form of defence.

Kuniyoshi /,ku:ni'jɒʃi/ Utagawa 1797–1861. Japanese printmaker. His series *108 Heroes of the Suikoden* depicts heroes of the Chinese classic *The Water Margin*. Kuniyoshi's dramatic, innovative style lent itself to warriors and fantasy, but his subjects also include landscapes and cats.

Kunlunshan /'kʊnlʊn 'ʃɑ:n/ mountain range on the edge of the great Tibetan plateau, China; 4,000 km/2,500 mi E–W; highest peak Muztag (7,282 m/23,900 ft).

Kunming /,kʊn'mɪŋ/ formerly **Yunnan** capital of Yunnan province, China, on Lake Dian Chi, about 2,000 m/6,300 ft above sea level; population (1986) 1,490,000. Industries include chemicals, textiles, and copper smelted with nearby hydroelectric power.

Kuomintang /,kwəʊmɪn'tæŋ/ original name of Chinese nationalist party, now known (outside Taiwan) as ◊Guomindang.

kurchatovium another name for the element ◊rutherfordium.

Kurd inhabitant of Kurdistan. Divided between more powerful states, the Kurds have nationalist aspirations; there are approximately 8 million in Turkey, 5 million in Iran, 4 million in Iraq, 500,000 in Syria, and 100,000 in the USSR. Some 1 million Kurds were made homeless and 25,000 killed as a result of chemical weapon attacks by Iraq 1984–89. The Kurdish language is a member of the Iranian branch of the Indo-European family and the Kurds are a non-Arab ethnic group.

There was an ill-fated attempt to set up an autonomous Kurdish state within the Ottoman Empire during the 1880s and the Treaty of Sèvres

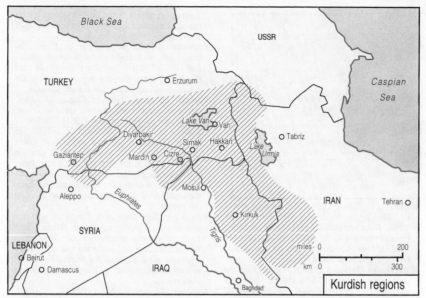

Kurdish regions

1920 provided a draft scheme for Kurdish independence. In Iran, the Kurds briefly achieved a Kurdish representative with Soviet backing 1946, were repressed under the shah, and when they revolted against the regime of Ayatollah Khomeini were savagely put down 1979–80. It was promised that the four provinces would be united in an autonomous unit; the Kurdish region, however, remains divided between more powerful states. In Iraq, Kurds were moved from north to south, a policy which led to revolts 1977. In 1988 Iraq was reported to have used chemical weapons to drive Kurds into Turkey. In Nov 1989 the Iraqi army completed the uprooting of Kurds from N Iraq, having moved an estimated 100,000–500,000 people to create an uninhabited 'security zone' on its borders with Iran and Turkey.

The Kurds are predominantly Sunni Muslims, although there are some Shi'ites in Iran. Kurds traditionally owe allegiance to their families, and larger groups are brought together under an agha, or lord. They are predominantly farmers, cultivating a wide range of crops and fruit. Kurdish professionals are found in many Middle Eastern cities.

kurdaitcha shoes shoes made of emu feathers, which leave no tracks. The were traditionally worn by Australian Aborigines when escaping their enemies.

Kurdistan /ˌkɜːdɪˈstɑːn/ or *Kordestan* hilly region in SW Asia in the neighbourhood of Mount Ararat, where the borders of Iran, Iraq, Syria, Turkey, and the USSR meet; area 192,000 sq km/74,600 sq mi; total population around 18 million.

Kure /ˈkuəreɪ/ naval base and port 32 km/20 mi SE of Hiroshima, on the S coast of Honshu, Japan; population (1980) 234,500. Industries include shipyards and engineering works.

Kuria Muria /ˈkuəriə ˈmuəriə/ group of five islands in the Arabian Sea, off the S coast of Oman; area 72 sq km/28 sq mi.

Kuril Islands /kuˈriːl/ chain of about 50 small islands stretching from the NE of Hokkaido, Japan, to the S of Kamchatka, USSR; area 14,765 sq km/5,700 sq mi; population (1970) 15,000. Some of them are of volcanic origin. Two of the Kurils are claimed by both Japan and the USSR.

The Kurils were discovered 1634 by a Russian navigator and were settled by Russians. Japan seized them 1875–1945, when under the Yalta agreement they were returned to the USSR. Japan still claims the southernmost (Etorfu and Kunashiri), and also the nearby small islands of Habomai and Shikotan (not part of the Kurils). The USSR agreed to the latter 1972, but the question

of Etorofu and Kunashiri prevents signature of a Japanese–Soviet peace treaty.

Kuropatkin /ˌkuərəˈpætkɪn/ Alexei Nikolaievich 1848–1921. Russian general. He made his reputation during the Russo-Turkish War 1877–78, was commander in chief in Manchuria 1903, and resigned after his defeat at Mukden in the ◊Russo-Japanese War. During World War I he commanded the armies on the N front until 1916.

Kurosawa /ˌkuərəˈsɑːwə/ Akira 1929– . Japanese director whose film *Rashomon* 1950 introduced Western audiences to Japanese cinema. Epics such as *Seven Samurai* 1954 combine spectacle with intimate human drama. His other films include *Drunken Angel* 1948, *Yojimbo* 1961, *Kagemusha* 1981, and *Ran* 1985.

Kuroshio /kəˈroʊʃiəʊ/ or *Japan Current* a warm ocean ◊current flowing from Japan to North America.

Kursk /kuəsk/ town and capital of Kursk region of the USSR; population (1987) 434,000. It dates from the 9th century. Industries include chemicals machinery, alcohol, and tobacco.

Kūt-al-Imāra /ˈkuːt æl ɪˈmɑːrə/ or *al Kūt* town in Iraq, on the river Tigris; population (1985) 58,600. It is a grain market and carpet-manufacturing centre. In World War I it was under siege by Turkish forces Dec 1915–Apr 1916, when the British garrison surrendered.

Kutch, Rann of /kʌtʃ/ salt, marshy area in Gujarat state, India, which forms two shallow lakes, the Great Rann and the Little Rann, in the wet season, and is a salt-covered desert in the dry. It takes its name from the former princely state of Kutch, which it adjoined. An international tribunal 1968 awarded 90% of the Rann of Kutch to India and 10% (about 800 sq km/300 sq mi) to Pakistan, the latter comprising almost all the elevated area above water the year round.

Kutuzov /kuˈtuːzɒf/ Mikhail Larionovich, Prince of Smolensk 1745–1813. Commander of the Russian forces in the Napoleonic Wars. He commanded an army corps at ◊Austerlitz, and the retreating army 1812. After the burning of Moscow he harried the French throughout their retreat, and later took command of the united Prussian armies.

Kuwait /kuˈweɪt/ country in SW Asia, bordered N and NW by Iraq, E by the Gulf, and S and SW by Saudi Arabia.
government The 1962 constitution was partly suspended by the emir 1976 and reinstated 1980. It vests executive power in the hands of the emir, who governs through an appointed prime minister and council of ministers. The current prime minister is the emir's eldest son, the crown prince. There is a single-chamber national assembly of

50 members, elected on a restricted suffrage for a four-year term. Political parties are not permitted and, despite the appearance of constitutional government, Kuwait is, in effect, a personal monarchy.
history The region was part of the Turkish ◊Ottoman Empire from the 16th century; the ruling family founded the sheikdom of Kuwait 1756. The ruler made a treaty with Britain 1899 enabling it to become a self-governing protectorate until it achieved full independence 1961.

Oil was first discovered 1938 and its large-scale exploitation began after 1945, transforming Kuwait City from a small fishing port into a thriving commercial centre. The oil revenues have enabled ambitious public works and education programmes to be undertaken. Sheik Abdullah al-Salem al-Sabah took the title of emir 1961 when he assumed full executive powers. He died 1965 and was succeeded by his brother, Sheik Sabah al-Salem al-Sabah. He, in turn, died 1977 and was succeeded by Crown Prince Jabir, who appointed Sheik Saad al-Abdullah al-Salem al-Sabah as his heir apparent. In Jan 1990 pro-democracy demonstrations were dispersed by the police.

Kuwait has used its considerable wealth not only to improve its infrastructure and social services but also to secure its borders, making, for example, substantial donations to Iraq, which in the past had made territorial claims on it. It has also been a strong supporter of the Arab cause generally.

Kuwait City /kuːˈweɪt/ (Arabic *Al Kuwayt*) formerly *Qurein* chief port and capital of the State of Kuwait, on the S shore of Kuwait Bay; population (1985) 44,300, plus the suburbs of Hawalli, population (1985) 145,100, Jahra, population (1985) 111,200, and as-Salimiya, population (1985) 153,400. Kuwait is a banking and investment centre.

Kuzbas /ˌkuːzˈbæs/ industrial area in Kemerovo region, S USSR, lying on the Tom river to the N of the Altai mountains. Development began in the 1930s. It takes its name from the old town of Kuznetsk.

Kuznets /ˈkʌznets/ Simon 1901–1985. Russian economist, who emigrated to the USA 1922. He developed theories of national income and economic growth, used to forecast the future, in *Economic Growth of Nations* 1971. Nobel prize 1971.

Kuznetsk Basin /kuːzˈnetsk/ industrial area in Kemorovo region, S USSR. Abbreviated to ◊Kuzbas.

Kuznetsov /ˌkuːznɪtˈsɒf/ Anatoli 1930–1979. Russian writer. His novels *Babi Yar* 1966, describing the wartime execution of Jews at Babi Yar, near Kiev, and *The Fire* 1969, about workers in a large metallurgical factory, were seen as anti-Soviet. He lived in Britain from 1969.

kW abbreviation for *kilowatt*.

Kwakiutl or *Kwa-Gulth* indigenous American people who live on both sides of the northern entrance to the Queen Charlotte Strait. Their language belongs to the Wakashan family.

Kwa Ndebele /ˌkwɑːndəˈbeɪli/ black homeland in Transvaal province, South Africa; achieved self-governing status 1981; population (1985) 235,800.

Kwangchow alternative name of ◊Guangzhou, city in China.

Kwangchu /ˌkwæŋˈdʒuː/ or *Kwangju* capital of South Cholla province, SW South Korea; population (1985) 906,000. It is at the centre of a rice-growing region. A museum in the city houses a huge collection of Chinese porcelain dredged up 1976 after lying for over 600 years on the ocean floor.

Kwangsi-Chuang alternative name of ◊Guanxi Zhuang, region of China.

Kwangtung alternative name of ◊Guangdong, province of China.

Kwannon or *Kannon* in Japanese Buddhism, a female form (known to the West as 'goddess of mercy') of the bodhisattva ◊Avalokiteśvara.

Kuwait
State of
(Dowlat al Kuwait)

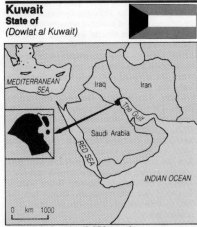

area 17,819 sq km/6,878 sq mi
capital Kuwait (also chief port)
physical hot desert
features oil revenues make it one of the world's best-equipped states in public works, and medical and educational services
head of state and government Jabir al-Ahmad al-Jabir al-Sabah from 1977
political system absolute monarchy
political parties none permitted
exports oil
currency Kuwaiti dinar (0.49 = £1 Feb 1990)
population (1988) 1,960,000 (40% Kuwaitis, 30% Palestinians); annual growth rate 5 5%
life expectancy men 70, women 74
language 78% Arabic, 10% Kurdish, 4% Farsi
religion Sunni Muslim, with Shi'ite minority
literacy 76% male/63% female (1985 est)
GNP $22 bn (1984); $11,431 per head of population
chronology
1961 Achieved full independence, with Sheikh Abdullah al-Salem al-Sabah as emir.
1965 Sheikh Abdullah died and was succeeded by his brother, Sheikh Sabah.
1977 Sheikh Sabah died and was succeeded by Crown Prince Jabir.
1990 Pro-democracy demonstrations suppressed.

Sometimes depicted with many arms extending compassion.

kwashiorkor Ghanaian name for the severe malnutrition common among children in W Africa, resulting in retarded growth.

Kwa Zulu black homeland in Natal province, South Africa; achieved self-governing status 1971; population (1985) 3,747,000.

Kweichow alternative name of ◊Guizhou, province of China.

Kweilin alternative name of ◊Guilin in China.

Kwik Cricket a form of ◊cricket devised for children. It is played with a soft ball and a major feature is that all players get a chance to bat and bowl.

KY abbreviation for ◊*Kentucky*.

Kyd /kɪd/ Thomas *c.*1557–1595. English dramatist, author in about 1588 of a bloody revenge tragedy *The Spanish Tragedy*, which anticipated elements present in Shakespeare's *Hamlet*.

Kyoga /kiˈəʊgə/ lake in central Uganda: area 4,425 sq km/1,709 sq mi. The Victoria Nile river passes through the lake.

Kyoto /kiˈəʊtəʊ/ former capital of Japan 794–1868 on Honshu island, linked by canal with Biwa Lake; population (1987) 1,469,000. Industries include silk weaving and manufacture, porcelain, bronze, and lacquer ware.

kyphosis an exaggerated outward curve of the upper spine. It is usually due to spinal disease, degeneration, or bad posture.

Kyprianou /ˌkɪpriəˈnuː/ Spyros 1932– . Cypriot politician. Foreign minister 1961–72, he founded the Democratic Front (DIKO) in 1976. He was president 1977–88.

Educated in Cyprus and the UK, he was called to the English Bar in 1954. He became secretary to Archbishop Makarios in London in 1952 and returned with him to Cyprus in 1959. On the death of Makarios in 1977 he became acting president and was then elected.

Kyrenia /kaɪˈriːniə/ port in Turkish-occupied Cyprus, about 20 km/12 mi N of Nicosia. Population (1985) 7,000.

Kyrie eleison (Greek 'Lord have mercy') the words spoken or sung at the beginning of the mass in the Catholic, Orthodox, and Anglican churches.

Kyushu /ˈkjuːʃuː/ most southerly of the main islands of Japan, separated from Shikoku and Honshu by Bungo Channel and Suo Bay, but connected to Honshu by bridge and rail tunnel
area 42,150 sq km/16,270 sq mi including about 370 small islands
capital Nagasaki
towns Fukuoka, Kumamoto, Kagoshima
physical mountainous, volcanic, with sub-tropical climate
features the active volcano Aso-take (1,592 m/5,225 ft) has the world's largest crater
products coal, gold, silver, iron, tin, rice, tea, timber
population (1986) 13,295,000.

Kyustendil /ˈkjuːstəndɪl/ town in SW Bulgaria, SW of Sofia, noted for its hot springs; population about 25,000.

Kyzyl-Kum /kɪˈziːl ˈkuːm/ desert in Kazakhstan and Uzbekistan, USSR, between the Sur-Darya and Amu-Darya rivers; area about 300,000 sq km/116,000 sq mi. It is being reclaimed for cultivation by irrigation and protective tree-planting.

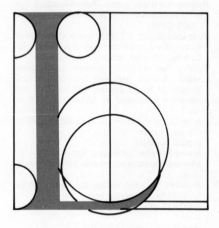

L twelfth letter of the Roman alphabet. The sound represented is one of the most stable in all languages; in some languages it tends to be lost between a back vowel and a consonant, as in English 'half', 'should', and so on.

L Roman numeral for 50; abbreviation for *learner* (driver).

l abbreviation for *litre*.

LA abbreviation for ◊*Louisiana; Los Angeles*.

La Condamine /læ ˌkɒndəˈmiːn/ Charles Marie de 1701–1774. French soldier and geographer who was sent by the French Academy of Sciences to Peru to measure the length of an arc of the meridien 1735–43. On his return journey he travelled the length of the Amazon, writing about the use of the nerve toxin curare, india rubber, and the advantages of inoculation.

laager term used by Boers in South Africa to describe an enclosed encampment; now more widely applied to the siege mentality of sections of the Afrikaner population.

Lab. abbreviation for *Labour* or *Labrador*.

labanotation a comprehensive system of accurate dance notation (*Kinetographie Laban* 1928) devised by Rudolf von Laban (1879–1958), dancer, choreographer, and dance theorist.

labelled compound a chemical compound in which a different ◊isotope (usually a radioactive one) of an atom is substituted for the usual one. Thus labelled, the path taken by the compound through a system can be followed, for instance by measuring the radiation emitted. This powerful and sensitive technique is used in medicine, chemistry (especially biochemistry), and industry.

labelling in sociology, defining or describing a person in terms of their behaviour; for example, describing someone who has broken a law as a criminal. Labelling theory deals with human interaction, behaviour, and control, particularly in the field of deviance. Social labelling has been seen as a form of social control in that labels affect both a person's self-image and other people's reactions. Crucial factors include who labels a person (for example, only a court can convict a criminal), and whether the label sticks.

labellum the lower petal of an orchid flower, which is a different shape from the two other lateral petals and gives the orchid its characteristic appearance.

The labellum is more elaborate and usually larger than the other petals, and it often has a distinctive patterning which encourages insects to land on it when visiting the flower. Sometimes it is extended backwards to form a hollow spur containing nectar.

Labor, Knights of in US history, a national labour organization founded by Philadelphia tailor Uriah Stephens 1869 and committed to cooperative enterprise, equal pay for both sexes, and an eight-hour day. The Knights grew rapidly in the mid-1880s under Terence V Powderly (1849–1924) but gave way to the ◊American Federation of Labor after 1886.

Labor Party in Australia, political party based on socialist principles. It was founded 1891 and first held office 1904. It formed governments 1929–31 and 1939–49, but in the intervening periods internal discord provoked splits, and reduced its effectiveness. It returned to power under Gough Whitlam 1972–75, and again under Bob Hawke from 1983.

Labour Day legal holiday in honour of workers. In the USA, it is celebrated on the first Monday in September. In many countries it coincides with ◊May Day.

labour market the market that determines the cost and conditions of the work force. This will depend on the demand of employers, the levels and availability of skills, and social conditions.

Labour Party UK political party based on socialist principles, originally formed to represent the working class. It was founded 1900 and first held office 1924. The first majority Labour government 1945–51 introduced ◊nationalization and the National Health Service, and expanded ◊social security. Labour was again in power 1964–70 and 1974–79. The party leader is elected by Labour members of Parliament. Neil Kinnock became leader 1983.

The Labour Party, the Trades Union Congress, and the cooperative movement together form the National Council of Labour, whose aims are to coordinate political activities and take joint action on specific issues.

Although the Scottish socialist Keir Hardie and John Burns, a workers' leader, entered Parliament independently as Labour Members 1892, it was not until 1900 that a conference representing the trade unions, the Independent Labour Party (ILP), and the ◊Fabian Society founded the Labour Party, known until 1906, when 29 seats were gained, as the ◊Labour Representation Committee. All but a pacifist minority of the Labour Party supported World War I, and in 1918 a socialist programme was first adopted, with local branches of the party set up to which individual members were admitted.

By 1922 the Labour Party was recognized as the official opposition, and in 1924 formed a minority government (with Liberal support) for a few months under the party's first secretary Ramsay MacDonald. A second minority government 1929 followed a conservative policy, and in 1931 MacDonald and other leaders, faced with a financial crisis, left the party to support the national government. The ILP seceded 1932. In 1936–39 there was internal dissension on foreign policy; the leadership's support of non-intervention in Spain was strongly and Stafford Cripps, Aneurin Bevan, and others were expelled for advocating an alliance of all left-wing parties against the Chamberlain government.

The Labour Party supported Churchill's wartime coalition, but then withdrew and took office for the first time as a majority government under Clement Attlee, party leader from 1935, after the 1945 elections. The welfare state was developed by nationalization of essential services and industries, a system of national insurance 1946, and the National Health Service 1948. Defeated 1951, Labour was split by disagreements on further nationalization, and unilateral or multilateral disarmament, but achieved unity under Hugh Gaitskell's leadership 1955–63.

Under Harold Wilson the party returned to power 1964–70 and, very narrowly, 1974–79. James Callaghan, who had succeeded Wilson 1976, was forced to a general election 1979 and lost. Michael Foot was elected to the leadership 1980; Neil Kinnock succeeded him 1983 after Labour had lost another general election. The party adopted a policy of unilateral nuclear disarmament 1986 and expelled the left-wing faction Militant Tendency, but rifts remained. Labour lost the 1987 general election, a major reason being their defence policy.

Labour Representation Committee a forerunner 1900–1906 of the British Labour Party. The committee was founded Feb 1900 after a resolution drafted by Ramsay ◊Macdonald and moved by the Amalgamated Society of Railway workers (now the National Union of Railwaymen) was carried at the 1899 Trades Union Congress (TUC). The resolution called for a special congress of the TUC parliamentary committee to campaign for more Labour members of Parliament. Ramsay MacDonald became its secretary. Following his efforts 29 Labour members of Parliament were elected in the 1906 general election, and the Labour Representation Committee was renamed the Labour Party.

labour theory of value in classical economics, the theory that the price (value) of a product directly reflects the amount of labour it involves. According to theory, if the price of a product falls, either the share of labour in that product has declined, or that expended in other goods has risen.

◊Marx adopted and developed the theory but it was not supported by all classical economists. ◊Malthus was a dissenter.

Labrador /ˈlæbrədɔː/ area of NE Canada, part of the province of Newfoundland, lying between Ungava Bay on the NW, the Atlantic on the E, and the Strait of Belle Isle on the SE; area 266,060 sq km/102,699 sq mi; population (1976) 33,052. It consists primarily of a gently sloping plateau with an irregular coastline of numerous bays, fjords, and inlets, and cliffs 60 m/200 ft to 120 m/400 ft high. Industries include fisheries, timber and pulp, and many minerals. Hydroelectric resources include Churchill Falls on Churchill River, where one of the world's largest underground power houses is situated. The Canadian Air Force base in Goose Bay is on land claimed by the Innu (or Montagnais-Naskapi) Indian people, who call themselves a sovereign nation (in 1989 numbering 9,500).

La Bruyère /ˌlæbruːˈjeə/ Jean de 1645–1696. French essayist. He was born in Paris, studied law, took a post in the revenue office, and in 1684 entered the service of the house of Condé. His *Caractères* 1688, satirical portraits of contemporaries, made him many enemies.

Labuan /ləˈbuːən/ a flat, wooded island off NW Borneo, a Federal Territory of East Malaysia; area 100 sq km/39 sq mi; population (1980) 12,000. Its chief town and port is Victoria, population 3,200. Labuan was ceded to Great Britain 1846, and from 1963 included in Sabah, Federation of Malaysia.

laburnum flowering tree *Laburnum anagyroides*, family Leguminosae, native to the mountainous parts of central Europe. The flowers, in long drooping clusters, are bright yellow and appear in early spring; some varieties have purple or reddish flowers. The seeds are poisonous.

lac resinous incrustation exuded by the female lac-insect *Coccus lacca*, which eventually covers the twigs of trees in India and the Far East. The gathered twigs are known as **stick-lac**, and yield a useful crimson dye; **shellac** is manufactured commercially by melting the separated resin and spreading it into thin layers or flakes.

Laccadive, Minicoy, and Amindivi Islands /ˈlækədɪv, ˈmɪnɪkɔɪ, ˌæmɪnˈdiːviː/ former name of Indian island group ◊Lakshadweep.

lace a delicate, decorative openwork textile fabric. *Needlepoint* or *point* laces (a development of embroidery) originated in Italy in the late 15th or early 16th centuries. Lace was first made from linen thread and sometimes also with gold, silver, or silk; cotton, wool, and synthetic fibres have been used more recently. The other chief variety of lace is *bobbin* or *pillow* ('true') lace, made by twisting threads together in pairs or groups, according to a pattern marked out by pins set in a cushion. It is said to have been invented by Barbara Uttmann (born 1514) of Saxony; elaborate patterns may require over a thousand bobbins. Lace is a European craft, with centres in Germany, France, Belgium, Italy, and England, such as Venice, Alençon, and Argentan for point lace, and Mechlin, Valenciennes, and Honiton for bobbin lace; both types are made at Brussels.

machine lace From 1589 various attempts were made at producing machine-made lace, and in 1809 John Heathcote achieved success with a bobbin net machine: the principles of this system are kept in modern machines making plain net. The earliest machine for making true lace, reproducing the movements of the workers' fingers, was invented in England by John Leavers in 1813. It had a wooden frame with mostly wooden moving parts, but worked on the same principle as the modern machines in Nottingham, England, the centre of machine-made lace.

La Ceiba /læ ˈseɪbə/ chief Atlantic port of Honduras; population (1985) 61,900.

lacewing insect of the families Hemerobiidae (the brown lacewings) and Chrysopidae (the green lacewings) of the order Neuroptera. Found throughout the world, they are so named because of the veining of their two pairs of semi-transparent wings, and have narrow bodies and long thin antennae. They are predators, especially on aphids. The eggs of the green lacewing are stalked.

Lachish /ˈleɪkɪʃ/ ancient city SW of Jerusalem, destroyed 589 BC, where inscribed potsherds have been found that throw light on Hebrew manuscripts and the early development of the alphabet.

Lachlan /ˈlæklən/ river in Australia which rises in the Blue Mountains, a tributary of the Murrumbidgee; length 1,485 km/920 mi.

Laclos /læˈkləʊ/ Pierre Choderlos de 1741–1803. French author. An army officer, he wrote a single novel in letter form, *Les Liaisons dangereuses/Dangerous Liaisons* 1782, an analysis of moral corruption.

La Condamine /læ ˌkɒndəˈmiːn/ a commune of Monaco.

lacquer a clear or coloured resinous varnish obtained from Oriental trees (*Toxicodendron vernici-flua*), and used for decorating furniture and art objects. It was developed in China, probably as early as the 4th century BC, and was later adopted in Japan.

lacrosse Canadian ball game, adopted from the North American Indians, and named from a fancied resemblance of the lacrosse stick to a bishop's crozier. Thongs across its curved end form a pocket to carry the small rubber ball.

The pitch is approximately 100 m/110 yd long and a minimum 55 m/60 yd wide in the men's game, which is played with ten players per side; the women's pitch is larger, and there are twelve players per side. The goals are just under 2 m/6 ft square, with loose nets.

World Championship first held in 1967 for men, 1969 for women

men	
1967	USA
1974	USA
1978	Canada
1982	USA
1986	USA
women	
1969	Great Britain
1974	USA
1978	Canada
1982	USA
1986	Australia
1989	United States

lactation the secretion of milk from the mammary glands of mammals. In late pregnancy, the cells lining the lobules inside the mammary glands begin extracting substances from the blood to produce milk. The supply of milk starts shortly after birth with the production of colostrum, a clear fluid consisting largely of water, protein, antibodies, and vitamins. The milk continues practically as long as the infant continues to suck.

lactic acid $CH_3CH(OH)CO_2H$ (modern name **hydroxypropanoic acid**) an organic acid, a colourless, almost odourless syrup, produced by certain bacteria during fermentation. It occurs in yoghurt, buttermilk, sour cream, wine, and certain plant extracts; it is also present in muscles when they are exercised hard, and in the stomach. It is used in food preservation, and the preparation of pharmaceuticals.

lactose a white sugar, found in solution in milk; it forms 5% of cow's milk. It is commercially prepared from the whey obtained in cheese-making. Like table sugar (sucrose), it is a disaccharide, consisting of two basic sugar units (monosaccharides), in this case, glucose and galactose. Unlike sucrose, it is tasteless.

Ladakh /ləˈdɑːk/ subsidiary range of the ◊Karakoram and district of NE Kashmir, India, on the border of Tibet; chief town Leh. After China occupied Tibet in 1951, it made claims on the area.

Ladd /læd/ Alan 1913–1964. US actor whose first leading role, the professional killer in *This Gun for Hire* 1942, made him a star. His career declined after the mid-1950s although his last role, in *The Carpetbaggers* 1964, was one of his best. His other films include *The Blue Dahlia* 1946 and *Shane* 1953.

Ladins /læˈdiːnz/ ethnic community (about 16,000) in the Dolomites whose language (Ladin) derives directly from Latin; they descend from the Etruscans and other early Italian tribes, and have links with the speakers of ◊Romansch.

Ladoga /ˈlædəgə/ (Russian *Ladozhskoye*) largest lake on the continent of Europe, in the USSR, just NE of Leningrad; area 18,400 sq km/7,100 sq mi. It receives the waters of the Svir, which drains Lake Onega, and other rivers, and runs to the Gulf of Finland by the river Neva.

Ladrones /læˈdrəʊnɪz/ Spanish name (meaning 'thieves') of the ◊Marianas archipelago.

Lady in the UK, the formal title of the daughter of an earl, marquis, or duke; and of any woman whose husband is above the rank of baronet or knight, as well as (by courtesy only) the wives of these latter ranks.

ladybird beetle of the family Coccinellidae, generally red or yellow in colour, with black spots. There are many species which, with their larvae, feed upon aphids and scale-insect pests.

Lady Day Christian festival (25 Mar) of the Annunciation of the Virgin Mary; until 1752 it was the beginning of the legal year in England, and it is still a ◊quarter day.

Ladysmith /ˈleɪdɪsmɪθ/ town in Natal, South Africa, 185 km/115 mi NW of Durban, near the Klip. It was besieged by the Boers, 2 Nov 1899–28 Feb 1900, during the South African War. Ladysmith was named in honour of the wife of Sir Henry ◊Smith, a colonial administrator.

lady's smock alternative name for the ◊cuckoo flower *Cardamine pratensis*.

Laënnec /leɪˈnek/ René Théophile Hyacinthe 1781–1826. French physician, inventor of the stethoscope 1814. He introduced the new diagnostic technique of auscultation (evaluating internal organs by listening with a stethoscope) in his book *Traité de l'auscultation médiaté* 1819, which quickly became a medical classic.

Laetrile patent name for an extract from the seeds of apricots, which was claimed as a cancer cure on no accepted evidence. In 1981 it was found to be of no effect against cancer.

Lafarge /ləˈfɑːʒ/ John 1835–1910. US painter and ecclesiastical designer. He is credited with the revival of stained glass in America, and also created woodcuts, watercolours, and murals.

Lafayette /ˌlæfeɪˈet/ Marie Joseph Gilbert de Motier, Marquis de Lafayette 1757–1834. French soldier and politician. He fought against Britain in the American War of Independence. During the French Revolution he sat in the National Assembly as a constitutional royalist, and in 1789 was given command of the National Guard. In 1792 he fled the country after attempting to restore the monarchy, and was imprisoned by the Austrians until 1797. He supported Napoleon during the Hundred Days, sat in the chamber of deputies as a Liberal from 1818, and played a leading part in the revolution of 1830.

He was a popular hero in the USA, and the towns of Lafayette in Louisiana, population (1980) 81,961, and in Indiana, population (1980) 43,011, are named after him.

Lafayette /ˌlæfaɪˈet/ Marie-Madeleine, Comtesse de Lafayette 1634–1693. French author. Her *Mémoires* of the French court are keenly observed, and her *La Princesse de Clèves* 1678 is the first French psychological novel and *roman à clef* (novel with a 'key') in that real-life characters (including ◊La Rochefoucauld, who was for many years her lover) are presented under fictitious names.

La Fontaine /ˌlæ fɒnˈteɪn/ Jean de 1621–1695. French poet. He was born at Château-Thierry, and from 1656 lived largely in Paris, the friend of Molière, Racine, and Boileau. His works include *Fables* 1668–94, and *Contes* 1665–74, a series of witty and bawdy tales in verse.

Lafontaine /ˌlæ fɒnˈteɪn/ Oskar 1943– . West German socialist politician, federal deputy chair of the Social Democrat Party (SPD) from 1987. Leader of the Saar regional branch of the SPD from 1977 and former mayor of Saarbrucken, he was dubbed 'Red Oskar' because of his radical views on defence and environmental issues. His attitude mellowed after becoming minister-president of Saarland in 1985. He is a likely future candidate for chancellor. He was shot and seriously wounded in 1990, at a political rally.

Laforgue /læˈfɔːg/ Jules 1860–1887. French poet, who pioneered ◊free verse and who greatly influenced later French and English writers.

lagan the legal term for wreckage lying on the ocean floor. See also ◊flotsam.

Lagash /ˈlɑːgəʃ/ Sumerian city north of Shatra, Iraq, of great importance under independent and semi-independent rulers from about 3000–2700 BC. Besides objects of high artistic value, it has provided about 30,000 clay tablets giving detailed information on temple administration. It was discovered 1877 and excavated by Ernest de Sarzec, then French consul in Basra.

lager a type of ◊beer.

Lagerkvist /ˈlɑːgəkvɪst/ Pär 1891–1974. Swedish author of lyric poetry, dramas, including *The Hangman* 1935, and novels, such as *Barabbas* 1950. Nobel prize 1951.

Lagerlöf /ˈlɑːgələːf/ Selma 1858–1940. Swedish novelist. She was originally a schoolteacher, and in 1891 published a collection of stories of peasant life, *Gösta Berling's Saga*. She was

Lahore *the Lahore Fort was largely reconstructed by the Mogul emperor Akbar, who reigned 1556–1605.*

the first woman to receive a Nobel prize, in 1909.

lagoon a coastal body of shallow salt water, usually with limited access to the sea. The term is normally used to describe the shallow sea area cut off by a ◊coral reef or barrier islands.

Lagos /'leɪgɒs/ chief port and former capital of Nigeria, located at the western end of an island in a lagoon and linked by bridges with the mainland via Iddo Island; population (1983) 1,097,000. Industries include chemicals, metal products, and fish.

◊Abuja was established as the new capital 1982.

Lagrange /læˈgrɒnʒ/ Joseph Louis 1736–1813. French mathematician, who predicted the existence of Lagrangian points 1772. His *Mécanique analytique* 1788 applied mathematical analysis, using principles established by Newton, to such problems as the movements of planets when affected by each other's gravitational force. He presided over the commission that introduced the metric system 1793.

Lagrangian points five points in space where a small body can remain in a stable orbit with two much more massive bodies. Three of the points, L1–L3, lie on a line joining the two bodies. The other two points, L4 and L5, which are the most stable, lie either side of the line. Their existence was predicted 1772 by Lagrange.

The ***Trojan asteroids*** lie at Lagrangian points L4 and L5 in Jupiter's orbit around the Sun. Clouds of dust and debris may lie at the Lagrangian points of the Moon's orbit around the Earth.

La Guardia /lə ˈgwɑːdiə/ Fiorello (Henrico) 1882–1947. US Republican politician, mayor of New York 1933–1945. Elected against the opposition of the powerful Tammany Hall Democratic Party organization, he cleaned up the administration, suppressed racketeering, and organized unemployment relief, slum-clearance schemes, and social services. Although nominally a Republican, he strongly supported Roosevelt's New Deal. La Guardia Airport, New York, is named after him.

La Hogue /lɑː ˈəʊg/ a naval battle fought off the Normandy coast in 1692 in which the combined British and Dutch fleets defeated the French.

Lahore /ləˈhɔː/ capital of the province of Punjab and second city of Pakistan; population (1981) 2,920,000. Industries include engineering, textiles, carpets, and chemicals. It is associated with Mogul rulers Akbar, Jahangir, and Aurangzeb, whose capital it was in the 16th–17th centuries.

Laibach /'laɪbæx/ German name of Ljubljana, a city in Yugoslavia.

Lailat ul-Barah Muslim festival, the ***Night of Forgiveness***, which takes place two weeks before the beginning of the fast of Ramadan (the ninth month of the Islamic year) and is a time for asking and granting forgiveness.

Lailat ul-Isra Wal Mi'raj Muslim festival that celebrates the prophet Muhammad's ◊Night Journey.

Lailat ul-Qadr Muslim festival, the ***Night of Power***, which celebrates the giving of the Koran to Muhammad. It usually falls at the end of Ramadan.

Laing /læŋ/ R(onald) D(avid) 1927–1989. Scottish psychoanalyst, originator of the 'social theory' of

mental illness, for example that ◊schizophrenia is promoted by family pressure for its members to conform to standards alien to themselves. His books include *The Divided Self* 1960 and *The Politics of the Family* 1971.

laissez-faire (French 'let alone') theory that the state should not intervene in economic affairs, except to break up a monopoly. The phrase originated with the Physiocrats, 18th-century French economists whose maxim was *laissez-faire et laissez-passer*, (that is, leave the individual alone and let commodities circulate freely). The degree to which intervention should take place is still one of the chief problems of modern economics, both in capitalist and in communist regimes. The Scottish economist Adam Smith justified the theory in *The Wealth of Nations* 1776.

Before the 17th century, control by the guild, local authorities, or the state, of wages, prices, employment, and the training of workmen, was taken for granted. As capitalist enterprises developed in the 16th and 17th centuries, entrepreneurs shook off the control of the guilds and local authorities. By the 18th century this process was complete. The reaction against *laissez-faire* began in the mid-19th century and found expression in labour legislation. This reaction was inspired partly by humanitarian protests against the social conditions created by the Industrial Revolution, partly by the wish to counter popular unrest by removing some of its causes.

The 20th century has seen an increasing degree of state intervention to promote social benefits, which after World War II in Europe was extended into the field of nationalization of leading industries and services. However, from the 1970s *laissez-faire* policies were again pursued in the UK and USA.

lake body of still water lying in depressed ground without direct communication with the sea. Lakes are common in formerly glaciated regions, along the courses of slow rivers, and in low land near the sea. The main classifications are by origin: ***glacial lakes***, formed by glacial scouring; ***barrier lakes***, formed by landslides and glacial moraines; ***crater lakes***, found in volcanoes; and ***tectonic lakes***, occurring in natural fissures.

Most lakes are freshwater, such as the Great Lakes in North America, but in hot regions where evaporation is excessive they may contain many salts, for example the Dead Sea. In the 20th century large artificial lakes have been created in connection with hydroelectric and other works. Some lakes have become polluted as a result of human activity. Sometimes ◊eutrophication (a state of overnourishment) occurs, when agricultural fertilizers leaching into lakes cause an explosion of aquatic life, which then depletes the lake's oxygen supply until it is no longer able to support life.

The World's Largest Lakes

Name and location	sq km	sq mi
Caspian Sea (USSR/Iran)	370,990	143,240
Superior (USA/Canada)	82,071	31,700
Victoria (Tanzania/ Kenya/Uganda)	69,463	26,820
Aral Sea (USSR)	64,500	24,904
Huron (USA/Canada)	59,547	23,000
Michigan (USA)	57,735	22,300
Tanganyika (Malawi/ Zaïre/Zambia/Burundi)	32,880	12,700
Baikal (USSR)	31,456	12,150
Great Bear (Canada)	31,316	12,096
Malawi (Tanzania/ Malawi/Mozambique)	28,867	11,150
Great Slave (Canada)	28,560	11,031
Erie (USA/Canada)	25,657	9,910
Winnipeg (Canada)	25,380	9,417
Ontario (USA/Canada)	19,547	7,550
Balkhash (USSR)	18,421	7,115
Ladoga (USSR)	17,695	6,835
Chad (Chad/Niger/Nigeria)	16,310	6,300
Maracaibo (Venezuela)	13,507	5,217

Lake /leɪk/ Veronica. Stage name of Constance Frances Marie Ockelman 1919–1973. US film actress, who co-starred with Alan Ladd in several films during the 1940s, including *The Blue Dahlia* 1946. Her other work includes *Sullivan's Travels* 1942 and *I Married a Witch* 1942.

Lake District region in Cumbria, England; area 1,800 sq km/700 sq mi. It embraces the the the principal English lakes separated by wild uplands rising to many peaks, including Scafell Pike 978 m/3,210 ft.

Windermere, in the SE, is connected with Rydal Water and Grasmere. The westerly Scafell range extends south to the Old Man of Coniston overlooking Coniston Water, and north to Wastwater. Ullswater lies in the NE of the district, with Hawes Water and Thirlmere nearby. The river Derwent flows north through Borrowdale forming Derwentwater Bassenthwaite. West of Borrowdale lie Buttermere, Crummock Water, and, beyond, Ennerdale Water.

The Lake District has associations with the writers Wordsworth, Coleridge, Southey, De Quincey, Ruskin, and Beatrix Potter, and was made a national park 1951.

lake dwelling a prehistoric village built on piles driven into the bottom of a lake. Such villages are found throughout Europe, in W Africa, South America, Borneo, and New Guinea. British examples include a lake village of the 1st centuries BC and AD excavated near Glastonbury, Somerset.

Lake Havasu City /'hævəsuː/ small town in Arizona, USA, which has been developed as a tourist resort. Old London Bridge was transported and reconstructed there in 1971.

lakh or *lac* or *lak* in India or Pakistan, the sum of 100,000 (rupees).

Lakshadweep /læk'ʃædwiːp/ group of 36 coral islands, 10 inhabited, in the Indian Ocean, 320 km/200 mi off the Malabar coast; area 32 sq km/12 sq mi; population (1981) 40,000. The administrative headquarters is on Kavaratti Island. Products include coir, copra, and fish. The religion is Muslim. The first Western visitor was Vasco da Gama 1499. They were British from 1877 until Indian independence, and created a Union Territory of the Republic of India 1956. Formerly known as the Laccadive, Minicoy, and Amindivi Islands, they were renamed Lakshadweep 1973.

Lakshmi /'lækʃmi/ Hindu goddess of wealth and beauty, consort of Vishnu; her festival is ◊Diwali.

Lalande /læ'lɑːnd/ Michel de 1657–1726. French organist and composer of church music for the court at Versailles.

La Línea /læ 'liːniə/ town and port on the isthmus of Algeciras Bay, S Spain, adjoining the frontier zone with Gibraltar; population (1981) 56,300.

Lalique /læ'liːk/ René 1860–1945. French designer of ◊Art Nouveau glass, jewellery, and house interiors.

Lallans /'lælənz/ a variant of 'lowlands' and a name for Lowland Scots, whether conceived as a language in its own right or as a northern dialect of English. Because of its rustic associations, Lallans has been known since the 18th century as 'the Doric', in contrast with the 'Attic' usage of Edinburgh ('the Athens of the North'). See ◊Scots language.

Lalo /'lɑːləʊ/ (Victor Antoine) Edouard 1823–1892. French composer. His Spanish ancestry and violin training are evident in the *Symphonie Espagnole* 1873 for violin and orchestra, and *Concerto for cello and orchestra* 1877. He also wrote an opera, *Le Roi d'Ys* 1887.

Lam /læm/ Wilfredo 1902–1982. Cuban abstract painter. Influenced by Surrealism in the 1930s (he lived in Paris 1937–41), he created a semi-abstract style using mysterious and sometimes menacing images and symbols mainly taken from Caribbean tradition. His *Jungle* series, for example, contains voodoo elements.

Lamaism the religion of Tibet and Mongolia, a form of Mahāyāna Buddhism. Buddhism was introduced

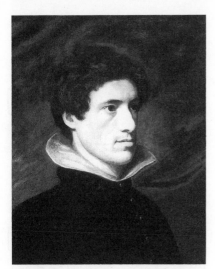

Lamb *English essayist and critic Charles Lamb collaborated with his sister Mary in* Tales from Shakespeare. *His portrait is by fellow essayist William Hazlitt.*

into Tibet AD 640, but the real founder of Lamaism was the Indian missionary Padma Sambhava who began his activity about 750. The head of the church is the ◊Dalai Lama, who is considered an incarnation of the Bodhisattva Avalokiteśvara. On the death of the Dalai Lama great care is taken in finding the infant in whom he has been reincarnated.

In the 15th century Tsongkhapa founded the sect of Geluk-Pa (virtuous), which has remained the most powerful organization in the country. The Dalai Lama, residing at the palace of Potala in Lhasa, exercised both spiritual and temporal authority as head of the Tibetan state until 1959, aided by the ◊Panchen Lama.

Before Chinese Communist rule, it was estimated that one in four of Tibet's male population was a Lamaist monk, but now their numbers are greatly reduced. Prayer-wheels and prayer-flags, on which were inscribed prayers, were formerly a common sight in the Tibetan countryside; when these were turned by hand or moved by the wind, great spiritual benefit was supposed to accrue.

La Mancha /læ ˈmæntʃə/ (Arabic *al mansha*, the dry land), former province of Spain now part of the autonomous region of Castilla-La Mancha; see under ◊Castile. Cervantes' *Don Quijote de la Mancha* 1605 begins there.

Lamarck /læˈmɑːk/ Jean Baptiste de 1744–1829. French naturalist, whose theory of evolution, known as **Lamarckism**, was based on the idea that ◊acquired characters are inherited. His works include *Philosophie Zoologique*/*Zoological Philosophy* 1809 and *Histoire naturelle des animaux sans vertèbres*/*Natural History of Invertebrate Animals* 1815–22.

Lamarckism a theory of evolution, now discredited, advocated during the early 19th century by Lamarck. It differed from the Darwinian theory of evolution in that it was based on the idea that ◊acquired characters were inherited: he argued that particular use of an organ or limb strengthens it, and that this development may be 'preserved by reproduction'. For example, he suggested that giraffes have long necks because they are continually stretching them to reach high leaves; according to the theory, giraffes that have lengthened their necks by stretching will pass this characteristic on to their offspring.

Lamartine /ˌlæmɑːˈtiːn/ Alphonse de 1790–1869. French poet. He wrote romantic poems, *Méditations* 1820, followed by *Nouvelles Méditations*/*New Meditations* 1823, *Harmonies* 1830, and others. His *Histoire des Girondins*/*History*

of the Girondins 1847 influenced the revolution of 1848.

Lamb /læm/ Charles 1775–1834. English essayist and critic. He collaborated with his sister Mary (1764–1847) on *Tales from Shakespeare* 1807, and his *Specimens of English Dramatic Poets* 1808 helped to revive interest in Elizabethan plays. As 'Elia' he contributed essays to the *London Magazine* from 1820 (collected 1823 and 1833).

Born in London, Lamb was educated at Christ's Hospital. He was a contemporary of ◊Coleridge, with whom he published some poetry in 1796. He was a clerk at India House 1792–1825, when he retired to Enfield. His sister Mary stabbed their mother to death in a fit of insanity 1796, and Charles cared for her between her periodic returns to an asylum.

Lamb /læm/ Willis 1913– . US physicist who revised the quantum theory of ◊Dirac. The hydrogen atom was thought to exist in either of two distinct states carrying equal energies. More sophisticated measurements by Lamb in 1947 demonstrated that the two energy levels were not equal. This discrepancy, since known as the Lamb shift, won for him the 1955 Nobel physics prize.

lambert unit of luminance (the light shining from a surface), equal to 1 ◊lumen per square centimetre. In scientific work the ◊candela per square metre is preferred.

Lambert /ˈlæmbət/ John 1619–1683. English general, a cavalry commander under Cromwell (at ◊Marston Moor, Preston, Dunbar, and Worcester). Lambert broke with him over the proposal to award Cromwell the royal title. After the Restoration he was imprisoned for life.

Lambeth /ˈlæmbəθ/ borough of S central Greater London

features Lambeth Palace (chief residence of the archbishop of Canterbury since 1197); Tradescant museum of gardening history; the ◊South Bank (including Royal Festival Hall, National Theatre); the Oval (headquarters of Surrey County Cricket Club from 1846) at Kennington, where the first England–Australia test match was played in 1880; Brixton Prison; Brixton had serious riots in 1981 and 1985

population (1981) 245,500.

Lambeth Conference meeting of bishops of the Anglican Communion every ten years, presided over by the archbishop of Canterbury; its decisions are not binding.

Lamburn /ˈlæmbɜːn/ Richmal Crompton. Full name of British writer Richmal ◊Crompton.

lamina in flowering plants (◊angiosperms), the blade of the ◊leaf on either side of the midrib. The lamina is generally thin and flattened, and is usually the primary organ of ◊photosynthesis. It has a network of veins through which water and nutrients are conducted. More generally, a lamina is any thin, flat plant structure, such as the ◊thallus of many seaweeds.

Lammas ('loaf-mass') medieval festival of harvest, celebrated 1 Aug. At one time it was an English ◊quarter day, and is still a quarter day in Scotland.

lammergeier bird of prey *Gypaetus barbatus*, also known as the bearded vulture, with a wingspan of 2.7 m/9 ft. It ranges over S Europe, N Africa, and Asia, in wild mountainous areas.

Lammermuir Hills /ˈlæməmjʊə/ a range of hills dividing Lothian and Borders regions, Scotland, from Gala Water to St Abb's Head.

Lamming /ˈlæmɪŋ/ George 1927– . Barbadian novelist, author of the autobiographical *In the Castle of my Skin* 1953, describing his upbringing in the small village where he was born. He later moved to London.

Lampedusa /ˌlæmpɪˈduːzə/ Giuseppe Tomasi di 1896–1957. Italian aristocrat, author of *The Leopard* 1958, a novel set in his native Sicily in the period after it was annexed by Garibaldi 1860, which chronicles the reactions of an aristocratic family to social and political upheavals.

lamprey eel-shaped jawless fish belonging to the family Petromyzontidae. Lampreys feed on other fish by fixing themselves by the round mouth to their host and boring into the flesh with their toothed tongue.

Lamu /ˈlɑːmuː/ island off the E coast of Kenya.

Lanark /ˈlænək/ formerly county town of Lanarkshire, Scotland; now capital of Clydesdale district, Strathclyde region; population (1981) 9,800. William Wallace once lived here, and later returned to burn the town and kill the English sheriff. *New Lanark* to the S, founded in 1785 by Robert Owen, was a socialist 'ideal village' experiment.

Lanarkshire /ˈlænəkʃə/ former inland county of Scotland, merged 1975 in the region of Strathclyde. The county town was Lanark.

Lancashire /ˈlæŋkəʃə/ county in NW England
area 3,040 sq km/1,173 sq mi
towns administrative headquarters Preston, which forms part of Central Lancashire New Town (together with Fulwood, Bamber Bridge, Leyland, and Chorley), Lancaster, Accrington, Blackburn, Burnley; ports Fleetwood and Heysham; seaside resorts Blackpool, Morecambe, and Southport
features river Ribble; Pennines; Forest of Bowland (moors and farming valleys)
products formerly a world centre of cotton manufacture, this has been replaced with newer varied industries
population (1987) 1,381,000
famous people Kathleen Ferrier, Gracie Fields, George Formby, Rex Harrison.

Lancaster /ˈlæŋkəstə/ city in Lancashire, England, on the river Lune; population (1983) 126,400. It was the former county town of Lancashire (now Preston). The university was founded 1964. Industries include textiles, floor coverings, furniture, plastics. There is a castle, which incorporates Roman work, and during the Civil War was captured by Cromwell.

Lancaster /ˈlæŋkəstə/ city in Pennsylvania, USA, 115 km/70 mi W of Philadelphia; population (1980) 54,700. It produces textiles and electrical goods. It was capital of the USA briefly in 1777.

Lancaster, Duchy and County Palatine of /ˈlæŋkəstə/ created 1351, and attached to the crown since 1399. The office of Chancellor of the Duchy is a sinecure without any responsibilities, usually held by a member of the Cabinet with a special role outside that of the regular ministries, for example, Harold Lever as financial adviser to the Wilson–Callaghan governments from 1974.

Lancaster /ˈlæŋkəstə/ 'Burt' (Burton Stephen) 1913– . US film actor, formerly an acrobat. A star from his first film, *The Killers* 1946, he proved himself adept both at action roles and more complex character parts in such films as *The Flame and the Arrow* 1950, *Elmer Gantry* 1960, and *The Leopard*/*Il Gattopardo* 1963.

Lancaster /'læŋkəstə/ Osbert 1908–1986. English cartoonist and writer. In 1939 he began producing daily 'pocket cartoons' for the *Daily Express*, in which he satirized current social mores through such characters as Maudie Littlehampton.

He was originally a book illustrator and muralist, and in the 1930s and 1940s produced several wittily debunking books on modern architecture (such as *Homes, Sweet Homes* 1939 and *Drayneflete Revisited* 1949), in which he introduced such facetious terms as Pont Street Dutch and Stockbroker's Tudor.

Lancaster House Agreement accord reached at a conference Sept 1979 at Lancaster House, London, between Britain and representative groups of Rhodesia, including the Rhodesian government under Ian Smith and black nationalist groups. The Agreement enabled a smooth transition to the independent state of Zimbabwe 1980.

Lancaster, House of English royal house, branch of the Plantagenets. It originated 1267 when Edmund (died 1296), the younger son of Henry III, was granted the earldom of Lancaster. Converted to a duchy for Henry of Grosmont (died 1361), it passed to John of Gaunt 1362 by his marriage to Blanche, Henry's daughter. John's son Henry IV established the royal dynasty of Lancaster 1399, and he was followed by two more Lancastrian kings, Henry V and Henry VI.

lancelet marine animal, genus *Amphioxus*, included in the ◊chordates, about 2.5 cm/1 in long. It has no skull, brain, eyes, heart, vertebral column, centralized brain, nor paired limbs, but there is a notochord (a supportive rod) which runs from end to end of the body, a tail, and a number of gillslits. Found in all seas, it burrows in the sand but when disturbed swims freely. Taxonomically it is significant since the notochord may be regarded as the precursor of the backbone (spinal column).

Lancelot of the Lake /'lɑːnslɒt/ in Arthurian legend the most celebrated of King Arthur's knights, the lover of Queen Guinevere. Originally a folkhero, he first appeared in the Arthurian cycle of tales in the 12th century.

Lanchow /ˌlænˈtʃau/ former name of ◊Lanzhou, city in China.

Lancret /lɒŋˈkreɪ/ Nicolas 1690–1743. French painter. His graceful *fêtes galantes* (festive groups of courtly figures in fancy dress) followed a theme made popular by Watteau. He also illustrated amorous scenes from the *Fables* of La Fontaine.

Lancs abbreviation for ◊*Lancashire*.

Land federal state (plural *Länder*) of West Germany or Austria.

Land /lænd/ Edwin 1909– . US inventor of the Polaroid camera 1947, which develops the film inside the camera and produces an instant photograph.

Landau /'lændau/ Lev 1908–1968. Russian theoretical physicist who made important contributions to most areas of twentieth century physics. He was awarded the 1962 Nobel physics prize for his work on liquid helium.

Landes /lɒnd/ sandy, low-lying area in SW France, along the Bay of Biscay, about 12,950 sq km/5,000 sq mi in extent. Formerly covered with furze and heath, it has in many parts been planted with pine and oak forests. It gives its name to a *département*, and extends into the *départements* of Gironde and Lot-et-Garonne. There is a testing range for rockets and missiles at Biscarosse, 72 km/45 mi SW of Bordeaux. There is an oilfield in Parentis-en-Born.

Land League Irish peasant organization, formed by Michael ◊Davitt 1879 to fight against evictions. Through its skilful use of the boycott against any man who took a farm from which another had been evicted, it forced Gladstone's government to introduce a law 1881 restricting rents and granting tenants security of tenure.

landlord and tenant or *lessor and lessee* in law, the relationship that exists when an owner of land or buildings (the landlord) gives to another (the tenant) the exclusive right of occupation for a definite limited period, whether it be a year, a term of years, a week, or a month. When the terms of the contract are embodied in a deed they are said to be covenants, and the whole agreement is termed a lease. In the UK there was traditionally freedom of contract between landlord and tenant, but wartime shortage of rented accommodation for lower-income groups led to abuse by unscrupulous landlords and from 1914 acts were passed affording protection for tenants against eviction and rent increases. The shortage was aggravated by World War II and from 1939 Rent Acts were passed greatly increasing the range of dwellings so protected. Extensive decontrol under the 1957 Rent Act led to hardship, and further legislation followed, notably the Rent Act of 1974, under which tenants of furnished and unfurnished premises were given equal security of tenure. The Housing Act of 1980 attempted to make it more attractive to landlords to let property, while still safeguarding the tenant, notably by creating a new category of tenure—the protected shorthold.

Landor /'lændɔ:/ Walter Savage 1775–1864. English poet and essayist. He lived much of his life abroad, dying in Florence, to which he had fled from a libel suit 1858. His works include the epic *Gebir* 1798 and the *Imaginary Conversations of Literary Men and Statesmen* 1824–29.

Landowska /læn'dɒfskə/ Wanda 1877–1959. Polish harpsichordist and scholar. She founded a school near Paris for the study of early music, and was for many years one of the few artists regularly performing on the harpsichord. In 1941 she moved to the USA.

land reform theory that ownership of land should be shared among the workers, the peasants and the agricultural workers.

Land Registry, HM an official body set up 1925 to register legal rights to land in England and Wales. There has been a gradual introduction, since 1925, of compulsory registration of land in different areas of the country. This requires the purchaser of land to register details of his or her title and all other rights (such as mortgages and ◊easements) relating to the land. Once registered, the title to the land is guaranteed by the Land Registry. This makes buying and selling of land easier and cheaper.

Landsat a series of satellites used for monitoring earth resources. The first was launched 1972.

Landseer /'lændsɪə/ Edwin Henry 1802–1873. British painter and sculptor. He achieved great popularity with sentimental studies of animals, and his *Monarch of the Glen* 1850 was intended for the House of Lords. His sculptures include the lions in Trafalgar Square, London, 1859.

Land's End /'lændz 'end/ promontory of W Cornwall, 15 km/9 mi WSW of Penzance, the most westerly point of England. An extension of Land's End is a group of dangerous rocks, the Longships, a mile out, marked by a lighthouse.

Landskrona /lændz'kru:nə/ town and port in Sweden, on the Sound, 32 km/20 mi N of Malmö; population (1983) 36,500. Industries include shipyards, machinery, chemicals and sugar refining. Carl XI defeated the Danes off Landskrona in 1677.

landslide a sudden downward movement of a mass of soil or rocks from a cliff or steep slope. Landslides happen when a slope becomes unstable, usually because the base has been undercut or certain boundaries of materials within the mass have become wet and slippery.

A *mudflow* happens when soil or loose material is soaked so that it no longer adheres to the slope; it forms a tongue of mud that reaches downhill from a semicircular hollow. A *slump* occurs when the material stays together as a large mass, or several smaller masses, and these may form a tilted steplike structure as they slide. A *landslip* is formed when ◊beds of rock dipping towards a cliff slide along a lower bed. Earthquakes may precipitate landslides.

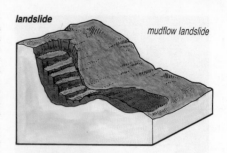

landslide

mudflow landslide

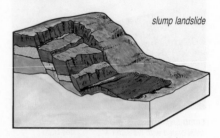

slump landslide

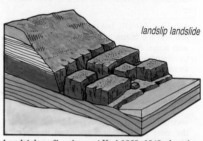

landslip landslide

Landsteiner /'lændstaɪnə/ Karl 1868–1943. Austrian immunologist, who discovered the ABO ◊blood group system 1900–02, and aided in the discovery of the Rhesus blood factors 1940. He also discovered the polio virus.

Landsteiner worked at the Vienna Pathology Laboratory, and the Rockefeller Institute for Medical Research, New York, where he was involved in the discovery of the MN blood groups in 1927. In 1936, he wrote *The Specificity of Serological Reactions*, which helped establish the science of immunology. He also developed a test for syphilis. Nobel Prize for Medicine 1930.

Landtag legislature of each of the *Länder* (states) that form the federal republics of West Germany and Austria.

Lane /leɪn/ Edward William 1801–1876. English traveller and translator, one of the earliest English travellers to Egypt to learn Arabic; his pseudo-scholarly writings, including *Manners and Customs of the Modern Egyptians* 1836, and an annotated translation of the *Arabian Nights* 1838–40, propagated a stereotyped image of the Arab world.

Lanfranc /'lænfræŋk/ *c.*1010–1089. Italian archbishop of Canterbury from 1070; he rebuilt the cathedral, replaced English clergy with Normans, enforced clerical celibacy, and separated the ecclesiastical from the secular courts.

Lanfranc was born in Pavia, Italy; he entered the monastery of Bec, Normandy, in 1042, where he opened a school which achieved international fame; St Anselm, later his successor, was his pupil there. His skill in theological controversy did much to secure the church's adoption of the doctrine of transubstantiation. He came over to England with William the Conqueror, whose adviser he was.

Lang /læŋ/ Andrew 1844–1912. Scottish historian and folklore scholar. His writings include historical works; anthropological essays, such as *Myth, Ritual and Religion* 1887 and *The Making of Religion* 1898, which involved him in controversy with ◊Frazer; novels; and a series of children's books, beginning with *The Blue Fairy Tale Book* 1889.

Lange *Former prime minister of New Zealand David Lange on a visit to London in 1988.*

Lang /læŋ/ Fritz 1890–1976. Austrian film director, born in Vienna. His German films include *Metropolis* 1927, *M* 1931, and the series of Dr Mabuse films, after which he fled from the Nazis to Hollywood 1936. His US films include *Fury* 1936, *You Only Live Once* 1937, and *The Big Heat* 1953.

Lange /ˈlɒŋi/ David (Russell) 1942– . New Zealand Labour Party prime minister 1983–89. Lange, a barrister, was elected to the House of Representatives 1977. Labour had a decisive win in the 1984 general election on a non-nuclear defence policy, which Lange immediately put into effect, despite criticism from the USA. He introduced a free-market economic policy and was re-elected 1987. He resigned Aug 1989 over a disagreement with his finance minister.

Langevin /lɒnʒ'væŋ/ Paul 1872–1946. French physicist who contributed to the studies of magnetism and X-ray emissions. During World War I he invented an apparatus for locating enemy submarines.

Langland /ˈlæŋlənd/ William c. 1332–c. 1400. English poet. Born in the W Midlands, he took minor orders, and in later life settled in London. His alliterative *Vision Concerning Piers Plowman* appeared in three versions between about 1362 and 1398, but some critics believe he was only responsible for the first of these. The poem forms a series of allegorical visions, in which Piers develops from the typical poor peasant to a symbol of Jesus, and condemns the social and moral evils of 14th-century England.

Langley /ˈlæŋli/ Samuel Pierpont 1834–1906. US inventor. His steam-driven aeroplane flew for 90 seconds in 1896, making the first flight by an engine-equipped aircraft. He was professor of physics and astronomy at the Western University of Pennsylvania 1866–87, and did valuable research on the infrared portions of the solar spectrum.

Langmuir /ˈlæŋmjʊə/ Irving 1881–1957. US scientist, who invented the mercury vapour pump for producing a high vacuum, and the atomic hydrogen welding process; he was also a pioneer of the thermionic valve. In 1932 he was awarded a Nobel prize for his work on surface chemistry.

Langobard alternative name for ◊Lombard, member of a Germanic people.

Langton /ˈlæŋtən/ Stephen c. 1150–1228. English priest. He studied in Paris, where he became chancellor of the university, and in 1206 was created a cardinal. When in 1207 Innocent III secured his election as archbishop of Canterbury, King John refused to recognize him, and Langton was not allowed to enter England until 1213. He supported the barons in their struggle against John, and was mainly responsible for ◊Magna Carta.

Langtry /ˈlæŋtri/ Lillie. Stage name of Emilie Charlotte le Breton 1853–1929. English actress, mistress of the future Edward VII. She was known

as the 'Jersey Lily' from her birthplace and considered to be one of the most beautiful women of her time.

She was the daughter of a rector, and married Edward Langtry (died 1897) 1874. She first appeared professionally in London 1881, and had her greatest success as Rosalind in Shakespeare's *As You Like It*. In 1899 she married Sir Hugo de Bathe.

language human communication through speech or writing, or both. Different nationalities typically have different languages or their own variations on a particular language. The term is also used to indicate systems of communication with language-like qualities, such as **animal language** (the way animals communicate), **body language** (gestures and expressions used to communicate ideas), and **computer languages** (such as BASIC and COBOL). One language may have various ◊dialects, which may be seen by those who use them as languages in their own right.

'A language' is any expression of language used by one or more communities for everyday purposes (the English language, the European languages, the Indo-European language family, the Japanese language, and so on).

Natural human language has a neurological basis centred on the left hemisphere of the brain, and expressed through two distinct mediums in most present-day societies: mouth and ear (the medium of sound, or **phonic medium**), and hand and eye (the medium of writing, or **graphic medium**). It appears to develop in children under normal circumstances, either as a unilingual or multi-lingual skill, crucially between the ages of one and five, and as a necessary interplay of innate and environmental factors. Any human child can learn any human language, under the appropriate conditions.

When forms of language are as distinct as Dutch and Arabic, it is obvious that they are different languages. When, however, they are mutually intelligible, as are Dutch and Flemish, a categorical distinction is harder to make. Rather than say that Dutch and Flemish are 'dialects' of a common Netherlandic language, Dutch and Flemish speakers may, for traditional reasons that include ethnic pride and political distinctness, prefer to talk about two distinct languages. To strengthen the differences among similar languages, groups may emphasize those differences (for example, the historical distancing of Portuguese from Castilian Spanish) or adopt different scripts (as in Urdu being written in Arabic script, Hindi in Devanagari script). From outside, Italian appears to be a single language; inside Italy, it is a standard variety resting on a base of many very distinct dialects. The terms 'language' and 'dialect' are not therefore easily defined and distinguished. English is today the dominant world language, but it has so many varieties (often mutually unintelligible) that scholars now talk about 'Englishes' and even 'the English languages' — all, however, united for international purposes by 'Standard English'.

Languedoc /ˌlɑːŋɡəˈdɒk/ former province of S France, lying between the Rhône, the Mediterranean, Guienne, and Gascony.

Languedoc-Roussillon /ˌlɑːŋɡəˈdɒk ˌruːsiːˈjɒn/ region of S France, comprising the *départements* of Aude, Gard, Hérault, Lozère, and Pyrénées-Orientales; area 27,400 sq km/10,576 sq mi; population (1986) 2,012,000. Its capital is Montpellier, and products include fruit, vegetables, wine, and cheese.

langur type of leaf-eating monkey that lives in trees in S Asia. It is related to the colobus monkey of Africa.

Lanier /ləˈnɪə/ Sidney 1842–1881. US flautist and poet. His *Poems* 1877 contain interesting metrical experiments, in accordance with the theories expounded in his *Science of English Verse* 1880, on the relation of verse to music.

lanolin a sticky, purified wax obtained from sheep's wool and used in cosmetics, soap, and leather preparation.

Lansbury /ˈlænzbəri/ George 1859–1940. British Labour politician, leader in the Commons 1931–35. In 1921, while Poplar borough mayor, he went to prison with most of the council rather than modify their policy of more generous unemployment relief. He was a member of Parliament 1910–12 and 1922–40; he was leader of the parliamentary Labour party 1931–35, but resigned (as a pacifist) in opposition to the party's militant response to the Italian invasion of Abyssinia (present-day Ethiopia).

Lansbury sat on Poplar borough council in London from 1903. He was member of Parliament for Bow 1910–12, when he resigned to force a by-election on the issue of votes for women, which he lost. He was editor of the *Daily Herald* 1912, carried it on as a weekly through World War I, and again as a daily until 1922. He edited *Lansbury's Labour Weekly* 1925–27.

Lansdowne /ˈlænzdaʊn/ Henry Charles, 5th Marquis of Lansdowne 1845–1927. British Liberal Unionist politician, governor-general of Canada 1883–88, viceroy of India 1888–93, war minister 1895–1900, and foreign secretary 1900–06. While at the Foreign Office he abandoned Britain's isolationist policy by forming an alliance with Japan and an entente cordiale with France. His letter of 1917 suggesting an offer of peace to Germany created a controversy.

Lansing /ˈlænsɪŋ/ capital of Michigan, USA, at the confluence of the Grand and Red Cedar rivers; population (1980) 472,000. Manufacturing includes motor vehicles, diesel engines, pumps, and furniture.

lanthanide one of the 15 chemically related elements of the lanthanide series. They are: lanthanum, cerium, praseodymium, neodymium, promethium, samarium, europium, gadolinium, terbium, dysprosium, holmium, erbium, thulium, ytterbium, and lutetium. The name ◊rare earth is also used for them, although it strictly means the oxides of these elements.

lanthanum in chemistry, a rare metallic element, symbol La, atomic number 57, relative atomic mass 138.9. It is the first element of the lanthanide series.

Lanzhou /ˌlænˈdʒəʊ/ formerly **Lanchow** capital of Gansu province, China, on the Yellow river, 190 km/120 mi south of the Great Wall; population (1986) 1,350,000. Industries include oil refining, chemicals, fertilizers, and synthetic rubber.

Lao a people who live along the Mekong river system. There are approximately 9,000,000 Lao in Thailand and 2,000,000 in Laos. The Lao language is a member of the Sino-Tibetan family.

Laoighis /liːʃ/ or **Laois** county in Leinster province, Republic of Ireland
area 1,720 sq km/664 sq mi
county town Portlaoise
physical flat except for the Slieve Bloom mountains in the NW
products sugarbeets, dairy products, woollens, agricultural machinery
population (1986) 53,000.

Laon /lɒŋ/ capital of Aisne *département*, Picardie, N France; 120 km/75 mi NE of Paris; population (1982) 29,000. It was the capital of France and a royal residence until the 10th century. It has a 12th-century cathedral.

Laos /laʊs/ landlocked country in SE Asia, bordered to the N by China, E by Vietnam, S by Cambodia, and W by Thailand.

government Laos became a republic Dec 1975 when the monarchy was abolished. The indirectly elected 264-member national congress of people's representatives appointed Prince Souphanouvong (1909–) as executive head of state (president) to be served by a cabinet (council of ministers) led by a prime minister. A 45-member supreme people's assembly, chaired by the president, was established to frame a new constitution. By 1986 a

Laos
People's Democratic Republic of
(Saathiaranagroat Prachhathippatay Prachhachhon Lao)

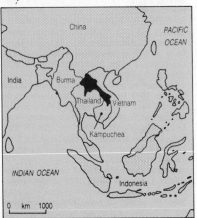

area 236,790 sq km/91,400 sq mi
capital Vientiane
towns Luang Prabang, the former royal capital
physical high mountains in the E; Mekong River in the W; jungle
features hydroelectric power from the Mekong is exported to Thailand; Plain of Jars, where a prehistoric people carved stone jars large enough to hold a person; once known as the Land of a Million Elephants

head of state Prince Souphanouvong from 1975; Phoumi Vongvichit acting president from 1986
head of government Kaysone Phomvihane from 1975
political system communism
exports tin, teak
currency new kip (1213.88 = £1 Feb 1990)
population (1989) 3,923,000; annual growth rate 2.6%
life expectancy men 48, women 51
language Lao
religion traditionally Theravada Buddhist
literacy 76% male/63% female (1985 est)
GNP $601 million (1983); $85 per head of population
chronology
1893–1945 Laos became a French protectorate.
1945 Temporarily occupied by Japan.
1946 Re-taken by France.
1950 Granted semi-autonomy in French Union.
1954 Full independence achieved.
1960 Right-wing government seized power.
1962 Coalition government established; civil war continued.
1973 Vientiane ceasefire agreement.
1975 Communist-dominated republic proclaimed with Prince Souphanouvong as head of state.
1987 Phoumi Vongvichit became acting president.
1988 Plans announced to withdraw 40% of the Vietnamese forces stationed in the country.
1989 First assembly elections since communist takeover.

minister and communist party leader, Kaysone Phomvihane.

The new administration, which inherited a poor, war-ravaged economy, attempted to reorganize the country along socialist lines, nationalizing businesses and industries and collectivizing agriculture. Faced with a food shortage and the flight of more than 250,000 refugees to Thailand, it modified its approach in 1979, introducing production incentives and allowing greater scope for the private sector. Further 'liberalization' followed from 1985 under the prompting of the Soviet leader Michail Gorbachev, with a new profit-related 'socialist business accounting system' being adopted. National elections were held in Mar 1989. Laos, now closely tied to the USSR and Vietnam (which has 40,000 troops stationed in Laos), still suffers from border skirmishes with rebels backed by Thailand in the S and China in the N. There have been attempts to improve relations with Thailand and China for economic reasons, and in Aug 1989 party-to-party relations were established with China after a ten-year break.

Lao Zi /ˌlauˈdziː/ c. 604–531 BC. Chinese philosopher, commonly regarded as the founder of ◊Taoism. Nothing certain is known of his life, and he is variously said to have lived in the 6th or the 4th century BC. The *Tao Tê Ching*, the Taoist scripture, is attributed to him but apparently dates from the 3rd century BC.

La Palma see under La ◊Palma, one of the Spanish Canary Islands.

La Pampa /læ ˈpæmpə/ province in Argentina; see under ◊Pampas.

laparotomy an exploratory operation within the abdomen. The use of laparotomy, as of other exploratory surgery, has decreased sharply with medical advances such as the various modes of scanning and the direct-viewing technique known as ◊endoscopy.

La Paz /læ ˈpæz/ city in Bolivia, 3,800 m/12,400 ft above sea level; population (1985) 992,600. Products include textiles and copper. Founded by the Spanish 1548, it has been the seat of government since about 1900.

lapis lazuli a rock containing the blue mineral lazurite in a matrix of white calcite with small amounts of other minerals. It occurs in silica-poor igneous rocks and metamorphic limestones found in Afghanistan, Siberia, Iran, and Chile. It was formerly used in the manufacture of ultramarine pigment.

Laplace /læˈplæs/ Pierre Simon, Marquis de Laplace 1749–1827. French astronomer and mathematician. Born in Normandy, he was appointed professor of mathematics at the Paris École Militaire 1767. In 1796, he theorized that the solar system originated from a cloud of gas (the nebular hypothesis). He studied the motion of the Moon and planets, and published a five-volume survey of ◊celestial mechanics, *Traité de méchanique céleste* 1799–1825. Among his mathematical achievements was the development of probability theory.

Lapland /ˈlæplænd/ region of Europe within the Arctic Circle in Norway, Sweden, Finland, and USSR, without political definition. Its chief resources are chromium, copper, iron, timber, hydroelectric power, and tourism. There are about 20,000 Lapps, who live by hunting, fishing, reindeer herding, and handicrafts.

La Plata /læ ˈplɑːtə/ capital of Buenos Aires province, Argentina; population (1980) 560,300. Industries include meat packing and petroleum refining. It was founded 1882.

La Plata, Río de /læ ˈplɑːtə/ or *River Plate* estuary in South America into which the rivers Paraná and Uruguay flow; length 320 km/200 mi and width up to 240 km/150 mi. The basin drains much of Argentina, Bolivia, Brazil, Uruguay, and Paraguay, who all cooperate in its development.

Laptev Sea /ˈlæptev/ part of the Arctic Ocean off the N coast of the USSR between Taimyr Peninsula and New Siberian Island.

draft document had ben completed, but remained the subject of government discussion. In the meantime, elections were finally held to the SPA, which was expanded to comprise 79 deputies elected for five-year terms and accorded the task of framing the economic plan and overseeing the work of state ministries. The controlling force and only political party in Laos is the Communist party (Lao People's Revolutionary Party), which is dominated by its 11-member Political Bureau and heads the broader Lao Front for National Reconstruction.

history Occupied from the 4th–5th centuries by immigrants from China, Laos came under Indian influence and adopted Buddhism during the 7th–11th centuries. As part of the ◊Khmer empire from the 11th–13th centuries, it experienced much artistic and architectural activity. From the 12th century, the country was invaded by the Lao from Thailand, who established small independent kingdoms and became Buddhists. Laos became an independent kingdom in the 14th century and was first visited by Europeans in the 17th century, becoming a French protectorate 1893–1945. After a brief period of Japanese occupation, France re-established control 1946 despite opposition from the Chinese-backed *Lao Issara* (Free Laos) nationalist movement. The country became semi-autonomous 1950, when, under the constitutional monarchy of the king of ◊Luang Prabang, it became an associated state of the French Union.

In 1954, after the Geneva Agreements, Laos gained full independence. Civil war broke out between two factions of former *Lao Issara* supporters: a moderate, royalist-neutralist group led by Prince Souvanna Phouma, which had supported the 1950 French compromise and was the recognized government for most of the country; and a more extreme Communist resistance group, the *Pathet Lao* (Land of the Lao), led by ex-Prince Souphanouvong (the half-brother of Prince Souvanna) and supported by China and the Vietminh, which controlled much of N Laos.

A coalition government was established after the 1957 Vientiane Agreement. This soon collapsed and in 1960 a third, right-wing force emerged when Gen Phoumi Nosavan, backed by the royal army, overthrew Souvanna Phouma and set up a pro-Western government headed by Prince Boun Gum. A new Geneva Agreement 1962 established a tripartite (right-left-neutral) government under the leadership of Prince Souvanna Phouma. Fighting continued, however, between the North Vietnamese–backed *Pathet Lao* and the US-backed neutralists and right wing, until the 1973 Vientiane Agreeement established a ceasefire line dividing the country NW to SE, giving the Communists two-thirds of the country including the Plain of Jars and the Bolovens Plateau in the south, but giving the Souvanna Phouma government two-thirds of the population. All foreign forces (North Vietnamese, Thai, and US) were to be withdrawn, and both sides received equal representation in Souvanna Phouma's provisional government 1974.

In 1975 the Communist *Pathet Lao* (renamed the Lao People's Front) seized power. King Savang Vatthana (1908–80), who had succeeded 1959, abdicated and Laos became a People's Democratic Republic under the presidency of Prince Souphanouvong. Prince Souvanna Phouma remained as an 'adviser' to the government, but the real controlling force was now the prime

La Paz La Paz, the seat of government in Bolivia.

laptop computer a portable ◊microcomputer, small enough to be used on the operator's lap. It consists of a single unit, incorporating a keyboard, ◊floppy disc or ◊hard disc drives, and a screen, the latter often forming a lid which folds back in use. The screen uses a liquid crystal or gas plasma display, rather than the bulkier and heavier cathode ray tubes found in most ◊VDUs. A typical laptop measures about 360 mm × 380 mm × 100 mm, and weighs between 3 and 7 kg.

lapwing bird *Vanellus vanellus* of the plover family, also known as the **green plover**, and from its call, as the **peewit**. Bottle-green above and white below, with a long thin crest and rounded wings, it is about 30 cm/1 ft long and inhabits moorland in Europe and Asia, making a nest scratched out of the ground.

Laramie /ˈlærəmi/ town in Wyoming, USA, on the Laramie Plains, a plateau 2,300 m/7,500 ft above sea level, bounded to the N and E by the Laramie Mountains; population (1980) 24,400. The Laramie River, on which it stands, is linked with the Missouri via the Platte. On the overland trail and Pony Express route, Laramie features in Western legend.

larceny in the UK, formerly the name for ◊theft. Until 1827 larceny was divided into 'grand larceny', punishable by death or transportation for life, and 'petty larceny', when the stolen articles were valued at less than a shilling (5p). In the USA these terms are still used.

larch tree, genus *Larix*, of the family Pinaceae. The common larch *Larix decidua* grows to 40 m/130 ft. It is one of the few ◊conifer trees to shed its leaves annually. The small needle-like leaves are replaced every year by new bright green foliage which later darkens. Closely resembling it is the tamarack *Larix laricina*, and both are timber trees. The golden larch *Pseudolarix amabilis*, a native of China, turns golden in autumn.

lard edible fat high in saturated fatty acids. It is prepared from pigs and used in margarine, soap, and ointment.

Larderello /ˌlɑːdəˈrɛləʊ/ site in the Tuscan hills, NE Italy, where the sulphur springs were used by the Romans for baths, and exploited for boric acid in the 18th–19th centuries. Since 1904 they have been used to generate electricity: the water reaches 220°C.

Lardner /ˈlɑːdnə/ Ring 1885–1933. US short story writer. A sporting correspondent especially keen on baseball, he based his characters on the people he met professionally. His collected volumes of short stories include *You Know Me, Al* 1916, *Round Up* 1929, and *Ring Lardner's Best Short Stories* 1938, all written in colloquial language.

Laredo /ləˈreɪdəʊ/ city on the Rio Grande river, Texas, USA; population (1980) 91,450. Indstries include oil refining and meat processing. **Nuevo Laredo**, Mexico, on the opposite bank, is a textile centre; population (1980) 203,300. There is much cross-border trade.

lares and *penates* in Roman mythology, spirits of the farm and of the store cupboard, often identified with the family ancestors, whose shrine was the centre of family worship in Roman homes.

Large Electron–Positron collider (LEP) the world's largest particle ◊accelerator, in operation from 1989 at the CERN laboratories near Geneva. It occupies a tunnel 3.8 m/12.5 ft wide and 27 km/16.7 mi long, which is buried 180 m/590 ft underground and forms a ring consisting of eight curved and eight straight sections. In 1989 the LEP was used to measure the mass and lifetime of the Z particle, carrier of the weak nuclear force.

Electrons and positrons enter the ring after passing through the Super Proton Synchrotron accelerator. They travel in opposite directions around the ring, guided by 3328 bending magnets and kept within tight beams by 1272 focusing magnets. As they pass through the straight sections, the particles are accelerated by a pulse of radio energy. Once sufficient energy is accumulated, the beams are allowed to collide. Four giant detectors are used to study the resulting shower of particles.

Largo Caballero /ˈlɑːgəʊ ˌkæbəˈjeərəʊ/ Francisco 1869–1946. Spanish socialist and leader of the Spanish Socialist Party (PSOE). He became prime minister of the popular-front government elected Feb 1936 and remained in office for the first ten months of the Civil War before being replaced by Juan Negrin (1887–1956) May 1937.

La Rioja /læ riˈɒxə/ region of N Spain; area 5,000 sq km/1,930 sq mi; population (1986) 263,000.

Larionov /ˌlæriˈɒnəf/ Mikhail Fedorovich 1881–1964. Russian painter, active in Paris from 1919. He pioneered a semi-abstract style known as **Rayonnism** with his wife Natalia ◊Goncharova, in which subjects appear to be deconstructed by rays of light from various sources. Larionov also produced stage sets for Diaghilev's *Ballets Russes* from 1915. In Paris he continued to work as a theatrical designer and book illustrator.

Larisa /ləˈrɪsə/ town in Thessaly, Greece, S of Mount Olympus; population (1981) 102,000. Products include textiles and agriculture.

lark songbird of the family Alaudidae, found mainly in the Old World, but also in North America. It is usually about 17 cm/7 in long, and nests in the open. The northern **skylark** *Alauda arvensis* breeds in Britain. Light-brown, 18 cm/7 in long, it nests on the ground, and sings as it rises almost vertically in the air.

Larkin /ˈlɑːkɪn/ Philip 1922–1985. English poet. His perfectionist, pessimistic verse includes *The North Ship* 1945, *The Whitsun Weddings* 1964, and *High Windows* 1974. He edited *The Oxford Book of 20th-Century English Verse* 1973. Born in Coventry, Larkin was educated at Oxford, and from 1955 was librarian at Hull University. He also wrote two novels.

larkspur plant of the genus ◊delphinium.

Larne /lɑːn/ seaport of County Antrim, N Ireland, on Lough Larne, terminus of sea routes to Stranraer, Liverpool, Dublin, and other places; population (1981) 18,200.

La Rochefoucauld /læ ˌrɒʃfuːˈkəʊ/ François, duc de La Rochefoucauld 1613–1680. French writer. *Réflexions, ou sentences et maximes morales/Reflections, or Moral Maxims* 1665 is a collection of brief, epigrammatic, and cynical observations on life and society, with the epigraph 'Our virtues are mostly our vices in disguise'. He was a lover of Mme de ◊Lafayette.

Born in Paris, he became a soldier, and took part in the ◊Fronde. His later years were divided between the court and literary society.

La Rochelle /ˌlæ rɒˈʃel/ fishing port in W France; population (1982) 102,000. It is the capital of Charente-Maritime *département*. Industries include shipbuilding, chemicals, and motor vehicles. A Huguenot stronghold, it was taken by Cardinal Richelieu in the siege of 1627–28.

Larousse /læˈruːs/ Pierre 1817–1875. French grammarian and lexicographer. His encyclopedic dictionary, the *Grand Dictionnaire universel du XIXème siècle/Great Universal 19th-Century Dictionary* 1865–76, was an influential work and continues in subsequent revisions.

Larsson /ˈlɑːsən/ Carl 1853–1919. Swedish painter, engraver, and illustrator. He is remembered for his watercolours of domestic life, delicately coloured and full of detail, illustrating his book *Ett Hem/A Home* 1899.

Lartigue /lɑːˈtiːg/ Jacques-Henri 1894–1986. French photographer. He began taking extraordinary and humorous photographs of his family at the age of seven, and went on to make ◊autochrome colour prints of women.

larva the stage between hatching and adulthood in those species in which the young have a different appearance and way of life from the adults. Examples include tadpoles (frogs) and caterpillars (butterflies). Larvae are typical of the invertebrates, and some (for example, shrimps) have two or more distinct larval stages. Among vertebrates, it is only the amphibians and some fish that have a larval stage.

The process whereby the larva changes into another stage, such as a pupa (chrysalis) or adult, is known as ◊metamorphosis.

laryngitis inflammation of the larynx, causing soreness of the throat, dry cough, and hoarseness. The acute form is due to a cold, excessive use of the voice, or inhalation of irritating smoke, and may cause the voice to be completely lost. With rest the inflammation usually subsides in a few days.

larynx in mammals, a cavity at the upper end of the trachea (windpipe), containing the vocal cords. It is stiffened with cartilage and lined with mucous membrane. Amphibians and reptiles have much simpler larynxes, with no vocal cords. Birds have a similar cavity, called the **syrinx**, found lower down the trachea, where it branches to form the bronchi. It is very complex, with well-developed vocal cords.

la Salle /lə ˈsæl/ René Robert Cavelier, Sieur de la Salle 1643–1687. French explorer. He made an epic voyage through North America, exploring the Mississippi River down to its mouth, and in 1682 founded Louisiana. When he returned with colonists, he failed to find the river mouth again, and was eventually murdered by his mutinous men.

lascar /ˈlæskə/ East Indian seaman. The word derives from the Persian *lashkar*, 'army', 'camp', and lascars were originally a class of ◊sepoy.

Las Casas /læs ˈkɑːsəs/ Bartolomé de 1474–1566. Spanish missionary, historian, and colonial reformer, known as **the Apostle of the Indies**. He was the first European to call for the abolition of Indian slavery in Latin America. He took part in the conquest of Cuba 1513, but subsequently worked for American Indian freedom in the Spanish colonies. *Apologetica historia de las Indias* (first published 1875–76) is his account of Indian traditions and his witnessing of Spanish oppression of the Indians.

Las Casas sailed to Hispaniola in the West Indies 1502 and was ordained priest there 1512. From Cuba he returned to Spain 1515 to plead for the Indian cause, winning the support of the Holy Roman emperor Charles V. In what is now Venezuela he unsuccessfully attempted to found a settlement of free Indians. In 1530, shortly before the conquest of Peru, he persuaded the Spanish government to forbid slavery there. In 1542 he became bishop of Chiapas in S Mexico. He returned finally to Spain 1547.

Lascaux /læsˈkəʊ/ cave system near Montignac in the Dordogne, SW France, discovered 1940. It has rich paintings of buffalo, horses, and red deer of the Upper Palaeolithic period, about 18,000 BC.

Lasdun /ˈlæzdən/ Denys 1914– . British architect. He designed the Royal College of Surgeons in Regent's Park, London 1960–64, some of the buildings at the University of East Anglia, Norwich, and the National Theatre 1976–77 on London's South Bank.

lapis lazuli The deep blue mineral lapis lazuli, a complex mixture of lazurite (sodium aluminium silicate) with other minerals, is the source of the pigment ultramarine.

Las Casas *Las Casas, Spanish missionary in the Americas who called for the abolition of Indian slavery.*

laser acronym for *Light Amplification by Stimulated Emission of Radiation*; a device for producing a narrow beam of light, capable of travelling over vast distances without dispersion, of being focused to give enormous power densities (10^8 watts per cm^2 for high-energy lasers), and operating on a principle similar to that of the ◊maser. Uses of lasers include communications (a laser beam can carry much more information than radio waves), cutting, drilling, welding, satellite tracking, medical and biological research, and surgery.

Many solid, liquid, and gaseous substances have been used for laser materials, including synthetic ruby crystal (used for the first extraction of laser light 1960, and giving a high-power pulsed output) and a helium–neon gas mixture, capable of continuous operation, but at a lower power.

A blue short-wave laser was developed in Japan 1988. Its expected application is in random access memory (◊RAM) and CD gramophone recording. A gallium arsenide chip, produced by IBM 1989, contains the world's smallest lasers in the form of cylinders of ◊semiconductor roughly one tenth of the thickness of a human hair; a million lasers can fit on a chip 1 cm/2.5 in square.

Sound wave vibrations from the window glass of a room can be picked up by a reflected laser

laser

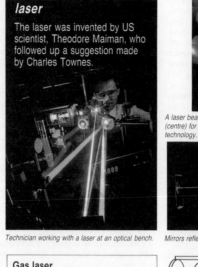

laser

The laser was invented by US scientist, Theodore Maiman, who followed up a suggestion made by Charles Townes.

A laser beam is used to check quartz windows (centre) for cleanliness, used in electro-optical technology.

Technician working with a laser at an optical bench.

Mirrors reflecting the beam of an argon ion laser.

Gas laser

(1) In a gas laser, electrons moving between the electrodes pass energy to gas atoms. An energised atom emits a ray of light.

(2) The ray hits another energised atom causing it to emit a further ray of light.

(3) The rays bounce between the mirrors at each end causing a build-up of light. Eventually the beam becomes strong enough to pass through the half-silvered mirror at one end, producing a laser beam.

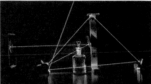
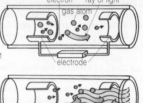
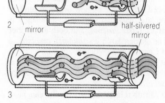

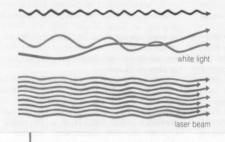

White light is a mixture of light waves of different wavelengths, corresponding to different colours. In a beam of white light, all the waves are out of step.

In a laser beam, all the waves are of the same wavelength, so the beam is a pure colour. All the waves in a laser beam are in step.

Laplace *Pierre Simon Laplace was called 'the French Newton' for his work on planetary orbits.*

beam. Lasers are also used as entertainment in theatres, concerts, and light shows.

laser printer a computer printer in which an image is formed by the action of a laser on a light-sensitive drum, then transferred to paper by means of an electrostatic charge. The image, which can be text or pictures, is made up of tiny dots, usually at a density of 120 per cm/300 per in.

laser surgery the use of intense light sources to cut, coagulate, and vaporize tissue. Less invasive than normal surgery, it destroys diseased tissue gently and allows quicker, more natural healing. It can be used with a flexible endoscope, to enable the surgeon to see the diseased area at which he or she needs to aim.

Lashio /ˈlæʃiəʊ/ town in the Shan state, Burma, about 200 km/125 mi NE of Mandalay; beginning of the Burma Road, constructed in 1938, to Kunming in China.

Laski /ˈlæski/ Harold 1893–1950. British political theorist. Professor of political science at the London School of Economics from 1926, he taught a modified Marxism, and published *A Grammar*

of Politics 1925 and *The American Presidency* 1940. He was chairman of the Labour Party 1945–46.

Las Palmas /læs ˈpælməs/ or **Las Palmas de Gran Canaria** tourist resort on the NE coast of Gran Canaria, Canary Islands; population (1986) 372,000. Products include sugar and bananas.

La Spezia /læ ˈspetsiə/ port in NW Italy, chief Italian naval base; population (1988) 107,000. Industries include shipbuilding, engineering, electrical goods, and textiles. The poet Shelley drowned in the Gulf of Spezia.

Lassa fever fever caused by a virus, first detected 1969, and spread by a species of rat found only in W Africa. There is no known cure, the survival rate being less than 50%.

Lassalle /læˈsæl/ Ferdinand 1825–1864. German socialist. He was imprisoned for his part in the ◊Revolution of 1848, during which he met ◊Marx, and in 1863 founded the General Association of German Workers (later the Social-Democratic Party). His publications include *The Working Man's Programme* 1862, and *The Open Letter*

lateral line system

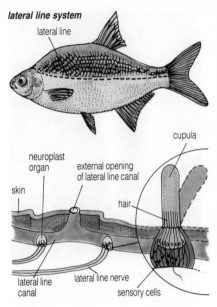

1863. He was killed in a duel arising from a love affair.

Lasseter's Reef /ˈlæsɪtəz ˈriːf/ legendary location of a rich gold-bearing area in Rawlinson Range, Western Australia, discovered by H B Lasseter 1897, but which he could never find again.

Lassus /ˈlæsəs/ (or *Lasso*) Roland de *c.* 1532–1594. Franco-Flemish composer. His works include polyphonic sacred music, songs, and madrigals, including settings of poems by his friend ◊Ronsard.

Las Vegas /læs ˈveɪɡəs/ city in Nevada, USA, known for its nightclubs and gambling casinos; population (1986) 202,000.

lat. abbreviation for ◊*latitude*.

Latakia /ˌlætəˈkiːə/ port with tobacco industries in NW Syria; population (1981) 197,000.

La Tène prehistoric settlement at the east end of Lake Neuchâtel, Switzerland, which has given its name to a culture of the Iron Age. The culture lasted from the 5th century BC to the Roman conquest; sites include Glastonbury Lake village, England.

latent heat in physics, heat that changes the state of a substance (for example, from solid to liquid) without changing its temperature.

lateral line system a system of sense organs in fishes and larval amphibians (tadpoles) which detects water movement. It usually consists of a row of interconnected pores on either side of the body and head.

Lateran Treaties a series of agreements that marked the reconciliation of the Italian state with the papacy 1929. They were hailed as a propaganda victory for the Fascist regime. The treaties involved recognition of the sovereignty of the ◊Vatican City State, the payment of an indemnity for papal possessions lost during unification in 1870, and agreement on the role of the Catholic church within the Italian state in the form of a concordat between Pope Pius XI and the dictator Mussolini.

laterite a red residual soil characteristic of tropical rain forests. It is formed by the weathering of basalts, granites, and shales and contains a high percentage of aluminium and iron hydroxides.

latex (Latin 'liquid') a lactiferous fluid of ◊angiosperm plants, an emulsion of various substances. Latex is exuded from the Para rubber tree and worked into rubber.

lathe a machine tool, used for *turning*. The workpiece to be machined is held and rotated, while cutting tools are moved against it. Modern lathes are driven by electric motors, which can drive the spindle carrying the workpiece at various speeds.

latifundium (Latin 'broad' + 'farm') in ancient Rome, a large agricultural estate designed to make maximum use of cheap labour, whether free workmen or slaves.

In present-day Italy, Spain, and South America, the term *latifondo* refers to a large agricultural estate worked by low-paid casual or semiservile labour in the interests of absentee landlords.

Latimer /ˈlætɪmə/ Hugh 1490–1555. English Christian church reformer and bishop. After his conversion to Protestantism 1524 he was imprisoned several times but was protected by Cardinal Wolsey and Henry VIII.

Latimer was appointed bishop of Worcester 1535, but resigned 1539. Under Edward VI his sermons denouncing social injustice won him great influence, but after the accession of Mary he was arrested 1553 and two years later burned at the stake in Oxford for heresy.

Latin /ˈlætɪn/ an Indo-European language of ancient Italy. Latin has passed through four influential phases: as the language of (1) Republican Rome, (2) the Roman Empire, (3) the Roman Catholic Church, and (4) W European culture, science, philosophy, and law during the Middle Ages and the Renaissance. During the third and fourth phases much Latin vocabulary entered the English language. It is the parent form of the ◊Romance languages, noted for its highly inflected grammar and conciseness of expression.

The direct influence of Latin in Europe has decreased since Renaissance times but is still considerable, and indirectly both the language and its classical literature still affect many modern languages and literatures. The insistence of Renaissance scholars upon an exact classical purity together with the rise of the European nation-states contributed to the decline of Latin as an international cultural medium.

Latin vocabulary has entered English in two major waves: as religious vocabulary from Anglo-Saxon times until the Reformation, and as the vocabulary of science, scholarship, and the law from the Middle Ages onward. In the 17th century the makers of English dictionaries deliberately converted Latin words into English, enlarging the already powerful French component of English vocabulary into the language of education and refinement, placing *fraternity* alongside 'brotherhood', *comprehend* beside 'understand', *feline* beside 'cat-like', and so on. Many 'Latin tags' are in regular use in English: *habeas corpus* ('you may have the body'), *ipse dixit* ('he said it himself'), *non sequitur* ('it does not follow'), and so on. English which consists of many Latin elements is 'Latinate', and often has a grandiose and even pompous quality.

Nowadays, with fewer students studying Latin in schools and universities, there is a tendency to make Latin words more conventionally English; for example, 'cactuses' rather than *cacti* as the plural of 'cactus'. This tendency is accompanied by some uncertainty about usage, for example, whether words like 'data' and 'media' are singular or plural.

Latin America countries of South and Central America (also including Mexico) in which Spanish, Portuguese, and French are spoken.

Latin literature only a few hymns and inscriptions survive from the earliest period of Latin literature before the 3rd century BC. Greek influence began with the work of Livius Andronicus (*c.* 284–204 BC) who translated the *Odyssey* and Greek plays into Latin. Naevius and Ennius both attempted epics on patriotic themes; the former used the native 'Saturnian' metre, but the latter introduced the Greek hexameter. Plautus and Terence successfully adapted Greek comedy to the Latin stage. Lucilius (190–103 BC) founded Latin verse satire, while the writings of Cato were the first important works in Latin prose.

In the *De Rerum Natura* of Lucretius, and the passionate lyrics of Catullus, Latin verse reached maturity. Cicero set a standard for Latin prose, in his orations, philosophical essays, and letters. To the same period belong the histories of Caesar.

The Augustan age (43 BC–AD 17) is usually regarded as the golden age of Latin literature. There is strong patriotic feeling in the work of the poets Virgil and Horace and the historian Livy, who belonged to Augustus's court circle. Virgil produced the one great Latin epic, the *Aeneid*, while Horace brought charm and polish to both the lyric and satire. Younger poets of the period were Ovid and the elegiac poets Tibullus and Propertius.

The 'silver age' of the Empire begins with the writers of Nero's reign: the Stoic philosopher Seneca, Lucan, author of the epic *Pharsalia*, the satirist Persius and, by far the greatest, the realistic novelist Petronius. Around the end of the 1st century and and at the beginning of the 2nd came the historian Tacitus and the satirist Juvenal; other writers of the period were the epigrammatist Martial, the scientist Pliny the Elder, the letter-writer Pliny the Younger, the critic Quintilian, the historian Suetonius, and the epic poet Statius.

The 2nd and 3rd centuries produced only one pagan writer of importance, the romancer Apuleius, but there were several able Christian writers, such as Tertullian, Cyprian, Arnobius (died 327), and Lactantius (died 325). In the 4th century there was something of a poetic revival, with Ausonius and Claudian, and the Christian poets Prudentius and St Ambrose. The Classical period ends, and the Middle Ages begin, with St Jerome's translation of the Bible, and St Augustine's *City of God*.

Throughout the Middle Ages Latin remained the language of the Church, and was normally employed for theology, philosophy, histories, and other learned works. Latin verse, adapted to rhyme and non-classical metres, was used both for hymns and the secular songs of the wandering scholars. Even after the Reformation, Latin retained its prestige as the international language of scholars, and was used as such by More, Bacon, Milton, and many others.

latitude and longitude angular distances defining position on the globe. *Latitude* (abbreviation lat.) is the angular distance of any point from the ◊equator, measured N or S along the Earth's curved surface, equalling the angle between the respective horizontal planes. It is measured in degrees, minutes, and seconds, each minute equalling one nautical mile (1.85 km/1.15 mi) in length. *Longitude* (abbreviation long.) is the angle between the terrestrial meridian through a place, and a standard meridian now taken at Greenwich, England. At the equator one degree of longitude measures approximately 113 km/70 mi.

For map making, latitude is based on the supposition that the Earth is an oblate spheroid. The difference between this (the geographical) and astronomical latitude is the correction necessary for local deviation of plumb line. All determinations of longitude are based on the Earth turning through 360° in 24 hours, or the Sun reaching 15° W each hour.

Latitudinarian in the Church of England from the 17th century, a member of a group of priests, which included J R Tillotson (1630–94, archbishop of Canterbury) and Edward Stillingfleet (1635–99, bishop of Worcester), who were willing to accept modifications of forms of church government and worship to accommodate Dissenters.

Latium /ˈleɪʃɪəm/ Latin name for ◊Lazio, a region of W central Italy.

La Tour /læˈtʊə/ Georges de 1593–1652. French painter active in Lorraine. He was patronized by the duke of Lorraine and perhaps also by Louis XIII. Many of his pictures are illuminated by a single source of light, with deep contrasts of light and shade. They range from religious paintings to genre scenes.

La Tour's style suggests a connection with the Dutch painters Honthorst and Terbrugghen who were followers of Caravaggio, but it is distinctive,

latitude and longitude

Point X lies on longitude 60°W

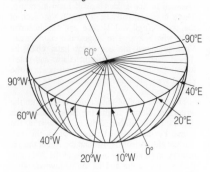

Point X lies on latitude 20°S

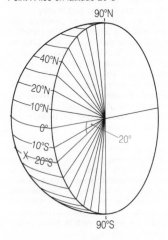

with fire or candlelight creating warm and glowing tones. His subjects include solitary women in domestic interiors, sometimes seated beside a table with a candle and a mirror.

La Trobe /lə 'trəʊb/ Charles Joseph 1801–1875. Australian administrator. He was superintendent of Port Phillip district 1839–51 and first lieutenant-governor of Victoria 1851–54. The Latrobe River is named after him, and flows generally SE through Victoria to Lake Wellington.

Lattakia /ˌlætəˈkiːə/ alternative form of ◊Latakia in Syria.

Latter-day Saint member of a US-based Christian sect, the ◊Mormons.

Latvia /ˈlætvɪə/ constituent republic of W USSR from 1940
area 63,700 sq km/24,595 sq mi
capital Riga
towns Daugavpils, Liepaja, Jelgava, Ventspils
physical lakes, marshes, wooded lowland
products meat and dairy products, communications equipment, consumer durables, motor-cycles, locomotives
population (1987) 2,647,000; Lett 54%, Russian 33%
language Latvian
religion mostly Lutheran Protestant with a Roman Catholic minority
recent history as in the other Baltic republics, there has been nationalist dissent since 1980, influenced by the Polish example and prompted by an influx of Russian workers and officials. In May 1990 the republic declared indepence from Moscow, subject to a 'transition period' for negotiation.

Latvian language the language of Latvia; with Lithuanian it is one of the two surviving members

Latvia

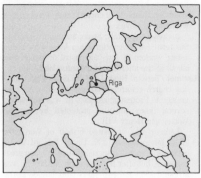

of the Baltic branch of the Indo-European language family.

Latynina /læˈtɪnɪnə/ Larissa Semyonovna 1935– . Soviet gymnast, winner of more Olympic medals than any person in any sport. She won 18 between 1956–64, including nine gold medals. She won a total of 12 individual Olympic and world championship gold medals.

Laud /lɔːd/ William 1573–1645. English priest. As archbishop of Canterbury from 1633, his High Church policy, support for Charles I's unparliamentary rule, censorship of the press, and persecution of the Puritans all aroused bitter opposition, while his strict enforcement of the statutes against enclosures and of laws regulating wages and prices alienated the propertied classes. His attempt to impose the use of the Prayer Book on the Scots precipitated the English ◊Civil War. Impeached by Parliament 1640, he was imprisoned in the Tower, condemned to death by a bill of ◊attainder, and beheaded.

laudanum alcoholic solution (tincture) of opium. Used formerly as a narcotic and for analgesia, it was available in the 19th century from pharmacists on demand.

Lauder /ˈlɔːdə/ Harry. Stage name of Hugh MacLennan 1870–1950. Scottish music-hall comedian and singer, who began his career as an 'Irish' comedian.

Lauderdale /ˈlɔːdədeɪl/ John Maitland, Duke of Lauderdale 1616–1682. Scottish politician. Formerly a zealous ◊Covenanter, he joined the Royalists 1647, and as high commissioner for Scotland 1667–1679 persecuted the Covenanters. He was created duke of Lauderdale 1672, and was a member of the ◊Cabal ministry 1667–73.

Laue /ˈlaʊə/ Max Theodor Felix 1879–1960. German physicist who was a pioneer in measuring the wavelength of X-rays by their diffraction through the closely spaced atoms in a crystal. His work led to the powerful technique now used to elucidate the structure of complex biological materials such as ◊DNA. He was awarded a Nobel prize 1914.

Laugharne /lɑːn/ village at the mouth of the river Towey, Dyfed, Wales. The home of the poet Dylan Thomas, it features in his work as 'Milk Wood'.

laughing jackass another name for ◊kookaburra.

Laughton /ˈlɔːtn/ Charles 1899–1962. English actor, who became a US citizen 1950. Initially a classical stage actor, his dramatic film roles included the king in *The Private Life of Henry VIII* 1933, Captain Bligh in *Mutiny on the Bounty* 1935, Quasimodo in *The Hunchback of Notre Dame* 1939, and Gracchus in *Spartacus* 1960.

Launceston /ˈlɔːnsəstən/ port in NE Tasmania, Australia, on the Tamar river; population (1986) 88,500. Founded in 1805, its industries include woollen blankets, saw milling, engineering, furniture and pottery making, and railway workshops.

laundrette a machine-operated self-service laundry. The first was opened in New York in 1945; the first British laundrette opened in Queensway, London, in 1949. Coin-operated laundrettes, without attendants, followed during the 1950s; other refinements included the tumble drier (UK 1959), and automatic dry cleaning (1964 in the UK).

Laud *A portrait of William Laud after a painting by Van Dyck.*

Laurasia /lɔːˈreɪʃə/ former land mass or supercontinent, consisting of what are now North America, Greenland, Europe, and Asia. It made up the northern half of ◊Pangaea, the 'world continent' that is thought to have existed between 250 and 200 million years ago. The southern half was ◊Gondwanaland.

laurel evergreen tree **sweet bay** *Laurus nobilis*, family Lauraceae, of which the aromatic leaves are used in cookery. Ornamental shrub laurels, for example **cherry laurel** *Prunus laurocerasus*, family Rosaceae, are poisonous. In classical times *L. nobilis* was used to make crowns for athletes, symbolizing victory.

Laurel and Hardy /ˈlɒrəl, ˈhɑːdi/ Stan Laurel (1890–1965) and Oliver Hardy (1892–1957) US film comedians (Laurel was English-born). Their films include many short silent films, as well as *Way Out West* 1937 and *A Chump at Oxford* 1940.

Laurence /ˈlɒrəns/ Margaret 1926–1987. Canadian writer, whose novels include *A Jest of God* 1966 and *The Diviners* 1974. She also wrote short stories set in Africa, where she lived for a time.

Laurier /ˈlɒrieɪ/ Wilfrid 1841–1919. Canadian politician, leader of the Liberal Party 1887–1919 and prime minister 1896–1911. The first French-Canadian to hold the office, he encouraged immigration into Canada from Europe and the USA, established a separate Canadian navy, and sent troops to help Britain in the Boer War.

Laughton *An actor with a wide dramatic range, Charles Laughton won an Academy Award for his performance in the film* The Private Life of Henry VIII *1933.*

laurustinus evergreen shrub *Viburnum tinus* of the family Caprifoliaceae, of Mediterranean origin. It has clusters of white flowers in the winter months.

Lausanne /ləʊˈzæn/ resort and capital of Vaud canton, W Switzerland, above the N shore of Lake Geneva; population (1987) 262,000. Industries include chocolate, scientific instruments, and publishing.

Lausanne, Treaty of peace settlement 1923 between Greece and Turkey after Turkey refused to accept the terms of the Treaty of Sèvres 1920, which would have made peace with the western allies. It involved the surrender by Greece of Smyrna (now Izmir) to Turkey and the enforced exchange of the Greek population of Smyrna for the Turkish population of Greece.

lava molten material that erupts from a ◊volcano and cools to form extrusive ◊igneous rock. A lava high in silica is viscous and sticky and does not flow far, whereas low-silica lava can flow for long distances.

Lava differs from its parent ◊magma in that the fluid 'fractionates' on its way to the surface of the Earth; that is, certain heavy or high-temperature minerals settle out and the constituent gases form bubbles and boil away into the atmosphere.

Laval /ləˈvæl/ Pierre 1883–1945. French right-wing politician. He was prime minister and foreign secretary 1931–32, and again 1935–36. In World War II he joined Pétain's Vichy government as vice-premier June 1940; dismissed Dec 1940, he was reinstated by Hitler's orders as head of the government and foreign minister 1942. After the war he was executed.

Laval, born near Vichy, entered the chamber of deputies 1914 as a Socialist, but after World War I moved towards the right. His second period as prime minister was marked by the ◊Hoare–Laval Pact for concessions to Italy in Abyssinia. His share in the deportation of French labour to Germany made him universally hated. On the Allied invasion he fled the country, but was arrested in Austria, tried for treason, and shot after trying to poison himself.

La Vallière /læ ˌvæliˈeə/ Louise de la Baume le Blanche, Duchesse de la Vallière 1644–1710. Mistress of the French king Louis XIV; she gave birth

lava Cooled lava of the pahoehoe type at Kilauea, Hawaii. The rope-like strands are formed during cooling by the movements of the liquid lava beneath the surface.

to four children 1661–74. She retired to a convent on her supersession by Mme de Montespan.

lavatory another name for a ◊toilet.

La Vendée see ◊Vendée, La.

lavender sweet-smelling herb, genus *Lavandula*, of the family Labiatae, a native of the W Mediterranean countries. The bushy low-growing *Lavandula angustifolia* has long, narrow, erect leaves of a silver-green colour. The flowers, borne on a terminal spike, vary in colour from lilac to deep purple and are covered with small fragrant oil glands. The oil is extensively used in pharmacy and perfumes.

laver red edible seaweed *Porphyra umbicalis*. Growing on the shore and below, attached to rocks and stones, it forms thin flat irregularly rounded sheets of tissue up to 20 cm/8 in across. It becomes almost black when dry.

Laver /ˈleɪvə/ 'Rod' (Rodney George) 1938– . Australian lawn tennis player. He was one of the greatest left-handed players, and the only player to perform the Grand Slam twice (1962 and 1969).

He won four Wimbledon singles titles, the Australian title three times, the US Open twice, and the French Open twice. He turned professional after winning Wimbledon 1962 but returned when the championships were opened to professionals 1968.

Lavoisier French chemist Antoine Lavoisier.

CAREER HIGHLIGHTS

Wimbledon
singles: 1961–62, 1968–69
doubles: 1971
mixed: 1959–60
US Open
singles: 1962, 1969
French Open
singles: 1962, 1969
doubles: 1961
mixed: 1961
Australian Open
singles: 1960, 1962, 1969
doubles: 1959–61, 1969

Lavery /ˈleɪvəri/ John 1856–1941. British portrait-painter of Edwardian society.

Lavoisier /læˈvwæzieɪ/ Antoine Laurent 1743–1794. French chemist. He proved that combustion needed only a part of 'air' which he called oxygen, thereby destroying the theory of phlogiston (an imaginary 'fire element' released during combustion). With Laplace, he showed that water was a compound of oxygen and hydrogen. In this way he established the modern basic rules of chemical combination.

Lavrentiev /læˈvrentief/ Mikhail 1900– . Soviet scientist, who developed the Akademgorodok ('Science City') in Novosibirsk, Russia from 1957. He was director of the Institute for Precision Mechanics and Computer Engineering from 1950.

law the body of rules and principles under which justice is administered or order enforced in a state. In western Europe there are two main systems: ◊Roman law, and ◊English law.

Roman law, first codified 450 BC and finalized under Justinian AD 528–534, advanced to a system of international law (*jus gentium*), applied in disputes between Romans and foreigners or provincials, or between provincials of different states. Church influence led to the adoption of Roman law all over western continental Europe, and it was spread to E Europe and parts of Asia by the French *Code Napoléon* in the 19th century. Scotland and Québec (because of their French links) and South Africa (because of its link with Holland) also have it as the basis of their systems.

English law derives from Anglo-Saxon customs, which were too entrenched to be broken by the Norman Conquest and still form the basis of the ◊common law (that is, common to the whole country) which by 1250 had been systematized by the royal judges. Alongside it there grew up a system of ◊*equity* developed in the Court of Chancery, where the Lord Chancellor considered petitions, and the ordinary rules were mitigated where their application would operate harshly in particular cases. In the 19th century there was major reform of the law (for example, the abolition of many capital offences, in which juries would not in any case convict) and of the complex system of courts

Laurel and Hardy The popular comic duo Laurel and Hardy, one of the most successful comedy teams in cinema history.

(see ◊law courts). Unique to English law are the **judicial precedents** whereby the reported decisions of the courts form a binding source of law for future decisions. In modified form English law was adopted by countries throughout the world came under English influence, including the USA.

Law /lɔ:/ Andrew Bonar 1858–1923. British Conservative politician, born in New Brunswick, Canada. He made a fortune in Scotland as a banker and iron-merchant, and entered Parliament 1900. Elected leader of the opposition 1911, he became colonial secretary in Asquith's coalition government 1915–16. Chancellor of the Exchequer 1916–19, and Lord Privy Seal 1919–21 in Lloyd George's coalition. He formed a Conservative Cabinet 1922, but resigned on health grounds.

Law /lɔ:/ William 1686–1761. English cleric. His ◊Jacobite opinions caused him to lose his fellowship at Emmanuel College, Cambridge, in 1714. His most famous work is *A Serious Call to a Devout and Holy Life* 1728, which influenced the ◊Wesleys.

Law Commissions in Britain, statutory bodies established 1965 (one for England and Wales and one for Scotland) which consider proposals for law reform and publish their findings. They also keep British law under constant review, looking for ways in which it can be simplified or finding obsolete laws that should be repealed.

law courts the bodies that adjudicate in legal disputes. Civil and criminal cases are usually dealt with by separate courts. In most countries there is a hierarchy of courts which provide an appeal system.

In England and Wales the court system was reorganized under the Courts Act 1971. The higher courts are: the **House of Lords** (the highest court for the whole of Britain), which deals with both civil and criminal appeals; the **Court of Appeal**, which is divided between criminal and civil appeal courts; the **High Court of Justice**, dealing with important civil cases; and the **Crown Court**, which handles serious criminal cases as well as certain civil cases.

The courts are organised in six circuits. The towns of each circuit are first-tier (High Court and Circuit Judges dealing with both criminal and civil cases), second-tier (High Court and Circuit Judges dealing with criminal cases only), or third-tier (Circuit Judges dealing with criminal cases only). Cases are allotted according to gravity among High Court and Circuit Judges and Recorders (part-time judges with the same jurisdiction as Circuit Judges). From 1971, solicitors were allowed for the first time to appear in and conduct cases at the level of the Crown Courts, and solicitors as well as barristers of ten years' standing became eligible for appointment as Recorders, who after five years become eligible as Circuit Judges. In 1989 a ◊Green Paper proposed (1) omitting the Bar's monopoly of higher courts, removing demarcation between barristers and solicitors; (2) cases to be taken on a 'no-win, no-fee' basis (as already happens in Scotland). In the UK 1989 there were 5,500 barristers and 47,000 solicitors.

The lower courts are: **County Courts**, dealing with minor civil cases, and served by Circuit Judges; **Magistrates' Courts**, dealing with minor criminal cases and served by ◊Justices of the Peace or Stipendiary (paid) Magistrates; and **Juvenile Courts**, held in separate buildings and presided over by specially qualified justices. There are also special courts, such as the Restrictive Practices Court and the Employment Appeal Tribunal.

In Scotland, the supreme civil court is the ◊Court of Session, with appeal to the House of Lords; the highest criminal court is the High Court of Justiciary, with no appeal to the House of Lords.

In the USA, the head of the federal judiciary is the Supreme Court which also hears appeals from

Lawrence The novelist and poet D H Lawrence.

the inferior federal courts and from the decisions of the highest state courts. The US Court of Appeals, organized in circuits, deals with appeals from the US District Courts in which civil and criminal cases are heard. State courts deal with civil and criminal cases involving state laws, the lowest being those of the justices of the peace.

Lawes /lɔ:z/ Henry 1596–1662. British composer, whose works include music for Milton's masque *Comus* 1634. His brother **William** (1602–45) was also a composer.

Lawes /lɔ:z/ John Bennet 1814–1900. English agriculturist, who patented the first artificial manure 'super-phosphate'. In 1843, he established the Rothamsted Experimental Station (Hertfordshire) at his birthplace.

Lawler /lɔ:lə/ Ray 1921– . Australian actor and playwright. He is best known for his play *The Summer of the Seventeenth Doll* 1955 about sugar-cane cutters, in which he played the lead role in the first production in Melbourne.

law lords in England, the ten Lords of Appeal in Ordinary who, together with the Lord Chancellor and other peers, make up the House of Lords in its judicial capacity.

Lawrence /ˈlɒrəns/ town in Massachusetts, USA; population (1980) 63,175. Industries include textiles, clothing, paper, and radio equipment. The town was established in 1845 to utilize power from the Merrimack Rapids on a site first settled in 1655.

Lawrence /ˈlɒrəns/ D(avid) H(erbert) 1885–1930. English writer, who in his work expressed his belief in emotion and the sexual impulse as creative and true to human nature. His novels include *Sons and Lovers* 1913, *The Rainbow* 1915, *Women in Love* 1921, and *Lady Chatterley's Lover* 1928. Lawrence also wrote short stories, for example 'The Woman Who Rode Away', and poetry.

Son of a Nottinghamshire miner, Lawrence studied at University College, Nottingham, and became a teacher. He achieved fame with the semi-autobiographical *Sons and Lovers*, which includes a portrayal of his mother (died 1911). In 1914 he married Frieda von Richthofen, ex-wife of his university professor, with whom he had run away 1912, and who was the model for Ursula Brangwen in *The Rainbow*, suppressed for obscenity, and its sequel *Women in Love*. His travels in search of health (he suffered from tuberculosis, from which he eventually died near Nice) prompted books such as *Mornings in Mexico* 1927. *Lady Chatterley's Lover* 1928 was banned as obscene in the UK until 1960.

Lawrence Miss Caroline Fry *Tate Gallery, London.*

Lawrence /ˈlɒrəns/ Ernest O(rlando) 1901–1958. US physicist. His invention of the cyclotron pioneered the production of artificial radioisotopes. He was professor of physics at the University of California, Berkeley, from 1930 and director of the Radiation Laboratory from 1936, which he built up into a large, brilliant school for research in nuclear physics. He was awarded a Nobel prize in 1939.

Lawrence /ˈlɒrəns/ Gertrude 1898–1952. English actress, who began as a dancer in the 1920s and later took leading roles in musical comedies. Her greatest successes were *Private Lives* 1930–31, written especially for her by Noël Coward, with whom she co-starred, and *The King and I* 1951.

Lawrence /ˈlɒrəns/ T(homas) E(dward) 1888–1935. soldier, known as 'Lawrence of Arabia'. Appointed to the military intelligence department in Cairo during World War 1, he took part in negotiations for an Arab revolt against the Turks, and in 1916 attached himself to the emir Faisal. He showed himself a guerrilla leader of genius, combining raids on Turkish communications with the stirring up of revolt among the Arabs. In 1935 he was killed in a motorcycle accident.

He was born in Wales, studied at Oxford, and during 1910–14 took part in archaeological expeditions to Syria and Mesopotamia. He joined the Royal Air Force in 1922 as an aircraftman under the name Ross, transferring to the tank corps under the name T E Shaw in 1923 when

Lawrence T E Lawrence, known as Lawrence of Arabia.

Lawson *former chancellor of the Exchequer, Nigel Lawson, at the Conservative Party Conference, 1985.*

his identity became known. He returned to the RAF in 1925, and adopted the name Shaw by deed poll in 1927. His account of the Arab revolt, *Seven Pillars of Wisdom* 1935 (published privately 1926), has been described as the last great romantic war book; *The Mint* 1955 was an account of life in the ranks.

Lawrence /'lɒrəns/ Thomas 1769–1830. British painter, the leading portraitist of his day. He became painter to George III in 1792 and president of the Royal Academy 1820. In addition to British royalty, he painted a series of European sovereigns and politicians (Waterloo Chamber, Windsor Castle, Berkshire) commissioned after the Allied victory at Waterloo.

Lawrence, St /'lɒrəns/ died 258. Christian martyr. Probably born in Spain, he became a deacon of Rome under Pope Sixtus II, and, when summoned to deliver the treasures of the church, displayed the beggars in his charge, for which he was broiled on a grid-iron. Feast day 10 Aug.

lawrencium a synthetic radioactive element, symbol Lr, atomic number 103. First synthesized in 1961, it was named after Ernest O Lawrence.

Lawson /'lɔːsən/ Nigel 1932– . British Conservative politician. A former financial journalist, he was financial secretary to the Treasury 1979–81, secretary of state for energy 1981–83, and chancellor of the Exchequer 1983. He resigned in 1989 after criticism of his policy of British membership of the ◊European Monetary System by government advisor Alan Walters.

law, the rule of the principle that law (as administered by the ordinary courts) is supreme and that all citizens (including members of the government) are equally subject to it and equally entitled to its protection.

laxative substance used to relieve constipation. Current medical opinion discourages regular or prolonged use. Regular exercise and a diet high in vegetable fibre is believed to be the best means of preventing and treating constipation.

Laxness /'læksnəs/ Halldor 1902– . Icelandic novelist, who wrote about Icelandic life in the style of the early sagas. Nobel prize 1955.

Layamon /'laɪəmən/ lived about 1200. English poet, author of the *Brut*, a chronicle of about 30,000 alliterative lines on the history of Britain from the legendary Brutus onwards, which gives the earliest version of the Arthurian story in English.

Layard /'leɪəd/ Austen Henry 1817–1894. British archaeologist. He travelled to the Middle East in 1839, conducted two expeditions to Nineveh and Babylon 1845–51, and sent to the UK the specimens forming the greater part of the Assyrian collection in the British Museum.

La'youn /lɑː'juːn/ capital of Western Sahara; population (1982) 97,000.

lay reader in the Church of England, an unordained member of the church who is permitted under licence from the bishop of the diocese to conduct some public services.

Lazarus in the New Testament (John 11), a friend of Jesus, raised by him from the dead. Lazarus is also the name of a beggar in a parable told by Jesus (Luke 16).

Lazarus /'læzərəs/ Emma 1849–1887. US poet, author of the poem on the base of the Statue of Liberty which includes the words: 'Give me your tired, your poor/Your huddled masses yearning to breathe free.'

Lazio /'lætsiəʊ/ (Roman *Latium*) region of W central Italy; area 17,200 sq km/6,639 sq mi; capital Rome; population (1988) 5,137,000. Products include olives, wine, chemicals, pharmaceuticals, and textiles. Home of the Latins from the 10th century BC, it was dominated by the Romans from the 4th century BC.

lb (Latin 'libra'.) abbreviation for *pound* (weight).

lbw abbreviation for *leg before wicket* (cricket).

lc in typography, the abbreviation for *lower case*, or 'small' letters, as opposed to capitals.

LCD abbreviation for ◊*liquid crystal display*.

L-dopa chemical, normally produced by the body, which is converted in the brain to dopamine, and is essential for local movement. It relieves the tremor and rigidity of ◊Parkinson's disease, but may have significant side effects, such as uncontrolled, writhing movements, extreme mood changes, and hallucinations. It is often given in combination with other drugs to improve its effectiveness at lower doses.

LDR a light-dependent resistor, or a resistor which conducts electricity better when light falls on it. LDRs are made from ◊semiconductors, such as cadmium sulphide, and are used in electric eye burglar alarms and light meters.

Lea /liː/ river rising in Bedfordshire, England, which joins the river Thames at Blackwell.

LEA in the UK, abbreviation for *local education authority*.

Leach /liːtʃ/ Bernard 1887–1979. British potter. His simple designs, inspired by a period of study in Japan, pioneered a revival of the art. He established the Leach Pottery at St Ives, Cornwall, in 1920.

leaching process by which substances are washed out of the ◊soil. Fertilizers leached out of the soil find their way into rivers and cause water ◊pollution. In tropical areas, leaching of the soil after ◊deforestation removes scarce nutrients and leads to a dramatic loss of soil fertility.

The leaching of soluble minerals in soils can lead to the formation of distinct horizons as different minerals are deposited at successively lower levels.

Leacock /'liːkɒk/ Stephen Butler 1869–1944. Canadian humorist, whose writings include *Literary*

Leach *Bernard Leach at work in his pottery in St Ives. His style owed much to his early studies in Japan.*

Lapses 1910, *Sunshine Sketches of a Little Town* 1912, and *Frenzied Fiction* 1918.

Born in Hampshire, he lived in Canada from 1876, and was head of the department of economics at McGill University, Montreal, 1908–36. He published works on politics and economics, and studies of Mark Twain and Dickens.

lead one of the four most used metallic elements, symbol Pb (Latin *plumbum*), atomic number 82, relative atomic mass 207.21. It is bluish-grey, and the heaviest, softest, and weakest of the common metals; it lacks elasticity and is a poor conductor of electricity, but is resistant to corrosion by acids. Lead is used as a shield for radioactive sources, and in ammunition, batteries, glass, ceramics, and alloys such as pewter and solder. Lead is a cumulative poison within the body, and lead water pipes and lead-based paints are a health hazard, as is the use of lead in 'anti-knock' petrol additives.

lead–acid cell a type of ◊accumulator (storage battery).

lead ore any of several minerals from which lead is extracted. The main primary ore is galena or lead sulphite PbS. This is unstable, and on prolonged exposure to the atmosphere it oxidizes into the minerals cerussite $PbCO_3$ and anglesite $PbSO_4$. Lead ores are usually associated with other metals, particularly silver—which can be mined at the same time—and zinc, which can cause problems during smelting.

Most commercial deposits of lead ore are in the form of veins, where hot fluids have leached the ore from cooling ◊igneous masses and deposited it in cracks in the surrounding country rock, and in thermal ◊metamorphic zones, where the heat of igneous intrusions has altered the minerals of surrounding rocks. Lead is mined in over 40 countries, but half of the world's output comes from the USA, the USSR, Canada, and Australia.

leaf lateral outgrowth on the stem of a plant, and in most species the primary organ of ◊photosynthesis. The chief leaf types are ◊cotyledons (seed leaves), scale-leaves (on underground stems), foliage leaves, and ◊bracts (in the axil of which a flower is produced). A *simple leaf* is undivided, as in the beech or oak. A *compound leaf* is composed of several leaflets, as in the blackberry, horse-chestnut, or ash tree (the latter being a ◊pinnate leaf). Leaves that fall in the autumn are termed *deciduous*, while evergreens are *persistent*.

Typically leaves are composed of three parts: the sheath or leaf-base, the petiole or stalk, and the ◊lamina or blade. The lamina has a network of veins through which water and nutrients are conducted. Structurally the leaf is made up of ◊mesophyll cells surrounded by the epidermis and usually, in addition, a waxy layer, termed the ◊cuticle, which prevents excessive evaporation of water from the leaf tissues by ◊transpiration. The epidermis is interrupted by small pores, or ◊stomata through which gas exchange occurs.

leaf-hopper numerous species of ◊bug of the family Cicadellidae. They feed on the sap of leaves. Each species feeds on a limited range of plants.

leaf insect insect of the order Phasmida, about 10 cm/4 in long, with a green, flattened body, remarkable for closely resembling the foliage on which it lives. It is most common in SE Asia.

League of Nations international organization formed after World War I to solve international disputes by arbitration. Established in Geneva, Switzerland, 1920, the League included representatives from states throughout the world, but was severely weakened by the US decision not to become a member, and had no power to enforce its decisions. It was dissolved 1946. Its subsidiaries included the *International Labour Organization* and the *Permanent Court of International Justice* in The Hague, Netherlands, both now under the auspices of the ◊United Nations.

The League of Nations was suggested in the US president Woodrow Wilson's 'Fourteen Points'

1917 as part of the peace settlement for World War I. The League covenant was drawn up by the Paris peace conference 1919 and incorporated into the Versailles and other peace treaties. The member states undertook to preserve the territorial integrity of all, and to submit international disputes to the League. There were a number of important subsidiary organizations:

International Labour Organization (ILO) formed 1919, based in Geneva and concerned primarily with working conditions and social welfare.

High Commission for Refugees (Nansen Office) created to assist refugees, primarily from the USSR and Eastern Europe. Built on the work of the Norwegian explorer Fridtjof Nansen as first high commissioner, the High Commission declined in importance after his death and the entry of the USSR to the League. It formed the basis for post-1945 refugee work by the United Nations.

Permanent Court of Justice created in The Hague 1921 and based on ideas for some form of international court put forward at the Hague congress 1907; now known as the International Court of Justice (see ◊United Nations).

The League enjoyed some success in the humanitarian field (international action against epidemics, drug traffic, and the slave trade), in organizing population exchanges after the Paris peace conferences had established new national boundaries, and in deferring arguments over disputed territories and former German colonies by mandating a League member to act as a caretaker of administration for a specified period of time, or until a permanent solution could be found. Mandates were created for Palestine (Britain), SW

***Leakey** British archaeologist Richard Leakey.*

Africa (South Africa), and the free city of Danzig (◊Gdańsk).

In the political and diplomatic field, the League was permanently hampered by internal rivalries and the necessity for unanimity in the decision-making process. No action was taken against Japan's aggression in Manchuria 1931; attempts to impose sanctions against Italy for the invasion of Ethiopia 1935–36 collapsed; no actions were taken when Germany annexed Austria and

Czechoslovakia, nor when Poland was invaded. Japan 1932 and Germany 1933 simply withdrew from the League and the expulsion of the USSR 1939 had no effect on the Russo-Finnish war. Long before the outbreak of World War II, diplomacy had abandoned international security and reverted to a system of direct negotiation and individual alliances.

Leakey /'li:ki/ Louis (Seymour Bazett) 1903–1972. British archaeologist, born in Kabete, Kenya. In 1958, with his wife Mary Leakey, he discovered gigantic animal fossils in ◊Olduvai Gorge, as well as many early remains of a human type.

Leakey /'li:ki/ Mary 1913– . British archaeologist. In 1948 she discovered, on Rusinga Island, Lake Victoria, E Africa, the prehistoric ape skull known as *Proconsul*, about 20 million years old; and human remains at Laetolil, to the south, about 3,750,000 years old.

Leakey /'li:ki/ Richard 1944– . British archaeologist, son of Louis and Mary Leakey. In 1972 he discovered at Lake Turkana, Kenya, an ape-form skull, estimated to be about 2.9 million years old; it had some human characteristics and a brain capacity of 800 cm³. In 1984 his team found an almost complete skeleton of *Homo erectus* some 1.6 million years old.

Leamington /'lemɪŋtən/ officially **Royal Leamington Spa** town and health resort in the West Midlands, England, on the river Leam, adjoining Warwick; population (1985) 56,500. The Royal Pump Room offers modern spa treatment.

Lean /li:n/ David 1908– . English film director. His films, noted for their atmospheric quality, include *Brief Encounter* 1946, *The Bridge on the River Kwai* 1957, *Lawrence of Arabia* 1962, and *A Passage to India* 1985.

Lear /lɪə/ Edward 1812–1888. English artist and humorist. His *Book of Nonsense* 1846 popularized the limerick. He first attracted attention by his paintings of birds, and later turned to landscapes. He travelled in Italy, Greece, Egypt, and India, publishing books on his travels with his own illustrations, and spent most of his later life in Italy.

learning theory in psychology, a theory about how an organism acquires new behaviours. Two main theories are classical and operant ◊conditioning.

leasehold in law, land or property held by a tenant (lessee) for a specified period, (unlike ◊freehold, outright ownership) usually at a rent from the landlord (lessor).

Under English law, houses and flats are often held on a lease for a period, such as 99 years, for which a lump sum is paid, plus an annual 'ground rent': the entire property reverts to the original owner at the end of the period. Under the Leasehold Reform Act of 1967, tenants were in many instances given the right to purchase the freehold or extend the lease of houses; and in the 1980s extension of the right to flats was under consideration, possibly in the form of **strata title**, a method used in Australia, where a building is subdivided (usually by voluntary agreement between landlord and tenants on payment of a capital sum) into 'strata', each comprising a standardized freehold (with specified rights, obligations, and rules of management). In 1987 the ◊Law Commission recommended a new type of land ownership called 'commonhold' which would give, in effect, freehold ownership of flats or business premises in shared buildings.

least action principle in science, the principle that nature 'chooses' the easiest path for moving objects, rays of light, and so on; also known in biology as the **parsimony principle**.

leather material prepared from the hides and skins of animals, by tanning with vegetable tannins and chromium salts. Leather is a durable and water-resistant material, and is used for bags, shoes, clothing, and upholstery. There are three main stages in the process of converting animal skin into leather: cleaning, tanning, and dressing.

Leatherhead /'leðəhed/ town in Surrey, England, SW of London, on the river Mole at the foot of

leaf

leaf margins

entire   serrate   dentate   incised   crenate   sinuate   scalloped   undulate

cross-section of a leaf

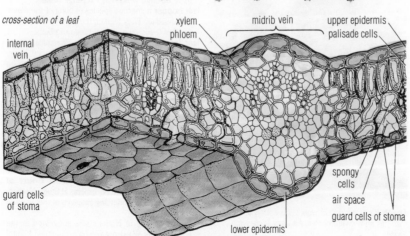

xylem
phloem
midrib vein
upper epidermis
palisade cells
internal vein
guard cells of stoma
spongy cells
air space
guard cells of stoma
lower epidermis

the N Downs; population (1985) 40,300. It has industrial research stations, the Thorndike Theatre (1968), and the Royal School for the Blind (1799).

leatherjacket the larva of the ◊crane-fly.

Leatherstocking Tales, The five US novels by James Fenimore Cooper, describing the ideal frontiersman Natty Bumppo, also known as Leatherstocking or Deerslayer: *The Pioneers* 1823, *The Last of the Mohicans* 1826, *The Prairie* 1827, *The Pathfinder* 1840, and *The Deerslayer* 1841. The novels follow (although not in order of publication) Natty's free life from youth before the American Revolution to death after the Louisiana Purchase.

leaven element inducing fermentation; applied to the yeast added to dough in bread making. It is used figuratively to describe any pervasive influence, usually in a good sense, although in the Old Testament it symbolized corruption, and unleavened bread was used in sacrifice.

Leaves of Grass collection of poems by the US writer Walt Whitman, published anonymously 1855 and augmented through many editions up to 1892. With its open metric and 'barbaric yawp', the book influenced subsequent US verse.

Leavis /'liːvɪs/ F(rank) R(aymond) 1895–1978. English literary critic, and co-founder (with his wife Q D Leavis) and editor of the controversial review *Scrutiny* 1932–53. He championed the work of D H Lawrence and James Joyce, and in 1962 attacked C P Snow's theory of 'Two Cultures'. His other works include *New Bearings in English Poetry* 1932 and *The Great Tradition* 1948. He was a lecturer at Cambridge university.

Leavitt /'levɪt/ Henrietta Swan 1868–1921. US astronomer, who in 1912 discovered the *period–luminosity law* that links the brightness of a ◊Cepheid variable star to its period of variation. This law allows astronomers to use Cepheid variables as 'standard candles' for measuring distances in space.

Lebanon /'lebənən/ country in W Asia, bordered N and E by Syria, S by Israel, and W by the Mediterranean.

government Under the 1926 constitution, amended 1927, 1929, 1943, and 1947, legislative power is held by the national assembly, whose 99 members are elected by universal adult suffrage, through a system of proportional representation, in order to give a fair reflection of all the country's religious groups. The assembly serves a four-year term. The president is elected by the assembly for a six-year term, and appoints a prime minister and cabinet who are collectively responsible to the assembly. Elections to the assembly were last held 1972 and its life has been extended at least six times until 1988. There are several political parties but membership of the national assembly is more easily recognized in terms of religious groupings. Under an unwritten agreement 1943 the president is Christian, the prime minister is Sunni Muslim, and the speaker of the national assembly is Shi'ite Muslim.

history The area now known as Lebanon was once occupied by ◊Phoenicia, an empire that flourished from the 5th century BC–1st century AD, when it came under Roman rule. Christianity was introduced during the Roman occupation, and Islam arrived with the Arabs 635. Lebanon was

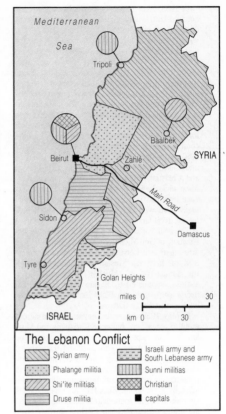

Mediterranean Sea

Tripoli

Baalbek

Beirut

Zahlé

SYRIA

Main Road

Sidon

Damascus

Tyre

Golan Heights

miles 0   30

km 0   30

ISRAEL

The Lebanon Conflict

▨ Syrian army	▨ Israeli army and South Lebanese army
⋮ Phalange militia	▥ Sunni militias
▨ Shi'ite militias	▨ Christian
═ Druse militia	■ capitals

Lebanon
Republic of
(al-Jumhouria al-Lubnaniya)

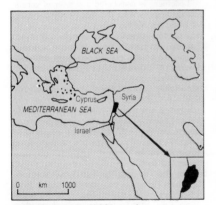

BLACK SEA

Cyprus   Syria

MEDITERRANEAN SEA

Israel

0   km   1000

area 10,452 sq km/4,034 sq mi

capital and port Beirut

towns ports Tripoli, Tyre, Sidon

physical valley N—S between mountain ranges

features few of the celebrated cedars of Lebanon remain; Mount Hermon; Chouf Mountains; archaeological sites at Baalbeck, Byblos, Tyre; until the civil war, the financial centre of the Middle East

head of state Elias Hwrawi from 1989.

heads of government Selim El-Hoss from 1989.

government emergent democratic republic

political parties Phalangist Party, Christian, radical, right-wing; Progressive Socialist Party (PSP), Druze, moderate, socialist; National Liberal Party (NLP), Maronite, centre-left; Parliamentary Democratic Front, Sunni Muslim, centrist; Lebanese Communist Party (PCL), nationalist, communist.

exports citrus and other fruit; industrial products to Arab neighbours

currency Lebanese pound (937.53 = £1 Feb 90)

population (1985 est) 3,500,000 (including

350,000 Palestinian refugees, many driven out, killed in fighting or massacred 1982–85); annual growth rate –0.1%

life expectancy men 63, women 67

language Arabic (official); French and English

religion Muslim 57% (Shi'ite 33%, Sunni 24%), Christian (Maronite and Orthodox) 40%, Druse 3%

literacy 86% male/69% female (1985 est)

GNP $3 bn (1983); $1,150 per head of population

chronology

1944 Full independence achieved.

1964 Palestine Liberation Organization (PLO) founded in Beirut.

1975 Outbreak of civil war between Christians and Muslims.

1976 Ceasefire agreed,

1978 Israel invaded S Lebanon in search of PLO fighters. International peacekeeping force established. Fighting broke out again.

1979 Part of S Lebanon declared an 'independent free Lebanon'.

1982 Bachir Gemayel became president, but was assassinated before he could assume office. His brother Amin Gemayel became president.

1983 Agreement reached for the withdrawal of Syrian and Israeli troops, but not honoured.

1984 Most of international peacekeeping force withdrawn.

1985 Lebanon nearing chaos, with many foreigners being taken hostage.

1987 Syrian troops sent into Beirut.

1988 Attempts to agree a Christian successor to Gemayel failed. His last act in office was to establish a military government; Selim El-Hoss set up a rival government, and the threat of partition hung over the country.

1989 Arab Peace Plan accepted by Muslims but rejected by Maronite Christians led by General Michel Aoun; National Assembly appointed Rene Muawad as president, in place of Aoun; Muawad killed by a car bomb, succeeded by Elias Hwrawi; Hwrawi formally made Selim El-Hoss prime minister; Aoun continued his defiance.

part of the Turkish Ottoman Empire from the 16th century, until administered by France under a League of Nations mandate 1920–41. It was declared independent 1941, became a republic 1943, and achieved full autonomy 1944.

Lebanon has a great variety of religions, including Christianity and many Islamic sects. For many years these coexisted peacefully, giving Lebanon a stability that enabled it, until the mid-1970s, to be a commercial and financial centre. Beirut's thriving business district was largely destroyed 1975–76, and Lebanon's role as an international trader has been greatly diminished.

After the establishment of Israel 1948, thousands of Palestinian refugees fled to Lebanon, and the ◊Palestine Liberation Organization (PLO) was founded in Beirut 1964 (its headquarters moved to Tunis 1982). The PLO presence in Lebanon has been the main reason for Israeli invasions and much of the subsequent civil strife. Fighting has been largely between left-wing Muslims, led by Kamul Joumblatt of the Progressive Socialist Party, and conservative Christian groups, mainly members of the Phalangist Party. There have also been differences between pro-Iranian traditional Muslims, such as the ◊Shi'ites, and and Syrian-backed deviationist Muslims, such as the ◊Druse.

In 1975 the fighting developed into full-scale civil war. A ceasefire was agreed 1976 but fighting began again 1978, when Israeli forces invaded Lebanon in search of PLO guerrillas. The UN secured Israel's agreement to a withdrawal and set up an international peacekeeping force, but to little avail. In 1979 Major Saad Haddad, a right-wing Lebanese army officer, with Israeli encouragement, declared an area of about 1,800 sq km/700 sq mi in S Lebanon an 'independent free Lebanon' and the following year Christian Phalangist soldiers took over an area N of Beirut. Throughout this turmoil the Lebanese government was virtually powerless. In 1982 Bachir Gemayel, youngest son of the founder of the Phalangist Party, became president. He was assassinated before he could assume office and his brother Amin took his place.

In 1983, after exhaustive talks between Lebanon and Israel, under US auspices, an agreement declared an end to hostilities and called for the withdrawal of all foreign forces from the country within three months. Syria refused to recognize the agreement and left about 40,000 troops, with about 7,000 PLO fighters, in N Lebanon. Israel responded by refusing to take its forces from the south. Meanwhile, a full-scale war began between Phalangist and Druse soldiers in the Chouf mountains, ending in a Christian defeat and the creation of a Druse-controlled mini-state. The multinational force was drawn gradually but unwillingly into the conflict until it was withdrawn in the spring of 1984. Attempts were made 1985 and 1986 to end the civil war but rifts within both Muslim and Christian groups have so far prevented it. Meanwhile Lebanon, and particularly Beirut, has seen its infrastructure and earlier prosperity virtually destroyed as it continues to be a battlefield for the rival factions.

The civil war in Beirut pits the E Beirut 'administration' of Gen Michel Aoun, backed by Christian army units and Lebanese militia forces (although 30% of them are Muslim), against the W Beirut 'administration' (Muslim) of Premier Selim al-Hoss, supported by Syrian army and Muslim militia allies, including Walid Jumblatt's Progressive Socialist Party (Druse).

In May 1989 the Arab League secured agreement to a ceasefire between Christians and Muslims and in Sept a peace plan was agreed by all exept Gen Aoun, who dissolved the national assembly. The assembly ignored him and in Nov elected the Maronite-Christian René Moawad as president instead of Aoun, but within days he was killed by a car bomb. Elias Hwrawi was made his successor and he immediately confirmed the acting prime minister, Selim El-Hoss, in that post. Despite being replaced as army commander in chief, Aoun continued to defy the constituted government.

Lebda /ˈlebdə/ former name of ◊Homs, a city in Syria near the river Orontes.

Lebedev /ˈlebɪdjef/ Peter Nikolaievich 1866–1912. Russian physicist. He proved by experiment, and then measured, the minute pressure which light exerts upon a physical body. Lebedev was professor at Moscow university 1892–1911, and his work confirmed ◊Maxwell's theoretical determination.

Lebensphilosophie (German) philosophy of life.

Lebensraum (German 'living space') theory developed by Hitler for the expansion of Germany into E Europe, and used by the Nazis to justify their annexation of neighbouring states on the grounds that Germany was overpopulated.

Leblanc /ləˈblɒŋ/ Nicolas 1742–1806. French chemist who in 1790 developed a process for making sodium carbonate (soda ash) from sodium chloride (common salt).

In the Leblanc process, salt was first converted into sodium sulphate by the action of sulphuric acid, which was then roasted with chalk or limestone (calcium carbonate) and coal to produce a mixture of sodium carbonate and sulphide. The carbonate was leached out with water and the solution crystallized. Leblanc devised this method of producing soda (for use in making glass, paper, soap, and various other chemicals) to win a prize offered in 1775 by the French Academy of Sciences, but the Revolutionary government granted him only a patent (1791), which they seized along with his factory three years later. A broken man, Leblanc committed suicide.

Lebowa /ləˈbəʊə/ black homeland in Transvaal province, South Africa; achieved self-governing status 1972; population (1985) 1,836,000.

Lebrun /ləˈbrɜːn/ Albert 1871–1950. French politician. He became president of the senate in 1931 and in 1932 was chosen as president of the republic. In 1940 he handed his powers over to Marshal Pétain.

Le Brun /ləˈbrɜːŋ/ Charles 1619–1690. French artist, painter to Louis XIV from 1662. In 1663 he became director of the French Academy and of the Gobelin factory, which produced art, tapestries, and furnishings for the new palace of Versailles. In the 1640s he studied under the painter Poussin in Rome. Returning to Paris in 1646, he worked on large decorative schemes including the *Galerie des glaces* (Hall of Mirrors) at Versailles. He also painted portraits.

Le Carré /lə ˈkæreɪ/ John. Pseudonym of David John Cornwell 1931– . His low-key realistic accounts of complex espionage include *The Spy Who Came in from the Cold* 1963, *Tinker Tailor Soldier Spy* 1974, *Smiley's People* 1980, and *The Little Drummer Girl* 1983. He was a member of the Foreign Service 1960–64.

Le Chatelier's principle or *Le Chatelier-Braun principle* in science, the principle that if a change in conditions is imposed on a system in equilibrium, the system will react to counteract that change and restore the equilibrium. First stated 1884 by French chemist Henri le Chatelier (1850–1936), it has been found to apply widely outside the field of chemistry.

lecithin a type of lipid (fat), containing nitrogen and phosphorus, which forms a vital part of the cell membranes of plant and animal cells. The name is from the Greek *lekithos*, (egg yolk), eggs being an important source of lecithin.

Leclair /ləˈkleə/ Jean-Marie 1697–1764. French violinist and composer. Originally a dancer and ballet-master, he composed ballet music, operas (*Scilla* and *Glaucus*), and violin concertos.

Leclanché /ləˈklɒnʃeɪ/ Georges 1839–1882. French engineer. In 1866 he invented a primary electrical ◊cell, which is still the basis of most dry batteries.

A Leclanché cell consists of a carbon rod (the positive pole) dipping into a mixture of powdered carbon and manganese (IV) oxide contained in a porous pot, which sits in a glass jar containing an ◊electrolyte (conducting medium) of ammonium chloride solution, into which dips a zinc electrode (negative pole). The cell produces a continuous current, the carbon mixture acting as a depolarizer, that is, preventing hydrogen bubbles from forming on the positive pole and increasing resistance. In a dry battery, the electrolyte is made in the form of a paste with starch.

Leconte de Lisle /ləˈkɒnt də ˈliːl/ Charles Marie René 1818–1894. French poet. He was born on

Le Carré English thriller writer John Le Carré spent four years in the British Foreign Service and used his experiences in The Spy Who Came in from the Cold 1963 and other novels of international espionage.

Réunion, settled in Paris 1846 and headed *Les* ◊*Parnassiens* 1866–76. His work drew inspiration from the ancient world, as in *Poèmes antiques/Antique Poems* 1852, *Poèmes barbares/Barbaric Poems* 1862, and *Poèmes tragiques/Tragic Poems* 1884.

Le Corbusier /lə ˌkɔːˈbjuːzieɪ/ Assumed name of Charles-Édouard Jeanneret 1887–1965. Swiss architect. His functionalist approach to town planning in industrial society, was based on the interrelation between modern machine forms and the techniques of modern architecture. His concept, *La Ville Radieuse*, developed in Marseille (1945–50) and Chandigarh, India, placed buildings and open spaces with related functions in a circular formation, with buildings based on standard-sized units mathematically calculated according to the proportions of the human figure.

He was originally a painter and engraver, but turned his attention to the problems of contemporary industrial society. *Vers une architecture* 1923 and *Le Modulor* 1948 have had worldwide influence on town planning and building design.

Lecouvreur /lə,kuːvˈrɜː/ Adrienne 1692–1730. French actress. She performed at the ◊Comédie Française, where she first appeared 1717. Her many admirers included the philosopher Voltaire and the army officer Maurice de Saxe; a rival mistress of the latter, the Duchesse de Bouillon, is thought to have poisoned her.

LED abbreviation for ◊*light-emitting diode*.

Leda /ˈliːdə/ in Greek mythology, wife of Tyndareus, by whom she was the mother of Clytemnestra. By Zeus, who came to her as a swan, she was the mother of Helen of Troy, and Castor and Pollux.

Lederberg /ˈledəbɜːg/ Joshua 1925– . US geneticist who showed that bacteria can reproduce sexually, combining genetic material so that offspring possess characteristics of both parent organisms.

Lederberg is considered a pioneer of genetic engineering, a science that relies on the possibility of artificially shuffling genes from cell to cell. He realised that bacteriophages (viruses that invade bacteria) can transfer genes from one bacterium to another, a discovery that led to the deliberate insertion by scientists of foreign genes into bacterial cells.

Ledru-Rollin /ləˈdruː rɒˈlæn/ Alexandre Auguste 1807–1874. French politician and contributor to the radical and socialist journal *La Réforme*. He became minister for home affairs in the provisional government formed 1848 after the overthrow of Louis Philippe and the creation of the Second Republic, but he opposed the elected president Louis Napoleon.

Le Duc Tho /ˈleɪ ˌdʊk ˈtəʊ/ 1911– . North Vietnamese diplomat, who was joint winner (with US secretary of state Kissinger) of the Nobel Peace Prize 1973 for his part in the negotiations to end the Vietnam War. He indefinitely postponed receiving the award.

Lee /liː/ Bruce. Stage name of Lee Yuen Kam 1941–1973. US 'Chinese Western' film actor, an expert in ◊kung fu who popularized the oriental martial arts in the West.

Lee /liː/ Christopher 1922– . British film actor, whose tall, gaunt figure was memorable in the title role of *Dracula* 1958 and its sequels. He has not lost his sinister image in subsequent Hollywood productions. His other films include *Hamlet* 1948, *The Mummy* 1959, *Julius Caesar* 1970, and *The Man with the Golden Gun* 1974.

Lee /liː/ Jennie, Baroness Lee 1904–1988. British socialist politician. She became a member of Parliament for the ◊Independent Labour Party at the age of 24, and in 1934 married Aneurin ◊Bevan. On the left wing of the Labour Party, she was on its National Executive Committee 1958–70 and was minister of education 1967–70, during which time she was responsible for founding the Open University 1969. She was made a baroness 1970.

Lee /liː/ Laurie 1914– . English writer, born near Stroud, Gloucestershire. His works include the autobiographical novel *Cider with Rosie* 1959, a classic evocation of childhood; nature poetry such as *The Bloom of Candles* 1947, and travel writing including *A Rose for Winter* 1955.

Lee /li:/ Nathaniel 1653–1692. English dramatist. From 1675 he wrote a number of extravagant tragedies, such as *The Rival Queens* 1677.

Lee /li:/ Robert E(dward) 1807–1870. US Confederate general in the ◊American Civil War, a military strategist. As military adviser to Jefferson ◊Davis, president of the Confederacy, and as commander of the army of N Virginia, he made several raids into Northern territory, but was defeated at Gettysburg and surrendered 1865 at Appomattox.

Lee, born in Virginia, was commissioned in 1829 and served in the Mexican War. In 1859 he suppressed John ◊Brown's raid on Harper's Ferry. On the outbreak of the Civil War in 1861 he joined the Confederate army of the Southern States, and in 1862 received the command of the army of N Virginia and won the Seven Days's Battle defending Richmond, Virginia, the Confederate capital, against Gen McClellan's Union forces. In 1863 Lee won victories at Fredericksburg and Chancellorsville, and in 1864 at Cold Harbor, but was besieged in Petersburg, June 1864–Apr 1865. He surrendered to Gen Grant 9 Apr 1865 at Appomattox courthouse.

Lee and Yang Tsung Dao (1926–) and Chen Ning (1922–) Chinese physicists who studied how parity operates at the nuclear level. They found no proof for the claim, made by ◊Wigner, that nuclear processes were indistinguishable from their mirror images, and that elementary particles made no distinction between left and right. In 1956 they predicted that parity was not conserved in weak interactions. Nobel prize 1957.

leech worm in the class Hirudinea. Leeches inhabit fresh water, and in tropical countries infest damp forests. As blood-sucking animals they are injurious to people and animals, to whom they attach themselves by means of a strong mouth adapted to sucking. Formerly, the medicinal leech *Hirudo medicinalis* was used extensively for 'bleeding' for a variety of ills. It still has some medicinal use, and is the source of the anti-coagulant hirudin.

Leech /li:tʃ/ John 1817–1864. British caricaturist. He illustrated many books, including Dickens's *A Christmas Carol*, and contributed 1841–64 about 3,000 humorous drawings and political cartoons to *Punch* magazine.

Leeds /li:dz/ city in W Yorkshire, England, on the river Aire; population (1984) 712,200. Industries include engineering, printing, chemicals, glass, and woollens.

Noted buildings include the Town Hall designed by Cuthbert Brodrick, Leeds University 1904, the

Lee *US Confederate general Robert E Lee. Siding with the Southern States in the Civil War, he won a number of battles 1862–63 before surrendering in 1865.*

Lee Kuan Yew *Singapore politician and premier Lee Kuan Yew, 1972.*

Art Gallery 1844, Temple Newsam (birthplace of Henry Darnley in 1545, now a museum), and the Cistercian Abbey of Kirkstall 1147. It is a centre of communications where road, rail and canal (to Liverpool and Goole) meet.

leek plant of the family Liliaceae. The cultivated leek is a variety of the wild *Allium ampeloprasum* of the Mediterranean area and Atlantic islands. The lower leaf-parts form the bulb, which is eaten as a vegetable. It is the national emblem of Wales.

Lee Kuan Yew /'li: ˌkwɑ:n 'ju:/ 1923– . Singapore politician, prime minister from 1959. Lee founded the anti-communist Socialist People's Action Party 1954 and entered the Singapore legislative assembly 1955. He was elected the country's first prime minister 1959, and took Singapore out of the Malaysian federation 1965.

Lee Teng-hui /'li: ˌtʌŋ 'hu:i/ 1923– . Taiwanese right-wing politician, vice president 1984–88, president and Kuomintang party leader from 1988. Lee, the country's first island-born leader, is viewed as a reforming technocrat.

Born in Tamsui, Taiwan, Lee taught for two decades as professor of economics at the National Taiwan University before becoming mayor of Taipei 1979. A member of the Kuomintang party and a protégé of Chiang Ching-kuo, he became vice president of Taiwan 1984 and succeeded to both the state presidency and Kuomintang leadership on Chiang's death Jan 1988. He has significantly accelerated the pace of liberalization and Taiwanization in the political sphere.

Leeuwarden /'leɪwɑ:dn/ city in the Netherlands, on the Ee river; population (1987) 85,200. It is capital of Friesland province. A marketing centre, it also makes gold and silver ware. After the draining of the Middelzee fenlands, the town changed from being a port to an agricultural market town. Notable buildings include the palace of the stadholders of Friesland and the church of St Jacob.

Leeuwenhoek /'leɪwənhu:k/ Anton van 1632–1723. Dutch pioneer of microscopic research. He ground his own lenses, some of which magnified up to 200 times. With these he was able to see individual red blood cells, sperm, and bacteria, achievements not repeated for more than a century.

Leeward Islands /'li:wəd/ (1) group of islands, part of the ◊Society Islands, in ◊French Polynesia, S Pacific; (2) general term for the northern half of the Lesser ◊Antilles in the West Indies; (3) former British colony in the West Indies (1871–1956) comprising Antigua, Montserrat, St Christopher/St Kitts-Nevis, Anguilla, and the Virgin Islands.

Le Fanu /'lefənu:/ (Joseph) Sheridan 1814–1873. Irish writer, born in Dublin. He wrote mystery novels and short stories, such as *The House by the Churchyard* 1863, *Uncle Silas* 1864, and *In a Glass Darkly* 1872.

Lefebvre /lə'fevrə/ Mgr Marcel 1905– . French Catholic priest. Ordained in 1929, he was a missionary and an archbishop in West Africa until

1962. He opposed the liberalizing reforms of the Second Vatican Council 1962–65 and formed the 'Priestly Cofraternity of Pius X'. In 1976, he was suspended by Pope Paul VI for continuing the unauthorized ordination of priests at his Swiss headquarters. His defiance continued and in June 1988 he was excommunicated by Pope John Paul II, in the first formal schism within the Roman Catholic Church since 1870.

Left Book Club book club formed in Britain 1936 to circulate to its members political books intended to counter the upsurge of fascism. Its founder was the publisher Victor ◊Gollancz. It produced mainly non-fiction, of which an example is George Orwell's *The Road to Wigan Pier* 1937. It was disbanded 1948.

left-handedness in humans, using the left hand more skilfully and in preference to the right hand for most actions. It occurs in about 9% of the population, predominantly males.

left-hand rule a rule used to recall which way a wire connected to a source of electricity will move when near a magnet. The thumb and first two fingers of the left hand are placed at right angles to each other. If the first finger is pointed in the direction of the magnetic field (from the N to the S pole of the magnet) and the second finger is pointed in the direction of the electric current (from the positive terminal to the negative terminal of the electric source), the thumb will point in the direction in which the wire will move.

left wing in politics, the socialist parties. The term originated in the French National Assembly 1789, where the nobles sat in the place of honour to the right of the president, and the commons sat to the left. It is also usual to speak of the right, left, and centre, when referring to the different elements composing a single party.

This arrangement has become customary in European parliaments, where the progressives sit on the left and the conservatives on the right.

legacy in law, a gift of personal property made by a testator in a ◊will and passing on the testator's death to the legatee. *Specific* legacies are definite named objects; a *general* legacy is a sum of money or item not specially identified; a *residuary* legacy is all the remainder of the deceased's personal estate after debts have been paid and the other legacies have been distributed.

legal aid public assistance with legal costs. In Britain it is given only to those below certain threshholds of income, only for certain cases, and may be for only part of the costs. It is administered by the Law Society and the Law Society of Scotland. Solicitors and barristers willing to do legal aid work belong to legal aid panels.

legal tender currency that must be accepted in payment of debt. Cheques and postal orders are not included. In most countries, limits are set on the amount of coinage, particularly of small denominations, that must legally be accepted.

legend (Latin *legere* 'to read') traditional or undocumented stories about famous people. The term was originally applied to the books of readings designed for use in Divine Service, and afterwards extended to the stories of saints read in monasteries. A collection of such stories was the 13th-century *Legenda Aurea* by Jacobus de Voragine.

Léger /le'ʒeɪ/ Fernand 1881–1955. French painter, associated with ◊Cubism. From around 1909 he evolved a characteristic style, composing abstract and semi-abstract works with cylindrical forms, reducing the human figure to robot components. Mechanical forms are constant themes in his work, including his designs for the Swedish Ballet 1921–22, murals, and the abstract film *Le Ballet mécanique/The Mechanical Ballet*.

Leghorn /'legho:n/ former English name for the Italian port ◊Livorno.

legionnaire's disease pneumonia-like disease, so called because it was first identified when it attacked a convention of US legionnaires (ex-servicemen) 1976. It is caused by the bacterium

Legionella pneumophila which breeds in warm water (for example in the cooling towers of air-conditioning systems). It is spread in minute water droplets, which may be inhaled.

Legitimist the party in France that continued to support the claims of the house of ◊Bourbon after the revolution of 1830. When the direct line became extinct 1883, the majority of the party transferred their allegiance to the house of Orléans.

Legnano, Battle of defeat of Holy Roman emperor Frederick I (Barbarossa) by members of the Lombard League 1176 at Legnano, NW of Milan. It was a major setback to the emperor's plans for imperial domination in Italy.

Le Guin /lə'gwɪn/ Ursula K(roeber) 1929– . US writer of science fiction and fantasy. Her novels include *The Left Hand of Darkness* 1969, which questions sex roles; the *Earthsea* trilogy 1968–72; and *The Dispossessed* 1974, which contrasts an anarchist and a capitalist society.

legume plant of the family Leguminosae (pea family), which has a pod containing dry fruits. Legumes are important in agriculture because their roots contain nitrogen-fixing bacteria that enrich the soil.

Leh capital of Ladakh region, E Kashmir, India, situated E of the Indus, 240 km/150 mi E of Srinagar. Leh is the nearest supply base to the Indian army outpost on the Siachen Glacier.

Lehár /leɪ'hɑː/ Franz 1870–1948. Hungarian composer. He wrote many operettas, among them *The Merry Widow* 1905, *The Count of Luxembourg* 1909, *Gypsy Love* 1910, and *The Land of Smiles* 1929. He also composed songs, marches, and a violin concerto.

Le Havre /lə 'hɑːvrə/ industrial port (engineering, chemicals, oil refining) in Normandy, NW France, on the Seine; population (1982) 255,000.

Lehmann /'leɪmən/ Lotte 1888–1976. German soprano. She excelled in Wagnerian operas and was an outstanding Marschallin in Richard ◊Strauss's *Der Rosenkavalier*.

Lehmann /'leɪmən/ Rosamond Nina 1903–1990. English novelist, whose books include *Invitation to the Waltz* 1932, *The Weather in the Streets* 1936, and *A Sea-Grape Tree* 1976. Once neglected as too romantic, her novels have regained popularity in the 1980s because of their sensitive portrayal of female adolescent experience.

Leibniz /'laɪbnɪts/ Gottfried Wilhelm 1646–1716. German mathematician and philosopher. Independently of, but concurrently with, Newton he developed ◊calculus. In his metaphysical works, such as *The Monadology* 1714, he argued that everything consisted of innumerable units, *monads*, whose individual properties determined their past, present, and future.

Monads, although independent of each other, interacted predictably; this meant that Christian faith and scientific reason need not be in conflict, and that 'this is the best of all possible worlds'. His optimism is satirized in Voltaire's *Candide* 1759.

Leicester /'lestə/ industrial city (food processing, hosiery, footwear, engineering, electronics, printing, plastics) and administrative headquarters of Leicestershire, England, on the river Soar; population (1983) 282,300.

Leicester /'lestə/ Robert Dudley, Earl of Leicester *c.* 1532–1588. English courtier. Son of the duke of Northumberland, he was created Earl of Leicester 1564. Queen Elizabeth I gave him command of the army sent to the Netherlands 1585–87, and of the forces prepared to resist the threat of Spanish invasion 1588.

His good looks won him the favour of Elizabeth, who might have married him if he had not been previously married to Amy Robsart. When his wife died 1560 by a fall downstairs, Dudley was suspected of murdering her. In 1576 he secretly married the widow of the Earl of Essex.

Leicestershire /'lestəʃə/ county in central England

area 2,550 sq km/984 sq mi

Leicester *The controversial favourite of Elizabeth I, Robert Dudley, Earl of Leicester.*

towns administrative headquarters Leicester; Loughborough, Melton Mowbray, Market Harborough

features Rutland district (formerly England's smallest county, with Oakham as its county town); Rutland Water, one of Europe's largest reservoirs; Charnwood Forest; Vale of Belvoir (under which are large coal deposits)

products horses, cattle, sheep, dairy products, coal

population (1987) 879,000

famous people C P Snow.

Leichhardt /'laɪkhɑːt/ Friedrich 1813–1848. Prussian-born Australian explorer. In 1843, he walked 965 km/600 mi from Sydney to Moreton Bay, Queensland, and in 1844 walked from Brisbane to Arnhem Land; he disappeared during a further expedition from Queensland 1848.

Leics abbreviation for ◊*Leicestershire*.

Leiden /'laɪdn/ or **Leyden** city in South Holland province, Netherlands; population (1988) 183,000. Industries include textiles and cigars. It has been a printing centre since 1580, with a university established since 1575. It is linked by canal to Haarlem, Amsterdam, and Rotterdam. The painters Rembrandt and Jan Steen were born here.

Leif Ericsson see ◊Ericsson, Leif.

Leigh /liː/ Mike 1943– . English playwright and director. He directs his own plays which evolve through improvisation before they are scripted; they include the comedies *Abigail's Party* 1977 and *Goose-Pimples* 1981. He wrote and directed the film *High Hopes* 1989.

Leigh /liː/ Vivien. Pseudonym of Vivien Mary Hartley 1913–1967. English actress, born in Darjeeling, India. She appeared on the stage in London and New York, and won Oscars for her performances as Scarlett O'Hara in *Gone With the Wind* 1939 and as Blanche du Bois in *A Streetcar Named Desire* 1951. She was married to Laurence Olivier 1940–60, and starred with him in the play *Antony and Cleopatra* 1951.

Leigh-Mallory /'liː 'mælərɪ/ Trafford 1892–1944. British air chief marshal in World War II. He took part in the Battle of Britain and was commander in chief of Allied air forces during the invasion of France.

Leighton /'leɪtn/ Frederic, Baron Leighton 1830–1896. English painter and sculptor. His historical subjects, especially classical scenes, were widely admired, for example *Captive Andromache* 1888 (Manchester City Art Gallery). Leighton's *Cimabue's Madonna Carried in Procession* 1855, was bought by Queen Victoria. He became president of the Royal Academy 1878 and was made a peer 1896. His house and studio near Holland Park, London, is now a Leighton museum.

Leinster /'lenstə/ SE province of the Republic of Ireland, comprising the counties of Carlow, Dublin, Kildare, Kilkenny, Laoighis, Longford, Louth, Meath, Offaly, Westmeath, Wexford, and Wicklow; area 19,630 sq km/7,577 sq mi; capital Dublin; population (1986) 1,850,000.

Leipzig /'laɪpzɪg/ capital of Leipzig county, East Germany, 145 km/90 mi SW of Berlin; population (1986) 552,000. Products include furs, leather goods, cloth, glass, cars, and musical instruments. The county of Leipzig has an area of 4,970 sq km/1,918 sq mi, and a population of 1,374,000.

leishmaniasis parasitic disease caused by microscopic protozoa (*Leishmania*), identified by William Leishman (1865–1926), and transmitted by sandflies. It may cause either localized infection or dangerous fever. It is prevalent in NE Africa and S Asia.

Leith /liːθ/ port in Scotland S of the Firth of Forth, incorporated in Edinburgh 1920. Leith was granted to Edinburgh as its port by Robert Bruce in 1329.

leitmotif (German 'leading motive') in music, a recurring theme or motive used to indicate a character or idea. ◊Wagner frequently used this technique in his operas.

Leitrim /'liːtrɪm/ county in Connacht province, Republic of Ireland, bounded on the NW by Donegal Bay

area 1,530 sq km/591 sq mi

county town Carrick-on-Shannon

features rivers Shannon, Bonet, Drowes and Duff

products potatoes, cattle, linen, woollens, pottery, coal, iron, lead

population (1986) 27,000.

Leix /liːʃ/ spelling used 1922–35 of ◊Laoighis, county of Ireland.

lek in biology, a closely spaced set of very small ◊territories each occupied by a single male during the mating season. Leks are found in the mating systems of several birds (for example, ruff and grouse) and a few antelopes. The lek is a traditional site where both males and females congregate during the breeding season. The males display to passing females in the hope of attracting them to mate. Once mated, the females go elsewhere to lay their eggs or complete gestation.

Leland /'liːlənd/ John 1506–1552. English antiquary, whose manuscripts have proved a valuable source for scholars. He became chaplain and librarian to Henry VIII, and during 1534–43 toured England collecting material for a history of English antiquities. The *Itinerary* was published in 1710.

Lely /'liːlɪ/ Peter. Adopted name of Pieter van der Faes 1618–1680. Dutch painter, active in England from 1641, who painted fashionable portraits in Baroque style. His subjects included Charles I, Cromwell, and Charles II. He painted a series of admirals, *Flagmen* (National Maritime Museum, Greenwich), and one of *The Windsor Beauties*

Leigh *English actress Vivien Leigh won an Academy Award for the role of Scarlett O'Hara in the Hollywood epic* Gone With the Wind *1939. She and Laurence Olivier were married in 1940 amid a blaze of publicity.*

Lely Dutch portrait artist Peter Lely was made Principal Painter to to King Charles II in 1661. This self-portrait was painted in about 1660.

(Hampton Court, Richmond), fashionable women of Charles II's court.

Lemaître /lə'meɪtrə/ Georges Edouard 1894–1966. Belgian cosmologist who proposed the ◊Big Bang theory of the origin of the universe 1927.

Born in Charleroi, he was ordained a priest 1922 before studying ◊astrophysics in England and the USA. Lemaître predicted that the entire Universe was expanding, which ◊Hubble confirmed, and suggested that the expansion had been started by an initial explosion, the Big Bang, a theory that is now generally accepted.

Léman, Lac /ˌlæk lə'mɒn/ French name for Lake ◊Geneva.

Le Mans industrial town in Sarthe *département*, France; population (1982) 150,000, conurbation 191,000. It has a ◊motor racing circuit where the annual endurance 24-hour race (established 1923) for sports cars and their prototypes is held.

Lemberg /'lembeək/ German name of ◊Lvov, city in USSR.

lemming small rodent found in northern latitudes. It is about 12 cm/5 in long, with thick brownish fur, small head, and short tail. Periodically, when their population exceeds the available food supply, lemmings undertake mass migrations.

Lemmon /'lemən/ 'Jack' (John Uhler III) 1925– . US character actor, often cast as the lead in comedy films such as *Some Like it Hot* 1959 but equally skilled at straight drama, as in *The China Syndrome* 1979.

Lemnos /'lemnɒs/ Greek island (Greek *Límnos*) in the N of the Aegean Sea
area 476 sq km/184 sq mi
towns Kastron, Mudros
physical of volcanic origin, rising to 430 m/1,411 ft

lemon

LeMond US cyclist Greg LeMond in the Tour de France, 1989.

products mulberries and other fruit, tobacco, sheep
population (1981) 15,700.

lemon fruit of the lemon tree *Citrus limon*. It may have originated in NW India, and was introduced into Europe by the Spanish Moors in the 12th or 13th century. It is now grown in Italy, Spain, California, Florida, South Africa, and Australia.

LeMond /lə'mɒnd/ Greg 1961– . US racing cyclist, the first American to win the Tour de France 1986.

A shooting incident in 1987 threatened to end his career but he made a remarkable comeback to regain his Tour de France title 1989 when he won by the smallest ever margin, seven seconds, from Laurent Fignon (France). He won the World Professional Road Race for the second time in 1989.

lemur many species of ◊primate inhabiting Madagascar and the Comoro Islands. They are arboreal animals, and some species are nocturnal. They can grow to 1.2 m/4 ft long, have large eyes, and long, bushy tails. They feed on fruit, insects, and small animals. Many are threatened with extinction owing to loss of their forest habitat and, in some cases, from hunting.

Lena /'liːnə/ longest river in Asiatic Russia, 4,400 km/2,730 mi, with numerous tributaries. Its source is near Lake Baikal and it empties into the Arctic Ocean through a delta 400 km/240 mi wide. It is ice-covered for half the year.

lemur fork-marked

Lendl Czech tennis player Ivan Lendl in the Liptons Tennis finals, which he won in 1989.

Le Nain family /lə 'næŋ/ French painters, the brothers **Antoine** (1588–1648), **Louis** (1593–1648) and **Mathieu** (1607–77). They were born in Laon, settled in Paris, and were among the original members of the French Academy in 1648. Attribution of work between them is uncertain. They chiefly painted sombre and dignified scenes of peasant life.

Lenard /'leɪnɑːt/ Phillip 1862–1947. German physicist who investigated the ◊photoelectric effect and cathode rays. Nobel prize 1905.

In later life he became obsessed with the need to produce a purely 'Aryan' physics free from the influence of ◊Einstein and other Jewish physicists.

Lenclos /lɒŋ'kləʊ/ Ninon de 1615–1705. French courtesan. As the recognized leader of Parisian society, she was the mistress in turn of many highly placed men, including Gen Condé and the writer La Rochefoucauld.

Lendl /'lendl/ Ivan 1960– . Czechoslovak lawn tennis player who is the top money winner of all time in the men's game. He has won seven Grand Slam singles titles, including the US and French titles three times each. He has won more than $14 million.

CAREER HIGHLIGHTS

US Championship 1985–87
French Championship 1984, 1986–87
Australian Championship 1989
Grand Prix Masters 1982–83, 1986–87.

lend-lease an act of the US congress Mar 1941 that gave the president power to order 'any defence article for the government of any country whose defence the president deemed vital to the defence of the USA'. During World War II, the USA negotiated many lend-lease agreements, most notably with Britain and the Soviet Union.

The aim of such agreements was to ignore trade balances between the participating countries during the war effort. Lend-lease was officially stopped Aug 1945, by which time goods and materials to the value of $42 billion had been traded in this way, of which the British Empire had received 65% and the Soviet Union 23% of the total.

Leng /leŋ/ Virginia 1955– . British showjumping rider, born in Malta. She has won world, European, and most major domestic championships.

She was a member of the successful British team at two world championships and was the individual champion in 1986 on *Priceless*. She won the European individual title twice, the Badminton horse trials twice, and Burghley on three occasions.

Lenin Communist political theorist and leader Vladimir Lenin with his family in 1922.

CAREER HIGHLIGHTS

World Championship 1986
European Championship 1985, 1989
Badminton Horse Trials 1985, 1989
Burghley Horse Trials 1983–84, 1986.

Lenglen /'lɒŋglen/ Suzanne 1899–1938. French tennis player, Wimbledon singles and doubles champion 1919–23 and 1925, and Olympic champion 1921. She became professional 1926. She also introduced modern sports clothes, designed by Jean ◊Patou.

Lenin /'lenɪn/ Vladimir Ilyich. Adopted name of Vladimir Ilyich Ulyanov 1870–1924. Soviet communist politician and theoretician. Active in the 1905 Revolution, Lenin had to leave Russia when it failed, settling in Switzerland 1914. He returned to Russia after the February revolution (see ◊Russian Revolution). In Nov 1917 he became leader of a Soviet government, concluded peace with Germany, and organized a successful resistance to White Russian (pro-Tsarist) uprisings and foreign intervention. His modification of traditional Marxist doctrine to fit conditions prevailing in Russia became known as **Marxism-Leninism**, the basis of communist ideology.

Lenin was born 22 Apr in Simbirsk (now renamed Ulyanovsk), on the river Volga, and became a lawyer in St Petersburg (now Leningrad). A Marxist from 1889, he was sent to Siberia for spreading revolutionary propaganda 1895–1900. He then edited the political paper *Iskra* ('The Spark') from abroad, and visited London several times. In *What Is to be Done?* 1902 he advocated a professional core of Social Democratic Party activists to spearhead the revolution in Russia, a suggestion accepted by the majority (*bolsheviki*) at the London party congress 1903. From Switzerland he attacked socialist support for World War I as for an 'imperialist' struggle, and wrote *Imperialism* 1917. After the renewed outbreak of revolution in Feb/Mar 1917, he returned to Russia in Apr. From the overthrow of the provisional government Nov 1917 until his death, Lenin effectively controlled the Soviet Union, although

Leningrad St Isaac's cathedral, Leningrad, USSR.

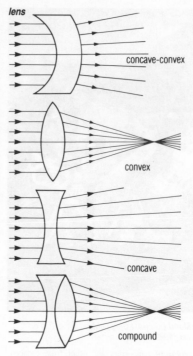

lens

concave-convex

convex

concave

compound

an assassination attempt 1918 injured his health. He founded the Third (Communist) ◊International 1919. Communism proving inadequate to put the country on its feet, he introduced the private-enterprise ◊New Economic Policy from 1921. His embalmed body is in a mausoleum in Red Square, Moscow.

Leninakan /ˌlenɪnə'kɑːn/ town in the Armenian Republic, USSR, 40 km/25 mi NW of Yerevan; population (1987) 228,000. Industries include textiles and engineering. It was founded 1837 as a fortress called Alexandropol, and virtually destroyed by an earthquake 1926 and again 1988.

Leningrad /'lenɪngræd/ capital of the Leningrad region, at the head of the Gulf of Finland; population (1987) 4,948,000. Industries include shipbuilding, machinery, chemicals, and textiles. Originally called St Petersburg, it was renamed Petrograd 1914, and Leningrad 1924.

Leninsk-Kuznetsky /'lenɪnsk kuz'netski/ town in Kemerovo region, S USSR, on the Inya river, 320 km/200 mi SSE of Tomsk; population (1985) 110,000. It is a mining centre in the Kuzbas, with a large iron and steel works; coal, iron, manganese, and other metals, and precious stones occur in the neighbourhood. Formerly Kolchugino, the town was renamed Leninsk-Kuznetsky in 1925.

Lennon /'lenən/ John 1940–1980. Rock singer and songwriter, former member of the ◊Beatles.

Leno /'liːnəʊ/ Dan 1861–1904. British comedian. Beginning as an acrobat, he became the idol of the music halls, and was considered the greatest of ◊pantomime 'dames'.

Le Nôtre /lə 'nəʊtrə/ André 1613–1700. French landscape gardener, creator of the gardens at Versailles and Les Tuileries.

Lens /lɒns/ coalmining town in Pas-de-Calais *département*, France; population (1982) 38,300, conurbation 327,000. During World War I it was in German occupation and close to the front line Oct 1914–Oct 1918, when the town and its mines were severely damaged. In World War II it was occupied by Germany May 1940–Sept 1944, but suffered less physical damage.

lens /lɒns/ in optics, a piece of a transparent material such as glass with two polished surfaces—one concave or convex, and the other plane, concave or convex—to modify rays of light. A convex lens converges the light and a concave lens diverges it. Lenses are essential

to spectacles, microscopes, telescopes, cameras, and almost all optical instruments.

The image formed by a single lens suffers from several defects or aberrations, notably spherical aberration in which a straight line becomes a curved image, and chromatic aberration in which an image in white light tends to have coloured edges. Aberrations are corrected by the use of compound lenses, which are built up from two or more lenses of different refractive index.

Lent in the Christian church, the 40-days period of fasting that precedes Easter, beginning on Ash Wednesday, but omitting Sundays.

Lenthall /'lentɔːl/ William 1591–1662. English lawyer. Speaker of the House of Commons in the ◊Long Parliament of 1640–60, he took an active part in the Restoration.

lenticel a small pore on the stems of woody plants or the trunks of trees. Lenticels are means of gas exchange between the stem interior and the atmosphere. They consist of loosely packed cells with many air spaces inbetween, and are easily seen on smooth-barked trees such as cherries, where they form horizontal lines on the trunk.

lentil annual plant *Lens culinaris* of the Leguminosae family. The plant, which resembles the vetch, grows 15–45 cm/6–18 in high, and has white, blue, or purplish flowers. The seeds, contained in pods about 1.6 cm/0.6 in long, are widely used as food. The commonest varieties are the greyish French lentil and the red Egyptian lentil.

Lenya /'leɪnjə/ Lotte. Adopted name of Karoline Blamauer 1905–1981. Austrian actress and singer She married Kurt ◊Weill in 1926 and appeared in several of the Brecht–Weill operas, notably *The Threepenny Opera* 1928.

Lenz's law in physics, law stating that the direction of an electromagnetically induced current (generated by moving a magnet near a wire or a wire in a magnetic field) will oppose the motion producing it. It is named after the German physicist Heinrich Friedrich Lenz (1804–65), who announced it in 1833.

Leo /'liːəʊ/ constellation of the zodiac, in the northern hemisphere near Ursa Major, through which the Sun passes from mid-Aug to mid-Sept. Its brightest star is first-magnitude Regulus, a blue-white star 85 light years away; Gamma Leonis is a double star. It represents a lion. In astrology, the dates for Leo are between about 23 July and 22 Aug (see ◊precession).

Leo III /'liːəʊ/ *the Isaurian* c. 680–740. Byzantine emperor and soldier. He seized the throne 717, successfully defended Constantinople against the Saracens 717–18, and attempted to suppress the use of images in church worship.

Leo /'liːəʊ/ thirteen popes, including:

Leo I St (the Great) c.390–461. Pope from 440 who helped to establish the Christian liturgy. Leo summoned the Chalcedon Council where his *Dogmatical Letter* was accepted as the voice of St Peter. Acting as ambassador to the emperor Valentinian III (425–455), Leo saved Rome from devastation by the Huns by buying off their king, Attila, with large sums of money.

Leo III c. 750–816. Pope from 795. After the withdrawal of the Byzantine emperors, the popes had become the real rulers in Rome. Leo III was forced to flee because of a conspiracy in Rome, and took refuge at the court of Charlemagne. He returned to Rome 799, and crowned Charlemagne emperor on Christmas Day 800, establishing the secular sovereignty of the pope over Rome under the suzerainty of the emperor.

Leo X Giovanni de' Medici 1475–1521. Pope from 1513. The son of Lorenzo the Magnificent of Florence, he was created a cardinal at 13. He bestowed on Henry VIII of England the title of Defender of the Faith, but later excommunicated him. A patron of the arts, he sponsored the rebuilding of St Peter's Church, Rome. He raised funds for this by selling indulgences, a sale that led the religious reformer Martin Luther to rebel against papal authority. He condemned Luther in

Leonardo da Vinci The Virgin and Child with St Anne and St John the Baptist (mid-1490s) National Gallery, London.

the bull *Exsurge domine* 1520 and excommunicated him 1521.

Leo XIII Gioacchino Pecci 1810–1903. Pope from 1878. After a successful career as a papal diplomat, he established good relations between the papacy and European powers, USA, and Japan. He remained intransigent in negotiations with the Italian government over the status of Rome, insisting that he keep control over part of it.

Leo encouraged foreign missions and emphasized the duty of the church in matters of social justice. His encyclical *Rerum novarum* 1891 pointed out the moral duties of employers towards workers.

León /leɪˈɒn/ city in W Nicaragua, population (1985) 101,000. Industries include textiles and food processing. Founded 1524, it was capital of Nicaragua until 1855.

León /leɪˈɒn/ city in Castilla-León, Spain; population (1986) 137,000. It was the capital of the kingdom of León 10th century–1230, when it was merged with Castile.

Leonard /ˈlenəd/ Sugar Ray 1956– . US boxer. In 1988 he became the first man to win world titles at five officially recognized weights. In 1976 he was Olympic light-welterweight champion and won his first professional title in 1979 when he beat Wilfred Benitez for the WBC welterweight title. He has since won titles at junior-middleweight (WBA version) 1981, middleweight (WBC) 1987, light-heavyweight (WBC) 1988, and super-middleweight (WBC) 1988. In 1989 he drew with Thomas Hearns.

Leonardo da Vinci /ˌliːəˈnɑːdəʊ də ˈvɪntʃi/ 1452–1519. Italian painter, sculptor, architect, engineer, and scientist, one of the greatest figures of the Italian Renaissance, active in Florence, Milan, and from 1516 in France. As state engineer and court painter to the duke of Milan, he produced the *Last Supper* mural about 1495 (Sta Maria delle Grazie, Milan), and on his return to Florence painted the *Mona Lisa* about 1503–06 (Louvre, Paris). His notebooks and drawings show an immensely inventive and enquiring mind, studying aspects of the natural world from anatomy to aerodynamics.

Leonardo was born at Vinci in Tuscany, and studied under ◊Verrocchio in Florence in the 1470s. His earliest dated work is a sketch of the Tuscan countryside 1473 (Uffizi, Florence); his early works include drawings, portraits, and religious scenes, such as the unfinished *Adoration of the Magi* (Uffizi). About 1482 he went to the court of Lodovico Sforza in Milan. In 1500 he returned to Florence (where he was architect and

engineer to Cesare Borgia in 1502), and then to Milan 1506. He went to France in 1516 and died at Château Cloux, near Amboise, on the Loire.

Apart from portraits, religious themes, and historical paintings, Leonardo's greatest legacies were his notebooks and drawings. He influenced many of his contemporary artists, including Michelangelo, Raphael, Giorgione, and Bramante.

Leoncavallo /ˌleɪɒnkəˈvæləʊ/ Ruggiero 1857–1919. Italian operatic composer, born in Naples. He played in restaurants, composing in his spare time, until in 1892 *Pagliacci* was performed. His other operas include *La Bohème* 1897 (contemporary with Puccini's version) and *Zaza* 1900.

León de los Aldamas /leɪˈɒn/ industrial city (leather goods, footwear) in central Mexico; population (1986) 947,000.

Leone /leɪˈəʊni/ Sergio 1928–1989. Italian film director, responsible for popularizing 'spaghetti' westerns (westerns made in Italy and Spain, usually with a US leading actor and a European supporting cast and film crew) and making a world star of Clint Eastwood. His films include *Per un Pugno di Dollari/A Fistful of Dollars* 1964, *Cera una Volta il West/Once upon a Time in the West* 1968, and *Cera una Volta il America/Once upon a Time in America* 1984.

Leonidas /liːˈɒnɪdæs/ died 480 BC. King of Sparta. He was killed after defending for three days the pass of ◊Thermopylae with 300 Spartans, 700 Thespians, and 400 Thebans against a huge Persian army.

Leonov /ljeˈɔːnɔːf/ Aleksei Arkhipovich 1934– . Soviet cosmonaut. In 1965 he was the first person to walk in space, from *Voskhod 2*.

Leonov /ljeˈɔːnɔːf/ Leonid 1899– . Russian novelist and playwright, whose works include the novels *The Badgers* 1925 and *The Thief* 1927, and the drama *The Orchards of Polovchansk* 1938.

leopard or **panther** member of the cat family *Panthera pardus*, found in Africa and Asia. The ground colour of the coat is golden and the black spots form rosettes, which differ according to the variety; black panthers are simply mutants and retain the patterning as a 'watered-silk' effect. The leopard is 1.5–2.5 m/5–8 ft long, including the tail, which may measure 1 m/3 ft.

The **snow leopard** or **ounce** *Panthera uncia*, which has irregular rosettes of much larger black spots on a light cream or grey ground, is a native of mountains in central Asia. The **clouded leopard** *Neofelis nebulosa* is rather smaller, about 1.75 m/5.8 ft overall, with large blotchy markings rather than rosettes, and found in SE Asia. There are seven subspecies, of which six are in danger of extinction, including the Amur leopard and the South Arabian leopard. One subspecies, the Zanzibar leopard, may already be extinct.

Leopardi /ˌleɪəʊˈpɑːdi/ Giacomo, Count Leopardi 1798–1837. Italian romantic poet. The first collection of his uniquely pessimistic poems, *Versi/Verses*, appeared 1824, and was followed by his philosophical *Operette Morali/Minor Moral Works* 1827, in prose, and *Canti/Lyrics* 1831.

Leopardi wrote many of his finest poems, including his patriotic odes, before he was 21. Throughout his life he was tormented by ill-health, by the consciousness of his deformity (he was hunch-backed), by loneliness and a succession of unhappy love-affairs, and by his 'cosmic pessimism' and failure to find consolation in any philosophy. After 1830 his life was divided between Florence, Rome, and Naples, where he died.

Leopold /ˈleɪəpəʊld/ three kings of Belgium:

Leopold I 1790–1865. King of Belgium from 1831, having been elected to the throne on the creation of an independent Belgium. Through his marriage, when prince of Saxe-Coburg, to Princess Charlotte Augusta, he was the uncle of Queen ◊Victoria, and exercised considerable influence over her.

Leopold II 1835–1909. King of Belgium from 1865, son of Leopold I. He financed the journalist

leopard

Stanley's explorations in Africa, which resulted in the foundation of the Congo Free State (now Zaïre), from which he extracted a huge fortune by ruthless exploitation.

Leopold III 1901–1983. King of Belgium from 1934, he surrendered to the Germans 1940. Postwar charges against his conduct led to a regency by his brother Charles, and his eventual abdication 1951 in favour of his son ◊Baudouin.

Leopold /ˈleɪəpəʊld/ two Holy Roman emperors:

Leopold I 1640–1705. Holy Roman emperor from 1658, in succession to his father Ferdinand III. He warred against Louis XIV of France and the Ottoman Empire.

Leopold II 1747–1792. Holy Roman emperor in succession to his brother Joseph II, he was the son of Empress Maria Theresa. His hostility to the French Revolution led to the outbreak of war a few weeks after his death.

Léopoldville /ˈliːəpəʊldvɪl/ former name (until 1966) of ◊Kinshasa, city in Zaïre.

Lepanto, Battle of /lɪˈpæntəʊ/ sea battle 7 Oct 1571, fought in the Mediterranean Gulf of Corinth off Lepanto (Italian name of the Greek port of *Naupaktos*), then in Turkish possession, between the Ottoman Empire and forces from Spain, Venice, Genoa, and the Papal States, jointly commanded by Don ◊John of Austria. The combined western fleets delivered a crushing blow to Muslim sea power. The Spanish writer Cervantes was wounded in the battle.

Le Pen /lə ˈpen/ Jean-Marie 1928– . French extreme right-wing politician. In 1972 he formed the French National Front, supporting immigrant repatriation and capital punishment; the party gained 10% of the national vote in the 1986 election. Le Pen was elected to the European Parliament 1984.

Le Pen served as a paratrooper in French Indochina and Algeria during the 1950s. He became a right-wing National Assembly deputy 1956. During the 1960s, he was connected with the extremist Organisation de l'Armée Secrète (OAS), devoted to perpetuating French rule in Algeria. The National Front has considerable support among underprivileged white youth but

Leopardi 19th-century Italian poet Giacomo Leopardi was tormented by his deformity, ill-health, and unhappy love affairs. His work is pessimistic, but of great lyrical beauty.

Lesotho
Kingdom of

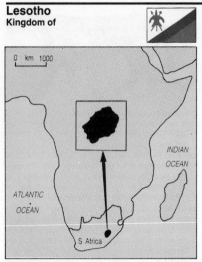

area 30,355 sq km/11,717 sq mi
capital Maseru
physical mountainous
features Lesotho is an enclave within South Africa
government military-controlled monarchy
head of state Moshoeshoe II from 1966
head of government Justin Lekhanya from 1986
political parties Basotho National Party (BNP), traditionalist, nationalist
exports wool, mohair, diamonds
currency maluti (4.33= £1 Feb 1990)
population (1987) 1,627,000; annual growth rate 2.5%
life expectancy men 46, women 52
language Sesotho and English (official)
religion Christian 70% (Roman Catholic 40%)
literacy 62% male/84% female (1985 est)
GNP $678.2 million (1981); $355 per head of population
chronology
1966 Basutoland achieved full independence within the Commonwealth as the Kingdom of Lesotho, with Chief Leabua Jonathan as prime minister.
1975 Members of the ruling party attacked by guerrillas backed by South Africa.
1986 South Africa imposed a border blockade, forcing the deportation of 60 African National Congress members.
1987 Gen Lekhanya ousted Chief Jonathan in a coup.

Le Pen's openly fascist statements caused his bid for the presidency 1988 to founder.

Lepenski Vir the site of Europe's oldest urban settlement (6th millennium BC), now submerged by an artificial lake on the Danube.

lepidoptera an order of insects, including ◊butterflies and ◊moths; the order consists of some 165,000 species. Both butterflies and moths have overlapping scales on their wings.

leprosy or *Hansen's disease* a chronic disease caused by a bacterium closely related to that of ◊tuberculosis. The infection attacks skin and nerves. Once common in many countries, leprosy is now confined almost entirely to the tropics. It is controlled with drugs.

There are two principal manifestations. *Lepromatous leprosy* is a contagious, progressive form distinguished by the appearance of raised blotches and lumps on the skin and thickening of the skin and nerves, with numbness, weakness, paralysis, and ultimately, deformity of the affected parts. In *tuberculoid leprosy*, sensation is lost in some areas of the skin; sometimes there is loss of pigmentation and of hair. The visible effects of long-standing leprosy (joint damage, paralysis, loss of fingers or toes) are due to nerve damage and injuries of which the sufferer may be unaware. Damage to the nerves remains, and the technique of using the patient's muscle material to encourage nerve re-growth is being explored.

Leptis Magna /ˈlɛptɪs ˈmæɡnə/ ruined city in Libya, 120 km/75 mi E of Tripoli. It was founded by the Phoenicians, then came under Carthage, and in 47 BC under Rome. Excavation in the 20th century revealed remains of fine Roman buildings.

lepton type of ◊elementary particle.

leptospirosis infectious disease of domestic animals, especially cattle, causing abortion; transmitted to humans, it causes meningitis and jaundice.

Le Puy /lə ˈpwiː/ capital of Haute-Loire *département*, Auvergne, SE France; population (1982) 26,000. It is dramatically situated on a rocky plateau; it has a 12th-century cathedral.

Lérida /ˈlɛrɪdə/ (Catalan *Lleida*) capital of Lérida province, N Spain, on the river Segre; 132 km/82 mi west of Barcelona; population (1986) 112,000. Industries include leather, paper, glass, and cloth. Lérida was captured by Caesar 49 BC. It has a palace of the kings of Aragon.

Lermontov /ˈlɛəməntɒf/ Mikhail Yurevich 1814–1841. Russian Romantic poet and novelist. In 1837 he was put into active military service in the Caucasus for a revolutionary poem on the death of Pushkin, which criticized Court values, and for participating in a duel. In 1838 he published the psychological novel *A Hero of Our Time* 1840 and a volume of poems *October* 1840.

Lerner /ˈlɜːnə/ Alan Jay 1918–1986. US lyricist, collaborator with Frederick ◊Loewe on musicals including *Brigadoon* 1947, *Paint Your Wagon* 1951, *My Fair Lady* 1956, *Gigi* 1958, and *Camelot* 1960.

Lerwick /ˈlɜːwɪk/ port in Shetland, Scotland; population (1985) 8,000. It is the administrative headquarters of Shetland. Main occupations include fishing and oil. Hand-knitted shawls are a speciality. A Viking tradition survives in the Jan festival of Up-Helly-Aa when a copy of a longship is burned.

Le Sage /lə ˈsɑːʒ/ Alan René 1668–1747. French novelist and dramatist. Born in Brittany, he abandoned law for literature. His novels include *Le Diable boîteux/The Devil upon Two Sticks* 1707 and his picaresque masterpiece *Gil Blas* 1715–1735, much indebted to Spanish originals.

lesbianism ◊homosexuality between women, so called from the Greek island of Lesbos (now Lesvos), the home of ◊Sappho the poet.

Lesbos /ˈlɛzbɒs/ ancient name of Lesvos, an island in the Aegean Sea.

lesion a general term used to denote any change in a body tissue that is a manifestation of disease or injury.

Les Misérables a novel by Victor Hugo, published 1862. On release from prison, Jean Valjean attempts to hide his past by assuming a series of false identities. He cares for a young girl, Cossette, who believes Valjean to be her father. When she marries he reveals the truth but dies a broken man.

Lesotho /lɪˈsuːtuː/ landlocked country in southern Africa, an enclave within South Africa.

government Lesotho is an independent monarchy within the Commonwealth. Its 1966 constitution was suspended, reinstated, and then suspended again, and all executive and legislative powers are now vested in the hereditary king, assisted by a six-member military council and a council of ministers. The constitution provides for a 99-member, single-chamber elected national assembly. The last elections were in 1973, when the Basotho National Party (BNP) won a majority of the seats. Elections due in 1985 were cancelled by the king because no candidates opposed the BNP, all of whose nominees were deemed to have been returned unopposed.

history The area now known as Lesotho was originally inhabited by the San, or Bushmen. During the 18th–19th centuries they were superseded by the Sotho, who were being driven southwards by the *Mfecane* ('the shaking-up of peoples') caused by the rise of the Zulu nation. Under the name of Basutoland, the Sotho nation was founded by Moshoeshoe I (1790–1870) from 1827, and at his request it became a British protectorate in 1868. It achieved internal self-government in 1965, with the paramount chief, Moshoeshoe II, as king, and was given full independence as Lesotho in 1966.

The BNP, a conservative group favouring limited cooperation with South Africa, held power from independence until 1986. Its leader, Chief Leabua Jonathan, became prime minister in 1966 and after 1970, when the king's powers were severely curtailed, the country was effectively under the prime minister's control. Since 1975 an organization called the Lesotho Liberation Army (LLA) has carried out a number of attacks on BNP members, with alleged South African support. South Africa, while denying complicity, has pointed out that Lesotho allowed the (until 1990) banned South African nationalist movement, the African National Congress (ANC), to use it as a base.

Economically, Lesotho is dependent on South Africa but has openly rejected the policy of apartheid. In retaliation, South Africa has tightened its border controls, causing food shortages in Lesotho. It has been alleged that South Africa has encouraged BNP dissenters to form a new party, the Basotho Democratic Alliance (BDA), and plotted with the BDA to overthrow the Lesotho government. Lesotho has also been under pressure from South Africa to sign a nonaggression pact, similar to the ◊Nkomati accord between South Africa and Mozambique, but the Lesotho government has refused to do so.

In 1986 South Africa imposed a border blockade, cutting off food and fuel supplies to Lesotho, and the government of Chief Jonathan was ousted and replaced in a coup led by Gen Justin Lekhanya. He announced that all executive and legislative powers would be vested in the king, ruling through a military council chaired by Gen Lekhanya, and a council of ministers. A week after the coup about 60 ANC members were deported to Zambia and on the same day the South African blockade was lifted. Although South Africa has denied playing any part in the coup, it is clear that it will find the new government more acceptable than the old. In February 1990 Maj-General Lenhanya announced that King Moshoeshoe had been stripped of his powers and gone into exile in Britain.

less developed country any country late in developing an industrial base, and dependent on cash crops and unprocessed minerals. The Group of 77 was established 1964 to pressure developed countries into giving greater aid to less developed countries.

The terms 'less developed' and 'developing' imply that industrial development is desirable or inevitable; many writers prefer ◊third world as opposed to 'industrial' countries; or 'South' and 'North'.

Lesseps /ˈlɛsəps/ Ferdinand, Vicomte de Lesseps 1805–1894. French engineer, constructor of the ◊Suez Canal 1859–69; he began the ◊Panama Canal 1879, but failed when he tried to construct it without locks.

Lessing /ˈlɛsɪŋ/ Doris (May) (born Taylor) 1919– . British novelist, born in Iran. Concerned with social and political themes, particularly the place of women in society, her work includes *The Grass is Singing* 1950, *The Golden Notebook* 1962, *The Good Terrorist* 1985, and the five-novel series *Children of Violence* 1952–69. She has also written an 'inner space fiction' series *Canopus in Argus Archives* 1979–83, and under the pen name 'Jane Somers', *The Diary of a Good Neighbour* 1981.

Lessing Political and social themes predominate in the work of novelist Doris Lessing.

Lessing /'lesɪŋ/ Gotthold Ephraim 1729–1781. German dramatist and critic. His plays include *Miss Sara Sampson* 1755, *Minna von Barnhelm* 1767, *Emilia Galotti* 1772, and the verse play *Nathan der Weise* 1779. His works of criticism *Laokoon* 1766 and *Hamburgische Dramaturgie* 1767–68 influenced German literature. *Laokoon* analysed the functions of poetry and the plastic arts; *Hamburgische Dramaturgie* reinterpreted Aristotle and attacked the restrictive form of French classical drama in favour of the freer approach of Shakespeare. He also produced many theological and philosophical writings.

Les Six (French 'the six') a group of French composers: Georges ◊Auric, Louis Durey (1888–1979), Arthur ◊Honegger, Darius ◊Milhaud, Francis ◊Poulenc, and Germaine Tailleferre (1892–1983). Formed in 1917, they were dedicated to producing works free from foreign influences and reflecting the contemporary world. They split up in the early 1920s.

Lesvos /'lezvɒs/ Greek island in the Aegean Sea, near the coast of Turkey
area 2,154 sq km/831 sq mi
capital Mytilene
products olives, wine, grain
population (1981) 104,620
history ancient name Lesbos; an Aeolian settlement, the home of ◊Alcaeus and ◊Sappho; conquered by the Turks from Genoa 1462; annexed to Greece 1913.

Letchworth /'letʃwəθ/ town in Hertfordshire, England, 56 km/35 mi NNW of London; population (1981) 31,835. Industries include clothing, furniture, scientific instruments, light metal goods, and printing. It was founded in 1903 as the first English ◊garden city.

Lethaby /'leθəbi/ William Richard 1857–1931. English architect. An assistant to Richard Norman Shaw, he embraced the principles of William Morris and Philip Webb in the ◊Arts and Crafts movement, and was co-founder and first director of the Central School of Arts and Crafts from 1894. He wrote a collection of essays entitled *Form in Civilization* 1922.

Lethe /'li:θi/ in Greek mythology, a river of the underworld whose waters, when drunk, brought forgetfulness of the past.

Le Touquet /lə 'tu:keɪ/ resort in N France, at the mouth of the river Canche; fashionable in the 1920s–30s.

letter a written or printed message, especially a personal communication. Letters are valuable as reflections of social conditions, literary, and political life. Legally, ownership of a letter (as a document) passes to the recipient, but the copyright remains with the writer.

Outstanding examples include:
ancient Cicero and Pliny, the Younger, and St Paul;
medieval Abelard and Héloïse (12th-century France), the Paston letters (15th-century England);
16th century Erasmus, Luther, Melanchthon, Spenser, Sidney;
17th century Donne, Milton, Cromwell, Dorothy Osborne, Wotton; Pascal, Mme de Sévigné (France);
18th century Pope, Walpole, Swift, Mary Wortley Montagu, Chesterfield, Cowper, Gray; Bossuet, Voltaire, Rousseau (France);
19th century Byron, Lamb, Keats, Fitzgerald, Stevenson; Emerson, J R Lowell (USA); George Sand, Saint-Beuve, Goncourt brothers (France); Schiller, Goethe (Germany); Gottfried Keller (Switzerland);
20th century T E Lawrence, G B Shaw and Ellen Terry, Katherine Mansfield; Rilke (Germany).

letterpress the method of printing from raised type, pioneered by Johannes ◊Gutenberg in Europe in the 1450s.

lettres de cachet /'letrə də 'kæʃeɪ/ French term for an order signed by the king and closed with his seal (*cachet*); especially an order under which persons might be imprisoned or banished without trial. They were used as a means of disposing of political opponents or criminals of high birth. The system was abolished during the French Revolution.

lettuce annual edible plant *Lactuca sativa*, family Compositae, believed to have been derived from the wild species *Lactuca serriola*. There are many varieties, including the cabbage lettuce, with round or loose heads, and the Cos lettuce, with long, upright heads.

leucite a silicate mineral, $KAlSi_2O_6$, occurring frequently in some potasssium-rich volcanic rocks. It is dull white to grey, and usually opaque. It is used as a source of potassium for fertilizer.

leucocyte a white blood cell. Leucocytes are part of the body's defences and give immunity against disease. There are several different types. Some (◊phagocytes and ◊macrophages) engulf invading microorganisms, others kill infected cells, while ◊lymphocytes produce more specific immune responses. Human blood contains about 11,000 leucocytes to the cubic millimetre — about one to every 500 red cells.

Leucocyte numbers may be reduced (leucopenia) by starvation, pernicious anaemia, and certain infections, such as typhoid and malaria. An increase in the numbers (leucocytosis) is a reaction to normal events such as digestion, exertion, and pregnancy, and to abnormal ones such as loss of blood, cancer, and most infections.

leukaemia any one of a group of cancerlike diseases of the blood cells, with widespread involvement of the bone marrow and other blood-forming tissue. The central feature is runaway production of white blood cells which are immature or in some way abnormal. These rogue cells, which lack the defensive capacity of healthy white cells, come to overwhelm the normal ones, leaving the victim vulnerable to infection. Abnormal functioning of the bone marrow also suppresses production of red blood cells and blood ◊platelets, resulting in ◊anaemia and a failure of the blood to clot.

Leukaemias are classified into acute or chronic, depending on their known rates of progression. They are also bracketed according to the type of white cell involved. Treatment is with radiotherapy and ◊cytotoxic drugs to suppress replication of abnormal cells, or by bone-marrow transplantation.

Levant /lɪ'vænt/ the E Mediterranean region, or more specifically, the coastal regions of Turkey-in-Asia, Syria, Lebanon, and Israel.

Le Vau /lə'vəʊ/ Louis 1612–1670. French architect, who drafted the plan of Versailles, and built the Louvre and Les Tuileries in Paris.

levee a naturally formed raised bank along the side of a river. When a river overflows its banks, the rate of flow in the flooded area is less than that in

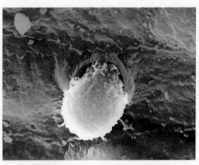

leucocyte False colour electron microscope view of a leucocyte passing through the thin layer of tissue that lines blood vessels. Leucocytes are transported around the body in the blood vessels but pass through the vessel walls into the other tissues as part of the body's defence system.

the channel, and silt is deposited. After the waters have withdrawn the silt is left as a bank that grows with successive floods. Eventually the river, contained by the levee, may be above the surface of the surrounding flood plain. Notable levees are found on the lower reaches of the Mississippi in the USA and the Po in Italy.

level or *spirit level* a simple instrument for finding horizontal level, used in surveying and building construction. It consists of a coloured liquid in a glass tube, in which a bubble is trapped. When the tube is horizontal, the bubble moves to the centre.

Levellers the democratic party in the English Revolution. They found wide support among Cromwell's New Model Army and the yeoman farmers, artisans, and small traders, and proved a powerful political force 1647–49. Their programme included the establishment of a republic, government by a parliament of one house elected by male suffrage, religious toleration, and sweeping social reforms. Mutinies by the Levellers in the army were suppressed by Cromwell in 1649. They were led by John ◊Lilburne.

Leven /'li:vən/ town in Fife region, Scotland; at the mouth of the river Leven, where it meets the Firth of Forth; population (1981) 8,600. It has timber, paper, and engineering industries.

Leven, Loch /'li:vən/ loch in Tayside region, Scotland; area 16 sq km/6 sq mi. It is drained by the river Leven, and has seven islands; Mary Queen of Scots was imprisoned 1567–68 on Castle Island. A national nature reserve since 1964. Leven is also the name of a sea loch in Strathclyde, Scotland.

Leven /'li:vən/ Alexander Leslie, 1st Earl of Leven *c.*1580–1661. Scottish general. He led the ◊Covenanters' army which invaded England in 1640, commanded the Scottish army sent to aid the English Puritans in 1643–46, and shared in the victory of Marston ◊Moor.

lever /'li:və/ a simple machine consisting of a rigid rod pivoted at a fulcrum, used for shifting or raising a heavy load or applying force in a similar way. Levers are classified into orders according to where the effort is applied, and the load-moving force developed, in relation to the position of the fulcrum.

A *first-order* lever has the load and the effort on opposite sides of the fulcrum, for example, a see-saw or pair of scissors. A *second-order* lever has the load and the effort on the same side of the fulcrum, with the load nearer the fulcrum, for example, a wheelbarrow or nutcrackers. A *third-order* lever has the effort nearer the fulcrum than the load with both on the same side of it, for example, a pair of tweezers or tongs. The mechanical advantage of a lever is the ratio of load to effort, equal to the perpendicular distance of the effort's line of action from the fulcrum divided by the distance to the load's line of action. Thus tweezers, for instance, have a

lever

first-order lever

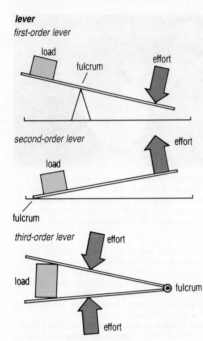

load fulcrum effort

second-order lever

load effort

fulcrum

third-order lever

effort

load fulcrum

effort

mechanical advantage of less than one.

Lever /ˈliːvə/ Charles James 1806–1872. Irish novelist. He wrote novels of Irish and army life, such as *Harry Lorrequer* 1837, *Charles O'Malley* 1840, and *Tom Burke of Ours* 1844.

leveraged buyout in business, the purchase of a controlling proportion of the shares of a company by its own management, financed almost exclusively by borrowing. It is so called because the ratio of a company's long-term debt to its equity (capital assets) is known as its 'leverage'.

Leverkusen /ˈleɪvəkuːzən/ river port in North Rhine-Westphalia, West Germany, 8 km/5 mi north of Cologne; population (1988) 155,000. It has iron, steel, and chemical industries.

Leverrier /ləˌveriˈeɪ/ Urbain Jean Joseph 1811–1877. French astronomer, who predicted the existence and position of Neptune.

Lévesque /leˈvek/ René 1922–1987. French-Canadian politician. In 1968 he founded the Parti Québecois, with the aim of an independent Québec, but a referendum rejected the proposal 1980. He was premier of Québec 1976–85.

Levi /ˈlevi/ Primo 1919–1987. Italian novelist. He joined the anti-Fascist resistance during World War II, was captured and sent to Auschwitz concentration camp. He wrote of these experiences in *Se questo e un uomo*/*If This is a Man* 1947.

leviathan in the Old Testament or Hebrew Bible, a mythical evil sea monster, identified by later commentators with the whale.

Levi-Montalcini /ˌlevi ˌmɒntælˈtʃiːni/ Rita 1909– . Italian neurologist who discovered nerve growth factor, a substance that controls how many cells make up the adult nervous system. Nobel prize 1986.

Levi-Montalcini studied at Turin and worked there until the Fascist anti-semitic laws forced her to go into hiding. She continued research into the nervous systems of chick embryos. After the war, she moved to the USA.

Lévi-Strauss /ˈlevi ˈstraʊs/ Claude 1908– . French anthropologist, who sought to find a universal structure governing all societies, reflected in the way myths are created. His works include *Tristes Tropiques* 1955, and *Mythologiques*/*Mythologies* 1964–71.

levitation counteraction of gravitational forces on a body. As claimed by medieval mystics, spiritualist mediums, and practitioners of transcendental meditation, it is unproven. In the laboratory it can be produced scientifically; for example, electrostatic force and acoustical waves have

been used to suspend water drops for microscopic study. It is also used in technology, for example, in magnetic levitation as in ◊maglev trains.

Levite in the Old Testament or Hebrew Bible, a member of one of the 12 peoples of Israel. Descended from Levi, a son of ◊Jacob, the Levites performed the lesser services of the Temple; the priesthood was confined to the descendants of Aaron, the brother of Moses.

Lewes /ˈluːɪs/ market town (administrative headquarters) in E Sussex, England, on the river Ouse; population (1981) 13,800. The Glyndebourne music festival is held nearby. Simon de Montfort defeated Henry III here in 1264; there is a house once belonging to Anne of Cleves, and a castle. The town is known for its 5th Nov celebrations.

Lewes /ˈluːɪs/ George Henry 1817–1878. English philosopher and critic. From acting he turned to literature and philosophy; his works include a *Biographical History of Philosophy* 1845–46, and *Life and Works of Goethe* 1855. He married in 1840, but left his wife in 1854 to form a life-long union with the writer Mary Ann Evans (George ◊Eliot), whom he had met in 1851.

Lewes, Battle of battle 1264 caused by the baronial opposition to Henry III, led by Simon de Montfort, earl of Leicester (1208–65). The king was defeated and captured at the battle.

The barons objected to Henry's patronage of French nobles in the English court, his weak foreign policy, and his support for the papacy against the Holy Roman Empire. In 1258, they forced him to issue the ◊Provisions of Oxford, and when he later refused to implement them, they revolted. They defeated and captured the king at Lewes in Sussex. Their revolt was broken by de Montfort's death and defeat at Evesham 1265.

Lewis /ˈluːɪs/ (William) Arthur 1915– . British economist, born on St Lucia, West Indies. He specialized in the economic problems of developing countries, as in *The Theory of Economic Growth* 1955, and shared a Nobel prize 1979.

Lewis /ˈluːɪs/ Carl (Frederick Carleton) 1961– . US athlete. At the 1984 Olympic Games he equalled Jesse ◊Owens' performance, winning gold medals in the 100 and 200 metres, sprint relay, and long jump. In the 1988 Olympics, he repeated his golds in the 100 metres and long jump, and won a silver in the 200 metres.

Lewis *US athlete Carl Lewis at the World Championships in Rome 1987.*

Lewis *US novelist Sinclair Lewis' depictions of small-town American life won him a Nobel prize 1930.*

CAREER HIGHLIGHTS

Olympic Games
gold:
100 metres 1984, 1988
200 metres 1984
4 x 100 metres relay 1984
long jump 1984, 1988
silver:
200 metres 1988
World Championships
gold:
100 metres 1983
4 x 100 metres relay 1983, 1987
long jump 1983, 1987
silver:
100 metres 1987.

Lewis Cecil Day see ◊Day Lewis.

Lewis /ˈluːɪs/ C(live) S(taples) 1898–1963. British academic and writer, born in Belfast. His books include the medieval study *The Allegory of Love* 1936, and the space fiction *Out of the Silent Planet* 1938. He was a committed Christian and wrote essays in popular theology such as *The Screwtape Letters* 1942 and *Mere Christianity* 1952; the autobiographical *Surprised by Joy* 1955; and a series of books of Christian allegory for children, set in the magic land of Narnia, including *The Lion, the Witch, and the Wardrobe* 1950.

Lewis /ˈluːɪs/ Jerry. Stage name of Joseph Levitch 1926– . US comic actor, formerly in partnership with Dean Martin (1946–1956). He enjoyed great commercial success as a solo performer and was revered by French critics, but his later films, such as *The Nutty Professor* 1963, were less well received in the USA.

Lewis /ˈluːɪs/ Jerry Lee 1935– . US rock-and-roll and country singer and pianist. His trademark was the 'pumping piano' style in hits such as 'Whole Lotta Shakin' Going On' and 'Great Balls of Fire' 1957; later recordings include 'What Made Milwaukee Famous' 1968.

Lewis /ˈluːɪs/ Matthew Gregory 1775–1818. British writer, known as 'Monk' Lewis from his popular terror romance *The Monk* 1795.

Lewis /ˈluːɪs/ Meriwether 1774–1809. US explorer. He was commissioned by president Thomas Jefferson to find a land route to the Pacific with William Clark (1770–1838). They followed the Missouri River to its source, crossed the Rocky Mountains (aided by an Indian girl, Sacajawea) and followed the Columbia River to the Pacific, then returned overland to St Louis 1804–06.

Formerly private secretary to President Jefferson, he was rewarded for his expedition with the governorship of the Louisiana Territory. His death, near Nashville, Tennessee, has been ascribed to suicide, but was more probably murder.

Lewis /ˈluːɪs/ (Harry) Sinclair 1885–1951. US novelist. He made a reputation with *Main Street* 1920,

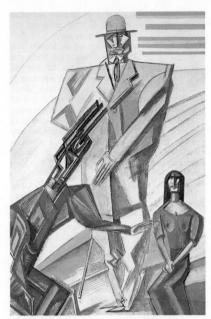

Lewis At the Seaside (1913), Victoria and Albert
Museum, London.

depicting American small-town life; *Babbitt* 1922, the
story of a real-estate dealer of the Midwest caught in
the conventions of his milieu; and *Arrowsmith* 1925,
a study of a scientist. Nobel prize 1930.

Born in Minnesota, he stayed for a time at
Upton Sinclair's socialist colony in New Jersey,
then became a freelance journalist. His later
books include *It Can't Happen Here* 1945, *Cass
Timberlane* 1945, and *The God-Seeker* 1949.

Lewis /'luːɪs/ (Percy) Wyndham 1886–1957.
English writer and artist, who pioneered ◊Vor-
ticism. He was noted for the hard and aggressive
style of both his writing and his painting. His literary works include the novels *Tarr* 1918 and *The
Childermass* 1928, the essay *Time and Western
Man* 1927, and autobiographies.

Born off Maine, in his father's yacht, he was
educated at the Slade art school and in Paris. On
returning to England he pioneered the new spirit
of art which his friend Ezra Pound called Vorticism;
he also edited *Blast*, a literary and artistic magazine
proclaiming its principles. Of his paintings, his portraits are especially memorable, such as those of
Edith Sitwell and T S Eliot. Although he has been
assessed by some as a leading spirit of the early
20th century, his support in the 1930s of Fascist
principles and Hitler alienated most critics.

Lewis US rock-and-roll singer Jerry Lee Lewis.

Lewisham /'luːɪʃəm/ borough of SE Greater London
features at Deptford shipbuilding yard (1512–1869),
Drake was knighted and Peter the Great worked
here; ◊Crystal Palace (re-erected at Sydenham in
1854) site now partly occupied by the National
Sports Centre; the poet James Elroy Flecker was
born here
population (1981) 233,225.

Lewis with Harris /'luːɪs/ largest island in the Outer
Hebrides; area 2,220 sq km/857 sq mi; popula-
tion (1981) 23,400. Its main town is Stornoway.
It is separated from NW Scotland by the Minch.
There are many lakes and peat moors. Harris is
famous for its tweeds.

Lewton /'luːtn/ Val. Stage name of Vladimir Ivan
Leventon 1904–1951. Russian-born US film producer, responsible for a series of atmospheric 'B'
horror films made for RKO in the 1940s, including
Cat People 1942 and *The Body Snatcher* 1946. He
co-wrote several of his films under the adopted
name of Carlos Keith.

Lexington /'leksɪŋtən/ town in Massachusetts,
USA; population (1981) 29,500. Industries include
printing and publishing. The Battle of Lexington
and Concord 1775 opened the War of ◊American
Independence. See also Paul ◊Revere.

Lexington-Fayette /'leksɪŋtən 'feɪət/ town in
Kentucky, USA, centre of the bluegrass coun-
try; population (1981) 204,160. Race horses are
bred in the area, and races and shows are held.
There is a tobacco market and the University of
Kentucky (1865).

ley an area of temporary grassland, sown to produce
grazing and hay or silage for a period of one to ten
years before being ploughed and cropped. Short-
term leys are often incorporated in systems of
crop rotation. A simple seven-year rotation, for
example, might include a three-year ley followed
by two years of wheat and then two years of
barley, before returning the land to temporary
grass once more. In this way, the cereal crops
can take advantage of the build-up of soil fertility
that occurs during the period under grass.

Leyden alternative form of ◊Leiden, city in the
Netherlands.

Leyden Lucas van see ◊Lucas van Leyden, Dutch
painter.

Leyland /'leɪlənd/ industrial town in Lancashire,
England; population (1981) 37,100. Industries include motor vehicles, paint and rubber. The Rover
Group (previously British Leyland), largest of British firms producing cars, buses, and lorries, has
its headquarters here.

LF in physics, abbreviation for *low ◊frequency*.

LH abbreviation for ◊*luteinizing hormone*.

Lhasa /'lɑːsə/ (the 'Forbidden City') capital of
the autonomous region of Tibet, China, at
5,000 m/16,400 ft; population (1982) 105,000.
Products include handicrafts and light industry.

Lhote /ləʊt/ André 1885–1962. French artist,
influential through his treatises on art. *Rugby*
(Musée d'Art Moderne, Paris) is an example of
his use of colour and geometric style.

liability in accounting, a financial obligation. Liabilities are placed alongside assets on a balance sheet
to show the wealth of the entity at a given date.

liana a woody, perennial climbing plant with very
long stems, which grows around trees up to the
canopy, where there is more sunlight. Lianas are
common in tropical rain forests, where individual stems may grow up to 70 m/255 ft long.
They have an unusual stem structure that allows

them to retain some flexibility, despite becoming
woody.

Liao /li'aʊ/ river in NE China, frozen Dec–Mar;
the main headstream rises in the mountains of
Inner Mongolia and flows E, then S to the Gulf
of Liaodong; length 1,450 km/900 mi.

Liaoning /li,aʊ'nɪŋ/ province of NE China
area 151,000 sq km/58,300 sq mi
capital Shenyang
towns Anshan, Fushun, Liaoyang
features it was developed by Japan 1905–45,
including the **Liaodong Peninsula** whose ports
had been conquered from the Russians, and the
province is one of China's most heavily industrialized areas
products cereals, coal, iron, salt, oil
population (1986) 37,260,000.

Liaoyang /li'aʊ 'jæŋ/ industrial city (engineering,
textiles) in Liaoning province; population (1970)
250,000. In 1904 Russia was defeated by Japan here.

Liaquat Ali Khan /'lɪəkwæt 'æli 'kɑːn/ 1895–1951.
Indian Muslim nationalist politician, prime minister
of Pakistan from independence 1947. The chief
lieutenant of Muhammad ◊Jinnah, he was a leader
of the Muslim League. He was assassinated.

Lib. abbreviation for *Liberal*.

Libau /'liːbaʊ/ German name of Latvian port
◊Liepaja.

Libby /'lɪbi/ Willard Frank 1908–1980. US chemist, whose development of ◊radiocarbon dating
1947 won him a Nobel prize 1960.

libel in law, defamation in a permanent form, such
as in a newspaper, book, or broadcast.

In English law a statement is defamatory if it
lowers the plaintiff in the estimate of right-thinking
people generally. Defences to libel are: to show
that the statement was true, or fair comment; or
to show that it was privileged (this applies, for example, to the reporting of statements made in Parliament or in a court); or, in certain circumstances,
making a formal apology. Libel actions are tried
by a judge with a jury, and the jury decides the
amount of the damages. In certain circumstances,
libel can also be a criminal offence. The stringency
of English libel law has been widely criticised as
limiting the freedom of the press. In the USA,
for example, the position is much more elastic,
particularly in criticism of public figures, when a
libel action can only succeed if the statement is
both false and deliberately malicious.

In the UK, the largest ever libel award of £5
million was made to Lord Aldington Dec 1989
after allegations that he was criminally responsible for the deaths of several thousand Yugoslavs
in 1945.

liberalism political and social theory that favours
parliamentary government, freedom of the press,
speech, and worship, the abolition of class privileges, a minimum of state interference in economic life, and international ◊free trade. It is
historically associated with the Liberal Party in
the UK and the Democratic Party in the USA.

Liberalism developed during the 17th–19th centuries as the distinctive theory of the industrial
and commercial classes in their struggle against
the power of the monarchy, the church, and the
feudal landowners. Economically it was associated
with ◊*laissez-faire*, or non-intervention. In the late
19th and early 20th centuries its ideas were modified by the acceptance of universal suffrage and
a certain amount of state intervention, in order
to ensure a minimum standard of living and to

Notable libel damages verdicts in the UK

Year	Case
1987	Jeffrey Archer v. News of the World: £500,000 for alleging a link between Mr Archer and a prostitute.
1988	Koo Stark v. Sunday People: £300,000 for alleging a liaison between Ms Stark and Prince Andrew of the UK.
1989	Sonia Sutcliffe v. Private Eye magazine: £600,000 for alleging that Mrs Sutcliffe exploited her husband's name following his conviction for multiple murder. (The amount was later reduced to £60,000 on appeal.)
1989	Lord Aldington v. Count Nikolai Tolstoy: £5 million for alleging that Lord Aldington was a war criminal.

remove extremes of poverty and wealth. The classical statement of liberal principles is found in *On Liberty* and other works of the British philosopher J S Mill.

Liberal Party in the UK, a political party, the successor to the ◊Whig Party, with an ideology of liberalism. In the 19th century it was the party of the left, representing the interests of commerce and industry. Its outstanding leaders were Palmerston, Gladstone, and Lloyd George. From 1914 it declined, and the rise of the Labour Party pushed the Liberals into the middle ground. The Liberals joined forces with the Social Democratic Party (SDP) for the 1983 and 1987 elections. In the 1987 election the Alliance, as they were jointly known, achieved 22 seats and 22.6% of votes. In 1988, a majority of the SDP voted to merge with the Liberals to form the Social and Liberal Democrats (called Liberal Democrats for short).

The term 'Liberal', used officially from about 1840 and unofficially from about 1815, marked the transfer of control from aristocrats to the more progressive industrialists, backed by supporters of the utilitarian reformer ◊Bentham, Nonconformists, and the middle classes. During the Liberals' first period of power 1830–41, they promoted parliamentary and municipal government reform and the abolition of slavery, but their ◊laissez-faire theories led to the harsh Poor Law of 1834. Except for two short periods the Liberals were in power 1846–66, but the only major change was the general adoption of ◊free trade. Liberal pressure forced Peel to repeal the Corn Laws 1846, thereby splitting the Tory party.

Extended franchise in 1867 and Gladstone's emergence as leader began a new phase, dominated by the Manchester school with a programme of 'peace, retrenchment, and reform'. Gladstone's 1868–74 government introduced many important reforms, including elementary education and vote by ballot. The party's left, mainly composed of working-class ◊Radicals led by Charles ◊Bradlaugh and Joseph ◊Chamberlain, repudiated *laissez-faire* and inclined towards republicanism, but the Liberals were split over Home Rule 1886 and many became the Liberal Unionists or joined the Conservatives. Except for 1892–95, the Liberals remained out of power until 1906, when, reinforced by Labour and Irish support, they returned with a huge

majority. Old-age pensions, National Insurance, limitation of the powers of the Lords, and the Irish Home Rule Bill followed.

Lloyd George's alliance with the Conservatives 1916–22 divided them between him and his predecessor Asquith, and although reunited 1923 the Liberals continued to lose votes. They briefly joined the National Government 1931–32. After World War II they were reduced to a handful of members of Parliament. A revival began under the leadership 1956–67 of Jo Grimond and continued under Jeremy Thorpe, who resigned after a period of controversy within the party 1976.

After a caretaker return by Grimond, David Steel became the first party leader in British politics to be elected by party members who were not MPs. In 1977–78 Steel entered into an agreement to support Labour in any vote of confidence in return for consultation on measures undertaken. He resigned 1988 and was replaced by Paddy Ashdown.

Liberal Party, Australian political party established 1944 by Robert Menzies, after a Labor landslide, and derived from the former United Australia Party. After the voters rejected Labor's extensive nationalization plans, the Liberals were in power 1949–72 and 1975–83, and were led in succession by H E Holt, J G Gorton, William McMahon (1908–), Billy Snedden (1926–), and Malcolm Fraser.

liberation theology Christian intellectual theory of Jesus' primary importance as the 'Liberator', personifying the poor and devoted to freeing them from oppression (Matthew 19:21, 25:35, 40). Initiated by the Peruvian priest Gustavo Gutierrez in *The Theology of Liberation* 1969, and enthusiastically, and sometimes violently, adopted in Latin America, it embodies a Marxist interpretation of the class struggle. One of its leaders is Leonardo Boff (1939–), a Brazilian Franciscan priest.

Liberator, the title given to Simón ◊Bolívar, South American revolutionary leader; also a title given to Daniel ◊O'Connell, Irish political leader.

Liberia /laɪˈbɪəriə/ country in W Africa, bounded to the N and NE by Guinea, E by the Ivory Coast, S and SW by the Atlantic, and NW by Sierra Leone.

government The 1984 constitution provides for a two-chamber national assembly consisting of a

26-member senate and a 64-member house of representatives, elected, like the president, by universal suffrage for a six-year term.

history The area now known as Liberia was bought by the American Colonization Society, a philanthropic organization active in the first half of the 19th century. The society's aim was to establish a settlement for liberated black slaves from the southern USA. The first settlers arrived in 1822, and Liberia was declared an independent republic in 1847. The new state suffered from financial difficulties, bankruptcy in 1909 bringing reorganization by US army officers. For almost 160 years the country's leaders were descended from the black American settlers, but the 1980 coup put Africans in power.

William Tubman was president from 1944 until his death in 1971 and was succeeded by Vice-President William R Tolbert (1913–1980), who was re-elected in 1975. In 1980 Tolbert was assassinated in a coup led by Master Sgt Samuel Doe (1952–), who suspended the constitution, banned all political parties and ruled through the People's Redemption Council (PRC). He proceeded to stamp out corruption in the public service, encountering considerable opposition and making enemies who were later to threaten his position.

A new constitution was approved by the PRC in 1983 and by national referendum in 1984. Political parties were again permitted, provided they registered with the Special Electoral Commission (SECOM). In 1984 Doe founded the National Democratic Party of Liberia (NDPL) and announced his intention to stand for the presidency. By 1985 there were 11 political parties, but they complained about the difficulties of the registration process and only three registered in time for the elections. Doe's party won clear majorities in both chambers, despite alleged election fraud, and he was pronounced president with 50.9% of the vote. In 1985 there was an unsuccessful attempt to unseat him. Doe alleged complicity by neighbouring Sierra Leone and dealt harshly with the coup leaders. There has been a gradual movement towards a pluralist political system, with a number of parties registering in opposition to the ruling NDPL, which, with growing economic problems, has threatened the stability of the Doe regime.

liberty in its medieval sense, a franchise, or collection of privileges, granted to an individual or community by the king, and the area over which this franchise extended.

Liberty /ˈlɪbəti/ Arthur Lasenby 1843–1917. shopkeeper and founder of a shop of the same name in Regent Street, London. Originally importing oriental goods, it gradually started selling British Arts and Crafts and Art Nouveau furniture, tableware, and fabrics. A draper's son, he trained at Farmer & Rogers' Cloak and Shawl Emporium and opened his own shop in 1875. Art Nouveau is sometimes still called *stile Liberty* in Italy.

liberty, equality, fraternity (*liberté, egalité, fraternité*) motto of the French republic from 1793. It was changed 1940–44 under the Vichy government to 'work, family, fatherland'.

LIBOR acronym for *London Interbank Offered Rates* loan rates for a specified period which are offered to first-class banks in the London interbank market. Banks link their lending to LIBOR as an alternative to the base lending rate when setting the rate for a fixed term, after which the rate may be adjusted.

Libra faint constellation of the zodiac, in the southern hemisphere near Scorpius. It represents the scales of justice. The Sun passes through Libra during Nov. In astrology, the dates for Libra are between about 23 Sept and 23 Oct (see ◊precession).

library a collection of information (usually in the form of books) held for common use. The earliest was at Nineveh in Babylonian times. The first public library was opened at Athens 330 BC. All ancient libraries were reference libraries; books could be

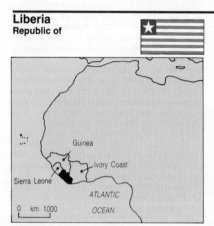

Liberia
Republic of

area 111,370 sq km/42,989 sq mi
capital Monrovia
physical forested highlands; swampy coast where six rivers end
features nominally the world's largest merchant navy because minimal controls make Liberia's a flag of convenience
head of state and government Samuel Kanyon Doe from 1980
political parties National Democratic party of

Liberia (NDLP), nationalist
government emergent democratic republic
exports iron ore, rubber, diamonds, coffee, cocoa, palm oil
currency Liberian dollar (1.70 = £1 Feb 1990)
population (1988) 2,436,000 (95% belonging to the indigenous peoples); annual growth rate 3.2%
life expectancy men 47, women 51
language English (official)
religion Muslim 20%, Christian 15%, traditional 65%
literacy 47% male/23% female (1985 est)
GNP $900 million (1983); $400 per head of population
chronology
1847 Founded as an independent republic.
1944 William Tubman elected president.
1971 Tubman died and was succeeded by William Tolbert.
1980 Tolbert assassinated in a coup led by Samuel Doe, who suspended the constitution and ruled through a People's Redemption Council (PRC).
1984 New constitution approved. National Democratic Party of Liberia (NDPL) founded by Doe.
1985 NDPL won decisive victory in general election. Unsuccessful coup against Doe.
1990 Gradual movement to more pluralist politics and economic problems threaten President Doe.

Libya
Socialist People's Libyan Arab State of the Masses
(al-Jamahiriya al-Arabiya al-Libya al-Shabiya al-Ishtirakiya al-Uzma)

area 1,759,540 sq km/679,182 sq mi
capital Tripoli
towns ports Benghazi, Misurata
physical desert; mountains in N and S
features Gulf of Sirte; rock paintings of about 3000 BC in the Fezzan; Roman city sites of Leptis Magna, Sabratha among others; the plan to pump water from below the Sahara to the coast risks exhaustion of a largely non-renewable supply

government one-party, socialist state
head of state and government Moamar Khaddhafi from 1969
political parties Arab Socialist Union (ASU), radical, left-wing
exports oil, natural gas
currency Libyan dinar (0.49 = £1 Feb 1990)
population (1986) 3,955,000 (including 500,000 foreign workers); annual growth rate 3.9%
life expectancy men 57, women 60
language Arabic
religion Sunni Muslim
literacy 60% (1985)
GDP $25 bn (1984); $7,000 per head of population
chronology
1951 Achieved independence as the United Kingdom of Libya, under King Idris.
1969 King deposed in a coup led by Col Moamar Khaddhafi. Revolution Command Council set up and the Arab Socialist Union (ASU) proclaimed the only legal party.
1972 Proposed federation of Libya, Syria, and Egypt abandoned.
1980 Proposed merger with Syria abandoned. Libyan troops began fighting in Chad.
1981 Proposed merger with Chad abandoned.
1986 US bombing of Khaddhafi's headquarters, following allegations of his complicity in guerrilla activities.
1988 Diplomatic relations with Chad restored.
1989 US accused Libya of building a chemical-weapons factory and shot down two Libyan planes; reconciliation with Egypt.

consulted but not borrowed.
Classification is usually by two major systems: Dewey Decimal Classification (now known as Universal Decimal Classification) invented by Melvil Dewey (1851–1931), and the Library of Congress system. Library cataloguing systems range from cards to microfiche and computer databases with on-line terminals. These frequently make use of ◊ISBN numbers and, for magazines and journals, ISSN numbers.

libretto (Italian 'little book') the text of an opera or other dramatic vocal work, or the scenario of a ballet.

Libreville /ˈliːbrəviːl/ capital of Gabon, on the estuary of the river Gabon; population (1985) 350,000. Products include timber, oil, and minerals. It was founded 1849 as a refuge for slaves freed by the French.

Libya /ˈlɪbiə/ country in N Africa, bordered to the N by the Mediterranean, E by Egypt, SE by the Sudan, S by Chad and Niger, and W by Algeria and Tunisia.

government The 1977 constitution created an Islamic socialist state and the government is designed to allow the greatest possible popular involvement, through a large congress and smaller secretariats and committees. There is a General People's Congress (GPC) of 1,112 members, which elects a secretary-general who was intended to be head of state. The GPC is serviced by a general secretariat, which is Libya's nearest equivalent to a legislature. The executive organ of the state is the General People's Committee, which replaces the structure of ministries that operated before the 1969 revolution. The Arab Socialist Union (ASU) is the only political party and, despite Libya's elaborately democratic structure, ultimate power rests with the party and the revolutionary leader, Col Khaddhafi.

history The area now known as Libya was successively under the domination of Phoenicia, Greece, Rome, the Vandals, and Byzantium, and from the 16th century was part of the Turkish Ottoman Empire. In 1911 it was conquered by Italy, becoming known as Libya from 1934. After being the scene of much fighting during World War II, in 1942 it was divided into three provinces: Fezzan, which was placed under French control; Cyrenaica

and Tripolitania, which were placed under British control. In 1951 it achieved independence as the United Kingdom of Libya, Muhammad Idris-as-Sanusi becoming King Idris.

The country enjoyed internal and external stability until a bloodless revolution 1969, led by young nationalist officers, deposed the king and proclaimed a Libyan Arab Republic. Power was vested in a Revolution Command Council (RCC), chaired by Col Moamer al-Khaddhafi, with the Arab Socialist Union (ASU) as the only political party. Khaddhafi soon began proposing schemes for Arab unity, none of which was permanently adopted. In 1972 he planned a federation of Libya, Syria, and Egypt, and later that year a merger between Libya and Egypt. In 1980 he proposed a union with Syria and in 1981 with Chad.

Khaddhafi tried to run the country on socialist Islamic lines, with people's committees pledged to socialism and the teachings of the Koran. The 1977 constitution made him secretary-general of the general secretariat of the GPC, but in 1979 he resigned the post in order to devote more time to 'preserving the revolution'. His attempts to establish himself as a leader of the Arab world have brought him into conflict with Western powers, particularly the USA. The Reagan administration objected to Libya's presence in Chad and its attempts to unseat the French-US-sponsored government of President Habré. The USA has linked Khaddhafi to worldwide terrorist activities, despite his denials of complicity, and the killing of a US soldier in a bomb attack in Berlin 1986 by an unidentified guerrilla group prompted a raid by US aircraft, some of them British-based, on Khaddhafi's personal headquarters, killing a number of civilians.

In Jan 1989 Khaddaffi resisted the urge to respond to the shooting-down of two of his fighters off the Libyan coast by the US navy and has worked steadily at improving external relations, particularly in the Arab world, effecting a reconciliation with Egypt in Oct 1989.

licence document issued by a government or other recognized authority conveying permission to the holder to do something otherwise prohibited, and designed to facilitate accurate records, the maintenance of order, and collection of revenue. In

Britain, examples are licences required for marriage, for driving, for keeping a gun, and for sale of intoxicating liquor. The term also refers to permission (in writing or not) granted by a private person, for example allowing use of his or her land for a particular event.

licensing laws laws governing the sale of alcoholic drinks. Most countries have some restrictions on the sale of alcoholic drinks, if not an outright ban, as in the case of Islamic countries.

In Britain, sales can only be made by pubs, restaurants, shops, and clubs which hold licences obtained from licensing justices. The hours during which alcoholic drinks can be sold are restricted, but they have been recently extended in England and Wales in line with Scotland. From August 1988 licensed premises can sell alcohol between 11am and 11pm Monday to Saturday, and 12 noon to 3pm and 7pm to 10.30pm on Sundays. These hours can be extended for particular occasions, by application to the licensing justices.

lichen organism of the group *Lichenes*, which consists of a fungus and an alga existing in a mutually beneficial relationship. Found on trees, rocks, and other substrates, lichen flourishes under very adverse conditions. Some lichens have food value, for example reindeer moss and Iceland moss; others give dyes such as litmus, or are used in medicine. They are sensitive to atmospheric pollution (see ◊indicator species).

Lichfield /ˈlɪtʃfiːld/ town in the Trent Valley, Staffordshire, England; population (1985) 26,310. The cathedral, 13th–14th centuries, has three spires. Samuel Johnson was born here.

Lichfield /ˈlɪtʃfiːld/ Patrick Anson, 5th Earl of Lichfield 1939– . British photographer, known for portraits of the rich and famous.

Lichtenstein /ˈlɪktənstaɪn/ Roy 1923– . US Pop artist. His reputation was made with an exhibition in New York 1962. He used advertising and comic-strip imagery, often focusing on popular ideals of romance and heroism, as in *Whaam!* 1963 (Tate Gallery, London).

Liddell Hart /ˈlɪdl ˈhɑːt/ Basil 1895–1970. British military scientist. He was an exponent of mechanized warfare, and his ideas were adopted in Germany 1935 in creating the 1st Panzer Division, combining motorized infantry and tanks. From 1937 he advised the UK War Office on army reorganization.

Lidice /ˈliːdɪtseɪ/ Czechoslovak mining village, replacing one destroyed by the Nazis 10 Jun 1942 as a reprisal for the assassination of ◊Heydrich. The men were shot, the women sent to concentration camps, and the children taken to Germany. The officer responsible was hanged 1946.

Lie /liː/ Trygve (Halvdan) 1896–1968. Norwegian Labour politician and diplomat. He became secretary of the Labour Party 1926. During the German occupation of Norway in World War II he was foreign minister in the exiled government 1941–46, when he helped retain the Norwegian fleet for the Allies. He became the first secretary-general of the United Nations 1946–53, when he resigned over Soviet opposition to his handling of the Korean War.

Liebig /ˈliːbɪɡ/ Justus, Baron von Liebig 1803–1873. German chemist, a major contributor to agricultural chemistry. He introduced the theory of ◊radicals, and discovered chloroform and chloral.

Liebknecht /ˈliːpknɛxt/ Karl 1871–1919. German socialist, father of Wilhelm Liebknecht. A founder of the German Communist Party, originally known as the Spartacus League (see ◊Spartacist), he led an unsuccessful revolt in Berlin 1919, and was murdered by army officers.

Liebknecht /ˈliːpknɛxt/ Wilhelm 1826–1900. German socialist, father of Karl Liebnecht. A friend of the communist theoretician Marx, with whom he took part in the ◊revolution of 1848 he was imprisoned for opposition to the Franco-Prussian War. He was the father of Karl Liebknecht.

Liechtenstein /ˈlɪktənstaɪn/ landlocked country in W central Europe, situated between Austria to the

Liechtenstein
Principality of

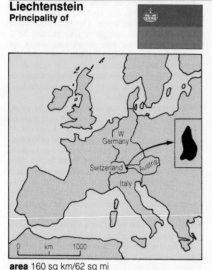

area 160 sq km/62 sq mi
capital Vaduz

physical Alpine; includes part of Rhine Valley
features only country in the world to take its name from its reigning family; most highly industrialized country
head of state Prince Hans Adam II from 1989
head of government Hans Brunhart from 1978
government constitutional monarchy
exports microchips, precision engineering, processed foods, postage stamps; easy tax laws make it a haven for foreign companies and banks
currency Swiss franc (2.53 = £1 Feb 1990)
population (1987) 27,700 (33% foreign); annual growth rate 1.4%
life expectancy men 65, women 73
language German
religion Roman Catholic
literacy 100% (1986)
GDP 1 bn Swiss francs (1984); $16,440 per head of population
chronology
1938 Prince Franz Josef II came to power.
1984 Vote extended to women in national elections.
1989 Prince Franz Joseph II died; Hans Adam II succeeded him as prince.

E, and Switzerland to the W.

government The 1921 constitution established a hereditary principality with a single-chamber parliament, the *Landtag*. The prince is formal and constitutional head of state. The *Landtag* has 25 members, 15 from the Upper Country and 10 from the Lower Country, elected for a four-year term through a system of proportional representation. The *Landtag* elects five people to form the government for its duration.

history Liechtenstein's history as a sovereign state began in 1342; its boundaries have been unchanged since 1434, and it has been known by its present name since 1719. Because of its small population of fewer than 30,000, it has found it convenient to associate itself with larger nations in international matters. For example, since 1923 it has shared a customs union with Switzerland, which since 1919 represents it abroad. Before this Austria undertook its diplomatic representation.

Liechtenstein is one of the world's richest countries, with an income per head of population greater than that of the USA, nearly twice that of the UK, and only slightly less than that of Switzerland. It has chosen not to be a full member of the United Nations but is represented in some UN specialist agencies. Prince Franz Josef II came to power in 1938, and although he retained the title, he passed the duties of prince to his heir, Hans Adam, in 1984. Franz Joseph II died in Oct 1989 and Hans Adam II immediately began to press strongly for the country to consider applying for full membership of the UN.

Despite the growing indications of change, Liechtenstein's political system remains innately conservative. Women did not achieve the right to vote in national elections until 1984 and were debarred from voting in three of the principality's 11 communes until Apr 1986.

Lied (German 'song') a musical setting of a poem, usually for solo voice and piano; referring to Romantic songs of Schubert, Schumann, Brahms, and Hugo Wolf.

lie detector popular name for a ◊polygraph.

Liège /liˈeɪʒ/ industrial city (weapons, textiles, paper, chemicals), capital of Liège province in Belgium, SE of Brussels, on the Meuse; population (1988) 200,000. The province of Liège has an area of 3,900 sq km/1,505 sq mi, and a population (1987) of 992,000.

liege in the feudal system, describing the allegiance owed by a vassal to his or her lord (the ◊liege lord).

lien in English law, the right to retain goods owned by another until the owner has satisfied a claim against him by the person in possession of the

goods. For example, the goods may have been provided as security for a debt.

Liepāja /liˈpaɪə/ (German *Libau*) naval and industrial port in the Republic of Latvia, USSR; population (1985) 112,000. The Knights of Livonia founded Liepāja in the 13th century. Industries include steel, engineering, textiles and clothing.

Lifar /liˈfɑː/ Serge 1905–1986. Russian dancer and choreographer. Born in Kiev, he studied under ◊Nijinsky, joined the Diaghilev company 1923, and was *maître de ballet* at the Paris Opéra 1930–44 and 1947–59.

A great experimenter, he produced his first ballet without music, *Icare*, in 1935, and published the same year the controversial *Le Manifeste du choréographie*. He developed the importance of the male dancer in his *Prometheus* 1929 and *Romeo and Juliet* (music by Prokofiev) 1955.

life the ability to grow, reproduce, and respond to such stimuli as light, heat, and sound. It is thought that life on Earth began about 4,000 million years ago. The earliest fossil evidence of life is thread-like chains of cells discovered 1980 in deposits in NW Australia that have been dated as 3,500 million years old.

It seems probable that the original atmosphere of Earth consisted of carbon dioxide, nitrogen, and water, and that complex organic molecules, such as ◊amino acids, were created when the atmosphere was bombarded by ultraviolet radiation or by lightning. Attempts to replicate these conditions in the laboratory have successfully shown that amino acids, purine and pyrimidine bases (◊base pairs in DNA), and other vital molecules can be created in this way.

It has also been suggested that life could have reached Earth from elsewhere in the universe in the form of complex organic molecules present in meteors or comets, but others argue that this is not really an alternative explanation because these primitive life forms must then have been created elsewhere by much the same process. Normally life is created by living organisms (a process called ◊biogenesis).

lifeboat a small land-based vessel specially built for rescuing swimmers in danger of drowning, or a boat carried aboard a larger ship in case of a need to abandon ship.

In the UK, The Royal National Lifeboat Institution (RNLI), founded 1824 at the instance of William Hillary, provides a voluntarily crewed and supported service. The US and Canadian Coast Guards are services of the governments. A modern RNLI boat is about 16 m/52 ft long and self-righting, so that it is virtually unsinkable. Inflatable lifeboats are used for inshore work.

life cycle in biology, the sequence of stages through which members of a given species pass. Most vertebrates have a simple life cycle consisting of ◊fertilization of sex cells or ◊gametes, a period of development as an ◊embryo, a period of juvenile growth after hatching or birth, an adulthood including ◊sexual reproduction, and finally death. Invertebrate life cycles are generally more complex and may involve major reconstitution of the individual's appearance (◊metamorphosis) and completely different styles of life. Plants have a special type of life cycle with two distinct phases, known as an ◊alternation of generations.

Thus dragonflies live an aquatic life as larvae and an aerial life during the adult phase. In many other invertebrates and protozoa there are several different stages in the life cycle, and in parasites these often occur in different host organisms.

life expectancy the average lifespan of a person at birth. It depends on nutrition, disease control, environmental contaminants, war, and living standards in general. In the UK, average life expectancy for both sexes currently stands at 75 and heart disease is the main cause of death. There is a marked difference between first world countries, which generally have an ageing population and third world countries, where life expectancy is much shorter. In Bangladesh life expectancy is currently 48; in Nigeria 49. In famine-prone Ethiopia it is only 41.

life insurance an insurance policy that pays money on the death of the holder. It is correctly called *assurance*, as the policy covers an inevitable occurrence, not a risk.

Life US weekly magazine of photo journalism, which recorded US and world events pictorially from 1936, when its owners, Time Inc., bought the title of an older magazine.

life sciences scientific study of the living world as a whole, a new synthesis of several traditional scientific disciplines including ◊biology, ◊zoology, and ◊botany, and newer, more specialized areas of study such as ◊biophysics and ◊sociobiology. This approach has led to many new ideas and discoveries, as well as to an emphasis on ◊ecology, the study of living organisms in their natural environment.

life table a way of summarizing the probability that an individual will give birth or die during successive periods of life. From this the proportion of individuals who survive from birth to any given age (*survivorship*) and the mean number of offspring produced (*net reproductive rate*) can be determined.

Insurance companies use life tables to estimate risks of death in order to set their premiums, while governments use them to determine future needs for education and health services.

LIFFE acronym for *London International Financial Futures Exchange*, one of the exchanges in London where ◊futures contracts are traded. It opened Sept 1982. It provides a worldwide exchange for futures dealers and investors, and began options trading 1985. It was a forerunner of the ◊Big Bang in bringing US-style 'open-house' dealing (as opposed to telephone dealing) to the UK.

Liffey /ˈlɪfi/ river in E Ireland, flowing from the Wicklow mountains to Dublin Bay; length 80 km/50 mi.

lift (US *elevator*) a device for lifting passengers and goods vertically, between the floors of a building. US inventor Elisha Graves ◊Otis developed the first passenger lift, installed 1857. The invention of the lift allowed the development of the ◊skyscraper from the 1880s.

Ligachev /ˈlɪɡətʃef/ Egor (Kuzmich) 1920– . Soviet politician. He joined the Communist Party 1944, and has been a member of the Politburo since 1985. He is regarded as the chief conservative ideologist, and the leader of conservative opposition to ◊President Gorbachev.

ligament a strong flexible connective tissue, made of the protein collagen, which joins bone to bone at moveable joints. Ligaments prevent bone dislocation (under normal circumstances), but permit joint flexion.

ligature 'thread' (nylon, gut, wire) tying a blood vessel, limb, or base of a tumour, used to stop the flow of blood or other fluid through it.

Ligeti /'lɪɡəti/ György (Sándor) 1923– . Hungarian-born Austrian composer who developed a dense, highly chromatic, polyphonic style in which melody and rhythm are sometimes lost in shifting blocks of sound. He achieved international prominence with *Atmosphères* 1961 and *Requiem* 1965, which were used for Kubrick's film epic *2001: A Space Odyssey*. Other works include an opera *Le Grand Macabre* 1978, and *Poème symphonique* 1962, for 100 metronomes.

Ligeti taught at the Budapest Academy of Music before moving to the West 1956, where he met avant-garde composers, including Stockhausen. He also worked briefly at the electronic studio in Cologne, West Germany (1957–8).

light ◊electromagnetic radiation in the visible range, having a wavelength, from about 400 nanometers in the extreme violet to about 770 nanometers in the extreme red. Light is considered to exhibit both particle and wave properties, and the fundamental particle or quantum of light is called the **photon**. The speed of light (and of all electromagnetic radiation) in a vacuum is approximately 300,000 km per second/186,000 miles per second, and is a universal constant denoted by *c*.

Newton was the first to discover, in 1666, that sunlight is composed of a mixture of light of all different colours in certain proportions and that it could be separated into its components by dispersion. Before his time it was supposed that dispersion of light produced colour instead of separating already existing colours.

The speed of light is allegedly the fastest speed in nature, but in 1971 a jet from the galaxy 3 273 was calculated as travelling at three times this speed, which should be impossible.

light-emitting diode (LED) a means of displaying symbols in electronic instruments and devices. An LED is made of ◊semiconductor material, such as gallium arsenide phosphide, that glows when electricity is passed through it. The first digital watches and calculators had LED displays, but now generally use ◊liquid crystal displays (LCD).

Lighthill /'laɪthɪl/ James 1924– . British mathematician, who specialized in the application of mathematics to high-speed aerodynamics and jet propulsion.

life expectancy

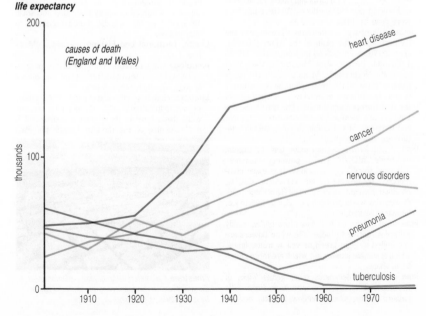

life table

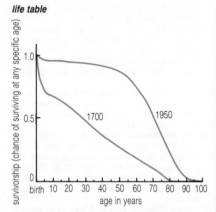

lighthouse structure carrying a powerful light to warn ships or aeroplanes that they are approaching land. The light is magnified and directed out to the horizon or up to the zenith by a series of mirrors or prisms. Increasingly lighthouses are powered by electricity and automated rather than staffed; the more recent models also emit radio signals. Only a minority of the remaining staffed lighthouses still use dissolved acetylene as a source of power.

Lights may be either flashing (the dark period exceeding the light) or rotating (the dark period being equal or less); fixed lights are liable to confusion. The pattern of lighting is individually varied so that ships or aircraft can identify the lighthouse.

Among early lighthouses were the Pharos of Alexandria (about 280 BC) and those built by the Romans at Ostia, Ravenna, Boulogne, and Dover. In England beacons burning in church towers served as lighthouses until the 17th century, and in the earliest lighthouses such as the Eddystone, first built 1698, open fires or candles were used. Where reefs or sandbanks made erection of a lighthouse impossible, lightvessels were often installed; increasingly these are replaced by fixed, small-scale lighthouses. Where it is impossible to instal a fixed structure, unattended lightbuoys equipped for up to a year's service may be used. In the UK, these are gradually being converted to solar power from acetylene gas in cylinders. In fog, sound signals are made (horns, sirens, explosives), and in the case of lightbuoys, fog bells and whistles are operated by the movement of the waves. In

lightning Lightning over wooded countryside, Derbyshire, England. A household light bulb would have to shine for 10,000 years to release the same amount of energy as a lightning bolt.

the UK there are three lighthouse authorities: Trinity House, the Northern Lighthouse Board, and Commissioners of Irish Lights. In the USA the supervisory authority is the Coast Guard.

In 1989 in Britain, there were 116 automated lighthouses, 58 staffed lighthouses, 112 minor automatics, 15 automated lightvessels, 2 automated lightfloats, 6 large automatic navigation buoys (lanbys), 601 buoys (of which 123 were unlit), and 13 beacons.

lightning high-voltage electrical discharge between two charged rainclouds or between a cloud and the Earth, caused by the build-up of electrical charges. Air in the path of lightning ionizes (becomes conducting), and expands; the accompanying noise is heard as thunder. Currents of 20,000 amps and temperatures of 30,000°C/54,000°F are common.

light pen in computing, an ◊input device resembling an ordinary pen, used to indicate locations on a computer screen. With certain computer-aided design (◊CAD) programs, the light pen can be used to instruct the computer to change the shape, size, position, and colours of sections of a screen image.

At its tip, the pen has a photoreceptor which emits signals as light from the screen passes beneath it. From the timing of this signal and a gridlike representation of the screen in the computer's memory, a computer program can calculate the position of the light pen.

light second unit of length, equal to the distance travelled by light in one second. It is equal to $2.997,925 \times 10^8$ m/$9.835,592 \times 10^8$ ft. See ◊light year.

light watt unit of radiant power (brightness of light). One light watt is the power required to produce a perceived brightness equal to that of light at a wavelength of 550 nm and 680 lumens.

light year in astronomy, the distance travelled by a beam of light in one calendar year, approximately 9.45 million million km/5.87 million million miles.

lignin a naturally occurring substance, produced by plants to strengthen their tissues. It is the essential ingredient of all wood, and is therefore of great commercial importance. It is difficult for ◊enzymes to attack lignin, so living organisms cannot digest wood, with the exception of a few specialized fungi and bacteria.

Chemically, lignin is made up of thousands of rings of carbon atoms joined together in a long chain. The way in which they are linked up varies along the chain.

lignite a type of ◊coal that is brown and fibrous, with a relatively low carbon content. In Scandinavia it is burned to generate power.

lignocaine short-term local anaesthetic injected into tissues or applied to skin. It is particularly effective for brief, invasive procedures such as dental care or insertion of a cannula (small tube) into a vein. Temporary paralysis (to prevent involuntary movement during eye surgery, for example) can be achieved by injection directly into the nerve serving the region.

Rapidly absorbed by mucous membranes (lining tissues), it may be sprayed into the nose or throat to allow comfortable insertion of instruments such as a bronchoscope or oesophagoscope during ◊endoscopy. Its action makes it a potent anti-arrhythmia drug as well. Given intravenously during or following a heart attack, it reduces the risk of irregular twitching of the ventricles.

Liguria /lɪˈgjuərɪə/ coastal region of NW Italy, which includes the resorts of the Italian Riviera, lying between the western Alps and the Mediterranean Gulf of Genoa. The region comprises the provinces of Genova, La Spezia, Imperia, and Savona, with a population (1988) of 1,750,000 and an area of 5,418 sq km/2,093 sq mi. Genoa is the chief town and port.

Likud alliance of right-wing Israeli political parties that defeated the Labor Party coalition in the May 1977 election, and brought Menachem Begin to power. In 1987, Likud were part of an uneasy national coalition with Labor, formed to solve Israel's economic crisis. In 1989, another coalition was formed under Shamir.

lilac flowering shrub *Syringa vulgaris*, family Oleaceae, bearing panicles of small, sweetly scented, white or purplish flowers.

Lilburne /ˈlɪlbɜːn/ John 1614–1657. English republican agitator. He was imprisoned 1638–40 for circulating Puritan pamphlets, fought in the Parliamentary army in the Civil War, and by his advocacy of a democratic republic won the leadership of the ◊Levellers.

In 1640, Oliver Cromwell made a speech in favour of Lilburne to get him released, and in 1641 Lilburne received an indemnity of £3,000. He rose to the rank of lieutenant-colonel in the army, but resigned 1645 due to the number of Presbyterians. In 1647 he was put in the Tower of London for accusations against Cromwell. He was banished 1652 and arrested again on his return in 1653. He was acquitted, but still imprisoned for 'the peace of the nation'. Harry Marten, the regicide, said of him, 'if the world was emptied of all but John Lilburne, Lilburne would quarrel with John, and John with Lilburne'.

Lilienthal /ˈliːliəntɑːl/ Otto 1848–1896. German aviation pioneer, who inspired the ◊Wright brothers. He made and successfully flew many gliders before he was killed in a glider crash.

Lilith /ˈlɪlɪθ/ in the Old Testament, Assyrian female demon of the night. According to the ◊Talmud, she was the wife of Adam before Eve's creation.

Lille /liːl/ (Flemish *Ryssel*) industrial city (textiles, chemicals, engineering, distilling), capital of Nord-Pas-de-Calais, France; population (1982) 174,000, metropolitan area 936,000. The world's first entirely automatic underground system was opened here 1982.

Lilongwe /lɪˈlɒŋgweɪ/ capital of Malawi since 1975; population (1985) 187,000. Products include tobacco and textiles.

lily plant of the genus *Lilium*, of which there are some 80 species, most with showy flowers growing from bulbs. The genus includes hyacinths, tulips, asparagus, and plants of the onion genus. The term is also applied to many lily-like plants of allied genera and families.

lily of the valley common garden plant *Convallaria majalis*, family Liliaceae, growing in woods in Europe, N Asia, and North America. The white flowers are strongly scented.

Lima /ˈliːmə/ capital of Peru, and industrial city (textiles, chemicals, glass, cement), with its port at Callao; population (1988) 418,000, metropolitan area 4,605,000. Founded by the conquistador Pizarro 1535, it was rebuilt after destruction by an earthquake 1746.

Survivals of the colonial period are the university 1551, cathedral 1746, government palace (the rebuilt palace of the viceroys), and the senate house (once the Inquisition).

Liman von Sanders /ˈliːmæn fɒn ˈsɑːndəz/ Otto 1855–1929. German general seconded to the Turkish army to become inspector-general and a Turkish field marshal in Dec 1913. This link between the Turks and the Germans caused great suspicion on the part of the French and Russians.

Limassol /ˈlɪməsɒl/ port in S Cyprus in Akrotiri Bay; population (1985) 120,000. Products include cigarettes and wine. Richard I married Berengaria of Navarre here 1191. The town's population increased rapidly with the influx of Greek Cypriot refugees following the Turkish invasion 1974.

limbo a West Indian dance in which the performer leans backwards from the knees to pass under a pole, which is lowered closer to the ground with each attempt. The world record has been unchanged since 1973 at 15.5 cm/6^1/8 in, although on roller skates the record is 13.3 cm/5^1/4 in.

limbo in Christian theology, a region for the souls of those who were not admitted to the divine vision. *Limbus infantum* was a place where unbaptized infants enjoyed inferior blessedness, and *limbus patrum* was where the prophets of the Old Testament dwelt. The word was first used in this sense in the 13th century by Thomas Aquinas.

Limbourg /ˈlæmˈbuə/ province of Belgium; capital Hasselt; area 2,400 sq km/926 sq mi; population (1987) 737,000.

Limbourg brothers Franco-Flemish painters, *Pol*, *Herman*, and *Jan* (Hennequin, Janneken), active in the late 14th and early 15th centuries, first in Paris, then at the ducal court of Burgundy. They produced richly detailed manuscript illuminations.

Patronized by Jean de Berri, duke of Burgundy, from about 1404, they illustrated two Books of ◊Hours that are masterpieces of the International Gothic style, the *Belles Heures* about 1408 (Metropolitan Museum of Art, New York), and *Les très riches Heures du Duc de Berri* about 1413–15 (Musée Condé, Chantilly). Their miniature paintings include a series of scenes representing the months, presenting almost a fairy-tale world of pinnacled castles with lords and ladies, full of detail and brilliant decorative effects. All three brothers were dead by 1416.

Limburg /ˈlɪmbɜːg/ southernmost province of the Netherlands in the plain of the Maas (Meuse); area 2,170 sq km/838 sq mi; population (1988) 1,095,000. Its capital is Maastricht, the oldest city in the Netherlands. Manufacture of chemicals has now replaced coal mining but the coal industry is still remembered at Kerkrade, alleged site of the first European coal mine. The marl soils of S Limburg are used in the manufacture of cement and fertilizer. Mixed arable farming and horticulture are also important.

lime or *quicklime* calcium oxide CaO or calcium hydroxide Ca(OH)^2. A white powdery substance, it is used to reduce soil acidity. It is made commercially by heating calcium carbonate, $CaCO_3$, obtained from limestone or chalk. Quicklime readily absorbs water to become calcium hydroxide, known as slaked lime.

lime small thorny bush *Citrus aurantifolia*, family Rutaceae, native to India. The white flowers are succeeded by light green or yellow fruits, limes, which resemble lemons but which are more globular in shape.

lime or *linden* deciduous tree, genus *Tilia*, of the family Tiliaceae. The **common lime** *Tilia vulgaris* bears greenish-yellow fragrant flowers in clusters on a winged stalk, succeeded by small bobbly fruits. It was the commonest tree in lowland regions of prehistoric England.

Limehouse /ˈlaɪmhaus/ district in E London; part of ◊Tower Hamlets.

Limerick /ˈlɪmərɪk/ county town of Limerick, Republic of Ireland, the main port of W Ireland, on the Shannon estuary; population (1986) 77,000. It was founded in the 12th century.

limerick five-line humorous verse, often nonsensical, which first appeared in England about 1820, and was popularized by Edward ◊Lear. An example is:

There was a young lady of Riga,
Who rode with a smile on a tiger;
They returned from the ride
With the lady inside,
And the smile on the face of the tiger.

Limerick /ˈlɪmərɪk/ county in SW Republic of Ireland, in Munster province
area 2,690 sq km/1,038 sq mi
county town Limerick
physical fertile, with hills in the south
products dairy products
population (1986) 164,000.

limestone a sedimentary rock composed chiefly of calcium carbonate $CaCO_3$, either derived from the shells of marine organisms or precipitated from solution, mostly in the ocean. Various types of limestone are used as building stone.

◊Marble is metamorphosed limestone. Certain so-called marbles are not marbles but fine-grained fossiliferous limestones that take an attractive polish. Caves commonly occur in limestone. ◊Karst is a type of limestone landscape.

limewater the common name for a dilute solution of slaked lime (calcium hydroxide Ca(OH)$_2$). In chemistry, it is used to detect the presence of carbon dioxide.

If a gas containing carbon dioxide is bubbled through limewater, the solution turns 'milky' owing to the formation of calcium carbonate ($CaCO^3$). Continued bubbling of the gas causes the limewater to clear again as the calcium carbonate is converted to the more soluble calcium hydrogen carbonate Ca(HCO$_3$)$_2$.

Limitation, Statutes of under English law, Acts of Parliament limiting the time within which legal action must be inaugurated. Actions for breach of contract and most other civil wrongs must be started within six years. Personal injury claims must usually be brought within three years.

limited company or *joint stock company* the usual type of company formation in the UK. It has its origins in the trading companies that began to proliferate in the 16th century. The capital of a limited company is divided into small units, and profits are distributed according to shareholding.

Limits, Territorial and Fishing see under ◊Maritime Law.

limnology study of lakes and other bodies of open fresh water, in terms of their plant and animal biology, and their physical properties.

Limoges /lɪˈmoʊʒ/ city and capital of Limousin, France; population (1982) 172,000. Fine enamels were made here in the medieval period, and it is the centre of the modern French porcelain

limestone Carboniferous limestone pavement near Ballynahowan, Ireland, showing the patterns caused by rain wearing away joints in the rock.

industry. Other industries include textiles, electrical equipment, and metal goods. The city was sacked by the Black Prince 1370.

limonite an iron ore, mostly poorly crystalline iron oxyhydroxide, but usually mixed with ◊hematite and other iron oxides. Also known as brown iron ore, it is often found in bog deposits.

Limousin /ˌliːmuːˈzæn/ former province and modern region of central France; area 16,900 sq km/6,544 sq mi; population (1986) 736,000. It consists of the *départements* of Corréze, Creuse, and Haute-Vienne. Chief town is Limoges. A thinly populated and largely unfertile region, it is crossed by the mountains of the Massif Central. Fruit and vegetables are produced in the more fertile lowlands. Kaolin is mined.

limpet type of mollusc. It has a conical shell, and adheres firmly to rocks by the disc-like foot. Limpets are marine animals, and leave their fixed position only to graze on seaweeds, always returning to the same spot. They are found in cooler waters of the Atlantic and Pacific. The common limpet *Patella vulgata* remains in the intertidal area.

Limpopo /lɪmˈpəʊpəʊ/ river in SE Africa, rising in the Transvaal and reaching the Indian Ocean in Mozambique; length 1,600 km/1,000 mi.

Linacre /ˈlɪnəkə/ Thomas *c.*1460–1524. English humanist, physician to Henry VIII from 1509, from whom he obtained a charter in 1518 to found the Royal College of Physicians, of which he was first president.

Lin Biao /ˌlɪnˈbjaʊ/ 1907–1971. Chinese politician and general. He joined the Communists 1927, became a commander of Mao Zedong's Red Army, and led the Northeast People's Liberation Army in the civil war after 1945. He became defence minister 1959, and as vice chairman of the party 1969, he was expected to be Mao's successor, but he lost favour, perhaps because of his control over the army. After an attempted coup failed, he was reported to have been killed in an aeroplane crash in Mongolia 17 Sept 1971.

Lincoln /ˈlɪŋkən/ industrial city in Lincolnshire, England; population (1981) 76,200. Manufacturing includes excavators, cranes, gas turbines, power units for oil platforms, and cosmetics. It was the flourishing Roman colony of Lindum, and had a big medieval wool trade. Paulinus built a church here in the 7th century, and the 11th–15th-century cathedral has the earliest Gothic work in Britain. The 12th-century High Bridge is the oldest in Britain still to have buildings on it.

Lincoln President of the USA during the Civil War, Abraham Lincoln. His main aim was to preserve the union and prevent the secession of the Southern states.

Lincolnshire

Lincoln /ˈlɪŋkən/ industrial city and capital of Nebraska, USA; population (1981) 172,000. Industries include engineering, oil refining, and food processing. It was known as Lancaster until 1867 when it was renamed after President Lincoln.

Lincoln /ˈlɪŋkən/ Abraham 1809–1865. 16th president of the USA 1861–65. In the US Civil War, his chief concern was the preservation of the Union from which the Confederate (Southern) slave states had seceded on his election. In 1863 he announced the freedom of the slaves with the **Emancipation Proclamation**. He was re-elected 1864 with victory for the North in sight, but assassinated at the end of the war.

Lincoln was born in a log cabin in Kentucky. Self-educated, he practised law from 1837 in Springfield, Illinois. He was a member of the state legislature 1832–42, and was known as *Honest Abe*. He joined the new Republican Party 1856, and was elected president 1860 on a minority vote. His refusal to concede to Confederate demands for the evacuation of the federal garrison at Fort Sumter, Charleston, South Carolina, precipitated the first hostilities of the Civil War. In the Gettysburg Address 1863, he declared the aims of preserving a 'nation conceived in liberty, and dedicated to the proposition that all men are created equal'. Re-elected with a large majority 1864 on a National Union ticket, he advocated a reconciliatory policy towards the South 'with malice towards none, with charity for all'. Five days after Gen Lee's surrender, Lincoln was shot in a theatre audience by an actor and Confederate sympathizer, John Wilkes ◊Booth.

Lincolnshire /ˈlɪŋkənʃə/ county in E England
area 5,890 sq km/2,274 sq mi
towns administrative headquarters Lincoln; resort Skegness
physical Lincoln Wolds, marshy coastline, the Fens in the SE, rivers Witham and Welland
features 16th-century Burghley House; Belton House, a Restoration mansion
products cattle, sheep, horses, cereals, flower bulbs, oil
population (1987) 575,000
famous people Isaac Newton, Alfred Tennyson, Margaret Thatcher.

Lincs abbreviation for *Lincolnshire*.

Lind /lɪnd/ Jenny 1820–1887. Swedish soprano of remarkable range, nicknamed the 'Swedish nightingale'.

Lindbergh /ˈlɪndbɜːg/ Charles (Augustus) 1902–1974. US aviator, who made the first solo non-stop flight across the Atlantic (New York–Paris) 1927 in the *Spirit of St Louis*.

linden another name for the ◊lime tree.

Lindisfarne /ˈlɪndɪsfɑːn/ site of monastery off the coast of Northumberland, England; see under ◊Holy Island.

Lindow Man the remains of an Iron Age man discovered in a peat bog at Lindow Marsh, Cheshire, UK, in 1984. The chemicals in the bog had kept the body in an excellent state of preservation.

'Pete Marsh', as the archeologists nicknamed him, had been knocked unconscious, strangled, and then had his throat cut before being thrown into the bog. He may have been a sacrificial victim, as Celtic peoples often threw offerings to the gods into rivers and marshes. His stomach contained part of an unleavened barley 'bannock' that might have been given as a sacrificial offering. His well-cared-for nails indicate that he might have been a Druid prince who became a willing sacrifice.

Lindsay /ˈlɪndzi/ (Nicholas) Vachel 1879–1931. US poet. He wandered the country, living by reciting his balladlike verse, including *General William Booth enters into Heaven* 1913, *The Congo* 1914, and *Johnny Appleseed*.

Lindsey, Parts of /ˈlɪndzi/ former administrative county within Lincolnshire, England. It was the largest of the three administrative divisions (or 'parts') of the county, with its headquarters at Lincoln. In 1974 Lindsey was divided between the new county of Humberside and a reduced Lincolnshire.

linear accelerator in physics, a machine in which charged ◊particles are accelerated (as in an ◊accelerator) to high speed in passing down a straight evacuated tube or waveguide by electromagnetic waves in the tube or by electric fields.

linear equation in mathematics, an equation involving two variables, of the general form $y = mx + c$, where m and c are constants. In ◊coordinate geometry, such an equation plotted using ◊Cartesian coordinates gives a straight-line graph of slope m; c is the value of y where the line crosses the y-axis. Linear equations can be used to describe the behaviour of buildings, bridges, trusses, and other static structures.

linear motor type of electric motor, an induction motor in which the stationary stator and moving armature are straight and parallel to each other (rather than being circular and one inside the other as in an ordinary induction motor). Linear motors are used, for example, to power sliding doors. There is a magnetic force between the stator and armature, and this has been used to support a vehicle, as in the experimental ◊maglev linear motor train.

linear programming in mathematics and economics, a set of techniques for finding the maxima or minima of certain variables governed by linear equations or inequalities. These maxima and minima are used to represent 'best' solutions

Lindbergh Pioneer US aviator, Charles Lindbergh. He was the first person to fly solo non-stop across the Atlantic.

in terms of goals such as maximizing profit or minimizing cost.

Line Islands /laɪn/ coral-island group in the Pacific ocean; population (1985) 2,500. Products include coconut and guano. Eight of the islands belong to Kiribati and two (Palmyra and Jarvis) are administered by the USA.

linen the yarn spun and the textile woven from ◊flax.

To get the longest possible fibres, flax is pulled, rather than cut by hand or machine, just as the seed bolls are beginning to set. After preliminary drying, it is steeped in water so that the fibre can be more easily separated from the wood of the stem, then hackled (combed), classified, drawn into continuous fibres, and spun. Bleaching, weaving, and finishing processes vary according to the final product, which can be sailcloth, canvas, sacking, cambric, or lawn. Because of the length of its fibre, linen yarn has twice the strength of cotton, and yet is superior in delicacy, so that it is especially suitable for lace making. It mixes well with synthetics.

line of force in physics, an imaginary line representing the direction of a magnetic field.

ling deepwater long-bodied fish *Molva molva* of the cod family found in the seas off NW Europe. It reaches 2 m/6 ft long and 20 kg/45 lb in weight.

ling another name for common ◊heather.

lingam in Hinduism, phallic emblem of ◊Siva, the *yoni* being the female equivalent.

lingua franca (Italian 'Frankish tongue') any language that is used as a means of communication by groups who do not themselves normally speak that language; for example, English is a lingua franca used by Japanese doing business in Finland, or Swedes in Saudi Arabia. The name comes from the mixture of French, Italian, Spanish, Greek, Turkish, and Arabic which was spoken around the Mediterranean from the time of the Crusades until the 18th century.

Many of the world's lingua francas are ◊pidgin languages, for example Bazaar Hindi (Hindustani), Bazaar Malay, and Neo-Melanesian (also known as Tok Pisin), the official language of Papua New Guinea.

linguistics the scientific study of language, from its origins, to the changing way it is pronounced (phonetics), derivation of words through various languages (etymology), development of meanings (semantics), and the arrangement and modifications of words to convey a message (grammar).

linkage in genetics, the association between two or more genes that tend to be inherited together because they are on the same chromosome. The closer together they are on the chromosome, the less likely they are to be separated by crossing over (one of the processes of ◊recombination) and they are then described as being 'tightly linked'.

Linköping /ˈlɪntʃɜːpɪŋ/ industrial town in SE Sweden; 172 km/107 mi SW of Stockholm; population (1986) 117,800. Industries include hosiery, aircraft and engines, and tobacco. It has a 12th-century cathedral.

Linlithgow /lɪnˈlɪθɡəʊ/ tourist centre in Lothian region, Scotland; population (1981) 9,600. Linlithgow Palace, now in ruins, was once a royal residence, and Mary Queen of Scots was born there.

Linlithgow /lɪnˈlɪθɡəʊ/ John Adrian Louis Hope, 1st Marquess Linlithgow 1860–1908. British administrator, son of the 6th earl of Hopetoun, first governor-general of Australia 1900–02.

Linlithgowshire /lɪnˈlɪθɡəʊʃə/ former name of West Lothian, now included in Lothian region, Scotland.

Linnaeus /lɪˈniːəs/ Carolus 1707–1778. Swedish naturalist and physician. His botanical work *Systema Naturae* 1758 contained his system for classifying plants into groups depending on the number of stamens in their flowers, providing a much-needed framework for identification. He also devised the concise and precise system for naming plants and animals, using one Latin (or Latinized)

word to represent the genus and a second to distinguish the species.

For example, in the Latin name of the daisy *Bellis perennis*, *Bellis* is the name of the genus to which the plant belongs, and *perennis* distinguishes the species from others of the same genus. By tradition the generic name always begins with a capital letter. The author who first described a particular species is often indicated after the name, for example, *Bellis perennis* Linnaeus, showing that the author was Linnaeus. See also ◊binomial classification, ◊taxonomy.

linnet bird of the finch family *Acanthis cannabina* common in Asia, NW Africa, and Europe. Mainly brown, the males have a crimson crown and breast in summer. It nests low in bushes and feeds on weed seeds and some insects. It is about 13 cm/5 in long, and a noted songster.

Linotype typesetting machine once universally used for newspaper work, which sets complete lines (slugs) of metal type. It was invented in the USA 1884 by German-born Ottmar ◊Mergenthaler.

Lin Piao /lɪn piˈaʊ/ alternative form of ◊Lin Biao.

linsang nocturnal, arboreal, and carnivorous mammal of the mongoose family, about 75 cm/2.5 ft long. It is native to Africa and SE Asia. The **African linsang** *Poiana richardsoni* is a long, low and lithe spotted animal about 33 cm/1.1 ft long with a 38 cm/1.25 ft tail. The two species of oriental linsang, genus *Prionodon*, of Asia are slightly bigger.

linseed seeds of the flax plant *Linum usitatissimum*, from which linseed oil is expressed, the residue being used as feeding cake for cattle. The oil is used in paint, wood treatments and varnishes, and in the manufacture of linoleum.

Linz /lɪnts/ industrial port (iron, steel, metalworking) on the river Danube in N Austria; population (1981) 199,900.

lion member of the cat family *Panthera leo*, now found only in Africa and NW India. The coat is tawny, the young having darker spot markings that usually disappear in the adult. The male has a heavy mane and a tuft at the end of the tail. Head and body measure about 2 m/6 ft, plus 1 m/3 ft of tail, the lioness being slightly smaller.

Lions produce litters of two to six cubs, and often live in prides of several adult males and females with several young. Capable of short bursts of speed, they skilfully collaborate in stalking herbivorous animals. Old lions whose teeth and strength are failing may resort to eating humans. 'Mountain lion' is a name for the ◊puma.

Lipari /ˈlɪpəri/ or *Aeolian Islands* volcanic group of seven islands off NE Sicily, including Lipari (on which is the capital of the same name), Stromboli (active volcano 926 m/3038 ft high) and Vulcano (also with an active volcano); area 114 sq km/44 sq mi. See ◊Aeolus.

Lipatti /lɪˈpæti/ Dinu 1917–1950. Romanian pianist, who perfected a small repertoire, notably Chopin. He died of leukaemia at 33.

Lipchitz /ˈlɪpʃɪts/ Jacques 1891–1973. Lithuanian-born sculptor, active in Paris from 1909; he emigrated to the USA 1941. One of the first Cubist sculptors.

Li Peng /ˈliː ˈpʌŋ/ 1928– . Chinese communist politician, a member of the Politburo from 1985, and head of government from 1987. He is the adopted son of the communist leader Zhou Enlai. During the pro-democracy demonstrations 1989 he supported the massacre of students by Chinese troops, and the subsequent executions of others.

Born at Chengdu in Sichuan province, the son of the writer Li Shouxun (who took part in the Nanchang rising 1927 and was executed 1930), Li was adopted by Zhou Enlai. He studied at the communist headquarters of Yanan 1941–47 and trained as a hydro-electric engineer at the Moscow Power Institute from 1948. He was appointed minister of the electric power industry 1981, a vice premier 1983, and prime minister 1987. In 1989 he launched the crackdown on pro-democracy demonstratio in Beiging that led

to the ◊massacre in ◊Tiananmen Square. He favours maintaining firm central and party control over the economy, and seeks improved relations with the USSR.

lipid one of a group of organic compounds soluble in solvents such as ethanol (alcohol), but not in water. They include oils, fats, waxes, steroids, carotenoids, and other fatty substances.

Lipmann /ˈlɪpmən/ Fritz 1899–1986. US biochemist. He investigated the means by which the cell acquires energy and highlighted the crucial role played by the energy rich phosphate molecule, adenosine triphosphate (ATP). For this and further work on metabolism, Lipmann shared the 1953 Nobel Physiology or Medicine Prize with Hans Krebs.

Li Po /ˌliːˈbəʊ/ 705–762. Chinese poet. He wrote in traditional forms, but his exuberance, the boldness of his imagination, and the intensity of his feeling have won him recognition as perhaps the greatest of all Chinese poets. Although he was mostly concerned with higher themes, he also celebrated the joys of drinking.

lipophilic (Greek 'fat-loving') in chemistry, a term describing ◊functional groups with an affinity for fats and oils.

lipophobic (Greek 'fat-hating') in chemistry, a term describing ◊functional groups that tend to repel fats and oils.

Lippe /ˈlɪpə/ river of N West Germany flowing into the Rhine; length 230 km/147 mi; also a former German state, now part of North Rhine-Westphalia.

Lippershey /ˈlɪpəʃaɪ/ Hans *c.* 1570–*c.* 1619. Dutch spectacle maker, credited with inventing the first telescope 1608.

Lippi /ˈlɪpi/ Filippino 1457–1504. Italian painter of the Florentine school, trained by Botticelli. He produced altarpieces and several fresco cycles, full of detail and drama, elegant and finely drawn. He was the son of Filippo Lippi. His frescoes, typical of late 15th-century Florentine work, can be found in Sta Maria sopra Minerva, Rome, in Sta Maria Novella, Florence, and elsewhere.

Lippi /ˈlɪpi/ Filippo 1406–1469. Italian painter, called *Fra* (Brother) Filippo, born in Florence and patronized by the Medici. He was a monk, and was tried in the 1450s for abducting a nun (the mother of his son Filippino). He painted many altarpieces, of Madonnas and groups of saints. His works include frescoes at Prato Cathedral from 1452 onwards and in Spoleto from 1466.

Lippizaner a breed of grey-white horse, named after its place of origin in Lippiza, Yugoslavia.

Lippmann /ˈlɪpmən/ Gabriel 1845–1921. French doctor, who invented the direct colour process in photography. He won the Nobel Prize for Physics in 1908.

liquefaction the process of converting a gas to a liquid. Liquefaction is normally associated with low temperatures and high pressures (see ◊condensation).

liquefied petroleum gas (LPG) liquid form of butane, propane, or pentane, produced by the distillation of petroleum during oil refining. At room temperature these substances are gases, although they can be easily liquefied and stored under pressure in metal containers. They are used for heating and cooking where other fuels are not available: camping stoves and cigarette lighters, for instance, often use liquefied butane as fuel.

liquid state of matter between a ◊solid and a ◊gas. A liquid forms a level surface and beneath the surface assumes the shape of its container. Its atoms do not occupy fixed postions as in a crystalline solid, nor do they have freedom of movement as in a gas. Unlike a gas, a liquid is difficult to compress since pressure applied at one point is equally transmitted throughout (Pascal's principle). ◊Hydraulics makes use of this property.

liquid air air that has been cooled so much that it has liquefied. This happens at temperatures below about –196°C. The various constituent gases including nitrogen, oxygen, argon, and neon can

liquid crystal display

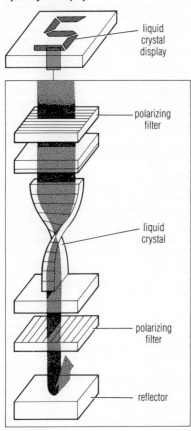

liquid crystal display

polarizing filter

liquid crystal

polarizing filter

reflector

be separated from liquid air by the technique of ◊fractionation.

Air is liquefied by the **Linde process**, in which air is alternately compressed, cooled, and expanded, the expansion resulting each time in a considerable reduction in temperature.

liquidation in economics, the termination of a company by converting all its assets into money to pay off its liabilities.

liquid crystal display (LCD) a display of numbers (for example in a calculator) or picture (such as on a pocket television screen) produced by molecules of an organic substance in a semi-liquid state. The display is a blank until the application of an electric field which 'twists' the molecules so that they reflect or transmit light falling on them.

liquidity in economics, the state of possessing sufficient money and/or assets to be able to pay off all liabilities. **Liquid assets** are those which may be converted quickly into cash, such as shares, as opposed to property.

liquorice perennial European herb *Glycyrrhiza glabra*, family Leguminosae. The long sweet root yields an extract made into a hard black paste, used in confectionery and medicines.

lira the standard Italian currency unit.

Lisboa /liːˈʒbɔːə/ Portuguese form of ◊Lisbon, capital of Portugal.

Lisbon /ˈlɪzbən/ (Portuguese **Lisboa**) city and capital of Portugal, in the SW on the tidal lake and estuary formed by the Tagus; population (1984) 808,000. Industries include steel, textiles, chemicals, pottery, shipbuilding, and fishing. It has been capital since 1260, and reached its peak of prosperity in the period of Portugal's empire during the 16th century.

Lisburn /ˈlɪzbɜːn/ cathedral city and market town in Antrim, N Ireland, on the river Lagan; population (1985) 87,900. It is noted for linen and furniture.

Lisieux /liːzˈjɜː/ town in Calvados *département*, France, to the SE of Caen; population (1982)

25,823. St Thérèse of Lisieux spent her religious life in the Carmelite convent here, and her tomb attracts pilgrims.

Lisp a computer-programming language for list processing used primarily in artificial-intelligence (AI) research. Developed in the 1960s, and until recently common only in university laboratories, Lisp is more popular in the USA than in Europe, where the language ◊Prolog is often preferred for AI work.

listed building in Britain, a building officially recognised as having historical or architectural interest and therefore legally protected from alteration or demolition. In England the listing is drawn up by the Secretary of State for the Environment under the advice of the English Heritage organization, which provides various resources for ◊architectural conservation.

There are about 500,000 listed buildings in England and around a million in Britain as a whole. Over the last 25 years the number of listed buildings has increased fivefold. In England they are divided into categories I, II*, II and III and in Scotland A, B and C. Grade I buildings, which are defined as being of 'exceptional interest', constitute less than 2% of entries on the list. Grade II* buildings constitute about 4% of entries. Grade III buildings are not legally protected and do not fall under the auspices of English Heritage. The listing system incorporates all pre-1700 buildings that have not been substantially altered, and almost all those built between 1700 and 1840.

Lister /ˈlɪstə/ Joseph, 1st Baron Lister 1827–1912. English surgeon, and founder of antiseptic surgery, influenced by Louis ◊Pasteur's work on bacteria. He introduced dressings soaked in carbolic acid and strict rules of hygiene to combat the increase in wound sepsis (the number of surgical operations had increased considerably, following the introduction of anaesthetics). Death rates, which had been more than 40%, fell dramatically. He was professor of surgery at Glasgow 1860–69, at Edinburgh 1869–77, and at King's College, London 1877–92. He was president of the Royal Society 1895–1900, and was created Baron Lister of Lyme Regis 1887.

listeriosis a disease of animals that may occasionally infect humans, caused by the bacterium *Listeria monocytogenes*. They breed at temperatures close to 0°C, which means they may flourish in precooked frozen meals if the cooking has not been thorough. Listeriosis causes inflammation of the brain and its surrounding membranes, but can be treated with penicillin.

Liszt /lɪst/ Franz 1811–1886. Hungarian pianist and composer. An outstanding virtuoso of the piano, he was an established concert artist by the age of 12. His expressive, romantic, and frequently chromatic works include piano music (*Transcendental Studies* 1851), symphonies, piano concertos, and organ music. Much of his music is programmatic; he also originated the symphonic poem.

Liszt was taught by his father, then by Czerny (1791–1857). He travelled widely in Europe, producing an opera *Don Sanche* in Paris at the age

Lisbon *The Bélem Towers, a fortress built in the 16th century by King Manuel I to protect the approaches to Lisbon.*

Lister *English surgeon Joseph Lister.*

of 14. As musical director and conductor at Weimar 1848–59, he was a champion of the music of Berlioz and Wagner.

Retiring to Rome, he turned again to his early love of religion, and in 1865 became a secular priest (adopting the title Abbé), but he continued to teach and give concert tours. Many of his compositions are lyrical, often technically difficult, piano works, including the *Liebesträume* and the *Hungarian Rhapsodies*, based on gypsy music. He also wrote an opera and a symphony; masses and oratorios; songs; and piano arrangements of works by Beethoven, Schubert, and Wagner among others. He died at Bayreuth.

Litani river rising near Baalbek in the Anti-Lebanon mountains of E Lebanon. It flows NE–SW through the Beqa'a Valley then E to the Meditarranean 8 km/5 mi N of Tyre. The Israelis invaded Lebanon as far as the Litani River in 1978.

litany in the Christian church, a form of prayer or supplication led by a priest with set responses by the congregation.

litchi or **lychee** tree *Litchi chinensis* of the family Sapindaceae. The delicately flavoured ovate fruit is encased in a brownish rough outer skin and has a hard seed. The litchi is native to S China, where it has been cultivated for 2,000 years.

literacy the ability to read and write. The level at which functional literacy is set rises as society becomes more complex, and it becomes increasingly difficult for an illiterate person to find work and cope with the other demands of everyday life.

literary criticism the establishment of principles governing literary composition, and the assessment of literary works. Contemporary criticism applies insights to literary works from structuralism, semiotics, feminism, Marxism, and psychoanalysis, whereas earlier criticism tended to deal with moral or political ideas, or with a literary work as a formal object independent of its creator.

Liszt *Franz Liszt, Romantic composer and pianist.*

The earliest systematic literary criticism was the *Poetics* of Aristotle; a later Greek critic was the author of the treatise *On the Sublime*, usually attributed to Longinus. Horace and Quintilian were influential Latin critics. The Italian Renaissance introduced humanist criticism, and the revival of classical scholarship exalted the authority of Aristotle and Horace. Like literature itself, European criticism then applied Neo-Classical, Romantic, and modern approaches.

literature words set apart in some way from ordinary everyday communication. In the ancient oral traditions, before stories and poems were written down, literature had a mainly public function—mythic and religious. As literary works came to be preserved in writing, and then, eventually, printed, their role became more private, as a vehicle for the exploration and expression of emotion and the human situation. Aesthetic criteria came increasingly to the fore; the English poet and critic Coleridge defined prose as words in their best order, and poetry as the 'best' words in the best order.

The distinction between ◊verse and ◊prose is not always clear cut, but in practice ◊poetry tends to be metrically formal (making it easier to memorize), whereas prose corresponds more closely to the patterns of ordinary speech. Poetry therefore had an early advantage over prose in the days before printing, which it has not relinquished until comparatively recently. Over the centuries poetry has taken on a wide range of forms, from the lengthy narrative such as the ◊epic to the lyric, expressing personal emotion in songlike form; from the ◊ballad, and the 14-line ◊sonnet, to the extreme conciseness of the 17-syllable Japanese ◊haiku. Prose came into its own in the West as a vehicle for imaginative literature with the rise of the modern ◊novel in the 18th century, and ◊fiction has since been divided into various genres such as the ◊historical novel, ◊detective fiction, ◊fantasy, and ◊science fiction.

See also the literature of particular countries, under English literature, French literature, Russian literature and so on.

lithification another term for ◊diagenesis.

lithium the lightest metallic element, symbol Li, atomic number 3, relative atomic mass 6.940. Lithium has a silvery lustre and tarnishes rapidly in air, so it is kept under naphtha. It is soft and ductile, and burns in air at 200°C. It is used as a reducing agent, in batteries, to harden alloys, and in producing tritium. Lithium compounds are used in medicine to treat depression.

Lithium was discovered by J A Arfvedson in 1817. Never occurring free in nature, it is nevertheless widely distributed, traces being found in nearly all igneous rocks and many mineral springs.

lithography in printing, graphic reproduction by a process originated by Aloys ◊Senefelder, in which a drawing is made with greasy pencil or crayon on an absorbent stone, which is then washed with a weak solution of nitric acid, then with water. The wet stone then repels any ink (which is greasy) applied to the surface, and the crayon attracts it, so that the drawing can be printed. Modern lithographic printing is used in book production, and has developed this basic principle into complex processes.

lithosphere the topmost layer of the Earth's structure, forming the jigsaw of plates that take part in the movements of ◊plate tectonics. The lithosphere comprises the ◊crust and a portion of the upper ◊mantle. It is regarded as being rigid and moves about on the semi-molten ◊asthenosphere. The lithosphere is about 75 km/47 mi thick.

Lithuania /ˌlɪθjuːˈeɪnɪə/ constituent republic of the W USSR from 1940
area 65,200 sq km/25,174 sq mi
capital Vilnius
towns Kaunas, Klaipeda
physical river Niemen; 25% forested; lakes, marshes, and complex sandy coastline

Lithuania

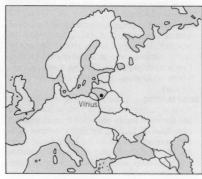

products bacon, dairy products, cereals, potatoes, heavy engineering, electrical goods, cement
population (1987) 3,641,000; 80% Lithuanian, 9% Russian, 8% Polish
language Lithuanian, an Indo-European tongue which has retained many ancient features and is related to Latvian; it is written in a Latin alphabet
religion only Soviet republic that is predominantly Roman Catholic
famous people Jacques Lipchitz
history formerly part of the Russian empire, Lithuania became an independent Soviet republic 1918, was overthrown by German, Polish, and nationalist Lituanians 1919, and a democratic republic was established. It was overthrown by a fascist coup 1926. In 1939 the USSR demanded military bases and in 1940 incorporated it as a constituent republic. As in the other Baltic republics, there has been nationalist dissent since 1980, influenced by the Polish example and prompted by the influx of Russian workers and officials. In Mar 1990 Lithuania unilaterally declared its independence; Moscow denied the declaration's validity and imposed an economic blockade.

Lithuanian language an Indo-European language spoken by the people of Lithuania that through its geographical isolation has retained many ancient features of the Indo-European language family. It acquired a written form in the 16th century, using the Latin alphabet, and is currently spoken by some 3–4 million people.

litmus dye obtained from lichens, and used as an indicator to test the acidic or alkaline nature of aqueous solutions; it turns red in the presence of acid, and blue in the presence of alkali.

litre metric unit of volume (abbreviation l), equal for all practical purposes to 1 dm³/1.76 pints. It was formerly defined as the volume occupied by 1 kg of pure water at 4°C at standard pressure, but this is slightly larger than one cubic decimetre.

Little Bighorn /ˈlɪtl ˈbɪɡhɔːn/ site in Montana, USA, of Gen George ◊Custer's defeat by the ◊Sioux Indians 25 June 1876 under chiefs ◊Crazy Horse and Sitting Bull, known as *Custer's last stand*.

Little Dipper another name for ◊Ursa Minor, the Little Bear. The name has also been applied to the stars in the ◊Pleiades open star cluster, the overall shape of the cluster being similar to that of the Plough, or Big Dipper.

Little Entente the name given to a series of alliances between Czechoslavakia, Romania and Yugoslavia (1920–21) for mutual security and the maintenance of existing frontiers. Reinforced by the Treaty of Belgrade 1929, the entente collapsed with Yugoslav cooperation with Germany 1935–38 and the Anglo-French abandonment of Czechoslovakia 1938.

Littlehampton /ˌlɪtlˈhæmptən/ seaside resort in W Sussex, England, at the mouth of the river Arun, 16 km/10 mi SE of Chichester; population (1981) 22,000.

Little Lord Fauntleroy novel for children by Frances Hodgson ◊Burnett, published in 1886. Cedric, a seven-year-old sporting a velvet suit and golden curls, lives in New York but discovers that his grandfather is an English earl who disinherited Cedric's father for marrying an American. The father dies, Cedric becomes Lord Fauntleroy and goes to live with his grandfather although his mother is ostracized. Under the boy's influence the grandfather mellows, improving the lot of his tenants and accepting Cedric's mother.

Little Review 1914–29 US literary magazine founded in Chicago by Margaret Anderson. It published many experimental figures including W B Yeats, Ezra Pound, T S Eliot, and William Carlos Williams, and was banned for publishing part of James Joyce's *Ulysses*. The *Little Review* was variously published in New York, Paris, and elsewhere.

Little Rock /ˈlɪtl rrɒk/ industrial city and capital of Arkansas, USA; population (1980) 394,000. Black/white integration of the schools caused riots here 1957 and was enforced by federal troops. In 1981–82 in the ◊Scopes monkey trial a federal judge ruled that a law requiring schools to teach ◊creationism as well as evolution was a violation of the constitutional separation of church and state.

Little Women a novel for children by Louisa M ◊Alcott published in 1868. It describes the daily life of a New England family of reduced circumstances, and the tensions and harmony between the four teenage daughters, Meg, Jo, Beth, and Amy. One of the most popular children's books ever written, it was followed by a sequel in 1869, entitled in England *Good Wives*.

Littlewood /ˈlɪtlwʊd/ Joan 1914– . English theatre director. She was responsible for many vigorous productions at the Theatre Royal, Stratford (London) 1953–75, such as *A Taste of Honey* 1959, *The Hostage* 1959–60, and *Oh, What a Lovely War* 1963.

liturgy in the Christian church, any service for public worship; the term was originally limited to the celebration of the ◊Eucharist.

Litvinov /lɪtˈviːnɒf/ Maxim 1876–1951. Soviet politician, commissioner for foreign affairs under Stalin from Jan 1931 until his removal from office in May 1939.

Liu Shaoqi /ˈljuː ˌʃaʊˈtʃ/ formerly *Liu Shao-chi* 1898–1969. Chinese communist politician, in effective control of government 1960–65. A labour organizer, he was a firm proponent of the Soviet line of development based around disciplined one-party control, the use of incentive gradings, and priority for industry over agriculture. This was opposed by Mao Zedong, but began to be implemented when Liu was in power as state president 1960–65. In 1967, during the Cultural Revolution, Liu was brought down.

The son of a Hunan peasant farmer, Liu attended the same local school as Mao. As a member of the Chinese Communist Party (CCP), he was sent to Moscow to study communism, and returned to Shanghai 1922. Mao yielded the title of president to him 1960, and after the failure of the Great Leap Forward to create effective agricultural communes, Liu introduced a recovery programme. This was successful, but was seen as a return to capitalism. He was stripped of his post and expelled from the CCP Apr 1969 and banished to Kaifeng in Henan province, where he died Nov 1969 after being locked in a disused bank vault. His political reputation was rehabilitated ten years later.

liver a large organ of vertebrates, which has many regulatory and storage functions. The human liver is situated in the upper abdomen, and weighs about 2 kg/4.5 lbs. It receives the products of digestion, converts glucose to glycogen (a long-chain carbohydrate used for storage), and breaks down fats. It removes excess amino acids from the blood, converting them to urea, which is excreted by the kidneys. The liver also synthesizes vitamins, produces bile and blood-clotting factors,

*Liverpool Robert Banks Jenkinson, 2nd Earl
Liverpool. The portrait is by Thomas Lawrence.*

and removes damaged red cells and toxins such as
alcohol from the blood.

Livermore Valley /'lɪvəmɔː/ valley in California,
USA, site of the Lawrence Livermore Laboratory.
Part of the University of California, it shares with
Los Alamos Laboratory, New Mexico, all US military research into nuclear warheads and atomic
explosives. It also conducts research into nuclear
fusion, using high-integrity lasers.

Liverpool /'lɪvəpuːl/ city, seaport, and dministra-
tive headquarters of Merseyside, NW England;
population (1984) 497,300. In the 19th and early
20th century, it exported the textiles of Lancashire and Yorkshire, and is the UK's chief Atlantic
port with miles of specialized, mechanized quays
on the river Mersey.

Liverpool /'lɪvəpuːl/ Robert Banks Jenkinson, 2nd
Earl Liverpool 1770–1825. British Tory politician.
He entered Parliament 1790, and was foreign
secretary 1801–03, home secretary 1804–06
and 1807–09, war minister 1809–12, and prime
minister 1812–27. His government conducted the
Napoleonic Wars to a successful conclusion, but
its ruthless suppression of freedom of speech and
of the press aroused such opposition that during
1815–20 revolution frequently seemed imminent.

liverwort plant of the class Hepaticae, related to
mosses, found growing in damp places. The main
sexual generation consists of a thallus, which may
be flat, green and lobed, like a small leaf, or leafy
and moss-like. The spore-bearing generation is
smaller, typically parasitic on the thallus, and
throws up a capsule from which spores are
spread.

livery companies the ◊guilds of the City of London. Their role is now social rather than industrial. Many administer charities, especially educational ones.

Livia Drusilla /'lɪvɪə druː'sɪlə/ 58 BC–AD 29. Roman empress, wife of ◊Augustus from 39 BC, she
was the mother by her first husband of ◊Tiberius
and engaged in intrigue to secure his succession to
the imperial crown. She remained politically active
to the end of her life.

Livingston /'lɪvɪŋstən/ industrial new town (electronics, engineering) in W Lothian, Scotland, established 1962; population (1985) 40,000.

Livingstone /'lɪvɪŋstən/ David 1813–1873. Scot-
tish missionary explorer. In 1841, he went to
Africa, reached Lake Ngami 1849, followed the
Zambezi to its mouth, saw the Victoria Falls 1855,

*Livingstone Scottish doctor and missionary David
Livingstone was the first European to explore many
parts of Central and East Africa.*

and went to East and Central Africa 1858–64,
reaching Lakes Shirwa and Malawi. From 1866,
he tried to find the source of the river Nile, and
reached Ujiji Oct 1871.

British explorer Henry Stanley joined Livingstone
in Ujiji, and the two explored Africa together.
Livingstone not only mapped a great deal of the
continent but also helped to end the slave trade
by Arabs. He died in Old Chitambo (in modern
Zambia) and was buried in Westminster Abbey,
London.

Livingstone /'lɪvɪŋstən/ formerly *Maramba* town
in Zambia; population (1987) 95,000. Founded
1905, it was named after the explorer David
Livingstone, and was capital of N Rhodesia
1907–35. Victoria Falls is nearby.

Livingstone /'lɪvɪŋstən/ Ken(neth) 1945– . Bri-
tish left-wing Labour politician. He joined the
Labour Party 1968, and was active in London
politics from 1971. As leader of the GLC from
1981 until its abolition 1986, he displayed outside
GLC headquarters current unemployment figures
so that they were clearly visible to MPs in the
Palace of Westminster across the river Thames.
He was elected to Parliament representing the
London constituency of Brent East 1987.

Living Theater experimental US theatre group
founded 1951 by Judith Malina and Julian Beck,
which mounted notable plays by Jack Gelber, John
Ashbery, and others, and the group production
Paradise Now 1968, considered to express the
spirit of the sixties.

Livonia /lɪ'vəʊnɪə/ former region in Europe on
the E coast of the Baltic Sea comprising most of
present-day Latvia and Estonia. Conquered and
converted to Christianity in the early 13th century by the Livonian Knights, a crusading order,
Livonia was independent until 1583, when it was
divided between Poland and Sweden. In 1710 it
was occupied by Russia, and in 1721 was ceded
to Peter the Great.

Livorno /lɪ'vɔːnəʊ/ (English 'Leghorn') industrial
port in W Italy; population (1988) 173,000. Industries include shipbuilding, distilling, and motor
vehicles. A fortress town since the 12th century, it
was developed by the Medici family; it has a naval
academy, and is also a resort.

Livy /'lɪvi/ Titus Livius 59 BC–AD 17. Roman historian, author of a *History of Rome* from the city's
foundation to 9 BC, based partly on legend. It
was composed of 142 books, of which 35 survive,
covering the periods from the arrival of Aeneas in
Italy to 293 BC and from 218–167 BC.

Li Xiannian /liː ʃi,æn ni'æn/ 1905– . Chinese politician, member of the Chinese Communist Party
(CCP) Politburo from 1956. He fell from favour

during the 1966–69 Cultural Revolution, but was
rehabilitated as finance minister 1973, supporting
cautious economic reform. He was state president
1983–88.

Li, born into a poor peasant family in Hubei
province, joined the CCP 1927 and served as
a political commissar during the Long March
of 1934–36. During the 1950s and early 1960s
he was vice premier to the State Council and
minister for finance and was inducted into the
CCP Politburo and secretariat in 1956 and 1958
respectively. He retains a seat on the Politburo's
standing committee and became chairman of the
the Chinese People's Political Consultative Conference (CPPCC).

lizard reptile of the suborder Lacertilia, belonging
with the snakes in the order Squamata. Lizards
are normally distinguishable from snakes by having four legs, movable eyelids, eardrums, and a
fleshy tongue, but some lizards are legless and
very snakelike in appearance. There are about
3,000 species of lizard worldwide.

Like other reptiles, they are most abundant in
the tropics, although the **common** or **viviparous
lizard** *Lacerta vivipara*, about 15 cm/6 in long,
lives in Europe as far north as the Arctic circle,
where it hibernates through the long winter. Like
many other species, it can shed its tail as a
defence, later regrowing it. There are some 20
families of lizards, including ◊geckos, ◊chamele-
ons, ◊skinks, ◊monitors, ◊agamas and ◊iguanas.
The **frilled lizard** *Chlamydosaurus kingi* of Australia has an erectile collar to frighten its enemies.
For flying lizard see ◊flying dragon.

Lizard Point /'lɪzəd/ most southerly point of England in Cornwall. The coast is broken into small
bays overlooked by two cliff lighthouses.

Ljubljana /luːb'ljɑːnə/ (German *Laibach*) capital and industrial city (textiles, chemicals, paper,
leather goods) of Slovenia, Yugoslavia; population
(1981) 305,200. It has a nuclear research centre
and is linked with S Austria by the Karawanken
road tunnel under the Alps (1979–83).

llama South American animal *Lama peruana*, about
1.2 m/4 ft high at the shoulder, a member of the
camel family. Llamas can be white, brown, or
dark, sometimes with spots or patches. They are
very hardy, and require little food or water. They
spit profusely when annoyed. Llamas are used in
Peru as beasts of burden, and also for their wool,
milk, and meat. The ◊alpaca is a related species.

Llanberis /ʃæn'berɪs/ village in Gwynedd, Wales,
point of departure for ascents of Mount Snowdon.

Llandaff /'lændəf/ town in S Glamorgan, Wales,
5 km/3 mi NW of Cardiff, of which it forms part.
The 12th-century cathedral, heavily restored,
contains Epstein's sculpture 'Christ in Majesty'.

Llandrindod Wells /ʃæn'drɪndɒd 'welz/ spa in
Powys, E Wales, administrative headquarters of
the county; population (1981) 4,186.

Llandudno /ʃæn'dɪdnəʊ/ resort and touring centre for N Wales, in Gwynedd. Great Orme's Head
is a spectacular limestone headland.

Llanelli /ʃæn'eʃi/ (formerly Llanelly) industrial
port in Dyfed, Wales; population (1981) 41,391.
Industries include tinplate and copper smelting.

Llanfair P G /'ʃænvaɪə/ village in Anglesey, Wales;
full name *Llanfairpwllgwyngyllgogerychwyr-
ndrobwllllantysiliogogogoch* (St Mary's church
in the hollow of the white hazel near the rapid
whirlpool of St Tysillio's church, by the red cave).

lizard

*frilled
lizard*

Lloyd George Portrait by William Orpen (1927) National Portrait Gallery, London.

Llewellyn /lʊˈwelɪn/ Richard. Pen name of Richard Vivian Llewellyn Lloyd 1907–1983. Welsh writer. *How Green Was My Valley* 1939, a novel about a S Wales mining family, was made into a play and a film.

Llewelyn /lʊˈwelɪn, Welsh ʃəˈwelɪn/ two kings of Wales:

Llewelyn I 1173–1240. King of Wales from 1194, who extended his rule to all Wales not in Norman hands, driving the English from N Wales 1212, and taking Shrewsbury 1215. During the early part of Henry III's reign, he was several times attacked by English armies. He was married to Joanna, illegitimate daughter of King John.

Llewelyn II *c.*1225–1282. King of Wales from 1246, grandson of Llewelyn I. In 1277 Edward I of England compelled Llewelyn to acknowledge him as overlord and to surrender S Wales. His death while leading a national uprising ended Welsh independence.

Lleyn /ˈʃiːn/ peninsula in Gwynedd, N Wales, between Cardigan Bay and Caernarvon Bay. It included the resort Pwllheli, and Bardsey Island at the tip of Peninsula Lleyn is the traditional burial place of 20,000 saints.

Lloyd /lɔɪd/ Harold 1893–1971. US film comedian, noted for his 'trademark' of spectacles with thick horn rims. He appeared from 1913 in silent and talking films.

Lloyd /lɔɪd/ Marie. Stage name of Matilda Alice Victoria Wood 1870–1922. English music-hall artist, whose Cockney songs embodied the music-hall traditions of 1890s comedy.

Lloyd /lɔɪd/ Selwyn; see ◊Selwyn Lloyd, British Conservative politician.

Lloyd George /ˈlɔɪd ˈdʒɔːdʒ/ David 1863–1945. Welsh Liberal politician, prime minister 1916–22. A pioneer of social reform, as chancellor of the Exchequer 1908–15 he introduced old-age pensions 1908 and health and unemployment insurance 1911. High unemployment, intervention in the Russian Civil War, and use of the ◊Black and Tans in Ireland eroded his support as prime minister, and creation of the Irish Free State 1921 and his pro-Greek policy against the Turks caused the collapse of his coalition government.

Lloyd George was born in Manchester, became a solicitor, and was member of Parliament for Caernarvon Boroughs from 1890. During the Boer War, he was prominent as a pro-Boer. His 1909 budget (with graduated direct taxes and taxing land values) provoked the Lords to reject it, and resulted in the Act of 1911 limiting their powers. He held ministerial posts during World War I until 1916 when there was an open breach between him and Prime Minister ◊Asquith, and he became prime minister of a coalition government. Securing a unified Allied command, he enabled the Allies to withstand the last German offensive and achieve victory. After World War I he had a major role in the Versailles peace treaty.

In the 1918 elections, he achieved a huge majority over Labour and Asquith's followers. He had become largely distrusted within his own party by 1922, and never regained power.

Lloyd's Register of Shipping an international society for the survey and classification of merchant shipping, which provides rules for the construction and maintenance of ships and their machinery. It was founded 1760.

It is governed by a large committee representing ship-owners, ship-builders, marine engineers, and underwriters. The register book, published annually, contains particulars of all known sea-going ships of 100 tonnes/98 tons gross and over.

Lloyd Webber /ˈlɔɪd ˈwebə/ Andrew 1948– . English composer. His early musicals, with lyrics by Tim Rice, include *Joseph and the Amazing Technicolor Dreamcoat* 1968; *Jesus Christ Superstar* 1970; and *Evita* 1978, based on the life of the Argentinian leader Eva Perón. He also wrote *Cats* 1981, *The Phantom of the Opera* 1986, and *Aspects of Love* 1989.

Llull /ljuːl/ Ramón 1232–1316. Catalan theologian and philosopher. In 1262, he became a monk and later a missionary in N Africa and Asia. He produced treatises on theology, mysticism, and chivalry in Catalan, Latin, and Arabic. His encyclopedic *Ars Magna* is a mechanical device for solving problems involving manipulation of fundamental Aristotelian categories. Llull died a martyr at Bugia, Algeria.

loa a spirit in voodoo. They may be male or female, and include Maman Brigitte, the loa of death and cemeteries, and Aida-Wedo, the rainbow snake. Believers may be under the protection of one particular loa.

loach carp-like freshwater fish, family Cobitidae, with a long narrow body, and no teeth in the small downward pointing mouth, which is surrounded by barbels. They are native to Asian and European waters. The European **stone loach** *Noemacheilus barbatulus*, has no scales and six barbels at the mouth.

Lobachevsky /ˌlɒbəˈtʃefski/ Nikolai Ivanovich 1792–1856. Russian mathematician, who concurrently with, but independently of, the Hungarian Janos Bolyai (1802–1860), founded non-Euclidean geometry in 1829. Lobachevsky published the first account of the subject in 1829, but his work went unrecognized until the German ◊Riemann's system was published.

lobby individual or ◊pressure group that sets out to influence government action. The lobby is prevalent in the USA, where the term originated in the 1830s from the practice of those wishing to influence state policy waiting for their electoral representative in the lobby of the Capitol. Under the UK lobby system, certain parliamentary journalists are given unofficial access to confidential news.

lobelia temperate and tropical genus of plants, family Lobeliaceae, with white to mauve flowers. They may grow to shrub size but are mostly small annual plants.

Lobengula /ˌləʊbənˈgjuːlə/ 1833–1894. King of Matabeleland (now part of Zimbabwe) 1870–93. After accepting British protection from internal and external threats to his leadership 1888, he came under increasing pressure from British mining interests to allow exploitation of goldfields near Bulawayo, and was overthrown 1893 by a military expedition organized by Cecil ◊Rhodes' South African Company.

Lobito /ləˈbiːtəʊ/ port in Angola; population (1970) 60,000. It is linked by rail with Beira in Mozambique, via the Zaïre and Zambia copperbelt.

lobotomy or *leucotomy* the cutting of a lobe. The term usually refers to the operation of *frontal lobotomy*, where the frontal lobes are disconnected from the rest of the brain by cutting the white matter that joins them. This may alleviate the condition of patients with severe depression, anxiety states or obsessive–compulsive disorders, but it is now rarely performed, and only on patients who have proved resistant to all other forms of treatment. See also ◊psychosurgery.

lobster marine member of the order Decapoda. Lobsters are grouped with the freshwater ◊crayfish in the suborder Reptantia ('walking'), though both lobsters and crayfish can also swim, using their fanlike tails. All have eyes on stalks and long antennae, and are mainly nocturnal. They scavenge and eat dead or dying fish.

True lobsters, family Homaridae, are distinguished by having very large 'claws' or pincers on their first pair of legs, and smaller ones on their second and third pairs. They include the **common lobster** *Homarus gammarus* found off Britain, which is bluish-black; the closely related **American lobster** *Homarus americanus*; and the **Norwegian lobster** *Nephrops norvegicus*, a small orange species.

Spiny lobsters, family Palinuridae, including the **spiny lobster** *Palinurus vulgaris* found off Britain, have no large pincers. They communicate by means of a serrated pad at the base of their antennae, the 'sound' being picked up by tufts of hair (not ears) on their fellow lobsters up to 60 m/180 ft away.

local government that part of government dealing mainly with matters concerning the inhabitants of a particular district or place, usually financed at least in part by local taxes. In the USA and UK local government has had comparatively large powers and responsibilities. England and Wales are divided into counties (Scotland into regions) and these are subdivided into districts.

In European countries such as France, West Germany, and the USSR, local government has tended historically to be more centrally controlled than in Britain, although German cities have a tradition of independent action, as exemplified in Berlin, and France from 1969 moved towards regional decentralization. In the USA the system shows evidence of the early type of settlement (for example in New England the town is the unit of local government, in the South the county, and in the N central states the combined county and township). A complication is the tendency to delegate power to special authorities in such fields as education. In Australia, although an integrated system similar to the British was planned, the scattered nature of settlement, apart from the major towns, has prevented implementation of any uniform tiered arrangement.

history The system of local government in England developed haphazardly; in the 18th century it varied in the towns between democratic survivals of the ◊guild system and the narrow rule of small oligarchies. The Municipal Reform Act 1835 established the rule of elected councils, although their actual powers remained small. In country areas local government remained in the hands of the justices of the peace (JPs) assembled in quarter sessions, until the Local Government Act 1888 set up county councils. These were given a measure of control over the internal local authorities, except the major bodies, which were constituted as county boroughs. The Local Government Act 1894 set up urban and rural district councils and, in the rural districts only, parish councils.

Under the Local Government Act 1972 the upper range of local government for England and Wales was established on a two-tier basis, with 46 ◊counties in England and eight in Wales. London and six other English cities were created metropolitan areas (their metropolitan county councils were abolished in 1986, and their already limited functions redistributed to *metropolitan district councils*), and the counties had ◊county councils. The counties were subdivided into districts (of which there are 300, each with a ◊district council, replacing the former county borough, borough, and urban and rural district councils) and then, in rural areas, into parishes and, in Wales, into 'communities' across the country, each again with its own council (see ◊parish council) dealing with local matters.

Under the Local Government Act 1974 a Commission for Local Administration for England and

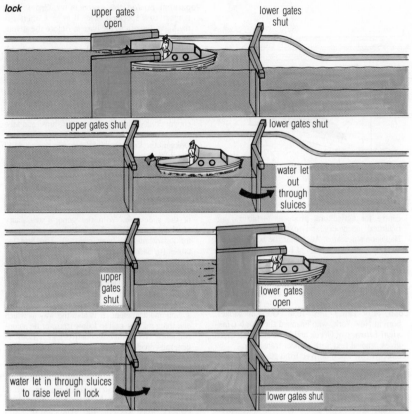

lock

upper gates open

lower gates shut

upper gates shut

lower gates shut

water let out through sluices

upper gates shut

lower gates open

water let in through sluices to raise level in lock

lower gates shut

Wales was set up, creating an **ombudsman** for complaints about local government.

Under the Local Government (Scotland) Act 1973 **Scotland** was divided into regions (nine) and island areas, rather than counties; these are subdivided into districts, which may in turn have subsidiary community councils, but the latter are not statutory bodies with claims on public funds as of right. **Northern Ireland** has a single-tier system of 26 district councils.

The activities of local government are financed largely by a local tax per head of population, known as the **community charge** or ◊**poll tax**, introduced 1989 in Scotland and 1990 in England and Wales. The poll tax replaced local property taxes known as ◊rates; it is subsidized by central government (see under ◊rate support grant). In the mid-1980s the Thatcher administration sought to remove many services from the aegis of local authorities and offer them for tender to private companies; thus in many areas school-meals provision was privatized, as were maintenance of council vehicles, street cleaning, and upkeep of parks and sports facilities. In 1987 a code of practice was issued to restrict the ability of local authorities to promote 'partisan' activities.

Local Group in astronomy, a cluster of about three dozen galaxies that includes our own. Like other groups of galaxies, the Local Group is held together by the gravitational attraction among its members, and does not expand with the expanding Universe. Its two largest galaxies are our own and the ◊Andromeda Galaxy; most of the others are small and faint.

local option the right granted by a government to the electors of each particular area to decide whether the sale of intoxicants shall be permitted. Such a system has been tried in certain states of the USA, in certain Canadian provinces, and in Norway and Sweden.

Locarno /ləˈkɑːnəʊ/ health resort in the Ticino canton of Switzerland on the north of Lago Maggiore, west of Bellinzona; population (1983) 15,300. Formerly in the duchy of Milan, it was captured by the Swiss in 1803.

Locarno, Pact of a series of diplomatic documents initialled in Locarno 16 Oct 1925 and formally signed in London 1 Dec 1925. The pact settled the question of French security, and the signatories—Britain, France, Belgium, Italy, and Germany—guaranteed the existing frontiers between Germany and France, and Germany and Belgium. The prime mover in the pact was British foreign secretary Austen Chamberlain. Following the signing of the pact, Germany was admitted to the League of Nations.

loc. cit. abbreviation for *loco citato* (Latin 'in the place cited').

Lochaber /lɒˈxɑːbə/ wild mountainous district of Highland region, Scotland, including Ben Nevis. Fort William is the chief town of the area. It is the site of large hydroelectric installations.

Lochner /ˈlɒxnə/ Stephan died 1451. German painter, active in Cologne, a master of the International Gothic style. Most of his work is still in Cologne, for example the *Virgin in the Rose Garden* (Wallraf-Richartz Museum).

Loch Ness /ˈlɒx ˈnes/ lake in Highland region, Scotland, forming part of the Caledonian Canal; 36 km/22.5 mi long, 229 m/754 ft deep. There have been unconfirmed reports of a **Loch Ness monster** since the 15th century.

lock a gated chamber installed in canals, rivers and seaways that allows boats to sail from one level to another. A lock has gates at each end, and a boat sails in through one gate when the levels are the same outside and inside. Then water is allowed in (or out) of the lock until the water level rises (or falls) to the new level outside the other gate.

lock and key devices that provide security, usually fitted to a door of some kind. In 1778 English locksmith Robert Barron made the forerunner of the modern **mortise lock**, which contains levers that the key must raise to an exact height before the bolt can be moved. The **Yale lock**, a pin-tumbler design, was invented by Linus Yale Jr 1865. More secure locks include **combination locks**, whose dial mechanism must be turned certain distances backwards and forwards to open, and **time locks**, which can be opened only at specific times.

Locks originated in the Far East over 4,000 years ago. The Romans developed the warded lock, which contains obstacles (wards) that the key must pass to turn.

Locke /lɒk/ John 1632–1704. English philosopher. His *Essay concerning Human Understanding* 1690 maintained that experience was the only source of knowledge (empiricism), and that 'we can have knowlege no farther than we have ideas' prompted by such experience. *Two Treatises on Government* 1690 was influential in forming modern ideas of liberal democracy.

Born in Somerset, he studied at Oxford, practised medicine, and in 1667 became secretary to the Earl of Shaftesbury. He consequently fell under suspicion as a Whig and in 1683 fled to Holland, where he lived until the 1688 revolution. In later life he published many works on philosophy, politics, theology, and economics; these include *Letters on Toleration* 1689–92, and *Some Thoughts concerning Education* 1693. His *Two Treatises on Government* supplied the classical statement of Whig theory, and enjoyed great influence in America and France. It supposed that governments derive their authority from popular consent (regarded as a 'contract'), so that a government may be rightly overthrown if it infringes such fundamental rights of the people as religious freedom. He believed that, at birth, the mind was a blank, and that all ideas came from sense impressions.

lockjaw former name for ◊tetanus.

locomotive a machine for hauling trains on railways. In 1804 Richard ◊Trevithick built the first locomotive, a steam engine on wheels. Locomotive design did not radically improve until George ◊Stephenson built the *Rocket* 1829, which featured a multitube boiler and blastpipe, standard in all following **steam locomotives**. Most modern locomotives are diesel or electric: **diesel locomotives** have a powerful diesel engine, and **electric locomotives** collect their power either from an overhead cable or a third rail alongside the ordinary track.

In a steam locomotive, fuel (usually coal, sometimes wood) is burned in a furnace. The hot gases and flames produced are drawn through tubes running through a huge water-filled boiler and heat up the water to steam. The steam is then fed to the cylinders, where it forces the pistons back and forth. Movement of the pistons is conveyed to the wheels by cranks and connecting rods.

Diesel locomotives have a powerful diesel engine, burning oil. The engine may drive a generator to produce electricity to power electric motors that turn the wheels, or the engine drives the wheels mechanically or through a hydraulic link. A number of **gas-turbine locomotives** are in use, in which a turbine spun by hot gases provides the power to drive the wheels.

Locke *English philosopher John Locke wrote* Two Treatises on Government *and* Essay Concerning Human Understanding. *The painting is by Dutch artist Herman Verelst (c. 1689).*

locomotive

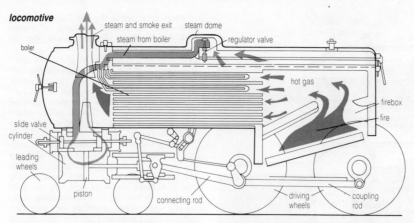

steam and smoke exit · steam dome
boiler · steam from boiler · regulator valve
steam dome
hot gas
firebox
fire
slide valve
cylinder
leading
wheels
piston · connecting rod · driving wheels · coupling rod

locus (Latin 'place') in mathematics, traditionally the path traced out by a moving point, but now defined as the set of all points on a curve satisfying given conditions. For example, the locus of a point that moves so that it is always at the same distance from another fixed point is a circle; the locus of a point that is always at the same distance from two fixed points is a straight line that perpendicularly bisects the line joining them.

locust swarming grasshopper, with short antennae and auditory organs on the abdomen, in the family Acrididae. As winged adults, flying in swarms, they may be carried by the wind hundreds of kilometres from their breeding grounds, and on landing devour all vegetation. Locusts occur in nearly every continent.

The *migratory locust Locusta migratoria* ranges from Europe to China, and even small swarms may cover several square kilometres, and weigh thousands of tonnes. Control by spreading poisoned food amongst the bands is very effective, but it is cheapest to spray concentrated insecticide solutions from aircraft over the insects or the vegetation on which they feed. They eat the equivalent of their own weight in a day, and, flying at night with the wind, may cover some 500 km/300 mi. The largest known swarm covered 1,036 sq km/400 sq mi, comprising approximately 40 thousand million insects.

locust tree alternative name for the ◊carob, small tree of the Mediterranean region.

lodestar or *loadstar* a star used in navigation or astronomy, especially ◊Polaris, the Pole Star.

Lodge /lɒdʒ/ David (John) 1935– . British novelist, short story writer, and critic. Much of his fiction concerns the role of Catholicism in mid-20th-century England, exploring the situation both through broad comedy and parody, as in *The British Museum is Falling Down* 1967, and realistically, as in *How Far Can You Go?* 1980.

Lodge /lɒdʒ/ Henry Cabot 1850–1924. US historian, Republican senator from 1893, and chairman of the Senate Foreign Relations Committee after World War I, who influenced the USA to stay out of the League of Nations 1920.

Lodge /lɒdʒ/ Henry Cabot Jr 1902–1985. US diplomat. He was Eisenhower's campaign manager, and US representative at the United Nations 1953–60. Ambassador to South Vietnam 1963–64 and 1965–67, he took over from Harriman as Nixon's negotiator in the Vietnam peace talks 1969. He was a grandson of the elder Henry Cabot Lodge.

Lodge /lɒdʒ/ Oliver Joseph 1851–1940. British physicist. He developed a system of wireless communication in 1894, and his work was influential in the development of radio receivers. He became greatly interested in psychic research after his son was killed in 1915.

Lodge /lɒdʒ/ Thomas c. 1558–1625. English author, whose romance *Rosalynde* 1590 was the basis of Shakespeare's *As You Like It.*

Lodi /ˈləʊdi/ town in Italy, 30 km/18 mi SE of Milan; population (1980) 46,000. It is a market

centre for agricultural produce; fertilizers, agricultural machinery and textiles are produced. Napoleon's defeat of Austria at the battle of Lodi in 1796 gave him control of Lombardy. Napoleon was first called Le Petit Caporal at Lodi.

Łódź /lɒdz/, Polish /wuːtʃ/ industrial town (textiles, machinery, dyes) in central Poland, 120 km/75 mi SW of Warsaw; population (1984) 849,000.

Loeb /lɜːb/ James 1867–1933. German banker, born in New York, who financed the *Loeb Classical Library* of Greek and Latin authors, which gives original text with parallel translation.

loess a yellow loam, derived from glacial meltwater deposits and accumulated by wind in periglacial regions during the ◊ice ages. It usually attains considerable depths, and the soil derived from it is very fertile. There are large deposits in central Europe (Hungary), China, and North America. Loess was first described 1821 in the Rhine area, and takes its name from a village in Alsace.

Loewe /ˈləʊi/ Frederick 1901–1988. US composer of musicals, born in Berlin. Son of an operatic tenor, he studied under Busoni, and in 1924 went with his father to the US. In 1942 he joined forces with the lyricist Alan Jay Lerner (1918–86), and their joint successes include *Brigadoon* 1947, *Paint Your Wagon* 1951, *My Fair Lady* 1956, *Gigi* 1958, and *Camelot* 1960.

Loewi /ˈlɜːvi/ Otto 1873–1961. German physiologist, whose work on the nervous system established that a chemical substance is responsible for the stimulation of one neurone by another. The substance was shown by the physiologist Henry ◊Dale to be acetylcholine, now known to be one of the most vital neurotransmitters. For this work Loewi and Dale were jointly awarded the Nobel Prize for Medicine.

Lofoten and Vesterålen /ˈləʊfəʊtn, ˈvestərəːlən/ island group off NW Norway; area 4,530 sq km/1,750 sq mi. Hinnoy, in the Vesterålens, is the largest island of Norway. The surrounding waters are rich in cod and herring. The *Maelström*, a large whirlpool hazardous to ships which gives its name to similar features elsewhere, occurs in one of the island channels.

Lofting /ˈlɒftɪŋ/ Hugh 1886–1947. English writer and illustrator of children's books, especially the 'Dr Dolittle' series, in which the hero can talk to animals. Lofting was born in Maidenhead, Berkshire, was originally a civil engineer, and went to the USA 1912.

log apparatus for measuring the speed of a ship; also the daily record of events on board a ship or aircraft. It originally consisted of a piece of weighted wood (log-chip) attached to a line with knots at equal intervals which was cast from the rear of a ship. The vessel's speed was estimated by timing the passage of the knots with a sand glass (like an egg-timer). Modern logs use electromagnetism and sonar.

log in mathematics, abbreviation for ◊logarithm.

loganberry hybrid between ◊blackberry and ◊raspberry with large, sweet, dull-red fruit.

logarithm or *log* the exponent or ◊index of a number to a specified base. If $b^a = x$, then a is the logarithm of x to the base b. Before the advent of cheap electronic calculators, multiplication and division could be simplified by being replaced with the addition and subtraction of logarithms.

For any two numbers x and y, $x \times y = b^a \times b^c = b^{a+c}$; hence we would add the logarithms of x and y, and look up this answer in antilogarithm tables. Tables of logarithms and antilogarithms are available (usually to the base 10) that show conversions of numbers into logarithms, and vice versa. For example, to multiply $6,560 \times 980$, one looks up the logarithms of the numbers — 3.8169 and 2.9912 — adds them together (6.8081), then looks up the antilogarithm of this to get the answer (6,428,000). *Natural* or *Naperian logarithms* are to the base e, an ◊irrational number equal to approximately 2.7183.

The principle of logarithms is also the basis of the slide rule. With the general availability of the electronic pocket calculator, the need for logarithms has been reduced. The first log tables (to base e) were published by the Scottish mathematician John Napier in 1614. Base-10 logs were introduced by the Englishman Henry Briggs (1561–1631) and Dutch mathematician Adriaen Vlacq (1600–1667).

logic a branch of philosophy that studies valid reasoning and argument. It is also the way in which one thing may be said to follow from, or be a consequence of, another (deductive logic). Logic is generally divided into the traditional formal logic of Aristotle, and the modern symbolic logic derived from Frege and Russell.

Aristotle's *Organon* is the founding work on logic, and Aristotelian methods as revived in the medieval church by Abelard in the 12th century were used in the synthesis of ideas aimed at in scholasticism. As befitted the spirit of the Renaissance, Bacon considered many of the general principles used as premises by the scholastics to be groundless; he envisaged that in natural philosophy principles worthy of investigation would emerge by 'inductive' logic, which works backward from the accumulated facts to the principle which accounts for them. The modern contribution to logic has been its mathematical expression by philosophers such as Boole, Frege, and Russell.

logical positivism the doctrine that the only meaningful propositions are those that can be verified empirically. Metaphysics, religion, and aesthetics are therefore meaningless. It was characteristic of the Vienna Circle in the 1920s and 1930s, and was influenced by Frege, Russell, and Wittgenstein.

logic gate the basic component of digital electronics, from which more complex circuits are built. There are seven main types of gate: Not, And, Or, Equivalence, Non-Equivalence (also called Exclusive Or, or Xor), Nand, and Nor. The type of gate determines how signals are processed. The process has close parallels in computer programming, where it forms the basis of binary logic.

Logo a computer-programming language designed to teach mathematical concepts. Developed about 1970 at the Massachusetts Institute of Technology, it became popular in schools and with home computer users because of its 'turtle graphics' feature. This allows the user to write programs that create line drawings on a computer screen, or drive a small mobile robot (a 'turtle' or a 'buggy') around the floor. It encourages the use of languages in a logical and structured way, leading to 'microworlds' in which problems can be solved by using a few standard solutions.

logos (Greek 'word') a term in Greek, Hebrew, and Christian philosophy and theology. It was used by Greek philosophers as the embodiment of 'reason' in the Universe. Under Greek influence the Jews came to conceive of 'Wisdom' as an aspect of God's activity. The Jewish philosopher ◊Philo (1st century AD) attempted to reconcile Platonic, Stoic, and Hebrew philosophy by identifying the logos with the Jewish idea of 'Wisdom'. Several of the New Testament writers took over Philo's conception of the logos, which they identified with Christ, and hence the second person of the Trinity.

Logron /lə'grəʊnjəʊ/ market town in La Rioja, N Spain, on the Ebro river; population (1986) 119,000. It is the centre of a wine region.

Lohengrin /'ləʊəngrɪn/ son of ◊Parsifal, hero of a late 13th-century legend, on which Wagner based his German opera *Lohengrin* 1847. Lohengrin married Princess Elsa, who broke his condition that she never ask his origin, and he returned to the temple of the ◊Holy Grail.

Loir /lwɑ:/ French river, rising N of Illiers in the *département* of Eure-et-Loir and flowing SE, then SW to join the Sarthe near Angers; 311 km/500 mi. It gives its name to the *départements* of Loir-et-Cher and Eure-et-Loir.

Loire /lwɑ:/ the longest river in France, rising in the Cévennes at 1,350 m/4,430 ft and flowing for 1,050 km/650 mi first north and then west until it reaches the Bay of Biscay at St Nazaire, passing Nevers, Orléans, Tours, and Nantes. It gives its name to the *départements* of Loire, Haute-Loire, Loire-Atlantique, Maine-et-Loire, Indre-et-Loire, and Saône-et-Loire. There are many chateaux and vineyards along its banks.

Loiret /lwɑ:'reɪ/ French river, 11 km/7 mi long. It rises near Olivet and joins the Loire 8 km/5 mi below Orléans. It gives its name to Loiret *département*.

Loki /'ləʊki/ in Norse mythology, one of the ◊Aesir, but the cause of dissension among the gods, and the slayer of ◊Balder. His children are the Midgard serpent Jörmungander which girdles the earth, the wolf Fenris, and Hela, goddess of death.

Lolita a novel by Nabokov, published 1955. It describes the infatuation of a middle-aged man for a precocious 12-year-old girl, and added the word 'nymphet' to the English language.

Lollard a follower of the English religious reformer John ◊Wycliffe in the 14th century. The Lollards condemned transubstantiation, advocated the diversion of ecclesiastical property to charitable uses, and denounced war and capital punishment. They were active from about 1377; after the passing of the statute *De Heretico Comburendo* ('The Necessity of Burning Heretics') 1401 many Lollards were burned, and in 1414 they raised an unsuccessful revolt in London.

The name is derived from the Dutch *lollaert* (mumbler), applied to earlier European groups on the Continent accused of combining pious pretentions with heretical belief. Lollardy lingered on in London and East Anglia, and in the 16th century became absorbed into the Protestant movement.

Greater London

London *The imposing keep of the Tower of London was built by Gundulf, William the Conqueror's bishop-architect, 1078–80.*

Lombard /'lɒmbɑ:d/ Carole. Stage name of Jane Alice Peters 1908–1942. US comedy film actress. Her successful career, which included starring roles in some of the best comedies of the 1930s, was tragically cut short by her death in a plane crash; her films include *Twentieth Century* 1934, *My Man Godfrey* 1936, and *To Be or Not To Be* 1942.

Lombard or *Langobard* member of a Germanic people who invaded Italy 568 and occupied Lombardy (named after them) and central Italy. Their capital was Monza. They were conquered by the Frankish ruler Charlemagne 774.

Lombard league an association of N Italian communes established 1164 to maintain their independence against the Holy Roman emperors' claims of sovereignty.

Supported by Milan and Pope Alexander III (1105–81), it defeated Frederick Barbarossa at Legnano in N Italy 1179, and effectively resisted Otto IV (1175–1218) and Frederick II, becoming the most powerful champion of the Guelph cause. Internal rivalries led to its dissolution in 1250.

Lombardy /'lɒmbədi/ (Italian *Lombardia*) region of N Italy, including Lake Como; capital Milan; area 23,900 sq km/9,225 sq mi; population (1988) 8,886,000. It is the country's chief industrial area (chemical, pharmaceuticals, engineering, textiles).

Lombok /'lɒmbɒk/ (Javanese 'chilli pepper') island of Indonesia, E of Java, one of the Sunda Islands; area 4,730 sq km/1,826 sq mi; population (1980) 1,957,000. Chief town is Mataram. It comprises a fertile plain between N and S mountain ranges.

Lombroso /lɒm'brəʊsəʊ/ Cesare 1836–1909. Italian criminologist. His major work is *L'uomo delinquente* 1889. He held the now discredited idea that there was a physically distinguishable criminal 'type'.

He became a professor of mental diseases at Pavia in 1862. Subsequently he held chairs in forensic medicine, psychiatry, and criminal anthropology at Turin.

Lomé /'ləʊmeɪ/ capital and port of Togo; population (1983) 366,000. It is a centre for gold, silver, and marble crafts; major industries include steel production and oil refining.

Lomé Convention convention 1975 that established economic cooperation between the EEC and African, Caribbean, and Pacific countries. It was renewed 1979 and 1985.

lomentum a type of ◊fruit, similar to a pod but constricted between the seeds. When ripe, it splits into one-seeded units, as seen, for example, in the fruit of sainfoin (*Onobrychis viciifolia*) and radish (*Raphanus raphanistrum*). It is a type of ◊schizocarp.

Lomond, Loch /'ləʊmənd/ largest freshwater Scottish lake, 37 km/21 mi long, area 70 sq km/27 sq mi, divided between Strathclyde and Central regions. It is overlooked by the mountain **Ben Lomond** 296.5 m/973 ft and linked to the Clyde estuary.

London, Museum of museum of London's history. It was formed by the amalgamation of the former Guildhall (Roman and medieval) and London (Tudor and later) Museums, housed from 1976 in a new building at the junction of London Wall and Aldersgate, near the Barbican.

London /'lʌndən/ the capital of England and the United Kingdom, on the river Thames; area 1,580 sq km/610 sq mi; population (1987) 6,770,000, larger metropolitan area about 9 million. The *City of London*, known as the 'square mile', area 677 acres, is the financial and commercial centre of the UK. ◊*Greater London* from 1965 comprises the City of London and 32 boroughs. Popular tourist attractions include the Tower of London, St Paul's Cathedral, Buckingham Palace, and Westminster Abbey. Roman Londinium was established soon after the Roman invasion 43 AD; in the 2nd century London became a walled city; by the 11th century, it was the main city of England and gradually extended beyond the walls to link with the originally separate Westminster.

The Tower of London was built by William the Conqueror on a Roman site, it houses the crown jewels and the royal armouries. Other features include 15th-century Guildhall; Mansion House (residence of the lord mayor); the Monument (a column designed by Wren) marking the site in Pudding Lane where the Great Fire of 1666 began; Barbican arts and conference centre; Central Criminal Court (Old Bailey) and the Inner and Middle Temples; markets including Covent Garden, Smithfield (meat), and Spitalfields (fruit and vegetables).

government There has since 1986 been no central authority for London; responsibility is divided between individual boroughs and central government.

The City of London has been governed by a corporation from the 12th century. Its structure and the electoral procedures for its common councillors and aldermen are medievally complex and it is headed by the lord mayor (who is, broadly speaking, nominated by the former and elected annually by the latter). After being sworn in at the Guildhall, he or she is presented the next day to the lord chief justice at the Royal Courts of Justice in Westminster, and the **Lord Mayor's Show** is a ceremonial procession there in Nov.

architecture London contains examples of all styles of English architecture since the 11th century. Examples include **Norman**: the White Tower, Tower of London; St Bartholomew's, Smithfield; the Temple Church. **Gothic**: Westminster Abbey; Westminster Hall; Lambeth Palace; Southwark Cathedral. **Tudor**: St James's Palace; Staple Inn, Holborn. **17th century**: Banqueting Hall, Whitehall (Inigo Jones); St Paul's, Kensington Palace, and many City churches (Wren). **18th century**: Somerset House (Chambers); St Martin-in-the-Fields; Buckingham Palace. **19th century**: British Museum (Neo-Classical); Houses of Parliament; Law Courts (Gothic); Westminster Cathedral (Byzantine). **20th century**: Lloyd's of London.

commerce and industry Important from Saxon times, the Port of London once dominated the Thames from Tower Bridge to Tilbury; its activity is now centred outside the metropolitan area, and downstream Tilbury has been extended to cope with container traffic. The prime economic importance of London is as a financial centre. There are various industries, mainly on the outskirts. There are also recording, broadcasting, television, and film studios; publishing companies, and the works and offices of the national press. Tourism is important. Some of the docks in the East End of London, once the busiest in the world, have been sold to the Docklands Development Corporation, which has built new houses, factories, and a railway.

education and entertainment Among its museums are the British, Victoria and Albert, Natural History, and Science museums, the National and Tate galleries. London University is the largest in Britain, while the Inns of Court have been the training school for lawyers since the 13th century. London has been the main centre of English drama ever since its first theatre was built by Burbage 1576.

London /ˈlʌndən/ city in SW Ontario, Canada, on the river Thames, 160 km/100 mi SW of Toronto; population (1986) 342,000. The centre of a farming district, it has tanneries, breweries, and factories making hosiery, radio and electrical equipment, leather and shoes. It dates from 1826 and is the seat of the University of Western Ontario. A Shakespeare festival is held in Stratford, about 30 km/18 mi to the northwest.

London /ˈlʌndən/ Jack (John Griffith) 1876–1916. US novelist, born in San Francisco. He is best known for adventure stories, for example, *The Call of the Wild* 1903, *The Sea Wolf* 1904, and *White Fang* 1906.

London County Council former administrative authority for London created 1888 by the Local Government Act; it incorporated parts of Kent, Surrey, and Middlesex in the metropolis. It was replaced by the Greater London Council 1964–86.

Londonderry /ˌlʌndənˈderi/ former name (until 1984) of the county and city of ◊Derry in Northern Ireland.

London Gazette twice-weekly publication (which first appeared in 1666) of official UK government announcements, service appointments, decorations, and so on.

London, Greater /ˈlʌndən/ official name for the City of London, which forms a self-governing enclave, and 32 surrounding boroughs; area 1,580 sq km/610 sq mi; population (1987) 6,770,000. Certain powers were exercised over this whole area by the Greater London Council (GLC) until its abolition 1986.

The surrounding boroughs are Barking and Dagenham, Barnet, Bexley, Brent, Bromley, Camden, Croydon, Ealing, Enfield, Greenwich, Hackney, Hammersmith and Fulham, Haringey, Harrow, Havering, Hillingdon, Hounslow, Islington, Kensington and Chelsea, Kingston upon Thames, Lambeth, Lewisham, Merton, Newham, Redbridge, Richmond upon Thames, Southwark, Sutton, Tower Hamlets, Waltham Forest, Wandsworth and Westminster.

London University university originated in 1826 with the founding of University College, to provide higher education free from religious tests. In 1836, a charter set up an examining body with power to grant degrees. London University threw open all degrees to women in 1878, the first British university to do so.

London Working Men's Association campaigning organization for political reform, founded June 1836 by William ◊Lovett and others, who in 1837 drew up the first version of the People's Charter (see ◊Chartism). It was founded in the belief that popular education, achieved through discussion and access to a cheap and honest press, was a means of obtaining political reform. By 1837 the LWMA had 100 members.

lone pair in chemistry, a pair of electrons in a bonding ◊atomic orbital that both belong to the atom itself, rather than having been paired by the sharing of electrons from different atoms. Such pairs can be involved in bonding with atoms that are deficient in electrons, forming **dative bonds**, in which both electrons in a bond are donated by one atom.

long. abbreviation for **longitude**; see ◊latitude and longitude.

Long /lɒŋ/ Huey 1893–1935. US Democratic politician, nicknamed 'the Kingfish', governor of Louisiana 1928–31, US senator for Louisiana 1930–35. A legendary public speaker, he was popular with poor white voters for his programme of social and economic reform, which he called the 'Share Our Wealth' programme, and which represented a significant challenge to Roosevelt's ◊New Deal, but his own extravagance, including the state capitol building at Baton Rouge built of bronze and marble, was widely criticized, and he was also accused of corruption. He was assassinated.

Long Beach /lɒŋ biːtʃ/ city in SW California, USA; population (1980) 361,334. It is a naval base and pleasure resort. Industries include oil refineries and aircraft. It forms part of the ◊Los Angeles conurbation.

Longchamp /ˈlɒŋʃɒm/ pleasure resort and racecourse in Paris, France, in the Bois de Boulogne. It is on the site of a former nunnery founded in 1260, suppressed 1790.

Longchamp French horseracing course situated at the Bois de Boulogne, near Paris. Most of the major races in France are run at Longchamp including the most prestigious open-age group race in Europe, the *Prix de L'Arc de Triomphe*, which attracts a top-quality field every October.

Long Day's Journey into Night US play by Eugene O'Neill, the harrowing tragedy of the theatrical Tyrone family, based on the author's own family. Written 1941 and published posthumously 1956, it has been repeatedly performed and made into a film.

Longfellow /ˈlɒŋˌfeləʊ/ Henry Wadsworth 1807–1882. US poet, born in Portland, Maine. He is remembered for ballads ('Excelsior' and 'The Wreck of the Hesperus'), the narrative *Evangeline* 1847, and his metrically haunting *The Song of* ◊*Hiawatha* 1855.

Longford /ˈlɒŋfəd/ county of Leinster province, Republic of Ireland
area 1,040 sq km/401 sq mi
county town Longford
features rivers Camlin and Inny; the Shannon marks the W boundary; several lakes
population (1986) 31,000.

Longford /ˈlɒŋfəd/ Frank (Francis Aungier) Pakenham, 7th Earl of Longford 1905– . Anglo-Irish Labour politician. He was brought up a Protestant but converted to Catholicism. He is an advocate of penal reform.

Longfellow US poet Henry Wadsworth Longfellow, author of The Song of Hiawatha, *photographed shortly before he died in 1882.*

He worked in the Conservative Party Economic Research Department 1930–32, then became a member of the Labour Party and held ministerial posts 1948–51 and 1964–68.

Longinus /lɒnˈdʒaɪnəs/ Cassius 213–273. Greek philosopher. He taught in Athens for many years. Adviser to ◊Zenobia of Palmyra, he instigated her revolt against Rome, and was put to death when she was captured.

Longinus /lɒnˈdʒaɪnəs/ Dionysius lived 1st century AD. Greek critic, author of a treatise *On the Sublime*, which influenced Dryden and Pope.

Long Island /ˌlɒŋ ˈaɪlənd/ island off the coast of Connecticut and New York, USA, separated from the mainland by Long Island Sound; area 3,627 sq km/1,400 sq mi. It includes two boroughs of New York City (Queens and Brooklyn), John F Kennedy airport, suburbs, and resorts.

It also has Brookhaven National Laboratory for atomic research, the world's largest automotive museum, the New York Aquarium, and a whaling museum. The popular pleasure resort of Coney Island is actually a peninsula in the SW, with a boardwalk 3 km/2 mi long.

longitude see ◊latitude and longitude.

Long March in Chinese history, the 10,000 km/6,000 mi trek undertaken 1934–35 by Mao Zedong and his communist forces from SE to NW China, under harassment from the Guomindang nationalist army.

Some 100,000 communists left Jiangxi, Mao's first headquarters, in Oct 1934 and 8,000 lasted the journey to arrive about a year later in Shaanxi, which became their new base. The march cemented Mao Zedong's control of the movement.

Long Parliament the English Parliament 1640–53 and 1659–60, which continued through the Civil War. After the Royalists withdrew in 1642, and the Presbyterian right was excluded in 1648, the remaining Rump ruled England until expelled by Cromwell in 1653. Reassembled 1659–60, the Long Parliament initiated the negotiations for the restoration of the monarchy.

Lonsdale /ˈlɒnzdeɪl/ Hugh Cecil Lowther, 5th Earl of Lonsdale 1857–1944. British sporting enthusiast. The Lonsdale Belts in boxing, first presented 1909, are named after him.

Lonsdale, an expert huntsman, steeplechaser, boxer, and yachtsman, was notorious for extramarital affairs, and was ordered to leave Britain by Queen Victoria after a scandal with actress Violet Cameron. As a result, he set off to the Arctic 1888 for 15 months, travelling by boat and sleigh through N Canada to Alaska. The collection of Inuit artefacts he brought back is now in the Museum of Mankind, London.

loofah fibrous skeleton of the fruit of *Luffa cylindrica*, family Cucurbitaceae, used as a bath sponge.

loom a weaving machine, first used to weave sheep's wool at least 7,000 years ago. A loom is a frame on which a set of lengthwise threads (warp) is strung. Then a second set of threads (weft), carried in a shuttle, is inserted at right-angles over and under the warp. In practice the warp threads are separated as appropriate, to create a gap, or shed, through which the shuttle can be passed in a straight line. The warp threads are moved by means of a harness. A device called a reed presses each new line of weave tight against the previous ones.

All looms have similar features, but on the modern power loom weaving takes place automatically at great speed. Mechanization of weaving began 1733 when John Kay invented the flying shuttle. A little over half a century later Edmund Cartwright introduced a steam-powered loom. Among recent developments are shuttleless looms, which work at very high speed, passing the weft through the warp by means of 'rapiers', and jets of air or water.

loon North American name for ◊diver.

Loos /ləʊs/ Adolf 1870–1933. Viennese architect. He rejected the ornamentation and curved lines of the Viennese *Jugendstil* (see ◊Art Nouveau). His most important buildings are private houses on Lake Geneva 1904 and the Steiner House in Vienna 1910, but his main importance is as a polemicist; for example the article *Ornament and Crime* 1908.

Loos /luːz/ Anita 1888–1981. US writer, author of the humorous fictitious diary ◊*Gentlemen Prefer Blondes* 1925.

loosestrife plant of the family Primulaceae, including the **yellow loosestrife** *Lysimachia vulgaris*, with spikes of yellow flowers, and the low-growing **creeping jenny** *Lysimachia nummularia*. The striking **purple loosestrife** *Lythrum saclicaria* belongs to the family Lythraceae.

Lope de Vega (Carpio) /ˈləʊpeɪ də ˈveɪɡə/ Felix 1562–1635. Spanish poet and dramatist, founder of modern Spanish drama. He was born in Madrid, served with the Armada 1588, and in 1613 took holy orders. He wrote epics, pastorals, odes, sonnets, and novels, and reputedly over 1,500 plays (of which 426 are still in existence), mostly tragi-comedies. He set out his views on drama in *Arte nuevo de hacer comedias/The New Art of Writing Plays* 1609, while re-affirming the classical form. *Fuenteovejuna* 1614 has been acclaimed as the first proletarian drama.

Lopes /ˈləʊpes/ Fernão *c.* 1380–1460. Portuguese medieval historian, whose *Crónicas/Chronicles* (begun 1434) relate vividly the history of the Portuguese monarchy between 1357 and 1411.

López /ˈləʊpes/ Carlos Antonio 1790–1862. Paraguayan dictator (in succession to his uncle José Francia) from 1840. He achieved some economic improvement; he was succeeded by his son Francisco López.

López /ˈləʊpes/ Francisco Solano 1827–1870. Paraguayan dictator in succession to his father Carlos López. He involved the country in a war with Brazil, Uruguay, and Argentina, during which approximately 80% of the population died.

Lopez /ˈləʊpez/ Nancy 1957– . US golfer, who turned professional 1977 and became in 1979 the first woman to win $200,000 in a season. She has twice won the US LPGA title and has won over 35 tour events.

Lop Nor /ˌlɒp ˈnɔː/ series of shallow salt lakes with shifting boundaries in the Taklimakan Shamo (desert) in Xinjiang Uyghur, NW China. Marco Polo visited Lop Nor, then a single lake of considerable extent, about 1273. The area is used for atomic tests.

loquat evergreen tree, *Eriobotrya japonica*, of the family Rosaceae, native to China and Japan and also known as the *Japan medlar*. The golden pear-shaped fruit has a delicate sweet-sour taste.

Lorca /ˈlɔːkə/ Federico García 1898–1936. Spanish poet and playwright, born in Granada. *Romancero gitano/Gipsy Ballad-book* 1928 shows the influence of the Andalusian songs of the area. In 1929–30 Lorca visited New York, and his experiences are reflected in *Poeta en Nuevo York*. He returned to Spain, founded a touring theatrical company, and wrote plays such as *Bodas de sangre/Blood Wedding* 1933 and *La casa de Bernarda Alba/The House of Bernarda Alba* 1936. His poems include a 'Lament' for the bullfighter Mejías. He was shot by the Falangists during the Spanish Civil War.

Lord in the UK, prefix used informally as alternative to the full title of a marquess, earl, or viscount; normally also in speaking of a baron, and as a courtesy title before the forename and surname of younger sons of dukes and marquesses.

Lord Advocate chief law officer of the Crown in Scotland.

Lord Chancellor in Britain, a government minister who is also head of the judiciary, and Speaker of the House of Lords.

Lord Howe Island /ˌlɔːd ˈhaʊ/ volcanic island and dependency of New South Wales, Australia, 700 km/435 mi NE of Sydney; area 15 sq km/6 sq mi; population (1984) 300. It is a popular resort.

lord-lieutenant in the UK, the Sovereign's representative in a county, who recommends magistrates for appointment.

lord mayor in the UK, ◊mayor of a city.

Lord's one of England's test match grounds and the headquarters of cricket's governing body, the Marylebone Cricket Club (MCC), since 1788 when the MCC was formed following the folding of the White Conduit Club.

The ground is named after Yorkshireman *Thomas Lord* (1757–1832) who developed the first site at Dorset Square in 1787. He moved the ground to a field at North Bank, Regent's Park, in 1811, and in 1814 developed the ground at its present site at St John's Wood. Lord's is also the home of the Middlesex cricket club.

Lords, House of the upper house of the UK ◊Parliament.

Lord's Prayer in the New Testament, prayer taught by Jesus to his disciples. It is sometimes called Our Father or Paternoster from the opening words in English and Latin.

Lord's Supper in the Christian church, another name for the ◊Eucharist.

Lorelei in Germanic folklore, a river nymph of the Rhine who lures sailors on to the rock where she sits combing her hair; a ◊siren. She features in several poems, including 'Die Lorelei' by the Romantic writer Heine. The **Lurlei** rock S of Koblenz is 130 m/430 ft high.

Loren /ˈlɔːrən/ Sophia. Stage name of Sofia Scicolone 1934– . Italian film actress who achieved fame under the guidance of her husband, producer Carlo Ponti. Her work includes *Aida* 1953, *The Key* 1958, *La Ciocara/Two Women* 1961, *Judith* 1965, and *Firepower* 1979.

Lorentz /ˈlɔːrənts/ Hendrik Antoon 1853–1928. Dutch physicist, winner (with his pupil Pieter Zeeman) of the Nobel Physics Prize 1902 for his work on the Zeeman effect.

Lorentz spent most of his career trying to develop and improve the ◊Maxwell electromagnetic theory. He also attempted to account for the anomalies of the ◊Michelson–Morley experiment by proposing, independently of ◊Fitzgerald that moving bodies contracted in their direction of motion. He took the matter further with his method of transforming space and time coordinates, later known as Lorentz transformations, which prepared the way for ◊Einstein's theory of ◊relativity.

Lorenz /ˈlɔːrənts/ Konrad 1903–1989. Austrian ethologist. Director of the Max Planck Institute for the Physiology of Behaviour in Bavaria 1955–73, he wrote the studies of ethology (animal behaviour) *King Solomon's Ring* 1952 and *On Aggression* 1966. In 1973 he shared a Nobel prize with N ◊Tinbergen and Karl von ◊Frisch.

Lorenz Austrian zoologist and biologist Konrad Lorenz, 1969.

Lorenz /ˈlɔːrənts/ Ludwig Valentine 1829–1891. Danish mathematician and physicist. He developed mathematical formulae to describe phenomena such as the relation between refraction of light and the density of a pure transparent substance, and the relation between a metal's electrical and thermal conductivity and temperature.

Lorenzetti /ˌlɔːrənˈzeti/ Ambrogio *c.* 1319–1347. Italian painter active in Siena and Florence. His allegorical frescoes *Good and Bad Government* 1337–39 (Palazzo Pubblico, Siena) include a detailed panoramic landscape, and a view of the city of Siena that shows an unusual mastery of spatial effects.

Lorenzetti /ˌlɔːrənˈzeti/ Pietro *c.* 1306–1345. Italian painter of the Sienese school, active in Assisi. His frescoes in the Franciscan basilica, Assisi reflect ◊Giotto's concern with mass and weight. He was the brother of Ambrogio Lorenzetti.

Lorestan alternative form of ◊Luristan, Iran.

Loreto /ləˈretəʊ/ town in the Marche region of central Italy; population (1981) 10,600. The town allegedly holds the Virgin Mary's house, carried there by angels from Nazareth; hence Our Lady of Loreto is the patron saint of aviators.

Lorient /ˌlɔːriˈɒn/ commercial and naval port in Brittany, NW France; population (1983) 104,000. Industries include fishing and shipbuilding.

lorikeet type of small, brightly coloured parrot, found in SE Asia and Australasia.

loris small Asian primate. Lorises are slow-moving, arboreal, and nocturnal. They have very large eyes and are tailless. They climb without leaping, gripping branches tightly and moving on or hanging below them.

The **slender loris** *Loris tardigradus* of S India and Sri Lanka is about 20 cm/8 in long. The tubbier **slow loris** *Nycticebus coucang* of SE Asia is 30 cm/1 ft. The angwantibo and potto are similar African forms.

Lorrain /lɒˈræn/ Claude 1600–1682. French painter; see ◊Claude Lorrain.

Lorraine /lɒˈreɪn/ former province and modern region of NE France in the upper reaches of the Meuse and Moselle rivers; bounded to the N by Belgium, Luxembourg, and West Germany and to the E by Alsace; area 23,600 sq km/9,095 sq mi; population (1986) 2,313,000. It consists of the *départements* of Meurthe-et-Moselle, Meuse, Moselle, and Vosges, and its capital is Nancy. There are deposits of coal, iron-ore and salt; grain, fruit and livestock are important. In 1871 the region was ceded to Germany as part of Alsace-Lorraine.

Lorraine, Cross of /lɒˈreɪn/ heraldic cross with double crossbars, emblem of the medieval French nationalist Joan of Arc. It was adopted by the Free French forces in World War II.

Lorre /ˈlɒri/ Peter. Stage name of Lazlo Löwenstein 1904–1964. Hungarian character actor, whose bulging eyes and sinister voice made him one of cinema's most memorable performers. He made several films in Germany before moving to Hollywood in 1935. He appeared

Losey Early in his career, US film director Joseph Losey was influenced by Brecht and worked with him.

in *M* 1931, *Mad Love* 1935, *The Maltese Falcon* 1941, *Casablanca* 1942, *Beat the Devil* 1953, and *The Raven* 1963.

lory type of Australasian, honey-eating ◊parrot that is brilliantly coloured.

Los Alamos /lɒs ˈæləmɒs/ town in New Mexico, USA, which has had a centre for atomic and space research since 1942. In World War II, the atom (nuclear fission) bomb was designed there (under ◊Oppenheimer), working on data from other research stations; the ◊hydrogen bomb was also developed there.

Los Angeles /lɒs ˈændʒəliːz/ city and port in SW California, USA; population of urban area (1980) 2,967,000, the metropolitan area of Los Angeles-Long Beach 9,478,000. Industries include aerospace, electronics, chemical, clothing, printing, and food-processing. Features include the suburb of Hollywood, centre of the film industry since 1911; the Hollywood Bowl concert arena; observatories at Mt Wilson and Mt Palomar; Disneyland; the Huntingdon Art Gallery and Library; and the Getty Museum.

It comprises Long Beach, Redondo Beach, Venice, Santa Monica, Burbank, Hollywood, Beverly Hills, Glendale, Pasadena, Pomona, and a number of other places.

Los Angeles /lɒs ˈæŋheles/ Victoria de 1923– . Spanish soprano. She is renowned for her interpretations of Spanish songs and for the roles of Manon and Madame Butterfly in Puccini's operas.

Losey /ˈləʊsi/ Joseph 1909–1984. US film director. Black-listed as a former Communist in the ◊McCarthy era, he settled in England, where his films included *The Servant* 1963 and *The Go-Between* 1971.

Lossiemouth /ˌlɒsiˈmaʊθ/ fishing port and resort in Grampian, Scotland; population (1981) 6,800. Ramsay MacDonald was born and buried here.

Lost Generation, the the disillusioned US literary generation of the 1920s, especially those who went to live in Paris. The phrase is attributed to the writer Gertrude Stein in Ernest Hemingway's novel of 1920s Paris, *The Sun Also Rises* 1926.

Lot /lɒt/ French river; see under ◊Gironde.

Lot in the Old Testament or Hebrew Bible, Abraham's nephew, who escaped the destruction of Sodom. Lot's wife was turned into a pillar of salt when she turned around to look at Sodom.

Lothair /ləʊˈθeə/ 825–869. King of Lotharingia (called after him, and later corrupted to Lorraine, now part of Alsace-Lorraine) from 855, when he inherited from his father, the Holy Roman

Lothian

emperor Lothair I, a district W of the Rhine, between the Jura mountains and the North Sea.

Lothair /ləʊˈθeə/ two Holy Roman emperors:

Lothair I 795–855. Holy Roman emperor from 817 in association with his father Louis I. On Louis' death, the empire was divided between Lothair and his brothers; Lothair took N Italy and the valleys of the rivers Rhône and Rhine.

Lothair II *c.*1070–1137. Holy Roman emperor from 1133 and German king from 1125. His election as emperor, opposed by the Hohenstaufens, was the start of the feud between ◊Guelph and Ghibelline.

Lothian /ˈləʊðiən/ region of Scotland
area 1,800 sq km/695 sq mi
towns administrative headquarters Edinburgh; Livingston
features Lammermuir, Moorfoot, and Pentland Hills; Bass Rock in the Firth of Forth, noted for seabirds
products bacon, vegetables, coal, whisky, engineering, electronics
population (1987) 744,000
famous people birthplace of R L Stevenson in Howard Place, Edinburgh.

lottery game of chance in which tickets sold may win a prize. In the UK lotteries are subject to strict government regulation. The largest lottery is the government-issued *Premium Savings Bonds* (from 1956), repayable at par without interest, but eligible for monthly prize-winning draws. In the USA state lotteries may bring a winner many millions, for example, in Illinois in 1984 one ticket brought a prize of $40 million.

Lotto /ˈlɒtəʊ/ Lorenzo *c.*1480–1556. Italian painter, born in Venice, active in Bergamo, Treviso, Venice, Ancona, and Rome. His early works were influenced by Giovanni Bellini; his mature style belongs to the High Renaissance. He painted dignified portraits, altarpieces, and frescoes.

lotus several different plants: those of the genus *Lotus*, family Leguminosae, including the bird's foot trefoil *Lotus corniculatus*; the shrub *Zizyphus lotus*, known to the ancient Greeks who used its fruit to make a type of bread and also a wine supposed to induce happy oblivion—hence *lotus-eaters*; the water-lily *Nymphaea lotus*, frequent in Egyptian art; and *Nelumbium nuciferum*, the sacred lotus of the Hindus, which floats, its flowerhead erect above the water.

Lotus motorcar company founded by Colin Chapman (1928–1982), who built his first racing car 1948, and also developed high-powered production saloons and sports cars, such as the Lotus-Cortina and Lotus Elan. Lotus has been one of the leading Grand Prix manufacturers since its first Grand Prix in 1960. Twice-world-champion Jim Clark had all his Grand Prix wins in a Lotus. The last Lotus world champion was Mario Andretti 1978.

Lotus 1–2–3 a popular ◊spreadsheet computer program, produced by Lotus Development

Corporation. It first appeared in 1982, and is credited with being one of the main reasons for the widespread acceptance of the IBM Personal Computer in businesses.

Lotus Sūtra an important scripture of Mahāyāna Buddhism, particularly in China and Japan. It is Buddha Śākyamuni's final teaching, emphasizing that everyone can attain Buddhahood with the help of bodhisattvas. The original is in Sanskrit (*Saddharmapundarīka Sūtra*) and thought to date to some time after 100 BC.

loudspeaker an electromechanical device that converts electrical signals into sound waves. It is used in all sound-reproducing systems such as radios, record players, tape recorders, and televisions.

The common type is the moving-coil speaker. Electrical signals from, for example, a radio are fed to a coil of fine wire wound around the top of a cone. The coil is surrounded by a magnet. When signals pass through it, the coil becomes an electromagnet, and so it moves, causing the cone to vibrate, which thus sets up sound waves.

Loughborough /ˈlʌfbərə/ industrial town in Leicestershire, England; population (1981) 47,647. Occupations include engineering, bell-founding, electrical goods, and knitwear. The university of technology was established 1966.

Louis, Prince of Battenberg /ˈluːi/ 1854–1921. German-born British admiral, who took British nationality 1917. He was First Sea Lord 1912–14, but was forced to resign because of anti-German sentiment. In 1917 he changed his name to Mountbatten, and was made marquess of Milford Haven. He was admiral of the fleet 1921.

Louis /ˈluːɪs/ Joe. Assumed name of Joseph Louis Barrow 1914–1981. US boxer, nicknamed 'the Brown Bomber'. He was world heavyweight champion 1937–49 and made a record 25 successful defences (a record for any weight).

Louis was the longest reigning world heavyweight champion at 11 years and 252 days before announcing his retirement 1949. He subsequently made a comeback and lost to Ezzard Charles in a world title fight 1950.

CAREER HIGHLIGHTS

Professional fights: 66
wins: 63
knockouts: 49
defeats: 3
1st professional fight: 4 July 1934 v. Jack Kracken (USA)
last professional fight: 26 Oct 1951 v. Rocky Marciano (USA)

Louis /ˈluːɪs/ Morris 1912–1962. US abstract painter. From Abstract Expressionism he turned to the colour-staining technique developed by Helen ◊Frankenthaler, using thinned-out acrylic paints poured on rough canvas to create the

loudspeaker

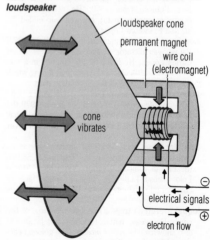

loudspeaker cone
permanent magnet
wire coil (electromagnet)
cone vibrates
electrical signals
electron flow

Louis XIV *A marble bust of the 'Sun King' Louis XIV of France, by Italian sculptor Bernini.*

illusion of vaporous layers of colour. The *Veil* paintings of the 1950s are examples.

Louis /'luːi/ eighteen kings of France:

Louis I *the Pious* 788–840. Holy Roman emperor from 814, when he succeeded his father Charlemagne.

Louis II *the Stammerer* 846–879. King of France from 877, son of Charles the Bald. He was dominated by the clergy and nobility, who exacted many concessions from him.

Louis III 863–882. King of N France from 879, while his brother Carloman (866–84) ruled S France. He was the son of Louis II. He countered a revolt of the nobility at the beginning of his reign, and his resistance to the Normans made him a hero of epic poems.

Louis IV (d'Outremer) 921–954. King of France from 936. His reign was marked by rebellion of nobles who refused to recognize his authority. As a result of his liberality they were able to build up powerful feudal lordships.

He was raised in England after his father Charles III, the Simple, had been overthrown 922 by Robert I. After the death of Raoul, Robert's brother-in-law and successor, Louis was chosen by the nobles to be king. He had difficulties with his vassal Hugh the Great, and skirmishes with Hungarians who had invaded S France.

Louis V 966–987. King of France from 986, last of the ◊Carolingian dynasty.

Louis VI *the Fat* 1081–1137. King of France from 1108. He led his army against feudal brigands, the English (under Henry I) and the Holy Roman Empire, temporarily consolidating his realm and extending it into Flanders. He was a benefactor to the church, and his advisers included Abbot ◊Suger.

Louis VII *c.* 1120–1180. King of France from 1137, who led the Second ◊Crusade.

Louis VIII 1187–1226. King of France from 1223, who was invited to become king of England in place of ◊John by the English barons, and unsuccessfully invaded England 1215–17.

Louis IX St 1214–1270. King of France from 1226, leader of the Seventh and Eighth ◊Crusades. He was defeated in the former by the Muslims, spending four years in captivity, and died in Tunis. He was canonized 1297.

Louis X *the Stubborn* 1289–1316. King of France who succeeded his father Philip IV 1314. His reign saw widespread noble discontent, which he countered by granting charters that guaranteed seignorial rights, although some historians claim that by using evasive tactics, he gave up nothing.

Louis XI 1423–1483. King of France from 1461. He broke the power of the nobility (headed by ◊Charles the Bold) by intrigue and military power.

Louis XII 1462–1515. King of France from 1499. He was duke of Orléans until he succeeded his cousin Charles VIII to the throne. His reign was devoted to Italian wars.

Louis XIII 1601–1643. King of France from 1610 (in succession to his father Henry IV), assuming royal power 1617. He was under the political control of ◊Richelieu 1624–42.

Louis XIV *the Sun King* 1638–1715. King of France from 1643, when he succeeded his father Louis XIII; his mother was Anne of Austria. Until 1661 France was ruled by the chief minister, Mazarin, but later Louis took absolute power, summed up in his saying *L'État c'est moi* ('I am the State'). Throughout his reign he was engaged in unsuccessful expansionist wars—1667–68, 1672–78, 1688–97, and 1701–13 (the War of the ◊Spanish Succession)—against various European alliances, always containing Britain and the Netherlands. He was a patron of the arts.

Greatest of his ministers was Colbert, whose work was undone by the king's military adventures. Louis attempted 1667–68 to annex the Spanish Netherlands, but was frustrated by an alliance of the Netherlands, Britain, and Sweden. Having detached Britain from the alliance, he invaded the Netherlands 1672, but the Dutch stood firm (led by William of Orange; see ◊William III of England) and despite the European alliance formed against France, achieved territorial gains at the Peace of Nijmegen 1678. When war was renewed 1688–97 between Louis and the Grand Alliance (including Britain), formed by William of Orange, the French were everywhere victorious on land, but the French fleet was almost destroyed at ◊La Hogue 1692. The acceptance by Louis of the Spanish throne 1700 (for his grandson) precipitated the War of the Spanish Succession, and the Treaty of Utrecht 1713 ended French supremacy in Europe. In 1660 Louis married the Infanta Maria Theresa of Spain, but he was greatly influenced by his mistresses, including Louise de ◊La Vallière, Mme de ◊Montespan, and Mme de ◊Maintenon.

Louis XV 1710–1774. King of France from 1715, with the Duke of Orléans as regent until 1723. He was the great-grandson of Louis XIV. Indolent and frivolous, Louis left government in the hands of his ministers, the Duke of Bourbon and Cardinal Fleury (1653–1743). On the latter's death he attempted to rule alone, but became entirely dominated by his mistresses, Mme de ◊Pompadour and Mme ◊Du Barry. His foreign policy led to Canada and India being lost to England.

Louis XVI 1754–1793. King of France from 1774, grandson of Louis XV, and son of Louis the Dauphin. He was dominated by his queen, ◊Marie Antoinette, and the finances fell into such confusion that in 1789 the ◊States General had to be summoned, and the ◊French Revolution began. Louis lost his personal popularity June 1791, when he attempted to flee the country (the Flight to Varennes) and in Aug 1792 the Parisians stormed the Tuileries palace and took the royal family prisoner. Deposed Sept 1792, Louis was tried in Dec, sentenced for treason Jan 1793, and guillotined.

Louis XVII 1785–1795. Nominal king of France, the son of Louis XVI. During the French Revolution he was imprisoned with his parents 1792, and probably died in prison.

Louis XVIII 1755–1824. King of France 1814–24, the younger brother of Louis XVI. He assumed the title of king 1795, having fled into exile 1791 during the French Revolution, but became king only on the fall of Napoleon I Apr 1814. Expelled during Napoleon's brief return (the 'hundred days') 1815, he returned after Napoleon's final defeat at Waterloo, pursuing a policy of calculated liberalism until ultra-royalist pressure became dominant after 1820.

Louisiana /luː,iːziˈænə/ state of the S USA; nickname Pelican State

area 135,900 sq km/52,457 sq mi

capital Baton Rouge

towns New Orleans, Shreveport, Lafayette, Lake Charles

Louisiana

features Mississippi delta

products rice, cotton, sugar, maize, oil, natural gas, sulphur, salt, processed foods, petroleum products, lumber, paper

population (1987) 4,461,000, which includes the Cajuns, descendants of 18th-century religious exiles from Canada, who speak a French dialect

famous people Louis Armstrong, Pierre Beauregard, Huey Long

history explored by La Salle; named after Louis XIV and claimed for France 1682; became Spanish 1762–1800; passed to the USA under the ◊Louisiana Purchase 1803; admitted to the Union as a state 1812.

Louisiana Purchase the sale by France in 1803 to the USA of an area covering about 2,144,000 sq km/828,000 sq mi, including the present-day states of Louisiana, Missouri, Arkansas, Iowa, Nebraska, North Dakota, South Dakota, and Oklahoma.

Louis Philippe /'luːi fɪ'liːp/ 1773–1850. King of France 1830–48. Son of Louis Philippe Joseph, Duke of Orléans 1747–93; both were known as *Philippe Égalité* from their support of the 1792 Revolution. He fled into exile 1793–1814, but became king after the 1830 revolution with the backing of the rich bourgeoisie. Corruption discredited his regime, and after his overthrow, he escaped to the UK and died there.

Louisville /'luːivɪl/ industrial city and river port on the Ohio, Kentucky, USA; population (1980) 655,000. Products include electrical goods, agricultural machinery, motor vehicles, tobacco, and baseball bats. It is noted for its Kentucky Fair and Exposition Center, and the Kentucky Derby. See also ◊horseracing.

Lourdes /luəd/ town in SW France with a Christian shrine to St ◊Bernadette which has a reputation for miraculous cures; population (1982) 18,000.

Lourenço Marques /ləˈrensəu ˈmɑːks/ former name of ◊Maputo, capital of Mozambique.

louse parasitic insect, order Anoplura, which lives on mammals. It has a flat, segmented body without wings, and a tube attached to the head, used for sucking blood from its host.

Some occur on humans including the head-louse *Pediculus capitis*, and the body-louse *Pediculus corporis*, a typhus carrier. Most mammals have their own varieties of lice. Biting-lice belong to a different order of insects, Mallophaga, and feed on skin, feathers, or hair.

Louth /lauð/ smallest county of the Republic of Ireland, in Leinster province; county town Dundalk; area 820 sq km/317 sq mi; population (1986) 92,000.

Louvain /luːˈvæn/ (Flemish *Leuven*) industrial town in Brabant province, central Belgium; population (1985) 85,000. Manufacturing includes fertilizers and food processing. Its university dates from 1425.

Louvre /'luːvrə/ French art gallery, former palace of the French kings, in Paris. It was converted by Napoleon to an art gallery 1793, and houses the sculpture *Venus de Milo* and Leonardo da Vinci's *Mona Lisa*.

Lovat /'lʌvət/ Simon Fraser, 12th Baron Lovat *c.* 1667–1747. Scottish ◊Jacobite. Throughout a political career lasting 50 years he constantly

Louvre US architect Pei Ieoh Ming designed the glass pyramid for the Louvre art gallery in Paris 1986–1988.

intrigued with both Jacobites and Whigs, and was beheaded for supporting the 1745 rebellion.

love-bird a small bird of the ◊parrot family.

Lovecraft /'lʌvkrɑːft/ H(oward) P(hillips) 1890 –1937. US writer of horror fiction, whose stories of hostile, supernatural forces, known collectively as the *Cthulhu Mythos*, have lent names and material to many other writers in the genre. Much of his work on this theme was collected in *The Outsider and Others* 1939.

love-in-a-mist perennial plant of S Europe *Nigella damascena*, family Ranunculaceae, with fern-like leaves, and delicate blue or white flowers.

Lovelace /'lʌvleɪs/ Richard 1618–1658. English poet. Imprisoned 1642 for petitioning for the restoration of royal rule, he wrote 'To Althea from Prison', and in a second term in jail 1648 revised his collection *Lucasta* 1649.

Lovell /'lʌvəl/ Bernard 1913– . British radio astronomer, director (until 1981) of ◊Jodrell Bank Experimental Station (now Nuffield radio astronomy laboratories).

During World War II he worked at the Telecommunications Research establishment (1939–45), and in 1951 became professor of radio astronomy at the University of Manchester. His books include *Radio Astronomy* 1951 and *The Exploration of Outer Space* 1961.

Low /ləʊ/ David 1891–1963. New Zealand-born British political cartoonist, creator (in newspapers such as the London *Evening Standard*), of Colonel Blimp, the TUC carthorse, and others.

Low Countries the region of Europe which consists of ◊Belgium and the ◊Netherlands, and usually includes ◊Luxembourg.

Lowell /'ləʊəl/ city in Massachusetts, USA; population (1980) 92,500. Industries include electronics, plastics, and chemicals. Once a textile centre, it was designated a national park in 1978 as a birthplace of the US industrial revolution.

Lowell /'ləʊəl/ Amy (Lawrence) 1874–1925. US poet, who succeeded Ezra Pound as leader of the ◊Imagists. Her works, in free verse, include *Sword-Blades and Poppy Seed* 1916.

Lowell /'ləʊəl/ J(ames) R(ussell) 1819–1891. US critic and poet whose works range from the didactic *The Vision of Sir Launfal* 1848 to satirical poems such as *The Biglow Papers* 1848.

Lowell /'ləʊəl/ Percival 1855–1916. US astronomer, who started the search for 'Planet X' beyond Neptune, which led to the discovery of Pluto. In 1894 he founded the Lowell Observatory at Flagstaff, Arizona, where he reported seeing 'canals' (now known to be an optical illusion) on the surface of Mars.

Lowell /'ləʊəl/ Robert (Traill Spence) 1917–1977. US poet whose work includes *Lord Weary's Castle* 1946 and *For the Union Dead* 1964. A Roman Catholic convert from 1940, he was imprisoned in 1943 as a conscientious objector.

Lower Austria (German *Niederösterreich*) largest federal state of Austria; drained by the Danube; area 19,200 sq km/7,411 sq mi; population (1987) 1,426,000. Its capital is St

Lowry Coming out of School *(1927), Tate Gallery, London.*

Pölten. In addition to wine, sugar-beet, and grain, there are reserves of oil. Manufactured products include textiles, chemicals, and metal goods.

Lower California English name for ◊Baja California, Mexico.

Lower Saxony /'sæksəni/ (German *Niedersachsen*) *Land* of N West Germany
area 47,400 sq km/18,296 sq mi
capital Hanover
towns Brunswick, Osnabrück, Oldenburg, Göttingen, Wolfsburg, Salzgitter, Hildesheim
features formed 1946 from Hanover, Oldenburg, Brunswick, and Schaumburg-Lippe; Lüneburg Heath; Harz mountains
products cereals, cars, machinery, electrical engineering
population (1988) 7,190,000
religion 75% Protestant, 20% Roman Catholic.

Lowestoft /'ləʊstɒft/ most easterly port in Britain, in Suffolk; population (1981) 55,000. The composer Benjamin Britten was born here.

Lowry /'laʊri/ L(aurence) S(tephen) 1887–1976. British painter. Born in Manchester, he lived mainly in nearby Salford. He painted northern industrial townscapes and town life. His characteristic style of matchstick figures and almost monochrome palette emerged in the 1920s.

Loy /lɔɪ/ Myrna. Stage name of Myrna Williams 1905– . US film actess who played Nora Charles in the *Thin Man* series (1943–47) co-starring

William Powell. Her other films include *The Mask of Fu Manchu* 1932 and *The Rains Came* 1939.

Loyalist member of the one-third of the US population remaining loyal to Britain in the War of ◊American Independence. Many went to Canada, especially E Ontario, after 1783. The term also refers to people in Northern Ireland who wish to remain part of the United Kingdom rather than unifying with the Republic of Ireland.

Loyola /lɔɪ'əʊlə/ founder of the Jesuits. See ◊Ignatius Loyola.

Lozère /ləʊ'zeə/ section of the Cévennes Mountains, S France. It rises in Finiels to 1,702 m/5,584 ft, and gives its name to a *département* in Languedoc-Roussillon region.

LPG abbreviation for *liquefied petroleum gas*.

LSD *l*ysergic acid *d*iethylamide, a psychedelic drug and a hallucinogen. Colourless, odourless, and easily synthesized, it is non-addictive, but its effects are unpredictable. Its use is illegal in most countries.

LSI *large-scale integration* the technology by which whole electrical circuits can be etched into a piece of semiconducting material just a few millimetres square. Most of today's electronics industry is based on LSI.

By the late 1960s a complete computer processor could be integrated on a single ◊silicon chip, and in 1971 the US electronics company Intel produced the first commercially available ◊microprocessor. ◊VLSI (very large-scale integration) results in even smaller chips.

Ltd abbreviation for *Limited*; see ◊private limited company.

Lualaba /ˌluːə'lɑːbə/ another name for the upper reaches of the river ◊Zaïre in Africa, as it flows N through Zaïre from near the Zambia border.

Luanda /luː'ændə/ formerly *Loanda* capital and industrial port (cotton, sugar, tobacco, timber, paper, oil) of Angola; population (1988) 1,200,000. It was founded 1575 and became a Portuguese colonial administrative centre as well as an outlet for slaves transported to Brazil.

Luang Prabang /luːˈæŋ prɑː'bæŋ/ or *Louangphraßbang* Buddhist religious centre in Laos, on the Mekong at the head of river navigation; population (1984) 44,244. It was the capital of the kingdom of Luang Prabang, incorporated in Laos in 1946, and the royal capital of Laos 1946–75.

Lubbers /'lʌbəs/ Rudolph (Frans Marie) 1939– . Netherlands politician. He became minister for economic affairs 1973 and prime minister 1983. He initially joined the family engineering business, Lubbers Hollandia.

Lübeck /'luːbek/ seaport of Schleswig-Holstein, West Germany, on the Baltic Sea, 60 km/37 mi NE of Hamburg; population (1988) 209,000. Founded

Lowell US poet Robert Lowell.

1143, it has five Gothic churches and a cathedral from 1173. Once head of the powerful ◊Hanseatic League, it later lost much of its trade to Hamburg and Bremen, but improved canal and port facilities helped it to retain its position as a centre of Baltic trade. Lübeck was a free state of both the Empire and the Weimar Republic. The name Lübeck is of Wendish origin and means 'lovely one'.

Lubetkin /luːˈbetkɪn/ Berthold 1901– . Russian architect, who settled in England in 1930. His pioneering designs include a block of flats in Highgate, London (Highpoint I, 1933–35), and the curvaceous Penguin Pool 1933 at London Zoo, restored 1989.

Lubitsch /ˈluːbɪtʃ/ Ernst 1892–1947. German film director, who worked in the USA from 1921. Starting as an actor in silent films in Berlin, he turned to writing and directing, including *Die Augen der Mummie Ma/The Eyes of the Mummy* 1918 and *Die Austernprinzessin/The Oyster Princess* 1919. In the USA he directed *The Marriage Circle* 1924 and, *The Student Prince* 1927. His sound films include *Design for Living* 1933, *Ninotchka* 1939, and *To Be or Not to Be* 1942.

Lublin /ˈlʊblɪn/ city in Poland, on the Bystrzyca river, 150 km/95 mi SE of Warsaw; population (1985) 324,000. Industries include textiles, engineering, aircraft, and electrical goods. A trading centre from the 10th century, it has an ancient citadel, 16th-century cathedral, and a university (1918). A council of workers and peasants proclaimed Poland's independence at Lublin in 1918; and a Russian-sponsored committee of national liberation, which proclaimed itself the provincial government of Poland at Lublin on 31 Dec 1944, was recognized by Russia five days later.

lubricant a substance used between moving surfaces to reduce friction. Carbon-based (organic) lubricants, commonly called grease and oil, are recovered from petroleum distillation. A solid lubricant is graphite (plumbago), either flaked or emulsified (colloidal) in water (aquadag) or oil (oildag). Semi-solid and liquid lubricants are more important, consisting of animal, vegetable, and mineral oils.

Extensive research has been carried out on chemical additives to lubricants, which can reduce corrosive wear, prevent the accumulation of 'cold sludge' (often the result of stop-start driving in city traffic jams), keep pace with the higher working temperatures of aviation gas turbines, or provide radiation-resistant greases for nuclear power plants. Silicon-based spray-on lubricants are also used domestically; they tend to attract dust and dirt less than carbon-based ones.

Lubumbashi /ˌluːbʊmˈbæʃi/ formerly (until 1986) *Elisabethville* town in Zaïre, on the Lualaba river; population (1984) 543,000. It is chief commercial centre of the Shaba copper-mining region.

Lucan /ˈluːkən/ John Bingham, 7th Earl of Lucan 1934– . British aristocrat and professional gambler. On 7 Nov 1974 his wife was attacked and their children's nanny murdered. No trace of Lucan has since been found, and no solution to the murder.

Lucan /ˈluːkən/ Marcus Annaeus Lucanus 39–65 AD. Latin poet, born in Cordova, a nephew of ◊Seneca and favourite of ◊Nero until the emperor became jealous of his verse. He then joined a republican conspiracy and committed suicide on its failure. His epic *Pharsalia* deals with the civil wars of ◊Caesar and ◊Pompey.

Lucas /ˈluːkəs/ George 1944– . US director and producer. His films, often on science fiction themes and using special effects, include *THX 1138* 1971, *American Graffiti* 1973, and the *Star Wars* trilogy 1977–83.

Lucas /ˈluːkəs/ Robert 1937– . US economist, leader of the Chicago University school of 'new classical' macroeconomics, which contends that wage and price adjustment is almost instantaneous and that the level of unemployment at any time must be the natural rate (it cannot be reduced by government action except

in the short term and at the cost of increasing inflation).

Lucas van Leyden /ˈluːkəs væn ˈlaɪdn/ 1494–1533. Dutch painter and printmaker, active in Leiden and Antwerp. He was a pioneer of Netherlandish genre scenes, for example *The Chess Players* (Staatliche Museen, West Berlin). His woodcuts and engravings were inspired by ◊Dürer, whom he met in Antwerp 1521. Lucas was an influence on ◊Rembrandt.

Lucca /ˈlʊkə/ city in NW Italy; population (1981) 91,246. It was an independent republic from 1160 until its absorption into Tuscany in 1847. The composer Puccini was born here.

Luce /luːs/ Henry Robinson 1898–1967. US publisher, founder of the magazine *Time* 1923, and of the pictorial weekly *Life* 1936. He married Clare ◊Boothe Luce.

lucerne /luːˈsɜːnn/ another name for the plant ◊alfalfa.

Lucerne /luːˈsɜːn/ (German *Luzern*) capital and tourist centre of Lucerne canton, Switzerland, on the Reuss where it flows out of Lake Lucerne; population (1987) 161,000. It developed around the Benedictine monastery, established about 750, and owes its prosperity to its position on the St Gotthard road and railway.

Lucerne, Lake /luːˈsɜːn/ (German *Luzern*) scenic lake in central Switzerland; area 114 sq km/ 44 sq mi.

Lucian /ˈluːsiən/ *c.* 125–*c.*190. Greek writer of satirical dialogues, in which he pours scorn on all religions. He was born at Samosata in Syria, and for a time was an advocate at Antioch, but later travelled before settling in Athens about 165. He occupied an official post in Egypt, where he died.

Lucifer (Latin 'bearer of light') in Christian theology, another name for the ◊devil, the leader of the angels that rebelled against God. Lucifer is also another name for the morning star (the planet ◊Venus).

Lucknow /ˈlʌknaʊ/ capital and industrial city (engineering, chemicals, textiles, many handicrafts) of the state of Uttar Pradesh, India; population (1981) 1,007,000. During the Indian Mutiny against British rule, it was besieged 2 Jul–16 Nov 1857.

Lucretia /luːˈkriːʃiə/ Roman woman, the wife of Collatinus, said to have committed suicide after being raped by Sextus, son of ◊Tarquinius Superbus. According to tradition, this incident led to the dethronement of Tarquinius and the establishment of the Roman Republic 509 BC.

Lucretius /luːˈkriːʃiəs/ (Titus Lucretius Carus) *c.* 99–55 BC. Roman poet and ◊Epicurean philosopher, whose *De Rerum Natura/On the Nature of Things* envisaged the whole universe as a combination of atoms, and had some concept of evolutionary theory. Animals were complex but initially quite fortuitous clusters of atoms, only certain combinations surviving to reproduce.

Lucullus /luːˈkʌləs/ Lucius Licinius 110–56 BC. Roman general and consul. As commander against ◊Mithridates of Pontus 74–66 he proved to be one of Rome's ablest generals and administrators, until superseded by Pompey. He then retired from politics. His wealth enabled him to live a life of luxury, and Lucullan feasts became legendary.

Lüda /ˌluːˈdɑː/ formerly *Hüta* industrial port (engineering, chemicals, textiles, oil refining, shipbuilding, food processing) in Liaoning, China, on Liaodong Peninsula, facing the Yellow Sea; population (1986) 4,500,000. It comprises the naval base of Lüshun (known under 19th-century Russian occupation as Port Arthur) and the commercial port of Dalien (formerly Talien/Dairen).

Both were leased to Russia (who needed an ice-free naval base) 1898, but were ceded to Japan after the ◊Russo-Japanese War; Lüshun was under Japanese siege Jun 1904–Jan 1905. After World War II Lüshun was occupied by Russian airborne troops (returned to China 1955) and Russia was granted shared facilities at Dalien (ended on the deterioration of Sino-Russian relations 1955).

Luddite one of a group of people involved in machine-wrecking riots in N England 1811–16. The organizer of the Luddites was referred to as General Ludd, but may not have existed. Many Luddites were hanged or transported.

The movement, which began in Nottinghamshire and spread to Lancashire, Cheshire, Derbyshire, Leicestershire, and Yorkshire, was primarily a revolt against the unemployment caused by the introduction of machines in the Industrial Revolution.

Ludendorff /ˈluːdndɔːf/ Erich von 1865–1937. German general, chief of staff to ◊Hindenburg in World War I, and responsible for the eastern-front victory at ◊Tannenberg 1914. After Hindenburg's appointment as chief of general staff and Ludendorff's as quartermaster-general 1916, he was also politically influential. He took part in the Nazi rising in Munich 1923, and sat in the Reichstag (parliament) as a right-wing Nationalist.

Lüderitz /ˈluːdərɪts/ port on Lüderitz Bay, SW Africa; population (1970) 6,500. It is a centre for diamond-mining. The town was formerly a German possession named after a German merchant who acquired land here in 1883.

Ludlow /ˈlʌdləʊ/ market town in Shropshire, England; on the river Teme, 42 km/26 mi S of Shrewsbury; population (1983) 8,130. Milton's masque *Comus* was presented at Ludlow Castle in 1634.

Ludwig /ˈlʊdvɪg/ Karl Friedrich Wilhelm 1816–1895. German physiologist who invented graphic methods of recording events within the body. Ludwig demonstrated conclusively that the circulation of the blood is purely mechanical in nature, and involves no occult vital forces. In the course of this work, he invented the kymograph, a rotating drum on which a stylus charts a continuous record of blood pressure and temperature. This was a forerunner of modern monitoring systems.

Ludwig /ˈlʊdvɪg/three kings of Bavaria:

Ludwig I 1786–1868. King of Bavaria 1825–48, succeeding his father Maximilian Joseph I. He made Munich an international cultural centre, but his association with the dancer Lola ◊Montez, who dictated his policies for a year, led to his abdication 1848.

Ludwig II 1845–1886. King of Bavaria from 1864, when he succeeded his father Maximilian II. He supported Austria during the Austro-Prussian War 1866, but brought Bavaria into the Franco-Prussian War as Prussia's ally, and in 1871 offered the German crown to the king of Prussia. He was the composer Wagner's patron, and built the Bayreuth theatre for him. Declared insane 1886, he drowned himself soon after.

Ludwig III 1845–1921. King of Bavaria 1913–1918, when he abdicated upon the formation of a republic.

Ludwigshafen /ˈluːdvɪgzˌhɑːfən/ city and Rhine river port, Rhineland-Palatinate, West Germany; population (1988) 152,000. Industries include chemicals, dyes, fertilizers, plastics, and textiles.

Luening /ˈluːnɪŋ/ Otto 1900– . US composer. He studied in Zurich, and privately with Busoni. In 1949 he joined the staff at Columbia University, and in 1951 began a series of pioneering compositions for instruments and tape, some in partnership with Vladimir Ussachevsky (*Incantation* 1952, *Poem in Cycles*, and *Bells* 1954). In 1959 he became co-director, with ◊Babbitt and Ussachevsky, of the Columbia-Princeton Electronic Music Center.

Luftwaffe German air force. In World War I and, as reorganized by the Nazi leader Goering 1933, in World War II, it also covered anti-aircraft defence and the launching of the flying bombs ◊V1, V2.

Lugano /luːˈgɑːnəʊ/ resort town on Lake Lugano, Switzerland; population (1980) 28,600.

Lugano, Lake /luːˈgɑːnəʊ/ lake partly in Italy, between lakes Maggiore and Como, and partly in Switzerland; area 49 sq km/19 sq mi.

Lugansk /luːˈgænsk/ former name of ◊Voroshilovgrad, (until 1935, and again 1958–70), Ukrainian Republic, USSR.

Lugard /luːˈgɑːd/ Frederick John Dealtry, 1st Baron Lugard 1858–1945. British colonial administrator. He served in the army 1878–89 and then worked for the British East Africa Company, for whom he took possession of Uganda in 1890. He went on to be high commissioner for N Nigeria 1900–07, governor of Hong Kong 1907–12, and governor general of Nigeria 1914–19. He received a barony in 1928.

luge a type of ◊toboggan.

Lugosi /luːˈgəʊsi/ Bela. Stage name of Bela Ferenc Blasko 1882–1956. Hungarian film actor who appeared in Hungarian and German films before going to Hollywood in 1921. His most famous role was *Dracula 1930*, followed by horror roles in *Son of Frankenstein* 1939, *The Body Snatcher* 1945, and *Bride of the Monster* 1956.

lugworm genus *Arenicola* of marine worms (also known as lobworms) that grow up to 25 cm/10 in long, and are common between tide-marks. They are useful for their cleansing and powdering of the sand, of which they may annually bring to the surface about 5,000 tonnes per hectare/1,900 tons per acre.

Lu Hsün /ˈluː ˈʃuːn/ former transcription of Chinese writer ◊Lu Xun.

Luik /laɪk/ Flemish name of ◊Liège, town in Belgium.

Lukács /ˈluːkɑːtʃ/ Georg 1885–1971. Hungarian philosopher, one of the founders of 'Western' or 'Hegelian' Marxism, a philosophical current opposed to the Marxism of the official communist movement.

In *History and Class Consciousness* 1923, he argued that the proletariat was the 'identical subject-object' of history. Under capitalism, social relations were 'reified' (turned into objective things), but the proletariat could grasp the social totality.

Lukács himself repudiated the book, and spent much of the rest of his life as an orthodox communist. He also made major contributions to Marxist aesthetics and literary theory. He believed, as a cultural relativist, that the most important art was that which reflected the historical movement of the time: for the 20th century, ◊socialist realism.

Luke, St /ˈluː ˈʃuːn/ 1st century AD. Traditionally the compiler of the third Gospel and of the Acts of the Apostles in the New Testament. He is the patron saint of painters; his emblem is a winged ox, and his feast day 18 Oct.

Luke is supposed to have been a Greek physician born in Antioch (Antakiyah, Turkey) and to have accompanied Paul after the ascension of Christ.

Luleå /ˈluːliɔː/ port in N Sweden, on the Gulf of Bothnia at the mouth of the river Luleə; population (1986) 66,500. It is the capital of Norrbotten county. Exports include iron ore and timber in ice-free months.

Lully /ˈluːliː/ Jean-Baptiste. Adopted name of Giovanni Battista Lulli 1632–1687. French composer of Italian origin who was court composer to Louis XIV. He composed music for the ballet, for Molière's plays, and established French opera with such works as *Alceste* 1674 and *Armide et Renaud* 1686. He was also a ballet dancer.

lumbago pain in the lower region of the back, usually due to strain or faulty posture. If it occurs with ◊sciatica, it may be due to pressure on spinal nerves by a displaced vertebra. Treatment includes rest, application of heat, and skilled manipulation (see ◊osteopathy). Surgery may be needed in rare cases.

lumbar puncture or *spinal tap* the insertion of a hollow needle between two lumbar (lower back) vertebrae to withdraw a sample of cerebrospinal fluid (CSF) for testing. Normally clear and colourless, the CSF acts as a fluid buffer for the brain and spinal nerves. Changes in its quantity, colour,

lung

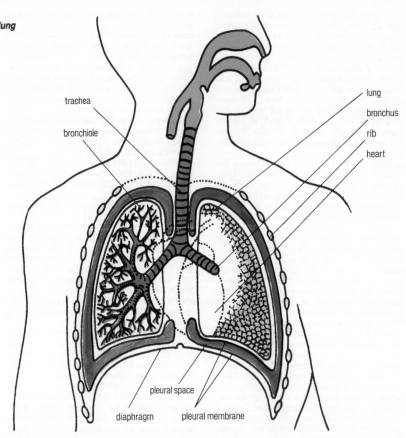

trachea
bronchiole
lung
bronchus
rib
heart
pleural space
diaphragm
pleural membrane

or composition may indicate neurological damage or disease.

Lumbini /lʊmˈbiːni/ birthplace of ◊Buddha in the foothills of the Himalayas near the Nepalese-Indian frontier. A sacred garden and shrine were established 1970 by the Nepalese government.

lumen SI unit (symbol lm) of luminous flux (the amount of light passing through an area per second). The lumen is defined in terms of the light falling on a unit area at a unit distance from a light source of luminous intensity of one ◊candela. One lumen at a wavelength of 5550 angstroms equals 0.0014706 watts.

Lumet /ˈluːmeɪ/ Sidney 1924– . US film director. His films, sometimes marked by a heavy-handed seriousness, have met with varying critical and commercial success. They include *Twelve Angry Men* 1957, *Fail Safe* 1964, *The Deadly Affair* 1967, and *Network* 1976.

Lumière /ˌluːmiˈeə/ Auguste Marie 1862–1954 and Louis Jean 1864–1948. French brothers who pioneered cinematography. In 1895 they patented their cinematograph, a combined camera and projector that operated at 16 frames per second, and opened the world's first cinema in Paris to show their films. The Lumière's first films were short static shots of everyday events such as *La Sorties des Usines Lumière* 1895 about workers leaving a factory and *L'Arroseur Arrosé* 1895, the world's first fiction film. Production was abandoned in 1900.

luminescence emission of light from a body when its atoms are excited by means other than raising its temperature. Short-lived luminescence is called fluorescence; longer-lived luminescence is called phosorescence.

When exposed to an external source of energy, the outer electrons in atoms of a luminescent substance absorb energy and 'jump' to a higher energy level. When these electrons 'jump' back to their former level they emit their excess energy as light. Many different exciting mechanisms are possible: visible light or some other ◊electromagnetic radiation (ultraviolet rays or X-rays), electron bombardment, chemical reactions, friction, and ◊radioactivity. Certain living organisms produce ◊bioluminescence.

luminous paint a preparation containing a mixture of pigment, oil, and a phosphorescent sulphide, usually calcium or barium. After exposure to light it appears luminous in the dark. The luminous paint used on watch faces is slightly radioactive and does not require exposure to light.

lumpenproletariat (German 'ragged proletariat') the poorest of the poor: beggars, tramps, and criminals (Marx).

Lumumba /lʊˈmʊmbə/ Patrice 1926–1961. Congolese politician, prime minister of Zaïre 1960. Imprisoned by the Belgians, but released in time to attend the conference giving the Congo independence 1960, he led the National Congolese Movement to victory in the subsequent general election. He was deposed in a coup d'état, and murdered some months later.

Lunardi /luːˈnɑːdi/ Vincenzo 1759–1806. Italian balloonist. He came to London as secretary to the Neapolitan ambassador, and made the first balloon flight in England from Moorfields in 1784.

Lund /lʊnd/ city in Malmöhus county, SW Sweden; 16 km/10 mi NE of Malmö; population (1986) 83,400. It has an 11th-century Romanesque cathedral and a university established 1666. The treaty of Lund was signed in 1676 after Carl XI had defeated the Danes.

Lundy /ˈlʌndi/ rocky island at the entrance to the Bristol Channel; 19 km/12 mi NW of Hartland Point, Devon, England; area 9.6 sq km/3.7 sq mi; population (1975) 40. Formerly used by pirates and privateers for a lair, it is now a National Trust bird sanctuary and the first British marine reserve (1987).

Lüneburg /ˈluːnəbɜːg/ town in Lower Saxony, West Germany; on the river Ilmenau; population (1985) 61,000. Industries include chemicals, paper, and iron works. It is a health resort.

Lüneburg Heath /ˈluːnəbɜːg/ (German *Lüneburger Heide*) site in Lower Saxony, West

lupin

Germany, between the Elbe and Aller rivers; It was here that more than a million German soldiers surrendered to Montgomery on 4 May 1945.

lung a large cavity of the body, used for gas exchange. Lungs are found in some slugs and snails, particularly those that live on land. Some fish (lungfish) and most tetrapod vertebrates have a pair of lungs, which occupy the thorax (the upper part of the trunk). Their function is to remove carbon dioxide dissolved in the blood and supply oxygen which is carried by ◊haemoglobin in red blood cells. The lung tissue, consisting of multitudes of air sacs and blood vessels, is very light and spongy.

Air is drawn into the lungs through the trachea and bronchi by the expansion of the ribs and the contraction of the diaphragm. The principal diseases of the lungs are tuberculosis, pneumonia, bronchitis, and cancer.

lungfish three genera of the order Dipnoi, found in Africa, South America, and Australia. They grow to about 2 m/6 ft, are eel shaped, long-lived, and in addition to gills have 'lungs' (modified swim bladders) with which they can breathe air in drought conditions. Lungfish are related to ◊coelacanth, and were abundant 350 million years ago.

Lunt /lʌnt/ Alfred 1893–1977. US actor. He went straight from school into the theatre, and in 1922 married Lynn ◊Fontanne with whom he subsequently co-starred in more than 30 successes. They formed a sophisticated comedy duo, and the New York Lunt-Fontanne theatre was named after them. Their shows included *Design for Living* by Noël Coward 1933, *There Shall Be No Night* 1940–41, and *The Visit* 1960.

Luo Guan-zhong /ˈluːəʊˌgwænˈdzɒŋ/ formerly *Luo Kuan-chung* 14th-century Chinese novelist, who reworked popular tales into *The Romance of the Three Kingdoms* and *The Water Margin*.

Luo Kuan-chung earlier form of ◊Luo Guan-zhong.

Luoyang /ˌluːəʊˈjæŋ/ (formerly Loyang) industrial city in Henan province; south of the Yellow river; population 1,114,000. Formerly the capital of China, industries include machinery and tractors.

Lupercalia Roman festival celebrated 15 Feb. It took place at the Lupercal, the cave where ◊Romulus and Remus were supposedly suckled by the wolf (*lupus*). Lupercalia included feasting, dancing, and sacrificing goats. Priests ran round the city carrying whips made from the hides of the sacrificed goats, a blow from which was believed to cure sterility in women.

lupin plant of the genus *Lupinus*, which comprises about 300 species. They are native to Mediterranean regions and parts of North and South America, and some species are naturalized in Britain. The spikes of pea-like flowers may be white, yellow, blue, or pink. *Lupinus albus* is cultivated in some places for cattle fodder, and for green manuring.

lupus in medicine, tuberculosis of the skin (lupus vulgaris). The organism produces ulcers which spread and eat away the underlying tissues. Treatment is primarily with standard antituberculous drugs, such as streptomycin, but ultraviolet light may also be used.

Lupus erythematosus has two forms: *discoid* seen as red, scaly patches on the skin; and,

disseminated or *systemic* LE, which may affect connective tissue anywhere in the body, often involving the internal organs. The latter is much more serious. Treatment is with ◊corticosteroids.

Lurçat /lʊəˈsɑː/ Jean 1892–1966. French artist influenced by the Cubists, who revived tapestry design, as in *Le Chant du Monde*.

Lurgan /ˈlɜːgən/ see ◊Craigavon, town in Northern Ireland.

Lurie /ˈlʊəri/ Alison 1926– . US novelist and critic. Her subtly written and satirical novels include *Imaginary Friends* 1967, *The War Between the Tates* 1974, and *Foreign Affairs* 1985, a tale of transatlantic relations, which won the Pulitzer Prize.

Luristan /ˌlʊərɪˈstɑːn/ or *Lorestan* mountainous province in W Iran; area 28,800 sq km/11,117 sq mi; population (1986) 1,367,000. The capital is Khorramabad. The province is inhabited by Lur tribes who live by their sheep and cattle. Excavation in the area has revealed a culture of the 8th–7th centuries BC with bronzes decorated with animal forms: its origins are uncertain.

Lusaka /luːˈsɑːkə/ capital of Zambia from 1964 (of N Rhodesia 1935–64), 370 km/230 mi NE of Livingstone; commercial and agricultural centre (flour mills, tobacco factories, vehicle assembly, plastics, printing); population (1987) 819,000.

Lüshun-Dalien /ˌluːˈʃuːn ˌdɑːˈlɪən/ see ◊Lüda, port in China.

Lusitania /ˌluːsɪˈteɪnɪə/ ocean liner sunk by a German submarine 7 May 1915 with the loss of 1,200 lives, including some Americans; its destruction helped bring the USA into World War I.

Lusitanian /ˌluːsɪˈteɪnɪən/ member of an ancient people of the Iberian peninsula, inhabiting an area roughly equivalent to modern Portugal. Conquered by Rome in 139 BC, the province of Lusitania rebelled periodically until final conquest by Pompey 73–72 BC.

lusophone the countries in which the ◊Portuguese language is spoken, or which were formerly ruled by Portugal.

Lü-ta /ˌluːˈtɑː/ former name of ◊Lüda, port in China.

lute family of stringed musical instruments of the 14th–18th centuries, including the mandore, theorbo, and chitarrone. They are pear-shaped and plucked with the fingers. Members of the lute family were used both as solo instruments and for vocal accompaniment, and were often played in addition to, or instead of, keyboard ◊continuo instruments in larger ensembles and in opera.

luteinizing hormone a ◊hormone produced by the pituitary gland. In males, it stimulates the testes to produce ◊androgens. In the female ◊menstrual cycle, it works together with follicle stimulating hormone to initiate production of egg cells by the ovary. If fertilization of the egg cell occurs, it plays an important part in maintaining the pregnancy by controlling the levels of oestrogen and progesterone in the body.

lutetium silvery-white metallic element, symbol Lu, atomic number 71, relative atomic mass 174.97. Lutetium is the last of the ◊lanthanide series, and is used in the 'cracking' or breakdown of petroleum, and in other chemical processes.

Luther /ˈluːθə/ Martin 1483–1546. German Christian church reformer, a founder of Protestantism. When a priest at the university of Wittenberg 1517, he attacked the sale of ◊indulgences in 95 theses and defied papal condemnation; the Holy Roman emperor Charles V summoned him to the Diet of Worms 1521, where he refused to retract his objections. After the drawing up of the Augsburg Confession 1530, he gradually retired from the Protestant leadership.

Luther was born in Eisleben, the son of a miner; he studied at the university of Erfurt, spent three years as a monk in the Augustinian convent there, and in 1507 was ordained priest. Shortly afterwards he attracted attention as a teacher and preacher at the university of Wittenberg; and in

1517, after returning from a visit to Rome, he attained nationwide celebrity for his denunciation of the Dominican monk J Tetzel (1455–1519), one of those sent out by the Pope to sell indulgences as a means of raising funds for the rebuilding of St Peter's Basilica in Rome.

On 31 Oct 1517, Luther nailed on the church door in Wittenberg a statement of 95 theses on indulgences, and in the next year he was summoned to Rome to defend his action. His reply was to attack the papal system even more strongly, and in 1520 he publicly burned in Wittenberg the papal bull that had been launched against him. On his way home from the imperial Diet of Worms he was taken into 'protective custody' by the elector of Saxony in the castle of Wartburg. Later he became estranged from the Dutch theologian Erasmus, who had formerly supported him in his attacks on papal authority, and engaged in violent controversies with political and religious opponents.

Formerly condemned by communism, Luther had by the 1980s been rehabilitated as a revolutionary socialist hero, and was claimed as patron saint by both East and West Germany.

Lutheranism a form of Protestant Christianity derived from the life and teaching of Martin Luther; it is sometimes called Evangelical to distinguish it from the other main branch of European Protestantism, the Reformed. The most generally accepted statement of Lutheranism is that of the *Augsburg Confession* 1530 but Luther's Shorter Catechism also carries great weight. It is the largest Protestant body, including some 80 million persons, of whom 40 million are in Germany, 19 million in Scandinavia, 8.5 million in the USA and Canada, with most of the remainder in central Europe.

It is the principal form of Protestantism in Germany, and is the national faith of Denmark, Norway, Sweden, Finland, and Iceland. The organization may be episcopal (Germany, Sweden) or synodal (the Netherlands and USA): the Lutheran World Federation has its headquarters in Geneva. Lutheranism is also very strong in the Midwestern USA where several churches were originally founded by German and Scandinavian immigrants.

Luthuli /luːˈtuːli/ or *Lutuli* Albert 1899–1967. South African politician, president of the African National Congress from 1952. Luthuli, a Zulu tribal chief, preached nonviolence and multiracialism. Arrested 1956, he was never actually tried for treason, although he suffered certain restrictions from 1959. He was under suspended sentence for burning his pass (an identity document required of non-white South Africans) when awarded the Nobel Peace Prize 1960.

Lutine British bullion ship, which sank in the North Sea 1799. Its bell, salvaged 1859, is at ◊Lloyd's. It is sounded once when a ship is missing and twice for good news.

Luton /ˈluːtn/ industrial town in Bedfordshire, England, 53 km/33 mi SW of Cambridge; population (1985) 165,000. Luton airport is a secondary one for London. Manufacturing includes cars, chemicals, electrical goods, ballbearings; and traditional manufacture of hats. Luton Hoo, a Robert Adam mansion, was built in 1762.

Lutoslawski /ˌluːtəʊˈswæfski/ Witold 1913– . Polish composer and conductor, born in Warsaw. His early music, dissonant and powerful (*First Symphony* 1947), was criticized by the communist government, so he adopted a more popular style. With the lifting of artistic repression, he quickly adopted avant-garde techniques, including improvisatory and aleatoric forms. He has written chamber, vocal, and orchestral music, including three symphonies, *Livre pour orchestre* 1968 and *Mi-parti* 1976.

Lutyens /ˈlʌtjənz/ (Agnes) Elisabeth 1906–1983. English composer. Her works, using the 12-tone system, are expressive and tightly organized, and include a substantial amount of chamber music,

Lutyens *The Midland Bank, Manchester, designed by Edwin Lutyens.*

stage, and orchestral works. Her choral and vocal works include a setting of ◊Wittgenstein's *Tractatus* and a cantata *The Tears of Night*. She was the daughter of Edwin Lutyens.

Lutyens /'lʌtjənz/ Edwin Landseer 1869–1944. English architect. His designs ranged from picturesque to Renaissance style country houses and ultimately evolved into a classical style as in the Cenotaph, London, and the Viceroy's House, New Delhi.

Lützen /'lʊtsən/ town in Halle county East Germany, SW of Leipzig, where in 1632 Gustavus Adolphus, king of Sweden, defeated the German commander Wallenstein in the Thirty Years' War; Gustavus was killed in the battle. Napoleon overcame the Russians and Prussians here in 1813.

lux SI unit (symbol lx) of illuminance (the light falling on an object). It is equivalent to the effect of an 'international candle' at a distance of 1 metre, and replaces the foot-candle (1 foot-candle = 10.76 lux).

Luxembourg, Palais du /'lʌksəmbɜːg/ palace in Paris, France, in which the Senate sits. Built 1615 for Marie de' Medici by Salomon de Brosse, it was later enlarged.

Luxembourg /'lʌksəmbɜːg/ capital of Luxembourg; population (1985) 76,000. The 16th-century Grand Ducal Palace, European Court of Justice, and European Parliament secretariat are situated here, but plenary sessions of the parliament are now held only in ◊Strasbourg. Products include steel, chemicals, textiles, and processed food.

Luxembourg /'lʌksəmbɜːg/ landlocked country in W Europe, bordered to the N and W by Belgium, E by West Germany, and S by France.

government Luxembourg is a hereditary and constitutional monarchy. The 1868 constitution, revised 1919 and 1956, provides for a single-chamber legislature, the 60-member chamber of deputies, elected by universal suffrage through a system of proportional representation, for a five-year term. There is also an advisory body called the Council of State, whose 21 members are appointed by the grand duke for life. Any of its decisions can be overruled by the chamber of deputies. The grand duke also appoints a prime minister and council of ministers who are collectively responsible to the chamber. The four main political parties are the Christian Social Party, the Socialist Party, the Democratic Party (or Liberals), and the Communist Party.

history Formerly part of the Holy Roman Empire, Luxembourg became a duchy 1354. From 1482 it was under ◊Habsburg control, and in 1797 was ceded, with Belgium, to France. The 1815 Treaty of Vienna made Luxembourg a grand duchy, ruled by the king of the Netherlands. In 1830 Belgium and Luxembourg revolted against Dutch rule; Belgium achieved independence 1839 and most of Luxembourg became part of it, the rest becoming independent in its own right 1848.

Although a small country, Luxembourg occupies an important position in W Europe, being a founder member of many international organizations, including the European Coal and Steel Community, the European Atomic Energy Commission, and the European Community. It formed an economic union with Belgium and the Netherlands 1948 (◊Benelux), which was the forerunner of wider European cooperation.

Grand Duchess Charlotte (1896–1985) abdicated 1964 after a reign of 45 years, and was succeeded by her son, Prince Jean. Proportional representation has resulted in a series of coalition governments. The Christian Social Party headed most of these from 1945–74, when its dominance was challenged by the Socialists. It regained pre-eminence 1979, and leads the current administration.

Luxembourg /'lʌksəmbɜːg/ province of Belgium; capital Arlon; area 4,400 sq km/1,698 sq mi; population (1987) 227,000.

Luxembourg Accord French-initiated agreement in 1966 that a decision of the Council of Ministers of the European Community may be vetoed by a member whose national interests are at stake.

Luxemburg /'lʌksəmbɜːg/ Rosa 1870–1919. Polish-born German communist, collaborator with Karl Liebknecht in founding the Spartacus League in 1918 (see ◊Spartacist), and murdered with him during the Jan 1919 Berlin workers' revolt.

Luxor /'lʌksɔː/ (Arabic *al-Uqsur*) village in Egypt on the E bank of the Nile near the ruins of ◊Thebes.

Lu Xun /:lu: 'ʃuːn/ pen name of Chon Shu-jêu 1881–1936. Chinese short story writer. His three volumes of satirically realistic stories, *Call to Arms*, *Wandering*, and *Old Tales Retold*, reveal the influence of Gogol. He is one of the most popular of modern Chinese writers.

Luzern /'luːt'seən/ German name of ◊Lucerne, town and lake in Switzerland.

Luxor *The temple of Queen Hatshepsut in Luxor, Egypt, showing a bust of the queen on one of the columns.*

Luzon /luːˈzɒn/ largest island of the ◊Philippines; area 108,130 sq km/41,750 sq mi; capital Quezon City; population (1970) 18,001,270. The chief city is Manila, capital of the Philippines. Products include rice, timber, and minerals. It has US military bases.

Lvov /lvɒf/ (Ukrainian *Lviv*) capital and industrial city of Lvov region in the Ukrainian Republic, USSR; population (1987) 767,000. Industries include textiles, metals, and engineering. The university was founded 1661. It was formerly an important centre on the Black Sea-Baltic trade route. Lvov, founded in the 13th century by a Galician prince (the name means city of Leo or Lev), was Polish 1340–1772, Austrian 1772–1919, Polish 1919–39, and annexed by the USSR 1945. The city was the site of violent nationalist demostrations in Oct 1989.

Luxembourg
Grand Duchy of
(Grand-Duché de Luxembourg)

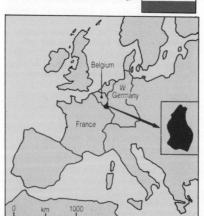

area 2,586 sq km/998 sq mi
capital Luxembourg
physical on the river Moselle; part of the Ardennes (Oesling) forest in the north
features Rupert Murdoch's television satellite Astra is based here

head of state Grand Duke Jean from 1964
head of government Jacques Santer from 1984
political system liberal democracy
political parties Christian Social Party (PCS), moderate, left-of-centre; Luxembourg Socialist Workers' Party (POSL), moderate, socialist; Democratic Party (PD), centre-left; Communist Party of Luxembourg, pro-European left-wing
exports pharmaceuticals, synthetic textiles; international banking is important; Luxembourg is economically linked with Belgium
currency Luxembourg franc (59.60 = £1 Feb 1990)
population (1989) 380,000; annual growth rate 0%
life expectancy men 68, women 74
language French (official); local Letzeburgesch; German
religion Roman Catholic
literacy 100% (1983)
GDP $3.8 bn (1981); $10,444 per head of population
chronology
1948 With Belgium and the Netherlands formed the Benelux customs union.
1958 Benelux became economic union.
1961 Prince Jean became acting head of state on behalf of his mother, Grand Duchess Charlotte.
1964 Grand Duchess Charlotte abdicated and Prince Jean became grand duke.

Lyell Scottish geologist Charles Lyell helped win acceptance for the theory of evolution with his Principles of Geology *1830–33, which asserted that the Earth's crust was gradually wrought through millennia of change.*

LW abbreviation for *long wave*, a radio wave with a wavelength of over 1000 m; one of the main wavebands into which radio frequency transmissions are divided.

LWM abbreviation for *low water mark*.

Lwów /lvuːf/ Polish form of ◊Lvov, city in Ukraine, USSR.

lycanthropy folk belief in human transformation to a ◊werewolf; or, in psychology, a delusion involving this belief.

Lyceum an ancient Athenian gymnasium and garden, with covered walks, where ◊Aristotle taught. It was SE of the city and named after the nearby temple of Apollo Lyceus.

Lyceum London theatre situated in Wellington Street, near the Strand. It was opened in 1809 (rebuilt 1834) and under the management of Henry ◊Irving (1878–1902), saw many of Ellen ◊Terry's triumphs.

lychee alternative spelling of ◊litchi.

Lycurgus /laɪ'kɜːɡəs/ Spartan lawgiver. He is said to have been a member of the royal house, who, while acting as regent, gave the Spartans their constitution and system of education. Many scholars believe him to be purely mythical.

Lydgate /'lɪdɡeɪt/ John *c.* 1370–*c.* 1450. English poet. He was a Benedictine monk, and later prior. His numerous works were often translations or adaptations, such as *Troy Book*, and *Falls of Princes*.

Born probably at Lydgate, Suffolk, he entered the Benedictine abbey of Bury St Edmunds, was ordained in 1397, and was prior of Hatfield Broadoak 1423–34. He was a friend of ◊Chaucer.

Lydia /'lɪdɪə/ ancient kingdom in Anatolia (7th–6th centuries BC), with its capital at Sardis. The Lydians were the first Western people to use standard coinage. Their last king, Croesus, was conquered by the Persians 546 BC.

Lyell /'laɪəl/ Charles 1797–1875. Scottish geologist. In his book *The Principles of Geology* 1830–33, he opposed ◊Cuvier's theory that the features of the Earth were formed by a series of catastrophes, and expounded ◊Hutton's view, known as ◊uniformitarianism, that past events were brought about by the same processes that occur today—a view that influenced Charles ◊Darwin's theory of evolution.

Lyell trained and practised as a lawyer, but retired from the law in 1827 and devoted himself full time to geology and writing. He implied that the Earth was much older than the 6,000 years of prevalent contemporary theory, and provided the first detailed description of the ◊Tertiary period. Although he only in old age accepted that species had changed through evolution, he nevertheless provided Darwin with a geological framework within which evolutionary theories could be placed. Darwin simply applied Lyell's geological method—explaining the past through what is observable in the present—to biology.

Lyly /'lɪli/ John *c.* 1553–1606. English playwright and author of the romance *Euphues, or the Anatomy of Wit* 1578. Its elaborate stylistic devices gave rise to the word 'euphuism' for an affected rhetorical style.

lyme disease a disease transmitted by tick bites which affects all the systems of the body. First described in 1977 following an outbreak in children living around Lyme, Conecticut, USA it is caused by the microorganism *Borrelia burgdorferi*, isolated by Burgdorfer and Barbour in the US in 1982. Untreated, the disease attacks the nervous system, heart, liver, kidney, eyes and joints, but responds to the antibiotic tetracycline. The tick which carries the disease, *Iricinus*, lives on deer, while *B. burgdorferi* relies upon mice during its life cycle.

Lyme Regis /'laɪm 'riːdʒɪs/ seaport and resort in Dorset, S England; population (1981) 3,500. The rebel duke of Monmouth landed here in 1685; and the Cobb (a massive stone pier) features in Jane Austen's *Persuasion* 1818 and John Fowles' *The French Lieutenant's Woman* 1969.

Lymington /'lɪmɪŋtən/ port and yachting centre in Hampshire, S England; 8 km/5 mi SW of Southampton; population (1981) 39,698. It has a ferry link with the Isle of Wight.

lymph the fluid found in the lymphatic system of vertebrates, which carries nutrients, oxygen, and white blood cells to the tissues, and waste matter away from them. It exudes from ◊capillaries into the tissue spaces between the cells and is made up of blood plasma, plus white cells.

Lymph is drained from the tissues by lymph capillaries which empty into larger lymph vessels (lymphatics). These lead to lymph nodes (small, round bodies chiefly situated in the neck, armpit, groin, thorax, and abdomen), which process the ◊lymphocytes produced by the bone marrow, and filter out harmful substances and bacteria. From the lymph nodes, vessels carry the lymph to the thoracic duct and the right lymphatic duct, which lead into the large veins in the neck. Some vertebrates, such as amphibians, have a lymph heart which pumps lymph through the lymph vessels.

lymph nodes small masses of lymphatic tissue in the body, which occur at various points along the major lymphatic vessels. Tonsils and adenoids are large lymph nodes. As the lymph fluid passes through them it is filtered, and bacteria and other

Lynn British singer Vera Lynn captured the hearts of the troops in World War II through her renditions of songs such as 'White Cliffs of Dover'.

microorganisms are engulfed by cells known as macrophages.

Lymph nodes are sometimes mistakenly called 'lymph glands', and the term 'swollen glands' refers to swelling of the lymph nodes caused by infection.

lymphocyte a type of white blood cell with a large nucleus, produced in the bone marrow. Most occur in the ◊lymph and blood, and around sites of infection. *B-lymphocytes* or ◊B cells are responsible for producing ◊antibodies. *T-lymphocytes* or ◊T-cells have several roles forming ◊immunity.

lymphokines chemical messengers produced by ◊lymphocytes that carry messages between the cells of the immune system (see ◊immunity). Examples include interferon, which initiates defensive reactions to viruses, and the interleukins, which activate specific immune cells.

Lynch /lɪntʃ/ 'Jack' (John) 1917– . Irish politician, born in Cork. A noted Gaelic footballer and a barrister, in 1948 he entered the parliament of the republic as a Fianna Fáil member, and was prime minister 1966–73 and 1977–79.

lynching the execution of an alleged offender by a summary court having no legal authority. In the USA it originated on the frontiers, where no regular courts existed. Later examples mostly occurred in the southern states, after the

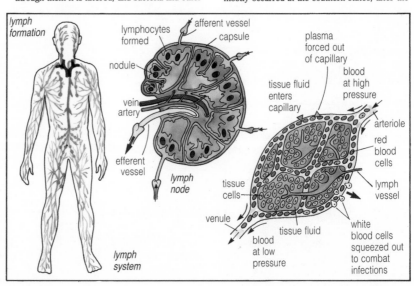

lymph formation

lymphocytes formed

afferent vessel

capsule

nodule

vein
artery

efferent vessel

lymph node

plasma forced out of capillary

tissue fluid enters capillary

blood at high pressure

arteriole

red blood cells

lymph vessel

tissue cells

venule

tissue fluid

blood at low pressure

white blood cells squeezed out to combat infections

lymph system

Civil War, and were racially motivated. During 1882–1900 the annual figure for the USA varied between 96 and 231, but it is today an exceptional occurrence.

Lynn /lɪn/ industrial city in Massachusetts, USA, on Massachusetts Bay; population (1980) 78,471. Founded as Saugus in 1629, it was renamed 1637 after King's Lynn, England.

Lynn /lɪn/ Vera 1917– . British singer, the 'Forces' Sweetheart' of World War II with 'We'll Meet Again' and 'White Cliffs of Dover', and in 1952 'Auf Wiederseh'n, Sweetheart'. Dame of the British Empire 1975.

lynx cat *Felis lynx* found in rocky and forested regions of North America and Europe. Larger than a wild cat, it has a short tail, tufted ears, and the long, silky fur is reddish brown or grey with dark spots. The US bobcat or bay lynx *Felix rufus* is a smaller relative. See also ◊caracal.

Lyon /'liːɒn/ (English *Lyons*) industrial city (textiles, chemicals, machinery, printing) and capital of Rhône *département*, Rhône-Alpes region, and third largest city of France, at the confluence of the Rhône and Saône, 275 km/170 mi NNW of Marseille; population (1982) 418,476, conurbation 1,221,000. Formerly a chief fortress of France, it was the ancient Lugdunum, taken by the Romans 43 BC.

Lyons /'liːɒn/ English form of ◊Lyon, city in France.

Lyons /'laɪənz/ Joseph 1848–1917. British entrepreneur, founder of the catering firm of J Lyons 1894. He popularized 'tea-shops', and the 'Corner Houses', incorporating several restaurants of varying types, were long a feature of London life. From the 1970s the firm moved into other fields of mass catering.

Lyons /'laɪənz/ Joseph Aloysius 1879–1939. Australian politician, founder of the United Australia Party 1931, prime minister 1931–39.

He was born in Tasmania and first elected to parliament in 1929. His wife *Dame Enid Lyons* (1897–) was the first woman member of the House of Representatives and of the federal cabinet.

lyophilization technical term for the ◊freeze-drying process used for foods and drugs, and in the preservation of organic archaeological remains.

Lyra small but prominent constellation of the northern hemisphere, representing the lyre of Orpheus. Its brightest star is Vega.

Epsilon Lyrae, the 'double double', is a system of four linked stars; Beta Lyrae is an eclipsing binary. The Ring Nebula, M57, is a ◊planetary nebula.

lyre stringed instrument of great antiquity. It consists of a soundbox with two curved arms extended upwards to a crosspiece to which four to ten strings are attached. It is played with a plectrum or the fingers. It originated in Asia, and was used in Greece and Egypt.

lyre-bird genus of Australian birds *Menura*. The male has a large lyre-shaped tail, brilliantly coloured. They nest on the ground, and feed on insects, worms, and snails.

Lysander /laɪ'sændə/ Spartan general. He brought the Peloponnesian War to a successful conclusion by capturing the Athenian fleet at Aegospotami 405 BC, and by starving Athens into surrender in the following year. He then aspired to make Sparta supreme in Greece and himself supreme in Sparta; he set up puppet governments in Athens and her former allies, and tried to secure for himself the Spartan kingship, but he was killed in battle with the Thebans.

Lysenko /lɪ'seŋkəʊ/ Trofim Denisovich 1898–1976. Soviet biologist, who believed in the inheritance of ◊acquired characters and used his position under Stalin to officially exclude ◊Mendel's theory of inheritance. He was removed from office after the fall of Khrushchev 1964.

Lysippus /laɪ'sɪpəs/ 4th century BC. Greek sculptor. He made a series of portraits of Alexander the Great (Roman copies survive) and is also known for the *Apoxyomenos*, an athlete (copy in the Vatican), and a colossal *Hercules* (lost).

lysis in biology, any process that destroys a cell by rupturing its lysis membrane (see under ◊lysosome).

Lysistrata a comedy by Aristophanes, produced 411 BC. The women of Athens, tired of war, refuse to make love to their husbands and occupy the Acropolis, to force a peace between the Athenians and the Spartans.

lysosome a structure, or organelle, inside a ◊cell, principally found in animal cells. Lysosomes contain enzymes that can break down proteins and other biological substances. They are bounded by a *lysis membrane* that resists the attack of these enzymes and thus protects the cell from them. They play a part in digestion, and in the white blood cells known as phagocytes the lysosyme enzymes attack ingested bacteria.

Lyte /laɪt/ Henry Francis 1793–1847. British cleric, author of the hymns 'Abide with me' and 'Praise, my soul, the King of Heaven'.

Lytham St Annes /'lɪðəm sənt 'ænz/ resort in Lancashire, England, on the river Ribble; 10 km/6 mi SE of Blackpool; population (1982) 39,641. It has a championship golf course.

Lytton /'lɪtn/ Edward George Earle Lytton Bulwer, 1st Baron Lytton of Knebworth 1803–1873. English writer. His novels successfully followed every turn of the public taste and include the Byronic *Pelham* 1828, *The Last Days of Pompeii* 1834, and *Rienzi* 1835. His plays include *Richelieu* 1838. He was Colonial Secretary 1858–59.

Lytton /'lɪtn/ Edward Robert Bulwer-Lytton, 1st Earl of Lytton 1831–1891. British diplomat, viceroy of India 1876–80, where he pursued a controversial 'forward' policy. Only son of the novelist, he was himself a poet under the pseudonym *Owen Meredith*, writing 'King Poppy' 1892 and other poems.

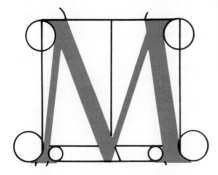

M the 13th letter of the Roman alphabet. It corresponds to the Greek *mu* and the Semitic *mem*, and is almost always sounded as a voiced labial nasal. Finally, or before consonants, it disappears in French, Portuguese, and other languages, leaving a trace in nasalization of the preceding vowel.

m abbreviation for *metre*.

M Roman numeral for *1,000*.

MA in education, abbreviation for *Master of Arts*.

Maas /mɑːs/ Dutch or Flemish name for the river ◊Meuse.

Maastricht /mɑːˈstrɪxt/ industrial city (metallurgy, textiles, pottery) and capital of the province of Limburg, Netherlands, on the river Maas, near the Dutch-Belgian frontier; population (1988) 160,000. Maastricht dates from Roman times.

Maazel /mɑːˈzel/ Lorin (Varencove) 1930– . US conductor and violinist. He studied the violin and made his debut as a conductor at the age of nine. He was conductor of the Cleveland Orchestra 1972–82 and the first US director of the Vienna State Opera.

Mabinogion, the (Welsh *mabinogi* 'instruction for young poets') a collection of medieval Welsh myths and folk tales put together in the mid-19th century and drawn from two manuscripts: *The White Book of Rhydderch* 1300–25 and *The Red Book of Hergest* 1375–1425.

The *Mabinogion* proper consists of four tales, three of which concern a hero named Pryderi. Other stories in the medieval source manuscripts touch on the legendary court of King ◊Arthur.

Mabuse /məˈbjuːz/ Jan. Adopted name of Jan Gossaert *c.*1478–*c.*1533. Flemish painter, active chiefly in Antwerp. His common name derives from his birthplace, Maubeuge. His visit to Italy in 1508 with Philip of Burgundy started a new vogue in Flanders for Italianate ornament and classical influence in painting, including sculptural nude figures.

Maazel US conductor Lorin Maazel made his debut as a conductor at the age of nine and as a violinist a few years later.

McAdam /məˈkædəm/ John Loudon 1756–1836. Scottish engineer. The word 'macadamizing' was coined for his system of constructing roads of broken granite.

macadamia edible nut from trees of the genus *Macadamia*, native to Queensland, Australia, family Proteaceae.

Macao /məˈkaʊ/ Portuguese possession on the south coast of China, about 65 km/40 mi west of Hong Kong, from which it is separated by the estuary of the Canton River; it consists of a peninsula and the islands of Taipa and Colôane.

area 17 sq km/7 sq mi

capital Macao, on the peninsula

features the peninsula is linked to Taipa by a bridge and to Colôane by a causeway, both 2 km long

government internal self-government with a consultative council and a legislative council under a Portuguese governor

currency pataca

population (1986) 426,000

language Cantonese; Portuguese (official)

religion Buddhist, with 6% Catholic minority

government under the constitution (organic statute) of 1976, Macao enjoys considerable political autonomy. The Portuguese president controls the colony's external affairs but appoints, in consultation with the local legislative assembly, a governor to exercise control over domestic matters. The governor works with a cabinet of five appointed secretaries and confers with a ten-member consultative council and a 17-member legislative council, both composed of a mixture of elected

Macao

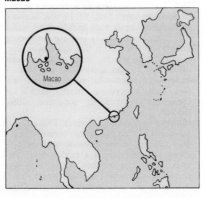

MacArthur US general Douglas MacArthur in 1945. He had been Allied commander in the SW Pacific area since 1942 and helped mastermind the defeat of Japan in World War II.

and nominated members. The legislative council frames internal legislation, but any bills passed by less than a two-thirds majority can be vetoed by the governor. A number of 'civic associations' and interest groups function, sending representatives to the legislative council.

history Macao was first established as a Portuguese trading and missionary post in the Far East 1537, and was leased from China 1557. It was annexed 1849 and recognized as a Portuguese colony by the Chinese government in a treaty 1887. The port declined in prosperity during the late 19th and early 20th centuries, as its harbour silted up and international trade was diverted to Hong Kong and the new treaty ports. The colony thus concentrated instead on local 'country trade' and became a centre for gambling and, later, tourism.

In 1951 Macao became an overseas province of Portugal, sending an elected representative to the Lisbon parliament. After the Portuguese revolution 1974, it became a 'special territory' and was granted considerable autonomy under a governor appointed by the Portuguese president.

In 1986 negotiations opened between the Portuguese and the Chinese government over the question of the return of Macao's sovereignty under similar 'one country, two systems' terms to those agreed by China and the UK for ◊Hong Kong. These negotiations proved successful and were concluded Apr 1987 by the signing of the Macao Pact, under which Portugal agreed to hand over sovereignty to the People's Republic Dec 1999, and China agreed in return to guarantee to maintain the port's capitalist economic and social system for at least 50 years.

macaque type of monkey of the genus *Macaca*. Various species of these medium-sized monkeys live in forests from the Far East to N Africa. The ◊rhesus and the ◊Barbary ape are part of this group. Macaques range from long-tailed to tailless types, and have well-developed cheek pouches to carry food.

MacArthur /məˈkɑːθə/ Douglas 1880–1964. US general in World War II, commander of US forces in the Far East and, from Mar 1942, of the Allied forces in the SW Pacific. After the surrender of Japan he commanded the Allied occupation forces there. During 1950 he commanded the UN forces in Korea, but in Apr 1951, after expressing views contrary to US and UN policy, he was relieved of all his commands by President Truman.

The son of an army officer, born in Arkansas, MacArthur became chief of staff 1930–35. He defended the Philippines against the Japanese

1941–42 and escaped to Australia. He was responsible for the reconquest of New Guinea 1942–45 and of the Philippines 1944–45, being appointed general of the army 1944. In the Korean War, he invaded the North until beaten back by Chinese troops; his threats to bomb China were seen as liable to start World War III and he was removed from command, but received a hero's welcome on his return to the USA.

MacArthur /məˈkɑːθə/ John 1767–1834. Australian colonist, a pioneer of sheep breeding and vine growing. He quarrelled with successive governors of New South Wales, and, when arrested by ◊Bligh, stirred up the **Rum Rebellion** 1808, in which Bligh was himself arrested and deposed.

Born in Devonshire, England, MacArthur went to Sydney in 1790, and began experiments in sheep breeding in 1794, subsequently importing from South Africa the merino strain. In later years he studied viticulture and planted vines from 1817, establishing the first commercial vineyard in Australia.

Macassar /məˈkæsə/ another name for ◊Ujung Pandang, port in the Celebes, Indonesia.

Macaulay /məˈkɔːli/ Rose 1881–1958. English novelist, The serious vein of her early novels changed to light satire in *Potterism* 1920 and *Keeping up Appearances* 1928. Her later books include *The Towers of Trebizond* 1956.

Macaulay /məˈkɔːli/ Thomas Babington, Baron Macaulay 1800–1859. English historian, essayist, poet, and politician, secretary of war 1839–41. His *History of England* in five volumes 1849–51 celebrates the Glorious Revolution of 1668 as the crowning achievement of the Whig party.

He entered Parliament as a liberal Whig in 1830. In India 1834–38, he redrafted the Indian penal code. He sat again in Parliament 1839–47 and 1852–56, and in 1857 accepted a peerage. His works include an essay on Milton 1825 published in the *Edinburgh Review*, a volume of verse, *Lays of Ancient Rome* 1842, and the *History of England* 1848–61 covering the years up to 1702.

macaw large, brilliantly coloured, long-tailed tropical American ◊parrot.

Macbeth /məkˈbeθ/ King of Scotland from 1040. The son of Findlaech, hereditary ruler of Moray, he was commander of the forces of Duncan I, King of Scotia, whom he killed in battle 1040. His reign was prosperous until Duncan's son Malcolm III led an invasion and killed him at Lumphanan. Shakespeare's tragedy *Macbeth* was based on the 16th-century historian ◊Holinshed's *Chronicles*.

Macbeth a tragedy by William Shakespeare, first performed 1605–06. Acting on a prophecy by three witches that he will be king of Scotland, Macbeth, a general of King Duncan, egged on by Lady Macbeth, murders Duncan and becomes king but is eventually killed by Macduff.

McBride Willie John 1940– . Irish Rugby Union player. He was capped 63 times by Ireland, and won a record 17 British Lions caps. He played on five Lions tours, 1962, 1966, 1968, 1971, and in 1974 as captain, when they returned from South Africa undefeated.

CAREER HIGHLIGHTS

British Lions tours:
1962 South Africa
1966 Australia and New Zealand
1968 South Africa
1971 Australia and New Zealand
1974 South Africa (captain)
1983 New Zealand (manager).

McCabe /məˈkeɪb/ John 1939– . English pianist and composer. His works include three symphonies; orchestral works, including *The Chagall Windows*; and songs.

Maccabees /ˈmækəbiːz/ Jewish family, sometimes known as the **Hasmonaeans**. It was founded by the priest Mattathias (died 166 BC) who, with his sons, led the struggle for Jewish independence against the Syrians in the 2nd century BC. This story is told in the book of Maccabees in the

McCarthy US senator Joe McCarthy exhibiting 'evidence' to the House of Representatives Un-American Activities Committee.

◊Apocrypha. Judas (died 161 BC) reconquered Jerusalem 165 BC, and Simon (died 135 BC) established Jewish independence 142 BC.

McCarran /məˈkærən/ Patrick 1876–1954. US Democrat politician. He became senator for Nevada 1932, and as an isolationist strongly opposed ◊lend-lease during World War II. He sponsored the McCarran-Walter Immigration and Nationality Act of 1952, which severely restricted entry and immigration to the USA; the act was amended 1965.

McCarthy /məˈkɑːθi/ Joseph R(aymond) 'Joe' 1909–1957. US right-wing Republican politician, whose unsubstantiated claim 1950 that the State Department had been infiltrated by Communists started a wave of anticommunist hysteria, wild accusations, and blacklists, which continued until he was discredited 1954.

A lawyer, McCarthy became senator for his native Wisconsin in 1946, and in Feb 1950 caused a sensation by claiming to hold a list of about 200 Communist Party members working in the State Department. This was in part inspired by the ◊Hiss case. McCarthy continued a witch-hunting campaign until 1954, when he turned his attention to the army, and it was shown that he and his aides had been falsifying evidence. By this time, however, many thousands of people in public life and the arts had been unofficially blacklisted as suspected Communists or fellow travellers (communist sympathizers). He gave his name to the practice of McCarthyism (making unsupported accusations).

McCarthy /məˈkɑːθi/ Mary (Therese) 1912–1989. US novelist and critic. Much of her work looks probingly at US society, for example the novels *The Groves of Academe* 1952, which describes the anticommunist witch-hunts of the time (see J ◊McCarthy), and *The Group* 1963, which follows the post-college careers of eight women.

McCartney Paul 1942– . Rock singer, songwriter, and bass guitarist, former member of the ◊Beatles, and leader of the pop group Wings 1971–81. His subsequent solo hits have included collaborations with Michael Jackson and Elvis Costello.

McClellan /məˈklelən/ George Brinton 1826–1885. US Civil War general, commander in chief of the Union forces 1861–62. He was dismissed by President Lincoln when he delayed five weeks in following up his victory over the Confederate general Lee at Antietam (see under ◊Civil War, American). He was the unsuccessful Democrat presidential candidate against Lincoln in 1864.

Macclesfield /ˈmækəlzfiːld/ industrial town (textiles, light engineering, paper, plastics) in Cheshire, NW England; population (1986) 151,800.

McClintock /məˈklɪntɒk/ Barbara 1902– . US geneticist, who concluded that ◊genes changed their position on the chromosome from generation to generation in a random way. This would explain how originally identical cells take on specialized functions as skin, muscle, bone, and nerve, and also how evolution could give

rise to the multiplicity of species. She worked at the Carnegie Institute, Cold Spring Harbor, New York.

McClintock /məˈklɪntɒk/ Francis Leopold 1819–1907. Irish polar explorer and admiral. He discovered the fate of the John ◊Franklin expedition and further explored the Canadian Arctic.

McClure /məˈklʊə/ Robert John le Mesurier 1807–1873. Irish-born British admiral and explorer. While on an expedition 1850–54 searching for John ◊Franklin, he was the first to pass through the Northwest Passage.

McCormick /məˈkɔːmɪk/ Cyrus Hall 1809–1884. US inventor of the reaping machine in 1831, which revolutionized 19th-century agriculture.

McCowen /məˈkaʊən/ Alec 1925– . British actor. His Shakespearean roles include Richard II and the Fool in *King Lear*; he is also noted for his dramatic one-man shows.

MacCready /məˈkriːdi/ Paul 1925– . US designer of the *Gossamer Condor* aircraft which made the first controlled flight by human power alone in 1977. His *Solar Challenger* flew from Paris to London under solar power; and in 1985 he constructed a powered replica of a ◊pterodactyl.

McCullers /məˈkʌləz/ Carson (Smith) 1917–1967. US novelist. Most of her writing (including her best-known novels *The Heart is a Lonely Hunter* 1940 and *Reflections in a Golden Eye* 1941) is set in the Southern states, where she was born, and deals with spiritual isolation, containing elements of sometimes macabre violence.

MacDermot /məkˈdɜːmət/ Galt 1928– . US composer. He wrote the rock musical *Hair* 1967, with lyrics by Gerome Ragni and James Rado. It opened in London 1968, the day stage censorship ended, and challenged conventional attitudes about sex, drugs, and the war in Vietnam.

McDiarmid /məkˈdɜːmɪd/ Hugh. Pen name of Christopher Murray Grieve 1892–1978. Scottish nationalist and Marxist poet. His works include *A Drunk Man looks at the Thistle* 1926 and two *Hymns to Lenin* 1930, 1935.

Macdonald /məkˈdɒnld/ John Alexander 1815–1891. Canadian Conservative politician. He was born in Glasgow but taken to Ontario as a child. In 1857 he became prime minister of Upper Canada. He took the leading part in the movement for federation, and in 1867 became the first prime minister of Canada. He was defeated 1873, but returned to office 1878, and retained it until his death.

Macdonald /məkˈdɒnld/ Flora 1722–1790. Scottish heroine who rescued Prince Charles Edward Stuart, the Young Pretender, after his defeat at Culloden in 1746. Disguising him as her maid, she escorted him from her home in the Hebrides to France. She was arrested, but released in 1747.

MacDonald /məkˈdɒnld/ (James) Ramsay 1866–1937. British Labour politician. He joined the ◊Independent Labour Party 1894, and became first secretary of the new Labour Party 1900. In Parliament he led the party 1906–14 and 1922–31, and was prime minister of the first two Labour governments, Jan–Oct 1924 and 1929–31, and of a coalition 1931–35, for which he left the party.

MacDonald was born in Scotland, the son of a labourer. He was elected to Parliament 1906, and led the party until 1914, when his opposition to World War I lost him the leadership. This he recovered 1922, and in Jan 1924 he formed a government dependent on the support of the Liberal Party. When this was withdrawn in Oct the same year, he was forced to resign. He returned to office 1929, again as leader of a minority government, which collapsed 1931 as a result of the economic crisis. MacDonald left the Labour Party to form a national government with backing from both Liberal and Conservative parties. He resigned the premiership 1935, remaining Lord President of the Council.

Macdonnell Ranges /ˌmækdəˈnel/ mountain range in central Australia, Northern Territory, with the town of Alice Springs; highest peak Mount Zeil 1,510 m/4,955 ft.

MacDowell /mək'dauəl/ Edward Alexander 1860–1908. US Romantic composer, influenced by ◊Liszt. His works include the *Indian Suite* 1896, and piano concertos and sonatas.

Macedonia ancient region of Greece, forming parts of modern Greece, Bulgaria, and Yugoslavia. Macedonia gained control of Greece after Philip II's victory at Chaeronea in 338 BC. His son, ◊Alexander the Great, conquered a vast empire. Macedonia became a Roman province in 146 BC.

Macedonia /ˌmæsɪ'dəʊnɪə/ (Greek **Makedhonia**) mountainous region of N Greece, bounded to the W and N by Albania and Yugoslavia; population (1981) 2,122,000; area 34,177 sq km/13,200 sq mi. Chief city is Thessaloniki. Fertile valleys produce grain, olives, grapes, tobacco and livestock. Mt Olympus rises to 2,918 m/9,570 ft on the border with Thessaly.

Macedonia /ˌmæsɪ'dəʊnɪə/ (Serbo-Croat **Makedonija**) a federal republic of Yugoslavia
area 25,700 sq km/9,920 sq mi
capital Skopje
physical mountainous; chief rivers Struma and Vardar
population (1981) 2,040,000, including 1,280,000 Macedonians, 380,000 Albanians, and 90,000 Turks
language Macedonian, closely allied to Bulgarian and written in Cyrillic
religion Macedonian Orthodox Christian
history Macedonia was an ancient country of SE Europe between Illyria, Thrace, and the Aegean Sea; settled by Slavs in the 6th century; conquered by Bulgars in the 7th century, by Byzantium 1014, by Serbia in the 14th century, and by the Ottoman Empire 1355; divided between Serbia, Bulgaria, and Greece after the Balkan Wars of 1912–13.

Maceió /ˌmæseɪ'əʊ/ industrial town (sugar, tobacco, textile, timber industries) in NE Brazil, capital of Alagoas state with its port at Jaraguá; population (1980) 375,800.

McEvoy /'mækɪvɔɪ/ Ambrose 1878–1927. British artist, watercolourist, and painter of delicate portraits of women.

McEwan /mə'kjuːən/ Ian 1948– . English novelist and short-story writer. His tightly written works often have sinister or macabre undertones and contain elements of violence and bizarre sexuality, as in the short stories *First Love, Last Rites* 1975. His novels include *The Comfort of Strangers* 1981 and *The Child in Time* 1987.

Macgillycuddy's Reeks /mə'gɪlɪˌkʌdiz 'riːks/ a range of mountains in SW Ireland lying W of Killarney, in County Kerry; includes Carrantuohill 1,041 m/3,414 ft, the highest peak in Ireland.

McGinley /mə'gɪnlɪ/ Phyllis 1905–1978. Canadian-born US writer of light verse. She became a contributor to the *New Yorker* magazine and published many collections of social satire. Her works include *One More Manhattan* 1937 and *The Love Letters of Phyllis McGinley* 1954.

McGonagall /mə'gɒnəgəl/ William 1830–1902. Scottish poet, noted for the unintentionally humorous effect of his extremely bad serious verse, for example, his poem on the Tay Bridge disaster of 1879.

Mach /mɑːk/ Ernst 1838–1916. Austrian philosopher and physicist. He was an empiricist, believing that science was a record of facts perceived by the senses, and that acceptance of a scientific law depended solely on its standing the practical test of use; he opposed concepts such as Newton's 'absolute motion'. He researched airflow, and ◊Mach numbers are named after him.

He was originally a professor of mathematics at Graz, and became professor of philosophy at Prague 1867–95 and Vienna 1895–1901.

Machado /mə'tʃɑːdəʊ/ Antonio 1875–1939. Spanish poet and dramatist. Born in Seville, he was inspired by the Castilian countryside

Machiavelli *Italian diplomat and writer Niccolò Machiavelli's reputation rests largely on his work* The Prince.

in his lyric verse, contained in *Campos de Castilla/Countryside of Castile* 1912.

Machado de Assis /mə'ʃɑːdəʊ di ə'siːs/ Joaquim Maria 1839–1908. Brazilian writer and poet. He is regarded as the greatest Brazilian novelist. His sceptical, ironic wit is well displayed in his 30 volumes of novels and short stories, including *Epitaph for a Small Winner* 1880 and *Dom Casmurro* 1900.

Machaut /mæ'ʃəʊ/ Guillaume de 1300–1377. French poet and composer. Born in Champagne, he was in the service of John of Bohemia for 30 years and, later, of King John the Good of France. He gave the forms of the *ballade* and *rondo* a new individuality and ensured their lasting popularity.

Machel /mæ'ʃel/ Samora 1933–1986. Mozambique nationalist leader, president 1975–86. Machel was active in the liberation front ◊Frelimo from its conception 1962, fighting for independence from Portugal. He became Frelimo leader 1966, and Mozambique's first president, from independence until his death in a plane crash near the South African border.

Machen /'mækɪn/ Arthur 1863–1947. Welsh author. Characterized by mystic symbolism and the supernatural, his writings include *House of Souls* 1906 and *Angels of Mons* 1915.

Machiavelli /ˌmækɪəveli/ Niccolò 1469–1527. Italian politician and author, whose name is now synonymous with cunning and cynical statecraft. In his most important political works, *Il principe/The Prince* 1513 and *Discorsi/Discourses* 1531, he discusses ways in which rulers can advance the interests of their states (and themselves) through an often amoral and opportunist manipulation of other people.

Machiavelli was born in Florence and was second chancellor to the republic 1498–1512. On the accession to power of the Medici 1512, he was arrested and imprisoned on a charge of conspiracy, but in 1513 released to exile in the country. *The Prince*, based on his observations of Cesare ◊Borgia, is a guide for the future prince of a unified Italian state. In *L'Arte della guerra/The Art of War* 1520 he outlined the provision of an army for the prince, and in *Historie fiorentine/History of Florence* he analysed the historical development of Florence until 1492. Among his later works are the comedies *La Mandragola/The Mandrake* 1524 and *Clizia*.

machine a device that allows a small force (the effort) to overcome a larger one (the load). There are three basic machines: the sloping or inclined plane, the lever, and wheel and axle. All other machines are combinations of these three basic types. Simple machines derived from the inclined

plane include the wedge and the screw; the spanner is derived from the lever; the pulley from the wheel.

The two important features of a machine are the mechanical advantage, which is the ratio load/effort, and the efficiency, which is the work done by the load divided by the work done by the effort; the latter is expressed as a percentage. In a perfect machine, with no friction, the efficiency is 100%. All practical machines have efficiencies of less than 100%, otherwise perpetual motion would be possible.

machine code in computing, the 'language' that the computer itself understands. In machine-code programs, instructions and storage locations are represented as binary numbers. a programmer writes programs in a high-level (easy-to-use) language, which are converted to machine code by a ◊compiler or ◊interpreter program within the computer.

machine gun a rapid-firing automatic gun. The forerunner of the modern machine gun was the Gatling (named after its US inventor R J Gatling 1818–1903), perfected in the USA in 1860 and used in the Civil War. It had a number of barrels arranged about a central axis, and the breech containing the reloading, ejection, and firing mechanism was rotated by hand, shots being fired through each barrel in turn.

The Maxim (named after its inventor, US-born British engineer H S Maxim 1840–1916) of 1884 was recoil-operated, but some later types have been gas-operated (Bren) or recoil assisted by gas (some versions of the Browning).

The **sub-machine-gun**, exploited by Chicago gangsters in the 1920s, was widely used in World War II; for instance, the Thompson, often called the Tommy gun. See ◊small arms.

machine politics the organization of a local political party to ensure its own election by controlling the electorate, and then to retain power through control of key committees and offices. The idea of machine politics was epitomized in the USA in the late 19th century, where it was used to control individual cities.

machine tool a power-driven machine for cutting and shaping metals. Machine tools have powerful electric motors to force cutting tools into the metal workpiece. They are made from hardened steel containing heat-resistant metals such as tungsten and chromium. The use of precision machine tools in ◊mass production assembly methods ensures that all duplicate parts produced are virtually identical.

Many machine tools now work automatically under computer control and are a key factor in factory ◊automation. The commonest machine tool is the ◊lathe, which shapes shafts and similar objects. A ◊milling machine cuts metal with a rotary toothed cutting wheel. Other machine tools cut, plane, grind, drill and polish.

Mach number ratio of the speed of a body to the speed of sound in the undisturbed medium through which the body travels. Mach 1 is reached when a body (especially an aircraft) has a velocity greater than that of sound ('passes the sound barrier'), namely 331 m sec^{-1}/1,087 ft sec^{-1} at sea level. Named after Austrian physicist Ernst Mach (1838–1916).

Machtpolitik (German) power politics.

Machu Picchu /'mɑːtʃuː 'piːktʃuː/ a ruined Inca city in Peru, built *c.* AD 1500, NW of Cuzco, discovered in 1911 by Hiram Bingham. It stands at the top of 300 m/1,000 ft high cliffs, and contains the well-preserved remains of houses and temples.

Macias Nguema /mə'siːəs əŋ'gweɪmə/ former name (until 1979) of ◊Bioko, an island of Equatorial Guinea in the Bight of Bonny, West Africa.

McIndoe /'mækɪndəʊ/ Archibald 1900–1960. New Zealand plastic surgeon. Born at Dunedin, New Zealand, he became famous in England during World War II for his remodelling of the faces of badly burned pilots, and formed the Guinea Pig Club for them.

Machu Picchu *Undiscovered by the Spanish, the Inca city of Machu Picchu remained hidden until the 20th century.*

MacInnes /məˈkɪnɪs/ Colin 1914–1976. English novelist, son of the novelist Angela Thirkell. He made a reputation with sharp depictions of London youth and subcultures of the 1950s, such as *City of Spades* 1957 and *Absolute Beginners* 1959.

Macintosh /ˈmækɪntɒʃ/ Charles 1766–1843. Scottish manufacturing chemist who invented a waterproof fabric lined with a rubber that was used for raincoats—hence 'mackintosh'. Other waterproofing processes have now largely superseded this method.

McKay /məˈkaɪ/ Heather Pamela (born Blundell) 1941– . Australian squash player. She won the British Open title an unprecedented 16 years in succession 1962–1977. She also won 14 consecutive Australian title 1960–1973 and was twice the World Open champion (inaugurated 1976). Between 1962 and 1980 she was unbeaten. She moved to Canada 1975 and became the country's outstanding racquetball player.

CAREER HIGHLIGHTS

World Open: 1976, 1979
British Open: 1962–77
Australian Open: 1960–73

Mackay of Clashfern Baron James Peter Hymers 1927– . Scottish lawyer and conservative politician. The son of a railway signalman, he won first class honours in mathematics and statistics and after a period of teaching and research switched to law, being called to the Bar in 1955. Ten years later he became a QC and in 1979 was unexpectedly made Lord Advocate for Scotland, and a life peer. He became Lord Chancellor in 1987, and in 1989 announced a reform package to end legal restrictive practices including prohibiting the barrister's monopoly of advocacy in the higher courts promoting the combination of the work of barristers and solicitors in 'mixed' practices, and allowing building societies and banks to do property conveyacing, formerly limited to solicitors. The plans met with fierce opposition.

Macke /ˈmækə/ August 1887–1914. German painter, a founder member of the ◊*Blaue Reiter* group in Munich. With Franz ◊Marc he developed a semi-abstract style comprising Cubist and Fauve characteristics.

Macke visited Paris in 1907. In 1909 he met Marc, and together they went to Paris 1912, where they encountered the abstract style of Robert Delaunay. In 1914 Macke visited Tunis with ◊Klee, and was inspired to paint a series of brightly coloured watercolours largely composed of geometrical shapes but still representational. He was killed in World War I.

McKellen /məˈkelən/ Ian 1939– . British actor, whose stage roles include Richard II and Edward II, and Mozart in the stage version of *Amadeus*. His films include *Priest of Love* 1982 and *Plenty* 1985.

Mackendrick /məˈkendrɪk/ Alexander 1912– . American born, Scottish director responsible for some of ◊Ealing studio's finest comedies, including *Whisky Galore* 1949 and *The Man in the White Suit* 1951. He later made several films in America like *Mandy* 1952 and *Sweet Smell of Success* 1957 before becoming a film lecturer.

Mackensen /ˈmækənzən/ August von 1849–1945. German field marshal. During ◊World War I he achieved the breakthrough at Gorlice and the conquest of Serbia 1915, and in 1916 played a major role in the overthrow of Romania. After the war Mackensen retained his popularity to become a folk hero of the German army.

Mackenzie /məˈkenzi/ Alexander *c.*1755–1820. British explorer and fur trader. In 1789, he was the first European to see the river, now part of N Canada, named after him. In 1792–93 he crossed the Rockies to the Pacific.

Mackenzie /məˈkenzi/ Compton 1883–1972. Scottish author. His parents were actors. He was educated at Magdalen College, Oxford University, and published his first novel *The Passionate Elopement* in 1911. Later works were *Carnival* 1912, *Sinister Street* 1913–14 (an autobiographical novel), and the comic *Whisky Galore* 1947. He published his autobiograaphy in ten 'octaves' (volumes) 1963–71.

Mackenzie /məˈkenzi/ William Lyon 1795–1861. Canadian politician, born in Scotland. He emigrated to Canada in 1820, and led the rebellion of 1837–38, an unsuccessful attempt to limit British rule and establish more democratic institutions in Canada. After its failure he lived in the USA until 1849, and in 1851–58 sat on the Canadian legislature as a Radical. He was grandfather of W L Mackenzie King, the Liberal prime minister.

Mackenzie River /məˈkenzi/ river in the Northwest Territories, Canada, flowing from Great Slave Lake NW to the Arctic Ocean; about 1,800 km/1,120 mi long. It is the main channel of the Finlay-Peace-Mackenzie system, 4,241 km/2,635 mi long. It was named after the British explorer Alexander Mackenzie, who saw it 1789.

mackerel pelagic fish *Scomber scombrus* found in the N Atlantic and Mediterranean. It is blue with irregular black bands down its sides, the latter and the under surface showing a metallic sheen. The largest of the mackerels is the tuna, which weighs up to 700 kg/1,550 lb, and the smallest is the common mackerel 0.7 kg/1.5 lb.

Mackerras /məˈkerəs/ Charles 1925– . Australian conductor. Known for his advocacy of the music of ◊Janáček, whom he has helped to popularize, he was conductor of the English National Opera 1970–78, and was knighted in 1979.

McKinley, Mount /məˈkɪnli/ peak in Alaska, USA, the highest in North America, 6,194 m/20,320 ft; named after US president William McKinley. See ◊Rocky Mountains.

McKinley /məˈkɪnli/ William 1843–1901. 25th president of the USA 1897–1901, a Republican. He was born in Ohio, and elected to Congress 1876. His period as president was marked by the USA's adoption of an imperialist policy, as exemplified by the Spanish-American War 1898 and the annexation of the Philippines. He was assassinated in Buffalo, New York.

Mackintosh /ˈmækɪntɒʃ/ Charles Rennie 1868–1928. Scottish ◊Art Nouveau architect, designer, and painter, who exercised considerable influence on European design. His work includes the Glasgow School of Art 1896.

Mackmurdo /məkˈmɜːdəʊ/ Arthur H 1851–1942. English designer and architect. He founded the Century Guild in 1882, a group of architects, artists, and designers inspired by William ◊Morris and John ◊Ruskin. His book and textile designs are forerunners of ◊Art Nouveau.

Maclaine /məˈkleɪn/ Shirley. Stage name of Shirley MacLean Beaty 1934– . US actress, sister of Warren Beatty. She has played both comedy and dramatic roles. Her many offscreen interests have limited her film appearances, which include *The Trouble with Harry* 1955, *The Apartment* 1960, and *Terms of Endearment* 1983.

McLaren racing car company, makers of the most successful Formula One Grand Prix car of the 1980s. The team was founded 1966 by the New Zealand driver Bruce McLaren, and by 1988 had won more than 80 Grand Prix races. McLaren was killed in an accident 1970, and Ron Dennis became the team manager. McLaren world champions have been: Emerson Fittipaldi 1974, James Hunt 1976, Nikki Lauda 1984, Alain Prost 1985, 1986, and 1989, and Ayrton Senna 1988.

Maclean /məˈkleɪn/ Alistair 1922–1987. Scottish adventure novelist. His first novel, *HMS Ulysses* 1955 was based on wartime experience. It was followed by *The Guns of Navarone* 1957, and other adventure novels. Many of his books were made into films.

Maclean /məˈkleɪn/ Donald 1913–1983. British spy, who worked for the USSR while in the UK civil service. He defected to the USSR 1951 together with Guy ◊Burgess.

Maclean, brought up in a strict Presbyterian family, was educated at Cambridge, where he was recruited by the Soviet ◊KGB. He worked for the UK Foreign Office in Washington 1944 and then Cairo 1948 before returning to London, becoming head of the American Department at the Foreign Office 1950.

Maclean /məˈkleɪn/ Fitzroy Hew 1911– . Scottish writer and diplomat, whose travels Russia and Central Asia inspired his *Eastern Approaches* 1949 and *A Person from England* 1958. During 1943–45 he commanded a unit giving aid to partisans in Yugoslavia.

MacLeish /məˈkliːʃ/ Archibald 1892–1982. US poet. He made his name with the poem 'Conquistador' 1932, which describes Cortés' march to the Aztec capital, but his later plays in verse, *Panic* 1935 and *Air Raid* 1938, deal with contemporary problems.

He was born in Illinois, was assistant secretary of state 1944–45, and helped to draft the constitution of UNESCO. From 1949–62 he was Boylston Professor of Rhetoric at Harvard, and his essays *Poetry and Opinion* 1950 reflect his feeling that a poet should be 'committed', expressing his outlook in his verse.

MacLennan /məˈklenən/ Robert (Adam Ross) 1936– . Scottish centrist politician. Member of Parliament for Caithness and Sutherland from 1966. He left the Labour Party for the Social Democrats (SDP) 1981, and was SDP leader 1988 during merger negotiations with the Liberals. He then became a member of the new Social and Liberal Democrats.

MacLennan was educated in Scotland, England and the USA, and called to the English Bar in 1962. When David Owen resigned the SDP leadership in 1988, MacLennan took over until the merger with the Liberal Party had been completed. He took a leading part in the negotiations.

Macleod /məˈklaʊd/ Iain Norman 1913–1970. British Conservative politician. As colonial secretary

McKellen *British actor Ian McKellen in the title role of the film* Walter.

Macmillan *Conservative prime minister Harold Macmillan, 1957.*

1959–61, he forwarded the independence of former British territories in Africa; he died in office as chancellor of the Exchequer.

Maclise /məˈkliːs/ Daniel 1806–1870. Irish painter, active in London from 1827. He drew caricatures of literary contemporaries, such as Dickens, and his historical paintings include *The Meeting of Wellington and Blücher after Waterloo* and *Death of Nelson* both 1860s (murals in the House of Lords, London).

McLuhan /məˈkluːən/ (Herbert) Marshall 1911–1980. Canadian theorist of communication, noted for his views on the effects of technology on modern society. He coined the phrase 'the medium is the message', meaning that the form rather than the content of information is crucial. His works include *The Gutenberg Galaxy* 1962 (in which he coined the phrase 'the global village' for the modern electronic society), *Understanding Media* 1964, and *The Medium is the Massage* (sic) 1967.

MacMahon /məkˈmɑːn/ Marie Edmé Patrice Maurice, Comte de MacMahon 1808–1893. Marshal of France. Captured at Sedan in 1870 during the Franco-Prussian War, he suppressed the ◊Paris Commune after his release, and as president of the republic 1873–79 worked for a royalist restoration until forced to resign.

Macmillan /məkˈmɪlən/ (Maurice) Harold, 1st Earl of Stockton 1894–1986. British Conservative politician. As minister of housing 1951–54 he achieved the construction of 300,000 new houses per year. He was chancellor of the Exchequer 1955–57, and became prime minister 1957 on Eden's resignation after the Suez crisis. At home, he furthered domestic expansion. Internationally, he attempted unsuccessfully to negotiate British entry to the European Community, and encouraged the transition to independence of British colonies in Africa.

As chancellor of the Exchequer 1955–57 he introduced Premium Savings Bonds. His realization of the 'wind of change' in Africa advanced the independence of former colonies. Macmillan, member of a family of publishers, entered Parliament as a Unionist 1924 and received his first ministerial post 1951; he became foreign secretary 1955 and then chancellor of the Exchequer. He led his party to victory in the 1959 elections on the slogan 'You've never had it so good' (the phrase was borrowed from a US election campaign; Macmillan first used it 1957 in a speech warning of the coming danger of inflation). Much of his career as prime minister was spent trying to maintain a UK nuclear weapon, and he was responsible for the purchase of US Polaris missiles 1962. His attempt to take the UK into the European Economic Community 1963 was blocked by the French president de Gaulle. Macmillan's ill health 1963 counteracted to some extent the effect at home of the Vassall spy case and the Profumo scandal. His nickname Supermac was coined by the cartoonist Vicky. He was awarded an earldom 1984.

McMillan /məkˈmɪlən/ Edwin Mattison 1907– . US physicist. In 1940, he discovered neptunium, the first transuranic element, by bombarding uranium with neutrons. In 1951, he shared a Nobel prize with ◊Seaborg for their discovery of transuranic elements. In 1943, he developed a method of overcoming the limitations of the cyclotron, the first ◊accelerator, for which he shared, 20 years later, an Atoms for Peace award with I Veksler, director of the Soviet Joint Institute for Nuclear Research, who had come to the same discovery independently. McMillan was professor at the University of California 1946–73.

MacMillan /məkˈmɪlən/ Kenneth 1929– . Scottish choreographer. After studying at the Sadler's Wells Ballet School he was director of the Royal Ballet 1970–77 and then principal choreographer.

He is renowned for his work with the Canadian dancer Lynn Seymour such as *La Baiser de la Fée* 1960 and *Anastasia* 1967–71. Other works include *Elite Syncopations* 1974 and *Mayerling* 1978. He was knighted in 1983.

MacMillan /məkˈmɪlən/ Kirkpatrick died 1878 Scottish blacksmith, who invented the bicycle in 1839. His invention consisted of a 'hobby-horse' that was fitted with treadles and propelled by pedalling.

MacNeice /məkˈniːs/ Louis 1907–1963. British poet, born in Belfast. He made his debut with *Blind Fireworks* 1929 and developed a polished ease of expression, reflecting his classical training, as in *Autumn Journal* 1939. Unlike many of his contemporaries, he was politically uncommitted. Later works include the play *The Dark Tower* 1947, written for radio, for which he also wrote features 1941–49; a verse translation of Goethe's *Faust*, and the radio play *The Administrator* 1961. He also translated the Greek classics.

Mâcon /ˈmɑːkɒn/ capital of the French *département* of Saône-et-Loire, on the Saône, 72 km/45 mi N of Lyons; population (1983) 39,000. It produces wine. Mâcon dates from ancient Gaul, when it was known as Matisco. The French writer Lamartine was born here.

McPhee /məkˈfiː/ Colin 1900–1964.. US composer. His studies of Balinese music 1934–36 produced two works, *Tabuh-tabuhan* for two pianos and orchestra 1936 and *Balinese CeremonialMusic* for two pianos 1940, which influenced ◊Cage and later generations of US composers.

Macpherson /məkˈfɜːsən/ James 1736–1796. Scottish writer and forger, author of *Fragments of Ancient Poetry collected in the Highlands of Scotland* 1760, followed by the epics *Fingal* 1761 and *Temora* 1763, which he claimed as the work of the 3rd-century bard ◊Ossian. After his death they were shown to be forgeries.

When challenged by Dr Samuel Johnson, Macpherson failed to produce his originals and a committee decided in 1797 that he had combined fragmentary materials with oral tradition. Nevertheless, the works of 'Ossian' influenced the development of the Romantic movement in Britain and in Europe.

Macquarie /məˈkwɒri/ Lachlan 1761–1834. Scottish administrator in Australia. He succeeded William ◊Bligh as governor of New South Wales in 1808, raised the demoralized settlement to prosperity, and did much to rehabilitate ex-convicts. In 1821 he returned to Britain in poor health, exhausted by struggles with his opponents. Lachlan River and Macquarie River and Island are named after him.

Macquarie Island is a Tasmanian dependency, some 1,370 km/850 mi SE of Hobart, and uninhabited except for an Australian government research station.

McQueen /məˈkwiːn/ Steve (Terrence Steven) 1930–1980. US actor. He was one of the most popular film stars of the 1960s and 1970s, admired for his portrayals of the strong, silent loner, and noted for performing his own stunt work. After television success in the 1950s he became a film star with *The Magnificent Seven* 1960. His films include *The Great Escape* 1963, *Bullitt* 1968, *Papillon* 1973, and *The Hunter* 1980.

McQueen *US actor Steve McQueen.*

macramé the art of making decorative fringes and lacework with knotted threads. The name comes from the Arabic word for 'striped cloth', which is often decorated in this way.

Macready /məˈkriːdi/ William Charles 1793–1873. British actor. He made his debut at Covent Garden, London, in 1816. Noted for his roles as Shakespeare's tragic heroes (Macbeth, Lear, and Hamlet), he was partly responsible for persuading the theatre to return to the original texts of Shakespeare and abandon the earlier, bowdlerized versions.

macro in computer programming, a new command created by combining a number of existing ones. For example, if the language has separate commands for obtaining data from the keyboard and for displaying data on the screen, the programmer might create a macro that performs both these tasks with one command. A *macro key* is a key on the keyboard that combines the effects of several individual key presses.

macrobiotics a dietary system of organically grown wholefoods. It originates in Zen Buddhism, and attempts to balance the principles of ◊yin and yang, which are regarded as present in various foods in different proportions.

macroeconomics the division of economics concerned with the study of whole (aggregate) economies or systems, including such aspects as government income and expenditure, the balance of payments, fiscal policy, investment, inflation, and unemployment. It seeks to understand the influence of all relevant economic factors on each other and thus to quantify and predict aggregate national income.

Modern macroeconomics takes much of its inspiration from the work of Keynes, whose *The General Theory of Employment, Interest, and Money* 1936 proposed that governments could prevent financial crises and unemployment by adjusting demand through control of credit and currency. *Keynesian macroeconomics* thus analyses aggregate supply and demand and holds that markets do not continuously 'clear' (quickly attain equilibrium between supply and demand) and may require intervention if objectives such as full employment are thought desirable. Keynesian macroeconomic formulations were generally accepted well in the post-war era and have been refined and extended by the *neo-Keynesian* school, which contends that in a recession the market will clear only very slowly and that full employment equilibrium may never return without significant demand management (by government). At the same time, however, *neo-classical* economics has experienced a recent resurgence, using tools from ◊microeconomics to challenge the central Keynesian assumption that resources

macrophage *Scanning electron micrograph of two macrophages on human lung tissue. The top one is the normal shape, covered with ruffles. The one below has elongated itself to engulf the particle at the left.*

may be underemployed and that full employment equilibrium requires state intervention. Another important school is **new classical** economics, which seeks to show the futility of Keynesian demand management policies and stresses instead the importance of **supply-side economics**, believing that the principal factor influencing growth of national output is the efficient allocation and use of labour and capital. A related school is that of the **Chicago monetarists** led by Milton ◊Friedman, who have revived the old idea that an increase in money supply leads inevitably to an increase in prices rather than in output; however, whereas the new classical school contends that wage and price adjustment is almost instantaneous and so the level of employment at any time must be the natural rate, the Chicago monetarists are more gradualist, believing that such adjustment may take some years.

macromolecule in chemistry, a very large molecule, generally of a polymer.

macrophage a type of white blood cell, or ◊leucocyte, found in all vertebrate animals. Macrophages specialize in the removal of bacteria and other microorganisms, or of cell debris after injury. Like phagocytes, they engulf foreign matter, but they are larger than phagocytes and have a longer life span. They are found throughout the body, but mainly in the lymph, connective tissues, and lungs; here they can also ingest dust, fibres, and other inhaled particles.

MacWhirter /mək'wɜːtə/ John 1839–1911. British landscape painter, whose works include *June in the Austrian Tyrol, Spindrift*, and watercolours.

McWhirter /mək'wɜːtə/ Norris 1925– . British editor and compiler, with his twin brother, **Ross McWhirter** (1925–1975), of the *Guinness Book of Records* from 1955.

MAD abbreviation for **mutual assured destruction**; the basis of the theory of ◊deterrence by possession of nuclear weapons.

mad cow disease popular name for ◊bovine spongiform encephalopathy (BSE).

Madagascar /ˌmædə'gæskə/ island in the Indian Ocean, off the coast of E Africa, about 400 km/280 mi from Mozambique.

government The 1975 constitution radically changed government structure and renamed the state the Democratic Republic of Madagascar. The constitution provides for a single-chamber national people's assembly of 137 members, elected by universal suffrage for a five-year term, and a president elected in the same way for a seven-year term. The president appoints and chairs a supreme revolutionary council (SRC), which acts as 'the guardian of the Malagasy Socialist Revolution'. A third of its members are nominated by the assembly and the rest are chosen by the president, who is also secretary-general of the political organization that embraces all the various party factions: the National Front for the Defence of the Malagasy Socialist Revolution (FNDR). Power therefore ultimately lies with the president's party. For day-to-day administration, the president appoints a prime minister and a council of ministers.

Madagascar
Democratic Republic of
(Repoblika Demokratika n'i Madagaskar)

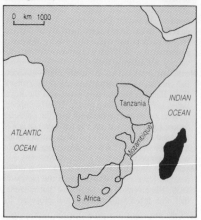

area 587,041 sq km/226,598 sq mi
capital Antananarivo
towns chief port Toamasina
physical central highlands; humid valleys and coastal plains
features one of the last places in the world to be inhabited, it evolved in isolation with unique animals, for example the lemur, now under threat from destruction of the forests
head of state and government Didier Ratsiraka from 1975

government one-party socialist republic
political parties National Front for the Defence of the Malagasy Socialist Revolution (FNDR)
exports coffee, sugar, spice, textiles
currency Malagasy franc (2,500 = £1 Mar 1989)
population (1988) 10,919,000; annual growth rate 2.8%
life expectancy men 49, women 50
language Malagasy (of the Malayo-Polynesian family, official); French and English
religion animist 50%, Christian 40%, Muslim 10%
literacy 74% male/62% female (1985 est)
GNP $2.7 bn (1983); $279 per head of population
chronology
1960 Achieved full independence, with Philibert Tsiranana as president.
1972 Army took control of the government.
1975 Martial law imposed under a national military directorate. New constitution proclaimed the Democratic Republic of Madagascar, with Didier Ratsiraka as president.
1976 Front-Line Revolutionary Organisation (AREMA) formed.
1977 National Front for the Defence of the Malagasy Socialist Revolution (FNDR) became the sole legal political organization.
1983 Ratsiraka re-elected, despite strong opposition from radical socialist National Movement for the Independence of Madagascar (MONIMA) under Monja Jaona.
1989 Ratsiraka re-elected for third term.

history Madagascar was first colonized over 2,000 years ago by Africans and Indonesians. They were joined from the 12th century by Muslim traders, and, from 1500, Europeans began to visit the island. Portuguese, Dutch, and English traders having given up, the French established a colony in the mid-17th century but fled after a massacre by local inhabitants. Madagascar was subsequently divided into small kingdoms until the late 18th century when, aided by traders and Christian missionaries, the Merina (the inhabitants of the highland area) united almost all the country under one ruler. In 1885 the country was made a French protectorate, though French control was not complete until 20 years later.

Madagascar remained loyal to Vichy France during World War II, but was taken by British forces 1942–43 and then handed over to the Free French. During the postwar period nationalist movements became active, and Madagascar became an autonomous state within the ◊French Community in 1958 and achieved full independence, as a republic, in 1960. Its history since independence has been greatly influenced by the competing interests of its two main ethnic groups, the coastal people, or *cotiers*, and the highland Merina.

The first president of the republic was Philibert Tsiranana, leader of the Social Democratic Party (PSD), which identified itself with the *cotiers*. In 1972 the army, representing the Merina, took control of the government and pursued a more nationalistic line than Tsiranana. This caused resentment among the *cotiers* and, with rising unemployment, led to a government crisis in 1975 which resulted in the imposition of martial law under a national military directorate, and the banning of all political parties. Later that year a new, socialist constitution was approved and Lieut-Comdr Didier Ratsiraka, a *cotier*, was elected president of the Democratic Republic of Madagascar. Political parties were permitted again and in 1976 the Front-Line Revolutionary Organization (AREMA) was formed by Ratsiraka as the nucleus of a single party for the state. By 1977 all political activity was concentrated in FNDR and all

the candidates for the national people's assembly were FNDR nominees.

In 1977 the National Movement for the Independence of Madagascar (MONIMA), a radical socialist party, withdrew from the FNDR and was declared illegal. MONIMA's leader, Monja Jaona, unsuccessfully challenged Ratsiraka for the presidency and, although his party did well in the capital, AREMA won 117 of the 137 assembly seats in the 1983 elections. Despite this overwhelming victory, social and political discontent has continued, particularly among the Merinas, who have openly demonstrated their opposition to the government. President Ratsiraka was re-elected with a 62% popular vote in Mar 1989, and in May AREMA won 120 of the 137 assembly seats.

Madame Bovary a novel by Flaubert, published in France 1857. It aroused controversy by its portrayal of a country doctor's wife driven to suicide by a series of unhappy love affairs.

Madeira /mə'dɪərə/ group of islands forming an autonomous region of Portugal off the NW coast of Africa, about 420 km/260 mi N of the Canary

Madeira

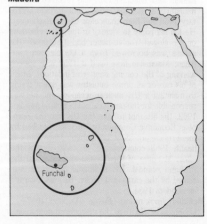

Madhya Pradesh

Islands. Madeira, the largest, and Porto Santo, are the only inhabited islands. The Desertas and Selvagens are uninhabited islets. Their mild climate makes them an all-year-round resort.

area 796 sq km/308 sq mi

capital Funchal, on Madeira

physical Pico Ruivo, on Madeira, is the highest mountain at 1,861 m/6,056 ft

products madeira (a fortified wine), sugar cane, fruit, fish, handicrafts

population (1986) 269,500

history Portuguese from the 15th century; occupied by Britain in 1801 and 1807–14. In 1980 Madeira gained partial autonomy but remains a Portuguese overseas territory.

Madeira River /məˈdɪərə/ river of W Brazil; length 3,250 km/2,020 mi. It is formed by the rivers Beni and Mamoré, and flows NE to join the Amazon.

Maderna /məˈdeənə/ Bruno 1920–1973. Italian composer and conductor. He studied with Malapiero and ◊Scherchen, and collaborated with ◊Berio in setting up an electronic studio in Milan. His compositions combine advanced techniques with an elegance of sound, and include a pioneering work for live and pre-recorded flute, *Musica su due dimensioni* 1952, numerous concertos, and the aleatoric *Aura* for orchestra 1974.

Madhya Bharat /ˈmʌdjə ˈbɑːrət/ state of India 1950–56. It was a union of 24 states of which Gwalior and ◊Indore were the most important. In 1956 Madhya Bharat was absorbed in Madhya Pradesh.

Madhya Pradesh /ˈmʌdjə prəˈdeʃ/ state of central India

area 442,800 sq km/170,921 sq mi

capital Bhopal

towns Indore, Jabalpur, Gwalior, Durg-Bhilainagar, Raipur, Ujjain,

features it is the largest of the states

products cotton, oilseed, sugar, textiles, engineering, paper, aluminium

population (1981) 52,132,000

language Hindi

history formed 1950 from the former British province of Central Provinces and Berar and the princely states of Makrai and Chattisgarh. In 1956 it lost some SW districts, including ◊Nagpur, and absorbed Bhopal, Madhya Bharat, and Vindhya Pradesh.

Madison /ˈmædɪsən/ capital of Wisconsin, USA, 193 km/120 mi NW of Chicago, between lakes Mendota and Monona; population (1980) 323,545;. products include agricultural machinery and medical equipment.

Madison /ˈmædɪsən/ James 1751–1836. 4th president of the USA 1809–17. In 1787 he became a member of the Philadelphia Constitutional Convention and took a leading part in drawing up the US constitution and the Bill of Rights. As secretary of state in Jefferson's government 1801–09, his main achievement was

the ◊Louisiana Purchase. He was elected president in 1808 and re-elected 1812. During his period of office the War of 1812 with Britain took place.

Madison Square Garden venue in New York, built as a boxing arena and also used for concerts. The current 'Garden' is the fourth to bear the name and staged its first boxing match in 1968. It is situated over Pensylvania Station on 7th Avenue, New York City.

The first 'Garden' had its roots in the 1870s when an Irishman called Gilmore gave concerts from a disused railway depot in Madison Square Park. It became known as Gilmore's Garden but when the former owner, circus proprietor Barnum, took it over again in 1880 he renamed it Madison Square Garden.

Madoc, Prince /ˈmædək/ legendary prince of Gwynedd, Wales, supposed to have discovered the Americas and been an ancestor of a group of light-skinned, Welsh-speaking Indians in the American West.

Madonna Italian name for the Virgin ◊Mary, meaning 'my lady'.

Madras /məˈdrɑːs/ industrial port (cotton, cement, chemicals, iron and steel) and capital of Tamil Nadu, India, on the Bay of Bengal; population (1981) 4,277,000. Fort St George 1639 remains from the East India Company when Madras was the chief port on the E coast. Madras was occupied by the French 1746–48, and shelled by the German ship *Emden* in 1914, the only place in India attacked in World War I.

Madras /məˈdrɑːs/ former name of Tamil ◊Nadu, state of India.

Madrid /məˈdrɪd/ industrial city (leather, chemicals, furniture, tobacco, paper) and capital of Spain and Madrid province; population (1986) 3,124,000. Built on an elevated plateau in the centre of the country, at 655 m/2,183 ft it is the highest capital city in Europe and has excesses of heat and cold. Madrid province has an area of 8,000 sq km/3,088 sq mi, and a population of 4,855,000. Madrid began as a Moorish citadel captured by Castile 1083, became important in the times of Charles V and Philip II and was designated capital 1561.

Features include the Real Academia de Bellas Artes 1752, the Prado Museum 1785, and the royal palace 1764. During the civil war Madrid was besieged by the Nationalists 7 Nov 1936–28 Mar 1939.

madrigal a form of secular song in four or five parts, usually sung without instrumental accompaniment. It originated in 14th-century Italy Madrigal composers include Andrea ◊Gabrieli, ◊Monteverdi, Thomas ◊Morley, and Orlando ◊Gibbons.

Madura /məˈdʊərə/ an island in Indonesia, off Surabaya, Java; one of the Sunda Islands

area 4,564 sq km/1,762 sq mi; with offshore islands, more than 5,000 sq km/2,000 sq mi

capital Pamekasan

features central hills rising to 4,800 m/1,545 ft; forested

products rice, tobacco, salt, cattle, fish

population (1970) 2,447,000

history See ◊Java.

Madurai /ˈmædjʊraɪ/ city in Tamil Nadu, India; site of the 16th–17th century Hindu temple of Sundareswara, and of Madurai University 1966; cotton industry; population (1981) 904,000.

Maeander /miˈændə/ anglicized form of the ancient Greek name of the river ◊Menderes in Turkey.

Maecenas /maɪˈsiːnəs/ Gaius Cilnius 69–8 BC. Roman patron of the arts who encouraged the work of ◊Horace and ◊Virgil.

maelstrom /ˈmeɪlstrɒm/ whirlpool off the ◊Lofoten Islands, Norway, also known as the Moskenesstraumen, which gave its name to whirlpools in general.

maenad in Greek mythology, a woman participant in the orgiastic rites of ◊Dionysus; maenads were also known as *Bacchae*.

Madurai An elaborate gateway to the Dravidian Meenakshi temple at Madurai, Tamil Nadu, built between the 16th and 17th centuries.

Maestricht alternative form of ◊Maastricht, city in the Netherlands.

Maeterlinck /ˈmeɪtəlɪŋk/ Maurice, Count Maeterlinck 1862–1949. Belgian poet and dramatist. His plays include *Pelléas et Mélisande* 1892, *L'Oiseau bleu/The Blue Bird* 1908, and *Le Bourgmestre de Stilmonde/The Burgomaster of Stilmonde* 1918, which celebrates Belgian resistance in World War I, a theme that caused his exile to the USA 1940. Nobel prize 1911.

Mafeking /ˈmæfɪkɪŋ/ former name of ◊Mafikeng, town in South Africa, incorporated into Bophuthatswana in 1980.

MAFF abbreviation for *Ministry of Agriculture, Fisheries and Food.*

Mafia /ˈmæfɪə/ secret society reputed to control organized crime such as gambling, loansharking, drug traffic, prostitution, and protection. It originated in 15th-century Sicily but now operates chiefly in large US cities.

In 19th-century Sicily the Mafia was employed by absentee landlords to manage their *latifundia* (landed estates), and through intimidation soon became the unofficial ruling group. In spite of loss of power on the *latifundia*, which were expropriated and divided among the peasants after World War II, the Mafia is still said to be powerful in Sicily. The Italian government has waged periodic campaigns of suppression, notably 1927, when the fascist leader Mussolini appointed Cesare Mori (1872–?) as prefect of Palermo. Mori's methods were, however, as suspect as those of the people he was arresting, and he was fired 1929. A further campaign was waged 1963–64.

The Mafia spread, mainly to the USA, through immigration. Organization is in 'families', each with its own boss or *capo*. Intimidation of witnesses, combined with a code of loyalty and secrecy, makes it difficult to bring criminal charges against its members. The Mafia, also known in the US as *Cosa Nostra*, features frequently in fiction, for example in the book and film *The Godfather* 1972.

Mafikeng /ˈmæfɪkɛŋ/ town (until 1980 Mafeking) in Bophuthatswana, South Africa; it was the capital of Bechuanaland, and the British officer Baden-Powell held it under Boer siege 12 Oct 1899–17 May 1900.

Magadan /ˌmægəˈdɑːn/ port for the gold mines in East Siberia, USSR, off the N shore of the Sea of Okhotsk; population (1985) 142,000.

Magadha /ˈmʌgədə/ a kingdom of ancient India, roughly corresponding to the middle and southern parts of modern ◊Bihar. It was the scene of many incidents in the life of Buddha, and was the seat of the Maurya dynasty, founded by Chandragupta in the 3rd century BC.

magazine a publication brought out periodically, typically containing articles, essays, reviews, illustrations, and so on. The first magazine in the UK was the *Compleat Library* 1691. The US *Reader's Digest* 1922, with editions in many different countries and languages, is the world's best-selling magazine.

The earliest illustrations were wood engravings; the half-tone process was invented 1882 and photogravure was used commercially from 1895. ◊Printing and paper-manufacturing techniques made great progress during the 19th century, making larger print runs possible. Advertising began to appear in magazines around 1800; it was a moderately important factor by 1850 and crucial to most magazines' finances by 1880. Specialist magazines for different interests and hobbies, and ◊comics, appeared in the 20th century.

In the UK distribution and sale of magazines is largely through newsagents' shops; in the USA postal subscriptions also account for a large percentage of sales. Publications that give details of television schedules regularly achieve the highest sales.

history Among the first magazines in Britain were the *Compleat Library* 1691 and the *Gentleman's Journal* 1692, which contained articles and book reviews. Notable successors, mainly with a mixture of political and literary comment, included R ◊Steele's *Tatler* 1709, J ◊Addison's *Spectator* 1711, E ◊Cave's *Gentleman's Magazine* 1731 (the first to use the word 'magazine' in this sense), the Radical John ◊Wilkes's *North Briton* 1762, the *Edinburgh Review* 1802, *Quarterly Review* 1806, *Blackwood's Magazine* 1817, and *Contemporary Review* 1866.

The 1930s saw the rise of the photojournalism magazines such as *Life* in the USA and the introduction of colour printing. The US pulp magazines of the 1930s and 1940s, specializing in crime fiction and science fiction, were breeding grounds for writers such as Raymond Chandler and Isaac Asimov. The development of cheap offset litho printing made possible the flourishing of the *underground press* in much of the western world in the 1960s, although it was limited by unorthodox distribution methods such as street sales. Prosecutions and economic recession largely killed the underground press; the main survivors are the satirical *Private Eye* 1961 and the London listings guide *Time Out* 1968 in Britain and the rock-music paper *Rolling Stone* 1968 in the USA.

women's magazines From the *Ladies' Mercury* 1693 until the first feminist publications of the late 1960s, the content of mass-circulation women's magazines in Britain was largely confined to the domestic sphere—housekeeping, recipes, beauty and fashion, advice columns, patterns—and gossip. In the late 18th century, women's magazines reflected society's temporary acceptance of women as intellectually equal to men, discussing public affairs and subjects of general interest, but by 1825 the trend had reversed. Throughout the 19th century the mildest expression of support for women's rights was enough to kill a magazine and often male editors saw their functions as instructing and improving women by moral teaching. Around 1900 publications for working women began to appear, lurid weekly novelettes known as penny dreadfuls. The first colour magazine for women in Britain, *Woman*, appeared in 1937.

Magdeburg /ˈmægdəbɜːg/ industrial city (vehicles, paper, chemicals, iron, steel, textiles, machinery) and port on the river Elbe, in East Germany, capital of Magdeburg county; population (1986) 289,000. Magdeburg was a member of the Hanseatic League, and has a 13th-century Gothic cathedral. Magdeburg county has an area of 11,530 sq km/4,451 sq mi, and a population of 1,250,000.

Magellan /məˈgelən/ Ferdinand 1480–1521. Portuguese navigator. In 1519 he set sail in the *Victoria* from Seville with the intention of reaching the East Indies by a westerly route. He sailed through the *Magellan Strait* at the tip of South America, crossed an ocean he named the Pacific, and in 1521 reached the Philippines, where he was killed in a battle with the islanders. His companions returned to Seville in 1522, completing the voyage under del ◊Cano.

Magellan was brought up at court and entered the royal service, but later transferred his services to Spain. He and his Malay slave, Enrique de Malacca, are considered the first circumnavigators of the globe, since they had once sailed from the Philippines to Europe. In 1964, the wreck of the *Concepcion* was thought to have been located off Leyte in the Philippines where it was abandoned.

Magellanic Clouds in astronomy, the two nearest galaxies. They are irregularly shaped, and appear as detached parts of the ◊Milky Way, in the southern constellations Dorado and Tucana.

The Large Magellanic Cloud is 160,000 light years away, and about a third the diameter of our galaxy; the Small Magellanic Cloud, 180,000 light years away, is about a fifth the diameter of our galaxy. They are named after the navigator Ferdinand Magellan, who first described them.

Magellan, Strait of /məˈgelən/ channel between South America and Tierra del Fuego, named after the navigator. It is 595 km/370 mi long, and joins the Atlantic and Pacific Oceans.

Magenta /məˈdʒentə/ town in Lombardy, Italy, 24 km/15 mi W of Milan, where France and Sardinia defeated Austria in 1859 during the struggle for Italian independence. Magenta dye was named in honour of the victory.

Maggiore, Lago /məˈdʒɔːreɪ/ lake partly in Italy, partly in Swiss canton of Ticino, with Locarno on its N shore; 63 km/39 mi long and up to 9 km/5.5 mi wide (area 212 sq km/82 sq mi), with fine scenery.

maggot the footless larvae of insects, a typical example being the larva of the blowfly which is deposited as an egg on flesh.

Maghreb /ˈmʌgrəb/ name for NW Africa (Arabic 'far west', 'sunset'). The Maghreb powers—Algeria, Libya, Morocco, Tunisia, and Western Sahara—agreed on economic coordination 1964–65, with Mauritania cooperating from 1970. Chad and Mali are sometimes included. See also ◊Mashraq.

magi /ˈmeɪdʒaɪ/ priests of the Zoroastrian religion of ancient Persia. The term is used in the New Testament of the Latin Vulgate Bible where the Authorized Version gives 'wise men'. The magi who came to visit the infant Christ with gifts of gold, frankincense, and myrrh (the *Adoration of the Magi*) were in later tradition described as 'the three kings'; their names were Caspar, Melchior, and Balthazar.

magic the art of controlling the forces of nature by supernatural means such as charms and ritual. The central ideas are that like produces like (**sympathetic magic**) and that influence carries by **contagion** or association; for example, by the former principle an enemy could be destroyed through an effigy, by the latter principle through personal items such as hair or nail clippings. See also ◊witchcraft.

It is now generally accepted that most early religious practices and most early art are of magical origin, and there are similarities betwen magic and the use of symbolism in religious ritual. Under Christianity existing magical rites were either suppressed (although they survived in modified form in folk custom and superstition) or replaced by those of the church itself. Those still practising the ancient rites were persecuted as witches.

magic bullet a term sometimes used for drugs that are specifically targeted on certain cells or tissues in the body, such as a small collection of cancerous cells (see ◊cancer) or cells that have been invaded by a virus. Such drugs can be made in various

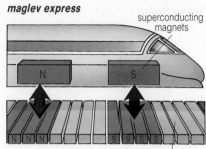

superconducting magnets

N   S

electromagnets

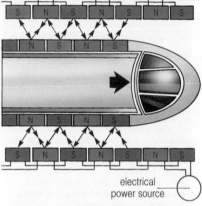

electrical power source

ways, but ◊monoclonal antibodies are increasingly being used to direct the drug to a specific target.

Magic Mountain, The a novel by Thomas Mann, published in Germany 1924. It is an ironic portrayal of the lives of inmates in a Swiss sanatorium, showing the futility of their sheltered existence.

magic numbers in atomic physics, the numbers of ◊neutrons or ◊protons (2, 8, 20, 28, 50, 82, 126) in the ◊nuclei of elements of outstanding stability such as lead and helium. There are accounted for by the neutrons and protons being arranged in completed 'layers' or 'shells'.

magic realism in literature, a fantastic situation realistically treated, as in the works of many Latin American writers, such as Isabel Allende, Jorge Luis Borges, García Márquez; pioneered in Europe by E T A Hoffman and Hesse; and practised in the UK by, among others, Angela Carter. The term was coined in the 1920s to describe German paintings.

magic square in mathematics, a square array of different numbers in which the rows, columns, and diagonals add up to the same total. A simple example employing the numbers 1 to 9, with a total of 15, is:

$$6\ 7\ 2$$
$$1\ 5\ 9$$
$$8\ 3\ 4$$

Maginot Line /ˈmæʒɪnəʊ/ French fortification system along the German frontier from Switzerland to Luxembourg built 1929–36 under the direction of the war minister, André Maginot. It consisted of semi-underground forts joined by underground passages, and protected by antitank defences; lighter fortifications continued the line to the sea. In 1940 the Germans pierced the Belgian frontier line and outflanked the Maginot Line.

magistrate in English law, a person who presides in a magistrates' court: either a ◊justice of the peace (with no legal qualifications, and unpaid) or a stipendiary magistrate. Stipendiary magistrates are paid, qualified lawyers largely used in London and major cities.

magistrates' court in England and Wales, a local law court that mainly deals with minor criminal

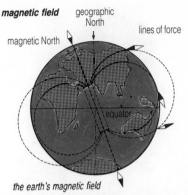

magnetic field

geographic North

magnetic North

lines of force

equator

the earth's magnetic field

cases, but also decides, in ◊committal proceedings, whether more serious criminal cases should be referred to the crown court. It deals with some civil matters, too, such as certain matrimonial proceedings. A magistrates' court consists of between two and seven lay justices of the peace (who are advised on the law by a clerk to the justices), or a single paid lawyer called a stipendiary magistrate.

maglev short for *mag*netic *lev*itation, a method of supporting, for example, a train above the track by magnetic forces.

magma molten material made up of solids and gases beneath the Earth's surface from which ◊igneous rocks are formed. Magma released by volcanoes is called ◊lava.

Magna Carta in English history, the charter granted by King John in 1215, traditionally seen as guaranteeing human rights against the excessive use of royal power. As a reply to the king's demands for excessive feudal dues and attacks on the privileges of the church, Archbishop Langton proposed to the barons the drawing up of a charter in 1213. John was forced to accept this at Runnymede (now in Surrey) on 15 Jun 1215.

Magna Carta begins by reaffirming the rights of the church. Certain clauses guard against infringements of feudal custom, for example, the king was prevented from making excessive demands for money from his barons without their consent. Others are designed to check extortions by officials or maladministration of justice, for example, no freeman to be arrested, imprisoned, or punished except by the judgment of his peers or the law of the land. The privileges of London and the cities were also guaranteed.

As feudalism declined Magna Carta lost its significance, and under the Tudors was almost forgotten. During the 17th century it was rediscovered and reinterpreted by the parliamentary party as a democratic document. Four original copies exist, one each in Salisbury and Lincoln cathedrals and two in the British Library.

magnesia common name for ◊magnesium oxide.

magnesium a light, white, fairly tough metallic element which burns with a bright flame. Symbol Mg, atomic number 12, relative atomic mass 24.32. It is widely distributed in its silicate, carbonate, and chloride forms. It is used in alloys, to strengthen aluminium for aircraft construction, and, with uranium, as a canning material in nuclear reactors. Its incendiary properties are used in flash photography, flares, and fireworks.

It was first found in Magnesia, a district in Thessaly, recognized as an element by J Black 1755, isolated by Humphry Davy 1808, and prepared in coherent form by A A B Bussy 1831.

magnesium oxide (also called *magnesia*) MgO white powder or colourless crystals, formed when magnesium is burned in air or oxygen. It is used to treat acidity of the stomach, and in some industrial processes.

magnet an object that forms a magnetic field (displays ◊magnetism).

magnetic field a region around a permanent magnet, or around a conductor carrying an electric current, in which a force acts on a moving charge or on a magnet placed in the field. The field can be represented by lines of force, which by convention link north and south poles and are parallel to the directions of a small compass needle placed on them. Its magnitude and direction are given by the ◊magnetic flux density, expressed in ◊teslas.

Experiments have confirmed that homing pigeons and some other animals rely on their perception of Earth's magnetic field for their sense of direction, and by 1979 it was suggested that humans to some extent share this sense.

magnetic flux a measurement of the strength of the magnetic field around electric currents and magnets. It is measured in ◊webers; one weber per square metre is equal to one tesla.

The amount of magnetic flux through an area equals the product of the area and the magnetic field strength at a point within that area.

magnetic pole the region on a magnet where the magnetic effects are strongest. Magnets (electromagnets as well as permanent magnets) always have two poles, called north and south. When a magnet is suspended freely, the north pole always points north and the south pole always points south.

Single magnetic poles, called *monopoles*, have never been observed, despite being searched for, although there is no theoretical reason why they could not exist. If monopoles were discovered it would have profound effects on the theory of quantum electrodynamics.

magnetic resonance imaging (MRI) a diagnostic scanning system based on the principles of nuclear magnetic resonance. MRI yields finely detailed three-dimensional images of structures within the body without exposing the patient to harmful radiation. The technique is useful for imaging the soft tissues of the body, such as the brain and the spinal cord.

Claimed as the biggest breakthrough in diagnostic imaging since the discovery of X-rays, MRI is a non-invasive technique using the principle that atomic nuclei in a strong magnetic field can be made to give off electromagnetic radiation, the characteristics of which depend on the environment of the nuclei.

magnetic storm in meteorology, a sudden disturbance affecting the Earth's magnetic field, causing anomalies in radio transmissions and magnetic compasses. It is probably caused by ◊sunspot activity.

magnetic tape a narrow plastic ribbon coated with an easily magnetizable material to record data. It is used in sound recording, audiovisual systems (videotape), and computing. For mass storage on commercial mainframe computers, large reel-to-reel tapes are used, but for the smaller mini- and microcomputers, tape cassettes and cartridges are more usual.

Magnetic tape was first used in *sound recording* 1947, and made overdubbing possible, unlike the direct-to-disc system it replaced. Two-track (stereo) tape was introduced in the 1950s and four-track in the early 1960s; modern studios use 16-, 24-, or 32-track tape, from which the tracks are mixed down to a stereo master tape.

In *computing*, magnetic tape was first used to record data and programs in 1951 as part of the UNIVAC 1 system. It was very popular as a storage medium for external memory in the 1950s–60s. Since then it has largely been replaced by magnetic discs. Information is recorded on the tape in binary form, with two different strengths of signal representing 1 and 0. It is quite common for around 20,000 bits of information to be recorded on each centimetre of tape and the tape drives of a mini- or mainframe computer can be capable of reading 5 metres of tape each second.

magnetism branch of physics dealing with the properties of ◊magnets and ◊magnetic fields. Magnetic fields are produced by moving charged particles; in electromagnets, electrons flow through a coil of wire connected to a battery; in magnets, spinning electrons within the atoms generate the field.

Substances differ in the extent to which they can be magnetized by an external field (susceptibility). Materials that can be strongly magnetized, such as iron, cobalt, and nickel, are said to be **ferromagnetic**. This is due to the formation of areas called domains in which atoms, weakly magnetic because of their spinning electrons, align to form areas of strong magnetism. Ferromagnetic materials lose their magnetism if heated to the Curie temperature. Most other materials are *paramagnetic*, being only weakly pulled toward a strong magnet. This is because their atoms have a low level of magnetism and do not form domains. *Diamagnetic* materials are weakly repelled by a magnet since electrons within their atoms act as electromagnets and reduce magnetism. *Antiferromagnetic* materials have a very low susceptibility that increases with temperature; a similar phenomenen in materials such as ferrites is called ferrimagnetism.

Apart from its universal application in dynamos, electric motors, and switch gears, magnetism is of considerable importance in modern science, for example in particle ◊accelerators for nuclear research, memory stores for computers, tape recorders, and ◊cryogenics.

magnetite a black iron ore, iron oxide (Fe_3O_4). Widely distributed, magnetite is found in nearly all igneous and metamorphic rocks. It is strongly magnetic and some deposits, called **lodestone**, are permanently magnetized. Lodestone has been used as a compass since the first millennium BC.

magneto a simple electric generator, often used to provide the electricity for the ignition system of motor cycles. It consists of a rotating magnet, which sets up an electric current in a coil.

magnetohydrodynamics (MHD) a field of science concerned with the behaviour of ionized gases in a magnetic field. Schemes have been developed that use MHD to generate electrical power.

magnetosphere the volume of space, surrounding a planet, controlled by the planet's magnetic field, and acting as a magnetic 'shell'. The Earth's extends 64,000 km/40,000 mi towards the Sun, but many times this distance on the side away from the Sun.

This is called a *magnetotail*. The outer edge of the magnetosphere is the *magnetopause*. Beyond this is a turbulent region, the *magnetosheath*, where the ◊solar wind is deflected around the magnetosphere. Inside the magnetosphere, atomic particles follow the Earth's lines of magnetic force. The magnetosphere contains the ◊Van Allen belts. Other planets have magnetospheres, notably Jupiter.

magnetron a ◊thermionic valve (vacuum tube) for generating very high-frequency oscillations, used in radar and to produce microwaves in a microwave oven.

Magnificat in the New Testament, the song of praise sung by Mary, the mother of Jesus, on her visit to her cousin Elizabeth shortly after the Annunciation; it is used in the liturgy of some Christian churches.

magnification a measure of the enlargement or reduction of an object in an imaging optical system. *Linear magnification* is the ratio of the size (height) of the image to that of the object. *Angular magnification* is the ratio of the angle subtended at the observer's eye by the image to the angle subtended by the object when viewed directly.

Magnitogorsk /mæg'niːtəʊgɔːsk/ industrial town (steel, motor vehicles, tractors, railway rolling stock) in Chelyabinsk region, USSR, on the E slopes of the Ural Mountains; population (1987) 430,000. It was developed in the 1930s to work iron, manganese, bauxite, and other metals in the district.

magnitude in astronomy, measure of the brightness of a star or other celestial object. Faint objects have larger magnitudes, sixth magnitude being

magnolia

the faintest visible to the naked eye under good conditions. The brightest objects have negative magnitudes. *Apparent magnitude* is the brightness of an object as seen from Earth, *absolute magnitude* the brightness at a standard distance of 10 parsecs (32.6 light years).

◊Sirius has a magnitude of −1.42. Each magnitude step is equal to a brightness difference of 2.512 times. The apparent magnitude of the Sun is −26.8, its absolute magnitude +4.8.

magnolia tree or shrub of the family Magnoliaceae, native to China, Japan, North America, and the Himalayas. Magnolias vary in height from 60 cm/2 ft to 30 m/150 ft. The large single flowers are white, rose, or purple.

Magnox an early type of nuclear reactor used in the UK, for example in Calder Hall, the world's first commercial nuclear power station. This type of reactor uses uranium fuel encased in tubes of magnesium alloy called Magnox. Carbon dioxide gas is used as a coolant to extract heat from the reactor core. See also ◊nuclear energy.

magnum opus (Latin) a great work of art or literature.

magpie genus of birds *Pica* in the crow family. It feeds on insects, snails, young birds, and carrion, and is found in Europe, Asia, N Africa, and W North America. The common magpie *Pica pica* has black and white plumage, the long tail having a metallic gloss.

Magritte /mə'griːt/ René 1898–1967. Belgian Surrealist painter. His paintings focus on visual paradoxes and everyday objects taken out of context. Recurring motifs include bowler hats, apples, and windows.

His first Surrealist works date from the mid-1920s. Magritte joined the other Surrealists in Paris 1927. Returning to Brussels in 1930, he painted murals for public buildings, and throughout his life created variations on themes of mystery treated with apparent literalism.

Magyar member of the largest ethnic group in Hungary, comprising 92% of the population. Magyars are of mixed Ugric and Turkic origin, and they arrived in Hungary towards the end of the 9th century.

Mahabad Kurdish town in Azerbaijan, W Iran, population (1983) 63,000. Occupied by Russian troops in 1941 it formed the centre of a short-lived Kurdish republic (1945–46) before being reoccupied by the Iranians. In the 1980s Mahabad was the focal point of resistance by Iranian Kurds against the Isalmic republic.

Mahābhārata /mə,haː'baːrətə/ (Sanskrit 'great poem of the Bharatas') Sanskrit Hindu epic consisting of 18 books probably composed in its present form about 300 BC. It forms with the *Rāmāyana* the two great epics of the Hindus. It deals with the fortunes of the rival families of the Kauravas and the Pandavas, and contains the ◊*Bhagavad-Gītā*, or *Song of the Blessed*, an episode in the sixth book.

Mahādeva (Sanskrit 'great god') a title given to the Hindu god ◊Siva.

Mahādevī (Sanskrit 'great goddess') a title given to Sakti, the consort of the Hindu god Siva. She is worshipped in many forms, including her more active manifestations as Kali or Durga and her peaceful form as Parvati.

Mahan /mə'hæn/ Alfred Thayer 1840–1914. US naval officer and military historian, author of *The Influence of Sea Power upon History* 1890, in which he propounded a global strategy based on the importance of sea power.

Mahan, an active naval officer during the American Civil War, became a lecturer in naval history and later president of Newport War College until his retirement in 1896. He argued that Britain held a strategic advantage over the central powers and predicted the defeat of the German navy in the World War I.

Maharashtra /,maːhə'ræʃtrə/ state in W central India
area 307,800 sq km/118,811 sq mi
capital Bombay
towns Pune, Nagpur, Ulhasnagar, Sholapur, Nasik, Thana, Kolhapur, Aurangabad, Sangli, Amravati,
features cave temples of Ajanta, containing 200 BC–7th century AD Buddhist murals and sculptures; Ellora cave temples 6th–9th century with Buddhist, Hindu, and Jain sculptures
products cotton, rice, groundnuts, sugar, minerals
population (1981) 62,694,000
language Marathi 50%
religion Hindu 80%, Parsee, Jain, and Sikh minorities
history formed 1960 from the southern part of the former Bombay state.

maharishi /,maːhə'riːʃi/ (Sanskrit *mahā* 'great', *rishi* 'sage') Hindu guru (teacher), or spiritual leader. The Maharishi Mahesh Yogi influenced the Beatles and other Westerners in the 1960s.

mahatma (Sanskrit 'great soul') title conferred on Mohandas K ◊Gandhi by his followers as the first great national Indian leader.

Mahāyāna /,maːhə'jaːnə/ (Sanskrit 'greater vehicle') one of the two major forms of ◊Buddhism, common in N Asia (China, Korea, Japan, and Tibet). Veneration of bodhisattvas is important in Mahāyāna, as is the idea that everyone has within them the seeds of Buddhahood.

A synthesis of Mahāyāna doctrines is found in the *Sūtra of the Golden Light*, stressing that people should obey reason (*prajñā*), which enables them to tell right from wrong; an act of self-sacrifice is the highest triumph of reason. The influential *Lotus Sūtra* describes the historical Buddha as only one manifestation of the eternal Buddha, the ultimate law (*dharma*) of the cosmos and the omnipresent and compassionate saviour.

Mahdi /'maːdi/ (Arabic 'he who is guided aright') in Islam, the title of a coming messiah who will establish the reign of justice on Earth. It has been assumed by many Muslim leaders, notably the Sudanese sheik Muhammad Ahmed (1848–85), who headed a revolt in 1881 against Egypt and in 1885 captured Khartoum.

Maharashtra

Mahler Austrian composer and conductor Gustav Mahler.

His great-grandson *Sadiq el Mahdi* (1936–), leader of the Umma party in the Sudan, was prime minister 1966–67. He was imprisoned 1969–74 for attempting to overthrow the military regime.

Mahfouz /maː'fuːz/ Naguib 1911– . Egyptian novelist and playwright. His novels, which deal with the urban working class, include a semi-autobiographical trilogy 1957, *Children of Gebelawi* 1959 (banned in Egypt because of its treatment of religious themes), and *Respected Sir* 1988. Nobel prize 1988.

mah-jong (Chinese 'sparrows') originally an ancient Chinese card game, dating from the Song dynasty 960–1279. It is now usually played by four people with 144 small ivory tiles, or 'dominoes', divided into six suits.

Mahler /'maːlə/ Alma (born Schindler) 1879–1964. Austrian pianist and critic. She was the daughter of the artist Anton Schindler and married the composer Gustav Mahler 1901.

Mahler /'maːlə/ Gustav 1860–1911. Austrian composer and conductor. His ten symphonies, the moving *Das Lied von der Erde/Song of the Earth* 1909, and his song cycles display a synthesis of Romanticism and new uses of chromatic harmonies and musical forms.

Mahler was born in Bohemia (now Czechoslovakia); he studied at the Vienna Conservatoire, and conducted in Prague, Leipzig, Budapest, and Hamburg 1891–97. He was director of the Vienna Court Opera from 1897 and conducted the New York Philharmonic from 1910.

Mahmud /maː'muːd/ two sultans of the Ottoman Empire:

Mahmud I 1696–1754. Ottoman sultan from 1730. After restoring order to the empire in Istanbul 1730, he suppressed the ◊Janissary rebellion 1731 and waged war against Persia 1731–46. He led successful wars against Austria and Russia, concluded by the Treaty of Belgrade 1739. He was a patron of the arts and also carried out reform of the army.

Mahmud II 1785–1839. Ottoman sultan from 1808 who attempted to westernize the declining empire, carrying out a series of far-reaching reforms of civil service and army. In 1826 he destroyed the ◊Janissaries. Wars against Russia 1807–12 led to losses of territory. The pressure for Greek independence after 1821 led to conflict with Britain, France, and Russia, leading to the destruction of the Ottoman fleet at the Battle of Navarino in 1829 and defeat in the Russo-Turkish war 1828–29, and he was forced to recognize Greek independence in 1830.

There was further disorder with the revolt in Egypt of Mehemet Ali (Muhammad Ali) 1831–32, which in turn led to temporary Ottoman-Russian

Mailer *US novelist and journalist Norman Mailer, photographed in 1965 on the balcony of his Brooklyn Heights apartment.*

peace. Attempts to control the rebellious provinces failed in 1839, resulting in effect in the granting of Egyptian autonomy.

mahogany timber from several genera of trees found in the Americas and Africa. Mahogany is a tropical hardwood obtained chiefly by rainforest logging. It has a warm red colour and takes a high polish.

True mahogany comes from trees of the genus *Swietenia* but other types come from the Spanish and Australian cedars, the Indian redwood, and other trees of the family Meliaceae, native to Africa and the E Indies.

Mahón /maːˈɒn/ or *Port Mahon* capital and port of the Spanish island of Minorca; population (1981) 21,900. Probably founded by the Carthaginians, it was in British occupation 1708–56 and 1762–82.

Mahratta or *Maratha* member of a people of Maharashtra, India. Their language is Marathi. In the 17th and 18th centuries the Mahratta formed a powerful military confederacy in rivalry with the Mogul emperors. The Afghan allies of the latter defeated them 1761, and, after a series of wars with the British 1779–1871, most of their territory was annexed.

Maia in Greek mythology, daughter of Atlas and mother of Hermes.

Maiden Castle /ˈmeɪdn ˈkɑːsəl/ a prehistoric hillfort and later earthworks on Fordington Hill, near Dorchester, Dorset, England. Ramparts, about 18 m/60 ft high, enclosed an area of 18 ha/45 acres. The site was inhabited from Neolithic times (about 2000 BC) and stormed by the Romans AD 43.

maidenhair fern *Adiantum capillus-veneris* with hairlike fronds terminating in small kidney-shaped, spore-bearing pinnules. It is widely distributed in the Americas, and is sometimes found in the British Isles.

maidenhair tree another name for ◊ginkgo, a genus of ornamental trees related to the conifers.

Maidenhead /ˈmeɪdnhed/ town in Berkshire, S England, 40 km/25 mi W of London, on the river Thames; boating centre; it manufactures computer software, plastics, pharmaceuticals, and has a printing industry. Population (1983) 48,473.

maid of honour in Britain, the closest attendant on a queen. They are chosen generally from the daughters and granddaughters of peers, but in the absence of another title bear that of Honourable.

The appointment dates from the Plantagenet kings and included a mistress of the robes (almost invariably a duchess) and ladies-in-waiting (officially styled 'ladies and women of the bedchamber').

Maidstone /ˈmeɪdstəʊn/ town in Kent, SE England, on the river Medway, administrative headquarters of the county; prison, law courts; population (1986) 133,700. Industries include agricultural machinery and paper. Maidstone has the ruins of All Saints' College 1260. The Elizabethan Chillington Manor is an art gallery and museum.

Maiduguri /ˌmaɪduˈɡʊəri/ capital of Borno state, NE Nigeria; population (1983) 230,900.

Maine

Maikop /maɪˈkɒp/ capital of Adyge autonomous region of the USSR on the river Bielaia, with timber mills, distilleries, tanneries, and tobacco and furniture factories; population (1985) 140,000. Oilfields, discovered in 1900, are linked by pipeline with Tapse on the Black Sea.

Mailer /ˈmeɪlə/ Norman 1923– . US writer and journalist. He gained wide attention with his novel of World War II *The Naked and the Dead* 1948. A social commentator in the US literary and political scene, he has run for mayor of New York and has expressed radical sexual views.

Other novels include *An American Dream* 1964. Journalism includes *Armies of the Night* 1968, about protest against the Vietnam War, and *The Executioner's Song* 1979 (Pulitzer Prize), about a convicted murderer on Death Row. Mailer has also ventured into filmmaking.

Maillart /maɪˈaː/ Ella 1903– . Swiss explorer whose six-month journey into Russian Turkestan was described in *Turkestan Solo* 1934. Subsequently she crossed the Gobi Desert with Peter Fleming, recounted in *Forbidden Journey* 1937.

Maillol /maɪˈɒl/ Aristide Joseph Bonaventure 1861–1944. French artist who turned to sculpture in the 1890s. His work is devoted to the human figure, particularly the female nude. It shows the influence of classical Greek art, but tends towards simplified rounded forms. Maillol was influenced by the ◊Nabis. A typical example of his work is *Fame* for the Cézanne monument in Aix-en-Provence.

mail order a type of business in which retail organizations sell their goods by post through catalogues.

Maimonides /maɪˈmɒnɪdiːz/ Moses (Moses Ben Maimon) 1135–1204. Jewish rabbi and philosopher, born in Córdoba, Spain. Known as one of the greatest Hebrew scholars, he attempted to reconcile faith and reason; his philosophical classic is *More nevukhim/The Guide to the Perplexed* 1176–91, which helped to introduce the theories of Aristotle into medieval philosophy.

He left Spain in 1160 to escape the persecution of the Jews and settled in Fez, and later in Cairo, where he was personal physician to Sultan Saladin. His codification of Jewish law is known as the *Mishneh Torah/The Torah Reviewed* 1180; he also formulated the **13 Principles**, which summarize the basic beliefs of Judaism.

Main /maɪn/ river in central West Germany, flowing through Frankfurt to join the river Rhine at Mainz. A canal links it with the Danube. Length 515 km/320 mi.

Maine /meɪn/ old French province bounded on the N by Normandy, on the W by Brittany, and on the S by Anjou. The modern *départements* of Sarthe and Mayenne approximately correspond with it.

Maine /meɪn/ French river, 11 km/7 mi long, formed by the junction of the Mayenne and Sarthe; it enters the Loire below Angers, and gives its name to Maine-et-Loire *département*.

Maine /meɪn/ northeasternmost state of the USA, largest of the New England states; nickname Pine Tree State
area 86,200 sq km/33,273 sq mi
capital Augusta
towns Portland, Lewiston, Bangor
physical Appalachian Mountains; Acadia National Park; 80% of the state is forested
products dairy and market garden produce, paper, pulp, timber, textiles; tourism and fishing are also important
population (1986) 1,174,000
famous people Longfellow, Edna St Vincent Millay, Kate Douglas Wiggin
history settled from 1623, it became a state 1820.

mainframe a large computer used for commercial data processing and other large-scale operations. Because of the increase in computing power, the distinction between the mainframe, ◊supercomputer, ◊minicomputer, and ◊microcomputer (personal computer) is becoming less important.

main sequence in astronomy, the part of the ◊Hertzsprung–Russell diagram that contains most of the stars, including the Sun. It runs diagonally from the top left of the diagram to the lower right. The most massive (and hence brightest) stars are at the top left, with the least massive (coolest) stars at the bottom right.

Main Street classic US satirical novel by Sinclair Lewis, published 1920, which made the small-town American Main Street the exemplification of enduring if simplistic US values.

maintenance in law, payments to support children or a spouse, under the terms of an agreement, or by a court order. In Britain, financial provision orders are made on divorce, but a court action can also be brought for maintenance without divorce proceedings. Applications for maintenance of illegitimate children are now treated in the same way as for legitimate children.

Maintenon /ˌmæntəˈnɒ̃/ Françoise d'Aubigné, Marquise de Maintenon 1653–1719. Second wife of Louis XIV of France from 1684, and widow of the writer Paul Scarron (1610–60). She was governess to the children of Mme de Montespan by Louis, and his mistress from 1667. She secretly married the king after the death of Queen Marie Thérèse in 1683. Her political influence was considerable, and, as a Catholic convert from Protestantism, her religious opinions were zealous.

Mainz /maɪnts/ (French *Mayence*) capital of Rhineland-Palatinate, West Germany, on the Rhine, 37 km/23 mi WSW of Frankfurt-am-Main; population (1988) 189,000. In Roman times it was a fortified camp and became the capital of Germania Superior. Printing was possibly invented here about 1448 by ◊Gutenberg.

maiolica or *majolica* a kind of enamelled ◊pottery, so named from the Italian form of Majorca, the

maize

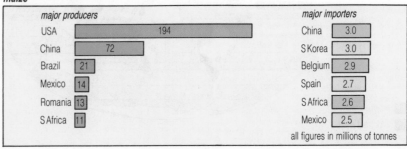

major producers		major importers	
USA	194	China	3.0
China	72	S Korea	3.0
Brazil	21	Belgium	2.9
Mexico	14	Spain	2.7
Romania	13	S Africa	2.6
S Africa	11	Mexico	2.5

all figures in millions of tonnes

Spanish island where such ware was originally made. The term is applied to the richly decorated enamel pottery produced in Italy in the 15th to 18th centuries.

Maitreya the Buddha to come, 'the kindly one', an important figure in all forms of Buddhism; he is known as *Mi-lo-fo* in China and *Miroku* in Japan. Buddhists believe that a Buddha appears from time to time to maintain knowledge of the true path; Maitreya is the next future Buddha.

maize (North American *corn*) plant *Zea mays* of the grass family. Grown extensively in all subtropical and warm temperate regions, its range has been extended to colder zones by hardy varieties developed in the 1960s. It is widely used as animal feed;sweetcorn, a variety of maize in which the sugar is not converted to starch, is a familiar vegetable, known as corn on the cob; other varieties are made into hominy, polenta, popcorn, and corn bread. It is used in corn oil and fermented to make alcohol; its stalks are made into paper and hardboard.

Major /ˈmeɪdʒə/ John 1943– . British Conservative politician, briefly foreign secretary 1989 and then chancellor of the Exchequer from 1989. Formerly a banker, he became Member of Parliament for Huntingdonshire in 1979 and joined the government in 1981, becoming deputy to Chancellor Nigel Lawson 1987. In 1989 Major was promoted to foreign secretary and, after Lawson's resignation, to chancellor, within the space of six months.

Major John Major, British chancellor of the Exchequer from 1989.

Majorca /məˈjɔːkə/ (Spanish *Mallorca*) largest of the ◊Balearic Islands, belonging to Spain, in the W Mediterranean
area 3,640 sq km/1,405 sq mi
capital Palma
maize

Makarios III Archbishop Makarios, president of Cyprus 1960–77.

features the highest mountain is Puig Mayor 1,445 m/4,741 ft
products olives, figs, oranges, wine, brandy, timber, sheep; tourism is the mainstay of the economy
population (1981) 561,215
history captured 797 by the Moors, it became the kingdom of Majorca 1276, and was united with Aragon in 1343.

major-general after the English Civil War, one of the officers appointed by Oliver Cromwell in 1655 to oversee the 12 military districts into which England had been divided. Their powers included organizing the militia, local government, and the collection of some taxes.

Makarios III /məˈkɑːrɪɒs/ 1913–1977. Cypriot politician, Greek Orthodox archbishop 1950–77. A leader of the Resistance organization ◊EOKA, he was exiled by the British to the Seychelles 1956–57 for supporting armed action to achieve union with Greece (*enosis*). He was president of the republic of Cyprus 1960–77 (briefly deposed by a Greek military coup Jul–Dec 1974).

Makarova /məˈkɑːrəvə/ Natalia 1940– . Russian ballerina. She danced with the Kirov Ballet 1959–70, then sought political asylum in the West. Her roles include the title role in *Giselle*, and Aurora in *The Sleeping Beauty*.

Makeyevka /məˈkeɪəfkə/ formerly (until 1931) *Dmitrievsk* city in the Donets Basin, SE Ukraine, USSR; population (1987) 455,000. Industries include coal, iron, steel, and chemicals.

Makhachkala /məˌkætʃkəˈlɑː/ formerly (until 1922) *Port Petrovsk* capital of Dagestan, USSR, on the Caspian Sea, ESE of Grozny, from which pipelines bring petroleum to Makhachkala's refineries; population (1987) 320,000. Other industries include shipbuilding, meat packing,

chemicals, matches, and cotton textiles.

Malabar Coast /ˈmæləbɑː ˈkəʊst/ the coastal area of Karnataka and Kerala states, India, lying between the Arabian Sea and the Western Ghats; about 65 km/40 mi W to E, 725 km/450 mi N to S. A fertile area with heavy rains, it produces food grains, coconuts, rubber, spices; teak, ebony, and other woods. Lagoons fringe the shore. A district of Tamil Nadu transferred in 1956 to Kerala was called Malabar Coast.

Malabo /məˈlɑːbəʊ/ port and capital of Equatorial Guinea, on the island of Bioko; population (1983) 15,253. It was founded in the 1820s by the British as Port Clarence. Under Spanish rule it was known as Santa Isabel (until 1973).

Malacca /məˈlækə/ or *Melaka* state of W Peninsular Malaysia; capital Malacca; area 1,700 sq km/656 sq mi; population (1980) 465,000 (about 70% Chinese). Products include rubber, tin, and wire. The town originated in the 13th century as a fishing village frequented by pirates, and later developed into a trading port. Portuguese from 1511, then Dutch from 1641, it was ceded to Britain 1824, becoming part of the Straits Settlements.

Malacca, Strait of /məˈlækə/ channel between Sumatra and the Malay Peninsula; length 965 km/600 mi; narrows to less than 38 km/24 mi wide. It carries all shipping between the Indian Ocean and the South China Sea.

malachite a common ◊copper ore, basic copper carbonate, $Cu_2CO_3(OH)_2$. It is a source of green pigment and is polished for use in jewellery, ornaments, and art objects.

Málaga /ˈmæləgə/ industrial seaport (sugar refining, distilling, brewing, olive-oil pressing, shipbuilding) and holiday resort in Andalusia, Spain; capital of Málaga province on the Mediterranean; population (1986) 595,000. Founded by the Phoenicians and taken by the Moors 711, Málaga was capital of the Moorish kingdom of Malaga from the 13th century until captured 1487 by Ferdinand and Isabella.

Malagasy inhabitant of Madagascar. Primarily rice farmers, they make use of both irrigated fields and swidden (temporary plot) methods. The language belongs to the Austronesian family and, despite Madagascar's proximity to Africa, contains only a small number of Bantu and Arabic loan words.

Malagasy Republic /ˌmæləˈgæsi/ former name (1958–75) of ◊Madagascar.

Malamud /ˈmæləmʌd/ Bernard 1914–1986. US novelist. He first attracted attention with *The Natural* 1952, taking a professional baseball player as his hero. Later works, often dealing with Jewish immigrant tradition, include *The Assistant* 1957, *The Fixer* 1966, *Dubin's Lives* 1979, and *God's Grace* 1982.

malapropism an amusing slip of the tongue, arising from the confusion of similar-sounding words. The term derives from the French *mal à propos* (inappropriate); historically, it is associated with Mrs Malaprop, a character in Sheridan's play *The Rivals* 1775, who was the pineapple (pinnacle) of perfection in such matters.

malaria infectious parasitic disease transmitted by mosquitoes, marked by periodic fever and an enlarged spleen, which affects some 200 million people a year on a recurring basis. When a female mosquito of the *Anopheles* genus bites a human with malaria, it takes in with the human blood the malaria parasite (*Plasmodium*). This matures within the insect, and is then transferred when the mosquito bites a new victim.

Inside the human body the parasite settles first in the liver, then multiplies to attack the red blood cells, when the symptoms of malaria become evident. Tests on a vaccine were begun in Nov 1986 in the USA. In Brazil a malaria epidemic broke out among new settlers in the Amazon region, with 287,000 cases 1983 and 500,000 cases 1988. The last recorded case of native malaria in England was 1918 in Kent.

Malatya /ˌmælətˈjɑː/ capital of a province of the

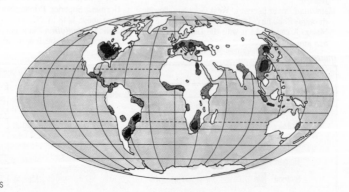

 major areas

 important areas

malaria

life cycle of the malaria parasite,
split between mosquito and human

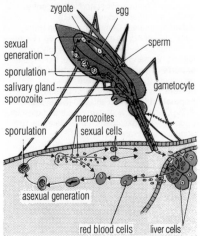

same name in E central Turkey, lying W of the
river Euphrates; population (1985) 251,000.

Malawi /məˈlɑːwi/ country in SE Africa, bordered N and NE by Tanzania, E, S and W by
Mozambique, and W by Zambia.

government The 1966 constitution provides for
a president elected for a five-year term, but was
amended in 1971 to make Hastings ◊Banda president for life. Malawi is a one-party state, all adults
being required to be members of the Malawi Congress Party (MCP). The single-chamber legislature, the national assembly, has 112 elected members, and the president may appoint any number
of additional members. He also appoints a cabinet
whose members are directly responsible to him.
Hastings Banda's system of personal, paternalistic
rule has not been seriously challenged in his 20
years of office. There are at least three opposition
groups which operate from outside Malawi.

history During the 15th–19th centuries the Malawi empire occupied roughly the southern part of
the region that makes up present-day Malawi. In
the 17th century the Portuguese were the first
Europeans to visit the area, but Britain intervened to stop them from annexing it and thereby
linking the Portuguese colonies of Angola and
Mozambique. The difficulty of the terrain, and
the warfare between the rival Yao and Ngoni
groups, long prevented penetration of the region
by outsiders, though David ◊Livingstone reached
Lake Malawi in 1859. In 1891 Britain annexed
the country, making it the British protectorate
of Nyasaland from 1907. Between 1953 and 1964
it was part of the Federation of Rhodesia and
Nyasaland, which comprised the territory that is
now Zimbabwe, Zambia, and Malawi.

Dr Hastings Banda, through the MCP, led a
campaign for independence and in 1963 the federation was dissolved. Nyasaland became independent as Malawi in 1964, and two years later
became a republic and a one-party state, with
Dr Banda as its first president. He has governed
his country in a very individual way, tolerating
no opposition, and his foreign policies have at
times been rather idiosyncratic. He astonished
his black African colleagues in 1967 by officially
recognizing the republic of South Africa, and in
1971 became the first African head of state to
visit that country. In 1976, however, he also recognized the communist government in Angola.

Banda keeps a tight control over his government colleagues and, as yet, no successor has
emerged. In 1977 he embarked upon a policy
of cautious liberalism, releasing some political
detainees and allowing greater press freedom.
His external policies are based on a mixture
of national self-interest and practical reality
and have enabled Malawi to live in reasonable

harmony with its neighbours.

Malawi, Lake /məˈlɑːwi/ or *Lake Nyasa* African lake, bordered by Malawi, Tanzania, and
Mozambique, formed in a section of the Great
◊Rift Valley. It is about 500 m/1,650 ft above sea
level and 560 km/350 mi long, with an area of
37,000 sq km/14,280 sq mi. It is intermittently
drained to the south by the river Shiré into the
Zambezi.

Malay person of Malay culture, comprising the majority population of the Malay peninsula and also
found in S Thailand, and coastal Sumatra and
Borneo.

Malay language a member of the Western or
Indonesian branch of the ◊Malayo-Polynesian
language family, used in the Malay peninsula and
many of the islands of Malaysia and Indonesia. The
Malay language can be written with either Arabic
or Roman scripts.

The dialect of the S Malay peninsula is the basis
of both standard Malay in Malaysia and Bahasa
Indonesia, the official language of Indonesia. Bazaar Malay is a widespread pidgin variety used for
trading and shopping.

Malayo-Polynesian or *Austronesian* a family of
languages spoken in Malaysia, the Indonesian
archipelago, parts of Indo-China, Taiwan, Madagascar, Melanesia, and Polynesia (excluding Australia and most of New Guinea). The group contains some 500 distinct languages, including Malay
in Malaysia, Bahasa in Indonesia, Fijian, Hawaiian,
and Maori.

Malay Peninsula /məˈleɪ/ southern projection of
the continent of Asia, lying between the Strait
of Malacca, which divides it from Sumatra, and
the China Sea. The northern portion is partly in
Burma, partly in Thailand; the south forms part
of ◊Malaysia. The island of Singapore lies off its
southern extremity.

Malaysia /məˈleɪziə/ country in SE Asia, comprising the Malay Peninsula, bordered to the N
by Thailand, and surrounded E, S, and W by
the South China Sea; and the states of Sabah
and Sarawak in the northern part of the island
of Borneo (S Borneo is part of Indonesia).

government Malaysia is a federation of 13
states: Johore, Kedah, Kelantan, Malacca,
Negri Sembilan, Pahang, Penang, Perak, Perlis,
Sabah, Sarawak, Selangor, and Trengganu. Each
has its own constitution, head of state, and

elected assembly, led by a chief minister and
cabinet, and legislates on matters outside the
federal parliament's sphere.

Under the 1957 constitution, a monarch is
elected for five-year terms by and from among
the hereditary rulers of Johore, Kedah, Kelantan,
Negri Sembilan, Pahang, Perak, Perlis, Selangor,
and Trengganu. The paramount ruler's powers are
similar to those of the British monarch, including
discretion in the appointment of a prime minister
and in granting a dissolution of parliament. Generally, the monarch acts on the advice of the prime
minister and cabinet, who wield effective power.

The two-chamber federal legislature or parliament is composed of a 68-member upper house
or senate, *Dewan Negara*, comprising 42 members appointed by the monarch and two members elected by each of the 13 state assemblies
for six-year terms, and a house of representatives, *Dewan Rakyat*, whose 177 members are
elected for five-year terms from single-member
constituencies by universal suffrage. The senate
can only delay bills already approved by the dominant house of representatives, whose majority
party or coalition provides the prime minister, who
governs with a cabinet selected from parliament.

Malaysia's principal party is the New United
Malays' National Organization (UMNO Baru),
which is oriented towards ethnic Malays. It leads
the National Front coalition, which is composed of
12 other parties, most importantly the Chinese-
oriented Malaysian Chinese Association (MCA),
and Gerakan Party, and the Indian-oriented Malaysian Indian Congress (MIC). The principal
opposition parties are the moderate, mainly Chinese, Democratic Action Party (DAP), the radical
Muslim Pan-Malayan Islamic Party (PAS), and
Spirit of 1946 (Semangat '46), a breakaway from
the UMNO. Smaller regional parties operate at
state level.

history The areas that compose present-day Malaysia were part of the Buddhist Sri Vijaya empire
in the 9th–14th centuries. This was overthrown
by Majapahit, Java's last Hindu kingdom. After
this period of Indian influence came the introduction of Islam, and a powerful Muslim empire
developed in the area. Its growth was checked
by the Portuguese conquest of Malacca in 1511.
In 1641 the Dutch ousted the Portuguese, and
the area came under British control from 1786,

Malawi

Republic of
(Malaŵi) former name
Nyasaland

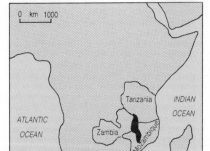

area 118,000 sq km/45,560 sq mi
capital Lilongwe
towns Blantyre-Limbe
physical occupies the mountainous west side
of Lake Malawi
features Livingstonia National Park on the Nyika
Plateau in the north, rich in orchids, arthropods,

elephants; Shiré Highlands, noted for tea and
tobacco, and rising to 1,750 m/5,750 ft.
head of state and government Hastings
Kamusu Banda from 1966 for life
government one-party republic
political parties Malawi Congress Party (MCP),
multi-racial, right-wing
exports tea, tobacco, cotton, groundnuts,
sugar
currency kwacha (4.42 = £1 Feb 1990)
population (1985) 7,059,000; annual
growth rate 3.1%; Malawi contains a refugee
population of about 500,000 in camps and
possibly as many settled among local people.
About 70,000 refugees crossed the border Sept
1986.
life expectancy men 44, women 46
language English (official); Chichewa
religion Christian 50%; Muslim 30%
literacy 52% male/31% female (1985 est)
GNP $1.1 bn (1984); $200 per head of
population
chronology
1964 Nyasaland achieved independence, within
the Commonwealth, as Malawi.
1966 Became a one-party republic, with
Hastings Banda as president.
1971 Banda was made president for life.
1977 Banda started a programme of moderate
liberalization, releasing some political detainees
and allowing greater freedom of the press.
1986–89 Influx of over 650,000 refugees from
Mozambique.

with a brief return to Dutch rule 1818–24. Britain succeeded in unifying its protectorates in Borneo and the Malay Peninsula after World War II, making them a crown colony under the name of the Federation of Malaya in 1948.

The Federation of Malaysia was formed 1963 by the union of the 11 states of the Federation of Malaya with the British crown colonies of N Borneo (then renamed Sabah) and Sarawak, and Singapore, which seceded from the federation in 1965. Since 1966 the 11 states on the Malay Peninsula have been known as West Malaysia, and Sabah and Sarawak as East Malaysia. The two regions are separated by 400 miles of the South China Sea. The establishment of the federation was opposed by guerrillas backed by Sukarno of Indonesia 1963–66, while the Philippines disputed the sovereignty of East Malaysia in 1968, through their claim on Sabah.

Tunku Abdul ◊Rahman was Malaysia's first prime minister 1963–69, and his multiracial style of government was successful until anti-Chinese riots in Kuala Lumpur in 1969 prompted the formation of an emergency administration. These riots followed a fall in support for the United Malays' National Organization (UMNO) in the federal election, and were indicative of Malay resentment of the economic success of the Chinese business community. They provoked the resignation of Tunku Abdul Rahman in 1970 and the creation by his successor, Tun Abdul Razak, of a broader National Front governing coalition, including previous opposition parties in its ranks. In addition, a 'new economic policy' was launched in 1971, with the aim of raising the percentage of Malay-owned businesses from 4% to 30% by 1990, and to extend the use of pro-Malay 'affirmative action' quota systems for university entrance and company employment. During the 1970s Malaysia enjoyed economic growth, but relations with the Chinese community became uneasy later in the decade as a result of the federal government's refusal to welcome Vietnamese refugees. Even more serious has been a revival in fundamentalist Islam in the west and north.

Dr Mahathir bin ◊Mohamad became the new leader of the UMNO and prime minister in 1981 and pursued a more narrowly Islamic and Malay strategy than his predecessors. He also launched an ambitious industrialization programme, seeking to emulate Japan. He was re-elected in 1982 and 1986, but has encountered opposition from his Malaysian Chinese Association coalition partners, Christian-Muslim conflict in Sabah, and slower economic growth as a result of the fall in world tin, rubber, and palm-oil prices. In 1987, in the wake of worsening Malay-Chinese relations, Dr Mahathir ordered the arrest of more than 100 prominent opposition activists, including the DAP's leader, Lim Kit Siang, and a tightening of press censorship. These moves precipitated a rift in the UMNO, with the former premier Tunku Abdul Rahman and former trade and industry minister Razaleigh Hamzah leaving to form a new multiracial party grouping, Semangat '46, in 1989. In 1988 a reconstituted New UMNO had been set up by Dr Mahathir following a high-court ruling that, as a result of irregularities in its 1987 leadership election, the existing UMNO was an 'unlawful body'. The prime minister also announced some relaxation of the 1971 ethnic Malaya (*bumiputra*) oriented 'new economic policy'—Malay equity ownership having reached only 18% by 1987—as part of the more concensual 'Malay unity' programme.

Malaysia joined ◊ASEAN in 1967 and originally adopted a pro-Western, anti-Communist position. During recent years, while close economic links have been developed with Japan and joint ventures encouraged, relations with the communist powers and with Islamic nations have also become closer.

Malcolm /ˈmælkəm/ four kings of Scotland, including:

Malcolm III called *Canmore* c. 1031–1093. King

Malaysia

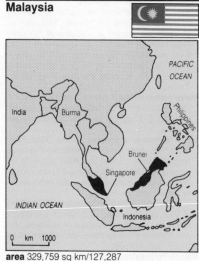

area 329,759 sq km/127,287 sq mi
capital Kuala Lumpur
towns Kuching in Sarawak and Kota Kinabalu in Sabah
physical comprises W Malaysia (the nine Malay states – Perlis, Kedah, Johore, Selangor, Perak, Negri Sembilan, Kelantan, Trengganu, Pahang – plus Penang and Malacca); and E Malaysia (Sarawak and Sabah); 75% of the area tropical jungle; a central mountain range; swamps in the E
head of state Rajah Azlan Muhibuddin Shah (sultan of Perak) from 1989
head of government Mahathir bin Mohamad from 1981
political system liberal democracy
political parties New United Malay's National Organization (UMNO Baru) Malay-orientated nationalist; Malaysian Chinese Association (MCA), Chinese-orientated conservative; Gerakan, Chinese-orientated left-of-centre; Malaysian Indian Congress (MIC), Indian-orientated; Democratic Action Party (DAP), left-of-centre multi-racial, though Chinese dominated; Pan-Malayan Islamic Party (PAS), Islamic; Semangat '46, moderate, multi-racial.
exports pineapples, palm oil, rubber, timber, petroleum (Sarawak), bauxite
currency ringgit (4.60 = £1 Feb 1990)
population (1988) 16,968,000 (Malaysian 47%, Chinese 32%, Indian 8%, and indigenous peoples – Dayaks, Ibans – of E Malaysia 10%); annual growth rate 2.5%
life expectancy men 65, women 69
language Malay (official, usually written in Arabic characters); in Sarawak English is also official
religion Muslim (official)
literacy 81% male/66% female (1985 est)
GNP $29.7 bn (1983); $714 per head of population
chronology
1963 Formation of federation of Malaysia.
1965 Secession of Singapore from federation.
1969 Anti-Chinese riots in Kuala Lumpur.
1971 Launch of Bumiputra 'new economic policy'.
1981 Election of Dr Mahathir bin Mohamad as prime minister.
1982 Mahathir bin Mohamad re-elected.
1986 Mahathir bin Mohamad re-elected.
1987 Arrest of opposition DAP leader as Malay-Chinese relations deteriorate.
1988 Split in ruling UMNO party over Mahathir's leadership style; new UMNO formed.
1989 Semangat '46 set up by former members of UMNO including ex-premier Tunku Abdul Rahman.

of Scotland from 1054, the son of Duncan I (died 1040); he was killed at Alnwick while invading Northumberland.

Malcolm X assumed name of Malcolm Little 1926–1965. US black nationalist leader. While serving a prison sentence for burglary (1946–53) he joined the ◊Black Muslims sect. On his release he campaigned for black separatism, condoning violence in self-defence, but in 1964 modified his views to found the Islamic-socialist Organization of Afro-American Unity, preaching racial solidarity. A year later he was assassinated by Black Muslim opponents while addressing a rally in Harlem, New York. His *Autobiography of Malcolm X* was published 1964.

Maldives /ˈmɔːldiːvz/ group of 1,196 islands in the N Indian Ocean, about 640 km/400 mi SW of Sri Lanka, only 203 of which are inhabited.
government The 1968 constitution provides for a single-chamber citizens' council (*Majilis*) of 48 members, and a president, nominated by the *Majilis* and elected by referendum. They all serve a five-year term. 40 of the *Majilis's* members are elected by universal suffrage and eight are appointed by the president, who appoints and leads a cabinet which is responsible to the *Majilis*. There are no political parties and women are precluded from holding office.
history The islands, under Muslim control from the 12th century, came under Portuguese rule in 1518. A dependency of Ceylon from 1645–1948, they were under British protection from 1887–1965 as the Maldive Islands, and became a republic in 1953. The sultan was restored in 1954 and then, three years after achieving full independence as Maldives, the islands returned to republican status in 1968.

Maldives became fully independent as a sultanate outside the Commonwealth in 1965, with Ibrahim Nasir as prime minister. Nasir became president when the sultan was deposed for the second time, in 1968, and the country became a republic. It rejoined the Commonwealth in 1982. Britain had an air-force staging post on the southern island of Gan 1956–75, and its closure meant a substantial loss of income. The president nevertheless refused a Soviet offer in 1977 to lease the former base, saying that he did not want it used for military purposes again, nor leased to a superpower.

In 1978 Nasir announced that he would not stand for re-election and the *Majilis* nominated Maumoon Abdul Gayoom, a member of Nasir's cabinet, as his successor. Nasir went to Singapore but was called back to answer charges of misusing government funds. He denied the charges and attempts to extradite him failed. Despite rumours of a plot to overthrow him, Gayoom was re-elected for a further five years in 1983. Under Gayoom economic growth accelerated, helped by an expansion in tourism. Overseas, Gayoom broadly adhered to his predecessor's policy of nonalignment, but also began to develop closer links with the Arab nations of the Middle East, and in 1985 rejoined the Commonwealth and was a founder member of the ◊SAARC. In Nov 1988, soon after being re-elected for a third term, Gayoom was briefly ousted in an attempted coup led by Abdullah Luthufi, an exiled businessman from the pro-secessional atoll of Adu, who had recruited a force of 200 Tamil mercenaries in Sri Lanka. Gayoom was restored to office following the intervention of Indian paratroops; 17 of those captured, including Luthufi, were sentenced to life imprisonment in 1989.

Maldon /ˈmɔːldən/ English market town in Essex, at the mouth of the river Chelmer; population (1981) 14,750. It was the scene of a battle in which the East Saxons were defeated by the Danes in 991, commemorated in the Anglo-Saxon

Maldives
Republic of
(Divehi Jumhuriya)

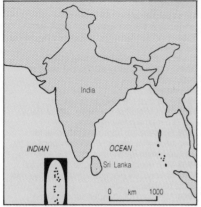

area 298 sq km/115 sq mi
capital Malé
physical comprises 1,200 coral islands grouped into 12 clusters of atolls, largely flat, none bigger than 13 sq km/5 sq mi
features only about 200 of the islands are inhabited
head of state and government Maumoon

Abdul Gayoom from 1978
political system authoritarian nationalism
political parties none; candidates elected on the basis of personal influence and clan loyalties
exports coconuts, copra, bonito (fish related to tuna); tourism
currency Rufiya (16.00 = £1 Feb 1990)
population (1988) 200,000; annual growth rate 3.2%
language Divehi (related to Sinhalese)
religion Islam
literacy 82% male/82% female (1977)
GNP $56 million (1983); $470 per head of population
chronology
1953 Originally a sultanate, the Maldive Islands became a republic within the Commonwealth.
1954 Sultanate restored.
1965 Achieved full independence outside the Commonwealth.
1968 Sultan deposed and a republic reinstated with Ibrahim Nasir as president.
1978 Nasir retired and was replaced by Maumoon Abdul Gayoom.
1983 Gayoom re-elected.
1985 Rejoined the Commonwealth.
1988 Gayoom re-elected. Coup attempt by mercenaries thought to have the backing of former president Nasir was foiled by Indian paratroops.

poem *The Battle of Maldon*.

Malé /'mɑːleɪ/ capital of the Maldives in the Indian Ocean; population (1985) 38,000. It trades in copra, breadfruit, and palm products.

Malebranche /mæl'brɒnʃ/ Nicolas 1638–1715. French philosopher. *De la Recherche de la Vérité/Search after Truth* 1674–78 was inspired by Descartes; he maintained that exact ideas of external objects are obtainable only through God. Born in Paris, he joined the Congregation of the Oratory in 1660.

Malenkov /'mælənkɒf/ Georgi Maximilianovich 1901–1988. Soviet prime minister 1953–55, Stalin's designated successor but abruptly ousted within two weeks of Stalin's death as Communist Party secretary by ◊Khrushchev, and replaced as prime minister in 1955 by ◊Bulganin.

Malenkov officially resigned on grounds of 'inadequate experience' and subsequently occupied minor party posts. He was expelled from the Central Committee 1957 and from the Communist Party 1961.

Malevich /'mælɪvɪtʃ/ Kasimir 1878–1935. Russian abstract painter, born in Kiev. In 1912 he visited Paris and became a Cubist, and in 1913 he launched his own abstract movement, ◊*Suprematism*. Later he returned to figurative themes treated in a semi-abstract style.

Malherbe /mæ'leəb/ François de 1555–1628. French poet and grammarian, born in Caen. He became court poet about 1605 under Henry IV and Louis XIII. He advocated reform of language and versification, and established the 12-syllable Alexandrine as the standard form of French verse.

Mali /'mɑːli/ landlocked country in NW Africa, bordered to the NE by Algeria, E by Niger, SE by Burkina Faso, S by the Ivory Coast, SW by Senegal and Guinea, and W and N by Mauritania.
government The 1974 constitution, amended in 1981 and 1985, provides for a one-party state, with a president elected by universal suffrage, and an 82-member national assembly elected from a party list for a three-year term. The president serves for six years and may be re-elected any

Mali
Republic of
(République du Mali)

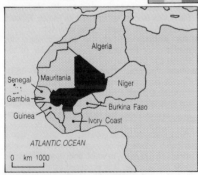

area 1,240,142 sq km/478,695 sq mi
capital Bamako
physical river Niger in S; savanna; part of the Sahara in N
features the old town of Timbuktu
head of state and government Moussa Traoré from 1968
political system one-party republic

political parties Malian People's Democratic Union (UDPM), nationalist
exports cotton, groundnuts, livestock
currency CFA franc (replacing Mali franc 1984) (485.00 = £1 Feb 1990)
population (1988) 7,784,000; annual growth rate 2.8%
life expectancy men 40, women 44
language French (official), Bambara
religion Sunni Muslim 65%, animist 35%
literacy 23% male/11% female (1985 est)
GNP $1.1 bn (1983); $140 per head of population
chronology
1959 With Senegal, formed the Federation of Mali.
1960 Became the independent Republic of Mali, with Mobido Keita as president.
1968 Keita replaced in an army coup by Moussa Traoré.
1974 New constitution made Mali a one-party state.
1976 New national party, the Malian People's Democratic Union, announced.
1983 Agreement between Mali and Guinea for eventual political and economic integration signed.

number of times. The party is the Malian People's Democratic Union (UDPM).

history From the 7th to the 11th century part of the ◊Ghana Empire, then of the Muslim ◊Mali empire, which flourished in NW Africa during the 7th–15th centuries, the area now known as Mali came under the rule of the ◊Songhai Empire during the 15th–16th centuries. In 1591 an invasion by Moroccan forces seeking to take over the W Sudanese gold trade destroyed the Songhai Empire and left the area divided into small kingdoms.

Because of its inland position, the region had little contact with Europeans, who were trading around the coast from the 16th century, and it was not until the 19th century that France, by means of treaties with local rulers, established colonies throughout most of NW Africa. As French Sudan, Mali was part of French West Africa from 1893. In 1959, with Senegal, it formed the Federation of Mali. In 1960 Senegal left and Mali became a fully independent republic.

Its first president, Modibo Keita, imposed an authoritarian socialist regime but his economic policies failed and he was removed in an army coup in 1968. The constitution was suspended, political activity was banned, and government was placed in the hands of a Military Committee for National Liberation (CMLN) with Lieut Moussa Traoré as president and head of state. In 1969 he became prime minister as well. He promised a return to civilian rule and in 1974 a new constitution made Mali a one-party state. A new party, the UDPM, was announced in 1976. Despite student opposition to a one-party state and army objections to civilian rule, Traoré successfully made the transition so that by 1979 Mali had a constitutional government, while ultimate power lay with the party and the military establishment.

In 1983 Mali and Guinea signed an agreement for eventual economic and political integration. In 1985 a border dispute with Burkina Faso resulted in a five-day conflict which was settled by the International Court of Justice.

malic acid $C_4H_6O_5$ an organic compound that can be extracted from apples, plums, cherries, grapes, and other fruits. It occurs in all living cells, though in smaller amounts, being one of the intermediates of ◊Krebs' cycle.

Mali Empire a Muslim empire in NW Africa during the 7th–15th centuries. Thriving on its trade in gold, it reached its peak in the 14th century under Mansa Musa (reigned 1312–37), when it occupied an area covering present-day Senegal, Gambia, Mali, and S Mauritania. Mali's territory was similar to (though larger than) that of the ◊Ghana Empire, and gave way in turn to the ◊Songhai Empire.

Malik /'mælɪk/ Yakob Alexandrovich 1906–1980. Soviet diplomat. He was permanent representative at the United Nations 1948–53 and 1968–76, and it was his walkout from the Security Council in Jan 1950 that allowed the authorization of UN intervention in Korea (see ◊Korean War).

Malines /mæ'liːn/ French name for ◊Mechelen, city in Belgium.

Malinovsky /ˌmælɪ'nɒfski/ Rodion Yakolevich 1898–1967. Russian soldier and politician. In World War II he fought at Stalingrad, commanded in Ukraine, and led the advance through the Balkans to capture Budapest 1945. He was minister of defence 1957–67.

Malinowski /ˌmælɪ'nɒfski/ Bronislaw 1884–1942. Polish anthropologist, one of the founders of the theory of ◊functionalism in the social sciences. His study of the peoples of the Trobriand Islands led him to see customs and practices in terms of their function in creating and maintaining social order.

Malipiero /ˌmælɪ'pjeərəʊ/ Gian Francesco 1882–1973. Italian composer and editor of ◊Monteverdi and ◊Vivaldi. His own works include operas based on Shakespeare's *Julius Caesar* 1934–35 and *Antony and Cleopatra* 1936–37 in a Neo-Classical style.

mallard common wild duck *Anas platyrhynchos* found almost worldwide and from which domestic ducks were bred. The male, which can grow to a length of 60 cm/2 ft, usually has a green head and brown breast, while the female is mottled brown. They are omnivorous.

Mallarmé /ˌmælɑːˈmeɪ/ Stéphane 1842–1898. French poet who founded the Symbolist school with Verlaine. His belief that poetry should be evocative and suggestive was reflected in *L'Après-midi d'un faune/Afternoon of a Faun* 1876, which inspired Debussy. Later publications are *Poésies complètes/Complete Poems* 1887, *Vers et prose/Verse and Prose* 1893, and the prose *Divagations/Digressions* 1897.

Malle /mæl/ Louis 1932– . French film director. After a period as assistant to Robert ◊Bresson, he directed *Les Amants/The Lovers* 1958, audacious in its time for its explicitness. His subsequent films, made in France and the USA, include *Zazie dans le metro* 1961, *Vive Maria* 1965, *Pretty Baby* 1978, *Atlantic City* 1980, and *Au Revoir les enfants* 1988.

mallee small trees and shrubs of the genus *Eucalyptus* with many small stems and thick underground roots that retain water. Before irrigation farming began it characterized the mallee region of NW Victoria, Australia.

Mallorca Spanish form of ◊Majorca, an island in the Mediterranean.

mallow flowering plant of the family Malvaceae, including the European **common mallow** *Malva sylvestris*; the **tree mallow** *Lavatera arborea*; and the **marsh mallow** *Althaea officinalis*. See also ◊hollyhock. Most have pink or purple flowers.

Malmaison /ˌmælmeɪˈzɒn/ chateau near Paris formerly belonging to the empress ◊Josephine, who died there.

Malmédy /ˈmælmədi/ town in Liège, E Belgium 40 km/25 mi S of Aachen, in the region of Eupen et Malmédy.

Malmö /ˈmælməʊ/ industrial port (shipbuilding, engineering, textiles) in SW Sweden; population (1988) 231,000.

Malory /ˈmæləri/ Thomas 15th century. English author of the prose romance *Le Morte d'Arthur* (about 1470). It is a translation from the French, modified by material from other sources, and deals with the exploits of King Arthur's knights of the Round Table and the quest for the Grail.

Malory's identity is uncertain. He is thought to have been the Warwickshire landowner of that name who was member of Parliament for Warwick in 1445, and in 1451 and 1452 was charged with rape, theft, and attempted murder. If that is so, he must have compiled *Morte d'Arthur* during his 20 years in Newgate prison.

Malpighi /mælˈpiːgi/ Marcello 1628–1694. Italian physiologist, who made many discoveries (still known by his name) in his microscope studies of animal and plant tissues.

Malplaquet, Battle of /ˌmælplæˈkeɪ/ victory in 1709 of the British, Dutch, and Austrian forces over the French forces during the War of the ◊Spanish Succession. The village of Malplaquet is in Nord *département*, France.

malpractice in US law, ◊negligence by a professional person, usually a doctor, which may lead to an action for damages by the client. Such legal actions are more common in the USA than in Britain, and result in doctors having high insurance costs which are reflected in higher fees charged to their patients.

Malraux /mælˈrəʊ/ André 1901–1976. French novelist. He became involved in the nationalist and communist revolution in China in the 1920s, reflected in *La Condition humaine/Man's Estate* 1933; *L'Espoir/Days of Hope* 1937 is set in Civil War Spain. He was minister of cultural affairs 1960–69.

malt in brewing, grain (barley, oats, or wheat) artificially germinated and then dried in a kiln. Malts are fermented to make beers or lagers, or fermented and then distilled to produce spirits

Malta
Republic of
(Repubblika Ta'Malta)

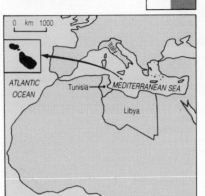

area 320 sq km/124 sq mi
capital Valletta
physical includes the island of Gozo 67 sq km/26 sq mi and Comino 2.5 sq km/1 sq mi
features large commercial dock facilities
head of state Vincent Tabone from 1989
head of government Edward Fenech Adami from 1987
political system liberal democracy
political parties Malta Labour Party (MLP), moderate, left-of-centre; Nationalist Party, Christian, centrist, pro-European
exports vegetables, knitwear, handmade lace,

plastics, electronic equipment
currency Maltese pound (0.55 = £1 Feb 1990)
population (1987) 346,000; annual growth rate 0.7%
life expectancy men 69, women 74
language Maltese (related to Arabic, with Phoenician survivals and influenced by Italian)
religion Roman Catholic
literacy 86% male/82% female (1985 est)
GNP $1.04 bn (1983); $2,036 per head of population
chronology
1942 Awarded the George Cross.
1955 Dom Mintoff of the Malta Labour Party (MLP) became prime minister.
1956 Referendum approved proposal for integration with the UK. Proposal opposed by the Nationalist Party.
1958 MLP rejected the integration proposal.
1962 Nationalists elected, with Borg Olivier as prime minister.
1964 Achieved full independence, within the Commonwealth. Ten-year defence and economic aid treaty with the UK signed.
1971 Mintoff re-elected. The 1964 treaty declared invalid and negotiations began for the leasing of the NATO base in Malta.
1972 Seven-year NATO agreement signed.
1974 Became a republic.
1984 Mintoff retired and was replaced by Mifsud Bonnici as prime minister and MLP leader.
1987 Edward Fenech Adami (Nationalist) became prime minister.
1989 Vincent Tabone elected president.

such as whisky.

Malta /ˈmɔːltə/ island in the Mediterranean, S of Sicily, E of Tunisia, and N of Libya.

government The 1974 constitution provides for a single-chamber legislature, the 65-member House of Representatives, elected by universal suffrage, through a system of proportional representation, for a five-year term. As formal head of state the president is elected by the House for a five-year term, and appoints a prime minister and cabinet, drawn from and collectively responsible to the House, which may be dissolved within its five-year term. A 1987 amendment to the constitution made provision for any party winning more than 50% of the votes in a general election to be guaranteed a majority of seats in the House of Representatives, regardless of the number of seats actually won.

history Malta was occupied in turn by Phoenicia, Greece, Carthage, and Rome, and fell to the Arabs 870. In 1090 the Norman Count Roger of Sicily conquered Malta, and it remained under Sicilian rule until the 16th century, when the Holy Roman Emperor Charles V handed it over to the Knights of ◊St John of Jerusalem 1530. After a Turkish attack 1565 the knights fortified the island, and held it until 1798, when they surrendered to Napoleon. After requesting British protection, Malta was annexed by Britain 1814, and became an important naval base. A vital link in World War II, Malta came under heavy attack and was awarded the ◊George Cross decoration.

The island was made self-governing 1947, and in 1955 Dom Mintoff, leader of the Malta Labour Party (MLP), became prime minister. In 1956 the MLP's proposal for integration with the UK was approved by a referendum but opposed by the conservative Nationalist Party, led by Dr Giorgio Borg Olivier. In 1958 Mintoff rejected the British proposals and resigned, causing a constitutional crisis. By 1961 both parties favoured independence, and talks began 1962, with Borg Olivier as prime minister.

Malta became a fully independent state within the Commonwealth and under the British crown

in 1964, having signed a ten-year military and economic aid treaty with the UK. In 1971 Mintoff and the MLP returned to power with a policy of international nonalignment. He declared the 1964 treaty invalid and began to negotiate a new arrangement for leasing the Maltese NATO base and obtaining the maximum economic benefit from it for his country.

A seven-year agreement was signed 1972. Malta became a republic 1974, and in the 1976 general election the MLP was returned with a reduced majority. It again won a narrow majority in the House of Representatives 1981, even though the Nationalists had a bigger share of the popular vote. As a result, Nationalist MPs refused to take up their seats for over a year. Relations between the two parties were also damaged by allegations of pro-government bias in the broadcasting service. At the end of 1984 Mintoff announced his retirement and Dr Mifsud Bonnici succeeded him as MLP leader and prime minister. The Nationalist Party was elected in 1987 and its leader, Edward Fenech Adami, became prime minister.

Malta, Knights of /ˈmɔːltə/ another name for members of the military-religious order of the Hospital of ◊St John of Jerusalem.

Malthus /ˈmælθəs/ Thomas Robert 1766–1834. English economist and cleric, whose *Essay on the Principle of Population* 1798 (revised 1803) argued for population control, since populations increase in geometric ratio, and food only in arithmetic ratio. He saw war, famine, and disease as necessary checks on population growth.

maltose a ◊disaccharide sugar with the molecular formula $C_{12}H_{22}O_{11}$, in which both monosaccharide units are glucose. It is produced by the enzymic hydrolysis of starch and is a major constituent of malt, produced in the early stages of beer and whisky manufacture.

malt tax in Britain, a tax on malt was first introduced 1697 on the use of malt in brewing. It supplemented the existing beer duty when a hop duty was imposed between 1711 and 1862. The malt tax was abolished 1880 when replaced by a tax on drinking beer.

Maluku (Moluccas)

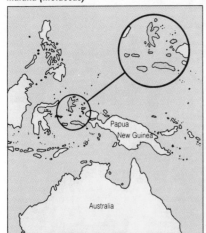

Maluku /məˈluːkuː/ or **Moluccas** group of Indonesian islands
area 74,500 sq km/28,764 sq mi
capital Ambon, on Amboina
population (1980) 1,411,000
history as the Spice Islands, they were formerly part of the Netherlands East Indies, and the S Moluccas attempted secession from the newly created Indonesian republic from 1949; exiles continue agitation in the Netherlands.

Malvern /ˈmɔːlvən/ English spa in Hereford and Worcester, on the E side of the *Malvern Hills*, which extend for about 16 km/10 mi, and have their high point in Worcester Beacon 425 m/1,395 ft; population (1981) 32,000. The *Malvern Festival* 1929–39, associated with Shaw and Elgar, was revived in 1977.

Malvinas /mælˈviːnəs/ Argentinian name for the ◊Falkland Islands.

mamba venomous snake of the cobra family found in Africa S of the Sahara. The *green mamba Dendroaspis angusticeps* is 1.5 m/5 ft long or more and lives in trees, feeding on birds and lizards. The *black mamba Dendroaspis polylepis* is the largest venomous snake in Africa, occasionally as much as 3.4 m/11 ft long, and spends more time on the ground.

Mameluke /ˈmæməluːk/ member of a powerful political class who dominated Egypt from the 13th century until their massacre in 1811 by Mehmet Ali.

The Mamelukes were originally descended from freed Turkish slaves. They formed the royal bodyguard in the 13th century, and in 1250 placed one of their own number on the throne. Mameluke sultans ruled Egypt until the Turkish conquest of 1517, and they remained the ruling class until 1811.

Mamet /ˈmæmɪt/ David 1947– . US playwright. His plays, with their vivid, freewheeling language and sense of ordinary US life, include *American Buffalo* 1977, *Sexual Perversity in Chicago* 1978, and *Glengary, Glen Ross* 1984.

mammal a vertebrate animal which suckles its young and has hair, lungs, and a four-chambered heart. Mammals maintain a constant body temperature in varied surroundings. Most mammals give birth to live young, but the platypus and echidna lay eggs. There are over 4,000 species, adapted to almost every conceivable way of life. The smallest shrew weighs only 2 g/0.07 oz, the largest whale up to 150 tonnes.

mammary gland in female mammals, milk-producing gland derived from epithelial cells underlying the skin, active only after the production of young. In all but monotremes (egg-laying mammals), the mammary glands terminate in teats which aid infant suckling. The number of glands and their position vary between species. In humans there are two, in cows four, and in pigs between ten and fourteen.

mammography an X-ray procedure used to detect breast cancer at an early stage.

Mammon an evil personification of wealth and greed; originally a Syrian god of riches, cited in the New Testament as opposed to the Christian god.

mammoth genus *Mammuthus* of extinct elephants whose remains are found worldwide. Some were half as tall again as modern species. The woolly mammoth *Elephas primigenius*, the size of an Indian elephant, had long fur, and large inward-curving tusks. Mammoths were abundant in N Europe in Pleistocene times.

Mammoth Cave huge limestone cavern in Mammoth Cave National Park 1936, Kentucky, USA. The main cave is 6.5 km/4 mi long, and rises to a height of 38 m/125 ft; it is known for its stalactites and stalagmites. Indian councils were once held here.

Mamoulian /məˈmuːliən/ Rouben 1898–1987. Armenian film director who lived in the USA from 1923. After several years on Broadway he turned to films, making the first sound version of *Dr Jekyll and Mr Hyde* 1932 and *Queen Christina* 1933. His later work includes *The Mark of Zorro* 1940 and *Silk Stockings* 1957.

Man. abbreviation for ◊*Manitoba*.

management process or technique of managing a business. Systems vary according to the type of organization, company, and objectives. In Europe, there has been a trend toward management by consensus, rather than by the individual.

Since the early 1970s, there has been a growing demand for learned management skills, such as those taught in the Harvard Business School (USA) and at the London Business School. By contrast, in Japan, such skills are learned on the job; employees tend to spend their careers with the same company and toward the end of it will acquire management status.

Managua /məˈnɑːgwə/ capital and chief industrial city of Nicaragua, on the lake of the same name; population (1985) 682,000. It has twice been destroyed by earthquake and rebuilt, in 1931 and 1972; it was also badly damaged during the civil war in the late 1970s.

manakin bird of the family Pipridae found in South and Central America, about 15 cm/ 6 in long and often brightly coloured. It feeds on berries and other small fruits.

Manama /məˈnɑːmə/ (Arabic *Al Manamah*) capital and free trade port of Bahrain, on Bahrain Island; handles oil and entrepôt trade; population (1988) 152,000.

manatee plant-eating aquatic mammal of the genus *Trichechus* belonging to the order Sirenia (sea cows). Manatees are found on the eastern coasts of tropical North and South America, and around West Africa. They are in danger of becoming extinct.

Manatees occur in fresh and sea water. Their forelimbs are flippers; their hindlimbs are absent, but they have a short, rounded and flattened tail which is used for propulsion.

Manaus /məˈnaʊs/ capital of Amazonas, Brazil, on the Rio Negro, near its confluence with the Amazon; population (1980) 612,000. It can be reached by sea-going vessels, although 1,600 km/1,000 mi from the Atlantic. Formerly a centre of the rubber trade, it developed as a tourist centre in the 1970s.

Manawatu /ˌmænəˈwɑːtuː/ river in North Island, New Zealand, rising in the Ruahine Range.
Manawatu Plain is a rich farming area, specializing in dairying and fat lamb production.

Mancha /ˈmæntʃə/ see ◊La Mancha, former province of Spain.

Manche, La /mɒnʃ/ French name for the English ◊Channel. It gives its name to a French *département*.

Manchester /ˈmæntʃɪstə/ port in NW England, on the river Irwell, 50 km/31 mi E of Liverpool. It is a manufacturing (textile machinery, chemicals, rubber, processed foods) and financial centre;

Greater Manchester

population (1985) 451,000. It is linked by the Manchester Ship Canal, built 1894, to the river Mersey and the sea.
features home of the Hallé Orchestra, the Northern College of Music, the Royal Exchange (built 1869, now a theatre), a town hall (by Alfred ◊Waterhouse), and a Cotton Exchange (now a leisure centre).
history originally a Roman camp, Manchester is mentioned in the Domesday Book, and already by the 13th century was a centre for the wool trade. Its damp climate made it ideal for cotton, introduced in the 16th century, and in the 19th century the Manchester area was a world centre of manufacture, using cotton imported from North America and India. After 1945 there was a sharp decline, and many disused mills were refurbished to provide alternative industrial uses.

Long a hub of ◊Radical thought, Manchester has always been a cultural and intellectual centre; it was the original home of the *Guardian* (founded as the *Manchester Guardian* 1821). Its pop-music scene flourished in the 1980s.

Manchester, Greater /ˈmæntʃɪstə/ former (1974–86) metropolitan county of NW England, replaced by a residuary body in 1986 which covers some of its former functions
area 1,290 sq km/498 sq mi
towns administrative headquarters Manchester; Bolton, Oldham, Rochdale, Salford, Stockport, and Wigan
features Manchester Ship Canal links it with the Mersey and the sea; Old Trafford cricket ground at Stretford, and the football ground of Manchester United
products industrial
population (1987) 2,580,000
famous people Anthony Burgess, John Dalton, Gracie Fields, James Joule, Emmeline Pankhurst.

Manchu ruling dynasty in China from 1644 until their overthrow in 1912. Originally a nomadic people from Manchuria, they established power through a series of successful invasions from the north.

Manchukuo /ˌmæntʃuːˈkwəʊ/ former Japanese puppet state in Manchuria 1932–45.

Manchuria /mænˈtʃʊəriə/ European name for the NE region of China. It was united with China by the ◊Manchu dynasty 1644, but as the Chinese Empire declined Japan and Russia were rivals for its control. The Russians were expelled after the ◊Russo-Japanese War, and in 1932 Japan consolidated its position by creating a puppet state, *Manchukuo*, which disintegrated on the defeat of Japan in World War II.

From the 17th century it was controlled by the Manchus, and a Manchu dynasty ruled China by conquest 1644–1912. Chinese colonization of Manchuria began in the 18th century (80% of the population by 1900). Manchukuo was ruled by the former Chinese emperor Henry ◊P'u-i; its capi-

Mandela *The African National Congress vice president, Nelson Mandela. A resonant symbol of the black struggle against South African apartheid, he is pictured shortly after his release from prison in 1990, ending 27 years of incarceration.*

Manet *A Bar at the Folies-Bergère (1882) Courtauld Collection, London.*

tal was Hsinking (modern Chinese Changchun). After World War II Japanese settlers were expelled. Manchuria comprises the provinces of Heilongjiang, Jilin, and Liaoning.

Mandaean a member of the only surviving Gnostic sect of Christianity (see ◊Gnosticism). The Mandaeans live near the Euphrates, S Iraq, and their sacred book is the *Ginza*.

mandala a symmetrical design in Hindu and Buddhist art, representing the universe; used in some forms of meditation.

Mandalay /ˌmændəˈleɪ/ chief town of Upper Myanmar, on the river Irrawaddy, about 495 km/370 mi N of Yangon; population (1983) 533,000.

Founded by King Mindon Min in 1857, it was capital of Burma 1857–85, and has many pagodas, temples, and monasteries.

Mandarin the standard form of the Chinese language. Historically it derives from the language spoken by *mandarins*, Chinese imperial officials, from the 7th century onwards. It is used by 70% of the population.

mandarin variety of the tangerine orange *Citrus reticulata*.

mandate in history, a territory whose administration was entrusted to Allied states by the League of Nations under the Treaty of Versailles after World War I. Mandated territories were former German and Turkish possessions (including Iraq, Syria, Lebanon, and Palestine). When the United Nations replaced the League of Nations in 1945, mandates that had not achieved independence became known as ◊trust territories.

In general, mandate means any official command; in politics also the right (given by the electors) of an elected government to carry out its programme of policies.

Mandela /mænˈdelə/ Nelson (Rolihlahla) 1918– . South African politician and lawyer. As organizer of the banned ◊African National Congress (ANC), he was acquitted of treason 1961, but was given a life sentence 1964 on charges of sabotage and plotting to overthrow the government. In prison he became a symbol of unity for the worldwide anti-apartheid movement. In Feb 1990 he was released, the ban on the ANC having been lifted.

Mandela /mænˈdelə/ Winnie (Nomzamo) 1934– . Civil-rights activist in South Africa and wife of Nelson Mandela. A leading spokesperson for the African National Congress during her husband's imprisonment 1964–90, she has been jailed

for a year and put under house arrest several times.

Mandelbrot /ˈmændəlˌbrɒt/ Benoit B 1924– . Polish-born US scientist who coined the term ◊fractal geometry' to describe 'self-similar' shape, a motif that repeats indefinitely, each time smaller.

Mandelshtam /ˈmændlʃtæm/ Osip Emilevich 1891–1938. Russian poet. Son of a Jewish merchant, he was sent to a concentration camp by the Communist authorities in the 1930s, and died there. His posthumously published work with its classic brevity established his reputation as one of the greatest modern Russian poets.

Mandeville /ˈmændɪvɪl/ John. Supposed author of a 14th-century travel manual for pilgrims to the Holy Land, originally written in French and probably the work of Jean d'Outremeuse of Liège. As well as references to real marvels such as the pyramids, there are tales of headless people with eyes in their shoulders, and other such fantastic inventions.

mandolin musical instrument with four or five pairs of strings. It is descended from the ◊lute, and takes its name from its almond-shaped body (Italian *mandorla* 'almond').

mandragora or **mandrake** genus of almost stemless plants with narcotic properties, of the family Solanaceae. They have large leaves, pale blue or violet flowers, and globose berries known as devil's apples. The humanoid shape of the root gave rise to the superstition that it shrieks when pulled from the ground.

mandrake another name for the plant ◊mandragora.

mandrill large W African ground-living monkey *Mandrillus sphinx*. The nose is bright red and the cheeks striped with blue. There are red callosities on the buttocks; the fur is brown, apart from a yellow beard. It has large canine teeth.

Manes /ˈmɑːneɪz/ in ancient Rome, the spirits of the dead, revered as lesser deities, or sometimes identified with the gods of the underworld.

Manet /ˈmæneɪ/ Edouard 1832–1883. French painter, active in Paris. Rebelling against the academic tradition, he developed a clear and unaffected Realist style. His work was an inspiration to the young Impressionists. His subjects were chiefly modern, such as *Un Bar aux Folies-Bergère*/*A Bar at the Folies-Bergère* 1882 (Courtauld Art Gallery, London).

Manet, born in Paris, trained under a history painter and was inspired by Goya and Velázquez but also by his near-contemporary Courbet. His *Déjeuner sur l'herbe*/*Picnic on the Grass* 1863 and *Olympia* 1865 (both Musée d'Orsay, Paris) offended conservative tastes in their matter-of-fact treatment of the nude body. He never exhibited with the Impressionists, although he was associated with them from the 1870s.

mangabey type of African monkey genus *Cercocebus* with long limbs and tail. It lives in tropical forests.

Mangalore /ˌmæŋɡəˈlɔː/ industrial port (textiles, timber, food-processing) at the mouth of the Netravati River in Karnataka, S India; population (1981) 306,000.

manganese a silvery-white metallic element, symbol Mn, atomic number 25, relative atomic mass 54.9. Manganese is among the most common metals in the Earth's crust and is used to make certain steels, as well as bronze, brass, and nickel alloys.

manganese ore any mineral from which manganese is produced. The main ores are the oxides, such as *pyrolusite*, MnO_2; *hausmannite*, Mn_3O_4; and *manganite*, $MnO(OH)$.

Manganese ores may accumulate in metamorphic rocks or as sedimentary deposits, frequently forming nodules on the sea floor (since the 1970s many schemes have been put forward to harvest deep-sea manganese nodules). The world's main producers are the USSR, South Africa, Brazil, Gabon, and India.

mangel wurzel or **mangold** variety of the common beet *Beta vulgaris* used chiefly as feed for cattle and sheep.

mango tree *Mangifera indica*, native to India but now widely cultivated for its oval fruits in other tropical and subtropical areas, for example the West Indies.

mangold another name for ◊mangel wurzel.

mangrove shrub or tree found in the muddy swamps of tropical coasts and estuaries where, by sending down aerial roots from its branches, it rapidly forms close-growing mangrove swamps. Its timber is impervious to water and resists marine worms.

Manhattan /mænˈhætn/ an island 20 km/12.5 mi long and 4 km/2.5 mi wide, lying between the Hudson and East rivers and forming a borough of the city of ◊New York, USA; population (1980) 1,428,000. It includes the Wall Street business centre and Broadway theatres.

Manhattan Project code name for the development of the ◊atom bomb in the USA in World War II,

mangrove *Mangrove swamp in Costa Rica. The extensive root system helps trap mud and silt. The trees are adapted to cope with the salt water that engulfs the roots each high tide.*

to which the physicists Fermi and Oppenheimer contributed.

manic depression a mental disorder characterized by recurring periods of ◊depression which may or may not alternate with periods of inappropriate elation (mania) or overactivity. Sufferers may be genetically predisposed to the condition.

Manichaeism religion founded by the prophet Mani (Latinized as Manichaeus, *c.*216–276). Despite persecution Manichaeism spread and flourished until about the 10th century. It held that the material world is an invasion of the realm of light by the powers of darkness: particles of goodness imprisoned in matter were to be rescued by messengers such as Jesus, and finally by Mani himself.

He proclaimed his creed in 241 at the Persian court. Returning from missions to China and India, he was put to death at the instigation of the Zoroastrian priesthood.

Manifest Destiny in US history, the belief that Americans had a providential mission to extend both their territory and their democratic processes westwards across the continent. The phrase was coined by journalist John L O'Sullivan in 1845. Reflecting this belief, Texas and California were shortly afterwards annexed by the USA.

Manila /məˈnɪlə/ industrial port (textiles, tobacco, distilling, chemicals, shipbuilding) and capital of the Philippines, on the island of Luzon; population (1980) 1,630,000, metropolitan area (including ◊Quezon City) 5,926,000.

history Manila was founded 1571 by Spain, captured by the USA 1898, and in 1945 during World War II the old city to the south of the river Pasig was reduced to rubble in fighting between US and Japanese troops. It was replaced as capital by Quezon City 1948–76.

manioc another name for the plant ◊cassava.

Manipur /ˌmʌnɪˈpʊə/ state of NE India
area 22,400 sq km/8,646 sq mi
capital Imphal
features Loktak Lake; original Indian home of polo
products grain, fruit, vegetables, sugar, textiles, cement
population (1981) 1,434,000
language Hindi
religion Hindu 70%
history administered from the state of Assam until 1947 when it became a Union Territory. It became a state 1972.

Man, Isle of /mæn/ island in the Irish Sea, a dependency of the British crown, but not part of the UK
area 570 sq km/220 sq mi
capital Douglas
towns Ramsey, Peel, Castletown
features Snaefell 620 m/2,035 ft; annual TT (Tourist Trophy) motorcycle races, gambling casinos, Britain's first free port, tax haven; tailless Manx cat; tourism, banking, and insurance are important
exports light engineering products
currency the island produces its own coins and notes in UK currency denominations
population (1986) 64,000
language English (Manx, nearer to Scottish than Irish Gaelic, has been almost extinct since the 1970s)
government crown-appointed lieutenant-governor, a legislative council, and the representative House of Keys, which together make up the Court of Tynwald, passing laws subject to the royal assent. Laws passed at Westminster only affect the island if specifically so provided
history Norwegian until 1266, when the island was ceded to Scotland; it came under UK administration 1765.

Manitoba /ˌmænɪˈtəʊbə/ prairie province of Canada
area 650,000 sq km/250,900 sq mi
capital Winnipeg

Manipur

INDIAN OCEAN

Manitoba

Winnipeg

features lakes Winnipeg, Winnipegosis, and Manitoba (area 4,700 sq km/1,814 sq mi); 50% forested
exports grain, manufactured foods, beverages, machinery, furs, fish, nickel, zinc, copper, and the world's largest caesium deposits
population (1986) 1,071,000
history known as Red River settlement until it joined Canada 1870, it was the site of the Riel Rebellion 1885. The area of the province was extended 1881 and 1912.

Manitoba, Lake /ˌmænɪˈtəʊbə/ lake in Manitoba province, Canada, which drains into Lake Winnipeg to the NE through the river Dauphin; area 4,700 sq km/1,800 sq mi.

Manizales /ˌmænɪˈsɑːles/ city in the Central Cordillera in W Colombia 2,150 m/7,000 ft above sea level, centre of a coffee-growing area; population (1985) 328,000. It is linked with Mariquita by the world's longest overhead cable transport system 72 km/45 mi.

Manley /ˈmænli/ Michael 1924– . Jamaican politician, prime minister 1972–80 and from 1989, adopting more moderate socialist policies. His father, **Norman Manley** (1893–1969), was founder of the People's National Party and prime minister 1959–62.

Mann /mæn/ Anthony. Adopted name of Emil Anton Bundmann 1906–1967. US film director who made a series of violent but intelligent 1950s Westerns starring James Stewart, such as *Winchester '73* 1950. He also directed one of the best film epics, *El Cid* 1961. His other films include *The Glenn Miller Story* 1954 and *A Dandy in Aspic* 1968.

Mann /mæn/ Heinrich 1871–1950. German novelist who fled to the USA in 1937 with his brother Thomas Mann. His books include a scathing trilogy dealing with the Kaiser's Germany *Das Kaiserreich/The Empire* 1918–25.

Mann /mæn/ Thomas 1875–1955. German novelist and critic, concerned with the theme of the artist's relation to society. His first novel was ◊*Buddenbrooks* 1901 which, followed by *Der Zauberberg/The Magic Mountain* 1924, led to a Nobel prize 1929. Later works include *Dr Faustus* 1947 and *Die Bekenntnisse des Hochstaplers Felix Krull/Confessions of Felix Krull* 1954. Notable among his short stories is *Der Tod in Venedig/Death in Venice* 1913.

Mann worked in an insurance office in Munich and on the staff of the periodical *Simplicissimus*. His opposition to the Nazi regime forced him to live abroad and in 1940 he became a US citizen. Among his other works are the biblical tetralogy on the theme of Joseph and his brothers 1933–44, and a number of short stories including *Tonio Kröger* 1903.

manna a sweetish exudation obtained from many trees such as the ash and larch, and used in medicine. The manna of the Bible is thought to have been from the tamarisk tree.

Mannerheim /ˈmænəheɪm/ Carl Gustav Emil von 1867–1951. Finnish general and politician, leader of the conservative forces in the civil war 1917–18 and regent 1918–19. He commanded the Finnish army 1939–40 and 1941–44, and was president of Finland 1944–46.

After the Russian Revolution 1917, a Red (socialist) militia was formed in Finland with Russian backing, and independence was declared in Dec. The Red forces were opposed by a White (counterrevolutionary) army led by Mannerheim, who in 1918 crushed the socialists with German assistance. In 1944, after leading the defence against Soviet invasion in two wars, he negotiated the peace settlement with the USSR and became president.

Mannerism in painting and architecture, a style characterized by a subtle but conscious breaking of the 'rules' of classical composition, for example, displaying the human body in a distorted pose, off-centre, and using harsh, non-blending colours. The term was coined by ◊Vasari and used to describe the 16th-century reaction to the peak of Renaissance classicism as achieved by Raphael, Leonardo, and early Michelangelo.

The effect is one of unsettling the viewer, who is expected to understand the norms that the Mannerist picture is deliberately violating. Strictly speaking, Mannerism is used to describe painters and architects in Italy (primarily Rome and Florence) during the years 1520 to 1575 beginning with, and largely derived from, the later works of Michelangelo in painting and architecture, and including the works of the painters Giovanni Rosso and Parmigianino, and the architect Giulio Romano, but the term has been extended to cover similar ideas in other arts and in other countries.

Manners family name of dukes of Rutland; seated at Belvoir Castle, Lincolnshire, England.

Mannheim /ˈmænhaɪm/ industrial city (heavy machinery, glass, earthenware, chemicals) on the Rhine in Baden-Württemberg, West Germany; population (1988) 295,000. The modern symphony orchestra, with its balance of instruments and the important role of the conductor, originated at Mannheim in the 18th century when the elector palatine assembled the finest players of his day.

Mannheim /ˈmænhaɪm/ Karl 1893–1947. Hungarian sociologist, who settled in the UK 1933. In *Ideology and Utopia* 1929 he argued that all knowledge, except in mathematics and physics, is ideological, a reflection of class interests and values; that there is no such thing as objective knowledge or absolute truth.

Mannheim distinguished between ruling class ideologies and those of utopian or revolutionary groups, arguing that knowledge is thus created by a continual power struggle between rival groups and ideas, Later works such as *Man and Society* 1940 analysed modern mass society in terms of its fragmentation and susceptibility to extremist ideas and totalitarian governments.

Manning /ˈmænɪŋ/ Henry Edward 1808–1892. English priest, one of the leaders of the Oxford Movement. In 1851 he was converted to Roman Catholicism, and in 1865 became archbishop of Westminster. He was created a cardinal 1875.

Manning /ˈmænɪŋ/ Olivia 1911–1980. British novelist. The best known of her books are semi-autobiographical and set during World War II. These include *The Great Fortune* 1960, *The Spoilt City* 1962, and *Friends and Heroes* 1965, forming the 'Balkan trilogy', and a later 'Levant trilogy'.

Manoel /mənˈwel/ two kings of Portugal:

Manoel I 1469–1521. King of Portugal from 1495, when he succeeded his uncle John II (1455–95). He was known as 'the Fortunate', because his reign was distinguished by the discoveries made by Portuguese navigators and the expansion of the Portuguese empire.

Manoel II 1889–1932. King of Portugal 1908–10. He ascended the throne on the assassination of his father, Carlos I, but was driven out by a revolution 1910, and lived in England.

manometer instrument for measuring the pressure of liquids (including human blood pressure) or gases. In its basic form, it is a U-tube partly filled with coloured liquid; pressure of a gas entering at

manometer

one side is measured by the level to which the liquid rises at the other.

manor basic economic unit in ◊feudalism in Europe, established under the Norman conquest in England. It consisted of the lord's house and cultivated land, land rented by free tenants, land held by villagers, common land, woodland, and waste land.

Here and there traces of the system survive in England—the common land may have become an area for public recreation—but the documents sometimes sold at auction and entitling the owner to be called 'lord of the manor' seldom have any rights attached to them.

Manpower Services Commission former name of the ◊Training Agency, UK organization for retraining the unemployed.

Mansart /mɒnˈsɑː/ Jules Hardouin 1646–1708. French architect of the palace of Versailles and Grand Trianon, and designer of the Place de Vendôme and the Place des Victoires, Paris.

Mansell /ˈmænsəl/ Nigel 1954– . English motor-racing driver. Runner-up in the world championship on two occasions.

He started his Formula One career with a Lotus 1980 and won the 1985 European Grand Prix. Drove for Williams 1985–88 and from 1989 for Ferrari. He has won 15 Grand Prix. He also completed one event as a single-handicap golfer on the European Professional Golfers Association (PGA) tour in 1989.

Mansfield /ˈmænsfiːld/ industrial town (textiles, shoes, machinery, chemicals, coal) in Nottinghamshire, England, on the river Maun, 22 km/14 mi N of Nottingham; population (1981) 59,000.

Mansfield /ˈmænzfiːld/ Jayne. Stage name of Vera Jayne Palmer 1933–1967. US actress who had a short career as a kind of living parody of Marilyn Monroe in films including *The Girl Can't Help It* 1956 and *Will Success Spoil Rock Hunter?* 1957.

Mansfield /ˈmænsfiːld/ Katherine. Pen name of Kathleen Beauchamp 1888–1923. New Zealand writer, who lived most of her life in England. Her delicate artistry emerges not only in her volumes of short stories, such as *In a German Pension* 1911, *Bliss* 1920 and *The Garden Party* 1923, but also in her *Letters* and *Journal*.

Born near Wellington, New Zealand, she was educated in London, to which she returned after a two-year visit home, where she published her earliest stories. She maried the critic John Middleton Murry in 1913.

mantis

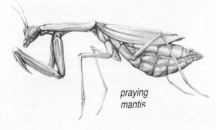

praying mantis

Mantegna The Agony in the Garden *(c.1455) National Gallery, London.*

manslaughter in English law, the unlawful killing of a human being in circumstances not so culpable as ◊murder; for example, when the killer suffers extreme provocation; is in some way mentally ill (diminished responsibility); did not intend to kill but did so accidentally in the course of another crime or by behaving with criminal recklessness; or is the survivor of a genuine suicide pact which involved killing the other person.

manslaughter, corporate in law, the crime of manslaughter in which the accused is alleged to be responsible for the deaths of many people. The first case of this kind in Britain was brought against Townsend Thoresen Ltd who operated the cross-Channel ferry *Herald of Free Enterprise* which sank in Mar 1987 off Zeebrugge, Belgium, with the loss of 193 lives.

Mans, Le /lə ˈmɒŋ/ town in France, site of an annual motor race; see ◊Le Mans.

Manson /ˈmænsən/ Patrick 1844–1922. Scottish physician, who showed that insects are responsible for the spread of diseases like elephantiasis and malaria.

Manson spent many years in practice in the Far East. On his return to London, he founded the School of Tropical Medicine. His work on malaria earned him the nickname 'Mosquito Manson'.

Manston /ˈmænstən/ RAF aerodrome in Kent, England, a major diversionary aerodrome for aircraft (civil or military) in distress.

Mansûra /mænˈsʊərə/ industrial town (cotton) and capital of Dakahlia province, NE Egypt, on the Damietta branch of the Nile; population (1983) 310,900. Mansûra was founded about 1220; St Louis IX, king of France, was imprisoned in the fortress while on a Crusade, 1250.

manta another name for the ◊devil ray, a large fish.

Mantegna /mænˈtenjə/ Andrea c.1431–1506. Italian Renaissance painter and engraver, active chiefly in Padua and Mantua, where some of his frescoes remain. Paintings such as *The Agony in the Garden* about 1455 (National Gallery, London) reveal a dramatic linear style, mastery of perspective, and strongly Classical architectural detail.

Mantegna was born in Vicenza. Early works include frescoes for the Eremitani Church in Padua (1440s, badly damaged). From 1460 he worked for Ludovico Gonzaga in Mantua, producing an outstanding fresco series in the Ducal Palace (1470s) and later *The Triumph of Caesar* (Hampton Court, near London). He was influenced by the sculptor Donatello and in turn influenced the Venetian painter Giovanni Bellini (his brother-in-law) and the German artist Dürer.

mantis insect of the family Mantidae, related to cockroaches. Some species can reach a length of 20 cm/8 in. There are about 2,000 species of mantis, mainly tropical.

The praying mantis *Mantis religiosa* has front legs adapted for grasping its prey; when at rest, the mantis appears to be praying, hence its name. The eggs are laid in Sept and hatch early in the following summer.

mantle the intermediate zone of the Earth between the ◊crust and the ◊core. It is thought

Mao Zedong *Chairman Mao with vice chair Lin Biao, who is holding the* Little Red Book *of Mao's thoughts.*

to consist of silicate minerals such as olivine and spinel.

The mantle is separated from the crust by the ◊Mohorovičić discontinuity, and from the core by the Gutenberg discontinuity. The patterns of seismic waves passing through it show that its uppermost as well as its lower layers are solid. However, from 72 km to 250 km/45 to 155 mi in depth is a zone through which seismic waves pass more slowly (the 'low-velocity zone'). The inference is that materials in this zone are close to their melting points and they are partly molten. The low-velocity zone is considered the ◊asthenosphere on which the solid lithosphere rides.

mantra in Hindu or Buddhist belief, a word repeatedly intoned to assist concentration and develop spiritual power; for example *om*, which represents the names of Brahma, Vishnu, and Siva. Followers of a guru may receive their own individual mantra.

Mantua /'mæntjuə/ (Italian *Mantova*) capital of Mantua province, Lombardy, Italy, on an island of a lagoon of the river Mincio, SW of Verona; industry (chemicals, brewing, printing); population (1981) 60,866. The poet Virgil was born near Mantua, which dates from Roman times; it has Gothic palaces and a cathedral founded in the 12th century.

Manu /'mɑːnuː/ in Hindu mythology, the founder of the human race, who was saved by ◊Brahma from a deluge.

Manutius /mə'njuːʃiəs/ Aldus 1450–1515. Italian printer, established in Venice (which he made the publishing centre of Europe) from 1490; he introduced italic type and was the first to print books in Greek.

Manx Gaelic a form of ◊Gaelic language.

Manzoni /mænd'zɔuni/ Alessandro, Count Manzoni 1785–1873. Italian poet and novelist, best known for his historical romance, *I promessi sposi*/*The Betrothed* 1825–27, set in Spanish-occupied Milan during the 17th century. Verdi's *Requiem* commemorates him.

Maoism form of communism based on the ideas and teachings of the Chinese communist leader ◊Mao Zedong. It involves an adaptation of ◊Marxism to suit conditions in China and apportions a much greater role for agriculture and the peasantry in the building of socialism, thus effectively bypassing the capitalist (industrial) stage envisaged by Marx.

Maori /'mɑuri/ member of a Polynesian people of New Zealand, who form about 10% of the population; (1986) 294,200. In recent years there has been increased Maori consciousness, and a demand for official status for the Maori language and review of the Waitangi Treaty of 1840 (under which the Maoris surrendered their lands to British sovereignty). The **Maori Unity Movement/Kotahitanga** was founded 1983 by Eva Rickard. The Maoris claim 70% of the country's land, and have secured a ruling that the fishing grounds of the far north belong solely to local tribes.

Maori language a member of the Polynesian branch of the Malayo-Polynesian language family, spoken by the Maori people of New Zealand. Only one-third use the language today, but efforts are being made to strengthen it after a long period of decline and official indifference.

In Maori, New Zealand is *Aotearoa* ('land of the long white cloud') and European settlers are *Pakeha*, a term often used by white New Zealanders when constrasting themselves with the Maori.

Mao Zedong /'mau dzɪ'dʌŋ/ or **Mao Tse-tung** 1893–1976. Chinese political leader and Marxist theoretician. A founder of the Chinese Communist Party (CCP) 1921, Mao soon emerged as its leader. He organized the ◊Long March 1934–36 and the war of liberation 1937–49, and headed the CCP and government until his death. His influence diminished with the failure of his 1958–60 ◊Great Leap Forward, but he emerged dominant again during the 1966–69 ◊Cultural Revolution. Mao adapted communism to Chinese conditions, as set out in the *Little Red Book*.

Mao, son of a peasant farmer in Hunan province, was once library assistant at Beijing University and a headmaster at Changsha. He became chief of CCP propaganda under the Guomindang (nationalist) leader Sun Yat-sen (Sun Zhong Shan) until sacked by Sun's successor Chiang Kai-shek (Jiang Jie Shi). In 1931–34 Mao set up a communist republic at Jiangxi and, with Zhu De, marshalled the Red Army in preparation for the Long March to Shaanxi. CCP chair from 1935, Mao secured an alliance with the Guomindang 1936–45. He built

up a people's republic at Yan'an 1936–47, where he married his third wife ◊Jiang Qing 1939. During the liberation war and civil wars, he successfully employed mobile, rural-based guerrilla tactics.

Mao served as party chair until his death Sept 1976 and as state president until 1959. After the damages of the Cultural Revolution, the Great Helmsman, as he was called, working with his prime minister Zhou Enlai, oversaw a period of reconstruction from 1970 until deteriorating health weakened his political grip in the final years.

Mao's writings and thoughts dominated the functioning of the People's Republic 1949–76. He stressed the need for rural rather than urban-based revolutions in Asia, for reducing rural-urban differences, and for perpetual revolution to prevent the emergence of new elites. Overseas, Mao helped precipitate the Sino-Soviet split 1960 and was a firm advocate of a ◊nonaligned Third World strategy. Since 1978, the leadership of Deng Xiaoping has reinterpreted Maoism and criticized its policy excesses, but many of Mao's ideas remain influential.

map a diagrammatic representation of an area, for example part of the Earth's surface, or the distribution of the stars. Modern maps of the Earth are

map projection

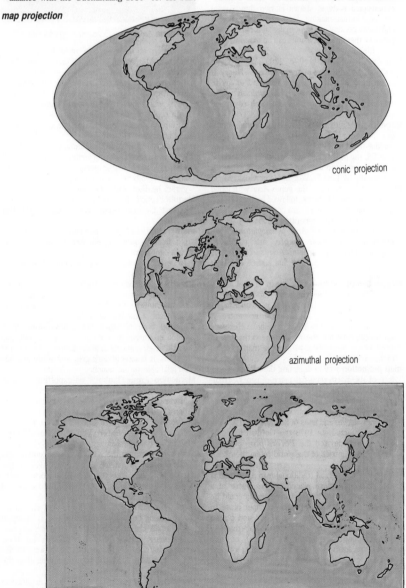

conic projection

azimuthal projection

cylindrical projection

Map
716

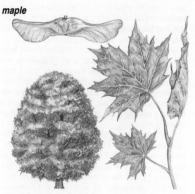

maple

made using aerial photography; a series of overlapping stereoscopic photographs is taken which can then be used to prepare a three-dimensional image.

Laser beams, microwaves, and infrared equipment are also used for land surveying, and satellite pictures make a valuable contribution when large areas are being mapped. Many different kinds of ◊map projection (the means by which a three-dimensional body is shown in two dimensions) are used in map-making. Detailed maps requiring constant updating are kept in digital form on computer so that minor revisions can be made without redrafting.

Map /mæp/ Walter *c.*1140–*c.* 1209. Welsh cleric and satirist who was in the service of Henry II as an itinerant justice in England, and envoy to Alexander III. His *De Nugis Curialium* was a collection of gossip and scandal from royal and ecclesiastical courts.

Mapai (Miphlegeth Poolei Israel) the Israeli Workers' Party or Labour Party, founded 1930. Its leading figure until 1965 was David Ben Gurion. In 1968, the party allied with two other democratic socialist parties to form the Israeli Labour Party, led initially by Levi Estikol and later Golda Meir.

maple deciduous tree of the genus *Acer* with lobed leaves and green flowers, followed by two-winged fruits, samaras. There are over 200 species, chiefly in northern temperate regions.

Acer campestre and *Acer pseudoplatanus*, the **sycamore** or **great maple**, are native to Europe. The sugar maple, *Acer saccharum*, is a North American species, and source of maple syrup.

Mappa Mundi a 13th-century map of the world, one of the best-known medieval world maps. It is circular, and shows Asia at the top, with Europe and Africa below, and Jerusalem at the centre. It was drawn by David de Bello, a canon at Hereford Cathedral, who left the map to the cathedral. In 1988 there were plans to sell the map to raise money for repairs.

map projection way of depicting the spherical surface of the Earth on a flat piece of paper. Traditional projections include the **conic, azimuthal,** and **cylindrical**. The weakness of these systems is that countries in different latitudes are disproportionately large, and lines of longitude and latitude appear distorted. In 1973 the German historian Arno Peters devised the **Peters projection** in which the countries of the world retain their relative areas.

The theory behind traditional map projection is that, if a light were placed at the centre of a transparent Earth, the surface features could be thrown as shadows on a piece of paper close to the surface. This paper may be flat and placed on a pole (azimuthal or zenithal), or may be rolled around the equator (cylindrical), or may be in the form of a tall cone resting on the equator (conical). The resulting maps differ from one another, distorting either area or direction, and each is suitable for a particular purpose. For example, projections distorting area the least are used for distribution maps, and those with least

Maradona *Argentinian footballer Diego Maradona.*

distortion of direction are used for navigation charts. ◊Mercator's projection dates from 1569.

Maputo /mə'puːtəʊ/ formerly (until 1975) *Lourenço Marques* capital of Mozambique, and Africa's second largest port, on Delagoa Bay; population (1986) 883,000. Linked by rail with Zimbabwe and South Africa, it is a major outlet for minerals, steel, textiles, processed foods, and furniture.

maquis type of vegetation common in many Mediterranean countries, consisting of scrub woodland with many low-growing tangled bushes and shrubs, typically including species of broom, gorse, heather, and rockrose.

Maquis French ◊Resistance movement that fought against German occupation during World War II.

mara rodent *Dolichotis patagona* of the guineapig family, occurring in Argentina, with long back limbs and a short tail. They can grow to 75 cm/2.5 ft long and are sometimes known as 'Patagonian cavies'.

Mara (Sanskrit 'killing') in Buddhism, a supernatural being who attempted to distract the Buddha from the meditations that led to his enlightenment. In Hinduism, a goddess of death.

marabou type of stork *Leptoptilos crumeniferus* found in Africa. It is about 120 cm/4 ft tall, has a bald head, and eats snakes, lizards, insects, and carrion. It is largely dark grey and white and has an inflatable throat pouch.

Maracaibo /ˌmærə'kaɪbəʊ/ oil-exporting port in Venezuela, on the channel connecting Lake Maracaibo with the Gulf of Venezuela; population (1981) 889,000.

Maracaibo, Lake /ˌmærə'kaɪbəʊ/ lake in a rich oil-producing region in NW Venezuela; area 14,000 sq km/5,400 sq mi.

Maracanã Stadium the world's largest football stadium, in Rio de Janeiro, Brazil, built 1950. It has a capacity of 175,000 but held a world record 199,854 spectators for the 1950 World Cup final between Brazil and Uruguay.

It has also been used for world championship boxing contests and hosted the 1954 world basketball championship. The local senior soccer teams of Rio use the stadium for their home matches. A feature of the ground is the 2.25 m/7 ft by 1.75 m/5 ft moat surrounding the pitch.

Maradona /ˌmærə'dɒnə/ Diego 1960– . Argentinian footballer who helped his country to win the ◊World Cup 1986.

He left South America for Barcelona, Spain, 1982 for a transfer fee of approximately £5 million. He moved to Napoli, Italy, for £6.9 million 1984, and contributed to their first Italian League title.

CAREER HIGHLIGHTS

World Cup: 1986
Italian League: 1987
Italian Cup: 1987
Spanish Cup: 1983

Marat /'mærɑː/ Jean Paul 1743–1793. French Revolutionary leader and journalist. He was elected in 1792 to the National Convention, where he carried on a long struggle with the ◊Girondins, ending in their overthrow in May 1793. In July he was murdered by Charlotte ◊Corday.

marathon athletics endurance race over 42.195 km/26 mi 385 yd. It was first included in the Olympic Games in Athens 1896. The distance varied until it was standardized in 1924. More recently races have been opened to wider participation, including social runners as well as those competing at senior level, for example the London Marathon from 1981.

The marathon derives its name from the story of Pheidippides, a Greek soldier who ran the distance of approximately 35 km/22 mi from the battlefield of Marathon to Athens with the news of a Greek victory over the Persians in 490 BC. The current marathon distance was first used at the 1908 Olympic Games when the race was increased by an extra 365 yards from the 26 miles (the distance from Windsor to London) so that the race would finish in front of the royal box at the White City stadium. Well-known marathons include the Boston Marathon 1897, New York Marathon 1970, and the Chicago Marathon 1977.

Marathon, Battle of /'mærəθən/ 490 BC. Fought between the Greeks, who were ultimately victorious, and invading Persians on the plain of Marathon, NE of Athens. Before the battle, news of the Persian destruction of the Greek city of Eretria was taken from Athens to Sparta by a courier, Pheidippides, who fell dead on arrival. His feat is commemorated by the **marathon race**.

marble metamorphosed ◊limestone that takes and retains a good polish; it is used in building and sculpture. Mineral impurities give it various colours and patterns; in its pure form it is white and consists almost entirely of calcite $CaCO_3$. Carrara, Italy, is known for white marble.

Marble Arch triumphal arch in London designed by John ◊Nash to commemorate Nelson's victories. Intended as a ceremonial entry to Buckingham Palace, in 1851 it was moved to Hyde Park at the end of Oxford Street.

Marat *The Death of Marat (1793) by Jacques-Louis David (Musée des Beaux Arts de Belgique, Brussels).*

Marburg /'mɑːbɜːg/ manufacturing town (chemicals, machinery, pottery) in Hessen, West Germany, on the river Lahn, 80 km/50 mi N of Frankfurt-am-Main; population (1984) 77,300. The university 1527 was founded as a centre of Protestant teaching. Luther and Zwingli disputed on religion at Marburg in 1529.

Marburg disease viral disease of central Africa, first occurring in Europe in 1967 among research workers in Germany working with African green monkeys, hence its common name **green monkey disease**. It is characterized by haemorrhage of the mucous membranes, fever, vomiting and diarrhoea; mortality is high.

Marc /mɑːk/ Franz 1880–1916. German Expressionist painter, associated with Kandinsky in founding the ◊*Blaue Reiter* movement. Animals played an essential part in his view of the world and bold semi-abstracts of red and blue horses are characteristic of his work.

Marceau /mɑːˈsəʊ/ Marcel 1923– . French mime artist. He is the creator of the clown-harlequin Bip and mime sequences such as 'Youth, Maturity, Old Age, and Death'.

Marchais /mɑːˈʃeɪ/ Georges 1920– . Leader of the French Communist Party (PCF) from 1972. Under his leadership, the party committed itself to a 'transition to socialism' by democratic means and entered into a union of the left with the Socialist Party (PS). This was severed 1977, and the PCF returned to a more orthodox pro-Moscow line, since when its share of the vote has decreased.

Marchais joined the PCF 1947 and worked his way up through the party organization to become its general secretary. He was a presidential candidate 1981, and sanctioned the PCF's participation in the Mitterrand government 1981–84. He remained leader of the PCF despite a fall in its national vote from 21% 1973 to 10% 1986.

Marchand /mɑːˈʃɒn/ Jean Baptiste 1863–1934. French general and explorer. In 1898, he headed an expedition in Africa from the French Congo, which occupied the town of Fashoda (now Kodok) on the White Nile. The subsequent arrival of British troops under Kitchener resulted in a crisis that nearly led to war between Britain and France.

Marche /'mɑːkeɪ/ region of E central Italy consisting of the provinces of Ancona, Ascoli Piceno, Macerata, and Pesaro e Urbino; capital Ancona; area 9,700 sq km/3,744 sq mi; population (1988) 1,429,000.

marches /'mɑːtʃɪz/ the boundary areas of England with Wales, and England with Scotland. In the Middle Ages these troubled frontier regions were held by lords of the marches, sometimes called

Marc Blue Horse *by Franz Marc (private collection).*

Marconi Italian inventor Guglielmo Marconi, whose pioneering work on wireless telegraphy earned him a Nobel prize in 1909.

marchiones and later earls of March. The 1st Earl of March of the Welsh marches was Roger de Mortimer (*c.*1286–1330); of the Scottish marches, Patrick Dunbar (died 1285).

Marcian /'mɑːʃən/ 396–457. Eastern Roman emperor 450–457. He was a general who married Pulcheria, sister of Theodosius II, and became emperor at the latter's death. He convened the Council of ◊Chalcedon in 451 and refused to pay tribute to Attila the Hun.

Marciano /ˌmɑːsiˈɑːnəʊ/ 'Rocky' (Rocco Francis Marchegiano) 1923–1969. US boxer, world heavyweight champion 1952–56. He retired after 49 professional fights, the only heavyweight champion to retire undefeated.

Born in Brockton, Massachussetts, he was known as the 'Brockton Blockbuster'. He knocked out 43 of his 49 opponents. Marciano was killed in a plane crash.

Marconi /mɑːˈkəʊni/ Guglielmo 1874–1937. Italian pioneer in the invention and development of wireless telegraphy. In 1895 he achieved wireless communication over more than a mile, and in England in 1896 he conducted successful experiments that led to the formation of the company that became Marconi's Wireless Telegraph Company Ltd. He shared the Nobel Prize for Physics 1909.

In 1898 he successfully transmitted signals across the English Channel, and in 1901 established communication with St John's, Newfoundland, from Poldhu in Cornwall, and in 1918 with Australia. Marconi was an Italian delegate to the Versailles peace conference in 1919 after World War I.

Marconi Scandal a scandal in 1912 in which UK chancellor Lloyd George and two other government ministers were found by a French newspaper to have dealt in shares of the US Marconi company shortly before it was announced that the Post Office had accepted the British Marconi company's bid to construct an imperial wireless chain. A parliamentary select committee, biased towards the Liberal government's interests, found that the other four wireless systems were technically inadequate and therefore the decision to adopt Marconi's tender was not the result of ministerial corruption. The scandal did irreparable harm to Lloyd George's reputation.

Marco Polo bridge incident a conflict 1937 between Chinese and Japanese Guangdong (formerly *Kwangtung*) army troops on the border of Japanese-controlled ◊Manchukuo and China which led to full-scale war between the two

states. It lasted until the Japanese surrender 1945.

Although initially only a minor skirmish, the conflict escalated because of the ambitions of the Kwangtung army to expand their control farther into China and the Chinese determination to oppose any further incursions.

Marcos /'mɑːkɒs/ Ferdinand 1917–1989. Filipino right-wing politician, president 1965–86, when he was forced into exile in Hawaii. He was backed by the USA when in power, but in 1988 US authorities indicted him and his wife for racketeering and embezzlement, and at her trial in 1990 she was accused of stealing 105 million.

Marcos was convicted while a law student 1939 of murdering a political opponent of his father, but eventually secured his own acquittal. In World War II he was a guerrilla fighter, survived Japanese prison camps of Bataan, and became president 1965. His regime became increasingly repressive, with the use of the secret marshals: anti-crime squads executing those only suspected of offences. He was overthrown and exiled 1986 by a popular front led by Corazón ◊Aquino, widow of a murdered opposition leader. A US grand jury investigating Marcos and his wife alleged that they had embezzled millions of dollars from the Philippines government, received bribes, and defrauded US banks. Marcos was too ill to stand trial, however, and died in Honolulu, Hawaii, Sept 1989.

Marcus Aurelius Antoninus /'mɑːkəs ɔːˈriːliː əs ˌæntəˈnaɪnəs/ AD 121–180. Roman emperor from 161 and Stoic philosopher. Although considered one of the best of the Roman emperors, he persecuted the Christians for political reasons. He wrote philosophical *Meditations*.

Born in Rome, he was adopted (at the same time as Lucius Aurelius Verus) by his uncle, the emperor Antoninus Pius, whom he succeeded in 161. He conceded an equal share in the rule to Lucius Verus (died 169). Marcus Aurelius spent much of his reign warring against the Germanic tribes and died in Pannonia, where he had gone to drive back the invading Marcomanni.

Marcuse /mɑːˈkuːzə/ Herbert 1898–1979. German political philosopher, in the US from 1934; his theories combining Marxism and Freudianism influenced radical thought in the 1960s. His books include *One-Dimensional Man* 1964.

Marcuse preached the overthrow of the existing social order by using the system's very tolerance to ensure its defeat but was not an advocate of violent revolution. A refugee from Hitler's Germany, he became professor at the University of California at San Diego 1965.

Mardi Gras (French 'fat Tuesday' from the custom of using up all the fat in the household before the beginning of ◊Lent) Shrove Tuesday. A festival was traditionally held on this day in Paris, and there are carnivals in many parts of the world, including New Orleans, Louisiana; Italy; and Brazil.

Marduk /'mɑːdʊk/ in Babylonian mythology, the sun god, creator of Earth and humans.

mare (plural *maria*) dark lowland plain on the Moon. The name comes from Latin 'sea', because these areas were once wrongly thought to be water.

Marengo, Battle of /məˈreŋgəʊ/ defeat of the Austrians by the French emperor Napoleon on 14 Jun 1800, as part of his Italian campaign, near the village of Marengo in Piedmont, Italy.

mare nostrum (Latin 'our sea') Roman name for the Mediterranean.

Margaret /'mɑːgrət/ 1282–1290. Queen of Scotland from 1285, known as *the Maid of Norway*. Margaret was the daughter of Eric II, king of Norway, and Princess Margaret of Scotland. When only two years of age she became queen of Scotland on the death of her grandfather, Alexander III, but died in the Orkneys on a voyage to her kingdom.

Margaret /'mɑːgrət/ (Rose) 1930– . Princess of the UK, younger daughter of George VI. In

1960 she married Anthony Armstrong-Jones, later created Lord Snowdon, but in 1976 they agreed to live apart, and were divorced 1978. Their children are *David, Viscount Linley* (1961–) and *Lady Sarah Armstrong-Jones* (1964–).

Margaret of Anjou /ɒnˈʒuː/ 1430–1482. Queen of England from 1445, wife of ◊Henry VI of England. After the outbreak of the Wars of the ◊Roses in 1455, she acted as the leader of the Lancastrians, but was defeated and captured at the battle of Tewkesbury 1471 by Edward IV.

Her one object had been to secure the succession of her son, Edward (born 1453), who was killed at Tewkesbury. After five years' imprisonment Margaret was allowed in 1476 to return to her native France, where she died in poverty.

Margaret, St /ˈmɑːɡrət/ 1045–1093. Queen of Scotland, the granddaughter of King Edmund Ironside of England. She went to Scotland after the Norman Conquest, and soon after married Malcolm III. The marriage of her daughter Matilda to Henry I united the Norman and English royal houses.

Through her influence the Lowlands, until then purely Celtic, became largely anglicized. She was canonized 1251 in recognition of her benefactions to the church.

margarine a butter substitute, made from animal fats and vegetable oils. The French chemist Hippolyte Mège-Mouriès invented margarine in 1889. Modern margarines are usually made with vegetable oils, such as sunflower oil, giving a product that is low in saturated fats; see ◊polyunsaturate.

Margate /ˈmɑːɡeɪt/ town and seaside resort on the N coast of Kent, SE England; industry (textiles, scientific instruments); population (1981) 53,280. It has a fine promenade and sands.

margay small wild cat *Felis wiedi* found from southern USA to South America in forested areas, where it hunts birds and small mammals. It is about 60 cm/2 ft long with a 40 cm/1.3 ft tail, has a rather rounded head, and black spots and blotches on a yellowish-brown coat.

marginal cost pricing in economics, the setting of a price based on the production cost plus the cost of producing another unit. In this way, the price of an item is kept to a minimum, reflecting only the extra cost of labour and materials.

Marginal cost pricing may be used by a company during a period of poor sales with the additional sales generated allowing it to remain operational without a reduction of the labour force.

marginal efficiency of capital in economics, effectively the rate of return on investment in a given business project compared with the rate of return if the capital were invested at prevailing interest rates.

marginal productivity in economics, the extra output gained by increasing a factor of production by one unit.

marginal utility in economics, the measure of additional satisfaction (utility) gained by a consumer who receives one additional unit of a product or service. The concept is used to explain why consumers buy more of a product when the price falls.

An individual's demand for a product is determined by the marginal utility (and the point at which he has sufficient quantity). The greater the supply of the item available to him, the smaller the marginal utility, supply is the main price determinant. In total utility, supply is the main price determinant. The total utility of diamonds is low because their use is mainly decorative, but because of their rarity, the price is high, and the marginal utility is high. On the other hand, the total utility of bread is high because it is essential, but its marginal utility may be very low because it is plentiful, making it much cheaper than diamonds.

margrave German title (equivalent of marquess) for the 'counts of the march', who guarded the frontier regions of the Holy Roman Empire from Charlemagne's time. Later the title was used by

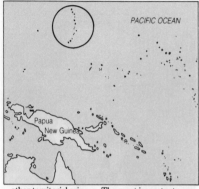

Marianas

PACIFIC OCEAN

Papua
New Guinea

other territorial princes. The most important were the margraves of Austria and of Brandenburg.

Margrethe II /mɑːˈɡreɪdə/ 1940– . Queen of Denmark from 1972, when she succeeded her father Frederick IX. In 1967, she married the French diplomat Count Henri de Laborde de Monpezat, who took the title Prince Hendrik. Her heir is Crown Prince Frederick (1968–).

marguerite plant *Leucanthemum vulgare*, family Compositae. It is a shrubby perennial and bears white daisylike flowers.

Marguerite of Navarre /ˌmɑːɡəˈriːt nævəˈ/ also known as *Margaret d'Angoulême* 1492–1549. Queen of Navarre from 1527, French poet, and author of the *Heptaméron* 1558, a collection of stories in imitation of Boccaccio's *Decameron*. The sister of Francis I of France, she was born in Angoulême. Her second husband 1527 was Henri d'Albret, king of Navarre.

Mari /ˈmɑːri/ autonomous republic of the USSR, E of Gorky and W of the Urals
area 23,200 sq km/8,900 sq mi
capital Yoshkar-Ola
features the Volga flows through the SW; 60% is forested
products timber, paper; grain, flax, potatoes, fruit
population (1985) 725,000; about 43% are ethnic Mari
history the Mari were conquered by Russia in 1552. Mari was made an autonomous region 1920, an autonomous republic 1936.

Mariana Islands /ˌmæriˈɑːnəz/ or *Marianas* archipelago in the NW Pacific, divided politically into ◊*Guam* and the *Northern Marianas*, a commonwealth in union with the USA of 16 mountainous islands, extending 560 km/350 mi north from Guam
area 480 sq km/185 sq mi
capital Garapan on Saipan
products sugar, coconuts, coffee
currency US dollar
population (1988) 21,000, mainly Micronesian
language 55% Chamorro, English
religion mainly Roman Catholic
government own constitutionally elected government
history sold to Germany by Spain 1899. The islands were mandated to Japan 1918, and taken by US Marines 1944–45 in World War II. They were under US trusteeship from 1947, and voted to become a Commonwealth of the USA 1975.

Mariana Trench the lowest region on the Earth's surface; the deepest part of the sea floor. The trench is 2,400 km/1,500 mi long and is situated 300 km/200 mi E of the Mariana Islands, in the NW Pacific Ocean. Its deepest part is the gorge known as the Challenger Deep, which extends 11,034 m/36,201 ft below sea level.

Marianne symbolic figure of the French republic, dating from the Revolution. Statues of her adorn public buildings in France. Her name combines those of the Virgin Mary and St Anne.

Mariánské Lázně /ˈmæriːənskeɪ ˈlɑːznɪeɪ/ (German *Marienbad*) spa town in Czechoslovakia,

internationally famous before World War II; population (1981) 17,950. The water of its springs, which contains ◊Glauber's salts, has been used medicinally since the 16th century.

Maria Theresa /məˈriːə təˈreɪzə/ 1717–1780. Empress of Austria from 1740, when she succeeded her father, the Holy Roman Emperor Charles VI; her claim to the throne was challenged and she became embroiled, first in the War of the ◊Austrian Succession 1740–48, then in the ◊Seven Years' War 1756–63; she remained in possession of Austria but lost Silesia. The rest of her reign was peaceful and, with her son Joseph II, she introduced social reforms.

She married her cousin Francis of Lorraine 1736, and on the death of her father became archduchess of Austria and queen of Hungary and Bohemia. Her claim was challenged by Charles of Bavaria, who was elected emperor 1742, while Frederick of Prussia occupied Silesia. The War of the Austrian Succession followed, in which Austria was allied with Britain, and Prussia with France; when it ended 1748, Maria Theresa retained her heritage, except that Frederick kept Silesia, while her husband had succeeded Charles as emperor 1745. Intent on recovering Silesia, she formed an alliance with France and Russia against Prussia; the Seven Years' War, which resulted, exhausted Europe and left the territorial position as before. After 1763 she pursued a consistently peaceful policy, concentrating on internal reforms; although her methods were despotic, she fostered education, codified the laws, and abolished torture. She also expelled the Jesuits. In these measures she was assisted by her son, Joseph II, who became emperor 1765, and succeeded her in the Habsburg domains.

Maribor /ˈmæribɔː/ (German *Marburg*) town and resort on the river Drave in Slovenia, Yugoslavia, with a 12th-century cathedral and some industry (boots and shoes, railway rolling stock); population (1981) 185,500. Maribor dates from Roman times.

Marie /məˈriː/ 1875–1938. Queen of Romania. She was the daughter of the Duke of Edinburgh, second son of Queen Victoria, and married Prince Ferdinand of Romania in 1893 (he was king 1922–27). She wrote a number of literary works, notably *Story of My Life* 1934–35. Her son Carol became king of Romania, and her daughters, Elisabeth and Marie, queens of Greece and Yugoslavia respectively.

Marie Antoinette /məˈriː ˌæntwəˈnet/ 1755–1793. Queen of France from 1774. She was the daughter of Empress Maria Theresa of Austria, and married ◊Louis XVI of France in 1770. With a reputation for frivolity and extravagance, she meddled in politics in the Austrian interest, and helped provoke the ◊French Revolution of 1789. She was tried for treason in Oct 1793 and guillotined.

Marie Antoinette influenced her husband to resist concessions in the early days of the Revolution, for example, ◊Mirabeau's plan for a constitutional settlement. She instigated the disastrous flight to Varennes, which discredited the monarchy, and welcomed foreign intervention against the Revolution, betraying French war strategy to the Austrians in 1792.

Marie de France /də ˈfrɒns/ *c.*1150–1215. French poet, thought to have been the half-sister of Henry II of England, and abbess of Shaftesbury 1181–1215. She wrote *Lais* (verse tales which dealt with Celtic and Arthurian themes) and *Ysopet*, a collection of fables.

Marie de' Medici /deɪ ˈmedɪtʃi/ 1573–1642. Queen of France, wife of Henry IV from 1600, and regent (after his murder) for their son Louis XIII. She left the government to her favourites, the Concinis, until in 1617 Louis XIII seized power and executed them. She was banished, but after she led a revolt in 1619, ◊Richelieu effected her reconciliation with her son, but when she attempted to oust him in 1630, she was exiled.

Marie Louise /luːˈiːz/ 1791–1847. Queen consort of Napoleon I from 1810 (after his divorce from Josephine), mother of Napoleon II. She was the daughter of Francis I of Austria (see Emperor ◊Francis II), and on Napoleon's fall returned to Austria. In 1815 she was granted the duchy of Parma.

Marienbad /ˈmærɪənbæd/ German name of ◊Mariánské Lázně, spa town in Czechoslovakia.

Mariette /ˌmæriˈet/ Auguste Ferdinand François 1821–1881. French egyptologist, whose discoveries from 1850 included the 'temple' between the paws of the Sphinx. He founded the Egyptian Museum in Cairo.

marigold several members of the family Compositae, including **pot marigold** *Calendula officinalis*, and the tropical American *Tagetes patula*, commonly known as **French marigold**.

marijuana the dried leaves and flowers of the hemp plant ◊cannabis, used as a drug.

marimba a type of bass ◊xylophone.

Marin /ˈmærɪn/ John 1870–1953. US painter, known for seascapes in watercolour and oil, influenced by Impressionism. He visited Europe 1905–11, and began his paintings of the Maine coast 1914.

Mariner spacecraft series of US space probes that explored the planets Mercury, Venus, and Mars 1962–75. *Mariner 1* (to Venus) had a failed launch. *Mariner 2* 1962 made the first fly-by of Venus, at 34,000 km/21,000 mi, confirmed the existence of ◊solar wind, and measured Venusian temperature. *Mariner 3* did not achieve its intended trajectory to Mars. *Mariner 4* 1965 passed Mars at a distance of 9,800 km/6,100 mi, and took photographs, revealing a dry, cratered surface. *Mariner 5* 1967 passed Venus at 4,000 km/2,500 mi, and measured Venusian temperature, atmosphere, mass, and diameter. *Mariners 6* and *7* 1969 photographed Mars' equator and southern hemisphere respectively, and also measured temperature, atmospheric pressure and composition, and diameter. *Mariner 8* (to Mars) had a failed launch. *Mariner 9* 1971 mapped the entire Martian surface, and photographed Mars' moons. Its photographs revealed the changing of the polar caps, and the extent of volcanism, canyons, and 'canals', which suggested that there once might have been water on Mars. *Mariner 10* 1974–75 took close-up photographs of Mercury and Venus, and measured temperature, radiation, and magnetic fields. Mariners 11 and 12 were renamed ◊Voyager probes 1 and 2.

marines a fighting force that operates both on land and at sea.

The **US Marine Corps** (1775) is constituted as an arm of the US Navy. It is made up of infantry and air support units trained and equipped for amphibious landings under fire. The British **Corps of Royal Marines** (1664) is primarily a military force also trained for fighting at sea, and providing commando units, landing craft, crews, and frogmen.

Marinetti /ˌmærɪˈneti/ Filippo Tommaso 1876–1944. Italian author, who in 1909 published the first manifesto of ◊Futurism, which called for a break with tradition in art, poetry, and the novel, and glorified the machine age.

Born at Alexandria, he illustrated his theories in *Mafarka le futuriste/Mafarka the Futurist* 1910, plays, and a volume on theatrical practice 1916. He recorded his World War I experiences in *Otto anime in una bomba* 1919, and welcomed Mussolini with *Futurismo e fascismo/Futurism and Fascism* 1924.

Marini /məˈriːni/ Marino 1901–1980. Italian sculptor. Influenced by ancient art, he developed a distinctive horse-and-rider theme and a dancers series, reducing the forms to an elemental simplicity. He also produced fine portraits in bronze.

marionette type of ◊puppet, a jointed figure controlled from above by wires or strings. Intricately

---

marjoram

flower detail

crafted marionettes were used in Burma and Ceylon and later at the courts of Italian princes in the 16th–18th centuries.

Mariotte /ˌmæriˈɒt/ Edme 1620–1684. French physicist and priest known for his statement in 1676 of ◊Boyle's law about the volume of gas, formulated in 1672. He had earlier, in 1660, discovered the eye's blind spot.

Maritain /ˌmærɪˈtæn/ Jacques 1882–1973. French philosopher. Originally a disciple of ◊Bergson, as in *La philosophie bergsonienne/Bergsonian Philosophy* 1914, he later became the best known of the Neo-Thomists applying the methods of Thomas ◊Aquinas to contemporary problems, for example *Introduction à la Philosophie/Introduction to Philosophy* 1920.

maritime law that part of the law dealing with the sea: in particular fishing areas, ships, and navigation. Seas are divided into **internal waters** governed by a state's internal laws (such as harbours, inlets); ◊**territorial waters** (the area of sea adjoining the coast over which a state claims rights); the **continental shelf** (the sea bed and subsoil which the coastal state is entitled to exploit beyond the territorial waters); and the **high seas**, where international law applies.

Maritime Trust UK body established in 1970 to discover, repair, and preserve ships of historic, scientific, or technical interest: its first president was the Duke of Edinburgh.

Maritsa /məˈrɪtsə/ (Greek **Hevros**; Turkish **Meric**) river, rising in the Rhodope Mountains, Bulgaria, which forms the Greco-Turkish frontier before entering the Aegean Sea near Enez; length 440 km/275 mi.

Mariupol /ˌmæriˈuːpəl/ former name (until 1948) of the port of ◊Zhdanov in the USSR.

Marius /ˈmeəriəs/ Gaius 155–86 BC. Roman military commander and politician. Born near Arpinum, he was elected consul seven times the first time in 107 BC. He defeated the Cimbri and the Teutons (Germanic tribes attacking Gaul and Italy) 102–101 BC. Marius tried to deprive Sulla of the command in the East against Mithridates and, as a result, civil war broke out in 88 BC. Sulla marched on Rome, and Marius fled to Africa, but later Cinna held Rome for Marius and together they created a reign of terror in Rome.

Marivaux /ˌmærɪˈvəʊ/ Pierre Carlet de Chamblain de 1688–1763. French novelist and dramatist. His sophisticated comedies include *Le Jeu de l'amour et du hasard/The Game of Love and Chance* 1730 and *Les Fausses confidences/False Confidences* 1737; his novel, *La Vie de Marianne/The Life of Marianne* 1731–41 has autobiographical elements. Marivaux gave the word *marivaudage* (over-subtle lovers' conversation) to the French language.

He was born and lived for most of his life in Paris, writing for both of the major Paris theatre companies: the ◊Comédie Française and the Comédie Italienne, which specialized in ◊commedia dell'arte.

---

marjoram aromatic herb of the Labiatae family. Wild marjoram *Origanum vulgare* is found both in Europe and Asia and has become naturalized in the Americas; the culinary sweet marjoram is *Origanum majorana*.

Mark Antony /ˈmɑːk ˈæntəni/ Antonius, Marcus 83–30 BC. Roman politician and soldier. He was tribune and later consul under Julius Caesar, serving under him in Gaul. In 44 BC he tried to secure for Caesar the title of king. After Caesar's assassination, he formed the Second Triumvirate with Octavian (◊Augustus) and Lepidus. In 42 he defeated Brutus and Cassius at Philippi. He took Egypt as his share of the empire and formed a liaison with ◊Cleopatra. In 40 he returned to Rome to marry Octavia, the sister of Augustus. In 32 the Senate declared war on Cleopatra. Antony was defeated by Augustus at the battle of Actium 31 BC. He returned to Egypt and committed suicide.

marketing promoting goods and services to consumers. Marketing has in the 20th century become an increasingly important determinant of company policy, influencing product development, pricing, methods of distribution, advertising, and promotion techniques. Marketing skills are increasingly taught in schools and colleges.

market maker in the UK, a stockbroker entitled to deal directly on the stock exchange. The role was created in Oct 1986, when the jobber (intermediary) disappeared from the stock exchange. Market makers trade in the dual capacity of broker and jobber.

Markevich /mɑːˈkjevɪtʃ/ Igor 1912–1983. Russian-born composer and conductor. He composed the ballet *L'Envol d'Icare* 1932, and the cantata *Le Paradis Perdu* 1933–35 to words by Milton. After World War II he concentrated on conducting.

markhor large wild goat *Capra falconeri*, with spirally twisted horns and long shaggy coat. It is found in the Himalayas.

Markievicz /ˈmɑːkjɪvɪtʃ/ Constance Georgina, Countess Markievicz (born Gore Booth) 1868–1927. Irish nationalist, who married the Polish count Markievicz in 1900. Her death sentence for taking part in the Easter Rising of 1916 was commuted, and after her release from prison in 1917 she was elected to the Westminster Parliament as a Sinn Féin candidate in 1918 (technically the first British woman member of Parliament), but did not take her seat.

Markov /ˈmɑːkɒv/ Andrei 1856–1922. Russian mathematician, formulator of the ◊Markov chain, an example of a stochastic process.

Mark Antony *A great orator and soldier, Mark Antony committed suicide after his defeat at the battle of Actium in 31 BC.*

Marlborough *John Churchill, 1st Duke of Marlborough, a portrait after Kneller.*

Markova /mɑːˈkəʊvə/ Alicia, adopted name of Lilian Alicia Marks 1910– . British ballet dancer. Trained by ◊Pavlova, she was ballerina with ◊Diaghilev's company 1925–29, was the first resident ballerina of the Vic-Wells Ballet 1933–35, partnered Anton ◊Dolin in their own Markova-Dolin Company 1935–37, and danced with the Ballet Russe de Monte Carlo 1938–41 and Ballet Theatre, USA, 1941–46. She is associated with the great classical ballets, especially *Giselle*.

Markov chain in statistics, an ordered sequence of discrete states (random variables) x_1, x_2, ..., x_i, ..., x_n such that the probability of x_i depends only on n and/or the state x_{i-1} which has preceded it. If independent of n, the chain is said to be homogeneous.

Marks /mɑːks/ Simon, 1st Baron of Broughton 1888–1964. English chain-store magnate. His father, Polish immigrant Michael Marks, had started a number of 'penny bazaars' with Yorkshireman Tom Spencer in 1887; Simon Marks entered the business in 1907 and built up a national chain of Marks and Spencer stores.

Mark, St /mɑːk/ lived 1st century AD. In the New Testament, Christian apostle and evangelist, whose name is given to the second Gospel. It was probably written 65–70 AD, and used by the authors of the first and third Gospels. He is the patron saint of Venice, and his emblem is a winged lion; feast day 25 Apr.

His first name was John, and his mother, Mary, was one of the first Christians in Jerusalem. He was a cousin of Barnabas, and accompanied Barnabas and Paul on their first missionary journey. He was a fellow worker with Paul in Rome, and later became Peter's interpreter after Paul's death. According to tradition he was the founder of the Christian church in Alexandria, and St Jerome says that he died and was buried there.

marl crumbling sedimentary rock, sometimes called ***clayey limestone***, including various types of calcareous ◊clays and argillaceous ◊limestones. Marls are often laid down in freshwater lakes and are usually soft, earthy, and of a white, grey, or brownish colour. They are used in cement-making and as fertilizer.

Marlborough /ˈmɔːlbrə/ market town in Wiltshire, England, 122 km/76 mi W of London, site of Marlborough College 1843, a public school.

Marlborough /ˈmɔːlbrə/ John Churchill, 1st Duke of Marlborough 1650–1722. English soldier, created a duke 1702 by Queen Anne. He was granted the Blenheim mansion in Oxfordshire in recognition of his services, which included defeating the French army outside Vienna in the Battle of ◊Blenheim 1704, during the War of the ◊Spanish Succession.

In 1688 he deserted his patron, James II, for William of Orange, but in 1692 fell into disfavour for Jacobite intrigue. He had married Sarah Jennings (1660–1744), confidante of the future Queen Anne, who created him a duke on her accession. He achieved further victories in Belgium at ◊Ramillies 1706 and ◊Oudenaarde 1708, and in France at ◊Malplaquet 1709. However, the return of the Tories to power and his wife's quarrel with the queen led to his dismissal in 1711 and his flight to Holland to avoid charges of corruption. He returned in 1714.

Marlborough House mansion in Pall Mall, London. Designed by Christopher ◊Wren, it was the 1st Duke of Marlborough's London home: later users include Edward VII (as Prince of Wales), Queen Mary (consort of George V), and from 1962 gatherings of Commonwealth members.

Marley /ˈmɑːli/ Bob (Robert Nesta) 1945–1980. Jamaican reggae singer, a Rastafarian whose songs, many of which were topical and political, popularized reggae in the UK and the USA in the 1970s. One of his best-known songs is 'No Woman No Cry'; his albums include *Natty Dread* 1975 and *Exodus* 1977.

marlin or ***spearfish*** several genera of fish, family Istiophoridae, order Perciformes. Some 2.5 m/7 ft long, they are found in warmer waters, have elongated snouts, and high-standing dorsal fins.

Marlowe /ˈmɑːləʊ/ Christopher 1564–1593. English poet and dramatist. His work includes the blank-verse plays *Tamburlaine the Great* about 1587, *The Jew of Malta* about 1589, *Edward II* and *Dr Faustus*, both about 1592, the poem *Hero and Leander* 1598, and a translation of Ovid's *Amores*.

Born in Canterbury, Marlowe was educated at Cambridge, where he is thought to have become a government agent. His life was turbulent, with a brief imprisonment in connection with a man's death in a brawl (of which he was cleared), and a charge of atheism (following statements by the playwright ◊Kyd under torture). He was murdered in a Deptford tavern, allegedly in a dispute over the bill, but it may have been a political killing.

Marmara /ˈmɑːmərə/ small inland sea separating Turkey in Europe from Turkey in Asia, connected through the Bosporus with the Black Sea, and through the Dardanelles with the Aegean; length 275 km/170 mi, breadth up to 80 km/50 mi.

Marmontel /ˌmɑːmɒnˈtel/ Jean François 1723–1799. French novelist and dramatist. He wrote

Marley *Reggae musician Bob Marley.*

tragedies and libretti, and contributed to the *Encyclopédie* (see ◊encyclopedia); in 1758 he obtained control of the journal *Le Mercure/The Mercury*, in which his *Contes moraux/Moral Studies* 1761 appeared. Other works include *Bélisaire/Belisarius* 1767, and *Les Incas/The Incas* 1777.

He was appointed historiographer of France 1771, secretary to the Académie 1783, and professor of history at the Lycée 1786, but retired in 1792 to write his *Mémoires d'un père/Memoirs of a Father* 1804.

marmoset small tree-dwelling monkey in the family Hapalidae found in South and Central America. Most species have characteristic tufted ears, bearlike claws, and a handsome tail, and some are fully grown when the body is only 18 cm/7 in. The tail is not prehensile. Best known is the common marmoset *Callithrix jacchus* of Brazil, often kept there as a pet.

marmot large burrowing rodent of the genus *Marmota* which eats plants and insects. They are found from the Alps to the Himalayas, and also in North America. Marmots live in colonies, make burrows, one to each family, and hibernate. In North America they are called woodchucks or groundhogs. *Marmota marmota* is the typical marmot of the Central European Alps.

Marne /mɑːn/ river in France which rises in the plateau of Langres and joins the Seine at Charenton near Paris; length 5,251 km/928 mi. It gives its name to the *départements* of Marne, Haute Marne, Seine-et-Marne, and Val de Marne; and to two battles of ◊World War I.

Marne, Battles of the /mɑːn/ in World War I, two unsuccessful German offensives: ***First Battle*** 6–9 Sept 1914, von Moltke's advance was halted by the British Expeditionary Force and the French under Foch; ***Second Battle*** 15 July–4 Aug 1918, Ludendorff's advance was defeated by British, French, and US troops under the French general Pétain, and German morale crumbled.

Maronite member of a Christian sect deriving from refugee Monothelites (Christian heretics) of the 7th century. They were subsequently united with the Roman Catholic Church, and number about 400,000 in Lebanon and Syria, with an equal number scattered overseas in S Europe and the Americas.

Maroon (Spanish *cimarrón* 'wild, untamed') freed or escaped African slave. They were organized and armed by the Spanish in Jamaica in the late 17th century and early 18th century. They harried the British with guerrilla tactics.

Marot /ˈmærəʊ/ Clément 1496–1544. French poet, best known for his translation of the *Psalms* 1539–43. His graceful, witty style has been a model for later writers of light verse.

Born at Cahors, he accompanied Francis I to Italy in 1524, and was taken prisoner at Pavia, but was soon released, and by 1528 was a salaried member of the royal household. Suspected of heresy, he fled to Turin, where he died.

Marprelate controversy a pamphleteering attack on the clergy of the Church of England made in 1588 and 1589 by a Puritan writer or writers, who took the pseudonym of ***Martin Marprelate***. The pamphlets were printed by John Penry, a Welsh Puritan. His press was seized, and he was charged with inciting rebellion and hanged in 1593.

Marquand /mɑːˈkwɒnd/ John Phillips 1893–1960. US writer. Originally known for a series of stories featuring the Japanese detective Mr Moto, he made a serious reputation with his gently satirical novels of Boston society: *The Late George Apley* 1937 and *H M Pulham, Esq* 1941.

Marquesas Islands /mɑːˈkeɪzəz/ (French *Îles Marquises*) island group in ◊French Polynesia, lying north of the Tuamotu Archipelago; area 1,270 sq km/490 sq mi; population (1983) 6,500. The administrative headquarters is Atuona on Hiva Oa. It was annexed by France 1842.

marquess or ***marquis*** title and rank of a nobleman who in the British peerage ranks below a duke and above an earl. The wife of a marquess is a marchioness.

The first English marquess was created in 1385, but the lords of the Scottish and Welsh 'marches' were known as *marchiones* before this date. The premier English marquess is the Marquess of Winchester (title created 1551).

Marquet /mɑː'keɪ/ Pierre Albert 1876–1947. French painter of landscapes and Parisian scenes, especially the Seine and its bridges. He was associated with the ◊Fauves, but soon developed a more conventional, naturalistic style.

marquetry the inlaying of different types of wood, bone, or ivory, usually on furniture, to create ornate patterns and pictures. *Parquetry* is the term used for geometrical inlaid patterns. The method is thought to have originated in Germany or Holland.

Marquette /mɑː'ket/ Jacques 1637–1675. French Jesuit missionary and explorer. He went to Canada in 1666, explored the upper lakes of the St Lawrence, and in 1673 with Louis Jolliet (1645–1700), set out on a voyage down the Mississippi on which they made the first accurate record of its course.

Márquez Gabriel García see ◊García Márquez, Colombian novelist.

Marquis /'mɑːkwɪs/ Don(ald Robert Perry) 1878–1937. US author. He is chiefly known for his humorous writing—*Old Soak* 1921, portraying a hard-drinking comic—and *archy and mehitabel* 1927, the typewritten verse adventures of a cockroach and a cat.

Marquises, Îles /mɑː'kiːz/ French form of ◊Marquesas Islands, part of ◊French Polynesia.

Marrakesh /ˌmærə'keʃ/ historic town in Morocco in the foothills of the Atlas mountains, about 210 km/130 mi south of Casablanca; population (1982) 549,000. It is a tourist centre, and has textile, leather, and food processing industries. Founded 1062, it has a medieval palace and mosques, and was formerly the capital of Morocco.

marram grass coarse perennial grass *Ammophila arenaria*, flourishing on sandy areas. Because of its tough, creeping rootstocks, it is widely used to hold coastal dunes in place.

Marrano one of the Spanish and Portuguese Jews converted by force to Christianity in the 14th and 15th centuries, many of whom secretly preserved their adherence to Judaism and carried out Jewish rites. Under the Spanish Inquisition thousands were burned at the stake.

marriage the legally or culturally sanctioned union of one man and one woman (monogamy); one man and two or more women (polygamy); one woman and two or more men (polyandry). The basis of marriage varies considerably in different societies (romantic love in the West; arranged marriages in some other societies), but most marriage ceremonies, contracts, or customs involve a set of rights and duties such as care and protection, and there is generallly an expectation that children will be born of the union to continue the family line.

In different cultures and communities there are various conventions and laws that limit the choice of a marriage partner.

restrictive factors include:

age limits, below which no marriage is valid (16 in the UK);

degrees of consanguinity or other special relationships within which marriage is either forbidden or enjoined;

economic factors such as ability to pay ◊bridewealth or a dowry;

rank, caste, or religious differences;

medical requirements, such as the blood tests of some states of the USA;

the necessity of obtaining parental, family, or community consent;

the negotiations of a marriage broker in some cultures, as in Japan or formerly among Jewish communities;

colour, for example, marriage was illegal until 1985 between 'European' and 'non-European' people in South Africa, and until 1967 was illegal between white and black people in some Southern US states, and between white and Asian people in some western states.

rights In Western cultures, social trends have led to increased legal equality for women within marriage: in England married women were not allowed to hold property in their own name until 1882; in California community property laws entail the equal division of all assets between the partners on divorce. Other legal changes have made ◊divorce easier, notably in the USA and increasingly in the UK, so that remarriage is more and more frequent for both sexes within the lifetime of the original partner.

law In England marriages can be effected according to the rites of the Church of England or those of other faiths, or in a superintendent registrar's office. In most other European countries and in the USA civil registration of marriage, as well as (or instead of) a religious ceremony, is obligatory. Common-law marriages (that is, cohabitation as man and wife without a legal ceremony) are recognized in, for example, Scotland, some states of the USA, and the USSR. As a step to international agreement on marriage law the United Nations in 1962 adopted a convention on consent to marriage, minimum age for marriage, and registration.

marrow trailing vine *Cucurbita pepo*, family Cucurbitaceae, producing large pulpy fruits, used as vegetables and in preserves; the young fruits of one variety are known as courgettes (USA zucchini).

Marryat /'mæriət/ Frederick 1792–1848. British naval officer and novelist, popularly known as Captain Marryat from his naval rank. He resigned from the Royal Navy in 1830 after the success of his first novel, *Frank Mildmay*. He wrote a number of popular adventure stories, including *Peter Simple* 1834, *Mr Midshipman Easy* 1836, and a series of children's books, of which the best known is *Children of the New Forest* 1847.

Mars /mɑːz/ in Roman mythology, the god of war, after whom the month of March is named. He is equivalent to the Greek Ares.

Mars /mɑːz/ the fourth planet from the Sun, average distance 227,800,000 km/141,500,000 mi. It revolves around the Sun in 687 Earth days, and has a rotation period of 24 hr 37 min. It is much smaller than Venus or Earth, with diameter 6,780 km/4,210 mi, and mass 0.11 that of Earth. Mars is slightly pear-shaped, with a low, level northern hemisphere, comparatively uncratered and geologically 'young', and a heavily cratered 'ancient' southern hemisphere.

The landscape is a dusty, red, eroded lava plain; red atmospheric dust whipped up by winds of up to 200 kph/125 mph account for the light pink sky. Mars has white polar caps (water ice and frozen carbon dioxide) which advance and retreat with the seasons. There are four enormous volcanoes near the equator, of which the largest

Mars *Mars as seen by the Viking spacecraft on its approach to the red planet.*

is Olympus Mons 24 km/15 m high, with a base 600 km/375 mi across, and a crater 65 km/40 mi wide. The atmosphere is 95% carbon dioxide, 3% nitrogen, 1.5% argon, and 0.15% oxygen. Recorded temperatures vary from –100°C to 0°C. The atmospheric pressure is 7 millibars, equivalent to the pressure 35 km/22 mi above Earth. No proof of life on Mars has been obtained. There are two small satellites: ◊Phobos and Deimos.

Mars may approach Earth to within 54,700,000 km/34,000,000 mi. The first human-made object to orbit another planet was ◊Mariner 9. ◊Vikings 1 and 2, which landed, also provided much information. Studies in 1985 showed that enough water might exist to sustain prolonged missions by space crews. To the east of the four volcanoes lies a high plateau cut by a system of valleys some 4,000 km/2,500 mi long, up to 200 km/120 mi wide and 6 km/4 mi deep; these features are apparently caused by faulting and wind erosion.

Marsala /mɑː'sɑːlə/ port in W Sicily, Italy, noted for export of sweet wine of the same name; population (1980) 85,000. The nationalist leader ◊Garibaldi landed here 1860.

marsala a type of dessert wine produced in Sicily which has a dark amber colour and burnt-sugar flavour. It is made with the addition of grape juice that has been cooked and reduced to one-third of its original volume.

Marseillaise, La /ˌmɑːseɪ'eɪz/ French national anthem; the words and music were composed in 1792 as a revolutionary song by the army officer Rouget de Lisle.

Marseille /mɑː'seɪ/ the chief seaport of France, industrial centre (chemicals, oil refining, metallurgy, shipbuilding, food processing), and capital of the *département* of Bouches-du-Rhône, on the Golfe du Lion, Mediterranean Sea; population (1982) 1,111,000.

It is surrounded by hills and connected with the river Rhône by a canal, and there are several offshore islands including ◊If. Its university was founded 1409.

history Marseille was founded by mariners of Phocaea in Asia Minor in 600 BC. Under the Romans it was a free city, and then, after suffering successive waves of invaders, became in the 13th century an independent republic, until included in France in 1481. Much of the old quarter was destroyed by Germany in 1943.

Marsenne /mɑː'sen/ Marin 1588–1648. French mathematician and philosopher who, from his base in Paris, did much to disseminate throughout Europe the main advances of French science. In mathematics he defined a particular form of ◊prime number, since referred to as a Mersenne prime.

Marsh /mɑːʃ/ Ngaio 1899–1982. New Zealand writer of detective fiction. Her first detective novel *A Man Lay Dead* 1934 introduced her protagonist Chief Inspector Roderick Alleyn.

marshal a title given in some countries to a high officer of state. Originally it meant one who tends horses, in particular one who shoes them.

The ◊Earl Marshal in England organizes state ceremonies; the office is hereditarily held by the duke of Norfolk. The corresponding officer in Scotland was the Earl Marischal.

marshal highest military rank in the British Royal Air Force. It corresponds to admiral of the fleet in the navy and field marshal in the army. In the French army the highest officers bear the designation of *maréchal de France*/marshal of France.

Marshall /'mɑːʃəl/ Alfred 1842–1924. English economist, professor of economics at Cambridge University 1885–1908. He was a founder of neoclassical economics, and stressed the power of supply and demand to generate equilibrium prices in markets, introducing the concept of elasticity of demand relative to price. His *Principles of Economics* 1890 remains perhaps the most influential textbook of neo-classical economics.

Marshall /'mɑːʃəl/ George Catlett 1880–1959. US general and diplomat. He was army chief of staff in World War II, secretary of state 1947–49, and secretary of defence Sept 1950–Sept 1951. He initiated the ◊*Marshall Plan* 1947 and received the Nobel Peace prize 1953.

Marshall, born in Pennsylvania, was commissioned in 1901, served in World War I, and in 1939 became chief of staff with the rank of general. On resigning in Nov 1945 he became ambassador to China, attempting to secure a coalition between the Nationalist and Communist forces against Japan. As defence secretary (a post never normally held by a soldier), he backed Truman's recall of MacArthur from Korea.

Marshall /ˈmɑːʃəl/ John 1755–1835. US jurist. As chief justice of the Supreme Court 1801–35, he established the power and independence of the Supreme Court. He laid down interpretations of the US constitution in a series of important decisions which have since become universally accepted.

Marshall /ˈmɑːʃəl/ John Ross 1912–1988. New Zealand National Party politician, noted for his negotiations of a free-trade agreement with Australia. He was deputy to K J Holyoake as prime minister and succeeded him Feb–Nov 1972.

Marshall Islands /ˈmɑːʃəl/ the Radak (13 islands) and Ralik (11 islands) chains in the W Pacific
area 180 sq km/69 sq mi
capital Majuro
features include two atolls used for US atombomb tests 1946–63, Eniwetok and Bikini (hence the name given to two-piece swimsuits which supposedly had an explosive impact)—radioactivity will last for 100 years, and the people have made claims for rehabilitation; and Kwajalein atoll (the largest) which has a US intercontinental missile range
products copra, phosphates, fish, tourism
population (1988) 41,000
government internally self-governing
recent history German 1906–19; administered by Japan until 1946, passed to the USA as part of the Pacific Islands Trust Territory 1947. They were used for many atomic bomb tests 1946–63, and the islanders are demanding compensation. In 1986 a compact of Free Association with the USA was signed, under which the islands manage their own internal and external affairs but the USA controls military activities in exchange for financial support.
currency US dollar
language English (official)
religion Christian and local faiths

Marshall Plan a programme of US financial aid to Europe, set up at the end of World War II, totalling $12,000 million 1948–52. Officially known as the European Recovery Programme, it was initiated by George ◊Marshall in a speech at Harvard in June 1947, but was in fact the work of a State Department group led by Dean ◊Acheson.

marsh gas a form of the gas ◊methane. It is produced in swamps and marshes by the action of bacteria.

marsh marigold plant *Caltha palustris* of the buttercup family Ranunculaceae, known as the kingcup in the UK and as the cowslip in the USA. It grows in moist sheltered spots, and has five-sepalled flowers of a brilliant yellow.

Marsilius of Padua /mɑːˈsɪlɪəs/ 1270–1342. Italian scholar and jurist. Born in Padua, he

marsh marigold

Marshall Islands

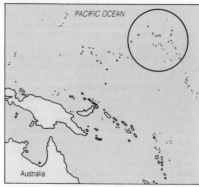

studied and taught at Paris, and in 1324 collaborated with John of Jandun in writing the *Defensor pacis/Defender of the Peace*, a plea for the subordination of the ecclesiastical to the secular power and for the right of the people to choose their own government. He played a part in the establishment of the Roman republic in 1328, and was made archbishop of Milan.

Marston Moor, Battle of /ˈmɑːstən ˈmʊə/ battle fought in the English Civil War on 2 July 1644 on Marston Moor, 11 km/7 mi W of York. The Royalists were completely defeated by the Parliamentarians and Scots.

The Royalist forces were commanded by Prince Rupert and the Duke of Newcastle; their opponents by Oliver Cromwell and Lord Leven. Lord Fairfax, on the right of the Parliamentarians, was routed, but Cromwell's cavalry charges were decisive.

marsupial (Greek *marsupion*, little purse or bag) mammal in which the female has a pouch where she carries her young for some considerable time after birth. Marsupials include the kangaroo, wombat, opossum, Tasmanian wolf, bandicoot, and wallaby.

Martello tower a type of tower for coastal defence. Formerly much used in Europe, many were built along the English coast, especially in Sussex and Kent, in 1804, as a defence against the threatened French invasion. The name is derived from a tower on Cape Mortella, Corsica, which was captured by the British with great difficulty in 1794, and was taken as a model. They are round towers of solid masonry, sometimes moated, with a flat roof for mounted guns.

marten small carnivorous mammal belonging to the weasel family Mustelidae, genus *Martes*. Martens live in North America, Europe, and Asia. The *pine marten Martes martes* has long brown fur and is about 75 cm/2.5 ft long. It is found in Britain.

The *stone* or *beech marten Martes foina* is lighter in colour. The *sable Martes zibellina* lives in E Siberia, and provides the most valued fur. The largest is the *fisher Martes pennanti*, with black fur and reaching 125 cm/4 ft, of North America.

Martens /ˈmɑːtəns/ Wilfried 1936– . Prime minister of Belgium from 1979, member of Social Christian Party (CVP). He was president of the Dutch-speaking CVP 1972–79 and, as prime minister, headed six coalition governments in the periods 1979–81, 1981–85, and from 1985.

Martha's Vineyard /ˈmɑːθəz ˈvɪnjəd/ island 32 km/20 mi long off the coast of Cape Cod, Massachusetts, USA; chief town Edgertown. It is the former home of whaling captains, and now a summer resort.

Martial /ˈmɑːʃəl/ (Marcus Valerius Martialis) AD 41–104. Latin epigrammatist. His poetry, often bawdy, reflects contemporary Roman life.

Born in Bilbilis, Spain, Martial settled in Rome in 64, where he lived by his literary and social gifts. He is renowned for correctness of diction, versification, and form.

martial arts styles of armed and unarmed combat developed in the East from ancient techniques and arts. Common martial arts include ◊aikido, ◊judo, ◊jujitsu, ◊karate, ◊kendo, and ◊kung fu.

martial law the replacement of civilian by military authorities in the maintenance of order. In Britain, the legal position of martial law is ill-defined but, in effect, when war or rebellion is in progress in an area, the military authorities are recognized as having powers to maintain order by summary means. In the USA martial law is usually proclaimed by the president or the government of a state in areas of the country where the civil authorities have been rendered unable to act, or to act with safety. Martial law, though neither in the constitution nor laid down in statutes, has frequently been used in the US, for example in Hawaii 1941–44 after the bombing of Pearl Harbor.

martin several genera of birds, related to the swallow, in the family Hirundinidae. The European house martin *Delichon urbica*, a summer migrant from Africa, is blue-black above and white below, distinguished from the swallow by its shorter, less forked tail.

The cuplike mud nest is usually constructed under the eaves of buildings. Best known of other species are the brownish European sand martin *Riparia riparia*, which tunnels to make a nest in sandy banks, also a migrant from Africa, and the purple martin of North America *Progne subis*, a handsome steely-blue bird which often nests in hollow trees.

Martin /ˈmɑːtɪn/ (Basil) Kingsley 1897–1969. English journalist who, as editor of the *New Statesman* 1931–60, made it the voice of controversy on the left.

Martin /ˈmɑːtɪn/ Archer John Porter 1910– . British biochemist, Nobel prizewinner for chemistry in 1952 for work with Richard Synge on paper chromatography in 1944.

Martin /ˈmɑːtɪn/ John 1789–1854. British Romantic painter of grandiose landscapes and ambitious religious subjects, such as *Belshazzar's Feast* (several versions).

Other examples are *The Great Day of His Wrath* and *The Plains of Heaven* (both Tate Gallery, London). Martin often worked on large canvases, and made mezzotints from his work, which were hugely popular in the early 19th century.

Martin /ˈmɑːtɪn/ Richard 1754–1834. Irish landowner and lawyer known as 'Humanity Martin'. He founded the British Royal Society for Prevention of Cruelty to Animals in 1824.

Martin /ˈmɑːtɪn/ Violet Florence 1862–1915. Irish novelist under the pen name Martin Ross. She collaborated with her cousin Edith Somerville on tales of Anglo-Irish provincial life, for example *Some Experiences of an Irish RM* 1899.

Martin V /ˈmɑːtɪn/ 1368–1431. Pope from 1417. A member of the Roman family of Colonna, he was elected during the Council of Constance, and ended the Great Schism between the rival popes of Rome and Avignon.

Martin du Gard /mɑːˈtæn djuː ˈɡɑː/ Roger 1881–1958. French novelist who realistically recorded the way of life of the bourgeoisie in the eight-volume *Les Thibault/The World of the Thibaults* 1922–40. Nobel prize 1937.

Martineau /ˈmɑːtɪnəʊ/ Harriet 1802–1876. English journalist, economist, and novelist, who wrote popular works on economics, children's stories, and articles in favour of the abolition of slavery.

Martineau /ˈmɑːtɪnəʊ/ James 1805–1900. British Unitarian minister and philosopher. A noted orator, he anticipated Anglican modernists in his theology.

Martinet /ˌmɑːtɪˈneɪ/ Jean French inspector-general of infantry under Louis XIV, whose constant drilling brought the army to a high degree of efficiency; hence the use of his name to mean a strict disciplinarian.

Martineau *English writer Harriet Martineau became a prominent literary figure for her writings on Unitarianism, political science, and the abolition of slavery.*

Martinez /mɑːˈtiːnes/ Maria Montoya 1890–1980. Pueblo Indian potter, who revived silvery black-on-black ware (made without the wheel) at San Ildefonso Pueblo, New Mexico, USA.

Martínez Ruiz /mɑːˈtiːneθ rruːˈiːθ/ José. Real name of ◊Azorín, Spanish author.

Martini /mɑːˈtiːni/ Simone *c.*1284–1344. Italian painter, one of the great masters of the Sienese school. A pupil of Duccio, he continued the graceful linear pattern of Sienese art, but introduced a fresh element of naturalism. His patrons included the city of Siena, the king of Naples, and the pope. Two of his frescoes are in the Palazzo Pubblico in Siena: the *Maestà* about 1315 and the horseback warrior *Guidoriccio da Fogliano* (the attribution of the latter is disputed). He died at the papal court in Avignon.

Martinique

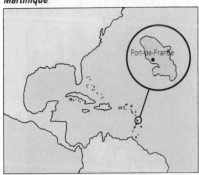

Martinique /ˌmɑːtɪˈniːk/ French island in the West Indies (Lesser Antilles)
area 1,079 sq km/417 sq mi
capital Fort-de-France
features several active volcanoes; Napoleon's empress Josephine was born in Martinique, and her childhood home is a museum
products sugar, cocoa, rum, bananas, pineapples
population (1984) 327,000
history Martinique was reached by Spanish navigators in 1493, and became a French colony in 1635; since 1972 it has been a French overseas region.

Martinmas in the Christian calendar, the feast of St Martin, 11 Nov. Fairs were frequently held on this day, at which farmworkers were hired.

In the Middle Ages it was also the day on which cattle were slaughtered and salted for winter consumption.

Martins Peter 1946– . Danish-born US dancer, choreographer, and director, principal dancer with the New York City Ballet from 1965 and its joint director from 1983.

Martins trained at the Royal Danish Ballet School, joining the company 1965, and the same year joined the New York City Ballet as a principal. He created roles in, among others, Robbins's *Goldberg Variations* 1971 and Balanchine's *Violin Concerto* and *Duo Concertant* both 1972, and choreographed, for example, *Calcium Night Light* 1978.

Martin, St /ˈmɑːtɪn/ 316–400. Bishop of Tours, France, from about 371, and founder of the first monastery in Gaul. He is usually represented as tearing his cloak to share it with a beggar. His feast day is Martinmas, 11 Nov.

Born in Pannonia, SE Europe, a soldier by profession, Martin was converted to Christianity, left the army, and lived for ten years as a recluse. After being elected bishop of Tours, he worked for the extinction of idolatry and the extension of monasticism in France.

Martin's Hundred /ˈmɑːtɪnz/ plantation town established in Virginia, USA (1619) and eliminated by an Indian massacre three years later. Its remains, the earliest extensive trace of British colonization in America, were discovered in 1970.

Martinu /ˈmɑːtɪnuː/ Bohuslav (Jan) 1890–1959. Czech composer, who studied in Paris. He left Czechoslovakia after the Nazi occupation of 1939. The quality of his music varies but at its best it is richly expressive and has great vitality. His works include the operas *Julietta* 1937 and *The Greek Passion* 1959, symphonies, and chamber music.

martyr (Greek 'witness') one who voluntarily suffers death for refusing to renounce their faith. The first recorded Christian martyr was St Stephen, who was killed in Jerusalem shortly after Jesus' alleged ascension to heaven.

Marvell /ˈmɑːvəl/ Andrew 1621–1678. English metaphysical poet and satirist. His poems include 'To His Coy Mistress' and 'Horatian Ode upon Cromwell's Return from Ireland'. He was committed to the Parliamentary cause, and was Member of Parliament for Hull from 1659. He devoted his last years mainly to verse satire and controversial prose works.

Marvin /ˈmɑːvɪn/ Lee 1924–1987. US film actor who began his career playing violent, often psychotic villains and progressed to playing violent, occasionally psychotic heroes. His work includes *The Big Heat* 1953, *The Killers* 1964, and *Cat Ballou* 1965.

Marx /mɑːks/ Karl (Heinrich) 1818–1883. German philosopher, economist, and social theorist, whose account of change through conflict is known as historical, or dialectical, materialism (see ◊Marxism). His ◊*Das Kapital/Capital* 1867–95 is the fundamental text of Marxist economics, and his systematic theses on class struggle, history, and the importance of economic factors in politics have exercised an enormous influence on later thinkers and political activists.

The son of a lawyer, he was born in Trier, and studied law and philosophy at Bonn and Berlin. During 1842–43, he edited the *Rheinische Zeitung/Rhineland Newspaper* until its suppression. In 1844 he began his life-long collaboration with ◊Engels, with whom he developed the Marxist philosophy, first formulated in their joint works, *Die heilige Familie/The Holy Family* 1844, and *Die deutsche Ideologie/German Ideology* 1846 (which contains the theory demonstrating the material basis of all human activity: 'Life is not determined by consciousness, but consciousness by life'), and Marx's *Misère de la philosophie/Poverty of Philosophy* 1847. Both joined the Communist League, a German refugee organization, and in 1847–48 they prepared its programme, *The Communist Manifesto*. During the 1848 revolution

Marx Brothers *US film comedians; from top left Zeppo, Groucho, Chico, and Harpo.*

Marx edited the *Neue Rheinische Zeitung/New Rhineland Newspaper*, until he was expelled from Prussia 1849.

He then settled in London, where he wrote *Die Klassenkämpfe in Frankreich/Class Struggles in France* 1849, *Die Achtzehnte Brumaire des Louis Bonaparte/The 18th Brumaire of Louis Bonaparte* 1852, *Zur Kritik der politischen Ökonomie/Critique of Political Economy* 1859, and his monumental work *Das Kapital/Capital*. In 1864 the International Working Men's Association was formed, whose policy Marx, as a member of the general council, largely controlled. Although he showed extraordinary tact in holding together its diverse elements, it collapsed 1872 due to Marx's disputes with the anarchists, including Bakunin. The second and third volumes of *Das Kapital* were edited from his notes by Engels, and published posthumously. Marx was buried at Highgate, London.

Marx's philosophical work owes much to the writings of Hegel, although he rejected Hegel's idealism, and was influenced by Feuerbach and Hess.

Marx Brothers US film comedians **Leonard 'Chico'** (from the 'chicks' (girls) he chased) 1891–1961; **Arthur 'Harpo'** (from the harp he played) 1893–1964; **Julius 'Groucho'** 1890–1977; **Milton 'Gummo'** (from his gumshoes or galoshes) 1894–1977, who left the team early on, and **Herbert 'Zeppo'** (born at the time of the first zeppelins) 1901–79, part of the team until 1934. Their films include *Animal Crackers* 1932, *Duck Soup* 1933, *A Night at the Opera* 1935, and *Go West* 1937.

Marxism philosophical system, developed by the 19th-century German social theorists ◊Marx and ◊Engels, also known as **dialectical materialism**, under which matter gives rise to mind (materialism) and all is subject to change (from dialectic; see ◊Hegel). As applied to history, it supposes that the succession of feudalism, capitalism, socialism, and finally the classless society is inevitable. The stubborn resistance of any existing system to change necessitates its complete overthrow in the **class struggle**—in the case of capitalism, by the proletariat—rather than gradual modification.

Social and political institutions progressively change their nature as economic developments transform material conditions. The orthodox belief is that each successive form is 'higher' than the last; perfect socialism is seen as the ultimate rational system, and it is alleged that the state would then wither away. Marxism has proved one of the most powerful and controversial theories in modern history, inspiring both dedicated exponents (Lenin, Trotsky, Stalin, Mao) and bitter opponents. It is the basis of ◊communism.

Mary /ˈmeəri/ in the New Testament, the mother of Jesus through divine intervention (see ◊Annunciation), wife of ◊Joseph. The Roman Catholic Church maintains belief in her ◊Immaculate Conception and bodily assumption into heaven, and venerates her as a mediator. Feast day 15 Aug.

Mary *Portrait of Mary Queen of Scots, after Nicholas Hilliard (c.1610) National Portrait Gallery, London.*

Traditionally her parents were elderly and named Joachim and Anna. Mary (Hebrew ***Miriam***) married Joseph and accompanied him to Bethlehem. Roman Catholic doctrine assumes that the brothers of Jesus were Joseph's sons by an earlier marriage, and that she remained a virgin. Pope Paul VI proclaimed her 'Mother of the Church' in 1964.

Mary /mɔˈriː/ town in Turkmenistan, S USSR, on the Murghab River; population (1985) 85,000. It is situated in a cotton-growing oasis in the Kara Kum desert, near where Alexander the Great founded a city (◊Merv).

Mary /ˈmeəri/ ***Queen of Scots*** 1542–1587. Queen of Scotland 1542–67. Also known as ***Mary Stuart***, she was the daughter of James V. Mary's connection with the English royal line from Henry VII made her a threat to Elizabeth I's hold on the English throne, particularly as she represented a champion of the Catholic cause. She was married three times. After her forced abdication she was imprisoned but escaped 1568 to England. Elizabeth I held her prisoner, while the Roman Catholics, who regarded Mary as rightful queen of England, formed many conspiracies to place her on the throne, and for complicity in one of these she was executed.

Mary's mother was the French Mary of Guise. Born in Linlithgow (now in Lothian region, Scotland), Mary was sent to France, where she married the dauphin, later Francis II. After his death she returned in 1561 to Scotland, which, during her absence, had turned Protestant. She married her cousin, the Earl of ◊Darnley, in 1565, but they soon quarrelled, and Darnley took part in the murder of Mary's secretary, ◊Rizzio. In 1567 Darnley was assassinated as the result of a conspiracy formed by the Earl of ◊Bothwell, possibly with Mary's connivance, and shortly after Bothwell married her. A rebellion followed; defeated at Carberry Hill, Mary abdicated and was imprisoned. She escaped in 1568, raised an army, and after its defeat at Langside fled to England, only to be imprisoned again. A plot against Elizabeth I devised by Anthony Babington led to her trial and execution at Fotheringay Castle in 1587.

Mary /ˈmeəri/ Duchess of Burgundy 1457–1482. Daughter of Charles the Bold. She married Maximilian of Austria 1477, thus bringing the Low Countries into the possession of the Habsburgs and, ultimately, of Spain.

Mary of Guise, or Mary of Lorraine 1515–1560. French wife of James V of Scotland from 1538, and from 1554 regent of Scotland for her daughter ◊Mary Queen of Scots. A Catholic, she moved from reconciliation with Scottish Protestants to repression, and died during a Protestant rebellion in Edinburgh.

Mary /ˈmeəri/ Queen 1867–1953. Consort of George V of the UK. The daughter of the Duke and Duchess of Teck, the latter a grand-daughter of George II, in 1891 she became engaged to the Duke of Clarence, eldest son of the Prince of Wales (later Edward VII). After his death 1892, she married 1893 his brother George, Duke of York, who succeeded to the throne 1910.

Mary /ˈmeəri/ two queens of England:

Mary I 1516–1558. Queen of England from 1553. She was born at Greenwich, the daughter of Henry VIII by Catherine of Aragon. When Edward VI died, she secured the crown without difficulty in spite of the conspiracy to substitute Lady Jane ◊Grey. In 1554 she married Philip II of Spain, and as a devout Catholic obtained the restoration of papal supremacy. She was succeeded by her half-sister Elizabeth 1. Although naturally humane, she sanctioned the persecution of Protestants which won her the nickname of ***Bloody Mary***.

Mary II 1662–1694. Queen of England, Scotland, and Ireland from 1688. She was the elder daughter of ◊James II, and in 1677 was married to her cousin, ◊William III of Orange. After the 1688 revolution she accepted the crown jointly with William. During his absences abroad she took charge of the government, and showed courage and resource when invasion seemed possible in 1690 and 1692.

Maryborough /ˈmeəribərə/ Australian coastal and market (grain, livestock) town in SE Queensland; industries (coal and gold-mining, iron, steel); population (1980) 21,000.

Maryborough /ˈmeəribərə/ see ◊Portlaoighise, town in the Republic of Ireland.

Maryland /ˈmeərilænd/ state of the E USA; nickname Old Line State or Free State
area 31,600 sq km/12,198 sq mi
capital Annapolis
towns Baltimore, Silver Spring, Dundalk, Bethesda
features Chesapeake Bay, an inlet of the Atlantic; horse racing (the Preakness Stakes at Baltimore); yacht racing at Annapolis; Fort Meade, a government electronic-listening centre
products fruit, cereals, tobacco, fish, oysters
population (1986) 4,463,000
famous people Francis Scott Key, Stephen Decatur, H L Mencken, Upton Sinclair
history one of the original Thirteen Colonies, first settled 1634; it became a state 1788.

Mary Magdalene, St /ˌmægdəˈliːni/ woman who according to the New Testament was present at the Crucifixion and was the first to meet the risen Jesus. She is often identified with the woman of St Luke's gospel who anointed Jesus' feet, and her symbol is a jar of ointment; feast day 22 July.

Mary of Modena /ˈmɒdɪnə/ 1658–1718. Queen consort of England and Scotland. She was the daughter of the Duke of Modena, Italy, and married James, Duke of York, later James II, in 1673. The birth of their son James Francis Edward Stuart was the signal for the revolution of 1688 which overthrew James II. Mary of Modena fled to France.

Mary Poppins a collection of children's stories by P(amela) L Travers (1906–), published in

Maryland

Mary of Modena *James II's consort, Mary of Modena, joined him in his refuge in France after the invasion of England by William of Orange. Her portrait is by the Dutch painter William Wissing c.1685.*

the UK 1934. They feature the eccentric Mary Poppins who looks after the children of the Banks family and entertains her charges by using her magical powers. Sequels include *Mary Poppins Comes Back* 1935.

Mary Rose greatest warship of Henry VIII of England, which sank off Southsea, Hampshire, on 19 July 1545. The wreck was located in 1971, and raised in 1982 for preservation in dry dock in Portsmouth harbour.

Masaccio /məˈzætʃəʊ/ (Tomaso di Giovanni di Simone Guidi) 1401–1428. Florentine painter, a leader of the early Italian Renaissance. His frescoes in Sta Maria del Carmine, Florence, 1425–28, which he painted with Masolino da Panicale (*c.* 1384–1447), show a decisive break with Gothic conventions. He was the first painter to apply the scientific laws of perspective, newly discovered by the architect Brunelleschi.

Masaccio's frescoes in the Brancacci Chapel of St Maria del Carmine include scenes from the life

Masaccio *The Virgin and Child (from the Pisa polyptych, 1426) National Gallery, London.*

Masaryk *Tomáš Masaryk, the first president of Czechoslovakia.*

of St Peter (notably *The Tribute Money*) and a moving account of *Adam and Eve's Expulsion from Paradise*. They have a monumental grandeur, without trace of Gothic decorative detail, unlike the work of his colleague and teacher Masolino. Masaccio's figures have solidity and weight, harking back to Giotto, and are clearly set in three-dimensional space.

Other works by Masaccio are the *Trinity* about 1428 (Sta Maria Novella, Florence) and the *Pisa polyptych* (National Gallery, London, Staatliche Museen, Berlin, and Museo di Capodimonte, Naples). Although his career marks a turning point in Italian art, he attracted few imitators (Fra Filippo Lippi's early style followed Masaccio).

Masada /məˈsɑːdə/ rock fortress 396 m/1,300 ft above the west shore of the Dead Sea, Israel. When besieged by the Romans AD 72, its population of 953 committed mass suicide.

Masai /ˈmɑːsaɪ/ member of an African people, whose territory was divided between Tanzania and Kenya. They were originally warriors and nomadic breeders of humped zebu cattle, but are now gradually adopting a more settled life. They speak a Nilotic language.

Masaryk /ˈmæsərɪk/ Jan (Garrigue) 1886–1948. Czech politician, son of Tomáš Masaryk. He was foreign minister from 1940, when the Czech government was exiled in London in World War II. He returned in 1945, retaining the post, but as a result of communist political pressure committed suicide.

Masaryk /ˈmæsərɪk/ Tomáš (Garrigue) 1850–1937. Czech nationalist politician. He directed the Czech revolutionary movement against the Austrian Empire, founding with Beneš and Stefanik the Czechoslovak National Council, and in 1918 was elected first president of the newly formed Czechoslovak Republic. Three times re-elected, he resigned in 1935 in favour of Beneš.

masc. in grammar, the abbreviation for *masculine*, see ◊gender.

Mascagni /mæsˈkɑːnji/ Pietro 1863–1945. Italian composer of the one-act opera *Cavalleria rusticana/Rustic Chivalry*, first produced in Rome in 1890.

Mascara /mæsˈkɑːrə/ town and wine-trade centre, 96 km/60 mi SE of Oran, Algeria; the headquarters of Abd-el-Kader (*c.*1807–83) who fought the French invasion of Algeria 1830–47, Mascara being captured 1841.

Masefield /ˈmeɪsfiːld/ John 1878–1967. English poet and novelist. His works include novels (*Sard Harker* 1924), critical works (*Badon Parchments* 1947), children's books (*The Box of Delights*

1935), and plays. He was Poet Laureate from 1930.

Masekela Hugh 1939– . South African trumpet player, in exile from 1960, who has recorded jazz, rock, and *mbaqanga*, or township jive. His albums include *Techno-Bush* 1984.

maser acronym for *m*icrowave *a*mplification by *s*timulated *e*mission of *r*adiation. In physics, it is a high-frequency microwave amplifier or oscillator. The signal to be amplified is used to stimulate unstable atoms into emitting energy at the same frequency. The principle has been extended to other parts of the electromagnetic spectrum, as for example in the ◊laser.

The two-level ammonia gas maser was first suggested in 1954 by C H Townes at Columbia University, New York, USA, and independently the same year by Basov and Prokhorov in the USSR. The solid-state three-level maser, the most sensitive amplifier known, was envisaged by Bloembergen in 1956 at Harvard. The ammonia maser is used as a frequency standard oscillator (see ◊clock), and the three-level maser as a receiver for satellite communications and radioastronomy.

Maserati Italian racing-car company, founded 1926 by the six Maserati brothers. The most outstanding Maserati was the 250F Grand Prix car, which the Argentinian Juan Manuel Fangio drove during his world-championship-winning year 1957. The company withdrew from Grand Prix racing at the end of 1957.

Maseru /məˈseəruː/ capital of Lesotho, South Africa, on the Caledon river; population (1986) 289,000. It is a centre for trade and diamond processing.

Mashhad /mæʃˈhæd/ or **Meshed** holy city of the Shi'ites, and industrial centre (carpets, textiles, leather goods), in NE Iran; population (1986) 1,464,000. It is the second largest city in Iran.

Mashonaland /məˈʃɒnəlænd/ E Zimbabwe, the land of the Shona people, now divided into three administrative regions. Granted to the British South Africa Company in 1889, it was united with Southern Rhodesia in 1923. The ◊Zimbabwe ruins are here. Prime Minister Robert Mugabe is a Shona.

Mashraq /mæʃˈrɑːk/ (Arabic 'east') the Arab countries of the E Mediterranean: Egypt, Sudan, Jordan, Syria, and Lebanon. The term is contrasted with ◊Maghreb, Arab countries of NW Africa.

Masirah Island /məˈsɪərə/ an island in the Arabian Sea, part of the sultanate of Oman, formerly used as an air staging post by British forces on their way to and from the Far East.

Masire /mæˈsɪəreɪ/ Quett Ketumile Joni 1925– . President of Botswana from 1980. He was a journalist before entering politics, sitting in the Bangwaketse Tribal Council and then the Legislative Council. In 1962, with Seretse ◊Khama, he founded the Botswana Democratic Party and in 1965 was made deputy prime minister. After independence, in 1966, he became vice president and, on Khama's death in 1980, president. Masire maintained his predecessor's policy of nonalignment and helped Botswana become one of the most stable states in Africa.

Maskelyne /ˈmæskəlɪn/ Nevil 1732–1811. English astronomer, who accurately measured the distance from the Earth to the Sun by observing a transit of Venus across the Sun's face 1769. In 1774, he measured the mass of the Earth by noting the deflection of a plumbline near Mount Schiehallion in Scotland. He was the fifth Astronomer Royal 1765–1811. He began publication 1766 of the *Nautical Almanac*, containing tables for navigators.

masochism a desire to subject oneself to physical or mental pain, humiliation, or punishment, for erotic pleasure, to alleviate guilt, or out of destructive impulses turned inwards. The term is derived from Leopold von ◊Sacher-Masoch.

Mason /ˈmeɪsən/ A(lfred) E(dward) W(oodley) 1865–1948. British novelist, famed for his tale

of cowardice redeemed in the Sudan, *The Four Feathers* 1902, and a series featuring the detective Hanaud of the Sûreté, including *At the Villa Rose* 1910.

Mason /ˈmeɪsən/ James 1909–1984. British actor who portrayed romantic villains in British films of the 1940s. After *Odd Man Out* 1947 he worked in the USA, notably in *A Star is Born* 1954. Other films include *The Wicked Lady* 1946, *Lolita* 1962, and *Cross of Iron* 1977.

Mason-Dixon Line in the USA, the boundary line between Maryland and Pennsylvania (latitude 39° 43′ 26.3′N), named after Charles Mason (1730–87) and Jeremiah Dixon (died 1777), English astronomers and surveyors who surveyed it 1763–67. It was popularly seen as dividing the North from the South.

masque a spectacular and essentially aristocratic entertainment with a fantastic or mythological theme in which music, dance, and extravagant costumes and scenic design were more important than plot. Originating in Italy, it reached its height of popularity at the English court between 1600 and 1640, with the collaboration of Ben ◊Jonson as writer and Inigo ◊Jones as stage designer.

The masque had great influence on the development of ballet and opera, and the elaborate frame in which it was performed developed into the proscenium arch.

mass in physics, the quantity of matter in a body. Mass determines the acceleration produced in a body by a given force acting on it, the acceleration being inversely proportional to the mass of the body. The mass also determines the force exerted on a body by ◊gravity on Earth, although this attraction varies slightly from place to place. In the SI system, the base unit of mass is the kilogram.

At a given place, equal masses experience equal gravitational forces, which are known as the weights of the bodies. Masses may, therefore, be compared by comparing the weights of bodies at the same place. The standard unit of mass to which all other masses are compared is a platinum-iridium cylinder of 1 kg.

Mass in Christianity, the celebration of the ◊Eucharist.

Mass in music, the setting of the invariable parts of the Christian Mass, that is *Kyrie, Gloria, Credo, Sanctus* with *Benedictus*, and *Agnus Dei*. A notable example is Bach's *Mass in B Minor*.

Massachusetts /ˌmæsəˈtʃuːsɪts/ New England state of the USA; nickname Bay State or Old Colony

area 21,500 sq km/8,299 sq mi

capital Boston

towns Worcester, Springfield, New Bedford, Brockton, Cambridge

features the two large Atlantic islands of Nantucket and Martha's Vineyard, former whaling centres; rivers Merrimac and Connecticut; University of Harvard 1636; Massachusetts Institute of Technology (MIT) 1861; Woods Hole Oceanographic Institute; Massachusetts Biotechnology Research

Massawa *Temperatures here may reach 46°C/115°F and water evaporates quickly. About 230,000 tonnes of salt are collected from these pans every year.*

Park to develop new products and processes; Norman Rockwell Museum at Stockbridge
products electronic and communications equipment, shoes, textiles, machine tools, building stone, cod
population (1985) 5,819,000
famous people Samuel Adams, Louisa May Alcott, Emily Dickinson, Emerson, Hawthorne, Poe, Revere, Thoreau, Whistler
history one of the original ◊Thirteen Colonies, it was first settled 1620 by the Pilgrims at Plymouth, and became a state 1788.

massage method of relieving muscle tension in the body by systematic stroking, pressing, and kneading. Increasingly popular as an aid to relaxation as well as in medical treatment. In *aromatherapy* massage is used in combination with stress-relieving aromatic oils.

Massawa /məˈsɑːwə/ chief port and naval base of Ethiopia, in Eritrea, on the Red Sea, with salt production and pearl fishing; population (1980) 33,000. It is one of the hottest inhabited spots in the world, the temperature reaching 37.8°C/100°F in May. Massawa was an Italian possession 1885–1941.

Masséna /ˌmæseɪˈnɑː/ André 1756–1817. Marshal of France. He served in the French Revolutionary Wars, and under the emperor Napoleon was created marshal 1804, duke of Rivoli 1808, and prince of Essling 1809. He was in command in Spain 1810–11 in the Peninsular War, and was defeated by British troops under Wellington.

mass-energy equation ◊Einstein's equation $E = mc^2$, denoting the equivalence of mass and energy, where E is the energy in joules, m is the mass in kilograms, and c is the speed of light, in vacuum, in metres per second.

Massenet /ˌmæsəˈneɪ/ Jules Emile Frédéric 1842–1912. French composer of opera, ballets, oratorios, and orchestral suites. His many operas include *Hérodiade* 1881, *Manon* 1884, *Le Cid* 1885, and *Thaïs* 1894; among other works is the orchestral suite *Scènes pittoresques* 1874.

Masses, the US left-wing magazine which printed many prominent radical writers 1911–17, including John Reed and Max Eastman. It was superseded by the *Liberator* 1918–25 and then by *New Masses*, which advanced the cause of proletarian writing through the Depression 1930s.

Massey /ˈmæsi/ Vincent 1887–1967. Canadian Liberal Party politician. He was the first Canadian to become governor general of Canada (1952–59). He helped to establish the Massey Foundation 1918 which funded the building of Massey College and the University of Toronto.

Massif Central /mæˈsiːf sɒnˈtrɑːl/ mountainous plateau region of S central France; area 93,000 sq km/36,000 sq mi, highest peak Puy de Sancy 1,886 m/6,188 ft. It is a source of hydroelectricity.

Massine /mæˈsiːn/ Léonide 1895–1979. Russian choreographer and dancer with the Ballets Russes. He was a creator of comedy in ballet and also symphonic ballet using concert music.

He succeeded ◊Fokine at the Ballets Russes and continued with the company after ◊Diaghilev's death, later working in both the USA and Europe. His works include the first Cubist-inspired ballet *Parade* 1917, *La Boutique Fantasque* 1919, and *The Three-Cornered Hat* 1919.

Massinger /ˈmæsɪndʒə/ Philip 1583–1640. English dramatist, author of *A New Way to Pay Old Debts* about 1625. He collaborated with ◊Fletcher and ◊Dekker, and has been credited with a share in writing Shakespeare's *Two Noble Kinsmen* and *Henry VIII*.

mass observation the study of the details of people's daily lives through observation and interview. A society of the name was founded in London in 1937 for the purpose, employing a panel of observers and a number of trained investigators, and publishing the results.

Masson /ˈmæsɒn/ André 1896–1987. French artist and writer, a leader of Surrealism until 1929. His interest in the unconscious led him to experiment with 'automatic' drawing—simple pen and ink work, and later multi-textured accretions of pigment, glue, and sand.

Masson left the Surrealist movement after a quarrel with the writer André Breton. During World War II he moved to the USA, then returned to France and later turned to landscape painting.

Massorah a collection of philological notes on the Hebrew text of the Old Testament. It was at first an oral tradition, but was committed to writing in the Aramaic language at Tiberias, Palestine, between the 6th and 9th centuries.

mass production the manufacture of goods on a large scale, a technique that aims for low unit cost and high sales. In modern factories mass production is achieved by a variety of means, such as the division and specialization of labour, and ◊mechanization. This speeds up production and allows the manufacture of near-identical or interchangeable parts. Such parts can then be assembled quickly into a finished product on an ◊assembly line.

The division of labour means that a job is divided into a number of steps, and then groups of workers are employed to carry them out, specializing and therefore becoming more skilled in certain activities. In this way they can produce much more than if they individually had to carry out all the stages of manufacture themselves. However, the system has been criticized for removing workers' involvement with the end product.

Many of the machines now used in factories are ◊robots: they work automatically under computer control. Such automation further streamlines production and raises output.

mass spectrometer in physics, an apparatus for analysing chemical composition. Positive ions (charged particles) of a substance are separated by an electromagnetic system, which permits accurate measurement of the relative concentrations of the various ionic masses present, particularly isotopes.

Master of the King's/Queen's Musick appointment to the British royal household, the holder composing appropriate music for state occasions. The first was Nicholas Lanier, appointed by Charles I in 1626; the composer Malcolm ◊Williamson was appointed in 1975.

Master of the Rolls title of an English judge ranking immediately below the Lord Chief Justice. He presides over the Court of Appeal, besides being responsible for ◊Chancery records and for the admission of solicitors.

Masters /ˈmɑːstəz/ Edgar Lee 1869–1950. US poet. In his *Spoon River Anthology* 1915, the people of a small town tell of their frustrated lives.

Masters /ˈmɑːstəz/ John 1914–1983. British novelist, born in Calcutta, who served in the Indian army 1934–47. A series deals with the Savage family throughout the period of the Raj, for example, *Nightrunners of Bengal* 1951, *The Deceivers* 1952, *Bhowani Junction* 1954.

mastiff British dog, usually fawn in colour, originally bred for sporting purposes. It has a large head, wide-set eyes, and broad muzzle. It can grow up to 90 cm/3 ft at the shoulder, and weigh 100 kg/220 lb.

mastodon primitive elephant, whose fossil remains have been discovered in all the continents except Australia, particularly in deposits from the Pleistocene Age in the USA and Canada. It resembled the modern elephant, but was lower and longer; its teeth suggest that it ate leaves in the primeval swamps and forests.

Mastroianni /ˌmæstrəʊˈjæni/ Marcello 1924– . Italian film actor, famous for his carefully understated roles as an unhappy romantic lover in such films as *La Dolce Vita* 1959 and *La Notte/The Night* 1961.

Masulipatnam /məˌsuːlɪpətˈnæm/ or **Manchilipatnam**, also **Bandar** Indian seaport (its name means fish town) in Andhra Pradesh, at the mouth of the N branch of the river Kistna; population (1981) 138,500.

Masurian Lakes /məˈsʊəriən/ lakes in Poland (former East Prussia) which in 1914–15 were the scene of battles in which the Germans defeated the Russians.

Matabeleland /ˌmætəˈbiːlilænd/ the W portion of Zimbabwe between the Zambezi and Nimpopo rivers, inhabited by the Ndebele people.
area 181,605 sq km/70,118 sq mi
towns Bulawayo
features rich plains watered by tributaries of the Zambezi and Limpopo, with mineral resources
language Matabele
famous people Joshua Nkomo
history Matabeleland was granted to the British South Africa Company 1889 and occupied 1893 after attacks on white settlements in Mashonaland; in 1923 it was included in Southern Rhodesia. It is now divided into two administrative regions.

Matadi /məˈtɑːdi/ chief port of Zaïre on the river Zaïre, 115 km/70 mi from its mouth, linked by oil pipelines with Kinshasa; population (1984) 144,700.

Mata Hari /ˈmɑːtə ˈhɑːri/ ('Eye of the Day'), stage name of Gertrud Margarete Zelle 1876–1917. Dutch courtesan, dancer, and probable spy. In World War I she appears to have been a double agent, in the pay of both France and Germany. She was shot by the French on espionage charges.

matamata South American freshwater turtle or terrapin *Chelys fimbriata* with a shell up to 40 cm/15 in long. The head is flattened, with a 'snorkel' nose, and the neck has many projections of skin. The movement of these in the water may attract prey, which the matamata catches by opening its mouth suddenly to produce an inrush of water.

Matanzas /məˈtænsəs/ industrial port (tanning, textiles, sugar) in NW Cuba; population (1986) 105,400. Founded 1693, it became a major centre of coffee, tobacco, and sugar production.

Matapan /ˌmætəˈpæn/ southernmost cape of mainland Greece, off which, on 28 Mar 1941, during World War II, a British fleet under Admiral Cunningham sank an Italian squadron.

match a small strip of wood or paper, tipped with combustible material for producing fire. Friction matches containing phosphorus were first made by John Walker of Stockton-on-Tees, England, about 1826.

A *safety match* is one in which the oxidizing agent and the combustible body are kept apart, the former being incorporated into the striking surface on the side of the box, the latter into the match.

maté dried leaves of the Brazilian holly *Ilex paraguensis*, an evergreen shrub akin to the common holly, that grows in Paraguay and Brazil. The roasted powdered leaves are made into a tea.

materialism the philosophical theory that there is nothing in existence over and above matter and matter in motion. Such a theory excludes the possibility of deities. It also sees mind as an attribute of the physical, denying idealist theories which see mind as something independent of body, for example Descartes' theory of 'thinking substance'.

Like most other philosophical ideas, materialism probably arose among the early Greek thinkers. The Stoics and the Epicureans were materialists, and so were the ancient Buddhists. Among modern materialists have been Hobbes, Diderot, d'Holbach, Büchner, and Haeckel; while Hume, J S Mill, Huxley, and Spencer showed materialist tendencies.

material product or *social product* system of national accounting used by socialist countries which includes all productive services but usually does not include non-public services and financial activities that would be included in conventional Western national accounts to give gross national product. GDP is a more comprehensive measure of a country's output.

mathematical induction a formal method of proof in which the proposition $P(n + 1)$ is proved true on the hypothesis that the proposition $P(n)$ is true. The proposition is then shown to be true for a particular value of n, say k, and therefore by induction the proposition must be true for $n = k + 1, k + 2, k + 3, \ldots$ In many cases $k = 1$, so the proposition is true for all positive integers.

mathematics the science of spatial and numerical relationships. The main divisions of **pure mathematics** include geometry, arithmetic, algebra, calculus, and trigonometry. Mechanics, statistics, numerical analysis, computing, the mathematical theories of astronomy, electricity, optics, thermodynamics, and atomic studies come under the heading of **applied mathematics**.

early history Prehistoric human beings probably learned to count at least up to 10 on their fingers. The Chinese, Hindus, Babylonians, and Egyptians all devised methods of counting and measuring which were of practical importance in their everyday lives. The first theoretical mathematician is held to be Thales of Melitus (c.580 BC), who is believed to have proposed the first theorems in plane geometry. His disciple ◊Pythagoras established geometry as a recognized science among the Greeks. The later school of Alexandrian geometers (4th and 3rd centuries BC) included ◊Euclid and ◊Archimedes. Our present decimal numerals are based on a Hindu-Arabic system which reached Europe about AD 100 from Arab mathematicians of the Middle East such as al-◊Khwarizmi.

Europe Western mathematics began to develop from the 15th century. Geometry was revitalized by the invention of coordinate geometry by Descartes 1637; Pascal and Fermat developed probability theory, Napier invented logarithms, and Newton and Leibniz developed calculus. In Russia, Lobachevsky rejected Euclid's parallelism and developed non-Euclidean geometry, a more developed form of which (by Riemann) was later utilized by Einstein in his relativity theory.

the present Higher mathematics has a powerful tool in the high-speed electronic computer, which can create and manipulate mathematical 'models' of various systems in science, technology, and commerce. Modern additions to school syllabuses such as sets, group theory, matrices, and graph theory are sometimes referred to as 'new' or 'modern' mathematics.

Mather /'mæðə/ Cotton 1663–1728. US theologian and writer. He was a Puritan minister in Boston, and wrote over 400 works of history, science, annals, and theology, including *Magnalia Christi American/The Great Works of Christ in America* 1702, a vast compendium of early New England history and experience. Mather appears to have supported the Salem witch-hunts.

Matilda /mə'tıldə/ 1102–1167. Claimant to the throne of England. On the death of her father, Henry I, in 1135, the barons elected her cousin Stephen to be king. Matilda invaded England 1139, and was crowned by her supporters 1141. Civil war ensued until in 1153 Stephen was finally

mathematical symbols

$a{\rightarrow}b$	a implies b
∞	infinity
lim	limiting value
$a{\sim}b$	numerical difference between a and b
$a{\approx}b$	a approximately equal to b
$a=b$	a equal to b
$a{\equiv}b$	a identical with b (for formulae only)
$a>b$	a greater than b
$a<b$	a smaller than b
$a{\neq}b$	a not equal to b
$b<a<c$	a greater than b and smaller than c, that is a lies between the values b & c but cannot equal either.
$a{\geq}b$	a equal to or greater than b, that is, a at least as great as b
$a{\leq}b$	a equal to or less than b, that is, a at most as great as b
$b{\leq}a{\leq}c$	a lies between the values b & c and could take the values b and c.
$\lvert a\rvert$	absolute value of a; this is always positive, for example $\lvert-5\rvert=5$
$+$	addition sign, positive
$-$	subtraction sign, negative
$\times$ or $\odot$	multiplication sign, times
$:$ or $\div$ or $/$	division sign, divided by
$a+b=c$	$a+b$, read as 'a plus b', denotes the addition of a and b. The result of the addition, c, is also known as the sum.
$\int$	indefinite integral
$_a\int^b f(x)dx$	definite integral, or integral between $x=a$ and $x=b$
$a-b=c$	$a-b$, read as 'a minus b', denotes subtraction of b from a.
	$a-b$, or c, is the difference. Subtraction is the opposite of addition.
$a{\times}b=c$	
$ab=c$	$a{\times}b$, read as 'a multiplied by b', denotes multiplication of a by b. $a{\times}b$, or c, is the product, a and b are factors of c.
$a.b=c$	
$a:b=c$	$a:c$, read as 'a divided by b', denotes division. a is the dividend, b is the divisor; $a:b$, or c, is the quotient.
$a{\div}b=c$	One aspect of division – repeated subtraction, is the opposite of multiplication – repeated addition.
$a/b=c$	In fractions, $\frac{a}{b}$ or a/b, a is the numerator (= dividend), b the denominator (= divisor).
$a^b=c$	a^b, read as 'a to the power b'; a is the base, b the exponent.
$^b\sqrt{a}=c$	$^b\sqrt{a}$, is the bth root of a, b being known as the root exponent. In the special case of $^2\sqrt{a}=c$, $^2\sqrt{a}$ or c is known as the square root of a, and the root exponent is usually omitted, that is, $^2\sqrt{a} = \sqrt{a}$.
e	exponential constant and is the base of natural (napierian) logarithms = 2.7182818284.......
π	ratio of the circumference of a circle to its diameter = 3.1415925535........

recognized as king, with Henry II (Matilda's son) as his successor.

Matilda was recognized during the reign of Henry I as his heir. She married first the Holy Roman emperor Henry V, and after his death Geoffrey Plantagenet, Count of Anjou (1113–51).

Matisse /mæ'ti:s/ Henri 1869–1954. French painter, sculptor, illustrator, and designer. He settled in the south of France in 1914. His work concentrates on designs that emphasize curvaceous surface patterns, linear arabesques, and brilliant colour. Subjects include odalisques (women of the harem), bathers, and dancers; later works include pure abstracts, as in his collages of coloured paper shapes and the designs 1949–51 for the decoration of a chapel for the Dominican convent in Vence, near Nice.

Matisse was one of the most original creative forces in early 20th-century art. In 1904 he worked with Signac in the south of France in a Neo-Impressionist style. The following year he was the foremost of the Fauve painters exhibiting at the Salon d'Automne, painting with bold brushstrokes, heavy impasto, and strong colours. He soon abandoned conventional perspective in his continued experiments with colour, and in 1910 an exhibition of Islamic art further influenced him towards the decorative. His murals of *The Dance* 1932–33 (Barnes Foundation, Merion, Pennsylvania) are characteristic.

Matlock /'mætlɒk/ spa town with warm springs, administrative headquarters of Derbyshire, England; population (1981) 21,000.

Mato Grosso /'mætəu 'grɒsəu/ (Portuguese 'dense forest') area of SW Brazil, now forming two states, with their capitals at Cuiaba and Campo Grande. The forests, now depleted, supplied rubber and rare timbers; diamonds and silver are mined.

matriarchy a form of social organization in which women head the family, and descent and relationship are reckoned through the female line. Matriarchy, often associated with polyandry (one wife with several husbands), occurs in certain parts of India, in the South Pacific, Central Africa, and among some North American Indian peoples. In **matrilineal** societies, powerful positions are usually held by men but acceded to through female kin.

matrix in mathematics, a square ($n \times n$) or rectangular ($m \times n$) array of elements (numbers or algebraic variables). They are a means of condensing information about mathematical systems, and can be used for, among other things, solving simultaneous linear equations and transformations.

Much early matrix theory was developed by the British mathematician Arthur ◊Cayley, although the term was first coined by his contemporary James Sylvester (1814–97).

matrix in biology, usually refers to the ◊extracellular matrix.

Matsudaira /ˌmæsuː'daɪrə/ Tsuneo 1877–1949. Japanese diplomat and politician who became the first chair of the Japanese Diet (parliament) after World War II.

Matsudaira negotiated for Japan at the London Naval Conference of 1930 and acted as imperial

Matterhorn *The Matterhorn, first climbed by the British mountaineer Edward Whymper in 1865. The mountain appears to be an isolated peak, but is actually the end of a ridge.*

household minister 1936–45, advising the emperor, but was unsuccessful in keeping Japan out of a war with the Western powers.

Matsue /'mætsəjeɪ/ city NW of Osaka on Honshu, Japan; population (1980) 135,500. It has remains of a magnificent castle, fine old tea houses, and the Izumo Grand Shrine (dating in its present form from 1744).

Matsukata /ˌmætsuːˈkaːtə/ Masayoshi 1835–1924. Prince of Japan. As a politician, he paved the way for the modernization of the Japanese economy in the 1880s.

Matsuoka /ˌmætsuˈəʊkə/ Yosuke 1880–1946. Japanese politician. As foreign minister 1927–29, he was largely responsible for the increasingly belligerent attitude towards China. His attempts to deal with Japan's worsening economic situation led to inflation and civil unrest.

Matsuyama /ˌmætsuˈjɑːmə/ largest city on Shikoku, Japan; industries (agricultural machinery, textiles, chemicals); population (1984) 418,000. There is a feudal fortress 1634.

Matsys /'mætsaɪs/ (also **Massys** or **Metsys**) Quentin 1464/65–1530. Flemish painter, born in Louvain, active in Antwerp. He is known for religious subjects such as the *Lamentation* 1511 (Musées Royaux, Antwerp) and portraits set against landscapes or realistic interiors.

Matsys may have visited Italy before 1520. His works include the *St Anne altarpiece* 1509 (Musées Royaux, Brussels) and a portrait of *Erasmus* 1517 (Museo Nazionale, Rome), which he presented to Thomas More.

matter in physics, the material of which all objects outside the mind are considered to be composed. The history of science and philosophy is largely taken up with accounts of theories of matter, ranging from the hard 'atoms' of Democritus to the 'waves' of modern quantum theory.

Matterhorn /'mætəhɔːn/ (French *le Cervin* Italian *il Cervino*) mountain peak in the Alps on the Swiss-Italian border; 4,478 m/14,690 ft. It was first climbed in 1865 by English mountaineer Edward Whymper (1840–1911); four members of his party of seven were killed when the rope broke during the descent.

Matthau /'mæθaʊ/ Walter. Stage name of Walter Matuschanskavasky 1922– . US character actor, impressive in both comedy and dramatic roles. He gained film stardom in the 1960s after his stage success in *The Odd Couple* (1965), and went on to act in, among others, *Kotch* 1971 and *Charley Varrick* 1973.

Matthews /'mæθjuːz/ Stanley 1915– . English footballer who played for Stoke City, Blackpool,

and England. He played nearly 700 Football League games, and won 54 international caps. He was the first European Footballer of the Year 1956.

An outstanding right-winger, he had the nickname 'the Wizard of the Dribble' because of his ball control. At the age of 38 he won an FA Cup Winners' medal when Blackpool beat Bolton Wanderers 4–3 by scoring three goals in the last 20 minutes. He was the first Footballer of the Year in 1948 (won again in 1963) and the first footballer to be knighted. He continued to play first-division football after the age of 50.

CAREER HIGHLIGHTS

Football League appearances: 698, goals: 71
International appearances: 54, goals: 11
FA Cup: 1953
Footballer of the Year: 1948, 1963
European Footballer of the Year: 1956.

Matthew, St /'maθju:/ Christian apostle and evangelist, the traditional author of the first Gospel. He is usually identified with Levi, who was a tax collector in the service of Herod Antipas, and was called by Jesus to be a disciple as he sat by the Lake of Galilee receiving customs dues. His emblem is a man with wings; feast day 21 Sept.

Matthias Corvinus /məˈθaɪəs kɔːˈvaɪnəs/ 1440–1490. King of Hungary from 1458. His aim of uniting Hungary, Austria, and Bohemia involved him in long wars with the Holy Roman emperor and the kings of Bohemia and Poland, during which he captured Vienna (1485) and made it his capital. His father was János ◊Hunyadi.

Mature /məˈtjʊə/ Victor 1915– . US actor, film star of the 1940s and early 1950s. He gave memorable performances in, among others, *My Darling Clementine* 1946, *Kiss of Death* 1947, and *Samson and Delilah* 1949.

matze (Yiddish) unleavened bread eaten during the ◊Passover.

Mauchly /'mɒxli/ John William 1907–1980. US physicist and engineer. He constructed 1946 the first general-purpose computer, the ENIAC, in collaboration with John Eckert (1919–). Their company was bought by Remington Rand 1950, and they built the Univac 1 computer 1951 for the US census. The idea for ENIAC grew out of the pair's work in World War II on ways of automating the calculation of artillery firing tables for the US Army.

Maudling /'mɔːdlɪŋ/ Reginald 1917–1979. British Conservative politician, chancellor of the Exchequer 1962–64, contender for the party leadership 1965, and home secretary 1970–72. He resigned when referred to during the bankruptcy proceedings of the architect John Poulsen, since (as home secretary) he would have been in charge of the Metropolitan Police investigating the case.

Maufe /'mɔːf/ Edward 1883–1974. British architect. His works include the Runnymede Memorial and Guildford Cathedral.

Mauger (pronounced *Major*) Ivan Gerald 1939– . New Zealand speedway star. He won the world individual title a record six times 1968–79.

CAREER HIGHLIGHTS

World Champion:
individual: 1968–70, 1972, 1977, 1979
pairs: 1969*–70
team: 1968, 1971–72, 1979
long track: 1971–72, 1976
British League Riders Champion: 1971, 1973
* championship unofficial 1968

Maugham /mɔːm/ (William) Somerset 1874–1965. English writer. His work includes the novels *Of Human Bondage* 1915, *The Moon and Sixpence* 1919, and *Cakes and Ale* 1930; short stories *The Trembling of a Leaf* 1921, *Ashenden* 1928; and plays *Lady Frederick* 1907, *Our Betters* 1923.

Born in Paris, he was educated at King's School, Canterbury and Heidelberg, then studied medicine at St Thomas's, London. During

Maugham *Somerset Maugham in 1931, a portrait by P Steegman in which the sitter is placed against the kind of exotic landscape that often formed the background of his stories.*

World War I he was a secret agent in Russia; his *Ashenden* spy stories are based on this experience.

Mau Mau name given by white settlers to a Kenyan secret guerrilla society with nationalist aims 1952–60, an offshoot of the Kikuyu Central Association banned in World War II. Attacks on other Kikuyu (about 1,000 killed) were far more common than on whites (about 100 killed).

Mauna Kea astronomical observatory in Hawaii, USA, built on a dormant volcano at 4,200 m/13,784 ft above sea level. Because of its elevation high above clouds, atmospheric moisture, and artificial lighting, Mauna Kea is ideal for infrared astronomy. The first telescope on the site was installed 1970.

Telescopes include the 2.24 m/88 in University of Hawaii reflector 1970. In 1979 three telescopes were erected: the 3.8 m/150 in United Kingdom Infrared Telescope (UKIRT) (also used for optical observations); the 3 m/120 in NASA Infrared Telescope Facility (IRTF); and the 3.6 m/142 in Canada-France-Hawaii Telescope (CFHT), designed for optical and infrared work. The 15 m/50 ft diameter UK/Netherlands James Clerk Maxwell Telescope (JCMT) is the world's largest telescope specifically designed to observe millimetre wave radiation from nebulae, stars, and galaxies. The JCMT is operated via satellite links by astronomers in Europe.

Work began 1986 on what will be the world's largest optical telescope, the *W M Keck Telescope*. It will have a primary mirror 10 m/33 ft across, unique in that it comprises 36 individual hexagonal segments joined together in a huge mosaic, each controlled and adjusted by computer to generate single images of the objects observed. The Keck Telescope will be built and operated jointly by the California Institute of Technology and the University of California.

Mauna Loa /ˌmaʊnəˈləʊə/ active volcano rising to a height of 4,169 m/13,678 ft on the Pacific island of Hawaii; it has numerous craters, including the second largest active crater in the world.

Maundy Thursday in the Christian church, the Thursday before Easter. The ceremony of washing the feet of pilgrims on that day was instituted in commemoration of Jesus' washing of the apostles' feet and observed from the 4th century until 1754.

In the UK it was performed by the English sovereigns until the time of William III, and *Maundy money* is still presented by the sovereign to poor people each year.

Maupassant /,məʊpæ'sɒŋ/ Guy de 1850–1893. French author who established a reputation with the short story 'Boule de Suif/Ball of Fat' 1880 and wrote some 300 short stories in all. His novels include *Une Vie/A Woman's Life* 1883 and *Bel-Ami* 1885.

Mauriac /,mɔːri'æk/ François 1885–1970. French novelist. His novel *Le Baiser au lépreux/A Kiss for the Leper* 1922 describes the conflict of an unhappy marriage. The irreconcilability of Christian practice and human nature are examined in *Fleuve de feu/River of Fire* 1923, *Le Désert de l'amour/The Desert of Love* 1925, and *Thérèse Desqueyroux* 1927. Nobel Prize for Literature 1952.

Maurice /'mɒrɪs/ (John) Frederick Denison 1805–1872. Anglican cleric from 1834, co-founder with Charles ◊Kingsley of the Christian Socialist movement. He was deprived of his professorships in English history, literature, and divinity at King's College, London, because his *Theological Essays* 1853 attacked the doctrine of eternal punishment; he became professor of moral philosophy at Cambridge 1866.

Maurist a congregation of French Benedictine Catholic monks, established in 1621 at the monastery of St Maur-sur-Loire. Subsequently its chief house was in Paris, and there the Maurist fathers carried on literary and historical work. In 1792 the congregation was suppressed.

Mauritania /,mɒrɪ'teɪnɪə/ country in NW Africa, bordered to the NE by Algeria, E and S by Mali, SW by Senegal, W by the Atlantic Ocean, and NW by Western Sahara.

government The 1961 constitution was suspended 1978 after a coup, and was replaced by a charter that gave executive and legislative power to a Military Committee for National Recovery (CMRN), which in 1979 became the Military Committee for National Salvation (CMSN). The chair of the CMSN is also president of the republic, prime minister, and minister of defence. The only political party, the Mauritanian People's Party (PPM), was banned 1978 and some of its exiled supporters now operate from Paris through the Alliance for a Democratic Mauritania (AMI), or from Dakar, in Senegal, through the Organization of Nationalist Mauritanians.

history Mauritania was the name of the Roman province of NW Africa, after the Mauri, a ◊Berber people who inhabited it. Berbers occupied the region during the 1st–3rd centuries AD, and it came under the control of the ◊Ghana Empire in the 7th–11th centuries. The Berbers were converted to Islam from the 8th century, and Islamic influence continued to dominate as the area was controlled by the ◊Almoravids and then the Arabs. French influence began in the 17th century, with the trade in gum arabic, and developed into colonization by the mid-18th century, when France gained control of S Mauritania.

In 1920 Mauritania became a French colony as part of French West Africa. It achieved internal self-government within the French Community 1958 and full independence 1960. Moktar Ould Daddah, leader of the PPM, became president 1961.

In 1975 Spain ceded Western Sahara to Mauritania and Morocco, leaving them to decide how to share it. Without consulting the Saharan people, Mauritania occupied the southern area, leaving the north to Morocco. A resistance movement developed against this occupation, the Popular Front for Liberation, or the Polisario Front, with Algerian backing, and Mauritania and Morocco found themselves engaged in a guerrilla war, forcing the two former rivals into a mutual defence pact. The conflict weakened Mauritania's economy and in 1978 President Daddah was deposed in a bloodless coup led

Mauritania
Islamic Republic of
(République Islamique de Mauritanie)

area 1,030,700 sq km/397,850 sq mi
capital Nouakchott
physical valley of river Senegal in south; the rest is arid
features includes part of the Sahara Desert
head of state and government Moaouia Ould Sidi Mohamed Taya from 1984
political system military republic
political parties no political parties allowed
exports iron ore, fish
currency ouguiya (142.25 = £1 Feb 1990)
population (1988) 1,894,000 (30% Arab Berber, 30% black Africans, 30% Haratine – descendants of black slaves, who remained slaves until 1980); annual growth rate 2.9%
life expectancy men 42, women 46
language Arabic (official), French
religion Sunni Muslim
literacy 2.9%
GDP $614 million (1984); $466 per head of population
chronology
1960 Achieved full independence, with Moktar Ould Daddah as president.
1975 Western Sahara ceded by Spain. Mauritania occupied the southern part and Morocco the rest. Polisario Front formed in Sahara to resist the occupation by Mauritania and Morocco.
1978 Daddah deposed in bloodless coup and replaced by Mohamed Khouni Ould Haidalla. Peace agreed with Polisario Front.
1981 Diplomatic relations with Morocco broken.
1984 Haidalla overthrown by Moaouia Ould Sidi Mohamed Taya. Polisario regime formally recognized.
1985 Relations with Morocco restored.
1989 Violent clashes between Mauritanians and Senegalese in Nouakchott and Dakar following dispute over border grazing rights. Arab-dominated government expels thousands of Africans into N Senegal. Earlier, governments agreed to repatriate each other's citizens (about 250,000).

by Col Mohamed Khouna Ould Haidalla. Peace with the Polisario was eventually agreed in Aug, allowing diplomatic relations with Algeria to be restored.

In Dec 1984, while Col Haidalla was attending a Franco-African summit meeting in Burundi, Col Moaouya Ould Sidi Ahmed Taya, a former prime minister, led a bloodless coup to overthrow him. Diplomatic relations with Morocco were broken 1981 and the situation worsened 1984 when Mauritania formally recognized the Polisario regime in Western Sahara. Normal relations were restored 1985. During 1989 there were a number of clashes with Senegalese in border areas and the presidents of the two countries met to try to resolve their differences.

Mauritius /mə'rɪʃəs/ Indian Ocean, E of Madagascar.

government Mauritius is an independent state within the Commonwealth, with a resident governor general as head of state, representing the British monarch. Its 1968 constitution, amended in 1969, provides for a single-chamber legislative assembly of up to 71 members, 62 elected by universal adult suffrage, plus the speaker and up to eight of the most successful non-elected candidates as 'additional' members. The governor general appoints the prime minister and a council of ministers who are collectively responsible to the assembly. Of a number of political parties, the three most significant are the Mauritius Labour Party (MLP), the Mauritius Socialist Movement (MSM), and the Mauritius Militant Movement (MMM).

history Uninhabited until the 16th century, the island was colonized on a small scale by the Dutch, who named it Mauricius after Prince Maurice of Nassau. They abandoned it in 1710, and in 1715 it was occupied by the French, who imported African slaves to work on their sugar-cane plantations. Mauritius was seized by Britain in 1810, and was formally ceded by the Treaty of Paris in 1814. The abolition of slavery in 1833 brought about the importation of indentured labourers from India, whose descendants now make up about 70% of the island's population. In 1957 Mauritius achieved internal self-government, and full independence within the Commonwealth in 1968.

Seewoosagur Ramgoolam, leader of the MLP, who had led the country since 1959, became its first prime minister. During the 1970s he led a succession of coalition governments and even in 1976, when the MMM became the assembly's largest single party, Ramgoolam formed another fragile coalition. Dissatisfaction with the government's economic policies led to Ramgoolam's defeat and the formation in 1982 of an MMM–Mauritius Socialist Party (PSM) coalition government led by Aneerood Jugnauth. Strains developed within the alliance, 12 MMM ministers resigned in 1983, and the coalition was dissolved. Jugnauth then founded the MSM, and the PSM was incorporated in the new party. A general election later that year resulted in an MSM–MLP–Mauritius Social Democratic Party (PMSD) coalition, which won 37 assembly seats. Jugnauth became prime minister on the understanding that Sir Seewoosagur Ramgoolam would be president if Mauritius became a republic. When the constitutional change failed to get legislative approval, Sir Seewoosagur Ramgoolam was appointed governor general in 1983. He died in 1985 and former finance minister, Sir Veersamy Ringadoo, replaced him.

Recent economic policies have cut inflation and unemployment, on the strength of which Aneerood Jugnauth was re-elected in an early general election in Aug 1987. Mauritius, which has no standing army, has pursued a moderately nonaligned foreign policy during recent years.

Maurois /mɔː'wɑː/ André. Pen name of Emile Herzog 1885–1967. French novelist and writer, whose works include the semi-autobiographical *Bernard Quesnay* 1926, and fictionalized biographies, such as *Ariel* 1923, a life of Shelley.

In World War I he was attached to the British Army, and the essays in *Les Silences du Colonel Bramble* 1918 give humorously sympathetic observations on the British character.

Mauroy /mɔː'wɑː/ Pierre 1928– . French socialist politician, prime minister 1981–84. He oversaw the introduction of a radical reflationary programme.

Mauroy worked for the FEN teachers' trade union and served as national secretary for the Young Socialists during the 1950s, rising in the ranks of the Socialist Party (PS) in the NE region. He entered the National Assembly in 1973 and was prime minister in the Mitterrand government of 1981, but was replaced by Fabius in July 1984.

Mauritius
State of

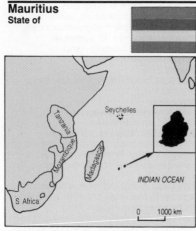

Seychelles

Tanzania

Mozambique

Madagascar

S Africa

INDIAN OCEAN

0   1000 km

area 2,040 sq km/787 sq mi; the island of Rodrigues is part of Mauritius and there are several small island dependencies
capital Port Louis
physical a mountainous, volcanic island surrounded by coral reefs
features geologically part of Gondwanaland, it has unusual wildlife including flying fox and ostrich; it was the home of the dodo (extinct from about 1680)
head of state Elizabeth II represented by Veerasamy Ringadoo from 1986
head of government Aneerood Jugnauth

from 1982
political system constitutional monarchy
political parties Mauritius Socialist Movement (MSM), moderate socialist-republican; Mauritius Labour Party (MLP), centrist Hindu-orientated; Mauritius Social Democratic Party (PMSD), conservative, Francophile; Mauritius Militant Movement (MMM), Marxist-republican.
exports sugar, knitted goods; tourism
currency Mauritius rupee (25.00 = £1 Feb 1990)
population (1987) 1,041,000; annual growth rate 1.9%
life expectancy men 64, women 69
language English (official); creole French
religion Hindu 45%, Christian 30%, Muslim 15%
literacy 89% male/77% female (1985 est)
GNP $957 million (1984); $1,240 per head of population
chronology
1968 Achieved full independence within the Commonwealth, with Seewoosagur Ramgoolam as prime minister.
1982 Aneerood Jugnauth prime minister.
1983 Jugnauth formed a new party, the Mauritius Socialist Movement, pledged to make Mauritius a republic within the Commonwealth, but Assembly refused. Ramgoolam appointed governor general. Jugnauth formed a new coalition government.
1985 Ramgoolam died, succeeded by Ringadoo.
1987 Jugnauth's coalition re-elected.

Maury /'mɔːri/ Matthew Fontaine 1806–1873. US naval officer, founder of the US Naval Oceanographic Office. His system of recording oceanographic data is still used today.

Maurya dynasty Indian dynasty *c.*321–*c.* 185 BC, founded by Chandragupta Maurya (321–*c.*279 BC) on the basis of a highly organized aristocracy, which ruled much of the Indian continent until the murder of the emperor Brhadratha in 185 BC and the creation of the Suringa dynasty. After the death of Emperor ◊Asoka, the empire was riven by dynastic disputes.

Mavor /'meɪvə/ O H Real name of the Scottish playwright James ◊Bridie.

Mawson /'mɔːsən/ Douglas 1882–1958. Australian explorer, born in Britain, who reached the magnetic South Pole on ◊Shackleton's expedition of 1907–09.
    Mawson led Antarctic expeditions 1911–14 and 1929–31. Australia's first permanent Antarctic base was named after him. He was professor of mineralogy at the University of Adelaide 1920–1953.

max. abbreviation for *maximum.*

Maxim /'mæksɪm/ Hiram Stevens 1840–1916. US-born (naturalized British) inventor of the first automatic machine gun in 1884.

Maximilian /ˌmæksɪ'mɪliən/ 1832–1867. Emperor of Mexico 1864–67. He accepted that title when the French emperor Napoleon III's troops occupied the country, but encountered resistance from the deposed president ◊Juárez. In 1866, after the French troops withdrew on the insistence the USA, Maximilian was captured by Mexican republicans and shot.

Maximilian I /ˌmæksɪ'mɪliən/ 1459–1519. Holy Roman emperor from 1493, the son of Emperor Frederick III. He had acquired the Low Countries through his marriage to Mary of Burgundy 1477; he married his son Philip I (the Handsome) to the heiress to the Spanish throne, and undertook long wars with Italy and Hungary in attempts to extend Habsburg power. He was the patron of the artist Dürer.

maximum and minimum in mathematics, points at which the slope of a curve representing a ◊function in ◊coordinate geometry changes from positive to negative (maximum), or from negative to positive

(minimum). A tangent to the curve at a maximum or minimum has zero gradient.
    Maxima and minima can be found by differentiating the function for the curve and setting the differential to zero (the value of the slope at the turning point). For example, differentiating the function for the ◊parabola $y = 2x^2 - 8x$ gives $dy/dx = 4x - 8$. Setting this equal to zero gives $x = 2$, so that $y = -8$ (found by substituting $x = 2$ into the parabola equation). Thus the function has a minimum at the point $(2, -8)$.

maxwell c.g.s. unit (symbol Mx) of magnetic flux (the strength of a ◊magnetic field in an area multiplied by the area). It is now replaced by the SI unit, the ◊weber (one maxwell = 10^{-8} weber). The maxwell is a very small unit, representing a single line of magnetic flux.

Maxwell /'mækswəl/ (Ian) Robert 1923– . Czech-born British publishing and newspaper proprietor, chief executive of Maxwell Communications Corporation, and owner of several UK national newspapers, including the *Daily Mirror*. He was Labour Member of Parliament for Buckingham 1964–70.

Maxwell /'mækswəl/ James Clerk 1831–1879. Scottish physicist. He contributed to every branch of physical science, particularly gases, optics, colour sensation, electricity, and magnetism. His theoretical work in magnetism prepared the way for wireless telegraphy and telephony.
    Born in Edinburgh, he was professor of natural philosophy at Aberdeen 1856–60, and then of physics and astronomy at London. In 1871, he became professor of experimental physics at Cambridge. His principal works include *Perception of Colour, Colour Blindness* 1860, *Theory of Heat* 1871, *Electricity and Magnetism* 1873, and *Matter and Motion* 1876.

Maxwell–Boltzmann distribution basic equation concerning the distribution of velocities of the molecules of a gas.

May /meɪ/ Thomas Erskine 1815–1886. English constitutional jurist. He was Clerk of the House of Commons from 1871 until 1886, when he was created Baron Farnborough. He wrote a practical *Treatise on the Law, Privileges, Proceedings, and Usage of Parliament* 1844, the authoritative work on parliamentary procedure.

maya (Sanskrit 'illusion') in Hindu philosophy, particularly in the *Vedānta*, the cosmos which Isvara, the personal expression of Brahman, or the ◊atman, has called into being. This is real, yet also an illusion, since its reality is not everlasting.

Maya /'maɪə/ member of an American Indian civilization originating in the Yucatán Peninsula about 2600 BC, with later sites in Mexico, Guatemala, and Belize, and enjoying a classical period AD 325–925, after which it declined. The Maya constructed stone buildings and stepped pyramids without metal tools; used hieroglyphic writing in manuscripts, of which only three survive; were skilled potters, weavers, and farmers; and regulated their rituals and warfare by observations of the planet Venus.

Mayagüez /'maɪəgwez/ port in W Puerto Rico with needlework industry and a US agricultural experimental station; population (1980) 96,200.

Mayakovsky /ˌmaɪə'kɒfski/ Vladimir 1893–1930. Russian futurist poet, who combined revolutionary propaganda with efforts to revolutionize poetic technique in his poems '150,000,000' 1920 and 'V I Lenin' 1924. His satiric play *The Bedbug* 1928 was taken in the West as an attack on philistinism in the USSR.

Mayan art art of the Central American civilization of the Maya, between about AD 300 and 900. Mayan figures have distinctive squat proportions and squared-off composition. Large, steeply inclined pyramids were built, for example at ◊Chichén Itzá, decorated with sculpture and inscription.
    Bonampak, Copan, Tikal, and Palenque were other sites of Mayan worship. In sculpture, human heads and giant reclining figures of Mayan deities are frequent motifs. A few intricately painted manuscripts survive (in the Museo de América, Madrid, for example).

May Day first day of May. In many countries it is a public holiday in honour of labour; see also ◊Labour Day. Traditionally the first day of summer. In parts of England it is still celebrated as a pre-Christian magical rite; for example, the dance around the maypole (an ancient fertility symbol).

Mayence /maɪ'ɒns/ French name for the West German city of ◊Mainz.

Mayenne /maɪ'en/ *département* of W France in Pays-de-Loire region
area 5,212 sq km/2,033 sq mi
capital Laval
features river Mayenne
products iron, slate; paper
population (1982) 271,184.

Mayenne /maɪ'en/ river in W France which gives its name to the *département* of Mayenne; length 200 km/125 mi. It rises in Orne, flows in a generally S direction through Mayenne and Maine-et-Loire, and joins the river Sarthe just above Angers to form the Maine.

Mayer /'maɪə/ Julius Robert von 1814–1878. German physicist who in 1842 anticipated ◊Joule in deriving the mechanical equivalent of heat, and

maximum and minimum

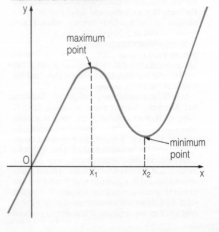

y

maximum point

minimum point

O x_1 x_2 x

Maurya dynasty

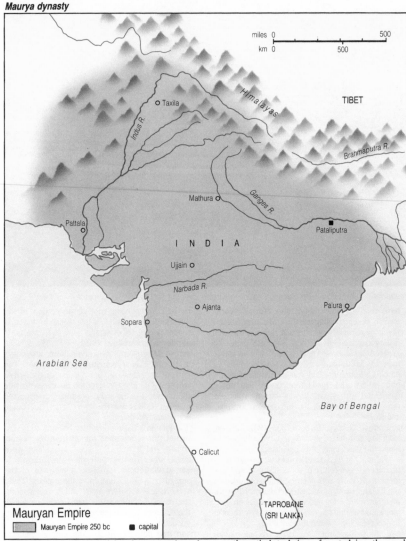

miles 0   500
km 0   500

TIBET

Taxila

Himalayas

Brahmaputra R.

Indus R.

Mathura

Ganges R.

Pataliputra

Pattala

I N D I A

Ujjain

Narbada R.

Ajanta

Palura

Sopara

Arabian Sea

Bay of Bengal

Calicut

TAPROBANE
(SRI LANKA)

Mauryan Empire

Mauryan Empire 250 bc   ■ capital

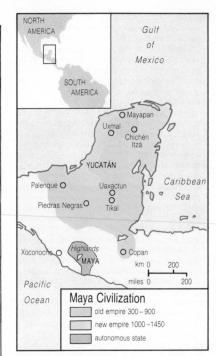

NORTH
AMERICA

Gulf
of
Mexico

SOUTH
AMERICA

Mayapan

Uxmal

Chichén
Itzá

YUCATÁN

Palenque

Uaxactun

Caribbean
Sea

Piedras Negras

Tikal

Xoconocho

Highlands
MAYA

Copan

km 0   200

Pacific
Ocean

miles 0   200

Maya Civilization

old empire 300–900

new empire 1000–1450

autonomous state

◊Helmholtz in the principle of conservation of energy.

Mayer Louis Burt. Adopted name of Eliezer Mayer 1885–1957. US film producer and distributor. He founded a production company in 1917 and in 1924 became vice president of the newly formed MGM. Something of a tyrant, he built up his studio into one of Hollywood's finest through the use of top talent and good judgement of audience tastes.

Mayer /ˈmeɪə/ Robert 1879–1985. British philanthropist who founded the Robert Mayer Concerts for Children and the Transatlantic Foundation Anglo-American Scholarships.

Mayerling /ˈmaɪəlɪŋ/ site near Vienna of the hunting lodge of Crown Prince ◊Rudolph of Austria, where he was found shot dead in 1889.

Mayfair /ˈmeɪfeə/ district of Westminster in London, England, vaguely defined as lying between Piccadilly and Oxford Street, and including Park Lane; formerly a fashionable residential district, but increasingly taken up by offices.

Mayflower the ship in which, in 1620, the ◊Pilgrims sailed from Plymouth, England, to found Plymouth in present-day Massachusetts, USA.

mayfly insect of the order Ephemeroptera (Greek *ephemeros* 'lasting for a day', an allusion to the very brief life of the adult). The larval stage is passed in water. The adult has transparent, net-veined wings.

Maynard Smith /ˈmeɪnɑːd ˈsmɪθ/ John 1920– . British biologist. He applied ◊game theory to animal behaviour, and developed the concept of the ◊ESS (evolutionarily stable strategy) as a

mathematical technique for studying the evolution of behaviour. His books include *The Theory of Evolution* and *Evolution and the Theory of Games*.

Maynooth /meɪˈnuːθ/ village in Kildare, Republic of Ireland, with a Roman Catholic training college for priests; population (1981) 3,388.

Mayo /ˈmeɪəʊ/ county in Connacht province, Republic of Ireland
area 5,400 sq km/2,084 sq mi
towns administrative town Castlebar
features Lough Conn; wild Atlantic coast scenery; Achill Island; the village of Knock, where two women claimed a vision of the Virgin with two saints 1897, now a site of pilgrimage
products sheep and cattle farming; fishing
population (1986) 115,000.

Mayo /ˈmeɪəʊ/ William James 1861–1939. US surgeon, founder, with his brother **Charles Horace Mayo** (1865–1939), of the Mayo Clinic for medical treatment 1889 in Rochester, Minnesota.

mayor /ˈmeɪəʊ/ title of head of urban administration. In England, Wales, and Northern Ireland, the mayor is the principal officer of a district council that has been granted district-borough status under royal charter. In certain cases the chair of a city council may have the right to be called **Lord Mayor** (a usage also followed by Australian cities). In the USA a mayor is the elected head of a city or town.

Parish councils that adopt the style of town councils have a chair known as the town mayor. In Scotland the equivalent officer is known as a

provost. The office of mayor was revived (for the first time since 1871) in Paris for Jacques Chirac in 1977.

Mayor of the Palace administrator of the ◊Merovingian royal court in the 7th century. After the death of Dagobert I (605–39) and the subsequent decline of the Merovingian kings, holders of this office became in effect rulers of the kingdom, and established a hereditary succession.

Mayotte /maɪˈɒt/ or **Mahore** island group of the ◊Comoros, off the E coast of Africa, a *collectivité territoriale* of France by its own wish. The two main islands are Grande Terre and Petite Terre.
area 374 sq km/144 sq mi
capital Dzaoudzi
products coffee, copra, vanilla, fishing
languages French, Swahili
population (1984) 59,000.
history a French colony 1843–1914, and later, with the Comoros, an overseas territory of France. In 1974, Mayotte voted to remain a French dependency.

mayweed several species of the daisy family, including the low annual **pineapple mayweed** *Matricaria matricarioides* and the **scentless mayweed** *Tripleurospermum inodorum*. Both thrive as weeds in arable and waste places. *M. matricarioides* bears tall, yellowish-green, button-like flowers and the whole plant smells of pineapple; *T. inodorum* produces flowers with a yellow disc and many white ray florets but has no scent.

Mayan art *A Chac Mool idol reclines at the centre of a former sacrifical altar in the city of Chichén Itzá. Chac Mools once held in their lap bowls the still-beating human hearts torn from living victims.*

Mazarin /ˌmæzəˈræŋ/ Jules 1602–1661. French politician, who succeeded Richelieu as chief minister of France in 1642. His attack on the power of the nobility led to the ◊Fronde and his temporary exile, but his diplomacy achieved a successful conclusion to the Thirty Years' War, and, in alliance with Cromwell during the British protectorate, he gained victory over Spain.

maze a deliberately labyrinthine arrangement of passages or paths. One of the earliest was the Cretan maze constructed by Daedalus, within which the Minotaur lived. The best-known maze in England is that at Hampton Court, near London, which dates from 1689.

Mazowiecki /ˌmæzɒvˈjetski/ Tadeusz 1927– . Polish politician, founder member of ◊Solidarity, and Poland's first postwar noncommunist prime minister from 1989. A former member of the Polish parliament 1961–70, he was debarred from reelection by the authorities after investigating the police massacre of Gdansk strikers. He became legal adviser to Lech ◊Walesa and, after a period of internment, edited the Solidarity newspaper *Tygodnik Solidarnosc*. In 1989 he became prime minister after the elections denied the communists their customary majority. A devout Catholic, he is a close friend of Pope John Paul II.

mazurka a lively national dance of Poland from the 16th century. In triple time, it is characterized by foot-stamping and heel-clicking, together with a turning movement.

Mazzini /mætˈsiːni/ Giuseppe 1805–1872. Italian nationalist. He was a member of the revolutionary society, the ◊Carbonari, and founded in exile the nationalist movement *Giovane Italia/Young Italy* 1832. Returning to Italy on the outbreak of the 1848 revolution, he headed a republican government established in Rome, but was forced into exile again on its overthrow 1849. He acted as a focus for the movement for Italian unity (see ◊Risorgimento).

Mazzini, born in Genoa, studied law. For his subversive activity with the Carbonari he was imprisoned 1830, then went to France, founding in Marseille the Young Italy movement, followed by an international revolutionary organization, Young Europe, 1834. For many years he lived in exile in France, Switzerland, and the UK, but returned to Italy (despite having been condemned to death in his absence by the Sardinian government) for the ◊revolution of 1848. He conducted the defence of Rome against French forces and when it failed he refused to join in the capitulation and returned to London, where he continued to agitate until his death in Geneva, Switzerland.

Mbabane /əmbɑːˈbɑːneɪ/ capital (since 1902) of Swaziland, 160 km/100 mi west of Maputo, in the Dalgeni Hills; population (1986) 38,000.

MBE abbreviation for *Member (of the Order) of the British Empire*.

Mboma another spelling of ◊Boma, Zaïrean port.

Mboya /əmˈbɔɪə/ Tom 1930–1969. Kenyan politician, a founder of the ◊Kenya African National Union (KANU), and minister of economic planning (opposed to nationalization) from 1964 until his assassination.

MCC abbreviation for *Marylebone Cricket Club*.

McDowell /məkˈdaʊəl/ Malcolm 1943– . British actor who played the rebellious hero in the film *If* 1969 and confirmed his acting abilities in Stanley Kubrick's *A Clockwork Orange* 1971.

MD abbreviation for *Doctor of Medicine*.

MDMA psychedelic drug, also known as ◊ecstasy.

ME abbreviation for ◊*Maine*.

ME abbreviation for *Middle English*, the period of the English language 1050–1550.

ME abbreviation for *myalgic encephalitis*, a debilitating condition still not universally accepted as a genuine disease. The condition is a diffuse one, with a range of symptoms including extreme fatigue, muscular pain, and weakness and anxiety attacks.

ME, sometimes known as post-viral fatigue syndrome, is not a new phenomenon. Outbreaks

meander *The river Cuckmere, Sussex, England, meanders over the flood plain near its mouth.*

have been documented for more than 50 years. Recent research suggests that ME may be the result of chronic viral infection, leaving the sufferer exhausted, debilitated, and with generally lowered resistance. There is no definitive treatment for ME.

mea culpa (Latin 'my fault') an admission of guilt.

mead /miːd/ drink made from honey and water fermented with yeast. It was known in ancient times, and was drunk by the Greeks, Britons, and Norse.

Mead /miːd/ George Herbert 1863–1931. US philosopher and social psychologist, who helped to found the philosophy of pragmatism.

He taught at the University of Chicago during its prominence as a centre of social scientific development in the early 20th century, and is regarded as the founder of ◊symbolic interactionism. His work on group interaction had a major influence on sociology, stimulating the development of role theory, ◊phenomenology, and ◊ethnomethodology.

Mead /miːd/ Margaret 1901–1978. US anthropologist, who challenged the conventions of Western society with *Coming of Age in Samoa* 1928.

Meade /miːd/ James Edward 1907– . British Keynesian economist. He shared a Nobel prize in 1977 for his work on trade and capital movements, and published a four-volume *Principles of Political Economy* 1965–76.

Meade /miːd/ Richard 1938– . British equestrian in three-day events. He won three Olympic gold medals 1968, 1972, and was twice a world champion. He is associated with some well-known horses, like Cornishman, Laureston and The Poacher, and has won all the sport's major honours.

CAREER HIGHLIGHTS

Olympic champion:
individual: 1972
team: 1968, 1972
World champion:
team: 1970, 1982
Badminton Horse Trials: 1970, 1982
Burghley Horse Trials: 1964

mean in mathematics, a measure of the average of a number of terms or quantities. The simple *arithmetic mean* is the average value of the quantities, that is, the sum of the quantities divided by their number. The *weighted mean* takes into account the frequency of the terms that are summed; it is calculated by multiplying each term by the number of times it occurs, summing the results and dividing this total by the total number of occurrences. The *geometric mean*

is the corresponding root of the product of the quantities. In statistics, it is a measure of central tendency of a set of data.

meander a loop-shaped curve in a river flowing across flat country. As a river flows, any curve in its course is accentuated by the current. The current is fastest on the outside of the curve where it cuts into the bank; on the curve's inside the current is slow and deposits any transported material. In this way the river changes its course across the floodplain.

A loop in a river's flow may become so accentuated that it becomes cut off from the normal course and forms an ◊oxbow lake. The word comes from the river ◊Menderes in Turkey.

mean deviation in statistics, a measure of the spread of a population from the ◊mean. Thus, if there are n observations with a mean of m, the mean deviation is the sum of the moduli of the differences of the observation values from m, divided by n.

mean free path in physics, the average distance travelled by a particle, atom, or molecule between successive collisions. It is of importance in the ◊kinetic theory of gases.

measles a virus disease (rubeola), spread by airborne infection. Symptoms are severe catarrh, small spots inside the mouth, and a raised, blotchy red rash appearing after about a week's incubation. Prevention is by vaccination. In the West it is not usually a serious disease, though serious complications may develop, but Third World children may suffer a high mortality.

In the UK a vaccination programme is under way, combining measles, mumps, and rubella (German measles) vaccine.

meat flesh of animals taken as food, in Western countries chiefly from cattle, sheep, pigs, and poultry. Major exporters include Argentina, Australia, New Zealand, Canada, USA, and Denmark (chiefly bacon). *Meat substitutes* are textured vegetable protein (TVP), usually ◊soya-based, extruded in fibres in the same way as plastics.

Meat is wasteful in production (the same area of grazing land would produce greater food value in cereal crops). Grazing lands take up more than 3,000 million hectares and produce around 140 million tonnes of meat per year, of which the developed nations in 1980 consumed 90 million tonnes, or 110 kg/242 lb per person in the USA, 75 kg/165 lb in the UK, 30 kg/66 lb in Japan, 6 kg/13 lb in Nigeria, and 1.1 kg/2.4 lb in India. Research suggests that, in a healthy diet, consumption of meat (especially with a high fat content) should not exceed the Japanese level.

Meath /miːð/ county in the province of Leinster, Republic of Ireland

area 2,340 sq km/903 sq mi

county town Trim

features Tara Hill, 155 m/509 ft high, was the site of a palace and coronation place of many kings of Ireland (abandoned in the 6th century) and St Patrick preached here.

products sheep, cattle

population (1986) 104,000.

meat-packing the preparation of meat for consumption, especially if it is to be transported long distances. The industry depends on refrigeration, which was invented in 1861.

The first commercial use of frozen meat was in a shipment from the US to London in 1874. Frozen meat was first depatched from Argentina to London in 1878, and from Australia in 1879. Chicago had the world's largest meat-packing plants until the stockyards closed in 1971.

Mecca /'mekə/ (Arabic *Makkah*) city in Saudi Arabia and, as birthplace of Muhammad, the holiest city of the Islamic world; population (1974) 367,000. In the centre of Mecca is the Great Mosque, in whose courtyard is the ◊Kaaba. It also contains the well Zam-Zam, associated by tradition with the biblical characters Hagar and Ishmael. Most pilgrims come via the port of ◊Jiddah.

mechanical advantage the amount by which a machine can magnify a force. It is the load (the weight lifted or moved by the machine) divided by the effort (the force use by the operator).

mechanical equivalent of heat in physics, a constant factor relating the calorie (the c.g.s. unit of heat) to the joule (the unit of mechanical energy), equal to 4.1868 joules per calorie. It is redundant in the SI system of units, which measures heat and all forms of energy in joules (so that the mechanical equivalent of heat is 1).

mechanics branch of applied mathematics dealing with the motions of bodies and the forces causing these motions, and also with the forces acting on bodies in ◊equilibrium. It is usually divided into ◊dynamics and ◊statics.

Quantum mechanics is the system based on the ◊quantum theory which has superseded Newtonian mechanics in the interpretation of physical phenomena on the atomic scale.

mechanization use of machines as a substitute for manual labour or the use of animals. Until the 1700s there were few machines available to help people in the home, on the land, or in industry. There were no factories, only cottage industries, in which people carried out work, such as weaving, in their own home for other people. The 1700s saw a long series of inventions, initially in the textile industry, that ushered in a machine age and brought about the ◊Industrial Revolution.

Among the first inventions in the textile industry were those made by John ◊Kay (flying shuttle, 1773), James ◊Hargreaves (spinning jenny, 1767), and Richard ◊Arkwright (water frame, 1769). Arkwright pioneered the modern mechanized factory system by installing many of his ◊spinning machines in one building and employing people to work them.

Mechelen /'mexələ/ (French *Malines*) industrial city (furniture, carpets, textiles) and market gardening centre in Antwerp province, N Belgium, which gave its name to Mechlin lace; population (1985) 76,120.

Mechnikov /'metʃnɪkɒf/ Elie 1845–1916. Russian scientist who discovered the function of white blood cells and ◊phagocytes. After leaving Russia and joining ◊Pasteur in Paris, he described how these 'scavenger cells' can attack the body itself (autoimmune disease).

Mecklenburg /'meklənbɜːg/ historic name of an area of the Baltic coast of Germany. It was formerly the two grand duchies of Mecklenburg-Schwerin and Mecklenburg-Strelitz, which became free states of the Weimar Republic 1918–34, and were joined 1946 (with part of Pomerania) to form a region of East Germany. In 1952 it was split into the counties of Rostock, Schwerin, and Neubrandenburg.

Medal of Honor in the US, the highest award for the navy (1861) and army (1862) for gallantry in action; presented by the president. Of differing design, both are bronze stars with the goddess Minerva encircled in their centres.

medals and decorations coinlike metal pieces, struck or cast to commemorate historic events; mark distinguished service, whether civil or military (in the latter case in connection with a particular battle, or for individual feats of courage, or for service over the period of a campaign); or as a badge of membership of an order of knighthood, society, or other special group.

Waterloo Medal British, established 1816; until the 19th century medals were awarded only to officers; this was the first to be issued to all ranks.

Armada medal issued by Elizabeth I following the defeat of the Armada; the first English commemorative medal

George Cross 1940 highest British civilian award for bravery, the medallion in the centre of the cross depicting St George and the Dragon

Iron Cross German, see under ◊knighthood

Légion d'honneur French, see under ◊knighthood

Medal of Honor highest award given in the US for the navy (1861) and army (1862) for gallantry in action; of differing design, both are bronze stars with the goddess Minerva encircled in their centres

Medal for Merit US civilian, 1942; recognizes exceptional conduct in the performance of outstanding service

Ordre National du Mérite French, civil and military, 1963, replacing earlier merit awards

Order of Merit British, see ◊Merit, Order of, and ◊knighthood

Order of the Purple Heart US military, established by Washington 1782, when it was of purple cloth (now made of bronze and enamel); revived by Hoover 1932, when it was issued to those wounded in action from World War I onward

Pour le Mérite German, instituted by Frederick the Great, military in 1740, and since 1842 for science and art

Presidential Medal of Freedom USA, highest peacetime civilian award since 1963

USSR Gold Star Medal Soviet Union, civilian and military

Victoria Cross British military, 1856

Medan /mə'dɑːn/ seaport and economic centre of the island of Sumatra, Indonesia; population (1980) 1,379,000. It trades in rubber, tobacco, and palm oil.

Medawar /'medəwə/ Peter (Brian) 1915–1987. Brazilian-born British immunologist, who, with ◊Burnet, discovered that the body's resistance to grafted tissue is undeveloped in the newborn child, and studied the way it is acquired.

Medawar's work has been vital in understanding the phenomenon of tissue rejection following ◊transplantation. Shared Nobel Prize for Medicine with Burnet 1960.

Mede /miːd/ member of a people of NW Iran who first appeared in the 9th century BC as tributaries to Assyria, with their capital at Ecbatana (now Hamadán). Allying themselves with Babylon, they destroyed the Assyrian capital of ◊Nineveh 612 BC, and extended their conquests into central Anatolia. In 550 BC they were overthrown by the Persians, with whom they rapidly merged.

Medea /mɪ'dɪə/ in Greek mythology, the sorceress daughter of the king of Colchis. When ◊Jason reached the court, she fell in love with him, helped him acquire the golden fleece, and they fled together. When Jason married Creusa, Medea killed his bride with the gift of a poisoned garment, and also killed her own two children by Jason.

Medea tragedy by Euripedes, produced 431 BC. It deals with the later part of the legend of Medea—her murder of Jason's bride and of her own children.

Medellín /,meðeɪ'iːn/ industrial town (textiles, chemicals, engineering, coffee) in the Central Cordillera, Colombia, 1,538 m/5,048 ft above sea level; population (1985) 2,069,000. It is a centre of the Colombian drug trade, and there has been considerable violence in the late 1980s. It has five universities.

median in mathematics, the middle number of an ordered group of numbers. If there is no middle number (because there is an even number of terms), the median is the ◊mean (average) of the two middle numbers.

meat

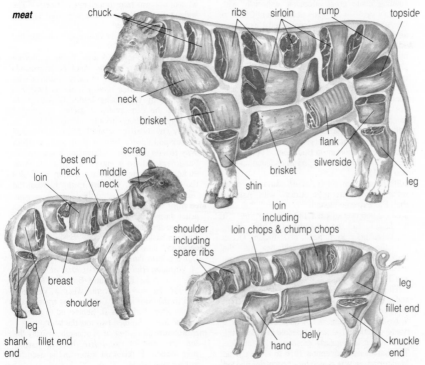

chuck — ribs — sirloin — rump — topside — neck — brisket — flank — silverside — brisket — shin — leg — scrag — best end neck — loin — middle neck — loin — breast — shoulder — shoulder including spare ribs — loin including loin chops & chump chops — leg — fillet end — hand — belly — knuckle end — leg — shank — fillet end

For example, the median of the group 2, 3, 7, 11, 12 is 7; that of 3, 4, 7, 9, 11, 13 is 8.

mediation a technical term in ◊Hegel's philosophy, and in Marxist philosophy influenced by Hegel, describing the way in which an entity is defined through its relations to other entities.

Medici /'medɪtʃi/ noble family of Florence, the city's rulers from 1434 until they died out 1737. Family members included ◊Catherine de' Medici, Pope ◊Leo X, Pope ◊Clement VII, ◊Marie de' Medici.

Medici Giovanni de' 1360–1429. Italian entrepreneur and banker, politically influential in Florence as a supporter of the popular party. He was the father of Cosimo de' Medici.

Medici Cosimo de' 1389–1464. Italian politician and banker. Regarded as the model for Machiavelli's *The Prince*, he dominated the government of Florence from 1434 and was a patron of the arts. He was succeeded by his inept son *Piero de' Medici* (1416–69).

Medici Lorenzo de' *the Magnificent* 1449–1492. Italian politician, ruler of Florence from 1469. He was also a poet and a generous patron of the arts.

Medici Cosimo de' 1519–1574. Italian politician, ruler of Florence; duke of Florence from 1537 and 1st grand duke of Tuscany from 1569.

Medici Ferdinand de' 1549–1609. Italian politician, grand duke of Tuscany from 1587.

medicine the science of preventing, diagnosing, alleviating, or curing disease, both physical and mental; also any substance used in the treatment of disease. The basis of medicine is anatomy (the structure and form of the body), and physiology (the study of the body's functions).

In the West, medicine increasingly relies on new drugs and sophisticated surgical techniques, while diagnosis of disease is more and more by non-invasive procedures. The time and cost of Western-type medical training makes it inaccessible to many parts of the Third World; where health care of this kind is provided it is often by auxiliary medical helpers trained in hygiene and the administration of a limited number of standard drugs for the prevalent diseases of a particular region.

medicine, alternative forms of medical treatment that do not use synthetic drugs or surgery in response to the symptoms of a disease, but aim to treat the patient as a whole (◊holism). The emphasis is on maintaining health (with diet and exercise) rather than waiting for the onset of illness. It may involve the use of herbal remedies and techniques such as ◊acupuncture, ◊homeopathy, and ◊osteopathy.

Some alternative treatments are increasingly accepted by orthodox medicine, but the absence of enforceable standards in some fields has led to the proliferation of eccentric or untrained practitioners.

medieval art painting and sculpture of the Middle Ages in Europe and parts of the Middle East, dating roughly from the 4th century to the emergence of the Renaissance in Italy in the 1400s. This includes early Christian, Byzantine, Celtic, Anglo-Saxon, and Carolingian art. The Romanesque was the first truly international style of medieval times, superseded by Gothic in the late 12th century. Religious sculpture, frescoes, and manuscript illumination proliferated; panel painting came only towards the end of the period.

early Christian art (3rd–5th centuries AD) When Christianity was made one of the official religions of the Roman state, churches were built and artistic traditions adapted to the portrayal of the new Christian saints and symbols. Roman burial chests (*sarcophagi*) were adopted by the Christians and their imagery of pagan myths gradually changed into biblical themes.

Byzantine style (4th century–1453) developed in the eastern empire, centred on Constantinople. The use of mosaic associated with Byzantine art also appears in church decoration in the West, for example in Ravenna. Churches there, built in the 5th and 6th centuries, present powerful religious images on walls and vaults in brilliant, glittering colour. Byzantine art soon froze into religious stereotypes and iconlike figures. The Byzantine style continued in icon painting, a strong theme in the art of Greece and Russia.

early medieval art (4th–10th centuries) S Europe was overrun by people from the north, and their art consisted mainly of portable objects, articles for personal use or adornment. They excelled in metalwork and jewellery, often in gold with garnet or enamel inlays, ornamented with highly stylized, animal-based interlace patterns. This type of ornament was translated into manuscript illumination produced in Christian monasteries, such as the decorated pages of the Northumbrian *Lindisfarne Gospels* (British Museum, London) 7th century, or the Celtic 8th-century *Book of Kells* (Trinity College, Dublin, Ireland).

Carolingian art (late 8th–early 9th centuries) Manuscript painting flourished in Charlemagne's empire, drawing its inspiration from the late Classical artistic traditions of the early Christian and Byzantine styles. Several monasteries produced richly illustrated prayer books and biblical texts.

Romanesque, or *Norman* (10th–12th centuries) Chiefly evident in church sculpture, on capitals and portals, and in manuscript illumination. Romanesque art combined naturalistic elements with the fantastic, poetical, and pattern-loving Celtic and Germanic tradition. Imaginary beasts and medieval warriors mingle with biblical themes. Fine examples remain throughout Europe, from N Spain and Italy to France, the Germanic lands of the Holy Roman Empire, and England. The Romanesque style arrived in Scandinavia in the late 11th century.

Gothic art (late 12th–15th centuries) As large cathedrals were built in Europe, sculptural decoration became more monumental and stained glass filled the tall windows, for example in Chartres Cathedral, France. Figures were also carved in wood. Court patronage produced exquisite small ivories, goldsmith's work, devotional books illustrated with miniatures, and tapestries depicting romantic tales. Panel painting, initially on a gold background, evolved in N Europe into the more realistic International Gothic style. In Italy fresco painting made great advances, especially with Giotto's cycle of the lives of Mary and Christ in the Arena Chapel, Padua (completed 1306), seen as proto-Renaissance.

Medina /me'di:nə/ (Arabic *Madinah*) Saudi Arabian city, about 355 km/220 mi N of Mecca; population (1974) 198,000. It is the second holiest city in the Islamic world, containing the tomb of Muhammad. It produces grain and fruit. It also contains the tombs of the caliphs or Muslim leaders Abu Bakr, Omar, and Fatima, Muhammad's daughter.

meditation act of spiritual contemplation, practised by members of many religions or as a secular exercise. It is important in Buddhism. The Sanskrit term is *dhyāna*. See also ◊transcendental meditation (TM).

Mediterranean /ˌmedɪtə'reɪnɪən/ inland sea separating Europe from N Africa, with Asia to the E; extreme length 3,700 km/2,300 mi; area 2,966,000 sq km/1,145,000 sq mi. It is linked to the Atlantic (at the Strait of Gibraltar), Red Sea, and Indian Ocean (by the Suez Canal), Black Sea (at the Dardanelles and Sea of Marmara). The main subdivisions are the Adriatic, Aegean, Ionian, and Tyrrhenian seas.

The Mediterranean is almost tideless, saltier and warmer than the Atlantic, and shallows from Sicily to Cape Bon (Africa) divide it into an E and W basin. It is endangered by human and industrial waste pollution; 100 million people live along the coast and it is regularly crossed by oil tankers. The Barcelona Convention 1976 to clean up the Mediterranean was signed by 17 countries and led

Mediterranean Sea

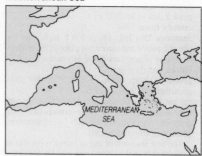

to a ban on dumping of mercury, cadmium, persistent plastics, DDT, crude oil, and hydrocarbons.

Mediterranean climate a climate characterized by hot dry summers and warm wet winters. Mediterranean zones are situated in either hemisphere on the western side of continents, between latitudes of 30° and 60°.

During the winter rain is brought by the ◊westerlies; in summer Mediterranean zones are under the influence of the ◊trade winds. The regions bordering the Mediterranean Sea, California, central Chile, the Cape of Good Hope, and parts of S Australia have such climates.

Medjugorje village in Bosnia, Yugoslavia, NW of Dubrovnik, where the Virgin Mary is alleged to have appeared to six schoolchildren in 1981.

The apparition was supposedly seen for several days running; large crowds claimed to see various 'signs', although not the Virgin herself. The same Hill of Vision was the site of a massacre of Orthodox Catholic Serbs by Roman Catholics in 1941.

medlar small European shrub or tree *Mespilus germanica* of the family Rosaceae. Native to SE Europe, it is widely cultivated for its fruit resembling a small brown-green pear or quince. These are palatable when decay has set in.

Médoc /mer'dɒk/ French district bordering the Gironde in Aquitaine region, N of Bordeaux. It is famed for its wines, Margaux and St Julien being two of the best-known varieties. Lesparre and Pauillac are the chief towns.

Medusa /mə'dju:zə/ in Greek mythology, a mortal woman who was transformed into a ◊Gorgon. The winged horse ◊Pegasus was supposed to have sprung from her blood.

medusa jellyfish stage in Cnidarian (coelenterate) life cycle.

Medvedev /mɪd'vjedef/ Vadim 1929– . Soviet politician. He was deputy chief of propaganda 1970–78, was in charge of party relations with communist countries 1986–88, and in 1988 was appointed by the Soviet leader Gorbachev to succeed the conservative Ligachev as head of ideology. He adheres to a firm Leninist line.

Medway /'medweɪ/ river of SE England, rising in Sussex and flowing through Kent and the *Medway towns* (Chatham, Gillingham, Rochester) to Sheerness, where it enters the Thames; about 96 km/60 mi long. In local tradition it divides the 'Men of Kent', who live to the E, from the 'Kentish Men', who live to the W.

Mee /mi:/ Margaret 1909–1988. English botanical artist. In the 1950s, she went to Brazil, where she depicted the many exotic species of plants in the Amazon basin.

Meegeren /'meɪɡərən/ Han van 1889–1947. Dutch painter famous for his forgeries, especially of Vermeer. His 'Vermeer' *Christ at Emmaus* was bought for Rotterdam's Boymans Museum in 1937. He was discovered when a 'Vermeer' sold to the Nazi leader Goering was traced back to him after World War II. Sentenced to a year's imprisonment, he died two months later.

meerschaum an aggregate of minerals, usually along the soft white mineral, *sepiolite*, hydrous magnesium silicate. It floats on water and is used for making pipe bowls.

medicine: chronology

c.400 BC	Hippocrates recognized disease had natural causes.
c.200 AD	Galen, the authority of the Middle Ages, consolidated the work of the Alexandrian doctors.
1543	Andreas Versalius gave the first accurate account of the human body.
1628	William Harvey discovered the circulation of the blood.
1768	John Hunter began the foundation of experimental and surgical pathology.
1785	Digitalis used to treat heart disease; the active ingredient was isolated 1904.
1798	Edward Jenner published his work on vaccination.
1877	Patrick Manson, Scottish parasitologist, worked on animal carriers of infectious diseases.
1882	Robert Koch isolated the tuberculosis bacillus.
1884	Edwin Klebs, German pathologist, isolated the diptheria bacillus.
1885	Louis Pasteur produced the rabies vaccine.
1890	Joseph Lister demonstrated antiseptic surgery.
1897	Martinus Beijerinck, Dutch botanist, discovered viruses.
1899	German doctor, Felix Hoffman, developed aspirin; Sigmund Freud founded psychiatry.
1910	Paul Ehrlich synthesized the first specific bacterial agent, salvarsan (cure for syphilis).
1922	Insulin was first used to treat diabetes.
1928	Sir Alexander Fleming discovered the antibiotic penicillin.
1930s	Electro-convulsive therapy (ECT) was developed.
1932	Gerhard Domagk, German bacteriologist and pathologist, began work on the sulphonamide drugs, a kind of antibiotic .
1940s	Lithium treatment for depression was developed.
1950	Proof of a link between cigarette smoking and lung cancer was established.
1950s	Major development of antidepressant drugs and beta blockers for heart disease; Medawar's work on the immune system.
1950–75	Manipulation of the molecules of synthetic chemicals, the main source of new drugs.
1953	Vaccine for polio developed by Jonas Salk.
1960s	Heart transplant surgery began with the work of Christiaan Barnard; new generation of minor tranquillizers called benzodiazepenes developed.
1971	Viroids, disease causing organisms even smaller than viruses, were isolated outside the living body.
1975	Nuclear medicine, for example positron emission tomography (Hounsfield), came into practical use.
1978	Birth of the first 'test-tube baby', Louise Brown, on 25 July in England.
1980s	AIDS (Acquired Immune Deficiency Syndrome) first recognized in the USA; recognition of the discovery of the transposable gene by Barbara McClintock, US geneticist.
1980	Smallpox eradicated by the World Health Organization.
1984	Vaccine for leprosy developed; discovery of the Human Immuno-deficiency Virus (HIV) responsible for AIDS, at the Institut Pasteur in Paris and in the USA.
1987	World's longest surviving heart transplant patient died in France, 18 years after his operation.
1989	Patient with Parkinson's disease first treated by graft of fetal brain tissue.

Meerut /'mɪərət/ industrial city (chemicals, soap, food processing) in Uttar Pradesh, N India; population (1981) 538,000. The ◊Indian Mutiny began here in 1857.

mega- prefix denoting multiplication by a million. For example, a megawatt (MW) is equivalent to a million watts.

megabyte in computing, a measure of the capacity of ◊memory or storage, equal to 1024 ◊kilobytes. It is also used, less precisely, to mean one million bytes.

megalith prehistoric stone monument of the late Neolithic or early Bronze Age. Megaliths include single, large uprights (*menhirs*, for example the Five Kings, Northumberland, England); *rows* (for example, Carnac, Brittany, France); *circles*, generally with a central 'altar stone' (for example Stonehenge, Wiltshire, England); and the remains of burial chambers with the covering earth removed, looking like a hut (*dolmens*, for example Kits Coty, Kent, England).

megamouth filter-feeding deep-sea shark *Megachasma pelagios*, first discovered 1976. It has a bulbous head with protruding jaws and blubbery lips, is 4.5 m/15 ft long, and weighs 750 kg/1,650 lb.

megapode large (70 cm/2.3 ft long) ground-living bird of the family Megapodidae, found mainly in Australia, but also in SE Asia. They lay their eggs in a pile of rotting vegetation 4 m/13 ft across, and the warmth from this provides the heat for incubation. The male bird feels the mound with his tongue and adjusts it to provide the correct temperature.

megatherium extinct giant ground sloth of America. Various species lived from about 7 million years ago until geologically recent times. They were plant-eaters, and some grew to 6 m/20 ft long.

megaton one million tons. Used with reference to the explosive power of a nuclear weapon, it is equivalent to the explosive force of one million tons of trinitrotoluene (TNT).

INDIAN OCEAN

Shillong

Meghalaya /,megə'leɪə/ state of NE India
area 22,500 sq km/8,685 sq mi
capital Shillong
features mainly agricultural and comprises tribal hill districts
products potatoes, cotton, jute, fruit
minerals coal, limestone, white clay, corundum, sillimanite
population (1981) 1,328,000, mainly Khasi, Jaintia, and Garo
religion Hindu 70%.
language various

Megiddo /mə'gɪdəʊ/ site of a fortress town in N Israel, where Thothmes III defeated the Canaanites about 1469 BC; the Old Testament figure Josiah was killed in battle about 609 BC; and in World War I the British field marshal Allenby broke the Turkish front 1918. It is identified with ◊Armageddon.

Mehemet Ali /mɪ'hemɪt 'ɑːli/ 1769–1849. Pasha (governor) of Egypt from 1805, and founder of the dynasty that ruled until 1953. An Albanian in the Ottoman service, he had originally been sent to Egypt to fight the French. As pasha, he established a European-style army and navy, fought his Turkish overlord 1831 and 1839, and conquered Sudan.

Mehta /'meɪtə/ Zubin 1936– . Indian conductor, director of the Israel Philharmonic Orchestra from 1968 (for life from 1981), and of the New York Philharmonic from 1978.

Meier /'maɪə/ Richard 1934– . US architect, whose white designs spring from the poetic modernism of the ◊Le Corbusier villas of the 1920s. His abstract style is at its most mature in the *Museum für Kunsthandwerk* (Museum of Arts and Crafts), Frankfurt, West Germany, which was completed 1984.

Earlier schemes are the Bronx Developmental Centre, New York (1970–76) and the Athenaeum–New Harmony (1974). He is the architect for the Getty Museum, Los Angeles.

Meiji era /'meɪdʒiː/ in Japanese history, the reign of Emperor ◊Mutsuhito 1867–1912.

Meikle /'miːkəl/ Andrew 1719–1811. Scottish millwright who in 1785 designed and built the first practical threshing machine for separating cereal grains from the husks.

Meinhof /'maɪnhɒf/ Ulrike 1934–1976. West German urban guerrilla, member of the ◊Baader-Meinhof gang in the 1970s.

A left-wing journalist, Meinhof was converted to the use of violence to achieve political change by the imprisoned Andreas Baader. She helped free Baader and they became joint leaders of the urban guerrilla organization the Red Army Faction. As the faction's chief ideologist, Meinhof was arrested in 1972 and, in 1974, sentenced to eight years' imprisonment. She committed suicide in 1976 in the Stammheim high-security prison.

Mein Kampf (German 'my struggle') book written by Adolf ◊Hitler 1924 during his jail sentence for his part in the abortive 1923 Munich beer-hall putsch. Part autobiography, part political philosophy, the book outlines Hitler's ideas of German expansion, anti-communism, and anti-Semitism.

meiosis in biology, a process of cell division in which the number of ◊chromosomes in the cell is halved. It only occurs in ◊eukaryotic cells, and is part of a life cycle that involves sexual reproduction, because it allows the genes of two parents to be combined without the total number of chromosomes increasing.

In many animals that are normally ◊diploid (having two sets of chromosomes per cell) meiosis occurs during formation of the ◊gametes (sex cells, sperm and egg), so that the gametes are

Meier *US architect Richard Meier's Museum für Kunsthandwerk (Museum of Arts and crafts, Frankfurt, West Germany, 1984).*

◊haploid (having only one set of chromosomes). When the gametes unite during ◊fertilization, the diploid condition is restored. In plants, meiosis occurs just before spore formation. Thus the spores are haploid and in lower plants such as mosses they develop into a haploid plant called a gametophyte which produces the gametes (see ◊alternation of generations). See also ◊mitosis.

Meir /meɪˈɪə/ Golda 1898–1978. Israeli Labour (*Mapai*) politician, born in Russia. She was foreign minister 1956–66 and prime minister 1969–74, resigning after criticism of the Israelis' lack of preparation for the 1973 Arab-Israeli War.

Meissen /ˈmaɪsən/ city in Dresden county, East Germany, on the river Elbe; known for Meissen or Dresden porcelain from 1710; population (1983) 38,908.

Meistersinger (German 'master singer') one of a group of German lyric poets, singers, and musicians of the 14th–16th centuries, who formed guilds for the revival of minstrelsy. Hans ◊Sachs was a Meistersinger, and Richard Wagner's opera, *Die Meistersinger von Nüremberg* 1868 depicts the tradition.

Meitner /ˈmaɪtnə/ Lise 1878–1968. Austrian physicist, the first to realize that ◊Hahn had inadvertently achieved the fission of uranium. Driven from Nazi Germany because of her Jewish origin, she later worked in Sweden. She refused to work on the atomic bomb.

Mekele capital of Tigray region, N Ethiopia. Population (1984) 62,000.

Meknès /mekˈnes/ (Spanish *Mequinez*) city in N Morocco, known for wine and carpetmaking; population (1981) 487,000. One of Morocco's four imperial cities, it was the capital until 1728, and is the site of the tomb of Sultan Moulay Ismail.

Mekong /ˌmiːˈkɒŋ/ river rising as the Za Qu in Tibet and flowing to the South China Sea, through a vast delta (about 200,000 sq km/77,000 sq mi); length 4,425 km/2,750 mi. It is being developed for irrigation and hydroelectricity by Cambodia, Laos, Thailand, and Vietnam.

Melaka /məˈlækə/ Malaysian form of ◊Malacca, state of peninsular Malaysia.

melaleuca tree tropical tree, also known as the paperbark *melaleuca leucadendron*, family Myrtaceae. The leaves produce *cajuput oil*, which has medicinal uses.

In favourable conditions, such as in the Florida Everglades, the tree reproduces rapidly. Attempts are being made to extirpate it because in a forest fire its crown becomes a ball of flame, accelerating the spread of the blaze in all directions.

Melanchthon /məˈlæŋkθən/ Philip. Assumed name of Philip Schwarzerd 1497–1560. German theologian who helped Luther prepare a German translation of the New Testament. In 1521 he issued the first systematic formulation of Protestant theology, and composed the *Confession of ◊Augsburg* 1530.

Melanesia /ˌmeləˈniːzɪə/ islands in the SW Pacific between Micronesia to the north and Polynesia to the east, embracing all the islands from the New Britain archipelago to Fiji.

Melanesian indigenous inhabitant of Melanesia.

Melanesian languages see ◊Malayo-Polynesian languages.

Meir Israeli politician and prime minister Golda Meir, 1970.

meiosis

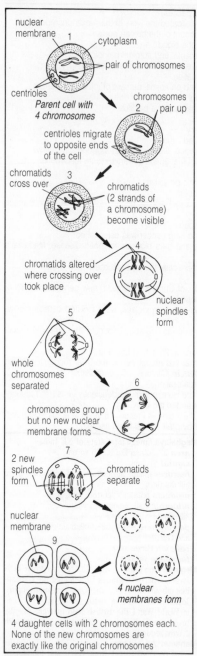

nuclear membrane — 1 — cytoplasm
centrioles — pair of chromosomes
Parent cell with 4 chromosomes
chromosomes pair up — 2
centrioles migrate to opposite ends of the cell
chromatids cross over — 3 — chromatids (2 strands of a chromosome) become visible
chromatids altered where crossing over took place — 4
nuclear spindles form
whole chromosomes separated — 5
chromosomes group but no new nuclear membrane forms — 6
2 new spindles form — 7 — chromatids separate
nuclear membrane — 8
9 — 4 nuclear membranes form

4 daughter cells with 2 chromosomes each. None of the new chromosomes are exactly like the original chromosomes

Melanesian pidgin English a form of ◊pidgin English.

melanism black coloration of animal bodies caused by large amounts of the pigment melanin. Melanin is of significance in insects, because melanic ones warm more rapidly in sunshine than pale ones, and can be more active in cool weather. A fall in temperature may stimulate such insects to produce more melanin. In industrial areas, dark insects and pigeons match sooty backgrounds and escape predation, but they are at a disadvantage in rural areas where they do not match their backgrounds. This is known as *industrial melanism*.

melanoma mole or growth containing the dark pigment melanin. Malignant melanoma is a type of skin cancer developing in association with a pre-existing mole. Once rare, this disease is now increasing, possibly due to depletion of the ozone layer, which provides some protection against ultraviolet radiation from the

Mekong River

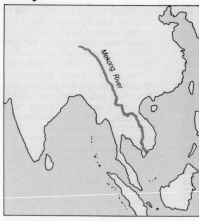

Sun. Most at risk are those with fair hair and light skin.

Melba /ˈmelbə/ Nellie, adopted name of Helen Porter Mitchell 1861–1931. Australian soprano. One of her finest roles was Donizetti's *Lucia*. *Peach melba* (half a peach plus vanilla ice cream and melba sauce, made from sweetened, fresh raspberries) and *melba toast* (crisp, thin toast) are named after her.

Melbourne /ˈmelbən/ capital of Victoria, Australia, near the mouth of the river Yarra; population (1986) 2,943,000. Industries include engineering, shipbuilding, electronics, chemicals, food processing, clothing, and textiles.

Founded 1835, it was named after Lord Melbourne 1837, grew in the wake of the gold rushes, and was the seat of the Commonwealth government 1901–27. It is the country's second largest city, with three universities, and is the site of the 1956 Olympics.

Melbourne /ˈmelbən/ William Lamb, 2nd Viscount 1779–1848. British Whig politician. Home secretary 1830–34, he was briefly prime minister in 1834 and again 1835–41. He was married 1805–25 to Lady Caroline Ponsonby (novelist Lady Caroline Lamb, 1785–1828). Accused in 1836 of seducing Caroline ◊Norton, he lost the favour of William IV, but was an adviser to the young Queen Victoria.

Melbourne Cup Australian horse race, raced over 3.2 km/2 mi at Flemington Park, Victoria, on the first Tuesday in November. It was inaugurated 1861.

Melchite or *Melkite* member of a Christian church in Syria, Egypt, Lebanon, and Israel. The Melchite Church was founded in Syria in the 6th–7th centuries after accepting Byzantine rule at the council of Chalcedon 451 (unlike the ◊Maronites). In 1754 some Melchites broke away to form a ◊Uniate Church with Rome; the remainder belong to the Orthodox Church.

Melanesia

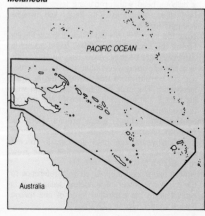

PACIFIC OCEAN

Australia

Melbourne *English politician Viscount Melbourne was a friend and mentor to Queen Victoria on her accession.*

Méliès Georges 1861–1938. French film pioneer, born in Paris. From 1896–1908 he made over 1,000 films, mostly fantasies, such as *Le Voyage dans la Lune/A Trip to the Moon* 1902. He developed trick effects such as slow motion, double exposure, and dissolves, and in 1897 built Europe's first film studio at Montreuil.

Melilla /me'lɪljə/ port and military base on the NE coast of Morocco; area 14 sq km/5 sq mi; population (1986) 56,000. It was captured by Spain 1496 and is still under Spanish rule. Also administered from Melilla are three other Spanish possessions: Peñón ('rock') de Velez de la Gomera, Peñón d'Alhucemas, and the Chaffarine Islands.

melitin (Greek 'bee') extract of honey-bee poison, a powerful antibiotic.

Mellon /'melən/ Andrew William 1855–1937. US financier who donated his art collection to found the National Gallery of Art, Washington DC, 1941. His son, **Paul Mellon** (1907–) was its president 1963–79. He funded Yale University's Centre for British Art, New Haven, Connecticut, and donated important works of art to both collections.

melodrama a play or film with romantic and sensational plot elements, often unsubtly acted. Originally it meant a play accompanied by music. The early melodramas used extravagant theatrical effects to heighten violent emotions and actions artificially. By the end of the 19th century, melodrama had become a popular genre of stage play. Today the term is often derogatory.

Beginning with the early work of ◊Goethe and ◊Schiller, melodrama was popularized in France by Pixérécourt, and first introduced to England in an unauthorized translation by Thomas Holcroft as *A Tale of Mystery* 1802. Melodramas were frequently played against a Gothic background of mountains or ruined castles.

melody in music, a sequence of notes forming a theme or tune.

melon twining plant of the family Cucurbitaceae. The musk melon *Cucumis melo* and the watermelon *Citrullus vulgaris* are two of the many edible varieties.

Melos /'miːlɒs/ (modern Greek *Mílos*) Greek island in the Aegean, one of the Cyclades; area 155 sq km/60 sq mi. The sculpture of *Venus de Milo* was discovered here 1820 (now in the Louvre). The capital is Plaka.

Melpomene /mel'pɒmənɪ/ in Greek mythology, the ◊Muse of tragedy.

Melrose /'melrəʊz/ town in Borders region, Scotland. The heart of King Robert the Bruce is buried her and the ruins of Melrose Abbey 1136 are commemorated in verse by Sir Walter Scott.

meltdown a very serious type of accident in a nuclear reactor. If the reactor's cooling system fails and a major part of the core reaches its melting point (about 2,900°C/5,200°F), the metal reactor vessel may also melt, burn through the concrete floor beneath and release radioactive material into the atmosphere through ◊fallout. A meltdown was narrowly avoided at Three Mile Island, Pennsylvania, USA, 1979, but occurred in a reactor at ◊Chernobyl 1986, spreading radioactive fallout over a large area of N Europe.

melting point the temperature at which a substance melts, or changes from a solid to liquid form. A pure substance under standard conditions of pressure (usually one atmosphere) has a definite melting point. If heat is supplied to a solid at its melting point, the temperature does not change until the melting process is complete. The melting point of ice is 0°C/32°F.

Melton Mowbray /'meltən 'məʊbreɪ/ market town in Leicestershire, England, on the river Eye; a hunting and horse-breeding centre known for pork pies and Stilton cheeses; population (1981) 29,500.

Melville /'melvɪl/ Henry Dundas, Viscount Melville 1742–1811. British Tory politician, born in Edinburgh. He entered Parliament 1774, and as home secretary 1791–94 persecuted the parliamentary reformers. His impeachment for malversation (misconduct) 1806 was the last in English history.

Melville /'melvɪl/ Herman 1819–1891. US writer, whose ◊*Moby-Dick* 1851 was inspired by his whaling experiences in the South Seas, the setting for other fiction, such as *Typee* 1846 and *Omoo* 1847. He published several volumes of verse, and short stories (*The Piazza Tales* 1856). *Billy Budd* was completed just before his death and published 1924.

Melville was born in Albany, New York. He took to the sea after his father went bankrupt, and struggled to make a literary living, working in the New York customs office 1866–85. A friend of Nathaniel Hawthorne, he explored the dark, troubled side of American experience in novels of unusual form and great philosophical power. He wrote no prose from 1857 until *Billy Budd*. He died in obscurity. *Moby-Dick* was filmed by John Huston 1956. *Billy Budd* was the basis of an opera by Benjamin Britten 1951, and made into a film 1962.

membrane in living things, a continuous layer, made up principally of fat molecules, which encloses a ◊cell or a part of a cell (organelle). Certain small molecules can pass through the cell membrane, but most must enter or leave the cell via channels in the membrane made up of special proteins. The ◊Golgi apparatus within the cell produces certain membranes.

In cell organelles, enzymes may be attached to the membrane at specific positions, often alongside other enzymes involved in the same process, like workers at a conveyor belt. Thus membranes help to make cellular processes more efficient.

Memel /'meɪməl/ German name for ◊Klaipeda, port in Lithuania, USSR.

memento mori (Latin) a reminder of death.

Memlinc /'memlɪŋk/ or **Memling** Hans *c.*1430–1494. Flemish painter, born near Frankfurt-am-Main, Germany, but active in Bruges. He painted religious subjects and portraits. Some of his works are in the Hospital of St John, Bruges, including the *Adoration of the Magi* 1479.

Memlinc is said to have been a pupil of van der Weyden, but his style is calmer and softer. He was town painter in Bruges 1475–87. His portraits include *Tommaso Portinari and his Wife* (Metropolitan Museum of Art, New York), and he decorated the *Shrine of St Ursula* 1489 (Hospital of St John, Bruges).

Memorial Day in the USA, a day of remembrance (formerly Decoration Day) instituted 1868 for those killed in the US Civil War. It is now observed as a public holiday on the last Monday in May in remembrance of all Americans killed in war.

Melville *Herman Melville, author of the classic American novel Moby-Dick.*

memory in computing, the part of a system used to store data and programs either permanently or temporarily. There are two main types: internal memory and external memory. Memory capacity is measured in ◊kilobytes or ◊megabytes.

Internal memory is either read-only (stored in ◊ROM, ◊PROM and ◊EPROM chips) or read/write (stored in ◊RAM chips). Read-only memory stores information that must be constantly available or accessed very quickly, and that is unlikely to be changed. It is non-volatile, that is, it is not lost when the computer is switched off. Read/write memory is volatile: it stores programs and data only while the computer is switched on. *External memory* is permanent, non-volatile memory employing storage devices which include magnetic discs (such as floppy discs, hard discs), magnetic tape (tape streamers, cassettes), laser discs including ◊CD-ROM (compact discs) and ◊bubble memory. By rapidly swapping blocks of information in and out of internal memory from external memory, the limited size of a computer's memory may artificially be increased.

memory ability to store and recall observations and sensations. Memory does not seem to be based in any particular part of the brain; it may depend on changes to the pathways followed by nerve impulses as they move through the brain. Memory can be improved by regular use as the connections between ◊nerve cells (neurons) become 'well-worn paths' in the brain. Events stored

Memlinc *St John the Baptist and St Lawrence, National Gallery, London.*

in **short-term memory** are forgotten quickly, whereas those in **long-term memory** can last for many years, enabling recognition of people and places over long periods of time. Human memory is not well understood.

Memphis /'memfɪs/ ruined city beside the Nile, 19 km/12 mi south of Cairo, Egypt. Once the centre of the worship of Ptah, it was the earliest capital of a united Egypt under King Menes about 3200 BC, but was superseded by Thebes under the new empire 1570 BC. It was later used as a stone quarry, but the 'cemetery city' of Sakkara survives, with the step pyramid built for King Zoser by ◊Imhotep, probably the world's oldest stone building.

Memphis /'memfɪs/ industrial city (pharmaceuticals, food processing, cotton, timber, tobacco) on the Mississippi River, in Tennessee, USA; population (1986) 960,000. It has recording studios and record companies (Sun 1953–68, Stax 1960–75); Graceland, the home of Elvis Presley, is a museum.

Menai Strait /'menaɪ/ channel of the Irish Sea, dividing Anglesey from the Welsh mainland; about 22 km/14 mi long, up to 3 km/2 mi wide. It is crossed by Telford's suspension bridge 1826 (reconstructed 1940) and Stephenson's tubular rail bridge 1850.

Menam /mi:'næm/ another name for the ◊Chao Phraya river, Thailand.

Menander /me'nændə/ c.342–291 BC. Greek comic dramatist, born in Athens. Of his 105 plays only fragments (many used as papier-mâché for Egyptian mummy cases) and Latin adaptations were known prior to the discovery 1957 of the *Dyscholos/The Bad-Tempered Man*.

Mencius /'menʃɪəs/ Latinized name of Mengzi c. 372–289 BC. Chinese philosopher and moralist, in the tradition of Confucius. Mencius considered that human nature was innately good, although this goodness required cultivation, and based his conception of morality on this conviction.

Born in Shantung (now Shandong) province, he was founder of a Confucian school. After 20 years' unsuccessful search for a ruler to put into practice his enlightened political programme, based on people's innate goodness, he retired. His teachings are preserved as the *Book of Mengzi*.

Mencken /'meŋkən/ H(enry) L(ouis) 1880–1956. US essayist and critic, known as 'the sage of Baltimore'. His unconventionally phrased, satiric contributions to *Smart Set* and *US Mercury* (both of which periodicals he edited) aroused great controversy. His book *The American Language* 1918 is often revised.

Mende person of the Mende culture, from central-east Sierra Leone and W Liberia. They number approximately 1 million, and their language belongs to the Niger-Congo family.

Mendel /'mendl/ Gregor Johann 1822–1884. Austrian biologist, founder of ◊genetics. His experiments with successive generations of peas gave the basis for his theory of particulate inheritance rather than blending, involving dominant and recessive characters. His results, published 1865–69, remained unrecognized until early this century. Mendel was abbot of the Augustinian abbey at Brünn (now Brno, Czechoslovakia) from 1868.

mendelevium an artificially made element, symbol Md, atomic number 101. One of the ◊actinide series, it is a radioactive element produced by bombardment of einsteinium-253.

Mendeleyev /,mendə'leɪef/ Dmitri Ivanovich 1834–1907. Russian chemist who framed the periodic law in chemistry which states that the chemical properties of the elements depend on their relative atomic masses. This law is the basis of the ◊periodic table of elements.

Mendelism in genetics, the theory of inheritance originally outlined by Gregor Mendel. He suggested that, in sexually reproducing species, all characteristics are inherited through indivisible

Mendelism

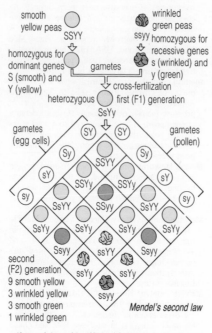

smooth yellow peas SSYY

wrinkled green peas ssyy

homozygous for dominant genes S (smooth) and Y (yellow)

homozygous for recessive genes s (wrinkled) and y (green)

gametes

cross-fertilization

heterozygous

first (F1) generation SsYy

gametes (egg cells)

gametes (pollen)

	SY	SY	Sy	sY	sy
SY	SSYY				
Sy		SSYy	SSYy		
sY		SsYY	SsYY	SsYy	
sy	SsYy	SsYy	SsYy	Ssyy

second (F2) generation
9 smooth yellow
3 wrinkled yellow
3 smooth green
1 wrinkled green

ssYY ssYy ssYy ssyy

Mendel's second law

'factors' (now identifed with ◊genes) contributed by each parent to its offspring.

Mendelssohn (-Bartholdy) /'mendlsən baː'tɒldi/ (Jakob Ludwig) Felix 1809–1847. German composer, also a pianist and conductor. Among his many works are *A Midsummer Night's Dream* 1827; the *Fingal's Cave* overture 1832; and five symphonies, which include the Reformation (1830), the Italian (1833), and the Scottish (1842). He also composed the violin concerto 1844; *Songs Without Words* 1832–45 for the piano; operas; and the oratorios *St Paul* 1836 and *Elijah* 1846.

Menderes /,mendə'res/ (Turkish *Büyük Menderes*) river in European Turkey, about 400 km/250 mi long, rising near Afyonkarahisar and flowing along a winding course into the Aegean. The word 'meander' is derived from the ancient Greek name for the river.

Mendes /'mendɪs/ Filho Francisco 'Chico' 1944– 1988. Brazilian environmentalist and labour leader. Opposed to the destruction of Brazil's rainforests, he organized itinerant rubber tappers into the Workers' Party (PT) and was assassinated.

Born in the NW Amazonian state of Acre, Mendes became an outspoken opponent of the destruction of Brazil's rainforests for cattle-ranching purposes, and received death threats from ranchers. (Rubber-tapping is sustainable rainforest use.) Mendes was awarded the UN Global 500 Ecology Prize in 1987.

Mendès-France /,mɒndes'frɒns/ Pierre 1907– 1982. French prime minister and foreign minister 1954–55. He extricated France from the war in Indochina, and prepared the way for Tunisian independence.

mendicant order religious order dependent on alms. In the Roman Catholic Church there are four orders of mendicant friars: Franciscans, Dominicans, Carmelites, and Augustinians. Hinduism has similar orders.

Mendoza /men'dəʊsə/ capital of the Argentine province of the same name; population (1980) 597,000. Founded 1561, it developed owing to its position on the Trans-Andean railway; it lies at the centre of a wine-producing area.

Mendoza /men'dəʊsə/ Antonio de c.1490–1552. First Spanish viceroy of New Spain (Mexico) 1535–51. He attempted to develop agriculture and mining and supported the church in its attempts to convert the Indians. The system he

established lasted until the 19th century. He was subsequently viceroy of Peru 1551–52.

Menelik II /'menəlɪk/ 1844–1913. Negus (emperor) of Abyssinia (now Ethiopia) from 1889. He defeated the Italians 1896 at ◊Adowa, and thereby retained the independence of his country.

Menem /'menem/ Carlos Saul 1935– . Argentinian politician, president from 1989; leader of the Peronist (Justice Party) movement. As president, he improved relations with the United Kingdom.

Menem, born in La Rioja province, joined the Justice Party while training to be a lawyer. In 1963 he was elected president of the party in La Rioja and in 1983 became governor. In 1989 he defeated the Radical Union Party (UCR) candidate and became president of Argentina. Despite anti-British speeches during the election campaign, President Menem soon declared a wish to resume normal diplomatic relations with the UK and to discuss the future of the Falkland Islands in a spirit of compromise.

Menes /'miːniːz/ c. 3200 BC. traditionally, the first king of the first dynasty of ancient Egypt. He is said to have founded Memphis and organized worship of the gods.

Mengistu /men'gɪstuː/ Haile Mariam 1937– . Ethiopian soldier and socialist politician, head of state from 1977 (president from 1987). As an officer in the Ethiopian army, he took part in the overthrow in 1974 of Emperor ◊Haile Selassie and in 1977 led another coup, becoming head of state. He was confronted with severe problems of drought and secessionist uprisings, but survived with help from the USSR and the West. In 1987 civilian rule was formally reintroduced, but with the Marxist-Leninist Workers' Party of Ethiopia the only legally permitted party.

Mengs /meŋs/ Anton Raffael 1728–1779. German Neo-Classical painter, born in Bohemia. He was court painter in Dresden 1745 and in Madrid 1761; he then worked alternately in Rome and Spain. The ceiling painting *Parnassus* 1761 (Villa Albani, Rome) is an example of his work.

Mengs's father was a miniature painter at the Dresden court and encouraged his son to specialize in portraiture. He was sent to Rome 1741. In 1755 he met the art connoisseur Johann Winckelmann (1717–68), a founder of Neo-Classicism; Mengs adopted his artistic ideals and wrote a treatise on *Beauty in Painting*. He worked in the Vatican 1772–73, then in Spain, and again in Rome from 1777.

menhir (Breton 'long stone') a prehistoric standing stone; see ◊megalith.

Ménière's disease (or syndrome) a recurring condition of the inner ear affecting mechanisms both of hearing and balance. It develops usually in the middle or later years. Symptoms, which include ringing in the ears, nausea, vertigo, and loss of balance, may be relieved by drugs.

Menindee /mə'nɪndi/ village and sheep centre on the Darling river in New South Wales, Australia. It is the centre of a scheme for conserving

Mendelssohn (-Bartholdy) *German composer and pianist Felix Mendelssohn.*

meniscus

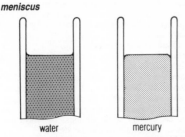

water   mercury

the waters of the Darling in **Menindee Lake** (155 sq km/60 sq mi) and other lakes nearby.

meningitis inflammation of the meninges (membranes) surrounding the brain caused by bacterial or viral infection. The severity of the disease varies from mild to rapidly lethal, and symptoms include fever, headache, nausea, neck stiffness, delirium, and (rarely) convulsions. Many common viruses can cause the occasional case of meningitis, although not usually in its more severe form. The treatment for viral meningitis is rest. Bacterial meningitis, though treatable by antibiotics, is a much more serious threat. Diagnosis is by ◊lumbar puncture.

meniscus in physics, the curved shape of the surface of a liquid in a thin tube, caused by the cohesive effects of ◊surface tension. Most liquids adopt a concave curvature (viewed from above), although with highly viscous liquids (such as mercury) the meniscus is convex. Meniscus is also the name of a concavo-convex or convexo-concave ◊lens.

Mennonite member of a Protestant Christian sect, originating in Zürich 1523. Members refuse to hold civil office or do military service, and reject infant baptism. They were later named Mennonites after Menno Simons (1496–1559), leader of a group in Holland.

When the Mennonites came under persecution, some settled in Germantown, Pennsylvania. The **Hutterian Brethren** (named after Jacob Hutter who died in 1536) hold substantially the same beliefs, and Hutterian principles are the basis of the ◊**Bruderhof**.

Menon /'menən/ Vengalil Krishnan 1897–1974. Indian politician, who was important in the Indian nationalist movement. He represented India at the United Nations 1952–62, and was defence minister 1957–62.

He was barrister of the Middle Temple in London, and Labour member of St Pancras Borough Council, London, 1934–47. He was secretary of the India League in the UK from 1929, and in 1947 was appointed Indian high commissioner in London. He became a member of the Indian parliament 1953, and minister without portfolio 1956. He was dismissed by Nehru 1962 when China invaded India after Menon's assurances to the contrary.

menopause in women, the cessation of reproductive ability, characterized by menstruation (see ◊menstrual cycle) becoming irregular and eventually ceasing. The onset is about the age of 50, but often varies greatly. Menopause is usually uneventful, but some women suffer from complications such as flushing, excessive bleeding, and nervous disorder. Since the 1950s, hormone replacement therapy (HRT), using ◊oestrogen alone or with ◊progesterone, has been developed to counteract such effects.

Long-term use of HRT is associated with an increased risk of cancer of the uterus, and shares with the contraceptive pill a risk of clot formation in the blood vessels, leading to possible stroke (pulmonary embolus). However, without HRT there is increased risk of ◊osteoporosis leading to broken bones, which may be indirectly fatal (for example, about 50% of women over 65 who fracture a hip die within 12 months of their accident). The menopause is also known as the 'change of life'.

menstrual cycle

menstruation   ovulation   egg dies if not fertilized

womb lining (endometrium is shed)   egg released from ovary   womb lining continues to thicken   corpus luteum breaks down

follicle maturing   ovulation   corpus luteum developing

oestrogens   progesterone

menstruation   menstruation

days   end of menstruation

1 2 3 4 5 6 7 8 9 10 11 12 13 14 15 16 17 18 19 20 21 22 23 24 25 26 27 28 1 2 3

start of menstruation   copulation could result in fertilization

menorah a seven-branched candlestick used in Jewish ritual, a symbol of Judaism and of the state of Israel.

Menorca /me'nɔːkə/ Spanish form of ◊Minorca, one of the Balearic Islands.

Menotti /me'nɒti/ Gian Carlo 1911– . Italian-born US composer. He wrote both the music and the libretti for operas, including *The Medium* 1946, *The Telephone* 1947, *The Consul* 1950, *Amahl and the Night Visitors* 1951 (the first opera to be written for television), and *The Saint of Bleecker Street* 1954. He has also written orchestral and chamber music.

Mensa International organization founded in the UK 1945 with membership limited to those passing an 'intelligence' test. Criticized by many who believe that intelligence is not satisfactorily measured by IQ tests alone.

Menshevik member of the minority (Russian *menshinstvo* 'minority') of the Russian Social Democratic Party, who split from the ◊Bolsheviks 1903. The Mensheviks believed in a large, loosely organized party, and that before socialist revolution could occur in Russia, capitalist society must develop further. During the Russian Revolution they had limited power and set up a government in Georgia, but were suppressed 1922.

Menotti US composer Gian Carlo Menotti.

mens sana in corpore sano (Latin) a healthy mind in a healthy body.

menstrual cycle the cycle that occurs in female mammals of reproductive age, in which the body is prepared for pregnancy. At the beginning of the cycle, a Graafian (egg) follicle develops in the ovary, and the inner wall of the uterus forms a soft spongy lining. The egg is released from the ovary, and the lining of the uterus becomes vascularized (filled with blood vessels). If fertilization does not occur, the corpus luteum (remains of the Graafian follicle) degenerates, and the uterine lining breaks down, and is shed. This is what causes the loss of blood that marks menstruation. The cycle then begins again. Human menstruation takes place from puberty to menopause, occurring about every 28 days.

The cycle is controlled by a number of ◊hormones, including ◊oestrogen and ◊progesterone. If fertilization occurs, the corpus luteum persists and goes on producing progesterone.

mental handicap impairment of intelligence. It can be very mild, but in more severe cases, it is associated with social problems and difficulties in living independently. People may be born with mental handicap or may acquire it through brain damage.

mental illness abnormal working of the mind. Since normal working cannot be defined, the borderline between mild mental illness and normality is a matter of opinion. Mild forms are known as **neuroses**, affecting the emotions, whereas more severe forms, the **psychoses**, distort conscious reasoning.

menthol peppermint camphor $C_{10}H_{19}OH$, an alcohol derivative of menthone. It occurs in peppermint and is responsible for the plant's odour.

Menton /mɒn'tɒn/ (Italian **Mentone**) resort on the French Riviera, close to the Italian frontier; population (1982) 22,234. It belonged to the princes of Monaco from the 14th century until briefly independent 1848–60, when the citizens voted to merge with France.

menu in computing, a list of options, displayed on screen, from which the user may make a choice. An example is the choice of services offered to the customer by a bank cash dispenser: withdrawal, deposit, balance, and statement.

Menuhin /'menjuɪn/ Yehudi 1916– . US violinist. A child prodigy, he achieved great depth of interpretation, and was often accompanied on the piano by his sister Hephzibah (1921–81). He conducted his own chamber orchestra and founded a school in Surrey, England, 1963 for training young musicians.

Menzies /'menzɪz/ Robert Gordon 1894–1978. Australian politician, leader of the United Australia

Mercalli scale

Value	Description
I	Only detected by instrument.
II	Felt by people resting.
III	Felt indoors; hanging objects swing; feels like passing traffic.
IV	Feels like passing heavy traffic; standing cars rock; windows, dishes, and doors rattle; wooden frames creak.
V	Felt outdoors; sleepers are woken; liquids spill; doors swing open.
VI	Felt by everybody; people stagger; windows break; trees and bushes rustle; weak palster cracks.
VII	Difficult to stand upright; noticed by vehicle drivers; plaster, loose bricks, tiles, and chimneys fall; bells ring.
VIII	Car steering affected; some collapse of masonry; chimney stacks and towers fall; branches break from trees; cracks in wet ground.
IX	General panic; serious damage to buildings; underground pipes break; cracks and subsidence in ground.
X	Most buildings destroyed; lamdslides; water thrown out of canals.
XI	Rails bent; underground pipes totally destoyed.
XII	Damage nearly total; rocks displaced; objects thrown into the air.

(now Liberal) Party and prime minister 1939–41 and 1949–66.

A Melbourne lawyer, he entered politics 1928, was attorney-general in the federal parliament 1934–39, and in 1939 succeeded Joseph Lyons as prime minister and leader of the United Australia Party, until 1941, when he resigned after colleagues were dissatisfied with his leadership of Australia's war effort. In 1949 he became prime minister of a Liberal–Country Party coalition government, and was re-elected 1951, 1954, 1955, 1958, 1961, and 1963. Knighted 1963, he was appointed Lord Warden of the Cinque Ports 1965, and retired as prime minister 1966. His critics argued that he did not show enough interest in Asia, and supported the US and white African regimes too uncritically. His defenders argued that he provided stability in domestic policy and national security.

Menzies /'menzɪz/ William Cameron 1896–1957. US art director of films, later a film director, who was one of Hollywood's most imaginative and talented designers. He was responsible for the sets of such films as *Gone With the Wind* 1939 and *Foreign Correspondent* 1940. His films as director include *Things to Come* 1936 and *Invaders from Mars* 1953.

Meo or *Miao* member of a SE Asian highland people (also known as Hmong). They are predominantly hill farmers, cultivating rice and maize, rearing pigs, and many are involved in growing the opium poppy. Their language belongs to the Sino-Tibetan family.

MEP abbreviation for *Member of the ◊European Parliament*.

Mephistopheles or *Mephisto* another name for the ◊devil, or an agent of the devil, associated with the ◊Faust legend.

Mequinez Spanish name for ◊Meknés, a town in Morocco.

Mercalli scale scale used to measure the intensity of an ◊earthquake. It differs from the ◊Richter scale, which measures *magnitude*. It is named after the Italian seismologist Giuseppe Mercalli (1850–1914). Intensity is a subjective value, based on observed phenomena, and varies from place to place with the same earthquake.

mercantilism economic theory, held in the 16th–18th centuries, that a nation's wealth (in the form of bullion or treasure) was the key to its prosperity. To this end, foreign trade should be regulated to obtain a surplus of exports over imports, and the state should intervene where necessary (for example subsidizing exports and taxing imports). The bullion theory of wealth was demolished by Adam ◊Smith in Book IV of *The Wealth of Nations* 1776.

Mercator /mɜ:'keɪtə/ Gerardus 1512–1594. Latinized form of the name of the Flemish map-maker Gerhard Kremer. He devised the first modern atlas, showing *Mercator's projection* in which the parallels and meridians on maps are drawn uniformly at 90°. It is often used for navigational charts, because compass courses can be drawn as straight lines, but the true area of countries is increasingly distorted the further N or S they are from the equator. For other types, see ◊map projection.

Mercedes-Benz German car-manufacturing company created by a merger of the Daimler and Benz factories 1926. The first cars to carry the Mercedes name were those built by Gottlieb ◊Daimler 1901. In the 1930s Mercedes-Benz dominated Grand Prix races. The W196, which made its debut 1954, was one of the finest racing cars of the postwar era. Following a disaster at Le Mans 1955, when 80 spectators lost their lives after an incident involving a Mercedes, the company withdrew from motor sport until 1989.

mercenary a soldier hired by the army of another country or by a private army. Mercenary military service originated in the 14th century, when cash payment on a regular basis was the only means of guaranteeing soldiers' loyalty. In the 20th century mercenaries have been common in wars and guerrilla activity in Asia, Africa, and Latin America.

Most famous of the mercenary armies was the *Great Company* of the 14th century, which was in effect a glorified protection racket, comprising some 10,000 knights of all nationalities and employing *condottieri*, or contractors, to serve the highest bidder. By the end of the 14th century, condottieri and *freelances* were an institutionalized aspect of warfare. In the 18th century, Swiss cantons and some German states regularly provided the French with troops for mercenary service as a means of raising money; they were regarded as the best forces in the French army. Britain employed 20,000 German mercenaries to make up its numbers during the Seven Years' War 1756–63 and used Hessian forces during the War of American Independence 1775–83.

Article 47 of the 1977 Additional Protocols to the Geneva Convention stipulates that 'a mercenary shall not have the right to be a combatant or a prisoner of war' but leaves a party to the Protocols the freedom to grant such status if so wished.

Mercer /'mɜ:sə/ David 1928–1980. British dramatist. He first became known for his television plays, including *A Suitable Case for Treatment* 1962, filmed as *Morgan*; stage plays include *After Haggerty* 1970.

Merchant /'mɜ:tʃənt/ Ismael 1936– . Indian film producer, known for his stylish collaborations with James ◊Ivory on films including *Shakespeare Wallah* 1965, *The Europeans* 1979, *Heat and Dust* 1983, *A Room with a View* 1986, and *Maurice* 1987.

merchant bank a bank that developed from merchant houses trading in various parts of the world. As such houses became known, they found that a remunerative way to finance trade was to accept bills of exchange from lesser-known traders. Originally developed in the UK in the 19th century, merchant banks now offer many of the services provided by the commercial banks.

Traditionally, the merchant banks have been situated in the City of London, but in recent years have been opened in major provincial cities and abroad.

merchant navy the passenger and cargo ships of a country. Most are owned by private companies (but in the USSR and other communist countries they are state-owned and closely associated with the navy). To avoid strict regulations on safety, union rules on crew wages, and so on, many ships are today registered under 'flags of convenience', that is, flags of countries that do not have such rules.

Types of ship include:

tramps either in home coastal trade, or carrying bulk cargoes worldwide;

tankers the largest ships afloat, up to 500,000 tonnes/492,000 tons and 380 m/1,245 ft long, and other vessels carrying specialized cargo;

cargo liners combining cargo and passenger traffic on short or world voyages. Passenger-only liners enjoyed a revival in the 1980s.

Most merchant ships are diesel-powered, but there have been attempts to revive sails (under automatic control) in combination with diesel to reduce costs, the first commercial venture being the Japanese *Aitoku Maru* 1980. Nuclear power was used in the *Savannah* 1959 (US), but problems with host ports mean that only the USSR builds such ships for 'internal' use, for example, Arctic icebreakers and the 26,400 tonne/26,000 ton N Pacific/Arctic barge carrier *Sevmorput* 1985.

Merchant of Venice, The a comedy by William Shakespeare, first performed 1596–97. Antonio, a rich merchant, borrows money from Shylock, a Jewish moneylender, promising a pound of flesh if the sum is not repaid; when Shylock presses his claim, the heroine, Portia, disguised as a lawyer, saves Antonio's life.

Merchants Adventurers trading company founded 1407 and consisting of guilds and traders in many N European ports. In direct opposition to the Hanseatic League, it came to control 75% of English overseas trade by 1550.

Mercia /'mɜ:sɪə/ an Anglo-Saxon kingdom that emerged in the 6th century. By the late 8th century it dominated all England south of the Humber, but from about 825 came under the power of ◊Wessex. Mercia eventually came to denote an area bounded by the Welsh border, the river Humber, East Anglia, and the river Thames.

Merckx /meəks/ Eddie 1945– . Belgian cyclist known as 'the Cannibal'. He won the Tour de France a joint record five times 1969–74.

Merckx turned professional 1966 and won his first classic race, the Milan–San Remo, the same year. He went on to win 24 classics as well as the three major tours (of Italy, Spain, and France) a total of 11 times. He was world professional road-race champion three times and in 1971 won a record 54 races in the season. He rode 50 winners in a season four times. He retired in 1977.

CAREER HIGHLIGHTS

Tour de France: 1969–72, 1974
Tour of Italy: 1968, 1970, 1972–74
Tour of Spain: 1973
world professional champion: 1967, 1971, 1974
world amateur champion: 1964.

Mercury /'mɜ:kjʊri/ Roman god, identified with the Greek Hermes, and like him represented with winged sandals and a winged staff entwined with snakes. He was the messenger of the gods.

mercury chemical element, the only common liquid metal at ordinary temperatures; symbol Hg, atomic number 80, relative atomic mass 200.61. It is a dense, mobile, silvery liquid (also called quicksilver), found free in nature. The chief source is the mineral cinnabar, HgS. Its alloys with other metals are called amalgams. It is used in drugs and chemicals, for mercury vapour lamps, arc rectifiers, power-control switches, barometers, and thermometers. It was known to the ancient Chinese and Hindus, and is found in Egyptian tombs of about 1500 BC.

Mercury /'mɜ:kjʊri/ in astronomy, the closest planet to the Sun, at an average distance of 58,000,000 km/36,000,000 mi. Its diameter is 4,880 km/3,030 mi, its mass 0.056 that of Earth. Mercury orbits the Sun every 88 days, and spins

Mercury Mariner 10 spacecraft photomosaic of the heavily cratered surface of Mercury, taken 29 March 1974.

on its axis every 59 days. On its sunward side the surface temperature reaches over 400°C, but on the 'night' side it falls to –170°C. Mercury has an atmosphere with minute traces of argon and helium. The US space probe Mariner 10 1974 discovered that its surface is cratered by meteorite impacts. Mercury has no moons.

Its largest known feature is the Caloris Basin, 1,400 km/870 mi wide. There are also cliffs hundreds of kilometres long and up to 4 km/2.5 mi high, thought to have been formed by the cooling of the planet billions of years ago. Inside is an iron core three-quarters of the planet's diameter, which produces a magnetic field 1% the strength of the Earth's.

mercury fulminate highly explosive compound used in detonators and percussion caps. It is a grey, sandy powder, and extremely poisonous.

Mercury project the US project to put a human in space in the one-seat Mercury spacecraft 1961–63. The first two Mercury flights, on Redstone rockets, were short flights to the edge of space and back. The orbital flights, beginning with the third in the series (made by ◊Glenn), were launched by Atlas rockets.

Meredith /ˈmɛrədɪθ/ George 1828–1909. English novelist and poet. He published the first realistic psychological novel *The Ordeal of Richard Feverel* 1859. Later works include *Evan Harrington* 1861, *The Egoist* 1879, *Diana of the Crossways* 1885, and *The Amazing Marriage* 1895. His best verse is in *Modern Love* 1862.

merengue a type of Latin American dance music with a lively 2/4 beat. Accordion and saxophone are prominent instruments, with ethnic percussion. It originated in the Dominican Republic and became popular in New York in the 1980s.

merganser type of diving duck with a sawbill for catching fish. It is widely distributed in the N hemisphere.

Mergenthaler /ˈmɜːɡən,tɑːlə/ Ottmar 1854–1899. German-American who invented a typesetting method. He went to the USA in 1872 and developed the first linotype machine (for casting metal type in complete lines) 1876–86.

merger the linking of two or more companies, either by creating a new organization by consolidating the original companies, or by absorption by one of the others. Unlike a takeover, which is not always a voluntary fusion of the parties, a merger is the result of an agreement.

There were many mergers in the UK preceding the Big Bang of 1986 designed to improve the competitiveness of companies.

Mérida /ˈmɛrɪðə/ capital of Yucatán state, Mexico, a centre of the sisal industry; population (1986) 580,000. It was founded 1542, and has a cathedral 1598. Its port on the Gulf of Mexico is Progreso.

meridian half a ◊great circle drawn on the Earth's surface passing through both poles and thus through all places with the same longitude. Terrestrial longitudes are usually measured from the Greenwich Meridian.

An astronomical meridian is a great circle passing through the celestial pole and the zenith (the point immediately overhead).

Mérimée /ˌmɛrɪˈmeɪ/ Prosper 1803–1870. French author. Among his works are the stories *Colomba* 1841, *Carmen* 1846, and the *Lettres à une inconnue/Letters to an Unknown Girl* 1873. Born in Paris, he entered the public service, and under Napoleon III was employed on unofficial diplomatic missions.

merino breed of sheep. Its close-set, silky wool is of extremely good quality. The merino, now found all over the world, is the breed on which the Australian wool industry is built.

Merionethshire /ˌmɛrɪˈɒnəθʃə/ former county of N Wales, included in the new county of Gwynedd 1974. Dolgellau was the administrative town.

meristem a region of plant tissue containing cells that are actively dividing to produce new tissues (or have the potential to do so). Meristems found in the tip of roots and stems, the apical meristems, are responsible for the growth in length of these organs.

The ◊cambium is a lateral meristem which is responsible for increase in girth in perenial plants. Some plants also have intercalary meristems, as in the stems of grasses, for example. These are responsible for their continued growth after cutting or grazing has removed the apical meristems of the shoots.

Meristem culture involves growing meristems taken from shoots on a nutrient-containing medium, and using them to grow new plants. It is used to progagate infertile plants or hybrids which do not breed true from seed, and to generate virus-free stock, since viruses rarely infect apical meristems.

meritocracy a system (of for example education or government) in which selection is by performance (in education, by competitive examinations), which therefore favours intelligence and ability rather than social position or wealth. The result is the creation of an elite group. The term was coined by Michael Young in his *The Rise of the Meritocracy* 1958.

Merit, Order of British order of chivalry, founded on the lines of an order of ◊knighthood.

Merleau-Ponty /mɛə,ləʊpɒnˈtiː/ Maurice 1908–1961. French philosopher, one of the most significant contributors to ◊phenomenology after ◊Husserl. He attempted to move beyond the notion of a pure experiencing consciousness, arguing in *The Phenomenology of Perception* 1945 that perception is intertwined with bodily awareness and with language. In his posthumous work, *The Visible and the Invisible* 1964 he argued that our experience is inherently ambiguous and elusive, and that the traditional concepts of philosophy are therefore inadequate to grasp it.

Merlin /ˈmɜːlɪn/ legendary magician and counsellor to King Arthur. Welsh bardic literature has a cycle of poems attributed to him, and he may have been a real person. He is said to have been buried in a cave in the park of Dynevor Castle, Dyfed.

merlin a small ◊falcon.

mermaid mythical sea creature (the male is a *merman*), having a human upper part, and a fish's tail. The dugong and seal are among suggested origins for the idea.

Meroe /ˈmɛrəʊi/ ancient city in Sudan, on the Nile near Khartoum, capital of Nubia from about 600 BC to AD 350. Tombs and inscriptions have been excavated, and iron-smelting slag heaps have been found.

Merovingian dynasty a Frankish dynasty, named after its founder, Merovech (5th century AD). His descendants ruled France from the time of Clovis (481–511) to 751.

Merrie England a book published 1893 by socialist journalist Robert Blatchford (1851–1943), calling nostalgically for an end to industrialism and a return to the rural way of life.

Mersey /ˈmɜːzi/ river in NW England; length 112 km/70 mi. Formed by the confluence of the Goyt and Etherow rivers, it flows W to join the Irish Sea at Liverpool Bay. It is linked to the Manchester Ship Canal.

Mersey beat a type of pop music of the mid-1960s that originated in the NW of England (also called the *Liverpool sound* or, elsewhere, ◊beat music), drawing on US styles. It was almost exclusively performed by all-male groups, of whom the most famous was the Beatles.

Merseyside /ˈmɜːzisaɪd/ former (1974–86) metropolitan county of NW England, replaced by a residuary body in 1986 which covers some of its former functions
area 650 sq km/251 sq mi
towns administrative headquarters Liverpool; Bootle, Birkenhead, St Helens, Wallasey, Southport
features river Mersey; Merseyside Innovation Centre (MIC), linked with Liverpool University and Polytechnic; Prescot Museum of clock and watch making; Speke Hall (Tudor), and Croxteth Hall and Country Park (a working country estate open to the public)
products chemicals, electrical goods, vehicles
population (1987) 1,457,000
famous people the Beatles

Mersin /meəˈsiːn/ or *İçel* Turkish industrial free port (chrome, copper, textiles, oil refining); population (1985) 314,000.

Merthyr Tydfil /ˈmɜːθə ˈtɪdvɪl/ industrial town (light engineering, electrical goods) in Mid Glamorgan, Wales, UK; population (1982) 60,000. It was formerly a centre of the Welsh coal and steel industries.

Merton /ˈmɜːtn/ borough of SW Greater London, including the districts of Wimbledon Merton, Mitcham, and Morden
features part of Wimbledon Common (includes Caesar's Camp—an Iron Age fort); All England Tennis Club 1877
population (1982) 166,600

Merv /meəf/ oasis in Soviet Turkmenistan, a centre of civilization from at least 1200 BC, and site of a town founded by Alexander the Great. Old Merv was destroyed by the emir of Bokhara 1787, and the modern town of Mary, founded by the Russians in 1885, lies 29 km/18 mi west.

mesa (Spanish 'table') a flat-topped steep-sided plateau, consisting of horizontal weak layers of rock topped by a resistant formation; particularly those found in the desert areas of the USA and Mexico. A small mesa is called a butte.

Mesa Verde /ˈmeɪsə ˈvɜːdi/ (Spanish 'green table') a wooded clifftop in Colorado, USA, with Pueblo dwellings, called the Cliff Palace, built into its side. Dating from about 1000 BC, with 200 rooms and 23 circular ceremonial chambers (kivas), it had an estimated population of about 400 people and was probably a regional centre.

mescalin drug derived from a turnip-shaped cactus (*Lophophora williamsii*), known locally as ◊peyote. The tops, which scarcely appear above ground, are dried and chewed, or added to alcoholic drinks.

Merseyside

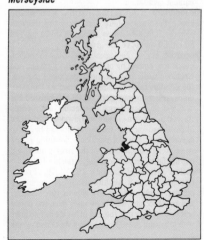

Mescalin is said to heighten the perceptions. It is used by some North American Indians in religious rites.

Meshed /meˈʃed/ a variant spelling of ◊Mashhad, a town in Iran.

Meskhetians community of Turkish descent who formerly inhabited Meskhetia, USSR, on the Turkish-Soviet border. They were deported by Stalin 1944 to Kazakhstan and Uzbekistan, and have campaigned since then for a return to their homeland. In June 1989 at least 70 were killed in pogroms directed against their community in the Ferghana Valley of Uzbekistan by the native Uzbeks.

Stalin distrusted the Meskhetians' potentially pro-Turk leanings; an estimated 30,000–50,000 of the 200,000 deported died in the process. In 1989 34,000 of the 160,000 living in Uzbekistan were evacuated after the pogroms, which resulted from the refusal of the Meskhetians, who are mostly Shia Muslims, to join with the predominantly Sunni Muslim Uzbeks in an anti-Soviet pan-Islamic Front.

Mesmer /ˈmesmə/ Friedrich Anton 1733–1815. Austrian physician, an early experimenter in ◊hypnosis, which was formerly (and popularly) called *mesmerism* after him.

He claimed to reduce people to trance state by consciously exerted 'animal magnetism', their willpower being entirely subordinated to his. Expelled by the police from Vienna, he created a sensation in Paris in 1778, but was denounced as a charlatan in 1785.

mesmerism former term for ◊hypnosis, after Friedrich Mesmer.

Mesolithic the Middle Stone Age period of ◊prehistory.

meson unstable fundamental particle with mass intermediate between those of the electron and the proton, found in cosmic radiation and emitted by nuclei under bombardment by very high-energy particles. Its existence was predicted in 1935 by Japanese physicist Hideki Yukawa (1907–1981).

mesophyll the tissue between the upper and lower epidermis of a leaf blade (lamina), consisting of parenchyma-like cells containing numerous ◊chloroplasts.

In many plants mesophyll is divided into two distinct layers. The *palisade mesophyll* is usually just below the upper epidermis and is composed of regular layers of elongated cells. Lying below them is the *spongy mesophyll*, composed of loosely arranged cells of irregular shape. This layer contains fewer chloroplasts and has many intercellular spaces for the diffusion of gases (required for ◊respiration and ◊photosynthesis), linked to the outside by means of ◊stomata.

Mesopotamia /ˌmesəpəˈteɪmɪə/ the land between the rivers Euphrates and Tigris, part of modern Iraq. Here the civilizations of Sumer and Babylon flourished, and some consider it the site of the earliest civilization.

mesosphere layer in the Earth's ◊atmosphere above the stratosphere and below the thermosphere. It lies between about 50 km/31 mi and 80 km/50 mi above the ground.

Mesozoic era of geological time 248–65 million years ago, consisting of the Triassic, Jurassic, and Cretaceous periods. At the beginning of the era, the continents were joined together as Pangaea, dinosaurs and other giant reptiles dominated the sea and air; and ferns, horsetails, and cycads thrived in a warm climate worldwide. By the end of the Mesozoic era, the continents had begun to assume their present positions, flowering plants were dominant and many of the large reptiles and marine fauna were becoming extinct.

Mesrine /mezˈriːn/ Jacques 1937–1979. French criminal. From a wealthy family, he became a burglar celebrated for his glib tongue, sadism, and bravado, and for his escapes from the police and prison. Towards the end of his life he had links with left-wing guerrillas. He was shot dead by the police.

Messager /ˌmesɑːˈʒeɪ/ André Charles Prosper 1853–1929. French composer and conductor. He studied under ◊Saint-Saëns. Messager composed light operas, such as *La Béarnaise* 1885 and *Véronique* 1898.

Messalina /ˌmesəˈliːnə/ Valeria c. AD 22–48. Third wife of the Roman emperor ◊Claudius, whom she dominated. She was notorious for her immorality, forcing a noble to marry her in AD 48, although still married to Claudius, who then had her executed.

Messerschmitt /ˈmesəʃmɪt/ Willy 1898–1978. German plane designer, whose ME-109 was a standard Luftwaffe fighter in World War II, and whose ME-262 (1942) was the first mass-produced jet fighter.

Messiaen /ˌmesiˈɒŋ/ Olivier 1908– . French composer and organist. His music is mystical in character, vividly coloured, and incorporates transcriptions of birdsong. Among his works are the *Quartet for the End of Time* 1941, the large-scale *Turangalîla Symphony* 1949, solo organ and piano pieces.

His theories of melody, harmony, and rhythm, drawing on medieval and oriental music, have inspired contemporary composers such as ◊Boulez and ◊Stockhausen.

messiah (from Hebrew 'anointed') a saviour or deliverer. Jews from the time of the Old Testament exile in Babylon have looked forward to the coming of a messiah. Christians believe that the messiah came in the person of ◊Jesus.

Messier /mesiˈeɪ/ Charles 1730–1817. French astronomer, who discovered 15 comets and in 1781 published a list of 103 star clusters and nebulae. Objects on this list are given M (for Messier) numbers which astronomers still use today, such as M1, the Crab Nebula, and M31, the Andromeda Galaxy.

Messina /meˈsiːnə/ city and port in NE Sicily; population (1988) 271,000. It produces soap, olive oil, wine, and pasta. Originally an ancient Greek settlement (Zancle), it was taken first by Carthage and then by Rome. It was rebuilt after an earthquake 1908.

Messina, Strait of /meˈsiːnə/ channel in the central Mediterranean separating Sicily from mainland Italy; in Greek legend a monster (Charybdis), who devoured ships, lived in the whirlpool on the Sicilian side, and another (Scylla), who devoured sailors, in the rock on the Italian side. The classical hero Odysseus passed safely between them.

Messrs abbreviation for *messieurs* (French 'sirs' or 'gentlemen') used in formal writing to address an organization or group of people.

Meštrović /ˈmeʃtrəvɪtʃ/ Ivan 1883–1962. Yugoslav sculptor, a naturalized American from 1954. His works include portrait busts of the sculptor Rodin (with whom he is often compared), President Hoover, and Pope Pius XI, and many public monuments.

metabolism the chemical processes of living organisms: a constant alternation of building up (*anabolism*) and breaking down (*catabolism*). For example, green plants build up complex organic substances from water, carbon dioxide, and mineral salts (photosynthesis); by digestion animals partially break down complex organic substances, ingested as food, and subsequently resynthesize them in their own bodies.

metal a type of element with certain chemical characteristics and physical properties. Metals are good conductors of heat and electricity; opaque, but reflect light well; malleable, which enables them to be cold-worked and rolled into sheets; and ductile, which permits them to be drawn into thin wires. Sixty to seventy metals are known.

Generally hard, metals are crystalline in their normal pure state, many of them mixing with one another to form alloys, whose properties depend on the proportions of their constituents. Their hardness, tensile strength, toughness, and brittleness may be varied by physical means such as heat-treatment or work-hardening, but their physical properties, such as melting point, coefficient of thermal expansion, and density, are constant. Their chemical properties are determined by the fact that, with the exception of gold, metals will, to a greater or lesser extent, readily lose one or more electrons to generate a ◊cation (positive ion).

The following are widely used in commerce: *precious metals*: gold, silver, mercury, platinum and the platinum metals, used principally in jewellery; *heavy metals*: iron, copper, zinc, tin and lead, the common metals of engineering; *rarer heavy metals*: nickel, cadmium, chromium, tungsten, molybdenum, manganese, cobalt, vanadium, antimony, and bismuth, used principally for alloying with the heavy metals; *light metals*: aluminium and magnesium; *alkali metals*: sodium, potassium and lithium; and *alkaline earth metals*: calcium, barium and strontium, used principally for chemical purposes.

Other metals have come to the fore because of special nuclear requirements, for example, technetium, produced in nuclear reactors, is corrosion-inhibiting; zirconium may replace aluminium and magnesium alloy in canning uranium in reactors.

metal detector an electronic device for detecting metal, usually below ground, developed from the wartime mine detector. In the head of the metal detector is a coil, which is part of an electronic circuit. The presence of metal causes the frequency of the signal in the circuit to change, setting up an audible note in the headphones worn by the user.

metal fatigue a condition in which metals fail or fracture under relatively light loads, when these loads are applied repeatedly. Structures that are subject to flexing, such as the airframes of aircraft, are prone to metal fatigue.

Metalious /məˈteɪlɪəs/ Grace (born Repentigny) 1924–1964. US novelist. She wrote many short stories but struck the headlines with *Peyton Place* 1958, an exposé of life in a small New England town.

metallic glass a substance produced from metallic materials (non-corrosive alloys rather than simple metals) in a liquid state which, by very rapid cooling, are prevented from reverting to their regular metallic structure. Instead they take on the properties of glass, while retaining the metallic properties of malleability and relatively good electrical conductivity.

metalloid (or *semimetal*) an element, such as arsenic, with some metallic properties; metalloids are thus usually electrically semiconducting. The term is also used for nonmetallic elements, such as carbon, which can form an alloy with a metal.

metallurgy the science and technology of metals. Extractive or *process metallurgy* is concerned with the extraction of metals from their ◊ores, and refining and adapting them for use. *Physical metallurgy* is concerned with their properties and application.

Metals can be extracted from their ores in three main ways: *dry processes* such as smelting, volatilization, or amalgamation—treatment with mercury; *wet processes* involving chemical reactions; and *electrolytic processes*, which work on the principle of ◊electrolysis.

The foundations of metallurgical art were laid about 3500 BC in Egypt, Mesopotamia, and India, where the art of ◊smelting metals from ores was discovered, starting with bronze. Later, gold, silver, copper, lead, and tin were worked. The smelting of iron appears to have been discovered about 1500 BC. The Romans hardened and tempered steel, using ◊heat treatment. From then until about AD 1400, advances in metallurgy were due to the Arabian chemists. ◊Cast iron began to be made in the 14th century (in a crude blast furnace). The demands of the Industrial Revolution led to an enormous increase in iron production, particularly of ◊wrought iron. The invention by Henry Bessemer of the ◊Bessemer process in 1856 made cheap steel

Metamorphic rocks

typical depth and temperature of formation	Main primary material (before metamorphosis)		
	shale with several minerals	sandstone with only quartz	limestone with only calcite
15 km/300°C	slate	quartzite	marble
20 km/400°C	schist		
25 km/780°C	gneiss		
30 km/600°C	hornfels	quartzite	marble

available for the first time, leading to its present widespread use.

metamorphic rock a rock altered in structure and composition by pressure, heat, or chemically active fluids after original formation. (If heat is sufficient to melt the original rock, technically it becomes an igneous rock upon cooling.)

metamorphism geological term referring to the changes in rocks of the Earth's crust caused by increasing pressure and temperature.

metamorphosis a period during the life cycle of many invertebrates, most amphibians, and some fish, during which the individual's body changes from one form to another through a major reconstitution of its tissues. For example, adult frogs are produced by metamorphosis from tadpoles, and butterflies are produced from caterpillars following metamorphosis within a pupa.

In classical thought and literature, metamorphosis is the transformation of a living being into another shape, either living or animate (for example ◊Niobe). The Roman poet ◊Ovid wrote influentially on this theme.

metaphor a figure of speech whose name in Greek means 'transfer' and implies the use of an analogy or close comparison between two things that are not normally treated as if they had anything in common. Metaphor is a common means of extending the uses and references of words. See also ◊simile.

If we call people cabbages or foxes, we are indicating that in our opinion they share certain qualities with those vegetables or animals: an inert quality in the case of cabbages, a cunning quality in the case of foxes, which may lead on to calling people 'foxy' and saying 'He really foxed them that time', meaning that he tricked them. If a scientist is doing research in the *field* of nuclear physics, the word 'field' results from comparison between scientists and farmers (who literally work in fields). Such usages are metaphorical.

metaphysical in English literature, a term applied to a group of 17th-century poets, whose work is characterized by conciseness, ingenious, often highly intricate wordplay, and striking imagery. The best-known exponents of this genre are John ◊Donne, George ◊Herbert, and Abraham ◊Cowley.

metaphysics a branch of philosophy that deals with first principles, especially 'being' (ontology) and 'knowing' (◊epistemology), and that is concerned with the ultimate nature of reality. It has been maintained that no certain knowledge of metaphysical questions is possible.

Epistemology, or the study of how we know, lies at the threshold of the subject. Metaphysics is concerned with the nature and origin of existence and of mind, the interaction between them; the meaning of time and space, causation, determinism and free will, personality and the self, arguments for belief in God, and human immortality. The foundations of metaphysics were laid by ◊Plato and ◊Aristotle. St Thomas ◊Aquinas, basing himself on Aristotle, produced a metaphysical structure that is accepted by the Catholic church. The subject has been advanced by Descartes, Spinoza, Leibniz, Berkeley, Hume, Locke, Kant, Hegel, Schopenhauer, and Marx; and in modern times by Bergson, Bradley, Croce, McTaggart, Whitehead, and Wittgenstein.

Metastasio /ˌmetəˈstæziəʊ/ pen name of Pietro Trapassi 1698–1782. Italian poet and the leading librettist of his day, creating 18th-century Italian *opera seria* (serious opera).

Metaxas /ˌmetækˈsæs/ Joannis 1870–1941. Greek soldier and politician, born in Ithaca. He restored ◊George II (1890–1947) as king of Greece, under whom he established a dictatorship as prime minister from 1936, and introduced several important economic and military reforms. He led resistance to the Italian invasion of Greece in 1941, refusing to abandon Greece's neutral position.

metazoa another name for animals. It reflects an earlier system of classification, in which there were two main divisions within the animal kingdom, the multicellular animals, or metazoa, and the single-celled 'animals' or protozoa. The ◊protozoa are not now included in the animal kingdom, so only the metazoa remain.

metempsychosis another name for ◊reincarnation.

meteor a flash of light in the sky, popularly known as a *shooting* or *falling star*, caused by a particle of dust, a *meteoroid*, entering the atmosphere at speeds up to 70 km/45 mi per second and burning up by friction. Several times each year the Earth encounters swarms of dust shed by comets, which give rise to a *meteor shower*. This usually comes from one particular point in the sky, after which the shower is named; the Perseid meteor shower in August appears in the constellation Perseus. A brilliant meteor is termed a *fireball*. Most meteoroids are smaller than grains of sand.

meteor-burst communications technique for sending messages by bouncing radio waves off the fiery tails of ◊meteors. High-speed computer-controlled equipment is used to sense the presence of a meteor and to broadcast a signal during the short time that the meteor races across the sky. The system, first suggested in the late 1920s, remained impracticable until data-compression techniques were developed,

metamorphosis *An adult green darner dragonfly perched on its empty larval skin after metamorphosis. The green darner is found throughout North America, on Hawaii, and the E coast of Africa.*

enabling messages to be sent in automatic high-speed bursts each time a meteor trail appeared. There are usually enough meteor trails in the sky at any time to permit continuous transmission of a message. The technique offers a communications link that is difficult to jam, undisturbed by storms on the Sun, and would not be affected by nuclear war.

meteorite a piece of rock or metal from space that reaches the surface of the Earth, Moon, or other body. Meteorites are thought to be fragments from asteroids, although some may be pieces from the heads of comets. Most are stony, although some are made of iron and a few have a mixed rock-iron composition. Meteor Crater in Arizona, about 1,200 m/4,000 ft in diameter and 200 m/650 ft deep, is the site of a meteorite impact about 50,000 years ago.

Thousands of meteorites hit the Earth each year, but most fall in the sea or in remote areas and are never recovered. The largest known meteorite is one composed of iron, weighing 60 tonnes, which lies where it fell in prehistoric times at Grootfontein, Namibia. Meteorites are slowed down by the Earth's atmosphere, but if they are moving fast enough they can form a ◊crater on impact.

meteorology the scientific observation and study of the ◊atmosphere, so that weather can be accurately forecasted. Data from meteorological stations and weather satellites is collated by computer at central agencies such as the Meteorological Office in Bracknell, near London, and a forecast and ◊weather maps based on current readings are issued at regular intervals.

At meteorological stations readings are taken of the factors determining weather conditions: atmospheric pressure, temperature, humidity, wind (using the ◊Beaufort scale), cloud cover (measuring both type of cloud and coverage), and precipitation such as rain, snow, and hail (measured at 12-hourly intervals). Satellites are used either to relay information transmitted from the Earth-based stations, or to send pictures of cloud development, indicating wind patterns, and snow and ice cover.

meter an instrument used for measurement; the term is often compounded with a prefix to denote a specific type of meter, for example, ammeter, voltmeter, flowmeter, or pedometer.

methanal HCHO (common name *formaldehyde*) a gas at ordinary temperatures, condensing to a liquid at –21°C. It has a powerful penetrating smell. Dissolved in water, it is used as a biological preservative. It is used in manufacture of plastics, dyes, foam (for example urea-formaldehyde foam, used in insulation), and in medicine.

methane the simplest hydrocarbon, CH_4, of the paraffin series. Colourless, odourless, and lighter than air, it burns with a bluish flame, and explodes when mixed with air or oxygen. It is the chief constituent of natural gas and also occurs in the explosive firedamp of coal mines, and in marsh gas formed from rotting vegetation, where spontaneous combustion produces the pale flame seen over marshland and known as will-o'-the-wisp or ignis fatuus.

Methane is responsible for 38% of the warming of the globe through the greenhouse effect, and the amount of methane in the air is predicted to double over the next 60 years.

methanogenic bacteria one of a group of primitive bacteria (◊archaebacteria). They give off methane gas as a by-product of their metabolism, and are common in sewage-treatment plants and hot springs, where the temperature is high and oxygen is absent.

methanoic acid HCOOH (common name *formic acid*) a colourless, slightly fuming liquid that melts at 8°C and boils at 101°C. It occurs in stinging ants, nettles, sweat, and pine needles, and is used in dyeing, tanning, and electroplating.

methanol CH_3OH (common name *methyl alcohol*) the simplest of the alcohols. It can be made by the dry distillation of wood (hence it is also known as wood alcohol), but is usually made from coal or natural gas. When pure, it is a colourless, flammable liquid with a pleasant odour, and is highly poisonous.

Methanol is used to produce formaldehyde (from which resins and plastics can be made), methyl-tert-butyl ether (MTB, a replacement for lead as an octane-booster in petrol), vinyl acetate (largely used in paint manufacture), and petrol.

Method the US adaptation of ◊Stanislavsky's teachings on acting and direction, in which importance is attached to the psychological building of a role rather than the technical side of its presentation. Emphasis is placed on improvisation, aiming for a spontaneous and realistic style of acting. One of the principal exponents of the Method was the US actor and director Lee Strasberg, who taught at the ◊Actors Studio in New York.

Methodism evangelical Protestant Christian movement which was founded by John ◊Wesley 1739 within the Church of England, but which became a separate body 1795. The church government is presbyterian in Britain and episcopal in the USA. In 1988 there were over 50 million Methodists.

Methodist doctrines are contained in Wesley's sermons and *Notes on the New Testament*. A series of doctrinal divisions in the early 19th century were reconciled by a conference in London 1932 which brought Wesleyan methodists, primitive methodists, and United methodists into the Methodist Church. Supreme authority is vested in the annual conference (50% ministers, 50% lay people; members are grouped under 'class leaders' and churches into 'circuits'.

Expansion in the 19th century in developing industrial areas enabled people to overcome economic depression or change by spiritual means. Its encouragement of thrift and simple living helped many to raise their economic status. Smaller Methodist groups such as the Primitive Methodists and the Methodist New Connexion provided leadership in early trades unionism in disproportion to their size. Mainstream Wesleyans at first were conservative but identified increasingly with Gladstonian liberalism in the second half of the 19th century.

Methodius, St /me'θəυdɪəs/ *c.*825–884. Greek Christian bishop, who with his brother ◊Cyril translated much of the Bible into Slavonic. Feast day 14 Feb.

Methuselah /mə'θju:zələ/ in the Old Testament, Hebrew patriarch who lived before the Flood; his supposed age of 969 years made him a byword for longevity.

methyl alcohol another name for ◊methanol.

methylated spirit alcohol that has been rendered undrinkable. It is used for industrial purposes and is free of duty. It is nevertheless drunk by some individuals, resulting eventually in death. One of the poisonous substances in it is methanol, or methyl alcohol, and this gives it its name. (The 'alcohol' of alcoholic drinks is ethanol.)

methyl benzene another name for ◊toluene.

metonymy a figure of speech whose Greek name suggests a transferred title. When people speak or write metonymically they work by association. They may refer to the theatrical profession as 'the stage', or call journalists 'the press'. See also ◊synecdoche.

metre SI unit (symbol m) of length, equivalent to 1.093 yards. It is defined by scientists as the length of the path travelled by light in a vacuum during a time interval of 1/299,792,458 of a second.

metre (US **meter**) in poetry, the arrangement of syllables and words, usually according to the number and type of feet in a line. See also ◊verse.

metric system system of weights and measures developed in France in the 18th century and recognized by other countries including the UK in the 19th century. In 1960 an international conference on weights and measures recommended

the universal adoption of a revised International System (Système International d'Unités, or SI), with seven prescribed 'base units', the metre 'm' for length, kilogram 'kg' for mass, second 's' for time, ampere 'A' for electric current, kelvin 'K' for thermodynamic temperature, candela 'cd' for luminous intensity, and mole 'mol' for quantity of matter.

Two supplementary units are included in the SI system—the radian (rad) and steradian (sr)—used to measure plane and solid angles. In addition, there are recognized derived units which can be expressed as simple products or divisions of powers of the basic units, with no other integers appearing in the expression, for example the watt.

Some non-SI units, well established and internationally recognized, remain in use in conjunction with SI: minute, hour and day in measuring time; multiples or submultiples of base or derived units which have long-established names, such as tonne for mass, the litre for volume; and specialist measures such as the metric carat for gemstones.

Prefixes used with metric units are tera (T) million million times; giga (G) billion (thousand million) times; mega (M) million times; kilo (k) thousand times; hecto (h) hundred times; deka (da) ten times; deci (d) tenth part; centi (c) hundreth part ; milli (m) thousandth part; micro (μ) millionth part; nano (n) billionth part ; pico (p) trillionth part; femto (f) quadrillionth part; atto (a) quintillionth part.

The metric system was made legal for most purposes in the UK and USA in the 19th century. The UK government agreed to the adoption of SI as the primary system of weights and measures in 1965, but compulsion was abandoned in 1978, although Britain will have to conform to European Community regulations. A Metric Act was passed in the USA in 1975.

Metro-Goldwyn-Mayer (MGM) US film-production company 1924–1970s, when it was taken over by United Artists. MGM was formed by the amalgamation of the Metro Picture Corporation, the Goldwyn Picture Corporation, and Louis B Mayer Pictures. One of the most powerful Hollywood studios of the 1930s to the 1950s, it produced such prestige films as *David Copperfield* 1935 and *The Wizard of Oz* 1939. Among its stars were Greta Garbo, James Stewart, and Elizabeth Taylor.

metronome a clockwork device, invented by Johann Maelzel in 1814, using a sliding weight to regulate the speed of a pendulum to assist in keeping time.

metropolitan (Greek 'mother-state, capital') in the Christian church generally, a bishop who has rule over other bishops (termed **suffragans**). In the Church of England, the archbishops of York and Canterbury are both metropolitans. In the Eastern Orthodox Church, a metropolitan has a rank between an archbishop and a ◊patriarch.

metropolitan county in England, a group of six counties (1974–86) established under the Local Government Act 1972 in the major urban areas outside London: Tyne and Wear, South Yorkshire, Merseyside, West Midlands, Greater Manchester, and West Yorkshire. Their elected assemblies were abolished 1986 when their areas of responsibility reverted to district councils.

Metropolitan Opera Company foremost opera company in the USA, founded 1883 in New York. The Metropolitan Opera House (opened 1883) was demolished 1966, and the company transferred to the Lincoln Center.

Metsu /'metsju:/ Gabriel 1629–1667. Dutch painter, born in Leiden, active in Amsterdam from 1657. His paintings resemble those of Terborch. His main subjects were genre scenes, usually with a few well-dressed figures. He excelled in rich glossy fabrics.

Metternich /'metənɪk/ Klemens (Wenzel Lothar), Prince von Metternich 1773–1859. Austrian foreign minister from 1809 until the 1848 revolution forced him to flee to the UK. At the Congress

Metternich *The architect of the 1815 Congress of Vienna, Austrian chancellor and foreign minister Prince von Metternich.*

of Vienna 1815 he advocated cooperation by the great powers to suppress democratic movements.

Metz /mets/ industrial city (shoes, metal goods, tobacco) in Lorraine region, NE France, on the Moselle river; population (1982) 186,000. Part of the Holy Roman Empire 870–1552, it became one of the great frontier fortresses of France, and was in German hands 1871–1918.

Meurthe /mɜːt/ river rising in the Vosges mountains in NE France and flowing in a NW direction to join the Moselle at Frouard, near Nancy; length 163 km/102 mi. It gives its name to the *département* of Meurthe-et-Moselle.

Meuse /mɜːz/ (Dutch **Maas**) river flowing through France, Belgium, and the Netherlands; length 900 km/560 mi. It was a line of battle in both World Wars.

Mewar /me'wɑː/ another name for ◊Udaipur, a city in Rajasthan, India.

Mexicali /ˌmeksɪ'kæli/ city in NW Mexico; population (1984) 500,000. It produces soap and cottonseed oil. The availability of cheap labour attracts many US companies (Hughes Aerospace, Rockwell International, and others).

Mexican Empire short-lived empire 1822–23 following the liberation of Mexico from Spain. The empire lasted only eight months, under the revolutionary leader ◊Iturbide.

When the French emperor Napoleon I put his brother Joseph on the Spanish throne in 1808, links between Spain and its colonies weakened and an independence movement grew in Mexico. There were several unsuccessful uprisings until, in 1821, Gen Agustín de Iturbide published a plan promising independence, protection for the church, and the establishment of a monarchy. As no European came forward, in 1822 he proclaimed himself emperor. Forced to abdicate, he went into exile; on his return to Mexico he was ordered shot by republican leaders Guadalupe Victoria and Santa Anna. Victoria became the first president of Mexico.

Mexican War war between the USA and Mexico 1846–48, begun when Gen Zachary Taylor invaded New Mexico. Mexico City was taken 1847, and under the Treaty of Guadaloupe-Hidalgo, Mexico lost Texas, New Mexico, and California (half its territory) to the USA for $15 million compensation.

Mexico /'meksɪkəʊ/ country in Central America, bordered N by the USA, E by the Gulf of Mexico, SE by Belize and Guatemala, and SW and W by the Pacific Ocean.

government Mexico is a federal republic of 31 states and a federal district, based in Mexico City. The constitution dates from 1917.

Mexico
United States of
(Estados Unidos Mexicanos)

area 1,958,201 sq km/755,866 sq mi
capital Mexico City
towns Guadalajara, Monterrey; port Veracruz
physical partly arid central highlands flanked by Sierra Madre mountain ranges E and W; tropical coastal plains
features frontier of 2,000 miles with USA; resorts Acapulco, Mexicali, Tijuana; Baja California peninsula; volcanoes, such as Popocatepetl; archaeological sites of pre-Spanish period
head of state and government Carlos Salinas de Gortari from 1988

government federal democratic republic
political parties Institutional Revolutionary Party (PRI), moderate, left-wing; National Action Party (PAN), moderate Christian socialist
exports silver, gold, lead, uranium, oil, natural gas, traditional handicrafts, fish, shellfish
currency peso (free rate 4,109.63 = £1 Mar 1989)
population (1989) 88,087,000 (a minority are *criollos* of Spanish descent, 12% are American Indian, and the majority are of mixed descent; 50% of the total are under 20 years of age); annual growth rate 2.6%
life expectancy men 64, women 68
language Spanish (official); Indian languages include Nahuatl, Maya, and Mixtec
religion Roman Catholic
literacy 92% male/88% female (1985)
GNP $168 bn (1983); $1,800 per head of population
chronology
1821 Mexico achieved independence from Spain.
1846–48 Mexico at war with US.
1848 Maya Indian revolt suppressed.
1917 New constitution introduced, designed to establish permanent democracy.
1983–84 Financial crisis.
1985 Institutional Revolutionary Party (PRI) returned to power. Earthquake in Mexico City.
1986 IMF loan agreement signed to keep the country solvent until at least 1988.
1988 The PRI candidate, Carlos Salinas Gotari elected president.

Mexico City *The ornate Metropolitan Cathedral (1573) which stands at the centre of Mexico City.*

Legislative power rests with a two-chamber national congress of senate, chamber of deputies, and directly elected president, all serving a six-year term. The president chooses the cabinet. The Senate has 64 members, each state and the federal district being represented by two senators. The Chamber has 400 members: 300 representing single-member constituencies and 100 elected by proportional representation so as to give due weight to minority parties. Members of Congress are elected by universal suffrage. Each state has an elected governor and chamber of deputies, elected for a six-year term.

Political parties must register and meet certain criteria in order to operate. The main parties are the Institutional Revolutionary Party (PRI) and the National Action Party (PAN).

history Mexico was the centre of the ◊Maya civilization, which existed in Central America from about 1500 BC until the Spanish conquest in the 16th century AD. Other inhabitants were the Toltecs and the Aztecs, who settled on the central plateau and whose last king, Montezuma II, was killed 1520 during the Spanish invasion.

In 1535 Mexico became the viceroyalty of New Spain. Spanish culture and Catholicism were established, and the country's natural resources were exploited. Colonial rule became increasingly oppressive; the struggle for independence began 1810, and Spanish rule was ended 1821. The ◊Mexican Empire followed 1922–23.

Mexico's early history as an independent nation was marked by civil and foreign wars, and was dominated until 1855 by the dictator Antonio López de ◊Santa Anna. The US annexation of Texas 1835 brought about the ◊Mexican War 1846–48, in the course of which Mexico suffered further losses, including New Mexico and California. Santa Anna was overthrown 1855 by Benito Juárez, whose liberal reforms included many anti-clerical measures.

In 1861, enticed by the offer of 30% of the proceeds, France planned to intervene in the recovery of 79 million francs owed to a Swiss banker by former Mexican president Miramon, who was overthrown and exiled by Juárez 1860.

Seeking to regain power, in 1862 Miramon appealed to Empress Eugénie, consort of Napoleon III, saying that steps must be taken against Juárez and his anti-Christian policies. Eugénie proposed Maximilian, the brother of Emperor Franz-Josef of Austria. Napoleon agreed, since the plan suited his colonial ambitions, and in 1864 Maximilian accepted the crown offered him by conservative opponents of Juárez. Juárez and his supporters continued to fight against this new branch of the Habsburg empire, and in 1867 the monarchy collapsed and Maximilian was executed.

There followed a capitalist dictatorship under Gen Porfirio Diaz, who gave the country stability but whose handling of the economy made him unpopular. He was overthrown 1910 by Madero, who re-established a liberal regime but was himself assassinated 1913. The 1910 revolution brought changes in land ownership, labour legislations, and reduction in the powers of the Roman Catholic Church.

The broadly based PRI has dominated Mexican politics since the 1920s, pursuing moderate, left-of-centre policies. Its popularity has been damaged in recent years by the country's poor economic performance and rising international debts. However, despite criticisms from vested-interest groups such as the trade unions and the church, the PRI scored a clear win in the 1985 elections. The government's problems grew worse later that year when an earthquake in Mexico City caused thousands of deaths and made hundreds of thousands homeless.

Mexico's foreign policy has been influenced by its proximity to the USA. At times the Mexican government has criticized US policy in Central America, and as a member, with Colombia, Panama, and Venezuela, of the ◊Contadora Group, has argued for the withdrawal of all foreign advisers from the region. Despite claims of frauds during the 1988 elections, the PRI candidate, Carlos Salinas de Gortari, was declared president by the electoral college.

Mexico City /ˈmeksɪkəʊ/ (Spanish *Ciudad de México*) capital, and industrial (iron, steel, chemicals, textiles) and cultural centre of Mexico, 2,255 m/7,400 ft above sea level on the southern edge of the central plateau; population (1986) 18,748,000. It is thought to be the most polluted city in the world.

Notable buildings include the 16th-century cathedral, the national palace, national library, Palace of Justice, and national university; the Ministry of Education has murals 1923–27 by Diego Rivera.

The city dates from about 1325, when the Aztec capital Tenochtitlán was begun on an island in Lake Texcoco. This city was levelled 1521 by the Spaniards, who in 1522 founded a new city on the site. It was the location of the 1968 Summer Olympics. In 1984, the explosion of a liquefied gas tank caused the deaths of over 450 people, and in 1985, over 2,000 were killed by a earthquake.

Meyerbeer /ˈmaɪəbeə/ Giacomo. Adopted name of Jakob Liebmann Beer 1791–1864. German composer. He is renowned for his spectacular operas, including *Robert le Diable* 1831 and *Les Huguenots* 1836. From 1826 he lived mainly in Paris, returning to Berlin after 1842 as musical director of the Royal Opera.

mezuzah in Judaism, a small box containing a parchment scroll inscribed with a prayer, the Shema, which is found on the doorpost of every room in a Jewish house except the bathroom.

mezzanine architectural term (derived from the diminutive of the Italian *mezzano*, middle) for a storey with a lower ceiling placed between two higher storeys, usually between the ground and first floors of a building.

mezzogiorno /ˌmetsəʊˈdʒɔːnəʊ/ (Italian 'midday') the hot, impoverished regions of S Italy.

mezzo-soprano female singing voice halfway between soprano and contralto.

mezzotint a print produced by a method of etching in density of tone rather than line, popular in the 18th and 19th centuries. A copper or steel plate is worked with a tool that raises a burr (rough edge), which will hold ink. The burr is then scraped away to produce a range of lighter tones.

MFA abbreviation for ◊*Multi-Fibre Arrangement.*

Mfecane in African history, a series of disturbances in the early 19th century among communities in what is today the eastern part of South Africa. They arose when chief ◊Shaka conquered the Nguni peoples between the Tugela and Pongola rivers, then created by conquest a centralized, militaristic Zulu kingdom from several communities, resulting in large-scale displacement of people.

mg abbreviation for *milligram*.

Mgr in the Roman Catholic Church, the abbreviation for *Monsignor*.

MHD abbreviation for ◊*magnetohydrodynamics*.

mho SI unit of electrical conductance, now called the ◊siemens; equivalent to a reciprocal ohm.

mi abbreviation for *mile*.

MI abbreviation for ◊*Michigan*.

Miami /maɪˈæmi/ city and port in Florida, USA; population (1984) 383,000. It is the hub of finance, trade, and air transport for Latin America and the Caribbean.

There has been an influx of immigrants from Cuba, Haiti, Mexico, and South America since 1959. It is also a centre for oceanographic research, and a tourist resort for its beaches.

Miandad /miˈændæd/ Javed 1957– . Pakistani test cricketer, his country's leading run-maker. He scored a century on his test debut in 1976 and has since gone on to be one of a handful of players to make 100 test appearances. He has captained his country. His highest score of 311 was made when he was aged 17.

CAREER HIGHLIGHTS

All First-Class Matches
runs 25,400
average 53.58
best 311 Karachi Whites v. National Bank 1974–75
Test Cricket
runs 7,422
average 57.09
best 280 not out v. India 1982–83

mica a group of silicate minerals that split easily into thin flakes along lines of weakness in their crystal structure (perfect basal cleavage). They are glossy, have a pearly lustre, and are found in many igneous and metamorphic rocks. Their good thermal and electrical insulation qualities make them valuable in industry.

Their chemical composition is complicated, but they are silicates with silicon-oxygen tetrahedra arranged in continuous sheets, with weak bonding between the layers, resulting in perfect cleavage. A common example of mica is muscovite (white mica), $KAl_2Si_3Al_{10}(OH)_2$.

Micah /ˈmaɪkə/ 8th century BC. In the Old Testament, a Hebrew prophet whose writings denounce the oppressive ruling class of Judah and demand justice.

Michael /ˈmaɪkəl/ in the Bible, an archangel, referred to as the guardian angel of Israel. In the New Testament Book of Revelation he leads the hosts of heaven to battle against Satan. In paintings he is depicted with a flaming sword and sometimes a pair of scales. Feast day 29 Sept (Michaelmas).

Michael /ˈmaɪkəl/ Mikhail Fyodorovich Romanov 1596–1645. Tsar of Russia from 1613. He was elected tsar by a national assembly, at a time of chaos and foreign invasion, and was the first of the house of Romanov, which ruled until 1917.

Michael /ˈmaɪkəl/ 1921– . King of Romania 1927–30 and 1940–47. The son of Carol II, he succeeded his grandfather as king 1927, but was displaced when his father returned from exile 1930. In 1940 he was proclaimed king again on his father's abdication, and in 1944 overthrew the fascist dictatorship of Ion Antonescu (1882–1946) and enabled Romania to share in the victory of the Allies at the end of the World War II. He abdicated and left Romania 1947.

michaelmas daisy popular name for species of ◊aster, family Compositae, and also for the sea aster or starwort.

Michaelmas Day in Christian church tradition, the festival of St Michael and all angels, observed 29 Sept, and one of the English ◊quarter days.

Michelangelo /ˌmaɪkəlˈændʒələu/ Buonarroti 1475–1564. Italian sculptor, painter, architect, and poet, active in his native Florence and in

Michelangelo *David (1501) Accademia, Florence.*

Rome. His giant talent dominated the High Renaissance. The marble *David* 1501–04 (Accademia, Florence) set a new standard in nude sculpture. His massive figure style was translated into fresco in the Sistine Chapel 1508–12 and 1536–41 (Vatican). Other works in Rome include the dome of St Peter's basilica.

Born near Florence, he was a student of Ghirlandaio and trained under the patronage of Lorenzo de' Medici. His patrons later included several popes and Medici princes. In 1496 he completed the *Pietà* (St Peter's, Rome), a technically brilliant piece that established his reputation. Also in Rome he began the great tomb of Pope Julius II: *The Slaves* (Louvre, Paris) and *Moses* (S Pietro in Vincoli, Rome) were sculpted for this unfinished

project. His grandiose scheme for the Sistine Chapel tells, on the ceiling, the Old Testament story from Genesis to the Deluge, and on the altar wall he later added a vast *Last Judgement*.

From 1516 to 1534 he was again in Florence, where his chief work was the design of the Medici sepulchral chapel in S Lorenzo. Back in Rome he became chief architect of St Peter's in 1547. His friendship with Vittoria Colonna (1492–1547), a noblewoman, inspired many of his sonnets and madrigals.

Michels /ˈmɪklz/ Robert 1876–1936. German social and political theorist. Originally a radical, he became a critic of socialism and Marxism, and in his last years supported Hitler and Mussolini. In *Political Parties* 1911 he propounded the **Iron Law of Oligarchy**, arguing that in any organization or society, even a democracy, there is a tendency towards rule by the few in the interests of the few, and that ideologies like socialism and communism were merely propaganda to control the masses. He believed that the rise of totalitarian governments—both fascist and communist—in the 1930s confirmed his analysis and proved that the masses were incapable of asserting their own interests.

Michelson /ˈmaɪkəlsən/ Albert Abraham 1852–1931. German-born US physicist. In conjunction with Edward Morley, he performed in 1887 the *Michelson–Morley experiment* to detect the motion of the Earth through the postulated ether (a medium believed to be necessary for the propagation of light). The failure of the experiment indicated the nonexistence of the ether, and led ◊Einstein to his theory of ◊relativity. Nobel prize 1907.

He invented the Michelson interferometer, made precise measurement of the speed of light, and from 1892 was professor of physics at the University of Chicago.

Michigan /ˈmɪʃɪgən/ state of the USA, bordered by the Great Lakes, Ohio, Indiana, Wisconsin, and Canada; nickname Great Lake State or Wolverine State
area 151,600 sq km/58,518 sq mi
capital Lansing
towns Detroit, Grand Rapids, Flint
features Lake Michigan; Porcupine Mountains; Muskegon, Grand, St Joseph, and Kalamazoo rivers; over 50% forested

Michelson *Albert Abraham Michelson's interferometer. The instrument was used to take measurements in the Michelson–Morley experiment designed to detect a difference in the velocities of light in directions parallel to and perpendicular to the motion of the Earth.*

Michigan

Lansing

products cars, iron, cement, oil
population (1986) 9,145,000
famous people George Custer, Edna Ferber, Henry Ford
history explored by the French from 1618, it became British 1763, and a US state 1837.

In 1973, 97% of the population were contaminated by PBB (poly-brominated biphenyl), a flame-retardant chemical inadvertently mixed with livestock feed.

Michigan, Lake /'mɪʃɪgən/ lake in north central USA, one of the Great Lakes; area 58,000 sq km/22,390 sq mi. Chicago and Milwaukee are its main ports. Lake Michigan is joined to Lake Huron by the Straits of Mackinac. Green Bay is the major inlet.

Mickiewicz /,mɪtski'evɪtʃ/ Adam 1798–1855. Polish revolutionary poet, whose *Pan Tadeusz* 1832–34 is Poland's national epic. He died at Constantinople while raising a Polish corps to fight against Russia in the Crimean War.

micro- prefix denoting one millionth part (symbol μ). For example a micrometre, μm, is one millionth of a metre.

microbe another name for ◊microorganism.

microbiological warfare use of harmful microbes as a weapon. See ◊biological warfare.

microbiology the study of organisms that can only be seen under the microscope, mostly single-celled organisms such as viruses, bacteria, protozoa, and yeasts. The practical applications of microbiology are in medicine (since many microorganisms cause disease); in brewing, baking, and so on, where the microorganisms carry out fermentation; and in genetic engineering, which is making microbiology an increasingly important field.

microchip popular name for the ◊silicon chip or ◊integrated circuit.

microcomputer or **micro** a small desktop or portable computer, typically designed to be used by one person at a time. Microcomputers are the smallest of the four classes of computer (the others are ◊supercomputer, ◊mainframe, and ◊minicomputer). Since the appearance in 1975 of the first commercially available microcomputer, the Altair 8800, micros have become widely accepted in commerce and industry.

microeconomics the division of economics concerned with the study of individual decision-making units within an economy: a consumer, firm, or industry. Unlike macroeconomics, it looks at how individual markets work and how individual producers and consumers make their choices and with what consequences. This is done by analysing how relevant prices of goods are determined and the quantities that will be bought and sold.

For simplicity, microeconomics begins by analysing a market in which there is **perfect competition**, a theoretical state which exists only when no individual producer or consumer can influence the market price. In the real world, there is always imperfect competition for various reasons (monopoly practices, barriers to trade, and so on), and microeconomics examines what effect these have on wages and prices.

Underlying these and other concerns of microeconomics is the concept of **optimality**, first advanced by Vilfredo ◊Pareto in the 19th century. Pareto's perception of the most efficient state of an economy, when there is no scope to reallocate resources without making someone worse off, has been extremely influential.

microfiche sheet of film on which printed text is photographically reduced. See ◊microform.

microform generic name for media on which text or images are photgraphically reduced. The main examples are **microfilm** (similar to the film in an ordinary camera) and **microfiche** (flat sheets of film, generally 105 mm × 148 mm, holding the equivalent of 420 A4 sheets). Microform has the advantages of low reproduction and storage costs, but it requires special devices for reading the text. It is widely used for archiving and for storing large volumes of text such as library catalogues.

microlight aircraft very light aircraft with a small engine, rather like a powered hang-glider.

micrometer instrument for measuring minute lengths or angles with great accuracy; different types of micrometer are used in astronomical and engineering work.

The type of micrometer used in astronomy consists of two fine wires, one fixed and the other movable, placed in the focal plane of a telescope; the movable wire is fixed on a sliding plate and can be positioned parallel to the other until the object appears between the wires. The movement is then indicated by a scale on the adjusting screw.

The **micrometer gauge**, of great value in engineering, has its adjustment effected by an extremely accurate fine-pitch screw (◊vernier).

micrometre one millionth of a ◊metre.

microminiaturization the reduction in size and weight of electronic components. The first size reduction in electronics was brought about by the introduction of the ◊transistor. Further reductions were achieved with ◊integrated circuits and the ◊silicon chip.

micron obsolete name for the ◊micrometre.

Micronesia /,maɪkrəʊ'ni:ziə/ islands in the Pacific Ocean lying N of ◊Melanesia, including the Federated States of Micronesia, Belau, Kiribati, the Mariana and Marshall Islands, Nauru, and Tuvalu.

Micronesia, Federated States of /,maɪkrəʊ'ni:ziə/ self-governing island group (Kosrae, Ponape, Truk, and Yap) in the W Pacific; capital Kolonia,

Micronesia

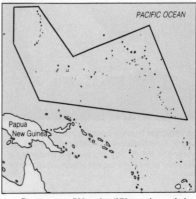

PACIFIC OCEAN

Papua New Guinea

on Ponape; area 700 sq km/270 sq mi; population (1988) 86,000. It is part of the US Trust Territory. Purchased by Germany from Spain 1898, they were occupied 1914 by Japan. They were captured by the USA in World War II, and became part of the US Trust Territory of the Pacific 1947. Micronesia became internally self-governing from 1979, and in free association with the USA from 1986 (there is US control of military activities in return for economic aid). The people are Micronesian and Polynesian, and the main languages are Kosrean, Ponapean, Trukese, and Yapese, although the official language is English.

Micronesian inhabitant of Micronesia. Their languages belong to the Austronesian family.

microorganism or **microbe** a living organism invisible to the naked eye but visible under a microscope. Most are single-celled; they include bacteria, protozoa, yeasts, viruses, and some algae.

microphone the first component in a sound-reproducing system, whereby the mechanical energy of sound waves is converted into electrical energy. One of the simplest is the telephone receiver mouthpiece, invented by Alexander Graham Bell in 1876; other types of microphone are used in broadcasting and sound-film apparatus.

Telephones have a **carbon microphone**, which reproduces only a narrow range of frequencies. For live music, a **moving-coil microphone** is often used. In it, a diaphragm that vibrates with sound waves moves a coil through a magnetic field, thus generating an electric current. The **ribbon microphone** combines the diaphragm and coil. The **condenser microphone** is most common in recording and works by a ◊capacitor.

microprocessor a computer's central processing unit (◊CPU) contained on a single ◊integrated circuit. The appearance of the first microprocessors in 1971 heralded the introduction of the microcomputer. The microprocessor has led to a dramatic fall in the size and cost of computers and to the introduction of ◊dedicated computers in washing machines, cars, and so on.

microscope instrument for magnification with high resolution for detail. Optical and electron microscopes are the ones chiefly in use; other types include acoustic and X-ray. In 1988 a scanning tunnelling microscope was used to photograph a single protein molecule for the first time. Laser microscopy is under development.

The **optical microscope** usually has two sets of glass lenses and an eyepiece. It was invented 1609 in the Netherlands by Zacharias Janssen (1580–c.1638).

The **electron microscope** (developed from 1932) passes a beam of electrons through a specimen instead of a beam of light, and, since these are not visible, replaces the eyepiece with a fluorescent screen or photographic plate; far higher magnification and resolution is possible than with the optical microscope.

The **scanning electron microscope** (SEM), developed in the mid-1960s, moves a fine beam of electrons over the surface of a specimen, the

micrometer

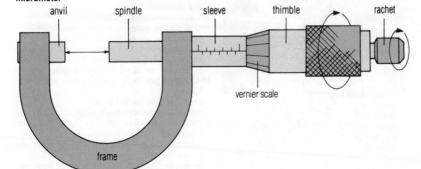

anvil   spindle   sleeve   thimble   rachet

vernier scale

frame

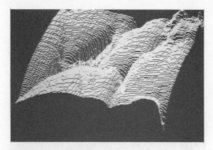

microscope *Scanning tunnelling microscope (STM) image, magnified about 250, 000 times, of a high purity gold surface. Scanning tunnelling microscopy is based on quantum mechanical effects and can reveal individual atoms.*

reflected electrons being collected to form the image. The specimen has to be in a vacuum chamber.

The *acoustic microscope* passes an acoustic (ultrahigh-frequency sound) wave through the specimen, the transmitted sound being used to form an image on a computer screen.

The *scanned-probe microscope* (developed in the late 1980s) runs a probe, with a tip so fine that it may consist only of a single atom, across the surface of the specimen, which requires no special preparation. In the scanning tunnelling microscope, an electric current that flows through the probe is used to construct an image of the specimen. In the atomic force microscope, the force felt by the probe is measured and used to form the image. These instruments can magnify a million times and give images of single atoms.

microtubules tiny tubes found in almost all cells with a nucleus. They help to define the shape of a cell by forming scaffolding for cilia and form fibres of mitotic spindle.

microwave an ◊electromagnetic wave with a wavelength in the range 0.1 to 30 cm (between radio waves and ◊infrared radiation). They are used in radar, as carrier waves in radio broadcasting, and in microwave heating and cooking.

microwave heating heating by means of ◊microwaves. Microwave ovens use this form of heating for the rapid cooking or reheating of foods, where heat is generated throughout the food simultaneously. Industrially, microwave heating is used for destroying insects in grain and enzymes in processed food; for pasteurizing and sterilizing liquids; and drying timber and paper.

Midas /'maɪdæs/ in Greek legend, a king of Phrygia who was granted the gift of converting all he touched to gold, and who, for preferring the music of Pan to that of Apollo, was given ass's ears by the latter.

MIDAS /'maɪdæs/ acronym for *Mi*ssile *D*efence *A*larm *S*ystem.

Mid-Atlantic Ridge the ◊ocean ridge, formed by the movement of plates described by ◊plate tectonics, that runs along the centre of the Atlantic Ocean, parallel to its edges, for some 14,000 km/8,800 mi, almost from the Arctic to the Antarctic.

The Mid-Atlantic Ridge is central because the ocean crust beneath the Atlantic Ocean has continually grown outwards from the ridge at a steady rate during the past 200 million years. Iceland straddles the ridge and was formed by volcanic outpourings.

Middelburg /'mɪdlbɜ:g/ industrial town (engineering, tobacco, furniture) in SW Netherlands, capital of Zeeland and former ◊Hanseatic town ; population (1985) 38,930. Its town hall dates from the 15th-century.

Middle Ages the period of European history between the fall of the Roman Empire in the 5th century and the Renaissance in the 15th. Among the period's distinctive features were the unity of W Europe within the Roman Catholic church, the feudal organization of political, social, and

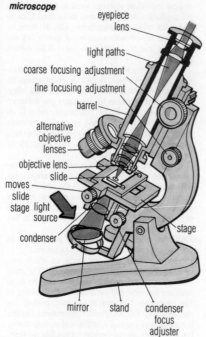

microscope

eyepiece lens

light paths

coarse focusing adjustment

fine focusing adjustment

barrel

alternative objective lenses

objective lens

slide

moves slide stage light source

condenser

stage

mirror   stand   condenser focus adjuster

economic relations, and the use of art for largely religious purposes.

It can be divided into three sub-periods:

The *early Middle Ages*, 5th–11th centuries, when Europe was settled by pagan Germanic tribes who adopted the vestiges of Roman institutions and traditions, were converted to Christianity by the church (which had preserved Latin culture after the fall of Rome), and who then founded feudal kingdoms;

The *High Middle Ages*, 12th–13th centuries, which saw the consolidation of feudal states,

Mid-Atlantic Ridge

Greenland

Iceland

North America

Reykjanes ridge

mid-Atlantic ridge

Europe

Newfoundland

fractures transverse to main mid-ocean ridge

mid-Atlantic ridge

Africa

South America

mid-Atlantic ridge

arrows indicate direction of spreading of material extruded from the mid-ocean ridge

Atlantic–Indian ridge

Falkland Islands

the expansion of European influence during the ◊Crusades, the flowering of ◊scholasticism and monasteries, and the growth of population and trade;

The *later Middle Ages*, 14th–15th centuries, when Europe was devastated by the ◊Black Death and incessant warfare, ◊feudalism was transformed under the influence of incipient nation-states and new modes of social and economic organization, and the first voyages of discovery were made.

middle C the white note at the centre of the piano keyboard, indicating the division between left and right-hand regions and corresponding to the treble and bass staves of printed music.

Middle East indeterminate area now usually taken to include the Balkan States, Egypt, and SW Asia. Until the 1940s, this area was generally called the Near East, and the term Middle East referred to the area from Iran to Burma.

Middle English the period of the ◊English language from about 1050 to 1550.

Middle Kingdom *Egyptian* a period of Egyptian history extending from the late 11th to the 13th dynasty (roughly 2040–1670 BC);

Chinese Chinese term for China and its empire up to 1912, describing its central position in the Far East.

Middlemarch A Study of Provincial Life a novel by George Eliot, published in England 1871–72. Set in the fictitious provincial town of Middlemarch, the novel has several interwoven plots played out against a background of social and political upheaval.

Middle Range or *Middleback range* mountain range in the NE of Eyre Peninsula, South Australia, about 65 km/40 mi long, parallel with the W coast of Spencer Gulf. Iron deposits are mined at Iron Baron, Iron Knob, and Iron Monarch.

Middlesbrough /'mɪdlzbrə/ industrial town and port on the Tees, Cleveland, England, commercial and cultural centre of the urban area formed by Stockton-on-Tees, Redcar, Billingham, Thornaby, and Eston; population (1983) 148,400. Formerly a centre of heavy industry, it diversified its products in the 1960s. It is the birthplace of the navigator Captain James Cook (1728–79).

Middlesex /'mɪdlseks/ former English county, absorbed by Greater London in 1965. Contained within the Thames basin, it provided good agricultural land before it was built over. It was settled in the 6th century by Saxons, and its name comes from its position between the kingdoms of the East and West Saxons. The name is still used, as in Middlesex County Cricket Club.

Middleton /'mɪdltən/ Thomas c.1570–1627. English dramatist. He produced numerous romantic plays, tragedies, and realistic comedies, both alone and in collaboration. The best-known are *A Fair Quarrel* and *The Changeling* 1622 with Rowley; *The Roaring Girl* with Dekker; and *Women Beware Women* 1621. His political satire *A Game at Chess* 1624 was concerned with the plots to unite the royal houses of England and Spain, and caused a furore with the authorities.

Middle Way the path to enlightenment, taught by Buddha, which avoids the extremes of indulgence and asceticism.

Middx abbreviation for ◊*Middlesex*.

midge popular name for many insects resembling ◊gnats, generally divided into biting midges (family Ceratopogonidae) that suck blood, and non-biting midges (family Chironomidae). The larvae of some midges are the 'bloodworms' of stagnant water.

Mid Glamorgan /'mɪd glə'mɔ:gən/ county in S Wales

area 1,020 sq km/394 sq mi

towns administrative headquarters Cardiff; resort Porthcawl; Aberdare, Merthyr Tydfil, Bridgend, Pontypridd

features Caerphilly Castle, with its water defences

products the north was formerly an important coal (Rhondda) and iron and steel area; Royal Mint

Mid Glamorgan

at Llantrisant; agriculture in the south; Caerphilly noted for mild cheese

population (1987) 535,000

language 8% Welsh, English.

MIDI abbreviation for *Musical Instrument Digital Interface*, a manufacturer's standard allowing different pieces of digital music equipment used in composing and recording to be freely connected.

The information-sending device (any electronic instrument) is called a controller and the reading device (such as a computer) the sequencer. Pitch, dynamics, decay rate, and stereo 'position' may all be transmitted via the interface.

Midi-Pyrénées /mɪˈdi: ˌpɪrəˈneɪ/ region of SW France; area 45,300 sq km/17,486 sq mi; population (1986) 2,355,000. Its capital is Toulouse, and it consists of the *départements* of Ariège, Aveyron, Haute-Garonne, Gers, Lot, Haute-Pyrénées, Tarn, and Tarn-et-Garonne. Towns include Montauban, Cahors, Rodez, and Lourdes. The region includes a number of spa towns, winter resorts, and prehistoric caves.

Midlands /ˈmɪdləndz/ area of England corresponding roughly to the Anglo-Saxon kingdom of ◊Mercia. *E Midlands* Derbyshire, Leicestershire, Northamptonshire, Nottinghamshire. *W Midlands* the former metropolitan county of ◊West Midlands created from parts of Staffordshire, Warwickshire, and Worcestershire; and (often included) *S Midlands* Bedfordshire, Buckinghamshire, and Oxfordshire.

In World War II, the E Midlands was worked for oil, and substantial finds were made in the 1980s; the oilbearing E Midlands Shelf extends into Yorkshire and Lincolnshire.

Midlothian /mɪdˈləʊðɪən/ former Scottish county S of the Firth of Forth, included 1975 in the region of Lothian; Edinburgh was the administrative headquarters.

midnight sun the constant appearance of the Sun (within the Arctic and Antarctic circles) above the ◊horizon during the summer.

Midrash /ˈmɪdræʃ/ (Hebrew 'inquiry') the ancient Jewish commentaries on the Bible, in the form of sermons in which allegory and legendary illustration are used. They were compiled mainly in Palestine between AD 400 and 1200.

midshipman a trainee naval officer. In the UK, a midshipman has either completed the first year at the Royal Naval College, Dartmouth, or is in his first year with the fleet, after which he becomes an acting sublieutenant. In the US students training at the naval academy are called midshipmen.

midsummer the summer ◊solstice, about 21 June. Midsummer's Day is 24 June, the Christian festival of St John the Baptist.

Midsummer Night's Dream, A a comedy by William Shakespeare, first performed 1595–96. Hermia, Lysander, Demetrius, and Helena in their various romantic endeavours are subjected to the playful

manipulations of the fairies Puck and Oberon in a wood near Athens. Titania, queen of the fairies, is similarly bewitched and falls in love with Bottom, a stupid weaver, whose head has been turned into that of an ass.

Midway Islands /ˈmɪdweɪ/ two islands in the Pacific, 1,800 km/1,120 mi NW of Honolulu; area 5 sq km/2 sq mi; population (1980) 500. They were annexed by the USA 1867, and are now administered by the US Navy. The naval *Battle of Midway* 3–6 June 1942, between the USA and Japan, was the turning point in the Pacific in World War II.

Midwest /ˌmɪdˈwest/ or *Middle West* a large area of N central USA. It is a loosely defined, but is generally taken to comprise the states of Ohio, Indiana, Illinois, Michigan, Iowa, Wisconsin, Minnesota, and sometimes Nebraska. It tends to be conservative socially and politically, and isolationist. Traditionally its economy is divided between agriculture and heavy industry.

midwifery the assistance of women in childbirth. Traditionally, it was undertaken by unqualified helpers, but today, in many developed countries, it is the province of the specialist.

Mies van der Rohe /ˈmiːs ˌvæn də ˈrəʊə/ Ludwig 1886–1969. German architect who practised in the USA from 1937. He was director of the ◊Bauhaus 1929–33. He became professor at the Illinois Technical Institute 1938–58, for which he designed new buildings on characteristically functional lines from 1941. He also designed the bronze-and-glass Seagram building in New York 1956–59.

Mifune /miːˈfuːneɪ/ Toshiro 1920– . Japanese actor who appeared in several films directed by ◊Kurosawa, including *Rashomon* 1950 and *Throne of Blood* 1957. He has also appeared in European and American films.

mignonette sweet-scented plant *Reseda odorata*, native to N Africa, bearing yellowish-green flowers in racemes (along the main stem), with abundant foliage. It was brought to England about 1752; related species are found in the wild.

migraine acute, sometimes incapacitating headaches that recur, often with advance symptoms such as flashing lights, and are accompanied by nausea. No cure has been discovered, but ◊ergotamine normally relieves the symptoms. Some sufferers learn to avoid particular foods (such as chocolate), which suggests an allergic factor.

migrant labour people who leave their homelands to work elsewhere, usually because of economic or political pressures.

The world's pool of legal and illegal immigrants is an important economic and social force. About 7 million migrants were employed in the Middle East during the 1970s and early 1980s, but the subsequent decline in jobs had severe financial

consequences for India and Sri Lanka, who supplied the workers. S Europe has also been a traditional source of migrant workers.

migration the movement, either seasonal or as part of a single life cycle, of certain animals, chiefly birds and fish, to distant breeding or feeding grounds.

The precise methods by which animals navigate and know where to go are still obscure. Birds have much sharper eyesight and better visual memory of ground clues than humans, but in long-distance flights appear to navigate by the Sun and stars, possibly in combination with a 'reading' of the Earth's magnetic field through an inbuilt 'magnetic compass', which is a tiny mass of tissue between the eye and brain in birds. Similar cells occur in 'homing' honeybees, and in certain bacteria which use it to determine which way is 'down'. Most striking, however, is the migration of young birds which have never flown a route before and are unaccompanied by adults. It is postulated that they may inherit as part of their genetic code an overall 'sky chart' of their journey which is triggered into use when they become aware of how the local sky pattern above the place in which they hatch fits into it. Similar theories have been advanced in the case of fish, such as eels and salmon, with whom vision obviously plays a less important role, but for whom currents and changes in the composition and temperature of the sea in particular locations may play a part, for example in enabling salmon to return to the precise river in which they were spawned. Migrations also occurs with land animals, for example, lemmings and antelope. Related to migration is the homing ability of pigeons, bees, and other creatures.

Mihailović /mɪˈhaɪləvɪtʃ/ Draza 1893–1946. Yugoslav soldier, leader of the guerrilla ◊Chetniks of World War II against the German occupation. His feud with Tito's communists led to the withdrawal of Allied support and that of his own exiled government from 1943. He turned for help to the Italians and Germans, and was eventually shot for treason.

mikado (Japanese 'honourable palace gate') title until 1867 of the Japanese emperor, when it was replaced by the term 'tennō' (heavenly sovereign).

Milan /mɪˈlæn/ (Italian *Milano*) industrial city (aircraft, cars, locomotives, textiles), financial and cultural centre, capital of Lombardy, Italy; population (1988) 1,479,000.

features The Gothic cathedral, built about 1450, crowned with pinnacles, can hold 40,000 worshippers; the Brera art gallery; the convent with Leonardo da Vinci's *Last Supper* 1495–97; La Scala opera house (Italian *Teatro alla Scala*) 1778; an annual trade fair.

history Settled by the Gauls in the 5th century BC, it was conquered by the Roman consul Marcellus 222 BC to become the Roman city of *Mediolanum*. Under Diocletian, in AD 286 Milan

migration

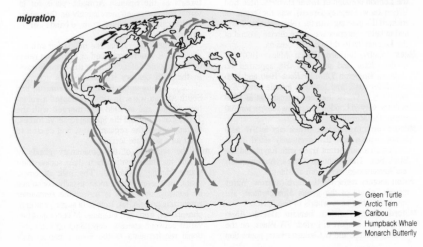

Green Turtle
Arctic Tern
Caribou
Humpback Whale
Monarch Butterfly

Milan *The Gothic cathedral, built about 1450, can hold up to 40,000 worshippers.*

was capital of the Western empire. Destroyed by Attila the Hun 452, and again by the Goths 539, the city regained its power through the political importance of its bishops. It became an autonomous commune 1045; then followed a long struggle for supremacy in Lombardy.

The city was taken by ◊Frederick I (Barbarossa) 1162; only in 1176 were his forces finally defeated, at the battle of Legnano. Milanese forces were again defeated by the emperor at the battle of Cortenuova 1237. In the Guelph-Ghibelline struggle the Visconti family emerged at the head of the Ghibelline faction; they gained power 1277, establishing a dynasty which lasted until 1450 when Francesco Sforza seized control and became duke. The Sforza court marked the highpoint of Milan as a cultural and artistic centre. Control of the city passed to Louis XII of France 1499, and in 1540 it was annexed by Spain, beginning a long decline. The city was ceded to Austria by the Treaty of ◊Utrecht 1714, and in the 18th century began a period of intellectual enlightenment. Milan was in 1796 taken by Napoleon, who made it the capital of the Cisalpine Republic 1799, and in 1805 capital of the kingdom of Italy until 1814, when it reverted to the Austrians. In 1848, Milan rebelled unsuccessfully (the *Cinque Giornate/Five Days*), and in 1859 was joined to Piedmont.

Milankovitch hypothesis the combination of factors governing the occurrence of ◊ice ages proposed in 1930 by the Yugoslavian geophysicist Milankovitch (1879–1958).

mildew minute fungi that appear as a destructive growth on plants, paper, leather, or wood, when exposed to damp; they form a thin white coating.

Mildura /mɪlˈdʊərə/ town in NW Victoria, Australia, on the Murray River, with food-processing industries; population (1985) 16,500.

mile imperial measure of length. A statute mile is equal to 1,760 yd (1.60934 km), and an international nautical mile is equal to 1,852 m/2,026 yd.

Mile End /ˈmaɪl ˈend/ area of the East End of London, in the district of Stepney, now part of the London borough of Tower Hamlets. Mile End Green (now Stepney Green) was the scene of Richard II's meeting with the rebel peasants 1381, and in later centuries was the exercise ground of the London 'trained bands', or ◊militia.

Miles /maɪlz/ Bernard (Baron Miles) 1907– . English actor and producer. He appeared on stage as Briggs in *Thunder Rock* 1940 and Iago in *Othello* 1942, and his films include *Great Expectations* 1947. He founded a trust that in 1959 built the City of London's first new theatre for 300 years, the Mermaid.

Miletus /mɪˈliːtəs/ ancient Greek city in SW Asia Minor, with a port that eventually silted up. It carried on an important trade with Egypt and the Black Sea. The scientists Thales, Anaximander, and Anaximenes were born at Miletus.

milfoil another name for the herb ◊yarrow. Water milfoils, plants of the genus *Miriophyllum*, are unrelated; they have whorls of fine leaves.

Milford Haven /ˈmɪlfəd ˈheɪvən/ (Welsh *Aberdaugleddau*) seaport in Dyfed, SW Wales, on the estuary of the E and W Cleddau rivers; population (1985) 14,000. It has oil refineries, and a terminal for giant tankers linked by pipeline with Llandarcy, near Swansea.

Milford Haven, Marquess of /ˈmɪlfəd ˈheɪvən/ title given in 1917 to Prince ◊Louis of Battenberg (1854–1921).

Milhaud /ˈmiːjəʊ/ Darius 1892–1974. French composer, a member of the group of composers known as ◊*Les Six*. Among his works are the operas *Christophe Colombe* 1928 and *Bolivar* 1943, and the jazz ballet *La Création du monde* 1923. He lived in both France and the US. He collaborated on ballets with Paul ◊Claudel. In 1940 he went to the USA as professor of music at Mills College, California, and became professor of composition at the National Conservatoire in Paris 1947. Much of his later work—which includes chamber, orchestral, and choral music—is polytonal.

miliaria itchy blisters formed in the skin condition ◊prickly heat.

Militant Tendency a faction formed within the British Labour Party, aligned with the publication *Militant*. It became active in the 1970s, with radical socialist policies based on Trotskyism (see ◊Trotsky), and gained some success in local government, for example in the inner-city area of Liverpool. In the mid-1980s the Labour Party considered it to be an organization within the party and banned it.

A number of senior Militants were expelled from the party in 1986, amid much legal conflict. The contested deselection of the incumbent Member of Parliament Frank Field as Labour candidate for Birkenhead, Lancashire, in 1990 led to renewed allegations of Militant infiltration of the Labour Party.

military-industrial complex the conjunction of the military establishment and the arms industry, both inflated by Cold War demands. The phrase was first used by US president and former general Dwight D Eisenhower in 1961 to warn Americans of the potential misplacement of power.

military law articles or regulations that apply to members of the armed forces.

militia a body of civilian soldiers, usually with some military training, who are on call in emergencies, distinct from professional soldiers. In Switzerland, the militia is the national defence force, and every able-bodied man is liable for service in it. In the UK the ◊*Territorial Army* and in the USA the ◊*National Guard* have supplanted earlier voluntary militias.

In England in the 9th century King Alfred established the first militia, or *fyrd*, in which every freeman was liable to serve. After the Norman Conquest a feudal levy was established in which landowners were responsible for raising the men required. This in turn led to the increasing use of the general levy by English kings to combat the growing power of the barons. In the 16th century, under such threats as the Spanish Armada, plans for internal defence relied increasingly on the militia, or what came to be called 'trained bands', of the general levy.

After the Restoration, the militia fell into neglect, but it was reorganized in 1757, and relied upon for home defence during the French wars. In the 19th century it extended its activities abroad, serving in the Peninsular, Crimean, and South African wars. In 1852 it adopted a volunteer status, and in 1908 was merged with the Territorial Army and the Special Reserve forces, to supplement the regular army, and ceased to exist as a separate force.

milk the secretion of the ◊mammary glands of female mammals, with which they suckle their young (during ◊lactation). The milk of cows, goats, or sheep is that most usually consumed by humans; over 85% is water, the remainder comprising protein, fat, lactose (a sugar), calcium, phosphorus, iron, and vitamins. Milk composition varies between species, depending on the nutritional requirements of the young; human milk

Mill *Educated by his father, John Stuart Mill was reading Plato and Demosthenes with ease at the age of ten. His* Autobiography *gives a painful account of the teaching methods that turned him against Utilitarianism.*

contains less protein and more lactose than that of cows.

milking machine a machine that uses suction to milk cows. The first milking machine was invented in the USA by L O Colvin in 1860. Later it was improved so that the suction was regularly released by a pulsating device, since it was found that continuous suction is harmful to the cow.

Milky Way the faint band of light crossing the night sky, consisting of stars in the plane of our galaxy. The name Milky Way is often used for the galaxy itself. It is a spiral ◊galaxy, about 100,000 light years in diameter, containing at least 100 billion stars. The Sun is in one of its spiral arms, about 25,000 light years from the centre.

The Milky Way is a member of a small cluster, the ◊Local Group. The densest parts, towards the centre, lie in the constellation Sagittarius. In places, the Milky Way is interrupted by lanes of dark dust that obscure light from the stars beyond, such as the Coalsack Nebula in Crux (the Southern Cross).

Mill /mɪl/ James 1773–1836. Scottish philosopher and political thinker who developed the theory of ◊utilitarianism. He is remembered for his political articles, and for the rigorous education he gave his son John Stuart Mill.

Born near Montrose, Mill moved to London 1802. Associated for most of his working life with the East India Company, he wrote a vast *History of British India* 1817–18. He was one of the founders of University College, London, together with his friend and fellow utilitarian Jeremy Bentham.

Mill /mɪl/ John Stuart 1806–1873. English philosopher and economist, who wrote *On Liberty* 1859, the classic philosophical defence of liberalism, and *Utilitarianism* 1863, a version of the 'greatest happiness for the greatest number' principle in ethics. His progressive views inspired *On the Subjection of Women* 1869. In his social philosophy, he gradually abandoned the Utilitarians' extreme individualism for an outlook akin to liberal socialism, while still laying great emphasis on the liberty of the individual; this change can be traced in the later editions of *Principles of Political Economy* 1848.

He was born in London, the son of James Mill (1773–1836), an eminent Utilitarian philosopher. In 1822 he entered the East India Company, where he remained until retiring in 1858. In 1826, as described in his *Autobiography* 1873, he passed through a mental crisis; he found his father's bleakly intellectual Utilitarianism emotionally unsatisfying, and abandoned it for a more

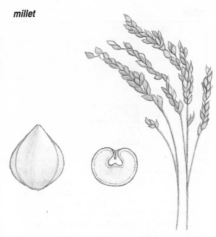

millet

Millais Christ in the House of His Parents *(1850) Tate Gallery, London.*

human philosophy influenced by Coleridge. In *Utilitarianism*, he states that actions are right if they bring about happiness and wrong if they bring about the reverse of happiness. *On Liberty* moved away from the utilitarian notion that individual liberty was necessary for economic and governmental efficiency and advanced the classical defence of individual freedom as a value in itself and the mark of a mature society. He sat in Parliament as a Radical 1865–68, and introduced a motion for women's suffrage. His philosophical and political writings include *A System of Logic* 1843 and *Considerations on Representative Government* 1861.

Millais /'mɪleɪ/ John Everett 1829–1896. British painter, a founder member of the ◊**Pre-Raphaelite Brotherhood** (PRB) in 1848. By the late 1850s he had dropped out of the PRB and his style became more fluent and less detailed.

One of his PRB works, *Christ in the House of His Parents* 1850 (Tate Gallery, London), caused an outcry on its first showing, since its realistic detail was considered unfitting to the sacred subject. In later works such as *The Boyhood of Raleigh* 1870 (Tate Gallery, London), Millais pursued light, popular subjects. He was elected president of the Royal Academy in 1896.

Millay /mɪ'leɪ/ Edna St Vincent 1892–1950. US poet who wrote emotional verse, including *Renascence* 1917 and *The Harp-Weaver* 1922.

millennium a period of 1,000 years. Some Christian sects, and Jehovah's Witnesses, believe that Jesus will return to govern the Earth in person at the next millennium, the 6001st year after the creation (as located by Archbishop Usher at 4004 BC).

This belief, *millenarianism*, also called chiliasm (from the Greek for 1,000), was widespread in the early days of Christianity. As hopes were disappointed, belief in the imminence of the second coming tended to fade, but millenarian views have been expressed at periods of great religious excitement, such as the Reformation.

Miller /'mɪlə/ Arthur 1915– . US playwright. His plays deal with family relationships and contemporary American values, and include *Death of a Salesman* 1949 and *The Crucible* 1953, based on the Salem witch trials and reflecting the communist witch-hunts of Senator ◊McCarthy. He was married 1956–61 to the film star Marilyn Monroe, for whom he wrote the film *The Misfits* 1960.

Among other plays are *All My Sons* 1947, *A View from the Bridge* 1955, and *After the Fall* 1964, based on his relationship with Monroe. He also wrote the television film *Playing for Time* 1980.

Miller /'mɪlə/ Glenn 1904–1944. US trombonist and, as bandleader, exponent of the big-band

swing sound from 1938. He composed his signature tune 'Moonlight Serenade' (a hit 1939). He disappeared without trace on a flight between England and France during World War II.

Miller /'mɪlə/ Henry 1891–1980. US writer. Years spent in the Paris underworld underpin his novels *Tropic of Cancer* 1934 and *Tropic of Capricorn* 1938. They were so outspoken that the former was banned in England until 1963, and the latter was published in the USA only in 1961.

Miller /'mɪlə/ Stanley 1930– . US chemist. In the early 1950s, under laboratory conditions, he tried to imitate the original conditions of the Earth's atmosphere (a mixture of methane, ammonia, and hydrogen), added an electrical discharge, and waited. After a few days he found that amino acids, the ingredients of protein, had been formed.

Miller /'mɪlə/ William 1801–1880. Welsh crystallographer, developer of a coordinate system capable of mapping the shapes and surfaces of crystals.

miller's thumb another name for ◊bullhead, a small fish.

millet type of grass, family Gramineae, of which the grains are used as a cereal food, and the stems as fodder. The most important types are *Panicum miliaceum*, extensively cultivated in the warmer parts of Europe, and *Sorghum bicolor*, also known as ◊durra.

Millet /mi:'leɪ/ Jean François 1814–1875. French painter, a leading member of the ◊Barbizon school, painting scenes of peasant life and landscapes. *The Angelus* 1859 (Musée d'Orsay, Paris) brought him great success and was widely reproduced in his day.

Millett /'mɪlɪt/ Kate 1934– . US radical feminist lecturer, writer, and sculptor, whose book *Sexual Politics* 1970 was a landmark in feminist thinking. She was a founding member of the **National Organization of Women** (NOW). Later books

Miller US playwright Arthur Miller, Sept 1956.

include *Flying* 1974, *The Prostitution Papers* 1976, and *Sita* 1977.

millibar unit of pressure, equal to one thousandth of a ◊bar.

Millikan /'mɪlɪkən/ Robert Andrews 1868–1953. US physicist, awarded a Nobel prize 1923 for his determination of the ◊electric charge on an electron by his oil-drop experiment (which took him five years up to 1913 to perfect).

He observed oil droplets, charged by external ◊radiation, falling under ◊gravity between two horizontal metal plates connected to a high-voltage supply. By varying the voltage, he was able to make the electrostatic field between the plates balance the gravitational field so that some droplets became stationary and floated. If a droplet of weight W is held stationary between plates separated by a distance d and carrying a potential difference V, the charge on the drop, e, is equal to Wd/V.

millilitre one thousandth of a litre (ml), equivalent to 1 cu cm (cc).

millimetre of mercury unit of pressure, used in medicine for measuring blood pressure, defined as the pressure exerted by a column of mercury one millimetre high, under the action of gravity.

Millin /'mɪlɪn/ Sarah Gertrude (born Liebson) 1889–1968. South African novelist, an opponent of racial discrimination, as seen in, for example, *God's Step-Children* 1924.

milling a metal machining method that uses a rotating toothed cutting wheel to shape a surface. The term also applies to grinding grain.

millipede arthropod of worldwide distribution, of the class Diplopoda. It has a segmented body, each segment usually bearing two pairs of legs, and the distinct head bears a pair of short clubbed antennae. Most are a few cm long; a few in the tropics are 30 cm/12 in.

Millipedes live in damp dark places, feeding mainly on rotting vegetation. Some species injure crops by feeding on tender roots, and some produce a poisonous secretion in defence. Certain orders have silk glands.

Mills /mɪlz/ C Wright 1916–1962. US sociologist, whose concern for humanity, ethical values, and individual freedom led him to criticize the US establishment.

Originally in the liberal tradition, Mills later adopted Weberian and even Marxist ideas. He aroused considerable popular interest in sociology with such works as *White Collar* 1951, *The Power Elite* 1956, depicting the US as ruled by businessmen, military experts, and politicians, and *Listen, Yankee* 1960.

Mills /mɪlz/ John 1908– . British actor, who appeared in films such as *In Which We Serve* 1942, *The Rocking Horse Winner* 1949, *The Wrong Box* 1966, and *Oh, What a Lovely War* 1969. He received an Oscar for *Ryan's Daughter* 1971.

Mills Brothers US vocal group who specialized in close-harmony vocal imitations of instruments,

millet

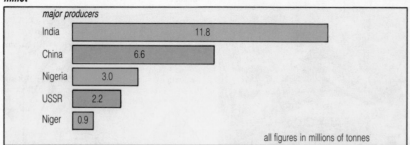

major producers

India	11.8
China	6.6
Nigeria	3.0
USSR	2.2
Niger	0.9

all figures in millions of tonnes

comprising Herbert Mills (1912–), Harry Mills (1913–82), John Mills (1889–1935), and Donald Mills (1915–). Formed 1922, the group first broadcast on radio in 1925, and continued to perform until the 1950s. Their 70 hits include 'Lazy River' 1948 and 'You Always Hurt the One You Love' 1944.

Mills Cross a type of ◊radio telescope consisting of two rows of aerials at right angles to each other, invented 1953 by the Australian radio-astronomer Bernard Mills. The cross-shape produces a narrow beam useful for pinpointing the positions of radio sources.

Milne /mɪln/ A(lan) A(lexander) 1882–1956. English writer. His books for children were based on the teddy bear and other toys of his son Christopher Robin (*Winnie-the-Pooh* 1926 and *The House at Pooh Corner* 1928). He also wrote children's verse (*When We Were Very Young* 1924 and *Now We Are Six* 1927) and plays, including an adaptation of Kenneth Grahame's *The Wind in the Willows* as *Toad of Toad Hall* 1929.

Milner /'mɪlnə/ Alfred, Viscount Milner 1854–1925. British colonial administrator. As governor of Cape Colony 1897–1901, he negotiated with ◊Kruger but did little to prevent the second ◊South African War; and as governor of the Transvaal and Orange River colonies 1902–05 after their annexation, he reorganized their administration. In 1916 he became a member of Lloyd George's war cabinet.

Milosevic /mɪ'lɒʃəvɪtʃ/ Slobodan 1941– . Serbian communist politician. A leading figure in the Yugoslavian Communist Party (LCY) in the republic of Serbia, he became Serbian party chief and president in 1986 and campaigned to reintegrate Kosovo and Vojvodina provinces into 'greater Serbia'.

He was educated at Belgrade University and rapidly rose up the ranks of the LCY in his home republic of Serbia, helped by his close political and business links to Ivan Stambolic, his predecessor as local party leader. Milosevic won popular support within Serbia for his assertive nationalist stance, encouraging street demonstrations in favour of the reintegration of Kosovo and Vojvodina autonomous provinces into the Serbian republic.

Milosz /'mi:wɒʃ/ Czeslaw 1911– . Polish writer, born in Lithuania. He became a diplomat before defecting and taking US nationality. His poetry in English translation includes *Selected Poems* 1973 and *Bells in Winter* 1978. Among his novels are *The Seizure of Power* 1955 and *The Issa Valley* 1981. Nobel prize 1980.

Milstein /'mɪlstaɪn/ César 1927– . Argentinian molecular biologist who developed monoclonal antibodies, giving immunity against specific diseases. He shared a Nobel prize 1984.

Milstein, who settled in Britain 1961, was engaged on research into the immune system at the Laboratory of Molecular Biology in Cambridge. He and his colleagues devised a means of accessing the immune system for purposes of research, diagnosis, and treatment. They developed monoclonal antibodies (MABs), cloned cells which, when introduced into the body, can be targeted to seek out sites of disease. The full potential of this breakthrough is still being investigated. However, MABs, which can be duplicated

in limitless quantities, are already in use to combat disease. Milstein shared the Nobel Prize for Medicine with two colleagues, George Kohler and Niels Jerne.

Milton /'mɪltən/ John 1608–1674. English poet. His early poems include the pastoral *L'allegro* and *Il penseroso* 1632, the masque *Comus* 1633, and the elegy *Lycidas* 1637. His later works include *Paradise Lost* 1667, *Paradise Regained* 1677, and the classic drama, *Samson Agonistes* 1677.

Born in London, Milton was educated at Christ's College, Cambridge (where he was known as 'the Lady of Christ's' for his fine features), and then devoted himself to study for his poetic career. His middle years were devoted to the Puritan cause and pamphleteering, including one advocating divorce, and another (*Areopagitica*) freedom of the press. From 1649 he was (Latin) secretary to the Council of State. His assistants (as his sight failed) included ◊Marvell. He married Mary Powell 1643, and their three daughters were later his somewhat unwilling scribes. After Mary's death 1652, the year of his total blindness, he married twice more, his second wife Catherine Woodcock dying in childbirth, while Elizabeth Minshull survived him for over half a century. He is buried in St Giles's, Cripplegate, London.

Milton Keynes /'mɪltən 'ki:nz/ industrial (engineering, electronics) new town in ◊Buckinghamshire, England; population (1983) 146,000. It was developed 1967 around the old village of the same name, following a grid design by Richard Llewelyn-Davies; it is the headquarters of the Open University.

Milwaukee /mɪl'wɔ:ki/ industrial (meatpacking, brewing, engineering, textiles) port in Wisconsin, USA, on Lake Michigan; population (1980)

1,207,000. It was founded by German immigrants in the 19th century.

mime a type of acting in which gestures, movements, and facial expressions replace speech. It has developed as a form of theatre, particularly in France, where ◊Marceau and ◊Barrault have continued the traditions established in the 19th century by Deburau and the practices of the ◊commedia dell'arte in Italy. In ancient Greece, mime was a crude, realistic comedy with dialogue and exaggerated gesture.

mimicry the imitation of one species (or group of species) by another. The most common form is *Batesian mimicry* (named after H W ◊Bates), where the mimic resembles a model that is poisonous or unpleasant to eat, and has ◊aposematic coloration; the mimic thus benefits from the fact that predators learn to avoid the model. Hoverflies that resemble bees or wasps are an example. Appearance is usually the basis for mimicry, but calls, songs, scents, and other signals can also be mimicked.

In *Mullerian mimicry*, two or more equally poisonous or distasteful species have a similar colour pattern, thereby reinforcing the warning each gives to predators. In some cases, mimicry is not for protection, but allows the mimic to prey on, or parasitize, the model.

mimosa plant of the family Leguminosae, found in tropical and subtropical regions. It ranges from herb to large tree size, and bears small, fluffy, golden ball-like flowers.

min. abbreviation for *minute* (time); *minimum*.

Minangkabau people of W Sumatra in Indonesia. In addition to approximately 3 million Minangkabau in W Sumatra, there are sizeable communities in the major Indonesian cities. The Minangkabau language belongs to the Austronesian family.

minaret a slender turret or tower attached to a Muslim mosque. It has one or more balconies, from which the *muezzin* calls the people to prayer five times a day.

Minas Gerais /'mi:nɒʒ ʒe'raɪs/ state in SE Brazil; major centre of the country's iron ore, coal, diamond and gold mining; area 587,172 sq km/226,794 sq mi; population (1980) 13,378,500; capital Belo Horizonte.

mind in philosophy, the presumed mental or physical being or faculty that enables a person to think, will, and feel; the seat of the intelligence and of

mimicry

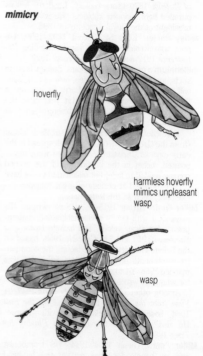

hoverfly

harmless hoverfly mimics unpleasant wasp

wasp

Milton *The 17th-century English poet John Milton.*

memory; sometimes only the cognitive or intellectual powers as distinguished from the will and the emotions.

Mind may be seen as synonymous with the merely random chemical reactions within the brain, or as a function of the brain as a whole, or (more traditionally) as existing independently of the physical brain, through which it expresses itself, or even as the only reality, matter being considered the creation of intelligence. The relation of mind to matter may be variously regarded. Traditionally, materialism identifies mental and physical phenomena equally in terms of matter and motion. Dualism holds that mind and matter exist independently side by side. Idealism maintains that mind is the ultimate reality, and that matter does not exist apart from it.

Mindanao /ˌmɪndəˈnaʊ/ the second-largest island of the Philippines
area 94,627 sq km/36,526 sq mi
towns Davao, Zamboanga
physical mountainous rainforest
features in 1971, an isolated people, the Tasaday, were reputedly first seen by others (this may be a hoax). The active volcano Apo reaches 2,954 m/9,600 ft, and Mindanao is subject to severe earthquakes. There is a Muslim guerrilla resistance movement
products pineapples, coffee, rice, coconut, rubber, hemp, timber, nickel, gold, steel, chemicals, fertilizer
population (1980) 10,905,250.

Minden /ˈmɪndən/ industrial town (tobacco, food processing) of North Rhine-Westphalia, West Germany, on the river Weser; population (1985) 80,000. The French were defeated here 1759 by an allied army from Britain, Hanover, and Brunswick, commanded by the duke of Brunswick.

Mindoro /mɪnˈdɔːrəʊ/ island of the Philippine Republic, S of Luzon
area 10,347 sq km 3,995 sq mi
towns Calapan
features Mount Halcon 2,590 m/8,500 ft
population (1980) 500,000.

Mindszenty /ˈmɪndsenti/ József 1892–1975. Roman Catholic primate of Hungary. He was imprisoned by the communist government 1949, but escaped 1956 to take refuge in the US legation. The pope persuaded him to go into exile in Austria 1971, and he was 'retired' when Hungary's relations with the Vatican improved 1974.

mine explosive charge on land or sea, or in the atmosphere, designed to be detonated by contact, vibration (for example from an enemy engine), magnetic influence, or a timing device. Countermeasures include metal detectors (useless for plastic types), specially equipped helicopters, and (at sea) ◊minesweepers.

mineral a naturally formed inorganic substance with a particular chemical composition and an ordered internal structure. Either in their perfect crystalline form or otherwise, minerals are the constituents of ◊rocks. In more general usage, a mineral is any substance economically valuable for mining (including coal and oil, despite their organic origins).

mineral dressing preparing a mineral ore for processing. Ore is seldom in a fit state to be processed when it is mined; it often contains unwanted rock and dirt. Therefore it is usually crushed into a uniform size, and then separated from the dirt, or gangue. This may be done magnetically (some iron ores), by washing (gold), by treatment with chemicals (copper ores), or by ◊flotation.

mineralogy the study of minerals. The classification of minerals is based chiefly on their chemical composition and the kind of chemical bonding that holds these atoms together. The mineralogist also studies their crystallographic and physical characters, occurrence, and mode of formation.

mineral oil oil obtained from mineral sources, for example, coal or petroleum, as distinct from oil obtained from vegetable or animal sources.

mineral salt in nutrition, a simple inorganic chemical that is required by living organisms. Plants usually obtain their mineral salts from the soil, while animals get theirs from their food. Important mineral salts include iron salts (needed by both plants and animals), magnesium salts (needed mainly by plants, to make chlorophyll), and calcium salts (needed by animals to make bone or shell).

mineral water water with mineral constituents gathered from the rocks over which it flows, and classified by these into earthy, brine, and oil mineral waters; or water with artificially added minerals and, sometimes, carbon dioxide.

Many people believe that mineral waters have curative powers, the types of these medicinal waters being: alkaline (Vichy), bitter (Seidlitz), salt (Droitwich), earthy (Bath), sulphurous (Aachen), and special varieties, such as barium (Harrogate). Perrier, named after Louis Perrier, the French doctor who first advocated its use, comes from the French village of Vergèze in W Provence. Supply of Perrier, formerly the most widely sold mineral water, were withdrawn temporarily Feb 1990 after traces of benzene, a cancer-causing chemical, were found in samples in the USA and Europe. Evian water comes from Haute-Savoie *département*, France, and Malvern water from Hereford and Worcester, England. Possible pollution of tap water in many areas of the UK led to greatly increased sales of mineral water in the 1980s.

Minerva /mɪˈnɜːvə/ in ancient Roman mythology, the goddess of intelligence, and of the handicrafts and arts, counterpart of the Greek ◊Athena. From the earliest days of ancient Rome, there was a temple to her on the Capitol.

minesweeper small naval vessel for locating and destroying mines at sea. A typical modern minesweeper weighs about 725 tonnes, and is built of reinforced plastic (immune to magnetic and acoustic mines). Remote-controlled miniature submarines may be used to lay charges next to the mines and destroy them.

Mingus /ˈmɪŋɡəs/ Charles 1922–1979. US bass player and composer. He was influential for his experimentation with atonality and dissonant effects, opening the way for the new style of free collective jazz improvisation of the 1960s.

Minhow /ˌmɪnˈhaʊ/ name in use 1934–43 for Foochow, now ◊Fuzhou, a town in SE China.

miniature painting (Latin *miniare* 'to paint with minium' (a red colour)) painting on a very small scale, notably early manuscript paintings, and later miniature portraits, sometimes set in jewelled cases. The art of manuscript painting was developed in classical times in the West, and revived in the Middle Ages. Several Islamic countries, for example Persia and India, developed strong traditions of manuscript art. Miniature portrait painting enjoyed a vogue in France and England in the 16th–19th centuries.

Jean Clouet and Holbein the Younger both practised the art for royal patrons. Later in the 16th century Nicholas Hilliard painted exclusively miniatures and set out the rules of this portrait style in his treatise *The Art of Limning*.

minicomputer a multi-user computer whose size and processing power are between those of a ◊mainframe and a ◊microcomputer.

Minicomputers are often found in medium-sized businesses, or university departments handling ◊database or other commercial programs, or running scientific or graphical applications that require much numerical computation.

Minimalism a movement beginning in the late 1960s in abstract art and music towards a severely simplified composition. In *painting*, it emphasized geometrical and elemental shapes. In *sculpture*, Carl André focused on industrial materials. In *music*, US live instrumental music from the late 1960s bases large-scale statements on layers of imperceptibly shifting repetitive patterns. Its major exponents are Steve ◊Reich and Philip ◊Glass.

The idea of hypnotic repetition is a feature of US music from the Balinese transcriptions of Colin ◊McPhee and the rhythmic experiments of ◊Nancarrow, to the tape music of Terry Riley (in *c*.1964).

minimum lending rate (MLR) in the UK, the rate of interest at which the Bank of England lends to the money market; see also ◊bank rate.

mining extraction of minerals from under the land or sea for industrial or domestic use. Exhaustion of traditionally accessible resources has led to development of new mining techniques, for example extraction of oil from under the North Sea and from land shale reserves. Technology is also under development for the exploitation of minerals from entirely new sources such as mud deposits and mineral nodules on the sea bed.

Mud deposits have been laid down by hot springs about 350°C: sea water penetrates beneath the ocean floor, and carries copper, silver, and zinc with it on its return. Such springs occur along the midocean ridges of the Atlantic and Pacific, and in the geological rift between Africa and Arabia under the Red Sea.

Mineral nodules form on the ocean bed and contain manganese, cobalt, copper, molybdenum, nickel; they stand out on the surface, and 'grow' by only a few millimetres every 100,000 years.

mink two species of carnivorous mammal of the weasel family, usually found in or near water. They have rich brown fur, and are up to 50 cm/1.6 ft long with bushy tails 20 cm/8 in long. They live in Eurasia and North America.

They produce an annual litter of six in their riverbank burrows. The demand for their fur led to the establishment from the 1930s of mink ranches, and production of varying shades.

Minneapolis /ˌmɪniˈæpəlɪs/ city in Minnesota, USA, forming with St Paul the Twin Cities area; population (1980) 371,000, metropolitan area 2,114,000.

The world's most powerful computers (Cray 2 supercomputer 1985) are built here, used for long-range weather forecasting, spacecraft design, code-breaking. The city centre is glass-covered against the difficult climate; there is an arts institute, symphony orchestra, Minnesota University, and Tyrone ◊Guthrie theatre.

Minnelli /mɪˈneli/ Liza 1946– . US actress and singer, daughter of Judy ◊Garland and the director Vincente Minnelli. She gave a star-making performance in the musical *Cabaret* 1972. Her subsequent films include *New York* 1977 and *Arthur* 1981.

Minnelli /mɪˈneli/ Vincente 1910–1986. US film director, who specialized in musicals and occasional melodramas. His best films, such as *Meet Me in St Louis* 1944 and *The Band Wagon* 1953, display a powerful visual flair.

Minnesinger any of a group of German lyric poets of the 12th and 13th centuries who, in their songs, dealt mainly with the theme of courtly love without revealing the identity of the object of their affections. Minnesingers included Dietmar von Aist, Friedrich von Hausen, Heinrich von Morungen, Reinmar, and Walther von der Vogelweide.

Minnesota /ˌmɪnɪˈsəʊtə/ state of the northern midwest USA; nickname North Star or Gopher State
area 218,700 sq km/84,418 sq mi
capital St Paul
towns Minneapolis, Duluth, Bloomington, Rochester
features sources of the Red, St Lawrence, and Mississippi rivers; Minnehaha Falls at Minneapolis; Mayo Clinic at Rochester
products cereals, potatoes, livestock, pulpwood, iron ore (60% of US output), farm and other machinery
population (1987) 4,246,000
famous people F Scott Fitzgerald, Sinclair Lewis, William and Charles Mayo
history the first Europeans to explore were French fur traders in the 17th century; part

mining

Since prehistoric times, humans have dug into the earth to obtain the materials needed to help sustain life. In the resources-hungry 20th century, power, mineral, and building needs are being met by an ever-increasing range of mining methods, allowing exploration and extraction wherever required.

Traditional ways of raising hand-hewn coal are being replaced by safer and more efficient computer-controlled operations. (1) MINOS, the Mine-Operating System, has a control centre on the surface. (2) FIDO continuously monitors underground teams. (3) MIDAS surveys seams and adjusts the shearer automatically. (4) IMPACT monitors the machinery, to save on maintenance and avoid breakdown. (5) Transport is also monitored to minimise delays. (6) Coal is graded and washed under electronic control.

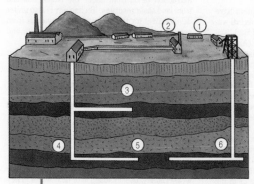

The discovery of oil and gas under the sea is not the only one to attract commercial exploitation. Mineral nodules have been found on the sea bed, and despite technical and legal problems, dredging of mineral-rich mud from the bottom of the Red Sea may soon be viable.

belt to main plant

crushing unit

pincers

In quarries and open-cast mines the ore is so near to the surface that it can be cut without tunnelling. Rocks released by blasting can be gathered, crushed, and fed onto conveyor belts to the main plant in one continuous process.

pre pilot mining vessel

sea water

electronic boxes

pump motor

mud pump

brine

sediment thickness meter

suction head

mud

was ceded to Britain 1763, and part passed to the USA under the Louisiana Purchase 1803; it became a territory 1849 and a state 1858.

minnow abundant small fish *Phoxinus phoxinus* of the carp family found in streams and ponds worldwide. Most species are small and dully coloured, but some are brightly coloured. They feed on larvae and insects.

Minoan civilization Bronze Age civilization on the Aegean island of Crete. The name is derived from Minos, the legendary king of Crete, reputed to be the son of the god Zeus. The civilization is divided into three main periods: early Minoan, about 3000–2200 BC, middle Minoan, about 2200–1580 BC; and late Minoan, about 1580–1100 BC. The Minoan language was deciphered by Michael ◊Ventris.

No palaeolithic remains have yet been found in Crete, but in the Neolithic Age some centuries before 3000 BC the island was inhabited by people coming probably from SW Asia Minor, and akin to the early Bronze Age inhabitants

of the Greek mainland. With the opening of the Bronze Age, about 3000 BC, the Minoan culture proper began. Each period was marked by cultural advances in copper and bronze weapons, pottery of increasingly intricate design, frescoes, and the construction of palaces and fine houses. About 1400 BC, in the late Minoan period, the civilization was suddenly destroyed by earthquake or war. A partial revival continued until about 1100.

In religion the Minoans seem to have worshipped principally a great mother goddess with whom was associated a young male god. The tales of Greek mythology about Rhea, the mother of Zeus, and the birth of Zeus himself in a Cretan cave seem to be based on Minoan religion.

minor the legal term for those under the age of majority, which varies from country to country but is usually between 18 and 21. In Britain (since 1970), the USA (from 1971 for voting, and in some states for all other purposes) and certain European countries the age of majority is 18. Most civic and legal rights and duties only

St. Paul

accrue at the age of majority; for example, the rights to vote, to make a will, and (usually) to make a fully binding contract, and the duty to act as a juror.

Minorca /mɪˈnɔːkə/ (Spanish **Menorca**) second largest of the ◊Balearic Islands in the Mediterranean
area 689 sq km/266 sq mi
towns Mahon, Ciudadela
products copper, lead, iron, tourism
population (1985) 55,500.

minor planet another name for an ◊asteroid.

Minos /ˈmaɪnɒs/ in Greek mythology, a king of Crete (son of ◊Zeus and ◊Europa).

Minotaur /ˈmaɪnətɔː/ in Greek mythology, a monster, half man and half bull, offspring of Pasiphaë, wife of King Minos of Crete, and a bull. It lived in the labyrinth at Knossos and its victims were seven girls and seven youths, sent in annual tribute by Athens, until ◊Theseus killed it, with the aid of Ariadne, the daughter of Minos.

Minsk /mɪnsk/ industrial city (machinery, textiles, leather; centre of the Soviet computer industry) and capital of the Byelorussian Republic, USSR; population (1987) 1,543,000.

Dating back to the 11th century and in turn held by Lithuania, Poland, Sweden, and Russia, Minsk was destroyed by Napoleon 1812 and the Germans 1944. In 1989 mass graves containing the remains of over 30,000 victims of mass evacuations carried out by Stalin between 1937–41 were uncovered in a forest outside the city.

Minsmere /ˈmɪnzmɪə/ coastal marshland bird reserve (1948) near Aldeburgh, Suffolk, attracting a greater number of species than any other in Britain, and noted for the Scrape, an artificial breeding habitat.

minster /ˈmɪnstə/ in the UK, a church formerly attached to a monastery, for example, York Minster. Originally the term meant a monastery, and in this sense it is often preserved in place names, such as Westminster.

mint in economics, a place where coins are made under government authority. In Britain, the official mint is the **Royal Mint**; the US equivalent is the **Bureau of the Mint**.

The UK Royal Mint also manufactures coinages, official medals and seals for Commonwealth and foreign countries. For centuries in the Tower of London, the Royal Mint was housed in a building on Tower Hill from 1810 until the new Royal Mint was opened at Llantrisant, near Cardiff, Mid Glamorgan, in 1968. The nominal head is the Master Worker and Warden, who is the chancellor of the Exchequer, but the actual chief is the Deputy Master and Comptroller, a permanent civil servant.

mint in botany, an aromatic plant, genus *Mentha*, of the family Labiatae, widely distributed in temperate regions. The plants have square stems, creeping rootstocks, and flowers, usually pink or purplish, that grow in a terminal spike. Mints include **garden mint** *Mentha spicata* and **peppermint** *Mentha piperita*.

Minto /ˈmɪntəʊ/ Gilbert, 4th Earl of 1845–1914. British colonial administrator who succeeded Curzon as viceroy of India, 1905–10. With John Morley, secretary of state for India, he co-sponsored the Morley Minto reforms of 1909. The reforms increased Indian representation in

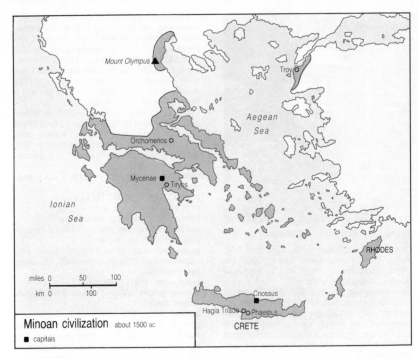

Minoan civilization about 1500 BC
■ capitals

Mount Olympus

Troy

Aegean Sea

Orchomenos

Mycenae
Tiryns

Ionian Sea

RHODES

miles 0 — 50 — 100
km 0 — 100

Cnossus
Hagia Triada Phaestus
CRETE

government at provincial level, but also created separate Muslim and Hindu electorates which, it was believed, helped the British Raj in the policy of divide and rule.

Mintoff /ˈmɪntɒf/ Dom (Dominic) 1916– . Labour prime minister of Malta 1971–84. He negotiated the removal of British and other foreign military bases 1971–79, and made treaties with Libya.

Minton /ˈmɪntən/ Thomas 1765–1836. English potter. He first worked at the Caughley porcelain works, but in 1789 established himself at Stoke-on-Trent as an engraver of designs (he originated the 'willow pattern') and in the 1790s founded a pottery there, producing high-quality bone china, including tableware.

minuet European courtly dance of the 17th century, later used with the trio as the third movement in a Classical symphony.

minute unit of time consisting of 60 seconds; also unit of angle equal to one sixtieth of a degree.

minuteman in weaponry, a US three-stage intercontinental ballistic missile with a range of about 8,000 km/5,000 mi. In US history, a member of the citizens' militia in New England who fought in the War of Independence; they pledged to be ready at a minute's notice.

Miocene fourth epoch of the Tertiary period of geological time, 25–5 million years ago. The name means 'middle recent'. At this time grasslands spread over the interior of continents, and hoofed mammals rapidly evolved.

mips *million instructions per second* in computing, a measure of the speed of a processor.

Miquelon Islands /ˈmiːkəlɒn/ small group of islands off the S coast of Newfoundland which with St Pierre form a French overseas *département*. See ◊St Pierre and Miquelon

area 216 sq km/83 sq mi

products cod; silver fox and mink are bred

population (with St Pierre, 1982) 6,045.

Mir (Russian 'peace') Soviet space station, the core of which was launched 20 Feb 1986. *Mir* is intended to be a permanently occupied space station.

Mir weighs almost 21 tonnes, is approximately 13.5 m/45 ft long, and has a maximum diameter of 4.15 m/14 ft. It carries a number of improvements over the earlier ◊Salyut series of space stations, including six docking ports; four of these can have scientific and technical modules attached to

them. The first of these was the *Kvant* (quantum) astrophysics module, launched 1987. This had two main sections: a main experimental module and a service module which would be separated in orbit. The experimental module was 5.8 m/19 ft long and had a maximum diameter matching that of *Mir*. When attached to the *Mir* core, *Kvant* added a further 40 cu m/1,413 cu ft of working space to that already there. Among the equipment carried by *Kvant* were several X-ray telescopes and an ultraviolet telescope.

mir (Russian 'world') in Russia before the 1917 Revolution, a self-governing village community, in which the peasants distributed land and collected taxes.

Mira or *Omicron Ceti* the brightest long-period pulsating ◊variable star, located in the constellation ◊Cetus. Mira was the first star discovered to vary in brightness over a regular period.

In 1596 Dutch astronomer David Fabricus noticed Mira as a third-magnitude object. Because it did not appear on any of the star charts available at the time, he mistook it for a ◊nova. The German astronomer Johann Bayer included it on his star atlas 1603 and designated it Omicron Ceti. The star vanished from view again, only to reappear within a year. Continued observation revealed a periodic variation between third or fourth magnitude and ninth magnitude over an average period of 331 days. Mira can sometimes reach second magnitude and once, in 1779, it almost attained first magnitude.

Mirabeau /ˈmɪrəbəʊ/ Honoré Gabriel Riqueti, Comte de 1749–1791. French politician, leader of the National Assembly in the French Revolution. He wanted to establish a parliamentary monarchy on the English model. From May 1790 he secretly acted as political adviser to the king.

Mirabeau was from a noble Provençal family. Before the French Revolution he had a stormy career, was three times imprisoned, and passed several years in exile. In 1789 he was elected to the States General as a representative of the third estate. His eloquence won him the leadership of the National Assembly; nevertheless, he was out of sympathy with the majority of the deputies, whom he regarded as mere theoreticians.

miracle an event that cannot be explained by the known laws of nature and is therefore attributed to divine intervention.

miracle play another name for ◊mystery play.

mirage the illusion seen in hot climates of water on the horizon, or of distant objects being enlarged. The effect is caused by the refraction, or bending, of light.

Light rays from the sky bend as they pass through the hot layers of air near the ground, so that they appear to come from the horizon. Because the light is from a blue sky, the horizon appears blue and watery. If, during the night, cold air collects near the ground, light can be bent in the opposite direction, so that objects below the horizon appear to float above it. In the same way, objects such as trees or rocks near the horizon can appear enlarged.

Miranda /mɪˈrændə/ Carmen. Stage name of Maria de Carmo Miranda da Cunha 1909–1955. Portuguese dancer and singer who lived in Brazil from her childhood. Successful in Brazilian films, she went to Hollywood 1939 via Broadway and appeared in over a dozen musicals, including *Down Argentine Way* 1940 and *The Gang's All Here* 1943.

Mirandola Italian 15th-century philosopher. See ◊Pico della Mirandola.

Mirlees /mɜːˈliːz/ Hope 1887–1978. British writer, whose fantasy novel *Lud-in-the-Mist* 1926 contrasts the supernatural with the real world.

Mirman /ˈmɜːmən/ Sophie 1956– . British entrepreneur, founder of the Sock Shop, launched on the US market in 1987.

Miró /mɪˈrəʊ/ Joan 1893–1983. Spanish Surrealist painter, born in Barcelona. In the mid-1920s he developed a distinctive abstract style with amoeba shapes, some linear, some highly coloured, generally floating on a plain ground.

During the 1930s his style became more sombre, and after World War II he produced larger abstracts. He experimented with sculpture and printmaking and produced ceramic murals (for example in the UNESCO building, Paris, 1958). He also designed sets for the ballet director Diaghilev.

Mirren /ˈmɪrən/ Helen 1946– . British actress, whose stage roles include Shakespearean ones, for example Lady Macbeth and Isabella in *Measure for Measure*. Her films include *The Long Good Friday* 1981 and *Cal* 1984.

mirror any polished surface that reflects light; often made from 'silvered' glass (in practice, a mercury alloy coating of glass). A plane (flat) mirror produces a same-size, erect 'virtual' image located behind the mirror at the same distance from it as the object is in front of it. A spherical concave mirror produces a reduced, inverted real image in front or an enlarged, erect virtual image behind it

Mirabeau As leader of the National Assembly, Honoré Gabriel Mirabeau sought to remodel rather than overthrow the French monarchy.

(as with a shaving mirror), depending on how close the object is to the mirror. A spherical convex mirror produces a reduced, erect virtual image behind it (as with a car's rear-view mirror).

In a plane mirror the light rays appear to come from behind the mirror but do not actually do so. The inverted real image from a spherical concave mirror is an image in which the rays of light pass through it. The ◊focal length *f* of a spherical mirror is half the radius of curvature; it is related to the image distance *v* and object distance *u* by the equation $1/v + 1/u = 1/f$.

MIRV abbreviation for *multiple independently targeted re-entry vehicle*, used in ◊nuclear warfare.

Mirzapur /ˌmɪəzə'pʊə/ city of Uttar Pradesh, India, on the river Ganges; a grain and cotton market, with bathing sites and temples on the river; population (1981) 127,785.

Misanthrope, The a comedy by Molière, first produced in France 1666. The play contrasts the noble ideals of Alceste with the worldliness of his lover Celimene.

miscarriage spontaneous expulsion of a fetus from the womb before it is capable of independent survival.

misdemeanour in English law, an obsolete term for an offence less serious than a ◊felony. In the USA, a misdemeanour is an offence punishable only by a fine or short term in prison, while a felony carries a term of imprisonment of a year or more.

mise en scène (French 'stage setting') in cinema, the composition and content of the frame in terms of background scenery, actors, costumes, props, and lighting.

misericord or *miserere* in architecture, a projection on the underside of a hinged seat of the choir stalls in a church, used as a rest for a priest when standing during long services. Misericords are often decorated with carvings.

Mishima /'mɪʃɪmə/ Yukio 1925–1970. Japanese novelist, whose work often deals with sexual desire and perversion, as in *Confessions of a Mask* 1949 and *The Temple of the Golden Pavilion* 1956. He committed hara-kiri (ritual suicide) as a demonstration against the corruption of the nation and the loss of the samurai warrior tradition.

Mishna /'mɪʃnə/ a collection of commentaries on written Hebrew law, consisting of discussions between rabbis handed down orally from their inception in AD 70 until about 200, when, with the Gemara, the discussions in schools of Palestine and Babylon on law, it was committed to writing to form the Talmud.

Miskito /mɪ'skiːtəʊ/ American Indian people of Central America, living mainly in the area that is now Nicaragua.

Miskolc /'mɪʃkɒlts/ industrial city (iron, steel, textiles, furniture, paper) in NE Hungary, on the river Sajo, 145 km/90 mi NE of Budapest; population (1988) 210,000.

Misr /'mɪsrə/ Egyptian name for ◊Egypt and for ◊Cairo.

misrelated participle see ◊participle.

missal in the Roman Catholic Church, a service book containing the complete office of Mass for the entire year. A simplified missal in the vernacular was introduced 1969 (obligatory from 1971): the first major reform since 1570.

missel thrush a type of ◊thrush.

missile rocket-propelled weapon, which may be nuclear-armed (see ◊nuclear warfare). Modern missiles are classified according to range into *intercontinental ballistic missiles* (ICBMs, capable of reaching targets over 5,500 km/3,400 mi), *intermediate-range* (1,100 km/680 mi–2,750 km/1,700 mi), and *short-range* (under 1,100 km/680 mi) missiles. The first long-range ballistic missiles used in warfare were the ◊V1 and V2 launched by Germany against Britain in World War II.

Outside the industrialized countries, 22 states had active ballistic-missile programmes by 1989, and 17 had deployed these weapons: Afghanistan,

Mishima *Japanese novelist Yukio Mishima 1970.*

Argentina, Brazil, Cuba, Egypt, India, Iran, Iraq, Israel, North Korea, South Korea, Libya, Pakistan, Saudi Arabia, South Africa, Syria, and Taiwan. Non-nuclear short-range missiles were used during the Iran–Iraq War 1980–88 against Iraqi cities. In the Falklands conflict 1982, smaller, conventionally armed *sea-skimming missiles* were used (the French Exocet) against British ships by the Argentine forces, and similar small missiles have been used against aircraft and ships elsewhere.

mission an organized attempt to spread a religion. Throughout its history Christianity has been the most influential missionary religion; Islam has also played a missionary role. Missionary activity in the Third World has frequently been criticized for its political, economic, and cultural effects on indigenous peoples.

history of Christian missions

1st–3rd centuries Christianity was spread throughout the Roman Empire by missionaries, including St Paul and Gregory I.

4th–8th centuries St Patrick, St Aidan, St Columba, St Boniface, and St Martin of Tours operated beyond the empire.

Middle Ages The Benedictine, Dominican, and Franciscan orders all engaged in missionary work.

16th century The foundation of the Jesuit order supplied such missionaries as Francis Xavier (1506–1552). Las Casas attempted to prevent Spanish oppression of American Indians.

17th century John Eliot (1604–1690) in North America thought the Mohicans were one of the lost tribes of Israel and translated the Bible into their language. The Society for Promoting Christian Knowledge (SPCK) was founded 1698.

18th century Many other Protestant churches founded missionary societies, including the Moravians 1732 and the Baptists 1792.

19th century Evangelical missionaries on Tahiti tried to keep Roman Catholics out by force. Baptist missionaries on Jamaica condemned drumming and dancing. George Selwyn (1809–1878), the first bishop of New Zealand, vainly opposed white confiscation of Maori lands. The China Inland Mission was founded 1865. In Africa renewed impetus came from the career of David Livingstone.

20th century Since the World Missionary Conference in Edinburgh, Scotland, 1910 there has been growing international cooperation. Christian mission has largely given way to the concept of partnership, with Third World countries sending members to, for example, Britain, and local churches having far greater control over the training and finance of missionaries sent to them.

Mississippi /ˌmɪsɪ'sɪpi/ river in the USA, the main arm of the great river system draining the USA between the Appalachian and the Rocky mountains. The length of the Mississippi is 3,780 km/2,350 mi; of the Mississippi/Missouri 6,020 km/3,740 mi.

The Mississippi rises in the lake region of N Minnesota, with St Anthony Falls at Minneapolis. Below the tributaries Minnesota, Wisconsin, Des Moines, and Illinois, the confluence of the Missouri and Mississippi occurs at St Louis. The river turns at the Ohio junction, passing Memphis, and takes in the St Francis, Arkansas, Yazoo, and Red tributaries before reaching its delta on the Gulf of Mexico beyond New Orleans.

In spring, warm air from the Gulf of Mexico collides with cold fronts from the north to create tornadoes along the Red River, a western tributary. The Spanish explorer Hernando de Soto reached a point on the Mississippi near present-day Memphis 1541.

Mississippi /ˌmɪsɪ'sɪpi/ state of the S USA; nickname Magnolia State
area 123,600 sq km/47,710 sq mi
capital Jackson
towns Biloxi, Meridian, Hattiesburg
features Mississippi river; Vicksburg National Military Park (Civil War site)
products cotton, sweet potatoes, sugar, rice, canned sea food at Biloxi, timber, pulp, oil, natural gas, chemicals
population (1985) 2,657,000
famous people William Faulkner, Elvis Presley, Eudora Welty
history settled in turn by French, English, and Spanish until passing under US control 1798; statehood achieved 1817. After secession from the Union during the Civil War, it was readmitted 1870.

Mississippian US term for the lower ◊Carboniferous period of geological time, named after the state of Mississippi.

Missolonghi /ˌmɪsə'lɒŋgi/ (Greek *Mesolóngion*) town in W Central Greece and Eubrea region, on the N shore of the Gulf of Patras; population (1981) 10,200. It was several times under siege by the Turks in the wars of 1822–26 and it was here that the British poet Byron died.

Missouri /mɪ'zʊəri/ state of the central USA; nickname Show Me State
area 180,600 sq km/69,712 sq mi
capital Jefferson City
towns St Louis, Kansas City, Springfield, Independence
features Mississippi and Missouri rivers; Pony Express Museum at St Joseph; birthplace of Jesse James; Mark Twain State Park; Harry S Truman Library at Independence
products meat and other processed food, aerospace and transport equipment, lead, clay, coal
population (1986) 5,066,000
famous people T S Eliot, Joseph Pulitzer, Mark Twain
history explored by de Soto 1541; acquired under the ◊Louisiana Purchase; achieved statehood 1821.

Missouri Compromise in US history, the solution by Congress (1820–21) of a sectional crisis caused by the 1819 request from Missouri for admission to the union as a slave state, despite its proximity to existing non-slave states. The compromise

Mississippi/Missouri Rivers

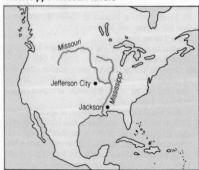

Mississippi

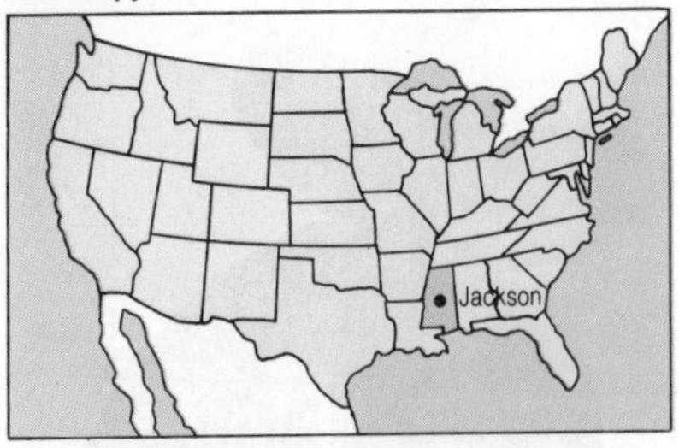

was the simultaneous admission of Maine as a non-slave state.

Missouri River /mɪˈzʊəri/ river in central USA, a tributary of the Mississippi, which it joins at St Louis; length 3,725 km/2,328 mi.

Mistinguett /ˌmiːstæŋˈget/ stage name of Jeanne Bourgeois 1873–1956. French actress and dancer. A leading music-hall artist in Paris from 1899, she appeared in revues at the Folies-Bergère, Casino de Paris, and Moulin Rouge. She was famous for the song 'Mon Homme' and her partnership with Maurice Chevalier.

mistletoe parasitic evergreen unisexual plant *Viscum album*, native to Europe. It grows on trees as a branched bush, with translucent white berries. Used in many Western countries as a Christmas decoration, it also featured in ◊Druidism.

The seeds of the European mistletoe are dispersed by birds, but the ***dwarf mistletoe*** *Arceuthobium* of North America shoots its seeds at 100 kph/60 mph as far as 15 m/16 yd. Mistletoes lose water more than ten times as fast as other plants to draw nutrients to them, and the dwarf mistletoe causes loss of 20 million cubic metres of wood fibre a year.

mistral cold, dry, northerly wind that occasionally blows during the winter on the Mediterranean coast of France. It has been known to reach a velocity of 145 kph/90 mph.

Mistral /mɪsˈtrɑːl/ Gabriela. Pen name of Lucila Godoy de Alcayaga 1889–1957. Chilean poet, who wrote *Sonnets of Death* 1915. Nobel Prize for Literature 1945. She was consul of Chile in Spain, and represented her country at the League of Nations and the United Nations.

Mitchell /ˈmɪtʃəl/ Arthur 1934– . US dancer, director of the Dance Theater of Harlem, which he founded with Karel Shook in 1968. Mitchell was a principal dancer with the New York City Ballet 1956–68, creating many roles in Balanchine's ballets.

Mitchell /ˈmɪtʃəl/ Juliet 1940– . British psychoanalyst and writer. She first came to public notice with an article in *New Left Review* 1966 entitled 'The Longest Revolution', one of the first attempts to combine socialism and feminism using Marxist theory to explain the reasons behind women's oppression. Her more recent publications, *Women's Estate* 1971 and *Psychoanalysis and Feminism* 1974, have had considerable influence on feminist thinking.

Mitchell /ˈmɪtʃəl/ Margaret 1900–1949. US novelist, born in Atlanta, Georgia, which is the setting for her one book *Gone With the Wind* 1936, a story of the US Civil War.

Missouri

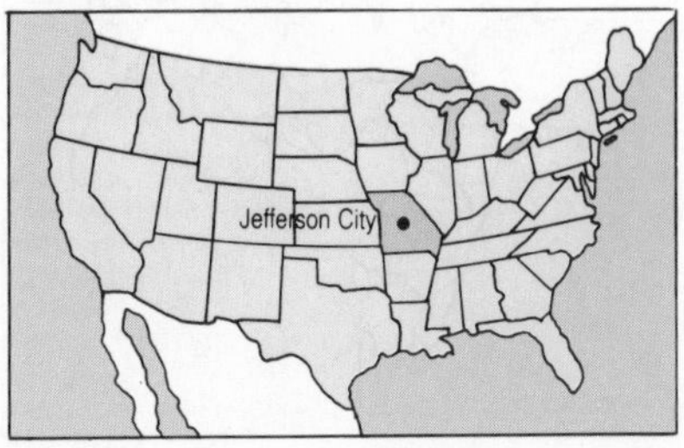

Mitchell /ˈmɪtʃəl/ Peter 1920– . British chemist. He received a Nobel prize in 1978 for work on the conservation of energy by plants during respiration and photosynthesis.

Mitchell /ˈmɪtʃəl/ R(eginald) J(oseph) 1895–1937. British aircraft designer, whose Spitfire fighter was a major factor in winning the Battle of Britain.

Mitchum /ˈmɪtʃəm/ Robert 1917– . US film actor, a star for over 30 years. His films include *Out of the Past* 1947, *The Night of the Hunter* 1955, and *Farewell My Lovely* 1975.

mite minute animal belonging to the Arachnida, related to spiders. Mites may be free-living scavengers or predators. Some are parasitic, such as the ***itch mite*** *Sarcoptes scabiei* which burrows in human skin, or the ***red mite*** *Dermanyssus gallinae* which sucks blood from poultry and other birds.

Mitford sisters /ˈmɪtfəd/ the six daughters of Lord Redesdale, including:
Nancy (1904–73), author of the semi-autobiographical *The Pursuit of Love* 1945 and *Love in a Cold Climate* 1949, and editor and part author of *Noblesse Oblige* 1956 elucidating 'U' (upper-class) and 'non-U' behaviour;
Diana (1910–) who married Oswald ◊Mosley;
Unity (1914–48), who became an admirer of Hitler; and
Jessica (1917–), author of the autobiographical *Hons and Rebels* 1960 and *The American Way of Death* 1963.

Mithraism the ancient Persian worship of Mithras. His cult was introduced into the Roman Empire in 68 BC, spread rapidly particularly among soldiers, and by about AD 250 rivalled Christianity in strength.

Mithras /ˈmɪθræs/ in Persian mythology, the god of light. Mithras represented the power of goodness, and promised his followers compensation for present evil after death. Mithras was said to have captured and killed the sacred bull, from whose blood all life sprang.

A bath in the blood of a sacrificed bull formed part of the initiation ceremony. In 1954 remains of a Roman temple dedicated to Mithras were discovered in the City of London.

Mithridates VI Eupator /ˌmɪθrɪˈdeɪtiːz/ known as ***the Great*** 132–63 BC. King of Pontus (NE Asia Minor, on the Black Sea) from 120 BC. He massacred 80,000 Romans in overrunning the rest of Asia Minor and went on to invade Greece. He was defeated by ◊Sulla in the First Mithridatic War 88–84; by ◊Lucullus in the Second 83–81; and by ◊Pompey in the Third 74–64. He was killed by a soldier at his own order rather than surrender.

Mitilíni /ˌmɪtɪˈliːni/ modern Greek name of ◊Mytilene, town on the island of Lesvos.

mitochondria rodlike or spherical bodies within ◊eukaryotic cells, containing enzymes responsible for energy production. They are thought to be derived from free-living bacteria that, at a very early stage in the history of life, invaded larger cells and took up a symbiotic way of life there. Each still contains its own small loop of DNA, and new mitochondria arise by division of existing ones.

mitosis in biology, the process of cell division. The genetic material of ◊eukaryotic cells is carried on a number of ◊chromosomes. To control their movements during cell division so that both new cells get a full set, a system of protein tubules, known as the spindle, organizes the chromosomes into position in the middle of the cell before they replicate. The spindle then controls the movement of chromosomes as the cell goes through the stages of division: ***interphase***, ***prophase***, ***metaphase***, ***anaphase***, and ***telophase***. See also ◊meiosis.

mitre in the Christian church, the headdress worn by bishops, cardinals, and mitred abbots at solemn services. There are mitres of many different shapes, but in the Western church they usually take the form of a tall cleft cap. The mitre worn by the pope is called a tiara.

Mithras *This marble head wearing a Phrygian cap was found in the excavation of London's temple of Mithras.*

Mitre /ˈmɪtreɪ/ Bartólomé 1821–1906. Argentinian president 1862–68. In 1852 he helped overthrow the dictatorial regime of Juan Manuel de Rosas and in 1861 unify Argentina. Mitre encouraged immigration and favoured growing commercial links with Europe. He is seen as a symbol of national unity.

Mitterrand /ˌmiːtəˈrɒŋ/ François 1916– . French socialist politician, president from 1981. He held ministerial posts in 11 governments 1947–1958. He founded the French Socialist Party (PS) 1971. In 1985 he introduced proportional representation, allegedly to weaken the growing opposition from left and right.

Mitterrand studied law and politics in Paris. During World War II he was prominent in the Resistance. He entered the National Assembly as a centre-left deputy for Nièvre. Opposed to Gen de Gaulle's creation of the Fifth Republic 1958, he formed the centre-left anti-Gaullist Federation of the Left in the 1960s. In 1971 he became leader of the new PS. An electoral union with the Communist Party 1972–77 established the PS as the most popular party in France.

Mitterrand was elected president 1981. His programme of reform was hampered by deteriorating economic conditions after 1983. When the socialists lost their majority Mar 1986, he was compelled to work with a right-wing prime minister, Chirac, and grew in popularity. He defeated Chirac to secure a second term in the presidential election May 1988.

Mitylene /ˌmɪtɪˈliːni/ alternative spelling of ◊Mytilene, Greek city on the island of Lesvos.

mitosis

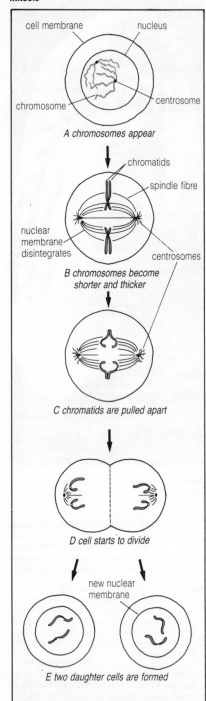

A chromosomes appear

chromatids

spindle fibre

nuclear membrane disintegrates

centrosomes

B chromosomes become shorter and thicker

C chromatids are pulled apart

D cell starts to divide

new nuclear membrane

E two daughter cells are formed

Mix 'Tom' (Thomas) 1880–1940. US actor, a cowboy star of silent films. At their best his films, such as *The Range Riders* 1910 and *King Cowboy* 1928, were fast-moving and full of impressive stunts.

mixed-ability teaching the practice of teaching children of all abilities in a single class. Mixed-ability teaching is normal practice in British primary schools but most secondary schools begin to divide children according to ability, either in sets or, more rarely, streams, as they approach public examinations at 16.

mixture in chemistry, a substance containing two or more compounds that still retain their separate physical and chemical properties. There is no chemical bonding between them and they can be separated from each other by physical means.

Mizoguchi /ˌmiːzəʊˈguːtʃi/ Kenji 1898–1956. Japanese film director whose *Ugetsu Monogatari* 1953 confirmed his international reputation. He also directed *Blood and Soul* 1923, *The Poppies* 1935, and *Street of Shame* 1956.

Mizoram /ˌmaɪzəˈræm/ state of NE India
area 21,100 sq km/8,145 sq mi
capital Aizawl
products rice, hand loom weaving
population (1981) 488,000
religion 84% Christian
history made a Union Territory 1972 from the Mizo Hills District of Assam. Rebels carried on a guerrilla war 1966–76, but in 1976 acknowledged Mizoram as an integral part of India. It became a state 1986.

mks system system of units in which the base units metre, kilogram, and second replace the centimetre, gram, and second of the ◊c.g.s. system. From it developed the ◊SI system.

It simplifies the incorporation of the electrical units into the metric system, and was incorporated in SI (see ◊SI units). For application to electrical and magnetic phenomena, the ampere was added, creating what was called the MKSA system.

ml abbreviation for *millilitre*.

Mladenov /mləˈdeɪnɒf/ Petar 1936– . Bulgarian Communist politician, secretary general of the Bulgarian Communist Party from Nov 1989 after the resignation of ◊Zhivkov.

MLR abbreviation for *minimum lending rate*.

mm abbreviation for *millimetre*.

Mmabatho /məˈbɑːtəʊ/ or *Sun City* capital of Bophuthatswana, South Africa; population (1985) 28,000. It is a casino resort frequented by many white South Africans.

mmHg abbreviation for *millimetre of mercury*.

MN abbreviation for ◊*Minnesota*.

MO abbreviation for ◊*Missouri*.

moa extinct kiwi-like bird, order Dinornithoformes, 19 species of which lived in New Zealand. They varied from 0.5 to 3.5 m/2–12 ft, with strong limbs, a long neck, and no wings. The last moa was killed in the 1800s. The Maoris used them as food, but the use of European firearms enabled them to be killed in too large numbers.

Moab /ˈməʊæb/ an ancient country in Jordan E of the S part of the river Jordan and the Dead Sea. The inhabitants were closely akin to the Hebrews in culture, language, and religion, but were often at war with them, as recorded in the Old Testament. Moab eventually fell to Arab invaders. The *Moabite Stone*, discovered in 1868 at Dhiban, dates from the 9th century BC and records the rising of Mesha, king of Moab, against Israel.

Mitterrand French socialist president François Mitterrand, May 1989.

Mix Film actor Tom Mix in the film Fighting for Gold 1919. He starred in more than 60 Westerns over 30 years.

moat a ditch, often filled with water, surrounding a building or garden. Some 5,000 moats exist in England alone, many dating from the 12th–13th centuries; some were built for defence and others as a status symbol.

Mobile /məʊˈbiːl/ industrial city (meat-packing, paper, cement, clothing, chemicals) and only seaport in Alabama, USA; population (1980) 443,500. Founded 1702 by the French a little to the north of the present city, Mobile was capital of the French colony of Louisiana until 1763. It was then British until 1780, and Spanish to 1813.

Möbius /ˈmɜːbiəs/ Augustus Ferdinand 1790–1868. German mathematician, inventor of the möbius strip and considered one of the founders of ◊topology.

möbius strip structure made by giving a half twist to a flat strip of paper and joining the ends together. It has certain strange properties, arising from the fact that it has only one edge and one side. If cut down the centre of the strip, instead of two new strips of paper, only one long strip is produced. It was invented by the German mathematician Augustus Möbius.

Mobutu /məˈbuːtuː/ Sese-Seko-Kuku-Ngbeandu-Wa-Z a-Banga 1930– . Zaïrean president from 1965. He assumed the presidency by coup, and created a unitary state under his centralized government. He abolished secret voting in elections 1976 in favour of a system of acclamation at mass rallies. His personal wealth is estimated at $3–4 billion, and more money is spent on the presidency than on the entire social-services budget. The harshness of some of

Mizoram

Aizawl

INDIAN OCEAN

Mobutu *President Mobutu of Zaïre.*

his policies has attracted widespread international criticism.

Mobutu Sese Seko Lake /mə'buːtuː 'seseɪ 'sekəʊ/ lake on the border of Uganda and Zaïre in the Great ◊Rift Valley; area 4,275 sq km/1,650 sq mi. The first European to see it was the British explorer Samuel ◊Baker, who named it Lake Albert after the Prince Consort. It was renamed 1973 by Zaïre's president Mobutu after himself.

Moby-Dick US novel by Herman Melville, published 1851. Its story of the conflict between the monomaniac Captain Ahab and the great white whale explores both the mystery and the destructiveness of nature's power.

Moçambique /ˌmuːsəmˈbiːkə/ the Portuguese name for ◊Mozambique.

Moche or ***Mochica*** a pre-Inca people who lived in the coastal area of Peru AD 100–800. Remains include massive platform tombs (*adobe*) and pottery.

In 1988 the burial of one of their warrior-priest rulers was discovered. He was nicknamed the 'Great Lord of Sipan', after the village near the site of his pyramid tomb (*huaca*). It contained a priceless treasure hoard, including a gold mask and ear pendants.

mockingbird American bird *Mimus polyglottos*, related to the thrushes, brownish grey, with white markings on the black wings and tail. It is remarkable for its ability to mimic.

mock orange deciduous shrub of the genus *Philadelphus*, family Philadelphaceae, including *Philadelphus coronarius* which has white, strongly scented flowers, resembling those of the orange; it is sometimes referred to as syringa.

mod a youth subculture that originated in London and Brighton in the early 1960s around the French view of the English; revived in the late 1970s. Mods were fashion-conscious, speedy, and upwardly mobile; they favoured scooters and soul music.

MOD abbreviation for *Ministry of ◊Defence*.

Model Parliament English parliament set up 1295 by Edward I; it was the first to include representatives from outside the clergy and aristocracy, and was established because Edward needed the support of the whole country against his opponents: Wales, France, and Scotland. His sole aim was to raise money for military purposes, and the parliament did not pass any legislation.

The parliament comprised archbishops, bishops, abbots, earls, and barons (all summoned by special writ, and forming the basis of the modern House of Lords); also present were the lower clergy (heads of chapters, archdeacons, two clerics from each diocese, and one from each cathedral) and representatives of the shires, cities, and boroughs (two knights from every shire, two representatives from each city, and two burghers from each borough).

modem (*mo*dulator-*dem*odulator) a device for transmitting data over telephone lines. The modem converts digital signals to analogue, and back again. Modems are used for linking remote terminals to central computers, and to enable computers to communicate with each other over long distances.

Modena /'mɒdɪnə/ city in Emilia, Italy, capital of the province of Modena, 37 km/23 mi NW of Bologna; population (1988) 177,000. It has a 12th-century cathedral, a 17th-century ducal palace, and a university 1683, noted for its medical and legal faculties.

Moderator in the Church of Scotland, the minister chosen to act as president of the annual General Assembly.

moderator in a nuclear reactor, the material such as graphite used to reduce the speed of neutrons. Neutrons produced by nuclear fission are fast-moving and must be slowed for them to initiate further fission, so that nuclear energy continues to be released, and at a controlled rate.

Slow neutrons are much more likely to cause ◊fission in a uranium-235 nucleus than to be captured in a U-238 (non-fissile uranium) nucleus. By using a moderator, a reactor can thus be made to work with fuel containing only a small proportion of U-235.

Modernism in the Church of England, a development of the 20th-century liberal church movement, which attempts to reconsider Christian beliefs in the light of modern scientific theories and historical methods, without abandoning the essential doctrines. Similar movements exist in many Nonconformist churches and in the Roman Catholic Church. Modernism was condemned by Pope Pius X in 1907.

Modernism in the arts, a general term used to describe various tendencies in the first three-quarters of the 20th century. It refers mainly to a conscious attempt to break away from the artistic traditions of the 19th century, and also to a concern with form and the exploration of technique as opposed to content and narrative.

In the visual arts, direct representationalism gave way to abstraction (see ◊abstract art); in literature, writers experimented with alternatives to orthodox sequential storytelling, such as ◊stream of consciousness; in music, the traditional concept of key was challenged by ◊atonality; and in architecture, functionalism ousted decorativeness as a central objective. Critics of Modernism have found in it an austerity that is seen as dehumanizing. Modernism as a movement is followed by ◊Post-Modernism.

Modern Jazz Quartet, the US jazz group specializing in group improvisation, formed 1952 (disbanded 1974 and re-formed 1981), led by pianist John Lewis (1920–), with Milt Jackson (1923–) on vibraphone, bass player Percy Heath (1923–), and as drummer first Kenny Clarke (1914–85) and later Connie Kay (1927–). Noted for elegance and mastery of form, they have sometimes been criticized for being too 'classical'.

Modigliani /ˌmɒdɪlˈjɑːni/ Amedeo 1884–1920. Italian artist, active in Paris from 1906. He painted and sculpted graceful nudes and portrait studies. His paintings have a distinctive soft, elongated, linear style.

Modigliani was born in Livorno. He was encouraged to sculpt by Brancusi, and his series of strictly simplified heads reflects a shared interest in archaic sculptural styles. The portrait of *Jeanne Hebuterne* 1919 (Guggenheim Museum, New York) is typical of his painting. His life was dramatic and dissolute, and he died of the combined effects of alcoholism, drug addiction, and tuberculosis.

modular course in education, a course, usually leading to a recognized qualification, which is divided into short and often optional units that are assessed as they are completed.

An accumulation of modular credits may then lead to the award of a qualification such as a degree, a BTEC diploma or a GCSE pass. Modular schemes are increasingly popular as a means of allowing students to take a wider range of subjects.

modulation in ◊radio, the intermittent change of frequency, or amplitude, of a radio carrier wave, in accordance with the audio-frequency, speaking voice, music, or other signal being transmitted. See ◊pulse-code modulation.

modulation in music, movement from one ◊key to another.

module in construction, a part that governs the form of the rest; for example, Japanese room sizes are traditionally governed by multiples of standard tatami floor mats; modern prefabricated buildings are mass-produced in a similar way. The components of a spacecraft are designed in coordination; for example, for the Apollo Moon landings the craft comprised a command module (for working, eating, sleeping), service module (electricity generators, oxygen supplies, manoeuvring rocket), and lunar module (to land and return the astronauts).

modulus in mathematics, the positive value of a ◊real number, irrespective of its sign, indicated by a pair of vertical lines. Thus |3| is 3; and |–5| is 5.

For a ◊complex number, the modulus is its distance to the origin when it is plotted on an Argand diagram, and can be calculated (without plotting) by applying ◊Pythagoras' theorem. In general, the modulus of the complex number $a + bi$ is $\sqrt{(a^2 + b^2)}$.

modus operandi (Latin) a method of operating.

modus vivendi (Latin 'way of living') a compromise between opposing points of view.

Mogadishu /ˌmɒgəˈdɪʃuː/ or ***Mugdisho*** capital and chief port of Somalia; population (1988) 1,000,000. It is a centre for oil refining, food processing, and uranium mining. It has mosques dating back to the 13th century, and a cathedral built 1925–28.

Mogilev /ˌmɒgɪlˈjɒf/ industrial city (tractors, clothing, chemicals, furniture) in the Byelorussian Republic, USSR, on the Dneiper, 193 km/120 mi east of Minsk; population (1987) 359,000. It was annexed by Russia from Sweden 1772.

Mogok /'məʊgɒk/ village in Burma, 114 km/71 mi NNE of Mandalay, known for its ruby and sapphire mines.

Mogul emperors N Indian dynasty 1526–1857, established by ◊Zahir ('Baber'). They were descendants of Tamerlane, the 14th-century Mongol leader, and ruled until the last Mogul emperor was

Modigliani Nude (c.1916) Courtauld Collection, London.

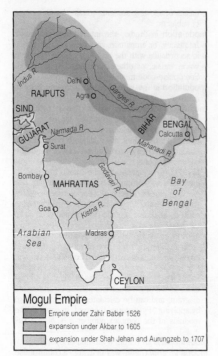

Mogul Empire

- Empire under Zahir Baber 1526
- expansion under Akbar to 1605
- expansion under Shah Jehan and Aurungzeb to 1707

dethroned and exiled by the British 1857; they included ◊Akbar, ◊Aurangzeb, and ◊Shah Jehan. They were Muslims.

MOH abbreviation for *Medical Officer of Health*.

Mohács, Battle of /ˈməʊhɑːtʃ/ Austro-Hungarian defeat of the Turks 1687 which effectively marked the end of Turkish expansion into Europe. It is also the site of a Turkish victory in 1526. Mohács is now a river port on the Danube in Hungary.

mohair hair of the Angora goat. The fine, white, lustrous fibre is manufactured into fabric. Commercial mohair is now obtained from cross-bred animals, pure-bred supplies being insufficient.

Mohamad /məˈhæməd/ Mahathir bin 1925– . Prime minister of Malaysia from 1981 and leader of the United Malays' National Organization (UMNO). His 'look east' economic policy emulates Japanese industrialization.

Mahathir bin Mohamad was elected to the House of Representatives 1964 and gained the support of the dominant UMNO's radical youth wing as an advocate of economic help to *bumiputras* (ethnic Malays) and as a proponent of a more Islamic social policy. Dr Mahathir held a number of ministerial posts from 1974 before being appointed prime minister and UMNO leader in 1981. He was re-elected 1986, but has alienated sections of UMNO by his authoritarian leadership.

Mohammed /məʊˈhæmɪd/ alternative form of ◊Muhammad, founder of Islam.

Mohammedanism misnomer for ◊Islam, the religion founded by Muhammad.

Mohawk North American Indian nation, part of the ◊Iroquois confederation.

Mohenjo Daro /məˈhendʒəʊ ˈdɑːrəʊ/ site of a city about 2500–1600 BC on the lower Indus, Pakistan, where excavations from the 1920s have revealed the ◊Indus Valley civilization. The most striking artistic remains are soapstone seals of elephants and snakes.

Mohican and Mohegan two closely related North American Indian peoples, akin to the Algonquins, who formerly occupied Connecticut and the Hudson Valley. James Fenimore ◊Cooper confused the two peoples.

Mohole US project for drilling a hole through the Earth's crust, so named from the ◊Mohorovičić discontinuity that marks the transition from crust to mantle. Initial tests were made in the Pacific in 1961, but the project was subsequently abandoned.

The cores that were brought up illuminated the geological history of the Earth and aided the development of geophysics.

Moholy-Nagy /ˈməʊhɔɪ ˈnɒdʒ/ Laszlo 1895–1946. US photographer, born in Hungary. He lived in Germany 1923–29, where he was a member of the Bauhaus school, and fled from the Nazis in 1935. Through the publication of his illuminating theories and practical experiments, he had great influence on 20th-century photography and design.

Mohorovičić discontinuity /ˌməʊhəˈrəʊvɪtʃɪtʃ/ also *Moho* or *M-discontinuity* boundary that separates the Earth's crust and mantle, marked by a rapid increase in the speed of earthquake waves. It follows the variations in the thickness of the crust and is found approximately 32 km/20 mi below the continents and about 10 km/6 mi below the oceans. It is named after the Yugoslav geophysicist Andrija Mohorovičić (1857–1936), who suspected its presence after analysing seismic waves from the Kulpa Valley earthquake 1909.

Mohs /məʊz/ Friedrich 1773–1839. German mineralogist, who in 1812 devised *Mohs' scale* of minerals, classified in order of relative hardness.

Mohs' scale scale of hardness for minerals (in ascending order): 1 talc; 2 gypsum; 3 calcite; 4 fluorite; 5 apatite; 6 orthoclase; 7 quartz; 8 topaz; 9 corundum; 10 diamond.

The scale is useful in mineral identification because any mineral will scratch any other mineral lower on the scale than itself, and similarly it will be scratched by any other mineral higher on the scale.

Moi /mɔɪ/ Daniel arap 1924– . Kenyan politician, president from 1978. Originally a teacher, he became minister of home affairs in 1964, vice president in 1967, and succeeded ◊Kenyatta as president.

Moissan /mwæˈsɒn/ Henri 1852–1907. French chemist. For his preparation of pure fluorine in 1886, Moissan was awarded the 1906 Nobel Chemistry Prize. He also attempted to create artificial diamonds by rapidly cooling mixtures of carbon heated to high temperatures. His claims of success were treated with suspicion.

Mojave Desert /məʊˈhɑːvi/ arid region in S California, USA, part of the Great Basin; area 38,500 sq km/15,000 sq mi.

Mokha /ˈməʊkə/ or *Mocha* seaport of N Yemen near the mouth of the Red Sea, once famed for its coffee exports. It has declined since the USSR built a new port near Hodeida. Population about 8,000.

moksha (Sanskrit 'liberation') in Hinduism, liberation from the cycle of reincarnation and from the illusion of ◊maya. In Buddhism, ◊enlightenment.

molar in chemistry, a molar ◊solution contains one ◊mole in grams of solute in one cubic decimetre of solution.

molarity the ◊concentration of a solution expressed as the number of ◊moles in grams of solute per cubic decimetre of solution.

molar volume the volume occupied by one ◊mole (the molecular mass in grams) of any gas at standard temperature and pressure, equal to 2.24136 $\times 10^{-2}$ m³.

molasses the drainings from raw cane sugar; the term is commonly used as a synonym for treacle. Molasses from sugar cane produces rum in fermentation; that from beet sugar gives alcohol.

Mold /məʊld/ market town in ◊Clwyd, Wales, on the river Alyn; population (1981) 8,555. It is the administrative headquarters of Clwyd and has two theatres.

Moldavia /mɒlˈdeɪviə/ constituent republic of the Soviet Union from 1940
area 33,700 sq km/13,012 sq mi
capital Kishinev
features ◊Black Earth region
products wine, tobacco, canned goods

Mohs scale

Number	Defining mineral	Other substances compared
1	talc	
2	gypsum	2½ fingernail
3	calcite	3½ copper coin
4	fluorite	
5	apatite	5½ steel blade
6	orthoclase	5¾ glass
7	quartz	7 steel file
8	topaz	
9	corundum	
10	diamond	

The scale is not regular: diamond, at number 10, the hardest natural substance, is 90 times harder in absolute terms than corundum, number 9.

population (1987) 4,185,000; 64% Moldavians (a branch of the Romanian people) Ukrainian 14%, Russian 13%, Gagauzi 4%, Jewish 2%
language Moldavian, allied to Romanian
religion Russian Orthodox
recent history formed from part of the former Moldavian Republic of the USSR (within Ukraine) and areas of Bessarabia ceded by Romania 1940, except the area bordering the Black Sea (added to Ukraine SSR). In 1988 a 'Popular Front' organization, the 'Democratic Movement for Perestroika' was formed in the republic, which has since campaigned for accelerated political reform and for the grant of official status for the Moldavian language. During 1989, following a decision by the republic's parliament to accede to the latter demand, there were a series of Russian–Moldavian clashes in Kishinev.

Moldavia /mɒlˈdeɪviə/ former principality in Eastern Europe, on the river Danube, occupying an area divided today between the Soviet republic of Moldavia and modern Romania. It was independent between the 14th and 16th centuries, when it became part of the Ottoman Empire. In 1940 the E part, Bessarabia, became part of the Soviet Union, whereas the W part remained in Romania.

mole burrowing mammal of the family Talpidae. Moles grow to 18 cm/7 in, and have acute senses of hearing, smell, and touch, but poor vision. They have strong, clawed front feet, and eat insects, grubs, and worms.

The common mole of Europe *Talpa europaea* has a thickset body about 18 cm/7 in with soft dark fur. Practically blind, it lives underground in circular grass-lined nests, and excavates extensive tunnels in its search for worms and grubs, throwing up the earth at intervals in molehills. The short muscular forelimbs and shovel-like feet are adapted for burrowing. Some members of the family are aquatic, such as the *Russian desman Desmana moschata*.

mole SI unit (symbol mol) of the amount of a substance. One mole of an element that exists as single atoms weighs as many grams as its ◊atomic number (so 1 mol of carbon weighs 12 g),

Moi Kenyan politician Daniel arap Moi has been president since 1978.

Moldavia

and it contains 6.022045×10^{23} atoms, which is ◊Avogadro's number.

One mole of a substance is defined as the amount of that substance that contains as many elementary entities (atoms, molecules, and so on) as there are atoms in 0.012 kg of the ◊isotope carbon-12.

mole a mechanical device for boring horizontal holes underground without the need for digging trenches. It is used for laying pipes and cables.

mole a person working subversively within an organization. The term has come to be used broadly for someone who gives out ('leaks') secret information in the public interest; it originally meant a person who spends several years working for a government department or a company with the intention of passing secrets to a rival or enemy.

The term was popularized in the novels of John Le Carré. In the UK it has been applied, for example, to the civil servants Sarah Tisdall, who leaked government information to the press, and Clive Ponting, who passed it in confidence to his Member of Parliament; his successful defence was that this was legal and his duty.

molecular biology the study of the molecular basis of life, including the biochemistry of molecules such as DNA, RNA, and proteins, and the structure and function of the various parts of living cells.

molecular clock the use of rates of ◊mutation in genetic material to calculate the length of time elapsed since two related species diverged from each other during evolution. The method can be based on comparisons of the DNA or of widely occurring proteins, such as haemoglobin.

Since mutations are thought to occur at a constant rate, the length of time that must have elapsed in order to produce the difference between two species can be estimated. This information can be compared with the evidence obtained from palaeontology to reconstruct evolutionary events.

molecular weight another name for ◊relative molecular mass.

molecule smallest particle of any substance that can exist freely yet still exhibit all the chemical properties of the substance. Molecules are composed of ◊atoms, ranging in size from one atom in, for example, a helium molecule, to the large ◊macromolecules found in polymers. Molecules cannot be split into smaller entities without changing the chemical nature of the substance concerned.

They are held together by electrovalent bonds, in which the atoms gain or lose electrons to form ions, or covalent bonds, in which electrons from each atom are shared in a new molecular orbital. The symbolic representation of a molecule is known as a formula. The presence of more than one atom is denoted by a subscript figure. For example, water (H_2O) contains two atoms of hydrogen.

According to the molecular or ◊kinetic theory of matter, molecules are in a state of constant motion, the extent of which depends on their temperature, and exert forces on one another.

Molecules were inferrable from ◊Avogadro's hypothesis 1811, but only became generally accepted in 1860 when proposed by Stanislao Cannizzaro (1826–1910).

Molière /ˈmɒliɛə/ Pen name of Jean Baptiste Poquelin 1622–1673. French satirical playwright from whose work modern French comedy developed. One of the founders of the Illustre Théâtre 1643, he was later its leading actor. In 1655 he wrote his first play, *L'Etourdi*, followed by *Les Précieuses ridicules* 1659. His satires include *L'Ecole des femmes* 1662, ◊*Le Misanthrope* 1666, *Le Bourgeois gentilhomme* 1670, and *Le Malade imaginaire* 1673.

Other satiric plays include *Tartuffe* 1664 (banned until 1697 for attacking the hypocrisy of the clergy), *Le Médecin malgré lui* 1666, and *Les Femmes Savantes* 1672. Molière's comedies, based on the exposure of hypocrisy and cant, made him vulnerable to many attacks (from which he was protected by Louis XIV) and marked a new departure in the French theatre away from reliance on classical Greek themes.

Molinos /mɒˈliːnɒs/ Miguel de 1640–1697. Spanish mystic and Roman Catholic priest. He settled in Rome and wrote in Italian several devotional works, including the *Guida spirituale/Spiritual Guide* 1675 which aroused the hostility of the Jesuits. In 1687 he was sentenced to life

Molière *French Playwright Molière died a day after performing the title role in his* Le Médecin malgré lui.

imprisonment. His doctrine is known as ◊quietism.

Molise /mɒˈliːzeɪ/ mainly agricultural region of S central Italy, comprising the provinces of Campobasso and Isernia; area 4,400 sq km/ 1,698 sq mi; population (1988) 335,000. Its capital is Campobasso.

mollusc invertebrate animal of the phylum Mollusca. The majority are marine animals, but some inhabit fresh water, and a few are terrestrial. They include shellfish, snails, slugs, and cuttles. The body is soft, limbless, and cold-blooded. There is no internal skeleton, but most species have a hard shell covering the body.

Molluscs vary in diet, the carnivorous species feeding chiefly upon other members of the class. Some are vegetarian. Reproduction is by means of eggs, and is sexual.

The shells of molluscs take a variety of forms, univalve (snail), bivalve (mussel), chambered (nautilus), and many other variations. In some cases, for example octopus and squid, the shell is internal. There is a fold of skin, the mantle, which covers the whole body or the back only, and secretes the calcareous substance forming the shell. The lower ventral surface forms the locomotory organ, or foot.

Molly Maguires, the in US history, a secret Irish coalminers' organization in the 1870s which staged strikes and used violence against coal-company officials and property in the anthracite fields of Pennsylvania, prefiguring a long period of turbulence in industrial relations. The movement was infiltrated by Pinkerton agents (detectives) and in 1876 trials led to convictions and executions.

Molnár /ˈməʊlnɑː/ Ferenc 1878–1952. Hungarian novelist and playwright. His play *Liliom* 1909 is a study of a circus barker, adapted as the musical *Carousel*.

Moloch /ˈməʊlɒk/ or *Molech* in the Old Testament, a Phoenician deity worshipped in Jerusalem in the 7th century BC, to whom live children were sacrificed by fire.

Molokai /ˌməʊləˈkaɪ/ mountainous island of Hawaii state, USA, SE of Oahu
area 673 sq km/259 sq mi
features Kamakou 1,512 m/4,960 ft is the highest peak;
population (1980) 6,049
history the island is famous as the site of a leper colony organized 1873–89 by Belgian missionary Joseph ◊De Veuster (Father Damien).

Molotov /ˈmɒlətɒf/ former name (1940–62) for the port of ◊Perm in USSR.

Molotov /ˈmɒlətɒf/ Vyacheslav Mikhailovich. Assumed name of V M Skryabin 1890–1986. Soviet communist politician. He was chair of the Council of People's Commissars (prime minister) 1930–41, and foreign minister 1939–49, during which period he negotiated a nonaggression treaty with Germany (the ◊Hitler–Stalin pact), and again 1953–56. In 1957 he was expelled from the government for Stalinist activities.

molecule

covalent bonding

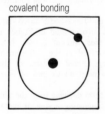

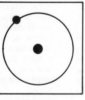

shared path of electron

proton   proton

atoms of hydrogen sharing electrons

7 electrons   1 electron
in outer ring   in outer ring

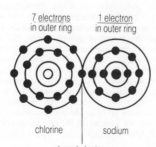

chlorine   sodium

shared electron

Sodium chloride Na Cl

ionic bonding

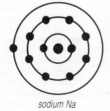

chlorine Cl   *sodium Na*

molluscs: classification

Phylum Mollusca

Class Monoplacophora	primitive marine forms, including Neopilina (2 species)
Class Amphineura	(1,150 species)
1 Aplacophora	wormlike marine forms
2 Polyplacophora	chitons, coat-of-mail shells
Class Gastropoda	snail-like molluscs, with single or no shell (9,000 species)
1 Prosobranchia	limpets, winkles, whelks
2 Opisthobranchia	seaslugs
3 Pulmonata	land and freshwater snails, slugs
Class Scaphopoda	tusk shells, marine burrowers (350 species)
Class Bivalvia	molluscs with a double (two-valved) shell (15,000 species); mussels, oysters, clams, cockles, scallops, tellins, razor shells, shipworms
Class Cephalopoda	molluscs with shell generally reduced, arms to capture prey, and beak-like mouth; body bilaterally symmetrical and nervous system well developed (750 species); squids, cuttlefish, octopuses, pearly nautilus, argonaut

Molotov cocktail or *petrol bomb* home-made weapon consisting of a bottle filled with petrol, plugged with a rag as a wick, ignited, and thrown as a grenade. Resistance groups during World War II named them after the Soviet foreign minister Molotov.

Moltke /'mɒltkə/ Helmuth Carl Bernhard, Count von Moltke 1800–1891. Prussian general. He entered the Prussian army 1821, became chief of the general staff 1857, and was responsible for the Prussian strategy in the wars with Denmark 1863–64, Austria 1866, and France 1870–71. He was created a count 1870 and a field marshal 1871.

Moltke /'mɒltkə/ Helmuth Johannes Ludwig von Moltke 1848–1916. German general (nephew of Count von Moltke, the Prussian general), chief of the German general staff 1906–14. His use of ◊Schlieffen's plan for a rapid victory on two fronts failed and he was superseded.

Moluccas /məʊ'lʌkəz/ another name for ◊Maluku, Indonesia.

molybdenite molybdenum sulphide, MoS_2, the chief ore mineral of molybdenum. It possesses a hexagonal crystal structure similar to graphite, has a blue metallic lustre, and is very soft (1–1.5 on Mohs' scale).

molybdenum a white metallic element, symbol Mo, atomic number 42, relative atomic mass 95.975. It is important in making special steels, and it is also used for electrodes (since it is easily welded to soda and Pyrex glass, and to other metals), and for filaments (alloyed with tungsten) in thermionic valves.

It has a melting point of 2,620°C, and is not found in the free state. As an aid to lubrication, molybdenum disulphide (MoS_2) greatly reduces surface friction between ferrous metals. Producing countries include Canada, the USA, and Norway.

Mombasa /mɒm'bæsə/ industrial port (oil refining, cement) in Kenya (serving also Uganda and Tanzania), built on Mombasa Island and adjacent mainland; population (1984) 481,000.

moment of a force in physics, product of the force and the perpendicular distance from the point to the line of action of the force; it measures the turning effect or torque produced by the force.

Monaco
Principality of

area 1.95 sq km/0.75 sq mi
capital Monaco-Ville
town Monte Carlo, noted for its film festival, motor races, and casino
physical steep slope
features surrounded landward by French territory, it is being expanded by filling in the sea; aquarium and oceanographic centre
head of state Rainier III from 1949
head of government Jean Ausseil from 1986
government constitutional monarchy under French protectorate
exports some light industry, but economy depends on tourism and gambling
currency French franc (9.70 = £1 Feb 1990)
population (1989) 29,000; annual growth rate –0.5%
language French
religion Roman Catholic
literacy 99% (1985)
chronology
1861 Became an independent state under French protection.
1918 France given a veto over succession to the throne.
1949 Prince Rainier III ascended the throne.

---

moment of inertia in physics, the sum of all the point masses of a rotating object multiplied by the squares of their respective distances from the axis of rotation. It is analagous to the ◊mass of a stationary object or one moving in a straight line.

In linear dynamics, Newton's second law of motion states that the force on a moving object F equals the products of its mass m and acceleration a ($F = ma$); the analogous equation in rotational dynamics is $T = IA$, where T is the torque (the turning effect of a force) that causes an angular acceleration A and I is the moment of inertia. For a given object, I depends on its shape and the position of its axis of rotation.

momentum in physics, the product of the mass of a body and its linear velocity; *angular momentum* (of a body in rotational motion) is the product of its moment of inertia and its angular velocity. The momentum of a body does not change unless it is acted on by an external force.

The law of conservation of momentum is one of the fundamental concepts of classical physics. It states that the total momentum of all bodies in a closed system is constant and unaffected by processes occurring within the system.

An orbiting body possesses angular momentum, this being the result of the combined effects of its orbital velocity, mass, and distance from the primary. Angular momentum is also a property of rotating bodies. The angular momentum of an object of mass m travelling at a velocity v in a circular orbit of radius R is expressed as mvR. Angular momentum is conserved, and should any of the values alter (such as the radius of orbit), the remainder will compensate to preserve the value of angular momentum, and that lost by one component is passed to another. An example is a rotating gas cloud: any large contracting gas cloud undergoes an increase in its axial rotation velocity to conserve angular momentum. Another example is a spinning ice skater. With outstretched arms, the skater spins only slowly, although the rate of spin increases dramatically when the arms are pulled in, redistributing the mass of the skater.

Momoh /'məʊməʊ/ Joseph Saidu 1937– . Sierra Leone soldier and politician, president from 1985. An army officer who became commander 1983, with the rank of major-general, he succeeded Siaka Stevens as president when he retired; Momoh was endorsed by Sierra Leone's one political party, the All-People's Congress (APC). He has dissociated himself from the policies of his predecessor, pledging to fight corruption and improve the economy.

Mona /'məʊnə/ Latin name for ◊Anglesey, island in Wales.

Monaco /'mɒnəkəʊ/ small sovereign state, forming an enclave in southern France, with the Mediterranean to the south.

government Under the 1911 constitution, modified 1917 and largely rewritten 1962, Monaco is a hereditary principality, but an earlier concept of attributing the prince with a divine right to rule has been deleted. Legislative power is shared between the prince and a single-chamber national council, with 18 members elected by universal suffrage for a five-year term. Executive power is formally vested in the prince but in practice is exercised by a four-member council of government.

There are no political parties as such but the 1983 and 1988 National Council elections were contested by the National and Democratic Union (UND), which, formed in 1962, supports Prince Rainier and captured all the Council's seats. A rival organization, the Democratic and Socialist Union, also contested the 1983 election but has since been dormant.

history Formerly part of the Roman empire, Monaco became a Genoese possession in the 12th century, and has been ruled since 1297 by the Grimaldi family. It was a Spanish protectorate 1542–1641, then came under French protection and during the French revolution was annexed by France. The ruling family were imprisoned (one was guillotined), but regained power after the 1814 Treaty of Paris. In 1815 Monaco became a protectorate of Sardinia but reverted to French protection in 1861. In 1940 it was occupied by Italy, and in 1943 by Germany, but was liberated in 1945.

Agreements between France and Monaco state that Monaco will be incorporated in France if the reigning prince dies without a male heir. France is closely involved in the government of Monaco, providing a civil servant, of the prince's choosing, to head its Council of Government.

monad a philosophical term deriving from the philosophy of Leibniz, suggesting a soul or metaphysical unit which has a self-contained life. The monads are independent of each other, but coordinated by a 'pre-established harmony'.

Monadnock /mə'nædnɒk/ a mountain in New Hampshire, USA, 1,063 m/3,186 ft high. The term Monadnock is also used to mean any isolated hill or mountain.

Monaghan /'mɒnəhən/ (Irish *Mhuineachain*) county of the NE Republic of Ireland, province of Ulster; area 1,290 sq km/498 sq mi; population (1986) 52,000. The county town is Monaghan. The county is low and rolling, and includes the rivers Finn and Blackwater. Products include cereals, linen, potatoes, and cattle.

Monarchianism a form of belief in the Christian Trinity which emphasizes the undifferentiated unity of God. It was common in the early 3rd century.

monarchy, succession to the in the UK, the people who are in line to ascend the throne in the event of the death of the person preceding them. See ◊Elizabeth II.

monasticism devotion to religious life under vows of poverty, chastity, and obedience, known to Judaism (for example ◊Essenes), Buddhism, and other religions, before Christianity. In Islam, the Sufis formed monastical orders from the 12th century.

3rd century The institution of monasticism is ascribed to St Anthony in Egypt, but the inauguration of communal life is attributed to his disciple, St Pachomius. Possibly communities for women (nuns, from Latin *nonna* 'elderly woman') preceded those for men, and most male orders have their female counterpart.

6th century Full adaptation to conditions in W Europe was made by St Benedict, his 'rule' being generally adopted.

10th century In 910 the foundation of Cluny began the system of orders whereby each monastery was subordinated to a central institution.

11th century During the Middle Ages other forms of monasticism were established, including the hermitlike Carthusians 1084 and the Augustinian Canons, who were clerics organized under a monastic system.

12th century The military Knights Templar and Knights Hospitallers of St John were formed.

13th century The four mendicant orders of friars—Franciscans, Dominicans, Carmelites, and Augustinians—were established, and monasticism reached the height of its influence.

16th century Monasticism was severely affected by the Reformation. A revival came with the foundation of orders dedicated to particular missions, such as the great weapon of the Counter-Reformation, the Society of Jesus (Jesuits) 1540.

18th century The French Revolution exercised a repressive influence.

20th century The trend in many orders is to modern dress, and involvement as 'workers' outside the monastery, despite disapproval by Pope John Paul II.

Monastir /ˌmɒnəˈstɪə/ Turkish name for the town of ◊Bitolj in S Yugoslavia; also coastal town in Tunisia, birthplace of the former president, Habib Bourguiba.

Monastir /ˌmɒnəˈstɪə/ resort town on the Mediterranean coast of Tunisia, 18 km/11 mi S of Sousse. Summer residence of the president of Tunisia.

monazite a mineral, $(Ce, La, Y, Th)PO_4$, yellow to red, valued as a source of ◊lanthanides or rare earths, including cerium and europium; generally found in placer deposit (alluvial) sands.

Mönchengladbach /ˌmʌnʃənˈɡlædbæk/ industrial city (textiles, machinery, paper) in North Rhine-Westphalia, West Germany, on the river Niers near Düsseldorf; population (1988) 255,000. It is the NATO headquarters for N Europe.

Monck /mʌŋk/ or **Monk**, George, 1st Duke of Albemarle 1608–1669. English soldier. During the Civil War he fought for King Charles I, but after being captured changed sides and took command of the Parliamentary forces in Ireland. Under the Commonwealth he became commander in chief in Scotland, and in 1660 he led his army into England and brought about the restoration of Charles II.

He served in Cromwell's Scottish campaign 1650, and at sea against the Netherlands 1652–53; he was created duke of Albemarle in 1660.

Mond /mɒnd/ Ludwig 1839–1909. German chemist who perfected a process for recovering sulphur during the manufacture of alkali.

In 1873, he helped to found the firm of Brunner, Mond and Co., which pioneered the British chemical industry. Mond was also instrumental in developing the Canadian nickel industry.

He moved to England in 1862, and became a British subject in 1867. His son Alfred Mond, 1st Baron Melchett (1868–1930) was a founder of Imperial Chemical Industries (ICI).

Mondale /ˈmɒndeɪl/ Walter 'Fritz' 1928– . US Democrat politician, unsuccessful presidential candidate 1984. He was a senator 1964–76 for his home state of Minnesota, and vice president to Jimmy Carter 1977–81. After losing the 1984 presidential election to Reagan, Mondale retired from national politics to resume his law practice.

Monday the second day of the week. The name derives from its having been considered sacred to the Moon (Old English *Mōnandaeg* and Latin *Lunae dies*).

Mondrian /ˈmɒndriɑːn/ Piet (Pieter Mondriaan) 1872–1944. Dutch painter, a pioneer of abstract art. He lived in Paris 1919–38, then in London, and from 1940 in New York. He was a founder member of the de ◊Stijl movement and chief exponent of Neo-Plasticism, a rigorous abstract style based on the use of simple geometric forms and pure colours.

In Paris from 1911 Mondrian was inspired by Cubism. He returned to the Netherlands during World War I, where he used a series of still lifes and landscapes to refine his ideas, ultimately developing a pure abstract style. His aesthetic theories were published in the journal *De Stijl* from 1917, in *Neoplasticism* 1920, and in the essay 'Plastic Art and Pure Plastic Art' 1937. From the New York period his *Broadway Boogie-Woogie* 1942–43 (Museum of Modern Art, New York) reflects a late preoccupation with jazz rhythms.

Monet /ˈmɒneɪ/ Claude 1840–1926. French painter, a pioneer of Impressionism and a lifelong exponent of its ideals; his painting *Impression, Sunrise* 1872 gave the movement its name. In the 1870s he began painting the same subjects at different times of day to explore the effects of light on colour and form; the *Haystacks* and *Rouen Cathedral* series followed in the 1890s, and from 1899 a series of *Water Lilies* painted in the garden of his house at Giverny in Normandy.

Monet was born in Paris. In Le Havre in the 1850s he was encouraged to paint by Boudin, and soon met Jongkind, whose light and airy seascapes were of lasting influence. From 1862 in Paris he shared a studio with Renoir, Sisley, and others, and they showed their work together at the First Impressionist Exhibition 1874.

Monet's work from the 1860s onwards reveals an obsession with the evanescent effects of light and colour, and from the late 1860s he painted in the classic Impressionist manner, juxtaposing brushstrokes of colour to create an effect of dappled, glowing light. His first series showed the Gare St Lazare in Paris with its puffing steam engines. Views of the water garden in Giverny gradually developed into large, increasingly abstract colour compositions. Between 1900 and 1909 he produced a series of water-lily mural panels for the French state (the Orangerie, Paris).

monetarism an economic policy, advocated by the economist Milton Friedman and others, which proposes control of a country's money supply to keep it in step with the country's ability to produce goods, with the aim of curbing inflation. Cutting government spending is advocated, and the long-term aim is to return as much of the economy as possible to the private sector allegedly in the interests of efficiency.

Additionally, credit is restricted by high interest rates, and industry is not cushioned against internal market forces or overseas competition (with the aim of preventing 'overmanning', 'restrictive' union practices, and 'excessive' wage demands). Unemployment may result, but monetarists claim, less than eventually occurs if Keynesian methods are adopted. Monetarist policies were widely adopted in the 1980s in response to the inflation problems caused by spiralling oil prices in 1979.

monetary policy an economic policy which sees control of both the money supply and liquidity as

Monet The Water Lily Pond *(1899)* National Gallery, London.

important determinants of the level of employment and inflation. By influencing interest rates, the policy aims to ease balance of payment problems.

money any common medium of exchange acceptable in payment for goods or services or for the settlement of debts. Money is usually coinage (invented by the Chinese in the second millennium BC) and paper notes (used by the Chinese from about AD 800). Recent developments such as the cheque and credit card fulfil many of the traditional functions of money.

money market an institution that deals in gold and foreign exchange, and securities in the short term. Long-term transactions are dealt with on the capital market. There is no physical market place, and many deals are made by telephone or telex.

money supply the quantity of money present in an economy at a given moment. Monetarists hold that a rapid increase in money supply inevitably provokes a rise in the rate of inflation.

In Britain there are several definitions of money supply. M0 was defined as notes and coins in circulation, together with the operational balance of clearing banks with the Bank of England. The M1 definition encompasses M0 plus current account deposits; M2, now rarely used, covers the M1 items plus deposit accounts; M3 covers M2 items plus all other deposits held by UK citizens and companies in the UK banking sector. In May 1987 the Bank of England introduced new terms including M4 (M3 plus building society deposits) and M5 (M4 plus Treasury bills and local authority deposits).

Mongol person of Mongol culture from Central Asia. Mongols, who comprise a number of distinct ethnic groups, live in the Mongolian People's Republic, the USSR, and China. The Mongol language belongs to the Altaic family.

The Mongols are primarily pastoral nomads, herding sheep, horses, cattle, and camels. Traditionally the Mongols moved with their animals in summer to the higher pastures, returning in winter to the lower steppes. The government of the Mongolian People's Republic now encourages more sedentary forms of pastoralism and winter quarters are often more permanent. About 60% of the Mongolian population live in felt-covered domed tents known as **gers**. Many Mongols are Buddhist, though the Mongolian government has been communist since 1924. During the 13th century AD, under Genghis Khan, the Mongols conquered Central Asia and attacked Eastern Europe. Kublai Khan, the grandson of Genghis Khan, was the first emperor of the Yuan Dynasty (1279–1368) in China.

Mongol Empire empire established by Genghis Khan, who extended his domains from Russia to N China and became khan of the Mongol tribes in 1206. His grandson Kublai Khan conquered China and used foreigners such as Marco Polo as well as subjects to administer his empire. In 1367 the Mongols lost China and suffered defeats

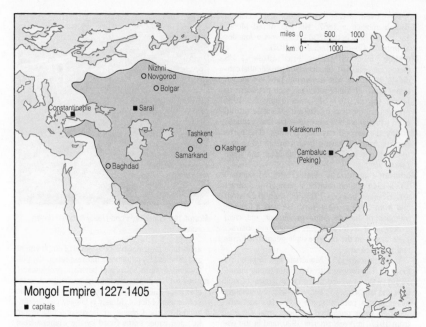

Mongol Empire 1227-1405
■ capitals

in the West in 1380; the empire broke up soon afterwards.

Mongolia /mɒŋˈɡəʊlɪə/ country in E Central Asia, bounded N by the USSR and S by China.

government Mongolia is a socialist state with, under the 1960 constitution, a single-chamber legislature, the 370-deputy People's Great Assembly *Ardyn Ih Hural*, elected by universal suffrage for five-year terms. The assembly meets annually and elects a nine-member policy-making presidium, whose chair functions as state president, to take over its functions between sittings. It also appoints a council of ministers to carry out day-to-day executive administration, and a state procurator, who heads the judicial system. Mongolia's controlling force and sole political party is the Mongol People's Revolutionary Party, headed by Jambyn Batmonh. This is organized on Communist lines and has a Congress, Central Committee, Secretariat and Politburo, all serving five-year terms.

history Formerly inhabited by nomads from N Asia, the area was united under Genghis Khan in 1206, and by the end of the 13th century was part of the vast Mongol empire which stretched right across Asia. From 1689 it was part of China.

After the revolution of 1911–12 Mongolia became autonomous under Jebsten Damba Khutukhtu (the Living Buddha). From 1915 it increasingly fell under Chinese influence and not until 1921, with the support of the USSR, were Mongolian nationalists able to cast off the Chinese yoke. In 1924 it adopted the Soviet system of government and, after proclaiming itself a People's Republic, launched a programme of 'defeudalization', involving the destruction of Lamaism. An armed uprising by antigovernment forces in 1932 was suppressed with Soviet assistance. China recognized its independence in 1946, but relations deteriorated as Outer Mongolia took the Soviet side in the Sino-Soviet dispute. In 1966 Outer Mongolia signed a 20-year friendship, cooperation and mutual-assistance pact with the USSR, and the thousands of Soviet troops based in the country caused China to see it as a Russian colony.

Isolated from the outside world during the 1970s, under the leadership of Yumjaagiyn Tsedenbal—the nation's dominant figure since 1958—Mongolia underwent great economic change as urban industries developed and settled agriculture on the collective system spread, with new areas being brought under cultivation. After the accession to power in the USSR of Mikhail Gorbachev, Outer Mongolia was encouraged to broaden its outside contacts. Cultural exchanges with China increased, diplomatic relations were established with the US, and between 1987 and 1990 the number of Soviet troops stationed in the country was reduced from 80,000 to 15,000. A Mongolian nationalist revival developed, with increasing study and use of the Mongolian script. Influenced by events in Eastern Europe, an opposition grouping, the Mongolian Democratic Union, was illegally formed in Dec 1989 by the Moscow University–educated Sanjasuren Zorig (1962–). During 1990, it spearheaded a campaign demanding greater democratization and the return of Tsedenbal, who had been exiled in Moscow since his deposition in 1984, to face trial.

Mongolia, Inner /mɒŋˈɡəʊlɪə/ (Chinese *Nei Mongol*) autonomous region of NE China from 1947
area 450,000 sq km/173,700 sq mi

Mongolia
Mongolian People's Republic
(*Bügd Nayramdakh Mongol Ard Uls*)

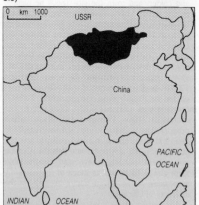

area 1,567,000 sq km/605,000 sq mi
capital Ulaanbaatar (formerly Ulan Bator)
towns Darkhan, Choybalsan
physical a high plateau with steppe (grasslands)
features Altai Mountains; salt lakes; part of Gobi Desert
head of state Jambyn Batmonh from 1984
head of government Dumagiin Sodnom from 1984

---

capital Hohhot
features strategic frontier area with USSR; known for Mongol herdsmen, now becoming settled farmers
physical grassland and desert
products cereals under irrigation; coal; reserves of rare earth oxides europium, and yttrium at Bayan Obo
population (1986) 20,290,000.

mongolism former name (now considered offensive) for ◊Down's syndrome.

Mongoloid a former racial classification, based on physical features, used to describe people of E Asian and North American origin; see ◊race.

mongoose carnivorous mammal of the family Viverridae. The **Indian mongoose** *Herpestes mungo* is greyish in colour, about 50 cm/1.5 ft long, with a long tail. It may be tamed, and is often kept for its ability to kill snakes. The **Egyptian mongoose** or **ichneumon** is larger.

monism in philosophy, the theory that reality is made up of only one substance. This view is usually contrasted with ◊dualism, which divides reality into two substances, matter and mind. Spinoza saw the one substance as God or Nature.

monitor type of lizard of the family Varanidae, found in Africa, S Asia, and Australasia. Monitors are generally large and carnivorous, with well-developed legs and claws, and a long powerful tail which can be swung in defence.

Monitors include the **Komodo dragon**, the largest of all lizards, and also the slimmer **Salvador's monitor** *Varanus salvadorii* which may reach 2.5 m/8 ft. Several other monitors, such as the **lace monitor** *Varanus varius* and the **perentie** *Varanus giganteus* of Australia and the **Nile monitor** *Varanus niloticus* of Africa, are up to 2 m/6 ft long.

Moniz /ˈmɒnɪz/ Antonio Egas 1874–1955. Portuguese neurologist, pioneer of prefrontal leucotomy (surgical separation of white fibres in the prefrontal lobe of the brain) to treat schizophrenia and paranoia; the treatment is today considered questionable. Nobel prize 1949.

monk member of a male religious order; see ◊monasticism.

Monk /mʌŋk/ Thelonious 1917–1982. US jazz pianist and composer. Working in Harlem, New York,

political system communism
exports meat and butter; varied minerals; furs
currency tugrik (5.71 = £1 Feb 1990)
population (1989) 2,093,000; annual growth rate 2.8%
life expectancy men 60, women 64
language Khalkha Mongolian (official), Chinese, Russian
religion formerly Tibetan Buddhist Lamaist, suppressed in the 1930s
literacy 93% male/85% female (1980 est)
GNP $1.8 bn (1983); $750 per head of population
chronology
1911 Outer Mongolia gained autonomy from China.
1915 Chinese sovereignty reasserted.
1921 Chinese rule finally overthrown with Soviet help.
1924 Mongolian People's Republic proclaimed.
1946 China recognized Mongolia's independence.
1966 20-year friendship, cooperation, and mutual-assistance pact signed with USSR. Deterioration in relations with China.
1984 Yumjaagiyn Tsedenbal, effective leader, deposed and replaced by Jambyn Batmonh.
1987 Soviet troop numbers reduced and Mongolia's external contacts broadened.
1989 Further major Soviet troop reductions.
1990 Democratization campaign launched by Mongolian Democratic Union; (Mar) entire politburo resigns following demands for reform

during the Depression, he took part in developing the jazz style known as *bebop* or *bop*. He became popular in the 1950s, and is remembered for numbers such as 'Round Midnight', 'Blue Monk', and 'Hackensack'.

monkey the smaller, mainly tree-dwelling primates, excluding humans and the anthropoid ◊apes.
Old World monkeys, family Cercopithecidae, of tropical Africa and Asia are distinguished by their close-set nostrils and differentiated thumbs, some also having cheek pouches and behinds with bare patches (callosities) of hardened skin. They include ◊baboons, ◊langurs, ◊macaques, and guenons.
New World monkeys of Central and South America are characterized by wide-set nostrils, and some have highly sensitive prehensile tails. They comprise:
(1) the family Cebidae, which includes the larger species: saki, ◊capuchin, squirrel, howler, and spider monkeys;
(2) the family Callithricidae, which includes the very small species, notably the ◊marmosets and tamarins.

monkey-puzzle tree or *Chilean pine* evergreen tree *Araucaria araucana*, native to Chile; it has whorled branches covered in prickly leaves of a leathery texture.

Monmouth /ˈmʌnməθ/ market town in Gwent, Wales; Henry V was born in the now-ruined castle.

Monmouth /ˈmʌnməθ/ James Scott, Duke of Monmouth 1649–1685. Claimant to the English crown, the natural son of Charles II and Lucy Walter. After James II's accession in 1685, he landed at Lyme Regis, Dorset, claimed the crown, and raised a rebellion, which was crushed at ◊Sedgemoor in Somerset. Monmouth was executed with 320 of his accomplices.
    When ◊James II converted to Catholicism, the Whig opposition attempted unsuccessfully to secure Monmouth the succession to the crown by the Exclusion Bill, and in 1684, having become implicated in a Whig conspiracy, he fled to Holland.

Monmouthshire /ˈmʌnməθʃə/ former county of Wales, which in 1974 became, minus a small strip on the border with Mid Glamorgan, the new county of *Gwent*.

Monnet /ˈmɒneɪ/ Jean 1888–1979. French economist. The originator of Churchill's offer of union between the UK and France in 1940, he devised and took charge of the French modernization programme under de Gaulle in 1945. In 1950 he produced the 'Shuman Plan' initiating the coordination of European coal and steel production in the European Coal and Steel Community (ECSC), which developed into the Common Market (EEC).

monocarpic or *hapaxanthic* describing plants that flower and produce fruit only once during their life cycle, after which they die. Most ◊annual plants and ◊biennial plants are monocarpic, but there are also a small number of monocarpic ◊perennial plants which flower just once, sometimes after as long as 90 years, dying shortly afterwards, for example, century plant (*Agave*) and some species of bamboo (*Bambusa*). See also ◊semelparity.

monoclonal antibodies antibodies produced by fusing an antibody-producing lymphocyte with a cancerous myeloma cell. The resulting fused cell, called a hybridoma, is immortal and can be used to produce large quantities of a single, specific antibody. By choosing antibodies which are directed against antigens found on cancer cells, and combining them with cytotoxic drugs, it is hoped to make so-called 'magic bullets' which will be able to pick out and kill cancers.
    It is the antigens on the outer cell walls of germs entering the body that provoke the production of antibodies as a first line of defence against disease. Antibodies 'recognize' these foreign antigens, and, in locking onto them, cause the release of chemical signals in the bloodstream to alert the immune

monkey-puzzle tree

system for further action. Monoclonal antibodies are purpose-grown copies of these natural antibodies, with the same ability to recognize specific antigens. Introduced into the body, they can be targeted at disease sites.
    The full potential of these biological missiles, developed by César ◊Milstein and others at Cambridge 1975, is still under investigation. However, they are already in use in blood-grouping, in pinpointing viruses and other sources of disease, in tracing cancer sites, and in developing vaccines.

monocotyledon angiosperm (flowering plant) with a single cotyledon, or seed leaf (as opposed to ◊dicotyledons, which have two). Monocotyledons usually have narrow leaves with parallel veins and smooth edges, and hollow or soft stems. Their flower parts are arranged in threes. Most are small plants such as orchids, grasses, and lilies, but some are trees such as palms.

Monod /ˈmɒnɒd/ Jacques 1910–1976. French biochemist who shared the 1965 Nobel Prize for Medicine (with two colleagues) for research in genetics and microbiology.

monody in music, declamation by accompanied solo voice, used at the turn of the 16th and 17th centuries.

monoecious having separate male and female flowers on the same plant. Maize (*Zea mays*), for example, has a tassel of male flowers at the top of the stalk and a group of female flowers (on the ear, or 'cob') lower down. Monoecy is a way of avoiding self-fertilization. ◊Dioecious plants have male and female flowers on separate plants.

monogamy the practice of having only one husband or wife at a time in ◊marriage.

monohybrid inheritance a pattern of inheritance seen in simple ◊genetics experiments, where the two animals (or two plants) being crossed are genetically identical except for one gene.
    This gene may code for some obvious external features such as seed colour, with one parent having green seeds and the other having yellow seeds. The offspring are monohybrids, that is, hybrids for one gene only, having received one copy of the gene from each parent. Known as the F1 generation, they are all identical, and usually resemble one parent, whose version of the gene (the dominant ◊allele) masks the effect of the other version (the recessive allele). Although the characteristic coded for by the recessive allele (for example, green seeds) completely disappears in this generation, it can reappear in offspring of the next generation if they have two recessive alleles. On average, this will occur in one out of four offspring from a cross between two of the monohybrids. The next generation (called F2) show a 3:1 ratio for the characteristic in question, 75% being like the original parent with the recessive allele. Gregor ◊Mendel first carried out experiments of this type (crossing varieties of artificially bred plants, such as peas) and they revealed the principles of genetics. The same basic mechanism underlies all inheritance, but in

most plants and animals there are so many genetic differences interacting to produce the external appearance (phenotype) that such simple, clear-cut patterns of inheritance are not evident.

Monophysite (Greek 'one-nature') a member of a group of Christian heretics of the 5th–7th centuries who taught that Jesus had one nature, in opposition to the orthodox doctrine laid down at the Council of Chalcedon in 451, that he had two natures, the human and the divine. Monophysitism developed as a reaction to ◊Nestorianism and led to the formal secession of the Coptic and Armenian churches from the rest of the Christian church. Monophysites survive today in Armenia, Syria, and Egypt.

Monopolies and Mergers Commission (MMC) UK government body re-established in 1973 under the Fair Trading Act and, since 1980, embracing the Competition Act. Its role is to investigate and report when there is a risk of creating a monopoly following a company merger or takeover, or when a newspaper or newspaper assets are transferred. It also investigates companies, nationalized industries, or local authorities which are suspected of operating in a non-competitive way. The US equivalent is the *Federal Trade Commission* (FTC).

monopoly in economics, the domination of a market for a particular product or service by a single company, which can therefore restrict competition and keep prices high. In practice, a company can be said to have a monopoly when it controls a significant proportion of the market (technically an ◊oligopoly).
    In the UK, monopoly was originally a royal grant of the sole right to manufacture or sell a certain article. The Fair Trading Act of 1973 defines a monopoly supplier as one having 'a quarter of the market', and the Monopolies and Mergers Commission controls any attempt to reach this position; in the USA 'antitrust laws' are similarly used. In communist countries the state itself has the overall monopoly; in capitalist ones some services such as transport or electricity supply may be state monopolies, but in the UK the Competition Act of 1980 covers both private monopolies and possible abuses in the public sector. A *monopsony* is a situation in which there is only one buyer, for example, most governments are the only legal purchasers of military equipment inside their countries.

monorail a railway that runs on a single rail. It was invented in 1882 to carry light loads, and when run by electricity was called a *telpher*.
    The Wuppertal Schwebebahn, which has been running in Germany since 1901, is a suspension monorail, where the passenger cars hang from an arm fixed to a trolley that runs along the rail. Most modern monorails are of the straddle type, where the passenger cars run on top of the rail. They are used to transport passengers between terminals at some airports.

monosaccharide or *simple sugar* a ◊carbohydrate that cannot be hydrolysed (split) into smaller carbohydrate units. Examples are glucose and fructose, both of which have the molecular formula $C_6H_{12}O_6$.

monosodium glutamate (MSG) $NaC_5H_8O_4$, the sodium salt of glutamic acid, an ◊amino acid found in proteins which has an important role in the metabolism of plants and animals. It is used to enhance the flavour of many packaged and fast foods, and in many Chinese dishes. Ill effects may arise from its overconsumption, and some people are very sensitive to it, even in small amounts.

monotheism the belief or doctrine that there is only one God, the opposite of polytheism. See also ◊religion.

Monothelite member of a group of Christian heretics of the 7th century who sought to reconcile the orthodox and ◊Monophysite theologies by maintaining that, while Christ possessed two natures, he had only one will. Monothelitism was condemned as a heresy by the Third Council of Constantinople 680.

monotreme member of the order Monotremata, the only living egg-laying mammals, found in Australasia. They include the echidna and platypus.

Monroe /mənˈrəʊ/ James 1758–1831. 5th president of the USA 1817–25, born in Virginia. He served in the War of Independence, was minister to France 1794–96, and in 1803 negotiated the ◊Louisiana Purchase. He was secretary of state 1811–17. His name is associated with the ◊Monroe Doctrine.

Monroe /mənˈrəʊ/ Marilyn. Stage name of Norma Jean Mortenson or Baker 1926–1962. US film actress, who made comedies such as *The Seven Year Itch* 1955, *Bus Stop* 1956, and *Some Like It Hot* 1959. Her second husband was baseball star Joe di Maggio, and her third Arthur ◊Miller.

Monroe Doctrine the declaration by President Monroe 1823 that any further European colonial ambitions in the W hemisphere would be threats to US peace and security, made in response to proposed European intervention against newly independent former Spanish colonies in South America. In return the USA would not interfere in European affairs. The doctrine, subsequently broadened, has been a recurrent theme in US foreign policy, although it has no basis in US or international law.

Monrovia /mɒnˈrəʊvɪə/ capital and port of Liberia; population (1985) 500,000. Industries include rubber, cement, and petrol processing.

It was founded 1821 for slaves repatriated from the USA. Originally called Christopolis, it was named after US president Monroe.

Mons /mɒnz/ (Flemish *Bergen*) industrial city (coalmining, textiles, sugar) and capital of the province of Hainaut, Belgium; population (1985) 90,500. The military headquarters of NATO is at nearby Chièvres-Casteau.

Monsarrat /ˈmɒnsəræt/ Nicholas 1910–1979. English novelist who served with the navy in the Battle of the ◊Atlantic, subject of *The Cruel Sea* 1951.

monsoon (Old Dutch 'monçon') a wind system that dominates the climate of a wide region, with seasonal reversals of direction; in particular, the wind in S Asia that blows towards the sea in winter and towards the land in summer, bringing heavy rain. The monsoon may cause destructive flooding all over India and SE Asia from Apr to Sept. Thousands of people are rendered homeless each year.

monstera or *Swiss cheese plant* evergreen climbing plant of the Arum family, Araceae, native to tropical America, cultivated as a house plant.

Monroe *James Monroe, remembered for the Monroe Doctrine, his warning to European nations not to interfere with the countries of the Americas.*

Monroe *Legendary film star Marilyn Monroe. Her vulnerability was part of her appeal.*

Areas between the veins of the leaves dry up, creating deep marginal notches and ultimately holes.

monstrance in the Roman Catholic Church, a vessel used from the 13th century to hold the Host (bread consecrated in the Eucharist) when exposed at benediction or in processions.

montage in cinema, the juxtaposition of several images or shots to produce an independent meaning. The term is also used more generally to describe the whole process of editing or a rapidly edited series of shots. It was coined by the Russian director ◊Eisenstein.

Montagnard member of a group in the legislative assembly and National Convention convened after the ◊French Revolution. They supported the more extreme aims of the revolution, and were destroyed as a political force after the fall of Robespierre 1794.

Montagu family name of dukes of Manchester.

Montagu /ˈmɒntəgju:/ Edward Douglas Scott, 3rd Baron Montagu of Beaulieu 1926– . British car enthusiast, founder of the Montagu Motor Museum at Beaulieu, Hampshire, and chair of English Heritage (Historic Buildings and Monuments Commission) from 1983.

Montagu /ˈmɒntəgju:/ Lady Mary Wortley (born Pierrepont) 1689–1762. British society hostess known for her witty and erudite letters. She had a quarrel with the writer Alexander Pope, her former friend and correspondent. She introduced inoculation against smallpox into Britain.

Montagu-Douglas-Scott family name of the dukes of Buccleuch; seated at Bowhill, Selkirk, Scotland; Boughton House, Northamptonshire, England; and Drumlanrig, Dumfriesshire, Scotland; descended from the Duke of ◊Monmouth.

Montaigne /mɒnˈteɪn/ Michel Eyquem de 1533–1592. French writer, regarded as the creator of the essay form. In 1580 he published the first two volumes of his *Essais*, the third volume appeared in 1588. Montaigne deals with all aspects of life from an urbanely sceptical viewpoint. Through the translation by John Florio in 1603 he influenced Shakespeare and other English writers.

Born at the Château de Montaigne, near Bordeaux, he studied law, and in 1554 became a counsellor of the Bordeaux *parlement*. Little is known of his earlier life, except that he regularly visited the court of Francis II and Paris. In 1571 he retired to his estates, relinquishing his magistracy. He toured Germany, Switzerland, and Italy 1580–81, returning on his election as mayor of Bordeaux, a post he held until 1585.

Montale /mɒnˈtɑ:li/ Eugenio 1896–1981. Italian poet and writer. His pessimistic poetry, for which he was awarded a Nobel prize in 1975, includes *Ossi di seppia/Cuttlefish bones* 1925 and

Le Occasioni/Occasions 1939. In 1989 it was revealed that much of his literary journalism, such as his regular column in the *Corriere della Sera* newspaper, was in fact written by an American, Henry Frost.

Montana /mɒnˈtænə/ state of the W USA on the Canadian border; nickname Treasure State
area 381,200 sq km/147,143 sq mi
capital Helena
towns Billings, Great Falls, Butte
features Missouri and Yellowstone rivers; Glacier National Park; Little Bighorn; Museum of the Plains Indian; the fourth largest state
physical mountainous forests in the west, rolling grasslands in the east
products wheat under irrigation, cattle, wool, copper, oil, natural gas
population (1986) 819,000
famous people Gary Cooper
history first settled 1809; influx of immigrants pursuing gold in the mid 19th century; became a state 1889.

Montana /mɒnˈtænə/ Joe 1956– . US footballer. He appeared in three winning Super Bowls with the San Francisco 49ers 1982, 1985, and 1989, winning the Most Valuable Player award in the first two, and setting a record for passing yardage 1989.

He graduated from Notre Dame college, where he led his team to the national college championship 1978. He suffered a serious back injury 1986, from which many people said he would never recover. He was the leading passer in the National Conference 1981, 1984, and 1985, and leading passer in the NFL 1987, setting league records for touchdowns thrown (31), and 22 consecutive completions. In the 1989 Super Bowl, he set a record for most passes without an interception (33).

Montand /mɒnˈtɒn/ Yves 1921– . French actor and singer who achieved fame in the thriller *La Salarie de la Peur/The Wages of Fear* 1953 and continued to be popular in French and American films, including *Let's Make Love* 1960 (with Marilyn Monroe), *Grand Prix* 1966, *Le Sauvage/The Savage* 1976, *Jean de Florette* 1986, *Manon des Sources* 1986.

Montanism movement within the early Christian church that strove to return to the purity of primitive Christianity. It originated in Phrygia in about 156 with the teaching of a prophet named Montanus. The theologian ◊Tertullian was a noted Montanist.

Montaubon /ˌmɒntəʊˈbɒn/ industrial town (porcelain, textiles) in the Midi-Pyrénées region, SW France, on the river Tarn; population (1982) 53,147. The painter Ingres was born here.

Mont Blanc /ˌmɒn ˈblɒŋ/ (Italian *Monte Bianco*) the highest mountain in the ◊Alps, between France and Italy; height 4,807 m/15,772 ft. It was first climbed 1786.

montbretia plant *Tritonia crocosmiflora*, family Iridaceae, with orange or reddish flowers on long stems.

Montcalm /mɒntˈkɑ:m/ Louis-Joseph de Montcalm-Gozon, Marquis de 1712–1759. French general, appointed military commander in Canada 1756. He won a succession of victories over the British during the French and Indian War, but was defeated in 1759 by ◊Wolfe at Québec, where both he and

Montana

Wolfe were killed; this battle marked the end of French rule in Canada.

Mont Cenis /ˌmɒn sə'niː/ pass in the Alps between Lyon, France and Turin, Italy at 2,082 m/6,831 ft.

Monte Bello Islands /'mɒnti 'beləʊ/ group of uninhabited islands in the Indian Ocean, off Western Australia, used by the UK for nuclear-weapons testing 1952; the largest of the group is Barrow Island.

Monte Carlo /'mɒnti 'kɑːləʊ/ a town and resort in ◊Monaco, known for its gambling; population (1982) 12,000.

Monte Cristo /'mɒnti 'krɪstəʊ/ a small uninhabited island 40 km/25 mi to the S of Elba, in the Tyrrhenian Sea; its name supplied a title for Dumas' hero in *The Count of Monte Cristo*.

Montego Bay /mɒn'tiːgəʊ 'beɪ/ port and resort on the NW coast of Jamaica; population (1982) 70,200.

Montélimar /mɒn'teɪlɪmɑː/ town in Drôme district, France; noted for the nougat to which its name is given; population (1982) 30,213.

Montenegro /ˌmɒnti'niːgrəʊ/ (Serbo-Croat **Crna Gora**) constituent republic of Yugoslavia
area 13,800 sq km/5,327 sq mi
capital Titograd
town Cetinje
features smallest of the republics; Skadarsko Jezero (Lake Scutari) shared with Albania
physical mountainous
population (1986) 620,000, including 400,000 Montenegrins, 80,000 Muslims, and 40,000 Albanians
language Serbian variant of Serbo-Croat
religion Serbian Orthodox
history part of ◊Serbia from the late 12th century, it became independent (under Venetian protection) after Serbia was defeated by the Turks 1389. It was forced to accept Turkish suzerainty in the late 15th century, but was never completely subdued by Turkey. It was ruled by Bishop Princes until 1851, when a monarchy was founded, and became a sovereign principality under the Treaty of Berlin 1878. It was overrun by Austria in World War I, and in 1918 voted after the deposition of King Nicholas to become part of the future Yugoslavia.

Prince Nicholas took the title of king 1910. Montenegro participated in the Balkan Wars.

Monterey /ˌmɒntə'reɪ/ fishing port on Monterey Bay in California, USA, once the state capital; population (1980) 27,500. It is the setting for Steinbeck's novels *Cannery Row* 1945 and *Tortilla Flat* 1935 dealing with migrant fruit workers.

Monterrey /ˌmɒntə'reɪ/ industrial city (iron, steel, textiles, chemicals, food processing) in NE Mexico; population (1986) 2,335,000.

Montespan /ˌmɒntes'pɒŋ/ Françoise-Athénais de Rochechouart, Marquise de Montespan 1641–1707. Mistress of Louis XIV of France from 1667. They had seven children, for whom she engaged the future Madame de ◊Maintenon as governess. She retired to a convent in 1691.

Montesquieu /ˌmɒntes'kjɜː/ Charles Louis de Secondat, baron de la Brède 1689–1755. French philosophical historian, author of the *Lettres Persanes/Persian Letters* 1721. *De l'Esprit des Lois/The Spirit of the Laws* 1748, a 31-volume philosophical disquisition on politics and sociology as well as legal matters, advocated the separation of powers within government, a doctrine that became the basis of liberal constitutions.

Born near Bordeaux, Montesquieu became adviser to the Bordeaux parliament 1714. After the success of *Lettres Persanes*, he adopted a literary career, writing *Considérations sur les Causes de la grandeur des Romains et de leur décadence/On the Causes of the Grandeur of the Romans and their Declension* 1734.

Montessori /ˌmɒnte'sɔːri/ Maria 1870–1952. Italian educationalist. From her experience with

Monteverdi *One of the great composers of operas, Claudio Monteverdi.*

mentally handicapped children, she developed the **Montessori method**, an educational system for all children based on a more informal approach, incorporating instructive play and allowing children to develop at their own pace.

Monteux /mɒn'tɜː/ Pierre 1875–1964. French conductor. Ravel's *Daphnis and Chloe* and Stravinsky's *Rite of Spring* were first performed under his direction. He conducted ◊Diaghilev's Ballets Russes 1911–14 and 1917, and the San Francisco Symphony Orchestra 1935–52.

Monteverdi /ˌmɒntɪ'veədi/ Claudio (Giovanni Antonio) 1567–1643. Italian composer. He contributed to the development of the opera with *Orfeo* 1607 and *The Coronation of Poppea* 1642. He also wrote madrigals, ◊motets, and sacred music, notably the *Vespers* 1610.

Montevideo /ˌmɒntɪvɪ'deɪəʊ/ capital and chief port (grain, meat products, hides) of Uruguay, on Río de la Plata; population (1985) 1,250,000. It was founded 1726.

Montez /'mɒntez/ Lola. Stage name of Maria Gilbert 1818–1861. Irish actress and dancer. She appeared on the stage as a Spanish dancer, and in 1847 became the mistress of King Ludwig I of Bavaria, whose policy she dictated for a year. Her liberal sympathies led to her banishment through Jesuit influence in 1848. She died in poverty in the US.

Montezuma II /ˌmɒntɪ'zuːmə/ 1466–1520. Aztec emperor 1502–20. When the Spanish conquistador Cortés invaded Mexico, Montezuma was imprisoned and killed during the Aztec attack on Cortés' force as it tried to leave Tenochtitlán, the Aztec capital city.

Montfort /'mɒntfət/ Simon de Montfort, Earl of Leicester *c.* 1208–1265. English politician and soldier. From 1258 he led the baronial opposition to Henry III's misrule during the second ◊Barons' War and in 1264 defeated and captured the king at Lewes, Sussex. In 1265, as head of government, he summoned the first parliament in which the towns were represented; he was killed at the Battle of Evesham during the last of the Barons' Wars.

Born in Normandy, the son of **Simon de Montfort** (*c.* 1160–1218) who led a crusade against the Albigenses, he arrived in England in 1230, married Henry III's sister, and was granted the earldom of Leicester.

Montgolfier /mɒŋ'gɒlfieɪ/ Joseph Michel 1740–1810 and Étienne Jacques 1745–1799. French brothers whose hot-air balloon was used for the first successful human flight 21 Nov 1783.

They were papermakers of Annonay, near Lyon, where on 5 June 1783 they first sent up

a balloon filled with hot air. After further experiments with wood-fuelled paper balloons, they went aloft themselves, in Paris. The Montgolfier experiments greatly stimulated scientific interest in aviation.

Montgomery /mənt'gʌməri/ market town in Powys, Wales; population about 1,000.

Montgomery /mənt'gaməri/ state capital of Alabama, USA; population (1980) 273,000. The **Montgomery Bus Boycott** 1955 began here when a black passenger, Rosa Parks, refused to give up her seat to a white. Led by Martin Luther King, it was a landmark in the civil-rights campaign. Alabama's bus-segregation laws were outlawed by the US Supreme Court 13 Nov 1956.

Montgomery /mənt'gaməri/ Bernard Law, 1st Viscount Montgomery of Alamein 1887–1976. British field marshal. In World War II he commanded the 8th Army in N Africa in the Second Battle of El ◊Alamein 1942. As commander of British troops in N Europe from 1944, he received the German surrender on 1945.

At the start of World War II he commanded part of the British Expeditionary Force in France 1939–40 and took part in the evacuation from Dunkirk. In Aug 1942 he took command of the 8th Army, then barring the German advance on Cairo; the victory of El Alamein in Oct turned the tide in N Africa and was followed by the expulsion of Field Marshal Rommel from Egypt and rapid Allied advance into Tunisia. In Feb 1943 his forces came under US general Eisenhower's command, and they took part in the conquest of Tunisia and Sicily and the invasion of Italy. He was promoted to field marshal in 1944. In 1948 Montgomery became permanent military chair of the Commanders-in-Chief Committee for W European defence, and 1951–58 was deputy Supreme Commander Europe.

Montgomery commanded the Allied armies during the opening phase of the invasion of France in June 1944, and from Aug the British and imperial troops that liberated the Netherlands, overran N Germany, and entered Denmark. At his 21st Army Group headquarters on Lüneberg Heath, he received the German surrender on 3 May 1945. He was in command of the British occupation force in Germany until Feb 1946, when he was appointed chief of the Imperial General Staff, and was that year created a viscount.

Montgomery /mənt'gʌməri/ Henry ('Robert') 1904–1981. US film actor of the 1930s and 1940s. He directed some of his later films, such as *Lady in the Lake* 1947, before leaving the cinema for television and politics. His other films include *Night Must Fall* 1937 and *Mr and Mrs Smith* 1941.

Montgomeryshire /mənt'gʌmrɪʃə/ former county of N Wales, included in Powys 1974.

month unit of time based on the motion of the Moon around the Earth. The time from one new or full Moon to the next (the **synodic month**) is 29.53 days. The time for the Moon to complete one orbit around the Earth relative to the stars, the **sidereal month** is 27.32 days. The **calendar month** is a human invention, devised to fit the calendar year.

Montherlant /ˌmɒntẽə'lɒŋ/ Henri de Millon 1896–1972. French author. He was a Nazi sympathizer. His novels, which are marked by an obsession with the physical, include *Aux Fontaines du désir/To the Fountains of Desire* 1927 and *Pitié pour les femmes/Pity for Women* 1936. His most critically acclaimed work is *Le Chaos et la nuit/Chaos and Night* 1963.

Monti /'mɒti/ Eugenio 1928– . Italian bobsleigh driver who won Olympic gold medals in two- and four-person bobs in 1968, and between 1957 and 1968 won 11 world titles.

His two-person successes were shared with the brakemen Renzo Alvera and Sergio Siorpaes, both Italian. On his retirement in 1968 Monti became manager to the Italian team.

Montgomery *The British field marshal, Viscount Montgomery of Alamein, advances in the turret of a tank during the attack on El Alamein, Oct 1942.*

CAREER HIGHLIGHTS

Olympic champion:
two-person 1968
four-person 1968
world champion:
two-person 1957–61, 1963, 1966, 1968
four-person 1960, 1961, 1968.

Montmartre /mɒm'mɑːtrə/ district of Paris, France, dominated by the basilica of Sacre Coeur 1875. It is situated in the N of the city on a 120 m/400 ft high hill.

Montoneros left-wing guerrillas in Argentina.

Montparnasse /,mɒmpɑː'næs/ district of Paris, France, frequented by artists and writers. The Pasteur Institute is also here.

Montpellier /mɒm'peliɛ/ industrial city (engineering, textiles, food processing, and a trade in wine and brandy), capital of ◊Languedoc-Roussillon, France; population (1982) 221,000. It is the birthplace of the philosopher Auguste Comte.

Montreal /,mɒntri'ɔːl/ inland port, industrial city (aircraft, chemicals, oil and petrochemicals, flour, sugar, brewing, meat packing) of Québec, Canada, on Montreal island at the junction of the Ottawa and St Lawrence rivers; population (1986) 2,921,000.
features Mont Réal (Mount Royal, 230 m/753 ft) overlooks the city; an artificial island in the St Lawrence (site of the international exhibition 1967); three universities; except for Paris, the world's largest French-speaking city
history Jacques ◊Cartier reached the site 1535, ◊Champlain established a trading post 1611, and the original Ville Marie (later renamed Montreal) was founded 1642 by Paul de Chomédy, Sieu de Maisonneuve (1612–76). It was the last town surrendered by France to Britain 1760. Nevertheless, when troops of the rebel Continental Congress occupied the city 1775–76, the citizens refused to be persuaded (even by a visit from Benjamin Franklin) to join the future USA in its revolt against Britain.

Montreux /mɒn'trɜː/ winter resort in W Switzerland on Lake Geneva; population (1980) 21,000. It is the site of the island rock fortress of Chillon, where François Bonivard (commemorated by the poet Byron), prior of the Abbey of St Victor, was imprisoned 1530–36 for his opposition to the Duke of Savoy. At the annual television festival (first held 1961), the premier award is the *Golden Rose of Montreux.*

Montreux, Convention of /mɒn'trɜː/ international agreement 1936 allowing Turkey to remilitarize the Dardenelles.

Montrose /mɒn'trəuz/ James Graham, 1st Marquess of Montrose 1612–1650. Scottish soldier. Son of the 4th earl of Montrose. He supported the ◊Covenanters against Charles I, but after 1640 changed sides. Defeated in 1645 at Philiphaugh, he escaped to Norway. Returning in 1650 to raise a revolt, he survived shipwreck only to

Montreal *The Hotel de Ville in Montreal.*

have his weakened forces defeated, and (having been betrayed to the Covenanters) was hanged in Edinburgh.

Mont St Michel /'mɒn ,sæm mɪ'ʃel/ islet in NW France converted to a peninsula by an artificial causeway; noted for its Benedictine monastery, founded 708.

Montserrat /'mɒntsəræt/ volcanic island in the West Indies, one of the Leeward group, a British crown colony; capital Plymouth; area 110 sq km/42 sq mi; population (1985) 12,000. Practically all buildings were destroyed by Hurricane Hugo Sept 1989.
Montserrat produces cotton, cotton-seed, coconuts, citrus and other fruits, and vegetables. Its first European visitor was Christopher ◊Columbus 1493, who named it after the mountain in Spain. It was first colonized by English and Irish settlers who moved from St Christopher 1632. The island became a British crown colony 1871.

Montserrat /,mɒntsə'ræt/ (Spanish *monte serrado*, 'serrated mountain') mountain in NE Spain, height 1,240 m/4,070 ft, so called because its uneven outline resembles the edge of a saw.

Monty Python's Flying Circus British satirical TV comedy series 1969–74, written and performed by John Cleese, Terry Jones, Michael Palin, Eric Idle, Graham Chapman, and the US animator Terry Gilliam. The series achieved cult status and the group made several films: *And Now for Something Completely Different* 1971, *Monty Python and the Holy Grail* 1975, *The Life of Brian* 1979, *The Meaning of Life* 1983. Individual members of the team have written, directed, and appeared in separate projects.

Monument, the in England, a tower commemorating the Great Fire of London 1666. It was designed by Christopher ◊Wren and completed in 1677. It stands near the site of the house in Pudding Lane where the conflagration began.

Monza /'mɒnzə/ town in N Italy, known for its motor racing circuit; population (1988) 123,000. Once the capital of the ◊Lombards, it preserves the Iron Crown of Lombardy in the 13th-century cathedral. Umberto I was assassinated here.

Moon, the the natural satellite of Earth, 3,476 km/2,160 mi in diameter, with a mass an eighth that of Earth. Its average distance from Earth is 384,400 km/238,900 mi, and it orbits every 27.32 days (the *sidereal month*). It spins on its axis so that it keeps one side permanently turned towards Earth. The Moon is thought to have no air or water.
The Moon is illuminated by sunlight, and goes through a cycle of phases from *new* (dark) via *first quarter* (half Moon) to Full and back again to new every 29.53 days (the *synodic month*, also known as a *lunation*). On its sunlit side temperatures reach 110°C, but during the two-week lunar night the surface temperature drops to –170°C.
The Moon's composition is rocky, with a surface heavily scarred by ◊meteorite impacts that have formed craters up to 240 km/150 mi across. Rocks brought back by astronauts show the Moon is 4.6 billion years old, the same age as Earth. It differs from Earth in that most of the Moon's

surface features were formed within the first billion years of its history when it was subjected to heavy bombardment by meteorites. The youngest craters are surrounded by bright rays of ejected rock. The largest scars have been filled by dark lava to produce the lowland plains known as seas or *maria* (see ◊mare). These dark patches form the familiar 'man-in-the-Moon' pattern.
The origin of the Moon is open to debate. Theories suggest that it split from the Earth; that it was a separate body captured by Earth's gravity; that it formed in orbit around Earth; or that it was formed from debris thrown off when a body the size of Mars struck Earth. Future exploration of the Moon by the Soviets and the Americans may provide information on lunar resources, using gamma-ray spectrometers, or detect water permafrost, which could be located at the permanently shadowed lunar poles.

moon in astronomy, any small body that orbits a planet. Mercury and Venus are the only planets in the solar system that do not have moons.

Moon /muːn/ Sun Myung 1920– . Korean industrialist and founder of the ◊Unification Church (*Moonies*) 1954. From 1973 he launched a major mission in the USA and elsewhere. The church has been criticized for its manipulative methods of recruiting and keeping members. He was convicted of tax fraud in the USA 1982.
Moon has allegedly been associated with extreme right-wing organizations, arms manufacture, and the Korean Central Intelligence Agency.

Moon /muːn/ William 1818–1894. English inventor of the Moon alphabet for the blind. Devised in 1847, it uses only nine symbols in different orientations. From 1983 it has been possible to write it with a miniature typewriter.

Moonie /'muːni/ town in SE Queensland, W of Brisbane, the site of Australia's first commercial oil strike; population (1961) approximately 100.

Moonie /'muːni/ popular name for a follower of the ◊Unification Church, a religious sect founded by Sun Myung Moon.

Moon probe spacecraft used to investigate the Moon. Early probes flew past the Moon or crash-landed on it, but later ones achieved soft landings or went into orbit. Soviet probes included the long Lunik/Luna series. US probes (Ranger, Surveyor, Lunar Orbiter) prepared the way for the Apollo crewed flights.
The first space probe to hit the Moon was the Soviet Lunik 2, on 13 Sept 1959 (Lunik 1 had missed the Moon eight months earlier). In Oct 1959, Lunik 3 sent back the first photographs of the Moon's far side. Lunik 9 was the first probe to soft-land on the Moon, on 3 Feb 1966, transmitting photographs of the surface to Earth. Lunik 16 was the first probe to return automatically to Earth carrying Moon samples, in Sept 1970, although by then Moon rocks had already been brought back by ◊Apollo astronauts. Lunik 17 landed in Nov 1970 carrying a lunar rover, Lunokhod, which was driven over the Moon's surface by remote control from Earth.
The first successful US Moon probe was Ranger 7, which took close-up photographs before it hit the Moon on 31 July 1964. Surveyor 1, on 2 June 1966, was the first US probe to soft-land on the lunar surface. It took photographs, and later Surveyors analysed the surface rocks. Between 1966 and 1967 a series of five Lunar Orbiters photographed the entire Moon in detail, in preparation for the Apollo landings.

moonstone a translucent, pearly variety of potassium sodium ◊feldspar, found in Sri Lanka and Myanmar, and distinguished by a blue, silvery, or red opalescent tint. It is valued as a gem.

Moor any of the Muslims who conquered Spain and occupied its southern part from 711 to 1492. They were of mixed Arab and Berber origin. The name (English form of Latin *Maurus*) was originally applied to an inhabitant of the Roman province of Mauritania, in NW Africa.

Moorcock /'mʊəkɒk/ Michael 1939– . English writer, associated with the 1960s new wave in science fiction, editor of the magazine *New Worlds* 1964–69. He wrote the Jerry Cornelius novels, collected as *The Cornelius Chronicles* 1977, and *Gloriana* 1978.

Moore /mʊə/ (Robert Frederick) 'Bobby' 1941– . British footballer. Captain of West Ham United and England, he led them to victory over West Germany in the 1966 World Cup final at Wembley Stadium.

Between 1962 and 1970 he played a record 108 games for England. He played the last of his 668 Football League games for Fulham against Blackburn Rovers in 1977, after a career spanning 19 years. He later played in Hong Kong before becoming a director of Southend United and in 1984 he became their manager.

CAREER HIGHLIGHTS

Football League appearances: 668
goals: 25
International appearances: goals: 2
World Cup: 1966
European Cup Winners Cup: 1965
FA Cup: 1964
Footballer of the Year: 1964

Moore /mʊə/ Dudley 1935– . British actor and comedian, formerly teamed with comedian Peter Cook, who became a Hollywood star after appearing in *10* 1979. His other films, mostly comedies, include *Bedazzled* 1968, *Arthur* 1981, and *Santa Claus* 1985.

Moore /mʊə/ G(eorge) E(dward) 1873–1958. British philosopher. Educated at Trinity College, Cambridge University, he was professor of philosophy at the university 1925–39, and edited the journal *Mind*, to which he contributed 1921–47. His books include *Principia Ethica* 1903, in which he attempted to analyse the moral question 'What is good?', and *Some Main Problems of Philosophy* 1953, but his chief influence was as a teacher.

Moore /mʊə/ George (Augustus) 1852–1933. Irish novelist, born in County Mayo. He studied art in Paris 1870, and published two volumes of poetry there. His first novel, *A Modern Lover* 1883, was sexually frank for its time and banned in some quarters. It was followed by others, including *Esther Waters* 1894.

Moore /mʊə/ Gerald 1899–1987. British pianist, renowned as an accompanist of singers, a role he raised to equal partnership.

Moore /mʊə/ Henry 1898–1986. British sculptor. His subjects include the reclining nude, mother and child groups, the warrior, and interlocking abstract forms. As an official war artist during World War II, he did a series of drawings of London's air-raid shelters. Many of his postwar works are in bronze or marble, including monumental semi-abstracts such as *Reclining Figure* 1957–58 (outside UNESCO, Paris), and often designed to be placed in landscape settings.

Moore, born in Yorkshire, studied at Leeds and the Royal College of Art, London, but claimed to have learned more from archaic South and Central American sculpture, and this is reflected in his work from the 1920s. By the early 1930s most of his main themes had emerged, and the Surrealists' preoccupation with organic forms in abstract works proved a strong influence; Moore's hollowed wooden shapes strung with wires (resembling those of Barbara ◊Hepworth) date from the late 1930s. Abstract work suggesting organic structures recurs after World War II, for example in the interwoven bonelike forms of the *Hill Arches* and the bronze *Sheep Pieces* 1970s, set in fields by his studio in Much Hadham, Hertfordshire.

Moore /mʊə/ (John) Jeremy 1928– . British major general of the Commando Forces, Royal Marines, 1979–82. He commanded the land forces in the UK's conflict with Argentina over the Falklands 1982.

Moore Family Group, *bronze (1949) Tate Gallery, London.*

Moore /mʊə/ John 1761–1809. British general, born in Glasgow. In 1808 he commanded the British army sent to Portugal in the Peninsular War. After advancing into Spain he had to retreat to Corunna in the NW, and was killed in the battle fought to cover the embarkation.

He entered the army in 1776, serving in the American and French Revolutionary Wars and against the Irish rebellion of 1798.

Moore /mʊə/ Marianne 1887–1972. US poet. She edited the literary magazine *Dial* 1925–29, and published volumes of witty and intellectual verse including *Observations* 1924, *What are Years* 1941, and *A Marianne Moore Reader* 1961.

Moore /mʊə/ Roger 1928– . British actor who starred in the television series *The Saint* 1962–70, and assumed the film role of James Bond in 1973 in *Live and Let Die*. His films include *Diane* 1955, *Gold* 1974, *The Wild Geese* 1978, and *Octopussy* 1983.

Moore /mʊə/ Thomas 1779–1852. Irish poet, born in Dublin. Among his works are the verse romance *Lalla Rookh* 1817 and the *Irish Melodies* 1807–35. These were set to music by John Stevenson 1807–35 and include 'The Minstrel Boy' and 'The Last Rose of Summer'.

moorhen bird *Gallinula chloropus* of the rail family, common in water of swamps, lakes, and ponds in Eurasia, Africa, and North and South America. It is about 33 cm/13 in long, mainly brown and grey, but with a red bill and forehead, and a vivid white underside to the tail. The big feet are not webbed or lobed, but the moorhen can swim well.

Moorhouse /'mʊəhaʊs/ Adrian 1964– . English swimmer who won the 100 metres breaststroke at the 1988 Seoul Olympics.

He has won gold medals at both the Commonwealth Games and the European Championships but was disqualified from first place for an illegal turn during the 1986 world championships.

CAREER HIGHLIGHTS

Olympic Games
100 m breaststroke 1988
Commonwealth Games
100 m breaststroke 1982
200 m breaststroke 1986
European Championships
200 m breaststroke 1983
100 m breaststroke 1985, 1987, 1989, 1990

Moorhouse /'mʊəhaʊs/ Geoffrey 1931– . British travel writer, born in Bolton, Lancashire. His books include *The Fearful Void* 1974, and (on cricket) *The Best-Loved Game* 1979.

moose North American name for ◊elk.

Moose Jaw /,muːs 'dʒɔː/ town in S Saskatchewan, Canada, with grain elevators, extensive stockyards, petroleum refineries; population (1985) 35,500.

moot a legal and administrative assembly found in nearly every community in medieval England.

moped a lightweight motorcycle with pedals. Early mopeds (like the autocycle) were like motorized bicycles, using the pedals to start the bike and assist propulsion uphill. The pedals have little function in many modern mopeds.

Moradabad /,mɔːrədə'bæd/ trading city in Uttar Pradesh, India, on the Ramganga river; produces textiles and engraved brassware; population (1981) 348,000. It was founded 1625 by Rustam Khan, and the Great Mosque dates from 1631.

moraine rocky debris or ◊till carried along and deposited by a ◊glacier. Material eroded from the side of a glaciated valley and carried along the glacier's edge is called lateral moraine; that worn from the valley floor and carried along the base of the glacier is called ground moraine. Rubble dropped at the foot of a melting glacier is called terminal moraine.

When two glaciers converge their lateral moraines unite to form a medial moraine. Debris that has fallen down crevasses and become embedded in the ice is termed englacial moraine; when this is exposed at the surface due to partial melting it becomes ablation moraine.

morality play didactic medieval verse drama, in part a development of the ◊mystery play (or miracle play), in which human characters are replaced by personified virtues and vices, the limited humorous elements being provided by the Devil. Morality plays flourished in the 15th century, the best-known example being *Everyman*. They exerted an influence on the development of Elizabethan drama and comedy.

Moral ReArmament (MRA) international anticommunist movement calling for 'moral and spiritual renewal'. It was founded by the Christian evangelist F N D Buchman in 1938.

Morandi /mɒ'rændi/ Giorgio 1890–1964. Italian still-life painter and etcher, whose subtle studies of bottles and jars convey a sense of calm and repose.

Moravia /mə'reɪvɪə/ (Czech *Morava*) district of central Europe, from 1960 two regions of Czechoslovakia:
South Moravia (Czech *Jihomoravský*)
area 15,030 sq km/5,802 sq mi
capital Brno
population (1986) 2,075,000
North Moravia (Czech *Severomoravský*)
area 11,070 sq km/4,273 sq mi
capital Ostrava
population (1986) 1,957,000
features (N and S) river Morava; 25% forested
products maize, grapes, wine in the south; wheat, barley, rye, flax, sugarbeet in the north; coal and iron
history part of the Avar territory since the 6th century; conquered by Charlemagne's Holy Roman Empire. In 874 the kingdom of Great Moravia was founded by the Slavic prince Sviatopluk, who ruled until 894. It was conquered by the Magyars 906, and became a fief of Bohemia 1029. It was passed to the Habsburgs 1526, and became an Austrian crown land 1849. It was incorporated in the new republic of Czechoslovakia 1918, forming a province until 1949.

Moravia /mə'reɪvɪə/ Alberto. Pen name of Alberto Pincherle 1907– . Italian novelist. His first successful novel was *Gli indifferenti/The Time of Indifference* 1929. However, its criticism of Mussolini's regime led to the government censoring his work until after World War II. Later books include *La romana/Woman of Rome* 1947, *La ciociara/Two Women* 1957, and *La noia/The Empty Canvas* 1961, a study of an artist's obsession with his model.

Moravian member of a Christian Protestant sect, the *Moravian Brethren*. It is an episcopal

Moravia *Italian writer, journalist, and critic Alberto Moravia is a leading figure in Italian intellectual and cultural life.*

church and was founded in Bohemia 1457 as an offshoot of the Hussite movement (see John ◊Huss). Its followers were persecuted in the 17th and 18th centuries. There are about 63,000 Moravians in the USA, and small congregations in the UK and the rest of Europe.

Persecution began 1620, and the Moravians were held together mainly by the leadership of their bishop, Comenius. Driven out of Bohemia in 1722, they spread over Germany and into England and North America. In 1732 missionary work was begun.

Moray Earl of Moray another spelling of ◊Murray, regent of Scotland 1567–70.

Moray Firth /'mʌri/ North Sea inlet in Scotland, between Burghead (Grampian) and Tarbat Ness (Highland region), 38 km/15 mi wide at its entrance. The town of Inverness is situated at the head of the Firth.

Morayshire /'mʌriʃə/ former county of NE Scotland, divided 1975 between Highland region (the SW section) and Grampian region (the NE); the county town was Elgin.

Morazán /,mɒrə'sɑːn/ Francisco 1792–1842. Central American politician, born in Honduras. He was elected president of the United Provinces of Central America in 1830. In the face of secessions he attempted to hold the union together by force but was driven out by the Guatemalan dictator Carrera. Morazán was eventually captured and executed in 1842.

Morbihan, Gulf of /,mɔːbi'ɒn/ seawater lake in ◊Brittany, W France, linked by a channel with the Bay of Biscay; area 104 sq km/40 sq mi. Morbihan is a Breton word meaning 'little sea' and the gulf gives its name to a *département*.

Mordovia /mɔː'dəuviə/ another name for ◊Mordvinia, republic of the USSR.

Mordvinia /mɔː'dvɪniə/ (or *Mordovia*) autonomous republic of central USSR
area 26,200 sq km/10,100 sq mi
capital Saransk
features river Sura on the E; forested in the W
products sugar beet, grains, potatoes; sheep and dairy farming; timber, furniture, and textiles
population (1986) 964,000
history Mordvinia was conquered by Russia during the 13th century. It was made an autonomous region 1930, and an Autonomous Soviet Socialist Republic 1934.

More /mɔː/ (St) Thomas 1478–1535. English politician and author. From 1509 he was favoured by ◊Henry VIII and employed on foreign embassies. He was a member of the privy council from 1518

and Lord Chancellor from 1529 but resigned over Henry's break with the pope. For refusing to accept the king as head of the church, he was executed. The title of his political book *Utopia* 1516 has come to mean any supposedly perfect society.

Son of a London judge, More studied at Oxford and law at Lincoln's Inn, London, and was influenced by the humanists John Colet and ◊Erasmus, who became a friend. In Parliament from 1504, he was made Speaker of the House of Commons in 1523. He was knighted in 1521, and on the fall of Cardinal Wolsey became Lord Chancellor, but resigned in 1532 because he could not agree with the king on his ecclesiastical policy and the marriage with Anne Boleyn. In 1534 he refused to take the oath of supremacy to Henry VIII as head of the church, and after a year's imprisonment in the Tower of London he was executed.

Among Thomas More's writings are the Latin *Utopia* 1516, sketching an ideal commonwealth; the English *Dialogue* 1528, a theological argument against the Reformation leader Tyndale; and a *History of Richard III*. He was also a patron of artists, including ◊Holbein. More was canonized in 1935.

More /mɔː/ Kenneth 1914–1982. British actor, a film star of the 1950s, cast as leading man in adventure films and light comedies such as *Genevieve* 1953, *Doctor in the House* 1954, and *Northwest Frontier*. His film career declined in the 1960s, although he played occasional character parts.

Moreau /mɔː'rəu/ Gustave 1826–1898. French Symbolist painter. His works are biblical, mythological, and literary scenes, richly coloured and detailed, and atmospheric.

Salome Dancing Before Herod 1876 attracted much attention when it was first exhibited. In the 1890s Moreau taught at the Ecole des Beaux-Arts in Paris, where his pupils included Matisse and Rouault. Much of his work is in the Musée Moreau, Paris.

Moreau /mɔː'rəu/ Jean Victor Marie 1763–1813. French general in the Revolutionary Wars who won a brilliant victory over the Austrians at ◊Hohenlinden 1800; as a republican he intrigued against Napoleon, and, when banished, joined the Allies and was killed at the Battle of Dresden.

Moreau /mɔː'rəu/ Jeanne 1928– . French actress who has appeared in international films, often in passionate roles. Her work includes *Les Amants/The Lovers* 1958, *Jules et Jim/Jules and Jim* 1961, *Chimes at Midnight* 1966, and *Querelle* 1982.

Morecambe /'mɔːkəm/ town and resort in Lancashire, England, on Morecambe Bay, conjoined with the port of Heysham, which has a ferry service to Ireland; joint population (1982) 43,000.

Morecambe Bay /'mɔːkəm 'beɪ/ inlet of the Irish Sea, between the Furness Peninsula (Cumbria) and Lancashire, England, with shallow sands. There are oil wells, and natural gas 50 km/30 mi offshore.

morel type of mushroom. The common morel, *Morchella esculenta*, grows abundantly in Europe and North America. The yellowish-brown edible

cap is much wrinkled and about 2.5 cm/1 in long. It is used for seasoning gravies, soups, and sauces.

mores (Latin) the customs and manners of a society.

Moresby /'mɔːzbi/ John 1830–1922. British naval explorer and author. He is remembered as the first European to visit the harbour in New Guinea, now known as Port Moresby.

Morgagni /mɔː'gænji/ Giovanni Battista 1682–1771. Italian anatomist. As professor of anatomy at Padua, Morgagni carried out large numbers of autopsies, and developed the view that disease was not an imbalance of the body's humours but a result of alterations in the organs. His work formed the basis of morbid anatomy and ◊pathology.

Morgan /'mɔːgən/ Henry *c.*1635–1688. Welsh buccaneer in the Caribbean. He made war against Spain, capturing and sacking Panama 1671. In 1674 he was knighted and appointed lieutenant-governor of Jamaica.

Morgan /'mɔːgən/ John Pierpont 1837–1913. US financier and investment banker whose company (sometimes criticized as 'the money trust') wielded great influence over US corporate economy after the Civil War, being instrumental in the formation of many trusts to stifle competition. He set up the US Steel Corporation in 1901.

Morgan /'mɔːgən/ Lewis Henry 1818–1881. US anthropologist. He studied American Indian culture, and was adopted by the Iroquois.

Morgan /'mɔːgən/ Thomas Hunt 1866–1945. US geneticist, awarded a Nobel prize 1933 for his pioneering studies in classical genetics. He was the first to work on the fruit fly, *Drosophila*, which has since become a major subject of genetic studies. He helped establish that the genes were located on the chromosomes, discovered sex chromosomes, and invented the techniques of genetic mapping.

Morgan le Fay in the romance and legend of ◊Arthur, an enchantress and healer, ruler of ◊Avalon and sister of the king, whom she tended after his final battle. In some versions of the legend she is responsible for the suspicions held by the king of his wife ◊Guinevere.

Morgenthau Plan proposals originated by Henry Morgenthau Jr (1891–1967), US secretary of the Treasury, for Germany after World War II, calling for the elimination of war industries in the Ruhr and Saar basins and the conversion of Germany 'into a country primarily agricultural and pastoral in character'. The plan had already been dropped by the time the Allied leaders Churchill, Roosevelt, and Stalin met at Yalta Feb 1945.

Morisco one of the Spanish Muslims and their descendants who accepted Christian baptism. They were all expelled from Spain in 1609.

Morisot /,mɒri'səu/ Berthe 1841–1895. French Impressionist painter, who specialized in pictures of women and children.

Morland /'mɔːlənd/ George 1763–1804. English painter whose picturesque country subjects became widely reproduced in engravings. He was an admirer of Dutch and Flemish painters of rustic life.

Morley Edward 1838–1923. US physicist who collaborated with ◊Michelson on the Michelson–Morley experiment 1887. In 1895 he established precise and accurate measurements of the densities of oxygen and hydrogen.

Morley /'mɔːli/ John, 1st Viscount Morley of Blackburn 1838–1923. British Liberal politician and writer. He entered Parliament in 1883, and was secretary for Ireland in 1886 and 1892–95. As secretary for India 1905–10, he prepared the way (with Viceroy Gilbert ◊Minto) for more representative government.

He was Lord President of the Council 1910–14, but resigned in protest against the declaration of war. He published lives of the philosophers Voltaire and Rousseau and the politicians Burke and Gladstone. He received a peerage in 1908.

More *Portrait of Thomas More after Hans Holbein (1527), National Portrait Gallery, London.*

Morocco
Kingdom of *(al-Mamlaka al-Maghrebia)*

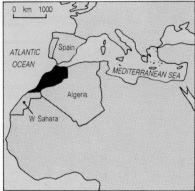

area 458,730 sq km/177,070 sq mi
capital Rabat
towns Marrakesh, Fez, Kenes; ports Casablanca, Tangier
physical mountain ranges NE–SW; plains in W
features Atlas Mountains; the towns Ceuta (from 1580), Melilla (from 1492), and three small coastal settlements are held by Spain; a tunnel across the Strait of Gibraltar to Spain was proposed 1985
head of state Hassan II from 1961
head of government Mohamed Karim Lamrani from 1984
government constitutional monarchy
political parties Constitutional Union (UC), right-wing; National Rally of Independents (RNI), royalist; Popular Movement (MP), moderate socialist; Istiqlal, nationalist, right-of-centre;

Socialist Union of Popular Forces (USFP), progressive socialist; National Democratic Party (PND), moderate, nationalist
economy dates, figs, cork, wood pulp, canned fish, phosphates, tourism
currency dirham (13.57 = £1 Feb 1990)
population (1989 est) 25,380,000; annual growth rate 2.5%
life expectancy men 57, women 60
language Arabic (official) 75%, Berber 25%, French, Spanish
religion Sunni Muslim
literacy 45% male/22% female (1985 est)
GNP $15.6 bn (1983); $800 per head of population
chronology
1956 Achieved independence from France as the Sultanate of Morocco.
1957 Sultan restyled king of Morocco.
1961 Hassan II came to the throne.
1969 Former Spanish province of Ifni returned to Morocco.
1972 Major revision of the constitution.
1975 Western Sahara ceded by Spain to Morocco and Mauritania.
1976 Guerrilla war in the Sahara by the Polisario Front. Sahrawi Arab Democratic Republic (SADR) established in Algiers. Diplomatic relations with Algeria broken.
1979 Mauritania signed a peace treaty with Polisario.
1983 Peace formula for the Sahara proposed by the Organization of African Unity (OAU) but not accepted by Morocco.
1984 Hassan signed an agreement for cooperation and mutual defence with Libya.
1987 Ceasefire agreed with Polisario but fighting continued.
1988 Diplomatic relations with Algeria restored.
1989 Diplomatic relations with Syria restored.

There are a number of political parties, the most significant being the Constitutional Union (UC), the National Rally of Independents (RNI), the Popular Movement (MP), Istiqlal, the Socialist Union of Popular Forces (USFP), and the National Democratic Party (PND).

history Originally occupied by ◊Berber tribes, the coastal regions of the area now known as Morocco were under Phoenician rule during the 10th–3rd centuries BC, and became a Roman colony in the 1st century AD. It was invaded in the 5th century by the ◊Vandals, in the 6th century by the Visigoths, and in the 7th century began to be conquered by the Arabs. From the 11th century the region was united under the ◊Almoravids, who ruled a Muslim empire that included Spain, Morocco, and Algeria. They were followed by the ◊Almohads, another Muslim dynasty, whose empire included Libya and Tunisia.

In the 15th century Portugal occupied the Moroccan port of Ceuta, but was defeated in 1578. Further European influence began in the 19th century, and was more lasting, with Morocco being divided in 1912 into French and Spanish protectorates. It became fully independent as the Sultanate of Morocco in 1956, under Mohammed V (sultan since 1927). The former Spanish protectorate joined the new state, with Tangier, which had previously been an international zone.

The sultan was restyled king of Morocco in 1957. After his death in 1961 he was succeeded by King Hassan II, who has survived several attempted coups and assassinations. Between 1960 and 1972 several constitutions were formulated in an attempt to balance personal royal rule with demands for greater democracy.

Hassan's reign has been dominated by the dispute over ◊Western Sahara, a former Spanish colony seen as historically Moroccan. In 1975 Spain ceded it to Morocco and Mauritania, leaving them to divide it. The inhabitants, who had not been consulted, reacted violently through an independence movement, the Polisario Front. Less than a year later, Morocco and Mauritania were involved in a guerrilla war.

With Algerian support, Polisario set up a government in exile in Algiers, the Sahrahwi Arab Democratic Republic (SADR). This prompted Hassan to sever diplomatic relations with Algeria in 1976. In 1979 Mauritania agreed a peace treaty with Polisario, and Morocco annexed the part of Western Sahara that Mauritania had vacated. Polisario reacted by intensifying its operations. In 1983 the Organization of African Unity (OAU) proposed a cease-fire, direct negotiations between Morocco and Polisario, and a referendum in Western Sahara. Morocco agreed but refused to deal directly with Polisario.

Although the war was costly, it allowed Hassan to capitalize on the patriotism it generated in his country. In 1984 he unexpectedly signed an agreement with Col Khaddhafi of Libya, who had been helping Polisario, for economic and political cooperation and mutual defence. Meanwhile, Morocco was becoming more isolated as SADR gained wider recognition. Towards the end of 1987 the Polisario guerrillas agreed a cease-fire and in Aug 1988 a United Nations peace plan was accepted, despite continued fighting in some areas. Full diplomatic relations with Algeria were restored in May 1988, and with Syria in Jan 1989.

Moroni /məˈrəuni/ capital of the Comoros Republic, on Njazídja (Grand Comore); population (1980) 20,000.

Morpheus /ˈmɔːfjuːs/ in Greek and Roman mythology, the god of dreams, son of Hypnos or Somnus, god of sleep.

morphine opium ◊alkaloid, prescribed for severe pain. Its use produces serious side effects, including nausea, constipation, tolerance, and addiction. Although it is a controlled substance in Britain, its effective ◊analgesia makes it highly valued in the treatment of terminal illness.

Morley /ˈmɔːli/ Malcolm 1931– . British painter, active in New York from 1964. He coined the term *Superrealism* for his work in the 1960s.

Morley /ˈmɔːli/ Robert 1908– . British actor and playwright, active in Britain and the US. His film work has been mainly character roles, including films such as *Marie Antoinette* 1938, *The African Queen* 1952, and *Oscar Wilde* 1960.

Morley /ˈmɔːli/ Thomas 1557–1602. English composer. A student of ◊Byrd, he became organist at St Paul's Cathedral, London, and obtained a monopoly on music printing. A composer of the English madrigal school, he also wrote sacred music, songs for Shakespeare's plays, and a musical textbook.

Mormon or *Latter-day Saint* member of a Christian sect, the *Church of Jesus Christ of Latter-day Saints*, founded at Fayette, New York, in 1830 by Joseph ◊Smith. According to Smith, Mormon was an ancient prophet in North America whose *Book of Mormon*, of which Smith claimed divine revelation, is accepted by Mormons as part of the Christian scriptures. In the 19th century the faction led by Brigham ◊Young was polygamous. It is a missionary church with headquarters in Utah and a worldwide membership of about 6 million.

Jesus is said to have appeared to an early native American people after his ascension to establish his church in the New World. The Mormon church claims to be a re-establishment of this by divine intervention. Their doctrines met with persecution, and Smith was killed in Illinois. Further settlements were rapidly established despite opposition, and Brigham Young and 12 apostles undertook the first foreign Mormon mission in the UK. In 1847 he led a westward migration of most of the church's members to the Valley of the Great Salt Lake. Young attributed the doctrine of plural marriage to the original founder, although Smith

is on record as condemning it. Polygamy was formally repudiated by the Utah Mormons 1890.

Most of the Mormons that remained in the Middle West (headquarters Independence, Missouri) accepted the founder's son Joseph Smith (1832–1914) as leader, adopted the name *Reorganized Church of Jesus Christ of Latter-day Saints*, and now claim to be the true successor of the original church. They do not accept the non-Christian doctrines proclaimed by Young.

morning glory plant *Ipomoea purpurea*, family Convolvulaceae, native to tropical America, with dazzling blue flowers. Small quantities of substances similar to ◊LSD are found in the seeds of one variety.

Moro /ˈmɔːrəu/ Aldo 1916–1978. Italian Christian Democrat politician. Prime minister 1963–68 and 1974–76, he was expected to become Italy's president, but he was kidnapped and shot by Red Brigade urban guerrillas.

Moroccan Crises two periods of international tension 1905 and 1911 following German objections to French expansion in Morocco. Their wider purpose was to break up the Anglo-French Entente 1904, but both crises served to reinforce the entente and isolate Germany.

Morocco /məˈrɒkəu/ country in N Africa, bordered N and NW by the Mediterranean, E and SE by Algeria, and S by Western Sahara.

government Morocco is an unusual constitutional monarchy in that the king, as well as being the formal head of state, presides over his appointed cabinet and has powers, under the 1972 constitution, to dismiss the prime minister and other ministers, as well as to dissolve the legislature. This consists of a 306-member chamber of representatives, serving a six-year term. 206 are directly elected by universal suffrage and 100 are chosen by an electoral college of local councillors and employers' and employees' representatives.

Morris *(left) William Morris, photographed by Abel Lewis (c.1880). (right) The* Strawberry Thief, *a design by Morris in printed cotton. It was patented 1883.*

morphogen one of a class of substances believed to be present in the growing embryo that control its growth pattern. It is thought that variations in the concentration of morphogens in different parts of the embryo cause them to grow at different rates.

morphology in biology, the study of the physical structure and form of organisms, in particular their soft tissues.

Morrigan in Celtic mythology, a goddess of war and death who could take the shape of a crow.

Morris /ˈmɒrɪs/ Henry 1889–1961. British educationalist. He inspired and oversaw the introduction of the 'village college' and ◊community school education, which he saw as regenerating rural life.

Through emphasis on providing a centre for continuing education and leisure activities for both adults and children on a single site, it has also proved influential in urban areas. He persuaded ◊Gropius, together with Maxwell Fry, to design the Village College at Impington, near Cambridge, 1939. He was chief education officer for Cambridgeshire 1922–54.

Morris /ˈmɒrɪs/ Thomas, Jr 1851–1875. British golfer. One of the first great champions, he was known as 'Young Tom' to distinguish him from his father (who was known as 'Old Tom'). Morris junior won the British Open four times 1868–72.

Morris /ˈmɒrɪs/ William 1834–1896. English designer, socialist, and poet, who shared the Pre-Raphaelite painters' fascination with medieval settings. His first book of verse was *The Defence of Guenevere* 1858. In 1862 he founded a firm for the manufacture of furniture, wallpapers, and the like, and in 1890 he set up the Kelmscott Press to print beautifully decorated books. The prose romances *A Dream of John Ball* 1888 and *News from Nowhere* 1891 reflect his socialist ideology. He also lectured on socialism.

William Morris was born in Walthamstow, London, and educated at Oxford, where he formed a lasting friendship with the Pre-Raphaelite artist ◊Burne-Jones and was influenced by the art critic Ruskin and the painter and poet ◊Rossetti. He abandoned his first profession, architecture, to study painting, but had a considerable influence on such architects as Lethaby and Philip ◊Webb. A founder of the Arts and Crafts movement, Morris did much to raise British craft standards.

He published several volumes of verse romances, notably *The Life and Death of Jason* 1867 and *The Earthly Paradise* 1868–70; a visit to Iceland 1871 inspired *Sigurd the Volsung* 1876 and general interest in the sagas. He joined the Social Democratic Federation 1883, but left it 1884 because he found it too moderate, and set up the Socialist League. To this period belong the critical and sociological studies *Signs of Change* 1888 and *Hopes and Fears for Art* 1892.

morris dance an English folk dance. In early times it was usually performed by six men, one of whom wore girl's clothing while another portrayed a horse. The others wore costumes decorated with bells. It probably originated in pre-Christian ritual dances and is still popular today in the UK and USA.

Morrison /ˈmɒrɪsən/ Herbert Stanley, Baron Morrison of Lambeth 1888–1965. British Labour politician. He was secretary of the London Labour Party 1915–45, and a member of the London County Council 1922–45. He entered Parliament in 1923, and in 1955 was defeated by Gaitskell in the contest for leadership of the party.

He was minister of transport 1929–31, home secretary 1940–45, Lord President of the Council and leader of the House of Commons 1945–51, and foreign secretary Mar–Oct 1951.

Morrison /ˈmɒrɪsən/ Toni 1931– . US novelist, whose fiction records black life in the South. Her works include *The Song of Solomon* 1978, *Tar Baby* 1981, and *Beloved* 1987, based on a true story about infanticide in Kentucky, which won the Pulitzer prize 1988.

Morse /mɔːs/ Samuel (Finley Breese) 1791–1872. US inventor. In 1835 he produced the first adequate electric ◊telegraph, and in 1843 was granted $30,000 by Congress for an experimental line between Washington and Baltimore. With his assistant Alexander Bain he invented the Morse code. He was also a respected portrait painter.

Morse code international code for transmitting messages by wire or radio using signals of short (dots) and long (dashes) duration, originated by Samuel Morse for use on his ◊telegraph.

The letters SOS (3 short, 3 long, 3 short) form the international distress signal, being distinctive and easily transmitted (popularly *Save our souls*). By radio telephone the distress call is 'Mayday', for similar reasons (popularly alleged to derive from French *m'aidez*, help me).

Morte D'Arthur, Le a series of episodes from the legendary life of King Arthur by Thomas Malory, completed 1470, regarded as the first great prose work in English literature. Only the last of the eight books composing the series is titled *Le Morte D'Arthur*.

mortgage a transfer of property—usually a house—as a security for repayment of a loan. The loan is normally repaid to a bank or building society over a period of years.

Mortimer /ˈmɔːtɪmə/ John 1923– . English barrister and writer. His works include the plays *The Dock Brief* 1958 and *A Voyage Round My Father* 1970, the novel *Paradise Postponed* 1985, and the television series *Rumpole of the Bailey*, from 1978, centred on a fictional barrister.

Mortimer /ˈmɔːtɪmə/ Roger de, 8th Baron of Wigmore and 1st Earl of March *c.*1287–1330. English politician and adventurer. He opposed Edward II and with Edward's queen, Isabella, led a rebellion against him 1326, bringing about his abdication. From 1327 Mortimer ruled England as the queen's lover, until Edward III had him executed.

A rebel, he was imprisoned by Edward II for two years before making his escape from the Tower of London to France. There he joined with the English queen, Isabella, who was conducting negotiations at the French court, and returned with her to England in 1326. Edward fled when they landed with their followers, and Mortimer secured Edward's deposition by Parliament. In

Morse *Samuel Morse invented the electric telegraph and developed a code system (Morse code) to send messages.*

1328 he was created Earl of March. He was popularly supposed responsible for Edward II's murder, and when the young Edward III had him seized while with the queen at Nottingham Castle, he was hanged, drawn, and quartered at Tyburn, London.

mortmain lands held by a corporate body, especially the church, in perpetual or inalienable tenure.

In the Middle Ages, alienation in mortmain, usually to a church in return for a ◊chantry foundation, deprived the feudal lord of his future incidents (payments due to him when the land changed ownership) and rights of wardship, and so attempts were often made to regulate the practice.

Morton /ˈmɔːtn/ Henry Vollam 1892–1979. English journalist and travel writer, author of the *In Search of …* series published during the 1950s. His earlier travel books include *The Heart of London* 1925, *In the Steps of the Master* 1934, and *Middle East* 1941.

Morton /ˈmɔːtn/ J(ohn) B(ingham) 1893–1979. British journalist, best known for the humorous column he contributed to the *Daily Express* 1924–76 under the pen name of **Beachcomber**.

Morton /ˈmɔːtn/ Jelly Roll. Stage name of Ferdinand Joseph La Menthe 1885–1941. US jazz pianist, singer, and composer. Influenced by Scott Joplin, he played a major part in the development of jazz from ragtime to swing by improvising and imposing his own personality on the music. His band from 1926 was called the Red Hot Peppers.

Morton /ˈmɔːtn/ William Thomas Green 1819–1868. US dentist who in 1846 introduced ether as an anaesthetic; his claim to be the first to do so was strongly disputed.

Morse code

A ·—	B —···	C —·—·	D —··	E ·	F ··—·
G ——·	H ····	I ··	J ·———	K —·—	L ·—··
M ——	N —·	O ———	P ·——·	Q ——·—	R ·—·
S ···	T —	U ··—	V ···—	W ·——	X —··—

| | | Y —·—— | Z ——·· | | |

| 1 ·———— | 2 ··——— | 3 ···—— | 4 ····— | 5 ····· |
| 6 —···· | 7 ——··· | 8 ———·· | 9 ————· | 0 ————— |

While searching for ways to avoid the pain of tooth extraction, he learned of the pain-killing effects of ether from C T Jackson, a chemist and physician. Morton realized the anaesthetic potential of the gas, and the two men patented the process and set about publicizing it. Morton's contribution to medicine lay in making the value of anaesthesia generally known and appreciated.

mosaic a design or picture, usually for a floor or wall, produced by inlay of small pieces of marble, glass, or other materials. Mosaic was commonly used by the Romans for their villas (for example Hadrian's Villa at Tivoli) and by the Byzantines.

The art was revived by the Italians during the 13th century, when it was used chiefly for the decoration of churches (for example San Vitale, ◊Ravenna). More recent examples of mosaic work can be seen in the hall of the Houses of Parliament and in Westminster Cathedral, London.

Moscow /ˈmɒskəʊ/ (Russian **Moskva**) capital of the USSR and of the Moskva region, on the Moskva river 640 km/400 mi SE of Leningrad; population (1987) 8,815,000. Its industries include machinery, electrical equipment, textiles, chemicals, and many food products.

features The 12th-century Kremlin (Citadel), at the centre of the city, is a walled enclosure containing a number of historic buildings, including three cathedrals, one of them the burial place of the tsars; the Ivan Veliki tower 90 m/300 ft, a famine-relief work commissioned by Boris Godunov 1600; various palaces, including the former imperial palace, museums, and the Tsar Kolokol, the world's largest bell (200 tonnes) 1735. The walls of the Kremlin are crowned by 18 towers and have five gates. Red Square, used for political demonstrations and processions, contains St Basil's Cathedral, the state department store GUM, and Lenin's tomb. The headquarters of the ◊KGB, with Lubyanka Prison behind it, is in Dzerzhinsky Square; the underground railway was opened 1935. Institutions include Moscow University 1755 and People's Friendship University (for foreign students) 1953; the ◊Academy of Sciences, which moved from Leningrad 1934; Tretyakov Gallery of Russian Art 1856; Bolshoi Theatre 1780 for opera and ballet; Moscow Art Theatre 1898; Moscow State Circus. Moscow is the seat of the patriarch of the Russian Orthodox Church. On the city outskirts is Star City (Zvezdnoy Gorodok), the Soviet space centre.

Moscow is the largest industrial centre of the USSR, linked with Stavropol by oil pipeline 480 km/300 mi, built 1957.

history Moscow, founded as the city-state of Muscovy 1127, was destroyed by the Mongols during the 13th century, but rebuilt 1294 by Prince Daniel (died 1303) as the capital of his principality. During the 14th century, it was under the rule of ◊Alexander Nevski, Ivan I (1304–41), and Dmitri Donskai (1350–89), and became the foremost political power in Russia, and its religious capital. It was burned in 1571 by the khan of the Crimea, and ravaged by fire in 1739, 1748, and 1753; in 1812 it was burned by its own citizens to save it from Napoleon's troops, or perhaps by accident. It became capital of the Russian Soviet

Federated Social Republic (RSFSR) 1918, and of the Union of Soviet Socialist Republics (USSR) 1922. In World War II Hitler's troops were within 20 mi of Moscow on the NW by Nov 1941, but the stubborn Russian defence and severe winter weather forced their withdrawal in Dec.

Moseley /ˈməʊzli/ Henry Gwyn-Jeffreys 1887–1915. English physicist who, 1913–14, devised the series of atomic numbers, leading to the modern ◊periodic table of the elements. He did valuable work on atomic structure.

Moselle /məʊˈzel/ or **Mosel** a river in W Europe some 515 km/320 mi long; it rises in the Vosges, France, and is canalized from Thionville to its confluence with the ◊Rhine at Koblenz in Germany. It gives its name to the *départements* of Moselle and Meurthe-et-Moselle in France.

Moses /ˈməʊzɪz/ *c.* 13th century BC. Hebrew lawgiver and judge who led the Israelites out of Egypt to the promised land of Canaan. On Mount Sinai he claimed to have received from Jehovah the **Ten Commandments** engraved on tablets of stone. The first five books of the Old Testament—in Judaism, the *Torah*—are ascribed to him.

According to the Torah, the infant Moses was hidden among the bulrushes on the banks of the Nile when the pharaoh commanded that all newborn male Hebrew children should be destroyed. He was found by a daughter of Pharaoh, who reared him. Eventually he became the leader of the Israelites in their *Exodus* from Egypt and their 40 years' wandering in the wilderness, and died at the age of 120, after having been allowed a glimpse of the Promised Land from Mount Pisgah.

Moses /ˈməʊzɪz/ Ed(win Corley) 1955– . US track athlete and 400 metres hurdler. Between 1977 and 1987 he ran 122 races without defeat.

He first broke the world record in 1976, and his time of 47.02 seconds set in 1983 still stood on 1 Jan 1990. He was twice Olympic champion (1976–1984) and twice world champion (1983–1987). He took the Olympic oath on behalf of competitors in Los Angeles 1984.

Moses /ˈməʊzɪz/ 'Grandma' (born Anna Mary Robertson) 1860–1961. US painter. She was self-taught, and began full-time painting in about 1927, after many years as a farmer's wife. She painted naive and colourful scenes from rural American life.

Mosi-oa-tunya /ˈməʊsi ˈəʊə ˈtuːnjə/ the African name for the ◊Victoria Falls of the Zambezi River.

Moskva /mʌskˈvɑː/ the Russian name for ◊Moscow, capital of the USSR.

Moslem alternative word for **Muslim**, a follower of ◊Islam.

Mosley /ˈməʊzli/ Oswald (Ernald) 1896–1980. British politician, founder of the British Union of Fascists (BUF). He was a Member of Parliament 1918–31, then led the BUF until his internment 1940–43, when he was released on health grounds. In 1946 Mosley was denounced when it became known that Italy had funded his prewar efforts to establish ◊fascism in Britain, but in 1948 he resumed fascist propaganda with his Union Movement, the revived BUF.

His first marriage was to a daughter of the Conservative politician Lord Curzon, his second to Diana Freeman-Mitford, one of the ◊Mitford sisters.

mosque (Arabic *mesjid*) in Islam, a place of worship. Chief features are: the dome; the minaret, a balconied turret from which the faithful are called to prayer; the *mihrab*, or prayer niche, in one of the interior walls, showing the direction of the holy city of Mecca; and an open court surrounded by porticoes.

The earliest mosques were based on the plan of Christian basilicas, although different influences contributed towards their architectural development. Mosques vary a great deal in style in various parts of the world.

mosquito fly of the family Culicidae. The female mosquito has needlelike mouthparts and sucks

blood before egg-laying. Males feed on plant juices. Some mosquitoes carry diseases such as ◊malaria.

Mosquito Coast the Caribbean coast of Honduras and Nicaragua, characterized by swamp, lagoons and tropical rain forest. A largely undeveloped territory occupied by Mosquito Indians, Garifunas and Zambos, many of whom speak English. Between 1823 and 1860 Britain maintained a protectorate over the Mosquito Coast which was ruled by a succession of 'Mosquito Kings'.

moss small non-flowering plant of the class Musci (10,000 species), forming with the ◊liverworts the order Bryophyta. The stem of each plant bears rhizoids which anchor it; there are no true roots. Leaves spirally arranged on its lower portion have sexual organs at their tip. Most mosses flourish best in damp conditions where other vegetation is thin. The peat or bog moss *Sphagnum* was formerly used for surgical dressings.

Moss gardens are popular in Japan; there is one at the Moss Temple, near Kyoto.

Mossadeq /ˈmɒsədek/ Muhammad 1880–1967. Iranian prime minister 1951–53. He instigated a dispute with the Anglo-Iranian Oil Company over the control of Iran's oil production, and when he failed in his attempt to overthrow the shah he was imprisoned. From 1956 he was under house arrest.

Mössbauer /ˈmɜːsˈbaʊə/ Rudolf 1929– . German physicist who discovered in 1958 that in certain conditions a nucleus can be stimulated to emit very sharply defined beams of gamma rays. This became known as the **Mössbauer effect**. Such a beam was used in 1960 to provide the first laboratory test of ◊Einstein's General Theory of Relativity. For his work on gamma rays Mössbauer shared the 1961 Nobel physics prize with ◊Hofstadter.

Mostaganem /mɒˌstægəˈnem/ industrial port (metal and cement) in NW Algeria, linked by pipeline with the natural gas fields at Hassi Messaoud; population (1982) 169,500. It was founded in the 11th century.

Mostar /ˈmɒstɑː/ industrial town (aluminium, tobacco) in Bosnia and Herzegovina, Yugoslavia, noted for its grapes and wines; population (1981) 110,000.

Mostel /mɒˈstell/ 'Zero' (Samuel Joel) 1915–1977. US comedian and actor, active mainly in the theatre. His film work includes *Panic in the Streets* 1950, *A Funny Thing Happened on the Way to the Forum* 1966, *The Producers* 1967, and *The Front* 1976.

Mosul /ˈməʊsəl/ industrial city (cement, textiles) and oil centre in Iraq, on the right bank of the Tigris, opposite the site of ancient ◊Nineveh; population (1985) 571,000. Once it manufactured the light cotton fabric *muslin*, which was named after it.

motel type of hotel, near a motorway or main road, in which each room is accessible from the car-parking area. The first motel was built 1925 by A Heinman in the USA.

motet a form of sacred, polyphonic music for unaccompanied voices that originated in 13th-century Europe.

moth one of the insects forming the greater part of the order Lepidoptera. The wings are covered with flat, microscopic scales. The mouthparts are formed into a sucking proboscis, but certain moths have no functional mouthparts, and rely upon stores of fat and other reserves built up during the caterpillar stage. In many cases the males are smaller and more brightly coloured than the females. At least 100,000 different species of moth are known.

Moths feed chiefly on the nectar of flowers, on honeydew and other fluid matter: some, like the hawk moths, frequent flowers and feed while hovering.

Female vapourer and winter moths have wings either absent or reduced to minute flaps. Moths vary greatly in size. The minute Nepticulidae

mosaic *A mosaic from the 1st or 2nd century AD from southern Italy.*

sometimes have a wingspread less than 3 mm, while the giant Noctuid or owlet moth *Erebus agrippina* measures about 280 mm/11 in across. The largest British moths are the death's head and convolvulus hawk moths, which have a wingspread ranging from 114 mm/4.5 in to 133 mm/5.25 in.

The larvae or caterpillars have a well-developed head, three thoracic and ten abdominal segments. Each thoracic segment bears a pair of short legs, ending in single claws; a pair of suckerlike abdominal feet is present on segments three to six and ten of the hind-body. In the family Geometridae the caterpillars bear the abdominal feet only on segments six and ten of the hind body. They move by a characteristic looping gait and are known as 'loopers', or geometers. Projecting from the middle of the lower lip of a caterpillar is a minute tube or spinneret, through which silk is emitted to make a cocoon within which the change to the pupa or chrysalis occurs. Silk glands are especially large in the ◊silkworm moth. Many caterpillars, including the geometers, which are sought by birds, are protected by their resemblance in both form and coloration to their immediate surroundings. Others, which are distasteful to such enemies, are brightly coloured or densely hairy.

The feeding caterpillars of many moths cause damage: the winter moth and the codling moth attack fruit trees; the Mediterranean flour moth infects flour mills; and several species of clothes moth eat natural fibres.

mother-of-pearl the smooth lustrous lining in the shells of pearl-bearing molluscs; see ◊pearl.

Motherwell and Wishaw /'mʌðəwəl 'wɪʃɔ:/ industrial town (Ravenscraig iron and steel works, coal mines) in Strathclyde, Scotland, SE of Glasgow; population (1981) 68,000. The two burghs were amalgamated in 1920.

motion picture the US term for film; see ◊cinema.

mot juste (French) the right word, just the word to suit the occasion.

motor a machine that provides mechanical power, particularly an ◊electric motor. Machines that burn fuel (petrol, diesel) are usually called engines.

motorboat small, water-borne craft for pleasure cruising or racing, powered by a petrol, diesel, or gas-turbine engine. Any boat not equipped as a motorboat may be converted by a detachable outboard motor. For increased speed, especially in racing, motorboat hulls are designed to skim the water (aquaplane) and reduce frictional resistance. Plastics, steel, and light alloys are now used in construction as well as the traditional wood.

In recent designs, drag is further reduced with hydrofins and ◊hydrofoils, which enable the hull to rise clear of the water at normal speeds. Notable events in motor or 'powerboat' racing include the American Gold Cup 1947 over a 145 km/90 mi course, and the Round-Britain race 1969.

motorcar another term for ◊car.

motorcycle or *motorbike* a two-wheeled vehicle propelled by a ◊petrol engine. The first successful motorized bicycle was built in France 1901, and British and US manufacturers first produced motorbikes 1903.

In 1868 Ernest and Pierre Michaux in France experimented with a steam-powered bicycle, but the steam power unit was too heavy and cumbersome. Gottlieb ◊Daimler, a German engineer, created the first motorcycle when he installed his lightweight petrol engine in a bicycle frame 1885. Daimler soon lost interest in two wheels in favour of four and went on to pioneer the ◊car.

The first really successful two-wheel design was devised by Michael and Eugene Werner in France 1901. They adopted the classic motorcycle layout with the engine low down between the wheels. Harley Davidson in the USA and Triumph in the UK began manufacture 1903. Road races like the Isle of Man TT (Tourist Trophy), established 1907, helped improve motorcycle design and it soon evolved into more or less its present form. Until the 1970s British manufacturers predominated but today Japanese motorcycles

dominante the world market, particularly Honda, Kawasaki, Suzuki, and Yamaha. They make a wide variety of machines, from ◊mopeds (lightweights with pedal assistance) to streamlined superbikes capable of speeds up to 250 kph/160 mph. There is still a smaller but thriving Italian motorcycle industy, making more specialist bikes. Laverda, Moto Guzzi, and Ducati continue to be popular Italian manufacturers.

The lightweight bikes are generally powered by a ◊two-stroke petrol engine, while bikes with an engine capacity of 250 cc upwards are generally ◊four-strokes, although many special-use larger bikes (such as those developed for off-road riding and racing) are two-stroke. Most motorcycles are air-cooled—their engines are surrounded by metal fins to offer a large surface area—although some have a water-cooling system similar to that of a car. Most small bikes have single-cylinder engines, but larger machines can have as many as six. The single-cylinder engine was popular in British manufacture, then the Japanese preferred developing multiple-cylinder models, but there has recently been some return to favouring single-cylinder engines. A revived British Norton racing motorcycle uses a Wankel (rotary) engine. In the majority of bikes a chain carries the drive from the engine to the rear wheel, though some machines are now fitted with shaft drive.

motorcycle racing racing of motorcycles. It has many different forms: *road racing* over open roads; *circuit racing* over purpose-built tracks; *speedway* over oval-shaped dirt tracks; *motocross* over natural terrain, incorporating hill climbs; and *trials*, also over natural terrain, but with the addition of artificial hazards.

The first motorcycle race was from Paris to Nantes and back 1906. The most famous road-race series is the Isle of Man Tourist Trophy (TT) races held over the island's roads; inaugurated 1907. For finely tuned production machines, there exists a season-long world championship Grand Prix series with various categories for machines with engine sizes 80 cc–500 cc.

motorcycle racing: recent winners

World Championships have been in existence since 1949. The ◊Blue Riband event is the 500 cc class.
1980 Kenny Roberts *(USA)*
1981 Marco Luchinelli *(Italy)*
1982 Franco Uncini *(Italy)*
1983 Freddie Spencer *(USA)*
1984 Eddie Lawson *(USA)*
1985 Freddie Spencer *(USA)*
1986 Eddie Lawson *(USA)*
1987 Wayne Gardner *(Australia)*
1988 Eddie Lawson *(USA)*
1989 Eddie Lawson *(USA)*

Isle of Man Tourist Trophy
1980 Graeme Crosby *(New Zealand)*
1981 Mick Grant *(Great Britain)*
1982 Norman Brown *(Great Britain)*
1983 Rob McElnea *(Great Britain)*
1984 Rob McElnea *(Great Britain)*
1985 Joey Dunlop *(Ireland)*
1986 Roger Burnett *(Great Britain)*
1987 Joey Dunlop *(Ireland)*
1988 Joey Dunlop *(Ireland)*
1989 Steve Hislop *(Great Britain)*.

motor effect the tendency of a wire carrying an electric current in a magnetic field to move. The direction of the movement is given by the ◊left-hand rule. This effect is used in the ◊electric motor. It also explains why streams of electrons produced, for instance, in a television tube can be directed by electromagnets.

motoring law the law affecting the use of vehicles on public roads. It covers the licensing of vehicles and drivers, and the criminal offences that can be committed by the owners and drivers of vehicles.

In Britain, all vehicles are subject to road tax and (when over a certain age) to an annual

safety check (MOT test). Anyone driving on a public road must have a valid driving licence for that kind of vehicle. There is a wide range of offences: from parking in the wrong place to causing death by dangerous driving. Offences are punishable by fixed penalties: fines; endorsement of the offender's driving licence; disqualification from driving for a period; or imprisonment, depending on the seriousness of the offence. Courts must disqualify drivers convicted of driving while affected by alcohol. Licence endorsements carry penalty points (the number depending on the seriousness of the offence) which are totted up. Once a driver acquires more than 12 points, the court must disqualify him or her from driving.

Many other countries deal with driving offences much more severely. In the USA, for example, pressure groups such as Mothers Against Drunk Drivers have succeeded in making the courts impose much more severe penalties.

motor nerves in anatomy, nerves which transmit impulses from the central nervous system to muscles or body organs. Motor nerves cause voluntary and involuntary muscle contractions, and stimulate glands to secrete hormones.

motor neurone disease incurable wasting disease in which the nerve cells controlling muscle action gradually die, causing progressive weakness and paralysis. It usually occurs in later life and may be caused by an abnormal protein retained within the nerve cells. Physicist Stephen Hawking is a sufferer, as was actor David Niven.

motor racing competitive racing of motor vehicles. It has forms as diverse as hill-climbing, stock-car racing, rallying, sports-car racing, and Formula One Grand Prix racing. The first race was from Paris to Rouen 1894.

Road races like the *Targa Florio* and *Mille Miglia* were tests of a driver's skill and a machine's durability in the 1920s and 1930s. The 24-hour endurance race at ◊Le Mans (1923) is now the foremost race for sports cars and prototypes.

Purpose-built circuits include: Brands Hatch, Brooklands (to 1939), and Silverstone, UK; Hockenheim, Nurburgring, Germany; Monza, Italy; Indianapolis, USA. Street circuits include Detroit, USA, and Monte Carlo, Monaco. In Grand Prix racing (instituted 1906) a world championship for drivers has been in existence since 1950, and for constructors since 1958. The first six drivers and cars in each race are awarded points from nine to one, and the accumulative total at the end of a season (normally 16 races) decides the winners.

Drivers include Juan Manuel Fangio (Argentina), Alberto Ascari (Italy), Stirling Moss (UK), Jim Clark (UK), Jackie Stewart (UK), Graham Hill (UK), Jack Brabham (Australia), Niki Lauda (Austria), and Alain Prost (France).

Specialist makes of car include Bugatti, BRM, Mercedes, Alfa Romeo, Ferrari, Lotus, Brabham, Williams, and McLaren. There are also races for modified mass-produced cars; time-checked events, often across continents, are popular, the toughest being the Safari Rally 1953 run every Easter.

motor racing: recent winners

World Driver's Championship first held 1950
1980 Alan Jones *(Australia)*
1981 Nelson Piquet *(Brazil)*
1982 Keke Rosberg *(Finland)*
1983 Nelson Piquet *(Brazil)*
1984 Niki Lauda *(Austria)*
1985 Alain Prost *(France)*
1986 Alain Prost *(France)*
1987 Nelson Piquet *(Brazil)*
1988 Ayrton Senna *(Brazil)*
1989 Alain Prost *(France)*

Le Mans Grand Prix d'Endurance
(Le Mans 24-Hour Race) first held 1923

1980 Jean-Pierre Jassuad *(France)*/Jean Rondeau *(France)*
1981 Jacky Ickx *(Belgium)*/Derek Bell *(UK)*
1982 Jacky Ickx *(Belgium)*/Derek Bell *(UK)*
1983 Vern Schuppan *(Austria)*/Al Holbert *(USA)*/Hurley Haywood *(USA)*
1984 Klaus Ludwig *(West Germany)*/Henri Pescarolo *(France)*
1985 Klaus Ludwig *(West Germany)*/'John Winter' *(West Germany)*/Paolo Barilla *(Italy)*
1986 Hans Stuck *(West Germany)*/Derek Bell *(UK)*/Al Holbert *(USA)*
1987 Hans Stuck *(West Germany)*/Derek Bell *(UK)*/Al Holbert *(USA)*
1988 Jan Lammers *(Holland)*/Johnny Dumfries *(UK)*/Andy Wallace *(UK)*
1989 Jochen Mass *(West Germany)*/Manuel Reuter *(West Germany)*/Stanley Dickens *(Sweden)*

Indianapolis 500 first held 1911
1980 Johnny Rutherford *(USA)*
1981 Bobby Unser *(USA)*
1982 Gordon Johncock *(USA)*
1983 Tom Sneva *(USA)*
1984 Rick Mears *(USA)*
1985 Danny Sullivan *(USA)*
1986 Bobby Rahal *(USA)*
1987 Al Unser *(USA)*
1988 Rick Mears *(USA)*
1989 Emerson Fittipaldi *(Brazil)*.

motorway a major road, called **freeway** in the USA, with traffic going in opposite directions on each side of a central strip. Features include: no parking, no crossings, controlled exits and entries, no sharp bends, and a higher speed limit than on normal roads.

The first motorway (85 km/53 mi) ran from Milan to Varèse and was completed 1924, and some 500 km/300 mi of motorway *(autostrada)* were built in Italy by 1939. The German *Autobahnen* reached 2,100 km/1,310 mi by 1942. Soon after World War II motorways were built in the USA, France, and Britain, and subsequently in other countries. The most ambitious building programme was in the USA, which by 1974 had 70,800 km/44,000 mi of motorway. In 1984 there were 2,792 km/1,735 mi of motorway in the UK.

Motown the first black-owned US record company, founded in Detroit (*motor town*) 1959 by Berry Gordy Jr (1929–). Its distinctive, upbeat sound (exemplified by the Four Tops and the ◊Supremes) was a major element in 1960s pop music.

The Motown sound was created by in-house producers and songwriters such as Smokey Robinson (1940–) and the team of Holland-Dozier-Holland; performers included Stevie Wonder, Marvin Gaye, and the Temptations. Its influence faded after the company's move to Los Angeles 1971, but it still provided a breeding ground for singers such as Lionel Richie (1950–) and Michael Jackson. Gordy sold Motown to the larger MCA company in 1988.

Mott /mɒt/ Nevill Francis 1905– . British physicist noted for his research on the electronic properties of metals, semiconductors, and noncrystalline materials. He shared the Nobel Prize for Physics 1977.

mouflon type of sheep *Ovis ammon* found wild in Cyprus, Corsica, and Sardinia. It has woolly underfur in winter, but this is covered by heavy guard hairs. The coat is brown, with white belly and rump. Males have strong curving horns. The mouflon lives in rough mountain areas.

mould mainly saprophytic ◊fungi living on foodstuffs and other organic matter, a few being parasitic on plants, animals, or each other. Many are of medical or industrial importance, for example penicillin.

moulding a common method of shaping plastics, clays, and glass. In *injection moulding*, molten plastic, for example, is injected into a water-cooled mould and takes the shape of the mould

motor racing *(Top left) Nigel Mansell at the Mexican Grand Prix, 1988. (Top right) Ayrton Senna at the Belgian Grand Prix, 1988.*

when it solidifies. In *blow moulding*, air is blown into a blob of molten plastic inside a hollow mould. In *compression moulding*, synthetic resin powder is simultaneously heated and pressed into a mould. When metals are used, the process is called ◊casting.

Moulins /muːˈlæn/ capital of the *département* of Allier, Auvergne, central France; industries (cutlery, textiles, glass); population (1982) 25,500. Moulin was capital of the old province of Bourbonnais 1368–1527.

Moulmein /maʊlˈmeɪn/ port and capital of Mon state in SE Burma, on the Salween estuary; population (1983) 202,967.

moulting the periodic shedding of the hair or fur of mammals, feathers of birds, or skin of reptiles. In mammals and birds, moulting is usually seasonal and is triggered by changes of day length.

The term is also often applied to the shedding of the ◊exoskeleton of arthropods, but this is more correctly called ◊ecdysis.

Moundbuilder a member of various North American Indian peoples who built earth mounds, linear and conical in shape, for tombs, platforms for chiefs' houses, and temples, from about 300 BC.

They carried out group labour projects under the rule of an elite. A major site is Monk's Mound in Mississippi. They were in decline by the time of the Spanish invasion, but traces of their culture live on in the folklore of the Choctaw and Cherokee Indians.

mountain a natural upward projection of the Earth's surface, higher and steeper than a hill. The process of mountain building (orogenesis) consists of volcanism, folding, faulting, and thrusting, resulting from the collision and welding together of two tectonic plates. This process deforms the rock and compresses the sediment between the two plates into mountain chains.

mountain ash or **rowan** flowering tree *Sorbus aucuparia* of the family Rosaceae. It grows to 50 ft/15 m, and has pinnate leaves and large clusters of whitish flowers, followed by scarlet berries.

mountaineering the art and practice of mountain climbing. For major peaks of the Himalayas it was formerly thought necessary to have elaborate support from Sherpas, fixed ropes, and oxygen at high altitudes ('siege- style' climbing). In the 1980s the 'Alpine style' was introduced. This dispenses with these aids, and relies on human ability to adapt Sherpa-style to high altitude.

In 1854 *Wetterhorn*, Switzerland, was climbed by Alfred Wills, thereby founding the sport; 1865 *Matterhorn*, Switzerland–Italy, by ◊Whymper; 1897 *Aconcagua*, Argentina, by Zurbriggen; 1938 *Eiger*, Switzerland (north face), by Heinrich Harrer; 1953 *Everest*, Nepál/Tibet, by ◊Hillary/◊Tenzing; 1981 *Kongur*, China by ◊Bonington.

mountain lion another name for ◊puma.

Mountbatten /maʊntˈbætn/ Louis, 1st Earl Mountbatten of Burma 1900–1979. British admiral. In World War II he became chief

of combined operations 1942 and commander in chief in SE Asia 1943. As last viceroy of India 1947 he oversaw the transition to independence, becoming first governor general of India until 1948. He was chief of UK Defence Staff 1959–65. Mountbatten was killed by an Irish Republican Army bomb aboard his yacht at Mullaghmore, County Sligo.

Mounties popular name for the Royal Canadian Mounted Police, known for their uniform of red jacket and broad-brimmed hat. Their Security Service, established 1950, was disbanded 1981, and replaced by the independent Canadian Security Intelligence Service.

Mount Isa /ˈaɪzə/ mining town (copper, lead, silver, zinc) in NW Queensland, Australia; population (1984) 25,000.

Mount Lofty Range /ˈlɒfti/ mountain range in SE South Australia; Mount Bryan 934 m/3,064 ft is the highest peak.

Mount Rushmore /ˈrʌʃmɔː/ mountain in the Black Hills, South Dakota, USA; height 1,890 m/6,203 ft. On its granite face are carved giant portrait heads of presidents Washington, Jefferson, Lincoln, and Theodore Roosevelt. The sculptor was Gutzon ◊Borglum.

Mount St Helens /seɪnt ˈhelənz/ volcanic mountain in Washington state, USA. When it erupted in 1980 after being quiescent since 1857, it devastated an area of 600 sq km /230 sq mi and its height was reduced from 2,950 m/9,682 ft to 2,560 m/8,402 ft.

Mount Vernon /ˈvɜːnən/ village in Virginia, USA, on the Potomac river, where George Washington lived 1752–99 and was buried on the family estate, now a national monument.

Mourning Becomes Electra 1931 trilogy of plays by Eugene O'Neill, bringing the Orestes legend (see ◊Agamemnon) to the world of 19th-century New England; considered among the greatest of modern US plays.

mouse in computing, an input device, used to control a pointer on a computer screen. It is about the size of a pack of playing cards, is connected to the computer by a wire, and incorporates one or more buttons that can be pressed. Moving the mouse across a desktop causes a corresponding movement of the pointer. In this way, the operator can manipulate objects on the screen and make menu selections.

mouse in zoology, many small rodents, particularly those of the family Muridae. The house mouse *Mus musculus* is distributed worldwide. It is 75

Mountbatten *Admiral Lord Louis Mountbatten 1943.*

mountain

Animals and plants that live on mountains are adapted to cope with low temperatures, strong winds, a thin, poor soil, and air with little oxygen.

With increasing altitude, the climate becomes bleaker. Temperature, for example, falls by roughly 1°C/2°F for every 150m/500ft. On high mountains near the equator, this usually produces distinct zones of vegetation (shown right) similar to those found as one travels from the tropics to the North Pole.

climatic zone	vegetation zone
latitude	altitude
arctic ice pack	
	snow line
tundra	low alpine vegetation
	tree line
boreal forests	coniferous forest
temperate forests	deciduous forest
tropical forests	tropical forest
equator	

Plants of the alpine zone are small, compact and low-growing to survive the cold, strong winds. Most are perennial, continuing their growth over several years. Mountain animals tend to stay on the high slopes and peaks throughout the year. Many have a thick protective coat, and some of the hoofed mammals have soft pads on their feet that help them to cling to rocks.

Alpine wildlife 1. Brown bear 2. Alpine marmot 3. Chamois 4. Peregrine falcon 5. Golden eagle 6. Ibex.

7. Windflowers and gentians bloom in spring and last just a few weeks.

mm/3 in long, with a naked tail of equal length, and a grey-brown body.

Common in Britain is the wood mouse *Apodemus sylvaticus*, richer in colour, and normally shy of human habitation. The tiny harvest mouse *Micromys minutus*, 65–75 mm/2.5–3 in long, makes spherical nests of straw supported on grass stems. *Jumping mice*, family Zapodidae, with enlarged back legs, live across the N hemisphere except in Britain.

mousebird bird of the order Coliiformes, including the single family (Coliidae) of small crested birds peculiar to Africa. They have hairlike feathers, long tails, and mouselike agility. The largest is the **blue-naped mousebird** *Colius macrourus*, about 35 cm/14 in long.

Moustier, Le /'muːstieɪ/ cave in the Dordogne, SW France, with prehistoric remains, giving the name **Mousterian** to the flint-tool culture of Neanderthal peoples; the earliest ritual burials are linked with Mousterian settlements.

mouth the cavity forming the entrance to the digestive tract. In mammals, it is also the entrance to the respiratory tract, and is enclosed by the jaws, cheeks, and palate.

mouth organ another name for ◊harmonica, a musical instrument.

movement in music, a section of a large work, such as a symphony, which is often complete in itself.

Mow Cop /'maʊ 'kɒp/ the site in England of an open-air religious gathering on 31 May 1807 that is considered to be the start of ◊Primitive Methodism. Mow Cop is a hill at the S end of the Pennines on the Cheshire-Staffordshire border and dominates the surrounding countryside. It remained a popular location for revivalist meetings.

Moyse /mwaːz/ Marcel 1889–1984. French flautist. Trained at the Paris Conservatoire, he made many recordings and was an influential teacher.

Mozambique /ˌməʊzəmˈbiːk/ country in SE Africa, bordered to the N by Zambia, Malawi, and Tanzania, E by the Indian Ocean, S by South Africa, and E by Swaziland and Zimbabwe.

government The 1975 constitution, revised 1978, provides for a one-party socialist state, based on the National Front for the Liberation of Mozambique (Frelimo). The president heads its political bureau and central committee secretariat. There is a 250-member People's Assembly, comprising 130 members of Frelimo's central committee plus 120 others from central and provincial governments, the armed forces, and citizens' representatives. The assembly is convened by the president and meets twice a year. Its functions are performed in its absence by a 15-member inner group, called the Permanent Commission, also convened and presided over by the president. Frelimo was formed in 1962 by a merger of three nationalist parties, the Mozambique National Democratic Union (UDENAMO), the Mozambique African Nationalist Union (MANU) and the African Union of Independent Mozambique (UNAMI). Frelimo was reconstituted in 1977 as a 'Marxist-Leninist vanguard party'.

history Mozambique's indigenous peoples are of Bantu origin. By the 10th century the Arabs had established themselves on the coast. The first European to reach Mozambique was Vasco da ◊Gama in 1498, and the country became a Portuguese colony in 1505. Portugal exploited Mozambique's resources of gold and ivory, and used it as a source of slave labour, both locally and overseas.

Guerrilla groups opposed Portuguese rule from the early 1960s, the various left-wing factions combining to form Frelimo. Its leader, Samora Machel, demanded complete independence, and in 1974 internal self-government was achieved, with Joaquim Chissano, a member of Frelimo's Central Committee, as prime minister.

Becoming president of an independent Mozambique in 1975, Machel was faced with the emigration of hundreds of thousands of Portuguese settlers, leaving no trained replacements in key economic positions. Two activities had been the mainstay of Mozambique's economy: transit traffic from South Africa and Rhodesia and the export of labour to South African mines. Although Machel supported the African National Congress (ANC) in South Africa, and the Patriotic Front in Rhodesia, he knew he must coexist and trade with his two white-governed neighbours. He put heavy pressure on the Patriotic Front for a settlement of the guerrilla war and this eventually bore fruit in the 1979 Lancaster House Agreement and the election victory of Robert Mugabe, a reliable friend of Mozambique, as leader of the newly independent Zimbabwe.

From 1980 Mozambique was faced with widespread drought, which affected most of southern Africa, and attacks by mercenaries, under the banner of the Mozambique National Resistance (Renamo), also known as the MNR, who were covertly but strongly backed by South Africa. The attacks concentrated on Mozambique's transport system.

Machel, showing considerable diplomatic skill, had by 1983 repaired relations with the USA, undertaken a successful European tour, and established himself as a respected African leader. In 1984 he signed the ◊Nkomati accord, under which South Africa agreed to deny facilities to the MNR, and Mozambique in return agreed not to provide bases for the banned ANC. Machel took steps to honour his side of the bargain but was doubtful about South Africa's good faith. In Oct 1986 he

mouse

Mozambique
People's Republic of (*República Popular de Moçambique*)

area 799,380 sq km/308,561 sq mi
capital and chief port Maputo
towns ports Beira, Nacala
physical mostly flat; mountains in W
features rivers Zambezi, Limpopo
head of state and government Joaquim Chissano from 1986

government one-party socialist republic
political parties National Front for the Liberation of Mozambique (Frelimo), Marxist-Leninist
exports sugar, cashews, tea, cotton, copra, sisal
currency metical (replaced escudo 1980) (1450.62 = £1 Sept 1987)
population (1989) 15,259,000 (mainly indigenous Bantu peoples; Portuguese 50,000); annual growth rate 2.8%
life expectancy men 44, women 46
language Portuguese (official)
religion animist 69%, Roman Catholic 21%, Muslim 10%
literacy 55% male/22% female (1985 est)
GDP $2.7 bn (1983); $220 per head of population
chronology
1962 Frelimo (liberation front) established.
1975 Full independence achieved as a socialist republic, with Samora Machel as president and Frelimo as the sole legal party.
1983 Re-establishment of good relations with Western powers.
1984 Nkomati Accord signed with South Africa.
1986 Machel killed in air crash, and succeeded by Joaquim Chissano.
1988 Tanzania announced complete withdrawal of its troops.
1989 Frelimo offered to abandon Marxist-Leninism; Chissano re-elected.

died in an air crash near the South African border. Despite the suspicious circumstances, an inquiry pronounced his death an accident.

The following month Frelimo's Central Committee elected former prime minister Joaquim Chissano as his successor. Chissano immediately pledged to carry on the policies of his predecessor. He strengthened the ties forged by Machel with Zimbabwe and Britain and in 1987 took the unprecedented step of requesting permission to attend the Commonwealth Heads of Government summit that year. Mozambique's economic problems were aggravated in 1987 by food shortages, after another year of drought. In 1988 President Chissano met South African state president Botha and later that year, as tension was reduced, Tanzanian troops were withdrawn from the country. In July 1989, at its annual conference, Frelimo offered to abandon Marxism-Leninism to achieve a national consensus and Chissano was re-elected president and party leader.

Mozart /'məʊtsɑːt/ Wolfgang Amadeus 1756–1791. Austrian composer and performer who showed astonishing precocity as a child and was an adult virtuoso. He was trained by his father, Leopold Mozart (1719–87). From an early age he composed prolifically, his works including 27 piano concertos, 23 string quartets, 35 violin sonatas, and more than 50 symphonies, including the E flat K543, G minor K550, and C major K551 ('Jupiter') symphonies, all composed in 1788. His operas include *Idomeneo* 1781, *Le Nozze di Figaro/The Marriage of Figaro* 1786, *Don Giovanni* 1787, *Così fan tutte/Thus Do All Women* 1790, and *Die Zauberflöte/The Magic Flute* 1791. Strongly influenced by ◊Haydn, Mozart's music marks the height of the Classical age in its purity of melody and form.

Mozart's career began when, with his sister, Maria Anna, he was taken on a number of tours 1762–79, visiting Vienna, the Rhineland, Holland, Paris, London, and Italy. Mozart not only gave public recitals, but had already begun to compose. In 1772 he was appointed master of the archbishop of Salzburg's court band. He found the post uncongenial, since he was treated as a servant, and in 1781 he was suddenly dismissed. From then on he lived mostly in Vienna, and married Constanze Weber in 1782. He supported himself as a pianist, composer, and teacher, but his lack of business acumen often

resulted in financial difficulties. His *Requiem*, unfinished at his death, was completed by a pupil. Mozart had been in failing health, and died impoverished. His works were catalogued chronologically by the musicologist Ludwig von Köchel (1800–77) 1862.

mp in chemistry, the abbreviation for *melting point*.

MP abbreviation for *Member of Parliament*.

mpg abbreviation for *miles per gallon*.

mph abbreviation for *miles per hour*.

MPLA (Portuguese *Movimento Popular de Libertacade Angola*, Popular Movement for the Liberation of Angola) socialist organization founded in the early 1950s that sought to free Angola from Portuguese rule 1961–75 before being involved in the civil war against its former allies ◊UNITA and ◊FNLA 1975–76. The MPLA took control of the country but UNITA guerrilla activity continues, supported by South Africa.

Mr title used before a name to show that the person is male; it is the abbreviation for *mister*. Mr was originally the abbreviation for 'master', and 'mister' is a corrupted pronunciation of the abbreviation.

MRBM abbreviation for *medium-range ballistic missile*.

Mrs title used before a name to show that the person is married and female; partly superseded by Ms, which does not indicate marital status. Pronounced 'missus', Mrs was originally an abbreviation for *mistress*.

Ms title used before a woman's name; pronounced 'miz'. Unlike Miss or Mrs, it can be used by married or unmarried women, and was introduced by the women's movement in the 1970s to avoid making this distinction.

MS abbreviation for ◊*Mississippi*.

MSc in education, abbreviation for *Master of Science*.

MSC abbreviation for *Manpower Services Commission*; see ◊Training Agency.

MS-DOS *Microsoft Disc Operating System* an ◊operating system, produced by the Microsoft Corporation, that is widely used on ◊microcomputers. A version called PC-DOS is sold by IBM specifically for their range of personal computers. MS-DOS and PC-DOS are usually referred to as Dos.

MS(S). abbreviation for *manuscript(s)*.

MT abbreviation for ◊*Montana*.

Mtwara /əm'twɑːrə/ deepwater seaport in S Tanzania, on Mtwara Bay; population (1978) 48,500. It was opened 1954.

MU abbreviation for *monetary unit*.

Mubarak /muː'baːræk/ Hosni 1928– . Egyptian politician, president from 1981. He commanded the air force 1972–75 (and was responsible for the initial victories in the Egyptian campaign of 1973 against Israel), when he became an active vice president to Sadat, and succeeded him on his assassination. He has continued to pursue Sadat's moderate policies, and has significantly increased the freedom of the press and of political association.

Muckrakers, the a movement of US writers and journalists about 1880–1914 who aimed to expose political, commercial, and corporate corruption, and record frankly the age of industrialism, urban poverty and degradation, unbridled business trusts, and conspicuous consumption. Novelists included Frank Norris, Theodore Dreiser, Jack London, and Upton Sinclair.

Main figures of the earlier period include Rebecca Harding Davis, Henry George (*Progress and Poverty* 1879), and Henry Demarest Lloyd (1847–1903). Later, with the growth of journals like *McClure's Magazine*, it included Lincoln Steffens (1866–1936) (*The Shame of the Cities* 1904), Ida M Tarbell, and Thorstein Veblen (*Theory of the Leisure Classes* 1904). Also associated with the Progressive movement in politics, it gave to both US literature and journalism a critical role it was to maintain.

mucous membrane thin skin found on all internal body surfaces of animals (for example, eyelids, breathing and digestive passages, genital tract). It secretes mucus, a moistening, lubricating, and protective fluid.

mucus a lubricating and protective fluid, secreted by ◊mucous membranes in many different parts of the body. In the gut, mucus smooths the passage of food and keeps potentially damaging digestive enzymes away from the gut lining. In the lungs, it traps airborne particles so that they can be expelled.

mudfish another name for ◊bowfin.

mudnesters Australian group of birds that make their nests from mud, including the apostle bird *Struthidea cinerea*, so called from its appearance in little flocks of about 12, the white-winged chough *Corcorax melanorhamphos*, and the magpie lark *Grallina cyanoleuca*.

mudpuppy brownish amphibian *Necturus maculosus*. It is about 20 cm/8 in long, and retains large external gills. It lives in streams in North America and eats fish, snails, and other invertebrates.

mudskipper type of fish, genus *Periophthalmus*, found in brackish water and shores in the tropics, except for the Americas. It can walk or climb over mudflats, using its strong pectoral fins as legs, and has eyes set close together on top of the head. It grows up to 30 cm/12 in long.

mudstone a fine-grained sedimentary rock made up of clay- to silt-sized particles (up to 0.0625 mm).

muezzin (Arabic) a person whose job it is to perform the call to prayer five times a day from the minaret of a Muslim mosque.

mufti a Muslim legal expert who guides the courts in their interpretation. In Turkey the **grand mufti** had supreme spiritual authority until the establishment of the republic in 1924.

Mugabe /muː'gɑːbi/ Robert (Gabriel) 1925– . Zimbabwean politician, prime minister from 1980 and president from 1987. He was in detention in Rhodesia for nationalist activities 1964–74, then carried on guerrilla warfare from Mozambique. As leader of ◊ZANU he was in alliance with Joshua ◊Nkomo of ZAPU from 1976, and the two parties merged 1987.

Muggeridge /'mʌgərɪdʒ/ Malcolm 1903– . British journalist. He worked for the *Guardian* and *Daily Telegraph*, and was editor of *Punch* 1953–57. *Chronicles of Wasted Time* 1972–73 is an autobiography.

mudskipper

mugwump in US political history, a colloquial name for the Republicans who voted in the 1884 presidential election for Grover Cleveland, the Democratic candidate, rather than for their Republican nominee, James G Blaine (1830–93); hence the modern meaning of one who refuses to follow the official party line.

Muhammad /məˈhæməd/ or **Mohammed, Mahomet** c.570–632. Founder of Islam, born in Mecca on the Arabian peninsula. In about 616 he claimed to be a prophet and that the *Koran* was revealed to him by God (it was later written down by his followers). He fled from persecution to the town now known as Medina in 622: the flight, *Hegira*, marks the beginning of the Islamic era.

Originally a shepherd and caravan conductor, he found leisure for meditation by his marriage with a wealthy widow in 595, and received his first revelation in 610. After some years of secret teaching, he openly declared himself the prophet of God, and, as the number of his followers increased, he was forced to flee to Medina. After the battle of Badr in 623, he was continuously victorious, entering Mecca as the recognized prophet of Arabia 630. The succession was troubled.

mujaheddin (Arabic *mujahid*, 'fighters', from *ji-had*, 'holy war') Islamic fundamentalist guerrillas of contemporary Afghanistan and Iran.

Mujibur Rahman /muːˈdʒiːbʊə/ Sheik 1921–1975. Bangladeshi nationalist politician, president 1975. He was arrested several times for campaigning for the autonomy of East Pakistan. He won the elections 1970 as leader of the Awami League, but was again arrested when negotiations with the Pakistan government broke down. After the civil war 1971, he became prime minister of the newly independent Bangladesh. He was presidential dictator Jan–Aug 1975, when he was assassinated.

Mukalla /mʊˈkælə/ seaport capital of the Hadhramaut coastal region of South Yemen; on the Gulf of Aden 480 km E of Aden; population(1984) 158,000.

Mukden /ˈmʊkdən/ former name of ◊Shenyang, city in China.

Mukden, Battle of /ˈmʊkdən/ the taking of Mukden (now Shenyang), NE China, the capital of the Manchu emperors, from Russian occupation by the Japanese, 20 Feb–10 Mar 1905, during the ◊Russo-Japanese War. Mukden was later the scene of a surprise attack 18 Sept 1931 by the Japanese on the Chinese garrison, which marked the beginning of their invasion of China.

mulberry tree, genus *Morus*, of the family Moraceae, consisting of a dozen species, including the *black mulberry Morus nigra*. It is native to W Asia, and has heart-shaped, toothed leaves, and spikes of whitish flowers. The fruit, made up of a cluster of small drupes, resembles a raspberry.

The leaves of the white mulberry *M. alba* are those used in feeding silkworms.

Mulberry Harbour a prefabricated floating harbour, used on D-day in World War II, to assist in the assault on the German-held French coast of Normandy.

Muldoon /mʌlˈduːn/ Robert David 1921– . New Zealand National Party politician, prime minister 1975–84.

A chartered accountant, he was minister of finance 1967–72, and in 1974 replaced John Marshall as leader of the National Party, after the latter had been criticized as insufficiently aggressive in opposition. He became prime minister in 1975 and pursued austere economic policies. He sought to introduce curbs on trade unions, and was a vigorous supporter of the Western alliance. He was defeated in the general election of 1984 and was succeeded as prime minister by the Labour Party's David Lange.

mule hybrid animal, usually the offspring of a male ass and a mare.

Mülheim an der Ruhr /ˈmjuːlhaɪm/ industrial city in North Rhine-Westphalia, West Germany, on the river Ruhr; population (1988) 170,000.

Mulhouse /mjʊˈluːz/ (German *Mülhausen*) industrial city (textiles, engineering, electrical goods) in Haut-Rhin *département*, Alsace, E France; population (1982) 221,000.

Mull /mʌl/ second largest island of the Inner Hebrides, Strathclyde, Scotland; area 950 sq km/367 sq mi; population (1981) 2,600. It is mountainous, and is separated from the mainland by the Sound of Mull. There is only one town, Tobermory. The economy is based on fishing, forestry, tourism, and some livestock.

mullah (Arabic 'master') a teacher, scholar, or religious leader of Islam. It is also a title of respect given to various other dignitaries who perform duties connected with the sacred law.

mullein plant of the genus *Verbascum*, family Scrophulariaceae. The *great mullein Verbascum thapsus* has lance-shaped leaves, 30 cm/12 in or more in length, covered in woolly down; in the second year of growth, a large spike of yellow flowers is produced. It is found in Europe and Asia, and is naturalized in North America.

Muller /ˈmʌlə/ Hermann 1890–1967. US geneticist who discovered the effect of radiation on genes by his work on fruit flies. Nobel prize 1946.

Müller /ˈmjuːlə/ Johannes Peter 1801–1858. German comparative anatomist whose studies of nerves and sense organs opened a new chapter in physiology by demonstrating the physical nature of sensory perception. His name is associated with a number of discoveries, including the Müllerian ducts in the mammalian fetus and the lymph heart in frogs.

Müller /ˈmjuːlə/ Paul 1899–1965. Swiss chemist awarded a Nobel prize in 1948 for his discovery of the first synthetic contact insecticide, DDT, in 1939.

mullet two types of fish. The *red mullet Mullus surmuletus* is found in the Mediterranean and warm Atlantic as far N as the English Channel. It is about 40 cm/16 in long, red with yellow stripes, and has long barbels round the mouth. The *grey mullet Crenimugil labrosus* lives in ponds and estuaries. It is greyish above, with longitudinal dark stripes, and grows to 60 cm/24 in.

Milliken /ˈmʌlɪkən/ Robert Sanderson 1896–1986. US chemist and physicist, who received the 1966 Nobel Prize for Chemistry for his development of the molecular orbital theory.

Mullingar /ˌmʌlɪŋˈɡɑː/ county town of Westmeath, Republic of Ireland; population (1983) 7,000. It is a cattle market and trout-fishing centre.

Mulock /ˈmjuːlɒk/ unmarried name of British novelist Dinah ◊Craik.

Mulready /ˈmʌlrɛdi/ William 1786–1863. Irish painter of rural scenes, active in England. In 1840 he designed the first penny-postage envelope, known as the *Mulready envelope*.

Mulroney /mʌlˈrəʊni/ Brian 1939– . Canadian politician. A former businessman, he replaced Joe Clark as Progressive Conservative party leader 1983, and achieved a landslide in the 1984 election to become prime minister. He won the 1988 election on a platform of free trade with the USA, but with a reduced majority.

Multan /ˌmʊlˈtɑːn/ industrial city (textiles, precision instruments, chemicals, pottery, jewellery) in Punjab province, central Pakistan, 205 km/190 mi SW of Lahore; population (1981) 732,000. It trades in grain, fruit, cotton, and wool. It is on a site inhabited since the time of Alexander the Great.

multicultural education education aimed at preparing children to live in a multiracial society by giving them an understanding of the culture and history of different ethnic groups.

The initiative for multicultural teaching in the UK rose out of the Swann Report 1985 against racism and racial disadvantage in schools.

Multi-Fibre Arrangement (MFA) a worldwide system of managed trade in textiles and clothing which came into force in 1974. It has been revised four times to take into account changing trends in production, consumption, and world trading conditions. MFA IV (1986–91) included silk, linen, ramie, and jute in an attempt to control trade in all products.

multilateralism trade among more than two countries without discrimination over origin or destination, and regardless of whether a large trade gap is involved.

Unlike ◊bilateralism, multilateralism does not require the trade flow between countries to be of the same value.

multinational corporation company or enterprise operating in several countries, usually defined as one that has 25% or more of its output capacity located outside its country of origin.

Such enterprises, many of them US-based, are seen in some quarters as posing a threat to individual national sovereignty and as exerting undue influence to secure favourable operating conditions.

multiple birth in humans, the production of more than two babies from one pregnancy. Multiple births can be caused by more than two eggs being produced and fertilized (often as the result of hormone therapy to assist pregnancy), or by a single fertilized egg dividing more than once before implantation.

multiple proportions, law of in chemistry, the principle that states that if two elements combine with each other to form more than one compound, then the ratio of the masses of one of them that combine with a particular mass of the other is a small whole number.

multiple sclerosis (MS) an incurable disease of the central nervous system, occurring in young or middle adulthood. It is characterized by degeneration of the myelin sheath which surrounds nerves in the brain and spinal cord. It is also known as disseminated sclerosis. Its cause is unknown.

Depending on where the demyelination occurs— which nerves are affected—the symptoms of MS can mimic almost any neurological disorder. Typically seen are unsteadiness, ◊ataxia, weakness, speech difficulties, and rapid involuntary movements of the eyes. The course of the disease is episodic, with frequent intervals of ◊remission.

multiplier in economics, the theoretical concept, formulated by J M Keynes, of the effect on national income or employment by an adjustment in overall demand. For example, investment by a company in a new plant will stimulate new income and expenditure, which will in turn generate new investment, and so on, so that the actual increase in national income may be several times greater than the original investment.

multistage rocket a rocket launch vehicle consisting of a number of rocket stages joined together, usually end to end. See ◊step rocket.

multitasking or *multiprogramming* in computing, a system in which one processor appears to run several different programs (or different parts of the same program) at the same time. All the programs are held in memory together, and each is allowed to run for a certain period, for example while other programs are waiting for a ◊peripheral device to work or for input from an operator. The ability to multitask depends on the ◊operating system rather than the type of computer.

Mulu /ˈmuːluː/ mountainous region in N Borneo near the border with Sabah. Its limestone cave system, one of the largest in the world, was explored by a Royal Geographical Society Expedition 1978.

Mumford /ˈmʌmfəd/ Lewis 1895–1990. US sociologist and writer on town planning. His books, including *Technics and Civilization* 1934 and *The Culture of Cities* 1938, discussed the rise of cities and proposed the creation of green belts around large conurbations.

mummers' play or *St George play* British folk drama enacted in dumb show by a masked cast, performed on Christmas Day to celebrate the death of the old year and its rebirth as the new year. The plot usually consists of a duel between St George and an infidel knight, in which one of them is killed but later revived by a doctor. Mummers' plays are still performed in some parts of Britain.

mummy human or animal body preserved after death, either naturally or artificially by drying or freezing (the science of ◊cryonics). Examples are mammoths preserved in glacial ice from 25,000 years ago; shrunken heads preserved by the ◊Jivaro people in South America; the mummies of ancient Egypt; and recent mummies, such as Lenin and Eva Perón.

mumps virus infection marked by fever and swelling of the parotid salivary glands (under the ear). It is usually minor in children, although meningitis is a possible complication. It may cause sterility in adult males.

Mumps is the most common form of ◊meningitis in children, but it follows a much milder course than bacterial meningitis, and a complete recovery is usual. Rarely, mumps meningitis may lead to deafness. An effective vaccine against mumps, measles, and rubella (MMR vaccine) is now offered to children aged 18 months.

Munch /muŋk/ Edvard 1863–1944. Norwegian painter. He studied in Paris and Berlin, and his best works date from 1892–1908, when he lived mainly in Germany. His paintings often focus on neurotic emotional states. The *Frieze of Life* 1890s, a sequence of highly charged, symbolic paintings, includes some of his favourite images, for example *Skriket/The Scream* 1893. He reused these in etchings, lithographs, and woodcuts.

Munch was influenced by van Gogh and Gauguin, but soon developed his own expressive style, reducing his compositions to broad areas of colour with sinuous contours emphasized by heavy brushstrokes, distorting faces and figures. His first show in Berlin 1892 made an enormous impact on young German artists. In 1908 he suffered a nervous breakdown and returned to Norway. Later works include a series of murals 1910–15 in the assembly halls of Oslo University.

München /ˈmunʃən/ German name of ◊Munich, city in West Germany.

Münchhausen /mun'tʃauzən/ Karl Friedrich, Freiherr (Baron) von 1720–1797. German soldier, born in Hanover. He served with the Russian army against the Turks, and after his retirement in 1760 told exaggerated stories of his campaigning adventures. This idiosyncrasy was utilized by the German writer Rudolph Erich Raspe (1737–94) in his extravagantly fictitious *Adventures of Baron Munchausen* 1785, which he wrote in English while living in London.

Münchhausen's syndrome an emotional disorder in which a patient feigns or invents symptoms in order to secure medical treatment. In some cases the patient will secretly ingest substances to produce real symptoms. It was named after the exaggerated tales of Baron Münchhausen.

Mungo, St another name for St ◊Kentigern, first bishop of Glasgow.

Munich /ˈmjuːnɪk/ (German *München*) industrial city (brewing, printing, precision instruments, machinery, electrical goods, textiles), capital of Bavaria, West Germany, on the river Isar; population (1986) 1,269,400.

features Munich owes many of its buildings and art treasures to the kings ◊Ludwig I and Maximilian II of Bavaria. The cathedral is late 15th century. The Alte Pinakothek contains paintings by old masters, the Neue Pinakothek, modern paintings; there is the Bavarian National Museum, the Bavarian State Library, and the Deutsches Museum (science and technology). The university, founded at Ingolstadt 1472, was transferred to Munich 1826; to the NE at Garching there is a nuclear research centre.

history Dating from the 12th century, Munich became the residence of the dukes of Wittelsbach in the 13th century, and the capital of independent Bavaria. It was the scene of the Nov revolution of 1918, the 'Soviet' republic of 1919, and the Hitler putsch of 1923. It became the centre of the Nazi movement, and the ◊Munich Agreement of 1938 was signed there. When the 1972 Summer Olympics were held in Munich, a number of Israeli athletes were killed by guerrillas.

Munich Agreement pact signed on 29 Sept 1938 by the leaders of the UK (N ◊Chamberlain), France (◊Daladier), Germany (Hitler), and Italy (Mussolini), under which Czechoslovakia was compelled to surrender its Sudeten-German districts (the **Sudetenland**) to Germany. Chamberlain claimed it would guarantee 'peace in our time', but it did not prevent Hitler from seizing the rest of Czechoslovakia in Mar 1939.

Most districts were not given the option of a plebiscite under the agreement. After World War II the Sudetenland was returned to Czechoslovakia, and over 2 million German-speaking people were expelled from the country.

Municipal Corporation Act UK act of Parliament 1835 that laid the foundations of modern local government. The act specified corporate towns where borough councils were elected by, and from among, rate-paying householders to undertake local government functions. Each council was to elect a watch committee that was responsible for appointing sufficient police constables to keep the peace.

Munnings /ˈmʌnɪŋz/ Alfred 1878–1959. British painter excelling in racing and hunting scenes. As president of the Royal Academy 1944–49 he was outspoken in his dislike of 'modern art'.

Munro /mən'rəu/ H(ugh) H(ector) British author who wrote under the pen name ◊Saki.

Munster /ˈmʌnstə/ southern province of Republic of Ireland, comprising the counties of Clare, Cork, Kerry, Limerick, North and South Tipperary, and Waterford; area 24,140 sq km/9,318 sq mi; population (1986) 1,019,000.

It was a kingdom until the 12th century, and was settled in plantations by the English from 1586.

Münster /ˈmunstə/ industrial city (wire, cement, iron, brewing and distilling) in North Rhine-Westphalia, NW West Germany, formerly the capital of Westphalia; population (1988) 268,000. The Treaty of Westphalia was signed simultaneously here and at Osnabrück 1648, ending the Thirty Years' War.

Its university was founded 1773. Badly damaged in World War II, its ancient buildings, including the 15th-century cathedral and town hall, have been restored or rebuilt.

Munternia /mʌn'tɜːniə/ Romanian name of ◊Wallachia, former province of Romania.

muntjac small deer, genus *Muntiacus*, found in SE Asia. The buck has short spiked antlers and two sharp canine teeth forming tusks. They are sometimes called 'barking deer' because of their voices.

Muntjac live mostly in dense vegetation and do not form herds. Some have escaped from parks in central England and become established in the wild.

mural painting (Latin *murus*, wall) the decoration of walls, vaults, and ceilings by means of ◊fresco, oil, ◊tempera, or ◊encaustic methods. Mural painters include Cimabue, Giotto, Masaccio, Ghirlandaio, and, in the 20th century, Diego Rivera.

Murasaki Shikibu /ˌmuərə'saːki ˈʃikibu/ *c.*978–*c.* 1015. Japanese writer, a lady at the court. Her masterpiece of fiction, *The Tale of Genji*, is one of the classic works of Japanese literature, and may be the world's first novel.

She was a member of the Fujiwara clan, but her own name is not known; scholars have given her the name Murasaki after a character in the book. It deals with upper-class life in Heian Japan, centring on the affairs of Prince Genji.

Murat /mjuə'raː/ Joachim 1767–1815. King of Naples from 1808. An officer in the French army, he was made king by Napoleon, but deserted him in 1813 in the vain hope that the Allies would recognize him. In 1815 he attempted unsuccessfully to make himself king of all Italy, but when he landed in Calabria in an attempt to gain the throne he was captured and shot.

Murcia /ˈmuəθiə/ industrial city (silk, metal, glass, textiles, pharmaceuticals), capital of the Spanish province of Murcia, on the river Segura; population (1986) 310,000. Murcia was founded 825 on the site of a Roman colony by 'Abd-ar-Rahman II, caliph of Cordoba. It has a university and 14th-century cathedral.

Murcia /ˈmuəθiə/ autonomous region of SE Spain; area 11,300 sq km/4,362 sq mi; population (1986) 1,014,000. It includes the cities Murcia and Cartagena, and produces esparto grass, lead, zinc, iron, and fruit.

murder unlawful killing of one person by another. In British law murder is committed only when the killer acts with malice aforethought, that is, intending either to kill or to cause serious injury, or realizing that this would probably result. In 1985 in Venezuela, 3.7% of male deaths were murders; in the USA, 1.6%; in the UK, 0.006%.

Munch The Sick Child *(1907)* Tate Gallery, London.

Münster The university of Münster, founded 1773 as the university of the province of Westphalia.

murder: statistics

homicide offences by relations and sex of victim: England and Wales 1988

relationship	male (%)	female (0%)
partner	6	37
relative	20	23
associate	27	22
unrelated	37	13
unresolved	10	5
total	100	100

If the killer can show provocation by the victim (action or words which would make a reasonable person lose their self-control) or diminished responsibility (an abnormal state of mind caused by illness, injury, or mental subnormality), the charge is reduced to the less serious crime of ◊manslaughter. Murder is punishable by life imprisonment. See also ◊homicide.

'Murders in the Rue Morgue, The' 1841 tale by the US writer Edgar Allan Poe, acknowledged as the first detective story. Poe's detective Auguste Dupin points to the clues leading to the solution of the macabre mystery in what Poe called a 'tale of ratiocination'.

Murdoch /'mɜːdɒk/ Iris 1919– . British novelist, born in Dublin. Her novels combine philosophical speculation with often outrageous situations and tangled human relationships. They include *The Sandcastle* 1957, *The Sea, The Sea* 1978, and *The Book and the Brotherhood* 1987.

A lecturer in philosophy, she became in 1948 a fellow of St Anne's College, Oxford University, and published *Sartre, Romantic Rationalist* 1953. Her novel *A Severed Head* 1961 was dramatized; others include *The Philosopher's Pupil* 1983.

Murdoch /'mɜːdɒk/ Rupert 1931– . Australian entrepreneur and newspaper owner, with interests in Australia, the UK, and the USA. Among his UK newspapers are the *Sun*, the *News of the World*, and *The Times*; in the USA, he has a 50% stake in 20th Century Fox, and he also owns publishing companies. He is chief executive of Sky Television, the UK's first satellite television service.

Murdock /'mɜːdɒk/ William 1754–1839. Scottish inventor who first used coal gas for domestic lighting. He illuminated his house and offices using coal gas in 1792, and in 1797 and 1798 he held public demonstrations of his invention.

Murger /mjʊəˈʒeə/ Henri 1822–1861. French writer, born in Paris. He studied painting, and in 1848 published *Scènes de la vie de bohème/Scenes of Bohemian Life*, which formed the basis of Puccini's opera *La Bohème*.

Murillo /mjʊəˈrɪləʊ/ Bartolomé Esteban 1617–1682. Spanish painter, active mainly in Seville. He painted sweetly sentimental pictures of the Immaculate Conception; he also specialized in studies of street urchins.

Murillo was born in Seville. Visiting Madrid in the 1640s, he was befriended by the court painter Velázquez. After his return to Seville he received many important commissions, chiefly religious. He founded the academy of painting in Seville 1660 with the help of Herrera the Younger.

Murmansk /mʊəˈmænsk/ seaport in NW USSR, on the Barents Sea; population (1987) 432,000. It is the largest city in the Arctic, the USSR's most important fishing port, and base of the icebreakers that keep the Northeast Passage open.

It is the centre of Soviet Lapland and the only port on the Soviet Arctic coast that is in use all year round. After the entry of the USSR into World War II in 1941, supplies from the UK and later from the USA were unloaded there.

Murnau /'mʊənaʊ/ F W. Assumed name of Friedrich Wilhelm Plumpe 1889–1931. German silent-film director, whose 'subjective' use of a moving camera to tell the story, through expressive images and without subtitles, in *Der letzte Mumm/The Last Laugh* 1924 made him famous.

Murdoch *Iris Murdoch has won numerous awards including the Booker prize 1978 for* The Sea, The Sea *and was again shortlisted for the award 1987 for* The Book and the Brotherhood.

Other films include *Nosferatu* 1922, a version of the Dracula story.

Murphy Audie 1924–1971. US actor and war hero, who starred mainly in low-budget Western films. His work includes *The Red Badge of Courage* 1951, *The Quiet American* 1958, and *The Unforgiven* 1960.

Murphy Dervla 1931– . Irish writer whose extensive travels have been recorded in books such as *Full Tilt* 1965.

Murray /'mʌri/ principal river of Australia, 2,575 km/1,600 mi long. It rises in the Australian Alps near Mount Kosciusko and flows west, forming the boundary between New South Wales and Victoria, and reaches the sea at Encounter Bay, South Australia. With its main tributary, the Darling, it is 3,750 km/2,330 mi long.

Its other tributaries include the Lachlan and the Murrumbidgee. The Dartmouth Dam 1979 in the Great Dividing Range supplies hydroelectric power and has drought-proofed the Murray river system, but irrigation (for grapes, citrus and stone fruits) and navigation schemes have led to soil salinization.

Murray family name of dukes of Atholl; seated at Blair Castle, Perthshire, Scotland.

Murray /'mʌri/ Gilbert 1866–1957. British scholar. Born in Sydney, Australia, he was taken to England in 1877, and was professor of Greek at Glasgow University 1889–99 and at Oxford 1908–36. Author of *History of Ancient Greek Literature* 1897, he became best known for verse translations of the Greek dramatists, especially Euripides, making the plays more accessible to modern readers. Order of Merit 1941.

Murray /'mʌri/ James Augustus Henry 1837–1915. Scottish philologist. He was the first editor of the *Oxford English Dictionary* (originally the *New English Dictionary*) from 1878 until his death; the first volume was published 1884.

Murray was born near Hawick. He was president of the Philological Society 1878–80 and 1882–84. He himself edited more than half the dictionary, working in a shed (nicknamed the Scriptorium) in his back garden.

Murray /'mʌri/ James Stuart, Earl of Murray, or Moray 1531–1570. Regent of Scotland from 1567, an illegitimate son of James V. Murray was one of the leaders of the Scottish Reformation, and after the deposition of his half-sister ◊Mary Queen of Scots, he became regent. He was assassinated by one of her supporters.

murray cod Australian freshwater fish *Maccullochella macquariensis*, which grows to about

2 m/6 ft. It is is named after the river in which it is found.

Murrayfield Scottish rugby ground and home of the national team. It staged its first international in 1925 when Scotland beat England 14–11. The capacity is approximately 70,000.

The ground was built on the site of the old Edinburgh Polo Ground at Murray's Field. The West Stand was added in the 1930s and the East Stand in the 1980s. Over 100,000 fans are reputed to have been in the ground for the match against Wales in 1975.

Murrumbidgee /ˌmʌrəmˈbɪdʒi/ river of New South Wales, Australia; length 1,690 km/1,050 mi. It rises in the Australian Alps, flows N to the Burrinjuck reservoir, and then W to meet the river ◊Murray.

Murry /'mʌri/ John Middleton 1889–1957. British writer. He produced studies of Dostoievsky, Keats, Blake, and Shakespeare, poetry, and an autobiographical novel, *Still Life* 1916. In 1913 he married Katherine ◊Mansfield, whose biography he wrote. He was a friend of D H Lawrence.

Musashi Miyamato. Japanese exponent of the martial arts, whose manual *A Book of Five Rings* on samurai strategy achieved immense popularity in the USA from 1974 when it appeared in translation. It was said that Japanese businessmen used it as a guide to success.

Muscat /'mʌskæt/ (Arabic *Masqat*) capital of Oman, E Arabia, adjoining the port of Matrah, which has a deepwater harbour; combined population (1982) 80,000. It produces natural gas and chemicals. Port Qabus is named after the sultan.

Muscat and Oman /'mʌskæt, əʊˈmɑːn/ the former name of ◊Oman, country in the Middle East.

muscle contractile animal tissue which produces locomotion and maintains the movement of body substances. Muscle is made of long cells which can contract to between one-half and one-third of their relaxed length. *Striped* muscles are activated by ◊motor nerves under voluntary control; they are attached to bones, except for those that form the tongue. *Involuntary* or *smooth* muscles are controlled by motor nerves of the ◊autonomic nervous system, and located in the gut, blood vessels, iris, and ducts. *Cardiac* muscle only occurs in the heart, and is also controlled by the autonomic nervous system.

muscular dystrophy any of a group of inherited muscle disorders marked by weakening and wasting of muscle. Muscle fibres degenerate, to be replaced by fatty tissue, although the nerve supply remains unimpaired.

The commonest form, Duchenne muscular dystrophy, strikes little boys, usually before the age of four. The child develops a waddling gait and an inward curvature (lordosis) of the lumbar spine. There is no cure, but physical treatments can minimize disability.

Muses in Greek mythology, the nine daughters of Zeus and Mnemosyne (goddess of memory) and inspirers of creative arts:

Calliope epic poetry;
Clio history;
Erato love poetry;
Euterpe lyric poetry;
Melpomene tragedy;
Polyhymnia hymns;
Terpsichore dance;
Thalia comedy;
Urania astronomy.

Museveni /muːˈsevəni/ Yoweri Kaguta 1945– . Ugandan general and politician, president from 1986. He led the opposition to Idi Amin's regime 1971–78 and was minister of defence 1979–80 but, unhappy with Milton Obote's autocratic leadership, formed the National Resistance Army (NRA), which helped to remove him. Museveni leads a broad-based coalition government.

Museveni was educated in Uganda and at the University of Dar es Salaam, Tanzania. He entered the army, eventually rising to the rank of general. Until Amin's removal Museveni led

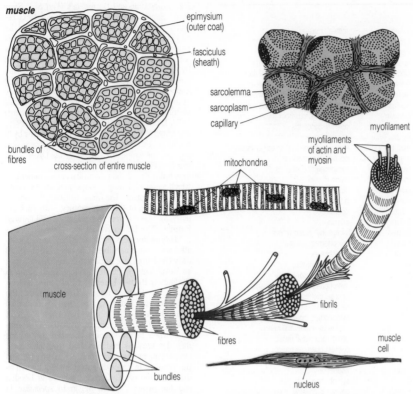

muscle

epimysium (outer coat)

fasciculus (sheath)

sarcolemma

sarcoplasm

capillary

myofilament

myofilaments of actin and myosin

mitochondria

bundles of fibres

cross-section of entire muscle

muscle

fibrils

fibres

muscle cell

bundles

nucleus

the anti-Amin Front for National Salvation. When Obote was ousted in a coup by Tito Okello 1985, Museveni entered into a brief power-sharing agreement with Okello, before taking over as president.

Musgrave /ˈmʌzgreɪv/ Thea 1928– . Scottish composer. Her works, in a conservative modern idiom, include concertos for horn, clarinet, and viola; string quartets; and operas, including *Mary, Queen of Scots* 1977.

Musgrave Ranges /ˈmʌzgreɪv/ Australian mountain ranges on the border between South Australia and the Northern Territory; the highest peak is Mount Woodruffe 1,525 m/5,000 ft. The area is an Aboriginal reserve.

mushroom fungus consisting of an upright stem and a spore-producing cap with radiating gills on the undersurface. There are many edible species belonging to the genus *Agaricus*, including the field mushroom *A. campestris*. See also ◊toadstool.

music the art of combining sounds into a unified whole, typically in accordance with fixed patterns and for an aesthetic purpose. Music is generally categorized as classical, ◊jazz, ◊pop music, ◊country and western, and so on.

The Greek word *mousikē* covered all the arts presided over by the Muses. The various civilizations of the ancient and modern world developed their own musical systems. Eastern music recognizes many more subdivisions of an interval than does Western music and also differs from Western music in that the absence, until recently, of written notation ruled out the composition of major developed works; it fostered melodic and rhythmic patterns, freely interpreted (as in the Indian *raga*) by virtuosos.

Western classical music

Middle Ages The documented history of Western music since Classical times begins with the liturgical music of the medieval Catholic church, derived from Greek and Hebrew antecedents. The four scales, or modes, to which the words of the liturgy were chanted were traditionally first set in order by St Ambrose in AD 384. St Gregory the Great added four more to the original Ambrosian modes, and this system forms the basis of Gregorian ◊plainsong still used in the Roman

Catholic Church. The organ was introduced in the 8th century, and in the 9th century harmonized music began to be used in churches with notation developing towards its present form. In the 11th century counterpoint was introduced, notably at the monastery of St Martial, Limoges, France, and in the late 12th century at Nôtre Dame in Paris (by Léonin and Perotin). In the late Middle Ages the Provençal and French ◊troubadours and court composers, such as Machaut, developed a secular music, derived from church and folk music (see also ◊Minnesingers).

The *15th and 16th centuries* in Europe saw the growth of contrapuntal or polyphonic music. One of the earliest composers was the Englishman John Dunstable, whose works inspired the French composer Guillaume Dufay, founder of the Flemish school; its members included Dufay's pupil Joannes Okeghem and the Renaissance composer Josquin Desprez. Other composers of this era were Palestrina from Italy, Roland de Lassus

from Flanders, Victoria from Spain, and Tallis and Byrd from England. ◊Madrigals were written during the Elizabethan age in England by such composers as Thomas Morley and Orlando Gibbons.

The *17th-century* Florentine Academy, a group of artists and writers, aimed to revive the principles of Greek tragedy. This led to the invention of dramatic recitative and the beginning of opera. Monteverdi was an early operatic composer; by the end of the century the form had evolved further in the hands of Alessandro Scarlatti in Italy and Jean-Baptiste Lully in France. In England the outstanding composer of the period was Purcell.

The early *18th century* was dominated by J S Bach and Handel. Bach was a master of harmony and counterpoint. Handel is renowned for his dramatic oratorios. Bach's sons, C P E Bach and J C Bach, reacted against contrapuntal forms and developed sonata form, the basis of the Classical sonata, quartet, and symphony. In these types of compositions mastery of style was achieved by the Viennese composers Haydn and Mozart. With Beethoven, music assumed new dynamic and expressive functions.

19th century Romantic music, represented in its early stages by Weber, Schubert, Schumann, Mendelssohn, and Chopin, tended to be subjectively emotional. Orchestral colour was increasingly exploited—particularly by Berlioz—and harmony became more chromatic. Nationalism became prominent at this time as evidenced by the intense Polish nationalism of Chopin; and the exploitation of Hungarian music by Liszt; the Russian Rimsky-Korsakov, Borodin, Mussorgsky, and, less typically, Tchaikovsky; and the works of the Czechs, Dvořák, Smetana; and the Norwegian Grieg. Revolutionary changes were brought by Wagner in the field of opera, although traditional Italian lyricism continued in the work of Rossini, Verdi, and Puccini. Wagner's contemporary, Brahms, stood for Classical discipline of form combined with Romantic feeling. The Belgian César Franck, with a newly chromatic idiom, also renewed the tradition of polyphonic writing.

20th century Around 1900 a reaction against romanticism became apparent in the impressionism of Debussy and Ravel, and exotic chromaticism of Stravinsky and Scriabin. In Austria and Germany, the tradition of Bruckner, Mahler, and Richard Strauss faced a disturbing new world of atonal expressionism in Schoenberg, Berg, and Webern. After World War I Neo-Classicism, represented by Stravinsky, Prokofiev, and Hindemith, attempted to restore 18th-century principles of objectivity and order while maintaining a distinctively 20th-century tone. In Paris ◊Les Six adopted a more relaxed style, while composers further from the

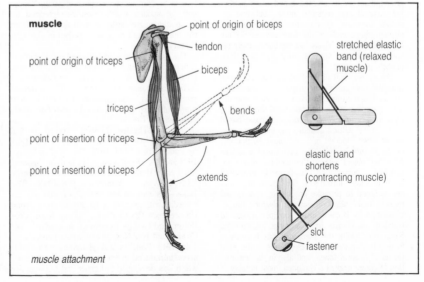

muscle

point of origin of biceps

tendon

point of origin of triceps

biceps

triceps

bends

point of insertion of triceps

point of insertion of biceps

extends

stretched elastic band (relaxed muscle)

elastic band shortens (contracting muscle)

slot

fastener

muscle attachment

music: great composers

Giovanni Palestrina	c.1525–1594	Italian	motets, masses
Claudio Monteverdi	1567–1643	Italian	operas, vocal music
Henry Purcell	1659–1695	English	vocal music, operas
Antonio Vivaldi	1678–1741	Italian	concertos, chamber music
George Frideric Handel	1685–1759	German	oratorios, operas, orchestral music
Johann Sebastian Bach	1685–1750	German	keyboard, choral music, concertos
Joseph Haydn	1732–1809	Austrian	symphonies, oratorios, chamber music
Wolfgang Amadeus Mozart	1756–1791	Austrian	symphonies, operas, chamber music
Ludwig van Beethoven	1770–1827	German	symphonies, chamber music, opera
Carl Maria von Weber	1786–1826	German	operas, concertos
Gioacchino Rossini	1792–1868	Italian	operas
Franz Schubert	1797–1828	Austrian	songs, symphonies, chamber music
Hector Berlioz	1803–1869	French	operas, symphonies
Felix Mendelssohn	1809–1847	German	symphonies, concertos
Frédéric Chopin	1810–1849	Polish	piano music
Robert Schumann	1810–1856	German	piano, vocal music, concertos
Franz Liszt	1811–1886	Hungarian	piano, orchestral music
Richard Wagner	1813–1883	German	operas
Giuseppe Verdi	1813–1901	Italian	operas
César Franck	1822–1890	Belgian	symphony, organ works
Bedrich Smetana	1824–1884	Czech	symphonies, operas
Anton Bruckner	1824–1896	Austrian	symphonies
Johann Strauss II	1825–1899	Austrian	waltzes, operettas
Johannes Brahms	1833–1897	German	symphonies, concertos
Camille Saint-Saëns	1835–1921	French	symphonies, concertos, operas
Modest Mussorgsky	1839–1881	Russian	operas, orchestral music
Peter Ilyich Tchaikovsky	1840–1893	Russian	ballet music, symphonies
Antonin Dvořák	1841–1904	Czech	symphonies, operas
Edvard Grieg	1843–1907	Norwegian	concertos, orchestral music
Nikolai Rimsky-Korsakov	1844–1908	Russian	opera, orchestral music
Leos Janáček	1854–1928	Czech	operas, chamber music
Edward Elgar	1857–1934	English	orchestral music
Giacomo Puccini	1858–1924	Italian	operas
Gustav Mahler	1860–1911	Czech	symphonies
Claude Debussy	1862–1918	French	operas, orchestral music
Richard Strauss	1864–1949	German	operas, orchestral music
Carl Nielsen	1865–1931	Danish	symphonies
Jean Sibelius	1865–1957	Finnish	symphonies, orchestral music
Sergei Rachmaninov	1873–1943	Russian	symphonies, concertos
Arnold Schoenberg	1874–1951	Austrian	operas, orchestral and chamber music
Maurice Ravel	1875–1937	French	piano, chamber music
Béla Bartók	1881–1945	Hungarian	operas, concertos
Igor Stravinsky	1882–1971	Russian	ballets, operas
Anton Webern	1883–1945	Austrian	chamber, vocal music
Alban Berg	1885–1935	Austrian	operas, chamber music
Sergei Prokofiev	1891–1953	Russian	symphonies, ballets
George Gershwin	1898–1937	American	musicals, operas
Dmitri Shostakovich	1906–1975	Russian	piano music
Olivier Messiaen	1908–	French	piano, organ, orchestral music
Benjamin Britten	1913–1976	English	vocal music, operas
Karlheinz Stockhausen	1928–	German	electronic, vocal music

cosmopolitan centres of Europe, such as Elgar, Delius, and Sibelius, continued loyal to the romantic symphonic tradition. The rise of radio and gramophone media created a new mass market for classical and romantic music, but one resistant to music by contemporary composers. Organizations such as the International Society for Contemporary Music became increasingly responsible for ensuring that music continued to be publicly performed.

The second half of the 20th century has seen dramatic changes in the nature of composition and in the instruments used to create sounds. The recording studio has facilitated the development of *musique concrète*/concrete music based on recorded natural sounds, and electronic music in which sounds are generated electrically, developments implying the creation of music as a finished object without the need for interpretation by live performers. Chance music, promoted by John Cage, introduced the notion of a music designed to provoke unforeseen results and thereby make new connections; aleatoric music, developed by Boulez, introduced performers to freedom of choice from a range of options. Since the 1960s the computer has become a focus of attention for developments in the synthesis of musical tones, and also in the automation of compositional techniques, most notably at

Stanford University and MIT in the USA, and at IRCAM in Paris.

musical 20th-century form of dramatic musical performance, combining elements of song, dance, and the spoken word, often characterized by lavish staging and large casts. It developed from the operettas and musical comedies of the 19th century.

The *operetta* is a light-hearted entertainment with extensive musical content: Jaques Offenbach, Johann Strauss, Franz Lehár, and Gilbert and Sullivan all composed operettas. The **musical comedy** is an anglicization of the French *opéra bouffe*, of which the first was *A Gaiety Girl* 1893, mounted by George Edwardes (1852–1915) at the Gaiety Theatre, London. Typical musical comedies of the 1920s were *Rose Marie* 1924 by Rudolf Friml 1879–1972; *The Student Prince* 1924 and *The Desert Song* 1926, both by Sigmund Romberg (1887–1951); and *No, No, Nanette* 1925 by Vincent Youmans (1898–1946). The 1930s–40s was an era of sophisticated musical comedies with many filmed examples and a strong US presence (Irving Berlin, Jerome Kern, Cole Porter, and George Gershwin). In England Noël Coward and Ivor Novello also wrote musicals.

In 1943 Rodgers and Hammerstein's *Oklahoma!* introduced an integration of plot and music, which was developed in Lerner and Loewe's *My*

Fair Lady 1956 and Bernstein's *West Side Story* 1957. Sandy Wilson's *The Boy Friend* 1953 revived the British musical and was followed by hits such as Lionel Bart's *Oliver!* 1960. Musicals began to branch into religious and political themes with *Oh What a Lovely War!* 1963, produced by Joan Littlewood and Charles Chiltern, and the Andrew Lloyd Webber musicals *Jesus Christ Superstar* 1970 and *Evita* 1978. Another category of musical, substituting a theme for conventional plotting, includes Stephen Sondheim's *Company* 1970, Hamlisch and Kleban's *A Chorus Line* 1975, and Lloyd Webber's *Cats* 1981, using verses by T S Eliot. In the 1980s 19th-century melodrama was popular, for example *Phantom of the Opera* 1986 and *Les Misérables* 1987.

music hall a British light theatrical entertainment, in which singers, dancers, comedians, and acrobats perform in 'turns'. The music hall's heyday was at the beginning of the 20th century, with such artistes as Marie Lloyd, Harry Lauder, and George Formby. The US equivalent is ◊vaudeville.

Many performers had a song they were associated with, such as Albert Chevalier (1861–1923) ('My Old Dutch'), or a character 'trademark', such as Vesta Tilley's immaculate masculine outfit as Burlington Bertie. Later stars of music hall included Sir George Robey, Gracie Fields, the Crazy Gang, Ted Ray, and the US comedian Danny Kaye.

history Music hall originated in the 17th century, when tavern-keepers acquired the organs that the Puritans had banished from churches. On certain nights organ music was played, and this resulted in a weekly entertainment known as the 'free and easy'. Certain theatres in London and the provinces then began to specialize in variety entertainment. With the advent of radio and television, music hall declined, but in the 1960s–70s there was a revival in working men's clubs and in pubs.

music theatre the staged performance of vocal music that deliberately sets out to get away from the grandiose style and scale of traditional opera.

Its origins can be traced to the 1920s and 1930s, to plays with music like Kurt Weill's *Mahagonny-Songspiel*, but it came into its own as a movement in the 1960s. It includes not just contemporary opera (such as Alexander Goehr's *Naboth's Vineyard* 1968) but also works like Peter Maxwell Davies' *Eight Songs for a Mad King* 1969.

Musil /'muːzɪl/ Robert 1880–1942. Austrian novelist, author of the unfinished *Der Mann ohne Eigenschaften/The Man without Qualities* (three volumes, 1930–43). Its hero shares the author's background of philosophical study and scientific and military training, and is preoccupied with the problems of the self viewed from a mystic but agnostic viewpoint.

musk perennial plant *Mimulus moschatus* of the family Scrophulariaceae; its small oblong leaves exude the musky scent from which it takes its name. Also any of several plants with a musky odour, including the **musk mallow** *Malva moschata* and the **musk rose** *Rosa moschata*.

musk deer small deer *Moschus moschiferus* native to mountains of central Asia. It is about 50 cm/20 in high, sure-footed, with large ears, no antlers or horns, and is solitary. It is hunted and farmed for the musk secreted by an abdominal gland, which is used as medicine or perfume.

musk ox hoofed mammal *Ovibos moschatus* native to the Arctic regions of North America. It displays characteristics of sheep and oxen, is about the size of a small domestic cow, and has long brown hair. At certain seasons it exhales a musky odour.

Its underwool (*qiviut*) is almost as fine as vicuna, and musk-ox farms have been established in Alaska, Québec, and Norway.

muskrat rodent *Ondatra zibethicus* about 30 cm/12 in long, living in watery regions of North America. It has webbed feet, a flattened tail, and shiny light-brown fur. It builds up a store of food, plastering it over with mud, for winter

musk ox

consumption. It is hunted for its fur (*musquash*).

Muslim or *Moslem* a follower of ◊Islam.

Muslim Brotherhood movement founded by members of the Sunni branch of Islam in Egypt in 1928. It aims at the establishment of a theocratic Islamic state and is headed by a 'supreme guide'. It is also active in Jordan, Sudan, and Syria.

mussel a number of bivalve molluscs, some of them edible, such as the *Mytilus edulis*, found in clusters attached to rocks around the N Atlantic and American coasts. It has a blue-black shell.

Freshwater pearl mussels, such as *Unio margaritiferus*, are found in some North American and European rivers. The green-lipped mussel, found only off New Zealand, produces an extract that is used in the treatment of arthritis.

Musset /mju:'seɪ/ Alfred de 1810–1857. French poet and playwright. He achieved success with the volume of poems *Contes d'Espagne et d'Italie/Stories of Spain and Italy* 1829. His *Confession d'un enfant du siècle/Confessions of a Child of the Century* 1835 recounts his broken relationship with George Sand.

Born in Paris, he abandoned the study of law and medicine to join the circle of Victor Hugo. Most typical of his work are the verse *Les Nuits/Nights* 1835–37 and the short plays *Comédies et proverbes/Comedies and Proverbs* 1840.

Mussolini /,mʊsə'li:ni/ Benito 1883–1945. Italian dictator 1925–43. As founder of the Fascist Movement (see ◊fascism) 1919 and prime minister from 1922, he became known as *Il Duce* 'the leader'. He invaded Ethiopia 1935–36, intervened in the Spanish Civil War 1936–39 in support of Franco, and conquered Albania 1939. In June 1940 Italy entered World War II supporting Hitler. Forced by military and domestic setbacks to resign 1943, Mussolini established a breakaway government in N Italy 1944–45, but was killed trying to flee the country.

Mussolini was born in the Romagna, the son of a blacksmith, and worked in early life as a teacher and journalist. He became active in the socialist movement, from which he was expelled 1914 for advocating Italian intervention in World War I. In 1919 he founded the Fascist Movement, whose programme combined violent nationalism with demagogic republican and anti-capitalist slogans, and launched a campaign of terrorism against the socialists. This movement was backed by many landowners and industrialists, and by the heads of the army and police, and in Oct 1922 Mussolini was in power as prime minister at the head of a coalition government. In 1925 he assumed dictatorial powers, and in 1926 all opposition parties were banned. During the years that followed, the entire political, legal, and education system was remodelled on Fascist lines.

Mussolini's *Blackshirt* followers were the forerunners of Hitler's Brownshirts, and his career of conquest drew him into close cooperation with Nazi Germany. They formed the ◊Axis alliance 1936. During World War II, Italian defeats in N Africa and Greece, the Allied invasion of Sicily, and discontent at home destroyed Mussolini's prestige, and in July 1943 he was compelled to resign by his own Fascist Grand Council. He was released from prison by German parachutists in

Sept, and set up a 'Republican Fascist' government in N Italy. In Apr 1945 he and his mistress, Clara Petacci, were captured at Lake Como by partisans while heading for the border, and shot. Their bodies were hung upside down and exposed to the execration of the mob in Milan.

Mussorgsky /mʊ'sɔ:gski/ Modest Petrovich 1839–1881. Russian composer, who was largely self-taught. His opera *Boris Godunov* was completed in 1869, although not produced in St Petersburg until 1874. Some of his works were 'revised' by ◊Rimsky-Korsakov, and only recently has their harsh and primitive beauty been recognized.

Born at Karevo, he resigned his commission in the army in 1858 to concentrate on music while working as a government clerk. A member of the group of nationalist composers, the Five, he was influenced by both folk music and literature. Among his other works are the incomplete operas *Khovanshchina* and *Sorochintsy Fair*, the orchestral *A Night on the Bare Mountain* 1867, the suite for piano *Pictures at an Exhibition* 1874, and many songs. Mussorgsky died in poverty, from alcoholism.

Mustafa Kemal /'mʊstəfə kə'ma:l/ Turkish leader, who assumed the name of ◊Atatürk.

mustard annual plant of the family Cruciferae. The seeds of black mustard *Brassica nigra* and white mustard *Sinapis alba* are used in the production of table mustard.

Black and white mustard are cultivated in Europe, North America, and England, where wild mustard or charlock *Sinapis arvensis* is also found. The seedlings of white mustard are used as a salad food. Mustard is frequently grown by farmers and ploughed in to enrich the soil.

Mustique /mʊ'sti:k/ an island in the Caribbean. See under ◊St Vincent and the Grenadines.

mutagen any substance that makes ◊mutation of genes more likely. A mutagen is likely to also act as a ◊carcinogen.

Mutare /mu:'ta:ri/ (former name to 1982 *Umtali*) industrial town (vehicle assembly, engineering, tobacco, textiles, paper) in E Zimbabwe, chief town of Manicaland province; population (1982) 69,621.

mutation in biology, a change in the genes produced by a change in the ◊DNA or ◊RNA that makes up the hereditary material of all living organisms. Mutations, the raw material of evolution, result from mistakes during replication (copying) of DNA molecules. Only a few improve the organism's performance and are therefore favoured by ◊natural selection. Mutation rates are increased by certain chemicals and by radiation.

Common mutations include the omission or insertion of a base (one of the chemical subunits of DNA), known as *point mutations*. Larger-scale mutations include removal of a whole segment of DNA or its inversion within the DNA strand. Not all mutations affect the organism, because there is a certain amount of redundancy in the genetic information. If a mutation is 'translated' from DNA into the protein that makes up the organism's structure, it may be in a nonfunctional part of the protein and thus have no detectable effect. This is known as a *neutral mutation*, and is important in ◊molecular-clock studies because

Mussolini *Benito Mussolini greeting Adolf Hitler at Florence railway station, Italy, October 1940.*

such mutations tend to accumulate gradually as time passes. Some mutations do affect functional parts of proteins, or genes that control protein production, and most of these are lethal to the organism.

mute in music, any device used to dampen the vibration of an instrument and so affect the tone. Brass instruments use plugs of metal or cardboard inserted in the bell, while orchestral strings apply a form of clamp to the bridge.

A cloth applied to the skin of a kettledrum, or inserted into the bell of a saxophone or clarinet, has a similar effect.

Muti /'mu:ti/ Riccardo 1941– . Italian conductor of the Philharmonia Orchestra, London, 1973–82, the Philadelphia Orchestra from 1981, and artistic director of La Scala, Milan, from 1986. He is known as a purist, devoted to carrying out a composer's intentions to the last detail.

mutiny a refusal by members of the armed forces to obey orders given by a (usually military) authority. It is the most serious breach of military discipline and may be punishable by death.

Effective mutinies in history include the ◊Indian Mutiny by Bengal troops against the British 1857 and the mutiny of some Russian soldiers in World War I who left the eastern front for home and helped to bring about the Russian Revolution of 1917. French and British soldiers in the trenches mutinied then, too. Several American units mutinied during the War of American Independence and the War of 1812.

In the UK the punishment, defined in the 1879 Army Discipline Act, can be death in serious cases; the last British soldier to be executed for mutiny was Private Jim Daly in India in 1920. The Incitement to Mutiny Act 1797 and Incitement to Disaffection Act 1934 were designed to prevent civilians from inciting members of the armed services to mutiny.

notable British mutinies
1789 Mutiny on the Bounty: Captain ◊Bligh cast adrift with 18 men.
1797 Spithead Mutiny (April–May): the Channel fleet mutinied for better wages and conditions; a wage increase was given and the king pardoned the mutineers.
1797 Nore Mutiny (May–June): mutineers (led by Richard Parker) demanded changes in the Articles of War and a say in the selection of officers. Parker, and 35 others, were executed.
1857 Indian Mutiny.
1914 Curragh Mutiny: British army officers refused to fight against Ulster volunteers.
1917 Etaples: mutiny by more than 1,000 British troops during World War I.
1919 North Russian campaign: mutiny by British forces refusing to fight against Bolsheviks.
1931 Invergordon: mutiny following wage cuts of 25% in the fleet; the cut was later reduced to 10%.
1944 Salerno: mutiny by 700 British reinforcements during World War II.

Mutiny Act in Britain, an act of Parliament, passed 1689 and re-enacted annually since then (since 1882 as part of the Army Acts), for the establishment and payment of a standing army. The act is intended to prevent an army from existing in peacetime without Parliament's consent.

Mutsuhito /,mu:tsu:'hi:təʊ/ 1852–1912 . Emperor of Japan from 1867, when he took the title *meiji tennō* ('enlightened sovereign'). During his reign Japan became a world military and naval power. He abolished the feudal system and discrimination against the lowest caste, established state schools, and introduced conscription, the Western calendar, and other measures in an attempt to modernize Japan, including a constitution 1889.

mutton bird any of a group of shearwaters and petrels that breed in burrows on Australasian islands. The young are very fat, and are killed for food and oil.

mutual fund another name for ◊unit trust, particularly in the USA.

Muzorewa *Zimbabwean politician and bishop of the Methodist Church, Abel Muzorewa, 1979.*

mutual induction in physics, the production of an electromotive force (emf) or voltage in an electric circuit caused by a changing ◊magnetic flux in a neighbouring circuit. The two circuits are often coils of wire, as in a transformer, and the size of the induced emf depends largely on the numbers of turns of wire in each of the coils.

mutualism or ◊symbiosis an association between two organisms of different species whereby both profit from the relationship.

Muybridge /ˈmaɪbrɪdʒ/ Eadweard. Adopted name of Edward James Muggeridge 1830–1904. British photographer. He made a series of animal locomotion photographs in the USA in the 1870s and proved that, when a horse trots, there are times when all its feet are off the ground. He also explored motion in birds and humans.

Muzorewa /ˌmuːzəˈreɪwə/ Abel (Tendekayi) 1925– . Zimbabwean politician and Methodist bishop. He was president of the African National Council 1971–85, and was prime minister of Rhodesia/Zimbabwe 1979. He was detained for a year in 1983–84. He is leader of the minority United Africa National Council (UANC).

Myanmar, Union of
Socialist Republic of the Union of *(Pyidaungsu Socialist Thammada Myanma Naingngandaw;* formerly **Burma)**

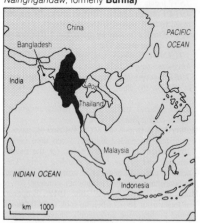

area 676,577 sq km/261,159 sq mi
capital and chief port Yangon (formerly Rangoon)
towns Mandalay, Karbe
physical over half is forested; rivers Irrawaddy and Chindwin; mountains in N, W, and E
head of state and government General Saw Maung from 1988

Muzorewa was educated at Methodist colleges in Rhodesia and Nashville, Tennessee.

MVD Soviet Ministry of Internal Affairs, name of the secret police 1946–53; now the ◊KGB.

Mwiiny /mwiːˈiːni/ Ali Hassan 1925– . Tanzanian socialist politician, president from 1985, when he succeeded Nyerere. He began a revival of private enterprise and control of state involvement and spending.

Myanmar /ˈbɜːmə/ formerly (until 1989) *Burma* country in SE Asia, bordered by India to the NW, China to the NE, Laos and Thailand to the SE, and the Bay of Bengal to the SW.

government Under the 1974 constitution, which was temporarily suspended in Sept 1988, Myanmar is a unitary republic. The highest organ of state power is the 489-member people's assembly (*Pyithu Hluttaw*), elected by universal suffrage every four years. The people's assembly elects the nation's executive, the 30-member state council, which has a representative from each of Myanmar's 14 states and divisions and is headed by a chair who acts as president. It also functions as the sole legislature and elects a council of ministers, headed by a prime minister, in charge of day-to-day administration. The controlling force and sole party in Myanmar is the National Unity Party (formerly the Socialist Programme Party).

history The Burmese date their era from AD 638, when they arrived from the region where China meets Tibet. By 850 they had organized a state in the centre of the plain at Pagan, and 1044–1287 maintained a hegemony over most of the area now known as Myanmar. In 1287 Kublai Khan's grandson Ye-su Timur occupied Burma after destroying the Pagan dynasty. After he withdrew, anarchy supervened. From about 1490–1750 the Toungoo dynasty maintained itself, with increasing difficulty; and in 1752 Alaungpaya reunited the country and founded Rangoon (now Yangon) as his capital. In a struggle with Britain 1824–26, his descendants lost the coastal strip from Chittagong to Cape Negrais. The second Burmese War 1852 resulted in the British annexation of Lower Burma, including Rangoon.

government military republic
political parties National Unity Party, military-socialist ruling party; National League for Democracy (NLD), pluralist opposition grouping
exports rice, rubber, jute, teak, jade, rubies, sapphires
currency kyat (10.77 = £1 Feb 1990)
population (1989) 39,893,000; annual growth rate 1.9%
life expectancy men 56, women 59
language Burmese
religion Hinayana Buddhist; religious centre Pagan
literacy 76% male/66% female (1980 est)
GDP $6.5 bn (1983); $174 per head of population
chronology
1886 United as province of British India.
1937 Became crown colony in the British Commonwealth.
1942–45 Occupied by Japan.
1948 Granted independence from Britain. Left the Commonwealth.
1962 Gen Ne Win assumed power in army coup.
1973–74 Adoption of presidential-style 'civilian' constitution.
1975 Formation of opposition National Democratic Front.
1988 Government resigned after violent demonstrations. Two changes of regime later, Gen Saw Maung seized power in a military coup in Sept with over 1,000 killed.
1989 Martial law declared; arrest of thousands of people, including advocates of democracy and human rights.

Thibaw, the last Burmese king, precipitated the third Burmese War 1885, and the British seized Upper Burma 1886. The country was united as a province of India until 1937, when it was made a crown colony with a degree of self-government.

Burma was occupied 1942–45 by Japan, under a government of anti-British nationalists. The nationalists, led by Aung San and U Nu, later founded the Anti-Fascist People's Freedom League (AFPFL). Burma was liberated 1945 and achieved full independence outside the Commonwealth 1948.

A parliamentary democracy was established under the socialist AFPFL led by Prime Minister U Nu. The republic was weakened by civil war between ◊Karens, communist guerrillas, and ethnic group separatists. Splits within the AFPFL forced the formation of an emergency caretaker government by Gen Ne Win (1911–) 1958–60, leading to a military coup 1962 and abolition of the parliamentary system. Ne Win became head of a revolutionary council and established a strong one-party state.

In 1974 a new presidential constitution was adopted and the revolutionary council was dissolved. The military leaders became civilian rulers. Ne Win became president and was re-elected 1978, before stepping down to be replaced by U San Yu (1918–) 1981.

The post-1962 government adopted a foreign policy of neutralist isolationism while at home it pursued its unique, self-reliant, Buddhist-influenced 'Burmese Way towards Socialism', founded upon state ownership in the commercial-industrial sector and strict agricultural price control. Internal opposition by armed separatist groups continued after 1962, causing the economy to deteriorate. The Burmese Communist Party, which received Chinese funding during the 1960s, established control over parts of the N; the Karen National Liberation Army in the SE; and the Kachin Independence Army in the NE. In 1975 the non-communist ethnic separatist groups joined together to form the broad National Democratic Front with the aim of creating a federal union. In 1974 and 1976 worsening economic conditions prompted a wave of food riots and in Sept 1987, with rice prices spiralling, student demonstrations broke out in Yangon. Worker's riots followed in the spring of 1988. Initially they were violently supressed, at the cost of several hundred lives. In the summer of 1988 San Yu and Ne Win, the leader of the ruling party, were forced to resign, as was the newly appointed president, Brig-Gen Sein Lwin, following the murder of 3,000 unarmed demonstrators. With the government control crumbling, as a widely supported pro-democracy movement swept the nation, the more reformist Maung Maung took over as president and free multi-party elections were promised 'within three months'. However, in Sept 1988 a military coup was staged by Gen Saw Maung, with the constitution being suspended, martial law imposed, and authority transferred to a 19-member State Law and Order Restoration Council. The new regime proceeded to pursue a more liberal economic course and to legalize the formation of political parties. Popular opposition leaders, including Suu Kyi (1945– , the daughter of the late Aung San) and U Nu, were harassed and debarred from standing in the elections that were promised in May 1990. Behind the scenes, Ne Win remained in control.

myasthenia gravis an uncommon condition in humans, characterized by loss of muscle power. The muscles tire rapidly and fail to respond to nervous stimulation requiring further effort. ◊Autoimmunity is the cause.

mycelium an interwoven mass of threadlike filaments or ◊hyphae, forming the main body of most fungi. The reproductive structures, or 'fruiting bodies', grow from this mycelium.

Mycenae ancient Greek city in the E Peloponnese, which gave its name to the Mycenaean (Bronze Age) civilization. Its peak was 1400–1200 BC,

Mycenae *The Lion Gate, the main entrance to the citadel.*

when the Cyclopean walls (using close-fitting stones) were erected. The city ceased to be inhabited after about 1120 BC.

Mycenaean civilization Bronze Age civilization that flourished in Crete, Cyprus, Greece, the Aegean Islands, and W Anatolia about 4000–1000 BC. During this period, magnificent architecture and sophisticated artefacts were produced.

Originating in Crete, it spread into Greece about 1600 BC, where it continued to thrive, with its centre at Mycenae, after the decline of Crete in about 1400. It was finally overthrown by the Dorian invasions, about 1100. The system of government was by kings, who also monopolized priestly functions. The Mycenaeans have been identified with the ◊Achaeans of Homer, and were among the besiegers at ◊Troy. They may also have been the marauding ◊sea peoples of Egyptian records. They used a form of Greek deciphered by Michael ◊Ventris. Their palaces were large and luxurious, and contained highly efficient sanitary arrangements. Commercial relations were maintained with Egypt. Pottery, frescoes, and metalwork reached a high artistic level. Evidence of the civilization was brought to light by the excavations of Heinrich ◊Schliemann at Troy, Mycenae, and Tiryns (a stronghold on the plain of Argolis) from 1870 onwards, and of Arthur ◊Evans in Crete from 1899.

mycorrhiza a mutually beneficial (mutualistic) association occurring between plant roots and a soil fungus. Mycorrhizal roots take up nutrients more efficiently, and the fungus benefits by obtaining carbohydrates from the tree.

An *ectotrophic mycorrhiza* occurs on many tree species, which usually grow much better as a result, especially in the seedling stage. Typically the roots become repeatedly branched and coral-like, penetrated by hyphae of a surrounding fungal ◊mycelium. In an *endotrophic mycorrhiza*, the growth of the fungus is mainly inside the root, as in orchids. Such plants do not usually grow properly, and may not even germinate, unless the appropriate fungus is present.

myelin sheath the insulating layer that surrounds nerve cells in vertebrate animals. It acts to speed up the passage of nerve impulses. The myelin is made up of fats and proteins and is formed from up to a hundred layers of membrane, laid down by special cells, the *Schwann cells*.

Myers /'maɪəz/ F(rederic) W(illiam) H(enry) 1843–1901. English psychic investigator and writer, coiner of the word 'telepathy'. He was a founder and one of the first presidents of the *Society for Psychical Research* (1900).

My Lai massacre the killing of 109 civilians in My Lai, a village in South Vietnam, by US troops in Mar 1968. An investigation in 1969 was followed by the conviction of Lt William Calley, commander of the platoon.

Sentenced to life imprisonment 1971, Calley was later released on parole. His superior officer was acquitted but the trial revealed a US Army policy of punitive tactics against civilians. News of the massacre contributed to domestic pressure for the USA to end its involvement in Vietnam.

mynah a number of starling species of birds, especially of SE Asia. The glossy black **hill mynah** *Gracula religiosa* of India is a realistic mimic of sounds and human speech.

myoglobin a globular protein, closely related to ◊haemoglobin, which is located in vertebrate muscle. Oxygen binds to myoglobin and is released only when the haemoglobin can no longer supply adequate oxygen to muscle cells.

myopia short-sightedness, caused either by an eyeball that is too long or a lens that is too strong. Nearby objects are sharply perceived, but distance vision is blurred.

myopia low-luminance poor night vision. About 20% of people have poor vision in twilight and nearly 50% in the dark. Low-luminance myopia does not show up in normal optical tests, but in 1989 a method was developed of measuring the degree of blurring by projecting images on a screen using a weak laser beam.

Myrdal /'mɜ:dɑ:l/ Gunnar 1898–1987. Swedish economist, author of many works on development economics. Nobel prize 1974.

myrmecophyte a plant that lives in association with a colony of ants, and possesses specialized organs in which the ants live. For example, *Myrmecodia*, an epiphytic plant from Malaysia, develops root tubers containing a network of cavities inhabited by ants.

Several species of *Acacia* from tropical America have specialized hollow thorns for the same purpose. This is probably a mutualistic (mutually beneficial) relationship, with the ants helping to protect the plant from other insect pests and in return receiving shelter.

Myron /'maɪrən/ *c.* 500–440 BC. Greek sculptor. His *Discobolus/Discus-Thrower* and *Athene and Marsyas*, much admired in his time, are known through Roman copies. They confirm his ancient reputation for brilliant composition and naturalism.

myrrh gum resin produced by a small tree, *Commiphora myrrha*, found in Abyssinia and Arabia. In ancient times it was used for incense and perfume, and in embalming.

myrtle evergreen shrub of the genus *Myrtus*, family Myrtaceae. The common Mediterranean myrtle *M. communis* has oval opposite leaves and white flowers followed by purple berries, all of which are fragrant.

Mysore /,maɪ'sɔ:/ or *Maisur* industrial city (engineering, silk) in ◊Karnataka, some 130 km/80 mi SW of Bangalore, India; population (1981) 476,000.

mystery play or *miracle play* a medieval religious drama based on stories from the Bible. Mystery plays were performed around the time of church festivals, reaching their height in Europe during the 15th and 16th centuries. A whole cycle running from the Creation to the Last Judgement was performed in separate scenes on mobile wagons by various town guilds.

Four English cycles survive: Coventry, Wakefield (or Townley), Chester, and York. Versions are still performed, such as the York cycle in York.

mystery religion any of various cults of the ancient world, open only to the initiated; for example the cults of Demeter (see ◊Eleusinian Mysteries), Dionysus, Cybele, Isis, and Mithras. Underlying some of them is a fertility ritual, in which a deity undergoes death and resurrection, and initiates feed on the flesh and blood to attain communion with the divine and ensure their own life beyond the grave. The influence of mystery religions on early Christianity was considerable.

mysticism religious belief based on personal spiritual experience, not necessarily involving an orthodox deity, though found in all the major religions; for example, kabbalism in Judaism, Sufism in Islam, and the bhakti movement in Hinduism.

3rd century Mysticism was first introduced to W Europe through Neo-Platonism, which was largely affected by Oriental schools of thought, and in its turn influenced the rise of Christian mysticism.

8th century Beginning of Sufism, an Islamic mystical movement.

11th–12th century Ramanuja, a Tamil Brahmin, taught that the way of devotion (*bhakti*) in Hinduism was superior to the way of knowledge.

13th century A kabbalistic movement in Judaism arose in S France and Spain.

14th–16th centuries Christian mystics of this era, when feudalism was breaking down in Germany, were Thomas à Kempis and Jacob Boehme. The Anabaptists were regarded as heretical. The Counter-Reformation produced Catholic mystics such as St Teresa and St John of the Cross.

17th century Quietism spread from Spain to France, while the Quakers (Friends) originated in the UK.

18th century Two great English mystics: William Law and William Blake. The scientific study of mysticism was begun by William James and others.

20th century A revival of mysticism in the UK and the USA was expressed in, for example, the works of the poet W B Yeats and the novelist Aldous Huxley, often drawing on Eastern religions and psychedelic experiences.

mythology the study and interpretation of the stories inherent in a given culture and how they relate to similar stories told in other cultures. These stories are of gods and other supernatural beings, with whom humans may have relationships, devised to explain the operation of the universe and human history.

Ancient mythologies, with the names of the chief god of each, include those of Egypt (Osiris), Greece (Zeus), Rome (Jupiter), India (Brahma), and the Teutonic peoples (Odin or Woden).

Mytilene /,mɪtɪ'li:ni/ (modern Greek *Mitilíni*) port, capital of the Greek island of Lesvos (to which the name Mytilene is sometimes applied) and a centre of sponge fishing; population (1981) 24,000.

myxoedema thyroid deficiency developing in adult life, most commonly in middle-aged women. The symptoms are loss of energy and appetite, inability to keep warm, mental dullness, and dry, puffy skin. It is completely reversed by giving the thyroid hormone known as thyroxine.

myxomatosis a contagious, usually fatal, virus infection of rabbits which causes much suffering. It is sometimes deliberately introduced to reduce the rabbit population.

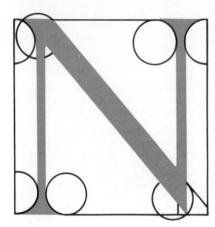

Nabokov *Born in Russia, Vladimir Nabokov was an exile for all his adult life. The theme of alienation runs throughout his work, and his best-known novel remains the controversial* Lolita *1955.*

N 14th letter of the Roman alphabet, representing when spoken an alveolar nasal sound. In several Romance languages it disappears in many cases, with nasalization of the preceding vowel.

n. abbreviation for ◊*noun*.

N abbreviation for *north*, ◊*newton*, and the symbol for *nitrogen*.

NAACP abbreviation for ◊*National Association for the Advancement of Colored People*, a US civil-rights organization.

NAAFI acronym for *Navy, Army, and Air Force Institutes* a non-profit-making association providing canteens for HM British Forces in the UK and abroad.

Nabis, les (Hebrew 'prophet') a group of French artists, active in the 1890s in Paris, united in their admiration of Gauguin — the mystic content of his work, the surface pattern and intense colour. In practice their work was decorative. ◊Bonnard and ◊Vuillard were members.

Nablus /'nɑ:bləs/ market town on the West Bank of the river Jordan, N of Jerusalem, the largest Palestinian town, after E Jerusalem, in Israeli occupation; population (1971) 64,000. Formerly Shechem, it was the ancient capital of Samaria, and a few ◊Samaritans remain. The British field marshal Allenby's defeat of the Turks here 1918 completed the conquest of Palestine.

Nabokov /nə'bəʊkɒf/ Vladimir 1899–1977. US writer who left his native Russia 1917, and began writing in English in the 1940s. His principal book is *Lolita* 1955, the story of the infatuation of the middle-aged Humbert Humbert with a precocious child of 12. His other books include *The Real Life of Sebastian Knight* 1945 and *Pnin* 1957.

He was born in St Petersburg, settled in the USA 1940, and became a US citizen 1945. He was professor of Russian literature at Cornell University 1948–59, producing a translation and commentary on *Eugene Onegin* 1963. He was also a lepidopterist (a collector of butterflies

and moths), a theme used in his book *Pale Fire* 1962.

Nacala /nə'kɑ:lə/ seaport in Nampula province, N Mozambique; a major outlet for minerals. It is linked by rail with Malawi.

Nachingwea /nə'tʃɪŋgweɪə/ military training base in Tanzania, about 360 km/225 mi south of Dar-es-Salaam. It was used by the guerrillas of Frelimo (Mozambique) 1964–75 and the African National Congress 1975–80.

Nadar /nə'dɑ:/ Adopted name of Gaspard-Félix Tournachon 1820–1910. French portrait photographer and caricaturist. He took the first aerial photographs (from a balloon 1858) and was the first to use artificial light.

Nader /'neɪdə/ Ralph 1934– . US lawyer. The 'scourge of corporate morality', he has led many consumer campaigns. His book *Unsafe at Any Speed* 1965 led to US car-safety legislation.

nadir the point in the sky vertically 'below' the observer (that is, beneath the Earth), and hence diametrically opposite to the **zenith**.

Nadir /'neɪdɪə/ Shah (Khan) *c.* 1880–1933. King of Afghanistan from 1929. Nadir played a key role in the 1919 Afghan War, but was subsequently forced into exile in France. He returned to Kabul in 1929 to seize the throne and embarked on an ambitious modernization programme. This alienated the Muslim clergy and in 1933 he was assassinated by fundamentalists. His successor as king was his son ◊Zahir Shah.

Naemen /'nɑ:mən/ Flemish form of ◊Namur, city in Belgium.

naevus a type of birthmark, colloquially known as a 'port-wine mark'. It is a bright-red-coloured area

Nader *US consumer campaigner Ralph Nader at a press conference, 1971.*

of the skin, consisting of a mass of small blood vessels.

A naevus of moderate size is harmless, and such marks are usually disguised cosmetically unless they are extremely disfiguring, when they can sometimes be treated by cutting out, by burning with an electric needle, by freezing with carbon dioxide snow, or by argon laser treatment.

Nafud desert area in Saudi Arabia to the south of the Syrian Desert.

Naga peoples who inhabit the highland region near the Indian-Myanmar border. These peoples do not possess a common name; some of the main groups are Ao, Konyak, Sangtam, Lhota, Sema, Rengma, Chang, and Angami. Their languages belong to the Sino-Tibetan family.

Nagaland /'nɑ:gəlænd/ state of NE India, bordering Myanmar on the east
area 16,721 sq km/6,456 sq mi
capital Kohima
products rice, tea, coffee, paper, sugar
population (1981) 775,000
history formerly part of Assam, it was seized by Britain from Burma (now Myanmar) 1826. The British sent 18 expeditions against the Naga peoples in the north 1832–87. After India attained independence 1947, there was Naga guerrilla activity against the Indian government; the state of Nagaland was established 1963 in response to demands for self-government, but fighting continued sporadically.

nagana animal sleeping sickness (see ◊tsetse).

Nagasaki /,nægə'sɑ:ki/ industrial port (coal, iron, shipbuilding) on Kyushu island, Japan; population (1987) 447,000. An atom bomb was dropped on it 9 Aug 1945.

Nagasaki was the only Japanese port open to European trade from the 16th century until other ports were opened 1859. Three days after ◊Hiroshima, the second atom bomb was dropped. Of Nagasaki's population of 212,000, 73,884 were killed and 76,796 injured, not counting the long-term victims of radiation.

Nagorno-Karabakh autonomous region (*oblast*) of the Soviet republic of ◊Azerbajian; population (1987) 180,000 (76% Armenian, 23% Azeri), the Christian Armenians forming an enclave within the predominantly Shi'ite Muslim Azerbaijan. Since Feb 1988 the region has been the site of ethnic conflicts between the two groups and the subject of violent disputes between Azerbaijan and the neighbouring republic of Armenia.
area 4,400 sq km/1,700 sq mi
capital Stepanakert
history an autonomous protectorate after the Russian revolution in 1917, Nagorno-Karabakh was annexed in 1923 to Azerbaijan against the wishes of the local population. Armenians in Nagorno-Karabakh felt discriminated against by the Azerbaijan republic. Inter-ethnic violence was provoked by the local council voting to transfer the region's administrative control to Armenia, and in response the area was placed under direct

rule from Moscow Jan–Nov 1989. During autumn 1989 the inter-republic conflict escalated, with Azerbaijan first imposing an economic blockade on Armenia, and then descending into civil war and threatening secession from the USSR, which resulted in 20,000 Soviet troops being sent to the republic. There have been large-scale cross-border migrations of Armenians from Azerbaijan and Azeris from Armenia, involving over 300,000 people.

Nagoya /nəˈgɔɪə/ industrial seaport (cars, textiles, clocks) on Honshu island, Japan; population (1987) 2,091,000. It has a shogun fortress 1610, and a noted Shinto shrine, *Atsuta Jingu*.

Nagpur /ˌnæɡˈpʊə/ industrial city (textiles, metals) in Maharashtra, India; population (1981) 1,298,000. The university was founded 1923.

Nagy /nɒdʒ/ Imre 1895–1958. Hungarian politician, prime minister 1953–55 and 1956. He led the Hungarian revolt against Soviet domination in 1956, for which he was executed.

Nagy, an Austro-Hungarian prisoner of war in Siberia during World War I, became a Soviet citizen after the Russian Revolution, and lived in the USSR 1930–44. In 1953, after Stalin's death, he became prime minister, introducing liberal measures such as encouraging the production of consumer goods, but was dismissed 1955 by hardline Stalinist premier Rákosi. Reappointed Oct 1956 during the Hungarian uprising, he began taking liberalization further than the Soviets wanted, for example announcing Hungarian withdrawal from the Warsaw Pact. Soviet troops entered Budapest, and Nagy was dismissed 4 Nov 1956. He was captured by the KGB and shot. His remains were relocated in Budapest, and in 1989 the Hungarian Supreme Court recognized his leadership of a legitimate government and quashed his conviction for treachery.

Naha /ˈnɑːhɑː/ chief port on Okinawa island, Japan; population (1984) 304,000.

Nahayan /ˌnɑːhəˈjaːn/ Sheikh Zayed bin Sultan al- 1918– . Emir of Abu Dhabi from 1969, when he deposed his brother, Sheikh Shakhbut. He was elected president of the supreme council of the United Arab Emirates (UAE) in 1971. Before 1969 he was governor of the eastern province of Abu Dhabi, one of seven ◊Trucial States in the Persian Gulf and Gulf of Oman, which were under British protection. He was unanimously re-elected emir in 1986.

Nahua indigenous people of central Mexico. The Nahua language, in the Uto-Aztecan family, is spoken by over a million people today.

Nahum /ˈneɪhəm/ 7th century BC. In the Old Testament, a Hebrew prophet, possibly born in Galilee, who forecast the destruction of Nineveh.

naiad in classical mythology, a water-nymph.

nail in biology, a hard, flat, flexible outgrowth of the digits of primates (humans, monkeys, and apes). Nails are derived from the ◊claws of ancestral primates.

Naipaul /ˈnaɪpɔːl/ V(idiadhar) S(urajprasad) 1932– . British writer, born in Trinidad of Hindu parents. His novels include *A House for Mr Biswas* 1961, *The Mimic Men* 1967, and *A Bend in the River* 1979. His brother **Shiva(dhar) Naipaul** (1940–85) was also a novelist (*Fireflies* 1970) and journalist.

Nairnshire /ˈneənʃə/ former county of Scotland, bounded on the north by the Moray Firth, included 1975 in the Highland region. The county town was Nairn.

Nairobi /naɪˈrəʊbi/ capital of Kenya, in the central highlands at 1,660 m/5,450 ft; population (1985) 1,100,000. It has light industry and food processing, and is the headquarters of the United Nations Environment Programme (UNEP).

Nairobi was founded 1899, and its university 1970. It has the International Louis Leakey Institute for African Prehistory 1977, and the International Primate Research Institute is nearby.

Najaf a holy city near the Euphrates in Iraq, 144 km/90 mi south of Baghdad.

Nairobi *Kimathi Street and the Hilton Hotel in Kenya's capital of Nairobi.*

Najibullah Ahmadzai 1947– . Afghan communist politician, a member of the Politburo from 1981, and leader of the ruling People's Democratic Party of Afghanistan (PDPA) from 1986, later entitled state president. His attempts to broaden the support of the PDPA regime had little success, but his government survived the following withdrawal of Soviet troops Feb 1989.

A Pusthtun (Pathan), Najibullah joined the communist PDPA 1965, allying with its gradualist Parcham (banner) faction, and was twice imprisoned for anti-government political activities during the 1960s and 1970s. After the Soviet invasion Dec 1979, Najibullah became head of the KHAD secret police and entered the PDPA Politburo 1981. He replaced Babrak Karmal as leader of the PDPA, and thus the nation, May 1986. His hold on power became imperilled 1989 following the withdrawal of the Soviet military forces.

Nakasone /ˌnækəˈsəʊneɪ/ Yasuhiro 1917– . Japanese conservative politician, leader of the Liberal Democratic Party (LDP) and prime minister 1982–87. He stepped up military spending and increased Japanese participation in international affairs, with closer ties to the USA. His reputation was tarnished by his involvement in the Recruit insider-trading scandal.

Nakasone was educated at Tokyo University. He held ministerial posts from 1967 and established his own faction within the conservative LDP. In 1982 he was elected president of the LDP and prime minister. He encouraged a less paternalist approach to economic management. Although embarrassed by the conviction of one of his supporters in the 1983 Lockheed corruption scandal, he was re-elected 1986 by a landslide.

Naked and the Dead, The 1948 debut novel by the US writer Norman Mailer, set on a Pacific island during combat in World War II, and displaying war not only as a battle with the enemy but as a psychic and political condition.

Nakhichevan autonomous republic forming part of Azerbaijan Republic, USSR, even though it is entirely outside the Azerbaijan boundary, being separated from it by the Armenian Republic; area 5,500 sq km/2,120 sq mi; population (1986) 272,000. Taken by Russia in 1828, it was annexed to the Azerbaijan Republic in 1924. 85% of the population are Muslim Azeris who maintain strong links with Iran to the south. Nakhichevan has been affected by the Armenia—Azerbaijan conflict; many Azeris have fled to Azerbaijan, and in Jan 1990 frontier posts and border fences with Iran were destroyed.

Najibullah *Afghan communist state president Najibullah Ahmadzai. Head of an embattled military regime, he has been faced, since 1989, by mujaheddin insurgency and attempted coups.*

Nakhodka /nəˈxɒdkə/ pacific port in E Siberia, USSR, on the sea of Japan, E of Vladivostok; population (1985) 150,000. US-caught fish, especially pollock, are processed by Soviet factory ships in a joint venture.

Nakuru, Lake a salt lake in the Great Rift Valley, Kenya.

Namaqualand /næˈmɑːkwələnd/ or **Namaland** near-desert area on the SW coast of Africa divided between Namibia and South Africa.

Great Namaqualand is in Namibia, north of the Orange River, area 388,500 sq km/150,000 sq mi; sparsely populated by the Nama, a Hottentot people.

Little Namaqualand is in Cape Province, South Africa, south of the Orange River, area 52,000 sq km/20,000 sq mi; copper and diamonds are mined here.

Namatjira /ˌnæməˈtʃɪərə/ Albert 1902–1959. Australian Aboriginal painter of watercolour landscapes of the Australian interior. Acclaimed after an exhibition in Melbourne in 1938, he died destitute.

Namib Desert coastal desert region in Namibia between the Kalahari Desert and the Atlantic Ocean. Its sand dunes are among the tallest in the world, reaching heights of 370 m/1,200 ft.

Namibia /nəˈmɪbɪə/ country in SW Africa, bounded on the N by Angola and Zambia, on the E by Botswana and South Africa, and on the W by the Atlantic Ocean. Much of the land is desert.

government A new constitution has been framed by the transitional 72-member constituent assembly, which was elected by proportional representation in Nov 1989. Unanimously approved in Feb 1990, it entrenches a multi-party system with an independent judiciary and bill of fundamental human rights. Executive authority is wielded by a president who may serve a maximum of two five-year terms.

history Annexed, with the exeption of the British/Cape Colony enclave of ◊Walvis Bay, by Germany 1884, it was occupied in World War I by South African forces under L Botha, and was mandated to South Africa 1920. South Africa did not accept the termination of the mandate by the United Nations 1966, although briefly accepting the principle of ultimate independence 1978 (UN Security Council Resolution 435); in 1968 the UN renamed the territory Namibia. South Africa's apartheid laws were extended to the

Namibia
formerly **South West Africa**

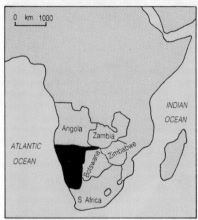

0 km 1000

INDIAN OCEAN

Angola
Zambia
ATLANTIC OCEAN
Botswana Zimbabwe
S Africa

area 824,300 sq km/318,262 sq mi
capital Windhoek
physical mainly desert; includes the enclave of Walvis Bay (area 1,120 sq km/432 sq mi) currently administered by South Africa
head of state and government Sam Nujoma from 1990
government democratic republic
political parties South West African People's Organization of Namibia (SWAPO), socialist Ovambo-orientated; Democratic Turnhalle Alliance (DTA), moderate, multi-racial coalition; United Democratic Front (UDF), disaffected ex-SWAPO members; National Christian Action (ACN), white conservative
exports diamonds, uranium
currency South African rand (4.33 = Feb 1990)

population (1988) 1,288,000 (85% black African, 6% European). There are 300,000 displaced families, 50,000 refugees, and 75,000 in SWAPO camps in exile
life expectancy black 40, white 69
language Afrikaans, German, English
religion 51% Lutheran, 19% Roman Catholic, 6% Dutch Reformed Church, 6% Anglican
literacy 38%
GDP $1,247m (1985); $1,084 per head of population
chronology
1884 German and British colonies established.
1915 German colony seized by South Africa.
1920 Administered by South Africa, under League of Nations mandate, as British South Africa (SWA).
1946 Full incorporation in South Africa refused by United Nations (UN).
1958 South West African People's Organization (SWAPO) set up to seek racial equality and full independence.
1966 South Africa's apartheid laws extended to the country.
1968 Redesignated Namibia by UN.
1978 UN Security Council Resolution 435 for the granting of full sovereignty accepted by South Africa and then rescinded.
1988 Peace talks between South Africa, Angola, and Cuba led to agreement on full independence for Namibia.
1989 Unexpected incursion by SWAPO guerrillas from Angola into Namibia threatened agreed timetable for independence from South Africa.
1990 Liberal multi-party 'independence' constitution adopted; Sam Nujoma elected president.

colony in 1966 and in opposition to such racial discrimination Sam ◊Nujoma, an Ovambu, led first a political (from 1958) and then (from mid-1960s) an armed resistance campaign for independence, forming the South West Africa People's Organization (SWAPO) and the People's Liberation Army of Namibia (PLAN). Following harassment, he was forced into exile in 1960, establishing guerrilla bases in Angola and Zambia. Military conflict in Namibia escalated from the mid-1970s as the Pretoria regime attempted to topple the new Marxist government in neighbouring Angola. In 1985 South Africa installed a puppet regime in Namibia, the Transitional Government of National Unity (TGNU), a multi-racial body, but including only one Ovambo minister. It attempted to reform the apartheid system but was internally divided between moderate reformist and conservative wings, and failed to secure UN recognition.

In 1988 progress was finally made towards a peace settlement in Namibia as a result of both South Africa and the USSR (via Cuba) tiring of the cost of their proxy military involvment in the civil wars of both the colony and neighbouring Angola. In Aug 1988 the South African and Angolan governments signed an agreement that provided for an immediate ceasefire, followed by the rapid withdrawal of South African forces from Angola and, during 1989, the phased withdrawal of Cuba's troops from Angola and South Africa's from Namibia. From Apr 1989, a UN peacekeeping force was stationed in Namibia to oversee the holding of multi-party elections in Nov. These were won by SWAPO, but its 57% share of the seats in the constituent assembly, which had the task of framing a new 'independence constitution', fell short of the two-thirds majority required for it to dominate the proceedings. As a consequence, a moderate multi-party constitution was adopted in Feb 1990. Sam Nujoma was unanimously elected Namibia's first president by the assembly on 16 Feb 1990, to be formally sworn in by the

UN secretary-general on independence day, 21 Mar 1990.

Nampo /ˌnæmˈpəʊ/ formerly (to 1947) **Chinnampo** city on the west coast of North Korea, 40 km/25 mi SW of Pyongyang; population (1984) 691,000.

Namur /nəˈmjʊə/ (Flemish **Namen**) industrial city (cutlery, porcelain, paper, iron, steel), capital of the province of Namur, in S Belgium, at the confluence of the Sambre and Meuse rivers; population (1988) 103,000. It was a strategic location during both world wars. The province of Namur has an area of 3,700 sq km/1,428 sq mi, and a population (1987) of 415,000.

Nanaimo /næˈnaɪməʊ/ coal-mining centre of British Columbia, Canada, on the E coast of Vancouver Island; population (1985) 50,500.

Nanak /ˈnɑːnək/ 1469–c. 1539. Indian guru and founder of Sikhism, a religion based on the unity of God and the equality of all human beings. He was strongly opposed to caste divisions.

Nana Sahib /ˈnɑːniː ˈsɑːb/ popular name for Dandhu Panth 1820–c. 1859. The adopted son of a former *peshwa* (chief minister) of the ◊Mahrattas in central India, he joined the rebels in the ◊Indian Mutiny 1857–58, and was responsible for the massacre at Kanpur when safe conducts given to British civilians were broken and many women and children massacred. After the failure of the mutiny he took refuge in Nepál.

Nancarrow /nænˈkærəʊ/ Conlon 1912– . US composer who settled in Mexico 1940. Using a player-piano as a form of synthesizer, punching the rolls by hand, he experimented with complicated combinations of rhythm and tempo, producing a series of studies that anticipated minimalism and brought him recognition in the 1970s.

Nancecuke /nænsˈkjːk/ site in Cornwall of a secret Ministry of Defence establishment until 1978. A branch of the Chemical Defence Establishment at ◊Porton Down, it was closed when Britain gave up chemical and biological weapons.

Nanchang /ˌnænˈtʃæŋ/ industrial (textiles, glass, porcelain, soap) capital of Jiangxi province, China,

about 260 km/160 mi SE of Wuhan; population (1986) 1,120,000. It is an important road and rail junction. It was originally a walled city built in the 12th century. The first Chinese Communist rising took place here 1 Aug 1927.

Nancy /ˈnɒnsi/ capital of the *département* of Meurthe-et-Moselle and of the region of Lorraine, France, on the river Meurthe 280 km/175 mi E of Paris; population (1982) 307,000. Nancy dates from the 11th century.

Nanda Devi /ˈnʌndə ˈdiːvi/ peak in the Himalayas, Uttar Pradesh, N India; height 7,817 m/25,645 ft. Until Kanchenjunga was absorbed into India, Nanda Devi was the country's highest mountain.

Nanga Parbat /ˈnʌŋgə ˈpɑːbæt/ peak in the Himalayan Karakoram mountains of Kashmir; height 8,126 m/26,660 ft.

Nanjing /ˌnænˈdʒɪŋ/ formerly **Nanking** capital of Jiangsu province, China, 270 km/165 mi NW of Shanghai; centre of industry (engineering, shipbuilding, oil refining), commerce, and communications; population (1986) 2,250,000. The bridge 1968 over the Chang Jiang river is the longest in China at 6,705 m/22,000 ft.

The city dates from the 2nd century BC, perhaps earlier. It received the name Nanjing ('southern capital') under the Ming dynasty (1368–1644), and was the capital of China 1368–1403, 1928–37, and 1946–49. Its university was founded 1888.

Nanking /ˌnænˈkɪŋ/ former name of ◊Nanjing, city in China.

Nanning /ˌnænˈnɪŋ/ industrial river port, capital of Guangxi autonomous region, China, on the You Jiang; population (1982) 866,000. It was an important supply town during the Vietnam war and the Sino-Vietnamese confrontation 1979.

nano- prefix used in ◊SI units of measurement, equivalent to one thousand millionth part (10⁻⁹). For example, a nanosecond is one thousand millionth of a second.

Nansen /ˈnænsən/ Fridtjof 1861–1930. Norwegian explorer and scientist. In 1893, he sailed to the Arctic in the *Fram*, which was deliberately allowed to drift N with an iceflow. Nansen, accompanied by F J Johansen, continued N on foot and reached 86° 14' N, the highest latitude then attained. After World War I, Nansen became League of Nations high commissioner for refugees. Nobel Peace Prize 1923.

He made his first voyage to Greenland waters in a sealing ship 1882, and in 1888–89 attempted to cross the Greenland icefield. He was professor of zoology and oceanography at the University of Christiania (now Oslo). Norwegian ambassador in London 1906–08. The *Nansen passport* issued to stateless persons is named after him.

Nanshan Islands /ˈnænˈʃæn/ Chinese name for the ◊Spratly Islands.

Nantes /nɒnt/ industrial port in W France on the Loire, capital of Pays de la Loire region; industries (oil, sugar refining, textiles, soap, tobacco); population (1982) 465,000. It has a cathedral 1434–1884 and a castle founded 938. It is the birthplace of the writer Jules Verne.

Nantes, Edict of decree by which Henry IV of France granted religious freedom to the ◊Huguenots 1598. It was revoked 1685 by Louis XIV.

Nantucket /nænˈtʌkɪt/ island and resort in Massachusetts, USA, S of Cape Cod, 120 sq km/46 sq mi. In the 18–19th centuries, Nantucket was a whaling port.

Napa /ˈnæpə/ capital of Napa country, California, USA; population (1980) 50,900; centre of the notable wine-producing Napa Valley situated to the NE of San Francisco.

napalm fuel used in flamethrowers and incendiary bombs. Produced from jellied petrol, it is a mixture of *na*phthenic and *palm*itic acids. Napalm causes extensive burns because it sticks to the skin even when aflame. It was widely used by the US Army during the Vietnam War.

naphtha term originally applied to naturally occurring liquid hydrocarbons, now used for the mixtures of hydrocarbons obtained by destructive distillation of petroleum, coal-tar, and shale oil. It is an important raw material for the petrochemical and plastics industries.

naphthalene $C_{10}H_8$ a solid, aromatic hydrocarbon obtained from coal-tar. A white, shiny, solid with a smell of moth-balls, it is used in making indigo and certain azo-dyes, and as a mild disinfectant and insecticide.

Napier /'neɪpɪə/ wool port in Hawke Bay on the E coast of North Island, New Zealand; population (1986) 52,000.

Napier /'neɪpɪə/ Charles James 1782–1853. British general. He conquered Sind in India (now a province of Pakistan) 1841–43 with a very small force and governed it until 1847. He was the first commander to mention men from the ranks in his dispatches.

Napier /'neɪpɪə/ John 1550–1617. Scottish mathematician who invented ◊logarithms 1614, and 'Napier's bones', an early logarithmic calculating device for multiplication and division.

Napier /'neɪpɪə/ Robert Cornelis, 1st Baron Napier of Magdala 1810–1890. British field marshal. Knighted for his services in relieving Lucknow during the Indian Mutiny, he took part in capturing Peking (Beijing) 1860 during the war against China in 1860. He stormed Magdala in the Abyssinian campaign 1868, was created a peer in the same year, was commander in chief in India 1870–76, and governor of Gibraltar 1876–82.

Naples /'neɪpəlz/ (Italian *Napoli*) industrial port (shipbuilding, cars, textiles, paper, food processing) and capital of Campania, Italy, on the Tyrrhenian Sea; population (1988) 1,201,000. To the south is the Isle of Capri, and behind the city is Mount Vesuvius, with the ruins of Pompeii at its foot.

Naples is the third largest city of Italy, and as a port second in importance only to Genoa. Buildings include the royal palace, the San Carlo Opera House, the Castel Nuovo 1283, and the university 1224.

The city began as the Greek colony Neapolis in the 6th century BC and was taken over by Romans 326 BC; it became part of the Kingdom of the Two ◊Sicilies 1140 and capital of the Kingdom of Naples 1282.

Naples, Kingdom of /'neɪpəlz/ the southern part of Italy, alternately independent and united with ◊Sicily in the Kingdom of the Two Sicilies.

Naples was united with Sicily 1140–1282, first under Norman rule 1130–94, then Hohenstaufen 1194–1266, then Angevin from 1268; apart from Sicily, but under continued Angevin rule to 1435; reunited with Sicily 1442–1503, under the house of Aragon to 1501; a Spanish Habsburg possession 1504–1707 and Austrian 1707–35; under Spanish Bourbon rule 1735–99. The *Neapolitan Republic* was established 1799 after Napoleon had left Italy for Egypt, but fell after five months to the forces of reaction under Cardinal Ruffo, with the British admiral Nelson blockading the city by sea; many prominent citizens were massacred after the capitulation. The Spanish Bourbons were restored 1799, 1802–05, and 1815–1860, when Naples joined the Kingdom of Italy.

Napoleon I /nə'pəʊlɪən/ Bonaparte 1769–1821. Emperor of the French 1804–14 and 1814–15. A general from 1796 in the ◊Revolutionary Wars, in 1799 he overthrew the Directory (see ◊French Revolution) and made himself dictator. From 1803 he conquered most of Europe, and installed his brothers as puppet kings (see ◊Bonaparte). After the Peninsular War and retreat from Moscow 1812, he was forced to abdicate 1814 and was banished to Elba. In Mar 1815 he reassumed power but was defeated at the ◊Waterloo and exiled to the island of St Helena. His internal administrative reforms are still evident in France.

Napoleon, born in Ajaccio, Corsica, received a commission in the artillery 1785 and first

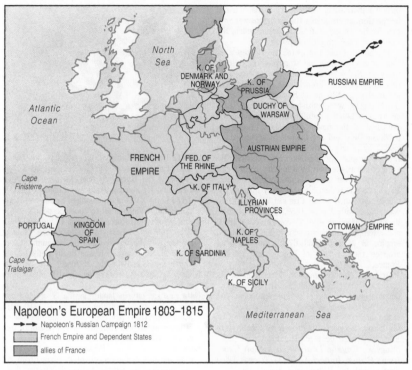

distinguished himself at the siege of ◊Toulon 1793. Having suppressed a royalist rising in Paris 1795, he was given command against the Austrians in Italy, and defeated them at Lodi, Arcole, and Rivoli 1796–97. Egypt, seen as a halfway house to India, was overrun, and Syria invaded, but his fleet was destroyed by the British admiral ◊Nelson at the Battle of the Nile. He returned to France to carry out a coup against the government of the Directory and establish his own dictatorship, nominally as First Consul. The Austrians were again defeated at Marengo 1800, and the coalition against France shattered, a truce being declared 1802. A plebiscite the same year made him consul for life. In 1804 a plebiscite made him emperor.

While retaining and extending the legal and educational reforms of the Jacobins, Napoleon replaced the democratic constitution established by the Revolution with a centralized despotism, and by his ◊concordat conciliated the Catholic church. The *Code Napoléon* is still the basis of French law.

Napoleon I Napoleon Crossing the Alps *(1800) by Jacques Louis David, Charlottenburg Castle, Berlin.*

War was renewed by Britain 1803, aided by Austria and Russia from 1805, and Prussia from 1806. Prevented by the navy from invading Britain, Napoleon drove Austria out of the war by victories at Ulm and Austerlitz 1805, and Prussia by the victory at Jena 1806. Then, after the battles of Eylau and Friedland, he formed an alliance with Russia at Tilsit 1807. Napoleon now forbade entry of British goods to Europe under the ◊Continental System, occupied Portugal, and in 1808 placed his brother Joseph on the Spanish throne. Both countries revolted, with British aid, and Austria attempted to re-enter the war, but was defeated at Wagram. In 1796 Napoleon had married ◊Josephine de Beauharnais, but in 1809, to assert his equality with the Habsburgs, he divorced her to marry the Austrian emperor's daughter, ◊Marie Louise.

When Russia failed to enforce the Continental System, Napoleon occupied Moscow, but his retreat in the bitter winter of 1812 encouraged Prussia and Austria to declare war again 1813, and he was defeated at Leipzig and driven from Germany. Despite his brilliant campaign on French soil, the Allies invaded Paris and compelled him to abdicate Apr 1814; he was banished to the island of Elba, off the west coast of Italy. In Mar 1815 he escaped and took power for a hundred days, with the aid of Marshal ◊Ney, but the UK and Prussia led an alliance against him at Waterloo, Belgium, in June. Surrendering to the British, he again abdicated, and was exiled to the island of St Helena, 1,900 km/1,200 mi west of Africa. His body was brought back 1840 to be interred in the Hôtel des Invalides, Paris.

Napoleon II /nə'pəʊlɪən/ 1811–1832. Title given by the Bonapartists to the son of Napoleon I and ◊Marie Louise; until 1814 he was known as *the king of Rome*, and after 1818 as the duke of Reichstadt. After his father's abdication 1814 he was taken to the Austrian court, where he spent the rest of his life.

Napoleon III /nə'pəʊlɪən/ 1808–1873. Emperor of the French 1852–70, known as *Louis-Napoleon*. After two attempted coups (1836 and 1840) he was jailed and went into exile, returning for the revolution of 1848, when he became president of the Second Republic, but soon turned authoritarian. In 1870 he was manoeuvred by the German chancellor Bismarck into war with Prussia; he was forced to surrender at Sedan, NE France, and the empire collapsed.

The son of Louis Bonaparte and Hortense de Beauharnais, brother and step-daughter respectively of Napoleon I, he led two unsuccessful revolts against the French king Louis Philippe, at Strasbourg 1836 and at Boulogne 1840. After the latter he was imprisoned. Escaping 1846, he lived in London until 1848. He was elected president of the newly established French republic in Dec, and set himself to secure a following by posing as the champion of order and religion against the revolutionary menace. He secured his re-election by a military coup d'état 1851, and a year later was proclaimed emperor. Hoping to strengthen his regime by military triumphs, he joined in the Crimean War 1854–55, waged war with Austria 1859, winning the Battle of Solferino, annexed Savoy and Nice 1860, and attempted unsuccessfully to found a vassal empire in Mexico 1863–67. In so doing he aroused the mistrust of Europe and isolated France.

At home, his regime was discredited by its notorious corruption; republican and socialist opposition grew, in spite of severe repression, and forced Napoleon, after 1860, to make concessions in the direction of parliamentary government. After losing the war with Prussia he withdrew to England, where he died. His son by Empress ◊Eugénie, *Eugène Louis Jean Joseph Napoleon, Prince Imperial* (1856–79), was killed fighting with the British army against the Zulus in Africa.

Napoleonic Wars 1803–15 a series of European wars that followed the ◊Revolutionary Wars.
1803 Britain renewed the war against France, following an appeal from the Maltese against Napoleon's seizure of the island.
1805 Napoleon's planned invasion of Britain from Boulogne ended by Nelson's victory at ◊*Trafalgar*; coalition formed by Britain, Austria, Russia, Sweden. Austria defeated at Ulm; Austria and Russia at ◊*Austerlitz*.
1806 Prussia, latest member of the coalition, defeated at Jena; Napoleon instituted an attempted blockade, the *Continental System*, to isolate Britain from Europe.
1807 Russia defeated at Eylau and Friedland and on making peace with Napoleon under the *Treaty of Tilsit* changed sides, agreeing to attack Sweden, and was forced to retreat.
1808 Napoleon's invasion of Portugal, and habit of installing his relatives as puppet kings, led to the ◊*Peninsular War*.
1809 Revived Austrian opposition to Napoleon was ended by defeat at ◊*Wagram*.
1812 The Continental System finally collapsed on its rejection by Russia, and Napoleon made the fatal decision to invade; he reached *Moscow* but was defeated by the Russian resistance, and by the bitter winter as he retreated through a countryside laid waste by the retreating Russians (380,000 French soldiers died).

Napoleon III *Emperor of the French 1852–70.*

narcissus

1813 Britain, Prussia, Russia, Austria, and Sweden formed a new coalition, which defeated Napoleon at the *Battle of the Nations*, Leipzig, Germany. He abdicated and was exiled to Elba.
1814 Louis XVIII became king of France, and the Congress of Vienna met to conclude peace.
1815 Napoleon returned to Paris. 16 June the British commander Wellington defeated the French marshal Ney at Quatre Bras (in Belgium, SE of Brussels), and Napoleon was finally defeated at *Waterloo*, S of Brussels, 18 June.

Napoli /ˈnɑːpəli/ Italian form of ◊Naples, city in Italy.

Nara /ˈnɑːrə/ city in Japan, in the S of Honshu island, the capital of the country AD 710–94; population (1984) 316,000. It was the birthplace of Japanese art and literature and is noted for its ancient wooden temples.

Narayan /nəˈraɪən/ Jaya Prakash 1902–1979. Veteran socialist and associate of Vinobha Bham in the Bhoodan movement for rural reforms that took place during the last years of the Raj. He was prominent in the protest movement against Indira Gandhi's emergency regime, 1975–77, and acted as umpire in the Janata leadership contest that followed Indira Gandhi's defeat in 1977.

Narbonne /ˌnɑːˈbɒn/ city in Aude *département*, S France; population (1983) 39,246. It was the chief town of S Gaul in Roman times and a port in medieval times.

narcissism in psychology, an exaggeration of normal self-respect and pride in oneself, which may amount to mental disorder when it precludes relationships with other people.

Narcissus /nɑːˈsɪsəs/ genus of bulbous plants of the family Amaryllidaceae, of which the best-known are the daffodil, jonquil, and narcissus.

Narcissus /nɑːˈsɪsəs/ in Greek mythology, a beautiful youth, who rejected the love of the nymph ◊Echo, and was condemned to fall in love with his own reflection in a pool. He pined away and in the place where he died a flower sprang up, which was named after him.

narcolepsy a rare disorder characterized by bouts of overwhelming sleepiness and loss of muscle power. It is controlled by drugs.

narcotic pain-relieving and sleep-inducing drug. The principal narcotics induce dependency, and include opium, its derivatives and synthetic modifications (such as morphine and heroin); alcohols (for example paraldehyde and ethyl alcohol); and barbiturates.

Nares /neəz/ George Strong 1831–1915. Scottish vice-admiral and explorer who sailed to the Canadian Arctic on an expedition in search of John ◊Franklin 1852, and again in 1876 when he discovered the Challenger Mountains. During 1872–76 he commanded the Challenger Expedition. His Arctic explorations are recounted in *Voyage to the Polar Seas* 1878.

Narmada River a river that rises in the Maikala range in Madhya Pradesh state, central India, and flows 1,245 km/778 mi WSW to the Gulf of Khambat, an inlet of the Arabian Sea. Forming the traditional boundary between Hindustan and Deccan, the Narmada is a holy river of the Hindus. India's Narmada Valley Project is one of the largest and most controversial river development projects in the world. Between 1990 and 2040 it is planned to build 30 major dams, 135 medium-sized

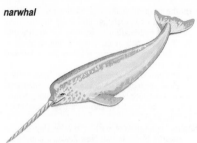

narwhal

dams and 3,000 smaller dams in a scheme that will involve moving 1 million of the valley's population of 20 million people.

Narnia, Chronicles of a series of seven books for children by C S ◊Lewis. The first, *The Lion, the Witch and the Wardrobe*, was published in 1950; in it children travel through a wardrobe into an imaginary country, Narnia. There the Christian story is re-enacted in a mythical context, the lion Aslan representing Christ. Further journeys into Narnia feature in the sequels *Prince Caspian* 1951, *The Voyage of the 'Dawn Treader'* 1952, *The Silver Chair* 1953, *The Horse and his Boy* 1954, *The Magician's Nephew* 1955, and *The Last Battle* 1956.

Narodnik member of a secret Russian political movement, active 1873–76 before its suppression by the tsarist authorities. Narodniks were largely university students, and their main purpose was to convert the peasantry to socialism.

Narragansett Bay /ˌnærəˈɡænsɪt/ Atlantic inlet, Rhode Island, USA. Running inland for 45 km/28 mi, it encloses a number of islands.

Narses /ˈnɑːsiːz/ *c.* 478–*c.* 573. Byzantine general. Originally a eunuch slave, he later became an official in the imperial treasury. He was joint commander with the Roman general Belisarius in Italy 538–39, and in 552 destroyed the Ostrogoths at Taginae in the Apennines.

Narvik /ˈnɑːvɪk/ seaport in Nordland county, N Norway, on Lofot Fjord, exporting iron ore from Swedish mines; population (1980) 19,500. To secure this ore supply Germany seized Narvik in Apr 1940. British, French, Polish, and Norwegian forces recaptured the port but had to abandon it on 10 Jun to cope with the worsening Allied situation elsewhere in Europe.

narwhal whale *Monodon monoceros*, found only in the Arctic Ocean. It grows to 5 m/16 ft long, has a grey and black body, a small head, and short flippers. The male has a single spirally fluted tusk which may be up to 2.7 m/9 ft long.

NASA *N*ational *A*eronautics and *S*pace Administration, the US government agency, founded 1958, for spaceflight and aeronautical research. Its headquarters are in Washington DC and its main installation is at the ◊Kennedy Space Center.

Naseby, Battle of /ˈneɪzbi/ decisive battle of the English Civil War 14 June 1645, when the Royalists led by Prince Rupert were defeated by Oliver Cromwell and Gen Fairfax. It is named after the nearby village of Naseby, 20 km/12 mi NW of Northampton.

Nash /næʃ/ (Richard) 'Beau' 1674–1762. British dandy. As master of ceremonies at Bath from 1705, he made the town the most fashionable watering-place in England, and introduced a polished code of manners into general use.

Nash /næʃ/ John 1752–1835. English architect. He laid out Regent's Park, London, and its approaches. From 1813–1820 he planned Regent Street (later rebuilt), repaired and enlarged Buckingham Palace (for which he designed Marble Arch), and rebuilt Brighton Pavilion in flamboyant oriental style.

Nash /næʃ/ John Northcote 1893–1977. English illustrator, landscape artist, and engraver. He was the brother of the artist Paul Nash.

Nash Battle of Britain *(Aug/Oct 1940) Imperial War Museum, London.*

Nash /næʃ/ Ogden 1902–1971. US poet. He published numerous volumes of humorous verse characterized by puns, light epigrams, and unorthodox rhymes.

Nash /næʃ/ Paul 1889–1946. English painter, an official war artist in World Wars I and II. In the 1930s he was one of a group of artists promoting avant-garde styles in the UK. Two of his most celebrated works are *Totes Meer/Dead Sea* (Tate Gallery, London) and *The Battle of Britain* (Imperial War Museum, London).

Nash(e) /næʃ/ Thomas 1567–1601. English poet, dramatist, and pamphleteer. Author of the first English picaresque novel, *The Unfortunate Traveller* 1594. Born in Suffolk, he settled in London about 1588, where he was rapidly drawn into the Martin ◊Marprelate controversy (a pamphleteering attack on the clergy of the Church of England by Puritans), and wrote at least three attacks on the Martinists. Among his other works are the satirical *Pierce Pennilesse* 1592, the religious *Christes Teares over Jerusalem* 1593, and the comedy *Summer's Last Will and Testament* 1592.

Nash /næʃ/ Walter 1882–1968. New Zealand Labour politician. He was born in England, and emigrated to New Zealand 1909. He held ministerial posts 1935–49, was prime minister 1957–60, and leader of the Labour Party until 1963.

Nashville /næʃvɪl/ port on the Cumberland river and capital of Tennessee, USA; population (1986) 931,000. It is a banking and commercial centre, and has large printing, music-publishing, and recording industries. Most of the Bibles in the USA are printed here, and it is the hub of the country-music business.

Nashville dates from 1778, and the Confederate army was defeated here in 1864 in the American Civil War.

Nasmyth /neɪsmɪθ/ Alexander 1758–1840. Scottish portrait and landscape painter. His portrait of the poet Robert Burns hangs in the Scottish National Gallery.

Nasmyth /neɪsmɪθ/ James 1808–1890. Scottish engineer and machine-tool manufacturer, whose many inventions included the steel hammer in 1839. At his factory near Manchester, he developed the steam hammer for making large steel forgings (the first of which was the propeller shaft for Brunel's steamship *Great Britain*).

Nassan agreement agreement signed 18 Dec 1962 whereby the USA provided Britain with Polaris missiles, marking a strengthening in Anglo-American relations.

Nassau /næsɔː/ capital and port of the Bahamas, on New Providence island; population (1980) 135,000. English settlers founded it 1629.

Nasser /næsə/ Gamal Abdel 1918–1970. Egyptian politician, prime minister 1954–56 and from 1956 president of Egypt (the United Arab Republic 1958–71). In 1952 he was the driving power behind the Neguib coup, which ended the monarchy. His nationalization of the Suez Canal 1956 (see ◊Suez Crisis) and his ambitions for an Egyptian-led Arab union led to disquiet in the Middle East (and in the West).

nastic movement a plant movement that is caused by an external stimulus, such as light or temperature, but which is directionally independent of its source, unlike ◊tropisms. Nastic movements occur due to changes in water pressure within specialized cells, or as a result of differing rates of growth in parts of the plant. Examples include the opening and closing of crocus flowers following an increase or decrease in temperature (**thermonasty**), and the opening and closing of evening primrose *Oenothera* flowers on exposure to dark and light (**photonasty**).

The leaf movements of a Venus fly trap following a tactile stimulus, and the rapid collapse of the sensitive plant's (*Mimosa pudica*) leaflets are examples of **haptonasty**. Sleep movements, where the leaves or flowers of some plants adopt a different position at night, are described as **nyctinasty**. Other types include **hydronasty**, in response to a change in the atmospheric humidity, and **chemonasty**, in response to a chemical stimulus.

Nasturtium genus of plants of the family Cruciferae, including **watercress**, *Nasturtium officinale*, a perennial aquatic plant of Europe and Asia, grown as a salad crop. It also includes plants of the South American Tropaeolaceae family, including the garden species, *Tropaeolum majus*, with orange or scarlet flowers, and *Tropaeolum minus*, which has smaller flowers.

Natal /nə'tæl/ province of South Africa, NE of Cape Province, bounded on the E by the Indian Ocean

area 91,785 sq km/35,429 sq mi

capital Pietermaritzburg

towns Durban

physical slopes from the Drakensberg to a fertile subtropical coastal plain

products sugar cane, black wattle (*Acacia mollissima*), maize, fruits, vegetables, tobacco, coal

population (1985) 2,145,000

history called Natal because Vasco da Gama reached it Christmas Day 1497; part of the British Cape Colony 1843–56, when it was made into a separate colony; Zululand was annexed to Natal 1897, and the districts of Vrijheid, Utrecht, and part of Wakkerstroom were transferred from the Transvaal to Natal 1903; the colony became a part of the Union of South Africa 1910.

Natal /nə'tæl/ industrial (textiles, salt refining) seaport in Brazil, capital of the state of Rio Grande do Norte; population (1980) 376,500. Natal was founded 1599 and became a city 1822.

Nasser *Egyptian politician and prime minister Gamal Abdel Nasser, Oct 1964.*

Nataraja ('Lord of the Dance') in Hinduism, a title of ◊Siva.

Natchez /nætʃɪz/ member of a North American Indian people of the Mississippi area, one of the ◊Moundbuilder group of peoples. They had a highly developed caste system, headed by a ruler priest (the 'Great Sun'), unusual in North America. This lasted until the near genocide of the Natchez by the French in 1731; only a few survive in Oklahoma.

Natchez /nætʃɪz/ trading centre in Mississippi, USA, on the bluffs above the Mississippi river; population (1980) 22,000. It has many houses of the pre-American Civil War period, and was important in the heyday of steamboat traffic.

national accounts the organization of a country's finances. In the UK the economy is divided into the ***public sector*** (central government, local authorities, and public corporations), the ***private sector*** (the personal and company sector), and the ***overseas sector*** (transactions between residents and non-residents of the UK).

The ◊public sector borrowing requirement (PSBR), as the state took over a larger and larger share of the economy, became a crucial factor in budgets of the UK and other countries in the 1970s. It is the deficit between the amount the public sector receives, from taxation and other sources, and the amount it needs to finance its activities. In the UK, central government revenue and expenditure is channelled through the Consolidated Fund, which meets expenditure out of revenue arising largely from taxation, and the National Loans Fund, which handles most of central government's domestic lending and borrowing.

national anthem a patriotic song for official occasions. The US national anthem, 'The Star-spangled banner', was written during the war of 1812 by Francis Scott ◊Key and was adopted officially in 1931. In Britain 'God Save the King/Queen' has been accepted as such since 1745, although both music and words are of much earlier origin. The German anthem 'Deutschland über Alles/Germany before everything' is sung to music by Haydn. The French national anthem, the ◊'Marseillaise', dates from 1792. The ◊'Internationale', adopted as the Soviet national anthem 1917, was replaced by the song 'Unbreakable Union of Freeborn Republics' 1944.

Countries within the Commonwealth retain 'God Save the King/Queen' as the 'royal anthem', adopting their own anthem as a mark of independence. These include 'Advance Australia Fair' 1974–76 and from 1984 'O Canada', written 1882 and adopted gradually through popular usage. The anthem of united Europe is Schiller's 'Ode to Joy' set by Beethoven in his Ninth Symphony.

National Army Museum official museum, established in 1960 in Chelsea, London, for the British, Indian, and colonial forces 1485–1914. The Imperial War Museum deals with the period from 1914.

national assistance in the UK, term used 1948–66 for a weekly allowance paid by the state to ensure a minimum income (◊supplementary benefit until 1988).

National Association for the Advancement of Colored People (NAACP) US civil-rights organization, dedicated to ending black inequality and segregation through nonviolent protest. Founded 1910, its first aim was to eradicate lynching. The NAACP campaigned to end segregation in state schools; it funded test cases which eventually led to the Supreme Court decision 1954 outlawing school segregation, although it was only through the ◊civil rights movement of the 1960s that desegregation was achieved. In 1987 it had about 500,000 members, black and white.

The NAACP was founded by a group of white liberals, including William Walling, Oswald Villard, the social worker Jane Addams, the philosopher John Dewey, and the novelist William Dean Howells. Most of the officials were white, but most of the members were drawn from the ranks of the black bourgeoisie. It merged with the Niagara Movement founded 1905 by W E B DuBois. During World War II its membership increased from 50,000 to 400,000. The organization has been criticized by militants and black separatists for its moderate stance and its commitment to integration. See also *history* under ◊black.

National Book League former name of ◊Book Trust.

National Country Party former name for the Australian ◊National Party.

National Curriculum a scheme set up by the UK government 1987 to establish a single course of study in ten subjects common to all primary and secondary state schools. The national curriculum is divided into three core subjects—English, maths, and science—and seven foundation subjects—geography, history, technology, a foreign language (for secondary school pupils), art, music, and physical education. There are four key stages, on completion of which the pupil's work is assessed. The stages are for ages 5–7, 7–11, 11–14, and 14–16.

The syllabus for each subject is proposed by a working party, which after consultation with the National Curriculum Council, consisting of 14 people from education, industry, and commerce, proposes a final report to the secretary of state for education, who publishes regulations setting out what is to be taught. The first final report was produced June 1988.

national debt debt incurred by the central government of a country to its own people and institutions, and also to overseas creditors. If it does not wish to raise taxes to finance its activities, a government can borrow from the public by means of selling interest-bearing bonds, for example, or from abroad. Traditionally, a major cause of incurring national debt was the cost of war but in recent decades governments have borrowed heavily in order to finance development or nationalization, to support an ailing currency, or to avoid raising taxes. On 31 Mar 1988 the UK national debt was £197,295 million, or £3,465 per head of population.

Government budgets are often planned with a deficit that is funded by overseas borrowing. In the 1980s most governments adopted monetary policies designed to limit their borrowing requirements, both to reduce the cost of servicing the debt and because borrowing money tends to cause inflation.

In Britain the national debt is managed by the Bank of England, under the control of the Treasury. The first issue of government stock in Britain was made 1693, to raise a loan of £1 million. Historically, increases of the national debt have been caused by wartime expenditure; thus after the War of the Spanish Succession 1701–14 it reached £54 million. By 1900 it had been brought down to £610 million but World War I forced it up, by 1920, to £7,828 million and World War II, by 1945, to £21,870,221,651. Since then other factors have increased the national debt, including nationalization expenditure and overseas borrowing to support the pound. However, as a proportion of gross domestic product, the national debt has fallen since 1945 and stabilized at about 40–45%. In the 1970s it stood at over £35,000 million. As a proportion of gross national product, net government debt in the UK has been falling steadily since 1975 when it stood at 58% and by 1988 it was only 45%. By contrast, in Italy, it continued to increase growing from 60% to 110% over the same period.

The US national debt, $2,436,453,269 in 1870, was $1,132,357,095 in 1905, but had risen to $24,299,321,467 by 1920 and it has since risen almost continuously, reaching $1,823,103 million in 1985. In the USA the net government debt as a proportion of gross national product rose steadily in the 1980s from only 19% in 1981 to 31% in 1988, as its borrowing increased to finance a huge influx of imported goods.

National Dock Labour Scheme in the UK a scheme that guaranteed continued employment and pay for dockworkers, even if there was no work to be done; some 9,000 dockworkers were registered under the scheme, which operated from 1947 until its abolition by the Thatcher government in 1989.

National Economic Development Council (NEDC) known as '*Neddy*', the UK forum for economic consultation between government, management, and trade unions. Established 1962, it examines the country's economic and industrial performance, in both the public and private sectors, and seeks agreement on ways to improve efficiency. Its role diminished during the 1980s.

National Front in the UK, extreme right-wing political party founded 1967. It was formed from a merger of the League of Empire Loyalists and the British National Party. In 1980 dissension arose and splinter groups formed. Electoral support in the 1983 and 1987 general elections was minimal. Some of its members had links with the National Socialist Movement of the 1960s (see ◊Nazi Party).

National Gallery London art gallery housing the British national collection of pictures by artists no longer living. It was founded in 1824, when Parliament voted £57,000 for the purchase of 38 pictures from the collection of John Julius, plus £3,000 for the maintenance of the building in Pall Mall, London, where they were housed. The present building in Trafalgar Square was designed by William Wilkins 1778–1839, and opened in 1838: there have been several extensions.

National Guard a ◊militia force recruited by each state of the USA. The volunteer National Guard units are under federal orders in emergencies, and are now an integral part of the US Army. The National Guard have been used against demonstrators; in May 1970 at Kent State University, Ohio, they killed four students who were protesting against the bombing of Cambodia by the USA.

National Health Service UK government medical scheme; see under ◊health service.

National Heritage Memorial Fund government fund established in Britain in 1980 to save the countryside, historic houses, and works of art, as a memorial to those who died on military service during World War II.

national income the total income of a state in one year, comprising both the wages of individuals and the profits of companies. It is equal to the value of the output of all goods and services during the same period. National income is equal to gross national product (the value of a country's total output) minus an allowance for replacement of ageing capital stock.

national insurance in the UK, state social security scheme which provides child allowances, maternity benefits, and payments to the unemployed, sick, and retired, and also covers medical treatment. It is paid for by weekly contributions from employees and employers.

National Insurance Act 1911. UK act of Parliament, introduced by Lloyd George, Liberal chancellor, which first provided insurance for workers against ill-health and unemployment.

Part I of the act introduced compulsory health insurance for all manual workers aged between 16 and 70 and non-manual workers with incomes below 50 a year who did not claim exemption. Part II of the act provided insurance against unemployment for 2 million workers but excluded domestic servants, agricultural workers, and non-manual workers exempt from Part I. The schemes were contributory, with employer, employee, and the state making regular contributions. The act provided for medical assistance and maternity benefits and supplemented recently introduced welfare provisions for disabilities and pensions.

nationalism in music, a 19th-century movement in which composers (such as Smetana and Grieg) included the folk material of their country in their works, projecting the national spirit and its expression.

nationalism in politics, a feeling of solidarity with other people sharing one's ethnic origins, traditional culture, or language; the term describes a movement that consciously aims to unify a nation or to liberate it from foreign rule. Nationalist movements became a potent factor in European politics from the 19th century; since 1900 nationalism has become a strong force in Asia and Africa, and in the late 1980s revived strongly in Eastern Europe.

Stimulated by the French Revolution, movements arose in the 19th century in favour of national unification in Germany and Italy, and advancing national independence in Italy, Ireland, Belgium, Hungary, Bohemia, Poland, and the Balkan states. Revival of interest in the national language, history, traditions, and culture has accompanied and influenced many political movements, for example in Ireland, Czechoslovakia, Poland, and Finland.

In the second half of the 20th century a strongly national literary and political movement has developed in Scotland and Wales.

nationalization policy of bringing a country's essential services and industries under public ownership. It was pursued, for example, by the UK Labour government 1945–51. In recent years the trend towards nationalization has slowed and in many countries (the UK, France, and Japan) reversed (◊privatization). Assets in the hands of foreign governments or companies may also be nationalized, for example Iran's oil industry (see ◊Abadan), the ◊Suez Canal, and US-owned fruit plantations in Guatemala, all in the 1950s.

In the UK acts were passed nationalizing the Bank of England, coal, and most hospitals in 1946; transport and electricity in 1947; gas in 1948; and iron and steel in 1949. In 1953 the succeeding Conservative government provided for the return of road haulage to private enterprise and for decentralization of the railways. It also denationalized iron and steel in 1953, but these were renationalized by the next Labour government in 1967. In 1977 Callaghan's Labour government nationalized the aircraft and shipbuilding industries.

National Liberal Foundation central organization of the British ◊Liberal party, established 1877 in Birmingham. The first president was Joseph Chamberlain.

national park land set aside and conserved for public enjoyment. The first was Yellowstone National Park, USA, established 1872. National parks include not only the most scenic places, but also places distinguished for their historic, prehistoric, or scientific interest, or for their superior recreational assets.

In England and Wales under the National Park Act 1949 the Peak District, Lake District, Snowdonia, and other areas of natural beauty were designated as national parks. Port Hacking, New South Wales, near Sydney, is Australia's chief national park. Of the 30 national parks in Canada, the most notable is Jasper, in the Rockies. The Kruger and Natal national parks were pioneer African examples. An innovation to preserve the national environment is the reservation of ◊wilderness areas, with no motorized traffic, no overflying aircraft, no hotels, hostels, shops or cafés, no industry, and the minimum of management.

National Party, Australian Australian political party representing the interests of the farmers and people of the smaller towns. It developed from about 1860 as the *National Country Party*, and holds the power balance between Liberals and Labour. It gained strength following the introduction of proportional representation 1918, and has been in coalition with the Liberals since 1949.

National Physical Laboratory (NPL) research establishment, set up 1900 at Teddington, England, under the control of the Department of Industry; the chair of the visiting committee is the president of the Royal Society. In 1944 it began work on a project to construct a digital computer, called the ACE (Automatic Computing Engine), one of the first ever built. It was completed in Nov 1950, embodying many of the ideas of Alan ◊Turing

National Portrait Gallery art gallery in London, containing individual portraits of distinguished British men and women. It was founded in 1856 and the present building in St Martin's Place, Trafalgar Square, opened in 1896. In addition to paintings, busts and photographs are displayed.

National Research Development Council UK corporation exploiting inventions derived from public or private sources, usually jointly with industrial firms. It was set up 1967 under the Development of Inventions Acts 1948–65.

National Rivers Authority UK environmental agency launched Sept 1989. It is responsible for managing water resources, investigating pollution controls, and taking over flood controls and land drainage from the former 10 regional water authorities of England and Wales.

National Savings several government savings schemes in the UK, including the National Savings Bank (NSB), which operates through the Post Office; National Savings Certificates; and British Savings Bonds.

national security adviser office of adviser on foreign affairs to the US president and head of the National Security Council, created by President Eisenhower 1953. The national security adviser in 1989 was Lt-Gen Brent Scowcroft, the author of a 1983 weapons report proposing MX missiles.

The office was originally a clerical post, but took on greater stature when held by McGeorge Bundy 1961–66, Walt Rostow 1966–69, and Henry ◊Kissinger 1969–75. ◊Brzezinski, appointed 1977, exceeded Secretary of State Vance in his influence on President Carter. President Reagan's adviser, Admiral John Poindexter, who succeeded Robert McFarlane (1937–) in 1985, was forced to resign 1986 because of scandal surrounding his part in the illicit sale of arms to Iran (see ◊Irangate). He was succeeded by Frank Carlucci (1930–), Lt-Gen Colin Powell (1937–), and Scowcroft.

National Security Agency (NSA) the largest and most secret of US intelligence agencies. Established 1952 to intercept foreign communications as well as to safeguard US transmissions, the NSA collects and analyses computer communications, telephone signals and other electronic data, and gathers intelligence. Known as the Puzzle Palace, its headquarters are at Fort Meade, Maryland (with a major facility at Menwith Hill, England).

The NSA was set up by a classified presidential memorandum and its very existence was not acknowledged until 1962. It operates outside normal channels of government accountability, and its budget (also secret) is thought to exceed several billion dollars. Fort Meade has several Cray supercomputers.

national security directive in the USA, secret decree issued by the president that can establish national policy and commit federal funds without the knowledge of Congress, under the National Security Act 1947. The National Security Council alone decides whether these directives may be made public; most are not. The directives have been criticized as unconstitutional, as they enable the executive branch of government to make laws.

history In 1950 President Truman issued a secret directive for covert operations to foment 'unrest and revolt' in the Eastern bloc. J F Kennedy authorized an invasion of Cuba by this means, and Lyndon Johnson approved military incursions into Laos during the Vietnam War. The US invasion of Grenada and the allocation of 19 million dollars for the CIA to start arming and training Contras in Central America were also authorized by national security directives. Reagan authorized some 300 such directives during his time in office, of which only about 50 have been made known.

National Socialism official name for the ◊Nazi movement in Germany; see also ◊fascism.

National Sound Archive department of the British Library. It now has over 750,000 discs and over 40,000 hours of tapes, ranging from birdsong to grand opera.

National Theatre British national theatre company established 1963, and the complex, opened 1976, that houses it on London's South Bank. The national theatre of France is the ◊Comédie Française, founded 1680.

National Trust British trust founded 1895 for the preservation of land and buildings of historic interest or beauty, incorporated by act of Parliament 1907. It is the largest private landowner in Britain. The National Trust for Scotland was established 1931.

National Westminster Tower building designed by Richard Seifert, located in the City of London, England. It is 183 m/600 ft high, making it London's tallest building, and has 49 storeys. It was completed in 1979 at a cost of £72 million.

native metal a mineral consisting of a metal uncombined with any other element. Copper and silver can be found as native metals.

nativity a Christian festival celebrating a birth: *Christmas* celebrated 25 Dec from AD 336 in memory of the birth of Jesus in Bethlehem; *Nativity of the Virgin Mary* celebrated 8 Sept by the Catholic and Eastern Orthodox churches; *Nativity of John the Baptist* celebrated 24 June by the Catholic, Eastern Orthodox, and Anglican churches.

NATO abbreviation for ◊*North Atlantic Treaty Organization*.

Natron, Lake a salt and soda lake in the Great Rift Valley, Kenya.

natural in music, a sign cancelling a sharp or flat. A *natural trumpet* or horn is an instrument without valves.

Natural Bridge a village in Virginia, USA, 185 km/115 mi W of Richmond. The nearby Cedar Creek is straddled by an arch of limestone 66 m/215 ft high and 27 m/90 ft wide.

Natural Environment Research Council (NERC) UK organization established by royal charter 1965 to undertake and support research in the earth sciences, to give advice both on exploiting natural resources and on protecting the environment, and to support education and training of scientists in these fields of study. Research areas include

geothermal energy, industrial pollution, waste disposal, satellite surveying, acid rain, biotechnology, atmospheric circulation, and climate. Research is carried out principally within the UK but also in Antarctica and in many developing countries. It comprises 13 research bodies: British Antarctic Survey, Freshwater Biological Association, British Geological Survey, Institute of Hydrology, Plymouth Marine Laboratory, Institute of Oceanographic Sciences Deacon Laboratory, Proudman Oceanographic Laboratory, Institute of Virology, Institute of Terrestrial Ecology, Scottish Marine Biological Association, Sea Mammal Research Unit, Unit of Comparative Plant Ecology, and the NERC Unit for Thematic Information Systems.

natural frequency the frequency at which a mechanical system will vibrate freely. A stretched string, for example, always vibrates at the same frequency when struck. This natural frequency depends upon the string's weight and tension.

More complicated systems, such as bridges, also vibrate with a fixed natural frequency. If a varying force with a frequency equal to the natural frequency is applied to such an object the vibrations can become violent, a phenomenon known as ◊resonance.

natural gas a mixture of flammable gases found in the Earth's crust, now one of the world's three main fossil fuels (with coal and oil). Natural gas is a mixture of ◊hydrocarbons, such as methane, ethane, butane, and propane. Before the gas is piped to homes, butane and propane are removed and liquefied to form 'bottled gas'. Natural gas is liquefied for transport and storage, and is therefore often used where other fuels are scarce and expensive.

Test flights of the first aircraft powered by liquefied natural gas began 1989. The craft, made in the USSR, will save 9 tonnes/8.9 tons of kerosene on a journey of 2,000 km/1,250 mi.

Natural History Museum the British Museum (Natural History) in London, containing the departments of zoology, entomology, geology, mineralogy, palaeontology, and botany. The museum is in a building designed by ◊Waterhouse and erected 1873–80 in South Kensington; it has no adminstrative connection with the British Museum. In 1985 the Natural History Museum was merged with the Geological Museum.

natural logarithms in mathematics, the exponent of a number expressed to base e, where e represents the ◊irrational number 2.71828. . . .

Nauru
Republic of

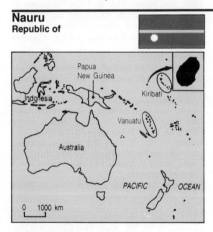

area 21 sq km/8 sq mi
capital Yaren
physical island country in W Pacific
features plateau circled by coral cliffs and sandy beach
head of state and government Hammer DeRoburt from 1987
political system liberal democracy
exports phosphates

currency Australian dollar (2.23 = £1 Feb 1990)
population (1989) 8,100 (mainly Polynesian; Chinese 8%, European 8%); annual growth rate 3.1%
language Nauruan (official), English
religion Protestant 45%
literacy 99%
GDP $155 million (1981); $21,400 per head of population
chronology
1888 Annexed by Germany.
1920 Administered by Australia, New Zealand, and UK until independence, except 1942–45, when it was occupied by Japan.
1968 Full independence achieved, with 'special member' Commonwealth status. Hammer DeRoburt elected president.
1976 Bernard Dowiyogo elected president.
1978 DeRoburt returned to power.
1986 DeRoburt briefly replaced as president by Kenneth Adeang.
1987 DeRoburt returned to power; Adeang established the Democratic Party of Nauru.
1989 DeRoburt defeated on no confidance motion and replaced by Kensas Aroi, who later resigned and was succeeded by Bernard Dowiyogo.

Natural ◊logarithms are also called Naperian logarithms, after their inventor, the Scottish mathematician John Napier.

natural selection the process whereby gene frequencies in a population change through certain organisms producing more descendants than others, because they are better able to survive and reproduce. The accumulated effect of natural selection is to produce ◊adaptations such as the thick coat of a polar bear or the spadelike forelimbs of a mole. It was recognized by Charles Darwin as the main process of ◊evolution.

nature the living world, including plants, animals, fungi, and all microorganisms, and naturally formed features of the landscape, such as mountains and rivers.

Nature Conservancy Council (NCC) UK government agency established by act of Parliament 1973 (Nature Conservancy created by royal charter 1949). It is responsible for designating and managing national nature reserves and other conservation areas, advising government ministers on policies, providing advice and information, and commissioning or undertaking relevant scientific research.

nature–nurture controversy or *environment-heredity controversy* a long-standing dispute among philosophers and psychologists over the relative importance of inheritance ('nature') and experience ('nurture').

nature reserve area set aside to protect a habitat and the wildlife that lives within it, with only restricted admission for the public. A nature reserve often provides a sanctuary for rare species. The world's largest is Etosha Reserve, Namibia; area 99,520 sq km/38,415 sq mi.

The National Parks Act 1949 gave powers to designate such areas in Britain to be placed in the charge of the ◊Nature Conservancy Council.

Naukratis city of Greek traders in ancient Egypt, in the Nile delta, rediscovered by the British archaeologist William ◊Petrie 1884.

Nauru /naʊˈruː/ island country in the SW Pacific, in ◊Polynesia, W of Kiribati.

government The constitution dates from independence in 1968. It provides for a single-chamber parliament of 18 members, elected by universal suffrage for a three-year term, and a president who is both head of state and head of government. The president and cabinet are elected by parliament and responsible to it. The size of the country allows a very intimate style of government, with the president combining several portfolios in a cabinet of only five. Voting in parliamentary elections is compulsory. Traditionally, members of parliament have been elected as independents and then grouped themselves into pro- and anti-government factions. In 1987, however, the Democratic Party of Nauru was formed by the then opposition leader, Kennan Adeang.

history The first Europeans, Britons, arrived 1798 and called it Pleasant Island. The German empire seized it 1888. Nauru was placed under Australian administration by the League of Nations in 1920, with the UK and New Zealand as co-trustees. Japan occupied and devastated Nauru 1942–45, destroying its mining facilities and deporting two-thirds of its population to Truk Atoll in ◊Micronesia, 1,600 km to the NW. In 1947 Nauru became a United Nations trust territory administered by Australia.

Internal self-government was granted 1966 and in 1968, on achieving full independence, Nauru became a 'special member' of the Commonwealth, which means that it does not have direct representation at meetings of heads of government. The head chief of Nauru, Hammer DeRoburt, was elected president in 1968 and re-elected until 1983 with one interruption, 1976–78, when Bernard Dowiyogo was president. The Dec 1986 elections resulted in a hung parliament and the need for fresh polls.

In the 1987 elections, DeRoburt secured a narrow majority. This prompted the defeated Kennan Adeang, who had briefly held power in 1986, to establish the Democratic Party of Nauru as a formal opposition grouping. In Aug 1989 Adeang secured the ousting of DeRoburt on a vote of no confidence and Kensas Aroi became president, with Adeang serving as finance minister in the new government. According to Australian government sources, Aroi was DeRoburt's 'unacknowledged natural son'. Four months later Aroi resigned on the grounds of ill health and in the subsequent election was defeated by Bernard Dowiyogo.

Nauru is attempting to sue its former trustees (New Zealand, the UK, and Australia) for removing nearly all the island's phosphate-rich soil 1922–68, leaving it barren. Nauru received $2.5 million for phosphate worth $65 million and had to pay Australia $20 million to keep the remaining soil. Nauru's residual phosphate supplies, which have earned $80 million a year, are set to run out in 1995 and an economic diversification programme has been launched.

nautical mile unit of distance used in navigation. In the UK it was formerly defined as 1,853 m/6,082 ft; the international nautical mile is now defined as 1,852 m.

nautilus /ˈnɔːtɪləs/ type of ◊cephalopod found in the Indian and Pacific oceans. The *pearly nautilus Nautilus pompilius* has a chambered spiral shell about 20 cm/8 in in diameter. Its body occupies the outer chamber. The nautilus has a large number of short, grasping tentacles surrounding a sharp beak.

The living nautilus is a representative of a group common 450 million years ago. Paper nautilus is an alternative name for the ◊argonaut, a type of octopus.

Nautilus is also the name of the world's first nuclear-powered submarine, launched by the US 1954. It sailed under the ice cap to the North Pole.

Navajo /ˈnævəhəʊ/ North American Indian people, related to the ◊Apache; population about 200,000. They were defeated by Kit ◊Carson and US troops 1864, and were rounded up and exiled. Their reservation, created 1868, is the largest in the USA (65,000 sq km/25,000 sq m), and is mainly in NE Arizona, but extends into NW New Mexico and SE Utah. They earn an income from uranium, natural gas, tourism, rugs and blankets, and silver and turquoise jewellery. They use sand painting to make temporary altars.

Navarino, Battle of /ˌnævəˈriːnəʊ/ a decisive naval action 20 Oct 1827 off Pylos in the Greek war of liberation that was won by the combined fleets of the English, French, and Russians under Vice-Admiral Edward Codrington (1770–1851) over the Turkish and Egyptian fleets. Navarino is the Italian and historic name of Pylos Bay, Greece, on the SW coast of the Peloponnese.

Navarre /nəˈvɑː/ (Spanish *Navarra*) autonomous mountain region of N Spain
area 10,400 sq km/4,014 sq mi
capital Pamplona
features Monte Adi 1,503 m/4,933 ft; rivers Ebro and its tributary the Arga
population (1986) 513,000
history part of the medieval kingdom of Navarre. Estella, to the SW, where Don Carlos was proclaimed king 1833, was a centre of agitation by the ◊Carlists.

Navarre, Kingdom of /nəˈvɑː/ former kingdom comprising the Spanish province of Navarre and part of the French *département* of Basses-Pyrénées. It resisted the Moorish conquest, and was independent until it became French 1284 on the marriage of Philip IV to the heiress of Navarre. In 1479 Ferdinand of Aragon annexed Spanish Navarre, with French Navarre going to Catherine of Foix (1483–1512), who kept the royal title. Her grandson became Henry IV of France, and Navarre was absorbed in the French crown lands 1620.

nave in architecture, the central part of a church, between the choir and the entrance.

navel a small indentation in the centre of the abdomen of mammals, the remains of the site of attachment of the ◊umbilical cord, which connects the fetus to the ◊placenta.

navigation the means of finding the position, course, and distance travelled by a ship, plane, or other craft. Traditional methods include the magnetic ◊compass and ◊sextant. Today the gyrocompass is usually used, together with highly sophisticated electronic methods, such as Decca, Loran, and Omega. These employ beacons that beam out radio signals. Satellite navigation employs satellites that broadcast time and position signals.

The US Global Positioning System, when complete, will feature 18 Navstar satellites that will enable users (including eventually motorists and walkers) to triangulate their position (from any three satellites) to within 15 m/50 ft.

Navigation Acts a series of acts passed from 1381 to protect English shipping from foreign competition, and to ensure monopoly trading between Britain and its colonies. The last was repealed 1849. The Navigation Acts helped to establish England as a major sea power. They ruined the Dutch merchant fleet in the 17th century, and were one of the causes of the War of ◊American Independence.

1650 'Commonwealth Ordinance' forbade foreign ships to trade in English colonies.

1651 Forbade the importation of goods except in English vessels or in vessels of the country of origin of the goods. This act led to the Anglo-Dutch War 1652–54.

1660 All colonial produce was required to be exported in English vessels.

1663 Colonies were prohibited from receiving goods in foreign (rather than English) vessels.

navigation, biological the ability of animals or insects to navigate. Although many animals navigate by following established routes or known landmarks, many animals can navigate without such aids; for example, birds can fly several thousand miles back to their nest site, over unknown terrain. Such feats may be based on compass information derived from the position of the Sun, Moon, or stars, or on the characteristic patterns of Earth's magnetic field.

Biological navigation refers to the ability to navigate both in long-distance ◊migrations and over shorter distances when foraging (for example, the honey bee finding its way from the hive to a nectar site and back). Where reliant on known landmarks, birds may home on features that can be seen from very great distances (such as the cloud caps that often form above isolated mid-ocean islands). Even smells can act as a landmark. Aquatic species like salmon are believed to learn the characteristic taste of the river where they hatch and return to it, often many years later.

Navratilova /ˌnævrætɪˈləʊvə/ Martina 1956– . Czechoslovak tennis player, who became a naturalized US citizen 1981. The most outstanding woman player of the 1980s, she has 52 Grand Slam victories, including 17 singles titles. She has won the Wimbledon singles title eight times, including six in succession 1982–87.

Navratilova was born in Prague, Czechoslovakia. She won her first Wimbledon title 1976 (doubles with Chris Evert). Between 1974 and 1988 she won 52 Grand Slam titles (singles and doubles) second only to Margaret ◊Court. Her first Grand Slam win was mixed doubles at the 1974 French Championship (with Ivan Molina, Colombia).

Navratilova *Martina Navratilova confirmed her position at the top of women's tennis by winning her sixth successive Wimbledon singles title in 1987. She equalled the record held by Helen Wills Moody.*

CAREER HIGHLIGHTS

Wimbledon
singles: 1978–79, 1982–87
doubles: 1976, 1979, 1981–84, 1986
mixed: 1985
US Open
singles: 1983–84, 1986–87
doubles: 1977–78, 1980, 1983–84, 1986–89
mixed: 1985, 1987
French Open
singles: 1982, 1984
doubles: 1975, 1982, 1984–88
mixed: 1974, 1985
Australian Open
singles: 1981, 1983, 1985
doubles: 1980, 1982–85, 1987–89

navy a fleet of ships, usually a nation's ◊warships and the organization to maintain them. The USSR have one of the world's largest merchant fleets, and the world's largest fishing, hydrographic, and oceanographic fleets, in which all ships have intelligence-gathering equipment. In the late 1980s, the UK had a force of small carriers, destroyers, frigates, and submarines.

5th century BC Naval power was an important factor in the struggle for supremacy in the Mediterranean; for example, the defeat of Persia by Greece at Salamis.

311 BC The first permanent naval organization was established by the Roman Empire with the appointment of navy commissioners to safeguard trade routes from pirates and eliminate the threat of rival sea power.

878 Alfred the Great of England overcame the Danes with a few king's ships, plus ships from the shires and some privileged coastal towns.

12th century Turkish invasions ended Byzantine dominance.

13th century The first French royal fleet was established by Louis IX. His admirals came from Genoa.

1339–1453 During the Hundred Years' War there was a great deal of cross-Channel raiding by England and France.

16th century Spain built a large navy for exploration and conquest in the early part of the century. In England, building on the beginnings made by his father Henry VII, Henry VIII raised a force that included a number of battleships, such as the *Mary Rose*, created the long-enduring administrative machinery of the Admiralty, and, by mounting

heavy guns low on a ship's side, revolutionized strategy by the use of the 'broadside'. Elizabeth I encouraged Drake, Frobisher, Hawkins, Raleigh, and other navigators to enlarge the empire.

1571 The Battle of Lepanto was one of the last to be fought with galleys, or oar-propelled ships.

1588 The defeat of the Spanish Armada began the decline of the sea power of Spain.

17th century There was a substantial development in naval power among the powers of N Europe; for example, in the Netherlands, which then founded an empire in the Americas and the East; France, where a strong fleet was built up by Richelieu and Louis XIV that maintained the links with possessions in India and North America; and England, comparatively briefly under Cromwell. In the late 17th century the British overtook the Dutch as the leading naval power.

1775–83 The US navy grew out of the coastal colonies' need to protect their harbours during the War of Independence, as well as the need to capture British war supplies. In late 1775 Washington prepared five schooners and a sloop, manned with army personnel, and sent them to prey on inbound supply vessels. By the time of the Declaration of Independence 1776 these were augmented by armed brigs and sloops from the various colonies. The hero of the period was John Paul Jones.

1805 Effectively reorganized by Pitt in time for the French Revolutionary Wars, the Royal Navy under Nelson won a victory over the French at Trafalgar, which ensured British naval supremacy for the rest of the 19th century.

19th century The US fleet was successful in actions against pirates off Tripoli 1803–05 and the British navy 1812–14, and rapidly expanded during the Civil War and again for the Spanish-American War 1898.

World War I Britain maintained naval supremacy in the face of German U-boat and surface threats.

1918–41 Between the wars the US fleet was developed to protect US trade routes, with an eye to the renewed German threat in the Atlantic and the danger from Japan in the Pacific.

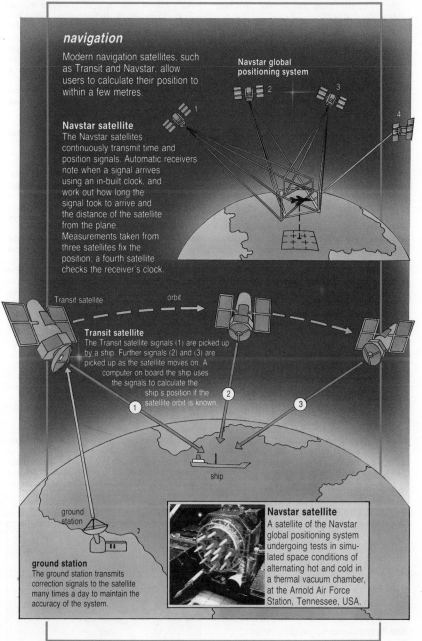

navigation

Modern navigation satellites, such as Transit and Navstar, allow users to calculate their position to within a few metres.

Navstar global positioning system

Navstar satellite
The Navstar satellites continuously transmit time and position signals. Automatic receivers note when a signal arrives using an in-built clock, and work out how long the signal took to arrive and the distance of the satellite from the plane. Measurements taken from three satellites fix the position: a fourth satellite checks the receiver's clock.

Transit satellite
orbit

Transit satellite
The Transit satellite signals (1) are picked up by a ship. Further signals (2) and (3) are picked up as the satellite moves on. A computer on board the ship uses the signals to calculate the ship's position if the satellite orbit is known.

ship

ground station
The ground station transmits correction signals to the satellite many times a day to maintain the accuracy of the system.

Navstar satellite
A satellite of the Navstar global positioning system undergoing tests in simulated space conditions of alternating hot and cold in a thermal vacuum chamber, at the Arnold Air Force Station, Tennessee, USA.

1950s After World War II the US fleet emerged as the world's most powerful.

1962 The Cuban missile crisis (when the USA forced the removal of Soviet missiles from Cuba) demonstrated the USSR's weakness at sea and led to its development under Admiral Sergei Gorshkov.

1980s The Soviet fleets (based in the Arctic, Baltic, Mediterranean, and Pacific) continued their expansion, becoming more powerful than the combined NATO forces. The new pattern of the Soviet navy reflected that of other fleets: over 400 submarines, many with Polaris-type missiles, and over 200 surface combat vessels (mostly of recent date) including helicopter carriers, cruisers, destroyers, and escort vessels. The USA maintained aircraft-carrier battle groups and recommissioned World War II battleships to give its fleet superior firepower, as well as the smaller support vessels.

Naxalite member of an Indian extremist communist movement named after the town of Naxalbari, W Bengal, where a peasant rising was suppressed 1967. The movement was founded by Charu Mazumdar (1915–72).

Naxos /'næksɒs/ an island of Greece, the largest of the Cyclades, area 453 sq km/175 sq mi. Known since early times for its wine, it was a centre for the worship of Bacchus, who, according to Greek mythology, found the deserted Ariadne on its shore and married her.

Nazareth /'næzərəθ/ town in Galilee, N Israel, SE of Haifa; population (1981) 64,000. According to the New Testament, it was the boyhood home of Jesus.

Nazarite a Hebrew under a vow, who in ancient times observed certain rules until it was fulfilled, for example not to cut his hair or to drink wine. ◊Samson and ◊Samuel were Nazarites for life.

Nazca /'næskə/ town south of Lima, Peru, near a plateau that has geometric linear markings interspersed with giant outlines of birds and animals. The markings were made by American Indians, possibly in the 6th century AD, and their function is thought to be ritual rather than astronomical.

Naze, the /neɪz/ headland on the coast of Essex, England, S of the port of Harwich; also the English name for Lindesnes, a cape in S Norway.

Nazi Party German ◊fascist political party. The name is derived from the full name, *Nationalsozialistiche Deutsche Arbeiterpartei* (National Socialist German Workers' Party). It was formed from the German Workers' Party (founded 1919), and led by Adolf ◊Hitler 1921–45. The ideology was based on racism, nationalism, and the supremacy of the state over the individual. During the 1930s, many similar parties were created throughout Europe, although only those of Austria and Sudetenland were of major importance. These parties collaborated with the German occupation of Europe 1939–45. After the Nazi atrocities of World War II (see ◊SS, ◊concentration camp), the party was banned in Germany, but there are parties with Nazi or neo-Nazi ideologies in many countries.

Nazi-Soviet pact see ◊Hitler–Stalin pact.

NB abbreviation for ◊*New Brunswick*; ◊*Nebraska*; *nota bene* (Latin 'note well').

Nazi Party *Brown-shirted girls giving the Nazi salute, 1940.*

NBS abbreviation for *National Bureau of Standards*, the US federal standards organization, to whose technical standards all US government procurement is based.

NC abbreviation for ◊*North Carolina*.

ND abbreviation for ◊*North Dakota*.

N'djamena /əndʒə'meɪnə/ capital of Chad, at the confluence of the Chari and Logone rivers, on the Cameroon border; population (1985) 511,700. Founded 1900 by the French at the junction of caravan routes, it was used 1903–12 as a military centre against the kingdoms of central Sudan. Its name until 1973 was Fort Lamy.

Ndola /ən'dəʊlə/ mining centre and chief city of the Copperbelt province of central Zambia; population (1987) 418,000.

N'Dour /ən'dʊə/ Youssou 1959– . Senegalese singer, songwriter, and musician whose fusion of traditional *mbalax* percussion music with bluesy Arab-style vocals, accompanied by African and electronic instruments, became popular in the West in the 1980s on albums such as *Immigrés* 1984 with the band Le Super Etoile de Dakar.

Neagh, Lough /neɪ/ lake in Northern Ireland, 25 km/15 mi W of Belfast; area 396 sq km/153 sq mi. It is the largest lake in the British Isles.

Neagle /'niːgəl/ Anna 1908–1986. British actress, whose films include *Nell Gwyn* 1934, *Victoria the Great* 1937, and *Odette* 1950. She was made a Dame of the British Empire in 1969.

Neale /niːl/ John Mason 1818–1866. Anglican cleric. He translated ancient and medieval hymns, including 'Jerusalem, the golden'.

Neanderthal hominid of the Palaeolithic period named from a skeleton found in Neanderthal valley near Dusseldorf, West Germany, in 1956. *Homo sapiens neanderthalensis* lived from about 100,000 to 40,000 years ago and was very similar to present-day people, being slightly smaller, stockier, and heavier-featured with prominent brow ridges and a strong jaw. They looked after their disabled and buried their dead carefully. They were replaced throughout Europe by, or possibly interbred with, modern *Homo sapiens sapiens*.

Near East term used until the 1940s to describe the area of the Balkan states, Egypt and SW Asia, now known as the ◊Middle East.

Neath /niːθ/ town in West Glamorgan, Wales, near the mouth of the river Neath; population (1984) 26,000. The Roman fort of Nidum was discovered nearby 1949; there are also remains of a Norman castle and abbey.

Nebraska /nə'bræskə/ plains state of the central USA; nickname Cornhusker State
area 200,400 sq km/77,354 sq mi
capital Lincoln
towns Omaha, Grand Island, North Platte
features Rocky Mountain foothills; tributaries of the Missouri; Boys' Town for the homeless near Omaha; the ranch of Buffalo Bill
products cereals, livestock, processed foods, fertilizers, oil, natural gas
population (1987) 1,594,000
famous people Fred Astaire, Willa Cather, Henry Fonda, Gerald Ford, Harold Lloyd, Malcolm X
history ceded to Spain by France 1763, retroceded to France 1801, and part of the ◊Louisiana Purchase 1803. It was first settled 1847, became a territory 1854, and a state 1867.

Nebraska

Nebuchadnezzar /,nebjʊkəd'nezə/ or *Nebuchadrezzar* II king of Babylonia from 604 BC. Shortly before his accession he defeated the Egyptians at Carchemish and brought Palestine and Syria into his empire. Judah revolted, with Egyptian assistance, 596 and 587–586 BC; on both occasions he captured Jerusalem and carried many Jews into captivity. He largely rebuilt Babylon and constructed the hanging gardens.

nebula a cloud of gas and dust in space. Nebulae are the birthplaces of stars. An *emission nebula*, such as the ◊Orion nebula, glows brightly because its gas is energized by stars that have formed within it. In a *reflection nebula*, starlight reflects off grains of dust in the nebula, such as surrounds the stars of the ◊Pleiades cluster. A *dark nebula* is a dense cloud, composed of molecular hydrogen, which partially or completely absorbs light behind it. Examples include the Coalsack nebula in ◊Crux, and the Horsehead nebula in Orion. Some nebulae are produced by gas thrown off from dying stars; see ◊planetary nebula; ◊supernova.

neck the structure between the head and the trunk in animals. In humans its bones are the upper seven vertebrae, and it has many powerful muscles which support and move the head. In front, it contains the pharynx and trachea, and behind these the oesophagus. Within it are the large arteries (carotid, temporal, maxillary) and veins (jugular) that supply the brain and head.

Necker /'nekə/ Jacques 1732–1804. French politician. As finance minister 1776–81, he attempted reforms, and was dismissed through Queen Marie Antoinette's influence. Recalled 1788, he persuaded Louis XVI to summon the States General (parliament), which earned him the hatred of the court, and in July 1789 he was banished. The outbreak of the French Revolution with the storming of the Bastille forced his reinstatement, but he resigned Sept 1790.

necrosis death of body tissue, usually due to bacterial poisoning or loss of blood supply.

nectar a sugary liquid secreted by some plants from a *nectary*, a specialized gland usually situated near the base of the flower. Nectar often accumulates in special pouches or spurs, not always in the same location as the nectary. It attracts insects, birds, bats, and other animals to the flower for ◊pollination, and is the raw material used by bees in the production of honey.

nectarine smooth, shiny-skinned peach, usually smaller than other peaches and with firmer flesh.

NEDC abbreviation for ◊*National Economic Development Council*.

née (French 'born') followed by a surname, indicates the name of a woman before marriage.

Needham /'niːdəm/ Joseph 1900– . British biochemist and sinologist known for his work on the history of Chinese science. He worked first as a biochemist concentrating mainly on problems in embryology. In the 1930s he learnt Chinese and

nebula *The Orion nebula is located 1,600 light years from Earth and its fan-shaped cloud is 15 light years across.*

began to collect material. The first volume of his *Science and Civilization in China* was published in 1954 and by 1989 15 volumes had appeared.

needlefish long thin-bodied fish of the ◊garfish type, with needle teeth.

Needles, the /'ni:dlz/ a group of rocks in the sea near the Isle of ◊Wight.

Nefertiti /ˌnefə'ti:ti/ or *Nofretète* 14th century BC. Queen of Egypt, who ruled *c.* 1372–1350 BC. She was the wife of the pharoah ◊Ikhnaton.

She disappeared from the records about 12 years after the marriage, and her name was defaced on monuments at some later date. In 1986 a small gold scarab bearing her name, inscribed within the royal cartouche which marks the name of a pharoah, was recovered from an ancient wreck which confirms that she briefly ruled in her own right.

negative/positive in photography, a reverse image, which when printed is again reversed, restoring the original scene. It was invented by ◊Talbot about 1834.

Negev /'negev/ desert in S Israel which tapers to the port of Eilat. It is fertile under irrigation, and minerals include oil and copper.

negligence in law, negligence consists in doing some act which a 'prudent and reasonable' person would not do, or omitting to do some act which such a person would do. Negligence may arise in respect of a person's duty towards an individual or towards other people in general. *Contributory negligence* is a defence sometimes raised where the defendant to an action for negligence claims that the plaintiff by his or her own negligence contributed to the cause of the action.

A person's duty towards an individual may cover parenthood, guardianship, trusteeship, or a contractual relationship; a person's duty towards other people may include the duties owed to the community, such as care upon the public highway, and the maintenance of structures in a safe condition.

Negri Sembilan /'negri sem'bi:lən/ state of S Peninsular Malaysia; area 6,646 sq km/2,565 sq mi; population (1980) 574,000. It is mainly mountainous; products include rice and rubber. The capital is Seremban.

Negro term formerly used to refer to a member of the indigenous people of Africa south of the Sahara, today distributed around the world. The term generally preferred today is ◊black.

Nehemiah /ˌni:ə'maɪə/ 5th century BC. Jewish governor of Judaea under Persian rule. He rebuilt Jerusalem's walls 444 BC, and made religious and social reforms.

Nehru /'neəru:/ Jawaharlal 1889–1964. Indian nationalist politician, prime minister from 1947. He was born in Allahabad and educated at a UK public school and Cambridge University. Before partition he led the socialist wing of the ◊Congress Party, and was second in influence only to Mahatma ◊Gandhi. He was imprisoned nine times 1921–45 for political activities. As prime minister from the creation of the dominion (later republic) of India Aug 1947, he originated the

Nehru *Pandit Jawaharlal Nehru (left) with Mohammed Ali Jinnah, the founder of Pakistan.*

Nelson *British admiral Horatio Nelson won the Battle of Trafalgar 1805, but was mortally wounded.*

idea of ◊nonalignment. His daughter was Indira Gandhi.

Neizvestny /neɪz'vestni/ Ernst 1926– . Russian artist and sculptor, who found fame when he had an argument with Khrushchev in 1962, and eventually left the country 1976. His works include a vast relief in the Moscow Institute of Electronics, and the Aswan monument, the tallest sculpture in the world.

Nejd /nedʒd/ region of central Arabia consisting chiefly of desert; area about 2,720,000 sq km/800,000 sq mi. It forms part of the kingdom of Saudi Arabia, and is inhabited by Bedouins. The capital is Riyadh.

Nekrasov /nɪ'kra:sɒf/ Nikolai Alekseevich 1821–1877. Russian poet and publisher. He espoused the cause of the freeing of the serfs, and identified himself with the peasants in such poems as 'Who Can Live Happy in Russia?' 1876.

Nelson /'nelsən/ Azumah 1958– . Ghanaian featherweight boxer, world champion from 1984.

Nelson won the 1978 Commonwealth Games at featherweight, the World Boxing Championship featherweight title in 1984, beating Wilfredo Gomez, and in 1988 captured the super-featherweight title by beating Mario Martinez.

Nelson /'nelsən/ Horatio, Viscount Nelson 1758–1805. English admiral. He joined the navy 1770. In the Revolutionary Wars against France he lost the sight in his right eye 1794, and his right arm 1797. He became a national hero, and rear-admiral, after the victory off Cape St Vincent, Portugal. In 1798 he tracked the French fleet to Aboukir Bay, and almost entirely destroyed it in the Battle of the Nile. In 1801 he won a decisive victory over Denmark at ◊Copenhagen, and in 1805, after two years of blockading Toulon, another over the Franco-Spanish fleet at ◊Trafalgar, near Gibraltar.

Nelson was born at Burnham Thorpe, Norfolk, where his father was rector. While serving in the West Indies he married Mrs Frances Nisbet. He was almost continuously on active service in the Mediterranean 1793–1800, and lingered at Naples for a year, during which he helped to crush a democratic uprising and fell completely under the influence of Lady ◊Hamilton. In 1800 he returned to England, and soon after separated from his wife. He was promoted to vice-admiral 1801, and sent to the Baltic to operate against the Danes, nominally as second-in-command; in fact, it was Nelson who was responsible for the victory of Copenhagen, and for negotiating peace with Denmark. On his return to England he was created a viscount.

In 1803 he received the Mediterranean command, and for nearly two years blockaded Toulon. When in 1805 his opponent, the French admiral Villeneuve (1763–1806), eluded him, Nelson pursued him to the West Indies and back, and on 21 Oct defeated the combined French and

Spanish fleets off Cape Trafalgar, 20 of the enemy ships being captured. Nelson himself was mortally wounded. He is buried in St Paul's Cathedral, London.

nematode unsegmented worm of the phylum Aschelminthes. Namatodes are pointed at both ends, with a tough, smooth outer skin. They include some soil and water forms, but a large number are parasites, such as the roundworms and pinworms that live in humans, or the eelworms that attack plant roots.

nem. con. abbreviation for *nemine contradicente* (Latin 'with no one opposing').

nem. diss. abbreviation for *nemine dissentiente* (Latin 'with no one dissenting').

Nemerov /'nemərɒv/ Howard 1920– . US poet, critic, and novelist. He published his poetry collection *Guide to the Ruins* 1950, a short story collection *A Commodity of Dreams* 1959, and in 1977 his *Collected Poems* won both the National Book Award and the Pulitzer Prize.

Nemesis in Greek mythology, the goddess of retribution, especially punishing hubris (Greek *hybris*), arrogant self-confidence.

nemesis theory theory of animal extinction, suggesting that a sister star to the Sun caused the extinction of groups of animals such as dinosaurs. The theory holds that the movement of this as yet undiscovered star disrupts the ◊Oort cloud of comets every 26 million years, resulting in the Earth suffering an increased bombardment from comets at these times. The theory was proposed in 1984 to explain the newly discovered layer of iridium—an element found in comets and meteorites—in rocks dating from the end of dinosaur times. However, many palaeontologists deny any evidence for a 26-million-year cycle of extinctions.

nemo me impune lacessit (Latin 'no one injures me with impunity') the motto of Scotland.

Nennius /'neniəs/ *c.* 800. Welsh historian, believed to be the author of a Latin *Historia Britonum*, which contains the earliest reference to King Arthur's wars against the Saxons.

neo- (Greek *neos* 'new') a new development of an older form, often in a different spirit. Examples include *Neo-Marxism* and *Neo-Classicism*.

Neo-Classical economics a school of economic thought based on the work of 19th-century economists such as Alfred Marshall, using ◊marginal theory to modify classical economic theories. Mathematics became extremely important, as did microeconomic theoretical systems. Neo-Classicists believed competition to be the regulator of economic activity which would establish equilibrium between output and consumption. Neo-Classical economics was largely superseded from the 1930s by the work of ◊Keynes.

Neo-Classicism movement in art and architecture in Europe and North America about 1750–1850, a revival of classical art, which superseded the Rococo style. It was partly inspired by the excavation of the Roman cities of Pompeii and Herculaneum. The architect Piranesi was an early Neo-Classicist; in sculpture ◊Canova and in painting ◊David were exponents. Others include Thorvaldsen (sculpture), Ingres (painting), Robert Adam (architecture), Flaxman (art).

neo-colonialism a disguised form of ◊imperialism, by which a country may grant independence to another country but continues to dominate it by control of markets for goods or raw materials. This system was analysed in the Ghanaian leader Kwame Nkrumah's book *Neo-Colonialism, the Last Stage of Imperialism* 1965.

Neo-Darwinism the modern theory of ◊evolution, built up since the 1930s by integrating ◊Darwin's theory of evolution through natural selection with the theory of genetic inheritance founded on the work of ◊Mendel.

Néo-Destour (New Socialist Destour Party) an offshoot of the conservative/liberal Tunisian Destour party that has held power since independence from France after its creation in 1934. Néo-Destour rose to prominence under the leadership of Habib ◊Bourguiba after 1937 and led the rebellion of 1953 which resulted in independence in 1956. Despite party splits during the early 1950s, it has consolidated its position as the country's sole political party.

Neo-Impressionism movement in French painting in the 1880s, an extension of the Impressionists' technique of placing small strokes of different colour side by side. Seurat was the chief exponent; his minute technique became known as *pointillism*. Signac and Pissarro practised the same style for a few years.

Neolithic last period of the ◊Stone Age, characterized by developed communities based on agriculture, and identified by sophisticated stone tools. In W Asia the earliest neolithic communities appeared about 9,000 BC. In Europe farming began in about 6,500 BC in the Balkans and Aegean.

There is evidence of human sacrifice at the neolithic village at Cayonu Tepesi in Turkey. In SW Britain a number of wooden trackways across the Somerset Levels date to around 4,000 BC, and show a sophisticated network of communications for these societies.

neon a chemically inert gaseous element, symbol Ne, atomic number 10, relative atomic mass 20.183. It is extracted by liquefaction and ◊fractionation. It glows bright orange-red in a ◊discharge tube, and is used in lights such as advertisement signs, and in lasers. Neon was discovered by British chemists, W Ramsay and M Travers 1898. It is present in the atmosphere in the proportion 18 parts per million (by volume).

neoplasm literally, a new growth. It is any lump or tumour, which may be benign or malignant (cancerous).

neoprene a ◊synthetic rubber, developed in the USA 1931. It is made from acetylene and hydrogen chloride, and is much more resistant to heat and petrol than ordinary rubber.

Neo-Realism a movement in Italian cinema that emerged in the 1940s. It is characterized by its naturalism, its social themes, and the visual authenticity achieved through location filming. Exponents included the directors de Sica, Visconti, and Rossellini.

neoteny in biology, the retention of some juvenile characteristics in an animal that seems otherwise mature. An example is provided by the axolotl, a salamander that can reproduce sexually although still in its larval form. It has been suggested that new species could arise in this way, and that our own species evolved from its apelike ancestors by neoteny, on the grounds that facially we resemble a young ape.

NEP abbreviation for the Soviet leader Lenin's ◊New Economic Policy.

Nepál /nɪ'pɔ:l/ landlocked country in the Himalayan mountain range, bounded to the N by Tibet, to the E by Sikkim, and to the S and W by India.
government Under the constitution of 1962, amended 1980, Nepál is ruled by a monarch. There is a tiered system of Panchayats (councils) and a one-chamber legislature, the *Rashtriya Panchayat* (National Assembly), of whose members 112 are directly elected every five years and 28 are nominated by the monarch, who may veto its decisions. The Panchayat debates and passes bills and elects a prime minister, who heads and, with the monarch, selects the cabinet. Executive power is exercised by the sovereign and cabinet.
history From one of a group of small principalities, the Gurkhas emerged to unite Nepál under King Prithivi Narayan Shah in 1768. In 1816, after the year-long Anglo-Nepáli 'Gurkha War', a British Resident was stationed in Katmandu and the kingdom became a British-dependent 'buffer-state'. The country was recognized as fully independent by Britain in 1923 although it remained bound by treaty obligations until 1947, the year of India's independence. Between 1846 and 1951 Nepál was ruled by a hereditary prime minister of the Rana

Nepál
(Sri Nepala Sarkar)

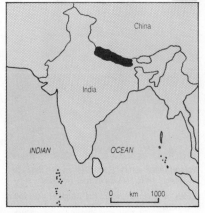

area 147,181 sq km/56,812 sq mi
capital Katmandu
physical descends from the Himalaya mountain range in the N to the river Ganges plain in the S
features Mt Everest, Mt Kangchenjunga
head of state King Birendra Bir Bikram Shah Dev from 1972
head of government Marich Man Singh Shrestha from 1986
government constitutional monarchy
political parties banned from 1961; four opposition parties function unofficially: the Communist Party of Nepál (CPN), Marxist-Leninist-Maoist; the Nepáli Congress Party (NCP), left-of-centre; the United Liberation Torchbearers and the Democratic Front, radical republican
exports jute, rice, timber
currency Nepálese rupee (48.31 = £1 Feb 1990)
population (1989) 18,760,000 (mainly known by the name of the predominant clan, the Gurkhas; the Sherpas are a Buddhist minority of NE Nepál); annual growth rate 2.3%
life expectancy men 47, women 45
language Nepáli
religion Hindu, with Buddhist minority
literacy 39% male/12% female (1985 est)
GNP $2.6 bn (1983); $140 per head of population
chronology
1768 Nepál emerged as unified kingdom.
1815–16 Anglo-Nepáli 'Gurkha War'; Nepál became a British-dependent 'buffer state'
1846–1951 Ruled by the Rana family.
1923 Independence from Britain recognized
1951 Monarchy restored.
1959 Constitution created elected legislature.
1960–61 Parliament dissolved by king and political parties banned.
1980 Constitutional referendum held following popular agitation.
1981 Direct elections held to national assembly.
1983 Overthrow of monarch-supported prime minister.
1986 New assembly elections returned a majority opposed to *panchayat* system.
1988 Strict curbs placed on opposition activity, with more than 100 supporters of banned opposition party arrested and tight censorship imposed.
1989 Border blockade imposed by India in treaty dispute.

family. The Ranas were overthrown in a revolution led by the Nepáli congress, and the monarchy, in the person of King Tribhuvan, was restored to power.

In 1959 King Mahendra Bir Bikram Shah, who had succeeded his father in 1955, promulgated the nation's first constitution and held elections. The Nepáli Congress Party leader B P Koirala became prime minister and proceeded to clash with the king over policy. King Mahendra thus dissolved parliament in Dec 1960 and issued a ban on political parties in Jan 1961. In Dec 1962 he introduced the new constitution with an indirectly elected assembly.

King Mahendra died in 1972. His son Birendra (1945–), faced with mounting agitation for political reform led by B P Koriala, held a referendum on the constitution. As a result, it was amended and the first elections to the National Assembly were held in May 1981. They led to the defeat of a third of the pro-government candidates and returned a more independently minded National Assembly, which in July 1983 unseated Prime Minister Surya Bahadur Thapa, despite his royal support, and installed in office Lokendra Bahadur Chand. Opposition to the banning of political parties has increased in recent years, with terrorist actions in Kathmandu in June 1985. In May 1986 elections to the National Assembly returned a majority of members opposed to the partyless *Panchayat* system and resulted in the replacement of Prime Minister Chand. Four opposition parties function unofficially: the Communist Party of Nepal, the Nepáli Congress Party, the United Liberation Torchbearers, and the Democratic Front.

In foreign affairs, Nepál has pursued a neutral, ◊nonaligned policy, seeking to create a 'zone of peace' in S Asia between India and China. In recent years commercial links with China have increased. This has been resented by India who, in 1989, imposed a partial blockade on Nepál's

borders as part of a dispute over the renegotiation of expired transit and trade duties.

nepenth or *nepenthes* a drug that makes people forget cares or worries, used by ◊Helen of Troy in ◊Homer's Odyssey.

neper unit used in telecommunications to express a ratio of powers and currents. It gives the attenuation of amplitudes as the natural logarithm of the ratio.

nephrectomy surgical removal of a kidney.

nephritis inflammation of the kidneys, usually due to bacterial infection. The degree of illness varies, and it may be acute or chronic, requiring a range of treatments from antibiotics to ◊dialysis.

nephron a microscopic unit in an animal's kidneys that forms urine. Each nephron consists of a filter cup surrounding a knot of blood capillaries and a long, narrow collecting tubule in close association with yet other capillaries. Waste materials and water pass from the bloodstream into the filter cup and essential minerals and some water are reabsorbed from the tubule back into the blood. The urine that is left eventually passes out from the body.

Neptune /'neptjuːn/ in Roman mythology, god of the sea, the equivalent of the Greek ◊Poseidon.

Neptune /'neptjuːn/ in astronomy, the eighth planet in average distance from the Sun. Neptune orbits the Sun every 164.8 years at an average distance of 4,497 million km/2,794 million mi. It is a giant gas (hydrogen, helium, methane) planet with a diameter of 48,600 km/30,200 mi and a mass 17.2 times that of Earth. It has three narrow rings enclosed in a disc of dust that may reach down to the Neptunian cloud tops. Its rotation period is 16 hours 3 minutes. Neptune has two named moons (Nereid and Triton), and six more discovered by Voyager 2 probes.

Neptune was located 1846 by Galle and D'Arrest after calculations by Adams and Leverrier had predicted its existence on the basis that another body must be disturbing the orbit of Uranus. The

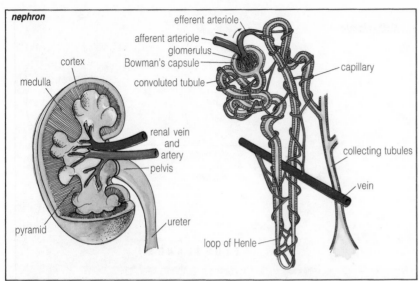

nephron

efferent arteriole
afferent arteriole
glomerulus
Bowman's capsule
convoluted tubule
cortex
medulla
renal vein and artery
pelvis
pyramid
ureter
capillary
collecting tubules
vein
loop of Henle

cameras of ◊Voyager probes, which passed Neptune Aug 1989, revealed a wide variety of cloud features. Notable among these were bright polar collars and broad bands in different shades of blue girdling Neptune's southern hemisphere. The blue colouring results from the absorption of red light by the methane in the atmosphere. Another cloud feature is an Earth-sized oval storm cloud, which has been named the Great Dark Spot, and has been likened to the Great Red Spot on Jupiter. Above and around it, cirrus-type clouds of frozen methane are forming and taking shape, with winds of up to 2,400 kph/1,500 mph. 'The Scooter' is so called because it is a cloud that travels around the planet at a faster rate than the other clouds. Neptune is believed to have a central rocky core covered by a of ice.

Nereid orbits every 360 days on a highly elliptical path; Triton orbits every 5.9 days in an east-to-west retrograde direction and is thought to be similar in nature to the planet Pluto.

neptunium an artificially made element, symbol Np, atomic number 93. Neptunium is a member of the actinide series produced in nuclear reactors by neutron bombardment of uranium. It is radioactive and chemically highly reactive.

NERC abbreviation for ◊**Natural Environment Research Council**.

Nereids in Greek mythology, 50 sea goddesses who sometimes mated with mortals. Their father was Nereus, a sea god, and their mother was Doris.

Nergal /'nɜːgæl/ Babylonian god of the sun, war, and pestilence, ruler of the underworld, symbolized by a winged lion.

Nernst /neənst/ Hermann 1864–1941. German physical chemist. Nernst's investigations, for which he won the 1920 Nobel Chemistry Prize,

were concerned with heat changes in chemical reactions. He proposed in 1906 the principle known variously as the Nernst heat theorem and the third law of thermodynamics. The law states that chemical changes at ◊absolute zero involve no change of ◊entropy.

Born in Briesen, Prussia, Nernst was professor of chemistry at Göttingen 1905, and Berlin. He suffered under the Nazi regime because two of his daughters married Jews.

Nero /'nɪərəʊ/ AD 37–68. Roman emperor from 54. Son of Domitius Ahenobarbus and Agrippina, he was adopted by Claudius, and succeeded him as emperor in 54. He was a poet, connoisseur of art, and performed publicly as an actor and singer. He is said to have murdered his stepfather ◊Claudius' son Britannicus, his own mother, his wives Octavia and Poppaea, and many others. After the great fire of Rome 64, he persecuted the Christians, who were suspected of causing it. Military revolt followed 68; the Senate condemned Nero to death, and he committed suicide.

Neruda /ne'ruːdə/ Pablo. Pen name of Neftalí Ricardo Reyes y Basualto 1904–1973. Chilean poet, diplomat, and communist leader. His work includes lyrics and the epic of the American continent *Canto General* 1950. He was consul

and ambassador to many countries as well as a senator 1945–48.

He went into exile 1948–52 but returned and became consul to France 1971–72. Nobel Prize for Literature 1971.

Nerva /'nɜːvə/ Marcus Cocceius Nerva *c.* AD 35–98. Roman emperor. He was proclaimed emperor on Domitian's death AD 96, and introduced state loans for farmers, family allowances, and allotments of land to poor citizens.

Nerval /neə'væl/ Gérard de. Pen name of Gérard Labrunie 1808–1855. French writer and poet, precursor of French ◊symbolism and ◊surrealism. His writings include the travelogue *Voyage en Orient* 1851; short stories, including the collection *Les Filles du feu* 1854; poetry; a novel *Aurélia* 1855, containing episodes of visionary psychosis; and drama. He lived a wandering life, with periodic insanity, and committed suicide.

nerve a strand of nerve cells enclosed in a sheath of connective tissue joining the ◊central nervous system with receptor and effector organs. A single nerve may contain both ◊motor and sensory nerve cells, but they act independently.

nerve cell an elongated cell (neuron), part of the ◊nervous system, that transmits electrical impulses. A nerve impulse is a travelling wave of chemical and electrical changes which affects the surface membrane of the nerve fibre. Sequential changes in the permeability of the membrane to positive sodium (Na^+) ions and potassium (K^+) ions produce electrical signals called action potentials. Impulses are received by the cell body and passed, as a pulse of electric charge, along the ◊axon. At the far end of the axon, there are ◊synapses where the impulse triggers the release of a chemical ◊neurotransmitter, which stimulates another nerve cell or the action of an effector organ (for example, a muscle). Nerve impulses travel quickly, in humans as fast as 160 m/525 ft per second along a nerve cell.

Nervi /'neəvi:/ Pier Luigi 1891–1979. Italian architect, who used soft steel mesh within concrete to give it flowing form, for example Turin exhibition hall 1949, the UNESCO building in Paris 1952, and the cathedral at New Norcia, near Perth, Australia 1960.

nerve cell

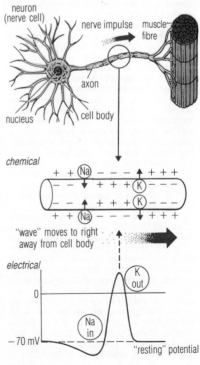

neuron (nerve cell)
nerve impulse
muscle fibre
axon
nucleus
cell body

chemical

$+$ $+$ (Na) $-$ $-$ $-$ $-$ $+$ $+$ $+$
$-$ $-$ $-$ $+$ $+$ $+$ (K) $-$ $-$
$-$ $-$ $-$ $+$ $+$ $+$ (K) $-$ $-$
$+$ $+$ (Na) $-$ $-$ $-$ $-$ $+$ $+$ $+$

"wave" moves to right away from cell body

electrical

0

K out

Na in

−70 mV

"resting" potential

K = potassium   Na = sodium

Neptune *False colour image of Neptune from Voyager 2 which, on 25 Aug 19 89, flew within 4,800 km/3,000 mi of Neptune, after a journey of 7,088 million km/4,430 million mi.*

Neruda *As a poet, Pablo Neruda of Chile identified with the working class from which he came, voicing the dreams and sorrows of his people.*

nervous system the system of interconnected ◊nerve cells of most invertebrates and all vertebrates. It comprises the ◊central and ◊autonomic nervous systems. It may be as simple as the nerve net of coelenterates (for example, jellyfish) or as complex as the mammalian nervous system, with a central nervous system comprising brain and spinal cord, and a peripheral nervous system connecting up with sensory organs, muscles, and glands.

Nesbit /'nezbɪt/ E(dith) 1858–1924. English author of children's books, including *The Story of the Treasure Seekers* 1899 and *The Railway Children* 1906. Her stories often have a humorous magical element, as in *Five Children and It* 1902. *The Treasure Seekers* is the first of several books about the realistically squabbling Bastable children. Nesbit was a Fabian socialist and supported her family by writing.

Ness, Loch /nes/ see ◊Loch Ness.

Nestlé /'neslei/ Henri 1814–1890. Swiss industrialist who established a milk-based baby-food factory in Vevey, Switzerland 1867, Farine Lactée Henri Nestlé. He abandoned all his interest in the business 1875. After various amalgamations and takeovers, the company once more took the name of Nestlé in 1947.

Nestorianism Christian doctrine held by the Syrian ecclesiastic Nestorius (died *c.* 457), patriarch of Constantinople 428–431. He asserted that Jesus had two natures, human and divine. He was banished for maintaining that Mary was the mother of the man Jesus only, and therefore should not be called the Mother of God. His followers survived as the Assyrian church in Syria, Iraq, Iran, and as the Christians of St Thomas in S India.

Netherlands, the /'neðələndz/ country in W Europe on the North Sea, bounded to the E by West Germany and to the S by Belgium.

government The Netherlands is a hereditary monarchy. Its constitution 1983, based on that of 1814, provides for a two-chamber legislature called the States-General, consisting of a First Chamber of 75 and a Second Chamber of 150. Members of the First Chamber are indirectly elected by representatives of 11 provincial councils for a six-year term, half retiring every three years, and Second Chamber members are elected by universal adult suffrage, through a system of proportional representation, for a four-year term. Legislation is introduced and bills amended in the Second Chamber, while the First has the right to approve or reject.

The monarch appoints a prime minister as head of government, and the prime minister chooses the cabinet. Cabinet members are not permitted to be members of the legislature but they may attend its meetings and take part in debates, and they are collectively responsible to it. There is also a council of state, the government's oldest advisory body, whose members are intended to represent a broad cross section of the country's life, and include former politicians, scholars, judges, and business people, all appointed for life. The sovereign is its formal president but appoints a vice president to chair it.

Although not a federal state, the Netherlands gives considerable autonomy to its 11 provinces, each of which has an appointed governor and an elected council.

history The land south of the Rhine, inhabited by ◊Celts and Germanic people, was brought under Roman rule by Julius Caesar as governor of ◊Gaul 51 BC. The ◊Franks followed, and their kings subdued the ◊Frisians and Saxons north of the Rhine in the 7th–8th centuries and imposed Christianity on them. After the empire of Charlemagne broke up, the local feudal lords, headed by the count of ◊Holland and the bishop of ◊Utrecht, became practically independent although they owed nominal allegiance to the German or Holy Roman Empire. Many Dutch towns during the Middle Ages became prosperous trading centres, usually ruled by small groups of merchants. In

Netherlands

the 15th century the Netherlands or Low Countries (Holland, Belgium, Flanders) passed to the dukes of Burgundy, and in 1504 to the Spanish Habsburgs.

The Dutch aspired to political freedom and Protestantism, and rebelled from 1568 against the tyranny of the Catholic Philip II of Spain. William the Silent, Prince of Orange, and his sons Maurice (1567–1625) and Frederick Henry (1584–1647) were the leaders of the revolt and of a confederation established in the north, the United Provinces, which repudiated Spain 1581. The south (now Belgium and Luxembourg) was reconquered by Spain, but not the north, and in 1648 its independence as the Dutch Republic was finally recognized under the Treaty of Westphalia. A long struggle followed between the Orangist or popular party, which favoured centralization under the Prince of Orange as chief magistrate or *stadholder*, and the oligarchical or states' rights party. The latter, headed by John de ◊Witt, seized control 1650, but ◊William of Orange (William III of England) recovered the *stadholderate* with the French invasion 1672.

Despite the long war of independence, during the early 17th century the Dutch led the world in trade, art, and science, and founded an empire in the East and West Indies. Commercial and colonial rivalries led to naval wars with England 1652–54, 1665–67, and 1672–74. Thereafter until 1713 Dutch history was dominated by a struggle with France under Louis XIV. These wars exhausted the Netherlands, which in the 18th century ceased to be a great power. The French revolutionary army was welcomed 1795,

and created the Batavian Republic. In 1806 Napoleon made his brother Louis king of Holland and 1810–13 annexed the country to France. The Congress of ◊Vienna united the N and S Netherlands under King William I (son of Prince William V of Orange) but the south broke away 1830 to become independent Belgium.

Under William I (reigned 1814–40), William II (1840–49), William III (1849–90), and Queen Wilhelmina (1890–1948), the Netherlands followed a path of strict neutrality, but its brutal occupation by Germany 1940–45 persuaded it to adopt a policy of cooperation with its neighbours. It became a member of the Western European Union, the North Atlantic Treaty Organization (NATO), the Benelux customs union, the European Coal and Steel Community, the European Atomic Energy Community (Euratom), and the European Community. In 1980 Queen Juliana, who had reigned since 1948, abdicated in favour of her eldest daughter, Beatrix.

The granting of independence to former colonies (Indonesia 1949, with the addition of W New Guinea 1963; Suriname 1975; see also ◊Netherlands Antilles) increased immigration and unemployment. All governments since 1945 have been coalitions, with the parties differing mainly over economic policies. The three most significant are the Christian Democratic Appeal (CDA, 54 seats in the Second Chamber 1986), the Labour Party (PvdA, 52 seats), and the liberal People's Party for Freedom and Democracy (VVD, 27 seats). The 1987 general election produced another coalition, led by Lubbers, but he resigned after opposition to his anti-pollution proposals. The Sept

Netherlands Antilles

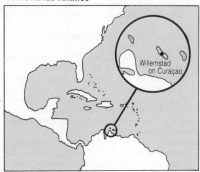

1989 general election produced little change and eventually Lubbers formed another CDA–PvdA-led coalition.

Netherlands Antilles /ˈneðələndz æn'tiliːz/ two groups of Caribbean islands, part of the Netherlands with full internal autonomy, comprising ◊Curaçao and Bonaire off the coast of Venezuela (◊Aruba is considered separately), and St Eustatius, Saba, and the S part of St Maarten in the Leeward Islands, 800 km/500 mi NE
area 797 sq km/308 sq mi
capital Willemstad on Curaçao
products oil from Venezuela is refined here; tourism
language Dutch (official), Papiamento, English
population (1983) 193,000.

Netherlands East Indies former name of ◊Indonesia (1798–1945).

netsuke toggle of ivory, wood, or other materials, made to secure a purse or tobacco pouch, for men wearing Japanese traditional costume. Made especially in the Edo period in Japan 1601–1867, the miniature sculptures are now valued as works of art.

nettle plants of the genus *Urtica*, family Urticaceae. Stinging hairs on the generally ovate leaves can penetrate the skin, causing inflammation. The *common nettle Urtica dioica* grows on waste ground in Europe and North America.

nettle-rash popular name for the skin disorder urticaria.

network in computing, a method of connecting computers so that they can share data and ◊peripheral devices such as printers. The main types are classified by the pattern of the connections, for example, star or ring network; or by the degree of geographical spread allowed, for example, local area networks (LANs) for communication within a room or building, and wide area networks (WANs) for more remote systems.

Netzahualcóyotl /ˌnetsəˌwælkə'jotl/ Mexican city lying to the south of Lake Texcoco, forming a suburb to the NE of Mexico City; population (1980) 1,341,200.

Neubrandenburg /nɔɪ'brændənbɜːg/ county in East Germany; capital Neubrandenburg; area 10,950 sq km/4,227 sq mi; population (1986) 619,000.

Neuchâtel /ˌnɜːʃæ'tel/ (German *Neuenburg*) capital of Neuchâtel canton in NW Switzerland, on Lake Neuchâtel, W of Berne; population (1980) 34,500. It has a Horological (clock) Research Laboratory.

Neumann /'nɔɪmæn/ Balthasar 1687–1753. German Rococo architect and military engineer, whose work includes the bishop's palace in Würzburg.

Neumann /vɒn 'njuːmən/ John von 1903–1957. Hungarian-born US scientist and mathematician, known for his pioneering work on computer design. He invented his celebrated 'rings of operators' (called von Neumann algebras) in the late 1930s, and also contributed to set theory, games theory, cybernetics (with his theory of

Neumann *Hungarian-born mathematician John von Neumann, who made important contributions to quantum physics, logic, metheoric*

self-reproducing automata), and the development of the atomic and hydrogen bombs.

He was born in Budapest and became an assistant professor of physical mathematics at Berlin University before moving to Princeton, USA, 1929, where he later became professor of mathematics. In the early 1940s he described a design for a stored-program computer.

neuralgia pain originating in a nerve. Trigeminal neuralgia is a severe pain on one side of the face.

neurasthenia an obsolete term for nervous exhaustion, covering mild ◊depression and various symptoms of ◊neurosis. Formerly thought to be a bodily malfunction, it is now generally considered to be mental in origin.

neuritis nerve inflammation caused by injury, poisoning, or disease.

neurology the branch of medicine concerned with disease of, or damage to, the brain, spinal cord, and peripheral nerves.

neuron another name for a ◊nerve cell.

neurosis in psychology, a general term referring to emotional disorders, such as anxiety, depression, and obsessions. The main disturbance tends to be one of mood; contact with reality is relatively unaffected, in contrast to ◊psychosis.

neuroticism a personality dimension described by

Netherlands
Kingdom of the
(Koninkrijk der Nederlanden), popularly referred to as **Holland**

area 41,900 sq km/16,178 sq mi
capital Amsterdam
towns The Hague (seat of government); chief port Rotterdam
physical almost completely flat; rivers Rhine, Schelde *(Scheldt)*, Maas; Frisian Islands
territories Aruba, Netherlands Antilles
features land reclamation has turned the former Zuider Zee inlet into the freshwater ijsselmeer
head of state Queen Beatrix Wilhelmina

Armgard from 1980
head of government Rudolph Lubbers from 1982
government constitutional monarchy
political parties Christian Democratic Appeal (CDA), Christian, right-of-centre; Labour party (PVdA), moderate, left-of-centre; People's Party for Freedom and Democracy (VVD), free enterprise, centrist
exports dairy products, flower bulbs, vegetables, petrochemicals, electronics
currency guilder (3.21 = £1 Feb 1990)
population (1988) 14,715,000 (including 300,000 of Dutch-Indonesian origin absorbed 1949–64 from former colonial possessions); annual growth rate 0.5%
life expectancy men 73, women 80
language Dutch
religion Roman Catholic 35%, Protestant 28%
literacy 99% (1985)
GNP $122.4 bn (1984); $9,175 per head of population
chronology
1940–45 Occupied by Germany during World War II.
1947 Joined Benelux Union.
1948 Queen Juliana succeeded Queen Wilhelmina to the throne.
1949 Founder member of NATO.
1958 Joined European Community.
1980 Queen Juliana abdicated in favour of her daughter Beatrix.
1981 Opposition to Cruise missiles averted their being sited on Dutch soil.
1989 Prime minister Lubbers resigned over ecological issue. General election and new Lubbers-led coalition.

Nevada

◊Eysenck. People with high neuroticism are worriers, emotional, and moody.

neurotoxin any substance that destroys nervous tissue.

neurotransmitter a chemical that diffuses across a ◊synapse, and thus transmits impulses between ◊nerve cells, or between nerve cells and effector organs (for example, muscles). Common neurotransmitters are norepinephrine (which also acts as a hormone) and acetylcholine, the latter being most frequent at junctions between nerve and muscle.

Neusiedler See /'nɔɪzi:dləzeɪ/ (Hungarian *Fertö Tó*) shallow lake in E Austria and NW Hungary, SE of Vienna; area 152 sq km/60 sq mi; the only steppe lake in Europe.

Neuss /nɔɪs/ industrial city in North Rhine-Westphalia, West Germany; population (1988) 144,000.

Neutra /'nɔɪtrɑ/ Richard Joseph 1892–1970. Austrian architect, who became a US citizen 1929. His works, often in impressive landscape settings, include Lovell Health House, Los Angeles, and Mathematics Park, Princeton.

neutrality the legal status of a country that decides not to take part in a war. Certain states, notably Switzerland and Austria, have opted for permanent neutrality. Neutrality always has a legal connotation. Neutrality towards the big power alliances is usually called *nonalignment* (see ◊nonaligned movement).

neutralization when the excess acid (or excess base) in a substance is reacted with added base (or added acid) in an amount so that the resulting substance is neither acidic nor basic. In theory neutralization involves adding acid or base as required to achieve ◊pH7. When the colour of an ◊indicator is used to test for neutralization, the final pH may differ from pH7 depending upon the indicator used.

neutrino a very small uncharged elementary particle of minute mass, very difficult to detect and of great penetrating power, emitted in all radioactive disintegrations that give rise to ◊beta rays. Nuclear reactors emit neutrinos.

neutron one of the three chief subatomic ◊particles (the others being the ◊proton and the ◊electron). Neutrons have about the same mass as protons but no electric charge, and occur in the nuclei of all ◊atoms except hydrogen. They contribute to the mass of atoms but do not affect their chemistry, which depends on the proton or electron numbers. For instance, ◊isotopes of a single element (with

New Brunswick

different masses) differ only in the number of neutrons in their nuclei and have identical chemical properties.

Outside a nucleus, a neutron is radioactive, decaying with a ◊half-life of about 12 minutes to give a proton and an electron. The neutron was discovered 1932 by the British chemist James ◊Chadwick.

neutron beam machine a nuclear reactor or accelerator producing a stream of neutrons, which can 'see' through metals. It is used in industry to check molecular changes in metal under stress.

neutron bomb hydrogen bomb that kills by radiation. See ◊nuclear warfare.

neutron star a very small, 'superdense' star composed mostly of ◊neutrons. They are thought to form when massive stars explode as ◊supernovae, during which the ◊protons and ◊electrons of the star's atoms merge to make neutrons. A neutron star may have the mass of up to three Suns, compressed into a globe only 20 km/12 mi in diameter. If its mass is any greater, its gravity will be so strong that it will shrink even further to become a ◊black hole. Being so small, neutron stars can spin very quickly. The rapidly 'flashing' radio stars called ◊pulsars are believed to be neutron stars.

Nevada /nɪ'vɑ:də/ state of the W USA; nickname Sagebrush, Silver, or Battleborn State
area 286,400 sq km/110,550 sq mi
capital Carson City
towns Las Vegas, Reno
physical Mojave Desert, Lake Tahoe, mountains and plateaus alternating with valleys
features legal gambling; Nuclear Rocket Development Station at Jackass Flats NW of Las Vegas: fallout from nuclear tests in the 1950s may have caused subsequent deaths, including that of John Wayne, who was filming there
products mercury, barite, gold, copper, oil, gaming machines
population (1987) 1,053,000
history ceded to the USA after the Mexican War 1848; first permanent settlement 1858; discovery of silver the same year led to rapid population growth; became a state 1864; huge water projects and military installations 20th century.

Nevers /nə've̩/ industrial town in Burgundy, central France, at the meeting of the Loire and Nièvre rivers; capital of the former province of Nivernais and the modern *département* of Nièvre; population (1982) 44,800.

New Age a type of instrumental pop music of the 1980s, often semi-acoustic or electronic; less insistent than rock.

New Amsterdam /'nju: 'æmstədæm/ town in Guyana, on the Berbice, founded by the Dutch; population (1980) 25,000. Also a former name (1624–64) of ◊New York.

Newark /'nju:ək/ largest city (industrial and commercial) of New Jersey, USA; industries (electrical equipment, machinery, chemicals, paints, canned meats); population (1980) 1,963,000. The city dates from 1666, when a settlement called Milford was made on the site.

Newark /'nju:ək/ market town in Nottinghamshire, England; population (1981) 24,000. It has the ruins of a 12th-century castle in which King John died.

Newbolt /'nju:bəʊlt/ Henry John 1862–1938. British poet and naval historian. His works include *The Year of Trafalgar* 1905 and *A Naval History of the War* 1920 on World War I. He is best remembered for his *Songs of the Sea* 1904 and *Songs of the Fleet* 1910 which were set to music by Stanford.

New Britain /nju: 'brɪtn/ largest island in the ◊Bismarck Archipelago, part of Papua New Guinea; capital Rabaul; population (1985) 253,000.

New Brunswick /nju: 'brʌnzwɪk/ maritime province of E Canada
area 73,400 sq km/28,332 sq mi

capital Fredericton
towns Saint John, Moncton
features Grand Lake, St John river; Bay of Fundy
products cereals; wood, paper; fish; lead, zinc, copper, oil and natural gas
population (1986) 710,000, 37% French-speaking
history first reached by Europeans (Cartier) 1534; explored by Champlain 1604; remained a French colony as part of Nova Scotia until ceded to England 1713; after American Revolution, many United Empire Loyalists settled there, and it became a province 1784; one of the original provinces of Confederation 1867.

Newbury /'nju:bəri/ market town in Berkshire, England; population (1981) 26,000. It is noted for its racecourse and training stables, nearby ◊Aldermaston, ◊Harwell and RAF ◊Greenham Common, and its electronics industries.

Newby /'nju:bi/ (George) Eric 1919– . British sailor and travel writer. His books include *A Short Walk in the Hindu Kush* 1958, *The Big Red Train Ride* 1978, *Slowly Down the Ganges* 1966, and *A Travellers Life* 1985.

New Caledonia /'nju: ˌkælɪ'dəʊniə/ island group in the S Pacific, a French overseas territory between Australia and the Fiji Islands
area 18,576 sq km/7,170 sq mi
capital Nouméa
physical fertile, surrounded by a barrier reef
products nickel (the world's third largest producer), chrome, iron
currency CFP franc
population (1983) 145,300, 43% Kanak (Melanesian), 37% European, 8% Wallisian, 5% Vietnamese and Indonesian, 4% Polynesian
language French (official)
religion Roman Catholic 60%, Protestant 30%
history New Caledonia was visited by Captain Cook 1774, and became French 1853. A general strike to gain local control of nickel mines 1974 was defeated. In 1981 the French socialist government promised moves towards independence. The 1985 elections resulted in control of most regions by Kanaks, but not the majority of seats. In 1986 the French conservative government reversed the reforms. The Kanaks boycotted a referendum Sept 1987 and a majority were in favour of remaining a French dependency. In 1989 the leader of the Socialist National Liberation front (the most prominent separatist group), Jean-Marie Tjibaou, was murdered.

Newcastle /'nju:kɑ:səl/ industrial port (iron, steel, chemicals, textiles, ships) in New South Wales, Australia; population (1986) 429,000. The nearby coalmines were discovered 1796. A penal settlement was founded 1804.

Newcastle /'nju:kɑ:səl/ Thomas Pelham-Holles, Duke of Newcastle 1693–1768. British Whig politician. He was secretary of state 1724–54, and then prime minister during the Seven Years' War, until 1762, although ◊Pitt the Elder (1st earl of Chatham) was mainly responsible for the conduct of the war.

Newcastle-under-Lyme /'nju:kɑ:səl ʌndə 'laɪm/ industrial town (coal, bricks and tiles, clothing) in Staffordshire, England; population (1981) 120,100. Keele University is nearby.

Newcastle-upon-Tyne /'nju:kɑ:səl əpɒn 'taɪn/ industrial port (coal, shipbuilding, marine and electrical engineering, chemicals, metals), commercial and cultural centre, in Tyne and Wear, NE England, administrative headquarters of Tyne and Wear and Northumberland; population (1981) 278,000.
features Parts are preserved of a castle built by Henry II 1172–77 on the site of an older castle; the cathedral is chiefly 14th-century; there is a 12th-century church, and the Guildhall 1658. Newcastle is connected with the neighbouring town of Gateshead by several bridges. The headquarters of the Ministry of Social Security is here.

history Chiefly known as a coaling centre, Newcastle first began to trade in coal in the 13th century. In 1826 ironworks were established by George ◊Stephenson, and the first engine used on the Stockton and Darlington railway was made at Newcastle.

Newcomen /'nju:kʌmən/ Thomas 1663–1729. English inventor of an early steam engine. He patented his 'fire engine' 1705, which was used for pumping water from mines until ◊Watt invented one with a separate condenser.

new criticism in literature, a 20th century US movement stressing the pre-eminence of the text without biographical and other external interpolation, but instead using techniques such as statistical counting. The term was coined by J E Spingarn in 1910.

New Deal in US history, programme introduced by President F D Roosevelt 1933 to counter the depression of 1929, including employment on public works, farm loans at low rates, and social reforms such as old-age and unemployment insurance, prevention of child labour, protection of employees against unfair practices by employers, and loans to local authorities for slum clearance. Many of its provisions were declared unconstitutional by the Supreme Court 1935–36, and full employment did not come until World War II.

The *Public Works Administration* was given $3.3 billion to spend on roads, public buildings, and similar developments (the ◊Tennessee Valley Authority was a separate project). The *Agricultural Adjustment Administration* raised agricultural prices by restriction of output. In 1935 Harry L ◊Hopkins was put in charge of a new agency, the *Works Progress Administration* (WPA), which in addition to taking over the public works created something of a cultural revolution with its federal theatre, writers', and arts projects. When the WPA was disbanded 1943 it had found employment for 8.5 million people.

The New Deal encouraged the growth of trade-union membership, brought previously unregulated areas of the US economy under federal control, and revitalized cultural life and community spirit. Although it did not succeed in restoring full prosperity, it did bring political stability to the industrial-capitalist system.

New Delhi see ◊Delhi, capital of India.

New Delhi city in the Union Territory of Delhi, designed by Lutyens; capital of India since 1912; population (1981) 273,000.

New Democratic Party (NDP) Canadian political party, moderately socialist, formed 1961 by a merger of the Labour Congress and the Cooperative Commonwealth Federation. Its leader from 1975, *Edward Broadbent* (1936–), resigned 1989. There are also provincial and territorial New Democratic Parties, which have formed governments in British Columbia, Saskatchewan, Manitoba, and Yukon.

New Economic Policy (NEP) economic policy of the USSR 1921–29 devised by the Soviet leader Lenin. Rather than requisitioning all agricultural produce above a stated subsistence allowance, the state requisitioned only a fixed proportion of the surplus; the rest could be traded freely by the peasant. The NEP thus reinstated a limited form of free-market trading. The state retained complete control of major industries.

The NEP was introduced in Mar 1921 after a series of peasant revolts and the ◊Kronstadt uprising. Aimed at re-establishing an alliance with the peasantry, it began as an agricultural measure to act as an incentive for peasants to produce more food. The policy was ended in 1928 by Stalin's first Five-Year Plan, which began the collectivization of agriculture.

New England region of NE USA, comprising the states of Maine, New Hampshire, Vermont, Massachusetts, Rhode Island, and Connecticut, originally settled by Pilgrims and Puritans from England. It is a geographic region rather than a political entity. The area is still heavily forested

Newfoundland and Labrador

and the economy relies on tourism as well as industry.

New England district of N New South Wales, Australia, especially the tableland area of Glen Innes and Armidale.

New English Art Club British society founded 1886 to secure better representation for younger painters than was given by the Royal Academy. It included ◊Sargent, Augustus ◊John, Paul ◊Nash, Rothenstein, and ◊Sickert.

New Forest ancient forest in S England: see under ◊Hampshire.

Newfoundland breed of dog, said to have originated in Newfoundland. Males can grow to 70 cm/2.3 ft tall, and weigh 65 kg/145 lbs, the females slightly smaller. They are gentle in temperament, and their fur is dense, flat and usually dull black. Dogs that are black and white or brown and white are called Landseers.

Newfoundland and Labrador /'nju:fənlənd, 'læbrədɔ:/ Canadian province on Atlantic Ocean
area 405,700 sq km/156,600 sq mi
capital St John's
towns Corner Brook, Gander
physical Newfoundland island and ◊Labrador on the mainland on the other side of the Straits of Belle Isle; rocky
features Grand Banks section of the continental shelf rich in cod; home of the Newfoundland and Labrador dogs
products newsprint, fish products, hydroelectric power, iron, copper, zinc, uranium, offshore oil
population (1986) 568,000
history colonized by Vikings about AD 1000; the English, under ◊Caboto, reached Newfoundland 1497; colony established 1583; France also made settlements and British sovereignty not recognized until 1713; internal self-government 1855; joined Canada 1949.

It was the first English colony, Humphrey ◊Gilbert taking possession 1583. France retained the offshore islands of St Pierre and Miquelon. In 1934, as Newfoundland had fallen into financial difficulties, administration was vested in a governor and a special commission. A 1948 referendum favoured federation with Canada.

Newgate /'nju:gɪt/ a prison in London, which stood on the site of the Old Bailey central criminal court. Originally a gatehouse (hence the name), it was established in the 12th century, rebuilt after the Great Fire of 1666 and again in 1780, and was demolished 1903. Public executions were held outside it 1783–1868. One of the cells is preserved in the Museum of London.

New General Catalogue a catalogue of star clusters and nebulae compiled by the Danish astronomer John Louis Emil Dreyer (1852–1926) and published 1888. Its main aim was to revise, correct, and expand upon the General Catalogue compiled by John Herschel which appeared 1864.

New Guinea /nju: 'gɪni/ island in the SW Pacific, N of Australia, comprising Papua New Guinea and Irian Jaya (administered by Indonesia); area 775,213 sq km/229,232 sq mi; population (1980) 1,174,000. Part of the Dutch East Indies from 1828, it was ceded by the UN to Indonesia 1963.

New Hampshire

Its tropical rainforest is under threat from logging companies and resettlement schemes.

Newham /'nju:əm/ borough of E Greater London, N of the Thames, includes East and West Ham
features former residents include Dick Turpin and Gerard Manley Hopkins; former Royal Victoria and Albert and King George V docks
population (1984) 209,400.

New Hampshire /nju: 'hæmpʃə/ state of the NE USA; nickname Granite State
area 24,000 sq km/9,264 sq mi
capital Concord
towns Manchester, Nashua
features White Mountains; Mount ◊Monadnock 1,063 m/3,489 ft; the state's ◊primary elections: no president has ever come to office without succeeding here
products electrical machinery, gravel, apples, maple syrup, livestock
population (1987) 1,057,000
famous people Mary Baker Eddy, Robert Frost
history first settled 1623, it was the first colony to declare its independence of Britain. It became a state 1788, one of the original Thirteen States.

Newhaven /nju: 'heɪvən/ port in E Sussex, SE England, with container facilities and cross-channel services to Dieppe, France; population (1985) 11,000.

New Haven /nju: 'heɪvən/ port town in Connecticut, USA, on Long Island Sound; population (1980) 418,000. *Yale University*, third oldest in the USA, was founded here 1701 and named after Elihu Yale (1648–1721), an early benefactor.

New Hebrides /nju: 'hebrɪdi:z/ former name (until 1980) of ◊Vanuatu.

Ne Win /,neɪ 'wɪn/ Maung Shu Maung, 'Brilliant Sun' 1911– . Burmese politician, ruler from 1962 to 1974, president 1984–81.

Active in the nationalist movement during the 1930s, Ne Win joined the Allied forces in the war against Japan in 1945 and held senior military posts before becoming prime minister in 1958. After leading a coup in 1962, he ruled the country as chair of the revolutionary council until 1974, when he became state president. Although he stepped down as president 1981, he continued to dominate political affairs as chair of the ruling Burma Socialist Programme Party (BSPP). His domestic 'Burmese Way to Socialism' policy programme brought the economy into serious decline, and Ne Win was forced to step down as BSPP leader 1988 after riots in Rangoon (now Yangon).

New Ireland Forum a meeting between politicians of the Irish Republic and Northern Ireland May 1983. It offered three potential solutions to the Northern Irish problem, but all were rejected by the UK the following year.

The Forum was the idea of John Hume (1923–), leader of the Northern Irish Social Democratic Labour Party, and brought together representatives of the three major political parties of the republic, including Fianna Fáil and Fine Gael. The Forum suggested three possibilities for a solution

New Jersey

New Mexico

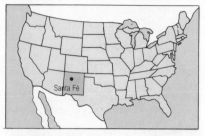

to the Northern Irish problem: unification under a nonsectarian constitution, a federation of North and South, or joint rule from London and Dublin. It recognized that any solution would have to be agreed by a majority in the North, which seemed unlikely. All three options were rejected by the UK government after talks between the British and Irish leaders, Thatcher and Garret FitzGerald, in Nov 1984 (known as the Anglo-Irish summit), although the talks led to improved communication between the two governments.

New Jersey /njuː ˈdʒɜːzi/ state of NE USA; nickname Garden State

area 20,200 sq km/7,797 sq mi

capital Trenton

towns Newark, Jersey City, Paterson, Elizabeth

features coastal resorts, including Atlantic City; Princeton University 1746; Walt Whitman's house in Camden

products asparagus, fruit, potatoes, tomatoes, poultry, chemicals, metal goods, electrical machinery, clothing

population (1985) 7,562,000

famous people Aaron Burr, James Fenimore Cooper, Stephen Crane, Thomas Edison, Alexander Hamilton, Thomas Paine, Paul Robeson, Frank Sinatra, Bruce Springsteen

history colonized in the 17th century by the Dutch, it was ceded to England 1664, and became a state 1787, one of the original Thirteen States.

New London /njuː ˈlʌndən/ naval base and yachting centre of SE Connecticut, USA; on Long Island Sound at the mouth of the river Thames.

newly industrialized country (NIC) a country that has in recent decades experienced a breakthrough into manufacturing and rapid export-led economic growth. The prime examples are Taiwan, Hong Kong, Singapore, and South Korea. Their economic development during the 1970s and 1980s was partly due to a rapid increase of manufactured goods in their exports.

Newlyn /ˈnjuːlɪn/ seaport near Penzance, Cornwall, England, which gives its name to the Newlyn School of artists 1880–90, including Stanhope Forbes (1857–1947). The Ordnance Survey relates heights in the UK to mean sea level here.

Newman /ˈnjuːmən/ John Henry 1801–1890. English Roman Catholic theologian. While still an Anglican, he wrote a series of *Tracts for the Times*, which gave their name to the Tractarian Movement (subsequently called the ◊Oxford Movement). He became a Catholic 1845 and was made a cardinal 1879. In 1864 his autobiography, *Apologia pro vita sua*, was published.

Newman, born in London, was ordained in the Church of England 1824, and in 1827 became vicar of St Mary's, Oxford. There he was influenced by the historian R H Froude and the Anglican priest Keble, and in 1833 published the first of the *Tracts for the Times*. They culminated in *Tract 90* 1841 which found the Thirty-Nine Articles of the Anglican church compatible with Roman Catholicism, and Newman was received into the Roman Catholic Church 1845. He was

rector of Dublin University 1854–58 and published his lectures on education as *The Idea of a University* 1873. His poem *The Dream of Gerontius* appeared 1866, and *The Grammar of Assent*, an analysis of the nature of belief, 1870. He wrote the hymn 'Lead, kindly light' 1833.

Newman /ˈnjuːmən/ Paul 1925– . US actor and director, Hollywood's leading male star of the 1960s and 1970s. His films include *The Hustler* 1962, *Butch Cassidy and the Sundance Kid* 1969, *The Sting* 1973, and *The Color of Money* 1986 (for which he won an Academy Award).

Newmarket /ˈnjuːmɑːkɪt/ town in Suffolk, E England, centre for horse racing since James I's reign, notably the One Thousand and Two Thousand Guineas, the Cambridgeshire, the Jockey Club Stakes and the Cesarewitch. It is the headquarters of the Jockey Club, and a bookmaker who is 'warned off Newmarket Heath' is banned from all British racecourses. The National Horseracing Museum 1983 and the National Stud are here.

New Mexico /njuː ˈmɛksɪkəʊ/ state of the SW USA; nickname Land of Enchantment

area 315,000 sq km/121,590 sq mi

capital Santa Fé

towns Albuquerque, Las Cruces, Roswell

physical more than 75% of the area is over 1,200 m/3,900 ft above sea level; plains, mountains, caverns

features Great Plains and Rocky Mountains; Rio Grande; Carlsbad Caverns, the largest known; Los Alamos atomic and space research centre; White Sands Missile Range (also used by Space Shuttle); Kiowa Ranch, site of D H Lawrence's Utopian colony in the Sangre de Christos mountains

products uranium, oil, natural gas, cotton, cereals, vegetables

population (1987) 1,500,000

famous people Kit Carson

history explored by Spain in the 16th century; most of it was ceded to the USA by Mexico 1848, and it became a state 1912.

New Model Army army created 1645 by Oliver Cromwell to support the cause of Parliament during the English ◊Civil War. It was characterized by organization and discipline. Thomas Fairfax was its first commander.

New Orleans /njuː ˈɔːlɪnz/ commercial and industrial city (banking, oil refining, rockets) and Mississippi river port in Louisiana, USA; population (1980) 557,500. It is the traditional birthplace of jazz.

Founded by the French in 1718, it still has a distinctive French Quarter and Mardi Gras celebrations. The Saturn rockets for Apollo spacecraft are built here. Dixieland jazz exponents still play at Preservation Hall. The Superdome sports palace is among the world's largest enclosed stadiums, and is adaptable to various games and expected audience size.

New Plymouth /njuː ˈplɪməθ/ port on the W coast of North Island, New Zealand; population (1983) 36,500. It lies at the centre of a dairy farming region; Taranaki gas fields are nearby.

Newport /ˈnjuːpɔːt/ river port, capital of the Isle of Wight, England; population (1981) 23,500. Charles I was imprisoned in nearby Carisbrooke Castle.

Newport /ˈnjuːpɔːt/ seaport in Gwent (administrative headquarters), Wales, on the river Usk, NW of Bristol; population (1983) 130,200. There is a steelworks at nearby Llanwern, and a high-tech complex at Cleppa Park. The Newport Transporter Bridge was built 1906.

Newport News /ˈnjuːpɔːt ˈnjuːz/ industrial city (engineering, shipbuilding) and port of SE Virginia, USA, at the mouth of the river James; population (1980) 144,903.

New Québec Crater (formerly *Chubb Crater*) crater discovered 1950 by a prospector, F W Chubb, in N Québec, 96 km/60 mi from Hudson Strait, Canada. Made by a meteor in prehistoric times, it is 411 m/1,350 ft deep, with its rim 168 m/550 ft above the local land level. In the centre is a lake (Crater Lake) 224 m/800 ft deep.

New River an artificial waterway constructed 1613 to bring water to London from Chadwell Springs in Hertfordshire to Islington, London, a distance of 61 km/38 mi. It was built by Hugh Myddleton; under his scheme, private individuals could pay to receive cleaner water than was available from the Thames or Fleet. It was largely rebuilt in the 19th century.

New Rochelle residential suburb of New York on Long Island Sound; population (1980) 70,800.

news agency agency handling news stories and photographs, which are then sold to newspapers and magazines. Major world agencies include Associated Press (AP), Agence France-Presse (AFP), United Press International (UPI), Telegraphic Agency of the Soviet Union (TASS), and Reuters.

Journalists write and edit their material on a VDT (visual display terminal), then press a button to transmit it to the agency headquarters. It is coded to queue at editor's desk in order of priority (such as flash or urgent) for worldwide distribution to individual newspapers. Third World countries dislike the dominance of the agencies, which are accused of 'Western bias', and have attempted to start their own system.

New South Wales /ˈnjuː saʊθ ˈweɪlz/ state of SE Australia

area 801,600 sq km/309,418 sq mi

capital Sydney

towns Newcastle, Wollongong, Broken Hill

physical Great Dividing Range (including Blue Mountains) and part of the Australian Alps (including Snowy Mountains and Mount Kosciusko); Murray, Darling, Murrumbidgee river system irrigates the Riverina district

features a major radio telescope at Parkes, and Siding Spring Mountain 859 m/2,817 ft, NW of Sydney, has telescopes that can observe the central sector of our galaxy. ◊Canberra forms an enclave within the state, and New South Wales administers the dependency of ◊Lord Howe Island

products cereals, fruit, sugar, tobacco, wool, meat, hides and skins, gold, silver, copper, tin, zinc, coal; hydroelectric power from the Snowy river

population (1987) 5,570,000; 60% living in Sydney

history convict settlement 1788–1850, and opened

New South Wales

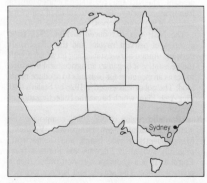

newt

to free settlement by 1819; received self-government 1856; became a state of the Commonwealth of Australia 1901. Since 1973 there has been decentralization to counteract the pull of Sydney, and the New England and Riverina districts have separatist movements. It was called New Wales by James ◊Cook, who landed at Botany Bay 1770 and thought that the coastline resembled that of Wales.

newspaper a daily or weekly publication in the form of folded sheets containing news and comment. News-sheets became commercial undertakings after the invention of printing and were introduced 1609 in Germany, 1616 in the Netherlands. In 1622 the first newspaper appeared in English, the *Weekly News*, edited by Nicholas Bourne and Thomas Archer. By 1645 there were 14 news weeklies on sale in London. Improved ◊printing (steam printing 1814, the rotary press 1846 USA and 1857 UK), newsprint (paper made from woodpulp, used in the UK from the 1880s), and a higher literacy rate led to the growth of newspapers. In recent years, production costs have fallen with the introduction of new technology. The oldest national newspaper in the UK is *The Observer* 1791; the highest circulation UK newspaper is the Sunday *News of the World* (over 5 million copies weekly).

history One of the earliest newspapers, the Roman *Acta Diurna*, said to have been started by the emperor Julius Caesar, contained announcements of marriages, deaths, and military appointments, and was posted up in public places. The first daily in the UK was the subsidized pro-government *Daily Courant* 1702. Arrests, seizure of papers, and prosecution for libel or breach of privilege were employed by the government against opposition publications, and taxes and restrictions were imposed 1700–1820 in direct relation to the growth of radical opinion. The last of these taxes, stamp duty, was abolished 1855.

A big breakthrough was the Linotype machine that cast whole lines of type, introduced in Britain 1896, and better train services made national breakfast-time circulation possible. There were nine evening papers in the London area at the end of the 19th century, and by 1920, 50% of British adults read a daily paper; by 1947, just before the introduction of television, the average adult read 1.2 daily papers and 2.3 Sunday papers; in 1975, only 49% of adults read a daily paper.

The first generation of press barons, ◊Beaverbrook, ◊Northcliffe, and ◊Rothermere in the UK, and ◊Hearst in the USA, used their power to propagate their own political opinions. Newspaper proprietors now may own papers that espouse conflicting viewpoints. For commercial reasons, diminishing choice and increasing monopoly occurs throughout Europe and the USA. Some countries, such as Sweden, have a system of government subsidies to encourage competition.

Newspapers in the first half of the 20th century reinforced the traditional class model of British society, being aimed at upper, middle, or working-class readers. During World War II and until 1958, newsprint rationing prevented market forces from killing off the weaker papers. Polarization into 'quality' and 'tabloid' newspapers followed. Sales of national newspapers that have closed, such as the *News Chronicle*, were over 1 million; they were popular with the public but not with advertisers. Papers with smaller circulation, such as *The Times* and the *Independent*, survive because their

readership is comparatively well off, so advertising space can be sold at higher rates. The *Guardian* is owned by a nonprofit trust. Colour supplements have proliferated since their introduction by some Sunday papers in the 1960s. The mass-circulation papers have huge sales boosted by lotteries and photographs of women in states of undress; their news content is small. Some of them claim not to be newspapers in the traditional sense; their editorial policy is to entertain rather than inform.

British newspapers cover a political spectrum from the moderate left to the far right. Investigative reporting is restricted by stringent laws of libel and contempt of court and by the Official Secrets Act. The Press Council was established 1953 to foster 'integrity and a sense of responsibility to the public', but has no power to enforce its recommendations. In Dec 1989 all major national newspapers agreed on a new code of conduct to prevent possible new legislation by instituting a right of reply, a readers representative and prompt correction of mistakes.

newt a salamander, one of the tailed ◊amphibians of the genus *Triturus*, found in Europe, Asia, and North America. The **smooth newt** *Triturus vulgaris* is about 5 cm/2 in long plus a 4 cm/1.6 in tail. It is olive, spotted in the breeding male, and the underside is orange with blotches. It eats small invertebrates and fish.

New Testament the second part of the ◊Bible, recognized by the Christian church from the 4th century as sacred doctrine. The New Testament includes the Gospels, which tell of the life and teachings of Jesus, the history of the early church, teachings of St Paul, and mystical writings. It was written in Greek during the 1st and 2nd centuries AD, and the individual sections have been ascribed to various authors.

newton /'njuːtn/ SI unit (symbol N) of ◊force. One newton is the force needed to accelerate an object with mass 1 kg by 1 metre per second per second. To accelerate a car weighing 1,000 kg from 0 to 60 mph in 30 seconds would take about 2.5×10^5 N.

Newton /'njuːtn/ Isaac 1642–1727. English physicist and mathematician, who discovered the law of gravity, created calculus, discovered that white light is composed of many colours, and developed the three standard laws of motion still in use today. During 1665–66, he discovered the binomial theorem, differential and integral calculus, and also began to investigate the phenomenon of gravitation. In 1685, he expounded his universal law of gravitation. His greatest work, *Philosophiae Naturalis Principia Mathematica*, was published in three volumes 1686–87, with the aid of Edmund ◊Halley.

Newton's universal law of gravitation was 'Every particle of matter in the universe attracts every other particle with a force whose direction is that of the line joining the two, and whose magnitude is directly as (proportional to) the product of the masses, and inversely as (proportional to) the square of their distance from each other'. His *Opticks* 1704 proved that white light could be separated by refraction, into various colours.

Newton *Portrait of Isaac Newton by Godfrey Kneller (1702) National Portrait Gallery, London.*

Newton laid the foundation of physics as a modern discipline. Born at Woolsthorpe, Lincolnshire, he was educated at Grantham grammar school and Trinity College, Cambridge, of which he became a Fellow in 1667. He was elected a Fellow of the Royal Society in 1672, and soon afterwards published his *New Theory about Light and Colours. De Motu corporum in gyrum/On the motion of bodies in orbit* was written in 1684. Newton resisted James II's attacks on the liberties of the universities, and sat in the parliaments of 1689 and 1701/1702 as a Whig. Appointed Warden of the Royal Mint in 1695, and Master in 1699, he carried through a reform of the coinage. He was elected president of the Royal Society in 1703, and was knighted in 1705. Most of the last 30 years of his life were taken up by studies and experiments in alchemy. He was buried in Westminster Abbey.

Newtonian physics ◊physics based on the concepts of Isaac Newton, before the formulation of ◊quantum theory or ◊relativity theory.

Newton's laws of motion in physics, three laws that form the basis of Newtonian mechanics. (1) Unless acted upon by a net force, a body at rest stays at rest, and a moving body continues moving at the same speed in the same straight line. (2) A net force applied to a body gives it a rate of change of ◊momentum proportional to the force and in the direction of the force. (3) When a body A exerts a force on a body B, B exerts an equal and opposite force on A, that is, to every action there is an equal and opposite reaction.

Newton's rings in optics, an ◊interference phenomenon seen (using white light) as concentric rings of spectral colours where light passes through a thin film of transparent medium, such as the wedge of air between a large-radius convex lens and a flat glass plate. With monochromatic light (light of a single wavelength), the rings take the form of alternate light and dark bands. They are caused by interference (interaction) between light rays reflected from the plate and those reflected from the curved surface of the lens.

new town in the UK, a town either newly established or greatly enlarged after World War II, when the population was rapidly expanding and city centres had either decayed or been destroyed. In 1976 the policy, which had been criticized for disrupting family groupings and local communities, destroying small shops and specialist industries, and leading to the decay of city centres, was abandoned.

In order to stimulate employment in depressed areas, 14 new towns were planned 1946–50, with populations of 25–60,000, among them Cwmbran and Peterlee, and eight near London to relieve congestion there. Another 15, with populations up to 250,000, were established 1951–75, but by then a static population and cuts in government spending halted their creation.

New Wave in pop music, a style that evolved parallel to punk in the second half of the 1970s. It shared the urban aggressive spirit but was musically and lyrically more sophisticated; examples are the early work of Elvis Costello in the UK and Talking Heads in the USA.

New Wave (French *nouvelle vague*) French literary movement of the 1950s, a cross-fertilization of the novel (Marguerite Duras, Alain Robbe-Grillet, Nathalie Sarraute) and film (directors

New York

New York *The New York skyline, showing the twin towers of the World Trade Center.*

Jean-Luc Godard, Alain Resnais and François Truffaut).

New World the Americas, so called by Europeans who reached them later than other continents. The term is used as an adjective to describe animals and plants that live in the western hemisphere.

New York /ˌnjuː 'jɔːk/ state of the NE USA; nickname Empire State
area 127,200 sq km/49,099 sq mi
capital Albany
towns New York, Buffalo, Rochester, Yonkers, Syracuse
physical Adirondack and Catskill mountains; Lake Placid; bordering on lakes Erie and Ontario; Hudson river; Niagara Falls; ◊Long Island
features West Point, site of the US Military Academy 1802; National Baseball Hall of Fame, Cooperstown; racing at Saratoga Springs; Corning Museum of Glass 1951, reputedly the world's finest collection, including a portrait head of Amenhotep II of the 15th century BC; Washington Irving's home at Philipsburg Manor; Fenimore House (J F ◊Cooper), Cooperstown; home of F D Roosevelt at Hyde Park, and the Roosevelt Library; home of Theodore Roosevelt; the Adirondacks are noted for their scenery and sporting facilities; Seneca and Cayuga lakes
products clothing, printing, Steuben glass, titanium concentrate, cereals, apples, maple syrup, poultry, meat, dairy products, wine
population (1985) 17,783,000
famous people Henry and William James, Herman Melville, Walt Whitman
history explored by Champlain and Hudson 1609, colonized by the Dutch from 1614, and annexed by the English 1664. The first constitution was adopted 1777, when New York became one of the original Thirteen States.

New York /ˌnjuː 'jɔːk/ largest city in USA, industrial port (printing, publishing, clothing), cultural and commercial centre in New York State, at the junction of the Hudson and East rivers; comprises the boroughs of the Bronx, Brooklyn, Manhattan, Queens, and Staten Island; population (1980) 9,081,000
features the Statue of Liberty stands on Liberty Island (called Bedloe's Island until 1956) in the inner harbour. Skyscrapers include the World Trade Center (412 m/1,350 ft), the Empire State Building (381 m/1,250 ft), and the Art Deco Chrysler Building. St Patrick's Cathedral is 19th-century Gothic. There are a number of notable art galleries, among them the Frick Collection, the Metropolitan Museum of Art (with a medieval crafts department, the ◊Cloisters), the Museum of Modern Art, and the Guggenheim, designed by Frank Lloyd Wright. Columbia University 1754 is the best known of a number of institutions of higher education. Central Park is the largest park
history the Italian navigator Giovanni da Verrazano (c. 1485–c. 1528) reached New York Bay 1524, and Henry Hudson explored it 1609. The Dutch established a settlement on Manhattan 1613, named New Amsterdam from 1626; this was captured by the English in 1664 and renamed New York. During the War of Independence, British troops occupied New York 1776–84; it was the capital of the USA

New Zealand

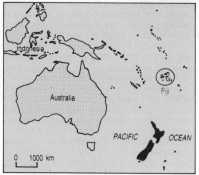

area 268,000 sq km/103,448 sq mi
capital Wellington
towns Hamilton, Palmerston North, Christchurch, Dunedin; ports Wellington, Auckland
physical comprises North Island, South Island, Stewart Island, Chatham Islands, and minor islands; mainly mountainous
overseas territories Tokelau (three atolls transferred 1926 from the former Gilbert and Ellice Islands colony); Niue Island (one of the Cook Islands, but separately administered from 1903: chief town Alafi); Cook Islands are internally self-governing, but share common citizenship with New Zealand; Ross Dependency is in Antarctica
features on North Island are Ruapehu, at 2,797 m/9,180 ft the highest of three active volcanoes, the geysers and hot springs of the Rotorua district, Lake Taupo (616 sq km/238 sq mi), source of Waikato River, and NE of the lake, Kaingaroa state forest, one of the world's largest planted forests. On South Island are the Southern Alps and Canterbury Plains, noted for sheep
head of state Elizabeth II from 1952 represented by Paul Reeves from 1985

head of government Geoffrey Palmer from 1989
government constitutional monarchy
political parties Labour Party, moderate, left-of-centre; New Zealand National Party, free enterprise, centre-right
exports lamb, beef, wool, leather, dairy products and other processed foods; kiwi fruit became a major export crop in the 1980s; seeds and breeding stock; timber, paper, pulp, light aircraft
currency New Zealand dollar (2.88 = £1 Feb 1990)
population (1989) 3,397,000 (including 270,000 Maoris and 60,000 other Polynesians; the whites are chiefly of British descent); annual growth rate 0.9%
life expectancy men 71, women 77
language English (official); Maori (the Lange government pledged to give it official status)
religion Protestant 50%, Roman Catholic 15%
literacy 99% (1984)
GNP $21.4 bn (1984); $7,916 per head of population
chronology
1947 Full independence within the Commonwealth confirmed by New Zealand parliament.
1972 National Party government replaced Labour Party, with Norman Kirk as prime minister.
1974 Kirk died and was replaced by Wallace Rowling.
1975 National Party returned, with Robert Muldoon as prime minister.
1984 Labour Party returned under David Lange.
1985 Non-nuclear defence policy created disagreements with France and the US.
1987 National Party declared support for the Labour government's non-nuclear policy. Lange re-elected. New Zealand officially became a 'friendly' rather than 'allied' country to the US because of its non-nuclear defence policy.
1988 Free-trade agreement with Australia signed.
1989 Lange resigned over economic row with finance minister, and was replaced by Geoffrey Palmer.

1785–89. The five boroughs were linked 1898 to give the city its present extent.

New Yorker, the sophisticated US weekly magazine founded 1925 by Harold Ross (1892–1951), noted for its long, well-informed general articles, literary fiction, and cartoons. It has nurtured many important writers, including Dorothy Parker, James Thurber, J D Salinger, John Updike, and S J Perelman.

As editor Ross was succeeded 1952 by William Shawn (1907–   ), who was replaced 1987 by Robert Gottlieb (1931–   ), then president of the publishing firm Knopf, the *New Yorker* having been bought 1985 by the Newhouse conglomerate, owners of Knopf.

New Zealand /ˌnjuː 'ziːlənd/ or *Aotearoa*, country in the S Pacific, SE of Australia.
government New Zealand is a constitutional monarchy. As in Britain, the constitution is the gradual product of legislation, much of it passed by Parliament in London. The governor-general represents the British monarch as formal head of state and appoints the prime minister, who chooses the cabinet. All ministers are drawn from and collectively responsible to the single-chamber legislature, the House of Representatives. This has 97 members, including four Maoris, elected by universal suffrage from single-member constituencies. It has a maximum life of three years and is subject to dissolution within that period.
history New Zealand was occupied by the ◊Polynesian ◊Maoris some time before the

14th century. ◊Tasman reached it 1642 but the Maoris would not let him land. ◊Cook explored the coasts 1769, 1773, and 1777. British missionaries began to arrive from 1815. By the Treaty of Waitangi 1840 the Maoris accepted British sovereignty; colonization began, and large-scale sheep farming was developed. The colony was granted self-government 1853. The Maoris resented the loss of their land and rose in revolt 1845–47 and 1860–72, until concessions were made, including representation in parliament. George Grey, governor 1845–53 and 1861–70 and Radical prime minister 1877–84, was largely responsible for the conciliation of the Maoris and the introduction of male suffrage.

The Conservatives held power 1879–90 and were succeeded by a Liberal government which ruled with trade-union support; this government introduced women's suffrage 1893 and old-age pensions 1898, and was a pioneer in labour legislation. After 1912 the Reform (formerly Conservative) Party regained power, and the trade unions broke with the Liberals to form the Labour Party. The Reform and Liberal parties united to become the National Party 1931. New Zealand became a dominion in the British Empire 1907 and was granted full independence 1931. New Zealand troops had served in the Boer War in South Africa, and more than 100,000 fought in World War I and II. Independence was formally accepted by the New Zealand legislature 1947.

The country has a record of political stability, with the centrist National Party holding office

New Zealand

physical

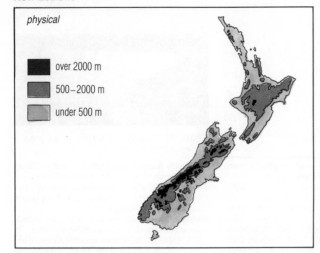

over 2000 m

500–2000 m

under 500 m

population

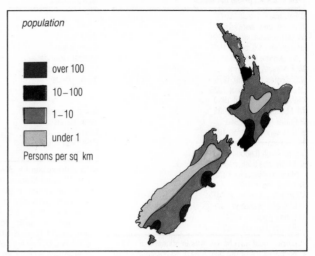

over 100

10–100

1–10

under 1

Persons per sq km

annual rainfall

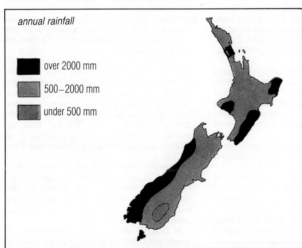

over 2000 mm

500–2000 mm

under 500 mm

land use

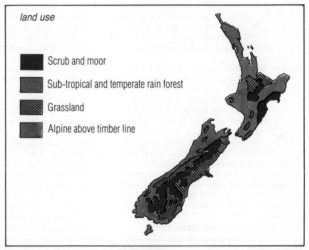

Scrub and moor

Sub-tropical and temperate rain forest

Grassland

Alpine above timber line

from the 1930s until it was replaced by a Labour Party administration, led by Norman Kirk, in 1972. During this period New Zealand built up a good social-security system. The economy was thriving at the time Kirk took office, but growing inflation was aggravated by the 1973–74 energy crisis which resulted in a balance-of-payments deficit. The Labour government's foreign-policy line was influenced by the UK's decision to join the European Community, which was likely to affect New Zealand's future exports. It began a phased withdrawal from some of the country's military commitments in SE Asia and established diplomatic relations with China. Norman Kirk died Aug 1974 and was succeeded by the finance minister, Wallace Rowling. The state of the economy worsened and in 1975 the National Party, led by Robert ◊Muldoon, was returned to power. However, the economy failed to revive and in 1984 Muldoon introduced controversial labour legislation. To renew his mandate, he called an early election but was swept out of office by the Labour Party.

The Labour Party elected Aug 1987 (with the same majority as in the previous parliament) had fought the election on a non-nuclear defence policy, which its leader David Lange immediately put into effect, forbidding any vessels carrying nuclear weapons or powered by nuclear energy from entering New Zealand's ports. This put a great strain on relations with the USA. In 1985 the trawler *Rainbow Warrior*, the flagship of the environmentalist pressure group ◊Greenpeace, which was monitoring nuclear tests in French Polynesia, was mined in Auckland harbour, with loss of life,

by French secret-service agents. The French prime minister eventually admitted responsibility and New Zealand demanded compensation.

There are currently seven active political parties. James McLay was leader of the National Party 1984–86, replaced by James Bolger. In the 1984 general election Labour won 56 seats in the House and the National Party 37. In July 1987 the National Party gave its support to the government in a bi-partisan non-nuclear policy, and as a result the US re-classified New Zealand as a 'friendly', rather than an 'allied' country. In Aug Lange was re-elected with a majority of 17. He later resigned and was replaced by Geoffrey Palmer.

New Zealand literature prose and poetry of New Zealand. Among interesting pioneer records are those of Edward Jerningham Wakefield and F E Maning; and *A First Year in Canterbury Settlement* by Samuel ◊Butler. Earliest of the popular poets was Thomas Bracken, author of the New Zealand national song, followed by native-born Jessie Mackay and W Pember Reeves, though the latter is better known as the author of the prose account of New Zealand *The Long White Cloud*; and Ursula Bethell (1874–1945). In the 20th century New Zealand literature gained an international appeal with the short stories of Katherine ◊Mansfield, produced an excellent exponent of detective fiction in Dame Ngaio ◊Marsh, and struck a specifically New Zealand note in *Tutira, the Story of a New Zealand Sheep Station* 1926, by W H Guthrie Smith (1861–1940). Poetry of a new quality was written by R A K Mason (1905–71) in the 1920s, and in the 1930s by a group of which A R D Fairburn (1904–57) with a witty

conversational turn, and Allen Curnow (1911–), poet, critic, and anthologist, are the most striking. In fiction the 1930s were remarkable for the short stories of Frank Sargeson (1903–) and Roderick Finlayson (1904–), and the talent of John Mulgan (1911–45), who is remembered both for his novel *Man Alone*, and for his posthumous factual account of the war in which he died, *Report on Experience* 1947. Kendrick Smithyman (1922–) struck a metaphysical note in poetry, James K Baxter (1926–) published fluent lyrics, and Janet Frame (1924–) has a brooding depth of meaning in such novels as *The Rainbirds* 1968, and *Intensive Care* 1970. In 1985 Keri Hulme (1947–) won the Booker Prize for her novel *The Bone People*.

Ney /neɪ/ Michael, Duke of Elchingen, Prince of Ney 1769–1815. Marshal of France under ◊Napoleon I, who commanded the rearguard of the French army during the retreat from Moscow, and for his personal courage was called 'the bravest of the brave'. When Napoleon returned from Elba, Ney was sent to arrest him, but instead deserted to him and fought at Waterloo. He was subsequently shot for treason.

The son of a cooper, he joined the army in 1788, and rose from the ranks. He served throughout the Revolutionary and Napoleonic Wars.

NF abbreviation for ◊*Newfoundland*.

Ngorongoro Crater /əŋˌgɒrəŋˈgɒrəʊ/ crater in the Tanzanian section of the African Great Rift Valley noted for its large numbers of wildebeests, gazelle, and zebra.

Ngugi wa Thiong'o /əŋˈguːgi wɑː θiˈɒŋgəʊ/ 1938– . Kenyan writer of essays, plays, short

New Zealand: prime ministers

J Ballance (Liberal) 1891
R J Seddon (Liberal) 1893
W Hall-Jones (Liberal) 1906
Joseph Ward (Liberal) 1906
T MacKenzie (Liberal) 1912
W F Massey (Reform) 1912
J G Coates (Reform) 1925
Joseph Ward (United) 1928
G W Forbes (United) 1930
M J Savage (Labour) 1935
P Fraser (Labour) 1940
S G Holland (National) 1949
K J Holyoake (National) 1957
Walter Nash (Labour) 1957
K J Holyoake (National) 1960
J Marshall (National) 1972
N Kirk (Labour) 1972
W Rowling (Labour) 1974
R Muldoon (National) 1975
D Lange (Labour) 1984
G Palmer (Labour) 1989

stories, and novels. He was imprisoned after the performance of the play *Ngaahika Ndeenda/I Will Marry When I Want* 1977, and lived in exile from 1982. His novels, written in English and Gikuyu, include *The River Between, Petals of Blood*, and *Caitaani Mutharaba-ini/Devil on the Cross*, and deal with colonial and post-independence oppression.

Nguyen Van Linh /'nu:jən væn 'lɪn/ 1914– . Vietnamese communist politician, member of the Politburo 1976–81 and from 1985; party leader from 1986. He began economic liberalization and troop withdrawal from Kampuchea and Laos.

Nguyen, born in North Vietnam, joined the anti-colonial Thanh Nien, a forerunner of the current Communist Party of Vietnam (CPV), in Haiphong 1929. He spent much of his subsequent party career in the South as a pragmatic reformer. He was a member of CPV's Politburo and secretariat 1976–81, suffered a temporary setback when party conservatives gained the ascendancy, and re-entered the Politburo 1985, becoming CPV leader Dec 1986.

NH abbreviation for ◊*New Hampshire*.

Nicaragua
Republic of
(República de Nicaragua)

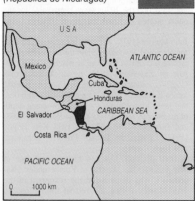

area 127,849 sq km/49,350 sq mi
capital Managua
towns chief port Corinto
physical volcanic mountain ranges; lakes Nicaragua and Managua
features largest state of Central America and most thinly populated
head of state and government from Apr 1990 Violeta Barios de Chamorro
political system emergent democracy
political parties Sandinista National Liberation Front (FSLN), Marxist-Leninist; Democratic Conservative Party (PCD), centrist; National

New Zealand

	Area in sq km
North Island	114,700
South Island	149,800
Chatham Islands	960
Stewart Island	1,750
minor islands	823
	268,033
Island Territories	
Cook Islands	290
Niue	260
Ross Dependency	450,000
Tokelau	10

NHS abbreviation for *National Health Service*, the UK state-financed ◊health service.

niacin one of the 'B group' ◊vitamins, deficiency of which gives rise to ◊pellagra. Niacin is the collective name for compounds that satisfy the dietary need for this function. Nicotinic acid ($C_5H_5N.COOH$) and nicotinamide ($C_5H_5N.CONH_2$) are both used by the body. Common natural sources are yeast, wheat, and meat.

Niagara Falls /naɪ'ægərə/ two waterfalls on the Niagara river, on the Canada–USA border, separated by Goat Island. The *American Falls* are 51 m/167 ft high, 330 m/1,080 ft wide; *Horseshoe Falls*, in Canada, are 49 m/160 ft high, 790 m/2,600 ft across.

On the west bank of the river is *Niagara Falls*, a city in Ontario, Canada; population (1986) 72,000, metropolitan area of Niagara Falls-St Catharines 343,000; on the east bank is *Niagara Falls*, New York State, USA; population (1980) 71,000. They have hydroelectric generating plants and tourism.

Niamey /,nɪə'meɪ/ river port and capital of Niger; population (1983) 399,000. It produces textiles, chemicals, pharmaceuticals, and foodstuffs.

Nibelungenlied anonymous 12th-century German epic poem, *Song of the Nibelungs*, derived from older sources. The composer Richard ◊Wagner made use of the legends in his *Ring* cycle.

◊Siegfried, possessor of the Nibelung treasure, marries Kriemhild (sister of Gunther of Worms)

Opposition Union (UNO), loose, US-backed coalition;
exports coffee, cotton, sugar
currency cordoba (68313.15 = £1 Feb 1990)
population (1989) 3,692,000 (70% mestizo, 15% Spanish descent, 10% Indian or black); annual growth rate 3.3%
life expectancy men 59, women 61
language Spanish (official)
religion Roman Catholic
literacy 61% male/60% female (1980 est)
GDP $3.4 bn (1983); $804 per head of population
chronology
1838 Achieved full independence.
1962 Sandinista National Liberation Front (FSLN) formed to fight Somoza regime.
1979 Somoza government ousted by FSLN.
1982 Subversive activity against the government promoted by the US. State of emergency declared.
1984 The US mined Nicaraguan harbours.
1985 Denunciation of Sandinista government by US president Reagan. FSLN, led by Daniel Ortega Saavedra, won big victory in assembly elections.
1987 Central American peace agreement co-signed by Nicaraguan leaders.
1988 Peace agreement failed. Nicaragua held talks with Contra rebel leaders. Hurricane left 180,000 people homeless.
1989 Demobilization of rebels and release of former Somozan supporters; cease-fire ended.
1990 FSLN defeated by UNO, a US-backed coalition; Violeta Chamorro president from Apr.

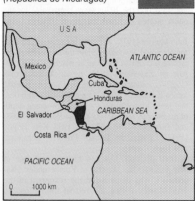

Niagara Falls The 300 m/1,000 ft-wide crest of the US section of the Niagara Falls.

and wins Brunhild as a bride for Gunther. However, Gunther's vassal Hagen murders Siegfried, and Kriemhild achieves revenge by marrying Etzel (Attila) of the Huns, at whose court both Hagen and Gunther are killed.

Nicaea, Council of /naɪ'siːə/ Christian church council held in Nicaea (modern Iznik, Turkey) in 325, called by the Roman emperor Constantine. It upheld the doctrine of the Trinity in the Nicene ◊Creed.

Nicaragua /,nɪkə'ræGjuə/, Spanish /,nɪkə'ra:gwə/ country in Central America, between the Pacific Ocean and the Caribbean, bounded N by Honduras and S by Costa Rica.

government The constitution dates from Jan 1987. The 96-member National Constituent Assembly is elected by universal suffrage through a system of proportional representation, and a president, also popularly elected, serves a six-year term, with the assistance of a vice president and an appointed cabinet. The two main parties are the Sandinista National Liberation Front (FSLN) and the Democratic Conservative Party (PCD).

history For early history, see ◊American Indian. The first European to reach Nicaragua was Gil Gonzalez de Avila 1522, who brought it under Spanish rule. It remained Spanish until 1821 and was then briefly united with Mexico. Nicaragua achieved full independence 1838.

In 1912, at the Nicaraguan government's request, the USA established military bases in the country. Their presence was opposed by a guerrilla group led by Augusto César Sandino. The USA withdrew its forces 1933 but not before it had set up and trained a national guard, commanded by a trusted nominee, Gen Anastasio Somoza. Sandino was assassinated 1934, reputedly on Somoza's orders, but some of his followers continued their guerrilla activity on a small scale.

The Somoza family began a near-dictatorial rule which was to last for over 40 years. During this time they developed wide business interests and amassed a huge personal fortune. Gen Anastasio Somoza was elected president 1936 and stayed in office until his assassination 1956, when he was succeeded by his son Luis. The left-wing FSLN, named after the former guerrilla leader, was formed 1962 with the object of overthrowing the Somozas by revolution. Luis Somoza was followed by his brother Anastasio, who headed an even more notorious regime. In 1979, after considerable violence and loss of life, Somoza was ousted and fled the country. The FSLN established a provisional junta of national reconstruction led by Daniel Ortega Saavedra, published a guarantee of civil rights, and appointed a council of state, prior to an elected national assembly and a new constitution.

Nicaragua's relations with the USA deteriorated rapidly with the election of President Reagan. He froze the package of economic assistance arranged by his predecessor, Jimmy Carter, alleging that the Sandinista government was supporting attempts to overthrow the administration in El Salvador. In Mar 1982 the Nicaraguan government declared a state of emergency in the wake of attacks on bridges and petroleum installations.

Nicholas II *Tsar Nicholas II of Russia in his youth.*

The Reagan administration embarked on a policy of destabilizing Nicaragua's government and economy by actively supporting the counter-revolutionary forces (the Contras), known to have executed prisoners, killed civilians, and engaged in forced conscription, and by covert ◊Central Intelligence Agency operations, including the mining of Nicaraguan harbours 1984. In Feb 1985 Reagan denounced Ortega's regime, saying that his objective was to 'remove it in the sense of its present structure'. In May 1986 Eden Pastora, a Contra leader, gave up the fight against the Sandinistas and was granted asylum in Costa Rica. The following month the US Congress approved $100 million in overt military aid to the Contras.

Political parties were operating again when a large number fought the 1984 election for the new national assembly. The FSLN won 61 seats and the PCD 14. In Aug 1987 a peace plan put forward by US President Reagan was rejected by Nicaragua and, instead, a Central American Peace Agreement, instigated by Costa Rican President Oscar Arias, was signed in Guatemala by leaders of Nicaragua, El Salvador, Guatemala, Honduras, and Costa Rica. In the Feb 1990 elections, President Daniel Ortega's FSLN was defeated by the National Opposition Union (UNO), a loose US-backed coalition led by Violeta Chamorro.

Nicaragua, Lake /ˌnɪkəˈrægwə/ lake in Nicaragua, the largest in Central America; area 8,250 sq km/3,185 sq mi.

Nicaraguan Revolution the revolt 1978–79 in Nicaragua, led by the socialist *Sandinistas* against the US-supported right-wing dictatorship established by Anastasio ◊Somoza. His son, President Anastasio (Debayle) Somoza, was forced into exile and assassinated in Paraguay 1980. The Sandinista National Liberation Front (FSLN) is named after Augusto César Sandino, a guerrilla leader killed by the US-trained National Guard 1934.

Nice /niːs/ city on the French Riviera; population (1982) 449,500. Founded in the 3rd century BC,

it repeatedly changed hands between France and the Duchy of Savoy from the 14th–19th centuries. In 1860 it was finally transferred to France.

There is an annual Battle of Flowers, and chocolate and perfume are made. Chapels in the nearby village of Vence have been decorated by Chagall and Matisse, and Nice has a Chagall museum.

Nicene Creed one of the fundamental creeds of Christianity, promulgated by the Council of ◊Nicaea 325.

niche in ecology, the 'place' occupied by a species in its habitat, including all chemical, physical, and biological components, such as the food supply, the time of day at which the species feeds, temperature, moisture, and the parts of the habitat that it uses (for example, trees or open grassland). Ecological theory holds that two species cannot occupy exactly the same niche and coexist; they will be in direct competition, and one will displace the other.

Nichiren /ˈnɪtʃɪren/ 1222–1282. Japanese Buddhist monk, founder of the sect that bears his name. It bases its beliefs on the *Lotus Sūtra*, which Nichiren held to be the only true revelation of the teachings of Buddha, and stresses the need for personal effort to attain enlightenment.

Nicholas /ˈnɪkələs/ two tsars of Russia:

Nicholas I 1796–1855. Tsar of Russia from 1825. His Balkan ambitions led to war with Turkey 1827–29 and the Crimean War 1853–56.

Nicholas II 1868–1918. Tsar of Russia 1894–1917. He was dominated by his wife, Princess Alix of Hessen, who was under the influence of ◊Rasputin. His mismanagement of the Russo-Japanese War and of internal affairs led to the revolution 1905, which he suppressed, although he was forced to grant limited constitutional reforms. He took Russia into World War I 1914, was forced to abdicate 1917, and was shot with his family by the Bolsheviks at Ekaterinburg July 1918.

Nicholas of Cusa /ˈkjuːzə/ 1401–1464. German philosopher, important in the transition from scholasticism to the philosophy of modern times. He argued that knowledge is learned ignorance (*docta ignorantia*), since God, the ultimate object of knowledge, is above the opposites by which human reason grasps the objects of nature. He also asserted that the universe is boundless, and has no circumference, thus breaking with Middle Ages cosmology.

Nicholas, St /ˈnɪkələs/ also known as *Santa Claus* 4th century. In the Christian church, patron saint of Russia, children, merchants, and sailors; bishop of Myra (now in Turkey). His legendary gifts of dowries for poor girls led to the custom of giving gifts to children on the eve of his feast day, 6 Dec, still retained in some countries, such as the Netherlands, although elsewhere now transferred to Christmas Day. His emblem is three balls.

Nicholson /ˈnɪkəlsən/ Ben 1894–1982. English abstract artist. After early experiments influenced by Cubism and de Stijl, he developed a style of geometrical reliefs, notably a series of white reliefs (from 1933).

Born in Denham, Buckinghamshire, son of William ◊Nicholson, he studied at the Slade, as well as in Europe and in California. He was awarded the Order of Merit 1968. He married the sculptor Barbara Hepworth.

Nicholson /ˈnɪkəlsən/ Jack 1937– . US film actor, who captured in the late 1960s the mood of non-conformist, uncertain young Americans in such films as *Easy Rider* 1969 and *Five Easy Pieces* 1970. He subsequently became a mainstream Hollywood star, appearing in *Chinatown* 1974, *One Flew over the Cuckoo's Nest* 1975, and *Batman* 1989.

Nicholson /ˈnɪkəlsən/ John 1822–1857. British general and colonial administrator in India, born in Ireland. He was administrative officer at Bannu in the Punjab 1851–56, and was allegedly noted for his justness of his rule. Promoted to brigadier general 1857 on the outbreak of the ◊Indian

Mutiny, he defeated resistance in the Punjab, but was killed during the storming of Delhi.

Nicholson /ˈnɪkəlsən/ William 1872–1949. English artist, noted for his development of the poster produced with his brother-in-law, James Pryde, as 'The Beggarstaff Brothers'. He was the father of Ben Nicholson.

nickel a lustrous white metallic element, symbol Ni, atomic number 28, relative atomic mass 58.71. It has a high melting point, low electrical and thermal conductivity, and can be magnetized. Nickel may be forged readily when hot, resists corrosion, and is tough, malleable, and ductile when cold. It is used in coinage and for electroplating and in alloys with iron, steel, copper, and chromium.

It was discovered by Cronstedt 1751, the name being an abbreviation of Swedish *kopparnickel* (false copper). Canada provides the most extensive deposits, which are usually extracted with copper. Finely divided nickel is used as a catalyst in the hydrogenation of vegetable oils.

nickel ore any mineral ore from which nickel is obtained. The main minerals are arsenides such as chloanthite ($NiAs_2$), and the sulphides millerite (NiS) and pentlandite ($(NI,Fe)_9S_8$, the commonest ore. The chief nickel-producing countries are Canada, the USSR, Cuba, and Australia.

Nicklaus /ˈnɪkləs/ Jack (William) 1940– . US golfer, nicknamed 'the Golden Bear'. He won a record 20 major titles, including 18 professional 'majors' 1962–86.

Born in Columbus, Ohio. Nicklaus played for the US Ryder Cup team six times 1969–81 and was non-playing captain 1983 and 1987 when the event was played over the course he designed at Muirfield Village, Ohio. He was voted the Golfer of the Century 1988.

CAREER HIGHLIGHTS

US Amateur: 1959, 1961
US Open: 1962, 1967, 1972, 1980
British Open: 1966, 1970, 1978
US Masters: 1963, 1965–66, 1972, 1975, 1986
US PGA: 1963, 1971, 1973, 1975, 1980
US Ryder Cup team: 1969, 1971, 1973, 1975, 1977.

Nicobar Islands /ˈnɪkəbɑː/ group of Indian islands, part of the Union Territory of ◊Andaman and Nicobar Islands.

Nicolle /nɪˈkɒl/ Charles 1866–1936. French bacteriologist whose discovery in 1909 that typhus is transmitted by the body louse made the armies of World War I introduce delousing as a compulsory part of the military routine.

His original observation was that typhus victims, once admitted to hospitals, did not infect the staff; he speculated that transmission must be via the skin or clothes, which were washed as standard procedure for new admissions. The experimental evidence was provided by infecting a healthy monkey using a louse recently fed on an infected chimpanzee.

Nicolson /ˈnɪkəlsən/ Harold 1886–1968. British diplomat and author. His works include biographies (*Lord Carnock* 1930, *Curzon: The Last Phase* 1934, and *King George V* 1952) and studies such as *Monarchy* 1962, as well as *Diaries and Letters* 1930–62. He married Victoria ◊Sackville-West in 1913.

Nicosia /ˌnɪkəˈsiːə/ capital of Cyprus, with leather, textile, and pottery industries; population (1987) 165,000. Nicosia was the residence of Lusignan kings of Cyprus 1192–1475. The Venetians, who took Cyprus 1489, surrounded Nicosia with a high wall, which still exists; it fell to the Turks 1571. It was again partly taken by the Turks in the invasion 1974. The Greek and Turkish sectors are separated by the Attila Line.

nicotine an ◊alkaloid (nitrogenous compound) obtained from the dried leaves of the tobacco plant *Nicotiana tabacum* and used as an insecticide. It is the component of cigarette smoke that causes bodily addiction.

Nicotine in its pure form is one of the most powerful poisons known. It is named after a

Nicholson *Versatile film actor Jack Nicholson as the Joker in Batman 1989.*

16th-century French diplomat, Jacques Nicot, who introduced tobacco to France. A colourless oil, soluble in water, it turns brown on exposure to the air.

Niebuhr /'niːbuə/ Barthold Georg 1776–1831. German historian. He was Prussian ambassador in Rome 1816–23, and professor of Roman history at Bonn until 1831. His three-volume *History of Rome* 1811–32 used a critical examination of original sources.

Niebuhr /'niːbuə/ Karsten 1733–1815. Danish map-maker, surveyor, and traveller, sent by the Danish government to explore the Arabian peninsula 1761–67.

Nietzsche *Friedrich Nietzsche's writings had a considerable influence on modern literature, philosophy, psychoanalysis, and religion, while his Superman has been considered a prototype for Hitler's ideal Aryan.*

Niebuhr /'niːbuə/ Reinhold 1892–1971. US Protestant Christian theologian. His *Moral Man and Immoral Society* 1932 reflected liberalism for biblical theology and attacked depersonalized industrial society.

Niederösterreich /'niːdər,ɜːstəraɪʃ/ German name for the federal state of ◊Lower Austria.

Niedersachsen /'niːdə,sæksən/ German name for the region of ◊Lower Saxony, West Germany.

nielsbohrium alternative name for the element ◊unnilpentium.

Niger
Republic of
(*République du Niger*)

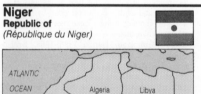

area 1,186,408 sq km/457,953 sq mi
capital Niamey
physical mountains in centre; arid except in S (savanna) and SW (river Niger)
features part of the Sahara Desert and subject to Sahel droughts

Nielsen /'niːlsən/ Carl (August) 1865–1931. Danish composer. His works show a progressive tonality, as in his opera *Saul and David* 1902 and six symphonies. He also composed concertos for violin 1911, clarinet 1928, chamber music, piano works, and songs.

Niemeyer /'niːmaɪə/ Oscar 1907– . Brazilian architect, joint designer of the United Nations headquarters in New York, and of many buildings in Brasilia.

Niemöller /'niːmɜːlə/ Martin 1892–1984. German Christian Protestant pastor. He was imprisoned in a concentration camp 1938–45 for campaigning against Nazism in the German church. and was president of the World Council of Churches 1961–68.

NIEO abbreviation for *New International Economic Order*.

Niepce /njeps/ Joseph Nicéphore 1765–1833. French pioneer of ◊photography.

Nietzsche /'niːtʃə/ Friedrich Wilhelm 1844–1900. German philosopher who rejected the accepted absolute moral values and the 'slave morality' of Christianity. He argued that 'God is dead' and therefore people were free to create their own values. His ideal was the *Übermensch*, or 'Superman', who would impose his will on the weak and worthless. Nietzsche claimed that knowledge is never objective, but always serves some interest or unconscious purpose.

His insights into the relation between thought and language had an important influence on philosophy. Although claimed as a precursor by Nazism, many of his views are incompatible with totalitarian ideology. He is a profoundly ambivalent thinker whose philosophy can be appropriated for many purposes.

Born in Röcken, Saxony, he attended Bonn and Leipzig universities and was professor of Greek at Basel 1869–80. He had abandoned theology for philology, and was influenced by the writings of Schopenhauer and the music of Wagner, of whom he became both friend and advocate. Both these attractions passed, however, and ill health caused his resignation from the university. He spent his later years in N Italy, in the Engadine, and in S France. He published *Morgenröte* 1880–81, *Die fröhliche Wissenschaft* 1881–82, *Also sprach Zarathustra* 1883–85, *Jenseits von Gut und Böse* 1885–86, *Genealogie der Moral* 1887, and *Ecce Homo* 1888. He suffered a permanent breakdown in 1889 from overwork and loneliness.

Nièvre /ni'eɪvrə/ river in central France, rising near Varzy and flowing 40 km/25 mi south to join the Loire at Nevers; it gives its name to a *département*.

Niger /'naɪdʒə/ third longest river in Africa, 4,185 km/2,600 mi from the highlands bordering

head of state and government Ali Seybou from 1987
government military republic
political parties banned from 1974
exports groundnuts, livestock, gum arabic, tin, uranium
currency CFA franc (485.00 = £1 Feb 1990)
population (1989) 7,444,000; annual growth rate 2.8%
life expectancy men 41, women 44
language French (official), Hausa, Djerma
religion Sunni Muslim 85%, animist 15%
literacy 19% male/9% female (1985 est)
GDP $2.3 bn (1982); $475 per head of population
chronology
1960 Achieved full independence from France with Hamani Diori elected president.
1974 Diori ousted in an army coup led by Seyni Kountché.
1977 Cooperation agreement signed with France.
1987 Kountché died and was replaced by the army commander-in-chief Ali Seybou.

Sierra Leone and Guinea NE through Mali, then SE through Niger and Nigeria to an inland delta on the Gulf of Guinea. Its flow has been badly affected by the expansion of the Sahara Desert.

It is sluggish and frequently floods its banks. It was explored by Mungo Park 1795–96.

Niger /'niːʒə/ landlocked country in W Africa, bounded to the N by Nigeria and Libya, to the E by Chad, to the S by Nigeria and Benin, and to the W by Burkina Faso and Mali.

government The 1960 constitution was suspended after a military coup in 1974 and Niger is now ruled by a supreme military council of army officers and a council of ministers appointed by the president, who is head of state as well as head of government and also combines the portfolios of interior and national defence. In a move towards greater democracy, the National Development Council, of 150 elected members, was reconstituted 1983 and given the task of drawing up a national charter. Since 1974 all political parties have been banned.

history Niger was part of ancient and medieval empires in ◊Africa. European explorers arrived in the late 18th century, and Tuareg people invaded the area from the N. France seized it from the Tuaregs 1904 and made it part of French West Africa, although fighting continued until 1922. It became a French overseas territory 1946 and an autonomous republic within the French Community 1958.

Niger achieved full independence in 1960, and Hamani Diori was elected president. Maintaining very close and cordial relations with France, Diori seemed to have established one of the most stable regimes in Africa, and the discovery of uranium deposits promised a sound economic future. However, a severe drought 1968–74 resulted in widespread civil disorder and in Apr 1974 Diori was ousted by the army led by the chief of staff, Lt-Col Seyni Kountché. Having suspended the constitution and established a military government with himself as president, he tried to restore the economy and negotiated a more equal relationship with France through a cooperation agreement 1977.

Still threatened by possible droughts and consequential unrest, Kountché has tried to widen his popular support by liberalizing his regime and releasing political prisoners, including former President Diori. More civilians have been introduced into the government with the prospect of an eventual return to constitutional rule. When Lt-Col Seyni Kountche died in 1987, the Supreme Military Council appointed Colonel Ali Seybou acting president.

Nigeria /naɪ'dʒɪərɪə/ country in W Africa on the Gulf of Guinea, bounded to the N by Niger, to the E by Chad and Cameroon, and to the W by Benin.

government The constitution is based on one of 1979, amended after military coups 1983 and 1985. The president is head of state, commander in chief of the armed forces, and chair of the 28-member Armed Forces Ruling Council (AFRC), composed of senior officers of the army and police force. The AFRC appoints the National Council of Ministers, which is also headed by the president.

Nigeria is a federal republic of 19 states. Each of the states has a military governor, appointed by the AFRC, who in turn appoints and leads a state executive council. There is also a coordinating federal body called the National Council of States, which includes the president and all the state governors. All political parties are now banned.

history Nigeria has been inhabited since at least 700 BC. In the 12th–14th centuries civilizations developed in the Yoruba area and in the Muslim N Portuguese and British slave traders raided from the 15th century (see ◊slavery).

◊Lagos was supposedly bought from a chief by British traders in 1861; in 1886 it became the colony and protectorate of Lagos. The Niger

Nigeria
Federal Republic of

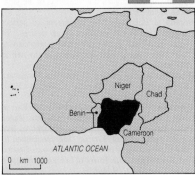

area 923,773 sq km/356,576 sq mi
capital Abuja; chief port Lagos
towns administrative headquarters Abuja;
Ibadan, Ogbomosho, Kano; ports Port
Harcourt, Warri, Calabar
physical the arid north becomes savanna and
farther south tropical rainforest, with mangrove
swamps along the coast; river Niger
features harmattan (a dry wind from the
Sahara); rich artistic heritage, for example
Benin bronzes
head of state and government Ibrahim
Babangida from 1985
government military republic
political parties Social Democratic Party
(SDP), left-of-centre; National Republican
Convention (NRC), right-of-centre

exports petroleum (richest African country in
oil resources), cocoa, groundnuts, palm oil,
cotton, rubber, tin
currency naira (13.33 = £1 Feb 1990)
population (1989) 115,152,000 (of three main
ethnic groups, Yoruba in the W, Ibo in the E,
and Hausa-Fulani in the N); annual growth
rate 3.3%
life expectancy men 47, women 50
language English (official), Hausa, Ibo, Yoruba
religion Sunni Muslim in the north, Christian in
the south
literacy 54% male/31% female (1985 est)
GDP $65 bn (1983); $750 per head of
population
chronology
1960 Achieved full independence within the
Commonwealth.
1963 Became a republic, with Nnamdi Azikiwe
as president.
1966 Military coup, followed by a counter-coup
led by Gen Yakubu Gowon. Slaughter of many
members of the Ibo tribe in the north.
1967 Conflict about oil revenues leads to
declaration of an independent state of Biafra
and outbreak of civil war.
1970 Surrender of Biafra and end of civil war.
1975 Gowon ousted in military coup; a second
coup puts Gen Obasanjo in power.
1979 Shehu Shagari becomes civilian
president.
1983 Shagari's government overthrown in coup
by Maj-Gen Buhari.
1985 Buhari replaced in a bloodless coup led
by Maj-Gen Ibrahim Babangida.
1989 Two new parties approved.

river valley was developed by the National African Company (later the Royal Niger Company),
which came to an end 1899, and in 1900 two
protectorates were set up: North Nigeria and
South Nigeria, with Lagos joined to South Nigeria
1906. Britain's largest African colony, Nigeria was
united 1914.

Nigeria became a federation 1954 and achieved
full independence, as a constitutional monarchy
within the Commonwealth, in 1960. In 1963 it
became a republic, based on a federal structure
so as to accommodate the many different ethnic
groups, which included the Ibo, the Yoruba, the
Aro, the Angas, and the Hausa. Nigeria's first
president was Dr Nnamdi Azikiwe, a banker and
proprietor of an influential newspaper group, who
had played a leading part in the movement for
independence. He came from the Ibo tribe. His
chief rival was Abubakar ◊Tafawa Balewa, who
was prime minister from 1957 until he was assassinated in a military coup in 1966. The coup had been
led mainly by Ibo junior officers from the E region,
which had become richer after the discovery of oil
there in 1958. The offices of president and prime
minister were suspended and it was announced
that the state's federal structure would be abandoned. Before this could be done, the new military
government was overturned in a counter-coup by
a mostly Christian group from the N, led by Col
Yakubu ◊Gowon. He re-established the federal
system and appointed a military governor for each
region. Soon afterwards tens of thousands of Ibos
in the N were killed.

In 1967 a conflict developed between Gowon
and the military governor of the E region,
Col Chukwuemeka Odumegwu-Ojukwu, about
the distribution of oil revenues, which resulted
in Ojukwu's declaration of an independent Ibo
state of Biafra. Gowon, after failing to pacify the
Ibos, ordered federal troops into the E region and a
civil war began, lasting until Jan 1970, when Biafra
surrendered to the federal forces. It was the first
modern war between black Africans and left the
economy gravely weakened. Warfare and famine
together took an estimated 1,000,000 lives.

In 1975, while he was out of the country,
Gowon was replaced in a bloodless coup led by
Brig Murtala Mohammad, but he was killed within
a month and replaced by Gen Olusegun Obasanjo.
He announced a gradual return to civilian rule
and in 1979 the leader of the National Party
of Nigeria, Shehu Shagari, became president. In
Dec 1983, with the economy suffering from
falling oil prices, Shagari's civilian government
was deposed in another bloodless coup, led by
Maj-Gen Muhammadu Buhari. In 1985 another
peaceful coup replaced Buhari with a new military
government, led by Maj-Gen Ibrahim Babangida,
the army Chief of Staff. At the end of the year an
attempted coup by rival officers was thwarted.

Babangida promised a return to a demo-
cratic civilian government in 1992 and in Oct 1989 the
Armed Forces Ruling Council (AFRC) approved
the formation of two parties, one to the left
and one to the right of the political spectrum.
Austerity measures, prescribed by the IMF in
response to economic assistance, created widespread dissatisfaction with the government early
in 1990.

nightingale songbird of the thrush family with a song
of great beauty, heard at night as well as by day.
About 16.5 cm/6.5 in long, it is dull brown, lighter
below, with a reddish-brown tail. It migrates to
Europe and winters in Africa. It feeds on insects
and small animals.

Nightingale /ˈnaɪtɪŋɡeɪl/ Florence 1820–1910.
English nurse, the founder of nursing as a profession. She took a team of nurses to Scutari
(now Üsküdar, Turkey) in 1854 and reduced the
◊Crimean War hospital death rate from 42% to
2%. In 1856 she founded the Nightingale School
and Home for Nurses in London.

Born in Florence, Italy, she trained in Germany
and France. She was the author of the classic
Notes on Nursing, and was awarded the Order
of Merit 1907.

nightjar nocturnal bird *Caprimulgus europaeus*, with
a large bristle-fringed gape that catches moths and
other flying insects in the air. About 28 cm/11 in
long, it is patterned in shades of brown, and well

Nightingale *A pencil drawing of Florence Nightingale
by George Scharf, 1857.*

camouflaged. It is a summer visitor to Europe, and
winters in tropical Africa.

Night Journey or *al-Miraj* (Arabic 'the ascent') in
Islam, the journey of the prophet Muhammad,
guided by the archangel Gabriel, from Mecca to
Jerusalem, where he met the earlier prophets,
including Adam, Moses, and Jesus; he then ascended to paradise, where he experienced the
majesty of Allah, and was also shown hell.

nightshade several plants in the family Solanaceae,
of which the best known are the black nightshade
Solanum nigrum, bittersweet or woody nightshade *Solanum dulcamara*, and deadly nightshade
or ◊belladonna.

Nihilist member of a group of Russian revolutionaries in the reign of Alexander II 1855–81. The
name, popularized by the writer Turgenev, means
one who approves of nothing (Latin *nihil*) belonging to the existing order. In 1878 the Nihilists
launched a guerrilla campaign leading to the murder of the tsar 1881.

Niigata /ˈniːiɡɑːtə/ industrial port (textiles, metals, oil refining, chemicals) in Chubu region,
Honshu island, Japan; population (1984) 459,000.

Nijinsky *The great Russian dancer and choreographer
Vaslav Nijinsky as 'Le Dieu Bleu' in 1912. He
rejected the forms of Classical ballet in favour of free
expression, and was famous for his combination of
power and grace.*

River Nile

Nijinsky /nɪ'dʒɪnski/ Vaslav 1890–1950. Russian dancer and choreographer. Noted for his powerful but graceful technique, he was a legendary member of ◊Diaghilev's Ballets Russes, for whom he choreographed Debussy's *L'Après-midi d'un faune* 1912 and *Jeux* 1913, and Stravinsky's *The Rite of Spring* 1913. He also took lead roles in ballets such as *Petrushka* 1911. He rejected conventional forms of classical ballet in favour of free expression. His sister was the choreographer Bronislava Nijinska.

Nijmegen /'naɪmeɪɡən/ industrial city (brewery, electrical engineering, leather, tobacco) in E Netherlands, on the river Waal; population (1988) 241,000. The Roman Noviomagus, Nijmegen was a free city of the Holy Roman Empire and a member of the Hanseatic League.

Nijmegen, Treaties of /'naɪmeɪɡən/ peace treaties 1678–79 between France on the one hand and the Netherlands, Spain, and the Holy Roman Empire on the other, ending the Third Dutch War.

Nike /'naɪkiː/ in Greek mythology, goddess of victory, represented as 'winged', as in the statue from Samothrace in the Louvre. One of the most beautiful architectural monuments of Athens was the temple of Nike Apteros.

Nikolayev /ˌnɪkə'laɪev/ port (with shipyards) and naval base on the Black Sea, in Ukraine, USSR; population (1987) 501,000.

nil desperandum (Latin) never despair.

Nile /naɪl/ river in Africa, the world's longest, 6,695 km/4,160 mi. The Blue Nile rises in Lake Tana, Ethiopia, the White Nile at Lake Victoria, and they join at Khartoum, Sudan. It enters the Mediterranean at a vast delta in N Egypt.

Its remotest headstream is the Luvironza, in Burundi. The Nile proper begins on leaving Lake Victoria above ◊Owen Falls. From Lake Victoria it flows over rocky country, and there are many cataracts and rapids, including the Murchison Falls, until it enters Lake Mobutu (Albert). From here it flows across flat country and in places spreads out to form lakes. At Lake No it is joined by the Bahr el Ghazal, and from this point to Khartoum it is called the White Nile. At Khartoum it is joined by the Blue Nile, which rises in the Ethiopian highlands, and 320 km/200 mi below Khartoum it is joined by the Atbara. From Khartoum to ◊Aswan there are six cataracts. The Nile is navigable to the second cataract, a distance of 1,545 km/960 mi. The delta of the Nile is 190 km/120 mi wide. From 1982 Nile water has been piped beneath the Suez Canal to irrigate ◊Sinai. The water level behind the Aswan Dam fell from 170 m/558 ft (1979) to 150 m/492 ft (1988), threatening Egypt's hydroelectric power generation.

Nile, Battle of the /naɪl/ alternative name for the Battle of Aboukir Bay 1 Aug 1798, in which Nelson defeated Napoleon's fleet, thus ending the projected French conquest of the Middle East.

nilgai large antelope *Boselaphus tragocamelus* native to India. The bull has short conical horns and is bluish-grey. The female is brown.

Nîmes /niːm/ capital of Gard *département*, Languedoc-Roussillon, S France; population (1982) 132,500. Roman remains include an amphitheatre dating from the 2nd century AD and the Pont du Gard (aqueduct). The city gives its name to the cloth known as denim (de Nîmes); it is the birthplace of the writer Alphonse Daudet.

Nimitz /'nɪmɪts/ Chester William 1885–1966. US admiral. During World War II, he reconquered the Solomon Islands 1942–43, Gilbert Islands 1943, and Marianas and Marshalls 1944, and signed the Japanese surrender as the US representative.

Nin /nɪn/ Anaïs 1903–1977. US novelist and diarist. Her extensive and impressionistic diaries, published 1966–76, reflect her interest in dreams, which along with psychoanalysis form recurring themes of her gently erotic novels (such as *House of Incest* 1936 and *A Spy in the House of Love* 1954).

Born in Paris, she started out as a model and dancer, but later took up the study of psychoanalysis. She emigrated to the USA in 1940, becoming a prominent member of the Greenwich Village literary society in New York.

Nineteen Eighty-Four a futuristic novel by George Orwell, published 1949, which tells of an individual's battle against, and eventual surrender to, a totalitarian state where Big Brother rules. It is a dystopia (the opposite of utopia) and many of the words and concepts in it have passed into common usage (newspeak, doublethink, thought police).

1992 popular name for the European Commission's aim to achieve a single market, without import tariffs or frontier controls, within Europe by 1992.

Nineteen Propositions demands presented by the English Parliament to Charles I 1642. They were designed to limit the powers of the crown, and their rejection represented the final breakdown of peaceful negotiations and the beginning of the Civil War.

Nineveh /'nɪnɪvə/ capital of the Assyrian Empire from the 8th century BC until its destruction by the Medes under King Cyaxares in 612 BC, as forecast by the Old Testament prophet Nahum. It was situated on the Tigris (opposite the modern city of Mosul, Iraq) and was adorned with splendid palaces.

Excavations from 1842 onwards by Emile Botta (1802–70), French consul in Iraq, and ◊Layard, brought to light the ruins of Nineveh (including the library of King Ashurbanipal) under the mounds, or tells, of Kuyunjik and Nebi Yunus.

Ningbo /ˌnɪŋ'bəʊ/ port (formerly Ningpo) and special economic zone in Zhejiang province, E China; industries (fishing, shipbuilding, high-tech); population (1984) 615,600. Already a centre of foreign trade under the Tang dynasty (618–907), it was one of the original treaty ports 1842.

Ningpo former name for ◊Ningbo, port in China.

Ningxia /'nɪŋʃɑː/ or *Ningxia Hui* autonomous region (formerly Ninghsia-Hui) of NW China
area 170,000 sq km/65,620 sq mi
capital Yinchuan
physical desert plateau
products cereals and rice under irrigation; coal
population (1986) 4,240,000, including many Muslims, and nomadic herders.

Niobe /'naɪəbi/ in Greek mythology, the daughter of Tantalus and wife of Amphion, the king of Thebes. Contemptuous of the mere two children of the goddess Leto, Apollo and Artemis, she died of grief when her own twelve offspring were killed by them in revenge, and was changed to stone by Zeus.

niobium light-grey metal closely allied to tantalum, symbol Nb, atomic number 41, relative atomic mass 92.91. Occurring in a number of rare minerals, it is generally obtained from an African ore, and is a valuable addition to stainless steels. It is also used for canning high-temperature nuclear fuel elements, for example in fast breeder-reactors, especially when liquid sodium is the coolant.

Formerly known in the USA as columbium, it was first prepared by Blomstrand in 1864, though discovered in an ore by Hatchett in 1801.

Nippon /'nɪpɒn/ English transliteration of the Japanese name for ◊Japan.

nirvana in Buddhism, the attainment of perfect serenity by the eradication of all desires. To some Buddhists it means complete annihilation, to others it means the absorption of the self in the infinite.

Niterci resort city on the E shore of Guanabara Bay opposite Rio de Janeiro; population (1980) 382,700.

Nithsdale /'nɪθsdeɪl/ William Maxwell, 5th Earl of Nithsdale 1676–1744. English ◊Jacobite leader who was captured at Preston, brought to trial in Westminster Hall, London, and condemned to death on 9 Feb 1716. With his wife's assistance he escaped from the Tower of London in woman's dress, and fled to Rome.

nitrate any salt of nitric acid, containing the NO$_3$ ion. Nitrates of various kinds are used in explosives, in the chemical industry, in curing meat (see ◊nitre), and as inorganic fertilizers.

Nitrates in the soil, whether naturally occurring or from inorganic or organic fertilizers, can be used by plants to make proteins and nucleic acids. Being soluble in water, nitrates are leached out by rain into streams and reservoirs. High levels are now found in drinking water, especially in arable areas. These are harmful to newborn babies, and it is possible that they contribute to stomach cancer, although the evidence for this is unproven. The UK current standard is 100 milligrams per litre, double the EC limits to be implemented by 1993.

nitre or *saltpetre*, potassium nitrate, KNO$_3$, a mineral found on and just under the ground in desert regions; used in explosives. Nitre occurs in Bihar, India, Iran, and Cape Province, South Africa. The salt was formerly used for the manufacture of gunpowder, but the supply of nitre for explosives is today largely met by making the salt from nitratine (also called Chile saltpetre, NaNO$_3$). Saltpetre is a ◊preservative and is widely used for curing meats.

nitric acid or *aqua fortis* HNO$_3$ an acid obtained by the oxidation of ammonia, or the action of sulphuric acid on potassium nitrate. It is a strong oxidizing agent, dissolves most metals, and is used for nitration and esterification of organic substances, for explosives, plastics, and dyes, and in making sulphuric acid and nitrates.

nitrification a process that takes place in soil when bacteria oxidize ammonia, turning it into nitrates. Nitrates can be absorbed by the roots of plants, so this is a vital stage in the ◊nitrogen cycle.

nitrite any salt or ester of nitrous acid containing the nitrite ion (NO$_2$). Nitrites are used as a preservative (for example, to prevent the growth of botulism spores) and as colouring in cured meats, such as bacon and sausages.

nitrocellulose a series of esters with 2–6 nitrate (NO$_3$) groups per molecule, made by the action of concentrated nitric acid on cellulose (for example cotton waste) in the presence of concentrated sulphuric acid. Those with five or more nitrate groups are explosive (gun cotton), but those with less were once used in lacquers, rayon, and plastics, especially coloured and photographic film, until replaced by non-inflammable cellulose acetate.

nitrogen a colourless, odourless, inert gas, symbol N, atomic number 7, relative atomic mass 14.008. Nitrogen is a constituent of many organic substances, particularly proteins. It is obtained for use in industry by liquefaction and ◊fractionation of air. Nitrogen is used in the Haber process to make ammonia, NH$_3$, and to provide an inert atmosphere for certain chemical reactions.

It was isolated by Daniel Rutherford (1749–1819) in 1772. There are an estimated 4 trillion tonnes of nitrogen in the atmosphere, or about 78% by volume. Many nitrogen compounds, for example nitric acid, nitrates, ammonia, and the oxides, are

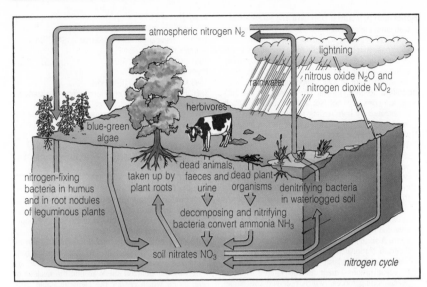

atmospheric nitrogen N$_2$

lightning

rainwater

nitrous oxide N$_2$O and nitrogen dioxide NO$_2$

herbivores

blue-green algae

nitrogen-fixing bacteria in humus and in root nodules of leguminous plants

taken up by plant roots

dead animals, faeces and dead plant organisms

denitrifying bacteria in waterlogged soil

decomposing and nitrifying bacteria convert ammonia NH$_3$

soil nitrates NO$_3$

nitrogen cycle

of importance in foods, drugs, fertilizers, dyes, and explosives. In nature, atmospheric nitrogen is 'fixed' by certain soil bacteria.

nitrogen cycle in ecology, the process of nitrogen passing through the ecosystem. Nitrogen, in the form of inorganic compounds (such as nitrates) in the soil, is absorbed by plants and turned into organic compounds (such as proteins) in plant tissue. A proportion of this nitrogen is eaten by ◊herbivores and used for their own biological processes, with some of this in turn being passed on to the carnivores, which feed on the herbivores. The nitrogen is ultimately returned to the soil as excreta and when organisms die and are converted back to inorganic form by bacterial ◊decomposers.

Although about 78% of the atmosphere is nitrogen, this cannot be used directly by most organisms. However, certain bacteria and cyanobacteria are capable of ◊nitrogen fixation; that is, they can extract nitrogen directly from the atmosphere and convert it to compounds such as nitrates that other organisms can use. Some nitrogen-fixing bacteria live mutually with leguminous plants (peas and beans) or other plants (for example, alder), where they form characteristic nodules on the roots. The presence of such plants greatly increases the nitrate content, and hence the fertility, of the soil.

nitrogen fixation the process by which nitrogen in the atmosphere is converted into nitrogenous compounds by the action of microorganisms, such as cyanobacteria and bacteria, in conjunction with certain ◊legumes. Several chemical processes reproduce nitrogen fixation to produce fertilizers; see ◊nitrogen cycle.

nitrogen oxides chemical compounds that contain only nitrogen and oxygen. They are all gases.
Nitrogen monoxide (NO) is a colourless gas released when metallic copper reacts with concentrated ◊nitric acid. On contact with air it is oxidized to **nitrogen dioxide**, which is a brown pungent gas that is harmful if inhaled. It is the commonest of the nitrogen oxides. If liquified, it gives a colourless solution (N$_2$O$_4$). It has been used in rocket fuels. *Nitrous oxide* (N$_2$O) is a colourless gas with a 'sweet' smell. It has been used as an anaesthetic, and is known familiarly as 'laughing gas'.

nitroglycerine a substance produced by the action of nitric and sulphuric acids on glycerol. It is very poisonous and explodes with great violence if heated in a confined space. It is used in the preparation of dynamite, cordite, and other high explosives.

nitrous acid (HNO$_2$) a weak acid which, in solution with water, decomposes quickly to form nitric acid and nitrogen dioxide.

Niue /'nju:eɪ/ coral island in the S Pacific, W of the Cook Islands; overseas territory of New Zealand
area 260 sq km/100 sq mi
towns port Alofi
products coconuts, passion fruit, honey
population (1988) 2,200
history inhabited by warriors who stopped Capt Cook from landing 1774; British protectorate 1900; annexed by New Zealand 1901; attained self-government in free association with New Zealand (with which there is common citizenship) 1974.

Niven /'nɪvən/ David 1909–1983. British actor, born in Scotland. His films include the Oscar-winning *Separate Tables* 1958 and *The Guns of Navarone* 1961. He published two volumes of autobiography, *The Moon's a Balloon* 1972 and *Bring on the Empty Horses* 1975.

Nixon /'nɪksən/ Richard (Milhous) 1913– . 37th president of the USA 1969–74, a Republican. He attracted attention as a member of the Un-American Activities Committee 1948, and was vice president to Eisenhower 1953–61. As president he was responsible for US withdrawal from Vietnam, and forged new links with China, but at home his culpability in the cover-up of the ◊Watergate scandal and the existence of a 'slush fund' for political machinations during his re-election campaign 1972 led to his resignation 1974 after being threatened with ◊impeachment.

Nixon *American politician and president of the USA 1968–74, Richard Nixon. He resigned while under threat of impeachment as a result of the Watergate affair.*

Of Quaker family, Nixon grew up in Whittier, California; he became a lawyer, entered Congress 1947, and in 1948, as a member of the Un-American Activities Committee, pressed for the investigation of Alger ◊Hiss, accused of being a spy. Nixon was senator for California from 1951 until elected vice president. He lost the presidential election 1960 to J F Kennedy, but in a 'law and order' campaign defeated Vice-President Humphrey 1968 in one of the most closely contested elections in US history.

In 1969 he formulated the Nixon Doctrine abandoning close involvement with Asian countries, but escalated the war in Cambodia by massive bombing. Re-elected 1972 in a landslide victory over George McGovern, he resigned 1974, the first US president to do so, under threat of impeachment on three counts: obstruction of the administration of justice in the investigation of Watergate; violation of constitutional rights of citizens, for example attempting to use the Internal Revenue Service, Federal Bureau of Investigation, and Central Intelligence Agency as a weapon against political opponents; and failure to produce 'papers and things' as ordered by the Judiciary Committee. He was granted a pardon 1974 by President Ford.

Nixon Doctrine political principle formulated in 1969 by US president Nixon, which abandoned policies of close involvement with Asian countries to avoid further armed conflicts such as that in Vietnam.

Nizhni-Novgorod /'nɪʒni 'nɒvgərɒd/ former name (until 1932) of the city of ◊Gorky in central USSR.

NJ abbreviation for ◊*New Jersey*.

Nkomati Accord a non-aggression treaty between South Africa and Mozambique concluded 1984, under which they agreed not to give material aid to opposition movements in each other's countries, which in effect meant that South Africa pledged itself not to support the Mozambique National Resistance (Renamo), while Mozambique was committed not to help the outlawed African National Congress (ANC).

Mozambique was forced to enter into the accord because of the state of its economy, and it proved to be a largely one-sided arrangement, with South Africa seldom honouring its obligations. Despite this, the two countries reiterated their commitments to it, and set up a joint security commission to keep the situation under review.

Nkomo /əŋ'kəuməu/ Joshua 1917– . Zimbabwean politician, president of ZAPU (Zimbabwe African People's Union) from 1961, and a leader of the black nationalist movement against the white Rhodesian regime. He was a member of Robert ◊Mugabe's cabinet 1980–82 and from 1987.

After completing his education in South Africa, Joshua Nkomo became a welfare officer on Rhodesian Railways and later organizing secretary of the Rhodesian African Railway Workers' Union. He entered politics 1950 and rose to become president of ZAPU. He was soon arrested, with other black African politicians, and was in detention

Nkomo *Zimbabwean politician and cabinet member Joshua Nkomo.*

Nkrumah The first president of Ghana, Kwame Nkrumah.

1963–74. After his release he joined forces with Robert Mugabe as a joint leader of the Patriotic Front 1976, opposing the white-dominated Smith regime. Nkomo took part in the Lancaster House Conference which led to Rhodesia's independence as the new state of Zimbabwe, and became a cabinet minister and vice president.

Nkrumah /əŋˈkruːmə/ Kwame 1909–1972. Ghanaian nationalist politician, prime minister of the Gold Coast 1952–57 and of independent Ghana 1957–60, and Ghana's first president 1960–66. His policy of 'African socialism' led to links with the communist bloc.

Originally a teacher, he studied later in both Britain and the USA, and on returning to Africa formed the Convention People's Party (CPP) 1949 with the aim of immediate self-government. He was imprisoned 1950 for incitement of illegal strikes, but was released the same year. As president he established an authoritarian regime and made Ghana a one-party (CPP) state 1964. He then dropped his stance of nonalignment and drew closer to the USSR and other communist countries. Deposed from the presidency while on a visit to Beijing 1966, he remained in exile in Guinea, where he was made a co-head of state, until his death, but was posthumously 'rehabilitated' 1973.

NKVD (Russian 'People's Commissariat of Internal Affairs') the Soviet secret police 1934–38, replaced by the ◊KGB. The NKVD was reponsible for Stalin's infamous ◊purges.

NM abbreviation for ◊*New Mexico*.

n.o. abbreviation for *not out* (cricket).

no. abbreviation for *number*.

Nō or *Noh* the classical, aristocratic Japanese drama, which developed in the 14th–16th centuries and is still performed. There is a repertory of some 250 pieces, of which five, one from each of the several classes devoted to different subjects, may be put on in a performance lasting a whole day. Dance, mime, music, and chanting develop the mythical or historical themes. All the actors are men, some of whom wear masks and elaborate costumes; scenery is limited. Nō influenced ◊kabuki drama.

Nō developed from popular rural entertainments and religious performances staged at shrines and temples by travelling companies. The leader of one of these troupes, Kan'ami (1333–84), and his son and successor Zeami (1363–1443/4) wrote a number of Nō plays and are regarded as the founders of the form. The plots often feature a ghost or demon seeking rest or revenge, but the aesthetics are those of Zen Buddhism. Symbolism and suggestion take precedence over action, and the slow, stylized dance is the most important element. Flute, drums, and chorus supply the music.

Noah /ˈnəʊə/ in the Old Testament or Hebrew Bible, the son of Lamech and father of Shem, Ham, and Japheth, who built an ark so that he and his family and specimens of all existing animals might survive the ◊Flood; there is also a Babylonian version of the tale.

Nobel /nəʊˈbel/ Alfred Bernhard 1833–1896. Swedish chemist and engineer. He invented dynamite 1867 and ballistite, a smokeless gunpower, 1889. He amassed a large fortune from the manufacture of explosives and the exploitation of the Baku oilfields in Russia. He left this fortune in trust for the endowment of five ◊Nobel prizes.

nobelium metallic, radioactive element of the ◊actinide series, symbol No, atomic number 102. It is obtained by bombarding curium, and was first produced 1958. It is named after Alfred Nobel.

Nobel prize annual international prize, first awarded 1901 under the will of Alfred Nobel, Swedish chemist, who invented dynamite. The interest on the Nobel fund is divided annually among the persons who have made the greatest contributions in the fields of physics, chemistry, medicine, literature, and world peace.

The first four are awarded by academic committees based in Sweden, while the peace prize is awarded by a committee of the Norwegian parliament. A sixth prize, for economics, financed by the Swedish National Bank, was first awarded 1969. The prizes have a large cash award and are given to organizations—such as the United Nations peacekeeping forces, which received the Nobel Peace Prize in 1988—as well as individuals.

Nobel Prize winners

Peace
1982 Alva Myrdal (Sweden), Alfonso Garcia Robles (Mexico)
1983 Lech Walesa (Poland)
1984 Bishop Desmond Tutu (South Africa)
1985 International Physicians for the Prevention of Nuclear War
1986 Elie Wiesel (USA)
1987 President Oscar Arias Sanchez (Costa Rica)
1988 The United Nations peacekeeping forces
1989 The Dalai Lama (Tibet)
Economics
1982 George J Stigler (USA)
1983 Gérard Debreu (USA)
1984 Richard Stone (UK)
1985 Franco Modigliani (USA)
1986 James Buchanan (USA)
1987 Robert Solow (USA)
1988 Maurice Allais (France)
1989 Trygve Haavelmo (Norway)
Physiology and Medicine
1982 Sune Bergström (Sweden), Bengt I Samuelson (Sweden), and John R Vane (UK)
1983 Barbara McClintock (USA)
1984 Niels K Jerne (Denmark), Georges Köhler (Germany) and Cesar Milstein (UK)
1985 Michael Brown (USA), and Joseph Goldstein (USA)
1986 Stanley Cohen (USA), and Rita Levi-Montalcini (USA)
1987 Susumu Tonegawa (Japan)
1988 Gertrude Elion (USA), George Hitchins (USA) and James Black (UK)
1989 Michael Bishop (USA), and Harold Varmus (USA)
Literature
1982 Gabriel García Marquez (Colombia)
1983 William Golding (UK)
1984 Jaroslav Seifert (Czechoslovakia)
1985 Claude Simon (France)
1986 Wole Soyinka (Nigeria)
1987 Joseph Brodsky (USSR/USA)
1988 Naguib Mahfouz (Egypt)
1989 Camilo Jose Cela (Spain)
Chemistry
1982 Aaron Klug (UK)
1983 Henry Taube (USA)
1984 Robert Bruce Merrifield (USA)
1985 Herbert Hauptman (USA), and Jerome Karle (USA)
1986 Dudley R Herschbach (USA), Yuan Lee (USA), and John Polanyi (Canada)
1987 Jean-Marie Lehn (France), Charles Pedersen (USA), and Donald Cram (USA)
1988 Johann Deisenhofer, Robert Huber, and Hartmut Michel (Germany)
1989 Sidney Altman (USA), Thomas Cech (USA)
Physics
1982 Kenneth G Wilson (USA)
1983 Subrahmanyan Chandrasekhar (USA), William A Fowler (USA)
1984 Carlo Rubbia (Italy), Simon van der Meer (Netherlands)
1985 Klaus von Klitzing (Germany)
1986 Ernst Ruska (Germany), Gerd Binnig (Switzerland), and Heinrich Rohrer (Switzerland)
1987 Georg Bednorz (Switzerland), and Alex Müller (Germany)
1988 Leon Lederman, Melvin Schwartz, and Jack Steinberger (USA)
1989 Norman Ramsey (USA), Hans Dehmelt (USA), and Wolfgang Paul (Germany)

nobility the ranks of society who originally enjoyed certain hereditary privileges. Their wealth was mainly derived from land. In many societies until the 20th century, they provided the elite personnel of government and the military.

noble gas structure the configuration of electrons in noble or ◊inert gases (helium, neon, argon, krypton, xenon, and radon). This is characterized by full electron shells around the nucleus of an atom, which render the element stable. Any ion, produced by the gain or loss of electrons, that achieves an electronic configuration similar to one of the inert gases is said to have a noble gas structure.

Noble Savage, the influential Enlightenment idea of the virtuous innocence of 'savage' peoples, often embodied in the American Indian, and celebrated by the writers J J Rousseau, Chateaubriand (in *Atala* 1801), and James Fenimore Cooper.

noblesse oblige (French 'nobility obliges') the aristocracy ought to behave honourably. The phrase is often used sarcastically to point out how removed this idea is from reality.

nocturne in music, a lyrical, dreamy piece, often for piano, introduced by John Field (1782–1837) and adopted by Chopin.

node a position in a ◊standing wave pattern at which there is no vibration. Points at which there is maximum vibration are called **antinodes**. Stretched strings, for example, can show nodes when they vibrate. Guitarists can produce special effects (◊harmonics) by touching a sounding string lightly to produce a node.

nodule in geology, a lump of mineral or other matter found within rocks or formed on the seabed surface; ◊mining technology is being developed to exploit them.

Noel-Baker /ˈnəʊəl ˈbeɪkə/ Philip John 1889–1982. British Labour politician. He was involved in drafting the charters of both the League of Nations and United Nations. He published *The Arms Race* 1958, and was awarded the Nobel Peace Prize 1959.

Nofretete alternative name for ◊Nefertiti, queen of Egypt.

Norfolk

Noriega *Panamanian leader General Manuel Noriega, who was deposed and seized by US troops in Dec 1989.*

Norman *Soprano Jessye Norman, celebrated for her powerful voice in opera and solo performances.*

Norman Invasion of England

dependency   ✕ battle

possessions (England after 1066)

Noguchi /nəʊˈguːtʃi/ Hideyo 1876–1928. Japanese bacteriologist, who studied syphilitic diseases, and discovered the parasite of yellow fever, a disease from which he died while working in British W Africa.

noise unwanted sound. Permanent, incurable loss of hearing can be caused by prolonged exposure to high noise levels (above 85 decibels). If the noise is in a narrow frequency band, temporary hearing loss can occur even though the level is below 85 decibels or exposure is only for short periods. Lower levels of noise are an irritant, but seem not to increase fatigue or affect efficiency to any great extent.

Roadside meter tests, introduced by the Ministry of Transport in Britain in 1968, allowed 87 decibels as the permitted limit for cars and 92 for lorries.

Nolan /ˈnəʊlən/ Sidney 1917– . Australian artist, who created atmospheric paintings of the outback, exploring themes from Australian history such as the life of the outlaw Ned Kelly and the folk heroine Mrs Fraser.

Nolde /ˈnɒldə/ Emil. Adopted name of Emil Hansen 1867–1956. German Expressionist painter. He studied in Paris and Dachau, joined the group of artists known as *die Brücke* 1906–07, and visited Polynesia 1913; he then became almost a recluse in NE Germany. Many of his themes were religious.

noli me tangere (Latin 'touch me not') in the Bible, the words spoken by Jesus to Mary Magdalene after the Resurrection (John 20:17); the title of many works of art depicting this scene; in botany, a plant of the genus *Impatiens*.

Nollekens /ˈnɒlɪkənz/ Joseph 1737–1823. English sculptor, specializing in portrait busts and memorials.

Nom Chinese-style characters used in writing the Vietnamese language. Nom characters were used from the 13th century for Vietnamese literature, but were replaced in the 19th century by a romanized script known as Quoc Ngu.

nom. in grammar, abbreviation for ◊*nominative*.

nom de plume (French 'pen name') a writer's pseudonym.

nominalism a trend in the medieval philosophy of scholasticism. In opposition to the Realists, who maintained that universals have a real existence, the Nominalists taught that they are mere names invented to describe the qualities of real things;

that is, classes of things have no independent reality. William of ◊Occam was a leading medieval exponent of nominalism. Controversy on the issue continued at intervals from the 11th to the 15th centuries.

nominative in the grammar of some inflected languages such as Latin, Russian, and Sanskrit, the form of a word used to indicate that a noun or pronoun is the subject of a finite verb.

nonaligned movement strategic and political position of neutrality ('nonalignment') towards major powers, specifically the USA and USSR. Although originally used by poorer states, the nonaligned position was later adopted by oil-producing nations.

The term was originally used by the Indian prime minister Nehru, and was adopted 1961 at an international conference in Belgrade, Yugoslavia, by the country's president Tito, in general opposition to colonialism, neo-colonialism, and imperialism, and to the dominance of dangerously conflicting East and West alliances. However, many members were in receipt of aid from either East or West or both, and some went to war with one another (Vietnam–Kampuchea, Ethiopia–Somalia).

Nonconformist in religion, originally a member of the Puritan section of the Church of England clergy who, in the Elizabethan age, refused to conform to certain practices, for example the wearing of the surplice and kneeling to receive Holy Communion. After 1662 the term was confined to those who left the church rather than conform to the Act of Uniformity requiring the use of the Prayer Book in all churches. It is now applied mainly to members of the Free churches.

Nonjurors priests of the Church of England who after the revolution of 1688 refused to take the oaths of allegiance to William and Mary. They continued to exist as a rival church for over a century, and consecrated their own bishops, the last of whom died 1805. Thomas Ken (1637–1711), William Law (1686–1761), and Jeremy ◊Collier were Nonjurors.

Nono /ˈnɔːnəʊ/ Luigi 1924– . Italian composer. His early vocal compositions have something of the spatial character of ◊Gabrieli, for example *Il Canto Sospeso* 1955–56. After the opera *Intolleranza* 1960 his style became increasingly expressionistic. His music is frequently polemical in subject matter and a number of works incorporate tape recorded elements.

nonrenewable resource natural resource, such as coal or oil, that takes thousands or millions of years

to form naturally and can therefore not be replaced once it is consumed. The main energy sources used by humans are nonrenewable resources.

non sequitur (Latin 'it does not follow') a statement that has little or no relevance to the one that preceded it.

Nordenskjöld /ˈnɔːdnʃəʊld/ Nils Adolf Erik 1832–1901. Swedish explorer. He made voyages to the Arctic with the geologist Torell and in 1878–79 discovered the Northeast Passage. He published the results of his voyages in a series of books, including *Voyage of the Vega round Asia and Europe* 1881.

Nordic ethnic designation formerly used to describe the Germanic peoples of Scandinavia.

Nord-Pas-de-Calais /ˈnɔː ˌpɑː də kæˈleɪ/ region of N France; area 12,400 sq km/4,786 sq mi; population (1986) 3,923,000. Its capital is Lille, and it consists of the *départements* of Nord and Pas-de-Calais.

Pas-de-Calais is the French term for the Strait of Dover.

Nore, the /nɔː/ sandbank at the mouth of the river Thames, England; site of the first lightship 1732.

Nore mutiny /nɔː/ British naval mutiny in 1797, caused by low pay and bad conditions.

Norfolk /ˈnɔːfək/ county on E coast of England
area 5,360 sq km/2,069 sq mi
towns administrative headquarters Norwich; King's Lynn, and resorts Great Yarmouth, Cromer, and Hunstanton
physical rivers Ouse, Yare, Bure, Waveney; the ◊Broads; Halvergate Marshes wildlife area
features traditional reed thatching; Grime's Graves (Neolithic flint mines); shrine of Our Lady of Walsingham, a medieval and modern centre of pilgrimage; Blickling Hall (Jacobean); residence of Elizabeth II at Sandringham (built 1869–71)
products cereals, turnips, sugar beet, turkeys, geese, offshore natural gas
population (1987) 736,000
famous people Fanny Burney, John Sell Cotman, John Crome ('Old Crome'), Rider Haggard, Thomas Paine.

Norfolk /ˈnɔːfək/ seaport in SE Virginia, USA, on the river Elizabeth, headquarters of the US Atlantic fleet; industries (shipbuilding, chemicals, motor vehicles); population (1980) 267,000.

Norfolk /ˈnɔːfək/ Miles Fitzalan-Howard, 17th Duke of Norfolk 1915– . Earl marshal of England, and premier duke and earl; seated at Arundel

Castle, Sussex. As earl marshal, he is responsible for the organization of ceremonial on major state occasions.

Norfolk Island /'nɔ:fək/ Pacific island territory of Australia, S of New Caledonia

area 40 sq km/15 sq mi

products citrus fruit, bananas; tourism is important

population (1986) 2,000

history reached by Cook 1774, settled 1856 by descendants of the mutineers of the *Bounty* (see ◊Bligh) from ◊Pitcairn Island; Australian territory from 1914, largely self-governing from 1979.

Noriega Manuel Antonio Morena 1940– . Panamanian general and politician, effective ruler of Panama from 1982 until arrested by the USA 1989 and detained for trial on drugs-trafficking charges.

Born in Panama City, he was commissioned in the National Guard 1962. He became intelligence chief 1970, and chief of staff 1982. He wielded considerable political power behind the scenes, which led to his enlistment by the CIA until charges of drugs trafficking discredited him. Relations with the USA deteriorated and in Dec 1989 President Bush ordered an invasion of Panama by 24,000 US troops that eventually resulted in Noriega's arrest and detention, pending trial, in the USA.

Norilsk /nə'rılsk/ world's most northerly industrial city (nickel, cobal, platinum, selenium, tellurium, gold, silver) in Siberia, USSR; population (1987) 181,000. The permafrost is 300 m/1,000 ft deep, and the winter temperature may be –55°C.

norm informal guideline about what is, or is not, considered normal social behaviour (as opposed to rules and laws, which are formal guidelines). Such shared values and expectations vary from one society to another and from one situation to another, and range from crucial taboos such as incest or cannibalism to trivial customs and traditions, such as the correct way to hold a fork. Norms are an integral part of any society's culture and of any group or organization's subculture, and a key part of social control and social order.

Norman /'nɔ:mən/ descendant of the Norsemen, to whose duke, Rollo, Normandy was granted by Charles III of France 911, and who adopted French language and culture. In the 11th and 12th centuries the Normans conquered England (under William the Conqueror), parts of Wales and Ireland, S Italy, Sicily, and Malta, settled in Scotland, and took a prominent part in the Crusades.

Norman /'nɔ:mən/ Greg 1955– . Australian golfer, nickname 'the Great White Shark'. After many wins in his home country, he was successful on the European PGA Tour before joining the US Tour. He has won the world match-play title three times.

CAREER HIGHLIGHTS

British Open: 1986
World Match-play Championship: 1980, 1983, 1986
Dunlop Masters: 1981–82
Canadian Open: 1984

Norman /'nɔ:mən/ Jessye 1945– . US soprano, born in Augusta, Georgia. She made her operatic debut at the Deutsche Oper, Berlin, 1969. She is noted for her interpretation of *Lieder*, as well as operatic roles, and for her powerful voice.

Norman /'nɔ:mən/ Montagu, 1st Baron Norman 1871–1950. British banker. Governor of the Bank of England 1920–44, he handled German reparations after World War I, and, by his advocacy of a return to the gold standard in 1925 and other policies, was held by many to have contributed to the economic depression of the 1930s.

Norman architecture /'nɔ:mən/ English term for ◊Romanesque, the style of architecture used in England 11th–12th centuries. Norman buildings are massive, with round arches (although trefoil arches are sometimes used for small openings). Buttresses are of slight projection, and vaults are barrel-roofed. Examples in England include the

Norman architecture *Norman tower at Hedingham, Essex, begun in the late 11th century. It is 22 m/72 ft high.*

Keep of the Tower of London, and parts of the cathedrals of Chichester, Gloucester, and Ely.

Normandy /'nɔ:məndi/ two regions of NW France: ◊Haute-Normandie and ◊Basse-Normandie. Its main towns are Alençon, Bayeux, Dieppe, Deauville, Lisieux, Le Havre, and Cherbourg. It was named after the Viking Northmen (Normans), people who conquered the area in the 9th century. As a French duchy it reached its peak under William the Conqueror and was noted for its centers of learning established by Lanfranc and St Anselm. Normandy was united with England 1100–35. England and France fought over it during the Hundred Years' War, England finally losing it 1449 to Charles VII. The Normandy beaches were the site of the Allied invasion on D-day, 6 June 1944. Features of Normandy include the painter Monet's restored home and garden at Giverny, Mont St Michel, Château Miromesnil, the birthplace of de Maupassant, Victor Hugo's house at Villequier, and ◊Calvados apple brandy.

Norman French the form of French used by the Normans in Normandy from the 10th century, and by the Norman ruling class in England after the Conquest. It remained the language of the court until the 15th century, the official language of the law courts until the 17th century, and is still used in the Channel Islands.

Norman yoke popular belief dating from the 17th century or earlier, and revived in Victorian times, that the Norman invasion and the imposition of feudalism on England destroyed a better, Saxon, system of government. In reality, the Normans were able to conquer England so easily because of its lack of an organized government.

Norn in Scandinavian mythology, any of three goddesses of fate — the goddess of the past (Urd), the goddess of the present (Verdandi), and the goddess of the future (Skuld).

Norris /'nɒrɪs/ Frank 1870–1902. US novelist. An influential Naturalist writer, he wrote *McTeague* 1899, about a brutish San Francisco dentist and the love of gold. He completed only two parts of his projected trilogy, the *Epic of Wheat: The Octopus* 1901, dealing with the struggles between wheat farmers, and *The Pit* 1903, describing the gamble of the Chicago wheat exchange.

Norseman early inhabitant of Norway. The term Norsemen is also applied to Scandinavian ◊Vikings who during the 8th–11th centuries raided and settled in Britain, Ireland, France, Russia, Iceland, and Greenland. The Norse religion (banned 1000) was recognized by the Icelandic government 1973.

North /nɔ:θ/ Frederick, 8th Lord North 1732–1792. British Tory politician. He entered Parliament in 1754, became chancellor of the Exchequer in 1767,

North *The policies of Lord North, largely dictated by George III and an influential circle of 'king's friends', precipitated the American Revolution.*

and was prime minister in a government of Tories and 'king's friends' from 1770. His hard line against the American colonies was supported by George III, but in 1782 he was forced to resign by the failure of his policy. In 1783 he returned to office in a coalition with ◊Fox, and after its defeat retired from politics.

North /nɔ:θ/ Oliver 1943– . US Marine. In 1981 he was inducted into the National Security Council (NSC), where he supervised the mining of Nicaraguan harbours 1983, an air-force bombing raid on Libya 1986, and an arms-for-hostages deal with Iran 1985 which, when uncovered in 1986 (◊Irangate), forced his dismissal and conviction on charges of obstructing Congress, mutilating government documents, and taking an illegal gratuity; he was fined $150,000.

He was born into a San Antonio, Texas, military family, and was a graduate of the US Naval College, Annapolis. He led a counter-insurgency Marine platoon in the Vietnam War 1968–69, winning a Silver Star and Purple Heart before returning home wounded. After working as a

North *US Marine Lt-Col Oliver North. A Vietnam war hero, he was the central figure in the Irangate scandal, overseeing 1985–86 a clandestine foreign policy network.*

North America

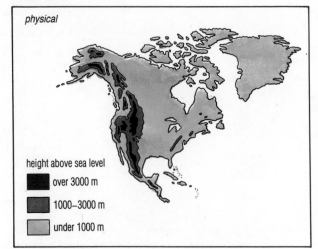

physical

height above sea level
◼ over 3000 m
▨ 1000–3000 m
▨ under 1000 m

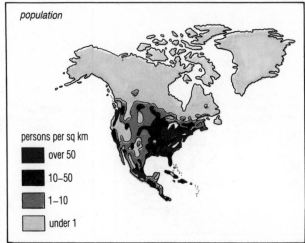

population

persons per sq km
◼ over 50
◼ 10–50
▨ 1–10
☐ under 1

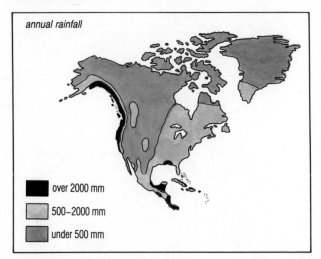

annual rainfall

◼ over 2000 mm
▨ 500–2000 mm
▨ under 500 mm

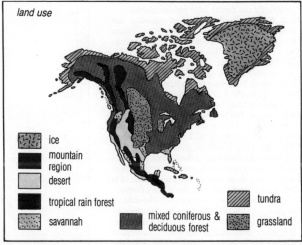

land use

▨ ice
◼ mountain region
☐ desert
◼ tropical rain forest
▨ savannah
▨ mixed coniferous & deciduous forest
▨ tundra
▨ grassland

Marine instructor, as well as participating in a number of overseas secret missions, he became the NSC deputy director for political military affairs.

North /nɔː.θ/ Thomas 1535–1601. English translator, whose version of ◊Plutarch's *Lives* 1579 was the source for Shakespeare's Roman plays.

Northallerton /nɔː'θælətən/ market town, administrative headquarters of North Yorkshire, England; industries (tanning and flour milling); population (1985) 13,800.

North America third largest of the continents (including Central America), and over twice the size of Europe
area 24,000,000 sq km/9,500,000 sq mi
largest cities (population over 1 million) Mexico City, New York, Chicago, Toronto, Los Angeles, Montreal, Guadalajara, Monterrey, Philadelphia, Houston, Guatemala City, Vancouver, Detroit
physical mountain belts to the E (Appalachians) and W (see ◊Cordilleras), the latter including the

North America: early history

Rocky Mountains and the Sierra Madre; coastal plain on the Gulf of Mexico, into which the Mississippi river system drains from the central Great Plains; the St Lawrence and the Great Lakes form a rough crescent (with the Great Bear and Great Slave lakes, and lakes Athabasca and Winnipeg) around the exposed rock of the great Canadian/Laurentian Shield, into which Hudson Bay breaks from the north
population (1981) 345 million; the aboriginal American Indian, Inuit, and Aleut peoples are now a minority within a population predominantly of European immigrant origin. Many Africans were brought in as part of the slave trade
language predominantly English, Spanish, French
features climatic range is wide from arctic in Alaska and N Canada (only above freezing Jun–Sept) to the tropical in Central America, and much of the W of USA is arid. There are also great extremes within the range, owing to the vast size of the land mass

exports the immensity of the US home market makes it less dependent on exports, and the USA's industrial and technological strength automatically tend to exert a pull on Canada, Mexico, and Central America. The continent is unique in being dominated in this way by a single power, which also exerts great influence over the general world economy
religion predominantly Christian, Jewish.

North American Indian indigenous inhabitant of North America. Many prefer to describe themselves as 'Native Americans' rather than 'American Indians', the latter term having arisen because Columbus believed he had reached the East Indies.

Northampton /nɔː'θæmptən/ county town of Northamptonshire, England; population (1984) 163,000. Boots and shoes (of which there is a museum) are still made, but engineering has superseded them as the chief industry; there is also food processing and brewing.

Northamptonshire /nɔː'θæmptənʃə/ county in central England
area 2,370 sq km/915 sq mi
towns administrative headquarters Northampton; Kettering
features river Nene; Canons Ashby, Tudor house, home of the Drydens for 400 years; churches with broached spires
products cereals, cattle
population (1987) 562,000
famous people John Dryden.

Northants abbreviation for *Northamptonshire*.

North Atlantic Drift warm ocean ◊current in the N Atlantic Ocean; the continuation of the ◊Gulf

c.35,000 BC	American Indians entered North America from Asia.
c.9000 BC	Marmes man, earliest human remains.
300	Earliest Moundbuilder sites.
C.AD 1000	Leif Ericsson reached North America.
12th–14th centuries	Height of the Moundbuilder and Pueblo cultures.
1492	12 Oct Columbus first sighted land in the Caribbean.
1497	Giovanni Caboto reached Canada.
1565	First Spanish settlements in Florida.
1585	First attempted English settlement in North Carolina.
1607	First permanent English settlement, Jamestown, Virginia.
	See also under ◊Alaska, ◊Canada, and ◊United States of America.

Northamptonshire

Stream. It flows E across the Atlantic and has a mellowing effect on the climate of W Europe, particularly the British Isles and Scandinavia.

North Atlantic Treaty agreement signed 4 Apr 1949 by Belgium, Canada, Denmark, France, Iceland, Italy, Luxembourg, Netherlands, Norway, Portugal, UK, USA; Greece, Turkey 1952; West Germany 1955; Spain 1982. They agreed that 'an armed attack against one or more of them in Europe or North America shall be considered an attack against them all'. The North Atlantic Treaty Organization (NATO) is based on this treaty.

North Atlantic Treaty Organization (NATO) association set up 1949 to provide for the collective defence of the major W European and North American states against the perceived threat from the USSR. Its chief body is the Council of Foreign Ministers (who have representatives in permanent session), and there is an international secretariat in Brussels, Belgium, and also the Military Committee consisting of the Chiefs of Staff. The military headquarters SHAPE (Supreme Headquarters Allied Powers, Europe) is in Chièvres, near Mons, Belgium. Both the Supreme Allied Commanders (Europe and Atlantic) are from the USA, but there is also an Allied Commander, Channel (a British admiral). In 1960 a permanent multinational *Allied Mobile Force* (AMF) was established to move immediately to any NATO country under threat of attack; headquarters in Heidelberg, West Germany.

France withdrew from the organization (not the alliance) 1966; Greece withdrew politically but not militarily 1974. In 1980 Turkey was opposed to Greek re-entry because of differences over rights in the Aegean Sea. NATO has encountered numerous problems since its inception over such issues as the hegemonial position of the USA, the presence in Europe of US nuclear weapons, burden sharing, and standardization of weapons. Its counterpart is the ◊Warsaw Pact.

North Brabant /ˈnɔːθ brəˈbænt/ (Dutch *Noord-Brabant*) southern province of the Netherlands, lying between the Maas (Meuse) and Belgium; area 4,940 sq km/1,907 sq mi; population (1988) 2,156,000. The capital is 's-Hertogenbosch.

North Carolina

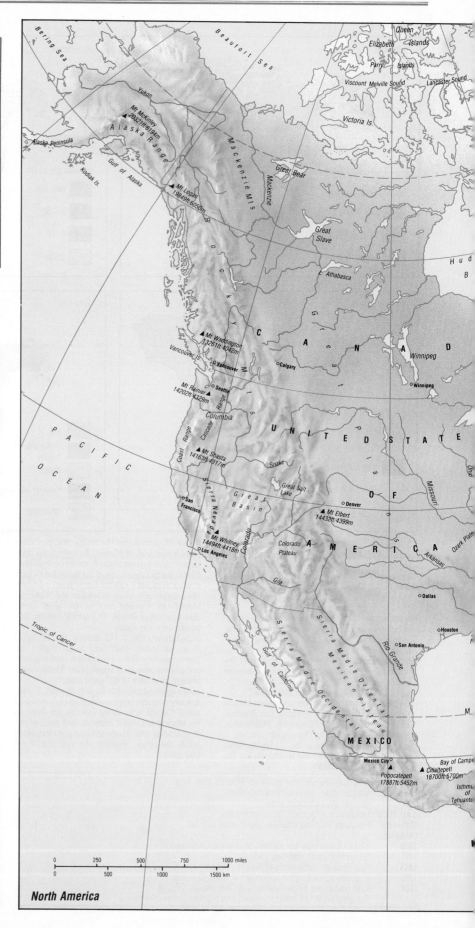

North America

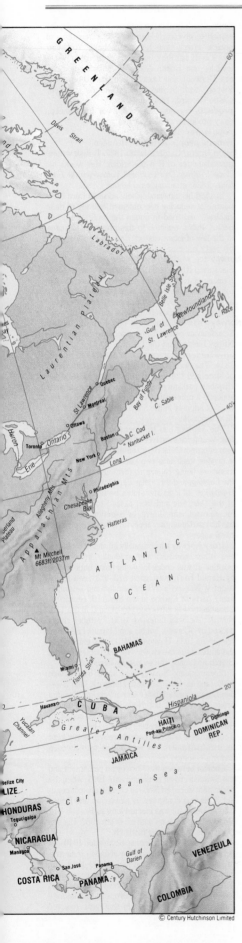

North Dakota

Former heathland is now under mixed farming. Towns such as Breda, Tilburg, and Eindhoven are centres of brewing, engineering, microelectronics, and textile manufacture.

North Cape (Norwegian *Nordkapp*) a cape in the Norwegian county of Finnmark; the most northerly point of Europe.

North Carolina /ˈnɔːθ ˌkærəˈlaɪnə/ state of the USA; nickname Tar Heel or Old North State
area 136,400 sq km/52,650 sq mi
capital Raleigh
towns Charlotte, Greensboro, Winston-Salem
features Appalachian Mountains (including Blue Ridge and Great Smoky Mountains); site of Fort Raleigh on Roanoke Island; Wright Brothers National Memorial at Kitty Hawk; the Research Triangle established 1956 (Duke University, University of North Carolina, and North Carolina State University) for high-tech industries
products tobacco, maize, soybeans, livestock, poultry, dairy products, textiles, clothing, furniture, computers, mica, feldspar, bricks
population (1986) 6,331,000
famous people Billy Graham, O Henry
history Walter Raleigh sent out 108 colonists from Plymouth 1585 under his cousin Richard Grenville, who established the first English settlement in the New World on Roanoke Island; the survivors were taken home by Drake 1586. Further attempts failed there, the settlers having disappeared without trace. The first permanent settlement was made 1663; it became one of the original Thirteen States 1789.

Northcliffe /ˈnɔːθklɪf/ Alfred Charles William Harmsworth, 1st Viscount Northcliffe 1865–1922. British newspaper proprietor, born in Dublin. Founding the *Daily Mail* 1896, he revolutionized popular journalism, and with the *Daily Mirror* 1903 originated the picture paper. In 1908 he also obtained control of *The Times*.

Northd abbreviation for ◊*Northumberland*.

North Dakota /ˈnɔːθ dəˈkəʊtə/ prairie state of the N USA; nickname Sioux or Flickertail State
area 183,100 sq km/70,677 sq mi
capital Bismarck
towns Fargo, Grand Forks, Minot
features fertile Red River Valley, Missouri Plateau; Badlands, so called because the pioneers had great difficulty in crossing them (including Theodore Roosevelt's Elkhorn Ranch)
products cereals, meat products, farm equipment, oil, coal
population (1984) 686,000
famous people Maxwell Anderson, Louis L'Amour
history acquired by the USA partly in the ◊Louisiana Purchase 1803, and partly by treaty with Britain 1813; it became a state 1889.

North-East Frontier Agency former name (until 1972) for ◊Arunachal Pradesh, territory of India.

North-East India area of India (Meghalaya, Assam, Mizoram, Tripura, Manipur, and Nagaland, and Arunachal Pradesh) linked with the rest of India only by a narrow corridor. There is opposition to immigration from Bangladesh and the rest of India, and demand for secession.

North-East Passage sea route from the N Atlantic, around Asia, to the N Pacific, pioneered by ◊Nordenskjöld 1878–79, and developed by the USSR in settling N Siberia from 1935. The USSR owns offshore islands, and claims it as

Northern Territory

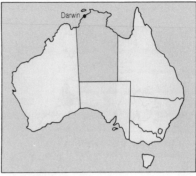

an internal waterway; the USA claims that it is international.

Northern Areas districts N of Azad Kashmir, directly administered by Pakistan but not merged with it. India and Azad Kashmir each claim them as part of disputed Kashmir. They include Baltistan, Gilgit and Skardu, and Hunza (an independent principality for 900 years until 1974).

Northern Ireland see ◊Ireland, Northern.

northern lights common name for the ◊aurora borealis.

Northern Rhodesia /ˈnɔːðən rəʊˈdiːʃə/ former name (until 1964) of ◊Zambia.

Northern Territory territory of Australia
area 1,346,200 sq km/519,633 sq mi
capital and chief port Darwin
towns Alice Springs
features mainly within the tropics, though with wide range of temperature; very low rainfall, but artesian bores are used; Macdonnell Ranges (Mt Zeil 1,510 m/4,956 ft); ◊Cocos and ◊Christmas Islands were included in the territory 1984
exports beef cattle, prawns, bauxite (Gove), gold and copper (Tennant Creek), uranium (Ranger)
population (1987) 157,000
government there is an administrator and legislative assembly, and the territory is also represented in the federal parliament
history originally part of New South Wales, it was annexed 1863 to South Australia, but 1911–78 (when self-government was granted) was under the control of the Commonwealth of Australia government. Mineral discoveries on land occupied by Aborigines led to a royalty agreement 1979.

North Holland (Dutch *Noord-Holland*) low-lying coastal province of the Netherlands occupying the peninsula jutting northwards between the North Sea and the Ijsselmeer; area 2,670 sq km/1,031 sq mi; population (1988) 2,353,000. Most of it is below sea-level, protected from the sea by a series of sand dunes and artificial dykes. The capital is Haarlem; other towns are Amsterdam, Hilversum, Den Helder, and the cheese centres Alkmaar and Edam. Famous for its bulbfields, the province also produces grain and vegetables.

North Korea see ◊Korea, North.

North Ossetian /ˈnɔːθ ɒˈsiːʃən/ area of the Caucasus, USSR; see ◊Ossetia.

North Pole the north point where an imaginary line penetrates the Earth's surface by the axis about which it revolves; see also ◊Poles and ◊Arctic.

North Rhine-Westphalia /ˈnɔːθ ˈraɪn westˈfeɪliə/ (German *Nordrhein-Westfalen*) administrative *Land* of West Germany
area 34,100 sq km/13,163 sq mi
capital Düsseldorf
towns Cologne, Essen, Dortmund, Duisburg, Bochum, Wuppertal, Bielefeld, Bonn, Gelsenkirchen, Münster, Mönchengladbach
features valley of the Rhine; Ruhr industrial district
products iron, steel, coal, lignite, electrical goods, fertilizers, synthetic textiles
population (1988) 16,700,000
religion Roman Catholic 53%, Protestant 42%

Northumberland

North Yorkshire

history see ◊Westphalia.

Northrop /'nɔ:θrəp/ John 1891–1987. US chemist. In the 1930s he crystallized a number of enzymes, including pepsin and trypsin, showing conclusively that they were proteins. He shared the 1946 Nobel Chemistry Prize with Wendell ◊Stanley and James ◊Sumner.

North Sea sea to the E of Britain and bounded by the coasts of Belgium, the Netherlands, Germany, Denmark, and Norway; area 523,000 sq km/202,000 sq mi; average depth 55 m/180 ft, greatest depth 660 m/2,165 ft. In the NE it joins the Norwegian Sea, and in the S it meets the Strait of Dover. It has fisheries, oil, and gas. For pollution, see ◊sewage disposal.

North Uist /'ju:ɪst/ an island of the Outer Hebrides, Scotland. Lochmaddy is the main port of entry. It produces tweeds and seaweed, and crofting is practised.

Northumberland /nɔ:'θʌmbələnd/ county in N England
area 5,030 sq km/1,942 sq mi
towns administrative headquarters Newcastle-upon-Tyne; Berwick-upon-Tweed, Hexham
features Cheviot Hills, rivers Tweed and upper Tyne of Northumberland National Park in the W; ◊Holy Island; ◊Farne Islands; part of Hadrian's Wall and Housestead's Fort; Alnwick and Bamburgh castles; Thomas ◊Bewick museum; large moorland areas are used for military manoeuvres
products sheep
population (1986) 301,000
famous people Thomas Bewick, Bobby Charlton.

Northumberland /nɔ:'θʌmbələnd/ John Dudley, Duke of Northumberland *c.*1502–1553. English politician, son of the privy councillor Edmund Dudley (beheaded 1510), raised to a dukedom in 1551, and chief minister until Edward VI's death 1553. He tried to place his daughter-in-law Lady Jane ◊Grey on the throne, and was executed on Mary's accession.

Northumbria /nɔ:'θʌmbriə/ Anglo-Saxon kingdom that covered NE England and SE Scotland, comprising the 6th-century kingdoms of Bernicia (Forth–Tees) and Deira (Tees–Humber), united in the 7th century. It accepted the supremacy of Wessex 827, and was conquered by the Danes in the late 9th century.

Influenced by Irish missionaries, it was a cultural and religious centre until the 8th century with priests such as Bede, Cuthbert, and Wilfrid.

North-West Frontier Province province of Pakistan; capital Peshawar; area 74,500 sq km/-28,757 sq mi; population (1985) 12,287,000. It was a province of British India 1901–47. It includes the strategic Khyber Pass, the site of constant struggle between the British Raj and the ◊Pathan warriors. In the 1980s it has

had to accommodate a stream of refugees from neighbouring Afghanistan.

Northwest Passage Atlantic–Pacific sea route around the north of Canada. Canada, which owns offshore islands, claims it as an internal waterway; the USA insists that it is an international waterway, and sent an icebreaker through without permission 1985.

Early explorers included ◊Frobisher and John Franklin, whose failure to return 1847 led to the organization of 39 expeditions in the next ten years. R McClune explored the passage 1850–53, though he did not cover the whole route by sea. ◊Amundsen was the first European to sail through.

Northwest Territories /'nɔ:θwest 'terɪtəriz/ territory of Canada
area 3,426,300 sq km/1,322,552 sq mi
capital Yellowknife
physical extends to the North Pole, to Hudson's Bay in the east, and in the west to the edge of the Canadian Shield
features Mackenzie river; Great Slave Lake and Great Bear Lake; Miles Canyon
products oil and natural gas, zinc, lead, gold, tungsten, silver
population (1986) 52,000, over 50% native peoples (Indian, Inuit)
history the area was the northern part of Rupert's Land, bought by the Canadian government from the Hudson's Bay Company 1869. An Act of 1952 placed the Northwest Territories under a commissioner acting at Ottawa under the Ministry of Northern Affairs and Natural Resources.

North Yorkshire /'jɔ:kʃə/ county in NE England
area 8,320 sq km/3,212 sq mi
towns administrative headquarters Northallerton; York, and the resorts of Harrogate, Scarborough, and Whitby
features England's largest county; including part of the Pennines, the Vale of York, and the Cleveland Hills and North Yorkshire Moors, which form a

Northwest Territories

national park (within the park are Fylingdales radar station to give early warning—four minutes—of nuclear attack, and Rievaulx abbey); Yorkshire Dales National Park (including Swaledale, Wensleydale, and Bolton Abbey in Wharfedale); rivers Derwent and Ouse; Fountains Abbey near Rippon, with Studley Royal Gardens attached; Castle Howard; York Minster
products cereals, wool and meat from sheep, dairy products, coal, electrical goods
population (1987) 706,000
famous people Alcuin, W H Auden.

Norton /'nɔ:tn/ Caroline 1808–1877. British writer, granddaughter of R B ◊Sheridan. Her works include *Undying One* 1830 and *Voice from the Factories* 1836, attacking child labour.

In 1836 her husband falsely accused Lord Melbourne of seducing her, obtained custody of their children, and tried to obtain the profits from her books. Public reaction to this prompted changes in the law of infant custody and married women's property rights.

Norway the world's largest ever passenger liner, measuring 316 m/1,037 ft long and with a gross tonnage of over 70,200 tonnes. It can carry 2,400 passengers. The *Norway* was launched originally as the *France* 1979, and renamed 1981 after purchase by Knut Kloster of Norway.

Norway /'nɔ:weɪ/ country in NW Europe, on the Scandinavian peninsula, bounded E by Sweden and NE by Finland and the USSR.
government Norway's constitution dates from 1814. The hereditary monarch is the formal head of state and the legislature consists of a single-chamber parliament, the *Storting*. The monarch appoints a prime minister and state council on the basis of support in the *Storting*, to which they are all responsible.

The *Storting* has 157 members, elected for a four-year term by universal suffrage through a system of proportional representation. Once elected, it divides itself into two parts, a quarter of the members being chosen to form an upper house, the *Lagting*, and the remainder a lower house, the *Odelsting*. All legislation must be first introduced in the *Odelsting* and then passed to the *Lagting* for approval, amendment, or rejection. Once a bill has had parliamentary approval it must receive the royal assent.
history Norway was originally inhabited by Lapps and other nomads, and gradually invaded by ◊Goths. It was under local chieftains until unified by Harald Fairhair (reigned 872–933) as a feudal country. Norway's ◊Vikings raided and settled in many parts of Europe in the 8th–11th centuries. Christianity was introduced by ◊Olaf II in the 11th century; he was defeated 1030 by rebel chiefs backed by ◊Canute, but his son Magnus I regained the throne 1035. Haakon IV (1217–63) established the authority of the crown over the nobles and the church and made the monarchy hereditary.

◊Denmark and Norway were united by marriage 1380, and in 1397 Norway, Denmark, and Sweden became united under one sovereign. Sweden broke away 1523 but Norway remained under Danish rule until 1814, when it was ceded to Sweden. Norway rebelled, Sweden invaded, and a compromise was reached whereby Norway kept its own parliament but was united with Sweden under a common monarch.

Conflict between the Norwegian parliament and the Swedish crown continued until 1905, when the parliament declared Norway completely independent. This was confirmed by plebiscite, and Prince Carl of Denmark was elected king as Haakon VII. He ruled for 52 years until his death 1957. His son ◊Olaf V is the reigning monarch.

The experience of German occupation 1940–45 persuaded the Norwegians to abandon their traditional neutral stance and join NATO 1949, the Nordic Council 1952, and the European Free Trade Area (EFTA) 1960. Norway was accepted into membership of the European Community 1972 but a referendum held that year rejected

Norway
Kingdom of
(Kongeriket Norge)

area 387,000 sq km/149,421 sq mi (includes Svalbard and Jan Mayen)
capital Oslo
towns Bergen, Trondheim
physical mountainous; forests cover 25% of area; extends north of Arctic Circle
territories dependencies in the Arctic (Svalbard and Jan Mayen) and in Antarctica (Bouvet and Peter I Island, and Queen Maud Land)
features beautiful fjords, including Hardanger and Sogne, the longest 185 km/115 mi and deepest 1,245 m/4,086 ft; glaciers in N; midnight sun and northern lights; great resources of hydroelectric power
head of state Olaf V from 1957
head of government Jan P Syse from 1989
government constitutional monarchy

political parties Norwegian Labour Party (DNA), moderate, left-of-centre; Conservative Party, progressive, right-of-centre; Christian People's Party (KrF), Christian, centre-left; Centre Party (SP), left-of-centre, rural-orientated
exports petrochemicals from North Sea oil and gas, paper, wood pulp, furniture, iron ore and other minerals, high-tech goods, sports goods, fish
currency krone (11.01 = £1 Feb 1990)
population (1989) 4,204,000; annual growth rate 0.3%
life expectancy men 73, women 80
language Riksmal (formal Dano-Norwegian) and Landsmal (based on the local dialects of Norway)
religion Evangelical Lutheran (endowed by state)
literacy 100% (1984)
GNP $56 bn (1982); $12,432 per head of population
chronology
1814 Independent from Denmark.
1905 Links with Sweden ended.
1940–45 Occupied by Germany.
1949 Joined NATO.
1952 Joined Nordic Council.
1957 King Haakon VII succeeded by his son, Olaf V.
1960 Joined EFTA.
1972 Accepted into membership of the European Community but application withdrawn after a referendum.
1988 Prime minister Gro Harlem Brundtland awarded Third World Prize.
1989 Brundtland defeated in elections. Jan P Syse became prime minister.

the proposal and the application was withdrawn. Its exploitation of North Sea oil and gas resources have given it a higher income per head of population than most of its European neighbours, and it has succeeded in maintaining good relations with the USSR without damaging its commitments in the West.

Norway has enjoyed stability under a series of coalition governments. In Nov 1988 Prime Minister Gro Harlem Brundtland was awarded the annual Third World Prize for her work on environmental issues but in the Sept 1989 election her party lost seats to the far right and the far left. Following a vote of no confidence, she resigned in Oct 1989 and was succeeded by the conservative Jan P Syse.

Norwegian Sea /nɔːˈwiːdʒən ˈsiː/ part of the ◊Arctic Ocean.

Norwich /ˈnɒrɪdʒ/ cathedral city in Norfolk, E England; population (1986) 121,600. Industries include shoes, clothing, chemicals, confectionery, engineering, and printing.

It has a Norman castle with a collection of paintings by the Norwich school (◊Cotman, ◊Crome); 15th-century Guildhall, medieval churches, Tudor houses, Georgian Assembly House. The Sainsbury Laboratory 1987, in association with the John Innes Institute, was founded to study the molecular foundations of pathogenicity.

Norwich /ˈnɒrɪdʒ/ 1st Viscount Norwich: title of (Alfred) Duff ◊Cooper.

nose in humans, the upper entrance of the respiratory tract; the organ of the sense of smell. The external part is divided down the middle by a septum of ◊cartilage. The nostrils contain plates of cartilage which can be moved by muscles and have a growth of stiff hairs at the margin to prevent foreign objects from entering. They contain cells sensitive to smell. The whole nasal cavity is lined with a ◊mucous membrane that warms and moistens the air and ejects dirt.

nosebleed bleeding from the nose. Although usually minor and easily controlled, the loss of blood may occasionally be so rapid as to be life-threatening,

particularly in small children. Most nosebleeds can be stopped by simply squeezing the nose for a few minutes, but in exceptional cases transfusion and the packing of the nose with ribbon gauze may be required.

nosocomial description of any infection acquired in hospital, whether its effects are seen during the patient's stay or following discharge.

nose

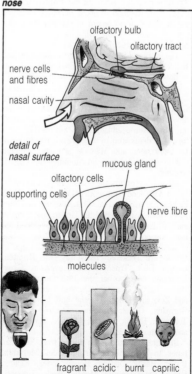

olfactory bulb
olfactory tract
nerve cells and fibres
nasal cavity
detail of nasal surface
mucous gland
olfactory cells
supporting cells
nerve fibre
molecules
fragrant   acidic   burnt   caprilic

Nottinghamshire

Widely prevalent in hospitals, nosocomial infections threaten patients who are seriously ill or whose immune systems have been suppressed. The threat is compounded by the tendency of some ◊pathogens to become drug-resistant.

Nostradamus /ˌnɒstrəˈdɑːməs/ Latinized name of Michel de Nôtredame 1503–1566. French physician and astrologer who was consulted by Catherine de' Medici and was physician to Charles IX. His book of prophesies in rhyme, *Centuries* 1555, has had a number of interpretations.

nostril in vertebrates, the opening of the nasal cavity, in which cells sensitive to smell are located. (In fish, these cells detect water-borne chemicals, so they are effectively organs of taste.) In those that have lungs (lungfish and tetrapod vertebrates), the nostrils also take in air. In humans, and most other mammals, the nostrils are located on a ◊nose.

notation in music, the use of symbols to represent individual sounds (such as the notes of the chromatic scale) so that they can be accurately interpreted and reproduced.

notation in dance, the recording of dances by symbols. There are several dance notation systems; prominent among them is ◊Labanotation.

note in music, the written symbol indicating pitch and duration, the sound of which is a tone.

notochord the stiff but flexible rod that lies between the gut and nerve cord of all embryonic and larval chordates, including the vertebrates. It forms the supporting structure of the adult amphioxus (a small eel-like creature), but in vertebrates it is replaced by the vertebral column, or spine.

Nott /nɒt/ John 1932– . British Conservative politician, minister for defence 1981–83 during the ◊Falkland Islands campaign against Argentina.

Nottingham /ˈnɒtɪŋəm/ industrial city (engineering, coalmining, cycles, textiles, knitwear, pharmaceuticals, tobacco, lace, electronics) and administrative headquarters of Nottinghamshire, England; population (1981) 217,080.

Features include the university 1881; the Playhouse (opened 1963) and the recently refurbished Theatre Royal. Nearby are Newstead Abbey, home of Byron, and D H Lawrence's home at Eastwood.

Nottinghamshire /ˈnɒtɪŋəmʃə/ county in central England
area 2,160 sq km/834 sq mi
towns administrative headquarters Nottingham; Mansfield, Worksop
features river Trent; the remaining areas of Sherwood Forest (home of ◊Robin Hood), formerly a royal hunting ground, are included in the 'Dukeries'; Cresswell Crags (remains of prehistoric humans); D H Lawrence commemorative walk from Eastwood (where he lived) to Old Brinsley Colliery
products cereals, cattle, sheep, light engineering, footwear, limestone, ironstone, oil

Nova Scotia

population (1987) 1,008,000
famous people D H Lawrence, Alan Sillitoe
history in World War II Nottinghamshire produced the only oil out of U-boat reach, and drilling revived in the 1980s.

Notts abbreviation for ◊Nottinghamshire.

Nouakchott /ˌnuːækˈʃɒt/ capital of Mauritania; population (1985) 500,000. Products include salt, cement, and insecticides.

Nouméa a port on the SW coast of New Caledonia; population (1983) 60,100.

noun the grammatical ◊part of speech referring to words that name a person, animal, object, quality, idea and so on. Nouns can refer to objects such as house, tree (concrete nouns); abstract ideas such as love, anger (abstract nouns); and in English many simple words are both noun and verb (jump, reign, rain). Adjectives are sometimes used as nouns (a local man, one of the locals).

A common noun does not begin with a capital letter (*child, cat*), whereas a proper noun does, because it is the name of a particular person, animal, or place (*John, Rover, London*). A concrete noun refers to things that can be sensed (*dog, box*), while an abstract noun relates to generalizations 'abstracted' from life as we observe it (*love, condition, illness*). A countable noun can have a plural form (*book: books*), while an uncountable noun or mass noun cannot (*dough*). Many English nouns can be used both countably and uncountably (*wine*: 'Have some wine; it's one of our best wines'). A collective noun is singular in form but refers to a group (*flock, group, committee*), and a compound noun is made up of two or more nouns (*blackbird, teapot, coffee jug, car-factory strike committee*). A verbal noun is formed from a verb (*run: running; build: building; regulate: regulation*).

nouvelle cuisine (French 'new cooking') a style of French cooking that avoids traditional rich sauces, emphasizing fresh ingredients with attractive presentation. The phrase was coined in the magazine *Harpers and Queen* in June 1975.

nova (plural *novae*) a faint star that suddenly erupts in brightness, becoming visible in binoculars or to the naked eye. Novae are believed to occur in close ◊double star systems, where gas from one star flows to a companion ◊white dwarf. The gas ignites, and is thrown off in an explosion, the star increasing in brightness by 10,000 times or more. Unlike a ◊supernova, the star is not completely disrupted by the outburst.

After a few weeks or months it subsides to its previous state; it may erupt many more times. The name comes from the Latin 'new', although novae are not new stars at all.

Novak /ˈnəʊvæk/ (Marilyn Pauline) Kim 1933– . US film actress who starred in such films as *Pal Joey* 1957, *Vertigo* 1958, *Kiss Me Stupid* 1964, and *The Legend of Lyla Clare* 1968.

Novalis /nəʊˈvɑːlɪs/ Pen name of Freiherr von Hardenburg 1772–1801. Pioneer German Romantic poet, who wrote *Hymnen an die Nacht/Hymns to the Night* 1800, prompted by the death of his fiancée Sophie von Kühn. He left two unfinished romances, *Die Lehrlinge zu Sais/The Novices of Sais* and *Heinrich von Ofterdingen*.

Nova Lisboa /ˈnəʊvə lɪzˈbəʊə/ former name (1928–73) for ◊Huambo, in Angola.

Nova Scotia /ˈnəʊvə ˈskəʊʃə/ province of E Canada
area 55,500 sq km/21,423 sq mi
capital and chief port Halifax
towns Dartmouth, Sydney
features Cabot Trail (Cape Breton Island), Alexander Graham Bell Museum, Fortress Louisbourg; Strait of Canso Superport is the largest deepwater harbour on the Atlantic coast of the continent
products coal, gypsum, dairy products, poultry, fruit, forest products, fish products (including scallop and lobster)
population (1986) 873,000
history England and France contended for possession of the territory until Nova Scotia (which then included present-day New Brunswick and Prince Edward Island) was ceded to Britain 1713; Cape Breton Island remained French until 1763.

Nova Scotia was visited by Caboto 1497. A French settlement was established 1604, but expelled 1613 by English colonists from Virginia. The name of the colony was changed from Acadia to Nova Scotia 1621. Nova Scotia was one of the four original provinces of the dominion of ◊Canada.

Novaya Zemlya /ˈnɑːvɪə ˈzemlɪə/ Arctic island group off the NE of the USSR; area 81,279 sq km/31,394 sq mi; population, a few Samoyed. It is rich in birds, seals, and walrus.

novel an extended fictitious prose narrative, often including some sense of the psychological development of the central characters and of their relationship with a broader world. The European novel is said to have originated in Greece in the 2nd century BC. The modern novel took its name and inspiration from the Italian *novella*, the short tale of varied character which became popular in the late 13th century. As the main form of narrative fiction in the 20th century, the novel is frequently classified according to genres and sub-genres such as the ◊historical novel, ◊detective fiction, ◊fantasy, and ◊science fiction.

Ancient Greek examples include the *Daphnis and Chloë* of Longus; almost the only surviving Latin example that could be called a novel is the *Golden Ass* of Apuleius, based on a Greek model. There is a similar, but until the 19th century independent, tradition of prose narrative including psychological development in the Far East, notably in Japan, with *The Tale of Genji* by Murasaki Shikibu (978–*c.*1015).

The works of the Italian writers Boccaccio and Bandello were translated into English in such collections as Painter's *Palace of Pleasure* 1566–67, which inspired the Elizabethan novelists, including Lyly, Sidney, Greene, Nash, and Lodge. In Spain, Cervantes's *Don Quixote* 1604 contributed to the development of the novel through its translation into other European languages, but the 17th century was dominated by the French romances of La Calprenède and Mlle de Scudéry, although Congreve and Aphra Behn continued the English tradition.

In the 18th century the realistic novel was established in England in the work of Defoe, Richardson, Fielding, Sterne, and Smollett. Walpole, and later Mary Shelley, developed the Gothic novel; in the early 19th century Sir Walter Scott developed the historical novel, and Jane Austen wrote 'novels of manners'. Novelists of the Victorian age in Britain are Dickens, Thackeray, the Brontës, George Eliot, Trollope, and Stevenson. Great European novelists of the 19th century were Hugo, Balzac, the two Dumas, George Sand, and Zola in France; Goethe and Jean Paul in Germany; Gogol, Turgenev, Dostoievsky, and Tolstoy in Russia; Cooper, Melville, Hawthorne, and Twain in the USA.

In Britain the transition period from Victorian times to the 20th century includes Meredith, Butler, Hardy, Gissing, Henry James, Kipling, Conrad, and George Moore, Wells, Bennett,

Novgorod The theatre, the monument to the thousandth anniversary of the foundation of the Russian state (862), and the cathedral of St Sophia (11th century) inside the Novgorod kremlin.

and Galsworthy. Slightly later are W Somerset Maugham, E M Forster, James Joyce, D H Lawrence, Ivy Compton-Burnett, and Virginia Woolf—the last four being particularly influential in the development of novel technique. Among those who began writing in the 1920s are J B Priestley, Richard Hughes, Aldous Huxley, Christopher Isherwood, Graham Greene, V S Pritchett, Evelyn Waugh; Elizabeth Bowen, Rose Macaulay, and Rosamund Lehmann. The 1930s produced Nigel Balchin, Joyce Cary, Lawrence Durrell, and George Orwell, and recent British writers include Anthony Powell, John Fowles, Kingsley Amis, Anthony Burgess, Iris Murdoch, Angela Carter, Doris Lessing, Salman Rushdie, and Martin Amis.

20th-century European novelists include (German) Lion Feuchtwanger, Thomas Mann, Franz Kafka, Ernst Wiechert, Stefan Zweig, Christa Wolff, Heinrich Böll, and Gunter Grass; (French) André Gide, Marcel Proust, Jules Romains, François Mauriac, and Alain Robbe-Grillet; (Italian) Gabriele d'Annunzio, Ignazio Silone, Alberto Moravia, Italo Calvino, and Primo Levi; (Russian) Maxim Gorky, Mikhail Sholokhov, Aleksei Tolstoi, Boris Pasternak, and Alexander Solzhenitsyn; (Spanish) Arturo Baréa, Pío Baroja and Ramón Pérez de Ayala. In the Americas contemporary novelists include (Latin American) Mario Vargas Llosa and Gabriel García Márquez; (Canadian) Morley Callaghan, Robertson Davies, and Margaret Atwood; and (US) Ernest Hemingway, William Faulkner, Bernard Malamud, Eudora Welty, Vladimir Nabokov, and Saul Bellow.

Novello /nəˈveləʊ/ Ivor. Adopted name of Ivor Novello Davies 1893–1951. Welsh composer and actor-manager. He wrote popular songs, such as 'Keep the Home Fires Burning', in World War I, and musicals in which he often appeared as the romantic lead, including *Glamorous Night* 1925, *The Dancing Years* 1939, and *Gay's the Word* 1951.

November criminals name given by right-wing nationalists in post-1918 Germany to the socialist politicians who had taken over the government after the abdication of Kaiser Wilhelm II and had signed the armistice with the Western Allies Nov 1918.

Noverre /nɒˈveə/ Jean-Georges 1727–1810. French choreographer, writer, and ballet reformer. He promoted ◊ballet d'action and simple, free movement, and is often considered the creator of modern Classical ballet. *Les Petits Riens* 1778 was one of his works.

Novgorod /ˈnɒvgərɒd/ industrial (chemicals, engineering, clothing, brewing) city on the Volkhov River, NW USSR, a major trading city in medieval times; population (1987) 228,000.

nuclear energy *The Sellafield nuclear plant, Cumbria, England. The nuclear-fuel-reprocessing plant is to the right of the dome.*

advanced gas-cooled reactor (AGR)

AGR under construction

Magnox reactor

Pressurized water reactor

electricity generation

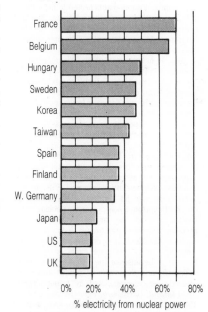

% electricity from nuclear power

Novgorod was the original capital of the Russian state, founded at the invitation of the people of the city by the Viking (Varangian) chieftain Rurik 862. The Viking merchants who went there quickly became fully assimilated into the native Slav population. In 912, the capital of the principality moved to Kiev, but this did little to harm Novgorod. It developed a strong municipal government run by the leaders of the craft guilds and, until the 13th century, flourished as a major commercial centre (with a monopoly on the Russian fur trade) for trade with Scandinavia, the Byzantine empire and the Muslim world. It became one of the principal members of the ◊Hanseatic League, but its economy had already started to decline. This was hastened during the 15th-century rule of the boyars, nobles who had seized power from the guilds 1416. It came under the control of Ivan the Great III 1478, and was sacked by Ivan the Terrible 1570.

Novgorod school Russian school of icon and mural painters, active from the late 14th to the 16th century in Novgorod. They were inspired by the work of the refugee Byzantine artist ◊Theophanes the Greek. Russian artists imitated his linear style, but this became increasingly stilted and mannered.

Novi Sad /ˈnɒvi ˈsɑːd/ industrial and commercial (pottery and cotton) city, capital of the autonomous province of Vojvodina, Yugoslavia on the river Danube; population (1981) 257,700. Products include leather, textiles, and tobacco.

Novocaine trade name of *procaine*, the first synthetic local anaesthetic, invented 1905. It has now been replaced by agents such as ◊lignocaine.

Novokuznetsk /ˌnɒvəkuzˈnetsk/ industrial city (steel, aluminium, chemicals) in the Kuzbas, S central USSR; population (1987) 589,000. It was called Stalinsk 1932–61.

Novorossiisk /ˌnɒvərɒˈsiːsk/ USSR Black Sea port and industrial (cement, metallurgy, food processing) city; population (1987) 179,000.

Novosibirsk /ˌnɒvəsɪˈbɪəsk/ industrial city (engineering, textiles, chemicals, food processing) in W Siberia, USSR on the river Ob; population (1987) 1,423,000. Winter lasts eight months here.

At Akademgorodok 'Science City', population 25,000, advanced research is carried on into Siberia's local problems.

Nowa Huta an industrial suburb of Kraków, on the Vistula River. It is the centre of Poland's steel industry.

Noyes /ˈnɔɪz/ Alfred 1880–1958. British poet, who wrote poems about the sea and the anthology favourites 'The Highwayman', 'Barrel Organ', and 'Go down to Kew in lilac-time...'.

NPA abbreviation for *New People's Army* (Philippines).

NS abbreviation for ◊*Nova Scotia*.

NSAID abbreviation for *non-steroidal anti-inflammatory drug*. It is effective in the long-term treatment of rheumatoid ◊arthritis and osteoarthritis, and acts to reduce swelling and pain in soft tissues. Bleeding into the digestive tract is a serious side effect; it should not be used by persons who have a peptic ulcer.

NSPCC abbreviation for *National Society for the Prevention of Cruelty to Children* (UK).

NSW abbreviation for ◊*New South Wales*.

NT abbreviation for ◊*Northern Territory*, Australia.

NTP (*Normal Temperature and Pressure*) former name for ◊*STP* (*Standard Temperature and Pressure*).

Nu, U (Thakin) /nuː/ 1907– . Burmese politician, prime minister for most of the period from 1948 to the military coup of 1962. Exiled abroad from 1966, U Nu returned to the country 1980 and, in 1988, helped found the National League for Democracy opposition movement.

Formerly a teacher, U Nu joined the Dobhama Asiayone (Our Burma) nationalist organization during the 1930s and was imprisoned by the British authorities at the start of World War II. He was released 1942, following Japan's invasion of Burma (now Myanmar), and appointed foreign minister in a puppet government. In 1945 he fought with the British against the Japanese and on independence became Burma's first prime minister. Excepting short breaks during 1956–57 and 1958–60, he remained in this post until Gen ◊Ne Win overthrew the parliamentary regime in 1962.

Nuba the peoples of the Nuba mountains, W of the White Nile, Sudan. Their languages belong to the Nubian branch of the Chari-Nile family.

Nubia /ˈnjuːbiə/ former African country now divided between Egypt and Sudan; it gives its name to the *Nubian Desert* S of Lake Nasser.

Ancient Egypt, which was briefly ruled by Nubian kings in the 8th–7th centuries BC, knew the N as Wawat and the S as Kush, with the dividing line roughly at Dongola. Egyptian building work in the area included ◊Abu Simbel, Philae, and a defensive chain of forts which established the lines of development of medieval fortification. Nubia's capital *c.* 600 BC–AD 350 was Meroe, near Khartoum. About 250–AD 550 most of Nubia was occupied by the *x-group people*, of whom little is known; their royal mound tombs (mistaken by earlier investigations for natural mounds created by wind erosion) were excavated by W B ◊Emery, and many horses and attendants were found to have been slaughtered to accompany the richly jewelled dead.

nuclear-arms verification the process of checking the number and types of nuclear weapons held by a country in accordance with negotiated limits. The chief means are:

reconnaissance satellites that detect submarines or weapon silos, using angled cameras to give three-dimensional pictures of installations, penetrating camouflage by means of scanners, and partially seeing through cloud and darkness by infrared devices;

telemetry, or radio transmission of instrument readings;

interception to get information on performance of weapons under test;

on-site inspection by experts visiting bases, launch sites, storage facilities, and test sites in another country;

radar tracking of missiles in flight;

seismic monitoring of underground tests, in the same way as with earthquakes. This is not accurate and on-site inspection is needed. Tests in the atmosphere, space, or the oceans are forbidden, and the ban is accepted because explosions are not only dangerous to all but immediately detectable.

nuclear energy energy from the inner core or ◊nucleus of the atom, as opposed to energy released in chemical processes, which is derived from the electrons surrounding the nucleus.

nuclear fission As in an atomic bomb, fission is achieved by allowing a ◊neutron to strike the nucleus of an atom of uranium-235, which then splits apart to release two or three other neutrons. If the uranium-235 is pure, a ◊chain reaction is set up when these neutrons in turn strike other nuclei. This happens very quickly, resulting in the burst of energy seen in the atomic bomb. However, the process can be controlled by absorbing excess neutrons in 'control rods' (which may be made of steel alloyed with boron), which is the method used in a ◊nuclear reactor.

nuclear fusion The process that occurs in the hydrogen bomb, and in the sun and other stars, whereby hydrogen nuclei fuse to form helium nuclei with an accompanying release of energy. Attempts to harness fusion for commercial power production have so far been unsuccessful, although machines such as the Joint European Torus (or ◊JET) have demonstrated that fusion power is theoretically feasible. In 1989 it was claimed that fusion could occur in a test tube at room temperature, but this was not confirmed.

nuclear physics the study of the properties of the nucleus of the ◊atom.

nuclear reactor device for producing ◊nuclear energy in a controlled manner. There are various types of reactor, all using nuclear fission. In a *gas-cooled reactor*, a circulating gas under pressure (such as carbon dioxide) removes heat from the core of the reactor, which usually contains natural uranium. The efficiency of the fission process is increased by slowing neutrons in the core by using a ◊moderator such as carbon. The reaction is controlled with neutron-absorbing rods made of boron. An *advanced gas-cooled reactor* (AGR) generally uses enriched uranium as its fuel. A *water-cooled reactor*, such as the steam-generating heavy water (deuterium oxide) reactor, has water circulating through the hot core. The water is converted to steam, which drives turbo-alternators for generating electricity. The most widely used reactor is the *pressurized-water reactor*, which contains a sealed system of pressurized water that is heated to form steam in heat exchangers in an external circuit. The *fast breeder reactor* has no moderator and uses fast neutrons to bring about fission. The *fast reactor* uses a mixture of plutonium and uranium oxide as fuel. It has no moderator. When operating, uranium is converted to plutonium, which can be extracted and used later as fuel. The fast breeder is so called because it produces more plutonium than it consumes. Heat is removed from the reactor by a coolant of liquid sodium. The world's largest fast breeder, the Superphénix, is at Creys-Malville in SW France, but the USSR has the most advanced programme.

nuclear accidents Public concern over the safety of nuclear reactors has been intensified by explosions and accidental release of radioactive materials. *Chernobyl*, Ukraine, USSR. In Apr 1986 there was an explosive leak, caused by overheating, from a non-pressurized boiling water reactor, one of the largest in Europe. The resulting clouds of radioactive material spread as far as Sweden; 31 people were killed in the explosion (many more are expected to die or become ill because of the long-term effects of radiation), and thousands of square kilometres of land were contaminated by fallout. *Three Mile Island*, Harrisburg, Pennsylvania, USA. In 1979, a combination of mechanical and electrical failure, as well as operator error, caused a pressurized water reactor to leak radioactive matter. *Church Rock*, New Mexico, USA. In July 1979, 100 million gallons of radioactive water containing uranium leaked from a pond into the Rio Purco, causing the water to become over 6,500 times as radioactive as safety standards allow for drinking water. *Ticonderoga*, 130 km/80 mi off the coast of Japan. In 1965 a US Navy Skyhawk jet bomber fell off the deck of this ship, sinking in 4,900 m/16,000 ft

of water. It carried a one-megaton hydrogen bomb. The accident was only revealed in 1989. *Windscale* (now Sellafield), Cumbria, England. In 1957, fire destroyed the core of a reactor, releasing large quantities of radioactive fumes into the atmosphere.

Concerns about safety have led to study of reactors incorporating process-inherent ultimate safety (PIVS), a safety system for the emergency cooling of a reactor by automatically flooding an overheated core with water. Other concerns about nuclear power centre on the difficulties of reprocessing nuclear fuel and disposing safely of nuclear waste, and the cost of nuclear power stations (especially of decommissioning a station at the end of its life).

In 1989, the UK government decided to postpone the construction of new nuclear power stations; in the USA, no new stations have been commissioned in over a decade; the Rancho Seco station, near Sacramento, California was closed by popular vote. Some countries, such as France and the USSR, are pressing ahead with their nuclear programmes.

nuclear warfare war involving the use of nuclear weapons. Nuclear-weapons research began in Britain 1940, but was transferred to the USA after it entered World War II. The research programme, known as the Manhattan Project, was directed by J Robert Oppenheimer. The worldwide total of nuclear weapons in 1989 was about 50,000, and the number of countries possessing nuclear weapons stood officially at five: USA, USSR, UK, France, and China. Many other nations were thought either to have a usable stockpile of these weapons (Israel, South Africa) or the ability to produce them quickly (India, Pakistan, and others).

atom bomb The original weapon relied on use of a chemical explosion to trigger a chain reaction. The first test explosion was at Alamogordo, New Mexico, 16 Jul 1945; the first use in war was by the USA against Japan 6 Aug 1945 over Hiroshima and three days later at Nagasaki.

hydrogen bomb A much more powerful weapon than the atom bomb, it relies on the release of thermonuclear energy by the condensation of hydrogen nuclei to helium nuclei (as happens in the Sun). The first detonation was at Eniwetok Atoll, Pacific Ocean, 1952 by the USA.

neutron bomb or enhanced radiation weapon (ERW) It is a very small hydrogen bomb that has relatively high radiation but relatively low blast, designed to kill (in up to six days) by a brief neutron radiation that leaves buildings and weaponry intact.

nuclear warfare

When the missiles have been launched into space, the individual warheads separate from the "bus" that carries them, and re-enter the atmosphere independently, each heading for a different target.

Nuclear methods of attack now include aircraft bombs, rocket-propelled missiles with nuclear warheads (long- or short-range, surface-to-surface, and surface-to-air), depth charges, and high-powered landmines ('atomic demolition munitions' to blast craters in the path of an advancing enemy army).

The major subjects of Soviet-US negotiation are *intercontinental ballistic missiles* (ICBMs) which have from 1968 been equipped with clusters of warheads (which can be directed to individual targets) and are known as multiple independently targetable re-entry vehicles (MIRVs). The 1980s US-designed MX (Peacekeeper) carries up to ten warheads in each missile. In 1980, the UK bought submarine-launched Trident missiles from the USA. Each warhead has eight independently targetable re-entry vehicles (each nuclear-armed) with a range of about 6,400 km/4,000 mi to eight separate targets within about 240 km/150 mi of the central aiming point.

Nuclear methods of defence include:
antiballistic missile (ABM) earth-based systems with two types of missile, one short-range with high acceleration, and one comparatively long-range for interception above the atmosphere; *Strategic Defense Initiative* (announced by the USA 1983 to be operative from 2000; popularly known as the 'Star Wars' programme) 'directed energy weapons' firing laser beams would be mounted on space stations, and by burning holes in incoming missiles would either collapse them or detonate their fuel tanks.

nuclear waste the toxic by-products of the nuclear energy industry. Reactor waste is of three types: high-level spent fuel, or the residue when nuclear fuel has been removed from a reactor and reprocessed; intermediate, which may be long- or short-lived; and low-level, but bulky, waste from reactors, which has only short-lived radioactivity. Disposal, by burial on land or at sea, raises problems of safety, environmental pollution, and security.

Waste from a site where uranium is mined or milled may have an active life of several thousand years. Sea disposal has occurred at many sites, for example 450 km/300 mi off Land's End, England, but there is no guarantee of the safety of this method of disposal, even for low-activity waste. There have been proposals to dispose of high-activity waste in old mines, granite formations, and specially constructed bunkers. The most hopeful proposed method is by vitrification into solid glass cylinders, which would be placed in titanium-cobalt alloy containers and deposited on dead planets in space. Beneath the sea the containers would start

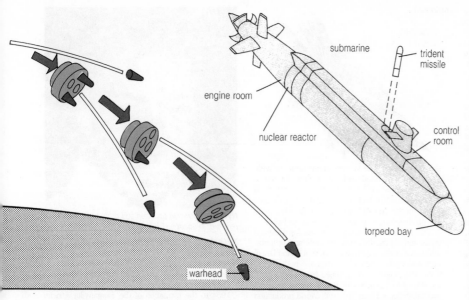

engine room
nuclear reactor
submarine
trident missile
control room
torpedo bay
warhead

to corrode after 1,000 years, and the cylinders themselves would dissolve within the next 1,000 years.

nuclear winter the expected effect of a widespread nuclear war. Besides the destruction caused by nuclear blasts and the subsequent radiation, it has been suggested that the atmosphere would be so full of dust, smoke, soot, and ash that the Sun's rays could not penetrate for a significant period of time, sufficient to eradicate most plant life on which other life depends. The cold would be intense, and a great increase in snow and ice worldwide would occur.

Once the ash finally settled, the Sun's rays would be reflected so much that there would not be enough heat to warm up the planet for some time. Insects, grasses, and sea life would have the best prospects of survival, as well as microorganisms.

nucleic acid a complex organic acid made up of a long chain of nucleotides. The two types, known as DNA (deoxyribonucleic acid) and RNA (ribonucleic acid), form the basis of heredity in living organisms. The nucleotides are made up of a sugar (deoxyribose or ribose), a phosphate group, and one of four purine or pyrimidine bases. The order of the bases along the nucleic acid strand contains the genetic 'message'.

nucleolus in biology, a structure found in the nucleus of ◊eukaryotic cells. It produces the RNA that makes up the ◊ribosomes, from instructions in the DNA.

nucleon a particle found inside the nucleus of an ◊atom, either a ◊proton or a ◊neutron.

nucleon number the number of nucleons (protons or neutrons) in the nucleus of a ◊atom. The nucleon number (also called the mass number) is the sum of the proton number and the neutron number. In symbols, such as $^{14}_{6}C$ that represent nuclear ◊isotopes, the lower, or subscript, number is the proton number. The upper, or superscript, number is the nucleon number.

nucleotide organic compound consisting of a purine (adenine or guanine) or a pyrimidine (thymine or cytosine) base linked to a sugar and a phosphate group. ◊DNA and ◊RNA are made up of long chains of nucleotides.

nucleus in physics, the positively charged central part of an ◊atom. Except for hydrogen, the nuclei contain ◊neutrons as well as ◊protons. Surrounding the nuclei are ◊electrons, which contain a negative charge equal to the protons, thus giving the atom a neutral charge.

nucleus in biology, the central part of a ◊eukaryotic cell, containing the chromosomes.

Nuffield /ˈnʌfiːld/ William Richard Morris, Viscount Nuffield 1877–1963. English manufacturer and philanthropist. Starting with a small cycle-repairing business, in 1910 he designed a car that could be produced cheaply, and built up Morris Motors Ltd at Cowley, Oxford. He endowed Nuffield College, Oxford, 1937 and the Nuffield Foundation 1943.

nugget piece of gold found as a lump of the ◊native ore. Nuggets occur in ◊alluvial deposits where river-borne particles of the metal have adhered to one another.

nuisance in law, interference with enjoyment of, or rights over, land. In English law there are two kinds of nuisance. *Private nuisance* affects a particular occupier of land, such as noise from a neighbour; the aggrieved occupier can apply for an ◊injunction and claim ◊damages. *Public nuisance* affects an indefinite number of members of the public, such as obstructing the highway; it is a criminal offence. In this case, individuals can only claim damages if they are affected more than the general public.

nuit blanche (French 'white night') a night without sleep.

Nujoma /nuːˈdʒəʊmə/ Sam 1929– . Namibian left-wing politician, leader of ◊SWAPO from 1959. He was exiled 1960 after founding SWAPO 1959 and controlled guerrillas from Angolan bases until the first free elections were held 1989, making Nujoma president designate.

Nukua'lofa /ˌnuːkuəˈləʊfə/ capital and port of Tonga on Tongatapu; population (1986) 29,000.

Nullarbor Plain /ˈnʌləbɔː/ (Latin *nullus arbor* 'no tree') arid coastal plateau area divided between W and S Australia; there is a network of caves beneath it. Atom-bomb experiments were carried out in the 1950s at Maralinga, an area in the NE bordering on the Great Victoria Desert.

nulli secundus (Latin) second to none.

Numa Pompilius /ˈnjuːmə pɒmˈpɪliəs/ legendary king of Rome *c.*716–*c.*679 BC, who succeeded Romulus, and was credited with the introduction of religious rites.

numbat Australian banded anteater *Myrmecobius fasciatus*. It is brown with white stripes on the back, and has a long tubular tongue to gather termites and ants. The body is about 25 cm/10 in long, and the tongue can be extended 10 cm/4 in.

number a symbol used in counting or measuring. In mathematics, there are various kinds of numbers. The everyday number system is the decimal system, using the base 10. ◊Real numbers include all rational numbers (integers, or whole numbers, and fractions), and irrational numbers (those not expressible as fractions). ◊Complex numbers include the real and unreal numbers (real-number multiples of the square root of –1). The ◊binary number system, used in computers, has 2 as its base.

The ordinary numerals, 0, 1, 2, 3, 4, 5, 6, 7, 8, 9, give a counting system which, in the denary system, continues 10, 11, 12, 13, and so on. These are whole numbers (positive integers), with fractions represented as, for example $^{1}/_{4}$, $^{1}/_{2}$, $^{3}/_{4}$, or as decimal fractions (0.25, 0.5, 0.75). They are also ◊rational numbers. Irrational numbers cannot be represented in this way and require symbols, such as $\sqrt{2}$, π, and e. They can be expressed numerically only as the (inexact) approximations 1.414, 3.142 and 2.718 (to three places of decimals) respectively. π and e are also examples of transcendental numbers, because they (unlike $\sqrt{2}$) cannot be derived by solving a ◊polynomial equation (an equation with one ◊variable quantity) with rational ◊coefficients (multiplying factors). Complex numbers, which include the real numbers (rational and irrational numbers) as well as unreal numbers, take the general form $a + bi$, where $i = \sqrt{-1}$ (that is, $i^2 = -1$), and a is the real part and bi is the unreal part.

history The ancient Egyptians, Greeks, Romans, and Babylonians all evolved number systems although none had a zero, which was introduced from India by way of Arab mathematicians in about the 6th century AD and allowed a place-value system to be devised on which the denary (counting in tens) system is based. Other number systems have since evolved and have found applications. For example, numbers to base two (binary numbers), using only 0 and 1, are commonly used in digital computers to represent the two-state 'on' or 'off' pulses of electricity. Binary numbers were first developed by Gottfried Leibniz in the late 17th century.

Numidia /njuːˈmɪdiə/ Roman N African territory 'nomads' land', now E ◊Algeria.

numismatics the study of ◊coins, and ◊medals and decorations.

nun (Latin *nonna* 'elderly woman') a woman belonging to a religious order under the vows of poverty, chastity, and obedience, and living under a particular rule. Christian convents are ruled by a superior (often elected), who is subject to the authority of the bishop of the diocese or sometimes directly to the pope. See ◊monasticism.

It is possible that the institution of Christian communities for nuns preceded the establishment of monasteries. The majority of the male orders have their female counterparts.

nunatak a mountain peak protruding through an ice sheet.

nuncio a diplomatic representative of the pope, performing the functions of a papal ambassador.

Nuneaton /nʌnˈiːtn/ market town in Warwickshire, England, on the river Anker, NE of Coventry; industries (ceramics, tiles and bricks); population (1984) 72,000.

Nunn /nʌn/ Trevor 1940– . British stage director, linked with the Royal Shakespeare Company from 1968. He received a Tony award (with John Caird) for his production of *Nicholas Nickleby* 1982 and for *Les Misérables* 1987.

Nuremberg /ˈnjʊərəmbɜːg/ (German *Nürnberg*) industrial city (electrical and other machinery, precision instruments, textiles, toys) in Bavaria, West Germany; population (1988) 467,000. From 1933 the Nuremberg rallies were held here, and in 1945 the Nuremberg trials of war criminals.

Created an imperial city 1219, it has an 11th–16th century fortress and many medieval buildings (restored after destruction of 75% of the city in World War II), including the home of Hans ◊Sachs, where the ◊Meistersingers met. The artist Dürer was born here.

Nuremberg rallies the annual meetings of the German ◊Nazi Party. They were characterized by extensive marches in party formations and mass rallies addressed by Nazi leaders such as Hitler and Goebbels.

Nuremberg trials after World War II, the trials of the 24 chief ◊Nazi war criminals Nov 1945–Oct 1946 by an international military tribunal consisting of four judges and four prosecutors: one of each from the UK, USA, USSR, and France. An appendix accused the German cabinet, general staff, high command, Nazi leadership corps, ◊SS, ◊Sturm Abteilung, and ◊Gestapo of criminal responsibility.

The main charges in the indictment were: (1) conspiracy to wage wars of aggression; (2) crimes against peace; (3) war crimes, for example, murder and ill-treatment of civilians and prisoners of war, deportation of civilians for slave labour, and killing of hostages; (4) crimes against humanity, for example, mass murder of the Jews and other peoples, and murder and ill-treatment of political opponents.

Of the accused, Krupp was too ill to be tried; Ley committed suicide during the trial, and ◊Bormann, who had fled, was sentenced to death in his absence. Fritsche, Schacht, and ◊Papen were acquitted. The other 18 were found guilty on one or more counts. ◊Hess, Walther Funk, and ◊Raeder were sentenced to life imprisonment, Shirach and Speer to 20 years, Neurath to 15 years, and Doenitz to 10 years. The remaining 11 men, sentenced to death by hanging, were ◊Goering (who committed suicide before he could be executed), ◊Ribbentrop, ◊Kaltenbrunner, ◊Rosenberg, Hans Frank, Wilhelm Frick, Fritz Sauckel, Arthur Seyss-Inquart, Julius Streicher, ◊Keitel, and ◊Jodl. The SS and Gestapo were declared criminal organizations.

Nureyev /njuˈreɪef/ Rudolf 1938– . Soviet dancer and choreographer. A soloist with the Kirov Ballet, he defected to the West 1961, where he was mainly associated with the Royal Ballet, and was Margot ◊Fonteyn's principal partner.

nursery rhyme jingle current among children. Usually limited to a couplet or quatrain with strongly marked rhythm and rhymes, nursery rhymes have often been handed down by oral tradition.

Some of the oldest nursery rhymes are connected with a traditional tune and accompanied the ancient ring games, for example, 'Here we go round the mulberry bush', which was part of the May Day festivities. Others contain fragments of incantations and other rites; others have a factual basis and commemorated popular figures, such as Jack Sprat and Jack Horner.

nursing supervision of health as well as care of the sick, the very young, the very old, and the disabled. Organized training first originated 1836 in Germany, and was developed in Britain by the work of Florence ◊Nightingale who, during the Crimean War, established standards of scientific, humanitarian care in military hospitals.

In ancient times very limited care was associated with some temples, and in Christian times nursing became associated with the religious orders until the Reformation brought it into secular hands in Protestant countries. Many varied qualifications are now available, standards being maintained by the National Boards (England, Scotland, Wales, and Northern Ireland) for Nursing, Midwifery and Health Visiting, and the Royal College of Nursing (1916) is the professional body. In the USA, although registration is the responsibility of individual states, an almost uniform standard has been established by the National League for Nursing (1952).

Nusa Tenggara /ˈnuːsə ttɛŋˈgɑːrə/ volcanic archipelago in Indonesia, also known as the *Lesser Sunda Islands*, including ◊Bali, ◊Lombok, and ◊Timor; area 73,144 sq km/28,241 sq mi. The islands form two provinces of Indonesia: *Nusu Tenggara Barat*, population (1980) 2,724,500; and *Nusu Tenggara Timur*, population (1980) 2,737,000.

nut the common name for a dry, single-seeded fruit that does not split open to release the seed. A nut is formed from more than one carpel, but only one seed becomes fully formed, the remainder aborting. The wall of the fruit, the pericarp, becomes hard and woody, forming the outer shell. Examples are the acorn, hazelnut, and

nuthatch

European nuthatch

sweet chestnut. The kernels of most nuts provide a concentrated food with about 50% fat and a protein content of 10–20%, though a few, such as chestnuts, are high in carbohydrates and have only a moderate (5%) protein content. Most nuts are produced by perennial trees and bushes.

The term also describes various hard-shelled fruits and seeds, including almonds and walnuts, which are really the stones of ◊drupes, and Brazil nuts and shelled peanuts, which are both seeds. While the majority are obtained from plantations, considerable quantities of Brazil and pecan nuts are still collected from the wild. World production in the mid-1980s was about 4 million tonnes a year. Nuts also provide edible and industrial oils.

nut and bolt a common method of fastening pieces of metal together. They came into use at the turn of the 19th century, following Henry Maudslay's invention of a precision screw-cutting ◊lathe.

nutation in astronomy, a slight 'nodding' of the Earth in space, caused by the varying gravitational pulls of the ◊Sun and ◊Moon. Nutation changes the angle of the Earth's axial tilt (average 23.5°) by about 9 seconds of arc to either side of its mean position, a complete side-to-side nodding taking just over 18.5 years.

nutation in botany, the spiral movement exhibited by the tips of certain stems during growth; it enables a climbing plant to find a suitable support. Nutation sometimes also occurs in tendrils and flower stalks.

nutcracker bird *Nucifraga caryocatactes* of the crow family, found in areas of coniferous forest in Asia and parts of Europe, particularly mountains. About 33 cm/1.1 ft long, it has speckled plumage and a powerful beak. It feeds on conifer seeds. Irregularly, there is a mass migration of nutcrackers from Siberia to W Europe.

nuthatch European bird *Sitta europaea* about the size of a sparrow, with a blue-grey back and buff breast. It is a climber, and feeds mainly on nuts. The nest is built in a hole in a tree, and five to eight white eggs with reddish-brown spots are laid in early summer.

nutmeg kernel of the seed of the evergreen tree *Myristica fragrans*, native to the Moluccas. Both the nutmeg and its secondary covering, known as *mace*, are used as a spice in cookery.

nutrition the science of food, and its effect on human and animal life health, and disease. Nutrition studies the basic nutrients required to sustain life, their bioavailability in foods and overall diet, and the effect of cooking and storage. *Malnutrition* is caused by underfeeding, found especially in Third World countries; an imbalanced diet, found everywhere; and over-feeding, found in more wealthy Western countries. Nutrition also studies feeds for farm animals, pets, and animals kept in captivity.

Nuuk /nuːk/ Greenlandic for ◊Godthaab, capital of Greenland.

NV abbreviation for ◊*Nevada*.

NY abbreviation for ◊*New York*.

nyala antelope *Tragelaphus angasi* found in the thick bush of S Africa. About 1 m/3 ft at the shoulder, it is greyish-brown with thin vertical white stripes. Males have horns up to 80 cm/2.6 ft long.

Nyasa /niˈæsə/ former name for Lake ◊Malawi.

Nyerere Tanzanian politician and premier Dr Julius Nyerere, in London, 1960.

Nyasaland /ˈniˈæsəlænd/ former name (until 1964) for ◊Malawi.

Nyerere /njəˈreəri/ Julius (Kambarage) 1922– . Tanzanian socialist politician, president 1964–85. Originally a teacher, he devoted himself from 1954 to the formation of the Tanganyika African National Union and subsequent campaigning for independence. He became chief minister 1960, was prime minister of Tanganyika 1961–62, president of the newly formed Tanganyika Republic 1962–64, first president of Tanzania 1964–85, and head of the Organization of African Unity 1984.

Nyers /njeəʃ/ Rezso 1923– . Hungarian socialist leader. As secretary of the ruling Hungarian Socialist Worker's Party's (HSWP) central committee 1962–74 and a member of its politburo 1966–74, he was the architect of Hungary's liberalizing economic reforms in 1968.

Born in Budapest, he worked as a printer and in 1940 joined the Hungarian Social Democratic Party, which, in 1948 was forcibly merged with the communists. He was removed from his HSWP posts in 1974 and his career remained at a standstill until 1988, when, with a new reform initiative underway, he was brought back into the politburo. He became head of the newly formed Hungarian Socialist Party 1989.

Nyíregyháza /ˈniːredʒˌhɑːzə/ market town in E Hungary; population (1988) 119,000. It trades in tobacco and vegetables.

Nykvist /ˈniːkvɪst/ Sven 1922– . Swedish director of photography, associated with the film director Ingmar Bergman. He worked frequently in the USA from the mid-1970s onwards. His films include *The Virgin Spring* 1960 (for Bergman), *Pretty Baby* 1978 (for Louis Mallé), and *Fanny and Alexander* 1982 (for Bergman).

nylon a synthetic fibre-forming plastic, which is similar in chemical structure to protein. It is used in the manufacture of toilet articles, textiles, and medical sutures. Nylon fibres are stronger and more elastic than silk, and relatively insensitive to moisture and mildew. Nylon is particularly suitable for hosiery and woven goods, simulating other materials such as silks and furs; it is also used in carpets. It was developed in the USA 1937 by the chemist W H Carothers and his associates.

nymph in Greek mythology, a guardian spirit of nature. *Hamadryads* or *dryads* guarded trees; *naiads*, springs and pools; *oreads*, hills and rocks; and *nereids*, the sea.

nymph in entomology, the immature form of insects which do not have a pupal stage, for example, grasshoppers and dragonflies. Nymphs generally resemble the adult (unlike larvae), but do not have fully formed reproductive organs or wings.

NZ abbreviation for ◊*New Zealand*.

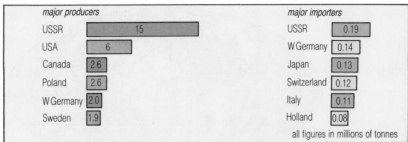

major producers		major importers	
USSR	15	USSR	0.19
USA	6	W Germany	0.14
Canada	2.6	Japan	0.13
Poland	2.6	Switzerland	0.12
W Germany	2.0	Italy	0.11
Sweden	1.9	Holland	0.08

all figures in millions of tonnes

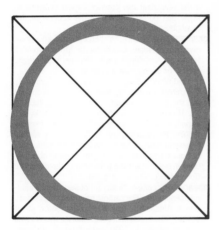

O 15th letter of the Roman alphabet, whose form was derived from the Semitic alphabet. In modern English it represents a wide range of sounds, from the diphthong ō (*so*) to the open sounds in *or*, and *on*, and the oo-sound in *wolf*.

o/a abbreviation for *on account*.

Oahu /əʊˈɑːhuː/ island of Hawaii, USA, in the N Pacific
area 1,525 sq km/589 sq mi
towns state capital Honolulu
physical formed by two extinct volcanoes
features Waikiki beach; Pearl Harbor naval base
products sugar, pineapples; tourism is important
population (1980) 762,000.

oak tree and shrub of the genus *Quercus*, family Fagaceae, with over 300 known species widely distributed in temperate zones. They are valuable for timber, the wood being durable and straight grained. Their fruits are called acorns.

Oak wilt, the result of a symbiotic partnership between a beetle and a fungus, resembles Dutch ◊elm disease and is virulent.

oak

The English oak *Quercus robur*, also found in Europe, grows to 36 m/120 ft with a girth of 15 m/50 ft. Other European varieties are the evergreen oak *Quercus ilex*, the Turkey oak *Quercus cerris*, and the cork oak *Quercus suber*, of the W Mediterranean region; valuable New World timber oaks are the white oak *Quercus alba* and the evergreen live oak *Quercus virginiana*.

Oakland /ˈəʊklənd/ industrial port (vehicles, textiles, chemicals, food processing, shipbuilding) in California, USA, on the E coast of San Francisco Bay; population (1980) 339,300. It is linked by bridge (1936) with San Francisco.

Oakley /ˈəʊkli/ Annie (Phoebe Annie Oakley Mozee) 1860–1926. US sharpshooter, member of Buffalo Bill's Wild West Show (see William ◊Cody).

Oak Ridge /ˈəʊk ˈrɪdʒ/ town in Tennessee, E USA, on the river Clinch, noted for the Oak Ridge National Laboratory 1943 which manufactures ◊plutonium for nuclear weapons; population (1980) 27,600.

Oaks horse race, one of the English classics, run at Epsom racecourse in June (normally two days after the ◊Derby), for three-year-old fillies only. The race is named after the Epsom home of the 12th Earl of Derby.

oarfish oceanic fish *Regalecus glesne*, in the family of ribbon-fishes. Occasionally up to 9 m/30 ft long, it has no scales, a small mouth, large eyes, and a compressed head.

oarweed large brown seaweeds (algae) found on the lower shore and below, also known as *kelps* or *tangles*, in particular *Laminaria digitata*. This species has fronds 1 to 2 m/3 to 6 ft long. Attached to it has a thick stalk and a frond divided into flat fingers.

OAS abbreviation for ◊Organization of American States.

oasis area of land made fertile by the presence of water near the surface in an otherwise arid region. The occurrence of oases affects the distribution of plants, animals, and people in the desert regions of the world.

Oastler /ˈəʊstlə/ Richard 1789–1861. English social reformer. He opposed child labour and the

oat

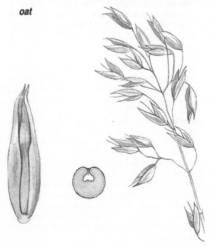

◊Poor Law 1834, and was largely responsible for securing the Factory Act 1833 and the Ten Hours Act 1847. He was born in Leeds, and was known as the 'Factory King'.

oat type of grass, genus *Avena*, and an important cereal food. The plant has long, narrow leaves and a stiff straw stem; the panicles of flowers, and later of grain, hang downward. The cultivated oat *Avena sativa* is produced for human and animal food.

In Europe, its importance has diminished because of the rapid decline of the working horse population, and of greater preference for higher-yielding barley as an animal feed.

Oates /əʊts/ Joyce Carol 1938– . US writer. Her novels, often containing surrealism and violence, include *A Garden of Earthly Delights* 1967 *Them* 1969, *Unholy Loves* 1979 and *A Bloodsmoor Romance* 1982.

Oates /əʊts/ Laurence Edward Grace 1880–1912. British Antarctic explorer, who accompanied ◊Scott on his second expedition to the South Pole. On the return journey, suffering from frostbite, he went out alone into the blizzard to die rather than delay the others.

Oates /əʊts/ Titus 1649–1705. British conspirator. A priest, he entered the Jesuit colleges at Valladolid, Spain, and St Omer, France, as a spy in 1677–78, and on his return to England announced he had discovered a 'Popish Plot' to murder Charles II and re-establish Catholicism. Although this story was almost entirely false, many innocent Roman Catholics were executed during 1678–80 on Oates's evidence. In 1685 he

TITUS OATES

Oates The fictitious 'Popish Plot' concocted by Titus Oates was supposed to involve the murder of the king, the burning of London, and slaughter of Protestants.

oat

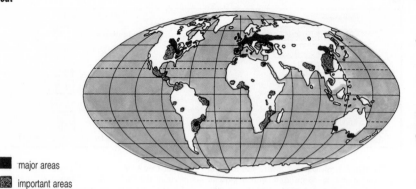

■ major areas

▒ important areas

was flogged, pilloried, and imprisoned for perjury. He was pardoned and granted a pension after the revolution of 1688.

oath a solemn promise to tell the truth or perform some duty, combined with an appeal to a deity or something held sacred.

In English courts witnesses normally swear to tell the truth holding a ◊New Testament in their right hand. People who object to the taking of oaths, such as ◊Quakers and atheists, give a solemn promise (◊affirmation) to tell the truth. A Jew swears holding the Pentateuch, with his or her head covered. Muslims and Hindus swear by their respective sacred books; a Chinese witness breaks a saucer before giving evidence. In the USA a witness raises his right hand in taking the oath.

OAU abbreviation for ◊Organization of African Unity.

Oaxaca /wəˈhɑːkə/ capital of a state of the same name in the Sierra Madre del Sur mountain range, central Mexico; population (1980) 157,300; former home town of presidents Benito Juárez and Porfirio Diaz; industries include food processing, textiles, and handicrafts.

Ob /ɒb/ river in Asiatic USSR, flowing 3,380 km/ 2,100 mi from the Altai mountains through the W Siberian Plain to the Gulf of Ob in the Arctic Ocean. With its main tributary, the **Irtysh**, it is 5,600 km/3,480 mi.

Although frozen for half the year, and subject to flooding, it is a major transportation route. Novosobirsk and Barnaul are the main ports.

ob. abbreviation for *obiit* (Latin 'he/she died').

Oban /ˈəʊbən/ seaport and resort in Strathclyde, W Scotland; population (1981) 8,000.

OBE Order of the British Empire, a British order of knighthood.

Obeid, El /ˈəʊbeɪd/ see ◊El Obeid, city in Sudan.

Oberammergau /ˌəʊbərˈæməgaʊ/ village in Bavaria, West Germany, where a Christian passion play has been performed every ten years (except during the world wars) since 1634 to commemorate the ending of the plague.

Oberammergau /ˌəʊbərˈæməgaʊ/ a town in Bavaria, West Germany, 72 km/45 mi SW of Munich. A Passion Play is performed here every 10 years. Population (1980) 5,000.

Oberhausen /ˈəʊbəˌhaʊzən/ industrial (metals, machinery, plastics, chemicals) and coalmining city in the Ruhr valley, North Rhine–Westphalia, West Germany; population (1988) 222,000.

Oberon /ˈəʊbərɒn/ king of the elves or fairies, and, according to a 13th-century French romance *Huon of Bordeaux*, an illegitimate son of Julius Caesar. Shakespeare used the character in *A Midsummer Night's Dream*.

Oberon /ˈəʊbərɒn/ Merle. Stage name of Estelle Merle O'Brien Thompson 1911–1979. Tasmanian-born British actress who starred in several Alexander Korda films, including *The Scarlet Pimpernel* 1935, and was briefly married to him. She played Cathy to Laurence Olivier's Heathcliff in *Wuthering Heights* 1939, and after 1940 worked successfully in the USA.

Oberösterreich /ˈəʊbərˌɜːstəraɪʃ/ German name for the federal state of ◊Upper Austria.

obesity condition of being overweight (generally, 20% or more above the desirable weight for your sex and height).

Obesity increases susceptibility to disease and strains the vital organs, and lessens life expectancy; it is remedied by healthy diet and exercise.

obi or *obeah* a form of witchcraft practised in the West Indies. It combines elements of Christianity and African religions, such as snake worship.

obiit (Latin 'he/she died') found, for example, in inscriptions on tombstones, followed by a date.

objective correlative phrase suggested by T S ◊Eliot in a discussion of Shakespeare's *Hamlet*. Recognizing that the hero's emotion in the play was somehow excessive and inexplicable, Eliot suggested that the dramatist must find an exact, sensuous equivalent, or 'objective correlative' for any emotion he wishes to express. He gave an example from *Macbeth* where Lady Macbeth's state of mind in the sleep walking scene is communicated to the audience by a skilful building up of images and actions.

object-oriented programming (OOP) a type of computer programming based on 'objects', in which data are closely linked to the procedures that operate on them. For example, a circle on the screen might be an object; it has data, such as a centre point and a radius, as well as procedures for moving it, erasing it, changing its size, and so on.

The technique originated with the Simula and Smalltalk languages in the 1960s and early 1970s, but it has now been incorporated into many general-purpose programming languages.

oboe a musical instrument of the ◊woodwind family. Played vertically, it is a wooden tube with a bell, is double-reeded, and has a yearning, poignant tone. Its range is almost three octaves.

Obote /əʊˈbəʊti/ (Apollo) Milton 1924– . Ugandan politician who led the independence movement from 1961. He became prime minister 1962 and was president 1966–71 and 1980–85, being overthrown by first Idi ◊Amin and then Brig Tito Okello.

Obraztsov /ˌɒbrəstˈsɒf/ Sergei 1901– . Russian puppeteer, head of the Moscow-based State Central Puppet Theatre, the world's largest puppet theatre (with a staff of 300). The repertoire was built up from 1923.

Obrenovich /əʊˈbrenəvɪtʃ/ Serbian dynasty that ruled 1816–42 and 1859–1903. The dynasty engaged in a feud with the rival house of Karageorgevich, which obtained the throne by the murder of the last Obrenovich 1903.

O'Brien /əʊˈbraɪən/ Angela Maxine ('Margaret') 1937– . US child actress, a star of the 1940s. She received a special Academy Award in 1944, but her career, including leading parts in *Lost Angel* 1943, *Meet Me in St Louis* 1944, and *The Secret Garden* 1949, did not survive into adolescence.

O'Brien /əʊˈbraɪən/ Willis H 1886–1962. US film animator and special effects man, responsible for one of the cinema's most memorable monsters, *King Kong* 1933.

obscenity laws in Britain, laws prohibiting the publishing of any material which tends to deprave or corrupt. Obscene material can be, for example, pornographic, violent, or encourage drug taking. Publishing includes distribution, sale, and hiring of the material. There is a defence of public good, if the defendant can produce expert evidence to show that publication was in the interest of, for example, art, science, or literature.

observation in science, the perception of a phenomenon, for example, examining the Moon through a telescope, watching mice to discover their mating habits, or seeing how a plant grows.

Traditionally observation was seen as entirely separate from theory, free from preconceptions and therefore important to the belief in ◊objectivity. However, as the above examples show, observations are ordered according to a pre-existing theory; for instance, one cannot observe mating behaviour without having decided what mating behaviour might look like. In addition many observations actually affect the behaviour of the observed (for instance, of mating mice).

observatory a site or facility for observation of natural phenomena. The earliest recorded observatory was at Alexandria, built by Ptolemy Soter, about 300 BC. The erection of observatories was revived in W Asia about AD 1000, and extended to Europe. The one built on Hveen island, Denmark 1576, for Tycho ◊Brahe, was elaborate, but survived only to 1597. It was followed by those at Paris 1667, Greenwich 1675, and Kew 1769. The modern observatory dates from the invention of the telescope. Most were near towns, but with the advent of big telescopes, clear skies, and hence high, remote sites, became essential. The most powerful optical telescopes covering the sky from the northern hemisphere are Mount ◊Palomar; Kitt Peak, Arizona; La Palma, Canary Islands; and Mount Semirodniki, Caucasus, USSR. ◊Radio astronomy observatories include ◊Jodrell Bank; the Mullard, Cambridge, England; ◊Arecibo; Effelsberg, West Germany; and ◊Parkes. In the 1970s optical telescopes were established at Cerro Tololo, Las Campanas, and La Silla, Chile; and ◊Siding Spring. Observatories are also carried on aircraft or sent into orbit as satellites, in space stations, and on the Space Shuttle.

obsession repetitive unwanted thought that is often recognized by the sufferer as being irrational, but which nevertheless causes distress. It can be associated with a compulsion where the individual feels an irresistible urge to carry out a repetitive series of actions. For example, a person excessively troubled by fears of contamination by dirt or disease may engage in continuous hand-washing.

obsidian a black or dark-coloured glassy volcanic rock, chemically similar to ◊granite, but formed by cooling rapidly on the Earth's surface at low pressure.

The glassy texture is the result of rapid cooling, which inhibits the growth of crystals. Obsidian was valued by the early civilizations of Mexico for making sharp-edged tools and ceremonial sculptures.

obstetrics the medical specialty concerned with the management of pregnancy, childbirth, and the immediate post-natal period.

O'Casey /əʊˈkeɪsi/ Sean. Adopted name of John Casey 1884–1964. Irish dramatist. His early plays are tragicomedies, blending realism with symbolism and poetic with vernacular speech: *The Shadow of a Gunman* 1922, *Juno and the Paycock* 1925, and *The Plough and the Stars* 1926. Later plays include *Red Roses for Me* 1946 and *The Drums of Father Ned* 1960.

He also wrote the anti-war drama *The Silver Tassie* 1929, *The Star Turns Red* 1940, *Oak Leaves and Lavender* 1947, and a six-volume autobiography.

Occam /ˈɒkəm/ or **Ockham**, William of *c.* 1300–1349. English philosopher, who revived the fundamentals of nominalism. He was born in Ockham, Surrey, and as a Franciscan monk, defended the doctrine of evangelical poverty against Pope John XXII, becoming known as the Invincible Doctor. He was imprisoned in Avignon, France, on charges of heresy in 1328 but escaped to Munich, Germany, where he died. The principle of reducing assumptions to the absolute minimum is known as *Occam's razor*.

Occitanie /ˌɒksɪtæˈniː/ area of S France; see ◊Languedoc-Roussillon.

occultation in astronomy, the temporary obscuring of a star by a body in the solar system. Occultations are used to provide information about changes in an orbit, and the structure of objects in space, such as radio sources.

The exact shapes and sizes of planets and asteroids can be found when they occult stars. The rings of Uranus were discovered when that planet occulted a star 1977.

occupational psychology the study of human behaviour at work. It includes dealing with problems in organizations, advising on management difficulties, and investigating the relationship between humans and machines (as in the design of aircraft controls). Another important area is ◊psychometrics and the use of assessment to assist in selection of personnel.

ocean great mass of salt water. Strictly speaking three oceans exist — ◊Atlantic, ◊Indian, and ◊Pacific — to which the Arctic is often added. They cover approximately 70% or 363,000,000 sq km/ 140,000,000 sq mi of the total surface area of the Earth

depth (average) 3,660 m/12,000 ft, but shallow ledges 180 m/600 ft run out from the continents, beyond which the continental slope reaches down to the ◊abyssal zone, the largest area, ranging from 2,000–6,000 m/6,500–19,500 ft. Only the ◊deep-sea trenches go deeper, the deepest recorded being 11,034 m/36,201 ft (by the *Vityaz*, USSR) in the Mariana Trench of the W Pacific 1957

features deep trenches (off E and SE Asia, and western South America), volcanic belts (in the W Pacific and E Indian Ocean), and ocean ridges (in the mid-Atlantic, E Pacific, and Indian Ocean)

temperature varies on the surface with latitude (–2°C to +29°C); decreases rapidly to 370 m/1,200 ft, then more slowly to 2,200 m/7,200 ft; and hardly at all beyond that

water contents salinity averages about 3%; minerals commercially extracted include bromine, magnesium, potassium, salt; those potentially recoverable include aluminium, calcium, copper, gold, manganese, silver.

oceanarium large display tank in which aquatic animals and plants live together much as they would in their natural environment.

An oceanarium was first created by the explorer and naturalist W Douglas Burden in 1938 in Florida, USA.

Oceania /ˌəʊʃiˈɑːniə/ the islands of the S Pacific (◊Micronesia, ◊Melanesia, ◊Polynesia). The term sometimes includes ◊Australasia and the ◊Malay archipelago, in which case it is considered as one of the seven continents.

Ocean Island /ˈəʊʃən/ another name for ◊Banaba, island in Kiribati.

oceanography the study of the oceans. It is a very wide science and its subdivisions deal with the individual ocean's extent and depth, the water's evolution and composition, its physics and chemistry, the bottom topography, currents and wind effects, tidal ranges, the biology, and the various aspects of human use.

ocean ridge topographical feature of the seabed indicating the presence of a constructive plate margin produced by the rise of magma to the surface, see ◊plate tectonics. It can rise many thousands of feet or metres above the surrounding abyssal plain.

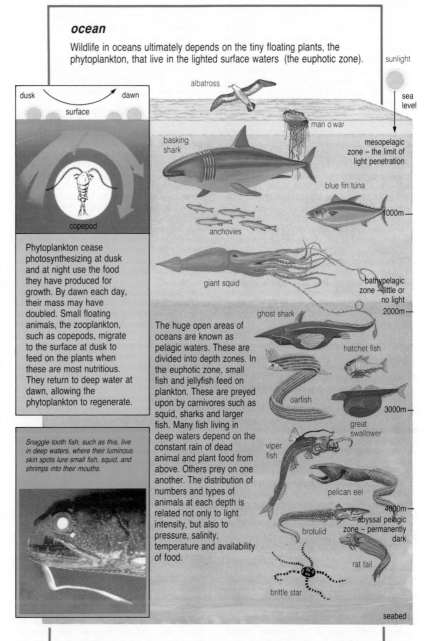

ocean

Wildlife in oceans ultimately depends on the tiny floating plants, the phytoplankton, that live in the lighted surface waters (the euphotic zone).

Phytoplankton cease photosynthesizing at dusk and at night use the food they have produced for growth. By dawn each day, their mass may have doubled. Small floating animals, the zooplankton, such as copepods, migrate to the surface at dusk to feed on the plants when these are most nutritious. They return to deep water at dawn, allowing the phytoplankton to regenerate.

Snaggle tooth fish, such as this, live in deep waters, where their luminous skin spots lure small fish, squid, and shrimps into their mouths.

The huge open areas of oceans are known as pelagic waters. These are divided into depth zones. In the euphotic zone, small fish and jellyfish feed on plankton. These are preyed upon by carnivores such as squid, sharks and larger fish. Many fish living in deep waters depend on the constant rain of dead animal and plant food from above. Others prey on one another. The distribution of numbers and types of animals at each depth is related not only to light intensity, but also to pressure, salinity, temperature and availability of food.

Ocean ridges usually have a ◊rift valley along their crests, indicating where the flanks are being pulled apart by the growth of the plates of the ◊lithosphere beneath. The crests are generally free of sediment; increasing depths of sediment are found with increasing distance down the flanks. Ocean ridges, such as the ◊Mid-Atlantic Ridge, consist of many segments offset along ◊faults.

ocean trench topographical feature of the seabed indicating the presence of a destructive plate margin (produced by the movements of ◊plate tectonics). The subduction or dragging downwards of one plate of the ◊lithosphere beneath another means that the ocean floor is pulled down.

Ocean trenches are found around the edge of the Pacific Ocean and the NE Indian Ocean; minor ones occur in the Caribbean and near the Falkland Islands. Ocean trenches represent the deepest parts of the ocean floor, the deepest being the ◊Mariana Trench which has a depth of 11,034 m/36,201 ft.

Oceanus /əʊˈsɪənəs/ in Greek mythology, the god (one of the ◊Titans) of a river supposed to encircle the earth. He was the progenitor of other river gods, and the nymphs of the seas and rivers.

ocelot wild ◊cat of Central and South America, up to 1 m/3 ft long with a 45 cm/1.5 ft tail. It weighs about 18 kg/40 lbs, and has a pale yellowish coat marked with longitudinal stripes and blotches. Hunted for its fur, it is close to extinction.

Ochoa /əʊˈtʃəʊə/ Severo 1905– . US biochemist. He discovered an enzyme able to assemble units of the ◊nucleic acid RNA in 1955, whilst working at New York University. For his work towards the synthesis of RNA Ochoa shared the 1959 Nobel Physiology or Medicine Prize with Arthur ◊Kornberg.

O'Connell /əʊˈkɒnl/ Daniel 1775–1847. Irish politician, called 'the Liberator'. In 1823 he founded the Catholic Association to press Roman Catholic claims. Although ineligible as a Roman Catholic to take his seat, he was elected MP for County

Clare 1828, and so forced the government to grant Catholic emancipation. In Parliament he cooperated with the Whigs in the hope of obtaining concessions until 1841, when he launched his campaign for repeal of the union.

His reserved and vacillating leadership and conservative outlook on social questions alienated his most active supporters, who broke away and formed the ◊Young Ireland movement.

O'Connor /əʊˈkɒnə/ Feargus 1794–1855. Irish parliamentary follower of Daniel ◊O'Connell. He sat in parliament 1832–35, and as editor of the *Northern Star* became an influential figure of the Chartist movement (see ◊Chartism).

O'Connor /əʊˈkɒnə/ Flannery 1925–1964. US novelist and story writer. Her works have a great sense of evil and sin, and often explore the religious sensibility of the Deep South. Her short stories include *A Good Man Is Hard to Find* 1955 and *Everything That Rises Must Converge* 1965.

Her novels are *Wise Blood* 1952 and *The Violent Bear It Away* 1960. She exemplifies the postwar revival of the ◊Gothic novel in southern US fiction.

OCR *optical character recognition* in computing, a technique whereby a program can understand words or figures by 'reading' a printed image of the text. The image is first input from paper by ◊scanning. The program then uses its knowledge of the shapes of characters to convert the image to a set of internal codes.

Once, OCR required specially designed characters such as the OCRA-B lettering, which appears on cheques, but current devices will recognize most standard typefaces and even handwriting.

octal number system a number system to the ◊base eight, used in computing, in which all numbers are made up of the digits 0 to 7. For example, decimal 8 is represented as octal 10, and decimal 17 as octal 21. See also ◊hexadecimal number system.

octane rating a numerical classification of petroleum fuels indicating their combustion characteristics.

The efficient running of an ◊internal combustion engine depends on the ignition of a petrol–air mixture at the correct time during the cycle of the engine. Higher-rated petrol burns faster than lower-rated fuels. The use of the correct grade must be matched to the engine.

Octans constellation in the southern hemisphere containing the southern celestial pole.

octave in music, a distance of eight notes as measured on the white notes of a piano keyboard. It corresponds to the consonance of first and second harmonics.

Octavian /ɒkˈteɪviən/ original name of ◊Augustus, the first Roman emperor.

October Revolution the second stage of the ◊Russian Revolution 1917.

Octobrists a group of Russian liberal constitutional politicians who accepted the reforming October Manifesto instituted by Tsar Nicholas II after the 1905 revolution and rejected more radical reforms.

octopus type of ◊cephalopod having a round or oval body, and eight arms with rows of suckers on each. They occur in all temperate and tropical seas, where they feed on crabs and other small animals. They can vary their coloration according to their background, and can swim with their arms or by a type of jet propulsion by means of their funnel. They are as intelligent as some vertebrates, and are not dangerous.

The common octopus *Octopus vulgaris* may reach 2 m/6 ft, and the giant octopus *Octopus apollyon* may span more than 10 m/32 ft. Octopuses are shy creatures who release clouds of ink when frightened.

Ocussi Ambeno /ɒˈkuːsi æmˈbeɪnəʊ/ until 1975, an exclave of the Portuguese colony of East Timor, on the N coast of Indonesian West Timor. The port is an outlet for rice, copra and sandalwood.

ODA abbreviation for ◊*Overseas Development Administration*.

ode lyric poem of complex form, originally chanted to a musical accompaniment. In Ancient Greece, exponents include Sappho, Pindar, Horace, and Catullus, and among English poets, Spenser, Milton, and Dryden.

Odense /ˈəʊdənsə/ industrial port on the island of Fyn, Denmark; population (1988) 174,000. Industries include shipbuilding, electrical goods, glass, and textiles. It is the birthplace of Hans Christian Andersen.

Oder /ˈəʊdə/ Polish *Odra* European river flowing N from Czechoslovakia to the Baltic Sea (the river Neisse is a tributary); length 885 km/550 mi.

Oder–Neisse Line /ˌəʊdəˈnaɪsə/ provisional border between Poland and East Germany agreed at the Potsdam Conference in 1945 at the end of World War II, named after the two rivers that form the frontier.

Odessa /əˈdesə/ seaport in Ukraine, USSR, on the Black Sea, capital of Odessa region; population (1987) 1,141,000. Products include chemicals, pharmaceuticals, and machinery. Odessa was founded by Catherine II 1795 near the site of an ancient Greek settlement. Occupied by Germany 1941–44, Odessa suffered severe damage under the Soviet scorched-earth policy and from German destruction.

Odets /əʊˈdets/ Clifford 1906–1963. US playwright, associated with the Group Theatre, whose plays include *Waiting for Lefty* 1935, *Awake and Sing* 1935, *Golden Boy* 1937, and *The Country Girl* 1950.

Odin /ˈəʊdɪn/ chief god of Scandinavian mythology, the *Woden* or *Wotan* of the Germanic peoples. A sky god, he is resident in Asgard, at the top of the world-tree, and receives the souls of heroic slain warriors from the Valkyries (the 'divine maidens') feasting with them in his great hall, Valhalla. The wife of Odin is Freya, or Frigga, and Thor is their son. Wednesday is named after him.

Odoacer /ˌɒdəʊˈeɪsə/ 433–493. King of Italy from 476, when he deposed Romulus Augustulus, the last Roman emperor. He was a leader of the barbarian mercenaries employed by Rome. He was overthrown and killed by Theodoric the Great, king of the Ostrogoths.

Odoyevsky /ˌɒdəˈjefski/ Vladimir 1804–1869. Russian writer whose works include tales of the supernatural, science fiction, satires, children's stories, and music criticism.

Odysseus /əˈdɪsjuːs/ the chief character of Homer's *Odyssey*, mentioned also in the *Iliad* as one of the foremost leaders of the Greek forces at the siege of Troy, noted for his courage and ingenuity. He is said to have been the ruler of the island of Ithaca.

Odyssey Greek epic poem in 24 books, probably written before 700 BC, attributed to Homer. It describes the voyage of Odysseus after the fall of Troy and the vengeance he takes on the suitors of his wife Penelope on his return. During his ten-year wanderings he has many adventures including encounters with the Cyclops, Circe, Scylla and Charybdis, and the Sirens.

OE abbreviation for *Old English*; see ◊English language.

OECD abbreviation for ◊*Organization for Economic Cooperation and Development*.

octopus

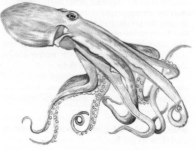

oedema waterlogging of the tissues due to excessive loss of plasma through the capillary walls into the tissues. It may be generalized (the condition once known as dropsy) or confined to one area, such as the ankles.

Oedema may be mechanical—the result of obstructed veins or heart failure—or it may be due to increased permeability of the capillary walls, as in kidney disease or malnutrition. Accumulation of fluid in the abdomen is known as ascites.

Oedipus /ˈiːdɪpəs/ in Greek legend, king of Thebes. Left to die at birth because his father Laius had been warned by an oracle that his son would kill him, he was saved and brought up by the king of Corinth. Oedipus killed Laius in a quarrel (without recognizing him) and married his mother Jocasta. After four children had been born, the truth was discovered. Jocasta hanged herself, Oedipus blinded himself, and as an exiled wanderer was guided by his daughter, Antigone.

Because Oedipus saved Thebes from the Sphinx, he was granted the Theban kingdom and Jocasta (wife of Laius and his own mother) as his wife. The Greek dramatist Sophocles used the story in two tragedies.

Oedipus complex in psychology, term coined by ◊Freud for the unconscious antagonism of a son to his father, whom he sees as a rival for his mother's affection. For a girl antagonistic to her mother for the same reason, the term is *Electra complex*.

Freud saw this as a universal part of childhood development, which in most children is resolved during late childhood. Contemporary theory places less importance on the Oedipus complex than did Freud and his followers.

Oedipus Tyrannus or *Oedipus the King* 409 BC and *Oedipus at Colonus* 401 BC two tragedies by Sophocles based on the legend of ◊Oedipus, King of Thebes.

OEEC abbreviation for *Organization for European Economic Cooperation*.

oersted c.g.s. unit (symbol Oe) of ◊magnetic field strength, now replaced by the SI unit ampere by metre. The Earth's magnetic field is about 1/2 oersted; the field near the poles of a small bar magnet is several hundred oersteds; and a powerful ◊electromagnet can have a field strength of 30,000 oersteds.

Oersted /ˈɜːsted/ Hans Christian 1777–1851. Danish physicist who founded the science of electromagnetism. In 1820 he discovered the ◊magnetic field associated with an electric current.

oesophagus the passage by which food travels from mouth to stomach. The human oesophagus is about 23 cm/9 in long. Its upper end is at the bottom of the ◊pharynx, immediately behind the windpipe.

oestrogen a group of hormones produced by the ◊ovaries of vertebrates, the term is also used for various synthetic hormones which mimic their effects. The principal oestrogen in mammals is oestradiol. Oestrogens promote the development of female secondary sexual characteristics in mammals, stimulate egg production, and prepare the lining of the uterus for pregnancy.

oestrus in mammals, the period during a female's reproductive cycle (also known as the oestrus cycle or ◊menstrual cycle) when mating is most likely to occur. It usually coincides with ovulation.

Offa /ˈɒfə/ died 796. King of Mercia, England, from 757. He conquered Essex, Kent, Sussex, and Surrey, defeated the Welsh and the West Saxons, and established Mercian supremacy over all England south of the river Humber.

Offaly /ˈɒfəli/ county of the Republic of Ireland, in the province of Leinster, between Galway on the west and Kildare on the east; area 2,000 sq km/772 sq mi; population (1986) 60,000.

Towns include the county town of Tullamore. Features include the rivers Shannon (along the W boundary), Brosna, Clodagh, and Broughill; the Slieve Bloom mountains in the SE.

Offa's Dyke /ˈɒfəz/ a defensive earthwork along the Welsh border, of which there are remains from the mouth of the river Dee to that of the river Severn. It represents the boundary secured by ◊Offa's wars with Wales.

Offenbach /'ɒfənbɑːk/ Jacques 1819–1880. French composer. He wrote light opera, initially for presentation at the Bouffes Parisiens. Among his works are *Orphée aux enfers*/*Orpheus in the Underworld* 1858, *La Belle Hélène* 1864, and *Les Contes d'Hoffmann*/*The Tales of Hoffmann* 1881.

Offenbach am Main /'ɒfənbæx æm 'maɪn/ city in Hessen, West Germany; population (1988) 107,000. It faces Frankfurt on the other side of the river Main.

office automation the introduction of computers and other electronic equipment, such as fax machines, to support an office routine. Increasingly, computers have been used to support administrative tasks such as document processing, filing, mail, and diary management; project planning and management accounting have also been computerized.

Official Secrets Act UK act of Parliament 1989, making disclosure of confidential material from government sources by employees subject to disciplinary procedures; it replaced Section 2 of an act of 1911, which had long been accused of being too wide ranging. It remains an absolute offence for a member or former member of the security and intelligence services (or those working closely with them) to disclose information about their work. There is no public-interest defence, and disclosure of information already in the public domain is still a crime. Journalists who repeat disclosures may also be prosecuted.

Prosecution under criminal law is reserved for material that the government claims is seriously harmful to national security. Any service member wishing to complain of misconduct within the service is allowed access to an independent counsellor, in turn with access to senior ministers. Investigations under special warrants, which are issued by the secretary of state in such cases as terrorism and organized crime, are also to be regarded as absolutely secret, but the act limits the circumstances of their operation, and there is an independent commissioner and tribunal to prevent abuse of such powers.

offset litho the most common method of ◊printing, which uses smooth printing plates. It works on the principle of ◊lithography, that grease and water repel one another. The printing plate is prepared using a photographic technique, resulting in a type image which attracts greasy printing ink. On the printing press the plate is wrapped around a cylinder and wetted and inked in turn. The ink adheres only to the type area, and this image is then transferred via an intermediate blanket cylinder to the paper.

O'Flaherty /əʊ'flɑːhəti/ Liam 1897–1984. Irish author whose novels of ◊Fenian activities in county Mayo include *The Neighbour's Wife* 1923, *The Informer* 1925, and *Land* 1946.

Ogaden /ˌɒɡə'den/ desert region in Harar province, SE Ethiopia, that borders on Somalia. It is a desert plateau, rising to 1,000 m/3,000 ft, inhabited mainly by Somali nomads practising arid farming. A claim to the area was made by Somalia in the 1960s, resulting in guerilla fighting that has continued intermittently. It is one of five new autonomous provinces created in Ethiopia 1987.

Ogallala Aquifer /ˌəʊɡə'lælə/ the largest source of groundwater in the USA, stretching from southern South Dakota to NW Texas. The over-exploitation of this water resource has resulted in the loss of over 18% of the irrigated farmland of Oklahoma and Texas in the period 1940–90.

Ogbomosho /ˌɒɡbə'məʊʃəʊ/ city and commercial centre in W Nigeria, 80 km/50 mi NE of Ibadan; population (1981) 590,600.

Ogden /'ɒɡdən/ C(harles) K(ay) 1889–1957. English writer and scholar. With I A ◊Richards he

Ohio

Columbus

developed the simplified form of English known as ◊Basic English. Together they wrote *Foundations of Aesthetics* 1921 and *The Meaning of Meaning* 1923.

Ogdon /'ɒɡdən/ John 1937–1989. English pianist, renowned for his interpretation of Chopin, Liszt, and Busoni. In 1962 he shared the Tchaikovsky award with Vladimir Ashkenazy in Moscow.

Oglethorpe /'əʊɡəlθɔːp/ James Edward 1696–1785. English soldier. He joined the Guards, and in 1732 obtained a charter for the colony of Georgia, intended as a refuge for debtors and for European Protestants.

OGPU former name 1923–34 of the Soviet secret police, the ◊KGB.

Ogun /'əʊɡʊn/ a state of SW Nigeria; population (1982) 2,473,300; area 16,762 sq km/6,474 sq mi; capital Abeokuta.

OH abbreviation for ◊*Ohio*.

O'Higgins /əʊ'hɪɡɪnz/ Bernardo 1778–1842. Chilean revolutionary, known as 'the Liberator of Chile'. He was a leader of the struggle for independence from Spanish rule 1810–17 and head of the first permanent national government 1817–23.

Ohio /əʊ'haɪəʊ/ river in the USA, 1,580 km/ 980 mi long; it is formed by the union of the Allegheny and Monongahela at Pittsburgh, Pennsylvania, and flows SW until it joins the river Mississippi at Cairo, Illinois.

Ohio /əʊ'haɪəʊ/ state of the midwest USA; nickname Buckeye State
area 107,100 sq km/41,341 sq mi
capital Columbus

towns Cleveland, Cincinnati, Dayton, Akron, Toledo, Youngstown, Canton
features Ohio river; Serpent Mound, a 1.3 m/4 ft embankment, 405 m/1,330 ft long, and about 5 m/18 ft across (built by ◊Hopewell Indians about 1st–2nd century BC)
products coal, cereals, livestock, machinery, chemicals, steel
population (1986) 10,752,000
famous people Thomas Edison, John Glenn, Paul Newman, Gen Sherman, Orville Wright; six presidents (Garfield, Grant, Harding, Harrison, Hayes, and McKinley)
history ceded to Britain by France 1763; first settled by Europeans 1788; state 1803.

ohm SI unit (symbol Ω) of electrical ◊resistance (the property of a substance that restricts the flow of electrons through it).

It was originally defined with reference to the resistance of a column of mercury, but is now taken as the resistance between two points when a potential difference of 1 volt between them produces a current of 1 amp.

Ohm /əʊm/ Georg Simon 1787–1854. German physicist who studied electricity and discovered the fundamental law that bears his name. The SI unit of electrical resistance is named after him, and the unit of conductance (the reverse of resistance) is called the mho, which is Ohm spelt backwards.

ohmic heating method of heating used in the food processing industry, in which an electric current is passed through foodstuffs to sterilize them before packing. The heating effect is similar to that obtained by microwaves in that electrical energy is transformed into heat throughout the whole volume of the food, not just at the surface. This makes the method suitable for heating foods containing chunks of meat or fruit. It is an alternative to in-can sterilization and has been used to produce canned foods such as meat chunks, prawns, baked beans, fruit, and vegetables.

OHMS abbreviation for *On Her (His) Majesty's Service*.

Ohm's law law proposed by Georg Ohm in 1827 that states that the steady electrical current in a metallic circuit is directly proportional to the constant total ◊electromotive force in the circuit.

ohmic heating *An ohmic heating system, in which liquid food is sterilized by passing an electric current through it.*

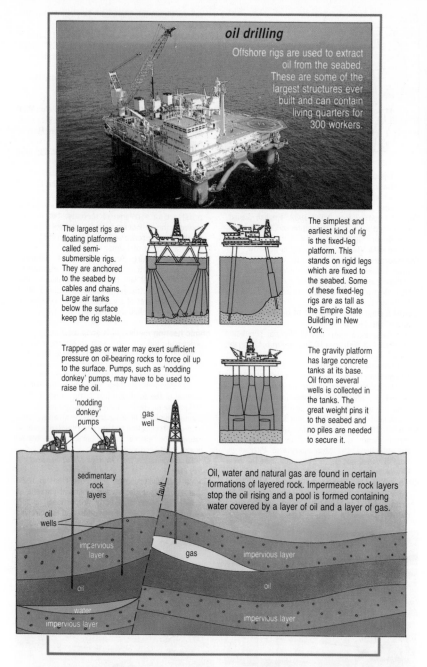

oil drilling

Offshore rigs are used to extract oil from the seabed. These are some of the largest structures ever built and can contain living quarters for 300 workers.

The largest rigs are floating platforms called semi-submersible rigs. They are anchored to the seabed by cables and chains. Large air tanks below the surface keep the rig stable.

The simplest and earliest kind of rig is the fixed-leg platform. This stands on rigid legs which are fixed to the seabed. Some of these fixed-leg rigs are as tall as the Empire State Building in New York.

Trapped gas or water may exert sufficient pressure on oil-bearing rocks to force oil up to the surface. Pumps, such as 'nodding donkey' pumps, may have to be used to raise the oil.

The gravity platform has large concrete tanks at its base. Oil from several wells is collected in the tanks. The great weight pins it to the seabed and no piles are needed to secure it.

'nodding donkey' pumps

gas well

sedimentary rock layers

fault

oil wells

impervious layer

gas

impervious layer

oil

oil

water

impervious layer

impervious layer

Oil, water and natural gas are found in certain formations of layered rock. Impermeable rock layers stop the oil rising and a pool is formed containing water covered by a layer of oil and a layer of gas.

oil Oil refinery at Stanlow near Ellesmere Port, Cheshire, UK.

If a current I flows between two points in a conductor across which the ◊potential difference (voltage) is E, then E/I is a constant (which is known as the ◊resistance, R, between the two points). Hence $E/I = R$. Equations relating E, I and R are often quoted as Ohm's law, but the term 'resistance' did not enter into the law as originally stated.

Ohrid, Lake /'ɒxrɪd/ a lake on the frontier between Albania and Yugoslavia; area 350 sq km/135 sq mi.

oil inflammable substance, usually insoluble in water, and chiefly composed of carbon and hydrogen. Oils may be solids (fats and waxes) or liquids. The three main types are: **essential oils**, used in perfumes and for flavouring; **fixed oils**, obtained from animals and plants; and **mineral oils**, obtained chiefly from the refining of ◊petroleum.
Essential oils are volatile liquids that have the odour of their plant source and are used in perfumes, flavouring essences, and in ◊aromatherapy.
Fixed oils are mixtures of ◊esters of fatty acids, of varying consistency, found in both animals (for example, fish oils) and plants (in nuts and seeds). They are used as food; to make soaps, paints, and varnishes; and for lubrication.

oil crop plant from which vegetable oils are pressed from the seeds. Cool temperate areas grow rapeseed and linseed; warm temperate regions produce sunflowers, olives, and soyabeans; tropical regions produce groundnuts (such as peanuts), palm oil, and coconuts. Some of the major vegetable oils, such as soyabean oil, peanut oil, and cottonseed oil, are derived from crops grown primarily for other purposes. Most vegetable oils are used as both edible oils and as ingredients in industrial products such as soaps, varnishes, printing inks, and paints.

oil palm type of ◊palm tree *Elaeis guineensis*, the fruit of which yields valuable oils, used as food or processed into margarine, soaps, and livestock feeds.

Oise /waːz/ European river that rises in the Ardennes plateau, Belgium, and flows through France in a SW direction for 300 km/186 mi to join the Seine about 65 km/40 mi below Paris. It gives its name to a French *département* in Picardie.

Oistrakh /'ɔɪstraːk/ David Fyodorovich 1908–1974. Soviet violinist, celebrated for performances of both standard and contemporary Russian repertoire. Shostakovich wrote both his violin concertos for him.

OK abbreviation for ◊Oklahoma.

okapi animal *Okapia johnstoni* of the giraffe family, though with much shorter legs and neck, found in the tropical rainforests of central Africa. Purplish brown with creamy face and black and white stripes on the legs and hindquarters, it is excellently camouflaged. Okapis have remained virtually unchanged for millions of years. Unknown to Europeans until 1901, only a few hundred are thought to survive.

Okavango Swamp /ˌɒkəˈvæŋgəʊ/ marshy area in NW Botswana, fed by the *Okavango River*, which rises in Angola.

Okayama /ˌɒkəˈjaːmə/ industrial port (textiles, cotton) in W Honshu, Japan; population (1987) 570,000. It has three Buddhist temples.

Okeechobee /ˌəʊkiˈtʃəʊbi/ lake in the N Everglades, Florida, USA; 65 km/40 mi long and 40 km/25 mi wide. The largest lake in southern USA.

O'Keeffe /əʊˈkiːf/ Georgia 1887–1986. US painter, based mainly in New York and New Mexico, known for her large, semi-abstract studies of flowers and skulls.

Her mature style stressed contours and subtle tonal transitions, and in paintings such as *Black Iris* 1926 (Metropolitan Museum of Art, New York) the subject is transformed into a powerful and erotic abstract image. In 1946 she settled in New Mexico, where the desert landscape inspired many of her paintings.

okapi

female okapi

Oklahoma

Oklahoma City

Okefenokee /ˌəʊkɪfɪˈnəʊki/ swamp in SE Georgia and NE Florida, USA, rich in alligators, bears, deer, and birds. Much of its 1700 sq km/660 sq mi forms a Natural Wildlife Refuge.

Okeghem /ˈɒkəgem/ Johannes (Jean d') c. 1420–1497. Flemish composer of church music, including masses and motets. He was court composer to Charles VII, Louis XI, and Charles VIII of France.

Okhotsk, Sea of /əʊˈxɒtsk/ arm of the N Pacific between the Kamchatka Peninsula and Sakhalin, and bordered southward by the Kurile Island; area 937,000 sq km/361,700 sq mi. Free of ice only in summer, it is often fogbound.

Okinawa /ˌɒkɪˈnɑːwə/ largest of the Japanese ◊Ryukyu Islands in the W Pacific
area 2,250 sq km/869 sq mi
capital Naha
population (1986) 1,190,000
history captured by the USA in the *Battle of Okinawa* 1 Apr–21 June 1945 with 47,000 US casualties (12,000 dead) and 60,000 Japanese (only a few hundred survived as prisoners); the island was returned to Japan 1972.

Oklahoma /ˌəʊkləˈhəʊmə/ state of the south central USA; nickname Sooner State
area 181,100 sq km/69,905 sq mi
capital Oklahoma City
towns Tulsa, Lawton, Norman, Enid
features Arkansas, Red, and Canadian rivers; Wichita and Ozark ranges; the Oklahoma panhandle is part of the Dust Bowl; the high plains have Indian reservations (Cherokee, Chickasaw, Choctaw, Creek, and Seminole)
products cereals, peanuts, cotton, livestock, oil, natural gas, helium, machinery and other metal products
population (1986) 3,305,000
famous people Woody Guthrie, Will Rogers
history the region was acquired by the ◊Louisiana Purchase 1803. Part of the present state formed the Territory of Oklahoma from 1890, and was thrown open to settlers with lotteries and other hurried distribution of land. Together with what remained of Indian Territory, it became a state 1907.

Oklahoma City /ˌəʊkləˈhəʊmə/ industrial city (oil refining, machinery, aircraft, telephone equipment), capital of Oklahoma, USA, on the Canadian river; population (1984) 443,500.

okra type of ◊hibiscus plant, with edible fruit known as *bhindi* or ladies' fingers.

Okubo /əʊˈkuːbəʊ/ Toshimichi 1831–1878. Japanese ◊samurai leader whose opposition to the Tokugawa shogunate made him a leader in the Meiji restoration (see ◊Mutsuhito) 1866–68.

Okuma /əʊˈkuːmə/ Shigenobu 1838–1922. Japanese politician and prime minister. He helped to found the Jiyuto (Liberal Party) 1881, and became prime minister briefly 1898 and again 1914, when he presided over Japanese pressure for territorial concessions in China, before retiring 1916.

Holding a series of ministerial appointments after the ◊Meiji restoration 1868, Okuma specialized in fiscal and constitutional reform.

Olaf /ˈəʊləf/ five kings of Norway, including:

Olaf I Tryggvesson 969–1000. King of Norway from his election 995. He began the conversion of Norway to Christianity, and was killed in a sea battle against the Danes and Swedes.

Olaf II Haraldsson 995–1030. King of Norway from 1015. He offended his subjects by his centralizing policy and zeal for Christianity, and was killed in battle by Norwegian rebel chiefs backed by ◊Canute of Denmark. He was declared the patron saint of Norway 1164.

Olaf V 1903– . King of Norway from 1957, when he succeeded his father Haakon VII.

Olazabal /ˌəʊləsəˈbæl/ Jose Maria 1966– . Spanish golfer, one of the leading players on the European circuit. After a distinguished amateur career he turned professional 1986. He was a member of the European Ryder Cup teams in 1987 and 1989.

He won the English amateur championship in 1984 and Youths title the following year. He finished second in the European money list in his second year as a professional.

Olbers /ˈɒlbəs/ Heinrich 1758–1840. German astronomer. A medical doctor, Olbers was a keen amateur astronomer and a founder member of the *Celestial Police*, a group of astronomers who attempted to locate a supposed 'missing planet' between Mars and Jupiter. During his search he discovered two ◊asteroids, Pallas 1802 and Vesta 1807. Credited to him are a number of comet discoveries together with a new method of calculating cometary orbits. He is also responsible for Olbers' paradox.

Olbers' paradox a question put forward 1826 by Heinrich Olbers, who asked: If the universe is infinite in extent and filled with stars, why is the sky dark at night? The answer is that the stars do not live infinitely long, so there is not enough starlight to fill the universe. A wrong answer, frequently given, is that the expansion of the universe weakens the starlight.

Olbrich /ˈɒlbrɪʃ/ Joseph Maria 1867–1908. Viennese architect who worked under Otto ◊Wagner and was opposed to the over-ornamentation of Art Nouveau. His major buildings, however, remain Art Nouveau in spirit: the Vienna Sezession 1897–98, the Hochzeitsturm 1907, and the Tietz department store in Düsseldorf, Germany.

old age the later years of life. The causes of progressive degeneration of bodily and mental processes associated with it are still not precisely known (see ◊ageing), but every one of the phenomena can occur at almost any age, and the process does not take place throughout the body at an equal speed. Normally, however, ageing begins after about 30. The arteries start to lose their elasticity, so that a greater strain is thrown upon the heart. The resulting gradual impairment of the blood supply is responsible for many of the changes, but between 30 and 60 there is a period of maturity in which ageing usually makes little progress. Research into the process of old age (*gerontology*) includes study of dietary factors, and the mechanisms behind structural changes in arteries and bones. *Geriatrics* is the branch of medicine dealing with old age and its diseases.

Old Bailey popular name for the Central Criminal Court in London, situated in a street of that name in the City of London, off Ludgate Hill.

Old Catholic one of various breakaway groups from Roman Catholicism, including those in Holland (such as the *Church of Utrecht*, who separated from Rome 1724 after accusations of ◊Jansenism) and groups in Austria, Czechoslovakia, Germany, and Switzerland, who rejected the proclamation of ◊papal infallibility of 1870. Old Catholic clergy are not celibate.

The Old Catholic Church entered full communion with the Church of England 1931. Anglican and Old Catholic bishops have joined in the consecration of new bishops so that their consecration can be traced back to the time of an undivided church.

Oldenbarnevelt /ˌəʊldənˈbɑːnəvelt/ Johan van 1547–1619. Dutch politician, a leading figure in the Netherlands' struggle for independence from Spain, who helped William I negotiate the Union of Utrecht 1579.

As leader of the Republican party he opposed the war policy of stadholder Maurice of Orange and negotiated a 12-year truce with Spain in 1609. His support of the Remonstrants (Arminians) in the religious strife against Maurice and the Gomarists (Cavinists) effected his downfall and he was arrested and executed.

Oldenburg /ˈəʊldənbɜːg/ industrial city in Lower Saxony, West Germany, on the river Hunte; population (1988) 139,000. It is linked by river and canal to the Ems and Wieser rivers.

Oldenburg /ˈəʊldənbɜːg/ Claes 1929– . US pop artist, known for *soft sculptures*, gigantic replicas of everyday objects and foods, made of stuffed canvas or vinyl.

Oldenburg /ˈəʊldənbɜːg/ Henry 1615–1677. German official who founded and edited the first-ever scientific periodical *Philosophical Transactions* and through his extensive correspondence, acted as a clearing house for the science of the day. He was born in Bremen and first appeared in London 1652 working as a Bremen agent and then a tutor. In 1663, he was appointed to the new post of Secretary to the Royal Society, a position he held until his death.

Old English another term for ◊Anglo-Saxon; see also ◊English language.

Oldfield /ˈəʊldfiːld/ Bruce 1950– . English fashion designer, who set up his own business 1975. His evening wear has been worn by the British royal family and other personalities.

Oldham /ˈəʊldəm/ industrial city in Greater Manchester, England; population (1981) 107,800. Industries include textiles and textile machinery, plastics, electrical goods, and electronic equipment.

Old Man of the Sea in the ◊Arabian Nights, a man who compels strangers to carry him until they drop, encountered by ◊Sinbad the Sailor on his fifth voyage. Sinbad escapes by getting him drunk. The Old Man of the Sea is also used in Greek mythology to describe ◊Proteus, an attendant of the sea god Poseidon.

Old Moore's Almanac annual publication in the UK containing prophecies of the events of the following year. It was first published 1700 under the title *Vox Stellarum/Voices of the Stars*, by Francis Moore (1657–c.1715).

Old Pretender nickname of ◊James Edward Stuart, the son of James II of England.

Old Sarum /ˈseərəm/ Iron Age hill-fort site near ◊Salisbury, England.

Old Stone Age art see under ◊ancient art.

Old Style a qualification, often abbreviated to 'OS', of dates before the year 1752 in England as quoted in later writers. In that year the ◊calendar in use in England was reformed by the omission of 11 days, in order to bring it into line with the more exact Gregorian system, and the beginning of the year was put back from 25 Mar to 1 Jan.

Old Testament Christian term for the Hebrew ◊Bible, which is the first part of the Christian Bible. It contains 39 (according to Christians) or 24 (according to Jews) books, which include the history of the Jews and their covenant with God, prophetical writings, and religious poetry. The first five books are traditionally ascribed to Moses and known as the Pentateuch (by Christians) or the Torah (by Jews).

The original language of the text was Hebrew, and dates from the 12th–2nd century BC. Its transmission was mainly oral, and the earliest known manuscripts containing part of the text are among the ◊Dead Sea Scrolls. The traditional text was compiled by rabbinical authorities around the 2nd century AD .

Old Trafford two sporting centres in Britain, both situated in Manchester. The *Old Trafford football ground* is the home of Manchester United FC and was opened in 1910. The record attendance is 76,692, its capacity now reduced to 56,385. It is one of the most modern grounds in

Britain. During the war it was heavily bombed and the team had to play at neighbouring Manchester City's Maine Road Ground. It was used for the 1966 World Cup competition and has also hosted the FA Cup Final and replays. The *Old Trafford cricket ground* was opened 1857 and has staged test matches regularly since 1884. The ground capacity is 40,000.

Olduvai Gorge /'ɒlduvaɪ 'gɔːdʒ/ deep cleft in the Serengeti steppe, Tanzania, where the ◊Leakeys found prehistoric stone tools in the 1930s. They discovered 1958–59 Pleistocene remains of prehumans and gigantic animals. The gorge has given its name to the *Olduvai culture*, a simple stone-tool culture of prehistoric hominids, dating from 2–0.5 million years ago.

The Pleistocene remains included sheep the size of a carthorse, pigs as big as a rhinoceros, and a gorilla-sized baboon. The skull of an early hominid (1.75 million years old) *Australopithecus boisei* (its huge teeth earned it the nickname 'Nutcracker Man'), was also found here, as well as remains of *Homo habilis* and primitive types of *Homo erectus*.

Old Vic /'əʊld 'vɪk/ theatre in S London, England, former home of the National Theatre (1963–76).

The theatre was founded 1818 as the Coburg. Taken over by Emma Cons 1880 (as the Royal Victoria Hall), it became a popular centre for opera and drama, and was affectionately dubbed the Old Vic. In 1898 Lilian Baylis, niece of Emma Cons, assumed the management, and in 1914 began a celebrated series of Shakespeare productions. Badly damaged in 1940 air raids, the Old Vic reopened 1950–81, becoming the temporary home of the National Theatre until the South Bank building was finished. It was completely refurbished 1985.

Old World the continents of the eastern hemisphere, so called because they were familiar to Europeans before the Americas. Used as an adjective to describe animals and plants that live in the eastern hemisphere.

oleander or *rose bay* evergreen Mediterranean shrub *Nerium oleander*, family Apocynaceae, with pink or white flowers and leaves which secrete the poison oleandrin.

olefin common name for ◊alkene.

O level, General Certificate of Education in the UK, formerly the examination usually taken at 16. It was superseded by the ◊GCSE 1988.

Olga, St /'ɒlgə/ died 969. The wife of Igor, the Scandinavian prince of Kiev. Her baptism around 955 was an important step in the Christianization of Russia.

Oligocene third epoch of the Tertiary period of geological time, 38–25 million years ago. The name, from Greek, means 'a little recent', referring to the presence of the remains of some modern types of animals existing at that time.

oligopoly in economics, a situation in which few companies control the major part of a particular market and concert their actions to perpetuate such control. This may include an agreement to fix prices (a ◊cartel).

oligosaccharide a ◊carbohydrate comprising a few ◊monosaccharide units linked together. It is a general term used to indicate that a carbohydrate is larger than a simple di- or trisaccharide but not as large as a polysaccharide.

Oliphant /'ɒlɪfənt/ Margaret 1828–1897. Scottish writer, author of over 100 novels, biographies, and numerous articles and essays. Her major work is the series *The Chronicles of Carlingford* 1863–66, including *The Perpetual Curate* and *Hester*.

Olivares /ˌɒlɪ'vɑːres/ Count-Duke of (born Gaspar de Guzmán) 1587–1645. Spanish prime minister 1621–43. He overstretched Spain in foreign affairs, and unsuccessfully attempted domestic reform. He committed Spain to recapturing the Netherlands and to involvement in the Thirty Years' War 1618–48, and his efforts to centralize power led to revolts in Catalonia and Portugal, which brought about his downfall.

Oliver *The British miniaturist Isaac Oliver, a popular figure at the court of James I. The miniature is a self-portrait, c.1590.*

olive evergreen tree *Olea europaea* of the family Oleaceae. Native to Asia but widely distributed in Mediterranean and subtropical areas, it grows up to 15 m/50 ft high, with twisted branches and opposite, lance-shaped leaves. The white flowers are followed by bluish-black oval fruits, which are eaten or pressed to make olive oil.

The oil, which is pale yellow and chiefly composed of glycerides, is widely consumed; it is also used in soaps and ointments, and as a lubricant.

olive branch an ancient symbol of peace; in the Bible (Genesis 9), an olive branch is brought back by the dove to Noah to show that the flood has abated.

olivenite basic copper arsenate, $Cu_2(AsO_4)(OH)$, occurring as a mineral in olive-green prisms.

Oliver /'ɒlɪvə/ Isaac *c.* 1556–1617. British painter of miniatures, originally a Huguenot refugee, who studied under Nicholas ◊Hilliard. He became a court artist in the reign of James I. Famous sitters include the poet John Donne.

Olives, Mount of /'ɒlɪvz/ a range of hills E of Jerusalem, important in the Christian religion: a former chapel (now a mosque) marks the traditional site of Jesus' ascension to heaven, and the Garden of Gethsemane was at its foot.

Olivier /ə'lɪvieɪ/ Laurence (Kerr), Baron Olivier 1907–1989. English actor and director. For many years associated with the Old Vic, he was director of the National Theatre company 1962–73. His stage roles include Henry V, Hamlet, Richard III, and Archie Rice in Osborne's *The Entertainer*. His acting and direction of filmed versions of Shakespeare's plays received critical acclaim, for example *Henry V* 1944 and *Hamlet* 1948.

Other films in which he appeared are *Wuthering Heights* 1939, *Rebecca* 1940, *Sleuth* 1972,

Marathon Man 1976, and *The Boys from Brazil* 1978. The Olivier Theatre (part of the National Theatre on the South Bank, London) is named after him.

olivine greenish mineral, magnesium iron silicate, $(Mg,Fe)_2SiO_4$. It is an important rock-forming mineral in such rocks as peridotite, gabbro, and basalt. Olivine is called *peridot* when pale green and transparent, and used in jewellery.

olm cave-dwelling aquatic salamander *Proteus anguinus* found along the E Adriatic seaboard in Italy and Yugoslavia. The 'adult' is permanently larval in form, about 25 cm/10 in long, with external gills. See ◊neoteny.

Olmos /'ɒlmɒs/ a small town on the edge of the Sechura Desert, NW Peru. It gives its name to the large scale Olmos Project which began in 1926 in an attempt to irrigate the desert plain and increase cotton and sugar cane production.

Olney /'əʊlni/ small town in Buckinghamshire, England, where every Shrove Tuesday local women run a pancake race.

Olomouc /'ɒləmaʊts/ industrial city in central Czechoslovakia, at the confluence of the Bystrice and Morava rivers; population (1986) 106,000. Industries include sugar refining, brewing, and metal goods.

Olson /'əʊlsən/ Charles 1910–1970. US poet, noted for his theories of 'composition by field' and his association with the Black Mountain school of poets. His chief works were his *Maximus* poems 1953–75, a striking attempt to extend the American epic poem beyond Pound's *Cantos* or W C Williams's *Paterson*.

Olsztyn /'ɒlʃtɪn/ formerly **Allenstein** industrial town in NE Poland at the centre of the Mazurian Lakes region; population (1985) 147,000. It was founded 1334 and was formerly in East Prussia.

Olympia /ə'lɪmpɪə/ sanctuary in the W Peloponnese, ancient Greece, with a temple of Zeus, and the stadium (for foot races, boxing, wrestling) and hippodrome (for chariot and horse races), where the original Olympic games were held.

Olympic Games sporting contests originally held in Olympia, ancient Greece, every four years during a sacred truce; records were kept from 776 BC. Women were forbidden to be present and the male contestants were naked. The ancient games were abolished AD 394. The modern games have been held every four years since 1896. Since 1924 there has been a separate winter games programme. From 1994 the winter and summer games are held two years apart.

The first modern games were held in Athens. They were revived by Frenchman Pierre de Fredi, Baron de Coubertin (1863–1937), and have been held every four years with the exception of 1916, 1940, and 1944, when the two world wars intervened. Special tenth-anniversary, intercalated, games were held in Athens 1906. At the first revived Games 311 competitors represented 13 nations in nine sports. At Seoul, South Korea, in 1988, nearly 10,000 athletes represented nearly 150 nations in 23 sports, plus demonstration sports like tenpin bowling, baseball, and tae

Olympic Games *Bas relief on the base of a statue c. 510 BC, Athens Museum, showing a pair of wrestlers practising, a runner in the start position, and a javelin thrower.*

kwon do (a form of martial arts). The Olympic flag bears the emblem of five coloured rings (red, yellow, blue, black, and green) which are said to represent the five continents.

Olympic venues

summer games/winter games
1896 Athens, Greece
1900 Paris, France
1904 St Louis, USA
1906 Athens, Greece
1908 London, England
1912 Stockholm, Sweden
1920 Antwerp, Belgium
1924 Paris, France/Chamonix, France
1928 Amsterdam, Holland/St Moritz, Switzerland
1932 Los Angeles, USA/Lake Placid, USA
1936 Berlin, Germany/Garmisch-Partenkirchen, Germany
1948 London, England/St Moritz, Switzerland
1952 Helsinki, Finland/Oslo, Norway
1956 Melbourne, Australia*/Cortina d'Ampezzo, Italy
1960 Rome, Italy/Squaw Valley, USA
1964 Tokyo, Japan/Innsbruck, Austria
1968 Mexico City, Mexico/Grenoble, France
1972 Munich, West Germany/Sapporo, Japan
1976 Montreal, Canada/Innsbruck, Austria
1980 Moscow, USSR/Lake Placid, USA
1984 Los Angeles, USA/Sarajevo, Yugoslavia
1988 Seoul, South Korea/Calgary, Canada
1992 Barcelona, Spain/Albertville, France
1994 Lillehammer, Norway (winter games)
*Because of quarantine restrictions, equestrian events were held in Stockholm, Sweden.

Olympus /ə'limpəs/ (Greek *Olimbos*) several mountains in Greece and elsewhere, the most famous being **Mount Olympus** in N Thessaly, Greece, 2,918 m/9,577 ft high. In ancient Greece it was considered the home of the gods.

OM abbreviation for ◊Order of Merit.

Om sacred word in Hinduism, used to begin prayers and placed at the beginning and end of books. It is composed of three syllables, symbolic of the Hindu Trimurti, or trinity of gods.

Omagh /'əumə/ county town of Tyrone, Northern Ireland, on the river Strule, 48 km/30 mi S of Londonderry; population (1981) 14,625.

Omaha /'əuməha:/ city in E Nebraska, USA, on the Missouri; population (1980) 314,000. It is a livestock-market centre, with food-processing and meat-packing industries.

Oman /əu'ma:n/ country on the Arabian peninsula, bounded to the W by the United Arab Emirates, Saudi Arabia, and South Yemen, and to the E by the Arabian Sea.
government Oman has no written constitution and the sultan has absolute power, ruling by decree. There is no legislature. The sultan takes advice from an appointed cabinet. There is also a consultative assembly of 55 nominated members. There are no political parties.
history For early history, see ◊Arabia. The city of ◊Muscat has long been an important trading post. The country was in Portugal's possession 1508–1658, and was then ruled by Persia until 1744. By the early 19th century, the state of Muscat and Oman was the most powerful in Arabia: it ruled Zanzibar until 1861 and also coastal parts of Persia and Pakistan.

In 1951 it became the independent sultanate of Muscat and Oman and signed a treaty of friendship with Britain. Said bin Taimur, who had been sultan since 1932, was overthrown by his son, Qaboos bin Said, in a bloodless coup 1970, and the country was renamed Oman. Qaboos embarked on a more liberal and expansionist policy than his father. The Popular Front for the Liberation of Oman has been fighting to overthrow the sultanate since 1965.

Oman's wealth is based on a few oil fields. Conflicts in neighbouring countries, such as the Yemen, Iran, Iraq, and Afghanistan, have not only emphasized the country's strategic importance but put its own security at risk. The sultan has tried to follow a path of nonalignment, maintaining close ties with the USA and other NATO

Oman
Sultanate of
formerly known as
Muscat and Oman

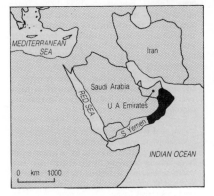

area 272,000 sq km/105,000 sq mi
capital Muscat
towns Salalah
physical mountains and a high arid plateau;
fertile coastal strip
features Jebel Akhdar highlands; Kuria Muria islands; Masirah Island is used in aerial reconnaissance of the Arabian Sea and Indian Ocean
head of state and government Qaboos bin Said from 1970
political system absolute monarchy
exports oil, dates, silverware
currency Omani rial (0.64 = £1 Feb 1990)
population (1989) 1,389,000; annual growth rate 4.7%
life expectancy men 51, women 54
language Arabic
religion Sunni Muslim
literacy 20% (1983)
GNP $7 bn (1983); $2,400 per head of population
chronology
1951 The Sultanate of Muscat and Oman achieved full independence. Treaty of friendship with Britain signed.
1970 After 38 years' rule, Sultan Said bin Taimur replaced in coup by his son Qaboos bin Said. Name changed to Sultanate of Oman.
1975 Left-wing rebels in the south defeated.
1982 Memorandum of Understanding with the UK signed, providing for consultation on international issues.

countries, but also keeping good relations with the USSR.

Omar /'əuma:/ 581–644. Adviser of the prophet Muhammad. In 634 he succeeded Abu Bakr as caliph (civic and religious leader of Islam), and conquered Syria, Palestine, Egypt, and Persia. He was assassinated by a slave. The Mosque of Omar in Jerusalem is attributed to him.

Omar Khayyam /'əuma: kəɪ'jæm/ c.1050–1123. Persian astronomer and poet. Born in Nishapur, he founded a school of astronomical research and assisted in reforming the calendar. The result of his observations was the *Jalālī* era, begun 1079. In the West, Omar Khayyam is chiefly known as a poet through ◊Fitzgerald's version of the *The Rubaiyat of Omar Khayyam* 1859.

Omayyad dynasty /əu'maiæd/ Arabian dynasty of the Islamic empire who reigned as caliphs 661–750. They were overthrown by Abbasids, but a member of the family escaped to Spain and in 756 assumed the title of emir of Córdoba. His dynasty, which took the title of caliph 929, ruled in Córdoba until the early 11th century.

ombudsman (Swedish 'commissioner') an official acting on behalf of the private citizen in investigating complaints against the government. The post is of Scandinavian origin; it was introduced in Sweden 1809, Denmark 1954, and Norway 1962, and spread to other countries from the 1960s.

The first Commonwealth country to appoint an ombudsman was New Zealand 1962; the UK followed 1966 with a parliamentary commissioner; and Hawaii was the first US state to appoint an ombudsman, 1967. The UK Local Government Act 1974 set up a local ombudsman, or commissioner for local administration, to investigate maladministration by local councils, police, health or water authorities. In the 1980s, ombudsmen have been appointed to private bodies such as banks (1986), insurance companies (1983), and building societies (1988).

Omdurman /,ɒmdə'ma:n/ city in Sudan, on the White Nile, a suburb of Khartoum; population (1983) 526,000. It was the residence of the Mahdi 1884–98. The Battle of Omdurman 1898 was a victory for British troops under Kitchener over the forces of the Mahdi.

Omega Workshop a group of early 20th-century English artists, led by Roger ◊Fry, who brought them together to design and make interiors, furnishings, and craft objects. The workshop, started in 1913, included members of the Bloomsbury Group, such as Vanessa Bell, Duncan Grant, Wyndham Lewis, and Henri Gaudier-Brzeska.

The articles they made were often primitive—both in design and execution—and brightly coloured. Some members of the workshop moved to Charleston, a house in the South Downs which they decorated and fitted out with their creations, but the workshop itself lasted only until 1920.

omnibus in literature, a collection of works by a writer, or works by various writers on a similar subject, reprinted in one volume; in technology, a road conveyance for several passengers, more commonly known as a bus.

omnivore an animal that feeds on both plant and animal material. Omnivores have digestive adaptations intermediate between those of ◊herbivores and ◊carnivores, with relatively unspecialized digestive systems and gut microorganisms that can digest a variety of foodstuffs.

Omsk /ɒmsk/ industrial city (agricultural and other machinery, food processing, sawmills, oil refining) in the USSR, capital of Omsk region, W Siberia; population (1987) 1,134,000. The refineries are linked with Tuimazy in Bashkiria by a 1,600 km/1,000 mi pipeline.

onager type of wild ass *Equus hemionus* found in W Asia. Onagers are sandy brown, lighter underneath, and about the size of a small horse.

Onassis /əu'næsis/ Aristotle (Socrates) 1906–1975. Turkish-born Greek shipowner. During the 1950s he was one of the first shipbuilders to build supertankers. In 1968 he married Jacqueline Kennedy, widow of US president John F Kennedy.

onchocerciasis or *river blindness* disease found in tropical Africa and Latin America. It is transmitted by bloodsucking blackflies, which infect the victim with parasitic worms, producing skin disorders and blindness.

oncogene a gene carried by a virus that induces a cell to divide abnormally, forming a ◊tumour. Oncogenes arise from mutations in genes (proto-oncogenes) found in all normal cells. They are usually also found in viruses that are capable of transforming normal cells to tumour cells. Such viruses are able to insert their oncogenes into the host cell's DNA, causing it to divide uncontrollably. More than one oncogene may be necessary to transform a cell in this way.

In 1989 US scientists J Michael Bishop and Harold Varmus were jointly awarded the Nobel prize for their concept of oncogenes, although credit for the discovery was claimed by a French cancer specialist, Dominique Stehelin.

oncology the branch of medicine concerned with the diagnosis and treatment of cancer.

ondes Martenot (French 'Martenot waves') electronic musical instrument invented by Maurice Martenot and first demonstrated in 1928. A melody of considerable range and voice-like timbre is produced by sliding a contact along a conductive ribbon, the left hand controlling the tone colour. In addition to inspiring works from Messiaen, Varkse, Jolivet and others, it has been in regular demand among composers of film and radio incidental music.

Onega, Lake /əʊ'neɪgə/ second largest lake in Europe, NE of Leningrad, partly in Karelia, USSR; area 9,600 sq km/3,710 sq mi. The **Onega canal**, along its south shore, is part of the Mariinsk system linking Leningrad with the river Volga.

Oneida /əʊ'naɪdə/ small town in New York State, USA, named after the Oneida people (a nation of the ◊Iroquois confederacy). It became known from 1848 for the **Oneida Community**, a religious sect which practised a form of 'complex marriage' until its dissolution 1879.

O'Neill /əʊ'niːl/ Eugene (Gladstone) 1888–1953. US playwright, the leading US dramatist between World Wars I and II. His plays include *Anna Christie* 1922, *Desire under the Elms* 1924, *The Iceman Cometh* 1946, and the posthumously produced autobiographical drama *Long Day's Journey into Night* 1956 (written 1940). Nobel prize 1936.

O'Neill was born in New York. He had varied experience as gold prospector, sailor, and actor. Other plays include *Beyond the Horizon* 1920, *The Great God Brown* 1925, *Strange Interlude* 1928 (which lasts five hours), *Mourning Becomes Electra* 1931 (a trilogy on the theme of Orestes from Greek mythology; see ◊Agamemnon), and *A Moon for the Misbegotten* 1947 (written 1943).

O'Neill /əʊ'niːl/ Terence, Baron O'Neill of the Maine 1914– . Northern Irish Unionist politician. In the Ulster government he was minister of finance 1956–63, prime minister 1963–69. He resigned when opposed by his party on measures to extend rights to Roman Catholics, including a universal franchise.

onion bulbous plant *Allium cepa* of the family Liliaceae. Cultivated from ancient times, it may have originated in Asia. The edible part is the bulb, containing an acrid volatile oil and having a strong flavour.

The onion is a biennial, the common species producing a bulb in the first season and seeds in the second.

online system in computing, a system that allows the computer to work interactively with its users,

O'Neill *Previously a sailor, gold prospector, actor, and reporter, US playwright Eugene O'Neill was awarded the Nobel Prize for Literature in 1936.*

responding to each instruction as it is given and prompting users for information when necessary, as opposed to a ◊batch system. Since the fall in the cost of computers in the 1970s, online operation has become increasingly attractive commercially.

Onnes /'ɒnəs/ Kamerlingh 1853–1926. Dutch physicist who worked mainly in the field of low temperature physics. In 1911 he discovered the phenomenon of ◊superconductivity, for which he was awarded the 1913 Nobel physics prize.

o.n.o. abbreviation for *or near(est) offer*.

onomatopoeia a ◊figure of speech whose Greek name means 'name-making', on the principle of copying natural sounds. Thus the word or name 'cuckoo' arises out of imitating the sound that the cuckoo makes.

Such words as *bang, crash, ripple, smash, splash,* and *thump* are said to be onomatopoeic. Onomatopoeia works differently in different languages, the English *bowwow* for a sound made by dogs being paralleled by the French *oua, oua*. Onomatopoeia may be built into prose or verse, as in 'a sudden sizzling sound', the 's' and 'z' sounds used to suggest frying.

Onsager /'ɒnsɑːgə/ Lars 1903–1976. Norwegian-born US physicist, whose discovery of the 'reciprocity relations of Onsager' in 1931 was vital to the production of nuclear energy. Nobel prize 1968.

Ont. abbreviation for ◊Ontario.

Ontario /ɒn'teərɪəʊ/ province of central Canada

area 1,068,600 sq km/412,480 sq mi

capital Toronto

towns Hamilton, Ottawa (federal capital), London, Windsor, Kitchener, St Catharines, Oshawa, Thunder Bay, Sudbury

features Black Creek Pioneer Village; ◊Niagara Falls; richest, chief manufacturing, most populated, and leading cultural province of English-speaking Canada

products nickel, iron, gold, forest products, motor vehicles, iron, steel, paper, chemicals, copper, uranium

population (1986) 9,114,000

history First explored by the French in the 17th century, it came under British control 1763 (Treaty of Paris). An attempt 1841 to form a merged province with French-speaking Québec failed, and Ontario became a separate province of Canada 1867.

Ontario, Lake /ɒn'teərɪəʊ/ smallest and easternmost of the Great Lakes, on the US-Canadian border; area 19,200 sq km/7,400 sq mi. It is connected to Lake Erie by the Welland Canal and the Niagara River, and drains into the St Lawrence River. Its main port is Toronto.

On the Road novel by Jack Kerouac, published in the USA 1955, exploring the freewheeling life of the ◊*beat generation* in the style of 'spontaneous bop prosody'.

ontogeny the process of development of a living organism, including the part of development that takes place after hatching or birth. The idea that 'ontogeny recapitulates phylogeny' (the development of an organism goes through the same stages as its evolutionary history), proposed by the German scientist Haeckel, is now discredited.

Ontario

Toronto

ontology that branch of philosophy concerned with the study of being. In the 20th century, ◊Heidegger distinguished between an 'ontological' enquiry (an enquiry into **Being**) and an 'ontic' enquiry (an enquiry into a specific kind of entity).

onus (Latin) a burden or responsibility.

onyx a semiprecious variety of chalcedonic ◊silica(SiO_2) in which the crystals are too fine to be detected microscopically (cryptocrystalline). It has straight parallel bands of different colours: milk-white, black, and red.

Sardonyx, an onyx variety, has layers of brown or red carnelian alternating with lighter layers of onyx. It can be carved into cameos.

oolite a limestone made up of tiny spherical carbonate particles called *ooliths*. Ooliths have a concentric structure with a diameter up to 2 mm/0.08 in. They were formed by chemical precipitation and accumulation on ancient sea floors.

The surface texture of oolites is rather like that of fish roe. The late Jurassic limestones of the British Isles are mostly oolitic in nature.

Oort /ɔːt/ Jan Hendrik 1900– . Dutch astronomer. In 1927, he calculated the mass and size of the galaxy, and the Sun's distance from its centre, from the observed movements of stars around the galaxy's centre. In 1950 Oort proposed that comets exist in a vast swarm, now called the **Oort Cloud**, at the edge of the solar system.

In 1944 Oort's student Hendrik van de Hulst calculated that hydrogen in space would emit radio waves at 21 cm/8.3 in wavelength, and in the 1950s Oort's team mapped the spiral structure of the galaxy from the radio waves given out by interstellar hydrogen.

oosphere another name for the female gamete or ◊ovum of certain plants such as algae.

Oostende /əʊst'endə/ Flemish form, meaning 'east end', of ◊Ostend.

ooze sediment of fine texture consisting mainly of organic matter found on the ocean floor at depths greater than 2,000 m/6,600 ft. Several kinds of ooze exist, each named after its constituents. *Siliceous ooze* is composed of the ◊silica shells of tiny marine plants (diatoms) and animals (radiolarians). *Calcareous ooze* is formed from the ◊calcite shells of microscopic animals (foraminifera) and floating algae (coccoliths).

opal a cryptocrystalline form of ◊silica (SiO_2), often occurring as stalactites and found in many types of rock. The common opal is translucent, milk-white, yellow, red, blue, or green, and lustrous. Precious opal is opalescent, the characteristic play of colours being caused by close-packed silica spheres diffracting light rays within the stone.

Opals are found in Hungary, New South Wales, Australia (black opals were first discovered there in 1905), and Mexico (noted for red fire opals).

Op art movement in modern art, popular in the 1960s. It uses scientifically based optical effects that confuse the spectator's eye. Precisely painted lines or dots are arranged in carefully regulated patterns that create an illusion of surface movement. Exponents include Victor Vasarely and Bridget Riley.

op. cit. abbreviation for *opere citato* (Latin 'in the work cited').

OPEC abbreviation for ◊*Organization of the Petroleum Exporting Countries*.

opencast mining or *open-pit mining* mining at the surface rather than underground. Coal, iron ore, and phosphates are often extracted by opencast mining. Often the mineral deposit is covered by soil, which must first be stripped off, usually by huge excavators such as walking draglines and bucketwheel excavators. The ore deposit is then broken up by explosives.

One of the largest excavations in the world has been made by opencast mining at the Bingham Canyon copper mine in Utah, USA, measuring 790 m/2,590 ft deep and 3.7 km/2.3 mi across.

Open College in the UK, an initiative launched by the Manpower Services Commission (now the ◊Training Commission) to enable people to gain and update technical and vocational skills by means of distance teaching, such as correspondence, radio, and television.

open-door policy economic philosophy of equal access by all nations to another nation's markets.

The term was suggested by US secretary of state John Jay Sept 1899 to allow all nations free access to trade with China, and hence a rejection of a sphere-of-influence agreement for Chinese trade.

open-hearth furnace once the most important method of steelmaking, now largely superseded by the ◊basic-oxygen process. The open-hearth furnace was developed in England by German-born William and Friedrich Siemens, and improved by Pierre and Emile Martin 1864. In the furnace, molten pig iron and scrap are packed into a shallow hearth and heated by overhead gas burners using preheated air.

open learning teaching available to students without pre-qualifications by means of flexible attendance at an institution, often including teaching by correspondence, radio, television, or tape, for example the Open University and Open College.

open shop factory or other business employing men and women not belonging to trade unions, as opposed to the ◊closed shop, which employs trade unionists only.

Open University an institution established in the UK 1969 to enable mature students without qualifications to study to degree level without regular attendance. Open University teaching is based on a mixture of correspondence courses, TV and radio lectures and demonstrations, personal tuition organized on a regional basis, and summer schools.

Announced by Harold Wilson 1963 as a 'university of the air', it was largely created by Jennie ◊Lee, minister for the arts, from 1965. There are now over 30 similar institutions in other countries, including Thailand and South Korea.

opera dramatic musical work in which singing takes the place of speech. In opera the music accompanying the action has paramount importance, although dancing and spectacular staging may also play their parts. Opera originated in late 16th-century Florence when a number of young poets and musicians attempted to reproduce in contemporary form the musical declamation, lyrical monologues, and choruses of classical Greek drama.

One of the earliest opera composers was Jacopo Peri (1561–1633), whose *Euridice* influenced Monteverdi. At first solely a court entertainment, opera soon became popular, and in 1637 the first public opera house was opened in Venice. In the later 17th century the elaborately conventional *aria*, designed to display the virtuosity of the singer, became predominant, overshadowing the dramatic element. Composers of this type of opera included Cavalli, Cesti, and Alessandro Scarlatti. In France opera was developed by Lully and Rameau, and in England by Purcell, but the Italian style retained its ascendance, as exemplified by Handel.

Comic opera (opera buffa) was developed in Italy by such composers as Pergolesi, while in England *The Beggar's Opera* 1728 by John Gay started the vogue of the *ballad opera*, using popular tunes and spoken dialogue. *Singspiel* was the German equivalent (although its music was newly composed). A lessening of artificiality began with Gluck, who insisted on the pre-eminence of the dramatic over the purely vocal element. Mozart learned much from Gluck in writing his serious operas, but excelled in Italian *opera buffa*. In works such as *The Magic Flute*, he laid the foundations of a purely German-language opera, using the *Singspiel* as a basis. This line was continued by Beethoven in *Fidelio* and by the work of Weber, in which the Romantic style appears for the first time in opera.

The Italian tradition, which placed the main stress on vocal display and melodic suavity (*bel canto*), continued unbroken into the 19th century

in the operas of Rossini, Donizetti, and Bellini. It is in the Romantic operas of Weber and Meyerbeer that the work of Wagner has its roots. Dominating the operatic scene of his time, Wagner attempted to create, in his 'music-dramas', a new art-form, and completely transformed the 19th-century conception of opera. In Italy, Verdi assimilated, in his mature work, much of the Wagnerian technique, without sacrificing the Italian virtues of vocal clarity and melody. This tradition was continued by Puccini. In French opera in the mid-19th century, represented by such composers as Delibes, Gounod, Saint-Saëns, and Massenet, the drama was subservient to the music. More serious artistic ideals were put into practice by Berlioz in *The Trojans*, but the merits of his work were largely unrecognized in his own time.

Bizet's *Carmen* began a trend towards realism in opera; his lead was followed in Italy by Mascagni, Leoncavallo, and Puccini. Debussy's *Pelléas and Melisande* represented a reaction against the over-emphatic emotionalism of Wagnerian opera. National operatic styles were developed in Russia by Glinka, Rimsky-Korsakov, Mussorgsky, Borodin, and Tchaikovsky, and in Bohemia by Smetana. Several composers of light opera emerged, including Sullivan, Lehár, Offenbach, and Johann Strauss. In the 20th century the Viennese school produced an outstanding opera in Berg's *Wozzeck*, and the Romanticism of Wagner was revived by Richard Strauss in *Der Rosenkavalier*.

Modern composers of opera include Gershwin, Menotti, Weill, Bernstein, and Stravinsky in the US; Tippett and Britten in the UK; Henze in Germany; Petrassi in Italy; and Prokofiev and Shostakovich in the USSR.

opera buffa (Italian 'comic opera') a type of humorous opera with characters taken from everyday life. The form began as a musical intermezzo in the 18th century and was then adopted in Italy and France for complete operas. An example is Rossini's *The Barber of Seville*.

opéra comique (French 'comic opera') opera that includes text to be spoken, not sung; Bizet's *Carmen* is an example. Of the two Paris opera houses in the 18th and 19th centuries, the *Opéra* (which aimed at setting a grand style) allowed no spoken dialogue, whereas the *Opéra Comique* did.

opera seria (Italian 'serious opera') a type of opera distinct from *opera buffa*, or humorous opera. Common in the 17th and 18th centuries, it tended towards formality. Examples include many of Handel's mythology-based operas.

operating system (OS) in computing, a program that controls the basic operation of a computer. A typical OS controls the ◊peripheral devices, organizes the filing system, provides a means of communicating with the operator, and runs other programs.

Many computers have their own operating system, but some are accepted standards. These include CP/M (by Digital Research) and MS-DOS (by Microsoft) for microcomputers, and Unix (by Bell Laboratories) for minicomputers.

operational amplifier a type of electronic circuit that is used to increase the size of an alternating voltage signal without distorting it.

They are used in a wide range of electronic measuring instruments. The name arose because they were originally designed to carry out mathematical operations and solve equations.

operations research a business discipline that uses logical analysis to find solutions to managerial and administrative problems, such as the allocation of resources, inventory control, competition, and the identification of information needed for decision-making.

Typically, a problem is identified by researchers and a model constructed; then solution techniques are applied to the model to solve the problems. Key skills required include mathematics, economics, and engineering, while the use of computers has become increasingly important.

Operations research was developed as a discipline in the UK during World War II in response to the need to improve efficiency of military systems. Its use spread, and by the 1950s methods were being adapted to improve management of industrial systems in the USA.

operetta a short amusing musical play, which may use spoken dialogue.

operon a group of genes that are found next to each other on a chromosome, and are turned on and off as an integrated unit. They usually produce enzymes that control different steps in the same biochemical pathway. Operons were discovered (by the French biochemists F Jacob and J Monod) in bacteria; they are less common in higher organisms where the control of metabolism is a more complex process.

Ophiuchus large constellation of the equatorial region of the sky, known as the serpent bearer. The Sun passes through Ophiuchus each Dec, although the constellation is not part of the zodiac. Ophiuchus contains ◊Barnard's Star.

ophthalmia inflammation of the eye. *Ophthalmia neonatorum* (newborn) is an acute inflammation of a baby's eyes at birth with the organism of gonorrhoea caught from the mother. *Sympathetic ophthalmia* is the diffuse inflammation of the sound eye that is apt to follow septic inflammation of the other.

ophthalmology the medical speciality concerned with diseases of the eye and its surrounding tissues.

Ophüls /'ɒphʊls/ Max. Adopted name of Max Oppenheimer 1902–1957. German film director. He moved to cinema from the theatre, and his work used intricate camera movements. He worked in Europe and the USA, attracting critical praise for films such as *Letter from an Unknown Woman* 1948 and *Lola Montes* 1955.

opiates, endogenous naturally produced chemicals in the body that have effects similar to morphine and other opiate drugs. They include ◊endorphins and ◊encephalins.

Opie /'əupi/ John 1761–1807. British artist. Born in St Agnes, Cornwall, he became famous as a portrait painter in London from 1780, later painting historical pictures such as *The Murder of Rizzio*.

Opie /'əupi/ Peter Mason 1918–1982 and Iona Margaret Balfour 1923– . Husband-and-wife team of folklorists who specialized in the myths and literature of childhood. Their books include the *Oxford Dictionary of Nursery Rhymes* 1951 and *The Lore and Language of Schoolchildren* 1959. In 1987 their collection of children's books was sold to the Bodleian library, Oxford, for £500,000.

opinion poll attempt to measure public opinion by taking a survey of the views of a representative sample of the electorate. The first accurately sampled opinion poll was carried out by the statistician George ◊Gallup during the US presidential election 1936. Opinion polls have encountered criticism on the grounds that their publication may influence the outcome of an election.

Rather than simply predicting how people will vote, poll results may alter voters' intentions, for example, by establishing one party as likely to win and making the voters wish to join the winning side, or by making the lead of one party seem so great that its supporters feel they need not bother to vote.

opium drug extracted from the unripe seeds of the opium poppy *Papaver somniferum* of SW Asia. An addictive narcotic, it contains several alkaloids, the most important being *morphine*, one of the most powerful natural painkillers and addictive narcotics known, and *codeine*, a milder painkiller.

Heroin is a synthetic derivative of morphine and even more powerful as a drug. Opium is still sometimes given as a tincture, dissolved in alcohol and known as *laudanum*.

Opium Wars wars waged in the mid-19th century by the UK against China to enforce the opening of Chinese ports to trade in opium. Opium from British India paid for Britain's imports from China, such as porcelain, silk, and, above all, tea, then obtainable in bulk only from China.

The *First Opium War 1839–42*, between Britain and China, resulted in the cession of Hong Kong to Britain and the opening of five treaty ports, licensed for foreign trade. Other European states were also subsequently given concessions.

A *Second Opium War 1856–60* followed between Britain and France in alliance against China, when there was further Chinese resistance, notably in Canton, one of the treaty ports. At its close the Summer Palace in Beijing was set on fire. China was forced to ratify the treaty of Tientsin 1858 which gave the European states even more trading privileges at the expense of the Chinese.

Opole /ɒ'pəʊleɪ/ industrial town in S Poland, on the river Oder; population (1983) 121,900. It is an agricultural centre, other occupations include textiles, chemicals, and cement.

Oporto /ə'pɔːtəʊ/ alternative form of ◊Porto in Portugal.

opossum the only marsupial native to North America, of the family Didelphidae. Opossums are arboreal, nocturnal animals, with prehensile tails, and hands and feet well adapted for grasping. They can grow to the size of a cat, and are carnivorous and insectivorous.

The *common opossum Didelphis marsupialis*, with yellowish-grey fur, has spread its range into North America. Most true opossums are confined to Central and South America, but the name is popularly applied to some of the similar animals (phalangers) found in Australia.

Oppenheimer /'ɒpən,haɪmə/ J(ulius) Robert 1904–1967. US physicist. As director of the Los Alamos Science Laboratory 1943–45, he was in charge of the development of the atomic bomb (the Manhattan Project). He objected to the development of the hydrogen bomb, and was declared a security risk 1953 by the US Atomic Energy Commission (AEG)

Oppenheimer was the son of a German immigrant. Before World War II he worked with the physicist Rutherford in Cambridge. He was rehabilitated by the AEG in 1963 when it granted him the Fermi award.

opportunity cost in economics, that which has been forgone in order to achieve an objective. A family may choose to buy a new television set and forgo their annual holiday; the holiday represents the opportunity cost.

In decision-making, economists prefer to look at the opportunity costs because it requires a rational

Oppenheimer US physicist J Robert Oppenheimer, who led the Manhattan Project to design the first atomic bomb, but later opposed work on the hydrogen bomb.

approach (all alternatives are examined), while an accountant's view of cost is more concerned with the way in which money is spent and the profit or loss that results.

opposition in astronomy, the moment at which the longitude of a body in the solar system differs from that of the Sun by 180°, so that it lies opposite the Sun in the sky and crosses the ◊meridian at about midnight. The term also applies to the alignment of the two bodies at this moment.

Although the ◊inferior planets cannot come to opposition, it is the best time for observation of the other planets as they can then be seen during the night.

Opposition, Leader of His/Her Majesty's in UK politics, official title (from 1937) of the leader of the largest opposition party in the House of Commons.

optical aberration see ◊aberration, optical.

optical computer a computer in which both light and electrical signals are used in the CPU (central processing unit). The technology is still not fully developed, but such a computer promises to be faster and less vulnerable to outside electrical interference than one that relies solely on electricity.

optical contouring computerized monitoring of a light pattern projected onto a patient to detect discrepancies in movements during breathing.

optical fibre very fine optically pure glass fibre through which light can be reflected to transmit an image or information from one end to the other. Bundles of such fibres are used in ◊endoscopes to inspect otherwise inaccessible parts of machines or of the living body. Optical fibres are increasingly being used to replace copper wire in telephone cables, the messages being coded as pulses of light rather than a fluctuating electric current. In 1989 a 2,700 km/1690 mi optical-fibre link was opened between Adelaide and Perth, Australia.

optical illusion a scene or picture that fools the eye. An example of a natural optical illusion is that the moon appears bigger when it is on the horizon than it does when it is high in the sky, owing to the ◊refraction of light rays by the Earth's atmosphere.

optical instrument a device that uses one or more ◊lenses or ◊mirrors to produce an image. See ◊eye, ◊microscope, ◊periscope, ◊projector, and ◊telescope.

optics scientific study of light and vision, for example shadows and mirror images, and lenses, microscopes, telescopes, and cameras. Light rays travel for all practical purposes in straight lines, although ◊Einstein has demonstrated that they may be 'bent' by a gravitational field. On striking a surface they are reflected or refracted with some absorption of energy, and the study of these facts is the subject of geometrical optics.

option in business, a contract giving the owner the right (as opposed to the obligation, as with futures contracts; see ◊futures trading) to buy or sell a specific quantity of a particular commodity or currency at a future date and at an agreed price, in return for a premium. The buyer or seller can

optical fibre Spray of glass optical fibres showing the pinpoint of light emerging at the tip of each fibre.

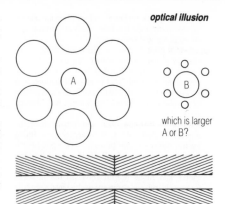

optical illusion

which is larger A or B?

are the two inner lines parallel?

decide not to exercise the option if it would prove disadvantageous.

opto-electronics a branch of electronics concerned with the development of devices (based on the semiconductor gallium arsenide) that respond not only to the ◊electrons of electronic data transmission, but also to ◊photons.

In 1989, scientists at IBM in the USA built a gallium arsenide microprocessor ('chip') containing 8,000 transistors and four photodetectors. The densest opto-electronic chip yet produced, this can detect and process data at a speed of 1 billion bits per second.

opus (Latin 'work') in music, a term, used with a figure, to indicate the numbering of a composer's works, usually in chronological order.

opus anglicanum (Latin 'English work') ecclesiastical embroidery made in England about AD 900–1500. It typically depicts birds and animals on highly coloured silks, using gold thread. It was popular throughout medieval Europe, being much in demand at the papal court.

Opus Dei /'əʊpəs 'deɪɪ/ (Latin 'God's work') a Roman Catholic institution aiming at the dissemination of the ideals of Christian perfection, particularly in intellectual and influential circles. Founded in Madrid in 1928, and still powerful in Spain, it is now international. Its members may be of either sex, and lay or clerical.

OR abbreviation for ◊*Oregon*.

oracle Greek sacred site where answers (also called oracles) were given by a deity to enquirers about future events; these were usually ambivalent, so that the deity was proven right whatever happened. The earliest was probably at Dodona (in ◊Epirus), where priests interpreted the sounds made by the sacred oaks of ◊Zeus, but the most celebrated was that of Apollo at ◊Delphi.

Oracle the ◊teletext system operated in Britain by Independent Television, introduced 1973. See also ◊Ceefax.

Oradea /ɒ'rɑːdiə/ or *Oradea-Mare* industrial city in Romania; on the river Koös; population (1983) 206,200. Industries include agricultural machinery, chemicals, non-ferrous metallurgy, leather goods, printing, glass, textiles, clothing, and brewing.

history Created seat of a bishopric by St Ladislas in 1083; destroyed by the Turks in 1241 and rebuilt. Many of its buildings date from the reign of Maria Theresa in the 18th century. It was ceded by Hungary to Romania in 1919, and held by Hungary 1940–45.

oral literature stories that are or have been transmitted in spoken form, such as public recitation, rather than through writing or printing. Most preliterate societies seem to have had a tradition of oral literature, including short 'folk tales', legends, proverbs, and riddles as well as longer narrative works; and most of the ancient epics—such as the Greek *Odyssey* and the Mesopotamian *Gilgamesh* —seem to have been composed and added to over many centuries before they were committed to writing.

Some ancient stories from oral traditions were not written down as literary works until the 19th century, such as the Finnish *Kalevala* (1822); many fairy tales, such as those collected in Germany by the Grimm brothers, also come into this category. The extent to which this sort of *folk literature* has been consciously embellished and altered, particularly in Europe in the 19th century for nationalistic purposes, is controversial.

Oran /ɔːˈrɑːn/ (Arabic *Wahran*) seaport in Algeria; population (1984) 663,500. Products include iron, textiles, footwear, and processed food. It was part of the Ottoman Empire except 1509–1708 and 1732–91 under Spanish rule.

history Oran was occupied by France in 1831. After the surrender of France to Germany in 1940, the French warships in the naval base of Mers-el-Kebir nearby were put out of action by the British navy to prevent them from falling into German hands.

orange evergreen tree of the genus *Citrus*, remarkable for bearing blossom and fruit at the same time. Thought to have originated in SE Asia, they are commercially cultivated in Spain, Israel, Brazil, South Africa, USA, and elsewhere. The *sweet orange Citrus sinensis* is the one commonly eaten fresh; the Jaffa, blood, and navel orange are varieties within this species.

Tangerines and mandarins belong to a related species *Citrus reticulata*. The *sour orange* or *Seville Citrus aurantium* is the bitter orange used in making marmalade. Oranges yield several essential oils.

Orange /ˈɒrɪndʒ/ town in New South Wales, Australia, 200 km/125 mi NW of Sydney; population (1984) 32,000. There is a woollen-textile industry based on local sheep flocks, and fruit is grown.

Orange /ˈɒrɪndʒ/ river in South Africa, rising on the Mont aux Sources in Lesotho and flowing W to the Atlantic; length 2,100 km/1,300 mi. It runs along the S boundary of the Orange Free State, and was named 1779 after William of Orange. Water from the Orange is diverted via the Orange–Fish River Tunnel 1975 to irrigate the semi-arid E Cape Province.

Orange /ˈɒrɪndʒ/ town in France, N of Avignon; population (1982) 27,500. It has the remains of a Roman theatre and arch. It was a medieval principality from which came the royal house of Orange.

Orange County /ˈɒrɪndʒ/ metropolitan area of S California, USA; area 2,075 sq km/801 sq mi; it adjoins Los Angeles County; population (1980) 1,932,700. Industries include aerospace and electronics. Oranges and strawberries are grown, Disneyland is here, and Santa Ana is the chief town.

Orange Free State /ˈɒrɪndʒ ˌfriː ˈsteɪt/ province of the Republic of South Africa
area 127,993 sq km/49,405 sq mi
capital Bloemfontein
features plain of the High Veld; Lesotho forms an enclave on the Natal–Cape Province border
products grain, wool, cattle, gold, oil from coal, cement, pharmaceuticals
population (1987) 1,863,000 (1,525,000 ethnic Africans)
history original settlements from 1810 were complemented by the ◊Great Trek, and it was recognized by Britain as independent 1854. Following the South African or Boer War 1899–1902, it was annexed by Britain until it entered the union as a province 1910.

Orange, House of /ˈɒrɪndʒ/ the royal family of the Netherlands. The title is derived from the small principality of Orange, in S France, held by the family from the 8th century to 1713. They held considerable possessions in the Netherlands, to which, after 1530, was added the German county of Nassau.

From the time of William the Silent (1533–1585) the family dominated Dutch history, bearing the title of stadholder for the greater part of the 17th and 18th centuries. The son of Stadholder

William V was made King William I by the Allies 1815.

Orangeman member of the Ulster Protestant *Orange Society* established 1795 in opposition to the United Irishmen and the Roman Catholic secret societies. It was a revival of the Orange Institution 1688, formed in support of William (III) of Orange, the anniversary of whose victory over the Catholic James II at the Battle of the Boyne 1690 is commemorated by Protestants in parades on 12 July.

Orange, Project /ˈɒrɪndʒ/ plan 1980 for a white South African 'homeland' (Projek Oranje) to be established on the border between Orange Free State and the Northern Cape. No black person would be allowed to live or work there.

orang-utan anthropoid ape *Pongo pygmaeus*, found solely in Borneo and Sumatra. Up to 1.65 m/5.5 ft in height, it is covered with long red-brown hair, and mainly lives a solitary, arboreal life, feeding chiefly on fruit. Now an endangered species, it is officially protected because its habitat is being systematically destroyed by deforestation.

Orang-utans are slow-moving and have been hunted for food, as well as by animal collectors. They are sometimes considered the most intelligent of the apes. The name means 'man of the forest'.

Orasul Stalin /ˈɔːrəsuːl ˈstɑːlɪn/ name 1948–56 of the Romanian town ◊Braşov.

Oratorian a member of the Roman Catholic order of secular priests, called in full *Congregation of the Oratory of St Philip Neri*, formally constituted by Philip Neri 1575 in Rome, and characterized by the degree of freedom allowed to individual communities. The churches of the Oratorians are noted for their music.

The order was first established in England by Cardinal Newman 1848, and in 1884 Brompton Oratory in London was opened.

oratorio musical setting of religious texts, scored for orchestra, chorus, and solo voices, on a scale more dramatic and larger than that of a cantata.

The term derives from St Philip Neri's Oratory in Rome, where settings of the *Laudi spirituali* were performed in the 16th century. The definitive form of oratorio began in the 17th century with Cavalieri, Carissimi, Alessandro Scarlatti, and Schütz, and reached perfection in such works as J S Bach's *Christmas Oratorio*, and Handel's *Messiah*. Other examples of oratorios are Haydn's *The Creation* and *The Seasons*, Mendelssohn's *Elijah*, and Elgar's *The Dream of Gerontius*.

Orbison /ˈɔːbɪsən/ Roy 1936–1988. US pop singer and songwriter, noted for his operatic ballad style on songs like 'Only The Lonely' 1960 and 'Running Scared' 1961.

Orbison, born in Texas, began in the mid-1950s as a rockabilly singer on Sun Records. He soon specialized in slow, dramatic numbers, but his biggest hit was the jaunty 'Oh, Pretty Woman'

1964. In the 1970s he turned to country material but made a pop comeback in 1988 as a member of the Travelin' Wilburys with Bob Dylan, George Harrison (ex-Beatles), Tom Petty (1952–), and Jeff Lynne (1947–). The last Orbison album, *Mystery Girl* 1989, was a posthumous success.

orbit the path of one body in space around another, such as the orbit of Earth around the Sun, or the Moon around Earth. When the two bodies are similar in mass, as in a ◊double star, both bodies move around their common centre of mass. The movement of objects in orbit follows ◊Kepler's laws, which apply to artificial satellites as well as to natural bodies.

As stated by the laws, the orbit of one body around another is an ellipse. The ellipse can be highly elongated, as are comet orbits around the Sun, or it may be almost circular, as are those of some planets. The closest point of a planet's orbit to the Sun is called *perihelion*; the most distant point is *aphelion*. (For a body orbiting the Earth, the closest and furthest points of the orbit are called *perigee* and *apogee*.)

orbital, atomic the region around the nucleus of an ◊atom (or, in a molecule, around several nuclei) in which an ◊electron is most likely to be found. According to ◊quantum theory, the position of an electron is uncertain; it may be found at any point. However, it is more likely to be found in some places than in others, and these make up the orbital.

An atom or molecule has numerous orbitals, each of which has a fixed size and shape. An orbital is characterized by three numbers – called *quantum numbers* – representing its energy (and hence size), its angular momentum (and hence shape), and its orientation. Each orbital can be occupied by one or two electrons (by two only if their spins are aligned in opposite directions).

orchestra group of musicians playing together in sections, each made up of a different instrument.

orbital, atomic

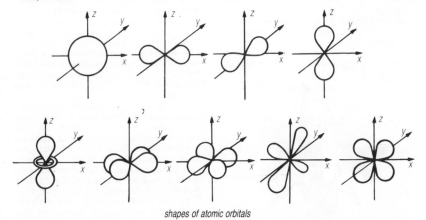

shapes of atomic orbitals

In contemporary Western music, an orchestra often refers to an ensemble containing the various bowed string instruments and sections of wind, brass, and percussion. The size and format may vary according to the needs of composers.

The term was originally used in Greek theatre for the semicircular space in front of the stage, and was adopted in 17th-century France to refer first to the space in front of the stage where musicians sat, and later to the musicians themselves.

The string section is commonly divided into two groups of violins (first and second), violas, cellos, and double basses. The woodwind section became standardized by the end of the 18th century, when it consisted of two each of flutes, oboes, clarinets, and bassoons, to which were later added piccolo, cor anglais, bass clarinet, and double bassoon. At that time, two timpani and two horns were also standard, and two trumpets were occasionally added. During the 19th century, the brass section was gradually expanded to include four horns, three trumpets, three trombones, and tuba. To the percussion section a third timpani was added, and from Turkey came the bass drum, side drum, cymbals, and triangle. One or more harps became common and, to maintain balance, the number of string instruments to a part also increased. Other instruments used in the orchestra include xylophone, ◊celesta, piano, and organ.

The term may also be applied to non-Western ensembles such as the Indonesian gamelan orchestra, consisting solely of percussion instruments, mainly tuned gongs and bells.

orchestration the scoring of a composition for orchestra.

orchid plant of the family Orchidaceae, which contains some 18,000 species, distributed throughout the world except in the coldest areas, and most numerous in damp equatorial regions. The flowers have three sepals and three petals and are sometimes solitary, but more usually borne in spikes, racemes, or panicles, either erect or drooping.

The lowest petal of each flower, the labellum, is usually large, and may be spurred, fringed, pouched, or crested. Many tropical orchids are epiphytes attached to trees, but temperate orchids commonly grow on the ground and include the spotted orchis *Dactylorhiza maculata* and other British species.

Orczy /ˈɔːtsi/ Baroness Emmusca 1865–1947. Hungarian-born British novelist, who wrote the historical adventure ◊*The Scarlet Pimpernel* 1905. The foppish Sir Percy Blakeney, the bold rescuer of victims of the French Revolution, appeared in many sequels.

ordeal, trial by in medieval times, method of testing guilt of an accused person based on a belief in heaven's protection of the innocent. Examples of such ordeals are walking barefoot over glowing ploughshares, dipping the hand into boiling water, and swallowing consecrated bread (causing the guilty to choke).

order in classical architecture, the ◊column (including capital, shaft, and base) and the entablature, considered as an architectural whole. The five orders are Doric, Ionic, Corinthian, Tuscan, and Composite.

The earliest order was the Doric (which had no base), which originated before the 5th century BC,

orchid

soon followed by the Ionic, which was first found in Asia Minor. The Corinthian (with leafs in the capitals) dates from the end of the 5th century BC, while the Composite appears first on the arch of Titus in Rome AD 82. No Tuscan columns survive from antiquity, although the order was thought to originate in Etruscan times. The five orders were described in detail by the Italian Sebastiano Serlio in his treatise on architecture 1537.

order in biological classification, a group of related ◊families. For example, the horse, rhinoceros, and tapir families are grouped in the order Perissodactyla, the odd-toed ungulates, because they all have either one or three toes on each foot. The names of orders are not shown in italic (unlike genus and species names) and by convention they all have the ending -formes (birds and fish), -a (mammals, amphibians, reptiles, and other animals), or -ales (fungi and plants). Related orders are grouped together in a ◊class.

order in council in the UK, an order issued by the sovereign with the advice of the Privy Council; in practice it is issued only on the advice of the cabinet. Acts of Parliament often provide for the issue of orders in council to regulate the detailed administration of their provisions.

Order of Merit British order of chivalry founded 1902 by Edward VII and limited in number to 24 at any one time.

ordinal number in mathematics, one of the series first, second, third, fourth,... Ordinal numbers relate to order, whereas ◊cardinal numbers (1, 2, 3, 4...) relate to quantity, or count.

ordination religious ceremony by which a person is accepted into the priesthood or monastic life in various religions. Within the Christian church, ordination authorizes a person to administer the sacraments. The Roman Catholic and Eastern Orthodox churches and the Church of England refuse to ordain women.

ordination of women Many Christian Protestant denominations, such as the Methodists and Baptists, ordain women as ministers, as do many churches in the Anglican Communion outside the UK. In 1988 the first female bishop was elected within the Anglican Communion (in Massachusetts, USA).

Ordnance Survey official state department for the mapping of Britain, established 1791; revision is continuous.

Ordovician period of geological time 505–438 million years ago; the second period of the ◊Palaeozoic era. Animal life was confined to the sea: reef-building algae and the first jawless fish are characteristic.

The period is named after the Ordovices, an ancient Welsh people, because the system of rocks formed in the Ordovician period was first studied in Wales.

ore a body of rock, a vein within it, or a deposit of sediment, worth mining for the economically valuable mineral it contains.

The term is usually applied to sources of metals. Hydrothermal ore deposits are formed from fluids, especially saline water, passing through fissures in the host rock at an elevated temperature. Examples are the 'porphyry copper' deposits of Chile and Bolivia, the submarine copper-zinc-iron sulphide deposits recently discovered on the East Pacific Rise, and the limestone lead-zinc deposits that occur in the southern USA and in the Pennines of Britain.

Other ores are concentrated by igneous processes, causing the ore metals to become segregated from a magma, for example, the chromite and platinum-metal-rich bands within the Bushveld, South Africa. Erosion and transportation in rivers of material from an existing rock source can lead to further concentration of heavy minerals in a deposit, for example, Malaysian tin deposits. Weathering of rocks in situ can result in residual metal-rich soils, such as the nickel-bearing laterites of New Caledonia.

Oregon /ˈɒrɪgən/ state of the NW USA, on the Pacific; nickname Beaver State
area 251,500 sq km/97,079 sq mi
capital Salem
towns Portland, Eugene
features fertile Willamette river valley; Columbia and Snake rivers; Crater Lake, deepest in the USA (589 m/1,933 ft); Coast and Cascade mountain ranges, the latter including Mount St Helens
products wheat, livestock, timber, gold, silver, nickel, electronics
population (1987) 2,690,000
famous people Linus Pauling
history the Oregon Trail (3,200 km/2,000 mi from Independence, Missouri, to the Columbia river) was the pioneer route across the USA 1841–60. Settled 1811 by the Pacific Fur Company, Oregon Territory included Washington until 1853; it became a state 1859.

Orel /ɔːˈriɒl/ industrial city in the USSR, capital of Orel region, on the river Oka 320 km/200 mi SSW of Moscow; population (1987) 335,000. Industries include engineering, textiles, and food stuffs. It is the birthplace of the writer Ivan Turgenev.

Orellana /ˌɒrelˈjɑːnə/ Francisco de 1511–1546. Spanish explorer who travelled with Francesco ◊Pizarro from Guayaquil, on the Pacific coast of South America, to Quito in the Andes. He was the first person known to have navigated the full length of the Amazon from the Napo River to the Atlantic Ocean (1541–43).

Orenburg /ˈɒrənbɜːg/ city in S central USSR, on the Ural river; population (1987) 537,000. It is a trading and mining centre and capital of Orenburg region. It dates from the early 18th century and was called Chkalov 1938–57 in honour of a long-distance flyer.

Orense /ɒˈrenseɪ/ town in NW Galicia, Spain, on the river Miño; population (1986) 102,000. It produces textiles, furniture, food products, and metal goods.

Oresteia, The a trilogy of plays by Aeschylus, which won first prize at the festival of Dionysus in 458 BC, *Agamemnon*, *Choephoroe*, and *Eumenides*. They describe the murder of Agamemnon by his wife Clytemnestra and the consequent vengeance of his son Orestes and daughter Electra.

Orestes /ɒˈrestiːz/ in Greek legend, the son of ◊Agamemnon and ◊Clytemnestra.

Öresund /ˌɜːrəˈsʊnd/ strait between Sweden and Denmark; in English called the ◊Sound.

orfe fish *Leuciscus idus* of the carp family. It grows up to 50 cm/1.7 ft, and feeds on small aquatic animals. Generally greyish-black, an ornamental variety is orange. It lives in rivers and lakes of Europe and NW Asia.

Orff /ɔːf/ Carl 1895–1982. German composer, an individual stylist whose work is characterized by sharp dissonances and percussion. Among his compositions are the scenic cantata *Carmina Burana* 1937 and the opera *Antigone* 1949.

Orford, 1st Earl of /ˈɔːfəd/ title of the British politician Robert ◊Walpole.

organ musical wind instrument of ancient origin. It produces sound from pipes of various sizes under applied pressure and has keyboard controls.

One note only is sounded by each pipe, but these are grouped into stops, which are ranks or scales of pipes prepared to 'speak' by a knob.

Oregon

These, in turn, form part of a sectional organ, one of the tonal divisions comprising the whole organ. These separate manuals are the great, swell, choir, solo, echo, and pedal organs, controlled by the player's hands and feet. By this grouping and subdivision, extremes of tone and volume are obtained.

It developed from the Panpipe and hydraulus, and is mentioned in writings as early as the 3rd century BC. Organs were imported to France from Byzantium in the 8th and 9th centuries, after which their manufacture in Europe began. The superseding of the old drawslides by the key system dates from the 11th–13th centuries, the first chromatic keyboard from 1361. The more recent designs date from 1809 when the composition pedal was introduced. Apart from its continued use in serious compositions and for church music, the organ has been adapted for light entertainment. The electric tone-wheel organ was invented 1934 by the US engineer Laurens Hammond (1895–1973). Other types of electric organ were developed in the 1960s. Electrically controlled organs substitute electrical impulses and relays for some of the air-pressure controls. These, such as the Hammond organs, built during the 1930s for the large cinemas of the period, include many special sound effects as well as colour displays. In electronic organs the notes are produced by electronic oscillators and are amplified at will.

organ in biology, part of a living body, such as the liver or brain, that has a distinctive function or set of functions.

Organ /ˈɔːɡən/ (Harold) Bryan 1935– . English portraitist, whose subjects include Harold Macmillan, Michael Tippett, Elton John, and the Prince and Princess of Wales.

organelle a discrete and specialized structure in a living cell; organelles include *mitochondria, chloroplasts, lysosomes, ribosomes*, and the *nucleus*.

organic chemistry the chemistry of carbon compounds, particularly the more complex carbon compounds. The basis of organic chemistry is the ability of carbon to form long chains of atoms, branching chains, rings, and other complex structures. In a typical organic compound, each carbon atom forms a bond with each of its neighbouring carbon atoms in the chain or ring, and two more with hydrogen atoms (carbon has a valency of four). Other atoms that may be involved in organic molecules include oxygen and nitrogen. Compounds containing only carbon and hydrogen are known as hydrocarbons.

Organic chemistry is largely the chemistry of a great variety of homologous series, in which the molecular formulae, when arranged in ascending order, form an arithmetical progression. The physical properties undergo a gradual change from one member to the next.

The chain of carbon atoms forming the backbone of an organic molecule may be built up from beginning to end without branching; or it may throw off branches at one or more points. This division of organic compounds is known as the *open-chain* or *aliphatic* compounds. Sometimes, however, the ropes of carbon atoms curl round and form rings. These constitute the second division of organic compounds, known as *closed-chain, ring,* or *cyclic* compounds. Other structural varieties are known.

Many organic compounds are made only by living organisms (for example proteins, carbohydrates), and it was once believed organic compounds could not be made by any other means. This was disproved when Wöhler synthesized urea, but the name 'organic' (that is 'living') chemistry has remained in use. Many organic compounds are derived from oil, which represents the chemical remains of millions of microscopic marine organisms.

In inorganic chemistry, a specific formula usually represents one substance only, but in organic chemistry, it is exceptional for a molecular

organic chemistry
common organic molecule groupings

formula	name	atomic bonding
CH_3	Methyl	
CH_2CH_3	Ethyl	
CC	Double bond	
CHO	Aldehyde	
CH_2OH	Alcohol	
CO	Ketone	
COOH	Acid	
CH_2NH_2	Amine	
C_6H_6	Benzene ring	

formula to represent only one substance. Substances having the same molecular formula are called *isomers*, and the relationship is known as *isomerism*.

Hydrocarbons form one of the most prolific of the many organic types; fuel oils are largely made up of hydrocarbons. Typical groups containing only carbon, hydrogen, and oxygen are alcohols, aldehydes, ketones, ethers, esters, and carbohydrates. Among groups containing nitrogen are amides, amines, nitro-compounds, amino-acids, proteins, purines, alkaloids, and many others, both natural and artificial. Other organic types contain sulphur, phosphorus, or halogen elements.

The most fundamental of all natural processes are oxidation, reduction, hydrolysis, condensation, polymerization, and molecular rearrangement. In nature, such changes are often brought about through the agency of promoters known as *enzymes*, which act as catalytic agents in promoting specific reactions. The most fundamental of all natural processes is *synthesis*, or building up. In living plant and animal organisms, the energy stored in carbohydrate molecules, derived originally from sunlight, is released by slow oxidation and utilized by the organisms. The complex carbohydrates thereby revert to carbon dioxide and water, from where they were built up with absorption of energy. Thus, a so-called carbon food cycle exists in nature. In a corresponding nitrogen food cycle, complex proteins are synthesized in nature from carbon dioxide, water, soil nitrates, and ammonium salts, and these proteins ultimately revert to the elementary raw materials

from which they came, with the discharge of their energy of chemical combination.

organic farming farming without the use of synthetic fertilizers (such as ◊nitrates and phosphates) or ◊pesticides (herbicides, insecticides and fungicides) or other agrochemicals (such as hormones, growth stimulants or fruit regulators).

In place of artificial fertilizers, compost, manure, seaweed or other substances derived from living things are used (hence the name organic'). Growing a crop of a nitrogen-fixing plant such as lucerne, then ploughing it back into the soil, also fertilizes the ground. Some organic farmers use naturally occurring chemicals such as nicotine or pyrethrum to kill pests, but control by nonchemical methods is preferred. Those methods include removal by hand, intercropping (planting with companion plants which deter pests), mechanical barriers to infestation, crop rotation, better cultivation methods, and ◊biological control. Weeds can be controlled by hoeing, mulching (covering with manure, straw or black plastic) or burning off. Organic farming methods produce food without pesticide residues and greatly reduce pollution of the environment. They are more labour intensive, and therefore more expensive, but use less fossil fuel. Soil structure is greatly improved by organic methods, and recent studies show that a conventional farm can lose four times as much soil through erosion as an organic farm, although the loss may not be immediately obvious.

Organisation de l'Armée Secrète (OAS) guerrilla organization formed 1961 by French settlers devoted to perpetuating their own rule in Algeria (Algérie Française). It collapsed on the imprisonment 1962–68 of its leader Gen Raoul Salan.

Organization for Economic Co-operation and Development (OECD) Paris-based international organization of 24 industrialized countries which coordinates member states' economic policy strategies. The OECD's subsidiary bodies include the International Energy Agency 1974, set up in the face of a world oil crisis.

It superseded the Organization for European Economic Co-operation (established 1948 to promote European recovery under the ◊Marshall Plan) 1961, when the USA and Canada became members and its scope was extended to include development aid. The OECD members are: Australia, Austria, Belgium, Canada, Denmark, Finland, France, Germany, Greece, Iceland, Ireland, Italy, Japan, Luxembourg, Netherlands, New Zealand, Norway, Portugal, Spain, Sweden, Switzerland, Turkey, UK, and USA.

Organization of African Unity (OAU) association established 1963 to eradicate colonialism and improve economic, cultural, and political cooperation in Africa; headquarters Addis Ababa, Ethiopia. The Secretary-General is Salim Ahmed Salim (Deputy Prime Minister of Tanzania). The French-speaking *Joint African and Mauritian Organization/Organisation Commune Africaine et Mauritienne: OCAM* (1962) works within the framework of the OAU for African solidarity; headquarters Yaoundé, Cameroon.

Organization of American States (OAS) association founded 1948 by a charter signed by representatives of 30 North, Central, and South American states. Canada held observer status from 1972 and became a full member 1989. It aims to maintain peace and solidarity within the hemisphere, and is also concerned with the social and economic development of Latin America. Its headquarters are in Washington, DC, USA. It is based on the International Union of American Republics 1890–1910 and Pan-American Union 1910–1948, set up to encourage friendly relations between countries of North and South America.

Organization of Central American States (*Organizacion de Estados Centro Americanos: ODECA*) international association promoting common economic, political, educational, and military aims in Central America. The first organization, established 1951, was superseded in 1962. Its members are Costa Rica, El Salvador, Guatemala, Honduras, and Nicaragua, provision being made for Panama to join at a later date. The permanent headquarters is in Guatemala City.

Organization of the Petroleum Exporting Countries (OPEC) body established 1960 to co-ordinate price and supply policies of oil-producing states, and also to improve the position of Third World states by forcing Western states to open their markets to the resultant products. Its concerted action in raising prices in the 1970s triggered worldwide recession but also lessened demand so that its influence was reduced by the mid-1980s. OPEC members in 1986 were: Algeria, Ecuador, Gabon, Indonesia, Iran, Iraq, Kuwait, Libya, Nigeria, Qatar, Saudi Arabia, United Arab Emirates, and Venezuela.

OPEC's importance in the world market was reflected in its ability to implement oil price rises from \$3 a barrel in 1973 to \$30 a barrel in 1980. In the 1980s, OPEC's dominant position was undermined by reduced demand for oil in industrialized countries, increased non-OPEC oil supplies, and production of alternative energy. These factors contributed to the dramatic fall in world oil prices to \$10 a barrel in July 1986 from \$28 at the beginning of the year, forcing OPEC to reduce its output.

organizer in embryology, a part of the embryo that causes changes to occur in another part, through ◊induction, thus 'organizing' development and ◊differentiation.

organum in music, a form of early medieval harmony in which voices move in parallel.

orienteering sport of cross-country running and route-finding. Competitors set off at one minute intervals and have to find their way, using map and compass, to various check points (approximately 0.8 km/0.5 mi apart), where their control cards are marked. World championships have been held since 1966. Orienteering was invented in Sweden by Maj Ernst Killander in 1918.

orienteering

World Championships first held 1966
individual (men/women)
1981 Oyvin Thon *(Norway)*/Annichen Kringstad *(Norway)*
1983 Morten Berglia *(Norway)*/Annichen Kringstad *(Norway)*
1985 Kari Sallinen *(Finland)*/Annichen Kringstad *(Norway)*
1987 Kent Olsson *(Sweden)*/Arja Hannus *(Sweden)*
1989 Peter Thoresen *(Norway)*/Marita Skogum *(Sweden)*
relay (men/women)
1979 Sweden/Finland
1981 Norway/Sweden
1983 Norway/Sweden
1985 Norway/Sweden
1987 Norway/Norway
1989 Norway/Sweden

origami art of folding paper into forms such as dolls and birds, originating in Japan in the 10th century.

Origen /ˈɒrɪdʒen/ *c.*185–*c.*254. Christian theologian, born in Alexandria, who produced a fancifully allegorical interpretation of the Bible. He castrated himself to ensure his celibacy.

original sin Christian doctrine that Adam's fall rendered humankind able to achieve salvation only through divine grace.

Orinoco /ˌɒrɪˈnəʊkəʊ/ river in N South America, flowing for about 2,400 km/1,500 mi through Venezuela and forming for about 320 km/200 mi the boundary with Colombia; tributaries include the Guaviare, Meta, Apure, Ventuari, Caura, and Caroni. It is navigable by large steamers for 1,125 km/700 mi from its Atlantic delta; rapids obstruct the upper river.

oriole brightly coloured songbird. In Africa and Eurasia, orioles belong to the family Oriolidae, such as the golden oriole *Oriolus oriolus*; in the Americas to the Icteridae, such as the bobolink and the Baltimore oriole.

Orissa

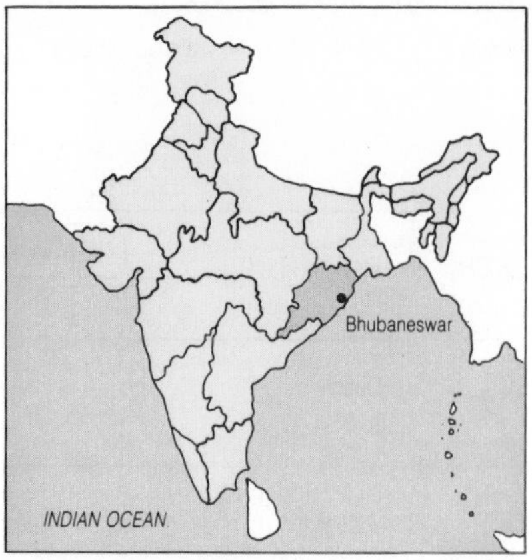

Orion in astronomy, a very prominent constellation in the equatorial region of the sky, representing the hunter of Greek mythology. It contains the bright stars Betelgeuse and Rigel, as well as a distinctive row of three stars that make up Orion's belt. Beneath the belt, marking the sword of Orion, is the Orion nebula; nearby is one of the most distinctive dark nebulae, the Horsehead.

Orion in Greek mythology, a giant of ◊Boeotia, famed as a hunter.

Orion nebula a luminous cloud of gas and dust 1,500 light years away, in the constellation Orion, from which stars are forming. It is about 15 light years in diameter, and contains enough gas to make a cluster of thousands of stars. At the nebula's centre is a group of hot young stars, called the ***Trapezium***, which make the surrounding gas glow. It is visible to the naked eye as a misty patch below the belt of Orion.

Orissa /ɒˈrɪsə/ state of NE India
area 155,800 sq km/60,139 sq mi
capital Bhubaneswar
towns Cuttack, Rourkela
features mainly agricultural; Chilka lake with fisheries and game; temple of Jagannath or Juggernaut at Puri
products rice, wheat, oilseed, sugar, timber, chromite, dolomite, graphite, iron
population (1981) 26,272,000
language Oriya (official)
religion Hindu 90%
history administered by the British 1803–1912 as a subdivision of Bengal, it joined with Bihar to become a province; in 1936 Orissa became a separate province and 1948–49 its area was almost doubled before its designation as a state 1950.

Orkney

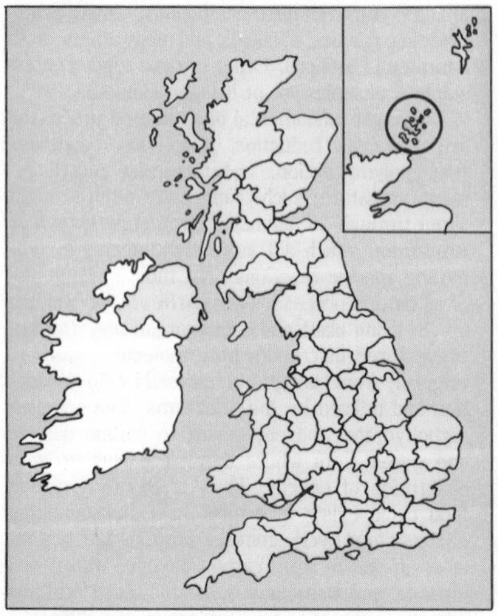

Orizaba /ˌɒrɪˈsɑːbə/ industrial city and resort in Veracruz state, Mexico; population (1980) 115,000. Industries include brewing, paper, and textiles. An earthquake in 1973 severely damaged it.

Orizaba /ˌɒrɪˈsɑːbə/ Spanish name for ◊Citlaltepec, mountain in Mexico.

Orkney Causeway construction in N Scotland put up in World War I, completed 1943, joining four of the Orkney Islands, built to protect the British fleet from intrusion through the eastern entrances to Scapa Flow. It links Kirkwall and the island by road.

Orkney Islands /ˈɔːkni/ island group off the NE coast of Scotland
area 970 sq km/375 sq mi
towns administrative headquarters Kirkwall, on Mainland (Pomona)
features comprises about 90 islands and islets, low-lying and treeless; population, long falling, has in recent years risen as their remoteness from the modern world attracts new settlers, for example Peter Maxwell Davies on Hoy; mild climate owing to the Gulf Stream; Skara Brae, a remarkably well-preserved Neolithic village on Mainland; Scapa Flow, between Mainland and Hoy, was a naval base in both world wars, and the German fleet scuttled itself here 21 June 1919
products fishing and farming, wind power (Burgar Hill has the world's most productive wind generator; blades 60 m/197 ft diameter)
population (1987) 19,000
history Harold I (Fairhair) of Norway conquered the islands 876; they were pledged to James III of Scotland 1468 for the dowry of Margaret of Denmark, and annexed by Scotland (the dowry unpaid) 1472.

Orkneys, South /ˈɔːkniz/ islands in the British Antarctic Territory; see ◊South Orkneys.

Orlando /ɔːˈlændəʊ/ industrial city in Florida, USA; population (1986) 148,000. Kennedy Space Center and Disney World are nearby. The city was named 1857 after Orlando Reeves, a soldier killed in a clash with Indians.

Orlando /ɔːˈlændəʊ/ Vittorio Emanuele 1860–1952. Italian politician, prime minister 1917–19. He attended the Paris Peace Conference after World War I, but dissatisfaction with his handling of the Adriatic settlement led to his resignation. He initially supported Mussolini, but was in retirement

Orkney Islands *The houses of the Neolithic village of Skara Brae are of drystone construction.*

1925–46, when he returned to the assembly and then the senate.

Orlando Furioso a poem by the Italian Renaissance writer Ariosto, published 1532 as a sequel to Boiardo's *Orlando Innamorato* 1441–94. The poem describes the unrequited love of Orlando for Angelica, set against the war between Saracens (Arabs) and Christians during Charlemagne's reign. It influenced Shakespeare, Byron, and Milton, and is considered to be the perfect poetic expression of the Italian Renaissance.

Orleanists French monarchist group that supported the Orléans branch of the royal family in opposition to the Bourbon Legitimists. Both groups were united in 1883 when the Bourbon line died out.

Orléans /ɔːˈlɑnz/ industrial city of France, on the river Loire; 115 km/70 mi SW of Paris; population (1982) 220,500. It is capital of Loiret *département*. Industries include engineering and food processing. Orléans, of pre-Roman origin and formerly the capital of the old province of Orléanais, is associated with Joan of Arc, who liberated it from English rule in 1429.

Orly /ˈɔːli/ a suburb of Paris in the *département* of Val-de-Marne; population (1982) 17,000. There is an international airport.

Ormandy /ˈɔːməndi/ Eugene 1899–1985. Hungarian-born US conductor. Originally a violin virtuoso, he championed ◊Rachmaninov and ◊Shostakovich and was music director of the Philadelphia Orchestra 1936–80.

ormolu (French *or moulu* 'ground gold') an alloy of copper, zinc, and sometimes tin, used for furniture decoration.

Ormonde /ˈɔːmənd/ James Butler, Duke of Ormonde 1610–1688. Irish general. He commanded the Royalist troops in Ireland 1641–50 during the Irish rebellion and the English Civil War, and was lord lieutenant 1644–47, 1661–69, and 1677–84. He was created a marquess in 1642 and a duke in 1661.

Ormuzd /ˈɔːmuzd/ another name for **Ahura Mazda**, the good god of ◊Zoroastrianism.

Orne /ɔːn/ French river rising E of Sées and flowing NW, then NE to the English Channel below Caen; 152 km/94 mi long. A ship canal runs alongside it from Caen to the sea at Ouistreham. The Orne gives its name to a *département* in Normandy; population (1982) 295,500.

ornithology in zoology, the study of birds. It covers scientific aspects relating to their structure and classification, their habits, song, flight, and their value to agriculture as destroyers of insect pests. It also covers the activities of people interested in birds.

This interest has led to the formation of societies for their protection, of which the Society for the Protection of Birds 1889 in Britain was the first; it received a royal charter 1904. The Audubon Society 1905 in the USA has similar aims. Other countries now have similar societies, and there is an International Council for Bird Preservation with its headquarters at the Natural History Museum, London. The headquarters of the British Trust for Ornithology is at Beech Grove, Tring, Hertfordshire. Migration, age, and pollution effects on birds are monitored by ringing (trained government-licensed operators fit numbered metal rings to captured specimens with a return address). Legislation in various countries to protect wild birds followed from a British act of Parliament 1880.

ornithophily the ◊pollination of flowers by birds. Ornithophilous flowers are typically brightly coloured, often red or orange. They produce large quantities of thin, watery nectar, and are scentless because most birds do not respond well to smell. They are found mostly in tropical areas, with hummingbirds being the most important pollinators in North and South America, and the sunbirds in Africa and Asia.

orogeny formation of mountains, by processes of volcanism, folding, faulting, and upthrusting (by the action of ◊plate tectonics).

Orontes /ɒˈrɒntiːz/ (Arabic *'Asi*) river flowing through Lebanon, Syria, and Turkey to the Mediterranean, and used mainly for irrigation; length 400 km/250 mi.

Orozco /ɒˈrɒskəʊ/ José Clemente 1883–1949. Mexican painter, known for his murals inspired by the Mexican revolution of 1910, such as the series in the Palace of Government, Guadalajara, 1949.

Orpen /ˈɔːpən/ William Newenham Montague 1878–1931. Irish artist. He studied at Dublin and London, became famous as a portraitist and genre artist, and was elected a member of the Royal Academy in 1919. Knighted 1918.

Orpheus /ˈɔːfjuːs/ mythical Greek poet and musician. The son of Apollo and a muse, he married Eurydice, who died from the bite of a snake. Orpheus went down to Hades to bring her back and her return to life was granted on condition that he walked ahead of her without looking back. He broke this condition, and Eurydice was irretrievably lost. In his grief, he despised the Maenad women of Thrace, and was torn in pieces by them.

Orphism ancient Greek mystery cult, of which the Orphic hymns formed part of the secret rites which, accompanied by a harsh lifestyle, were aimed at securing immortality. Remains of an Orphic temple were found 1980 at Hungerford, Berkshire, England.

Orr /ɔː/ Robert 'Bobby' 1948– . Canadian hockey player, who played for the Boston Bruins (1967–76) and the Chicago Blackhawks (1976–79) of the National Hockey League. He was voted the best defence every year 1967–75, and was Most Valuable Player 1970–72. He was the first defence to score 100 points in a season, and won the scoring leader 1970 and 1975.

orrery a mechanical device for demonstrating the motions of the heavenly bodies. Invented about 1710 by George Graham, it was named after his patron, the 4th Earl of Orrery. It is the forerunner of the modern ◊planetarium.

orris root the underground stem of a species of iris grown in S Europe. Violet-scented, it is used in perfumery.

Orsini /ɔːˈsiːni/ Felice 1819–1858. Italian political activist, a member of the ◊Carbonari secret revolutionary group, who attempted unsuccessfully to assassinate Napoleon III in Paris Jan 1858. He was subsequently executed, but the Orsini affair awakened Napoleon's interest in Italy and led to a secret alliance with Piedmont at Pilombières 1858, directed against Italy.

Orsk /ɔːsk/ industrial city in the USSR, at the junction of the Or and Ural rivers; population (1987) 273,000. Industries include mining, oil refining, locomotives, and aluminium. Its refineries are fed by a pipeline from Guriev. The town was originally a fortress.

Ortega (Saavedra) /ɔːˈteɪɡə/ Daniel 1945– . Nicaraguan socialist politician, head of state from 1981. He was a member of the Sandinista Liberation Front (FSLN) which overthrew the regime of Anastasio Somoza 1979. US-sponsored ◊Contra guerillas opposed his government from 1982.

A participant in underground activities against the Somoza regime from an early age, Ortega was imprisoned and tortured several times. He became a member of the national directorate of the FSLN and fought in the two-year campaign for the ◊Nicaraguan Revolution. Ortega became a member of the junta of national reconstruction, and its coordinator two years later. In the Feb 1990 elections, Ortega lost the presidency to US-backed Violeta Chamorro.

Ortega y Gasset /ɔːˈteɪɡə iː gæˈset/ José 1883–1955. Spanish philosopher and critic. He considered communism and fascism the cause of the downfall of western civilization. His *Toward a Philosophy of History* 1941 contains philosophical reflections on the state, and an interpretation of the meaning of human history.

orthochromatic a photographic film or paper of decreased sensitivity, that can be processed with a red safelight. Using it, blue objects appear lighter and red ones darker because of increased blue sensitivity.

orthodontics branch of ◊dentistry, mainly dealing with correction of malocclusion (faulty position of teeth).

Orthodox Church or *Eastern Orthodox Church* or *Greek Orthodox Church* a federation of self-governing Christian churches mainly found in E Europe and parts of Asia. The centre of worship is the Eucharist. There is a married clergy, except for bishops; the Immaculate Conception is not accepted. The highest rank in the church is that of Ecumenical Patriarch, or Bishop of Istanbul. There are approximately 130 million adherents.

The church's teaching is based on the Bible, and the Nicene ◊Creed, as modified by the Council of Constantinople 381, is the only confession of faith used. The celebration of the Eucharist has changed little since the 6th century. The ritual is elaborate, and accompanied by singing in which both men and women take part, but no instrumental music is used. Besides the seven sacraments, the prayer book contains many other services for daily life. During the marriage service the bride and groom are crowned.

Its adherents include Greeks, Russians, Romanians, Serbians, Bulgarians, Georgians, and Albanians. In the last 200 years the Orthodox Church has spread into China, Korea, Japan, and Alaska, as well as among the people of Siberia and central Asia. Some of the churches were founded by the apostles and their disciples; all conduct services in their own languages and follow their own customs and traditions, but are in full communion with one another. There are many monasteries, for example Mount Athos in Greece, which has flourished since the 10th century. The senior church of Eastern Christendom is that of Constantinople (Istanbul).

orthopaedics the branch of medicine concerned with the surgery of bones and joints.

ortolan bird *Emberiza hortulana* of the bunting family, common in Europe and W Asia, migrating to Africa in the winter. It is brownish, with a grey head, and nests on the ground.

Orton /ˈɔːtn/ Joe 1933–1967. English dramatist of black comedies in which surreal and violent action takes place in genteel and unlikely settings. Plays include *Entertaining Mr Sloane* 1964, *Loot* 1966, and *What the Butler Saw* 1968. His diaries deal frankly with his personal life. He was murdered by his lover Kenneth Halliwell.

Orvieto /ˌɔːviˈetəʊ/ town in Umbria, Italy, NE of Lake Bolsena, population (1981) 22,800. Built on the site of Volsinii, an Etruscan town destroyed by the Romans 280 BC, Orvieto has many Etruscan remains. The name is from Latin *Urbs Vetus*, 'old town'.

Orwell /ˈɔːwel/ George. Pen name of Eric Arthur Blair 1903–1950. English author. His books include the satire *Animal Farm* 1945, which included such sayings as 'All animals are equal, but some are more equal than others', and the prophetic *Nineteen Eighty-Four* 1949, portraying state control of existence carried to the ultimate extent. Other works include *Down and Out in Paris and London* 1933 and *Homage to Catalonia* 1938.

Born in India, he was educated in England, and for five years served in the Burmese police force, an experience reflected in the novel *Burmese Days* 1935. Life as a dishwasher and tramp were related in *Down and Out in Paris and London* and service for the Republican cause in the Spanish Civil War in *Homage to Catalonia*. He also wrote numerous essays.

oryx type of large African desert antelope with large horns. The Arabian oryx *Oryx leucoryx* was extinct in the wild, but bred in captivity and has been successfully reintroduced into the wild. The scimitar-horned oryx of the Sahara is also rare. Beisa oryx in east Africa and gemsbok in the Kalahari are more common. In profile the two

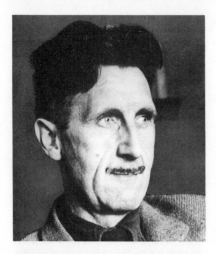

Orwell English novelist and essayist George Orwell.

long horns appear as one, which may have given rise to the legend of the unicorn.

OS/2 a single-user computer ◊operating system, produced jointly by Microsoft Corporation and IBM, for use on large microcomputers. Its main features are ◊multi-tasking and the ability to access large amounts of internal ◊memory.

Osaka /əʊˈsɑːkə/ industrial port (iron, steel, shipbuilding, chemicals, textiles) on Honshu island; population (1987) 2,546,000, metropolitan area 8,000,000. It is the oldest city of Japan, and was at times the seat of government in the 4th–8th centuries.

Lying on a plain sheltered by hills and opening on to Osaka bay, Osaka is honeycombed with waterways. It is a tourist centre for Kyoto and the Seto Inland Sea, and linked with Tokyo by fast electric train 200 kph/124 mph. An underground shopping and leisure centre 1951 has been used as a model for others throughout Japan. It was a mercantile centre in the 18th century, and in the 20th century set the pace for Japan's revolution based on light industries.

Osborne /ˈɒzbɔːn/ Dorothy 1627–1695. English letter-writer. In 1655 she married Sir William Temple (1628–99), to whom she wrote her letters, written 1652–54, but first published 1888.

Osborne /ˈɒzbɔːn/ John (James) 1929– . English dramatist. He was one of the first ◊Angry Young Men of British theatre with his debut play, *Look Back in Anger* 1956. Other plays include *The Entertainer* 1957, *Luther* 1960, and *Watch It Come Down* 1976.

Osborne House preferred residence of Queen Victoria, for whom it was built 1845, on the Isle of Wight, England. It was presented to the nation by Edward VII.

Osborne Judgement UK legal ruling of 1909 that prevented ◊trade unions from using membership subscriptions to finance the Labour Party. In 1913 the judgement was negated by the Trade Union Act which permitted them to raise political levies and provide financial support to the Labour Party.

Oscar in cinema, popular name for ◊Academy Award.

Oscar /ˈɒskə/ two kings of Sweden and Norway:

Oscar I 1799–1859. King of Sweden and Norway from 1844, when he succeeded his father, Charles XIV. He established freedom of the press, and supported Denmark against Germany 1848.

Oscar II 1829–1907. King of Sweden and Norway 1872–1905, king of Sweden until 1907. He was the younger son of Oscar I, and succeeded his brother Charles XV. He was an international arbitrator in Samoa, Venezuela, and the Anglo-American dispute. He fought hard to prevent the separation of his two kingdoms but relinquished the throne of Norway to Haakon VII in 1905.

oscillating universe in astronomy, a theory that states that the gravitational attraction of the mass within the universe will eventually slow down and stop the expansion of the universe. The outward motions of the galaxies will then be reversed, eventually resulting in a 'Big Crunch' where all the matter in the universe would be contracted into a small volume of high density. This could undergo a further ◊Big Bang, thereby creating another expansion phase. The theory suggests that the universe would alternately expand and collapse through alternate Big Bangs and Big Crunches.

oscillator generator producing a desired oscillation (vibration). There are many types of oscillator for different purposes, involving various arrangements of valves or components such as ◊transistors, ◊inductors, ◊capacitors, and ◊resistors. It is an essential part of a radio transmitter, generating the high-frequency carrier signal necessary for radio communication.

The ◊frequency is often controlled by the vibrations set up in a crystal, for example, quartz.

oscillograph instrument for recording oscillations, electrical or mechanical. An *oscilloscope* shows variations in electrical potential on the screen of a ◊cathode-ray tube, by means of deflection of a beam of ◊electrons.

Oshima /ˈəʊʃɪmə/ Nagisa 1932– . Japanese film director, whose violent and sexually explicit *In the Realm of the Senses/Ai No Corrida* 1977 has been one of cinema's most controversial films. His other work includes *Death by Hanging* 1968 and *Merry Christmas Mr Lawrence* 1983, which starred the singer David Bowie.

Oshogbo /ɒˈʃɒɡbəʊ/ city and trading centre on the river Niger, in W Nigeria, 200 km/125 mi NE of Lagos; population (1986) 405,000. Industries include cotton and brewing.

osier tree or shrub of the willow genus *Salix*, cultivated for basket making, in particular *Salix viminalis*.

Osijek /ˈɒsiek/ (German *Esseg*) industrial port in Croatia, Yugoslavia, on the river Drava; population (1981) 158,800. Industries include textiles, chemicals, and electrical goods.

Osiris /əʊˈsaɪrɪs/ ancient Egyptian god, the embodiment of goodness, ruled the underworld, after being killed by ◊Set. The sister-wife of Osiris was ◊Isis or Hathor and their son ◊Horus captured his father's murderer.

Under ◊Ptolemy I's Graeco-Egyptian empire Osiris was developed (as a means of uniting his Greek and Egyptian subjects) into *Serapis* (Osiris+Apis, the latter being the bull-god of Memphis who carried the dead to the tomb), elements of the cults of Zeus and Hades being included, which did not please the Egyptians; the greatest temple of Serapis was the Serapeum in Alexandria. The cult of Osiris, and that of Isis, later spread to Rome.

Oslo /ˈɒzləʊ/ capital and industrial port (textiles, engineering, timber) of Norway; population (1988) 454,000. The first recorded settlement was made by Harald III, but after a fire 1624, it was entirely replanned by Christian IV and renamed *Christiania* 1624–1924.

The port is built at the head of Oslo fjord, which is kept open in winter by icebreakers. There is a Viking museum, 13th-century Akershus Castle, a 17th-century cathedral, and the National Gallery includes many paintings by Munch.

Osman I /ˈɒzmən/ or *Othman I* 1259–1326. Turkish ruler from 1299. He began his career in the service of the ◊Seljuk Turks, but in 1299 he set up a kingdom of his own in Bithynia, NW Asia, and assumed the title of sultan. He conquered a great part of Anatolia, so founding a Turkish empire. His successors were known as 'sons of Osman', from which the term ◊*Ottoman Empire* is derived.

osmium a bluish-white, hard, crystalline metallic element, very heavy and infusible, symbol Os, atomic number 76, relative atomic mass 190.2. It is used for lamp filaments, with iridium to form a very hard alloy suitable for pen-nibs and fine machine bearings, and as a catalyst.

It is found in platinum-bearing river sands, and with iridium in osmiridium. Heated in air, it gives off a pungently irritating poisonous vapour. It was discovered in 1803 by British chemist, Smithson Tennant (1761–1815).

osmoregulation the process whereby the water content of living organisms is maintained at a constant level. If the water balance is disrupted, the concentration of salts will be too high or too low, and vital functions, such as nerve conduction, will be adversely affected.

In mammals, loss of water by evaporation is counteracted by increased intake and by mechanisms in the kidneys that enhance the rate at which water is resorbed before urine production. Both these responses are mediated by hormones, primarily those of the adrenal cortex (see ◊adrenal gland).

osmosis movement of solvent (liquid) through a semipermeable membrane separating solutions of different concentrations. The solvent passes from the more dilute solution to the more concentrated solution until the two concentrations are equal. Many cell membranes behave as semipermeable membranes, and osmosis is an important mechanism in the transport of fluids in living organisms, for example in the transport of water from the roots up the stems of plants.

Applying external pressure to the solution on the more concentrated side arrests osmosis, and is a measure of the osmotic pressure of the solution.

Fish have protective mechanisms to counteract osmosis, which would otherwise cause fluid transport between the body of the animal and the surrounding water (outwards in saltwater fish, inwards in freshwater ones).

Osnabrück /ˌɒznəˈbrʊk/ industrial city in Lower Saxony, West Germany; 115 km/71 mi W of Hanover; population (1988) 154,000. Industries include engineering, iron, steel, textiles, clothing, paper, and food processing. Before World War II, Osnabrück had some noted examples of Gothic and Renaissance architecture.

Osnabrück bishopric was founded by Charlemagne 783. The Treaty of Westphalia was signed at Osnabrück and Münster 1648, ending the Thirty Years' War. A type of rough fabric, *osnaburg*, was originally made here.

osprey bird of prey *Pandion haliaetus*, known in North America from its diet as the fish hawk. Dark brown above and a striking white below, it measures 60 cm/2 ft with a 2 m/6 ft wingspan.

Once extinct in Britain, it is now breeding again in Scotland. The 'osprey plumes' of the milliner are those of the egret.

Ossa /ˈɒsə/ mountain in Thessaly, Greece; height 1,978 m/6,490 ft. Two of Poseidon's giant sons were said to have tried to dislodge the gods from

osmosis

before osmosis

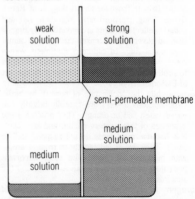

after osmosis

Olympus by piling nearby Mount Pelion on top of Ossa to scale the great mountain.

Ossa, Mount /ˈɒsə/ the highest peak on the island of Tasmania, Australia; height 1,617 m/5,250 ft.

Ossetia /ɒˈsiːʃə/ area of the Caucasus, home of the Ossets, who speak the Iranian language Ossetic, and who were conquered by the Russians in 1802. It has been the scene of Osset-Georgian inter-ethnic conflict from 1989. Some live in the *North Ossetian* Autonomous Republic of the SW USSR; area 8,000 sq km/3,088 sq mi; population (1985) 613,000; capital Ordzhonikidze. The rest live in the *South Ossetian* autonomous region of the Georgian Republic, population (1984) 98,000; capital Tshkinvali. The Ossets have demanded that South Ossetia be upgraded to an autonomous republic as a preliminary to reunification with north Ossetia.

Ossian /ˈɒsiən/ (Celtic *Oisin*) legendary Irish hero, invented by the Scottish writer James ◊Macpherson. He is sometimes represented as the son of ◊Finn Mac Cumhaill, about 250, and as having lived to tell the tales of Finn and the Ulster heroes to St Patrick, about 400. The publication 1760 of Macpherson's poems, attributed to Ossian, made Ossian's name familiar throughout Europe.

ossification the process whereby bone is formed in vertebrate animals by special cells (*osteoblasts*) that secrete layers of ◊extracellular matrix on the surface of the existing ◊cartilage. This matrix is then converted to bone by the deposition within it of calcium phosphate crystals.

Ossory /ˈɒsəri/ ancient kingdom, lasting until 1110, in Leinster, Ireland; the name is preserved in existent Church of Ireland and Roman Catholic bishoprics.

Ostade /ɒsˈtɑːdə/ Adriaen van 1610–1685. Dutch painter and engraver, best known for pictures of tavern scenes and village fairs. A native of Haarlem, Ostade may have studied under Frans Hals. His brother, *Isaac van Ostade* (1621–49), excelled in winter landscapes and roadside and farmyard scenes.

Östberg /ˈɜːstbɜːg/ Ragnar 1866–1945. Swedish architect, who designed the City Hall, Stockholm, Sweden (1911–23).

Ostend /ɒstˈend/ Flemish *Oostende* seaport and pleasure resort in W Flanders, Belgium; 108 km/67 mi NW of Brussels; population (1985) 69,000. There are large docks, and the Belgian fishing fleet has its headquarters here. Ferry links to Dover and Folkestone, England.

osteoarthritis degenerative disease of the joints in later life, sometimes resulting in disabling stiffness and wasting of muscles.

Formerly thought to be due to wear and tear, it has been shown to be less common in the physically active. It appears to be linked with crystal deposits, in the form of calcium phosphate, in cartilage, a discovery which suggests hope of eventual prevention.

osteology part of the science of ◊anatomy, dealing with bones and their uses.

osteomalacia a softening of the bones, a condition caused by lack of vitamin D in adult life. It results in pain and cramping, bone deformity, and a tendency to spontaneous fracture.

osteomyelitis infection of bone, with spread of pus along the marrow cavity. Now quite rare, it may ensue from a compound fracture (where broken bone protrudes through the skin), or from infectious disease elsewhere in the body.

The symptoms are high fever, severe illness, and pain over the limb. If the infection is at the surface of the bone it may quickly form an abscess; if it is deep in the bone marrow it may spread into the circulation and lead to blood poisoning. Most cases can be treated with antibiotics, but sometimes surgery is needed.

osteopathy system of alternative medical practice that relies on physical manipulation to treat mechanical stress. It claims to relieve not only postural problems and muscle pain, but asthma and other disorders.

osteoporosis thinning and weakening of bone substance. It is common in older people, affecting more women than men. It may occur in women whose ovaries have been removed unless hormone replacement therapy (HRT) is instituted. Osteoporosis may occur as a side effect of long-term treatment with ◊corticosteroids.

Ostia /ˈɒstiə/ ancient Roman town near the mouth of the Tiber. Founded about 330 BC, it was the port of Rome and had become a major commercial centre by the 2nd century AD. It was abandoned in the 9th century. The present-day seaside resort, *Ostia Mare*, is situated nearby.

ostinato (Italian 'obstinate') a persistently repeated melodic or rhythmic figure.

Ostpolitik (German 'eastern policy') West German chancellor ◊Brandt's policy of reconciliation with the communist bloc from 1971, pursued to a modified extent by his successors Schmidt and Kohl.

ostracism ancient Athenian political device to preserve public order. Votes on pieces of broken pot (Greek *ostrakon*) were used to exile unpopular politicians for ten years.

Ostrava /ˈɒstrəvə/ industrial city (iron works, furnaces, coal, chemicals) in Czechoslovakia, capital of Severomoravsky region, NE of Brno; population (1984) 324,000.

ostrich flightless bird *Struthio camelus* found in Africa. The male may be about 2.5 m/8 ft tall and weigh 135 kg/300 lb, and is the largest living bird. It has exceptionally strong legs and feet (two-toed) which enable it to run at high speed, and are also used in defence. It lives in family groups of one cock with several hens. Ostriches are bred, especially in South Africa, for leather and also for their tail feathers.

Ostrogoth member of a branch of the E Germanic people, the ◊Goths.

Ostrovsky /ɒˈstrɒfski/ Alexander Nikolaevich 1823–1886. Russian playwright, founder of the modern Russian theatre. He dealt satirically with the manners of the middle class in numerous plays, for example *A Family Affair* 1850. His fairy-tale play *The Snow Maiden* 1873 inspired the composers Tchaikovsky and Rimsky-Korsakov.

Ostwald /ˈɒstvælt/ Wilhelm 1853–1932. German chemist whose work on catalysts laid the foundations of the petrochemical and other industries. Nobel prize 1909.

Oswald, St /ˈɒzwəld/ *c.* 605–642. King of Northumbria from 634, after killing the Welsh king Cadwallon. Oswald had become a Christian convert during exile on the Scottish island of Iona. With the help of St Aidan he furthered the spread of Christianity until he was defeated and killed by King Penda of Mercia. Feast day 9 Aug.

Oswestry /ˈɒzwəstri/ market town in Shropshire, England; population (1981) 12,400. Industries include agricultural machinery and plastics. The church is dedicated to St ◊Oswald, killed here in 642.

Oswiecim (German ◊*Auschwitz*) town in S Poland, site of the World War II concentration and extermination camp.

OT abbreviation for ◊*Old Testament*.

Otago /əʊˈtɑːgəʊ/ a peninsula and coastal plain on South Island, New Zealand, constituting a district; area 64,230 sq km/ 25,220 sq mi; chief cities include Dunedin and Invercargill.

Otaru /əʊˈtɑːruː/ fishing port on W coast of Hokkaido, Japan, with paper mills; processes fish and makes sake; population (1984) 179,000.

Othello a tragedy by William Shakespeare, first performed 1604–05. Othello, a commander in the Venetian army, is persuaded by Iago that his wife Desdemona is having an affair with his friend Cassio. Othello murders Desdemona; on discovering her innocence, he kills himself.

Othman /ɒˈθmɑːn/ *c.* 574–656. Arabian caliph (leader of the Islamic empire) from 644, when he was elected; he was a son-in-law of the prophet Muhammad. Under his rule the Arabs became a naval power and captured Cyprus, but Othman's personal weaknesses led to his assassination. He was responsible for the final editing of the Koran, the sacred book of Islam.

Othman I another name for the Turkish sultan ◊Osman 1.

Otho I /ˈəʊθəʊ/ 1815–1867. King of Greece 1832–62. As the 17-year-old son of King Ludwig I of Bavaria, he was selected by the European powers as the first king of independent Greece. He was overthrown by a popular revolt.

Otis /ˈəʊtɪs/ Elisha Graves 1811–1861. US engineer, who developed a lift that incorporated a safety device, making it acceptable for passenger use in the first skyscrapers. The device, invented 1852, consisted of vertical ratchets on the sides of the lift shaft into which spring-loaded catches would engage and 'lock' the lift in position in the event of cable failure.

otitis inflammation of the ear. *Otitis externa*, occurring in the outer ear canal, is easily treated with antibiotics. Inflamed conditions of the middle ear (*otitis media*) or inner ear (*otitis interna*) are more serious, carrying the risk of deafness and infection of the brain.

O'Toole /əʊˈtuːl/ Peter 1932– . British actor who made his name as *Lawrence of Arabia* 1962, and remained a star in films such as *Beckett* 1964 and *The Lion in Winter* 1968 until the early 1970s. Subsequent appearances were few and poorly received by critics until *The Stuntman* 1978.

otosclerosis overgrowth of bone in the middle ear causing progressive deafness. This inherited condition is gradual in onset, developing usually before middle age. It is twice as common in women.

The middle ear cavity houses the sound conduction mechanism called the ossicular chain, consisting of three tiny bones (ossicles) which magnify vibrations received at the eardrum for onward transmission to the inner ear. In otosclerosis, extraneous growth of bone immobilizes the chain, preventing the conduction of sound. Surgery is necessary to remove the diseased bone and reconstruct the ossicular chain.

Otranto /ɒˈtræntəʊ/ seaport in Puglia, Italy, on the *Strait of Otranto*; population (1981) 5,000. It has Greek and Roman remains, a ruined castle (the inspiration for Horace Walpole's novel *The Castle of Otranto* 1764), and a castle begun 1080. The port is linked by ferry with Corfu.

Ottawa /ˈɒtəwə/ capital of Canada, in E Ontario, on the hills overlooking the Ottawa river, and divided by the Rideau Canal into the Upper

ostrich

(western) and Lower (eastern) Town; population (1986) 301,000, metropolitan area (with adjoining Hull, Québec) 819,000. Industries include timber, pulp and paper, engineering, food processing, and publishing. It was founded 1826–32 as Bytown, in honour of John By (1781–1836) whose army engineers were building the Rideau Canal. It was renamed 1854 after the Outaouac Indians.

Features include the National Museum, National Art Gallery, Observatory, Rideau Hall (the governor-general's residence), and the National Arts Centre 1969 (with an orchestra, and English/French theatre). In 1858 it was chosen by Queen Victoria as the country's capital.

Ottawa agreements the trade agreements concluded at the Imperial Economic Conference, held in Ottawa 1932, between Britain and its dependent territories. The Dominions agreed to lower their preferential tariffs on British manufactures, while Britain admitted almost all Dominion produce free of duty, granted preferences to the rest, and increased duties on foreign imports competing with Dominion produce.

otter aquatic carnivore of the weasel family found on all continents except Australia. It has thick, brown fur, a long, flattened tail, short limbs, and webbed toes. It is social, playful, and agile. It sometimes lies on its back in the water, resting a stone on its chest, on which it breaks shellfish.

The otter of Europe and Asia *Lutra lutra* has a broad head, elongated body covered by grey-brown fur, short legs, and webbed feet. Including a 45 cm/1.5 ft tail, it measures over 1 m/3.5 ft. It lives on fish. There are a number of American species, including the larger *Lutra canadensis* of North America, the sea otter *Enhydra lutris* of the N Pacific, and the giant otter of South America.

In the UK, they have been hunted to near-extinction for their fur, but are slowly making a recovery with the aid of protective legislation.

Otto /'ɒtəʊ/ Nikolaus August 1832–1891. German engineer, who in 1876 patented an effective internal combustion engine.

Otto /'ɒtəʊ/ four Holy Roman emperors, including:

Otto I 912–973. Holy Roman emperor from 936. He restored the power of the empire, asserted his authority over the pope and the nobles, ended the Magyar menace by his victory at the Lechfeld 955, and refounded the East Mark, or Austria, as a barrier against them.

otter

Otto IV *c.* 1182–1218. Holy Roman emperor, elected 1198. He engaged in controversy with Pope Innocent III, and was defeated by the Pope's ally, Philip of France, at Bouvines 1214.

Otto cycle another name for the ◊four-stroke cycle, introduced by the German engineer Nikolaus Otto in 1876. It improved upon existing engine cycles by compressing the fuel mixture before it was ignited.

Ottoman Empire /'ɒtəmən/ Muslim empire of the Turks 1300–1920, the successor of the ◊Seljuk Empire. It was founded by ◊Osman I and reached its height with ◊Suleiman in the 16th century. Its capital was Istanbul (formerly Constantinople). At its greatest extent its bounds were Europe as far as Hungary, part of S Russia, Iran, the Palestinian coastline, Egypt, and N Africa. From the 17th century it was in decline. There was an attempted revival and reform under the Young Turk party 1908, but the regime crumbled when Turkey took the German side in World War I. The sultanate was abolished by Atatürk 1922; the last sultan was Muhammad VI.

Otway /'ɒtweɪ/ Thomas 1652–1685. English dramatist. His plays include the tragedies *Alcibiades* 1675, *Don Carlos* 1676, *The Orphan* 1680, and *Venice Preserv'd* 1682.

Otztal Alps /'ɒːtstɑːl/ a range of the Alps in Italy and Austria, rising to 3,774 m/12,382 ft at Wildspitze, Austria's second highest peak.

OU abbreviation for ◊*Open University*.

Ouagadougou /,wægə'duːguː/ capital and industrial centre of Burkina Faso; population (1985) 442,000. Products include textiles, vegetable oil, and soap.

Oudenaarde /'uːdənɑːd/ small town of E Flanders, W Belgium, on the Scheldt, 28 km/18 mi SSW of Ghent; population (1982) 27,200. It is noted for its tapestries and carpet-weaving.

Oudenaarde was the site of the victory by the British, Dutch, and Austrians over the French in 1708 during the War of Spanish Succession.

Oudh /aʊd/ region of N India, now part of Uttar Pradesh. An independent kingdom before it fell under Mogul rule, Oudh regained independence 1732–1856, when it was annexed by Britain. Its capital was Lucknow, centre of the ◊Indian Mutiny 1857–58. In 1877 it was joined with Agra, from 1902 as the United Provinces of Agra and Oudh, renamed Uttar Pradesh 1950.

Ouessant /'wesɒn/ French form of ◊Ushant, an island W of Brittany.

Oughtred /'uːtrɪd/ William 1575–1660. English mathematician. He is credited as the inventor of the slide rule 1622. His major work *Clavis mathematicae*/*The Key to Mathematics* 1631 was a survey of the entire body of mathematical knowledge of his day. It introduced the '×' symbol for multiplication, as well as the symbols for *sin, cos*, and *tan*.

Ouida /'wiːdə/ pen name of Marie Louise de la Ramée 1839–1908. British romantic novelist whose novels included *Under Two Flags* 1867 and *Moths* 1880.

Oujda /uːʒ'dɑː/ industrial and commercial city (lead and coalmining) in N Morocco, near the border with Algeria; population (1982) 471,000. It trades in wool, grain, and fruit.

Oulu /'əʊluː/ (Swedish *Uleåborg*) industrial port (saw mills, tanneries, shipyards) in W Finland, on the Gulf of Bothnia; population (1986) 97,900. It was originally a Swedish fortress 1375.

ounce snow leopard *Panthera uncia*, which lives in the mountains of central Asia. It has light cream or grey fur with large black spots, and is similar in size to the leopard.

ounce unit of weight, the 16th part of an ◊avoirdupois pound, equal to 437.5 grains (28.3 g); also the 12th part of a pound troy, equal to 480 grains. The **fluid ounce** is a measure of capacity, in the UK equivalent to one twentieth of a pint.

Ouse /uːz/ name of several British rivers:

The **Great Ouse** rises in Northamptonshire and winds its way across 250 km/160 mi to enter the Wash north of King's Lynn. A huge sluice across the Great Ouse, near King's Lynn, was built as part of extensive flood-control works 1959.

The **Little Ouse** flows for 38 km/24 mi along part of the Norfolk/Suffolk border and is a tributary of the Great Ouse.

The Yorkshire **Ouse** is formed by the junction of the Ure and Swale near Boroughbridge, and joins the Trent to form the Humber.

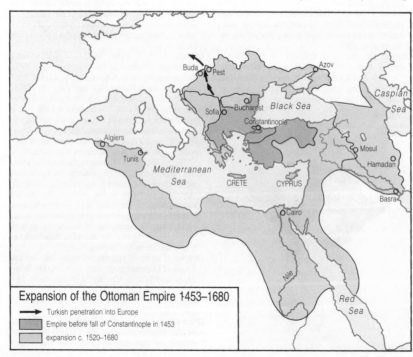

Expansion of the Ottoman Empire 1453–1680

→ Turkish penetration into Europe

▮ Empire before fall of Constantinople in 1453

▯ expansion c. 1520–1680

Oughtred *William Oughtred is an example of the learning and intellectual achievement of the clergy of his time: his* Clavis mathematicae *was a survey of the entire body of mathematical knowledge of his day.*

The Sussex *Ouse* rises between Horsham and Cuckfield, and flows through the S Downs to enter the English Channel at Newhaven.

ousel or *ouzel* ancient name of the blackbird. The ring ouzel *Turdus torquatus* is similar to a blackbird, but has a white band across the breast. It is found in Europe in mountainous and rocky country. Water ouzel is another name for the ◊dipper.

Ousmane /uːˈsmɑːn/ Sembene 1923– . Senegalese writer and film director. His novels, written in French, include *Le Docker Noir* 1956, about his experiences as a union leader in Marseille, *Les bouts de bois/ God's Bits of Wood* 1960, *Le Mandat/The Money Order*, and *Xala*, the last two of which he made into films.

Ouspensky /uːˈspenski/ Peter 1878–1947. Russian mystic. Originally a scientist, he became a disciple of ◊Gurdjieff and expanded his ideas in terms of other dimensions of space and time, for example in *Tertium Organum* 1912.

outback the immense inland region of Australia. Its main inhabitants are Aborigines, miners (including opals), and cattlemen. Its harsh beauty has been recorded by artists such as Sidney Nolan.

outlawry in medieval England, a declaration that a criminal was outside the protection of the law, with his or her lands and goods forfeited to the Crown, and all civil rights being set aside. It was a lucrative royal 'privilege'; ◊Magna Carta restricted its use and under Edward III it was further modified. Some outlaws became popular heroes, for example, ◊Robin Hood.

output device in computing, any device for displaying, in a form intelligible to the user, the results of processing done by a computer. The most common output devices are the VDU (visual display unit, or screen) and the printer.

Outram /ˈuːtrəm/ James 1803–1863. British general, born in Derbyshire. He entered the Indian Army in 1819, served in the Afghan and Sikh wars, and commanded in the Persian campaign of 1857. On the outbreak of the ◊Indian Mutiny he co-operated with Gen Henry Havelock (1795–1857) to raise the siege of Lucknow, and held the city until relieved by Sir Colin Campbell (later Baron ◊Clyde).

outré (French) extreme, beyond the bounds of acceptability.

Outsider, The French *L'Etranger* a novel by Albert Camus, published 1942. A man is sentenced to death, ostensibly for murder, but as much for his failure to conform to the values of a hypocritical society.

Oval, the cricket ground in Kennington, London, England, the home of Surrey County Cricket Club. It was the venue for the first test match between England and Australia 1880.

Ovamboland /aʊˈvæmbəʊlænd/ region of N Namibia stretching along the Namibia-Angola frontier; the scene of conflict between SWAPO guerrillas and South Africa forces in the 1970s and 1980s.

ovary in female animals, the organ which generates the ◊ovum. In humans, the ovaries are two whitish rounded bodies about 25 mm/1 in by 35 mm/1.5 in, located in the abdomen near the ends of the ◊Fallopian tubes. Every month, from puberty to the onset of the menopause, an ovum is released from the ovary. This is called ovulation, and forms part of the ◊menstrual cycle. In botany, an ovary is the expanded basal portion of the ◊carpel of flowering plants, containing one or more ◊ovules. It is hollow with a thick wall to protect the ovules. Following fertilization of the ovum, it develops into the fruit wall or pericarp.

The ovaries of female animals secrete the hormones responsible for the secondary sexual characteristics of the female, such as smooth, hairless facial skin and enlarged breasts.

In botany, the relative position of the ovary to the other floral parts is often an important character in classification; it may be either inferior or superior, depending on whether the petals and sepals are inserted above or below.

Ovens River /ˈʌvənz/ river in Victoria, Australia, a tributary of the Murray.

overdraft in banking, a loan facility on a current account. It allows the account holder to overdraw on his or her account up to a certain limit and for a specified time, and interest is payable on the amount borrowed. An overdraft is a cheaper form of borrowing than the credit options that major credit-card companies offer.

overhead in economics, fixed costs in a business which do not vary in the short term. These might include property rental, heating and lighting, insurance, and administration costs.

Overijssel /ˌəʊvərˈaɪsəl/ province of the E central Netherlands; capital Zwolle; area 3,340 sq km/1,289 sq mi; population (1988) 1,010,000. It is generally flat, and contains the rivers Ijssel and Vecht. Products include sheep, cattle, and dairy products.

overlander one of the Australian drovers in the 19th century who opened up new territory by driving their cattle to new stations, or to market, before the establishment of regular stock routes.

overland telegraph the cable erected 1870–72 linking Port Augusta in South Australia and Darwin in Northern Territory, and the latter by undersea cable to Java; it ended the communications isolation of the Australian continent.

Overlord, Operation the Allied invasion of Normandy 6 June 1944 during World War II.

Overseas Development Administration (ODA) UK official body that deals with development assistance to overseas countries, including financial aid on concessionary terms and technical assistance, usually in the form of sending specialists abroad and giving training in the UK.

overtone a note that has a frequency or pitch that is a multiple of the fundamental frequency, the sounding body's ◊natural frequency. Each sound source produces a unique set of overtones, which gives the source its quality or timbre.

overture a piece of instrumental music, usually preceding an opera. There are also overtures to suites and plays, ballets, and 'concert' overtures, such as Elgar's *Cockaigne* and John Ireland's descriptive *London Overture*.

The use of an overture in opera began during the 17th century; the 'Italian' overture consisting of two quick movements separated by a slow one, and the 'French' of a quick movement between two in slower tempo.

Ovid /ˈɒvɪd/ Full name Publius Ovidius Naso 43–17 BC. Roman poet. His poetry deals mainly with the themes of love (*Amores*, *Ars amatoria*), mythology (*Metamorphoses*), and exile (*Tristia*).

Born at Sulmo, Ovid studied rhetoric in Rome in preparation for a legal career, but soon turned to literature. In 8 BC he was banished by Augustus to Tomi, on the Black Sea, where he died. This punishment, supposedly for his immoral *Ars amatoria*, was probably because of some connection with Julia, the profligate daughter of Augustus.

Oviedo /ˌɒviˈeɪdəʊ/ industrial city (textiles, metal goods, pharmaceuticals, matches, chocolate, sugar) and capital of Asturias region, Spain, 25 km/16 mi south of the Bay of Biscay; population (1986) 191,000.

ovipary a method of animal reproduction in which eggs are laid by the female and develop outside her body, in contrast to ovovivipary and vivipary. It is the most common form of reproduction.

ovovivipary a method of animal reproduction in which fertilized eggs develop within the female (unlike ovipary), and the embryo gains no nutritional substances from the female (unlike vivipary). It occurs in some invertebrates, fish, and reptiles.

ovulation in female animals, the process of making and releasing egg cells. In mammals it occurs as part of the ◊menstrual cycle.

ovule a structure found in seed plants that develops into a seed after fertilization. It consists of an ◊embryo sac containing the female gamete (ovum or egg cell), surrounded by nutritive tissue, the nucellus. Outside this there are one or two coverings that provide protection, developing into the testa or seed coat following fertilization.

In flowering plants (◊angiosperms) the ovule is within an ◊ovary, but in ◊gymnosperms (conifers and their allies) the ovules are borne on the surface of an ovuliferous (or ovule-bearing) scale, usually within a ◊cone, and are not enclosed by an ovary.

ovum the female gamete (sex cell) before fertilization. In animals, it is called an egg, and is produced in the ovaries. In plants, where it is also known as an egg cell or oosphere, the ovum is produced in an ovule. The ovum is non-motile. It must be fertilized by a male gamete before it can develop further, except in cases of ◊parthenogenesis.

Owen /ˈəʊɪn/ David 1938– . British politician, originally a doctor. He entered Parliament 1966, and was Labour foreign secretary 1977–79. In 1981 he was one of the founders of the ◊Social Democratic Party (SDP), and in 1983 became its leader. Opposed to the decision of the majority of the party to merge with the Liberals 1987, Owen stood down, but emerged 1988 as leader of a rump SDP, which survived until 1990.

Owen Richard 1804–1892. British anatomist and palaeontologist. He attacked the theory of natural selection and in 1860 published an anonymous and damaging review of Charles ◊Darwin's work. He was Director of the Natural History Museum, London, 1856–1883 and was responsible for the first public exhibition of dinosaurs.

Owen /ˈəʊɪn/ Robert 1771–1858. British socialist, born in Wales. In 1800 he became manager of a mill at New Lanark, Scotland, where by improving working and housing conditions and providing schools he created a model community. His ideas stimulated the ◊co-operative movement.

From 1817 Owen proposed that 'villages of co-operation', self-supporting communities run on socialist lines, should be founded; these, he believed, would ultimately replace private ownership. His later attempt to run such a community in the USA failed.

Owen /ˈəʊɪn/ Wilfred 1893–1918. English poet. His verse, owing much to the encouragement of Siegfried ◊Sassoon, expresses his hatred of war, for example *Anthem for Doomed Youth*, published 1921.

Owen Falls /ˈəʊɪn/ waterfall in Uganda on the White Nile, 4 km/2.5 mi below the point at which the river leaves Lake Victoria. A dam, built 1949–60, provides hydroelectricity for Uganda and Kenya, and helps to control the flood waters.

Owens /ˈəʊɪnz/ (James Cleveland) 'Jesse' 1913–1980. US track and field athlete, who excelled in the sprints, hurdles, and the long jump. At the 1936 Olympics he won four gold medals.

Owen *Socialist reformer Robert Owen.*

Owens *US track and field athlete Jesse Owens during an exhibition of the long jump at White City, 1936.*

The Nazi leader Hitler is said to have stormed out of the stadium at the 1936 Berlin Olympic Games, in disgust at the black man's triumph. Owens held the world long jump record for 25 years 1935–60. At Ann Arbor, Michigan, on 25 May 1935 he broke six world records in less than an hour.

CAREER HIGHLIGHTS

Olympic Games—gold:
100 Metres (1936), 200 Metres (1936), 4x100 Metres Relay (1936), Long Jump (1936)
World Records:
100 Metres: 1936
100 Yards: 1935, 1936
200 Metres : 1935
220 Yards: 1935
200 Metres Hurdles: 1935
220 Yards Hurdles: 1935
4x100 Metres Relay: 1936 (US National team)
Long Jump: 1935

owl bird of the order Strigiformes, found worldwide. They are mainly nocturnal birds of prey, with mobile heads, soundless flight, acute hearing, and forward-facing eyes, set round with rayed feathers. All species lay white eggs, and begin incubation as soon as the first is laid. They disgorge indigestible remains of their prey in pellets (castings).

They comprise two families: *typical owls* family Strigidae, of which there are about 120 species; and *barn owls* family Tytonidae, of which there are 10 species.

The *tawny owl Strix aluco* is a brown-flecked species of Europe and the Middle East; the *little owl Athene noctua* is the Greek symbol of wisdom and bird of ◊Athena, found widely near human homes; the *snowy owl Nyctea scandiaca* lives in the Arctic; the largest of the owls are the *eagle owl Bubo bubo* of Eurasia, and *powerful owl Ninox strenua* of Australia, both up to 0.75 m/2.25 ft long; the world-wide *barn owl Tyto alba* was formerly common in Britain, but is now diminished by pesticides and loss of habitat. In Malaysia, it is used for rat control.

Some species of owl are in danger of extinction. Island species such as the New Zealand laughing owl and the Madagascan grass owl are most at risk.

Owl and the Nightingale an early Middle English poem, written about 1200, which takes the form of an argument between an owl, who may represent wisdom and respectability, and a nightingale, who may symbolize gaiety and ◊courtly love.

ox the castrated male of domestic species of cattle, used in Third World countries for ploughing and other agricultural purposes, also the extinct wild ox or aurochs of Europe, and living wild species.

oxalic acid $(COOH)_2 \cdot 2H_2O$ a white, poisonous solid, soluble in water, alcohol, and ether. Oxalic acid is found in rhubarb, and its salts (oxalates) occur in wood sorrel and other plants. It is used in the leather and textile industries, in dyeing and bleaching, ink manufacture, metal polishes, and for removing rust and ink stains.

owl

barn owl

oxbow lake curved lake found on the flood plain of a river. Oxbows are caused by the loops of ◊meanders being cut off at times of flood and the river subsequently adopting a shorter course. In the USA, the term ◊bayou is often used.

Oxbridge generic term for Oxford and Cambridge, the two oldest universities in the UK. They are still distinctive because of their ancient collegiate structure, their separate entrance procedures, and their high proportion of students from private schools.

Oxenstjerna /ˈʊksənˌʃeənə/ Axel Gustafsson, Count Oxenstjerna 1583–1654. Swedish politician, chancellor from 1612. He pursued Gustavus Adolphus's foreign policy, acted as regent for Queen Christina, and conducted the Thirty Years' War to a successful conclusion.

OXFAM (*Ox*ford Committee for *Fam*ine Relief) charity established in the UK 1942 by Canon Theodore Richard Milford (1896–1987), initially to assist the starving people of Greece and subsequently to relieve poverty and famine worldwide.

Oxford and Asquith, Earl of title of British Liberal politician Herbert Henry ◊Asquith.

Oxford English see ◊English language.

Oxford Group an early name for the ◊Moral Rearmament movement.

Oxford Movement also known as *Tractarian Movement* or *Catholic Revival* a movement that attempted to revive Catholic religion in the Church of England. Cardinal Newman dated the movement from ◊Keble's sermon in Oxford 1833. The Oxford Movement by the turn of the century had transformed the face of the Anglican communion, and is represented today by Anglo-Catholicism.

Oxfordshire /ˈɒksfədʃə/ county in S central England
area 2,610 sq km/1,007 sq mi
towns administrative headquarters Oxford; Abingdon, Banbury, Henley-on-Thames, Witney, Woodstock
features river Thames and tributaries; Cotswolds and Chiltern Hills; Vale of the White Horse (chalk hill figure 114 m/374 ft long); Oxford University; Europe's major fusion project JET (Joint European Torus) is being built at the UK Atomic Energy Authority's fusion laboratories at Culham
products cereals, cars, paper, bricks, cement
population (1987) 578,000
famous people Flora Thompson.

Oxford University oldest British university, established during the 12th century, the earliest existing college being founded 1249. After suffering from land confiscation during the Reformation, it was reorganized by Elizabeth I 1571. Besides the colleges, notable academic buildings are the Bodleian Library (including the New Bodleian, opened 1946, with a capacity of 5 million books), the Divinity School, and the Sheldonian Theatre. The university is governed by the Congregation of the University; Convocation, composed of masters and doctors, has a delaying power. Normal business is conducted by the Hebdomadal Council. In 1985 there were 9,000 undergraduates and 3,000 postgraduates.

Oxfordshire

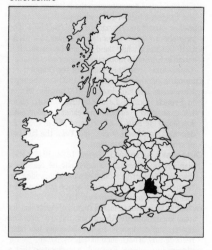

Oxford colleges

1249 University
c.1263 Balliol
1264 Merton
c.1278 St Edmund Hall
1314 Exeter
1326 Oriel
1340 The Queen's
1379 New
1427 Lincoln
1438 All Souls
1458 Magdalen
1509 Brasenose
1517 Corpus Christi
1546 Christ Church
1555 St John's
1555 Trinity
1571 Jesus
1612 Wadham
1624 Pembroke
1714 Worcester
1740 Hertford
1870 Keble
1878 Lady Margaret Hall
1879 Somerville
1879 St Anne's
1886 St Hugh's
1893 St Hilda's
1928 St Peter's
1937 Nuffield
1950 St Anthony's
1962 Linacre
1962 St Catherine's
1965 St Cross
1966 Wolfson
1979 Green

oxidation in chemistry, the loss of ◊electrons, gain of oxygen, or loss of hydrogen by an atom, ion, or molecule during a chemical reaction.

Oxidation may be brought about by reaction with another compound (oxidizing agent), which simultaneously undergoes ◊reduction, or electrically at the anode (positive terminal) of an electric cell.

oxide a compound of oxygen and another element, frequently produced by burning the element or a compound of it in air or oxygen.

Oxides of metals are normally ◊bases and will react with an acid to produce a ◊salt in which the metal forms the cation (positive ion). Some of them will also react with a strong alkali to produce a salt in which the metal is part of a complex anion (negative ion; see ◊amphoteric). Most oxides of non-metals are acidic (dissolve in water to form an ◊acid). Some oxides display no pronounced acidic or basic properties.

oxlip see under ◊cowslip.

Oxon. abbreviation for *Oxoniensis* (Latin 'of Oxford').

oxpecker African bird, genus *Buphagus*, of the starling family. It clambers about the bodies of large mammals, feeding on ticks and other parasites. Its vigilance may help to warn the host of approaching dangers.

Oxus /'ɒksəs/ ancient name of ◊Amu Darya, river in USSR.

oxyacetylene torch a gas torch that burns acetylene in pure oxygen, producing a high-temperature (3,000°C) flame. It is widely used in welding to fuse metals. In the cutting torch, a jet of oxygen burns through metal already melted by the oxyacetylene flame.

oxygen (Greek *oxys* 'acid' *genes* 'forming') a colourless, odourless, tasteless, gaseous element, slightly soluble in water, symbol O, atomic number 8, relative atomic mass 16.00. The only gas able to support respiration, it is just as essential for almost all combustion, and is used in high-temperature welding and improving blast-furnace working.

Oxygen is obtained by ◊fractionation of liquid air, by electrolysis of water, or by heating manganese dioxide with potassium chlorate. It is very reactive, and combines with all other elements, except the inert gases and fluorine, in the process of oxidation.

It was identified by the British chemist J Priestley 1774 by heating mercuric oxide using the Sun's rays and a burning glass, and independently in the same year by the Swedish chemist C W Scheele (1742–86). It is the most abundant element on the Earth's surface, and makes up nearly one-half of the total material on the surface of the Earth – 21% by volume of the atmosphere, nearly 50% by weight of the rocks, and 89% by weight of the water. Liquefied oxygen is pale blue and magnetic and is used as a rocket fuel.

oxygen debt a physiological state produced by vigorous exercise, in which the lungs cannot supply all the oxygen that the muscles need.

Oxygen is required for the release of energy from food molecules (aerobic ◊respiration). Instead of breaking food molecules down fully, muscle cells switch to a form of partial breakdown that does not require oxygen (anaerobic respiration) so that they can continue to generate energy. This partial breakdown produces ◊lactic acid, which results in a sensation of fatigue when it reaches certain levels in the muscles and the blood. Once the vigorous muscle movements cease, the body breaks down the lactic acid, using up extra oxygen to do so. Panting after exercise is an automatic reaction to 'pay off' the oxygen debt.

oxymoron (Greek 'sharply dull' or 'pointedly foolish') a ◊figure of speech, the combination of two or more words that are normally opposites, in order to startle. 'Bittersweet' is an oxymoron, as are 'cruel to be kind' and 'beloved enemy'.

oxytocin a hormone that stimulates the uterus in late pregnancy to initiate and sustain labour. After birth, it stimulates the uterine muscles to contract, reducing bleeding at the site where the placenta was attached.

It is also secreted during lactation. Intravenous injections may be given to induce labour, improve contractions, or control haemorrhage after birth. Oxytocin sprayed in the nose a few minutes before nursing improves milk production.

oyster bivalve ◊mollusc with the upper valve flat, the lower concave, hinged by an elastic ligament. The mantle, lying against the shell, protects the inner body, which includes respirative, digestive, and reproductive organs. Oysters are distinguished by their change of sex, which may alternate annually or more frequently, and by the number of their eggs—a female may discharge up to a million eggs during a spawning period.

Among the species commercially exploited for food are the European oyster *Ostrea edulis*, and the North American *Ostrea virginica* of the Atlantic coast. The former is larviparous (eggs and larvae remain in the mantle cavity for a period before release) and the latter oviparous (eggs are discharged straight into the water). Oyster farming

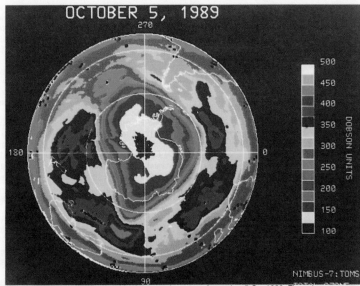

ozone Satellite map showing the 'hole' in the ozone layer over Antarctica, 5 Oct 1989. The colours represent Dobson units, a measure of atmospheric ozone, as shown on the colour scale on the right.

is increasingly practised, the beds being specially cleansed for the easy setting of the free-swimming larvae (known as 'spats'), and the oysters later properly spaced for growth and fattened.

◊Pearls are not obtained from members of the true oyster family. There are oyster beds at Whitstable, Kent, and Colchester, Essex, England.

oyster catcher wading bird related to the plovers. The common oyster catcher of European coasts, *Haemotopus ostralegus*, is black and white, with a long red beak to open shellfish.

oz abbreviation for ◊ounce.

Ozal /əʊ'zaːl/ Turgut 1927– . Turkish Islamic right-wing politician, prime minister 1983–89, president from 1989.

Born in Malatya, E central Turkey, and educated in Istanbul, he entered goverment service then worked for the World Bank 1971–79. In 1980 he was deputy to prime minister Bulent Ulusu, under the military regime of Kenan Evren, and, when political pluralism returned in 1983, he founded the Islamic, right-of-centre Motherland Party (ANAP) and led it to victory in the elections of that year. In the 1987 general election he retained his majority and in Nov 1989 replaced Evren as Turkey's first civilian president for 30 years.

Ozal President of Turkey Turgat Ozal. He is the country's first civilian head of state since 1960.

ozalid process a copying process used, for example, to produce printing proofs from film images. The film is placed on top of chemically treated paper, and then exposed to ultraviolet light. The image is developed using ammonia.

Ozark Mountains /'əʊzaːk/ area in USA (shared by Arkansas, Illinois, Kansas, Mississippi, Oklahoma) of ridges, valleys and streams, highest point only 700 m/2,300 ft; area 130,000 sq km/ 50,000 sq mi.

ozone O_3 a highly reactive blue gas, comprising three atoms of oxygen. It is formed when the molecule of the stable form of oxygen (O_2) is split by ultraviolet radiation or electrical discharge. It forms a layer in the upper atmosphere, which protects life on Earth from ultraviolet rays, a cause of skin cancer. At lower levels it contributes to the ◊greenhouse effect.

At ground level, ozone can cause asthma attacks, stunted growth in plants, and corrosion of certain materials. It is produced by the action of sunlight on car exhaust fumes, and is a major air pollutant in hot summers. Ozone is a powerful oxidizing agent and is used industrially in bleaching and air-conditioning.

A continent-sized hole has formed over Antarctica as a result of damage to the ozone layer caused by ◊chlorofluorocarbons. In 1989 ozone depletion was 50% over the Antarctic compared to 3% over the Arctic. On the surface, ozone is so dangerous that the US Environment Protection Agency recommends people should not be exposed for more than one hour a day to ozone levels of 120 parts per billion, while the World Health Organization recommends a lower 76–100ppb. It is known that even at levels of 60ppb ozone causes respiratory problems.

Ozu /'əʊzuː/ Yasujiro 1903–1963. Japanese film director, who became known in the West only in his last years. *Tokyo Monogatari/Tokyo Story* 1953 illustrates his typical low camera angles and his theme of middle-class family life.

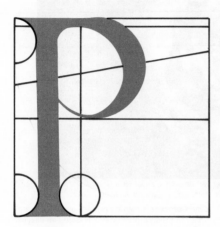

P 16th letter of the Roman alphabet. In Semitic languages, in Greek, and in Latin *p* had much of the same sound as it normally has today in English when final, or when following *s* at the beginning of a word, the sound of an unvoiced labial stop. In other positions in English, and especially when initial, *p* is aspirated.

p in music, the abbreviation for *piano* (Italian 'softly').

p(p). abbreviation for *page(s)*.

P2 Italian masonic lodge implicated in a number of political and financial scandals during the 1980s.

p.a. abbreviation for *per annum* (Latin 'yearly').

PA abbreviation for ◊*Pennsylvania*.

Paarl a town on the Great Berg River, Cape Province, South Africa; population (1980) 71,300. It is the centre of a noted wine-producing area, 50 km/31 mi NE of Cape Town. Nelson Mandela served the last days of his imprisonment at the Victor Vester prison near here.

Pabst /pɑ:pst/G(eorg) W(ilhelm) 1885–1967. German film director, whose films include *Die Büchse der Pandora/Pandora's Box, Das Tagebuch einer Verlorenen/The Diary of a Lost Girl* both 1929 and starring Louise ◊Brooks, and *Die Dreigroschenoper/The Threepenny Opera* 1931.

paca large nocturnal, burrowing ◊rodent of Central and South America, about 60 cm/2 ft long.

Pacaraima, Sierra /ˌpækəˈraɪmə/ mountain range along the Brazil–Venezuela frontier, extending into Guyana; length 620 km/385 mi. Highest point *Mount Roraima* a plateau about 50 sq km/20 sq mi, 2,629 m/8,625 ft above sea level, surrounded by 300 m/1,000 ft cliffs, at the conjunction of the three countries. Formed 300 million years ago, it has a largely unique fauna and flora, because of its isolation, consisting only of grasses, bushes, flowers, insects, and small amphibians.

pace (Latin) with deference to, followed by a name, used to acknowledge contradiction of the person named.

pacemaker a medical device fitted to patients whose hearts beat irregularly. It delivers minute electric shocks to stimulate the heart muscles at certain times. The latest ones are powered by radioactive isotopes for long life, and are implanted in the patient's body.

Pachomius, St /pəˈkəʊmiəs/ 292–346. Egyptian Christian, the founder of the first Christian monastery, near Dendera on the river Nile. Originally for ◊Copts, the monastic movement soon spread to include Greeks.

Pacific Islands /pəˈsɪfɪk ˈaɪləndz/ United Nations trust territory in the W Pacific comprising over 2,000 islands and atolls, under Japanese mandate 1919–47, and administered by the USA 1947–80, when all its members, the ◊Carolines, ◊Marianas (except ◊Guam), and ◊Marshall Islands, became independent.

Pacific Ocean world's largest ocean, extending from Antarctica to the Bering Strait; area 166,242,500 sq km/64,170,000 sq mi; average depth 4,188 m/13,749 ft; greatest depth of any ocean 11,034 m/36,210 ft in the ◊Mariana Trench.

Pacific Security Treaty military alliance agreement between Australia, New Zealand, and USA, signed 1951 (see ◊ANZUS).

Pacific War war 1879–83 by an alliance of Bolivia and Peru against Chile. Chile seized Antofagasta and the coast between the mouths of the rivers Loa and Paposo, rendering Bolivia landlocked, and also annexed the southern Peruvian coastline from Arica to the mouth of the Loa, with the nitrate fields of the Atacama Desert.

Bolivia has since tried to regain Pacific access, either by a corridor across its former Antofagasta province or by a twin port with Arica at the end of the rail link from La Paz. Brazil supports the Bolivian claims, which would facilitate its own transcontinental traffic.

pacifism belief that violence, even in self-defence, is unjustifiable under any condition, and that arbitration is preferable to war as a means of solving disputes.

Pacifist sentiment before and during World War I persuaded many to become conscientious objectors and refuse to fight, even when conscripted. They were imprisoned and in some cases executed. As a result of the carnage in the war, pacifism became stronger in the 1920s and 1930s, with organizations like the Peace Pledge Union in Britain. During World War II, conscientious objectors who refused to bear arms were often placed in noncombatant units such as the British Pioneer Corps, or in medical units.

In the East, pacifism has roots in Buddhism, and nonviolent action was used by ◊Gandhi in the struggle for Indian independence.

Pacino /pətʃiːno/ Al(berto) 1940– . US actor who played moody roles in films such as *The Godfather* 1972 and *Scarface* 1983.

pact of steel the military alliance between Nazi Germany and Fascist Italy, instituted 1939.

Padang /ˈpɑːdæŋ/ port on the W coast of Sumatra, Indonesia; population (1980) 481,000. The Dutch secured trading rights here 1663. The port trades in copra, coffee, and rubber.

Paddington Bear a bear who features in a series of children's stories by British writer Michael Bond (1926–), beginning with *A Bear called Paddington* 1958. He is found abandoned on Paddington Station in London by the Brown family, who adopt him; he likes marmalade sandwiches and customarily wears a hat, duffel-coat, and wellington boots.

Paderborn /ˌpɑːdəˈbɔːn/ market town in North Rhine-Westphalia, West Germany; population (1988) 110,000. Industries include leather goods, metal products, and precision instruments. It was the seat of a bishopric in Charlemagne's time, and later became a member of the Hanseatic League.

Paderewski /ˌpædəˈrefski/ Ignacy Jan 1860–1941. Polish pianist, composer, and politician. After his debut in Vienna 1887 he became celebrated in Europe and the USA as an exponent of Chopin. During World War I he helped to organize the Polish army in France; in 1919 he became prime

minister of the newly independent Poland, which he represented at the Peace Conference, but continuing opposition forced him to resign the same year. He resumed a musical career 1922, was president of the Polish National Council in Paris 1940, and died in New York.

padre (Italian 'father') a priest.

Padua /ˈpædjuə/ (Italian *Padova*) city in N Italy, 45 km/28 mi W of Venice; population (1988) 224,000. The astronomer Galileo taught at the university, founded 1222.

The 13th-century Palazzo della Ragione, the basilica of S Antonio, and the botanical garden 1545 are notable. It is the birthplace of the historian Livy and the painter Andrea Mantegna.

paediatrics or *pediatrics* the medical speciality concerned with the care of children.

paedomorphosis in biology, an alternative term for ◊neoteny.

Paestum /ˈpiːstəm/ ancient Greek city, near Salerno in S Italy. It was founded about 600 BC as the Greek colony Posidonia, and a number of Doric temples remain.

Pagalu /pəˈgɑːluː/ former name (1973–79) of ◊Annobón, island in Equatorial Guinea.

Pagan archaeological site in Burma (now Myanmar) with the ruins of the former capital (founded 847, taken by Kublai Khan 1287). These include Buddhist temples with wall paintings of the great period of Burmese art (11th–13th centuries).

Paganini /ˌpægəˈniːni/ Niccolò 1782–1840. Italian violinist and composer, a soloist from the age of nine. His works for the violin ingeniously exploit the potential of the instrument.

Page /peɪdʒ/ Earle (Christmas Grafton) 1880–1961. Australian politician, leader of the Country Party 1920–39 and briefly prime minister in Apr 1939. He represented Australia in the British war cabinet 1941–42 and was minister of health 1949–55.

Page /peɪdʒ/ Frederick Handley 1885–1962. British aircraft engineer, founder of one of the earliest aircraft-manufacturing companies 1909 and designer of long-range civil aeroplanes and multi-engined bombers in both world wars, such as the Halifax, flown in World War II.

pageant originally the wagon on which medieval ◊mystery plays were performed. The term was later applied to the street procession of songs, dances, and historical tableaux that became fashionable during the 1920s.

The open-air entertainment ◊son et lumière is related to the pageant.

paging in computing, a way of increasing the apparent memory capacity of a machine. See ◊virtual memory.

Pagnol /pɑːŋɔl/ Marcel 1895–1974. French film director, author, and playwright, whose work includes *Fanny* 1932 and *Manon des Sources* 1953. He regarded the cinema as recorded theatre; thus his films, although strong on character and

Paganini A drawing by Ingres of the Italian violinist and composer Paganini.

background, fail to exploit the medium fully as an independent art form.

Pago Pago /ˈpɑːŋgəʊ ˈpɑːŋgəʊ/ chief port of American Samoa on the island of Tutuila; population (1980) 3,060. Formerly a naval coaling station, it was acquired by the USA under a commercial treaty with the local king 1872.

Pahang /pəˈhʌŋ/ state of E Peninsular Malaysia; capital Kuantan; area 36,000 sq km/13,896 sq mi; population (1980) 799,000. It is mountainous and forested, and produces rubber, tin, gold, and timber. There is a port at Tanjung Gelang. Pahang is ruled by a sultan.

Pahlavi dynasty Iranian dynasty founded by Riza Khan (1877–1944), an army officer who seized control of the government 1921, and was proclaimed shah 1925. During World War II Britain and the USSR were nervous of his German sympathies, and occupied Iran 1941–46. They compelled him to abdicate in favour of his son Mohammed Riza Shah Pahlavi, who was deposed in the Islamic revolution 1979.

Pahsien /pɑːˈʃjen/ another name for ◊Chongqing, port in SW China.

pain special sense that has evolved to give an awareness of harmful effects on the body. It may be triggered by stimuli such as trauma, inflammation, and heat. The sensation of pain is transmitted by separate nerves from that of fine touch, so that it is possible in diseases such as syringomyelia to have no sense of pain in a limb, yet maintain a normal sense of touch. Such an anaesthetic limb is at great risk of infection via unnoticed cuts and abrasions.

A message to the brain travels along the nerves as electrical impulses. When these reach the gap between one nerve and another, chemicals govern whether this gap is bridged, and may also either increase or decrease the attention the message receives, or modify its intensity in either direction. The main type of transmitter is known simply by an initial as 'substance P', a neuropeptide concentrated in a certain area of the spinal cord. Substance P has been found in fish, and there is also evidence that the same substances that cause pain in humans, for example, bee venom, cause a similar reaction in insects, for instance spiders.

Painkillers include ◊aspirin, ◊morphine, ◊codeine, paracetamol, and synthetic versions of the natural pain inhibitors, the encephalins and endorphins, which avoid the side-effects of all the others.

Paine /peɪn/ Thomas 1737–1809. English left-wing political writer, active in the American and French revolutions. His influential pamphlets include *Common Sense* 1776, *The Rights of Man* 1791, and *The Age of Reason* 1793. He advocated republicanism, deism, the abolition of slavery, and the emancipation of women.

Paine, born in Thetford, Norfolk, was a friend of Benjamin Franklin and went to America 1774, where he published several republican pamphlets and fought for the colonists in the War of Independence. In 1787 he returned to Britain. *The Rights of Man* is an answer to the conservative

Paine *Portrait after George Romney of the English political writer Thomas Paine (c.1880), National Portrait Gallery, London.*

Pakistan
Islamic Republic of

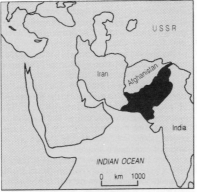

area 796,100 sq km/307,295 sq mi; one-third of Kashmir is under Pakistani control
capital Islamabad
towns Karachi (largest city and port), Lahore
physical fertile plains; Indus river; Himalaya mountains in the N
features the 'five rivers' (Indus, Jhelum, Chenab, Ravi and Sutlej) feed one of the world's largest irrigation systems; K2; Khyber Pass; sites of the Indus Valley civilization
head of state Ghulam Ishaq Khan from 1988
head of government Benazir Bhutto from 1988
government emergent democracy
political parties Pakistan People's Party (PPP), moderate, Islamic, socialist; Islamic Democratic Alliance (IJI), including the Pakistan Muslim League (PML), Islamic conservative; Mohajir National Movement (MQM), Sind-based Mohajir settlers
exports cotton textiles, rice, leather, carpets
currency Pakistan rupee (36.20 = £1 Feb 1990)
population (1989) 110,358,000 (66% Punjabi, 13% Sindhi); annual growth rate 3.1%
life expectancy men 51, women 49
language Urdu and English (official); Punjabi
religion Sunni Muslim 75%, Shi'ite Muslim 20%, Hindu 4%
literacy 40% male/19% female (1985 est)
GDP $35 bn (1983); $280 per head of population
chronology
1947 Pakistan formed following partition of India.
1956 Proclaimed a republic.
1958 Military rule imposed by Gen Ayub Khan.
1969 Power transferred to Gen Yahya Khan.
1971 Secession of East Pakistan (Bangladesh). After civil war, power was transferred to Zulfiqar Ali Bhutto.
1977 Bhutto overthrown in military coup by Gen Zia ul-haq. Martial law imposed.
1979 Bhutto executed.
1981 Opposition Movement for Restoration of Democracy formed. Islamization process pushed forward.
1985 Non-party elections held, amended constitution adopted, martial law and ban on political parties lifted.
1986 Agitation for free elections launched by Benazir Bhutto, daughter of Zulfiqar Ali Bhutto
1988 Zia introduced Islamic legal code, the *Shariah*. He was killed in a military air crash in Aug, and Benazir Bhutto was elected prime minister in Nov.
1989 Pakistan rejoined the Commonwealth.
1990 Army mobilized in support of Muslim separatists in Indian Kashmir (Apr).

theorist Burke's *Reflections on the Revolution in France*. In 1792, Paine was indicted for treason and escaped to France, to represent Calais in the National Convention. Narrowly escaping the guillotine, he regained his seat after the fall of Robespierre. Paine returned to the USA 1802, and died in New York.

paint material used to give a protective and decorative finish to surfaces. Paints consist of a pigment suspended in a vehicle, or binder, sometimes with added solvents. It is the vehicle that dries and hardens to form an adhesive film of paint. Among the most common kinds are cellulose paints (or lacquers), oil-based paints, emulsion paints, and special types such as enamels and primers.

Lacquers consist of a synthetic resin (such as an acrylic resin or cellulose acetate) dissolved in a volatile organic solvent, which evaporates rapidly to give a very quick-drying paint. A typical *oil-based paint* has a vehicle of a natural drying oil (such as linseed oil) or a synthetic alkyl resin, containing a prime pigment of iron, lead, titanium, or zinc oxide, to which coloured pigments may be added. The finish—gloss, semi-matt, or matt—depends on the amount of inert pigment (such as clay or silicates). Oil-based paints can be thinned, and brushes cleaned, in a solvent such as turpentine or white spirit (a petroleum product). *Emulsion paints*, sometimes called latex paints, consist of pigments dispersed in a water-based emulsion of a polymer (such as polyvinyl chloride [PVC] or acrylic resin). They can be thinned with water, which can also be used to wash the paint out of brushes and rollers. *Enamels* have little pigment, and they dry to an extremely hard, high-gloss film. *Primers* for the first coat on wood or metal, on the other hand, have a high pigment content (as do undercoat paints). Aluminium or bronze powder may be used for priming or finishing objects made of metal.

painting the application of colour, pigment, or paint to a surface. The chief methods of painting are:
tempera emulsion painting, with a gelatinous (for example egg yolk) rather than oil base; known in ancient Egypt
fresco watercolour painting on plaster walls; the palace of Knossos, Crete, contains examples from about 2,000 BC
ink developed in China from calligraphy in the Sung period and became highly popular in Japan from the 15th century
oil ground pigments in linseed, walnut, or other oil; spread from N to S Europe in the 15th century
watercolour pigments combined with gum arabic and glycerine, which are diluted with water; the method was developed in the 15th–17th centuries from wash drawings
acrylic synthetic pigments developed after World War II; the colours are very hard and brilliant.

For the history of painting see under ◊ancient art; ◊medieval art; ◊Chinese art, and so on. Individual painters and art movements are listed alphabetically.

Pakhtoonistan /pɑːkˌtuːnɪˈstɑːn/ independent state desired by the ◊Pathan people.

Pakistan /ˌpɑːkɪˈstɑːn/ country in S Asia, stretching from the Himalayas to the Arabian Sea, bounded to the W by Iran, to the NW by Afghanistan, to the NE by China, and to the E by India.
government The 1973 constitution, suspended 1977, has been restored in part and amended 1985 to make the president the dominant political figure. Primary power resides with the central government, headed by an executive president who is elected for five-year terms by a joint sitting of the federal legislature. Day-to-day administration is performed by a prime minister (drawn from the National Assembly) and cabinet appointed by the president. Since the death of Gen Zia in 1988 and the election of Benazir Bhutto, power has shifted

from the president to the prime minister in what has become a dual administration.

Pakistan is a federal republic comprising four provinces: Sind, Punjab, North-West Frontier Province, and Baluchistan, administered by appointed governors and local governments drawn from elected provincial assemblies; ◊Tribal Areas, which are administered by the centre; and the Federal Capital Territory of Islamabad. The federal legislature (*Majlis i-Shura*) comprises two chambers, a lower house (National Assembly) composed of 207 members directly elected for five-year terms by universal suffrage as well as 20 women and 10 minority group appointees, and an upper chamber (Senate) composed of 87 members elected, a third at a time, for six-year terms by provincial assemblies and tribal areas following a quota system. The National Assembly has sole jurisdiction over financial affairs.

history For history before 1947, see ◊Indus Valley Civilization and ◊India. The name Pakistan for a Muslim division of British India was put forward 1930; it was made up by Choudhary Rahmat Ali (1897–1951) from the names of the predominantly Muslim parts of the subcontinent: *P*unjab, the *A*fghan NW Frontier, *K*ashmir, *S*ind, and Baluchi*stan*. *Pak* means 'pure' in Urdu and *stan* means 'land'. Fear of domination by the Hindu majority in India led in 1940 to a serious demand for a separate Muslim state, which delayed for some years India's independence. In 1947 British India was divided into two dominions, India and Pakistan.

Ater the death of its leader ◊Jinnah 1948, Pakistan remained as a dominion with the British monarch as head of state until being declared a republic Mar 1956. Its new constitution was abrogated Oct 1958, and military rule imposed through a coup by Gen Muhammad Ayub Khan. The country experienced rapid economic growth during the 1960s but regional tension mounted between demographically dominant East Pakistan and West Pakistan, where political and military power was concentrated.

After serious strikes and riots Mar 1969, Gen Ayub Khan stepped down and was replaced by the commander-in-chief, Gen Agha Muhammad Yahya Khan. Pakistan's first elections with universal suffrage were held Dec 1970 to elect an assembly to frame a new constitution. Sheikh ◊Mujib ur-Rahman's Awami League, which proposed autonomy, gained a majority of seats in East Pakistan and the Pakistan People's Party (or PPP) in West Pakistan. East Pakistan declared its independence from the West Mar 1971, precipitating a civil war. India intervened on East Pakistan's side Dec 1971, and the independent republic of ◊Bangladesh emerged.

Gen Yahya Khan resigned, passing power in (West) Pakistan to the People's Party leader Zulfiqar Ali ◊Bhutto, who introduced a new federal parliamentary constitution (Apr 1973) and a socialist economic programme of land reform and nationalization. From the mid-1970s the Sind-based Bhutto faced deteriorating economic conditions and growing regional opposition, particularly from Baluchistan and from ◊Pathans campaigning for an independent Pakhtoonistan. Bhutto won a majority in the Mar 1977 Assembly elections, but was accused of ballot-rigging by the Pakistan National Alliance opposition. Riots ensued and after four months of unrest, the Punjabi Muslim army Chief of Staff, Gen ◊Zia ul-Haq, seized power in a bloodless coup July 1977. Martial law was imposed; Bhutto was imprisoned for alleged murder and hanged Apr 1979.

After the Dec 1979 Soviet invasion of ◊Afghanistan, over 2 million refugees poured into Pakistan, which became the recipient of US aid. The economy also relied on remittances from workers in the Middle East. Between 1979 and 1981 Gen Zia imposed severe restrictions on political activity. He introduced a broad Islamization programme aimed at deepening his support base and appeasing Islamic fundamentalists. This was opposed by middle-class professionals and by the Shi'ite minority. In Mar

1981, nine banned opposition parties, including the People's Party of Pakistan, formed the Movement for the Restoration of Democracy alliance to campaign for a return to parliamentary government. The military government responded by arresting several hundred opposition politicians. A renewed democracy campaign 1983 resulted in considerable anti-government violence in Sind province. From 1982, however, Gen Zia slowly began enlarging the civilian element in his government and in Dec 1984 he held a successful referendum on the Islamization process, which was taken to legitimize his continuing as president for a further five-year term. In Feb 1985, direct elections were held to the National and Provincial assemblies, but on a non-party basis. The opposition boycotted the poll, as they had done in Dec, resulting in a turnout of only 53%. A new civilian cabinet was nevertheless formed and an amended constitution adopted.

In Dec 1985, martial law and the ban on political parties were lifted, military courts were abolished, and military administrators stepped down in favour of civilians. A government was formed by the Pagaro faction of the Pakistan Muslim League led by Mohammad Khan Junejo, which supported, and was subservient to Gen Zia. Benazir ◊Bhutto (1953–), the daughter of Zulfiqar Ali Bhutto and leader of the PPP, returned from self-exile in London Apr 1986 to launch popular campaign for immediate open elections. Riots erupted in Lahore, Karachi, and rural Sind, where troops were sent in, and PPP leaders were arrested.

In May 1988, concerned with the deteriorating state of the economy and anxious to accelerate the Islamization process, president Zia dismissed the Junejo government and dissolved the National Assembly and provincial legislatures, promising fresh elections within 90 days. Ruling by ordinance, Zia decreed, in July 1988, that the Sharia, the Islamic legal code, would immediately become the country's supreme law. A month later, the president was killed, along with senior army officers, in a military air crash near Bahawalpur.

Sabotage was suspected. Ghulam Ishaq Khan, the senate's elderly chair, succeeded as president, but in the free multi-party elections held in Nov 1988 the PPP, which had moved towards the centre in its policy stance, emerged as the largest single party, with 45% of the National Assembly's elective seats. After forging a coalition with the Mohajir National Movement (MQM), Benazir Bhutto was sworn in as prime minister in Dec 1988, and Ghulam Ishaq Khan was elected as president. The new Bhutto administration pledged itself to a free-market economic programme, support of the Afhgan mujaheddin, and to leave untouched the military budget. In Oct 1989 the MQM withdrew from the ruling coalition and allied itself with the opposition Islamic Democratic Alliance. The Bhutto government narrowly survived a vote of no confidence a month later.

In foreign affairs, Pakistan's relations with India have been strained since independence, with border wars over Kashmir 1965 and East Pakistan 1971. It left the Commonwealth 1972, when the new state of Bangladesh was accepted, but rejoined in 1989. As a result of shared hostility to India, Pakistan has been allied with China since the 1950s; in recent years it has developed close relations with the USA, while at the same time joining the ◊nonaligned movement (1979) and drawing closer to the Islamic states of the Middle East and Africa.

Pakula /pə'ku:lə/ Alan J 1928– . US film director, formerly a producer, whose best films are among the finest of 1970s cinema and include *Klute* 1971 and *All the President's Men* 1976. His later work includes *Sophie's Choice* 1982.

Palaeocene first epoch of the Tertiary period of geological time, 65–55 million years ago. Many types of mammals spread rapidly after the disappearance of the great reptiles of the Mesozoic. The name means 'the ancient part of the early recent'.

Palaeolithic earliest division of the Stone Age; see ◊prehistory.

palaeontology in geology, the study of ancient life that encompasses the structure of ancient organisms and their environment, evolution, and ecology, as revealed by their ◊fossils.

The practical aspects of palaeontology are based on using the presence of different fossils to date particular rock strata and to identify rocks that were laid down under particular conditions, for instance giving rise to the formation of oil. The term *palaeontology* was first used in 1834, during the period when the first ◊dinosaur remains were discovered.

Palaeozoic era of geological time 590–248 million years ago. It comprises the Cambrian, Ordovician, Silurian, Devonian, Carboniferous, and Permian periods. The Cambrian, Ordovician, and Silurian constitute the Lower Palaeozoic; the Devonian, Carboniferous, and Permian make up the Upper Palaeozoic. The era includes the evolution of multicellular life forms in the sea; the invasion of land by plants and animals; and the evolution of fish, amphibians, and early reptiles. The continents were very different from the present ones but, towards the end of the era, all were joined together as a single world continent called ◊Pangaea. The earliest identifiable fossils date from this era. The climate was mostly warm with short ice ages.

Palamas /'pæləməs/ Kostes 1859–1943. Greek poet. He enriched the Greek vernacular as a literary language by his use of it, particularly in his poetry, such as *Songs of my Fatherland* 1886 and *The Flute of the King* 1910, which expresses his vivid awareness of Greek history.

Palamedes Greek mythological hero and inventor of writing. His name means 'Contriver'. He exposed ◊Odysseus's pretence of madness before the Greek expedition sailed to ◊Troy and in revenge was falsely denounced as a traitor by Odysseus, and stoned to death by the Greek army.

Palance /paləns/ Jack. Stage name of Walter Jack Palahnuik 1920– . US film actor, often cast as a villain. His films include *Shane* 1953 and *Batman* 1989.

palate in mammals, the ceiling of the mouth. The bony front part is the hard palate, the muscular rear part the soft palate. Incomplete fusion of the palate causes interference with speech.

Palatinate /pə'lætineit/ a historic division of Germany, dating from before the 8th century. It was ruled by a *count palatine* (a count with royal prerogatives) and varied in size.

When it was attached to Bavaria 1815 it consisted of two separate parts: Rhenish (or Lower) Palatinate on the Rhine (capital Heidelberg), and Upper Palatinate (capital Amberg on the Vils) 210 km/130 mi to the E. In 1946 Rhenish Palatinate became an administrative division of the *Land* (West German region) of Rhineland-Palatinate with its capital at Neustadt; Upper Palatinate remained an administrative division of Bavaria with its capital at Regensburg.

Palau /pə'lau/ former name (until 1981) of the Republic of ◊Belau.

Paldiski /'pɑ:ldiski/ small, ice-free port in Estonia, a Soviet naval base 40 km/25 mi W of Tallinn at the entrance to the Gulf of Finland.

Palembang /pə'lembæŋ/ oil-refining city in Indonesia, capital of S Sumatra province; population (1980) 786,000. Palembang was the capital of a sultanate when the Dutch established a trading station there 1616.

Palermo /pə'leəməu/ capital and seaport of Sicily; population (1988) 729,000. Industries include shipbuilding, steel, glass, and chemicals. It was founded by the Phoenicians 8th century BC.

Palestine /'pælistain/ (Arabic *Falastin* 'Philistines') (also called the *Holy Land* because of its links with Judaism, Christianity, and Islam) the area between the Mediterranean and the river Jordan, with Lebanon to the north and Sinai to the south. It was in ancient times dominated in turn by Egypt, Assyria, Babylonia, Persia, Macedonia, the Ptolemies, the Seleucids, and the Roman and Byzantine empires. Today it forms part of Israel. The Palestinian people (about 500,000 in the West Bank, E Jerusalem, and the Gaza Strip; 1,200,000 in Jordan; 1,200,000 in Israel; 300,000 in Lebanon; and 100,000 in the USA) are descendants of the people of ◊Canaan.

Palestine Liberation Organization (PLO) organization founded 1964 to bring about an independent state of Palestine. It is formed of several distinct groupings, the chief of which is al-◊Fatah, led by Yasser ◊Arafat, the president of the PLO since 1969. To achieve its ends it has pursued diplomatic initiatives, but also operates as a guerrilla army. In 1988, the Palestine National Council voted to create a state of Palestine, but at the same time endorsed United Nations resolution 242, recognizing Israel's right to exist.

Beirut became PLO headquarters 1970–71 after its defeat in the Jordanian civil war. In 1974 the PLO became the first non-government delegation to be admitted to a session of the United Nations General Assembly. When Israel invaded Lebanon 1982 it had to abandon its headquarters there; it moved on to Tunis and in 1986 to Baghdad. PLO members who remained in Lebanon after the expulsion were later drawn into the internal conflict; see ◊Arab-Israeli Wars. In 1986 Jordan suspended 'political coordination' with the PLO and expelled Arafat's deputy, dealing instead directly with Palestinians in Israeli-occupied territories.

Palestrina /ˌpælɪˈstriːnə/ Giovanni Pierluigi da 1525–1594. Italian composer of secular and sacred choral music. Apart from motets and madrigals, he also wrote 105 masses, including *Missa Papae Marcelli*.

Paley /ˈpeɪli/ Grace 1922– . US short-story writer and critic. Her stories express Jewish and feminist experience with bitter humour, as in *The Little Disturbances of Man* 1960 and *Later the Same Day* 1985.

Pali /ˈpɑːli/ an ancient Indo-European language of N India, related to Sanskrit, and a classical language of Buddhism.

Palissy /ˌpælɪˈsiː/ Bernard 1510–1589. French potter, noted for his richly coloured rustic pottery, such as dishes with realistic modelled fish and reptiles or with the network piercing. He was favoured by Catherine de' Medici but was imprisoned in the ◊Bastille as a Huguenot in 1588, and died there.

Palk Strait a channel separating SE India from the island of Sri Lanka; 53 km/33 mi at its widest point.

Palladio /pəˈlɑːdɪəʊ/ Andrea 1518–1580. Italian architect. His country houses (for example, Malcontenta, and the Villa Rotonda near Vicenza) were designed from 1540 for patrician families of the Venetian Republic.

These buildings influenced Neo-Classical architecture, such as Washington's home at Mount Vernon, USA, the palace of Tsarskoe Selo in Russia, and Prior Park, England.

palladium in Greek mythology, an image of Pallas ◊Athene, supposed to be a gift from Zeus to the city of Troy. According to legend, the city could not be captured while the image remained. It was stolen by Odysseus and Diomedes, and was later alleged to have been taken to Rome by Aeneas.

palladium in chemistry, a white metal of the platinum family, symbol Pd, atomic number 46, relative atomic mass 106.4. Palladium does not tarnish in air, can absorb up to 3,000 times its volume of hydrogen, and is used as a catalyst. Other uses include springs in clocks and watches, parts of delicate balances and surgical instruments, dental fillings, and as an alloy with gold to make white gold.

It was discovered 1803 by British physicist William Wollaston (1766–1828), and found in platinum ore in Brazil, California (USA), and the Urals (USSR), and in nickel ores of Canada. It is also a non-radioactive product of a slow-neutron nuclear reactor.

Pallas a title of the goddess ◊Athene in Greek mythology and religion.

palliative in medicine, treatment given to relieve symptoms rather than to cure the underlying cause. In conditions that will resolve of their own accord

(for instance, the common cold) or are incurable, the entire treatment may be palliative.

pallium a woven vestment worn by the pope and by Catholic primates and archbishops. It is Y-shaped, falling across the shoulders back and front.

palm plant of the family Palmae, characterized by a single tall stem bearing a thick cluster of large palmate or pinnate leaves at the top. The majority of the numerous species are tropical or subtropical. Some, such as the coconut, date, sago, and oil palms, are important economically.

Palma, La /ˈpælmə/ one of the ◊Canary Islands, Spain

area 730 sq km/282 sq mi

capital Santa Cruz de la Palma

features forested

products wine, fruit, honey, silk; tourism is important

population (1981) 77,000.

Palma /ˈpælmə/ (Spanish *Palma de Mallorca*) industrial port (textiles, cement, paper, pottery), resort, and capital of the Balearic Islands, Spain, on Majorca; population (1986) 321,000. Palma was founded 276 BC as a Roman colony.

Palmas, Las /ˈpælməs/ port in the Canary Islands; see ◊Las Palmas.

Palm Beach /ˈpɑːm ˈbiːtʃ/ winter resort in Florida, USA, on an island between Lake Worth and the Atlantic; population (1980) 9,730.

Palme /ˈpɑːnə/(Sven) Olof 1927–1986. Swedish social-democratic politician, prime minister 1969–76 and 1982–86. He entered government 1963, holding several posts before becoming leader of the Social Democratic Labour Party (SAP) 1969. He was assassinated Feb 1986.

Palme, educated in Sweden and the USA, joined the SAP 1949 and became secretary to the prime minister 1954. He led the SAP youth movement 1955–61. As prime minister he carried out constitutional reforms, turning the Riksdag into a single-chamber parliament and stripping the monarch of power.

Palmer /ˈpɑːmə/ Arnold (Daniel) 1929– . US golfer, who helped to popularize the game in the USA in the 1950s and 1960s. He won the Masters 1958, 1960, 1962, and 1964; the US Open 1960; and the British Open 1961 and 1962.

Born in Pennsylvania, he won the US amateur title 1954, and went on to win all the world major professional trophies except the US PGA championship. In the 1980s he enjoyed a successful career on the US Seniors Tour.

CAREER HIGHLIGHTS

US Open: 1960
British Open: 1961–62
Masters: 1958, 1960, 1962, 1964
World Match-Play: 1964, 1967
US Ryder Cup: 1961, 1963*, 1965, 1967, 1971, 1973, 1975**
* playing captain; ** non-playing captain

Palmer /ˈpɑːmə/ Geoffrey Winston Russell 1942– . New Zealand Labour politician, prime minister from 1989, deputy prime minister and attorney-general 1984–89.

A graduate of Victoria University, Wellington, Palmer was a law lecturer in the USA and New Zealand before entering politics, becoming Labour member for Christchurch in the House of Representatives 1979. He succeeded David ◊Lange on Lange's resignation as prime minister.

Palmer /ˈpɑːmə/ Samuel 1805–1881. British painter and etcher. He lived 1826–35 in Shoreham, Kent, with a group of artists who were all followers of William Blake and called themselves *the Ancients*. Palmer's expressive landscape style during that period reflected a strongly spiritual inspiration.

Palmerston /ˈpɑːməstən/ Henry John Temple, 3rd Viscount Palmerston 1784–1865. British politician. Initially a Tory, in Parliament from 1807, he was secretary-at-war 1809–28. He broke with the Tories 1830 and sat in the Whig cabinets of 1830–34, 1835–41, and 1846–51 as foreign secretary. He was prime minister 1855–58 (when he rectified

Aberdeen's mismanagement of the Crimean War, suppressed the Indian Mutiny, and carried through the Second Opium War) and 1859–65 (when he almost involved Britain in the US Civil War on the side of the South).

Palmerston succeeded to an Irish peerage 1802. He served under five Tory prime ministers before joining the Whigs. His foreign policy was marked by distrust of France and Russia, against whose designs he backed the independence of Belgium and Turkey. He became home secretary in the coalition government of 1852, and prime minister on its fall, and was responsible for the warship ◊*Alabama* going to the Confederate side in the American Civil War. He was popular with the people and made good use of the press, but his high-handed attitude annoyed Queen Victoria and other ministers.

Palmerston North /ˈpɑːməstən ˈnɔːθ/ town on the SW coast of North Island, New Zealand; industries (textiles, dairy produce, electrical goods); population (1986) 67,400.

Palm Springs /ˈpɑːm ˈsprɪŋz/ resort and spa in S California, USA, about 160 km/100 mi E of Los Angeles; population (1980) 32,300.

Palm Sunday in the Christian calendar, the Sunday before Easter, and first day of Holy Week, which commemorates Jesus' entry into Jerusalem, when the crowd strewed palm leaves in his path.

Palmyra /pælˈmaɪrə/ ancient city and oasis in the desert of Syria, about 240 km/150 mi NE of Damascus. Palmyra, the biblical Tadmor, was flourishing by about 300 BC. It was destroyed AD 272 after Queen Zenobia had led a revolt against the Romans. Extensive temple ruins exist, and on the site is a village called Tadmur.

Palmyra /pælˈmaɪrə/ coral atoll 1,600 km/1,000 mi SW of Hawaii, in the Line Islands, S Pacific, purchased by the USA from a Hawaiian family 1979 for the storage of highly radioactive nuclear waste from 1986.

Palo Alto city in California, USA, situated SE of San Francisco at the centre of the high-tech region known as 'Silicon Valley'; site of Stanford University.

Palomar, Mount /ˈpæləmɑː/ the location of an observatory, 80 km/50 mi NE of San Diego, California, USA, with a 5 m/200 in diameter reflector, the Hale. It was dedicated 1948.

Palumbo /pəˈlʌmbəʊ/ Peter 1935– . British property developer. Appointed chair of the Arts Council 1988, he advocated a close partnership between public and private funding of the arts, and a greater role for the regions. His planned Mies van

Palmerston *During his lifelong career at the forefront of British politics as foreign secretary, home secretary, and prime minister, Palmerston was popular with the people but incurred enmity abroad with his bellicose foreign policy and the displeasure of Queen Victoria with his imperious attitude.*

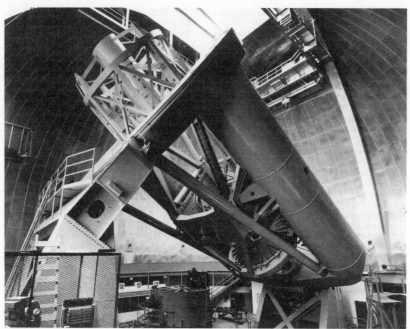

Palomar, Mount *The 200-inch Hale telescope shown pointing north at the Palomar Observatory, California. When it was dedicated in 1948, it was the largest optical telescope in the world.*

der Rohe skyscraper beside the Mansion House, London, was condemned by Prince Charles as 'a giant glass stump'.

Pamirs /pə'mɪəz/ central Asian plateau mainly in the USSR, but extending into China and Afghanistan, traversed by mountain ranges. Its highest peak is Mount Communism (Kommunizma Pik 7,495 m/24,600 ft) in the Akademiya Nauk range, the highest mountain in the USSR.

Pampas /'pæmpəz/ flat, treeless, Argentinian plains, lying between the Andes and the Atlantic, and rising gradually from the coast to the lower slopes of the mountains. The E Pampas contain large cattle ranches and the flax- and grain-growing area of Argentina; the W Pampas are arid and unproductive.

pampas grass grass, genus *Cortaderia*, native to South America. *Cortaderia argentea* is grown in gardens, and has tall leaves and large panicles of white flowers.

Pamplona /pæm'pləʊnə/ industrial city (wine, leather, shoes, textiles) in Navarre, N Spain, on the Arga river; population (1986) 184,000. A pre-Roman town, it was rebuilt by Pompey 68 BC, captured by the Visigoths 476, sacked by Charlemagne 778, became the capital of Navarre, and was taken by Wellington in the Peninsular War 1813. An annual running of bulls takes place in the streets every July.

Pamyat (Russian 'memory') nationalist Russian popular movement. Founded 1979 as a cultural and historical group attached to the Soviet Ministry of Aviation Industry, it grew from the mid-1980s, propounding a violently conservative and anti-Semitic Russian nationalist message.

Pan /pæn/ in Greek mythology, god (Roman *Sylvanus*) of flocks and herds, shown as a man with the horns, ears, and hoofs of a goat, and playing a shepherd's pipe.

panacea a remedy for all known disease; a cure-all.

Pan-Africanist Congress (PAC) militant South African nationalist group, which broke away from the African National Congress 1959. More radical than the ANC, the Pan-Africanist Congress has a black-only policy for Africa. Its military wing is called Poqo ('we alone'). Since the 1970s, it has been weakened by internal dissent.

In Mar 1960, the PAC organized a campaign of protest against South African pass laws, which resulted in the ◊Sharpeville massacre; the following month, the PAC was declared an illegal organization by the South African government. It continued guerrilla activities against South Africa from bases in Botswana, and was unbanned 1990.

Panama /ˌpænə'mɑː/ country in Central America, on a narrow isthmus between the Caribbean and the Pacific Ocean, bounded to the W by Costa Rica and to the E by Colombia.

government The constitution was revised 1983, when a new, single-chamber legislative assembly of 67 members, elected by universal suffrage for a five-year term, was created. The president, elected in the same way for a similar period of office, is assisted by two elected vice presidents and an appointed cabinet.

Panama is divided into nine provinces, each with its own governor, appointed by the president. There are also three Indian reservations, which enjoy a high degree of self-government.

history For early history, see ◊American Indian. Panama was visited by Christopher ◊Columbus 1502. Vasco Núñez de ◊Balboa 'discovered' the Pacific from the Darien isthmus 1513. Spanish settlements were sacked by Francis ◊Drake 1572–95 and Henry ◊Morgan 1668–71; Morgan destroyed the old city of Panama, which dated from 1519. Remains of Fort St Andrews, built by Scottish settlers 1698–1701, were discovered 1976. Panama remained part of the viceroyalties of Peru and New Granada until 1821, when it gained independence from Spain and joined Gran Colombia.

Panama achieved full independence 1903 with US support, which at the same time bought the rights to build the Panama Canal and was given control of a ten-mile-wide strip of territory, known as the Canal Zone, in perpetuity. Panama was guaranteed US protection and an annuity. In 1939 Panama's protectorate status was ended by mutual agreement, and in 1977 two treaties were signed by Panama's president (1968–78), Gen Omar Torrijos Herara, and US President Carter. One transferred ownership of the canal to Panama and the other guaranteed its subsequent neutrality, with the conditions that only Panamanian forces would be stationed in the zone, and that the USA would have the right to use force to keep the canal open if it became obstructed.

The 1980s saw a deterioration in the state of Panama's economy, with opposition to the austerity measures that the government introduced to try to halt the decline. There are a large number of political organizations, the most significant being represented in the assembly by two coalitions, the centre-right National Democratic Union (Unade), which won 40 seats in the 1984 general election,

Panama
Republic of
(República de Panamá)

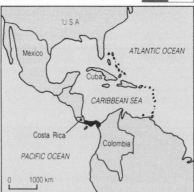

area 77,100 sq km/29,768 sq mi
capital Panama City
towns Cristóbal, Balboa, Colón
physical mountain ranges; tropical rainforest
features Panama Canal; Barro Colorado Island in Gatun Lake (the reservoir which supplies the canal), a tropical forest reserve since 1923; Smithsonian Tropical Research Institute
head of state and government Guillermo Endara from 1989
government emergent democratic republic
political parties Democratic Revolutionary Party (PRD), right-wing; Labour Party (PALA), right-of-centre; Republican Party (PR), right-wing; National Liberal Republican Movement (MOLIRENA), left-of-centre; Authentic Panama

Party (PPA), centrist; Christian Democratic Party (PDC), centre-left
exports bananas, petroleum products, copper from one of the world's largest deposits, shrimps
currency balboa (1.70 = £1 Feb 1990)
population (1989) 2,370,000; annual growth rate 2.2%
life expectancy men 69, women 73
language Spanish
religion Roman Catholic
literacy 89% male/88% female (1985)
GDP $4.1 bn (1983); $1,116 per head of population
chronology
1903 Became independent from Colombia.
1974 Agreement to negotiate a full transfer of the Panama Canal from the US to Panama.
1977 US-Panama treaties transfer the canal to Panama, with the US guaranteeing its protection and an annual payment.
1984 Nicolas Ardito Barletta elected president, but army commander-in-chief Gen Manuel Noriega in effective control.
1985 Barletta resigned to be replaced by Eric Arturo del Valle.
1987 Noriega resisted calls for his removal, despite suspension of US military and economic aid.
1988 Trying to dismiss Noriega, del Valle was replaced by Manuel Solis Palma. Noriega, charged with drug smuggling by a US federal court, declared a state of emergency.
1989 Assembly elections declared invalid after complaints of fraud. US invaded Panama and Noriega eventually surrendered. Guillermo Endara installed as president.

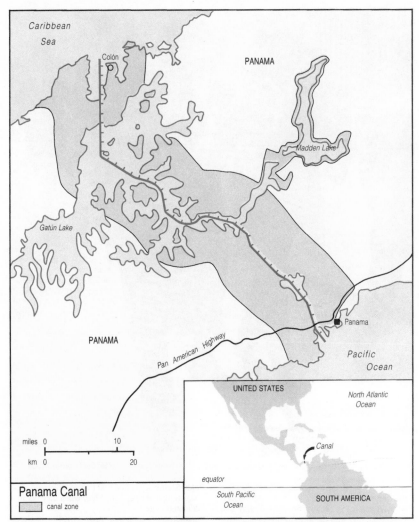

Panama Canal

canal zone

and the centre-left Democratic Opposition Alliance (ADO), which won 27 seats. After a very close result, Dr Nicolas Ardito Barletta, the Democratic Revolutionary Party (PRD) candidate, was declared president, but in 1985 he resigned, amid speculation that he had been forced to do so by the commander of the National Guard. Relations between Panama and the USA deteriorated with the departure of President Barletta, and the Reagan administration cut and later suspended its financial aid.

Barletta was succeeded by Eric Arturo del Valle, but the country was from 1983 effectively ruled by the army commander in chief, Gen Manuel Noriega. In 1987 he was accused of corruption, election rigging, involvement in the cocaine trade, and the murder of a political opponent. Political parties, labour and student unions, and business groups united as the National Civic Crusade to campaign for his removal; demonstrations were suppressed by riot police. In July 1987 Noriega

panda

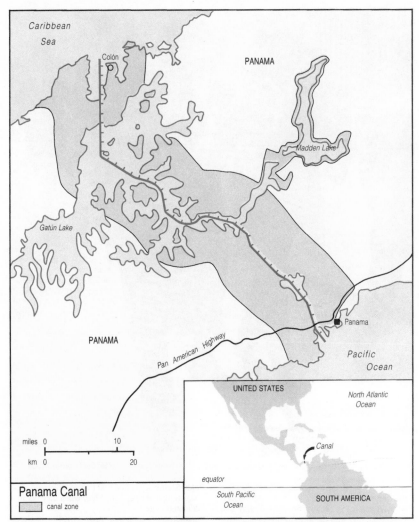

*lesser
panda*

successfully resisted calls for his removal, despite the suspension of US military and economic aid. He declared the May 1989 assembly elections invalid and in Sept Francisco Rodriguez, with army backing, was made president. In the following month an attempted coup against Noriega was put down. In Dec 1989, after mounting harassment of Americans in the Canal Zone, US president Bush ordered troops to invade the country with the declared object of arresting Noriega and bringing him to trial. Noriega sought refuge in the Vatican embassy but eventually surrendered and was taken to the USA to answer charges relating to drug trafficking. The US authorities installed Guillermo Endara as president.

Panama Canal /ˌpænəˈmɑː/ canal across the Panama isthmus in Central America, connecting the Pacific and Atlantic oceans; length 80 km/ 50 mi, with 12 locks. Built by the USA 1904–14 after an unsuccessful attempt by the French, it was formally opened 1920. The *Panama Canal Zone* was acquired 'in perpetuity' by the USA 1903, comprising land extending about 5 km/3 mi on either side of the canal. The Zone passed to Panama 1979, but the USA retains control of the management and defence of the canal itself until 1999, and the use of about 25% of the Zone's former land area.

Panama City /ˌpænəˈmɑː/ capital of the Republic of Panama, near the Pacific end of the Panama Canal; population (1980) 386,000. Products include chemicals, plastics, and clothing. An earlier Panama, to the NE, founded 1519, was destroyed 1671, and the city was founded on the present site 1673.

Pan-American Highway road linking the USA with Central and South America; length 25,300 km/ 15,700 mi. Starting from the US-Canadian frontier (where it links with the Alaska Highway), it runs through San Francisco, Los Angeles, and Mexico City to Panama City, then down the W side of South America to Valparaiso, Chile, where it crosses the Andes and goes to Buenos Aires, Argentina. The road was first planned 1923.

Pan-American Union former name 1910–48 of the ◊Organization of American States.

Panay /pæˈnaɪ/ one of the Philippine islands, lying between Mindoro and Negros
area 11,515 sq km/4,446 sq mi
capital Iloilo
features mountainous, 2,215 m/7,265 ft in Madiaás
products rice, sugar, pineapples, bananas, copra; copper
history seized by Spain 1569; occupied by Japan 1942–45.

Panchen Lama /ˈpɑːntʃən ˈlɑːmə/ 10th incarnation 1935–1989. Tibetan spiritual leader, second in importance to the ◊Dalai Lama. A protégé of the Chinese since childhood, he is not indisputably recognized. When the Dalai Lama left Tibet 1959, the Panchen Lama was deputed by the Chinese to take over, but was stripped of power in 1964 for refusing to denounce the Dalai Lama. He did not appear again in public until 1978.

panchromatic in photography, a highly sensitive black-and-white film made to render all visible spectral colours in correct grey tones. It is always developed in total darkness.

pancreas in vertebrates, a gland between the spleen and the duodenum. When stimulated by ◊secretin, it secretes enzymes into the duodenum which digest starch, proteins, and fats. In humans, it is about 18 cm/7 in long, and lies behind and below the stomach. It contains groups of cells called the *islets of Langerhans*, which secrete the hormones insulin and glucagon that regulate the blood sugar level.

panda mammal of NW China and Tibet. The *giant panda Ailuropoda melanoleuca* has black and white fur with black eye patches, and feeds solely on bamboo shoots. It can grow up to 1.5 m/4.5 ft long, and weigh up to 140 kg/300 lbs. The *lesser panda Ailurus fulgens*, 50 cm/1.5 ft long, is black and chestnut, with a long tail. Destruction of their natural habitats have made their extinction possible in the wild. There is dispute as to whether they should be included in the bear family or racoon family, or classified as a family of their own.

The panda is the symbol of the Worldwide Fund for Nature (formerly the World Wildlife Fund), and the focus of conservation efforts.

Pandora /pænˈdɔːrə/ in Greek mythology, the first woman. Zeus sent her to Earth with a box of evils (to counteract the blessings brought to mortals by ◊Prometheus's gift of fire); she opened it, and they all flew out. Only hope was left inside as a consolation.

Pangaea /pænˈdziːə/ or *Pangea* world continent, named by Alfred ◊Wegener, that may have existed between 250 and 200 million years ago, made up of all the continental masses. It may be regarded as a combination of ◊Laurasia in the north and ◊Gondwanaland in the south, the rest of Earth being covered by the ◊Panthalassa ocean.

Pan-Germanism a movement that developed during the 19th century to encourage unity between German-speaking peoples in Austria, the Netherlands, Flanders, Luxembourg, and Switzerland. Encouraged by the unification of Germany after 1871, the movement became increasingly influential in the period up to 1914.

Pan-Germanism also had an impact in Belgium (Flemish separatism) and in Poland during World War I. Despite the defeat of Germany in 1919, its ideas were revived under Hitler's plans to expand through Europe.

pangolin or *scaly anteater* African and Asian toothless, long-tailed mammal, order Pholidota, up to 1 m/3 ft long. The upper part of the body is covered with horny plates for defence. It is nocturnal, and eats ants and termites.

Panipat /'pɑːnɪpət/ town in Punjab, India; scene of three decisive battles: 1526, when Baber (1483–1530), great-grandson of Tamerlane, defeated the emperor of Delhi and founded the ◊Mogul Empire; 1556, won by his descendant ◊Akbar; 1761, when the ◊Mahrattas were defeated by ◊Ahmad Shah of Afghanistan.

Panjshir Valley /'pəŋdzɪr 'vali/the valley of the river Panjshir which rises in the Panjshir range to the N of Kabul, E Afghanistan. It has been the chief centre of Mujaheddin rebel resistance against the Soviet-backed Najibullah government since 1979.

Pankhurst /'pæŋkhɜːst/ Emmeline (born Goulden) 1858–1928. English suffragette. Founder of the Women's Social and Political Union 1903, she launched the militant suffragette campaign 1905. In 1926 she joined the Conservative Party, and was a prospective parliamentary candidate.

She was supported by her daughters *Christabel Pankhurst* (1880–1958), the political leader of the movement, and *Sylvia Pankhurst* (1882–1960).

pansy perennial garden flower, also known as *heartsease*, derived from the European wild pansy *Viola tricolor*, and including many different varieties and strains. The flowers are usually purple, yellow, cream, or a mixture, and there are many highly developed varieties bred for size, colour, or special markings.

Pantanal a large area of swamp land in the Mato Grosso of SW Brazil, occupying 220,000 sq km/8,4975 sq mi in the upper reaches of the Paraguay river; one of the world's great wildlife refuges; 1,370 sq km/530 sq mi were designated as national park in 1981.

Pantelleria /,pæntelə'rɪə/ volcanic island in the Mediterranean, 100 km/62 mi SW of Sicily and part of that region of Italy

area 115 sq km/45 sq mi

town Pantelleria

products sheep, fruit, olives, capers

population (1981) 7,800

history Pantelleria has drystone dwellings dating from prehistoric times. The Romans called it *Cossyra* and sent people into exile there. Strategically placed, the island has been much fought over. It was strongly fortified by Mussolini in World War II, and surrendered to the Allies 11 June 1943.

Panthalassa ocean that may have covered the surface of the Earth not occupied by the world continent ◊Pangaea between 250 and 200 million years ago.

pantheism (Greek *pan*, all; *theos*, God) a mode of thought that regards God as omnipresent, identical to the universe or nature. It is expressed in Egyptian religion and Brahmanism; stoicism, Neo-Platonism, Judaism, Christianity, and Islam can be interpreted in pantheistic terms. Pantheistic philosophers have included Bruno, Spinoza, Fichte, Schelling, and Hegel.

pantheon originally a temple for worshipping all the gods, such as that in ancient Rome, rebuilt by ◊Hadrian and still used as a church. In more recent times, it is a building where famous people are buried (Panthéon, Paris).

panther another name for ◊leopard.

pantomime in the British theatre, a traditional Christmas entertainment with its origins in the harlequin spectacle of the 18th century and burlesque of the 19th century, which gave rise to the tradition of the principal boy being played by an

pansy

Pankhurst *The suffragette Emmeline Pankhurst under arrest after demonstrating outside Buckingham Palace 1914.*

actress and the dame by an actor. The harlequin's role diminished altogether as themes developed on folktales such as *The Sleeping Beauty* and *Cinderella*, and with the introduction of additional material such as popular songs, topical comedy, and audience participation.

After World War II, pantomimes on ice became popular. The term 'pantomime' was also applied to Roman dumbshows performed by a masked actor, to 18th-century ballets with mythical themes, and, in 19th-century France, to the wordless Pierrot plays from which modern ◊mime developed.

pantothenic acid (chemical formula $C_9H_{17}NO_5$) one of the water-soluble B ◊vitamins, occurring widely throughout a normal diet. There is no specific deficiency disease associated with pantothenic acid but it is known to be involved in the breakdown of fats and carbohydrates.

Panufnik /'panufnɪk/ Andrzei 1914– . Polish composer and conductor. A pupil of Weingartner, he came to Britain in 1954. His music is based on an intense working out of small motifs.

panzer German mechanized divisions and regiments in World War II, used in connection with armoured vehicles, mainly tanks.

Paolozzi /'paolodzi/ Eduardo 1924– . British sculptor, a major force in the Pop art movement in London in the mid-1950s. He typically uses bronze casts of pieces of machinery to create robot-like structures.

papacy the office of the ◊pope or bishop of Rome, as head of the Roman Catholic Church.

papal infallibility doctrine formulated by the Roman Catholic Vatican Council 1870, which stated that the pope, when speaking officially on certain doctrinal or moral matters, was protected from error by God, and such rulings could therefore not be challenged.

Papal States area of central Italy in which the pope was temporal ruler 756–1870, when Italy became a united state.

Papandreou /'papəŋdreu/ Andreas 1919– . Greek socialist politician, founder of the Pan-Hellenic Socialist Movement (PASOK), and prime minister 1981–89. In 1989 he became implicated in the 'Koskotas affair', the alleged embezzlement and diversion of funds to the Greek government of $200 million from the Bank of Crete, headed by George Koskotas. The scandal caused him to lose the 1989 election.

Son of a former prime minister, he studied law in Athens and at Harvard. He was director of the Centre for Economic Research in Athens 1961–64, and economic adviser to the Bank of Greece. He was imprisoned Apr–Dec 1967 for his political activities, after which he founded PASOK. After another spell in overseas universities, he returned to Greece 1974. He was leader of the opposition 1977–81, and became Greece's first socialist prime minister. He was re-elected 1985. Nine officials of PASOK resigned because of the 'Koskotas affair'.

papaya another name for ◊pawpaw, a tropical tree.

Papeete /,pɑːpiˈeɪti/ capital and port of French Polynesia on the NW coast of Tahiti; population (1983) 79,000. Products include vanilla, copra, and mother-of-pearl.

Papen /'pɑːpən/ Franz von 1879–1969. German right-wing politician. As chancellor 1932, he negotiated the Nazi–Conservative alliance that made Hitler chancellor 1933. He was envoy to Austria 1934–38 and ambassador to Turkey 1939–44. Although acquitted at the ◊Nuremberg trials, he was imprisoned by a German denazification court for three years.

paper a sheet of vegetable fibre. The name comes from ◊papyrus, a form of writing material made from

paper making

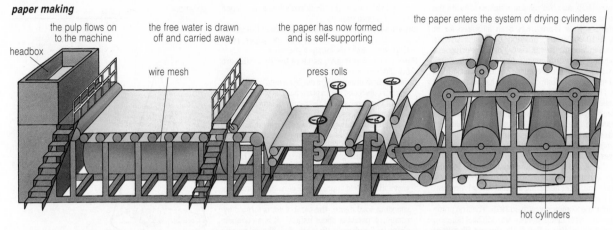

the pulp flows on to the machine

the free water is drawn off and carried away

the paper has now formed and is self-supporting

the paper enters the system of drying cylinders

headbox

wire mesh

press rolls

hot cylinders

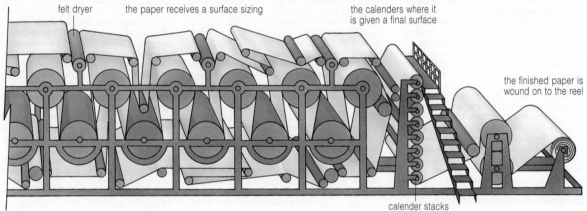

felt dryer

the paper receives a surface sizing

the calenders where it is given a final surface

the finished paper is wound on to the reel

calender stacks

water reed, used in ancient Egypt. The invention of true paper, originally made of pulped fishing nets and rags, is credited to Tsai Lun, Chinese minister of agriculture, AD 105.

Its use gradually spread from the 8th century and the first English paper mill was established at Stevenage in the 15th century.

With the spread of literacy there was a great increase in the demand for paper. Production by hand of single sheets could not keep pace with this demand and led to the invention, by Louis Robert in 1799, of a machine to produce a continuous reel of paper. Today most paper is made from ◊woodpulp on a ◊Foudrinier machine. Recycling avoids some of the enormous waste of trees. Apart from its obvious uses in writing, printing, and packaging, paper is today also employed in towels and toilet tissues, hardboard, and insulating panels; and in electrical work as an insulator.

Papandreou Greek former prime minister Andreas Papandreou in Brussels, Feb 1988.

In 1988 Britain used about 1.9 million tonnes of newsprint, which was about 22% of total paper usage. Domestic paper production was approximately 1 million tonnes in 1989, and imported paper cost £600 million a year.

paper sizes standard European sizes for paper, designated by a letter (A, B, or C) and a number (0–6). The letter indicates the size of the basic sheet at manufacture; the number is how many times it has been folded. A4 is obtained by folding in half an A3 sheet, which is half an A2 sheet, and so on.

Paphos /'pæfos/ resort town on the SW coast of Cyprus; population (1985) 23,200; capital of Cyprus in Roman times and the legendary birthplace of Aphrodite who rose out of the sea; archaeological remains include the 2,300-year-old underground 'Tombs of the Kings', the Roman villa of Dionysos and the 7th-century Byzantine castle.

papier mâché a craft technique that involves building up layer upon layer of pasted paper, which is then baked or left to harden. Used for trays, decorative objects, and even furniture, it is often painted, lacquered, or decorated with mother of pearl.

Papineau /,pæpɪ'nəʊ/ Louis Joseph 1786–1871. Canadian politician. He led a mission to England to protest against the planned union of Lower Canada (Québec) and Upper Canada (Ontario), and demanded economic reform and an elected provincial legislature. In 1835 he gained the co-operation of William Lyon ◊Mackenzie in Upper Canada, and in 1837 organized an unsuccessful rebellion of the French against British rule in Lower Canada. He fled the country, but returned 1847 to sit in the United Canadian legislature until 1854.

Papp /pæp/ Joseph 1921– . US theatre director, and founder of the New York Shakespeare Festival 1954, free to the public and held in an open-air theatre in Central Park. He also founded the New York Public Theatre 1967, an off-Broadway forum for new talent.

Productions directed by Papp include *The Merchant of Venice* and a musical version of *The Two Gentlemen of Verona* (Tony award 1972). The New York Public Theatre staged the first productions of the musicals *Hair* 1967 and *A Chorus Line* 1975. Many of Papp's productions transferred to Broadway.

pappus (plural *pappi*) in botany a modified ◊calyx comprising a ring of fine, silky hairs, or sometimes scales or small teeth, which persists after fertilization. Pappi are found in members of the daisy family (Compositae) such as the dandelions (*Taraxacum*), where they form a parachute-like structure that aids dispersal of the fruit.

Papua /'pɑːpuə/ original name of the island of New Guinea, but latterly its SE section, now part of ◊Papua New Guinea.

Papuan a speaker of a Papuan language. These languages are spoken mainly on the island of New Guinea, though some are used in New Britain and the Solomon Islands.

Papua New Guinea /'pɑːpuə ,njuː 'gɪnɪ/ country in the SW Pacific, comprising the E part of the island of New Guinea, the New Guinea islands, the Admiralty islands, and part of the Solomon islands.

government The British monarch is the formal head of state, represented by a resident governor-general. The governor-general appoints the prime minister and cabinet, who are drawn from and responsible to the parliament.

The constitution from 1975 provides for a single-chamber legislature, the National Parliament, consisting of 109 members elected by universal suffrage for a five-year term, 89 representing local single-member constituencies and 20 provincial constituencies. Although Papua New Guinea is not a federal state, it has 20 provincial governments with a fair degree of autonomy. Out of about 12 political parties, the Papua New Guinea Party (Pangu Pati), People's Democratic Movement (PDM), National

Party (NP), and Melanesian Alliance (MA) are the most significant.

history New Guinea has been inhabited for at least 10,000 years, probably by Asians arriving from Indonesia. It was visited by the Portuguese explorer Jorge de Menezes about 1526 and by Dutch traders in the 17th century. The Dutch East India Company took control of the W half of the island and in 1828 it became part of the Netherlands East Indies. In 1884 the SE was claimed by Britain, the N by Germany; the British part, Papua, was transferred to Australia 1905 and the German part after World War I, when Australia was granted a League of Nations mandate and then a trusteeship over the area.

Once freed from Japanese occupation in 1945, the two territories were jointly administered by Australia and, after achieving internal self-government as Papua New Guinea, became fully independent, within the Commonwealth, in 1975. The first prime minister after independence was Michael Somare, leader of the Pangu Pati (PP). Despite allegations of incompetence, he held office until 1980, when Julius Chan, leader of the People's Progress Party, succeeded him. Somare returned to power in 1982, but in 1985 he lost a no-confidence motion in parliament and was replaced by Paias Wingti, leader of the breakaway People's Democratic Movement (PDM), with former prime minister Chan as his deputy. In Aug 1987 Prime Minister Wingti returned to power with a slender majority of three votes. He announced a more independent foreign policy of good relations with the USSR, USA, Japan, and China. In July 1988, following shifts in coalition alliances, Wingti lost a no-confidence vote and was replaced as prime minister by the former foreign minister and PP's new leader, Rabbie Namaliu. Somare became foreign minister in the new six-party coalition government. Faced with a deteriorating internal law and order situation—soldiers rioting in Port Moresby in Feb 1989 over inadequate pay increases—the government imposed a state of emergency on ◊Bougainville island from June 1989 because of the growing strength there of the guerrilla separatist movement, which had

forced the closure of the island's Panguna copper mine a month earlier.

papyrus type of paper made by the ancient Egyptians from the stem of the papyrus or paper reed *Cyperus papyrus* family Cyperaceae.

Pará /pə'rɑː/ alternative name of the Brazilian port ◊Belém.

parabola in mathematics, a curve formed by cutting a right circular cone with a plane parallel to the sloping side of the cone; one of the family of curves known as ◊conic sections.

It can also be defined as a path traced out by a point that moves in such a way that the distance from a fixed point (focus) is equal to its distance from a fixed straight line (directrix); it thus has an ◊eccentricity of 1.

The trajectories of missiles within the Earth's gravitational field approximate closely to parabolas (ignoring the effect of air resistance). The corresponding solid figure, the paraboloid, is formed by rotating a parabola about its axis. It is a common shape for headlamp reflectors, dish-shaped microwave and radar aerials, and for radiotelescopes, since a source of radiation placed at the focus of a paraboloidal reflector is propagated as a parallel beam.

Paracels /,pærə'selz/ (Chinese *Xisha*/Vietnamese *Hoang Sa*/) group of about 130 small islands in the S China Sea. Situated in an oil-bearing area, they were occupied by China following a skirmish with Vietnam 1974.

Paracelsus /,pærə'selsəs/ Adopted name of Theophrastus Bombastus von Hohenheim 1493–1541. Swiss physician, alchemist, and scientist. He developed the idea that minerals and chemicals might have medical uses (iatrochemistry). He introduced the use of ◊laudanum (which he named) for painkilling purposes. Although Paracelsus was something of a charlatan, and his books contain much mystical nonsense, his rejection of the ancients and insistence on the value of experimentation make him an important figure in early science.

He lectured in Basel on the need for observational experience rather than traditional lore in medicine: he made a public bonfire of the works

parabola   directrix   D   F   P

of his predecessors Avicenna and ◊Galen. He was the disseminator in Europe of the medieval Islamic alchemists' theory that matter is composed of only three elements: salt, sulphur, and mercury.

paracentesis the evacuation of unwanted fluid from a body tissue or cavity by means of a drainage tube.

paracetamol analgesic, particularly effective for musculoskeletal pain. It is as effective as aspirin in reducing fever, and less irritating to the stomach, but has little anti-inflammatory action. An overdose can cause severe, often irreversible, liver damage.

parachute umbrella-shaped device, used to slow down the descent of a human being, or supplies, from a plane or missile to a safe speed for landing, or sometimes to aid (through braking) the landing of a plane or missile itself. It consists of some two dozen panels of nylon with shroud lines to a harness. Modern designs enable the parachutist to exercise considerable control of direction, as in ◊skydiving.

Leonardo da Vinci sketched a parachute design, but the first descent, from a balloon, was not made until 1797 by Garnerin, and the first from an aircraft by Berry 1912. In *parascending*, the parachuting procedure is reversed, the canopy (parafoil) to which the person is attached being towed behind a vehicle to achieve an ascent.

paradigm all those factors, both scientific and otherwise, that influence the research of the scientist. The term, first used by the US historian of science T S ◊Kuhn, has subsequently spread to social studies and politics.

paradise (Persian 'pleasure garden') in various religions, a place or state of happiness. Examples are the Garden of Eden and the Messianic kingdom; the Islamic paradise of the Koran is a place of sensual pleasure.

Paradise Lost an epic poem by John Milton, first published 1667. The poem describes the Fall of Man and the battle between God and Satan, as enacted through the story of Adam and Eve in the Garden of Paradise. A sequel, *Paradise Regained*, was published 1671.

paraffin a general term for hydrocarbons of the paraffin series, general formula $C_nH_{2n} + _2$. The lower members are gases, such as methane (marsh or natural gas). The middle ones (mainly liquid) form the basis of petrol (gasolene), kerosene, and lubricating oils, while the higher ones (paraffin waxes) are used in ointment and cosmetic bases. The fuel commonly sold as paraffin in Britain is more correctly called kerosene.

Paraguay /,pærə'gwaɪ/ landlocked country in South America, bounded to the NE by Brazil, to the S by Argentina, and to the NW by Bolivia.

government The 1967 constitution provides for a president and a two-chamber legislature, the National Congress, consisting of the Senate and

Papua New Guinea

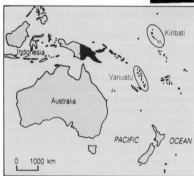

Kiribati
Indonesia
Vanuatu
Australia
PACIFIC OCEAN
0   1000 km

area 462,840 sq km/178,656 sq mi
capital Port Moresby (on E New Guinea)
physical mountains in centre; thickly forested
features wholly within the tropics, with annual rainfall 100 cm/39 in; rare birds of paradise, the world's largest butterfly, orchids
head of state Elizabeth II, represented by Kingsford Dibela from 1983
head of government Rabbie Namaliu from 1988
government constitutional monarchy
political parties Papua New Guinea Party - (Pangu Pati: PP), urban- and coastal-orientated nationalist; People's Democratic Movement (PDM), 1985 breakaway from the PP; National Party (NP), highlands-based; Melanesian

Alliance (MA), Bougainville-based autonomy; People's Progress Party (PPP), conservative
exports copra, coconut oil, palm oil, tea, copper
currency kina (1.64 = £1 Feb 1990)
population (1989) 3,613,000 (including Papuans, Melanesians, Pygmies, and various minorities); annual growth rate 2.6%
life expectancy men 51, women 53
language English (official); pidgin English
religion Protestant 33%, Roman Catholic 18%, local faiths
literacy 55% male/36% female (1985 est)
GNP $2.5 bn (1983); $480 per head of population
chronology
1883 Annexed by Queensland, became known as the Australian Territory of Papua.
1884 NE New Guinea annexed by Germany; SE claimed by Britain.
1914 NE New Guinea occupied by Australia.
1921–42 Held as a League of Nations mandate.
1942–45 Occupied by Japan.
1975 Achieved full independence, within the Commonwealth, with Michael Somare as prime minister.
1980 Julius Chan became prime minister.
1982 Somare returned to power.
1985 Somare challenged by deputy prime minister, Paias Wingti, who later formed a five-party coalition government.
1988 Wingti defeated on no-confidence vote and replaced by Rabbie Namaliu, who established a six-party coalition government.
1989 State of emergency imposed in Bougainville in response to separatist violence.

Chamber of Deputies, all elected by universal suffrage for a five-year term. The president appoints and leads the cabinet, which is called the Council of Ministers.

The Senate has 30 members and the Chamber 60, and the party winning the largest number of votes in the congressional elections is allocated two-thirds of the seats in each chamber. A law passed in 1981 prescribes that a political party must have a minimum of 10,000 members, and must contest at least a third of the constituencies before it can operate.

history For early history, see ◊American Indian. The Guaraní Indians had a settled agricultural civilization before the arrival of Europeans: Sebastian ◊Cabot 1526–30, followed by Spanish colonists, who founded the city of Asunción 1537. From about 1600–1767, when they were expelled, Jesuit missionaries administered much of the country. It became a province subordinate to the Spanish viceroyalty of Peru, then from 1776 part of the viceroyalty of Buenos Aires, and in 1811 Paraguay declared its independence.

The first president was J G R Francia (ruled 1816–40), a despot; he was followed by his nephew C A López and in 1862 by his son F S López, who involved Paraguay in a war with Brazil, Argentina, and Uruguay. Paraguay was invaded and López killed at Aquidabán 1870. When the war was finally over the population consisted mainly of women and children. Recovery was slow with many revolutions. Continuing disputes with Bolivia over the frontier in the torrid Chaco zone of the north flared up into war 1932–35; arbitration by the USA and five South American republics reached a peace settlement 1938.

Since 1940 Paraguay has been mostly under the control of military governments led by strong, autocratic leaders. Gen Morinigo was president 1940–47 and Gen Alfredo Stroessner 1954–89. During the US presidency of Jimmy Carter the Stroessner regime came under strong criticism for its violation of human rights and this resulted in some tempering of the general's ruthless rule. Criticism by the Reagan administration was less noticeable. Stroessner maintained his supremacy by ensuring that the armed forces and business community shared in the spoils of office, and by preventing opposition groups from coalescing into a credible challenge. In the 1983 Congress elections the National Republican Party, led by the president, with the largest number of votes, automatically secured 20 Senate and 40 Chamber seats. The Radical Liberal Party came second, with six Senate and 13 Chamber seats.

Stroessner sought and won an eighth consecutive term only to be ousted, in Feb 1989, by Gen Andrés Rodriguez who, in May 1989, was elected president. The Colorado party was also successful in the congressional elections.

parakeet small ◊parrot.

paraldehyde common name for ◊ethanal trimer.

parallax the change in the apparent position of an object against its background when viewed from two different positions. In astronomy, nearby stars show a shift owing to parallax when viewed from different positions on the Earth's orbit around the Sun. A star's parallax is used to deduce its distance.

Nearer bodies such as the Moon, Sun, and planets also show a parallax caused by the motion of the Earth. *Diurnal parallax* is caused by the Earth's rotation.

parallel circuit an electrical circuit in which the components are connected side by side. The current flowing in the circuit is shared by the components.

parallel computing or *parallel processing* an emerging computer technology that allows more than one computation at the same time. Currently, this means having a few computer processors working in parallel, but in future the number could run to thousands or millions.

The technique, which involves breaking down computations into small parts and performing thousands of them simultaneously rather than in a linear sequence, offers the prospect of a vast improvement in working speed.

parallel lines and parallel planes in mathematics, straight lines or planes that always remain the same perpendicular distance from one another no matter how far they are extended. This is a principle of Euclidean geometry. Some non-Euclidean geometries,

parallax

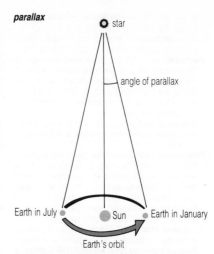

such as elliptical and hyperbolic geometry, however, reject Euclid's parallel axiom.

parallelogram in mathematics, a quadrilateral (four-sided plane figure) with opposite pairs of sides equal in length and parallel, and opposite angles equal. In the special case when all four sides are equal in length, the parallelogram is known as a rhombus, and when the internal angles are right angles, it is a rectangle or square.

The diagonals of a parallelogram bisect each other. Its area is the product of the length of one side and the perpendicular distance between these two parallel sides.

parallelogram of forces in physics and applied mathematics, a method of calculating the resultant (combined effect) of two different forces acting together on an object. Because a force has both magnitude and direction it is a ◊vector quantity and can be represented by a straight line. A second force acting at the same point in a different direction is represented by another line drawn at an angle

parallelogram

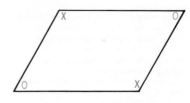

(i) opposite sides & angles are equal

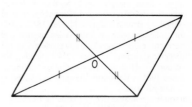

(ii) diagonals bisect each other at 0.

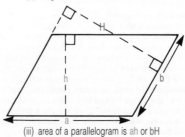

(iii) area of a parallelogram is ah or bH

Paraguay
Republic of
(República del Paraguay)

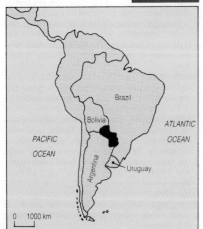

area 406,752 sq km/157,006 sq mi
capital Asunción
town port Concepción
physical mostly flat; divided by river Paraguay; river Paraná in the south
features Itaipú dam on border with Brazil; Gran Chaco plain with huge swamps
head of state and government Andrés Rodríguez from 1989
government military republic

political parties National Republican Association (Colorado Party), right-of-centre; Liberal Party (PL), right-of-centre; Radical Liberal Party (PLR), centrist
exports cotton, soya beans, timber, tung oil, maté
currency guaraní (2177.49 = £1 Feb 1990)
population (1989) 4,518,000 (95% of mixed Guaraní Indian-Spanish descent); annual growth rate 3.0%
life expectancy men 63, women 68
language Spanish (official), spoken by 6%; Guaraní 40%; remainder bilingual
religion Roman Catholic
literacy 91% male/85% female (1985 est)
GDP $5.6 bn (1983); $1,614 per head of population
chronology
1811 Independent from Spain.
1865–70 At war with Argentina, Brazil, and Uruguay. Much territory lost.
1932–35 Much territory won from Bolivia during the Chaco War.
1940–48 Gen Higino Morinigo president.
1948–54 Political instability with six different presidents.
1954 Gen Alfredo Stroessner seized power. He was subsequently re-elected seven times, despite increasing opposition and accusations of human-rights violations.
1989 Stroessner ousted in coup led by Gen Andrés Rodríguez. Rodríguez and the Colorado Party won presidential and congressional elections.

to the first. By completing the parallelogram (of which the two lines are sides) a diagonal may be drawn from the original angle to the opposite corner to represent the resultant force vector.

paralysis loss of voluntary movement due to failure of nerve impulses to reach the muscles involved. It may result from almost any disorder of the nervous system, including brain or spinal-cord injury, stroke, and progressive conditions such as tumour or multiple sclerosis.

Infantile paralysis is an old-fashioned term for ◊polio; *paralysis agitans* is ◊Parkinson's disease.

Paramaribo /ˌpærə'mærɪbəʊ/ port and capital of Suriname, South America, 24 km/15 mi from the sea on the river Surinam; population (1980) 193,000. Products include coffee, fruit, timber, and bauxite. It was founded by the French on an Indian village 1540, made capital of British Surinam 1650, and placed under Dutch rule 1816.

Paramount Studios US film production and distribution company, founded 1912 as the Famous Players Film Company by Adolph Zukor (1873–1976). In 1914 it merged with the distribution company Paramount Pictures. A major studio from the silent days of cinema, Paramount was adept at discovering new talent and Cecil B de Mille made many of his films for the studio. Despite its success, the company was often in financial trouble and in 1966 was taken over by Gulf and Western Industries. In recent years it has produced such successful films as *Grease* 1978 and *Raiders of the Lost Ark* 1981.

Paraná /ˌpærə'nɑː/ river in South America, formed by the confluence of the Rio Grande and Paranaiba; the Paraguay joins it at Corrientes, and it flows into the Rio de la Plata with the Uruguay; length 4,500 km/2,800 mi. It is used for hydroelectric power by Argentina, Brazil, and Paraguay.

Paraná /ˌpærə'nɑː/ industrial port (flour mills, meat canneries) and capital of Entre Rios province in E Argentina, on the Paraná river, 560 km/350 mi NW of Buenos Aires; population (1980) 160,000.

paranoia mental disorder marked by a single-channelled delusion, for example, that the patient is someone of great importance or the subject of a conspiracy.

paraplegia paralysis of the lower limbs, usually due to spinal injury.

parapsychology study of phenomena, for example, extra-sensory perception, which are not within (Greek *para* 'beyond') the range explicable by established science. The faculty allegedly responsible for them, and common to humans and other animals, is known as *psi*.

Parapsychological phenomena include: *mediumship*, supposed contact with the spirits of the dead, usually via an intermediate 'guide' in the other world; *precognition*, foreknowledge of events, as in 'second sight'; *telekinesis*, movement of objects from one position to another by human mental concentration; and *telepathy*, a term coined by British essayist Myers (1843–1901) for 'communication of impressions of any kind from one mind to another, independently of the recognized channels of sense'. Most scientists are sceptical, but a chair of parapsychology was established 1984 at Edinburgh University, endowed by Arthur ◊Koestler.

paraquat a non-selective herbicide (1,1-dimethyl-4,4-dipyridylium). Although quickly degraded by soil microorganisms, it is deadly to human beings if ingested.

parasite an organism that lives on or in another organism (called the 'host'), feeding on the host without immediately killing it, and dependent on it to some degree. Parasites that live inside the host, such as liver flukes and tapeworms, are called *endoparasites*; those that live on the outside, such as fleas and lice, are called *ectoparasites*.

parathyroid a small ◊endocrine gland. Two parathyroid glands are located behind the ◊thyroid gland of most vertebrates. They secrete parathyroid hormone, which regulates the amount of calcium in the blood.

paratyphoid fever an infective fever, similar to typhoid but milder and less dangerous.

Parcae in Roman mythology, the three Fates of ancient Rome, whose Greek counterparts are the Moirai.

Parc des Princes French sports stadium and home of national rugby union team. It has also staged international association football and is the home for Paris's two senior football teams, Paris St Germain and Racing Club.

It was used for France's first rugby international in 1905. After World War I it fell into disuse but a new stadium was built on the old site and in 1973 it was the venue for international rugby for the first time in more than 50 years.

Paré /'pæreɪ/ Ambroise 1509–1590. French surgeon who introduced modern principles into wound treatment. As a military surgeon, Paré developed new ways of treating wounds and amputations. He abandoned the practice of cauterization (sealing with heat), using balms and soothing lotions instead. He also used ligatures to tie off blood vessels.

His methods greatly reduced the death rate among the wounded. Paré eventually became chief surgeon to Charles IX. He also made important contributions to dentistry and childbirth, and invented an artificial hand.

parenchyma a plant tissue composed of loosely packed, more or less spherical cells, with thin cellulose walls. Although parenchyma often has no specialized function, it is usually present in large amounts, forming a packing or ground tissue. It usually has many intercellular spaces.

parental care in biology, the time and energy spent by a parent in order to rear its offspring to maturity. Among animals, it ranges from the simple provision of a food supply for the young which are abandoned after the eggs are laid (for example, many wasps) to feeding and protection of the young after hatching or birth, as in birds and mammals. In the more social species, parental care may include the teaching of skills, such as female cats teaching their kittens to hunt.

parent governor an elected parent representative on the governing body of a state school. The 1980 ◊Education Act in the UK made it mandatory for all state schools to include parent governors, in line with the existing practice of some local education authorities. The 1986 Education Act increased parental representation.

parent–teacher association (PTA) group attached to a school consisting of parents and teachers who support the school by fund raising. In the UK, PTAs are organized into a national federation, the National Confederation of PTAs, which increasingly acts as a pressure group for state schools.

Pareto /pə'reɪtəʊ/ Vilfredo 1848–1923. Italian economist and political philosopher, born in Paris. He produced the first account of society as a self-regulating and interdependent system that operates independently of human attempts at voluntary control. A vigorous opponent of socialism and liberalism, Pareto justified inequality of income on the grounds of his empirical observation (*Pareto's*

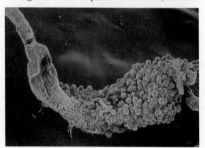

parasite *False-colour electron microscope view of the stomach of a female* Anopheles *mosquito infected with the malaria parasite* Plasmodium. *The parasites eventually spread to the salivary gland and are transmitted to humans when the mosquito takes a blood meal.*

law) that income distribution remained constant whatever efforts were made to change it.

A founder of welfare economics, he put forward a concept of 'optimality' which contends that optimum conditions exist in an economic system if no-one can be made better off without at least one other person becoming worse off.

Paris /'pærɪs/ port and capital of France, on the River Seine; *département* in the Île de France region; area 105 sq km/40.5 sq mi; population (1982, metropolitan area) 8,707,000. Products include metal, leather, and luxury goods; chemicals, glass, and tobacco. The Champs-Élysées leading to the Arc de Triomphe, the Place de la Concorde, and the Eiffel Tower are among the city's features. Paris was the centre of the revolutions of 1789–94, 1830, and 1848.

Paris /'pærɪs/ in Greek legend, a prince of Troy whose abduction of Helen, wife of King Menelaus of Sparta, caused the Trojan war.

Paris /'pærɪs/ Henri d'Orléans, Comte de Paris 1908– . Head of the royal house of France. He served in the Foreign Legion under an assumed name 1939–40, and in 1950, on the repeal of the *loi d'exil* 1886 banning pretenders to the French throne, returned to live in France.

Paris /'pærɪs/ Matthew *c.* 1200–1259. English chronicler. He entered St Albans Abbey 1217, and wrote a history of England up to 1259.

Paris Club an international forum dating from the 1950s for the rescheduling of debts granted or guaranteed by official bilateral creditors; it has no fixed membership nor an institutional structure. In the 1980s it has been closely involved in seeking solutions to the serious debt crises affecting many developing countries.

Paris Commune two periods of government in France:

The Paris municipal government 1789–94 was established after the storming of the Bastille, and remained powerful in the French Revolution until the fall of Robespierre 1794.

The provisional national government 18 Mar–May 1871 was formed while Paris was besieged by the Germans. It consisted of socialists and left-wing republicans, and is often considered the first socialist government in history. Elected after the right-wing National Assembly at Versailles tried to disarm the National Guard, it fell when the Versailles troops captured Paris and massacred 20,000–30,000 people 21–28 May.

parish the smallest territorial subdivision in Christian church administration, served by a parish church.

Its origins lay in early medieval Italian cities, and by the 12th century, most of Christian Europe was divided into parishes. The parish has often been the centre of community life, especially in rural areas.

parish council unit of local government in England and Wales, based on church parishes. In Wales they are commonly called *community councils*.

They provide and maintain monuments, playing fields, footpaths, and churchyards, administer local charities, may impose a limited local rate, are elected every four years and function in parishes of 200 or more electors. Parish councils were established by the Local Government Act 1894, but most of their legal powers were abolished by the 1972 Local Government Act.

Paris-Plage /pæ'riː'plɑːʒ/ fashionable resort in Nord-Pas-de-Calais region, N France, adjoining ◊Le Touquet.

Paris, Treaty of any of various peace treaties signed in Paris; they include:

1763 ending the ◊Seven Years' War
1783 recognizing ◊American Independence
1814 and *1815* following the abdication and final defeat of ◊Napoleon I
1856 ending the ◊Crimean War
1898 ending the ◊Spanish-American War
1919–20 the conference preparing the Treaty of ◊Versailles at the end of World War I was held in Paris

Paris *(Top left) the Pompidou Centre of art and culture (1977). (Top right) the Basilica of Sacré Coeur (1919).*

1946 after World War II the peace treaties between the ◊Allies and Italy, Romania, Hungary, Bulgaria, and Finland

1973 concluding the ◊Vietnam War.

parity in economics, equality of price, rate of exchange, wages, and buying power. Parity ratios may be used in the setting of wages to establish similar status to different work groups. Parity in international exchange rates means that those on a par with each other share similar buying power. In the USA, agricultural output prices are regulated by a parity system.

parity the state of a number, being either even or odd. In computing, a parity ◊bit is sometimes added to numbers to help ensure accuracy. The bit is chosen so that the total number of 1s, including the extra bit, is always of the same parity.

Park /pɑːk/ Merle 1937– . British ballerina, born in Rhodesia. She joined Sadler's Wells 1954, and by 1959 was a principal soloist with the Royal Ballet. She combined elegance with sympathetic appeal in such roles as Cinderella.

Park /pɑːk/ Mungo 1771–1806. Scottish surgeon and explorer. He traced the course of the Niger 1795–97 and probably drowned during a second

expedition in 1805–06. He published *Travels in the Interior of Africa* 1799.

Park Chung Hee /ˈpɑːk ˌtʃʊŋˈhiː/ 1917–1979. President of South Korea 1963–79. Under his rule South Korea had the world's fastest-growing economy and the wealth was widely distributed, but recession and his increasing authoritarianism led to his assassination 1979.

Parker /ˈpɑːkə/ 'Charlie', 'Bird', 'Yardbird' (Charles Christopher) 1920–1955. US alto saxophonist and jazz composer, associated with the trumpeter Dizzy Gillespie in developing the bebop style. His mastery of improvisation inspired performers on all jazz instruments.

Parker /ˈpɑːkə/ Dorothy (born Rothschild) 1893–1967. US writer and wit. She reviewed for the magazines *Vanity Fair* and the *New Yorker*, and wrote wittily ironic verses, collected in several volumes including *Not So Deep As a Well* 1940, and short stories.

Parker /ˈpɑːkə/ Matthew 1504–1575. English cleric. He was converted to Protestantism at Cambridge. He received high preferment under Henry VIII and Edward VI, and as archbishop of Canterbury from 1559 was largely responsible for the Elizabethan religious settlement (the formal establishment of the Church of England).

Parkes /pɑːks/ the site in New South Wales of the Australian National Radio Astronomy Observatory, featuring a radio telescope of 64 m/210 ft aperture, run by the Commonwealth Scientific and Industrial Research Organization.

Parkes /pɑːks/ Henry 1815–1896. Australian politician, born in the UK. He promoted education and the cause of federation, and suggested the official name 'Commonwealth of Australia'. He was five times premier of New South Wales 1872–91. Parkes, New South Wales, is named after him.

Parkinson /ˈpɑːkɪnsən/ Cecil (Edward) 1931– . British Conservative politician. He was chair of the party 1981–83, and became minister for trade and industry, but resigned Oct 1984 following disclosure of an affair with his secretary. In 1987 he rejoined the cabinet as secretary of state for energy, and in 1989 became the transport secretary.

Parkinson /ˈpɑːkɪnsən/ Cyril Northcote 1909– . British historian, celebrated for his study of public and business administration *Parkinson's Law* 1958, which included the dictum: 'Work expands to fill the time available for its completion.'

Parkinson /ˈpɑːkɪnsən/ James 1755–1824. British neurologist, who first described Parkinson's disease.

Parkinson's disease or *Parkinsonism, paralysis agitans* a degenerative disease of the brain characterized by slowness and loss of mobility, muscular rigidity, tremor, and speech difficulties. It is a progressive condition, mainly seen in people over the age of 50.

Parkinson's disease destroys a group of cells called the *substantia nigra* ('black substance') in the upper part of the ◊brainstem. These cells are concerned with the production of a neurotransmitter known as dopamine, which is essential to the control of voluntary movement. It is the almost total loss of these cells, and of their chemical product, which produces such disabling effects. The introduction of ◊L-dopa in the 1960s seemed at first the answer to Parkinson's disease. However, it became obvious that long-term use of the drug brings considerable problems. At best, it postpones the terminal phase of the disease. Brain grafts with dopamine-producing cells were pioneered in the early 1980s, and recently there have been attempts to graft Parkinson's patients with fetal brain tissue. In 1989 a large US study showed that the drug deprenyl may slow the rate at which disability progresses in patients with early Parkinson's disease.

Parkman /ˈpɑːkmən/ Francis 1823–1893. US historian and traveller, whose work chronicles the European exploration and conquest of North America, in such books as *The California and Oregon Trail* 1849 and *La Salle and the Discovery of the Great West* 1879.

Parkman viewed the defeat by England of the French at Québec 1759 (described in his *Montcalm and Wolfe* 1884) as the turning point of North American history, insofar as it swung the balance of power in North America towards the British colonies which would form the USA.

Paris Commune *Scenes of destruction under the provisional socialist government. This statue of Napoleon had been on top of the Column Vendôme.*

Parker *A virtuoso on the alto saxophone, Charlie Parker was able to improvise on any theme, from traditional ballads and lullabies to rhythmic blues numbers such as 'Now's the Time', 'Chi Chi', and 'Parker's Mood'.*

parliament the legislative body of a country. The world's oldest parliament is the Icelandic Althing from about 930. The UK parliament is usually dated from 1265. The Supreme Soviet of the USSR, with 1,500 members, may be the world's largest legislature.

In the UK, Parliament is the supreme legislature, comprising the House of Commons and the House of Lords. There are 650 Members of Parliament in the commons, each representing a geographical constituency. The origins of Parliament are in the 13th century, but its powers were not established until the late 17th century. The powers of the Lords were curtailed 1911, and the duration of parliaments was fixed at five years, but any parliament may extend its own life, as happened during both world wars. It meets in the Palace of Westminster, London.

history Parliament originated under the Norman kings as the Great Council of royal tenants-in-chief, to which in the 13th century representatives of the shires were sometimes summoned. The parliament summoned by Simon de Montfort 1265 (as head of government in the Barons' War) set a precedent by including representatives of the boroughs as well as the shires. Under Edward III the burgesses and knights of the shires began to meet separately from the barons, thus forming the House of Commons.

By the 15th century Parliament had acquired the right to legislate, vote, and appropriate supplies, examine public accounts, and impeach royal ministers. The powers of Parliament were much diminished under the Yorkists and Tudors but under Elizabeth I a new spirit of independence appeared.

The revolutions of 1640 and 1688 established parliamentary control over the executive and judiciary, and finally abolished all royal claim to tax or legislate without parliamentary consent. During these struggles the two great parties (Whig and Tory) emerged, and after 1688 it became customary for the sovereign to choose ministers from the party dominant in the Commons.

The English Parliament was united with the Scottish 1707, and with the Irish 1801–1922. The franchise was extended to the middle classes 1832, to the urban working classes 1867, to agricultural labourers 1884, and to women 1918 and 1928. The duration of parliaments was fixed at three years 1694, at seven 1716, and at five 1911. Payment of MPs was introduced 1911.

The *House of Lords* comprises the *temporal peers*: all hereditary peers of England created to 1707, all hereditary peers of Great Britain created 1707–1800, and all hereditary peers of the UK from 1801 onwards; all hereditary Scottish peers (under the Peerage Act 1963); all peeresses in their own right (under the same act); all life peers (both the ◊law lords and those created under the Life Peerages Act 1958); and the *spiritual peers*: the two archbishops and 24 of the bishops (London, Durham, and Winchester by right, and the rest by seniority). Since the Parliament Act 1911 the powers of the Lords have been restricted in that they may delay a bill passed by the Commons but not reject it. The Lords are presided over by the Lord Chancellor.

The *House of Commons* is presided over by the Speaker. Constituencies are kept under continuous review by the Parliamentary Boundary Commissions 1944. Proceedings in the House of Commons were televised from Nov 1989.

A *public bill* that has been passed is an ◊act of Parliament.

parliamentary paper in UK politics, an official document, such as a White Paper or report of a select committee, which is prepared for the information of Members of Parliament.

Parliament, European governing body of the European Community; see ◊European Parliament.

Parliament, Houses of the building where the UK legislative assembly meets. The present Houses of Parliament in London, designed in Gothic Revival style by the architects Charles Barry and A W Pugin, were built 1840–60, the previous building

having burned down 1834. It incorporates portions of the medieval Palace of Westminster.

The Commons debating chamber was destroyed by incendiary bombs 1941: the rebuilt chamber (opened 1950) is the work of G G Scott and preserves its former character.

Parma /ˈpɑːmə/ city in Emilia-Romagna, N Italy; industries (food processing, textiles, engineering); population (1988) 175,000. Founded by the Etruscans, it was the capital of the duchy of Parma 1545–1860. It has given its name to Parmesan cheese.

Parmenides /pɑːˈmenɪdiːz/ *c.*510–450 BC. Greek pre-Socratic philosopher, head of the Eleatic school (so called after Elea in S Italy). Against Heraclitus's doctrine of Becoming, Parmenides advanced the view that nonexistence was impossible, that everything was permanently in a state of being. Despite evidence of the senses to the contrary, motion and change is illusory, in fact, logically impossible, because it would imply a contradiction. Parmenides saw speculation and reason as more important than the evidence of the senses.

Parmigianino /ˈpɑːrmənʤɪnə/ Francesco 1503–1540. Italian painter and etcher, active in Parma and elsewhere. He painted religious subjects and portraits in a Mannerist style, with elongated figures.

Parnassiens, Les /ˌpɑːnæsˈjæŋ/ school of French poets including Leconte de Lisle, Mallarmé, and Verlaine, which flourished 1866–76. Named from the review *Parnasse Contemporain*, it advocated 'art for art's sake' in opposition to the ideas of the Romantics.

Parnassus /pɑːˈnæsəs/ mountain in central Greece; height 2,457 m/8,064 ft, revered as the abode of Apollo and the Muses. Delphi lies on its southern flank.

Parnell /pɑːˈnel/ Charles Stewart 1846–1891. Irish nationalist politician. He supported a policy of obstruction and violence to attain Home Rule, and became the president of the Nationalist Party 1877. In 1879 he approved the ◊Land League, and his attitude led to his imprisonment 1881. His career was ruined 1890 when he was cited as co-respondent in a divorce case.

Parnell, born in County Wicklow, was elected Member of Parliament for Meath 1875. He welcomed Gladstone's ◊Home Rule Bill, and continued his agitation after its defeat 1886. In 1887 his reputation suffered from an unfounded accusation by *The Times* of complicity in the murder of Lord Frederick ◊Cavendish. Three years later came the adultery scandal, and for fear of losing the support of Gladstone, Parnell's party deposed him.

parody in literature and the other arts, a work that imitates the style of another work, usually with mocking or comic intent; it is related to ◊satire.

Parr /pɑː/ Catherine 1512–1548. Sixth wife of Henry VIII of England. She had already lost two husbands when in 1543 she married Henry VIII. She survived him, and in 1547 married Lord Seymour of Sudeley (1508–49).

Parramatta /ˌpærəˈmætə/ river, W arm of Port Jackson, New South Wales, Australia. It is 24 km/15 mi long and is lined with industrial suburbs of Sydney: Balmain, Drummoyne, Concord, Parramatta, Ermington and Rydalmere, Ryde, and Hunter's Hill.

parrot bird of the order Psittaciformes, abundant in the tropics, especially in Australia and South America. The smaller species are commonly referred to as parakeets. They are mainly vegetarian, and range in size from the 8.5 cm/3.5 in pygmy parrot to the 100 cm/40 in Amazon parrot. The plumage is very colourful, and the call is commonly a harsh screech. The talent for imitating human speech is marked in the grey parrot *Psittacus erithacus* of Africa.

Several species are endangered. One of the rarest is the imperial parrot, found only in Dominica in the Caribbean, which is threatened by deforestation. In 1986, 600,000 parrots were caught and sold.

Parry /ˈpæri/ Charles Hubert Hastings 1848–1918. English composer. His works include songs, motets,

Parnell As chair of the Home Rule party and militant campaigner for Irish self-government, Parnell earned the nickname of 'uncrowned king of Ireland'.

and the setting of Milton's 'Blest Pair of Sirens' and Blake's 'Jerusalem'.

Parry /ˈpæri/ William Edward 1790–1855. English admiral and Arctic explorer. He made detailed charts during explorations of the Northwest Passage 1819–20, 1821–23, and 1824–25. He made an attempt to reach the North Pole 1827. The Parry Islands, Northwest Territories, Canada, are named after him.

parsec in astronomy, a unit used for distances to stars and galaxies. One parsec is equal to 3.2617 ◊light years, 2.063 × 10⁵ ◊astronomical units, and 3.086 × 10¹³ km.

It is the distance at which a star would have a ◊parallax (apparent shift in position) of one second of arc when viewed from two points the same distance apart as the Earth's distance from the Sun.

Parsee or *Parsi* a follower of the religion ◊Zoroastrianism. The Parsees fled from Persia after its conquest by the Arabs, and settled in India in the 8th century AD. About 100,000 Parsees now live mainly in Bombay State.

Parsifal in Germanic legend, the father of ◊Lohengrin and one of the knights who sought the Holy Grail.

parsley biennial herb *Petroselinum crispum*, cultivated for flavouring. Up to 45 cm/1.5 ft high, it has pinnate, aromatic leaves and yellow umbelliferous flowers.

parsnip temperate Eurasian biennial *Pastinaca sativa*, family Umbelliferae, with a fleshy edible root.

Parsons /ˈpɑːsənz/ Charles Algernon 1854–1931. English engineer who invented the Parsons steam ◊turbine 1884, a landmark in marine engineering and later universally used in electricity generation (to drive an alternator).

Parsons /ˈpɑːsənz/ Talcott 1902–1979. US sociologist, who attempted to integrate all the social sciences into a science of human action. He was professor of sociology at Harvard University from

Parr Portrait of Catherine Parr by an unknown artist (c.1545), National Portrait Gallery, London.

parrot

grey parrot

1931 until his death, and author of over 150 books and articles. His theory of structural functionalism dominated US sociology from the 1940s to the 1960s, and as an attempt to explain social order and individual behaviour it was a major step in establishing sociology as an academic and scientific discipline.

part. in grammar, the abbreviation for ◊*participle*.

parthenocarpy in botany, the formation of fruits without seeds. This phenomenon, of no obvious benefit to the plant, occurs naturally in some plants, such as bananas. It can also be induced in some fruit crops, either by breeding or by applying certain plant hormones.

parthenogenesis the development of an ovum (egg) without any genetic contribution from a male. Parthenogenesis is the normal means of reproduction in some plants (for example, dandelions) and animals (for example, certain fish). Some sexually reproducing species, such as aphids, show parthenogenesis at some stage in their life cycle.

In most cases, there is no fertilization at all, but in a few the stimulus of being fertilized by a sperm is needed to initiate development, although the male's chromosomes are not absorbed into the nucleus of the ovum. Parthenogenesis can be artificially induced in many animals (such as rabbits) by cooling, pricking, or applying acid to an egg.

Parthenon /ˈpɑːθənɒn/ temple of Athena Parthenos ('the Virgin') on the Acropolis at Athens; built 447–438 BC under the supervision of Phidias, and the most perfect example of Doric architecture (by Callicrates and Ictinus). In turn a Christian church and Turkish mosque, it was then used as a gunpowder store, and reduced to ruins when the Venetians bombarded the Acropolis 1687. Greek sculptures from the Parthenon were removed by Lord Elgin in the early 19th century; popularly known as the ◊Elgin marbles.

parsley

flower

seed heads

Parthia /ˈpɑːθɪə/ ancient country in W Asia in what is now NE Iran, capital Ctesiphon. Originating about 248 BC, it reached the peak of its power under Mithridates I in the 2nd century BC, and was annexed to Persia under the Sassanids AD 226. Parthian horsemen feigned retreat and shot their arrows unexpectedly backwards, hence 'Parthian shot', a remark delivered in parting.

participle a form of the verb, in English either a *present participle* ending in -*ing* (for example, 'working' in 'They were working', 'working men', and 'a hard-working team') or a *past participle* ending in -*ed* in regular verbs (for example, 'train*ed*' in 'They have been trained well', 'trained soldiers', and 'a well-trained team').

In irregular verbs the past participle has a special form (for example, drive/*driven*; light/*lit*, burn/*burned, burnt*). The participle is also used to open such constructions as 'Coming down the stairs, she paused and...' and 'Angered by the news, he...'. Such constructions, when not logically formed, have amusing or ambiguous results. 'Driving along a country road, a stone broke my windscreen' suggests that the stone was driving along the road. This illogical usage is a **misrelated participle**; a **dangling** or **hanging participle** has nothing at all to relate to: 'While driving along a country road there was a loud noise under the car.' Such sentences need to be completely reexpressed, except in some well-established usages where the participle can stand alone (for example, 'Taking all things into consideration, your actions were justified').

particle physics the study of elementary particles that make up all atoms. Atoms are made up of positively charged protons and, except for hydrogen, neutrons (which have no charge) in the nucleus, surrounded by negatively charged electrons. Nuclei do not split apart easily; they usually need to be bombarded by particles such as protons, raised to very high kinetic energies by particle accelerators.

Pioneering research took place at the Cavendish laboratory, Cambridge, England. In 1895, J J Thomson discovered that all atoms contain identical, negatively charged particles (**electrons**) which could easily be freed. By 1913, Rutherford had shown that electrons surround a very small, positively charged **nucleus**, thus, the nucleus of a hydrogen atom consists of a single positively charged particle, a **proton** (identified by Chadwick in 1932). The nuclei of other elements are made up of protons and uncharged particles called **neutrons**.

1932 also saw the discovery of a particle, predicted by ◊Dirac, with the mass of an electron, but an equal and opposite charge—the *positron*. This was the first example of an **antiparticle**; it is now believed that almost all particles have corresponding antiparticles. The following year, ◊Pauli argued that a hitherto unsuspected particle must accompany electrons in beta-emission; the so-called **electron-neutrino**. Neutrino radiation is extremely penetrating.

particles and fundamental forces By the mid-1930s, four fundamental kinds of ◊force had been identified. The **electromagnetic force** acts between all particles with electric charge, and was

Parthenon The west front of the Parthenon, on the Acropolis in Athens, Greece.

throught to be related to the exchange between the particles of **photons**, packets of electromagnetic radiation. The **strong force** (holding quarks together to form protons and neutrons, and binding these particles together inside the nucleus) is transmitted by the exchange of particles called **gluons** between quarks and antiquarks. Theoretical work on the **weak force** (responsible for beta radioactivity of the Sun) began with ◊Fermi in the 1930s; current theory suggests the exchange during weak interactions of **W** and **Z particles** with masses some 100 times that of the proton. The existence of W and Z particles was confirmed in 1983 at ◊CERN. The fourth fundamental force, **gravity**, is experienced by all particles; the projected go-between particles have been dubbed **gravitons**.

leptons and quarks The electron and electron neutrinos are examples of **leptons**—particles with half-integral spin that 'feel' the weak, but not the strong force. There are known to be two more electron-like leptons plus their neutrinos: the **muon** (found by US physicist Carl Anderson in cosmic radiation in 1937), and the **tauon**, a surprise discovery of the 1970s.

hadrons (particles that 'feel' the strong force) started to turn up in bewildering profusion in experiments in the 1950s and 1960s. They are classified into ◊**mesons**, with whole-number or zero spins, and **baryons**, with half-integral spins. It was shown in the early 1960s that if hadrons of the same spin are represented as points on suitable charts, simple patterns are formed. This symmetry enabled a hitherto unknown particle, the **omega-minus**, to be predicted from a gap in one of the patterns; it duly turned up in experiments. In 1964, Gell-Mann and Zweig suggested that all hadrons were built from just three types or **flavours** of a new particle with half-integral spin and charge of magnitude either $1/3$ or $2/3$ that of an electron, which Gell-Mann christened the **quark**. Mesons are quark–antiquark pairs (spins either add to 1 or cancel to zero) and baryons are quark triplets. To account for new mesons such as the **psi** the number of quark flavours had risen to six by 1985.

particle, subatomic a particle that is smaller than an ◊atom. The ◊proton, ◊electron, and ◊neutrino are the only stable particles. The ◊neutron is stable only when in the atomic nucleus. Over 200 other unstable particles are known from experiments with particle ◊accelerators and ◊cosmic radiation. All decay rapidly into other particles and are characterized by such properties as their mass, charge, spin, and lifetime. Particles that are influenced by the 'strong' nuclear force are known as hadrons. These are divided into heavy particles, baryons, which include the proton and neutron, and intermediate-mass particles, mesons. Light particles that are influenced by the 'weak' nuclear force are known as leptons.

particle, subatomic The drift chamber of the Mark II particle detector at the Stanford Linear Accelerator centre in California, which allows physicists to study the tracks of subatomic particles.

partisan member of an armed group that operates behind enemy lines or in occupied territories during wars. The name 'partisans' was first given to armed bands of Russians who operated against Napoleon's army in Russia during 1812, but has since been used to describe Russian, Yugoslav, and Polish ◊Resistance groups against the Germans during World War II.

Partisan Review US intellectual and literary magazine, founded 1934 to express Marxist principles. In the later 1930s it departed from the orthodox line, committed itself to Modernist literature, and during the 1950s printed many of the major writers and critics of the time, including Saul Bellow, Mary McCarthy, and Lionel Trilling (1905–75).

partnership in English law, two or more persons carrying on a common business for shared profit. The business can be of any kind, for instance solicitors, shop owners or window cleaners. A partnership differs from a limited company in that the individuals remain separate in identity and are not protected by limited liability, so that each partner is personally responsible for any debts of the partnership. Absolute mutual trust is therefore essential.

part of speech a category of words, as defined in the ◊grammar of Western languages which has described Greek and Latin over the centuries since classical times. The 'part of speech' of a word is its grammatical function. The four major parts of speech are the ◊noun, ◊verb, ◊adjective, and ◊adverb; the minor parts of speech vary according to schools of grammatical theory, but include the ◊article, ◊conjunction, ◊preposition, and ◊pronoun.

In languages like Greek and Latin the part of speech of a word tends to be invariable (usually marked by an ending or inflection); in English, it is much harder to recognize the function of a word simply by its form. Some English words may have only one function (for example, *and* as a conjunction). Others, however, may have several functions (for example, *fancy*, which is a noun in the phrase 'flights of fancy', a verb in 'Fancy that!', and an adjective in 'a fancy hat').

partridge gamebird of the family Phasianidae which includes pheasants and quail. Two species common in the UK are the grey partridge *Perdix perdix*, with mottled brown back, grey speckled breast, and patches of chestnut on the sides, and the French partridge *Alectoris rufa*, distinguished by its red legs, bill, and eyelids. The back is plain brown, the throat white edged with black, and the sides barred chestnut and black.

Partridge /'pɑːtrɪdʒ/ Eric 1894–1979. New Zealand lexicographer. He studied at Oxford University after serving in World War I and settled in England to write a number of dictionaries including *A Dictionary of Slang and Unconventional English* 1934 and 1970, and *Dictionary of the Underworld, British and American* 1950.

Parvati in Hindu mythology, the consort of Siva in one of her gentler manifestations, and the mother of Ganesa; she is said to be the daughter of the Himalayas.

parvenu (French 'arrived') a social upstart.

Pasadena /,pæsə'diːnə/ city in SW California, USA, part of the ◊Los Angeles conurbation; population (1980) 118,500. On 1 Jan the East–West football game is held here in the 85,000-seat Rose Bowl. The California Institute of Technology (Caltech) owns the Hale Observatories (which include the Mount Palomar telescope) and is linked with the Jet Propulsion Laboratories.

PASCAL a high-level computer-programming language. Designed by Niklaus Wirth (1934–) in the 1960s as an aid to teaching programming, it is still widely used as such in universities, but is also recognized as a good general-purpose programming language.

pascal SI unit (symbol Pa) of pressure, equal to 1 newton per square metre. It replaces ◊bars and millibars (10^5 Pa = 1 bar). It is named after the French scientist Blaise Pascal.

Pascal's triangle

```
                    1
                 1     1
              1     2     1
           1     3     3     1
        1     4     6     4     1
     1     5    10    10     5     1
  1     6    15    20    15     6     1
1     7    21    35    35    21     7     1
```

Pascal /'pæskæl/ Blaise 1623–1662. French philosopher and mathematician. He contributed to the development of hydraulics, the ◊calculus, and the mathematical theory of ◊probability.

In mathematics, Pascal is known for his work on conic sections and, with Pierre de Fermat, the probability theory. In physics, Pascal's chief work concerned fluid pressure and hydraulics. ***Pascal's principle*** states that the pressure everywhere in a fluid is the same, so that pressure applied at one point is transmitted equally to all parts of the container. This is the principle of the hydraulic press and jack.

Pascal's triangle is a triangular array of numbers in which each number is the sum of the pair of numbers above it. Plotted at equal distances along a horizontal axis, the numbers in the rows give the binomial probability distribution with equal probability of success and failure, such as when tossing fair coins.

In 1654, he went into the ◊Jansenist monastery of Port Royal and defended the Jansenists against the ◊Jesuits in his *Lettres Provinciales* 1656. His *Pensées* 1670 was part of an unfinished defence of the Christian religion.

Pas-de-Calais /,pɑːdə'kæleɪ/ French name for the ◊Strait of Dover and of the French *département* bordering it, of which Arras is the capital and Calais the chief port. See also ◊Nord-Pas-de-Calais.

pas de deux a dance for two performers. A *grand pas de deux* is danced by the prima ballerina and the premier danseur.

Pashto or *Pushtu* an Indo-European language, officially that of Afghanistan, and also spoken in another dialect in N Pakistan.

Pasiphae in Greek mythology, wife of ◊Minos and mother of ◊Phaedra and of the ◊Minotaur, the offspring of her sexual union with a bull sent from the sea by the god ◊Poseidon.

Pasmore /'pɑːsmɔː/ Victor 1908– . British painter, a member of the Euston Road School in the 1930s. He painted landscapes and, from 1947, abstract paintings and constructions (reviving the early ideas of the Constructivists).

Pasolini /,pæsə'liːni/ Pier Paolo 1922–1975. Italian poet, novelist, and film director, an influential figure of the post-war years. His writings (making much use of first Friulan and later Roman dialect) include the novels *Ragazzi di vita*/*The Ragazzi* 1955 and *Una vita violenta*/*A Violent Life* 1959. Among his films are *Il vangelo secondo Mateo*/*The Gospel According to St Matthew* 1964 and *I racconti de Canterbury*/*The Canterbury Tales* 1972.

Many of his works are coloured by his experience of life in the poor districts of Rome, where he lived from 1950, and illustrate the decadence and inequality of society from his Marxist viewpoint.

pasque flower plant *Pulsatilla vulgaris* of the buttercup family. A low-growing hairy perennial, it has feathery leaves and large purple bell-shaped flowers which start erect then droop. Found in Europe and Asia, it is characteristic of grassland on limy soil.

Passau /'pæsaʊ/ town in SE Bavaria, West Germany, at the junction of the Inn and Ilz with the Danube. The *Treaty of Passau* 1552 between Maurice, elector of Saxony, and the future emperor Ferdinand I allowed the Lutherans full religious liberty, and prepared the way for the Peace of Augsburg: see ◊Reformation.

Passchendaele /'pæʃəndeɪl/ village in W Flanders, Belgium, near Ypres. The Passchendaele ridge

---

before Ypres was the object of a costly and unsuccessful British offensive in World War I, July–Nov 1917; British casualties numbered nearly 400,000.

passé (French) out of date.

Passfield /'pɑːsfiːld/ Baron Passfield title of the Fabian socialist Sidney ◊Webb.

passim (Latin 'in many places') indicates that a reference occurs repeatedly throughout the work.

passion flower climbing plant of the tropical American genus *Passiflora*, family Passifloraceae. It bears distinctive flowerheads comprised of a saucer-shaped petal base, a fringe-like corona and a central stalk bearing the stamens and ovary. Some species produce edible fruit.

passion play play representing the death and resurrection of a god, such as Osiris, Dionysus, or Jesus; it has its origins in medieval ◊mystery plays. Traditionally, a passion play takes place every ten years at ◊Oberammergau, West Germany.

Pass Laws South African laws that required the black population to carry passbooks (identity documents) at all times and severely restricted freedom of movement. The laws, a major cause of discontent, formed a central part of the policies of ◊apartheid. They were repealed 1986.

Passover in Judaism, a spring festival, dating from ancient times, which commemorates the exodus from Egypt.

passport document issued by a government authorizing the bearer to go abroad and guaranteeing the bearer the state's protection. Some countries require an intending visitor to obtain a special endorsement or visa. From 1978 the member states of the European Community have begun to introduce a common passsport.

Passy /'pæsi/ Frédéric 1822–1912. French economist, who shared the first Nobel peace prize 1901 with J H Dunant. He founded the International League for Permanent Peace 1867, and was co-founder, with the English politician William R Cremer (1828–1908), of the Inter-Parliamentary Conferences on Peace and on Arbitration 1889.

Pasternak /'pæstənæk/ Boris Leonidovich 1890–1960. Russian poet and novelist. His volumes of lyric poems include *A Twin Cloud* 1914, and *On Early Trains* 1943, and he translated Shakespeare's tragedies. His novel ◊*Dr Zhivago* 1957, was followed by a Nobel prize (which he declined).

Pasteur /'pæstɜː/ Louis 1822–1895. French chemist and microbiologist who discovered that fermentation was caused by microorganisms. He also developed a vaccine for ◊rabies, which led to the foundation of the Institut Pasteur in Paris 1888.

Pasteur saved the French silkworm industry by identifying two microbial diseases that were decimating the worms. He discovered the pathogens responsible for ◊anthrax and chicken cholera, and developed vaccines for these diseases. He inspired his pupil ◊Lister's work in antiseptic surgery. Pasteurization is based on his discoveries. See also ◊food technology.

pasteurization treatment of food to reduce the number of microorganisms it contains and so

Pasteur *French chemist and scientist Louis Pasteur.*

pasteurization

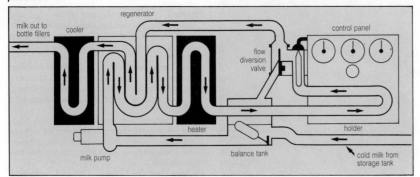

protect consumers from disease. Harmful bacteria are killed and the development of others is delayed. For milk, the method involves heating it to 72°C/161°F for 15 seconds follwed by rapid cooling to 10°C/50°F or lower.

The experiments of Louis Pasteur on wine and beer in the 1850s and 1860s showed how heat treatment slowed the multiplication of bacteria and thereby the process of souring. Pasteurization of milk made headway in the dairy industries of Scandinavia and the USA before 1900 because of the realization that it also killed off bacteria associated with the diseases of tuberculosis, typhoid, diptheria, and dysentery.

In Britain, progress was slower but with encouragement from the 1922 Milk and Dairies Act the number of milk-processing plants gradually increased in the years before the World War II. In the 1990s nearly all liquid milk sold in the UK is heat treated and available in pasteurized, sterilized, or ultra-heat-treated (UHT) form. UHT milk is heated to at least 132°C/269°F for one second to give it a shelf life of several months.

pastiche in the arts, a work which imitates another's style, or a medley composed of fragments from an original. The intention is normally homage, rather than ridicule as in parody.

Paston family family of Norfolk, England, whose correspondence and documents (known as the Paston letters) for 1422–1509 throw valuable light on the period.

pastoral staff a staff shaped like a shepherd's crook carried by Christian cardinals and bishops on certain formal occasions as a sign of office.

past participle see ◊participle.

Patagonia /ˌpætə'gəʊniə/ geographic area of South America, south of latitude 40° S, with sheep farming, and coal and oil resources. Sighted by Magellan 1520, it was claimed by both Argentina and Chile until divided between them 1881.

patchouli soft-wooded shrub *Pogostemon heyneanus*, family Labiateae, source of the perfume patchouli.

Patel Vallabhbhai Jhaverbhai 1875–1950. Indian nationalist politician. A fervent follower of Gandhi, he participated in the Satyagraha (the struggle for Indian independence by nonviolent, noncooperative means) at Kaira 1918, and later became home minister in Nehru's first government after independence.

He was a member of the right wing of the Indian National Congress and supported the conservative opposition to the reform of Hindu law as it applied to the lack of rights of Hindu women.

paten flat dish of gold or silver used in the Christian church for holding the consecrated bread at the Eucharist.

patent or *letters patent* documents conferring the exclusive right to make, use, and sell an invention for a limited period. Ideas are not eligible, neither is anything not new. The earliest known patent for an invention in England is dated 1449 (granted by Henry VI for making stained glass for Eton College).

The London Patent Office protects patents (in the UK only) for 20 years. The European Patent Office (established in Munich, with a branch in The Hague, 1977) grants patents in 16 European countries (protection in each country being the same as provided by its own internal law), also covering designs and trade marks. In the USA the period of patent is only 17 years. In 1987 the USA began issuing patents for new animal forms (new types of livestock and assorted organisms) being created by gene splitting. See also ◊Frankenstein law.

Pater /'peɪtə/ Walter Horatio 1839–1894. English critic. A stylist and supporter of 'art for art's sake', he published *Studies in the History of the Renaissance* 1873, *Marius the Epicurean* 1885, *Imaginary Portraits* 1887, and other works.

Paternoster /ˌpætə'nɒstə/ (Latin 'Our father') in the Roman Catholic Church, the Lord's Prayer. The opening words of the Latin version are *Pater noster*.

Paterson /'pætəsən/ 'Banjo' (Andrew Barton) 1864–1941. Australian journalist, author of volumes of light verse and 'Waltzing Matilda', adapted from a traditional song.

Pathan /pə'tɑːn/ Muslim people of NW Pakistan and Afghanistan. Formerly a constant threat to the British Raj, the Pakistani Pathans now claim independence, with the Afghani Pathans, in their own state of Pakhtoonistan.

Pathé Charles 1863–1957. French film pioneer, who began his career selling projectors in 1896 and with the profits formed Pathé Frères with his brothers. In 1901 he embarked on film production and by 1908 had becomed the world's biggest producer, with branches worldwide. He also developed an early colour process and established a weekly newsreel, *Pathé Journal*. World War I disrupted his enterprises and by 1918 he was gradually forced out of business by foreign competition.

pathetic fallacy the illusion that natural events and objects are controlled by human emotions, so that in some way they express human sorrow or joy. The phrase was invented by John Ruskin in *Modern Painters* describing the ascription of human feelings to the outside world.

pathogen (Greek 'disease producing') in medicine, a bacterium or virus that causes disease. Most pathogens are ◊parasites, and the diseases they cause are incidental to their search for food or shelter inside the host. Nonparasitic organisms, such as soil bacteria or those living in our gut and feeding on waste foodstuffs, can also become pathogenic to a person whose immune system or liver is damaged. The larger parasites that can cause disease, such as nematode worms, are not usually described as pathogens.

pathology the medical specialty concerned with the study of disease processes.

Patiala /ˌpʌti'ɑːlə/ city in E Punjab, India; industries (textile and metalwork); population (1981) 206,254.

Patinir /ˌpɑːti'nɪə/ (also Patenier, Patinier) Joachim c.1485–c.1524. Flemish painter, active in Antwerp, whose inspired landscape backgrounds dominated his religious subjects. He is known to have worked with Matsys and to have painted landscape backgrounds for other artists' works.

Patmore /'pætmɔː/ Coventry 1823–1896. British poet and critic. He was a librarian at the British Museum 1846–66, and as one of the Pre-Raphaelites achieved fame with the poem *The Angel in the House* 1854–63 and the collection of odes *The Unknown Eros* 1877.

Patmos /'pætmɒs/ Greek island in the Aegean, one of the Dodecanese; the chief town is Hora. St John is said to have written the New Testament Book of Revelation while in exile here.

Patna /'pætnə/ capital of Bihar state, India, on the Ganges; population (1981) 916,000. It has remains of a hall built by the emperor Asoka in the 3rd century BC.

Paton /'peɪtn/ Alan 1903–1988. South African writer. His novel *Cry, the Beloved Country* 1948 focused on the racial inequality in South Africa.

Born in Pietermaritzburg, he became first a schoolmaster and in 1935 principal of a reformatory near Johannesburg, which he ran on enlightened lines.

Patou /pæ'tuː/ Jean 1880–1936. French designer of sporting clothes (as worn by Suzanne ◊Lenglen) from 1922 and bias-cut white satin evening dresses 1929; and creator of the perfume Joy 1926.

Patras /'pætrəs/ (Greek *Patrai*) industrial city (hydroelectric installations; textiles and paper) in the NW Peloponnese, Greece, on the Gulf of Patras; population (1981) 141,500. The ancient *Patrae*, it is the only one of the 12 cities of ◊Achaea to survive.

patriarch (Greek 'ruler of a family') in the Old Testament or Hebrew Bible, one of the ancestors of the human race, and especially those of the Jews from Adam to the sons of Jacob. In the Eastern Orthodox Church, the term refers to the leader of a national church.

patricians /pə'trɪʃənz/ privileged class in ancient Rome, descended from the original citizens. After the 4th century BC the rights formerly exercised by the patricians alone were made available to the ◊plebeians, and patrician descent became only a matter of prestige.

Patrick, St /'pætrɪk/ 389–c.461. Patron saint of Ireland. Born in Britain, probably in S Wales, he was carried off by pirates to six years' slavery in Antrim before escaping either to Britain or Gaul—his poor Latin suggests the former—to train as a missionary. He is variously said to have landed again in Ireland 432 or 456, and his work was a vital factor in the spread of Christian influence there. His symbols are snakes and shamrocks; feast day 17 Mar.

Patrick is credited with founding the diocese of Armagh, of which he was bishop, though this was probably the work of a 'lost apostle' (Palladius or Secundinus). Of his writings only his *Confessio* and an *Epistola* survive.

patronage the right of appointment to an office or position in politics and the church; or sponsorship of the arts. In the arts, patronage takes the form of sponsorship or support, formerly by individuals (often royal or noble) or by the church. In this century, patrons have tended to be the state and (increasingly) private industry.

In Britain, where it was nicknamed 'Old Corruption', patronage existed in the 16th century, but was most common from the restoration of 1660 to the 19th century, when it was used to manage elections and ensure party support. Patronage was used not only for the preferment of friends, but also as a means of social justice, often favouring, for example, the families of those in adversity. Political patronage has largely been replaced by a system of meritocracy (in which selection is by open competition rather than by personal recommendation).

Ecclesiastical patronage was the right of selecting a person to a living or benefice, termed an advowson. ***Salaried patronage*** was the nomination to a salaried post: at court, in government, the Church of England, the civil service, the armed services, or to the East India Company. The Northcote-Trevelyan report on the civil service 1854 advised the replacement of patronage in the civil service by open competitive examination, although its recommendations were carried out only later in the century. Commissions in the

British army were bought and sold openly until the practice was abolished in 1871. Church livings were bought and sold as late as 1874.

Patronage survives today in the political honours system (awards granted to party supporters) and the appointment of university professors, leaders of national corporations and government bodies, and so on, which is often by invitation rather than by formal application. Selection on the grounds of justice rather than solely on the basis of ability lives on today with the practice of positive ◊discrimination.

Patten Chris(topher Francis) 1944– . British Conservative politician, environment secretary from 1989. A former director of the Conservative Party research department, he held junior ministerial posts under Margaret Thatcher, despite his reputation of being to the left of the party. Patten's 'green' credentials and presentational skills made him the obvious choice to replace Nicholas Ridley as environment secretary.

Patterson /ˈpætəsən/ Harry 1929– . English novelist, born in Newcastle. He has written many thrillers under his own name, including *Dillinger* 1983, as well as under the pseudonym Jack Higgins, including *The Eagle Has Landed* 1975.

Patti /ˈpæti/ Adelina 1843–1919. Anglo-Italian soprano renowned for her performances of Lucia in *Lucia di Lammermoor* and Amina in *La sonnambula*. At the age of 62 she was persuaded out of retirement to make a number of gramophone recordings, one of the first opera singers to be recorded.

Patton /ˈpætn/ George (Smith) 1885–1945. US general in World War II, known as 'Blood and Guts'. He commanded the 2nd Armoured Division 1940, and in 1942 led the Western Task Force that landed at Casablanca, Morocco. After commanding the 7th Army, he led the 3rd Army across France and into Germany, and in 1945 took over the 15th Army.

Pau /pəʊ/ industrial city (electrochemical and metallurgical) and resort, capital of Pyrénées-Atlantiques *département* in Aquitaine, SW France, near the Spanish border; population (1982) 131,500. It is the centre of the ◊Basque area of France, and there has been guerrilla activity.

Paul /pɔːl/ Elliot Harold 1891–1958. US author. His books include the travel book *The Narrow Street/The Last Time I Saw Paris* 1942.

Paul /pɔːl/ Les. Adopted name of Lester Polfuss 1915– . US inventor of the solid-body electric guitar in the early 1940s, and a pioneer of recording techniques including overdubbing and electronic echo. The **Gibson Les Paul guitar** was first marketed 1952 (the first commercial solid-body guitar was made by Leo ◊Fender). As a guitarist in the late 1940s and the 1950s he recorded with the singer Mary Ford (1928–77).

Paul /pɔːl/ 1901–1964. King of the Hellenes from 1947, when he succeeded his brother George II. He was the son of Constantine I. He married in 1938 Princess Frederika (1917–), daughter of the Duke of Brunswick, whose involvement in politics brought her under attack.

Paul /pɔːl/ six popes, including:

Paul VI, Giovanni Battista Montini 1897–1978. Pope from 1963. His encyclical *Humanae Vitae/Of Human Life* 1968 reaffirmed the church's traditional teaching on birth control, thus following the minority report of the commission originally appointed by Pope John, rather than the majority view.

He was born near Brescia, Italy. He spent more than 25 years in the Secretariat of State under Pius XI and Pius XII before becoming archbishop of Milan in 1954. In 1958 he was created a cardinal by Pope John, and in 1963 he succeeded him as pope, taking the name of Paul as a symbol of ecumenical unity.

Paul I /pɔːl/ 1754–1801. Tsar of Russia from 1796, in succession to his mother Catherine II. Mentally unstable, he pursued an erratic foreign policy, and was assassinated.

Pauli /ˈpaʊli/ Wolfgang 1900–1958. Austrian physicist, who originated *Pauli's exclusion principle*:

Patton *An accomplished fencer, sailor, airplane pilot, and athlete, US general Patton demanded rigorous standards of individual fitness and unit training of his troops during World War II.*

in a given system no two electrons, protons, neutrons, or other elementary particles of half-integrated spin can be characterized by the same set of ◊quantum numbers. He also predicted the existence of neutrinos. He won the Nobel prize 1945 for his work on atomic structure.

Pauling /ˈpɔːlɪŋ/ Linus Carl 1901– . US chemist, noted for his fundamental work on the nature of the chemical bond and on the discovery of the helical structure of many proteins. Nobel Prize for Chemistry 1954. An outspoken opponent of nuclear testing, he also received the Nobel Peace Prize in 1962.

Paulinus /pɔːˈlaɪnəs/ died 644. Roman missionary to Britain who joined St ◊Augustine in Kent 601, converted the Northumbrians 625, and became the first archbishop of York. Excavations 1978 revealed a church he built in Lincoln.

Paul, St /pɔːl/ AD *c.*3–*c.*68. Christian missionary and martyr; in the New Testament, one of the apostles and author of 13 epistles. He is said to have been converted by a vision on the road to Damascus. His emblems are a sword and a book; feast day 29 June.

The Jewish form of his name is Saul. He was born in Tarsus (now in Turkey), son of well-to-do Pharisees, and had Roman citizenship. Originally opposed to Christianity, he took part in the stoning of St Stephen. After his conversion he made great missionary journeys, for example to ◊Philippi and ◊Ephesus, becoming known as the Apostle of the Gentiles (non-Jews). On his return to Jerusalem, he was arrested, appealed to Caesar, and (as a citizen) was sent to Rome for trial about 57 or 59. After two years in prison, he may have been released before his final arrest and execution under the emperor Nero.

St Paul's theology was rigorous on such questions as sin and atonement, and his views on the role of women were adopted by Christian church generally.

Paulus /ˈpaʊlʊs/ Friedrich von 1890–1957. German field marshal in World War II, commander of the forces that besieged Stalingrad (now Volgograd) in the USSR 1942–43; he was captured and gave evidence at the Nuremberg trials before settling in East Germany.

Pausanias /pɔːˈseɪniæs/ 2nd century AD. Greek geographer, author of a valuably accurate description of Greece compiled from his own travels,

Description of Greece, also translated as *Itinerary of Greece*.

Pavarotti /ˌpævəˈrɒti/ Luciano 1935– . Italian tenor, whose operatic roles have included Rodolfo in *La Bohème*, Cavaradossi in *Tosca*, the Duke of Mantua in *Rigoletto*, and Nemorino in *L'Elisir d'amore*.

Pavia, Battle of /pəˈviːə/ battle 1525 between France and the Holy Roman Empire. The Habsburg emperor Charles V defeated and captured Francis I; it signified the onset of Habsburg dominance in Italy.

Pavlov /ˈpævlɒv/ Ivan Petrovich 1849–1936. Russian physiologist who studied conditioned reflexes in animals. His work influenced behavioural theory (see ◊behaviourism) and ◊learning theory. See also ◊conditioning.

Pavlova /ˈpævləvə/ Anna 1881–1931. Russian dancer. Prima ballerina of the Imperial Ballet from 1906, she left Russia 1913, and went on to become one of the world's most famous Classical ballerinas. With London as her home, she toured extensively with her own company, influencing dancers worldwide with roles such as ◊Fokine's *The Dying Swan* solo 1905.

pawnbroker one who lends money on the security of goods held. The traditional sign of the premises is three gold balls, the symbol used in front of the houses of the medieval Lombard merchants.

pawpaw or **papaya** tropical tree *Carica papaya*, originating in South America and grown in many tropical countries. The edible fruits resemble a melon, with orange-coloured flesh and numerous blackish seeds in the central cavity; they may weigh up to 9 kg/20 lb. The fruit juice or the tree sap are often used to tenderize meat.

In the USA, pawpaw is the plant *Asimina triloba*, which has an unpleasant odour but carries edible oval berries 75 mm/3 in long.

Pax Roman goddess of peace; Greek counterpart ◊Irene.

Paxton /ˈpækstən/ Joseph 1801–1865. English architect, garden superintendent to the Duke of Devonshire from 1826 and designer of the Great Exhibition building 1851 (◊Crystal Palace), revolutionary in its structural use of glass and iron.

PAYE (Pay As You Earn) in the UK, a system of tax collection in which a proportional amount of income tax is deducted on a regular basis by the employer before wages are paid to the Inland Revenue, reliefs due being notified to the employer by a code number for each employee. In the USA it is called withholding tax.

It was introduced in Britain in 1944 to spread the tax burden over the year for the increasing number of wage-earners becoming liable.

paymaster-general head of the Paymaster-General's Office, the British government department (established 1835) that acts as paying agent for most other departments.

Paysandú /ˌpaɪsænˈduː/ city in Uruguay, capital of Paysandú department, on the river Uruguay; population (1985) 74,000. Tinned meat is the main product. The city dates from 1772, and is linked by bridge 1976 with Puerto Colón in Argentina.

Pays de la Loire /peɪˈiː də lɑː ˈlwɑː/ agricultural region of W France, comprising the *départements* of Loire-Atlantique, Maine-et-Loire, Mayenne, Sarthe, and Vendée; capital Nantes; area 32,100 sq km/12,391 sq mi; population (1986) 3,018,000. Industries include shipbuilding and wine.

Paz /pɑːs/ (Estenssoro) Victor 1907– . President of Bolivia 1952–56, 1960–64, and from 1985. He founded and led the **Movimiento Nacionalista Revolucionario** which seized power 1952. His regime extended the vote to Indians, nationalized the country's largest tin mines, and embarked on a major programme of agrarian reform.

After holding a number of financial posts he entered politics in the 1930s and in 1942 founded the National Revolutionary Movement (MNR). In exile in Argentina, during one of Bolivia's many periods of military rule, he returned in 1951 and became president in 1952. He immediately embarked on a programme of political reform, retaining the presidency until 1956 and being re-elected (1960–64) and again in 1985, returning from near-retirement, at the age of 77. During his long career he was Bolivian ambassador in London (1956–59) and a professor at London University (1966).

Paz /pɑːs/ Octavio 1914– . Mexican poet, whose *Sun Stone* 1957 is a personal statement taking the ◊Aztec Calendar Stone as its basic symbol.

PC abbreviation for *police constable*; *Privy Councillor*; *personal computer*.

PCB abbreviation for ◊*polychlorinated biphenyl*; ◊*printed circuit board*.

PCP abbreviation for *phencyclidine*, a drug popularly known as ◊angel dust.

pea climbing plant *Pisum sativum*, family Leguminosae, with pods of edible seeds. The **sweet pea** *Lathyrus odoratus* is grown for its scented flowers.

Peace /piːs/ river formed in British Columbia, Canada, by the union at Finlay Forks of the Finlay and Parsnip rivers and flowing through the Rockies and across Alberta to join the river Slave just N of Lake Athabasca; length 1,600 km/1,000 mi.

Peace Corps a body of trained men and women, established in the USA by President Kennedy 1961, providing skilled workers for the developing countries, especially in the fields of teaching, agriculture, and health. Living among the country's inhabitants, volunteers are paid only a small allowance to cover their basic needs and maintain health. The Peace Corps was inspired by the British programme Voluntary Service Overseas.

peace movement the collective opposition to war. The Western peace movements of the 1980s can trace their origins to the ◊pacifists of the 19th century and conscientious objectors during World War I. The campaigns after World War II have tended to concentrate on nuclear weapons, but there are numerous organizations, some wholly pacifist, some merely opposed to escalation.

In the UK, the Peace Pledge Union may be the oldest organization in the peace movement, the ◊Campaign for Nuclear Disarmament the largest, and the ◊Greenham Common women the most publicized.

peach tree *Prunus persica*, family Rosaceae. It has ovate leaves and small, usually pink flowers. The yellowish edible fruits have thick velvety skins; the ◊nectarine is a smooth-skinned variety.

peacock bird of the pheasant family, native to S Asia. The common peacock *Pavo cristatus* is rather larger than a pheasant. The male has a large fan-shaped tail, brightly coloured with blue, green, and purple 'eyes' on a chestnut ground. The peahen is brown with a small tail.

Peacock /ˈpiːkɒk/ Thomas Love 1785–1866. English satirical novelist and poet. His works include *Headlong Hall* 1816, *Nightmare Abbey* 1818, *Crotchet Castle* 1831, and *Gryll Grange* 1831.

Peak District /piːk/ tableland of the S Pennines in NW Derbyshire, England. It is a tourist region and a national park (1951). The highest point is Kinder Scout 636 m/2,088 ft.

Peake /piːk/ Mervyn (Lawrence) 1911–1968. English writer and illustrator, born in China. His novels include the grotesque fantasy trilogy *Titus Groan* 1946, *Gormenghast* 1950, and *Titus Alone* 1959.

Peale /piːl/ Charles Willson 1741–1827. American artist, head of a large family of painters. His portraits of leading figures in the War of Independence include the earliest known portrait of Washington 1772.

peanut another name for ◊groundnut.

pear tree *Pyrus communis*, family Rosaceae, native to temperate regions of Eurasia. It has a succulent edible fruit, less hardy than the apple.

pearl calcareous substance (nacre) secreted by many molluscs, and deposited in thin layers on the inside of the shell around a parasite, a grain of sand, or some other irritant body. After several years of the mantle (the layer of tissue between the shell and the body mass) secreting this calcium carbonate, a pearl is formed.

Although commercially valuable pearls are obtained from freshwater mussels and oysters, the precious pearl comes from the various species of *Margaritifera* found in tropical waters off N and W Australia, the Californian coast, the Persian Gulf, and in the Indian Ocean.

Artificial pearls were first cultivated in Japan in 1893. A tiny bead of shell from a clam, plus a small piece of membrane from another pearl oyster's mantle (to stimulate the secretion of nacre) is inserted in oysters kept in cages in the sea for three years, and then the pearls are harvested.

Pearl Harbor /ˈpɜːl ˈhɑːbə/ US Pacific naval base in Oahu, Hawaii, USA, the scene of a Japanese attack 7 Dec 1941, which brought the USA into World War II. It took place while Japanese envoys were holding so-called peace talks in Washington. More than 2,000 US servicemen were killed, and a large part of the US Pacific fleet was destroyed or damaged during the attack.

The local commanders Admiral Kummel and Lt-Gen Short were relieved of their posts and held responsible for the fact that the base was totally unprepared at the time of the attack, but recent information indicates that warnings of the attack given to the USA (by British intelligence and others) were withheld from Kummel and Short by President Roosevelt. US public opinion was very much against entering the war, and Roosevelt wanted an excuse to change popular sentiments and take the USA into the war.

Pears /pɪəz/ Peter 1910–1986. English tenor. A co-founder with ◊Britten of the Aldeburgh Festival, he was closely associated with the composer's work and played the title role in *Peter Grimes*.

Pearse /pɪəs/ Patrick Henry 1879–1916. Irish poet prominent in the Gaelic revival, a leader of the ◊Easter Rising 1916. Proclaimed president of the provisional government, he was court-martialled and shot after its suppression.

Pearson /ˈpɪəsən/ Karl 1857–1936. British statistician, who followed ◊Galton in introducing statistics and probability into genetics, and developed the concept of eugenics (improving the human race by selective breeding). He introduced the term ◊standard deviation into statistics.

Pearson /ˈpɪəsən/ Lester Bowles 1897–1972. Canadian politician, leader of the Liberal Party from 1958, prime minister 1963–68. As foreign minister 1948–57, he effectively represented Canada at the United Nations. Nobel Peace Prize 1957.

He served as president of the General Assembly 1952–53 and helped to create the UN Emergency Force (UNEF) that policed Sinai following the Egypt–Israel war of 1956. As prime minister, Pearson led the way to formulating a national medicare law.

Peary /ˈpɪəri/ Robert Edwin 1856–1920. US polar explorer who, after several unsuccessful attempts, became the first person to reach the North Pole on 6 Apr 1909. In 1988 an astronomer claimed Peary's measurements were incorrect.

Peary sailed to Cape Sheridan in the *Roosevelt* with his aide Matthew Henson, and they then made a sledge journey to the Pole.

Peasants' Revolt the rising of the English peasantry June 1381. Following the Black Death, there was a shortage of agricultural workers, which led to higher wages. The Statute of Labourers was enacted 1351, attempting to return wages to pre-plague levels. When a poll tax was enforced 1379, riots broke out all over England, especially in Essex and Kent. Led by Wat ◊Tyler and John ◊Ball, the rebels sacked Canterbury, and marched to London, where they continued plundering, burning John of Gaunt's palace at the Savoy, and taking the prisons at Newgate and Fleet. The young king Richard II attempted to appease the mob, who demanded an end to serfdom and feudalism. The rebels then took the Tower of London and murdered Archbishop Sudbury and Robert Hales. Again the king attempted to make peace at Smithfield, and Wat Tyler was stabbed to death by William Walworth, the Lord Mayor of London. The king made concessions to the

rebels, and they dispersed, but the concessions were revoked immediately.

peat fibrous organic substance found in ◊bogs and formed by the incomplete decomposition of plants such as sphagnum moss. The USSR, Canada, Finland, Ireland, and other places have large deposits, which have been dried and used as fuel from ancient times. Peat can also be used as a soil additive.

A number of ancient corpses, thought to have been the result of ritual murders, have been found preserved in peat bogs, mainly in Scandinavia. In 1984, Lindow Man was found in mainland Britain, near Wilmslow, Cheshire, dating from about 500 BC.

pecan nut-producing tree *Carya pecan*, native to S USA and N Mexico, and now widely cultivated. The tree grows to over 45 m/150 ft, and the edible nuts are smooth-shelled, the kernel resembling a smoothly ovate walnut.

peccary tropical American genus of piglike animals *Tayassu*, having a gland in the middle of the back which secretes a strong-smelling substance. They are blackish in colour, covered with bristles, and have tusks which point downwards. Adults reach a height of 40 cm/16 in, and a weight of 25 kg/60 lbs.

Pechenga /ˈpetʃɪŋə/ (Finnish **Petsamo**) ice-free fishing port in Murmansk, USSR, on the Barents Sea. Russia ceded Pechenga to Finland 1920 but recovered it under the 1947 peace treaty.

Pechora /pɪˈtʃɔːrə/ river in the USSR, rising in the N Urals. It carries coal, timber, and furs (June–Sept) to the Barents Sea 1,800 km/1,125 mi to the N.

Peck Eldred Gregory 1916– . US actor. One of Hollywood's most enduring stars, he was often cast as a decent man of great moral and physical strength, as in *The Old Gringo* 1989. His other films include *Spellbound* 1945 and *To Kill a Mockingbird* 1962.

Peckinpah Sam 1925–1985. US film director, often of westerns, usually associated with slow-motion, blood-spurting violence. His films, such as *The Wild Bunch* 1969, exhibit a thoughtful, if depressing, view of the world.

Pécs /peɪtʃ/ city in SW Hungary, the centre of a coalmining area on the Yugoslavia frontier; population (1988) 182,000. Industries include metal, leather, and wine. The town dates from Roman times, and was under Turkish rule 1543–1686.

pedicel the stalk of an individual flower, which attaches it to the main floral axis, often developing in the axil of a bract.

pediment in architecture, the triangular part crowning the fronts of buildings in classic styles. The pediment was a distinctive feature of Greek temples.

pedometer small portable instrument for measuring the approximate distance covered by its wearer. Each step taken by the walker sets in motion a swinging weight within the instrument, causing the mechanism to rotate, and the number of rotations are registered on the instrument face.

Pedro /ˈpedrəʊ/ two emperors of Brazil:

Pedro I 1798–1834. Emperor of Brazil 1822–31. The son of John VI of Portugal, he escaped to Brazil on Napoleon's invasion, and was appointed regent 1821. He proclaimed Brazil independent 1822 and was crowned emperor, but abdicated 1831 and returned to Portugal.

Pedro II 1825–1891. Emperor of Brazil 1831–89. He proved an enlightened ruler, but his antislavery measures alienated the landowners, who compelled him to abdicate.

Peeblesshire /ˈpiːbəlzʃə/ former county of S Scotland, included from 1975 in Borders region; Peebles was the county town.

Peel /piːl/ fishing port in the Isle of Man, 19 km/12 mi NW of Douglas.

Peel /piːl/ Robert 1788–1850. British Conservative politician. As home secretary 1822–27 and 1828–30, he founded the modern police force and in 1829 introduced Roman Catholic emancipation. He was prime minister 1834–35 and 1841–46, when his repeal of the ◊Corn Laws

Peel *A portrait of Robert Peel, founder of the police force, by H W Pickersgill.*

caused him and his followers to break with the party.

Peel, born in Lancashire, entered Parliament as a Tory 1809. After the passing of the Reform Bill 1832, which he had resisted, he reformed the Tories under the name of Conservative Party, on a basis of accepting necessary reforms and seeking middle-class support. He fell from prime ministerial office because his repeal of the Corn Laws 1846 was opposed by the majority of his party. He and his followers then formed a third party standing between the Liberals and Conservatives; the majority of the Peelites, including Gladstone, subsequently joined the Liberals.

Peele /pi:l/ George 1558–1597. English dramatist. He wrote a pastoral, *The Arraignment of Paris* 1584; a fantastic comedy, *The Old Wives' Tale* 1595; and a tragedy, *David and Bethsabe* 1599.

Peenemünde /,peɪnə'mʊndə/ fishing village in East Germany, used from 1937 by the Germans to develop the V2 rockets used in World War II.

peepul an Indian tree. See under ◊fig and ◊bo tree.

peerage in the UK, holders of the titles of duke, marquess, earl, viscount, and baron. Some of these titles may be held by a woman in default of a male heir. In the later 19th century they were augmented by the Lords of Appeal in Ordinary (life peers), and from 1958 by a number of specially created life peers of either sex (usually long-standing members of the Commons). Since 1963 peers have been able to disclaim their titles (for example Lord Home and Tony Benn), usually to take a seat in the Commons (where peers are disqualified from membership).

peer group in the social sciences, people who have a common identity based on such characteristics as similar social status, interests, age, or ethnic group. The concept has proved useful in analysing the power and influence of workmates, school friends, and ethnic and religious groups in socialization and social behaviour.

Pegasus /'pegəsəs/ in astronomy, a constellation of the northern hemisphere, near Cygnus, representing the winged horse of Greek mythology.

Pegasus /'pegəsəs/ in Greek mythology, the winged horse which sprang from the blood of Medusa. Hippocrene, the spring of the Muses on Mount Helicon, is said to have sprung from a blow of his hoof. He was transformed to a constellation.

pegmatite an extremely coarse-grained igneous rock found in veins usually associated with large granite masses.

Pegu /pe'gu:/ city in S Burma, on the river Pegu, NE of Rangoon; population (1983) 254,762. It was founded AD 573 and is noted for the Shwemawdaw pagoda.

Péguy /peɪ'gi:/ Charles 1873–1914. French Catholic socialist, who established a socialist publishing

house in Paris. From 1900 he published on political topics *Les Cahiers de la Quinzaine/Fortnightly Notebooks* and poetry, including *Le Mystère de la charité de Jeanne d'Arc/The Mystery of the Charity of Joan of Arc* 1897.

Pei /'peɪ/ Ieoh Ming 1917– . Chinese Modernist/high-tech architect, who became a US citizen 1948. His buildings include Dallas City Hall, Texas; East Building, National Gallery of Art, Washington DC, 1978; John F Kennedy Library Complex and the John Hancock tower, Boston 1979; the Bank of China Tower, Hong Kong, 1987; and a glass pyramid in front of the Louvre, Paris, 1989.

Peiping /,peɪ'pɪŋ/ name, meaning 'northern peace', 1928–49 of ◊Beijing in China.

Peipus, Lake /'paɪpəs/ (Estonian **Peipsi**, Russian **Chudskoye**) lake on the Estonian border in the USSR. Alexander Nevski defeated the Teutonic Knights on its frozen surface 1242.

Peirce /pɪəs/ Charles Sanders 1839–1914. US philosopher, founder of ◊pragmatism, who argued that genuine conceptual distinctions must be correlated with some difference of practical effect. He wrote extensively on the logic of scientific enquiry, suggesting that truth could be conceived of as the object of an ultimate consensus.

pekan or **fisher marten** North American marten (carnivorous mammal) about 1.2 m/4 ft long, with a doglike face, and brown fur with white patches on the chest.

Peking /,beɪ'dʒɪŋ/ former name of ◊*Beijing*, capital of China.

pekingese long-haired toy dog with a flat skull and flat face. It was first bred at the Chinese court as the 'imperial lion dog'. The first specimens brought to Britain were those taken during the Opium Wars when the Summer Palace in Beijing was looted 1860.

Peking man early type of human, *Homo Erectus*. Carbon dating indicates that they lived between 500,000 and 1,500,000 years ago. A skull was found near Beijing (formerly Peking) 1927, sent to the USA 1941 and disappeared; others have since been found.

Pelagius /pe'leɪdʒiəs/ 360–420. British theologian. He went to Rome about 400, and taught that every person possesses free will, denying Augustine's doctrines of predestination and original sin. Cleared of heresy by a synod in Jerusalem 415, he was later condemned by the pope and the emperor.

pelargonium flowering plant of the genus *Pelargonium*, grown extensively in gardens, where it is familiarly known as *geranium*. It is related to the true geranium, being also a member of the family Geraniaceae. Ancestors of the garden hybrids came from S Africa.

Pelé Adopted name of Edson Arantes do Nascimento 1940– . Brazilian footballer. A prolific goal scorer, he appeared in four World Cup competitions 1958–70 and won three medals.

He spent most of his career with the Brazilian team Santos before playing with the New York Cosmos in the USA. He played inside left.

CAREER HIGHLIGHTS

first-class appearances: 1,363
first-class goals: 1,281
World Cup winner: 1958, 1962, 1970
Brazilian Cup: 1962–64, 1968
World Club Championship: 1962–63

Pelée, Mont /pə'leɪ/ volcano on the island of Martinique; height 1,258 m/4,428 ft. It destroyed the town of St Pierre during its eruption 1902.

Pelham /'peləm/ Henry 1696–1754. British Whig politician. He held a succession of offices in Walpole's cabinet 1721–42, and was prime minister 1743–54.

pelican type of water bird remarkable for the pouch beneath the bill used as a fishing net and temporary store for its catches of fish. Some species grow up to 1.8 m/6 ft, and have wingspans of 3 m/10 ft.

They include the pinkish common pelican *Pelicanus onocrotalus* of Europe, Asia, and Africa; the Australian black-backed pelican *Pelicanus*

conspicillatus; and the American brown pelican *Pelicanus occidentalis*, which is marine, and dives for its food.

Pelion mountain in Thessaly, Greece, near Mount ◊Ossa; height 1,548 m/5,079 ft. In Greek mythology it was the home of the ◊centaurs.

pellagra a disease of subtropical countries in which the staple food is maize, due to deficiency of nicotinic acid (one of the B vitamins), which is contained in protein foods and yeast.

pellitory-of-the-wall plant *Parietaria judaica* of the nettle family, found growing in cracks in walls and rocks and also on banks, in W and S Europe. It is much branched, softly hairy, and up to 1 m/3 ft high. The stems are reddish, the leaves lance-shaped, and the greenish male and female flowers are separate but on the same plant.

Peloponnese /,peləpə'ni:s/ (Greek **Peloponnesos**) peninsula forming the S part of Greece; area 21,549 sq km/8,318 sq mi; population (1981) 1,012,500. It is joined to the mainland by the narrow isthmus of Corinth, and is divided into the nomes of Argolis, Arcadia, Achaea, Elis, Corinth, Lakonia, and Messenia, representing its seven ancient states.

Peloponnesian War conflict between Athens and Sparta and their allies, 431–404 BC, originating in suspicions about the 'empire-building' ambitions of Pericles. It was ended by ◊Lysander's destruction of the political power of Athens.

pelota or **jai alai** 'merry festival' very fast ball game (means 'ball') of Basque derivation, popular in Latin American countries. It is played in a walled court, or *cancha*, and resembles squash, but the players use a long, curved, wickerwork basket, or *cesta*, strapped to the hand, to hurl the ball (about the size of a baseball) against the walls.

Peltier effect in physics, a change in temperature at the junction of two different metals produced when an electric current flows through them. The extent of the change depends on what the conducting metals are, and the nature of change (rise or fall in temperature) depends on the direction of current flow. It is the reverse of the ◊Seebeck effect. It is named after the French physicist Jean Charles Peltier (1785–1845) who discovered it 1834.

Pemba /'pembə/ coral island in the Indian Ocean, 48 km/30 mi NE of Zanzibar, and forming with it part of Tanzania
area 984 sq km/380 sq mi
capital Chake Chake
products cloves, copra
population (1985) 257,000.

Pembroke /'pembrʊk/ seaport and engineering centre in Dyfed, Wales; population (1981) 15,600. Henry VII was born in Pembroke Castle.

Pembrokeshire /'pembrʊkʃə/ former extreme SW county of Wales, which became part of Dyfed 1974; the county town was Haverfordwest.

pemmican preparation of dried fatless beef or venison pressed into cubes, once used as a food by Arctic explorers and North American Indians.

PEN (abbreviation for Poets, Playwrights, Editors, Essayist, Novelists) literary association established 1921 by C A ('Sappho') Dawson Scott, to promote international understanding between writers.

penance a Roman Catholic sacrament, involving ◊confession of sins and the reception of absolution, and works performed or punishment self-inflicted in atonement for sin. Penance is worked out now in terms of good deeds rather than routine repetition of prayers.

Penang /pɪ'næŋ/ (Malay **Pulau Pinang**) state in W Peninsular Malaysia, formed of Penang Island, Province Wellesley, and the Dindings on the mainland; area 1,030 sq km/398 sq mi; capital Penang (George Town); population (1980) 955,000. Penang Island was bought from Britain from the ruler of Kedah 1785; Province Wellesley was acquired 1800.

Penarlag /,penɑ:'lɑːg/ Welsh name of ◊Hawarden, town in Clwyd, Wales.

penates /pe'nɑːteɪz/ the household gods of a Roman family. See ◊lares and penates.

Penda /'pendə/ c. 577–654. King of Mercia from about 632. He raised Mercia to a powerful kingdom, and defeated and killed two Northumbrian kings, Edwin 632 and ◊Oswald 641. He was killed in battle by Oswy, king of Northumbria.

Penderecki /,pendə'retski/ Krzystof 1933– . Polish composer. His Expressionist works, such as the *Threnody for the Victims of Hiroshima* 1961 for strings, employ cluster and percusssion effects. He later turned to religious subjects and a more orthodox style, as in the *Magnificat* 1974 and the *Polish Requiem* 1980–83.

Pendlebury /'pendlbəri/ John Devitt Stringfellow 1904–1941. British archaeologist. Working with his wife, he became the world's leading expert on Crete. In World War II he was deputed to prepare guerrilla resistance on the island, was wounded during the German invasion, and shot by his captors.

Pendleton Act in US history, a civil-service reform bill 1883 sponsored by senator George Pendleton (1825–1889) of Ohio that was designed to curb the power of patronage exercised by new administrations over a swelling federal bureaucracy. Initially about 10% of civil-service appointments were made subject to competitive examinations administered by an independent Civil Service Commission.

pendulum a weight (called a 'bob') swinging at the end of a rod or cord.

The regularity of a pendulum's swing was used in making the first really accurate clocks in the 17th century. Pendulums can be used for measuring the acceleration due to gravity (an important constant in physics), and in prospecting for oils and minerals. Specialized pendulums are used to measure velocities (ballistic pendulum) and to demonstrate the Earth's rotation (Foucault's pendulum).

Penelope /pə'neləpi/ in Greek legend, wife of ◊Odysseus. During his absence after the siege of Troy she kept her many suitors at bay by asking them to wait until she had woven a shroud for her father-in-law, but undid her work nightly. When Odysseus returned, he killed her suitors.

penetration technology the development of missiles which have low radar, infrared and optical signatures, and can penetrate an enemy's defences undetected. In 1980 the USA announced that it had developed such piloted aircraft, known as Stealth. In 1989 two out of three tests failed, and the cost of the Stealth had risen to $500 million each.

penguin flightless, marine bird, usually black and white, found in the southern hemisphere. They range in size from 40 cm/1.6 ft to 1.2 m/4 ft tall, and have thick feathers to protect them from the intense cold. They are awkward on land, but their wings have evolved into flippers, making them excellent swimmers. Penguins congregate to breed in 'rookeries', and often spend many months incubating their eggs while their mates are out at sea feeding.

penguin

Largest is the **emperor penguin** *Aptenodytes forsteri* 1.2 m/4 ft tall, whose single annual egg is brooded by the male in the warmth of a flap of his body skin, so that it rests on his feet. Among the small species is the **jackass penguin** *Spheniscus demerss*, which lays two eggs in a scraped hollow in the ground. Jackass penguins have declined in numbers, at first because of egg-collecting by humans, but more recently owing to overfishing, which deprives them of food, and to oil spills near their breeding colonies.

penicillin an ◊antibiotic, produced by fungus *Penicillium notatum*. The first antibiotic to be discovered, it kills a broad spectrum of bacteria, many of which cause disease in humans.

Its use is limited, however, by increasing resistance of ◊pathogens and allergic reaction in patients. Since 1941, numerous other members of the penicillin family have been discovered, which are more selective against, or resistant to, specific microorganisms.

peninsula tongue of land surrounded on three sides by water but still attached to a larger landmass. Florida, USA, is an example.

Peninsular War war 1808–14 caused by the French emperor Napoleon's invasion of Portugal and Spain. British expeditionary forces, combined with Spanish and Portuguese resistance, succeeded in defeating the French at Vimeiro 1808, Talavera 1809, ◊Salamanca 1812, and Vittoria 1813. The results were inconclusive, and the war was ended by Napoleon's abdication.

1807 Portugal was occupied by the French.

1808 Napoleon placed his brother Joseph Bonaparte on the Spanish throne. Armed revolts followed all over Spain and Portugal. A British force under Sir Arthur Wellesley was sent to Portugal and defeated the French at Vimeiro; Wellesley was then superseded, and the French were allowed to withdraw.

1809 Wellesley took a new army to Portugal, and advanced on Madrid, but after defeating the French at Talavera had to retreat.

1810–11 Wellesley (now Viscount Wellington) stood on the defensive.

1812 Wellington won another victory at ◊*Salamanca*, occupied Madrid, and forced the French to evacuate S Spain.

1813 Wellington's victory at *Vittoria* drove the French from Spain.

1814 Wellington invaded S France. The war was ended by Napoleon's abdication.

penis male reproductive organ, used for internal fertilization; it transfers sperm to the female reproductive tract. In mammals, the penis is made erect by vessels which fill with blood, and in most mammals (but not men) is stiffened by a bone. It also contains the urethra, through which urine is passed. Snakes and lizards have two penises, other reptiles only one. A few birds, mainly ducks and geese, also have a type of penis, as do snails, barnacles, and some other invertebrates. Many insects have a rigid, non-erectile male organ, usually referred to as an intromittent organ.

Penn /pen/ Irving 1917– . US fashion, advertising, portrait, editorial, and fine art photographer.

penicillin Penicillium notatum *is a species of fungus that was used as an early source of the antibiotic pencillin.*

In 1948 he took the first of many journeys to Africa and the Far East, resulting in a series of portrait photographs of local people, avoiding sophisticated technique. He was associated for many years with *Vogue* magazine in the USA.

Penn /pen/ William 1644–1718. English Quaker, born in London. He joined the Quakers 1667, and in 1681 obtained a grant of land in America, in settlement of a debt owed by the king to his father, on which he established the colony of Pennsylvania as a refuge for the persecuted Quakers.

Penney /'peni/ William 1909– . British scientist. He worked at Los Alamos 1944–45, designed the first British atomic bomb, and developed the advanced gas-cooled nuclear reactor used in some power stations.

Pennines /'penaɪnz/ mountain system, 'the backbone of England', broken by a gap through which the river Aire flows to the E and the Ribble to the W; length (Scottish border to the Peaks in Derbyshire) 400 km/250 mi.

Pennsylvania /,pensɪl'veɪnɪə/ state of NE USA; nickname Keystone State
area 117,400 sq km/45,316 sq mi
capital Harrisburg
towns Philadelphia, Pittsburgh, Erie, Allentown, Scranton
features Allegheny mountains; Ohio, Susquehanna, and Delaware rivers; University of Pennsylvania is one of the leading research campuses in the USA
products mushrooms, fruit, flowers, cereals, tobacco, meat, poultry, dairy products, anthracite, electrical equipment
population (1986) 11,889,000
famous people Marian Anderson, Maxwell Anderson, Stephen Foster, Benjamin Franklin, George C Marshall, Robert E Peary, Gertrude Stein, John Updike
history founded and named by William ◊Penn 1682, following a land grant by Charles II. It was one of the original Thirteen States. There was a breakdown at the Three Mile Island nuclear reactor plant in Harrisburg 1979.

Pennsylvanian US term for the upper ◊Carboniferous period of geological time, named after the US state.

pennyroyal perennial plant *Mentha pulegium*, with oblong leaves and whorls of purplish flowers. It is found growing in wet places on sandy soil.

Pensacola /,pensə'kəʊlə/ port in NW Florida, USA, on the Gulf of Mexico, with a large naval air-training station; industries (chemicals, synthetic fibres, paper); population (1984) 60,500. Pensacola was founded by the Spanish 1696.

pension an organized form of saving for retirement. Pension schemes, which may be government-run or privately administered, involve regular payment for a qualifying period; when the person retires, a payment is made each week from the invested pension fund. Pension funds have today become influential investors in major industries. In the UK, the age at which pensions become payable is 65 for men and 60 for women.

pentadactyl limb the typical limb of the mammals, birds, reptiles and amphibians. These ◊vertebrates are all descended from primitive amphibians whose immediate ancestors were fleshy-finned fish.

The limb which evolved in those amphibians had three parts: a 'hand/foot' with five digits

Pennsylvania

(fingers/toes), a lower limb containing two bones, and an upper limb containing one bone. This basic pattern has persisted in all the terrestrial vertebrates, and those aquatic vertebrates (such as seals) which are descended from them. Natural selection has modified the pattern to fit different ways of life. In flying animals (birds and bats) it is greatly altered and in some vertebrates, such as whales and snakes, the limbs are greatly reduced or lost. Pentadactyl limbs of different species are an example of ◊homologous organs.

Pentagon the headquarters of the US Department of Defense, Arlington, Virginia. One of the world's largest office buildings (five-sided with a pentagonal central court), it houses the administrative and command headquarters for the US armed forces and has become synonymous with the defence-establishment bureaucracy.

Pentagon Papers a top-secret US Defense Department report on the history of US involvement in the Vietnam War that was leaked to the *New York Times* by Daniel Ellsberg June 1971, fuelling the anti-war movement. President Nixon tried to stop publication, but the Supreme Court ruled in favour of the press.

pentanol $C_5H_{11}OH$ (common name ***amyl alcohol***) in chemistry, a clear colourless oily liquid, usually having a characteristic choking odour.

Pentateuch Greek (and Christian) name for the first five books of the Bible, ascribed to Moses, and called the ***Torah*** by Jews.

pentathlon a five-sport competition. Modern pentathlon consists of former military training pursuits: swimming, fencing, running, horsemanship, and shooting. It was formerly a five-event track and field competition for women, superseded by the ◊heptathlon 1981.

Pentecost Jewish festival (50th day after ◊Passover) celebrating the end of the Palestinian grain harvest; in the Christian church, day on which the apostles experienced inspiration of the Holy Spirit, and commemorated on Whit Sunday.

Pentecostal movement Christian revivalist movement inspired by the baptism in the Holy Spirit with 'speaking in tongues' experienced by the apostles at the time of Pentecost. It represents a reaction against rigid theology and formal worship of the traditional churches. Pentecostalists believe in the literal word of the Bible and disapprove of alcohol, tobacco, dancing, theatre, and so on. It is an intensely missionary faith, and recruitment has been rapid since the 1960s: worldwide membership is more than 10 million.

The Pentecostal movement dates from 4 Apr 1906 when members of the congregation of the Azusa Street Mission in Los Angeles experienced 'baptism in the Spirit'. From this phenomenon it is sometimes also known as the Tongues movement. The services are informal, with gospel music and exclamations of 'Hallelujah'.

The movement spread, and took hold in revivalist areas of Wales and N England, but was less successful there than in Scandinavia, South America, and South Africa. In the USA, where the largest grouping is the Assemblies of God, members of the movement total more than 0.5 million. It has been spoken of as the 'third force' in Christendom, and a serious challenge to Roman Catholicism and traditional Protestantism.

Pentland Firth /'pentlənd 'fɜ:θ/ the channel separating the Orkney Islands from N Scotland.

Penza /'penzə/ industrial city (sawmills, bicycles, watches, calculating machines, textiles) in the USSR, capital of Penza region, 560 km/350 mi SE of Moscow, at the junction of the Penza and Sura rivers; population (1987) 540,000. It was founded as a fort 1663.

Penzance /pen'zæns/ seaport for the Scilly Isles and resort in Cornwall, SW England, on Mount's Bay; population (1981) 19,500. It now incorporates the seaport of ◊Newlyn.

peony or ***paeony*** perennial plant of the family Paeoniaceae, remarkable for its brilliant flowers. Most popular are the common peony *Paeonia*

officinalis, the white peony *Paeonia lactiflora*, and the taller tree peony *Paeonia suffruticosa*.

People's Charter the key document of ◊Chartism, a movement for reform of the British political system in the 1830s. It was used to mobilize working-class support following the restricted extension of the franchise specified by the 1832 Reform Act. It was drawn up in Feb 1837.

The campaign failed but within 70 years four of its six objectives; (universal male suffrage, abolition of property qualifications for Members of Parliament, payment of MPs) and voting by secret ballot had been realized.

Peoria /pi'ɔ:riə/ city in central Illinois, USA, on the river Illinois, a transport, mining, and agricultural centre; population (1980) 366,000. Fort Crève Coeur was built here by the French explorer La Salle 1680 and became a trading centre. The first US settlers arrived 1818 and the town was known as Fort Clark until 1825. In US comedy, Peoria is the epitome of a small town.

Pepin /'pepin/ ***the Short*** c. 714–c. 768. King of the Franks from 751. The son of Charles Martel, he acted as ◊mayor of the palace to the last Merovingian king, Childeric III, deposed him and assumed the royal title himself, founding the ◊Carolingian line.

pepper climbing plant *Piper nigrum* native to the E Indies. When gathered green, the berries are crushed to produce the seeds for the condiment black pepper. When the berries are ripe the seeds are removed, and the outer skin discarded to produce white pepper. Sweet pepper comes from the ◊capsicum plant.

peppermint perennial herb *Mentha piperita*, with ovate aromatic leaves, and purple flowers. Oil of peppermint is used in medicine and confectionery.

peptide a molecule comprising two or more ◊amino acid molecules (not necessarily different) joined by ***peptide bonds***, whereby the acid group of one acid is linked to the amino group of the other (–CO.NH–). The number of amino acid molecules in the peptide is indicated by reference to it as a di-, tri-, or polypeptide (two, three, or many amino acids).

Proteins are built up of interacting polypeptide chains with various types of bonds occurring between the chains. Incomplete hydrolysis (splitting up) of a protein yields a mixture of peptides, examination of which helps to determine the sequence in which the amino acids occur within the protein.

Pepusch /'peipuʃ/ Johann Christoph 1667–1752. German composer who settled in England about 1700. He contributed to John Gay's ballad operas *The Beggar's Opera* and *Polly*.

Pepys /pi:ps/ Samuel 1633–1703. English diarist. His diary, written 1659–69 (when his sight failed) in shorthand, was a unique record of both the daily life of the period and the intimate feelings of the man. It was not deciphered until 1825.

He was born in London, entered the navy office 1660, and was secretary to the Admiralty 1672–79, when he was imprisoned in the Tower on suspicion of being connected with the Popish Plot (see Titus ◊Oates). He was then reinstated 1684 and finally demoted, after the 1688 Revolution, for suspected disaffection.

Perak /'peərə/ state of W Peninsular Malaysia; capital Ipoh; area 21,000 sq km/8,106 sq mi; population (1980) 1,805,000. It produces tin and rubber. The government is a sultanate. The other important town is Taiping.

percentage a way of representing a number as a ◊fraction of 100. Thus 45 per cent (45%) equals $45/100$, and 45% of 20 is $45/100 \times 20 = 9$.

In general, if a quantity x changes to y, the percentage change is $100(x-y)/x$. Thus, if the number of people in a room changes from 40 to 50, the percentage increase is $(100 \times 10)/40 = 25\%$. To express a fraction as a percentage, its denominator must first be converted to 100, for example, $1/8 = 12.5/100 = 12.5\%$. The use of percentages often makes it easier to compare fractions that do not have a common denominator.

The percentage sign is thought to have been derived as an economy measure when recording in the old 'counting houses'. $25/100$ of a cargo would take two lines of parchment and hence the 100 denominator was put alongside the 25 and re-arranged to %.

Perceval /'pɜ:sivəl/ Spencer 1762–1812. British Tory politician. He became chancellor of the Exchequer 1807 and prime minister 1809. He was shot in the lobby of the House of Commons 1812 by a merchant who blamed government measures for his bankruptcy.

perch freshwater fish, genus Perca, found in Europe, Asia, and North America. They have varied shapes, and are usually a greenish colour. They are very prolific, spawning when three years old, and have voracious appetites.

The common perch *Perca fluviatilis* is olive green or yellowish in colour, with dark vertical bands. It can be 50 cm/1.6 ft long but is usually less. It is a predator found in still water and rivers. The American yellow perch *Perca flavescens* is slightly smaller.

Perchlike fishes form the largest order of bony fishes, the Perciformes, with some 8,000 species. This order includes the sea breams, cichlids, damselfishes, mullets, barracudas, wrasses, and gobies.

percussion instrument musical instrument played by being struck with the hand or a beater. Percussion instruments can be divided into those that can be tuned to produce a sound of definite pitch, and those without pitch.

Examples of tuned percussion instruments include:
kettledrum a hemisperical bowl of metal with a membrane stretched across the top, tuned by screwtaps around the rim
tubular bells suspended on a frame
glockenspiel (German '*bell play*') a small keyboard of steel bars
xylophone similar to a glockenspiel, but with wooden rather than metal bars.

Instruments without definite pitch include:
snare drum with a membrane across both ends, and a 'snare' that rattles against the underside when the drum is beaten
bass drum, which produces the lowest sound in the orchestra
tambourine a wooden hoop with a membrane stretched across it, and with metal jingles inserted in the sides
triangle a suspended triangular-shaped steel bar, played by striking it with a separate bar of steel. The sound produced can be clearly percieved even when played agianst a full orchestra
cymbals two brass dishes struck together
castanets two hollow shells of wood struck together
gong a suspended disc of metal struck with a soft hammer.

Percy /'pɜ:si/ family name of dukes of Northumberland; seated at Alnwick Castle, Northumberland, England.

Pepys *Portrait by John Hayls (1666), National Portrait Gallery, London.*

percussion instrument

bass drum

kettle drum

tambourine

snare drum

glockenspiel

tubular bells

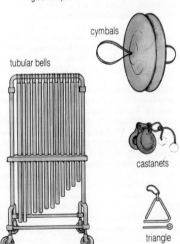

cymbals

castanets

triangle

Percy /'pɜːsi/ Henry 'Hotspur' 1364–1403. English soldier, son of the 1st Earl of Northumberland. In repelling a border raid, he defeated the Scots at Homildon Hill in Durham 1402, and was killed at the battle of Shrewsbury while in revolt against Henry IV.

Percy /'pɜːsi/ Thomas 1729–1811. English scholar and bishop of Dromore from 1782. He discovered a manuscript collection of songs, ballads, and romances, from which he published a selection as *Reliques of Ancient English Poetry* 1765, influential in the Romantic revival.

Pereira capital of Risaralda department, central Colombia, situated at an altitude of 1,463 m/ 4,800 ft, overlooking the fertile Cauca valley west of Bogota; population (1985) 390,000. Founded 1863, the city has developed into an important centre of the country's coffee and cattle industries.

Perelman /'perəlmən/ S(idney) J(oseph) 1904– 1979. US humorist, born in New York. He wrote for the *New Yorker* magazine, and film scripts for the Marx Brothers. He shared the Academy Award for the film script *Around the World in 80 Days* 1956.

perennating organ in plants, that part of a ◊biennial plant or herbaceous ◊perennial that allows it to survive the winter, usually a root, tuber, rhizome, bulb, or corm.

perennial plant a plant that lives for more than two years. Herbaceous perennials have aerial stems and leaves which die each autumn, and they survive the winter by means of an underground storage (perennating) organ, such as a bulb or rhizome. Trees and shrubs, or woody perennials, have stems which persist above ground throughout the year, and may be either ◊deciduous or ◊evergreen. See also ◊annual plant, ◊biennial plant.

Peres /'peres/ Shimon 1923–   . Israeli socialist politician, prime minister 1984–86. Peres emigrated from Poland to Palestine 1934, but was educated in the USA. In 1959 he was elected to the Knesset (Israeli parliament). He became leader of the Labour Party 1977. Peres was prime minister under a power-sharing agreement with the leader of the Consolidation Party (Likud), Yitzhak ◊Shamir.

perestroika (Russian 'restructuring') in Soviet politics, the wide-ranging economic and government reforms initiated during Gorbachev's leadership of the Soviet state and its institutions. It is also the title of a book by Gorbachev 1987.

Originally, in the economic sphere, perestroika was conceived as involving the 'switching onto a track of intensive development' by automation and improved labour efficiency. It has evolved, however, to increasingly attend to market indicators and incentives ('market socialism') and a gradual dismantlement of the Stalinist central planning system, with decision-taking authority being devolved to self-financing enterprises.

Pérez de Cuéllar /'peres də 'kweɪjɑː/ Javier 1920–   . Peruvian diplomat. A delegate to the first United Nations general assembly 1946–47, he held several ambassadorial posts and was appointed secretary-general of the UN 1982.

Pérez Galdós /'peresp gæl'dɒs/ Benito 1843–1920. Spanish novelist, born in the Canary Islands. His works include the 46 historical novels in the cycle *Episodios nacionales* and the 21-novel cycle *Novelas españolas contemporáneos*, which includes *Doña Perfecta* 1876 and the epic *Fortunata y Jacinta* 1886–87, his masterpiece. In scale he has been compared to Balzac and Dickens.

perfect competition see ◊competition, perfect.

Pérez de Cuéllar *Peruvian diplomat and secretary-general of the United Nations since 1982, Javier Pérez de Cuéllar, Mexico City, 1984.*

Pericles *Bust of Pericles found near Tivoli, Italy, 1781. Under his rule, Greek culture reached its finest expression.*

performance art staged artistic events, sometimes including music, painting, and sculpture. The events, which originated in the 1950s, are akin to happenings but less spontaneous.

perfume fragrant essence used to scent the body, cosmetics, and candles. More than 100 natural aromatic chemicals may be blended from a range of 60,000 flowers, leaves, fruits, seeds, woods, barks, resins, and roots, combined by natural animal fixatives and various synthetics, the latter increasingly used even in expensive products.

Favoured ingredients include ◊balsam, ◊civet, hyacinth, ◊jasmine, lily of the valley, musk (from the ◊musk deer), orange blossom, rose, and tuberose. Culture of the cells of such plants, on membranes that are constantly bathed in a solution to carry the essential oils away for separation, is now being adopted to reduce costs.

Perga /'pɜːgə/ ruined city of Pamphylia, 16 km/ 10 mi NE of Adalia, Turkey, noted for its local cult of Artemis. It was visited by the apostle St Paul.

Pergamum /'pɜːgəməm/ ancient Greek city in W Asia Minor, which became the capital of an independent kingdom 283 BC. As the ally of Rome it achieved great political importance in the 2nd century BC, and became a centre of art and culture. Close to its site is the modern Turkish town of Bergama.

peri in Persian myth, a beautiful, harmless being, ranking between angels and evil spirits. Peris were ruled by Eblis, greatest of evil spirits.

Peri /'peəri/ Jacopo 1561–1633. Italian composer, who served the ◊Medici family. His experimental melodic opera *Euridice* 1600 established the opera form and influenced Monteverdi. His first opera, *Dafne* 1597, is now lost.

perianth a collective term for the outer whorls of the ◊flower, which protect the reproductive parts during development. In most ◊dicotyledons the perianth is composed of two distinct whorls, the calyx of ◊sepals and the corolla of ◊petals, whereas in many ◊monocotyledons they are indistinguishable and the segments of the perianth are then known individually as tepals.

periastron in astronomy, the point at which an object travelling in an elliptical orbit around a star is at its closest to the star; compare ◊apastron.

pericarp the wall of a ◊fruit. It encloses the seeds and is derived from the ◊ovary wall. In fruits such as the acorn, the pericarp becomes dry and hardened, forming a shell around the seed. In fleshy fruits the pericarp is typically made up of three distinct layers. The *epicarp* or *exocarp* forms the tough outer skin of the fruits, while the *mesocarp* is often fleshy and forms the middle layers. The innermost layer or *endocarp*, which surrounds the seeds may be membranous, or may be thickened and hard, as in the ◊drupe (stone) of cherries, plums, and apricots.

Pericles /'perɪkliːz/ *c.*490–429 BC. Athenian politician, who dominated the city's affairs from 461 BC (as leader of the democratic party), and under whom Greek culture reached its height. He created a confederation of cities under the leadership of Athens, but the disasters of the ◊Peloponnesian War led to his overthrow 430 BC. Although quickly reinstated, he died soon after.

peridot a gem variety of the mineral ◊olivine. *Peridotite* is an ultrabasic (silica-poor) ◊igneous rock that consists almost entirely of olivine.

peridotite a rock consisting largely of the mineral olivine; pyroxene and other minerals may also be present. Peridotite is an ultrabasic rock containing less than 45% silica by weight. It is believed to be one of the rock types making up the Earth's upper mantle, and is sometimes brought from the depths to the surface by major movements, or as inclusions in lavas.

perigee the point at which an object, travelling in an elliptical orbit around the Earth, is at its closest to the Earth.

Périgueux /ˌperɪ'gɜː/ capital of Dordogne *département*, Aquitaine, France, on the river Isle, 127 km/79 mi ENE of Bordeaux; trading centre for wine and truffles; population (1982) 35,392. The Byzantine cathedral dates from 984.

perihelion the point at which an object, travelling in an elliptical orbit around the Sun, is at its closest to the Sun.

Perim /'perɪm/ island in the strait of Bab-el-Mandeb, the S entrance to the Red Sea; part of South Yemen; area 13 sq km/5 sq mi.

perinatal relating to the period shortly before, during, and after the birth of a child.

period a punctuation mark (.). The term 'period' is universally understood in English, and is the preferred usage in North America; the term 'full stop' is the preferred form in the UK. Traditionally, the period has two functions: to mark the end of a properly formed sentence, and to indicate that a word has been abbreviated.

In present-day practice these functions continue, but in such contexts as fictional dialogue and advertising, periods often follow phrases and incomplete sentences, in order to represent speech more faithfully or for purposes of emphasis. Such abbreviations as acronyms are unlikely to have periods (NATO rather than N.A.T.O.), and contractions may or may not have periods, according to the stylistic preference of the writer (for instance, 'Mr Greene' or 'Mr. Greene', as preferred).

period another name for menstruation; see ◊menstrual cycle.

period in physics, the time taken for one complete cycle of a repeated sequence of events. For example, the time taken for a pendulum to swing from side to side and back again is the period of the pendulum.

periodic table of the elements a classification of the elements following the statement by Mendeleyev 1869 that 'the properties of elements are in periodic dependence upon their atomic weight'. Today elements are arranged in sequence according to their ◊atomic numbers, and classified into nine vertical groups (groups I–VIII plus the ◊transition elements) and seven horizontal periods. There are striking similarities in the chemical properties of the elements in each of the main groups, and a gradation of properties along the periods. These are dependent on the electronic and nuclear structure of atoms of the elements. The table has been used to predict the existence of as yet unknown ◊transuranic elements.

periodontal disease formerly known as *pyorrhoea* disease of the supporting tissues of the teeth caused

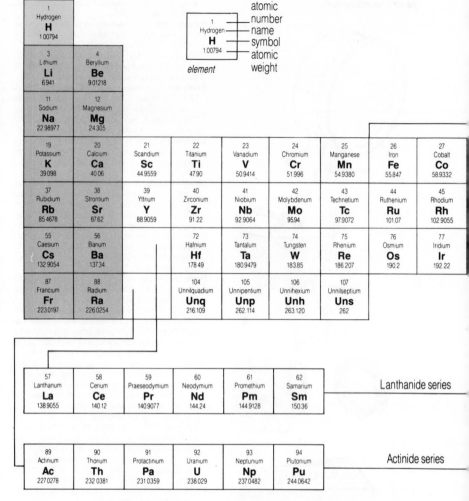

by the accumulation of plaque; the gums recede, and the teeth become loose and may eventually drop out.

peripheral device in computing, any item of equipment attached to and controlled by a computer. Peripherals are typically for input from and output to the user (for example, a keyboard or printer), storing data (for example, a disc drive), communications (such as a modem) or for performing physical tasks (such as a robot).

periscope optical instrument designed for observation from a concealed position. In its basic form, it consists of a tube with parallel mirrors at each end inclined at 45° to its axis. It attained prominence in naval and military operations of World War I.

peristalsis contractions that pass along tubular organs, such as the intestines, in waves produced by the contraction of smooth ◊muscle. The same term describes the wavelike motion of earthworms and other invertebrates, in which part of the body contracts as another part elongates.

peritoneum the tissue lining the abdominal cavity and digestive organs of vertebrates.

peritonitis inflammation within the peritoneum, due to infection or other irritation. It is sometimes seen following a burst appendix. Peritonitis would quickly prove fatal without treatment.

periwinkle in botany, trailing blue-flowered evergreen plants of the genus *Vinca*, family Apocynaceae.

The related *Madagascar periwinkle Catharanthus roseus* produces chemicals that inhibit the division of cells and are used to treat leukaemia.

periwinkle in zoology, a snail-like marine mollusc found on the shores of Europe and E North America. It has a conical spiral shell, and feeds on algae.

perjury the offence of deliberately making a false statement on ◊oath (or ◊affirmation) when appearing as a witness in legal proceedings, on a point material to the question at issue. In Britain it is punishable by a fine, imprisonment up to seven years, or both.

Perkin /'pɜːkɪn/ William Henry 1838–1907. British chemist. In 1856 he discovered the mauve dye that originated the aniline dye industry.

Perkins /'pɜːkɪnz/ Anthony 1932– . US film actor who played the mother-fixated psychopath Norman Bates in *Psycho* 1960.

Perkins Gilman /'pɜːkɪnz 'gɪlmən/ Charlotte 1860–1935. US feminist socialist poet, novelist, and historian, author of *Women and Economics*, proposing the ending of the division between 'men's work' and 'women's work' by abolishing housework. From 1909 to 1916 she wrote and published a magazine *The Forerunner* in which her feminist Utopian novel *Herland* 1915 was serialized.

Perlis /'pɜːlɪs/ border state of Peninsular Malaysia, NW Malaysia; capital Kangar; area 800 sq km/309 sq mi; population (1980) 148,000. It produced rubber, rice, coconuts, and tin. Perlis is ruled by a raja. It was transferred by Siam to Britain 1909.

Perm /pɜːm/ industrial city (shipbuilding, oil refining, aircraft, chemicals, sawmills), capital of Perm region, USSR, on the Kama near the Ural mountains; population (1987) 1,075,000. It was called Molotov 1940–57.

permafrost condition in which a deep layer of soil does not thaw out during the summer but remains at below 0°C/32°F for at least two years, despite thawing of the soil above. It is claimed that 26% of the world's land surface is permafrost.

periodic table of the elements

					2 Helium **He** 4.00260
5 Boron **B** 10.81	6 Carbon **C** 12.011	7 Nitrogen **N** 14.0067	8 Oxygen **O** 15.9994	9 Fluorine **F** 18.99840	10 Neon **Ne** 20.179
13 Aluminium **Al** 26.98154	14 Silicon **Si** 28.086	15 Phosphorus **P** 30.97376P	16 Sulphur **S** 32.06	17 Chlorine **Cl** 35.453	18 Argon **Ar** 39.948

28 Nickel **Ni** 58.70	29 Copper **Cu** 63.546	30 Zinc **Zn** 65.38	31 Gallium **Ga** 69.72	32 Germanium **Ge** 72.59	33 Arsenic **As** 74.9216	34 Selenium **Se** 78.96	35 Bromine **Br** 79.904	36 Krypton **Kr** 83.80
46 Palladium **Pd** 106.4	47 Silver **Ag** 107.868	48 Cadmium **Cd** 112.40	49 Indium **In** 114.82	50 Tin **Sn** 118.69	51 Antimony **Sb** 121.75	52 Tellurium **Te** 127.75	53 Iodine **I** 126.9045	54 Xenon **Xe** 131.30
78 Platinum **Pt** 195.09	79 Gold **Au** 196.9665	80 Mercury **Hg** 200.59	81 Thallium **Tl** 204.37	82 Lead **Pb** 207.37	83 Bismuth **Bi** 207.2	84 Polonium **Po** 210	85 Astatine **At** 211	86 Radon **Rn** 222.0176

63 Europium **Eu** 151.96	64 Gadolinium **Gd** 157.25	65 Terbium **Tb** 158.9254	66 Dysprosium **Dy** 162.50	67 Holmium **Ho** 164.9304	68 Erbium **Er** 167.26	69 Thulium **Tm** 168.9342	70 Ytterbium **Yb** 173.04	71 Lutetium **Lu** 174.97
95 Americium **Am** 243.0614	96 Curium **Cm** 247.0703	97 Berkelium **Bk** 247.0703	98 Californium **Cf** 251.0786	99 Einsteinium **Es** 252.0828	100 Fermium **Fm** 257.0951	101 Mendelvium **Md** 258.0986	012 Nobelium **No** 259.1009	103 Lawrencium **Lr** 260.1054

Permafrost gives rise to a poorly drained form of grassland typical of N Canada, Siberia, and Alaska known as ◊tundra.

Permian period of geological time 286–248 million years ago, the last period of the Palaeozoic era. Its end was marked by a significant change in marine life, including the extinction of many corals and trilobites. Deserts were widespread, and terrestrial amphibians and mammal-like reptiles flourished. Cone-bearing plants (gymnosperms) came to prominence.

permutation in mathematics, a specified arrangement of a group of objects. It is the arrangement of *a* distinct objects taken *b* at a time in all possible orders. It is given by $a!/(a − b)!$, where '!' stands for ◊factorial. For example, the number of permutations of four letters taken from any group of six different letters is $6!/2! = (1 × 2 × 3 × 4 × 5 × 6)/(1 × 2) = 360$.

The theoretical number of four-letter 'words' that can be made from an alphabet of 26 letters is $26!/22! = 358,800$. See also ◊combination.

Pernambuco /ˌpɜːnæmˈbuːkəʊ/ state of NE Brazil, on the Atlantic

area 98,281 sq km/37,946 sq mi

capital Recife (former name Pernambuco)

features highlands; the coast is low and humid

population (1985) 6,776,000.

Perón /peˈrɒn/ 'Evita' (Maria Eva) (born Duarte) 1919–1952. Argentinian populist leader, born in Buenos Aires. A successful radio actress, in 1945 she married Juan Perón. After he became president she virtually ran the health and labour ministries, and did a lot of charitable work. In 1951 she stood for the post of vice president, but was opposed by the army and withdrew; she died of cancer soon afterwards.

Perón /peˈrɒn/ (María Estela) Isabel (born Martínez) 1931– . President of Argentina 1974–76, and third wife of Juan Perón. She succeeded him after he died in office, but labour unrest, inflation, and political violence pushed the country to the brink of chaos. Accused of corruption, she was held under house arrest for five years. She went into exile in Spain.

Perón /peˈrɒn/ Juan (Domingo) 1895–1974. Argentine politician, dictator 1946–55 and from 1973 until his death. He took part in the military coup 1943, and his popularity with the *descamisados* ('shirtless ones') led to his election as president 1946. He instituted social reforms, but encountered economic difficulties. After the death of his second wife Eva Perón he lost popularity, and was deposed in a military coup 1955. He returned from exile to the presidency 1973, but died in office 1974, and was succeeded by his third wife Isabel Perón.

Perotin the Great *c.*1160–*c.*1220. French composer. His church music has a timeless quality and introduced new concepts of harmony and part-writing to traditional organum.

Perpendicular a period of English Gothic architecture lasting from the end of the 14th century to the mid-16th century. It is characterized by window tracery consisting chiefly of vertical members, two or four arc arches, lavishly decorated vaults and use of traceried panels. Examples include the choir and cloister of Gloucester Cathedral, and King's College Chapel, Cambridge.

perpetual motion idea that a machine can be designed and constructed in such a way that, once started, it will continue in motion indefinitely without requiring any further input of energy (motive power). Such a device contradicts the two laws of thermodynamics that state that (a) energy can neither be created nor destroyed (the law of conservation of energy), and (b) heat cannot by itself flow from a cooler to a hotter object. As a result, all practical (real) machines require a continuous supply of energy, and no heat engine is able to convert all the heat into useful work.

Perpignan /ˌpɜːpiːnˈjɒŋ/ market town (olives, fruit, wine) and resort, capital of the Pyrénées-Orientales *département* of France, just off the Mediterranean coast, near the Spanish border; population (1982) 138,000. Overlooking Perpignan is the castle of the counts of Roussillon.

per pro abbreviation for *per procurationem* (Latin 'by the agency of').

Perrault /peˈrəʊ/ Charles 1628–1703. French author of the fairy tales *Contes de ma mère l'oye/ Mother Goose's Fairy Tales* 1697, including 'Sleeping Beauty', 'Red Riding Hood', 'Blue Beard', 'Puss in Boots', and 'Cinderella'.

Perrin Jean 1870–1942. French physicist who produced the crucial evidence that finally established the atomic nature of matter. Assuming the atomic hypothesis, Perrin demonstrated how the phenomenon of ◊Brownian movement could be used to derive precise values of ◊Avrogrado's number. He won the 1926 Nobel physics prize.

perry alcoholic liquor made from pears, produced mainly in Normandy and the English West Country.

Perry /ˈperi/ Frederick John 1909– . English lawn-tennis player, the last Briton to win the men's singles at Wimbledon 1936. He also won the world table-tennis title 1929. He later became a television commentator.

CAREER HIGHLIGHTS

lawn tennis
Wimbledon
singles: 1934–36
French Open
singles: 1935
doubles: 1933
Australian Open
singles: 1934
doubles: 1934
US Open
singles: 1933–34, 1936
table tennis
World Championships
singles: 1929
English Championships
doubles: 1928–30

Perón Eva (Evita) Perón used her talents as a broadcaster and speaker to gain support for her husband Juan Perón, the Argentinian leader.

Perry /'peri/ Matthew Calbraith 1794–1858. US naval officer, commander of the expedition of 1853 that reopened communication between Japan and the outside world after 250 years' isolation. Evident military superiority enabled him to negotiate the *Treaty of Kanagawa* 1854 giving the USA trading rights with Japan.

per se (Latin) in itself.

Perse /pɜːs/ Saint-John. Pen name of Alexis Saint-Léger 1887–1975. French poet and diplomat, a US citizen from 1940. His first book of verse, *Eloges* 1911, reflects the ambience of the West Indies, where he was born and raised. His later works include *Anabase* 1924, an epic poem translated by T S Eliot in 1930. Nobel prize 1960.

Entering the foreign service in 1914, he was secretary-general 1933–40. He then emigrated permanently to the USA, and was deprived of French citizenship by the Vichy government.

Persephone /pɜː'sefəni/ Greek goddess, the daughter of Zeus and Demeter. She was carried off to the underworld by Pluto, who later agreed that she should spend six months of the year with her mother. The myth symbolizes the growth and decay of vegetation.

Persepolis /pɜː'sepəlɪs/ ancient capital of the Persian Empire, 65 km/40 mi NE of Shiraz. It was burned down after its capture in 331 BC by Alexander the Great.

Perseus /'pɜːsjuːs/ in Greek mythology, son of Zeus and Danaë. He slew ◊Medusa, the Gorgon; rescued ◊Andromeda; and became king of Tiryns.

Perseus /'pɜːsjuːs/ in astronomy, a constellation of the northern hemisphere, near Cassiopeia, representing the mythological hero. The eye of the decapitated Gorgon is represented by the variable star Algol. Perseus lies in the Milky Way and contains the Double Cluster, a twin cluster of stars. Every August the Perseid meteor shower radiates from its northern part.

Pershing /'pɜːʃɪŋ/ John Joseph 1860–1948. US general. He served in the Spanish War 1898, the Philippines 1899–1903, and Mexico 1916–17. He commanded the US Expeditionary Force sent to France 1917–18.

Persia, ancient kingdom in SW Asia. The early Persians were a nomadic Aryan people that migrated through the Caucasus to the Iranian plateau.

7th century BC The Persians were established in the present region of Fars, which then belonged to the Assyrians.

550 ◊Cyrus the Great overthrew the empire of the Medes, to whom the Persians had been subject, and founded the Persian Empire.

539 Having conquered all Anatolia, Cyrus added Babylonia (including Syria and Palestine) to his empire.

529–485 ◊Darius I organized an efficient centralized system of administration and extended Persian rule east into Afghanistan and NW India and as far north as the Danube, but the empire was weakened by internal dynastic struggles.

499–449 The ◊*Persian Wars* with Greece ended Persian domination of the ancient world.

331 Alexander the Great drove the Persians under Darius III (died 330 BC) into retreat at Arbela on the Tigris, marking the end of the Persian Empire and the beginning of the Hellenistic period under the Seleucids.

AD 226 The ◊Sassanian Empire was established in Persia, and annexed Parthia.

637 Arabs took the capital, Ctesiphon, and introduced Islam in place of Zoroastrianism.
For modern history see ◊Iran.

Persian inhabitant of Persia (Iran). The Persians claim descent from Aryans who are thought to have migrated from S Russia around 2000 BC. The Persian language belongs to the Indo-Iranian branch of the Indo-European family.

Persian art see under ◊ancient art: art of early civilizations.

Persian Gulf or *Arabian Gulf* a large shallow inlet of the Arabian Sea; area 233,000 sq km/90,000 sq mi.

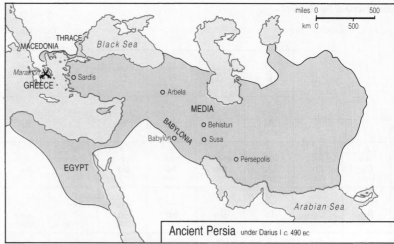

Ancient Persia under Darius I c. 490 BC

It divides the Arabian peninsula from Iran, and is linked by the Strait of Hormuz and the Gulf of Oman to the Arabian Sea. Oilfields surround it in the Gulf States of Bahrain, Iran, Iraq, Kuwait, Oman, Qatar, Saudi Arabia, and the United Arab Emirates.

Persian language a member of the Indo-Iranian branch of the Indo-European language family and the official language of the state once known as Persia but now called Iran. Persian is known to its own speakers as *Farsi*, the language of the province of Fars (Persia proper). It is written in the Arabic script, from right to left, and has a large mixture of Arabic religious, philosophical, and technical vocabulary.

Persian literature before the Arab conquest is represented by the sacred books of ◊Zoroastrianism known as the Avesta and later translated into Pahlavi, in which language there also appeared various secular writings. After the conquest the use of Arabic became widespread. The Persian language was revived during the 9th century and the following centuries saw a succession of brilliant poets including the epic writer Firdawsi, the didactic S'adi (1184–1291), the mystic Rumi (1207–73), the lyrical Hafiz, and Jami who combined the gifts of his predecessors and is considered the last of the classical poets. Omar Khayyam, who is well known outside Persia, is less considered there. In the 16th and 17th centuries many of the best writers worked in India, still using classical forms and themes, and it was not until the revolutionary movements and contact with the West during the 20th century that Persian literature developed further.

Persian Wars a series of conflicts between the Greeks and the Persians 499–449 BC. The eventual victory of Greece marked the end of

Perry Matthew Perry, whose expedition to Japan 1853 led to the Treaty of Kanagawa enabling Europe and the USA to trade with Japan.

Persian domination of the ancient world and the beginning of Greek supremacy.

499 Revolt of the Ionian Greeks against Persian rule.

490 Darius I of Persia defeated at Marathon.

480 Xerxes I victorious at Thermopylae (narrow pass from Thessaly to Locris, which Leonidas, king of Sparta, and 1,000 men defended to the death against the Persians); Athens was captured, but the Greek navy was victorious at ◊Salamis.

479 Greeks under Spartan general Pausanias (died c. 470) victorious at Plataea, driving the Persians from the country.

persicaria plant *Polygonum persicaria* of the dock family, found growing in waste places and arable land, often near water. Sprawling, with lance-shaped, black-spotted leaves, it bears spikes of pink flowers. *Pale persicaria Polygonum lapathifolium* is slightly larger, with pale dots on the leaves, and heads of usually white flowers.

persimmon or *Virginian date plum* tree *Diospyros virginiana* of the family Ebenaceae, native to North America. Some 12 m/40 ft high, the persimmon has alternate oval leaves, and yellow-green unisexual flowers. The small, sweet, orange fruits are edible. The Japanese persimmon *Diospyros kaki* has larger fruits and is widely cultivated.

personal computer (PC) another name for ◊microcomputer. The term is also used, more specifically, to mean the IBM Personal Computer and machines based on it.

The first IBM PC was introduced in 1981; it had 64 kilobytes of random access memory (RAM) and one floppy-disc drive. It was followed in 1983 by the XT (with a hard-disc drive) and in 1984 by the AT (based on a more powerful ◊microprocessor). Many manufacturers have copied the basic design, which is now regarded as a standard for business microcomputers.

personal equity plan (PEP) investment scheme introduced in the UK 1987. Shares of public companies listed on the UK stock exchange are purchased by PEP managers on behalf of their clients. Up to certain limits, individuals may purchase such shares and, provided they hold them for at least a year, enjoy any capital gains and reinvested dividends tax-free.

personality an individual's characteristic way of behaving across a wide range of situations. Two broad dimensions of personality are ◊extroversion and ◊neuroticism. A number of more specific personal traits have also been described, including ◊psychopathy (antisocial behaviour).

personification a ◊figure of speech in which animals, plants, objects, and ideas are treated as if they were human or alive ('Clouds chased each other across the face of the moon'; 'Nature smiled on their work and gave it her blessing'; 'The future beckoned eagerly to them').

Perspex trade name for a clear tough plastic first produced 1930. It is widely used for watch glasses, advertising signs, domestic baths, motorboat windshields and protective shields. Its chemical name is polymethylmethacrylate (PMMA). It is manufactured under other names: Plexiglas (in the USA), Oroglas (in Europe), and Lucite.

perspiration the excretion of water and dissolved substances from the ◊sweat glands of the skin of mammals. Perspiration has two main functions: body cooling by the evaporation of water from the skin surface, and excretion of waste products such as salts.

Perth /pɜːθ/ industrial town in Tayside, E Scotland, on the river Tay; population (1981) 42,000. It was the capital of Scotland from the 12th century until James I of Scotland was assassinated here 1437.

Perth /pɜːθ/ capital of Western Australia, with its port at nearby Fremantle on the Swan river; population (1986) 1,025,300. Products include textiles, cement, furniture, and vehicles. It was founded 1829, and is the commercial and cultural centre of the state.

Perthshire /'pɜːθʃə/ former inland county of central Scotland, of which the major part was included in Tayside 1975, the SW being included in Central region; Perth was the administrative headquarters.

Peru /pə'ruː/ country in South America, on the Pacific, bounded to the N by Ecuador and Colombia, to the E by Brazil and Bolivia, and to the S by Chile.

government The 1980 constitution provides for a president who is head of both state and government, elected by universal suffrage for a five-year term, and governing with an appointed council of ministers.

The two-chamber legislature, the National Congress, comprises a 60-member Senate and a 180-member Chamber of Deputies, also popularly elected for five years. Senators are elected on a national basis but members of the Chamber are elected, through a system of proportional representation, from local constituencies. The two main political parties are the democratic left-wing American Popular Revolutionary Alliance (APRA), and the alliance of six left-wing parties, the Unified Left (IU).

history For early history, see ◊American Indian. The ◊Chimu culture flourished from about 1200 and was gradually superseded by the ◊Inca empire, building on 800 years of Andean civilization and covering a large part of South America. Civil war had weakened the Incas when the conquistador ◊Pizarro arrived from Spain 1532, raiding, looting, and enslaving the people. He executed the last of the Inca emperors, Atahualpa, 1533. Before Pizarro's assassination 1541, Spanish rule was firmly established.

A native revolt by ◊Tupac Amaru 1780 failed, and during the successful rebellions by the European settlers in other Spanish possessions in South America 1810–22, Peru remained the Spanish government's headquarters; it was the last to achieve independence 1824. It attempted union with Bolivia 1836–39. It fought a naval war against Spain 1864–66, and in the ◊Pacific War against Chile 1879–83 over the nitrate fields of the Atacama Desert, Peru was defeated and lost three provinces (one, Tacna, was returned 1929). Other boundary disputes were settled by arbitration 1902 with Bolivia, 1927 with Colombia, and 1942 with Ecuador. Peru declared war on Germany and Japan Feb 1945.

Peru was ruled by right-wing dictatorships from the mid-1920s until 1945 when free elections returned. Although Peru's oldest political organization, APRA, was the largest party in Congress, it was constantly thwarted by smaller conservative groups, anxious to protect their business interests. APRA was founded in the 1920s to fight imperialism throughout South America but Peru was the only country where it became established.

In 1948 a group of army officers led by Gen Manuel Odría ousted the elected government, temporarily banned APRA and installed a military junta. Odría became president 1950 and remained

in power until 1956. In 1963 military rule ended and Fernando Belaúnde Terry, the joint candidate of the Popular Action (AP) and Christian Democrats (PDC) parties, won the presidency, while APRA took the largest share of the Chamber of Deputies seats.

After economic problems and industrial unrest, Belaúnde was deposed in a bloodless coup 1968 and the army returned to government led by Gen Velasco Alvarado. Velasco introduced land reform, with private estates being turned into cooperative farms, but he failed to return any land to Indian peasant communities, and the Maoist guerrillas of Sendero Luminoso became increasingly active in the Indian region of S Peru.

Another bloodless coup, 1975, brought in Gen Morales Bermúdez. He called elections for the presidency and both chambers of Congress May 1980 and Belaúnde was re-elected. Belaúnde embarked on a programme of agrarian and industrial reform but at the end of his presidency, in 1985, the country was again in a state of economic and social crisis. His constitutionally elected successor was the young Social Democrat, Alan García Pérez, who embarked on cleansing the army and police of the old guard. By Feb 1986 about 1,400 had elected to retire. After trying to expand the economy with price and exchange controls, in July 1987 he announced his intention to nationalize the banks and insurance companies, but delayed the move in Aug, after a vigorous campaign against the proposal.

García Pérez has declared his support for the Sandinista government in Nicaragua and criticized US policy throughout Latin America.

Peru Current formerly known as *Humboldt Current* cold ocean ◊current flowing north from the Antarctic along the W coast of South America to S Ecuador, then west. It reduces the coastal temperature, making the W slopes of the Andes arid because winds are already chilled and dry when they meet the coast.

Peru
Republic of
(República del Perú)

area 1,285,200 sq km/496,093 sq mi
capital Lima, including port of Callao
towns Arequipa, Iquitos, Chiclayo
physical Andes mountains N–S cover 27%; Amazon river-basin jungle in NE
features Lake Titicaca; Peru Current; Atacama Desert; monuments of the Chimu and Inca civilizations
head of state and government Alan García Pérez from 1985
government democratic republic
political parties American Popular Revolutionary Alliance (APRA), moderate, left-wing; United Left (IU), left-wing
exports coffee, alpaca, llama and vicuna wool,

Perugia /pə'ruːdʒə/ capital of Umbria, Italy, 520 m/1,700 ft above the Tiber, about 137 km/85 mi north of Rome; population (1988) 148,000. Its industries include textiles, liqueurs, and chocolate. One of the 12 cities of Etruria, it surrendered to Rome 309 BC. There is a university 1276, municipal palace 1281, and a 15th-century cathedral.

Perugino /,peru:'dʒiːnəʊ/ Pietro. Assumed name of Pietro Vannucci 1445/50–1523. Italian painter, active chiefly in Perugia, the teacher of Raphael, who absorbed his soft and graceful figure style. Perugino produced paintings for the lower walls of the Sistine Chapel 1481 (Vatican), and in 1500 decorated the Sala del Cambio in Perugia.

Perutz /pə'ruːts/ Max 1914– . Austrian-born British biochemist, who shared the Nobel chemistry prize 1962 with John Kendrew for work on the structure of the haemoglobin molecule.

Perutz moved to Britain in 1936 to work with John Bernal (1901–1971) at Cambridge University. After internment in Canada as an alien during World War II he returned to Cambridge and completed his research in 1959.

perverting the course of justice in English law, the criminal offence of acting in such a way as to prevent justice being done. Examples are tampering with evidence, misleading the police or a court, and threatening witnesses or jurors.

Pesach the Jewish festival of ◊Passover.

Pescadores /,peskə'dɔːrɪz/ (Chinese *Penghu*) group of about 60 islands off Taiwan, of which they form a dependency; area 130 sq km/50 sq mi.

Pescara /pe'skɑːrə/ town in Abruzzi, E Italy, at the mouth of the Pescara river, on the Adriatic; population (1988) 131,000. Hydroelectric installations supply Rome with electricity. It is linked to Yugoslavia by ferry.

peseta the standard currency of Spain.

Peshawar /pə'ʃaʊə/ capital of North-West Frontier Province, Pakistan, 18 km/11 mi E of the Khyber

---

fish meal, lead, copper, iron, oil
currency inti (21834.40 = £1 Feb 1990)
population (1989) 21,792,000 (46% American Indian, mainly Quechua and Aymara; 43% of mixed Spanish-American Indian descent); annual growth rate 2.6%
life expectancy men 57, women 61
language Spanish 68%, Quechua 27% (both official), Aymará 3%
religion Roman Catholic
literacy 91% male/78% female (1985 est)
GNP $18.6 bn (1983); $655 per head of population
chronology
1824 Achieved independence from Spain, the last South American country to do so.
1902 Boundary dispute with Bolivia settled.
1927 Boundary dispute with Colombia settled.
1942 Boundary dispute with Ecuador settled.
1948 Army coup, led by Gen Manuel Odria, installed a military government.
1963 Return to civilian rule, with Fernando Belaúnde Terry as president.
1968 Return of military government in a bloodless coup led by Gen Juan Velasco Alvarado.
1975 Velasco replaced, in a bloodless coup, by Gen Morales Bermúdez.
1980 Return to civilian rule, with Fernando Belaúnde as president.
1981 Boundary dispute with Ecuador renewed.
1985 Belaúnde succeeded by Social Democrat Alan García Pérez.
1987 President García delayed the nationalization of Peru's banks after a vigorous campaign against the proposal.
1988 García under pressure to seek help from the International Monetary Fund.
1989 The International Development Bank suspended credit to Peru because it was six months behind in debt payments. The annual inflation rate to Apr was 4,329%.

Pass; population (1981) 555,000. Products include textiles, leather, and copper.

pessary a device for administering drugs locally to the vagina. It is a suitably shaped solid body, made usually from glycerine or oil of theobromine, which melts within the vagina to release the contained drug, for example a contraceptive, antibiotic, or antifungal agent.

Pessoa /pəˈsəʊə/ Fernando 1888–1935. Portuguese poet. Born in Lisbon, he was brought up in South Africa, and was bilingual in English and Portuguese. He wrote under three assumed names (which he called 'heteronyms': Alvaro de Campos, Ricardo Reis, and Alberto Caeiro), for each of whom he invented a biography.

pest in biology, any insect, fungus, rodent, or other living organism that has a harmful effect on human beings, other than those that directly cause human diseases. Most pests damage crops or livestock, but the term also covers those that damage buildings, destroy food stores, and spread disease.

Pestalozzi /ˌpestəˈlɒtsi/ Johann Heinrich 1746–1827. Swiss educationalist who advocated Rousseau's 'natural' principles (of natural development and the power of example), and described his own theories in *Wie Gertrude ihre Kinder lehrt/How Gertrude Teaches her Children* 1801. He stressed the importance of mother and home in a child's education. *International Children's Villages* named after him have been established, for example Sedlescombe, East Sussex, UK.

pesticide chemical used in farming and gardening to combat pests and diseases. Pesticides are of three main types—insecticides (to kill insects), fungicides (to kill fungal diseases), and herbicides (to kill weeds). The safest pesticides are those made from plants, such as the insecticides pyrethrum and derris. More potent are synthetic products, such as chlorinated hydrocarbons. These products, including DDT and dieldrin, are highly toxic to wildlife and human beings (there are around 4,000 cases of acute pesticide poisoning a year in the UK), so their use is now declining. Safer pesticides such as malathion are based on organic phosphorus compounds. In 1985, 400 different chemicals were approved in the UK for use as pesticides.

pet animal kept for companionship and occasionally for status. Research suggests that interaction with pets induces relaxation (slower heart rate and lower blood pressure). In 16th–17th century Europe, keeping animals in this way was thought suggestive of witchcraft.

Pétain /peˈtæn/ Henri Philippe 1856–1951. French general and right-wing politician. His defence of Verdun 1916 during World War I made him a national hero. In World War II he became prime minister June 1940 and signed an armistice with Germany. Removing the seat of government to ◊Vichy, he established an authoritarian regime. He was imprisoned after the war.

In 1917 Pétain was created French commander in chief, although he became subordinate to Marshal Foch 1918. He suppressed a rebellion in Morocco 1925–26. As a member of the Higher Council of National Defence he advocated a purely defensive military policy, and was strongly conservative in politics. On the Allied invasion he was taken to Germany, but returned 1945 and was sentenced to death for treason, the sentence being commuted to life imprisonment.

petal part of a flower whose function is to attract pollinators such as insects or birds. Petals are frequently large and brightly coloured, and may also be scented. Some have a nectary at the base and markings on the petal surface, known as ◊honey guides, to direct pollinators to the source of the nectar. In wind-pollinated plants, however, the petals are usually small and insignificant, and sometimes absent altogether. Petals are derived from modified leaves, and are known collectively as a ◊corolla.

Some insect-pollinated plants also have inconspicuous petals, with large colourful ◊bracts or ◊sepals taking over their role, or strong scents that attract pollinators such as flies unaided.

Peter /ˈpiːtə/ Laurence J 1910–1990. Canadian writer and teacher, author (with Raymond Hull) of *The Peter Principle* 1969, in which he outlined the theory that people tend to be promoted into positions for which they are incompetent.

Peter /ˈpiːtə/ three tsars of Russia:

Peter I *the Great* 1672–1725. Tsar of Russia from 1682 on the death of his brother Tsar Feodor, he assumed control of the government 1689. He attempted to reorganize the country on Western lines; the army was modernized, a fleet was built, the administrative and legal systems were remodelled, education was encouraged, and the church was brought under state control. On the Baltic coast, where he had conquered territory from Sweden, Peter built his new capital, St Petersburg (now Leningrad).

After a successful campaign against the Ottoman Empire 1696, he visited Holland and Britain to study Western techniques, and worked in Dutch and English shipyards. In order to secure an outlet to the Baltic, Peter undertook a war with Sweden 1700–21, which resulted in the acquisition of Estonia and parts of Latvia and Finland. A war with Persia 1722–23 added Baku to Russia.

Peter II 1715–1730. Tsar of Russia from 1727. Son of Peter the Great, he had been passed over in favour of Catherine I 1725, but succeeded her 1727. He died of smallpox.

Peter III 1728–1762. Tsar of Russia 1762. Weak-minded son of Peter I's eldest daughter, Anne, he was adopted 1741 by his aunt ◊Elizabeth and at her command married the future Catherine II 1745. He was deposed in favour of his wife, and probably murdered by her lover Alexius Orlov.

Peter I /ˈpiːtə/ 1844–1921. King of Serbia from 1903. He was the son of Prince Alexander Karageorgevich, and was elected king when the last Obrenovich king was murdered 1903. He took part in the retreat of the Serbian army 1915, and in 1918 was proclaimed first king of the Serbs, Croats, and Slovenes.

Peter II /ˈpiːtə/ 1923–1970. King of Yugoslavia 1934–45. He succeeded his father, Alexander I, and assumed the royal power after the overthrow of the regency 1941. He escaped to the UK after the German invasion, and married Princess Alexandra of Greece 1944. He was dethroned 1945.

Peterborough /ˈpiːtəbərə/ city in Cambridgeshire, England, noted for its 12th-century cathedral; population (1981) 115,400. It was designated a new town 1967. Nearby Flag Fen disclosed 1985 a well-preserved Bronze Age settlement of 660 BC.

Peter Damian, St /ˈpiːtə ˈdeɪmɪən/ real name Pietro Damianai 1007–1072. Italian monk who was associated in the initiation of clerical reform with Pope Gregory VII.

Peterhead /ˌpiːtəˈhed/ industrial seaport (fishing, shipbuilding, light engineering, whisky distilling, woollens) in Grampian, Scotland, 54 km/33 mi NE of Aberdeen; population (1981) 17,015. The Old Pretender landed here 1715. The harbour is used by service industries for North Sea oil.

Peter I Island /ˈpiːtə/ uninhabited island in the Bellingshausen Sea, Antarctica, belonging to Norway since 1931; area 180 sq km/69 sq mi.

Peterlee /ˌpiːtəˈliː/ new town in County Durham, England, established 1948; population (1981) 22,750. It was named after Peter Lee, first Labour chair of a county council.

Peter Lombard /ˈpiːtə ˈlɒmbɑːd/ 1100–1160. Italian Christian theologian whose *Sententiarum libri quatuor* considerably influenced Catholic doctrine.

Peterloo massacre name given, in analogy with the Battle of Waterloo, to the events in St Peter's Fields, Manchester, England, 16 Aug 1819, when an open-air meeting in support of parliamentary reform was charged by yeomanry and hussars. Eleven people were killed and 500 wounded.

Peter Pan or *The Boy Who Wouldn't Grow Up* a play for children by J M ◊Barrie, first performed in 1904. Peter Pan, an orphan with magical powers, arrives in the night nursery of the Darling children, Wendy, John and Michael. He teaches them to fly and introduces them to the Never Never Land inhabited by fantastic characters, including the fairy Tinkerbell, the Lost Boys and the pirate Captain Hook. The play was followed by a story, *Peter Pan in Kensington Gardens* 1906, and a book of the play 1911.

Peter Rabbit full title *The Tale of Peter Rabbit* first of the children's stories written and illustrated by English author Beatrix ◊Potter, published in 1900. The series, which included *The Tailor of Gloucester* 1902; *The Tale of Mrs Tiggy Winkle* 1904; *The Tale of Jeremy Fisher* 1906, and a sequel to Peter Rabbit *The Tale of the Flopsy Bunnies* 1909, were based on her observation of family pets and the wildlife around her home in the English Lake District.

Peter, St /ˈpiːtə/ died AD 64. Christian martyr, the author of two epistles in the New Testament and leader of the apostles. Tradition has it that he later settled in Rome; he is regarded as the first bishop of Rome, whose mantle the pope inherits. His emblem is two keys; feast day 29 June.

Originally a fisherman of Capernaum, on the Sea of Galilee, Peter may have been a follower of John the Baptist, and was the first to acknowledge Jesus as the Messiah. His real name was Simon, but he was nicknamed Cephas ('Peter', from the Greek for 'rock') by Jesus as being the rock on which he founded his church. Peter is said to have been crucified under the emperor Nero. Bones excavated from under the Basilica of St Peter's in the Vatican 1968 were accepted as his by Pope Paul VI.

Peter's pence in the Roman Catholic Church, voluntary annual contribution to papal administrative costs; during the 10th–16th centuries it was a compulsory levy of one penny per household.

Peter the Hermit /ˈpiːtə/ 1050–1115. French priest whose eloquent preaching of the First ◊Crusade sent thousands of peasants marching against the Turks, who massacred them in Asia Minor. Peter escaped and accompanied the main body of crusaders to Jerusalem.

petiole in botany, the stalk attaching the leaf blade, or ◊lamina, to the stem. Typically it is continuous with the midrib of the leaf and attached to the base of the lamina, but occasionally it is attached to the lower surface of the lamina (a peltate leaf), as in the nasturtium. Petioles that are flattened and leaf-like are termed phyllodes. Leaves that lack a petiole are said to be ◊sessile.

Petipa /pəˌtiːˈpɑː/ Marius 1818–1910. French choreographer. For the Imperial Ballet in Russia he created masterpieces such as *La Bayadère* 1877, *The Sleeping Beauty* 1890, *Swan Lake* 1895 (with Ivanov), and *Raymonda* 1898, which are still performed.

Petit Alexis 1791–1820. French physicist, co-discoverer of *Dulong and Petit's law*, which states that the ◊specific heat capacity of an element is inversely proportional to its ◊atomic mass.

petition of right in British law, the procedure whereby, before the passing of the ◊Crown Proceedings Act 1947, a subject petitioned for legal relief against the crown, for example for money due under a contract, or for property of which the crown had taken possession. The most famous petition of right was that presented by Parliament and accepted by Charles I in 1628, declaring illegal taxation without parliamentary consent, imprisonment without trial, billeting of soldiers on private persons, and use of martial law.

petit point another name for *tent stitch*. A type of embroidery used on canvas for upholstery and cushions, common in the 18th century.

Petőfi /ˈpetɜːfi/ Sándor 1823–1849. Hungarian nationalist poet. He published his first volume of poems 1844. He expressed his revolutionary ideas in the semi-autobiographical poem 'The Apostle', and died fighting the Austrians in the battle of Segesvár.

Peter I *A portrait engraved from a painting by I Kupetsky in 1737. One of the boats built by Peter the Great is preserved in the National Maritime Museum in London.*

Petra /'petrə/ (Arabic **Wadi Musa**) ruined city carved out of the red rock at a site in modern Jordan, on the eastern slopes of the Wadi el Araba, 90 km/56 mi S of the Dead Sea. An Edomite stronghold and capital of the Nabataeans in the 2nd century, it was captured by the Roman emperor Trajan AD 106 and wrecked by the Arabs in the 7th century. It was forgotten in Europe until 1812 when the Swiss traveller J L Burckhardt came across it.

Petrarch /'petrɑ:k/ (Italian **Petrarca**) Francesco 1304–1374. Italian poet, born in Arezzo, a devotee of the Classical tradition. His *Il Canzoniere* were sonnets in praise of his idealized love 'Laura', whom he first saw 1327. She was a married woman, who refused to become his mistress and died of plague 1348.

From 1337 he often stayed in secluded study at his home at Vaucluse, near Avignon, and, eager to restore the glories of Rome, wanted to return the papacy there from Avignon. He was a friend of ◊Boccaccio, and supported ◊Rienzi's republic 1347.

petrel two families of seabirds (Procellariidae and Hydrobatidae) which include albatrosses, fulmars, and shearwaters.

Most familiar is the storm petrel of the N Atlantic *Hydrobates pelagicus*, also known as Mother Carey's chicken. Seldom coming to land except to breed, they lay a single egg in holes among the rocks. They are sooty black with a white patch on the tail.

Like other ground-nesting or burrow-nesting seabirds, petrels are vulnerable to predators such as rats that take eggs and nestlings. Several island species are in danger of extinction, including the Bermuda petrel (or cahow) and the Madeira gadfly petrel.

Petrie /'pi:tri/ (William Matthew) Flinders 1853–1942. English archaeologist, who excavated sites in Egypt (the pyramids at Giza, the temple at Tanis, the Greek city of Naucratis in the Nile delta, Tell el Amarna, Naquada, Abydos, and Memphis) and Palestine from 1880. He was a grandson of the explorer Matthew Flinders.

petrochemical a chemical derived from the processing of ◊petroleum. The *petrochemical industry* is a term embracing those industrial manufacturing processes that obtain their raw materials from the processing of petroleum.

petrodollars in economics, dollar earnings of nations that make up the ◊Organization of Petroleum Exporting Countries (OPEC).

Petrograd /'petrəgræd/ name 1914–24 of ◊Leningrad, city in the USSR.

petrol a mixture of hydrocarbons derived from petroleum, mainly used as a fuel for internal combustion engines. It is colourless and highly volatile. In the USA, petrol is called gasoline.

petrol engine the most commonly used source of power for cars and motorcycles, introduced by the German engineers Gottlieb Daimler and Karl Benz 1885. The petrol engine is a complex piece of machinery made up of about 150 moving parts. It is a reciprocating piston engine, in which a number of pistons move up and down in cylinders. The motion of the pistons drive round a crankshaft, at the end of which is a heavy flywheel. From the flywheel the power is transferred to the car's driving wheels via the transmission system of clutch, gearbox, and final drive.

The parts of the petrol engine can be subdivided into a number of systems. The *fuel system* pumps fuel from the petrol tank into (usually) the carburettor. There it mixes with air and is sucked into the engine cylinders. The *ignition system* supplies the sparks to ignite the fuel mixture in the cylinders. By means of an ignition coil and contact breaker, it boosts the 12-volt battery voltage to pulses of 18,000 volts or more. These go via a ◊distributor to the ◊spark plugs in the cylinders, where they create the sparks. Ignition of the fuel in the cylinders produces temperatures of 700°C or more, and the engine must be cooled to prevent overheating. Most engines have a *water-cooling system*, in which water circulates through channels in the cylinder block and extracts the heat. It flows through pipes in a radiator, which are cooled by air. A few cars and most motorbikes are air-cooled, the cylinders being surrounded by many fins to present a large surface area to the air. The *lubrication system* also removes some heat, but its main job is to lubricate the moving parts with oil. Throughout the system oil is pumped under pressure to the camshaft, crankshaft, and valve-operating gear.

petroleum a natural oil, a thick greenish-brown liquid found underground in permeable rocks. Petroleum consists of hydrocarbons mixed with oxygen, sulphur, and other elements in varying proportions. It is thought to be derived from organic material that has been converted by, first, bacterial action, then heat and pressure, but its origin may be chemical rather than biological. From crude petroleum, various products are made by distillation and other processes, for example, fuel oil, gasoline (petrol), kerosene, diesel, lubricating oil, paraffin wax, and petroleum jelly.

Petroleum is often found in association with natural gas (mainly methane). It occurs in anticlines and other traps below impervious rock layers. Oil may flow naturally from wells under gas pressure from above or water pressure from below, causing it to rise up the borehole, but many wells require artificial means to bring the oil to the surface.

The occurrence of petroleum was known in ancient times, but the exploitation of oil fields began with the first commercial well in Pennsylvania 1859. The USA led production until the 1960s, when the Middle East became dominant, with immense reserves that led to worldwide dependence on cheap oil for transport and industry. In 1961 the Organization of the Petroleum Exporting Countries (OPEC) was established to avoid exploitation of member countries; after OPEC's price rises in 1973, the International Energy Agency (IEA) was established 1974 to protect the interests of oil-consuming countries.

Petroleum products and chemicals are used in large quantities in the manufacture of detergents, artificial fibres, plastics, insecticides, fertilizers, pharmaceuticals, toiletries, and synthetic rubber. Aviation fuel is a volatile form of petrol.

petrel

Madeiran fork-tailed petrel

Pollution is created by the spilling or burning of petroleum fuel. The transport of oil can lead to major catastrophes—for example, the *Torrey Canyon* tanker lost off SW England, 1967, which led to an agreement by the international oil companies 1968 to pay compensation for massive shore pollution. The 1989 spill in Alaska from the *Exxon Valdez* threatened the area's fragile environment, despite clean-up efforts.

Drilling for oil can also involve risk. The Piper Alpha drilling rig in the North Sea caught on fire July 1988, killing many workers.

A new kind of bacterium was developed during the 1970s in the USA, capable of 'eating' oil as a means of countering oil spills. Its creation gave rise to the so-called ◊Frankenstein law.

petrology branch of ◊geology that deals with the study of rocks, their mineral compositions, and their origins.

Petronius /pə'trəʊniəs/ Gaius, known as Petronius Arbiter Roman author of a licentious romance *Satyricon*. He was a companion of the emperor Nero, and supervisor of his pleasures.

Petropavlovsk /ˌpetrəʊpæv'lɒvsk/ industrial city (flour, agricultural machinery, leather) in the Kazakh Republic, USSR, on the Ishim river, the Trans-Siberian railway, and the Transkazakh line, opened 1953; population (1987) 233,000. A former caravan station, it was founded as a Russian fortress 1782.

Petropavlovsk-Kamchatskiy Pacific seaport and Soviet naval base on the E coast of the Kamchatka peninsula, USSR; population (1987) 252,000.

Petrópolis /pe'trɒpəlis/ hill resort in SE Brazil, founded by Pedro II; population (1980) 149,427.

Petrovsk /pɪ'trɒvsk/ former name (until 1921) of the Soviet port ◊Makhachkala.

Petrozavodsk /ˌpetrəʊzə'vɒdsk/ industrial city (metal goods, cement, prefabricated houses, sawmills), capital of Karelia Republic, USSR, on the W shore of Lake Onega; population (1987) 264,000. Peter the Great established the township 1703 as an ironworking centre; it was named Petrozavodsk 1777.

Petsamo /'petsəməʊ/ Finnish name of the Murmansk port ◊Pechenga.

Pevensey /'pevənsi/ English village in Sussex, 8 km/5 mi NE of Eastbourne, the site of William the Conqueror's landing 1066. The walls remain of the Roman fortress of Anderida, later a Norman castle, and prepared against German invasion in World War II.

Pevsner /'pevznə/ Nikolaus 1902–1983. Anglo-German art historian. Born in Leipzig, he fled from the Nazis to England. He became an authority on architecture, especially English. In his series *The Buildings of England* 1951–74, he achieved a first-hand report on every notable building in the country.

pewter an ◊alloy of tin and lead, known for centuries, once widely used for domestic utensils but now used mainly for ornamental ware.

peyote cactus *Lophopora williamsii* of Mexico and southern USA. Its white/pink flowers contain the hallucinogen **mescalin**, which is used by American Indians in religious ceremonies.

Pfalz /pfælts/ German name of the historic division of Germany, the ◊Palatinate.

Pforzheim /'pfɔ:tshaɪm/ city in Baden-Württemberg, West Germany, 26 km/16 mi SE of Karlsruhe, with goldsmith industries; population (1988) 105,000. It was a Roman settlement, and the residence of the ◊margraves of Baden 1300–1565.

pH a scale for measuring acidity or alkalinity. A pH of 7.0 indicates neutrality, below 7 is acid, while above 7 is alkaline. The scale runs from 0 to 14. Strong acids, as used in car batteries, have a pH of about 2; acidic fruits such as citrus fruits are about pH 4. Fertile soils have a pH of about 6.5 to 7.0, while weak alkalis such as soap are 9 to 10. Corrosive alkalis such as lye are pH 13.

Phaedra in Greek mythology a Cretan, daughter of Minos and Pasiphae, married to ◊Theseus of Athens. Her adulterous passion for her stepson ◊Hippolytus leads to her death in plays by Euripides and Seneca, adapted by Racine.

Phaedrus *c*.15 BC–*c*. AD 50. Roman fable writer, born in Macedonia. He was born a slave and freed by Augustus. The allusions in his fables (modelled on those of Aesop) caused him to be brought to trial by a minister of Tiberius. He was popular in medieval times.

Phaethon /ˈfeɪəθən/ in Greek mythology, the son of ◊Helios, who was allowed for one day to drive the chariot of the Sun. Losing control of the horses, he almost set the Earth on fire, and was killed by Zeus with a thunderbolt.

phage another name for a bacteriophage, a ◊virus that attacks bacteria.

phagocyte a type of white blood cell, or ◊leucocyte, that can engulf a bacterium or other invading microorganism. Phagocytes are found in blood, lymph, and other body tissues, where they also ingest foreign matter and dead tissue. A ◊macrophage differs in size and life span.

Phalangist member of a Lebanese military organization, since 1958 the political and military force of the ◊Maronite Church in Lebanon. Its unbending right-wing policies and resistance to the introduction of democratic institutions helped contribute to the the civil war in Lebanon.

The ***Phalanges Libanaises*** was founded 1936 by Pierre Gemayel after seeing the discipline and authoritarianism of Nazi Germany. Its initial aim was to protect the Maronite position in Lebanon; in 1958 it entered the political arena to oppose growing Arab nationalism. It today forms the largest Lebanese political group.

Phalaris /ˈfælərɪs/ 570–554 BC. Tyrant of the Greek colony of Acragas (Arrgigento) in Sicily. He is said to have built a hollow bronze bull in which his victims were roasted alive. He was killed in a people's revolt.

petroleum

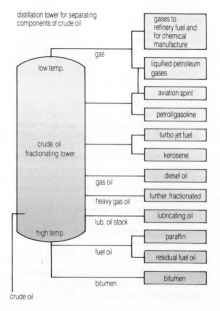

distillation tower for separating components of crude oil

gas — low temp.

crude oil fractionating tower

gas oil

heavy gas oil

lub. oil stock

high temp.

fuel oil

bitumen

crude oil

gas — gases to refinery fuel and for chemical manufacture

liquified petroleum gases

aviation spirit

petrol/gasoline

turbo jet fuel

kerosene

diesel oil

further fractionated

lubricating oil

paraffin

residual fuel oil

bitumen

The *Letters of Phalaris* attributed to him were proved by the scholar Richard ◊Bentley to be a forgery of the 2nd century AD.

phalarope genus of seabirds related to plovers and resembling sandpipers. They are native to North America, Britain, and polar regions of Europe.

The red-necked *Phalaropus ilobatus* and grey *Phalaropus fulicarius* visit Britain from the Arctic; *Phalaropus tricolor* is exclusively North American. The male is courted by the female and hatches the eggs. The female is larger and more colourful.

phallus (in Hinduism ◊lingam) a model of the male sexual organ, used in fertility rituals in ancient Greece and Anatolia, India, and many other parts of the world.

phanerogam obsolete term for plants that bear flowers or cones and reproduce by means of seeds, that is ◊angiosperms and ◊gymnosperms, or ◊seed plants. Plants such as mosses, fungi, and ferns were known as **cryptogams**.

Phanerozoic (Greek *phanero* 'visible') eon in Earth history, consisting of the most recent 590 million years. It comprises the Palaeozoic, Mesozoic, and Cenozoic eras. The vast majority of fossils come from this eon, owing to the evolution of hard shells and internal skeletons. The name means 'interval of well-displayed life'.

Pharaoh /ˈfeərəʊ/ Hebrew form of the Egyptian royal title Per-'o. This term, meaning 'great house', was originally applied to the royal household, and after about 950 BC to the king.

Pharisee member of a Jewish sect that arose in the 2nd century BC in protest against all movements towards compromise with Hellenistic culture. They were devout adherents of the law, both as found in the Torah and in the oral tradition known as the Mishnah.

They were opposed by the Saducees on several grounds: the Saducees did not acknowledge the Mishnah; the Pharisees opposed Greek and Roman rule of their country; and the Pharisees held a number of beliefs, such as the existence of hell, angels, and demons, the resurrection of the dead, and the future coming of the Messiah, not found in the Torah.

The Pharisees rejected political action, and in the 1st century AD the left wing of their followers, the **Zealots**, broke away to pursue a revolutionary nationalist policy. After the fall of Jerusalem, Pharisee ideas became the basis of orthodox Judaism.

pharmacology study of the origins, applications, and effects of chemical substances on living organisms. Products of the pharmaceutical industry range from aspirin to anti-cancer agents.

A wide range of resources (human and plant molecular biology, newly discovered soil-grown moulds, genetically engineered compounds, monoclonal antibiotics) is employed in the search for new drugs.

pharynx the interior of the throat, the cavity at the back of the mouth. Its walls are made of muscle strengthened with a fibrous layer and lined with mucous membrane. It has an opening into the back of each nostril, and downwards into the gullet and (through the epiglottis) into the windpipe. On each side, the Eustachian tube leads from it to the middle ear. The upper part (naso-pharynx) is an airway, but the remainder is a passage for food. Inflammation of the pharynx is named pharyngitis.

phase a physical state of matter: for example, ice and liquid water are different phases of water; a mixture of the two is termed a two-phase system.

phase in astronomy, the apparent shape of the Moon or a planet when all or part of its illuminated hemisphere is facing Earth. The Moon undergoes a full cycle of phases from new (when between Earth and the Sun) through first quarter (when at 90° eastern elongation from the Sun), full (when opposite the Sun), and last quarter (when at 90° western elongation from the Sun). The ◊inferior planets can also undergo a full cycle of phases, as can an asteroid passing inside the Earth's orbit.

The Moon is gibbous (more than half but less than fully illuminated) when between first quarter and full or full and last quarter. Mars can appear gibbous at quadrature (when it is at right angles to the Sun in the sky). The gibbous appearance of Jupiter is barely noticeable.

phase in physics, a stage in an oscillatory motion, such as a wave motion: two waves are in phase when their peaks and their troughs coincide. Otherwise, there is a **phase difference**, which has important consequences in ◊interference phenomena and ◊alternating current electricity.

PhD abbreviation for ***Doctor of Philosophy***.

pheasant bird of the family Phasianidae, which also includes quail and peafowl. The plumage of the male **common pheasant** *Phasianus colchicus* is richly tinted with brownish-green, yellow, and red markings, but the female is a camouflaged brownish colour. The nest is made in the ground, and the male is polygamous.

According to legend, pheasants were introduced from Asia to Europe by the Argonauts, who brought them from the banks of the river Phasis. They have also been introduced to North America. Pheasants were introduced to Britain in the 11th century by the Normans.

Among the more exotically beautiful pheasants of other genera, often kept as ornamental birds, are the **golden pheasant** *Chrysolophus pictus* from China and the **argus pheasant** of Malaysia *Argusianus argus*, which has metallic spots or 'eyes' on the wings.

phenol a member of a group of aromatic chemical compounds with weakly acidic properties, which are characterized by a hydroxyl (-OH) group attached directly to an aromatic ring. The simplest of the phenols, derived from benzene, is also known as phenol. It is sometimes called **carbolic acid** and can be extracted from coal tar. Pure phenol consists of colourless, needle-shaped crystals which readily take up moisture from the atmosphere. It has a strong and characteristic smell and was once used as an antiseptic. It is, however, toxic by absorption through the skin.

phenomena in philosophy, a technical term used in ◊Kant's philosophy, describing things as they appear to us, rather than as they are in themselves.

phenomenalism a philosophical position that argues that statements about objects can be reduced to statements about what is perceived or perceivable. Thus J S Mill defined material objects as 'permanent possibilities of sensation'. Phenomenalism is closely connected with certain forms of ◊empiricism.

phenomenology the philosophical perspective, founded by Husserl, that in the social sciences concentrates on phenomena as objects of perception (rather than as facts or occurrences which exist independently) in attempting to examine the ways people think about and interpret the world around them. It has been practised by the philosophers Heidegger, Sartre, and Merleau-Ponty.

In contrast to positivism or 'scientific' philosophy, phenomenology sees reality as essentially relative and subjective, and uses such tools as ethnomethodology and symbolic interactionism to focus on the structure of everyday life.

phenotype in genetics, the traits actually displayed by an organism. The phenotype is not a direct reflection of the ◊genotype because some alleles are masked by the presence of other, dominant alleles (see ◊dominance). The phenotype is further modified by the effects of the environment (for example, poor food stunting growth).

phenylketonuria condition arising from genetic causes, in which the liver of a child cannot control the level of phenylalanine (found in protein foods) in the bloodstream in the normal way by excretion in the urine. It is controlled by special diet.

pheromone chemical signal that is emitted (like an odour) by one animal and affects the behaviour of others. Pheromones are used by many animal species to attract mates.

Phidias /ˈfɪdiæs/ mid-5th century BC. Greek sculptor, one of the most influential of classical times.

phenol

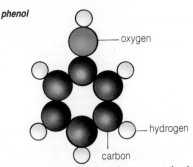

He supervised the sculptural programme for the Parthenon (most of it preserved in the British Museum, London, and known as the *Elgin marbles*). He also executed the colossal statue of Zeus at Olympia, one of the Seven Wonders of the World. He was a friend of the political leader Pericles, who made him superintendent of public works in Athens.

Phil. abbreviation for ◊*Philadelphia*.

Philadelphia /ˌfɪləˈdelfɪə/ industrial city and port on the Delaware river in Pennsylvania, USA; population (1980) 1,688,000, metropolitan area 3,700,000. Products include refined oil, chemicals, textiles, processed food, printing and publishing. Founded 1682 as the 'city of brotherly love', it was the first capital of the USA 1790–1800.

Philae /ˈfaɪliː/ island in the Nile, Egypt, above the first rapids, famed for the beauty of its temple of Isis (founded about 350 BC and in use until the 6th century AD). In 1977 the temple was re-erected on the nearby island of Agilkia above the flooding caused by the Aswan Dam.

philately the collection and study of postage stamps. It originated as a hobby in France about 1860.

Many countries earn extra revenue and cater to the philatelist by issuing sets of stamps to commemorate special events, anniversaries, and so on. There are many specialized fields of collection, from particular countries to specimens that have some defect; for example, contemporary issues that accidentally remain unperforated.

Philby /ˈfɪlbi/ 'Kim' (Harold) 1912–1988. British intelligence officer from 1940 and Soviet agent from 1933. He was liaison officer in Washington 1949–51, when he was asked to resign. Named in 1963 as having warned Guy Burgess and Donald Maclean (similarly double agents) that their activities were known, he fled to the USSR, and became a Soviet citizen and general in the KGB. A fourth member of the ring was Anthony ◊Blunt.

Philby /ˈfɪlbi/ Harry St John Bridger 1885–1960. British explorer. As chief of the British political mission to central Arabia 1917–18, he was the first European to visit the southern provinces of Najd. He wrote *The Empty Quarter* 1933, and *Forty Years in the Wilderness* 1957.

Philharmonic Society a group of people organized for the advancement of music; the term is derived from Greek 'love of harmony'. The Royal Philharmonic Society was founded in London in 1813 by the pianist Johann Baptist Cramer (1771–1858) for the purpose of improving musical standards by means of orchestral concerts organized on a subscription basis. Another Philharmonic Society was founded in New York in 1842.

Philip /ˈfɪlɪp/ Duke of Edinburgh 1921– . Prince of the UK, husband of Elizabeth II, and a grandson of George I of Greece and a great-great-grandson of Queen Victoria. He was born in Corfu, raised in England, and educated at Gordonstoun and Dartmouth Naval College. During World War II he served in the Mediterranean, taking part in the battle of Matapan, and in the Pacific.

A naturalized British subject, taking the surname Mountbatten Mar 1947, he married Princess Elizabeth in Westminster Abbey 20 Nov 1947, having the previous day received the title Duke of Edinburgh. In 1956 he founded the Duke of Edinburgh's Award Scheme to encourage creative achievement among young people. He was created a prince of the UK 1957, and awarded the Order of Merit 1968.

Philip /ˈfɪlɪp/ six kings of France, including:

Philip II (Philip Augustus) 1165–1223. King of France from 1180. He waged war in turn against the English kings Henry II, Richard I (with whom he also went on the Third Crusade), and John (against whom he won the decisive battle of Bouvines in Flanders 1214) to evict them from their French possessions, and establish a strong monarchy.

Philip IV *the Fair* 1268–1314. King of France from 1285. He engaged in a feud with Pope Boniface VIII, and made him a prisoner 1303. Clement V (1264–1314), elected pope through Philip's influence, moved to Avignon, and collaborated with Philip to suppress the ◊Templars, a powerful order of knights. Philip allied with the Scots against England, and invaded Flanders.

Philip VI 1293–1350. King of France from 1328, first of the house of Valois, elected by the barons on the death of his cousin, Charles IV. His claim was challenged by Edward III of England, who defeated him at Crécy 1346.

Philip II of Macedon /ˈfɪlɪp/ 382–336 BC. King of ◊Macedonia from 359 BC. He seized the throne from his nephew, for whom he was regent, conquered the Greek city-states, and formed them into a league whose forces could be united against Persia. He was assassinated while he was planning this expedition, and was succeeded by his son ◊Alexander the Great. His tomb was discovered at Vergina, N Greece, in 1978.

Philip /ˈfɪlɪp/ five kings of Spain, including:

Philip I *the Handsome* 1478–1506. King of Castile from 1504, through his marriage 1496 to Joanna the Mad (1479–1555). He was the son of the Holy Roman emperor Maximilian I.

Philip II 1527–1598. King of Spain from 1556. He was born at Valladolid, the son of the Habsburg emperor Charles V, and in 1554 married Queen Mary of England. On his father's abdication 1556 he inherited Spain, the Netherlands, and the Spanish possessions in Italy and the Americas, and in 1580 annexed Portugal. His intolerance and lack of understanding of the Netherlanders drove them into revolt. Political and religious reasons combined to involve him in war with England and, after 1589, with France. The defeat of the ◊Spanish Armada marked the beginning of the decline of Spanish power.

Philip V 1683–1746. King of Spain from 1700. A grandson of Louis XIV of France, he was the first Bourbon king of Spain. He was not recognized by the major European powers until 1713. See ◊Spanish Succession, War of the.

Philip Neri, St /ˈnɪəri/ 1515–1595. Italian Roman Catholic priest who organized the Congregation of the Oratory (see ◊Oratorian). He built the oratory over the church of St Jerome, Rome, where prayer meetings were held and scenes from the Bible performed with music, originating the musical form ◊oratorio. Feast day 26 May.

Philippeville /ˈfɪlɪpvɪl/ former name (until 1962) of Algerian port of ◊Skikda.

Philippi /fɪˈlɪpaɪ/ ancient city of Macedonia founded by Philip of Macedon 358 BC. Near Philippi, Mark Antony and Augustus defeated Brutus and Cassius 42 BC. It was the first European town where St Paul preached (about AD 53), founding the congregation to which he addressed the Epistle to the Philippians.

Philippines /ˈfɪlɪpiːnz/ country on an archipelago between the Pacific Ocean to the E and the South China Sea to the W.

government The constitution was approved by plebiscite in Feb 1987. It provides for a US-style executive president who is elected for a non-renewable six-year term and a two-chamber legislature or congress: a 24-member Senate and 250-member House of Representatives, with similar respective powers to their counterparts in the USA. Senators are elected in national-level contests for six-year terms (a maximum of two consecutive

Philip II *Philip II, King of Spain 1556–98.*

terms). Representatives serve three-year terms (up to a maximum of three consecutive), with 200 being directly elected at the district level and up to a further 50 being appointed by the president from lists of 'minority groups'. The president appoints an executive cabinet, but, as in the USA, while being unable to directly introduce legislation may impose vetoes on congressional bills that can only be overridden by two-thirds majorities in each chamber. There is also a Bill of Rights and 15-member Supreme Court.

history The people of the Philippine islands probably came from the ◊Malay Peninsula. They were semi-nomadic hunters and fisherfolk when the first European arrived, ◊Magellan, 1521, followed by conquering Spanish forces in 1565. Roman Catholicism was introduced during the reign of ◊Philip II (after whom the islands were named), replacing Islam, which had been spread by Arab traders and missionaries.

During the 19th century there were a series of armed nationalist revolts. These continued after the islands were ceded by Spain to the USA in 1898, and increasing self-government was granted in 1916 and 1935. The Philippines were occupied by Japan 1942–45, before becoming a fully independent republic in 1946. A succession of presidents drawn from the islands' wealthy estate-owning elite followed, who did little to improve the lot of the ordinary peasant.

In 1965 President Diosdado Macapagal was defeated by Ferdinand ◊Marcos, the leader of the Nationalist Party. Marcos initiated rapid economic development and some land reform. He was re-elected in 1969, but encountered growing opposition from communist insurgents and Muslim separatists in the S. A high rate of population growth aggravated poverty and unemployment. Some months before his second term had been completed, Marcos declared martial law, suspended the constitution and began to rule by decree. Intermittent referenda allowed him to retain power. Marcos's authoritarian leadership was criticized for corruption and in 1977 the opposition leader, Benigno Aquino, was jailed under sentence of death for alleged subversion. In 1978 martial law was relaxed, the 1972 ban on political parties was lifted and elections for an interim National Assembly were held, resulting in an overwhelming victory for Marcos.

In Jan 1981 martial law was lifted completely and hundreds of political prisoners released. Marcos then won approval, by referendum, for a partial return to democratic government with himself as president, working with a prime minister and executive council. Political and economic conditions deteriorated, communist guerrilla insurgency escalated, unemployment climbed to over 30% and the national debt increased. In 1983 Benigno Aquino, allowed to travel to the USA for medical treatment, was shot dead on his arrival at Manila airport. A commission of inquiry reported that Aquino had been killed by the military guard escorting him as part of a broader conspiracy.

National Assembly elections were held in May 1984, amid violence and widespread claims of corruption, and although the government party stayed in power, the opposition registered significant gains. Early in 1986 the main anti-Marcos

Philippines
Republic of the
(Republika ng Pilipinas)

area 300,000 sq km/115,800 sq mi
capital Manila (on Luzon)
towns Quezon City
ports Cebu, Davao (on Mindanao) and Iloilu
physical comprises over 7,000 islands, with volcanic mountain ranges traversing the main chain N–S, and 50% of the area still forested. The largest islands are **Luzon** 108,172 sq km/41,754 sq mi and **Mindanao** 94,227 sq km/36,372 sq mi; others include Samar, Negros, Palawan, Panay, Mindoro, Leyte, Cebu, and the Sulu group
features Luzon, is the site of Clark Field, US air base used as a logistical base in the Vietnam War, and Subic Bay, US naval base; Mindanao has active volcano Apo (2,855 m/9,370 ft) and mountainous rainforest
head of state and government Corazón Aquino from 1986
government emergent democracy

political parties People's Power, including the PDP-Laban Party and the Liberal Party, centrist pro-Aquino; Nationalist Party, Union for National Action (UNA), and Grand Alliance for Democracy (GAD), conservative opposition groupings; Mindanao Alliance, Mindanao Island-based decentralist body
exports sugar, copra and coconut oil, timber, iron ore and copper concentrates
currency peso (37.00 = £1 Feb 1990)
population (1989) 61,971,000 (93% Malaysian); annual growth rate 2.4%
life expectancy men 60, women 64
language Filipino (based on Malay dialect Tagalog), but English and Spanish are widespread **religion** Roman Catholic 84%, Protestant 9%, Muslim 5%
literacy 86% male/85% female (1985 est)
GNP $16 bn (1984); $772 per head of population
chronology
1542 Named the Philippines by Spanish explorers.
1565 Conquered by Spain.
1898 Ceded to the US.
1935 Grant of internal self-government.
1942–45 Japanese occupation.
1946 Independence granted.
1965 Ferdinand Marcos elected president.
1983 Murder of Benigno Aquino.
1986 Overthrow of Marcos by Corazón Aquino's People's Power movement.
1987 'Freedom constitution' adopted; People's Power won majority in congressional elections. Attempted right-wing coup suppressed. Communist guerrillas active. Government in rightward swing.
1988 Diluted land-reform act gave favourable compensation to large estateholders.
1989 Failure of referendum on southern autonomy; attempted coup foiled with US air support.

movement, United Nationalist Democratic Organization (UNIDO), chose Corazón ◊Aquino, Benigno's widow, despite her political inexperience, to contest new elections for the presidency which Marcos had been persuaded to hold as a means of maintaining vital US economic and diplomatic support.

The campaign resulted in over 100 deaths, and large-scale electoral fraud was witnessed by international observers. On 16 Feb 1986 the National Assembly declared Marcos the winner, a result disputed by an independent electoral watchdog, the National Citizens' Movement for Free Elections (Namfrel). Corazón Aquino began a non-violent protest, termed 'people's power', which gathered massive popular support, backed by the Roman Catholic church, and President Marcos came under strong international pressure, particularly from the USA, to stand down. On 22 Feb 1986 the army, led by Chief of Staff Lt-Gen Fidel Ramos and defence minister Juan Enrile, declared its support for Aquino and on 25 Feb Marcos left for exile in Hawaii, where he died in Sept 1989.

On assuming the presidency, Corazón Aquino dissolved the pro-Marcos National Assembly. She proceeded to govern in a conciliatory fashion, working with a coalition cabinet team comprising opposition politicians and senior military figures. She freed 500 political prisoners and granted an amnesty to the New People's Army (NPA) communist guerrillas in an effort to end the 17-year-old insurgency, and introduced a major rural-employment economic programme, with land reforms opposed by property owners.

The new administration endured a series of attempted coups by pro-Marcos supporters and faced serious opposition from Juan Enrile, dismissed in Nov 1986. In Feb 1987 a new 'freedom constitution' was overwhelmingly approved in a national plebiscite. This gave Aquino a mandate to rule as president until 30 June 1992. In the

subsequent congressional elections, held in May 1987, Aquino's People's Power coalition won over 90% of the elected seats. However, in August 1987 the government was rocked by a coup attempt led by Col Gregorio 'Gringo' Honasan, an army officer closely linked with Enrile, which claimed 53 lives. In response, Aquino effected a major cabinet reshuffle in Sept 1987 that signalled a shift to the right in the government's policy, with tougher measures being instituted towards the NPA and the Land Reform Act 1988 being diluted. Vice President Salvador Laurel, the former leader of UNIDO, was replaced as foreign minister. In Aug 1988 Laurel formed a new right-of-centre opposition force, the Union for National Action (UNA) and become president of the revived Nationalist Party in May 1989. Aquino endured a further reverse in Nov 1989 when a regional referendum proposing the merging of the 13 southern provinces, including ◊Mindanao, into an 'automonous region' was rejected. This initiative had been made in an attempt to end the two decades long Muslim separatist struggle led by Moro National Liberation Front (MNLF).

Since becoming president, Corazón Aquino has enjoyed firm backing from the USA. In Dec 1989 US air support was provided to help foil a further Honasan-planned coup attempt. Since 1947 the USA has had major naval and air bases on ◊Luzon Island, at Subic Bay and Clark Field respectively. The leases for these bases are due to expire in 1991 but are likely to be extended.

Philip, St 1st century AD. In the New Testament, one of the 12 apostles. He was an inhabitant of Bethsaida (N Israel), and is said to have worked as a missionary in Anatolia. Feast day 3 May.

Philip the Good /'fɪlɪp/ 1396–1467. Duke of Burgundy from 1419. He engaged in the Hundred Years' War as an ally of England until he made peace with the French at the Council of Arras 1435. He made the Netherlands a centre of art and learning.

Philistine /'fɪlɪstaɪn/ member of a people of non-Semitic origin (possibly from Asia Minor) who founded city states on the Palestinian coastal plain in the 12th century BC, adopting a Semitic language and religion. They were at war with the Israelites in the 11th–10th centuries BC (hence the pejorative use of their name in Hebrew records for anyone uncivilized in intellectual and artistic terms).

Phillip /'fɪlɪp/ Arthur 1738–1814. British vice admiral, founder and governor of the convict settlement at Sydney, Australia, 1788–1792, and hence founder of New South Wales.

Phillipa of Hainault /'fɪlɪpə, 'heɪnɔːt/ 1311–1369. Daughter of William III Count of Holland; wife of King Edward III of England, whom she married in York Minster 1328, and by whom she had 12 children (including Edward the Black Prince, Lionel Duke of Clarence, John Duke of Lancaster, Edmund Duke of York, and Thomas Duke of Gloucester). She was admired for her clemency and successfully pleaded for the lives of the six burghers of Calais who surrendered to to save the town from destruction 1347. Queen's College, Oxford, was founded in her honour and established by Royal Charter 1341.

Phillips /'fɪlipz/ Anton 1874–1951. Dutch industrialist. The electronics firm Philips Bulb and Radio Works was founded by his brother Gerard Philips in Eindhoven 1891. Anton served as chair of the company 1921–51, during which time the firm became the largest producer of electrical goods outside the USA.

Phillips curve a graph showing the relationship between percentage changes in wages and unemployment, and indicating that wages rise faster during periods of low unemployment as employers compete for labour. The implication is that the dual objectives of low unemployment and low inflation are inconsistent. The concept has been widely questioned since the early 1960s because of the apparent instability of the wages/unemployment relationship. It was developed by the British economist A(lban) W(illiam) Phillips (1914–75), who plotted graphically wage and unemployment changes between 1861 and 1957.

Philoctetes in Greek mythology, a hero in the Trojan War, who killed Paris using one of the poisoned arrows of Heracles.

On his way to the Trojan War, Philoctetes was bitten by a serpent and abandoned by his companions on the island of Lemnos. His friends came back to fetch him ten years later when they learned that the Trojan War could only be won by the arrows of Heracles, held by Philoctetes. He used one of them to kill Paris, and soon afterwards the Greeks captured Troy.

Philo Judaeus /'faɪləʊ dʒuːˈdiːəs/ (lived 1st century AD) Jewish philosopher of Alexandria, who in AD 40 undertook a mission to Caligula to protest against the emperor's claim to divine honours. In his writings Philo Judaeus attempts to reconcile Judaism with Platonic and Stoic ideas.

philology (Greek 'love of language') in historical ◊linguistics, it refers to the study of the development of languages. It is also an obsolete term for the study of literature.

In this sense the scholars of Alexandria, who edited Homer, were philologists. The Renaissance gave great impetus to this kind of study. Dutch scholars took the lead in the 17th century and Richard Bentley (1662–1742) made significant contributions in England. From the study of Sanskrit there arose at the beginning of the 19th century, under Franz Bopp's (1791–1867) leadership, what is called comparative philology, originally mainly concerned with the ◊Indo-European family of languages, while the Romantic movement greatly inspired the establishment of national philology.

philosophy (Greek 'love of wisdom') branch of learning that includes metaphysics (the nature of Being), epistemology (theory of knowledge), logic (study of valid inference), ethics, and aesthetics. Originally, philosophy included all intellectual endeavour, but

philosophy: the great philosophers

Name	Dates	Nationality	Representative Work
Heraclitus	c.544–483 BC	Greek	On Nature
Parmenides	c.510–450 BC	Greek	fragments
Socrates	469–399 BC	Greek	—
Plato	428–347 BC	Greek	Republic; Phaedo
Aristotle	384–322 BC	Greek	Nichomachean Ethics; Metaphysics
Epicurus	341–270 BC	Greek	fragments
Lucretius	c.99–55 BC	Roman	On the Nature of Things
Plotinus	AD 205–270	Greek	Enneads
Augustine	354–430	N African	Confessions; City of God
Aquinas	c.1225–1274	Italian	Summa Theologies
Duns Scotus	c.1266–1308	Scottish	Opus Oxoniense
William of Occam	c.1285–1349	English	Commentary of the Sentences
Nicholas of Cusa	1401–1464	German	De Docta Ignorantia
Giordano Bruno	1548–1600	Italian	De la Causa, Principio e Uno
Bacon	1561–1626	English	Novum Organum; The Advancement of Learning
Hobbes	1588–1679	English	Leviathan
Descartes	1596–1650	French	Discourse on Method; Meditations on the First Philosophy
Pascal	1623–1662	French	Pensées
Spinoza	1632–1677	Dutch	Ethics
Locke	1632–1704	English	Essay Concerning Human Understanding
Leibniz	1646–1716	German	The Monadology
Vico	1668–1744	Italian	The New Science
Berkeley	1685–1753	Irish	A Treatise Concerning the Principles of Human Knowledge
Hume	1711–1776	Scottish	A Treatise of Human Nature
Rousseau	1712–1778	French	The Social Contract
Diderot	1713–1784	French	D'Alembert's Dream
Kant	1724–1804	German	The Critique of Pure Reason
Fichte	1762–1814	German	The Science of Knowledge
Hegel	1770–1831	German	The Phenomenology of Spirit
Schelling	1775–1854	German	System of Transcendental Idealism
Schopenhauer	1788–1860	German	The World as Will and Idea
Comte	1798–1857	French	Cours de philosophie positive
Mill	1806–1873	English	Utilitarianism
Kierkegaard	1813–1855	Danish	Concept of Dread
Marx	1818–1883	German	Economic and Philosophical Manuscripts
Dilthey	1833–1911	German	The Rise of Hermeneutics
Pierce	1839–1914	US	How to Make our Ideas Clear
Nietzsche	1844–1900	German	Thus Spake Zarathustra
Bergson	1859–1941	French	Creative Evolution
Husserl	1859–1938	German	Logical Investigations
Russell	1872–1970	English	Principia Mathematica
Lukács	1885–1971	Hungarian	History and Class Consciousness
Wittgenstein	1889–1951	Austrian	Tractatus Logico-Philosophicus; Philosophical Investigations
Heidegger	1889–1976	German	Being and Time
Gadamer	1900–	German	Truth and Method
Sartre	1905–1980	French	Being and Nothingness
Merleau Ponty	1908–1961	French	The Phenomenology of Perception
Quine	1908–	US	Word and Object
Foucault	1926–1984	French	The Order of Things

over time traditional branches of philosophy have acquired their own status as separate areas of study. Philosophy is concerned with fundamental problems, including the nature of mind and matter, perception, self, free will, causation, time and space, and the existence of moral judgements, which cannot be resolved by a specific method. Contemporary philosophers are inclined to think of philosophy as an investigation of the fundamental assumptions that govern our ways of understanding and acting in the world.

Oldest of all philosophical systems is the Vedic system c.2500 BC, but like many other Eastern systems it rests on a primarily mystic basis. The first scientific system originated in Greece in the 6th century BC with the Milesian school (Thales, Anaximander, Anaximenes). Both they and later pre-Socratics (Pythagoras, Xenophon, Parmenides, Zeno of Elea, Empedocles, Anaxagoras, Heraclitus, Democritus) were lively theorists, and ideas such as atomism, developed by Democritus, occur in later schemes of thought. In the 5th century Socrates, foremost among the teachers known as the Sophists, laid the foundation of ethics; Plato evolved a system of universal ideas; Aristotle developed logic. Later schools include Epicureanism (Epicurus), stoicism (Zeno) and scepticism (Pyrrho); the eclectics—not a school, they selected what appealed to them from various systems (Cicero and Seneca)—and the neo-Platonists, infusing a mystic element into the system of Plato (Philo, Plotinus and, as disciple, Julian the Apostate).

The close of the Athenian schools of philosophy by Justinian AD 529 marks the end of ancient philosophy, though many of its teachers moved eastwards; Greek thought emerges in Muslim philosophers such as Avicenna and Averroes, and the Jewish Maimonides. For the West the work of Aristotle was transmitted through Boethius. Study by medieval scholastic philosophers, mainly concerned with the reconciliation of ancient philosophy with Christian belief, began in the 9th century with John Scotus Erigena and includes Anselm, Abelard, Albertus Magnus, Thomas Aquinas, his opponent Duns Scotus, and William of Occam.

In the 17th century Descartes, with his rationalist determination to doubt, and faith in mathematical proof, marks the beginning of modern philosophy, and was followed by Spinoza, Leibniz, and Hobbes; but the empiricists, principally an 18th-century English school (Locke, Berkeley, Hume), turned instead to physics as indicating what can be known and how, and led up to the transcendental criticism of Kant. In the early 19th century classical German idealism (Fichte, Schelling, Hegel) repudiated Kant's limitation of human knowledge; and in France Comte developed the positivist thought which attracted Mill and Spencer. Notable also in the 19th century are the pessimistic atheism of Schopenhauer; the dialectical materialism of Marx and Engels; the work of Nietzsche and Kierkegaard, which led towards 20th-century existentialism; the pragmatism of William James and Dewey; and the

absolute idealism at the turn of the century of the neo-Hegelians (Bradley, Royce).

Among 20th-century movements are the logical positivism of the Vienna circle (Carnap, Popper, Ayer); the creative evolution of Bergson; neo-Thomism, the revival of the medieval philosophy of Aquinas (Maritain); existentialism (Heidegger, Jaspers, Sartre); the phenomenology of Husserl, who influenced Ryle; and realism (Russell, Moore, Broad, Wittgenstein). 20th-century philosophers have paid great attention to the nature and limits of language, particularly in relation to the language used to formulate philosophical problems.

Phiz /fɪz/ pseudonym of Hablot Knight Browne 1815–1882. British artist. He illustrated the greater part of the *Pickwick Papers* and other works by Dickens, as well as novels by C J Lever and Harrison Ainsworth (1805–82).

phlebitis inflammation of a vein. It is sometimes associated with blockage by a blood clot (◊thrombosis), in which case it is more accurately described as thrombophlebitis.

It may occur as a result of the hormonal changes associated with pregnancy, owing to long-term use of the contraceptive pill, or following prolonged immobility (which is why post-operative patients are mobilized as soon as possible after surgery). If a major vein is involved, nearly always in a leg, the part beyond the blockage swells, and may remain engorged for weeks. Treatment is with ◊anticoagulant drugs and sometimes surgery.

phlebotomy the practice of blood-letting; withdrawing blood from a vein.

phloem a tissue found in vascular plants whose main function is to conduct sugars and other food materials from the leaves, where they are produced, to all other parts of the plant.

Phloem is composed of sieve elements and their associated companion cells, together with some ◊sclerenchyma and ◊parenchyma cell types. Sieve elements are long, thin-walled cells joined end to end forming sieve tubes; large pores in the end walls allow the continuous passage of nutrients. Phloem is usually found in association with ◊xylem, the water-conducting tissue, but unlike the latter it is a living tissue.

phlogiston a hypothetical substance formerly believed to have been produced when something burns. The term was invented by G Stahl (1660–1734). The phlogiston theory has now been replaced by a corresponding theory of oxygen gain/loss.

phlox plant, genus *Phlox*, native to Siberia and North America. They are half-hardy annuals cultivated from *Phlox drummondii*, with lanceolate (tapering), opposite leaves, and red, white, or mauve flowers.

Phnom Penh /'nɒm 'pen/ capital of Cambodia, on the Mekong, 210 km/130 mi NW of Saigon; population (1981) 400,000. Industries include textiles and food-processing.

phobia an excessive irrational fear of an object or situation, for example agoraphobia (fear of open spaces and crowded places), acrophobia (fear of heights), claustrophobia (fear of enclosed places). Behaviour therapy is one form of treatment.

Phobos one of the two moons of Mars, discovered 1877 by the US astronomer Asaph Hall. It is an irregularly shaped lump of rock, cratered by ◊meteorite impacts. Phobos is $27 \times 21 \times 19$ km/$17 \times 13 \times 12$ mi across, and orbits Mars every 0.32 days at a height of 9,400 km/5,840 mi. It is thought to be an asteroid captured by Mars' gravity.

Phoenicia /fə'nɪʃiə/ ancient Greek name for N ◊Canaan on the E coast of the Mediterranean. The Phoenicians lived about 1200–332 BC, were seafaring traders and artisans, and are said to have circumnavigated Africa and established colonies in Cyprus, N Africa (for example Carthage), Malta, Sicily, and Spain. Their cities (Tyre, Sidon, and Byblos were the main ones) were independent states ruled by hereditary kings but dominated by merchant ruling classes. The fall of Tyre to Alexander the Great ended the separate history of Phoenicia.

The Phoenicians occupied the seaboard of Lebanon and Syria, N of Mount Carmel. Their exports included Tyrian purple cloth, furniture (from the timber of Lebanon), and jewellery. Documents found 1929 at Ugarit on the Syrian coast give much information on their civilization, and their deities included ◊Baal, Astarte or ◊Ishtar, and ◊Moloch. Competition from the colonies combined with attacks by the Sea Peoples, the Assyrians, and the Greeks on the cities in Phoenicia led to their ultimate decline.

phoenix /'fiːnɪks/ mythical Egyptian bird that burned itself to death on a pyre every 500 years, and rose rejuvenated from the ashes.

Phoenix /'fiːnɪks/ capital of Arizona, USA; industrial city (steel, aluminium, electrical goods, food processing) and tourist centre on the Salt river; population (1986) 882,000.

Phoenix Islands /'fiːnɪks/ group of eight islands in the South Pacific, included in Kiribati; total land area 18 sq km/11 sq mi. Drought has rendered them all uninhabitable.

Phoenix Park Murders the murder of several prominent members of the British government in Phoenix Park, Dublin on 6 May 1882. It threatened the co-operation between the Liberal government and the Irish nationalist members at Westminster, which had been secured by the ◊Kilmainham Treaty.

It began with the stabbing of Thomas Burke, the permanent undersecretary for Ireland and Frederick Cavendish, chief secretary to the viceroy. A murderous campaign was continued by the Irish National Invincibles until some members turned queen's evidence.

phon unit of loudness, equal to the value in decibels of an equally loud tone with frequency 1000 Hz. The higher the frequency, the louder a noise sounds for the same decibel value; thus an 80-decibel tone with a frequency of 20 Hz sounds as loud as 20 decibels at 1000 Hz, and the phon value of both tones is 20. An aircraft engine has a loudness of around 140 phons.

phonetics the identification, description, and classification of sounds used in articulate speech. These sounds are codified in the International Phonetic Alphabet (a highly modifed version of the Roman alphabet).

A **phoneme** is the range of sound that can be substituted without change of meaning in the words of a particular language, for example; 'r' and 'l' form a single phoneme in Japanese, but are two distinct phonemes in English.

phoney war the period in World War II between Oct 1939 when the Germans had defeated Poland, and Apr 1940 when the invasions of Denmark and Norway took place. During this time there were few signs of hostilities in Western Europe, indeed, Hitler made some attempts to arrange a peace settlement with Britain and France.

phonograph the name Thomas ◊Edison gave to his sound-recording apparatus, which developed into the ◊record player.

phosphate any salt or ester of ◊phosphoric acid. Incomplete neutralization of phosphoric acid gives rise to acid phosphates (see ◊acid salts and ◊buffer).

phosphorescence *An organic chemist working with phosphorescing solutions.*

Photography

1515	Leonardo da Vinci described the camera obscura.
1750	The painter Canaletto used a camera obscura as an aid to his painting in Venice.
1790	Thomas Wedgwood in England made photograms—placing objects on leather, sensitized by using silver nitrate.
1826	Nicephore Niépce 1765–1833, a French doctor, produced the world's first photograph from nature on pewter plates with a camera obscura and an eight-hour exposure.
1835	Niépce and L J M Daguerre produced the first *Daguerreotype* camera photograph.
1839	Daguerre was awarded an annuity by the French government and his process given to the world.
1841	Fox ◊Talbot's Calotype process was patented—the first multi-copy method of photography using a negative/positive process, sensitized with silver iodide.
1844	Fox Talbot published the first photographic book, *The Pencil of Nature*.
1845	Hill and Adamson began to use Calotypes for portraits in Edinburgh.
1851	Fox Talbot used a one-thousandth of a second exposure to demonstrate high-speed photography.
1855	Roger Fenton made documentary photographs of the Crimean war from a specially constructed caravan with portable darkroom.
1859	Nadar in Paris made photographs underground using battery-powered arc lights.
1860	Queen Victoria was photographed by Mayall. Abraham Lincoln was photographed by Matthew Brady for political campaigning.
1861	Single-lens reflex-plate camera patented by Thomas Sutton.
1862	Nadar took aerial photographs over Paris.
1870	Julia Margaret Cameron used long lenses for her distinctive portraits.
1878	In the USA Eadweard Muybridge analysed the movements of animals through sequential photographs, using a series of cameras.
1880	A silver bromide emulsion was fixed with hypo. Photographs were first reproduced in newspapers in New York using the half-tone engraving process. The first twin-lens reflex camera was produced in London.
1889	Eastman Company in the USA produced the Kodak No. 1 camera and roll film, facilitating universal, hand-held snapshots.
1902	In Germany Deckel invented a prototype leaf shutter and Zeiss introduced the Tessar lens.
1904	The Autochrome colour process was patented by the Lumière brothers.
1905	Alfred Stieglitz opened the gallery '291' in New York promoting photography. Lewis Hine used photography to expose the exploitation of children in US factories, causing protective laws to be passed.
1907	The autochrome process began to be factory-produced.
1914	Oskar Barnack designed a prototype Leica camera for Leitz in Germany.
1924	Leitz launched the first 35-mm camera, the Leica, delayed because of World War I. It became very popular with photo-journalists because it was quiet, small, dependable, and had a range of lenses and accessories.
1929	Rolleiflex produced a twin-lens reflex camera in Germany.
1935	In the USA, Mannes and Godowsky invented Kodachrome transparency film, which has great acutance and rich colour quality. Electronic flash was invented in the USA. Social documentary photography received wide attention through the photographs of Dorothea Lange, Margaret Bourke-White, Arthur Rothstein, Walker Evans and others taken for the Farm Security Administration of the plight of the poor tenant farmers in the Mid-west.
1936	*Life* magazine, noted for photo-journalism, was first published in the USA.
1938	*Picture Post* magazine was introduced in the UK.
1940	Multigrade enlarging paper by Ilford was made available in the UK.
1945	The 'Zone system' of exposure estimation was published in the book *Exposure Record* by Ansel Adams.
1947	Polaroid black and white instant process film invented by Dr Edwin Land, who set up the Polaroid corporation in Boston, Massachusetts. Principles of holography demonstrated in England by Dennis Gabor.
1955	Kodak introduced Tri-X, a black and white 200 ASA film.
1959	The zoom lens invented in Germany by Voigtlander.
1960	Laser invented in the USA, making holography possible. Polacolor, a self-processing colour film, introduced by Polaroid, using a 60-second colour film and dye diffusion technique.
1963	Cibachrome, paper and chemicals for printing directly from transparencies, was made available by Ciba-Geigy of Switzerland. One of the most permanent processes, it is marketed by Ilford in the UK.
1969	Photographs taken on the Moon by US astronauts.
1972	SX70 system, a single-lens reflex camera with instant prints, produced by Polaroid.
1980	Ansel Adams sold an original print *Moonrise:Hernandez* for $45,000, a record price, in the USA. Voyager 1 sent photographs of Saturn back to Earth across space.
1985	Minolta Corporation in Japan introduced the Minolta 7000—the world's first body-integral autofocus single-lens reflex camera.

Phosphates are used as fertilizers, and lead to the development of healthy root systems. They are involved in many biochemical processes, often as part of complex molecules (see ◊ATP).

phosphor a substance that gives out visible light when it is illuminated by a beam of electrons or ultraviolet light. The television screen is coated on the inside with phosphors which glow when beams of electrons strike them. Fluorescent lamp tubes are also phosphor-coated.

phosphorescence in physics, the emission of light by certain substances after they have absorbed energy, whether from visible light, other electromagnetic radiation such as ultraviolet rays or X-rays, or cathode rays (a beam of electrons). When the stimulating energy is removed phosphorescence ceases, although it may persist for a short time after (unlike ◊fluorescence, which stops immediately).

The most common uses of phosphorescent substances, called phosphors, are as light-emitting coatings on the inside of television screens, in so-called fluorescent lamps and tubes, in day-glo paints, and as optical brighteners in detergents.

phosphoric acid an acid derived from phosphorus and oxygen. Its commonest form (H_3PO_4) is also known as orthophosphoric acid, and is produced by the action of phosphorus pentoxide (P_2O_5) on water. It is used in rust removers and for rust-proofing iron and steel.

phosphorus an element, symbol P, atomic number 15, relative atomic mass 30.975. It occurs in several forms, the commonest being white phosphorus (a waxy solid emitting a greenish glow in air, burning spontaneously to phosphorus pentoxide, and very poisonous) and red phosphorus (neither igniting spontaneously nor poisonous). It is used in fertilizers, in matches, in the prevention of scale and corrosion in pipes and boiler tubes, and in certain organic chemicals.

It was first identified by the German alchemist Hennig Brand in 1669. Production of phosphorus and its compounds has greatly increased since World War II.

photocell or **photoelectric cell** device for measuring or detecting light or other electromagnetic radiation.

In a **photoemissive** cell, the radiation causes electrons to be emitted and a current to flow (◊photoelectric effect); a **photovoltaic** cell causes an ◊electromotive force to be generated in the presence of light across the boundary of two substances. A **photoconductive** cell, which is semiconductor-based, increases its conductivity when exposed to electromagnetic radiation. They are used for photographers' exposure meters, burglar and fire alarms, automatic doors, and in solar arrays.

photochemical reaction any chemical reaction in which light is produced or light initiates the reaction. Light can initiate reactions by exciting atoms or molecules and making them more reactive: the light energy becomes converted to chemical energy.

This type of reaction is seen in the bleaching of dyes or the yellowing of paper by sunlight. It is harnessed by plants in ◊photosynthesis and by humans in ◊photography. Chemical reactions that produce light are most commonly seen when materials are burned. Light-emitting reactions are used by living organisms in ◊bioluminescence. One photochemical reaction is the action of sunlight on car exhaust fumes, which results in the production of ◊ozone. Some large cities, such as Los Angeles, and Santiago, Chile, now suffer serious pollution forming photochemical smog.

photocopier machine that uses some form of photographic process to reproduce copies of documents. Most modern photocopiers, as pioneered by the Xerox Corporation (USA), use electrostatic photocopying, or xerography ('dry writing'). This employs a drum coated with a light-sensitive material such as selenium, which holds a pattern of static electricity charges corresponding to the dark areas of an image projected on to the drum by a lens. Finely divided pigment (toner) of opposite electric charge sticks to the charged areas of the drum, and is transferred to a sheet of paper which is heated briefly to melt the toner and stick it to the paper.

Additional facilities include enlargement and reduction, copying on both sides of the sheet of paper, and copying in colour.

photoelectric effect in physics, the emission of ◊electrons from a metallic surface when it is struck by ◊photons (quanta of electromagnetic radiation), usually those of visible light or ultraviolet radiation.

photofit system aiding the identification of wanted persons. Witnesses select photographs of a single feature (hair, eyes, nose, mouth), their choices resulting in a composite likeness that is then rephotographed and circulated. It is a sophisticated development by Jacques Penry 1970 for Scotland Yard of the ◊identikit system.

photogram a picture produced on photographic material by exposing it to light, but without using a camera.

photography a process for producing images on sensitized materials by various forms of radiant energy, including visible light, ultraviolet, infrared, X-rays; radioactive radiation and electron beam.

photogravure ◊printing process that uses a plate prepared photographically, covered with a pattern of recessed cells in which the ink is held. See ◊gravure.

photosynthesis

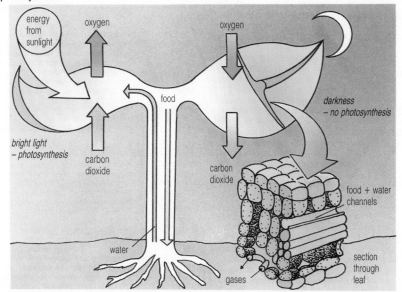

photometer an instrument that measures luminous intensity. Bunsen's greasespot photometer 1844 compares the intensity of a light source with a known source by each illuminating half of a translucent area. Modern photometers use ◊photocells, as in a photographer's exposure meter. A photomultiplier can also be used as a photometer.

photomultiplier an instrument that detects low levels of electromagnetic radiation (usually visible light or ◊infrared radiation) and amplifies it to produce a detectable signal.

One type resembles a ◊photocell with an additional series of coated ◊electrodes (dynodes) between the ◊cathode and ◊anode. Radiation striking the cathode releases electrons (primary emission) which hit the first dynode, producing yet more electrons (◊secondary emission) which strike the second dynode. This produces a measurable signal up to 100 million times larger than the original signal eventually leaving the anode. Similar devices, called image intensifiers, are used in television camera tubes that 'see' in the dark.

photon in physics, the smallest 'package', 'particle', or quantum of energy in which ◊light, or any other form of electromagnetic radiation, is emitted; a type of ◊photon.

photoperiodism a biological mechanism that controls the timing of certain activities by responding to changes in day length. The flowering of many plants is initiated in this way. Photoperiodism in plants is regulated by a light-sensitive pigment, **phytochrome**. The breeding seasons of many temperate animals are also triggered by increasing or declining day length, as part of their ◊biorhythms.

Autumn-flowering plants (for example, chrysanthemum and soyabean) and autumn-breeding mammals (such as goats and deer) require days that are shorter than a critical length; spring-flowering and spring-breeding ones (such as radish and lettuce; birds) are triggered by longer days.

photosphere the visible surface of the Sun, which emits light and heat. About 300 km/200 mi deep, it consists of incandescent gas at a temperature of 5,360K.

Rising cells of hot gas produce a mottling of the photosphere known as **granulation**, each granule being about 1,000 km/620 mi in diameter. The photosphere is often marked by large, dark patches called ◊sunspots.

photosynthesis the process by which green plants, photosynthetic bacteria and cyanobacteria utilize light energy from the Sun to produce food molecules (◊carbohydrates) from carbon dioxide and water. There are two stages. During the **light reaction** sunlight is used to split water (H_2O) into oxygen (O_2), protons (hydrogen ions, H^+) and electrons, and oxygen is given off as a by-product. In the second stage **dark reaction**, where sunlight is not required, the protons and electrons are used to convert carbon dioxide (CO_2) into carbohydrates (CH_2O). Photosynthesis depends on the ability of ◊chlorophyll to capture the energy of sunlight and use it to split water molecules.

Other pigments, such as ◊carotenoids, are also involved in capturing light energy and passing it on to chlorophyll. Photosynthesis by cyanobacteria was responsible for the appearance of oxygen in the Earth's atmosphere 2,500 million years ago, and photosynthesis by plants maintains the oxygen level today.

phrase structure grammar a theory of language structure which proposes that a given language has several different potential sentence patterns, consisting of various sorts of phrase, which can be expanded in various ways.

For example, the sentence 'the girl opened the door' contains a noun phrase 'the girl', and a verb phrase 'opened the door'; the verb phrase can be further analysed into a verb 'opened' and noun phrase 'the door'; and so on.

phrenology theory of the Viennese physician Dr Franz Josef ◊Gall that the skull shape revealed measurable psychological and intellectual features. Modern science discredits it.

Phrygia /'frɪdʒɪə/ former kingdom of W Asia covering the Anatolian tableland. It was inhabited in ancient times by an Indo-European people, and achieved great prosperity in the 8th century BC under a line of kings bearing in turn the names Gordius and Midas, but then fell under Lydian rule. From Phrygia the cult of ◊Cybele was introduced into Greece and Rome.

Phryne /'fraɪnɪ/ Greek courtesan of the 4th century BC, famed for her beauty. She is said to have been the model for the Aphrodite of Cnidos by the Athenian sculptor Praxiteles.

phylacteries in Judaism, another name for ◊tefillin.

phyllite a ◊metamorphic rock produced under increasing temperature and pressure, in which mica crystals are aligned so that the rock splits along their plane of orientation, the resulting break being shiny and smooth. It is intermediate between slate and schist.

phyllotaxis the arrangement of leaves on a plant stem. Leaves are nearly always arranged in a regular pattern and in the majority of plants they are inserted singly, either in a **spiral** arrangement up the stem, or on **alternate** sides. Other principal forms are opposite leaves, where two arise from the same node, and whorled, where three or more arise from the same node.

phylloxera a genus of aphid-like lice. The species *Phylloxera vitifolia*, a native of North America, attacks grape vines, laying its eggs under the bark. European vines are especially susceptible and many French vineyards suffered by the arrival of the pest in Europe in the 19th century; most European vines are now grafted on to rootstock of the American vine, which is not as susceptible to the disease. The phylloxera bug (hemipteran) may be destroyed by spraying with carbon disulphide or petroleum.

phylogeny the historical sequence of changes that occurs in a given species during the course of evolution. It used to be erroneously associated with ontogeny (the process of development of a living organism).

phylum (plural *phyla*) a major grouping in biological classification. Mammals, birds, reptiles, amphibians, and fish belong to the phylum Chordata; the phylum Mollusca consists of snails, slugs, mussels and clams, squid and octopuses; the phylum Porifera contains sponges, and the phylum Echinodermata includes starfish, sea urchins, and sea cucumbers. Among plants there are between four and nine phyla depending on the classification used; all flowering plants belong to a single phylum, Angiospermata, and all conifers to another, Gymnospermata. Related phyla are grouped together in a ◊kingdom; phyla are subdivided into ◊classes.

physical change in chemistry, a change to a substance that does not produce a new chemical substance and that can be easily reversed. Boiling and melting are physical changes.

physics the branch of science concerned with the ultimate laws that govern the structure of the universe, and forms of matter and energy and their interactions. For convenience, physics is often divided into branches such as nuclear physics, solid and liquid state physics, electricity, electronics, magnetism, optics, acoustics, heat, and thermodynamics. Before this century, physics was known as *natural philosophy*.

piano or *pianoforte* a stringed musical instrument, played by felt-covered hammers activated from a keyboard, and capable of soft (piano) or loud (forte) tones, hence its name.

It was introduced in 1709 by Bartolommeo Christofori, a harpsichord-maker of Padua, and uses a clever mechanism to make the keyboard touch-sensitive. Extensively developed during the 18th century, it attracted admiration among many composers, although it was not until 1768 that J C Bach gave one of the first public recitals on the instrument. Further improvements in the keyboard action and tone by makers such as Broadwood, Erard, and Graf, together with a rapid expansion of published music by Haydn, Beethoven, Schubert and others, led to the development of the powerfully resonant concert grand and the mass production of smaller upright pianos for the home.

The *player piano* is designed to reproduce key-actions recorded on a perforated paper roll. The concert *Duo-Art* reproducing piano encoded more detailed information, such that audiences were unable to distinguish a live performance form a reproduced performance.

Piano /'piænɔ/ Renzo 1937– . Italian architect who designed (with Richard ◊Rogers) the Pompidou Centre, Paris, completed 1977. Among his other buildings are the Kansai Airport, Osaka, Japan, and a sports stadium in Bari, Italy, both using new materials and making imaginative use of civil-engineering techniques.

Piazzi /'pi'ætsi/ Giuseppe 1746–1826. Italian astronomer, director of Palermo Observatory. In 1801 he discovered the first asteroid, which he named ◊Ceres.

Picabia /'pi'ka:biə/ Francis 1879–1953. French painter, a Cubist from 1909. On his second visit to New York, 1915–16, he joined with Marcel Duchamp in the Dadaist revolt and later took the movement to Barcelona. He associated with the

physics: landmarks

c.400 BC	The first 'atomic' theory was put forward by Democritus.
c.250 BC	Archimedes' principle of buoyancy was established.
1600 AD	Magnetism was described by English physicist and physician William Gilbert (1544–1603).
c.1610	The principle of falling bodies descending to Earth at the same speed was established by Galileo.
1642	The principles of hydraulics were put forward by French mathematician, physicist, and philosopher Blaise Pascal (1623–62).
1643	The mercury barometer was invented by Italian physicist Evangelista Torricelli (1608–47).
1656	The pendulum clock was invented by Dutch physicist and astronomer Christiaan Huygens (1629–95).
c.1665	Newton put forward the law of gravity, stating that the Earth exerts a constant force on falling bodies.
1677	The simple microscope was invented by Dutch microscopist Antoni van Leeuwenhoek (1632–1723).
1690	The wave theory of light was propounded by Huygens.
1704	The corpuscular theory of light was put forward by Newton.
1714	The mercury thermometer was invented by German physicist (Gabriel) Daniel Fahrenheit.
1771	The link between nerve action and electricity was discovered by Italian anatomist and physiologist Luigi Galvani (1737–98).
1795	The metric system was adopted in France.
1798	The link between heat and friction was discovered by American-British physicist Count Benjamin Thomson Rumford (1753–1814).
1800	Volta invented the Voltaic cell.
1808	The 'modern' atomic theory was propounded by British physicist and chemist John Dalton (1766–1844).
1811	Avogadro's hypothesis relating volumes and numbers of molecules of gases was proposed by Italian physicist and chemist Amedeo Avogadro (1776–1856).
1815	Refraction of light was explained by French physicist Augustin Fresnel (1788–1827).
1819	The discovery of electromagnetism was made by Danish physicist Hans Oersted (1777–1851).
1821	The dynamo principle was described by British physicist and chemist Michael Faraday (1791–1867); the thermocouple was discovered by German physicist Thomas Seebeck (1770–1831).
1827	*Ohm's law* was established by German physicist GS Ohm; Brownian motion resulting from molecular vibrations was observed by British botanist Robert Brown (1773–1858).
1831	Electromagnetic induction was discovered by Faraday.
1842	The principle of conservation of energy was observed by German physician and physicist Julius von Mayer (1814–78).
c.1847	The mechanical equivalent of heat was described by Joule.
1849	A measurement of speed of light was put forward by French physicist Armand Fizeau (1819–96).
1851	The rotation of the Earth was demonstrated by Foucault.
1859	Spectrographic analysis was made by German chemist Robert Bunsen (1811–99) and German physicist Gustav Kirchhoff (1824–87).
1861	Osmosis was discovered.
1873	Light was conceived as electromagnetic radiation by British physicist James Clerk Maxwell.
1877	A theory of sound as vibrations in an elastic medium was propounded by British physicist John Rayleigh (1842–1919).
1887	The existence of radio waves was predicted by Hertz.
1895	X-rays were discovered by German physicist Wilhelm Röntgen (1845–1923).
1896	The discovery of radioactivity was made by French physicist Antoine Becquerel (1852–1908).
1897	The electron was discovered by J J Thomson.
1899	Rutherford discovered alpha and beta rays.
1900	Quantum theory was propounded by Planck; the discovery of gamma rays was made by French physicist Paul-Ulrich Villard (1860–1934).
1902	Heaviside discovered the ionosphere.
1904	The theory of radioactivity was put forward by Rutherford and British chemist Frederick Soddy (1877–1966).
1905	Einstein propounded his *special theory of relativity*.
1911	The discovery of the atomic nucleus was made by Rutherford.
1915	Einstein put forward his *general theory of relativity*; X-ray crystallography was discovered by William and Lawrence Bragg.
1922	The orbiting electron atomic theory was propounded by Bohr.
1924	Appleton made his study of the Heaviside layer.
1927	The uncertainty principle of atomic physics was established by German physicist Werner Heisenberg (1901–76).
1928	Wave mechanics was introduced by Schrödinger.
1931	The cyclotron was developed by American physicist Ernest Lawrence (1901–58).
1932	The discovery of the neutron was made by Chadwick; the electron microscope was developed by Soviet-American physicist Vladimir Zworykin (1889–1982).
1933	The position, the antiparticle of the electron, was discovered by Millikan.
1934	Artificial radioactivity was developed by Frédéric and Irène Joliot-Curie.
1939	The discovery of nuclear fission was made by Hahn and German chemist Fritz Strassman (1902–).
1942	The first controlled nuclear chain reaction was achieved by Fermi.
1956	The neutrino, a fundamental particle, was discovered.
1960	The Mössbauer effect of atom emissions was discovered by German physicist Rudolf Mössbauer (1929–); the first maser was developed by American physicist Theodore Maiman (1927–).
1963	Maiman developed the first laser (a term for light amplification by stimulated emission of radiation).

Surrealists for a time. His work was generally provocative and experimental.

Picardie /'pıkədi/ (English *Picardy*) region of N France, including Aisne, Oise, and Somme *départements*; area 19,400 sq km/7,488 sq mi; population (1986) 1,774,000. Industries include chemicals and metals. It was a major battlefield in World War I.

picaresque (Spanish *picaro* 'rogue') in literature, a genre of novels which take for their heroes

rogues and villains, telling their story in a series of loosely linked episodes. Examples include Defoe's *Moll Flanders*, Fielding's *Tom Jones*, and Twain's *Huckleberry Finn*.

Picasso /'pı'kæsɔʊ/ Pablo 1881–1973. Spanish artist, active chiefly in France, one of the most inventive and prolific talents in 20th century art.

Born in Málaga, son of an art teacher, José Ruiz Blasco, and an Andalusian mother, Maria Picasso López; he discontinued use of the name Ruiz in

1898. He was a mature artist at ten, and at 16 was holding his first exhibition. In 1900 he made an initial visit to Paris, where he was to settle, and during his Blue Period 1901–04 painted mystic distorted figures in blue tones; a brief, more supple Rose Period 1905–06 followed, but in 1907 he completed the revolutionary *Les Demoiselles d'Avignon* by which ◊Cubism was fully launched. Picasso has also been regarded as the founder of ◊Surrealism, but his subsequent development included by turns Classicism, Romanticism, ◊Realism ◊Expressionism, ◊Abstractionism, and ◊Naturalism, and ranged through ceramics, sculpture, sets for ballet (for example *Parade* in 1917 for Diaghilev), book illustrations (such as Ovid's *Metamorphoses*), portraits (Stravinsky, Valéry, and others),and the mural *Guernica* 1937 (Casón del Buen Retiro, Madrid), a comment on the bombing of civilians in the Spanish Civil War. He continued to paint into his 80s.

Piccard /pɪˈkɑː/ August 1884–1962. Swiss scientist. In 1931–32, he and his twin brother Jean Félix made ascents to 16,800 m/55,000 ft in a balloon of his own design, resulting in important discoveries concerning stratospheric phenomena such as ◊cosmic rays. He also built and used, with his son Jacques Ernest, bathyscaphes for research under the sea.

piccolo a woodwind instrument, the smallest member of the ◊flute family.

picketing a gathering of workers and their trade union representatives, usually at the entrance to their place of work, to try to persuade others to support them in an industrial dispute.

Pickford /ˈpɪkfəd/ Mary. Adopted name of Gladys Smith 1893–1979. US silent film actress, born in Toronto, Canada. As a child she toured with various road companies, started her film career 1909, and in 1919 formed United Artists with Charlie Chaplin, D W Griffith, and her second husband (1920–36) Douglas Fairbanks. She often appeared as a young girl, even when she was well into her twenties. The public did not like her talking films, and she retired 1933. She was known as 'America's Sweetheart'.

Pico della Mirandola /ˈpiːkəʊ ˌdelə mɪˈrændələ/ Count Giovanni 1463–1494. Italian mystic philosopher. Born at Mirandola, of which his father was prince, he studied Hebrew, Chaldean, and Arabic, showing particular interest in the Jewish and theosophical system, the ◊Kabbala. His attempt to reconcile the religious base of Christianity, Islam, and the ancient world earned Pope Alexander VI's disapproval.

picric acid $C_6H_2(NO_2)_3OH$ a yellow crystalline solid (modern name 2,4,6-trinitrophenol). It is a strong acid, which is used to dye wool and silks yellow, for the treatment of burns, and in the manufacture of explosives.

Pict Roman term for a member of the peoples of N Scotland, possibly meaning 'painted' (tattooed). Of pre-Celtic origin, and speaking a non-Celtic language, the Picts were united with the Celtic Scots under the rule of Kenneth MacAlpin 844.

Picton /ˈpɪktən/ small port at the NE extremity of South Island, New Zealand, with a ferry to Wellington, North Island.

PID abbreviation for *pelvic inflammatory disease*, an increasingly common gynaecological condition. It is characterized by lower abdominal pain, malaise, and fever; menstruation may be disrupted; infertility may result. The bacterium *Chlamydia trachomatis* has been implicated in a high proportion of cases. The incidence of the disease is twice as high in women using intrauterine contraceptive devices (IUDs).

PID is potentially life-threatening, and, while mild episodes usually respond to antibiotics, surgery may be necessary in cases of severe or recurrent pelvic infection.

pidgin English /ˈpɪdʒɪn ˈɪŋglɪʃ/ originally a trade jargon or contact language between the British and the Chinese in the 19th century, but now commonly and loosely used to mean any kind of 'broken' or 'native' version of the English language.

Pidgin is believed to have been a Chinese pronunciation of the English word 'business' (hence the expression, 'This isn't my pigeon'). There have been many forms of pidgin English, often with common elements because of the wide range of contacts made by commercial shipping (see ◊pidgin languages). The original pidgin English of the Chinese ports combined words of English with a rough-and-ready Chinese grammatical structure. Melanesian pidgin English (also known as *Tok Pisin*) combines English and the syntax of local Melanesian languages. For example, the English pronoun 'we' becomes both *yumi* (you and me), and *mifela* (me and fellow, excluding you).

pidgin languages trade jargons, contact languages, or lingua francas arising in ports and markets where people of different linguistic backgrounds meet for commercial and other purposes.

Generally, a pidgin comes into existence to answer short-term needs, for example Korean Bamboo English as used during the Korean War. Unless there is a reason for extending the life of such a hybrid form (in the case of Korean Bamboo English combining elements of English, Korean, and Japanese), it will fade away when the need passes. Usually a pidgin is a rough-and-ready blend of the vocabulary of one (often dominant) language with the syntax or grammar of one or more other groups (usually in a dependent position). ◊Pidgin English in various parts of the world, *français petit negre*, and bazaar Hindi or Hindustani are examples of pidgins which have served long-term purposes, to the extent of being acquired by children as one of their everyday languages. See also ◊Creole languages.

pièce de résistance (French) the most outstanding item in a collection; the main dish of a meal.

Pieck /piːk/ Wilhelm 1876–1960. German communist politician. He was a leader of the 1919 Spartacist revolt and a founder of the Socialist Unity Party 1946. From 1949 he was president of East Germany; the office was abolished on his death.

pied-à-terre (French 'foot on the ground') a convenient second home, usually small and in a town or city.

Piedmont /ˈpiːdmɒnt/ (Italian *Piemonte*) region of N Italy, bordering Switzerland on the north and France on the west, and surrounded, except on the east, by the Alps and the Apennines; area 25,400 sq km/9,804 sq mi; population (1988) 4,377,000. Its capital is Turin, and towns include Alessandria, Asti, Vercelli, and Novara. It also includes the fertile Po river valley. Products include fruit, grain, cattle, cars, and textiles. The movement for the unification of Italy started in the 19th century in Piedmont, under the house of Savoy.

Piero della Francesca Baptism of Christ (c.1439), National Gallery, London.

pier a structure built out into the sea from the coastline for use as a landing place or promenade. The first British pier was built at Ryde, Isle of Wight, in 1814. Eugenius Birch (1818–1883) designed the West Pier, Brighton 1866 (339 m/1,115 ft); Margate Pier, 1856; and the North Pier, Blackpool 1863.

Piercy /ˈpɪəsi/ Marge 1937– . US novelist. Her fiction looks at social life and the world of the liberated woman. Novels include the utopian *Woman on the Edge of Time* 1979 and *Fly Away Home* 1984.

Piero della Francesca /piˈeərəʊ ˌdelə frænˈtʃeskə/ c.1420–1492. Italian painter, active in Arezzo and Urbino. His work has a solemn stillness and unusually solid figures, luminous colour and compositional harmony. It includes a fresco series, *The Legend of the True Cross* (S Francesco, Arezzo), begun about 1452. Piero wrote two treatises, one on mathematics, one on the laws of perspective in painting.

Piero di Cosimo /piˈeərəʊ di: ˈkɒzɪməʊ/ c.1462–1521. Italian painter, noted for inventive pictures of mythological subjects, often featuring fauns and centaurs. He also painted portraits.

Pietermaritzburg /ˌpiːtəˈmærɪtsbɜːg/ industrial city (footwear, furniture, aluminium, rubber, brewing), capital from 1842 of Natal, South Africa; population (1980) 179,000. Founded 1838 by Boer trekkers from the Cape, it was named after their leaders, Piet Retief and Gert Maritz, killed by the Zulus.

Pietism religious movement within Lutheranism in the 17th century which emphasized spiritual and devotional Christianity.

It was founded by Philipp Jakob Spener (1635–1705), a minister in Frankfurt, Germany, who emphasized devotional meetings for 'groups of the Elect' rather than biblical learning; he wrote the *Pia Desideria* 1675. The movement was for many years associated with the University of Halle (founded 1694), Germany.

pietra dura (Italian 'hard stone') an Italian technique of inlaying furniture with semi-precious stone, such as agate or quartz, in different colours to create pictures or patterns.

Pietro /piˈetrəʊ/ Berrettini da Cortona 1596–1669. Italian painter and architect, a major influence in the development of Roman High Baroque. His huge fresco *Allegory of Divine Providence* 1633–39 (Barberini Palace, Rome) glorifies his patron the pope and the Barberini family, and gives a convincing illusion of reality.

pig

large white

saddle back

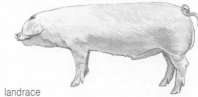

landrace

piezoelectric effect property of some crystals, for example, ◊quartz, which develop an electromotive force or voltage across opposite faces when subjected to a mechanical strain, and, conversely, which alter in size when subjected to an electromotive force. Piezoelectric crystal ◊oscillators are used as frequency standards (for example, replacing balance wheels in watches), and for producing ◊ultrasound. The crystals are also used in gramophone pick-ups, transducers in ultrasonics, and in certain gas lighters.

pig hoofed mammal of family Suidae. The European *wild boar Sus scrofa* is the ancestor of domesticated breeds; it is 1.5 m/4.5 ft long and 1 m/3 ft high, with formidable tusks, but not naturally aggressive. Pigs are omnivorous, and have simple stomachs and thick hides.

Other wild pigs include the ◊*babirusa*, and the ◊*wart hog*. The farming of domesticated pigs was practised in China at least 9,000 years ago, and was a common feature of ancient Greek and Roman agriculture. Numerous breeds evolved over the centuries, many of which have all but disappeared in more recent times with the development of intensive rearing systems; however, different environments and requirements have ensured the continuation of a variety of types. The Berkshire and Tamworth are now rare in the UK, but still widespread in Australia and New Zealand. Modern indoor rearing methods often favour the Large White and the Landrace, of British and Swedish origin respectively; the Welsh and the British Saddleback have the necessary hardy characteristics for outdoor systems. Over the last 30 years, hybrid pigs, produced by crossing two or more breeds, have become popular for their heavy lean carcasses. Porker pigs are slaughtered at about 70 kg/155 lb liveweight, baconers at 95 kg/210 lb and the heavy hogs, whose meat goes into the manufacture of such items as sausages and pork pies, at 115 kg/250 lb.

Pigalle Jean Baptiste 1714–1785. French sculptor. In 1744 he made the marble *Mercury* (Louvre, Paris), a lively, naturalistic work. His subjects ranged from the intimate to the formal, and included portraits.

Pigalle studied in Rome 1736–39. In Paris he gained the patronage of Madame de Pompadour, the mistress of Louis XV. His works include *Venus, Love and Friendship* 1758 (Louvre), a nude statue of *Voltaire* 1776 (Institut de France, Paris), and the grandiose *Tomb of Marechal de Saxe* 1753 (Strasbourg).

pigeon any member of the family Columbidae, sometimes also called doves, distinguished by their large crops which, becoming glandular in the breeding season, secrete a milky fluid ('pigeon's milk') which aids digestion of food for the young. They are found worldwide.

There are many species: domesticated varieties (pouter, fantail, homer) derive from the rock dove *Columba livia*. Similar is the stock-dove *Columba oenas*, but the wood-pigeon *Columba palumbus* is much larger and has white patches on the neck. The American species include the mourning-doves, which, like the European turtle-doves, live much of the time on the ground. The *collared dove Streptopelia decaocto* has multiplied greatly in Europe since it first arrived from central Asia 1930. It lives in urban areas as well as the countryside. The fruit pigeons of Australia and the Malay regions are beautifully coloured. In the USA, there were once millions of passenger pigeons *Ectopistes migratorius*, but they have been extinct since 1914.

pigeon racing sport of racing pigeons against a clock. The birds are taken from their loft(s) and transported to a starting point, often hundreds of miles away. They have to return to their loft and a special clock times their arrival.

In Britain the National Homing Union dates from 1896. Elizabeth II has a flight of pigeons which is looked after by a racing manager.

Piggott Lester 1935– . English jockey. He was regarded as a brilliant tactician and adopted a unique high riding style. A champion jockey 11

Piggott *Last weigh-in for champion jockey Lester Piggott after the final Handicap Stakes, Nottingham, 29 Oct 1985. He rode more than 4,000 winners, many of them in the classic races in Britain, France, and the USA.*

times 1960–1982, he rode a record nine ◊Derby winners.

He was associated with such great horses as Nijinsky, Sir Ivor, Roberto, Empery, and The Minstrel. Piggott won all the major races including all the English classics. He retired from riding 1985 and took up training. In 1987 he was imprisoned for tax evasion.

CAREER HIGHLIGHTS

Champion Jockey: 1960, 1964–71, 1981–82
Derby: 1954, 1957, 1960, 1968, 1970, 1972, 1976–77, 1983 *Oaks:* 1957, 1959, 1966, 1975, 1981, 1984,
St Leger: 1960–61, 1967–68, 1970–72, 1984
1,000 Guineas: 1970, 1981
2,000 Guineas: 1957, 1968, 1970, 1985

Pigou /'pɪguː/ Arthur Cecil 1877–1959. British economist, whose notion of the 'real balance effect' (the 'Pigou effect') contended that employment was stimulated by a fall in prices, because the latter increased liquid wealth and thus demand for goods and services.

pika or *mouse-hare* small mammal of the family Ochotonidae, belonging to the order Lagomorpha (rabbits and hares). Pikas have short rounded ears, and most species are about 20 cm/8 in long, with greyish-brown fur and no visible tail. They live in mountainous regions of Asia and North America. The warning call is a sharp whistle. They are vegetarian, and in late summer cut grasses and other plants and place them in piles to dry as hay, which is then stored for the winter.

pike long, thin, freshwater fish *Esox lucius* family Esocidae, of Europe, Asia, and North America; it is a voracious feeder and may reach 2.2 m/7 ft, and 9 kg/20 lbs. Other types of pike include muskellunges and pickerels.

pike-perch freshwater fish *Stizostedion lucioperca*, related to the perch, common in Europe, W Asia, and North America. It reaches over 1 m/3 ft.

Pikes Peak /'paɪks 'piːk/ mountain in the Rampart range of the Rocky Mountains, Colorado, USA; height 4,300 m/14,110 ft.

Pilate /'paɪlət/ Pontius early 1st century AD. Roman procurator of Judaea AD 26–36. Unsympathetic to the Jews, his actions several times provoked riots,

and in AD 36 he was recalled to Rome after brutal suppression of a Samaritan uprising. The New Testament Gospels describe his reluctant ordering of Jesus' crucifixion, but there has been considerable debate about his actual role in it; many believe that pressure was put on him by Jewish conservative priests. The Greek historian Eusebius says he committed suicide, but Coptic tradition says he was martyred as a Christian.

pilchard fish *Sardina pilchardus* of the herring family. Bluish-green above and silvery beneath, it grows to 25 cm/10 in long. It is most abundant in the W Mediterranean.

pilgrimage journey to sacred places inspired by religious devotion. For Hindus the holy places include Varanasi and the purifying river Ganges; for Buddhists the places connected with the crises of Buddha's career; for the ancient Greeks the shrines at Delphi and Ephesus among others; for the Jews, the sanctuary at Jerusalem; and for Muslims, Mecca. The great centres of Christian pilgrimages have been, or are, Jerusalem, Rome, the tomb of St James of Compostela in Spain, the shrine of Becket, Canterbury, England, and the holy places at La Salette and Lourdes in France.

Among Christians, pilgrimages were common by the 2nd century, and as a direct result of the established necessity of making pilgrimages there arose numerous hospices catering for pilgrims, the religious orders of knighthood, and the Crusades. The three major centres of pilgrimage in medieval England were Canterbury, Bury (the shrine of St Edmund), and Walsingham, Norfolk. Walsingham is still a site of pilgrimage each Easter.

Pilgrimage of Grace a rebellion against Henry VIII of England 1536–37, originating in Yorkshire and Lincolnshire. The rising, headed by Robert Aske (died 1537), was directed against the policies of the monarch (such as the dissolution of the monasteries and the effects of ◊enclosure).

At its peak, the rebels controlled York and included the archbishop there among their number. A truce was arranged in Dec and the insurrection dispersed, but the rebels' demands were not met, and a further revolt broke out in 1537, which was suppressed with severity, with the execution of over 200 of the rebels.

Pilgrims the emigrants who sailed from Plymouth, Devon, England, in the *Mayflower* 16 Sept 1620 to found the first colony in New England at New Plymouth, Massachusetts. Of the 102 passengers fewer than a quarter were Puritan refugees.

The Pilgrims originally set sail in the *Mayflower* and *Speedwell* from Southampton 5 Aug 1620, but had to put into Dartmouth when the latter needed repair. Bad weather then drove them into Plymouth Sound, where the *Speedwell* was abandoned. They landed at Cape Cod in Dec, and about half their number died over the winter before they received help from the Indians; the survivors celebrated ◊Thanksgiving autumn 1621.

The voyage was duplicated 1957 with *Mayflower II*, a replica presented by Britain and now at New Plymouth, Massachusetts.

Pilgrim's Progress an allegory by John Bunyan, published 1678–84, which describes a man's journey through life to the Celestial City. On his way through the Slough of Despond, the House Beautiful, Vanity Fair, Doubting Castle, and other landmarks, Christian meets a number of allegorical figures.

Pilgrims' Way track running from Winchester to Canterbury, England, which was the route of medieval pilgrims visiting the shrine of Thomas à Becket. Some 195 km/120 mi long, the Pilgrims' Way can still be traced for most of its of its length.

Pilgrim Trust British charity established 1930 by the US philanthropist Edward Harkness (1874–1940) to further social and educational welfare in Britain and to preserve its national heritage.

Pill, the a commonly used term for the contraceptive pill, based on female hormones. The combined pill, which contains oestrogen and progesterone, stops the production of eggs, and makes the mucus produced by the cervix hostile to sperm. It is the most effective form of contraception apart from sterilization, being over 99% effective.

The mini-pill or progesterone-only pill prevents implantation of a fertilized egg into the wall of the uterus. The mini-pill has a slightly higher failure rate, especially if not taken at the same time each day, but has fewer side-effects and is considered safer for long-term use. Possible side-effects of the Pill include migraine or headache and high blood pressure. More seriously, oestrogen-containing pills can slightly increase the risk of a blood clot forming in the blood vessels. This risk is increased in women over 35 if they smoke. Controversy surrounds other possible health effects of taking the Pill. The evidence for a link with breast cancer is slight, and the Pill protects women from cancer of the ovaries and womb.

pillory instrument of punishment consisting of a wooden frame set on a post, with holes in which the prisoner's head and hands were secured. Bystanders threw whatever was available at the miscreant. Its use was abolished in England 1837.

Pilobolous Dance Theater US troupe whimsically named after a light-sensitive fungus. Its members collectively choreograph surreal body-sculptures with a mixture of dance, gymnastics and mime.

pilotfish small sea fish *Naucrates ductor*, which hides below sharks, turtles, or boats, using the shade as a base from which to prey on smaller fish. It is found in all warm oceans and grows to about 36 cm/1.2 ft.

Pilsen /ˈpɪlzən/ German form of Czechoslovakian town of ◊Plzeň.

Pilsudski /pɪlˈsʊdski/ Joseph 1867–1935. Polish nationalist politician, dictator from 1926. Born in Russian Poland, he founded the Polish Socialist Party 1892, and was twice imprisoned for anti-Russian activities. During World War I he commanded a Polish force to fight for Germany, but fell under suspicion of intriguing with the Allies, and in 1917–18 was imprisoned by the Germans. When Poland became independent he was elected chief of state, and led an unsuccessful Polish attack on the USSR 1920. He retired 1923, but in 1926 led a military coup which established his dictatorship until his death.

Piltdown man /ˈpɪltdaʊn/ skull fragments 'discovered' by Charles Dawson (died 1916) at Piltdown, E Sussex 1913, and believed to be the earliest European human remains until proved a hoax 1953 (the jaw was that of an orang-utan). The most likely perpetrator was Samuel Woodhead, a lawyer friend of Dawson, who was an amateur palaeontologist.

pimento or *allspice* tree found in tropical parts of the New World. The dried fruits of the species *Pimenta dioica* are used as a spice.

pimpernel plant of the genus *Anagallis*, family Primulaceae. The scarlet pimpernel *A. arvensis* grows in cornfields, the flowers opening only in full sunshine. It is naturalized in North America.

Pincus /ˈpɪŋkəs/ Gregory Goodwin 1903–1967. US biologist who devised the contraceptive pill in the 1950s together with Min Chueh Chang and John Rock.

As a result of studying the physiology of reproduction, Pincus conceived the idea of using synthetic ◊hormones to mimic the condition of pregnancy in women. This effectively prevents impregnation.

Pindar c. 552–442 BC. Greek poet, born near Thebes. He is noted for his choral lyrics, 'Pindaric Odes', written in honour of victors of athletic games.

Pindling /ˈpɪndlɪŋ/ Lynden (Oscar) 1930– . Bahamian prime minister from 1967. After studying law in London, he returned to the island to join the newly formed Progressive Liberal Party, and then became the first black prime minister of the Bahamas.

Pindus Mountains /ˈpɪndəs/ (Greek **Pindhos Oros**) range in NW Greece and Albania, between Epirus and Thessaly: highest point Smolikas 2,633 m/8,638 ft.

pine evergreen resinous tree of the genus *Pinus* with some 70–100 species, belonging to the Pinaceae, the largest family of conifers. The Scots pine *Pinus*

sylvestris is grown commercially for soft timber and its yield of turpentine, tar, and pitch.

The oldest living species is probably the bristlecone pine *Pinus aristata*, native to California, of which some specimens are said to be 4,600 years old.

pineal body or *pineal gland* an outgrowth of the vertebrate brain. In some lower vertebrates, this develops a lens and retina, which show it to be derived from an eye, or pair of eyes, situated on the top of the head in ancestral vertebrates. The pineal still detects light (through the skull) in some fish, lizards, and birds. In fish that can change colour to match the background, the pineal perceives the light level and controls the colour change. In birds, the pineal detects changes in daylight and stimulates breeding behaviour as spring approaches.

Mammals also have a pineal gland, but it is located within the brain. It secretes a hormone-like substance, melatonin, which may influence rhythms of activity. In humans, it is a small piece of tissue attached to the posterior wall of the third ventricle of the brain.

pineapple plant *Ananas comosus*, native to South and Central America, but now cultivated in many other tropical areas, such as Hawaii and Queensland, Australia. The mauvish flowers are produced midway in the second year, and subsequently consolidate with their bracts into a fleshy fruit.

For export to world markets the fruits are cut unripe and lack the sweet juiciness typical of the tinned pineapple (usually the smoother-skinned Cayenne variety), which is allowed to mature fully.

pine marten type of ◊marten, a small mammal.

Pinero /pɪˈnɪərəʊ/ Arthur Wing 1855–1934. British dramatist. A leading exponent of the 'well-made' play, he enjoyed huge contemporary success with his farces, beginning with *The Magistrate* 1885. More substantial social drama followed with *The Second Mrs Tanqueray* 1893, and comedies including *Trelawny of the 'Wells'* 1898.

pink perennial plant of the genus *Dianthus*, including the maiden pink *Dianthus deltoides* found in dry grassy places. The stems have characteristically swollen nodes and the flowers range in colour from white through pink to purple. Garden forms include carnations, sweet williams, and baby's breath *Gypsophila paniculata*.

Pinkerton /ˈpɪŋkətən/ Allan 1819–1884. US detective, born in Glasgow. In 1852 he founded *Pinkerton's National Detective Agency*, and built up the federal secret service from the espionage system he developed during the US Civil War.

Pink Floyd British psychedelic rock group, formed 1965. The original members were Syd Barrett (1946–), Roger Waters (1944–), Richard Wright (1945–), and Nick Mason (1945–). Their albums include *The Dark Side of the Moon* 1973 and *The Wall* 1979, with its spin-off film starring Bob Geldof.

Pinkie, Battle of /ˈpɪŋki/ battle on 10 Sept 1547 near Musselburgh, Lothian, Scotland, in which the Scots were defeated by the English under the duke of Somerset.

pinna in botany, the primary division of a ◊pinnate leaf.

pinnate leaf a leaf that is divided up into many small leaflets, arranged in rows along either side of a midrib, as in ash tree (*Fraxinus*). It is a type of compound ◊leaf. Each leaflet is known as a *pinna*, and where the pinnae are themselves divided, the secondary divisions are known as pinnules.

Pinocchio a fantasy for children by Carlo ◊Collodi published in Italy 1883 and in English translation 1892. It tells the story of a wooden puppet that assumes the characteristics of a human boy. He has a long nose that grows every time he tells a lie. A Walt Disney cartoon film, based on Collodi's story, was released in 1940 and brought the character to a much wider audience.

Pinochet (Ugarte) /ˈpiːnəʊʃeɪ uːˈɡɑːteɪ/ Augusto 1915– . Military ruler of Chile from 1973, when

a CIA-backed coup ousted and killed president Salvador Allende. Pinochet took over the presidency and ruled ruthlessly, crushing all opposition. He was voted out of power when general elections were held in 1989 but remains head of the armed forces until 1997.

pint imperial liquid or dry measure equal to 20 fluid ounces, 1/2 of a quart, 1/8 of a gallon, or 0.568 litre. In the US, a liquid pint is equal to 0.473 litre, while a dry pint is equal to 0.550 litre.

Pinter /ˈpɪntə/ Harold 1930– . English writer, originally an actor. He specializes in the tragicomedy of the breakdown of communication, broadly in the tradition of the Theatre of the ◊Absurd, for example *The Birthday Party* 1958 and *The Caretaker* 1960. Later plays include *The Homecoming* 1965, *Old Times* 1971, *Betrayal* 1978, and *Mountain Language* 1988.

Pinter's work is known for its pauses, allowing the audience to read between the lines. He writes for radio and television, and his screenplays include *The Go-Between* 1969 and *The French Lieutenant's Woman* 1982.

Pinturicchio /ˌpɪntuˈrɪkiəʊ/ (or Pintoricchio). Pseudonym of Bernardino di Betti c.1454–1513. Italian painter, active in Rome, Perugia, and Siena. His chief works are the frescoes in the Borgia Apartments in the Vatican, 1490s, and in the Piccolomini Library of Siena Cathedral, 1503–08. He may have assisted ◊Perugino in decorating the Sistine Chapel, Rome.

pinworm ◊nematode worm *Enterobius vermicularis*, an intestinal parasite of humans.

Pinyin the Chinese phonetic alphabet approved 1956, and used from 1979 in transcribing all names of people and places from the Chinese language into foreign languages using the Roman alphabet. For example, Chou En-lai becomes Zhou Enlai, Hua Kuo-feng becomes Hua Guofeng, Teng Hsiao-ping becomes Deng Xiaoping, Peking becomes Beijing.

Pioneer probes a series of US space probes 1958–78. Pioneers 1 to 3, launched 1958, were intended Moon probes, but Pioneer 2's launch failed, and 1 and 3 failed to reach their target, although they did measure the ◊Van Allen belts. Pioneer 4 began to orbit the Sun after passing the Moon. Pioneer 5, launched 1960, was the first of a series to study the solar wind between the planets. Pioneers 6 (1965), 7 (1966), 8 (1967), and 9 (1968) monitored solar activity.

Pioneer 10, launched Mar 1972, was the first probe to reach Jupiter (Dec 1973) and to leave the solar system 1983. Pioneer 11, launched Apr 1973, passed Jupiter Dec 1974, and was the first probe to reach Saturn (Sept 1979), before also leaving the solar system. Pioneers 10 and 11 carry plaques containing messages from Earth in case they are found by other civilizations among the stars. Pioneer Venus probes were launched May and Aug 1978. One orbited Venus, and the other dropped three probes onto the surface. In early 1990 Pioneer 10 was 7.1 billion km from the Sun. Both it and Pioneer 11 were still returning data-measurements of starlight intensity to Earth.

Piozzi /pɪˈɒtsi/ Hester Lynch (born Salusbury) 1741–1821. Welsh writer. She published *Anecdotes of the late Samuel Johnson* 1786 and their correspondence 1788. Johnson had been a constant visitor to her house in Streatham, London, when she was married to her first husband, Henry Thrale, but after Thrale's death Johnson was alienated by her marriage to the musician Gabriel Piozzi. *Thraliana*, her diaries and notebooks of the years 1766–1809, was published 1942.

pipefish fish related to seahorses but long and thin like a length of pipe. The *great pipefish Syngnathus acus* grows up to 50 cm/1.6 ft, and the male has a brood pouch for eggs and developing young.

pipeline a pipe for carrying water, oil, gas, or other material over long distances. They are widely used in water-supply and oil- and gas-distribution schemes. The USA has over 300,000 km/200,000 mi of oil pipelines alone.

piranha

red
piranha

Piranesi The 18th-century Italian architect Giambattista Piranesi engraved Roman antiquities on copper and worked on a great series of etchings of the Rome of his day compared with Rome in ancient times. This etching is one of the Carceri d'Invenzione.

and treatment of his plays anticipated the work of Brecht, O'Neill, Anouilh, and Genet. Nobel Prize for Literature 1934.

Piranesi /ˌpɪrəˈneɪzi/ Gimabattista 1720–1778. Italian architect, most influential for his powerful etchings of Roman antiquities and as a theorist of architecture, advocating imaginative use of Roman models. Only one of his designs was built, Sta Maria del Priorato, Rome.

piranha South American freshwater fish, genus *Serrusalmus*. It can grow to 60 cm/2 ft long. It has razor-sharp teeth, and some species may rapidly devour animals, especially if attracted by blood.

Piran, St *c.* AD 500. Christian missionary sent to Cornwall by St Patrick. There are remains of his oratory at Perranzabuloe, and he is the patron saint of Cornwall and its nationalist movement; feast day 5 Mar.

pirate radio in the UK, illegal radio broadcasting set up to promote an alternative to the state-owned monopoly. The early pirate radio stations broadcast from ships offshore, outside territorial waters; the first was Radio Atlanta (later Radio Caroline), set up in 1964.

Pirithous /paɪˈriθoʊʊs/ in Greek mythology, king of the ◊Lapiths, and friend of ◊Theseus. His marriage with Hippodamia was the occasion of a battle between the Lapiths and their guests, the ◊Centaurs, which is a recurrent subject of Greek art.

pirouette in dance, a movement comprising a complete turn of the body on one leg with the other raised.

Pirquet /pɪəˈkeɪ/ Clemens von 1874–1929. Austrian paediatrician and pioneer in the study of allergy.

Pisa /ˈpiːzə/ city in Tuscany, Italy; population (1988) 104,000. The Leaning Tower is 55 m/180 ft high and about 5 m/16.5 ft out of perpendicular. It has foundations only about 3 m/10 ft deep and is the campanile of Pisa's 11th–12th-century cathedral (with a pulpit by Giovanni Pisano); university 1338.

Pisa The Leaning Tower of Pisa in Italy is 55 m/180 ft high and about 5 m/16.5 ft out of perpendicular.

One of the longest is the Trans-Alaskan Pipeline in Alaska.

Piper /ˈpaɪpə/ John 1903– . British painter and designer. He painted mostly traditional Romantic views of landscape and architecture. As an official war artist he painted damaged buildings in a melancholy vein. He also designed theatre sets and stained-glass windows (Coventry Cathedral; Catholic Cathedral, Liverpool).

pipette a device for the accurate measurement of a known volume of liquid, usually for transfer from one container to another, used in chemistry and biology laboratories.

A conventional pipette is a glass tube, often with an enlarged bulb, which is calibrated in one or more positions. Liquid is drawn into the pipette by suction, to the desired calibration mark. The release of liquid is controlled by careful pressure of the forefinger over the upper end of the tube, or by a plunger or rubber bulb.

pipit any of several birds in the family Motacillidae, related to the wagtails. The European meadow pipit *Anthus pratensis* is about the size of a sparrow and streaky brown, but has a slender bill. It lives in open country and feeds on the ground.

pique (French) a feeling of slight irritation or resentment.

piracy the taking of a ship, aircraft, or any of its contents, from lawful ownership, punishable under

international law by the court of any country where the pirate may be found or taken. The contemporary equivalent is ◊hijacking. Piracy is also used to describe infringement of ◊copyright.

Algiers (see ◊corsairs), the West Indies (see ◊buccaneers), the coast of Trucial Oman (the Pirate Coast), Chinese and Malay waters, and such hideouts as Lundy Island, SW England, were long pirate haunts, but modern communications and the complexities of supplying and servicing modern vessels tend to eliminate piracy. Between the 16th and 18th centuries, the Barbary states of N Africa (Morocco, Algiers, Tunis, and Tripoli) were called the Pirate States.

Piraeus /paɪˈriːəs/ port of both ancient and modern ◊Athens and main port of Greece, on the Gulf of Aegina; population (1981) 196,400. Constructed as the port of Athens about 493 BC, it was linked with that city by the Long Walls about 460 BC. After the destruction of Athens by Sulla 86 BC, Piraeus declined. Modern Piraeus is an industrial suburb of Athens.

Pirandello /ˌpɪrənˈdeɪoʊ/ Luigi 1867–1936. Italian writer. The novel *Il fu Mattia Pascal/The Late Mattia Pascal* 1904 was highly acclaimed, along with many short stories. His plays include *La Morsa/The Vice* 1912, *Sei personaggi in cerca d'autore/Six Characters in Search of an Author* 1921, and *Enrico IV/Henry IV* 1922. The theme

Pisa was a maritime republic in the 11th–12th centuries. The scientist Galileo was born there.

Pisanello /ˌpiːzəˈneləʊ/ nickname of Antonio Pisano c. 1395–1455/56. Italian artist active in Verona, Venice, Naples, Rome, and elsewhere. His panel paintings reveal a rich International Gothic style; his frescoes are largely lost. He was also an outstanding portrait medallist.

His frescoes in the Palazzo Ducale in Mantua were rediscovered after World War II.

Pisano /piːˈsɑːnəʊ/ family of Italian sculptors, father and son, Nicola (died ? 1284) and his son Giovanni (died after 1314). They made decorated marble pulpits in churches in Pisa, Siena, and Pistoia. Giovanni also created figures for Pisa's baptistery and designed the façade of Siena Cathedral.

Pisano /piːˈsɑːnəʊ/ Andrea c.1290–1348. Italian sculptor, who made the earliest bronze doors for the Baptistery of Florence Cathedral, completed 1336.

Pisces faint constellation of the zodiac, mainly in the northern hemisphere near Pegasus, represented by two fish tied together by their tails. Pisces contains the **vernal ◊equinox**, the point at which the Sun's path around the sky (the ◊ecliptic) crosses the celestial equator. The Sun reaches this point around Mar 21 each year as it passes through Pisces from mid-Mar to late Apr. In **astrology**, the dates for Pisces are between about 19 Feb and 20 Mar (see ◊precession).

Piscis Austrinus constellation of the southern hemisphere. Its brightest star is ◊Fomalhaut.

Pisistratus /paɪˈsɪstrətəs/ c. 605–527 BC. Athenian politician. Although of noble family, he assumed the leadership of the peasant party, and seized power 561 BC. He was twice expelled, but recovered power from 541 BC until his death. Ruling as a dictator under constitutional forms, he was the first to have the Homeric poems written down, and founded Greek drama by introducing the Dionysiac peasant festivals into Athens.

Pissarro /pɪˈsɑːrəʊ/ Camille 1831–1903. French Impressionist painter, born in the West Indies. He went to Paris in 1855, met Corot, then Monet, and soon became a leading member of the Impressionist group. He experimented with various styles, including ◊Pointillism, in the 1880s.

His son **Lucien Pissarro** (1863–1944) worked in the same style for a time; he settled in the UK from 1890.

pistachio deciduous Eurasian tree *Pistacia vera*, family Anacardiaceae, with edible green nuts which are eaten salted or used to flavour foods.

pistil a general term describing the female part of a flower, either referring to one single ◊carpel or a group of several fused carpels.

Pistoia /pɪˈstɔɪə/ city in Tuscany, Italy, 16 km/10 mi NW of Florence; industries (steel, small arms, paper, pasta, olive oil); population (1982) 92,500. Pistoia was the site of the Roman rebel Catiline's defeat 62 BC. It is surrounded by walls (1302) and has a 12th-century cathedral.

pistol small ◊firearm designed for one-hand use. Pistols were in use from the early 15th century.

The problem of firing more than once without reloading was tackled by using many combinations of multiple barrels, both stationary and revolving. A breech-loading, multi-chambered revolver of as early as 1650 still survives; the first practical solution, however, was Samuel Colt's six-gun 1847. Behind a single barrel, a short six-chambered cylinder was rotated by cocking the hammer and a fresh round brought into place. The automatic pistol, operated by gas or recoil, was introduced in Germany in the 1890s. Both revolvers and automatics are in widespread military use.

piston a barrel-shaped device used in reciprocating engines (◊steam, ◊petrol, ◊diesel) to harness power. Pistons are driven up and down in cylinders by expanding steam or hot gases. They pass on their motion via a connecting rod and crank to a ◊crankshaft, which turns the driving wheels. In a pump or ◊compressor, the role of the piston is reversed, being used to move gases and liquids.

Piston /ˈpɪstən/ Walter (Hamor) 1894–1976. US composer and teacher. He wrote a number of textbooks, including *Harmony* 1941 and *Orchestration* 1955. His Neo-Classical works include eight symphonies, a number of concertos, chamber music, the orchestral suite *Three New England Sketches* 1959, and the ballet *The Incredible Flautist* 1938.

Pitcairn Islands /ˈpɪtkeən/ British colony in Polynesia, 5,300 km/3,300 mi NE of New Zealand
area 27 sq km/10 sq mi
capital Adamstown
features in the group are the uninhabited Henderson Islands, an unspoiled coral atoll with a rare ecology, and tiny Ducie and Oeno, annexed by Britain in 1902
exports fruit and souvenirs to passing ships
population (1982) 54
language English
government the governor is the British high commissioner in New Zealand
history the islands were first settled by nine mutineers from the *Bounty* together with some Tahitians, their occupation remaining unknown until 1808.

pitch in chemistry, a black substance, hard when cold, but liquid when hot, used as a sealant on roofs. It is made by the destructive distillation of wood or coal tar.

pitch in music, the position of a note in the scale, dependent on the frequency of the predominant sound wave. In **standard pitch**, A above middle C has a frequency of 440 Hz. **Perfect pitch** is an ability to name or reproduce any note heard or asked for; it does not necessarily imply high musical ability.

pitchblende an ore consisting mainly of uranium oxide U_3O_8, but also containing a radioactive salt of radium $RaBr_2$. It was first separated by Marie and Pierre Curie in 1898.

pitcher plant insectivorous plant of the genus *Nepenthes*, the leaves of which are shaped like a pitcher and filled with a fluid that traps insects.

Pitman /ˈpɪtmən/ Isaac 1813–1897. English teacher and inventor of Pitman's shorthand. He studied Samuel Taylor's scheme for shorthand writing, and in 1837 published his own system, *Stenographic Soundhand*, fast and accurate, and adapted for use in many languages.

A simplified *Pitman Script*, combining letters and signs, was devised 1971 by Emily D Smith. His grandson **(Isaac) James Pitman** (1901–85) devised the 44-letter *Initial Teaching Alphabet* in the 1960s to help children to read.

Pitot tube an instrument that measures fluid (gas and liquid) flow. It is used to measure the speed of aircraft, and works by sensing pressure differences in different directions in the airstream. It was invented in the 1730s by the Frenchman Henri Pitot (1695–1771).

Pitt /pɪt/ William, the Elder, 1st Earl of Chatham 1708–1778. British Whig politician, 'the Great Commoner'. As paymaster of the forces 1746–55, he broke with tradition by refusing to enrich himself; he was dismissed for attacking Newcastle, the prime minister. He served effectively as prime minister in coalition governments 1756–61 (successfully conducting the Seven Years' War) and 1766–68.

Entering Parliament 1735, Pitt led the Patriot faction opposed to the Whig prime minister Walpole and attacked Walpole's successor, Carteret, for his conduct of the War of the Austrian Succession. Recalled by popular demand to form a government on the outbreak of the Seven Years' War 1756, he was forced to form a coalition with Newcastle 1757. A 'year of victories' ensued 1759, and the French were expelled from India and Canada. In 1761 Pitt wished to escalate the war by a declaration of war on Spain, George III disagreed and Pitt resigned, but was again recalled to form an all-party government 1766. He championed the Americans against the king, though rejecting independence, and collapsed during his last speech in the House of Lords—opposing the withdrawal of British troops—and died a month later.

Pitt *Politician and orator William Pitt the Elder, Lord Chatham, known as 'the Great Commoner'.*

Pitt /pɪt/ William, the Younger 1759–1806. British Tory prime minister 1783–1801 and 1804–06. He raised the importance of the House of Commons and clamped down on corruption, carried out fiscal reforms and union with Ireland. He attempted to keep Britain at peace but underestimated the importance of the French Revolution and became embroiled in wars with France from 1793; he died on hearing of Napoleon's victory at Austerlitz.

Son of William Pitt the Elder, he entered Cambridge University at 14 and Parliament at 22. He was the Whig Shelburne's chancellor of the Exchequer 1782–83, and with the support of the Tories and king's friends became Britain's youngest prime minister 1783. He reorganized the country's finances and negotiated reciprocal tariff reduction with France. In 1793, however, the new French republic declared war and England fared badly. His policy in Ireland led to the 1798 revolt, and he tried to solve the Irish question by the Act of Union 1800, but George III rejected the Catholic emancipation Pitt had promised as a condition, and Pitt resigned 1801.

On his return to office 1804, he organized an alliance with Austria, Russia, and Sweden against Napoleon, which was shattered at Austerlitz. In declining health, he died on hearing the news, saying: 'Oh, my country! How I leave my country!' He was buried in Westminster Abbey.

pitta songless bird of the genus *Pitta*. Some 20 species are native to SE Asia, W Africa, and Australia. They have round bodies, big heads, and are often brightly coloured. They live on the ground and in low undergrowth, and can run from danger.

pittance in medieval monasteries, a small dish of food, distributed by a monk called the pittancer,

Pitt *William Pitt the Younger entered Parliament at the age of 22 and two years later became England's youngest prime minister.*

either to sick monks or to celebrate a feast day.

Pitt-Rivers /ˈpɪt ˈrɪvəz/ Augustus Henry 1827–1900. English general and archaeologist. He made a series of model archaeological excavations on his estate in Wiltshire, England, being among the first to recognize the value of everyday objects as well as art treasures. The *Pitt-Rivers Museum*, Oxford, contains some of his collection.

Pittsburgh /ˈpɪtsbɜːɡ/ industrial city (machinery and chemicals) and inland port, where the Allegheny and Monongahela join to form the Ohio River in Pennsylvania, USA; population (1980) 423,940; metropolitan area 2,264,000. Established by the French as Fort Duquesne 1750, the site was taken by the British 1758 and renamed Fort Pitt.

pituitary gland the most important of the ◊endocrine glands of vertebrates, situated in the centre of the brain. The anterior lobe secretes hormones, some of which control the activities of other glands (thyroid, gonads, and adrenal cortex); others are direct-acting hormones affecting milk secretion, and controlling growth. Secretions of the posterior lobe control body water balance, and contraction of the uterus. The posterior lobe is regulated by the ◊hypothalamus, and thus forms a link between the nervous and hormonal systems.

Piura capital of the department of the same name in the arid NW of Peru, situated on the Piura river, 160 km/100 mi SW of Punta Pariñas; population (1981) 186,000. It is the most westerly point in South America, and was founded 1532 by the conquistadors left behind by Pizarro. Cotton is grown in the surrounding area.

Pius /ˈpaɪəs/ twelve popes, including:

Pius IV 1499–1565. Pope from 1559, of the Medici family. He reassembled the Council of Trent (see Counter-Reformation under ◊Reformation) and completed its work 1563.

Pius V 1504–1572. Pope from 1566, who excommunicated Elizabeth I of England, and organized the expedition against the Turks that won the victory of ◊Lepanto.

Pius VI (Giovanni Angelo Braschi) 1717–1799. Pope from 1775. He strongly opposed the French Revolution, and died a prisoner in French hands.

Pius VII 1742–1823. Pope from 1800. He concluded a ◊concordat with France 1801 and took part in Napoleon's coronation, but relations became strained. Napoleon annexed the papal states, and Pius was imprisoned 1809–14. After his return to Rome 1814 he revived the Jesuit order.

Pius IX 1792–1878. Pope from 1846. He never accepted the incorporation of the Papal States and of Rome in the kingdom of Italy, and proclaimed the dogmas of the Immaculate Conception of the Virgin 1854 and papal infallibility 1870; his pontificate was the longest in history.

Pius X (Giuseppe Melchiore Sarto) 1835–1914. Pope from 1903, canonized 1954, who condemned Modernism (see under ◊Christianity) in a manifesto 1907.

Pius XI (Achille Ratti) 1857–1939. Pope from 1922, he signed the ◊concordat with Mussolini 1929.

Pius XII (Eugenio Pacelli) 1876–1958. Pope from 1939. He proclaimed the dogma of the bodily assumption of the Virgin Mary 1950 and in 1951 restated the doctrine (strongly criticized by many) that the life of an infant must not be sacrificed to save a mother in labour. He was also widely criticized for failing to speak out against atrocities committed by the Germans during World War II.

pixel (contraction of 'picture element') a single dot on a computer screen. All screen images are made up of a collection of pixels, with each pixel being either off (dark) or on (illuminated, possibly in colour). The number of pixels available determines the screen's resolution. Typical resolutions of microcomputer screens vary from 320 × 200 pixels to 640 × 480 pixels, but screens with over 1,000 × 1,000 pixels are now quite common for graphic (pictorial) displays.

Pizarro /pɪˈzɑːrəʊ/ Francisco c. 1475–1541. Spanish conquistador who took part in the expeditions of

Place A tailor by trade, Francis Place was responsible for repealing the Combination Acts which had made trade unionism illegal.

Balboa and others. In 1526–27 he explored the NW coast of South America, and conquered Peru 1531 with 180 followers. The Inca king Atahualpa was seized and murdered. In 1535 Pizarro founded Lima. Internal feuding led to Pizarro's assassination.

His half-brother *Gonzalo Pizarro* (c. 1505–48) explored the region east of Quito 1541–42. He made himself governor of Peru 1544, but was defeated and executed.

pizzicato (Italian 'pinched') in music, an instruction to pluck a bowed stringed instrument (such as the violin) with the fingers.

Plaatje /ˈplɑːtʃi/ Solomon 1876–1932. Pioneer South African writer and nationalist who was the first secretary-general and founder of the ◊African National Congress 1912.

Place /pleɪs/ Francis 1771–1854. English Radical. He showed great powers as a political organizer, and made Westminster a centre of Radicalism. He secured the repeal of the anti-union Combination Acts 1824.

placebo (Latin 'I will please') a harmless substance, often called a 'sugar pill', that has no chemotherapeutic value and yet produces physiological changes.

placenta

network of blood vessels in placenta

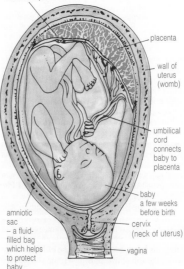

placenta

wall of uterus (womb)

umbilical cord connects baby to placenta

baby a few weeks before birth

amniotic sac – a fluid-filled bag which helps to protect baby

cervix (neck of uterus)

vagina

Its use in medicine is limited to drugs trials, where it is given alongside the substance being tested, to compare effects. The 'placebo effect', first named in 1945, demonstrates the control 'mind' exerts over 'matter', including causing changes in blood pressure, analgesia, and rates of healing.

placenta the organ composed of maternal and embryonic tissue which attaches the developing ◊embryo or ◊fetus of placental mammals to the ◊uterus. Oxygen, nutrients, and waste products are exchanged between maternal and fetal blood over the placental membrane, but the two blood systems are not in direct contact. The placenta also produces hormones which regulate the progress of pregnancy. It is shed as part of the afterbirth.

The tissue in plants that joins the ovary to the ovules is also called a placenta.

placer deposit a detrital concentration of an economically important mineral, especially gold, but also other minerals such as cassiterite, chromite, and platinum metals. The mineral grains become concentrated during transport by water or wind because they are more dense than other detrital minerals such as quartz, and (like quartz) they are relatively resistant to chemical breakdown. Examples are the Witwatersrand gold deposits of South Africa, which are gold- and uranium-bearing conglomerates laid down by ancient rivers, and the placer tin deposits of the Malay Peninsula.

plague disease transmitted by fleas (carried by the black ◊rat) which infect the sufferer with the bacillus *Pasturella pestis*. An early symptom is swelling of lymph nodes, usually in the armpit and groin; such swellings are called 'buboes', hence 'bubonic' plague. It causes virulent blood poisoning and the death rate is high.

Plague epidemics include the ◊Black Death and the Great Plague of London 1665. Other and more virulent forms of plague are septicaemic and pneumonic; the latter was fatal before the introduction of sulpha drugs and antibiotics.

plaice fish *Pleuronectes platessa* belonging to the flat-fish group, abundant in the N Atlantic. It is white beneath and brownish with orange spots on the 'eyed' side. It can grow to 75 cm/2.5 ft long, and weighs about 2 kg/4.5 lbs.

Plaid Cymru /ˈplaɪd ˈkʌmri/ (Welsh 'Party of Wales') Welsh nationalist political party established 1925, dedicated to an independent Wales. In 1966 the first Plaid Cymru Member of Parliament was elected.

plain or *grassland* land, usually flat, upon which grass predominates. The plains cover large areas of the Earth's surface, especially between the deserts

Planck One of the founders of 20th-century physics and formulator of the quantum theory, Max Planck was professor of theoretical physics at Berlin University.

plain

Animals of the plains depend on grasses and occasional trees for sustenance. Plant-eaters graze (feed on growing grass), browse (eat leaves, twigs and sparse vegetation), or forage (rummage for bulbs, roots and fruits). They are preyed upon by the meat-eaters.

African plain (savannah) wildlife and plants. 1. Baboon 2. Acacia tree 3. Eland 4. Low-growing shrubs 5. Giraffe 6. Elephant 7. Steenbok 8. Topi 9. Warthog 10. Weaver bird nests 11. Termite mound 12. Baobab tree 13. Lions 14. Rhinoceros

Russian plain (steppe) wildlife and plants. 1. Shrubs and small trees 2. Grass snake 3. Lemmings 4. Field voles 5. Saiga antelope 6. Suslik 7. Marbled polecat 8. Black-bellied hamster

In temperate grasslands, where winter temperatures can fall far below freezing and summer temperatures rise to 40°C/104°F, many of the animals survive by living underground in burrows. In tropical grasslands, the climate is less extreme. Here a great variety of plants grow, and provide food for many more types of animals. The African grasslands support the world's largest wildlife populations.

of the tropics and the rainforests of the equator, and have rain in one season only. In such regions the climate belts move north and south during the year, bringing rainforest conditions at one time and desert conditions at another. Examples include the

plane

North European Plain, the High Plains of the USA and Canada, and the Russian Plain also known as the ◊steppe.

Plains Indian any of the North American Indians of the High Plains, which run over 3,000 km/2,000 mi from Alberta to Texas. The various groups are Blackfoot, Cheyenne, Comanche, Pawnee, and the Dakota or Sioux.

plainsong ancient chant of the Christian church first codified by Ambrose, bishop of Milan, and then by Pope Gregory in the 6th century. See ◊Gregorian chant.

Planck /plæŋk/ Max 1858–1947. German physicist who framed the quantum theory 1900.

He was appointed to the chair of physics at Kiel 1885 and Berlin 1889. Much of his early work was in thermodynamics. From 1930 to 1937, he was president of the Kaiser Wilhelm Institute. He was awarded the Nobel Prize for Physics 1918, and became a Fellow of the Royal Society in 1926.

Planck's constant in physics, a fundamental constant (symbol h) that is the energy of one quantum of electromagnetic radiation (the smallest possible 'packet' of energy; see ◊quantum theory) divided by the frequency of the radiation. Its value is 6.626196×10^{-34} joule seconds.

plane tree of the genus *Platanus*. Species include the oriental plane *Platanus orientalis*, a favourite plantation tree of the Greeks and Romans; the hybrid London plane *P. x hispanica*, with palmate, usually five-lobed leaves; and the American plane or buttonwood *P. occidentalis*. All species have pendulous burrlike fruits and are capable of growing to 30 m/100 ft high.

planet a large body in orbit around a star, made of rock, metal, or gas. There are nine planets in the ◊solar system.

The inner four, called the *terrestrial planets*, are small and rocky, and include our planet Earth. The outer planets, with the exception of Pluto, are large balls of liquid and gas; the largest is Jupiter, which contains more than twice as much mass as all the other planets combined. Planets do not produce light, but reflect the light of their parent star.

planetarium optical projection device by means of which the motions of stars and planets are reproduced on a domed ceiling representing the sky.

planetary nebula a shell of gas thrown off by a star at the end of its life. Planetary nebulae have nothing to do with planets. They were named by William Herschel, who thought their rounded shape resembled the disc of a planet. After a star such as the Sun has expanded to become a ◊red giant, its outer layers are ejected into space to form a planetary nebula, leaving the core as a ◊white dwarf at the centre.

planimeter simple integrating instrument for measuring the area of a plane surface. It consists of two hinged arms: one is kept fixed and the other is traced round the boundary of the area. This actuates a small graduated wheel; the area is calculated from the wheel's change in position.

plankton small, often microscopic, forms of plant and animal life that drift in fresh or salt water, and are a source of food for larger animals.

plant an organism that carries out ◊photosynthesis, has cellulose cell walls and complex ◊eukaryotic cells and is immobile. A few parasitic plants have lost the ability to photosynthesize, but are still considered to be plants. See under ◊plant classification.

Plants are autotrophs, that is, they make carbohydrates from water and carbon dioxide, and are the primary producers in all food chains, so that all

planets

Planet	Main constituents	Atmosphere	Average distance from Sun in millions of km	Time for one orbit in Earth-years	Diameter in thousands of km	Average density if density of water is 1 unit
Mercury	rocky, ferrous	–	5.8	0.24	4.9	5.4
Venus	rocky, ferrous	carbon dioxide	108	0.61	12.1	5.2
Earth	rocky, ferrous	nitrogen, oxygen	150	1.00	12.8	5.5
Mars	rocky	carbon dioxide	228	1.88	6.8	3.9
Jupiter	liquid hydrogen, helium	–	778	11.86	142.8	1.3
Saturn	hydrogen, helium	–	1,427	29.50	120.0	0.7
Uranus	icy, hydrogen, helium	hydrogen, helium	2,875	84.00	51.1	1.2
Neptune	icy, hydrogen, helium	hydrogen, helium	4,496	164.80	49.5	1.7
Pluto	icy, rocky	methane	5,900	248.40	4.0	about 1

plant

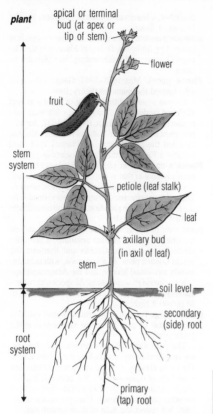

apical or terminal bud (at apex or tip of stem)

flower

fruit

stem system

petiole (leaf stalk)

leaf

axillary bud (in axil of leaf)

stem

soil level

secondary (side) root

root system

primary (tap) root

animal life is dependent on them. They play a vital part in the carbon cycle, removing carbon dioxide from the atmosphere and generating oxygen. The study of plants is known as botany.

Many of the lower plants (the algae and bryophytes) consist of a simple body, or thallus, upon which the organs of reproduction are borne. Simplest of all are the threadlike algae, for example *Spirogyra*, which consist of a chain of cells. The seaweeds (algae) and mosses and liverworts (bryophytes) represent a further development, with simple, multicellular bodies that have specially modified areas in which the reproductive organs are carried. Higher in the morphological scale are the ferns, club mosses, and horsetails (pteridophytes). Ferns produce leaflike fronds bearing sporangia on their undersurface in which the spores are carried. The spores are freed and germinate to produce small independent bodies carrying the sexual organs; thus the fern, like other pteridophytes and some seaweeds, has two quite separate generations in its life cycle; see ◊alternation of generations.

The spermatophytes have special supportive water-conducting tissues, which identify them as vascular plants. This group includes all seed plants, that is the gymnosperms (conifers, yews, cycads, and ginkgo) and the angiosperms (flowering plants).

The seed plants are the largest group, and structurally the most complex. They are usually divided into three parts, root, stem, and leaves. Stems grow above or below ground. Their cellular structure is designed to carry water and salts from the roots to the leaves in the ◊xylem, and sugars from the leaves to the roots in the ◊phloem. The leaves manufacture the food of the plant by means of photosynthesis, which occurs in the ◊chloroplasts they contain. Flowers and cones are modified leaves arranged in groups and enclosing the reproductive organs from which the fruits and seeds result.

Plantagenet English royal house, reigning 1154–1399, whose name comes from the nickname of Geoffrey, Count of Anjou (1113–51), father of Henry II, who often wore a sprig of broom, *planta genista*, in his hat. In the 1450s,

Richard, duke of York, revived it as a surname to emphasize his superior claim to the throne over Henry VI.

plantain plants of the genus *Plantago*. The great plantain *Plantago major* has oval leaves, grooved stalks and spikes of green flowers with purple anthers followed by seeds, which are used in bird food. Some species are troublesome lawn weeds. Various types of ◊banana are also known as plantains.

plant classification the taxonomy or ◊classification of plants. Originally the plant ◊kingdom included bacteria, diatoms, dinoflagellates, fungi, and slime moulds, but, these are not now thought of as plants. The groups that are always classified as plants are the bryophytes (mosses and liverworts), pteridophytes

(ferns, horsetails, and clubmosses), gymnosperms (conifers, yews, cycads, and ginkgos), and angiosperms (flowering plants). The angiosperms are split into monocotyledons (for example, orchids, grasses, lilies) and dicotyledons (for example, oak, buttercup, geranium, and daisy).

The basis of plant classification was established by ◊Linnaeus. Among the angiosperms, it is largely based on the number and arrangement of the flower parts.

The unicellular algae, such as *Chlamydomonas*, are often now put with the protists instead of the plants, and some classification schemes even classify the multicellular algae (seaweeds and freshwater weeds) in a new kingdom, the Protoctista, along with the protists.

plant classification

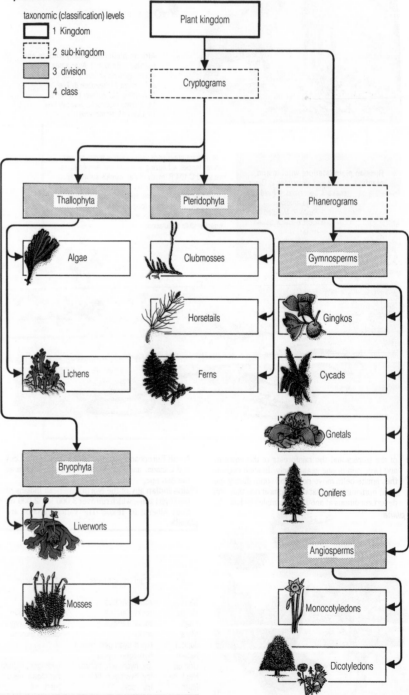

taxonomic (classification) levels
1 Kingdom
2 sub-kingdom
3 division
4 class

Plant kingdom

Cryptograms

Thallophyta

Pteridophyta

Phanerograms

Algae

Clubmosses

Gymnosperms

Horsetails

Gingkos

Lichens

Ferns

Cycads

Gnetals

Bryophyta

Conifers

Liverworts

Angiosperms

Mosses

Monocotyledons

Dicotyledons

plant hormone a substance produced by a plant that has a marked effect on its growth, flowering, leaf-fall, fruit-ripening, or some other process. Examples include *auxin*, *gibberellin*, *ethylene*, and *cytokin*.

Unlike animal hormones, these substances are not produced by a particular area of the plant body and they may be less specific in their effects. It has therefore been suggested that they should not be described as hormones at all.

plasma in biology, the liquid part of the blood.

plasma in physics, an ionized gas produced at extremely high temperatures, as in the Sun and other stars, and which contains positive and negative charges in approximately equal numbers. It is affected by a magnetic field, and is a good electrical conductor.

plasmapheresis the removal from the body of large quantities of whole blood and its fractionization by centrifugal force in a continuous flow cell separator. Once separated, the elements of the blood are isolated and available for specific treatment. Restored blood is then returned to the venous system of the patient.

plasmid a small, mobile piece of ◊DNA found in ◊bacteria and used in ◊genetic engineering.

Plassey, Battle of /'plæsi/ a victory in India 1757 for the British under Clive over Suraj-ud-Dowlah, nawab of Bengal, near a village in W Bengal, on the Bhagirathi River, 50 km/31 mi NNW of Krishnagar. By 1801 the site of the battle had been eaten away by the river.

plaster of Paris a form of calcium sulphate, mixed with water for making casts and moulds.

plastic any of the stable synthetic materials that are fluid at some stage in their manufacture, when they can be shaped, and that later set to rigid or semi-rigid solids. Plastics today are chiefly derived from petroleum. Most are polymers, made up of long chains of identical molecules.

Processed by extrusion, injection-moulding, vacuum-forming and compression, they emerge in consistencies ranging from hard and inflexible to soft and rubbery. They replace an increasing number of natural substances, being lightweight, easy to clean, durable, and capable of being rendered very strong, for example by the addition of carbon fibres, for building aircraft and other engineering projects.

Thermoplastics soften when warmed, then re-harden as they cool. Examples of thermoplastics include polystyrene, a clear plastic used in kitchen utensils or (when expanded into a 'foam' by gas injection) in insulation and ceiling tiles; polyethylene or polythene, used for containers and wrapping; and polyvinyl chloride (PVC), used for drainpipes, floor tiles, audio discs, shoes, and handbags.

Thermosets remain rigid once set, and do not soften when warmed. They include bakelite, used in electrical insulation and telephone receivers; epoxy resins, used in paints and varnishes, to laminate wood, and as adhesives; polyesters, used in synthetic textile fibres and, with glass fibre reinforcement, in car bodies and boat hulls; and polyurethane, prepared in liquid form as a paint or varnish, and in foam form for upholstery and in lining materials (where it may be a fire hazard). One group of plastics, the silicones, are chemically inert, have good electrical properties, and repel water. Silicones find use in silicone rubber, paints, electrical insulation materials, laminates, waterproofing for walls, and stain-resistant textiles.

Biodegradable plastics are being developed; other plastics cannot be broken down by microorganisms, so cannot easily be disposed of. Incineration leads to the release of toxic fumes, unless carried out at very high temperatures.

Plasticine trade name for an oil-based plastic material used in modelling. It was invented 1897 for children but is also used by architects and engineers; the earliest space suits were modelled in Plasticine.

Plasticine is also used as a landing point in jumping events (human and equestrian), because it marks clearly and is easily smoothed; as a means of

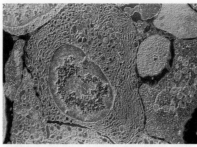

plasma False-colour electron microscope view of a human plasmocyte (plasma cell). Plasmocytes are mature lymphocytes or white blood cells which synthesize and secrete the antibodies of the immune system.

deadening the noise of explosives in demolition practice; and, in combination with lead, as ballast in small boats.

plastic surgery branch of surgery concerned with the repair of congenital disfigurement and the reconstruction of tissues damaged by disease or injury. The aim is to achieve good functional and cosmetic results. Relatively little plastic surgery is undertaken purely for cosmetic reasons.

plastid a general name for a cell ◊organelle of plants that is enclosed by a double membrane and contains a series of internal membranes and vesicles. Plastids contain DNA and are produced by division of existing plastids. They can be classified into two main groups, the *chromoplasts*, which contain pigments such as ◊carotenes and ◊chlorophyll, and the *leucoplasts*, which are colourless; however, the distinction between the two is not always clear-cut.

◊Chloroplasts are the major type of chromoplast. They contain chlorophyll, are responsible for the green coloration of most plants, and perform ◊photosynthesis. Other chromoplasts give the flower petals or the fruits their distinctive colour. Leucoplasts are important food-storage bodies and include amyloplasts, found in the roots of many plants, which store large amounts of starch.

Plataea, Battle of battle 479 BC, in which the Greeks defeated the Persians during the ◊Persian Wars.

plateau an elevated area of fairly flat land, or a mountainous region in which the peaks are at the same height. An *intermontane plateau* is one surrounded by mountains. A *piedmont plateau* is one that lies between the mountains and low-lying land. A *continental plateau* rises abruptly from low-lying lands or the sea.

platelet a tiny 'cell' found in the blood, which helps it to clot. Platelets are not true cells, but membrane-bound cell fragments which bud off from large cells in the bone marrow.

Plate, River /pleɪt/ English name of Río de ◊la Plata, estuary in South America.

plate tectonics concept that attributes ◊continental drift and ◊seafloor spreading to the continual formation and destruction of the outermost layer of the Earth. This layer is seen as consisting of major and minor plates, curved to the planet's spherical shape and with a jigsaw fit to one another. Convection currents within the Earth's mantle produce upwellings of new material along joint lines at the surface, forming ridges (for example the ◊mid-Atlantic ridge). The new material extends the plates, and these move away from the ridges. Where two plates collide, one overrides the other and the lower is absorbed back into the mantle. These 'subduction zones' occur in the ocean trenches.

The moving plates consist of the Earth's ◊crust and the topmost solid layer of mantle, together called the ◊lithosphere. The plates move on a mobile layer of the mantle called the ◊asthenosphere. Some plates carry only ocean crust, others also carry continental crust. Only ocean crust is formed at mid-ocean ridges. The continents take little part in the generation and destruction of the

plate material and are carried along passively on the moving plates.

The concept of continental drift was first put forward in 1915 by the German geophysicist Alfred Wegener; plate tectonics was formulated in the mid-1960s and has gained widespread acceptance among earth scientists.

Plath /plæθ/ Sylvia 1932–1963. US poet and novelist. Plath's powerful, highly personal poems, often expressing a sense of desolation, are distinguished by their intensity and sharp imagery. Collections include *The Colossus* 1960, *Ariel* 1965, published after her death, and *Collected Poems* 1982. Her autobiographical novel, *The Bell Jar* 1961, deals with the events surrounding a young woman's emotional breakdown.

Born in Boston, Massachusetts, she attended Smith College and was awarded a Fulbright scholarship to study at Cambridge University, England, where she met the poet Ted Hughes, whom she married 1956; they separated in 1962. She committed suicide while living in London.

platinum a metallic element, symbol Pt, atomic number 78, relative atomic mass 195.09. It is greyish-white, untarnishable in air, and very resistant to heat and strong acids. Both pure and as an alloy, it is used extensively in jewellery, dentistry, and the chemical industry (in finely divided form, platinum acts as a catalyst). In combination with organic compounds, platinum has been found effective in treating various types of cancer, including those of the testis and ovary. In industry, it is employed for switch contacts because of its durability, in car exhaust systems, where it helps the conversion of car fumes to nontoxic gases, and is valuable in scientific apparatus because platinum wires can be sealed gas-tight.

Platinum occurs as the metal; alloyed with iridium, osmium and other similar metals; and with gold and iron, especially in the Urals (USSR), and in S Africa, Canada, and the USA.

Plato /'pleɪtəʊ/ *c.* 428–347 BC. Greek philosopher, pupil of Socrates, teacher of Aristotle, and founder of the Academy. He was the author of philosophical dialogues on such topics as metaphysics, ethics, and politics. Central to his teachings is the notion of Forms, which are located outside the everyday world, timeless, motionless, and absolutely real.

His philosophy has influenced Christianity and European culture, directly and through Augustine, the Florentine Platonists during the Renaissance, and countless others. Born of a noble family, he entered politics on the aristocratic side, and in philosophy became a follower of Socrates. He travelled widely after Socrates's death, and founded the educational establishment, the Academy, in order to train a new ruling class.

Of his work, some 30 dialogues survive, intended for performance either to his pupils or to the public. The principal figure in these ethical and philosophical debates is Socrates and the early ones employ the Socratic method, in which he asks questions and traps the students into contradicting themselves, for example, *Iron*, on poetry. Other dialogues include the *Symposium*, on love, *Phaedo*, on immortality, and *Apology and Crito*, on Socrates' trial and death. It is impossible to say whether Plato's Socrates is a faithful representation of the real man or an articulation of Plato's own thought. Plato's philosophy rejects scientific rationalism (establishing facts through experiment) in favour of arguments, because mind, not matter, is fundamental, and material objects are merely imperfect copies of abstract and eternal 'ideas'. His political philosophy is expounded in two treatises, *The Republic* and *The Laws*, both of which describe ideal states (see also under ◊Utopia). Platonic love is inspired by a person's best qualities and seeks their development.

platypus monotreme mammal *Ornithorhynchus anatinus*, found in Tasmania and E Australia. Semi-aquatic, it has naked jaws resembling a duck's beak, small eyes, and no external ears. It lives in long burrows along river banks, where it lays two eggs in a rough nest. It feeds on water worms and insects, and when full-grown is 60 cm/2 ft long.

Plautus /ˈplɔːtəs/ *c.*254–184 BC. Roman dramatist, born in Umbria, who settled in Rome and worked in a bakery before achieving success as a dramatist. He wrote at least 56 comedies, freely adapted from Greek originals, of which 20 survive. Shakespeare based *The Comedy of Errors* on his *Menaechmi*.

Player /ˈpleɪə/ Gary 1935– . South African golfer, who won major championships in three decades and the first British Open 1959. A match-play specialist, he won the world title five times.

His total of nine 'majors' is the fourth (equal) best of all time. He is noted for wearing all-black outfits. In the 1980s he was a successful Seniors player.

CAREER HIGHLIGHTS

British Open: 1959, 1968, 1974
US Open: 1965
US Masters: 1961, 1974, 1978
US PGA: 1962, 1972
World Match-play: 1965–66, 1968, 1971, 1973

Playfair /ˈpleɪfeə/ William Henry 1790–1857. Scottish Neo-Classical architect responsible for much of the design of Edinburgh New Town in the early 19th century. His Royal Scottish Academy 1822 and National Gallery of Scotland 1850 in Greek style helped to make Edinburgh the 'Athens of the North'.

plate tectonics

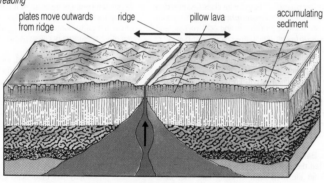

sea floor spreading

plates move outwards from ridge — ridge — pillow lava — accumulating sediment

rising magma

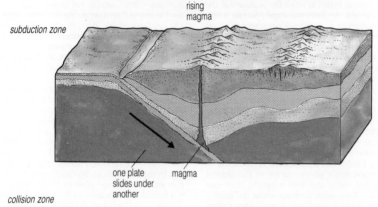

subduction zone

one plate slides under another — magma

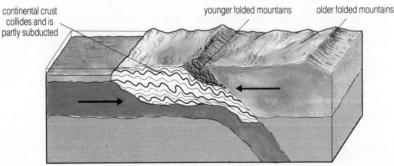

collision zone

continental crust collides and is partly subducted — younger folded mountains — older folded mountains

playgroup in the UK, a voluntary, usually part-time pre-school group, run by parents or sometimes by charitable organizations, to provide nursery education for children from three to five.

Playgroups were started in the 1960s in response to a national shortage of places in maintained nursery education. By the 1980s, they were catering for 450,000 children annually, with training and advice services organized nationally by the Pre-School Playgroups Association.

playing cards a set of small pieces of card with different markings, used in playing games. A standard set consists of 52 cards divided into four suits: hearts, clubs, diamonds, and spades. Within each suit there are 13 cards: numbered two to ten, three picture (or court) cards (jack, queen, and king) and the ace.

Playing cards probably originated in China or India, and first appeared in Europe in 14th-century Italy as the 78 cards (22 emblematic, including 'the hanged man', and 56 numerals) of the ◊tarot cards, used both for gaming and in fortune-telling. However, in the 15th century they were reduced to the standard pack of 52 for most games, which include bridge, whist, poker, rummy, and cribbage.

plc abbreviation for ◊*public limited company*.

pleadings in English law, documents exchanged between the parties to court actions, which set out the facts that form the basis of the case they intend to present in court, and (where relevant)

platypus

stating what damages or other remedy they are claiming.

Pleasance /ˈplezəns/ Donald 1919– . English actor. He has been acclaimed for roles in Pirandello's *The Rules of the Game*, in Pinter's *The Caretaker*, and also in the title role of the film *Dr Crippen* 1962, conveying the sinister aspect of the outcast from society. Other films include *THX 1138* 1971 and *The Eagle has Landed* 1976.

plebeian a member of the unprivileged class in ancient Rome, composed of aliens, freed slaves, and their descendants. During the 5th–4th centuries BC plebeians waged a long struggle to win political and social equality with the patricians, eventually securing admission to the offices formerly reserved for patricians.

plebiscite ◊referendum or direct vote by all the electors of a country or district on a specific question. Since the 18th century it has been employed on many occasions to decide to what country a particular area should belong, for example, in Upper Silesia and elsewhere after World War I, and in the Saar 1935.

Pléiade, La /pleɪˈɑːd/ group of seven poets in 16th-century France led by Pierre Ronsard, who were inspired by Classical models to improve French verse. They were so called from the seven stars of the Pleiades group.

Pleiades /ˈplaɪədiːz/ in astronomy, a star cluster about 400 light years away in the constellation Taurus, representing the Seven Sisters of Greek mythology. Its brightest stars (highly luminous, very young blue-white giants only a few million years old) are visible to the naked eye, but there are many fainter ones.

The stars of Pleiades are still surrounded by traces of the reflection ◊nebula from which they formed, visible on long-exposure photographs.

Pleiades /ˈplaɪədiːz/ in Greek mythology, seven daughters of ◊Atlas, who asked to be changed to a cluster of stars to escape the pursuit of ◊Orion.

pleiotropy a process whereby a given gene influences several different observed characteristics of an organism.

Pleasance The mild demeanour of Donald Pleasance reveals little of his sinister acting career. Dr Crippen and Count Dracula are but two of the evil characters he has portrayed.

Pleistocene first epoch of the Quaternary period of geological time, beginning 1.8 million years ago and ending 10,000 years ago. Glaciers were abundant during the ◊Ice Age, and humans evolved into modern *Homo sapiens* appeared about 100,000 years ago.

Plekhanov Georgi Valentinovich 1857–1918. Russian Marxist revolutionary and theorist, founder of the Menshevik party. He led the first ◊populist demonstration in St Petersburg, and left for exile 1880. He became a Marxist and, with Lenin, edited the newspaper *Iskra* ('spark'). In 1903 his opposition to Lenin led to the Bolshevik-Menshevik split. In 1917 he returned to Russia.

Plenty, Bay of /'plenti/ broad inlet on the NE coast of North Island, New Zealand, with the port of Tauranga. One of the first canoes bringing Maori immigrants landed here about 1350.

Plesetsk /plɪ'setsk/ a rocket-launching site, 170 km/105 mi south of Archangel, USSR. From here the USSR has launched unpiloted satellites since 1966.

Plethon /'pleθɒn/ George Gemisthos 1353–1452. Byzantine philosopher, who taught for many years at Mistra in Asia Minor. A Platonist, he maintained a resolutely anti-Christian stance, and was the inspiration for many of the ideas of the 15th-century Florentine Platonic Academy.

pleurisy inflammation of the pleura, the secreting membrane which covers the lungs, and lines the space in which they rest. Nearly always due to bacterial or viral infection, it renders breathing painful.

The two surfaces move easily on one another, being lubricated by small quantities of fluid. When it is inflamed the surfaces may dry up or stick together, making breathing difficult and painful. A large volume of fluid may collect in the pleural cavity, the space between the two surfaces. Pus in the pleural cavity is called empyema. Pleurisy occurs in pneumonia and tuberculosis, but may also be a consequence of scarlet fever or rheumatism.

Pleven /'plevən/ industrial town (textiles, machinery, ceramics) in N Bulgaria; population (1987) 134,000. In the Russo-Turkish War 1877, Pleven surrendered to the Russians after a siege of five months.

Plimsoll /'plɪmsəl/ Samuel 1824–1898. English social reformer, born in Bristol. He sat in Parliament as a Radical 1868–80, and through his efforts the Merchant Shipping Act was passed in 1876, providing for Board of Trade inspection of ships, and the compulsory painting of a *Plimsoll line*.

Plimsoll line a loading marking painted on the hull of ships, first suggested by Samuel Plimsoll. It shows the safe levels to which the hull can sink in waters at various times.

Plimsoll line

TF	Tropical fresh water
F	Fresh water
T	Tropical salt water
S	Salt water in Summer
W	Salt water in Winter
WNA	Winter in North Atlantic
LR	Lloyd's Register

Pliny the Elder /'plɪni/ (Gaius Plinius Secundus) *c.* AD 23–79. Roman scientist and historian; only his works on astronomy, geography, and natural history survive. He was killed in an eruption of Vesuvius.

Pliny the Younger /'plɪni/ (Gaius Plinius Caecilius Secundus) *c.* 61–113. Roman administrator, nephew of Pliny the Elder, whose correspondence is of great interest. Among his surviving letters are those describing the eruption of Vesuvius, his uncle's death, and his correspondence with the emperor ◊Trajan.

Pliocene ('almost recent') fifth and last epoch of the Tertiary period of geological time, 5–1.8 million years ago. Human-like apes ('australopithecines') evolved in Africa.

Plisetskaya /plɪ'setskiə/ Maya 1925– . Soviet ballerina and actress. She attended the Moscow Bolshoi Ballet School and succeeded Ulanova as prima ballerina of the Bolshoi Ballet.

PLO abbreviation for ◊*Palestine Liberation Organization*

Ploeşti /plɔɪ'eʃt/ industrial city (textiles, paper, petrochemicals; oil centre) in SE Romania; population (1985) 234,000.

Plomer /'pluːmə/ William 1903–1973. South African novelist, author of *Turbot Wolfe*, an early criticism of South African attitudes to race. He settled in London in 1929, and wrote two autobiographical volumes.

plotter an ◊output device that draws pictures or diagrams under computer control. They are often used for producing business charts, architectural plans and enginering drawings. *Flatbed plotters* move a pen up and down across a flat drawing surface, while *roller plotters* roll the drawing paper past the pen as it moves from side to side.

Plough, the in astronomy, a popular name for the most prominent part of the constellation ◊Ursa Major.

plough the most important agricultural implement, used for tilling the soil. The plough dates from about 3500 BC, when oxen were used to pull a simple wooden blade, or ard. In about 500 BC the iron share came into use.

By about AD 1000 horses as well as oxen were being used to pull wheeled ploughs, equipped with a plowshare for cutting a furrow, a blade for forming the walls of the furrow (called a coulter), and a mouldboard to turn a furrow. Steam ploughs came into use in some areas in the 1860s, superseded half a century later by tractor-drawn ploughs. The present plough consists of many 'bottoms', each comprising a curved ploughshare and angled mouldboard. The bottom is designed so that it slices into the ground and turns the soil over.

Plovdiv /'plɒvdɪv/ industrial city (textiles, chemicals, leather, tobacco) in Bulgaria, on the Maritsa; population (1987) 357,000. Conquered by Philip of Macedon in the 4th century BC, it was known as Philippopolis (Philip's city).

plover wading bird of the family Charadriidae, found worldwide. They are usually black or brown above, and white below. They have short bills.

plough Camel pulling a plough on Lanzarote, one of the Canary Islands.

The European *golden plover* Pluviatilis *apricaria*, of heathland and sea coast, is about 28 cm/11 in long. The *ringed plover* Charadrius *hiaticula*, with a black and white face, and black band on the throat, is found on British shores, but largest of the ringed plovers is the killdeer *Charadrius vociferus*, so called because of its cry.

plum tree *Prunus domestica*, bearing an edible fruit. There are many varieties, including the Victoria, Czar, egg-plum, greengage, and damson; the sloe *Prunus spinosa* is closely related. The dried plum is known as a prune.

plumbago an alternative name for the mineral ◊graphite.

plumule the part of a seed embryo which develops into the shoot, bearing the first true leaves of the plant.

plur. in grammar, the abbreviation for *plural*.

pluralism in political science, the view that decision-making in contemporary liberal democracies is the outcome of competition among several interest groups in a political system characterized by free elections, representative institutions, and open access to the organs of power. This concept is opposed by corporatist and other approaches that perceive power to be centralized in the state and its principal elites.

pluralism in philosophy, the belief that reality consists of several different elements, not just two—matter and mind—as in ◊dualism.

plus ça change, plus c'est la même chose (French) the more things change, the more they stay the same.

Plutarch /'pluːtɑːk/ *c.* 46–120 BC. Greek biographer, born at Chaeronea. He lectured on philosophy at Rome, and was appointed procurator of Greece by Hadrian. His *Parallel Lives* comprise biographies of pairs of Greek and Roman soldiers and politicians, followed by comparisons between the two. Thomas North's 1579 translation inspired Shakespeare's Roman plays.

Pluto /'pluːtəʊ/ in astronomy, the smallest and outermost planet, located by Clyde ◊Tombaugh 1930. It orbits the Sun every 248.5 years at an average distance of 5,360,000,000 km/3,600,000,000 mi. Its elliptical orbit occasionally takes it within the orbit of Neptune, such as 1979–99. Pluto has a diameter of about 3,000 km/2,000 mi, and a mass about 0.005 that of Earth. It is of low density, composed of rock and ice, with frozen methane on its surface. Charon, Pluto's moon, was discovered 1978.

Charon is about 1,000 km/600 mi in diameter and orbits the planet at a height of about 20,000 km/12,500 mi every 6.39 days—the same time that Pluto takes to spin on its axis. It remains permanently above the same place on Pluto. Some astronomers have suggested that Pluto was a former moon of Neptune that escaped.

Pluto /'pluːtəʊ/ in Roman mythology, the lord of Hades, the underworld. He was the brother of Jupiter and Neptune.

plutonic rock an ◊igneous rock derived from magma that has cooled and solidified deep in the crust of the Earth; granites and gabbros are examples of plutonic rocks.

plutonium a synthetic element, a silvery metal, symbol Pu, atomic number 94, relative atomic mass 242. Its most stable isotope, Pu-239 (discovered 1941), has a half-life of 24,000 years, undergoes nuclear fission, and is usually made in reactors by bombarding U-238 with neutrons. It is used in atom bombs, in reactors, and for enriching the abundant U-238. It has awkward physical properties, and is poisonous to animals, being absorbed into bone marrow.

It was first produced 1940, by Glenn Seaborg and his co-workers at the University of California at Berkeley, by bombarding uranium with deuterons. It has the lowest level of human tolerance of any radioactive carcinogen. It burns spontaneously in the presence of air to form plutonium dioxide, which forms a fine dust and clings to surfaces. One peaceful use is to power heart pacemakers.

Plymouth /'plɪməθ/ city and seaport in Devon, England, at the mouth of the river Plym, with dockyard, barracks, and naval base at Devonport; population (1981) 244,000.

The city rises N from the Hoe headland where tradition has it that ◊Drake played bowls before leaving to fight the Spanish Armada. John ◊Hawkins, Drake, and the ◊Pilgrims in *Mayflower* sailed from Plymouth Sound. The city centre was reconstructed after heavy bombing in World War II.

Plymouth Brethren a fundamentalist Christian Protestant sect characterized by extreme simplicity of belief, founded in Dublin about 1827 by the Reverend John Nelson Darby (1800–82). An assembly was held in Plymouth 1831 to celebrate its arrival in England, but by 1848 the movement had split into 'Open' and 'Close' Brethren. The latter refuse communion with all those not of their persuasion. The Plymouth Brethren are mainly found in the fishing villages of NE Scotland.

Plynlimon /plɪn'lɪmən/ mountain in Powys, Wales, with three summits, the highest is 752 m/2,468 ft.

plywood a manufactured wood widely used in building. It is made up of thin sheets, or plies, of wood, which are stuck together so that the grain (direction of the wood fibres) of one sheet is at right-angles to the grain of the plies on either side. This construction gives plywood equal strength in every direction.

Plzeň /'pɪlzən/ (German *Pilsen*) industrial city (heavy machinery, cars, beer) in W Czechoslovakia, capital of Západočeský region; 84 km/52 mi SW of Prague; population (1984) 174,000.

p.m. abbreviation for *post meridiem* (Latin 'after noon').

PM abbreviation for *Prime Minister*.

pneumatic drill a drill operated by compressed air, used in mining and tunnelling, for drilling shot-holes (for explosives), and in road mending for breaking up pavements. It contains an air-operated piston which delivers hammer blows to the drill ◊bit many times a second. The French engineer Germain Sommeiller (1815–71) developed the pneumatic drill 1861 for tunnelling in the Alps.

pneumatophore an erect root that rises up above the soil or water and promotes gaseous exchange. Pneumatophores, or breathing roots, are formed by certain swamp-dwelling trees, such as mangroves, since there is little oxygen available to the roots in waterlogged conditions. They have numerous pores or ◊lenticels over their surface, allowing gas exchange.

pneumoconiosis disease of the lungs caused by dust, especially from coal, which causes the lung to become fibrous. The victim has difficulty breathing.

pneumonectomy surgical removal of a lung.

pneumonia inflammation of the lungs due to bacterial or viral infection. It is characterized by a build-up of fluid in the alveoli, the clustered air sacs (at the end of the air passages) where oxygen exchange takes place.

With widespread availability of antibiotics, fulminating pneumonia is much less common than it was. However, it remains a dire threat to patients whose immune systems are suppressed (including transplant recipients, and AIDS and cancer victims) and to those who are critically ill or injured.

pneumothorax the presence of air in the pleural cavity, between a lung and the chest wall. It may be due to penetrating injury of the lung, lung disease, or it may arise without apparent cause. Prevented from expanding normally, the lung is liable to collapse.

Pnom Penh /'nɒm 'pen/ alternative form of ◊Phnom Penh, capital of Cambodia.

Po /pəʊ/ longest river in Italy, flowing from the Cottian Alps to the Adriatic; length 668 km/415 mi. Its valley is fertile and contains natural gas. The river is heavily polluted with nitrates, phosphates, and arsenic.

PO abbreviation for *Post Office*.

Pobeda, Pik /pɒb'jedə/ highest peak in the ◊Tian Shan mountain range on the Soviet-Chinese border; at 7,439 m/24,406 ft, it is the second highest mountain in the USSR.

Pocahontas /ˌpɒkə'hɒntəs/ *c.*1595–1617. American Indian princess alleged to have saved the life of John Smith, the English colonist, when he was captured by her father Powhatan. She married an Englishman, and has many modern US descendants. She died in Gravesend, Kent.

pochard type of diving duck found in Europe and North America. The male common pochard *Aythya ferina* has a red head, black breast, whitish body and wings with black markings, and is about 45 cm/1.5 ft long. The female is greyish-brown, with greyish-white below.

The *canvas-back Aythya valisineria*, is a related New World species.

Po Chu-i former transliteration of ◊Bo Zhu Yi, Chinese poet.

pod in botany, a type of ◊fruit that is characteristic of plants belonging to the Leguminosae family, such as peas and beans (technical name *legume*). It develops from a single ◊carpel and splits down both sides when ripe to release the seeds.

In certain species the seeds may be ejected explosively due to uneven drying of the fruit wall, which sets up tensions within the fruit. The name 'legume' is also used for crops of the pea and bean family. 'Grain legume' refers to those that are grown for their dried seeds, such as lentils, chick peas, and soybeans.

podesta in the Italian ◊communes, the highest civic official, appointed by the leading citizens, and often holding great power.

Podgorica or *Podgoritsa* /'pɒdgərɪtsə/ former name (until 1946) of ◊Titograd, city in Yugoslavia.

Podolsk /pə'dɒlsk/ industrial city (oil refining, machinery, cables, cement, ceramics) in the USSR, 40 km/25 mi SW of Moscow; population (1987) 209,000.

podzol or *podsol* type of soil found predominantly under coniferous forests and moorlands in cool regions where rainfall exceeds evaporation. The constant downward movement of water leaches nutrients from the upper layers, making podzols poor agricultural soils.

The leaching of minerals such as iron and aluminium leads to the formation of a bleached zone, often also depleted of clay. These minerals can accumulate lower down the soil profile to form a hard, impermeable layer which restricts the drainage of water through the soil.

Poe /pəʊ/ Edgar Allan 1809–1849. US writer and poet. His short stories are renowned for their horrific atmosphere (as in 'The Fall of the House of Usher' 1839) and acute reasoning (for example, 'The Gold Bug' 1843 and 'The Murders in the Rue Morgue' 1841, in which the investigators Legrand and Dupin anticipate Conan Doyle's Sherlock Holmes). His poems include 'The Raven' 1844. His novel, *The Narrative of Arthur Gordon Pym of Nantucket* 1838, has attracted critical attention recently.

Poe *Daguerreotype of US writer Edgar Allan Poe.*

Born in Boston, he was orphaned 1811, and joined the army but was court-martialled for neglect of duty. He failed to earn a living by writing, became addicted to alcohol, and in 1847 lost his wife (commemorated in his poem *Annabel Lee*). His verse, of haunting lyric beauty, influenced the French Symbolists (for example, *Ulalume* and *The Bells*).

Poet Laureate poet of the British royal household, so called because of the laurel wreath awarded to eminent poets in the Graeco-Roman world. Early poets with unofficial status were Chaucer, Skelton, Spenser, Daniel, and Jonson. There is a stipend of £70 a year, plus £27 in lieu of the traditional butt of sack (cask of wine).

Poets Laureate

1638	William Davenant
1668	John Dryden
1689	Thomas Shadwell
1692	Nahum Tate
1715	Nicholas Rowe
1718	Laurence Eusden
1730	Colley Cibber
1757	William Whitehead
1785	Thomas Warton
1790	Henry Pye
1813	Robert Southey
1843	William Wordsworth
1850	Alfred, Lord Tennyson
1896	Alfred Austin
1913	Robert Bridges
1930	John Masefield
1968	Cecil Day Lewis
1972	John Betjeman
1984	Ted Hughes

poetry the imaginative expression of emotion, thought, or narrative, often in metrical form, and often in figurative language. Poetry has traditionally been distinguished from prose (ordinary written language) by rhyme or rhythmical arrangement of words, although the distinction is not always clear cut.

Poetry is often described as lyric, or songlike poetry (sonnet, ode, elegy, pastoral), and narrative, or story-telling (ballad, lay, epic). Poetic form has also been used as a vehicle for satire, parody, and expositions of philosophical, religious, and practical subjects.

Poetry (Chicago) US literary magazine, founded by Harriet Monroe, with Ezra Pound as foreign editor. It introduced many major modern poets, including T S Eliot, Wallace Stevens, W C Williams, Marianne Moore, and Carl Sandburg, and printed the manifesto of Imagism. With many subsequent editors, it survives still.

pogrom (Russian 'destruction') an unprovoked persecution or extermination of an ethnic group, particularly Jews, carried out with official connivance. The Russian pogroms began 1881, and were common throughout the country. Later there were pogroms in E Europe and in Germany under Hitler.

poikilothermy the condition in which an animal's body temperature is largely dependent on the temperature of the air or water in which it lives. It is characteristic of all animals except birds and mammals, which maintain their body temperatures by ◊homeothermy. Poikilotherms have some means of warming themselves up, such as basking in the sun, or shivering, and can cool themselves down by sheltering from the sun under ◊a rock or by bathing in water. See ◊homeotherms ('warm-blooded animals').

Poikilotherms are often referred to as 'cold-blooded animals', but this is not really correct: their blood may be as warm as their surroundings, which means it may be warmer than the blood of birds and mammals, for example, in very hot climates.

Poincaré /'pwæŋkæreɪ/ Jules Henri 1854–1912. French mathematician, who developed the theory of differential equations and was a pioneer in ◊relativity theory. He also published the first paper devoted entirely to ◊topology.

Poincaré /'pwæŋkæreɪ/ Raymond Nicolas Landry 1860–1934. French politician, prime minister 1912–13, president 1913–20, and again prime minister 1922–24 (when he ordered the occupation of the Ruhr, Germany) and 1926–29. He was a cousin of the mathematician Jules Henri Poincaré.

Poindexter /'pɔːɪndeksta/ John (Marlan) 1936– . US rear admiral and Republican government official. In 1981 he joined the Reagan administration's National Security Council (NSC) and became national security adviser 1985. As a result of the ◊Irangate scandal, Poindexter was forced to resign 1986, along with his assistant, Oliver North.

A doctor in nuclear physics, Poindexter served in the US Navy before becoming deputy head of naval educational training 1978–81. He worked closely with the NSC head, Robert McFarlane, from 1983, and took over when McFarlane left Dec 1985. Poindexter retired from the navy Dec 1987, awaiting prosecution on charges arising out of Irangate. He was found guilty on all counts Apr 1990.

poinsettia winter flowering shrub *Euphorbia pulcherrima*, also known as Mexican flame-leaf and Christmas-flower, with large red leaves encircling small greenish-yellow flowers. It is native to Mexico and tropical America and is a popular pot plant in North America and Europe.

pointe (French 'toe of shoe') in dance, the tip of the toe. A dancer *sur les pointes* is dancing on her toes in blocked shoes, as popularized by Marie ◊Taglioni 1832.

Pointe-Noire /'pwænt 'nwɑː/ chief port of the Congo, formerly (1950–58) the capital; population (1984) 297,000. Industries include oil refining and shipbuilding.

pointer breed of dog, often white mixed with black, tan, or dark brown, about 60 cm/2 ft tall, and weighing 28 kg/62 lbs. They were bred to scent the position of game and indicate it by standing, nose pointed towards it, often with one foot raised, in silence.

Pointillism technique in oil painting developed in the 1880s by the Neo-Impressionist Seurat. He used small dabs of pure colour laid side by side to create an impression of shimmering light when viewed from a distance.

pointillism in music, a form of 1950s ◊serialism in which melody and harmony are replaced by complexes of isolated tones.

point of sale in business premises, the point where a sale is transacted, for example, a supermarket checkout. In conjunction with electronic funds transfer, point of sale is part of the terminology of 'cashless shopping', enabling buyers to transfer funds directly from their bank accounts to the shop's (◊EFTPOS).

poise c.g.s. unit (symbol P) of dynamic ◊viscosity (the property of liquids that determines how readily they flow). For most liquids the centipoise (one hundredth of a poise) is used. Water at 20°C has a viscosity of 1.002 centipoise.

Poiseuille's formula in physics, a relationship describing the rate of flow of a fluid through a narrow tube. For a capillary (very narrow) tube of length l and radius r with a pressure difference p between its ends, and a liquid of ◊viscosity η, the velocity of flow expressed as the volume per second is $\pi p r^4/8l\eta$. The formula was devised 1843 by the French physicist Jean Louis Poiseuille (1799–1869).

poison a chemical substance that when introduced into or applied to the body is capable of injuring health or destroying life.

The majority of poisons may be divided into **corrosives**, for example, sulphuric, nitric, hydrochloric acids, caustic soda, and corrosive sublimate, which burn and destroy the parts with which they come into contact; **irritants** such as arsenic, copper sulphate, zinc chloride, silver nitrate, and green vitriol, which have an irritating effect on the stomach and bowels; **narcotics**, for example, opium, prussic acid, potassium cyanide, chloroform, carbon monoxide, which affect the brain and spinal

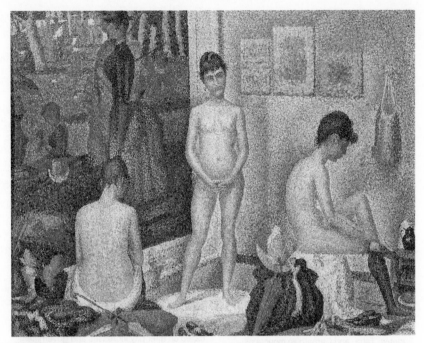
Pointillism George Seurat's *Poseuses, Artemis, Luxembourg*. His painstakingly minute technique evolved from Impressionist brushwork, but was also based on scientific knowledge of the effects of colour.

cord, inducing a stupor; **narcotico-irritants** which combine intense irritations and finally act as narcotics, for example, carbolic acid, foxglove, henbane, deadly nightshade (belladonna), tobacco, and many other substances of plant origin.

In non-corrosive poisoning every effort is made to remove the poison from the system as soon as possible, for example, usually by vomiting induced by an emetic. For some corrosive and irritant poisons there are chemical antidotes, but for recently developed poisons in a new category, for example, ◊paraquat, which produce proliferative changes in the system, there is no antidote.

In most countries the sale of poison is carefully controlled by law, and, in general, only qualified and registered pharmacists and medical practitioners may dispense them.

poison pill in business, a tactic to avoid hostile takeover by making the target unattractive. For example, a company may give a certain class of shareholders the right to have their shares redeemed at a very good price in the event of the company being taken over, thus involving potential predator in considerable extra cost.

Poisson /'pwæsɒn/ Siméon Denis 1781–1840. French applied mathematician. In probability theory he formulated the *Poisson distribution*, which is widely used in probability calculations. He published four treatises and several papers on aspects of physics, including mechanics, heat, electricity and magnetism, elasticity and astronomy.

Poitevin in English history, relating to the reigns of King John and King Henry III; derived from the region of France south of the Loire (Poitou), controlled by the English for most of this period.

Poitier /'pwɒtieɪ/ Sidney 1924– . US actor and film director, the first black actor to become a star in Hollywood. His films as an actor included *In the Heat of the Night* 1967, and as director *Stir Crazy* 1980.

Poitiers /'pwɒtieɪ/ capital of Poitou-Charentes, W France; population (1982) 103,200; products include chemicals and clothing. The Merovingian king Clovis defeated the Visigoths under Alaric here 507; ◊Charles Martel stemmed the Saracen advance 732, and ◊Edward the Black Prince defeated the French 1356.

Poitou-Charentes /pwɑːˈtuː ʃæˈrɒnt/ region of W central France, comprising the *départements* of

Charente, Charente-Maritime, Deux-Sèvres, and Vienne; capital Poitiers; area 25,800 sq km/9,959 sq mi; population (1986) 1,584,000. The region is noted for the celebrated brandy produced at Cognac.

poker card game of US origin, in which two to eight people play (usually for stakes), and try to obtain a hand of five cards ranking higher than those of their opponents. The one with the best scoring hand wins the central pool.

Poland /'pəʊlənd/ country in E Europe, bounded to the E by the USSR, to the S by Czechoslovakia, and to the W by East Germany.

government Under the constitution of 1952, Poland has a two-chamber legislature, comprising a 460-member lower assembly, the *Sejm* (parliament), and a 100-member upper chamber, the Senate. 253 (55%) of the *Sejm's* seats have, initially, been reserved for contests between candidates from the Patriotic Movement for National Rebirth (PRON), the Polish United Workers party (PUWP) (Communist Party) broad front organization; 46 (10%) for a national list of dignitaries; and the remaining 161 (35%) for non-PRON candidates. A two-ballot majority 'run off' voting system is employed and terms are for four years. The Senate's members are elected in free, multi-party contests. The *Sejm* passes bills, adopts the state budget and economic plan, and appoints a 24-member executive council of ministers, headed by a chair, or prime minister. The Senate has the power of veto in specified areas, which can be overriden by a two-thirds *Sejm* vote. Both chambers jointly elect, for a six-year term, a French-style executive state president who is responsible for military and foreign affairs and has the authority to dissolve parliament, call referenda, veto bills, and impose martial law. It has been promised that when the current assembly-elected president has served his full term, the next chief executive will be directly elected by the public and the *Sejm* will be fully opened to multi-party competition for its seats. At the local level, there are elected people's councils in each of the country's 49 provinces (*voivod*ships).

history In the 10th century the Polish tribes were first united under one Christian ruler, Mieczyslaw. Mongols devastated the country 1241, and thereafter German and Jewish refugees settled among the ◊Slav population. The first parliament met 1331, and Casimir the Great (1333–1370) raised

Poland
Polish Republic

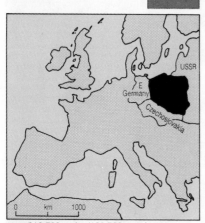

area 312,700 sq km/120,733 sq mi
capital Warsaw
towns Lódź, Kraków, Wroclaw, Poznań, Katowice, Bydgoszcz, Lublin; ports Gdánsk, Szczecin, Gdynia
physical comprises part of the great plain of Europe; Vistula, Oder, and Neisse rivers; Sudeten, Tatra, and Carpathian mountains
head of government Tadeusz Mazowiecki from 1989
government socialist pluralist republic
political parties Social Democratic Party of the Polish Republic, the 1990 successor to the Polish United Worker's Party (PUWP), formerly Marxist-Leninist, now social democratic; Union of Social Democrats, radical breakaway from the PUWP formed 1990; Solidaårnosc (Solidarity) Parliamentary Club (OKP), anti-communist coalition
exports coal, softwood timber, chemicals, machinery, ships
currency zloty (16061 = £1 Feb 1990)
population (1989) 38,389,000; annual growth rate 0.9%
life expectancy men 67, women 75
language Polish, a member of the western branch of the Slavonic family
religion Roman Catholic 93%
literacy 99.3% male/98.3% female (1978)
GNP $110 bn (1984); $2,750 per head of population

chronology
1918 Poland revived as independent republic.
1939 German invasion and occupation.
1944 Germans driven out by Soviet force.
1945 Polish boundaries redrawn at Potsdam Conference.
1947 Communist people's republic proclaimed.
1956 Poznań riots. Gomulka installed as Polish United Workers' Party (PUWP) leader.
1970 Gomulka replaced by Gierek after Gdańsk riots.
1980 Emergence of Solidarity free trade union following Gdańsk disturbances.
1981 Imposition of martial law by Gen Jaruzelski.
1983 Ending of martial law.
1984 Amnesty for political prisoners.
1985 Zbigniew Messner became prime minister.
1987 Referendum on economic reform rejected.
1988 Solidarity strikes and demonstrations were called off after pay increases and government agreement to hold a church-state-union conference. Messner resigned and was replaced by the reformist Mieczyslaw Rakowski.
1989 Historic agreement to re-legalize Solidarity and introduce new socialist pluralist constitution following Church-state-union round table negotiations (Apr). Solidarity sweep board in national assembly elections (June). Zaruzelski elected president (July). 'Grand coalition' formed headed by Solidarity's Mazowiecki (Sept).
1990 PUWP dissolved and replaced by new Social Democrat Party and breakaway Union of Social Democrats (Jan).

the country to a high level of prosperity. Under the Jagellion dynasty (1386–1572) Poland became a great power, the largest country in Europe when it was united with Lithuania (1569–1776). Elected kings followed the death of the last Jagellion, a reactionary nobility wielded much power, and Poland's strength declined. But Stephen Bathory defeated Ivan the Terrible of Russia 1581 and in 1683 John III Sobieski forced the Turks to raise their siege of Vienna. In the mid-17th century a war against Russia, Sweden, and Brandenburg ended in the complete defeat of Poland, from which it never recovered.

Wars with the Ottoman Empire, dissension among the nobles, quarrels at the election of every king, the continuance of serfdom, and the persecution of Protestants and Greek Orthodox Catholics laid the country open to interference by Austria, Russia, and Prussia, ending with partition 1772, and again 1793, when Prussia and Russia seized further areas. A patriotic rising led by Tadeusz Kosciuszko was defeated, and Russia and Prussia occupied the rest of the country 1795. The Congress of Vienna rearranged the division 1815 and reconstituted the Russian portion as a kingdom under the tsar. Risings 1830 and 1863 led to intensified repression and an increased attempt to Russianize the population.

Poland was revived as an independent republic 1918 under the leadership of Jósef ◊Pilsudski, the founder of the PPS, taking advantage of the USSR's internal upheaval to advance into Lithuania and Ukraine before the Polish troops were driven back by the Red Army. Poland and the USSR then agreed on a frontier E of the ◊Curzon Line. Politically, the initial post-independence years were characterized

by instability, 14 multi-party coalition governments holding power 1918–26. Pilsudski seized complete power in a coup and proceeded to govern in an increasingly authoritarian manner until his death in 1935. He was succeeded by a military regime headed by Smigly-Rydz. In Apr 1939 the UK and France concluded a pact with Poland to render military aid if it was attacked, and at the beginning of Sept Germany invaded (see ◊World War II). During the war, Western Poland was incorporated into the Nazi Reich, while the remainder, after a brief Soviet occupation of the E (1940–41), was treated as a colony. The country endured the full brunt of Nazi barbarism: a third of the educated elite were 'liquidated' and, in all, six million Poles lost their lives, half of them Jews slaughtered in concentration camps.

A treaty between Poland and the USSR Aug 1945 (ratified 1946) established Poland's eastern frontier at the Curzon Line. Poland lost 181,350 sq km/70,000 sq mi in the east to the USSR but gained 101,000 sq km/39,000 sq mi in the west from Germany. After elections, a 'people's republic' was established Feb 1947 and Poland joined ◊Comecon 1949 and the ◊Warsaw Pact 1955, remaining under close Soviet supervision, with the Soviet marshal Rokossovsky serving as minister for war 1949–56. A harsh Stalinist form of rule was instituted under the leadership of Boleslaw Bierut (1892–1956), involving rural collectivization, the persecution of Catholic church opposition, and the arrest of Cardinal Stefan Wyszynski 1953. In June 1956, serious strikes and riots, leading to 53 deaths, broke out in Poznan in opposition to Soviet 'exploitation' and food shortages. The more pragmatic Wladyslaw ◊Gomulka took over

as PUWP leader, reintroduced private farming and released Cardinal Wyszynski.

A further outbreak of strikes and rioting in Gdansk, Gdynia, and Szczecin Dec 1970 followed sudden food-price rises. This led to Gomulka's replacement as PUWP leader by the Silesia party boss Edward ◊Gierek, whose programme aimed at raising living standards and consumer-goods production. The country's foreign debt grew and food prices again triggered strikes and demonstrations June 1976. Opposition to the Gierek regime, which was accused of corruption, mounted 1979 after a visit to his homeland by the recently elected pope ◊John Paul II. Strikes in Warsaw 1980, following a poor harvest and meat-price rises, rapidly spread across the country. The government attempted to appease workers by entering into pay negotiations with unofficial strike committees, but at the Gdansk shipyards demands emerged for permission to form free, independent trade unions. The government conceded the right to strike, and in Gdansk 1980 the Solidarity (Solidarność) union was formed under the leadership of Lech ◊Walesa.

In Sept 1980, the ailing Gierek was replaced as PUWP leader by Stanislaw Kania, but unrest continued as the 10-million member Solidarity campaigned for a five-day working week and established a rural section. With food shortages mounting and PUWP control slipping, Kania was replaced as PUWP leader Oct 1981 by the prime minister, Gen Wojciech ◊Jaruzelski; the Soviet army was active on Poland's borders; and martial law was imposed 13 Dec 1981. Trade-union activity was banned, the leaders of Solidarity arrested, a night curfew imposed, and the Military Council of National Salvation established, headed by Jaruzelski. Five months of severe repression ensued, resulting in 15 deaths and 10,000 arrests. The USA imposed economic sanctions.

In June 1982, curfew restrictions were eased, prompting further serious rioting in Aug. In Nov Walesa was released and in Dec 1982 martial law was suspended (lifted 1983). The pope visited Poland 1983 and called for conciliation. The authorities responded by dissolving the Military Council and granting an amnesty to political prisoners and activists. In 1984, 35,000 prisoners and detainees were released on the 40th anniversary of the People's Republic, and the US relaxed its economic sanctions.

The Jaruzelski administration pursued pragmatic reform, including liberalization of the electoral system. Conditions remained tense, however, strained by the murder of Father Jerzy Popieluszko, a pro-Solidarity priest, by security-force members 1984; by the continued ban on Solidarity; and by a threat (withdrawn 1986) to try Walesa for slandering state electoral officials. Economic conditions and farm output slowly improved, but Poland's foreign debt remained huge. In Sept 1986, with the release of further prominent dissidents and the establishment of the broad new Consultative Council, the Jaruzelski administration sought to regain the public's trust. However, in Nov 1987 the regime failed to gain the necessary level (50% of the electorate) of support for a referendum on further liberalization reforms. During the following year the nation's shipyards, coalmines, ports, and steelworks were paralysed by a wave of Solidarity-led strikes for higher wages to offset the effect of recent price rises. With its economic strategy in tatters, the government of prime minister Zbigniew Messner resigned, being replaced, in Dec 1988, by a new administration headed by the reformist communist Mieczyslaw Rakowski, and the PUWP's politburo was infused with a new clutch of technocrats. Following six weeks of PUWP-Solidarity-Church negotiations, a historic accord was reached in Apr 1989 under whose terms Solidarity was re-legalized, the formation of opposition political associations tolerated, legal rights conferred upon the Catholic Church, the state's media monopoly lifted, and a new 'socialist pluralist' constitution adopted. In the subsequent national assembly elections, which were held in

June 1989, Solidarity captured all but one of *Sejm* and Senate seats that they were entitled to contest. In Sept 1989 a grand 'coalition' was formed with Tadeusz ◊Mazowiecki, editor of Solidarity's newspaper, taking over as prime minister. Jaruzelski continued as president, being re-elected in July. The new government, which attracted generous financial aid from Western powers, particularly the USA and West Germany, proceeded to set about dismantling the command economy and encouraging the private sector: a stock exchange was opened in Oct 1989, meat rationing ended, foreign 'inward investment' sought, the zloty drastically devalued, and a privatization programme launched. A tough ◊IMF-approved austerity programme was also instituted in an effort to solve the problem of supra-500% hyperinflation.

Polanski /pə'lænski/ Roman 1933– . Polish film director, born in Paris. He suffered a traumatic childhood in Nazi-occupied Poland, and later his wife, actress Sharon Tate, was the victim of murder by the Charles Manson 'family'. His tragic personal life is reflected in a fascination with horror and violence in his work. His films include *Repulsion* 1965, *Cul de Sac* 1966, *Rosemary's Baby* 1968, *Tess* 1979, and *Frantic* 1988.

polar coordinates in mathematics, a way of defining the position of a point in terms of its distance *r* from a fixed point (the origin) and its angle Θ to a fixed line or axis. The coordinates of the point are (*r*, Θ).

Often the angle is measured in ◊radians, rather than degrees. The system is useful for defining positions on a plane in programming the operations of, for example, computer-controlled cloth- and metal-cutting machines.

Polaris or *Pole Star* or *North Star* the bright star closest to the north celestial pole, and the brightest star in the constellation Ursa Minor. Its position is indicated by the 'pointers' in ◊Ursa Major. Polaris is a yellow ◊supergiant about 700 light years away.

It currently lies within 1 degree of the north celestial pole; ◊precession (Earth's axial wobble) will bring Polaris closest to the celestial pole (less than half a degree away) about AD 2100. It is also known as Alpha Ursae Minoris.

polarized light ordinary light which can be regarded as electromagnetic vibrations at right angles to the line of propagation but in different planes. Light is said to be polarized when the vibrations take place in one particular plane. Polarized light is used to test the strength of sugar solutions, to measure stresses in transparent materials, and to prevent glare.

Ordinary light may be plane-polarized by reflection from a polished surface or by passing it through a Nicol prism or a synthetic polarizing film such as Polaroid.

Polaroid camera an instant-picture camera, invented by Edwin Land in the USA 1947. The original camera produced black-and-white prints in about one minute. Modern cameras can produce black-and-white prints in a few seconds, and colour prints in less than a minute. An advanced model has automatic focusing and exposure. It ejects a piece of film immediately after the picture has been taken. The film consists of layers of emulsion and colour dyes together with a pod of chemical developer. When the film is ejected the pod bursts, and processing begins in the light.

polar reversal changeover in polarity of the Earth's magnetic poles. Studies of the magnetism retained in rocks at the time of their formation have shown that in the past the Earth's north magnetic pole repeatedly became the south magnetic pole, and vice versa.

Polar reversal seems to be relatively frequent, taking place three or four times every million years. The last occasion was 700,000 years ago. Distinctive sequences of magnetic reversals are used in dating rock formations. Movements of the Earth's molten core are thought to be responsible for both the Earth's magnetic field and its reversal.

It is calculated that in about 1,200 years' time the north magnetic pole will become the south magnetic pole.

Pole /pəul/ Reginald 1500–1558. English cardinal from 1536, who returned from Rome as papal legatee on the accession of Mary in order to readmit England to the Catholic church. He succeeded Cranmer as archbishop of Canterbury 1556.

polecat species of weasel *Mustela putorius* with a brown back and dark belly. The body is about 50 cm/20 in long and it has a strong smell. It is native to Asia, Europe, and North America.

Almost extinct in Britain around 1915, the polecat has since increased in numbers. A ferret is a domesticated polecat.

poles geographic north and south points of the axis about which the Earth rotates. The magnetic poles are the points towards which a freely suspended magnetic needle will point; however, they vary continually.

In 1985 the magnetic north pole was some 350 km/218 mi NW of Resolute Bay, Northwest Territories, Canada. It moves northwards about 10 km/6 mi each year, although it can vary in a day about 80 km/50 mi from its average position. It is relocated every decade in order to update navigational charts. It is thought that periodic changes in the Earth's core cause a reversal of the magnetic poles (see ◊polar reversal). Many animals, including migrating birds and fish, are believed to orientate themselves partly using the Earth's magnetic field. A permanent scientific base collects data at the South Pole.

Pole Star ◊Polaris, the northern pole star. There is no bright star near the southern celestial pole.

police civil law-and-order force. In the UK it is under the Home Office, with 56 autonomous police forces, generally organized on a county basis; mutual aid is given in circumstances such as mass picketing in the 1984–85 miners' strike, but there is no national police force or police riot unit (such as the French CRS riot squad). The predecessors of these forces were the ineffective medieval watch and London's Bow Street runners, introduced 1749 by Henry ◊Fielding which formed a model for the London police force established by ◊Peel's government 1829 (hence 'peelers' or 'bobbies'); the system was introduced throughout the country from 1856.

Landmarks include: *Criminal Investigation Department* detective branch of the London Metropolitan Police (New Scotland Yard) 1878, recruited from the uniformed branch (such departments now exist in all UK forces); women police 1919; motorcycle patrols 1921; two-way radio cars 1927; personal radio on the beat 1965; and *Special Patrol Groups* (SPG) 1970, squads of experienced officers concentrating on a specific problem (New York has the similar Tactical Patrol Force). Unlike most other police forces, the British are armed only on special occasions, but arms issues grow more frequent. In 1985 London had one police officer for every 268 citizens.

Foreign police forces include the Garda Síochána in the Republic of Ireland, Carabinieri in Italy, Guardia Civil in Spain, the Royal Canadian Mounted Police ('Mounties') in Canada, Police Nationale (under the Ministry of the Interior) for the cities and Gendarmerie (part of the army) elsewhere in France.

Police Complaints Authority in the UK, a statutory body, set up 1984, which supervises the investigation of complaints against the police. It can order disciplinary action to be taken against police officers. It superseded the Police Complaints Board.

Policy Research, Institute for British left-wing think-tank established in 1988 with Baroness Blackstone as chair of the board of trustees. It was designed to set the agenda for a future Labour government and challenge the conservative government's belief in the advantages of the free market economy.

polio (poliomyelitis) a virus infection of the central nervous system affecting nerves that activate muscles. The disease used to be known as infantile paralysis. The World Health Organization expects that polio will be eradicated by 2000.

The polio virus is a common one, and mostly its effects are confined to the throat and intestine, as in flu or a mild digestive upset. There may also be muscle stiffness in the neck and back. Paralysis is seen in about 1% of cases, and the disease is life-threatening only if the muscles of the throat and chest are affected. Cases of this kind, once entombed in an 'iron lung', are today maintained on a respirator. Two kinds of vaccine are available, one injected (see ◊Salk) and one given by mouth.

Polish Corridor strip of land, designated under the Treaty of ◊Versailles 1919 to give Poland access to the Baltic. It cut off East Prussia from the rest of Germany. It was absorbed when Poland took over the southern part of East Prussia 1945.

Polish language a member of the Slavonic branch of the Indo-European language family, spoken mainly in Poland. Polish is written in the Roman and not the Cyrillic alphabet and its standard form is based on the dialect of Poznań in W Poland.

Politburo contraction of 'political bureau', a subcommittee (known as the Praesidium 1952–66) of the Central Committee of the Communist Party in the USSR and some other communist states, which lays down party policy. It consists of 12 voting and 6 candidate (non-voting) members.

Politian /pp'lɪʃən/ (Angelo Poliziano) Pen name of Angelo Ambrogini 1454–1494. Italian poet, playwright, and exponent of humanist ideals; he was tutor to Lorenzo de ◊Medici's children, professor at the University of Florence, and wrote commentaries and essays on classical authors.

political action committee (PAC) US organization which raises funds for political candidates and in return commits them to a particular policy. It also spends money on changing public opinion. There were 3,500 PACs in 1984, and they controlled 25% of all funds spent in elections for ◊Congress.

Polk /pəuk/ James Knox 1795–1849. 11th president of the USA from 1845, a Democrat, born in North Carolina. He admitted Texas to the Union, and forced the war on Mexico that resulted in the annexation of California and New Mexico.

polka folk dance in lively two-four time. The basic step is a hop followed by three short steps. It originated in Bohemia and spread with German immigrants to the USA, becoming a style of Texas country music. From about 1830 it was fashionable in European society.

pollack marine fish *Pollachius pollachius* of the cod family, growing to 75 cm/2.5 ft, and found inshore.

Pollaiuolo /pp,laιu:ʹəulɔu/ Antonio c. 1432–1498 and Piero c.1441–1496. Italian artists, active in Florence. Both brothers were painters, sculptors, goldsmiths, engravers, and designers. Antonio is said to have been the first Renaissance artist to make a serious study of anatomy. The *Martyrdom of St Sebastian* 1475 (National Gallery, London) is considered a joint work.

The brothers also executed two papal monuments in St Peter's basilica, Rome. The best-known individual works are Piero's set of *Virtues* in Florence and Antonio's engraving *The Battle of the Nude Gods* about 1465. Antonio's work places a strong emphasis on the musculature of the human figure in various activities.

pollarding a type of pruning whereby the young branches of a tree are severely cut back, about 6–12 ft/2–4 m above the ground, to produce a stump-like trunk with a rounded, bushy head of thin new branches. It is often practised on willows, where the new branches or 'poles' are cut at intervals of a year or more, and used for fencing and firewood. Pollarding is also used to restrict the height of many street trees. See also ◊coppicing.

pollen the grains formed by seed plants that contain the male gametes. In ◊angiosperms pollen is produced within ◊anthers, in most ◊gymnosperms it is produced in male ◊cones. A pollen grain is typically yellow and, when mature, has a hard outer wall. Pollen of insect-pollinated plants (see ◊pollination) is often sticky and spiny, and larger than the smooth, light grains produced by wind-pollinated species.

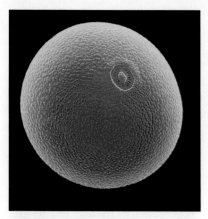

pollen *Electron-microscope picture of a pollen grain from cocksfoot grass, which is wind-pollinated.*

The outer wall of pollen grains from both insect-pollinated and wind-pollinated plants is often elaborately sculptured with ridges or spines so distinctive that individual species or genera of plants can be recognized from their pollen. Since pollen is extremely resistant to decay, much important information on the vegetation of earlier times can be gained from the study of fossil pollen. The study of pollen grains is known as palynology.

pollen tube an outgrowth from a pollen grain that grows towards the ◊ovule, following germination of the grain on the stigma. In ◊angiosperms (flowering plants) the pollen tube reaches the ovule by growing down through the ◊style, carrying the male gametes inside. The gametes are discharged into the ovule and one fertilizes the egg cell.

pollination the process by which fertilization occurs in the sexual reproduction of higher plants. The male ◊gametes are contained in ◊pollen grains, which must be transferred from the ◊anther to the ◊stigma in ◊angiosperms, and from the male cone to the female cone in ◊gymnosperms. Self-pollination occurs when pollen is transferred to a stigma of the same flower, or to another flower on the same plant; cross-pollination occurs when pollen is transferred to another plant. This involves external pollen-carrying agents, such as wind (see ◊anemophily), water, insects, birds (see ◊ornithophily), bats, and other small mammals.

Animal pollinators carry the pollen on their bodies and are attracted to the flower by scent, or by the sight of the petals. Most flowers are adapted for pollination by one particular agent only. Those that rely on animals generally produce nectar, a sugary liquid, or surplus pollen, or both, on which the pollinator feeds. Thus the relationship between pollinator and plant is an example of mutualism, in which both benefit. However, in some plants, the pollinator receives no benefit (as in ◊pseudocopulation), while in others, nectar may be removed by animals that do not effect pollination.

Pollination of flowering plants also leads to the formation of the ◊endosperm, for which a second male gamete is needed; the process is known as ***double fertilization***.

pollinium a group of pollen grains which is transported as a single unit during pollination. Pollinia are common in orchids.

Pollock /ˈpɒlək/ Jackson 1912–1956. US painter, a pioneer of Abstract Expressionism and the foremost exponent of the dripping and splashing technique ***action painting***, a style he developed around 1946.

In the early 1940s Pollock moved from a vivid Expressionist style, influenced by Mexican muralists such as Siqueiros and by Surrealism, towards a semi-abstract style. The paintings of this period are colourful and vigorous, using jumbled signs or symbols like enigmatic graffiti. He moved on to the more violently expressive abstract style, placing large canvases on the studio floor and dripping or hurling his paint on top of them. He was soon recognized as the leading Abstract Expressionist, and continued to develop his style, producing even larger canvases in the 1950s.

poll tax or ***community charge*** tax levied on every individual, without reference to their income or property. Being simple to administer, it was among the earliest sorts of tax (introduced in England 1377), but because of its indiscriminate nature (it is a regressive tax, in that it falls proportionately more on poorer people) it has often proved unpopular. It contributed to the ◊Peasants' Revolt 1381 and was abolished in England 1698. In the USA it survived longer but in 1964 its use was declared unconstitutional in federal elections because of its frequent abuse as a tool for disenfranchising blacks.

Poll tax was introduced by the UK Conservative government in Scotland 1 Apr 1989, and in England and Wales 1 Apr 1990, replacing the property-based local taxation (◊rates). Amendments to the tax are being considered in the wake of widespread opposition and regional demonstrations, in particular the Central London anti-poll tax rally Mar 1990 (which culminated in police-civilian violence and high-street looting).

pollution the harmful effect on the environment of by-products of human activity, principally industrial and agricultural processes, for example noise, smoke, gases, chemical effluents in seas and rivers, indestructible pesticides, sewage (see ◊sewage disposal), and household waste. Pollution contributes to the ◊greenhouse effect, and heavily polluted areas may eventually become uninhabitable.

Pollution control involves higher production costs for the industries concerned, but failure to implement adequate controls may result in long-term environmental damage and an increase in the incidence of diseases such as cancer.

Natural disasters may also cause pollution; volcanic eruptions, for example, cause ash to be ejected into the atmosphere and deposited on the land surface.

In the UK 1987 air pollution caused by carbon monoxide emission from road transport was measured at 5.26 million tonnes. In Feb 1990 the UK had failed to apply 21 European Community Laws on air and water pollution and faced prosecution before the European Court of Justice on 31 of the 160 EC directives in force.

Pollux in Greek mythology, the twin brother of ◊Castor.

Pollux brightest star in the constellation Gemini, and the 17th brightest star in the sky. Pollux is a yellowish star with a true luminosity 35 times that of the Sun. It is 35 light years away.

polo game played between two teams of four on horseback, which originated in Iran, spread to India and was first played in England 1869. A game lasts about an hour, divided into 'chukkas' of 7 1/2 minutes. A small ball is struck with the side of a mallet through goals at each end of the ground.

The rules were evolved by the Hurlingham Club 1875. Noted surviving British clubs are Roehampton, London, and Cowdray Park, Sussex, but the game is most popular in India.

Polo /ˈpəʊləʊ/ Marco 1254–1324. Venetian traveller and writer. He travelled overland to China 1271–75, and served under the emperor Kublai Khan until he returned to Europe by sea 1292–95. He was then captured while fighting for Venice against Genoa, and in prison wrote an account of his travels.

polonaise a Polish dance in stately three-four time, which was common in 18th-century Europe. Chopin developed the polonaise as a pianistic form.

polonium a radioactive element, symbol Po, atomic number 84, relative atomic mass 210. Polonium occurs naturally, but only in minute quantities. It has the largest number of isotopes of any element. One potential use for polonium is as a lightweight power source in satellites.

It was the first radioactive element to be isolated, by Marie and Pierre Curie in 1898 (in pitchblende residues), and was named after Marie Curie's native Poland.

pollen

pollen grains land on stigma

stigma

style

1

ovary

male nucleus in pollen tube

2

pollen tube grows into ovary

3

male nucleus reaches egg cell

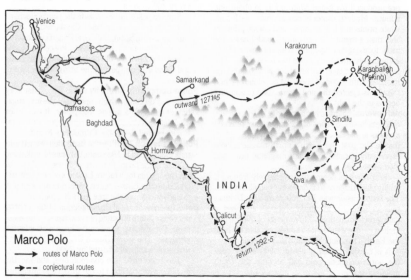

Marco Polo

→ routes of Marco Polo

⇢ conjectural routes

Venice

Karakorum

Karanbalish (Peking)

Samarkand

Damascus

outward 1271–5

Baghdad

Hormuz

Sindifu

INDIA

Ava

Calicut

return 1292–5

Pol Pot /pol'pot/ (also known as Saloth Sar, Tol Saut, and Pol Porth) 1925– . Cambodian politician and communist leader, in power 1975–79. He became a member of the anti-French resistance under Ho Chi Minh in the 1940s and a member of the communist party. As leader of the Khmer Rouge, he overthrew the government of Gen Lon Nol 1975 and proclaimed a republic of Democratic Kampuchea with himself as prime minister. The policies of the Pol Pot government were to evacuate cities and put people to work in the countryside. The Khmer Rouge also carried out a systematic extermination of the educated and middle classes before the regime was overthrown by a Vietnamese invasion 1979. Since then, Pol Pot has led a resistance group against the Vietnamese although he has been tried and convicted, in absentia, of genocide.

Poltava /pol'ta:və/ industrial city (machinery, foodstuffs, clothing) in Ukraine, USSR, capital of Poltava region, on the river Vorskla; population (1987) 309,000. Peter the Great defeated ◊Charles XII of Sweden here 1709.

poltergeist (German 'noisy ghost') unexplained phenomenon that invisibly moves objects or hurls them about, starts fires, or causes other mischief.

polyandry system whereby a woman has more than one husband at the same time. It is found in many parts of the world, for example, in Madagascar, Malaysia, and certain Pacific isles, and among certain Inuit and South American Indian groups. In Tibet and certain parts of India polyandry takes the form of the marriage of one woman to several brothers.

polyanthus garden variety of ◊primrose, with multiple flowers on one stalk, bred in a variety of colours.

Polybius /pə'lɪbɪəs/ *c.* 201–120 BC. Greek politician and historian. He was involved with the ◊Achaean League against the Romans and, following the defeat of the Macedonians at Pydna in 168 BC, he was taken as a political hostage to Rome. He returned to Greece in 151 and was present at the capture of Carthage by his friend Scipio in 146. His history of Rome in 40 books, covering the years 220–146, has largely disappeared.

Polycarp, St /'pɒlɪkɑ:p/ *c.* 69–*c.* 155. Christian martyr allegedly converted by St John the Evangelist. As bishop of Smyrna (modern Izmir, Turkey), for over 40 years he carried on a vigorous struggle against various heresies, and was burned alive at a public festival; feast day 26 Jan.

polychlorinated biphenyls (PCBs) a group of dangerous industrial chemicals, valuable for their fire-resisting qualities, but an environmental hazard because of persistent toxicity. Since 1973, their use has been limited by international agreement.

polyester a type of thermosetting plastic, used in making synthetic fibres, such as Dacron and Terylene, resins, and constructional plastics. With glass fibre added as reinforcement, polyesters are used in car bodies and boat hulls.

polyethylene a polymer of the gas ethylene (now called ethene, C_2H_4), best known under the tradename Polythene. It is a tough, white translucent waxy thermoplastic (it can be repeatedly softened by heating). It is used for packaging, bottles, toys, electric cable, pipes and tubing.

It is produced in two forms: low-density polyethylene, made by high-pressure polymerization of ethylene gas, and high-density polyethylene, which is made at lower pressure using catalysts. This form, first made by German chemist ◊Ziegler, is more rigid at low temperatures and softens at higher temperatures than the low-density type.

polygamy the practice of having more than one husband or wife at the same time. It is found among many peoples, and is common in Africa. Normally it is confined to chiefs and nobles, as among ancient Egyptians, Teutons, Irish, and Slavs. Islam limits a man's legal wives to four. Certain Christian sects, for example, the Anabaptists of Münster, Germany, and the Mormons, have practised polygamy.

polygon in geometry, a plane (two-dimensional) figure with three or more straight-line sides. Common polygons have their own names, which define the number of sides (for example, triangle, quadrilateral, pentagon).

These are all convex polygons, having no interior angle greater than 180°. In general, the more sides a polygon has, the larger the sum of its internal angles and, in the case of a convex polygon, the more closely it approximates to a circle.

polygraph or *polygram* an instrument that records graphically certain body activities, such as thoracic and abdominal respiration, blood pressure, pulse rate, and galvanic skin response (changes in electrical resistance of the skin). Changes in these activities when a person answers a question may indicate that the person is lying.

polyhedron in geometry, a solid figure with four or more plane faces. The more faces there are on a polyhedron, the more closely it approximates to a sphere. Knowledge of the properties of polyhedra is important in crystallography and stereochemistry in determining the shapes of crystals and molecules.

There are only five types of regular polyhedra (with all faces the same size and shape), as was deduced by early Greek mathematicians; they are the tetrahedron (four equilateral triangular faces), cube (six square faces), octahedron (eight equilateral triangles), dodecahedron (12 regular pentagons) and icosahedron (20 equilateral triangles).

Polyhymnia in Greek mythology, the ◊Muse of singing, mime, and sacred dance.

Polykleitos 5th century BC. Greek sculptor, whose *Spear Carrier* 450–40 BC (Roman copies survive) exemplifies the naturalism and harmonious proportions of his work. He created the legendary colossal statue of *Hera* in Argos, in ivory and gold.

polymer a compound made up of large molecules composed of many repeated simple units (**monomers**). There are many polymers, both natural (cellulose, chitin, lignin) and synthetic (polyethylene and nylon, types of plastic).

polymerization the chemical union of two or more (usually small) molecules of the same kind to form a new compound.

There are three types: *addition polymerization*, simple multiples of the same compound; *condensation polymerization*, in which molecules are joined together by the elimination of water; and *co-polymerization*, in which the polymer is built up from two or more different types of molecules.

polymorphism in genetics, the coexistence of several distinctly different types in a ◊population. Examples include the different blood groups in humans, and different colour forms in some butterflies.

Polynesia /ˌpɒlɪ'niːzɪə/ those islands of Oceania E of 170° E latitude, including Hawaii, Kiribati, Tuvalu, Fiji, Tonga, Tokelau, Samoa, Cook Islands, and French Polynesia.

Polynesian indigenous inhabitant of Polynesia. The Polynesian languages belong to the Austronesian family.

Polynesian languages see ◊Malayo-Polynesian languages.

polynomial in mathematics, algebraic expression that has only one ◊variable (denoted by a letter). A polynomial of degree one, that is, whose highest ◊power of x is 1, as in $2x + 1$, is called a linear polynomial; $3x^2 +$

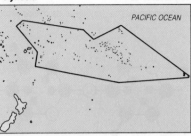

Polynesia

PACIFIC OCEAN

$2x + 1$ is quadratic; $4x^3 + 3x^2 + 2x + 1$ is cubic.

polyp or *polypus* small 'stalked' benign tumour, most usually found on mucous membrane of the nose and bowel. Intestinal polyps are usually removed, as some have been found to be precursors of cancer.

polypeptide a long-chain ◊peptide.

polyphony music combining two or more 'voices' or parts, each with an individual melody.

polyploid in genetics, possessing three or more sets of chromosomes in cases where the normal complement is two sets (◊diploid). Polyploidy arises spontaneously and is common in plants (especially among the angiosperms), but rare in animals. Many crop plants are natural polyploids, including wheat, which has four sets of chromosomes per cell (durum wheat) or six sets (bread wheat). Plant breeders can induce the formation of polyploids by treatment with a chemical, colchicine.

Matings between polyploid individuals and normal diploid ones are invariably sterile. Hence, an individual which develops polyploidy through a genetic aberration can initially only reproduce vegetatively, by parthenogenesis, or by self-fertilization (modes of reproduction that are common only among plants). Once a polyploid population is established, however, they can reproduce sexually. An example is cord-grass *spartina anglica* which is a polyploid of a European grass and a related North American grass, accidentally introduced. The resulting polyploid has spread dramatically.

polysaccharide a long-chain ◊carbohydrate made up of hundreds or thousands of linked simple sugars (monosaccharides) such as glucose and closely related molecules.

The polysaccharides are natural polymers. They either act as energy-rich food stores in plants (starch) and animals (glycogen), or have structural roles in the plant cell wall (cellulose, pectin) or the tough outer skeleton of insects and similar creatures (chitin). See also ◊carbohydrate.

polystyrene a type of ◊plastic.

polytechnic in the UK, an institution for further education offering courses mainly at degree level and concentrating on full-time vocational courses, although many polytechnics provide a wide range of part-time courses at advanced levels. From Apr 1989 the 29 polytechnics in England became independent corporations.

From Apr 1989 public funds became the responsibility of the new Polytechnics and Colleges Funding Council; polytechnic staff ceased to be local government employees and became employed by their own polytechnics; buildings worth around £3 billion were transferred from local government to polytechnics.

Academic validation of courses is carried out by the Council for National Academic Awards. In 1981 there were 127,000 full-time students at 30 polytechnics.

polytheism the worship of many gods, as opposed to monotheism (belief in one god). Examples are the religions of ancient Egypt, Babylon, Greece, Rome, and Mexico, and modern Hinduism.

Polythene trade name for a variety of ◊polyethylene.

polytonality in music, the simultaneous use of more than one ◊key. A combination of two keys is bitonality.

polygon

	number of sides	sum of interior angles (degrees)
triangle	3	180
quadrilateral	4	360
pentagon	5	540
hexagon	6	720
heptagon	7	900
octagon	8	1,080
decagon	10	1,440
duodecagon	12	1,800
icosagon	20	3,240

polysaccharide

glucose molecules linked to form polysaccharide glycogen (animal starch)

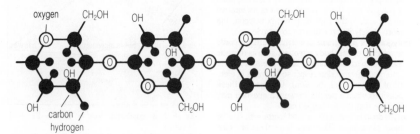

polyunsaturate a type of triglyceride (◊fat or oil) in which the long carbon chains of the ◊fatty acids contain several double bonds. By contrast, the carbon chains of saturated fats (such as lard) contain only single bonds.

The more double bonds the chains contain, the lower the melting point of the triglyceride. Unsaturated chains with several double bonds produce oils, such as vegetable and fish oils, which are liquids at room temperature. Saturated fats, with no double bonds, are solids at room temperature. The polyunsaturated fats used for margarines are produced by taking a vegetable or fish oil and turning some of the double bonds to single bonds, so that the product is semi-solid at room temperature. This is done by bubbling hydrogen through the oil in the presence of a catalyst, such as platinum. The catalyst is later removed. Medical evidence suggests that polyunsaturated fats are less likely to contribute to cardiovascular disease than saturated fats, but there is also some evidence that they may have adverse effects on health. Monounsaturated oils, such as olive oil, with a single double bond, are probably healthier than either saturated or polunsaturated fats. Butter contains both saturated and unsaturated fats, together with ◊cholesterol, which also plays a role in heart disease.

polyurethane a type of ◊plastic.

polyvinyl chloride (PVC) a type of ◊plastic.

pome a type of ◊pseudocarp, or false fruit, typical of certain plants belonging to the Rosaceae family. The outer skin and fleshy tissues are developed from the ◊receptacle after fertilization and the five ◊carpels (the true fruit) form the 'core' of the pome which surrounds the seeds. Examples of pomes are apples, pears, and quinces.

pomegranate fruit of a deciduous shrub or small tree *Punica granatum*, native to SW Asia but cultivated widely in tropical and subtropical areas. The seeds of the reddish-yellow fruit are eaten fresh or made into wine.

Pomerania /ˌpɒməˈreɪniə/ (Polish *Pomorze*, German *Pommern*) region along the south shore of the Baltic Sea, including the island of Rügen, forming part of Poland and (west of the Oder-Neisse line) East Germany from 1945. The chief port is Gdansk. It was formerly part of Germany.

pomeranian small breed of dog, about 15 cm/6 in, and 3 kg/6.5 lbs. It has long straight hair with a neck frill, and the tail is carried over the back.

Pomfret /ˈpʌmfrɪt/ an old form of ◊Pontefract, a town in Yorkshire, England.

Pommern /ˈpɒmən/ German form of ◊Pomerania, former province of Germany.

Pomona /pəˈməʊnə/ in Roman mythology, goddess of fruit trees.

Pomorze /pɒˈmɒʒeɪ/ Polish form of ◊Pomerania, region of N Europe, now largely in Poland.

Pompadour /ˈpɒmpəduə/ Jeanne Antoinette Poisson, Marquise de Pompadour 1721–1764. Mistress of ◊Louis XV of France from 1744, born in Paris. She largely dictated the government's ill-fated policy of reversing France's anti-Austrian policy for an anti-Prussian one. She acted as the patron of the Enlightenment philosophers Voltaire and Diderot.

Pompeii /pɒmˈpeɪiː/ ancient city in Italy, near ◊Vesuvius, 21 km/13 mi SE of Naples. In 63 AD an earthquake destroyed much of the city, which had been a Roman port and pleasure resort; it was completely buried beneath volcanic ash when Vesuvius erupted AD 79. Over 2,000 people were killed. Pompeii was rediscovered 1748 and the systematic excavation begun 1763 still continues.

Pompey /ˈpɒmpi/ the Great (Gnaeus Pompeius Magnus) 106–48 BC. Roman soldier and politician. Originally a supporter of ◊Sulla and the aristocratic party, he joined the democrats when he became consul with ◊Crassus 70 BC. He defeated ◊Mithridates VI of Pontus, and annexed Syria and Palestine. In 60 BC he formed the First Triumvirate with Julius ◊Caesar (whose daughter Julia he married) and Crassus, and when it broke down after 53 BC he returned to the aristocratic party. On the outbreak of civil war 49 BC he withdrew to Greece, was defeated by Caesar at Pharsalus 48 BC, and was murdered in Egypt.

Pompidou /ˌpɒmpɪˈduː/ Georges 1911–1974. French conservative politician, president from 1969. An adviser on Gen de Gaulle's staff 1944–46, he held administrative posts until he became director-general of the French House of Rothschild 1954, and even then continued in close association with de Gaulle. In 1962 he became prime minister, but resigned after the Gaullist victory in the elections 1968, and was elected to the presidency on de Gaulle's resignation.

Ponce /ˈpɒnseɪ/ industrial port (textiles, sugar, rum) in S Puerto Rico, USA; population (1980) 189,000; named after the Spanish explorer ◊Ponce de León.

Ponce de León /ˈpɒnseɪ deɪ leɪˈɒn/ Juan *c.* 1460–1521. Spanish soldier and explorer. He is believed to have sailed with Columbus 1493, and served 1502–04 in Hispaniola. He conquered Puerto Rico 1508, and was made governor 1509. In 1513 he was the first European to reach Florida.

He returned to Spain 1514 to report his 'discovery' of Florida (which he thought was an island), and was given permission by King Ferdinand to colonize it. In the attempt, he received an arrow wound of which he died in Cuba.

Poncelet /ˈpɒnsəleɪ/ Jean 1788–1867. French mathematician, who worked on projective geometry. His book, started in 1814 and completed 1822, deals with the properties of plane figures unchanged when projected.

Pompeii *The streets of the Roman resort of Pompeii were filled with volcanic ash, stones, and poisonous gases when nearby Vesuvius erupted AD 79. The town was lost under the ash for nearly 1,700 years.*

Pondicherry /ˌpɒndɪˈtʃeri/ Union Territory of SE India; area 480 sq km/185 sq mi; population (1981) 604,000. Its capital is Pondicherry, and products include rice, groundnuts, cotton, and sugar. Pondicherry was founded by France 1674 and changed hands several times between French, Dutch, and British before being returned to France 1814 at the close of the Napoleonic wars. Together with Karaikal, Yanam, and Mahé (on the Malabar Coast) it formed a French colony until 1954 when all were transferred to the government of India; since 1962 they have formed the Union Territory of Pondicherry. Languages spoken include French, English, Tamil, Telegu, and Malayalam.

pond-skater water ◊bug that rows itself across the surface by using its middle legs. It feeds on smaller insects.

pondweed aquatic plant of the genus *Potamogeton* that either floats on the water or is submerged. The leaves of the floating pondweed are broad and leathery, whereas leaves of the submerged form are narrower and translucent; the flowers grow in green spikes.

Ponta Delgada /ˈpɒntə delˈgɑːdə/ port, resort, and chief commercial centre of the Portuguese ◊Azores, on São Miguel; population (1981) 22,200.

Pontefract /ˈpɒntɪfrækt/ town in Wakefield borough, W Yorkshire, N England, 34 km/21 mi SW of York; population (1981) 33,000. Produces coal and confectionery (liquorice Pontefract cakes). Features include the remains of the Norman castle where Richard II died.

Pontiac /ˈpɒntiæk/ *c.* 1720–1769. North American Indian, chief of the Ottawa from 1755. In 1763–64 he led the 'Conspiracy of Pontiac' in an attempt to stop British encroachment on Indian lands. He achieved remarkable success against overwhelming odds, but eventually signed a peace treaty 1766, and was murdered by an Illinois Indian at the instigation of a British trader.

Pontiac /ˈpɒntiæk/ a motor-manufacturing city in Michigan, USA, 38 km/24 mi NW of Detroit; population (1980) 76,700.

Pontine Marshes /ˈpɒntaɪn/ formerly malarial marshes in Latium Italy, near the coast 40 km/25 mi SE of Rome. They defied the attempts of the Romans to drain them, and it was not until 1926, under Mussolini's administration, that they were brought into cultivation. Products include cereals, fruit and vines, and sugar beet.

Pontormo /pɒnˈtɔːməʊ/ Jacopo Carucci 1494–1557. Italian painter, active in Florence. He developed a dramatic Mannerist style, with lurid colours.

Pontormo worked in ◊Andrea del Sarto's workshop from 1512. An early work, *Joseph in Egypt* about 1515 (National Gallery, London), is already Mannerist. His mature style is demonstrated in *The Deposition* about 1525 (Sta Felicità, Florence), an extraordinary composition of interlocked figures, with rosy pinks, lime yellows, and pale apple greens illuminating the scene. The same distinctive colours occur in the series of frescoes 1522–25 for the Certosa monastery outside Florence.

Pontus /ˈpɒntəs/ kingdom of NE Asia Minor on the Black Sea from about 300–65 BC when its greatest ruler, ◊Mithridates VI, was defeated by ◊Pompey.

Pontypool /ˌpɒntəˈpuːl/ industrial town in Torfaen district, Gwent, SE Wales, on the Afon Llwyd, 15 km/9 mi N of Newport; population (1981) 36,761. Products include coal, iron and steel goods, tinplate glass, synthetic textiles, and scientific instruments.

Pontypridd /ˌpɒntəˈpriːð/ industrial town (coal mining, chain and cable works, light industry on the Treforest trading estate) in Taff-Ely district, Mid Glamorgan, S Wales; population (1981) 33,134.

pony small horse under 1.47 m/58 in (14.2 hands) shoulder height.

Although of Celtic origin, all the pony breeds have been crossed with thoroughbred and Arab stock, except for the smallest—the hardy Shetland—less than 105 cm/42 in. Other British breeds, including the small Exmoor and Dartmoor, the slightly larger

New Forest, and the large Welsh cob, are found elsewhere in Europe and the East.

poodle breed of dog, including standard (above 38 cm/15 in at shoulder), miniature (below 38 cm/15 in), and toy (below 28 cm/11 in) types. The long curly coat, usually cut into an elaborate style, is usually either black or white, although greys and browns are also bred.

The poodle probably originated in Russia, was naturalized in Germany, where it was used as a sporting dog and gained its name (from the German *pudeln*, to splash), and became a luxury dog in France.

pool game derived from ◊billiards and played in many different forms. Originally popular in the USA, it is now also played in Europe.

It is played with balls of different colours, each of which is numbered. The neutral ball (black) is the number 8 ball. The best-known form of pool is *8-ball pool* in which players have to pot all their own balls before the opponent, and then must sink the 8-ball to win the game. Other forms include potting balls in numerical order, or potting a nominated ball into a nominated pocket.

Poole /pu:l/ industrial town (chemicals, engineering, boatbuilding, confectionery, pottery from local clay) and yachting centre on Poole harbour, Dorset, S England, 8 km/5 mi W of Bournemouth; population (1984) 123,000.

The first Scout camp was held 1907 on Brownsea Island in the harbour, which is now owned by the National Trust. Furzey Island, also within the harbour, is part of Wytch Farm, Britain's largest onshore oil development.

Pool Malebo /'pu:l mə'li:bəu/ lake on the border between the Congo and Zaïre, formed by a widening of the Zaïre river, 560 km/350 mi from its mouth.

Poona /'pu:nə/ former spelling of ◊Pune, city in India.

poor law English system for poor relief, established by the Poor Relief Act 1601. Each parish was responsible for its own poor, paid for by a parish tax. It was reformed in the 19th century, parish functions being transferred to the Poor Law Commissioners 1834 and eventually to the Ministry of Health 1914. It is now superseded by rights to benefit payments, administered by the Department of Social Security.

Pop Iggy. Stage name of James Osterberg 1947– . US rock singer and songwriter, initially known as *Iggy Stooge* with a seminal garage band called the Stooges (1967–74), noted for his self-destructive proto-punk performances. David Bowie contributed as producer and composer to *The Idiot* 1977, *Lust for Life* 1977, and *Blah, Blah, Blah* 1986.

Pop art movement of young artists in the mid-1950s and 1960s, reacting against the elitism of abstract art. Pop art used popular imagery drawn from advertising, comic strips, film, and television. It originated in the UK 1956 with Richard Hamilton, Peter Blake (1932–), and others, and broke through in the USA with the paintings of flags and numbers by Jasper Johns 1958 and Andy Warhol's first series of soup cans 1962.

Pop art was so named by the British critic Lawrence Alloway (1926–). Richard Hamilton described it in 1957 as 'popular, transient, expendable, low-cost, mass-produced, young, witty, sexy, gimmicky, glamorous, and big business'. The artists often used repeating images and quoted from others' work. Among them were Lichtenstein and Oldenburg in the USA, and in the UK Hockney briefly experimented with the genre.

pope /pəup/ the bishop of Rome as head of the Roman Catholic Church, which claims him as the spiritual descendant of St Peter. Elected by the Sacred College of Cardinals, a pope dates his pontificate from his coronation with the tiara, or triple crown, at St Peter's Basilica, Rome. The pope had great political power in Europe from the early Middle Ages until the Reformation.

history
11th–13th centuries The papacy enjoyed its greatest temporal power under Gregory VII and Innocent III.
1309–78 The papacy came under French control (headquarters Avignon rather than Rome), 'the Babylonian Captivity'.
1378–1417 The 'Great Schism' followed, with rival popes in Avignon and Rome.
16th century Papal political power further declined with the withdrawal of allegiance by the Protestant states at the Reformation.
1870 The Papal States in central Italy, which had been under the pope's direct rule from 756, merged with the newly united Italian state. At the Vatican Council the doctrine of papal infallibility was proclaimed.
1929 The Lateran Treaty recognized papal territorial sovereignty even in Italy only within the Vatican City.
1978 John Paul II became the first non-Italian pope since 1542.
1982 A commission of the Roman Catholic and Anglican churches agreed that in any union between them, the pope would be 'universal primate'.

Pope /pəup/ Alexander 1688–1744. English poet and satirist. He established his reputation with the precocious *Pastorals* 1709 and *Essay on Criticism* 1711, which were followed by a parody of the heroic epic *The Rape of the Lock* 1712–14, and 'Eloisa to Abelard' 1717. Other works include a highly Neo-Classical translation of Homer's *Iliad* and *Odyssey* 1715–26.

He had a biting wit, which he expressed in the form of heroic couplets. As a Catholic, he was subject to discrimination, and his life was embittered by a deformity of the spine. The success of his translations made it possible for him to settle in Twickenham from 1719, but his edition of Shakespeare attracted scholarly ridicule, for which he revenged himself by a satire on scholarly dullness, the *Dunciad* 1728. His philosophy, including *An Essay on Man* 1733–34 and *Moral Essays* 1731–35, was influenced by ◊Bolingbroke. His finest mature productions are his *Imitations of the Satires of Horace* 1733–38 and his personal letters. Among his friends were the writers Swift, Arbuthnot, and Gay. His line 'A little learning is a dangerous thing' is often misquoted.

Popish Plot a supposed plot to murder Charles II; see under Titus ◊Oates.

poplar deciduous tree of the genus *Populus* with characteristically broad leaves. Most species are

Pope *English poet and satirist Alexander Pope was also a keen landscape gardener, who devoted much of his time to cultivating a garden and grotto on his estate in Twickenham. The painting is by William Hoare c. 1739.*

tall; they are often grown as windbreaks in commercial orchards.

The *white poplar Populus alba* has a smooth grey trunk and leaves with white undersides. Other varieties are the *aspen Populus tremula, grey poplar Populus canescens,* and *black poplar Populus nigra.* The latter was the only poplar in England in medieval times, but is increasingly rare, with fewer than 1,000 trees remaining in Britain. It is distinctive for its bark, the most ragged of any British tree, and for its tall, leaning trunk.

poplin a strong fabric, originally with a warp of silk and a weft of worsted, but now usually made from cotton, in a plain weave with a finely corded surface.

pop music short for *popular music*, umbrella term for modern music not classifiable as jazz or classical. Pop became distinct from folk music with the advent of sound-recording techniques, and incorporated blues, country and western, and music hall; electronic amplification and other technological innovations have played a large part in the creation of new styles. The traditional format is a song of roughly three minutes with verse, chorus, and middle eight bars.

1910s The singer Al Jolson was one of the first recording stars. Ragtime was still popular.
1920s In the USA Paul Whiteman and his orchestra, the country singer Jimmie Rodgers (1897–1933), the blues; in the UK the singer Al Bowlly (1899–1941, born in Mozambique).
1930s The crooner Bing Crosby, vocal groups such as the Andrews Sisters, and swing bands.
1940s Rhythm and blues evolved in the USA while Frank Sinatra was a teen idol and Glenn Miller played dance music; the UK preferred singers such as Vera Lynn.
1950s In the USA *doo-wop* (a vocal group style based on a cappella street-corner singing), *rockabilly*, and the rise of *rock and roll* (Elvis Presley, Chuck Berry). British pop records were often cover versions of US originals.
1960s The Beatles and *Mersey beat* transcended UK borders, followed by the Rolling Stones. *Hard rock* (the Who, Led Zeppelin). *Art rock* (Genesis, Yes). In the USA *surf music* (group harmony vocals or fast, loud, guitar-based instrumentals). *Motown, folk rock* (the Byrds, Bob Dylan), *blues rock* (Jimi Hendrix, Janis Joplin). *Psychedelic rock* evolved from 1966 on both sides of the Atlantic (Pink Floyd, the Doors, Jefferson Airplane).
1970s First *glitter rock* (David Bowie), *heavy metal*, and *disco* (dance music with a very emphatic, mechanical beat); in the UK also *pub rock* (a return to basics, focusing on live performance). From 1976 *punk*; the US term *New Wave* encompassed bands not entirely within the punk idiom (Talking Heads, Elvis Costello).
1980s Punk continued as *hardcore* or mutated into *gothic*; dance music developed regional US variants: *hip-hop* (New York), *go-go* (Washington DC), and *house* (Chicago). Live audiences grew, leading to anthemic *stadium rock* (U2, Bruce Springsteen) and increasingly elaborate stage performances (Michael Jackson, Prince). An interest in worldwide *roots music* sparked new fusions.

Popocatépetl /ˌpɒpəˌkætə'petl/ (Aztec 'smoking mountain') volcano in central Mexico, 50 km/30 mi SE of Mexico City; 5,340 m/17,526 ft. It last erupted 1920.

Popov /'pɒpɒv/ Alexander 1859–1905. Russian physicist who devised the first ◊aerial, in advance of ◊Marconi (although he did not use it for radio communication), and a detector for radio waves.

Popper /'pɒpə/ Karl (Raimund) 1902– . Austrian philosopher of science. His theory of falsificationism says that although scientific generalizations cannot be conclusively verified, they can be conclusively falsified by a counterinstance, and therefore science is not certain knowledge, but a series of 'conjectures and refutations', approaching, though never reaching, a definitive truth. For Popper, psychoanalysis and Marxism are unfalsifiable and therefore unscientific.

population

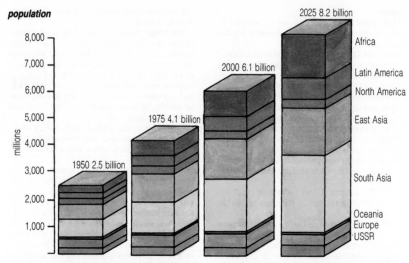

His major work on the philosophy of science is *The Logic of Scientific Discovery* 1935. Other works include *The Poverty of Historicism* 1957 (about the philosophy of social science), *Conjectures and Refutations* 1963, and *Objective Knowledge* 1972.

Born and educated in Vienna, Popper was naturalized British 1945 and was professor of logic and scientific method at the London School of Economics 1949–69. He opposes Wittgenstein's view that philosophical problems are merely pseudo-problems. Popper's view of scientific practice has been criticized by T S ◊Kuhn and other writers.

poppy plant of the genus *Papaver* that bears brightly coloured, often dark-centred, flowers and yields a milky sap. Species include the crimson field *Papaver rhoeas* and ◊opium poppies, found in Europe and Asia. Closely related are the Californian poppy *Eschscholzia californica*, and the yellow-horned or sea poppy *Glaucium flavum*.

popular front a political alliance of liberals, socialists, communists, and other centre and left-wing parties against fascism. This policy was proposed by the Communist International 1935, and was adopted in France and Spain, where popular-front governments were elected 1936; that in France was overthrown 1938, and in Spain 1939. In Britain a popular-front policy was advocated by Sir Stafford Cripps and others, but rejected by the Labour Party. The resistance movements in the occupied countries during World War II represented a revival of the popular-front idea, and in postwar politics the term tends to recur whenever a strong right-wing party can be counterbalanced only by an alliance of those on the left.

population in biology and ecology, a group of animals of one species, living in a certain area and able to interbreed; the members of a given species in a ◊community of living things.

population cycle in biology, regular fluctuations in the size of a population, as seen in lemmings, for example. Such cycles are often caused by density-dependent mortality: high mortality due to overcrowding causes a sudden decline in the population, which then gradually builds up again. Population cycles may also result from an interaction between a predator and its prey.

population genetics the branch of genetics that studies the way in which the frequencies of different ◊alleles in populations of organisms change, as a result of natural selection and other processes, to give rise to evolution.

Populism in US history, a late 19th-century political movement that developed out of farmers' protests against economic hardship. The Populist, or People's, Party was founded 1892 and fielded several presidential candidates. It failed, however, to reverse increasing industrialization and the relative decline of agriculture in the USA.

porcelain (hardpaste) type of ◊ceramic material characterized by its hardness, ringing sound when struck, translucence, and shining finish, like that of a cowrie shell (Italian *porcellana*). It is made of kaolin and petuntse (fusible feldspar consisting chiefly of quartz, and reduced to a fine, white powder) and was first developed in China.

porcupine ◊rodent with sharp quills on its body. Porcupines of the family Hystricidae are terrestrial in habit. They are characterized by long spines in the coat. The colouring is brown with black and white quills.

North American porcupines, family Erethizontidae, differ from the Old World varieties by living in trees and having a prehensile tail and much shorter spines.

porcupine fish another name for ◊globefish.

Porgy and Bess classic US folk opera 1935 by George and Ira Gershwin, based on the novel *Porgy* 1925 by DuBose Heyward, a story of the black residents of Catfish Row in Charleston, South Carolina.

Pori /'pɔːri/ (Swedish *Björneborg*) ice-free industrial port (nickel and copper refining, sawmills, paper, textiles) on the Gulf of Bothnia, SW Finland; population (1985) 79,000. A deepwater harbour was opened in 1985.

pornography obscene literature, pictures, photos, or films of no artistic merit, intended only to arouse sexual desire.

Standards of what is obscene and whether a particular work has artistic value are subjective, hence there is often difficulty in determining whether a work violates obscenity laws.

porphyria rare hereditary metabolic disorder that may cause mental confusion. Other symptoms, for example, excessive growth of hair, contraction of muscles to reveal the teeth, sensitivity to sunlight, and a need for blood infusions, have been suggested as the basis for vampirism and werewolf legends.

It is known as the 'royal disease' because sufferers included Mary Queen of Scots, James I, and (controversially) George III.

porphyry any ◊igneous rock containing large crystals in a finer matrix.

porpoise smallest member of the whale group, distinguished from the dolphin by not having a 'beak', and being smaller. It can grow to 1.8 m/6 ft long, and feeds on fish and crustaceans.

Porritt /'pɒrɪt/ Jonathon 1950– . British environmental campaigner, director of ◊Friends of the Earth from 1984. He has stood for election in both British and European elections as an Ecology (Green) Party candidate.

Porsche racing and road car first built 1948 by Ferdinand Porsche, an engineer with Daimler-Benz before becoming a designer with the Auto-Union racing team in 1930. His son, Terry, formed the Porsche Company 1948 and produced Grand Prix cars, sports cars, and prototypes.

Their Formula One racing car was not successful and it was at sports-car and Can-Am racing that they proved to be more dominant.

Porsche /pɔː∫/ Ferdinand 1875–1951. German car designer. Among his designs were the Volkswagen (German 'people's car'), marketed after World War II, and Porsche sports cars.

Porson /'pɔːsən/ Richard 1759–1808. British classical scholar, professor of Greek at Cambridge from 1792 and editor of ◊Aeschylus and ◊Euripides.

port sweet, fortified (with brandy) dessert wine (red, tawny, or white), from grapes grown in the Douro basin of Portugal and exported from Porto, hence the name.

Port Adelaide /'pɔːt 'ædɪleɪd/ industrial port (cement, chemicals) in South Australia, on Gulf St Vincent, 11 km/7 mi NW of Adelaide; population (1985) 37,000.

Port Arthur /'pɔːt 'ɑːθə/ industrial deepwater port (oil refining, shipbuilding, brass, chemicals) in Texas, USA, 24 km/15 mi SE of Beaumont; population (1980) 61,000. Founded 1895, it gained importance with the discovery of petroleum near Beaumont in 1901.

Port Arthur /'pɔːt 'ɑːθə/ former name (until 1905) of the port and naval base of Lushun in NE China. Scene of a naval engagement between Japan and Russia in 1904.

population

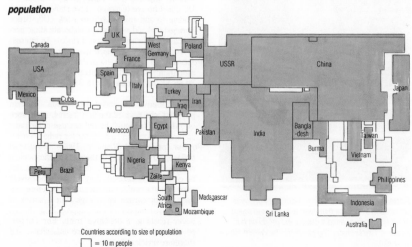

Countries according to size of population
☐ = 10 m people

porcupine

North American porcupine

Port Augusta /ɔːˈgʌstə/ port (trading in wool and grain) in South Australia, at the head of Spencer Gulf, NNW of Adelaide; population (1985) 17,000. Base for the Royal Flying Doctor Service.

Port-au-Prince /ˌpɔːtəʊˈprɪns/ capital and industrial port (sugar, rum, textiles, plastics) of Haiti; population (1982) 763,000.

Port Darwin /ˌpɔːt ˈdɑːwɪn/ port serving ◊Darwin, capital of Northern Territory, Australia.

Port Elizabeth /ɪˈlɪzəbəθ/ industrial port (engineering, steel, food processing) in Cape province, South Africa, about 710 km/440 mi E of Cape Town on Algoa Bay; population (1980) 492,140.

Porter /ˈpɔːtə/ Cole (Albert) 1892–1964. US composer and lyricist of musical comedies. His shows, many of which were made into films, include *The Gay Divorcee* 1932 and *Kiss Me Kate* 1948.

Porter /ˈpɔːtə/ Edwin Stanton 1869–1941. US director of silent films, a pioneer of his time. His 1903 film *The Great Train Robbery* lasted 12 minutes, which for the period was extremely long, and contained an early use of the close-up. More concerned with the technical than the artistic side of his films, which include *The Teddy Bears* 1907 and *The Final Pardon* 1912, Porter abandoned film-making 1916.

Porter /ˈpɔːtə/ Eric 1928– . English actor. His numerous classical roles include title parts in *Uncle Vanya*, *Volpone*, and *King Lear*; on television he played Soames in *The Forsyte Saga*.

Porter /ˈpɔːtə/ Katherine Anne 1890–1980. US writer, born in Texas. She published three volumes of short stories between 1930 and 1944, and the allegorical novel *Ship of Fools* 1962.

Porter /ˈpɔːtə/ Rodney 1917–1985. British biochemist. In 1962 Porter proposed a structure for the antibody, gamma globulin (IgG) in which the molecule was seen as consisting of four chains. Porter was awarded, with Gerald ◊Edelman, the 1972 Nobel Physiology or Medicine Prize.

Port Harcourt /ˈhɑːkɔːt/ port (trading in coal, palm oil, and groundnuts) and capital of Rivers state in SE Nigeria, on the river Bonny in the Niger delta; population (1983) 296,200. It is also an industrial centre producing refined mineral oil, aluminium sheet, tyres, and paints.

Port Kelang /kəˈlæŋ/ Malaysian rubber port (Port Swettenham until 1971) on the Strait of Malacca, 40 km/25 mi SW of Kuala Lumpur. Population (1980) 192,080.

Portland /ˈpɔːtlənd/ industrial port (aluminium, paper, timber, lumber machinery, electronics) and capital of Multnomah county, NW Oregon, USA; on the Columbia river, 173 km/108 mi from the sea, at its confluence with the Willamette river; population (1980) 366,400.

Portland /ˈpɔːtlənd/ industrial port (shipbuilding) and largest city of Maine, USA, on Casco Bay, SE of Sebago Lake; population (1980) 61,500. Birthplace of the poet Longfellow.

Portland /ˈpɔːtlənd/ William Bentinck, 1st Earl of Portland 1649–1709. Dutch politician who accompanied William of Orange to England 1688, and was created an earl 1689. He served in William's campaigns.

Portland /ˈpɔːtlənd/ William Henry Cavendish Bentinck, 3rd Duke of Portland 1738–1809. British politician, originally a Whig, who in 1783 became nominal prime minister in the Fox–North coalition government. During the French Revolution he joined the Tories, and was prime minister 1807–09.

Portland, Isle of /ˈpɔːtlənd/ rocky peninsula off Dorset, S England, joined to the mainland by the ◊Chesil Bank. Portland Castle was built by Henry VIII 1520; Portland harbour is a naval base; building stone is still quarried.

Port Louis /ˈpɔːt ˈluːi/ capital of Mauritius, on the island's NW coast; population (1987) 139,000. Exports include sugar, textiles, watches, and electronic goods.

Port Mahon /pɔːt mɑːˈɒn/ port serving ◊Mahon on the Spanish island of Minorca.

Portmeirion /pɔːtˈmeəriən/ holiday resort in Gwynedd, Wales, built by the architect Clough

Williams-Ellis in Italianate fantasy style; setting of the 1967 cult television series *The Prisoner.*

Port Moresby /ˈmɔːzbi/ capital and port of Papua New Guinea on the S coast of New Guinea; population (1987) 152,000.

Porto /əʊˈpɔːtəʊ/ (English *Oporto*) industrial city (textiles, leather, pottery) in Portugal, on the Douro, 5 km/3 mi from its mouth; population (1984) 327,000. It exports port. It is the second largest city in Portugal, and has a 12th-century cathedral.

Pôrto Alegre /ˈpɔːtəʊ æˈleɪgri/ port and capital of Rio Grande do Sul state, S Brazil; population (1986) 2,705,000. It is a freshwater port for ocean-going vessels, and is Brazil's major commercial centre.

Port-of-Spain /ˈpɔːt əv ˈspeɪn/ port and capital of Trinidad and Tobago, on Trinidad; population (1988) 58,000.

Porton Down /ˈpɔːtn ˈdaʊn/ site of the Chemical Defence Establishment (CDE) of the Ministry of Defence in Wiltshire, SW England. Its prime role is to conduct research into means of protection from chemical attack.

Porto Novo /ˈpɔːtəʊ ˈnəʊvəʊ/ capital of Benin, W Africa; population (1982) 208,258. It was a former Portuguese centre for the slave and tobacco trade with Brazil, and became a French protectorate 1863.

Porto Rico /ˈpɔːtəʊ ˈriːkəʊ/ name until 1932 of ◊Puerto Rico, US island in the Caribbean.

Port Phillip Bay /ˈfɪlɪp/ inlet off Bass Strait, Victoria, Australia, on which Melbourne stands.

Port Pirie /ˈpɪri/ industrial port (smelting of ores from the Broken Hill mines, and chemicals) in S Australia; population (1985) 16,030.

Port Rashid /ræˈʃiːd/ port serving ◊Dubai in the United Arab Emirates.

Port Royal /ˌpɔːt ˈrɔɪəl/ former capital of ◊Jamaica, at the entrance to Kingston harbour.

Port Royal /ˌpɔːt ˈrɔɪəl/ former Cistercian convent, SW of Paris, founded in 1204. In 1626 its inmates were moved to Paris, and the buildings were taken over by a male community which became a centre of Jansenist teaching. During the second half of the 17th century it was subject to periodic persecutions (◊Jansenism being unpopular with the French authorities) and finally in 1709 was dispersed; the following year the buildings were destroyed by order of Louis XIV.

Port Said /saɪd/ port in Egypt, on reclaimed land at the N end of the ◊Suez Canal; population (1983) 364,000. During the 1967 Arab-Israel war the city was damaged and the canal was blocked; Port Said was evacuated by 1969, but by 1975 had been largely reconstructed.

Portsmouth /ˈpɔːtsməθ/ city and naval port in Hampshire, England, opposite the Isle of Wight; population (1981) 179,500.

Portsmouth /ˈpɔːtsməθ/ port in Rockingham county, SE New Hampshire, USA, on the estuary of the river Piscataqua; population (1980) 26,000. The naval base on Seavy's Island specializes in submarine construction and maintenance. Founded in 1623, Portsmouth was the state capital 1679–1775. The treaty ending the Russo-Japanese War was signed here 1905.

Portsmouth /ˈpɔːtsməθ/ port and independent city in SE Virginia, USA, on the Elizabeth River, seat of a US navy yard and training centre, population (1980) 104,577. It also makes textiles, chemicals, fertilizers, raises oysters, and trades in tobacco and cotton.

Portsmouth /ˈpɔːtsməθ/ Louise de Kéroualle, Duchess of Portsmouth 1649–1734. Mistress of Charles II of Britain, a Frenchwoman who came to England as Louis XIV's agent 1670, and was hated by the public.

Port Sunlight a model village built 1888 by W H Lever (1851–1925) for workers at the Lever Brothers soap factory at Birkenhead near Liverpool, NW England. Designed for a population of 3,000, and covering an area of 320 ha/130 acres, it includes an art gallery, church, library, and social hall.

Port Swettenham /ˈswetnəm/ former name of ◊Port Kelang, port in Peninsular Malaysia.

Port Talbot /ˈtɔːlbət/ industrial port (tinplate and steel strip mill) in W Glamorgan, Wales; population (1981) 47,500.

Portugal /ˈpɔːtjʊgəl/ country in SW Europe, on the Atlantic, bounded to the N and E by Spain.

government The 1976 constitution, revised 1982, provides for a president, elected by universal suffrage for a five-year term, and a single-chamber, 250-member assembly, similarly elected and serving a four-year term. The president, an active politician rather than a figurehead, appoints a prime minister who chooses the council of ministers, responsible to the assembly. A council of state, chaired by the president, acts as a supreme national advisory body.

history Portugal originated in the 11th century as a country subject to ◊León, while the south was ruled by the ◊Moors. It became an independent monarchy in the reign of Alfonso I (1128–85), who captured Lisbon 1147. Alfonso III (1248–79) expelled the Moors. During the 13th century the *Cortes*, an assembly representing nobles, clergy, and cities, began to meet and secured control of taxation. A commercial treaty with England was signed 1294 and an alliance established 1373. During the 15th century Portuguese mariners explored the African coast, opened the sea route to India, and reached Brazil, and colonists followed in the 16th century.

In 1580 Philip II of Spain seized the crown. The Portuguese rebelled against Spanish rule 1640, placed the house of Braganza on the throne, and after a long war forced Spain to recognize their independence 1668. Portugal fought as the ally of Britain in the War of the Spanish Succession. France invaded Portugal 1807–11 (see ◊Peninsular War). A strong democratic movement developed and after a civil war 1828–34, constitutional government was established. Carlos I was assassinated 1908; his son Manuel II was driven from the country by a revolution 1910 and a republic was proclaimed.

Portugal remained economically weak and corrupt until the start of the dictatorship of Dr Antonio de Oliveira ◊Salazar, prime minister from 1928. Social conditions were improved at the cost of personal liberties.

Salazar was succeeded as prime minister 1968 by Dr Marcello Caetano, who proved unable to liberalize the political system or deal with the costly wars in Portugal's colonies of Angola and Mozambique. Criticisms of his administration led to a military coup Apr 1974 to 'save the nation from government'. The Junta of National Salvation was set up, headed by Gen Antonio Ribeiro de Spinola. He became president a month later, with a military colleague replacing the civilian prime minister.

The new president promised liberal reforms, but after disagreements within the Junta, Spinola resigned Sept 1974 and was replaced by Gen Francisco da Costa Gomes. In 1975 there was a swing to the left among the military and President Gomes narrowly avoided a communist coup by collaborating with the leader of the moderate Socialist Party (PS), Mario ◊Soares. In 1976 Portugal's first free assembly elections in 50 years were held. The PS won 36% of the vote and Soares formed a minority government. The army chief, Gen Antonio Ramalho ◊Eanes, won the presidency, with the support of centre and left-of-centre parties.

After surviving precariously for over two years, Soares resigned 1978. A period of political instability followed, with five prime ministers in two and a half years, until, in Dec 1980, President Eanes invited Dr Francisco Balsema a co-founder of the Social Democratic Party (PSD), to form a centre-party coalition. Dr Balsema survived many challenges to his leadership, and in Aug 1982 the assembly approved his draft of a new constitution, which would reduce the powers of the president and move the country to a fully civilian government. In 1983 Soares entered a coalition with the PSD, whose leader was now the former finance minister, Professor Aníbal Cavaco Silva. In June 1985 the PS-PSD coalition broke up and a premature general election was called. Cavaco Silva formed a minority government, and was able to form a majority government after a landslide victory for the PSD July 1987. He has increased economic growth and raised living standards, and favours a free market and privatization.

In the 1986 presidential election Soares won a surprising victory to become Portugal's first civilian president for 60 years. He promised a more open and cooperative presidency. Portugal entered the European Community 1986, and is a committed member of NATO. In July 1987 the Social Democrats won an absolute majority in parliament, with the PRD and Communists both losing seats.

Portugal: former colonies

Name	Colonized	Independent
Brazil	1532	1822
Uruguay	1533	1828
Mozambique	1505	1975
Angola	1941	1975

Portuguese East Africa former name of ◊Mozambique.

Portuguese Guinea /'gɪni/ former name of ◊Guinea-Bissau.

Portuguese language a member of the Romance branch of the Indo-European language family, the national language of Portugal, closely related to Spanish and strongly influenced by Arabic. It is also spoken in Brazil, Angola, Mozambique, and other former Portuguese colonies.

Portuguese literature under Provençal influence, medieval Portuguese literature produced popular ballads and troubadour songs, and the Renaissance stimulated the outstanding work of the dramatist Gil Vicente, and the lyric and epic poet Camöens. In the 17th and 18th centuries there was a decline to

Portugal
Republic of
(República Portuguesa)

area 92,000 sq km/35,521 sq mi (including Azores and Madeira)
capital Lisbon
towns Coimbra, ports Porto, Setúbal
physical mountainous in the N, plains in the S
features rivers Minho, Douro, Tagus, Guadiana; Serra da Estrélla
head of state Mario Alberto Nobre Lopes Soares from 1986
head of government Cavaco Silva from 1985
government democratic republic
political parties Social Democratic Party (PSD), moderate, left-of-centre; Socialist Party (PS), progressive socialist; Democratic Renewal Party (PRD), centre-left; Democratic Social Centre Party (CDS) , moderate, left-of-centre
exports port wine, olive oil, resin, cork, sardines, textiles, pottery, pulpwood

currency escudo (251.45 = £1 Feb 1990)
population (1989) 10,240,000; annual growth rate 0.7%
life expectancy men 68, women 75
language Portuguese, one of the Romance languages, ultimately derived from Latin, but considerably influenced later by Arabic
religion Roman Catholic
literacy 89% male/80% female (1985)
GDP $19.4 bn (1984); $1,930 per head of population
chronology
1928–68 Military dictatorship under Antonio de Oliveira Salazar.
1968 Salazar succeeded by Marcello Caetano.
1974 Caetano removed in a military coup led by Gen Antonio Ribeiro de Spinola. Spinola was then replaced by Gen Fransisco da Costa Gomes.
1975 African colonies became independent.
1976 New constitution, providing for a gradual return to civilian rule, adopted. Minority government appointed, led by the Socialist Party leader Mario Soares.
1978 Soares resigned.
1980 Francisco Balsema formed a centre-party coalition after two and a half years of political instability.
1982 Draft of new constitution approved, reducing the powers of the presidency.
1983 Centre-left coalition government formed.
1985 Cavaco Silva became prime minister.
1986 Mario Soares elected first civilian president for 60 years. Portugal joined European Community.
1987 Soares re-elected with large majority.
1988 Portugal joined the Western European Union.
1989 Constitution amended to allow state undertakings to be denationalised.

formality, but the *Letters of a Portuguese Nun*, supposed to have been written by Marianna Alcoforado, were a poignant exception, and found echoes in the modern revolutionary period. No single figure has achieved international acclaim among the varied writers of the 19th and 20th centuries, although there is a lively tradition of writing in Brazil, and Angola developed its own school of Portuguese-African poetry.

Portuguese man-of-war coelenterate with the appearance of a large jellyfish. There is a gas-filled float on the surface, below which hang feeding, stinging, and reproductive individuals. The float can be 30 cm/1 ft long.

Portuguese West Africa former name of ◊Angola.

Poseidon /pə'saɪdn/ Greek god (Roman Neptune), the brother of Zeus and Pluto. The brothers dethroned their father, Kronos, and divided his realm, Poseidon taking the sea; he was also worshipped as god of earthquakes. His son was ◊Triton.

Posen /'pəʊzən/ German form of ◊Poznań, city in Poland.

Poseidon *The Temple of Poseidon (northeast corner), Cape Sounion, Greece .*

positivism a theory associated with the French philosopher Comte (1798–1857), and ◊empiricism, which confines genuine knowledge within the bounds of science and observation. The theory is hostile to theology and to metaphysics which oversteps this boundary. ***Logical positivism*** developed in the 1920s. It rejected any metaphysical world beyond everyday science and common sense, and confined statements to those of formal logic or mathematics. It was influential through the work of A J Ayer and the Vienna circle.

On the basis of positivism, Comte constructed his 'Religion of Humanity', in which the object of adoration was the Great Being, that is, the personification of humanity as a whole.

positron an ◊elementary particle, produced in some radioactive ◊decay processes, which is similar in every respect to an ◊electron, except that it carries a positive ◊electric charge. It is thus the ◊antiparticle to the electron. When a positron and electron collide they anihilate each other to produce gamma radiation.

positron emission tomography (PET) a technique that enables doctors to observe the operation of the human body by following the progress of a radioactive chemical that has been inhaled or injected. PET scanners pinpoint the location of the chemical by bombarding the body with low energy ◊gamma radiation. The technique has been used to study a wide range of diseases including schizophrenia, Alzheimer's disease, and Parkinson's disease.

possum Australian name for many of the smaller marsupials found in Australia (shortened form of opossum). The tiny ***honey possum*** *Tarsipes spencerae* has a long tongue to take nectar from flowers. The big ***gliding possum*** *Schoinobates volans* can glide 100 m/300 ft or more on the huge membrane stretched between front and back limbs. The ***brush possum*** *Trichosurus vulpecula* has become very common in New Zealand after being introduced.

postal service the system for delivering mail. In Britain regular permanent systems were not created until the emergence of modern nation state. Henry VIII in 1516 appointed Brian Tuke as Master of the Posts, to maintain a regular service on the main roads from London. Postmasters (usually innkeepers) passed the mail to the next post, and supplied horses for the royal couriers; private people wishing to send letters or to travel themselves 'post haste' were permitted to use the service. Private services were discouraged to avoid losing revenue for the state service and assisting treasonable activities, the latter point being stressed by the act establishing the Post Office, passed under ◊Cromwell in 1657. Mail coaches first ran in 1784, and in 1840 Rowland Hill's prepaid penny postage stamp, for any distance within the UK, led to a massive increase in use. Services were extended to registered post 1841; post boxes 1855 (see Anthony ◊Trollope); savings bank 1861; postcards 1870; postal orders 1881, parcel post 1883, air mail 1911, telephone 1912, data processing by computer 1967, and giro 1968. In 1969 the original General Post Office ceased to be a government department, and was split into two, the Post Office and ◊British Telecom. International cooperation is through the Universal Postal Union, 1875, at Berne.

postcard a card with space for a written message that can be sent through the mail without an envelope. The postcard's inventor was Emmanual Hermann, of Vienna, who in 1869 proposed a 'postal telegram', sent at a lower fee than a normal letter with an envelope. The first picture postcard was produced 1894.

The postcard, typically 14×9 cm/5.5×3.5 in, rapidly gained popularity after the introduction of the picture postcard. From 1902 the address could be written on the back, leaving the whole of the front for the illustration. Subjects included topographical views, reproductions of paintings, photographs of film stars, and sentimental drawings; common in Britain was the seaside comic postcard, typically illustrated by Donald McGill (1875–1962).

poster advertising announcement for public display, often illustrated, first produced in France during the mid-19th century, when colour ◊lithography came into its own.

Poster artists include Jules Chéret, Millais, Toulouse-Lautrec, and Charles Dana Gibson. Poster art flourished again in the 1960s, with an emphasis on psychedelic art and artists such as Rick Griffin, Peter Max, and Stanley Mouse in the USA; Michael English and Martin Sharp in the UK.

Post-Impressionism Paul Gauguin's Ea Haere la Oe Go! (1893), Hermitage, Leningrad. The Post-Impressionists were passionate in their pursuit of meaning in art. Gauguin found a new world of symbolism in the South Sea Islands.

poste restante (French) a system whereby mail is sent to a certain post office and kept there until collected by the addressee.

post hoc, ergo propter hoc (Latin) after this, therefore on account of this.

Post-Impressionism the various styles of painting that followed Impressionism in the 1880s and 1890s. The term was first used by the British critic Roger Fry in 1911 to describe the works of Cézanne, van Gogh, and Gauguin. These painters moved away from the spontaneity of Impressionism, attempting to give their work more serious meaning and permanence.

Post-Modernism a late 20th-century movement in the arts that rejects the preoccupation of ◊Modernism with form and technique rather than content. In the visual arts, and in architecture, it uses an amalgam of styles from the past, such as the classical and the baroque, whose slightly off-key familiarity has a more immediate appeal than the austerities of Modernism.

post mortem (Latin 'after death') dissection of a dead body to determine the cause of death. It is also known as an ◊autopsy.

Post Office (PO) a government department or authority with responsibility for postal services and telecommunications.

In the UK, the first Master of the Post was appointed 1516 with a limited brief, and in 1635, there was a royal proclamation 'for the settling of the letter office in England and Scotland', establishing the first public service. The service developed and expanded rapidly, with financial services being provided by the 18th century. It has responsibility for paying out social security and collecting revenue for state insurance schemes. Post Office activities were divided 1981 to separate telecommunications activities, and in 1984, these were privatized, and a new company, British Telecom, was established.

post scriptum (abbreviation PS; Latin) something written below the signature on a letter.

potash general name for any potassium-containing mineral, most often applied to potassium carbonate (K_2CO_3). Potash, originally made by roasting plants to ashes in earthenware pots, is commercially produced from the mineral sylvite (potassium chloride, KCl) and is used mainly in making artificial fertilizers, glass, and soap.

The potassium content of soils and fertilizers is also commonly expressed as potash, although usually meaning potassium oxide (K_2O).

potassium metallic element of the alkali group, symbol K, atomic number 19, relative atomic mass 39.1. It is a soft, silvery-bright metal which reacts violently with water, forming potassium hydroxide and hydrogen; this ignites and burns spontaneously with a violet flame. The element is therefore kept under kerosene or naphtha. The salts are important as essential constituents of fertilizers. Alloyed with sodium, it may be used as a coolant in nuclear reactors.

Widely distributed in nature in combination with other elements, it is found in salt deposits (carnallite and kainite) and minerals (feldspar, greensand, alunite, leucite), and forms 2.9% of the Earth's solid crust. It was discovered 1807 by Humphry Davy by electrolysis of caustic potash (KOH), the first instance of a metal being isolated by an electric current.

potato perennial plant *Solanum tuberosum*, family Solanaceae, with edible tuberous roots that are rich in starch. Used by the Andean Indians for at least 2,000 years before the Spanish Conquest, the potato was introduced to Europe by the mid-16th century, and reputedly to England by Walter Raleigh. In Ireland, the potato famine in 1845, caused by a parasitic fungus, resulted in many thousands of deaths, and led to large-scale emigration to the USA. See also ***sweet potato*** under ◊yam.

Potchefstroom /ˈpɒtʃəfstrəʊm/ oldest town in the Transvaal, South Africa on the river Mooi, founded by ◊Boers trekking from the Cape 1838. It is the centre of a large cattle-rearing area.

poteen Irish alcoholic liquor traditionally made from potatoes, or barley and yeast, in illicit stills.

Potemkin /pəˈtemkɪn/ Grigory Aleksandrovich, Prince Potemkin 1739–1791. Russian politician. He entered the army and attracted the notice of Catherine II, whose friendship he kept throughout his life. He was an active adminstrator who reformed the army, built the Black Sea Fleet, conquered the Crimea, developed S Russia, and founded the Kherson arsenal 1788 (the first Russian naval base on the Black Sea).

potential difference see ◊potential, electric

potential, electric the relative electrical state of an object. A charged ◊conductor, for example, has a higher potential than the earth, whose potential is taken by convention to be zero. An electric ◊cell has a potential in terms to e.m.f. (◊electromotive force) which can make current flow in an external circuit. The difference in potential between two points—the potential difference—is expressed in ◊volts; that is, a 12V battery has a potential difference of 12 volts between its negative and positive terminals.

potential energy ◊energy possessed by an object by virtue of its position or state. It is contrasted with ◊kinetic energy.

potentiometer in physics, an electrical ◊resistor that can be divided so as to compare or measure voltages. A simple type consists of a length of uniform resistance wire (about 1 m/3 ft long) carrying a constant current provided by a cell connected across the ends of the wire. The source of potential difference (voltage) to be measured is connected (to oppose the cell) between one end of the wire, through a ◊galvanometer (instrument for measuring small currents), to a contact free to slide along the wire. The sliding contact is moved until the galvanometer shows no deflection. The ratio of the length of potentiometer wire in the galvanometer circuit to the total length of wire is then equal to the ratio of the unknown potential difference to that of the cell. In radio circuits, any rotary variable resistance (such as volume control) may be referred to as a potentiometer.

Potomac /pəˈtəʊmək/ river in W Virginia, Virginia and Maryland states, USA, rising in the Allegheny mountains, and flowing SE through Washington, DC, into Chesapeake Bay. It is formed by the junction of the N Potomac, about 153 km/95 mi long, and S Potomac, about 209 km/130 mi long, and is itself 459 km/285 mi long.

Potosí /ˌpɒtəʊˈsiː/ town in SW Bolivia, standing on the Cerro de Potosí slopes at 4,020 m/13,189 ft, it is among the highest towns in the world; population (1982) 103,000. Silver, tin, lead, and copper are mined here. It was founded by Spaniards 1545; during the 17th and 18th centuries it was the chief silver mining town and most important city in South America.

potpourri mixture of dried flowers and leaves, for example, rose petals, lavender, and verbena, used to scent the air.

Potsdam /ˈpɒtsdæm/ capital of Potsdam county, East Germany, on the river Havel W of Berlin; population (1986) 140,000. Products include textiles, pharmaceuticals, and electrical goods. The New Palace 1763–70 and Sans Souci were both built by Frederick the Great, and Hitler's Third Reich was proclaimed in the garrison church 21 Mar 1933. The Potsdam Conference took place here. Potsdam county has an area of 12,570 sq km/4,852 sq mi, and a population of 1,120,000.

Potsdam Conference conference held at Potsdam (in what is now East Germany) July 1945 between representatives of the USA, the UK, and the USSR. They established the political and economic principles governing the treatment of Germany in the initial period of Allied control at the end of World War II, and sent an ultimatum to Japan demanding unconditional surrender on pain of utter destruction.

Potter /ˈpɒtə/ Beatrix 1866–1943. English writer and illustrator of children's books, beginning with *Peter Rabbit* 1900; her diaries, written in a secret

Potter Although she grew up in London, Beatrix Potter was always interested in nature. Her classic picture books began as a series of letters to children.

code, were translated and published 1966. Her Lake District home is a museum.

Potter /'pɒtə/ Paulus 1625–1654. Dutch painter, active in Delft, The Hague, and Amsterdam. He is known for paintings of animals, such as *The Young Bull* 1647 (Mauritshuis, The Hague).

Potter /'pɒtə/ Stephen 1900–1969. British author of humorous studies in how to outwit and outshine others, including *Gamesmanship* 1947, *Lifemanship* 1950, and *One Upmanship* 1952.

Potteries, the /'pɒtəriz/ the centre of the china and earthenware industry in England, lying in the upper Trent basin of N Staffordshire. Wedgwood and Minton are factory names associated with the Potteries, which cover the area around Stoke-on-Trent, and include the formerly separate towns of Burslem, Hanley, Longton, Fenton, and Tunstall.

pottery a type of ◊ceramic ware in domestic and ornamental use ranging from opaque and porous earthenware through translucent bone china (5% calcined bone) to finest ◊porcelain.

pottery and porcelain ◊ceramics in domestic and ornamental use including:

earthenware made of porous clay and fired, whether unglazed (when it remains porous, for example, flowerpots, winecoolers) or glazed (most tableware).

stoneware made of non-porous clay with a high silica content, fired at high temperature, which is very hard.

bone china (softpaste) semi-porcelain made of 5% bone ash and ◊china clay; first made in the West in imitation of Chinese porcelain.

porcelain (hardpaste) characterized by its hardness, ringing sound when struck, translucence, and shining finish, like that of a cowrie shell (Italian *porcellana*); made of kaolin and petuntse (fusible feldspar consisting chiefly of quartz, and reduced to a fine, white powder); first developed in China.

BC 10,000 earliest known pottery in Japan

c.5000 potter's wheel developed by the Egyptians

c.600–450 black and red figured vases from Greece

AD 6th century fine quality stoneware developed in China, as the forerunner of porcelain

7–10th century Tang porcelain in China

10–13th century Song porcelain in China

14–17th century Ming porcelain in China; Hispano-Moresque ware

16th century Majolica Italian tin-glazed earthenware with painted decoration, often large dishes with figures;

faience (from ◊Faenza) name applied both to this and delftware

17th century Chinese porcelain first imported to the West; it was soon brought in large quantities

poultry

a battery hen

(for example, the Nanking Cargo) as a ballast in tea clippers;

delftware tin-glazed earthenware brought to perfection in ◊Delft, especially the white with blue decoration, also copied in England

18th century Dresden in 1710 the first European hardpaste porcelain was made in Dresden by Böttger 1682–1719; the factory later transferred to Meissen

Sèvres from 1769 hardpaste porcelain as well as softpaste made in ◊Sèvres, France, remarkable for its ground colours;

*Wedgwood c.*1760 cream-coloured earthenware perfected (superseding delftware) by ◊Wedgwood; he also devised stoneware, typically with white decoration in Neo-Classical designs on a blue ground, still among the wares made in Barlaston, Staffordshire, England;

English softpaste made *c.*1745–1810, first in Chelsea, later in Bow, Derby, and Worcester.

English hardpaste first made in Plymouth 1768–70, and Bristol 1770–81, when the stock was removed to New Hall in Staffordshire;

*bone china c.*1789 first produced by Josiah Spode (1754–1827); Coalport, near Shrewsbury, and ◊Minton followed as did all English tableware of this type from 1815

19th century large-scale production of fine wares, in Britain notably ◊Royal Worcester from 1862, and Royal (Crown) Derby from 1876

20th century there has been a revival in the craft of the individual potter, for example, Bernard Leach, Lucie Rie.

potto arboreal, nocturnal, African mammal *Perodicticus potto* belonging to the loris family of primates. It has a thick body, strong limbs, grasping feet and hands, and grows to 40 cm/16 in long. It has horny spines along its backbone, which it uses in self-defence. It climbs slowly, and eats insects, snails, fruit, and leaves.

poujadist member of an extreme right-wing political movement in France led by Pierre Poujade (1920–) which was prominent in French politics 1954–58. Known in France as the Union de Défence des Commerçants et Artisands, it won 52 seats in the national election 1956. Its voting strength came mainly from the lower-middle-class and petit-bourgeois sections of society but the return of ◊de Gaulle to power 1958, and the foundation of the Fifth Republic led to a rapid decline in the movement's fortunes.

Poulenc /'puːlæŋk/ Francis (Jean Marcel) 1899–1963. French composer and pianist. A self-taught composer of witty and irreverent music, he was a member of the group of French composers known as ◊Les Six. Among his many works are the operas *Les Mamelles de Tirésias* 1947 and *Dialogues des Carmélites* 1957, and the ballet *Les Biches* 1923.

Poulsen /'pəulsən/ Valdemar 1869–1942. Danish engineer who in 1900 was the first to demonstrate that sound could be recorded magnetically—originally on a moving steel wire or tape; this was the forerunner of the tape recorder.

poultry domestic birds such as ducks, geese, turkeys, and chickens.

Good egg-laying breeds of chicken are Leghorns, Minorcas, Marans, and Anconas; varieties most suitable for eating are Dorkings and Indian Game; those useful for both purposes are Orpingtons, Rhode Island Reds, Wyandottes, and Plymouth Rocks. Most farm poultry are hybrids, selectively bred for certain characteristics, including feathers and down.

Since World War II, the development of battery-produced eggs and intensive breeding of broiler fowls and turkeys has roused a public outcry against 'factory' methods of farming. The birds are often kept in small cages constantly, have their beaks amputated to prevent pecking of their neighbours, and are given food full of growth hormones and antibacterial drugs, which eventually make their way up the food chain to humans. Factory farming has led to a growing interest in deep-litter and free-range systems, although these only account for a small percentage of total production.

Factory farming has doubled egg yields and increased the availability of poultry meat. In 1988, over 450 million chickens and 30 million turkeys were sold in the UK for meat.

POUM acronym for *Partido Obrero de Unificación Marxista* ('Workers' Marxist Union Party') a small Spanish anti-Stalinist communist party led by Andrés Nin and Joaquín Maurín, prominent during the Spanish Civil War. Since Republican Spain received most of its external help from the USSR, the Spanish communist party used this to force the suppression of the POUM in 1937. POUM supporters included George Orwell, who chronicled events in his book *Homage to Catalonia*.

pound imperial unit (symbol lb) of mass. The commonly used avoirdupois pound, also called the *imperial standard pound* (7,000 grains/0.45 kg), differs from the *troy pound* (5,760 grains/0.37 kg), which is used for weighing precious metals. It derives from the Roman *libra*, which weighed 0.327 kg.

pound British standard monetary unit, issued as a gold sovereign before 1914, as a note 1914–83, and as a circular yellow metal alloy coin from 1983. The edge inscriptions are: 1983 *Decus et tutamen* 'An ornament and a safeguard'; 1984 (Scottish) *Nemo me impune lacessit* 'No one injures me with impunity'; 1985 (Welsh) *Pleidiol wyf i'm gwlad* 'True am I to my country', from the national anthem.

The *green pound* is the European Community exchange rate for conversion of EC farm prices to sterling. The pound sterling is also the unit of currency in Egypt, the Falkland Islands, Gibraltar, Lebanon, Malta, St Helena, Sudan, and Syria.

Pound /paund/ Ezra 1885–1972. US poet, who lived in London from 1908. His verse *Personae* and *Exultations* 1909 established the principles of

Pound US poet Ezra Pound founded the Imagist movement and influenced W B Yeats and James Joyce, but his mental instability led to 13 years in a psychiatric hospital.

the ◊Imagist movement. His largest Modern work was the series of *Cantos* 1925–1969 (intended to number 100), which attempted a massive re-appraisal of history.

In Paris 1921–25, he was a friend of US writers Gertrude Stein and Hemingway, and then settled in Rapallo, Italy. His anti-Semitism and sympathy with the fascist dictator Mussolini led him to broadcast from Italy in World War II, and he was arrested by US troops 1945. Found unfit to plead, he was confined in a mental hospital until 1958.

His first completely Modern poem was *Hugh Selwyn Mauberley* 1920. He also wrote versions of Old English, Provençal, Chinese, ancient Egyptian, and other verse.

poundal imperial unit (symbol pdl) of force, now replaced in the SI system by the ◊newton. One poundal = 0.1383 newtons. It is defined as the force necessary to accelerate a mass of 1 lb by 1 ft per second per second.

Poussin /puːˈsæŋ/ Nicolas 1594–1665. French painter, active chiefly in Rome; court painter to Louis XIII 1640–43. He was one of France's foremost landscape painters in the 17th century. He painted mythological and literary scenes in a strongly classical style, for example *Rape of the Sabine Women* about 1636–37 (Metropolitan Museum of Art, New York).

Poussin went to Rome 1624 and studied Roman sculpture in the studio of ◊Domenichino. His style reflects painstaking preparation: he made small wax models of the figures in his paintings, experimenting with different compositions and lighting. Colour was subordinate to line.

poverty the condition that exists when the basic needs of human beings are not being met, particularly shelter, food, and clothing.

In many countries, poverty is common and persistent, being reflected in poor nutrition, low life expectancy, and high levels of infant mortality. It may result from a country's complete lack of resources, and an inability to achieve economic development.

Many different definitions of poverty exist, since there is little agreement on the standard of living (known as the *poverty level*) considered to be the minimum adequate level by the majority of people.

Poverty Bay /ˈpɒvəti ˈbeɪ/ inlet on the E coast of North Island, New Zealand, on which the port of Gisborne stands. Captain ◊Cook made his first landing here 1769.

powder metallurgy a method of shaping heat-resistant metals such as tungsten. Metal powder is pressed into a mould and then sintered (heated to very high temperatures).

Powell /ˈpaʊəl/ (John) Enoch 1912– . British Conservative politician. He was minister of health 1960–63, and contested the party leadership 1965. In 1968 he made a speech against immigration that led to his dismissal from the shadow cabinet. He resigned from the party 1974, and was Official Unionist Party member for South Down, Northern Ireland 1974–87.

Powell /ˈpaʊəl/ Anthony (Dymoke) 1905– . English novelist, who wrote the monumental series of 12 volumes *A Dance to the Music of Time* 1951–75, which begins shortly after World War I and chronicles a period of 50 years in the lives of Nicholas Jenkins and his circle of upper-class friends.

Powell /ˈpaʊəl/ Cecil Frank 1903–1969. English physicist, awarded a Nobel prize 1950 for his use of photographic emulsion as a method of tracking charged nuclear particles.

Powell /ˈpaʊəl/ Michael 1905–1990. English film director, who collaborated with screenwriter Emeric Pressburger (1902–88). Their work, often criticized for extravagance, is richly imaginative, and includes the films *A Matter of Life and Death* 1946 and *Black Narcissus* 1947.

Powell /ˈpaʊəl/ William 1892–1984. US film actor who co-starred with Myrna Loy in the *Thin Man* series of films 1934–1947. He also played leading roles in *My Man Godfrey* 1936, *Life with*

Father 1947, and *Mister Roberts* 1955. He retired 1955.

power in mathematics, power, also called an index or exponent, is denoted by a superior small numeral. A number or symbol raised to the power 2, that is, multiplied by itself, is said to be squared (for example, 3^2, x^2) and something raised to the power three is said to be cubed (for example, 2^3, y^3).

power in physics, the rate of doing work or consuming energy. It is measured in watts, or other units of work per unit time.

powerboat a ◊motorboat used for racing.

power of attorney in English law, legal authority to act on behalf of another, for a specific transaction, or for a particular period. From 1986 powers of attorney may, in certain circumstances, remain valid when the person who granted the power subsequently becomes mentally incapable.

power station building where electrical power is generated (see ◊electricity). The largest in Europe is the Drax near Selby, Yorkshire, which supplies 10% of Britain's electricity.

Powys /ˈpaʊɪs/ county in central Wales
area 5,080 sq km/1,961 sq mi
towns administrative headquarters Llandrindod Wells
features Brecon Beacons National Park, Black mountains, rivers Wye and Severn, which both rise on Plynlimon (see ◊Dyfed); Lake Vyrnwy, artificial reservoir supplying Liverpool and Birmingham, and same size as Lake ◊Bala; alternative technology centre near Machynlleth
products agriculture, dairy cattle, sheep
population (1987) 113,000
language 20% Welsh, rest English.

Powys /ˈpaʊɪs/ John Cowper 1872–1963. English novelist. His mystic and erotic books include *Wolf Solent* 1929 and *A Glastonbury Romance* 1933. He was one of three brothers (*Theodore Francis Powys* 1875–1953 and *Llewelyn Powys* 1884–1939), all writers.

Poynter /ˈpɔɪntə/ Edward John 1836–1919. British artist, first head of the Slade School of Fine Art, London, 1871–75, and president of the Royal Academy in succession to ◊Millais. He produced decorous nudes, mosaic panels for Westminster Palace 1870, and scenes from ancient Greece and Rome.

Poznań /ˈpɒznæn/ (German *Posen*) industrial city (machinery, aircraft, beer) in W Poland; population (1985) 553,000. Settled by German immigrants 1253, it passed to Prussia 1793, but was restored to Poland 1919.

Pozsgay /ˈpɒzɡaɪ/ Imre 1933– . Hungarian socialist politician, presidential candidate for the Hungarian Socialist Party from 1989. Influential in the democratization of Hungary 1988–89, he was rejected by the electorate in the parliamentary elections of Mar 1990, coming a poor third in his constituency.

Pozsgay joined the ruling Hungarian Socialist Workers' Party (HSWP) 1950 and was a lecturer in Marxism-Leninism and an ideology chief in Bacs county 1957–70. He was minister of education and culture from 1976, before becoming head of the Patriotic People's Front umbrella organization 1982. Noted for his reformist social-democratic instincts, he was brought into the HSWP Politburo in 1988 as a move towards political pluralism began. Having publicly declared that 'communism does not work', he helped remould the HSWP into the new Hungarian Socialist Party 1989 and was selected as its candidate for the presidency.

Pozzuoli /ˌpɒtsuˈəʊli/ port in Campania, S Italy, W of Naples; population (1981) 71,000. It is shaken by some 25 earthquakes a day, 60% of its buildings are uninhabitable, and an eventual major disaster seems inevitable.

pp abbreviation for *per procurationem* (Latin 'by proxy'); in music, the abbreviation for *pianissimo* (Italian 'very softly').

PR abbreviation for *public relations*, or ◊*proportional representation*.

Prado /ˈprɑːdəʊ/ Spanish art gallery (*Réal Museo de Pintura del Prado*/Royal Picture Gallery of the

Powys

Prado), containing the national collection of pictures, founded by Charles III in 1785.

praemunire title of three English acts of Parliament passed 1353, 1365, and 1393, aimed to prevent appeal to the pope against the power of the king, and therefore an early demonstration of independence from Rome. The statutes were opposed by English bishops.

praesidium the executive committee of the Supreme Soviet in the USSR; the ◊Politburo was known as the praesidium 1952–66.

praetor in ancient Rome, a magistrate, elected annually, who assisted the ◊consuls and presided over the civil courts. After a year in office, a praetor would act as a provincial governor for a further year. The number of praetors was finally increased to eight.

pragmatism a philosophical tradition that interprets truth in terms of the practical effects of what is believed, and in particular the usefulness of these effects. The US philosopher Peirce is often accounted the founder of pragmatism; it was further advanced by William James.

Prague /prɑːɡ/ (Czech *Praha*) city and capital of Czechoslovakia on the river Vltava; population (1985) 1,190,000. Industries include cars and aircraft, chemicals, paper and printing, clothing, brewing, and food processing. It became the capital 1918.

Praha /ˈprɑːhɑː/ Czech name for ◊Prague.

Praia /ˈpraɪə/ port and capital of the Republic of Cape Verde, on the island of São Tiago (Santiago); population (1980) 37,500. Industries include fishing and shipping.

prairie the central North American plain, formerly grass-covered, extending over most of the region between the Rockies on the west and the Great Lakes and Ohio river on the east.

prairie dog a burrowing rodent. See ◊marmot.

Prakrit /ˈprɑːkrɪt/ a general name for the ancient Indo-European dialects of N India, contrasted with the sacred classical language Sanskrit. The word is itself Sanskrit, meaning 'natural', as opposed to *Sanskrit*, which means 'perfected'. The Prakrits are considered to be the ancestors of such modern N Indian languages as Hindi, Punjabi, and Bengali.

Prasad /prəˈsɑːd/ Rajendra 1884–1963. Bihari lawyer, politician, and follower of Mohandas Gandhi in Bihar. Prior to World War II, he succeeded Subhas Chandra Bose as national president of the Indian National Congress. He went on to become India's first president after independence.

praseodymium a silver-white metallic element, symbol Pr, atomic number 59, relative atomic mass 140.098. It is a member of the lanthanide series of elements, and occurs naturally in monazite and bastnasite. It is used in carbon-arc lights and as a pigment in glass.

Prato /ˈprɑːtəʊ/ industrial town (woollens) in Tuscany, central Italy; population (1988) 165,000.

The 12th-century cathedral has works of art by Donatello, Filippo Lippi, and Andrea della Robbia.

prawn shrimplike member of the suborder Natantia ('swimming'), order Decapoda, as contrasted with lobsters and crayfish, which are able to 'walk'. The *common prawn Leander serratus*, of temperate seas has a long saw-edged spike or rostrum just in front of its eyes, and antennae much longer than its body length. It is distinguished from the shrimp not only by its larger size, but by having pincers on its second pair of legs.

Praxiteles /præk'sɪtəliːz/ mid-4th century BC. Greek sculptor, active in Athens. His *Aphrodite of Knidos* about 350 BC (known through Roman copies) is thought to have initiated the tradition of life-size freestanding female nudes in Greek sculpture.

prayer address to divine power, ranging from a magical formula to attain a desired end, to selfless communication in meditation. Within Christianity the Catholic and Orthodox churches sanction prayer to the Virgin Mary, angels, and saints as intercessors, whereas Protestantism limits prayer to God alone.

preadaptation in biology, the fortuitous possession of a character that allows an organism to exploit a new situation. In many cases, the character evolves to solve a particular problem that a species encounters in its preferred habitat, but once evolved may allow the organism to exploit an entirely different situation. Thus the ability to extract oxygen directly from the air evolved in some early fishes, probably in response to life in stagnant, deoxygenated pools; this later made it possible for their descendants to spend time on land, so giving rise eventually to the air-breathing amphibians.

Precambrian in geology, the time from the formation of Earth (4.6 billion years ago) up to 590 million years ago. Its boundary with the succeeding Cambrian period marks the time when animals first developed hard outer parts (exoskeletons) and so left abundant fossil remains. It comprises about 85% of geological time and is divided into two periods: the Archaean and the Proterozoic.

precedent the ◊common law principle that, in deciding a particular case, judges are bound to follow any applicable principles of law laid down by superior courts in earlier reported cases.

precession a slow wobble of the Earth on its axis, like that of a spinning top. The gravitational pulls of the Sun and Moon on the Earth's equatorial bulge cause the Earth's axis to trace out a circle on the sky every 25,360 years. The position of the celestial poles (see ◊celestial sphere) is constantly changing owing to precession, as are the positions of the equinoxes (the points at which the celestial equator intersects the Sun's path around the sky). The *precession of the equinoxes* means that there is a slow but steady drift in the coordinates of objects on the celestial sphere; this is why the dates of the astrological signs of the zodiac no longer correspond to the times of year when the Sun actually passes through the constellations. For example, the Sun passes through Leo from mid-Aug to mid-Sept, but the astrological dates for Leo are between about 23 July and 22 Aug.

precipitation meteorological term for water that falls to the Earth from the atmosphere. It includes ◊rain, ◊snow, sleet, ◊hail, ◊dew, and ◊frost.

predestination in Christian theology, the doctrine asserting that God has determined all events beforehand, including the ultimate salvation or damnation of the individual human soul. Today Christianity in general accepts that humanity has free will, though some forms, such as Calvinism, believe that salvation can only be attained by the gift of God. The concept of predestination is also found in Islam.

The theory of predestination caused the early-5th-century controversy between Augustine of Hippo, who claimed the absolute determination of choice by God, and Pelagius, who upheld the doctrine of free will. Luther and Calvin adopted the Augustinian view at the Reformation, although

in differing degrees, but ◊Arminius adopted the Pelagian standpoint.

pref. in grammar, abbreviation for *prefix*.

prefect French government official who, under the centralized Napoleonic system 1800–1984, was responsible for enforcing government policy in each *département* and *région*. In 1984 prefects were replaced by presidents of elected councils (see *government* under ◊France).

prefix a letter or group of letters that can be added to the beginning of a word to make a new word.

pregnancy in humans, the period during which a fetus grows within the womb. It begins at conception and ends at birth, and the normal length is 40 weeks. Menstruation usually stops on conception. About one in five pregnancies fails, but most of these failures occur very early on, so the woman may notice only that her period is late. After the second month, the breasts become tense and tender, and the areas round the nipples become darker. Enlargement of the uterus can be felt at about the end of the third month, and thereafter the abdomen enlarges progressively. Pregnancy in animals is called ◊gestation.

Occasionally the fertilized egg implants not in the womb but in the ◊fallopian tube, leading to an ectopic ('out of place') pregnancy. This will cause the woman severe abdominal pain and vaginal bleeding. If the growing fetus ruptures the tube, life-threatening shock may ensue.

prehistoric art art of prehistoric cultures; see under ◊ancient art.

prehistoric life the diverse organisms that inhabited Earth from the origin of life about 3.5 billion years ago to the time when humans began to keep written records about 3500 BC. During the course of evolution, new forms of life developed and other forms, including the dinosaurs, became extinct. Prehistoric life evolved over this vast timespan from simple bacterialike cells in the oceans to shellfish, fishes, insects, plants, amphibians, reptiles, birds, and mammals. On a geological timescale human beings are thought to have evolved relatively recently, perhaps about 4 million years ago, although the dating is a matter of some debate. See also ◊geological time.

prehistory human cultures before the use of writing. The classification system was devised 1816 by the Danish archaeologist Christian Thomsen, and is based on the materials used by early humans for tools and weapons.

Stone Age Flint was predominant; divided into:
Old Stone Age (Palaeolithic) 3,500,000–5000 BC, in which the tools were chipped into shape; it includes ◊Neanderthal and ◊Cro-Magnon people; the only domesticated animals were dogs. Cave paintings were produced 20,000–8,000 years ago in many parts of the world, for example, ◊Altamira, Spain; ◊Lascaux, France; central Sahara; India; and Australia;
Middle Stone Age (Mesolithic) and *New Stone Age* (Neolithic), when tools were ground and polished, and, in Neolithic times, agriculture and domestication of cattle and sheep were practised. A Stone Age culture survived in Australia until the 19th century.

Bronze Age Period of bronze tools and weapons beginning approximately 6000 BC in the Far East, and continuing in the Middle East until about 1200 BC; in Britain it lasted about 2000–500 BC, and in Africa the transition from stone tools to iron was direct. The heroes of the Greek poet Homer lived in the Bronze Age.

Iron Age Iron was hardened by the addition of carbon, so that it superseded bronze for tools and weapons; in the Old World generally from about 1000 BC.

prelude in music, a composition intended as the preface to further music, to set a mood for a stage work, as in Wagner's *Lohengrin*; as used by Chopin, a short piano work.

Premadasa Ranasinghe 1924– . Sri Lankan politician, a United National Party member of parliament from 1960, prime minister from 1978, and president

from 1988, having gained popularity through overseeing a major house building and poverty-alleviation programme.

From a slum background and a member of the dhobi (laundryworkers') caste, Premadasa was elected deputy mayor of Colombo 1955. He served successively as minister of local government from 1968, UNP Chief Whip from 1970, and leader of the House from 1977, before being appointed prime minister. He was elected president Dec 1988. He

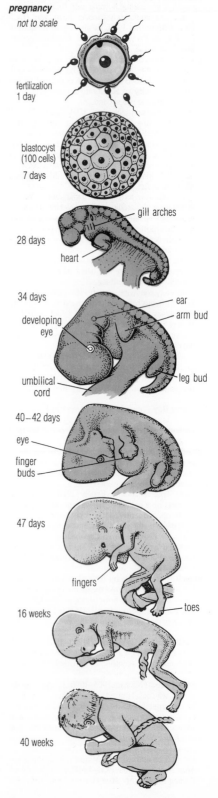

pregnancy

not to scale

fertilization
1 day

blastocyst
(100 cells)
7 days

gill arches

28 days

heart

34 days

ear

developing
eye

arm bud

leg bud

umbilical
cord

40–42 days

eye

finger
buds

47 days

fingers

toes

16 weeks

40 weeks

opposed the 1987 Indo-Sri Lankan peace-keeping agreement aimed at solving the Tamil crisis.

prematurity the condition of an infant born before term. In obstetrics, an infant whose birth weight is less than 2.5 kg/5.5 lbs is described as premature.

Premature babies are often at risk. They lose heat quickly because they lack an insulating layer of fat beneath the skin; there may also be breathing difficulties. In hospitals with advanced technology, special care baby units (SCBUs) can save babies born as early as 24 weeks.

premedication combination of drugs given before surgery to prepare a patient for general anaesthesia.

One component (an ◊anticholinergic) dries excess secretions produced by the airways when a tube is passed down the trachea, and during inhalation of anaesthetic gases. Other substances act to relax muscles, reduce anxiety, and relieve pain.

premenstrual tension (PMT) popular name for *premenstrual syndrome*, a medical condition comprising a number of physical or emotional features that occur cyclically before menstruation, and which disappear with the onset of menstruation itself. Symptoms include mood changes, breast tenderness, a feeling of bloatedness, and headache.

Preminger /'premɪŋgə/ Otto (Ludwig) 1906–1986. US film producer, director, and actor. Born in Vienna, he went to the USA 1935. He directed *Margin for Error* 1942, *Laura* 1944, *The Moon is Blue* 1953, *The Man With the Golden Arm* 1955, *Anatomy of a Murder* 1959, *Skidoo!* 1968, and *Rosebud* 1974. His films are characterized by an intricate technique of story-telling, and a masterly use of the wide screen and the travelling camera.

Premium Savings Bond British government bond introduced in 1956 whose purchaser is eligible for a prize-winning lottery. The prize money is funded from interest payable on the bond.

Premonstratensian a Roman Catholic monastic order founded 1120 by St Norbert (*c.* 1080–1134), a German bishop, at Prémontré, N France. Members were known as White Canons. The rule was a stricter version of that of the Augustinian Canons.

Prempeh I /'prempeɪ/ chief of the Ashanti people in W Africa. He became king 1888, and later opposed British attempts to take over the region. He was deported and in 1900 the Ashanti were defeated. He returned to Kumasi (capital of the Ashanti region) 1924 as chief of the people.

Prenderghast /'prendəgaːst/ Maurice 1859–1924. US painter who created a decorative watercolour style, using small translucent pools of colour, inspired by the Impressionists.

He studied in Paris in the 1890s and was influenced by the ◊Nabis painters Bonnard and Vuillard. In 1898 he visited Italy. *Umbrellas in the Rain, Venice* 1899 (Museum of Fine Arts, Boston, Massachusetts) is typical.

preparatory school a fee-paying independent school. In the UK, it is a junior school which prepares students for entry to a senior school at about age 13. In the USA, it is a school which prepares children for university entrance at about age 18.

preposition a grammatical ◊part of speech coming before a noun or pronoun in order to show a location ('in', 'on'), time ('during'), or some other relationship (for example figurative relationships in phrases like 'by heart' or 'on time').

In the sentence 'Put the book on the table' *on* is a preposition governing the noun 'table' and relates the verb 'put' to the phrase 'the table', indicating where the book should go. Some words of English that are often prepositional in function may, however, be used adverbially, as in the sentences, 'He picked the book up' and 'He picked up the book', in which the ordering is different but the meaning the same. In such cases *up* is called an *adverbial particle* and the form 'pick up' is a *phrasal verb*.

Pre-Raphaelite Brotherhood group of British painters 1848–53: Dante Gabriel Rossetti, John Everett Millais, and Holman Hunt were founder members. They aimed to paint serious subjects, to study nature closely, and to shun the influence of painterly

styles post-Raphael. Their subjects were mainly biblical and literary, painted with obsessive naturalism. Artists associated with the group include Burne-Jones and William Morris.

Presbyterianism system of Christian Protestant church government, expounded during the Reformation by John Calvin, which gives its name to the established Church of Scotland, and is also practised in England, Ireland, Switzerland, North America, and elsewhere. There is no compulsory form of worship and each congregation is governed by presbyters or elders (clerical or lay), who are of equal rank. Congregations are grouped in presbyteries, synods, and general assemblies.

Prescott /'preskət/ John Leslie 1938– . British Labour Party politician, a member of the ◊Kinnock shadow cabinet.

A former merchant seaman and trade-union official, he became member of Parliament for Hull East and, in 1975, a member of the European Parliament, despite being opposed to Britain's membership of the European Community. A strong parliamentary debater and television performer, he is sometimes critical of his colleagues. In 1988 he unsuccessfully challenged Roy Hattersley for the deputy leadership.

Prescott /'preskət/ William Hickling 1796–1859. US historian, author of *History of the Reign of Ferdinand and Isabella, the Catholic* 1838, *History of the Conquest of Mexico* 1843, and *History of the Conquest of Peru* 1847.

prescription in English law, the legal acquisition of title or right (such as an ◊easement) by uninterrupted use or possession.

prescription in medicine, an order written in a recognized form by a practitioner of medicine, dentistry, or veterinary surgery to a pharmacist for a preparation of drugs to be used in treatment.

By tradition it is written in Latin, except for the directions addressed to the patient. It consists of (1) the superscription *recipe* (take), contracted to R; (2) the inscription or body, containing the names and quantities of the drugs to be dispensed; (3) the subscription, or directions to the pharmacist; (4) the signature, consisting of the contraction *Signa*, followed by directions to the patient; and (5) the patient's name, the date, and the practitioner's name.

present participle see ◊participle.

preservatives food ◊additives used to inhibit the growth of bacteria, yeasts, mould, and other

Pre-Raphaelite Brotherhood Dante Gabriel Rossetti's La Ghirlandata (1873), Guildhall Art Gallery, London. Minute detail and a vivid use of colour mark this portrait as a work of the Pre-Raphaelite Brotherhood.

microorganisms to extend the shelf-life of foods. The term sometimes refers to ◊antioxidants as well. All preservatives are potentially damaging to health if eaten in sufficient quantity. Both the amount used, and the foods in which they can be used, are restricted by law.

Alternatives to preservatives include faster turnover of food stocks, refrigeration, better hygiene in preparation, sterilization, and pasteurization (see ◊food technology).

president the usual title of the head of state in a republic; the power of the office may range from the equivalent of a constitutional monarch to the actual head of the government. For presidents of the USA, see ◊United States of America.

presidential medal of freedom highest peacetime civilian award in the USA, instituted 1963, conferred annually on Independence Day by the president on those making significant contributions to the 'quality of American life'. It replaced the Medal of Freedom awarded from 1945 for acts and service aiding US security.

Presley /'prezli/ Elvis (Aaron) 1935–1977. US singer and guitarist, born in Tupelo, Mississippi. With his recordings for Sun Records in Memphis, Tennessee, 1954–55 and early hits such as 'Heartbreak Hotel' 1956, 'Hound Dog' 1956, and 'Love Me Tender' 1956, he created an individual vocal style, influenced by Southern blues, gospel music, country music, and rhythm and blues.

press the news media. See under ◊newspaper.

Pressburg /'presbʊək/ German name of ◊Bratislava, city in Czechoslovakia.

Pressburger /'presbɜːgə/ Emeric 1902–1988. Hungarian director, producer, and screenwriter, known for his partnership with Michael ◊Powell.

Press Council in the UK, organization (established 1953) that aims to preserve the freedom of the press, to maintain standards, consider complaints, and report on monopoly developments.

In 1989 there were 1,484 complaints to the Press Council, of which 26 were upheld.

press gang method used to recruit soldiers and sailors into the British armed forces in the 18th and early 19th centuries. In effect it was a form of kidnapping carried out by the services or their agents, often with the aid of armed men.

pressure in physics, force per unit area. In a fluid (liquid or gas) pressure increases with depth. At the edge of Earth's atmosphere, pressure is zero whereas at ground level it is about 1013.25 millibars (or 1 atmosphere). Pressure at a depth *h* in a fluid of density *d* is equal to *hdg*, where *g* is the acceleration due to ◊gravity. The SI unit of pressure is the ◊pascal (◊newton per square metre), equal to 0.01 millibars. Pressure has also been measured using a mercury column (see ◊Torricelli); 1 atmosphere equals 760 mm of mercury.

pressure cooker a closed pot in which food is cooked in water under pressure. Under pressure water boils at a higher temperature than normal boiling point (100°C/212°F), and therefore cooks

Presley Elvis Presley, for many years the most popular pop singer in the world.

food quicker. The modern pressure cooker has a quick-sealing lid and a safety valve, which can be adjusted to vary the steam pressure inside.

The French scientist Denis Papin invented the pressure cooker in England in 1679.

pressure group or *interest group* or *lobby* group that puts pressure on governments or parties to ensure laws and treatment favourable to its own interest. Pressure groups have played an increasingly prominent role in contemporary Western democracies. In general they fall into two types: groups concerned with a single issue, such as nuclear disarmament, and groups attempting to promote their own interest, such as oil producers.

Prestel the ◊viewdata service provided by British Telecom (BT), which provides information on the television screen via the telephone network. BT pioneered the service 1975.

Prester John /ˈprestə ˈdʒɒn/ legendary Christian prince who, in the 12th–13th centuries, was believed to rule a powerful empire in Asia. In the 14th–16th centuries, Prester John was identified with the king of Ethiopia.

Preston /ˈprestən/ industrial seaport (textiles, chemicals, electrical goods, aircraft and shipbuilding), adminstrative headquarters of Lancashire, NW England, on the river Ribble 34 km/21 mi S of Lancaster; population (1983) 125,000. Cromwell defeated the Royalists at Preston in 1648. It is the birthplace of Richard Arkwright, inventor of cotton-spinning machinery.

Prestonpans, Battle of /ˌprestənˈpænz/ Prince ◊Charles Edward Stuart's Jacobite forces defeated the English in 1745 at Prestonpans, a town in Lothian region, E Scotland.

Prestwick /ˈprestwɪk/ town in Strathclyde, SW Scotland; population (1985) 13,532. Industries include engineering and aerospace engineering. The international airport is linked with a ◊free port.

prêt-à-porter (French) ready-to-wear.

pretender a claimant to a throne. In British history, the term is widely used to describe the Old Pretender (◊James Francis Edward Stuart) and the Young Pretender (◊Charles Edward Stuart).

Pretoria /prɪˈtɔːrɪə/ administrative capital of the Republic of South Africa from 1910 and capital of Transvaal province from 1860; population (1985) 741,300. Industries include engineering, chemicals, iron, and steel. Founded 1855, it was named after Boer leader Andries Pretorius (1799–1853).

Previn /ˈprevɪn/ André (George) 1929– . US conductor and composer, born in Berlin. After a period working as a composer and arranger in the US film industry, he concentrated on conducting. He was principal conductor of the London Symphony Orchestra 1968–79. He was appointed music director of Britain's Royal Philharmonic Orchestra 1985 (a post he relinquished the following year, staying on as principal conductor), and of the Los Angeles Philharmonic in 1986.

Prévost d'Exiles /preˈvəʊ degˈziːl/ Antoine François 1697–1763. French novelist, known as Abbé Prévost, who sandwiched a military career into his life as a monk. His *Manon Lescaut* 1731 inspired operas by Massenet and Puccini.

Priam in Greek mythology, the last king of Troy. He was killed by Pyrrhus, son of Achilles, when Greeks entered the city of Troy concealed in a wooden horse.

Priapus /praɪˈeɪpəs/ Greek god of garden fertility, son of Dionysus and Aphrodite, represented as grotesquely ugly, with an exaggerated phallus. He was also a god of gardens, where his image was frequently used as a scarecrow.

Pribilof Islands /ˈprɪbɪlɒf/ group of four islands in the Bering Sea, of volcanic origin, 320 km/200 mi SW of Bristol Bay, Alaska, USA. Named after Gerasim Pribilof who reached them in 1786, they were sold by Russia to the USA in 1867 with Alaska, of which they form part. They were made a fur-seal reservation in 1868.

Price /praɪs/ Vincent 1911– . US actor, star of horror films including *House of Wax* 1953 and *The Fall of the House of Usher* 1960.

prickly heat inflammation of the sweat glands; a disorder caused by excessive sweating. Small itchy blisters (or miliaria) are formed but quickly dry up and heal.

prickly pear cactus of the genus *Opuntia*, native to Central and South America, especially Mexico and Chile, but naturalized in S Europe, N Africa, and Australia where it is a pest. The common prickly pear *Opuntia vulgaris* is low-growing, with bright yellow flowers, and prickly, oval fruit; the flesh and seeds of the peeled fruit have a pleasant taste.

Pride and Prejudice a novel by Jane Austen, published in the UK 1813. Mr and Mrs Bennet, whose property is due to pass to a male cousin, William Collins, are anxious to secure good marriage settlements for their five daughters. Central to the story is the romance between the witty Elizabeth Bennet and the proud Mr Darcy.

Pride's purge the removal of about 100 Royalists and Presbyterians of the English House of Commons from Parliament by a detachment of soldiers led by Col Thomas Pride (died 1658) in 1648. They were accused of negotiating with Charles I and were seen as unreliable by the army. The remaining members were termed the ◊Rump and voted in favour of the king's trial.

Pride (a former London drayman or brewer who rose to be a colonel in the Parliamentary army) acted as one of the judges at the trial and also signed the king's death warrant. He opposed the plan to make Cromwell king.

Priestley /ˈpriːstli/ J(ohn) B(oynton) 1894–1984. English novelist and playwright. His first success was a novel about travelling theatre, *The Good Companions* 1929. He followed it with a realist novel about London life, *Angel Pavement* 1930; later books include *Lost Empires* 1965 and *The Image Men* 1968. As a playwright he was often preoccupied with theories of time, as in *An Inspector Calls* 1945, but had also a gift for family comedy, for example, *When We Are Married* 1938. He was also noted for his wartime broadcasts and literary criticism, such as *Literature and Western Man* 1960.

Priestley /ˈpriːstli/ Joseph 1733–1804. English chemist, who identified oxygen 1774.

A Unitarian minister, he was elected Fellow of the Royal Society 1766. In 1791 his chapel and house in Birmingham were sacked by a mob because of his support for the French Revolution. In 1794 he emigrated to the USA.

priest's hole hiding place in private homes for Catholic priests in the 16th–17th centuries when there were penal laws against them in Britain. Many still exist, for example at Speke Hall, near Liverpool.

Prigogine /prɪˈgəʊzɪn/ Ilya 1917– . Russian-born Belgian chemist who, as a highly original theoretician, has made major contributions to the field of ◊thermodynamics for which work he was awarded the Nobel physics prize 1977. Earlier theories had considered systems at or about equilibrium. Prigogine began to study 'dissipative' or non-equilibrium structures frequently found in biological and chemical reactions.

prima facie (Latin) at first sight.

primary in presidential election campaigns in the USA, an election to decide the candidates for the major parties. Held in some 35 states, primaries begin with New Hampshire in Feb and continue until June, and operate under varying complex rules. Generally speaking, the number of votes received by a candidate governs the number of delegates who will vote for that person at the national conventions in July/Aug, when the final choice of candidate for both Democratic and Republican parties is made.

primary education the education of children between the ages of 5 and 11 in the state school system in England and Wales, and up to 12 in Scotland.

primate in zoology, member of the order of mammals that includes monkeys, apes, and humans, as well as lemurs, bushbabies, lorises, and tarsiers. Generally, they have forward-directed eyes, gripping hands and feet, and opposable thumbs and big toes. They tend to have nails rather than claws, with gripping pads on

the ends of the digits, all adaptations to the climbing mode of life.

primate in the Christian church, the official title of archbishops. The archbishop of Canterbury is the Primate of All England, and the archbishop of York the Primate of England.

prime minister or *premier* head of a parliamentary government, usually the leader of the largest party. The first in Britain is usually considered to have been Robert ◊Walpole, but the office was not officially recognized until 1905. In some countries, such as Australia, a distinction is drawn between the prime minister of the whole country, and the premier of an individual state. In countries with an executive president, such as France, the prime minister is of lesser standing.

prime number a number that can be divided only by 1 or itself, that is, having no other factors. There is an infinite number of primes, the first ten of which are 2, 3, 5, 7, 11, 13, 17, 19, 23 and 29. The number 2 is the only even prime (because all other even numbers have 2 as a factor).

Over the centuries mathematicians have sought general methods (algorithms) for calculating primes, from Eratosthenes's sieve to programs on powerful computers. Eratosthenes's method (dating from about 200 BC) is to write in sequence all numbers from 2, then, starting with 2, underline every second number, thus eliminating numbers that can be divided by 2. Next, starting with 3, cross out every third number (whether or not they are underlined), thus eliminating numbers divisible by 3. Continue the process for 5, 7, and so on. Numbers that remain are primes.

In 1989 researchers at Amdahl Corporation, Sunnyvale, California, calculated the largest known prime number. It has 65,087 digits, and is more than a trillion trillion trillion times as large as the previous record holder. It took over a year of computation to locate the number and prove it was a prime.

prime rate the rate charged by commercial banks to their best customers. It is the base rate on which other rates are calculated according to the risk involved. Only borrowers who have the highest credit rating qualify for the prime rate.

Primitive Methodism Protestant Christian movement, an offshoot of Wesleyan ◊Methodism, that emerged in England 1811 when evangelical enthusiasts organized camp meetings at places such as ◊Mow Cop 1807. Inspired by American example, open-air sermons were accompanied by prayers and hymn singing. In 1932 the Primitive Methodists became a constituent of a unified Methodist church.

Hugh Bourne (1772–1852) and William Clowes, who were both expelled from the Wesleyan Methodist circuit for participating in camp meetings, formed a missionary campaign that led to the development of Primitive Methodist circuits in central, eastern and northern England. They

Priestley Known for discovering oxygen, Joseph Priestley was also a Presbyterian minister and a political radical.

Prime Ministers of Britain

Sir Robert Walpole	(Whig)	1721
Earl of Wilmington	(Whig)	1742
Henry Pelham	(Whig)	1743
Duke of Newcastle	(Whig)	1754
Duke of Devonshire	(Whig)	1756
Duke of Newcastle	(Whig)	1757
Earl of Bute	(Tory)	1762
George Grenville	(Whig)	1763
Marquess of Rockingham	(Whig)	1765
Duke of Grafton	(Whig)	1766
Lord North	(Tory)	1770
Marquess of Rockingham	(Whig)	1782
Earl of Shelbourne	(Whig)	1782
Duke of Portland	(Coalition)	1783
William Pitt	(Tory)	1783
Henry Addington	(Tory)	1801
William Pitt	(Tory)	1804
Lord Grenville	(Whig)	1806
Duke of Portland	(Tory)	1807
Spencer Percival	(Tory)	1809
Earl of Liverpool	(Tory)	1812
George Canning	(Tory)	1827
Viscount Goderich	(Tory)	1827
Duke of Wellington	(Tory)	1828
Earl Grey	(Whig)	1830
Viscount Melbourne	(Whig)	1834
Sir Robert Peel	(Conservative)	1834
Viscount Melbourne	(Whig)	1835
Sir Robert Peel	(Conservative)	1841
Lord J Russell	(Liberal)	1846
Earl of Derby	(Conservative)	1852
Lord Aberdeen	(Peelite)	1852
Viscount Palmerston	(Liberal)	1855
Earl of Derby	(Conservative)	1858
Viscount Palmerston	(Liberal)	1859
Lord J Russell	(Liberal)	1865
Earl of Derby	(Conservative)	1866
Benjamin Disraeli	(Conserative)	1868
W E Gladstone	(Liberal)	1868
Benjamin Disraeli	(Conserative)	1874
W E Gladstone	(Liberal)	1880
Marquess of Salisbury	(Conservative)	1885
W E Gladstone	(Liberal)	1886
Marquess of Salisbury	(Conservative)	1886
W E Gladstone	(Liberal)	1892
Earl of Roseberry	(Liberal)	1894
Marquess of Salisbury	(Conservative)	1895
Sir H Campbell-Bannerman	(Liberal)	1905
H H Asquith	(Liberal)	1908
H H Asquith	(Coalition)	1915
D Lloyd George	(Coalition)	1916
A Bonar Law	(Conservative)	1922
Stanley Baldwin	(Conservative)	1923
Ramsay MacDonald	(Labour)	1924
Stanley Baldwin	(Conservative)	1924
Ramsay MacDonald	(Labour)	1929
Ramsay MacDonald	(National)	1931
Stanley Baldwin	(National)	1935
N Chamberlain	(National)	1937
Sir Winston Churchill	(Coalition)	1940
Clement Attlee	(Labour)	1945
Sir Winston Churchill	(Conservative)	1951
Sir Anthony Eden	(Conservative)	1955
Harold Macmillan	(Conservative)	1957
Sir Alec Douglas-Home	(Conservative)	1963
Harold Wilson	(Labour)	1964
Edward Heath	(Conservative)	1970
Harold Wilson	(Labour)	1974
James Callaghan	(Labour)	1976
Margaret Thatcher	(Conservative)	1979

gained a strong following in working-class mining and agricultural communities, and concentrated on villages and towns rather than major urban centres. Primitive Methodism as a separate sect was exported to the USA in 1829 and then to Canada, Australia, New Zealand, South Africa, and Nigeria.

Primitivism influence on modern art (Kirchner, Modigliani, Picasso, and others) of aboriginal cultures of Africa, Australia, the Americas, and also of Western folk art.

Primo de Rivera /ˈpriːməʊ deɪ rɪˈveərə/ Miguel 1870–1930. Spanish soldier and politician, dictator from 1923 as well as premier from 1925. He was captain-general of Catalonia when he led a coup against the ineffective monarchy and became virtual dictator of Spain with the support of Alfonso XIII. He resigned 1930.

Primorye territory of the Russian Soviet Federal Socialist Republic in SE Siberia on the Sea of Japan; area 165,900 sq km/64,079 sq mi; population(1985) 2,136,000. The capital is Vladivostok. Timber and coal are produced.

primrose woodland plant *Primula vulgaris*, common to Europe, bearing pale yellow flowers in spring. Related to it is the cowslip, and the false oxlip is a hybrid of the two.

prince a royal or noble title. In Rome and medieval Italy it was used as the title of certain officials, for example, *princeps senatus* (Latin 'leader of the Senate'). The title was granted to the king's sons in 15th century France, and in England from Henry VII's time. The British sovereign's eldest son is normally created Prince of Wales.

Prince /prɪns/ (Harold) Hal 1928– . US director of musicals such as *Cabaret* 1968 and *Follies* 1971 on Broadway in New York, and *Evita* 1978 and *Sweeney Todd* 1980 in London's West End.

Prince /prɪns/ stage name of Prince Rogers Nelson 1958– . US pop musician, who composes, arranges, and produces his own records, and often plays all the instruments. His albums, including *1999* 1982 and *Purple Rain* 1984, contain elements of rock, funk, and jazz.

He was born in Minneapolis, Minnesota. His band, the Revolution, broke up after four years in 1986. His hits include 'Little Red Corvette' from *1999*, 'Kiss' from *Parade* 1986, and 'Sign O' The Times' 1987.

Prince Edward Island /ˈedwəd/ province of E Canada
area 5,700 sq km/2,200 sq mi
capital Charlottetown
features named after Prince Edward of Kent, father of Queen Victoria; PEI National Park; Summerside Lobster Carnival
products potatoes, dairy products, lobsters, oysters, farm vehicles
population (1986) 127,000
history first recorded visit by Cartier 1534, who called it Isle St-Jean; settled by French; taken by British 1758; annexed to Nova Scotia 1763; separate colony 1769; settled by Scottish 1803; joined Confederation 1873.

In the late 1980s, there was controversy about whether to build a bridge to the mainland.

Prince Imperial title of ◊Eugène, son of Emperor Napoleon III of France.

Prince Rupert /ˈruːpət/ fishing port at the mouth of the Skeena river in British Columbia, Canada, on Kaien Island, W side of Tsimpsean peninsula; population (1983) 16,786.

princess royal title borne only by the eldest daughter of the British sovereign, granted by royal declaration. It was first borne by Mary, eldest daughter of Charles I, probably in imitation of the French court where the eldest daughter of the king was styled 'Madame Royale'. The title is currently held by Princess Anne.

Princeton /ˈprɪnstən/ borough in Mercer county, W central New Jersey, USA, 80 km/50 mi SW of New York; population (1983) 12,035. The seat of Princeton University, founded 1746 at Elizabethtown and moved to Princeton 1756;

Princetown /ˈprɪnstaʊn/ village on the W of Dartmoor, Devon, SW England, containing Dartmoor prison, opened 1809.

Prince William Sound a channel in the Gulf of Alaska, extending 200 km/125 mi NW from Kayak Island. In Mar 1989 the oil tanker *Exxon Valdez* ran aground here, spilling 12 million gallons of crude oil in what was reckoned to be the world's greatest oil pollution disaster.

print a picture or design that is printed using a plate (block, stone, or sheet) that holds ink or colour; for different techniques, see ◊engraving. The oldest type of print is the woodcut, common in medieval Europe, followed by line engraving (from the 15th century), and etching (from the 17th); coloured woodblock prints flourished in Japan from the 18th century. ◊Lithography was invented 1796.

The German artist Dürer created outstanding woodcuts and line engravings, and the Dutch painter Rembrandt was one of the first major artists to produce etchings.

printed circuit board (PCB) an electrical circuit created by laying (printing) 'tracks' of a conductor such as copper onto one or both sides of an insulating board. The PCB was invented 1936 by the Austrian scientist Paul Eisler, and was first used on a large scale 1948.

Components such as integrated circuits (chips), resistors, and capacitors can be soldered to the surface of the board (surface-mounted) or, more commonly, attached by inserting their connecting pins or wires into holes drilled in the board.

printer in computing, an output device for producing printed copies of text or graphics. Types include the *daisywheel*, which produces good-quality text but no graphics; the *dot matrix*, which creates character patterns from a matrix of small dots, producing text and graphics; and the ◊*laser printer*, which produces high-quality text and graphics.

Prince *US pop star Prince in concert, 1986.*

Prince Edward Island

printing

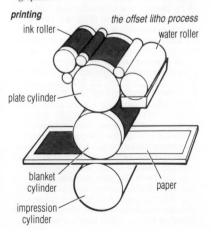

the offset litho process
ink roller
water roller
plate cylinder
blanket cylinder
paper
impression cylinder

printed circuit board

A typical microcomputer PCB

serial and
parallel interfaces

edge connector

ROM
(rent-only
memory)

microprocessor
(CPU)
central
processing
unit

RAM
(random
-access
memory)

RF modulator
radio
frequency

ULA
(uncommitted logic
array)

expansion ports

---

printing the reproduction of text or illustrative material on paper, as in books or newspapers, or on an increasing variety of materials, for example on tins and plastic containers. The first printing used moveable type and hand operated presses, but much current printing is effected by electronically controlled machinery. Current printing processes include ◊offset litho, ◊gravure print, and electronic phototypesetting.

In China the art of printing from a single wooden block was known in the 6th century AD, and moveable type was being used by the 11th century. In Europe printing was unknown for another three centuries, and it was only in the 15th century that moveable type was re-invented, traditionally by Johannes ◊Gutenberg in Germany. William ◊Caxton introduced printing to England. There was no further substantial advance until, in the 19th century, steam power replaced hand-operation of the presses, making possible long 'runs', and hand-composition of type (each tiny metal letter was taken from the case and placed individually in the narrow stick that carried one line of text) was replaced by machines operated by a keyboard.

The *Linotype*, used in newspapers (it produced a line of type in a solid slug) was invented by Ottmar Mergenthaler 1886, and the *Monotype*, used in bookwork (it produced a series of individual characters, which could be hand-corrected) by Tolbert Lanston (1844–1913) in the USA 1889. Important as these inventions were, they represented no fundamental change, but simply a faster method of carrying out the same basic operations. The actual printing process still involved pressing inked raised type onto paper, a method called ◊letterpress.

In the 1960s this form of printing began to face increasing competition from ◊*offset litho*, a method that prints from an inked flat surface, while high-circulation magazines were printed by the ◊*gravure* method, which uses recessed plates.

The introduction of electronic phototypesetting machines, also in the 1960s, allowed the entire process of setting and correction to be done in the same way as a copy-typist operates, thus eliminating the composing room, and leaving only the making of plates and the running of the presses to be done traditionally.

By the 1970s the final steps were taken to plateless printing, using various processes, such as a computer-controlled laser beam, or continuous jets of ink acoustically broken up into tiny equal-sized drops, which are electrostatically charged under computer control.

prion an exceptionally small microorganism, a hundred times smaller than a virus. Composed of protein, and without any detectable amount of nucleic acid (genetic material), it is thought to cause diseases such as scrapie in sheep, and some degenerative diseases of the nervous system in humans. How it can operate without nucleic acid is not yet known. The prion was claimed to have been discovered at the University of California 1982.

prior, prioress in a Christian religious community, the deputy of either an abbot or abbess, responsible for discipline. In certain Roman Catholic orders, it is the principal of a monastery or convent.

Prior /ˈpraɪə/ James 1927– . British Conservative politician. He held ministerial posts from 1970. As employment secretary he curbed trade-union activity with the Employment Act 1980, and was Northern Ireland secretary 1981–84. After his resignation 1984 he became chair of the General Electric Company (GEC).

Prior /ˈpraɪə/ Matthew 1664–1721. British poet and diplomat. He was associated under the Whigs with the negotiation of the treaty of Ryswick 1697 ending the war with France and under the Tories with that of Utrecht 1714 ('Matt's Peace') ending the War of the Spanish Succession, but on the Whigs' return to power he was imprisoned by the government leader Walpole 1715–17. His gift as a poet was for light occasional verses.

Pripet /ˈpriːpɪt/ (Russian *Pripyat*) river in W Soviet Union, a tributary of the Dnieper, which it joins 80 km/50 mi above Kiev, Ukraine, after a course of about 800 km/500 mi. The *Pripet marshes* near Pinsk were of strategic importance in both world wars.

prism in mathematics, a solid figure whose cross-section is constant in planes drawn perpendicular to its axis. A cylinder is a prism with a circular cross-section.

prism in optics, a triangular block of transparent material (plastic, glass, silica) commonly used to 'bend' a ray of light or split a beam into its spectral colours. Prisms are used like mirrors to define the optical path in binoculars, camera viewfinders, and periscopes. The dispersive property of prisms is used in the ◊spectroscope.

prison place of confinement for those convicted of contravening the laws of the state; most countries claim to aim at rehabilitation. The average number of people in prison in the UK (1987) was 56,400, with almost 20% of these under the age of 21. About 22% were on ◊remand (awaiting trial or sentence). Because of overcrowding in prisons, almost 2,000 prisoners were held in police cells (1988). 55% of male prisoners and 34% of female prisoners were reconvicted within two years of being discharged from prison (1984). The US prison population (1988) was 800,000.

Experiments have been made in Britain and elsewhere in 'open prisons' without bars, release of prisoners to work in ordinary jobs outside the prison in the final stages of their sentence, and aftercare on release. Attempts to deal with the increasing number of young offenders include from 1982 accommodation in community homes in the case of minor offences, with (in more serious cases) 'short, sharp shock' treatment in detention centres (although the latter was subsequently found to have little effect on reconviction rates).

history, UK

late 18th century Growth of criminal prisons as opposed to places of detention for those awaiting trial or confined for political reasons. Previously criminals had commonly been sentenced to death, mutilation, or transportation rather than imprisonment. One of the greatest reformers in Britain was John Howard, whose Prison Act 1778 established the principle of separate confinement combined with work in an attempt at reform (it was eventually carried out when Pentonville prison was built 1842).

prism White light passing through a prism is split into its constituent wavelengths, forming the colours of the rainbow.

19th century The Quaker Elizabeth Fry campaigned against the appalling conditions in early 19th-century prisons. Penal servitude was introduced 1857, as an additional deterrent, after the refusal of the colonies to accept transported convicts.

1948 Penal servitude and hard labour were finally abolished by the Criminal Justice Act 1948, so that there is only one form of prison sentence, namely imprisonment.

1967 Under the Criminal Justice Act 1967 courts may suspend prison sentences of two years or less, and, unless the offender has previously been in prison or borstal, will normally do so; that is, the sentence comes into effect only if another offence is committed. Persistent offenders may receive an extended sentence for the protection of the public. After serving one-third of their sentence (minimum 12 months), selected prisoners may be released on parole.

1972 The Criminal Justice Act 1972 required the courts to consider information about an offender before sentencing them to prison for the first time, and introduced the concept of *community service* to replace prison for nonviolent offenders, and of day-training centres for the social education under intensive supervision of those who could not integrate well into society.

remand prison In the UK 1987, 59,000 people were remanded. Nearly half were eventually either found not guilty or given a non-custodial sentence. Two-thirds of all women remanded were freed after trial. In the mid-1970s remand prisoners made up about 12% of the prison population in England and Wales. In 1989 this figure was 23%. The average waiting time for remand prisoners is now eight weeks. In Scotland there is a strict 110-day limit.

Priština /ˈpriːʃtɪnɑ/ capital of Kosovo autonomous province, S Serbia, Yugoslavia; population (1981) 216,000.

Pritchett /ˈprɪtʃɪt/ V(ictor) S(awdon) 1900– . English short story writer, novelist, and critic, with an often witty and satirical style. His critical works include *The Living Novel* 1946 and a biography of the French novelist Balzac.

privacy the right of the individual to be free from secret surveillance (by scientific devices or other means) and from the disclosure to unauthorized persons of personal data, as accumulated in computer data banks. Always an issue complicated by considerations of state security, public welfare (in the case of criminal activity), and other factors, it has been rendered more complex by present-day technology.

computer data All Western countries now have computerized-data protection. In the USA the Privacy Act 1974 requires that there should be no secret databanks and that agencies handling data must ensure their reliability and prevent misuse (information gained for one purpose must not be used for another). The public must be able to find out what is recorded and how it is used, and be able to correct it. In Britain under the Data Protection Act 1984 a register is kept of all businesses and organizations that store and process personal information, and they are subject to a code of practice set out in the act.

media In the UK, a bill to curb invasions of privacy by the media failed to reach the statute book in 1989. It would have enabled legal action against publication, or attempted publication, of private information without consent. In the USA the media have a working rule that private information is made public only concerning those who have entered public life, such as politicians, entertainers, and athletes.

private enterprise business unit where economic activities are in private hands and are carried on for private profit, as opposed to national, municipal, or cooperative ownership.

privateer a privately owned and armed ship commissioned by a state to attack enemy vessels. The crews of such ships were, in effect, legalized pirates; they were not paid but received a share of the spoils. Privateering existed from ancient times

until the 19th century, when it was declared illegal by the Declaration of Paris 1856.

private limited company a registered company which has limited liability (the shareholders cannot lose more than their original shareholdings), and a minimum of two shareholders and a maximum of fifty. It cannot offer its shares or debentures to the public and their transfer is restricted; a shareholder may relinquish shares with the permission of the other shareholders.

private school alternative name for a fee-paying independent school.

privatization the selling or transfer into private hands of state-owned or public assets and services (nationalized industries). Privatization of services takes place by the contracting out to private firms of the rendering of services previously supplied by public authorities. The proponents of privatization argue for the public benefit from its theoretically greater efficiency in a competitive market, and the release of resources for more appropriate use by government. Those against privatization believe that it removes a country's assets from all the people to a minority, whereas public utilities such as gas and water become private monopolies, and that a profit-making state-owned company raises revenue for the government.

In many cases the trend towards privatization was prompted by dissatisfaction with the high level of subsidies being given to often inefficient state enterprise. The term 'privatization' is used even when the state retains a majority share of an enterprise.

The policy has been pursued by the post-1979 Conservative administration in Britain, and by recent governments in France, Japan (Nippon Telegraph and Telephone Corporation 1985, Japan Railways 1987, Japan Air Lines 1987), Italy, and elsewhere. By 1988 the practice had spread worldwide with communist countries such as China and Cuba selling off housing to private tenants.

Industries in Britain privatized since 1979:

British Telecom
British Gas Corporation
British National Oil Corporation
British Airways
British Airports Authority
British Aerospace
British Shipbuilders
British Steel
British Transport Docks Board
British Water Board
National Freight Company
Enterprise Oil

privet evergreen shrubs of the genus *Ligustrum*, family Oleaceae, with dark green leaves, including the wild *common privet Ligustrum vulgare*, with white flowers and black berries, and *hedge privet Ligustrum ovalifolium*.

Privy Council originally the chief royal officials of the Norman kings in Britain, which under the Tudors and early Stuarts became the chief governing body. It was replaced from 1688 by the ◊cabinet, originally a committee of the council, and the council itself now retains only formal powers, in issuing royal proclamations and orders-in-council. Cabinet ministers are automatically members, and it is presided over by the Lord President of the Council. The *Judicial Committee of the Privy Council*, once a final court of appeal for members of the Commonwealth, is almost completely obsolete.

privy purse the personal expenditure of the British sovereign, which derives from his/her own resources (as distinct from the ◊civil list which now finances only expenses incurred in pursuance of official functions and duties). The office that deals with this expenditure is also known as the Privy Purse.

Privy Seal, Lord until 1884, the UK officer of state in charge of the royal seal to prevent its misuse. The honorary title is now held by a senior cabinet minister who has special nondepartmental duties.

Prix Goncourt French literary prize for fiction, given by the Académie ◊Goncourt from 1903.

probability the likelihood or chance an event will occur, often expressed as odds, or in mathematics, numerically as a fraction or decimal. In general, the probability that *n* particular events will happen out of a total of *m* possible events is *n/m*. A certainty has a probability of 1; an impossibility has a probability of 0. Empirical probability is defined as the number of successful events divided by the total possible number of events.

In tossing an unbiased coin, the chance that it will land heads is the same as the chance that it will land tails, that is, 1 to 1 or even; mathematically this probability is expressed as $1/2$ or 0.5. The odds against any chosen number coming up on the roll of an unbiased die are 6 to 1; the probability is $1/6$ or 0.1666.... If two dice are rolled there are $6 \times 6 = 36$ different possible combinations. The probability of a double (two numbers the same) is $1/6$ since there are six doubles in the 36 events: (1,1) (2,2) (3,3) (4,4) (5,5) (6,6). Probability (double) $6/36 = 1/6$.

Probability theory was developed by the French mathematicians Pascal and Fermat in the 17th century, initially in response to a request to calculate the odds of being dealt various hands at cards. Today probability plays a major part in the mathematics of atomic theory, and finds application in insurance and statistical studies.

probate formal proof of a will. In the UK, if its validity is unquestioned, it is proven in 'common form'; the executor, in the absence of other interested parties, obtains at a probate registry a grant upon their own oath. Otherwise, it must be proved in 'solemn form': its validity established at a probate court (in the Chancery Division of the High Court), those concerned being made parties to the action.

probation in law, the placing of offenders under supervision in the community, as an alternative to prison. Juveniles are no longer placed on probation, but under a 'supervision' order.

procedure in computing, a small part of a computer program, which performs a specific task, such as clearing the screen or sorting a file. In some programming languages, there is an overlap between procedures, ◊functions and ◊subroutines. Careful use of procedures is an element of ◊structured programming. A *procedural language* such as ◊BASIC is one where the programmer describes a task in terms of how it is to be done, as opposed to a *declarative language* such as Prolog, where it is described in terms of the required result.

processing cycle in computing, the sequence of steps performed repeatedly by a computer in the execution of a program. The computer's ◊CPU (central processing unit) continuously works through a loop of fetching a program instruction from the memory, fetching any data it needs, operating on the data, and storing the result in the memory, before it fetches another program instruction.

processor in computing, another name for the central processing unit (◊CPU) or ◊microprocessor of a computer.

proconsul Roman ◊consul who went on to govern a province when his term ended.

Proconsul the prehistoric ape whose skull was found on Rusinga Island in Lake Victoria (Nyanza), E Africa, by Mary ◊Leakey. It is believed to be 20 million years old.

Procrustes /prəʊˈkrʌstiːz/ (Greek 'the stretcher') in Greek mythology, a robber who tied his victims to a bed; if they were too tall for it, he cut off the ends of their legs, and if they were too short he stretched them.

procurator fiscal officer of a Scottish sheriff's court who (combining the role of public prosecutor and coroner) inquires into suspicious deaths and carries out the preliminary questioning of witnesses to crime.

Procyon the eighth-brightest star in the sky, and the brightest in the constellation Canis Minor. Procyon is a white star 11.3 light years away, with a mass of 1.7 Suns. It has a ◊white dwarf companion that orbits it every 40 years.

productivity, biological in an ecosystem, the amount of material in the ◊food chain produced by the primary producers (plants) that is available for consumption by animals. Plants turn carbon dioxide gas into sugars and other complex carbon compounds by means of photosynthesis. Their net productivity is defined as the quantity of carbon compounds formed, less the quantity used up by the respiration of the plant itself.

profit-sharing a system whereby an employer pays the workers a fixed share of the company's profits. It originated in France in the early 19th century, and was widely practised for a time within the cooperative movement.

Profumo /prə'fju:məʊ/ John (Dennis) 1915– . British Conservative politician, secretary of state for war 1960–June 1963, when he resigned on the disclosure of his involvement with Christine Keeler, mistress also of a Soviet naval attaché. In 1982 Profumo became administrator of the social and educational settlement Toynbee Hall in London.

progesterone a hormone that occurs in vertebrates. In mammals, it regulates the menstrual cycle and pregnancy.

prognosis in medicine, prediction of the course or outcome of illness or injury, especially the chance of recovery.

programme music music that tells a story, depicts a scene or painting, or illustrates a literary or philosophical idea, such as Richard Strauss' *Don Juan*.

programming in computing, the activity of writing instructions in a programming language for the control of a computer. Applications programming is for end-user programs, such as accounts programs or word-processing packages. Systems programming is for operating systems and the like, which are concerned more with the internal workings of the computer.

There are several programming styles:

Procedural programming, in which programs are written as lists of instructions which the computer obeys in sequence, is by far the most popular. It is the 'natural' style, closely matching the computer's own sequential operation.

Declarative programming, such as in the programming language Prolog, does not describe how to solve a problem, but rather describes the logical structure of the problem. Running such a program is more like proving an assertion than following a procedure.

Functional programming is a style based largely on the definition of functions. There are very few functional programming languages, Hope and ML being the most widely used, though many more conventional languages (for example C) make extensive use of functions.

Object-oriented programming, the most recently developed style, involves viewing a program as a collection of objects that behave in certain ways when they are passed certain 'messages'. For example, an object might be defined to represent a table of figures which will be displayed on screen when a 'display' message is received.

programming language in computing, a special notation in which instructions for controlling a computer are written. Programming languages are designed to be easy for people to write and read, but must be capable of being mechanically translated (by a ◊compiler or ◊interpreter) into the ◊machine code that the computer can execute.

program trading buying and selling a group of shares using a computer program to generate orders automatically whenever there is an appreciable movement in prices.

One form in use in the USA in 1989 was *index arbitrage* in which a program traded automatically whenever there was a difference between New York and Chicago prices of an equivalent number of shares. Program trading comprised some 14% of daily trading on the New York Stock Exchange by volume in Sept 1989 but was widely criticized for lessening market stability.

progression sequence of numbers each formed by a specific relationship to its predecessor. An

arithmetical progression has numbers which increase or decrease by a common sum or difference (for example 2, 4, 6, 8), a *geometric progression* has numbers each bearing a fixed ratio to its predecessor (for example 3, 6, 12, 24), and a *harmonic progression* is a sequence with numbers whose ◊reciprocals are in arithmetical progression, for example 1, 1/2, 1/3, 1/4.

progressive education teaching methods that take as their starting point children's own aptitudes and interests, and encourage them to follow their own investigations and lines of inquiry.

Progressivism in US history, the name of both a reform movement and a political party, active in the two decades before World War I. Mainly middle-class and urban-based, Progressives secured legislation at national, state, and local levels to improve the democratic system, working conditions, and welfare provision.

Prohibition in US history, the period 1920–33 when alcohol was illegal, and which represented the culmination of a long campaign by church and women's organizations, temperance societies, and the Anti-Saloon League. This led to bootlegging (the illegal distribution of liquor, often illicitly distilled), to the financial advantage of organized crime, and public opinion insisted on repeal 1933.

The prohibition amendment to the US constitution is known as the Volstead Act, after the congressman who introduced it.

projection see ◊map projection.

projector an apparatus that projects a picture onto a screen. In a *slide projector*, a lamp shines a light through the photographic slide or transparency, and a projection ◊lens throws an enlarged image of the slide onto the screen. A *ciné projector* has similar optics, but incorporates a mechanism that holds the film still while light is shone through each frame (picture). A shutter covers the film when it moves between frames.

prokaryote in biology, an organism whose cells lack organelles (specialized structures such as nuclei, mitochondria, and chloroplasts). The prokaryotes comprise the *bacteria* and *cyanobacteria*; all other organisms are eukaryotes.

Prokhorov /'proxərof/ Aleksandr 1916– . Russian physicist whose fundamental work on microwaves in 1955 led to the construction of the first practical ◊maser by ◊Townes, for which they shared the 1964 Nobel physics prize.

Prokofiev /prə'kɒfief/ Sergey (Sergeyevich) 1891–1953. Soviet composer. His music includes operas such as *The Love of Three Oranges* 1921; ballets for ◊Diaghilev, including *Romeo and Juliet* 1935; seven symphonies including the *Classical Symphony* 1916–17; music for films; piano and violin concertos; songs and cantatas (for example, that composed for the 30th anniversary of the October Revolution); and *Peter and the Wolf* 1936.

Prokopyevsk /prə'kɒpjefsk/ chief coalmining city of the Kuzbas, Siberia, USSR, on the river Aba; population (1987) 278,000.

prolapse the displacement of an organ due to the effects of strain in weakening the supporting tissues. The term is most often used with regard to the rectum (due to chronic bowel problems), or the uterus (following several pregnancies).

proletariat in Marxist theory, those classes in society that possess no property, and therefore depend on the sale of their labour or expertise (as opposed to the capitalists or bourgeoisie, who own the means of production, and the petty bourgeoisie, or working small-property owners). They are usually divided into the industrial, the agricultural, and the intellectual proletariat.

The term is derived from Latin *proletarii*, the class possessing no property, whose contribution to the state was considered to be their offspring, *proles*.

Prolog in computing, a programming language based on logic. Invented at the University of Marseille, France, 1971, it did not achieve widespread use until more than ten years later. It

is used mainly for ◊artificial intelligence programming.

PROM (programmable *r*ead-only *m*emory) in computing, a memory device in the form of a silicon chip that can be programmed to hold information permanently. PROM chips are empty of information when manufactured, unlike ROM chips, which have their memories built into them. Other memory devices are ◊EPROM and ◊RAM.

promenade concert originally a concert in which the audience walked about, now in the UK the name of any one of an annual BBC series (the Proms) at the Royal Albert Hall, London, at which part of the audience stands. They were originated by Henry Wood 1895.

Prometheus /prə'mi:θju:s/ in Greek mythology, a ◊Titan who stole fire from heaven for the human race. In revenge, Zeus had him chained to a rock with an eagle preying on his liver, until he was rescued by ◊Hercules.

promethium an element of the ◊rare earth group, symbol Pm, atomic number 61. Several isotopes have been reported, obtained by fission of uranium or by neutron bombardment of neodymium. Its existence in nature is unconfirmed.

prominence a bright cloud of gas projecting from the Sun into space 100,000 km/60,000 mi or more. *Quiescent prominences* last for months, and are held in place by magnetic fields in the Sun's corona. *Surge prominences* shoot gas into space at speeds of 1,000 km/600 mi per sec. *Loop prominences* are gases falling back to the Sun's surface after a solar ◊flare.

promissory note a written promise to pay on demand, or at a fixed future time, a specific sum of money to a named person or bearer. Like a cheque, it is negotiable if endorsed by the payee. A commercial paper is a form of promissory note that can be bought and sold. These forms of payment are usually issued by large corporations at times when credit is otherwise difficult to obtain.

pronghorn hoofed herbivorous mammal *Antilocapra americana* of the W USA. It is light brown, and about 1 m/3 ft high. It sheds its horns annually, and can reach speeds of 100 kph/60 mph. The loss of prairies to agriculture, combined with excessive hunting, has brought this unique animal close to extinction.

pronoun a grammatical ◊part of speech that is used in place of a noun, usually to save repetition of the noun for example 'The people arrived around nine o'clock. *They* behaved as though we were expecting *them*').

'They', 'them', 'he', and 'she' are *personal pronouns* (representing people); 'this/these', and 'that/those' are *demonstrative pronouns* (demonstrating or point to something: this book and not that book. Words like 'that' and 'who' can be *relative pronouns* in sentences like 'She said that she was coming' and 'Tell me who did it' relating one clause to another), and 'myself' and 'himself' are *reflexive pronouns* (reflecting back to a person, as in 'He did it himself').

pronghorn

pronunciation the way in which words are rendered into human speech sounds; either a language as a whole ('French pronunciation') or a particular word or name ('what is the pronunciation of *allophony*?'). The pronunciation of languages forms the academic subject of ◊**phonetics**.

A particular speaker's pronunciation of his or her language or other languages is an *accent*. The pronunciation of individual words in English is a matter of convention rather than absolute correctness; notoriously, it cannot be predicted from the spelling. The pronunciations of foreign words shown in the *Hutchinson Encyclopedia* are established English versions, where these exist; otherwise, they are acceptable renderings of the foreign-language pronunciation into English sounds.

proof spirit a numerical scale used to indicate the alcohol content of an alcoholic drink. Proof spirit (or 100% proof spirit) acquired its name from a solution of alcohol in water which, when used to moisten gunpowder, contained just enough alcohol to permit it to burn.

The degrees proof of an acoholic drink is based more accurately on the specific gravity of an aqueous solution containing the same amount of alcohol as the drink. Whisky containing 40% alcohol, by volume, is 70 degrees proof.

propaganda literally, the spreading of information, used particularly with reference to the promotion of a religious or political doctrine. The word has acquired pejorative connotations because of its association with the use of propaganda by Nazi Germany and other regimes.

propane a gaseous hydrocarbon (C_3H_8) found in petroleum and used as fuel.

propanol another name for ◊propyl alcohol.

propanone ($CH_3)_2CO$ (common name *acetone*) in chemistry, a colourless inflammable liquid used extensively as a solvent, as in nail-varnish remover. It boils at 56.5°C, mixes with water in all proportions, and has a characteristic odour.

propellant the substance burned in a rocket for propulsion. Two propellants are used; oxidizer and fuel are stored in separate tanks and pumped independently into the combustion chamber. Liquid oxygen (oxidizer) and liquid hydrogen (fuel) are common propellants, used for example in the Space Shuttle main engines.

propeller a screw-like device used to propel ships and some aeroplanes. A propeller has a number of curved blades, and accelerates fluid (liquid or gas) backwards when it rotates. Reaction to this backward movement of fluid sets up a propulsive thrust forwards. The marine screw propeller was developed by Francis Pettit Smith in Britain and Swedish-born John Ericsson in the USA.

propene CH_3CHCH_2 (common name *propylene*) second member of the alkene series of hydrocarbons. A gas, it is widely used by industry to make organic chemicals, including polypropylene plastics.

propenoic acid CH_2CHCO_2H (common name *acrylic acid*) obtained from the aldehyde propenal (acrolein) derived from glycerol or fats. Glass-like thermoplastic resins are made by polymerizing ◊esters of propenoic acid or methyl propenoic acid, and used for transparent components, lenses, and dentures. Other acrylic compounds are used for adhesives, artificial fibres, and artists' acrylic paint.

proper motion the gradual change in the position of a star that results from its motion in orbit around the galaxy. Proper motions are slight, undetectable to the naked eye, but can be accurately measured on telescopic photographs taken many years apart. ◊Barnard's Star is the star with the largest proper motion, 10.3 ◊arc seconds per year.

properties in chemistry, the characteristics a substance possesses by virtue of its composition. *Physical properties* of a substance can be measured by physical means, for example boiling point, melting point, hardness, elasticity, colour, and physical state. *Chemical properties* are the way it reacts with other substances; whether it is acidic or basic, an oxidizing or a

reducing agent, a salt, or stable to heat, for example.

Propertius /prə'pɜːʃəs/ Sextus *c.* 47–15 BC. Roman elegiac poet, a member of ◊Maecenas' circle, who wrote of his love for his mistress 'Cynthia'.

property the right to control the use of a thing (such as land, a building, a work of art, or a computer program). In English law, a distinction is made between *real property*, which involves a degree of geographical fixity, and *personal property*, which does not. Property is never absolute, since any society places limits on an individual's property (such as the right to transfer that property to another). Different societies have held widely varying interpretations of the nature of property and the extent of the rights of the owner of that property.

The debate about private and public property began with the Greeks. For Plato, an essential prerequisite for the guardians of his *Republic* was that they owned no property, while Aristotle saw private property as an equally important prerequisite of political participation. The Creation myth in the Bible was interpreted variously as a state of original communism destroyed by the Fall (by Thomas More in his *Utopia* 1516), and hence a justification of the monastic ideal, in which property is held in common, or as justifying the institution of private property, since Adam was granted dominion over all things in Eden. Locke argued that property rights to a thing are acquired by expending labour on it. Adam Smith saw property as a consequence of the transition of society from an initial state of hunting (in which property did not exist) to one of flock-rearing (which depended on property for its existence). Marx contrasted an Asiatic mode of production, a mythical age in which all property was held in common, with the situation under capitalism in which the only 'property' of the worker, labour, was appropriated by the capitalist. One of Marx's achievements was to reawaken the debate over property in terms that are still being used today.

prophet a person thought to speak from divine inspiration or who foretells the future. In Islam, ◊Muhammad is believed to be the last and greatest of a long line of prophets beginning with Adam and including Moses (both in the Old Testament or Hebrew Bible) and Jesus.

In the Bible, one of the succession of saints and seers who preached and prophesied in the Hebrew kingdoms in Palestine from the 8th century BC until the suppression of Jewish independence in 586 BC, and possibly later. The chief prophets were Elijah, Amos, Hosea, and Isaiah. The prophetic books of the Old Testament constitute a division of the Hebrew Bible.

prophylaxis any measure taken to prevent disease, including exercise and ◊vaccination. Prophylactic (preventive) medicine is an increasing aspect of public health provision.

proportion two variable quantities *x* and *y* are proportional if, for all values of *x*, $y = kx$, where k is a constant. This means that if *x* increases, *y* increases in a linear fashion. A graph of *x* against *y* would be a straight line passing through the origin (the point $x = 0$, $y = 0$). *y* is inversely proportional to *x* if the graph of *y* against $1/x$ is a straight line through the origin. The corresponding equation is $y = k/x$. Many laws of science relate quantities that are proportional (for example ◊Boyle's Law).

proportional representation (PR) electoral system in which distribution of party seats corresponds to their proportion of the total ◊votes cast, and minority votes are not wasted, (as opposed to a simple majority, or 'first past the post', system). Forms include:

party list or additional member system (AMS). As recommended by the Hansard Society 1976 for introduction in Britain, three-quarters of the members would be elected in single-member constituencies on the traditional majority-vote system, and the remaining seats be allocated according to the overall number of votes cast for each party (a variant of this is used in West Germany).

single transferable vote (STV), in which candidates are numbered in order of preference by the voter, and any votes surplus to the minimum required for a candidate to win are transferred to second preferences, as are second-preference votes from the successive candidates at the bottom of the poll until the required number of elected candidates is achieved (this is in use in the Republic of Ireland).

In France 1985 it was proposed to introduce a system under which, after ruling out parties with less than a 5% poll in each *département*, the votes for the rest would be divided by the number of seats to obtain an electoral quotient (for example, if the quotient were 15,000 votes, party A with 30,000 votes would win two seats, and party B with 12,000 would win none); unallocated seats would be distributed in a second round when each party's poll would be divided by the number of seats it had already won, plus one (that is, party A would now be credited with only 10,000 votes; party B, having won no seat so far, would be credited with its original 12,000, and so gain a seat).

prop root or *stilt root* a modified root that grows from the lower part of a stem or trunk down to the ground, providing a plant with extra support. Prop roots are common on some woody plants, such as mangroves, and also occur on a few herbaceous plants, such as maize. *Buttress roots* are a type of prop root found at the base of tree trunks, extended and flattened along the upper edge to form massive triangular buttresses; they are common on tropical trees.

propyl alcohol usually a mixture of two isomeric compounds, normal propyl alcohol and isopropyl alcohol ($CH_3CHOHCH_3$). The former is also known as 1-propanol, and the latter as 2-propanol. It is a colourless liquid which can be mixed with water, and is used in perfumery.

propylene common name for ◊propene.

pro rata (Latin) in proportion.

prose spoken or written language without metrical regularity; in literature, prose corresponds more closely to the patterns of everyday speech than ◊poetry. In modern literature, however, the distinction between verse and prose is not always clear cut.

In Western literature prose was traditionally used for what today is usually called nonfiction; that is, history, biography, essays, and so on, while verse was used for imaginative literature. Prose came into its own as a vehicle for ◊fiction with the rise of the modern ◊novel in the 18th century.

Prosecution Service, Crown body established by the Prosecution of Offences Act 1985, responsible for prosecuting all criminal offences in England and Wales. It is headed by the Director of Public Prosecutions (DPP), and brings England and Wales in line with Scotland (see ◊procurator fiscal) in having a prosecution service independent of the police.

In most cases the decision to prosecute is made on the basis of evidence presented by the police to local crown prosecutors in each of 43 police authority areas. The DPP had previously taken action (under the guidance of the attorney general) only in cases of special difficulty or importance.

Proserpina Roman equivalent of ◊Persephone, goddess of the underworld.

Prost Alain 1955– . French motor-racing driver. He won 39 races from 153 starts, and was world champion 1985, 1986, and 1989.

He raced in Formula One events from 1980. He had his first Grand Prix win 1981 (French GP) driving a Renault. In 1984 he began driving for McLaren.

CAREER HIGHLIGHTS

World champion: 1985 (Marlboro-McLaren), 1986 (Marlboro-McLaren), 1989 (Marlboro-Honda)
Formula One Grand Prix races: 153 wins; 39 (record)
1st Grand Prix: 1980 Argentine GP (McLaren)

prostaglandin a complex fatty acid that acts as a messenger substance between cells. Effects include stimulating the contraction of smooth muscle (for example, of the womb during birth), regulating the

Prost *French motor racing driver Alain Prost in the Formula One series of the Grand Prix season, 1989.*

production of stomach acid, and modifying hormonal activity. In excess, prostaglandins may produce inflammatory disorders such as arthritis. Synthetic prostaglandins are used to induce labour in humans and domestic animals.

The actions of substances such as aspirin are due to inhibition of prostaglandin synthesis.

prostate gland a gland surrounding, and opening into, the urethra at the base of the penis of male mammals. The prostate gland produces an alkaline fluid, which is released during ejaculation; this fluid activates sperm, and prevents their clumping together.

prosthesis replacement of a body part with an artificial substitute. Prostheses in the form of artificial limbs, such as metal hooks for hands and wooden legs, have been used for centuries, although modern artificial limbs are more natural-looking and comfortable to wear. The recently developed study of ◊bionics uses myoelectric, or bionic, arms, which are electronically operated and worked by minute electrical impulses from body muscles. Other prostheses include hearing aids, false teeth and eyes, and for the heart, a ◊pacemaker, and plastic heart valves and blood vessels.

prostitution receipt of money for sexual acts. Society's attitude towards it varies according to place

prosthesis

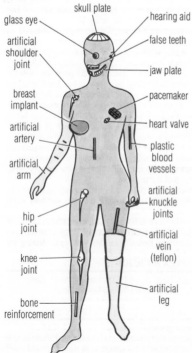

and period. In some countries, tolerance is combined with licensing of brothels and health checks on the prostitutes. In the UK a compromise system makes it legal to be a prostitute, but soliciting for customers publicly, keeping a brothel, living on 'immoral earnings', and 'procuring' (arranging to make someone into a prostitute) are illegal.

The English Collective of Prostitutes is an organization that represents the interests of prostitutes. US organizations include COYOTE (Call Off Your Old Tired Ethic).

protactinium a rare element, symbol Pa, atomic number 91, relative atomic mass 231.04. One of the actinide series of elements, it is present in very small quantities in pitchblende.

protandry in a flower, the state where the male reproductive organs reach maturity before those of the female. This is a common method of avoiding self-fertilization. See also ◊protogyny.

protectionism in economics, the imposition of heavy duties or import quotas by a government as a means of discouraging the import of foreign goods likely to compete with domestic products. The opposite practice is ◊free trade.

protectorate formerly in international law, a small state under the direct or indirect control of a larger one. The 20th-century equivalent was a ◊trust territory. In English history the rule of Oliver and Richard ◊Cromwell 1653–59 is referred to as the Protectorate.

protein a long-chain molecule composed of amino acids joined by ◊peptide bonds. Proteins are essential to all living organisms. As ***enzymes*** they regulate all aspects of metabolism. Structural proteins such as ***keratin*** and ***collagen*** make up the skin, claws, bones, tendons, and ligaments, while ***muscle*** proteins produce movement, ***haemoglobin*** transports oxygen, and ***membrane*** proteins regulate the movement of substances into and out of cells. For humans, protein is an essential part of the diet, and is found in greatest quantity in soya beans and other grain legumes, meat, eggs, and cheese.

pro tem(pore) (Latin) for the time being.

Proterozoic period of geological time, 2.5 billion to 590 million years ago, the second division of the Precambrian era. It is defined as the time of simple life, since many rocks dating from this eon show traces of biological activity, and some contain the fossils of bacteria and algae.

Protestantism one of the main divisions of Christianity, which emerged from Roman Catholicism at the ◊Reformation. The chief denominations are the Anglican Communion, Baptists, Lutherans, Methodists, Pentecostal Movement, and Presbyterians, with a total membership of about 320 million.

Protestantism takes its name from the protest of Luther and his supporters at the Diet of Spires 1529 against the decision to reaffirm the edict of the Diet of Worms against the Reformation. The ecumenical movement of the 20th century has unsuccessfully attempted to reunite various

Protestant denominations and, to some extent, the Protestant churches and the Catholic church. From the 1970s there was a revival of interest in Christianity among young people which was not necessarily connected to the established churches.

Proteus in Greek mythology an old man, the warden of the sea beasts of Poseidon, who possessed the gift of prophecy, but could transform himself to any form he chose to evade questioning.

prothallus the short-lived gametophyte of many ferns and other ◊pteridophytes. It bears either the male or female sex organs, or both. Typically it is a small, green, flattened structure which is anchored in the soil by several ◊rhizoids and needs damp comditions to survive. The reproductive organs are borne on the lower surface close to the soil. See also ◊alternation of generations.

protist in biology, a single-celled organism which has a ◊eukaryotic cell, but which is not member of the plant, fungal, or animal kingdoms. The main protists are ◊protozoa.

Single-celled photosynthetic organisms, such as diatoms and dinoflagellates, are classified as protists or algae. Recently the term has also been used for members of the kingdom Protoctista, which features in certain five-kingdom classifications of the living world. This kingdom may include slime moulds, all algae (seaweeds as well as unicellular forms), and protozoa.

protocol in computing, an agreed set of standards for the transfer of data between different devices. They cover transmission speed, format of data, and the signals required to synchronize the transfer. See also ◊interface.

Protocols of Zion forged document containing supposed plans for Jewish world conquest alleged to have been submitted by ◊Herzl to the first Zionist Congress at Basel 1897, and published in Russia 1905. They were proved to be a forgery by *The Times* 1921, but were used by Hitler in his anti-Semitic campaign.

protogyny in a flower, the state where the female reproductive organs reach maturity before those of the male. Like ◊protandry, this is a method of avoiding self-fertilization, but it is much less common.

proton (Greek 'first') positively charged subatomic particle, a fundamental constituent of any atomic ◊nucleus. Their lifespan is effectively infinite.

protonema the young ◊gametophyte of a moss, which develops from a germinating spore (see ◊alternation of generations). Typically it is a green, branched, threadlike structure which grows over the soil surface bearing several buds that develop into the characteristic adult moss plants.

proton number the number, sometimes called the ***atomic number***, of protons in the nucleus of an ◊atom. Adding the proton number to the number of neutrons in the nucleus (the neutron number) produces the ◊nucleon number.

Proton rocket a Soviet space rocket introduced 1965, used to launch heavy satellites, space probes, and the Salyut and Mir space stations. Proton consists

protein

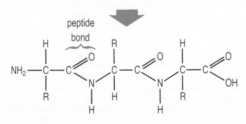

amino acids, where R is one of many possible side chains

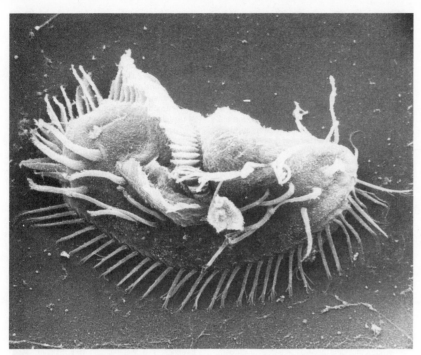

protozoa *Scanning electron micrograph of ciliate protozoa Oxtricha. They are microscopic, unicellular, and free-living; they are highly evolved and contain two kinds of nucleus. The cilia that decorate the bodies help in locomotion and feeding.*

of up to four stages as necessary. It has never been used to launch people into space.

protoplasm the contents of a living ◊cell. Strictly speaking it includes all the discrete structures (organelles) in a cell, but it is often used simply to mean the jelly-like material in which these float. The contents of a cell outside the nucleus are called ◊cytoplasm.

prototype in technology, any of the first few machines of a new design. Prototypes are tested for performance, reliability, economy, and safety; then the main design can be modified before full-scale production begins.

protozoa a group of single-celled organisms without rigid cell walls. Some, such as amoeba, ingest other cells, but most are ◊saprotrophs or parasites. The group is polyphyletic (containing organisms which have different evolutionary origins).

Proudhon /pru:'dɒn/ Pierre Joseph 1809–1865. French anarchist, born in Besançon. He sat in the Constituent Assembly of 1848, was imprisoned for three years, and had to go into exile in Brussels. He published *Qu'est-ce que la propriété/What is Property?* 1840 and *Philosophie de la misère/Philosophy of Poverty* 1846. His most noted dictum is 'property is theft'.

Proust /pru:st/ Joseph Louis 1754–1826. French chemist. He was the first to state the principle of constant composition of compounds—that compounds consist of the same proportions of elements wherever found.

Proust /pru:st/ Marcel 1871–1922. French novelist and critic. The autobiographical novel *À la recherche du temps perdu/Remembrance of Things Past* 1913 is the expression of his childhood memories coaxed from his subconscious; it is also a precise reflection of life in provincial France at the end of the 19th century.

Proust was a delicate, asthmatic child, and although he moved in fashionable Parisian society in his youth, he shut himself away after the death of his parents 1904–05 in a cork-lined room in his Paris flat.

Prout William 1785–1850. British chemist. In 1815 Prout, a London physician, published his hypothesis that the atomic weight of every atom was an exact and integral multiple of the hydrogen atom.

The discovery of ◊isotopes in the 20th century established Prout's Hypothesis.

Provençal language a member of the Romance branch of the Indo-European language family, spoken in and around Provence in SE France. It is now regarded as a dialect or patois.

During the Middle Ages it was in competition with French and was the language of the troubadours. It had a strong literary influence on such neighbouring languages as Italian, Spanish, and Portuguese. Since the 19th century attempts have been made to revive it as a literary language.

Provençal literature Provençal literature originated in the 10th century, and flowered in the 12th century with the work of the ◊troubadours. After the decline of the troubadours in the 13th century, Provençal disappeared as a literary medium from the 14th until the 19th century, when Jacques Jasmin (1798–1864) and others paved the way for the Félibrige group of poets, of whom the greatest are Joseph Roumanille (1818–91), Frédéric Mistral (1830–1914), and Félix Gras (1844–1901).

Provence-Alpes-Côte d'Azur /prə'vɒns ˌkəut dæ'zjuə/ region of SE France, comprising the *départements* of Alpes-de-Haute-Provence, Hautes-Alpes, Alpes-Maritimes, Bouches-du Rhône, Var, and Vaucluse; area 31,400 sq km/12,120 sq mi; capital Marseille; population (1986) 4,059,000. The *Côte d'Azur*, on the Mediterranean, is a tourist centre. Provence was an independent kingdom in the 10th century, and the area still has its own language, Provençal.

Proverbs a book of the Hebrew Bible (and Christian Old Testament), traditionally ascribed to ◊Solomon. The Proverbs form a series of maxims on moral and ethical matters.

Providence /'prɒvɪdəns/ industrial port (jewellery, silverware, textiles and textile machinery, watches, chemicals meat packing), capital of Rhode Island, USA, on the Providence river, 43 km/27 mi from the Atlantic; population (1980) 919,000. Providence was settled by Roger Williams 1636.

Provincetown Players group of US actors, producers, and playwrights formed 1915 in Provincetown, Cape Cod, Massachusetts; they later moved to New York. Mounting new plays by Eugene O'Neill, Theodore Dreiser,

e e cummings, and others, they opened the door to US experimental theatre.

Provisions of Oxford provisions issued by Henry III of England 1258 under pressure from Simon de Montfort (1208–65) and the baronial opposition. They provided for the establishment of a baronial council to run the government, carry out reforms, and keep a check on royal power.

provost chief magistrate of a Scottish burgh, approximate equivalent of an English mayor.

Proxima Centauri the closest star to the Sun, 4.3 light years away. It is a faint ◊red dwarf, visible only with a telescope, and is a member of the Alpha Centauri triple star system. It is called Proxima because it is about 0.1 light years closer to us than its two partners.

proxy in law, a person authorized to stand in another's place; also the document conferring this right. The term usually refers to voting at meetings, but there may be marriages by proxy.

Prudhoe Bay /'prʌdəu 'beɪ/ a bay in N ◊Alaska. A pipeline links oil fields with the Gulf of Alaska to the S.

Prud'hon /pru:don/ Pierre 1758–1823. French Romantic painter. He became drawing instructor and court painter to the Emperor Napoleon's wives.

After winning the Prix de Rome 1784, Prud'hon visited Italy but, unlike his contemporary David, he was unaffected by the Neo-Classical vogue; his style is indebted to ◊Correggio.

Prunus genus of trees of the northern hemisphere, family Rosaceae, producing fruit with a fleshy, edible pericarp. The genus includes plums, peaches, apricots, almonds, and cherries.

Prussia /'prʌʃə/ a N German state 1618–1945. It was an independent kingdom until 1867 when it became a dominant part of the North German Confederation and part of the German Empire 1871 under the Prussian King Wilhelm I. West Prussia became part of Poland under the ◊Versailles Treaty and East Prussia was largely incorporated into the USSR after 1945.

1618 Formed by the union of ◊Brandenburg and the duchy of Prussia (established 1525).

1640–88 The country's military power was founded by ◊Frederick William, the 'Great Elector'.

1701 Prussia became a kingdom under Frederick I.

1713–40 Frederick William I expanded the army.

1740–86 Silesia, East Frisia, and West Prussia were annexed by ◊Frederick II the Great.

Proust *During the 1890s, around the time this photograph was taken, Marcel Proust moved in the most fashionable Parisian circles, but shortly afterwards he became a virtual recluse, dedicating his time to his autobiographical novel, A la recherche du temps perdu.*

Prussia

● Berlin

1806 ◊Frederick William III was defeated at Jena by Napoleon.

1815 After the Congress of Vienna Prussia regained its lost territories and also acquired lands in the Rhineland and Saxony.

1848 Affected by the ◊revolutions of 1848.

1864 War with Denmark resulted in the acquisition of Schleswig and Holstein.

1866 After the defeat of Austria, Prussia formed the North German Confederation with the territories of Hanover, Nassau, Frankfurt-am-Main, and Hesse-Cassel.

1918 Prussia became a republic after World War I.

1932 Prussia lost its local independence in Hitler's Germany and came under the control of the Reich.

1946 After World War II the Allies abolished the state altogether, dividing its territories among East and West Germany, Poland, and the USSR.

prussic acid an old name for ◊hydrocyanic acid.

Prut a river that rises in the Carpathian Mountains of SW Ukraine and flows 900 km/565 mi to meet the Danube at Reni. For part of its course it follows the E frontier of Romania.

Prynne /prɪn/ William 1600–1669. English Puritan. He published in 1632 *Histriomastix*, a work attacking stage plays; it contained aspersions on the Queen, for which he was pilloried and lost his ears. In 1637 he was again pilloried and branded for an attack on the bishops. He opposed the execution of Charles I, and actively supported the Restoration.

Przemysl /ˈpʃɛmɪsʊ/ industrial city (timber, ceramics, flour milling, tanning, distilling, food processing, gas, engineering) in SE Poland; population (1981) 62,000.

history Founded in the 8th century, it belonged alternately to Poland and Kiev in the 10th–14th centuries. An Austrian territory 1722–1919, it was a frontier fortress besieged by Soviet troops Sept 1914–Mar 1915, and was occupied by the Germans June 1941–July 1944.

Przhevalsky /pʃeˈvælski/ Nikolai Mikhailovitch 1839–1888. Russian explorer and soldier. In 1870 he crossed the Gobi Desert to Beijing and then went on to the upper reaches of the Chang Jiang River. His attempts to penetrate Tibet as far as Lhasa failed on three occasions, but he continued to explore the mountain regions between Tibet and Mongolia, where he made collections of plants and animals, including a wild camel and a wild horse.

The Kirghiz town of Karakol on the eastern shores of Lake Issyk Kul where he died was renamed Przhevalsky in 1889.

PS abbreviation for *post scriptum* (Latin 'after writing').

psalm a sacred poem or song of praise. The Book of Psalms in the Hebrew Bible (Christian Old Testament) is divided into five books containing 150 psalms. They are traditionally ascribed to David, the second king of Israel.

PSBR abbreviation for ◊*public-sector borrowing requirement*.

pseudocarp a fruitlike structure that incorporates tissue that is not derived from the ovary wall. The additional tissues may be derived from floral parts such as the ◊receptacle and ◊calyx. For example, the coloured, fleshy part of a strawberry develops from the receptacle and the true fruits are small

◊achenes—the 'pips' embedded in its outer surface. Rose hips are a type of pseudocarp that consists of a hollow, fleshy receptacle containing a number of achenes within. Different types of pseudocarp include pineapples, figs, apples, and pears.

A *coenocarpium* is a fleshy, multiple pseudocarp derived from an ◊inflorescence rather than a single flower. The pineapple has a thickened central axis surrounded by fleshy tissues derived from the receptacles and floral parts of many flowers. A fig is a type of pseudocarp called a *syconium*, formed from a hollow receptacle with small flowers attached to the inner wall. After fertilization the ovaries of the female flowers develop into one-seeded achenes. Apples and pears are ◊pomes, another type of pseudocarp.

pseudocopulation the attempted copulation by a male insect with a flower. It results in ◊pollination of the flower and is common in the orchid family, where the flowers of many species resemble a particular species of female bee. When a male bee attempts to mate with a flower, the pollinia (groups of pollen grains) stick to its body. They are transferred to the stigma of another flower when the insect attempts copulation again.

PSFD abbreviation for public sector financial deficit; see under ◊public sector borrowing requirement.

psi in parapsychology, a hypothetical facility common to humans and other animals said to be responsible for extra-sensory perception (ESP) and telekinesis.

Psilocybe genus of mushroom with hallucinogenic properties, including the Mexican sacred mushroom *Psilocybe mexicana* which contains compounds with effects similar to LSD. A related species *Psilocybe semilanceata* is found in Britain.

psittacosis virus disease, contracted by humans from birds (especially parrots), which may result in pneumonia.

Pskov /pskɒf/ industrial city (food processing, leather) in USSR, on the Velikaya river, SW of Leningrad; population (1987) 202,000. Dating from 965, it was independent 1348–1510, when it became Russian.

psoriasis chronic skin inflammation resulting in raised, red, scaly patches, usually on the scalp, back, arms, and legs. The attacks are recurrent, but sometimes disappear of their own accord. Tar preparations are used to treat it. Psoriasis may be accompanied by a form of arthritis.

Psyche /ˈsaɪki/ late Greek personification of the soul as a winged girl or young woman. The goddess Aphrodite was so jealous of Psyche's beauty that she ordered her son Eros, the god of love, to make her fall in love with the worst of men, but he fell in love with her himself.

psychedelic rock or *acid rock* a type of pop music, with advanced electronic equipment for both light and sound, which began about 1966. The free-form improvisations and light shows of the hippie years had by the 1980s become stadium performances with lasers and other special effects.

psychiatry the branch of medicine dealing with the diagnosis and treatment of mental disorder.

In practice there is considerable overlap between psychiatry and ◊clinical psychology, the fundamental difference being that psychiatrists are trained medical doctors (holding an MD degree) and may therefore prescribe drugs, whereas psychologists may hold a PhD but do not need a medical qualification to practise. See also ◊psychology.

psychic a person allegedly possessed of parapsychological, or paranormal, powers.

psychoanalysis a theory and treatment method for neuroses, developed by ◊Freud. The main treatment method involves the free association of ideas, and interpretation. It is typically expensive and prolonged and there is controversy about its effectiveness.

It emphasizes the impact of early childhood sexuality and experiences, which are stored in the unconscious and can lead to the development of adult emotional problems. Modern approaches,

drawing from Freud's ideas, tend to be briefer and problem-focused.

psychology the systematic study of human and animal behaviour. The first psychology laboratory was founded 1879 by Wilhelm ◊Wundt in Leipzig, Germany. The subject includes diverse areas of study and application, among them the roles of instinct, heredity, environment and culture; the processes of sensation, perception, learning and memory; the bases of motivation and emotion; and the functioning of thought, intelligence and language.

◊Experimental psychology emphasizes the application of rigorous and objective scientific methods to the study of a wide range of mental processes and behaviour, whereas social psychology concerns the study of individuals within their social environment; for example, within groups and organizations. This has led to the development of related fields such as ◊occupational psychology, which studies human behaviour at work, and ◊educational psychology. Clinical psychology concerns the understanding and treatment of health problems, particularly mental disorders, such as anxiety, phobias, or depression; treatment may include ◊behaviour therapy, ◊cognitive therapy, ◊counselling, ◊psychoanalysis, or some combination of these.

Influential psychologists have included Gustav Fechner (1801–87 founder of psychophysics); Wolfgang Köhler (1887–1967), one of the ◊gestalt or 'whole' psychologists; Sigmund Freud and his associates Jung, Adler, and Rorschach; William James, Jean Piaget; Carl Rogers; Hans Eysenck; J B Watson, and B F Skinner. Modern studies have been diverse, for example the psychological causes of obesity; the nature of religious experience; and the underachievement of women seen as resulting from social pressures. Other related subjects are the nature of sleep and dreams, and possible extensions of the senses, which leads to the more controversial ground of ◊parapsychology.

psychometrics the measurement of mental processes. This includes intelligence and aptitude testing to help in job selection and in the clinical assessment of cognitive deficiencies resulting from brain damage.

psychopathy a personality disorder characterized by chronic antisocial behaviour (violating the rights of others, often violently) and an absence of feelings of guilt about the behaviour.

pseudocopulation

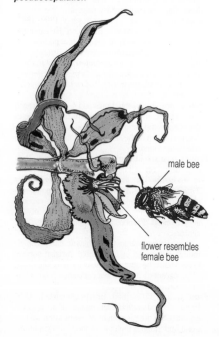

male bee

flower resembles female bee

psychology: chronology

1879	Wilhelm Wundt founded the first psychological laboratory, in Leipzig.
1890	William James published the first comprehensive psychology text, *Principles of Psychology*.
1895	Freud's first book on psychoanalysis was published.
1896	The first clinical psychology clinic was founded by Witner at the University of Pennsylvania.
1903	Pavlov reported his early study on conditioned reflexes in animals.
1905	Binet and Simon developed the first effective intelligence test.
1908	A first textbook of social psychology was published by William McDougall.
1913	J B Watson published his influential work *Behaviourism*.
1926	Jean Piaget presented his first book on child development.
1947	Eysenck published *Dimensions of Personality*, a large-scale study of neuroticism and extraversion.
1953	Skinner's *Science of Human Behaviour*, a text of operant conditioning, was published.
1957	Chomsky's *Syntactic Structures*, which stimulated the development of psycholinguistics, the study of language processes, was published.
1963	Milgram's studies of compliance with authority indicated conditions under which individuals behave cruelly to others when instructed to do so.
1967	Neisser's *Cognitive Psychology* marked renewed interest in the study of cognition after years in which behaviourism had been dominant.
1972	Newell and Simon simulated human problem-solving abilities by computer; an example of artificial intelligence.
1989	Jeffrey Masson attacked the fundamental principles of Freudian analytic psychotherapy in his book *Against Therapy*.

Because the term has been misused to refer to any severe mental disorder, many psychologists now prefer the term 'antisocial personality disorder'.

psychosis or **psychotic disorder** a general term for a serious mental disorder where the individual commonly loses contact with reality and may experience hallucinations (seeing or hearing things that do not exist) or delusions (fixed false beliefs). For example, in a paranoid psychosis, an individual may believe that others are plotting against him or her. A major type of psychosis is ◊schizophrenia.

psychosomatic a description of any physical symptom or disease arising from emotional or mental factors.

The term 'psychosomatic' has been applied to many conditions, including asthma, migraine, ◊hypertension, and peptic ulceration. Whereas it is unlikely that these and other conditions are wholly due to psychological factors, emotional states such as anxiety or depression do have a distinct influence on the frequency and severity of illness.

psychosurgery operation to achieve some mental effect, for example *leucotomy*/(US)*lobotomy* the separation of the white fibres in the prefrontal lobe of the brain, as a means of relieving a deep state of anxiety. It is irreversible, the degree of personality change is not predictable, and its justification is disputed.

psychotherapy treatment approaches for mental problems which involve talking rather than surgery or drugs. Examples include ◊behaviour therapy, ◊cognitive therapy, and ◊psychoanalysis.

psychotic disorder another name for ◊psychosis.

pt abbreviation for *pint*.

Ptah Egyptian god, the divine potter, a personification of the creative force. He was worshipped at ◊Memphis, and often portrayed as a mummified man. He was the father of ◊Imhotep.

ptarmigan a type of ◊grouse *Lagopus mutus* found in N Europe. About 36 cm/1.2 ft long, it has a white coat in winter.

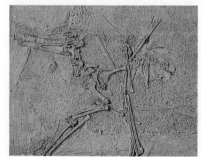

pterodactyl *Fossil remains of a pterodactyl, discovered in Württemberg, West Germany.*

pteridophyte a simple type of ◊vascular plant. The pteridophytes comprise four classes: the Psilosida, including the most primitive vascular plants, found mainly in the tropics; the Lycopsida, including the clubmosses and *Selaginella*; the Sphenopsida, including the horsetails; and the Pteropsida, including the ferns. They are mainly terrestrial, non-flowering plants characterized by the presence of a vascular system, the possession of true stems, roots, and leaves, and by a marked ◊alternation of generations, with the sporophyte forming the dominant generation in the life-cycle. They do not produce seeds.

The pteridophytes formed a large and dominant flora during the Carboniferous period, but many are now known only from fossils.

pterodactyl extinct flying reptile of the order Pterosauria, existing in the Mesozoic age. Pterosaurs were formerly assumed to be smooth-skinned gliders, but recent discoveries show that at least some were furry, probably warm-blooded, and may have had muscle fibres and blood vessels on their wings, stiffened by moving the hind legs, thus allowing controlled and strong flapping flight. They ranged from starling size to the largest with 17 m/50 ft wingspan.

PTFE (*poly*tetra*fluoro*ethylene) a tough, waxlike, heat-resistant plastic, also known by the trade name Teflon, much used for the coating on nonstick kitchenware.

PTO abbreviation for *please turn over*.

Ptolemy /ˈtɒləmi/ (Claudius Ptolemaeus) *c.* AD 100–170 Egyptian astronomer and geographer, who worked in Alexandria. The *Almagest* developed the theory that Earth is the centre of the universe, with the Sun, Moon, and stars revolving around it. In 1543 ◊Copernicus disproved the ***Ptolemaic system***. Ptolemy's *Geography* was a standard source of information until the 16th century.

Ptolemy /ˈtɒləmi/ dynasty of kings of Macedonian origin who ruled Egypt over a period of 300 years; they included:

Ptolemy I *c.*367–283 BC. Ruler of Egypt from 323 BC, king from 304. He was one of ◊Alexander the Great's generals, and possibly his half-brother (see also ◊Thaïs). He established the library at Alexandria.

Ptolemy XIII 63–47 BC. Joint ruler of Egypt with his sister-wife Cleopatra; she put him to death.

ptomaine group of toxic chemical substances produced as a result of decomposition.

puberty stage in human development when the individual becomes sexually mature. It may occur from the age of ten upwards. The sexual organs take on their adult form and pubic hair grows. In girls, menstruation begins, and the breasts develop; in boys, the voice breaks and becomes deeper, and a beard develops.

pubes the lowest part of the front of the human trunk, the region where the external generative organs are situated. The underlying bony structure, the pubic

arch, is formed by the union in the midline of the two pubic bones, which are the front portions of the hip bones. In women it is more prominent than in men, to allow more room for the passage of the child's head at birth, and carries a pad of fat and connective tissue, the mons veneris (mountain of Venus), for its protection.

Public Against Violence (Slovak *Verejnosť Proti Násil'u*) the Slovak half of the Czechoslovak democratic movement, counterpart of the Czech organization ◊Civic Forum.

public corporation a company structure that is similar in organization to a public limited company but with no shareholder rights. Such corporations are established to carry out state-owned activities, but are financially independent of the state and are run by a board. The first public corporation to be formed in the UK was the Central Electricity Board in the 1920s.

After World War II, a number of industries were nationalized, and new public corporations established. Since the late 1970s, however, there has been a growing incidence of ◊privatization, and many previously nationalized activities have been returned to the private sector, becoming public limited companies.

Public Health Acts 1848, 1872, 1875 in the UK, legislation enacted by Parliament to deal with squalor and disease and to establish a code of sanitary law. The first act, in 1848, established a central board of health with three members who were responsible to Parliament to impose local boards of health in districts where the death rate was above the national average and made provision for other local boards of health to be established by petition. The 1872 act made it obligatory for every local authority to appoint a medical officer of health. The 1875 act consolidated previous acts and provided a comprehensive code for public health.

public house or *pub* a building licensed for consumption of liquor. In Britain a pub is either 'free' (when the licensee has free choice of suppliers) or, more often, 'tied' to a brewery company owning the house.

public inquiry in English law, a legal investigation where witnesses are called and evidence is produced in a similar fashion to a court of law. Inquiries may be held as part of legal procedure, or into a matter of public importance.

Inquiries that are part of certain legal procedures, such as where planning permission is disputed, or where an inquiry is required by an act of Parliament, are headed by an inspector appointed by the secretary of state concerned, who then makes a decision based on the inspector's report (although this report is not binding). The longest and most expensive inquiry ever held was the Sizewell B nuclear-plant inquiry, which lasted for two and a quarter years. Inquiries into a matter of public importance are usually headed by a senior judge. Examples include the **Scarman inquiry** following inner city riots in 1981, an inquiry into the King's Cross underground fire 1987, and an inquiry into child abuse in Cleveland in 1988.

public lending right (PLR) method of paying a royalty to authors when books are borrowed from libraries, similar to a royalty on performance of a play or piece of music. Payment to the copyright holder for such borrowings was introduced in Australia 1974 and in the UK 1984.

public limited company (plc) a registered company in which shares and debentures may be offered to the public. It must have a minimum of seven shareholders and there is no upper limit. The company's financial records must be available for any member of the public to scrutinize, and the company's name must carry the words 'public limited company' or initials *plc*. A public company can raise enormous financial resources to fuel its development and expansion by inviting the public to buy shares.

Public Order Act UK act of Parliament 1986 to control ◊riots.

public school in England, a fee-paying independent school. In Scotland, the USA, and many other

English-speaking countries, a 'public' school is a state-maintained school, and independent schools are generally known as 'private' schools.

Some English public schools (for example Eton, Harrow, Rugby, Winchester) are ancient foundations, usually originally intended for poor male scholars; others developed in the 18–19th centuries. Among those for girls are Roedean and Benenden. Many public schools are coeducational in the sixth form. Some discipline (less than formerly) is in the hands of senior boys/girls (prefects). Originally, UK public schools stressed a classical education, character training, and sports, but the curriculum is now closely allied to state education although with generally a wider range of subjects offered, and a lower pupil-to-teacher ratio.

public-sector borrowing requirement (PSBR) amount of money needed by a government to cover any deficit in financing its own activities, including loans to local authorities and public corporations, and also the funds raised by local authorities and public corporations from other sources.

The PSBR is financed chiefly by sales of debt to the public outside the banking system (gilt-edged stocks, national savings, and local-authority stocks and bonds), by external transactions with other countries, and by borrowing from the banking system. In the UK, after the 1986 budget this measure was changed to the *public sector financial deficit (PSFD)*, which is net of the asset sales due to privatization thought to distort the PSBR.

public spending expenditure by government, covering national military, health, education, infrastructure, and other projects, and the cost of servicing overseas borrowing. An important source of revenue to cover public expenditure is taxation. Most countries present their plans for spending in their annual budgets.

publishing the production of books for sale. The publisher arranges for the commissioning, editing, printing, binding, and distribution to booksellers or bookclubs. Although all rights in a book may be purchased by the publisher for a single outright fee, it is more usual and generally fairer to publisher and author if a fixed royalty is paid on every copy sold, in return for the exclusive right to publish in an agreed territory. In Britain many leading publishers are members of the Publishers' Association.

Puccini Striving for perfection in the drama of his operas as much as in the scores, Puccini drove his librettists Giacosa and Illica to produce 'a libretto that would move the world'. The libretti of his masterpieces Madame Butterfly and Tosca are models of their kind.

Puccini /puˈtʃiːni/ Giacomo (Antonio Domenico Michele Secondo Maria) 1858–1924. Italian opera composer whose music shows a strong gift for melody and dramatic effect. His realist works include *Manon Lescaut* 1893, *La Bohème* 1896, *Tosca* 1900, *Madame Butterfly* 1904, and the unfinished *Turandot* 1926.

puddle clay clay, with sand or gravel, which has had water added and mixed thoroughly so that it becomes watertight. The term was coined 1762 by the canal builder James Brindley, although its use in dams goes back to Roman times.

Pudovkin /puːˈdɒfkɪn/ Vsevolod Illationovich 1893–1953. Russian film director, whose films include the silent *Mother* 1926, *The End of St Petersburg* 1927, and *Storm over Asia* 1928; and the sound films *Deserter* 1933 and *Suvorov* 1941.

Puebla (de Zaragoza) /ˈpweblə deɪ ˌsærəˈɡɒsə/ industrial city (textiles, sugar refining, metallurgy, hand-crafted pottery and tiles) and capital of Puebla state, S central Mexico; population (1986) 1,218,000. Founded 1535 as Pueblo de los Angeles, it was later renamed after Gen de Zaragoza, who defeated the French here 1862.

Pueblo /ˈpweɪbləʊ/ (Spanish *pueblos*, villages) generic name for North American Indians of SW North America including the ◊Hopi.

Pueblo /ˈpweɪbləʊ/ US intelligence vessel captured by the North Koreans Jan 1968, allegedly within their territorial waters. The crew, but not the ship, were released Dec 1968. A naval court recommended no disciplinary action.

puerperal relating to childbirth.

puerperal fever infection of the genital tract of the mother after childbirth that formerly often resulted in fatal blood poisoning, but which is now treated by antibiotics.

Puerto Rico, Commonwealth of /ˈpweətəʊ ˈriːkəʊ/ easternmost island of the Greater Antilles, situated between the US Virgin Islands and the Dominican Republic

area 9,000 sq km/3,475 sq mi

capital San Juan

towns ports Mayagüez, Ponce

features highest per capita income in Latin America

exports sugar, tobacco, rum, pineapples, textiles, plastics, chemicals, processed foods

currency US dollar

population (1980) 3,197,000, 67% urban

language Spanish and English (official)

religion Roman Catholic

government under the constitution of 1952, similar to that of the USA, with a governor elected for four years, and a legislative assembly with a senate and house of representatives

history visited 1493 by Columbus; annexed by Spain 1509; ceded to the USA after the ◊Spanish-American War 1898; achieved Commonwealth status with local self-government 1952. This was confirmed in preference to independence by a referendum 1967, but there is an independence movement, and another wishing incorporation as a state of the USA.

Puerto Sandino a major port on the Pacific W coast of Nicaragua, known as Puerto Somoza until 1979.

puff adder a type of ◊adder.

puffball globulous fruiting body of certain ◊fungi which cracks with maturity, releasing the enclosed spores, for example the **common puffball** *Lycoperdon perlatum*.

puffer fish a fish of the family Tetraodontidae. As a means of defence it inflates its body with air or water until it becomes spherical and the skin spines become erect. Puffer fish are mainly found in warm waters, where they feed on molluscs, crustaceans, and coral. They vary in size, up to 50 cm/20 in long.

The skin of some puffer fish is poisonous (25 times more toxic than cyanide), but they are prized as a delicacy (fugu) in Japan after the poison has been removed. Nevertheless about a hundred dead diners are recorded each year.

puffin seabird *Fratercula arctica* of the ◊auk family, found in the N Atlantic. It is about 30 cm/1 ft long, with a white face and front, red legs, and a large deep bill, very brightly coloured in summer. It has short wings and webbed feet. It is a poor flyer, but an excellent swimmer. It nests in rock crevices, or makes burrows, and lays a single egg.

pug breed of small dog with short wrinkled face, chunky body, and tail curled over the hip.

Puget Pierre 1620–1694. French Baroque sculptor who developed a powerful and expressive style. He created a muscular statue of the tyrant *Milo of Croton* 1672–82 (Louvre, Paris) for the garden of the palace of Versailles.

Puget worked in Italy 1640–43 and was influenced by ◊Michelangelo and ◊Pietro da Cortona. After 1682 he failed to gain further court patronage because of his stubborn temperament and his severe style.

Puget Sound an inlet of the Pacific Ocean on the W coast of Washington state, USA.

Pugin /ˈpjuːdʒɪn/ Augustus Welby Northmore 1812–1852. English architect, collaborator with ◊Barry in the detailed design of the Houses of Parliament. He did much to revive Gothic architecture in England.

Puglia /əˈpjuːliə/ (English *Apulia*) region of Italy, the south eastern 'heel'; area 19,300 sq km/7,450 sq mi; capital Bari, population (1988) 4,043,000. Products include wheat, grapes, almonds, olives, and vegetables. The main industrial centre is Taranto.

P'u-i /ˈpuː ˈjiː/ (formerly *Pu-Yi*) Henry 1906–1967. Last emperor of China (as Hsuan Tung) from 1908 until his deposition 1912; he was restored for a week 1917. He was president 1932–34 and emperor 1934–45 of the Japanese puppet state of Manchukuo (see ◊Manchuria). Captured by Soviet troops, he was returned to China 1949 and put on trial 1950. Pardoned by Mao Zedong 1959, he became a worker in a botanical garden in Beijing.

pūjā worship, in Hinduism, Buddhism, and Jainism.

Pula /ˈpuːlə/ commercial and naval port in W Croatia, Yugoslavia, on the Adriatic coast; population (1981) 77,278. A Roman naval base, *Colonia Pietas Julia*, it was seized by Venice in 1148, passed to Austria 1815, to Italy 1919, and Yugoslavia 1947. It has a Roman theatre, and a castle and cathedral constructed under Venetian rule. There is an annual film festival.

Pulitzer /ˈpʊlɪtsə/ Joseph 1847–1911. US newspaper proprietor, born in Hungary. He acquired the *New York World* 1883 and in 1903 founded the school of journalism at Columbia University, which awards the annual Pulitzer prizes in journalism and letters.

pulley

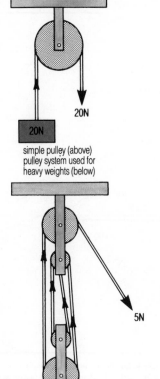

20N

20N

simple pulley (above)
pulley system used for
heavy weights (below)

5N

20N N = newton,
a unit of force

Pulitzer Prize for Fiction

1970	Jean Stafford *Collected Stories*
1972	Wallace Stegner *Angle of Repose*
1973	Eudora Welty *The Optimist's Daughter*
1975	Michael Shaara *The Killer Angels*
1976	Saul Bellow *Humboldt's Gift*
1978	James Alan McPherson *Elbow Room*
1979	John Cheever *The Stories of John Cheever*
1980	Norman Mailer *The Executioner's Song*
1981	John Kennedy Toole *A Confederacy of Dunces*
1982	John Updike *Rabbit is Rich*
1983	Alice Walker *The Color Purple*
1984	William Kennedy *Ironweed*
1985	Alison Lurie *Foreign Affairs*
1986	Larry McMurtry *Lonesome Dove*
1987	Peter Taylor *A Summons to Memphis*
1988	Toni Morrison *Beloved*
1989	Anne Tyler *Breathing Lessons*

pulley a simple machine consisting of a grooved wheel round which rope or chain can be run. A simple pulley serves only to change the direction of the applied effort (as in a simple hoist for raising loads). The use of more than one pulley results in a mechanical advantage, so that a given effort can raise a heavier load.

The mechanical advantage depends on the arrangement of the pulleys. For instance, a block and tackle arrangement with three ropes supporting the load will lift it with 1/3 of the effort needed to lift it directly (if friction is ignored), giving a mechanical advantage of 3.

Pullman /ˈpʊlman/ George 1831–1901. US engineer who developed the Pullman railway car. In an attempt to improve the standard of comfort of rail travel, he built his first Pioneer Sleeping Car 1863. He formed the Pullman Palace Car Company 1867 and in 1881 the town of Pullman, Illinois, was built for his workers.

pulmonary pertaining to the ◊lungs.

pulsar a celestial source that emits pulses of energy at regular intervals, ranging from a few seconds to small fractions of a second. They were discovered 1967, and are thought to be rapidly rotating ◊neutron stars, which flash at radio and other wavelengths as they spin. Over 300 radio pulsars are now known in our galaxy, although a million may exist.

Two pulsars, one in the ◊Crab Nebula and one in the constellation ◊Vela, give out flashes of visible light. Pulsars gradually slow down as they get older, and eventually the flashes fade. *X-ray pulsars* are caused by hot gas falling on to a spinning neutron star in a ◊binary system. They were discovered at the Mullard Radio Astronomy Observatory, Cambridge, England, by Jocelyn Bell, a member of a team under Antony ◊Hewish.

pulse crop such as peas and beans. They are grown primarily for their seeds, which provide a concentrated source of vegetable protein, and make a vital contribution to human diets in poor countries where meat is scarce. Soya beans are the major temperate protein crop in the West; most are used for oil production or for animal feed. In Asia, most are processed into soya milk and beancurd. Peanuts dominate pulse production in the tropical world and are generally consumed as human food.

Pulses play a useful role in ◊crop rotations as they help to raise soil nitrogen levels as well as acting as break crops. In the mid-1980s, world production was about 50 million tonnes a year.

pulse impulse transmitted by the heartbeat throughout the arterial systems of vertebrates. When the heart muscle contracts, it forces blood into the ◊aorta. Because the arteries are elastic, the sudden rise of pressure causes a throb or sudden swelling through them. The actual flow of the blood is about 60 cm/2 ft a second in humans. The pulse rate is generally about 70 per minute. The pulse can be felt where the artery is near the surface, such as the wrist or the neck.

pulse-code modulation method of converting a continuous electrical signal (such as that produced by a microphone) into a series of pulses (a digital signal) for transmission along a telephone line.

In a process called ◊digital sampling, the continuous signal is sampled thousands of times a second and each part of the signal given a number related to its strength when sampled. The numbers are then converted into ◊binary code and transmitted as a series of pulses. At the receiving end the process is reversed. The advantages of the system arise because noise (static) on the line can easily be distinguished from the signal and removed; hence it is possible to send error-free messages. This has led to increasing use of the system in telephone, telegraph and computer systems since its adoption in the 1960s. It is well suited to transmission along ◊optical fibres.

puma large wild cat found in the Americas, also called cougar or mountain lion. Tawny-coated, it is 1.5 m/4.5 ft long with a 90 cm/3 ft tail. They have been hunted nearly to extinction.

pumice a light volcanic rock produced by the frothing action of expanding gases during the solidification of lava. It has the texture of a hard sponge and is used as an abrasive.

pump a device for moving liquids and gases, or compressing gases. Some pumps, such as the traditional *lift-pump* used to raise water from wells, work by a reciprocating (up-and-down) action. Movement of a piston in a cylinder with a one-way valve creates a partial vacuum in the cylinder, thereby sucking water into it. *Gear pumps*, used to pump oil in a car's lubrication system, have two meshing gears which rotate inside a housing, and the teeth move the oil. *Rotary pumps* contain a rotor with vanes projecting from it inside a casing, sweeping the oil round as they move.

pumped storage a type of hydroelectric plant that uses surplus electricity to pump water back into a high-level reservoir. In normal working the water flows from this reservoir through the ◊turbines to generate power for feeding into the national grid. At times of low power demand, electricity is taken from the grid to turn the turbines into pumps which then pump water back again. This ensures that there is always a maximum 'head' of water in the reservoir to give the maximum output when required.

pumpkin type of marrow *Cucurbita pepo* of the family Cucurbitaceae. The large spherical fruit has a thick, orange rind, pulpy flesh, and many seeds.

pun a ◊figure of speech, a play on words or double meaning that is technically known as *paronomasia* (Greek: 'adapted meaning'). Double meaning can be accidental or deliberate, often resulting from homonymy or the multiple meaning of words; puns, however, are intended as jokes or as clever and compact remarks.

The success of a pun is often a matter of taste; if an ominous horoscope is called a 'horrorscope' or a genetic experiment is characterized as producing 'designer genes', this may or may not be regarded as witty, useful, or relevant. Puns may depend on either the sound or the look of a word, or may require some modification of the words in question to produce their effect (for example, a political meeting described as 'coming apart at the themes', echoing 'seams').

Punch (Italian *Punchinello*) the male character in the traditional ◊puppet play *Punch and Judy*, a humpbacked, hooknosed figure who fights with his wife, Judy.

Punch generally overcomes or outwits all opponents. The play is performed by means of glove puppets, manipulated by a single operator concealed in a portable canvas stage frame, who uses a squeaky voice for Punch. Punch originated in Italy, and was probably introduced to England at the time of the Restoration.

The British satirical magazine *Punch* was founded 1841.

punch drink of Indian origin, made of spirits, fruit juice, sugar, spice, and hot water.

punched card in computing, an early form of data storage and input, now almost obsolete. The 80-column card was widely used in the 1960s and 1970s. This was a thin card, measuring 190 x 84 mm, holding up to 80 characters of data encoded as small rectangular holes.

The punched card was invented by Joseph-Marie Jacquard (1752–1834) in about 1801 to control weaving looms. The first data processing machine using punched cards was developed by Herman ◊Hollerith in the 1880s for the US census.

punctuated equilibrium model an evolutionary theory developed by Niles Eldridge and Stephen Gould 1972 to explain discontinuities in the fossil record. It claims that periods of rapid change alternate with periods of relative stability (stasis), and that the appearance of new lineages is a separate process from the gradual evolution of adaptive changes within a species.

The pattern of stasis and more rapid change is now widely accepted, but the second part of the theory remains unsubstantiated.

punctuation the system of conventional signs (*punctuation marks*) and spaces by means of which written and printed language is organized so as to be as readable, clear, and logical as possible.

It contributes to the effective layout of visual language; if a work is not adequately punctuated there may be problems of ambiguity and unclear association among words. There are preferred styles in the punctuation of a language like English, and conventions of punctuation also differ from language to language. In English, some people prefer a fuller use of punctuation, while others punctuate more lightly; comparably, the use of punctuation will vary according to the kind of passage being produced: a personal letter, a newspaper article, and a technical report all being laid out and punctuated in distinctive ways.

The standard punctuation marks and conventions are the ◊period (full stop or point), ◊comma, ◊colon, ◊semicolon, ◊exclamation mark (or point), ◊question mark, ◊apostrophe, ◊asterisk, ◊hyphen, and ◊parenthesis (including

Punjab

Chandigarh

INDIAN OCEAN

dashes, brackets, and the use of parenthetical commas).

Pune /ˈpuːnə/ formerly **Poona** city in Maharashtra, India; population (1985) 1,685,000. Products include chemicals, rice, sugar, cotton, paper, and jewellery.

Punic (Latin *Punicus* 'a Phoenician') relating to ◊Carthage, ancient city in N Africa founded by the Phoenicians.

Punic Wars three wars between ◊Rome and ◊Carthage:
First 264–241 BC, resulted in the defeat of the Carthaginians under ◊Hamilcar Barca and the cession of Sicily to Rome;
Second 218–201 BC, Hannibal invaded Italy, defeated the Romans under ◊Fabius Maximus at Cannae, but was finally defeated by ◊Scipio at Zama (now in Algeria);
Third 149–146 BC, ended in the destruction of Carthage, and her possessions becoming the Roman province of Africa.

Punjab /ˌpʌnˈdʒɑːb/ Sanskrit name meaning 'five rivers' (the Indus tributaries Jhelum, Chnab, Ravi, Beas, and Sutlej). It was a former state of British India, now divided between India and Pakistan. Punjab was annexed by Britain 1849, after the Sikh Wars 1845–46 and 1848–49, and formed into a province with its capital at Lahore. Under the British, W Punjab was extensively irrigated, and land was granted to Indians who had served in the British army.

Punjab /ˌpʌnˈdʒɑːb/ state of NW India
area 50,400 sq km/19,454 sq miles
capital Chandigarh
towns Amritsar
features mainly agricultural, crops chiefly under irrigation; longest life expectancy rates in India (59 for women, 64 for men); Harappa, see Indus ◊Valley civilization
population (1981) 16,670,000
language Punjabi
religion Sikhism 60%, Hinduism 30%; there is friction between the two groups.

Punjab /ˌpʌnˈdʒɑːb/ state of NE Pakistan
area 205,344 sq km/79,263 sq mi
capital Lahore
features wheat cultivations (by irrigation)
population (1981) 47,292,000
language Punjabi, Urdu
religion Muslim.

Punjabi inhabitant of Punjab. The Punjabi language belongs to the Indo-Iranian branch of the Indo-European family.

Punjabi language a member of the Indo-Iranian branch of the Indo-European language family, spoken in the Punjab provinces of India and Pakistan. It is considered by some to be a variety of Hindi, by others to be a distinct language.

punk a movement of disaffected youth of the late l970s, manifesting itself in fashions and music designed to shock or intimidate. *Punk rock* stressed aggressive performance within a three-chord, three-minute format, for example, the Sex

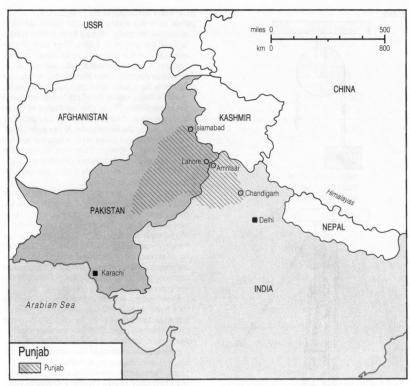

Punjab
▨ Punjab

Pistols 1975–78, the Slits 1977–82, and Johnny Thunders (with the Heartbreakers from 1975).

Punta Arenas /ˈpʊntə əˈreɪnəs/ seaport (trading in meat, wool, and oil), in Chile, capital of Magallanes province, on Magellan Strait, most southerly town on the American mainland; population (1982) 99,000. The name means 'sandy point' in Spanish.

pupa the non-feeding, largely immobile stage of some insect life cycles, in which larval tissues are broken down, and adult tissues and structures are formed.
In many insects, it is *exarate*, with the appendages (legs, antennae, wings) visible outside the pupal (chrysalis) case, but in butterflies and moths, it is *obtect*, with the appendages developing inside the pupal case.

puppet figure manipulated on a small stage, usually by an unseen operator. The earliest known puppets are from 10th-century BC China. The types include *finger* or *glove puppets* (such as ◊Punch); *string marionettes* (which reached a high artistic level in ancient Burma and Sri Lanka and in Italian princely courts 16th–18th centuries, and for which the composer Haydn wrote his operetta *Dido* 1778); *shadow silhouettes* (operated by rods and seen on a lit screen, as in Java); and *bunraku* (devised in Osaka, Japan), in which three or four black-clad operators on stage may combine to work each puppet about 1 m/3 ft high.
During the 16th and 17th centuries puppet shows became popular with European aristocracy and puppets were extensively used as vehicles for caricature and satire until the 19th century, when they were offered as amusements for children in parks. In the 1920s ◊Obraztsov founded the Puppet Theatre in Moscow. Later in the 20th century interest was revived by television; for example, *The Muppet Show* in the 1970s.
In Britain the satirical TV programme *Spitting Image* features puppets caricaturing famous people; these are created by Fluck and Law.

Purana one of a number of sacred Hindu writings dealing with ancient times and events, and dating from the 4th century AD onwards. The 18 main texts include the *Vishnu Purāna* and *Bhāgavata*, which encourage devotion to Vishnu, especially in his incarnation as Krishna.

Purbeck, Isle of /ˈpɜːbek/ a peninsula in the county of ◊Dorset, S England. Purbeck marble and china clay are obtained from the 'isle', which includes Corfe Castle and Swanage.

Purcell /ˈpɜːsəl/ Henry 1659–1695. English Baroque composer. His work can be highly expressive, for example, the opera *Dido and Aeneas* 1689 and music for Dryden's *King Arthur* 1691 and for *The Fairy Queen* 1692. He wrote more than 500 works, ranging from secular operas and incidental music for plays to cantatas and church music.

Purchas /ˈpɜːtʃɪs/ Samuel 1577–1626. English compiler of travel books, rector of St Martin's Ludgate, 1614–26. His collection *Purchas, his Pilgrimage* 1613, was followed by another in 1619, and in 1625 by *Hakluytus Posthumus or Purchas his Pilgrimes*, based on papers left by Hakluyt.

purchasing-power parity a system for comparing standards of living between different countries. Comparing the gross domestic product of different countries involves first converting them to a

Purcell *Henry Purcell, whose work marks the high point of Baroque music in England.*

common currency (usually US dollars or sterling), a conversion which is subject to large fluctuations with variations in exchange rates. Purchasing power parity aims to overcome this by measuring how much money in the currency of those countries is required to buy a comparable range of goods and services.

purdah (Persian and Hindu 'curtain') the seclusion of women practised by some Islamic and Hindu peoples. It had begun to disappear with the adoption of Western culture, but the fundamentalism of the 1980s revived it, for example, the wearing of the ◊chador, an all-enveloping black mantle, in Iran. The Koran actually requests only 'modesty' in dress.

Pure Land Buddhism the dominant form of Buddhism in China and Japan. It emphasizes faith in and love of Buddha, in particular Amitābha (Amida in Japan, Amituofo in China), the ideal 'Buddha of boundless light', who has vowed that all believers who call on his name will be reborn in his Pure Land, or Western Paradise. This also applies to women, who had been debarred from attaining salvation through monastic life. There are over 16 million Pure Land Buddhists in Japan.

Amidism developed in China in the 3rd century, where the Pure Land school was, according to tradition, founded by the monk Hui Yuan (334–417); it spread in Japan from the 10th century. The basic teachings are found in the *Sukhāvati vyū ha*/*Pure Land Sūtra*. The prayer *Namu Amida Butsu* or *Nembutsu* was in some sects repeated for several hours a day. The *True Pure Land* school (Jōdo Shinshū), founded by the Japanese monk Shinran (1173–1262), held that a single, sincere invocation was enough and rejected monastic discipline and the worship of all other Buddhas; this has become the largest school.

purgative or *laxative* a drug to ease or accelerate the emptying of the bowels, such as Epsom salts, senna, or castor oil. With a diet containing enough fibre, such aids should not normally be necessary.

purgatory in Roman Catholic belief, a purificatory state or place for the souls of those who have died in a state of grace to expiate their venial sins.

purge the removal of suspected opponents, especially by Joseph Stalin in the USSR during the 1930s. The purges were carried out by the secret police against political opponents, Communist Party members, minorities, civil servants, and large sections of the armed forces' officer corps. Some 10 million people were executed or deported to labour camps 1934–38.

Puri /'puəri/ town in Orissa, E India, with a statue of Jagganath or Vishnu, one of the three gods of ◊Hinduism, dating from about 318, which is annually taken in procession on a large vehicle (hence the word 'juggernaut'). Devotees formerly threw themselves beneath its wheels.

Purim Jewish festival celebrated in Feb or Mar, commemorating ◊Esther, who saved the Jews from destruction.

The festival includes a complete reding of the Book of Esther in the synagogue, during which the listeners react with stamping, whistling, and hissing to the names of the main characters.

Puritan from 1564, a member of the Church of England who wished to eliminate Roman Catholic survivals in ritual, or substitute a presbyterian for an episcopal form of church government. The term also covers the separatists who withdrew from the church altogether. The Puritans were identified with the parliamentary opposition under James I and Charles I, and after the Restoration were driven from the church, and more usually known as ◊Dissenters or ◊Nonconformists.

Purple Heart, order of the the earliest US military award for distinguished service beyond the call of duty, established by Washington 1782. Made of purple cloth bound at the edges, it was worn on the facings over the left breast. After the American Revolution it lapsed until revived by President Hoover 1932, when it was issued to those wounded

Pushkin *Portrait of Aleksandr Pushkin by Vasily Tropinin, dated 1827.*

in World War II and subsequently. The present Purple Heart is of bronze and enamel.

purple heart slang term for a stimulant purple heart-shaped pill used by many young people, especially mods, in the 1960s in Britain.

purpura spontaneous bleeding beneath the skin localized in spots. It may be harmless, as sometimes with the elderly, or linked with disease.

pus yellowish liquid which forms in the body as a result of bacterial attack; it includes white blood cells (leucocytes) 'killed in battle' with the bacteria, plasma, and broken-down tissue cells. An enclosed collection of pus is an abscess.

Pusan /pu:'sæn/ or *Busan* chief industrial port of South Korea (textiles, rubber, salt, fishing); population (1985) 3,517,000. It was invaded by the Japanese 1592, and opened to foreign trade 1883.

Pusey /'pju:zi/ Edward Bouverie 1800–1882. English Church of England priest from 1828. In 1835 he joined J H ◊Newman in issuing the *Tracts for the Times*. After Newman's conversion to Catholicism, Pusey became leader of the High Church Party or Puseyites, striving until his death to keep them from conversion.

Pushkin /'puʃkin/ town NW of Leningrad, USSR; population 80,000. Founded by Peter the Great as Tsarskoe Selo ('tsar's village') 1708, it has a number of imperial summer palaces, restored after German troops devastated the town 1941–44. In the 1920s it was renamed Detskoe Selo ('children's village') but since 1937 it has been known as Pushkin, the poet having been educated at the school which is now a museum commemorating him.

Pushkin /'puʃkin/ Aleksandr 1799–1837. Russian poet and writer. He was exiled 1820 for his political verse, and in 1824 was in trouble for his atheistic opinions. He wrote ballads such as *The Gypsies* 1827, and the novel in verse ◊*Eugene Onegin* 1823–31. Other works include the tragic drama *Boris Godunov* 1825 and the prose pieces *The Captain's Daughter* 1836 and *The Queen of Spades* 1834. Pushkin's range was enormous, and his willingness to experiment freed later Russian writers from many of the archaic conventions of the literature of his time.

Pushtu /'pʌʃtu:/ another name for the ◊Pashto language.

Puss in Boots fairy tale, included in Charles ◊Perrault's collection. The youngest son of a poor miller inherits nothing from his father but a talking cat. By ingenuity and occasional magic the cat enables the hero to become rich, noble, and the husband of a princess.

putrefaction decomposition of organic matter by microorganisms.

putsch Swiss German term for a violent seizure of political power, such as Hitler and Ludendorff's abortive beer-hall putsch Nov 1923, which attempted to overthrow the Bavarian government.

Puttnam /'pʌtnəm/ David Terence 1941– . English film producer, influential in reviving the British

film industry internationally. Films include *Chariots of Fire* 1981 and *The Killing Fields* 1984.

Puvis de Chavannes /pju:'vi:s də ʃæ'væn/ Pierre Cécile 1824–1898. French Symbolist painter. His major works are vast decorative schemes, mainly on mythological and allegorical subjects, for public buildings such as the Panthéon and Hôtel de Ville in Paris. His work influenced Gauguin.

The Boston Public Library, Massachusetts, also has his murals. His *Poor Fisherman* 1881 (Louvre, Paris) was a much admired smaller Symbolist work.

Puy, Le see ◊Le Puy, town in France.

Pu-Yi former name of the last Chinese emperor Henry ◊P'u-i.

PVC polyvinylchloride, a type of ◊plastic.

Pwllheli /puʃ'heli/ resort in Gwynedd, Wales; the Welsh National Party, Plaid Cymru, was founded here 1925.

PWR (*p*ressurized *w*ater *r*eactor) a nuclear reactor design used in nuclear power stations in many countries, and in nuclear-powered submarines. In the PWR water under pressure is the coolant and ◊moderator. It circulates through a steam generator, where its heat boils water to provide steam to drive power ◊turbines.

pyelitis inflammation of the renal pelvis, the central part of the kidney where urine accumulates before discharge. Caused by bacterial infection, it is more common in women.

Pygmalion /pig'meiliən/ in Greek legend, a king of Cyprus who fell in love with an ivory statue he had carved, and when Aphrodite brought it to life as Galatea, he married her.

Pygmy /'pigmi/ member of the small-statured peoples of equatorial Africa (Negrillos) and SE Asia and Melanesia (Negritos).

Pyke /paik/ Margaret 1893–1966. British birth-control campaigner. In the early 1930s she became secretary of the National Birth Control Association (later the Family Planning Association, FPA), and campaigned vigorously to get local councils to set up family-planning clinics. She became chair of the FPA in 1954.

Pylos /'pailos/ port in SW Greece where the battle of ◊Navarino was fought.

Pym /pim/ Barbara 1913–1980. English novelist, born in Shropshire, whose novels include *Some Tame Gazelle* 1950, *The Sweet Dove Died* 1978, and *A Few Green Leaves* 1980.

Pym /pim/ Francis 1922– . British Conservative politician. He was defence secretary 1979–81, and

Pym *English politician John Pym, painted in 1641, on the eve of the Civil War. Pym played a leading role in the impeachment of ministers Strafford and Laud and of King Charles I, all of whom were eventually beheaded.*

pyramid

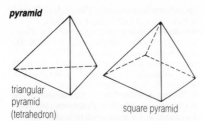

triangular pyramid (tetrahedron)

square pyramid

succeeded Carrington as foreign minister 1982, but was dismissed in the post-election reshuffle 1983.

Pym /pɪm/ John 1584–1643. English parliamentarian, largely responsible for the ◊Petition of Right 1628. As leader of the Puritan opposition in the ◊Long Parliament from 1640, he moved the impeachment of Charles I's advisers Strafford and Laud, drew up the ◊Grand Remonstrance, and was the chief of five Members of Parliament Charles I wanted arrested 1642. The five took refuge in the City, from which they emerged triumphant when the king left London.

Pynchon /'pɪntʃən/ Thomas 1937– . US novelist, who creates a bizarre, labyrinthine world in his books, which include *V* 1963, *The Crying of Lot 49* 1966, *Gravity's Rainbow* 1973, and *Vineland* 1989.

Pyongyang /ˌpjɒŋˈjæŋ/ capital and industrial city (coal, iron, steel, textiles, chemicals) of North Korea; population (1984) 2,640,000.

pyorrhoea former name for gum disease, now known as periodontal disease.

pyramid in geometry, a solid figure with triangular side-faces meeting at a common vertex (point) and with a ◊polygon as its base. The volume of a pyramid, no matter how many faces it has, is equal to the area of the base multiplied by one-third of the perpendicular height.

A pyramid with a triangular base is called a tetrahedron; the Egyptian pyramids have square bases.

pyramid pyramidal building used in ancient Egypt to enclose a royal tomb, for example the Great Pyramid of Khufu/Cheops at Gizah, near Cairo; 230 m/755 ft square and 147 m/481 ft high. In Babylon and Assyria broadly stepped pyramids (ziggurats) were used as the base for a shrine to a god: the Tower of Babel (see also ◊Babylon) was probably one of these. Pyramidal temple mounds were also built by the ◊Aztecs and ◊Mayas, for example at Chichen Itza and Cholula, near Mexico City, which is the world's largest in ground area (300 m/990 ft base, 60 m/195 ft high).

pyramid of numbers in ecology, a diagram that shows how many plants and animals there are at different levels in a ◊food chain.

There are always far fewer individuals at the bottom of the chain than at the top, because only about 10% of the food an animal eats is turned into flesh, so the amount of food flowing through the chain drops at each step. In a pyramid of numbers, the primary producers (usually plants) are represented at the bottom by a broad band, the plant-eaters are shown above by a narrower band, and the animals that prey on them by a narrower band still. At the top of the pyramid are the 'top carnivores' such as lions and sharks, which are present in the smallest number.

Pyramus and Thisbe /'pɪrəməs, 'θɪzbi/ legendary Babylonian lovers whose story was retold by ◊Ovid. Pursued by a lioness, Thisbe lost her veil, and when Pyramus arrived at their meeting-place, he found it bloodstained. Assuming Thisbe was dead, he stabbed himself, and she, on finding his body, killed herself. In *A Midsummer Night's Dream*, the 'rude mechanicals' perform the story as a farce for the nobles.

Pyrenees /ˌpɪrəˈniːz/ (French *Pyrénées*; Spanish *Pirineos*) mountain range in SW Europe between France and Spain; length about 435 km/270 mi; highest peak Aneto (French *Néthon*) 3,404 m/11,172 ft. ◊Andorra is entirely within the range. Hydroelectric power has encouraged industrial development in the foothills.

pyrethrum popular name for some flowers of the genus *Chrysanthemum*, family Compositae. The ornamental species *Chrysanthemum coccineum*, and hybrids derived from it, are commonly grown in gardens. Pyrethrum powder is a powerful contact herbicide for aphids and mosquitoes.

pyridine C_5H_5N a heterocyclic compound (see ◊cyclic compounds). It is a liquid with a sickly smell, and occurs in coal tar. It is soluble in water, acts as a strong base, and is used as a solvent, particularly in the manufacture of plastics.

pyridoxine $C_8H_{11}NO_3$ also called ◊vitamin B6. There is no clearly identifiable disease associated with deficiency but its absence from the diet can give rise to malfunction of the central nervous system and general skin disorders. Good sources are liver, meat, milk, and cereal grains. Related compounds may also show vitamin B6 activity.

pyrite a common iron ore, iron sulphide FeS_2; also called *fool's gold* because of its yellow metallic lustre. Pyrite has a hardness of 6–6.5 on the Mohs' scale. It is used in the production of sulphuric acid.

pyrogallol trihydroxybenzene, a derivative of benzene $C_6H_3OH_3$, prepared from gallic acid, and used in gas analysis for the measurement of oxygen, because its alkaline solution turns black as it rapidly absorbs oxygen. It is also used in photograph development.

pyrometer type of ◊thermometer used for measuring high temperatures.

pyroxene any one of a group of minerals, silicates of calcium, iron, and magnesium with a general formula $XYSi_2O_6$, found in igneous and metamorphic rocks. The internal structure is based on single chains of silicon and oxygen. Diopside ($X=Ca, Y=Mg$) and augite ($X=Ca, Y=Mg, Fe, Al$) are common pyroxenes.

Jadeite ($NaAlSi_2O_6$), which is considered the more valuable form of jade, is also a pyroxene.

Pyrrho /'pɪrəʊ/ *c.* 360–*c.* 270 BC. Greek philosopher, founder of ◊Scepticism, who maintained that since certainty was impossible, peace of mind lay in renouncing all claims to knowledge.

Pyrrhus /'pɪrəs/ *c.* 318–272 BC. King of ◊Epirus from 307, who invaded Italy 280, as an ally of the Tarentines against Rome. He twice defeated the Romans but with such heavy losses that a 'Pyrrhic victory' has come to mean a victory not worth winning. He returned to Greece 275 after his defeat at Beneventum, and was killed in a riot in Argos.

Pythagoras /paɪˈθægərəs/ *c.* 580–500 BC. Greek mathematician and philosopher, who formulated Pythagoras' theorem.

Much of his work concerned numbers, to which he assigned mystical properties. For example, he classified numbers into triangular ones (1, 3, 6, 10,...), which can be represented as a triangular array, and square ones (1, 4, 9, 16,...), which form squares. He also observed that any two adjacent

Pythagoras' theorem

for right-angled triangles

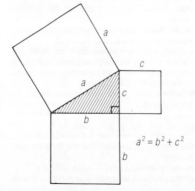

$a^2 = b^2 + c^2$

triangular numbers add to a square number (for example, 1 + 3 = 4, 3 + 6 = 9, 6 + 10 = 16,...).

Pythagoras was the founder of a politically influential religious brotherhood in Croton, S Italy (suppressed in the 5th century). Its tenets included immortality of the soul and ◊transmigration.

Pythagoras' theorem in geometry, theorem stating that in a right-angled triangle, the area of the square on the hypotenuse (the longest side) is equal to the sum of the areas of the squares drawn on the other two sides. If the hypotenuse is h units long and the lengths of the other sides are a and b, then $h^2 = a^2 + b^2$.

The theorem provides a way of calculating the length of any side of a right-angled triangle if the lengths of the other two sides are known. It is also used to determine certain trigonometrical relationships such as $sin^2 θ + cos^2 θ = 1$.

Pythagorus of Rhegium 5th century BC. Greek sculptor. He was born on Samos and settled in Rhegium (Reggio di Calabria), Italy. He made statues of athletes and is said to have surpassed his contemporary Myron in this field.

Pytheas /'pɪθɪəs/ 4th century BC. Greek navigator from Marseille who explored the coast of W Europe at least as far N as Denmark, sailed around Britain, and reached ◊Thule (possibly the Shetlands).

Pythian Games /'pɪθɪən/ ancient Greek festival in honour of ◊Apollo, celebrated near Delphi every four years.

Pythias /'pɪθɪæs/ in Greek legend, a Pythagorean whose friend Damon offered his own life as security when Pythias was condemned to death by a tyrant.

python type of constricting snake found in the tropics of Africa, Asia, and Australia, related to the boas but laying eggs rather than producing living young. Some species are small, but the reticulated python of SE Asia can grow to 10 m/33 ft.

pyx (Latin 'box') the container used in the Roman Catholic Church for the reservation of the wafers of the sacrament.

The *Trial of the Pyx* is the test of coinage by a goldsmith, at the hall of the Goldsmiths' Company, London, and is so called because of the box in which specimens of coinage are stored.

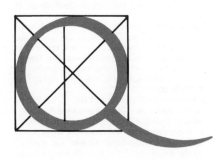

Q 17th letter of the alphabet, representing *koppa* of the earliest Greek alphabet. In Latin, as in English, it is always followed by *u: qu*, pronounced *kw*.

Qaboos /kəˈbuːs/ bin Saidq 1940– . Sultan of Oman. The 14th descendant of the Albusaid family, opposed to the conservative views of his father, in 1970 he overthrew him, in a bloodless coup, and assumed the sultanship. Since then he has followed more liberal and expansionist policies, while maintaining his country's position of international nonalignment.

Qaddafi alternative form of ◊Khaddhafi, Libyan leader.

Qadisiya, Battle of battle fought in S Iraq 637. A Muslim Arab force defeated a larger Zoroastrian Persian army and ended the ◊Sassanian Empire. The defeat is still resented in Iran, where modern Muslim Arab nationalism threatens to break up the Iranian state.

qat shrub *Catha edulis* related to coffee; the leaves are chewed as a mild narcotic in some Arab countries. Its use was banned in ◊Somalia 1983.

Qatar /ˈkætɑː/ country in the Middle East, occupying Qatar peninsula in the Arabian Gulf, bounded to the SW by Saudi Arabia and to the S by United Arab Emirates.
government A provisional constitution adopted 1970 confirmed Qatar as an absolute monarchy, with the emir holding all executive and legislative powers. The emir appoints and heads a council of ministers. An advisory council of 30 was established 1972, with limited powers to question ministers. There are no political parties.
history For early history, see ◊Arabia. Qatar, which used to be under ◊Bahrain's control, has had a treaty with Britain since 1868. It was part of the ◊Ottoman Empire from 1872 until World War I. The British government gave formal recognition 1916 to Sheikh Abdullah al-Thani as Qatar's ruler, guaranteeing protection in return for an influence over the country's external affairs.

In 1968 Britain announced its intention of withdrawing its forces from the Persian Gulf area by 1981, and Qatar, having failed in an attempt to form an association with other Gulf states, became fully independent 1 Sept 1971. A new treaty of friendship with Britain replaced the former arrangements.

In 1972, while the emir, Sheik Ahmad, was out of the country, his cousin, the crown prince, Sheik Khalifa, led a bloodless coup; already prime minister, he declared himself also emir. He embarked on an ambitious programme of social and economic reform, curbing the extravagances of the royal family. Qatar has good relations with most of its neighbours and is regarded as one of the more stable and moderate Arab states.

Qattara Depression /kəˈtɑːrə/ tract of the Western Desert, Egypt, up to 125 m/400 ft below sea level. Its very soft sand makes it virtually impassable to vehicles, and it protected the left flank of the Allied armies before and during the battle of ◊Alamein 1942. Area 20,000 sq km/7,500 sq mi.

QB abbreviation for *Queen's Bench.*

QC abbreviation for ◊*Queen's Counsel.*

QED abbreviation for *quod erat demonstrandum* (Latin 'which was to be proved').

qiblah the direction which Muslims face in prayer: the direction of Mecca. In every mosque this is marked by a niche (mihrab) in the wall.

Qin dynasty /tʃɪn/ Chinese imperial dynasty 221–206 BC. ◊Shi Huangdi was its most noted emperor.

Qingdao /ˌtʃɪŋˈdaʊ/ formerly *Tsingtao* industrial port and summer resort in Shandong province, E China; population (1984) 1,229,500. Industries include brewing.

Qinghai /ˌtʃɪŋˈhaɪ/ formerly *Tsinghai* province of NW China
area 721,000 sq km/278,306 sq mi
capital Xining
features mainly desert, with nomadic herders
products oil, livestock, medical products
population (1986) 4,120,000, including many Tibetans and other minorities

Qisarya /kiːˈsɑːriə/ Mediterranean port north of Tel Aviv-Jaffa, Israel; there are underwater remains of Herod the Great's port of Caesarea.

Qld abbreviation for ◊*Queensland.*

Qom /kʊm/ or *Qum* holy city of Shi'ite Muslims, in central Iran, 145 km/90 mi south of Tehran; population (1986) 551,000. The Islamic academy of Madresseh Faizieh 1920 became the headquarters of Ayatollah ◊Khomeini.

quadrathon a sports event in which the competitors must swim two miles, walk 30 miles, cycle 100 miles, and run 26.2 miles (a marathon) within 22 hours.

quadratic equation in mathematics, a polynomial equation of second degree (that is, an equation containing as its highest power the square of a single unknown variable, such as x). The general formula of such equations is $ax^2 + bx + c = 0$, in which a, b, and c are real numbers, and only the coefficient a cannot equal 0. In ◊coordinate geometry, a quadratic function represents a ◊parabola.

Depending on the value of the discriminant $b^2 - 4ac$, the roots (solutions) of a quadratic equation are either two real, two equal or two complex roots (when $b^2 - 4ac > 0$, two distinct real roots; when $b^2 - 4ac = 0$, two equal real roots; when $b^2 - 4ac < 0$, two distinct complex roots). Some quadratic equations can be solved by factorization, or the values of x can be found by using the formula for the general solution $x = [-b \pm \sqrt{(b^2 - 4ac)}]/2a$.

quadrature the position of the Moon or an outer planet where a line between it and Earth makes a right angle with a line joining Earth to the Sun.

quadrille a square dance for four or more couples, or the music for the dance, which alternates between two and four beats in a bar.

quadrivium in medieval education, the four advanced liberal arts (arithmetic, geometry, astronomy, and music) which were studied after mastery of the trivium.

Quadruple Alliance in European history, three military alliances of four nations:
the Quadruple Alliance 1718 of Austria, Britain, France, and the United Provinces (Netherlands), to prevent Spain from annexing Sardinia and Sicily;
the Quadruple Alliance 1813 of Austria, Britain, Prussia, and Russia, aimed at defeating the French emperor Napoleon; renewed 1815 and 1818. See Congress of ◊Vienna.
the Quadruple Alliance 1834 of Britain, France, Portugal, and Spain, guaranteeing the constitutional monarchies of Spain and Portugal against rebels in the Carlist War.

quaestor a Roman magistrate whose duties were mainly concerned with public finances. The quaestors originated as assistants to the consuls. Both urban and military quaestors existed, the latter being attached to the commanding generals in the provinces.

quagga South African wild horse which became extinct in the 1880s. It was brown, with a white tail and legs, and a striped head and neck.

Quai d'Orsay /ˈkeɪ dɔːˈseɪ/ part of the left bank of the Seine in Paris, where the French Foreign Office and other government buildings are situated. The

---

Qatar
State of
(Dawlat Qatar)

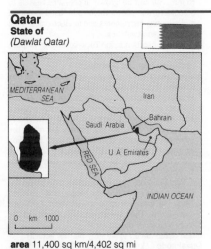

area 11,400 sq km/4,402 sq mi
capital and chief port Doha
towns Dukhan, centre of oil production
physical mostly flat desert
features negligible rain and surface water, so that only 3% is fertile, but irrigation allows self-sufficiency in fruit and vegetables; rich oil discoveries since World War II
head of state and government Sheik Khalifa bin Hamad al-Thani from 1972
government absolute monarchy
political parties none
exports oil, natural gas, petrochemicals, fertilizers, iron, steel
currency riyal (6.1881 = £1 Feb 1990)
population (1989) 342,000 (half in Doha); annual growth rate 6.8%
life expectancy men 65, women 70
language Arabic
religion Sunni Muslim
literacy 60% (1985)
GNP $5.9 bn (1983); $35,000 per head of population
chronology
1970 Constitution adopted, confirming the emirate as an absolute monarchy.
1971 Achieved full independence. New treaty of friendship with the UK signed.
1972 Emir Sheik Ahmad replaced in a bloodless coup, by his cousin, Crown Prince Sheik Khalifa.

name has become synonymous with the Foreign Office itself.

quail smallest species of the partridge family. The common quail *Coturnix coturnix* is about 18 cm/7 in long, reddish-brown, with a white throat and yellowish belly. It is found in Europe, Asia, and Africa, and has been introduced to North America.

Quaker popular name, originally derogatory, for a member of the Society of ◊Friends.

quango British term coined as an acronym from *qua*si-*a*utonomous *n*on-*g*overnmental *o*rganization, for example the Equal Opportunities Commission (1975). Quangos are nominally independent, but rely on government funding. Many (such as the Location of Offices Bureau) were abolished by the Thatcher government from 1979.

Quant /kwɒnt/ Mary 1934– . British fashion designer. Her Chelsea boutique, Bazaar, achieved a revolution in women's clothing and make-up, which epitomized the 'swinging London' of the 1960s.

quantity theory of money economic theory claiming that an increase in the amount of money in circulation causes a proportionate increase in prices.

The theory dates from the 17th century and was elaborated by the US economist Irving Fisher (1867–1947). Supported and developed by Milton Friedman, it forms the theoretical basis of modern ◊monetarism.

Quantrill /'kwɒntrɪl/ William Clarke 1837–1865. US criminal, who became leader of a guerrilla unit on the Confederate side in the Civil War. Frank and Jesse ◊James were among his aides.

quant. suff. abbreviation for *quantum sufficit* (Latin 'as much as suffices').

quantum number in physics, one of a set of four numbers that uniquely characterize an ◊electron and its state in an ◊atom. The *principal quantum number* n (= 1, 2, 3, and so on) defines the electron's main energy level. The *orbital quantum number* l (= $n - 1$, $n - 2$, and so on to 0) relates to angular momentum. The *magnetic quantum number* m (= l, $l - 1$, $l - 2$, and so on to 0 and then on to … $-(l - 2)$, $-(l - 1)$ and $-l$) describes the energies of electrons in a magnetic field. The *spin quantum number* m^s (= $+1/2$ or $-1/2$) gives the spin direction of the electron.

The principal quantum number, defining the electron's energy level, corresponds to shells (energy levels) also known by their spectroscopic designations K, L, M, and so on. The orbital quantum number gives rise to a series of subshells designated s, p, d, f, and so on, of slightly different energy levels. The magnetic quantum number allows further subdivision of the subshells (making three subdivisions p_x, p_y and p_z in the p subshell, for example, of the same energy level). No two electrons in an atom can have the same set of quantum numbers (the ◊Pauli exclusion principle).

quantum theory in physics, the theory that many quantities, such as ◊energy, cannot have a continuous range of values, but only a number of discrete (particular) ones, because they are packaged in 'quanta of energy'. Just as earlier theory showed how light, generally seen as a wave motion, could also in some ways be seen as composed of discrete particles (◊photons), quantum mechanics shows how atomic particles like electrons may also be seen as having wave-like properties. Quantum mechanics is the basis of particle physics, modern theoretical chemistry, and the solid-state physics which describes the behaviour of the silicon chips used in computers.

The theory began with the work of Max ◊Planck 1900 on radiated energy, and was extended by ◊Einstein to electromagnetic radiation generally, including ◊light. Niels ◊Bohr used it to explain the ◊spectrum of light emitted by excited hydrogen atoms. Later work by ◊Schrödinger, ◊Heisenberg, ◊Dirac, and others elaborated the theory to what is called quantum mechanics (or wave mechanics).

quarantine (from French *quarantaine* 40 days) any period for which people, animals, or vessels may be detained in isolation when suspected of carrying

quartz Well-formed crystals of quartz, which are pyramidal in shape. These crystals are a pure form of quartz, so they are colourless.

contagious disease. In some countries, imported animals are still quarantined to prevent the spread of ◊rabies.

quark any of at least five hypothetical ◊elementary particles that, together with their antiparticles, are believed to be fundamental constituents of mesons and baryons.

quart imperial liquid or dry measure, equal to 2 pints or 1.136 litres. In the USA, a liquid quart is equal to 0.946 litres, while a dry quart is equal to 1.101 litres.

quarter day in the financial year, any of the four dates on which such payments as ground rents become due: in England 25 Mar (Lady Day), 24 Jun (Midsummer Day), 29 Sept (Michaelmas), and 25 Dec (Christmas Day).

quarter session former local criminal court in England, replaced 1972 by crown courts (see also ◊law courts).

quartz a crystalline form of ◊silica SiO_2, one of the most abundant minerals of the Earth's crust (12% by volume). Quartz occurs in many different kinds of rock, including sandstone and granite. It ranks 7 on the Mohs' scale of hardness and is resistant to chemical or mechanical breakdown. Quartzes vary according to the size and purity of their crystals. Crystals of pure quartz are coarse, colourless, and transparent, and this form is usually called rock crystal. Impure coloured varieties, often used as gemstones, include ◊agate, citrine quartz and ◊amethyst. Quartz is used in ornamental work and industry, where its reaction to electricity makes it valuable in electronic instruments (see ◊piezoelectric effect). Quartz can also be made synthetically.

Natural crystals that would take million of years to form can now be 'grown' in pressure vessels to a standard that allows them to be used in optical and scientific instruments and in electronics, such as quartz wristwatches.

quartzite a ◊metamorphic rock consisting of pure quartz sandstone that has recrystallized under increasing heat and pressure.

quasar (abbreviation of *qua*si-stell*ar*) in astronomy, an object that appears star-like. Quasars are thought to be the brilliant centres of distant galaxies, caused by stars and gas falling towards an immense ◊black hole at the galaxy's centre. Quasar light shows a large ◊red shift, placing quasars far off in the Universe, the most distant lying over 10 billion light years away. Although quasars are small, with diameters of less than a light year, they give out as much energy as hundreds of galaxies.

Some quasars emit radio waves (see ◊radio astronomy), which is how they were first identified 1963, but most are radio-quiet. About 3,000 are now known. They are important in studies of the early history of the universe.

quasi (Latin 'as if') apparently but not actually.

Quasimodo /ˌkwɑːzɪˈməʊdəʊ/ Salvatore 1901–1968. Italian poet. His first book *Acque e terre/Waters and Land* appeared 1930. Later books, including *Nuove poesie/New Poetry* 1942, and *Il falso e vero verde/The False and True Green* 1956, reflect a growing preoccupation with

contemporary political and social problems. Nobel prize 1959.

quassia trees native to tropical parts of the Americas, with a bitter bark and wood, including *Quassia amara*, family Simaroubaceae. The heartwood is a source of quassiin, an infusion of which was formerly used as a tonic; it is now used in insecticides.

Quaternary period of geological time that began 1.8 million years ago and is still in process. It is divided into the ◊Pleistocene and ◊Holocene epochs.

Quatre Bras, Battle of /ˈkætrə ˈbrɑː/ battle fought 16 June 1815 during the Napoleonic Wars, in which the British commander Wellington defeated French forces under Marshal Ney. It is named after a hamlet in Brabant, Belgium, 32 km/20 mi SE of Brussels.

Quayle /kweɪl/ Anthony 1913– . English actor and director. From 1948–56 he directed at the Shakespeare Memorial Theatre, and appeared as Falstaff in *Henry IV*, Petruchio in *The Taming of the Shrew*, and the title role in *Othello*. He played nonclassical parts in *Galileo*, *Sleuth*, and *Old World*.

Quayle /kweɪl/ (J) Dan(forth) 1947– . US Republican politician, an Indiana congressman from 1977, senator from 1981, vice president from 1989.

Born into a rich and influential Indianapolis newspaper-owning family, Quayle was admitted to the Indiana bar 1974, and was elected to the House of Representatives 1977 and to the Senate 1981. When George Bush ran for president 1988, he selected Quayle as his running mate, admiring his conservative views and believing that Quayle could deliver the youth vote. This choice encountered heavy criticism because of Quayle's limited political experience and his association with a fundamentalist Christian group. Much was made of his earlier enlistment in the Indiana National Guard, which meant that he avoided action overseas during the Vietnam War.

Que. abbreviation for ◊*Québec*.

Québec /kwɪˈbek/ capital and industrial port (textiles, leather, timber, paper, printing and publishing) of Québec province, on the St Lawrence river, Canada; population (1986) 165,000, metropolitan area 603,000. It was founded 1608.

It was founded by the French explorer Samuel de ◊Champlain, and was a French colony 1608–1763. The British, under Gen ◊Wolfe, captured Québec 1759 after a battle on the nearby Plains of Abraham; both Wolfe and the French commander (◊Montcalm) were killed. Québec is a centre of French culture, and there are two universities, Laval 1663 (oldest in North America) and Québec 1969. Its picturesque old town survives below the citadel about 110 m/360 ft above the St Lawrence river.

Quayle Vice president of the USA from 1989, Dan Quayle.

Quebec

Québec /kwɪˈbek/ province of E Canada
area 1,540,700 sq km/594,710 sq mi
capital Québec
towns Montreal, Laval, Sherbrooke, Verdun, Hull, Trois-Rivières
features immense water-power resources, for example the James Bay project
products iron, copper, gold, zinc, cereals, potatoes, paper, textiles, fish, maple syrup (70% of world's output)
population (1986) 6,540,000
language French is the only official language since 1974, although 17% speak English. Language laws 1989 prohibit the use of English on street signs
history known as New France 1534–1763; captured by the British, and became province of Québec 1763–90, Lower Canada 1791–1846, Canada East 1846–67; one of the original provinces 1867; nationalist feelings 1960s (despite existing safeguards for Québec's French-derived civil law, customs, religion, and language) led to the foundation of the Parti Québecois by René Lévesque 1968; uprising by Québec Liberation Front (FLQ) separatists 1970; referendum on 'sovereignty-association' (separation) defeated 1980; Robert Bourassa and Liberals returned to power 1985, and enacted restrictive English-language legislation.

Québec Conference two conferences of Allied leaders in the city of Québec during World War II. The *first conference* 1943 approved the British admiral Mountbatten as supreme Allied commander in SE Asia and made plans for the invasion of France, for which the US general Eisenhower was to be supreme commander. The *second conference* Sept 1944 adopted plans for intensified air attacks on Germany, created a unified strategy against Japan, and established a postwar policy for a defeated Germany.

quebracho /keɪˈbrɑːtʃəʊ/ several South American trees, family Anacardiaceae, with very hard wood, especially the *red quebracho Schinopsis lorentzii* used in tanning.

Quechua /ˈketʃwə/ also *Quichua* or *Kechua* South American Indians of the Andean regions, whose ancestors include the Incas. The Quechua language is the second official language of Peru, and is also spoken in Ecuador.

Queen Anne style style popular in England 1700–20, characterized by plain, simple lines, particularly in silver and furniture.

Queen Charlotte Islands /ˈʃɑːlət/ archipelago about 160 km/100 mi off the coast of ◊British Columbia, W Canada, of which it forms part; area 9,790 sq km/3,780 sq mi; population 2,500. Graham and Moresby are the largest of about 150 islands. There are timber and fishing industries.

Queen Maud Land /ˈmɔːd/ a region of Antarctica W of Enderby Land, claimed by Norway since 1939.

Queens /kwinz/ a borough and county at the W end of Long Island, New York City, USA; population (1980) 1,891,300.

Queen's Award British award for industrial excellence established in 1965 as the Queen's Award to Industry, and replaced from 1976 by two separate awards, for export achievement and for technological achievement. Made to organizations, not individuals, the Queen's Award entitles the holder

Queensland

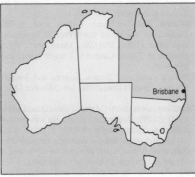

to display a special emblem for five years. Awards are made annually in April.

Queensberry /ˈkwiːnzbəri/ John Sholto Douglas, 8th Marquess of Queensberry 1844–1900. British patron of boxing. In 1867 he formulated the *Queensberry Rules* which form the basis of modern-day boxing rules.

A keen all-round sportsman, Douglas was an expert horseman and excelled at steeplechasing. He rode the ◊Aintree Grand National course. He was the father of Lord Alfred ◊Douglas.

Queen's Counsel (QC) in England, a barrister appointed to senior rank by the Lord Chancellor. When the monarch is a king the term is *King's Counsel*. A QC wears a silk gown, and takes precedence over a junior member of the Bar.

Queen's County /ˈkwiːnz/ former name of ◊Laois, county in the Republic of Ireland.

Queen's English see ◊English language.

Queensland /ˈkwiːnzlænd/ state in NE Australia
area 1,727,200 sq km/666,699 sq mi
capital Brisbane
towns Gold Coast-Tweed, Townsville, Sunshine Coast, Toowoomba, Cairns
features Great Dividing Range, including Mount Bartle Frere 1,657 m/5,438 ft; Great Barrier Reef (collection of coral reefs and islands about 2,000 km/1,250 mi long off the E coast; City of Gold Coast holiday area in the south, population 120,000; Mount Isa mining area
exports sugar, pineapples, beef, cotton, wool, tobacco, copper, gold, silver, lead, zinc, coal, nickel, bauxite, uranium, natural gas
population (1987) 2,650,000
history part of New South Wales until 1859, it then became self-governing.

Queen's Proctor in England, the official representing the crown in matrimonial, probate and admiralty cases. The Queen's Proctor's chief function is to intervene in divorce proceedings if it is discovered that material facts have been concealed from the court or that there has been collusion. When the monarch is a king the term is King's Proctor.

Queenstown /ˈkwiːnztaʊn/ former name (1849–1922) of ◊Cóbh, port in the Republic of Ireland.

Quemoy /keˈmɔɪ/ island off the SE coast of China, and administered by Taiwan; area 130 sq km/50 sq mi; Matsu 40 sq km/17 sq mi; population (1982) 57,847. When the islands were shelled from the mainland in 1960, the USA declared they would be defended if attacked.

quenching a kind of ◊heat treatment used to harden metals. They are heated to a certain temperature and then quickly plunged into cold water or oil.

Queneau /keˈnəʊ/ Raymond 1903–1976. French surrealist poet and humorous novelist, author of *Zazie dans le Métro/Zazie in the Metro* 1959, portraying a precocious young Parisian woman.

question mark a punctuation mark (?), used to indicate enquiry or doubt. When indicating enquiry, it is placed at the end of a *direct question* ('Who is coming?') but never at the end of an *indirect question* ('He asked us who was coming'). When indicating doubt, it usually appears between brackets, to show that a writer or editor is puzzled or uncertain about a statement or quotation.

Quetelet /ˈketˈleɪ/ Lambert Adolphe Jacques 1796–1874. Belgian statistician, a pioneer of modern statistical methods. He developed tests for the validity of statistical information, and gathered statistical data of many kinds. From his work on sociological data comes the concept of the 'average person'.

Quetta /ˈkwetə/ summer resort and capital of Baluchistan, W Pakistan; population (1981) 281,000. It was linked to Shikarpur by a gas pipeline in 1982.

quetzal long-tailed Central American bird. The male is brightly coloured, with green, red, blue, and white feathers, and is about 1.3 m/4.3 ft long including tail. The female is smaller and lacks the tail and plumage. It eats fruit, insects, and small frogs and lizards. It is the national emblem of Guatemala, and was considered sacred by the Mayans and the Aztecs. The quetzal's forest habitat is rapidly being destroyed, and hunting of birds for trophies or souvenirs also threatens its survival.

Quetzalcoatl /ˌketsəlkəʊˈætl/ feathered serpent god of air and water in the pre-Columbian ◊Aztec and ◊Toltec cultures of Central America. In legendary human form, he was said to have been fair-skinned and bearded, and to have reigned on Earth during a golden age. He disappeared across the sea, with a promise to return; ◊Cortés exploited the coincidence of description when he invaded. Ruins of one of his temples survive at Teotihuacán in Mexico.

Quevedo y Villegas /keˈveɪdəʊ iː viːˈjeɪgəs/ Francisco Gómez de 1580–1645. Spanish novelist and satirist. His picaresque novel *La Vida del Buscón/The Life of a Scoundrel* 1626 follows the tradition of the roguish hero who has a series of episodic adventures. *Sueis/Visions* 1627 is a brilliant series of satirical portraits of contemporary society.

Quezon City /ˈkeɪsɒn ˈsɪti/ former capital of the Philippines 1948–76, NE part of metropolitan ◊Manila, on Luzon Island; population (1980) 1,166,000.

quetzal

It was named after the Philippines' first president, Manuel Luis Quezon (1878–1944).

Qufu /ˌtʃuːˈfuː/ or **Chufu** town in Shandong province, China; population 27,000. It is the birthplace of Kong Zi (◊Confucius) and the site of the Great Temple of Confucius.

Quiberon /ˌkiːbəˈrɒn/ peninsula and coastal town in Brittany, NW France; in 1759 the British admiral ◊Hawke defeated a French fleet (under Conflans) in Quiberon Bay.

quicksilver former name for the element ◊mercury.

quid pro quo (Latin 'something for something') an exchange of one thing in return for another.

quietism a religious attitude, displayed periodically in the history of Christianity, consisting of passive contemplation and meditation to achieve union with God. The founder of modern quietism was the Spanish priest ◊Molinos who published a *Guida Spirituale/Spiritual Guide* 1675.

quilt a padded bed-cover or the method used to make padded covers or clothing. The padding is made by sewing a layer of wool or other stuffing between two outer pieces of material in patterns, often diamond shapes or floral motifs.

Quilts have been made in the home for centuries throughout Europe and more recently in the USA. They are sometimes decorated with patchwork or embroidery.

Quilter /ˈkwɪltə/ Roger 1877–1953. English composer. He wrote song settings of ◊Tennyson and ◊Shakespeare, including 'Now Sleeps the Crimson Petal' 1904 and 'To Daisies' 1906, and the *Children's Overture* 1920.

Quimby /ˈkwɪmbi/ Fred(erick) 1886–1965. US film producer, in charge of MGM's short films department 1926–56. Among the cartoons produced by this department were the *Tom and Jerry* series and those directed by Tex ◊Avery.

Quimper /kæmˈpeə/ town in Brittany, NW France, on the river Odet; population (1982) 60,162; a centre for the manufacture of decorative pottery since the 16th century.

quince tree *Cydonia oblonga*, family Rosaceae, native to W Asia. The bitter, yellow, pear-shaped fruit is used in preserves.

Quine /kwaɪn/ Willard Van Orman 1908– . US philosopher and logician. In *Two Dogmas of Empiricism* 1951, he argued against the analytic/synthetic distinction. In *Word and Object* 1960, he put forward the thesis of radical untranslatability, the view that a sentence can always be regarded as referring to many different things. He was professor of philosophy at Harvard.

quinine an antimalarial drug, the first that was effective for its treatment. Peruvian Indians taught French missionaries how to use the bark of the cinchona tree 1630, but quinine was not isolated for another two centuries.

Other drugs have since been developed with fewer side effects, but quinine is still valuable in the treatment of particularly resistant strains of malaria.

Quinn /kwɪn/ Anthony 1915– . Mexican actor, in films from 1935. Famous for the title role in *Zorba the Greek* 1964, he later often played variations on this larger-than-life character.

quince

Quinquagesima (Latin 'fiftieth') in the Christian church calendar, the Sunday before Lent and 50 days before Easter.

Quintana Roo /kɪnˈtɑːnə ˈrəʊəʊ/ state in SE Mexico, on the E of the ◊Yucatán peninsula, population (1980) 226,000. There are ◊Maya remains at Tulum; Cancun is a major resort and free port.

Quintero /kɪnterəʊ/ Serafín Alvarez and Joaquín Alvarez. Spanish dramatists; see ◊Alvarez Quintero.

Quintilian /kwɪnˈtɪliən/ (Marcus Fabius Quintilianus) *c.* AD 35–95. Roman rhetorician. He was born at Calgurris, Spain, taught rhetoric in Rome from AD 68, and composed the *Institutio Oratorio/The Education of an Orator*, in which he advocated a simple and sincere style of public speaking.

quipu (Quechua 'knot') a device used by the ◊Incas of ancient Peru to record numerical information, consisting of a set of knotted cords of one or several colours. Among its chief applications were the recording of granary and warehouse stores.

Quirinal /ˈkwɪrɪnəl/ one of the seven hills on which ancient Rome was built. Its summit is occupied by a palace built 1574 as a summer residence for the pope and occupied 1870–1946 by the kings of Italy. The name Quirinal is derived from that of Quirinus, local god of the ◊Sabines.

Quisling /ˈkwɪzlɪŋ/ Vidkun 1887–1945. Norwegian politician. Leader from 1933 of the Norwegian Fascist Party, he aided the Nazi invasion 1940 by delaying mobilization and urging non-resistance. He was made premier by Hitler 1942, and was arrested and shot as a traitor by the Norwegians 1945. His name became a generic term for a traitor who aids an occupying force.

Quito /ˈkiːtəʊ/ capital and industrial city (textiles, chemicals, leather, gold, silver) of Ecuador, about 3,000 m/9,850 ft above sea level; population (1982) 1,110,250. It was an ancient settlement, taken by the Incas about 1470 and by the Spanish 1534. It has a temperate climate all year round.

Quixote, Don novel by the Spanish writer ◊Cervantes, with a hero of the same name.

Qum alternative spelling of ◊Qom, city of Iran.

Qumran /ˈkuːmrɑːn/ or **Khirbet Qumran** ruined site, excavated from 1951, in the foothills on NW shores of the Dead Sea in Jordan. Originally an Iron Age fort (6th century BC) it was occupied in the late 2nd century BC by a monastic community, the ◊Essenes, until the buildings were burned down AD 68. The monastery library contained the *Dead Sea Scrolls*, discovered 1947; the scrolls had been hidden for safekeeping and never reclaimed.

quod erat demonstrandum (abbreviation QED; Latin 'which was to be proved') added at the end of a geometry proof.

quod vide (abbreviation qv; Latin 'which see') indicates a cross-reference.

quoits game in which a rubber ring (quoit) is thrown towards an iron hob from a point 16.5 m/54 ft distant. A 'ringer', a quoit landing over the hob, gains two points, and one landing nearest the hob, within a circle 1 m/3 ft in diameter, gains one point.

quorum a minimum number of members required to be present for the proceedings of an assembly to be valid. The actual number of people required for a quorum may vary.

quota in international trade, a limitation on the quantities exported or imported. Restrictions may be imposed forcibly or voluntarily. The justification of quotas include protection of a home industry from an influx of cheap goods, prevention of a heavy outflow of goods (usually raw materials) because there are insufficient numbers to meet domestic demand, allowance for a new industry to develop before it is exposed to demand, or prevention of a decline in the world price of a particular commodity.

quo vadis? (Latin) where are you going?

qv abbreviation for ◊*quod vide*.

QwaQwa /ˈkwɑːkwɑː/ a black homeland of South Africa which achieved self-governing status in 1974; population (1985) 181,600.

R 18th letter of the alphabet, corresponding to the Semitic *resh* and Greek *rho*. A liquid, pronounced with the tip of the tongue on the palate, it is sometimes 'trilled' by vibration of the tongue, especially in Scotland, but in S England r is often weak when used medially and silent finally.

RA abbreviation for *Royal Academy* of Art, London, founded 1768.

Rabat /rə'bɑːt/ capital of Morocco, industrial port (cotton textiles, carpets, leather goods) on the Atlantic coast, 177 km/110 mi W of Fez; population (1982) 519,000, Rabat-Salé 842,000. It is named after its original *ribat* or fortified monastery.

Rabaul /rɑːˈbaʊl/ largest port (trading in copra and cocoa) of Papua New Guinea, on the volcanic island of New Britain, SW Pacific; population (1980) 14,954. It was destroyed by British bombing after its occupation by the Japanese in 1942, but rebuilt.

rabbi the chief religious minister of a synagogue; the spiritual leader of a Jewish congregation; or a scholar of Judaic law and ritual.

rabbit greyish-brown, long-eared, burrowing mammal *Oryctolagus cuniculus* of the family Leporidae in the order Lagomorpha (with hares and pikas). It has legs and feet adapted for running and hopping, large front teeth, and can grow up to 40 cm/16 in long. It is native to Europe and N Africa, but is now found worldwide.

It produces several large litters in a year, and lives in groups of interconnected underground burrows called 'warrens'. Introduced into England in the 11th century, rabbits were originally delicate animals but they subsequently flourished until the virus disease myxomatosis was introduced in 1953 as a means of controlling the population (see ◊biological control). The North American equivalent of the species is the woodland *cottontail Silvilagus floridanus*. Rabbits are bred for meat and for fur, the pelts usually being treated to resemble more expensive furs.

Rabelais /ˈræbəleɪ/ François 1495–1553. French satirist, monk, and physician, whose name has become synonymous with bawdy humour. He was educated in the Renaissance humanist tradition and was the author of satirical allegories, *La Vie inestimable de Gargantua/The Inestimable Life of Gargantua* 1535 and *Faits et dits héroïques du grand Pantagruel/Deeds and Sayings of the Great Pantagruel* 1533, the story of two giants (father and son) Gargantua and Pantagruel.

Rabi /ˈrɑːbɪ/ Isidor Isaac 1898–1988. US physicist who developed techniques to measure the strength of weak magnetic fields with astonishing accuracy. These fields are generated when charged elementary particles, such as the electron, spin about their axis. The work won for him the Nobel physics prize in 1944.

rabies disease of the central nervous system which can afflict all warm-blooded creatures. It is almost invariably fatal once symptoms have developed. Its transmission to a human being is almost always by a bite from a rabid dog.

After an incubation period which may vary from 10 days to more than a year, symptoms of fever, muscle spasm, and delirium develop. As the disease progresses, the mere sight of water is enough to provoke convulsions and paralysis; hence, the alternative name for rabies, hydrophobia (fear of water). Death is usual within four to five days. Injections of rabies vaccine and antiserum may save someone bitten by a rabid animal from developing the disease (see also ◊quarantine). Louis ◊Pasteur was the first to produce an effective vaccine, and the Pasteur Institute was founded to treat the disease. As a control measure for foxes and other wild animals, vaccination (by bait) is recommended, rather than destruction. In France, foxes are now vaccinated against rabies by distributing capsules by helicopter.

Rabin /ræˈbiːn/ Itzhak 1922– . Israeli prime minister who succeeded Golda Meir 1974–77.

Rabuka /ræmˈbuːkə/ Sitiveni 1948– . Fijian soldier and politician. Trained at Sandhurst, he was made a colonel in the Fijian army, after serving with the UN in Lebanon. In 1987 he staged a coup against the Indian-led coalition government and declared a republic. Although the prime minister, Kamisese Mara, was subsequently reinstated, Rabuka remained an influential figure behind the scenes.

RAC abbreviation for the British *Royal Automobile Club*.

raccoon omnivorous nocturnal mammal of the Americas. The common raccoon *Procyon lotor* is about 60 cm/2 ft long, with a grey-brown body, a black and white ringed tail, and a black 'mask' around its eyes. The crab-eating raccoon *Procyon cancrivorus* of South America is slightly smaller, and has shorter fur.

race in anthropology, term sometimes applied to a physically distinctive group of people, on the basis of difference from other groups in skin colour, head shape, hair type, and physique. Formerly anthropologists divided the human race into three hypothetical racial groups: Caucasoid, Mongoloid, and Negroid. However, scientific studies have failed to indicate any absolute confirmation of genetic racial divisions. Many anthropologists today thus completely reject the concept of race, and social scientists tend to prefer the term ethnic group (see ◊ethnicity).

raccoon

Racine The tragedies of Racine are part of the great flowering of dramatic and poetic writing in 17th-century France. His subjects came from Greek mythology and he observed the rules of classical Greek drama.

Rachel /ˈreɪʃəl/ in the Old Testament, the favourite wife of ◊Jacob, and mother of ◊Joseph and Benjamin.

Rachel /ræˈʃel/ stage name of Elizabeth Félix 1821–1858. French tragic actress who excelled in fierce, passionate roles, particularly Racine's *Phèdre*, which she took on tour to Europe, the USA, and Russia.

Rachmaninov /rækˈmænɪnɒf/ Sergei (Vasilevich) 1873–1943. Russian composer, conductor, and pianist. After the 1917 Revolution he went to the USA. His dramatically emotional Romantic music has a strong melodic basis and includes operas, such as *Francesca da Rimini* 1906, three symphonies, four piano concertos, piano pieces, and songs. Among his other works are the *Prelude in C-sharp Minor* 1892 and *Rhapsody on a Theme of Paganini* 1934 for piano and orchestra.

racial disadvantage a situation in which children from ethnic minority groups perform less well than they should because of a foreign or hostile environment.

The Swann Report 1986 found that this was the case in British schools and recommended methods of combating racial disadvantage, and local authorities are increasingly adopting anti-racist policies and attempting to give their curricula a ◊multi-cultural dimension.

Racine /ræˈsiːn/ Jean 1639–1699. French dramatist and exponent of the classical tragedy in French drama. Most of his tragedies have women in the title role, for example *Andromaque* 1667, *Iphigénie* 1674, and *Phèdre* 1677. After the contemporary failure of the latter he no longer wrote for the secular stage, but influenced by Madame de ◊Maintenon wrote two religious dramas, *Esther* 1689 and *Athalie* 1691, which achieved posthumous success.

racism or *racialism* a belief in, or set of implicit assumptions about, the superiority of one's own ◊race or ethnic group, often accompanied by prejudice against members of an ethnic group different from one's own. Racism may be used to justify ◊discrimination, verbal or physical abuse, or even genocide, as in Nazi Germany.

Many social scientists believe that even where there is no overt discrimination, racism exists as an unconscious attitude in many individuals and societies, based on a ◊stereotype or preconceived idea about different ethnic groups, which is damaging to individuals (both perpetrators and victims) and to society as a whole. See also ◊ethnicity.

rackets (US form *racquets*) indoor game played on an enclosed court. It is regarded as the forerunner to many racket and ball games.

Although first played in the Middle Ages, it developed in the 18th century and was played against the walls of London buildings. The Fleet Prison was a popular venue. It is played on a court usually 18.3 m/60 ft long by 9.1 m/30 ft wide, by two or four persons each with a racket about 75 cm/2.5 ft long, weighing 255 grammes/9 oz. The ball is 25 mm/1 in in diameter and weighs 28 grammes/1 oz. Play begins from a service box, one of which is marked at each side of mid-court, and the ball must hit above a 2.75 m/9 ft line on the end wall. After service it may be played anywhere above a 68.5 cm/27 in high line on the end wall, the general rules of tennis applying thereafter. See also ◊squash.

rack railway a railway used in mountainous regions, which uses a toothed pinion running in a toothed rack to provide traction. The rack usually runs between the rails. Ordinary wheels lose their grip even on quite shallow gradients, but rack railways, like that on Mount Pilatus in Switzerland, can climb slopes as steep as 1 in 2.1.

rad (abbreviation of *radiation unit*) SI unit of absorbed dose of radiation. It is the dose when 1 kg of matter absorbs 0.01 joule of energy. Different types of radiation cause different amounts of damage for the same absorbed dose; the *dose equivalent* is measured in ◊rems.

radar (from *ra*dio *d*irection *a*nd *r*anging) a means of locating an object in space, direction finding, and navigation using high-frequency radio waves. Essential to navigation in darkness, cloud, and fog, it can be thwarted in warfare by: aircraft and missiles with a modified shape which reduces their radar cross-section; radar-absorbent paints; and electronic jamming. A countermeasure in pinpointing small targets is the use of ◊laser 'radar' instead of ◊microwaves. Chains of ground radar stations are used to warn of enemy attack, for example, North Warning System 1985, consisting of 52 stations across the Canadian Arctic and N Alaska. Radar is also used in ◊meteorology and ◊astronomy.

The direction of an object is ascertained by transmitting a beam of short-wavelength (1–100 cm/$^1\!/_2$–40 in) short-pulse radio waves, and picking up the reflected beam; and the distance by timing the journey of the radio waves (travelling at the speed of light) there and back.

radar astronomy the bouncing of radio waves off objects in the solar system, and reception and analysis of the 'echoes'. Radar contact with the Moon was first made 1945 and with Venus 1961. The travel time for radio reflections allows the distances of objects to be determined accurately. Analysis of the reflected beam reveals the rotation period and allows the object's surface to be mapped. The rotation periods of Venus and Mercury were first determined by radar. Radar maps of Venus were obtained first by Earth-based radar, and subsequently by orbiting spacecraft.

Radcliffe /'rædklɪf/ Anne (born Ward) 1764–1823. English novelist, a chief exponent of the ◊Gothic novel or 'romance of terror', for example, *The Mysteries of Udolpho* 1794.

Radha in the Hindu epic ◊*Mahābhārata*, the wife of a cowherd who leaves her husband for love of Krishna (an incarnation of the god Vishnu). Her devotion to Krishna is seen by the mystical *bhakti* movement as the ideal of the love between humans and God.

radial circuit a type of circuit used in household electric wiring in which all electrical appliances are connected via cables that radiate out from the main supply point or fuse box. In more modern systems, the appliances are connected in a ring, or ◊ring circuit, with each end of the ring connected to the fusebox.

radian in mathematics, an alternative unit to the ◊degree for measuring angles. It is the angle at the centre of a circle when the centre is joined to the two ends of an arc (part of the circumference) equal in length to the radius of the circle. There are 2π (approximately 6.284) radians in a full circle (360°).

1 radian is approximately 57°, and 1° is $\pi/180$ or approximately 0.0175 radians. Radians are

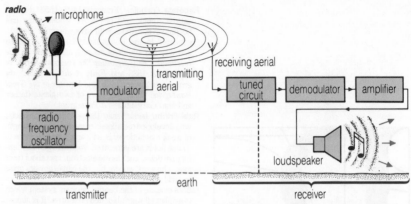

radio

microphone

transmitting aerial

receiving aerial

radio frequency oscillator

modulator

tuned circuit

demodulator

amplifier

loudspeaker

earth

transmitter

receiver

commonly used to specify angles in ◊polar coordinates.

radiation in physics, the emission of radiant ◊energy as ◊particles or waves, for example, sound, light, alpha particles, and beta particles.

radiation biology the study of how living things are affected by radioactive (ionizing) emissions (see ◊radioactivity), and by electromagnetic (non-ionizing) radiation (◊electromagnetic waves). Both are potentially harmful and can cause leukaemia and other cancers; even low levels of radioactivity are very dangerous. Both can be used therapeutically, for example to treat cancer, when the radiation dose is very carefully controlled (*radio therapy* or *X-ray therapy*).

Radioactive emissions are more harmful. Exposure to high levels produces radiation burns and radiation sickness, plus genetic damage (resulting in birth defects) and cancers in the longer term. Exposure to low-level ionizing radiation can also cause genetic damage and cancers, particularly leukaemia.

Electromagnetic radiation is usually harmful only if exposure is to high-energy emissions, for example close to powerful radio transmitters or near radar-wave sources. Such exposure can cause organ damage, cataracts, loss of hearing, leukaemia, and other cancers, or premature ageing. It may also affect the nervous system and brain, distorting their electrical nerve signals and leading to depression, disorientiation, headaches, and other symptoms. Individual sensitivity varies and some people are affected by electrical equipment such as televisions, computers, and refrigerators.

radiation sickness sickness resulting from overlong exposure to radiation, including X-rays, gamma-rays, neutrons and other nuclear radiation. Such radiation ionizes atoms in the body and causes nausea, vomiting, diarrhoea, and other symptoms. The body cells themselves may be damaged, even by relatively small doses, causing ◊leukaemia, and genetic changes may also be induced.

radiation units units of measurement for radioactivity and radiation doses. Continued use of the units introduced earlier this century (the ◊curie, rad, ◊rem, and ◊roentgen) has been approved while the derived SI units become familiar. 1 curie = 3.7×10^{10} ◊becquerels (activity); 1 rad = 10^{-2} ◊gray (absorbed dose); 1 rem = 10^{-2} ◊sievert (dose equivalent); 1 roentgen = 2.58×10^{-4} coulomb/kg (exposure to ionizing radiation). The average radiation exposure per person per year in the USA is 0.1 REM, of which 50% is derived from naturally occurring radon.

Radić /'rɑːdɪtʃ/ Stjepan 1871–1928. Yugoslav nationalist politician, born near Fiume. He led the Croat national movement within the Austro-Hungarian Empire, and supported union with Serbia 1919. His opposition to Serbian supremacy within Yugoslavia led to his murder in the parliament house.

radical in chemistry, a group of atoms (for example the methyl radical, $-CH_3$) forming part of a molecule, which takes part in chemical reactions without disintegration, yet often cannot exist alone.

radical in politics, anyone with opinions more extreme than the main current of a country's major political party or parties. It is more often applied to those with left-wing opinions. From the 1970s the term was also applied to right-wingers such as Enoch Powell.

Radical in Britain, a supporter of parliamentary reform before the Reform Bill 1832. As a group the Radicals later became the progressive wing of the Liberal Party. During the 1860s (led by Cobden, Bright, and J S Mill) they campaigned for extension of the franchise, free trade, and ◊laissez-faire, but after 1870, under the leadership of J Chamberlain and Dilke, they adopted a republican and semi-socialist programme. With the growth of ◊socialism in the later 19th century, Radicalism ceased to exist as an organized movement.

radicle the part of a plant embryo that develops into the primary root. Usually it emerges from the seed before the embryonic shoot, or ◊plumule, its tip protected by a root cap, or calyptra, as it pushes through the soil. The radicle may form the basis of the entire root system, or it may be replaced by adventitious (positioned on the stem) roots.

radio the transmission and reception of radio waves. In radio transmission a microphone converts ◊sound waves (pressure variations in the air) into an audiofrequency electrical signal which is then picked up by a receiving aerial and fed to a loudspeaker which reproduces sound waves.

The theory of ◊electromagnetic waves was first developed by James Clerk ◊Maxwell 1864, given practical confirmation in the laboratory 1888 by Heinrich ◊Hertz, and put to practical use by ◊Marconi, who in 1901 achieved reception of a signal in Newfoundland transmitted from Poldhu in Cornwall. To carry the transmitted electrical signal an ◊oscillator produces a carrier wave of high frequency; different stations are allocated different transmitting carrier frequencies. A modulator superimposes the audiofrequency signal on the carrier. There are two main ways of doing this: amplitude modulation (AM), used for long- and medium-wave broadcasts, in which the strength of the carrier is made to fluctuate in time with the audio signal; and frequency modulation (FM), as used for VHF broadcasts, in which the frequency of the carrier is made to fluctuate. The transmitting aerial emits the modulated electromagnetic waves which travel outwards from it.

In radio reception a receiving aerial picks up minute voltages in response to the waves sent out by a transmitter. A tuned circuit selects a particular frequency, usually by means of variable ◊capacitor connected across a coil of wire. A demodulator disentangles the audio signal from the carrier, which is now discarded, having served its purpose. An amplifier boosts the audio signal for feeding to the loudspeaker which reproduces sound waves.

radioactive decay the process of continuous disintegration undergone by the nuclei of radioactive elements, such as radium and various isotopes of uranium and the transuranic elements. Certain lighter artificially created isotopes also undergo radioactive decay. The associated radiation consists of alpha rays, beta rays, or gamma rays (or a combination of these) and it takes place with a characteristic half-life, which is the time taken for half of any mass of a radioactive isotope to decay completely. The original nucleotide is known as the parent substance, and the product is a daughter nucleotide (which may or may not be radioactive).

Radioactive Incident Monitoring Network (RIM NET) a monitoring network at 46 (to be raised to about 90) Meteorological Office sites throughout the UK. It feeds into a central computer, and was installed in 1989 to record contamination levels from nuclear incidents such as the ◊Chernobyl disaster.

radioactive tracer a radioactive isotope used in a labelled compound; see ◊tracer.

radioactive waste any waste that emits radiation in excess of the background level. See ◊nuclear waste.

radioactivity the spontaneous emission of radiation from the nuclei of atoms of certain substances, termed radioactive. The radiation is of three main types: *alpha particles*, fast-moving particles containing two protons and two neutrons, equivalent to helium nuclei; *beta particles*, fast-moving electrons; and *gamma rays*, high-energy highly penetrating protons. Beta and gamma radiation are both damaging to body tissues, but are especially dangerous if a radioactive substance is ingested or inhaled.

radio astronomy the study of radio waves emitted naturally by objects in space, by means of a ◊radio telescope. Radio emission comes from hot gas (*thermal radiation*), electrons spiralling in magnetic fields (*synchroton radiation*), and specific wavelengths (*lines*) emitted by atoms and molecules in space, such as the 21 cm/8 in line emitted by hydrogen gas. Radio astronomy began 1932 when Karl ◊Jansky detected radio waves from the centre of our galaxy, but the subject did not develop until after World War II.

Astronomers have mapped the spiral structure of the galaxy from the radio waves given out by interstellar gas, and they have detected many individual radio sources within our galaxy and beyond.

Among radio sources in our galaxy are the remains of ◊supernova explosions, such as the ◊Crab Nebula and ◊pulsars. Short-wavelength radio waves have been detected from complex molecules in dense clouds of gas where stars are forming. Searches have been undertaken for signals from other civilizations in the galaxy, so far without success.

Strong sources of radio waves beyond our galaxy include ◊radio galaxies and ◊quasars. Their existence far off in the universe demonstrates how the universe has evolved with time. Radio astronomers have also detected weak *background radiation* thought to be from the ◊Big Bang explosion that marked the birth of the universe. Radio astronomy has greatly improved our understanding of the evolution of stars, the structure of galaxies, and the origin of the universe.

radio beacon a radio transmitter in a fixed location, used in marine and aerial navigation. Ships and aircraft pinpoint their position by reference to the signals given out by two or more beacons.

radiocarbon dating or *carbon dating* a method of dating organic materials (for example bone, wood). Plants take up carbon dioxide gas from the atmosphere and convert it into their tissues, and some of that carbon dioxide contains the radioactive isotope of carbon, carbon-14. On death, the plant ceases to take up carbon-14 and that already taken up decays at a known rate, allowing the time which has elapsed since the plant died. Animals take the carbon-14 into their bodies from eating plant tissues and their remains can be similarly dated. After 120,000 years so little carbon-14 is left that it is difficult to get accurate results.

radio, cellular the use of a series of short-range transmitters at the centre of adjacent cells (each about 4 km/2.5 mi in diameter), using the same frequencies over and over again throughout the area covered. It is used for personal communication among subscribers via car telephones and portable units.

radiochemistry the chemical study of radioactive isotopes and their compounds (whether produced from naturally radioactive or irradiated materials) and their use in the study of other chemical processes.

When such isotopes are used in labelled compounds, they enable the biochemical functioning of different parts of the living body to be observed, and can help in the testing of new drugs, showing where the drug goes in the body and how long it stays there. They are also important in diagnosis, for example cancer, fetal abnormalities, and heart disease.

radio frequencies and wavelengths classification of, see ◊electromagnetic waves.

radio galaxy a galaxy that is a strong source of electromagnetic waves of radio wavelengths. All galaxies, including our own, emit some radio waves, but radio galaxies are up to a million times more powerful.

In many cases the strongest radio emission comes not from the visible galaxy but from two clouds, invisible in an optical telescope, that can extend for millions of light years either side of the galaxy. This double structure at radio wavelengths is also shown by some ◊quasars, suggesting a close relationship between the two types of object. In both cases, the source of energy is thought to be a massive black hole at the centre. Some radio galaxies are thought to result from two galaxies in collision or recently merged.

radiography a branch of science concerned with the use of radiation (particularly ◊X-rays) to produce images on photographic film or fluorescent screens. X-rays penetrate matter according to its nature, density, and thickness. In doing so they can cast shadows on photographic film, producing a radiograph. Radiography is widely used in medicine for examining bones and tissues and in industry for examining solid materials to check welded seams in pipelines, for example.

radioisotope or *radioactive ◊isotope* a radioactive form of an element. Most radioisotopes are made by bombarding an ordinary inactive material with neutrons in the core of a nuclear reactor. The radiations given off are easy to detect (hence their use as ◊tracers), can in some instances penetrate substantial thicknesses of materials, and may have profound effects on living matter. Radioisotopes are used in many fields of medicine, industry, agriculture, and research.

radiosonde a balloon carrying a radio transmitter, used to 'sound' or measure conditions in the atmosphere. It carries instruments to measure temperature, pressure, and humidity. A radar target is often attached, allowing it to be tracked.

radio telescope an instrument for detecting radio waves from the universe. Radio telescopes usually consist of a metal bowl which collects and focuses radio waves the way a concave mirror collects and focuses light waves. Other radio telescopes are shaped like long troughs, while some consist of simple rod-shaped aerials. Radio telescopes are much larger than optical telescopes, because the wavelengths they are detecting are much longer than the wavelength of light. A large dish such as that at ◊Jodrell Bank can see the radio sky less clearly than a small optical telescope sees the visible sky. The largest single dish is 305 m/1,000 ft across, at Arecibo, Puerto Rico.

Interferometry is a technique in which the output from two dishes is combined to give better resolution of detail than with a single dish. *Very long baseline interferometry* (VBLI) uses radio telescopes spread across the world to resolve minute details of radio sources. In *aperture synthesis*, several dishes are linked together to simulate the performance of a very large single dish. This technique was pioneered by Martin ◊Ryle at Cambridge, England, site of a radio telescope consisting of eight dishes in a line 5 km/3 mi long. The Very Large Array in New Mexico consists of 27 dishes arranged in a Y-shape, which simulates the performance of a single dish 27 km/17 mi in diameter.

radiotherapy the treatment of disease by ◊radiation from X-ray machines or radioactive sources. Radiation, which reduces the activity of dividing cells, is of special value for its effect on malignant tissues, certain non-malignant tumours, and some diseases of the skin. Generally speaking, the rays of the ordinary diagnostic X-ray machine are not penetrating enough to be very efficient in treatment, and for this purpose more powerful machines are required, operating from 10,000 to over 30 million volts. The lower-voltage machines are similar to conventional X-ray machines; the higher-voltage ones may be of special design, for example, linear accelerators and betatrons. Much radiation is now given using artificially produced ◊radio isotopes. Radioactive cobalt is the most useful, as this produces gamma rays (highly penetrating), and machines with sources of this material are used instead of very high-energy X-ray machines. Similarly certain radioactive substances may be administered to patients, for example, radioactive iodine for thyroid disease. Radium, formerly widely used for radiotherapy, has now been supplanted by more easily obtainable artificially produced substances.

radish annual herb *Raphanus sativus*, family Cruciferae, grown for its fleshy, pungent, edible root, which is usually reddish, but sometimes white or black.

radium (Latin *radius* 'ray') white, luminescent, metallic element, symbol Rd, atomic number 88, relative atomic mass 226.02. It is found in pitchblende in small quantities and in other uranium ores. Radium is used in radiotherapy, to treat cancer, and in luminous paints.

Radium bromide was first separated by Marie and Pierre Curie in 1898, but the element itself was only isolated 1911 (by Marie Curie and A L Debierne). It is now obtained commercially from pitchblende reserves in Czechoslovakia, E Africa and Colorado, USA.

Radium Hill /'reɪdiəm/ mining site SW of Broken Hill, New South Wales, Australia, formerly a source of radium and uranium.

Radnorshire /'rædnəʃə/ former border county of Wales, merged with Powys 1974. Presteign was the county town.

Radom /'rɑːdɒm/ industrial city (flour-milling, brewing, tobacco, leather, bicycles, machinery; iron works) in Poland, 96 km/60 mi S of Warsaw; population (1985) 214,000. Radom became Austrian 1795, Russian 1825, and was returned to Poland 1919.

radon radioactive gaseous element, symbol Rn, atomic number 86. One of the inert gases, it is produced from the radioactive decay of radium, thorium, and actinium. It occurs naturally in the soil, especially in areas rich in granite, including Cornwall and Devon. It is used in radiotherapy as a source of alpha particles. Radon was discovered in 1900 by German chemist Friedrich Dorn (1848–1916), but only isolated eight years later.

Raeburn /'reɪbɜːn/ Henry 1756–1823. Scottish portrait painter, active mainly in Edinburgh. He developed a technique of painting with broad brushstrokes directly on the canvas without preparatory drawing. He was appointed painter to George IV 1823. Between 1784 and 1787 he visited London and then Italy. *The Reverend Robert Walker Skating* (National Gallery, Edinburgh) is a popular work.

Raeder /'reɪdə/ Erich 1876–1960. German admiral. Chief of Staff in World War I, he became head of the navy in 1928, but was dismissed by Hitler in 1943 because of his failure to prevent Allied Arctic convoys from reaching the USSR. Sentenced to life imprisonment at the Nuremberg Trials of war criminals, he was released on grounds of ill health in 1955.

RAF abbreviation for ◊*Royal Air Force*.

rafflesia

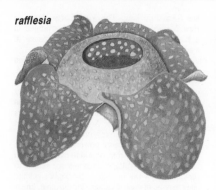

Rafelson /'reɪfəlsən/ 'Bob' (Robert) 1934– . US film director who gained critical acclaim for his second film, *Five Easy Pieces* 1971. His other films include *Head* 1968, *The Postman Always Rings Twice* 1981, and *Black Widow* 1987.

Raffles /'ræfəlz/ Thomas Stamford 1781–1826. British colonial administrator, born in Jamaica. He served in the East India Company, took part in the capture of Java from the Dutch 1811, and while governor of Sumatra 1818–23 was responsible for the acquisition and foundation of Singapore 1819. He was a founder and first president of the Zoological Society, London.

rafflesia parasitic plant without stems, family Rafflesiaceae, native to Malaysia. There are 14 species, several of which are endangered by logging of the forests where they grow. The largest flowers in the world are produced by *Rafflesia arnoldiana*. About 1 m/3 ft across, they exude a smell of rotting flesh, which attracts flies to pollinate them.

Rafsanjani /,ræfsændʒa:'ni:/ Hojatolesl am Ali Akbar Hashemi 1934– . Iranian cleric and politician. After training as a ◊mullah under Ayatollah ◊Khomeini at the holy city of Qom, he acquired considerable wealth through his construction business but kept in touch with his exiled mentor. When the Ayatollah returned after the revolution of 1979–80 Rafsanjani became the eminent speaker of the Iranian parliament and, after Khomeini's death in 1989, state president and effective political leader.

Raft /rɑːft/ George. Stage name of George Ranft 1895–1980. US film actor, usually cast as a gangster (as in *Scarface* 1932). His later work included *Some Like it Hot* 1959.

raga (Sanskrit *rāga* 'tone' or 'colour') in Indian music, a scale of notes and style of ornament for music associated with a particular mood or time of day; the equivalent term in rhythm is *tala*. A choice of raga and tala forms the basis of improvised music; however, a written composition may also be based on (and called) a raga.

Raglan /'ræglən/ FitzRoy James Henry Somerset, 1st Baron Raglan 1788–1855. English general. He took part in the Peninsular War under Wellington, and lost his right arm at Waterloo. He commanded the British forces in the Crimean War from 1854. The *raglan sleeve*, cut right up to the neckline with no shoulder seam, is named after him.

Ragnarök (German *Götterdämmerung*) in Norse mythology, the ultimate cataclysmic battle between gods and forces of evil from which a new order will come.

ragtime syncopated music ('ragged time') in two-four rhythm, usually played on piano. It developed in the USA among black musicians in the late 19th century; it was influenced by folk tradition, minstrel shows, and marching bands, and later merged into jazz. Scott ◊Joplin was a leading writer of ragtime pieces, called rags.

Ragusa /rə'guːzə/ town in Sicily, Italy, 54 km/34 mi SW of Syracuse; textile industries; population (1981) 64,492. It stands over 450 m/1,500 ft above the river Ragusa, and there are ancient tombs in caves nearby.

Ragusa /rə'guːzə/ Italian name (to 1918) for the Yugoslavian town of ◊Dubrovnik. Its English name

Rafsanjani President of Iran Ali Akbar Rafsanjani. He is viewed as the most pragmatic and influential member of Iran's post-Khomeini collective leadership.

was *Arrogosa*, from which the word 'argosy' is derived, because of the town's fame for its trading fleets while under Turkish rule in the 16th century.

ragwort perennial plant *Senecio jacobaea*, family ◊Compositae, prolific on waste ground; it has bright yellow flowers and is poisonous.

Rahere /'reɪhɪə/ minstrel and favourite of Henry I of England. After recovering from malaria while on a pilgrimage to Rome, in 1123 he founded St Bartholomew's priory and St Bartholomew's hospital in London.

Rahman Sheikh Mujibur. Bangladeshi politican; see ◊Mujibur Rahman, Sheikh.

Rahman /'rɑːmən/ Tunku Abdul 1903– . Malaysian politician, first prime minister of independent Malaya 1957–63 and of Malaysia 1963–70. Born at Kuala Keda, the son of the sultan and his sixth wife, a Thai princess, the Tunku studied law in England. After returning to Malaysia he founded the Alliance party 1952. The party was successful in the 1955 elections, and the Tunku became prime minister of Malaya on gaining independence 1957, continuing when Malaya became part of Malaysia 1963. His achievement was to bring together the Malay, Chinese, and Indian peoples within the Alliance party, but in the 1960s he was accused of showing bias towards Malays. Ethnic riots followed in Kuala Lumpur 1969 and, after many attempts to restore better relations, the Tunku retired 1970. He has recently voiced criticism of the authoritarian leadership of Mahathir bin Mohamad.

raï Algerian type of pop music developed in the 1970s from the Bedouin song form *melhoun*, using synthesizers and electronic drums.

Raikes /reɪks/ Robert 1735–1811. English printer who started the first Sunday school (for religious purposes) in Gloucester 1780 and who stimulated the growth of weekday voluntary 'ragged schools' for poor children.

rail any bird of the family Rallidae, including corncrakes, coots, moorhens, and gallinules. Many oceanic islands have their own species of rail, often flightless, such as the Guam rail and Auckland Island rail. Several of these species have declined sharply, usually because of introduced predators such as rats and cats.

railway method of transport in which trains convey passengers and goods along a twin rail track. Following the work of English steam pioneers such as ◊Watt, George ◊Stephenson built the first public steam railway, from Stockton to Darlington, 1825. This heralded extensive railway building in Britain as well as in Europe and North America, providing a fast and economic means of transport and communication nationally for the first time. After World War II steam was replaced by electric and diesel engines. At the same time growth in car ownership and air services rapidly destroyed the supremacy of the railways.

railways: chronology

1500s	Tramways—wooden tracks along which trolleys ran—were in use in mines.
1804	Richard Trevithick in England built the first steam locomotive, and ran it on the track at the Pen-y-darren ironworks in S Wales.
1825	George Stephenson built the first public railway to carry steam trains—the Stockton and Darlington line.
1829	Stephenson designed his locomotive *Rocket*.
1830	Stephenson completed the Liverpool and Manchester Railway, the first steam passenger line. The first US-built locomotive, *Best Friend of Charleston*, went into service on the South Carolina Railroad.
1835	Germany pioneered steam railways in Europe, using *Der Adler*, a locomotive built by Stephenson.
1863	The Scotsman Robert Fairlie patented a locomotive with pivoting driving bogies, allowing tight curves in the track (this was later applied particularly in the Garratt locomotives). London opened the world's first underground railway.
1869	The first US transcontinental railway was completed at Promontory, Utah, when the Union Pacific and the Central Pacific Railroads met. George Westinghouse (USA) invented the compressed-air brake.
1879	Werner von Siemens demonstrated an electric train in Germany. Volk's Electric Railway along the Brighton seafront was the world's first public electric railway.
1883	Charles Lartique built the first monorail, in Ireland.
1885	The trans-Canada continental railway was completed, from Montreal in the east to Port Moody, British Columbia in the west.
1890	The first electric underground railway opened in London.
1901	The world's most successful monorail, the Wuppertal Schwebebahn, went into service.
1912	The first diesel locomotive took to the rails in Germany.
1938	The British steam locomotive *Mallard* set a steam rail speed record of 201 kph/125 mph.
1941	Swiss Federal Railways introduced a gas-turbine locomotive.
1964	Japan National Railways inaugurated the 515 km/320 mi New Tokaido line between Osaka and Tokyo, on which ran the 210 kph/130 mph 'bullet' trains.
1973	British Rail's High Speed Train (HST) set a diesel rail speed record of 229 kph/142 mph.
1979	Japan National Railways' maglev test vehicle ML-500 attained a speed of 517 kph/321 mph.
1981	France's TGV superfast trains began operation between Paris and Lyons, regularly attaining a peak speed of 270 kph/168 mph.
1987	France and the UK began work on the Channel Tunnel, a railway link connecting the two countries, running beneath the English Channel.
1989	A new world rail speed record of 482.4 kph/298 mph was established by a French TGV train.

railway (Top left) A replica of Robert Stephenson's Rocket; the original was built for the Rainhill Trials in 1829. (Top right) The French TGV is one of the fastest passenger trains, travelling at speeds of 260 kph. (Bottom left) A locomotive on the line between Guayaquil and Quito in Ecuador, the last steamworked crossing of the Andes.

Four years after building the first steam railway, Stephenson opened the first steam passenger line, inaugurating it with his locomotive *Rocket*, which achieved speeds of 50 kph/30 mph. The railway building that followed resulted in 250 separate companies in Britain, which resolved into four systems 1921 and became the nationalized British Railways 1948, known as British Rail from 1965.

European railways developed quickly during the 19th century, and in the USA and Canada the growth of railways made full exploitation of the central and western territories possible as well as enabling the North to win the American Civil War.

With the growth of car ownership and government encouraged road haulage after World War II, and the demise of steam, rising costs on the railways meant higher fares and fewer passengers along with declining freight traffic. During the 1960s and 1970s many rural rail services closed down. From the 1970s national railway companies began investing in faster inter-city services: in the UK, the diesel high speed train (HST) was introduced; elsewhere such trains run on specially built tracks such as the ◊Shinkansen (Japan) and ◊TGV (France) networks.

Railway Children, The a novel for children by E ◊Nesbit, published 1906. Three children move with their mother to a country cottage after their father is suddenly taken away, and the adventures centre around the railway that runs past their home. Each day the children wave to an old gentleman on a passing train and enlist his help to secure the release of their father from wrongful imprisonment.

rain technically termed *precipitation* separate drops of water that fall to the Earth's surface from clouds. The drops are formed by the accumulation of droplets that condense from water vapour in the air.

The condensation is usually brought about by cooling, either when the air rises over a mountain range or when, being a warm air mass, it rises above a cooler air mass.

rainbow arch in the sky of the colours of the ◊spectrum formed by the refraction and reflection of the sun's rays through rain or mist. Its cause was discovered by ◊Theodoric of Freiburg in the 14th century.

rainbow alliance from the mid-1980s; a loose, left-of-centre political grouping of disparate elements, encompassing sections of society that are traditionally politically under-represented, such as non-white ethnic groups. Its aims include promoting minority rights and equal opportunities.

It is a direct translation of French *Arc-en-Ciel*, a name applied in 1984 to an alliance of 20 Euro-MPs from various countries who supported Green environmental policies.

Raine /reɪn/ Kathleen 1908– . English poet. Her volumes of poetry include *Stone and Flower* 1943 and *The Lost Country* 1971, and reflect both the Northumberland landscape of her upbringing and the religious feeling which led her to the Roman Catholic church 1944.

rainforest dense forest found on or near the ◊equator where the climate is hot and wet. Over half the tropical rainforests are in Central and South America, the rest in SE Asia and Africa. Although covering approximately 8% of the Earth's land surface, they comprise about 50% of all growing wood on the planet, and harbour at least 40% of the Earth's species (plants and animals). Rainforests are being destroyed at an increasing rate as their valuable timber is harvested and land cleared for agriculture, causing problems of ◊deforestation, soil ◊erosion, and flooding. By 1990 50% of the world's rainforest had been removed.

Rainforests can be divided into the following kinds: tropical, montane, upper montane or cloud, mangrove, and subtropical. They are characterized by a great diversity of species, usually of tall broad-leafed evergreen trees, with many climbing vines and ferns, some of which are an important source of raw materials for medicines. Rainforests comprise some of the most complex and diverse ecosystems on the planet and help to regulate global weather patterns. When deforestation occurs, the microclimate of the mature forest disappears; soil erosion and flooding become major problems since rainforests protect the shallow tropical soils.

Clearing of the rainforests may lead to a global warming of the atmosphere, and contribute to the ◊greenhouse effect. Deforestation also causes the salt level in the ground to rise to the surface, making the land unsuitable for farming or ranching.

Rainier /rəˈnɪə/ mountain in the ◊Cascade Range, Washington State, USA; 4,392 m/14,415 ft, crowned by 14 glaciers and carrying dense forests on its slopes. It is a quiescent volcano. Mount Rainier national park was dedicated 1899.

Rainier III /ˈreɪnɪeɪ/ 1923– . Prince of ◊Monaco from 1949. He was married to the US film actress Grace Kelly.

Rais /reɪ/ Gilles de 1404–1440. French marshal who fought alongside Joan of Arc. In 1440 he was hanged for the torture and murder of 140 children, but the court proceedings were irregular. He is the historical basis of the ◊Bluebeard character.

raisin a dried grape; used for eating, baking, and the confection trade, the chief kinds are the common raisin, the sultana or seedless raisin, and the currant. They are produced in the Mediterranean area, California, and Australia.

raison d'être (French) a reason for existence.

Rajasthan /ˌrɑːdʒəˈstɑːn/ state of NW India
area 342,200 sq km/132,089 sq mi
capital Jaipur
features includes the larger part of the Thar Desert, where India's first nuclear test was carried out
products oilseed, cotton, sugar, asbestos, copper, textiles, cement, glass
population (1981) 34,103,000
language Rajasthani, Hindi
religion Hindu 90%, Muslim 3%
history formed 1948, enlarged 1956.

Rajneesh meditation a form of meditation based on the teachings of the Indian Shree Rajneesh (born Chaadra Mohan Jain), established in the early 1970s. Until 1989 he called himself *Bhagwan* (Hindi 'God'). His followers, who number about half a million worldwide, regard themselves as

Sannyas, or Hindu ascetics; they wear orange robes and carry a string of prayer beads. They are not expected to observe any specific prohibitions but to be guided by their instincts.

Rajneesh initially set up an ashram, or religious community, in Poona, NW India. He gained many followers, both Indian and Western, but his teachings also created considerable opposition, and in 1981 the Bhagwan moved his ashram to Oregon, USA, calling himself 'guru of the rich'. He was deported in 1985 after pleading guilty to immigration fraud.

He teaches that there is a basic energy in the world, bio-energy, and that individuals can release this by *dynamic meditation*, which involves breathing exercises and explosive physical activity. His followers are encouraged to live in large groups, so that children may grow up in contact with a variety of people. Rajneesh died 1990.

Rajput /ˈrɑːdʒpʊt/ Indian Hindus, predominantly soldiers and landowners, widespread over N India. The Rajput states of W India are now merged in Rajasthan. The Rana family (ruling aristocracy of Nepál until 1951) is also Rajput.

Rajshahi /rɑːdʒˈʃɑːhi/ capital of Rajshahi region, W Bangladesh; population (1981) 254,000. It trades in timber and vegetable oil.

Raleigh /ˈrɔːli/ industrial city (food processing, electrical machinery, textiles), capital of North Carolina, USA; population (1980) 148,000.

Raleigh /ˈrɔːli/ or *Ralegh* Walter c. 1552–1618. English adventurer. He made colonizing and exploring voyages to North America 1584–87 and South America 1595, and naval attacks on Spanish ports. He was imprisoned by James I 1603–16 and executed on his return from an unsuccessful final expedition to South America.

Raleigh was born in Devon. He was knighted 1584, and made several attempts 1584–87 to

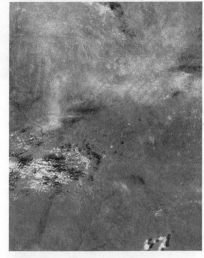

rainforest Satellite image of the rainforest surrounding the Rondonia Development Project in western Brazil. The image shows the extensive deforestation associated with farm settlement spreading from a central road (running left to right). Deforested areas appear blue or white; dense vegetation is red.

rainforest

tropical rainforest habitat

Along the equator rising hot air draws winds in from the north and south. These winds, known as trade winds, are wet and their moisture falls as torrential rain as the air rises. The ensuing hot wet conditions encourage the prolific growth of thousands of plant species, giving rise to the tropical rainforest. The varied and abundant species of plant support many different species of animal. The rain runs off into huge rivers, such as the Amazon, the Zaïre and the Mekong.

The tropical rainforest runs in a belt along the equator, broken only by mountain ranges.

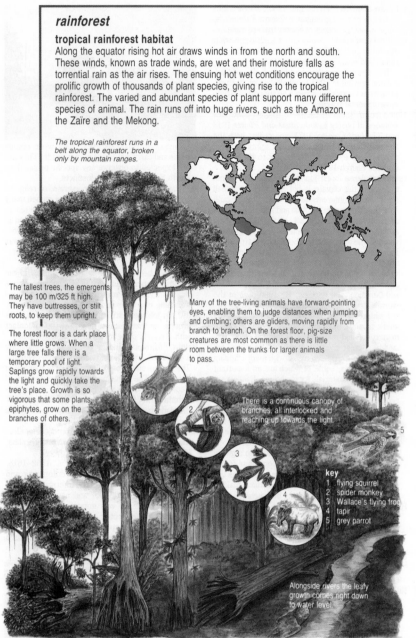

The tallest trees, the emergents may be 100 m/325 ft high. They have buttresses, or stilt roots, to keep them upright.

The forest floor is a dark place where little grows. When a large tree falls there is a temporary pool of light. Saplings grow rapidly towards the light and quickly take the tree's place. Growth is so vigorous that some plants, epiphytes, grow on the branches of others.

Many of the tree-living animals have forward-pointing eyes, enabling them to judge distances when jumping and climbing; others are gliders, moving rapidly from branch to branch. On the forest floor, pig-size creatures are most common as there is little room between the trunks for larger animals to pass.

There is a continuous canopy of branches, all interlocked and reaching up towards the light.

key
1   flying squirrel
2   spider monkey
3   Wallace's flying frog
4   tapir
5   grey parrot

Alongside rivers the leafy growth comes right down to water level

Rajasthan

Jaipur

INDIAN OCEAN

Ramakrishna claimed that mystical experience was the ultimate aim of religions, and that all religions which led to this goal were equally valid.

Ramakrishna's most important follower, Swami Vivekananda (1863–1902), set up the Ramakrishna Society 1887, which now has centres for education, welfare, and religious teaching throughout India and beyond.

Raman /'rɑːmən/ Venkata 1888–1970. Indian physicist who in 1928 discovered what became known as the *Raman effect*: the scattering of monochromatic light when passed through a transparent substance. Awarded a Nobel prize in 1930, in 1948 he became director of the Raman Research Institute and national research professor of physics.

Ramat Gan /rɑːmɑːt gɑːn/ industrial city (textiles, food processing) in W Israel, NE of Tel Aviv; population (1987) 116,000. It was established 1921.

Rāmāyana /rɑːˈmaɪənə/ Sanskrit epic *c.* 300 BC, in which Rama (an incarnation of the god Vishnu) and his friend Hanuman (the monkey chieftain) strive to recover Rama's wife, Sita, abducted by demon king Ravana.

Rambert /'rɒmbeə/ Marie. Adopted name of Cyvia Rambam 1888–1982. British ballet dancer and teacher born in Warsaw, Poland, who became a British citizen 1918. One of the major innovative and influential figures in modern ballet, she was with the Diaghilev ballet 1912–13, opened the Rambert School 1920, and in 1926 founded the Ballet Rambert which she directed (renamed Rambert Dance Company 1987).

Ramblers' Association society founded in Britain in 1935 to conserve the countryside and ensure that footpaths remain open.

Rambouillet /ˌrɒmbuːˈjeɪ/ town in the S of the forest of Rambouillet, SW of Paris, France;

establish a colony in 'Virginia' (now ◊North Carolina, USA). In 1595 he led an expedition to South America (described in his *Discovery of Guiana*) and distinguished himself in expeditions against Spain in Cádiz 1596 and the Azores 1597. After James I's accession 1603 he was condemned to death on a charge of conspiracy, but was reprieved and imprisoned in the Tower of London, where he wrote his unfinished *History of the World*. Released 1616 to lead a gold-seeking expedition to the Orinoco River in South America, which failed disastrously, he was beheaded on his return under his former sentence.

Raleigh, Fort /'rɔːli/ site of the first English settlement in America, at the N end of Roanoke Island, North Carolina, USA, to which in 1585 Walter Raleigh sent 108 colonists from Plymouth, England, under his cousin Richard Grenville. In 1586 Francis Drake took the dissatisfied survivors back to England. The outline fortifications are preserved.

RAM *random-access memory* in computing, a form of storage frequently used for the internal

◊memory of microcomputers. It is made up of a collection of ◊integrated circuits (chips). Unlike ◊ROM, RAM can be both read from and written to by the computer, but its contents are lost when the power is switched off. Today's microcomputers have up to eight megabytes of RAM.

Rama incarnation of ◊Vishnu, the supreme spirit of Hinduism. He is the hero of the epic poem, the *Rāmāyana*, and he is regarded as an example of morality and virtue.

Ramadan in the ◊Muslim calendar, the ninth month of the Muslim year. Throughout Ramadan a strict fast is observed during the hours of daylight; Muslims are encouraged to read the whole Koran as a commemoration of the Night of Power, which falls during the month, and is when Muslims believe Muhammad first received his revelations from the angel Gabriel.

Ramakrishna /ˌrɑːməˈkrɪʃnə/ 1834–1886. Hindu sage, teacher, and mystic (one dedicated to achieving oneness with or a direct experience of God or some force beyond the normal world).

Raleigh *Portrait of Sir Walter Raleigh by Nicholas Hilliard (c.1585) National Portrait Gallery, London.*

Rambert *As teacher and promoter to many leading dancers, choreographers, and stage designers, Marie Rambert was one of modern ballet's most influential figures.*

population (1985) 22,500. The former royal château is now the presidential summer residence. A breed of fine-woolled sheep is named after the town.

Rambouillet /ˌrɒmbuːˈjeɪ/ Catherine de Vivonne, Marquise de Rambouillet 1588–1665. French society hostess, whose salon at the Hôtel de Rambouillet in Paris included the writers Descartes, La Rochefoucauld, and Mme de Sévigné. The salon was ridiculed by the dramatist Molière in his *Les Précieuses ridicules* 1659.

Ram Das /ˈrɑːm dɑːs/ 1534–1581. Indian religious leader, fourth guru (teacher) of Sikhism 1574–81, who founded the Sikh holy city of Amritsar.

Rameau /ræˈməʊ/ Jean-Philippe 1683–1764. French organist and composer. He wrote *Treatise on Harmony* 1722 and his varied works include keyboard and vocal music and many operas, such as *Castor and Pollux* 1737.

Ramée /rɑːˈmeɪ/ Louise de la. Real name of British novelist ◊Ouida.

Ramillies, Battle of /ˈræmɪliz/ battle in which the British commander Marlborough defeated the French 23 May 1706, during the War of the ◊Spanish Succession, at a village in Brabant, Belgium, 21 km/13 mi N of Namur.

ramjet a simple kind of ◊jet engine used in some guided missiles. It only comes into operation at high speeds. Air is then 'rammed' into the combustion chamber, into which fuel is sprayed and ignited.

Ram Mohun Roy /ˈrɑːm ˈməʊhʊn ˈrɔɪ/ 1774–1833. Indian religious reformer, founder 1830 of ◊Brahma Samaj, a mystic cult.

Ramphal /ˈræmfɑːl/ Shridath Surendranath ('Sonny') 1928– . Guyanese politician. He was minister of foreign affairs and justice 1972–75, and became secretary-general of the British Commonwealth 1975. He studied at the University of London and Harvard Law School.

Rampling /ˈræmplɪŋ/ Charlotte 1945– . British actress, whose sometimes controversial films include *Georgy Girl* 1966, *The Night Porter/ Il Portiere di Notti* 1974, and *Farewell My Lovely* 1975.

Ramsay /ˈræmzi/ Allan 1686–1758. Scottish poet, born in Lanarkshire. He became a wig-maker and then a bookseller in Edinburgh. He published *The Tea-Table Miscellany* 1724–37, and *The Evergreen* 1724, collections of ancient and modern Scottish songs, including revivals of the work of such poets as ◊Dunbar and ◊Henryson.

Ramsay /ˈræmzi/ Allan 1713–1784. Scottish portrait painter. After studying in Edinburgh and Italy, he established himself as a portraitist in London, and

became painter to George III in 1760. He was the son of the poet Allan Ramsay. Portraits include *The Artist's Wife* about 1755 (National Gallery, Edinburgh).

Ramsay /ˈræmzi/ William 1852–1916. Scottish chemist who, with Lord Rayleigh, discovered argon 1894. In 1895 Ramsay manufactured helium, and in 1898, in cooperation with Morris Travers, identified neon, krypton, and xenon. In 1903 with Frederick Soddy, he noted the transmutation of radium into helium, which led to the discovery of the density and atomic weight of radium. Nobel prize 1904.

Ramses /ˈræmsiːz/ or *Rameses* eleven kings of ancient Egypt, including:

Ramses II or *Rameses II*. King of Egypt about 1304–1236 BC, the son of Seti I. He campaigned successfully against the Hittites, and built two rock temples at ◊Abu Simbel in Upper Egypt.

Ramses III or *Rameses III*. King of Egypt about 1200–1168 BC. He won a naval victory over the Philistines and other peoples, and asserted his suzerainty over Palestine.

Ramsgate /ˈræmzgeɪt/ seaside resort and cross-Channel port in the Isle of Thanet, Kent, SE England; population (1981) 39,642. There is a maritime museum. The architect Pugin built a home there, and is buried in the church next door (St Augustine's).

Rance /rɑːns/ river in Brittany, NW France, flowing into the English Channel between Dinard and St Malo, where a dam built 1960–67 (with a lock for ships) uses the 13 m/44 ft tides to feed the world's first successful tidal power station.

Rand /rænd/ an abbreviation for the Witwatersrand, a gold-bearing ridge in Transvaal, South Africa, extending for about 65 km/40 mi W and E of Johannesburg. Gold was first found there in 1854.

rand the unit of South Africa's decimal currency.

Rand /rænd/ Ayn. Adopted name of Alice Rosenbaum 1905–1982. US novelist of Russian origin. Her novel *The Fountainhead* 1943, describing an architect who destroys his masterpiece rather than see it altered, displays her influential blend of virulent anti-communism and fervent belief in individual enterprise.

random number one of a series of numbers which has no detectable pattern. They are used in ◊computer simulation and ◊computer games. It is impossible for an ordinary computer to generate true random numbers, but various techniques are available for obtaining pseudo-random numbers, these being close enough to true randomness for most purposes.

rangefinder instrument for determining the range or distance of an object from the observer;

Ramsay *After returning from study in Italy, the Scottish artist Allan Ramsay became a favourite of George III. The picture is a self-portrait, c. 1739.*

Ramses II *The temple of Ramses II at Abu Simbel, showing the head of a giant statue.*

used to focus a camera or to sight a gun accurately.

Rangoon /ˌrænˈguːn/ former name (until 1989) of ◊Yangon, capital of Myanmar.

Ranjit Singh /ˈrændʒɪt ˈsɪŋ/ 1780–1839. Indian maharajah. He succeeded his father as a minor Sikh leader 1792, and created a Sikh army that conquered Kashmir and the Punjab. In alliance with the British, he established himself as 'Lion of the Punjab', ruler of the strongest of the independent Indian states.

Rank /ræŋk/ Joseph Arthur 1888–1972. British film magnate. Having entered films in 1933 to promote the Methodist cause, he proceeded to gain control of much of the industry through takeovers and forming new businesses. The Rank Organization still owns the Odeon chain of cinemas and Pinewood Studios, although film is now a minor part of its activities.

Ransom /ˈrænsəm/ John Crowe 1888–1974. US poet and critic, born in Tennessee. He published his romantic but anti-rhetorical verse in, for example, *Poems About God* 1919, *Chills and Fever* 1924, *Selected Verse* 1947. As a critic and teacher he was a powerful figure in the movement of New Criticism, which shaped much literary theory from the 1940s to the 1960s.

Ransome /ˈrænsəm/ Arthur 1884–1967. English journalist (correspondent in Russia for the *Daily News* during World War I and the Revolution) and writer of adventure stories for children, such as *Swallows and Amazons* 1930 and *Peter Duck* 1932.

Ransome /ˈrænsəm/ Robert 1753–1830. English ironfounder and agricultural engineer, whose business earned a worldwide reputation in the 19th and 20th centuries. He introduced factory methods for the production of an improved range of ploughs from 1789. The firm remained at the forefront of advances in agricultural mechanization in connection with steam engines, threshing machines, and lawnmowers.

Rao /raʊ/ Raja 1909– . Indian writer, born at Hassan, Karnataka. He studied at Montpellier and the Sorbonne in France. He wrote about Indian independence from the perspective of a village in S India in *Kanthapura* 1938 and later, in *The Serpent and the Rope* 1960, about a young cosmopolitan intellectual seeking enlightenment. Collections of stories include *The Cow of the Barricades* 1947 and *The Policeman and the Rose* 1978.

Raoult /rɑːˈuː/ Francois 1830–1901. French chemist. In 1882, while working at the University of

Grenoble, Raoult formulated one of the basic laws of chemistry. Raoult's law enabled the molecular weight of a substance to be determined by noting how much of the substance was required to depress the freezing point of a solvent by a certain amount.

Rapallo /rə'pæləʊ/ port and winter resort in Liguria, NW Italy, 24 km/15 mi SE of Genoa on the Gulf of Rapallo; population (1981) 29,300. Treaties were signed here 1920 (settling the common frontiers of Italy and Yugoslavia) and 1922 (cancelling German and Russian counter-claims for indemnities for World War I).

Rapa Nui /'rɑːpə 'nuːi/ another name for ◊Easter Island, an island in the Pacific.

rape in botany, two plant species of the mustard family, *Brassica rapa* and *Brassica napus*, grown for their seeds which yield a pungent edible oil. The **common turnip** is a variety of the former, and the **swede turnip** of the latter.

rape in law, sexual intercourse without the consent of the subject. Most cases of rape are of women by men. From 1976 in the UK the victim's name may not be published, her sex history should not be in question, and her 'absence of consent' rather than (as previously required) proof of her 'resistance to violence' is the criterion of the crime. The anonymity of the accused is also preserved unless he is convicted. In 1985, there were 22,900 reported cases of sexual assault in the UK. However, since victims are often unwilling to report what has happened, it is thought that there are perhaps ten times as many rapes as the reported figure.

Raphael /'ræfeɪəl 'sænziəʊ/ (Raffaello Sanzio) 1483–1520. Italian painter, one of the greatest of the High Renaissance, active in Perugia, Florence, and Rome (from 1508), where he painted frescoes in the Vatican and for secular patrons. His harmoniously composed religious and mythological scenes were enormously influential; his portraits enhance his sitter's character and express dignity. Many of his designs were engraved. Much of his later work was the product of his studio.

Raphael was born in Urbino, the son of Giovanni Santi (died 1494), a court painter. In 1499 he went to Perugia, where he worked with ◊Perugino, whose graceful style is reflected in Raphael's *Marriage of the Virgin* (Brera, Milan). This work also shows his early concern for harmonious disposition of figures in the pictorial space. In Florence 1504–08 he studied the works of Leonardo da Vinci, Michelangelo, Masaccio, and Fra Bartolommeo. His paintings of this period include the *Ansidei Madonna* (National Gallery, London).

Next, Pope Julius II commissioned him to decorate the papal apartments (the Stanze) in the Vatican. In Raphael's first fresco series there, *The School of Athens* 1509 is a complex but classically composed grouping of Greek philosophers and mathematicians, centred on the figures of Plato and Aristotle. A second series of frescoes, 1511–14, includes the dramatic and richly coloured *Mass of Bolsena*.

Raphael *An Allegory* 'Vision of a Knight' *(c.1504) National Gallery, London.*

Raphael was increasingly flooded with commissions. Within the next few years he produced delightful mythological frescoes in the Villa Farnesina in Rome (1511–12), cartoons for tapestries for the Sistine Chapel, Vatican (Victoria and Albert Museum, London), and the *Sistine Madonna* about 1512 (Gemäldegalerie, Dresden, East Germany). One of his pupils was ◊Giulio Romano.

Rapid Deployment Force former name (until 1983) of ◊US Central Command, a military strike force.

rap music a rapid, rhythmic chant over a prerecorded repetitive backing track. Rap emerged in New York 1979 as part of the ◊hip-hop culture, although the usually macho, swaggering lyrics have roots in ritual boasts and insults.

rare earth oxide of elements of the lanthanide series. They are found only in certain rare minerals. The term is sometimes also used for the lanthanide elements themselves.

rare gas another name for ◊inert gas.

Ras al Khaimah /'ræs æl 'xaɪmə/ or **Ra's al Khaymah** an emirate on the Persian Gulf; area 1,690 sq km/652 sq mi; population (1980) 73,700. Products include oil, pharmaceuticals and cement. It is one of the seven members of the ◊United Arab Emirates.

Rashdun the 'rightly guided ones', the first four caliphs (heads) of Islam: Abu Bakr, Umar, Uthman, and Ali.

raspberry prickly cane-plant *Rubus idaeus* of the Rosaceae family, with white flowers followed by red fruits. These are eaten fresh and used for jam and wine.

Rasputin /ræs'pjuːtɪn/ (Russian 'dissolute') Gregory Efimovich 1871–1916. Siberian wandering 'holy man', the illiterate son of a peasant. He acquired influence over the tsarina ◊Alexandra, wife of ◊Nicholas II, because of her faith in his power to cure her son of his haemophilia, and he was able to make political and ecclesiastical appointments. His abuse of power and his notorious debauchery (reputedly including the tsarina) led to his being murdered by a group of nobles, who (when poison had no effect) dumped him in the river Neva after shooting him.

Rastafarianism religion originating in the West Indies, based on the ideas of Marcus ◊Garvey, who preached that the only way for black people to escape their poverty and oppression was to return to Africa. When Haile Selassie (**Ras Tafari**, the Lion of Judah) was crowned emperor of Ethiopia 1930, this was seen as a fulfilment of prophecy and Rastafarians acknowledged him as the Messiah, the incarnation of God (**Jah**). The use of ganja (marijuana) is a sacrament. There are no churches. There were about one million Rastafarians by 1990.

Rastafarians identify themselves with the Chosen People, the Israelites, of the Bible. Ethiopia is seen as the promised land, while all countries outside Africa, and their cultures and institutions, are **Babylon**, the place of exile. Rastafarians use a distinct language, in particular using the term 'I and I' for 'we' to stress unity. Many Rastafarians do not cut their hair, because of Biblical injunctions against this, but wear their hair in long dreadlocks, often covered in woollen hats in the Rastafarian colours of red, green, and gold. Food laws are very strict: for example, no pork or shellfish, no salt, milk, or coffee. The term *I-tal* is used for food as close as possible to its natural state. Medicines should be made from natural herbs. Meetings are held regularly for prayer, discussion, and celebration, and at intervals there is a very large meeting, or Nyabingi.

Rastatt, Treaty of in 1714, a treaty signed by Austria and France which supplemented the ◊Treaty of Utrecht, and helped to end the War of the ◊Spanish Succession.

rat various large rodents, particularly the large members of the family Muridae. They usually have pointed snouts and scaly tails.

The brown rat *Rattus norvegicus* is about 200 mm/8 in with a tail of almost equal length. It is

believed to have originated in central Asia, and is now found worldwide after being transported from Europe by ships. The black rat *Rattus rattus*, reponsible for the ◊plague, is smaller than the brown rat, but has larger ears, and a longer, more pointed snout. They do not interbreed with the brown rats.

rates in the UK, tax levied on residential, industrial, and commercial property by local authorities to cover their expenditure (see ◊county council, ◊local government). The rate for a household with several wage-earners may be identical with that for a single person of retirement age, and rebates are given to ratepayers whose income falls below a certain level. The Thatcher government (1979–) curbed high-spending councils by cutting the government supplementary grant aid to them and limiting the level of rate that could be levied (*ratecapping*), and in 1989–90 replaced the rate with a *community charge* or ◊poll tax on each individual. In Jan 1990 the UK government revised all valuations of business property in England and Wales as part of its new Uniform Business Rate. All commercial property users will pay 34.8% of the valuation. Rates were revalued proportionately higher in the south than the north.

rate support grant in the UK, an amount of money made available annually by central government to supplement rates as a source of income for local government. Introduced 1967, it consists of a resources element, giving help to local authorities with small resources; a needs element, based on population size; and a domestic element, to reimburse local authorities for rate reductions for domestic ratepayers. From 1979 the system has been used as a method of curbing local authority spending by reducing or withholding the grant.

Already in the 19th century the government was giving such help—by 1888 grants accounted for 14% of local revenue—and in 1929 the system was formalized, a block grant replacing various specific grants. This was modified 1948 (exchequer equalization grant) and 1958 (rate deficiency grant).

Rathbone /'ræθbəʊn/ (Philip St John) Basil 1892–1967. South African-born British character actor, one of the cinema's great villains; he also played Sherlock Holmes (the fictional detective created by Arthur Conan Doyle) in several films. He worked mainly in Hollywood, in films such as *The Adventures of Robin Hood* 1938 and *The Hound of the Baskervilles* 1939.

Rathenau /'rɑːtənaʊ/ Walther 1867–1922. German politician. He was a leading industrialist, and was appointed economic director during World War I, developing a system of economic planning in combination with capitalism. After the war he founded the Democratic Party, and became foreign minister 1922. The same year he signed the Rapallo Treaty of Friendship with the USSR, cancelling German and Soviet counter-claims for indemnities for World War I, and soon after was murdered by right-wing fanatics.

Rathlin /'ræθlɪn/ island off the N Irish coast, in Antrim; St Columba founded a church there in the 6th century, and in 1306 Robert Bruce hid there after his defeat by the English at Methven.

rationalism in theology, the belief that human reason rather than divine revelation is the correct means of ascertaining truth and regulating behaviour. In philosophy, rationalism takes the view that self-evident propositions deduced by reason are the sole basis of all knowledge (disregarding experience of the senses). It is usually contrasted with empiricism, which argues that all knowledge must ultimately be derived from the senses.

Following the work of the philosophers Descartes and Spinoza, rationalism developed through Leibniz, had an impact all over Europe in the 18th and 19th centuries, and extended to the USA.

rationalized units units for which the defining equations conform to the geometry of the system. Equations involving circular symmetry contain the factor 2π; those involving spherical symmetry 4π. ◊SI units are rationalized, ◊c.g.s. units are not.

rational number in mathematics, any number that can be expressed as an exact fraction (with a denominator not equal to 0), that is, as $a \div b$ where a, b are integers. For example 2, 1/4, ¹⁵/4, ⁻³/5 are all rational numbers, whereas π (= 3.141592...) is not. Numbers such as π are called ◊irrational numbers.

Ratisbon /ˈrætɪzbɒn/ English name for the West German city of ◊Regensburg.

ratite bird with a breastbone without the keel to which flight muscles are attached, for example, ostrich, rhea, emu, cassowary, and kiwi.

rat-tail or **grenadier** fish of the family Macrouridae. They have stout heads and bodies, and long tapering tails. They are common in deep oceanic waters on the continental slopes. Some species have a light-emitting organ in front of the anus. Also known as rat-tails are some of the ◊chimaeras.

Rattigan /ˈrætɪgən/ Terence 1911–1977. English playwright. His play *Ross* 1960 was based on T E Lawrence (Lawrence of Arabia). Rattigan's work ranges from the comedy *French Without Tears* 1936 to the psychological intensity of *The Winslow Boy* 1945. Other plays include *The Browning Version* 1948 and *Separate Tables* 1954.

Rattle /ˈrætl/ Simon 1955– . English conductor. Principal conductor of the Birmingham Symphony Orchestra from 1980, he is noted for his eclectic range and for interpretations of Mahler and Sibelius.

rattlesnake snake of the North American genus *Crotalus*, and related genera, distinguished by the horny flat rings of the tail, which rattle when vibrated as a warning to attackers. They can grow to 2.5 m/8 ft long. The venom injected by some rattlesnakes can be fatal.

Ratushinskaya /ˌrætuːˈʃɪnskəjə/ Irina 1954– . Soviet dissident poet. Sentenced 1983 to seven years in a labour camp plus five years in internal exile for criticism of the Soviet regime, she was released 1986. Her strongly Christian work includes *Grey is the Colour of Hope* 1988.

Rau /rau/ Johannes 1931– . West German socialist politician, member of the Social Democratic Party (SPD).

The son of a Protestant pastor, Rau began work as a salesman for a church publishing company before joining the SPD. He became state premier of North Rhine-Westphalia 1978. In Jan 1987 he stood for chancellor but was defeated by the incumbent conservative coalition.

Raunkiaer system of classification a scheme devised by the Danish ecologist Christen Raunkiaer (1860–1938) whereby plants are divided into groups according to the position of their ◊perennating buds in relation to the soil surface. For example, plants in cold areas, such as the tundra, generally have their buds protected below ground, whereas in hot,

Rattle *Simon Rattle conducting the Birmingham Symphony Orchestra.*

diamond backed rattle snake

tropical areas they are above ground and freely exposed. This method of plant classification is useful for comparing vegetation types in different parts of the world.

The main divisions are **phanerophytes** with buds situated well above the ground, **chamaephytes** with buds borne within 25 cm/10 in of the soil surface, **hemicryptophytes** with buds at or immediately below the soil surface, and **cryptophytes** with their buds either beneath the soil (**geophyte**) or below water (**hydrophyte**).

Rauschenberg /ˈrauʃənbɜːg/ Robert 1925– . US Pop artist, a creator of happenings (art in live performance) and incongruous multimedia works such as *Monogram* 1959 (Moderna Museet, Stockholm), a car tyre around the body of a stuffed goat daubed with paint. Rauschenberg also produced collages. In the 1960s he returned to painting and used the silk-screen printing process to transfer images to canvas.

Ravana in the Hindu epic *Rāmāyana*, the demon king of Lankā (Sri Lanka) who abducted Sita, the wife of Rama.

Ravel /ræˈvel/ (Joseph) Maurice 1875–1937. French composer. His work is characterized by its sensuousness, unresolved dissonances, and 'tone colour'. Examples are the piano pieces *Pavane pour une infante défunte* 1899 and *Jeux d'eau* 1901, and the ballets *Daphnis et Chloë* 1912 and *Boléro* 1928.

raven bird *Corvus corax* of the crow family. It is about 60 cm/2 ft long, and has black, lustrous plumage. It is a scavenger, found only in the northern hemisphere.

Ravenna /rəˈvenə/ historical city and industrial port (petrochemical works) in Emilia-Romagna, Italy; population (1988) 136,000. It lies in a marshy plain and is known for its Byzantine churches with superb mosaics.

Ravenna was a Roman port and naval station, and capital of the W Roman emperors 404–93; of ◊Theodoric the Great 493–526; and later of the Byzantine exarchs (bishops) 539–750. The British poet Byron lived for some months in Ravenna, home of Countess Guiccioli, during the years 1819–21.

Raven, The a famous US poem, written 1845 by Edgar Allan Poe, about a bereaved poet haunted by a raven which sonorously warns 'Nevermore'.

Ravi /ˈrɑːviː/ river in the Indian subcontinent, a tributary of the ◊Indus. It rises in India, forms the boundary between India and Pakistan for some 95 km/70 mi, and enters Pakistan above Lahore, the chief town on its 725 km/450 mi course. It is an important source of water for the Punjab irrigation canal system.

Rawalpindi /rɔːlˈpɪndi/ city in Punjab province, Pakistan, in the foothills of the Himalayas; population (1981) 928,400. Industries include oil refining, iron, chemicals, and furniture.

Rawlinson /ˈrɔːlɪnsən/ Henry Creswicke 1810–1895. English orientalist and political agent in Baghdad in the Ottoman Empire from 1844. He deciphered the Babylonian and Old Persian scripts of ◊Darius I's trilingual inscription at Behistun, Persia, continued the excavation work of A H ◊Layard, and published a *History of Assyria* 1852.

Rawls /rɔːlz/ John 1921– . US philosopher. In *A Theory of Justice* 1971, he revived the concept of the ◊'social contract', and its enforcement by civil disobedience.

Rawsthorne /ˈrɔːsθɔːn/ Alan 1905–1971. British composer. His *Theme and Variations* for two violins 1938 was followed by other tersely energetic works including *Symphonic Studies* 1939, the

overture *Street Corner* 1944, *Concerto for Strings* 1950, and a vigorously inventive sonata for violin and piano, 1959.

ray cartilaginous fish with a flattened body, wing-like pectoral fins, and a tail like a whip.

Types of rays include the stingray, which has a serrated, poisonous spine on the tail, and the ◊torpedo fish.

Ray /reɪ/ John 1627–1705. English naturalist who devised a classification system accounting for nearly 18,000 plant species. It was the first system to divide flowering plants into ◊monocotyledons and ◊dicotyledons, with additional divisions made on the basis of leaf and flower characters and fruit types.

Ray /reɪ/ Man. Adopted name of Emmanuel Rudnitsky 1890–1976. US photographer, painter, and sculptor, active mainly in France; associated with the Dada movement. His pictures often showed Surrealist images like the photograph *Le Violon d'Ingres* 1924.

Ray was born in Philadelphia, but lived in Paris from 1921 (in Los Angeles 1940–51). He began as a painter and took up photography in 1915, the year he first met the Dada artist Duchamp in New York. In 1922 he invented the **rayograph**, a black and white image obtained by placing objects on sensitized photographic paper; he also made much use of the technique of **solarization** (partly reversing the tones on a photograph). His photographs include portraits of many artists and writers.

Ray /reɪ/ Nicholas. Adopted name of Raymond Nicholas Kienzle 1911–1979. US film director, critically acclaimed for his socially aware dramas such as *Rebel Without a Cause* 1955. His later epics, such as *King of Kings* 1961, were less successful.

Ray /reɪ/ Satyajit 1921– . Indian film director, renowned for his trilogy of life in his native Bengal: *Pather Panchali*, *Unvanquished*, and *The World of Apu* 1955–59. Later films include *The Chess Players* 1977 and *The Home and the World* 1984.

Rayleigh /ˈreɪli/ John W Strutt, 3rd Baron Rayleigh 1842–1919. British physicist who wrote the standard *Treatise on Sound*, experimented in optics and microscopy, and, with William Ramsay, discovered argon. He was professor of experimental physics at Cambridge 1879–84, and was president of the Royal Society 1905–08, when he became chancellor of Cambridge University. In 1904 he received a Nobel prize.

Raynaud's disease a condition in which the blood supply to the extremities is reduced by periodic spasm of the blood vessels on exposure to cold. It is most often seen in young women.

Attacks are usually brought on by cold or by emotional factors. Typically the hands and/or feet take on a corpse-like pallor, changing to blue as the circulation begins to return; initial numbness is replaced by a tingling or burning sensation. Drugs may be necessary to control the condition, particularly in severe cases where there is risk of gangrene.

rayon artificial silk made from ◊cellulose. A common type is ◊viscose, which consists of regenerated filaments of pure cellulose. Acetate and triacetate are kinds of rayon consisting of filaments of cellulose acetate and triacetate.

razor a sharpened metallic blade used to remove facial or body hair. Razors were known in the Bronze Age. The safety razor was patented by William Henson in 1847; a disposable version was produced by King ◊Gillette at the start of the 20th century. The earliest electric razors date from the 1920s.

razorbill N Atlantic seabird *Alca torda*, of the auk family, which breeds on cliffs, and migrates to the Mediterranean in winter. It has a curved beak, and is black above and white below. It uses its wings as paddles when diving.

razorshell or **razor-fish** two genera *Ensis* and *Solen* of bivalve molluscs, with narrow elongated shells, resembling an old-fashioned razor handle and delicately coloured. They are found in sand among rocks.

RC abbreviation for ◊*Red Cross*; *Roman Catholic*.

re abbreviation for Latin 'with regard to'.

reaction in chemistry, the coming together of two or more atoms, ions or molecules resulting in a ◊chemical change. The nature of the reaction is portrayed by a chemical equation.

reaction principle principle stated by ◊Newton as his third law of motion: to every action, there is an equal and opposite reaction. In other words, a force acting in one direction is always accompanied by an equal force acting in the opposite direction. This explains how ◊jet and rocket propulsion works, and why a gun recoils after firing.

Reader's Digest world's best-selling magazine, founded 1922 in the USA to publish condensed articles and books, usually of an uplifting and often conservative kind, along with in-house features. It has editions in many different languages.

Reading /ˈredɪŋ/ industrial town (biscuits, electronics) on the river Thames, administrative headquarters of Berkshire, England; university 1892; population (1985) 138,000. An agricultural and horticultural centre. It was extensively rebuilt after World War II. Oscar ◊Wilde spent two years in Reading jail.

Reading /ˈredɪŋ/ industrial city (textiles, special steels) in Pennsylvania, USA; population (1980) 78,686.

Reagan /ˈreɪgən/ Ronald (Wilson) 1911– . US Republican politician, governor of California 1966–74, president 1981–89. A former Hollywood actor, Reagan was a hawkish and popular president. He withstood criticism of his interventionist foreign policy, but failed to confront a mounting trade deficit. He was succeeded by George ◊Bush. He unsuccessfully contested the Republican presidential nomination 1968 and 1976, and defeated ◊Carter in the 1980 election, and ◊Mondale 1984. He adopted an aggressive policy in Central America, attempting to overthrow the government of Nicaragua, and invading ◊Grenada 1983. In 1987, ◊Irangate was investigated by the Tower Commission; Reagan regretted that US/Iran negotiations had become an 'arms for hostages deal', but denied knowledge of resultant funds being illegally sent to the Contras in Nicaragua. He increased military spending (increasing the national budget deficit to record levels), cut social programmes, introduced deregulation of domestic markets, and cut taxes. His ◊Strategic Defense Initiative, announced 1983, has proven controversial due to the cost and unfeasibility.

Reagan was born in Tampico, Illinois, the son of a shoe salesman who was bankrupted during the Depression. He became a Hollywood actor 1937 and appeared in 50 films, including *Bedtime for Bonzo* 1951 and *The Killers* 1964. As president of the Screen Actors' Guild 1947–52, he became a conservative, critical of the bureaucratic stifling of free enterprise, and named names before the House Un-American Activities Committee. He joined the Republican Party 1962, and his term as governor of California was marked by battles against students. Having lost the Republican presidential nomination 1968 and 1976 to Nixon and Ford respectively, Reagan won it 1980 and defeated President Carter. He was wounded in an assassination attempt 1981. The invasion of Grenada generated a revival of national patriotism, and Reagan was re-elected by a landslide 1984. His insistence on militarizing space through the Strategic Defense Initiative, popularly called Star Wars, prevented a disarmament agreement when he met the Soviet leader ◊Gorbachev 1985 and 1986, but a 4% reduction in nuclear weapons was agreed 1987. In 1986, he ordered the bombing of Tripoli, Libya, in retaliation for the killing of a US soldier in Berlin.

realism In medieval philosophy, the theory that 'universals' have existence, not simply as names for entities, but entities in their own right. It

Realism *Gustave Courbet's* The Stonebreakers *1849 (formerly Dresden State Museum, destroyed in World War II).*

is thus opposed to nominalism. In contemporary philosophy, the term stands for the doctrine that there is an intuitively appreciated reality apart from what is presented to the consciousness. It is opposed to idealism.

Realist philosophers include C D Broad and (although their views were later modified) Bertrand Russell and G E Moore; Wittgenstein has been an important later influence.

Realism in the arts and literature, an unadorned, naturalistic approach to the subject matter. The term may also refer to a movement in mid-19th-century European art, a reaction against Romantic and Classical idealization and a rejection of conventional academic subjects, such as mythology, history, and sublime landscapes.

The painters Courbet and Daumier represent 19th-century Realism in France: both chose to paint scenes from contemporary life, using their art to expose injustice in society. Courbet shocked the public by exhibiting large canvases that focused on ordinary people.

real number in mathematics, any ◊rational (which include the integers) or ◊irrational number. Real numbers exclude ◊imaginary numbers, found in ◊complex numbers of the general form $a + bi$ where $i = \sqrt{-1}$, although these do include a real component a.

Realpolitik (German 'politics of realism') term coined 1853 to describe ◊Bismarck's policies during the 1848 revolutions: the pragmatic pursuit of self-interest and power, backed up by force when necessary.

Reagan *Ronald Reagan, US president 1981–89.*

real presence or ***transubstantiation*** in Christianity, the belief that there are present in the properly consecrated Eucharist the body and blood of Jesus. It is held by Roman Catholics, and in some sense by Anglo-Catholics.

real tennis racket and ball game played in France, from about the 12th century, over a central net in an indoor court, but with a sloping roof let into each end and one side of the court, against which the ball may be hit. The term real in this sense means 'royal', not 'genuine'. Basic scoring is as for 'lawn' ◊tennis, but with various modifications. The oldest court still in use is at Hampton Court, Richmond, W London, where it was installed by Henry VIII.

real-time system in computing, a program that responds to events in the world as they happen, as, for example, an automatic pilot program in an aircraft must respond instantly to correct course deviations. Process control, robotics, games, and many military applications are examples of real-time systems.

Reardon /ˈrɪədən/ Ray 1932– . Welsh snooker player. One of the leading players of the 1970s, he was six times world champion 1970–78.

recall a process by which voters can demand the dismissal from office of elected officials, as in some states of the USA.

Récamier /ˌreɪkæmˈjeɪ/ Jeanne Françoise 1777–1849. French society hostess, born in Lyons. At the age of 15 she married Jacques Récamier, an elderly banker, and held a salon of literary and political celebrities.

received pronunciation (RP) see ◊English language.

receiver in law, a person appointed by a court to collect and manage the assets of an individual, company, or partnership in serious financial difficulties. In the case of bankruptcy, the assets may be sold and distributed by a receiver to creditors. In France, a receiver is known as a syndic, and in Germany as an administrator.

receptacle the enlarged end of a flower stalk to which the floral parts are attached. Normally the receptacle is rounded but in some plants it is flattened or cup-shaped. The term is also used for the region on that part of some seaweeds which becomes swollen at certain times of the year and bears the reproductive organs.

recession in economics, a fall in business activity lasting more than a few months, causing stagnation in a country's output. A serious recession is called a *slump*.

recessive in genetics, an allele that can only produce a detectable effect on the organism bearing it when both chromosomes carry it, that is, when the same allele has been inherited from both parents. The individual is then said to be homozygous. In a heterozygous individual, the effect of a recessive allele will be masked by a dominant allele (see ◊dominance).

réchauffé (French 're-heated') warmed-up (as for leftover food); old, stale.

recherché (French 'sought after') rare.

Recife /re'siːfə/ industrial seaport (cotton textiles, sugar refining, fruit canning, flour milling) and naval base in Brazil, capital of Pernambuco state, at the mouth of the river Capibaribe; population (1980) 1,184,215. It was founded 1504.

reciprocal in mathematics, of a quantity, that quantity divided into 1. Thus the reciprocal of 2 is $1/2$ (= 0.5); of $2/3$ is $3/2$; of x^2 is $1/x^2$ or x^{-2}.

recitative in opera, on-pitch speech-like declamation of narrative episodes.

Recklinghausen /'reklɪŋ,haʊzən/ industrial town (coal, iron, chemicals, textiles, engineering) in North Rhine-Westphalia, West Germany, 24 km/15 mi NW of Dortmund; population (1988) 118,000. It is said to have been founded by Charlemagne.

recombination in genetics, any process which recombines or 'shuffles' the genetic material, so increasing genetic variation in the offspring. The two main processes of recombination are ◊*cross-ing over* (in which chromosome pairs exchange segments), and the random reassortment of the chromosomes that occurs during ◊*meiosis*, when each gamete (sperm or egg) receives only one of each chromosome pair.

Reconquista (Spanish 'reconquest') the Christian defeat of the Muslims 9th–15th centuries, and their expulsion from Spain. Spain was conquered by the Muslims between 711 and 728, and its reconquest began with Galicia, Leon, and Castile. By the 13th century, only Granada was left in Muslim hands, but disunity within the Christian kingdoms meant that it was not conquered until 1492, when it fell to ◊Ferdinand and Isabella.

Reconstruction in US history, the period 1865–77 after the Civil War during which the nation was reunited under the federal government after the defeat of the Southern Confederacy. The emancipated slaves were assisted in finding work, shelter, and lost relatives through federal agencies. Amendments to the US constitution, and to southern state constitutions, conferred equal civil and political rights on blacks, though many southern states, opposed to these radical Republican measures, still practised discrimination and segregation. Reconstruction paved the way for the modernization of the South, but failed to ensure racial equality, and the former slaves remained, in most cases,
* landless labourers.

recorder in the English legal system, a part-time judge who usually sits in the ◊Crown Courts in less serious cases but may also sit in the county courts or the High Court. They are chosen from barristers of standing and also, since the Courts Act of 1971, from solicitors. Recorders may eventually become circuit judges.

recorder in music, an instrument of the ◊woodwind family, blown through one end, in which different notes are obtained by covering the holes in the instrument. They are played in a consort (ensemble) of matching tone and comprise sopranino, descant, treble, and bass.

The descant, adopted into the orchestra, was gradually superseded by the flute, being revived as a school music instrument. The full consort has since been re-established for performing early music.

recording the process of storing information, or the information store itself. Sounds and pictures can be stored on discs or tape. The gramophone record stores music or speech as a spiral groove on a plastic disc and the sounds are reproduced by a record player. The ◊compact disc produces a more faithful reproduction of the original sounds. In ◊tape recording, sounds are stored as a magnetic pattern on plastic tape. The best quality reproduction is achieved using ◊digital audio tape. Pictures can be recorded on magnetic tape in a similar way by using a ◊videotape recorder. The video equivalent of a compact disc is the video disc.

Record Office, Public a government office containing the English national records since the Norman Conquest, brought together from courts of law and government departments, including the Domesday Book, the Gunpowder Plot papers, and the log of HMS *Victory* at Trafalgar. It was established 1838 in Chancery Lane, London; records from the 18th century onwards have been housed at Kew, London, since 1976.

record player device for reproducing sound recorded, usually in a spiral groove on a disc or record. A motor-driven turntable rotates the record at a constant speed, and a stylus or needle on the head of a pick-up is made to vibrate by the undulations in the record groove. These vibrations are then converted to electrical signals by a ◊transducer in the head (often a ◊piezoelectric crystal). After amplification, the signals pass to one or more loudspeakers which convert them into sound.

The pioneers of the record player were ◊Edison, with his ◊phonograph, and Emile Berliner (1851–1929), who invented the disc record 1896. More recent developments are stereophonic sound and digital recording on compact disc. In digital recording the signals picked up by the microphone are converted into precise numerical values by computer. These values, which represent the original sound wave form exactly, are recorded on compact disc. When it is played back by ◊laser, the exact values are retrieved. When fed via an amplifier to a loudspeaker, sound waves exactly like the original ones are recreated.

Recruit scandal a scandal in post-war Japanese history. The Recruit company was accused in July 1988 of illegal stock trading, but the affair widened as increasing numbers of senior government politicians were implicated, for example, Prime Minister Noboru Takeshita was accused in 1989 of receiving 'political donations', as well as bribery and fraud.

rectangle a quadrilateral (four-sided figure) with opposite sides equal and parallel, and with each interior angle a right angle (90°). Its area A is the product of the length l and breadth b; that is, $A = l \times b$. A rectangle with all four sides equal is a ◊square. A rectangle is a special case of a ◊parallelogram. The diagonals of a rectangle bisect each other.

rectifier device which is necessary for obtaining one-directional current (DC) from an alternating source of supply (AC). Types include plate rectifiers, thermionic ◊diodes, and ◊semiconductor diodes.

rector Anglican priest, formerly entitled to the whole of the ◊tithes levied in the parish, as opposed to a *vicar* (Latin 'deputy') who was only entitled to part.

rectum the lowest part of the digestive tract of animals, which stores faeces prior to elimination (defecation).

recursion in computing, a technique whereby a ◊function or ◊procedure calls itself, enabling a complex problem to be broken down into simpler

steps. For example, a function which returns the factorial of a number, n, would obtain its result by multiplying n by the factorial of n–1.

recycling the processing of industrial and household waste (such as paper, glass, and some metals) so that it can be reused, thus saving expenditure on scarce raw materials, slowing down the depletion of nonrenewable resources, and helping to reduce pollution.

red informal term for a leftist, revolutionary, or communist, which originated in the 19th century in the form 'red republican', meaning a republican who favoured a social as well as a political revolution, generally by armed violence. Red is the colour adopted by socialist parties.

Red and the Black, The French *Le Rouge et le noir* a novel by Stendhal, published 1830. Julien Sorel, a carpenter's son, pursues social advancement by dishonourable means. Marriage to a marquis's daughter, a title, and an army commission are within his grasp when revelation of his murky past by a former lover destroys him.

Red Army former name of the army of the USSR. It developed from the Red Guards, volunteers who carried out the Bolshevik revolution, and received its name because it fought under the red flag. It was officially renamed the *Soviet Army* 1946. The Chinese revolutionary army was also called the Red Army.

Red Badge of Courage, The classic US novel of the American Civil War published 1895 by Stephen Crane, the story of the youth Henry Fleming, his cowardice, courage, and final sense of personal victory.

red blood cell or *erythrocyte* an oxygen-transporting cell of the ◊blood. They are the most numerous type of blood cell and contain the red pigment haemoglobin. Mammalian erythrocytes are disc-like with a depression in the centre and no nucleus; those of other vertebrates are oval and nucleated.

Redbridge /'redbrɪdʒ/ borough of NE Greater London, including Ilford, Wanstead, and Woodford, and parts of Chigwell and Dagenham

features part of Epping Forest; Hainault Forest

population (1981) 225,300.

Red Brigades Italian *Brigate rosse* extreme left-wing guerrilla groups active in Italy during the 1970s and early 1980s. They were implicated in many kidnappings and killings, including that of Christian Democrat leader Aldo Moro 1978.

Red Cross, the international relief agency founded by the Geneva Convention 1864 at the instigation of the Swiss doctor Henri ◊Dunant to assist the wounded and prisoners in war. Its symbol is a symmetrical red cross on a white ground. In addition to dealing with associated problems of war, such as refugees and the care of the disabled, the Red Cross is increasingly concerned with victims of natural disasters—floods, earthquakes, epidemics, and accidents.

recycling *Crushed car bodies ready for recycling of the metal.*

Prompted by war horrors described by Dunant, the Geneva Convention laid down principles to ensure the safety of ambulances, hospitals, stores, and personnel distinguished by the Red Cross emblem. The Muslim equivalent is the **Red Crescent**.

The British Red Cross Society was founded 1870, and incorporated 1908. It works in close association with the St John Ambulance Association.

redcurrant in botany, a type of ◊currant.

Redding /ˈrɛdɪŋ/ Otis 1941–1967. US soul singer and songwriter. He had a number of hits in the mid-1960s such as 'My Girl' 1965, 'Respect' 1967, and '(Sittin' on the) Dock of the Bay' 1968, released after his death in a plane crash.

Redditch /ˈrɛdɪtʃ/ industrial town (needles, fishing tackle, car and aircraft components, cycles, motorcycles, electrical equipment) in Hereford and Worcester, England; population (1981) 66,854. Developed from 1965 as a new town to take Birmingham's overspill.

Red Duster colloquial name for the Red Ensign, flag of the British merchant navy. First used in 1674, it was shared with the Royal Navy until 1864, when it became the exclusive symbol of merchant ships.

red dwarf star that is cool, faint, and small (about ¹/₁₀ the mass and diameter of the Sun). They burn slowly, and have estimated lifetimes of 100 billion years. Red dwarfs may be the most abundant type of star, but are difficult to see because they are so faint. Two of the closest stars to the Sun, ◊Proxima Centauri and ◊Barnard's Star, are red dwarfs.

red flag the international symbol of socialism. In France it was used as a revolutionary emblem from 1792 onward, and was adopted officially as its flag by the Paris Commune of 1871. Since the revolution of Nov 1917, it has been the national flag of the USSR; as such it bears a golden hammer and sickle crossed, symbolizing the unity of the industrial workers and peasants, under a gold-rimmed five-pointed star, signifying peace between the five continents. The British Labour Party anthem, called 'The Red Flag', was written by Jim ◊Connell in 1889.

Redford /ˈrɛdfəd/ (Charles) Robert 1937– . US actor and film director. His first starring role was in *Butch Cassidy and the Sundance Kid* 1969, and his other films as an actor include *All the President's Men* 1976 and *Out of Africa* 1985. He directed *Ordinary People* 1980 and *The Milagro Beanfield War* 1988.

red giant a large bright star, with a cool surface. It is thought to represent a late stage in the evolution of a star like the Sun, as it runs out of hydrogen fuel at its centre. Red giants have diameters between 10 and 100 times that of the Sun. They are very bright because they are so large, although their surface temperature is lower than that of the Sun, about 2,000–3,000K.

Redgrave /ˈrɛdɡreɪv/ Michael 1908–1985. British actor. His stage roles included Hamlet and Lear (Shakespeare), Uncle Vanya (Chekhov), and the schoolmaster in Rattigan's *The Browning Version*. He also appeared in films. He was the father of Vanessa and Lynn Redgrave, both actresses.

Redgrave /ˈrɛdɡreɪv/ Vanessa 1937– . British actress. She has played Shakespeare's Lady Macbeth and Cleopatra on the stage, and the title role in the film *Julia* 1976 (Academy Award). She is active in left-wing politics. Daughter of Michael Redgrave.

Red Guards armed workers who took part in the ◊Russian Revolution of 1917. The name was also given to the school and college students, wearing red armbands, active in the Cultural Revolution in China 1966–68.

red-hot poker plant of the African genus *Kniphofia*, family Liliaceae, in particular *Kniphofia uvaria*, with a flame-red spike of flowers.

Redmond /ˈrɛdmənd/ John Edward 1856–1918. Irish politician, Parnell's successor as leader of the Nationalist Party 1890–1916. The 1910 elections saw him holding the balance of power in the House of Commons, and he secured the introduction of a ◊Home Rule bill, hotly opposed by Protestant Ulster.

red-hot poker

Redmond supported the British cause on the outbreak of World War I, and the bill was passed, but its operation suspended until the war's end. The growth of the nationalist party Sinn Féin (the political wing of the Irish Republican Army) and the 1916 Easter Rising ended his hopes and his power.

Redon /rəˈdɒn/ Odilon 1840–1916. French Symbolist painter. He used fantastic symbols and images, sometimes mythological. From the 1890s he also produced still lifes and landscapes. His work was much admired by the Surrealists.

Redon made his reputation as a Symbolist in Paris around 1880. Initially he worked mostly in black and white, but from 1890, in oils and pastels, he used colour in a way that recalled Impressionist work. The head of Orpheus is a recurring motif in his work.

Redoubt, Mount /rɪˈdaʊt/ an active volcanic peak rising to 3,140 m/10,197 ft W of Cook inlet in S Alaska, USA. There have been recent eruptions in 1966 and 1989.

Redouté /ˌreduːˈteɪ/ Pierre Joseph 1759–1840. French flower painter patronized by Empress Josephine and the Bourbon court. He taught flower drawing at the Museum of Natural History in Paris and produced volumes of delicate, highly detailed flowers, notably *Les Roses* 1817–24.

red pepper red fruit of the ◊capsicum.

Red Riding Hood traditional European fairy story. Little Red Riding Hood is on her way to visit her sick grandmother when she meets a wolf. After discovering where she is going he gets there before her, and eats and impersonates the grandmother. In Charles Perrault's version (1697) Red Riding Hood is eaten too, but later writers introduced a woodcutter to rescue her.

Red River western tributary of the ◊Mississippi, USA, so called because of the reddish soil sediment it carries. The stretch that forms the Texas-Oklahoma border is known as Tornado Alley because of the tornadoes caused by the collision in spring of warm air from the Gulf of Mexico with cold fronts from the north.

Red River river in N Vietnam, 500 km/310 mi long, which flows into the Gulf of Tonkin. Its extensive delta is a main centre of population.

Redruth /ˌrɛdˈruːθ/ town in Cornwall, England, part of the combined town of ◊Camborne-Redruth.

Red Scare in US history, a campaign against radicals and dissenters that took place in the aftermath of World War I and the Russian revolution, and during a period of labour disorders and violence in the USA. Mainly middle-class and urban-based progressives secured legislation at national, state, and local levels to improve the democratic system, working conditions, and welfare provision.

Red Sea submerged section of the Great Rift Valley (2,000 km/1,200 mi long and up to 320 km/200 mi wide). Egypt, Sudan, and Ethiopia (in Africa) and Saudi Arabia (Asia) are on its shores.

redshank wading bird *Tringa totanus* of N Europe and Asia, a type of sandpiper. It nests in swampy areas, although most winter in the south. It is greyish and speckled black, and has long red legs.

red shift in astronomy, the lengthening of the wavelengths of light from an object as a result of the object's motion away from us. It is an example of the ◊Doppler effect. The red shift in light from galaxies is evidence that the universe is expanding.

Lengthening wavelengths causes them to move or shift towards the red end of the ◊spectrum, hence the name. The amount of red shift can be measured by the displacement of lines in an object's spectrum. By measuring the amount of red shift in light from stars and galaxies, astronomers can tell how quickly these objects are moving away from us. A strong gravitational field can also produce a red shift in light; this is termed *gravitational red shift*.

redstart bird of the genus Phoenicurus. A member of the thrush family, it winters in Africa and spends the summer in Eurasia. The male has a dark grey head (with white mark on the forehead and black face) and back, brown wings with lighter underparts, and a red tail. The American redstart *Setophaga ruticilla* belongs to a different family.

Redstone rocket a short-range US military missile, modified for use as a space launcher. Redstone rockets launched the first two ◊Mercury flights. A modified Redstone, Juno 1, launched the first US satellite, Explorer 1.

red tape a derogatory term for bureaucratic methods, derived from the fastening for departmental bundles of documents in Britain.

Red Terror term used by opponents to describe the Bolshevik seizure and retention of power in Russia after Oct 1917.

reduction in chemistry, the gain of ◊electrons, loss of oxygen, or gain of hydrogen by an atom, ion, or molecule during a chemical reaction.

Reduction may be brought about by reaction with another compound, which is simultaneously oxidized (reducing agent), or electrically at the cathode (negative terminal) of an electric cell.

red shift

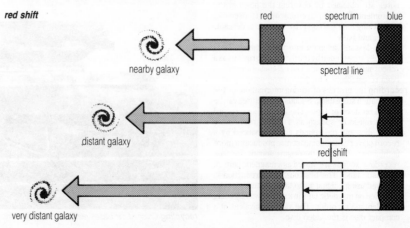

redundancy rights in British law, the rights of employees to a payment (linked to the length of their employment) if they lose their jobs because they are no longer needed. The statutory right was introduced in 1965, but payments are often made in excess of the statutory scheme.

redwing type of thrush *Turdus iliacus*, smaller than the song thrush, with reddish wing and body markings. It breeds in the north of Europe and Asia, flying south in winter.

redwood giant coniferous tree. See ◊sequoia.

reed various perennial aquatic grasses, in particular several species of the genus *Phragmites*; also the stalk of any of these plants. The common reed *Phragmites australis* attains 3 m/10 ft, having stiff, erect leaves, and straight stems bearing a plume of purplish flowers.

Reed /riːd/ Carol 1906–1976. British film producer and director, an influential figure in the British film industry of the 1940s. His films include *Odd Man Out* 1947, *The Fallen Idol* and *The Third Man* both 1950, and *Our Man in Havana* 1959.

Reed /riːd/ Ishmael 1938– . US novelist. His experimental, parodic, satirical novels exploit traditions taken from jazz and voodoo, and include *The Free-Lance Pallbearers* 1967, *Mumbo Jumbo* 1972, and *Reckless Eyeballing* 1986.

Reed /riːd/ Lou 1942– . US rock singer, songwriter, and former member (1965–70) of the seminal New York garage band **the Velvet Underground**. His solo work deals largely with urban alienation and angst, and includes the albums *Berlin* 1973, *Street Hassle* 1978, and *New York* 1989.

Reed /riːd/ Oliver 1938– . British actor, nephew of the director Carol Reed. He became a star through such films as *Oliver!* 1968, *Women in Love* 1969, *The Devils* 1971, and *Castaway* 1987.

reel in cinema, a plastic or metal spool used for winding and storing film. As the size of reels became standardized it came to refer to the running time of the film; a standard 35 mm reel holds 313 m/900 ft of film, which runs for ten minutes when projected at 24 frames per second; hence a 'two-reeler' was a film lasting 20 minutes. Modern projectors can, however, hold bigger reels, so this second definition no longer applies.

Rees-Mogg /ˌriːsˈmɒg/ Lord William 1928– . British journalist, editor of *The Times* 1967–81, chair of the Arts Council 1982–89, and from 1988 chair of the ◊Broadcasting Standards Council.

reeve in Anglo-Saxon England, an official charged with the administration of a shire or burgh, fulfilling similar functions to the later sheriff. After the Norman Conquest, the term tended to be restricted to the person elected by the villeins to oversee the work of the manor and to communicate with the manorial lord.

Reeves /riːvz/ William Pember 1857–1932. New Zealand politician and writer. He was New Zealand minister of education 1891–96, and director of the London School of Economics 1908–19. He wrote poetry and the classic description of New Zealand, *Long White Cloud* 1898.

referee in sport, the official in charge of a game.

referee in law, a member of the court of referees appointed by the House of Commons to give judgment on petitions against private bills; also one of the three officials to whom cases before the high court may be submitted.

referee in science, one who reads and comments on a scientific paper before its publication, normally a scientist of at least equal standing to the author(s).

referendum the procedure whereby a decision on proposed legislation is referred to the electorate for settlement by direct vote of all the people. It is most frequently employed in Switzerland, the first country to use it, but has also been used in Australia, New Zealand, Québec, and certain states of the USA. It was used in the UK for the first time 1975 on the issue of membership of the European Community. Critics argue that referenda undermine parliamentary authority, but

they do allow the elector to participate directly in decision-making. A similar device is the **recall**, whereby voters are given the opportunity of demanding the dismissal from office of officials. See also ◊initiative.

refining a process that purifies or converts something into a more useful form. Metals usually need refining after they have been extracted from their ores by such processes as ◊smelting. Petroleum, or crude oil, needs refining before it can be used; the process involves ◊fractionation, the separation of the substance into separate components or 'fractions'.

Electrolytic refining methods use the principle of ◊electrolysis to purify metals. When refining petroleum, or crude oil, subsequent refinery processes to fractionation serve to convert the heavier fractions into more useful lighter products. The most important of these is ◊cracking. Other processes include ◊polymerization, hydrogenation, and reforming.

reflection deflection of waves, such as ◊light or ◊sound waves, when they hit a surface. The **law of reflection** states that the angle of incidence (the angle between the ray and a perpendicular line drawn to the surface) is equal to the angle of reflection (the angle between the reflected ray and a perpendicular to the surface).

reflex an automatic response to a particular stimulus, controlled by the ◊nervous system. The receptor (for example, a sense organ) and the effector (such as a muscle) are linked directly (via the spinal ganglia or the lower brain, in vertebrates), making responses to stimuli very rapid. Reflex actions are more common in simple animals.

In animals with well-developed ◊central nervous systems, reflex actions can often be modified by other nerves that are under voluntary control. For example, humans learn to control the reflex that leads the bladder to be emptied as soon as it becomes full.

reflex anal dilatation a controversial method of diagnosing anal abuse in children, which was at the centre of speculation in Cleveland, NE England, in 1987 (see ◊child abuse). Repeated anal abuse stretches and damages the anal sphincter, with the result that when the anus is gently stretched apart during the test, it continues to dilate as a reflex action. The normal anal sphincter remains tightly closed.

reflex camera a camera that uses a mirror and prisms to reflect light passing through the lens into the viewfinder, showing the photographer the exact scene which is being shot. When the shutter button is released the mirror springs out of the way, allowing light to reach the film. The commonest type is the single-lens reflex (◊SLR) camera. The twin-lens reflex (◊TLR) camera has two lenses; one has a mirror for viewing, the other is used for exposing the film.

Reform Acts 1832, 1867, and 1884; in the UK, legislation that extended voting rights and redistributed parliamentary seats.

The 1832 act abolished pocket and ◊rotten boroughs, which had formed unrepresentative constituencies, redistributed seats on a more

equitable basis in the counties, and formed some new boroughs. The franchise was extended to male householders in property worth £10 a year or more in the boroughs and to owners of freehold property worth £2 a year, £10 copyholders or £50 leaseholders in the counties. The 1867 act redistributed seats from corrupt and small boroughs to the counties and large urban areas. It also extended the franchise in boroughs to adult male heads of households, and in counties to males who owned, or held on long leases, land worth £5 a year or occupied land worth £12 on which they paid poor rates. The 1884 act extended the franchise to male agricultural labourers.

The growth of the electorate in 19th-century Britain

year	UK voters	approximate percentage of population enfranchised
1831	515,920	2%
1833	809,374	3%
1866	1,367,845	5%
1869	2,445,847	8%
1883	3,155,143	9%
1886	5,674,964	16%

Reformation movement in Christianity (anticipated from the 12th century by the Waldenses, Lollards, and Hussites) to reform the Catholic Church. It became effective in the 16th century when the absolute monarchies gave it support by challenging the political power of the papacy and confiscating church wealth.

1517 The German priest Luther's protest against the sale of ◊indulgences began the Reformation in Europe.

1519 Zwingli led the Reformation in Switzerland.

1529 The term 'Protestant' was first used.

1533 Henry VIII renounced papal supremacy and proclaimed himself head of the Church of England.

1541 The French theologian Calvin established Presbyterianism in Geneva, Switzerland.

1559 The Protestant John Knox returned from exile to found the Church of Scotland.

1545–1563 The **Counter-Reformation** was initiated by the Roman Catholic Church at the **Council of Trent**. It aimed at reforming abuses and regaining the lost ground by using moral persuasion and extending the Spanish Inquisition to other countries.

mid-17th century The present European alignment had been reached, with the separation of Catholic and Protestant churches.

refraction in physics, the bending of ◊light when it passes from one medium to another. Refraction occurs because light travels at different velocities in diferent media. The **refractive index** of a material indicates by how much light is bent.

refractive index in physics, a measure of the refraction of a ray of light as it passes from one transparent medium to another. If the angle of incidence is *i* and the angle of refraction is *r*, the refractive index *n* = sin *i*/sin *r*. It is also equal to the speed of light in the first medium divided by the speed of light in the second, and it varies with the wavelength of the light.

refractory (of a material) able to resist high temperature, for example ◊ceramics made from clay,

reflection

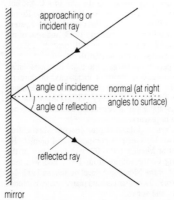

approaching or incident ray

angle of incidence

normal (at right angles to surface)

angle of reflection

reflected ray

mirror

refraction

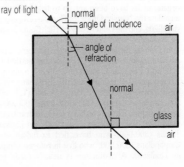

ray of light

normal

angle of incidence

air

angle of refraction

normal

glass

air

refrigeration

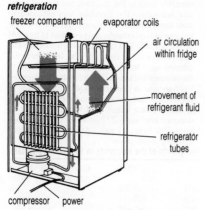

freezer compartment — evaporator coils

air circulation within fridge

movement of refrigerant fluid

refrigerator tubes

compressor — power

minerals, or other earthy materials. Furnaces are lined with silica and dolomite. Alumina (aluminium oxide) is an excellent refractory, often used for the bodies of spark plugs. Titanium and tungsten are often called refractory metals because they are temperature resistant. ◊Cermets are refractory materials made up of ceramics and metals.

refrigeration the use of technology to transfer heat from cold to warm, against the normal temperature gradient, so that a body can remain substantially colder than its surroundings. Refrigeration equipment is used for the chilling and deep freezing of food (see ◊food technology), and in air conditioners and industrial processes.

Refrigeration is commonly achieved by a vapour-compression cycle, in which a suitable chemical (the refrigerant) travels through a long circuit of tubing, during which it changes from a vapour to a liquid and back again. A compression chamber makes it condense, and thus give out heat. In another part of the circuit, called the evaporator coils, the pressure is much lower, so the refrigerant evaporates, absorbing heat as it does so. The evaporation process takes place near the central part of the refrigerator, which therefore becomes colder, while the compression process takes place near a ventilation grille, transferring the heat to the air outside. The most commonly used refrigerants in modern systems were ◊chlorofluorocarbons, but these are now being replaced by coolants that do not damage the ozone layer.

refugee in general, a person fleeing from a problem such as political, religious, or military persecution. At present there are an estimated 15 million refugees worldwide, whose resettlement and welfare are the responsibility of the United Nations.

Major refugee movements in 20th-century Europe include: Jews from Russia 1881–1914 and again after the Revolution, White Russians from the Soviet Union after 1917, Jews from Germany 1933–45, and the widespread displacement of peoples after World War II.

Elsewhere, the Palestinians represent the longest-running refugee problem, and many people left Vietnam (the *boat people*) after the victory of the North over the South. Refugee movements created by natural disasters and famine have been widespread throughout the world, most notably in Ethiopia and Sudan. Since 1920, international organizations have been set up to help refugees, including the Nansen Office for Russian refugees in the 1920s, and the United Nations High Commission for Refugees since 1945.

In 1990 the largest single refugee groupings are: Afghans (about 6 million, temporarily settled in Iran and Pakistan); Palestinians (2.3 million); Ethiopians (1.3 million, mostly Eritreans who have moved to Sudan); Mozambicans (1.2 million, displaced mostly to Malawi); Iraqis (600,000, predominantly Kurds who have settled in Iran); Somalis (400,000); Sudanese (400,000); Sri Lankan Tamils (300,000, who have fled to India); and Cambodians (300,000, who live in refugee camps in Thailand). A distinction is usually made by

Western nations between 'political' and so-called 'economic' refugees, particularly when the refugees come from low-income countries (see ◊boat people).

regalia or *crown jewels* symbols of royal authority. The British set (except for the Ampulla and the Anointing Spoon) were broken up at the time of ◊Cromwell, and now date from the ◊Restoration. In 1671 Colonel ◊Blood attempted to steal them, but was captured, then pardoned and pensioned by Charles II. They are kept in the Tower of London in the Crown Jewel House (1967).

Major items include St Edward's Crown; the Imperial State Crown; the jewelled Sword of State, used only at the Coronation; the Sword of State used at the opening of Parliament and on other state occasions; the Curtana (Sword of Mercy); the Swords of Temporal and Spiritual Justice; the Orb; the Royal Sceptre or Sceptre with the Cross (containing the great Star of Africa, cut from the Cullinan diamond); the Rod with the Dove; St Edward's Staff; the Spurs; the Coronation Ring (the 'Wedding Ring of England'); the Armills (gold bracelets, given by the Commonwealth countries in 1953 for the coronation of Elizabeth II); the Ampulla (which contains oil for the anointing); and the Anointing Spoon.

Regan /'riːgən/ Donald 1918– . US Republican political adviser to Ronald ◊Reagan. He was secretary of the Treasury 1981–85, and chief of White House staff 1985–87, when he was forced to resign because of widespread belief of his complicity in the ◊Irangate scandal.

regelation phenomenon in which water re-freezes to ice after it has been melted by pressure, at a temperature below the freezing point of water. Pressure makes an ice skate, for example, form a film of water that re-forms ice after the skater has passed.

Regency in Britain, the years 1811–20 during which ◊George IV (then Prince of Wales) acted as regent for his father ◊George III.

Regency style style of architecture popular in England during the late 18th and early 19th centuries. The style is characterized by its restrained simplicity and its imitation of ancient classical architecture, especially Greek. Architects of this period include Decimus Burton (1800–81), Henry Holland (1746–1806), and John ◊Nash.

regeneration in biology, the regrowth of a new organ or tissue after the loss or removal of the original. It is common in plants, where a new individual can often be produced from a 'cutting' of the original. In animals, regeneration of major organs is limited to lower organisms; certain lizards can regrow their tails if these are lost, and new flatworms can grow from a tiny fragment of an old one. In mammals, regeneration is limited to the repair of tissue in wound-healing, and the regrowth of peripheral nerves following damage.

Regensburg /'reɪgənsbuək/ city in Bavaria, West Germany, on the Danube at its confluence with the Regen, 100 km/63 mi NE of Munich; population (1988) 124,000. It has many medieval buildings, including a Gothic cathedral 1275–1530.

Regensburg stands on the site of a Celtic settlement dating from 500 BC. It became the Roman *Castra Regina* AD 179, the capital of the Eastern Frankish Empire, a free city 1245, and seat of the German *Diet* (parliament) 16th century–1806. It was included in Bavaria 1810.

regent person discharging the royal functions during a sovereign's minority or incapacity, or during a lengthy absence from the country. In England since the time of Henry VIII, Parliament has always appointed a regent or council of regency when necessary.

Reger /'reɪgə/ (Johann Baptist Joseph) Max(imilian) 1873–1916. German composer and pianist. He taught at Munich 1905–07, was professor at the Leipzig Conservatoire from 1907, and was conductor of the Meiningen ducal orchestra 1911–14. His works include organ and piano music, chamber music, and songs.

reggae the predominant form of West Indian popular music of the 1970s and 1980s, characterized by a heavily accented onbeat. The lyrics often refer to Rastafarianism. Musicians include Bob Marley (1945–81), Lee 'Scratch' Perry (1940–) (performer and producer), and the group Black Uhuru (1974–).

Reggio di Calabria /'redʒəu di: kə'læbriə/ industrial centre (farm machinery, olive oil, perfume) of Calabria, S Italy; population (1988) 179,000. It was founded by Greeks about 720 BC.

Reggio nell'Emilia /'redʒəu nel e'miːljə/ chief town of the province of the same name in Emilia-Romagna region, N Italy; population (1987) 130,000. It was here in 1797 that the Congress of the cities of Emilia adopted the tricolour flag that was later to become the national flag of Italy.

Regina /rə'dʒaɪnə/ industrial city (oil refining, cement, steel, farm machinery, fertilizers), capital of Saskatchewan, Canada; population (1986) 175,000. It was founded 1882 as *Pile O'Bones*, and renamed in honour of Queen Victoria of England.

Regional Crime Squad in the UK, a local police force that deals with serious crime; see under ◊Scotland Yard, New.

register in computing, a fast type of memory, often built into the computer's central processing unit (CPU). Some registers are reserved for special tasks, such as keeping track of the next command to be executed; others are used for holding frequently used data and for storing intermediate results.

Regulus brightest star in the constellation Leo, and the 21st-brightest star in the sky. Regulus has a true luminosity 160 times that of the Sun, and is 85 light years away.

Rehnquist /'renkwɪst/ William 1924– . Chief justice of the US ◊Supreme Court. Active within the Republican Party, he was appointed head of the office of legal counsel by President ◊Nixon in 1969 and controversially defended such measures as pre-trial detention and wiretapping.

He became an associate justice of the Supreme Court in 1972 and chief justice in 1986. Under his leadership, the court has established a reputation for conservative rulings on such issues as abortion and capital punishment.

Rehoboam King of Judah about 932–915 BC, son of Solomon. Under his rule the Jewish nation split into the two kingdoms of *Israel* and *Judah*. Ten of the tribes revolted against him and took Jeroboam as their ruler, leaving him only the tribes of Judah and Benjamin.

Rehoboth Gebiet /rɪ'həubəθ/ a district of Namibia to the south of Windhoek; area 32,168 sq km/ 12,420 sq mi; chief town Rehoboth. The area is occupied by the Basters, a mixed race of European-Nama descent.

Reich (German 'empire') three periods in history. The First Reich was the Holy Roman Empire 962–1806, the Second Reich the German Empire 1871–1918, and the ◊Third Reich Nazi Germany 1933–45.

Reich /raɪk/ Steve 1936– . US composer. His minimalist music consists of simple patterns carefully superimposed and modified to highlight constantly changing melodies and rhythms; examples are *Phase Patterns* for four electronic organs 1970, *Music for Mallet Instruments, Voices, and Organ* 1973, and *Music for Percussion and Keyboards* 1984.

Reich /raɪk/ Wilhelm 1897–1957. Austrian doctor, who emigrated to the USA 1939. He combined ◊Marxism and ◊psychoanalysis to advocate sexual freedom, for example in *Die Sexuelle Revolution/The Sexual Revolution* 1936–45, and *Die Funktion des Orgasmus/The Function of the Orgasm* 1948. Reich died in prison following committal for contempt of court.

Reichstadt, Duke of /'raɪkʃtæt/ title of ◊Napoleon II, son of Napoleon I.

Reichstag /'raɪkstaːg/ German parliament building and lower legislative house during the German Empire 1871–1918 and Weimar Republic 1919–33.

Reichstag Fire the burning of the German parliament building in Berlin 27 Feb 1933, less than a month after the Nazi leader Hitler became chancellor. The fire was used as a justification for the suspension of many constitutional guarantees, and also as an excuse to attack the communists. There is still debate over Nazi involvement in the crime, not least because they were the main beneficiaries.

Although three Bulgarians—◊Dimitrov, Popov, and Tanev—and a German, Torgler, were all indicted and tried at Leipzig, only a Dutch communist, Marinus van der Lubbe, was convicted, after being found at the scene of the crime and confessing.

Reichstein /ˈraɪkstaɪn/ Tadeus 1897– . Swiss biochemist who investigated the chemical activity of the adrenal glands. By 1946 Reichstein had identified a large number of steroids secreted by the adrenal cortex, some of which would later be used in the treatment of Addison's disease. Reichstein shared the 1950 Nobel physiology or medicine prize with Edward ◊Kendall and Philip Hench (1896–1965).

Reid /riːd/ Thomas 1710–1796. Scottish mathematician and philosopher. His *Enquiry into the Human Mind on the Principles of Common Sense* 1764 attempted to counter the sceptical conclusions of Hume. He believed that the existence of the material world and the human soul is self-evident 'by the consent of ages and nations, of the learned and unlearned'.

reification the alleged social process whereby relations between human beings are transformed into impersonal relations between things. Georg Lukacs, in *History and Class Consciousness* 1923, analyses this process as characteristic of capitalist society. Later Marxists have developed this analysis, thus extending Marx's early critique of alienation in the *Paris Manuscripts* 1844.

Reigate /ˈraɪgɪt/ town in Surrey, England, at the foot of the North Downs; population (1981) 52,554. With Redhill it forms a residential suburb of London.

Reims /riːmz/ (English *Rheims*) capital of Champagne-Ardenne region, France; population (1982) 199,000. It is the centre of the champagne industry, and has textile industries. It was known in Roman times as *Durocorturum*. From 987 all but six French kings were crowned here. Ceded to England 1420 under the Treaty of Troyes, it was retaken by Joan of Arc, who had Charles VII consecrated in the 13th-century cathedral. The German High Command formally surrendered here to Eisenhower 7 May 1945.

reincarnation the belief that after death the human soul or the spirit of a plant or animal may live again in another human or animal. It is part of the teachings of many religions and philosophies, for example ancient Egyptian and Greek (the philosophies of Pythagoras and Plato), Buddhism, Hinduism, Jainism, certain Christian heresies (such as the Cathars), and theosophy. It is also referred to as *transmigration* or metempsychosis.

reindeer (North American *caribou*) deer *Rangifer tarandus* of arctic and subarctic regions, common to both eastern and western hemispheres. About 120 cm/4 ft at the shoulder, it has a thick, brownish coat and broad hoofs well adapted to travel over snow. It is the only deer in which both sexes have antlers; up to 150 cm/5 ft long, they are shed in winter.

The Scandinavian reindeer has been domesticated by the Lapps for centuries. There are two types of North American caribou: the large woodland caribou of the more southerly region, and the barren-ground caribou of the north. Reindeer migrate southward in winter, moving in large herds. They eat grass, small plants, and lichens.

Reinhardt /ˈraɪnhɑːt/ 'Django' (Jean Baptiste) 1910–1953. Belgian jazz guitarist and composer, who was co-leader, with Stephane Grappelli, of Quintet de Hot Club de France 1934–1939.

Reinhardt /ˈraɪnhɑːt/ Max 1873–1943. Austrian producer and director, whose expressionist style was widely influential in German theatre and film during the 1920s and 1930s. Directors such as Murnau and Lubitsch and actors such as Dietrich worked with him. He co-directed the US film *A Midsummer Night's Dream* 1935.

In 1920 Reinhardt founded the Salzburg Festival. When the Nazis came to power, he lost his theatres and, after touring Europe as a guest director, went to the USA, where he produced and directed. He founded an acting school and theatre workshop in Hollywood.

Reisz /raɪs/ Karel 1926– . Czechoslovak film director who lived in Britain from 1938, originally a writer and film critic. His first feature film, *Saturday Night and Sunday Morning* 1960, was a critical and commercial success. His other work includes *Morgan* 1966, *The French Lieutenant's Woman* 1981, and *Sweet Dreams* 1986.

Rélamur Réné de 1683–1757. French metallurgist and entomologist who wrote a definitive work on the early steel industry as well as the first books on entomology. His work, published in 1722, described how to convert iron into steel and laid the foundations of the modern steel industry. He produced a six-volume work between 1734 and 1742 on the natural history of insects.

relational database in computing, a type of ◊database in which data are viewed as a collection of linked tables. It is the most popular of the three basic database models, the others being **network** and **hierarchical**.

relative atomic mass the mass of an atom. It depends on the number of protons and neutrons in the atom, the electrons having negligible mass. It is calculated relative to one twelfth the mass of an atom of carbon-12. If more than one ◊isotope of the element is present, the relative atomic mass is calculated by taking an average that takes account of the relative proportions of each isotope, resulting in values that are not whole numbers. The term **atomic weight**, although commonly used, is strictly speaking incorrect.

relative biological effectiveness (RBE) the relative damage caused to living tissue by different types of radiation. Some radiations do much more damage than others; alpha particles, for example, cause 20 times as much destruction as electrons (beta particles).

The RBE is defined as the ratio of the absorbed dose of a standard amount of radiation to the absorbed dose of 200 kV X-rays that produces the same amount of biological damage.

relative density or **specific gravity** in physics, the density (at 20°C) of a solid or liquid relative to (or divided by) the maximum density of water (at 4°C). The relative density of a gas is its density divided by the density of hydrogen (or sometimes dry air) at the same temperature and pressure.

relative humidity in physics, the concentration of water vapour in the air. It is expressed as a percentage of its moisture content to the moisture content of the air if it were saturated with water at the same temperature and pressure. The higher the temperature the more water vapour the air can hold.

relative molecular mass the mass of a molecule, calculated relative to one twelfth the mass of an atom of carbon-12. It is found by adding the relative atomic masses of the atoms that make up the molecule. The term **molecular weight** is often used, but strictly this is incorrect.

reindeer

relativism a philosophical position that denies the possibility of objective truth independent of some specific social or historical context, or conceptual framework.

relativity two theories propounded by Albert ◊Einstein concerning the nature of space and time.

special theory (1905) Starting with the premises that (1) the laws of nature are the same for all observers in unaccelerated motion, and (2) the speed of light is independent of the motion of its source, Einstein postulated that the time interval between two events was longer for an observer in whose frame of reference the events occur in different places than for the observer for whom they occur at the same place.

general theory of relativity (1915) The geometrical properties of space-time were to be conceived as modified locally by the presence of a body with mass. A planet's orbit around the Sun (as observed in three-dimensional space) arises from its natural trajectory in modified space-time; there is no need to invoke, as Newton did, a force of ◊gravity coming from the Sun and acting on the planet. Einstein's theory predicted slight differences in the orbits of the planets from Newton's theory, which were observable in the case of Mercury. The new theory also said light rays should bend when they pass by a massive object, owing to the object's effect on local space-time. The predicted bending of starlight was observed during the eclipse of the Sun 1919, when light from distant stars passing close to the Sun was not masked by sunlight.

Einstein showed that for consistency with premises (1) and (2), the principles of dynamics as established by ◊Newton needed modification; the most celebrated new result was the equation $E = mc^2$, which expresses an equivalence between mass (m) and ◊energy (E), c being the speed of light in a vacuum. Although since modified in detail, general relativity remains central to modern ◊astrophysics and ◊cosmology; it predicts, for example, the possibility of ◊black holes. General relativity theory was inspired by the simple idea that it is impossible in a small region to distinguish between acceleration and gravitation effects (as in a lift one feels heavier when the lift accelerates upwards), but the mathematical development of the idea is formidable. Such is not the case for the special theory, which a non-expert can follow up to $E = mc^2$ and beyond.

relay in physics, an electromagnetic switch. A small current passing through a coil of wire wound round an iron core attracts an ◊armature whose movement closes a pair of sprung contacts to complete a secondary circuit, which can be carrying a large current. The solid-state equivalent is a thyristor switching device.

relic a part of some divine or saintly person, or something closely associated with them. Christian examples include the arm of St Teresa of Avila, the blood of St Januarius, and the ◊True Cross. Buddhist relics include the funeral ashes of the historic Buddha, placed in a number of stupas or burial mounds.

In medieval times relics were fiercely fought for, and there were a vast number of fakes. The cult was condemned by Protestant reformers but upheld by the Roman Catholic Church at the Council of Trent in the mid-16th century. Parallel nonreligious examples of the phenomenon include the display of the preserved body of Lenin in Moscow, USSR.

relief in architecture, a term applied to carved figures and other forms that project from the background. The Italian terms *basso-rilievo* (low relief), *mezzo-rilievo* (middle relief), and *alto-rilievo* (high relief) are used according to the extent to which the sculpture projects. The French term *bas-relief* is commonly used for low relief.

religion (Latin *religare* 'to bind'; perhaps humans to God) code of belief or philosophy, which often involves the worship of a ◊God or gods. Belief in a supernatural power is not essential (absent in, for example, Buddhism and Confucianism),

Religious Festivals

Date	Festival	Religion	Event Commemorated
6 Jan	Epiphany	Western Christian	coming of the Magi
6–7 Jan	Christmas	Orthodox Christian	birth of Jesus
18–19 Jan	Epiphany	Orthodox Christian	coming of the Magi
Jan–Feb	New Year	Chinese	return of kitchen god to heaven
Feb–Mar	Shrove Tuesday	Christian	day before Lent
	Ash Wednesday	Christian	first day of Lent
	Purim	Jewish	story of Esther
	Mahashivaratri	Hindu	Siva
Mar–Apr	Palm Sunday	Western Christian	Jesus's entry into Jerusalem
	Good Friday	Western Christian	crucifixion of Jesus
	Easter Sunday	Western Christian	resurrection of Jesus
	Passover	Jewish	escape from slavery in Egypt
	Holi	Hindu	Krishna
	Holi Mohalla	Sikh	(coincides with Holi)
	Rama Naumi	Hindu	birth of Rama
	Ching Ming	Chinese	remembrance of the dead
13 Apr	Baisakhi	Sikh	founding of the Kalsa
Apr–May	Easter	Orthodox Christian	death and resurrection of Jesus
May–June	Shavuot	Jewish	giving of ten comandmments to Moses
	Pentecost (Whitsun)	Western Christian	Jesus's followers receiving the Holy Spirit
	Wesak	Buddhist	day of Buddha's birth, enlightenment and death
	Martyrdom of Guru Arjan	Sikh	death of fifth guru of Sikhism
June	Dragon Boat Festival	Chinese	Chinese martyr
	Pentecost	Orthodox Christian	Jesus's followers receiving the Holy Spirit
July	Dhammacakka	Buddhist	preaching of Buddha's first sermon
Aug	Raksha Bandhan	Hindu	family
Aug–Sept	Janmashtami	Hindu	birthday of Khrishna
Sept	Moon Festival	Chinese	Chinese hero
Sept–Oct	Rosh Hashana	Jewish	start of Jewish New Year
	Yom Kippur	Jewish	day of atonement
	Succot	Jewish	Israelites' time in the wilderness
Oct	Dusshera	Hindu	goddess Devi
Oct–Nov	Divali	Hindu	goddess Lakshmi
	Divali	Sikh	release of Guru Hargobind from prison
Nov	Guru Nanak's Birthday	Sikh	founder of Sikhism
Nov–Dec	Bodhi Day	Buddhist (Mahayana)	Buddha's enlightenment
Dec	Hanukkah	Jewish	recapture of Temple of Jerusalem
	Winter Festival	Chinese	time of feasting
25 Dec	Christmas	Western Christian	birth of Jesus
Dec–Jan	Birthday of Guru Gobind Sind	Sikh	last (tenth) human guru of Sikhism
	Martyrdom of Guru Tegh Bahadur	Sikh	ninth guru of Sikhism

but faithful adherence is usually considered to be rewarded, for example by escape from human existence (Buddhism), by a future existence (Christianity, Islam), or by worldly benefit (Sōka Gakkai Buddhism).

Among the chief religions are: *ancient and pantheist* religions of Babylonia, Assyria, Egypt, Greece, and Rome; *oriental* Hinduism, Buddhism, Jainism, Parseeism, Confucianism, Taoism, and Shinto; *'religions of a book'* Judaism, Christianity (the principal divisions are Roman Catholic, Eastern Orthodox, and Protestant), and Islam (Muhammadanism, the principal divisions are Sunni and Shi'ite); *combined derivation* such as the Baha'is, the Unification Church, and Mormonism. *Comparative religion* studies the various faiths impartially, but often with the hope of finding common ground, to solve the practical problems of competing claims of unique truth or inspiration. The earliest known attempt at a philosophy of religious beliefs is contained in fragments written by Xenophones in Greece 6th century BC, and later Herodotus and Aristotle contributed to the study. In 17th-century China, Jesuit theologies conducted comparative studies. Towards the end of the 18th century English missionary schools in Calcutta compared the Bible with sacred Indian texts. The work of Charles Darwin in natural history and the growth of anthropology stimulated the investigation of religious beliefs, notably by the Sanskrit scholar Max Müller (1823–1900) and the Scottish anthropologists James Frazer and Andrew Lang.

religious education (RE) the formal teaching of religion in schools.

In voluntary-aided church schools in the UK, RE syllabuses are permitted to follow the specific teachings of the church concerned; in other state schools, the syllabus is agreed between representatives of the local churches and the education authority. Until the introduction of the National Curriculum, RE was the only compulsory subject. The law allows parents to withdraw their children from RE on conscientious grounds.

In the USA, religious education within the doctrines of a particular church is prohibited in public (state-maintained) schools, because of the separation of church and state guaranteed under the first amendment to the constitution; however, the study of comparative religion is permitted.

REM US four-piece rock group formed 1980 in Georgia. Their songs are characterized by melodic bass lines, driving guitar, and evocative lyrics partly buried in the mix.

rem abbreviation of *roentgen equivalent man* SI unit of radiation dose equivalent. Some types of radiation do more damage than others for the same absorbed dose; the equivalent dose in rems is equal to the dose in ◊rads multiplied by the ◊relative biological effectiveness. Humans can absorb up to 25 rems without immediate ill effects; 100 rems may produce radiation sickness; and more than 800 rems causes death.

Remarque /rə'ma:k/ Erich Maria 1898–1970. German novelist, a soldier in World War I, whose *All Quiet on the Western Front* 1929 led to his being deprived of German nationality. He lived in Switzerland 1929–39, and then in the USA.

Rembrandt /'rembrænt/ Harmensz van Rijn 1606–1669. Dutch painter and etcher, one of the most prolific and influential artists in Europe of the 17th century. Between 1629 and 1669 he painted some 60 penetrating self-portraits. He also painted religious subjects, and produced about 300 etchings and over 1,000 drawings. His group portraits include *The Anatomy Lesson of Dr Tulp* 1632 (Mauritshuis, The Hague) and *The Night Watch* 1642 (Rijksmuseum, Amsterdam).

After studying in Leiden and for a few months in Amsterdam (with a history painter), Rembrandt began his career 1625 in Leiden, where his work reflected knowledge of ◊Elsheimer and ◊Caravaggio among others. He settled permanently in Amsterdam 1631, and obtained many commissions for portraits from wealthy merchants. The *Self-Portrait with Saskia* (his wife, Saskia van Uylenburgh) about 1634 (Gemäldegalerie, Dresden, East Germany) displays their prosperity in warm tones and rich, glittering textiles.

Saskia died 1642 and that year Rembrandt's fortunes began to decline (he eventually became bankrupt 1656). His work became more sombre and with deeper emotional content, and his portraits were increasingly melancholy, for example *Jan Six* 1654 (Six Collection, Amsterdam). From 1660 onward he lived with Hendrickje Stoffels, but he outlived her, and in 1668 his only surviving child, Titus, died too. Rembrandt had many pupils, including Dou and Fabritius.

remedial education special classes, or teaching strategies, that aim to help children with learning difficulties to catch up with children within the normal range of achievement.

Remembrance Sunday (known until 1945 as *Armistice Day*) in the UK, national day of remembrance for those killed in both world wars and later conflicts, on the second Sunday of Nov. In Canada 11 Nov is *Remembrance Day*. The US equivalent is ◊Veterans Day.

Remembrance Sunday is observed by a two-minute silence at the time of the signature of the armistice with Germany: 11:00 am, 11 Nov 1918 (although since 1956 the day of commemoration has been the Sunday). There are ceremonies at the Cenotaph in Whitehall, London, and elsewhere. 'Flanders poppies', symbolic of the blood shed, are sold in aid of war invalids and their dependants.

Remington /'remɪŋtən/ Frederic 1861–1909. US sculptor, painter, and illustrator. His exploratory trips to the American West inspired lively images of cowboys and horses, such as his sculpture *Off the Range* (Corcoran Gallery of Art, Washington DC).

Remington /'remɪŋtən/ Philo 1816–1889. US inventor of the typewriter and breech-loading rifle that bear his name. He began manufacturing typewriters 1873, using the patent of Christopher Sholes (1819–1890), and made improvements that resulted five years later in the first machine with a shift key, thus providing lower-case letters as well as capital letters. The Remington rifle and carbine, which had a falling block breech and a tubular magazine, were developed in collaboration with his father.

remission in medicine, temporary disappearance of symptoms during the course of a disease.

Rembrandt Girl Leaning on a Windowsill *(1645) Dulwich Picture Gallery, London.*

remittance man in the 19th century, a man living in a British colony (especially Australia), on money sent (remitted) to him from England, on condition that he did not return. This exile was imposed by the family because of some transgression.

remora warm-water fish that has an adhesive disc on the head, by which it attaches itself to whales, sharks, and turtles. These provide the remora with shelter, transport, and food in the form of parasites on the host's skin.

remote sensing gathering and recording information from a distance, developed as a result of space technology. Space probes send back photographs and data about planets as distant as Neptune. Satellites such as *Landsat* have surveyed all of the Earth's surface from orbit. Computer processing of data obtained by their scanning instruments, and the application of false-colours have made it possible to reveal surface features invisible in ordinary light. This has proved valuable in agriculture, forestry, and urban planning, and has led to the discovery of new deposits of minerals.

Remscheid /'remʃaɪt/ industrial city in North Rhine-Westphalia, West Germany, where stainless steel implements are manufactured; population (1988) 121,000.

REM sleep acronym for *rapid-eye-movement sleep* a phase of sleep that recurs several times nightly in humans and is associated with dreaming. The eyes flicker quickly beneath closed lids.

Renaissance the period and intellectual movement in European cultural history that is traditionally seen as ending the Middle Ages and beginning modern times. The Renaissance started in Italy in the 14th century, and flourished in W Europe until about the 17th century. The term 'Renaissance', to describe the period of time, was first used in the 18th century.

The aim of Renaissance education was to produce the 'complete human being' (**Renaissance man**), conversant in the humanities, mathematics and science (including their application in war), the arts and crafts, and athletics and sport; to enlarge the bounds of learning and geographical knowledge; to encourage the growth of scepticism and free-thought, and the study and imitation of Greek and Latin literature and art. The revival of interest in classical Greek and Roman culture inspired artists such as Leonardo da Vinci, Michelangelo, and Dürer, writers such as Petrarch, and prose writers such as Boccaccio; and scientists and explorers proliferated.

The beginning of the Italian Renaissance is usually dated in the 14th century with the writers Petrarch and Boccaccio. The invention of printing (mid-15th century), and geographical discoveries helped spread the new spirit. Biblical criticism by the Dutch humanist Erasmus and others contributed to the Reformation, but the Counter-Reformation almost extinguished the movement in 16th-century Italy. In the visual arts Renaissance painting and sculpture later moved towards ◊Mannerism.

Figures of the Renaissance include the politician Machiavelli, the poets Ariosto and Tasso, the philosopher Bruno, the physicist Galileo, and the artists Benvenuto, Michelangelo, Cellini, and Raphael in Italy; the writers Rabelais and Montaigne in France, Cervantes in Spain, and Camoëns in Portugal; the astronomer Copernicus in Poland; and the politicians More and Bacon, and the writers Sidney, Marlowe, and Shakespeare in England.

Especially in Italy, where the ideals of the Renaissance were considered to have been fulfilled by the great masters, the period 1490–1520 is known as the **High Renaissance**, and painting of the period described as **High Renaissance Classicism**.

Renaissance art movement in European art of the 15th and 16th centuries. It began in Florence, Italy, with the rise of a spirit of humanism and a new appreciation of the classical past. In painting and sculpture this led to greater naturalism and interest in anatomy and perspective. Renaissance art peaked around 1500 with the careers of Leonardo da Vinci, Raphael,

Michelangelo, and Titian in Italy and Dürer in Germany.

The Renaissance was heralded by the work of the early 14th-century painter Giotto in Florence, and in the early 15th century a handful of outstanding innovative artists emerged there: Masaccio in painting, Donatello in sculpture, and Brunelleschi in architecture. At the same time the humanist philosopher, artist, and writer Alberti recorded many of the new ideas in his treatises on painting, sculpture, and architecture. These ideas soon became widespread in Italy, and many new centres of patronage formed. In the 16th century Rome superseded Florence as chief centre of activity and innovation, and it became the capital of the High Renaissance.

In N Europe the Renaissance spirit is apparent in the painting of the van Eyck brothers in the early 15th century. Later, Dürer demonstrated a scientific and enquiring mind and through his travels in Italy brought many Renaissance ideas back to Germany. Hans Holbein the Younger brought some of the concerns of Renaissance art to England in the 16th century, but it was not until the 17th century that English taste was significantly affected.

renal pertaining to the kidneys.

Renault /'renəʊ/ Mary. Pen name of Mary Challans 1905–1983. English novelist who recreated the world of ancient Greece, with a trilogy on ◊Theseus and two novels on ◊Alexander: *Fire from Heaven* 1970 and *The Persian Boy* 1972.

Rendell /'rendl/ Ruth 1930– . English novelist and short-story writer, author of a detective series featuring Chief Inspector Wexford; her psychological crime novels explore the minds of people who commit murder, often through obsession or social inadequacy, as in *A Demon in my View* 1976 and *Heartstones* 1987.

René /rə'neɪ/ France-Albert 1935– . Seychelles politician, president from 1987. In 1964 René founded the left-wing Seychelles People's United Party (SPUP), pressing for complete independence. When this was achieved, in 1976, he became prime minister and James Mancham, leader of the Seychelles Democratic Party (SDP), became president. René seized the presidency in 1977 and set up a one-party state. He has since followed a non-nuclear policy of nonalignment and has survived several attempts to remove him.

renewable resource natural resource that is replaced by natural processes in a reasonable amount of time. Soil, water, forests, plants, and animals are all renewable resources as long as they are properly conserved. Solar, wind, wave, and geothermal energies are based on renewable resources.

Renfrew /'renfru:/ town on the Clyde, in Strathclyde, 8 km/5 mi NW of Glasgow, Scotland; population (1981) 21,396. It was formerly the county town of Renfrewshire.

Renfrewshire /'renfru:ʃə/ former county of W central Scotland, bordering the Firth of Clyde. It was merged with the region of Strathclyde in 1975. The county town was Renfrew.

Reni /'reɪni/ Guido 1575–1642. Italian painter, active in Bologna and Rome (about 1600–14), whose work includes the fresco *Phoebus and the Hours Preceded by Aurora* 1613 (Casino Rospigliosi, Rome). His successful workshop in Bologna produced numerous idealized religious images, including Madonnas.

Rennes /ren/ industrial city (oil refining, chemicals, electronics, cars) and capital of Ille-et-Vilaine *département*, W France, at the confluence of the Ille and Vilaine, 56 km/35 mi SE of St Malo; population (1982) 234,000. It was the old capital of Brittany. Its university specializes in Breton culture. The second ◊Dreyfus trial was held here 1899.

rennet an extract, traditionally obtained from a calf's stomach, that contains the enzyme rennin, used to coagulate milk in the cheesemaking process. The enzyme can now be chemically produced.

Rennie /'reni/ John 1761–1821. Scottish engineer who built the old Waterloo Bridge and old London Bridge (reconstructed in Arizona, USA,

Rennie studied at Edinburgh University and then worked for James ◊Watt from 1784. He started his own engineering business about 1791, and built bridges (Waterloo bridge, London, 1810–17), canals, dams (Rudyard dam, Staffordshire, 1800), and harbours.

Reno /'ri:nəʊ/ city in Nevada, USA, known for gambling and easy divorces; population (1984) 112,000.

Renoir /'renwɑ:/ Jean 1894–1979. French film director, son of the painter Auguste Renoir, whose films include *La Grande Illusion/Grand Illusion* 1937, and *Règle du Jeu/The Rules of the Game* 1939.

Renoir /'renwɑ:/ Pierre-Auguste 1841–1919. French Impressionist painter. He met Monet and Sisley in the early 1860s and together they formed the nucleus of the Impressionist movement. He developed a lively, colourful painting style with feathery brushwork and painted many voluptuous female nudes, such as *The Bathers* about 1884–87 (Philadelphia Museum of Art, USA). In his later years he turned to sculpture.

Born in Limoges, Renoir originally trained as a porcelain painter. He joined an academic studio 1861, and the first strong influences on his style were the Rococo artists Boucher and Watteau and the Realist Courbet, but in the late 1860s Impressionism made its impact and Renoir began to work out of doors. Painting with Monet, he produced many pictures of people at leisure by the river Seine. From 1879 he made several journeys abroad, to N Africa, the Channel Islands, Italy, and later to the UK, the Netherlands, Spain, and Germany. After his Italian visit of 1881 he moved towards a more Classical structure in his work, notably in *Les Parapluies/Umbrellas* about 1881–84 (National Gallery, London). In 1906 he settled in the south of France. Many of his sculptures are monumental female nudes not unlike those of ◊Maillol.

Rentenmark currency introduced in Germany at the end of 1923 by the president of the Reichsbank, Hjalmar Schacht (1877–1970), to replace old Reichsmarks which had been rendered worthless by inflation.

As Germany had no appreciable gold reserves, the currency was guaranteed against the assets of the country, namely land and railways. Schacht's success in stabilizing the currency was largely due to the population's willingness to trust the new Rentenmark.

Renoir Les Parapluies/Umbrellas *(about 1881–84) National Gallery, London.*

reparation indemnity paid by countries that start wars in which they are defeated, as by Germany in both world wars.

Repin /rɪ'piːn/ Ilya Yefimovich 1844–1930. Russian painter. His work includes dramatic studies, such as *Barge Haulers on the Volga* 1873 and portraits, including Tolstoy and Mussorgsky.

replication in biology, the production of copies of the genetic material, DNA; it occurs during cell division (◊mitosis and ◊meiosis), and depends for accuracy on the ◊base pair.

reply, right of the right of a member of the public to respond to a media statement. A statutory right of reply, enforceable by a Press Commission, as exists in many Western European countries, failed to reach the statute book in the UK in 1989. At present there is no legal provision in the UK that any correction should receive the same prominence as the original statement and legal aid is not available in defamation cases, so that only the wealthy are able to sue. However, the major newspapers signed a Code of Practice in 1989 that promised some public protection.

Representation of the People Acts a series of UK acts of Parliament from 1867 that extended voting rights, creating universal suffrage in 1928.

The 1867 and 1884 acts are known as the second and third ◊Reform Acts. The 1918 act gave the vote to men over the age of 21 and women over the age of 30, and the 1928 act extended the vote to women over the age of 21. Certain people had the right to more than one vote; this was abolished by the 1948 act. The 1969 act reduced the minimum age of voting to 18.

repression in psychology, the unconscious process said to protect a person from ideas, impulses, or memories that would threaten emotional stability were they to become conscious.

reprieve the legal temporary suspension of the execution of a sentence of a criminal court. It is usually associated with the death penalty. It is distinct from a pardon (extinguishing the sentence) and commutation (alteration) of a sentence (for example, from death to life imprisonment).

reproduction the process by which a living organism produces other organisms similar to itself. There are two kinds: ◊asexual reproduction and ◊sexual reproduction.

reproduction rate or *fecundity* in ecology, the rate at which a population or species reproduces itself.

reptile class of vertebrates (Reptilia) including snakes, lizards, crocodiles, turtles, and tortoises. They breathe by means of lungs; this distinguishes them from ◊amphibians, the larvae of which breathe through gills. They are cold-blooded, produced from eggs, and the skin is usually covered with scales. The metabolism is slow, and in some cases (some large snakes) intervals between meals may be months. Reptiles date back over 300 million years.

Many extinct forms are known, including the orders Pterosauria, Rhynchocephalia (containing one living form, the ◊tuatara lizard), Plesiosauria, Ichthyosauria, and Dinosauria. The chief living orders are the Chelonia (tortoises and turtles), Crocodilia (alligators and crocodiles), and Squamata, divided into three sub-orders: Lacertilia (lizards), Rhiptoglossa (chameleons); Ophidia (snakes).

Repton /'reptən/ Humphrey 1752–1818. English garden designer, who coined the term 'landscape gardening'. He worked for some years in partnership with John ◊Nash. Repton preferred more formal landscaping than Lancelot ◊Brown, and was responsible for the landscaping of some 200 gardens and parks.

republic a country where the head of state is not a monarch, either hereditary or elected, but usually a president whose role may or may not include political functions.

Republic, The a treatise by the Greek philosopher Plato in which the voice of ◊Socrates is used to describe the ideal state, where the cultivation of truth, beauty, and goodness achieves perfection.

Republican Party one of the USA's two main political parties, formed 1854 by a coalition of ◊slavery opponents, who elected their first president, Abraham ◊Lincoln, in 1860. The early Republican Party supported protective tariffs and favoured genuine settlers (homesteaders) over land speculators. Towards the end of the century the Republican Party was identified with US imperialism and industrial expansion. With few intermissions, the Republican Party controlled the legislature from the 1860s until defeated by the New Deal Democrats 1932. After an isolationist period before World War II, the Republican Party adopted an active foreign policy under ◊Nixon and ◊Ford, but the latter was defeated by Carter in the presidential election 1976. However, the party enjoyed landslide presidential victories for ◊Reagan and also carried the Senate 1980–86. ◊Bush won the 1988 election, but faced the prospect of a Democratic Senate and Congress.

Conservative tendencies and an antagonism of the legislature to the executive came to the fore after Lincoln's assassination, when Andrew Johnson, his Democratic and Southern successor, was impeached, and Gen ◊Grant was elected to the presidency 1868 and 1872. In the bitter period following the Civil War the party was divided into those who considered the South a beaten nation and those who wished to reintegrate the South into the country as a whole, but Grant carried through a liberal reconstruction policy in the South.

It became divided during Theodore ◊Roosevelt's attempts at regulation and control of big business, and in forming the short-lived Progressive Party 1912, Roosevelt effectively removed the liberal influence from the Republican Party.

The Republican Party remained in eclipse until the election of ◊Eisenhower 1952, more a personal triumph than that of the party, whose control of Congress was soon lost and not regained by the next Republican president, ◊Nixon, 1968.

requiem in the Roman Catholic church, a mass for the dead. Musical settings include those by Palestrina, Mozart, Berlioz, and Verdi.

reredos ornamental screen or wall-facing, behind a church altar.

research the primary activity in science, a combination of theory and experimentation directed towards finding scientific explanations of phenomena. It is commonly classified into two types: *pure research*, involving theories with little apparent relevance to human concerns; and *applied research*, concerned with finding solutions to problems of social importance, for instance in medicine and engineering. The two types are linked in that theories developed from pure research may eventually be found to be of great value to society.

Scientific research is most often funded by government and industry, and so a nation's wealth and priorities are likely to have a strong influence on the kind of work undertaken.

reserpine tranquillizer derived from the SE Asian plant *serpent wood Rauwolfia serpentina*, also used to treat hypertension.

reserve currency in economics, a country's holding of internationally acceptable means of payment (major foreign currencies or gold); central banks also hold the ultimate reserve of money for their domestic banking sector. On the asset side of company balance sheets, undistributed profits are listed as reserves.

residue in chemistry, a substance or mixture of substances remaining in the original container after the removal of one or more components by a separation process.

The non-volatile substance left in a container after ◊evaporation of liquid, the solid left behind after removal of liquid by filtration, and the substances left in a distillation flask after removal of components by ◊distillation, are all residues.

resin substance exuded from pines, firs, and other trees in gummy drops that harden in air. Varnishes are common products of the hard resins, and ointments come from the soft resins.

Rosin is the solid residue of distilled turpentine, a soft resin. The name 'resin' is also given to many synthetic products, used in adhesives, plastics, and varnishes, with similar characteristics, and manufactured by ◊polymerization.

resistance in physics, that property of a substance which restricts the flow of electricity through it, associated with conversion of electrical energy to heat; also the magnitude of this property. Resistance depends on many factors, such as the nature of the material, its temperature, dimensions, and thermal properties; degree of impurity; the nature and state of illumination of the surface; and the frequency and magnitude of the current. The practical unit of resistance is the ◊ohm.

resistance movement an opposition movement in a country occupied by an enemy or colonial power. During World War II, resistance in E Europe took the form of ◊guerrilla warfare, for example in Yugoslavia, Greece, Poland, and by ◊partisan bands behind the German lines in the USSR. In more industrialized countries, such as France (where the underground movement was called the *maquis*), Belgium, and Czechoslovakia, sabotage in factories and on the railways, propaganda, and the assassination of Germans and collaborators were more important.

Most resistance movements in World War II were based on an alliance of all anti-fascist parties, but there was internal conflict between those elements more intent on defeat of the enemy, and those who aimed at establishing communist regimes, as in Yugoslavia and Greece.

After World War II the same methods were used in Palestine, South America, and European colonial possessions in Africa and Asia to unsettle established regimes.

resistor in physics, any component in an electrical circuit used to introduce ◊resistance to a current. Resistors are often made from wire-wound coils or pieces of carbon. ◊Rheostats and ◊potentiometers are variable resistors.

Resnais /re'ne/ Alain 1922– . French film director, whose work is characterized by the themes of memory and unconventional concepts of time. His films include *Hiroshima mon amour* 1959, *L'Année dernière à Marienbad*/*Last Year at Marienbad* 1961 and *Providence* 1977.

resonance a rapid and uncontrolled increase in the size of a vibration when the vibrating object is subject to a force varying at its ◊natural frequency. In a trombone, for example, the length of the air column in the instrument is adjusted until it resonates with the note being sounded. Resonance effects are also produced by many electrical circuits. Tuning a radio, for example, is done by adjusting the natural frequency of the receiver circuit until it coincides with the frequency of the radio waves falling on the aerial.

Resonance has many physical applications. Children use it to increase the size of the movement on a swing, by giving a push at the same point during each swing. Soldiers marching across a bridge in step could cause the bridge to vibrate violently if the frequency of their steps coincided with its natural frequency. Resonance was the cause of the collapse of the Tacoma Narrows bridge, USA, in 1940 when the frequency of the wind coincided with the natural frequency of the bridge.

resources general term for materials that can be used to satisfy human wants. Because human wants are diverse and extend from basic physical requirements, such as food and shelter, to ill-defined aesthetic needs, resources encompass a vast range of items. The intellectual resources of a society—its ideas and technologies—determine which aspects of the environment meet that society's needs, and therefore become resources. For example, in the 19th century uranium was used only in the manufacture of coloured glass. Today, with the advent of nuclear technology, it is a military and energy resource. Resources are often categorized into *human resources*, such as labour, supplies, and skills,

respiration

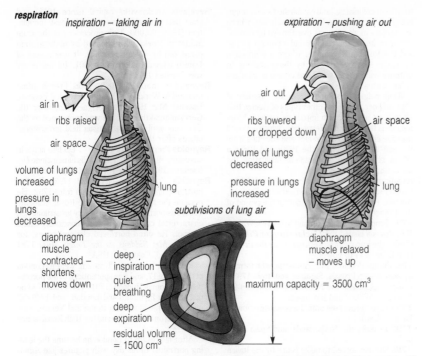

inspiration – taking air in

air in
ribs raised
air space
volume of lungs increased
pressure in lungs decreased
diaphragm muscle contracted – shortens, moves down
lung

expiration – pushing air out

air out
ribs lowered or dropped down
air space
volume of lungs decreased
pressure in lungs increased
lung
diaphragm muscle relaxed – moves up

subdivisions of lung air

deep inspiration
quiet breathing
deep expiration
residual volume = 1500 cm³
maximum capacity = 3500 cm³

and **natural resources**, such as climate, fossil fuels, and water. Natural resources are divided into ◊nonrenewable resources and ◊renewable resources.

Nonrenewable resources include minerals such as coal, copper ores, and diamonds, which exist in strictly limited quantities. Once consumed they will not be replenished within the likely time span of human history. In contrast, water supplies, timber, food crops, and similar resources can, if managed properly, provide a steady yield virtually forever; they are therefore replenishable or renewable resources. Inappropriate use of renewable resources can lead to their destruction, as for example the cutting down of rainforests. Some renewable resources, such as wind or solar energy, are continuous; supply is largely independent of people's actions.

Demands for resources made by rich nations are causing concern among many people who feel that the present and future demands of industrial societies cannot be sustained for more than a century or two, and that at the expense of the Third World and the environment. Other authorities believe that new technologies will emerge, enabling resources currently of little importance to replace those being exhausted.

Respighi /res'pi:gi/ Ottorino 1879–1936. Italian composer, a student of ◊Rimsky-Korsakov, whose works include the symphonic poems *The Fountains of Rome* 1917 and *The Pines of Rome* 1924 (incorporating the recorded song of a nightingale), operas, and chamber music.

respiration the biochemical process whereby food molecules are progressively broken down to release energy in the form of ◊ATP. In most organisms this is an aerobic process (oxygen is required). In all higher organisms, respiration occurs in the ◊mitochondria. Respiration is also used to mean breathing, although this is more accurately described as ◊gas exchange.

respiratory distress syndrome (RDS) formerly *hyaline membrane disease* a condition in which a newborn baby's lungs are insufficiently expanded to permit adequate oxygenation. Premature babies are most at risk. Normal inflation of the lungs requires the presence of a substance called surfactant to reduce the surface tension of the alveoli (air sacs) in the lungs. In premature babies, surfactant is deficient. As a result, the breathing is rapid, laboured, and shallow, and there is the likelihood of ◊asphyxia. Such babies survive with the aid of intravenous fluids and oxygen, sometimes with assisted ventilation.

response time in computing, the delay between entering a command and seeing its effect.

rest mass in physics, the mass of a particle at rest or moving at only a low velocity compared with that of light. According to the theory of ◊relativity, at very high velocities, there is a relativistic effect that increases the mass of the particle.

Restoration in English history, the period when the monarchy, in the person of Charles II, was re-established after the fall of the ◊Protectorate 1660.

Restoration comedy style of English theatre, dating from the Restoration. It witnessed the first appearance of women on the English stage, most notably in the 'breeches part', specially created in order to costume the actress in male attire, thus revealing her figure to its best advantage. The genre placed much emphasis on sexual antics. Examples include Wycherley's *The Country Wife* 1675, Congreve's *The Way of the World* 1700, and Farquhar's *The Beaux' Strategem* 1707.

restrictive trade practices agreements between people in a particular trade or business which keep the cost of goods or services artificially high (for example an agreement to restrict output) or provide barriers to outsiders entering the trade or business. In British law these agreements are void unless they are registered with the Office of Fair Trading and are shown not to be contrary to the public interest.

resurrection in Christian, Jewish, and Muslim belief, the rising from the dead that all souls will experience at the Last Judgment. The Resurrection also refers to Jesus rising from the dead on the third day after his crucifixion, which is a central belief of Christianity, celebrated at Easter.

resuscitation steps taken to revive anyone on the brink of death. The most successful technique for life-threatening emergencies, such as electrocution, near-drowning, or heart attack, is mouth-to-mouth resuscitation. Medical and paramedical staff are trained in cardiopulmonary resuscitation: the use of specialized equipment and techniques to restart the breathing and/or heart beat, and stabilize the patient long enough for more definitive treatment to be applied.

retail sale of goods and services to a consumer. The retailer is the last link in the distribution chain.

A retailer's purchases are usually made from a wholesaler.

The large range of retail outlets include vending machines, street pedlars, specialized shops, department stores, supermarkets, and co-operative stores. These are supplemented by auctions, door-to-door selling, telephone selling, and mail order.

retail price index (RPI) an indicator of variations in the ◊cost of living.

retail price maintenance (RPM) in the UK, exceptions to the general rule that shops can charge whatever price they choose for goods. The main areas where RPM applies are books (where the Net Book Agreement prevents booksellers charging less than the publisher's price) and some pharmaceutical products.

retriever type of dog. The commonest breeds are the Labrador retriever, large, smooth-coated, and usually black or yellow; and the golden retriever, with either flat or wavy coat. They can grow to 60 cm/2 ft high, and weigh 40 kg/90 lbs. They were traditionally used for retrieving game.

retrovirus a type of ◊virus containing the genetic material ◊RNA rather than the more usual ◊DNA.

For the virus to express itself and multiply within an infected cell, its RNA must be converted to DNA. It does this by using a built-in enzyme known as reverse transcriptase (since the transfer of genetic information from DNA to RNA is known as ◊transcription, and retroviruses do the reverse of this). Retroviruses include those causing ◊AIDS and other infections of the immune system. See ◊immunity.

Retz /res/ Jean François Paul de Gondi, Cardinal de Retz 1614–1679. French politician. A priest with political ambitions, he stirred up and largely led the insurrection of the ◊Fronde. After a period of imprisonment and exile he was restored to favour 1662 and created abbot of St Denis.

Réunion /,reɪu:n'jɒŋ/ French island of the Mascarenes group, in the Indian Ocean, 650 km/400 mi E of Madagascar, and 180 km/110 mi SW of Mauritius
area 2,512 sq km/970 sq mi
capital St Denis
physical forested, rising in Piton de Neiges to 3,069 m/10,072 ft
features administers five uninhabited islands also claimed by Madagascar
products sugar, maize, vanilla, tobacco, rum
population (1987) 565,000
history the first European visitors were the Portuguese 1513; annexed by Louis XIII of

resuscitation *A patient's-eye view of a doctor ready to resuscitate someone after a severe heart attack.*

Réunion

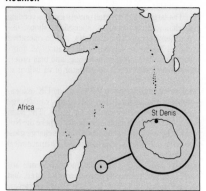

France 1642; overseas *département* of France 1946; overseas region 1972.

Reus /ˈreɪus/ industrial city with an international airport in Catalonia, E Spain, 10 km/6 mi NW of Tarragona.

Reuter /ˈrɔɪtə/ Paul Julius, Baron de Reuter 1816–1899. German founder of Reuters international news agency. He began a continental pigeon post 1849, and in 1851 he set up a news agency in London. In 1858 he persuaded the press to use his news telegrams, and the service became worldwide.

The agency became a private trust 1916, and was taken over by the Newspaper Proprietors' Association 1926–41. It became a public company 1984.

Reval /ˈreɪvæl/ former name of the Soviet port of ◊Tallinn.

Revans /ˈrevənz/ Reginald William 1907– . British management expert, originator of the 'action learning' method of management improvement, for example, that each department of a firm probes the problem-avoiding system of some other department until the circle is completed, with resultant improved productivity.

Revelation last book of the New Testament, traditionally attributed to the author of the Gospel of St John but now generally held to be the work of another writer. It describes a vision of the end of the world, of the Last Judgment, and of a new heaven and earth ruled by God from Jerusalem.

revenons à nos moutons (French 'let us return to our sheep') let us get back to the subject.

revenue sharing in the USA, federal aid to state and local government allocated under the State and Local Fiscal Assistance Act 1972.

Revere /rəˈvɪə/ Paul 1735–1818. American nationalist, a Boston silversmith, who carried the news of the approach of British troops to Lexington and Concord (see ◊American Independence, War of) on the night of 18 Apr 1775. Longfellow's poem 'Paul Revere's Ride' commemorates the event.

Revere's silver *Sons of Liberty* punchbowl 1768 (Museum of Fine Arts, Boston, USA) is his best-known piece. He also produced propaganda prints exposing British atrocities in the war.

reverse takeover in business, a ◊takeover situation where a company sells itself to another, to avoid being itself the target of a purchase by an unwelcome predator.

revisionism a political theory derived from Marxism that moderates one or more of the basic tenets of Marx, and which is hence condemned by orthodox Marxists. The first noted Marxist revisionist was Eduard Bernstein, who in Germany in the 1890s questioned the inevitability of a breakdown in capitalism. After World War II the term became widely used by established Communist parties, both in E Europe and Asia, to condemn movements (whether more or less radical) that threatened the official party policy.

revolution any rapid, far-reaching, or violent change in the political, social, or economic structure of society. It has usually been applied to different forms of political change: the American Revolution (War of Independence), where colonists broke free from their colonial ties and established a sovereign, independent state; the French Revolution, where an absolute monarchy was overthrown by opposition from inside the country and a popular rising; and the Russian Revolution, where a repressive monarchy was overthrown by those seeking to institute widespread social and economic changes in line with a socialist model.

While political revolutions are often associated with violence, there are other types of change that often have just as much impact on society. Most notable is the Industrial Revolution, which imposed massive changes on economies and societies from the mid-18th century. In the 1970s and 1980s a silicon revolution was identified, facilitating the increasing use of computers.

Revolutionary Wars a series of wars 1791–1802 between France and the combined armies of England, Austria, Prussia, and others, during the period of the French Revolution.

1791 Emperor ◊Leopold II and Frederick William II of Prussia issued the **Declaration of Pillnitz** inviting the European powers to restore the French king Louis XVI to power.

1792 France declared war on Austria, who formed a coalition with Prussia, Sardinia, and (from 1793), Britain, Spain, and the Netherlands; victories for France at ◊Valmy and Jemappes.

1793 French reverses until the reorganization by Lazare ◊Carnot.

1795 Prussia, the Netherlands, and Spain made peace.

1796 Sardinia forced to make peace by the Italian campaign of ◊Napoleon I, then a commander.

1797 Austria compelled to peace under the Treaty of ◊Campo-Formio.

1798 Napoleon's fleet, after its capture of Malta, was defeated by the British admiral ◊Nelson in Egypt at the **Battle of the Nile** (Aboukir Bay), and Napoleon had to return to France without his army; William Pitt the Younger, Britain's prime minister, organized a new coalition with Russia, Austria, Naples, Portugal, and Turkey.

1798–99 The coalition mounted its major campaign in Italy (under the Russian field marshal ◊Suvorov), but dissension led to the withdrawal of Russia.

1799 Napoleon, on his return from Egypt, reorganized the French army.

1800 14 June Austrian army defeated by Napoleon at Marengo in NW Italy, and again on 3 Dec (by Gen ◊Moreau) at Hohenlinden near Munich.

1801 Austria made peace under the Treaty of Lunéville; Sir Ralph ◊Abercromby defeated the French army by land in Egypt at the Battle of Alexandria, but was himself killed.

1802 Peace of Amiens truce between France and Britain, followed by the Napoleonic Wars.

revolutions of 1848 a series of revolts in various parts of Europe against monarchical rule. While some of the revolutionaries had republican ideas, many more were motivated by economic grievances. The revolution began in France and then spread to Italy, the Austrian Empire, and to Germany, where the short-lived ◊Frankfurt Parliament put forward ideas about political unity in Germany. None of the revolutions enjoyed any lasting success, and most were violently suppressed within a few months.

revolver a small hand gun with a revolving chamber that holds the bullets.

revue a stage presentation involving short satirical and topical items in the form of songs, sketches, and monologues; it originated in the late 19th century.

In Britain the first revue seems to have been *Under the Clock* 1893 by Seymour Hicks (1871–1949) and Charles Brookfield. The 1920s revues were spectacular entertainments, but the 'intimate revue' became increasingly popular, employing writers such as Noël Coward. During the 1960s the satirical revue took off with the Cambridge Footlights' production *Beyond the Fringe*, establishing the revue tradition among the young and at fringe theatrical events.

Reykjavik /ˈreɪkjəviːk/ capital (since 1918) and chief port of Iceland, on the SW coast; population (1988) 93,000. Fish processing is the main industry. Reykjavik is heated by underground mains fed by volcanic springs. It was a seat of Danish administration from 1801. Its university was founded 1911.

Reynaud /reɪˈnəu/ Paul 1878–1966. French prime minister in World War II, who succeeded Edouard Daladier Mar 1940, but resigned June after the German breakthrough. He was imprisoned by the Germans until 1945, and again held government offices after the war.

Reynolds /ˈrenldz/ Burt 1936– . US film actor in adventure films and comedies. His films include *Deliverance* 1972, *Hustle* 1975, and *City Heat* 1984.

Reynolds /ˈrenldz/ Joshua 1723–1792. English portrait painter, active in London from 1752. He became the first president of the Royal Academy 1768. His portraits display a facility for striking and characterful compositions in a consciously grand manner. He often borrowed classical poses, for example *Mrs Siddons as the Tragic Muse* 1784 (San Marino, California, USA).

Reynolds, born near Plymouth, went to London at the age of 17, and was apprenticed to the portrait painter Thomas Hudson (1701–79). From 1743 he practised in Plymouth and London, and 1749–52 completed his studies in Rome and Venice, concentrating on the antique and the High Renaissance masters.

After his return to London he became the leading portraitist of his day with pictures like *Admiral Keppel* 1753–54 (National Maritime Museum, London). His *Discourses on Art* 1769–91 contain his theories on the aims of academic art.

Reynolds /ˈrenldz/ Osborne 1842–1912. British physicist and engineer who studied ◊fluid flow, and devised the Reynolds number, which relates to turbulence in flowing fluids.

RGB *red-green-blue* a method of connecting a colour screen to a computer, involving three separate signals: red, green, and blue. All the colours displayed by the screen can be made up from these three component colours.

rhapsody in music, an instrumental ◊fantasia, often based on folk melodies, such as Lizst's *Hungarian Rhapsodies* 1853–54.

In ancient Greece, rhapsodes were a class of reciters of epic poems, especially those of ◊Homer, who performed at festivals. The title means 'stitchers of songs'.

rhe unit of fluidity equal to the reciprocal of the ◊poise.

rhea flightless bird, family Rheidae, found only in South America. There are two species: *Rhea americana* and the smaller *Pterocnemia pennata*. They differ from the ostrich in having a feathered neck and head and three-toed feet, no plume-like tail feathers, and in their smaller size (up to 1.5 m/5 ft high, and 25 kg/55 lbs).

Rhea in Greek mythology, a fertility goddess, one of the Titans, wife of Kronos and mother of several gods, including Zeus.

Rhee /riː/ Syngman 1875–1965. Korean right-wing politician. A rebel under Chinese and Japanese rule, he became president of South Korea from 1948 until riots forced him to resign and leave the country 1960.

Rheims /riːmz/ English version of ◊Reims.

Rheinland-Pfalz /ˈraɪnlænt ˈpfælts/ German name for the ◊Rhineland-Palatinate region, West Germany.

rhenium metallic element: symbol Re, atomic number 75, relative atomic mass 186.22. It was identified 1925 by Noddack, Tacke, and Berg in the minerals columbite, tantalite, and wolframite. It is a hard grey metal, used in thermocouples (electric temperature-measuring devices) and as a catalyst.

rheostat in physics, a variable ◊resistor, usually consisting of a high-resistance wire-wound coil with a sliding contact. The circular type in electronics (which can be used, for example, as the

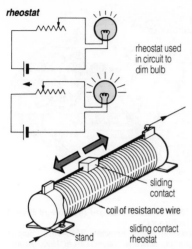

rheostat

rheostat used in circuit to dim bulb

sliding contact

coil of resistance wire

sliding contact rheostat

stand

volume control of an amplifier) is also known as a ◊potentiometer.

rhesus or **bandar** macaque monkey *Macaca mulatta*, found in N India and SE Asia. It has long, straight, brown-grey hair, pinkish face, and red buttocks. It can grow up to 60 cm/2 ft long, with a 20 cm/8 in tail.

rhesus factor a ◊protein on the surface of red blood cells of humans, which is involved in the rhesus blood group system. Most individuals possess the main rhesus factor (Rh+), but those without (Rh−) will produce ◊antibodies if they come into contact with it. The name comes from rhesus monkeys, in whose blood rhesus factors were first found.

If an Rh− mother carries an Rh+ fetus, she may produce antibodies if fetal blood crosses the ◊placenta. This is not normally a problem with the first infant because antibodies are only produced slowly. However, the antibodies continue to build up after birth, and a second Rh+ child may be attacked by antibodies passing from mother to fetus, and cause the child to contract anaemia, heart failure, or brain damage. In such cases, the blood of the infant has to be changed for Rh− blood. Alternatively, the problem can be alleviated by giving the mother anti-Rh globulin just after the first pregnancy, preventing the formation of antibodies.

rhetoric traditionally, the art of the orator (in Greek, *rhetor*) or of public speaking and debate. Rhetorical skills are valued in such occupations as politics, the law, preaching, and broadcasting.

Accomplished rhetoricians need not be sincere in what they say; they should, however, be effective, or at least entertaining. Nowadays, 'rhetoric' is often a pejorative term (for example, 'Cut the rhetoric and tell us what you really think').

rhetorical question a question, often used by public speakers and debaters, which either does not require an answer or for which the speaker intends to provide his or her own answer ('where else in the world can we find such brave young men as these?').

rheumatic fever or *acute rheumatism* an acute illness characterized by fever and painful swelling of joints. Some victims also experience involuntary movements of the limbs and head, a form of chorea.

Rheumatic fever, which strikes mainly children and young adults, is always preceded by a streptococcal infection such as ◊scarlet fever or a severe sore throat, usually occurring a couple of weeks beforehand. It is treated with bed-rest, antibiotics, and analgesics. The condition may give rise to disease of the heart valve.

rheumatism a general term for a variety of ailments associated with inflammation of the joints and muscles. Acute rheumatism is better known as *rheumatic fever*.

River Rhine

Rhine /raɪn/ (German **Rhein**, French **Rhin**) European river rising in Switzerland and reaching the North Sea via West Germany and the Netherlands; length 1,320 km/820 mi. Tributaries include the Moselle and the Ruhr. The Rhine is linked with the Mediterranean by the Rhine-Rhône Waterway, and with the Black Sea by the Rhine-Main-Danube Waterway.

The *Lorelei* is a rock in the river in Rhineland-Palatinate, West Germany, with a remarkable echo; the German poet Brentano gave currency to the legend of a siren who lured sailors to death with her song, also subject of a poem by Heine.

Rhine /raɪn/ Joseph Banks 1895–1980. US parapsychologist. His work at Duke University, North Carolina, involving controlled laboratory experiments in telepathy, clairvoyance, precognition, and psychokinesis, described in *Extra-Sensory Perception* 1934 made ESP a common term. See also ◊parapsychology.

Rhineland-Palatinate /ˈraɪnlænd pəˈlætɪnət/ (German *Rheinland-Pfalz*) administrative region (German *Land*) of West Germany
area 19,800 sq km/7,643 sq mi
capital Mainz
towns Ludwigshafen, Koblenz, Trier, Worms
physical wooded mountain country, river valleys of Rhine and Moselle
products wine (75% of German output), tobacco, chemicals, machinery, leather goods, pottery
population (1988) 3,611,000
history formed 1946 of the Rhenish ◊Palatinate and parts of Hessen, Rhine province, and Hessen-Nassau.

rhinoceros hoofed mammal of the family Rhinocerotidae. The one-horned Indian rhinoceros *Rhinoceros unicornis* is up to 2 m/6 ft at the shoulder, with a tubercled skin, folded into shield-like pieces; the African black rhinoceros *Diceros bicornis* is 1.5 m/5 ft high, with a prehensile upper lip for feeding on shrubs; the broad-lipped or 'white' rhinoceros *Ceratotherium simum* is actually slaty-grey, with a squarish mouth for browsing grass. The latter two are smooth-skinned and two-horned. They are solitary and vegetarian, with poor eyesight but excellent hearing and smell. Needless slaughter has led to the near extinction of all species of rhinoceros, particularly the Sumatran rhinoceros and Javan rhinoceros.

rhinoceros

Sumatran rhinoceros

Rhode Island

rhizoid a hair-like outgrowth found on the ◊gametophyte generation of ferns, mosses and liverworts. Rhizoids anchor the plant to the substrate, and can absorb water and nutrients. They may be composed of many cells, as in mosses, where they are usually brownish, or unicellular, as in liverworts, where they are usually colourless. Rhizoids fulfil the same functions as the ◊roots of higher plants but are simpler in construction.

rhizome a horizontal underground plant stem. It is a ◊perennating organ in some species, where it is generally thick and fleshy, while in other species it is mainly a means of ◊vegetative reproduction, and is therefore long and slender, with buds all along it that send up new plants. The potato is a rhizome that has two distinct parts, the tuber being the swollen end of a long, cord-like rhizome. See also ◊rootstock.

rhm (abbreviation for *roentgen–metre–hour*) unit of effective strength of a radioactive source that produces gamma rays. It is used for substances for which it is difficult to establish radioactive disintegration rates.

Rhode Island /rəʊd ˈaɪlənd/ smallest state of the USA, in New England; nickname Little Rhody or the Ocean State
area 3,100 sq km/1,197 sq mi
capital Providence
towns Cranston, Woonsocket
features Narragansett Bay runs inland 45 km/28 mi
products apples, potatoes, poultry (especially Rhode Island Reds), dairy products, jewellery (30% of the workforce), textiles, silverware, machinery, rubber, plastics, electronics
population (1987) 986,000
history founded 1636 by Roger Williams, exiled from Massachusetts Bay colony for religious dissent; one of the original Thirteen States.

Rhodes /rəʊdz/ (Greek *Rodhos*) Greek island, largest of the Dodecanese, in the E Aegean Sea
area 1,412 sq km/545 sq mi
capital Rhodes
products grapes, olives
population (1981) 88,000
history settled by Greeks about 1000 BC; ◊Colossus of Rhodes (fell 224 BC) was one of the ◊Seven Wonders of the World; held by the Knights Hospitallers of St John 1306–1522; taken from Turkish rule by the Italian occupation 1912; ceded to Greece 1947.

Rhodes /rəʊdz/ Cecil (John) 1853–1902. South African politician, born in the UK, prime minister of Cape Colony 1890–96. Aiming at the formation of a South African federation and of a block of British territory from the Cape to Cairo, he was responsible for the annexation of Bechuanaland (now Botswana) in 1885, and formed the British South Africa Company in 1889, which occupied Mashonaland and Matabeleland, thus forming *Rhodesia* (now Zambia and Zimbabwe).

Rhodes went to Natal in 1870. As head of De Beers Consolidated Mines and Goldfields of South Africa Ltd, he amassed a large fortune. He entered the Cape legislature in 1881, and became prime minister in 1890, but the discovery of his complicity in the ◊Jameson Raid forced him to resign in 1896. Advocating Anglo-Afrikaner cooperation, he was less alive to the rights of black Africans, despite the final 1898 wording of his dictum: 'Equal rights for every civilized man south of the Zambezi'.

The *Rhodes scholarships* were founded at Oxford University, UK, under his will, for students from the Commonwealth, USA, and Germany.

Rhodes /rəʊdz/ Wilfred 1877–1973. English cricketer. He was the game's most prolific wicket-taker, taking 4,187 wickets 1898–1930, and also scoring 39,802 first class runs.

Playing for Yorkshire Rhodes made a record 763 appearances in the county championship. He took 100 wickets in a season 23 times and completed the 'double' of 1,000 runs and 100 wickets in a season 16 times (both records). When he played his 58th and final game for England, against West Indies 1930, he was over 52 years old, the oldest ever test cricketer.

CAREER HIGHLIGHTS

All First Class Matches
Runs: 39,802; Average: 30.83
Best: 267 not out Yorkshire v. Leicestershire, 1921
Wickets: 4,187; Average: 16.71
Best: 9–24 C I Thornton's XI v. Australians, 1899
Test Cricket
Runs: 2,325; Average: 30.19
Best: 179 v. Australia, 1911–12
Wickets: 127; Average: 26.96
Best: 8–68 v. Australia, 1903–04

Rhodes /rəʊdz/ Zandra 1940– . English fashion designer, known for the extravagant fantasy and luxury of her dress creations.

Rhodesia /rəʊˈdiːʃə/ former name of ◊Zambia (North Rhodesia) and ◊Zimbabwe (South Rhodesia).

rhodium (from Greek *rhodon*, 'rose') a silvery-white metal of the platinum family; symbol Rh, atomic number 45, atomic weight 102.91. It is used in thermocouples and in electroplating, and gives a corrosion-free, highly polished surface, superior to that of chromium.

Rhodium was discovered 1803 by the British chemist William Wollaston (1766–1828). Its salts form red solutions, and occurs with platinum in river sands in the Urals and the Americas.

rhododendron evergreen and deciduous shrub of the genus *Rhododendron*, family Ericaceae. The leaves are often dark and leathery, and the large racemes of flowers occur in all colours except blue. They thrive on acid soils.

Rhodope Mountains /ˈrɒdəpi/ a range of mountains on the frontier between Greece and Bulgaria, rising to 2,925 m/9,497 ft at Musala.

rhombus a diamond-shaped plane figure, a parallelogram with four equal sides (opposite sides are equal in length and parallel) and no internal angle which is a right angle (otherwise it is a square). Its diagonals bisect each other at right angles. The area of a rhombus is half the product of the lengths of the two diagonals.

Rhondda /ˈrɒnðə/ industrial town in Mid Glamorgan, Wales; population (1981) 81,725. Light industries have replaced coalmining, formerly the main source of employment.

Rhône /rəʊn/ river of S Europe; length 810 km/500 mi. It rises in Switzerland and flows through Lake Geneva to Lyons in France, where at its confluence with the Saône the upper limit of navigation is reached. The river turns due south, passes Vienne and Avignon, and takes in the Isère and other tributaries. Near Arles it divides into the *Grand* and *Petit Rhône*, flowing respectively SE and SW into the Mediterranean west of Marseille.

Here it forms a two-armed delta; the area between the tributaries is the ◊Camargue, a desolate marsh. The Rhône is harnessed for hydroelectric power, the chief dam being at Genissiat in Ain *département*, constructed 1938–48. Between

rice

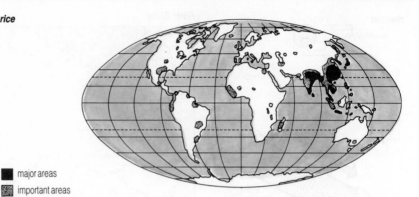

■ major areas
▨ important areas

Vienne and Avignon it flows through a major wine-producing area.

Rhône-Alpes /ˈrəʊn ˈælps/ region of E France in the upper reaches of the Rhône; area 43,700 sq km/16,868 sq mi; population (1986) 5,154,000. It consists of the *départements* of Ain, Ardèche, Drôme, Isère, Loire, Rhône, Savoie, and Haute-Savoie. The chief town is Lyon. There are several notable wine-producing areas including Chenas, Fleurie, and Beaujolais. Industrial products include chemicals, textiles, and motor vehicles.

rhubarb perennial plant *Rheum rhaponticum*, family Polygonaceae, grown for its pink edible leaf stalks. The leaves are poisonous.

Rhyl /rɪl/ seaside holiday resort in Clwyd, N Wales; population (1980) 23,000.

rhyme identity of sound, usually in the endings of lines of verse, such as 'wing' and 'sing'. Avoided in Japanese, it is a common literary device in other Asian and European languages. Rhyme first appeared in Europe in late Latin poetry, but was not used in classical Greek and Latin.

rhyolite an ◊igneous rock, the fine-grained volcanic (extrusive) equivalent of granite.

Rhys /riːs/ Jean 1894–1979. British novelist, born in Dominica. Her works include *Wide Sargasso Sea* 1966, a recreation of the life of Rochester's mad wife in *Jane Eyre* by Charlotte Brontë.

rhythm and blues (R & B) a term covering a type of US popular music of the 1940s–60s, replacing the tag 'race music'. The music drew on swing and jump-jazz rhythms and blues vocals and was a progenitor of rock and roll. It diversified into soul, funk, and other styles. Singers include Bo Diddley (1928–), Jackie Wilson (1934–84), and Etta James (c. 1938–).

rhythm method a method of natural contraception that works by avoiding intercourse when the woman is producing egg cells (ovulating). The time of ovulation can be worked out by the calendar (counting days from the last period), by temperature changes, or by inspection of the cervical mucus. All these methods are unreliable because it is possible for ovulation to occur at any stage of the menstrual cycle.

RI abbreviation for ◊*Rhode Island*.

ria long narrow sea inlet, usually branching and surrounded by hills. A ria is deeper and wider towards its mouth, unlike a ◊fjord. It is formed by the flooding of a river valley due to either a rise in sea level or a lowering of a landmass.

rib a long, often curved bone that extends laterally from the ◊spine in vertebrates. Fish and some reptiles have ribs along most of the spine, but in mammals they are found in the chest only. In humans, there are 12 pairs of ribs. The ribs protect the lungs and heart, and allow the chest to expand and contract easily.

At the rear, each pair is joined to one of the vertebrae of the spine. The upper seven are joined by ◊cartilage directly to the breast bone (sternum). The next three are joined by cartilage to the rib above. The last two ('floating ribs') are not attached; they end in the muscles of the back.

RIBA abbreviation for *Royal Institute of British Architects*.

Ribalta /rɪˈbæltə/ Francisco 1565–1628. Spanish painter, active in Valencia from 1599. Around 1615 he developed a dramatic Baroque style using extreme effects of light and shade (recalling ◊Caravaggio), as in *St Bernard Embracing Christ* about 1620–28 (Prado, Madrid).

Ribbentrop /ˈrɪbəntrɒp/ Joachim von. 1893–1946. German Nazi leader, born in the Rhineland. He joined the Nazi Party 1932, acted as Hitler's adviser on foreign affairs, and was German ambassador to Britain 1936–38 and foreign minister 1938–45. He was tried at Nuremberg as a war criminal 1946 and hanged.

Ribbentrop-Molotov pact see ◊Hitler-Stalin pact.

Ribble /ˈrɪbəl/ river in N England; length 120 km/75 mi. From its source in the Pennine hills, N Yorkshire, it flows S and SW past Preston, Lancashire, to join the Irish Sea.

Ribera /rɪˈbɪərə/ José (Jusepe) de 1591–1652. Spanish painter, active in Italy from 1616 under the patronage of the viceroys of Naples. His early work shows the impact of Caravaggio, but his colours gradually lightened. He painted many full-length saints and mythological figures, and genre scenes, which he produced without preliminary drawing.

riboflavin a ◊vitamin of the B complex (B₂) whose absence in the diet causes stunted growth.

ribonucleic acid the full name of ◊RNA.

ribosome in biology, the protein-making machinery of the cell. Ribosomes are made of proteins and a special type of ◊RNA, ribosomal RNA. They receive messenger RNA (copied from the ◊DNA) and ◊amino acids, and 'translate' the messenger RNA by using its chemically coded instructions to link amino acids in a specific order, to make a strand of a particular protein.

Ricardo /rɪˈkɑːdəʊ/ David 1772–1823. English economist, author of *Principles of Political Economy* 1817. Among his discoveries were the principle of ◊comparative advantage (that countries can benefit by specializing in goods they produce efficiently and trading internationally to buy others), and the law of diminishing returns (that continued increments of capital and labour applied to a given quantity of land will eventually show a declining rate of increase in output).

rice principal cereal of the wet regions of the tropics; derived from grass of the species *Oryza sativa*, probably native to India and SE Asia. The yield is very large, and rice is said to be the staple food of one-third of the world population.

cultivation Rice takes 150–200 days to mature in warm, wet conditions. During its growing period, it needs to be flooded either by the heavy monsoon rains or by adequate irrigation. This restricts the cultivation of swamp rice, the usual kind, to level land and terraces. A poorer variety, known as hill rice, is grown on hillsides. Outside Asia, there is some rice production in the Po valley of Italy, and in the US in Louisiana, the Carolinas, and California.

nutrition Rice contains 8–9% protein. Brown, or unhusked, rice has valuable B-vitamins that are lost

rice

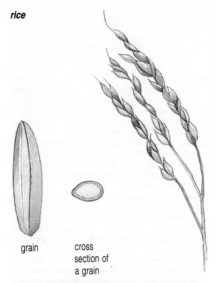

grain   cross
section of
a grain

rice

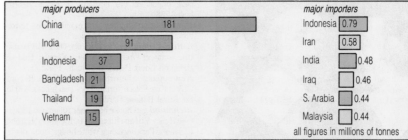

major producers		major importers	
China	181	Indonesia	0.79
India	91	Iran	0.58
Indonesia	37	India	0.48
Bangladesh	21	Iraq	0.46
Thailand	19	S. Arabia	0.44
Vietnam	15	Malaysia	0.44
		all figures in millions of tonnes	

in husking or polishing. Most of the the rice eaten in the world is, however, sold in polished form.

history Rice has been cultivated since prehistoric days in the East. New varieties with greatly increased protein content have been developed by gamma radiation for commercial cultivation, and yields are higher than ever before (see ◊green revolution).

byproducts Rice husks when burned provide a ◊silica ash that, mixed with lime, produces an excellent cement.

Rice /raɪs/ Elmer 1892–1967. US playwright. His works include *The Adding Machine* 1923 and *Street Scene* 1929, which won a Pulitzer Prize and was made into an opera by Kurt Weill. Many of his plays deal with such economic and political issues as the Depression (*We, the People* 1933) and racism (*American Landscape* 1939).

Rice-Davies /ˌraɪs ˈdeɪvɪs/ Mandy (Marilyn) 1944– . English model. She achieved notoriety in 1963 following the revelations of the affair between her friend Christine ◊Keeler and war minister John ◊Profumo and his subsequent resignation.

Rich /rɪtʃ/ Adrienne 1929– . US radical feminist poet, writer, and critic. Her poetry is both subjective and political, concerned with female consciousness, peace, and gay rights. Her works include *The Fact of a Doorframe: Poems Selected and New* 1984 and *On Lies, Secrets and Silence* 1979.

In the 1960s her poetry was closely involved with the student and anti-war movements in the USA but since then she has concerned herself with women's issues. In 1974, when given the National Book Award, she declined to accept it as an individual but with Alice Walker and Audrey Rich accepted it on behalf of all women.

Richard /ˈrɪtʃəd/ Cliff. Stage name of Harry Roger Webb 1940– . English pop singer. In the late 1950s he was influenced by Elvis Presley, but became a Christian family entertainer, continuing to have hits in the UK through the 1980s. His original backing group was *the Shadows* (1958–68 and later re-formed).

Richard /ˈrɪtʃəd/ three kings of England:

Richard I *the Lionheart* (French *Coeur-de-Lion*) 1157–1199. King of England from 1189. He was the third son of Henry II, against whom he twice rebelled. In the third ◊Crusade 1191–92 he won victories at Cyprus, Acre, and Arsuf (against ◊Saladin), but failed to recover Jerusalem. While returning overland he was captured by the Duke of Austria, who handed him over to the emperor Henry VI, and he was held prisoner until a large ransom was raised. His later years were spent in warfare in France, and he was killed while besieging Châlus. Himself a poet, he became a hero of legends after his death. He was succeeded by his brother John.

Richard II 1367–1400. King of England from 1377, effectively from 1389, son of Edward the Black Prince. He reigned in conflict with Parliament; they executed some of his associates 1388 and he some of the opposing barons 1397, whereupon he made himself absolute. Two years later, forced to abdicate in favour of ◊Henry IV, he was jailed and probably assassinated.

Richard was born in Bordeaux. He succeeded his grandfather Edward III when only ten, the government being in the hands of a council of regency. His fondness for favourites resulted in conflicts with Parliament, and in 1388 the baronial party headed by the Duke of Gloucester had many of his friends executed. Richard recovered control 1389, and ruled moderately until 1397, when he had Gloucester murdered and his other leading opponents executed or banished, and assumed absolute power. In 1399 his cousin Henry Bolingbroke, Duke of Hereford (later Henry IV), returned from exile to lead a revolt; Richard II was deposed by Parliament and imprisoned in Pontefract Castle, where he died mysteriously.

Richard III 1452–1485. King of England from 1483. The son of Richard, Duke of York, he was created duke of Gloucester by his brother Edward IV, and distinguished himself in the Wars of the ◊Roses. On Edward's death 1483 he became protector to his nephew Edward V, and soon secured the crown on the plea that Edward IV's sons were illegitimate. He proved a capable ruler, but the suspicion that he had murdered Edward V and his brother undermined his popularity. In 1485 Henry, Earl of Richmond (later ◊Henry VII), raised a rebellion, and Richard III was defeated and killed at ◊Bosworth. Scholars now tend to minimize the evidence for his crimes as Tudor propaganda.

Richard of Wallingford /ˈrɪtʃəd/ 1292–1335. English mathematician, abbot of St Albans from 1326. He was a pioneer of trigonometry, and designed measuring instruments.

Richards /ˈrɪtʃədz/ Frank. Pen name of Charles Harold St John Hamilton 1875–1961. English writer for the children's papers *Magnet* and *Gem*, who invented Greyfriars public school and the fat boy Billy Bunter.

Richards /ˈrɪtʃədz/ Gordon 1905–1986. English jockey who was champion on the flat a record 26 times 1925–1953.

He started riding 1920 and rode 4,870 winners from 21,834 mounts before retiring 1954 and taking up training. He rode the winners of all the classic races but only once won the ◊Derby on Pinza 1953. In 1947 he rode a record 269 winners in a season and in 1933 at Nottingham/Chepstow he rode 11 consecutive winners.

CAREER HIGHLIGHTS

Derby: 1953
Oaks: 1930, 1942
St Leger 1930, 1937, 1940, 1942, 1944
1,000 Guineas: 1942, 1948, 1951
2,000 Guineas: 1938, 1942, 1947
Champion Jockey: 1925, 1927–29, 1931–40, 1942–53

Richards /ˈrɪtʃədz/ I(vor) A(rmstrong) 1893–1979. English literary critic. He collaborated with C K ◊Ogden and wrote *Principles of Literary Criticism* 1924. In 1939 he went to Harvard, USA, where he taught detailed attention to the text and had a strong influence on contemporary US literary criticism.

Richards /ˈrɪtʃədz/ Theodore 1868–1928. US chemist. Working at Harvard University, Boston, for much of his career, Richards concentrated upon determining as accurately as possible the atomic weights of a large number of elements. He was awarded the 1914 Nobel Chemistry Prize.

Richardson /ˈrɪtʃədsən/ Dorothy 1873–1957. English novelist whose works were collected under the title *Pilgrimage* 1938. She used the 'stream of consciousness' technique to great effect and has been linked with Virginia ◊Woolf in creating a specifically feminine genre. Woolf credited her as having invented 'the psychological sentence of the feminine gender'.

Richardson /ˈrɪtʃədsən/ Harry Hobson 1838–1886. US architect, who designed buildings in a Romanesque style derived from that of N Spain. He had a strong influence on Louis ◊Sullivan.

Richardson /ˈrɪtʃədsən/ Henry Handel. Pen name of Ethel Henrietta Richardson 1880–1946. Australian novelist. Born in Melbourne, she left Australia when only 18. Her work *The Fortunes of Richard Mahony* 1917–29 reflects her father's life.

Richardson /ˈrɪtʃədsən/ Owen Williams 1879–1959. British physicist. He studied the emission of electricity from hot bodies, giving the name ◊thermionics to the subject. At Cambridge, he worked under J J ◊Thomson in the Cavendish Laboratory, and received a Nobel prize 1928.

Richardson /ˈrɪtʃədsən/ Ralph (David) 1902–1983. English actor. He played many stage parts, including Falstaff (Shakespeare), Peer Gynt (Ibsen), and Cyrano de Bergerac (Rostand). He shared the management of the Old Vic theatre with Laurence Olivier 1944–50.

Later stage successes include *Home* 1970 and *No Man's Land* 1976. His films include *Things to*

Richard III Portrait by an unknown artist (c. 1518–23) Royal Collection, Windsor.

Richelieu *A triple portrait of Cardinal Richelieu by Philippe de Champaigne. An inscription on the back says that it was painted for the use of the sculptor Franchesco Mochi in Rome and the right-hand profile is marked as 'the better of the two'.*

Come 1936, *Richard III* 1956, *Our Man in Havana* 1959, *The Wrong Box* 1966, *The Bed Sitting Room* 1969, and *O Lucky Man!* 1973.

Richardson /ˈrɪtʃədsən/ Samuel 1689–1761. English novelist, one of the founders of the modern novel. *Pamela* 1740–41, written in the form of a series of letters, and containing much dramatic conversation, achieved a sensational vogue all across Europe, and was followed by *Clarissa* 1747–48, and *Sir Charles Grandison* 1753–54.

Born in Derbyshire, he was brought up in London and apprenticed to a printer. He set up his own business in London 1719, becoming printer to the House of Commons. All his six young children died, followed by his wife 1731, which permanently affected his health.

Richardson /ˈrɪtʃədsən/ Tony 1928– . English director and producer. With George Devine he established the English Stage Company 1955 at the Royal Court Theatre, with productions such as *Look Back in Anger* 1956. His films include *Saturday Night and Sunday Morning* 1960, *A Taste of Honey* 1961, *Tom Jones* 1963, *Dead Cert* 1974, and *Joseph Andrews* 1977. He is the father of the actress Natasha Richardson.

Richborough /ˈrɪtʃbərə/ (Roman *Rutupiae*) former port in Kent, England; now marooned in salt marshes, it was militarily reactivated in both world wars.

Richelieu /ˈriːʃljɜː/ Armand Jean du Plessis de 1585–1642. French cardinal and politician, chief minister from 1624. He aimed to make the monarchy absolute; he ruthlessly crushed opposition by the nobility, and destroyed the political power of the ◊Huguenots, while leaving them religious freedom. Abroad he sought to establish French supremacy by breaking the power of the Habsburgs; he therefore supported the Swedish king Gustavus Adolphus and the German Protestant princes against Austria, and in 1635 brought France into the Thirty Years' War.

Born in Paris of a noble family, he entered the church, and was created bishop of Luçon 1606 and a cardinal 1622. Through the influence of ◊Marie de' Medici he became ◊Louis XIII's chief minister 1624, a position he retained until his death. His secretary Père ◊Joseph was the original Grey Eminence.

Richler /ˈrɪtʃlə/ Mordecai 1931– . Canadian novelist, born in Montreal. His novels, written in a witty, acerbic style, include *The Apprenticeship of Duddy Kravitz* 1959 and *St Urbain's Horseman* 1971.

Richmond /ˈrɪtʃmənd/ capital of Virginia, USA; population (1980) 219,000. It is the centre of the Virginian tobacco trade. It was the capital of the ◊Confederacy 1861–65, and a museum commemorates the writer Edgar Allan Poe, who grew up here.

Richmond /ˈrɪtʃmənd/ town in N Yorkshire, England; population (1971) 7,245. It has a theatre built 1788.

Richmond-upon-Thames /ˈrɪtʃmənd əpɒn ˈtemz/ borough of SW Greater London

features Hampton Garrick Villa; Old Court House (the architect Wren's last home), Faraday House; Hampton Court Palace and Bushy Park;

Kew outhoused departments of the Public Record Office; Kew Palace (former royal residence), within the Royal Botanic Gardens;

Richmond gatehouse of former Richmond Palace (see Henry VIII and Elizabeth I), Richmond Hill and Richmond Park (including White Lodge, home of the Royal Ballet School); Ham House (17th century); *Teddington* highest tidal point of the Thames; National Physical Laboratory;

Twickenham Kneller Hall (Royal Military School of Music); Marble Hill House (Palladian home of the Duchess of Suffolk, mistress of George II); Strawberry Hill (home of Horace Walpole); Twickenham Rugby Ground; Alexander Pope is buried in the church;

population (1981) 157,867.

Richter /ˈrɪktə/ Burton 1931– . US high energy physicist who, in the 1960s, designed the Stanford Positron Accelerating Ring (SPEAR). In 1974 Richter used SPEAR to produce a new particle, later named the ψ (psi) particle, thought to be formed from the charmed quark postulated by Sheldon ◊Glashow. Richter shared the 1976 Nobel Physics Prize with Samuel ◊Ting.

Richter /ˈrɪktə/ Charles Francis 1900–1985. US seismologist, deviser of the ◊Richter scale used to measure the strength of the waves from earthquakes.

Richter /ˈrɪʃtə/ Johann Paul Friedrich 1763–1825. German author, commonly known as Jean Paul. He created a series of comic eccentrics in works such as the romance *Titan* 1800–03 and *Die Flegeljahre/The Awkward Age* 1804–05.

Richter /ˈrɪxtə/ Sviatoslav (Teofilovich) 1915– . Russian pianist, an outstanding interpreter of Schubert, Schumann, Rachmaninov, and Prokofiev.

Richter scale scale based on measurement of seismic waves, used to determine the magnitude of an ◊earthquake at the epicentre. The magnitude of an earthquake differs from the intensity, measured by the ◊Mercalli scale, which is subjective and varies from place to place for the same earthquake.

The magnitude is a function of the total amount of energy released, and each point on the Richter scale represents a tenfold increase in energy over the previous point. It is named after US seismologist, Charles Richter.

Richthofen /ˈrɪʃthəʊfən/ Ferdinand Baron von 1833–1905. German geographer and traveller who carried out extensive studies in China 1867–70 and subsequently explored Java, Thailand, Myanmar (Burma), Japan, and California.

Richthofen *German air ace Baron von Richthofen (centre) during World War I with his 11th Chasing Squadron, 'Richthofen's Flying Circus'.*

Richthofen /ˈrɪʃthəʊfən/ Manfred, Freiherr von (the 'Red Baron') 1892–1918. German aviator. In World War I he commanded the 11th Chasing Squadron, known as *Richthofen's Flying Circus*, and shot down 80 aircraft before being killed in action.

ricin an extremely toxic extract from the seeds of the ◊castor oil plant. When combined with ◊monoclonal antibodies, ricin can attack cancer cells, particularly in the treatment of lymphoma and leukaemia. Ricin was used to assassinate the Bulgarian dissident Georgi Markov in London 1978.

rickets defective growth of bone in children due to lack of vitamin D. The bones, which do not harden adequately, are bent out of shape. Renal rickets, also a condition of malformed bone, is associated with kidney disease.

Ridgeway, the grassy track dating from prehistoric times that runs along the Berkshire Downs in S England from White Horse Hill to near Streatley.

Riding /ˈraɪdɪŋ/ Laura 1901– . US poet, a member of the Fugitive Group of poets, which flourished in the Southern US 1915–28. She went to England in 1926 and worked with the writer Robert Graves. She published her *Collected Poems* in 1938 wrote no more verse, but turned to linguistics in order to analyse the expression of 'truth'.

Ridley /ˈrɪdli/ Nicholas *c.*1500–1555. English Protestant bishop. He became chaplain to Henry VIII 1541, and bishop of London 1550. He took an active part in the Reformation and supported Lady Jane Grey's claim to the throne. After Mary's accession he was arrested and burned as a heretic.

Ridley /ˈrɪdli/ Nicholas 1929– . British Conservative politician, and cabinet minister. After a period in industry he became active as a 'dry' right winger in the Conservative Party: a 'Thatcherite' before Margaret ◊Thatcher had brought the term to public attention. He served under Harold Macmillan, Edward Heath and Alec Douglas-Home, but did not become a member of the cabinet until 1983. His apparent disdain for public opinion caused his transfer, in 1989, from the politically sensitive Department of the Environment to that of Trade and Industry.

Rie /riː/ Lucie 1902– . Austrian-born potter who worked in England from the 1930s. Her pottery, exhibited all over the world, is simple and pure in form, showing a debt to Bernard ◊Leach.

Riefenstahl /ˈriːfənʃtaːl/ Leni 1902– . German filmmaker. Her film of the Nazi rallies at Nuremberg *Triumph des Willens/Triumph of the Will* 1934, vividly illustrated Hitler's charismatic appeal but tainted her career. After World War II her work was blacklisted by the Allies until 1952.

She trained as a dancer, appearing in films in the 1920s, but in the early 1930s formed her own production company, and directed and starred in *Das blaue Licht/The Blue Light* 1932. She also made a two-part documentary of the 1936 Berlin Olympics (*Olympiad: Fest der Volker/Festival of the Nations* and *Olympiad: Fest der Schönheit/Festival of Beauty*). Unable to pursue her film career after being blacklisted, she turned to photography, and is known for the volumes of photographs that have come out of her visits to Africa, such as *The Last of the Nuba* 1973 and *Mein Afrika/My Africa* 1982.

Riel /riˈel/ Louis 1844–1885. French-Canadian rebel, a champion of the Métis (an Indian-French people); he established a provisional government in Winnipeg in an unsuccessful revolt 1869–70 and was hanged for treason after leading a second revolt in Saskatchewan 1885.

Riemann /ˈriːmæn/ Georg Friedrich Bernhard 1826–1866. German mathematician whose system of non-Euclidean geometry, thought at the time to be a mere mathematical curiosity, was used by Einstein to develop his General Theory of ◊Relativity.

Rienzi /riˈenzi/ Cola di *c.* 1313–1354. Italian political reformer. In 1347, he tried to re-establish the forms of an ancient Roman republic. His second attempt seven years later ended with his assassination.

rift valley

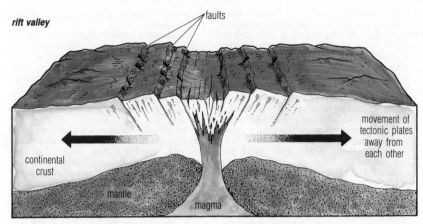

faults

movement of tectonic plates away from each other

continental crust

mantle

magma

Riesman /ˈriːsmən/ David 1909– . US sociologist, author of *The Lonely Crowd: A Study of the Changing American Character* 1950.

Rietvelt /ˈriːtfelt/ Gerrit Thomas 1888–1964. Dutch architect, an exponent of De ◊Stijl. He designed the Schroeder House at Utrecht 1924; he is also well known for colourful, minimalist chair design.

Rif, Er /rɪf/ mountain range about 290 km/180 mi long on the Mediterranean seaboard of Morocco.

Riff ◊Berber people of N Morocco, who under ◊Abd el-Krim long resisted the Spaniards and French.

rifle a ◊firearm that has spiral grooves (rifling) in its barrel. When a bullet is fired, the rifling makes it spin, thereby improving accuracy. Rifled guns came into use in the 16th century.

rift valley valley formed by the subsidence of a block of the Earth's ◊crust between two or more parallel ◊faults. Rift valleys are steep-sided and form where the crust is being pulled apart, as at ◊ocean ridges, or in the Great ◊Rift Valley of E Africa.

Rift Valley, Great /rɪft/ volcanic valley formed 10–20 million years ago by a crack in the Earth's crust, and running about 6,400 km/4,000 mi from the Jordan valley in Syria through the Red Sea to Mozambique in SE Africa. At some points its traces have been lost by erosion, but elsewhere such as S Kenya, cliffs rise thousands of metres. It is marked by a series of lakes, including Lake Turkana (formerly Lake Rudolph) and volcanoes, such as Mount Kilimanjaro.

Rift Valley fever virus disease originating south of the Sahara. Hosted by sheep and cattle, it is spread by mosquitoes, and a virulent strain reached Egypt 1977.

Riga /ˈriːgə/ capital and port of Latvian Republic, USSR; population (1987) 900,000. A member of the ◊Hanseatic League from 1282, Riga has belonged in turn to Poland 1582, Sweden 1621, and Russia 1710. It was the capital of independent Latvia 1918–40, and was occupied by Germany 1941–44, before being annexed by the USSR.

Rigaud /ˈriːgəʊ/ Hyacinthe 1659–1743. French portraitist, court painter to Louis XIV from 1688. His portrait of *Louis XIV* 1701 (Louvre, Paris) is characteristically majestic, with the elegant figure of the king enveloped in ermine and drapery.

Richter scale

value	relative amount of energy released	examples
1		
2		
3		
4	1	Carlisle, 1979
5	30	San Francisco, 1979 New England, 1979 Wrexham, Wales 1990
6	100	San Fernando, 1971
7	30,000	Chimbote, 1970 San Francisco, 1989
8	1,000,000	Tangshan, 1976 San Francisco, 1906 Lisbon, 1755 Alaska, 1964

Rigel the brightest star in the constellation Orion. It is a blue-white supergiant, with an estimated diameter of over 50 Suns. It is 900 light years away, and is 50,000 times more luminous than our Sun. It is the seventh-brightest star in the sky.

Rigg /rɪg/ Diana 1938– . English actress. Her stage roles include Héloïse in *Abelard and Héloïse* 1970, and television roles include Emma Peel in *The Avengers* 1965–67 and Lady Deadlock in *Bleak House* 1985. She became the hostess for *Mystery Theater* on US public TV 1989.

right-angled triangle a triangle in which one of the angles is a right angle (90°). It is the basic form of triangle for defining trigonometrical ratios (for example, sine, cosine, and tangent) and for which ◊Pythagoras' theorem holds true. The longest side of a right-angled triangle is called the hypotenuse.

Its area is equal to half the product of the lengths of the two shorter sides. A triangle constructed with its hypotenuse as the diameter of a circle with its opposite vertex (corner) on the circumference is a right-angled triangle. This is a fundamental theorem in geometry, first credited to the Greek mathematician Thales about 580 BC.

right ascension in astronomy, the coordinate on the ◊celestial sphere that corresponds to longitude on the surface of the Earth. It is measured in hours, minutes, and seconds eastwards from the point where the Sun's path, the ecliptic, intersects the celestial equator; this point is called the **vernal equinox**.

right of way the right to pass over land belonging to another, such as a public right of way which can be: a footpath; bridlepath, with horses permitted; or road, where vehicles are permitted. Other rights of way are licences (where personal permission is given) and ◊easements. In English law public rights of way are acquired by long use, by specific grant, or by statute. They are shown in definitive maps (which are conclusive evidence of the existence of the rights of way) maintained by the relevant local authority.

rights issue in finance, new shares offered to existing shareholders to raise new capital. Shareholders receive a discount on the market price while the company benefits from not having the costs of a re-launch of the new issue.

The amount of shares offered depends on the capital the company needs. In a 'one for one rights issue', a shareholder is offered one share for each that he already holds. For companies this is the cheapest way of raising more capital.

Rights of Man and the Citizen, Declaration of historic French document. According to the statement of the French National Assembly 1789, it provides for: representation in the legislature; equality before the law; equality of opportunity; freedom from arbitrary imprisonment; freedom of speech and religion; taxation in proportion to ability to pay; and security of property. In 1946 were added equal rights for women; right to work, join a union, and strike; leisure, social security, and support in old age; and free education.

right wing the more conservative or reactionary section of a political party or spectrum. It originated in the French national assembly 1789, where the nobles sat in the place of honour on the president's right, whereas the commons were on his left (hence ◊left wing).

Rigi /ˈriːgi/ mountain in central Switzerland, between lakes Lauerz, Lucerne, and Zug; height 1,800 m/5,908 ft.

rigor the medical term for shivering. *Rigor mortis* is the stiffness which ensues in a corpse soon after death.

Rigveda the oldest of the ◊Vedas, the chief sacred writings of Hinduism. It consists of hymns to the Aryan gods, such as Indra, and to nature gods.

Rijeka /riˈekə/ industrial port (oil refining, distilling, paper, tobacco, chemicals) in NW Yugoslavia; population (1983) 193,044.

history It has changed hands many times, and after being seized by Gabriele ◊d'Annunzio 1919, was annexed by Italy 1924 (Italian *Fiume*). It was ceded back to Yugoslavia 1949.

Riley /ˈraɪli/ Bridget (Louise) 1931– . British Op art painter. In the early 1960s she invented her characteristic style, arranging hard-edged black-and-white dots or lines in regular patterns that created disturbing effects of scintillating light and movement. *Fission* 1963 (Museum of Modern Art, New York) is an example of this style. She introduced colour in the late 1960s and experimented with silk-screen prints on Plexiglas.

Rilke /ˈrɪlkə/ Rainer Maria 1875–1926. Austrian writer, born in Prague. His prose works include the semi-autobiographical *Die Aufzeichnungen des Malte Laurids Brigge/Notebook of Malte Laurids Brigge* 1910, and his poetical works *Die Sonnette an Orpheus/Sonnets to Orpheus* 1923 and *Duisener Elegien/Duino Elegies* 1923. His verse is characterized by a form of mystic pantheism that seeks to achieve a state of ecstasy in which existence can be apprehended as a whole.

Rimbaud /ˈræmbəʊ/ (Jean Nicolas) Arthur 1854–1891. French Symbolist poet. His verse was chiefly written before the age of 20 notably *Les Illuminations* published 1886. From 1871 he lived with ◊Verlaine. Although the association ended after Verlaine attempted to shoot him, it was Verlaine's analysis of Rimbaud's work 1884 that first brought him recognition. Rimbaud then travelled widely, working as a trader in N Africa 1880–91.

Rimini /ˈrɪmɪni/ industrial port (pasta, footwear, textiles, furniture) and holiday resort in Emilia-Romagna, Italy; population (1988) 131,000.

Its name in Roman times was *Ariminum*, and it was the terminus of the Flaminian Way from Rome. In World War II it formed the eastern strongpoint of the German 'Gothic' defence line, and was badly damaged in the severe fighting Sept 1944, when it was taken by the Allies.

Rimsky-Korsakov /ˈrɪmski ˈkɔːsəkɒf/ Nikolay Andreyevich 1844–1908. Russian composer. He used Russian folk idiom and rhythms in his Romantic compositions and published a text on orchestration. His operas include *The Maid of Pskov* 1873, *The Snow Maiden* 1882, *Mozart and Salieri* 1898, and *The Golden Cockerel* 1907, a satirical attack on despotism that was banned until 1909.

Other works include the symphonic poem *Sadko* 1867, the programme symphony *Antar* 1869, and the symphonic suite *Scheherazade* 1888. He also completed works by other composers, for example, ◊Mussorgsky's *Boris Godunov*.

rinderpest viral form of cattle diarrhoea which can be fatal. Almost eliminated in the 1960s, it revived in Africa in the 1980s.

Rineanna /ˈrɪnjənə/ the Irish name of Shannon Airport, County Clare.

ring circuit a household electrical circuit in which appliances are connected in series to form a ring with each end of the ring connected to the power supply.

ring ouzel see ◊ousel.

Río de Janeiro The Sugar Loaf peak in Rio de Janeiro.

ringworm a fungus infection of the skin, usually of the scalp and feet (athlete's foot). It is treated with ◊antifungal preparations.

Rintelen /ˈrɪntələn/ Fritz von. German spy. He led a spy ring in the USA during World War I, sabotaging the shipment of Allied munitions until captured in 1915.

Rinzai (Chinese **Lin-ch'i**) a school of Zen Buddhism introduced to Japan from China in the 12th century by the monk Eisai and others. It emphasizes rigorous monastic discipline and sudden enlightenment by meditation on a *kōan* (paradoxical question).

Río de Janeiro /ˈriːəʊ də ʒəˈnɪərəʊ/ port and resort in Brazil; population (1980) 5,091,000, metropolitan area 10,217,000. The name commemorates the arrival of Portuguese explorers 1 Jan 1502, but there is in fact no river. Sugar Loaf Mountain stands at the entrance to the harbour. It was the capital of Brazil 1822–1960.

Some colonial churches and other buildings survive; there are modern boulevards, including the Avenida Rio Branco, and Copacabana is a luxurious beachside suburb.

Rio de Oro /ˈriːəʊ deɪ ˈɔːrəʊ/ former district in the south of the province of Spanish ◊Sahara. See ◊Western Sahara.

Río Grande /ˈriːəʊ ˈɡrændi/ river rising in the Rockies in S Colorado, USA, and flowing south to the Gulf of Mexico, where it is reduced to a trickle by irrigation demands on its upper reaches; length 3,050 km/1,900 mi. Its last 2,400 km/1,500 mi form the US-Mexican border.

Rio Grande do Norte /ˈriːuː ˈɡrʌndi duː ˈnɔːti/ state of NE Brazil; capital Natal; area 53,000 sq km/20,460 sq mi; population (1980) 1,900,750.

Riom /riˈɒm/ town on the river Ambène, in the Puy-de-Dôme *département* of central France. In World War II, it was the scene Feb–Apr 1942 of the 'war guilt' trials of several prominent Frenchmen by the ◊Vichy government. The accused included the former prime ministers ◊Blum and ◊Daladier, and Gen ◊Gamelin. The occasion turned into a wrangle over the reasons for French unpreparedness for war, and at the German dictator Hitler's instigation, the court was dissolved. The defendants remained in prison until released by the Allies 1945.

Río Muni /ˈriːəʊ ˈmuːni/ the mainland portion of ◊Equatorial Guinea.

Río Negro /ˈriːəʊ ˈneɪɡrəʊ/ river in South America, rising in E Colombia and joining the Amazon at Manáus, Brazil; length 2,250 km/1,400 mi.

Riopelle /ˌriːəʊˈpel/ Jean Paul 1923– . Canadian artist, active in Paris from 1946. In the 1950s he developed an Abstract Expressionist style and produced colourful impasto (with paint applied in a thick mass) paintings and sculptures. *Encounter*

1956 (Wallraf-Richartz Museum, Cologne, West Germany) is a typically rough-textured canvas.

riot disturbance caused by a potentially violent mob. In the UK, riots formerly suppressed under the ◊Riot Act are now governed by the Public Order Act 1986, which created a range of statutory offences (most of which were previously common law offences): riot, violent disorder (similar to riot but requiring only three people and no common purpose), affray (fights), threatening behaviour (shouting abuse), and disorderly conduct (minor acts of hooliganism). Methods of riot control include plastic bullets, stun bags (soft canvas pouches filled with buckshot which spread out in flight), water cannon, and CS gas (tear gas).

The UK Public Order Act was instituted in response to several inner-city riots in the early 1980s, and it greatly extends police powers to control marches and demonstrations by rerouting them, restricting their size and duration, or by making arrests. Under the Act a person is guilty of riot if in a crowd of 12 or more, threatening violence; the maximum sentence is ten years' imprisonment.

Riots in Britain include the Spitalfields weavers's riot 1736, the ◊Gordon riots 1780, the Newport riots 1839, and riots over the Reform Bill in Hyde Park, London, 1866; in the 1980s inner-city riots occurred in Toxteth, Liverpool; St Paul's, Bristol; Broadwater Farm, Tottenham, and Brixton, London; and in 1990 rioting took place in London and several other cities after demonstrations against the ◊poll tax.

Riot Act in the UK, an act passed 1714 to suppress the ◊Jacobite disorders. If three or more persons assembled unlawfully to the disturbance of the public peace, a magistrate could read a proclamation ordering them to disperse ('reading the Riot Act'), after which they might be dispersed by force. It was superseded by the 1986 ◊Public Order Act.

Río Tinto /ˈriːəʊ ˈtɪntəʊ/ town in Andalusia, Spain; population (1983) 8,400. Its copper mines, first exploited by the Phoenicians, are now almost worked out.

river

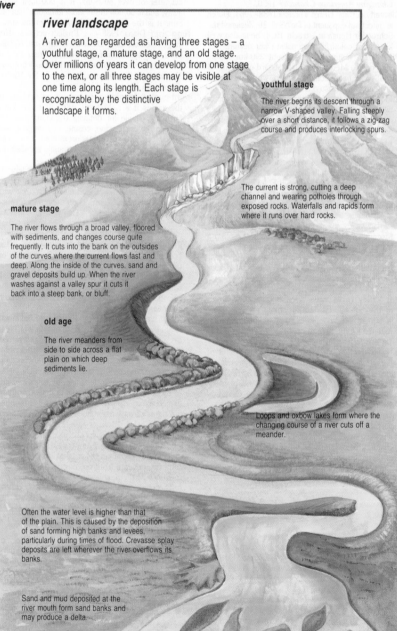

river landscape

A river can be regarded as having three stages – a youthful stage, a mature stage, and an old stage. Over millions of years it can develop from one stage to the next, or all three stages may be visible at one time along its length. Each stage is recognizable by the distinctive landscape it forms.

youthful stage

The river begins its descent through a narrow V-shaped valley. Falling steeply over a short distance, it follows a zig-zag course and produces interlocking spurs.

The current is strong, cutting a deep channel and wearing potholes through exposed rocks. Waterfalls and rapids form where it runs over hard rocks.

mature stage

The river flows through a broad valley, floored with sediments, and changes course quite frequently. It cuts into the bank on the outsides of the curves where the current flows fast and deep. Along the inside of the curves, sand and gravel deposits build up. When the river washes against a valley spur it cuts it back into a steep bank, or bluff.

old age

The river meanders from side to side across a flat plain on which deep sediments lie.

Loops and oxbow lakes form where the changing course of a river cuts off a meander.

Often the water level is higher than that of the plain. This is caused by the deposition of sand forming high banks and levees, particularly during times of flood. Crevasse splay deposits are left wherever the river overflows its banks.

Sand and mud deposited at the river mouth form sand banks and may produce a delta.

Major rivers

Name and location	km	mi
Nile (NE Africa)	6,695	4,160
Amazon (South America)	6,570	4,080
Chiang Jiang (China)	6,300	3,900
Mississippi-Missouri (USA)	6,020	3,740
Ob-Irtysh (USSR)	5,600	3,480
Huang He (China)	5,464	3,395
Zaïre (Africa)	4,500	2,800
Mekong (Asia)	4,425	2,750
Amur (Asia)	4,416	2,744
Lena (USSR)	4,400	2,730
Mackenzie (Canada)	4,241	2,635
Niger (Africa)	4,185	2,600
Yenisei (USSR)	4,100	2,550
Mississippi (USA)	3,779	2,348
Madeira (Brazil)	3,240	2,013
Sao Francisco (Brazil)	3,199	1,988
Yukon (USA)	3,185	1,979
Indus (Tibet/Pakistan)	3,180	1,975
Rio Grande (USA/Mexico)	3,050	1,900
Purus (Brazil)	2,993	1,860
Parana (Brazil)	2,940	1,827
Danube (Europe)	2,858	1,776
Brahmaputra (Asia)	2,850	1,770
Japura (Brazil)	2,816	1,750
Salween (Burma/China)	2,816	1,750
Euphrates (Iraq)	2,735	1,700
Tocantins (Brazil)	2,699	1,677
Zambezi (Africa)	2,650	1,650
Paraguay (Paraguay)	2,591	1,610
Orinoco (Venezuela)	2,600	1,600
Amu-Dar'ya (USSR)	2,540	1,578
Murray (SE Australia)	2,520	1,566
Ganges (India/Bangladesh)	2,510	1,560

RIP abbreviation for *requiescat in pace* (Latin 'may he/she rest in peace').

Ripon /'rɪpən/ city and market town in N Yorkshire, England; population (1981) 11,952. There is a cathedral 1154–1520; and the nearby 12th-century ruins of Fountains Abbey are among the finest monastic ruins in Europe.

ripple tank in physics, a shallow water-filled tray used to demonstrate various properties of waves, such as reflection, refraction, diffraction, and interference.

Rip Van Winkle legendary US character invented by Washington Irving in his 1819 tale of a man who falls into a magical 20-year sleep, and wakes to find he has slumbered through the War of Independence.

RISC (*r*educed *i*nstruction-*s*et *c*omputer) in computing, a kind of processor on a single silicon chip that is faster and more powerful than others in common use today. By reducing the range of operations the processor can carry out, the chips are able to optimize those operations to execute more quickly. Computers based on RISC chips became commercially available in the late 1980s but are less widespread than traditional processors.

risk capital or *venture capital* finance provided by venture capital companies, individuals, and merchant banks, for medium or long-term business ventures which are not their own, and in which there is a strong element of risk. In recent years, there has been a large growth in the number of UK companies specializing in providing venture capital.

Risorgimento movement for Italian national unity and independence from 1815. Uprisings failed 1848–49, but with French help, a war against Austria, including the Battle of Solferino 1859, led to the foundation of an Italian kingdom 1861. Unification was finally completed with the addition of Venetia 1866 and the Papal States 1870. Leading figures in the movement included ◊Cavour, ◊Mazzini, and ◊Garibaldi.

Ritter /'rɪtə/ (Woodward Maurice) 'Tex' 1905–1974. US singer and actor, popular as a singing cowboy in 'B' films in the 1930s and 1940s. He sang the title song to *High Noon* 1952, and his other films include *Sing Cowboy Sing* 1937 and *Arizona Trail* 1943.

ritualization in ethology, the stereotype that occurs in certain behaviour patterns when these are incorporated into displays. For example, the exaggerated and stylized head toss of the golden-eye drake during courtship is a ritualization of the bathing movement used to wet the feathers; its duration and form have become fixed. Ritualization may make displays clearly recognizable, so ensuring that individuals mate only with members of their own species.

Riva del Garda /'riːvə del 'gɑːdə/ town on Lake Garda, Italy, where the Prix Italia broadcasting festival has been held since 1948.

river long water course that flows down a slope along a bed between banks.

It originates at a point called its *source*, and enters a sea or lake at its *mouth*. Along its length it may be joined by smaller rivers called *tributaries*. A river and its tributaries form a *river system*.

Rivera /rɪ'veərə/ Diego 1886–1957. Mexican painter, active in Europe until 1921. He received many public commissions for murals exalting the Mexican revolution. A vast cycle on historical themes (National Palace, Mexico City) was begun 1929. In the 1930s he visited the USA and produced murals in the Rockefeller Center, New York (later overpainted because he included a portrait of Lenin).

Rivera /rɪ'veərə/ Primo de. Spanish politician; see ◊Primo de Rivera.

river blindness or *onchocerciasis* a type of blindness (caused by a parasitic worm) prevalent in Third World countries.

Riverina /ˌrɪvə'riːnə/ district of New South Wales, Australia, between the Lachlan and Murray rivers, through which runs the Murrumbidgee. On fertile land, artificially irrigated from the three rivers, wool, wheat, and fruit are produced.

Riverside /'rɪvəsaɪd/ city in California, USA, on the Santa Ana river east of Los Angeles; population (1980) 170,500. Founded 1870. It is the centre of a citrus-growing district and has a citrus research station: the seedless orange was developed at Riverside in 1873.

riveting a method of joining metal plates. A metal pin called a rivet, which has a head at one end, is inserted into matching holes in two overlapping plates and then the other end is struck and formed into another head, holding the plates tight. Riveting is used in building construction, boilermaking, and shipbuilding.

Riviera /ˌrɪvi'eərə/ the Mediterranean coast of France and Italy from Marseille to La Spezia. The most exclusive section, with the finest climate, is the ◊Côte d'Azur, Menton–St Tropez, which includes Monaco. It has the highest property prices in the world.

Rix /rɪks/ Brian 1924– . British actor and manager. He became known for his series of farces at London's Whitehall Theatre, notably *Dry Rot* 1954–58. He made several films for cinema and television, including *A Roof Over My Head* 1977, and is responsible for promoting mentally handicapped charities.

Riyadh /'riːæd/ (Arabic *Ar Riyad*) capital of Saudi Arabia and of the Central Province, formerly the sultanate of Nejd, in an oasis, connected by rail with Damman on the Arabian Gulf; population (1986) 1,500,000. Outside the city are date gardens irrigated from deep wells. There is a large royal palace, and Islamic university 1950.

Rizzio /'rɪtsɪəʊ/ David 1533–1566. Italian adventurer at the court of Mary, Queen of Scots. After her marriage to ◊Darnley, Rizzio's influence over her incited her husband's jealousy, and he was murdered by Darnley and his friends.

RKO Radio Keith Orpheum US film production and distribution company, formed 1928 as a result of a series of mergers and acquisitions. It was the most financially unstable of the major Hollywood studios, despite the success of many of its films, including *King Kong* 1933 and the series of musicals starring Fred Astaire and Ginger Rogers. In 1948, Howard ◊Hughes bought the studio and

accelerated its decline through poor management. The company ceased production 1953.

RN abbreviation for *Royal Navy*; see under ◊navy.

RNA *ribonucleic acid* nucleic acid involved in the process of translating ◊DNA, the genetic material into proteins. It is usually single-stranded, unlike DNA, and consists of a large number of nucleotides strung together, each of which comprises the sugar ribose and one of four bases (uracil, cytosine, adenine, or guanine). RNA is copied from DNA by the formation of ◊base pairs, with uracil taking the place of thymine. Although RNA is normally associated only with the process of protein synthesis, it makes up the hereditary material itself in some viruses, such as ◊retroviruses.

RNA occurs in three major forms, each with a different function in the synthesis of protein molecules. *Messenger RNA* (mRNA) acts as the template for protein synthesis. Each ◊codon (a set of three bases) on the RNA molecule is matched up with the corresponding amino acid, in accordance with the ◊genetic code. This process (translation) takes place in the ribosomes, which are made up of proteins and *ribosomal RNA* (rRNA). *Transfer RNA* (tRNA) is responsible for combining with specific amino acids, and then matching up a special 'anticodon' sequence of its own with a codon on the mRNA. This is how the genetic code is translated.

RNLI abbreviation for *Royal National Lifeboat Institution*.

roach freshwater fish *Rutilus rutilus* of N Europe, dark green above, whitish below, and with reddish lower fins. It grows to 35 cm/1.2 ft.

Roach /rəʊtʃ/ Hal 1892– . US film producer, usually of comedies, active from the 1910s to the 1940s. He worked with ◊Laurel and Hardy, and also produced films for Harold Lloyd and Charley Chase. His work includes *The Music Box* 1932, *Way Out West* 1936, and *Of Mice and Men* 1939.

roadrunner bird *Geococcyx californianus* of the ◊cuckoo family. It can run 25 kph/15 mph, and is native to the SW USA.

Roanoke /'rəʊənəʊk/ (American Indian 'shell money') industrial city (railway repairs, chemicals, steel goods, furniture, textiles) in Virginia, USA, on the Roanoke river; population (1980) 100,500. Founded in 1834 as Big Lick, it was a small village until 1881 when the repair shops of the Virginia Railway were set up here, after which it developed rapidly.

Robbe-Grillet /'rɒb griː'jeɪ/ Alain 1922– . French writer, the leading theorist of *le nouveau roman* ('the new novel'), for example his own *Les Gommes/The Erasers* 1953, *La Jalousie/Jealousy* 1957, and *Dans le labyrinthe/In the Labyrinth* 1959, which concentrates on detailed description of physical objects. He also wrote the script for the film *L'Année dernière à Marienbad/Last Year in Marienbad* 1961. Robbe-Grillet qualified as an agronomist and worked in Africa and the West Indies as a research biologist before turning to writing.

Robben Island /'rɒbɪn/ a notorious prison island in Table Bay, Cape Town, South Africa.

robbery in English law, a variety of ◊theft: stealing from the person, using force, or the threat of force, to intimidate the victim. The maximum penalty is life imprisonment.

Robbia, della /'rɒbiə/ Italian family of sculptors and architects, active in Florence. *Luca della Robbia* (1400–82) created a number of important works in

roadrunner

greater roadrunner

Florence, notably the marble *cantoria* (singing gallery) in the cathedral 1431–38 (Museo del Duomo), with lively groups of choristers. Luca also developed a characteristic style of glazed terracotta work.

Andrea della Robbia (1435–1525), Luca's nephew and pupil, and Andrea's sons continued the family business, inheriting the formula for the vitreous terracotta glaze. The blue and white medallions of foundling children 1463–66 on the Ospedale degli Innocenti, Florence, are well known. Many later works are more elaborate and highly coloured, such as the frieze 1522 on the façade of the Ospedale del Ceppo, Pistoia.

Robbins /ˈrɒbɪnz/ Jerome 1918– . US dancer and choreographer. He choreographed the musicals *The King and I* 1951, *West Side Story* 1957, and *Fiddler on the Roof* 1964. Robbins was ballet master of the New York City Ballet 1969–83, when he became joint ballet master-in-chief.

First a chorus boy on Broadway, then a soloist with the newly formed American Ballet Theater 1941–46, Robbins was associate director of the New York City Ballet 1949–59. Among his ballets are *Fancy Free* 1940 (adapted with Leonard Bernstein into the musical *On the Town* 1944). He also choreographed *Facsimile* 1946 and *The Age of Anxiety* 1950 (again with Bernstein).

Robert /ˈrɒbət/ two dukes of Normandy:

Robert I *the Devil* Duke of Normandy from 1028. He was the father of William the Conqueror, and is the hero of several romances; he was legendary for his cruelty.

Robert II *c.* 1054–1134. Eldest son of ◊William I (the Conqueror), succeeding him as duke of Normandy (but not on the English throne) 1087. His brother ◊William II ascended the English throne, and they warred until 1096, allowing Robert to take part in the First Crusade. When his other brother ◊Henry I claimed the English throne 1100, Robert contested the claim and invaded England unsuccessfully 1101. Henry invaded Normandy 1106, and captured Robert, who remained a prisoner in England until his death.

Robert /ˈrɒbət/ three kings of Scotland:

Robert I *Robert the Bruce* /bruːs/ 1274–1329. King of Scotland from 1306, and grandson of Robert de ◊Bruce. He shared in the national uprising led by William ◊Wallace, and, after Wallace's execution 1305, rose once more against Edward I of England, and was crowned at Scone 1306. He defeated Edward II at ◊Bannockburn 1314. In 1328 the treaty of Northampton recognized Scotland's independence and Robert as king.

Robert II 1316–1390. King of Scotland from 1371. He was the son of Walter (1293–1326), steward of Scotland, who married Marjory, daughter of Robert I. He was the first king of the house of Stuart.

Robert III *c.* 1340–1406. King of Scotland from 1390, son of Robert II. He was unable to control the nobles, and the government fell largely into the hands of his brother, Robert, duke of Albany (*c.* 1340–1420).

Roberts /ˈrɒbəts/ Bartholomew 1682–1722. British merchant-navy captain who joined his captors when taken by pirates in 1718. He became the most financially successful of all the sea rovers until surprised and killed in battle by the British navy.

Roberts /ˈrɒbəts/ David 1796–1864. Scottish painter whose oriental paintings were the result of several trips to the Middle East.

Roberts progressed from interior decorator to scene painter at Drury Lane Theatre, London, while making a name for himself with picturesque views of London and French cathedrals. From 1831 he travelled to Europe and the Middle East producing topographical views. Many of these were published in books including the six-volume *The Holy Land, Syria, Idumea, Arabia, Egypt & Nubia* 1842–49.

Roberts /ˈrɒbəts/ Frederick Sleigh, 1st Earl Roberts 1832–1914. British field marshal, known as 'Bobs'. During the Afghan War of 1878–80 he occupied Kabul, and during the Second South African War

Robert I *Robert I of Scotland, called Robert the Bruce, was crowned king in 1306.*

(1899–1902) he made possible the annexation of the Transvaal and Orange Free State.

Born in India, Roberts joined the Bengal Artillery in 1851, and served through the Indian Mutiny, receiving the VC, and the Abyssinian campaign of 1867–68. After serving in Afghanistan and making a victorious march to Kandahar, he became commander in chief in India 1885–93 and in Ireland 1895–99. He then received the command in South Africa, where he occupied Bloemfontein and Pretoria.

Roberts /ˈrɒbəts/ 'Tom' (Thomas William) 1856–1931. Australian painter, born in England, founder of the *Heidelberg School* which introduced Impressionism to Australia. He painted scenes of pioneering life.

Roberts arrived in Australia in 1869, returning to Europe to study 1881–85. He received official commissions, including one to paint the opening of the first Australian federal parliament, but is better known for his scenes of pioneering life.

Robertson /ˈrɒbətsən/ Thomas William 1829–1871. English dramatist. Initially an actor, he had his first success as a dramatist with *David Garrick* 1864, which set a new, realistic trend in English drama of the time; later plays included *Society* 1865 and *Caste* 1867.

Robeson /ˈrəʊbsən/ Paul 1898–1976. US bass singer and actor. He graduated from Columbia University as a lawyer, but limited opportunities for blacks led him instead to the stage. He appeared in *The Emperor Jones* 1924 and *Showboat* 1928, in which he sang 'Ol' Man River'. He played *Othello* in 1930, and his films include *Sanders of the River* 1935 and *King Solomon's Mines* 1937. An ardent advocate of black rights, he had his passport withdrawn 1950–58 because of his association with left-wing movements. He then left the USA to live in England.

Robespierre /ˈrəʊbzpjeə/ Maximilien François Marie Isidore de 1758–1794. French politician in the ◊French Revolution. As leader of the ◊Jacobins in the National Convention he supported the execution of Louis XVI and the overthrow of the ◊Girondins, and in Jul 1793 was elected to the Committee of Public Safety. A year later he was guillotined; many believe that he was a scapegoat for the Reign of ◊Terror since he only ordered 72 executions personally (see ◊terror, reign of).

Robespierre, a lawyer, was elected to the National Assembly of 1789–91. His defence of democratic principles made him popular in Paris, while his disinterestedness won him the nickname of 'the Incorruptible'. His zeal for social reform and his attacks on the excesses of the extremists made him enemies on both right and left; a conspiracy was formed against him, and in July 1794 he was

Robeson *US singer and actor Paul Robeson testifies before a committee in Washington, June 1948.*

overthrown and executed by those who actually perpetrated the Reign of Terror.

robin migratory song-bird *Erithacus rubecula* of the thrush family, found in Europe, W Asia, Africa, and the Azores. About 13 cm/5 in long, both sexes are olive brown, with a red breast. The nest is constructed in a sheltered place, and from five to seven white freckled eggs are laid. The larger North American robin belongs to the same family. In Australia members of several unrelated genera have been given the familiar name, and may have white, yellowish, or red breasts.

Robin Hood legendary English outlaw and champion of the poor against the rich. He is said to have lived in Sherwood Forest, Nottinghamshire, during the reign of Richard I (King of England 1189–99). He feuded with the Sheriff of Nottingham, accompanied by Maid Marian and a band of followers, known as his 'merry men'. He appears in ballads from the 13th century, but his first datable appearance is in Langland's *Piers Plowman* about 1377.

Robinson /ˈrɒbɪnsən/ Edward G. Stage name of Emanuel Goldenberg 1893–1973. US film actor, born in Romania, he emigrated with his family to the USA 1903. He was noted for his gangster roles, such as *Little Caesar* 1930. Other films include *Dr Ehrlich's Magic Bullet* 1940, *Double Indemnity* 1944, *The Ten Commandments* 1956, and *Soylent Green* 1973.

Robinson /ˈrɒbɪnsən/ Edwin Arlington 1869–1935. US poet. His verse, dealing mainly with psychological themes in a narrative style, includes *The Children of the Night* 1897, which established his reputation, and *The Man Who Died Twice* 1924.

Robinson /ˈrɒbɪnsən/ Henry Crabb 1775–1867. English writer, whose diaries, journals, and letters are a valuable source of information on his friends ◊Lamb, ◊Coleridge, ◊Wordsworth, and ◊Southey.

Robinson /ˈrɒbɪnsən/ Joan (Violet) 1903–1983. British economist who introduced Marxism to Keynesian economic theory. She expanded her analysis in *Economics of Perfect Competition* 1933.

Robinson /ˈrɒbɪnsən/ John Arthur Thomas 1919–1983. British Anglican cleric, bishop of Woolwich 1959–69. A left-wing Modernist, he wrote *Honest to God* 1963, which was interpreted as denying a personal God.

Robinson /ˈrɒbɪnsən/ Robert 1886–1975. English chemist, Nobel prizewinner 1947 for his research on the structure of many natural products, for example alkaloids. He formulated the electronic theory now used in organic chemistry.

Robinson /ˈrɒbɪnsən/ 'Sugar' Ray. Assumed name of Walker Smith 1920–1989. US boxer, world welterweight champion 1945–51, defending his title five times. He defeated Jake LaMotta 1951 to take the middleweight title. He lost the title six times and won it seven times. He had 202 fights, and fought until the age of 45.

robot

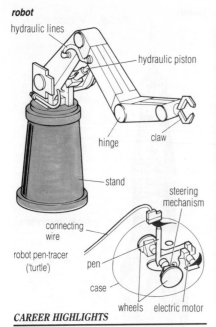

hydraulic lines

hydraulic piston

hinge   claw

stand

steering mechanism

connecting wire

robot pen-tracer ('turtle')

pen

case

wheels   electric motor

CAREER HIGHLIGHTS

Total fights: 202
Wins: 175
Draws: 6
Defeats: 19
No Contests: 2

Robinson /'rɒbɪnsən/ W(illiam) Heath 1872–1944. British cartoonist and illustrator, known for his humorous drawings of bizarre machinery for performing simple tasks, such as raising one's hat. Clumsy designs are often described as a 'Heath Robinson' contraption.

Robinson Crusoe *The Life and strange and surprising Adventures of Robinson Crusoe* a novel by Daniel Defoe, published 1719, in which the hero is shipwrecked on an island and survives for years by his own ingenuity until rescued; based on the adventures of Alexander ◊Selkirk. The book had many imitators and is the first major English novel.

robot any computer-controlled machine that can be taught or programmed to do work. The most common types are mechanical 'arms'; when fixed to the floor or a workbench, they perform functions such as paint spraying or assembling parts in factories. Others include computer-controlled

Robinson W Heath Robinson's illustration of Professor Branestawm's invention for peeling potatoes.

robot Robots welding car bodies on the assembly lines of the Mazda car plant, Hiroshima, Japan.

vehicles for carrying materials, and a miscellany of devices from cruise missiles, deep-sea and space-exploration craft to robotic toys.

Records of mechanical people and animals having been built go back more than 2000 years, bolstered by the fabulous creations of popular myth. However, it is only since the advent of the computer that the true robot has emerged.

Rob Roy /'rɒb 'rɔɪ/ nickname of Robert MacGregor 1671–1734. Scottish Highland ◊Jacobite outlaw. After losing his estates, he lived by cattle theft and extortion. Captured, he was sentenced to transportation but pardoned 1727. He is a central character in Walter Scott's historical novel *Rob Roy* 1817.

Robson /'rɒbsən/ Flora 1902–1984. English actress. Her successes included Queen Elizabeth in the film *Fire Over England* 1931 and Mrs Alving in Ibsen's *Ghosts* 1959.

Rocard /'rɒka:/ Michel 1930– . French socialist politician. A former radical, he joined the Socialist Party (PS) 1973, emerging as leader of its moderate social-democratic wing. He held ministerial office under Mitterrand 1981–85, and was appointed prime minister 1988.

Rocard trained at the prestigious École National d'Administration, where he was a classmate of Jacques Chirac. He became leader of the radical Unified Socialist Party (PSU) 1967, standing as its presidential candidate 1969.

Having gone over to the PS, he challenged Francois for the party's presidential nomination 1981. After serving as minister of planning and regional development 1981–83 and of agriculture 1983–85 in the ensuing Mitterrand administration, he resigned Apr 1985 in opposition to the government's introduction of proportional representation. In May 1988, however, as part of a strategy termed 'opening to the centre', the popular Rocard was appointed prime minister by Mitterrand.

Rochdale /'rɒtʃdeɪl/ industrial town (textiles, machinery, asbestos) in Greater Manchester, England, on the river Roch 16 km/10 mi NE of Manchester; population (1981) 92,704. The so-called Rochdale Pioneers founded the first Co-operative Society in England, in Toad Lane, Rochdale, 1844. The popular singer Gracie Fields was born here and a theatre is named after her.

Roche /'rəʊʃ/ Stephen 1959– . Irish cyclist. One of the outstanding riders on the continent in the 1980s, he was the first British winner of the Tour de France in 1987 and the first English-speaking

winner of the Tour of Italy the same year, as well as the 1987 world professional road race champion.

Rochefort /ˌrəʊʃ'fɔ:/ industrial port (metal goods, machinery) in W France, SE of La Rochelle and 15 km/9 mi from the mouth of the Charente; population (1982) 27,716. The port dates from 1666 and it was from here that Napoleon embarked for Plymouth on the *Bellerophon* on his way to final exile in 1815.

Rochelle, La /rɒ'ʃel/ see ◊La Rochelle, port in W France.

Rochester /'rɒtʃɪstə/ industrial city (flour, Kodak films and cameras) in New York State, USA, on the Genesee river south of Lake Ontario; population (1980) 970,000. Its university was founded 1850.

Rochester /'rɒtʃɪstə/ commercial centre with dairy and food-processing industries in Minnesota, USA; population (1980) 57,890. The Mayo Clinic is here.

Rochester /'rɒtʃɪstə/ John Wilmot, 2nd Earl of Rochester 1647–1680. English poet and courtier. He fought gallantly at sea against the Dutch, but chiefly led a debauched life at the court of Charles II. He wrote graceful (but often obscene) lyrics, and his *A Satire against Mankind* 1675 rivals Swift. He was patron of John Dryden.

Rochester upon Medway /'rɒtʃɪstə, 'medweɪ/ city in Kent, England; population (1983, with Chatham and Strood) 146,200. There is a 12th-century Norman castle keep, a 12th–15th-century cathedral, and many timbered buildings. A Dickens centre 1982 commemorates the town's many links with the novelist. The first borstal was near Rochester.

rochet in the Christian church, a vestment worn mainly by Catholic and Anglican bishops and abbots. The Catholic rochet reaches to the knee, while the Anglican rochet is ankle length.

rock constituent of the Earth's crust, composed of mineral particles and/or materials of organic origin consolidated into a hard mass as ◊igneous, ◊sedimentary, or ◊metamorphic rocks.

Igneous rock is made from molten lava or magma solidifying on or beneath the Earth's surface, for example, basalt, dolerite, granite, obsidian; *metamorphic rock* is formed by changes in existing igneous or sedimentary rocks under high pressure or temperature, or chemical action, for example from limestone to marble.

Rockall /'rɒkɔ:l/ British islet in the Atlantic, 24 m/80 ft across and 22 m/65 ft high, part of the Hatton-Rockall bank, and 370 km/230 mi west of North Uist in the Hebrides. The bank is part of a fragment of Greenland that broke away 60 million years ago. It is in a potentially rich oil/gas area. A party of British marines landed in 1955

Rochester The poet John Wilmot, 2nd Earl of Rochester, was a member of the profligate set at the court of Charles II. He was patron to John Dryden and is remembered for his bawdy wit.

rock climbing *Rock climbing in Scotland.*

formally to annex Rockall, but Denmark, Iceland, and Ireland challenge Britain's claims for mineral, oil, and fishing rights. The ***Rockall Trough*** between Rockall and Ireland, 250 km/155 mi wide and up to 3,000 m/10,000 ft deep, forms an ideal marine laboratory.

rock and roll a type of pop music born of a fusion of rhythm and blues and country and western, and based on electric guitar and drums. In the mid-1950s, with the death of Elvis Presley, it became the heartbeat of Western teenage rebellion. It found perhaps its purest form in late-1950s ***rockabilly***; the blanket term 'rock' later came to comprise a multitude of styles.

The term was popularized by US disc jockey Alan Freed (1922–65) from 1951. Influential rock-and-roll singers and songwriters of the 1950s included Chuck ◊Berry, Buddy ◊Holly, and Gene Vincent (1935–71).

rock climbing sport originally an integral part of mountaineering. It began as a form of training for Alpine expeditions and is now divided into three categories: the ***outcrop climb*** for climbs of up to 30 m/100 ft; the ***crag climb*** on cliffs of 30 m–300 m/100–1,000 ft, and the ***big wall climb***, which is the nearest thing to Alpine climbing, but without the hazards of snow and ice.

Rockefeller /ˈrɒkəˌfelə/ John D(avison) 1839–1937. US millionaire, founder of Standard Oil 1870 (which achieved control of 90% of US refineries by 1882). The activities of the Standard Oil Trusts led to an outcry against monopolies and the passing of the Sherman Anti-Trust Act of 1890. A lawsuit of 1892 prompted the dissolution of the Trust, only for it to be refounded in 1899 as a holding company. In 1911, this was also declared illegal by the Supreme Court.

He founded the philanthropic ***Rockefeller Foundation*** 1913, to which his son John D(avison) Rockefeller Jr (1874–1960) devoted his life.

rocket projectile driven by the reaction of gases produced by a fast-burning fuel. Unlike the jet engine, which is also a reaction engine, the rocket carries its own oxygen supply to burn its fuel and is totally independent of any surrounding atmosphere. As rockets are the only form of propulsion available which can function in a vacuum, they are essential to exploration of outer space. Multi-stage, or ◊step rockets have to be used, consisting of a number of rockets joined together. In warfare, the head of the rocket carries an explosive device.

Rockets have been valued as fireworks over the last seven centuries, but their intensive development as a means of propulsion to high altitudes, carrying payloads, started only in the inter-war years with the state-supported work in Germany (primarily by Werner ◊von Braun) and of Professor R H Goddard (1882–1945) in the USA.

Two main kinds of rockets are used: one burns liquid propellants, the other solid propellants. The fireworks rocket uses gunpowder as a solid propellant. The ◊space shuttle's solid rocket boosters use a mixture of powdered aluminium in a synthetic rubber binder. Most rockets, however, have liquid propellants, which are more powerful and easier to

control. Liquid hydrogen and kerosene are common fuels, while liquid oxygen is the most common oxygen-provider, or oxidizer. One of the biggest rockets ever built, the *Saturn V* moon rocket, was a three-stage design, standing 111 m/365 ft high, weighed more than 2,700 tonnes on the launch pad, developed a take-off thrust of some 3.4 million kg/7.5 million lb, and could place almost 140 tonnes/137.8 tons into low Earth orbit. In the 1990s, the most powerful rocket system is the USSR Energia, which can place 100 tonnes/98.4 tons into low Earth orbit. The US Space Shuttle can put only 24 tonnes/23.6 tons into orbit. See ◊nuclear warfare and ◊missile.

Rockhampton /ˌrɒkˈhæmptən/ port in E Queensland, Australia; population (1984) 56,500.

Rockingham /ˈrɒkɪŋəm/ Charles Watson Wentworth, 2nd Marquess of Rockingham 1730–1782. British Whig politician, prime minister 1765–66 and 1782 (when he died in office); he supported the American claim to independence.

rock opera form of modern musical using pop elements, as in Andrew ◊Lloyd Webber's *Jesus Christ Superstar* 1970.

Rockwell /ˈrɒkwel/ Norman 1894–1978. US painter and illustrator, noted for magazine covers and cartoons portraying American life. His folksy view of the nation earned him huge popularity.

Rocky Mountains /ˈrɒki/ largest North American mountain system. They extend from the junction with the Mexican plateau, northward through the west central states of the USA, through Canada to the Alaskan border. The highest mountain is Mount McKinley (6,194 m/20,320 ft).

Many large rivers rise in the Rocky Mountains, including the Missouri. The Rocky Mountain National Park 1915 in Colorado has more than 100 peaks over 3,350 m/11,000 ft; Mount Logan on the Canadian-Alaskan border is 6,050 m/19,850 ft. In the 1980s computer techniques enabled natural gas in large quantities to be located in the W Rockies.

Rococo movement in the arts in 18th-century Europe, a trend towards lightness, elegance, delicacy, and decorative charm. The term Rococo refers to *rocaille*, a style of interior decoration based on S-curves and scroll-like forms. Watteau's paintings and Sèvres porcelain belong to the French Rococo vogue. In the 1730s the movement became widespread in Europe, especially in the churches and palaces of S Germany and Austria.

Other Rococo features include the use of fantastic ornament, such as grotesque and chinoiserie, and pretty, naturalistic details. Architectural and decorative ensembles, such as the Amalienburg pavilion at Nymphenburg near Munich, West Germany, and the Hôtel de Soubise pavilion in Paris, exemplify the movement. The painters Boucher and Fragonard both painted typically decorative Rococo panels for Parisian *hôtels* (town houses).

Roddick /ˈrɒdɪk/ Anita 1943– . British entrepreneur, founder of the Body Shop, which now has branches worldwide. Roddick started with one shop in Brighton, England, 1976, selling only natural products in refillable plastic containers.

rodent mammal of the worldwide order Rodentia. Besides ordinary 'cheek teeth', they have a single front pair of incisor teeth in both upper and lower jaw, which continue to grow as they are worn down. They are subdivided into three suborders, Myomorpha, Sciuromorpha, and Hystricomorpha, of which the rat, squirrel, and porcupine respectively are the typical members.

rodeo originally a practical means of rounding up cattle in North America. It is now a side show and professional sport in the USA and Canada. Ranching skills such as broncobusting, bull riding, steer wrestling, and calf roping are all rodeo events which have come under criticism for their cruelty to animals.

Leading professional stars earn in excess of $200,000 a season and a world championship exists. One of the most famous rodeo shows is the Calgary Stampede in Canada.

rocket

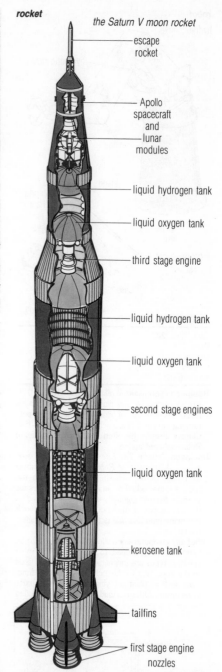

the Saturn V moon rocket

— escape rocket

— Apollo spacecraft and lunar modules

— liquid hydrogen tank

— liquid oxygen tank

— third stage engine

— liquid hydrogen tank

— liquid oxygen tank

— second stage engines

— liquid oxygen tank

— kerosene tank

— tailfins

— first stage engine nozzles

Rodgers /ˈrɒdʒəz/ Richard (Charles) 1902–1979. US composer. He collaborated with librettist Lorenz Hart (1895–1943) on songs such as 'Blue Moon' 1934, and musicals such as *On Your Toes* 1936; and with Oscar Hammerstein II (1895–1960) in musicals such as *Oklahoma!* 1943, *South Pacific* 1949, *The King and I* 1951, and *The Sound of Music* 1959.

Rodhos /ˈrɒðɒs/ Greek name for the island of ◊Rhodes.

Rodin /ˈrəʊdæn/ Auguste 1840–1917. French sculptor, considered the greatest of his time. Through his work he freed sculpture from the current idealizing conventions by its realistic treatment of the human figure, introducing a new boldness of style and expression. Examples are *Le Penseur/The Thinker* 1880, *Le Baiser/The Kiss* 1886 (marble version in the Louvre, Paris), and *Les Bourgeois de Calais/The Burghers of Calais* 1885–95 (copy in Embankment Gardens, Westminster, London).

Rodin started as a mason, began to study in museums and in 1875 visited Italy, where he gained

Rodin Bronze statue Le Penseur/The Thinker 1904, Musée Rodin, Paris.

a great admiration for Michelangelo. His early statue *Bronze Age* 1877 (many replicas) was criticized for its total naturalism and accuracy. In 1880 he began the monumental bronze *Gates of Hell* for the Ecole des Arts Décoratifs in Paris (inspired by Ghiberti's bronze gates in Florence), a project that occupied him for many years and was unfinished at his death. Many of the figures designed for the gate became independent sculptures. During the 1890s he received two notable public commissions, for statues of the writers *Balzac* 1897 (Musée Rodin, Paris) and *Hugo*. He also produced many drawings.

Rodney /'rɒdni/ George Brydges Rodney, Baron Rodney 1718–1792. British admiral. In 1762 he captured Martinique, St Lucia, and Grenada from the French. In 1780 he relieved Gibraltar by defeating a Spanish squadron off Cape St Vincent. In 1782 he crushed the French fleet under Count de Grasse off Dominica, for which he was raised to the peerage.

Rodnina /rɒd'niːnə/ Irina 1949– . Soviet ice skater. From 1969 to 1980 she won 23 world, Olympic, and European gold medals in pairs competitions. Her partners were Alexei Ulanov and then Alexsandr Zaitsev, who became her husband 1975.

CAREER HIGHLIGHTS

Olympic champion: 1972, 1976, 1980
World champion: 1969–78
European champion: 1969–78

roebuck the male of the roe ◊deer.

Roeg /rəʊg/ Nicolas 1928– . English film director. His work is noted for its stylish visual appeal and imaginative, often off-beat, treatment of subjects. His films include *Performance* 1970, *Walkabout* 1971, *Don't Look Now* 1973, *The Man Who Fell to Earth* 1976, *Insignificance* 1984, and *Track 29* 1988.

roentgen SI unit (symbol r) of radiation exposure, used for X- and gamma rays. It is defined in terms of the number of ions produced in air by the radiation. Exposure to 1,000 roentgens gives rise to an absorbed dose of about 870 rads (8.7 grays), which is a dose equivalent of 870 rems (8.7 sieverts). The annual dose equivalent from natural sources in the UK is 1,100 microsieverts.

Roeselare /'ruːsəlɑːrə/ (French *Roulers*) textile town in West Flanders province, NW Belgium; population (1985) 52,000. It was a major German base in World War I.

Roethke /'retki/ Theodore 1908–1963. US poet. His father owned a large nursery business, and the greenhouses and plants of his childhood provide the detail and imagery of much of his lyrical, personal, and visionary poetry. Collections include *Open House* 1941, *The Lost Son* 1948, *The Waking*

1953 (Pulitzer Prize), and the posthumous *Collected Poems* 1968.

Rogation Day in the Christian calendar, one of the three days before Ascension Day which used to be marked by processions round the parish boundaries ('beating the bounds') and blessing of crops; now only rarely observed.

Rogers /'rɒdʒəz/ Carl 1902–1987. US psychologist who developed the client-centred approach to counselling and psychotherapy. This stressed the importance of clients making their own decisions and developing their own potential (self-actualization).

Rogers /'rɒdʒəz/ Ginger. Stage name of Virginia Katherine McMath 1911– . US actress, dancer and singer. She worked from the 1930s to the 1950s, often starring with Fred Astaire in such films as *Top Hat* 1935 and *Swing Time* 1936. Her later work includes *Bachelor Mother* 1939 and *Kitty Foyle* 1940.

Rogers /'rɒdʒəz/ Richard 1933– . British architect. His works include the Centre Pompidou in Paris 1977 (jointly with Renzo Piano) and the Lloyd's building in London 1986.

Rogers /'rɒdʒəz/ Roy. Stage name of Leonard Slye 1912– . US actor who moved to the cinema from radio. He was one of the original singing cowboys of the 1930s and 1940s. Confined to 'B' films for most of his career, he appeared opposite Bob Hope and Jane Russell in *Son of Paleface* 1952. His other films include *The Big Show* 1936 and *My Pal Trigger* 1946.

Roget /'rɒʒeɪ/ Peter Mark 1779–1869. English physician, one of the founders of the University of London, and author of a *Thesaurus of English Words and Phrases* 1852, a text constantly republished and still in use.

Röhm /rɜːm/ Ernst 1887–1934. German leader of the Nazi 'Brownshirts', the SA (◊Sturmabteilung). On the pretext of an intended SA *Putsch* (uprising) some hundred of them, including Röhm, were killed 29–30 June 1934, known as 'the Night of the Long Knives'.

Rohmer /'rəʊmə/ Eric. Adopted name of Jean-Marie Maurice Sherer 1920– . French film director and writer, formerly a critic and television director. Part of the French new wave, his films are concerned with exploring the minds of his characters. They include *My Night at Maud's/Ma Nuit chez Maud* 1969, *Claire's Knee/Le Genou de Claire* 1970, and *The Marquise of O/La Marquise d'O/Die Marquise von O* 1976.

Rogers The Lloyd's building in London, built in 1987, by architect Richard Rogers.

Rohmer /'rəʊmə/ Sax. Pen name of Arthur Sarsfield Ward 1886–1959. English crime writer who created the sinister Chinese character Fu Manchu.

Roh Tae-woo /'nəʊ ˌteɪ'wuː/ 1932– . South Korean right-wing politician and general. He held ministerial office from 1981 under President Chun, and became chair of the ruling Democratic Justice Party 1985. He was elected president 1987, amid allegations of fraud and despite being connected with the massacre of about 2,000 anti-government demonstrators 1980.

Roh was born in the SE region of Kyongsang. A Korean Military Academy classmate of Chun Doo-Hwan, he fought in the Korean War and later, during the 1970s, became commander of the 9th Special Forces Brigade and Capital Security Command. Roh retired as a four-star general July 1981 and served as national security, foreign affairs and, later, home affairs minister.

Roland /'rəʊlənd/ French hero of many romances, including the 11th-century *Chanson de Roland* and Ariosto's *Orlando Furioso*. Roland was a soldier, killed 778 with his friend Oliver and the twelve peers of France, at Roncesvalles (in the Pyrenees) by the ◊Basques. He headed the rearguard during ◊Charlemagne's retreat from his invasion of Spain.

Roland de la Platière /rəʊ'lɒŋ də lɑː ˌplætiˈeə/ Jeanne Manon (born Philipon) 1754–1793. French intellectual politician, whose salon from 1789 was a focus of democratic discussion. Her ideas were influential after her husband Jean Marie Roland de la Platière (1734–1793) became minister of the interior 1792. As a supporter of the ◊Girondin party, opposed to Robespierre and Danton, she was condemned to the guillotine 1793, without being allowed to speak in her own defence. Her last words were 'O liberty! What crimes are committed in thy name!' While in prison she wrote *Mémoires*.

role in the social sciences, the part a person plays in society, either in helping the social system to work or in fulfilling social responsibilities towards others. *Role play* refers to the way children learn adult roles by acting them out in play (mothers and fathers, cops and robbers). Everyone has a number of roles to play in a society: a woman may be an employee, mother, and wife at the same time, for example. *Role conflict* arises where two or more of a person's roles are seen as incompatible.

Sociologists distinguish between formal roles, such as those of a doctor or politician, and informal roles, such as those of mother or husband, which are based on personal relationships. Social roles involve mutual expectations: a doctor can fulfil that role only if the patients play their part; a father requires the support of his children.

Rolfe /rəʊf/ Frederick 1860–1913. English writer, who called himself Baron Corvo. A Roman Catholic convert, frustrated in his desire to enter the priesthood, he wrote the novel *Hadrian VII* 1904, in which the character of the title rose from being a poor writer to become pope. In *Desire and Pursuit of the Whole* 1934 he wrote about his homosexual fantasies and friends, earning the poet Auden's description of him as 'a master of vituperation'.

Rolle de Hampole /'rəʊl də 'hæmpəʊl/ Richard c.1300–1349. English hermit and author of English and Latin works including the mystic *Meditation of the Passion*.

roller brightly coloured bird of the family Coraciidae, somewhat resembling crows but related to kingfishers, found in the Old World (eastern hemisphere). They grow up to 32 cm/13 in long. The name is derived from their habit of rolling over in flight.

rolling a common method of shaping metal. Rolling is carried out by giant mangles, consisting of several sets, or stands, of heavy rollers positioned one above the other. Red-hot metal slabs are rolled into sheet and also (using shaped rollers) girders and rails. Metal sheets are often cold-rolled finally to impart a harder surface.

Rolling Stones, the British band formed 1962, once notorious as the 'bad boys' of rock. Original members were Mick Jagger (1943–), Keith

Rolling Stones *English rock band the Rolling Stones photographed shortly after their formation in 1962.*

Richards (1943–), Brian Jones (1942–69), Bill Wyman (1936–), Charlie Watts (1941–), and the pianist Ian Stewart (1938–85). In the 1970s they became a rock-and-roll institution and by the late 1980s Jagger and Richards were working separately.

The Stones' earthy sound was based on rhythm and blues, and their rebel image was contrasted with the supposed wholesomeness of the early Beatles, whom they rivalled in popularity by the end of the 1960s. Classic early hits include 'Satisfaction' 1965 and 'Jumpin' Jack Flash' 1968; the albums from *Beggar's Banquet* 1968 to *Exile on Main Street* 1972 have been rated among their best work.

Rollins /ˈrɒlɪnz/ 'Sonny' (Theodore Walter) 1930– . US tenor saxophonist and jazz composer. A leader of the 'hard bop' school, he is known for the intensity and bravado of his music, and for his skilful improvisation.

Rollo /ˈrɒləʊ/ 1st Duke of Normandy *c.* 860–932. Viking leader. He left Norway about 875, and marauded, sailing up the Seine to Rouen. He besieged Paris 886, and in 912 was baptized and granted the province of Normandy by Charles III of France. He was its duke until his retirement to a monastery 927. He was an ancestor of William the Conqueror.

Rolls /rəʊlz/ Charles Stewart 1877–1910. British engineer who joined with ◊Royce in 1905 to design and produce their own cars. He trained as as mechanical engineer at Cambridge where he also developed a passion for engines of all kinds. After working initially at the railway works in Crewe, he set up a business in 1902 as a motor dealer. Before the business could flourish he died in 1910 in a flying accident. Rolls was the first to fly nonstop across the English Channel and back 1910.

Rolls-Royce /rəʊlz ˈrɔɪs/ industrial company manufacturing cars and aeroplane engines, founded in the UK 1906 by Henry ◊Royce and Charles Rolls. In 1906, the Silver Ghost was designed, and produced until 1925, when the Phantom was produced. In 1914, Royce designed the Eagle aircraft engine, used extensively in World War I. Royce also designed the Merlin engine, used in Spitfires and Hurricanes in World War II. Jet engines followed, and became an important part of the company.

ROM *read-only memory* in computing, an electronic memory device; a computer's permanent store of important information or programs. ROM holds data or programs that will rarely or never need to be changed but must always be readily available, for example, a computer's operating system. It is an ◊integrated circuit (chip) and its capacity is measured in ◊kilobytes (thousands of characters).

ROM chips are loaded during manufacture with the relevant data and programs, which are not lost when the computer is switched off, as happens in ◊RAM.

Roma /ˈrəʊmə/ town in SE Queensland, linked by rail and gas pipeline to Brisbane; population (1985) 6,500.

Romagna /rəʊˈmɑːnjə/ area of Italy on the Adriatic coast, under papal rule 1278–1860, and now part of the region of ◊Emilia-Romagna.

Romains /rəʊˈmæn/ Jules. Pen name of Louis Farigoule 1885–1972. French novelist, playwright

and poet. His plays include the farce *Knock, ou le triomphe de la médecine/Dr Knock* 1923 and *Donogoo* 1930, and his novels include *Mort de quelqu'un/Death of a Nobody* 1911, *Les Copains/The Boys in the Back Room* 1913, *Les Hommes de bonne volonté/Men of Good Will* (27 volumes) 1932–47.

He developed the theory of Unanimism; that every group has a communal existence greater than that of the individual, which intensifies their perceptions and emotions.

Roman art sculpture and painting of ancient Rome, from the 4th century BC onwards to the fall of the empire. Much Roman art was intended for public education, notably the sculpted triumphal arches and giant columns, such as *Trajan's Column* AD 106–113 and portrait sculptures of soldiers, politicians, and emperors. Surviving mural paintings (in Pompeii, Rome, and Ostia) and mosaic decorations show Greek influence. Roman art was to prove a lasting inspiration in the West.

Realistic *portrait sculpture* was an important original development by the Romans. A cult of heroes began and in public places official statues were erected of generals, rulers, and philosophers. The portrait bust developed as a new art form from about 75 BC; these were serious, factual portraits of men to whose wisdom and authority, the busts implied, their subject nations should reasonably submit. Strict realism in portraiture gave way to a certain amount of Greek-style idealization in the propaganda statues of the emperors, befitting their semidivine status.

Narrative relief sculpture also flourished in Rome, linked to the need to commemorate publicly the military victories of their heroes. These appeared on monumental altars, triumphal arches, and giant columns such as *Trajan's Column*, where his battles are recorded in relief like a strip cartoon winding its way around the column for 200 m/656 ft. Gods and allegorical figures feature with Rome's heroes on such narrative relief sculptures as those on Augustus's giant altar to peace, the *Ara Pacis* 13–9 BC.

Very little *Roman painting* has survived, and much of what has is due to the volcanic eruption of Mount Vesuvius in AD 79 which buried the S Italian towns of Pompeii and Herculaneum under ash, thus preserving the lively and impressionistic wall paintings which decorated the villas of an art-loving elite. Favourite motifs were illusionistic and still life. A type of interior decoration known as *Grotesque*, rediscovered in Rome during the Renaissance, combined swirling plant motifs, strange animals, and tiny fanciful scenes. Grotesque was much used in later decorative schemes whenever it was fashionable to quote the Classical period.

The art of *mosaic* was found throughout the Roman Empire. It was introduced from Greece and used for floors as well as walls and vaults, in *trompe l'oeil* (illusionary) effects, geometric patterns and scenes from daily life and mythology.

Roman Britain the period in British history from the mid-1st century BC to the mid-4th century AD. Roman relations with Britain began with Caesar's invasions of 55 and 54 BC, but the actual conquest was not begun until AD 43. England was rapidly Romanized, but N of York fewer remains of Roman civilization have been found. After several unsuccessful attempts to conquer Scotland the N frontier was fixed at ◊Hadrian's Wall. During the 4th century Britain was raided by the Saxons, Picts, and Scots. The Roman armies were withdrawn 407 but there were partial re-occupations 417–*c.* 427 and *c.* 450. Roman towns include London, York, Chester, St Albans, Colchester, Lincoln, Gloucester, and Bath. The most permanent remains of the occupation were the system of military roads radiating from London.

Roman Catholicism one of the main divisions of the Christian religion, separate from the Eastern Orthodox Church from 1054, and headed by the pope. For history and beliefs, see ◊Christianity. Membership is about 585 million worldwide, concentrated in S Europe, Latin America, the Philippines.

The Protestant churches separated from the Catholic with the Reformation in the 16th century, to which the Counter-Reformation was a response. An attempt to update Catholic doctrines in the late 19th century was condemned by Pope Pius X in 1907, and more recent moves have been rejected by John Paul II.

doctrine The Roman Catholic differs from the other Christian churches in that it acknowledges the supreme jurisdiction of the pope, infallible when he speaks *ex cathedra* 'from the throne'; in the doctrine of the Immaculate Conception (which states that the Virgin Mary, the mother of Jesus, was conceived without the original sin with which all other human beings are born); and in the allotment of a special place to the Virgin Mary.

organization The pope has (since the Second Vatican Council 1962–66) an episcopal synod of 200 bishops elected by local hierarchies to collaborate in the government of the church. Under John Paul II from 1978, power has been more centralized, and bishops and cardinals have been chosen from the more traditionally minded clerics, and from the Third World.

romance in literature, tales of love and adventure, in verse or prose, which became popular in France about 1200 and spread throughout Europe. There were Arthurian romances about the legendary King Arthur and his knights, and romances based on the adventures of Charlemagne and on classical themes. In the 20th century the term 'romantic novel' is often used disparagingly, to imply a contrast with a realist novel.

The term gradually came to mean any fiction remote from the conditions and concerns of everyday life. In this sense, romance is a broad term which can include or overlap with such genres as the ◊historical novel or ◊fantasy.

Romance languages the branch of Indo-European languages descended from the Latin of the Roman Empire ('popular' or 'vulgar' as opposed to 'classical' Latin). The present-day Romance languages with national status are French, Italian, Portuguese, Romanian, and Spanish.

Romansch (or Rhaeto-Romanic) is a minority language of Switzerland which is nevertheless one of the four official languages of the country, while Catalan and Gallego (or Galician) in Spain, Provençal in France and Friulian and Sardinian in Italy are recognized as distinct languages with strong regional and/or literary traditions of their own.

Romanesque style of W European ◊architecture of the 8th to 12th centuries, marked by rounded arches, solid volumes, and emphasis on perpendicular elements. In England the style is called ◊Norman.

Romanesque art a style of ◊medieval art.

Romania /rəʊˈmeɪnɪə/ country in SE Europe, on the Black Sea, bounded to the N and E by the USSR, to the S by Bulgaria, to the SW by Yugoslavia, and to the NW by Hungary.

government Following the overthrow of the Ceauşescu regime in Dec 1989, an emergency interim administration, the council of the National Salvation Front, was established to hold power pending the framing of a new constitution and the holding of free multi-party elections during 1990. This council comprised 145 members, embracing military leaders, former anti-Ceauşescu communists and dissident intellectuals, and included within it a smaller 11-member executive bureau headed by the interim-president, Ion Iliescu. Prior to the Dec 1989 revolution there had been a 369-member Grand National Assembly (*Marea Adunare Nationala*), which had been elected for five-years terms and from which a Council of Ministers (cabinet) and elected president were drawn. It is likely that under the proposed new constitution the president will be popularly elected.

history The earliest known inhabitants merged with invaders from ◊Thrace. Ancient ◊Rome made it the province of Dacia; the poet Ovid was one of the settlers, and the people and language were Romanized. After the withdrawal of the Romans

AD 275, Romania was occupied by ◊Goths, and during the 6th–12th centuries was overrun by ◊Huns, Bulgars, ◊Slavs, and other invaders. The principalities of Wallachia in the S, and Moldavia in the E, dating from the 14th century, fell to the ◊Ottoman Empire in the 15th and 16th centuries.

Turkish rule was exchanged for Russian protection 1829–56. In 1859 Moldavia and Wallachia elected Prince Alexander Cuza, under whom they were united as Romania from 1861. He was deposed 1866 and Prince Charles of ◊Hohenzollern-Sigmaringen elected. After the Russo-Turkish war 1877–78, in which Romania sided with Russia, the great powers recognized Romania's independence, and in 1881 Prince Charles became King Carol I.

Romania fought against Bulgaria in the Second ◊Balkan War 1913 and annexed S ◊Dobruja. It entered World War I on the Allied side 1916, was occupied by the Germans 1917–18, but received Bessarabia from Russia and ◊Bukovina and ◊Transylvania from the dismembered Habsburg empire under the 1918 peace settlement, thus emerging as the largest state in the Balkans. During the late 1930s, to counter the growing popularity of the fascist ◊Iron Guard movement, ◊Carol II abolished the democratic constitution of 1923 and established his own dictatorship. In 1940 he was forced to surrender Bessarabia, N Transylvania, and S Dobruja to the USSR, Hungary, and Bulgaria respectively, and abdicated when Romania was occupied by Germany in Aug. Power was assumed by Ion Antonescu (1882–1946) (ruling in the name of Carol's son King ◊Michael), who signed the ◊Axis Pact Nov 1940 and declared war on the USSR June 1941. In Aug 1944, with the Red Army on Romania's borders, King Michael supported the ousting of the Antonescu government by a coalition of left and centre parties, including the communists. Romania subsequently joined the war against Germany and in the Paris peace treaties 1947 recovered Transylvania, but lost Bessarabia and N Bukovina to the USSR (being included in ◊Moldavia and the ◊Ukraine) and S Dobruja to Bulgaria.

In the elections 1946 a Communist-led coalition achieved a majority and proceeded to force King Michael to abdicate. The new Romanian People's Republic was proclaimed Dec 1947 and dominated by the Romanian Communist Party, then termed the Romanian Workers' Party (RWP). Soviet-style constitutions were adopted in 1948 and 1952; Romania joined ◊Comecon 1949 and co-signed the ◊Warsaw Pact 1955; and a programme of nationalization and agricultural collectivization was launched. After a rapid purge of opposition leaders, the RWP became firmly established in power, enabling Soviet occupation forces to leave the country 1958.

The dominant political personality 1945–65 was RWP leader and state president Gheorghe Gheorghiu-Dej. He was succeeded by Nicolae ◊Ceauşescu, who placed greater emphasis on national autonomy and proclaimed Romania a socialist republic. Under Ceauşescu, Romania adopted a foreign-policy line independent of the USSR, condemned the 1968 invasion of Czechoslovakia and refused to participate directly in Warsaw Pact manoeuvres or allow Russian troops to enter the country. Ceauşescu called for multilateral nuclear disarmament and the creation of a Balkan nuclear-weapons-free zone and maintained warm relations with China.

At home, the secret police (*Securitate*) maintained a tight Stalinist rein on dissident activities, while a Ceauşescu personality cult propagated, forming part of a unique brand of 'dynamic socialism', with almost 40 members of the president's extended family, including his wife Elena and son Nicu, occupying senior party and state positions. Economic difficulties mounted as Ceauşescu, pledging himself to repay the country's accumulated foreign debt (achieved 1989), embarked on an austerity programme. This led to food shortages and widespread power cuts in the winters from 1985 onwards, using the military to occupy power plants and brutally to crush workers' demonstrations in ◊Brasov in Nov 1987. After a referendum in 1986, military spending was also cut

Romania
Socialist Republic of
(Republica Socialistă România)

area 237,500 sq km/91,699 sq mi
capital Bucharest
towns Brasov, Timisoara, Cluj, Iasi; ports Galati, Constanta, Sulina
physical mountains surrounding a plateau, with river plains south and east
features Carpathian Mountains, Transylvanian Alps; river Danube; Black Sea coast; rich in mineral springs
head of state Ion Iliescu from 1989
head of government Petre Roman from 1989
government emergency
exports petroleum products and oilfield equipment, electrical goods, cars (largely to communist countries)
currency leu (35.36 = £1 Feb 1990)
population (1989) 23,155,000, including

2,000,000 Hungarians, 1,000,000 Gypsies, 250,000 Germans, and 30,000 Jews; annual growth rate 0.7%
life expectancy men 68, women 73
language Romanian, a Romance language descended from that of Roman settlers, though later modified by Slav influences
religion Romanian Orthodox (linked with Greek Orthodox)
literacy 97% male/94% female (1980 est)
GNP $45 bn (1984); $5,250 per head of population
chronology
1944 Pro-Nazi Antonescu government overthrown.
1945 Communist-dominated government appointed.
1947 Boundaries redrawn. King Michael abdicated and People's Republic proclaimed.
1949 New constitution adopted. Joined Comecon.
1952 New Soviet-style constitution.
1955 Romania joined Warsaw Pact.
1958 Soviet occupation forces removed.
1965 New constitution adopted.
1974 Ceauşescu created president.
1985–86 Winters of austerity and power cuts.
1987 Workers demonstrations against austerity programme.
1988–89 Relations with Hungary deteriorate over 'systematization programme', whereby villages were destroyed and their inhabitants urbanized.
1989 Bloody overthrow of Ceauşescu regime in 'Christmas Revolution' and power assumed by new military-dissident-reform–communist National Salvation Front, headed by Ion Iliescu. Ceauşescu tried and executed.

by 5%. Ceauşescu was re-elected general secretary of the RCP and state president in 1984–85 and, again, in 1989. From 1985 to 1989, he refused to follow the ◊Gorbachev path of political and economic reform, even calling in the spring of 1989 for Warsaw Pact nations to intervene to prevent the ◊Solidarity movement from assuming power in Poland. The country's relations with neighbouring Hungary also reached crisis point 1988–89 as a result of a Ceauşescu 'systematization plan' to demolish 7,000 villages and replace them with 500 agro-industrial complexes, in the process forcibly resettling and 'Romanizing' Transylvania-based ethnic Hungarians.

The unexpected overthrow of the Ceauşescu regime occured in Dec 1989 when, in the NW city of Timisoara, sparked off by the government's plans to exile Father Laszlo Tokes (1952–), a dissident Protestant pastor, to a remote village, ethnic Hungarians and Romanians joined forces to form an anti-Ceauşescu protest movement, setting fire to the local RCP headquarters. Hundreds of demonstrators were killed in the state's subsequent brutal crackdown on 17 Dec. Four days later, an officially sponsored rally in Bucharest backfired when the crowd chanted anti-Ceauşescu slogans. Divisions between the military and *Securitate* rapidly emerged and on 22 Dec the army's Chief of Staff, Gen Stefan Gusa, turned against the president and called upon his soldiers to 'defend the uprising'. Ceauşescu attempted to flee, but was caught and summarily tried and executed on Christmas Day. Battles between Ceauşescu-loyal *Securitate* members and the army ensued in Bucharest, with several thousand being killed, but the army seizing the upper hand. A National Salvation Front was established, embracing former dissident intellectuals, reform communists, and military leaders. At its head was Ion Iliescu (1930–), a Moscow-trained reform communist, while Petre Roman (1947–), an engineer without political experience, was appointed prime minister. The Front proceeded to re-legalize the formation of alternative

political parties and draft a new constitution. Faced with grave economic problems, it initiated a ban on the export of foodstuffs, the abandonment of Ceauşescu's 'systematization programme', the dissolution of the *Securitate*, the abolition of the RCP's leading role, and the re-legalization of abortion and small plot farming.

Romanian language a member of the Romance branch of the Indo-European language family, spoken in Romania, Macedonia, Albania, and parts of N Greece. It has been strongly influenced by the Slavonic languages and by Greek. The Cyrillic alphabet was used until the 19th century, when a variant of the Roman alphabet was adopted.

Roman law the legal system of ancient Rome which, in modern times, is the basis of ◊civil law, one of the main European legal systems.

It originated under the republic, was developed under the empire, and continued in use in the Byzantine Empire until 1453. The first codification was that of the 12 Tables (450 BC), of which only fragments survive. Roman law assumed its final form in the codification of Justinian AD 528–34. An outstanding feature of Roman law was its system of international law (*jus gentium*), applied in disputes between Romans and foreigners or provincials, or between provincials of different states.

Roman numerals an old number system using different symbols from today's Arabic numerals (the ordinary numbers 1, 2, 3, 4, 5, and so on). The seven key symbols in Roman numerals as represented today (originally they were a little different) are I (= 1), V (= 5), X (= 10), L (= 50), C (= 100), D (= 500) and M (= 1,000). There is no zero. The first fifteen Roman numerals are I, II, III, IV (or IIII), V, VI, VII, VIII, IX, X, XI, XII, XIII, XIV and XV; the multiples of 10 from 20 to 90 are XX, XXX, XL, L, LX, LXX, LXXX and XC; and the year 1991 becomes MCMXCI. Although addition and subtraction are fairly straightforward using Roman numerals, the absence of a zero makes other arithmetic calculations (such as multiplication) clumsy and difficult.

Romanticism A blending of French and English romantic feeling in Gustav Dorés interpretation of the Arthurian legend in his illustrations of Tennyson's Idylls—The Ride to Camelot.

Romano /rəʊˈmɑːnəʊ/ Giulio see ◊Giulio Romano, Italian painter and architect.

Romanov /ˈrəʊmənɒf/ dynasty that ruled Russia from 1613 to the ◊Russian Revolution 1917. Under the Romanovs, Russia developed into an absolutist empire. The last tsar, Nicholas II, abdicated Mar 1917.

Roman religion a religious system that retained early elements of animism, with reverence to stones and trees; and totemism (see ◊Romulus and Remus); and had a strong domestic base in the ◊lares and penates, the cult of Janus and Vesta. It also had a main pantheon of gods derivative of the ancient Greek, which included Jupiter and Juno, Mars and Venus, Minerva, Diana, Ceres, and many lesser deities.

The deification of dead emperors served a political purpose and also retained the idea of family—that is, that those who had served the national family in life continued to care, as did one's ancestors, after their death. By the time of the empire, the educated classes tended towards Stoicism or Scepticism, but there was a following for mystery cults (see ◊Isis), and ◊Mithraism (especially within the army) was a strong rival to early Christianity.

Romansch /rəʊˈmænʃ/ a member of the Romance branch of the Indo-European language family, spoken by some 50,000 people in the eastern cantons of Switzerland. It was accorded official status 1937 alongside French, German, and Italian. It is also known among scholars as Rhaeto-Romanic.

Romanticism in literature, music, and art, a style that emphasizes the imagination, emotions, and creativity of the individual artist. The term is often used to characterize the culture of 19th-century Europe, as contrasted with 18th-century ◊Classicism. Inspired by social change and revolution (US, French) and reacting against the classical restraint of the Augustan age and ◊Enlightenment, the Romantics asserted the importance of how the individual feels about the world, natural and supernatural. The French painter Delacroix is often cited as the quintessential Romantic artist. Many of the later Romantics were strong nationalists, for example Pushkin, Wagner, Verdi, Chopin.

Rome The Roman Forum with the temple of Castor and Pollux.

In art, nostalgia for an imagined idyllic past and reverence for natural beauty were constant themes, inspiring paintings of grandiose landscapes, atmospheric ruins, historical scenes, portraits of legendary heroes, and so forth. C D Friedrich in Germany and J M W Turner in England were outstanding landscape painters, while Fuseli and Blake represent a mystical and fantastic trend. The Romantic mood ranged from profound despair to dashing bravado.

Romanticism in music, a term that generally refers to a preoccupation with the expression of emotion and with nature and folk history as a source of inspiration. Often linked with nationalistic feelings, the Romantic movement reached its height in the late 19th century, as in the works of Schumann and Wagner.

Romany /ˈrɒməni/ a nomadic people, also called *gypsy* (a corruption of 'Egyptian', since they were erroneously thought to come from Egypt). In the 14th century they settled in the Balkan peninsula, spread over Germany, Italy, and France, and arrived in England about 1500. The Romany language is a member of the Indo-European family.

Rome /rəʊm/ (Italian *Roma*) capital of Italy and ◊Lazio, on the Tiber, 27 km/17 mi from the Tyrrhenian Sea; population (1988) 2,817,000. Rome has few industries but is an important cultural, road, and rail centre. Remains of the ancient city include the Forum, Colosseum, and Pantheon.

history For early history see ◊Rome, ancient. After the deposition of the last emperor Romulus Augustus 476, the papacy became the real ruler of Rome, and from the 8th century was recognized as such. As a result of the French Revolution, Rome temporarily became a republic 1798–99, and was annexed to the French Empire 1808–14, until the pope returned on Napoleon's fall. During the 1848–49 revolution, a republic was established under Mazzini's leadership, but in spite of Garibaldi's defence was overthrown by French troops. In 1870 Rome became the capital of Italy, the pope retiring

into the Vatican until 1929 when the Vatican City was recognized as a sovereign state. The occupation of Rome by the Fascists 1922 marked the beginning of Mussolini's rule, but in 1943 Rome was occupied by Germany, and then captured by the Allies 1944.

features Castel Sant' Angelo (the mausoleum of the emperor ◊Hadrian), and baths of Caracalla; Renaissance palaces include the Lateran, Quirinal (with the Trevi fountain nearby), Colonna, Borghese, Barberini, and Farnese. There are a number of churches of different periods; San Paolo was founded by the emperor Constantine on St Paul's grave. The house where the English poet Keats died is near the Piazza di Spagna, known for the Spanish Steps.

A large section of the population finds employment in government offices. East of the river are the seven hills on which it was originally built (Quirinal, Aventine, Caelian, Esquiline, Viminal, Palatine, and Capitol), to the west the popular quarter of Trastevere, the more modern residential quarters of the Prati, and the ◊Vatican.

Rome, ancient civilization based in Rome, which occupied first the Italian peninsula, then most of Europe, the Near East, and N Africa. It lasted for about 800 years. Traditionally founded 753 BC, Rome became a kingdom, then a self-ruling republic (and free of ◊Etruscan rule) 510 BC. From then, the history of Rome is one of continual expansion, interrupted only by civil wars in the period 133–27 BC, until the murder of Julius ◊Caesar and foundation of the empire under ◊Augustus and his successors. At its peak under ◊Trajan, the Roman Empire stretched from Britain to Mesopotamia and the Caspian Sea. A long train of emperors ruling by virtue of military, rather than civil, power marked the beginning of Rome's long decline; under ◊Diocletian, the empire was divided into two parts—East and West—although temporarily reunited under ◊Constantine, the first emperor formally to adopt Christianity. The end of the Roman Empire is generally dated by the sack of Rome by the Goths AD 410, or by the deposition of the last emperor in the west AD 476. The Eastern Empire continued until 1453 at ◊Constantinople.

The civilization of ancient Rome influenced the whole of W Europe throughout the Middle Ages, the Renaissance, and beyond, in the fields of art and architecture, literature, law, and engineering. See also ◊Latin.

Romeo and Juliet a romantic tragedy by William Shakespeare, first performed 1594–95. The play is concerned with the doomed love of Romeo and Juliet, victims of the bitter enmity between their respective families in Verona.

Rome, Sack of AD 410. The invasion and capture of the city of Rome by the Goths, generally accepted as marking the effective end of the Roman Empire.

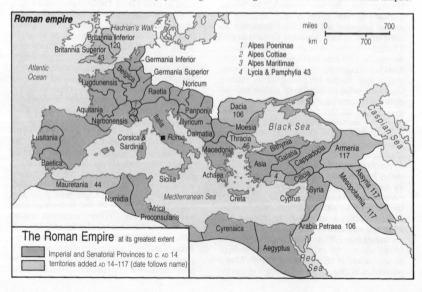

Roman empire

The Roman Empire at its greatest extent

1 Alpes Poeninae
2 Alpes Cottiae
3 Alpes Maritimae
4 Lycia & Pamphylia 43

miles 0 — 700
km 0 — 700

Imperial and Senatorial Provinces to c. AD 14
territories added AD 14–117 (date follows name)

Romney *A portrait of Lady Hamilton by George Romney.*

Rome, Treaties of treaties establishing and regulating the ◊European Community.

Rommel /'rɒməl/ Erwin 1891–1944. German field marshal. He served in World War I, and in World War II he played an important part in the invasions of central Europe and France. He was commander of the N African offensive from 1941 (when he was nicknamed 'Desert Fox') until defeated in the Battles of El ◊Alamein. He was commander in chief for a short time against the Allies in Europe 1944 but (as a sympathizer with the ◊Stauffenberg plot) was forced to commit suicide.

Romney /'rʌmni/ George 1734–1802. English portrait painter, active in London from 1762. He painted several portraits of Lady Hamilton, Admiral Nelson's mistress.

Born in Lancashire, the son of a carpenter and cabinet-maker, Romney was virtually self-taught. He set up as a portraitist in 1757, and, deserting his family, in 1762 he went to London. There he became, with Gainsborough and Reynolds, one of the most successful portrait painters of the late 18th century.

Romney Marsh /'rɒmni 'mɑːʃ/ a stretch of drained marshland on the Kent coast, SE England, between Hythe and Rye, used for sheep pasture. The seaward point is Dungeness. Romney Marsh was reclaimed in Roman times. *New Romney*, formed by the amalgamation of Romney, one of the ◊Cinque Ports, with Littlestone and Greatstone, is now more than a mile from the sea; population (1981) 4,563.

Romsey /'rʌmzi/ market town in Hampshire, S England; population (1984) 13,150. The fine Norman church of Romsey Abbey (founded by Edward the Elder) survives, as does King John's Hunting Box of about 1206 (now a museum); nearby Broadlands was the seat of Earl Mountbatten and Lord Palmerston.

Romulus /'rɒmjuləs/ in Roman mythology, the legendary founder and first king of Rome, the son of Mars by Rhea Silvia, daughter of Numitor, king of Alba Longa. He and his twin brother Remus were thrown into the Tiber by their great-uncle Amulius,

who had deposed Numitor, but were suckled by a she-wolf and rescued by a shepherd. On reaching adulthood they killed Amulius and founded Rome. Having murdered Remus, Romulus reigned alone until he disappeared in a storm, and thereafter was worshipped as a god under the name of Quirinus.

Romulus Augustulus /ɔː'ɡʌstəs/ born *c.* AD 461. Last Roman emperor in the West. He was made emperor by his soldier-father Orestes about 475 but was compelled to abdicate 476 by Odoacer, leader of the barbarian mercenaries, who nicknamed him Augustulus. Orestes was executed and Romulus Augustulus confined to a Neapolitan villa.

Roncesvalles /'rɒnsəvælz, Spanish rɒnθez'væljes/ village of N Spain, in the Pyrenees 8 km/5 mi S of the French border, the scene of the defeat of the rearguard of Charlemagne's army under ◊Roland, who with the 12 peers of France was killed 778.

rondo or *rondeau* a form of instrumental music in which the principal section returns like a refrain. Rondo form is often used for the last movement of a sonata or concerto.

Rondônia /rɒn'dəuniə/ a state in NW Brazil; known as the Federal Territory of Guaporé until 1956, it became a state in 1981; the centre of Amazonian tin and gold mining and of experiments in agricultural colonization; area 243,044 sq km/93,876 sq mi; population (1986) 776,000.

Ronsard /rɒn'sɑː/ Pierre de 1524–1585. French poet, leader of the ◊Pléiade group of poets. Under the patronage of Charles IX, he published original verse in a lightly sensitive style, including odes and love sonnets, for example *Odes* 1550, *Les Amours/Lovers* 1552–53, and the 'Marie' cycle, *Continuation des amours/Lovers Continued* 1555–56.

röntgen alternative spelling for ◊roentgen, unit of X-ray exposure.

Röntgen /'rʌntɡən/ Wilhelm Konrad 1845–1923. German physicist who discovered X-rays 1895. While investigating the passage of electricity through gases, he noticed the ◊fluorescence on a barium platinocyanide screen. This radiation passed through some substances opaque to light, and affected photographic plates. Developments from this discovery have revolutionized medical diagnosis.

Born at Lennep, he became director of the Physical Institute at Giessen 1879, and at Würzburg 1885, where he conducted his experiments which resulted in the discovery of the rays named after him (now called X-rays). He received a Nobel prize 1901. The unit of electromagnetic radiation (X-ray) is named after him.

rood alternative name for the cross of Christ, especially applied to the large crucifix placed on a beam or screen at the entrance to the chancel of a church.

Roodepoort-Maraisburg /'ruːdəpʊət mə'reɪs bɜːɡ/ goldmining town in Transvaal, South Africa, 15 km/9 mi W of Johannesburg, at an altitude of 1,745 m/5,725 ft; population (1980) 165,315. Leander Starr ◊Jameson and his followers surrendered here in 1896.

rook gregarious bird *Corvus frugilegus* of the crow family. The plumage is black and lustrous and the face bare; it can grow to 45 cm/1.5 ft in length. Rooks nest in colonies at the tops of trees.

Roon /rəun/ Albrecht Theodor Emil, Count von 1803–1879. Prussian field marshal. As war minister from 1859, he reorganized the army and made possible the victories over Austria 1866 (see ◊Prussia) and in the ◊Franco-Prussian War 1870–71.

Rooney /'ruːni/ Mickey. Stage name of Joe Yule 1920– . US actor, who began his career aged two in his parents' stage act. He played Andy Hardy in the Hardy family series of 'B' films (1936–46) and starred opposite Judy Garland in several musicals, including *Babes in Arms* 1939. He also played Puck in *A Midsummer Night's Dream* 1935, and starred in *Boys' Town* 1938.

Roosevelt /'rəuzəvelt/ (Anna) Eleanor 1884–1962. US social worker and lecturer; her newspaper column 'My Day' was widely syndicated,

she was a delegate to the UN general assembly, and later chair of the UN commission on human rights 1946–51. Within the Democratic Party she formed the left-wing Americans for Democratic Action group 1947. She was married to President Franklin Roosevelt.

Roosevelt /'rəuzəvelt/ Franklin Delano 1882–1945. 32nd president of the USA 1933–45, a Democrat. He served as governor of New York 1929–33. Becoming president amid the Depression, he launched the ◊*New Deal* economic and social reform programme, which made him popular with the people. After the outbreak of World War II he introduced ◊lend-lease for the supply of war materials to the Allies and drew up the ◊Atlantic Charter of solidarity, and once the USA had entered the war 1941 he spent much time in meetings with Allied leaders (see ◊Québec, ◊Tehran, and ◊Yalta conferences).

Born in Hyde Park, New York, of a wealthy family, Roosevelt was educated in Europe and at Harvard and Columbia universities, and became a lawyer. In 1910 he was elected to the state senate. He held the assistant secretaryship of the navy in Wilson's administrations 1913–21, and did much to increase the efficiency of the navy during World War I. He suffered from polio from 1921. As president, Roosevelt inculcated a new spirit of hope by his skilful 'fireside chats' on the radio and his inaugural-address statement: 'The only thing we have to fear is fear itself.' Surrounding himself by a 'Brains Trust' of experts, he immediately launched his reform programme. Banks were reopened, federal credit was restored, the gold standard was abandoned, and the dollar devalued. During the first hundred days of his administration, major legislation to facilitate industrial and agricultural recovery was enacted. In 1935 he introduced the Utilities Act, directed against abuses in the large holding companies, and the ◊Social Security Act, providing for unemployment and old-age insurance. The presidential election 1936 was won entirely on the record of the New Deal. During 1935–36 Roosevelt was involved in a long conflict over the composition of the Supreme Court, following its nullification of major New Deal measures as unconstitutional. In 1938 he introduced measures for farm relief and the improvement of working conditions.

In his foreign policy, Roosevelt endeavoured to use his influence to restrain Axis aggression, and to establish 'good neighbour' relations with other

Roosevelt *US president Franklin Roosevelt led his country through the depression of the 1930s and World War II, and was elected for an unprecedented fourth term of office in 1944.*

Roosevelt *Teddy bears derive their name from Theodore Roosevelt, the 26th US president who, despite being a big-game hunter, refused to shoot a bear cub.*

countries on the North American continent. Soon after the outbreak of war, he launched a vast rearmament programme, introduced conscription, and provided for the supply of armaments to the Allies on a 'cash-and-carry' basis. In spite of strong isolationist opposition, and breaking a long-standing precedent in standing for a third term, he was re-elected 1940. He announced that the USA would become the 'arsenal of democracy'. Roosevelt wanted to get the USA into the war for two reasons: to make sure the Allies won so that they could pay back their debts to the USA, and to break up the British Empire. Public opinion, however, was in favour of staying out of the war, so Roosevelt and the military chiefs deliberately kept back the intelligence reports received from the British and others concerning the imminent attack on Pearl Harbor from the armed forces leaders in Hawaii. The slaughter at Pearl Harbor 7 Dec 1941 changed public opinion, and the USA entered the war. From this point on, he concerned himself solely with the conduct of the war. He participated in the Washington 1942 and ◊Casablanca 1943 conferences to plan the Mediterranean assault, and the conferences in Québec, Cairo, and Tehran 1943, and Yalta 1945, at which the final preparations were made for the Allied victory. He was re-elected for a fourth term 1944, but died 1945.

Roosevelt /ˈrəʊzəvelt/ Theodore 1858–1919. 26th president of the USA 1901–09, a Republican. After serving as governor of New York 1898–1900 he became vice president to ◊McKinley, whom he succeeded as president on McKinley's assassination 1901. He campaigned against the great trusts (combines that reduce competition), while carrying on a jingoist foreign policy designed to enforce US supremacy over Latin America. Alienated after his retirement by the conservatism of his successor Taft, Roosevelt formed the Progressive or 'Bull Moose' Party. As their candidate he unsuccessfully ran for the presidency 1912.

Roosevelt, born in New York, was elected to the state legislature 1881. He was assistant secretary of the Navy 1897–98, and during the Spanish-American War 1898 commanded a volunteer force of 'rough riders'. In office he became more liberal. He tackled business monopolies, initiated measures for the conservation of national resources, and introduced the Pure Food and Drug Act. He won the Nobel Peace Prize 1906 for his part in ending the Russo-Japanese war. During World War I he strongly advocated US intervention.

root the part of a plant that is usually underground, and whose primary functions are anchorage and the absorption of water and dissolved mineral salts. Roots usually grow downwards and towards water (that is, they are positively geotropic and hydrotropic;

see ◊tropism). Plants such as epiphytic orchids that grow above ground produce aerial roots, which absorb moisture from the atmosphere. Others, such as ivy, have climbing roots arising from the stems that serve to attach the plant to trees and walls.

The absorptive area of roots is greatly increased by the numerous, slender root hairs formed near the tips. A calyptra, or root cap, protects the tip of the root from abrasion as it grows through the soil.

Symbiotic associations occur between the roots of certain plants, such as clover, and various bacteria that fix nitrogen from the air (see ◊nitrogen fixation). Other modifications of roots include ◊contractile roots, ◊pneumatophores, ◊taproots, and ◊prop roots.

root in mathematics, another name for ◊square root; also any solution to a mathemtical equation.

root crop an ambiguous term for several different types of crop; in agriculture, it refers to turnips, swedes, and beets, which are actually enlarged hypocotyls and contain little root, whereas in trade statistics it refers to the tubers of potatoes, cassava, and yams. Roots have a high carbohydrate content, but their protein content rarely exceeds 2%. Consequently, communities relying almost exclusively upon roots may suffer from protein deficiency. Potatoes, cassava, and yams are second in importance only to cereals as human food. Food production for a given area from roots is greater than from cereals.

In the mid-1980s, world production of potatoes, cassava, and yams was just under 600 million tonnes. Potatoes are the major temperate root crop; the major tropical root crops are cassava (a shrub that produces starchy tubers), yams, and sweet potatoes. Root crops are also used as animal feed, and may be processed to produce starch, glue, and alcohol. In England the earliest root crops were grown about 1650.

root hair a tubular outgrowth from a cell on the surface of a plant root. It is a delicate structure, which survives for a few days only and does not develop into a root. New root hairs are continually being formed near the root tip to replace the ones that are lost. The majority of land plants possess root hairs, which serve greatly to increase the surface area available for the absorption of water and mineral salts from the soil. The layer of the root's epidermis that produces root hairs is known as the piliferous layer.

root-mean-square (RMS) value obtained by taking the square root of the mean (average) of the squares of a set of values; for example the RMS value of four quantities a, b, c, and d is $\sqrt{[(a^2 + b^2 + c^2 + d^2)/4]}$. For an alternating current (AC), the RMS value is equal to the peak value divided by the square root of 2.

roots music or **world music** term originally denoting ◊reggae, later encompassing any music indigenous to a particular culture. Examples are W African *mbalax*, E African *soukous*, S African *mbaqanga*, French Antillean *zouk*, Javanese gamelan, Latin American salsa, Cajun music, and European folk music.

rootstock another name for ◊rhizome.

rope stout cordage with circumference over 2.5 cm/ 1 in. Rope is made similarly to thread or twine, by twisting yarns together to form strands, which are then in turn twisted around one another in the direction opposite to that of the yarns. Although ◊hemp is still used to make rope, nylon is increasingly used.

Roquefort-sur-Soulzon /ˈrɒkfɔː sjuə suːlˈzɒ/ village in Aveyron *département*, France; population (1982) 880. It gives its name to a strong cheese made of sheep's and goats' milk and matured in caves.

Roraima, Mount /rɔːˈraɪmə/ plateau in the ◊Pacaraima range in South America, rising to 2,875 m/9,432 ft on the Brazil, Guyana, Venezuela frontier.

rorqual whale of the genus *Balaenoptera*. They are large, long, fin whales with pleated throats. The **blue whale** *B. musculus* is the largest of all animals, measuring 30 m/100 ft and more. The

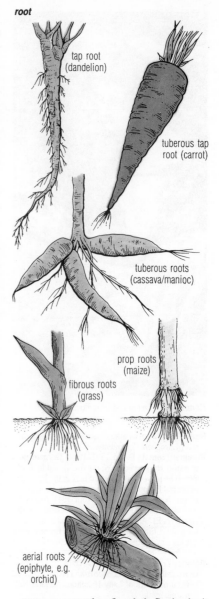

root

tap root (dandelion)

tuberous tap root (carrot)

tuberous roots (cassava/manioc)

prop roots (maize)

fibrous roots (grass)

aerial roots (epiphyte, e.g. orchid)

common rorqual or fin whale *B. physalus* is slate-coloured and not quite so long.

Rorschach test in psychiatry, a method of diagnosis involving the use of ink-blot patterns which subjects are asked to interpret, to help indicate personality type, degree of intelligence, and emotional stability. It was invented by the Swiss psychiatrist Hermann Rorschach (1884–1922).

Rosa /ˈrəʊzə/ Salvator 1615–1673. Italian painter, etcher, poet, and musician, active in Florence 1640–49 and subsequently in Rome. He created wild, romantic, and sometimes macabre landscapes, seascapes, and battle scenes. He also wrote verse satires.

Born near Naples, Rosa spent much of his youth travelling in S Italy. He first settled in Rome in 1639, and established a reputation as a landscape painter. In Florence he worked for the ruling Medici family.

Rosario /rəʊˈsɑːriəʊ/ industrial river port (sugar refining, meat packing, maté processing) in Argentina, 280 km/175 mi NW of Buenos Aires, on the Paraná; population (1980) 955,000. It was founded 1725.

rosary string of beads used in a number of religions, including Buddhism, Christianity, and Islam. The term also refers to a form of prayer used by Catholics, consisting of 150 ◊Ave Marias and 15

rose

◊Paternosters and Glorias, or to a string of 165 beads for keeping count of these prayers; it is linked with the adoration of the Virgin Mary.

Roscellinus /ˌrɒsəˈlaɪnəs/ Johannes *c.* 1050–*c.* 1122. Medieval philosopher, regarded as the founder of ◊scholasticism because of his defence of ◊nominalism (the idea that classes of things are simply names and have no objective reality) against ◊Anselm.

Roscius Gallus /ˈrɒskiəs ˈgæləs/ Quintus *c.* 126–62 BC. Roman actor, originally a slave, so gifted that his name became proverbial for a great actor.

Roscoff /ˈrɒskɒf/ a port on the Brittany coast of France with a ferry link to Plymouth in England; population (1982) 4,000.

Roscommon /rɒsˈkɒmən/ county of the Republic of Ireland in the province of Connacht
area 2,460 sq km/950 sq mi
towns county town Roscommon
physical bounded on the east by the river Shannon; lakes Gara, Key, Allen; rich pastures
features remains of a castle put up in the 13th century by English settlers. The name, originally Ros-Comain, means 'wood around a monastery'
population (1986) 55,000.

rose shrubs and climbers of the genus *Rosa*, family Rosaceae. Numerous cultivated forms have been derived from the sweet briar *Rosa rubiginosa* and the dog-rose *R. canina*. There are many climbing varieties, but the forms more commonly cultivated are bush roses, and standards which are cultivated roses grafted on to a briar stem.

By a Royal National Rose Society ruling in 1979, as received by the World Federation of Rose Societies, the hybrid tea was renamed the larger flowered rose, and the floribunda became the cluster-flower rose. Individual names, such as Peace, were unchanged.

Roseau /rəʊˈzəʊ/ formerly *Charlotte Town* capital of ◊Dominica, West Indies; population (1981) 20,000.

Rosebery /ˈrəʊzbəri/ Archibald Philip Primrose, 5th Earl of Rosebery 1847–1929. British Liberal politician. He was commissioner of works 1885, and foreign secretary 1886 and 1892–94, when he succeeded Gladstone as prime minister, but his government survived less than a year. After 1896 his imperialist views gradually placed him further away from the mainstream of the Liberal Party.

Roseirks /rɒˈseərəs/ a port at the head of navigation of the Blue Nile in Sudan. A hydro-electric scheme here provides the country with 70% of its electrical power.

rosemary evergreen shrub *Rosemarinus officinalis*, native to the Mediterranean and W Asia, with small scented leaves. It is widely cultivated as a culinary herb, and for the aromatic oil extracted from the clusters of pale purple flowers.

Rosenberg /ˈrəʊzənbɜːg/ Alfred 1893–1946. German politician, born in Tallinn, Estonia. He became the chief Nazi ideologist, and was Reich minister for eastern occupied territories 1941–44. He was tried at Nuremberg 1946 as a war criminal and hanged.

Rosenberg /ˈrəʊzənbɜːg/ Isaac 1890–1918. English poet of the World War I period. Trained as an artist at the Slade school in London, Rosenberg enlisted in the army 1915. He wrote about the horror of life on the front line, as in 'Break of Day in the Trenches'.

Like that of his contemporary Wilfred Owen, Rosenberg's work is now ranked with the finest World War I poems, although he was largely unpublished during his lifetime. After serving for 20 months in the front line, he was killed on the Somme.

Rosenberg /ˈrəʊzənbɜːg/ Julius 1918–53 and Ethel 1915–1953. US married couple, accused of being leaders of a nuclear-espionage ring passing information to the USSR; both were executed.

Roses, Wars of the name given in the 19th century by novelist Walter Scott to civil wars in England 1455–85 between the houses of ◊Lancaster (badge, red rose) and ◊York (badge, white rose):
1455 Opened with battle of St Albans 22 May, a Yorkist victory (◊Henry VI made prisoner).
1459–61 War renewed until ◊Edward IV, having become king, confirmed his position by a victory at Towton 29 Mar 1461.
1470 ◊Warwick (who had helped Edward to the throne) allied instead with Henry VI's widow, ◊Margaret of Anjou, but was defeated by Edward at Barnet 14 Apr and by Margaret at Tewkesbury 4 May.
1485 Yorkist regime ended with the defeat of ◊Richard III by the future ◊Henry VII at ◊Bosworth 22 Aug.

Rose Theatre former London theatre near Southwark Bridge where many of Shakespeare's plays were performed. The excavation and preservation of the remains of the theatre, discovered in 1989, caused controversy between government bodies and archaeologists.

It was built in 1587 by the impressario Philip Henslowe (*c.* 1550–1616), who managed it to 1603; the theatre was the site of the first performances of Shakespeare's plays *Henry VI* and *Titus Andronicus*.

Rosetta Stone a slab of basalt with inscriptions from 197 BC, found near the town of Rosetta, Egypt, 1799. It has the same text in Greek as in the hieroglyphic and demotic scripts, and was the key to deciphering other Egyptian inscriptions.

Discovered during the French Revolutionary Wars by one of Napoleon's officers in the town now called Rashid, in the Nile Delta, the Rosetta Stone was captured by the British 1801, and placed in the British Museum 1802. Demotic is a cursive script (for quick writing) derived from Egyptian hieratic, which in turn is a more easily written form of hieroglyphic.

Rosh Hashanah the two-day holiday that marks the start of the Jewish New Year (first new moon after the autumn equinox), traditionally announced by blowing a ram's horn.

Rosicrucians a group of early 17th-century philosophers, who claimed occult powers and employed the terminology of ◊alchemy to expound their mystical doctrines (said to derive from ◊Paracelsus). The name comes from books published in 1614 and 1615, attributed to Christian Rosenkreutz ('rosy cross'), most probably a pen name, but allegedly a writer living around 1460. Several societies have been founded in Britain and the USA that claim to be their successors, such as the Rosicrucian Fraternity (1614 in Germany, 1861 in USA).

Roskilde /ˈrɒskɪlə/ port at the S end of Roskilde Fjord, Zealand, Denmark; population (1981) 39,659; capital of the country from the 10th century until 1443.

Ross /rɒs/ James Clark 1800–1862. English explorer who discovered the magnetic North Pole 1831. He also went to the Antarctic 1839; Ross Island, Ross Sea, and Ross Dependency are named after him.

He is associated with ◊Parry and his uncle John Ross in Arctic exploration.

Ross /rɒs/ John 1777–1856. Scottish rear-admiral and explorer. He served in wars with France and made voyages of Arctic exploration in 1818, 1829–33, and 1850.

Ross /rɒs/ Martin. Pen name of Violet Florence ◊Martin, Irish novelist.

Ross /rɒs/ Ronald 1857–1932. British physician and bacteriologist, born in India. From 1881–99, he served in the Indian medical service, and 1895–98 identified the *Anopheles* mosquito as being responsible for the spread of malaria. Nobel prize 1902.

Ross and Cromarty /rɒs, ˈkrɒməti/ former county of Scotland. In 1975 Lewis, in the Outer ◊Hebrides, became part of the ◊Western Isles, and the mainland area was included in ◊Highland region. Dingwall was the administrative headquarters.

Ross Dependency /rɒs/ all the Antarctic islands and territories between 160° E and 150° W longitude and south of 60° S latitude; it includes Edward VII Land, Ross Sea and its islands, and parts of Victoria Land
area 450,000 sq km/173,700 sq mi
features the **Ross Ice Shelf** or Barrier is a permanent layer of ice across the Ross Sea about 425 m/1,400 ft thick
population there are a few scientific bases with about 250 staff, 12 of whom are present during winter
history given to New Zealand 1923. It is probable that marine organisms beneath the ice shelf had been undisturbed from the Pleistocene period until drillings were made 1976.

Rossellini /ˌrɒsəˈliːni/ Roberto 1906–1977. Italian film director. His World War II theme trilogy of films, *Roma Città aperta*/*Rome, Open City* 1945, *Paisà*/*Paisan* 1946, and *Germania Anno Zero*/*Germany Year Zero* 1947 are considered landmarks in postwar European cinema.

Rossetti /rəˈzeti/ Christina Georgina 1830–1894. English poet, sister of Dante Rossetti, and a devout High Anglican (see ◊Oxford movement). Her verse includes *Goblin Market and Other Poems* 1862 and expresses unfulfilled spiritual yearning and frustrated love. She was a skilful technician and made use of irregular rhyme and line length.

Rossetti /rəˈzeti/ Dante Gabriel 1828–1882. British painter and poet, a founder member of the ◊**Pre-Raphaelite Brotherhood** (PRB) in 1848.

rosemary

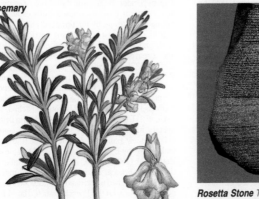

Rosetta Stone *The Rosetta Stone, discovered in 1799, with inscriptions dating from 197 BC.*

Rossetti *Poet and painter, Dante Gabriel Rossetti was a central figure in the Pre-Raphaelite movement. Many of his portraits feature his wife Elizabeth Siddal, who died two years after their marriage. He buried the manuscripts of his poems in her coffin but exhumed them seven years later.*

Apart from romantic medieval scenes, he produced dozens of idealized portraits of women. His verse includes 'The Blessed Damozel' 1850. His sister was the poet Christina Rossetti.

Rossetti, the son of an exiled Italian, formed the PRB with the painters Millais and Hunt, but soon developed a broader style and a personal subject matter, related to his poetry. He was a friend of the critic Ruskin, who helped establish his reputation as a painter, and of William Morris and his wife Jane, who became Rossetti's lover and the subject of much of his work. His *Poems* 1870 were recovered from the grave of his wife **Elizabeth Siddal** (1834–62, also a painter, whom he had married in 1860), and were attacked as of 'the fleshly school of poetry'.

Rossini /rɒ'siːni/ Gioachino (Antonio) 1792–1868. Italian composer. His first success was the opera *Tancredi* 1813. In 1816 his 'opera buffa' *Il barbiere di Siviglia/The Barber of Seville* was produced in Rome. During his fertile composition period 1815–23, he produced 20 operas, and created (with ◊Donizetti and ◊Bellini) the 19th-century Italian operatic style. After *Guillaume Tell/William Tell* 1829 he gave up writing opera and his later years were spent in Bologna and Paris.

Among the works of this period are the *Stabat Mater* 1842, and the piano music arranged for ballet by ◊Respighi as *La Boutique fantasque/The Fantastic Toyshop* 1919.

Ross Island /rɒs/ name of two islands in Antarctica:

Ross Island in Weddell Sea, discovered 1903 by the Swedish explorer Nordenskjöld, area about 3,885 sq km/1,500 sq mi;

Ross Island in Ross Sea, discovered 1841 by the British explorer James Ross, area about 6,475 sq km/2,500 sq mi, with the research stations Roos (New Zealand) and McMurdo (USA), and Mount Erebus 3,794 m/12,520 ft, the world's southernmost active volcano. Its lake of molten lava may provide a window on the ◊magma beneath the earth's crust which fuels volcanoes.

Rosslare /rɒs'leə/ port in County Wexford, Republic of Ireland, 15 km/9 mi SE of Wexford; population (1980) 600; the Irish terminus of the steamer route from Fishguard from 1906. It was founded by the English 1210.

Ross Sea /rɒs/ Antarctic inlet of the S Pacific. See also ◊Ross Dependency and ◊Ross Island.

Rostand /rɒs'tɒn/ Edmond 1869–1918. French dramatist, who wrote *Cyrano de Bergerac* 1897 and *L'Aiglon* 1900 (based on the life of Napoleon III), in which Sarah Bernhardt played a leading role.

Rostock /'rɒstɒk/ industrial port (electronics, fish processing, ship repair) and capital of Rostock county, on the river Warnow, in East Germany, 13 km/8 mi south of the Baltic; population (1986) 246,000. Founded 1189 in the 14th century it became a powerful member of the ◊Hanseatic League. Rostock county has an area of 7,080 sq km/2,733 sq mi, and a population of 903,000.

Rostov-on-Don /'rɒstɒv ɒn 'dɒn/ industrial port (shipbuilding, tobacco, cars, locomotives, textiles) in SW USSR, capital of Rostov region, on the river Don, 23 km/14 mi E of the Sea of Azov; population (1987) 1,004,000. Rostov dates from 1761, and is linked by river and canal with Volgograd on the Volga.

Rostropovich /ˌrɒstrə'pəʊvɪtʃ/ Mstislav 1927– . Russian cellist and conductor, deprived of Soviet citizenship in 1978 because of his sympathies with political dissidents. Prokofiev, Shostakovich, Khachaturian, and Britten wrote pieces for him. Since 1977 he has directed the National Symphony Orchestra, Washington, DC.

Rosyth /rə'saɪθ/ a naval base and dockyard used for nuclear submarine refits, in Fife, Scotland, built 1909 on the N shore of the Firth of Forth; population (1980) 6,500.

Rota /'rəʊtə/ naval base near ◊Cádiz, Spain.

Rotary Club philanthropic society of business and professional people; founded by US lawyer Paul Harris (1878–1947) in Chicago 1905. It is now international, with some 750,000 members.

Roth /rɒθ/ Philip 1933– . US novelist, noted for his portrayals of modern Jewish-American life. His books include *Goodbye Columbus* 1959; *Portnoy's Complaint* 1969; and a series of novels about a writer, Nathan Zuckerman, including *The Ghost Writer* 1979, *Zuckerman Unbound* 1981, and *The Anatomy Lesson* 1984.

Rothamsted /'rɒθəmsted/ an agricultural research centre in Hertfordshire, England, NW of St Albans.

Rothenburg /'rəʊtnbʊək/ town in Bavaria, West Germany, 65 km/40 mi west of Nuremberg; population (1978) 13,000. It is noted for its medieval buildings, churches, and walls.

Rotherham /'rɒðərəm/ industrial town (pottery, glass, coal) in South Yorkshire, England, on the river Don, NE of Sheffield; population (1981) 81,988.

Rothermere /'rɒðəmɪə/ Viscount 1868–1940. British newspaper proprietor, brother of Viscount ◊Northcliffe.

Rothko /'rɒθkəʊ/ Mark 1903–1970. US painter, born in Russia, an Abstract Expressionist and a pioneer of *Colour Field* painting (abstract, dominated by areas of unmodulated, strong colour).

Rothko produced a number of series of paintings in the 1950s and 1960s, including one at Harvard University, Cambridge, Massachusetts; one for the Tate Gallery, London; and his own favourite 1967–69 for a chapel in Houston, Texas.

Rothschild /'rɒθstʃaɪld/ a European family, noted for its activity in the financial world for two centuries. Mayer Anselm (1744–1812) set up as a moneylender in Frankfurt-am-Main, Germany, and important business houses were established throughout Europe by his ten children.

Nathan Mayer (1777–1836) settled in England, and his grandson Nathaniel (1840–1915) was created a baron in 1885. Lionel Walter (1868–1937) succeeded his father as 2nd Baron Rothschild and was a noted naturalist. His daughter Miriam (1908–) is an entomologist, famous for her studies of fleas. The 2nd baron's nephew, Nathaniel (1910–1990), 3rd Baron Rothschild, was a scientist. During World War II he worked in British military intelligence. He was head of the central policy-review staff in the Cabinet Office (the 'think tank' set up by Edward Heath) 1970–74. James de Rothschild (1878–1957), originally a member of the French branch, but who became a naturalized Briton, bequeathed to the nation Waddesdon Manor, near Aylesbury. Of the French branch, Baron Eric de Rothschild (1940–) owns Château Lafitte

and Baron Philippe de Rothschild (1902–) owns Château Mouton-Rothschild, both leading claret-producing properties in Pauillac, SW France.

rotifer any of the tiny invertebrates, also called 'wheel animalcules', of the phylum Aschelminthes. Mainly freshwater, some marine, rotifers have a ring of cilia that carries food to the mouth and also provides propulsion. Smallest of multicellular animals, few reach 0.05 cm/0.02 in.

Rotorua /ˌrəʊtə'ruːə/ town with medicinal hot springs and active volcanoes in North Island, New Zealand, near Lake Rotorua; population (1985) 52,000.

rotten borough an English parliamentary constituency, before the Great Reform Act 1832, that returned members to Parliament in spite of having small numbers of electors. Such a borough could easily be manipulated by those with sufficient money or influence.

Rotterdam /'rɒtədæm/ industrial port (brewing, distilling, shipbuilding, sugar and petroleum refining, margarine, tobacco) in the Netherlands and one of the foremost ocean cargo ports in the world, in the Rhine-Maas delta, linked by canal 1866–90 with the North Sea; population (1988) 1,036,000.

Rotterdam dates from the 12th century or earlier, but the centre was destroyed by German air attack 1940, and rebuilt; its notable art collections were saved. The philosopher Erasmus was born here. The university was founded 1973.

Rottweiler breed of guard dog originating from Rottweil in S Germany. Large and powerful, it needs regular exercise, and has not proved successful as a pet.

Rouault /ruː'əʊ/ Georges 1871–1958. French painter, etcher, illustrator, and designer. Early in his career he was associated with the ◊Fauves, but created his own style using heavy, dark colours and bold brushwork. His subjects included sad clowns, prostitutes, and evil lawyers; from about 1940 he painted mainly religious works.

Rouault was born in Paris, the son of a cabinet-maker. He was apprenticed to a stained-glass-maker; later he studied under the Symbolist painter Gustave Moreau and became curator of Moreau's studio. *The Prostitute* 1906 (Musée Nationale d'Art Moderne, Paris) and *The Face of Christ* 1933 (Musée des Beaux-Arts, Ghent, Belgium) represent extremes of Rouault's painting style. He also produced illustrations, designed tapestries, stained glass, and sets for Diaghilev's Ballets Russes, and in 1948 he published a series of etchings, *Miserere*.

Roubaix /ruː'beɪ/ town in Nord-Pay-de-Calais, N France, adjacent to Lille, population (1982) 102,000; important centre of French woollen textile production.

Roubiliac /ˌruːbɪ'jæk/ or **Roubillac**, Louis François c.1705–1762. French sculptor, a Huguenot who fled religious persecution to settle in England 1732. He became a leading sculptor of the day, creating a statue of Handel for Vauxhall Gardens 1737 (Victoria and Albert Museum, London) and teaching at St Martin's Lane Academy from 1745.

He also produced lively statues of historic figures, such as Newton, and an outstanding funerary monument, the *Tomb of Lady Elizabeth Nightingale* 1761 (Westminster Abbey, London).

Rouen /ruː'ɒn/ industrial port (cotton textiles, electronics, distilling, oil refining) on the Seine, capital of Haute-Normandie, NW France; population (1982) 380,000.

history Rouen was capital of ◊Normandy from 912. Lost by King ◊John 1204, it returned briefly to English possession 1419–49; Joan of Arc was burned in the square 1431. The novelist Flaubert was born here, and the hospital where his father was chief surgeon is now a Flaubert museum.

Rouget de Lisle /ruː'ʒeɪ də 'liːl/ Claude-Joseph 1760–1836. French army officer, who composed, while at Strasbourg in 1792, the 'Marseillaise', the French national anthem.

Roulers /ruː'leɪ/ French name of ◊Roeselare, town in Belgium.

roulette a gambling game of chance in which the players bet on a ball landing in the correct segment (numbered 0–36 and alternately coloured red and black) on a rotating wheel.

Bets can be made on a single number, double numbers, three, four, six, eight, twelve or twenty-four numbers. Naturally the odds are reduced the more numbers are selected. Bets can also be made on the number being odd or evens, between 1 and 18 or 19 and 36, or it being red or black. In each of those cases even odds are given. The advantage is with the banker, however, because the zero (0) gives all stakes to the bank unless a player bets on 0. The play is under the control of a croupier.

rounders bat and ball game similar to ◊baseball but played on a much smaller pitch. The first reference to rounders is in 1744.

Roundhead a member of the Parliamentary party during the English Civil War 1640–60, opposing the royalist Cavaliers. The term referred to the short hair then worn only by the lower classes.

roup contagious respiratory disease of poultry and game. Caused by unhealthy conditions, it is characterized by swelling of the head and purulent catarrh.

Rousseau /ruːˈsəʊ/ (Etienne-Pierre) Théodore 1812–1867. French landscape painter of the ◊Barbizon School. Born in Paris, he came under the influence of the British landscape painters Constable and Bonington, sketched from nature in many parts of France, and settled in Barbizon in 1848. He painted oppressive, gloomy, Romantic landscapes.

Rousseau /ruːˈsəʊ/ Henri 'Le Douanier' 1844–1910. French painter, a self-taught naive artist. His subjects included scenes of the Parisian suburbs and exotic junglescapes, painted with painstaking detail, for example *Surprised! Tropical Storm with a Tiger* 1891 (National Gallery, London).

Rousseau served in the army for some years, then became a toll collector (hence *Le Douanier*, 'the customs official'), and finally took up full-time painting in 1885. He exhibited at the Salon des Indépendants from 1886 to 1910 and was associated with the group led by Picasso and the poet Apollinaire, but his position was unique. As a naive painter, and a naive and pompous person, he was considered ridiculous, yet admired for his inimitable style.

Rousseau /ruːˈsəʊ/ Jean-Jacques 1712–1778. French social philosopher and writer, born in Geneva. *Discourses on the Origins of Inequality* 1754 made him famous, denouncing civilized society and postulating the paradox of the superiority of the 'noble savage'. *Social Contract* 1762 emphasized the rights of the people over those of the government, and stated that a government could be legitimately overthrown if it failed to express the general will of the people. It was a significant influence on the French Revolution. In the novel *Emile* 1762 he outlined a new theory of education, based on natural development and the power of example, to elicit the unspoiled nature and abilities of children. *Confessions*, published posthumously 1782, was a frank account of his occasionally immoral life, and was a founding work of autobiography.

Rovaniemi /ˈrɒvənjeɪmɪ/ capital of Lappi province, N Finland, and chief town of Finnish Lapland, situated just S of the Arctic Circle; population (1986) 32,769. After World War II the town was rebuilt by the architect Alvar Aalto who laid out the main streets in the form of a reindeer's antlers.

rowan another name for the ◊mountain ash tree.

Rowbotham /ˈrəʊbɒtəm/ Sheila 1943– . British socialist feminist, historian, lecturer, and writer. Her pamphlet *Women's Liberation and the New Politics* 1970 laid down fundamental approaches and demands of the emerging British women's movement.

Rowbotham first taught in schools and then became involved with the Workers Educational Association. An active socialist since the early 1960s, she has contributed to several left-wing journals. Other publications include *Hidden from*

Rousseau Jean-Jacques Rousseau, whose writings struck fear into despotic governments throughout Europe.

History and *Women's Consciousness, Man's World* both 1973, and *Beyond the Fragments* 1979.

Rowe /rəʊ/ Nicholas 1674–1718. English playwright and poet, whose dramas include *The Fair Penitent* 1702 and *Jane Shore* 1714, in which Mrs Siddons played. He edited Shakespeare, and was Poet Laureate from 1715.

rowing propulsion of a boat by oars, either by one rower with two oars (sculling) or by crews (two, four, or eight persons) with one oar each, often with a coxswain (steering).

Doggett's Coat and Badge 1715, begun for Thames watermen, and the first English race, still survives. Rowing as a sport began with the English Leander Club, 1817, followed by the Castle Garden boat club, USA, 1834. Chief annual races in the UK are the ◊Boat Race; Thames head of the river race; and the events of ◊Henley royal regatta, also a major international event. In the USA the Harvard–Yale boat race is held on the Thames at New London, and the Poughkeepsie regatta is a premier event.

Rowing: recent winners

World Championship first held 1962 for men, 1974 for women

men—single sculls
1981 Peter-Michael Kolbe *(West Germany)*
1982 Rudiger Reiche *(East Germany)*
1983 Peter-Michael Kolbe *(West Germany)*
1985 Pertti Karppinen *(Finland)*
1986 Peter-Michael Kolbe *(West Germany)*
1987 Thomas Lange *(East Germany)*
1989 Thomas Lange *(East Germany)*
women—single sculls
1981 Sanda Toma *(Romania)*
1982 Irina Fetisova *(USSR)*
1983 Jutta Hampe *(East Germany)*
1985 Cornelia Linse *(East Germany)*
1986 Jutta Hampe *(East Germany)*
1987 Magdalena Georgeyeva *(Bulgaria)*
1989 Elisabeta Lipa *(Romania)*

rowan

The Boat Race first held 1829, rowed annually between Putney and Mortlake by crews from the Oxford and Cambridge University rowing clubs
1986 Cambridge
1987 Oxford
1988 Oxford
1989 Oxford
1990 Oxford
wins
Cambridge 69, Oxford 66
Doggett's Coat and Badge first held 1715, the oldest continuous sporting trophy still regularly contested
1981 W Hickman
1982 G Anness
1983 P Hickman
1984 S McCarthy
1985 R B Spencer
1986 C Woodward-Fisher
1987 C Spencer
1988 G Hayes
1989 R Humphrey

Rowlandson /ˈrəʊləndsən/ Thomas 1756–1827. English painter and illustrator, a caricaturist of Georgian social life. His *Tour of Dr Syntax in Search of the Picturesque* 1809 and its two sequels 1812–21 proved very popular.

Rowlandson studied at the Royal Academy schools and in Paris. Impoverished by gambling, he turned from portrait painting to caricature around 1780. Other works include *The Dance of Death* 1815–16 and illustrations for the novelists Smollett, Goldsmith, and Sterne.

Rowley /ˈrəʊlɪ/ William *c.* 1585–*c.* 1642. English actor and dramatist, collaborator with ◊Middleton in *The Changeling* 1621 and with ◊Dekker and ◊Ford in *The Witch of Edmonton* published 1658.

Rowling /ˈrəʊlɪŋ/ Wallace 'Bill' 1927– . New Zealand Labour politician, party leader 1969–75, prime minister 1974–75.

Rowntree /ˈraʊntriː/ Benjamin Seebohm 1871–1954. British entrepreneur and philanthropist. Much of the money he acquired as chair (1925–41) of the family firm of confectioners, H I Rowntree, he used to fund investigations into social conditions. His writings include *Poverty* 1900. The three *Rowntree Trusts*, which were founded by his father *Joseph Rowntree* (1836–1295) in 1904, fund research into housing, social care and social policy, support projects relating to social justice, and give grants to pressure groups working in these areas.

Rowntree joined the York-based family business in 1889 after studying at Owens College (later the University of Manchester). The introduction of company pensions (1906), a five-day working week (1919), and an employee profit-sharing scheme (1923) gave him a reputation as an enlightened and paternalistic employer. An associate of David Lloyd George, he was director of the welfare department of the Ministry of Munitions during World War I.

His pioneering study of working-class households in York 1897–98, published as *Poverty*, was a landmark in empirical sociology; it showed that 28% of the population fell below an arbitrary level of minimum income, and 16% experienced 'primary poverty'. Rowntree also wrote on gambling, unemployment, and business organization.

Rowse /raʊs/ A(lfred) L(eslie) 1903– . English popular historian. He published a biography of Shakespeare 1963, and in 1973 controversially identified the 'Dark Lady' of Shakespeare's sonnets as Emilia Lanier, half-Italian daughter of a court musician, with whom the Bard is alleged to have had an affair 1593–95.

Roxburgh /ˈrɒksbərə/ former border county of Scotland, included in 1975 in Borders region. A mainly upland area, where sheep are raised, it includes the fringes of the Cheviot hills. Jedburgh was the county town.

Roy /rɔɪ/ Manabendra Nakh 1887–1954. Founder of the Indian Communist Party in exile in Tashkent 1920. Expelled from the Comintern 1929, he returned to India and was imprisoned for five years. A steadfast communist, he finally became

Rowlandson *This vigorous watercolour by the English artist Thomas Rowlandson is a typical example of his Dr Syntax series. This drawing is from the first series which appeared in 1809,* Tour of Dr Syntax in Search of the Picturesque, *for which William Combe wrote accompanying verses. It was a parody of popular picturesque travels of the day.*

disillusioned after World War II and developed his ideas on practical humanism.

Roy /rɔɪ/ Rajah Ram Rohan 1770–1833. Bengali religious and social reformer. He was founder of the Brahma Samaj sect, which formulated the creed of neo-Hinduism akin to Christian Unitarianism. He died in England 1833 as emissary of the Great Mogul, who was still nominal sovereign in India.

Royal Academy of Arts British society founded by George III in London in 1768 to encourage painting, sculpture, and architecture; its first president was Joshua ◊Reynolds. It is now housed in Old Burlington House, Piccadilly. There is an annual summer exhibition for contemporary artists, and tuition is provided for students at Royal Academy schools.

Royal Academy of Dramatic Art (RADA) British college founded by Herbert Beerbohm Tree 1904 to train young actors. Since 1905 its headquarters have been in Gower Street, London. A royal charter was granted 1920.

Royal Academy of Music British senior music school in London, founded in 1822, which provides a full-time complete musical education.

Royal Aeronautical Society the oldest British aviation body, formed 1866. Its members discussed and explored the possibilities of flight long before its successful achievement.

Royal Agricultural Society of England the premier association in England for the agricultural industry. Founded in 1839, the Society is today based at the National Agricultural Centre, Stoneleigh, Warwickshire, where it holds a four-day agricultural show every July.

Royal Air Force (RAF) the ◊air force of Britain. The RAF was formed 1918 by the merger of the Royal Naval Air Service and the Royal Flying Corps.

Royal Assent in the UK, formal consent given by a British sovereign to the passage of a bill through Parliament, after which it becomes an ◊act of Parliament. The last instance of a royal refusal was the rejection of the Scottish Militia Bill of 1702 by Queen Anne.

Royal Ballet title under which the British Sadler's Wells Ballet (at Covent Garden), Sadler's Wells Theatre Ballet, and the Sadler's Wells Ballet School were incorporated 1956.

Royal Botanic Gardens, Kew botanic gardens in Richmond, Surrey, England, popularly known as ◊Kew Gardens.

Royal British Legion full name of the ◊British Legion, a nonpolitical body promoting the welfare of war veterans and their dependants.

Royal Canadian Mounted Police (RCMP) Canadian national police force, known as the ◊Mounties.

Royal College of Music British college providing full-time complete musical education. Founded in 1883, it is in Kensington, W London.

royal commission in the UK and Canada, a group of people appointed by the government (nominally appointed by the sovereign) to investigate a matter of public concern and make recommendations on any actions to be taken in connection with it, including changes in the law. In cases where agreement on recommendations cannot be reached, a minority report can be submitted by dissenters. No royal commissions have been set up by the Thatcher administration since its election 1979. Royal commissions are usually chaired by someone eminent in public life, often someone favourable to the government's position.

Royal Greenwich Observatory the national astronomical observatory of the UK, founded 1675 at Greenwich, E London, England, to provide navigational information for seamen. After World War II, it was moved to Herstmonceux Castle, Sussex; in 1990 it was transferred to Cambridge. It also operates telescopes on La Palma in the

Canary Islands, including the 4.2 m/165 in William Herschel Telescope, commissioned 1987.

It was founded by King Charles II. The eminence of the observatory's work meant that Greenwich Time and the Greenwich Meridian were adopted as international standards of reference 1884.

Royal Horticultural Society British society established 1804 for the improvement of horticulture. The annual Chelsea Flower Show, held in the grounds of the Royal Hospital, London, is also a social event, and there is also a flower show held at Vincent Square. There are gardens, orchards, and trial grounds at Wisley, Surrey, and the Lindley Library has one of the world's finest horticultural collections.

royal household the personal staff of a sovereign. In Britain the chief officers are the Lord Chamberlain, the Lord Steward, and the Master of the Horse. The other principal members of the royal family also maintain their own households.

Royal Institution of Great Britain organization for the promotion, diffusion, and extension of science and knowledge, founded in London 1799 by the Anglo-American physicist Count Rumford (1753–1814). ◊Faraday and ◊Davy were among its directors.

Royal Marines British military force trained for amphibious warfare. See under ◊Marines.

Royal Military Academy officer training college popularly known as ◊Sandhurst.

Royal Opera House the leading British opera house, Covent Garden, London; the original theatre opened 1732 and the present building dates from 1858.

Royal Shakespeare Company (RSC) British professional theatre company that performs Shakespearean and other plays. It was founded 1961 from the company at the Shakespeare Memorial Theatre 1932 (now the Royal Shakespeare Theatre) in Stratford-upon-Avon, Warwickshire, England.

The RSC initially presented mainly Shakespeare at Stratford; these productions were usually transferred to the Aldwych Theatre, London, where it also performed modern plays and non-Shakespearean classics. In 1982 it moved into a permanent London headquarters at the Barbican. A second large theatre in Stratford, the Swan, opened 1986 with an auditorium similar to theatres of Shakespeare's day.

The first director of the RSC was Peter Hall. In 1968 Trevor Nunn replaced him, and in 1986 Nunn was succeeded by Terry Hands. Adrian Noble became director 1990.

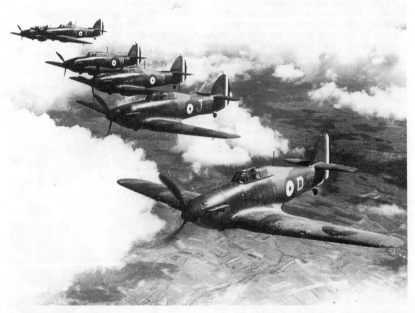

Royal Air Force *Hawker Mark I Hurricanes, flying in formation over France, 1940.*

Royal Society the oldest and premier scientific society in Britain, originating 1645 and chartered 1660; Christopher ◊Wren and Isaac ◊Newton were prominent early members. Its Scottish equivalent is the Royal Society of Edinburgh 1783.

The headquarters of the Royal Society is in Carlton House Terrace, London; the Royal Society of Edinburgh is in George Street.

Royal Society for the Prevention of Cruelty to Animals (RSPCA) British organization formed 1824 to safeguard the welfare of animals; it promotes legislation, has an inspectorate to secure enforcement of existing laws, and runs clinics.

royalty in law, payment to the owner for rights to use or exploit literary or artistic copyrights and patent rights in new inventions of all kinds. Oil, gas, and other mineral deposits are also subject to royalty payments, but in these cases, royalties are paid by the owners (often government) to the exploiters of the deposits.

royal-warrant holder a British commercial firm whose products are supplied to the royal family, and which is authorized to display a royal crest.

Royal Worcester Porcelain Factory see ◊Worcester Porcelain Factory.

Royce /rɔɪs/ (Frederick) Henry 1863–1933. British engineer, who so impressed Charles Stewart ◊Rolls by the car he built for his own personal use 1904 that ◊Rolls-Royce Ltd was formed 1906 to produce cars and engines.

RPI abbreviation for *retail price index*; see ◊cost of living.

rpm abbreviation for *revolutions per minute*.

RSFSR abbreviation for ◊*Russian Soviet Federal Socialist Republic*, the largest constituent republic of the USSR.

RSPB abbreviation for the *Royal Society for the Protection of Birds*; see ◊birdwatching.

RSPCA abbreviation for ◊*Royal Society for the Prevention of Cruelty to Animals*.

RSV abbreviation for *Revised Standard Version* of the ◊Bible.

RSVP abbreviation for *répondez s'il vous plaît* (French 'please reply').

Rt Hon. abbreviation for *Right Honourable*, the title of British members of Parliament.

Ruahine /ˌruːəˈhiːni/ mountain range in North Island, New Zealand.

Ruanda alternative spelling of ◊Rwanda, country in central Africa.

Ruapehu /ˌruːəˈpeɪhuː/ volcano in New Zealand, SW of Lake Taupo; the highest peak in North Island, 2,797 m/9,175 ft.

ruat coelum (Latin 'though the heavens may fall') whatever happens.

Rub' al Khali /ˈrub æl ˈkɑːli/ (Arabic 'empty quarter') vast sandy desert in S Saudi Arabia; area 650,000 sq km/250,000 sq mi. The British explorer Bertram Thomas (1892–1950) was the first European to cross it 1930–31.

rubato (from *tempo rubato*, Italian 'robbed time') in music, a pushing or dragging against the beat for extra expressive effect.

rubber coagulated latex of a great range of plants, mainly from the New World. Most important is Para rubber, which derives from the tree *Hevea brasiliensis*. It was introduced from Brazil to SE Asia, where most of the world supply is now produced, the chief exporters being Malaysia, Indonesia, Sri Lanka, Cambodia, Thailand, Sarawak, and Brunei. At about seven years the tree, which may grow to 20 m/60 ft, is ready for 'tapping'. Small incisions are made in the trunk and the latex drips into collecting cups.

Other sources of rubber are: Ceara rubber, and *Taraxacum Koksagyz*, or Russian dandelion, which grows in temperate climates and can yield about 45 kg/100 lb of rubber per tonne of roots, and guayule *Parthenium argentatum* which grows in SW USA and Mexico.

In the 20th century world production of rubber has increased a hundredfold, and World War II stimulated the production of synthetic rubber to replace the supplies from Malaysian sources overrun by the Japanese. There are an infinite variety of synthetic rubbers adapted to special purposes, but overwhelmingly the most important economically is SBR (styrene-butadene rubber). Cheaper than natural rubber, it is preferable for some purposes, for example, car-tyre treads, where its higher abrasion-resistance is useful, and is either blended with natural rubber or used alone for industrial moulding and extrusions, shoe soles, hosepipes, and latex foam.

rubber another name for a ◊condom.

rubber plant Asiatic tree *Ficus elastica*, family Moraceae, producing latex in its stem. With shiny, leathery, oval leaves, young plants are grown in the West as pot plants.

Rubbra /ˈrʌbrə/ Edmund 1901–1986. British composer. He studied under ◊Holst and was a master of contrapuntal writing, as exemplified in his study *Counterpoint* 1960. His compositions include 11 symphonies, chamber music, and songs.

rubella technical term for ◊German measles.

Rubens /ˈruːbɪnz/ Peter Paul 1577–1640. Flemish painter, who became court painter to the archduke Albert and his wife Isabella in Antwerp. After a few years in Italy, he brought the exuberance of Italian Baroque to N Europe, creating, with an army of assistants, innumerable religious and allegorical paintings for churches and palaces. These show mastery of drama in large compositions, and love of rich colour and fleshy nudes. He also painted portraits and, in his last years, landscapes.

Rubens entered the Antwerp painters' guild 1598 and went to Italy in 1600, studying artists of the High Renaissance. In 1603 he visited Spain, and in Madrid painted many portraits of the Spanish nobility. From 1604 to 1608 he was in Italy again, and in 1609 he settled in Antwerp and was appointed court painter. His *Raising of the Cross* 1610 and *Descent from the Cross* 1611–14, both in Antwerp Cathedral, show his brilliant painterly style. He went to France 1620, commissioned by the regent Marie de' Medici to produce a cycle of 21 enormous canvases allegorizing her life (Louvre, Paris). In 1628 he again went to Madrid, where he met the painter Velázquez. In 1629–30 he was in London as diplomatic envoy to Charles I, and painted the ceiling of the Banqueting House in Whitehall.

Rubens's portraits range from intimate pictures of his second wife such as *Hélène Fourment in a Fur Wrap* about 1638 (Kunsthistorisches Museum, Vienna) to dozens of portraits of royalty.

Rubicon /ˈruːbɪkən/ ancient name of the small river flowing into the Adriatic which, under the Roman Republic, marked the boundary between Italy proper and Cisalpine Gaul. When ◊Caesar led his army across it 49 BC he therefore declared war on the republic; hence to 'cross the Rubicon' means to take an irrevocable step. It is believed to be the present-day Fiumicino, which rises in the Etruscan Apennines 16 km/10 mi WNW of San Marino and enters the Adriatic 16 km/10 mi NW of Rimini.

rubidium element of the alkali group, symbol Rb, atomic number 37, relative atomic mass 85.48. It is a soft, white metal which tarnishes instantly in air and ignites spontaneously. Discovered spectroscopically by Bunsen and Kirchoff in the mineral lepidolite, it is slightly radioactive, and is used as a photo-sensor.

Rubik /ˈruːbɪk/ Erno 1944– . Hungarian architect, who invented the *Rubik cube*, a multicoloured puzzle which can be manipulated and rearranged in only one correct way, but about 43 trillion wrong ones. Intended to help his students understand three-dimensional design, it became a world craze.

Rubinstein /ˈruːbɪnstaɪn/ Artur 1887–1982. Polish-American pianist. He studied in Warsaw and Berlin, and appeared with the world's major symphony orchestras, specializing in the music of Chopin, Debussy, and Spanish composers.

Rubinstein /ˈruːbɪnstaɪn/ Helena 1882–1965. Polish tycoon, who emigrated to Australia 1902, where she started up a face-cream business. She moved to

Rubens The Descent from the Cross (*c.1611*) *Courtauld Collection, London.*

Europe 1904, and later to the USA, opening salons in London, Paris, and New York.

Rublev /ruːˈblɒf/ (Rublyov) *c.* 1370–1430. Russian icon painter. Only one documented work survives, the *Holy Trinity* about 1411 (Tretyakov Gallery, Moscow). This shows a basically Byzantine style, but with a gentler expression.

He is known to have worked with ◊Theophanes the Greek in the Cathedral of the Annunciation in Moscow. In later life Rublev became a monk. The director Tarkovsky made a film of his life 1966.

ruby the red transparent gem variety of the mineral ◊corundum Al₂O₃, aluminium oxide. Small amounts of chromium oxide, Cr_2O_3, substituting for aluminium oxide, give ruby its colour. Natural rubies are found mainly in Burma, but rubies can also be produced artificially and such synthetic stones are used in ◊lasers.

Ruda Sbląska /ˈruːdə ˈʃlɒnskə/ town in Silesia, Poland, with metallurgical industries, created 1959 by a merger of Ruda and Nowy Butom; population (1984) 163,000. Silesia's oldest mine is nearby.

rudd freshwater fish *Scardinius erythrophthalmus*, common in lakes and slow rivers of Europe. Brownish-green above and silvery below, with red fins and golden eyes, it can reach a length of 45 cm/1.5 ft, and a weight of 1 kg/2.2 lbs.

Rude /ruːd/ François 1784–1855. French Romantic sculptor. He produced the low-relief scene on the Arc de Triomphe, Paris, showing the capped figure of Liberty leading the revolutionaries (1833, known as *The Volunteers of 1792* or *The Marseillaise*).

Rude was a supporter of Napoleon, along with the painter David, and in 1814 both artists went into exile in Brussels for some years. Rude's other works include a bust of *David* 1831 (Louvre, Paris) and the monument *Napoleon Awakening to Immortality* 1854 (Louvre, Paris).

Rudolf /ˈruːdɒlf/ former name of Lake ◊Turkana in E Africa.

Rudolph /ˈruːdɒlf/ 1858–1889. Crown prince of Austria, the only son of Emperor Franz Joseph. From an early age he showed progressive views which brought him into conflict with his father. He conceived and helped to write a history of the Austro-Hungarian empire. In 1881, he married Princess Stephanie of Belgium, and they had one daughter, Elizabeth. In 1889 he and his mistress, Baroness Marie Vetsera, were found shot in his hunting lodge at Mayerling, near Vienna. The official verdict was suicide, although there were rumours that it was perpetrated by Jesuits, Hungarian nobles, or the baroness's husband.

Rudolph /'ruːdɒlf/ two Holy Roman emperors:

Rudolph I 1218–1291. Holy Roman emperor from 1273. Originally count of Habsburg, he was the first Habsburg emperor, and expanded his dynasty by investing his sons with the duchies of Austria and Styria.

Rudolph II 1552–1612. Holy Roman emperor from 1576, when he succeeded his father Maximilian II. His policies led to unrest in Hungary and Bohemia, which led to the surrender of Hungary to his brother Matthias 1608, and religious freedom for Bohemia.

Rudra early Hindu storm god, most of whose attributes were later taken over by ◊Siva.

rue shrubby perennial herb *Ruta graveolens*, family Rutaceae, native to S Europe and temperate Asia. It bears clusters of yellow flowers. An oil extracted from the strongly scented blue-green leaves is used in perfumery.

Rueil-Malmaison /ruːˈeɪ ˌmælmeɪˈzɒŋ/ NW suburb of Paris, France. The chateau of Malmaison, now a museum, was a favourite residence of Napoleon, and Empress Josephine retired here on her divorce.

ruff bird *Philomachus pugnax* of the snipe family. The name is taken from the frill of erectile feathers developed in breeding-time round the neck of the male. The ruff is found across N Europe and Asia, and migrates south in winter.

Rugby /'rʌgbi/ market town and railway junction in Warwickshire, England; population (1981) 59,500. Rugby School 1567 established its reputation under Thomas ◊Arnold. Rugby football originated here.

rugby a game that originated at Rugby school, England, 1823 when a boy, William Webb Ellis, picked up the ball and ran with it while playing football (now soccer). Rugby is played with an oval ball. It is now played in two forms: *Rugby League* and *Rugby Union*.

Rugby League the professional form of Rugby football founded in England 1895 as the Northern Union, when a dispute about pay caused northern clubs to break away from the Rugby Football Union. The game is similar to ◊Rugby Union but the number of players was reduced from 15 to 13 in 1906, and the scrum now plays a less important role as rule changes now made the game more open and fast-moving.

Rugby League: champions

1980 Hull Kingston Rovers
1981 Widnes
1982 Hull
1983 Featherstone Rovers
1984 Widnes
1985 Wigan
1986 Castleford
1987 Halifax
1988 Wigan
1989 Wigan
Premiership Trophy introduced at the end of the 1974–75 season; a knockout competition involving the top eight clubs in the first division
1980 Widnes
1981 Hull Kingston Rovers
1982 Hull Kingston Rovers
1983 Widnes
1984 Hull Kingston Rovers
1985 St Helens
1986 Warrington
1987 Wigan
1988 Widnes
1989 Widnes

Rugby Union the amateur form of Rugby football, in which there are 15 players on each side. 'Tries' are scored by 'touching down' the ball beyond the goal-line or by kicking goals from penalties. The Rugby Football Union was formed 1871 and has its headquarters at Twickenham, Middlesex. The first World Cup was held in Australia and New Zealand 1987, and was won by New Zealand.

Rugby Union: champions

International championship instituted 1884, it is now a tournament between England, France, Ireland, Scotland, and Wales
1980 England
1981 France
1982 Ireland
1983 France and Ireland
1984 Scotland
1985 Ireland
1986 France
1987 France
1988 France and Wales
1989 France
County championship inaugurated 1889
1980 Lancashire
1981 Northumberland
1982 Lancashire
1983 Gloucestershire
1984 Gloucestershire
1985 Middlesex
1986 Warwickshire
1987 Yorkshire
1988 Lancashire
1989 Durham
Pilkington Cup formerly the *John Player Special Cup* the English club knockout tournament, first held 1971–72
1980 Leicester
1981 Leicester
1982 Gloucester and Moseley
1983 Bristol
1984 Bath
1985 Bath
1986 Bath
1987 Bath
1988 Harlequins
1989 Bath

Rügen /'ruːgən/ island in the Baltic, part of Rostock county of East Germany; it is a holiday centre, linked by causeway to the mainland; chief town Bergen.

Ruhr /ruə/ river in West Germany; it rises in the Rothaargebirge and flows west to join the Rhine at Duisburg. The *Ruhr valley* (228 km/142 mi), a metropolitan industrial area (petrochemicals, cars; iron and steel at Duisburg and Dortmund) was formerly a coalmining centre.

The area was occupied by French and Belgian troops 1923–25 in an unsuccessful attempt to force Germany to pay reparations laid down in the Treaty of Versailles. During World War II the Ruhr district was severely bombed. Allied control of the area from 1945 came to an end with the setting-up of the European Coal and Steel Community 1952.

Ruisdael /'raɪzdɑːl/ or **Ruysdael** Jacob van *c.* 1628–1682. Dutch landscape painter, active in Amsterdam from about 1655. He painted rural scenes near his native town of Haarlem and in Germany, and excelled in depicting gnarled and weatherbeaten trees. The few figures in his pictures were painted by other artists.

Ruisdael was born in Haarlem, where he probably worked with his uncle, the landscape painter *Salomon van Ruysdael* (*c.* 1600–70). Jacob is considered the greatest realist landscape painter in Dutch art. ◊Hobbema was one of his pupils.

rule of law the doctrine that no individual, however powerful, is above the law. The principle had a significant influence on attempts to restrain the arbitrary use of power by rulers and on the growth of legally enforceable human rights in many Western countries. It is often used as a justification for separating legislative from judicial power.

rule of the road convention or law that governs the side of the road on which traffic drives. In Britain, this states that vehicles should be kept to the left of the road or be liable for any ensuing damage. The reverse applies nearly everywhere else in the world, all traffic keeping to the right which is also the rule at sea, and for two ships crossing, when the one having the other on its starboard must give way.

rum spirit fermented and distilled from sugar cane. Scummings from the sugar-pans produce the best rum, molasses the lowest grade.

Rum /rʌm/ or **Rhum** island of the Inner Hebrides, Highland region, Scotland, area 110 sq km/42 sq mi, a nature reserve from 1957. Haskeval is 741 m/2,432 ft high.

Rumania /ruːˈmeɪnɪə/ alternative spelling of ◊Romania.

Rumford /'rʌmfəd/ Benjamin Thompson, Count Rumford 1753–1814. American-born British physicist. In 1798, he published his theory that heat is a mode of motion, not a substance.

Rumford spied for the British in the War of American Independence, and was forced to flee from America to England 1776. He travelled in Europe, and was created a count of the Holy Roman Empire for services to the elector of Bavaria 1791. He founded the Royal Institute in London 1799.

ruminant general name for an even-toed hoofed mammal with a rumen, the 'first stomach' of the complex digestive system. Plant food is stored and fermented before being brought back to the mouth for chewing (chewing the cud), and then is swallowed to the next stomach. Ruminants include cattle, antelopes, goats, deer, and giraffes.

Rum Jungle /rʌm 'ʒʌŋgl/ uranium mining centre in the NW of Northern Territory, Australia.

rummy card game in which the players try to obtain either cards of the same denomination, or in sequence in the same suit, to score. It probably derives from mahjong.

Rump, the English parliament formed between Dec 1648 and Nov 1653 after ◊Pride's Purge of the ◊Long Parliament to ensure a majority in favour of trying Charles I. It was dismissed 1653 by Cromwell, who replaced it with the ◊Barebones Parliament. Reinstated after the Protectorate ended 1659 and the full membership of the Long Parliament restored by ◊Monk 1660, it dissolved itself shortly afterwards and was replaced by the Convention Parliament which brought about the restoration of the monarchy.

Runcie /'rʌnsi/ Robert (Alexander Kennedy) 1921– . English cleric, archbishop of Canterbury from 1980, the first to be appointed on the suggestion of the Church Crown Appointments Commission (formed 1977) rather than by political consultation. He favours ecclesiastical remarriage for the divorced and the eventual introduction of the ordination of women. He announced his retirement in 1990.

Runcorn /'rʌŋkɔːn/ industrial town (chemicals) in Cheshire, England, 24 km/15 mi up the Mersey estuary from Liverpool; population (1983) 64,600. As a new town it has received Merseyside overspill from 1964.

Rundstedt /'rʊndstet/ Karl Rudolf Gerd von 1875–1953. German field marshal in World War II. Largely responsible for the German breakthrough in France 1940, he was defeated on the Ukrainian front 1941. As commander in chief in France from 1942, he resisted the Allied invasion 1944, and in Dec launched the temporarily successful Ardennes offensive. He was captured, but in 1949 war-crime charges were dropped owing to his ill-health.

rune a character in the oldest Germanic script, chiefly adapted from the Latin alphabet, the earliest examples being from the 3rd century, and found in Denmark. Runes were scratched on wood, metal, stone, or bone.

Runge /'rʊgə/ Philipp Otto 1770–1810. German Romantic painter, whose portraits, particularly of children, have a remarkable clarity and openness. He also illustrated fairy tales by the brothers Grimm.

runner in botany, an aerial stem which produces new plants, a type of ◊stolon.

Runnymede /'rʌnimiːd/ a meadow on the S bank of the Thames near Egham, Surrey, England, where on 15 June 1215 King John put his seal to ◊Magna Carta.

Runyon /'rʌnjən/ Damon 1884–1946. US sports and crime reporter in New York, whose short

runner

foliage leaf

flower

flower bud

terminal bud

adventitious roots

secondary root

prostrate stem 'runner'

tap root

stories *Guys and Dolls* 1932 deal wryly with the seamier side of the city's life in his own invented jargon.

Rupert /'ru:pət/ Prince 1619–1682. English Royalist general and admiral, born in Prague, son of the Elector Palatine Frederick V (1596–1632) and James I's daughter Elizabeth. Defeated by Cromwell at ◊Marston Moor and ◊Naseby in the Civil War, he commanded a privateering fleet 1649–52, until routed by Admiral Robert Blake, and, returning after the Restoration, was a distinguished admiral in the Dutch Wars. He founded the ◊Hudson's Bay Company.

Rupert's Land /'ru:pəts lænd/ area of N Canada, of which Prince ◊Rupert was the first governor. Granted to the ◊Hudson's Bay Company 1670, it was later split among Québec, Ontario, Manitoba, and the Northwest Territories.

rupture synonym for ◊hernia.

Ruse /'ru:seɪ/ (Anglicized name **Rustchuk**) Danube port in Bulgaria, linked by rail and road bridge with Giurgiu in Romania; population (1987) 191,000.

rush plants of the genus *Juncus*, family Juncaceae, found in wet places in cold and temperate regions. The common rush has hollow stems which have been used for mat-making and baskets since ancient times.

Rushdie /'ruʃdi/ (Ahmed) Salman 1947– . British writer, born in India of a Muslim family. His novel *The Satanic Verses* 1988 (the title refers to verses deleted from the Koran) offended many Muslims with alleged blasphemy. In 1989 the Ayatollah Khomeini of Iran called for Rushdie and his publishers to be killed.

Rupert *Prince Rupert, Royalist general and admiral in the English Civil War. His portrait is from the studio of Lely, c. 1670.*

Rushdie was born in Bombay and later lived in Pakistan before moving to the UK. His earlier novels in the magic-realist style include *Midnight's Children*, which deals with India from the date of independence and won the Booker Prize, and *Shame* 1983, set in an imaginary parallel of Pakistan. The furore caused by *The Satanic Verses* led to the withdrawal of British diplomats from Iran. In India and elsewhere, many people were killed in demonstrations against the book and Rushdie was forced to go into hiding.

rus in urbe (Latin 'the country in the city') an urban retreat where one could imagine oneself in the countryside. The phrase is from Martial's *Epigrams*.

Rusk /rʌsk/ Dean 1909– . US Democratic politician. He was secretary of state to presidents Kennedy and Johnson 1961–69, and became unpopular through his involvement with the ◊Vietnam War.

During World War II he fought in Burma and China, and became deputy Chief of Staff of US forces. After the war he served in the Department of State, and as assistant secretary of state for Far Eastern affairs was prominent in ◊Korean War negotiations.

Ruskin /'rʌskɪn/ John 1819–1900. British art critic and social critic. He published five volumes of *Modern Painters* 1843–60, *The Seven Lamps of Architecture* 1849, in which he stated his philosophy of art, and *The Stones of Venice* 1851–53, in which he drew moral lessons from architectural history. His writings hastened the appreciation of painters considered unorthodox at the time, such as ◊Turner and the ◊Pre-Raphaelite Brotherhood. His later writings were concerned with social and economic problems.

Born in London, only child of a prosperous wine-merchant, Ruskin was able to travel widely and was educated at Oxford. The first volume of *Modern Painters* appeared 1843. In 1848 he married Euphemia 'Effie' Chalmers Gray, but the marriage proved a failure; six years later she secured a decree of nullity and later married the painter Millais.

The fifth and final volume of *Modern Painters* appeared in 1860, and the remaining years of Ruskin's life were devoted to social and economic problems, in which he adopted an individual and radical outlook exalting the 'craftsman'. He became increasingly isolated in his views. To this period belong a series of lectures and pamphlets (*Unto this Last* 1860, *Sesame and Lilies* 1865 on the duties of men and women, *The Crown of Wild Olive* 1866). Ruskin was Slade professor of art at Oxford 1869–79, and he made a number of social experiments, such as St George's Guild, for the establishment of an industry on socialist lines. His last years were spent at Brantwood, Cumbria.

Ruskin College was founded in Oxford 1899 by an American, Walter Vrooman, to provide education in the social sciences for working people. It is supported by trade unions and other organizations.

Russ /rʌs/ Joanna 1937– . US writer of feminist science fiction, exemplified by the novel *The Female Man* 1975. Her short stories have been collected in *The Zanzibar Cat* 1983.

Russell /'rʌsəl/ Bertrand (Arthur William), 3rd Earl 1872–1970. English philosopher and mathematician, who contributed to the development of modern mathematical logic, and wrote about social issues. His works include *Principia Mathematica* 1910–13 (with A N Whitehead), in which he attempted to show that mathematics could be reduced to a branch of logic; *The Problems of Philosophy* 1912; and *A History of Western Philosophy* 1946. He was an outspoken liberal pacifist.

The grandson of Prime Minister John Russell, he was educated at Trinity College, Cambridge, where he specialized in mathematics and became a lecturer 1895. Russell's pacifist attitude in World War I lost him the lectureship, and he was imprisoned for six months for an article he wrote in a pacifist journal. His *Introduction to Mathematical Philosophy* 1919 was written in prison. He and

Ruskin *John Ruskin, the art critic who championed Turner and became a pessimistic observer of contemporary society.*

his wife ran a progressive school 1927–32. After visits to the USSR and China, he went to the USA 1938 and taught at many universities. In 1940, a US court disqualified him from teaching at City College of New York because of his liberal moral views. He later returned to England, and was a fellow of Trinity College. He was a life-long pacifist except during World War II. From 1949 he advocated nuclear disarmament and until 1963 was on the Committee of 100, an offshoot of the Campaign for Nuclear Disarmament.

Among his other works are *Principles of Mathematics* 1903, *Principles of Social Reconstruction* 1917, *Marriage and Morals* 1929, *An Enquiry into Meaning and Truth* 1940, *New Hopes for a Changing World* 1951, and *Autobiography* 1967–69.

Russell /'rʌsəl/ Charles Taze 1852–1916. US religious figure, founder of the ◊Jehovah's Witness sect 1872.

Russell /'rʌsəl/ Dora (Winifred) (born Black) 1894–1986. English feminist, who married Bertrand ◊Russell 1921. The 'openness' of their marriage (she subsequently had children by another man) was a matter of controversy. She was a founder member of the National Council for Civil Liberties.

She was educated at Girton College, Cambridge, of which she became a Fellow. In 1927 the Russells founded the progressive Beacon Hill School in Hampshire. After World War II she actively supported the Campaign for Nuclear Disarmament.

Russell /'rʌsəl/ George William 1867–1935. Irish poet and essayist. An ardent nationalist, he helped found the Irish national theatre, and his poetry, published under the pseudonym 'AE', includes *Gods of War* 1915, and reflects his interest in mysticism and theosophy.

Russell /'rʌsəl/ Jane 1921– . US actress who was discovered by producer Howard Hughes. Her first film, *The Outlaw* 1943, was not properly released for several years owing to censorship problems. Her other films include *The Paleface* 1948, *Gentlemen Prefer Blondes* 1953, and *The Revolt of Mamie Stover* 1957. She retired in 1970.

Russell /'rʌsəl/ John 1795–1883. British 'sporting parson', who bred the short-legged, smooth-coated Jack Russell terrier.

Russell /'rʌsəl/ John Peter 1858–1931. Australian artist. Having met Tom ◊Roberts while sailing to England, he became a member of the French Post-Impressionist group.

Russell /'rʌsəl/ John, 1st Earl Russell 1792–1878. British Liberal politician, son of the 6th Duke of Bedford. He entered the House of Commons 1813, and supported Catholic emancipation and the Reform Bill. He held cabinet posts 1830–41, became prime minister 1846–52, and was again a cabinet minister until becoming prime minister again 1865–66. He retired after the defeat of his Reform Bill 1866.

As foreign secretary in Aberdeen's coalition 1852 and in Palmerston's second government 1859–65, Russell assisted Italy's struggle for unity, although his indecisive policies on Poland, Denmark, and the American Civil War provoked much criticism. He received an earldom 1861. He had a strained relationship with Palmerston.

Russell /ˈrʌsəl/ Ken 1927– . English film director, whose films include *Women in Love* 1969, *Altered States* 1979, and *Salome's Last Dance* 1988.

He is often criticized for self-indulgence; some consider his work to contain gratuitous sex and violence, but others have high regard for its vitality and imagination. Other films include *The Music Lovers* 1971, *The Devils* 1971, *Tommy* 1975, *Lisztomania* 1975, and *Gothic* 1986.

Russell /ˈrʌsəl/ Lord William 1639–1683. British Whig politician. Son of the 1st Duke of Bedford, he was among the founders of the Whig Party, and actively supported attempts in Parliament to exclude the Roman Catholic James II from succeeding to the throne. In 1683 he was accused, on dubious evidence, of complicity in the ◊Rye House Plot to murder Charles II, and was executed.

Russell /ˈrʌsəl/ William Howard 1821–1907. British journalist, born in Ireland. He acted as *The Times*'s correspondent during the ◊Crimean War, and created a sensation by his exposure of the mismanagement of the campaign.

Russia /ˈrʌʃə/ originally the name of the pre-revolutionary Russian Empire (until 1917), and now accurately restricted to the ◊Russian Soviet Federal Socialist Republic only. It is incorrectly used to refer to the whole of the present ◊Union of Soviet Socialist Republics.

Russian art painting and other products of the visual arts made in Russia and later in the USSR. From the 10th to the 17th century Russian art was dominated by the Eastern Orthodox Church and much influenced by various styles of Byzantine art. Painters such as Andrei Rublev produced icons, images of holy figures which were often considered precious. By the 17th century European influence had grown strong and in the 18th century the tsars imported European sculptors and painters. Early Russian Modernism 1910–30 anticipated Western trends but was then suppressed in favour of art geared to the sentimental glorification of workers.

Russian history the southern steppes of Russia were originally inhabited by nomadic peoples, and the northern forests by Slavonic peoples, who slowly spread southwards.

9th–10th centuries Viking chieftains established their own rule in Novgorod, Kiev, and other cities.

10th–12th centuries Kiev temporarily united the Russian peoples into an empire. Christianity was introduced from Constantinople 988.

13th century The Mongols (the Golden Horde) overran the southern steppes, compelling the Russian princes to pay tribute.

14th century Byelorussia and Ukraine came under Polish rule.

1462–1505 Ivan III, prince of Moscow, threw off the Mongol yoke and united the northwest.

1547–84 Ivan IV assumed the title of tsar and conquered Kazan and Astrakhan. During his reign the colonization of Siberia began.

1613 The first Romanov tsar was elected after a period of anarchy.

1667 Following a Cossack revolt, E Ukraine was reunited with Russia.

1682–1725 Peter I (the Great) modernized the administration and army, founded a navy, introduced Western education, and wrested the Baltic seaboard from Sweden. By 1700 the colonization of Siberia had reached the Pacific.

1762–96 Catherine II (the Great) annexed the Crimea and part of Poland, and recovered W Ukraine and White Russia.

1798–1814 Russia intervened in the Revolutionary and Napoleonic Wars (1798–1801, 1805–07), and after repelling Napoleon's invasion took part in his overthrow (1812–14).

1827–29 War with Turkey resulted from Russian attempts to dominate the Balkans.

1853–56 The ◊Crimean War.

1858–60 The treaties of Aigun 1858 and Peking 1860 were imposed on China, annexing territories north of the Amur and east of the Ussuri rivers.

1861 Serfdom was abolished. A rapid development of industry followed, revolutionary ideas spread, and a working-class movement developed.

1877–78 Balkan war with Turkey.

1898 The Social Democratic Party was founded.

1904–05 The occupation of Manchuria resulted in war with Japan.

1905 A revolution, although suppressed, compelled the tsar to accept a parliament with limited powers.

1914 Russo-German rivalries in the Balkans, which had brought Russia into an alliance with France 1895 and Britain 1907, were one of the causes of the outbreak of World War I.

1917 The ◊Russian Revolution.

For subsequent history, see ◊Union of Soviet Socialist Republics.

Russian language a member of the Slavonic branch of the Indo-European language family. The people of Russia proper refer to it as 'Great Russian', in contrast to Ukrainian (which they call 'Little Russian') and the language of Byelorussia ('White Russian'). It is written in the Cyrillic alphabet and is the standard means of communication throughout the USSR.

Russian literature literary works produced in Russia and later in the USSR. The earliest productions of Russian literature are sermons and chronicles and the unique prose poem 'Tale of the Armament of Igor', belonging to the period in the 11th and 12th centuries when the centre of literary culture was Kiev. By the close of the 14th century leadership had passed to Moscow, which was isolated from developments in the West until the 18th century: noteworthy in this period are the political letters of Ivan the Terrible, the religious writings of the priest Avvakum (1620–81), the first to use vernacular Slavonic (rather than the elaborate Church

Russian Soviet Federal Socialist Republic

Autonomous Soviet Socialist Republic

	Capital	Area sq km
Bashkir	Ufa	143,600
*Buryat	Ulan-Udé	351,300
Checheno-Ingush	Grozny	19,300
Chuvash	Cheboksary	18,300
Dagestan	Makhachkala	50,300
Kabardino-Balkar	Nalchik	12,500
Kalmyk	Elista	75,900
Karelian	Petrozavodsk	172,400
Komi	Syktyvkar	415,900
Mari	Yoshkar-Ola	23,200
Mordvinian	Saransk	26,200
N. Ossetian	Ordzhonikidze	8,000
Tatar	Kazan	68,000
*Tuva	Kizyl	170,500
Udmurt	Izhevsk	42,100
*Yakut	Yakutsk	3,103,000

Autonomous Regions:

Adyge	Maikop	7,600
Karachai-Cherkess	Cherkesk	14,100
Gorno-Altai	Gorno-Altaisk	92,600
*Jewish	Birobijan	36,000
*Khakass	Abakan	61,900

*In Asia

Slavonic language) in literature, and traditional oral folk-poems dealing with legendary and historical heroes which were collected in the 18th and 19th centuries.

Modern Russian literature begins with Mikhail Lomonosov (1711–65), who fused elements of Church Slavonic with colloquial Russian to create an effective written medium. Greatest of these earlier writers, working directly under French influence, were the fabulist Ivan Krylov (1768–1844) and the historian Nikolai Karamzin (1765–1826). Poetry reached its greatest height with Alexander Pushkin and the tempestuously Byronic Mikhail Lermontov, while prose was dominated by Nikolai Gogol. Typical of the intellectual unrest of the mid-19th century is the prose writer Alexander Herzen, known for his memoirs.

The golden age of the 19th-century Russian novel produced works by novelists such as Ivan Turgenev, Ivan Goncharov, Fyodor Dostoievsky, and Leo Tolstoy. In their wake came the humorous Nikolai Leskov (1831–95), the morbid Vsevolod Garshin (1855–88), and Vladimir Korolenko (1853–1921), and in drama the innovative genius of Anton Chekhov. Maxim Gorky rose above the pervasive pessimism of the 1880s and he had followers in Alexander Kuprin (1870–1938) and Ivan Bunin; in contrast are the depressingly negative Leonid Andreyev and Mikhail Artsybashev. To the more mystic school of thought belong the novelist Dmitri Merezhkovsky (1865–1941) and the poet philosopher Vladimir Soloviev (1853–1900), who moulded the thought of the greatest of the Symbolist poets, Alexander Blok. Many writers left the country at the Revolution, but in the 1920s two groups emerged: the militantly socialist LEF (Left Front of the Arts) led by the Futurist Mayakovsky, and the fellow travellers of NEP (New Economic Policy) including Boris Pilnyak (1894–1938), Pasternak, Alexei Tolstoy, and Ehrenburg. Literary standards sank to a very low ebb during the first five-year plan (1928–32), when facts were compulsorily falsified to present a rosy view of contemporary life in the effort to fortify socialism, but the novelist Sholokhov and poets Mandelshtam, Akhmatova, and Nikolai Tikhonov (1896–) were notable. More freedom was allowed by the subsequent Realism, for example Simonov and the work of the poet Alexander Tvardovsky (1910–71).

During World War II censorship was again severe until the thaw after Stalin's death, when Vladimir Dudintsev published his *Not by Bread Alone* 1956, but was then soon renewed. Landmarks were the controversy over the award of a Nobel prize to Pasternak, the public statements by the poet

Russian rulers 1547–1917

House of Rurik

Ivan 'the Terrible'	1547–84
Theodore I	1548–98
Irina	1598

House of Gudonov

Boris Gudonov	1598–1605
Theodore II	1605

Usurpers

Dimitri III	1605–06
Basil IV	1606–10

Interregnum	1610–1613

House of Romanov

Michael Romanov	1613–45
Alexis	1645–76
Theodore III	1676–82
Peter I 'Peter the Great' and Ivan V (brothers)	1682–96
Peter I 'Peter the Great', (Tsar)	1689–1721
(Emperor)	1721–25
Catherine I	1725–27
Peter II	1727–30
Anna Ivanovna	1730–40
Ivan VI	1740–41
Elizabeth	1741–62
Peter III	1762
Catherine II 'Catherine the Great'	1762–96
Paul I	1796–1801
Alexander I	1801–25
Nicholas I	1825–55
Alexander II	1855–81
Alexander III	1881–94
Nicholas II	1894–1917

Russian Soviet Federal Socialist Republic

Yevtushenko, and the imprisonment in 1966 of the novelists Andrei Sinyavsky (1926–) and Yuli Daniel (1926–) for smuggling their works abroad for publication. Others fled the country, such as Anatoly Kuznetsov (1929–), whose novel *The Fire* 1969 obliquely criticized the regime, and Solzhenitsyn, who found a different kind of disillusion in the West. To evade censorship there was also a resort to allegory, for example Vasili Aksyonov's *The Steel Bird* 1979 grotesquely satirizing dictatorship. Among those apart from all politics was the popular nonsense-verse writer Kornei Chukovsky. The intellectual and cultural thaw under premier Gorbachev will no doubt bring about revaluations and new discoveries of writers from the 1930s onwards.

Russian Revolution the two revolutions of Feb and Oct 1917 (Julian calendar) which began with the overthrow of the Romanov dynasty and ended with the establishment of a Soviet state. The *February Revolution* (Mar Western calendar) arose because of food and fuel shortages, the repressive nature of the tsarist government, and military incompetence in World War I. Riots in Petrograd led to the abdication of Tsar Nicholas II and the formation of a provisional government under Prince Lvov. They had little support as troops, communications, and transport were controlled by the Petrograd workers' and soldiers' council (soviet). ◊Lenin returned to Russia in Apr as head of the ◊Bolsheviks. Kerensky replaced Lvov as head of government in July. During this period, the Bolsheviks gained control of the soviets, and advocated land reform (under the slogan 'All power to the Soviets') and an end to the war.

The *October Revolution* was a coup on the night of 25–26 Oct (6–7 Nov Western calendar). Bolshevik workers and sailors seized the government buildings and the Winter Palace, Petrograd. The second All-Russian Congress of Soviets, which met the following day, proclaimed itself the new government of Russia, and Lenin became leader. Bolsheviks soon took control of the cities, established worker control in factories, and nationalized the banks. The ◊Cheka (secret police) was set up to silence the opposition. The government concluded peace with Germany through the Treaty of ◊Brest-Litovsk, but civil war broke out as anti-Bolshevik elements within the army attempted to seize power. The war lasted until 1920, when the Red Army, organized by ◊Trotsky, finally overcame 'White' opposition, but with huge losses.

Russian Soviet Federal Socialist Republic (Russian *Rossiyskaya*) (RSFSR) constituent republic of the USSR
area 17,075,000 sq km/6,592,658 sq mi
capital Moscow
towns Leningrad, Gorky, Rostov-on-Don, Volgograd
physical largest of the Soviet republics, it occupies about three-quarters of the USSR, and includes the fertile Black Earth district; extensive forests; the Ural Mountains with large mineral resources
features the heavily industrialized area around Moscow; and Siberia; it includes 16 autonomous republics
products three-quarters of the agricultural and industrial output of the USSR
population (1987) 145,311,000; 83% Russian
language Great Russian
religion traditionally Russian Orthodox

recent history see ◊Union of Soviet Socialist Republics.
Autonomous Soviet Socialist Republics (capitals in brackets): Bashkir (Ufa); Buryat (Ulan-Udé); Checheno-Ingush (Grozny); Chuvash (Cheboksary); Dagestan (Makhachkala); Kabardino-Balkar (Nalchik); Kalmyk (Elista); Karelia (Petrozavodsk); Komi (Syktyvkar); Mari (Yoshkar-Ola); Mordovia (Saransk); North Ossetia (Ordzhonikidze); Tatar (Kazan); Tuva (Kizyl); Udmurt (Izhevsk); Yakut (Yakutsk).

Russo-Japanese War war between Russia and Japan 1904–05, which arose from conflicting ambitions in Korea and ◊Manchuria, especially the Russian occupation of Port Arthur (modern Lüda) 1896 and of the Amur province 1900. Japan successfully besieged Port Arthur May 1904–Jan 1905, took Mukden 29 Feb–10 Mar, and on 27 May defeated the Russian Baltic fleet, which had sailed halfway around the world to Tsushima Strait. A peace was signed in Portsmouth, New Hampshire, USA, 23 Aug 1905. Russia surrendered its lease on Port Arthur, ceded S Sakhalin to Japan, evacuated Manchuria, and recognized Japan's interests in Korea.

russula type of fungus of the genus *Russula*, comprising many species. They are medium to large toadstools with flattened caps, and many are brightly coloured.

Russula emetica is a common species found in damp places under conifers. Up to 9 cm/3.5 in across, the cap is scarlet, fading to cherry, and the gills are white. This toadstool tastes acrid and causes vomiting eaten raw, but some russulas are edible.

rust in chemistry, a reddish-brown oxide of iron (hydrated iron (III) or ferric oxide, $Fe_2O_3.H_2O$) formed by the action of moisture and oxygen on the metal.

Paints which penetrate beneath any moisture, and plastic compounds which combine with existing rust to form a protective coating, are used to avoid rusting.

rust in botany, common name for the minute parasitic fungi of the order Uredinales, which appear on the leaves of their hosts as orange-red spots, later becoming darker. The best-known is the wheat rust *Puccinia graminis*.

Rust /rʊst/ Mathias 1968– . West German aviator, who in May 1987 piloted a light Cessna 172 turboprop plane from Finland to Moscow, landing in Red Square. Found guilty of 'malicious hooliganism', he served 14 months of a four-year prison sentence.

His exploit, carefully timed to take place on the USSR's 'national border guards' day', highlighted serious deficiencies in the Soviet air-defence system and led to the dismissal of the defence minister. Rust, despite pleading that his actions had been designed to promote world peace, was sentenced to four years' imprisonment by the Soviet authorities. After serving 14 months in a KGB prison in Lefortovo, he was released and sent home as a humanitarian gesture by the Gorbachev administration.

Ruth /ruːθ/ in the Old Testament or Hebrew Bible, Moabite (see ◊Moab) ancestress of David (king of Israel) by her second marriage to Boaz. When her first husband died, she preferred to stay with her mother-in-law, Naomi, rather than return to her own people.

Ruth /ruːθ/ George Herman 'Babe' 1895–1948. US baseball player, regarded by many as the greatest of all time. He played in ten ◊World Series and made 714 home runs, a record that stood from 1935 to 1974.

Ruth started playing 1914 as a pitcher for the Boston Braves before moving to the Boston Red Sox later that year. He joined the New York Yankees 1920 and became one of the best batters in the game. He hit 60 home runs in the 1927 season (a record beaten 1961 by Roger Maris). He is still the holder of the record for most bases in a season (457 in 1921). Yankee Stadium is known as 'the stadium Ruth

Rutherford *New Zealand physicist Ernest Rutherford (right) with J Ratcliffe in Cambridge, 1935.*

built' because of the money he brought into the club.

CAREER HIGHLIGHTS

Games: 2,502
Runs: 2,174
Home Runs: 714
Average: 342
World Series wins: 1915–16, 1918, 1923, 1927–28, 1932

Ruthenia /ruːˈθiːniə/ or *Carpathian Ukraine* region of central Europe, on the south slopes of the Carpathian mountains, home of the Ruthenes or Russniaks. Dominated by Hungary from 10th century, it was part of Austria-Hungary until World War I. Divided among Czechoslovakia, Poland, and Romania 1918, it was independent for a single day in 1938, immediately occupied by Hungary, captured by the USSR 1944, and from 1945–47 was incorporated into Ukraine Republic, USSR.

ruthenium element, symbol Ru, atomic number 44, relative atomic mass 101.06. It is a hard blue-white metal, a member of the platinum group, and is used to harden platinum and palladium for use in electrical contacts. It is also a versatile catalyst.

Rutherford /ˈrʌðəfəd/ Ernest 1871–1937. New Zealand physicist, a pioneer of modern atomic science. His main research was in the field of radioactivity, and he discovered alpha, beta, and gamma rays. He was the first to recognize the nuclear nature of the atom, and named the nucleus.

Rutherford *British actress Margaret Rutherford who specialized in eccentric character parts both on stage and in films.*

Rwanda
Republic of
(Republika y'u Rwanda)

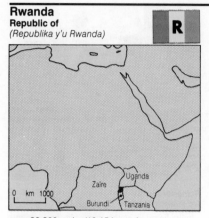

area 26,300 sq km/10,154 sq mi
capital Kigali
physical high savanna and hills, with volcanic mountains in NW
features part of lake Kivu; highest peak Mount Karisimbi 4,507 m/14,792 ft; Kagera river (whose headwaters are the source of the Nile) and National Park
head of state and government Juvenal Habyarimana from 1973
government one-party military republic
political parties National Revolutionary Development (MRND), nationalistic, socialist
exports coffee, tea, pyrethrum, tin, tungsten
currency franc (129.48 = £1 Feb 1990)
population (1989) 7,276,000 (Hutu 90%, Tutsi 9%); annual growth rate 3.3%
life expectancy men 45, women 48
language Kinyarwanda (a Bantu language), French
religion Christian (mainly Catholic) 54%, animist 45%, Muslim 1%
literacy 61% male/33% female (1985 est)
GNP $1.7 bn (1984); $270 per head of population
chronology
1962 Rwanda achieved full independence as the Republic of Rwanda, with Gregoire Kayibanda as president.
1962–65 Tribal warfare between the Hutu and the Tutsi.
1972 Renewal of tribal fighting.
1973 Kayibanda ousted in a military coup led by Maj-Gen Juvenal Habyarimana.
1978 New constitution approved but Rwanda remained a military-controlled state.

He was awarded the Nobel prize 1908, and in 1931 was created Baron Rutherford of Nelson, New Zealand.

Rutherford /'rʌðəfəd/ Margaret 1892–1972. British film and theatre actress who specialized in playing formidable yet jovially eccentric roles. She played Agatha Christie's Miss Marple in four films in the early 1960s and won an Academy Award for her role in *The VIPs* 1963.

rutherfordium artificially made element, symbol Rf, atomic number 104, named after Ernest Rutherford, but known in the USSR as kurchatovium (after scientist Igor Kurchatov). It is radioactive, with a very short half-life, only 70 seconds for the most stable of the isotopes. It is now renamed unnilquadium.

rutile naturally occurring crystalline form of titanium (IV) oxide, TiO_2, from which titanium is extracted. It is also used as a pigment which gives a brilliant white to paint, paper, and plastics. The coastal sands of E and W Australia are a major source.

Rutland /'rʌtlənd/ formerly the smallest English county, now part of ◊Leicestershire.

Ruwenzori /,ru:ən'zɔːri/ a mountain range on the frontier between Zaïre and Uganda, rising to 5,119 m/16,794 ft at Mt Stanley.

Jacob van see ◊Ruisdael.

Ruyter /'raɪtə/ Michael Adrianszoon de 1607–1676. Dutch admiral, who led his country's fleet in the wars against England. On 1–4 June 1666 he forced the British fleet under Rupert and Albemarle to retire into the Thames, but on 25 July was heavily defeated off the North Foreland, Kent. In 1667 he sailed up the Medway to burn three men-of-war at Chatham, and captured others. Ruyter was mortally wounded in an action against the French fleet off Messina, and died at Syracuse, Sicily.

Ruzicka /'ru:ʒɪtʃkə/ Leopold Stephen 1887–1976. Swiss chemist. Born in Yugoslavia, Ruzicka settled in Switzerland in 1929. He began research on such natural compounds as musk and civet. In the 1930s he investigated sex hormones, and in 1934 succeeded in extracting the male hormone androsterone from 31,815 l/56,000 pt of urine and in synthesizing it. Ruzicka, along with Butenandt, shared the 1939 Nobel Chemistry Prize.

Rwanda /ru:'ændə/ landlocked country in central Africa, bounded to the N by Uganda, to the E by Tanzania, to the S by Burundi, and to the W by Zaïre.

government The 1978 constitution provides for a president and a single-chamber legislature, the National Development Council, all elected by universal adult suffrage for a five-year term.

The president appoints and leads a council of ministers.

Rwanda is a one-party state, the sole legal party being the National Revolutionary Development Movement (MRND), whose leader is the president.

history For early history, see ◊Africa. The population comprises two ethnic groups: the agrarian Hutu, over 80%, were dominated by the pastoral Tutsi; there are also a few Pygmies.

Rwanda used to be linked to the neigbouring state of Burundi, 1891–1919 within the empire of German East Africa, and then under Belgian administration as a League of Nations mandate, then as a United Nations trust territory.

In 1961 the monarchy was abolished and Ruanda, as it was then called, became a republic. It achieved full independence 1962 as Rwanda, with Gregoire Kayibanda as its first president. Fighting broke out 1959 between the Hutu and the Tutsi, resulting in the loss of some 20,000 lives before an uneasy peace was agreed 1965.

Kayibanda was re-elected president 1969 but by the end of 1972 the civil warfare had restarted and in 1973 the head of the National Guard, Major-Gen Juvenal Habyarimana, led a bloodless coup, ousting Kayibanda and establishing a military government. Meetings of the legislature were suspended and the MRND was formed as the only legally permitted political organization. A referendum held at the end of 1978 approved a new constitution, but military rule continued.

Rwanda's population density has led to soil erosion and cultivation of all arable land, and dependence on foreign aid.

Ryan /'raɪən/ Robert 1909–1973. US theatre and film actor, equally impressive in leading and character roles. His films include *Woman on the Beach* 1947, *The Set-Up* 1949, and *The Wild Bunch* 1969.

rye

grain

cross section of a grain

Ryazan /rɪ'zæn/ industrial city (agricultural machinery, leather, shoes) dating from the 13th century, capital of Ryazan region, USSR, on the river Oka near Moscow; population (1987) 508,000.

Rybinsk /'rɪbɪnsk/ port and industrial city (engineering) on the Volga, NE of Moscow in the Russian Soviet Federal Socialist Republic. Between 1984 and 1988 it was named Andropov after a president of the Soviet Union; population (1987) 254,000.

Rydberg constant in physics, a constant that relates atomic spectra to the ◊spectrum of hydrogen. Its value is 1.0977×10^7 per metre.

Ryde /raɪd/ English resort on the NE coast of the Isle of Wight, on the Solent opposite Portsmouth, with which there is steamer and hovercraft connection.

Ryder Cup golf tournament for professional men's teams from the USA and Europe. It is played every two years and the match is made up of a series of singles, foursomes, and fourballs played over three days.

Named after businessman Samuel Ryder who donated the trophy 1927, the tournament is played alternately in the USA and Great Britain. The match was between the USA and Great Britain 1927–71; USA vs. Great Britain and Ireland 1973–77, and USA vs. Europe from 1979.

Ryder Cup: winners

USA: 1927, 1931, 1935, 1937, 1947, 1949, 1951, 1953, 1955, 1959, 1961, 1963, 1965, 1967, 1971, 1973, 1975, 1977, 1979, 1981, 1983
Great Britain: 1929, 1933, 1957
Europe: 1985, 1987
Drawn: 1969, 1989

Rye /raɪ/ town in East Sussex, England, noted for its literary associations; population (1985) 4,490. It was formerly a flourishing port (and one of the ◊Cinque Ports), but silt washed down by the river Rother has left it 3 km/2 mi inland. The novelist Henry James lived here; another writer, E F Benson

rye

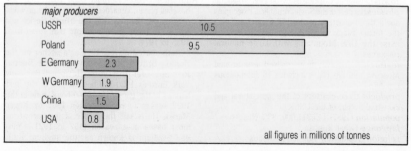

major producers	
USSR	10.5
Poland	9.5
E Germany	2.3
W Germany	1.9
China	1.5
USA	0.8

all figures in millions of tonnes

(who was mayor of Rye 1934–37), later lived in James' house.

rye a grain cereal *Secale cereale* grown extensively in N Europe. The flour is used to make black bread. In Britain, rye is grown principally as a forage crop, but the grain is used in the production of crispbread and some health cereals.

rye-grass perennial, rather wiry grass, *Lolium perenne*, common in pastures and waste places. It grows up to 60 cm/2 ft high, flowers in midsummer, and sends up abundant nutritious leaves, good for cattle. It is a Eurasian species but has been introduced to Australia and North America.

Rye House Plot conspiracy 1683 by English Whig extremists who had failed to stop the accession of the Catholic Charles II to the throne. They intended to murder Charles and his brother James, Duke of York, at Rye House, Hoddesdon, Hertfordshire, but the plot was betrayed. The Duke of ◊Monmouth was involved, and alleged co-conspirators, including Lord William ◊Russell and Algernon Sidney (1622–83) were executed for complicity.

Ryle /raɪl/ Gilbert 1900–1976. British philosopher. His *The Concept of Mind* 1949 set out to show that the distinction between an inner and outer world in philosophy and psychology cannot be sustained. He ridiculed the mind-body dualism of ◊Descartes as the doctrine of 'the Ghost in the Machine'.

Ryle /raɪl/ Martin 1918–1984. English radio-astronomer. At the Mullard Radio Astronomy Observatory, Cambridge, he developed the technique of sky-mapping using 'aperture synthesis', combining smaller dish aerials to give the characteristics of one large one. His work on the distribution of radio sources in the universe brought confirmation of the ◊Big Bang theory.

Rysbrack /'rɪzbræk/ John Michael 1694–1770. British sculptor, born in Antwerp, the Netherlands. He settled in England in 1720 and produced portrait busts and tombs in Westminster Abbey. He also created the equestrian statue of William III in Queen Square, Bristol.

Ryukyu Islands /ri'u:kju:/ southernmost island group of Japan, stretching towards Taiwan and including Okinawa, Miyako, and Ishigaki
area 2,254 sq km/870 sq mi
capital Naha on Okinawa
features 73 islands, some uninhabited; subject to typhoons

products sugar, pineapples, fish
population (1985) 1,179,000
history originally an independent kingdom; ruled by China from the late 14th century until seized by Japan 1609; taken by USA 1945 (see under ◊Okinawa); northernmost group, Oshima, restored to Japan 1953, the rest 1972.

Ryzhkov /rɪʒ'kɒf/ Nikolai Ivanovich 1929– . Soviet communist politician. He held governmental and party posts from 1975 before being brought into the Politburo and made prime minister 1985 by Gorbachev. A low-profile technocrat, Ryzhkov is viewed as a more cautious and centralist reformer than Gorbachev.

An engineering graduate from the Urals Polytechnic in Sverdlovsk, Ryzhkov became foreman of a local smelting works, and rose to become head of the giant Uralmash engineering conglomerate. A member of the Communist Party from 1959, he became deputy minister for heavy engineering 1975. He then served as first deputy chair of Gosplan 1979–82 and Central Committee secretary for economics 1982–85.

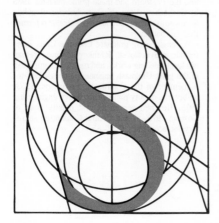

S 19th letter in the English alphabet, and its principal sibilant. It represents an alveolar fricative, either voiceless (sing) or voiced (roses).

S abbreviation for **south**.

SA abbreviation for ◊*South Africa*; ◊*South Australia*.

Saar /sɑː/ (French *Sarre*) river in W Europe; it rises in the Vosges mountains, in France, and flows 240 km/149 mi N to join the Moselle river in West Germany. Its valley is noted for vineyards.

Saarbrücken /zɑːˈbrʊkən/ city on the Saar, West Germany; population (1988) 184,000. It is situated on a large coalfield, and is an industrial centre (engineering, optical equipment). It has been the capital of Saarland since 1919.

SAARC abbreviation for *South Asian Association for Regional Cooperation*.

Saarinen /ˈsɑːrɪnən/ Eero 1910–1961. Finnish-born US architect. His works include the US embassy, London, the TWA terminal, New York, and Dulles Airport, Washington DC. He collaborated on a number of projects with his father, Eliel Saarinen.

Saarinen /ˈsɑːrɪnən/ Eliel 1873–1950. Finnish architect and town planner, founder of the Finnish Romantic school. In 1923 he emigrated to the USA, where he contributed to US skyscraper design by his work in Chicago, and later turned to functionalism.

Saarland /ˈsɑːlænd/ (French *Sarre*) *Land* (state) of West Germany, crossed NW–S by the river Saar. Saarland is one-third forest.
area 2,570 sq km/992 sq mi
capital Saarbrücken
products former flourishing coal and steel industries survive only by government subsidy; cereals and other crops; cattle, pigs, poultry
population (1988) 1,034,000
history in 1919, the Saar district was administered by France under the auspices of the League of Nations; a plebiscite returned it to Germany

1935; Hitler gave it the name Saarbrücken; part of the French zone of occupation 1945; economic union with France 1947; returned to Germany 1957; it is the smallest and poorest of the West German *Länder*.

Sabah /ˈsɑːbə/ self-governing state of the federation of Malaysia, occupying NE Borneo, forming (with Sarawak) East Malaysia; area 73,613 sq km/28,415 sq mi; population (1984) 1,177,000, of which the Kadazans form the largest ethnic group at 30%; also included are 250,000 immigrants from Indonesia and the Philippines. Its capital is Kota Kinabalu (formerly Jesselton), and its exports include hardwoods (quarter of the world's supplies), rubber, fish, cocoa, palm oil, copper, copra, and hemp. It is chiefly mountainous (highest peak Mount Kinabalu 4,098 m/13,450 ft) and forested. The languages are Malay (official) and English, the religions Sunni Muslim and Christian (the Kadazans, among whom there is unrest about increasing Muslim dominance). Its government consists of a constitutional head of state with a chief minister, cabinet, and legislative assembly. In 1877–78 the Sultan of Sulu made concessions to the North Borneo Company, which was eventually consolidated with Labuan as a British colony 1946, and became the state of Sabah within Malaysia 1963. The Philippines have advanced territorial claims on Sabah 1962 and 1968 on the grounds that the original cession by the Sultan was illegal, Spain having been sovereign in the area.

Sabatier /səˈbætieɪ/ Paul 1854–1951. French chemist. He found in 1897 that if a mixture of ethylene and hydrogen was passed over a column of heated nickel, the ethylene changed into ethane. Further work revealed that nickel could be used to catalyze numerous chemical reactions. Sabatier shared the 1912 Nobel Chemistry Prize with François ◊Grignard.

Sabatini /ˌsæbəˈtiːni/ Gabriela 1970– . Argentine tennis player who in 1986 became the youngest Wimbledon semifinalist for 99 years. She was ranked number three in the world behind Steffi Graf and Martina Navratilova in 1989 after capturing the Italian Open title.

Sabbatarianism belief held by some Protestant Christians in the strict observance of the Sabbath, Sunday, following the fourth commandment of the ◊Bible. It began in the 17th century.

Sabbatarianism has taken various forms, including an insistence on the Sabbath lasting a full 24 hours; prohibiting sports and games and the buying and selling of goods on the Sabbath; and ignoring public holidays when they fall on a Sunday.

Sabbath (Hebrew *shābath*, 'to rest') the seventh day of the week, regarded as a sacred day of rest; in Judaism, from sunset Friday to sunset Saturday; in Christianity, Sunday (or, in some sects, Saturday).

sabin unit of sound absorption, used in architecture. One sabin is the absorption of 0.093 sq m/1 sq ft

of a perfectly absorbing surface (an open window).

Sabin /ˈseɪbɪn/ Albert 1906– . Polish-born US microbiologist, whose involvement in the anti-polio campaigns led to the development of a new, highly effective live vaccine.

The earlier vaccine, developed by the physicist Jonas ◊Salk, was based on heat-killed viruses. Sabin was convinced that a live form would be longer-lasting and more effective, and he succeeded in weakening the virus so that it lost its virulence. The vaccine can be orally administered.

Sabine a member of an ancient people of central Italy, conquered by the Romans and amalgamated with them in the 3rd century BC. The so-called rape of the Sabine women—a mythical attempt by ◊Romulus in the early days of Rome to carry off the Sabine women to colonise the new city—is frequently depicted in art.

sable a carnivorous, nocturnal type of marten *Martes zibellina*, about 50 cm/20 in long, and usually brown. It is native to N Eurasian forests, but now found mainly in E Siberia.

Sabu /ˈsɑːbuː/ Stage name of Sabu Dastagir 1924–1963. Indian child actor, memorable as the hero of *The Thief of Baghdad* 1940. He acted in Britain and the USA until the 1950s. His other films include *Elephant Boy* 1937 and *Black Narcissus* 1947.

saccharide the scientific term for a ◊sugar molecule. Saccharides can be joined together in long chains to form ◊polysaccharides.

saccharin sweet, white solid, ortho-sulpho benzimide, $C_7H_5NO_3S$, which is substituted for sugar as a slimming aid. In massive quantities it causes cancer in rats, but investigations in the USA led to no conclusive findings on its effect on humans.

Sacco-Vanzetti case /ˈsækəʊ vænˈzeti/ murder trial in Massachusetts, USA, 1920–21. Italian immigrants Nicola Sacco (1891–1927) and Bartolomeo Vanzetti (1888–1927) were convicted of murder during an alleged robbery. The conviction was upheld on appeal, with application for retrial denied. Prolonged controversy delayed execution until 1927. In 1977 the verdict was declared unjust because of the judge's prejudice against the accuseds' anarchist views.

Sacher /ˈzæxə/ Paul 1906– . Swiss conductor. In 1926 he founded the Basle Chamber Orchestra, for which he has commissioned a succession of works from contemporary composers including Bartok, Stravinsky, and Britten.

Sacher-Masoch /ˈzæxəˈmɑːzɒx/ Leopold von 1836–1895. Austrian novelist. His books dealt with the sexual pleasures to be obtained by having pain inflicted on oneself, hence ◊masochism.

Sachlichkeit (German) objectivity, matter-of-factness.

Sacco-Vanzetti case *The Italian-American anarchists, Sacco and Vanzetti, entering a Massachusetts courthouse during their trial for murder, 1920–21.*

Sachs /zæks/ Hans 1494–1576. German poet and composer who worked as a master shoemaker in Nuremberg. He composed 4,275 *Meisterlieder/mastersongs*, and figures prominently in ◊Wagner's opera *Die Meistersinger/The Mastersingers*.

Sachsen /'zæksən/ German form of ◊Saxony, former kingdom and state of Germany.

sackbut musical instrument of the ◊brass family, a form of trombone, commonly in use from the 14th century.

Sackville /'sækvɪl/ Thomas, 1st Earl of Dorset 1536–1608. English poet, collaborator with Thomas Norton on *Gorboduc* 1561, written in blank verse and one of the earliest English tragedies.

Sackville-West /'sækvɪl'west/ Victoria ('Vita') 1892–1962. British poet and novelist, wife of Harold ◊Nicolson from 1913; *Portrait of a Marriage* 1973 by their son Nigel Nicolson described their married life. Her novels include *The Edwardians* 1930 and *All Passion Spent* 1931; she also wrote the pastoral poem *The Land* 1926. The fine gardens around her home at Sissinghurst, Kent, were created by her.

sacrament in Christian usage, observances forming the visible sign of inward grace. In the Roman Catholic Church there are seven sacraments: baptism, Holy Communion (Eucharist or mass), confirmation, rite of reconciliation (confession and penance), holy orders, matrimony, and the anointing of the sick; only the first two are held to be sacraments by certain Protestant churches.

Sacramento /sækrə'mentəʊ/ industrial port and capital (since 1854) of California, USA, 130 km /80 mi NE of San Francisco; population (1980) 276,000, metropolitan area 796,000. It stands on the Sacramento river, which flows 615 km/382 mi through Sacramento Valley to San Francisco Bay. Industries include the manufacture of detergents and jet aircraft, and food processing, especially almonds, peaches, and pears. It was founded as Fort Sutter 1848 on land bought by John Sutter 1839. Its old town has been restored.

sacred cow anything that is considered above criticism. In Hinduism, cows are sacred and must not be killed. Dairy cows in India (1981) totalled 23,425,000.

Sacred Thread ceremony Hindu initiation ceremony which is a passage to maturity for boys of the upper three castes, usually aged between five and twelve. It is regarded as a second birth; the castes whose males are entitled to undergo the ceremony are called 'twice born'.

Sadat /sə'dæt/ Anwar 1918–1981. Egyptian politician. Succeeding ◊Nasser as president 1970, he restored morale by his handling of the Egyptian campaign in the 1973 war against Israel. In 1974 his plan for economic, social, and political reform to transform Egypt was unanimously adopted in a referendum. In 1977 he visited Israel to reconcile

Sadat President Anwar Sadat of Egypt, Oct 1970.

the two countries, and shared the Nobel Peace Prize with Israeli prime minister Menachem Begin 1978. He was assassinated by Islamic fundamentalists.

Sadducee a member of an ancient Jewish sect opposed to the Pharisees. Sadducees denied the immortality of the soul and maintained the religious law in all its strictness.

Sade /saːd/ Marquis de 1740–1814. French soldier and author. He was imprisoned for sexual offences, and finally committed to an asylum. He wrote plays and novels dealing explicitly with a variety of sexual practices, including ◊sadism.

sadhu in Hinduism, a wandering holy man who devotes himself to the goal of *moksha*, or liberation from the cycle of reincarnation.

S'adi or Saadi /saː'diː/ Pen name of Sheikh Moslih Addin *c.* 1184–*c.* 1291. Persian poet, author of *Bustan/Tree-garden* and *Gulistan/Flower-garden*.

sadism a tendency to derive pleasure (usually sexual) from inflicting physical or mental pain on others. The term is derived from the Marquis de ◊Sade.

Sadler's Wells /'sædləz 'welz/ a theatre in Islington, N London, England. It was originally a music hall. Lilian Baylis later developed a theatre on the site 1931 as a northern annexe to the ◊Old Vic. For many years it housed the Sadler's Wells Opera Company, which moved to the London Coliseum 1969 (renamed English National Opera Company 1974) and the Sadler's Wells Ballet, which later became the ◊Royal Ballet and moved from London to Birmingham (Hippodrome) Aug 1989.

Sadowa, Battle of or *Battle of Königgrätz* Prussian victory over the Austrian army 13 km/8 mi NW of Hradec Kralove (German *Königgrätz*) 3 July 1866, ending the ◊Seven Weeks' War. It confirmed Prussian hegemony over the German states, and led to the formation of the North German Confederation 1867. It is named after the nearby village of Sadowa (Czech *Sadová*) in Czechoslovakia.

s.a.e. abbreviation for *stamped addressed envelope*.

safety glass glass that does not splinter into sharp pieces when smashed. *Toughened glass* is made by heating a glass sheet and then rapidly cooling it with a blast of cold air; it shatters into rounded pieces when smashed. *Laminated glass* is a 'sandwich' of a clear plastic film between two glass sheets; when this is struck, it simply cracks, the plastic holding the glass in place.

safety lamp a portable lamp designed for use in places where flammable gases such as methane may be encountered, for example in coal mines. The electric head lamp used as a miner's working light has the bulb and contacts in protected enclosures. The flame safety lamp, now used primarily for gas detection, has the wick enclosed within a strong glass cylinder surmounted by wire gauzes. Humphrey ◊Davy 1815 and

George ◊Stephenson each invented flame safety lamps.

Saffir–Simpson damage-potential scale scale of potential damage from wind and sea when a hurricane is in progress. 1 is minimal damage, 5 is catastrophic.

safflower Asian plant *Carthamus tinctorius*, family Compositae. It is thistlelike, and widely grown for the oil from its seeds which is used in cooking, margarine, and paints and varnishes; the seed residue is used as cattle feed.

saffron plant *Crocus sativus*, probably native to SW Asia, and formerly widely cultivated in Europe; also the dried orange-yellow ◊stigmas of its purple flowers, used for colouring and flavouring.

Safi /sæ'fiː/ Atlantic port in Tensift province, NW Morocco; population (1981) 256,000. It exports phosphates and has fertilizer plants, sardine factories, and boat building yards.

saga prose narrative written down in the 11th–13th centuries in Norway and Iceland. The sagas range from family chronicles, such as the *Landnamabok* of Ari (1067–1148) to legendary and anonymous ones such as the *Njala* saga.

Other sagas include the *Heimskringla* of Snorri Sturluson celebrating Norwegian kings (1178–1241), the *Sturlunga* of Sturla Thordsson (1214–84), and the legendary and anonymous *Laxdaela* and *Grettla* sagas.

Sagamihara /sə·gɑːmɪ'hɑːrə/ city on the island of Honshu, Japan, with a large silkworm industry; population (1987) 489,000.

Sagan /'seɪgən/ Carl 1934– . US physicist and astronomer, known for his popular science writings. His books include *The Cosmic Connection* 1973, and *Broca's Brain* 1979; he also presented the television series *Cosmos* 1980.

Sagan /sæ'gɒn/ Françoise 1935– . French novelist. Her studies of love relationships include *Bonjour Tristesse/Hello Sadness* 1954, *Un Certain Sourire/A Certain Smile* 1956, and *Aimez-vous Brahms?/Do You Like Brahms?* 1959.

Sagarmatha /sægə'mɑːtə/ Nepalese name for Mount Everest, 'the Goddess of the Universe', and the official name of the 1,240 sq km/476 sq mi Himalayan national park established 1976.

sage perennial herb *Salvia officinalis* with grey-green aromatic leaves used for flavouring. It grows up to 50 cm/1.6 ft high, and has bluish-lilac or pink flowers.

Sagittarius zodiac constellation representing a centaur aiming a bow and arrow at neighbouring Scorpius. The Sun passes through Sagittarius from mid-Dec to mid-Jan, including the winter solstice, when it is farthest south of the equator. The constellation contains many nebulae and ◊globular clusters, and open ◊star clusters. The centre of the galaxy is marked by the radio source Sagittarius A. In *astrology*, the dates for Sagittarius are between about 22 Nov and 21 Dec (see ◊precession).

sago the starchy material obtained from the pith of the sago palm *Metroxylon sagu*. It forms a nutritious food, and is used for manufacturing glucose, and sizing textiles.

sage

Sacramento The State capitol, where the legislature meets, in California's capital city. Built 1860–69 in fine classical style, it stands in parkland.

St Christopher (St Kitts)-Nevis

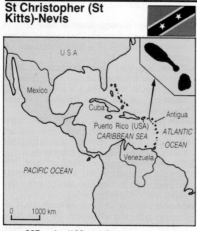

area 267 sq km/103 sq mi
capital Basseterre (on St Kitts)
towns Nevis (chief town of Nevis)
physical two islands in the Lesser Antilles
features St Kitts was the first of the British West Indian islands to be colonized
head of state Elizabeth II from 1983 represented by Clement Athelston Arrindell
head of government Kennedy Alphonse Simmonds from 1980
government federal constitutional monarchy
political parties People's Action Movement (PAM), centre-right; Nevis Reformation Party (NRP), Nevis-separatist; Labour Party, moderate, left-of-centre
exports sugar, molasses, cotton; tourism is important
currency East Caribbean dollar (4.59 = £1 Feb 1990)
population (1989) 40,000; annual growth rate 2.3%
language English
religion Christian
literacy 90% (1984)
GNP $40 million (1983)
chronology
1967 St Christopher, Nevis, and Anguilla were granted internal self-government, within the Commonwealth, with Robert Bradshaw, Labour Party leader, as prime minister.
1971 Anguilla left the federation.
1978 Bradshaw died and was succeeded by Paul Southwell.
1979 Southwell died and was succeeded by Lee L Moore.
1980 Coalition government led by Kennedy Simmonds.
1983 St Christopher-Nevis achieved full independence within the Commonwealth.
1984 Coalition government re-elected.
1989 Prime minister Simmonds won a third successive term.

Saguenay /ˌsæɡəˈneɪ/ river in Québec, Canada, used for hydroelectric power as it flows from Lac St Jean SE to the St Lawrence estuary; length 765 km/475 mi.

Sahara /səˈhɑːrə/ the largest desert in the world, occupying 5,500,000 sq km/2,123,000 sq mi of N Africa from the Atlantic to the Nile, covering W Egypt, part of W Sudan, large parts of Mauritania, Mali, Niger, and Chad, and southern parts of Morocco, Algeria, Tunisia, and Libya. Small areas in Algeria and Tunisia are below sea level, but it is mainly a plateau with a central mountain system, including the Ahaggar Mountains in Algeria, the Aïr Massif in Niger and the Tibesti Massif in Chad, of which the highest peak is Emi Koussi 3,415 m/11,208 ft. The area of the Sahara has expanded by 650,000 sq km/251,000 sq mi in the last half century, but reafforestation is being attempted in certain areas.

Oases punctuate the caravan routes, now modern roads. Resources include oil and gas in the north. Satellite observations have established a pattern of dried-up rivers below the surface, which existed two million years ago. Cave paintings confirm that 4,000 years ago running rivers and animal life existed.

Sahel /ˈsɑːhel/ (Arabic *sahil* 'coast') marginal area to the south of the Sahara, from Senegal to Somalia, where the desert has extended because of a population explosion, poor agricultural practice, destruction of scrub, and climatic change.

Saida /ˈsaɪdə/ ancient **Sidon** port in Lebanon; population (1980) 24,740. It stands at the end of the Trans-Arabian oil pipeline from Saudi Arabia. Sidon was the chief city of ◊Phoenicia, a bitter rival of Tyre about 1400–701 BC, when it was conquered by ◊Sennacherib. Later a Roman city, it was taken by the Arabs AD 637, and fought over during the Crusades.

saiga antelope *Saiga tartarica* of E European and W Asian steppes and deserts. Buff-coloured, whitish in winter, it stands 75 cm/2.5 ft at the shoulder, with a body about 1.5 m/5 ft long. Its nose is unusually large and swollen, an adaptation which may help warm and moisten the air inhaled, and keep out the desert dust. The saiga can run at 80 kph/50 mph.

Only the male has horns, which are straight and up to 30 cm/1 ft long. Once a vanishing species but now protected, the saiga has returned to some areas, and herds of thousands migrate with the changing seasons.

Saigon /saɪˈɡɒn/ former name (until 1976) of ◊Ho Chi Minh City, Vietnam.

Saigon, Battle of /saɪˈɡɒn/ during the Vietnam War, battle 29 Jan–23 Feb 1968, when 5,000 Vietcong were expelled by South Vietnamese and US forces. The city was finally taken by North Vietnamese forces 30 Apr 1975, after South Vietnamese withdrawal from the central highlands.

saint person eminently pious, especially one certified so in the Roman Catholic or Eastern Orthodox Church by ◊canonization. In the revised Calendar of Saints 1970 only 58 saints were regarded as of worldwide importance. The term is also used in Buddhism for individuals who have led a virtuous and holy life, such as Kukai (775–835), founder of the Japanese Shingon sect of Buddhism. For individual saints, see under forename, for example ◊Paul, St.

The lives of thousands of saints have been collected by the Bollandists, a group of Belgian Jesuits. In 1970 Pope Paul VI revised the calendar of saints' days: excluded were Barbara, Catherine, Christopher, and Ursula (as probably nonexistent); optional veneration might be given to George, Januarius, Nicholas (Santa Claus), and Vitus; insertions for obligatory veneration include St Thomas More and the Uganda martyrs.

St Albans /sənt ˈɔːlbənz/ city in Hertfordshire, England, on the river Ver, 40 km/25 mi NW of London; population (1981) 51,000. The cathedral was founded 793 in honour of St ◊Alban; nearby are the ruins of the Roman city of Verulamium on Watling Street.

St Albans, Battle of /sənt ˈɔːlbənz/ first battle in the English ◊Wars of the Roses, on 22 May 1455 at St Albans, Hertfordshire; a victory for the house of York.

St Augustine /seɪnt ˈɔːɡəstiːn/ port and holiday resort in Florida, USA; population (1980) 12,000. Founded by the Spanish 1565, it was burned by ◊Drake 1586, and ceded to the USA 1821. It includes the oldest house (late 16th century) and oldest masonry fort, Castillo de San Marcos (1672), in the USA.

St Austell /sənt ˈɔːstəl/ market town in Cornwall, England, 22 km/14 mi NE of Truro; population (1981) 36,500 (with Fowey, with which it is administered). It is the centre of the China clay area which supplies the Staffordshire potteries.

St Bartholomew, Massacre of /bɑːˈθɒləmjuː/ religious murder of ◊Huguenots in Paris, 24 Aug–17 Sept 1572, and until 3 Oct in the provinces. When ◊Catherine de' Medici's plot to have ◊Coligny assassinated failed, she resolved to have all the Huguenot leaders killed, persuading her son Charles IX it was in the interests of public safety. 25,000 people were believed to have been killed. Catherine received congratulations from all the Catholic powers, and the pope ordered a medal to be struck.

St Bernard /ˈbɜːnəd/ type of dog 70 cm/2.5 ft high at the shoulder, weight about 70 kg/150 lbs. They are squarely built, with pendulous ears and lips, large feet, and drooping lower eyelids. They are usually orange and white.

They are named after the monks of St Bernard, who kept them for finding lost travellers in the Alps and to act as guides.

St Bernard Passes /sənt ˈbɜːnəd/ the **Great** and **Little St Bernard Passes**, passes through the ◊Alps.

St Christopher (St Kitts)-Nevis /sənt ˈkrɪstəfə ˈniːvɪs/ country in the West Indies, in the Leeward Islands.

government The islands of St Christopher and Nevis form a federal state within the Commonwealth. The constitution dates from independence in 1983. The governor-general is the formal head of state, representing the British monarch, and appoints the prime minister and cabinet, who are drawn from and responsible to the assembly.

There is a single-chamber national assembly of 14 members, 11 elected by universal suffrage and three appointed by the governor-general, two on the advice of the prime minister and one on the advice of the leader of the opposition. There are three main political parties, the People's Action Movement (PAM), the Nevis Reformation Party (NRP), and the Labour Party.

Nevis Island has its own assembly of five elected and three nominated members, a prime minister and cabinet and a deputy governor-general. It has the option to secede in certain conditions.

history The original ◊American Indian inhabitants were Caribs. St Christopher (then called Liamuiga) and Nevis were named by Christopher ◊Columbus in 1493. St Christopher became Britain's first West Indian colony 1623, and Nevis was settled soon afterwards. France also claimed ownership until 1713. Sugar plantations were worked by slaves.

The islands were part of the Leeward Islands Federation 1871–1956, and a single colony with the British Virgin Islands until 1960. In 1967 St Christopher (often called St Kitts), Nevis and Anguilla attained internal self-government within the Commonwealth as associated states and Robert Bradshaw, leader of the Labour Party, became the first prime minister. In 1970 the NRP was formed, calling for separation for Nevis, and the following year Anguilla, disagreeing with the government in St Christopher, chose to return to being a British dependency.

Bradshaw died in 1978 and was succeeded by his deputy, Paul Southwell. He died the following year to be replaced by Lee L Moore. The 1980 general election produced a hung assembly and, although Labour won more than 50% of the popular vote, a PAM-NRP coalition government was formed, with the PAM leader, Dr Kennedy Simmonds, as prime minister.

On 1 Sept 1983 St Christopher and Nevis became independent. In the 1984 general election the PAM-NRP coalition was decisively returned to office. In the 1989 general election, PAM won six of the eleven elective seats in the National assembly and Dr Kennedy Simmonds continued in office.

St-Cloud /sæŋ 'klu:/ town in the Ile de France region, France; population about 29,000. The château, linked with Marie Antoinette and Napoleon, was demolished 1781, but the park remains. It is the site of the ◊Sèvres porcelain factory.

St David's /sənt' deɪvɪdz/ (Welsh **Tyddewi**) 'village' city in Dyfed, Wales. Its cathedral, founded by St ◊David, was rebuilt 1180–1522.

St-Denis /ˌsæn dəˈniː/ industrial town, a northern suburb of Paris, France; population (1983) 96,000. ◊Abelard was a monk at the famous 12th-century Gothic abbey, which contains many tombs of French kings.

St Dunstan's /sənt 'dʌnstənz/ British organization for those blinded in war service, founded in 1915 by newspaper proprietor Arthur Pearson (1866–1921), who had himself become blind in 1910.

Sainte-Beuve /sænt'bɜ:v/ Charles Augustin 1804–1869. French critic. He contributed to the *Revue des deux mondes/Review of the Two Worlds* from 1831. His articles on French literature appeared as *Causeries du lundi/Monday Chats* 1851–62, and his *Port Royal* 1840–59 is a study of ◊Jansenism.

St Elias Mountains /ˌseɪnt ɪˈlaɪəs/ mountain range on Alaska-Canada border; Mount Logan 6,050 m/19,850 ft, Canada's highest mountain, is its highest peak.

St Elmo's fire bluish, flame-like electrical discharge, which occurs above ships' masts or about an aircraft in stormy weather. Although high voltage, it is low current and therefore harmless. St Elmo (or St Erasmus) is the patron saint of sailors.

Saint-Étienne /ˌsænt etˈjen/ city in S central France, capital of Loire *département*, Rhônes-Alpes region; population (1982) 317,000. Industries include the manufacture of aircraft engines, electronics, and chemicals, and it is the site of a school of mining, established 1816.

Saint-Exupéry /ˌsænt ekˌsjuːpəˈriː/ Antoine de 1900–1944. French author, who wrote the autobiographical *Vol de nuit/Night Flight* 1931 and *Terre des hommes/Wind, Sand, and Stars* 1939. His *Le petit prince/The Little Prince* 1943, a children's book, is also an adult allegory.

St Gallen /sæŋ'gæl/ (German **Sankt Gallen**) town in NE Switzerland; population (1987) 126,000. Industries include natural and synthetic textiles. It was founded in the 7th century by the Irish missionary St Gall, and the Benedictine abbey library has many medieval manuscripts.

Saint-Gaudens /ˌseɪntˈgɔːdnz/ Augustus 1848–1907. US sculptor born in Ireland. His monuments include the granite and bronze *Adams memorial* 1891 (Rock Creek Cemetery, Washington DC); he also sculpted portraits.

St George's /sənt 'dʒɔːdʒɪz/ port and capital of ◊Grenada; population (1981) 4,800, urban area 29,000.

St George's Channel /sənt 'dʒɔːdʒɪz/ stretch of water between SW Wales and SE Ireland, linking the Irish Sea with the Atlantic. It is 160 km/100 mi long, and 80–150 km/50–90 mi wide. It is also the name of a channel between New Britain and New Ireland, Papua New Guinea.

St Germain-en-Laye, Treaty of /ˌsæn ʒeəˈmæŋ ɒn 'leɪ/ 1919 treaty condemning the war between Austria and the Allies, signed at St Germain-en-Laye, a town 21 km/13 mi W of Paris. Representatives of the USA signed it, but because the US Senate failed to ratify the Treaty of ◊Versailles, the Treaty of St Germain was not submitted to it. The USA made a separate peace with Austria in 1921.

St Gotthard Pass /sənt 'gɒtəd/ a pass through the Swiss ◊Alps, at an altitude of 2,000 m/6,500 ft.

St Helena /ˌsent ɪˈliːnə/ island in the S Atlantic, 1,900 km/1,200 mi W of Africa, area 122 sq km/47 sq mi; population (1985) 5,900. Its capital is Jamestown, and it exports fish and timber. Ascension and Tristan da Cunha are dependencies.

St Helena

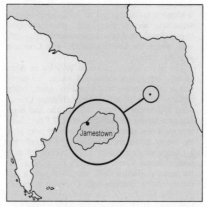

St Helena became a British possession 1673, and a colony 1834. Napoleon died in exile here 1821. Native to St Helena is the Giant Earwig *Labidura herculeana*, which is up to 8 cm/3 in long, the largest species of earwig in the world.

St Helens /sənt 'helənz/ town in Merseyside, England, 19 km/12 mi NE of Liverpool, and connected to the Mersey by canal; population (1981) 99,000. It is an important centre for the manufacture of sheet glass.

St Helier /sənt 'heliə/ resort and capital of Jersey, Channel Islands; population (1981) 25,700. The 'States of Jersey', the island legislature, sits here in the *salle des états*.

St Ives /sənt 'aɪvz/ fishing port and resort in Cornwall; population (1981) 10,000. Its artists' colony, founded by W Sickert and James Whistler, later included Naum Gabo, Barbara ◊Hepworth (a museum and sculpture gardens commemorate her), and Ben Nicholson.

St James's Palace /sənt 'dʒeɪmzɪz/ a palace in Pall Mall, London, a royal residence 1698–1837.

Saint John /seɪnt 'dʒɒn/ largest city of New Brunswick, Canada, on the Saint John river; population (1986) 121,000. It is a fishing port, and has shipbuilding, timber, fish processing, and textiles industries. Founded by the French as Saint-Jean 1635, it was taken by the British 1758.

St John, Order of (full title *Knights Hospitallers of St John of Jerusalem*) oldest order of Christian chivalry, named from the hospital at Jerusalem founded about 1048 by merchants of Amalfi for pilgrims, whose travel routes the knights defended from the Muslims. Today there are about 8,000 knights (male and female), and the Grand Master is the world's highest ranking Roman Catholic lay person.

On being forced to leave Palestine, the knights went to Cyprus 1291, to Rhodes 1309, and to Malta (granted to them by Emperor Charles V) 1530. Expelled by Napoleon (on his way to Egypt) 1798, they established their headquarters in Rome (Palazzo di Malta).

St John's /seɪnt 'dʒɒnz/ capital and chief port of Newfoundland, Canada; population (1986) 96,000, urban area 162,000. The main industry is cod fish processing.

It was founded by Humphrey ◊Gilbert 1582. Marconi's first trans-Atlantic radio message was received on Signal Hill 1901. Memorial University was founded 1925.

St John's /sənt 'dʒɒnz/ port and capital of Antigua and Barbuda, on Antigua; population (1982) 30,000.

St John's Wood /sənt ˌdʒɒnz 'wʊd/ residential suburb of NW London. It is the site of Lord's cricket ground, headquarters of the Marylebone Cricket Club (MCC).

Saint-Just /sænt'ʒuːst/ Louis Antoine Léon Florelle de 1767–1794. French revolutionary. A close associate of ◊Robespierre, he became a member of the Committee of Public Safety 1793, and was guillotined.

St Kilda /sənt 'kɪldə/ three mountainous islands, the most westerly of the Outer Hebrides, 200 km/124 mi west of the Scottish mainland; area 16 sq km/6 sq mi. They were populated from prehistory until 1930, and are now a nature reserve.

St Kitts-Nevis /sənt 'kɪts 'niːvɪs/ contracted form of ◊St Christopher-Nevis.

Saint-Laurent /ˌsæn ləʊˈrɒŋ/ Yves (Henri Donat Mathieu) 1936– . French couturier, partner to ◊Dior from 1954 and his successor 1957. He opened his own fashion house 1962.

St Lawrence /seɪnt 'lɒrəns/ river in E North America. From ports on the ◊Great Lakes, it forms, with linking canals (which also give great hydro-electric capacity to the river), the *St Lawrence*

St Lucia

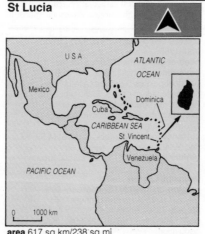

area 617 sq km/238 sq mi
capital Castries
physical mountainous; mainly tropical forest
features volcanic in origin; second largest of the Windward group
head of state Elizabeth II from 1979 represented by Vincent Floissac from 1987
head of government John G M Compton from 1982
government constitutional monarchy
political parties United Worker's Party (UWP), moderate, left-of-centre; St Lucia Labour Party (SLP), moderate, left-of-centre; Progressive Labour Party (PLP), moderate, left-of-centre
exports bananas, cocoa, copra; tourism is important
currency East Caribbean dollar (4.59 = £1 Feb 1990)
population (1989) 128,000; annual growth rate 1.2%
language English
religion Roman Catholic 90%
literacy 78% (1984)
GNP $133 million (1982); $698 per head of population
chronology
1967 Granted internal self-government as a West Indies associated state.
1979 Achieved full independence within the Commonwealth, with John Compton, leader of the United Workers' Party (UWP), as prime minister. Allan Louisy, leader of the Saint Lucia Labour Party (SLP), replaced Compton as prime minister.
1981 Louisy resigned and was replaced by Winston Cenac.
1982 Compton returned to power at the head of a UWP government.
1987 Compton re-elected with reduced majority.

Seaway for ocean-going ships, ending in the *Gulf of St Lawrence*. It is 1,050 km/650 mi long, and is ice-bound for four months annually.

St Leger horse race held at Doncaster, England every September. It is a flat race over 2.8 km/1.7 mi, and is the last of the season. First held 1776, it is the oldest of the English classic races. Because of damage to the course, the 1989 race was held at Ayr, the first time Scotland had staged a classic.

St Leonards /'lenədz/ seaside town near ◊Hastings, England.

St Lô /sæn 'ləʊ/ market town in Normandy, France, on the river Vire; population (1982) 24,800. In World War II it was almost entirely destroyed 10–18 Jul 1944, when US forces captured it from the Germans.

St Louis /seɪnt 'luːɪs/ city in Missouri, USA, on the Mississippi River; population (1980) 453,000, metropolitan area 2,356,000. Its industries include aerospace equipment, aircraft, vehicles, chemicals, electrical goods, steel, and beer.

Founded as a French trading post 1764, it passed to the USA 1803 under the ◊Louisiana Purchase. The Gateway Arch 1965 is a memorial by Eliel ◊Saarinen to the pioneers of the West.

Saint Lucia /sənt 'luːʃə/ country in the West Indies, one of the Windward Islands.

government The constitution dates from independence in 1979. The governor-general is the formal head of state, representing the British monarch. The governor-general appoints a prime minister and cabinet, drawn from and responsible to the House of Assembly.

There is a two-chamber parliament comprising the Senate, of 11 appointed members, and the House of Assembly, of 17 members, elected from single-member constituencies by universal suffrage. Six senators are appointed by the governor-general on the advice of the prime minister, three on the advice of the leader of the opposition, and two after wider consultation. Parliament has a life of five years.

There are three active political parties, the United Workers' Party (UWP), the St Lucia Labour Party (SLP) and the Progressive Labour Party (PLP).

history The early inhabitants were Carib Indians. ◊Columbus arrived 1502. The island was settled by the French 1635, who introduced ◊slavery, and ceded to Britain 1803.

Saint Lucia was a colony within the Windward Islands federal system until 1960, and acquired internal self-government 1967 as a West Indies

associated state. The leader of the UWP, John Compton, became prime minister. In 1975 the associated states agreed to seek independence separately and in Feb 1979, after prolonged negotiations, St Lucia achieved full independence within the Commonwealth, with Compton as prime minister.

The SLP came to power in 1979 led by Allan Louisy, but a split developed within the party and in 1981 Louisy was forced to resign, being replaced by the attorney general, Winston Cenac. Soon afterwards George Odlum, who had been Louisy's deputy, left with two other SLP members to form a new party, the PLP. For the next year the Cenac government had to fight off calls for a change of government which culminated in a general strike. Cenac eventually resigned and in the general election 1982 the UWP won a decisive victory, enabling John Compton to return as prime minister. In new elections in Apr 1987, Compton's UWP was only narrowly returned by a 9:8 majority over the SLP.

St-Malo /sæm mɑ:'ləʊ/ seaport and resort in the Ille-et-Vilaine *département*, W France, on the Rance estuary; population (1985) 47,500. It took its name from the Welshman Maclou (*c.* 640), who was bishop there.

St Michael and St George British orders of ◊knighthood.

St Michael's Mount /sənt 'maɪkəlz/ island in Mount's Bay, Cornwall, England, linked to the mainland by a causeway.

St Moritz /sæm mɒ'rɪts/ winter sports centre in SE Switzerland, which contains the Cresta Run (built 1885) for toboggans, bobsleighs, and luges. It was the site of the Winter Olympics 1928 and 1948.

St-Nazaire /sæn næ'zɑ:/ industrial seaport in Pays de la Loire region, France; population (1982) 130,000. It stands at the mouth of the river Loire, and in World War II was used as a German submarine base. Industries include shipbuilding, engineering, and food canning.

St-Omer /sænt əʊ'meə/ town in Pas-de-Calais *département*, France, 42 km/26 mi SE of Calais; population (1985) 15,500. From 1914–16, it was the site of British general headquarters in World War I.

St Paul /seɪnt 'pɔ:l/ capital and industrial city of Minnesota, USA, adjacent to ◊Minneapolis; population (1980) 270,000. Industries include electronics, publishing and printing, petrochemicals, cosmetics, and meat-packing.

St Paul's Cathedral cathedral church of the City of London, and the largest Protestant church in

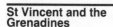

Saint-Simon Ahead of his time , the Comte de Saint-Simon advocated a 'meritocracy', the equality of women, and a plan to link the Atlantic and Pacific by canal.

England. A Norman building, which had replaced the original Saxon church, was burned down in the Great Fire 1666; the present cathedral, designed by Christopher ◊Wren, was built 1675–1710.

St Peter Port /sənt 'pi:tə 'pɔ:t/ only town of Guernsey, Channel Islands; population 16,000.

St Petersburg /'pi:təzbɜ:g/ former name of the city of ◊Leningrad, USSR.

St Petersburg /'pi:təzbɜ:g/ seaside resort and industrial city (space technology), W Florida, USA; population (1986) 243,000. It is across Tampa Bay from ◊Tampa.

Saint-Pierre /sæmpi'eə/ Jacques Henri Bernadin de 1737–1814. French author of the sentimental romance *Paul et Virginie* 1789.

St Pierre and Miquelon /sæmpi'eə 'mi:kəlɒn/ territorial collectivity of France, eight small islands off the south coast of Newfoundland, Canada

area St Pierre group 26 sq km/10 sq mi; Miquelon-Langlade group 216 sq km/83 sq mi

capital St Pierre

features the last surviving remnant of France's North American empire

products fish

currency French franc

population (1987) 6,300

language French

religion Roman Catholic

government French-appointed commissioner and elected local council; one representative in the National Assembly in France

history settled 17th century by Breton and Basque fishermen; French territory 1816–1976; overseas *département* until 1985; violent protests 1989 when France tried to impose its claim to a 200-mile fishing zone around the islands; Canada maintains that there is only a 12-mile zone.

St Quentin /sæn kɒn'tæn/ town on the river Somme, Picardie, N France; population (1985) 69,000. It was the site of a Prussian defeat of the French 1871, and was almost obliterated in World War I. It is linked by canal to the industrial centres of Belgium and Germany. Its traditional textile production has been replaced by chemicals and metalworks.

Saint-Saëns /sæn'sɒns/ (Charles) Camille 1835–1921. French composer, pianist and organist.

St Vincent and the Grenadines

area 388 sq km/150 sq mi, including Northern Grenadines 43 sq km/17 sq mi
capital Kingstown
physical volcanic mountains, thickly forested
features Mustique, one of the Grenadines, is an exclusive holiday resort
head of state Elizabeth II from 1979

represented by Joseph Lambert Eustace from 1985
head of government James Mitchell from 1984
government constitutional monarchy
political parties New Democratic Party (NDP), moderate, left-of-centre; St Vincent Labour Party (SVLP), moderate, left-of-centre
exports bananas, tarros, sweet potatoes, arrowroot, copra
currency Eastern Caribbean dollar (4.59 = £1 Feb 1990)
population (1987) 113,000; annual growth rate –4%
language English
religion Christian (47% Anglican, 28% Methodist, 13% Roman Catholic)
literacy 85% (1981)
GNP $90 million (1983); $250 per head of population
chronology
1969 Granted internal self-government.
1979 Achieved full independence within the Commonwealth, with Milton Cato as prime minister.
1984 James Mitchell replaced Cato as prime minister.
1989 Mitchell decisively re-elected.

Among his many lyrical Romantic pieces are concertos, the symphonic poem *Danse macabre* 1875, the opera *Samson et Dalila* 1877, and the orchestral *Carnaval des animaux*/*Carnival of the Animals* 1886.

Saint-Simon /ˌsænsiˈmɒn/ Claude Henri, Comte de 1760–1825. French socialist, who fought in the American War of Independence and was imprisoned during the French Revolution. He advocated an atheist society ruled by technicians and industrialists in *Du Système industrielle*/*The Industrial System* 1821.

Saint-Simon /ˌsænsiˈmɒn/ Louis de Rouvroy, Duc de 1675–1755. French soldier, courtier, and politician, whose *Mémoires* 1691–1723 are unrivalled as a description of the French court.

St Tropez /ˌsæn trəʊˈpeɪ/ fishing port on the French Côte d'Azur; population (1985) 6,250. It became popular as a resort in the 1960s.

St Valentine's Day Massacre the murder in Chicago, USA, of seven unarmed members of the 'Bugs' Moran gang on 14 Feb 1929 by members of Al Capone's gang disguised as policemen. The killings testified to the intensity of gangland warfare for the control of the trade in illicit liquor during ◊prohibition.

St Vincent /sənt ˈvɪnsənt/ cape of the Algarve region of SW Portugal off which England defeated the French and Spanish fleets 1797.

Saint Vincent and the Grenadines /sənt ˈvɪnsənt, ˌgrenəˈdiːnz/ country in the Windward Islands, West Indies.

government The constitution dates from independence in 1979. The head of state is a resident governor-general representing the British monarch. The governor-general appoints a prime minister and cabinet, drawn from and responsible to the Assembly.

There is a single-chamber legislature, the House of Assembly, with 19 members, of which 13 are elected by universal suffrage, four appointed by the governor-general on the advice of the prime minister and two on the advice of the leader of the opposition. The Assembly has a life of five years.

There are a number of political parties, the most significant being the moderately left-of-centre New Democratic Party (NDP) and the St Vincent Labour Party (SVLP).

history The original inhabitants were Carib Indians. ◊Columbus landed on St Vincent 1498. Claimed and settled by Britain and France, with African labour (see ◊slavery), the islands were ceded to Britain in 1783.

Collectively known as St Vincent, the islands were part of the West Indies Federation until 1962 and acquired internal self-government in 1969 as an associated state. They achieved full independence, within the Commonwealth, as St Vincent and the Grenadines, in Oct 1979.

Until the 1980s two parties dominated politics in the islands, the SVLP and the People's Political Party (PPP). Milton Cato, SVLP leader, was prime minister at independence but his leadership was challenged in 1981 when a decline in the economy and his attempts to introduce new industrial-relations legislation resulted in a general strike. Cato survived mainly because of divisions in the opposition parties, and in 1984 the centrist NDP, led by an SVLP defector and former prime minister, James Mitchell, won a surprising victory.

Saint Vincent Gulf /sənt ˈvɪnsənt/ inlet of the Southern Ocean on which Adelaide, South Australia stands. It is named after Adam John Jervis, 1st Earl of St Vincent (1735–1823).

St Vitus' dance former name for the disease ◊chorea. St Vitus, martyred under the Roman emperor, ◊Diocletian, was the patron saint of dancers.

Sakai /sɑːˈkaɪ/ city on the island of Honshu, Japan; population (1987) 808,000. Industries include engineering, aluminium, and chemicals.

Sakhalin /ˌsæxəˈliːn/ (Japanese *Karafuto*) island in the Pacific, north of Japan, which since 1947

salamander

fire salamander

forms with the ◊Kurils a region of the USSR; capital Yuzhno-Sakhalinsk (Japanese *Toyohara*); area 74,000 sq km/28,564 sq mi; population (1981) 650,000, including aboriginal ◊Ainu and Gilyaks. There are two parallel mountain ranges, rising to over 1,525 m/5,000 ft, which extend throughout its length, 965 km/600 mi. The economy is based on dairy farming, leguminous crops, oats, barley, and sugar beet. In the milder south, there is also timber, rice, wheat, fish, and some oil and coal. The island was settled by both Russians and Japanese from the 17th century. In 1875 the south was ceded by Japan to Russia, but Japan regained it 1905, only to cede it again 1945. It has a missile base.

Sakharov /ˈsækərɒv/ Andrei Dmitrievich 1921–1989. Soviet physicist, known both as the 'father of the Soviet H-bomb' and as an outspoken human-rights campaigner. Nobel Peace Prize 1975. He was elected to the Congress of the USSR People's Deputies (CUPD) 1989, where he emerged as leader of its radical reform grouping.

Sakharov was exempted from military service because of his skill at physics. In 1948 he joined Igor Tamm in developing the hydrogen bomb. He later protested against Soviet nuclear tests and was a founder of the Soviet Human Rights Committee. In 1980, he was arrested and sent to internal exile in Gorky, following his criticism of Soviet action in Afghanistan. At the end of 1986, he was freed from exile and allowed to return to Moscow and resume his place in the Soviet Academy of Sciences.

Saki /ˈsɑːki/ pen name of H(ugh) H(ector) Munro 1870–1916. Burmese-born British writer of ingeniously witty and bizarre short stories, often with surprise endings. He also wrote two novels *The Unbearable Bassington* 1912 and *When William Came* 1913.

Sakkara /səˈkɑːrə/ or *Saqqara* a village in Egypt, 16 km/10 mi south of Cairo, with 20 pyramids, of which the oldest (Third dynasty) is the 'Step Pyramid' designed by ◊Imhotep, whose own tomb here was the nucleus of the Aesklepieion, a centre of healing in the ancient world.

Sakti the female principle in ◊Hinduism.

Šakyamuni the historical ◊Buddha, called *Shaka* in Japan.

Saladin /ˈsælədɪn/ or *Sala-ud-din* 1138–1193. Sultan of Egypt from 1175, in succession to the Atabeg of Mosul, on whose behalf he conquered Egypt 1164–74. He subsequently conquered Syria 1174–87, and precipitated the third ◊Crusade by his recovery of Jerusalem from the Christians 1187. Renowned for knightly courtesy, Saladin made peace with Richard I of England 1192. He was a Kurd.

Salado /səˈlɑːdəʊ/ two rivers of Argentina, both rising in the Andes, and about 1,600 km/1,000 mi long. *Salado del Norte* or *Juramento* flows from the Andes to join the Paraná; the *Salado del Sud* or *Desaguadero* joins the Colorado and flows into the Atlantic south of Bahía Blanca.

Salam /səˈlɑːm/ Abdus 1926– . Pakistani physicist known for his work on fundamental ◊forces. In 1979 he was the first from his country to receive a Nobel prize.

Abdus Salam became a scientist by accident, when he won a scholarship to Cambridge in 1945 from the Punjab Small Peasants' welfare fund; he had intended to join the Indian civil service. He

Salamis *The early Byzantine gymnasium at Salamis. Once the chief city of ancient Cyprus, Salamis had a Christian community founded by Paul and Barnabas.*

subsequently worked on the structure of matter at the Cavendish Laboratory, Oxford, and elaborated the theory unifying fundamental forces in 1967. His ideas were verified experimentally at CERN in 1973.

Salamanca /ˌsæləˈmæŋkə/ city in Castilla-León, W Spain, on the river Tormes, 260 km/162 mi NW of Madrid; population (1986) 167,000. It produces pharmaceuticals and wool. Its university was founded about 1230. It has a superbly designed square, the Plaza Mayor.

Salamanca, Battle of /ˌsæləˈmæŋkə/ the British commander Wellington's victory over the French army in the ◊Peninsular War, 22 July 1812.

salamander any tailed amphibian, family Salamandridae, of the order *Caudata*, which lives in the northern hemisphere. The European *spotted* or *fire salamander Salamandra salamandra*, is black with bright yellow, orange, or red markings, and up to 20 cm/8 in long. Other types include the *giant salamander* of Japan *Andrias japonicus*, 1.5 m/5 ft long, and the *Mexican salamander Ambystoma mexicanum*, or ◊axolotl.

Salamis /ˈsæləmɪs/ island off Piraeus, the port of ◊Athens, Greece; area 101 sq km/39 sq mi; population (1981) 19,000. The town of Salamis, on the W coast, is a naval station.

Salamis ancient city on the E coast of Cyprus, the capital under the early Ptolemies, until its harbour silted up about 200 BC, when it was succeeded by Paphos in the SW.

Salamis, Battle of /ˈsæləmɪs/ naval battle off the coast of the island of Salamis in which the Greeks defeated the Persians 480 BC.

sal ammoniac an old name for ◊ammonium chloride.

Salang Highway /ˈsɑːlæŋ/ the main N–S route between Kabul, capital of Afghanistan, and the Soviet frontier; length 422 km/264 mi. The high-altitude *Salang Pass* and *Salang Tunnel* cross a natural break in the Hindu Kush mountains about 100 km/60 mi N of Kabul. This supply route was a major target of the Mujaheddin resistance fighters during the Soviet occupation of Afghanistan.

salat the daily prayers that are one of the Five Pillars of ◊Islam.

Muslims are required to pray five times a day, the first prayer being before dawn and the last after dusk. Prayer must be preceded by ritual washing and may be said in any clean place, facing the direction of Mecca. The prayers, which are recited in Arabic, follow a fixed series of words and movements.

Salazar /ˌsælə'zɑː/ Antonio de Oliveira 1889–1970. Portuguese prime minister 1932–68, exercising a virtual dictatorship. A corporative constitution on the Italian model was introduced 1933, and until 1945 Salazar's National Union, founded 1930, remained the only legal party. Salazar was also foreign minister 1936–47, and during World War II maintained Portuguese neutrality.

Sale /seɪl/ residential suburb of Manchester, England; population (1981) 57,824.

Sale /seɪl/ town in Victoria, Australia, linked by canal via the Gippsland Lake to Bass Strait; population (1981) 13,000. It has benefited from the Strait deposits of oil and natural gas, and the brown coal to the south. The town was named after the British general Robert Sale (1782–1845).

Salem /'seɪləm/ industrial city (iron mining, and textiles) in Tamil Nadu, India; population (1981) 515,000.

Salem /'seɪləm/ city and manufacturing centre in Massachusetts, USA, 24 km/15 mi NE of Boston; population (1980) 38,300. It was the site of witch trials, 1692, which ended in the execution of 19 people.

Salem /'seɪləm/ city in NW Oregon, USA, settled about 1840 and made state capital 1859; population (1980) 89,200. There are food processing and high-tech industries.

Salerno /sə'leənəʊ/ port in Campania, SW Italy, 48 km/30 mi SE of Naples; population (1988) 154,000. It was founded by the Romans about 194 BC, destroyed by Charlemagne, and sacked by Holy Roman Emperor Henry VI 1194. The temple ruins of the ancient Greek city of ◊*Paestum*, with some of the earliest Greek paintings known, are nearby. The university (1150–1817, revived 1944) and Salerno's medical school have been famous since medieval times.

Salford /'sɔːlfəd/ industrial city in Greater Manchester, England, on the river Irwell; population (1981) 98,000. Industries include engineering, electrical goods, textiles, and chemicals.

Salic law a law adopted in the Middle Ages by several European royal houses, excluding women from succession to the throne. In Sweden 1980 such a provision was abrogated to allow Princess Victoria to become crown princess. The name derives mistakenly from the Salian or northern division of the Franks who were supposed to have practised it.

salicylic acid the active chemical constituent of aspirin. The acid and its salts (salicylates) occur naturally in many plants; concentrated sources include willow bark and oil of wintergreen.

When purified, salicylic acid is a white solid, $C_6H_4(OH)(COOH)$, which crystallizes into prismatic needles at 159°C. It is used as an antiseptic, in food preparation, dyestuffs, and in the preparation of aspirin.

Salieri /ˌsæli'eəri/ Antonio 1750–1825. Italian composer. He taught Beethoven, Schubert, and Liszt, and was the musical rival of Mozart at the Emperor's court in Vienna.

Salinas de Gortiari /sə'liːnəs də ˌgɔːti'ɑːri/ Carlos 1948– . Mexican politician, president from 1988.

Educated in Mexico and the USA, he taught at Harvard and in Mexico before joining the government in 1971 and thereafter held a number of posts, mostly in the economic sphere. A member of the dominant Institutional Revolutionary Party (PRI), and a former finance minister, he narrowly won the 1988 presidential election, despite allegations of fraud.

Salinger /'sælɪndʒə/ J(erome) D(avid) 1919– . US writer of the novel of adolescence *The Catcher*

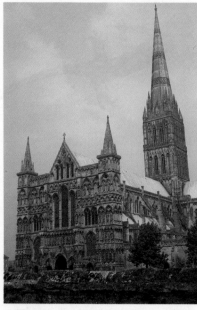

Salisbury *Salisbury cathedral has the highest spire in England at 123 m/404 ft.*

in the Rye 1951 and stories of a Jewish family, including *Franny and Zooey* 1961.

Salisbury /'sɔːlzbəri/ city in Wiltshire, England, 135 km/84 mi SW of London; population (1981) 35,355. The cathedral of St Mary, built 1220–66, is an example of Early English architecture; its decorated spire 123 m/404 ft is the highest in England. The cathedral library contains one of only four copies of the *Magna Carta* map. Salisbury is an agricultural centre, and industries include brewing and carpet manufacture. Another name for it is New Sarum, Sarum being a medieval Latin corruption of the ancient Romano-British name Sorbiodonum. Old Sarum, on a 90 m/300 ft hill to the north, was deserted when New Sarum was founded 1220, but was later again inhabited; it was brought within the town boundary 1953.

Salisbury /'sɔːlzbəri/ former name (until 1980) of ◊Harare, capital of Zimbabwe.

Salisbury /'sɔːlzbəri/ Robert Cecil, 1st Earl of Salisbury. Title conferred on Robert ◊Cecil, secretary of state to Elizabeth I of England.

Salisbury /'sɔːlzbəri/ Robert Arthur Talbot Gascoyne-Cecil, 3rd Marquess of Salisbury 1830–1903. British Conservative politician. He entered the Commons 1853 and succeeded to his title 1868. As foreign secretary 1878–80, he took part in the Congress of Berlin, and as prime minister 1885–86, 1886–92, and 1895–1902 gave his main attention to foreign policy, remaining also as foreign secretary for most of this time.

Salisbury /'sɔːlzbəri/ Robert Arthur James Gascoyne-Cecil, 5th Marquess of Salisbury 1893–1972. British Conservative politician. He was Dominions secretary 1940–42 and 1943–45, Colonial secretary 1942, Lord Privy Seal 1942–43 and 1951–52, and Lord President of the Council 1952–57.

Salisbury Plain /'sɔːlzbəri/ a 775 sq km/300 sq mi area of open downland between Salisbury and Devizes in Wiltshire, England. It rises to 235 m/770 ft in Westbury Down, and includes ◊Stonehenge. For many years it has been a military training area.

saliva a secretion which aids the swallowing and digestion of food in the mouth. In some animals, it contains the ◊enzyme ptyalin which digests starch, and in bloodsucking animals contains ◊anticoagulants.

Salk /sɔːlk/ Jonas Edward 1914– . US physician and microbiologist. In 1954, he developed the original vaccine which led to virtual eradication

of ◊polio in developed countries. He was director of the Salk Institute for Biological Studies, University of California, San Diego 1963–75.

Sallinen /'sælɪnen/ Tyko 1879–1955. Finnish Expressionist painter. Absorbing Fauve influences on visits to France 1909 and 1914, he created visionary works relating partly to his childhood experiences of religion. He also painted Finnish landscape and peasant life.

Sallust /'sæləst/ Gaius Sallustius Crispus 86–*c.* 34 BC. Roman historian, a supporter of Julius ◊Caesar. He wrote accounts of Catiline's conspiracy and the Jugurthine War in an epigrammatic style.

salmon fish of the family Salmonidae. The normal colour is silvery with a few dark spots, but the colour changes at the spawning season. Salmon live in the sea, but return to spawn in the place they were spawned, often overcoming great obstacles to get there.

The spawning season is between Sept and Jan, although they occasionally spawn at other times. The orange eggs, about 6 mm/0.25 in diameter, are laid on the river bed, fertilized by the male, and then covered with gravel by the female. The incubation period is from five weeks to five months. The young hatched fish are known as *alevins*, and when they begin feeding, they are called *parr*. At about two years old, the coat becomes silvery, and the young parr are then *smolts*. When the young fish return to the river to spawn between three and three and a half years of age, they are called *grilse*.

Salmon are increasingly 'farmed' in cages, and 'ranched' (selectively bred, hatched, and fed before release to the sea). Stocking rivers indiscriminately with hatchery fish may destroy the precision of their homing instinct by interbreeding between those originating in different rivers.

Salmonella a very varied group of bacteria. They can be divided into three broad groups. One of these causes typhoid and paratyphoid fevers, while a second group causes Salmonella ◊food poisoning, which is characterized by stomach pains, vomiting, diarrhoea, and headache. It can be fatal in elderly people, but others usually recover in a few days without antibiotics. Most cases are caused by contaminated animal products, especially poultry meat.

Human carriers of the disease may be well themselves but pass the bacteria on to others through unhygienic preparation of food. Domestic pets can also carry the bacteria while appearing healthy.

Salome 1st century AD. In the New Testament, granddaughter of the king of Judea, Herod the Great. Rewarded for her skill in dancing, she requested the head of John the Baptist from her stepfather ◊Herod Antipas.

Salonika /ˌsælə'naɪkə, sə'lɒnɪkə/ English name for ◊Thessaloniki, a port in Greece.

Salop /'sæləp/ abbreviation and former official name (1972–80) for ◊Shropshire, county in England.

salsa a Latin big-band dance music popularized by Puerto Ricans in New York in the 1980s and

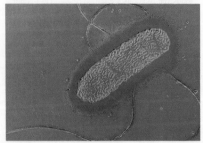

Salmonella *False-colour electron microscope view of the bacterium* Salmonella enteritidis, *a cause of food poisoning. Outbreaks of salmonella poisoning have been associated with infected chicken eggs (×8,700).*

by, among others, the Panamanian singer Rubén Blades (1948–).

salsify hardy biennial *Tragopogon porrifolius*, family Compositae, often called **vegetable oyster**; its white fleshy roots and spring shoots are eaten as vegetables.

SALT abbreviation for ◊**Strategic Arms Limitation Talks**, a series of US-Soviet negotiations 1969–79.

salt in chemistry, the general term for compounds formed by the attraction between anions and cations (positively and negatively charged ions). **Common salt** is sodium chloride (see ◊salt, common).

A salt may be produced by chemical reaction between an acid and a base, or by the displacement of hydrogen from an acid by a metal (see ◊displacement activity). As a solid, the ions normally adopt a regular arrangement to form ◊crystals. Some salts only form stable crystals as hydrates (when combined with water). A salt readily dissolves in water to give an electrolyte (a solution that conducts electricity).

saltation (Latin *saltare* 'to leap') the idea that an abrupt genetic change can occur in an individual, which then gives rise to a new species. The idea has now been largely discredited, although the appearance of ◊polyploid individuals can be considered an example.

salt, common sodium chloride (NaCl), found disolved in sea water and as rock salt (halite) in large deposits and salt domes. Common salt is used extensively in the food industry as a preservative and for flavouring, and in the chemical industry to make chlorine and sodium.

While common salt is an essential part of our diet, some medical experts believe that excess salt, largely from processed food, can lead to high blood pressure and increased risk of heart attacks.

Salt Lake City /ˈsɔːlt ˌleɪk ˈsɪti/ capital of Utah, USA, on the river Jordan, 18 km/11 mi SE of the Great Salt Lake; population (1982) 164,000. Founded 1847, it is the headquarters of the ◊Mormon Church. Mining, construction, and other industries are being replaced by high technology.

Salton Sea /ˈsɔːltən/ brine lake in SE California, USA, area 650 sq km/250 sq mi, accidentally created in the early 20th century during irrigation works from the Colorado river. It is used to generate electricity; see ◊solar ponds.

saltpetre former name for potassium nitrate, KNO₃, the compound used in making gunpowder (from about 1500). It occurs naturally, being deposited during dry periods in places with warm climates such as India.

saluki breed of dog, also called **gazelle hound**. It resembles the greyhound, is about 65 cm/26 in high, and has a silky coat, which is usually fawn, cream, or white. It is descended from the hound of the African desert Bedouins.

Salt Lake City The Mormon tabernacle was dedicated in 1893 and took forty years to build.

Salvador /ˌsælvəˈdɔː/ port and naval base in Bahia state, NE Brazil, on the inner side of a peninsula separating Todos Santos Bay from the Atlantic; population (1985) 2,126,000. Products include cocoa, tobacco, and sugar. Founded 1510, it was the capital of Brazil 1549–1763.

Salvador, El /elˈsælvədɔː/ republic in Central America; see ◊El Salvador.

salvage saving or rescue, either as a whole or in part, of any property threatened with destruction, especially at sea. The term is used more specifically for compensation payable to those who, by voluntary effort, have saved a ship and/or its cargo and passengers from complete loss through shipwreck, fire, or enemy action.

Salvarsan an organic compound, the first specific antibacterial agent. Because of its destructive effect on *Spirochaeta pallida*, it was used in the treatment of syphilis before the development of modern antibiotics.

It was discovered by Paul ◊Ehrlich in 1909. Another name for it is 606, referring to the number of experiments performed by Ehrlich in its discovery.

Salvation Army Christian evangelical, social-service, and social-reform organization, originating 1865 in London, England, with the work of William ◊Booth. Originally called the Christian Revival Association, it was renamed the East London Christian Mission in 1870 and from 1878 has been known as the Salvation Army, now a worldwide organization. It has military titles for its officials, is renowned for its brass bands, and its weekly journal is the *War Cry*.

sal volatile another name for ◊smelling salts.

Salween /ˈsælwiːn/ river rising in E Tibet and flowing 2,800 km/1,740 mi through Burma to the Andaman Sea; it has many rapids.

Salyut (Russian 'salute') a series of seven space stations launched by the USSR 1971–82. Salyut was cylindrical in shape, 15 m/50 ft long, and weighed 19 tonnes. It housed two or three cosmonauts at a time, for missions lasting up to eight months.

Salyut 1 was launched 19 Apr 1971. It was occupied for 23 days in June 1971 by a crew of three, who died during their return to Earth when their ◊Soyuz ferry craft depressurized. Salyut 2, in 1973, broke up in orbit before occupation. The first fully successful Salyut mission was a 14-day visit to Salyut 3 in July 1974. In 1986, the Salyut series was superseded by ◊Mir, an improved design capable of being enlarged by additional modules sent up from Earth.

Crews observed Earth and the sky, and carried out processing of materials in weightlessness.

Salzburg /ˈsæltsbɜːg/ capital of the state of Salzburg, W Austria, on the river Salzach, in W Austria; population (1981) 139,400. The city is dominated by the Hohensalzburg fortress. It is the seat of an archbishopric founded by St Boniface about 700 and has a 17th-century cathedral. Industries include stock rearing, dairy farming, forestry, and tourism.

Salzburg federal province of Austria; area 7,200 sq km/2,779 sq mi; population (1987) 462,000. Its capital is Salzburg.

Salzedo /sælˈzeɪdəʊ/ Carlos 1885–1961. French-born harpist and composer. He studied in Paris and moved to New York, where he later co-founded the International Composers' Guild. He did much to promote the harp as a concert instrument, and invented many unusual sounds.

Salzgitter /ˈzælts-gɪtə/ city in Lower Saxony, West Germany; population (1988) 105,000.

samara in botany, a winged fruit, a type of ◊achene.

Samara /səˈmɑːrə/ name until 1935 of ◊Kuibyshev, a port in the USSR.

Samaria /səˈmeəriə/ region of ancient Israel. The town of Samaria (modern **Sebastiyeh**) on the W bank of the river Jordan was the capital of Israel 10th–8th centuries BC, renamed Sebarte by Herod the Great. Extensive remains have been excavated.

Samaritan descendant of the colonists forced to settle in Samaria by the Assyrians, after the destruction of the Israelite kingdom 722 BC. Samaritans adopted Judaism, but rejected all sacred books except the Pentateuch, and regarded their temple on Mount Gerizim as the true sanctuary.

Samaritans /səˈmærɪtənz/ voluntary organization aiding those tempted to suicide or despair, established in 1953 in the UK. Groups of lay people, often consulting with psychiatrists, psychotherapists, and doctors, offer friendship and counselling to those using their emergency telephone numbers, day or night.

The Samaritans were founded at St Stephen's Church, Walbrook, London, by the rector, Chad Varah (1911–), and subsequently extended throughout Britain and overseas. They are inspired by the story of the 'good Samaritan' of the New Testament, who aided the injured traveller who had been attacked and robbed, instead of 'walking by on the other side of the road'.

Samarkand /ˌsæməˈkænd/ city in Uzbek Republic, USSR, capital of Samarkand region, near the river Zerafshan, 217 km/135 mi E of Bukhara; population (1987) 388,000. It was the capital of the empire of ◊Tamerlane, and was once an important city on the ◊Silk Road.

Tamerlane is buried here, and the splendours of his city have been restored. It was occupied by the Russians in 1868. It remained a centre of Muslim culture until the Russian Revolution. Industries include cotton-ginning and silk manufacture, and engineering.

Samarra /səˈmærə/ ancient town in Iraq, on the river Tigris, 105 km/65 mi NW of Baghdad; population (1970) 62,000. Founded 836 by the Abbasid Caliph Motassim, it was the Abbasid capital until 876, and is a place of pilgrimage for ◊Shi'ite Muslims.

samizdat (Russian 'self-published') material circulated underground to evade censorship, for example reviews of Solzhenitsyn's banned novel *August, 1914* 1972 in E Europe before the 1989 uprisings.

Samoa /səˈməʊə/ volcanic island chain in the SW Pacific. It is divided into Western ◊Samoa and American ◊Samoa.

Samoa, American /səˈməʊə/ group of islands 4,200 km/2,610 miles south of Hawaii, an unincorporated territory of the USA.
area 200 sq km/77 sq mi
capital Fagatogo on Tutuila
features five volcanic islands, including Tutuila, Tau, and Swain's Island, and two coral atolls. National park (1988) includes prehistoric village of Saua, virgin rainforest, flying foxes
exports canned tuna, handicrafts
currency US dollar
population (1981) 34,000
language Samoan and English
religion Christian
government as a non-self-governing territory of the USA, under Governor A P Lutali, it is administered by the US Department of the Interior
history the islands were acquired by the United States Dec 1899 by agreement with Britain and Germany under the Treaty of Berlin. A constitution was adopted 1960 and revised 1967.

Samoa, Western /səˈməʊə/ country in the SW Pacific, in ◊Polynesia, NE of Fiji.
government Western Samoa is an independent state within the Commonwealth. The 1962 constitution provides for a parliamentary system of government, with a constitutional head of state, a single-chamber legislative assembly, and a prime minister and cabinet drawn from and responsible to the assembly. The head of state is normally elected by the assembly for a five-year term but the present holder of the office has been elected for life. The head of state appoints the prime minister and cabinet on the basis of assembly support.

The assembly (*Fono*) has 47 members, including 45 Samoans, who are elected by clan chiefs (holders of Matai titles) in 41 territorial constituencies, and two, usually European, members who are elected from individual voter's roles. The assembly has a life of three years.

history The first Europeans to reach the island group of Samoa, 1722, were Dutch. In the 19th century Germany, the UK and the US had conflicting interests in the islands, sometimes called the Navigators' Islands, and administered them jointly 1889–99, when they were divided into American ◊Samoa and Western Samoa. Western Samoa was a German colony until World War I, and from 1920 was administered by New Zealand, first as a League of Nations mandate and from 1946 as a United Nations trust territory.

Western Samoa was granted internal self-government gradually until it achieved full independence, within the Commonwealth, on 1 Jan 1962. The office of head of state was held jointly by two traditional rulers, but on the death of one of them, the other, Malietoa Tanumafili II, became the sole head of state for life. The prime minister at the time of independence was Fiame Mata Afa Mulinu'u. He lost power 1970 but regained it 1973 until his death 1975. In 1976 the first prime minister who was not of royal blood was elected, Tupuola Taisi Efi.

In 1979 the previously unorganized opposition politicians came together to form the Human Rights Protection Party (HRPP) and it won the 1982 election, Va'ai Kolone becoming prime minister. Later that year he was removed because of alleged voting malpractices and replaced by Tupuola Efi. Efi resigned a few months later when his budget was not approved, and was replaced by the new HRPP leader, Tofilau Eti Alesana. The HRPP won a decisive victory in the Feb 1985 general election, securing 31 *Fono* seats, and Tofilau Eti Alesana continued as prime minister. At the end of the year he resigned because of opposition to his budget proposals, which resulted in large-scale defections from the HRPP. The head of state refused to call another election and Va'ai Kolone returned to lead a government that comprised independents as well as members of Tupuola Taisi Efi's (*Tupua Tamasese*) newly formed Christian Democratic Party (CDP). The

general election of Feb 1988 produced a hung parliament with Tofilau Eti Alesana as the new premier.

Samos /'seɪmɒs, Greek 'sɑːmɒs/ Greek island in the Aegean Sea, about 1.5 km/1 mi off the W coast of Turkey; area 476 sq km/184 sq mi; capital Limén Vathéos; population (1981) 31,600. Mountainous but fertile, it produces wine and olive oil. The mathematician Pythagoras was born here. The modern town of Teganion is on the site of the ancient city of Samos, which was destroyed by Darius I of Persia.

samovar (Russian 'self-boiling') an urn, heated by charcoal, used for making tea.

samoyed breed of dog, originating in Siberia. It is about 25 kg/60 lbs, and 50 cm/1.9 ft in height. It resembles a chow, but has a more pointed face and a white coat.

samphire also known as *glasswort* or *sea asparagus* perennial plant *Crithmum maritimum* found on sea cliffs in Europe. The aromatic leaves are fleshy and sharply pointed; the flowers grow in yellow-green umbels. It is used in salads, or pickled.

Samson /'sæmsən/ in the Old Testament or Hebrew Bible, a hero of Israel. He was renowned for exploits of strength against the Philistines, which ended when his mistress Delilah cut off his hair, as told in the Old Testament Book of Judges.

Samsun /'sæm'suːn/ Black Sea port and capital of a province of the same name in N Turkey; situated at the mouth of the Murat river in a tobacco-growing area; site of the ancient city of Amisus; population (1985) 280,000.

Samuel /'sæmjuəl/ in the Old Testament or Hebrew Bible, the last of the judges who ruled the ancient Israelites before their adoption of a monarchy, and the first of the prophets; the two books bearing his name cover the story of Samuel and the reigns of kings Saul and David.

Samuelson /'sæmjuəlsən/ Paul 1915– . US economist. He became professor at the Massachusetts Institute of Technology 1940, and was awarded a Nobel prize 1970 for his application of scientific analysis to economic theory. His

books include *Economics* 1948, a classic textbook, and *Linear Programming and Economic Analysis* 1958.

samurai feudal military caste in Japan from the mid-12th century until 1869, when the feudal system was abolished and all samurai pensioned off by the government. A samurai was an armed retainer of a *daimyō* (large landowner) with specific duties and privileges, and a strict code of honour. A *rōnin* was a samurai without feudal allegiance.

From the 16th century commoners were not allowed to carry swords, whereas samurai had two swords, and the higher class of samurai were permitted to fight on horseback. It is estimated that 8% of the population belonged to samurai families. A financial depression from about 1700 caused serious hardship to the samurai, beginning a gradual disintegration of their traditions and prestige, accelerated by the fall of the Tokugawa shogunate 1868, in which they had assisted. Under the new Meiji emperor they were stripped of their role and many rebelled. Their last rising was the *Satsuma Rebellion* 1877–78 in which 40,000 samurai took part.

San Hottentot name for hunter-gatherers of the Kalahari Desert. Found in Botswana, SW Africa and South Africa, they number approximately 50,000. Their languages belong to the Khoisan family.

San'a /sæ'nɑː/ capital of North Yemen, SW Arabia, 320 km/200 mi north of Aden; population (1986) 427,000. A walled city, with fine mosques and traditional architecture, it is rapidly being modernized.

San Andreas fault /·sæn æn'dreɪəs/ a geological fault line stretching for 1,125 km/700 mi in a NW–SE direction through the state of California, USA.

Two sections of the Earth's crust meet at the San Andreas fault and friction is created as the coastal Pacific plate moves NW, rubbing against the American continental plate which is moving slowly SE. The relative movement is only about 5 cm/2 in per year, which means that Los Angeles

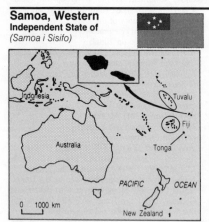

Samoa, Western
Independent State of
(Samoa i Sisifo)

area 2,830 sq km/1,093 sq mi
capital Apia on Upolu
physical comprises islands of Savai'i and Upolu, with two smaller islands and islets; mountain ranges on the main islands
features huge lava flows on Savai'i have cut down the area available for agriculture
head of state King Malietoa Tanumafili II from 1962
head of government Tofilau Eti Alesana from 1988
government liberal democracy
political parties Human Rights Protection Party (HRPP), led by Tofilau Eti Alesana; the Va'ai

Kolone Group (VKG); Christian Democratic Party (CDP), led by Tupuola Taisi Efi. All the parties are personality-based groupings
exports copra, bananas, cocoa; tourism is important
currency taia (3.88 = £1 Feb 1990)
population (1989) 169,000; annual growth rate 1.1%
language English and Samoan (official)
religion Christian
literacy 90% (1983)
GDP $65 million (1978); $400 per head of population
chronology
1959 Local government elected.
1961 Referendum favoured independence.
1962 Achieved full independence within the Commonwealth, with Fiame Mata'afa Mulinu'u as prime minister.
1975 Mata'afa died and was succeeded by Tupuola Taisi Efi, the first non-royal prime minister.
1982 Va'ai Kolone became prime minister, but was replaced the same year by Tupuola Efi. When the assembly failed to approve his budget, Tupuola Efi resigned and was replaced by Tofilau Eti Alesana.
1985 At the end of the year Tofilau Eti resigned over his budget proposals and the head of state refused to call a general election, inviting Va'ai Kolombe to return to lead the government.
1988 Elections produced a hung parliament, with first Tupuola Efi as prime minister and then Tofilau Eti.

San'a A view of the old city. A majority of the inhabitants still live within the city walls.

will reach San Francisco's latitude in 10 million years' time. The friction caused by this tectonic movement gives rise to periodic earthquakes.

San Antonio /ˌsæn ænˈtəʊniəʊ/ city in S Texas, USA; population (1980) 1,070,000. A commercial and financial centre, industries include aircraft maintenance, oil refining, and meat packing. Founded 1718, it grew up round the site of the ◊Alamo fort.

San Bernardino /ˈsæn ˌbɜːnəˈdiːnəʊ/ city in California, USA, 80 km/50 mi E of Los Angeles; population (1980) 119,000, metropolitan area 703,000. It was founded 1851 by Mormons.

San Cristóbal /ˌsæn krɪsˈtəʊbæl/ capital of Tachira state, W Venezuela, near the Colombian border; population (1981) 199,000. It was founded by the Spanish 1561, and stands on the ◊Pan-American Highway.

sanction measure used to enforce international law, such as the attempted economic boycott of Italy during the Abyssinian War by the League of Nations; of Rhodesia, after its unilateral declaration of independence, by the United Nations; and the call for measures against South Africa on human rights grounds by the United Nations and other organizations from 1985.

Sanctorius /sæŋkˈtɔːrɪəs/ Sanctorius 1561–1636. Italian physiologist who pioneered the study of ◊metabolism, and invented the clinical thermometer and a device for measuring pulse rate.

Sanctorius introduced quantitative methods into medicine. For 30 years, he weighed both himself and his food, drink, and waste products. He determined that over half of normal weight loss is due to 'insensible perspiration'.

sanctuary (Latin *sanctuarium* 'sacred place') a place of refuge from persecution or prosecution, usually in or near a place of worship. The custom of offering sanctuary in specific places goes back to ancient times and was widespread in Europe in the Middle Ages. In the 1980s in the UK, Christian churches, a Sikh temple, and a Hindu temple were all used as sanctuaries.

The ancient Hebrews established six separate towns of refuge, and the Greek temple of Diana at Ephesus provided sanctuary within a radius of two stadia (about 434 m/475 yd). In Roman temples the sanctuary was the *cella* (inner room), in which stood the statue of the god worshipped there.

In the Middle Ages a person who crossed the threshold of a church was under the protection of God. The right to sanctuary was generally honoured by the church and endured by the state. In legend and medieval art, hunted stags took sanctuary in church porticoes. At Beverly Minster in E Yorkshire, England, the privilege extended a mile and a half around the church; the closer to the centre of this zone the fugitives got, the more sinful it was to remove them. Beverley accumulated numbers of permanent sanctuary claimants, and they were absorbed into the life of the minster. A similar process took place at Westminster Abbey, London. The sanctuary there, next to the cloisters, developed into something like a small town, with shops and workshops, bringing in useful revenue.

In England the right of a criminal to seek sanctuary was removed by legislation 1623 and again 1697, though for civil offenders it remained until 1723. Immunity was valid for 40 days only, after which the claimant must either surrender, become an outlaw, or go into permanent exile. Viraj Mendis, a Sri Lankan illegal immigrant, claimed sanctuary for two years until Jan 1989, before police stormed the church in Manchester where he was living and he was deported.

sand loose grains of rock, sized 0.02–2.00 mm/0.0008–0.0800 in in diameter, consisting chiefly of ◊quartz, but owing their varying colour to mixtures of other minerals. It is used in cement-making, as an abrasive, in glass-making, and for other purposes.

Sands are classified into marine, freshwater, glacial, and terrestrial. Some 'light' soils contain up to 50% sand. Sands may eventually consolidate into ◊sandstone.

Sand /sɒnd/ George. Pen name of Amandine Aurore Lucie Dupin 1804–1876. French author, whose prolific literary output was often autobiographical. After nine years of marriage, she left her husband in 1831, and, while living in Paris as a writer, had love affairs with Alfred de ◊Musset, ◊Chopin, and others. Her first novel *Indiana* 1832 was a plea for women's right to independence.

Other novels include *La mare au diable*/*The Devil's Pool* 1846 and *La petite Fadette*/*The Little Fairy* 1848. In 1848 she retired to the château of Nohant, in central France.

sandbar ridge of sand built up by the currents across the mouth of a river or bay. A sandbar may be entirely underwater or it may form an elongated island that breaks the surface. A sandbar stretching out from a headland is a **sand spit**.

Sandburg /ˈsændbɜːg/ Carl August 1878–1967. US poet. His poetry celebrates ordinary US life, as in *Chicago Poems* 1916, and *The People, Yes* 1936. *Always the Young Strangers* 1953 is an autobiography. Both his poetry and his biography of Abraham Lincoln won Pulitzer prizes.

Sandby /ˈsændbi/ Paul 1725–1809. English watercolour painter. He specialized in Classical landscapes, using both watercolour and opaque bodycolour, and introduced ◊aquatint to England.

Sanders /ˈsɑːndəz/ George 1906–1972. Russianborn British actor, usually cast as a smooth-talking cad. Most of his film career was spent in the USA where he starred in such films as *Rebecca* 1940, *The Moon and Sixpence* 1942, and *The Picture of Dorian Gray* 1944.

sandgrouse bird of the family Pteroclidae, related to the pigeons. It lives in warm, dry areas of Europe and Africa and has long wings, short legs, and hard skin.

Sandgrouse may travel long distances to water to drink, and some carry water back to their young by soaking the breast feathers.

sandhopper crustacean *Talitrus saltator* about 1.6 cm/0.6 in long, without a shell. It is found above the high-tide mark on seashores. The term is also used to refer to some other amphipod crustaceans.

Sandhurst /ˈsændhɜːst/ popular name for the Royal Military Academy, the British military officer training college near the village of Sandhurst, Berkshire, founded 1799. Its motto is 'Serve to Lead'.

Sand French novelist George Sand. Her affairs with a succession of artists and poets provided the inspiration for much of her work.

sandstone Torridonian sandstone rock, shaped by the action of the waves at Loch Broom, Scotland. The layers in the rock are clearly visible.

San Diego /ˌsæn diˈeɪgəʊ/ city and military and naval base in California, USA; population (1980) 1,704,000. Industries include bio-medical technology, aircraft missiles, and fish canning. ◊Tijuana adjoins San Diego across the Mexican border.

sandpiper type of bird belonging to the snipe family Scolopacidae. The **common sandpiper** *Tringa hypoleucos* is a small graceful bird with long slender bill and short tail, drab above and white below. It is common in the N hemisphere.

Sandringham House private residence of the British sovereign, built 1863 by the Prince of Wales (afterwards Edward VII) 1869–71.

The house is built on the estate the prince had bought in Norfolk, NE of Kings Lynn, in 1863. It is named after the nearby village of Sandringham. George V and George VI both died in the house, and Elizabeth II completely modernized both it and the estate.

sandstone ◊sedimentary rocks formed from the consolidation of sand, with sand-sized grains (0.0625–2 mm/0.0025–0.08 in) in a matrix or cement. The principal component is quartz. Sandstones are classified according to the matrix or cement material (whether derived from clay or silt, for example as calcareous sandstone; ferruginous sandstone; siliceous sandstone).

Sandwich /ˈsænwɪtʃ/ resort and market town in Kent, England; population (1981) 4,184. It has many medieval buildings, and was one of the ◊Cinque ports, but recession of the sea has left the harbour useless since the 16th century.

Sandwich /ˈsænwɪtʃ/ John Montagu, 4th Earl of Sandwich 1718–1792. British politician. He was an inept First Lord of the Admiralty 1771–82 during the American War of Independence, his corrupt practices being held to blame for the British navy's inadequacies.

San Francisco Powell Street in San Francisco, USA.

The Sandwich Islands were named after him, as are sandwiches, which he invented so that he could eat without leaving the gaming table.

Sandwich Islands /'sænwɪtʃ/ former name of ◊Hawaii, a group of islands in the Pacific.

Sandys /sændz/ Original name of British politician Baron ◊Duncan-Sandys.

San Francisco /ˌsæn frænˈsɪskəʊ/ chief Pacific port of the USA, in California; population (1982) 691,637, metropolitan area of San Francisco-Oakland 3,192,000. The city stands on a peninsula, south of the Golden Gate 1937, the world's second longest single-span bridge, 1,280 m/4,200 ft. The strait gives access to San Francisco Bay. Industries include meat-packing, fruit canning, printing and publishing, and the manufacture of metal goods.

history In 1578 Sir Francis Drake's flagship, the *Golden Hind*, stopped near San Francisco on its voyage round the world. San Francisco was occupied in 1846 during the war with Mexico, and in 1906 was almost destroyed by an earthquake which killed 452 people. It was the site of the drawing up of the United Nations Charter in 1945, and of the signing of the peace treaty between the Western Allies and Japan in 1951.

Sanger /'sæŋə/ Frederick 1918– . English biochemist, the first to win a Nobel prize for chemistry twice: 1958 for determining the structure of insulin, and 1980 for his work on the chemical structure of genes.

Sanger worked throughout his life at Cambridge university. His second Nobel prize was shared with two US scientists, Paul Berg and Walter Gilbert, for establishing methods of determining the sequence of nucleotides strung together along strands of DNA.

sang froid (French 'cold blood') coolness, composure.

Sangha in Buddhism, the monastic orders, one of the Three Treasures of Buddhism (the other two are Buddha and the law, or dharma). The term Sangha is sometimes used more generally by Mahāyāna Buddhists to include all believers.

Sanhedrin supreme Jewish court at Jerusalem (2nd century BC–1st century AD) headed by the high priest.

San José /'sæn həʊˈzeɪ/ capital of Costa Rica; population (1984) 245,370. Products include coffee, cocoa, and sugar cane. Founded in 1737, it has been capital since 1823.

San José /'sæn həʊˈzeɪ/ city in Santa Clara Valley, California, USA; population (1980) 1,244,000. Industries include aerospace research and development, electronics, flowers, fruit canning, and wine making. It was the first capital of California 1849–51.

San Juan /'sæn ˈwɑːn/ capital of Puerto Rico; population (1980) 434,850. It is a port and industrial city. Products include sugar, rum, and cigars.

San Luis Potosí /'sæn luːˈiːs ˌpɒtəʊˈsiː/ silver-mining city and capital of San Luis Potosí state, central Mexico; population (1986) 602,000. Founded 1586 as a Franciscan mission, it was the colonial administrative headquarters and has fine buildings of the period.

San Marino /'sæn məˈriːnəʊ/ landlocked country within N central Italy.

government San Marino has no formal constitution. The single-chamber Great and General Council has 60 members, elected by universal suffrage for a five-year term. The council elects two of its members, one representing the capital and one the country, to serve a six-month period as captain's regent. Together they share the duties of head of state and head of government. They preside over a cabinet of ten, elected by the Council for a five-year term, called the Congress of State.

The country is divided into nine 'castles', which correspond to the original nine parishes of the republic. Each castle is governed by a castle captain and an auxiliary council, both serving a one-year term.

history San Marino claims to be the world's oldest republic, founded by St Marinus in the 4th century; it is the only city state to remain after the unification of Italy in the 19th century. It has had a treaty of friendship with Italy since 1862. Women had no vote until 1960.

San Marino's multi-party system mirrors that of the larger country that surrounds it. For the past 40 years it has been governed by a series of left-wing coalitions, the current one, the 'grand coalition', which comprises the Communists (PCS), and Christian Democrats (PDCS), dates from July 1986. At the May 1988 council election the PDCS secured 27 seats and the PCS 18, while the opposition Socialist Unionist Party (PSU) captured eight and the Socialist Party (PPS) seven seats.

San Martín /'sæn mɑːˈtiːn/ José de San Martín 1778–1850. South American nationalist. Born in Argentina, he served in the Spanish army during the Peninsular War, but after 1812 he devoted himself to the South American struggle for independence, playing a large part in the liberation of Argentina, Chile, and Peru from Spanish rule.

sannyasin in Hinduism, a person who has renounced worldly goods to live a life of asceticism and seek *moksha*, or liberation from reincarnation, through meditation and prayer.

San Pedro Sula /sæn ˈpedrəʊ ˈsuːlə/ main industrial and commercial city in NW Honduras, the

second largest city in the country; population (1986) 400,000. It trades in bananas, coffee, sugar, and timber, and manufactures textiles, plastics, furniture, and cement.

San Salvador /'sæn ˈsælvədɔː/ capital of El Salvador 48 km/30 mi from the Pacific, at the foot of San Salvador volcano 2,548 m/8,360 ft; population (1984) 453,000. Industries include food processing and textiles. Since its foundation 1525, it has suffered from several earthquakes.

sans-culotte (French 'without knee breeches') in the French Revolution a member of the working classes, who wore trousers, as opposed to the aristocracy and bourgeoisie, who wore knee breeches.

San Sebastián /'sæn sɪˈbæstiən/ port and resort in the Basque Country, Spain; population (1986) 180,000. It was formerly the summer residence of the Spanish court.

Sanskrit /'sænskrɪt/ the dominant classical language of the Indian subcontinent, a member of the Indo-Iranian group of the Indo-European language family, and the sacred language of Hinduism. The oldest form of Sanskrit is *Vedic*, the variety used in the Vedas and Upanishads (*c.* 1500–700 BC).

Classical Sanskrit was systematized by Panini and other grammarians in the latter part of the first millennium BC and became fixed as the spoken and written language of culture, philosophy, mathematics, law, and medicine. It is written in devanagari script and is the language of the two great Hindu epics, the *Mahābhārata* and the *Rāmāyana*, as well as many other classical and later works. Sanskrit vocabulary has not only influenced the languages of India, Thailand and Indonesia, but has also enriched several European languages, including English, with such words as *guru*, *karma*, *mahatma*, *pundit*, *swami*, and *yoga*, all relating to Hindu religion and philosophy.

sans souci (French) without cares or worries.

Santa Ana /'sæntə ˈænə/ commercial city in NW El Salvador, the second largest city in the country; population (1980) 205,000. It trades in coffee and sugar.

Santa Ana /'sæntə ˈænə/ periodic warm Californian ◊wind.

Santa Anna /'sæntəˈænə/ Antonio Lopez de Santa Anna 1795–1876. Mexican revolutionary. A leader in achieving independence from Spain in 1821, he pursued a chequered career of victory and defeat and was in and out of office as president or dictator for the rest of his life; he led the attack on the ◊Alamo in Texas 1836.

Santa Barbara /'bɑːbərə/ town in S California, USA; population (1980) 74,414. It is the site of a campus of the University of California. The Santa Ynez mountains are to the north. Vandenburg air force base is 80 km/50 mi to the northwest.

Santa Claus /klɔːz/ another name for Father Christmas; see under St ◊Nicholas.

Santa Cruz de la Sierra /ˌsæntə ˈkruːz de lə ˈsierə/ capital of Santa Cruz department in E Bolivia, the second largest city in the country; population (1982) 377,000. Sugar cane and cattle were the chief base of local industry until newly discovered oil and natural gas led to phenomenal growth.

Santa Cruz de Tenerife /ˌsæntə ˈkruːz də ˌtenəriːf/ capital of Tenerife and of the Canary Islands; population (1986) 211,000. It is a fuelling port and cable centre. Industry also includes oil refining, pharmaceuticals, and trade in fruit. Santa Cruz was bombarded by Blake 1657, and by Nelson 1797—the action in which he lost his arm.

Santa Fé /'sæntə ˈfeɪ/ capital of New Mexico, USA, on the river Santa Fé, 65 km/40 mi west of Las Vegas; population (1980) 48,935, many Spanish-speaking. A number of buildings date from the Spanish period, including a palace 1609–10; the cathedral 1869 is on the site of a monastery built 1622. Santa Fé is noted for American Indian jewellery and textiles; its chief industry is tourism. It is the oldest state capital in the USA.

Santa Fé /'sæntə ˈfeɪ/ capital of Santa Fé province, Argentina, on the Salado river 153 km/95 mi

---

San Marino
Most Serene Republic of
(Repubblica di San Marino)

area 60 sq km/23 sq mi
capital San Marino
physical on the slope of Mount Titano

features completely surrounded by Italian territory; one of the world's smallest states
head of state and government two captains-regent, elected for a six-month period
government direct democracy
political parties San Marino Christian Democrat Party (PDCS), right-of-centre; San Marino Communist Party (PCS), moderate Euro-communist; Socialist Unity Party (PSU) and Socialist Party (PSS), both left-of-centre
exports wine, ceramics, paint, chemicals
currency Italian lira (2,116 = £1 Feb 1990)
population (1989) 23,000; annual growth rate 3%
language Italian
religion Roman Catholic
literacy 97% (1985)
chronology
1862 Treaty with Italy signed, recognizing its independence and providing for its protection.
1947–86 Governed by a series of left-wing and centre-left coalitions.
1986 Formation of Communist and Christian Democrat 'grand coalition'.

Santiago *The Opera House in Santiago, Chile.*

north of Rosario; population (1980) 287,000. It has shipyards and exports timber, cattle, and wool. It was founded 1573, and the 1853 constitution was adopted here.

Santa Fé Trail US trade route 1821–80 from Independence, Missouri, to Santa Fé, New Mexico.

Santander /ˌsæntænˈdeə/ port on the Bay of Biscay, Cantabria, Spain; population (1986) 189,000. Industries include chemicals, textiles, vehicles, and shipyards. It was sacked by ◊Soult 1808, and was largely rebuilt after a fire 1941. Palaeolithic cave wall paintings of bison, wild boar, and deer were discovered at the nearby *Altamira* site 1879.

Santayana /ˌsæntiˈænə/ George 1863–1952. US philosopher and critic. His books include *The Life of Reason* 1905–06, *The Realm of Truth* 1937, *Background of My Life* 1945, volumes of poems, and the best-selling novel *The Last Puritan* 1935. Born in Spain, he graduated at Harvard, where he taught the history of philosophy 1889–1911.

Sant'Elia /sænˈtelɪə/ Antonio 1888–1916. Italian architect. His drawings convey a Futurist vision of a metropolis with skyscrapers, traffic lanes, and streamlined factories.

Santiago /ˌsæntiˈɑːgəʊ/ capital of Chile; population (1987) 4,858,000. Industries include textiles, chemicals, and food processing. It was founded 1541, and is famous for its broad avenues.

Santiago de Compostela /ˌsæntiˈɑːgəʊ deɪ ˌkɒmpɒsˈtelə/ city in Galicia, Spain; population (1986) 104,000. The 11th-century cathedral was reputedly built over the grave of Sant Iago el Mayor (St ◊James the Great), patron saint of Spain, and was one of the most popular places for medieval pilgrimage.

Santiago de Cuba /ˌsæntiˈɑːgəʊ deɪ ˈkiːbə/ port on the S coast of Cuba; population (1986) 359,000. Industries include sugar, rum, and cigars.

Santiago de los Caballeros /ˌsæntiˈɑːgəʊ deɪ lɒs ˌkæbælˈjeərɒs/ second largest city in the Dominican Republic; population (1982) 395,000. It is a trading and processing centre.

Santo Domingo /ˌsæntəʊ dəˈmɪŋgəʊ/ capital and chief sea port of the Dominican Republic; population (1982) 1,600,000. Founded in 1496 by Bartolomeo, brother of Christopher Columbus, it is the oldest colonial city in the Americas. Its cathedral was built 1515–40.

Santos /ˈsæntɒs/ coffee-exporting port in SE Brazil, 72 km/45 mi SE of São Paulo; population (1980) 411,000. The footballer Pélé played here for many years.

Sânusî /səˈnuːsi/ Sidi Muhammad ibn 'Ali as- 1787–1859. Algerian-born Muslim religious reformer. He preached a return to the puritanism of early Islam and met with much success in Libya, where he made Jaghbub his centre and founded the sect called after him.

San Yu /ˈsænˈjuː/ 1919– . Burmese politician. A member of the Revolutionary Council which came to power 1962, he became president 1981 and

São Tomé e Príncipe
Democratic Republic of

⬚ ★ ★

area 1,000 sq km/386 sq mi
capital São Tomé
physical comprises the two main islands and several smaller ones, all of volcanic origin; thickly forested and fertile
head of state and government Manuel Pinto da Costa from 1975

government one-party socialist republic
political parties Movement for the Liberation of São Tomé and Príncipe (MLSTP), nationalistic socialist
exports cocoa, copra, coffee, palm oil and kernels
currency dobra (180.01 = £1 Feb 1989)
population (1989) 114,000; annual growth rate 2.5%
language Portuguese
religion Roman Catholic
literacy 73% male/42% female (1981)
GNP $31 million (1983); $261 per head of population
chronology
1471 Discovered by Portuguese.
1522–1973 A province of Portugal.
1973 Granted internal self-government.
1975 Achieved full independence, with Manuel Pinto da Costa as president.
1984 Formally declared itself a nonaligned state.
1987 President now popularly elected.
1988 Unsuccessful coup attempt against Pinto da Costa.

was re-elected 1985. He was forced to resign July 1988, along with Ne Win, after riots in Rangoon (now Yangon).

Saône /səʊn/ river in E France, rising in the Vosges mountains and flowing 480 km/300 mi to join the Rhône at Lyon.

São Paulo /sau ˈpauləʊ/ city in Brazil, 72 km/44 mi NW of its port Santos; population (1980) 7,034,000, metropolitan area 15,280,000. It is 900 m/3,000 ft above sea level, and 2° S of the Tropic of Capricorn. It is South America's leading industrial city, producing electronics, steel, and chemicals, has meat-packing plants, and is the centre of Brazil's coffee trade. It originated as a Jesuit mission in 1554,

São Tomé /saʊn tɒˈmeɪ/ port and capital of São Tomé e Príncipe, on São Tomé island, Gulf of Guinea; population (1984) 35,000.

São Tomé e Príncipe /saʊn tuˈmeɪ, ˈprɪnsɪpə/ country in the Gulf of Guinea, off the coast of W Africa.

government The 1982 constitution describes the Movement for the Liberation of São Tomé e Príncipe (MLSTP) as the leading political force in the nation and the National People's Assembly as the supreme organ of the state. It has 40 members, all MLSTP nominees, elected by people's district assemblies for a five-year term. The president is also nominated by the MLSTP and elected for a five-year term by popular vote.

history The islands were uninhabited until the arrival of the Portuguese 1471, who brought convicts and exiled Jews to work on sugar plantations. Later on ◊slavery became the main trade, and in the 19th century forced labour was used on coffee and cocoa plantations.

As a Portuguese colony, São Tomé e Príncipe was given internal self-government 1973. After the military coup in Portugal 1974, the new government in Lisbon formally recognized the liberation movement, MLSTP, led by Dr Manuel Pinto da Costa, as the sole representative of the people of the islands and granted full independence July 1975. Dr da Costa became the first president and in Dec a National People's Assembly was elected. During the first few years of his presidency there were several unsuccessful attempts to depose him and small opposition groups still operate from outside the country, mainly in Lisbon.

With a worsening economy, da Costa began to reassess his country's international links, which had made it too dependent on the Eastern bloc and, in consequence, isolated from the West. In 1984 he proclaimed that in future São Tomé e Príncipe would be a ◊nonaligned state, and the number of Angolan, Cuban, and Soviet advisers

in the country was sharply reduced. Gradually São Tomé e Príncipe has turned more towards nearby African states such as Gabon, Cameroon, and Equatorial Guinea, as well as maintaining its links with Lisbon. In 1987 the constitution was amended, making the president subject to election by popular vote, and in Mar 1988 an attempted coup against him was foiled.

sap fluid exuded by certain plants, for example the rubber tree and opium poppy. The sap contains alkaloids, protein, and starch.

saponification in chemistry, the ◊hydrolysis (splitting) of an ◊ester by treatment with a strong alkali, resulting in the liberation of the alcohol from which the ester had been derived and a salt of the constituent fatty acid. The process is used in the manufacture of soap.

sapphire the deep blue, transparent gem variety of the mineral ◊corundum Al_2O_3, aluminium oxide. Small amounts of iron and titanium give it its colour. A corundum gem of any colour except red (which is a ruby) can be called a sapphire—for example, yellow sapphire.

Sappho /ˈsæfəʊ/ *c.* 612–580 BC. Greek lyric poet, friend of the poet ◊Alcaeus, and leader of a female literary coterie at Mytilene (modern *Lesvos*, hence ◊lesbianism); legend says she committed suicide when her love for the boatman Phaon

sapphire *Macrophotograph of sapphire, also known as corundum.*

was unrequited. Only fragments of her poems have survived.

Sapporo /sə'pɔːrəʊ/ capital of ◊Hokkaido, Japan; population (1987) 1,555,000. Industries include rubber and food processing. It is a winter sports centre, and was the site of the 1972 Winter Olympics. The university was founded 1918. Giant figures are sculpted in ice at the annual snow festival.

saprophyte in botany, an obsolete term for a saprotroph.

saprotroph (formerly **saprophyte**) an organism that feeds on the products (such as excreta) or dead bodies of others. They include most fungi (the rest being parasites), many bacteria and protozoa, animals such as dung beetles and vultures, and a few unusual plants, including several orchids. Saprotrophs cannot make food for themselves, so they are a type of ◊heterotroph. They are useful scavengers, and in sewage farms and refuse dumps break down organic matter into nutrients easily assimilable by green plants.

Saracen ancient Greek and Roman term for an Arab, used in the Middle Ages by Europeans for all Muslims. The equivalent term used in Spain was Moor.

Saragossa /ˌsærə'gɒsə/ English spelling of ◊Zaragoza, city in Aragon, Spain.

Sarajevo /ˌsærə'jeɪvəʊ/ capital of Bosnia and Herzegovina, Yugoslavia; population (1982) 449,000. Industries include engineering, brewing, chemicals, carpets, and ceramics. It was the site of the 1984 Winter Olympics. A Bosnian, Gavrilo Princip, assassinated Archduke ◊Francis Ferdinand here 1914, thereby precipitating World War I.

Saratoga Springs /ˈsærətəʊgə ˈsprɪŋz/ city and spa in New York State, USA, population (1980) 23,906. In 1777 the British general John ◊Burgoyne was defeated in two engagements nearby during the War of American Independence.

Saratov /sə'rɑːtɒf/ industrial port (chemicals, oil refining) on the Volga in the European Russian Soviet Socialist Republic; population(1987) 918,000. It was established in the 1590s as a fortress to protect the Volga trade route.

Sarawak /sə'rɑːwæk/ state of Malaysia, on the NW corner of the island of Borneo; capital Kuching; area 124,400 sq km/48,018 sq mi; population (1986) 1,550,000. It has a tropical climate, and produces timber, oil, rice, pepper, rubber, and coconuts. Sarawak was granted by the Sultan of Brunei to James Brooke 1841, who became 'Rajah of Sarawak'. It was a British protectorate from 1888 until captured by the Japanese in World War II. It was a Crown Colony 1946–63, when it became part of Malaysia.

sarcoma a type of malignant ◊tumour arising from the fat, muscles, bones, cartilage, or blood and lymph vessels and connective tissues. Sarcomas are much less common than ◊carcinoma.

sard or **sardonyx** a yellow or red-brown variety of ◊onyx.

Sardinia

sardine any of several small fish in the herring family.

Sardinia /sɑː'dɪniə/ (Italian **Sardegna**) mountainous island, special autonomous region of Italy; area 24,100 sq km/9,303 sq mi; population (1988) 1,651,000. Its capital is Cagliari, and it exports cork and petrochemicals. It is the second largest Mediterranean island, and includes Costa Smeralda (Emerald Coast) tourist area in the northeast and *nuraghi* (fortified Bronze Age dwellings). After centuries of foreign rule, it became linked 1720 with Piedmont, and this dual kingdom became the basis of a united Italy 1861.

Sardou /sɑː'duː/ Victorien 1831–1908. French dramatist. He wrote plays with roles for Sarah Bernhardt and Henry Irving, for example *Fédora* 1882, *Madame Sans-Gêne* 1893, and *La Tosca* 1887 (the basis for the opera by Puccini). G B ◊Shaw coined the expression 'Sardoodledom' to express his disgust with the contrivances of the 'well-made' play—a genre of which Sardou was the leading exponent.

Sargasso Sea /sɑː'gæsəʊ/ part of the N Atlantic (between 40° and 80° W and 25° and 30° N) left static by circling ocean currents, and covered with floating weed *Sargassum natans*.

Sargent /'sɑːdʒənt/ (Harold) Malcolm (Watts) 1895–1967. British conductor. From 1923 he was professor at the Royal College of Music, was chief conductor of the BBC Symphony Orchestra 1950–57, and continued as chief guest conductor and conductor-in-chief of the Henry Wood ◊promenade concerts. He had an easy, polished style.

Sargent /'sɑːdʒənt/ John Singer 1856–1925. US portrait painter. Born in Florence of American parents, he studied there and in Paris, then settled in London around 1885. He was a prolific and highly fashionable painter.

Sargent left Paris after a scandal concerning his décolleté portrait *Madame Gautreau* 1884. Later subjects included the actress Ellen Terry, President Theodore Roosevelt, and the writer Robert Louis Stevenson. His works show skill, verve, and sometimes superficial brilliance.

Sargeson /'sɑːdʒsən/ Frank 1903–1982. New Zealand writer of short stories and novels including *The Hangover* 1967 and *Man of England Now* 1972.

Sargon /'sɑːgɒn/ two Mesopotamian kings:

Sargon I king of Akkad *c.*2370–2230 BC, and founder of the first Babylonian empire. His story resembles that of Moses in that he was said to have been found floating in a cradle on the river Euphrates.

Sargon II died 705 BC. King of Assyria from 722 BC, who assumed the name of his famous predecessor. To keep conquered peoples from rising against him, he had whole populations moved from their homelands, including the Israelites from Samaria.

Sark /sɑːk/ one of the ◊Channel Islands, 10 km/6 mi E of Guernsey; area 5 sq km/2 sq mi; there is no town or village. It is divided into Great and Little Sark, linked by an isthmus, and is of great natural beauty. The Seigneurie of Sark was established by Elizabeth I, the ruler being known as Seigneur/Dame, and has its own parliament, the Chief Pleas. There is no income tax and cars are forbidden; immigration is controlled.

Sarmatian a member of an Indo-European nomadic people who slowly ousted the ◊Scythians from what is now S European USSR from the mid-3rd century BC and gave way to the ◊Goths by the 3rd century AD.

Sarney /'sɑːneɪ/ José 1930– . President of Brazil 1985–89, member of the Brazilian Democratic Movement (PMDB). Sarney was elected vice president in 1985 and within months, on the death of President Neves, became head of state. Despite earlier involvement with the repressive military regime, he and his party won a convincing victory in the 1986 general election. He was succeeded 1989 by Ferdinand Color of the Party for National Reconstruction.

Saroyan /sə'rɔɪən/ William 1908–1981. US author. He is best known for short stories, such as *The*

Daring Young Man on the Flying Trapeze 1934, idealizing the hopes and sentiments of the 'little man'. His plays include *The Time of Your Life* 1939 and *Talking to You* 1962.

Sarraute /sæ'rəʊt/ Nathalie 1920– . Russian-born French novelist whose books include *Portrait d'un inconnu/Portrait of a Man Unknown* 1948, *Les Fruits d'or/The Golden Fruits* 1964, and *Vous les entendez?/Do You Hear Them?* 1972. An exponent of the *nouveau roman*, Sarraute bypasses plot, character, and style for the half-conscious interaction of minds.

sarsaparilla drink prepared from the long twisted roots of plants in the genus *Smilax*, native to Central and South America.

Sartre /'sɑːtrə/ Jean-Paul 1905–1980. French author and philosopher, one of the leading proponents of ◊existentialism in post-war philosophy. He published his first novel *La Nausée/Nausea* 1937, followed by the trilogy *Les Chemins de la liberté/Roads to Freedom* 1944–45, and many plays, including *Huis Clos/In Camera* 1944. *L'Être et le néant/Being and Nothingness* 1943, his first major philosophical work, is important for its radical doctrine of human freedom. In the later work *Critique de la raison dialectique/Critique of Dialectical Reason* 1960 he tried to produce a fusion of existentialism and Marxism.

He was born in Paris, and was the lifelong companion of the feminist writer Simone de Beauvoir. During World War II he was a prisoner for nine months, and on his return from Germany joined the Resistance. As a founder of modern existentialism, he edited its journal *Les Temps modernes/Modern Times*, and expressed its tenets in his novels and plays. According to Sartre, people's awareness of their own freedom takes the form of anxiety, and they therefore attempt to flee from this awareness into what he terms *mauvaise foi* ('bad faith'); this is the theory he put forward in *L'Etre et le néant/Being and Nothingness*. In *Crime Passionel* 1948 he attacked aspects of communism, while remaining generally sympathetic. In his later work Sartre became more sensitive to the social constraints on people's actions. Sartre refused the Nobel Prize for Literature 1964 for 'personal reasons', but allegedly changed his mind later, saying he wanted it, or the money.

Sarum /'seərəm/ former settlement from which the modern city of ◊Salisbury, Wiltshire, England, developed.

Sary-Shagan /'sɑːri ʃə'gɑːn/ weapons-testing area in Kazakhstan, USSR, near the Chinese border. In 1980 testing of beam weapons was detected there.

SAS abbreviation for ◊*Special Air Service*; also for *Scandinavian Airlines System*.

Sasebo /'sɑːsebəʊ/ seaport and naval base on the W coast of Kyushu, Japan; population (1985) 251,000.

Sask. abbreviation for ◊Saskatchewan.

Saskatchewan /sæ'skætʃəwən/ (Cree *Kis-is-ska-tche-wan* 'swift flowing') province of W Canada
area 652,300 sq km/251,788 sq mi
capital Regina
towns Saskatoon, Moose Jaw, Prince Albert

Saskatchewan

Regina

satellite Satellite image of North America showing cloud-free skies over much of the continent.

physical prairies in the south; to the north forests, lakes and subarctic tundra
products more than 60% of Canada's wheat; oil, natural gas, uranium, zinc, potash (world's largest reserves), copper, the only western reserves of helium outside the USA
population (1986) 1,010,000
history French trading posts established about 1750; owned by Hudson's Bay Company, first permanent settlement 1774; ceded to Canadian government 1870 as part of Northwest Territories; became a province 1905.

Saskatoon /ˌsæskəˈtuːn/ city in Saskatchewan, Canada; population (1986) 201,000. Industries include cement, oil refining, chemicals, and metal goods. The university was founded 1907.

Sassanian Empire /səˈseɪniən/ Persian empire founded AD 224 by Ardashir, a chieftain in the area of modern Fars in Iran, who had taken over ◊Parthia; it was named for his grandfather, Sasan. The capital was Ctesiphon, near modern ◊Baghdad. After a rapid period of expansion, when it contested supremacy with Rome, it was destroyed in 637 by Muslim Arabs at the Battle of ◊Qadisiya.

Sassari /ˈsæsəri/ capital of the province of the same name, in the NW corner of Sardinia, Italy; population (1987) 121,000. Every May the town is the scene of the Sardinian Cavalcade, the greatest festival on the island.

Sassau-Nguesso /ˌsæsaʊŋˈgesəʊ/ Denis 1943– . Congolese socialist politician, president from 1979. He progressively consolidated his position within the ruling left-wing Congolese Labour Party (PCT) and the country, at the same time improving relations with France and the USA.

Sassoon /səˈsuːn/ Siegfried 1886–1967. English writer, author of the autobiography *Memoirs of a Foxhunting Man* 1928. His *War Poems* 1919 express the disillusionment of his generation.

Educated at Cambridge, Sassoon enlisted in the army 1915, serving in France and Palestine. He published many volumes of poems and three novels.

sat in Hinduism, true existence or reality: the converse of illusion (*maya*).

Satellite: the largest planetary satellites

Satan a name for the ◊devil.

satellite any small body that orbits a larger one, either natural or artificial. Natural satellites that orbit planets are called moons. The first ***artificial satellite***, Sputnik 1, was launched into orbit around the Earth by the USSR 1957. Artificial satellites are used for scientific purposes, communications, weather forecasting, and military purposes. The largest artificial satellites can be seen by the naked eye.

At any time there are several thousand artificial satellites orbiting the Earth, including active satellites, those that have ended their working lives, and discarded sections of rockets. Artificial satellites eventually re-enter the Earth's atmosphere. Usually they burn up by friction, but sometimes debris falls to the Earth's surface, as with ◊Skylab.

The USA launched 23 nuclear-powered satellites 1961–77, of which four malfunctioned. The Star Wars programme entails sending as many as 100 nuclear reactors into space. The USSR has launched 39 nuclear reactors on orbiting satellites since 1965, of which six have malfunctioned.

More than 70,000 pieces of space junk, ranging from disabled satellites to tiny metal fragments, are careering round the Earth. The amount of waste is likely to increase, as the waste particles in orbit are continually colliding and fragmenting further.

satellite, applications the uses to which artificial satellites are put. These include:
scientific experiments and observation Many astronomical observations are best taken above the disturbing effect of the atmosphere. Satellite observations have been carried out by IRAS (Infrared Astronomical Satellite, 1983), which made a complete infrared survey of the skies, and Solar Max (1980), which observed solar flares. The Hipparchos satellite, launched 1989, is expected to measure the positions of the stars with unprecedented accuracy. Medical experiments are carried out aboard crewed satellites, such as the Soviet Mir and the UD Skylab.
reconnaisance and mapping applications Apart from military use and routine mapmaking,

satellite Satellite receiving dish at the Pleumeur-Bodou receiving station in Brittany, France. The dish is 32 m/105 ft across, and weighs 290 tonnes/285 tons.

the US Landsat, the French SPOT, and the equivalent USSR satellites have provided much useful information about water sources and drainage, vegetation, land use, geological structures, oil and mineral locations, and snow and ice.
weather monitoring The US NOAA series of satellites, and others launched by the European space agency, Japan, and India, provide continuous worldwide observation of the atmosphere.
navigation The US Global Positioning System, when complete in 1993, will feature 18 Navstar satellites that will enable users (including walkers and motorists) to find their position to within 1.5 m/4.5 ft. The Transit system, launched in the 1960s, with 12 satellites in orbit, locates users to within 100 m/328 ft.
communications A complete worldwide communications network is now provided by satellites such as the US-run ◊Intelsat system.

satellite television transmission of broadcast signals through artificial communications satellites. Mainly positioned in ◊geostationary orbit, satellites have been used since the 1960s to relay television pictures around the world. Higher-power satellites have more recently been developed to broadcast signals to cable systems or directly to people's homes (DBS).

Direct broadcasting began in the UK Feb 1989 with the introduction of Rupert Murdoch's Sky Television service; its rival British Satellite Broadcasting (BSB) went on the air early in 1990.

satellite town new town planned and built to serve a particular local industry, or as a dormitory or overspill town for people who work in a nearby metropolis. New towns in Britain include Port Sunlight near Birkenhead (Cheshire), built to house workers at Lever Brothers soap factories. More recent examples include Welwyn Garden City (1948), Cumbernauld (1955), and Milton Keynes (1967).

Other new towns include Letchworth (Hertfordshire), established in 1903, Basildon (1949), Corby (1950), Harlow (1947). There are 31 such towns in the UK planned by a government-financed corporation, in cooperation with the local authority. When they are completed, control passes to the New Town Commission. Their populations will range from 50,000 (Welwyn) to 250,000 (Milton Keynes) by the end of the century. Problems once caused by lack of social amenities for early arrivals are now overcome by basing a new town on an existing centre.

Satie /ˈsæti:/ Erik (Alfred Leslie) 1866–1925. French composer. His piano pieces, such as *Gymnopédies* 1888, often combine wit and melancholy. His orchestral works include *Parade* 1917,

Satellite: the largest planetary satellites

Planet	Satellite	Diameter in km	Mean distance from centre of primary in km	Orbital period in days	Reciprocal mass (planet = 1)
Jupiter	Ganymede	5,270	1,070,000	7.16	12,800
Saturn	Titan	5,150	1,221,900	15.95	4,200
Jupiter	Callisto	4,820	1,880,000	16.69	17,700
Jupiter	Io	3,630	421,600	1.77	21,400
Earth	Moon	3,476	384,400	27.32	81.3
Jupiter	Europa	3,132	670,900	3.55	39,000
Neptune	Triton	2,720	354,000	5.88	750

amongst whose sound effects is a typewriter. He was the mentor of the group of composers known as ◊*Les Six*.

satire a poem or piece of prose, which uses wit, humour, or irony, often through ◊allegory or extended metaphor, to ridicule human pretensions or expose social evils. Satire is related to *parody* in its intention to mock, but satire tends to be more subtle and to mock an attitude or a belief, whereas parody tends to mock a particular work such as a poem by imitating its style, often with purely comic intent.

The Roman poets Juvenal and Horace wrote Satires, and the form became popular in Europe in the 17th and 18th centuries, used by Voltaire in France and by Pope and Swift in England. Both satire and parody are designed to appeal to the intellect rather than the emotions; and both, to be effective, require a knowledge of the original attitude, person, or work that is being mocked (although much satire, such as *Gulliver's Travels* by Swift, can also be enjoyed simply on a literal level).

Sato /'sɑːtəʊ/ Eisaku 1901–1975. Japanese politician. He opposed the policies of Hayato Ikeda (1899–1965) in the Liberal Democratic Party, and succeeded him as prime minister 1964–72, pledged to a more independent foreign policy. He shared a Nobel Peace Prize in 1974 for his rejection of nuclear weapons. His brother *Nobosuke Kishi* (1896–1987) was prime minister of Japan 1957–60.

satori in Zen Buddhism, awakening, the experience of sudden ◊enlightenment.

satrap title of a provincial governor in ancient Persia. The Persian Empire was divided between some 20 of these under Darius I, each owing allegiance only to the king. Later the term was used to describe any local ruler, often in a derogatory way.

satsuma small, hardy, loose-skinned orange *Citrus reticulata* of the tangerine family. The fruit withstands cold conditions well. It originated in Japan.

saturated solution in physics, a solution obtained when a solvent (liquid) can dissolve no more of a solute (usually a solid) at a particular temperature. Normally, a slight fall in temperature causes some of the solute to crystallize out of solution. If this does not happen, the phenomenon is called supercooling, and the solution is said to be *supersaturated*.

Saturday Evening Post popular US magazine, specializing in family reading and known for its folksy Norman Rockwell covers. Founded 1821, it was transformed into its modern character by G H Lorimer and then remodelled again in the 1960s.

Saturn in astronomy, the second largest planet in the solar system, sixth from the Sun, and encircled by bright rings. Viewed through a telescope it is white, but appears lemon-coloured when seen at closer range. Saturn orbits the Sun every 29.46 years at an average distance of 1,427,000,000 km/886,700,000 mi. Its equatorial diameter is 120,000 km/75,000 mi, but its polar diameter is 12,000 km/7,450 mi smaller, a result of its fast rotation and low density (70% of water, the lowest of any planet). Saturn spins on its axis every 10 hr 14 min at its equator, slowing to 10 hr 40 min at high latitudes. Its mass is 95 times that of Earth, and its magnetic field 1,000 times stronger. Saturn is believed to have a small core of rock and iron, encased in ice and topped by a deep layer of liquid hydrogen. There are over 20 known moons, its largest being ◊Titan. The visible rings, made of ice and rock, are 275,000 km/170,000 mi rim to rim, but only 100 m/300 ft thick. The ◊Voyager probes showed that the rings actually consist of thousands of closely spaced ringlets, looking like the grooves in a gramophone record.

Like Jupiter, Saturn's visible surface consists of swirling clouds, probably made of frozen ammonia at a temperature of –170°C, although the markings in the clouds are not as prominent as Jupiter's. The space probes Voyager 1 and 2 found winds reaching 1,800 kph/1,100 mph.

From Earth, Saturn's rings appear to be divided into three main sections. Ring A, the outermost, is separated from ring B, the brightest, by the Cassini division (named after its discoverer ◊Cassini), 3,000 km/2,000 mi wide; the inner, transparent ring C is also called the Crepe Ring. Each ringlet of the rings is made of a swarm of particles of ice and rock, a few centimetres to a few metres in diameter. Outside the A ring is the narrow and faint F ring, which the Voyagers showed to be twisted or braided. The rings of Saturn could be the remains of a shattered moon, or they may always have existed in their present form.

The Voyagers photographed numerous small moons orbiting Saturn, taking the known total to over 20, more than for any other planet. The largest moon, Titan, has a dense atmosphere. Saturn's major satellites, in order of mean distance from the planet, are:

Mimas mean distance 186,000 km/116,000 mi, diameter 390 km/245 mi;

Enceladus mean distance 238,000 km/147,900 mi, diameter 500 km/310 mi;

Tethys mean distance 295,000 km/183,300 mi, diameter 1,050 km/650 mi;

Dione mean distance 370,000 km/230,000 mi, diameter 1,120 km/700 mi;

Rhea mean distance 527,000 km/327,000 mi, diameter 1,530 km/950 mi;

Titan mean distance 1,222,000 km/759,000 mi, diameter 5,150 km/3,200 mi;

Hyperion mean distance 1,483,000 km/922,000 mi, shape irregular 370 × 280 × 225 km/230 × 175 × 140 mi;

Iapetus mean distance 3,500,000 km/2,200,000 mi, diameter 1,440 km/895 mi;

Phoebe mean distance 12,950,000 km/8,047,000 mi, diameter 160 km/100 mi.

Saturn in Roman mythology, the god of agriculture (Greek *Kronos*), whose period of rule was the ancient Golden Age. He was dethroned by his sons Jupiter, Neptune, and Pluto. At his festival, the Saturnalia in Dec, gifts were exchanged, and slaves were briefly treated as their masters' equals.

Saturn rocket a family of large US rockets, developed by Wernher von Braun for the ◊Apollo project. The two-stage Saturn IB was used for launching Apollo spacecraft into orbit around the Earth. The three-stage Saturn V sent Apollo spacecraft to the Moon, and launched the ◊Skylab space station. The lift-off thrust of a Saturn V was 3,500 tonnes. After Apollo and Skylab, the Saturn rockets were retired in favour of the ◊space shuttle.

satyagraha (Sanskrit 'grasping the truth') nonviolent resistance, especially to British rule in India, as employed by Mahatma ◊Gandhi from 1918; the idea owes much to the Russian writer Tolstoy.

satyr in Greek mythology, a woodland creature characterized by pointed ears, two horns on the forehead, and a tail, who attended Dionysus. Roman writers confused satyrs with goat-footed fauns.

Saudi Arabia /'saʊdɪ əˈreɪbɪə/ country on the Arabian peninsula, stretching from the Red Sea to the Arabian Gulf, bounded to the N by Jordan, Iraq, and Kuwait, to the E by Qatar and United Arab Emirates, to the SE by Oman, and to the S by North and South Yemen.

government Saudi Arabia is an absolute monarchy with no written constitution, no legislature and no political parties. The king rules, in accordance with Islamic law, by decree. He appoints and heads a council of ministers, whose decisions are the result of a majority vote but always subject to the ultimate sanction of the king.

history For early history, see ◊Arabia. The sultanate of Nejd in the interior came under Turkish rule in the 18th century. Present-day Saudi Arabia is almost entirely the creation of King Ibn Saud who, after the dissolution of the ◊Ottoman Empire in 1918, fought rival Arab rulers until, in 1926, he had established himself as the undisputed king of the Hejaz and sultan of Nejd. In 1932 Nejd and Hejaz became the United Kingdom of Saudi Arabia.

Oil was discovered in the 1930s and commercially exploited from the 1940s and became the basis of the country's great prosperity. Ibn Saud died 1953 and was succeeded by his eldest son, Saud. During King Saud's reign relations between Saudi Arabia and Egypt became strained and criticisms of the king within the royal family grew until in 1964 he abdicated in favour of his brother Faisal. Under King Faisal, Saudi Arabia became a leader among Arab oil producers.

In 1975 Faisal was assassinated by one of his nephews, and his half-brother Khalid succeeded him. Khalid was in failing health and increasingly relied on his brother Fahd to perform the duties of government. King Khalid died of a heart attack in 1982 and was succeeded by Fahd.

Saudi Arabia has drawn up proposals for a permanent settlement of the Arab-Israeli dispute and given financial support to Iraq in its war with Iran. The Gulf War has also prompted it to buy advanced missiles from the USA. Islamic fundamentalists have staged demonstrations in ◊Mecca in 1979 and 1987, leading to violence and worsening relations with Iran.

Saturn *A colour-enhanced image of Saturn from the space probe Voyager 1 in 1980, at a range of 34 million km/21 million mi.*

Saudi Arabia
Kingdom of
(al-Mamlaka al-'Arabiya as-Sa'udiya)

area 2,200,518 sq km/849,400 sq mi
capital Riyadh
towns Mecca, Medina; ports Jidda, Dammam
physical desert, sloping to the Persian Gulf from a height of 2,750 m/9,000 ft in the W
features Nafud desert in the N, and the Rub'al Khali (Empty Quarter) in the S, area 650,000 sq km/250,000 sq mi

head of state and government King Fahd Ibn Abdul Aziz from 1982
government absolute monarchy
political parties none
exports oil
currency rial (6.37 = £1 Feb 1990)
population (1989) 12,678,000 (16% nomadic); annual growth rate 4.2%
life expectancy men 59, women 63
language Arabic
religion Sunni Muslim, with a Shi'ite minority in the E
literacy 34% male/12% female (1980 est)
GDP $110.5 bn (1983); $11,500 per head of population
chronology
1926–32 Territories united and kingdom established.
1953 King ibn-Saud died and was succeeded by his eldest son, Saud.
1964 King Saud forced to abdicate and was succeeded by his brother Faisal.
1975 King Faisal assassinated by a nephew and succeeded by his half-brother Khalid.
1982 King Khalid died suddenly of a heart attack and was succeeded by his brother Crown Prince Fahd, who had effectively been ruling the country for some years because of King Khalid's ill health.

Saul /sɔːl/ died *c*.1010 BC. In the Old Testament or Hebrew Bible, the first king of Israel, who was anointed by Samuel and warred successfully against the Ammonites and Philistines (neighbouring peoples). He turned against Samuel and committed suicide as his mind became unbalanced.

Sault Ste Marie /ˈsuː seɪnt məˈriː/ twin industrial ports on the Canadian/US border, one in Ontario and one in Michigan; population (1981) 82,902 and (1980) 14,448 respectively. They stand at the falls (French *sault*) in St Mary's river, which links lakes Superior and Huron. The falls are bypassed by canals. Industries include steel, pulp, and agricultural trade.

Saumur /səʊˈmjʊə/ town in Maine-et-Loire *département*, France, on the river Loire; population (1985) 34,000. The area is famous for its sparkling wines. The cavalry school, founded 1768, has since 1942 also been a training school for the French armed forces.

sauna a type of bath causing perspiration by means of dry heat. It consists of a small room in which the temperature is raised to about 90°C/200°F. The bather typically stays in it for only a few minutes and then follows it with a cold shower or swim. Saunas are popular in health clubs and sports centres.

The modern sauna derives from a Finnish dry-heat bath in which small quantities of steam could be produced by throwing cold water over hot stones; this was traditionally followed by a beating of the skin with birch twigs to stimulate the circulation, and a plunge into the lake or snow outdoors.

Saunders /ˈsɔːndəz/ Cicely 1918– . English philanthropist, founder of the modern hospice movement, which aims to provide a caring and comfortable environment in which people with terminal illnesses can die.

She was the medical director of St Christopher's Hospice in Sydenham, S London, 1967–85, and later became its chair. She wrote *Care of the Dying* 1960.

Saunders /ˈsɔːndəz/ Clarence 1881–1953. US retailer, who opened the first self-service supermarket, Piggly-Wiggly, in Memphis, Tennessee, 1919.

Saussure /də səʊˈsjʊə/ Horace de 1740–1799. Swiss geologist who made the earliest detailed and first-hand study of the Alps. He was a physicist at the University of Geneva. The results of his Alpine survey appeared in his classic work *Voyages des Alpes/Travels in the Alps* 1779–86.

Sauternes /səʊˈtɜːn/ a sweet white table wine produced in the Gironde *département*, SW France. It takes its name from the village of Sauternes.

Savage /ˈsævɪdʒ/ Michael Joseph 1872–1940. New Zealand Labour politician. As prime minister 1935–40, he introduced much social-security legislation.

savanna or *savannah* extensive open tropical grasslands, with scattered trees and shrubs. Savannas cover large areas of Africa, South America, and N Australia.

The name was originally given by Spaniards to the treeless plains of the tropical South American prairies. Most of North America's savannahs have been built over.

Savannah /səˈvænə/ city and port of Georgia, USA, 29 km/18 mi from the mouth of the Savannah river; population (1980) 226,000. Founded 1733, Savannah was the first city in the USA to be laid out in geometrically regular blocks. It exports cotton, and produces cottonseed oil, fertilizers, and machinery. The *Savannah*, the first steam-powered ship to cross the Atlantic, was built here; most of the 25-day journey, in 1819, was made under sail. The first nuclear-powered merchant ship, launched by the USA 1959, was given the same name.

Savery /ˈseɪvəri/ Thomas *c*.1650–1715. British engineer who invented the steam-driven water pump, precursor of the steam engine, in 1696. The pump used a boiler to raise steam, which was condensed (in a separate condenser) by an external spray of cold water. The partial vacuum created sucked water up a pipe from the mine shaft; steam pressure was then used to force the water away, after which the cycle was repeated. Savery patented his invention in 1698.

Savimbi /səˈvɪmbi/ Jonas 1934– . Angolan soldier and revolutionary, founder of the National Union for the Total Independence of Angola (UNITA).

The struggle for independence from Portugal escalated in 1961 into a civil war. In 1966 Savimbi founded the right-wing UNITA, which he led against the left-wing People's Movement for the Liberation of Angola (MPLA), led by Agostinho Neto. Neto, with Soviet and Cuban support, became president when independence was achieved in 1975, while UNITA, assisted by South Africa, continued its fight. A ceasefire was agreed in June

Savimbi *Angolan guerrilla leader Jonas Savimbi, whose UNITA rebels have waged a fierce armed struggle against Angola's left-wing regime since 1975.*

1989, but fighting continued, and the truce was abandoned after two months.

savings unspent income, after deduction of tax. In economics, a distinction is made between ◊investment, involving the purchase of capital goods, such as buying a house, and saving (where capital goods are not directly purchased, for example, buying shares).

savings and loan association in the USA, an institution which makes loans for home improvements, construction, and purchase. It also offers financial services such as insurance and annuities. It is not solely dependent on individual deposits for funds but may borrow from other institutions and on ◊money markets.

Savings and loan associations originated as building societies in the 17th century to facilitate house purchase. They later spread to many other countries.

savoir faire (French) knowing what to do, how to behave.

Savonarola /ˌsævənəˈrəʊlə/ Girolamo 1452–1498. Italian reformer, a Dominican friar. His crusade against political and religious corruption won him huge popularity, and in 1494 he led a revolt in Florence that expelled the ruling Medici

Savonarola *Italian Dominican monk Savonarola established a democratic republic in Florence. His portrait is by Fra Bartolommeo.*

family and established a democratic republic. His denunciations of Pope ◊Alexander VI led to his excommunication in 1497, and in 1498 he was arrested, tortured, hanged, and burned for heresy.

Savoy /sə'vɔɪ/ area of France between the Alps, Lake Geneva, and the river Rhône. A medieval duchy, it was formed into the *départements* of Savoie and Haute-Savoie, in Rhône-Alpes region.
history Savoy was a duchy from the 14th century, with the capital Chambéry. In 1720 it became a province of the kingdom of Sardinia which, with Nice, was ceded to France in 1860 by Victor Emmanuel II (king of Italy from 1861) in return for French assistance in driving the Austrians from Italy.

Saw /sɔː/ Maung 1929– . Burmese soldier and politician. Appointed head of the armed forces in 1985 by ◊Ne Win, in 1988 he led a coup to remove Ne Win's successor, Maung Maung, and became leader of an emergency military government.

Sawchuk /'sɔːtʃʌk/ 'Terry' (Terrance Gordon) 1929–1970. Canadian ice-hockey player, often regarded as the greatest goaltender of all time. He played for Detroit, Boston, Toronto, Los Angeles, and New York Rangers 1950–67, and holds the National Hockey League (NHL) record of 103 shut-outs (games in which he did not concede a goal).

sawfish fish of the ◊ray order. The *common sawfish Pristis pectinatus*, family Pristidae, is more than 6 m/19 ft long. It resembles a shark and has some 24 teeth along an elongated snout (2 m/6 ft) which can be used as a weapon.

sawfly type of insect of the order Hymenoptera, related to bees, wasps, and ants, but lacking a 'waist' on the body. The egg-laying tube (ovipositor) of the female has a saw edge, which she uses to make a slit in a plant stem to lay her eggs.

Some species have sharp ovipositors that can drill into wood, such as the black and yellow European '*wood wasp*' *Uroceras gigas*, about 4 cm/1.5 in long, which bores into conifers.

Saxe /sæks/ French form of ◊Saxony, former kingdom of Germany.

Saxe /sæks/ Maurice, Comte de 1696–1750. Soldier, illegitimate son of the Elector of Saxony, who served under Prince Eugène of Savoy and was created marshal of France in 1743 for his exploits in the War of the Austrian Succession.

Saxe-Coburg-Gotha /'sæks 'kəʊbɜːg 'gəʊtə/ Saxon duchy. Albert, the Prince Consort of Queen Victoria, was a son of the 1st Duke (Ernest I 1784–1844), who was succeeded by Albert's elder brother, Ernest II (1818–93). It remained the name of the British royal house until 1917, when it was changed to Windsor.

saxhorn a family of brass musical instruments played with valves, invented by the Belgian Adolphe Sax (1814–94) in 1845.

saxifrage plant of the family Saxifragaceae, occuring in rocky, mountainous, and alpine situations. London Pride *Saxifraga umbrosa × spathularis* is a common garden hybrid, with rosettes of fleshy leaves and clusters of white to pink star-shaped flowers.

Saxon member of a Teutonic people who invaded Britain in the early Middle Ages; see under ◊Anglo-Saxon.

Saxony /'sæksəni/ (German *Sachsen*) former kingdom in Germany, which is now the modern region of Leipzig, Dresden, and Karl-Marx-Stadt (Chemnitz), East Germany. Saxony lay between Prussia, Bavaria, and Bohemia; Dresden was the capital. The name is derived from its Saxon inhabitants whose territories originally reached as far west as the Rhine, covering most of the administrative *Land* of Lower Saxony, West Germany, formed 1946. Saxony was conquered by Charlemagne 792, and became a dukedom 814. It was divided in two by the Congress of Vienna 1815, and incorporated in the German Empire 1871.
792 Saxony was conquered by Charlemagne.

814 When Charlemagne's empire broke up after his death, Saxony became a dukedom.
13th century It became an electorate (that is, ruled by an elector).
1483 Martin Luther was born in Saxony, and the Reformation originated here.
1618–48 Saxony suffered much in the Thirty Years' War.
18th century It became a kingdom.
1815 Because Saxony had supported Napoleon I, half the kingdom was given to Prussia by the Congress of Vienna, becoming the Prussian province of Saxony.
1866 The remaining kingdom joined the North German Confederation.
1871 Incorporated in the German Empire.
1918 At the end of World War I the king abdicated and Saxony became one of the federal states of the German Republic.
1946 After World War II, Saxony was made a new administrative *Land* of East Germany as ◊Saxony-Anhalt.
1952 Saxony-Anhalt was merged with Leipzig region.

Saxony-Anhalt /'sæksəni 'ænhælt/ former *Land* (administrative region) of East Germany, 1946–52. It consisted of Anhalt, a former duchy and state, and most of the former Prussian province of Saxony.

saxophone a large family of wind instruments combining woodwind and brass features, the single reed of the clarinet and the wide bore of the bugle. Patented in 1846 by Adolphe Sax, a Belgian instrument maker, the saxophone is a lively and versatile instrument that has played a prominent part in the history of jazz. Four of the original eight sizes remain in common use: soprano, alto, tenor, and baritone. The soprano is usually straight, the others curved back at the mouthpiece end, and with an upturned bell.

Sayan Mountains /saɪ'æn/ range in the SE USSR, on the Mongolian border; the highest peak is Munku Sardik 3,489 m/11,451 ft. The mountains have coal, gold, silver, graphite, and lead resources.

Sayers /'seɪəz/ Dorothy L(eigh) 1893–1957. English writer of crime novels featuring detective Lord Peter Wimsey and heroine Harriet Vane, including *Strong Poison* 1930, *The Nine Tailors* 1934, and *Gaudy Night* 1935. She also wrote religious plays for radio, and translations of Dante.

Say's law in economics, the 'law of markets' enunciated by Jean-Baptiste Say (1767–1832) to the effect that supply creates its own demand and that resources can never be under-used.

Widely accepted by classical economists, the 'law' was regarded as erroneous by J M Keynes in his analysis of the depression in Britain during the 1920s and 1930s.

SBS acronym for *Special Boat Service*, the British navy's equivalent of the ◊Special Air Service.

sc. abbreviation for *scilicet* (Latin 'let it be understood').

SC abbreviation for ◊*South Carolina*.

scabies contagious infection of the skin caused by the mite *Sarcoptes scaboi*. Treatment is by antiparasitic creams and lotions.

scabious Mediterranean plant of the family Dipsacaceae, with many small, usually blue, flowers borne in a single head on a tall stalk. The *small scabious Scabiosa columbaria* and the *field scabious Knautia arvensis* are common species.

Scafell Pike /ˌskɔː'fel/ highest mountain in England, 978 m/3,210 ft. It is in Cumbria in the Lake District and is separated from Scafell 964 m/3,164 ft by a ridge called Mickledore. The summit of Scafell Pike was presented to the National Trust by the third Lord Leconfield, as a war memorial, in 1919.

scalar quantity in mathematics and science, a quantity that has magnitude but no direction, as distinct from a ◊vector quantity, which has a direction as well as a magnitude. Temperature, mass, and volume are scalar quantities.

scalawag or *scallywag* in US history, a derogatory term for white Southerners who, during and after the Civil War of 1861–65, supported the Republican Party, and black emancipation and enfranchisement.

scale in music, a sequence of pitches that establishes a key, and in some respects the character of a composition. A scale is defined by its starting note and may be *major* or *minor* depending on the order of intervals. A *chromatic* scale is the full range of 12 notes: it has no key because there is no fixed starting point. A *whole-tone* scale is a six-note scale and is also indeterminate in key: only two are possible. A *diatonic* scale has seven notes, a *pentatonic* scale has five.

scale insect small ◊bug, superfamily Cocceidea, that feeds on plants. Some species are major pests, for example the citrus mealy bug, which attacks citrus fruits in America. The female is often wingless and legless, attached to a plant by the head and with the body covered with a waxy scale. The rare males are winged.

scallop marine ◊mollusc of the family Pectinidae, with a bivalve fan-shaped shell. Scallops use 'jet propulsion' to move through the water to escape predators such as starfish. The *St James's shell Pecten jacobaeus* was used as a badge by medieval pilgrims to ◊Santiago de Compostela.

scampi (Italian 'shrimps') small lobster *Nephrops norwegicus*, which grows to 15 cm/6 in long.

Scandinavia /ˌskændɪ'neɪvɪə/ peninsula in NW Europe, comprising Norway and Sweden; politically and culturally it also includes Denmark and Finland.

Scandinavian inhabitant of Scandinavia (Denmark, Norway, Sweden, and Iceland). The Scandinavian languages, including Faroese, belong to the Indo-European family.

scandium a scarce metallic element, symbol Sc, atomic number 21, relative atomic mass 44.96. It is one of the lanthanide series of elements and was discovered in 1879 in the Scandinavian mineral euxenite.

scanner a device, usually electronic, used to sense and reproduce an image. In medicine, scanners are used in diagnosis to provide images of internal organs.

scanning in medicine, the non-invasive examination of body organs to detect abnormalities of structure or function. Detectable waves, for example ◊ultrasound, magnetic, or ◊X-rays, are passed through the part to be scanned. Their absorption pattern is recorded, analysed by computer, and displayed pictorially on a screen.

scanning tunnelling microscope (STM) a microscope that produces a magnified image using a tiny tungsten probe, with a tip so fine that it may consist of a single atom, which moves across a specimen. The probe tip moves so close to the specimen surface that electrons jump (or tunnel) across the gap between the tip and the surface.

The magnitude of the electron flow (current) depends on the distance from the tip to the surface, and so by measuring the current, the contours of the surface can be determined. These can be used to form an image on a computer screen of the surface, with individual atoms resolved.

Scapa Flow /'skɑːpə 'fləʊ/ expanse of sea in the Orkney Islands, Scotland, until 1957 a base of the Royal Navy. It was the main base of the Grand Fleet during World War I, and in 1919 was the scene of the scuttling of 71 surrendered German warships.

scapolite a group of white or greyish minerals, silicates of sodium, aluminium, and calcium, common in metamorphosed limestones and forming at high temperatures and pressures.

scarab a dung-beetle of the family Scarabeidae. The *Scarabeus sacer* was revered by the ancient Egyptians as the symbol of resurrection.

Scarborough /'skɑːbərə/ spa and holiday resort in N Yorkshire, England; population (1985) 50,000. A ruined Norman castle overlooks the town, which is a touring centre for the Yorkshire Moors.

Scargill /'skɑːgɪl/ Arthur 1938– . British trade-union leader. Elected president of the National Union of Miners (NUM) 1981, he embarked on a collision course with the Conservative government of Margaret Thatcher. The damaging strike of 1984–85 split the miners's movement.

Scargill became a miner on leaving school and was soon a union and political activist, in the Young Communist League 1955–62 and then a member of the Labour Party from 1966 and president of the Yorkshire miners's union 1973–81. He became a fiery and effective orator. During the long miners's strike he was criticized for not seeking an early NUM ballot to support the strike decision.

Scarlatti /skɑːˈlætɪ/ (Giuseppe) Domenico 1685–1757. Italian composer, eldest son of Alessandro Scarlatti, who lived most of his life in Portugal and Spain in the service of the Queen of Spain. He wrote highly original harpsichord sonatas.

Scarlatti /skɑːˈlætɪ/ (Pietro) Alessandro (Gaspare) 1660–1725. Italian Baroque composer, Master of the Chapel at the court of Naples, who developed the opera form (◊arias interspersed with ◊recitative). He composed more than 100 operas, including *Tigrane* 1715, as well as church music and oratorios.

scarlet fever or *scarlatina* an infectious disease caused by the bacterium *Streptococcus pyogenes*. It is marked by a sore throat and a bright red rash spreading from the upper to the lower part of the body. The rash is followed by the skin peeling in flakes. It is treated with antibiotics.

Scarlet Pimpernel, The a historical adventure novel by Baroness Orczy published in the UK 1905. Set in Paris during the Reign of Terror (1793–94), it describes the exploits of a group of Britons, the League of the Scarlet Pimpernel, and particularly their leader, Sir Percy Blakeney, who save aristocrats from the Revolution.

scarp and dip in geology, the two slopes formed when a sedimentary bed outcrops as a landscape feature. The scarp is the slope that cuts across the bedding plane; the dip is the opposite slope which follows the bedding plane. The scarp is usually steep, while the dip is a gentle slope.

scent gland a gland that opens at the skin surface of animals, producing odorous compounds which are used in communication (◊pheromones).

Scepticism an ancient philosophical view that absolute knowledge of things is ultimately unobtainable, hence the only proper attitude is to suspend judgment. Its origins lay in the teachings of the Greek philosopher Pyrrho, who maintained that peace of mind lay in renouncing all claims to knowledge.

It was taken up in a less extreme form by the Greek ◊Academy in the 3rd and 2nd centuries BC. Academic sceptics claimed that although truth is finally unknowable, a balance of probabilities can be used for coming to decisions. The most radical form of scepticism is known as ◊solipsism, which maintains that the self is the only thing that can be known to exist.

Schadenfreude (German) malicious enjoyment at the misfortunes of others.

Schaffhausen /'ʃæfˌhaʊzən/ town in N Switzerland; population (1980) 34,250. Industries include the manufacture of watches, chemicals, and textiles. The Rhine falls here in a series of cascades 60 m/197 ft high.

Scheele /'ʃeɪlə/ Karl 1742–1786. Swedish chemist and pharmacist. In the book *Experiments on Air and Fire* 1777, he argued that the atmosphere was composed of two gases. One, which supported combustion (oxygen), he called 'fire air', and the other, which inhibited combustion (nitrogen), he called 'vitiated air'. He thus anticipated Joseph ◊Priestley in his discovery of oxygen by two years.

Scheer /ʃeə/ Reinhard 1863–1928. German admiral in World War I, commander of the High Sea Fleet in 1916 at the Battle of Jutland.

Scheherazade the storyteller in the ◊*Arabian Nights*.

Scheldt /skelt/ (Dutch **Schelde** French **Escaut**) river rising in Aisne *département*, N France and flowing 400 km/250 mi to join the North Sea south of Walcheren, in the Netherlands. Antwerp is the chief town on the Scheldt.

Schelling /'ʃelɪŋ/ Friedrich Wilhelm Joseph 1775–1854. German philosopher, who began as a follower of Fichte, but moved away from subjective ◊idealism towards a 'philosophy of identity' (*Identitätsphilosophie*), in which subject and object are seen as united in the absolute. His early philosophy influenced ◊Hegel, but his later work criticizes Hegel, arguing that being necessarily precedes thought.

scheltopusik another name for the glass snake.

Schenectady /skəˈnektədi/ industrial city on the river Mohawk, New York State, USA; population (1980) 67,972. It dates from 1662, and produces electrical goods.

Scherchen /'ʃeəʃən/ Hermann 1891–1966. German conductor. He collaborated with ◊Schoenberg, and in 1919 founded the journal *Melos* to promote contemporary music. He moved to Switzerland in 1933, and was active as a conductor and teacher. He also wrote two texts, *Handbook of Conducting* and *The Nature of Music*. During the 1950s he founded a music publishing house, Ars Viva Verlag, and an electronic studio at Gravesano.

scherzo (Italian 'joke') in music, a lively piece, usually in rapid triple (3/4) time; often used for the third movement of a symphony, sonata, or quartet.

Scheveningen /'sxeɪfənɪŋə/ seaside resort and northern suburbs of The ◊Hague, Netherlands. There is a ferry link with Great Yarmouth, England.

Schiaparelli /ˌskjæpəˈreli/ Elsa 1896–1973. Italian couturier and knitwear designer. Her innovative fashion ideas included padded shoulders, sophisticated colours ('shocking pink'), and the pioneering use of zips and synthetic fabrics.

Schiaparelli /ˌskjæpəˈreli/ Giovanni (Virginio) 1835–1910. Italian astronomer, who discovered the so-called 'Martian canals'. Among his achievements were studies of ancient and medieval astronomy, the discovery of asteroid 69 (Hesperia) Apr 1861, observation of double stars, and the discovery of the connection between comets and meteors. In 1877 he first drew attention to the linear markings on Mars, which gave rise to the 'Martian canal' controversy. These markings are now known to be optical effects and not real lines.

Schick test injection of a small quantity of diphtheria toxin to ascertain whether a person is immune to the disease or not. In the latter case, a local inflammation appears.

Schiedam /ˌsxiːˈdæm/ port in Zuid-Holland province, SW Netherlands, on the river Meuse, 5 km/3 mi west of Rotterdam; population (1987) 69,350. It is famous for its gin.

Schiele /'ʃiːlə/ Egon 1890–1918. Austrian Expressionist artist. Originally a landscape painter, he was strongly influenced by Art Nouveau and developed a contorted linear style. His subject matter included portraits and nudes. In 1911 he was arrested for alleged obscenity.

Schiller /'ʃɪlə/ Johann Christoph Friedrich von 1759–1805. German dramatist, poet, and historian. He wrote *Sturm und Drang* (storm and stress) verse and plays, including the dramatic trilogy *Wallenstein* 1798–99. Much of his work concerns the desire for political freedom and for the avoidance of mediocrity.

A qualified surgeon, after the success of the play *Die Räuber/The Robbers* 1781, he devoted himself to literature and completed his tragedies *Fiesko/Fiasco* and *Kabale und Liebe/Love and Intrigue* 1783. Moving to Weimar in 1787, he wrote his more mature blank-verse drama *Don Carlos* and the hymn 'An die Freude/Ode to Joy',

later used by ◊Beethoven in his ninth symphony. As professor of history at Jena from 1789, he completed a history of the Thirty Years' War and developed a close friendship with ◊Goethe after early antagonism. His essays on aesthetics include the piece of literary criticism *Über naive und sentimentalische Dichtung/Naive and Sentimental Poetry*. Schiller became the foremost German dramatist with his classic dramas *Wallenstein*, *Maria Stuart* 1800, *Die Jungfrau von Orleans/The Maid of Orleans* 1801, and *Wilhelm Tell/William Tell* 1804.

Schinkel /'ʃɪnkəl/ Karl Friedrich 1781–1841. Prussian Neo-Classical architect. Major works include the Old Museum, Berlin, 1823–30, the Nikolaikirche in Potsdam 1830–37, and the Roman Bath 1833 in the park of Potsdam.

schipperke /'ʃɪpəki/ (Dutch 'little boatman' from its use on canal barges) tailless watchdog, bred in Belgium. It has black fur and erect ears, is about 30 cm/1 ft high, and weighs about 7 kg/16 lbs.

schism a formal split over a doctrinal difference between religious believers, as in the Roman Catholic Church in the ◊Great Schism; that of the Old Catholics in 1870 over the doctrine of papal infallibility; and over use of the Latin Tridentine mass 1988.

schist a foliated (laminated) ◊metamorphic rock arranged in parallel layers of ◊minerals—for example, mica, which easily splits off into thin plates.

schistosomiasis another name for ◊bilharzia.

schizocarp a type of dry ◊fruit that develops from two or more carpels, and which splits, when mature, to form separate one-seeded units known as mericarps. The mericarps may be dehiscent, splitting open to release the seed when ripe, as in *Geranium*, or indehiscent, as in mallow *Malva* and plants of the Umbelliferae family, such as the carrot *Daucus carota* and parsnip *Pastinaca sativa*.

schizophrenia a mental disorder, a psychosis of unknown origin, which can lead to profound changes in personality and behaviour including paranoia and hallucinations. Treatments include drugs, family therapy, stress reduction, and rehabilitation.

Schlegel /'ʃleɪgəl/ August Wilhelm von 1767–1845. German Romantic author, translator of Shakespeare, whose *Über dramatische Kunst und Literatur/ Lectures on Dramatic Art and Literature* 1809–11 broke down the formalism of the old classical criteria of literary composition. Friedrich von Schlegel was his brother.

Schlegel /'ʃleɪgəl/ Friedrich von 1772–1829. German critic, who (with his brother August) was a founder of the Romantic movement, and a pioneer in the comparative study of languages.

Schlesinger /'ʃlesɪndʒə/ John 1926– . British film and television director, responsible for such British films as *Billy Liar* 1963 and *Darling* 1965. His first US film, *Midnight Cowboy* 1969, was a big commercial success and was followed by *Sunday, Bloody Sunday* 1971, *Marathon Man* 1976, and *Yanks* 1979.

Schleswig-Holstein /'ʃlezwɪg 'hɒlstaɪn/ *Land* (state) of West Germany
area 15,700 sq km/6,060 sq mi
capital Kiel
towns Lübeck, Flensburg, Schleswig
features river Elbe, Kiel Canal, Heligoland
products shipbuilding, mechanical and electrical engineering, food processing
population (1988) 2,613,000
religion Protestant 87%; Catholic 6%
history Schleswig (Danish *Slesvig*) and Holstein were two duchies held by the kings of Denmark from 1460, but were not part of the kingdom; a number of the inhabitants were German, and Holstein was a member of the Confederation of the Rhine formed 1815. Possession of the duchies had long been disputed by Prussia, and when Frederick VII of Denmark died without an heir 1863, Prussia, supported by Austria, fought and

defeated the Danes 1864, and in 1866 annexed the two duchies. A plebiscite held 1920 gave the northern part of Schleswig to Denmark, which made it the province of Haderslev and Aabenraa; the rest, with Holstein, remained part of Germany.

Schlieffen Plan military plan produced by chief of the German general staff Gen Count Alfred von Schlieffen (1833–1913) Dec 1905, which formed the basis of German military planning before World War I, and which inspired Hitler's plans for the conquest of W Europe in World War II. It involved a simultaneous attack on Russia and France, the object being to defeat France quickly and then deploy all available resources against the Russians.

Schliemann /ˈʃliːmən/ Heinrich 1822–1890. German archaeologist. He earned a fortune as a businessman, retiring in 1863 to pursue his life-long ambition to discover a historical basis for Homer's Illiad. In 1871 he began excavating at Hissarlik, Turkey, which yielded the ruins of nine consecutive cities and was indeed the site of Troy. His later excavations were at Mycenae 1874–76, where he discovered the ruins of the ◊Mycenaean civilization.

Schluter /ˈsluːtə/ Poul Holmskov 1929– . Danish right-wing politician, leader of the Conservative People's Party (KF) from 1974 and prime minister from 1982. Having joined the KF in his youth, he trained as a lawyer and then entered the Danish parliament (Folketing) in 1964. His centre-right coalition survived the 1987 election and was reconstituted, with Liberal support, in 1988.

Schmidt /ʃmɪt/ Helmut 1918– . West German socialist politician, member of the Social Democratic Party (SPD), chancellor 1974–83. As chancellor, Schmidt introduced social reforms and continued Brandt's policy of ◊Ostpolitik. With the French president Giscard d'Estaing, Schmidt introduced annual world and European economic summits. He was a firm supporter of ◊NATO and of the deployment of US nuclear missiles in West Germany during the early 1980s.

Schmidt was elected to the *Bundestag* (federal parliament) in 1953. He was interior minister 1961–65, defence minister 1969–72, and finance minister 1972–74. He became federal chancellor (prime minister) on Willy ◊Brandt's resignation in 1974. Re-elected 1980, he was defeated in the *Bundestag* in 1982 following the switch of allegiance by the SPD's coalition allies, the Free Democratic Party. Schmidt retired from federal politics at the general election of 1983, having encountered growing opposition from the SPD's left wing, who opposed his stance on military and economic issues.

Schmidt-Rottluff /ʃmɪt ˈrɒtluf/ Karl 1884–1974. German Expressionist painter and printmaker, a founder member of *die ◊Brücke* in Dresden 1905, active in Berlin from 1911. Influenced by van Gogh and the Fauves, he developed a vigorous style of brushwork and a bold palette. He painted portraits and landscapes, and produced numerous woodcuts and lithographs.

Schnabel /ˈʃnɑːbəl/ Artur 1882–1951. Austrian pianist, teacher, and composer. He taught music at the Berlin State Academy 1925–30, but settled in the USA in 1939, where he composed symphonies and piano works. He excelled at playing Beethoven and trained many pianists.

Schneider /ˈʃnaɪdə/ Romy. Stage name of Rosemarie Albach-Retty 1938–1982. Austrian film actress who starred in *Boccaccio '70* 1962, *Le Procès/Der Prozess* 1962, and *Ludwig* 1972.

Schoenberg /ˈʃɜːnbɜːg/ Arnold (Franz Walter) 1874–1951. Austro-Hungarian composer, a US citizen from 1941. After Romantic early work such as *Verklärte Nacht* 1899 and the *Gurrelieder/Songs of Gurra* 1900–11, he experimented with ◊atonality, producing such works as *Pierrot Lunaire* 1912 before developing the **12-tone system** of musical composition. This was further developed by his pupils ◊Berg and ◊Webern.

Schnabel Austrian pianist Artur Schnabel made his debut at the age of eight. With the arrival of the Nazi regime he emigrated to the USA, where he became known for his interpretation of the German classics.

After World War I he wrote several Neo-Classical works for chamber ensembles. He taught at the Berlin State Academy 1925–33. Driven from Germany by the Nazis, he settled in the US 1933, where he influenced music scoring for films. Later works include the opera *Moses and Aron* 1932–51.

scholasticism the theological and philosophical system of Christian Europe in the medieval period as studied in the schools. Scholasticism sought to integrate Christian teaching with Platonic and Aristotelian philosophy.

John Scotus (Erigena) is regarded as the founder, but the succession of 'Schoolmen', as scholastic philosophers were called, opened with Roscellinus at the end of the 11th century, when as a supporter of nominalism he was countered by Anselm, the champion of realism. The controversy over ◊universals thus begun continued for several centuries. William of Champeaux, Abélard, the English monk Alexander of Hales (died 1222), Albertus Magnus, and Peter Lombard played prominent parts, but more significant were Thomas Aquinas, whose writings became the classical textbooks of Catholic doctrine, and the Franciscan Duns Scotus. The last major scholastic philosopher was William of Occam, who, in the first half of the 14th century, restated nominalism.

In the 20th century there has been a revival of interest in scholasticism, in the writings of Jacques Maritian (1882–1973) and other Catholic scholars.

Schopenhauer /ˈʃəʊpənˌhaʊə/ Arthur 1788–1860. German philosopher, whose *The World*

Schoenberg Arnold Schoenberg teaching at the University of California.

Schubert Franz Schubert, whose songs include 'An die Musik/To music'.

as Will and Idea 1818 expounded an atheistic and pessimistic world view: an irrational will is considered as the inner principle of the world, producing an ever-frustrated cycle of desire, of which the only escape is aesthetic contemplation, or absorption into nothingness.

This theory struck a responsive chord in the philosopher Nietzsche, the composer Wagner, the German novelist Thomas Mann, and the English writer Thomas Hardy.

Schreiner /ˈʃraɪnə/ Olive 1862–1920. South African novelist and supporter of women's rights. Her autobiographical *The Story of an African Farm* 1883 describes life on the South African veld.

Schrödinger /ˈʃrɜːdɪŋə/ Erwin 1887–1961. Austrian physicist who advanced the study of wave mechanics (see ◊quantum theory). Born in Vienna, he became senior professor at the Dublin Institute for Advanced Studies 1940. He shared (with ◊Dirac) a Nobel prize 1933.

Schubert /ˈʃuːbət/ Franz (Peter) 1797–1828. Austrian composer. His eight symphonies include the incomplete eighth in B minor (the 'Unfinished') and the 'Great' in C major 1829. He wrote chamber and piano music, including the 'Trout Quintet', and over 600 *lieder* (songs) combining the romantic expression of emotion with pure melody. They include the cycles *Die schöne Müllerin/The Beautiful Maid of the Mill* 1823 and *Die Winterreise/The Winter Journey* 1827.

Schumacher /ˈʃuːmækə/ Ernst Friedrich 'Fritz' 1911–1977. German writer and economist, whose *Small is Beautiful: Economics as if People Mattered* 1973 makes a case for small-scale economic growth without great capital expenditure.

Schuman /ˈʃuːmɒn/ Robert 1886–1963. French politician. He was prime minister 1947–48, and as foreign minister 1948–53 he proposed in May 1950 a common market for coal and steel (the **Schuman Plan**), which was established as the European Coal and Steel Community 1952, the basis of the European Community.

Schumann /ˈʃuːmən/ Clara (Josephine) (born Wieck) 1819–1896. German pianist. Born in Leipzig, she married Robert Schumann in 1840 (her father had been his piano teacher). During his life and after his death she was devoted to popularizing his work, appearing frequently in European concert halls.

Schumann /ˈʃuːmən/ Robert Alexander 1810–1856. German Romantic composer. His songs and short piano pieces show simplicity combined with an ability to portray mood and emotion. Among his compositions are four symphonies, a violin concerto, a piano concerto, sonatas, and song cycles such as *Dichterliebe/Poet's Love* 1840. ◊Mendelssohn championed many of his works.

Schumpeter /ˈʃʊmpeɪtə/ Joseph A(lois) 1883–1950. US economist and sociologist, born in Austria. In *Capitalism, Socialism and Democracy* 1942 he contended that Western capitalism, impelled by its very success, was evolving into a form of socialism because firms would become increasingly large and their managements increasingly divorced from ownership, while social trends were undermining the traditional motives for entrepreneurial accumulation of wealth.

Schuschnigg /ˈʃuʃnɪg/ Kurt von 1897–1977. Austrian chancellor 1934, in succession to ◊Dollfuss. In Feb 1938 he was forced to accept a Nazi minister of the interior, and a month later Austria was occupied and annexed by Germany. He was imprisoned in Germany until 1945, when he went to the USA.

Schütz /ʃʊtz/ Heinrich 1585–1672. German composer, musical director to the Elector of Saxony from 1614. His works include *The Seven Last Words* about 1645, *Musicalische Exequien* 1636, and the *Deutsche Magnificat/German Magnificat* 1671.

Schwarzkopf /ˈʃvɑːtskɒpf/ Elisabeth 1915– . German soprano, known for her dramatic interpretation of operatic roles, such as Elvira in *Don Giovanni* and the Marschallin in *Der Rosenkavalier*, as well as songs.

Schwarzwald /ˈʃvɑːtsvælt/ German name for the ◊Black Forest, coniferous forest in West Germany.

Schweitzer /ˈʃvaɪtsə/ Albert 1875–1965. French theologian, organist, and missionary surgeon. He founded the hospital at Lambaréné in Gabon in 1913, giving organ recitals to support his work there. He wrote a life of Bach and *Von reimarus zu Wrede/The Quest for the Historical Jesus* 1906 and was awarded the Nobel Peace Prize in 1952 for his teaching of 'reverence for life'.

Schwerin /ʃveˈriːn/ capital of Schwerin county, East Germany; population (1986) 128,000. Industries include the manufacture of machinery and chemicals. It was formerly the capital of ◊Mecklenburg and earlier of Mecklenburg-Schwerin. Schwerin county has an area of 8,670 sq km/3,347 sq mi, and a population of 592,000.

Schwinger /ˈʃwɪŋə/ Julian 1918– . US quantum physicist. His research concerned the behaviour of charged particles in electrical fields. This work, expressed entirely through mathematics, combines elements from quantum theory and relativity theory.

Described as the 'physicist in knee pants', he entered college in New York at the age of 15, transferred to Columbia University and graduated at 17. At the age of 29 he became Harvard University's youngest full professor.

Schwitters /ˈʃvɪtəz/ Kurt 1887–1948. German artist, a member of the Dada movement. He moved to Norway in 1937 and to the UK in 1940. From 1918 he developed a variation on collage,

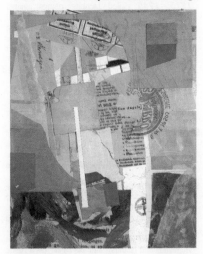

Schwitters Opened by Customs (1937–38) Tate Gallery, London.

using discarded rubbish such as buttons and bus tickets to create pictures and structures.

He called these art works *Merz*, and produced a magazine called *Merz* from 1923. Later he created *Merzbau*, extensive constructions of wood and scrap, most of which were destroyed.

Schwyz /ʃviːts/ capital of Schwyz canton, Switzerland; population (1980) 12,100. Schwyz was one of the three original cantons of the Swiss Confederation 1291, which gave its name to the whole country about 1450.

Sciascia /ˈʃæʃə/ Leonardo 1921–1989. Sicilian novelist, who used the detective novel to explore the hidden workings of Sicilian life, for example in *Il giorno della civetta/Mafia Vendetta* 1961.

sciatica persistent pain in the leg, along the sciatic nerve and its branches. Causes of sciatica include inflammation of the nerve itself, or pressure on, or inflammation of, a nerve root leading out of the lower spine.

science (Latin *scientia* 'knowledge') any systematic field of study or body of knowledge that aims, through experiment, observation, and deduction, to produce reliable explanation of phenomena, with reference to the material and physical world. Science is divided into separate areas of study, such as astronomy, biology, chemistry, mathematics, and physics, although more recently attempts have been made to combine traditionally separate disciplines under such headings as ◊life sciences and ◊earth sciences. These areas are sometimes jointly referred to as the **natural sciences**. The **physical sciences** comprise mathematics, physics, and chemistry. The application of science for practical purposes is called **technology**. **Social science** is the systematic study of human behaviour, and includes such areas as anthropology, economics, psychology, and sociology.

One area of contemporary debate is whether the social-science disciplines are actually sciences; that is, whether the study of human beings is capable of scientific precision or prediction in the same way as natural science is seen to be. For example, in 1982 the British government challenged the name of the Social Science Research Council, arguing instead for use of the term 'social studies'.

Activities such as healing, star-watching, and engineering have been practised in many societies since ancient times. Pure science, especially physics (formerly called natural philosophy), had traditionally been the main area of study for philosophers. The European scientific revolution between about 1650 and 1800 replaced speculative philosophy with a new combination of observation, experimentation, and rationality.

Today scientific research involves an interaction between tradition, experiment and observation, and deduction. The subject area called *philosophy of science* investigates the nature of this complex interaction, and the extent of its ability to gain access to the truth about the material world. It has long been recognized that induction from observation cannot give explanations based on logic. In the 20th century ◊Popper has described ◊scientific method as a rigorous experimental testing of a scientist's ideas or hypotheses (see ◊hypothesis). The origin and role of these ideas, and their interdependence with observation, have been examined, for example by the US thinker Kuhn, who places them in a historical and sociological setting. The *sociology of science* investigates how scientific theories and laws are produced, and questions the possibility of ◊objectivity in any scientific endeavour. One controversial aspect is the undermining of scientific realism and its replacement by scientific relativism, as described by ◊Feyerabend. Questions concerning the proper use of science and the role of science education are also restructuring this field of study.

science fiction or **speculative fiction** also known as **SF** or **sci-fi** genre of fiction and film with an

imaginary scientific and technological basis. It is sometimes held to have its roots in the works of Mary Shelley, notably *Frankenstein* 1818. Often taking its ideas and concerns from current ideas in science and the social sciences, SF aims to shake up standard perceptions of reality.

SF works often deal with alternative realities, future histories, robots, aliens, utopias and dystopias (often satiric), space and time travel, natural or human-made disasters, and psychic powers. Early practitioners were Jules Verne and H G Wells. In the 20th century the US pulp-magazine tradition of SF produced writers such as Arthur C Clarke, Isaac Asimov, Robert Heinlein, and Frank Herbert; a consensus of 'pure storytelling' and traditional values was disrupted by writers associated with the British magazine *New Worlds* (Brian Aldiss, Michael Moorcock, J G Ballard) and by younger US writers (Joanna Russ, Ursula Le Guin, Thomas Disch, Gene Wolfe) who used the form for serious literary purposes and for political and sexual radicalism. Thriving SF traditions, only partly influenced by the Anglo-American one, exist in France, Germany, and Eastern Europe, especially the USSR. In the 1980s the cyberpunk school spread from the USA, spearheaded by William Gibson and Bruce Sterling (1954–).

SF writers include James Tiptree Jr (Alice Sheldon 1915–87, US), Philip K Dick, John Brunner (1934– , UK), Samuel Delany (1942– ,US), Stanislaw Lem (1921– , Poland) Boris and Arkady Strugatsky (1931– , and 1925– , USSR), Harlan Ellison (1934–), Damon Knight (1922–), John Campbell (1910–71), and Frederik Pohl (1919–); the last four all US editors and anthologists).

Many mainstream writers have written SF, including Aldous Huxley (*Brave New World* 1932), George Orwell (*Nineteen Eighty-Four* 1949), and Doris Lessing.

Science Museum British museum of science and technology in South Kensington, London. Founded in 1853 as the National Museum of Science and Industry, it houses exhibits from all areas of science.

science park site on which high-technology industrial businesses are housed near a university, so that they can benefit from the research expertise of the university's scientists. Science parks originated in the USA in the 1950s. By 1985 the UK had 13.

scientific law in science, principles which are taken to be universally applicable.

Laws (for instance ◊Boyle's law, ◊Newton's laws of motion) form the basic theoretical structure of the physical sciences, so that the rejection of a law by the scientific community is an almost inconceivable event. On occasion a law may be modified, as was the case when Einstein showed that Newton's laws of motion do not apply to objects travelling at speeds close to that of light.

Scientology (Latin *scire* 'to know' and Greek *logos* 'branch of learning') an 'applied religious philosophy' based on ◊dianetics, founded in California in 1954 by L Ron ◊Hubbard as the **Church of Scientology**. It claims to 'increase man's spiritual awareness', but its methods of recruiting and retaining converts have been criticized. Its headquarters from 1959 have been in Sussex, England.

scilicet (Latin) namely, that is.

scilla bulbous plant of the family Liliaceae, bearing blue, pink, or white flowers, and including the spring squill *Scilla verna*.

Scilly Islands /ˈsɪli/ group of 140 islands and islets lying 40 km/25 mi SW of Land's End, England; administered by the Duchy of Cornwall; area 16 sq km/6.3 sq mi; population (1981) 1,850. The five inhabited islands are *St Mary's*, the largest, on which is Hugh Town, capital of the Scillies; *Tresco*, the second largest, with subtropical gardens; *St Martin's*, noted for beautiful shells; *St Agnes*, and *Bryher*.

Products include vegetables and flowers and tourism is important. The islands have remains of Bronze Age settlements. The numerous wreck sites off the islands include many of Sir Cloudesley ◊Shovell's fleet in 1707. The Isles of Scilly are an important birdwatching centre with breeding sea birds in the summer and rare migrants in the spring and autumn.

scintillation counter an instrument for measuring very low levels of radiation. The radiation strikes a scintillator (a device which outputs a unit of light when a charged elementary particle collides with it), whose small light output is 'amplified' by a ◊photomultiplier; the current pulses of its output are in turn counted or summed by a scaler.

Scipio Africanus Major /'skɪpiəu ˌæfrɪ'kɑːnəs 'meɪdzə/ 237–*c*.183 BC. Roman general. He defeated the Carthaginians in Spain 210–206 BC, invaded Africa 204 BC, and defeated Hannibal at Zama 202 BC.

Scipio Africanus Minor /'skɪpiəu ˌæfrɪ'kɑːnəs 'maɪnə/ *c*.185–129 BC. Roman general, the adopted grandson of Scipio Africanus Major, also known as *Scipio Aemilianus*. He destroyed Carthage in 146 BC, and subdued Spain 134 BC. He was opposed to his brothers-in-law, the Gracchi (see under ◊Gracchus), and his wife is thought to have shared in his murder.

Scipio Publius Cornelius /'skɪpiəu/ died 211 BC. Roman general, father of Scipio Africanus Major. Elected consul 218, during the 2nd Punic War, he was defeated by Hannibal at Ticinus and killed by the Carthaginians in Spain.

SCLC abbreviation for US civil-rights organization ◊*Southern Christian Leadership Conference*.

sclerenchyma a plant tissue whose function is to strengthen and support, composed of thick-walled cells that are heavily lignified (toughened). On maturity the cell inside dies, and only the cell walls remain.

Sclerenchyma may be made up of one or two types of cells: *Sclereids* can occur singly or in small clusters, and are often found in the hard shells of fruits, in seed coats, bark, and the stem cortex. *Fibres*, frequently grouped in bundles, are elongated cells, often with pointed ends, associated with the vascular tissue (◊xylem and ◊phloem) of the plant.

Some fibres provide useful materials, such as flax from *Linum usitatissimum* and hemp from *Cannabis sativa*.

sclerosis disease of the nervous system; see ◊multiple sclerosis.

Scofield /'skəʊfiːld/ Paul 1922– . English actor. His wide-ranging lead roles include the drunken priest in Greene's *The Power and the Glory*,

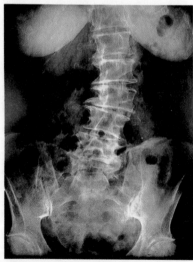

scoliosis X-ray of the lumbar spine of a woman, aged 80, showing a prominent scoliosis (lateral curve).

Harry in Pinter's *The Homecoming*, and Salieri in Shaffer's *Amadeus*. He appeared as Sir Thomas More in both stage and film versions of *A Man for All Seasons*.

scoliosis curvature of the spine. Correction by operations to insert bone grafts (thus creating only a rigid spine) has been replaced by insertion of an electronic stimulative device in the lower back to contract the muscles.

Scone /skuːn/ village in Tayside, Scotland, N of Perth. Most of the Scottish kings were crowned in its former ancient palace on the *Stone of Destiny* (now in the Coronation Chair at Westminster, London).

Scopes monkey trial trial held in Dayton, Tennessee, USA, 1925. John T Scopes, a science teacher at the high (secondary) school, was accused of teaching, contrary to a law of the state, Darwin's theory of evolution. He was fined $100, but this was waived on a technical point. The defence counsel was Clarence Darrow and the prosecutor William Jennings Bryan.

scopolamine another name for ◊hyoscine, a sedative drug.

scorched earth in warfare, the policy of burning and destroying everything that might be of use to an invading army, especially the crops in the fields. It was used to great effect in Russia in 1812 against the invasion of the French emperor Napoleon and again during World War II to hinder the advance of German forces in 1941.

Scorpio another term for ◊Scorpius.

scorpion member of the order Scorpiones, class Arachnida. Common in the tropics and sub-tropics, the scorpion has a segmented body with a long tail ending in a poisonous sting, though the venom is not usually fatal to a healthy adult. Some species reach 25 cm/10 in. They produce live young rather than eggs, and hunt chiefly by night.

scorpion fly insect of the order Mecoptera. They have a characteristic downturned beak with jaws at the tip, and many males have a turned-up tail, giving them their common name. Most feed on insects or carrion. They are an ancient group with relatively few living representatives.

Scorpius or *Scorpio* zodiac constellation in the southern hemisphere, representing a scorpion. The Sun passes briefly through Scorpius in the last week of Nov. The heart of the scorpion is marked by the red supergiant star Antares. Scorpius contains rich Milky Way star fields, plus the strongest ◊X-ray source in the sky, Scorpius X-1. In *astrology*, the dates for Scorpius are between about 24 Oct and 21 Nov (see ◊precession).

Scorsese /skɔː'seɪzi/ Martin 1942– . US director, whose films concentrate on complex characterization and the theme of alienation. His work includes *Taxi Driver* 1976, *Raging Bull* 1979, *After Hours* 1987, and *The Last Temptation of Christ* 1988.

Scotland /'skɒtlənd/ country in N Europe, part of the British Isles
area 78,470 sq km/30,297 sq mi
capital Edinburgh
towns Glasgow, Dundee, Aberdeen
features the Highlands in the north (see ◊Grampian Mountains); central Lowlands, including valleys of the Clyde and Forth, with most of the country's population and industries; Southern Uplands (including the ◊Lammermuir Hills); and islands of the Orkneys, Shetlands, and Western Isles

scorpion

industry electronics, aero and marine engines, oil, natural gas, chemicals, textiles, clothing, printing, paper, food processing, tourism
currency pound sterling
population (1987) 5,113,000
language English; Gaelic spoken by 1.3%, mainly in the Highlands
religion Presbyterian (Church of Scotland), Roman Catholic
famous people Robert Bruce, Walter Scott, Robert Burns, Robert Louis Stevenson, Adam Smith
government Scotland sends members to the UK Parliament at Westminster. Local government is on similar lines to that of England (see under ◊provost), but there is a differing legal system (see ◊Scots Law).

Scotland, history for early history, see also ◊Britain, ancient; ◊Celt; ◊Pict.
4th century BC Celts reached British Isles.
1st century AD Romans prevented by Picts from penetrating far into Scotland.
5th–6th centuries Christianity introduced from Ireland.
9th century Kenneth MacAlpin united kingdoms of Scotland.
946 Malcolm I conquered Strathclyde.
1015 Malcolm II conquered Lothian.
1263 Defeat of Haakon, king of Norway, at Battle of Largs.
1266 Scotland gained Hebrides from Norway at Treaty of Perth.
1292 Scottish throne granted by Edward I (attempting to annex Scotland) to John Baliol.
1297 Defeat of England at Stirling Bridge by Wallace.
1314 Robert Bruce defeated English at Bannockburn.
1328 Scottish independence recognized by England.
1371 First Stuart king, Robert II.
1513 James IV killed at Battle of Flodden.
1540s–1550s Knox introduced Calvinism to Scotland.
1565 Mary Queen of Scots married Darnley.
1566 Rizzio murdered.
1567 Darnley murdered.
1568 Mary fled to England.
1578 James VI took over government.
1587 Mary beheaded.
1592 Presbyterianism established.
1603 James VI became James I of England.
1638 Scottish rebellion against England.
1643 Solemn League and Covenant.
1651–1660 Cromwell conquered Scotland.
1679 Covenanters defeated at Bothwell Brig.
1689 Jacobites defeated at Killiecrankie.
1692 Massacre of Glencoe.
1707 Act of Union with England.
1715, 1745 Failed Jacobite risings against England.
18th and 19th centuries Highland Clearances: tenant farmers evicted to make way for sheep.
1945 First Scottish member of Parliament elected.
1979 Referendum rejected Scottish directly elected assembly.
1989 Local rates replaced by 'poll tax' despite wide opposition.
1990 350,000 warrants issued by Mar for nonpayment of poll tax.

Scotland Yard, New headquarters of the ◊Criminal Investigation Department (CID) of the London Metropolitan Police, established in 1878. It is named from its original location in Scotland Yard off Whitehall.

Scots language the form of the English language as traditionally spoken and written in Scotland, regarded by some scholars as a distinct language.

It is also known as *Inglis* (now archaic, and a variant of 'English'), ◊*Lallans* ('Lowlands'), *Lowland Scots* (in contrast with the Gaelic of the Highlands and Islands), and '*the Doric*' (as a rustic language in contrast with the 'Attic' or 'Athenian' language of Edinburgh's literati, especially in the

Scotland: regions

Regions	Administrative headquarters	Area sq km
Borders	Newtown St Boswells	4,662
Central	Stirling	2,590
Dumfries and Galloway	Dumfries	6,475
Fife	Glenrothes	1,308
Grampian	Aberdeen	8,550
Highland	Inverness	26,136
Lothian	Edinburgh	1,756
Strathclyde	Glasgow	13,856
Tayside	Dundee	7,668
Island Authorities:		
Orkney	Kirkwall	974
Shetland	Berwick	1,427
Western Islands	Stornoway	2,901
		78,303

18th century). It is also often referred to as 'Broad Scots' in contrast to the anglicized language of the middle classes.

Scots derives from the Northumbrian dialect of Anglo-Saxon or Old English, and has been spoken in SE Scotland since the 7th century. During the Middle Ages it spread to the far north, blending with the Norn dialects of Orkney and Shetland (once distinct varieties of Norse). Scots has been a literary language since the 14th century, with a wide range of poetry, ballads, and prose records, including two national epic poems: Barbour's *Bruce* and Blind Harry's *Wallace*. With the transfer of the court to England upon the Union of the Crowns in 1603 and the dissemination of the King James Bible, Scots ceased to be a national and court language in the 17th century, but has retained its vitality among the general population and in various literary and linguistic revivals.

Scots law the legal system of Scotland. Owing to its separate development, Scotland has a system differing from the rest of the UK, being based on ◊civil law. Its continued separate existence was guaranteed by the Act of Union with England in 1707.

In the latter part of the 20th century England adopted some features already existing in Scots law, for example, majority jury verdicts, and the replacement of police prosecution by a system of public prosecution (see under ◊procurator fiscal). There is no separate system of ◊equity. The supreme civil court is the House of Lords, below which comes the ◊Court of Session, and then the ◊sheriff court (in some respects similar to the English county court, but with criminal as well as civil jurisdiction). More serious criminal cases are heard by the High Court of Justiciary which also sits as a Court of Criminal Appeal (with no appeal to the Lords). Juries have 15 members, and a verdict of 'not proven' can be given. There is no coroner, enquiries into deaths being undertaken by the procurator fiscal.

Scott /skɒt/ (George) Gilbert 1811–1878. English architect. As the leading practical architect in the mid-19th-century Gothic revival in England, Scott was responsible for the building or restoration of many public buildings, including the Albert Memorial, the Foreign Office, and St Pancras Station, all in London.

Scott /skɒt/ George C(ampbell) 1927– . US actor who played mostly tough, authoritarian film roles. His work includes *Dr Strangelove* 1964, *Patton* 1970, *The Hospital* 1971, and *Firestarter* 1984.

Scott /skɒt/ Giles Gilbert 1880–1960. English architect, grandson of George Gilbert Scott. He designed Liverpool Anglican Cathedral, Cambridge University Library, and Waterloo Bridge, London 1945. He supervised the rebuilding of the House of Commons after World War II.

Scott /skɒt/ Paul (Mark) 1920–1978. English novelist, author of *The Raj Quartet* comprising

Scotland: kings and queens

(from the unification of Scotland to the union of the crowns of Scotland and England)

Celtic kings	Year of accession
Malcolm II	1005
Duncan I	1034
Macbeth	1040
Malcolm III Canmore	1057
Donald Ban (restored)	1095
Edgar	1097
Alexander I	1107
David I	1124
Malcolm IV	1153
William the Lion	1165
Alexander II	1214
Alexander III	1249
Margaret of Norway	1286–90
English Domination	
John Balliol	1292–96
Annexed to England	*1296–1306*
House of Bruce	
Robert I Bruce	1306
David II	1329
House of Stuart	
Robert II	1371
Robert III	1390
James I	1406
James II	1437
James III	1460
James IV	1488
James V	1513
Mary	1542
James VI	1567
Union of Crowns	*1603*

The Jewel in the Crown 1966, *The Day of the Scorpion* 1968, *The Towers of Silence* 1972 and *A Division of the Spoils* 1975, dealing with the British Raj in India.

Scott /skɒt/ Peter (Markham) 1909–1989. British naturalist, artist, and explorer, founder of the Wildfowl Trust at Slimbridge, Gloucestershire, England, and a founder of the World Wildlife Fund (now World Wide Fund for Nature).

Scott's paintings were usually either portraits or bird studies. He published many books on birds and an autobiography *The Eye of the Wind* 1961. He was the son of the Antarctic explorer R F Scott.

Scott /skɒt/ Randolph. Stage name of Randolph Crane 1903–1987. US actor. He began his career in romantic films before becoming one of Hollywood's greatest Western stars in the 1930s. His films include *Roberta* 1934, *Jesse James* 1939, and *Ride the High Country* 1962.

Scott /skɒt/ Robert Falcon, known as *Scott of the Antarctic* 1868–1912. English explorer, who

Scott *Robert Falcon Scott writing his journal during his second, fateful expedition to the Antarctic 1910–12.*

Scott *Despite the success of his Waverley novels, Sir Walter Scott's last years were marred by frantic literary efforts to pay off his creditors.*

commanded two Antarctic expeditions, 1901–04 and 1910–12. On 18 Jan 1912 he reached the South Pole, shortly after ◊Amundsen, but on the return journey he and his companions died in a blizzard only a few miles from their base camp. His journal was recovered and published in 1913. With Scott on the final expedition were Wilson, ◊Oates, Bowers, and Evans.

Scott /skɒt/ Walter 1771–1832. Scottish novelist and poet. His first works were translations of German ballads, followed by poems such as 'The Lady of the Lake' 1810 and 'Lord of the Isles' 1815. He gained a European reputation for his historical novels such as *Heart of Midlothian* 1818, *Ivanhoe* 1819, and *The Fair Maid of Perth* 1828. His last years were marked by frantic writing to pay off his debts after the bankruptcy of his publishing company in 1826.

Scottish inhabitant of Scotland, part of Britain; or person of Scottish descent. Although English is the main language, the Scots language (*Lallans*) is also spoken. Scottish Gaelic is spoken by 1.3%, mainly in the Highlands. Norse elements are found in the dialect of Shetland.

Scottish Gaelic language see ◊Gaelic language.

Scottish Gaelic literature the earliest examples of Scottish Gaelic prose belong to the period 1000–1150, but the most important early original composition is the history of the MacDonalds in the Red and Black Books at Clanranald. The first printed book in Scottish Gaelic was a translation of Knox's Prayer Book in 1567. Prose Gaelic is at its best in the folk tales, proverbs, and essays by writers such as Norman MacLeod in the 19th century and Donald Lamont in the 20th. Scottish Gaelic poetry falls into two main categories. The older, syllabic verse was composed by professional bards. The chief sources of our knowledge of this are the Book of the Dean of Lismore (16th century), which is also the main early source for the Ossianic ballads; the panegyrics in the Books of Clanranald; and the Fernaig manuscript. Modern Scottish Gaelic stressed poetry began in the 17th century but reached its zenith during the Jacobite period with Alexander MacDonald, Duncan Macintyre, Rob Donn, and Dugald Buchanan. Only William Livingstone (1808–70) kept alive the old nationalistic spirit in the 19th century. During and after World War II a new school emerged, including Somhairle MacGilleathain, George Campbell-Hay, and Ruaraidh MacThómais.

Scout member of a worldwide youth organization that emphasizes character, citizenship, and outdoor life. It was founded (as the Boy Scouts) in England 1908 by Robert ◊Baden-Powell. His book *Scouting for Boys* 1908 led to the incorporation in the UK of the Boy Scout Association by royal charter in 1912. There are four branches: Beaver Scouts (aged 6–8), Cub Scouts (aged 8–10 1/2), Scouts (10 1/2–15 1/2), and Venture Scouts (15 1/2–20).

Around a third of all Venture Scouts are girls and in 1990 younger girls were first admitted to the Scouts (see also ◊Girl Guides). In 1987 there were 560,000 Cubs and Scouts and 640,000 Brownies and Guides. In 1966 the rules of the Boy Scout Association (now the Scout Association) were revised to embody a more adult and 20th-century image, and the dress was updated; for example, the traditional shorts were exchanged for long trousers.

Scrabble board game for two to four players, based on the crossword puzzle, in which 'letter' counters of varying point values are used to form words.

scrambling circuit in radio-telephony, a transmitting circuit which renders signals unintelligible unless received by the corresponding unscrambling circuit.

Scranton /'skræntən/ industrial city on the Lackawanna River, Pennsylvania, USA; population (1980) 88,117. Anthracite is mined nearby.

scraper an earth-moving machine used in road construction. Self-propelled or hauled by a ◊bulldozer, a scraper consists of an open bowl, with a cutting blade at the lower front edge. When moving, the blade bites into the soil, which is forced into the bowl.

scrapie fatal disease of sheep and goats, which attacks the central nervous system, causing deterioration of the brain cells. It is believed to be caused by a submicroscopic organism known as a prion and may be related to ◊bovine spongiform encephalopathy, the disease of cattle known as 'mad cow disease'.

screamer South American marsh-dwelling bird of the family Anhimidae; there are only three species. They are about 80 cm/2.6 ft long, with short curved beaks, dark plumage, spurs on the front of the wings, and a crest or a horn on the head.

It wades in wet forests and marshes, but the feet are scarcely webbed. Screamers are related to ducks and are placed in the same order of birds, the Anseriformes.

screening a form of preventative medicine that involves testing large numbers of apparently healthy people to detect early signs of disease.

screw thread cylindrical or tapering piece of metal or plastic (or formerly wood) with a helical groove cut into it. Each turn of a screw moves it forward or backwards by a distance equal to the pitch (the spacing between neighbouring threads).

Its mechanical advantage equals 2 r/P; where P is the pitch and r is the radius of the thread. Thus the mechanical advantage of a tapering wood screw, for example, increases as it is rotated into the wood.

Scriabin /skri'æbɪn/ alternative transcription of the name of the Russian composer ◊Skryabin.

Scribe member of an ancient Jewish group, both priests and laypersons, who studied the law of Moses and sat in the ◊Sanhedrin (supreme court). In the New Testament they are associated with the ◊Pharisees.

Scribe /skri:b/ Augustin Eugène 1791–1861. French dramatist. He achieved recognition with *Une Nuit de la garde nationale/Night of the National Guard* 1815, and with numerous assistants produced many plays of technical merit but little profundity, including *Bertrand et Raton/The School for Politicians* 1833.

scrip issue or *subscription certificate* in finance, a free issue of new shares to existing shareholders based on their holdings. It does not involve the raising of new capital as in a ◊rights issue.

scrofula tuberculosis of the ◊lymph glands.

scrub bird Australian bird, genus *Atrichornis*, of which there are two species, both about 18 cm/7 in long, rather wrenlike but long-tailed. Scrub birds are good mimics.

Scudamore Champion jockey Peter Scudamore.

The noisy **scrub bird** *Atrichornis clamosus* was feared to be extinct, but was rediscovered, although numbers are still low.

Scudamore /skju:dəmɔ:/ Peter 1958– . British National Hunt jockey. He was champion jockey 1982 (shared with John Francome) and 1986–89. In the 1988–89 season he became the third jockey to ride 1,000 National Hunt winners; in Feb 1989 he became the first jockey to ride 150 winners in a season and went on to increase his total to 221.

Scullin /'skʌlɪn/ James Henry 1876–1953. Australian Labor politician. He was leader of the Federal Parliamentary Labor Party 1928–35, and prime minister and minister of industry 1929–31.

sculpture the artistic shaping in relief or in the round of materials such as wood, stone, metal, and, more recently, plastic and other synthetics. All ancient civilizations, including the Assyrian, Egyptian, Indian, Chinese, and Maya, have left examples of sculpture. Traditional European sculpture descends through that of Greece, Rome, and Renaissance Italy. The indigenous tradition of sculpture in Africa (see ◊African art), South America, and the Caribbean has particularly influenced modern sculpture.

In the 20th century Alexander ◊Calder invented the *mobile*, in which the suspended components move spontaneously with the currents of air. An extension is the *structure vivante*, in which a mechanism produces a prearranged pattern produced by magnets, lenses, bubbles, and so on, accompanied by sound; leading exponents are Bury, Soto, and Takis. Another development has been the sculpture garden, for example, Hakone open-air museum in Japan and the Grizedale Forest sculpture project in the Lake District, England.

World-famous sculptors include:

Ancient Greek Phidias, Praxiteles

Renaissance Donatello, Verrochio, della Robbia, Michelangelo

Baroque Bernini, Falconet, Houdon, Grinling Gibbons

Neo-Classical Canova, Flaxman

20th-century American Lipchitz, Calder, David Smith

20th-century British Epstein, Henry Moore, Hepworth, Reg Butler, Caro

20th-century European Arp, Gaudier-Brzeska, Rodin, Maillol, Picasso, Mestrovic, Brancusi, Marini, Giacometti, Gabo, and Neizvestny.

Scunthorpe /'skʌnθɔ:p/ industrial town in Humberside, England, 39 km/24 mi W of Grimsby; population (1981) 66,047. It has one of Europe's largest iron and steel works, which have been greatly expanded with EC help.

scurvy a disease caused by lack of vitamin C which is contained in fresh vegetables, fruit, and milk.

The signs are bleeding into the skin, swelling of the gums, and drying up of the skin and hair. Treatment is by giving the vitamin.

scurvy grass plant *Cochlearia officinalis* of the cabbage family, growing on salt marshes and banks by the sea. Shoots may grow low, or more erect up to 50 cm/2.6 ft, with rather fleshy heart-shaped leaves; flowers are white or mauve and four-petalled. The edible, sharp-tasting leaves are a good source of vitamin C and were formerly eaten by sailors as a cure for scurvy.

scutage in medieval Europe, a feudal tax imposed on knights as a substitute for military service.

It developed from fines for non-attendance at musters under the Carolingians, but in England by the 12th century it had become a purely fiscal measure designed to raise money for the finance of mercenary armies, reflecting the decline in the military significance of feudalism.

Scylla and Charybdis /'sɪlə, kə'rɪbdɪs/ in classical mythology, a sea-monster and a whirlpool, between which Odysseus had to sail. Later writers located them in the Straits of Messina, between Sicily and Italy.

scythe harvesting tool with long wooden handle and sharp, curving blade. It is similar to a ◊sickle. The scythe was in common use in the Middle East and Europe from the dawn of agriculture until the early 20th century, by which time it had generally been replaced by machinery.

Until the beginning of the 19th century, the scythe was used in the hayfield for cutting grass, but thereafter was applied to cereal crops as well, because it was capable of a faster work rate than the sickle. One man could mow 1 acre/0.4 hectares of wheat in a day with a scythe. Behind him came a team of workers to gather and bind the crop into sheaves and stand them in groups, or stooks, across the field.

Scythia /'sɪðɪə/ region N of the Black Sea between the Carpathian mountains and the river Don, inhabited by the Scythians 7th–1st centuries BC. From the middle of the 4th century BC the Scythians were slowly superseded by the Sarmatians. They produced ornaments and vases in gold and electrum with animal decoration.

SD abbreviation for ◊*South Dakota*.

SDI abbreviation for ◊*Strategic Defense Initiative*.

SDLP abbreviation for ◊*Social Democratic and Labour Party* (Northern Ireland).

SDP abbreviation for ◊*Social Democratic Party*.

SDR abbreviation for ◊*special drawing right*.

sea anemone invertebrate sea-dwelling animal of the class Cnidaria with a tubelike body attached by the base to a rock or shell. The other end has an open 'mouth' surrounded by stinging tentacles, which capture crustaceans and other small organisms. Many sea anemones are beautifully coloured, especially those in tropical waters.

Seaborg /'si:bɔ:g/ Glenn Theodore 1912– . US nuclear chemist. He was awarded a Nobel prize in 1951 for his discoveries of transuranic elements, and for production of the radio-isotope uranium 233.

sea cucumber echinoderm of the class Holothuroidea with a cylindrical body that is tough-skinned, knobbed, or spiny. The body may be several feet in length. Sea cucumbers are sometimes called 'cotton-spinners' from the sticky filaments they eject from the anus in self-defence.

seafloor spreading growth of the ocean ◊crust outwards (sideways) from mid-ocean ridges. The concept of seafloor spreading has been combined with that of continental drift and incorporated into ◊plate tectonics.

Seafloor spreading was proposed by US geologist Harry Hess in 1962, based on his observations of mid-ocean ridges and the relative youth of all ocean beds. In 1963, British geophysicists F Vine and D Matthews observed that the floor of the Atlantic Ocean was made up of rocks that could be arranged in strips, each strip being magnetized either normally or reversely (due to changes in the

sea-horse

Earth's polarity when the North Pole becomes the South Pole and vice versa, termed ◊polar reversal). These strips were parallel and formed identical patterns on both sides of the mid-ocean ridge. The inference was that each strip was formed at some stage in geological time when the magnetic field was polarized in a certain way. The seafloor magnetic-reversal patterns could be matched to dated magnetic reversals found in terrestrial rock. It could then be shown that new rock forms continuously and spreads away from the mid-ocean ridges, with the oldest rock located farthest away from the midline.

Confirmation came when sediments were discovered to be deeper further away from the oceanic ridge, because they had been in existence longer and had more time to accumulate sediment.

seagull see ◊gull.

Seagull, The a play by Anton Chekhov, first produced in Russia 1896. It studies the jealousy between a mother and son, the son's vain search for identity, and his ultimate suicide.

Seaham /'si:əm/ seaport in Durham, England, 8 km/5 mi south of Sunderland; population (1983) 23,000. Coal mines and engineering were developed from the 19th century. The poet Byron married Anne Isabella Milbanke at Seaham Hall nearby.

sea-horse fish of one of several genera, of which *Hippocampus* is typical. The body is small and compressed and covered with bony plates raised into tubercles or spines. The tail is prehensile, and the tubular mouth sucks in small animals as food.

seakale perennial plant *Crambe maritima* of the family Cruciferae. In Europe the young shoots are cultivated as a vegetable.

seal marine mammal of the family Phocidae. Seals have a streamlined body with thick blubber for insulation, no external earflaps and small front flippers. The hind flippers provide the thrust for swimming, but they cannot be brought under the body for walking on land. They feed on fish, squid, or crustaceans, and are common in Arctic and Antarctic waters, but are also found in Mediterranean, Caribbean, and Hawaiian waters. For seal hunting, see ◊sealing.

True seals include the **grey seal** *Halichoerus grypus*, which grows to 2.7 m/9 ft, and whose main population is around British coasts, and the shorter-nosed **common seal** *Phoca vitulina*, found in coastal regions over much of the N hemisphere. The largest seal is the **Southern elephant seal** *Mirounga leonina*, which can be 6 m/20 ft long and weigh 4 tonnes; the smallest

seal

Mediterranean monk seal

is the **Baikal seal** *Pusa sibirica*, only 1.2 m/4 ft long and the only seal to live entirely in fresh water. The rarest seals are the monk seals, the only species to live in warmer waters. The Caribbean monk seal may already be extinct, and the Mediterranean and Hawaiian species are both endangered, mainly owing to disturbance by humans. The ◊sea lion is closely related to the seal.

They are killed for their skins in Canada and Scandinavia, but conservationists have campaigned with some effect to stop the practice. In 1988–89 a seal plague in the North Sea killed more than 17,000 seals. It's ultimate cause was a previously unknown virus identified by UK scientists in Oct 1988 and named phocine distemper virus, or PDV. The blooms of toxic algae, reported along the coasts of Sweden and southern Norway during the start of the epidemic, may also have contributed the severity of the plague. Toxic algae blooms have been implicated in the deaths of humpback whales and dolphins along the east coast of the USA.

seal a mark or impression made in a block of wax to authenticate letters and documents. Seals were used in ancient China and are still used in China, Korea, and Japan. In medieval England, the **great seal** of the nation was kept by the chancellor. The **privy seal** of the monarch was initially kept for less serious matters, but by the 14th century it had become the most important seal.

sea law laws dealing with fishing areas, ships, and navigation; see ◊maritime law.

sea-lily deep-water echinoderm of the class Crinoidea. The rayed, cup-like body is borne on a stalk, and has feathery arms in multiples of five encircling the mouth.

sealing the hunting of seals. Seals are killed for blubber and for their skins, which are made into coats or capes, in Canada and Scandinavia. Conservationists have campaigned to stop the practice.

sea lion marine mammal of the family Otariidae which also includes the fur seals. This streamlined animal has large fore flippers which it uses to row itself through the water. The hind flippers can be turned beneath the body to walk on land. A small earflap is present.

There are two species of sea lion in the northern hemisphere, three in the south. They feed on fish, squid, and crustaceans. **Steller's sealion** *Eumetopias jubatus* lives in the N Pacific, large numbers breeding on the Aleutian Islands. Males may be up to 3.4 m/11 ft long, with a thick neck with the characteristic mane, and weigh up to one tonne. Females are one-third the weight. The **Californian sea lion** *Zalophus californianus* only reaches 2.3 m/7 ft, and is the species most often seen in zoos and as a 'performing seal'.

Sealyham breed of terrier dog, named after the place in Pembrokeshire where it originated as a cross of the Welsh and Jack Russell terriers.

Sea Peoples unidentified seafaring warriors who may have been ◊Achaeans, Etruscans, or ◊Philistines, who ravaged and settled the Mediterranean coasts in the 12th–13th centuries BC. They were defeated by Ramses III of Egypt 1191.

seaplane an aeroplane capable of taking off from, and alighting on, water. There are two major types, float-planes and flying-boats. The float-plane is similar to an ordinary aeroplane but has

floats in place of wheels; the flying-boat has a broad hull shaped like a boat, and may also have floats attached to the wing tips. Seaplanes depend on smooth water for a good landing and since World War II few have been built.

sea-potato yellow-brown sea-urchin *Echinocardium cordatum* covered in short spines, and found burrowing in sand from the lower shore downwards.

searching in computing, techniques for extracting a specific item from a large body of data, such as a file or table. The method used depends on how the data are organized. For example, a binary search, which requires the data to be in sequence, involves first deciding which half of the data contains the required item, then which quarter, then which eighth, and so on until the item is found.

Searle /sɜ:l/ Ronald 1920– . British cartoonist and illustrator, who created the schoolgirls of St Trinian's in 1941 and has made numerous cartoons of cats.

Sears Tower skyscraper in Chicago, USA, rising 110 storeys to a height of 443 m/1,454 ft. 'Topped out' in 1973, it was then the world's tallest building. It is the headquarters of Sears, Roebuck & Co, and provides office accommodation for more than 16,000 people.

sea-slug marine gastropod mollusc in which the shell is reduced or absent. Nudibranch sea-slugs include some very colourful forms, especially in the tropics. Tentacles on the back help take in oxygen. They are largely carnivorous, feeding on hydroids and sponges. Most are under 2.5 cm/1 in long, and live on the sea bottom or on vegetation, although some live in open waters.

British species include the shore-living **common grey sea-slug** *Aeolidia papillosa* up to 8 cm/3 in and the yellow **sea-lemon** *Archidoris pseudoargus*.

season climatic type, at any place, associated with a particular time of the year. The change in seasons is mainly due to the change in attitude of the Earth's axis in relation to the Sun, and hence the position of the Sun in the sky at a particular place. In temperate latitudes four seasons are recognized: spring, summer, autumn (fall), and winter. Tropical regions have two seasons—the wet and the dry. Monsoon areas around the Indian Ocean have three seasons: the cold, the hot, and the rainy.

The northern temperate latitudes have summer when the southern temperate latitudes have winter, and vice versa. During winter, the Sun is low in the sky and has less heating effect because of the oblique angle of incidence and because the sunlight has further to travel through the atmosphere. The differences between the seasons are more marked inland than near the coast, where the sea has a moderating effect on temperatures. In polar regions the change between summer and winter is abrupt; spring and autumn are hardly perceivable. In tropical regions, the belt of rain associated with the trade winds moves N and S with the Sun, as do the dry conditions associated with the belts of high pressure near the tropics. The monsoon's three seasons result from the influence of the Indian Ocean on the surrounding land mass of Asia in that area.

season

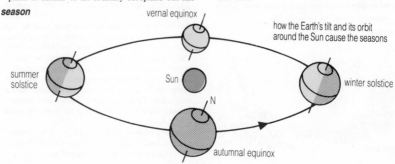

how the Earth's tilt and its orbit around the Sun cause the seasons

seasonal adjustment in statistics, an adjustment of figures designed to take into account influences which are purely seasonal, and relevant only for a short time. The resulting figures are then thought to reflect long-term trends more accurately.

seasonal affective disorder (SAD) a type of recurrent depression characterized by an increased incidence at a particular time of year. One type of seasonal affective disorder increases in incidence in autumn and winter, and is associated with increased sleeping and appetite.

It has been suggested that seasonal affective disorder may be caused by a change in the release of melatonin, a hormone secreted in response to the diurnal variation in light and dark.

seasonal unemployment unemployment arising from the seasonal nature of some economic activities. An example is agriculture, which uses a smaller labour force in winter.

Seasonal employment can be created, however, as in the example of the retail sector in Western countries over the Christmas period.

season, London the period May–July when it was considered fashionable to take up residence in London. Young women made their social debut (hence debutantes) by being presented to their sovereign at court in a special white dress and headdress—a custom abandoned in 1959.

sea-squirt ◊chordate of the class Ascidiacea. The adult is a pouch-shaped animal attached to a rock or other base, and drawing in food-carrying water through one siphon, and expelling it through another after straining through the gills. The young are free-swimming tadpole-shaped organisms.

SEATO abbreviation for ◊*Southeast Asia Treaty Organization*.

Seattle /si'ætl/ port (grain, timber, fruit, fish) of the state of Washington, USA, situated between Puget Sound and Lake Washington; population (1980) 493,846, metropolitan area (with Everett) 1,601,000. It is a centre for the manufacture of jet aircraft (Boeing), and also has shipbuilding, food processing, and paper industries.

There are two universities, Washington (1861) and Seattle (1891). First settled 1851, as the nearest port for Alaska, Seattle grew in the late 19th century under the impetus of the Gold Rush. It is named after the Indian Sealth.

sea-urchin a type of echinoderm with a globular body enclosed with plates of lime and covered with spines. Sometimes the spines are holding-organs, and they also assist in locomotion. Sea-urchins feed on seaweed and the animals frequenting them, and some are edible.

seaweed common name for a vast collection of lower plant forms belonging to the ◊algae and found growing from about high-water mark to depths of 100–200 m/300–600 ft. The plants have stalks or fronds, sometimes with air bladders to keep them afloat, and are green, blue-green, red, or brown.

Many have traditionally been gathered for food, such as purple laver *Porphyra umbilicalis*, green laver *Ulva lactuca*, and carragheen moss *Chondrus crispus*. From the 1960s–70s, seaweeds have been farmed, and the alginates extracted are used in convenience foods, ice-cream, and animal feed, as well as in toothpaste, soap, and the manufacture of iodine and glass.

Seawise Giant the biggest ship ever built (1979), a huge oil tanker of 564,739 tonnes deadweight

seaweed

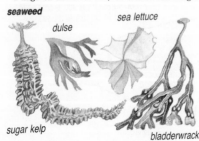

dulse

sea lettuce

sugar kelp

bladderwrack

SECANT OF AN ANGLE

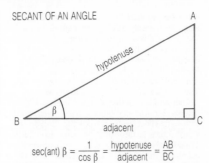

hypotenuse

β

B

adjacent

C

A

$$\sec(\text{ant}) \; \beta = \frac{1}{\cos \beta} = \frac{\text{hypotenuse}}{\text{adjacent}} = \frac{AB}{BC}$$

with a length of 458.5 m/1,504 ft, a beam (width) of 68.9 m/226 ft, and a draught of 24.6 m/80 ft.

Sebastiano del Piombo /sɪˈbæstiˈɑːnəʊ del piˈɒmbəʊ/ *c.*1485–1547. Italian painter, born in Venice. He moved to Rome in 1511, where his friendship with Michelangelo (and rivalry with Raphael) inspired him to his greatest works, such as *The Raising of Lazarus* 1517–19 (National Gallery, London). He also painted powerful portraits.

One of the greatest Venetian painters of the High Renaissance, Sebastiano was a pupil of ◊Giorgione. Michelangelo encouraged him and provided designs for his work, including *The Flagellation* (San Pietro in Montorio, Rome).

Sebastian, St /sɪˈbæstiən/ died *c.*288. Roman soldier, traditionally a member of Emperor Diocletian's bodyguard until his Christian faith was discovered. He was martyred by being shot with arrows; feast day 20 Jan.

Sebastopol /sɪˈbæstəpɒl/ alternative spelling of ◊Sevastopol, port in the USSR.

sec or **s** abbreviation for *second* (time).

secant in trigonometry, the function of an angle in a right-angled triangle obtained by dividing the length of the hypotenuse (the longest side) by the length of the side adjacent to the angle. It is the ◊reciprocal of the cosine (*sec = 1/cos*).

Secchi /ˈseki/ Pietro Angelo 1818–1878. Italian astronomer who did pioneering work in astrophysics, notably the classification of stellar spectra into four classes based on their colour and spectral characteristics. He was the first to classify solar ◊prominences as either quiescent or eruptive, and the first to describe solar ◊spicules.

secession (Latin *secessio*) in politics, the withdrawal from a federation of states by one or more of its members, as in the secession of the Confederate states from the Northern states in the USA 1860.

second basic ◊SI unit of time, one-sixtieth of a minute. It is defined as the duration of 9,192,631,770 periods of the radiation corresponding to the transition between two hyperfine levels of the ground state of the caesium-133 isotope.

secondary education in the UK, education from the age of 11 (12 in Scotland) until school-leaving at 16 or later.

secondary emission in physics, an emission of electrons from a surface of certain substances when they are struck by electrons or other particles from an external source. See also ◊photomultiplier.

secondary growth or *secondary thickening* the increase in diameter of the roots and stems of certain plants (notably shrubs and trees) that results from the production of new cells by the ◊cambium. It provides the plant with additional mechanical support and new conducting cells, the secondary ◊xylem and ◊phloem. Secondary growth is generally confined to ◊gymnosperms and, among the ◊angiosperms, to the dicotyledons. With just a few exceptions, the monocotyledons (grasses, lilies) exhibit only primary growth, resulting from cell division at the apical ◊meristems.

secondary market market for resale of purchase of shares, bonds, and commodities outside of organized stock exchanges and primary markets.

secondary modern school in the UK a secondary school that normally takes children who have failed to gain a ◊grammar school place, in those few areas which retain academic selection at 11 or 12.

secondary sexual character in biology, an external feature of an organism which is characteristic of its gender (male or female), but not the genitalia themselves. They include facial hair in men and breasts in women, combs in cockerells, brightly coloured plumage in many male birds, and manes in male lions. In many cases, they are involved in displays and contests for mates and have evolved by ◊sexual selection. Their development is stimulated by sex hormones.

Second World War another name for ◊World War II, 1939–45.

secrétaire (French) a small writing desk.

secretary bird long-legged, mainly grey-plumaged bird of prey *Sagittarius serpentarius*, about 1.2 m/4 ft tall, with an erectile head crest. It is protected in southern Africa because it eats poisonous snakes.

It gets its name from the fact that its head crest supposedly looks like a pen behind a clerk's ear. It is the only member of its family Sagittaridae, order Falconiformes.

secretary of state originally the title was given under Elizabeth I of England to each of two officials conducting the royal correspondence. In the UK a title held by a number of the more important ministers, for example, the secretary of state for foreign and commonwealth affairs. In the USA the secretary of state deals with foreign affairs.

Secret Garden, The a novel for children by English-born Frances Hodgson ◊Burnett published in the USA 1911. Mary, a spoilt, sickly orphan, is sent from India to England to live at the house of her uncle, a deformed recluse. Her cultivation of the secret garden from a forgotten wilderness helps to transform her health and outlook and leads her to effect a similar change in her cousin Colin, who believed himself to be an invalid.

secretin a ◊hormone produced by the small intestine of vertebrates which stimulates the production of digestive secretions by the pancreas and liver.

secretion in biology, any substance (normally a fluid) produced by a cell or specialized gland, for example, sweat, saliva, enzymes, and hormones. The process whereby the substance is discharged from the cell is also known as secretion.

Secret Service government ◊intelligence organization.

secret society society with membership by invitation only, often involving initiation rites, secret rituals, and dire punishments for those who break the code. Often founded for religious reasons or mutual benefit, some have become the province of corrupt politicians or gangsters, like the ◊Mafia, ◊Ku Klux Klan, ◊Opus Dei, and the ◊Triad.

sect a small ideological group, usually religious in nature, claiming a monopoly of access to truth or salvation.

Sects are usually highly exclusive. They demand strict conformity, total commitment to their code of behaviour, and complete personal involvement, sometimes to the point of rejecting mainstream society altogether in terms of attachments, names, possessions, and family. Most sects are short-lived, either because their appeal dies out and their members return to mainstream society, or because their appeal spreads and they become part of mainstream society (for example, Christianity).

secularization the process through which religious thinking, practice, and institutions lose their social significance. The concept is based on the theory, held by some sociologists, that as societies become industrialized their religious morals, values, and institutions give way to secular ones.

secular variable in astronomy, a star that, according to comparisons with ancient observations, has either increased or decreased substantially (and permanently) in brightness over the intervening centuries.

An example is Megrez (Delta Ursae Majoris), the faintest star in Ursa Major. According to 16th-century Danish astronomer Tycho Brahe, Megrez was of second magnitude although the 2nd-century astronomer Ptolemy ranked it as somewhat fainter. Its current magnitude is 3.3. It is unlikely that Megrez or any of the other secular variables has actually changed in brightness, and it seems either that the older values were subject to observational error, or that astronomers have misinterpreted those observations.

Secunderabad /saˈkʌndərəbæd/ northern suburb of Hyderabad city, Andhra Pradesh, India, separated from the rest of the city by the Hussain Sagar lake; population (1981) 144,287. Formerly a separate town, it was founded as a British army cantonment, with a parade ground where 7,000 troops could be exercised. It was by experiments at Secunderabad that Ronald ◊Ross established that malaria is carried by the anopheles mosquito.

Securities and Exchange Commission (SEC) official US agency created in 1934 to ensure full disclosure to the investing public and protection against malpractice in the securities (stocks and shares) and financial markets (such as insider trading).

Securities and Investment Board UK body with the overall responsibility for policing financial dealings in the City of London. Introduced in 1987 following the deregulation process of the so-called ◊Big Bang, it acts as an umbrella organization to such self-regulating bodies as the Stock Exchange.

Sedan /sɪˈdæn/ town on the river Meuse, in Ardennes *département*, NE France; population (1982) 24,535. Industries include textiles and dyestuffs; the town's prosperity dates from the 16th–17th centuries, when it was a ◊Huguenot centre. In 1870 Sedan was the scene of Napoleon III's surrender to Germany during the ◊Franco-Prussian War. It was the focal point of the German advance into France 1940.

sedan chair an enclosed chair for one passenger carried on poles by two bearers. Said to have been invented at Sedan, France, it was used in Europe in the 17th and 18th centuries.

sedative drug (minor tranquillizer) with a calming effect. It will induce sleep in larger doses.

Seddon /ˈsedn/ Richard John 1845–1906. New Zealand Liberal politician, prime minister 1893–1906.

seder meal that forms part of the Jewish festival of Passover, or Pesach.

sedge perennial grass-like plants of the genus *Carex*, family Cyperaceae, with three-cornered solid stems, common on wet and marshy ground.

Sedgemoor, Battle of /ˈsedʒmʊə/ battle that took place on 6 July 1685, on a tract of marshy land 5 km/3 mi SE of Bridgwater, Somerset, England, in which ◊Monmouth's rebellion was crushed by the forces of James II of England.

sediment any loose material that has 'settled'—deposited from suspension in water, ice, or air, generally as the water current or wind speed decreases. Typical sediments are, in order of increasing coarseness, clay, mud, silt, sand, gravel, pebbles, cobbles, and boulders.

Sediments differ from sedimentary rocks in which deposits are fused together in a solid mass of rock by a process called ◊diagenesis. Gravels are cemented into ◊conglomerates, rock screes into ◊breccias; sands become sandstones; muds become mudstones or shales; peat is transformed into coal.

sedimentary rock a rock formed by the accumulation and cementation of deposits that have been laid down by water, wind, ice, or gravity. Sedimentary rocks cover more than two-thirds of the Earth's surface and comprise three major categories: *clastic, chemically precipitated*, and *organic*. Clastic sediments are the largest group and are composed of fragments of pre-existing rocks; they include clays, sands, and gravels. Chemical precipitates include limestones

such as chalk, and evaporated deposits such as gypsum and halite (rock-salt). Coal, oil shale, and limestone made of fossil material are examples of organic sedimentary rocks.

Most sedimentary rocks show distinct layering (stratification), caused by alterations in composition or by changes in rock type. These strata may become folded or fractured by the movement of the Earth's crust, a process known as **deformation**.

sedition in the UK, the offence of inciting unlawful opposition to the crown and government. Unlike ◊treason, sedition does not carry the death penalty.

It includes attempting to bring into contempt or hatred the person of the reigning monarch, the lawfully established government, or either house of Parliament; inciting a change of government by other than lawful means; and raising discontent between different sections of the sovereign's subjects. Today any criticism aimed at reform is allowable.

Seebeck effect in physics, the generation of a voltage in a circuit containing two different metals, or semiconductors, by keeping the junctions between them at different temperatures. Discovered by the German physicist Thomas Seebeck (1770–1831), it is also called the thermoelectric effect, and is the basis of the ◊thermocouple. It is the opposite of the ◊Peltier effect (in which current flow causes a temperature difference between junctions of different metals).

seed the reproductive structure of higher plants (◊angiosperms and ◊gymnosperms). It develops from a fertilized ovule and consists of an embryo and a food store, surrounded and protected by an outer seed coat, called the testa. The food store is contained either in a specialized nutritive tissue, the ◊endosperm, or in the ◊cotyledons of the embryo itself. In angiosperms the seed is enclosed within a ◊fruit, whereas in gymnosperms it is usually naked and unprotected, once shed from the female cone. Following ◊germination the seed develops into a new plant.

Seeds may be dispersed from the parent plant in a number of different ways. Agents of dispersal include animals, as with ◊burrs and fleshy edible fruits and wind, where the seed or fruit may be winged or plumed. Water can disperse seeds or fruits that float, and various mechanical devices may eject seeds from the fruit, as in some pods or ◊legumes.

There may be a delay in the germination of some seeds to ensure that growth occurs under favourable conditions (see ◊after-ripening,

seed

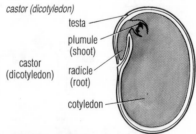

castor (dicotyledon)

testa
plumule (shoot)
castor (dicotyledon)
radicle (root)
cotyledon

maize (monocotyledon)

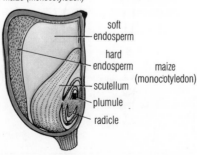

soft endosperm
hard endosperm
maize (monocotyledon)
scutellum
plumule
radicle

◊dormancy). Most seeds remain viable for at least 15 years if dried to about 5% water and kept at −20 centigrade although 20% of them will not survive this process.

seed drill a machine for sowing cereals and other seeds, developed by Jethro ◊Tull in England 1701, although simple seeding devices were known in Babylon 2000 BC.

The seed is stored in a hopper and delivered by tubes into furrows made in the ground by a set of blades called coulters attached in front. A ◊harrow is drawn behind the drill to cover up the seeds.

seed plant any seed-bearing plant; also known as a **spermatophyte**. The seed plants are subdivided into two classes, the ◊angiosperms, or flowering plants, and the ◊gymnosperms, principally the cycads and conifers. Together, they comprise the major types of vegetation found on land.

Angiosperms are the largest, most advanced, and most successful group of plants at the present time, occupying a highly diverse range of habitats. There are estimated to be about 250,000 different species. Gymnosperms differ from angiosperms in their ovules which are borne unprotected (not within an ◊ovary) on the scales of their cones. The arrangement of the reproductive organs, and their more simplified internal tissue structure, also distinguishes them from the flowering plants. In contrast to the gymnosperms, the ovules of angiosperms are enclosed within an ovary and many species have developed highly specialized reproductive structures, associated with ◊pollination by insects, birds, or bats.

Seeger /ˈsiːgə/ Pete 1919– . US folk singer and songwriter of anti-war protest songs, such as 'Where Have All The Flowers Gone?' 1956 and 'If I Had A Hammer' 1949.

Seeger was active in left-wing politics from the late 1930s and was a victim of the witchhunt of Senator ◊McCarthy in the 1950s. As a member of the vocal group *The Weavers* 1948–58, he popularized songs of diverse ethnic origin and had several top-ten hits.

Seeland /ˈzeːlænt/ German form of ◊Sjælland, the main island of Denmark.

Seferis /səˈfeərɪs/ George, assumed name of Greek poet-diplomat Georgios Seferiades 1900–1971. Ambassador to Lebanon 1953–57 and then to the UK 1957–62, he did much to help resolve the Cyprus crisis. He published his first volume of lyrics 1931 and his *Collected Poems* 1950. Nobel prize 1963.

Segovia /sɪˈɡəʊviə/ town in Castilla-León, central Spain; population (1981) 50,760. Thread, fertilizer, and chemicals are produced. It has a Roman aqueduct with 118 arches in current use, and the Moorish ◊alcázar was the palace of the monarchs of Castile. Isabella of Castile was crowned here 1474.

Segovia /sɪˈɡəʊviə/ Andrés 1893–1987. Spanish virtuoso guitarist, for whom works were composed by De ◊Falla, ◊Villa-Lobos, and others.

Segrè /seˈɡreɪ/ Emilio 1905–1989. Italian physicist settled in the USA, who in 1955 discovered antiproton, a new form of ◊antimatter. He shared the 1959 Nobel prize for physics with Owen Chamberlain. Segrè had earlier discovered the first synthetic element technetium (atomic number 43) in 1937.

Seifert /ˈsiːfət/ Jaroslav 1901–1986. Czech poet, who won state prizes, but became an original member of the Charter 77 human-rights movement. Works include *Mozart in Prague* 1970 and *Umbrella from Piccadilly* 1978. Nobel prize 1984.

Seikan Tunnel /ˈseɪkæn/ the world's largest underwater tunnel, opened 1988, linking the Japanese islands of Hokkaido and Honshu which are separated by the Tsungaru Strait; length 51.7 km/32.3 mi.

Seine /seɪn/ French river rising on the Langres plateau NW of Dijon, and flowing 774 km/472 mi in a NW direction to join the English Channel near Le Havre, passing through Paris and Rouen.

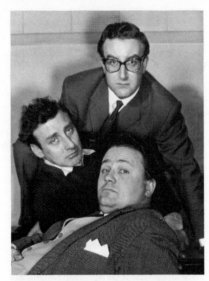

Sellers *Comedians Peter Sellers (top centre), Spike Milligan (left), and Harry Secombe (bottom right), three members of* The Goon Show, *which was broadcast on radio 1949–60.*

seismology study of earthquakes and how their shock waves travel through the Earth. By examining the global pattern of waves produced by an earthquake, seismologists can deduce the nature of the materials through which they have passed. This leads to an understanding of the Earth's internal structure.

On a smaller scale artificial earthquake waves, generated by explosions or mechanical vibrators, can be used to search for subsurface features in, for example, oil or mineral exploration.

Sekhmet /'sekmet/ ancient Egyptian goddess of heat and fire. She was represented with the head of a lioness, and worshipped at Memphis as the wife of Ptah.

Sekondi-Takoradi /ˌsekən'di: ˌtɑːkə'rɑːdi/ seaport of Ghana; population (1982) 123,700. The old port was founded by the Dutch. Takoradi has an artificial harbour, opened 1928. Railway engineering, boat building, and cigarette manufacture are important.

Selangor /sə'læŋə/ state of the Federation of Malaysia; area 7,956 sq km/3,071 sq mi; population (1980) 1,516,000. It was under British protection from 1874, and was a Federated State 1895–1946. The capital was transferred to Shah Alam from Kuala Lumpur 1973. Klang is the seat of the Sultan and a centre for rubber-growing and tin-mining, and Port Klang (formerly Port Keland and, in 1971, Port Swettenham) exports tin.

Selbourne /'selbɔːn/ village in Hampshire, England, 8 km/5 mi SE of Alton. Gilbert White, author of *The Natural History of Selbourne* 1789, was born here. The Selbourne Society (founded 1885) promotes the study of wildlife.

Selby /'selbi/ town on the river Ouse, North Yorkshire, England; population (1981) 10,726. The nearby Selby coalfield, discovered 1967, consists of 2,000 million tonnes of pure coal.

Selden /'seldən/ John 1584–1654. English antiquarian and opponent of Charles I's claim to ◊divine right, for which he was twice imprisoned. His *Table Talk* 1689 consists of short essays on political and religious questions.

select committee any of several long-standing committees of the UK House of Commons, such as the Environment Committee, and the Treasury and Civil Service Committee. These were intended to restore parliamentary control of the executive, improve the quality of legislation, and scrutinize public spending and the work of government departments. Select committees represent the major parliamentary reform of the 20th century, and a possible means—through their all-party

membership—of avoiding the automatic repeal of one government's measures by its successor.

The former Estimates Committee, called the Expenditure Committee from 1970, was replaced in 1979 by 14 separate committees, each with a more specialized function. Departmental ministers attend to answer questions, and if information is withheld on a matter of wide concern, a debate of the whole House may be called.

Selene /sɪ'liːni/ in Greek mythology, the goddess of the Moon. She was the daughter of Titan, and the sister of Helios and Eos. In later times she was identified with ◊Artemis.

selenium an element, symbol Se, atomic number 34, atomic weight 78.96, associated with telurium and the sulphur family. It occurs as selenides and in many sulphide ores, and is used in making red glasses and enamels. As a semiconductor it is used extensively in photocells and rectifiers.

It exists in several allotropic forms, the grey being a conductor of electricity when illuminated and its conductivity increasing markedly with the brightness of the incident light. Selenium was discovered by Berzelius 1817.

Seleucus I /sə'luːkəs/ Nicator *c.*358–280 BC. Macedonian general under Alexander the Great and founder of the *Seleucid Empire*. After Alexander's death 323 BC, Seleucus became governor, and then ruler of Babylonia 321, founding the city of Seleucia on the river Tigris. He conquered Syria and had himself crowned king 306, but his

semaphore

expansionist policies brought him into conflict with the Ptolemies, and he was assassinated by Ptolemy Ceraunus. He was succeeded by his son Antiochus I.

self-induction or *self-inductance* in physics, the creation of a back e.m.f. (◊electromotive force) in a coil because of variations in the current flowing through it.

Selfridge /'selfrɪdʒ/ Harry Gordon 1857–1947. US entrepreneur, who in 1909 founded Selfridges in London, the first large department store in Britain.

Seljuk Empire empire of the Turkish people, converted to Islam from the 7th century, under the leadership of the invading Tatars or Seljuk Turks. The Seljuk Empire 1055–1243 included all Anatolia and most of Syria. It was succeeded by the Ottoman Empire.

Selkirk /'selkɜːk/ Alexander 1676–1721. Scottish sailor marooned 1704–09 in the Juan Fernández Islands in the S Pacific. His story inspired Daniel Defoe to write *Robinson Crusoe*.

Selkirkshire /'selkɜːkʃə/ former inland county of Scotland, included in the Borders region 1975. The adminstrative headquarters was Selkirk.

Sellafield site of a nuclear power station on the coast of Cumbria, NW England. It was formerly known as Windscale.

Sellers /'seləz/ Peter 1925–1980. English comedian and film actor, whose ability as a mimic often allowed him to take several parts. He made

flags are red and yellow

A B C D E
F G H I J
K L M N O
P Q R S T
U V W X Y
Z   attention   numerals follow   error   front

his name in the British radio comedy series *Goon Show* 1949–60, and his films include *Dr Strangelove* 1964, *Being There* 1979, and five *Pink Panther* films 1964–78 (as the bumbling Inspector Clouseau).

seller's market market in which sellers prosper because there is a strong demand for their goods or services, thus pushing up the price.

Selous /sə'luː/ Frederick Courtney 1851–1917. British explorer and writer. His pioneer journey in the present-day Zambia and Zimbabwe area opened up the country to Europeans. He fought in the first Matabele War (1893) and was killed in the E African campaign in World War I.

selvas equatorial rainforest, such as that in the Amazon basin in South America.

Selwyn Lloyd /'selwɪn 'lɔɪd/ John, Baron 1904–1978. British Conservative politician. He was foreign secretary 1955–60, and chancellor of the Exchequer 1960–62, responsible for the creation of the National Economic Development Council, but the unpopularity of his policy of wage restraint in an attempt to defeat inflation forced his resignation. He was Speaker of the House of Commons 1971–76.

Selznick /'selznɪk/ David O(liver) 1902–1965. US film producer. His independent company Selznick International made such films as *King Kong* 1933, *Gone With the Wind* 1939, *Rebecca* 1940, and *Duel in the Sun* 1946.

semantics branch of ◊linguistics dealing with the meaning of words.

semaphore a visual signalling code in which the relative positions of two movable pointers or hand-held flags stand for different letters or numbers. The system is used by ships at sea and for railway signals.

Semarang /sə'mɑːræŋ/ port in N Java, Indonesia; population (1980) 1,027,000. There is a ship-building industry and exports include coffee, teak, sugar, tobacco, kapok, and petroleum from nearby oilfields.

Semele /'semɪli/ in Greek mythology, mother of Dionysus by Zeus. At Hera's suggestion she demanded that Zeus should appear to her in all his glory, but when he did so she was consumed by lightning.

semelparity in biology, the occurrence of a single act of reproduction during an organism's lifetime. Most semelparous species produce very large numbers of offspring when they do reproduce, and normally die soon afterwards. Examples include the Pacific salmon and the pine looper moth. Many plants are semelparous, or ◊monocarpic. Repeated reproduction is called iteroparity.

Semenov /sə'mjɒnɒf/ Nikoly 1896–   Russian physical chemist who made significant contributions to the study of chemical chain reactions. Working mainly in Leningrad at the Institute for Chemical Physics, in 1956 he became the first Russian to gain the Nobel chemistry prize which he shared with ◊Hinshelwood.

semicircular canal one of three looped tubes which form part of the labyrinth in the inner ◊ear. They are filled with fluid and detect changes in the position of the head, contributing to the sense of balance.

semicolon a punctuation mark (;) with a function halfway between the separation of sentence from sentence by means of a full stop or period (.) and the gentler separation provided by a comma (,).

Rather than the abrupt *We saw Mark last night. It was good to see him again*, and the casual (and often condemned) *We saw Mark last night, it was good to see him again*, the semicolon reflects a link between a two-part statement and is traditionally considered good style: *We saw Mark last night; it was good to see him again*.

semiconductor a crystalline material with an electrical conductivity between that of metals (good) and insulators (poor).

semiology or *semiotics* the study of the function of signs and symbols in human communication, both in language and by various non-linguistic means.

Beginning with the notion of the Swiss linguist Ferdinand de Saussure (1857–1913) that no word or other sign (**signifier**) is intrinsically linked with its meaning (**signified**), it was developed as a scientific discipline, especially by ◊Lévi-Strauss and ◊Barthes.

Modern semiotics has combined with structuralism in order to explore the 'production' of meaning in language and other sign systems, and has emphasized the conventional nature of this production.

semiotics another word for ◊semiology.

Semipalatinsk /ˌsemɪpə'lætɪnsk/ town in Kazakh Republic, USSR, on the river Irtysh; population (1987) 330,000. It was founded 1718 as a Russian frontier post, and moved to its present site 1776. Industries include meat-packing, tanning, and flour-milling, and the region produces nickel and chromium. The Kvzyl Kum atomic weapon testing ground is nearby.

Semiramis /se'mɪrəmɪs/ lived *c*.800 BC. Assyrian queen, later identified with the chief Assyrian goddess ◊Ishtar.

Semite a member of one of the ancient peoples of the Near and Middle East, traditionally said to be descended from Shem, a son of Noah in the Bible. Ancient Semitic peoples include the Israelites, Ammonites, Moabites, Edomites, Babylonians, Assyrians, Chaldaeans, Carthaginians, Phoenicians, and Canaanites. The Semitic peoples founded the religions of Judaism, Christianity, and Islam.

Semitic languages /sɪ'mɪtɪk/ a branch of the ◊Hamito-Semitic family of languages.

Semmelweis /'seməlvaɪs/ Ignaz Philipp 1818–1865. Hungarian obstetrician who pioneered ◊asepsis.

Semmelweis was an obstetric assistant at the General Hospital in Vienna at a time when 10% of women were dying of puerperal (childbed) fever. He realized that the cause was infectious matter carried on the hands of doctors treating the women after handling corpses in the post-mortem room. He introduced aseptic methods (hand-washing in chlorinated lime), and mortality fell to almost zero. Semmelweis was sacked for his efforts, which were not widely adopted. It was left to ◊Lister to reintroduce aseptic procedures.

Semtex a plastic explosive, manufactured in Czechoslovakia. It is safe to handle (it can only be ignited by a detonator), and difficult to trace, since it has no smell. It has been used by extremist groups in the Middle East and by the IRA in Northern Ireland.

Half a kilogram of Semtex is thought to have been the cause of an explosion that destroyed a

Pan-American Boeing 747 in flight over Lockerbie, Scotland, in Dec 1988, killing 270 people.

Senanayake /ˌsenə'naɪəkə/ Don Stephen 1884–1952. First prime minister of independent Sri Lanka (formerly Ceylon) 1947–52.

Senanayake /ˌsenə'naɪəkə/ Dudley 1911–1973. Prime minister of Sri Lanka 1952–53, 1960, and 1965–70; son of Don Senanayake.

Senate the Roman 'council of elders'. Originally consisting of the heads of patrician families, it was recruited from ex-magistrates and persons who had rendered notable public service, but was periodically purged by the censors. Although nominally advisory, it controlled finance and foreign policy.

The **US senate** consists of 100 members, two from each state, elected for a six-year term. The term also refers to the upper house of the Canadian parliament, equivalent to the House of Lords, and to the upper chambers of Italy and France. It is also given to the governing bodies in some universities.

Sendai /ˈsendaɪ/ city in Tojoku region, NE Honshu, Japan; population (1987) 686,000. Industries include metal goods (a Metal Museum was established 1975), textiles, pottery, and food processing.

Sendak /'sendæk/ Maurice 1928–   . US illustrator, born in New York, whose deliberately archaic children's book illustrations include *Where the Wild Things Are* 1963, *In the Night Kitchen* 1970, and *Outside Over There* 1981 (all of which books he also wrote).

Seneca /'senɪkə/ Lucius Annaeus *c*.4 BC–AD 65. Roman Stoic playwright, author of essays and nine tragedies. Born at Córdoba, Spain, he was Nero's tutor, but lost favour after his accession and was ordered to commit suicide. His tragedies were accepted as classical models by 16th-century dramatists.

Seneca Falls Convention in US history, a meeting in New York State July 1848 of women campaigning for greater rights. A Declaration of Sentiments, paraphrasing the US Declaration of Independence, called for female suffrage, equal educational and employment opportunities, and more legal rights.

Senefelder /'zeɪnə-feldə/ Alois 1771–1834. German engraver, born in Prague. He is considered the founder of ◊lithography.

Senegal /ˌsenɪ'gɔːl/ river in W Africa, formed by the confluence of the Bafing and the Bakhoy and flowing 1,125 km/700 mi NW and W to join the Atlantic near St Louis, Senegal. In 1968 the Organization of Riparian States of the River Senegal (Guinea, Mali, Mauretania, and Senegal)

Sendak *Condemned as disturbing by some parents and teachers, the strange creatures portrayed in* Where the Wild Things Are *by Maurice Sendak nonetheless convey extremely well the dreams and imaginings of childhood.*

was formed to develop the river valley, including a dam for hydroelectric power and irrigation at Joina Falls in Mali; its headquarters is in Dakar. The river gives its name to the Republic of Senegal.

Senegal /ˌsenɪˈɡɔːl/ country in W Africa, on the Atlantic, bounded to the N by Mauritania, to the E by Mali, to the S by Guinea and Guinea-Bissau, and enclosing Gambia on three sides.

government The constitution of 1963, amended, provides for a single-chamber legislature, the 120 member National Assembly, and a president who is head of state and head of government. The assembly and president are elected at the same time by universal suffrage to serve a five-year term. The president appoints and leads a council of ministers. The Senegalese Socialist Party (PS) is dominant.

Senegal's ten regions enjoy a high degree of autonomy, each having its own appointed governor and elected assembly and controlling a separate budget.

history For early history, see ◊Africa. Portuguese explorers arrived in the 15th century, and French settlers in the 17th. Senegal had a French governor from 1854, became part of French West Africa 1895, and a territory 1946.

Senegal became an independent republic in Sept 1960, with Leopold Sedar Senghor, leader of the Senegalese Progresssive Union (UPS), as its first president. Senghor was also prime minister 1962–70. UPS was the only legal party from 1966 until in Dec 1976 it was reconstituted as PS and two opposition parties were legally registered. In 1978 Senghor was decisively re-elected.

Senghor retired at the end of 1980 and was succeeded by Abdou Diouf, who declared an amnesty for political offenders and permitted more parties to register. In the 1983 elections PS won 111 of the assembly seats and the main opposition, the Senegalese Democratic Party (PDS), eight seats. Later that year Diouf tightened control of his party and the government, abolishing the post of prime minister. This met open opposition, sometimes violent, but he and the PS remained firmly in power.

Senegal
Republic of
(République du Sénégal)

ATLANTIC
OCEAN

Mauritania | Mali
Gambia
G Bissau | Guinea

0 km 1000

area 196,200 sq km/75,753 sq mi
capital and chief port Dakar
towns Thies, Kaolack
physical plains; swamp and tropical forest in SW
features river Senegal; The Gambia forms an enclave within Senegal
head of state and government Abdou Diouf from 1981
government emergent socialist deomocratic republic
political parties Senegalese Socialist Party (PS), democratic socialist; Senegalese Democratic Party (PDS), left-of-centre
exports groundnuts, cotton, fish, phosphates
currency CFA franc (485.00 = £1 Feb 1990)

In 1980 Senegal sent troops to the Gambia to protect it against a suspected Libyan invasion, and it intervened again in 1981 to thwart an attempted coup. As the two countries came closer together, they agreed on an eventual merger and the confederation of Senegambia came into being in Feb 1982. Senegal has always maintained close links with France, allowing it to retain military bases. In the Feb 1988 elections Diouf was re-elected president with 73% of the vote, but his ruling party had a slightly reduced majority in the National Assembly. In Apr 1989 border disputes led to a severance of diplomatic relations with neighbouring Mauritania, with more than 450 people killed during violent clashes between Senegalese and Mauretanians. Over 50,000 people were repatriated from both countries May 1989. In Aug formal recognition was given at the ending of the unsuccessful federation with the Gambia, Senegambia.

senescence in biology, the deterioration in physical and reproductive capacities associated with old age. See ◊ageing.

Senghor /sɒŋˈɡɔː/ Léopold 1906– . First president of independent Senegal 1960–80.

senile dementia a general term associated with old age; see ◊dementia.

Senna /ˈsenə/ Ayrton 1960– . Brazilian motor-racing driver. He had his first Grand Prix win in the 1985 Portuguese Grand Prix, has since surpassed Jim Clark's record for most pole positions, and in 1988 was world champion, winning a championship record eight races.

CAREER HIGHLIGHTS

World Champion: 1988
Grand Prix Wins:
1985: Portuguese, Belgian
1986: Spanish, Detroit
1987: Monaco, United States
1988: San Marino, Canadian, United States, British, German, Hungarian, Belgian, Japanese
1989: San Marino, Monaco, Mexico

Sennacherib /sɪˈnækərɪb/ died 681 BC. King of Assyria from 705. Son of ◊Sargon II, he rebuilt the city of Nineveh on a grand scale, sacked

population (1989) 7,704,000; annual growth rate 2.6%
life expectancy men 42, women 45
language French (official)
religion Muslim 80%, Christian 10% (chiefly Roman Catholic), animist 10%
literacy 37% male/19% female (1985 est)
GNP $2.7 bn (1983); $342 per head of population
chronology
1659 Became a French colony.
1854–65 Interior occupied.
1902 Became a territory of French West Africa.
1959 Formed the Federation of Mali with French Sudan.
1960 Achieved full independence, but withdrew from the federation. Léopold Sedar Senghor, leader of the Sengalese Progressive Union (UPS), became president.
1966 UPS declared the only legal party.
1974 Pluralist system re-established.
1976 UPS reconstituted as the Sengalese Socialist Party (PS). Prime Minister Abdou Diouf nominated as Senghor's successor.
1980 Senghor resigned and was succeeded by Diouf. Troops sent to defend The Gambia.
1981 Military help again sent to The Gambia.
1982 Confederation of Senegambia came into effect.
1983 Diouf re-elected. Post of prime minister abolished.
1988 Diouf decisively re-elected.
1989 Violent clashes between Senegalese and Mauritanians in Dakar and Nouakchott, killing more than 450 people. Over 50,000 people repatriated from both countries June. Senegambia federation abandoned.

Babylon 689, and crushed ◊Hezekiah, king of Judah, though failing to take Jerusalem. He was assassinated by his sons, and one of them, Esarhaddon, succeeded him.

Sennar /seˈnɑː/ town about 260 km/160 mi SE of Khartoum, on the Blue Nile, Sudan Republic; population (1972) 10,000. Nearby is the Sennar Dam 1926, part of the Gezira irrigation scheme.

Sennett /ˈsenɪt/ Mack. Stage name of Michael Sinnott 1880–1960. US film producer, originally an actor, responsible for such 1920s slapstick silent comedians as the Keystone Kops, 'Fatty' Arbuckle, and Charlie Chaplin. He did not make the transition to sound with much enthusiasm and retired 1935. His films include *Tillie's Punctured Romance 1914*, *The Shriek of Araby* 1923, and *The Barber Shop* (sound) 1933.

Sens /sɒns/ town in Yonne *département*, Burgundy, France; population (1982) 26,961. Its 12th–16th-century cathedral is one of the earliest in the Gothic style in France.

sense organ any organ that an animal uses to gain information about its surroundings. All sense organs have specialized receptors (such as light receptors in an eye) and some means of translating their response into a nerve impulse that travels to the brain. The main human sense organs are the eye, which detects light and colour (different wavelengths of light), the ear, which detects sound (vibrations of the air) and gravity, the nose, which detects some of the chemical molecules in the air, and the tongue which detects some of the chemicals in food, giving a sense of taste. There are also many small sense organs in the skin, including pain sensors, temperature sensors, and pressure sensors, contributing to our sense of touch.

Research suggests that our noses may also be sensitive to magnetic forces, giving us an innate 'sense of direction'. This sense is well developed in other animals, as are a variety of senses that we do not share. Some animals can detect small electric discharges, underwater vibrations, minute vibrations of the ground, or sounds that are below (infrasound) or above (ultrasound) our range of hearing. Sensitivity to light varies greatly. Most mammals cannot distinguish different colours, whereas some birds can detect the polarization of light. Many insects can see light in the ultraviolet range, which is beyond our spectrum, while snakes can form images of infrared radiation (radiant heat). In many animals, light is also detected by another organ, the pineal gland, which 'sees' light filtering through the skull, and measures the length of the day to keep track of the seasons.

Seoul /səʊl/ or *Sŏul* capital of South Korea, near the Han river, and with its chief port at Inchon; population (1985) 9,646,000. Industries include engineering, textiles, and food processing.

It was the capital of Korea 1392–1910, and has a 14th-century palace, and four universities. It was the site of the 1988 Summer Olympics.

sepal part of a flower, usually green, which surrounds and protects the flower in bud. The sepals are derived from modified leaves, and collectively known as the ◊calyx.

In some plants, such as the marsh marigold *Caltha palustris*, where the true ◊petals are absent, the sepals are brightly coloured and petal-like, taking over the role of attracting insect pollinators to the flower.

separation of powers an approach to limiting the powers of government by separating governmental functions into the executive, legislative, and judiciary. The concept has its fullest practical expression in the constitution of the USA.

Sephardim /sɪˈfɑːdɪm/ Jews descended from those expelled from Spain and Portugal in the 15th century, or from those forcibly converted to Christianity (Marranos) at that time. Many settled in N Africa, and some in other Mediterranean countries or in England.

sepoy an Indian soldier in the service of the British or Indian army in the days of British rule in India. The Indian Mutiny 1857–58 was thus known as the Sepoy Mutiny or Rebellion.

sepsis a general term for infection either on the surface of the body or within.

septicaemia ◊blood poisoning, the spread of ◊sepsis due to bacteria circulating in the bloodstream.

Septuagesima in the Christian church calendar, the third Sunday before Lent; the 70th day before Easter.

Septuagint (Latin *septuagint* 'seventy') the oldest Greek version of the Old Testament or Hebrew Bible, traditionally made by 70 scholars.

seq. abbreviation for *sequens* (Latin 'following').

sequoia two species of conifer in the family Taxodiaceae, native to California, USA. The redwood *Sequoia sempervivens* is a long-lived timber tree, and one variety, the Howard Libbey redwood, is the world's tallest tree at 110 m/361 ft, with a circumference of 13.4 m/44 ft. The *Sequoiadendron giganteum* is the world's largest tree, up to 30 m/100 ft in circumference at the base, and almost as tall as the redwood. It is also, except for the bristlecone pine, the oldest living tree, some specimens having lived more than 3,000 years.

Sequoya /sə'kwɔɪə/ George Guess 1770–1843. American Indian scholar and leader. After serving with the US army in the Creek War 1813–14, he made a study of his own Cherokee language and created a syllabary which was approved by the Cherokee council 1821. This helped thousands of Indians towards literacy and resulted in the publication of books and newspapers in their own language.

Sequoya went on to write down ancient tribal history. In later life he became a political representative of the Western tribes in Washington, negotiating for the Indians when the US government forced resettlement in Indian territory in the 1830s. A type of giant redwood tree is named after Sequoya, as is a national park in California.

Serang /sə'ræŋ/ alternative form of ◊Ceram, an Indonesian island.

seraph (plural **seraphim**) in Christian and Judaic belief, an ◊angel of the highest order. They are mentioned in the book of Isaiah in the Old Testament.

Serapis /'serəpɪs/ ancient Greek-Egyptian god, a combination of Hades and Osiris, invented by the Ptolemies; his finest temple was the Serapeum in Alexandria.

Serbia /'sɜːbiə/ (Serbo-Croat *Srbija*) constituent republic of Yugoslavia, which includes Kosovo and Vojvodina

area 88,400 sq km/34,122 sq mi

capital Belgrade

features includes the autonomous provinces of ◊*Kosovo*, capital Priština, of which the predominantly Albanian population demands unification with Albania; and ◊*Vojvodina*, capital Novi Sad, largest town Subotica, with a predominantly Serbian population.

sequoia

California redwood

physical fertile Danube plains in the north, and mountainous in the south

population (1986) 9,660,000

language the Serbian variant of Serbo-Croat, sometimes written in Cyrillic script

religion Serbian Orthodox

history the Serbs settled in the Balkans 7th century, and became Christians 9th century. They were united as one kingdom about 1169, and under Stephen Dushan (1331–55) founded an empire covering most of the Balkans. After their defeat at Kosovo 1389 they came under the domination of the Turks, who annexed Serbia 1459. Uprisings 1804–16, led by Kara George and Milosh Obrenovich, forced the Turks to recognize Serbia as an autonomous prinicipality under Milosh. The assassination of Kara George on Obrenovich's orders gave rise to a long feud between the two houses. After a war with Turkey 1876–78, Serbia became an independent kingdom. On the assassination of the last Obrenovich 1903 the Karageorgevich dynasty came to the throne. The two Balkan Wars 1912–13 greatly enlarged Serbia's territory at the expense of Turkey and Bulgaria. Serbia's designs on Bosnia and Herzegovina, backed by Russia, led to friction with Austria, culminating in the outbreak of war 1914. Serbia was completely overrun 1915–16, and was occupied until 1918, when it became the nucleus of the new kingdom of the Serbs, Croats, and Slovenes, later ◊Yugoslavia. There is still rivalry between Croats and Serbs. Slobodan Milosevic was elected president May 1989.

SERC abbreviation for *Science and Engineering Research Council*.

sere a type of plant ◊succession developing in a particular habitat. A *lithosere* is a succession starting on the surface of bare rock. A *hydrosere* is a succession in shallow freshwater, beginning with planktonic vegetation and the growth of pondweeds and other aquatic plants, and ending with the development of swamp. A *plagiosere* is the sequence of communities that develops following the clearing of the existing vegetation.

serenade a musical piece for chamber orchestra or wind instruments in several movements, originally intended for evening entertainment, such as Mozart's *Eine kleine Nachtmusik/A Little Night Music*.

serfdom the legal and economic status of peasants under ◊feudalism. Serfs could not be sold like slaves, but they were not free to leave their lord's estate. They had to work his land without pay for a number of days every week. Serfs also had to perform extra labour at harvest time and other busy seasons, and to pay tribute in kind; in return they were allowed to cultivate a portion of the estate for their own benefit. In England serfdom died out between the 14th and 17th centuries, but it lasted in France until 1789, in Russia until 1861, and in most European countries until the early 19th century.

Sergel /'seəgəl/ Johan Tobias 1740–1814. Swedish Neo-Classical sculptor, active mainly in Stockholm. His portraits include *Gustaf III* (Royal Palace, Stockholm) and he made terracotta figures such as *Mars and Venus* (Nationalmuseum, Stockholm).

Sergius, St /'sɜːdʒiəs/ of Radonezh 1314–1392. Patron saint of Russia, who founded the Eastern Orthodox monastery of the Blessed Trinity near Moscow 1334. Mediator among Russian feudal princes, he inspired the victory of Dmitri, Grand Duke of Moscow, over the Tatar khan Mamai at Kulikovo, on the upper Don, 1380.

serialism in music, an alternative name for the ◊twelve-tone system of composition. It usually refers to post-1950 compositions in which further aspects such as dynamics, durations, and attacks are brought under serial control. These other series may consist of fewer than 12 degrees while some pitch series can go higher.

series circuit an electric circuit in which the components are connected end to end, so that the current flows through them all one after the other.

Seringapatam /sə'rɪŋgəpə'tæm/ town in Karnataka, India, on an island in the Cauvery. It was the capital of Mysore State 1610–1799, when it was taken from the Sultan of Mysore, Tipu Sahib, by the British general Cornwallis.

Serlio /'seəliəʊ/ Sebastiano 1475–1554. Italian architect and painter, author of *L'Architettura* 1537–51, which set down practical rules for the use of the Classical orders, and was used by architects of the Neo-Classical style throughout Europe.

Serota /sə'rəʊtə/ Nicholas Andrew 1946– . British art-gallery director. He made his reputation as director of the Whitechapel Art Gallery from 1976 to 1987, when he became director of the Tate Gallery, London.

Serpens constellation of the equatorial region of the sky, representing a serpent coiled around the body of Ophiuchus. It is the only constellation divided into two halves, *Serpens Caput*, the head (on one side of Ophiuchus), and *Serpens Cauda*, the tail (on the other side). Its main feature is the Eagle Nebula.

serpentine a group of minerals, hydrous magnesium silicate, $Mg_3Si_2O_5(OH)_4$, occurring in soft ◊metamorphic rocks and usually dark green. The fibrous form *chrysotile* is a source of asbestos; another form is *antigorite*. Serpentine minerals are mainly derived from the hydrous alteration of ultrabasic rocks during metamorphism. Rare snake-patterned forms are used in ornamental carving.

Serpent Mound defensive embankment built by Hopewell Indians 2nd–1st centuries BC in Ohio, USA. It is 405 m/1,330 ft long, 1.3 m/4 ft high, and about 6 m/19 ft across.

SERPS abbreviation for State Earnings-Related Pension Schemes, the UK state ◊pension scheme. Pension schemes operated by private companies may now be run in conjunction with SERPS; if they are, they are called 'contracted in', and part of an employee's National Insurance contributions go towards the pension, which is linked to final salary.

serum a clear fluid that remains after blood clots. It is blood plasma with the anti-coagulant proteins removed, and contains ◊antibodies and other proteins, as well as the fats and sugars of the blood. It can be produced synthetically, and is used to protect against disease.

serval African wildcat *Felis serval*. It is a slender, long-limbed cat, about 1 m/3 ft long, with a yellowish-brown, black-spotted coat. It has large, sensitive ears, with which it locates its prey, mainly birds and rodents.

Servan-Schreiber /seə'vɒn ʃraɪ'beə/ Jean Jacques 1924– . French Radical politician, and founder of the magazine *L'Express* 1953. *Le Défi americain* 1967 maintained that US economic and technological dominance would be challenged only by a united left-wing Europe. He was president of the Radical Party 1971–75 and 1977–79.

Servetus /sɜː'viːtəs/ Michael 1511–1553. Spanish Christian theologian and Anabaptist. He was burned alive by the church reformer Calvin in Geneva, Switzerland, for his unitarian views. As a physician, he was a pioneer in the study of the circulation of the blood.

Service /'sɜːvɪs/ Robert William 1874–1938. Canadian author, born in England. He was popular for his ballads of the Yukon in the days of the Gold Rush, for example 'The Shooting of Dan McGrew' 1907.

service industry commercial activity that provides and charges for various services to customers (as opposed to manufacturing or supplying goods), such as restaurants, the tourist industry, cleaning, hotels, and the retail trade (shops and supermarkets).

With the decline in the manufacturing sector in many Western countries, such as Britain, service industries have gained importance and have become major employers of labour.

services, armed the air, sea, and land forces of a country; see ◊army; ◊navy; ◊air force; also called the armed forces.

history, UK The army and navy can be traced back to the locally raised forces that prevented King Alfred's Wessex from being overrun by the Danes. All three armed services are professionals, with no conscript element. The *Royal Navy* is known as the Senior Service, because of its formal origin under Henry VIII, whereas no permanent standing *army* was raised until the time of Charles II (see also ◊marines). The ◊Territorial Army is a back-up force of volunteers. The ◊*Royal Air Force* was formed 1918. ◊*Women's services* originated in World War I.

service tree deciduous Eurasian tree *Sorbus domestica*, family Rosaceae, with alternate leaves, white flowers, and small oval fruit. The wild service tree *Sorbus torminalis* has lobed leaves.

servo system an automatic control system used in aircraft, motor cars, and other complex machines. A specific input, such as moving a lever or joystick, causes a specific output, such as feeding current to an electric motor that moves, for example, the rudder of the aircraft.

At the same time the position of the rudder is detected and fed back to the central control, so that small adjustments can continually be made to maintain the desired course.

sesame annual plant *Sesamum indicum* of the family Pedaliaceas, probably native to SE Asia. It produces oily seeds used for food and soap making.

sessile in botany, a leaf, flower, or fruit that lacks a stalk and sits directly on the stem, as with the acorns of sessile oak *Quercus petraea*. In zoology, it is an animal that normally stays in the same place, such as a barnacle or mussel. The term is also applied to the eyes of crustaceans when these lack stalks and sit directly on the head.

Session, Court of one of the civil courts in Scotland.

Sessions /'seʃənz/ Roger (Huntingdon) 1896–1985. US composer, whose dense and dissonant works include *The Black Maskers* incidental music 1923, eight symphonies, and *Concerto for Orchestra* 1971.

Set in Egyptian mythology, the god of night, the desert, and of all evils. He was the murderer of ◊Osiris, and is portrayed as a grotesque animal.

set in mathematics, any collection of defined things (elements), provided the elements are distinct and that there is a rule to decide whether an element is a member of a set. It is usually denoted by a capital letter and indicated by curly brackets { }.

For example $L = \{$letters of the alphabet$\}$ represents the set that consists of all the letters of the alphabet. The symbol ϵ stands for 'is a member of'; thus $p \epsilon L$ means that p belongs to the set consisting of all letters. $4 \notin L$ means that 4 does not belong to the set consisting of all letters. The

oblique stroke passes through the 'is a member of' symbol to cancel it.

types of sets A *finite set* has a limited number of members, such as {letters of the alphabet}; an *infinite set* has an unlimited number of members, such as all whole numbers); an *empty* or *null set* has no members, such as the number of people who have swum across the Atlantic Ocean, written as { } or Ø; a *single-element set* has only one member, such as days of the week beginning with M, written as {Monday}. *Equal sets* have the same members; for example if $W = \{$days of the week$\}$ and $S = \{$Sunday, Monday, Tuesday, Wednesday, Thursday, Friday, Saturday$\}$, their equality is written $W = S$. Sets with the same number of members are *equivalent sets*; sets with some members in common are *intersecting sets* (red playing cards and face cards of the same pack); sets with no members in common are *disjoint sets* (minerals and vegetables); sets contained within others are *subsets* (vowels and letters of the alphabet). These types are often illustrated by a ◊Venn diagram.

Sète /seɪt/ town on the Mediterranean coast of France, in Hérault *département*, SW of Montpellier; population (1982) 40,466. It is a seaport, and handles fish, wine, brandy, and chemicals. It was founded 1666 as an outlet to the Canal du Midi.

Seton /'siːtn/ Ernest Thompson, born Ernest Seton Thompson. 1860–1946. Canadian author and naturalist, born in England. He illustrated his own books with drawings of animals. He was the founder of the ◊Woodcraft Folk youth movement.

Seto Naikai /'setəʊ 'naɪkəɪ/ (Japanese 'inland sea') a narrow body of water almost enclosed by the islands of Honshu, Shikoku, and Kyushu. It is both a transport artery and a national park (1934) with 3,000 islands.

setter breed of gun dog, about 60 cm/2 ft high, and weighing about 25 kg/55 lbs. It has a long, smooth coat, a feathered tail, and a spaniel-like face. They are called 'setters' because they were trained in crouching or 'setting' on the sight of game to be pursued.

The *Irish setter* is a rich red, the *English setter* is usually white with black, tan, or liver markings, and the *Gordon setter* is black and brown.

setting in UK education, the practice of dividing pupils into ability groups for each subject.

Settlement, Act of in Britain, a law passed 1701 during the reign of King William III, designed to ensure a Protestant succession to the throne by excluding the Roman Catholic descendants of James II in favour of the Protestant House

of Hanover. Elizabeth II still reigns under this Act.

settlement out of court a compromise reached between the parties to a legal dispute. Most civil legal actions are settled out of court, reducing legal costs, and avoiding the uncertainty of the outcome of a trial.

Seurat /'sɜːrɑː/ Georges 1859–1891. French artist. He originated, with ◊Signac, the Neo-Impressionist technique of ◊*Pointillism* (painting with small dabs rather than long brushstrokes), in part inspired by 19th-century theories of colour and vision. He also departed from Impressionism by evolving a more formal type of composition.

Seurat's compositions were based on the proportions of the ◊golden section rather than aiming to capture fleeting moments of light and movement. Outstanding examples of his work are *La Baignade/The Bathers, Asnières* 1884 (National Gallery, London) and *Sunday on the Island of La Grande Jatte* 1886 (Art Institute of Chicago).

Sevastopol /sɪ'væstəpəl/ or *Sebastopol* port, resort, and fortress in the Crimea, Ukraine Republic, USSR; population (1987) 350,000. It is the base of the Soviet Black Sea fleet, and also has shipyards and a wine-making industry. Founded by Catherine II 1784, it was successfully besieged by the English and French in the Crimean War (Oct 1854–Sept 1855), and in World War II by the Germans (Nov 1941–July 1942), but was retaken by the Soviets 1944.

seven deadly sins in Christian theology, anger, avarice, envy, gluttony, lust, pride, and sloth.

Sevenoaks /'sevənəʊks/ town in Kent, England. It lies 32 km/20 mi SE of London, population (1980) 19,000. Nearby are the 17th-century houses of Knole and ◊Chevening. Its seven oaks were blown down in a hurricane 1987, and subsequent attempts to replant them have been foiled by vandals.

Seventh Day Adventist a member of the Protestant Christian religious sect of the same name. The group has its main following in the USA, and distinctive tenets are that Saturday is the Sabbath and that Jesus' second coming is imminent.

Seven Weeks' War war 1866 between Austria and Prussia, engineered by the German chancellor Bismarck. It was nominally over the possession of ◊Schleswig-Holstein, but it was actually to confirm Prussia's superseding Austria as the leading German state. The Battle of ◊Sadowa was the culmination of von ◊Moltke's victories.

Seven Wonders of the World in antiquity, the pyramids of Egypt, the hanging gardens of Babylon, the temple of Artemis at Ephesus, the statue of Zeus at Olympia, the mausoleum

set

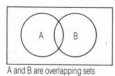
A and B are overlapping sets

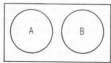
A and B are disjoint sets

A is the subset of B

Seurat The Bathers, Asnières (1883–84) National Gallery, London.

at Halicarnassus, the Colossus of Rhodes, and the Pharos (lighthouse) at Alexandria.

Seven Years' War war 1756–63 between Britain and Prussia on the one hand, and France, Austria, Spain, and Russia on the other. Politically, Britain gained control of many of France's colonies, including Canada. Fighting against great odds, Frederick II of Prussia was eventually successful, establishing Prussia as one of the great European powers.

severe combined immune deficiency (SCID) rare condition in which a baby is born without the body's normal defences against infection. The child must be kept within a transparent plastic tent until a matched donor can provide a bone-marrow transplant.

Severin /'sevərɪn/ Tim 1940– . Writer, historian, and traveller who re-enacted 'classic' voyages. In 1961 he led a motorcycle team along the Marco Polo route in Asia and four years later canoed the length of the Mississippi. His Jason Voyage followed the ancient route of the Argonauts in search of the Golden Fleece 1984; and a journey on horseback retraced the route to the Middle East taken by the Crusaders 1987–88.

Severn /'sevən/ river of Wales and England, rising on the NE side of Plynlimmon, N Wales, and flowing 338 km/210 mi through Shrewsbury, Worcester, and Gloucester to the Bristol Channel. The **Severn bore** is a tidal wave up to 2 m/6 ft high.

S England and S Wales are linked near Chepstow by a rail tunnel 1873–85, and road bridge 1966. A barrage has been proposed (seaward of Cardiff and Weston-super-Mare) which would be the world's largest tidal power-generating project; it would 16 km/10 mi across, and would produce 5% of the UK's electricity. It would also improve dock developments in Cardiff and Bristol.

Severus /sɪ'vɪərəs/ Lucius Septimus AD 146–211. Roman emperor. Born in N Africa, he held a command on the Danube when in AD 193 the emperor Pertinax was murdered. Proclaimed emperor by his troops, Severus proved an able administrator; he was the only African to become emperor. He died at York while campaigning in Britain against the Caledonians.

Severus of Antioch /sɪ'vɪərəs, 'æntɪɒk/ AD 467–538. Christian bishop, one of the originators of the **Monophysite** heresy. As patriarch of Antioch (from 512), Severus was the leader of opposition to the Council of Chalcedon 451, an attempt to unite factions of the early church, by insisting that Christ existed in one nature only. He was condemned by the emperor Justin I in 518, and left Antioch for Alexandria, never to return.

Seveso /sɪ'veɪsəʊ/ town in Lombardy, Italy, site of a factory manufacturing the herbicide hexachlorophene. In 1976 one of the by-products escaped in a cloud that contaminated the area, resulting in severe chloracne and deformed births.

Sévigné /ˌseɪviː'njeɪ/ Marie de Rabutin-Chantal, Marquise de Sévigné 1626–1696. French writer. In her letters to her daughter, the Comtesse de Grignan, she gives a vivid picture of contemporary customs and events.

Seville /sɪ'vɪl/ (Spanish **Sevilla**) city in Andalucia, Spain, on the Guadalquivir river, 96 km/60 mi of Cádiz; population (1986) 668,000. Industries include machinery, spirits, porcelain, pharmaceuticals, silk, and tobacco.

Formerly the centre of a Moorish kingdom, it has a 12th-century Alcázar palace, a 15th–16th-century Gothic cathedral, and a university 1502. Seville was the birthplace of the artists ◊Murillo and Velázquez.

Sèvre /'seɪvrə/ two French rivers from which the *département* of Deux Sèvres takes its name. The **Sèvre Nantaise** joins the Loire at Nantes; the **Sèvre Niortaise** flows into the Bay of Biscay.

Sèvres /'seɪvrə/ town in the Île de France region of France; now a Paris suburb, population about 21,000. The state porcelain factory was established in the park of ◊St-Cloud 1756, and

Seville Seville cathedral (1401–1520), the largest medieval cathedral in Europe, occupies the site of a Moorish mosque. The Giralda or bell tower, was probably built as a symbol of Moorish power.

it is also the site of a national museum of ceramics.

Sèvres /'seɪvrə/ fine porcelain produced at a factory in Sèvres, France since the early 18th century. It is characterized by the use of intensely coloured backgrounds (such as pink and royal blue), against which flowers are painted in elaborately embellished frames, often in gold. It became popular after the patronage of Louis XV's mistress, Madame de ◊Pompadour.

Sèvres, Treaty of the last of the treaties that ended World War I. Negotiated between the Allied powers and the Ottoman Empire, it was finalised in Aug 1920 but never ratified by the Turkish government.

The treaty reduced the size of Turkey by making concessions to the Greeks, Kurds, and Armenians, as well as ending Turkish control of Arab lands. Its terms were rejected by the newly

Sèvres A characteristic piece of Sèvres porcelain.

created nationalist government and the treaty was never ratified. It was superseded by the ◊Treaty of Lausanne in 1923.

sewage disposal the disposal of human excreta and other waterborne waste products from houses, streets, and factories. Conveyed through sewers to sewage works, sewage has to undergo a series of treatments to be acceptable for discharge into rivers or the sea, according to various local laws and ordinances.

In the industrialized countries of the West, most industries are responsible for disposing of their own wastes. Government agencies establish industrial waste-disposal standards. In most countries, sewage works for residential areas are the responsibility of local authorities. The solid waste (sludge) may be spread over fields as a fertilizer or, in a few countries, dumped at sea.

Raw sewage, or sewage that has not been treated properly, is one serious source of water pollution. A significant proportion of bathing beaches in densely populated regions have unacceptably high bacterial content, largely as a result of untreated sewage being discharged into rivers and the sea.

The use of raw sewage as a fertilizer (long practised in China) has the drawback that disease-causing microorganisms can survive in the soil and be transferred to people or animals by consumption of subsequent crops.

In 1987, Britain dumped more than 4,700 tonnes of sewage sludge into the North Sea, and 4,200 tonnes into the Irish Sea and other coastal areas. Also dumped in British coastal waters, other than the Irish Sea, were 6,462 tonnes of zinc, 2,887 tonnes of lead, 1,306 tonnes of chromium, and 8 tonnes of arsenic. Dumped into the Irish Sea were 916 tonnes of zinc, 297 tonnes of lead, 200 tonnes of chromium, and 1 tonne of arsenic.

Sewell /'sjuːəl/ Anna 1820–1878. English author, whose only published work tells the life story of a horse, *Black Beauty* 1877. Although now read as a children's book, it was written to encourage sympathetic treatment of horses by adults.

sewing machine apparatus for the mechanical sewing of cloth, leather, and other materials by a needle, powered by hand, treadle, or belted electric motor. The popular lockstitch machine, using a double thread, was invented independently in the USA by both Walter Hunt 1834 and Elias Howe 1846. Howe's machine was the basis of the machine patented 1851 by Isaac ◊Singer. In the latest, microprocessor-controlled sewing machines, as many as 25 different stitching patterns can be selected by pushbutton.

sex determination the process by which the sex of an organism is determined. In many species, the sex of an individual is dictated by the two sex chromosomes (X and Y) it receives from its parents. In mammals, some plants, and a few insects, males are XY and females XX; in birds, reptiles, some amphibians, and butterflies the reverse is the case. In bees and wasps, males are produced from unfertilized eggs, females from fertilized eggs. Environmental factors can affect some fish and reptiles, such as turtles, where sex is influenced by the temperature at which the eggs are kept before hatching.

Most fish have a very flexible system of sex determination, which can be affected by external factors. For example, in wrasse all individuals develop into females, but the largest individual in each area or school changes sex to become the local breeding male.

sexism belief in (or set of implicit assumptions about) the superiority of one's own sex, often accompanied by a ◊stereotype or preconceived idea about the opposite sex. Sexism may also be accompanied by ◊discrimination on the basis of sex, generally as practised by men against women.

The term, coined by analogy with racism, was first used in the 1960s by feminist writers to describe language or behaviour that implied women's inferiority. Examples include the contentious

sewing machine

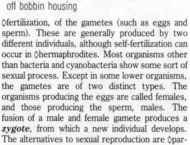

needle

upper thread

material

1 2 3 4 5 6

platten

lower thread

bobbin bobbin housing

bobbin housing rotates and catches upper thread

upper thread slips off bobbin housing

completed stitch

use of male pronouns to describe both men and women, and the assumption that some jobs are typically performed only by one sex.

sex linkage in genetics, the tendency for certain characteristics to occur exclusively, or predominantly, in one sex only. Human examples include red-green colour blindness and haemophilia, both found predominantly in males. In both cases, these characteristics are recessive (see ◊recessivity) and are determined by genes on the ◊X chromosome.

Since females possess two X chromosomes, any such recessive ◊allele on one of them is likely to be masked by the corresponding allele on the other. In males (who have only one X chromosome paired with an inert Y chromosome) any gene on the X chromosome will automatically be expressed. Colour blindness and haemophilia can appear in females, but only if they are ◊homozygous for these traits, due to inbreeding for example.

Sex Pistols, the UK punk rock group (1975–78) who became notorious under the guidance of their manager, Malcolm McLaren. They released one album, *Never Mind the Bollocks, Here's the Sex Pistols* 1977. Members included Johnny Rotten (real name John Lydon, 1956–) and Sid Vicious (John Ritchie, 1957–79).

sextant navigational instrument for determining latitude by measuring the angle between some heavenly body and the horizon. Invented by John Hadley (1682–1744) in 1730, it can only be used in clear weather.

When the horizon is viewed through the right-hand side **horizon glass**, which is partly clear and partly mirrored, the light from a star can be seen at the same time in the mirrored left-hand side by adjusting an **index mirror**. The angle of the star to the horizon can then be read on a calibrated scale.

Sexton /'sekstən/ Anne 1928–1974. US poet. She studied with Robert Lowell and wrote similarly confessional poetry, as in *All My Pretty Ones* 1962. She committed suicide, and her *Complete Poems* appeared posthumously 1981.

sexual reproduction a reproductive process in living creatures which requires the union, or

sextant

simplified diagram of a sextant

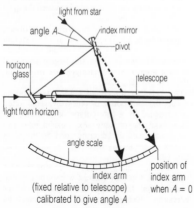

light from star

angle A

index mirror

pivot

horizon glass

telescope

light from horizon

angle scale

index arm (fixed relative to telescope) calibrated to give angle A

position of index arm when A = 0

◊fertilization, of the gametes (such as eggs and sperm). These are generally produced by two different individuals, although self-fertilization can occur in ◊hermaphrodites. Most organisms other than bacteria and cyanobacteria show some sort of sexual process. Except in some lower organisms, the gametes are of two distinct types. The organisms producing the eggs are called females, and those producing the sperm, males. The fusion of a male and female gamete produces a **zygote**, from which a new individual develops. The alternatives to sexual reproduction are ◊parthenogenesis and ◊spores.

sexual selection a process similar to ◊natural selection but relating exclusively to success in finding a mate for the purpose of sexual reproduction and producing offspring. Sexual selection occurs when one sex (usually but not always the female) invests more effort in producing young than the other. Members of the other sex compete for access to this limited resource (usually males competing for the chance to mate with females). Sexual selection often favours features that increase a male's attractiveness to females (such as the pheasant's 'tail') or enable males to fight with one another (such as a deer's antlers). More subtly, it can produce hormonal effects by which the male makes the female unreceptive to other males, causes the abortion of foetuses already conceived, or removes the sperm of males who have already mated with a female.

Seychelles /seɪ'ʃelz/ country in the Indian Ocean, off E Africa, N of Madagascar.

sexual reproduction

female reproductive system

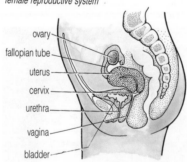

ovary

fallopian tube

uterus

cervix

urethra

vagina

bladder

male reproductive system

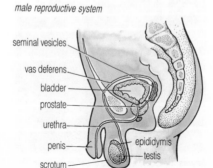

seminal vesicles

vas deferens

bladder

prostate

urethra

penis

scrotum

epididymis

testis

government Seychelles is a republic within the Commonwealth. The constitution of 1979 makes Seychelles a one-party state, the party being the Seychelles People's Progresssive Front (SPPF). The president, who is both head of state and head of government, and the single-chamber legislature, the National Assembly, both serve a five-year term. The president and 23 of the 25 assembly members are elected by universal suffrage, and two are appointed by the president.

history For early history, see ◊Africa. The islands were probably visited by the Portuguese about 1500 and became a French colony 1744. Seychelles was ceded to Britain by France in 1814 and was ruled as part of ◊Mauritius until it became a Crown Colony in 1903.

In the 1960s several political parties were formed, campaigning for independence, the most significant being the Seychelles Democratic Party (SDP), led by James Mancham, and the Seychelles People's United Party (SPUP), led by Albert René. René demanded complete independence while Mancham favoured integration with Britain. In 1975 internal self-government was agreed. The two parties then formed a coalition government with Mancham as prime minister. In June 1976 Seychelles became an independent republic within the Commonwealth, with Mancham as president and René as prime minister.

The following year René staged an armed coup while Mancham was attending a Commonwealth conference in London, and declared himself president. After a brief suspension of the constitution, a new one was adopted, creating a one-party state, with the SPUP being renamed the Seychelles People's Progressive Front. René, as the only candidate, was formally elected president in 1979 and then re-elected in 1984 and 1989. There have been several unsuccessful attempts to overthrow him, the last reported in 1987.

René has followed a policy of nonalignment and has forbidden the use of port facilities to vessels carrying nuclear weapons. He has maintained close links with Tanzania, which has provided military support.

Seyfert galaxy a type of galaxy whose small, bright centre is caused by hot gas moving at high speed around a massive central object, possibly a ◊black hole. Almost all Seyferts are spiral galaxies. They seem to be closely related to ◊quasars, but are about 100 times fainter. They are named after discoverer Carl Seyfert (1911–60).

Seymour family names of dukes of Somerset (seated at Maiden Bradley, Wilts), and marquesses of Hertford (seated at Ragley Hall, Warwicks); first came to prominence through the marriage of Jane Seymour to Henry VIII.

Seymour /'siːmɔː/ Jane c.1509–1537. Third wife of Henry VIII, whom she married in 1536. She died soon after the birth of her son Edward VI.

Seymour /'siːmɒ/ Lynn 1939– . Canadian-born ballerina of rare dramatic quality. She was principal dancer of the Royal Ballet from 1959 and artistic director of the Munich State Opera Ballet 1978–80.

Sezession (German 'secession') various groups of German and Austrian artists in the 1890s who 'seceded' from official academic art institutions in order to found modern schools of painting. The first was in Munich, 1892; the next, linked with the paintings of Gustav ◊Klimt, was the Vienna Sezession 1897; the Berlin Sezession followed in 1899.

In 1910 the members of the group *die* ◊*Brücke* formed the **Neue Sezession** when they were rejected by Berlin's first Sezession.

Sfax /sfæks/ (Arabic **Safaqis**) port and second largest city in Tunisia; population (1984) 232,000. It is the capital of Sfax district, on the Gulf of Gabès, and lies about 240 km/150 mi SE of Tunis. Industries include leather, soap, and carpets; there are also salt works and phosphate workings nearby. Exports include phosphates, olive oil, dates, almonds, esparto grass, and sponges.

Seychelles

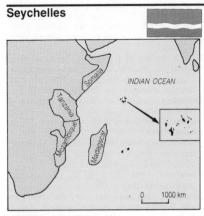

INDIAN OCEAN

Somalia

Tanzania

Mozambique

Madagascar

0   1000 km

area 453 sq km/175 sq mi
capital Victoria on Mahé
physical comprises two distinct island groups, one concentrated, the other widely scattered, totalling over 100 islands and islets
features the unique 'double coconut'
head of state and government France-Albert René from 1977
government one-party socialist republic
political parties Seychelles People's Progressive Front (SPPF), nationalistic socialist
exports copra, cinnamon; tourism is important
currency Seychelles rupee (9.21 = £1 Feb 1990)
population (1989) 70,000; annual growth rate 0.6%
language creole, spoken by 95%, English and French (all official)
religion Christian (Roman Catholic 90%)
literacy 60% (1983)
GDP $143 million (1982); $1,030 per head of population
chronology
1970 Constitutional conference in London on future status of Seychelles. James Mancham, leader of the Seychelles Democratic Party (SDP), argued for full independence, while France-Albert René, leader of the Seychelles People's United Party (SPUP), favoured full integration with the UK.
1975 Internal self-government granted.
1976 Full independence achieved as a republic within the Commonwealth, with Mancham as president.
1977 René ousted Mancham in an armed coup and took over the presidency.
1979 New constitution adopted, making the SPUP, restyled the Seychelles People's Progressive Front (SPPF), the only legal party.
1981 Attempted coup by South African mercenaries thwarted.
1984 René re-elected.
1987 Coup attempt foiled.
1989 René re-elected.

Sforza /ˈsfɔːtsə/ Italian family that ruled the duchy of Milan 1450–99 and 1522–35. Their court was a centre of Renaissance culture, and *Ludovico Sforza* (1451–1508) was patron of the artist ◊Leonardo da Vinci.

SFSR abbreviation for *Soviet Federal Socialist Republic.*

's Gravenhage /sˌxrɑːvənˈhɑːxə/ Dutch name for The ◊Hague.

Shaanxi /ˌʃɑːnˈʃiː/ formerly *Shensi* province of NW China
area 195,800 sq km/75,579 sq mi
capital Xian
physical mountains; Huang He valley, one of the earliest settled areas of China
products iron, steel, mining, textiles, fruit, tea, rice, wheat
population (1986) 30,430,000.

Shaba /ˈʃɑːbə/ formerly (until 1972) *Katanga* region of ◊Zaïre; area 496,965 sq km/191,828 sq mi; population (1984) 3,874,000. Its main town is ◊Lubumbashi, formerly Elisabethville.

Shache /ˌʃɑːˈtʃeɪ/ alternative name for ◊Yarkand, a city in China.

shackle unit of length, used at sea for measuring cable or chain. One shackle is 15 fathoms (90 ft/27 m).

Shackleton /ˈʃækəltən/ Ernest 1874–1922. Irish Antarctic explorer. In 1907–09, he commanded an expedition that reached 88° 23' S latitude, located the magnetic South Pole, and climbed Mount ◊Erebus.

He was a member of Scott's Antarctic expedition 1901–04, and also commanded the expedition 1914–16, which hoped to cross the Antarctic, when he had to abandon his ship, the *Endurance*, crushed in the ice of the Weddell Sea. He died on board the *Quest* on his fourth expedition 1921–22 to the Antarctic.

shad marine fish, largest (2.7 kg/6 lbs) of the herring family. They migrate in shoals to breed in rivers. They are Atlantic fish but have been introduced to the Pacific.

Shadow Cabinet the chief members of the British parliamentary opposition, each of whom is responsible for commenting on the policies and performance of a government ministry.

shaduf a machine for lifting water, consisting typically of a long wooden pole acting as a lever, with a weight at one end. The other end is positioned over a well, for example. The shaduf was in use in ancient Egypt, and is still used in Arab countries today.

Shadwell /ˈʃædwəl/ Thomas 1642–1692. English dramatist and poet. His plays include *Epsom-Wells* 1672 and *Bury-Fair* 1689. He was involved in a violent feud with the poet ◊Dryden, whom he attacked in 'The Medal of John Bayes' 1682 and succeeded as Poet Laureate.

SHAEF abbreviation for *Supreme Headquarters Allied Expeditionary Force* World War II military centre established 15 Feb 1944 in London, where final plans for the Allied invasion of Europe (under US general Eisenhower) were worked out.

Shaffer /ˈʃæfə/ Peter 1926– . English playwright. His plays include *Five Finger Exercise* 1958, the historical epic *The Royal Hunt of the Sun* 1964, *Equus* 1973, and *Amadeus* 1979 about the composer Mozart.

Shaftesbury /ˈʃɑːftsbəri/ market town and agricultural centre in Dorset, England, 30 km/19 mi SW of Salisbury; population (1985) 6,000. King Alfred is said to have founded an abbey on the site 880; Canute died at Shaftesbury 1035.

Shaftesbury /ˈʃɑːftsbəri/ Anthony Ashley Cooper, 1st Earl of Shaftesbury 1621–1683. English politician, a supporter of the Restoration of the monarchy. He became lord chancellor in 1672, but went into opposition in 1673 and began to organize the ◊Whig Party. He headed the demand for the exclusion of the future James II from the succession, secured the passing of the ◊Habeas Corpus Act in 1679 and, when accused of treason in 1681, fled to Holland.

Shaftesbury /ˈʃɑːftsbəri/ Anthony Ashley Cooper, 3rd Earl of Shaftesbury 1671–1713. English philosopher, author of *Characteristics of Men, Manners, Opinions, and Times* 1711 and other ethical speculations.

Shaftesbury /ˈʃɑːftsbəri/ Anthony Ashley Cooper, 7th Earl of Shaftesbury 1801–1885. British Tory politician. He strongly supported the Ten Hours Act of 1847 and other factory legislation, including the 1842 act forbidding the employment of women and children underground in mines. He was also associated with the movement to provide free education for the poor.

shag type of small ◊cormorant, *Phalacrocorax aristotelis*.

shah /ʃɑː/ (more formally, *Shahanshah* 'king of kings') traditional title of ancient Persian rulers, and also of those of the recent ◊Pahlavi dynasty in Iran.

Shah Jehan /ˈʃɑː dʒəˈhɑːn/ 1592–1666. ◊Mogul emperor of India from 1627, when he succeeded his father Jehangir. From 1658 he was a prisoner of his son Aurangzeb. He built the ◊Taj Mahal.

Shahn /ʃɑːn/ Ben 1898–1969. US artist, born in Lithuania, a Social Realist painter. His work included drawings and paintings on the ◊Dreyfus case and ◊Sacco and Vanzetti. As a mural painter he worked at the Rockefeller Center, New York (with the Mexican artist Diego Rivera), and the Federal Security Building, Washington, 1940–42.

Shaka /ˈʃɑːɡə/ or *Chaka* 1787–1828. Zulu leader who formed a Zulu empire in South Africa. He seized power from his half-brother 1816, and embarked on a campaign to unite the Nguni (the area that today forms the South African province of Natal), initiating the period of warfare known as the ◊Mfecane.

Shaker a member of the Christian sect of the *United Society of Believers in Christ's Second Appearing*, so-called because of their ecstatic shakings in worship. The movement was founded by James and Jane Wardley in England about 1747, and taken to North America 1774 by Ann Lee (1736–84). They anticipated modern spiritualist beliefs, but their doctrine of celibacy led to their virtual extinction. *Shaker furniture* has been admired in the 20th century for its simple and robust design.

Shakespeare /ˈʃeɪkspɪə/ William 1564–1616. English dramatist and poet. Established in London by 1589 as an actor and a playwright, he was England's unrivalled dramatist until his death, and is considered the greatest English playwright. His plays, written in blank verse, can be broadly divided into lyric plays, including ◊*Romeo and Juliet* and ◊*Midsummer Night's Dream*; comedies, including *Comedy of Errors, As You Like It, Much Ado About Nothing*, and *Measure For Measure*; historical plays, such as *Henry VI* (in three parts), *Richard III*, and *Henry IV* (in two parts), which

Shah Jehan *Mogul portrait of Shah Jehan by an unknown artist (c.1632–33), Victoria and Albert Museum, London.*

Shakespeare *Portrait attributed to John Taylor (c.1610) National Portrait Gallery, London.*

often showed cynical political wisdom; and tragedies, such as ◊Hamlet, ◊Macbeth, and ◊King Lear. He also wrote numerous sonnets.

Born in Stratford-on-Avon, the son of a wool dealer, he was educated at the grammar school, and in 1582 married Anne Hathaway. They had a daughter, Susanna, in 1583, and twins Hamnet (died 1596) and Judith in 1595. Early plays, written around 1589–93, were the tragedy *Titus Andronicus*; the comedies *The Comedy of Errors, The Taming of the Shrew*, and *Two Gentlemen of Verona*; the three parts of *Henry VI*; and *Richard III*. About 1593 he came under the patronage of the Earl of ◊Southampton, to whom he dedicated his long poems *Venus and Adonis* 1593 and *The Rape of Lucrece* 1594; he also wrote for him the comedy *Love's Labour's Lost*, satirizing ◊Raleigh's circle, and seems to have dedicated to him his sonnets written around 1593–96, in which the mysterious 'Dark Lady' appears.

From 1594 Shakespeare was a member of the Chamberlain's (later the King's) company of players, and had no rival as a dramatist, writing, for example, the lyric plays *Romeo and Juliet, A Midsummer Night's Dream*, and *Richard II* 1594–95, followed by *King John* and *The Merchant of Venice* in 1596. The Falstaff plays of 1597–99—*Henry IV* (parts I and II), *Henry V*, and *The Merry Wives of Windsor* (said to have been written at the request of Elizabeth I)— brought his fame to its height. He wrote *Julius Caesar* 1599. The period ended with the lyrically witty *Much Ado about Nothing, As You Like It*, and *Twelfth Night* about 1598–1601.

With *Hamlet* begins the period of the great tragedies, 1601–08: *Othello, Macbeth, King Lear, Timon of Athens, Antony and Cleopatra*, and *Coriolanus*. This 'darker' period is also reflected in the comedies *Troilus and Cressida, All's Well that Ends Well*, and *Measure for Measure* around 1601–04.

It is thought that Shakespeare was only part author of *Pericles*, which is grouped with the other plays of around 1608–11—*Cymbeline, The Winter's Tale*, and *The Tempest*—as the mature romance or 'reconciliation' plays of the end of his career. During 1613 it is thought that Shakespeare collaborated with Fletcher on *Henry VIII* and *Two Noble Kinsmen*. He had already retired to Stratford in about 1610, where he died on 23 Apr 1616.

For the first 200 years after his death, Shakespeare's plays were frequently performed in cut or revised form (Nahum Tate's *King Lear* was given a happy ending), and it was not until the 19th century, with the critical assessment of Coleridge and ◊Hazlitt, that the original texts were restored.

Shakhty /'ʃæxti/ town in the Donbas region of the Russian Soviet Federal Socialist Republic, 80 km/50 mi NE of Rostov; population (1987)

Shakespeare: the plays

Title	Performed
Early Plays	
Henry VI Part I	1589–92
Henry VI Part II	1589–92
Henry VI Part III	1589–92
The Comedy of Errors	1592–93
The Taming of the Shrew	1593–94
Titus Andronicus	1593–94
The Two Gentlemen of Verona	1594–95
Love's Labour's Lost	1594–95
Romeo and Juliet	1594–95
Histories	
Richard III	1592–93
Richard II	1593–96
King John	1596–97
Henry IV Part I	1597–98
Henry IV Part II	1597–98
Henry V	1599
Roman Plays	
Julius Caesar	1599–1600
Antony and Cleopatra	1607–08
Coriolanus	1607–08
The 'Great' or 'Middle' Comedies	
A Midsummer Night's Dream	1595–96
The Merchant of Venice	1596–97
Much Ado About Nothing	1598–99
As You Like It	1599–1600
The Merry Wives of Windsor	1600–01
Twelfth Night	1601–02
The Great Tragedies	
Hamlet	1600–01
Othello	1604–05
King Lear	1605–06
Macbeth	1605–06
Timon of Athens	1607–08
The 'Dark' Comedies	
Troilus and Cressida	1601–02
All's Well That Ends Well	1602–03
Measure for Measure	1604–05
Late Plays	
Pericles	1608–09
Cymbeline	1609–10
The Winter's Tale	1610–11
The Tempest	1611–12
Henry VIII	1612–13

225,000. Industries include anthracite mining, stone quarrying, textiles, leather, and metal goods. It was known as Aleksandrovsk Grushevskii until 1921.

shale a fine-grained and finely-laminated ◊sedimentary rock composed of silt and clay that parts easily along bedding planes. It differs from mudstone in that the latter splits into flakes. Oil shale contains kerogen, a solid bituminous material that yields ◊petroleum when heated.

shallot type of onion *Allium cepa* in which bulbs multiply freely; used for cooking and in pickles.

Shalmaneser /,ʃælmə'niːzə/ five Assyrian kings including:

Shalmaneser III King of Assyria 859–824 BC, who pursued an aggressive policy, and brought Babylon and Israel under the domination of Assyria.

shaman a ritual figure who acts as intermediary between society and the supernatural world in many indigenous cultures of Asia, Africa, and the Americas. Also known as a *medicine man, seer* or *sorcerer*, the shaman uses magic powers to cure illness and control good and evil spirits.

Shamir /ʃæ'mɪə/ Yitzhak 1915– . Israeli politician, born in Poland; foreign minister under Menachem Begin 1980–83, prime minister 1983–84, and again foreign minister in the ◊Peres unity government from 1984. In Oct 1986, he and Peres exchanged positions, Shamir becoming prime minister and Peres taking over as foreign minister. He was re-elected 1989. Shamir was a leader of the ◊Stern Gang guerrillas during the British mandate rule of Palestine.

shamrock several trifoliate plants of the family Leguminosae. One is said to have been used by St Patrick to illustrate the doctrine of the Holy Trinity, and it was made the national badge of Ireland.

Shan a member of a people of the mountainous borderlands between Thailand, Burma, and China. They are related to the Laos and Thais, and their language belongs to the Sino-Tibetan family.

Shandong /,ʃæn'dʌŋ/ or *Shantung* province of NE China
area 153,300 sq km/59,174 sq mi
capital Jinan
towns ports Yantai, Weihai, Qingdao, Shigiusuo
features crossed by the Huang He river and the ◊Grand Canal; Shandong Peninsula
products cereals, cotton, wild silk, varied minerals
population (1986) 77,760,000.

Shanghai /,ʃæŋ'haɪ/ port on the Huang-pu and Wusong rivers, Jiangsu province, China, 24 km/15 mi from the Chang Jiang estuary; population (1986) 6,980,000, the largest city in China. The municipality of Shanghai has an area of 5,800 sq km/2,239 sq mi and a population of 12,320,000. Industries include textiles, paper, chemicals, steel, agricultural machinery, precision instruments, shipbuilding, flour and vegetable-oil milling, and oil refining. It handles about 50% of China's imports and exports.

Shanghai is reckoned to be the most heavily populated area in the world with an average of 6 sq m/65 sq ft of living space and 2.2 sq m/ 2.6 sq yd of road per person.
features Famous buildings include the Jade Buddha Temple 1882; the former home of the revolutionary ◊Sun Yat-sen; the house where the First National Congress of the Communist Party of China met secretly in 1921; and the house, museum, and tomb of the writer Lu Xun.
history Shanghai was a city from 1360, but became important only after 1842, when the treaty of Nanking opened it to foreign trade. The international settlement then developed, which remained the commercial centre of the city after the departure of European interests 1943–46.

Shankar /'ʃæŋkaː/ Ravi 1920– . Indian composer and musician. A virtuoso of the ◊sitar, he has composed film music and founded music schools in Bombay and Los Angeles.

Shankara 799–833. Hindu philosopher who wrote commentaries on some of the major Hindu scriptures, as well as hymns and essays on religious ideas. Shankara was responsible for the final form of the Advaita Vedanta school of Hindu philosophy, which teaches that Brahman, the supreme being, is all that exists in the universe; everything else is illusion. Shankara was fiercely opposed to Buddhism and may have influenced its decline in India.

Shannon /'ʃænən/ longest river in Ireland, rising in County Cavan and flowing 260 km/161 mi through Loughs Allen and Ree and past Athlone, to reach the Atlantic through a wide estuary below Limerick. It is also the major source of electric power in the republic, with hydroelectric installations at and above Ardnacrusha, 5 km/3 mi N of Limerick.

Shannon /'ʃænən/ Claude Elwood 1916– . US mathematician, whose paper *The Mathematical Theory of Communication* 1948 marks the beginning of the science of information theory. He

Shanghai *The commercial centre of Shanghai, China.*

argued that information and ◊entropy are analogous, and obtained a quantitive measure of the amount of information in a given message.

Shansi /ˌʃænˈsiː/ alternative transcription of the Chinese province of ◊Shanxi.

Shantou /ˌʃænˈtaʊ/ or **Swatow** port and industrial city in SE China; population (1970) 400,000. It was opened as a special foreign trade area 1979.

Shantung /ˌʃænˈtʌŋ/ alternative transcription of the Chinese province of ◊Shandong.

Shanxi /ˌʃænˈʃiː/ or **Shansi** province of NE China
area 157,100 sq km/60,641 sq mi
capital Taiyuan
features a drought-ridden plateau, partly surrounded by the ◊Great Wall; the province saw the outbreak of the Boxer Rising
products coal, iron, fruit
population (1986) 26,550,000.

Shaoshan /ˌʃaʊˈʃæn/ the birthplace in the Chinese province of Hunan of the Communist leader Mao Zedong.

SHAPE abbreviation for *Supreme Headquarters Allied Powers Europe*, situated near Mons, Belgium, and the headquarters of NATO's *Supreme Allied Commander Europe* (SACEUR).

Shapiro /ʃəˈpɪərəʊ/ Karl 1913– . US poet. He was born in Baltimore, and his work includes the striking *V Letter* 1945, written after service in World War II.

Shapley /ˈʃæpli/ Harlow 1885–1972. US astronomer, whose study of ◊globular clusters showed that they were arranged in a halo around the galaxy, and that the galaxy was much larger than previously thought. He realized that the Sun was not at the centre of the galaxy as then assumed, but two-thirds of the way out to the rim.

share in finance, that part of the capital of a company held by a member (shareholder). Shares may be numbered and are issued as units of definite face value; shareholders are not always called on to pay the full face value of their shares, though they bind themselves to do so.

Preference shares carry a fixed rate of dividend and have first claim on the profits of the company; ordinary shares have second claim, and if profits have been good may attract a higher dividend than the preference shares; *deferred shares* rank for dividend only after the rights of preference and ordinary shareholders have been satisfied. Fully paid-up shares can be converted by the company into stock. In 1988 20.5% of the population over 16 in the UK owned shares, 25% in the USA, and 23% in Japan.

Shari'a the law of ◊Islam believed by Muslims to be based on divine revelation, and drawn from a number of sources, including the Koran, the Hadith and the consensus of the Muslim community. From the latter part of the 19th century, the role of the Shari'a courts in the majority of Muslim countries began to be taken over by secular courts, and the Shari'a to be largely restricted to family law.

Sharif /ʃæˈriːf/ Omar. Stage name of Michael Shalhoub 1932– . Egyptian actor, in international films after his successful appearance in *Lawrence of Arabia* 1962. His other films include *Dr Zhivago* 1965 and *Funny Girl* 1968.

Sharjah /ˈʃɑːdʒə/ or **Shariqah** third largest of the seven member states of the ◊United Arab Emirates, situated on the Arabian Gulf NE of Dubai; area 2,600 sq km/1,004 sq mi; population (1985) 269,000. Since 1952 it has included the small state of Kalba. In 1974 oil was discovered offshore. Industries include ship repairing, cement, paint, and metal products.

shark the bigger members of the Pleurotremata, a large group of marine fish with cartilaginous skeletons. They are found worldwide. They have streamlined bodies and high-speed manoeuvrability, and their eyes, though lacking acuity of vision or sense of colour, are highly sensitive to light. Their sense of smell is so acute that one-third of the brain is given up to interpreting its signals; it can detect blood in the water up to 1 km/0.6 mi

away. They also respond to electrical charges emanating from other animals.

Species include the 'maneater' **white shark** *Carcharodon carcharias* of tropical waters, which reaches about 12 m/40 ft; the **basking shark** *Cetorhinus maximus* of temperate seas, which reaches a similar size, but eats only marine organisms; and the equally harmless **whale shark** *Rhinocodon typus*, which, at 18 m/60 ft, is the largest living fish. Sharks have remained virtually unchanged for millions of years.

Relatively few attacks on humans are pursued to a fatal conclusion, and research suggests that they are not searching for food, but attempting to repel 'rivals' from their territory. Game fishing for 'sport', the eradication of sharks in swimming and recreation areas, and their industrial exploitation as a source of leather, oil, and protein have reduced their numbers.

Sharon /ˈʃeərən/ coastal plain in Israel between Haifa and Tel Aviv, and a sub-district of Central district; area 348 sq km/134 sq mi; population (1983) 190,400. It has been noted since ancient times for its fertility.

sharp in music, sounding higher in pitch than the indicated note value, or than expected. A sharp sign in front of a written note indicates that it is to be raised by a semitone. It is cancelled by a natural sign.

Sharp /ʃɑːp/ Cecil (James) 1859–1924. English collector and compiler of folk dance and song. His work ensured that the English folk-music revival became established in school music throughout the English-speaking world.

He travelled the country to record and save from extinction the folk-song tradition, for example *English Folk Song* 1907 (two volumes). In the USA he tracked down survivals of English song in the Appalachian Mountains and elsewhere.

Sharp /ʃɑːp/ Granville 1735–1813. English philanthropist. He was prominent in the anti-slavery movement and in 1772 secured a legal decision 'that as soon as any slave sets foot on English territory he becomes free'.

Sharpeville /ˈʃɑːpvɪl/ black township in South Africa, 65 km/40 mi S of Johannesburg and N of Vereeniging; 69 people were killed here when police fired on a crowd of demonstrators on 21 Mar 1960, during a campaign launched by the Pan-Africanist Congress against the pass laws (laws requiring nonwhite South Africans to carry identity papers).

On the anniversary of the massacre in 1985, during funerals of protesters against unemployment who had been killed, 19 people were shot by the police at Langa near Port Elizabeth.

Sharpey-Schäfer /ˈʃɑːpi ˈʃeɪfə/ Edward Albert 1850–1935. English physiologist and one of the founders of endocrinology. He made important discoveries relating to ◊adrenaline, and to the ◊pituitary and other ◊endocrine or ductless glands. He also devised a method of artificial respiration that improved on existing techniques.

Shasta, Mount /ˈʃæstə/ dormant volcano rising to a height of 4,317 m/14,162 ft in the Cascade Range, N California, USA.

Shastri /ˈʃæstri/ Lal Bahadur 1904–1966. Indian politician, who held various ministerial posts after independence, and succeeded Nehru as prime minister of India 1964. He campaigned for national integration, and secured a declaration of peace with Pakistan at the Tashkent peace conference 1966.

Before independence, he was imprisoned several times for civil disobedience. Because of his small stature, he was known as 'the Sparrow'.

Shatt-al-Arab /ˈʃæt æl ˈærəb/ (Persian **Arvand**) the waterway formed by the confluence of the rivers ◊Euphrates and ◊Tigris; length 190 km/120 mi to the Persian Gulf. Basra, Khorramshahr, and Abadan stand on it.

Its lower reaches form a border of disputed demarcation between Iran and Iraq. In 1975, the two countries agreed on the deepest water line as the frontier, but Iraq repudiated this 1980; the dispute was a factor in the Iran–Iraq war 1980–88.

Shaw /ʃɔː/ George Bernard 1856–1950. Irish dramatist. He was also a critic and novelist, and an early member of the socialist ◊Fabian Society. His plays combine comedy with political, philosophical, and polemic aspects, aiming to make an impact on his audience's social conscience as well as their emotions. They include *Arms and the Man* 1894, *The Devil's Disciple* 1897, *Man and Superman* 1905, *Pygmalion* 1913, and *St Joan* 1924. Nobel prize 1925.

Born in Dublin, the son of a civil servant, Shaw came to London in 1876, where he became a brilliant debater and supporter of the Fabians, and worked as a music and drama critic. He wrote five unsuccessful novels before in 1892 his first play, *Widowers' Houses*, was produced. Attacking slum landlords, it allied him with the realistic, political, and polemical movement in the theatre, pointing to people's responsibility to improve themselves and their social environment.

The volume *Plays: Pleasant and Unpleasant* 1898 also included *The Philanderer; Mrs Warren's Profession*, dealing with prostitution and banned until 1902; and *Arms and the Man* about war. *Three Plays for Puritans* 1901 contained *The Devil's Disciple, Caesar and Cleopatra* (a companion piece to the play by Shakespeare), and *Captain Brassbound's Conversion*, written for the actress Ellen ◊Terry. *Man and Superman* 1903 expounds his ideas of evolution by following the character of Don Juan into hell for a debate with the devil.

The 'anti-romantic' comedy *Pygmalion*, first performed 1913, was written for the actress Mrs Patrick ◊Campbell (and later converted to a musical as *My Fair Lady*). Later plays included *Heartbreak House* 1917, *Back to Methuselah* 1921, and the historical *St Joan* 1924.

Altogether Shaw wrote more than 50 plays and became a byword for wit. His theories were further explained in the voluminous prefaces to the plays, and in books such as *The Intelligent Woman's Guide to Socialism and Capitalism* 1928. He was also an unsuccessful advocate of spelling reform, and a prolific letter-writer.

Shaw /ʃɔː/ (Richard) Norman 1831–1912. British architect. He was the leader of the trend away from Gothic and Tudor styles back to Georgian lines. His buildings include Swan House, Chelsea, 1876.

shawm an early form of oboe.

Shchedrin /ʃtʃiˈdriːn/ N. Pen name of Mikhail Evgrafovich Saltykov 1826–1889. Russian writer, whose works include *Fables* 1884–85, in which he depicts misplaced 'good intentions', and the novel *The Golovlevs* 1880. He was a satirist of pessimistic outlook. He was exiled for seven years for an early story which proved too liberal for the authorities, but later held official posts.

Shearer /ˈʃɪərə/ (Edith) Norma 1900–1983. Canadian actress who starred in such films as *Private Lives* 1931, *Romeo and Juliet* 1936, and *Marie Antoinette* 1938, in which she played the title role. She was married to MGM executive Irving Thalberg.

shearwater sea bird related to petrels and albatrosses. The Manx shearwater *Puffinus puffinus* is the only species that breeds in Britain.

sheath another name for a ◊condom.

Sheba /ˈʃiːbə/ ancient name for South ◊Yemen (Sha'abijah). It was once renowned for gold and spices. According to the Old Testament, its queen

shark

great white shark

visited Solomon; the former Ethiopian royal house traced its descent from their union.

Shechem /'ʃiːkem/ ancient town in Palestine, capital of Samaria. In the Old Testament, it is the traditional burial place of Joseph; nearby is Jacob's well. Shechem was destroyed about AD 67 by the Roman emperor Vespasian; on its site stands Nablus (a corruption of Neapolis) built by ◊Hadrian.

sheep genus *Ovis* of ruminant hoofed mammals of the family Bovidae. Wild species survive in the uplands of central Asia, and their domesticated descendants are reared worldwide for meat, wool, milk, and cheese, and for rotation on arable land to maintain its fertility.

Over 50 breeds of sheep have evolved in the UK, and many more worldwide, to suit different requirements and a range of geographical and climatic conditions. Only a proportion of the UK breeds are now in full commercial use. They are grouped into three principal categories. The hardy **upland** breeds like the Scottish Blackface and Welsh Mountain are able to survive in a bleak and rugged environment. The **shortwool** varieties like the Down breeds of Hampshire and Suffolk are well adapted to thrive on the lush grassland of lowland areas. **Longwool** breeds like the Leicesters and Border Leicesters were originally valued for their coarse, heavy fleeces, but are now more important for crossing with hill-sheep flocks to produce fat lambs. In 1989 there were 41 million sheep in Britain.

sheepdog rough-coated breed of dog. The Old English sheepdog is grey or blue-grey, with white markings, and is about 56 cm/22 in tall at the shoulder. The Shetland sheepdog is much smaller, 36 cm/14 in tall, and shaped more like a long-coated collie. Sheepdogs were fomerly used by shepherds and farmers to tend sheep. Border collies are now considered the best breed for this job.

sheep

Scottish
blackface

Dorset
down

Suffolk

Welsh
mountain

Sheerness /ˌʃɪəˈnes/ seaport and resort on the Isle of ◊Sheppey, Kent, England; population (1981) 11,250. Situated at the confluence of the Thames and Medway, it was originally a fortress 1660, and was briefly held by the Dutch admiral de Ruyter 1667. It was a royal dockyard until 1960.

Sheffield /'ʃefiːld/ industrial city on the Don river, South Yorkshire, England; population (1986) 538,700. From the 12th century, iron smelting was the chief industry, and by the 14th century Sheffield cutlery, silverware, and plate were famous. During the Industrial Revolution the iron and steel industries developed rapidly. It now produces alloys and special steels, cutlery of all kinds, permanent magnets, drills, and precision tools. Other industries include electroplating, type-founding, and the manufacture of optical glass.

The parish church of St Peter and St Paul (14th–15th centuries) is the cathedral of Sheffield bishopric established 1914. Mary Queen of Scots was imprisoned at Sheffield 1570–84, part of the time in the Norman castle, which was captured by the Parliamentarians 1644 and subsequently destroyed. There are two art galleries; Cutlers' Hall; Ruskin museum, opened 1877 and revived 1985; and a theatre, The Crucible 1971; there is also a university 1905, and a polytechnic 1969. The city is a touring centre for the Peak District. The headquarters of the National Union of Mineworkers are in Sheffield.

Sheffield Outrages in British history, sensational reports in the national press 1866 exemplifying summary justice exercised by trade unions to secure subscriptions and obtain compliance with rules by threats, removal of tools, sabotage of equipment at work, and assaults.

Dramatic accounts of action taken against a strike-breaking worker in the cutlery trade led to a Royal Commission inquiry into trade-union activity. This coincided with a campaign by trade unionists to obtain the reform of the Master and Servant Law, which discriminated between employer and employee in cases of breach of contract. The result was publication of Majority and Minority Reports that were sympathetic to the legalization of trade unions. This was implemented in the Trade Union Act 1871 and ◊Criminal Law Amendment Act 1871.

sheik the leader or chief of an Arab family or village.

Shelburne /'ʃelbən/ William Petty FitzMaurice, 2nd Earl of Shelburne 1737–1805. British Whig politician. He was an opponent of George III's American policy, and as prime minister in 1783, he concluded peace with the USA. He was created Marquess of Lansdowne in 1784.

shelduck duck *Tadorna tadorna* with dark green head and red bill, with the rest of the plumage strikingly marked in black, white, and chestnut. Widely distributed in Europe and Asia, it lays 10–12 white eggs in rabbit burrows in sandy coasts, and is usually seen on estuary mudflats.

shelf sea relatively shallow sea, usually no deeper than 200 m/650 ft, overlying the continental shelf around the coastlines. Most fishing and marine mineral exploitations are carried out in shelf seas.

shellac a resin derived from secretions of the ◊lac insect.

Shelley /'ʃeli/ Mary Wollstonecraft 1797–1851. English writer, the daughter of Mary Wollstonecraft and William Godwin. In 1814 she eloped with the poet Percy Bysshe Shelley, whom she married in 1816. Her novels include ◊*Frankenstein* 1818, *The Last Man* 1826, and *Valperga* 1823.

Shelley /'ʃeli/ Percy Bysshe 1792–1822. English lyric poet, a leading figure in the Romantic movement. Expelled from Oxford for atheism, he fought all his life against religion and for political freedom. This is reflected in his early poems such as *Queen Mab* 1813. He later wrote tragedies including *The Cenci* 1818, lyric dramas such as *Prometheus Unbound* 1820, and lyrical poems such as 'Ode to the West Wind'. He drowned while sailing in Italy.

Born near Horsham, Sussex, he was educated at Eton school and University College, Oxford, where his collaboration in a pamphlet *The Necessity of Atheism* 1811 caused his expulsion. While living in London he fell in love with 16-year-old Harriet Westbrook, whom he married 1811. He visited Ireland and Wales writing pamphlets defending vegetarianism and political freedom, and in 1813 published privately *Queen Mab*, a poem with political freedom as its theme. Meanwhile he had become estranged from his wife and in 1814 left England with Mary Wollstonecraft Godwin, whom he married after Harriet had drowned herself 1816. *Alastor*, written 1815, was followed by the epic *The Revolt of Islam*, and by 1818 Shelley was living in Italy. Here he produced the tragedy *The Cenci*; the satire on Wordsworth, *Peter Bell the Third* 1819; and the lyric drama *Prometheus Unbound* 1820. Other works of the period are 'Ode to the West Wind' 1819; 'The Cloud' and 'The Skylark', both 1820; 'The Sensitive Plant' and 'The Witch of Atlas'; 'Epipsychidion' and, on the death of the poet Keats, 'Adonais' 1821; the lyric drama *Hellas* 1822; and the prose *Defence of Poetry* 1821. In July 1822 Shelley was drowned while sailing near La Spezia, and his ashes were buried in Rome.

shellfish popular name for molluscs and crustaceans, including the whelk and periwinkle, mussel, oyster, lobster, crab, and shrimp.

shell shock or *combat neurosis* any of the various forms of mental disorder that affect soldiers exposed to heavy explosions or extreme ◊stress. Shell shock was first diagnosed during World War I.

Shema Jewish prayer from the Torah, recited every morning and evening, which affirms the special relationship of the Jews with God.

Shenandoah /ˌʃenənˈdəʊə/ river in Virginia, USA, a tributary of the Potomac, which it joins at Harper's Ferry. ◊Sheridan laid waste the Shenandoah valley in the American Civil War.

Shensi /ˌʃenˈsiː/ former name for the Chinese province of ◊Shanxi.

Shenstone /'ʃenstən/ William 1714–1763. English poet and essayist whose poems include *Poems upon Various Occasions* 1737, the Spenserian *Schoolmistress* 1742, elegies, odes, songs, and ballads.

Shelley *Expelled from Oxford at 19, Percy Bysshe Shelley eloped to Switzerland with Mary Wollstonecraft, and died by drowning before he was 30.*

Shenyang /ˌʃenˈjæŋ/ industrial city and capital of Liaoning province, China; population (1986) 4,200,000. It was the capital of the Manchu emperors 1644–1912. Their tombs are nearby.

Historically known as Mukden, it was taken from Russian occupation by the Japanese in the Battle of Mukden 20 Feb–10 Mar 1905, and was again taken by the Japanese 1931.

Shenzen /ˌʃʌnˈdzʌn/ a Special Economic Zone established in 1980 opposite Hong Kong on the coast of Guangdong province, S China. Its status provided much of the driving force of its spectacular development in the 1980s when its population rose from 20,000 in 1980 to 600,000 in 1989. Part of the population is 'rotated' newcomers from other provinces who return to their homes after a few years spent learning foreign business techniques.

Shepard /ˈʃepəd/ Alan (Bartlett) 1923– . US astronaut, the fifth person to walk on the Moon. He was the first American in space, as pilot of the suborbital Mercury-Redstone 3 mission on board the Freedom 7 capsule May 1961, and commanded the Apollo 14 lunar landing mission 1971.

Shepard /ˈʃepəd/ E(rnest) H(oward) 1879–1976. British illustrator of books by A A Milne (*Winnie-the-Pooh* 1926) and Kenneth Grahame (*The Wind in the Willows* 1908).

Shepard /ˈʃepəd/ Sam 1943– . US dramatist and actor. His work combines colloquial American dialogue with striking visual imagery, and includes *The Tooth of Crime* 1972 and *Buried Child* 1978, for which he won the Pulitzer Prize. He has acted in a number of films, including *The Right Stuff* 1983, *Fool for Love* 1986, based on his play of the same name, and *Steel Magnolias* 1989.

shepherd's purse annual plant *Capsella bursa-pastoris* of the Cruciferae family, distributed worldwide in temperate zones. It is a persistent weed with white flowers followed by heart-shaped, seed-containing pouches from which its name derives.

Sheppard /ˈʃepəd/ Jack 1702–1724. English criminal. Born in Stepney, E London, he was an apprentice carpenter, but turned to theft and became a popular hero by four escapes from prison. He was finally caught and hanged.

Sheppey /ˈʃepi/ island off the N coast of Kent, England; area 80 sq km/31 sq mi; population about 27,000. Situated at the mouth of the river Medway, it is linked with the mainland by Kingsferry road and rail bridge over the Swale, completed 1960. The resort and port of Sheerness is here.

Shepard Winnie-the-Pooh and Piglet in search of the Woozle; one of E H Shepard's illustrations to Winnie-the-Pooh *1926.*

Sheraton /ˈʃerətən/ Thomas c. 1751–1806. English designer of elegant inlaid furniture, as in his *Cabinet-maker's and Upholsterer's Drawing Book* 1791. He was influenced by his predecessors ◊Hepplewhite and ◊Chippendale.

Sheridan /ˈʃerɪdən/ Philip Henry 1831–1888. US Union general in the American Civil War. Gen Ulysses S ◊Grant gave him command of his cavalry in 1864, and soon after of the army of the Shenandoah Valley, Virginia, which he cleared of Confederates. In the final stage of the war, Sheridan forced Gen Lee to retreat to Appomattox, and surrender.

Sheridan /ˈʃerɪdən/ Richard Brinsley 1751–1816. English dramatist and politician, born in Dublin. His social comedies include *The Rivals* 1775, celebrated for the character of Mrs Malaprop, *The School for Scandal* 1777, and *The Critic* 1779. In 1776 he became lessee of the Drury Lane Theatre. He became a member of Parliament in 1780.

He entered Parliament as an adherent of ◊Fox. A noted orator, he directed the impeachment of the former governor-general of India, Warren Hastings, and was treasurer to the Navy 1806–07. His last years were clouded by the burning down of his theatre in 1809, the loss of his parliamentary seat in 1812, and by financial ruin and mental breakdown.

sheriff (Old English *scīr* 'shire', *gerēfa* 'reeve') in England and Wales, the crown's chief executive officer in a county for ceremonial purposes; in Scotland, the equivalent of the English county-court judge, but also dealing with criminal cases; and in the USA the popularly elected head law-enforcement officer of a county, combining judicial authority with administrative duties.

In England, the office (elective until Edward II) dates from before the Norman Conquest. The sheriff, who is appointed annually by royal patent, and is chosen from the leading landowners, acts as returning officer for parliamentary elections, and attends the judges on circuit. The duties of keeping prisoners in safe custody, preparing panels of jurors for assizes, and executing writs, are supervised by the under-sheriff. The City of London has two sheriffs elected by members of the ◊livery companies.

Holmes, Sherlock fictitious private detective, created by the English writer Arthur Conan ◊Doyle in *A Study in Scarlet* 1887 and recurring in novels and stories until 1914. Holmes's ability to make inferences from slight clues always astonishes the narrator, Dr Watson.

The criminal mastermind against whom Holmes repeatedly pits his wits is Professor James Moriarty. Holmes is regularly portrayed at his home, 221b Baker Street, London, where he plays the violin and has bouts of determined action interspersed by lethargy and drug-taking. His characteristic pipe and deerstalker hat were the addition of an illustrator.

Sherman /ˈʃɜːmən/ William Tecumseh 1820–1891. US Union general in the American Civil War. In 1864 he captured and burned Atlanta, from where he marched to the sea, laying Georgia waste, and then drove the Confederates northwards. He was US Army Chief of Staff 1869–83.

Sherman was born in Ohio, received a command in the Federal army on the Mississippi front early in the war, and collaborated with Gen U S ◊Grant in the Vicksburg campaign.

Sherman Anti-Trust Act in US history, an act of Congress 1890, named after senator John Sherman (1823–1900) of Ohio, designed to prevent powerful corporations from monopolizing industries and restraining trade for their own benefit. Relatively few prosecutions of such trusts were successful under the act.

Sherpa /ˈʃɜːpə/ member of a people in NE Nepál of Mongolian origin, renowned for their mountaineering skill. A Sherpa, Tenzing Norgay, was one of the first two men to conquer Mount Everest.

Sherriff /ˈʃerɪf/ R(obert) C(edric) 1896–1975. British dramatist, remembered for his antiheroic war

play *Journey's End* 1929. Later plays include *Badger's Green* 1930 and *Home at Seven* 1950.

Sherrington /ˈʃerɪŋtən/ Charles Scott 1857–1952. English neurophysiologist, who studied the structure and function of the nervous system. *The Integrative Action of the Nervous System* 1906 formulated the principles of reflex action. Nobel Prize for Medicine (with E D ◊Adrian) 1932.

's-Hertogenbosch /seə,təʊxənˈbɒs/ (French *Bois-le-Duc*) capital of North Brabant, Netherlands, on the river Meuse, 45 km/28 mi SE of Utrecht; population (1988) 193,000. It has a Gothic cathedral, and was the birthplace of the painter Hieronymus Bosch.

Sherwood /ˈʃɜːwʊd/ Robert 1896–1955. US dramatist. His plays include *The Petrified Forest* 1934 (Humphrey ◊Bogart starred in the play and the film), *Idiot's Delight* 1936, *Abe Lincoln in Illinois* 1938, and *There Shall Be No Night* 1940. For each of the last three he received a Pulitzer prize.

Sherwood Forest /ˈʃɜːwʊd/ a hilly stretch of parkland in W Nottinghamshire, England, area about 520 sq km/200 sq mi. Formerly a royal forest, it is associated with the legendary ◊Robin Hood.

Shetland Islands /ˈʃetlənd/ islands off N coast of Scotland

area 1,400 sq km/541 sq mi

towns administrative headquarters Lerwick, on Mainland, largest of 19 inhabited islands

physical comprise over 100 islands; Muckle Flugga (latitude 60° 51⎪ ⎪N) is the most northerly of the British Isles

products Europe's largest oil port is Sullom Voe, Mainland; processed fish, handknits from Fair Isle and Unst, miniature ponies

population (1987) 22,000

language the dialect is derived from Norse, the islands having been a Norse dependency from the 8th century until 1472.

Shevardnadze /ˌʃevədˈnɑːdzə/ Edvard 1928– . Soviet politician. A supporter of ◊Gorbachev, he was first secretary of the Georgian Communist Party from 1972, and an advocate of economic reform. In 1985 he became foreign minister and a member of the Politburo, and has worked for détente and disarmament.

SHF in physics, abbreviation for **superhigh** ◊**frequency**.

Shiah alternative form of **Shi'ite**, one of the two main sorts of ◊Islam.

Shidehara /ˌʃɪdeɪˈhɑːrə/ Kijuro 1872–1951. Japanese politician and diplomat who, as foreign minister 1924–27 and 1929–31, promoted conciliation with China, and economic rather than military expansion. In 1945 he was recognized by the USA as prime minister and acted as speaker of the Japanese Diet (parliament) until his death.

Shetland

shield in geology, another name for ◊craton, the ancient core of a continent.

shield any material used to reduce the amount of radiation (electrostatic, electromagnetic, heat, nuclear) reaching from one region of space to another, or any material used as a protection against falling debris, as in tunnelling. Electrical conductors are used for electrostatic shields, soft iron for electromagnetic shields, and poor conductors of heat for heat shields. Heavy materials such as lead and concrete are used for protection against X-ray and nuclear radiation. See also ◊biological shield and ◊heat shield.

Shihchiachuang former name for the city of ◊Shijiazhuang in China.

Shi Huangdi /ˈʃiː ˌhwæŋdiː/ (formerly **Shih Huang Ti**) 259–210 BC. Emperor of China. He succeeded to the throne of the state of Qin in 246 BC, and reunited the country as an empire by 228 BC. He burned almost all existing books in 213 BC to destroy ties with the past; built the ◊Great Wall; and was buried in a tomb complex guarded by 10,000 individualized, life-size pottery warriors (excavated in the 1980s).

He had so overextended his power that the dynasty and the empire collapsed at the death of his feeble successor in 207 BC.

Shi'ite /ˈʃiːaɪt/ or **Shia** member of a sect of ◊Islam who believe that ◊Ali was ◊Muhammad's first true successor. They are doctrinally opposed to the ◊Sunni Muslims. Holy men have greater authority in the Shi'ite sect than in the Sunni sect. They are prominent in Iran and Lebanon, and are also found in Iraq and Bahrain. Breakaway sub-sects include the **Alawite** sect, to which the ruling party in Syria belongs; and the **Ismaili** sect, with the Aga Khan IV (1936–) as its spiritual head.

Shijiazhuang /ˌʃiːˌdʒɪəˈdʒwæŋ/ or **Shihchiachuang** city and major railway junction in Hebei province, China; population (1986) 1,160,000. Industries include textiles, chemicals, printing, and light engineering.

Shikoku /ʃiːˈkɒkuː/ smallest of the four main islands of Japan, S of Honshu, E of Kyushu; area 18,800 sq km/7,257 sq mi; population (1986) 4,226,000; chief town Matsuyama. Products include rice, wheat, soya, sugar cane, orchard fruits, salt, and copper.

It has a mild climate and annual rainfall in the south can reach 266 cm/105 in. The highest point is Mount Ishizuchi (1,980 m/6,498 ft). A suspension bridge links Shikoku to Awajishima Island over the Naruto whirlpool in the ◊Seto Naikai (Inland Sea).

Shillelagh /ʃɪˈleɪlə/ village in county Wicklow, Republic of Ireland, which gives its name to a rough cudgel of oak or blackthorn. The district was once covered by the Shillelagh Wood, which supplied oak roofing for St Patrick's cathedral in Dublin.

Shillong /ʃɪˈlɒŋ/ capital of Meghalaya state, NE India; population (1981) 109,244. It was the former capital of Assam.

Shilton /ˈʃɪltən/ Peter 1949– . English international footballer, an outstanding goalkeeper. His career began in the 1960s.

He has played for the following English clubs: Leicester City, Stoke City, Nottingham Forest, Southampton, and Derby County. He has made more than 850 Football League appearances, which is an all-time record, and won a record number of England caps.

CAREER HIGHLIGHTS

Football League 1978
Football League Cup 1979
European Cup 1979–80
European Super Cup 1980

Shimonoseki /ˌʃɪmənəʊˈseki/ seaport in the extreme SW of Honshu, Japan; population (1985) 269,000. It was opened to foreign trade 1890. The first of the ◊Sino-Japanese Wars ended with a treaty signed at Shimonoseki 1895. Industries include fishing, shipbuilding, engineering, textiles, and chemicals.

shingles common name for ◊herpes zoster.

Shinkansen (Japanese 'New Trunk Line') the fast railway network operated by Japanese Railways, on which the bullet trains run. The network, opened 1964, uses specially built straight and level track, on which average speeds of 160 kph/100 mph are attained.

Shinto the indigenous religion of Japan. It mingles an empathetic oneness with natural forces and loyalty to the reigning dynasty as descendants of the Sun goddess, Amaterasu-Omikami. Traditional Shinto stressed obedience and devotion to the emperor and an aggressive nationalistic aspect was developed by the Meiji rulers. Modern Shinto has discarded these aspects.

Shinto is the Chinese transliteration of the Japanese **Kami-no-Michi**, the Way or Doctrine of the Gods. Its holiest shrine is at Ise, near Kyoto, where in the temple of the Sun goddess is preserved the mirror that she is supposed to have given to Jimmu, the first emperor, in the 7th century BC. Sectarian Shinto consists of 130 sects; the sects are officially recognized but not state-supported (as was state Shinto until its disestablishment after World War II and Emperor Hirohito's disavowal of his divinity 1946).

shinty a winter game popular in the Scottish Highlands. Played between teams of 12 players with sticks and a ball, it resembles ◊hurling.

ship large sea-going vessel. The Greeks, Phoenicians, Romans, and Vikings used ships extensively for exploration and warfare. The 14th century was the era of European exploration by sailing ship, largely aided by the invention of the compass. In the 15th century Britain's Royal Navy was first formed, but in the 16th–19th centuries Spanish and Dutch ships reigned supreme. The ultimate sailing ships, the fast tea clippers, were built in the 19th century, at the same time as iron was first used for some shipbuilding instead of wood. Steam-propelled ships of the late 19th century were followed by compound engine and turbine-propelled boats from the early 20th century.

The Greeks and Phoenicians built wooden ships, propelled by oar or sail. The Romans and Carthaginians fought in galleys equipped with rams and several tiers of rowers. The oak ships of the Vikings were built for rough seas and propelled by oars and sail. The fleet of Richard the Lionheart was largely of sail. The invention of the compass in the 14th century led to exploration by sailing ship, resulting in the discovery of 'new worlds'. In the 15th Henry VIII built the *Great Harry*, the first double-decked English warship. In the 16th century ships were short and high-sterned, and despite Pett's three-decker in the 17th century, English ships did not bear comparison with the Spanish and Dutch until the era of Robert Seppings, a shipbuilding pioneer in the early 19th century. In the 1840s iron began replacing wood in shipbuilding, ◊Brunel's *Great Britain* 1845 being the pioneering vessel.

The USA and Britain experimented with steam propulsion as the 19th century opened. The paddle-wheel-propelled *Comet* appeared 1812, the Canadian *Royal William* crossed the Atlantic 1833, and the English *Great Western* steamed from Bristol to New York 1838. Pettit Smith applied the screw to the *Archimedes* 1839, and after 1850 the paddle wheel became obsolete. The introduction of the compound engine and turbine, the latter 1902, completed the revolution in propulsion until the advent of nuclear-powered vessels after World War II, chiefly submarines. More recently ◊hovercraft and ◊hydrofoil boats have been developed for specialized purposes, such as short-distance ferries. Sailing ships in automated form for cargo purposes are also planned.

ship money tax for support of the navy, levied on the coastal districts of England in the Middle Ages. Ship money was declared illegal by Parliament 1641. Charles I's attempts to levy it on the whole country in 1634–36, without parliamentary consent and in time of peace, aroused strong opposition from the member of Parliament John Hampden and others, who refused to pay.

Shiraz /ˈʃɪəˈræz/ ancient walled city of S Iran, the capital of Fars province; population (1986) 848,000. It is noted for wines, carpets, and silverwork, and for its many mosques.

shire a county in Britain. **The Shires** are the Midland counties of England.

Shiré Highlands /ˈʃɪəreɪ/ an upland area of S Malawi, E of the Shiré River; height up to 1,750 m/5,800 ft. Tea and tobacco are grown there.

Shizuoka /ˌʃiːzuːˈəʊkə/ town in Chubo region, Honshu, Japan; population (1985) 468,000. Industries include metal and food processing, and especially tea.

Shkodër /ˈʃkəʊdə/ (Italian **Scutari**) town on the Bojana, NW Albania, SE of Lake Shkodër, 19 km/12 mi from the Adriatic; population (1983) 71,000. Industries include woollens and cement. During World War I it was occupied by Austria 1916–18; and during World War II by Italy.

shock circulatory failure or sudden fall of blood pressure, resulting in pallor, sweating, fast (but weak) pulse, and possibly complete collapse. Causes include disease, injury, and psychological trauma.

In shock, the blood vessels dilate and the pressure falls below that necessary to supply the tissues of the body, especially the brain. Treatment is by drugs, rest, and, in the case of severe blood loss, restoration of the normal circulating volume.

shock absorber common name for a ◊damper.

Shockley /ˈʃɒkli/ William 1910–1989. US physicist and amateur geneticist, who worked with ◊Bardeen and ◊Brattain on the invention of the ◊transistor. They were jointly awarded a Nobel prize 1956. During the 1970s Shockley was severely criticized for his claim that blacks were genetically inferior to whites in terms of intelligence.

shoebill or **whale-headed stork** large, grey, long-legged, swamp-dwelling African bird *Balaeniceps rex*. Up to 1.5 m/5 ft tall, it has a large wide beak 20 cm/8 in long, with which it scoops fish, molluscs, reptiles, and carrion out of the mud.

Shoemaker /ˈʃuːmeɪkə/ William Lee 'Bill' 1931– US jockey, whose career 1949–89 was outstandingly successful. He rode 8,830 winners from nearly 40,000 mounts and his earnings exceeded $123 million. He was the leading US jockey ten times. Standing 1.5 m/4 ft 11 in tall he weighed about 43 kg/95 lb.

CAREER HIGHLIGHTS

US Triple Crown wins
Kentucky Derby: 1955, 1959, 1965, 1986
Preakness Stakes: 1963, 1967
Belmont Stakes: 1957, 1959, 1962, 1967, 1975
Leading US money winner: 1951, 1953–54, 1958–64

shofar in Judaism, a ram's horn blown in the synagogue as a call to repentance at the festivals of Rosh Hashanah and Yom Kippur.

shogi Japanese board game. It probably derives from the same Indian sources as chess, but is more complex.

shogun in Japanese history, the hereditary commander in chief of the army. Though nominally subject to the emperor, he was the real ruler of Japan 1192–1867, when the emperor reassumed power.

Shogun is an abbreviation of the official title *Seii-Tai-Shōgun*, 'barbarian-subduing commander', first given to one of the imperial guards for his subjugation of the Ainu people 794. Yoritomo Minamoto (died 1199) seized power 1185 and was granted the title 1192, and from then on shoguns were military dictators of the Minamoto or Fujiwara clan; the Tokugawa shoguns took over 1603–1868.

Sholapur /ˈʃəʊləˈpʊə/ town in Maharashtra state, India; population (1981) 514,860. Industries include textiles, leather goods, and chemicals.

Sholokhov /'ʃɒləkɒf/ Russian /'ʃɒləxəf/ Mikhail Aleksandrovich 1905–1984. Soviet novelist. His *And Quiet Flows the Don* 1926–40 depicts the Don Cossacks through World War I and the Russian Revolution. Nobel prize 1965.

Shona person of Shona culture, making up approximately 80% of the population of Zimbabwe. They also occupy the land between the Save and Pungure rivers in Mozambique, and smaller groups are found in South Africa, Botswana, and Zambia. The Shona language belongs to the Bantu branch of the Niger-Congo family.

shoot in botany, a general term for parts of a vascular plant growing above ground, comprising a stem bearing leaves, buds, and flowers. The shoot develops from the ◊plumule of the embryo.

shop a building for the retail sale of goods. Until the late 19th century, shop development had been almost static, but with the growth of manufactured goods and the concentration of population in big towns came the development of the department store and the chain store.

The world's first department store was the Bon Marché in Paris 1852. Macy's opened in the US 1858, Whiteleys in the UK 1863, and Wertheim in Germany 1870. The main innovation was goods at set prices.

The chain stores took the form of many shops scattered in different towns or counties, able to buy wholesale in such quantities that prices could be lowered below those of smaller competitors. As a development of wholesale purchase came direct links with factories producing goods, often under the same ownership, which further cut costs, and even the elimination of the shop itself by direct mail or ◊mail order.

Self-service originated in the USA many years earlier by Clarence Saunders. It developed rapidly after World War II as a result of staff shortages and labour costs, and was introduced in supermarkets for groceries and in hypermarkets outside towns. In the USA in the 1970s there developed the 'controlled shopping environment' of an air-conditioned enclosed mall of up to 250 shops in carpeted arcades, often on several levels, with music, free parking, cinemas, restaurants, and childcare facilities, for example, Woodfield Mall, Chicago. The idea was adopted in the UK and elsewhere.

Trading stamps, originating in Britain about 1851, were developed in the USA and re-exported to the UK (Green Shield) in 1958, but became a casualty of the recession and changed shopping habits in the late 1970s. They were reintroduced in 1987. Gradually being introduced are *direct debit* from a customer's bank account by use of a plastic card inserted in a computer terminal at the point of sale (an example of ◊EFTPOS), and laser check-outs, which automatically 'read' a bar code on the packaging of the goods and deliver an itemized bill to the customer, as well as recording for the store the deduction of the item from shelf stock.

shop steward trade union representative in a 'shop', or department of a factory, who recruits for the union, inspects contribution cards, and reports grievances to the district committee. This form of organization originated in the engineering industry and has spread to all large industrial undertakings.

short circuit a direct connection between two points in an electrical circuit. A large current flows through the short circuit, bypassing the rest of the circuit. The large current flowing may cause the circuit to overheat dangerously.

shorthand any system of rapid writing, such as the abbreviations practised by the Greeks and Romans. The first perfecter of an entirely phonetic system was Isaac ◊Pitman, by which system speeds of about 300 words a minute are said to be attainable.

The earliest shorthand system to be based on the alphabet was that of John Willis published 1603. Later alphabetic systems were devised by Thomas Shelton 1630 (used by the diarist Pepys) and Thomas Burney 1750, used by Charles Dickens as a reporter.

Stenotype machines, using selective keyboards enabling several word contractions to be printed at a time, are equally speedy and accurate. Abbreviations used can be transferred by the operator to a television screen, enabling the deaf to follow the spoken word.

Short Parliament the English Parliament that was summoned by Charles I on 13 Apr 1640 to raise funds for his war against the Scots. It was succeeded later in the year by the ◊Long Parliament.

short story a short work of prose fiction, which typically either sets up and resolves a single narrative point or which depicts a mood or an atmosphere. Short story writers include Chekhov, Kipling, Maupassant, Mansfield, Henry, Saki, and Borges.

short tennis a variation of lawn tennis. It is played on a smaller court, largely by schoolchildren. It can be played indoors or outdoors.

Shostakovich /ˌʃɒstə'kəʊvɪtʃ/ Dmitry (Dmitriyevich) 1906–1975. Soviet composer. His music, tonal, expressive, and sometimes highly dramatic, has not always been to official Soviet taste. He wrote 15 symphonies, chamber music, ballets, and operas, the latter including *Lady Macbeth of Mtsensk* 1934, which was suppressed as 'too divorced from the proletariat', but revived as *Katerina Izmaylova* 1963.

shot put or *putting the shot* in athletics, the sport of throwing (from the shoulder) a round weight, the 'shot', 7.26 kg/16 lb for men, and 4 kg/8.8 lb for women from a circle 2.13 m/7 ft in diameter boarded 10 cm/4 in high.

shoveler fresh-water duck *Anas clypeata*, so named from its long and broad flattened beak. Spending the summer in N Europe or North America, it winters further south. The male has a green head, white and brown body plumage, and can grow up to 50 cm/1.7 ft long. The female is speckled brown.

Shovell /'ʃʌvəl/ Cloudesley *c.*1650–1707. English admiral who took part, with George Rooke (1650–1709), in the capture of Gibraltar 1704. In 1707 his flagship *Association* was wrecked off the Isles of Scilly and he was strangled for his rings by an islander when he came ashore.

show trial public and well-reported trials of people usually accused of crimes against the state. In the USSR in the 1930s and 1940s Stalin carried out show trials against economic saboteurs, Communist Party members, army officers and even members of the Bolshevik leadership.

Shrapnel /'ʃræpnəl/ Henry 1761–1842. British army officer who invented shells containing bullets, to increase the spread of casualties, first used 1804; hence the word *shrapnel* to describe shell fragments.

Shreveport /'ʃriːvpɔːt/ port on the Red river, Louisiana, USA; population (1980) 205,800. Industries include oil, natural gas, steel, telephone equipment, glass, and timber. It was founded 1836, and named after Henry Shreeve, a riverboat captain who cleared a giant log jam.

shrew insectivorous mammal of the family Soricidae, found in Eurasia and the Americas. It is mouse-like, but with a long nose and pointed teeth. Its high metabolic rate means that it must eat almost constantly. The *common shrew Sorex araneus* is about 7.5 cm/3 in long. The *pigmy shrew Sorex minutus* is only about 50 cm/2 in long.

Shrewsbury, Earl of /'ʃrəʊzbəri/ title in the peerage of England, held by the family of Talbot since 1442. It is the premier earldom of England.

Shrewsbury /'ʃrəʊzbəri/ market town on the river Severn, Shropshire, England; population (1985) 87,300. It is the administrative headquarters of the county. To the east is the site of the Roman city of Viroconium (larger than Pompeii). In the 5th century, as Pengwern, Shrewsbury was capital of the kingdom of Powys, which later became part of Mercia. In the battle of Shrewsbury 1403, Henry IV defeated the rebels led by Hotspur (Sir Henry ◊Percy).

shrike 'butcher-bird' of the family Laniidae, of which there are over 70 species, living mostly in Africa, but also in Eurasia and North America. They often impale insects and small vertebrates on thorns. They can grow to 35 cm/14 in long, and have grey, black, or brown plumage.

shrimp a crustacean related to the ◊prawn. It has a cylindrical, semi-transparent body, with ten jointed legs. Some shrimps grow as large as 25 cm/10 in long.

The European *common shrimp Crangon vulgaris* is greenish, translucent, has its first pair of legs ending in pincers, possesses no rostrum (the beaklike structure which extends forward from the head in some crustaceans), and has comparatively shorter antennae than the prawn.

Shostakovich *Soviet composer Dmitry Shostakovich pictured in his study in 1954.*

Shropshire /ˈʃrɒpʃə/ county in W England
area 3,490 sq km/1,347 sq mi
towns administrative headquarters Shrewsbury; Telford, Oswestry, Ludlow
features on the Welsh border, it is bisected NW to SE by the Severn; the name is sometimes abbreviated to *Salop*, and was officially so known from 1974 until local protest reversed the decision 1980; Ellesmere is the largest of several lakes in the SW; and the Clee Hills rise to about 610 m/1,800 ft in the SW; Ironbridge Gorge open-air museum of industrial archaeology includes the Iron Bridge 1779
products chiefly agricultural: sheep and cattle
population (1987) 397,000.

shroud of Turin see ◊Turin shroud.

Shrove Tuesday in the Christian calendar, the day before the beginning of Lent. It is also known as *Mardi Gras* and, in the UK, *Pancake Day*, for the custom of eating rich things before the Lenten fast.

shrub a perennial, woody plant that typically produces several separate stems, at or near ground level, rather than the single trunk of most trees. A shrub is usually smaller than a tree, but there is no clear distinction between large shrubs and small trees.

Shultz /ʃults/ George P 1920– . US Republican politician, economics adviser to President ◊Reagan 1980–82, and secretary of state 1982–89.

Shultz taught as a labour economist at the University of Chicago before serving in the 1968–74 ◊Nixon administration, including secretary of Labor 1969–70 and secretary of the Treasury 1972–74. As State Department secretary, he was in charge of the formulation of US foreign policy. He was pragmatic and moderate, against the opposition of Defence Secretary Caspar ◊Weinberger.

Shute /ʃuːt/ Nevil. Pen name of Nevil Shute Norway 1899–1960. English novelist, who wrote *A Town Like Alice* 1949 and *On the Beach* 1957.

shuttle diplomacy a form of international diplomacy prominent in the 1970s where an independent mediator would travel between belligerent parties in order to try and achieve a compromise solution.

SI abbreviation for *Système International (d'Unités)* (French 'International System (of Metric Units)'). See ◊SI units.

Siachen Glacier /siˈætʃen/ Himalayan glacier at an altitude of 5,236 m/17,000 ft in the Karakoram mountains of N Kashmir. Occupied by Indian forces 1984, the glacier has been the focal point of a territorial dispute between India and Pakistan since independence 1947. Three wars in 1947, 1965, and 1971 resulted in the establishment of a temporary boundary between the two countries through the province of Jammu and Kashmir, but the accords failed to define a frontier in the farthest reaches of N Kashmir. Pakistan responded to the

Shropshire

1984 Indian action by sending troops to the heights of the nearby Baltoro Glacier.

sial in geochemistry and geophysics, term denoting the substance of the Earth's continental ◊crust, as distinct from the ◊sima of the ocean crust. The name is derived from *si*lica and *al*umina, its two main chemical constituents.

Sialkot /siˈælkɒt/ city in Punjab province, E Pakistan; population (1981) 302,000. Industries include the manufacture of surgical and sports goods, metalware, carpets, textiles, and leather goods.

siamang the largest ◊gibbon *Symphalangus syndactylus*, native to Malaysia and Sumatra. Siamangs have a large throat pouch to amplify the voice, making the territorial 'song' extremely loud. They are black-haired, up to 90 cm/3 ft tall, with very long arms (a span of 150 cm/5 ft).

Sian /ˌsiːˈæn/ former name of ◊Xian, China.

Sibelius /sɪˈbeɪliəs/ Jean (Christian) 1865–1957. Finnish composer. His works include nationalistic symphonic poems such as *En Saga* 1893 and *Finlandia* 1900, violin concerto 1904, and seven symphonies.

He studied the violin and composition at Helsinki and went on to Berlin and Vienna. In 1940 he abruptly ceased composing and spent the rest of his life as a recluse.

Siberia /saɪˈbɪəriə/ Asiatic region of the USSR, extending from the Urals to the Pacific
area 12,050,000 sq km/4,650,000 sq mi
towns Novosibirsk, Omsk, Krasnoyarsk, Irkutsk
features long and extremely cold winters
products hydroelectric power from rivers Lena, Ob, and Yenisei; forestry; mineral resources, including gold, diamonds, oil, natural gas, iron, copper, nickel, cobalt
history overrun by Russia 17th century, it was used from the 18th to exile political and criminal prisoners. The first *Trans-Siberian Railway* 1892–1905 from Leningrad (via Omsk, Novosibirsk, Irkutsk and Khabarovsk) to Vladivostok, approximately 8,700 km/5,400 mi, began to open it up.

Sibley /ˈsɪbli/ Antoinette 1939– . British dancer. Joining the Royal Ballet 1956, she became senior soloist 1960. Her roles included Odette/Odile, Giselle, and the betrayed girl in *The Rake's Progress*.

Sibyl /ˈsɪbɪl/ in Roman mythology, priestess of Apollo. She offered to sell ◊Tarquinius nine collections of prophecies, the *Sibylline Books*, but the price was too high. When she had destroyed all but three, he bought those for the identical price, and these were kept for consultation in emergency at Rome.

sic (Latin 'thus', 'so') sometimes found in brackets within a printed quotation to show that an apparent error is in the original.

Sichuan /ˌsɪtʃˈwɑːn/ formerly *Szechwan* province of central China
area 569,000 sq km/219,634 sq mi
capital Chengdu
towns Chongqing
features surrounded by mountains, it was the headquarters of the Nationalist government 1937–45, and China's nuclear research centres are here; it is China's most populous administrative area
products rice, coal, oil, natural gas
population (1986) 103,200,000.

Sicily /ˈsɪsəli/ (Italian *Sicilia*) largest Mediterranean island, an autonomous region of Italy; area 25,700 sq km/9,920 sq mi; population (1988) 5,141,000. Its capital is Palermo, and towns include the ports of Catania, Messina, Syracuse, and Marsala. It exports Marsala wine, olives, citrus, refined oil and petrochemicals, pharmaceuticals, potash, asphalt, and marble. The autonomous region of Sicily also includes the islands of ◊Lipari, Egadi, Ustica, and ◊Pantelleria. Etna, 3,323 m/10,906 ft high, is the highest volcano in Europe; its last major eruption was in 1971.

Conquered by most of the major powers of the ancient world, Sicily flourished under the Greeks

who colonized it during the 8th–5th centuries BC. It was invaded by Carthage, and became part of the Roman empire 241 BC–AD 476. In the Middle Ages it was ruled successively by the Arabs; by the Normans 1059–1194, who established the *Kingdom of the Two Sicilies* (that is, Sicily and the southern part of Italy); by the German emperors; and then by the Angevins, until the popular revolt known as the *Sicilian Vespers* 1282. Spanish rule was invited and continued in varying forms, with a temporary displacement of the Spanish Bourbons by Napoleon, until ◊Garibaldi's invasion 1860 resulted in the two Sicilies being united with Italy 1861.

Sickert /ˈsɪkət/ Walter (Richard) 1860–1942. British artist. His Impressionist cityscapes of London and Venice, portraits, and domestic interiors capture subtleties of tone and light, often with a melancholy air.

Sickert, in London from 1868, was born in Munich, the son of a Danish painter, and studied art at the Slade School. He established friendships with the artists Whistler and Degas. His work inspired the ◊Camden Town Group; examples include *Ennui* about 1913 (Tate Gallery, London).

sickle harvesting tool of ancient origin characterized by a curving blade with serrated cutting edge and short wooden handle. It was widely used in the Middle East and Europe for cutting wheat, barley, and oats from about 10,000 BC to the 19th century.

sickle-cell disease a hereditary blood disorder common among people of black African descent. It is characterized by distortion and fragility of the red blood cells, which are lost too rapidly from the circulation. This results in ◊anaemia. A curious effect of sickle-cell disease is to give protection against ◊malaria.

Siddons /ˈsɪdnz/ Sarah 1755–1831. Welsh actress. Her majestic presence made her most suited to tragic and heroic roles such as Lady Macbeth, Zara in Congreve's *The Mourning Bride*, and Constance in *King John*.

She toured the provinces with the company of Roger Kemble, her father, until she appeared in London to immediate acclaim. Her first success in Otway's *Venice Preserv'd* 1774 led to her appearing with ◊Garrick at Drury Lane. She continued with success until her retirement 1812.

sidereal period the orbital period of a body relative to the stars.

sidewinder type of rattlesnake *Crotalus cerastes* which lives in the deserts of the SW USA and Mexico, and moves by throwing its coils into a

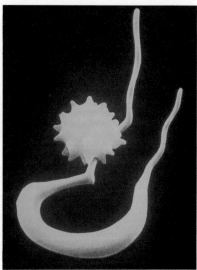

sickle-cell disease Scanning electron micrograph of the abnormal type of red blood cell that causes sickle-cell anaemia.

sideways 'jump' across the sand. It can grow up to 75 cm/2.5 ft long.

Sidi Barrâni /'sɪdi bəˈrɑːni/ coastal settlement in Egypt, about 370 km/230 mi W of Alexandria, the scene of much fighting 1940–42 during World War II.

Sidi-Bel-Abbès /'sɪdi 'bel æ'bes/ trading city in Algeria; population (1983) 187,000. Because of its strategic position, it was the headquarters of the French Foreign Legion until 1962.

Siding Spring Mountain peak 400 km/250 mi NW of Sydney, site of the 3.9 m/154 in *Anglo-Australian Telescope*, opened 1974, which was the first big telescope to be fully computer-controlled. It is one of the most powerful telescopes in the southern hemisphere.

Sidmouth, Viscount title of Henry ◊Addington, British Tory prime minister 1801–04.

Sidney /'sɪdni/ Philip 1554–1586. English poet and soldier, author of the sonnet sequence *Astrophel and Stella* 1591, *Arcadia* 1590, a prose romance, and *Apologie for Poetrie* 1595, the earliest work of English literary criticism. He was born in Penshurst, Kent. He entered Parliament 1581, and was knighted 1583. In 1585 he was made governor of Flushing in the Netherlands, and died at Zutphen, fighting the Spaniards.

Sidon /'saɪdn/ alternative name for ◊Saida, Lebanon.

Siegel /'siːgəl/ Don(ald) 1912– . US film director who made thrillers, Westerns, and police dramas. He also directed *Invasion of the Body Snatchers* 1956. His other films include *Madigan* 1968, *Dirty Harry* 1971, and *The Shootist* 1976.

Siegen /'ziːgən/ city in North Rhine-Westphalia, West Germany; population (1988) 107,000.

Siegfried /'siːgfriːd/, /'ziːkfriːt/ legendary Germanic hero, also known as ◊Sigurd. It is uncertain whether his story has a historical basis, but it was current about AD 700. A version is in the German *Nibelungenlied*.

Siegfried Line in World War I the defensive line established 1918 by the Germans in France; in World War II the name given by the Allies to the West Wall, the German defensive line established along its western frontier, from the Netherlands to Switzerland.

Siemens /'siːmənz/ family of four brothers, creators of a vast industrial empire. The eldest, *Ernst Werner von Siemens* (1812–92), founded the original electrical firm of Siemens und Halske 1847 and made many advances in telegraphy. *William (Karl Wilhelm)* (1823–83) perfected the open-hearth production of steel (now superseded), pioneered the development of the electric locomotive, the laying of transoceanic cables, and improvements in the electric generator.

siemens /'siːmənz/ SI unit (symbol S) of electrical conductance, the reciprocal of the ◊impedance of an electrical circuit. It was formerly called the mho or reciprocal ohm.

Siena /si'enə/ city in Tuscany, Italy; population (1985) 60,670. Founded by the Etruscans, it has medieval architecture by ◊Pisano and Donatello,

Sidney *Renaissance man Philip Sidney was a poet, politician, courtier, and soldier.*

Sierra Leone
Republic of

area 73,300 sq km/28,301 sq mi
capital Freetown
towns Bo, Kenema, Makeni
physical mountains in east; hills and forest; coastal mangrove swamps
features hot and humid climate (3,500 mm/138 in rainfall annually)
head of state and government Joseph Saidu Momoh from 1985
government one-party republic
political parties All People's Congress (APC), moderate socialist
exports palm kernels, cocoa, coffee, ginger, diamonds, bauxite, rutile
currency leone (200.89 = £1 Feb 1990)
population (1989) 4,318,000; annual growth rate 1.8%
life expectancy men 33, women 36
language English (official); local languages
religion Muslim 60%, animist 30%
literacy 38% male/21% female (1985 est)
GNP $1.2 bn (1983); $176 per head of population
chronology
1961 Achieved full independence as a constitutional monarchy within the Commonwealth, with Milton Margai, leader of the Sierra Leone People's Party (SLPP), as prime minister.
1964 Milton succeeded by his half-brother Albert Margai.
1967 General election results disputed by the army, who set up a National Reformation Council and forced the governor general to leave.
1968 Another army revolt made Siaka Stevens, leader of the All-People's Congress (APC), prime minister.
1971 New constitution adopted, making Sierra Leone a republic, with Stevens as president.
1978 APC declared the only legal party. Stevens sworn in for another seven-year term.
1985 Stevens retired at the age of 80 and was succeeded by Maj-Gen Joseph Momoh.
1989 Attempted coup against Momoh foiled.

including a 13th-century Gothic cathedral, and many examples of the Sienese school of painting which flourished from the 13th–16th century. The *Palio* ('banner', in reference to the prize) is a horse race in the main square, held annually since the Middle Ages.

Sienkiewicz /ˌʃeŋki'eɪvɪtʃ/ Henryk 1846–1916. Polish author. His books include *Quo Vadis?* 1895, set in Rome at the time of Nero, and the 17th-century historical trilogy *With Fire and Sword, The Deluge*, and *Pan Michael* 1890–93.

Sierra Leone /si'erə li'əʊn/ country in W Africa, on the Atlantic, bounded to the N and E by Guinea and to the SE by Liberia.

government The 1978 constitution makes Sierra Leone a one-party state, the party being the All People's Congress (APC). The constitution also provides for a president, who is both head of state and head of government, and a single-chamber legislature, the House of Representatives. The House has 127 members, 105 elected for five years by universal suffrage, 12 paramount chiefs, one for each district, and 10 additional members appointed by the president. The president, who is also leader and secretary general of the APC, is endorsed by the party as the sole candidate and then popularly elected for a seven-year term. The president appoints a cabinet and two vice presidents.

history For early history, see ◊Africa. Freetown, the capital, was founded by Britain 1787 for homeless Africans rescued from ◊slavery. Sierra Leone became a British colony 1808.

Sierra Leone achieved full independence, as a constitutional monarchy within the Commonwealth, in 1962, with Milton Margai, leader of the Sierra Leone People's Party (SLPP), as prime minister. He died in 1964 and was succeeded by his half-brother, Albert Margai. The 1967 general election was won by the APC, led by Siaka Stevens, but the result was disputed by the army, which assumed control and temporarily forced the governor-general to leave the country. In 1968 another army revolt brought back Stevens as prime minister and in 1971, after the constitution had been changed to make Sierra Leone a republic, he became president. He was re-elected in 1976 and the APC, having won the 1977 general election by a big margin, began to demand the creation of a one-party state. To this end, a new constitution

was approved by referendum in 1978, and Stevens was sworn in as president.

Stevens, who was now 80, did not run in 1985 and the APC endorsed the commander of the army, Maj-Gen Joseph Momoh, as the sole candidate for the party leadership and presidency. Momoh appointed a civilian cabinet and dissociated himself from the policies of his predecessor, who had been criticized for failing to prevent corruption within his administration. The last elections for the House of Representatives were held in May 1982 but annulled because of alleged irregularities. It was reported in Oct 1989 that an attempted coup against the government had been put down.

Sierra Madre /si'erə 'mɑːdreɪ/ chief mountain system of Mexico, consisting of three ranges, enclosing the central plateau of the country; highest point Pico de Orizaba 5,700 m/18,700 ft. The Sierra Madre del Sur ('of the south') runs along the SW Pacific coast.

Sierra Nevada /si'erə nɪ'vɑːdə/ mountain range of S Spain; highest point Mulhacén 3,481 m/ 11,425 ft.

Sierra Nevada /si'erə nɪ'vɑːdə/ mountain range in E California, USA; highest point Mount Whitney 4,418 m/14,500 ft. It includes the King's Canyon, Sequoia, and Yosemite Valley national parks.

sievert SI unit (symbol Sv) of dose equivalent. It is defined as the absorbed dose of ionizing radiation (with certain dimensionless factors to account for different types of radiation causing different effects in biological tissue) of 1 joule per kilogram. One sievert = 100 ◊rem.

Siger of Brabant /'siːgə, brə'bænt/ 1240–1282. Medieval philosopher, a follower of ◊Averroes, who taught at the University of Paris, and whose distinguishing between reason and Christian faith led to his works being condemned as heretical 1270. He refused to recant and was imprisoned. He was murdered while in prison.

sight the detection of light by an ◊eye, which can form images of the outside world.

Sigismund /'sɪgɪsmənd/ 1368–1437. Holy Roman emperor from 1411. He convened and presided over the council of Constance 1414–18, where he promised protection to the religious reformer ◊Huss, but imprisoned him after his condemnation for heresy, and acquiesced in his burning. King of Bohemia from 1419, he led the military campaign against the Hussites. He was the younger brother of Emperor Wenceslas (1361–1419).

Sigma Octantis the star closest to the south celestial pole (see ◊celestial sphere), in effect the southern equivalent of ◊Polaris, although far less conspicuous. Situated just less than 1° from the south celestial pole, Sigma Octantis is 120 light years away.

Signac /siːnˈjæk/ Paul 1863–1935. French artist. In 1884 he joined with ◊Seurat in founding the Société des Artistes Indépendants and developing the technique of ◊*Pointillism*.

Signac, born in Paris, was initially influenced by the great Impressionist Monet. He laid down the theory of Neo-Impressionism in his book *De Delacroix au Néo-Impressionisme* 1899. From the 1890s he developed a stronger and brighter palette. He and Matisse painted together in the south of France 1904–05.

signal a sign, gesture, sound, or action that conveys information. Examples include the use of flags (◊semaphore), light (traffic and railway signals), radio telephony, radio telegraphy (◊Morse code), and electricity (telecommunications and computer networks).

The International Code of Signals used by shipping was drawn up by an international committee and published 1931. The codes and abbreviations used by aircraft are dealt with by the International Civil Aviation Organization, established 1944.

Signorelli /ˌsiːnjəˈreli/ Luca c. 1450–1523. Italian painter, active in central Italy. About 1483 he was called to the Vatican to complete frescoes on the walls of the Sistine Chapel.

He produced large frescoes in Orvieto Cathedral, where he devoted a number of scenes to *The Last Judgment* 1499–1504. The style is sculptural and dramatic, reflecting late 15th-century Florentine trends, but Signorelli's work is especially imaginative. He settled in Cortona and ran a large workshop there producing altarpieces.

Sigurd in Norse mythology, a hero who appears in both the ◊*Nibelungenlied* (under his German name of ◊Siegfried) and the ◊*Edda*.

Sihanouk /ˌsiːəˈnuːk/ Norodom 1922– . Cambodian politician, king 1941–55, prime minister 1955–70, when his government was overthrown by a military coup led by Lon Nol. With Pol Pot's resistance front, he overthrew Lon Nol 1975, and again became prime minister 1975–76, when he was forced to resign by the Khmer Rouge.

Educated in Vietnam and Paris, he was elected king of Cambodia 1941. He abdicated 1955 in favour of his father, founded the Popular Socialist Community and governed as prime minister 1955–70.

After he was deposed in 1970, Sihanouk established a government in exile in Beijing and formed a joint resistance front with Pol Pot. This movement succeeded in overthrowing Lon Nol Apr 1975 and Sihanouk was reappointed head of state, but in Apr 1976 he was forced to resign by the communist Khmer Rouge leadership. Now living in North Korea, he became the recognized leader of the Democratic Kampuchea government in exile 1982.

Sikhism religion professed by 16 million Indians, living mainly in the Punjab. Sikhism was founded by Nanak (1469–c. 1539). Sikhs believe in a single God who is the immortal creator of the universe and who has never been incarnate in any form, and in the equality of all human beings; Sikhism is strongly opposed to caste divisions. Their holy book is the ◊*Guru Granth Sahib*. The *Khalsa* ('pure'), the company of the faithful, wear the five Ks: *kes*, long hair; *kangha*, a comb; *kirpan*, a sword; *kachh*, short trousers; and *kara*, a steel bracelet. Sikh men take the last name 'Singh' ('lion') and women 'Kaur' ('princess').

beliefs Human beings can make themselves ready to find God by prayer and meditation but can achieve closeness to God only as a result of God's *nadar* (grace). Sikhs believe in ◊reincarnation and

Sikkim

Gangtok

INDIAN OCEAN

that the ten human gurus were teachers through whom the spirit of Guru Nanak was passed on to live today in the *Guru Granth Sahib* and the *Khalsa*.

practice Sikhs do not have a specific holy day, but hold their main services on the day of rest of the country in which they are living. Daily prayer is important in Sikhism, and the gurdwara functions as a social as well as religious centre; it contains a kitchen, the *langar*, where all, male and female, Sikh and non-Sikh, may eat together as equals. Sikh women take the same role as men in religious observances; for example, in reading from the *Guru Granth Sahib* at the gurdwara. Festivals in honour of the ten human gurus include a complete reading of the *Guru Granth Sahib*; Sikhs also celebrate at the time of some of the major Hindu festivals, but their emphasis is on aspects of Sikh belief and the example of the gurus. Sikhs avoid the use of all nonmedicinal drugs and, in particular, tobacco.

history On Nanak's death he was followed as guru by a succession of leaders who converted the Sikhs (the word means 'disciple') into a military confraternity which established itself as a political power. The last of the gurus, Guru Gobind Singh (1666–1708), instituted the *Khanda-di-Pahul* ('baptism of the sword') and established the Khalsa. Gobind Singh was assassinated by a Muslim 1708, and since then the *Guru Granth Sahib* has taken the place of a leader.

Upon the partition of India many Sikhs migrated from W to E Punjab, and in 1966 the efforts of Sant Fateh Singh (c.1911–72) led to the creation of a Sikh state within India by partition of the Punjab. However, the Akali separatist movement agitates for a completely independent Sikh state, Khalistan, and a revival of fundamentalist belief was headed from 1978 by Sant Jarnail Singh Bhindranwale (1947–84), killed in the siege of the Golden Temple, ◊Amritsar. In retaliation for this, the Indian prime minister Indira Gandhi was assassinated in Oct of the same year by her Sikh bodyguards. Heavy rioting followed, in which 1,000 Sikhs were killed. Mrs Gandhi's successor, Rajiv Gandhi, reached an agreement for the election of a popular government in the Punjab and for state representatives to the Indian parliament with the moderate Sikh leader Sant Harchand Singh Longowal, who was himself killed 1985 by Sikh extremists.

Sikh Wars two wars in India between the Sikhs and the British:

First Sikh War 1845–46 following an invasion of British India by Punjabi Sikhs. The Sikhs were defeated and part of their territory annexed.

Second Sikh War 1848–49 arising from a Sikh revolt in Multan. They were defeated and the British annexed the Punjab.

Si-Kiang /ˈʃiː kiˈæŋ/ former name of ◊Xi Jiang, Chinese river.

Sikkim /ˈsɪkɪm/ or *Denjong* state of NE India; formerly a protected state, it was absorbed by

India 1975, the monarchy being abolished. China does not recognize India's sovereignty
area 7,300 sq km/2,818 mi
capital Gangtok
features Mount Kangchenjunga; wildlife including birds, butterflies, and orchids
products rice, grain, tea, fruit, soyabeans, carpets, cigarettes, lead, zinc, copper
population (1981) 316,000
language Bhutia, Lepecha, Khaskura (Nepáli) (all official)
religion Mahayana Buddhism, Hinduism.

Sikorski /sɪˈkɔːski/ Wladyslaw 1881–1943. Polish general and politician. In 1909, he formed the nationalist military organization which during World War I fought for the central powers. He was prime minister 1922–23 and war minister 1923–25. In Sept 1939 he became prime minister of the exiled Polish government, which transferred to London 1940. He was killed in an air crash.

Sikorski was born in Galicia, and served in the Russian war 1920. The intransigence of his government was a cause of Anglo-Russian friction, but allegations that his death was not accidental are unsubstantiated.

Sikorsky /sɪˈkɔːski/ Igor 1889–1972. Ukrainian engineer, who built the first successful helicopter. He emigrated to the USA 1918 where he first constructed multi-engined flying boats. His first helicopter (the VS300) flew 1939 and a commercial version (the R3) went into production 1943.

silage fodder preserved through controlled fermentation in a silo, an airtight structure that presses green crops. The term also refers to stacked crops that may be preserved indefinitely.

Silbury Hill /ˈsɪlbəri/ steep, rounded artificial mound (40 m/130 ft high) of the Bronze Age 2660 BC, in Wiltshire, near ◊Avebury, England. Excavation has shown it not to be a barrow (grave), as was previously thought.

Silchester /ˈsɪltʃɪstə/ archaeological site, a major town in Roman Britain. It is 10 km/6 mi N of Basingstoke, Hampshire.

silencer (North American *muffler*) a device in the exhaust system of cars and motorbikes. Gases leave the engine at supersonic speeds, and the exhaust system and silencer are designed to slow them down, thereby silencing them.

Some silencers use baffle plates (plates with holes, which disrupt the airflow), others use perforated tubes and an expansion box (a large chamber which slows down airflow).

Silenus /saɪˈliːnəs/ in Greek mythology, the son of Hermes, or Pan, and companion of ◊Dionysus. He is portrayed as a jovial old man, usually drunk.

Silesia /saɪˈliːziə/ long-disputed region of Europe, Austrian 1675–1745; Prussian/German 1745–1919 (following its seizure by ◊Frederick II); and in 1919 divided among newly formed Czechoslovakia, revived Poland, and Germany, which retained the major part. In 1945 all German Silesia east of the Oder–Neisse line was transferred to Polish administration; about 10 million inhabitants of German origin, both here and in Czechoslovak Silesia, were expelled.

The chief towns (with their German names) are: Wroclaw (Breslau), Katowice (Kattowitz), Zabrze (Hindenburg), Chorzow (Königshütte), Gliwice (Gleiwitz), and Bytom (Beuthen) in Poland, and Opava (Troppau) in Czechoslovakia.

silhouette a profile or shadow portrait filled in with black or a dark colour. A popular pictorial technique in the late 18th and early 19th centuries, it was named after Etienne de Silhouette (1709–67), a French finance minister who made paper cut-outs as a hobby.

silica silicon dioxide, SiO_2, the composition of the most common mineral group, of which the most familiar form is quartz. Other silica forms are ◊chalcedony, chert, opal, tridymite, and cristobalite. Chalcedony includes some semiprecious forms: gem varieties include agate, onyx, sardonyx, carnelian, and tiger's eye.

silicate a compound containing silicon and oxygen combined together as a negative ion (◊anion), together with one or more metal ◊cations.

Common natural silicates are sands (common sand is the oxide of silicon known as silica). Glass is a manufactured complex polysilicate material in which other elements (boron in borosilicate glass) have been incorporated.

silicon a non-metallic element, symbol Si, atomic number 14, relative atomic mass 78.09. It is used in glass-making, as a hardener in steel alloys, and in silicon chips for microcomputers.

Silicones are synthetic polymers based on a chain of oxygen and silicon atoms. They are types of plastic.

silicon chip an ◊integrated circuit with microscopically small electrical components on a piece of silicon crystal only a few millimetres square. Often with more than a million components, it is mounted in a rectangular plastic package and linked via gold wires to metal pins so that it can be connected to a printed circuit board for electronic devices such as computers, calculators, televisions, car dashboards, and domestic appliances.

Silicon Valley nickname given to Santa Clara county, California, since the 1950s the site of many high-technology electronic firms, whose prosperity is based on the silicon chip.

silicosis disease of miners and stone cutters who inhale flint dust, which makes lung tissue fibrous, less capable of aerating the blood, and less resistant to tuberculosis.

silk fine soft thread produced by the larva of the ◊silkworm moth, and used in the manufacture of textiles. The introduction of synthetics originally harmed the silk industry, but rising standards of living have produced an increased demand for real silk. China and Japan are the largest silk producers.

Silk Road ancient route by which silk was brought from China to Europe in return for trade goods; it ran via the Gobi Desert, Samarkand, Mount Ararat, and Transylvania.

silk-screen printing or *serigraphy* a method of printing based on stencilling. It can be used to print on most surfaces, including paper, plastic, cloth, and wood. A stencil (either paper or photographic) is attached to a finely meshed silk screen which has been stretched on a wooden frame, so that the ink only passes through to the paper beneath where

silicon chip False-colour microscope image of a computer memory chip. The tiny circuit components and interconnections are etched onto the chip during manufacture.

the image is required. Alternatively the design can be painted directly on to the screen with varnish. A series of screens can be used to add successive layers of colour to the design.

The process was developed in the early 20th century for comercial use and adopted by many artists from the 1930s onwards.

silkworm usually the larva of the *common silkworm moth Bombyx mori*. After hatching from the egg and maturing on the leaves of white mulberry trees (or a synthetic substitute), it 'spins' a protective cocoon of fine silk thread 275 m/900 ft long. It is killed before it can emerge as a moth to keep the thread intact, and several threads are combined to form the commercial silk thread woven into textiles.

Other moths produce different fibres, such as *tussah* from *Antheraea mylitta*. The raising of silkworms is called *sericulture* and began in China about 2,000 BC. Chromosome engineering and artificial selection practised in Japan have led to the development of different types of silkworm for different fibres.

Sillitoe /ˈsɪlɪtəʊ/ Alan 1928– . English novelist, who wrote *Saturday Night and Sunday Morning* 1958, about a working-class man in Nottingham, Sillitoe's hometown. He also wrote *The Loneliness of the Long Distance Runner* 1959, *Life Goes On* 1985, many other novels, and poems, plays, and children's books.

Sills /sɪlz/ Beverly 1929– . US operatic soprano. She sang with touring companies and joined the New York City Opera in 1955. In 1979 she became director of New York City Opera and retired from the stage in 1980.

silo in farming, an airtight tower in which ◊silage is made by the fermentation of freshly cut grass and other forage crops. In military technology, a silo is an underground chamber for housing and launching a ballistic missile.

Silone /sɪˈləʊneɪ/ Ignazio. Pen name of Secondo Tranquilli 1900–1978. Italian novelist. His novel *Fontamara* 1933 deals with the hopes and disillusionment of a peasant village from a socialist viewpoint. Other works include *Una manciata di more*/*A Handful of Blackberries* 1952.

Silurian period of geological time 438–408 million years ago, the third period of the Palaeozoic era. Silurian sediments are mostly marine, and consist of shales and limestone. The first land plants began to evolve during this period, and there were many jawless fish.

Silvanus /sɪlˈveɪnəs/ a Roman woodland deity identified in later times with ◊Pan.

silver lustrous metal, extremely malleable and ductile, symbol Ag (Latin *argentum*), atomic number 47, relative atomic mass 107.873. The chief ores are sulphides, from which the metal is extracted by smelting with lead. It is one of the best metallic conductors of both heat and electricity, and its most important compounds are the chloride and bromide which darken on exposure to light, the basis of photographic emulsions. Silver is used for tableware, jewellery, coinage, electrical contacts, electroplating, and as a solder. It has been known since prehistoric times. The world's greatest producer of silver is Mexico (approximately 40 million troy ounces per year), followed by the USA, Canada, Peru, the USSR, Australia, and Japan.

silver age period of Latin literature after the death of ◊Augustus, with writing rather too florid and rhetorical for modern taste; authors included Seneca, Juvenal, and Suetonius.

silverfish wingless insect, a type of ◊bristletail.

Silverstone Britain's premier motor-racing circuit. It is situated near Towcester, Northamptonshire, and was built on a disused airfield after World War II. It staged the first world championship Grand Prix on 13 May 1950, and became the permanent home of the British Grand Prix in 1987. Major features include the Becketts, Stowe and Club corners, the Abbey and Maggotts curves, the Hangar straight, and Woodcote.

Sim /sɪm/ Alastair 1900–1976. Scottish actor, usually in comedies. Possessed of a marvellously expressive face, he was ideally cast in eccentric roles, as in the title role in *Scrooge* 1951. His other films include *Inspector Hornleigh* 1939, *Green for Danger* 1945, and *The Belles of St Trinians* 1954.

sima in geochemistry and geophysics, term denoting the substance of the Earth's ocean ◊crust, as distinct from the ◊sial of the continent crust. The name is derived from *si*lica and *ma*gnesia, its two main chemical constituents.

Simenon /ˈsiːmənɒŋ/ Georges 1903–1989. Belgian crime writer. Initially a pulp fiction writer, in 1931 he created Inspector Maigret of the Paris Sûreté who appeared in a series of detective novels.

Simeon Stylites, St /ˈsɪmiən staɪˈlaɪtiːz/ *c.* 390–459. Syrian Christian ascetic, who practised his ideal of self-denial by living for 37 years on a platform on top of a high pillar. Feast day 5 Jan.

Simferopol /ˌsɪmfəˈrəʊpɒl/ city in the Crimea, Ukraine, USSR; population (1987) 338,000. Industries include the manufacture of soap and tobacco. It is on the site of the Tatar town of Ak-Mechet, conquered by the Russians 1783 and renamed.

simile a ◊figure of speech whose Latin name means 'likeness' and which in English uses the conjunctions 'like' and 'as' to express imaginative comparisons ('run like the devil'; 'as deaf as a post'). It is sometimes confused with ◊metaphor.

Not every comparison that uses these words is a simile; for example, 'The city of Bristol is like Bordeaux' simply and literally compares two ports. In 'The city of Bristol is like a fine old ship' a more imaginative comparison (not city with city, but city with ship) creates an analogical link between less obvious contexts, and is a simile.

Simla /ˈsɪmlə/ capital of Himachal Pradesh state, India, 2,300 m/7,500 ft above sea level, population (1980) 70,604. It was the summer administrative capital of British India 1864–1947.

Simmons /ˈsɪmənz/ Jean 1929– . British actress who starred in the films *Black Narcissus* 1947,

Simenon Georges Simenon, novelist of the world of crime.

Guys and Dolls 1955, and *Spartacus* 1960. She worked in Hollywood from the 1950s onwards, and retired in the early 1970s.

Simon /ˈsaɪmən/ (Marvin) Neil 1927– . US playwright. His stage plays (which were made into films) include the wryly comic *Barefoot in the Park* 1963, *The Odd Couple* 1965, and *The Sunshine Boys* 1972, and the more serious, autobiographical *Brighton Beach Memoirs* 1983 and *Biloxi Blues* 1985. He has also written screenplays and co-written musicals, including *Sweet Charity* 1966, *Promises, Promises* 1968, and *They're Playing Our Song* 1978.

Simon /siːˈmɒn/ Claude 1913– . French novelist. Originally an artist, he abandoned the 'time structure' in such novels as *La Route de Flandres/The Flanders Road* 1960, *Le Palace* 1962, and *Histoire* 1967. His later novels include *Les Géorgiques* 1981 and *L'Acacia* 1989. Nobel prize 1985.

Simon /ˈsaɪmən/ Herbert 1916– . US social scientist. He researched decision-making in business corporations, and argued that maximum profit was seldom the chief motive. Nobel Prize for Economics 1978.

Simon /ˈsaɪmən/ John Allsebrook, Viscount Simon 1873–1954. British Liberal politician. He was home secretary 1915–16, but resigned over the issue of conscription. He was foreign secretary 1931–35, home secretary again 1935–37, chancellor of the Exchequer 1937–40, and lord chancellor 1940–45.

Simon /ˈsaɪmən/ Paul 1942– . US pop singer and songwriter. In a folk-rock duo with Art Garfunkel (1942–), he had hits such as 'Mrs Robinson' 1968 and 'Bridge Over Troubled Water' 1970. His solo work includes the album *Graceland* 1986, for which he drew on Cajun and African music.

Simone Martini. Sienese painter; see ◊Martini, Simone.

Simonstown /ˈsaɪmənztaʊn/ naval base established in 1814 on False Bay, 37 km/23 mi S of Cape Town, South Africa.

si monumentum requiris, circumspice (Latin 'if you seek his monument, look about you') the epitaph of Christopher Wren in St Paul's Cathedral, London.

simony in the Christian church, the buying and selling of church preferments, now usually regarded as a sin. The term is derived from *Simon Magus* (Acts 8) who offered money to the Apostles for the power of the Holy Ghost.

simple harmonic motion (SHM) oscillatory or vibrational motion in which an object (or point) moves so that its acceleration towards a central point is proportional to its distance from it. A simple example is a pendulum, which also demonstrates another feature of SHM, that the maximum deflection is the same on each side of the central point.

A graph of the varying distance with respect to time is a sine curve, a characteristic of the oscillating current or voltage of an alternating current (AC), which is another example of SHM.

Simplon /ˈsæmplɒn/ (Italian *Sempione*) Alpine pass Switzerland–Italy. The road was built by Napoleon 1800–05, and the Simplon Tunnel 1906, 19.8 km/12.3 mi, is one of Europe's longest.

Simpson /ˈsɪmpsən/ (Cedric) Keith 1907–1985. British forensic scientist, head of department at Guy's Hospital, London, 1962–72. His evidence sent John Haig (the acid bath murderer) and Neville Heath to the gallows. In 1965 he identified the first 'battered baby' murder in England.

Simpson /ˈsɪmpsən/ James Young 1811–1870. British physician who was largely instrumental in the introduction of chloroform as an anaesthetic in 1847.

Simpson /ˈsɪmpsən/ N(orman) F(rederick) 1919– . British dramatist. His plays *A Resounding Tinkle* 1957, *The Hole* 1958, and *One Way Pendulum* 1959 show the logical development of an abnormal situation, and belong to the Theatre of the ◊Absurd. He also wrote a novel, *Harry Bleachbaker* 1976.

Simpson /ˈsɪmpsən/ Wallis Warfield, Duchess of Windsor 1896–1986. US socialite, twice divorced, who married the Duke of Windsor (formerly ◊Edward VIII) 1937, after his abdication.

Simpson Desert /ˈsɪmpsən/ desert area in Australia, chiefly in Northern Territory; area 145,000 sq km/56,000 sq mi. It was named after a president of the South Australian Geographical Society who financed its exploration.

simultaneous equations in mathematics, one of two or more algebraic equations that contain two or more unknown quantities which may have a unique solution. For example, in the case of two linear equations with two unknown variables, such as (i) $x + 3y = 6$ and (ii) $3y - 2x = 4$, the solution will be those unique values of x and y that are valid for both equations. Linear simultaneous equations can be solved by using algebraic manipulation to eliminate one of the variables, ◊coordinate geometry, or matrices (see ◊matrix).

One method of solution is first to eliminate one of the variables, for example, in the case above, by substituting for x in equation (ii) the value $6 - 3y$ obtained by rearranging equation (i); or by multiplying equation (i) by 2 (to give $2x + 6y = 12$) and adding this new equation to equation (ii) to give $9y = 16$, which is easily solved. Another method is by plotting the equations on a graph, because the two equations represent straight lines in coordinate geometry and the coordinates of their point of intersection are the values of x and y that are true for both of them. A third method of solving linear simultaneous equations involves manipulating matrices. If the equations represent either two parallel lines or the same line, then there will be no solutions or an infinity of solutions respectively.

sin disobedience to the will of God or the gods, as revealed in the moral code laid down by a particular religion. In Roman Catholic theology, a distinction is made between *mortal sins*, which, if unforgiven, result in damnation, and *venial sins*, which are less serious. In Islam, the one unforgivable sin is *shirk*, denial that Allah is the only god.

In Christian belief, humanity is in a state of *original sin* and therefore in need of redemption through the crucifixion of Jesus. The sacrament of ◊penance is seen as an earthly punishment for sin.

Sinai /ˈsaɪnaɪ/ Egyptian peninsula, at the head of the Red Sea; area 65,000 sq km/25,000 sq mi. Resources include oil, natural gas, manganese, and coal; irrigation water from the Nile is carried under the Suez Canal.

Sinai was occupied by Israel 1967–82. After the Battle of Sinai 1973, Israel began a gradual withdrawal from the area, under the disengagement agreement 1975, and the Camp David peace treaty 1979, and restored the whole of Sinai to Egyptian control by Apr 1982. Egypt established a religious complex (Jewish-Muslim-Christian) at Mount Sinai 1979.

Sinai, Mount /ˈsaɪnaɪ/ mountain near the tip of the Sinai Peninsula (Gebel Mûsa, 2,285 m/7,500 ft). In the Old Testament, this is allegedly where ◊Moses received the Ten Commandments from Jehovah.

Sinai, Battle of /ˈsaɪnaɪ/ battle 6–24 Oct 1973 which took place during the Yom Kippur War between Israel and Egypt. In one of the longest tank battles ever, the Israelis crossed the Suez canal 16 Oct cutting off the Egyptian 3rd Army.

Sinan /ˈsɪnɑːn/ 1489–1588. Ottoman architect, chief architect from 1538 to ◊Suleiman the Magnificent. Among the hundreds of buildings he designed are the Suleimaniye in Istanbul, a mosque complex, and the Topkapi Saray, palace of the Sultan (now a museum).

Sinatra /sɪˈnɑːtrə/ Frank (Francis Albert) 1915– . US singer and film actor. He achieved fame with the Tommy Dorsey band with songs such as 'Night and Day' and 'You'd Be So Nice To Come Home To'. After a slump in his career, he established

Sinatra US singer and film actor Frank Sinatra.

himself as an actor. *From Here to Eternity* 1953 won him an Academy Award. His later songs include 'My Way'.

Sinbad the Sailor or *Sindbad* in the ◊Arabian Nights, an adventurer who makes seven eventful voyages. He encounters the ◊Old Man of the Sea and, on his second voyage, is carried aloft by the roc, a giant bird.

Sinclair /ˈsɪŋkleə/ Clive 1940– . British electronics engineer, who produced the first widely available pocket calculator, pocket and wristwatch televisions, a series of popular home computers, and the innovative but commercially disastrous 'C5' personal transport (a low cycle-like three-wheeled device powered by a washing-machine motor).

Sinclair /ˈsɪŋkleə/ Upton 1878–1968. US novelist. His concern for social reforms is reflected in *The Jungle* 1906, which exposed the horrors of the Chicago stockyards and led to a change in food-processing laws, *Boston* 1928, and his Lanny Budd series 1940–53, including *Dragon's Teeth* 1942, which won a Pulitzer Prize.

Sind /sɪnd/ province of SE Pakistan, mainly in the Indus delta
area 140,914 sq km/54,393 sq mi
capital and chief seaport Karachi
population (1981) 19,029,000
language 60% Sindi; others include Urdu, Punjabi, Baluchi, Puhsto
features Sukkur Barrage, which enables water form the Indus river to be used for irrigation
history annexed 1843, it became a province of British India, and part of Pakistan on independence. There is agitation for its creation as a separate state, Sindhudesh.

Sinden /ˈsɪndən/ Donald 1923– . English actor, noted for his resonant voice and versatility. His roles range from Shakespearean tragedies to light comedies such as *There's a Girl in My Soup*, *Present Laughter*, and the television series *Two's Company*.

Sinding /ˈsɪndɪŋ/ Christian (August) 1856–1941. Norwegian composer. His works include four symphonies, piano pieces (including *Rustle of Spring*), and songs. His brothers Otto (1842–1909) and Stephan (1846–1922) were painter and sculptor, respectively.

sine in trigonometry, a function of an angle in a right-angled triangle defined as the ratio of the length of the side opposite the angle to the length of the hypotenuse (the longest side).

Various properties in physics vary sinusoidally, that is, they can be represented diagramatically by a sine wave (a graph obtained by plotting values of angles against the values of their sines). Examples include ◊simple harmonic motion, such as the way alternating current (AC) electricity varies with time.

sine die (Latin 'without a day being appointed') indefinitely.

sine qua non (Latin 'without which not') absolutely essential.

sinfonietta an orchestral work that is of a shorter, lighter nature than a ◊symphony.

sing. abbreviation for *singular*.

SINE OF AN ANGLE

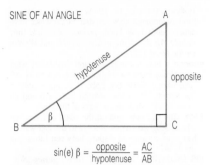

$$\sin(e)\ \beta = \frac{\text{opposite}}{\text{hypotenuse}} = \frac{AC}{AB}$$

sine wave

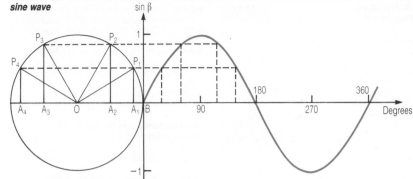

Note: $B\hat{O}P_4 = 180° - B\hat{O}P_1$ $\Rightarrow \sin B\hat{O}P_4 = \sin B\hat{O}P_1$
$B\hat{O}P_3 = 180° - B\hat{O}P_2$ $\&\ \sin B\hat{O}P_3 = \sin B\hat{O}P_2$

Singapore /ˌsɪŋəˈpɔː/ country in SE Asia, off the tip of the Malay Peninsula.

government Singapore has a single-tier system of government. The constitution of 1965 has provided for a one-chamber parliament, whose 81 members are elected for five-year terms by universal suffrage from single-member constituencies on a first-past-the-post basis. Parliament debates and votes on legislation and elects, for a four-year term, a ceremonial head of state (president). Executive power is held by a prime minister and cabinet drawn from the majority party within parliament. The dominant party in Singapore since independence has been the conservative People's Action Party.

history For early history, see ◊Malay Peninsula. Singapore was leased as a trading post in 1819 from the sultan of Johore by the British East India Company, on the advice of Stamford ◊Raffles, at a time when it was a swampy jungle. It passed to the crown in 1858 and formed part of the ◊Straits Settlements 1867–1942.

During World War II, Singapore functioned as a vital British military base in the Far East. Designed to be invulnerable to naval attack, it was invaded by land and occupied by Japan Feb 1942–Sept 1945. Singapore became a separate British crown colony in 1946 and fully self-governing, with ◊Lee Kuan Yew as prime minister, from 1959. It joined the Federation of ◊Malaysia in 1963, but seceded in 1965, alleging discrimination against the federation's Chinese members. A new independent republic of Singapore was thus formed in Sept 1965, which remained within the Commonwealth.

The new republic's internal political affairs were dominated by Prime Minister Lee Kuan Yew's People's Action Party, which gained a monopoly of all parliamentary seats in the elections between 1968 and 1980. Under Lee's stewardship, Singapore has developed rapidly as a commercial and financial entrepot and as a centre for new export industries. Today its inhabitants enjoy the highest standard of living in Asia outside Japan and Brunei.

Singapore *Singapore's city skyline.*

During the early 1980s, as the pace of economic growth briefly slowed, opposition to the Lee regime began to surface, with support for the PAP falling from 76% to 63% in the Dec 1984 election and two opposition deputies winning parliamentary seats for the first time. Lee responded by taking a firmer line against dissent, with J B Jeyaretnam, the Workers' Party leader, being conveniently found guilty of perjury in Nov 1986 and deprived of his parliamentary seat. Support for the PAP held steady, at 62%, in the Sept 1988 election and the opposition won only one seat. After the election, Lee announced that he intended to retire as prime minister by the end of 1990, handing over to his deputy, Goh Chok Tong. Plans were also unveiled to create a new position of elected executive president.

Singapore allied itself closely with the USA 1965–74. Since the mid-1970s, however, it has pursued a neutralist foreign policy and improved its relations with China. It is a member of ◊ASEAN.

Singapore City /ˌsɪŋəˈpɔː/ capital of Singapore, on the SE coast of the island of Singapore; population (1980) 2,413,945. It is an important oil refining centre and port.

Singer /'sɪŋə/ Isaac Bashevis 1904– . Polish novelist and short story writer. His works, written in Yiddish, often portray traditional Jewish life in Poland, and the loneliness of old age. They include *Gimpel the Fool* 1957, *The Slave* 1960, *Shosha* 1978, and *Old Love* 1979. Nobel prize 1978.

Singer /'sɪŋə/ Isaac Merit 1811–1875. US inventor of domestic and industrial sewing machines. Within a few years of opening his first factory 1851, he became the world's largest manufacturer (despite charges of patent infringement by Elias ◊Howe), and by the late 1860s more than 100,000 Singer sewing machines were in use in the USA alone. To make his machines available to the widest market, Singer became the first manufacturer to offer attractive hire-purchase terms.

Singh /sɪŋ/ Vishwanath Pratap 1931– . Indian politician, prime minister from 1989. As a member of the Congress (I) Party, he held ministerial posts under Indira Gandhi and Rajiv Gandhi, and from 1984 led an anti-corruption drive. When

Singer *Polish novelist and short-story writer Isaac Bashevis Singer.*

he unearthed an arms-sales scandal in 1988, he was ousted from the government and party and formed a broad-based opposition alliance, the *Janata Dal*, which won the 1989 election.

Singh was born in Allahabad, the son of a local raja. He was minister of commerce 1976–77 and 1983, Uttar Pradesh chief minister 1980–82, minister of finance 1984–86, and of defence 1986–87, when he discovered the embarrassing Bofors scandal. Respected for his probity and sense of principle, Singh emerged as one of the most popular politicians in India.

Singh, Gobind see ◊Gobind Singh, Sikh guru.

single sideband transmission radio wave transmission using either the frequency band above the carrier wave frequency, or below, instead of both (as now).

Sing Sing /'sɪŋ sɪŋ/ name until 1901 of the village of Ossining, New York, with a state prison of that name from 1825 (rebuilt 1930).

singularity in astrophysics, the point at the centre of a ◊black hole at which it is predicted that the infinite gravitational forces will compress the infalling mass of the collapsing star to infinite density. It is a point in space-time at which the known laws of physics break down.

Sinhalese member of the majority population of Sri Lanka. The Sinhalese language belongs to the Indo-Iranian branch of the Indo-European family.

Sining /ˌʃiːˈnɪŋ/ former name of the city of ◊Xining, Tsinghai province, W central China.

sinking fund money set aside for the repayment of debt. For a company, a sinking fund is used to allow annually for ◊depreciation; in the case of a nation, a sinking fund pays off a part of the national debt.

Singer *Inventor of the sewing machine, Isaac Merit Singer. He succeeded in mass-producing and selling them around the world.*

Singapore
Republic of

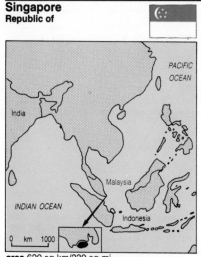

area 620 sq km/239 sq mi
capital Singapore City in the south of the
island, a major world port and financial centre,
founded by Stamford Raffles
physical comprises Singapore Island, which is
low and flat, and 57 small islands
features Singapore Island is joined to
the mainland by a causeway across the
Strait of Johore; temperature ranges only
24°–31°C/75°–88°F
head of state Wee Kim Wee from 1985
head of government Lee Kuan Yew from 1959
government liberal democratic republic

political parties People's Action Party (PAP)
conservative; Worker's Party (WP), socialist;
Singapore Democratic Party (SDP), liberal
pluralist
exports electronics, petroleum products,
rubber, machinery, vehicles
currency Singapore dollar (3.16 = £1 Feb
1990)
population (1989) 2,668,000 (Chinese
75%, Malay 14%, Tamil 7%); annual growth
rate 1.2%
life expectancy men 69, women 75
language Malay, Chinese, Tamil, and English
(all official)
religion Buddhist, Taoist, Muslim, Hindu,
Christian
literacy 93% male/79% female (1985 est)
GNP $17.9 bn (1984); $6,526 per head of
population
chronology
1819 Singapore leased to British East India
Company.
1858 Placed under Crown rule.
1942 Invaded and occupied by Japan.
1945 Japanese removed by British forces.
1959 Independence granted from Britain; Lee
Kuan Yew became prime minister.
1963 Joined new Federation of Malaysia.
1965 Left federation to become independent
republic.
1984 Opposition made advances in
parliamentary elections.
1986 Opposition leader convicted of perjury,
debarred from standing for election.
1988 The ruling conservative party elected to
all but one of the available assembly seats.

Sinn Féin /ʃin ˈfein/ Irish nationalist party
('We ourselves'), founded by Arthur Griffith
(1872–1922) in 1905; in 1917 ◊de Valera became its president. It is the political wing of
the Irish Republican Army, and is similarly split
between comparative moderates and extremists.
In 1985 it gained representation in 17 out of 26
district councils in Northern Ireland.

Sino-Japanese Wars wars waged by Japan against
China to expand to the mainland.
First Sino-Japanese War 1894–95. Under the
treaty of Shimonoseki, Japan secured the 'independence' of Korea, cession of Taiwan and the
nearby Pescadores Islands, and the Liaodong
peninsula (for a naval base). France, Germany,
and Russia pressured Japan into returning the
last-named, which Russia occupied 1896 to establish Port Arthur (now Lüda); this led to the
Russo-Japanese War 1904–05.
Second Sino-Japanese War 1931–45.
1931–32 The Japanese occupied Manchuria,
which they formed into the puppet state of
Manchukuo. They also attacked Shanghai, and
moved into NE China.
1937 Chinese leaders Chiang Kai-shek and Mao
Zedong allied to fight the Japanese; war was renewed as the Japanese overran NE China and
seized Shanghai and Nanjing.
1938 Japanese capture of Wuhan and Guangzhou
was followed by the transfer of the Chinese
capital to Chongqing; a period of stalemate followed.
1941 Japanese attack on the USA (see ◊Pearl
Harbor) led to the extension of lend-lease aid to
China and US entry into war against Japan and
its allies.
1944 A Japanese offensive threatened Chongqing.
1945 Chinese received the Japanese surrender
at Nanjing in Sept, after the Allies had concluded
World War II.

Sinuiju /ˌsinwiːˈdʒuː/ capital of North Pyongan
province, near the mouth of the Yalu river,
North Korea; population (1984) 754,000. It was
founded 1910.

sinusitis painful inflammation of one of the sinuses,
or air spaces, that surround the nasal passages.

Most cases clear with antibiotics and nasal de-
congestants, but some require surgical drainage.
It most frequently involves the maxillary sinuses,
within the cheek bones, to produce pain around
the eyes, toothache, and a nasal discharge.

Sioux /suː/ principal group of the Dakota family
of North American ◊Plains Indians, now found in
South Dakota and Nebraska. They defeated Gen
George Custer at Little Bighorn, Montana (under
chiefs Crazy Horse and Sitting Bull); as a result,
Congress abrogated the Fort Laramie treaty of
1868 (which had given the Indians a large area in
the Black Hills of Dakota). Gold, uranium, coal,
oil and natural gas are found there, and the Sioux
were awarded $160 million compensation 1980.

Sioux Falls /ˈsuː ˈfɔːlz/ largest city in South
Dakota, USA; population (1980) 81,343. Its industry (electrical goods and agricultural machinery) is powered by the Big Sioux river over the
Sioux Falls 30 m/100 ft.

siphon a tube in the form of an inverted U with
unequal arms. When it is filled with liquid and the
shorter arm is placed in a tank or reservoir, liquid
flows out of the longer arm provided that its exit
is below the level of the surface of the liquid in
the tank.

It works on the principle that the pressure at the
liquid surface is atmospheric pressure, whereas at
the lower end of the longer arm it is less than
atmospheric pressure, causing flow to occur.

siren in Greek mythology, a sea nymph who lured
sailors on to rocks by her singing. ◊Odysseus, in
order to hear the sirens safely, tied himself to the
mast and stuffed his crew's ears with wax; the
Argonauts escaped them because the singing of
Orpheus surpassed that of the sirens.

Sirius or *Dog Star* the brightest star in the sky,
8.7 light years away in the constellation Canis
Major. Sirius is a white star with a mass of 2.35
Suns, diameter 1.8 times that of the Sun, and a
luminosity of 23 Suns. It is orbited every 50 years
by a white dwarf, Sirius B.

Sirk /sɜːk/ Douglas. Assumed name of Claus
Detlef Sierck 1900–1987. Danish film director,
who studied in Germany but left 1937 because
of the Nazi regime, and eventually went to

Hollywood. During the 1950s he made a series of
lurid melodramas about capitalist USA which have
subsequently been highly praised by critics; they
include *All that Heaven Allows* 1956 and *Written
on the Wind* 1957.

sirocco a hot, normally dry and dust-laden wind
that blows from the highland of Africa to N Africa, Malta, Sicily, and Italy. It occurs mainly in
the spring. The name sirocco has been applied
to southerly winds in the east of the USA.

Sirte, Gulf of /ˈsɜːti/ gulf off the coast of Libya, on
which Benghazi stands. Access to the gulf waters
has been a cause of dispute between Libya and
the USA.

SIS abbreviation for *Special Intelligence Service.*

sisal strong fibre made from various species of
◊agave, such as *Agave sisalina.*

siskin greenish-yellow bird *Carduelis spinus* in the
finch family Fringillidae, about 12 cm/5 in long,
found in Eurasia.

Sisley /ˈsizli/ Alfred 1839–1899. French Impressionist painter, known for his views of Port-Marly
and the Seine, which he painted during floods
in 1876.

Sisley studied in an academic studio in Paris,
where he met Monet and Renoir. They took part
in the First Impressionist Exhibition 1874. Unlike
that of most other Impressionists, Sisley's style
developed slowly and surely, without obviously
changeful periods. He was almost exclusively a
landscape painter.

Sistine Chapel a chapel in the Vatican, Rome, begun
under Pope Sixtus IV in 1473 by Giovanni del Dolci,
and decorated by (among others) Michelangelo.
It houses the conclave that meets to select a
new pope.

Built to the proportions of Solomon's temple
in the Old Testament (its height one-half and its
width one-third of its length), it has frescoes on
the walls (emphasizing the authority and legality
of the papacy) by ◊Botticelli, ◊Ghirlandaio, and on
the altar wall and ceiling by ◊Michelangelo.

Sisulu /sɪˈsuːluː/ Walter 1912– . South African
civil-rights activist, the first full-time secretary
general of the ANC (African National Congress),
in 1964, with Nelson Mandela. He was imprisoned
in the 1964 ◊Rivonia Trial for opposition to the
apartheid system and released, at the age of 77,
as a gesture of reform by President F W ◊De
Klerk 1989.

Sisyphus /ˈsisifəs/ in Greek mythology, king of
Corinth who, after his evil life, was condemned
in the underworld to roll a huge stone uphill,
which always fell back before he could reach
the top.

Sita in Hinduism, the wife of Rama, an avatar (manifestation) of the god Vishnu; a character in the

siphon

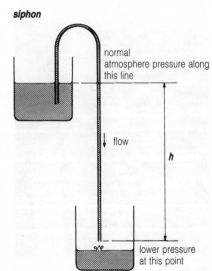

normal
atmosphere pressure along
this line

flow

h

lower pressure
at this point

Sitting Bull Sioux Indian chief Sitting Bull, who fought a rearguard action against white incursions into Indian lands. He defeated General Custer at the Battle of Little Big Horn.

◊*Rāmāyana* epic, characterized by chastity and kindness.

sitar Indian stringed instrument, having a pear-shaped body, long neck, and an additional gourd resonator at the opposite end. A principal solo instrument, it has seven metal strings extending over movable frets and two concealed strings that provide a continuous singing drone.

sitatunga herbivorous antelope *Tragelaphus spekei* found in several swamp regions in Central Africa. The hooves are long and splayed to help progress on soft surfaces. They are up to about 1.2 m/4 ft high at the shoulder; the males have thick horns up to 90 cm/3 ft long. Males are dark greyish-brown, females and young are chestnut, all with whitish markings on the rather shaggy fur.

Sitting Bull /'sɪtɪŋ 'bʊl/ *c.*1834–1893. North American Indian chief who led the ◊Sioux onslaught against Gen ◊Custer.

Sitwell /'sɪtwəl/ Edith 1887–1964. English poet, whose series of poems *Façade* was performed as recitations to the specially written music of ◊Walton from 1923.

Sitwell /'sɪtwəl/ Osbert 1892–1969. English poet and author, elder brother of Edith and Sacheverell Sitwell.

Sitwell /'sɪtwəl/ Sacheverell 1897–1988. English poet and art critic. His work includes *Southern Baroque Art* 1924 and *British Architects and Craftsmen* 1945; poetry; and prose miscellanies such as *Of Sacred and Profane Love* 1940 and *Splendour and Miseries* 1943.

SI units (French *Système International d'Unités*) standard system of scientific units used by scientists worldwide. Originally proposed in 1960, it replaces the ◊m.k.s., ◊c.g.s., and ◊f.p.s. systems. It is based on seven basic units: the metre (m) for length, kilogram (kg) for weight, second (s) for time, ampere (A) for electrical current, kelvin (K) for temperature, mole (mol) for amount of substance, and candela (cd) for luminosity.

Siva /'ʃiːvə/ or **Shiva** in Hinduism, the third chief god (with Brahma and Vishnu). As Mahadeva (great lord), he is the creator, symbolized by the phallic *lingam*, who restores what as Mahakala

Siva *Nataraja: Siva as Lord of the Dance. A bronze statue from Madras State, probably Tanjore-Pudukottai region. It is of the Chola dynasty, which ruled in the 10th century AD.*

he destroys. He is often sculpted as Nataraja, performing his fruitful cosmic dance. His consort or female principle (*sakti*) is Parvati, otherwise known as Durga or Kali.

Six, the the original six signatory countries to the Treaty of Rome which created the ◊European Community.

Six Acts in British history, acts of Parliament passed 1819 by Lord Liverpool's Tory administration to curtail political radicalism in the aftermath of the ◊Peterloo massacre and during a period of agitation for reform when ◊habeas corpus was suspended and the powers of magistrates extended.

The acts curtailed the rights of the accused by stipulating trial within a year; increased the penalties for seditious libel; imposed a newspaper stamp duty on all pamphlets and circulars containing news; specified strict limitations on public meetings; banned training with guns and other arms; and empowered magistrates to search and seize arms.

skating British skaters Christopher Dean and Jayne Torvill present Barnum on Ice at the World Championships, Helsinki, 1983.

ice-skating: recent winners

World Championship

men
1980 Jan Hoffman *(East Germany)*
1981 Scott Hamilton *(USA)*
1982 Scott Hamilton *(USA)*
1983 Scott Hamilton *(USA)*
1984 Scott Hamilton *(USA)*
1985 Alexsander Fadeev *(USSR)*
1986 Brian Boitano *(USA)*
1987 Brian Orser *(Canada)*
1988 Brian Boitano *(USA)*
1989 Kurt Browning *(Canada)*

women
1980 Annett Potzsch *(East Germany)*
1981 Denise Beillmann *(Switzerland)*
1982 Elaine Zayak *(USA)*
1983 Rosalynn Sumners *(USA)*
1984 Katerina Witt *(East Germany)*
1985 Katerina Witt *(East Germany)*
1986 Debi Thomas *(USA)*
1987 Katerina Witt *(East Germany)*
1988 Katerina Witt *(East Germany)*
1989 Midoria Ito *(Japan)*

pairs
1980 Sergei Shakrai and Marina Tcherkasova *(USSR)*
1981 Igor Lisovsky and Irina Vorobyeva *(USSR)*
1982 Tassilo Thierbach and Sabine Baess *(East Germany)*
1983 Oleg Vasiliev and Yelena Valova *(USSR)*
1984 Paul Martini and Barbara Underhill *(Canada)*
1985 Oleg Vasiliev and Yelena Valova *(USSR)*
1986 Sergei Grinkov and Ekaterina Gordeeva *(USSR)*
1987 Sergei Grinkov and Ekaterina Gordeeva *(USSR)*
1988 Oleg Vasilyev and Yelena Valova *(USSR)*
1989 Sergei Grinkov and Ekaterina Gordeeva *(USSR)*

ice dance
1980 Andras Sallay and Krisztine Regoczy *(Hungary)*
1981 Christopher Dean and Jayne Torvill *(Great Britain)*
1982 Christopher Dean and Jayne Torvill *(Great Britain)*
1983 Christopher Dean and Jayne Torvill *(Great Britain)*
1984 Christopher Dean and Jayne Torvill *(Great Britain)*
1985 Andrei Bukin and Natalia Bestemianova *(USSR)*
1986 Andrei Bukin and Natalia Bestemianova *(USSR*
1987 Andrei Bukin and Natalia Bestemianova *(USSR)*
1988 Andrei Bukin and Natalia Bestemianova *(USSR)*
1989 Sergei Ponamarenko and Marina Klimova *(USSR)*

Six Articles an act introduced by Henry VIII in England in 1539, to settle disputes over dogma in the English Church. The articles affirmed belief in transubstantiation, communion in one kind only, auricular confession, monastic vows, celibacy of the clergy, and private masses; those who rejected transubstantiation were to be burned at the stake. The act was repealed in 1547, replaced by 42 articles in 1551, and by an act of Thirty-Nine Articles in 1571.

Six Counties the six counties which form Northern Ireland, namely Antrim, Armagh, Down, Fermanagh, Londonderry, and Tyrone.

Six, Les a group of French 20th-century composers; see ◊*Les Six*.

sixth form in UK education, an inclusive term used for pupils who study for one or two years beyond school-leaving age in order to gain ◊A Level or other post-15 qualifications.

Sixtus /'sɪkstəs/ five popes, including:

Sixtus IV 1414–1484. Pope from 1471. He built the Sistine Chapel in the Vatican, which is named after him.

Sixtus V 1521–1590. Pope from 1585, who supported the Spanish Armada against Britain and the Catholic League against Henry IV of France.

SJ abbreviation for *Society of Jesus* (see ◊Jesuits).

Sjælland /'ʃelənd/ or *Zealand* the main island of ◊Denmark, on which Copenhagen is situated; area 7,000 sq km/2,700 sq mi; population (1970) 2,130,000. It is low-lying with an irregular coastline. The chief industry is dairy farming.

Skagerrak /'skægəræk/ arm of the North Sea between the S coast of Norway and the N coast of

skeleton

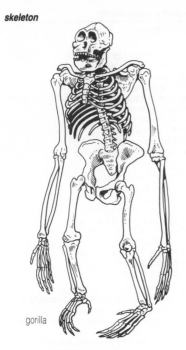

gorilla

fish (perch)

crab
(carapace and exoskeleton)

stag beetle (exoskeleton)

skate several species of flatfish of the ray group. The **common skate** *Raja batis* is up to 1.8 m/6 ft, greyish, with black specks. The egg-cases ('mermaids's purses') are often washed ashore by the tide.

skateboard single flexible board mounted on wheels, and steerable by weight positioning. As a land alternative to surfing, skateboards developed in California in the 1960s and became a worldwide craze in the 1970s. Skateboarding is practised in urban environments and enjoyed a revival in the late 1980s.

skating self-propulsion on ice by means of bladed skates, or on other surfaces by skates with small rollers. The chief competitive events are figure skating, for singles or pairs, ice-dancing, and simple speed skating.

Ice-skating became possible as a world sport from the opening of the first artificial ice rink in London, England, 1876. The first world ice-skating championships were held 1896. *Figure skating* includes both compulsory figures and freestyle combinations to music; *ice-dancing* is increasingly a choreographed combination of ballet and popular dance movements welded to an artistic whole, exemplified by John Curry and the team of Jayne Torvill and Christopher Dean.

The roller skate was the invention of James L Plympton, who opened the first rink at Newport, Rhode Island, USA, 1866; events are as for ice-skating.

Skegness /ˌskegˈnes/ holiday resort on the coast of Lincolnshire, England; population (1985) 14,553. It was the site of the first ◊Butlin holiday camp.

skeleton the rigid or semi-rigid framework, composed of bone, cartilage, chitin, and calcium carbonate or silica, found in all vertebrate animals and some invertebrates. It supports the animal's body, as well as protecting the internal organs and providing anchorage points for the muscles.

It may be internal, forming an ◊*endoskeleton*, or external, forming an ◊*exoskeleton*. Another type of skeleton, found in invertebrates such as earthworms, is the *hydrostatic skeleton*. This gains partial rigidity from fluid enclosed within a body cavity. Because the fluid cannot be compressed, contraction of one part of the body results in extension of another part, giving peristaltic motion.

Skelmersdale /ˈskelməzdeɪl/ town in Lancashire, England, west of Wigan; population (1985) 41,800. It was developed as a 'new town' from 1962, with many light industries, including electronics, engineering, and textiles.

skiing: recent winners

Alpine World Cup
men—overall
1980 Andreas Wenzel *(Liechtenstein)*
1981 Phil Mahre *(USA)*
1982 Phil Mahre *(USA)*
1983 Phil Mahre *(USA)*
1984 Pirmin Zurbriggen *(Switzerland)*
1985 Marc Girardelli *(Luxembourg)*
1986 Marc Girardelli *(Luxembourg)*
1987 Pirmin Zurbriggen *(Switzerland)*
1988 Pirmin Zurbriggen *(Switzerland)*
1989 Marc Girardelli *(Luxembourg)*
women
1980 Hanni Wenzel *(Liechtenstein)*
1981 Marie-Therese Nadig *(Switzerland)*
1982 Erika Hess *(Switzerland)*
1983 Tamara McKinney *(USA)*
1984 Erika Hess *(Switzerland)*
1985 Michela Figini *(Switzerland)*
1986 Maria Walliser *(Switzerland)*
1987 Maria Walliser *(Switzerland)*
1988 Michela Figini *(Switzerland)*
1989 Vreni Schneider *(Switzerland)*

Skelton /ˈskeltən/ John *c.* 1460–1529. English poet, who was tutor to the future Henry VIII. His satirical poetry includes the rumbustious *The Tunnyng of Elynor Rummynge* 1516, and political attacks on Wolsey, such as *Colyn Cloute* 1522.

Skiddaw /ˈskɪdɔː/ mountain (930 m/3,052 ft) in Cumbria, England; in the Lake District, north of Keswick.

skiffle a style of British popular music, introduced by the singer and banjo player Lonnie Donegan (1931–) in 1956, using improvised percussion instruments such as tea chests and washboards.

skiing self-propulsion on snow by means of elongated runners for the feet, slightly bent upward at the tip. As a sport, events include downhill (with speeds up to 125 km/80 mi per hour); slalom, in which a series of turns between flags have to be negotiated; cross-country racing; and ski jumping, when jumps of over 150 m/400 ft are achieved from ramps up to 90 m/295 ft high.

Skiing was known from about 3000 BC, but developed into a sport only from 1896 when it became possible to manoeuvre more accurately. The *Fédération Internationale des Skieurs* (1924) is linked with the Ski Club of Great Britain (1924), the Canadian Amateur Ski Association (1920), and the National Ski Association of America (1904).

Skikda /ˈskɪkdɑː/ trading port in Algeria; population (1983) 141,000. Products include wine, citrus, and vegetables. It was founded by the

Denmark. In May 1916 it was the scene of the Battle of ◊Jutland.

Skåne /ˈskɔːnə/ or **Scania** area of S Sweden. It is a densely populated and fertile agricultural region, comprising the counties of Malmöhus and Kristianstad. Malmö and Hälsingborg are important centres. It was under Danish rule until ceded to Sweden 1658.

Skara Brae /ˈskærə ˈbreɪ/ preserved Neolithic village in the Orkney Islands, Scotland, on Mainland.

skiing Swiss skier Pirmin Zurbriggen at the World Championships 1989.

skin

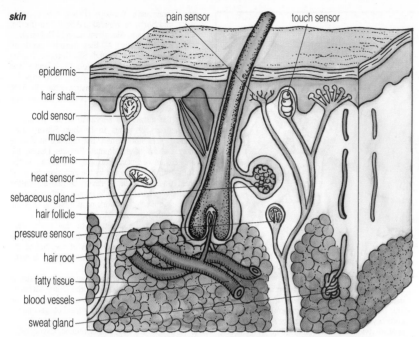

pain sensor   touch sensor
epidermis
hair shaft
cold sensor
muscle
dermis
heat sensor
sebaceous gland
hair follicle
pressure sensor
hair root
fatty tissue
blood vessels
sweat gland

French 1838 as Philippeville, and renamed after independence 1962.

skin the covering of the body of a vertebrate. In mammals, its outer layer (epidermis) is dead and protective, and the cells of this are constantly being rubbed away and replaced from below. The lower layer (dermis) contains blood vessels, nerves, hair roots, and the sweat and sebaceous glands, and is supported by a network of fibrous and elastic cells.

Skin grafting is the repair of injured skin by placing pieces of skin taken from elsewhere on the body so that the cells may multiply and cover it. The study of skin is called dermatology.

skink lizard of the family Scincidae, a large family of about 700 species found throughout the tropics and subtropics. The body is usually long, and the legs reduced. Some are actually legless and rather snake-like. Many are good burrowers, or can 'swim' through sand, like the *sandfish* genus *Scincus* of N Africa. Some skinks lay eggs, others bear live young.

Skinks include the *three-toed skink Chalcides chalcides* of S Europe and NW Africa, up to 40 cm/1.3 ft long, of which half is tail, and the *stump-tailed skink Tiligua rugosus* of Australia, which stores fat in its triangular tail, looks the same at either end, and feeds on fruit as well as small animals.

Skinner /'skɪnə/ B(urrhus) F(rederic) 1903– . US psychologist, a radical behaviourist who rejects mental concepts, seeing the organism as a 'black box' where internal processes are not important in predicting behaviour. He studied operant conditioning and stressed that behaviour is shaped and maintained by its consequences. His radical approach rejected almost all previous psychology; his text *Science and Human Behaviour* 1953 contains no references and no bibliography.

Skipton /'skɪptən/ industrial (engineering) town in North Yorkshire, England; population (1981) 13,246.

skittles or *ninepins* game in which nine wooden pins, arranged in a diamond-shaped frame at the end of an alley, are knocked down in two rolls from the other end of the alley with a wooden ball. Two or more players can compete. Skittles resembles ◊tenpin bowling. A smaller version *table skittles* is played indoors on a table using a pivoted ball attached to a pole by a chain.

Skolimowski /ˌskɒlɪ'mɒfski/ Jerzy 1938– . Polish film director, formerly a writer, active both in his native country and Western Europe. His films include *Deep End* 1970, *The Shout* 1978, and *Moonlighting* 1982.

Skopje /'skɒpjeɪ/ capital and industrial city of Macedonia, Yugoslavia; population (1981) 506,547. Industries include iron, steel, chromium mining, and food processing.

It stands on the site of an ancient town destroyed by earthquake in the 5th century, and was taken in the 13th century by the Serbian king Milutin, who made it his capital. Again destroyed by earthquake 1963, Skopje was rebuilt on a safer nearby site. It is an Islamic centre.

Skryabin /skri'æbin/ Alexander (Nikolayevich) 1872–1915. Russian composer and pianist. His powerfully emotional tone poems, such as *Prometheus* 1911, and symphonies, such as *Divine Poem* 1903, employed unusual harmonies.

skua dark-coloured gull-like seabird living in arctic and antarctic waters. Skuas can grow up to 60 cm/2 ft long, and are good fliers. They are aggressive scavengers, and will seldom fish for themselves but force gulls to disgorge their catch, and will also eat chicks of other birds. The largest species is the *great skua Stercorarius skua* of the N Atlantic, 60 cm/2 ft long and dark brown on the upper parts.

skull in vertebrates, the collection of flat and irregularly shaped bones (or cartilage) that encloses and protects the brain. In mammals, the skull consists of 22 plates of bone joined by sutures. The floor of the skull is pierced by a large hole for the spinal cord and a number of smaller apertures through which other nerves and blood vessels pass.

The bones of the face hold the upper teeth, enclose the sinuses, and form the framework for the eyes, nose, and mouth. The lower jaw is hinged to the middle of the skull at its lower edge. The plate at the back of the head is jointed at its lower edge with the upper section of the spine. Inside, the skull has various shallow cavities into which fit different parts of the brain.

skunk North American mammal of the weasel family. The *common skunk Mephitis mephitis* has a long, arched body, short legs, a bushy tail, and black fur with white streaks on the back. In self-defence, it discharges a foul-smelling fluid.

skydiving the sport of freefalling from an aircraft at up to 3,650 m/12,000 ft, performing aerobatics, and opening a parachute when 600 m/2,000 ft from the ground.

Skye /skaɪ/ largest island of the Inner Hebrides, Scotland; area 1,740 sq km/672 sq mi; population (1981) 8,000. It is separated from the mainland by the Sound of Sleat. The chief port is Portree. The economy is based on crofting, tourism, and livestock. Bonnie Prince Charlie (◊Charles Edward Stuart) took refuge here after ◊Culloden.

Skylab US space station, launched 14 May 1973, made from the adapted upper stage of a Saturn V rocket. At 75 tonnes, it was the heaviest object ever put into space, and was 25.6 m/84 ft long. Skylab contained a workshop for carrying out experiments in weightlessness, an observatory for monitoring the Sun, and cameras for photographing Earth's surface.

Damaged during launch, it had to be repaired by the first crew of astronauts. Three crews, each of three astronauts, occupied Skylab for periods of up to 84 days, at that time a record duration for

Skylab *A close-up view of the Skylab space station cluster, taken from the command module during the 'fly–around' inspection.*

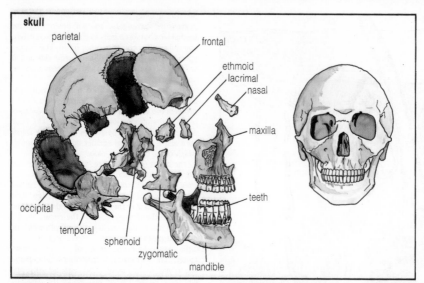

skull

parietal
frontal
ethmoid
lacrimal
nasal
maxilla
teeth
occipital
temporal
sphenoid
zygomatic
mandible

human spaceflight. Skylab finally fell to Earth on 11 July 1979, dropping debris on the outback of Western Australia.

skylark a type of ◊lark.

Skyros /'skaɪrɒs/ or *Skiros* Greek island, one of the ◊Sporades; area 209 sq km/81 sq mi. It is noted for its furniture and weaving. Rubert Brooke is buried here.

skyscraper a building so tall that it appears to 'scrape the sky', developed 1868 in New York, USA, where land prices were high and the geology suited to such methods of construction. Skyscrapers are now found in cities throughout the world. The world's tallest free-standing structure is the CN (Canadian National) Tower, Toronto, 555 m/1,821 ft.

In Manhattan, New York, are the Empire State Building (1931), 102 storeys and 381 m/1,250 ft high, and the twin towers of the World Trade Center 415 m/1,361 ft, but these were surpassed by the Sears Tower (1973) 443 m/1,454 ft in Chicago. Chicago was the home of the first skyscraper, the Home Insurance Building (1885), which was built ten storeys high with an iron and steel frame. A rigid steel frame is the key to skyscraper construction, taking all the building loads. The walls simply 'hang' from the frame (curtain walling), and they can thus be made from relatively flimsy materials such as glass and aluminium.

Slade /sleɪd/ Felix 1790–1868. British art collector, born in London. He bequeathed most of his art collection to the British Museum and endowed Slade professorships in fine art at Oxford, Cambridge, and University College, London. The *Slade School of Fine Arts* is a branch of the latter.

slaked lime calcium hydroxide, $Ca(OH)_2$, which is produced by adding water to quicklime (calcium oxide, CaO). Much heat is given out and the solid crumbles as it absorbs water. A solution of slaked lime is called ◊limewater.

slander spoken defamatory statement, although if broadcast on radio or television it constitutes ◊libel. In the UK slanders are generally only actionable if pecuniary loss has been suffered except where, for example, the slander imputes that a person is incapable of his or her profession. As in the case of libel, the slander must be made to some person other than the person defamed for it to be actionable.

slang extremely informal language usage. It is not usually accepted in formal speech or writing, and includes expressions that may be impolite or taboo in conventional terms.

Forms of slang such as army slang or Cockney rhyming slang are often extended into more general use because social conditions make them fashionable or people have grown accustomed to using them. Some types of slang are highly transient; others may last across generations, and gain currency in the standard language. Because slang is often vivid, suggestive, and linked with subjects such as defecation, urination, sex, blasphemy, and getting drunk, many people find it offensive. It is, however, pervasive in its influence and effects.

Slapton Sands beach in Devon, England, where during World War II, on the night of 27/28 Apr 1944 a convoy of landing craft carrying US troops on a pre-D-day exercise was by chance attacked by German E-boats (fast, armed boats). There were nearly 1,000 casualties, but the incident was not made public in case the Germans realized that Normandy was the intended Allied landing place, rather than the Pas-de-Calais.

slate a fine-grained, usually grey metamorphic rock that splits readily into thin slabs along its ◊cleavage plane. It is the metamorphic equivalent of ◊shale.

Slate is highly resistant to atmospheric conditions and can be used for writing on with chalk (actually gypsum). Quarrying slate takes such skill and time that it is now seldom used for roof and sill material except in restoring historic buildings.

Slav a member of an Indo-European people, speaking Slavonic languages, whose ancestors included the ◊Sarmatians and ◊Scythians. They fall into three groups: Eastern (Russians, Byelorussians, and Ukrainians); Western (Poles, Czechs, Slovaks, and Sorbs or Wends) and Southern (Serbs, Croats, Slovenes, Macedonians, and Bulgars).

By the 7th century AD they were the predominant population of E and SE Europe. During the 9th century they adopted Christianity, and in the course of the Middle Ages were expelled from what is now East Germany. After the 16th century they settled in Siberia on an increasingly large scale.

slavery the involuntary servitude of one person to another or one group to another. Slavery goes back to prehistoric times, but declined in Europe after the fall of the Roman Empire. During the imperialism of Spain, Portugal, and Britain in the 16th–18th centuries and in the American South in the 17th–19th centuries, slavery became a mainstay of an agricultural factory economy, with millions of Africans abducted to work on plantations in North and South America. Millions more died in the process, but the profits from this trade were enormous. Slavery was abolished in the British Empire 1833 and in the USA at the end of the Civil War 1863–65, but continues illegally in some countries.

Chattel slavery involves outright ownership of the slave by a master, but there are forms of partial slavery where an individual is tied to the land, or to another person, by legal obligations, as in ◊serfdom.

As a social and economic institution, slavery originated in the times when humans adopted sedentary farming methods of subsistence rather than more mobile forms of hunting and gathering. Slave labour became commonplace in ancient Greece and Rome, when it was used to cultivate large estates and to meet the demand for personal servants in the towns. Slaves were created through the capture of enemies, through birth to slave parents, through sale into slavery by free parents, and as a means of punishment.

After the fall of the Roman Empire in the 5th century, slavery persisted in Arab lands and in central Europe, where many Slavs were captured and taken as slaves to Germany (hence the derivation of the word). In Spain and Portugal, where the reconquest of the peninsula from the Moors in the 15th century created an acute shortage of labour, captured Muslims were enslaved. They were soon followed by slaves from Africa, imported by the Portuguese prince Henry the Navigator after 1444. Slaves were used for a wide range of tasks, and a regular trade in slaves was established between the Guinea Coast and the slave markets of the Iberian peninsula.

Slavery became of major economic importance after the 16th century with the European conquest of

skyscraper

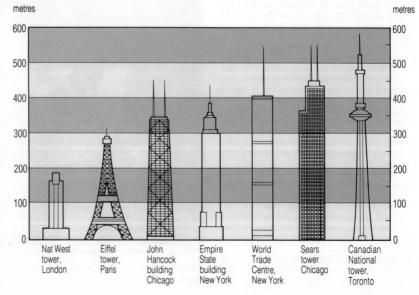

metres

600
500
400
300
200
100
0

Nat West tower, London | Eiffel tower, Paris | John Hancock building Chicago | Empire State building New York | World Trade Centre, New York | Sears tower Chicago | Canadian National tower, Toronto

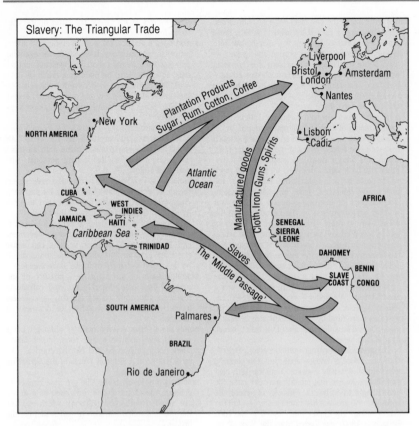

Slavery: The Triangular Trade

South and Central America. Needing a labour force but finding the indigenous inhabitants unwilling or unable to cooperate, the Spanish and Portuguese conquerors used ever-increasing numbers of slaves drawn from Africa. These slaves had a great impact on the sugar and coffee plantations. A lucrative triangular trade was established with alcohol, firearms, and textiles being shipped from Europe to be traded for slaves in Africa. The slaves would then be shipped to South or Central America where they would be traded for staples such as molasses and later raw cotton. In 1619 the first black slaves landed in an English colony in North America (Virginia). The huge profits became an important element in the British economy and the West Indian trade in general. It has been estimated that the British slave trade alone shipped 2 million slaves from Africa to the West Indies between 1680 and 1786. The total slave trade to the Americas in the single year of 1790 may have exceeded 70,000. According to another estimate, during the nearly 400 years of the slave trade, a total of 15 million slaves were delivered to buyers and some 40 million Africans lost their lives in the dreaded 'middle crossing'.

Anti-slavery movements and changes in the political and economic structure of Europe helped to bring about the abolition of slavery in most of Europe during the later 18th and early 19th century, followed by abolition in overseas territories somewhat later.

Only in the Southern states of the USA did slavery persist as a major, if not essential, component of the economy—providing the labour force for the cotton and other plantations. While the Northern states abolished slavery in the 1787–1804 period, the Southern states insisted on protecting the institution. Slavery became an issue in the economic struggles between Southern plantation owners and Northern industrialists in the first half of the 19th century, a struggle that culminated in the American Civil War.

Despite the common perception to the contrary, the war was not fought primarily on the slavery issue. Abraham Lincoln, however, saw the political advantages of promising freedom for Southern slaves, and the Emancipation Proclamation was enacted in 1863. This was reinforced after the war by the 13th, 14th, and 15th amendments to the US constitution (1865, 1868, and 1870), which abolished slavery altogether and guaranteed citizenship and civil rights to former slaves. Apart from the moral issues, there has also been debate on the economic efficiency of slavery as a system of production in the USA. It has been argued that plantation owners might have been better off employing labour, although the effect of emancipating vast numbers of slaves could, and did, have enormous political and social repercussions in the Reconstruction period following the Civil Wars after 1865.

Although outlawed in most countries of the world, various forms of slavery continue to exist—as evidenced by the steps taken by international organizations such as the League of Nations between the world wars and the United Nations since 1945 to curb such practices.

The 1926 League of Nations Slavery Convention was adopted by the UN 1953. Slavery was officially abolished in Saudi Arabia in 1963, and in Mauritania not until 1980. It was reported in Dec 1988 that slaves were being sold in Sudan. In 1989 China launched a national campaign against the abduction and sale of women and children. In Shaanxi province 2,000 such cases were uncovered in 1989 and in Sichuan 7,000 cases in 1990.

Slavkov /ˈslæfkɒf/ Czech name of ♦Austerlitz.

Slavonic languages or *Slavic languages* a branch of the Indo-European language family spoken in Central and Eastern Europe, the Balkans, and parts of N Asia. The family comprises the *southern group* (Serbo-Croat, Slovene, and Macedonian in Yugoslavia, and Bulgarian in Bulgaria); the *western group* (Czech and Slovak in Czechoslovakia, Sorbian in East Germany, and Polish and its related dialects); and the *eastern group* (Russian, Ukrainian, and Byelorussian in the USSR).

There is such a high degree of uniformity among the Slavonic languages that scholars speak of a 'dialect continuum' in which the users of one variety understand tolerably well much of what is said in other varieties. Some Slavonic languages, like Polish, are written in the Roman alphabet while others, like Russian, use the Cyrillic alphabet.

Slavophile intellectual and political group in 19th-century Russia which promoted the idea of an Eastern orientation for the empire in opposition to those who wanted the country to adopt Western methods and ideas of development.

SLBM abbreviation for *submarine-launched ballistic missile*; see ♦nuclear warfare.

SLD abbreviation for ♦*Social and Liberal Democrats*.

sleep a state of reduced awareness and activity that occurs at regular intervals in most mammals and birds, though there is considerable variation in the amount of time spent sleeping. Sleep differs from hibernation in occurring daily rather than seasonally, and involving less drastic reductions in metabolism. People deprived of sleep become irritable, uncoordinated, forgetful, hallucinatory, and even psychotic.

In humans sleep is linked with hormone levels and specific brain electrical activity, including delta waves, quite different from the brain's waking activity. REM (rapid eye movement) phases, associated with dreams, occur at regular intervals during sleep, when the eyes move rapidly below closed lids.

Sleep /sliːp/ Wayne 1948– . British dancer who was principal dancer with the Royal Ballet 1973–83 and formed his own company, Dash, in 1980.

sleeping pill a hypnotic, which may be anxiolytic (reduce anxiety) in smaller doses.

sleeping sickness an infectious disease of tropical Africa. Early symptoms include fever, headache, and chills, followed by ♦anaemia and joint pains. Later, the disease attacks the central nervous system, causing drowsiness, lethargy, and, if left untreated, death. Control is by eradication of the tsetse fly which transmits the disease to humans.

sleet precipitation consisting of a mixture of water and ice. In the UK, the term is usually applied to partly melted falling snow or hail. In the USA, it often describes frozen raindrops or snow that has melted and refrozen.

slide rule mathematical instrument with pairs of logarithmic sliding scales, used for rapid calculations, including multiplication, division, and the extraction of square roots.

It was invented 1622 by William Oughtred (1575–1660). A later version was devised by the French army officer Amédée Mannheim (1831–1906).

Sligo /ˈslaɪɡəʊ/ county in the province of Connacht, Republic of Ireland, situated on the Atlantic coast of NW Ireland; area 1,800 sq km/695 sq mi; population (1986) 56,000. The county town is Sligo; there is livestock and dairy farming.

Slim /slɪm/ William Joseph, 1st Viscount Slim 1891–1970. British field marshal in World War II. A veteran of Gallipoli, Turkey, in World War I, he commanded the 14th 'forgotten' army 1943–45, stemming the Japanese invasion of India at Imphal and Kohima, and then recovered Burma. He was governor general of Australia 1953–60.

slime mould or *myxomycete* an extraordinary organism which shows some features of ♦fungi and some of ♦protozoa. Slime moulds are not closely related to any other group, although they are often classed, for convenience, with the fungi.

Cellular slime moulds go through a phase of living as single cells, looking like amoebae, and feed by engulfing the bacteria found in rotting wood, dung, or damp soil. When a food supply is exhausted, up to 100,000 of these amoebae form into a colony resembling a single sluglike animal and migrate to a fresh source of bacteria. The colony then takes on the aspect of a fungus, and forms long-stalked fruiting bodies which release spores. These germinate to release amoebae, which repeat the life cycle.

Plasmodial slime moulds have a more complex life cycle involving sexual reproduction. They form a slimy mass of protoplasm with no internal cell walls, which slowly spreads over the bark or branches of trees.

Sloane /sləʊn/ Hans 1660–1753. British physician, born in County Down, Ireland. He settled in London, and in 1721 founded the Chelsea Physic Garden, London. He was president of the Royal College of Physicians 1719–35, and in 1727 succeeded Newton as president of the Royal Society. His library, which he bequeathed to the nation, formed the nucleus of the British Museum.

sloe fruit of the ◊blackthorn.

sloth South American mammal, about 70 cm/2.3 ft long, of the order Edentata. Sloths are greyish brown and have small rounded heads, rudimentary tails, and prolonged forelimbs. Each foot has long curved claws adapted to clinging upside down from trees. They are vegetarian.

Species include the **three-toed sloth** or **ai** *Bradypus tridactylus*, and the **two-toed sloth** *Choloepus didactylus* of northern South America.

Slough /slaʊ/ industrial town (pharmaceuticals, electronics, engineering) in Berkshire, England, near Windsor; population (1981) 97,000.

Slovakia /sləʊ'vaːkiə/ region in the east of Czechoslovakia settled in the 5th–6th centuries by Slavs; occupied by the Magyars in the 10th century; part of the kingdom of Hungary until 1918, when it became a province of ◊Czechoslovakia. Slovakia was a puppet state under German domination 1939–45, and was abolished as an administrative division in 1949. Its capital and chief town was Bratislava.

Slovene a member of the Slav people of Slovenia, and parts of the Austrian Alpine provinces of Styria and Carinthia; their language resembles Serbo-Croat. Austria and Yugoslavia disagree over the rights of Slovenes in S Carinthia.

Slovenia /sləʊ'viːniə/ or *Slovenija* constituent republic of NW Yugoslavia
area 20,300 sq km/7,836 sq mi
capital Ljubljana
physical mountainous; rivers Sava and Drava
features the wealthiest republic: contains 7% of the population of Yugoslavia, but produces 15% of Yugoslavia's GNP
products grain, sugarbeet, livestock, timber, cotton and woollen textiles, steel, vehicles
population (1986) 1,930,000, including 1,710,000 Slovenes
language Slovene, resembling Serbo-Croat, written in Roman characters
religion Roman Catholic
history settled by the Slovenes 6th century; until 1918 it was the Austrian province of Carniola; an autonomous republic of Yugoslavia 1946. In Sept 1989 it voted to give itself the right to secede from Yugoslavia.

slow-worm harmless species of lizard *Anguis fragilis*, common in Europe. Superficially resembling a snake, it is distinguished by its small mouth and movable eyelids. It is about 30 cm/1 ft long, and eats worms and slugs.

SLR abbreviation for *single-lens reflex*, a type of camera in which the image is seen in the lens used for taking the photo.

slug air-breathing gastropod related to snails, but with absent or much reduced shell. The **grey field slug** *Deroceras reticulatum* is a common British species, and a pest to crops and garden plants.

slug obsolete unit of mass, equal to 14.6 kg/32.17 lb. It is the mass that will have an acceleration of 1 foot per second per second when under a force of 1 pound weight.

Sluter /'sluːtə/ Claus c. 1380–1406. N European sculptor, probably of Dutch origin, active in Dijon, France. His work, in an expressive Gothic style, includes the *Well of Moses* c. 1395–1403 (now in the grounds of a hospital in Dijon) and the kneeling mourners, or *gisants*, for the tomb of his patron Philip the Bold, duke of Burgundy (Dijon Museum and Cleveland Museum, Ohio).

smack slang term for ◊heroin, an addictive depressant drug.

small arms one of the two main divisions of firearms, guns that can be carried by hand. The first small arms were portable handguns in use in the late 14th century, supported on the ground and ignited by hand. Modern small arms range from breech-loading single shot rifles and shotguns to sophisticated automatic and semi-automatic weapons. In 1980, there were 11,522 deaths in the USA caused by hand-held guns; in the UK, there were 8.

The matchlock, evolved during the 15th century, used a match of tow and saltpetre gripped by an S-shaped lever which was rocked towards the touch hole with one finger, enabling the gun to be held, aimed, and fired in much the same way as today. Front and back sights, followed by a curved stock which could be held against the shoulder (in the hackbut or Hookgun), gave increased precision. The difficulty of keeping a match alight in wet weather was overcome by the introduction of the wheel lock, in about 1515, in which a shower of sparks was produced by a spring-drawn steel wheel struck by iron pyrites. This cumbrous and expensive mechanism evolved into the simpler flintlock in about 1625, operated by flint striking steel and in general use for 200 years until a dramatic advance, the 'percussion cap', invented in 1810 by a sport-loving Scottish cleric, Alexander Forsyth (1769–1843), removed the need for external igniters. Henceforth, weapons were fired by a small explosive detonator placed behind or within the base of the bullet, struck by a built-in hammer.

The principles of rifling, breech loading, and the repeater, although known since the 16th century, were not successfully exploited until the 19th century. It was known that imparting a spin made the bullet's flight truer, but the difficulty of making the bullet bite the grooves had until then prevented the use of rifling. The Baker rifle, issued to the Rifle Brigade in 1800, was loaded from the front of the barrel (muzzle), and had a mallet for hammering the bullets into the grooves.

The first breech loader was Von Dreyse's 'needle gun', issued to the Prussian army in 1842, in which the detonator was incorporated with the cartridge. By 1870 breech-loading was in general use, being quicker, and sweeping the barrel out after each firing. An early rifle with bolt action was the Lee-Metford 1887, followed by the Lee-Enfield, both having a magazine beneath the breech, containing a number of cartridges. A modified model is still used by the British army. US developments favoured the repeater (such as the Winchester) in which the fired case was extracted and ejected, the hammer cocked, and a new charge inserted into the chamber, all by one reciprocation of a finger lever. In the semi-automatic, part of the explosion energy performs the same operations: the Garand, used by the US army, is of this type. Completely automatic weapons were adopted during World War II. From 1954 the British army standardized upon the Belgian FN 30, which is gas operated and can fire shots singly or automatically at 650–700 rounds per minute.

small claims court in the USA, a court that deals with small civil claims, using a simple procedure. In Britain, similar bodies introduced experimentally in London and Manchester have now ceased. The term is sometimes used for the arbitration procedure in county courts in the UK, where a simplified procedure applies for small claims.

smallpox contagious viral disease, marked by fever and skin eruptions leaving pitted scars. Widespread vaccination programmes have almost eradicated this disease.

It was endemic in Europe until the development of vaccination, and remained so in Asia, where a virulent form of the disease (variola major) entailed a fatality rate of 30% until the World Health Organization campaign from 1967, which resulted in its eradication by 1980. The virus now survives only in storage in various research institutes.

Smart /smaːt/ Christopher 1722–1771. English poet. In 1756 he was confined to an asylum, where he wrote his poems *A Song to David* and *Jubilate*

Agno/Rejoice in the Lamb, the latter appreciated today for its surrealism.

smart card a plastic card with an embedded microprocessor and memory. It can store, for example, personal data, identification, and bank account details, to enable it to be used as a credit or debit card. The card can be 'loaded' with credits that are then spent electronically, and reloaded as needed. Possible other uses range from hotel door 'keys' to passports.

The smart card was invented by French journalist Juan Moreno in 1974. By the year 2000 it will be possible to make cards with as much computing power as the leading personal computers of 1990.

smell a sense that responds to chemical molecules in the air. It works by having receptors for particular chemical groups, into which the airborne chemicals must fit to trigger a message to the brain.

A sense of smell is used to detect food and to communicate with other animals (see ◊pheromone and ◊scent gland). Aquatic animals can sense chemicals in water, but whether this sense should be described as 'smell' or 'taste' is debatable.

smelling salts or *sal volatile* a mixture of ammonium carbonate, bicarbonate, and carbamate together with other strong smelling substances; formerly used as a restorative for dizziness or fainting.

smelt small fish, usually marine, although some species are freshwater, and some live in lakes. They occur in Europe and North America. The most common European smelt is the **sparling** *Osmerus eperlanus*.

smelting processing a metallic ore in a furnace to produce the metal. Oxide ores such as iron ore are smelted with coke (carbon), which reduces the ore into metal and also provides fuel for the process.

A substance such as limestone is often added during smelting to facilitate the melting process and to form a slag, which dissolves many of the impurities present.

Smersh formerly the main administration of counter-intelligence in the USSR, established 1942. It was a subsection of the ◊KGB.

Smetana /'smetənə/ Bedřich 1824–1884. Czech composer, whose music has a distinct national character, for example, the operas *The Bartered Bride* 1866, *Dalibor* 1868, and the symphonic suite *My Country* 1875–80. He conducted the National Theatre of Prague 1866–74.

Smiles /smaɪlz/ Samuel 1812–1904. Scottish writer, author of the popular Victorian didactic work *Self Help* 1859.

Smirke /smɜːk/ Robert 1780–1867. English Classical architect, designer of the British Museum, London (1823–47).

Smith /smɪθ/ Adam 1723–1790. Scottish economist, often regarded as the founder of modern political economy. His *The Wealth of Nations* 1776 defined national wealth in terms of labour. The cause of wealth is explained by the **division of labour** – dividing a production process into several repetitive operations, each carried out by different workers. Smith advocated the free working of individual enterprise, and the necessity of 'free trade'.

He was born in Kirkcaldy, and was professor of moral philosophy at Glasgow 1752–63. He published *Theory of Moral Sentiments* 1759.

Smith /smɪθ/ Bessie 1894–1937. US jazz and blues singer, born in Chattanooga, Tennessee. She established herself in the 1920s, but her popularity waned in the Depression, and she died after a car crash when she was refused admission to a whites-only hospital. She was known as the Empress of the Blues.

Smith /smɪθ/ David 1906–1965. US sculptor and painter, whose work made a lasting impact on sculpture after World War II. He trained as a steel welder in a car factory. His pieces are large openwork metal abstracts.

Smith turned first to painting and then, about 1930, to sculpture. Using welded steel, he created

Smith Adam Smith, Scottish economist and author of The Wealth of Nations.

abstract structures influenced by the metal sculptures of Picasso. In the 1940s and 1950s he developed a more linear style. The *Cubi* series of totemlike abstracts, some of them painted, were designed to be placed in the open air.

Smith /smɪθ/ Henry George Wakelyn 1787–1860. British general. He served in the Peninsular War. Subsequently he fought in South Africa and India, and was governor of Cape Colony 1847–52. The towns of Ladysmith and Harrismith, South Africa, are named after his wife and himself respectively.

Smith /smɪθ/ Ian Douglas 1919– . Rhodesian politician. He was a founder of the Rhodesian Front 1962 and prime minister 1964–1979. In 1965 he made a unilateral declaration of Rhodesia's independence, and despite United Nations sanctions maintained his regime with tenacity. In 1979 he was succeeded as prime minister by Bishop Abel Muzorewa, when the country was renamed Zimbabwe. He was suspended from the Zimbabwe parliament in Apr 1987 and resigned in May as head of the white opposition party.

Smith /smɪθ/ John 1580–1631. English colonist. After an adventurous early life he took part in the colonization of Virginia, acting as president of the North American colony 1608–09. He explored New England in 1614, which he named, and published pamphlets on America and an autobiography. During an expedition among the American Indians his life is said to have been saved by ◊Pocahontas, whom he married.

Smith /smɪθ/ John Maynard 1920– . British biologist, see ◊Maynard Smith, John.

Smith /smɪθ/ Joseph 1805–1844. US founder of the ◊Mormon religious sect. Smith, born in Vermont, received his first religious call in 1820, and in 1827 claimed to have been granted the revelation of the *Book of Mormon* (an ancient prophet), inscribed on gold plates and concealed a thousand years before in a hill near Palmyra, New York State. He founded the Church of Jesus Christ of Latter-day Saints in Fayette, New York, 1830. The Mormons were persecuted for their beliefs and Smith was killed in Illinois.

Smith /smɪθ/ Maggie (Margaret Natalie) 1934– . English actress. Her roles include the title part (winning an Oscar) in the film *The Prime of Miss Jean Brodie* 1969. Other films include *California Suite* 1978, *A Private Function* 1984, and *A Room with a View* 1986.

Smith /smɪθ/ Matthew 1879–1960. British artist, known for his exuberant treatment of nudes, luscious fruits and flowers, and landscapes.

Smith /smɪθ/ Ross Macpherson 1892–1922 and Keith Macpherson Smith 1890–1955. Australian aviators and brothers, who made the first England-to-Australia flight 1919.

Smith British actress Maggie Smith playing the title role in the film The Prime of Miss Jean Brodie 1969.

Smith /smɪθ/ 'Stevie' (Florence Margaret) 1902–1971. British poet, noted for eccentrically direct verse, whose books include *Novel on Yellow Paper* 1936, and the volumes of poems *A Good Time was had by All* 1937, and *Not Waving but Drowning* 1957.

Smith /smɪθ/ William 1769–1839. British geologist, the founder of English geology. Working as a canal engineer, he noticed while supervising excavations that different beds of rock could be identified by their fossils, and so established the basis of ◊stratigraphy. He also produced the first geological maps of England and Wales.

Smithfield /'smɪθfiːld/ site of a meat market 1868 and poultry and provision market 1889, in the City of London, England. Formerly an open space, it was the scene of the murder of Wat ◊Tyler 1381, and the execution of many Protestant martyrs in the 16th century. The annual Bartholomew Fair was held here 1614–1855.

Smithson /'smɪθsən/ James 1765–1829. British chemist and mineralogist. The *Smithsonian Institute* in Washington DC, USA, was established in 1846, following his bequest of $100,000 for this purpose, and includes a museum, art gallery, zoo park, and astrophysical observatory.

Smiths, the English four-piece rock group (1982–87) from Manchester. Their songs, with lyrics by singer Morrissey (1959–) and tunes by guitarist Johnny Marr (1964–), drew on diverse sources such as rockabilly, Mersey beat, and the Byrds, with confessional humour and images of urban desolation.

smoker vent on the ocean floor, associated with an ◊ocean ridge, through which hot, mineral-rich groundwater erupts into the sea, forming thick clouds of suspension. The clouds may be dark or light, depending on the mineral content, thus producing 'white smokers' or 'black smokers'.

Seawater percolating through the sediments and crust is heated in the active area beneath and dissolves minerals from the hot rocks. As the charged water is returned to the ocean, the sudden cooling causes these minerals to precipitate from solution, so forming the suspension.

smoking inhaling the fumes from burning leaves, generally tobacco, in the form of ◊cigarettes, pipes, and cigars. The practice can be habit-forming and is dangerous to health. A direct link between lung cancer and smoking was established in 1950; there are also links between smoking and respiratory and coronary heart diseases. In the West, smoking is now forbidden in many public places because of the risk of *passive smoking*, the inhaling of fumes from other people's cigarettes.

Manufacturers have attempted to filter out harmful substances such as tar and nicotine, and to use milder tobaccos, and governments have carried out extensive anti-smoking advertising campaigns. In the UK and the USA all cigarette packaging must carry a government health warning, and television advertising of cigarettes is forbidden.

Smolensk /smə'lensk/ city on the river Dnieper, W USSR; population (1987) 338,000. Industries include textiles, distilling, and flour milling. It was founded 882 as the chief town of a Slavic tribe, and captured by Napoleon 1812. The Germans took the city 1941, and it was liberated by the Soviets 1943. Nearby is ◊*Katyn Forest*.

Smollett /'smɒlɪt/ Tobias George 1721–1771. Scottish novelist, who wrote the picaresque novels *Roderick Random* 1748, *Peregrine Pickle* 1751, *Ferdinand Count Fathom* 1753, *Sir Lancelot Greaves* 1760–62, and *Humphrey Clinker* 1771.

smuggling the illegal import or export of prohibited goods or the evasion of customs duties on dutiable goods. Smuggling has a long tradition in most border and coastal regions; goods smuggled include tobacco, spirits, diamonds, gold, and illegal drugs.

Restrictions on imports, originally a means of preventing debasement of coinage (for example, in 14th-century England) were later used for raising revenue, mainly on luxury goods, and led to a flourishing period of smuggling during the 18th century in goods such as wine, brandy, tea, tobacco, and lace.

Until the mid-19th century the islanders of Scilly, UK, poor in natural resources, thought little of the round trip to France in their long boats to bring back contraband. Smuggling is still one of the two principal industries of the state of Andorra.

smut parasitic ◊fungus, which infects flowering plants, particularly cereals.

Smuts /smʌts/ Jan Christian 1870–1950. South African politician, field marshal, and lawyer; prime minister 1919–24 and 1939–48. He supported the Allies in both world wars and was a member of the British imperial war cabinet 1917–18.

During the Second ◊South African War Smuts commanded the Boer forces in his native Cape Colony. He subsequently worked for reconciliation between the Boers and the British and on the establishment of the Union became minister of the interior 1910–12 and defence minister 1910–20. During World War I he commanded the South African forces in East Africa 1916–17. He was prime minister 1919–24, and minister of justice 1933–39, and on the outbreak of World War II succeeded Gen Hertzog as premier. He was created a field marshal in 1941 and received the Order of Merit in 1947. Although more of an internationalist than his contemporaries, Smuts was a segregationalist, voting in favour of legislation that took away black rights and land ownership.

Smyrna /'smɜːnə/ former name of the Turkish port of ◊Izmir.

Smyth /smaɪθ/ Ethel (Mary) 1858–1944. English composer who studied in Leipzig. Her works include the *Mass in D* 1893 and operas *The Wreckers* 1906 and *The Boatswain's Mate* 1916. In 1911 she was imprisoned as an advocate of women's suffrage.

Smythson /'smaɪðsən/ Robert 1535–1614. English architect, freemason of the Elizabethan country houses, including Longleat (1568–75), Wollaton Hall (1580–88), and Hardwick Hall (1590–97). Their castle-like silhouettes, symmetry, and large gridded windows are a uniquely romantic, English version of classicism.

Snaefell /,sneɪ'fel/ highest mountain in the Isle of ◊Man, 620 m/2,035 ft.

snail air-breathing gastropod mollusc, with a spiral shell. There are thousands of species, on land and in water.

The typical snails of the genus *Helix* have two species in Europe. The *common garden snail Helix aspersa* is very destructive to plants. The *Roman snail Helix pomatia* is 'corralled' for the gourmet food market. Overcollection has depleted the population. The French eat as much as 5 kg of snails per head each year.

Snake /sneɪk/ tributary of the Columbia river, in the NW USA; length 1,670 km/1,038 mi. It flows 65 km/40 mi through Hell's Canyon, one of the deepest gorges in the world.

snake reptile of the suborder Serpentes of the order Squamata, which also includes lizards. Snakes are characterized by an elongated limbless body, possibly evolved because of subterranean ancestors. One of the striking internal modifications is the absence or greatly reduced size of the left lung. The skin is covered in scales, which are markedly wider underneath where they form. There are 3,000 species found in the tropic and temperate zones, but none in New Zealand, Ireland, Iceland, and near the poles. Only three species are found in Britain: the adder, smooth snake, and grass snake.

In all except a few species, scales are an essential aid to locomotion. A snake is helpless on glass where scales can effect no 'grip' on the surface; progression may be undulant, 'concertina', or creeping, or a combination of these. Detailed vision is limited at a distance, though movement is immediately seen; hearing is restricted to ground vibrations (sound waves are not perceived); the sense of touch is acute; besides the sense of smell through the nasal passages, the flickering tongue picks up airborne particles which are then passed to special organs in the mouth for investigation; and some (rattlesnakes) have a cavity between eye and nostril which is sensitive to infrared rays (useful in locating warm-blooded prey in the dark). All snakes are carnivorous, and often camouflaged for better concealment in hunting as well as for their own protection. Some are oviparous and others ovoviviparous, that is, the eggs are retained in the oviducts until development is complete; in both cases the young are immediately self-sufficient.

The majority of snakes belong to the Colubridae, chiefly harmless, such as the common grass snake of Europe, but including the deadly African boomslang *Dispholidus typus*. The venomous families include the Elapidae comprising the true ◊cobras, the New World coral snakes, and the Australian taipan, copper-head, and death adder; the Viperidae (see ◊viper), and the Hydrophiidae, aquatic sea-snakes. Antisera against snakebite (made from the venom) are expensive to prepare and store, and specific to one snake species, so that experiments have been made with more widely valid treatment, for example, trypsin, a powerful protein-degrading enzyme, effective against the cobra/mamba group. Among the more primitive snakes are the Boidae, which still show links with the lizards and include the boa constrictor, anaconda, and python. These kill by constriction but their victims are usually comparatively small animals.

snapdragon perennial herbaceous plant of the genus *Antirrhinum*, family Scrophulariaceae, with spikes of brightly coloured two-lipped flowers. They are common garden flowers.

Snell /snel/ Willebrord 1581–1626. Dutch mathematician and physicist who devised the basic law of refraction, known as *Snell's law*, in 1621. This states that the ratio between the sine of the angle of incidence and the sine of the angle of refraction is constant. The laws describing the reflection of light were well known in antiquity but the principles governing the refraction of light were little understood. Snell's law was published by ◊Descartes in 1637.

snellen unit expressing the visual power of the ◊eye.

snipe European marsh bird of the family Scolopacidae, order Charadriiformes; species include *common snipe Gallinago gallinago*, and the rare *great snipe Gallinago media*, of which the males hold spring gatherings to show their prowess. It is closely related to the ◊woodcock.

snooker indoor game derived from ◊billiards (via ◊pool). It is played with 22 balls: 15 red, one each of yellow, green, brown, blue, pink and black, and a white cueball. Red balls when potted are worth one point while the coloured balls have ascending values from two points for the yellow to seven points for the black.

The game was invented by British army officers serving with the Devonshire Regiment in Jubbulpore, India, in 1875 and derived from the game of black pool. It did not gain popularity until the 1920s when Joe ◊Davis introduced new techniques. Since then it has become one of the biggest television sports in the UK and it is gaining popularity across Europe and the Far East. A season-long series of ranking tournaments culminates in the World Professional Championship at the Crucible Theatre, Sheffield, England, every Apr/May.

Snooker: recent winners

World Professional Championship first held 1927	
1980	Cliff Thorburn (Canada)
1981	Steve Davis (England)
1982	Alex Higgins (Northern Ireland)
1983	Steve Davis (England)
1984	Steve Davis (England)
1985	Dennis Taylor (Northern Ireland)
1986	Joe Johnson (England)
1987	Steve Davis (England)
1988	Steve Davis (England)
1989	Steve Davis (England)
World Amateur Championship instituted 1963	
1980	Jimmy White (England)
1982	Terry Parsons (Wales)
1984	O B Agrawal (India)
1985	Paul Mifsud (Malta)
1986	Paul Mifsud (Malta)
1987	Darren Morgan (Wales)
1988	James Wattana (Thailand)
1989	Ken Doherty (Republic of Ireland)

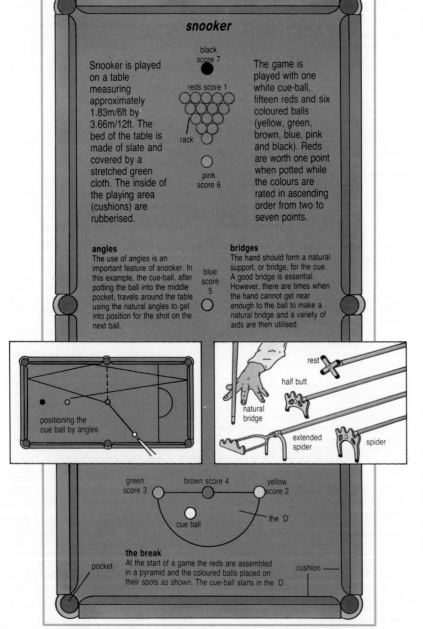

snooker

Snooker is played on a table measuring approximately 1.83m/6ft by 3.66m/12ft. The bed of the table is made of slate and covered by a stretched green cloth. The inside of the playing area (cushions) are rubberised.

black score 7
reds score 1
rack
pink score 6

The game is played with one white cue-ball, fifteen reds and six coloured balls (yellow, green, brown, blue, pink and black). Reds are worth one point when potted while the colours are rated in ascending order from two to seven points.

blue score 5

angles
The use of angles is an important feature of snooker. In this example, the cue-ball, after potting the ball into the middle pocket, travels around the table using the natural angles to get into position for the shot on the next ball.

bridges
The hand should form a natural support, or bridge, for the cue. A good bridge is essential. However, there are times when the hand cannot get near enough to the ball to make a natural bridge and a variety of aids are then utilised.

positioning the cue ball by angles

rest
half butt
natural bridge
extended spider
spider

green score 3
brown score 4
yellow score 2
cue ball
the 'D'

the break
At the start of a game the reds are assembled in a pyramid and the coloured balls placed on their spots as shown. The cue-ball starts in the 'D'.

pocket
cushion

snoring a loud noise during sleep made by vibration of the soft palate (the rear part of the roof of the mouth) caused by streams of air entering the nose and mouth at the same time. It is most common when the nose is partially blocked.

snow /snəʊ/ precipitation in the form of flaked particles caused by the condensation in air of excess water vapour below freezing point. Light reflecting in the crystals, which have a basic hexagonal (six-sided) geometry, gives the snow a white appearance.

Snow /snəʊ/ C(harles) P(ercy), Baron Snow 1905–1980. English novelist and physicist. He held government scientific posts in World War II and 1964–66. His sequence of novels *Strangers and Brothers* 1940–64 portrayed English life from 1920 onwards. His *Two Cultures* (Cambridge Rede lecture 1959) discussed the absence of communication between literary and scientific intellectuals in the West, and added the phrase 'the two cultures' to the language.

Snowden /'snəʊdn/ Philip, 1st Viscount Snowden 1864–1937. British right-wing Labour politician, chancellor of the Exchequer 1924 and 1929–31. He entered the coalition National Government in 1931 as Lord Privy Seal, but resigned in 1932.

Snowdon /'snəʊdn/ highest mountain in Wales, 1,085 m/3,560 ft above sea level. It consists of a cluster of five peaks. At the foot of Snowdon are the Llanberis, Aberglaslyn, and Rhyd-ddu passes. A rack railway ascends to the summit from Llanberis. Snowdonia, the surrounding mountain system, was made a National Park 1951.

Snowdon /'snəʊdn/ Anthony Armstrong-Jones, Earl of Snowdon 1930– . English portrait photographer, who married Princess Margaret in 1960, and was divorced in 1978.

snowdrop bulbous plant *Galanthus nivalis*, family Amaryllidaceae, with white bell-shaped flowers, tinged with green, in early spring.

snow leopard a type of ◊leopard.

Snow White traditional European fairy tale. Snow White is a princess persecuted by her jealous stepmother. Taking refuge in a remote cottage inhabited by seven dwarfs, she is tricked by the disguised queen into eating a poisoned apple. She is woken from apparent death by a prince.

Snowy Mountains /'snəʊi/ range in the Australian Alps, chiefly in New South Wales, near which Snowy River rises; both river and mountains are known for a hydroelectric and irrigation system.

snuff finely powdered ◊tobacco for sniffing up the nostrils as a stimulant or sedative. Snuff taking was common in 17th-century England and the Netherlands, and spread in the 18th century to other parts of Europe, but was superseded by cigarette smoking.

Snyders /'snaɪdəs/ Frans 1579–1657. Flemish painter of hunting scenes and still lifes. Based in Antwerp, he was a pupil of ◊Brueghel the Younger and later assisted ◊Rubens and worked with ◊Jordaens. In 1608–09 he travelled in Italy. He excelled at painting fur, feathers, and animals fighting.

Soames /səʊmz/ Christopher, Baron Soames 1920–1987. British Conservative politician. He held ministerial posts 1958–64, was vice president of the Commission of the European Communities 1973–77 and governor of (Southern) Rhodesia in the period of its transition to independence as Zimbabwe, Dec 1979–Apr 1980. He was created a life peer 1978.

Soane /səʊn/ John 1753–1837. English architect, whose individual Neo-Classical designs anticipated

snowdrop

snow *Snow crystal showing characteristic hexagonal symmetry.*

modern taste. His buildings include his own house in Lincoln's Inn Fields, London, now the Soane Museum. Little remains of his extensive work at the Bank of England, London.

soap a mixture of the sodium salts of various fatty acids: palmitic, stearic, or oleic acid. It is made by the action of caustic soda or caustic potash on fats of animal or vegetable origin. Soap makes grease and dirt disperse in water in a similar manner to a ◊detergent.

Soap was mentioned by Galen in the 2nd century for washing the body, although the Romans seem to have washed with a mixture of sand and oil. Soap was manufactured in Britain from the 14th century, and better-quality soap was imported from Castile or Venice. The Soapmakers' Company, London, was incorporated 1638. Soap was taxed in England from the time of Cromwell in the 17th century to 1853.

soap opera a television series or radio melodrama. It originated in the USA as a series of daytime programmes sponsored by washing-powder manufacturers. The popularity of the genre has led to soap operas being shown at peak viewing times. Television soap operas include: *Coronation Street* (UK, 1960–); *Crossroads* (UK, 1964–88); *Dallas* (USA, 1978–); *Dynasty* (USA, 1981–); *EastEnders* (UK, 1985–).

soapstone a type of rock from which ◊talc is derived.

Soares /'swɑːres/ Mario 1924– . Portuguese politician. Exiled in 1970, he returned to Portugal in 1974, and as leader of the Portuguese Socialist Party (PSP) was prime minister 1976–78. He resigned as party leader in 1980, but in 1986 he was elected Portugal's first socialist president.

Sobers /'səʊbəz/ (Garfield St Aubrun) 'Gary' 1936– . West Indian test cricketer. One of the game's great all-rounders, he scored more than 8,000 test runs, took over 200 wickets, held more than 100 catches, and holds the record for the highest test innings, 365 not out.

Sobers started playing first-class cricket in 1952. He played English county cricket with Nottinghamshire and while playing for them against Glamorgan at Swansea in 1968 he established a world record by scoring six 6s in one over. The unfortunate bowler was Malcolm Nash. Sobers was knighted for his services to cricket 1975. He played for West Indies 93 times.

CAREER HIGHLIGHTS

All First Class Cricket
Runs: 28,315
Average: 54.87
Best: 365 not out West Indies v Pakistan 1957–58
Wickets: 1,043
Average: 27.74
Best: 9–49 West Indies v Kent 1966
Test cricket
Runs: 8,032
Average: 57.78
Best: 365 not out v Pakistan 1957–58
Wickets: 235
Average: 34.03
Best: 6–73 v Australia 1968–69

Sobieski /sɒb'jeski/ John alternative name for ◊John III, king of Poland.

soca Latin Caribbean music, a mixture of *so*ul and *ca*lypso.

socage Anglo-Saxon term for the free tenure of land by the peasantry. Sokemen, holders of land by this tenure, formed the upper stratum of peasant society at the time of the ◊Domesday Book.

Sochi /'sɒtʃi/ seaside resort in the USSR, on the Black Sea; population (1987) 317,000. In 1976 it became the world's first 'no smoking' city.

Social and Liberal Democrats official name for the British political party formed 1988 from the former Liberal Party and most of the Social Democratic Party. Its leader (from July 1988) is Paddy ◊Ashdown. The common name for the party is the **Democrats**, which was agreed at the party conference Sept 1988.

social behaviour in zoology, behaviour concerned with altering the behaviour of other individuals of the same species. Social behaviour allows animals to live in groups and form alliances within their group. It may be aggressive or submissive (for example, cowering and other signals of appeasement), or designed to establish bonds (such as social grooming or preening).

The social behaviour of mammals and birds is generally more complex than that of lower organisms, and involves relationships with individually recognized animals. Thus, courtship displays allow individuals to choose appropriate mates and form the bonds necessary for successful reproduction. In the social systems of bees, wasps, ants, and termites, an individual's status and relationships with others is largely determined by its biological form, as a member of a caste of workers, soldiers or reproductives; see ◊eusociality.

social contract the idea that government authority derives originally from an agreement between ruler and ruled in which the former agrees to provide order in return for obedience from the latter. It has been used to support either absolutism (◊Hobbes) or democracy (◊Locke, ◊Rousseau). The term was revived in the UK in 1974 when a head-on clash between the Conservative government and the trade unions resulted in a general election which enabled a Labour government to take power. It now denotes an unofficial agreement (hence also called 'social compact') between a government and organized labour that, in return

Sobers *West Indian test cricketer Gary Sobers.*

for control of prices, rents, and so on, the unions would refrain from economically disruptive wage demands.

social credit theory, put forward by C H Douglas (1879–1952), that economic crises are caused by bank control of money, which leads to shortage of purchasing power. His remedy was payment of a 'social dividend'. There have been provincial social-credit governments in Canada, but the central government has always vetoed the plan.

social democracy a political ideology of belief in the gradual evolution of a democratic ◊socialism within existing political structures. The earliest was the German *Sozialdemokratische Partei* (SPD), today one of the two major West German parties, created in 1875 from August Bebel's earlier German Social Democratic Workers' Party, itself founded 1869. The British Labour Party is in the social democratic tradition.

Social Democratic Federation (SDF) in British history, a socialist society, founded as the Democratic Federation in 1881 and renamed in 1884. It was led by H M Hyndman (1842–1921), a former conservative journalist and stockbroker who claimed Karl ◊Marx as his inspiration without obtaining recognition from his mentor. In 1911 it became the British Socialist Party. The SDF organized meetings and marches for the unemployed that led to some clashes with police in central London in 1886 and 1887.

Social Democratic Labour Party (SDLP) Northern Irish left-wing political party, formed in 1970. It aims ultimately at Irish unification, but distances itself from the violent tactics of the Irish Republican Army (IRA), adopting a constitutional, conciliatory role. The SDLP, led by John Hume (1937–), was responsible for setting up the ◊New Ireland Forum in 1983.

Social Democratic Party (SDP) British political party formed 1981 by Labour Members of Parliament Roy Jenkins (its first leader), David Owen (leader from 1983), Shirley Williams, and William Rodgers, who resigned from the Labour Party and took a more centrist position. The 1983 and 1987 general elections were fought in alliance with the Liberal Party as the ***Liberal/SDP Alliance*** (1983, six seats, 11.6% of the vote; 1987, five seats, 9.8% of the vote). A merger of the two parties was voted for by the SDP 1987, and the new party became the ◊Social and Liberal Democrats. David Owen resigned the leadership during the negotiations concerning the merger and was replaced by Robert Maclennan, but continued to lead a separate SDP with two other MPs. In 1989 the SDP abandoned the attempt to operate as a national party, and planned to contest only certain electoral seats. In June 1990, Owen and a majority of members voted to wind up the party.

socialism movement aiming to establish a classless society by substituting public for private ownership of the means of production, distribution, and exchange. The term has been used to describe positions as widely apart as anarchism and social democracy. Socialist ideas appeared in classical times; in early Christianity; among later Christian sects such as the ◊Anabaptists and ◊Diggers; and, in the 18th and early 19th centuries, were put forward as systematic political aims by ◊Rousseau, ◊Saint Simon, ◊Fourier, ◊Owen, ◊Marx, and ◊Engels.

In the later 19th century socialist parties arose in most European countries; for example, in Britain the ◊Independent Labour Party. This period, when in Russia the Bolsheviks were reviving, witnessed a reaction against Marxism, typified by the ◊Fabian Society in Britain and the German Revisionists, which appealed to popular nationalism and solved economic problems by similar means of state control of the economy, but in the general interests of private capital.

The late 19th and early 20th centuries saw a division between those who reacted against Marxism leading to social-democratic parties and those

who emphasized the original revolutionary significance of Marx's teachings. Weakened by these divisions, the second ◊International (founded in 1889) collapsed in 1914, right-wing socialists in all countries supporting participation in World War I while the left opposed it. The Russian Revolution removed socialism from the sphere of theory to that of practice, and was followed in 1919 by the foundation of the Third International, which completed the division between right and left. This lack of unity, in spite of the temporary successes of the popular fronts in France and Spain in 1936–38, facilitated the rise of fascism and National Socialism (◊Nazism).

After World War II socialist and communist parties tended to formal union in Eastern Europe, although the rigid communist control that ensued was later modified in some respects in, for example, Poland, Romania, and Yugoslavia. Subsequent tendencies to broaden communism were suppressed in Hungary (1956) and Czechoslovakia (1968). In Western Europe, however, a communist takeover of the Portuguese revolution failed 1975–76, and elsewhere, as in France under ◊Mitterrand, attempts at socialist–communist cooperation petered out. Most countries in Western Europe have a strong socialist party, for example, in West Germany the Social Democratic Party and in Britain the ◊Labour Party.

'socialism in one country' concept proposed by ◊Stalin in 1924. In contrast to ◊Trotsky's theory of the permanent revolution, Stalin suggested that the emphasis be changed away from promoting revolutions abroad to the idea of building socialism, economically and politically, in the USSR without help from other countries.

socialist realism artistic doctrine set up by the USSR during the 1930s setting out the optimistic, socialist terms in which society should be portrayed in works of art (including music and painting as well as prose fiction).

The policy was used as a form of censorship of artists whose work, it was felt, did not follow the approved Stalinist party line, or was too 'Modern'. The policy was relaxed after Stalin's death, but remains in force. Artists whose work was censured in this way include the composer Shostakovich, and the writers Solzhenitsyn and Sholokhov.

socialization the process, beginning in childhood, by which a person learns how to become a member of a particular society, learning its norms, customs, laws, and ways of living. The main agents of socialization are the family, school, peer groups, work, religion, and the mass media. The main methods of socialization are direct instruction, rewards and punishment, imitation, experimentation, role play, and interaction.

Some agents of socialization, such as the family and the peer group, may conflict with each others, offering alternative goals, values, and styles of behaviour. Socialization is of particular interest to psychologists, anthropologists, and sociologists, but there are diverse opinions about its power and importance.

social mobility the movement of groups and individuals up and down the social scale. The extent or range of social mobility varies in different societies. Individual social mobility may occur through education, marriage, talent, and so on; group mobility usually occurs through change in the occupational structure caused by new technological or economic developments.

The caste system of India and the feudalism of medieval Europe are cited as examples of closed societies, where little social mobility was possible; the class system of Western industrial societies is considered relatively open and flexible.

Social Realism in painting, the branch of Realism concerned with poverty and deprivation. The French artist Courbet provides a 19th-century example of the genre. Subsequently, in the USA, the Ashcan school and Ben Shahn are among those described as Social Realists.

social science the group of academic disciplines which investigate how and why people behave the way they do, as individuals and in groups. The term originated with the 19th-century French thinker Auguste ◊Comte. The academic social sciences are generally listed as sociology, economics, anthropology, political science, and psychology.

Western thought about society has been influenced by the ideas and insights of such great theorists as Plato and Aristotle, Machiavelli, Rousseau, Hobbes, and Locke. The study of society, however, can be traced to the great intellectual period of the 18th century called the Enlightenment, and to the industrial and political revolutions of the 18th and 19th centuries, to the moral philosophy of ◊positivism. Comte attempted to establish the study of society as a scientific discipline, capable of precision and prediction in the same way as natural science, but it overlaps extensively with such subject areas as history, geography, law, philosophy, and even biology. And although some thinkers—such as Marx—have attempted to synthesize the study of society within one theory, none has yet achieved what Einstein has done for physics or Darwin for biology. A current debate is whether the study of people can or should be a science.

social security state provision of financial aid to alleviate poverty. The term 'social security' was first applied officially in the USA, in the Social Security Act 1935. It was first used officially in Britain 1944, and following the ◊Beveridge Report 1942 a series of acts was passed from 1945 to widen the scope of social security. Basic entitlements of those paying National Insurance contributions in Britain include an old-age pension, unemployment benefit, widow's pension, and payment during a period of sickness in one's working life. Other benefits include family credit, child benefit, and attendance allowance for those looking after sick or disabled people. Entitlements under National Insurance, such as unemployment benefit, are paid at flat rates regardless of need; other benefits, such as income support, are 'means-tested', that is, claimants' income must be below a certain level. Most payments, with the exception of unemployment benefit, are made by the Department of Social Security (DSS).

In the USA the term 'social security' usually refers specifically to old-age pensions, which have a contributory element, unlike 'welfare'. The federal government is responsible for social security (Medicare, retirement, survivors', and disability insurance); unemployment insurance is covered by a joint federal-state system for industrial workers, but few in agriculture are covered; and welfare benefits are the responsibility of individual states, with some federal assistance.

The concept of such payments developed in the later 19th century in Europe, for example compulsory social insurance in Germany from 1883; non-contributory old-age pensions in Britain from 1909; and compulsory health and unemployment insurance in Britain from 1911. The US social-security legislation was passed to enable the federal government to cope with the effects of the Depression of 1929.

The income-support scheme, known originally as national assistance, was called supplementary benefit 1966–88. Family credit was known as family income supplement, and child benefit was known until 1977 as family allowance. In 1987–88 further changes in the social-security system included the abolition of death and maternity grants, to be replaced by means-tested payments from a new Social Fund; and the replacement of maternity allowances by statutory maternity pay, paid by employers, not the DSS.

society the organization of people into groups. Social science, in particular sociology, is the study of human behaviour in a social context. Various aspects of society are discussed under ◊class, ◊community, ◊culture, ◊kinship, ◊norms, ◊role, ◊socialization, and ◊status.

Society Islands /səˈsaɪəti/ (French *Archipel de la Société*) an archipelago in ◊French Polynesia, divided into Windward Islands and Leeward Islands; area 1,685 sq km/650 sq mi; population (1983) 142,000. The administrative headquarters is Papeete on ◊Tahiti. The *Windward Islands* (French *Îles du Vent*) have an area of 1,200 sq km/460 sq mi, and a population (1983) 123,000. They comprise Tahiti, Moorea (area 132 sq km/51 sq mi; population 7,000), Maio (or Tubuai Manu; 9 sq km/3.5 sq mi; population 200), and the smaller Tetiaroa and Mehetia. The *Leeward Islands* (French *Îles sous le Vent*) have an area of 404 sq km/156 sq mi, and a population of 19,000. They comprise the volcanic islands of Raiatea (including the main town of Uturoa), Huahine, Bora-Bora, Maupiti, Tahaa, and four small atolls. Claimed by France 1768, the group became a French protectorate 1843, and a colony 1880.

Socinianism form of 17th-century Christian belief which rejects such traditional doctrines as the Trinity and original sin, named after *Socinus*, the Latinized name of Lelio Francesco Maria Sozzini (1525–62), Italian Protestant theologian. It is an early form of ◊Unitarianism.

His views on the nature of Christ were developed by his nephew, Fausto Paolo Sozzini (1539–1604), who also taught pacifist and anarchist doctrines akin to Tolstoy's. Socinianism denies the divinity of Jesus but emphasizes his virtues.

sociobiology the study of the biological basis of all social behaviour, including the application of ◊population genetics to the evolution of behaviour. It builds on the concept of ◊inclusive fitness. Contrary to some popular interpretations, it does not assume that all behaviour is genetically determined.

The New Zealand biologist W D Hamilton introduced the concept of inclusive fitness, which emphasizes that the evolutionary function of behaviour is to allow an organism to contribute as many of its own ◊alleles as it can to future generations: this idea is encapsulated in the British zoologist Dawkins's notion of the 'selfish gene'.

sociology the systematic study of society, in particular of social order and social change, social conflict and social problems. It studies institutions such as the family, law, and the church, as well as concepts such as norm, role, and culture. Sociology attempts to study people in their social environment according to certain underlying moral, philosophical, and political codes of behaviour.

Sociology today reflects a variety of perspectives and traditions. Its focus tends to be an contemporary industrial society, sometimes comparing it with pre-industrial society, and occasionally drawing on such related disciplines as history, geography, politics, economics, psychology, and anthropology. Its concerns range from theories of social order and change to detailed analyses of small groups, individuals, and the routines of daily life. The relation between theory and method is one part of the current debate about whether sociology is or should be a science, and whether it can or should be free of ideology.

Socotra /səʊˈkəʊtrə/ Yemeni island in the Indian Ocean; capital Tamridah; area 3,500 sq km/1,351 sq mi. Under British protection from 1886, it became part of South Yemen 1967, and is used as a military base by the USSR.

Socrates /ˈsɒkrətiːz/ *c.* 469–399 BC. Athenian philosopher. He wrote nothing but was immortalized in the dialogues of his pupil, Plato. In his desire to combat the scepticism of the ◊sophists, Socrates asserted the possibility of genuine knowledge. In ethics, he put forward the view that the good person never knowingly does wrong. True knowledge emerges through dialogue and systematic questioning, and an abandoning of uncritical claims to knowledge.

The effect of Socrates' teaching was disruptive since he opposed tyranny. Accused in 399 on charges of impiety and corruption of youth, he was condemned by the Athenian authorities to die by drinking hemlock.

Socratic method way of teaching used by Socrates, in which he aimed to guide pupils to clear thinking on ethics and politics by asking questions and then exposing their inconsistencies in cross-examination. This method was effective against the sophists.

soda ash former name for sodium carbonate (Na_2CO_3).

soda lime mixture of calcium hydroxide and sodium hydroxide or potassium hydroxide, used in medicine and as a drying agent.

Soddy /ˈsɒdi/ Frederick 1877–1956. English physical chemist, pioneer of research into atomic disintegration, who coined the term 'isotope'. Nobel prize 1921.

His works include *Chemistry of the Radio-Elements* 1912–14, *The Interpretation of the Atom* 1932, and *The Story of Atomic Energy* 1949. After his chemical discoveries, Soddy spent some 40 years developing a theory of 'energy economics', which he called 'Cartesian economics'. He argued for the abolition of debt and compound interest, the nationalization of credit, and a new theory of value based on the quantity of energy contained in a thing, believing that as a scientist he was able to see through the errors of economists.

Söderberg /ˈsəʊdəˌberi/ Hjalmar (Eric Fredrik) 1869–1941. Swedish writer. His work includes the novels *Förvillelser* 1895, *Martin Bircks ungdom* 1901, *Doktor Glas/Dr Glass* 1906, and the play *Gertrud* 1906.

sodium a metallic element, symbol Na (Latin *natrium*), atomic number 11, relative atomic mass 22.991. It is a soft, bright, silvery, reactive metal tarnishing quickly on exposure to air, and reacting violently with water to form sodium hydroxide. Important sodium compounds include common salt, sodium carbonate (Na_2CO_3, washing soda), and hydrogencarbonate ($NaHCO_3$, bicarbonate of soda), sodium hydroxide or caustic soda (NaOH), sodium nitrate or Chile saltpetre ($NaNO_3$, fertilizer), sodium thiosulphate or hypo ($Na_2S_2O_3$, photographic fixer).

Its commonest form is sodium chloride (NaCl, common salt). Sodium metal is used to a limited extent in spectroscopy, in discharge lamps, and alloyed with potassium as a heat-transfer medium in nuclear reactors. Sodium compounds are of the widest industrial importance and thousands of tonnes are manufactured annually. First isolated by Sir Humphry Davy in 1807, it is found abundantly in combination. An artificial isotope of sodium is used as a tracer in the human body.

Sodom and Gomorrah /ˈsɒdəm, gəˈmɒrə/ two ancient cities in the Dead Sea area of the Middle East, recorded in the Old Testament or Hebrew Bible (Genesis) as destroyed by fire and brimstone for their wickedness.

Sofia /ˈsəʊfiə/ or *Sofiya* capital of Bulgaria since 1878; population (1987) 1,129,000. Industries include textiles, rubber, machinery, and electrical equipment. It lies at the foot of the Vitosha Mountains.

softball a form of baseball played with similar equipment. The two main differences are the distances between the bases (60 ft/18.29 m) and that the ball is pitched underhand in softball. There are two forms of softball, fast pitch and slow pitch; in the latter the ball must be delivered to home plate in an arc that must not be less than 2.4 m/8 ft at its height.

soft currency a vulnerable currency that tends to fall in value on foreign-exchange markets because of political or economic uncertainty. Governments are unwilling to hold soft currencies in their foreign-exchange reserves, preferring strong or hard currencies, which are easily convertible.

software in computing, a collection of programs and procedures for making a computer perform a specific task, as opposed to ◊hardware, which is the machine itself. Software is created by programmers and either distributed on a suitable medium, such as the ◊floppy disc, or built into the computer in the form of ◊firmware. Examples of software include ◊operating systems, ◊compilers, and application programs such as payrolls. No computer can function without some form of software.

software project lifecycle in computing, the various stages of development in the writing of a major program (software), from the identification of a requirement to the installation, maintainance, and support of the finished program. The process includes ◊systems analysis and ◊systems design.

softwood a coniferous tree, or the wood from it. In general this type of wood is softer and easier to work, but in some cases less durable, than wood from ◊deciduous trees.

Sogne Fjord /ˈsɒŋnə ˈfiːɔːd/ longest and deepest fjord in ◊Norway, 185 km/115 mi long and 1,245 m/4,080 ft deep.

Soho /ˈsəʊhəʊ/ district of London, England, which houses the offices of publishing, film, and recording companies; restaurants; nightclubs; and a decreasing number of sexshops.

soil loose covering of broken rocky material and decaying organic matter overlying the bedrock of the Earth's surface. Various types of soil develop under different conditions: deep soils form in warm wet climates and in valleys; shallow soils form in cool dry areas and on slopes. *Pedology*, the study of soil, is significant because of the relative importance of different soil types to agriculture. The organic content of soil is widely variable, ranging from zero in some desert soils to almost 100% in peats.

Soil Association pioneer British ecological organization founded 1945, which campaigns against pesticides and promotes organic farming.

soil creep gradual movement of soil down a slope. As each soil particle is dislodged by a raindrop it moves slightly further downhill. This eventually results in a mass downward movement of soil on the slope.

Manifestations of soil creep are the formation of terracettes (steplike ridges along the hillside), leaning walls and telegraph poles, and trees

Sociology: chronology

1830	Auguste Comte coined the term 'sociology'.
1845	Friedrich Engels published *The Condition of the Working Classes in England*.
1887	The first volume of Karl Marx's *Das Kapital/Capital* was published.
1892	The first academic department of sociology was established, at the University of Chicago.
1895	Emile Durkheim published *The Rules of Sociological Method*.
1905	The American Sociological Society was founded in Chicago.
1913	Durkheim was appointed the first professor of sociology at the Sorbonne in Paris.
1913	Publication of Husserl's *Phenomenological Philosphy*.
1919	Max Weber was appointed professor of sociology at Munich University.
1920s–1930s	The Chicago School developed as a centre for urban sociology.
1922	Publication of Weber's *Economy and Society*.
1923	The Institute of Social Research was founded at Frankfurt University.
1923	The Japanese Sociological Society was founded in Tokyo.
1931	Talcott Parsons was appointed professor of sociology at Harvard University.
1934	Karl Popper's *The Logic of Scientific Discovery* was published.
1939	Parsons's *The Structure of Social Action* was published.
1949	The International Sociological Association was founded, sponsored by UNESCO.

that grow in a curve to counteract progressive leaning.

soil mechanics a branch of engineering that studies the nature and properties of the soil. Soil is investigated during construction work to ensure that it has the mechanical properties necessary to support the foundations of dams, bridges, and roads.

Soissons /'swæsɒn/ market town in Picardie region, N France; population (1982) 32,000. The chief industry is metallurgy. In 486 ◊Clovis defeated the Gallo-Romans here, ending their rule in France.

Sokol Czechoslovak educational and athletic organization founded in 1862, which plays an important part in public life. The movement also flourishes in Poland, Bulgaria, Yugoslavia, and other Slav countries. Until 1948 it was nonpolitical.

Sokoto /'səʊkətəʊ/ trading centre and capital of Sokoto state, NW Nigeria; population (1983) 148,000.

Sokoto /'səʊkətəʊ/ state in Nigeria, established 1976; capital Sokoto; area 102,500 sq km/39,565 sq mi; population (1984) 7,609,000. It was a ◊Fula sultanate from the 16th century until occupied by the British 1903.

sol a colloidal suspension of very small solid particles in a liquid that retains the physical properties of a liquid (see ◊colloid).

solan goose another name for the ◊gannet.

solar energy energy derived from the Sun's radiation. Solar heaters have industrial or domestic uses. They usually consist of a black (heat-absorbing) panel containing pipes through which air or water, heated by the Sun, is circulated, either by thermal ◊convection or by a pump. Solar energy may also be harnessed indirectly using solar cells made of panels of ◊semiconductor material (usually silicon) which generate electricity when illuminated by sunlight. Although it is difficult to generate a high output from solar energy compared

solar energy *Solar dishes at the Themis experimental solar-power station at Targassone in the French Pyrénées.*

to sources such as nuclear or fossil-fuel energy, it is an important non-polluting and renewable energy source used as far north as Scandinavia as well as in Mediterranean countries.

A solar furnace, such as that built in 1970 at Odeillo in the French Pyrénées, has thousands of mirrors to focus the Sun's rays; it produces uncontaminated intensive heat for industrial and scientific or experimental purposes. Advanced schemes have been proposed that will use giant solar reflectors in space that would harness ◊solar energy and beam it down to earth in the form of ◊microwaves. Despite their low running costs, their high installation cost and low power output have meant that solar cells have found few applications outside space probes and artificial satellites. Solar heating is, however, widely used for domestic purposes in many Mediterranean and Scandinavian countries.

solar pond natural or artificial 'pond', for example the Dead Sea, in which salt becomes more soluble in the Sun's heat. Water at the bottom becomes saltier and hotter, and is insulated by the less salty water layer at the top. Temperatures at the

bottom reach about 100°C/212°F and can be used to generate electricity.

solar radiation radiation given off by the Sun, consisting mainly of visible light, ◊ultraviolet radiation, and ◊infrared radiation, although the whole spectrum of ◊electromagnetic waves is present, from radio waves to X-rays. High-energy charged particles such as electrons are also emitted, especially from solar ◊flares. When these reach the Earth, they cause magnetic storms (disruptions of the Earth's magnetic field), which interfere with radio communications.

solar system the Sun and all the bodies orbiting around it: the nine planets (Mercury, Venus, Earth, Mars, Jupiter, Saturn, Uranus, Neptune, and Pluto), their moons, asteroids, and comets. It is thought to have formed from a cloud of gas and dust in space about 4,600 million years ago. The Sun contains 99% of the mass of the solar system. The edge of the solar system is not clearly defined, marked only by the limit of the Sun's gravitational influence, which extends about 1.5 light years, almost halfway to the nearest star.

solar wind a stream of atomic particles, mostly protons and electrons, from the Sun's corona, flowing outwards at speeds of between 300 km/186 mi and 1,000 km/621 mi per second.

The fastest streams come from 'holes' in the Sun's corona that lie over areas where there is no surface activity. The solar wind pushes the gas of comets' tails away from the Sun, and 'gusts' in the solar wind cause geomagnetic disturbances and aurorae on Earth.

solder alloy used for joining metals such as copper, its common alloys (brass and bronze) and tin-plated steel as used for making food cans. Soft solders (usually alloys of tin and lead, sometimes with added antimony) melt at low temperatures (about 200°C), and are widely used in the electrical industry for joining copper wires. Hard solders, such as silver solder (an alloy of copper, silver and zinc), melt at much higher temperatures, and form a much stronger joint. Brazing is another method of joining metals.

A necessary preliminary to making any solder joint is thorough cleaning of the surfaces of the metal to be joined (to remove oxide) and the use of a flux (to prevent the heat applied to melt the solder from re-oxidizing the metal).

sole flatfish found in temperate and tropical waters. The **common sol** *Solea solea*, also called **Dover sole**, is found in the southern seas of NW Europe. Up to 50 cm/1.6 ft long, it is a prized food fish, as is the **sand** or **French sole** *Pegusa lascaris* further south.

solenodon rare insectivorous shrew-like mammal, genus *Solenodon*. There are two species, one each on Cuba and Hispaniola, and they are threatened with extinction owing to introduced predators. They are about 30 cm/1 ft long with a 25 cm/10 in tail, slow-moving, and produce venomous saliva.

solenoid a coil of wire, usually cylindrical, in which a magnetic field is created by passing an electric current through it (see ◊electromagnet). This field can be used to move an iron rod placed on its axis. Mechanical valves attached to the rod can be operated by switching the current on or off, so converting electrical energy into mechanical energy. Solenoids are used to relay energy from the battery of a car to the starter motor by means of the ignition switch.

Solent, the /'səʊlənt/ channel between the coast of Hampshire, England, and the Isle of ◊Wight. It is now a yachting centre.

sole trader or **sole proprietor** one person who runs a business, receiving all profits and responsible for all liabilities. Many small businesses are sole traders.

sol-fa short for **tonic sol-fa**, a method of teaching music, usually singing, systematized by John Curwen (1816–1880). The notes of a scale are named by syllables (doh, ray, me, fah, soh, lah, te, with the ◊key indicated) to simplify singing by sight.

solar system

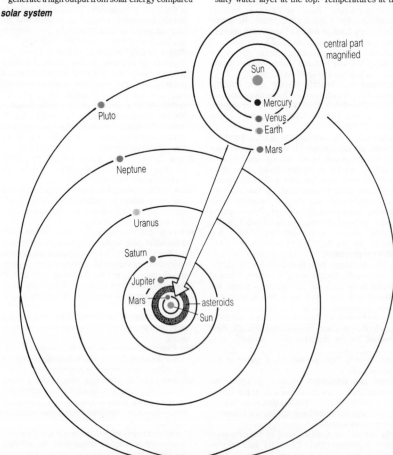

Pluto • Neptune • Uranus • Saturn • Jupiter • Mars • Sun • asteroids

central part magnified

Sun • Mercury • Venus • Earth • Mars

Solferino, Battle of /ˌsɒlfəˈriːnəʊ/ Napoleon III's victory over the Austrians 1859, at a village near Verona, N Italy, 8 km/5 mi S of Lake Garda.

solicitor in the UK, a member of one of the two branches of the English legal profession, the other being a ◊barrister. A solicitor is a lawyer who provides all-round legal services (making wills, winding up estates, conveyancing, divorce, and litigation). A solicitor cannot appear in court at crown court level, but must brief a barrister on behalf of his or her client. Solicitors may become circuit judges and recorders. In the USA the general term is lawyer or attorney.

Solicitor General in the UK, a law officer of the crown, deputy to the ◊Attorney General, a political appointee with ministerial rank.

solid in physics, a state of matter which holds its own shape (as opposed to a liquid, which takes up the shape of its container, or a gas, which totally fills its container). According to ◊kinetic theory, the atoms or molecules in a solid are not free to move but merely vibrate about fixed positions, such as those in crystal lattices.

Solidarity (Polish *Solidarność*) the national confederation of independent trade unions in Poland, formed under the leadership of Lech ◊Walesa Sept 1980. An illegal organization from 1981 to 1989, it now heads the Polish government.

Solidarity emerged from a summer of industrial disputes caused by the Polish government's attempts to raise food prices. The strikers created a trade-union movement independent of the Communist Party, and protracted negotiations with the government led to recognition of Solidarity in exchange for an acceptance of the leading role of the Communist Party in Poland. Continuing unrest and divisions in Solidarity's leadership led to the declaration of martial law in Dec 1981; the union was banned and its leaders were arrested. Walensa was released Dec 1982, and Solidarity continued to function as an underground organization. It was re-legalized Apr 1989 following a further wave of strikes under its direction and round-table talks with the governmemt. In the elections of June 1989 it won almost every seat open to it, and formed the senior partner in a 'grand coalition' government formed Sept 1989 with Tadeusz ◊Mazowiecki as prime minister.

Solidarity's achievements inspired the successful 'people power' movements in other E European countries during 1989, as well as the formation of more independent labour unions in the USSR.

solidification change of state of a substance from liquid or vapour to solid on cooling. It is the opposite of melting or sublimation.

solid-state circuit a circuit where all the components (resistors, capacitors, transistors, and diodes) and interconnections are made at the same time, and by the same processes, in or on one piece of single-crystal silicon. The small size of this construction accounts for its use in electronics for space vehicles and aircraft. See also ◊integrated circuit and ◊silicon chip.

Solingen /ˈzəʊlɪŋən/ city in North Rhine-Westphalia, West Germany; population (1988) 158,000. It was once famous for swords, but today produces high-quality steel for razor blades and cutlery.

solipsism in philosophy, a view which maintains that the self is the only thing that can be known to exist. It is an extreme form of ◊scepticism. The solipsist sees himself or herself as the only individual in existence, assuming other people to be a reflection of his or her own consciousness.

soliton nonlinear wave that does not widen and disperse in the normal way. Such behaviour is characteristic of the waves of ◊energy that constitute the particles of atomic physics, and the mathematical equations that sum up the behaviour of solitons are being used to further research in nuclear fusion and superconductivity.

It is so named from a *solitary* wave seen on a canal by Scottish engineer John Scott Russell (1808–1882), who raced after it on his horse. Before he lost it, it had moved on for over a mile as a smooth, raised, and rounded form, rather than widening and dispersing.

Solomon /ˈsɒləmən/ c. 974–c.937 BC. In the Old Testament or Hebrew Bible, king of Israel, son of David by Bathsheba. He was famed for his wisdom, the much later biblical Proverbs, Ecclesiastes, and Song of Songs being attributed to him. He built the temple in Jerusalem with the aid of heavy taxation and forced labour. The so-called *King Solomon's Mines* at Aqaba, Jordan (copper and iron), are of later date.

government constitutional monarchy
political parties People's Alliance Party (PAP), centre-left; Solomon Islands United Party (SIUPA), right-of-centre
exports palm oil, copra, rice, timber
currency Solomon Island dollar (4.11 = £1 Feb 1990)
population (1989) 314,000 (the majority Melanesian); annual growth rate 3.9%
language English (official)
religion Christian
literacy 13% (1980)
GDP $160 million (1983); $628 per head of population
chronology
1978 Achieved full independence within the Commonwealth, with Peter Kenilorea as prime minister.
1981 Solomon Mamaloni replaced Kenilorea as prime minister.
1984 Kenilorea returned to power, heading a coalition government.
1986 Kenilorea resigned after allegations of corruption, and was replaced by his deputy, Ezekiel Alebua.
1988 Kenilorea back as deputy prime minister. The Solomon Islands joined Vanuatu and Papua New Guinea to form the Spearhead Group, aiming to preserve Melanesian cultural traditions and secure independence for the French territory of New Caledonia.
1989 Solomon Mamaloni (People's Action Party) returned as prime minister and formed PAP-dominated coalition.

Solomon Islands /ˈsɒləmən/ country in the W Pacific, E of New Guinea, comprising many hundreds of islands, the largest of which is Guadalcanal.

government The constitution dates from 1978 and creates a constitutional monarchy within the Commonwealth, with a resident governor-general representing the UK monarch as head of state. There is a single-chamber legislature, the National Parliament, with 38 members elected by universal suffrage for a four-year term. The governor-general appoints a prime minister and cabinet drawn from and collectively responsible to the parliament.

The two main political parties are the Solomon Islands United Party (SIUPA) and the People's Alliance Party (PAP).

history The islands, which are inhabited by Melanesians, were sighted by a 1568 expedition from Peru led by the Spanish navigator Álvaro de Mendaña. They became a British protectorate in the 1890s.

The Solomon Islands were given internal self-government 1976, with Peter Kenilorea, leader of the SIUP, as chief minister. He became prime minister when they achieved full independence, within the Commonwealth, in 1978. In 1981 he was replaced by Solomon Mamaloni of the People's Progressive Party. Kenilorea had been unable to devolve power to the regions while preserving the unity of the state, but Mamaloni created five ministerial posts specifically for provincial affairs.

In the 1984 general election SIUPA won 13 seats and the opposition, now PAP, 12. Sir Peter Kenilorea, as he had become, was put back into office at the head of a coalition government. He immediately abolished the five provincial ministries. After narrowly surviving a series of no confidence motions, he resigned again as prime minister in Dec 1986, following allegations that he had accepted US$47,000 of French aid to repair cyclone damage to his home village in Malaita province. Kenilorea remained in the cabinet of his successor, Ezekiel Alebua, a fellow SIUPA member and became deputy prime minister from Feb 1988. In the general election of Feb 1989 support for the SIUPA halved to six seats and the PAP, led by Mamaloni, re-emerged, with 14 seats, as the dominant party. Mamaloni formed a coalition government that promised to reform the constitution so as to establish a republic and also to reduce the influence of 'foreign aid personnel'.

In its external relations, the Solomon Islands, under the SIUPA administrations, has pursued a moderate pro-Western course. However, during the 1981–84 Mamaloni administrations relations with the USA were strained by the government's refusal to allow nuclear-powered warships within the islands' territorial waters. In pursuance of a new, broader 'Pacific strategy', the Solomon Islands joined Papua New Guinea and Vanuatu in forming the Spearhead Group Mar 1988, with the aim of preserving ◊Melanesian cultural traditions and securing independence for the French dependency of ◊New Caledonia.

Solomon's seal perennial plant *Polygonatum multiflorum*, family Liliaceae, found growing in moist shady woodland areas. It has bell-like white flowers drooping from the leaf axils of its arching stems, followed by blue-black berries.

Solon /ˈsəʊlɒn/ c. 638–558 BC. Athenian statesman. As one of the chief magistrates about 594 BC, he carried out the revision of the constitution that laid the foundations of Athenian democracy.

Soloviev /ˌsɒləvˈjɒf/ Vladimir Sergeyevich 1853–1900. Russian philosopher and poet, whose blending of Neo-Platonism and Christian mysticism attempted to link all aspects of human experience in a doctrine of divine wisdom. His theories, expressed in poems and essays, influenced Symbolist writers such as ◊Blok.

solstice either of the points at which the Sun is farthest north or south of the celestial equator each year. The *summer solstice*, when the Sun is

---

Solomon Islands

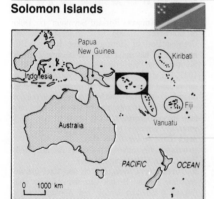

area 27,600 sq km/10,656 sq mi
capital Honiara on Guadalcanal
physical comprises all but the northernmost islands (which belong to Papua New Guinea) of a Melanesian archipelago that stretches nearly 1,500 km/900 mi. The largest is Guadalcanal (area 6,500 sq km/2,510 sq mi); others are Malaita, San Cristobal, New Georgia, Santa Isabel, Choiseul; mainly mountainous and forested
features rivers ideal for hydroelectric power
head of state Elizabeth II, represented by George Lepping from 1988
head of government Solomon Mamaloni from 1989

Somalia
Democratic Republic of
(Jamhuriyadda Dimugradiga Somaliya)

area 637,700 sq km/246,220 sq mi
capital Mogadishu
towns Hargeisa, Kismayu; port Berbera
physical mainly flat, with hills in the north
features many of the people are nomadic raisers of livestock
head of state and government Mohamed Siad Barre from 1969
government one-party socialist republic
political parties Somali Revolutionary Socialist Party (SRSP), nationalistic socialist
exports livestock, skins, hides, bananas
currency Somali shilling (698.02 = £1 Feb 1990)
population (1989) 8,552,000 (including 1 million refugees from W Somalia); annual growth rate 4.1%
life expectancy men 39, women 43
language Somali (national language), Arabic (also official), Italian, English
religion Sunni Muslim
literacy 18% male/6% female (1985 est)
GNP $1.2 bn (1983); less than $500 per head of population
chronology
1960 Achieved full independence.
1963 Border dispute with Kenya, diplomatic relations with the UK broken.
1968 Diplomatic relations with the UK restored.
1969 Following the assassination of the president, the army seized power. Maj-Gen Mohamed Siad Barre suspended the constitution and set up a Supreme Revolutionary Council.
1978 Defeated in eight-month war with Ethiopia.
1979 New constitution for a socialist one-party state adopted.
1987 Barre re-elected.
1989 Dissatisfaction with government and increased guerrilla activity in the N.

farthest north, occurs around June 21; the *winter solstice* around Dec 22.

Solti /ˈʃɒlti/ Georg 1912– . Hungarian-born British conductor. He was music director at Covent Garden 1961–71, and became director of the Chicago Symphony Orchestra 1969. He was also principal conductor of the London Philharmonic Orchestra 1979–83.

solubility in physics, a measure of the amount of solute (usually a solid or gas) that will dissolve in a given amount of solvent (usually a liquid) at a particular temperature. Solubility may be expressed as grams of solute per 100 grams of solvent or, for a gas, in parts per million of solvent. In ordinary terms, each is a way of expressing maximum possible concentration.

solute a substance that is dissolved in another substance (see ◊solution).

solution two or more substances mixed to form a single, homogenous phase. One of the substances is the *solvent* and the others (*solutes*) are said to be dissolved in it.

The constituents of a solution may be solid, liquid, or gaseous. The solvent is normally the substance that is present in greatest quantity, although when one of them is a liquid this is considered to be the solvent even if it is not the major substance.

Solvay process industrial process for the manufacture of sodium carbonate. It is a multi-stage process in which carbon dioxide is generated from limestone and passed through ◊brine saturated with ammonia. Sodium hydrogen carbonate is isolated and heated to yield sodium carbonate. All intermediate by-products are recycled so that the only ultimate by-product is calcium chloride.

solvent a substance, usually a liquid, that will dissolve another substance (see ◊solution).

Solway Firth /ˈsɒlweɪ/ inlet of the Irish Sea, formed by the estuaries of the Eden and the Esk, at the western end of the border between England and Scotland.

Solyman I alternative form of ◊Suleiman, Ottoman sultan.

Solzhenitsyn /ˌsɒlʒəˈnɪtsɪn/ Alexander (Isayevich) 1918– . Soviet novelist, a US citizen from 1974. After military service, he was in prison and exile 1945–57 for anti-Stalinist comments. Much of his writing is semi-autobiographical and highly critical of the system; for example, *One Day in the Life of Ivan Denisovich* 1962 deals with the labour camps under Stalin, and *The Gulag Archipelago* 1973 is an exposé of the whole Soviet camp network. This led to his expulsion from the USSR 1974.

He was awarded a Nobel prize in 1970. Other works include *The First Circle* and *Cancer Ward* both 1968. His autobiography, *The Oak and the Calf*, appeared 1980. He has adopted a Christian position, and his criticism of Western materialism is also stringent.

soma Indian intoxicating drink made from the fermented sap of the *Asclepias acida* plant. It was sacrificed to the Hindu god ◊Indra. Some have argued that the plant was in fact a hallucogenic mushroom.

Somali person of Somali culture from the Horn of Africa. Although the majority of Somalis live in the Somali Republic, there are Somali minorities in Ethiopia and Kenya. Their language belongs to the Cushitic branch of the Afro-Asiatic family.

Somalia /səˈmɑːlɪə/ country in the Horn of Africa, on the Indian Ocean.

government The 1979 constitution defines Somalia as a socialist state with power in the hands of the Somali Revolutionary Socialist Party (SRSP). As in most socialist states, the party and the state system operate alongside each other, with the president bestriding both. The president is chosen by the party as head of state and head of government and is secretary general of the party and president of its politburo. Party policy is formulated by the 51-member central committee, operating through 13 bureaux and sanctioned by the politburo. A council of ministers, appointed by the president, implements these policies. In the 177-member People's Assembly, six are presidential nominees and 171 elected by secret ballot for a five-year term from a single list of candidates approved by the party.

history For early history, see ◊Africa. Somalia developed around Arab trading posts which grew into sultanates. A British protectorate of Somaliland was established 1884–87 and Somalia, an Italian protectorate, 1889. The latter was a colony from 1927 and incorporated into Italian East Africa 1936; it came under British military rule 1941–50, when as a UN trusteeship it was again administered by Italy.

Somalia became a fully independent republic in 1960 through a merger of the two former colonial territories. Since then Somalia has been involved in disputes with its neighbours because of its insistence on the right of all Somalis to self-determination, wherever they have settled.

This has applied particularly to those living in the Ogaden district of Ethiopia and in NE Kenya. A dispute over the border with Kenya resulted in a break in diplomatic relations with Britain 1963–68. The dispute with Ethiopia led to an eight-month war in 1978, in which Somalia was defeated by Ethiopian troops assisted by Soviet and Cuban weapons and advisers. Some 1.5 million refugees entered Somalia, and guerrilla fighting continues in Ogaden. There was a rapprochement with Kenya in 1984 and, in 1986, the first meeting for ten years between the Somalian and Ethiopian leaders.

The first president of Somalia was Aden Abdullah Osman, and he was succeeded in 1967 by Dr Abdirashid Ali Shermarke of the Somali Youth League (SYL), which had become the dominant political party. In Oct 1969 President Shermarke was assassinated and the army seized power under the commander in chief, Maj-Gen Mohamed Siad Barre. He suspended the 1960 constitution, dissolved the national assembly, banned all political parties, and formed a military government. In 1970 he declared Somalia a socialist state.

In 1976 the junta transferred power to the newly created SRSP and three years later the constitution for a one-party state was adopted. Some unofficial opposition groups operate outside the country, from Ethiopia and London. Over the next few years Barre consolidated his position by increasing the influence of his own clan and reducing that of his northern rival, despite often violent opposition. He was re-elected in Jan 1987. Dissatisfaction with Barre's government, particularly in the northern region, contained the threat of civil war.

Somaliland /səˈmɑːlilænd/ region of Somali-speaking peoples in E Africa including the former British Somaliland Protectorate (established 1887), and Italian Somaliland (made a colony 1927, conquered by Britain 1941 and administered by Britain until 1950), which both became independent 1960 as the Somali Democratic Republic, the official name for ◊Somalia; and former French Somaliland which was established 1892, became known as the Territory of the Afars and Issas 1967, and became independent as ◊Djibouti 1977.

Somerset /ˈsʌməset/ family name of the dukes of Beaufort; seated at Badminton, Gloucestershire; descended in an illegitimate line from King Edward III.

Somerset /ˈsʌməset/ Edward Seymour, 1st Duke of Somerset *c.* 1506–1552. English politician. Created Earl of Hertford, after Henry VIII's marriage to his sister Jane, he became Duke of Somerset and Protector (regent) for Edward VI in 1547. His attempt to check ◊enclosure (the transfer of land from common to private ownership) offended landowners and his moderation in religion upset the Protestants, and he was beheaded on a fake treason charge in 1552.

Somerset /ˈsʌməset/ county in SW England
area 3,451 sq km/1,365 sq mi
towns administrative headquarters Taunton; Wells, Bridgwater, Glastonbury, Yeovil
features rivers Avon, Parret, and Exe; marshy coastline on the Bristol Channel; Mendip Hills (including Cheddar Gorge and Wookey Hole, a series of limestone caves where Old Stone Age flint implements and bones of extinct animals have been found); Quantock Hills; ◊Exmoor
products dairy products, and cider
population (1986) 450,800
famous people Henry Fielding.

Somerset House government office in the Strand, London, built 1775. It is used by the Inland Revenue, Principal Probate Registry, where wills are kept, and by the University of London. Somerset House is also the new home of the Courtauld Galleries.

The river facade was designed by William ◊Chambers. The General Register Office (births, marriages, and deaths), formerly at Somerset House, was merged with the Government Social Survey Department as the Office of Population

Somerset As protector of England from 1547 during the minority of Edward VI, Edward Seymour, Duke of Somerset, instigated the first Book of Common Prayer. He fell from power in 1549 and was executed 1552.

Censuses and Surveys in 1970, and transferred to St Catherine's House, also in the Strand.

Somerville /'sʌməvɪl/ Edith Oenone 1861–1949. Irish novelist, best known for her stories of Irish life written jointly with her cousin, Violet Martin ('Martin Ross'). Their works include *Some Experiences of an Irish RM* 1890.

Somerville /'sʌməvɪl/ Mary (born Fairfax) 1780–1872. Scottish scientific writer, who produced several widely used textbooks, despite having just one year of formal education. Somerville College, Oxford, is named after her. Her main works were *Mechanism of the Heavens* 1831 (a translation of ◊Laplace's treatise on celestial mechanics), *On the Connexion of Physical Sciences* 1834, *Physical Geography* 1848 and *On Molecular and Microscopic Science* 1869.

Somme /sɒm/ river in N France, on which Amiens and Abbeville stand; length 240 km/150 mi. It rises in Aisne *département* and flows west through Somme *département* to the English Channel.

Somme, Battle of the /sɒm/ Allied offensive in World War I July–Nov 1916 at Beaumont-Hamel-Chaulnes, on the river Somme in N France, during which severe losses were suffered by both sides. It was the first battle in which tanks were used. The German offensive around St Quentin Mar–Apr 1918 is sometimes called the Second Battle of the Somme.

Sommeiler /'sɒməleɪ/ Germain 1815–1871. French engineer who built the Mont Cenis Tunnel,

Somerset

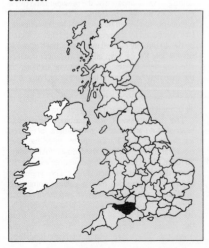

12 km/7 mi long, between Switzerland and France. The tunnel was drilled with his invention the ◊pneumatic drill.

Sommerfeld /'zɒməfelt/ Arnold 1868–1951. German physicist, who showed that the difficulties with the ◊Bohr model of the atom, in which electrons move around a central nucleus in circular orbits, could be overcome by supposing that electrons adopted elliptical orbits.

Somoza Debayle /sə'məʊsə/ Anastasio 1925–1980. Nicaraguan soldier and politician, president 1967–72 and 1974–79. The second son of Anastasio Somoza García, he succeeded his brother Luis Somoza Debayle (1922–1967; president 1956–63) as president of Nicaragua in 1967, to head an even more oppressive regime. He was removed by Sandinista guerrillas in 1979, and assassinated in Paraguay 1980.

Somoza García /sə'məʊsə/ Anastasio 1896–1956. Nicaraguan soldier and politician, president 1937–47 and 1950–56. A protégé of the USA, who wanted a reliable ally to protect their interests in Central America, he was virtual dictator of Nicaragua from 1937 until his assassination in 1956. He exiled most of his political opponents and amassed a considerable fortune in land and businesses. Members of his family retained control of the country until 1979, when they were overthrown by popular forces.

sonar or *echo-sounder* a method of locating underwater objects by the reflection of ultrasonic waves. The time taken for an acoustic beam to travel to the object and back to the source enables the distance to be found since the velocity of sound in water is known. The process was developed 1920.

The process is similar to that used in ◊radar. In World War I, an Allied Submarine Detection Investigation Committee was set up and an apparatus for detecting the presence of enemy U-boats beneath the sea surface by the use of ultrasonic echoes was perfected around 1920. It was named ASDIC, from its initials of the body responsible for it. In 1963, the name was changed, to accord with NATO practice, to sonar (*so*und *na*vigation and *r*anging).

sonata (Italian 'sounded') a piece of instrumental music written for a soloist or a small ensemble and consisting of a series of related movements.

sonata form in music, the structure of a movement, typically involving division into exposition, development, and recapitulation sections. It is the framework for much classical music, including ◊sonatas, ◊symphonies, and ◊concertos.

Sondheim /'sɒndhaɪm/ Stephen (Joshua) 1930– . US composer and lyricist. He wrote the witty and sophisticated lyrics of Leonard Bernstein's *West*

Somerville Scottish scientific writer Mary Somerville, portrayed by James Swinton. Somerville College, Oxford, one of the first women's colleges, is named after her.

Side Story 1957 and composed musicals, including *A Little Night Music* 1973, *Pacific Overtures* 1976, *Sweeney Todd* 1979, *Into the Woods* 1987, and *Sunday in the Park with George* 1989.

sone unit of subjective loudness. A tone of 40 decibels above the threshold of hearing with a frequency of 1000 hertz is defined as 1 sone; any sound that seems twice as loud as this has a value of 2 sones, and so on. A loudness of 1 sone corresponds to 40 ◊phons.

son et lumière (French 'sound and light') the outdoor night-time dramatization of the history of a notable building, monument, town, and so on, using theatrical lighting effects, sound effects, music, and narration; invented by Paul Robert Houdin, curator of the Château de Chambord.

song composition for one or more singers, often with instrumental accompaniment, such as madrigals and chansons. Common forms include folk song and ballad. The term *song* is used for secular music, whereas motet and cantata tend to be forms of sacred music.

song cycle a sequence of songs related in mood and sung as a group, used by romantic composers such as Schubert, Schumann, and Hugo Wolf.

Songhai Empire /ˌsɒŋ'gaɪ/ a former kingdom of NW Africa, founded in the 8th century, which developed into a powerful Muslim empire under the rule of Sonni Ali (reigned 1464–92). It superseded ◊Mali and extended its territory, occupying an area that includes present-day Senegal, Gambia, Mali, and parts of Mauretania, Niger, and Nigeria. In 1591 it was invaded and overthrown by Morocco.

'Song of Myself' the longest poem in Walt Whitman's ◊*Leaves of Grass*, relating the poet, the 'single separate person', to the democratic 'en masse'. It was regularly revised from its original form of 1855 to incorporate new experience and 'cosmic sensations'.

sonic boom a noise like a thunderclap that occurs when an aircraft passes through the ◊sound barrier, or begins to travel faster than the speed of sound. It is caused by shock waves set up by the aircraft.

sonnet fourteen-line poem of Italian origin introduced to England by Sir Thomas ◊Wyatt in the form used by Petrarch (rhyming *abba abba cdcdcd* or *cdecde*), as followed by Milton and Wordsworth; Shakespeare used the form *abab cdcd efef gg.*

sonoluminescence emission of light by a liquid that is subjected to high-frequency sound waves. The rapid changes of pressure induced by the sound cause minute bubbles to form in the liquid, which then collapse. Light is emitted at the final stage of the collapse, probably because it squeezes and heats gas inside the bubbles.

Sons of Liberty in American colonial history, the name adopted by those colonists opposing the ◊Stamp Act of 1765. Merchants, lawyers, farmers, artisans and labourers joined what was an early instance of concerted resistance to British rule, causing the repeal of the Act Mar 1766.

Sontag /'sɒntæg/ Susan 1933– . US critic, novelist, and screenwriter. Her novel *The Benefactor* appeared in 1963, and she established herself as a critic with the influential cultural essays of *Against Interpretation* 1966 and *Styles of Radical Will* 1969. More recent studies, showing the influence of French structuralism, are *On Photography* 1976 and the powerful *Illness as Metaphor* 1978.

Soochow /ˌsuː'tʃaʊ/ former transliteration for the Chinese city of ◊Suzhou.

Soong Ching-ling /suːn ˌtʃɪŋ'lɪŋ/ 1892–1981. Chinese politician, wife of the Guomindang founder ◊Sun Yat-sen; she remained a prominent figure in Chinese politics after his death, being vice chair of the republic from 1959, but came under attack 1967 during the Cultural Revolution. After the death of Zhu De (1886–1976), she served as acting head of state.

Sophia /sə'faɪə/ Electress of Hanover 1630–1714. Twelfth child of Frederick V, elector palatine of the Rhine and king of Bohemia, and Elizabeth, daughter of James I of England. She married the Elector of Hanover 1658. Widowed in 1698, she was recognized in the succession to the English throne 1701, and when Queen Anne died without issue in 1714, her son George I founded the Hanoverian dynasty.

sophist (Greek 'wise man') one of a group of 5th-century BC lecturers on culture, rhetoric, and politics. Sceptical about the possibility of achieving genuine knowledge, they applied bogus reasoning and were concerned with winning arguments rather than establishing the truth. ◊Plato regarded them as dishonest and *sophistry* came to mean fallacious reasoning.

Sophocles /'sɒfəkliːz/ 495–406 BC. Greek dramatist who, with Aeschylus and Euripides, is one of the three great tragedians. He modified the form of tragedy by introducing a third actor and developing stage scenery. He wrote some 120 plays, of which seven tragedies survive. These are *Antigone* 441, *Oedipus Tyrannus, Electra, Ajax, Trachiniae, Philoctetes* 409, and *Oedipus at Colonus* 401.

Sophocles lived in Athens at the time of ◊Pericles, a period of great prosperity. He was a popular man and the friend of ◊Herodotus. In his tragedies human will plays a greater part than that of the gods, as in the plays of Aeschylus, and his characters are generally heroic. This is perhaps what he meant when he said of Euripides 'He paints men as they are' and of himself 'I paint men as they ought to be'. A large fragment of a satyric play (a tragedy treated in a grotesquely comic fashion) *Ichneutae* also survives.

soprano in music, the highest range of female voice.

Sopwith /'sɒpwɪθ/ Thomas Octave Murdoch 1888–1989. English designer of the Sopwith Camel biplane, used in World War I, and joint developer of the Hawker Hurricane fighter plane used in World War II.

From a Northumbrian engineering family, Sopwith gained a pilot's licence in 1910 and soon after set a British aerial duration record for a flight of three hours 12 minutes. In 1912 he founded the Sopwith Aviation Company, which in 1920 he wound up and reopened as the Hawker Company, after the chief test pilot Harry Hawker. The Hawker Company was responsible for the Hawker Hart bomber, the Hurricane, and eventually the ◊Harrier jump jet.

sorbic acid a tasteless acid found in the fruit of the rowan or mountain ash, widely used in the preservation of food, for example cider, wine, soft drinks, animal feedstuffs, bread, and cheese.

Sorbonne /sɔː'bɒn/ common name for the University of Paris, originally a theological institute founded 1253 by Robert de Sorbon, chaplain to Louis IX.

Richelieu ordered the reconstruction of the buildings in 1626, which were again rebuilt in 1885. In 1808, the Sorbonne became the seat of the Académie of Paris and of the University of Paris. It is the most prestigious French university.

Sorbus genus of deciduous trees and shrubs of the northern hemisphere, family Rosaceae, including ◊mountain ash, ◊whitebeam, and ◊service tree.

Sorel /sɒ'rel/ Georges 1847–1922. French philosopher, who believed that socialism could only come about through a general strike; his theory of the need for a 'myth' to sway the body of the people was used by fascists.

Sørensen /'sɜːrənsən/ Søren 1868–1939. Danish chemist, who in 1909 introduced the concept of using a ◊pH scale as a measure of the acidity of a solution. On Sørensen's scale, still used today, a pH of 7 is neutral; higher numbers represent alkalinity, and lower numbers acidity.

sorghum also called *great millet* or *guinea-corn* cereal grass, native to Africa but cultivated widely in India, China, USA, and S Europe. The seeds are used for making bread.

sorority a building providing accommmodation for university women in the USA; the men's equivalent is a fraternity.

sorrel (Old French *sur* 'sour') species of plants in the genus *Rumex*, family Polygonaceae. *Rumex acetosa* is grown for its bitter salad leaves.

Sorrento /sɒ'rentəʊ/ town on the Gulf of Naples, SW Italy; population (1981) 17,301. It has been a resort since Roman times.

sorting in computing, techniques for arranging data in sequence. The choice of sorting method involves a compromise between running time, memory usage, and complexity.

Methods include *selection sorting*, where the smallest item is found and exchanged with the first item, the second smallest exchanged with the second item, and so on; *bubble sorting*, where adjacent items are continually exchanged until the data are in sequence; and *insertion sorting*, where each item is placed in the correct position and subsequent items moved down to make a place for it.

sorus in ferns, a group of sporangia, the reproductive structures that produce ◊spores. They occur on the lower surface of fern fronds.

SOS internationally recognized distress signal, using letters of the ◊Morse code.

Sosnowiec /sɒ'snɒvjets/ chief city of the Darowa coal region in the Upper Silesian province of Katowice, S Poland; population (1985) 255,000.

soul according to many religions, an intangible part of a human being that survives the death of the physical body.

Judaism, Christianity, and Islam all teach that at the end of the world each soul will be judged and assigned to heaven or hell on its merits. In other religions, such as Hinduism, the soul is thought to undergo ◊reincarnation until the individual reaches enlightenment and is freed from the cycle of rebirth. According to the teachings of Buddhism, no permanent self or soul exists.

soul music style of ◊rhythm and blues, influenced by gospel music, and sung by, among others, Sam Cooke (1931–1964), Aretha Franklin (1942–   ), and Al Green (1946–   ).

Soult /suːlt/ Nicolas Jean de Dieu 1769–1851. Marshal of France. He held commands in Spain in the Peninsular War, when he sacked the port of Santander 1808, and was chief of staff at the Battle of ◊Waterloo. He was war minister 1830–40.

sound physiological sensation received by the ear, originating in a vibration (pressure variation in the air), which communicates itself to the air, and travels in every direction, spreading out as an expanding sphere. All sound waves in air travel with a speed dependent on the temperature; under ordinary conditions, this is about 330 m/1,070 ft per second. The pitch of the sound depends on the number of vibrations imposed on the air per second, but the speed is unaffected. The loudness of a sound is dependent primarily on the amplitude of the vibration of the air.

The lowest note audible to a human being has a frequency of about 26 ◊hertz (vibrations per second), and the highest one of about 18,000 Hz; the lower limit of this range varies little with the person's age, but the upper range falls steadily from adolescence onwards.

Sound, the /saʊnd/ strait dividing SW Sweden from Denmark and linking the ◊Kattegat and the Baltic; length 113 km/70 mi; width between 5 km/3 mi and 60 km/37 mi.

sound barrier the concept that the speed of sound, or sonic speed, (about 1,220 kph/760 mph at sea level) constitutes a speed limit to flight through the atmosphere, since a badly designed aircraft suffers severe buffeting at near sonic speed owing to the formation of shock waves. US test pilot Chuck Yeager first flew through the 'barrier' in 1947 in a Bell X-1 rocket plane. Now, by careful design, aircraft such as Concorde can fly at supersonic speed with ease, though they create in their wake a ◊sonic boom.

sound synthesis the generation of sound (usually music) by electronic ◊synthesizer.

sound track a band at one side of a cine film on which the accompanying sound is recorded. Usually it

takes the form of an optical track (a pattern of light and shade). The pattern is produced on the film when signals from the recording microphone are made to vary the intensity of a light beam. During playback, a light is shone through the track onto a photocell, which converts the pattern of light falling on it into appropriate electrical signals. These signals are then fed to loudspeakers to recreate the original sounds.

soupçon (French 'suspicion') a very small amount, a dash.

Souphanouvong /,suːfænuː'vɒŋ/ Prince 1912–   . Laotian politician, president 1975–86. After an abortive revolt against French rule 1945, he led the guerrilla organization Pathet Lao, and in 1975 became first president of the Republic of Laos. He resigned after suffering a stroke.

source language in computing, the language in which programs are originally written, as opposed to ◊machine code, which is the form in which they are carried out by the computer. The translation from source language to machine code is done by a ◊compiler or ◊interpreter program within the computer.

Sousa /'suːzə/ John Philip 1854–1932. US bandmaster and composer of marches, such as 'The Stars and Stripes Forever!' 1897.

sousaphone a form of large bass ◊tuba, suggested by US bandmaster John Sousa, designed to wrap round the player in a circle and having a forward-facing bell.

South, the historically, in the USA, the states south of the ◊Mason-Dixon line, with an agrarian economy based on plantations worked by slaves, which seceded from the Union at the beginning of the US Civil War, becoming the ◊Confederacy. The term is now loosely applied in a geographic and cultural sense, with Texas often regarded as part of the Southwest rather than the South.

South Africa /saʊθ 'æfrɪkə/ country on the S tip of Africa, bounded to the N by Namibia, Botswana, and Zimbabwe, and to the NE by Swaziland and Mozambique.

government The 1984 constitution is based on racial discrimination. The legislature and government are dominated by the descendants of Europeans, termed Whites in the context of ◊apartheid. There is only conditional participation in government for non-Whites, in the form of Coloureds, or persons of mixed European and African descent, and Asians. Black Africans are still completely unrepresented at national level.

The three-chamber parliament consists of the House of Assembly, for Whites, the House of Representatives, for Coloureds, and the House of Delegates, for Indians. The House of Assembly has 178 members, 166 elected by universal White suffrage, four nominated by the president on the basis of one for each province, and eight elected by the 166. The House of Representatives has 85 members, 80 elected by universal Coloured suffrage, two nominated by the president and three elected by the 80. The House of Delegates has 45 members, 40 elected by universal Indian suffrage, two nominated by the president, and three elected by the 40 directly elected members. Each house is responsible for its 'own affairs', meaning matters affecting only Whites, Coloureds, or Indians, as the case may be. General legislation applying to all races, including Black Africans, has to be approved by all three houses and the president. Members of all three houses serve a five-year term.

The state president, who combines the roles of head of state and head of government, is elected for the duration of Parliament by an 88-member electoral college: 50 from the House of Assembly, 25 from the House of Representatives and 13 from the House of Delegates. The president appoints and presides over a cabinet dominated by Whites, and is advised by an appointed council of 60 members: 20 from the House of Assembly, 10 from the House of Representatives, 5 from the House of Delegates, and 25 chosen by the president. There are also 3 advisory ministers' councils: one for the whole country, one for the Coloured community, and one for the Indians.

Each of South Africa's four provinces has an adminstrator, appointed by the president, and an elected provincial council.

history for early history, see ◊Africa. The area was originally inhabited by Bushmen and Hottentots. Bantus, including Sotho, Swazi, Xhosa, and Zulu, settled there before the 17th century. The ◊Cape of Good Hope was rounded by Bartolomeu ◊Diaz 1488; the coast of Natal was sighted by Vasco da ◊Gama 1497. The Dutch East India Company founded Cape Town 1652 as a port of call on the way to the Indies.

Occupied by Britain 1795 and 1806, Cape Town and the hinterland were purchased by Britain 1814 for £6 million. Britons also settled in ◊Natal, on the coast near ◊Durban, 1824. In 1836 some 10,000 Dutch, wishing to escape from British rule, set out north on the Great Trek and founded the republic of ◊Transvaal and the ◊Orange Free State; they also settled in N Natal, which became part of Cape Colony 1844 and a separate colony 1856. The Orange Free State was annexed by Britain 1848 but became independent 1854.

The discovery of diamonds at Kimberley, Cape Colony, 1867, and of gold in Transvaal 1886, attracted prospectors, who came in conflict with the Dutch farmers, the ◊Boers. Britain attempted to occupy Transvaal 1877–81 but withdrew after a severe defeat at Majuba (see ◊South African Wars). Denial of citizenship rights to the migrant miners (*uitlanders*) in Transvaal, and the imperialist ambitions of Cecil ◊Rhodes and others, led to the Jameson Raid (see L S ◊Jameson) and the Boer War 1899–1902 (see ◊South African Wars), won by Britain.

In 1910 the Union of South Africa was formed, comprising the provinces of Cape of Good Hope, Natal, Orange Free State, and Transvaal. A Boer rebellion on the outbreak of ◊World War I was speedily crushed by ◊Smuts. South Africa occupied German SW Africa (see ◊Namibia). Between the wars the union was alternately governed by the republican nationalists under ◊Hertzog and the South African Party under Smuts, who supported the Commonwealth connection. Hertzog wanted South Africa to be neutral in ◊World War II, but Smuts took over as premier and South African troops fought with the Allies.

The NP came to power 1948 and has ruled South Africa ever since. Its leader, Daniel Malan, initiated the policy of apartheid, attempting to justify it as 'separate but equal' development. In fact, all but the White minority is denied a voice in the nation's affairs. In the 1950s the ◊African National Congress (ANC) led a campaign of civil disobedience until it and other similar movements were, in 1960, declared illegal, and in 1964 the ANC leader Nelson Mandela was sentenced to life imprisonment for alleged sabotage. He has become a central symbol of Black opposition to the apartheid regime.

Malan was succeeded 1958 by Hendrik ◊Verwoerd, who withdrew from the Commonwealth rather than abandon apartheid, and the Union became the Republic of South Africa 1961. Verwoerd was assassinated 1966 but his successor, B J ◊Vorster, pursued the same policy. Pass laws restricting the movement of Blacks within the country had been introduced, causing international outrage, and ten 'homelands' (Bantustans; see ◊Black national state) were established to contain particular ethnic groups. By the 1980s thousands of the apartheid regime's opponents had been imprisoned without trial and more than 3,000,000 people had been forcibly resettled in Black townships. International condemnation of police brutality followed the news of the death in detention of the Black community leader Steve Biko 1977. Despite all this, the NP continued to increase its majority at each election, with the White opposition parties failing to make any significant impact. The Progressive Federal Party is the main opposition party, calling for a federal constitution based on regional rather than race differences, and led by Colin Eglin; and the New Republic Party favours racial power sharing.

In 1978 Vorster resigned and was succeeded by Pieter W ◊Botha. He embarked on constitutional reform to involve Coloureds and Asians, but not Blacks, in the governmental process. This led to a clash within the NP and in Mar 1982 Dr Adries Treurnicht, leader of the hardline (*verkrampte*) wing, and 15 other extremists were expelled. They later formed a new party, the Conservative Party of South Africa (CPSA). Although there were considerable doubts about Botha's proposals in the Coloured and Indian communities as well as among the Whites, they were approved by 66% of the voters in an all-White referendum and came into effect Sept 1984. In 1985 a number of apartheid laws were amended or repealed, including the ban on sexual relations or marriage between people of different races and the ban on mixed racial membership of political parties, but the underlying inequalities in the system remained and dissatisfaction of the Black community grew. In the 1986 cabinet of 21, including Botha, there were 19 Whites, one Coloured, and one Indian. The main Coloured parties are the Labour Party of South Africa, led by the Rev Allan Hendrickse, and the People's Congress Party. The main Indian parties are the National People's Party, led by Amichand Rajbani, and the Solidarity Party, led by Dr J N Reddy.

In May 1986 South Africa attacked what it claimed to be guerrilla strongholds in Botswana, Zambia, and Zimbabwe. The exiled ANC leader Oliver ◊Tambo was receiving increasing moral support in meetings with politicians throughout the world, and Winnie ◊Mandela, during her husband's continuing imprisonment, was not afraid to condemn the system publicly. Non-violent resistance was advocated by Bishop ◊Tutu, the ◊Inkatha movement, and others. A state of emergency was declared June 1986, a few days before the tenth anniversary of the first ◊Soweto uprising, marked by a strike in which millions of Blacks participated. Serious rioting broke out in the townships and was met with police violence, causing hundreds of deaths.

Abroad, calls for economic ◊sanctions against South Africa grew during 1985 and 1986. At the

South Africa
Republic of (Afrikaans
Republiek van Suid-Afrika)

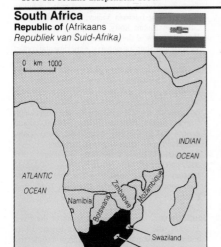

area 1,223,181 sq km/433,678 sq mi
capital Cape Town (legislative), Pretoria (administrative)
towns Johannesburg, Bloemfontein; ports Cape Town, Durban, Port Elizabeth, East London
physical a plateau
territories Prince Edward Island in the Antarctic
features Drakensberg Mountains, Table Mountain, Limpopo and Orange rivers; the Veld and the Karroo; part of Kalahari Desert; Kruger National Park, largest in the world
head of state and government F W de Klerk from 1989
government racialist, nationalist republic
political parties White: National Party (NP), right-of-centre, racialist; Conservative Party of South Africa (CPSA), extreme-right, racialist; Democratic Party (DP), left-of-centre, multi-racial. Coloureds: Labour Party of South Africa, left-of-centre; People's Congress Party, right-of-centre. Indian: National People's Party, right-of-centre; Solidarity Party, left-of-centre. Black: African National Congress (ANC), left-wing, anti-apartheid
exports maize, sugar, fruit; wool; gold, platinum (world's largest producer), diamonds
currency rand (commercial rate 4.33 = £1 Feb 1990)
population (1989) 35,625,000 (68% black, of whom the largest nations are the Zulu, Xhosa, Sotho, and Tswana, 18% white, 10% of mixed

ancestry, and 3% Asiatic); annual growth rate 2.5%
life expectancy men 55, women 55
language Afrikaans and English (both official); various Bantu languages
religion Christian; largest denomination is the Nederduits Gereformeerde Kerk/Dutch Reformed Church. Congregations are segregated
literacy 81% male/81% female (1980 est), ranging from 98% whites to 50% blacks
GNP $76.8 bn (1983); $1,296 per head of population
chronology
1910 Union of South Africa formed from two British colonies and two Boer republics.
1912 African National Congress (ANC) formed.
1948 Apartheid system of racial discrimination initiated by Daniel Malan.
1955 Freedom Charter adopted by African National Congress (ANC).
1958 Malan succeeded as prime minister by Hendrik Verwoerd.
1960 ANC banned.
1961 South Africa withdrew from the Commonwealth and became a republic.
1962 ANC leader Nelson Mandela jailed.
1964 Mandela, Walter Sisulu, Govan Mbeki, and five other ANC leaders sentenced to life imprisonment.
1966 Verwoerd assassinated and succeeded by B J Vorster.
1976 Soweto uprising.
1977 Death in custody of Pan African Congress activist Steve Biko.
1978 Vorster resigned and was replaced by Pieter W Botha.
1984 New constitution adopted, giving segregated representation to coloureds and Asians and making Botha president. Nonaggression pact with Mozambique signed but not observed.
1985 Growth of violence in black townships.
1986 Commonwealth agreed on limited sanctions. US Congress voted to impose sanctions. Several multinational companies announced closure of their South African operations.
1987 The government formally acknowledged the presence of its military forces in Angola.
1988 Peace agreement with Angola and Cuba, recognising independence for Namibia.
1989 Botha gave up NP leadership and state presidency. Democratic Party (DP) launched. F W de Klerk became president. Walter Sisulu and other ANC activists released
1990 Nelson Mandela released. ANC legalized.

Heads of Commonwealth conference 1985 the Eminent Persons' Group (EPG) of Commonwealth politicians was conceived to investigate the likelihood of change in South Africa without sanctions. In July 1986 the EPG reported that there were no signs of genuine liberalization. Reluctantly, Britain's prime minister, Margaret Thatcher, agreed to limited measures. Some Commonwealth countries, noticeably Australia and Canada, took additional independent action. The US Congress eventually forced President Reagan to move in the same direction. The decisions by individual multinational companies to close down their South African operations (see ◊disinvestment) may, in the long term, have the greatest effect.

At the end of 1988 South Africa signed a peace agreement with Angola and Cuba, which included the acceptance of Namibia's independence, and in 1989, under UN supervision, free elections took place there. In Feb 1989 state president Botha suffered a stroke that forced him to give up the NP leadership and later the presidency. He was succeeded in both roles by F W de Klerk, who promised major constitutional reforms. Meanwhile the non-racialist Democratic Party was launched, advocating universal adult suffrage, and made significant progress in the Sept 1989 whites-only assembly elections. Despite de Klerk's release of the veteran ANC activist Walter Sisulu and some of his colleagues in Oct 1989, the new president's promises of political reform were treated with scepticism by the opposition until he announced the lifting of the ban on the ANC, followed, on 11 Feb 1990, by the release of Nelson Mandela. With growing opposition from the extreme right-wing activists, the abandonment of apartheid and the establishment of a fully democratic political system will require considerable skill from both de Klerk and Mandela.

South Africa: provinces

Province	Capital	Area in sq km
Cape of Good Hope	Cape Town	721,000
Natal	Pietermaritzburg	86,965
Transvaal	Pretoria	286,064
Orange Free State	Bloemfontein	129,152
		1,223181

South African literature the founder of South African literature in English was Thomas Pringle (1789–1834), who published lyric poetry and the prose *Narrative of a Residence in South Africa*. The finest of the more recent poets are Roy Campbell and Francis C Slater (1876–1959). The first work of South African fiction to achieve fame outside the country was Olive Schreiner's *Story of an African Farm* 1833; later writers include Sarah G Millin, Pauline Smith (*The Little Karoo*), William Plomer (1903–73), Laurens van der Post, Alan Paton, Nadine Gordimer, and playwright Athol Fugard.

Original writing in ◊Afrikaans developed rapidly after the South African War, and includes the lyricists C L Leipoldt, J F E Celliers, and E N Marais (1872–1936); the satirical sketch and story writer C J Langenhoven, and the student of wildlife 'Sangiro' (A A Peinhar), author of *The Adventures of a Lion Family*, which became popular in English translation. In more recent years the intellectual barriers imposed by South Africa's isolation have prevented its writers from becoming more widely known, but there has been much spirited work, including that of the novelists André P Brink and Etienne Leroux, and the poet Ingrid Jonker.

Notable black writings include the autobiographical *Down Second Avenue* 1959, by Ezekiel Mphahlele (1919–); and the drama *The Rhythm of Violence* 1964, by Lewis Nkosi (1936–).

South African Wars two wars between the Boers (settlers of Dutch origin) and the British; essentially fought for the gold and diamonds of the Transvaal.

The *War of 1881* was triggered by the attempt of the Boers of the ◊Transvaal to reassert the independence surrendered 1877 in return for British aid against African peoples. The British were defeated at Majuba, and the Transvaal again became independent.

The *War of 1899–1902*, also known as the *Boer War*, was preceded by the armed ◊Jameson Raid into the Boer Transvaal; a failed attempt, inspired by the Cape Colony prime minister Rhodes, to precipitate a revolt against Kruger, the Transvaal president. The *uitlanders* (non-Boer immigrants) were still not given the vote by the Boers, negotiations failed, and the Boers invaded British territory, besieging Ladysmith, Mafeking (now Mafikeng), and Kimberley.

British commander ◊Kitchener countered Boer guerrilla warfare by putting the noncombatants who supported them into concentration camps (about 26,000 women and children died of sickness). The war ended with the Peace of Vereeniging when the Boers surrendered.

South America /'sauθ ə'merɪkə/ fourth largest of the continents, nearly twice as large as Europe
area 17,854,000 sq km/6,893,429 sq mi
largest cities (over 3.5 million inhabitants) Buenos Aires, São Paulo, Rio de Janeiro, Bogotá, Santiago, Lima, Caracas
features Andes in the west, Brazilian and Guiana highlands; central plains from the Orinoco basin to Patagonia; Parana–Paraguay–Uruguay system flowing to form the La Plata estuary; Amazon river basin, with its remaining great forests, with their rich fauna and flora
exports coffee, cocoa, sugar, bananas, oranges, wine, meat and fish products, cotton, wool, handicrafts, minerals including oil, silver, iron ore, copper
population (1985) 263,300,000, originally ◊American Indians, who survive chiefly in Bolivia, Peru, and Ecuador, and are increasing in number; in addition there are many mestizo (people of mixed Spanish or Portuguese and Indian ancestry) elsewhere; many people originally from Europe, largely Spanish, Italian, and Portuguese; and many of African descent, originally imported as slaves
language many American Indian languages, Spanish, Portuguese is the chief language in Brazil
religion Roman Catholic; American Indian beliefs
history for the archaic and later American Indian cultures, see ◊American Indian
16th century Arrival of Europeans, with the Spanish (◊Pizarro) and Portuguese conquest; the American Indians were mainly assimilated, or, where considered unsuitable for slave labour, killed and replaced by imported slaves from Africa.
18th century Revolt of ◊Túpac Amaru.
19th century Napoleon's toppling of the Spanish throne opened the way for the liberation of its colonies (led by ◊Bolívar and ◊San Martín). Brazil became peacefully independent. Large-scale European immigration took place (Hispanic, Italian, and German). Interstate wars took a heavy toll, for example, the Paraguay War (see under ◊Paraguay) and ◊Pacific War.
20th century Rapid industrialization and high population growth. In the 1980s heavy indebtedness incurred to fund economic expansion led to an inability to meet interest payments in the world slump.
1946–55 Perón president in Argentina.
1970–73 Elected socialist regime under Salvador Allende in Chile, overthrown by military backed by the US Central Intelligence Agency.
1982 Falklands War between the UK and Argentina.

Southampton /sauθ'hæmptən/ port in Hampshire, England; population (1981) 204,604. Industries include engineering, chemicals, plastics, flour-milling, and tobacco; it is also a passenger and container port.

The *Mayflower* set sail from here en route to North America 1620, as did the *Titanic* on its fateful maiden voyage 1912. There is a university, established 1952.

Southampton /sauθ'hæmptən/ Henry Wriothesley, 3rd Earl of Southampton 1573–1624. English courtier, patron of Shakespeare who dedicated *Venus and Adonis* and *The Rape of Lucrece* to him, and may have addressed him in the sonnets.

South Arabia, Federation of /'sauθ ə'reɪbɪə/ former grouping (1959–67) of Arab emirates and sheikdoms, joined by ◊Aden 1963. The western part of the area was claimed by ◊Yemen, and sporadic fighting and terrorism from 1964 led to British withdrawal 1967, and the proclamation of the Republic of South Yemen.

South Asia Regional Cooperation Committee (SARCC) organization established 1983 by India, Pakistan, Bangladesh, Nepál, Sri Lanka, Bhutan and the Maldives to cover agriculture, telecommunications, health, population, sport, art, and culture.

South Australia /'sauθ ɒs'treɪlɪə/ state of the Commonwealth of Australia
area 984,000 sq km/379,824 sq mi
capital and chief port Adelaide
towns Whyalla, Mount Gambier
features Murray Valley irrigated area, including wine-growing Barossa Valley; Lakes ◊Eyre and ◊Torrens; Mount Lofty, Musgrave and Flinders Ranges; parts of the ◊Nullarbor Plain, and Great Victoria and Simpson deserts; experimental rocket range in the arid north at Woomera; and at Maralinga British nuclear tests were made 1963 in which Aborigines were said to have died
products meat and wool (80% of area cattle and sheep grazing), wines and spirits, dried and canned fruit, iron (Middleback Range), coal (Leigh Creek), copper, uranium (Roxby Downs), oil and natural gas in the NE, lead, zinc, iron, opals, household and electrical goods, vehicles
population (1987) 1,388,000, including 13,300 Aborigines
history possibly known to the Dutch in the 16th century; surveyed by ◊Tasman 1644; first European settlement 1834; province 1836; state 1901.

South Bank an area of London south of the river Thames, the site of the Festival of Britain 1951, and now a cultural centre. Buildings include the Royal Festival Hall 1951 (Robert Matthew and Leslie Martin) and the National Theatre 1976 (Denys Lasdun), all connected by a series of walkways.

South Bend /'sauθ 'bend/ city on the St Joseph river, N Indiana, USA; population (1980) 110,000. Industries include the manufacture of agricultural machinery, cars, and aircraft equipment.

South Carolina /'sauθ ˌkærə'laɪnə/ state of the SE USA; nickname Palmetto State
area 80,600 sq km/31,112 sq mi
capital Columbia
towns Charleston, Greenville-Spartanburg
physical large areas of woodland; subtropical climate in coastal areas
products tobacco, cotton, fruit, soybeans, meat, textiles, clothing, paper, woodpulp, furniture, bricks, chemicals, machinery
population (1988) 3,493,000
famous people John C Calhoun
history first Spanish settlers 1526; Charles I gave the area (known as Carolina) to Robert Heath (1575–1649), attorney general 1629; Declaration of Independence, one of the original Thirteen States 1776; joined the Confederacy 1860; re-admitted to Union 1868.

South Dakota /'sauθ də'kəutə/ state of the USA; nickname Coyote or Sunshine State
area 199,800 sq km/77,123 sq mi
capital Pierre
towns Sioux Falls, Rapid City, Aberdeen
physical Great Plains; Black Hills (which include granite Mount Rushmore, on whose face giant relief portrait heads of former presidents Washington, Jefferson, Lincoln, and T Roosevelt are carved); Badlands

South America

Southend-on-Sea /ˌsaʊθ'end ɒn 'si:/ resort in Essex, England; population (1981) 157,100. Industries include light engineering and boat-building. The shallow water of the Thames estuary enabled the building of a pier 2 km/1.25 mi long.

Southend-on-Sea /ˌsaʊθ'end ɒn 'si:/ resort in Essex, England; population (1981) 157,100. Industries include light engineering and boat-building. The shallow water of the Thames estuary enabled the building of a pier 2 km/1.25 mi long.

Southern and Antarctic Territories French overseas territory created 1955. It comprises the islands of *St Paul* and *Amsterdam* (67 sq km/26 sq mi); the *Kerguelen* and *Crozet* Islands (7,515 sq km/2,901 sq mi); and *Adélie Land* on Antarctica itself (432,000 sq km/165,500 sq mi). All are uninhabited, except for research stations.

Southern Christian Leadership Conference (SCLC) US civil-rights organization founded 1957 by Martin Luther ◊King and led by him until his assassination 1968. It advocated nonviolence and passive resistance, and sponsored the 1963 march on Washington DC that focused national attention on the civil-rights movement.

Southern Cross popular name for the constellation ◊Crux.

Southerne /'sʌðən/ Thomas 1660–1746. English playwright and poet, author of the tragi-comedies *Oroonoko* 1695–96 and *The Fatal Marriage* 1694.

southern lights common name for the ◊aurora australis, coloured light in southern skies.

Southern US fiction part of a long tradition of fiction and belles lettres in the US South since Edgar Allan Poe, often distinctively different from other US fiction. In the 20th century a remarkable literary revival began, exemplified by the work of Ellen Glasgow and William Faulkner, dealing with the experience of a defeated agrarian region with proud traditions. The Southern Gothic school includes Flannery O'Connor and Carson McCullers.

Writers of the 19th century include William Gilmore Simms, Joel Chandler Harris, and George Washington Cable. Among 20th-century writers are Thomas Wolfe, Robert Penn Warren, Katherine Anne Porter, Eudora Welty, William Styron, and, on a lesser level, Margaret Mitchell, author of *Gone With the Wind* 1936.

Southey /'saʊði/ Robert 1774–1843. English poet and author, friend of Coleridge and Wordsworth. In 1813 he became Poet Laureate, but his verse is little read today. He is better known for his *Life of Nelson* 1813, and his letters. He abandoned his early revolutionary views, and from 1808 contributed regularly to the Tory *Quarterly Review*.

South Georgia /'saʊθ 'dʒɔ:dʒə/ island in the S Atlantic, a British crown colony administered with the South Sandwich Islands; area 3,757 sq km/1,450 sq mi. South Georgia lies 1,300 km/800 mi SE of the Falkland Islands, of which it was a dependency until 1985. The British Antarctic Survey has a station on nearby Bird Island.

South Georgia was visited by Captain James Cook 1775. The explorer Edward Shackleton is buried there. The chief settlement, Grytviken, was established as a whaling station 1904 and abandoned 1966; it was reoccupied by a small military garrison after the Falklands War 1982.

South Australia

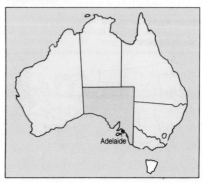

products cereals, livestock, gold (greatest USA producer)
population (1986) 708,000
famous people Crazy Horse, Sitting Bull, Ernest O Lawrence
history claimed by French 18th century; first white settlements 1794; state 1889.

Southeast Asia Treaty Organization (SEATO) former collective defence system analogous to NATO, established 1954. Participating countries were Australia, France, New Zealand, Pakistan, the Philippines, Thailand, the UK, and the USA, with Vietnam, Cambodia, and Laos as protocol states. It originated in ◊ANZUS. After the Vietnam War, SEATO was phased out by 1977 and its nonmilitary aspects assumed by the ◊Association of Southeast Asian Nations (ASEAN).

South East Cape most southerly point of Australia, in Tasmania.

South America Map

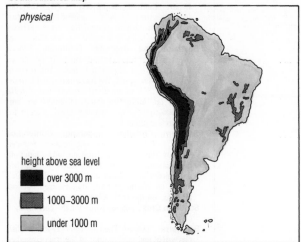

physical

height above sea level
- ■ over 3000 m
- ▨ 1000–3000 m
- ▢ under 1000 m

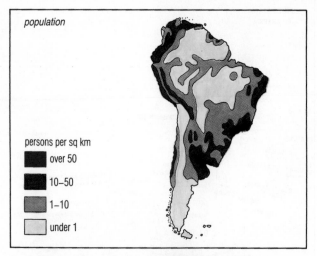

population

persons per sq km
- ■ over 50
- ■ 10–50
- ▨ 1–10
- ▢ under 1

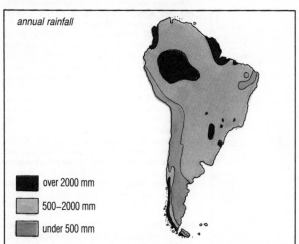

annual rainfall

- ■ over 2000 mm
- ▨ 500–2000 mm
- ▨ under 500 mm

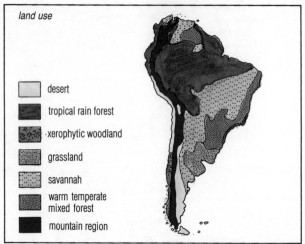

land use

- ▢ desert
- ▨ tropical rain forest
- ▨ xerophytic woodland
- ▨ grassland
- ▨ savannah
- ▨ warm temperate mixed forest
- ■ mountain region

South Glamorgan /ˈsaʊθ ˌɡləˈmɔːɡən/ county in S Wales
area 420 sq km/162 sq mi
towns administrative headquarters Cardiff; Barry, Penarth
features fertile Vale of Glamorgan; Welsh Folk Museum at St Fagans, near Cardiff
products dairy farming, industry (steel, plastics, engineering) in the Cardiff area
population (1987) 400,000
language 6% Welsh; English.

South Holland (Dutch *Zuid-Holland*) low-lying coastal province of the Netherlands; area 2,910 sq km/1,123 sq mi; population (1988) 3,208,000. The capital is The Hague. Noted for its bulbfields and glasshouses, the province also includes part of the Randstadt conurbation with major ports at Rotterdam and the Hook of Holland. Dairy cattle are reared; there are petroleum refineries at Rotterdam, and distilleries at Schiedam.

South Korea see ◊Korea, South.

Southland Plain /ˈsaʊθlænd/ plain on S South Island, New Zealand, on which Invercargill stands. It is an agricultural area with sheep and dairy farming.

South Orkney Islands /ˈsaʊθ ˈɔːkni/ group of barren, uninhabited islands in ◊British Antarctic Territory, SE of Cape Horn; area 620 sq km/240 sq mi. They were discovered by George Powell 1821.

South Sandwich Islands /ˈsaʊθ ˈsænwɪtʃ/ actively volcanic uninhabited British Dependent Territory; area 337 sq km/130 sq mi. Along with ◊South Georgia, 750 km/470 mi to the NW, it is administered from the Falkland Islands. They were claimed by Capt Cook 1775, and annexed by the UK 1908 and 1917. They were first formally claimed by Argentina 1948. In Dec 1976, 50 Argentine 'scientists' landed on Southern Thule, and were removed June 1982. There is an ice-free port off Cumberland Bay.

South Sea Bubble a financial crisis in Britain in 1720. The South Sea Company, founded 1711, which had a monopoly of trade with South America, offered in 1719 to take over more than half the national debt in return for further concessions. Its £100 shares rapidly rose to £1,000, and an orgy of speculation followed. When the 'bubble' burst, thousands were ruined. The discovery that cabinet ministers had been guilty of corruption led to a political crisis. Horace Walpole became prime minister, protected the royal family and members of the government from scandal, and restored financial confidence.

South Shetland Islands /ˈsaʊθ ˈʃetləndz/ archipelago of 12 uninhabited islands in the

South Glamorgan

South Carolina

Columbia

South Dakota

Pierre

South Atlantic, forming part of ◊British Antarctic Territory; area 4,622 sq km/1,785 sq mi.

South Shields /'saʊθ 'ʃiːldz/ manufacturing port in Tyne and Wear, England, on the Tyne estuary, east of Gateshead; population (1981) 87,000. Products include electrical goods, cables, and chemicals.

South Uist /'saʊθ 'juːɪst/ an island in the Outer Hebrides, Scotland, separated from North Uist by the island of Benbecula. There is a guided-missile range here.

Southwark /'sʌðək/ borough of S London, England; population (1986) 215,000. It is the site of the Globe Theatre (built on Bankside 1599 by Burbage, Shakespeare, and others, and burned down 1613); the 12th-century Southwark Cathedral; the George Inn (last galleried inn in London); the Imperial War Museum; Dulwich College and Picture Gallery, and the Horniman Museum.

South West Africa /'saʊθ ,west 'æfrɪkə/ former name (until 1968) of ◊Namibia.

South Yorkshire /'saʊθ 'jɔːkʃə/ metropolitan county of England, created 1976, originally administered by an elected council; its powers reverted to district councils from 1986
area 1,560 sq km/602 sq mi
towns administrative headquarters Barnsley; Sheffield, Doncaster
features river Don; part of Peak District National Park
products all the main towns are metal-working centres; coal, dairy, sheep, arable farming
population (1987) 1,296,000.

Soutine /suː'tiːn/ Chaim 1894–1943. Lithuanian-born French Expressionist artist. He painted landscapes and portraits, including many of painters active in Paris in the 1920s and 1930s. He had a distorted style, using thick application of paint (impasto) and brilliant colours.

sovereign British gold coin, introduced by Henry VII, which became the standard monetary unit in 1817. Minting ceased for currency purposes in the UK in 1914, but the sovereign continued to be used as 'unofficial' currency in the Middle East. It was minted for the last time in 1987 and has now been replaced by the *Britannia*.

The value is notionally £1, but the actual value is that of the weight of the gold at current rates. Like the Mexican 50-peso piece, South African krugerrand, and Soviet chervonetz of 10 roubles, sovereigns are bought by investors suspicious of falling values of paper currencies.

sovereignty absolute authority within a given territory. The possession of sovereignty is taken to be the distinguishing feature of the state, as against other forms of community. The term has an internal aspect, in that it refers to the ultimate source of authority within a state such as a parliament or monarch, and an external aspect, where it denotes the independence of the state from any outside authority.

Sovetsk /sɒv'jetsk/ town in Kaliningrad region, USSR. In 1807 Napoleon signed peace treaties with Prussia and Russia here. Until 1945 it was known as Tilsit, and was part of East Prussia.

soviet (Russian 'council') originally a strike committee elected by Russian workers in the 1905 revolution; in 1917 these were set up by peasants, soldiers, and factory workers. The soviets sent delegates to the All-Russian Congress of Soviets to represent their opinions to a future government. They were later taken over by the ◊Bolsheviks.

Soviet Central Asia formerly *Turkestan* an area consisting of the ◊Kazakh, ◊Uzbek, ◊Tadzhik, ◊Turkmen, and ◊Kirghiz Soviet Socialist Republics of the USSR.

These were conquered by Russia as recently as 1866–73, and until 1917 were divided into the Khanate of Khiva, the Emirate of Bokhara, and the Governor-Generalship of Turkestan. The Soviet government became firmly established 1919, and in 1920, the Khan of Khiva and the Emir of Bokhara were overthrown, and People's Republics set up. Turkestan became an Autonomous Soviet Socialist Republic 1921. Boundaries were redistributed 1925 along nationalist lines, and Uzbekistan, Tadzhikistan, and Turkmenistan became republics of the USSR, along with Bokhara and Khiva. The area populated by Kazakhs were united with Kazakhstan, which became a Union Republic 1936, the same year as Kirghizia. Shortfalls in agricultural production led to the establishment in 1962 of a Central Asian Bureau to strengthen centralized control by the Party Praesidium in Moscow. These republics are the home of the majority of Soviet Muslims, and strong nationalist sentiment persists.

Soviet Far East geographical, not administrative, division of Asiatic USSR, on the Pacific coast. It includes the Amur, Lower Amur, Kamchatka, and Sakhalin regions, and Khabarovsk and Maritime territories.

Soviet Union /'səʊviət 'juːniən/ alternative name for ◊Union of Soviet Socialist Republics (USSR).

sovkhoz state-owned farm in the USSR where the workers are state employees. The sovkhoz can be contrasted with the **kolkhoz** where the farm is run by a collective (see ◊collective farm).

Soweto /sə'weɪtəʊ/ (*So*uth *We*st *To*wnship) township in South Africa, SW of Johannesburg; population (1983) 915,872. It has experienced civil unrest over the years owing to the apartheid regime.

It began as a shanty town in the 1930s and is now the largest black city in South Africa, but until 1976 its population could have status only as temporary residents, serving as a workforce for Johannesburg. There were serious riots in June 1976, sparked by a ruling that Afrikaans be used in African schools there. Reforms followed but riots flared up again in 1985, and continued into the late 1980s.

soya bean leguminous plant *Glycine max*, native to E Asia, in particular Japan and China. Originally grown as a forage crop, it is increasingly used for human consumption in cooking oils and margarine, as a flour, or processed and extruded as textured vegetable protein (TVP).

Soyer /swɑː'jeɪ/ Alexis Benoît 1809–1858. French chef who worked in England. Soyer was chef at the Reform Club, London, and visited the Crimea to advise on nutrition for the British army. He was a prolific author of books of everyday recipes, such as *Shilling Cookery for the People* 1855.

Soyinka /ʃɔɪ'ɪŋkə/ Wole 1934– . Nigerian author, who was a political prisoner in Nigeria 1967–69. His works include the play *The Lion and the Jewel* 1963, his prison memoirs *The Man Died* 1972, and *Aké, The Years of Childhood* 1982, an autobiography. He was the first African to receive the Nobel Prize for Literature, in 1986.

Soyuz (Russian 'union') Soviet spacecraft, capable of carrying up to three cosmonauts. Soyuz consists of three parts: a rear section containing engines; the central crew compartment; and a forward compartment that gives additional room for working and living space. They are used for ferrying crews up to space stations.

On its first flight Apr 1967 it crashed, killing the lone pilot, Vladimir Komarov. The Soyuz 11 1971 had three deaths on re-entry.

Spa /spɑː/ town in Liège province, Belgium; population (1982) 9,600. Famous since the 14th century for its mineral springs, it has given its name to similar centres elsewhere.

Spaak /spɑːk/ Paul-Henri 1899–1972. Belgian socialist politician. From 1936 to 1966 he held office almost continuously as foreign minister or prime minister. He was an ardent advocate of international peace.

space the void that exists above Earth's atmosphere. Above 120 km/75 mi, very little atmosphere remains, so objects can continue to move quickly without extra energy. The space between the planets is not entirely empty, but

South Yorkshire

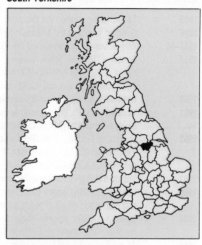

filled with the tenuous gas of the ◊solar wind as well as dust specks.

The space between stars is also filled with thin gas and dust. There is even evidence of highly rarefied gas in the space between clusters of galaxies, and also between individual galaxies.

Spacek /'speɪsek/ 'Sissy' (Mary Elizabeth) 1949– . US film actress who starred in *Badlands* 1973 and *Carrie* 1976, in which she played a repressed telekinetic teenager. Her other films include *Coal Miner's Daughter* 1979 and *Missing* 1982.

Spacelab a small space station built by the European Space Agency, carried in the cargo bay of the Space Shuttle, in which it remains throughout each flight, returning to Earth with the Shuttle. Spacelab consists of a pressurized module in which astronauts can work, and a series of *pallets*, open to the vacuum of space, on which equipment is mounted.

Spacelab is used for astronomy, Earth observation, and experiments utilizing the conditions of weightlessness and vacuum in orbit. The pressurized module can be flown with or without pallets, or the pallets can be flown on their own, in which case the astronauts remain in the Shuttle's own crew compartment. All the sections of Spacelab can be reused many times. The first Spacelab mission, consisting of a pressurized module and pallets, lasted ten days in Nov–Dec 1983.

space probe any instrumented object sent beyond Earth to other parts of the solar system, and on into deep space. The first probe was the Soviet Lunik 1, which flew past the Moon 1959. Other

Soutine The Road up the Hill *(c.1924)* Tate Gallery, London.

space research chronology

1903	Tsiolkovsky published the first practical paper on astronautics.
1926	Goddard launched the first liquid fuel rocket.
1937–45	Werner von Braun developed the V2 rocket.
1957	Sputnik 1 (Russian 'fellow-traveller': USSR), the first space satellite, orbited Earth at a height of 229–898 km/142–558 mi in 96.2 min on 4 Oct; Sputnik 2 (USSR), was launched 3 Nov carrying a live dog 'Laika' (died on board 10 Nov).
1958	Explorer 1 (USA), the first US satellite, 31 Jan discovered Van Allen radiation belts.
1961	Vostok 1 (USSR), first manned spaceship (Yuri Gagarin), was recovered on 12 Apr after a single orbit at a height of 175–142 km/109–88 mi in 89.1 min.
1962	Friendship 7 (USA); John Glenn was the first American in orbit round the Earth on 20 Feb; Telstar (USA), a communications satellite, sent the first live television transmission between USA and Europe.
1963	Vostok 6 (USSR); Valentina Tereshkova was the first woman in space 16–19 Jun.
1966	Venera 3 (USSR), space probe, launched Nov 1965, crash-landed on Venus 1 Mar, the first man-made object to reach another planet.
1967	Soyuz 1 (USSR); Vladimir Komarov was the first man to be killed in space research when his ship crash-landed on Earth on 24 Apr.
1969	Apollo-Saturn 11 (USA) was launched 16–24 Jul; Neil Armstrong was the first man to walk on the moon.
1970	Luna 17 (USSR) was launched 10 Nov; its unmanned lunar vehicle, *Lunokhod*, took photos and made soil analyses on the Moon.
1971	Salyut 1 (USSR), the first orbital space station, was established 19 Apr; it was visited by the Soyuz 11 manned spacecraft.
1971–2	Mariner 9 (USA) was the first space probe to orbit another planet, when it circled Mars.
1972	Pioneer 10 (USA), Earth's first starship, was launched 3 Mar; it reached Jupiter 1973; in 1983 it made its first passage of the asteroid belt, reached Neptune, and passed on into the first voyage beyond the solar system. Apollo 17 (USA) was launched Dec.
1973	Skylab 2 (USA), the first US orbital space station, was established.
1975	Apollo 18 (USA), 15–24 Jul, made a joint flight with Soyuz 19 (USSR), in a link-up in space.
1976	Viking 1 (USA), unmanned spacecraft, was launched 20 Aug 1975; it reached Mars, the spacecraft lander touching down on 20 Jul 1976; Viking 2 (USA) was launched 9 Sept 1975, its lander touching down on Mars 3 Sept 1976.
1977	Voyager 1 (USA), launched 5 Sept 1977, and Voyager 2 (USA), launched 20 Aug, both unmanned spacecraft, reached Jupiter Jan/Jul 1979, Uranus 1986, and are expected to reach Neptune 1989.
1979	Ariane (European Space Agency satellite launcher) was launched.
1981	Space Shuttle (USA), first re-usable manned spacecraft, was launched 12 Apr.
1982	Venera 13 and 14 (USSR) landed on Venus; soil samples indicated that the surface is similar to Earth's volcanic rock.
1986	Space Shuttle (USA) exploded shortly after launch killing all seven crew members. The space probe *Giotto* showed Halley's comet to be one of the darkest objects ever detected in the solar system, with an irregular nucleus 14.5 km/9 mi x 3km/ 2 mi. Voyager 2 reached Uranus and found it to have six more moons than was previously thought, making 12 known moons in all.

Space Shuttle Columbia *can carry into orbit loads of up to 29 tonnes in a cargo bay measuring 4.5 m × 18 m/15 ft × 60 ft, and bring back payloads of up to 14 tonnes.*

were postponed until **Discovery** was launched 29 Sept 1988. At the end of the 1980s, an average of $375 million dollars were spent on each Space Shuttle mission.

space sickness or ***space adaptation syndrome*** a feeling of nausea, sometimes accompanied by vomiting, experienced by about 40% of all astronauts during their first few days in space. It is akin to travel sickness, and is thought to be caused by confusion of the body's balancing mechanism, located in the inner ear, by weightlessness. The sensation passes after a week or so as the body adapts.

space station any large structure designed for human occupation in space for extended periods of time. Space stations are used for carrying out astronomical observations and surveys of Earth, as well as for biological studies and the processing of materials in weightlessness. The first space station was ◊Salyut 1, and the USA has launched ◊Skylab. The USA plans to build a larger space

probes include ◊Giotto, ◊Mariner, the ◊Moon probes, ◊Pioneer, ◊Viking, and ◊Voyager.

Space Shuttle reusable US crewed spacecraft, first launched 12 Apr 1981. It takes off vertically like a conventional rocket, but glides back to land on a runway. The Space Shuttle orbiter, the part that goes into space, is 37.2 m/122 ft long and weighs 68 tonnes. Two to eight crew members occupy the orbiter's nose section, and missions last up to ten days. In its cargo bay the orbiter can carry up to 29 tonnes of satellites, scientific equipment, ◊Spacelab, or military payloads. In 1986 the Space Shuttle *Challenger* blew up on take-off, killing all seven crew members.

At launch, the Shuttle's three main engines are fed with liquid fuel from a cylindrical tank attached to the orbiter; this tank is discarded shortly before the Shuttle reaches orbit. Two additional solid-fuel boosters provide the main thrust for launch, but are jettisoned after two minutes. Four orbiters were built: *Columbia, Challenger, Discovery,* and *Atlantis. Challenger* was destroyed in a mid-air explosion just over a minute into its tenth launch

28 Jan 1986, killing all seven crew members. The inquiry showed that the cold weather had made the rocket unsafe, and that it was launched because of the pressure put on the ground crew by the companies who were using the Shuttle. Flights

Soyuz *The crew of Soviet spacecraft Soyuz 37 before launch on 23 July 1980. On the left is Soviet cosmonaut Viktor Gorbatko and on the right is Pham Tuan, the first Vietnamese to fly in space.*

Space Shuttle *Lift-off of the Space Shuttle* Atlantis *18 Oct 1989, carrying a crew of five and the spacecraft* Galileo, *which was safely sent on its way to Jupiter.*

station in orbit during the 1990s, in cooperation with other countries.

space suit a protective suit worn by astronauts in space. It provides an insulated, air-conditioned cocoon in which astronauts can live and work for hours at a time while outside the spacecraft. Inside the suit is a cooling garment which keeps the body at a comfortable temperature even during vigorous work. The suit provides air to breathe, and removes exhaled carbon dioxide and moisture. The suit's outer layers insulate the occupant from the extremes of hot and cold in space (–150°C in the shade to +180°C in sunlight), and from the impact of small meteorites. Some space suits have a jet-propelled backpack, which the astronaut can use to move about.

space-time in physics, combination of space and time used in the theory of ◊relativity. When developing relativity, Einstein showed that time was in many respects like an extra dimension (or direction) to space. Space and time can thus be considered as entwined into a single entity, rather than two separate things.

Space-time is considered to have four dimensions: three of space and one of time. In relativity theory, events are described as occurring at points in space-time. The ***general theory of relativity*** describes how space-time is distorted by the presence of material bodies, an effect that we observe as gravity.

spadix a type of ◊inflorescence consisting of a long fleshy axis bearing many small, stalkless flowers. It is partially enclosed by a large bract or ◊spathe. A spadix is characteristic of plants belonging to the family Araceae, including arum lilies *Zantedeschia aethiopica*.

Spain /speɪn/ country in SW Europe, on the Iberian Peninsula between the Atlantic and the Mediterranean, bounded to the N by France and to the W by Portugal.

government The 1978 constitution puts a hereditary monarch as formal head of state. The monarch appoints a prime minister, called president of government, and a council of ministers, all responsible to the national assembly, *las Cortes Generales*. The *Cortes* consists of two chambers, the Chamber of Deputies, with 350 members, and the Senate, with 208. Deputies are elected by universal suffrage through a system of proportional representation, and 208 of the senators are directly elected to represent the whole country and 49 to represent the regions. All serve a four-year term.

Spain has developed a regional self-government, whereby each of the 50 provinces has its own council (*Diputación Provincial*) and civil governor. The devolution process was extended 1979 when 17 autonomous communities were approved, each with a parliament elected for a four-year term.

history Pre-Roman Spain was inhabited by Iberians, ◊Basques, ◊Celts, and Celtiberians. ◊Greece and ◊Phoenicia established colonies on the coast from the 7th century BC; ◊Carthage dominated from the 5th century, trying to found an empire in the SE. This was conquered by ancient ◊Rome about 200 BC and after a long struggle all Spain was absorbed into the Roman Empire. At the invitation of Rome the Visigoths (see ◊Goths) set up a kingdom in Spain from the beginning of the 5th century AD until the invasion by the ◊Moors 711. Christian resistance held out in the north and by 1250 they had reconquered all Spain except ◊Granada. During this struggle a number of small kingdoms were formed, all of which by the 13th century had been absorbed by ◊Castile and ◊Aragon. The marriage of ◊Ferdinand of Aragon to Isabella of Castile 1469 united their domains on their accession 1479. The conquest of Granada 1492 completed the unification of Spain.

Under Ferdinand and Isabella, Charles I (see ◊Charles V of the ◊Holy Roman Empire), and ◊Philip II, Spain became one of the greatest powers in the world. The discoveries of ◊Columbus, made on behalf of Spain, were followed by the conquest of most of Central and

Spain 1270-1492

South America. Naples and Sicily were annexed 1503, Milan 1535, Portugal 1580, and Charles I inherited the Netherlands, but with the revolt in the Netherlands and the defeat of the Armada 1588, Spain's power began to decline. The loss of civil and religious freedom, constant wars, inflation, a corrupt bureaucracy, and the expulsion of the Jews and Moors undermined the economy.

Spain
(España)

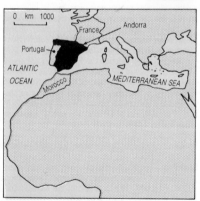

area 499,700 sq km/192,884 sq mi
capital Madrid
towns Bilbao, Valencia, Zaragoza, Murcia; ports Barcelona, Seville, Málaga
physical a central plateau with mountain ranges; lowlands in the south
features includes Balearic and Canary Islands, and Ceuta and Melilla on N African coast; rivers Ebro, Douro, Tagus, Guadiana, Guadalquivir; Iberian Plateau (Meseta); Pyrenees, Cantabrian Mountains, Andalusian Mountains, Sierra Nevada
head of state Juan Carlos I from 1975
head of government Felipe González Marquez from 1982
government constitutional monarchy
political parties Socialist Worker's Party (PSOE), democratic socialist; Popular Alliance (AP), centre-right; Christian Democrats (DC), centrist; Liberal Party (PL), left-of-centre

By the peace of Utrecht that concluded the War of the ◊Spanish Succession 1713, Spain lost Naples, Sicily, Milan, Gibraltar, and its last possessions in the Netherlands.

The 18th century saw reforms and economic progress, but Spain became involved in the ◊Revolutionary and ◊Napoleonic wars, first as the ally, then as the opponent of France.

exports citrus, grapes, pomegranates, vegetables, wine (especially sherry), olive oil, tinned fruit and fish, iron ore, cork, cars and other vehicles, leather goods, ceramics
currency peseta (183.95 = £1 Feb 1990)
population (1989) 39,784,000; annual growth rate 0.6%
life expectancy men 71, women 78
language Spanish (Castilian, official), but regional languages are recognized within their own boundaries (Basque, Catalan, Galician, Valencian, and Majorcan are the chief examples)
religion Roman Catholic (there are restrictions on the practice of Protestantism)
literacy 97% male/92% female (1985 est)
GDP $160.4 bn (1984); $5,500 per head of population
chronology
1947 Gen Franco announced there would be a return to the monarchy after his death, with Prince Juan Carlos as his successor.
1975 Franco died and was succeeded by King Juan Carlos I as head of state.
1978 New constitution adopted, with Adolfo Suárez, leader of the Democratic Centre Party, as prime minister.
1981 Suárez resigned and was succeeded by his deputy, Calvo-Sotelo. Attempted military coup thwarted.
1982 Socialist Workers' Party (PSOE), led by Felipe González, won a sweeping electoral victory. Basque separatist organization (ETA) stepped up its guerrilla campaign.
1985 ETA's campaign spread to holiday resorts.
1986 Referendum confirmed NATO membership. Spain joined the European Community.
1988 Spain joined the Western European Union. PSOE lost seats, holding only parity after general election.
1989 Talks between government and ETA collapsed and truce ended.

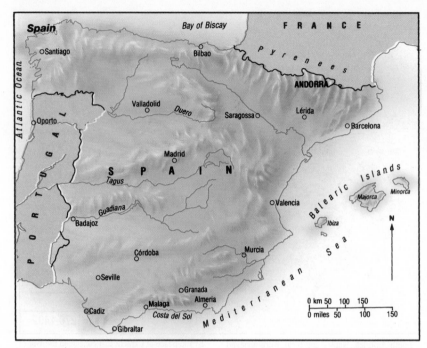

France occupied Spain 1808 and was expelled with British assistance 1814. Throughout the 19th century conflict raged between monarchists and liberals; revolutions and civil wars took place 1820–23, 1833–39, and 1868, besides many minor revolts, and a republic was temporarily established 1873–74.

Spain lost its American colonies between 1810 and 1830 and after the ◊Spanish-American War 1898 ceded Cuba and the Philippines to the USA.

Republicanism, socialism, and anarchism grew after 1900; ◊Primo de Rivera's dictatorship 1923–30 failed to preserve the monarchy under ◊Alfonso XIII, and in 1931 a republic was established. In 1936 the Popular Front, a centre-left alliance, took office and introduced agrarian and other reforms that aroused the opposition of the landlords and the Catholic church. A military rebellion led by Gen Francisco ◊Franco resulted in the Spanish ◊Civil War 1936–39. Franco was supported by the German Nazis and Italian Fascists, and won the war, establishing a military dictatorship.

In 1947 Franco allowed the revival of a legislature with limited powers, and announced that after his death the monarchy would be restored, naming the grandson of the last monarch, Prince Juan Carlos de Bourbon, as his successor. Franco died 1975 and King Juan Carlos became head of state. There followed a slow but steady progress to democratic government, with the new constitution endorsed by referendum 1978.

Spain faced two main internal problems, the demands for independence by regional extremists and the possibility of a right-wing military coup. The aims of the ruling Democratic Centre Party (UCD), led by Adolfo Suárez, included a devolution of power to the regions (Basque, Catalonia, and eventually Andalusia), entry into NATO, and membership of the European Community. In 1981 Suárez suddenly resigned and was succeeded by his deputy, Calvo Sotelo. He was immediately confronted with an attempted army coup in Madrid, while at the same time the military commander of Valencia declared a state of emergency there and sent tanks out on the streets. Both uprisings failed, and the two leaders were tried and imprisoned. Sotelo's decision to take Spain into NATO was widely criticized and, after defections from the party, he was forced to call a general election Oct 1982. The result was

a sweeping victory for the PSOE, led by Felipe Gonzalez.

The Basque separatist organization, ETA, had stepped up its campaign for independence with widespread terrorist activity, spreading in 1985 to the Mediterranean holiday resorts and threatening Spain's lucrative tourist industry. In 1985 unemployment reached 22%.

The PSOE had fought the election on a policy of taking Spain out of NATO and carrying out extensive nationalization. Once in office, however, Gonzalez showed himself to be a pragmatist. His nationalization programme was highly selective and he left the decision on NATO to a referendum. In Jan 1986 Spain became a full member of the European Community and in Mar the referendum showed popular support for remaining in NATO. In the July 1986 election the PSOE won 184 seats in the Chamber of Deputies and Gonzalez returned for another term as prime minister. In Nov 1988 Spain, with Portugal, became a member of the ◊Western European Union (WEU). In the Nov 1989 general election PSOE won only 175 seats in the 350-member National Assembly but retained power under prime minister Gonzales.

Spalato /'spɑːlətəʊ/ Italian name for ◊Split, a port in Yugoslavia.

Spalding /'spɔːldɪŋ/ market town on the river Welland, in Lincolnshire, England; population (1981) 18,000. The bulb farms are famous and there is a flower festival in May.

Spallanzani /ˌspælənt'sɑːni/ Lazzaro 1729–1799. Italian priest and biologist. He disproved the theory that microbes spontaneously generate out of rotten food, by showing that they would not grow in flasks of broth that had been boiled for 30 minutes and then sealed.

Spandau /'ʃpændaʊ/ suburb of West Berlin, Germany. The chief war criminals condemned at the Nuremberg Trials in 1946 were imprisoned in the fortress there. The last of them was the Nazi leader Rudolf Hess, and the prison was demolished following his death in 1987.

spaniel type of dog, characterized by large, drooping ears and a long, silky coat. The *Clumber spaniel*, weighing up to 32 kg/70 lb, takes its name from the estate of the duke of Newcastle, who imported them from France; it is white with lemon markings. The *cocker* (English and American) is smaller (12 kg/25 lb, 40 cm/15 in tall), and of various colours. The *springer* (English and Welsh), about 20 kg/45 lb and 50 cm/20 in tall, is so

called because of its use for 'springing' game. The *Sussex spaniel* is believed to be the oldest variety, weighs 20 kg/45 lb, is 40 cm/15 in tall, and is a golden liver colour. Toy spaniels include the *King Charles, Japanese, Tibetan,* and *Pekingese*.

Spanish inhabitant of Spain or person of Spanish descent. The Spanish language, Castilian, originated in the kingdoms of Castile and Aragon. The Catalan and Basque languages are also spoken in Spain.

Spanish-American War war 1898 by Cuban revolutionaries (with US backing) against Spanish rule. The Treaty of Paris ceded Cuba, the Philippines, Guam, and Puerto Rico to the USA.

Spanish architecture the architecture of Spain has been influenced by both Classical and Islamic traditions. Styles include *Roman* (3rd–5th century); *Asturian* (9th century), taking its name from the district in NW Spain which was unconquered by the Moors; *Mozarabic* (9th–11th century), a style of Spanish Christian architecture, showing the influence of Islamic architecture; *Romanesque* (11th and 12th centuries); *Gothic* (13th–16th century); *Renaissance* (15th–17th century), which is based on Italian models; **Baroque** (17th–18th century), a style which reached its peak in the fantastic designs of Churriguera and his followers; **Neo-Classical** (18th and 19th centuries); **Modern** Oscar Niemeyer and Antonio ◊Gaudí.

Spanish Armada the fleet sent by Philip II of Spain against England in 1588. Consisting of 130 ships, it sailed from Lisbon, and carried on a running fight up the Channel with the English fleet of 197 small ships under Howard of Effingham and Francis ◊Drake. The Armada anchored off Calais, but was forced to put to sea by fireships, and a general action followed off Gravelines. What remained of the Armada escaped round the N of Scotland and W of Ireland, suffering many losses by storm and shipwreck on the way. Only about half the original fleet returned to Spain.

Spanish art
painting:
late 15th–16th centuries Italian and Flemish influences contributed to Spanish Renaissance painting. The painters of this period include Bartolomé Bermejo (1440–95), Alonzo Sánchez Coello (1515–90), Luis de Vargas (1502–68), Francisco de Herrera the Elder, Juan de Juanes (1523–79), Juan Navarrette (1526–79), Luis de Morales (1509–86), and El Greco.
17th century The leading Spanish artist was Velázquez.
18th century Goya was to exert a great influence on European art of the following century.
20th century Painters include the Cubist Juan Gris, the Surrealists Joan Miró and Salvador Dali, and Pablo Picasso, widely regarded as the most innovative painter of the century.
sculpture Spanish sculptors include Berruguete (c. 1488–1561), El Greco, Montañes (1568–1649), Alonso Cano (1601–67), Julio González (1876–1942), and Pablo Picasso.

Spanish Civil War 1936–39. See ◊Civil War, Spanish.

Spanish fly another name for blister ◊beetle.

Spanish Guinea /ˈspænɪʃ ˈgɪnɪ/ former name of the Republic of ◊Equatorial Guinea.

Spanish language a member of the Romance branch of the Indo-European language family, traditionally known as Castilian and originally spoken only in NE Spain. As the language of the court it has been the standard and literary language of the Spanish state since the 13th century. It is now a world language, spoken in all South and Central American countries, except Brazil, Guyana, Suriname and French Guiana, as well as in the Philippines.

Castilian Spanish has never succeeded in supplanting such regional languages as Basque, Gallego or Galician, and Catalan. Because of the long Muslim dominance of the S Iberian peninsula, Spanish has been influenced by Arabic. Words in English of Spanish origin include *bronco, cargo, galleon, mosquito, ranch,* and *sherry.*

Spanish literature of the classical epics, the 12th-century *El cantar de Mio Cid* is the only complete example. The founder of Castilian prose was King Alfonso X, El Sabio (the Wise), who also wrote lyric poetry in the Galician dialect. The first true poet was the 14th-century satirist, Juan Ruiz (c. 1283–1350), archpriest of Hita. To the 15th century belong the Marquis of Santillana (Íñigo López de Mendoza), poet, critic, and collector of proverbs; chivalric romances, for example, the *Amadis de Gaula*; ballads dealing with the struggle against the Moors; and the *Celestina*, a novel in dramatic form. The flowering of verse drama began with Lope de Rueda (died 1565), and reached its height with Lope de Vega and Calderón de la Barca. In poetry the golden age of the 15th–16th centuries produced the lyrical Garcilaso de la Vega; the patriotic Fernando de Herrera (1534–97); the mystics Santa Teresa and Luis de León; the elaborate style of Luis de Góngora (1561–1627), who popularized the decadent 'gongorism'; and the biting satire of Francisco

de Quevedo. In fiction there developed the pastoral romance, for example, Jorge de Montemayor's *Diana*; the picaresque novel, established by the anonymous *Lazarillo de Tormes*; and the work of Cervantes. In the 18th century the Benedictine Benito J Feijoo introduced scientific thought to Spain, and French influence emerged in the comedies of Leandro F de Moratín (1760–1828) and others. Typical of the romantic era were the poets and dramatists Angel de Saavedra (Duque de Rivas) (1791–1865) and José Zorilla (1817–93); and the lyricist José de Espronceda (1810–42). Among 19th-century novelists are Pedro de Alarcón (1833–91), Emilia, condesa de Pardo Bazán (1852–1921), and Vicente Blasco Ibáñez (1867–1928); a 19th-century dramatist is José Echegaray (1832–1916).

The 'Generation of 1898' included the philosophers Miguel de Unamuno (1864–1936) and José Ortega y Gasset (1883–1955); the novelist Pío Baroja (1872–1956); the prose-writer Azorín (José Martínez Ruiz, 1874–1967); and the Nobel prizewinning poet Juan Ramón Jiménez (1881–1958). The next generation included novelist Camilo José Cela (1916–); the poets Antonio Machado (1875–1939), Rafael Alberti (1902–), Luis Cernuda (1902–63), and the Nobel prizewinner Vincente Aleixandre (1898–); and the dramatists Jacinto Benavente (1866–1954), the brothers Quintero, and—the most striking—F García Lorca. The Civil War and the strict censorship of the Franco government disrupted mid-20th century literary life, but later names include the novelists Rafael Sánchez Ferlosio (1927–) and Juan Goytisolo (1931–); and the poets Blas de Otero (1916–) and José Hierro (1922–).

Spanish Main term often used to describe the Caribbean in the 16th–17th centuries, but more properly the South American mainland between the river Orinoco and Panama.

Spanish Sahara /ˈspænɪʃ səˈhɑːrə/ former name for the ◊Western Sahara.

Spanish Succession, War of the a war 1701–14 between Britain, Austria, the Netherlands, Portugal, and Denmark (the Allies) and France, Spain, and Bavaria. It was caused by Louis XIV's acceptance of the Spanish throne on behalf of his grandson, Philip V of Spain, in defiance of the Partition Treaty of 1700, under which it would have passed to Archduke Charles of Austria (later Holy Roman emperor Charles VI).

Peace was made by the Treaties of Utrecht 1713 and Rastatt 1714. Philip V was recognized as king of Spain, thus founding the Spanish branch of the Bourbon dynasty. Britain received Gibraltar, Minorca, and Nova Scotia; and Austria received Belgium, Milan, and Naples.
1704 The French marched on Vienna to try to end the war, but were defeated at **Blenheim** by ◊Marlborough and ◊Eugène of Savoy.
1705 The Allies invaded Spain, twice occupying Madrid but failing to hold it.
1706 Marlborough was victorious over the French (under Villeroi) at **Ramillies** 23 May, in Brabant, Belgium.
1708 Marlborough and Eugène were victorious over the French (under the Duke of Burgundy and ◊Vendôme) at **Oudenaarde** (near Ghent, Belgium) 30 Jun–11 July.
1709 Marlborough was victorious with Eugène over the French (under Villars) at **Malplaquet** 11 Sept.
1713 Treaties of Utrecht and *1714* Rastat under which the Allies recognized Philip as King of Spain, but Gibraltar, Minorca, and Nova Scotia were ceded to Britain, and Belgium, Milan, and Naples to Austria.

Spanish Town /ˈspænɪʃ taʊn/ town in Middlesex county, Jamaica; population (1982) 89,000. Founded by Diego Columbus about 1525, it was the capital of Jamaica 1535–1871.

Spark /spɑːk/ Muriel 1918– . Scottish novelist. She is a Catholic convert, and her works have an

enigmatic satire: *The Ballad of Peckham Rye* 1960, *The Prime of Miss Jean Brodie* 1961, and *The Only Problem* 1984.

spark chamber electronic device for recording tracks of atomic ◊particles. In combination with a stack of photographic plates, a spark chamber enables the point where an interaction has taken place to be located to within a cubic centimetre. At its simplest, it consists of two smooth thread-like ◊electrodes which are positioned 1–2 cm apart, the space between being filled by gas.

spark plug a plug that produces an electric spark in the cylinder of a petrol engine to ignite the fuel mixture. It consists essentially of two electrodes insulated from one another. High-voltage (18,000 V) electricity is fed to a central electrode via the distributor. At the base of the electrode, inside the cylinder, the electricity jumps to another electrode earthed to the engine body, and creates a spark. See also ◊ignition coil.

sparrow term for many small thick-beaked birds. They are generally brown and grey, up to 18 cm/7 in long, and are found worldwide.

The Eurasian *house sparrow Passer domesticus*, family Ploceidae, of the order Passeriformes, has spread almost worldwide. It has brown-black marked plumage, and black chest and eye-stripe in the male. It is inconspicuous, intelligent, and adaptable, with a cheery chirp and untidy nesting habits. For hedge sparrow see ◊dunnock.

sparrow-hawk woodland bird of prey *Accipiter nisus* found in Eurasia and N Africa. It has a long tail and short wings. The male grows to 28 cm/1.1 ft long, and the female 38 cm/1.5 ft. It hunts small birds.

Sparta /ˈspɑːtə/ ancient Greek city-state in the S Peloponnese (near Sparte), developed from Dorian settlements in the 10th century BC. The Spartans, known for their military discipline and austerity, took part in the Persian and Peloponnesian wars.

The Dorians formed the ruling race in Sparta, the original inhabitants being divided into *perioeci* (tributaries without political rights) and helots or serfs. The state was ruled by two hereditary kings, and under the constitution attributed to Lycurgus all citizens were trained for war from childhood; hence the Spartans became proverbial for their indifference to pain or death, their contempt for luxury and the arts, and their harsh treatment of the helots. They distinguished themselves in the ◊Persian and ◊Peloponnesian wars, but defeat by the Thebans in 371 BC marked the start of their decline. The ancient city was destroyed by the Visigoths in AD 396.

Spartacist member of a group of left-wing radicals in Germany at the end of World War I, founders of the *Spartacus League*, which became the German Communist party in 1919. The league participated in the Berlin workers' revolt of Jan 1919 which was suppressed by the Freikorps on the orders of the socialist government. The agitation ended with the murder of Spartacist leaders Karl ◊Liebknecht and Rosa ◊Luxemburg.

Spartacus /ˈspɑːtəkəs/ died 71 BC. Thracian gladiator who in 73 BC led a revolt of gladiators and slaves at Capua. He was eventually caught by ◊Crassus and crucifed.

Spartakiad sports games held every four years in the USSR (so named from ancient Sparta's stress on physical fitness for state service), in which about 10,000 Soviet athletes compete (foreigners were admitted from 1979).

spastic a person with ◊cerebral palsy. The term is also applied generally to limbs with impaired movement, stiffness, and resistance to passive movement.

spathe in flowers, the single large bract surrounding the type of inflorescence known as a ◊spadix. It is sometimes brightly coloured and petal-like, as in the brilliant scarlet spathe of the flamingo plant *Anthurium andreanum* from South America; this serves to attract insects.

spa town a town with a spring, the water of which, it is claimed, has the power to cure illness and restore health. Spa towns in England include

Harrogate, Tunbridge Wells, Epsom, and Bath; the earliest spas date from the late 16th century, though it was only in the following century that they became widespread. They seem to have developed from the medieval belief in holy wells. Only eight spas remained in 1945, including Leamington and Bath.

speakeasy a bar that illegally sold alcohol during the ◊Prohibition period in the USA. The term is probably derived from the need to speak quickly or quietly to the doorkeeper in order to gain admission.

Speaker the presiding officer charged with the preservation of order in the legislatures of various countries. In the UK the Speaker in the House of Lords is the Lord Chancellor; in the House of Commons the Speaker is elected for each parliament, usually on an agreed basis among the parties, but often holds the office for many years. The original appointment dates from 1377.

Spear /spɪə/ Ruskin 1911–1990. British artist, whose portraits include Laurence Olivier (as Macbeth), Francis Bacon, and satirical representations of Margaret Thatcher.

spearmint perennial herb *Mentha spicata*, with aromatic leaves and spikes of purple flowers, used as an accompaniment to lamb and for flavouring dishes.

Special Air Service (SAS) specialist British regiment recruited mainly from Parachute Regiment volunteers. It has served in Malaysia, Oman, Northern Ireland, and against international terrorists, as in the siege of the Iranian embassy in London 1980.

The SAS was founded by Col David Stirling in N Africa 1942–45 and revived from 1952. Its headquarters is at Bradbury Lines near Hereford on the Welsh border. Members are anonymous. Their motto is 'Who dares wins' under a winged dagger.

Special Branch section of the British police originally established 1883 to deal with Irish Fenian activists. All 42 police forces in Britain now have their own Special Branches. They act as the executive arm of MI5 (British intelligence) in its duty of preventing or investigating espionage, subversion and sabotage; carry out duties at air and sea ports in respect of naturalization and immigration, and provide armed bodyguards for public figures.

special constable in the UK, a part-time volunteer who supplements local police forces as required. Special constables were established by the Special Constabulary Act 1831. They number some 16,000. They have no extra powers other than normal rights as citizens, although they wear a police-style uniform. They work alongside the police at football matches, demonstrations, and similar events.

special drawing right (SDR) the right of a member state of the ◊International Monetary Fund to apply for money to finance its balance of payments deficit. Originally, the SDR was linked to gold and the US dollar. After 1974 SDRs were defined in terms of a 'basket' of the 16 currencies of countries doing 1% or more of the world's trade. In 1981 the SDR was simplified to a weighted average of US dollars, French francs, German marks, Japanese yen and UK sterling.

special education education, often in separate 'special schools', for children with specific physical or mental problems or disabilities. In the UK, the 1981 Education Act encouraged local authorities to integrate as many children with special needs into mainstream schools as was practicable but did not recommend the complete closure of special schools.

special relationship the belief that ties of common language, culture, and shared aims of the defence of democratic principles should sustain a political relationship between the USA and the UK, and that the same would not apply to relationships between the USA and other European states.

Close cooperation in the sharing of nuclear-weapons technology has usually been cited as evidence of this bond, whereas the belated entry of the USA into both world wars in support of the UK has been interpreted as proof of its limitations in the light of political realities. Despite the special relationship, differences of opinion have occurred, largely reflecting the role of the USA as a superpower with concomitant global views compared to that of Britain as an increasingly European-oriented state.

speciation the emergence of a new species during evolutionary history. One cause of speciation is the geographical separation of populations of the parent species, followed by their reproductive isolation, so that they no longer produce viable offspring unless they interbreed. Other, less common causes are ◊assortative mating and the establishment of a ◊polyploid population.

species in biology, a distinguishable group of organisms, which resemble each other or consist of a few distinctive types (as in ◊polymorphism), and which can all interbreed (actually or potentially) to produce fertile offspring. Species are the lowest level in the system of biological classification. elv Related species are grouped together in a genus. Within a species there are usually two or more separate ◊populations, which may in time become distinctive enough to be designated subspecies or varieties, and could eventually give rise to new species, through ◊speciation. Around 1.4 million species have been identified so far, of which 750,000 are insects, 250,000 are plants, and 41,000 are vertebrates. In tropical regions there are roughly two species for each temperate-zone species. It is estimated that one species becomes extinct every day through habitat destruction.

A *native* species has existed in England at least from prehistoric times; a *naturalized* species is known to have been introduced by humans from their mother country, but now maintains itself; while an *exotic* species requires human intervention to survive.

specific gravity alternative term for ◊relative density.

specific heat capacity in physics, quantity of heat required to raise unit mass (1 kg) of a substance by one ◊kelvin (1°C). The unit of specific heat capacity in the SI system is the ◊joule per kilogram kelvin (J kg^{-1} K^{-1}).

speckle interferometry technique whereby large telescopes can achieve high resolution of astronomical objects despite the adverse effects of the atmosphere through which light from the object under study must pass. A long-exposure photograph is formed from many individual images, or 'speckles'; which together form the final picture. The technique was introduced by the French astronomer Antoine Labeyrie 1970.

spectacles a pair of lenses fitted in a frame and worn in front of the eyes to correct or assist defective vision. Common defects of the eye corrected by spectacle lenses are short sight (myopia) by using concave (spherical) lenses, long sight (hypermetropia) by using convex (spherical) lenses, and astigmatism by using cylindrical lenses.

Spherical and cylindrical lenses may be combined in one lens. For convenience bifocal spectacles provide for correction both at a distance and for reading by combining two lenses of different curvatures in one piece of glass.

Spectacles are said to have been invented in the 13th century by a Florentine monk. Few people found the need for spectacles until printing was invented, when the demand for them increased rapidly. It is not known when spectacles were introduced into England, but in 1629 Charles I granted a charter to the Spectacle Makers' Guild. Using photosensitive glass, lenses can be produced which darken in glare and return to normal in ordinary light conditions. See also ◊contact lens.

Spector /'spɛktə/ Phil 1940– . US record producer, known for the *Wall of Sound*, created using a large orchestra, distinguishing his work in the early 1960s with vocal groups such as the Crystals and the Ronettes. He withdrew into semi-retirement in 1966.

spectroscopy in physics, the study of spectra (see ◊spectrum) associated with atoms or molecules in solid, liquid, or gaseous phase. Spectroscopy can be used to identify unknown compounds and is an invaluable tool to scientists, industry (especially pharmaceuticals for purity checks), and medical workers.

Emission spectroscopy is the study of the characteristic series of sharp lines in the spectrum produced when an ◊element is heated. Thus an unknown mixture can be analysed for its component elements. Related is *absorption spectroscopy,* dealing with atoms and molecules as they absorb energy in a characteristic way. Again, dark lines can be used for analysis. More detailed structural information can be obtained by using *infrared spectroscopy* (concerned with molecular vibrations) or *nuclear magnetic resonance (NMR) spectroscopy* (concerned with interactions between adjacent atomic nuclei).

spectrum (plural *spectra*) in physics, an arrangement of frequencies or wavelengths when electromagnetic radiations are separated into their constituent parts. Visible light is part of the electromagnetic spectrum and most sources emit waves over a range of wavelengths: that can be broken up or 'dispersed'; white light can be separated into red, orange, yellow, green, blue, indigo, and violet.

There are many types of spectra, both emission and absorption, for radiation and particles, used in ◊spectroscopy. An incandescent body gives rise to a *continuous spectrum* where the dispersed radiation is distributed uninterruptedly over a range of wavelengths. An element gives a *line spectrum*—one or more bright discrete lines at characteristic wavelengths. Molecular gases give *band spectra* in which there are groups of close-packed lines shaded in one direction of wavelength. In an *absorption spectrum* dark lines or spaces replace the characteristic bright lines of the absorbing medium. The *mass spectrum* of an element is obtained from a mass spectrograph and shows the relative proportions of its constituent ◊isotopes.

The visible spectrum was first studied by ◊Newton, who showed in 1672 how white light could be broken up into different colours.

speculative action law cases taken on a 'no win, no fee' basis, legal in the USA and Scotland, but not in England. In 1989 the Lord Chancellor proposed that this should be introduced into English law, although not on an American-style contingency basis where lawyers take a percentage of the court's award.

speculum (plural *specula*) an instrument to aid examination of an opening into the body, for example the nose or vagina. The speculum allows the opening to be widened, permitting the passage of instruments. Many specula also have built-in electric lamps to illuminate the cavity being examined.

Spee /ʃpeɪ/ Maximilian, Count von Spee 1861–1914. German admiral, born in Copenhagen. He went down with his flagship in the 1914 battle of the Falkland Islands, and the *Graf Spee* battleship was named after him.

speech recognition in computing, techniques whereby a computer can understand ordinary speech. Spoken words are divided into 'frames', each lasting about one-thirtieth of a second, which are converted to a waveform. These are then compared with a series of stored frames to determine the most likely word. Research into speech recognition started 1938, but the technology became sufficiently developed for commercial applications only in the late 1980s.

The three types are: *separate word recognition* for distinguishing up to several hundred separately spoken words; *connected speech recognition* for speech where there is a short pause between words; and *continuous speech recognition* for normal but carefully articulated speech.

speech synthesis a computer-based technology for the generation of speech. A speech synthesizer is controlled by a computer, which supplies strings of codes representing basic speech sounds (phonemes) and these together make up words. Speech-synthesis applications include children's toys, car and aircraft warning systems, and talking books for the blind.

speed the rate at which something moves. Speed in kilometres per hour is calculated by dividing the distance travelled in kilometres by the time taken in hours. Speed is a ◊scalar quantity, as the direction of motion is not involved. This makes it different from velocity, which is a ◊vector quantity.

speed common name for ◊amphetamine, a stimulant drug.

speed of light the speed at which light and other ◊electromagnetic waves travel through empty space. Its value is 299,792,458 metres per second/186,281 miles per second. The speed of light is the highest speed possible, according to the theory of ◊relativity, and its value is independent of the motion of its source and of the observer. It is impossible to accelerate any material body to this speed because it would require an infinite amount of energy.

speed of sound the speed at which sound travels through a medium, such as air or water. In air at a temperature of 0°C (32°F), the speed of sound is 331 metres per second/1,087 feet per second. At higher temperatures, the speed of sound is greater; at 18°C (64°F) it is 342 metres per second/1,123 feet per second. It is greater in liquids and solids; for example, in water it is around 1,440 metres per second/4,724 feet per second, depending on the temperature.

speedometer instrument attached to the gear-box of a vehicle by a flexible drive, which indicates the speed of the vehicle in miles or kilometres per hour on a dial easily visible to the driver.

speedway the sport of motorcycle racing on a dirt track. Four riders compete in each heat over four laps. A series of heats make up a match or competition. In Britain there are two leagues, the British League and the National League. World championships exist for individuals, pairs, four-rider teams, long-track racing, and ice speedway.

The first organized races were in Australia 1923 and the first track in Britain was at Droylsden, near Manchester, 1927.

Speedway: World Championships

Individual
1980 Mike Lee *(England)*
1981 Bruce Penhall *(USA)*
1982 Bruce Penhall *(USA)*
1983 Egon Müller *(West Germany)*
1984 Erik Gundersen *(Denmark)*
1985 Erik Gundersen *(Denmark)*
1986 Hans Nielsen *(Denmark)*
1987 Hans Nielsen *(Denmark)*
1988 Erik Gundersen *(Denmark)*
1989 Hans Nielsen *(Denmark)*
Pairs first held 1970
1980 Dave Jessup and Peter Collins *(England)*
1981 Bruce Penhall and Bobby Schwartz *(USA)*
1982 Dennis Sigalos and Bobby Schwartz *(USA)*
1983 Kenny Carter and Peter Collins *(England)*
1984 Peter Collins and Chris Morton *(England)*
1985 Erik Gundersen and Tommy Knudsen *(Denmark)*
1986 Erik Gundersen and Hans Nielsen *(Denmark)*
1987 Erik Gundersen and Hans Nielsen *(Denmark)*
1988 Erik Gundersen and Hans Nielsen *(Denmark)*
1989 Erik Gundersen and Hans Nielsen *(Denmark)*
Team
1980 England
1981 Denmark
1982 USA
1983 Denmark
1984 Denmark
1985 Denmark
1986 Denmark
1987 Denmark
1988 Denmark
1989 England

speedwell flowering plant, genus *Veronica*, of the figwort family. Of the many wild species, most are low-growing with small bluish flowers. The creeping **Common speedwell** *Veronica officinalis* grows in dry grassy places, heathland and open woods throughout Europe, with oval leaves and spikes of lilac flowers.

Speenhamland system method of poor relief in England started by Berkshire magistrates in 1795, whereby wages were supplemented from the poor-rates. However, it encouraged the payment of low wages and was superseded by the 1834 ◊Poor Law.

Speke /spiːk/ John Hanning 1827–1864. British explorer. He joined ◊Burton in an African expedition in which they reached Lake Tanganyika 1858 and Speke went on to be the first European to see Lake ◊Victoria 1858.

His claim that it was the source of the Nile was disputed by Burton, even after Speke and Grant made a second confirming expedition 1860–63. Speke accidentally shot himself, in England, the day before he was due to debate the matter publicly with Burton.

speleology scientific study of caves, their origin, development, physical structure, flora, fauna, folklore, exploration, mapping, photography, cave-diving, and rescue work. *Potholing*, which involves following the course of underground rivers or streams, has become a popular sport.

Speleology first developed in France in the late 19th century, where the Société de Spéléologie was founded in 1895.

Spence /spens/ Basil 1907–1976. British architect. He was professor of architecture at the Royal Academy, London, 1961–68, and his works include Coventry Cathedral, Sussex University, and the British embassy in Rome.

Spencer /ˈspensə/ Herbert 1820–1903. British philosopher. He wrote *Social Statics* 1851, expounding his *laissez-faire* views on social and political problems, *Principles of Psychology* 1855, and *Education* 1861. In 1862 he began his ten-volume *System of Synthetic Philosophy*, in which he extended ◊Darwin's theory of evolution to the entire field of human knowledge. The chief of the ten volumes are *First Principles* 1862 and *Principles* of biology, psychology, sociology, and ethics. Other works are *The Study of Sociology*, *Man v. the State*, *Essays*, and an autobiography.

Spencer /ˈspensə/ Stanley 1891–1959. British painter. He was born and lived in Cookham-on-Thames, Berkshire, and recreated the Christian story in a Cookham setting. His detailed, dreamlike compositions had little regard for perspective and used generalized human figures.

Examples are *Christ Carrying the Cross* 1920 and *Resurrection* (both Tate Gallery, London) and murals of army life for the oratory of All Souls' at Burghclere in Berkshire.

Spencer-Churchill family name of the dukes of Marlborough, whose main seat is Blenheim Palace, Oxfordshire, England.

Spender /ˈspendə/ Stephen (Harold) 1909– . English poet and critic. His earlier poetry has a left-wing political content, as in *Twenty Poems* 1930, *Vienna* 1934, *The Still Centre* 1939, and *Poems of Dedication* 1946. Other works include the verse drama *Trial of a Judge* 1938, the autobiography *World within World* 1951, and translations. His *Journals 1939–83* were published 1985.

Educated at University College, Oxford, he founded with Cyril Connolly the magazine *Horizon* (of which he was co-editor 1939–41) and 1953–67 was co-editor of *Encounter*. He became professor of English at University College, London, in 1970.

Spengler /ˈʃpeŋlə/ Oswald 1880–1936. German philosopher, whose *Decline of the West* 1918 argued that civilizations go through natural cycles of growth and decay. He was admired by the Nazis.

Spenser /ˈspensə/ Edmund *c.* 1552–1599. English poet, who has been called the 'poet's poet'

because of his rich imagery and command of versification. He is known for his moral allegory *The Faerie Queene*, of which six books survive (three published 1590 and three 1596). Other books include *The Shepheard's Calendar* 1579, *Astrophel* 1586, the love sonnets in *Amoretti* and the *Epithalamion* 1595.

Born in London and educated at Cambridge, in 1580 he became secretary to the Lord Deputy in Ireland, and at Kilcolman Castle completed the first three books of *The Faerie Queene* (Elizabeth I being the 'Faerie Queene'). In 1598 Kilcolman Castle was burned down by rebels, and Spenser with his family narrowly escaped. He died in London, and was buried in Westminster Abbey.

sperm in biology, the male ◊gamete of animals. Each sperm cell has a head capsule containing a nucleus, a middle portion containing ◊mitochondria (which provide energy), and a long tail (flagellum). In most animals, the sperm are motile, and are propelled by a long flagellum, but in some (such as crabs and lobsters) they are non-motile. The term sometimes applies to the motile male gametes (◊antherozoids) of lower plants.

spermaceti glistening waxlike substance, not a true oil, contained in the cells of the huge, almost rectangular 'case' in the head of the sperm whale, amounting to about 2.5 tonnes. It rapidly changes in density according to temperature. It was formerly used in lubricants and cosmetics, but in 1980 a blend of fatty acids and esters from tallow and coconut oil was developed as a substitute.

spermatophore small, nutrient-rich packet of ◊sperm produced in invertebrates, newts and cephalopods.

spermatophyte in botany, another name for a ◊seed plant.

spermicide a cream, jelly, pessary, or other preparation that kills the sperm cells in semen. Spermicides are used for contraceptive purposes, usually in combination with a ◊condom or ◊diaphragm. Sponges impregnated with spermicide have been developed but are not yet in widespread use. Spermicide used alone is only 75% effective in preventing pregnancy.

Sperry /ˈsperi/ Elmer Ambrose 1860–1930. US engineer who developed various devices using ◊gyroscopes, such as gyrostabilizers (for ships and torpedoes) and gyro-controlled autopilots.

The first gyrostabilizers dated from 1912, and during World War I Sperry designed a pilotless aircraft that could carry up to 450 kg/990 lb of explosives a distance of 160 km/100 mi (the first flying bomb) under gyroscopic control. By the mid-1930s Sperry autopilots were standard equipment on most large ships.

Spey /speɪ/ river in Highland and Grampian regions, Scotland, rising SE of Fort Augustus, and flowing 172 km/107 mi to the Moray Firth

Spencer Christ Carrying the Cross *(1920)* Tate Gallery, London.

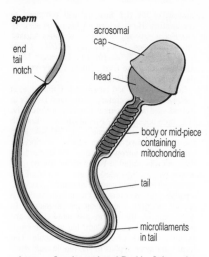

sperm

end
tail
notch

acrosomal
cap

head

body or mid-piece
containing
mitochondria

tail

microfilaments
in tail

between Lossiemouth and Buckie. It has salmon fisheries at its mouth.

Speyer /ˈʃpaɪə/ (English *Spires*) ancient city on the Rhine, in Rhineland-Palatinate, West Germany, 26 km/16 mi south of Mannheim; population (1983) 43,000. It was at the *Diet of Spires* 1529 that Protestantism received its name.

SPF abbreviation for *South Pacific Forum*.

sphalerite the chief ore of zinc, composed of zinc sulphide with a small proportion of iron, formula $(Zn,Fe)S$. It is brown with a non-metallic lustre unless an appreciable amount of iron is present (up to 26% by weight). Sphalerite usually occurs in ore veins in limestones, where it is often associated with galena. It crystallizes in the cubic system but does not normally form perfect cubes.

sphere in mathematics, a circular solid figure with all points on its surface the same distance from the centre. For a sphere of radius *r*, the volume $V = 4/3\pi r^3$ and the surface area $A = 4\pi r^2$.

Sphinx a mythological creature, represented in Egyptian, Assyrian and Greek art as a lion with a human head. In Greek myth the Sphinx was female, and killed travellers who failed to answer a riddle; she killed herself when ◊Oedipus gave the right answer.

sphygmomanometer instrument for measuring blood pressure, particularly of the arteries. Consisting of an inflatable arm cuff joined by a rubber tube to a column of mercury scale, it is used, together with a stethoscope, to measure blood pressure.

Spica brightest star in the constellation Virgo, and the 16th brightest star in the sky. Spica has a true luminosity of over 2,000 times that of the Sun, and is 275 light years away. It is also a spectroscopic ◊binary star, the components of which orbit each other every 4.014 days.

spice any aromatic vegetable substance used as a condiment and for flavouring food. Spices are obtained from tropical plants, and include pepper, nutmeg, ginger, and cinnamon. They have little food value, but increase the appetite, and may facilitate digestion.

Spice Islands /spaɪs/ former name of the ◊Moluccas, a group of islands in the Malay Archipelago.

spicules, solar in astronomy, short-lived jets of hot gas in the upper ◊chromosphere of the Sun. Spiky in appearance, they move at high velocities along lines of magnetic force to which they owe their shapes. Spicules are usually seen to form at about 45° to the vertical, and appear to disperse material into the ◊corona.

spider jointed-legged animal of the class Arachnida. Unlike insects, the head and breast are merged to form the cephalothorax, connected to the abdomen by a characteristic narrow waist. There are eight legs, and up to eight eyes. On the undersurface of the abdomen are spinnerets which exude a viscid fluid. This hardens on exposure

Sphinx *The avenue of ram sphinxes at the temple of Karnak in Luxor, Egypt.*

to the air to form silky threads, used to spin webs in which the spider nests and catches its prey. Its fangs inject substances to subdue and digest prey, the juices of which are then sucked in by the spider.

Species of particular interest include the *common garden spider Araneus diadematus*, which spins webs of remarkable beauty; the *zebra spider Salticus scenicus*, a longer-sighted species which stalks its prey and has pads on its feet which enable it to walk even on glass; the poisonous ◊tarantula and ◊black widow; the *water spider Argyroneta aquatica*, which fills a 'diving bell' home with air trapped on the hairs of the body; and the largest members of the group, the *bird-eating spider Mygale* of South America, with a body some 5 cm/2 in long and a leg-span of 30 cm/1 ft.

Spider venom is a powerful toxin which paralyses its prey. In 1989 it was claimed that it's use might help to prevent the development of epilepsy and Alzheimer's disease.

Spielberg /ˈspiːlbɜːg/ Steven 1947– . US director, whose successful films include *Jaws* 1975, *Close Encounters of the Third Kind* 1977, *Raiders of the Lost Ark* 1981, and *ET* 1982.

spikelet in botany, one of the units of a grass ◊inflorescence. It comprises a slender axis on which one or more flowers are borne. Each individual flower or floret has a pair of scalelike bracts, the glumes, and is enclosed by a membranous lemma and a thin, narrow palea, which may be extended into a long, slender bristle, or *awn*.

spikenard Himalayan plant *Nardostachys jatamansi*, family Valerianaceae; its underground stems give a perfume used in Eastern aromatic oils.

Spillane /spɪˈleɪn/ 'Mickey' (Frank Morrison) 1918– . US crime novelist. He began by writing for pulp magazines and became known for violent crime novels featuring his 'one-man police force' hero Mike Hammer; for example, *Vengeance is Mine* 1950 and *The Long Wait* 1951.

spina bifida a congenital defect in which part of the spinal cord and its membranes are exposed due to incomplete development of the spine.

Spina bifida, usually present in the lower back, varies in severity. The most seriously affected babies may be paralysed below the waist. There is also a risk of mental retardation from hydrocephalus, which is often associated with spina bifida. Surgery is performed to close the spinal lesion shortly after birth.

spinach annual plant *Spinacia oleracea* of the family Chenopodiaceae. A native of Asia, it is cultivated for its leaves which are eaten as a vegetable.

spinal cord a major component of the ◊central nervous system in *vertebrates*. It is enclosed by the bones of the ◊spine and links the peripheral nervous system to the brain.

spine the backbone of vertebrates. In most mammals, it contains 26 small bones called *vertebrae*, which enclose and protect the spinal cord (which links the peripheral nervous system to the brain). The spine connects with the skull, ribs, back muscles, and pelvis.

There are 7 cervical vertebrae, in the neck; 12 thoracic, in the upper trunk; 5 lumbar, in the lower back; the sacrum (consisting of 5 rudimentary vertebrae fused together, joined to the hip bones); and the coccyx (4 vertebrae, fused into the tailbone). The spine in humans has four curves (front to rear), which allow for the increased size of the chest and pelvic cavities, and permit springing, to minimize jolting of the internal organs.

spinel a group of 'mixed oxide' minerals consisting mainly of the oxides of magnesium and aluminium, $MgAl_2O_4$ and $FeAl_2O_4$. Spinels crystallize in the cubic system, forming octahedral crystals. They are found in high-temperature igneous and metamorphic rocks. The aluminium oxide spinel contains gem varieties, such as the ruby spinels of Sri Lanka and Myanmar (Burma).

spinet a keyboard instrument, similar to a harpsichord but smaller, which has only one string for each note.

spinning the art of drawing out and twisting fibres (originally wool or flax) into threads, by hand or machine. Synthetic fibres are extruded as a liquid through the holes of a spinneret.

spinning machine machine for spinning—drawing out fibres and twisting them into a long thread, or yarn. Spinning was originally done by hand, then with the spinning wheel, and in about 1767 James ◊Hargreaves in England built the spinning jenny, a machine that could spin 8, then 16, bobbins at once. Later came Samuel ◊Crompton's spinning mule 1779, which has a moving carriage carrying the spindles and is still used today.

Also used is the ring-spinning frame introduced in the USA in 1828 where sets of rollers moving at different speeds draw out finer and finer thread, which is twisted and wound onto rotating bobbins. Originally, some 9,000 years ago, spinning was done by hand using a distaff (a cleft stick holding a bundle of fibres) and a weighted spindle, which was spun to twist the thread. In the 1300s the spinning wheel appeared in Europe, though it had been used earlier in the East. It provided a way of turning the spindle mechanically. By the next century, the wheel was both spinning and winding the yarn onto a bobbin, but further mechanical development did not come until the 18th century.

Spinoza /spɪˈnəʊzə/ Benedict or Baruch 1632–1677. Dutch philosopher who believed in a rationalistic pantheism that owed much to Descartes' mathematical appreciation of the universe. Mind and matter are two modes of an infinite substance which he called God or Nature, good and evil being relative. He was a determinist, believing that human action was motivated by self-preservation.

Ethics 1677 is his main work. *A Treatise on Religious and Political Philosophy* 1670 was the only one of his works published during his life, and was attacked by Christians. He was excommunicated by the Jewish community in Amsterdam on charges of heretical thought and practice 1656. He was a lens-grinder by trade.

spiracle in insects, the opening of a ◊trachea, through which oxygen enters the body and carbon dioxide is expelled. In cartilaginous fish, the same name is given to a circular opening that marks the remains of the first gill slit. In tetrapod vertebrates, the spiracle has evolved into the

Spielberg *US film director Steven Spielberg.*

spine

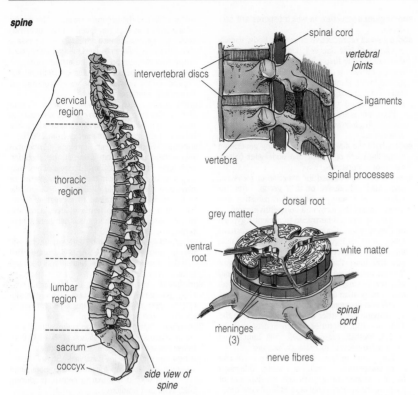

intervertebral discs

spinal cord

vertebral joints

ligaments

vertebra

spinal processes

cervical region

thoracic region

lumbar region

sacrum

coccyx

side view of spine

grey matter

dorsal root

ventral root

white matter

spinal cord

meninges (3)

nerve fibres

Eustachian tube, which connects the middle ear cavity with the pharynx.

spiraea herbaceous plant and shrubs of the genus *Spiraea*, family Rosaceae, which includes many cultivated species with ornamental panicles of flowers.

spiral a common curve such as that traced by a flat coil of rope. Various kinds of spiral can be generated mathematically, for example, an equiangular or logarithmic spiral (in which a tangent at any point on the curve always makes the same angle with it) and an ◊involute. It also occurs in nature as a normal consequence of accelerating growth, such as the spiral shape of the shells of snails and some other molluscs.

Spires /spɪə/ or /ˈspaɪəz/ English name for the German city of ◊Speyer.

spirits of salts an old name for ◊hydrochloric acid.

spiritualism a belief in the survival of the human personality and in communication between the living and those who have 'passed on'. The spiritualist movement originated in the USA in 1848. Adherents to this religious denomination practise *mediumship*, which claims to allow clairvoyant knowledge of distant events and spirit healing. The writer Arthur Conan Doyle and the Victorian prime minister Gladstone were converts.

In the UK the Society for Psychical Research was founded in 1882 by W H Myers and Henry Sidgwick to investigate the claims of spiritualism. Spiritualists include D D Home, the scientists Oliver Lodge and William Crookes, and Air Marshal Lord Dowding.

spit ◊sandbar (sand ridge) projecting into a body of water and growing out from land, deposited by a current carrying material from one direction to another across the mouth of an inlet.

Spitalfields /ˈspɪtlfiːldz/ district in the Greater London borough of ◊Tower Hamlets. It was once the home of ◊Huguenot silk weavers.

Spithead /ˌspɪtˈhed/ a roadstead between the mainland of England and the Isle of ◊Wight. The name is often applied to the entire eastern area of the ◊Solent.

Spitsbergen /ˈspɪts,bɜːgən/ the main island in the Norwegian archipelago of ◊Svalbard.

Spitz /spɪts/ Mark Andrew 1950– . US swimmer. He won a record seven gold medals at the 1972 Olympic Games, all in world record times.

He won 11 Olympic medals in total (four in 1968) and set 26 world records 1967–72. After retiring in 1972 he became a movie actor and two of his films were candidates for 'The Worst of Hollywood'.

CAREER HIGHLIGHTS

Olympic medals

Gold
4 x 100 metres freestyle relay 1968, 1972
4 x 200 metres freestyle relay 1968, 1972
4 x 100 metres medley relay 1972
100 metres freestyle 1972
200 metres freestyle 1972
100 metres butterfly 1972
200 metres butterfly 1972
Silver
100 metres butterfly 1968
Bronze
100 metres freestyle 1968.

Spinoza *Dutch philosopher Benedict Spinoza.*

spleen organ in vertebrates, part of the lymphatic system, which helps to process ◊lymphocytes. It also regulates the number of red blood cells in circulation by destroying old cells, and stores iron. It is situated behind the stomach.

splenectomy surgical removal of the spleen.

Split /splɪt/ (Italian *Spalato*) port in Yugoslavia, on the Adriatic; population (1981) 236,000. Industries include engineering, cement, and textiles, and it is also a tourist resort.

The Roman emperor Diocletian retired here in 305.

Spock /spɒk/ Benjamin McLane 1903– . US paediatrician and writer on child care. His *Common Sense Book of Baby and Child Care* 1946 urged less rigidity in bringing up children than had been advised by previous generations of writers on the subject, but was misunderstood as advocating complete permissiveness.

In his later work he stressed that his commonsense approach had not implied rejecting all discipline, but that his main aim was to give parents the confidence to trust their own judgement, rather than relying on books by experts who did not know a particular child. He has been an active peace campaigner.

Spode /spəʊd/ Josiah 1754–1827. English potter, son of Josiah Spode the elder (an apprentice of Thomas Whieldon who started his own works at Stoke-on-Trent 1770), and his successor in the new firm in 1797. He developed bone porcelain (bone ash, china stone, and china clay) around 1800, which was produced at all English factories in the 19th century, and became potter to King George III in 1806.

spoils system in the USA, the granting of offices and favours among the supporters of a party in office. The spoils system, a type of ◊patronage, was used by Jefferson, and was enlarged in scope by the 1820 Tenure of Office Act, which gave the president and Senate the power to reappoint posts that were the gift of the government after each four-yearly election. The practice remained common in the 20th century in US local government.

The term is derived from a speech after an election victory by Secretary of State William Marcy: 'To the victor belong the spoils of the enemy.'

Spokane /spəʊˈkæn/ city on the Spokane river, E Washington, USA; population (1980) 341,000. It is situated in a mining, timber, and rich agricultural area, and is the seat of Gonzaga University 1887.

Spoleto /spəˈleɪtəʊ/ town in Umbria, central Italy; population (1985) 37,000. There is an annual opera and drama festival established by Gian Carlo ◊Menotti. It was a papal possession 1220–1860, and has Roman remains and medieval churches.

sponge very simple animal of the phylum Porifera, usually marine. A sponge has a hollow body, its cavity lined by cells bearing flagellae, whose whiplike movements keep water circulating, bringing a stream of food particles. The body walls are strengthened with protein (as in the bath-sponge) or small spikes of silica.

sponsorship a form of advertising in sports, popular music, and the arts. Sponsorship became an important source of finance for sport in the 1970s, and takes several forms. Many companies sponsor sporting events, while others give money to individuals who wear the company's logo or motifs while performing. Rock tours are also commonly sponsored by advertisers, although some performers refuse in principle to endorse a product in this way. Major art exhibitions are often sponsored by large companies.

spontaneous generation the erroneous belief that living organisms can arise spontaneously from non-living matter, which survived until the mid-19th century, when the French chemist Louis Pasteur demonstrated that a nutrient broth would not generate microorganisms if it was adequately sterilized. The theory of ◊biogenesis holds that spontaneous generation cannot occur.

spore The earthstar Geastrum triplex *is so called because its outer covering splits into a star shape. A water droplet has just landed on top of the fungus, inducing it to expel a spore cloud.*

spooling in computing, a process in which information to be printed is temporarily stored in a file, the actual printing being carried out later. It is used to prevent a relatively slow printer from holding up the system at critical times, and to enable several computers or programs to share one printer.

spoonbill type of bird, of the family Threskiornithidae, characterized by a long, flat bill, dilated at the tip in the shape of a spoon. They are usually white, and up to 90 cm/3 ft tall. *The Eurasian spoonbill Platalea leucorodia* is found in shallow open water which it sifts for food.

spoonerism a form of expression not unlike a slip of the tongue, arising from the exchange of elements in a flow of words. The result can often be amusing and even ridiculous (for example 'a troop of Boy Scouts' becoming 'a scoop of Boy Trouts'). William Spooner (1844–1930) gave his name to the phenomenon.

Sporades /'spɒrədiːz/ island group in the Aegean Sea. The chief island of the *Northern Sporades* is ◊Skyros. The *Southern Sporades* are more usually referred to as the ◊Dodecanes.

sporangium a structure in which ◊spores are produced.

spore a small reproductive or resting body, usually consisting of just one cell. Unlike a ◊gamete, it does not need to fuse with another cell in order to develop into a new organism. Spores are produced by the lower plants, most fungi, some bacteria, and certain protozoa. They are generally light and easily dispersed by wind movements.

Plant spores are haploid and are produced by the sporophyte, following meiosis; see ◊alternation of generations.

sporophyte the diploid spore-producing generation in the life cycle of a plant that undergoes ◊alternation of generations.

sport an activity pursued for exercise or pleasure, performed individually or in a group, often involving the testing of physical capabilities and usually taking the form of a competitive game.

Many sports can be traced to ancient Egyptian or Greek times. Coursing was believed to have taken place in Egypt in 3000 BC, using Saluki dogs. Wrestling certainly took place in what is now Iraq more than 4,000 years ago; a form of hockey was played in Egypt about 2050 BC and falconry, boxing, athletics, and fencing were all played more than 4,000 years ago.

The real development of the majority of sports as competitions, rather than pastimes, was in the 18th and 19th centuries, when sports such as cricket, football, rugby football, golf, tennis, and many more became increasingly popular.

The advent of television has led to more and more competitions within each sport. Television has also helped the growth and development of some sports; darts, snooker, and bowls are three examples.

SPQR abbreviation for *Senatus Populusque Romanus*, Latin 'the Senate and People of Rome'.

spreadsheet in computing, a program that mimics a sheet of ruled paper, divided into columns and rows. The user enters values in the sheet, then instructs the program to perform some operation on them, such as totalling a column or finding the average of a series of numbers. Highly complex numerical analyses may be built up from these simple steps.

Spreadsheets are widely used in business for forecasting and financial control. The frst spreadsheet program, VisiCalc, appeared 1979.

spring a device, usually a metal coil, which returns to its original shape when stretched or compressed. Springs are used in some machines (such as clocks) to store energy, which can be released at a controlled rate. In other machines (such as engines) they are used to close valves.

In vehicle suspension systems springs are used to cushion passengers from road shocks. These springs are used in conjunction with ◊dampers, to limit their amount of travel.

spring in geology, a natural flow of water from the ground, formed at the point of intersection of the water table and the ground's surface. The source of water is rain that has fallen on the overlying rocks and percolated through. During its passage the water may have dissolved mineral substances which may then be precipitated at the spring.

A spring may be continuous or intermittent, and depends on the position of the water table and the topography (surface features).

Spring /sprɪŋ/ Richard 1950– . Irish Labour Party leader from 1982, who entered into coalition with ◊FitzGerald's Fine Gael 1982 as deputy prime minister (and minister for energy from 1983).

springbok South African antelope *Antidorcas marsupialis* about 80 cm/2.6 ft at the shoulder, with head and body 1.3 m/4 ft long. They may leap 3 m/10 ft or more in the air when startled or playing, and have a fold of skin along the middle of the back which is raised to a crest in alarm. They once migrated in herds of over a million, but are now found only in small numbers where protected.

Springfield /'sprɪŋfiːld/ capital and agricultural and mining centre of Illinois, USA; population (1980) 176,000. President Abraham Lincoln was born and is buried here.

Springfield /'sprɪŋfiːld/ city in Massachusetts, USA; population (1980) 531,000. It was the site (1794–1968) of the US arsenal and armoury, known for the Springfield rifle.

Springfield /'sprɪŋfiːld/ city and agricultural centre in Missouri, USA; population (1980) 133,000. Industries include engineering and textiles.

Springs /sprɪŋz/ city in Transvaal, South Africa, 40 km/25 mi east of Johannesburg; population (1980) 154,000. It is a mining centre, producing gold, coal, and uranium.

Springsteen /'sprɪŋstiːn/ Bruce 1949– . US rock singer, songwriter, and guitarist, born in New Jersey. His music combines melodies in traditional rock idiom and reflective lyrics of working-class life on albums such as *Born to Run* 1975 and *Born in the USA* 1984 and in concerts with the E Street Band.

spruce coniferous tree of the genus *Picea*, found over much of the northern hemisphere. Pyramidal in shape, spruces have harsh needles and drooping leathery cones. Some are important forestry trees, such as the *Sitka spruce Picea sitchensis* originally from W North America, and the *Norway spruce* or *Christmas tree Picea abies*.

Spurs, Battle of the a victory 1513 over the French, at Guinegate, NW France, by Henry VII of England; the name emphasizes the speed of the French retreat.

Sputnik (Russian 'fellow traveller') a series of ten Soviet Earth-orbiting satellites. *Sputnik 1* was the first artificial satellite, launched 4 Oct 1957. It weighed 84 kg/185 lb, with a 58 cm/23 in diameter, and carried only a simple radio transmitter which allowed scientists to track it as it orbited Earth. It burned up in the atmosphere 92 days later. *Sputnik 2*, launched 3 Nov 1957, weighed about 500 kg/1,100 lb including the dog Laika, the first living creature in space. Unfortunately, there was no way to return the dog to Earth, and it died in space. *Sputnik 3*

springbok

spring

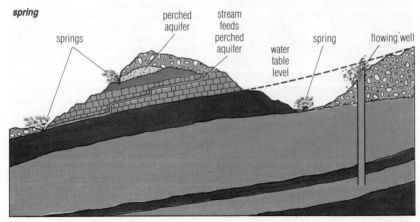

springs

perched aquifer

stream feeds perched aquifer

water table level

spring

flowing well

was launched 15 May 1958 and weighed about 1,300 kg/2,900 lb.

Spycatcher the controversial memoirs (published 1987) of former UK intelligence officer Peter ◊Wright. The Law Lords unanimously rejected the UK government's attempt to prevent allegations of MI5 misconduct being reported in the British media.

sq abbreviation for *square* (measure).

SQL *Structured Query Language* in computing, a language designed for use with ◊relational databases. Although it can be used by programmers in the same way as other languages, it is often used as a means for programs to communicate among themselves. Typically, one program (called the 'client') uses SQL to request data from a database 'server'.

square in geometry, a quadrilateral (four-sided) plane figure with all sides equal and each angle a rightangle. Its diagonals also bisect each other at rightangles. The area A of a square is the length l of one side multiplied by itself; $A = l^2$. Similarly, any quantity multiplied by itself, is also a square, represented by an index (power) of 2; for example, $4^2 = 16$ and $6.8^2 = 46.24$.

An algebraic term is squared by doubling its index, and squaring its coefficient if it has one; for example, $(x^2)^2 = x^4$ and $(6y^3)^2 = 36y^6$. A number which has a whole number as its ◊square root is known as a *perfect square*; for example, 25, 144 and 54,756 are perfect squares (with roots of 5, 12 and 234, respectively).

square root in mathematics, a number that when squared (multiplied by itself) equals another given number. For example, the square root of 25 (written $\sqrt{25}$) is ±5, because $5 \times 5 = 25$, and $(-5) \times (-5) = 25$. As an ◊index, a square root is represented by $1/2$, for example, $16^{1/2} = 4$.

Negative numbers (less than 0) do not have square roots that are ◊real numbers. Their roots are represented by ◊complex numbers, in which the square root of –1 is given the symbol i (that is, $\pm i^2 = -1$). Thus the square root of –4 is $\sqrt{[(-1) \times 4]} = \sqrt{-1} \times \sqrt{4} = 2i$.

squash game played on an enclosed court and derived from ◊rackets. Usually played by two players, it became a popular sport in the 1970s and then a fitness craze as well as a competitive sport.

The court is 9.75 m/32 ft long and 6.40 m/21 ft wide. Players use rackets and a small 'squashy' rubber ball. The ball is hit against a wall (the front wall) and when serving must be above a line 1.83 m/6 ft high. Thereafter the ball must be hit alternately against the front wall, within certain limitations, but rebounds off the other three walls are permitted. The object is to win points by playing shots the opponent cannot return to the wall. Squash was first played at Harrow school in 1817. The Squash Rackets Association was formed in 1928.

Springsteen US rock singer, songwriter, and guitarist Bruce Springsteen.

Squash: recent winners

World Open championship
men
1980 Geoff Hunt *(Australia)*
1981 Jahangir Khan *(Pakistan)*
1982 Jahangir Khan *(Pakistan)*
1983 Jahangir Khan *(Pakistan)*
1984 Jahangir Khan *(Pakistan)*
1985 Jahangir Khan *(Pakistan)*
1986 Ross Norman *(New Zealand)*
1987 Jansher Khan *(Pakistan)*
1988 Jahangir Khan *(Pakistan)*
1989 Jansher Khan *(Pakistan)*
women
1981 Rhonda Thorne *(Australia)*
1983 Vicky Cardwell *(Australia)*
1985 Sue Devoy *(New Zealand)*
1987 Sue Devoy *(New Zealand)*
1989 Martine Le Moignan *(Great Britain)*

squatter person illegally occupying someone else's property, for example, some of the urban homeless in contemporary Britain making use of vacant houses. In 19th-century Australia and New Zealand squatters were legal tenants of crown grazing land. The term was used there as synonymous with pastoralist or grazier, without an illegal imputation. Those who survived droughts and held on to their wealth established a politically powerful 'squattocracy', and built elegant mansions. As closer agricultural settlement spread at the end of the century, their influence waned.

In the UK from the 1970s the word became applied to those taking over publicly or privately owned empty houses and other premises, either on grounds of homelessness or as a political manoeuvre. Legislation was enacted to introduce a special speedy court procedure for removing squatters. Squatters commit a criminal offence if they take over property where there is a 'residential occupier'; for example, by moving in while the owner is on holiday.

squill bulb-forming perennial plant of the genus *Scilla*, family Liliaceae, found growing in dry places near the sea in W Europe. Cultivated species usually bear blue flowers either singly or in clusters at the top of the stem.

The *Spring squill Scilla verna* has narrow grasslike leaves, sometimes curled; violet-blue six-petalled flowers appear in early summer, two to 12 on a dense spike. The *autumn squill Scilla autumnalis* is somewhat similar, but flowers in autumn before the emergence of leaves.

squint or *strabismus* a common condition, in which one eye deviates in any direction. A squint may be convergent (with the bad eye turned inward), divergent (outward), or, in rare cases, vertical.

There are two types of squint: paralytic, arising from disease or damage involving the extra-ocular muscles or their nerve supply; and non-paralytic, which may be inherited or due to some refractive error within the eye. Non-paralytic (or concomitant) squint is the typical condition seen in small children. It is treated by corrective eye-wear, exercises for the eye muscles, or corrective surgery to the muscles.

squirrel bushy-tailed rodent of the family Sciuridae. They are about 20 cm/8 in long and generally live in trees, but some are ground dwellers. They are found worldwide except for Australia, Madagascar, and polar regions.

The *red squirrel Sciurus vulgaris* is found throughout Europe and N Asia. It is about 23 cm/9 in long (plus 18 cm/7 in tail), with red fur and bushy tail. It rears its young in stick nests, or 'dreys'. Although it is less active in winter, it does not hibernate, burying nuts as a winter store. In Britain, the red squirrel has been replaced in most areas by the introduced *grey squirrel Sciurus carolinensis* from North America. Ground squirrels or *gophers* make networks of tunnels in open ground, and carry their food in cheek pouches. *Prairie dogs* and ◊marmots are of the same family. There are also a number of genera

spruce

of *flying squirrels*, mostly Asian, but some in E Europe and North America, which can glide between trees on skin stretched between front and back limbs.

Sr abbreviation for *senior*.

Sri Lanka /ˌsriː ˈlæŋkə/ island in the Indian Ocean, off the SE coast of India.

government Under the 1978 constitution, the head of state and chief executive is the president, directly elected by universal suffrage for six-year terms. A two-term limit applies and voting is by the single transferable vote system. The president appoints and dismisses cabinet ministers, including the prime minister, may hold selected portfolios and dissolve parliament. Parliament, which is known as the National State Assembly, is a single-chamber body with supreme legislative authority. There are 225 members, directly elected by a complex system of proportional representation for six-year terms. A two-thirds parliamentary majority is required to alter the constitution.

history The aboriginal people, the Veddas (of whom a few may remain in jungle areas), were conquered about 550 BC by the Sinhalese from N India under their first king, Vijaya. In the 3rd century BC the island became a world centre of Buddhism. The spice trade brought Arabs, who called the island Serendip, and Europeans, who called it Ceylon. Portugal established settlements 1505, taken over by the Netherlands 1658 and by Britain 1796. Ceylon was ceded to Britain 1802 and became a crown colony.

Under British rule Tamils from S India (Hindus who had been settled in the north and east for centuries) took up English education and progressed rapidly in administrative careers. Many more Tamils immigrated to work on the tea and rubber plantations developed in central Sri Lanka near Kandy. Conflicts between the Sinhalese majority and the Tamils surfaced during the 1920s as nationalist politics developed. In 1931, universal suffrage was introduced for an elected legislature and executive council in which power was shared with the British, and in Feb 1948 independence was achieved.

Between 1948 and 1972, Sri Lanka remained a dominion within the British Commonwealth with a titular governor-general. The United National Party (UNP), led consecutively by Don and Dudley ◊Senanayake, held power until 1956, when the radical socialist and more narrowly Sinhalese Sri Lanka Freedom Party (SLFP), led by Solomon

squirrel

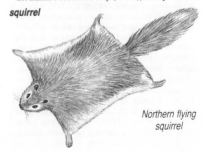

Northern flying squirrel

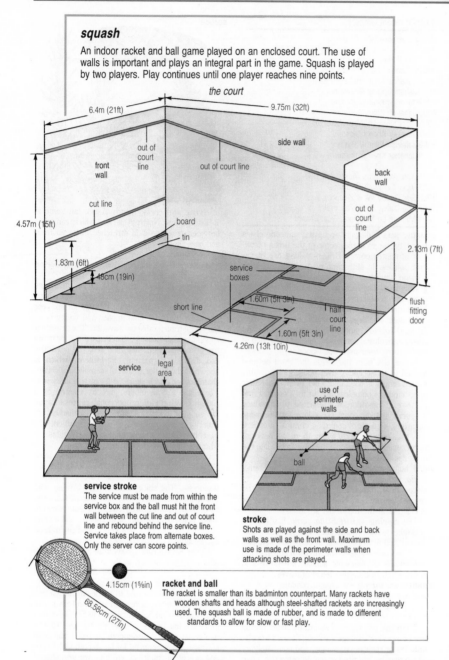

squash

An indoor racket and ball game played on an enclosed court. The use of walls is important and plays an integral part in the game. Squash is played by two players. Play continues until one player reaches nine points.

the court

6.4m (21ft) | 9.75m (32ft)

out of court line
front wall
side wall
out of court line
back wall
cut line
board
tin
4.57m (15ft)
out of court line
2.13m (7ft)
1.83m (6ft)
48cm (19in)
service boxes
short line
1.60m (5ft 3in)
half court line
flush fitting door
1.60m (5ft 3in)
4.26m (13ft 10in)

service
legal area

service stroke
The service must be made from within the service box and the ball must hit the front wall between the cut line and out of court line and rebound behind the service line. Service takes place from alternate boxes. Only the server can score points.

use of perimeter walls
ball

stroke
Shots are played against the side and back walls as well as the front wall. Maximum use is made of the perimeter walls when attacking shots are played.

4.15cm (1⅝in)
68.58cm (27in)

racket and ball
The racket is smaller than its badminton counterpart. Many rackets have wooden shafts and heads although steel-shafted rackets are increasingly used. The squash ball is made of rubber, and is made to different standards to allow for slow or fast play.

◊Bandaranaike, gained electoral victory and established Sinhalese rather than English as the official language to be used for entrance to universities and the civil service. This precipitated Tamil riots, culminating in the prime minister's assassination by a Buddhist monk Sept 1959. Bandaranaike's widow, Sirimavo, became prime minister and held office until 1977, except for UNP interludes 1960 and 1965–70. She implemented a radical economic programme of nationalization and land reform, a pro-Sinhalese educational and employment policy, and an independent nonaligned military policy.

In 1972 the Senate upper chamber was abolished and the new national name Sri Lanka ('Resplendent Island') adopted. Economic conditions deteriorated, spawning a serious wave of strikes 1976, while Tamil complaints of discrimination bred a separatist movement calling for the creation of an independent Tamil state (Eelam) in the north and east. The Tamil United Liberation Front (TULF) coalition was formed 1976 to campaign for this goal and emerged as the second-largest party in parliament from

the elections July 1977, easily won by the UNP led by Junius Jayawardene. The new government remodelled the 1972 constitution and introduced a new freer-market economic programme, which recorded initial success. In Oct 1980 Sirimavo Bandaranaike was deprived of her civil rights for six years for alleged abuses of power. The guerrilla activities of the Liberation Tigers of Tamil Eelam in the N and E provoked the frequent imposition of a state of emergency. In 1982 Jayawardene was re-elected president and the life of parliament was prolonged by referendum.

The violence escalated 1983, causing the deaths of over 400 people, mainly Tamils in the Jaffna area. This prompted legislation outlawing separatist organizations, including the TULF. The near civil war has cost thousands of lives and blighted the country's economy; the tourist industry has collapsed, foreign investment dried up, and aid donors have become reluctant to prop up a government seemingly bent on imposing a military solution. All-party talks with Indian mediation repeatedly failed to solve the Tamil dispute,

but in July 1987, amid protest riots, with several demonstrators killed by police, President Jayawardene, and the Indian prime minister Rajiv ◊Gandhi signed a peace pact. It proposed to make Tamil and English official languages, create a semi-autonomous homeland for the Tamils in the N and E, recognize the Tigers (once disarmed) as their representatives, and hold a referendum 1988 in the E province, which has pockets of Sinhalese and 32% Muslims. To police this agreement, a 7,000-strong Indian Peace Keeping Force (IPKF) was despatched to the Tiger-controlled Jaffna area. The Tamil Tigers put down their weapons and agreed to talks with the Sri Lankan government Apr 1989.

This employment of Indian troops served to fan unrest among the Sinhala community, who viewed the July 1987 Colombo Accord as a 'sell–out' to Tamil interests. Protest riots erupted in the S around Colombo and senior UNP politicians, including President Jayawardene, were targeted for assassination by the resurfaced Sinhala-Marxist guerrilla organization, the People's Liberation Front (JVP). In the N, despite an additional 50,000 reinforcements being sent, the IPKF failed to capture the Tiger's leader Velupillai Prabhakaran, who continued to wage a guerrilla war from fresh bases in the rural east.

Jayawardene being unable, under the terms of the constitution, to seek a second term, prime minister Ranasinghe ◊Premadasa stood for the governing party in the presidential election of Dec 1989 and defeated the SLFP's Sirimavo Bandaranaike, who called for the immediate withdrawal of the IPKF in a campaign that was marred by JVP-induced violence. A member of the lowly *dhobi* (washerman) caste, Premadasa was the country's first national leader not to be drawn from the priviledged *Goyigama* elite. The state of emergency, which had been imposed in May 1983, was temporarily lifted for the National Assembly elections that followed in Feb 1989 and in which the UNP secured a narrow overall majority. After the election, finance minister Dingri Banda Wijetunge was appointed prime minister and proceeded, with President Premadasa, to work for national reconciliation. Round-table negotiations were held with Tiger leaders in June 1989 and in Sept 1989 agreement was reached with India that the IPKF would be withdrawn by Apr 1990. Despite these moves the civil war, with its two fronts in the N and S, continued, with the death toll exeeding 1,000

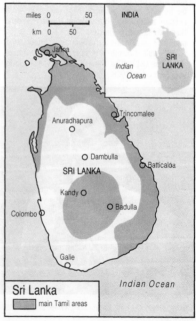

Sri Lanka
main Tamil areas

Sri Lanka
Democratic Socialist Republic of (former name **Ceylon**)
Prajathanrika Samajawadi Janarajaya Sri Lanka

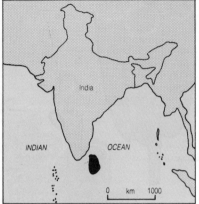

area 65,600 sq km/25,328 sq mi

capital and chief port Colombo

towns Kandy; ports Jaffna, Galle, Negombo, Trincomalee

physical flat in the N and around the coast; hills and mountains in the S

features Adam's Peak; ruined cities of Anuradhapura, Polonnaruwa

head of state Ranasinghe Premadsa from 1989

head of government Dingiri Banda Wijetunge from 1989

government liberal democratic republic

political parties United National Party (UNP), right-of-centre; Sri Lanka Freedom Party (SLFP), left-of-centre; Tamil United Liberation Front (TULF), Tamil autonomy; Eelam People's Revolutionary Liberation Front (EPLRF), Indian-backed Tamil-secessionist *Tamil Tigers*; People's Liberation Front (JVP), Sinhala-extremist organization, banned from 1983

exports tea, rubber, coconut products, plumbago, sapphires, rubies, precious stones

currency Sri Lanka rupee (67.80 = £1 Feb 1990)

population (1989) 17,541,000 (including 2,500,000 Tamils); annual growth rate 1.8%

life expectancy men 67, women 70

language Sinhalese (official, but English and Tamil are national languages)

religion Buddhist 67% (official), Hindu 18%

literacy 91% male/83% female (1985 est)

GNP $5.3 bn (1984); $340 per head of population

chronology

1948 Independence from Britain achieved (as Ceylon).

1956 Sinhalese established as official language.

1959 Assassination of Prime Minister Solomon Bandaranaike.

1972 Socialist Republic of Sri Lanka proclaimed.

1978 Presidential constitution adopted by new Jayawardene government.

1983 Tamil guerrilla violence escalated; state of emergency imposed.

1987 Violence continued despite ceasefire policed by Indian troops.

1988 Left-wing guerrilla campaign against the Indo-Sri Lankan peace pact. Prime Minister Premadasa elected president amid allegations of fraud.

1989 Premadasa became president; Wijetunge, prime minister. Leaders of the TULF and JVP assassinated. India agreed to withdraw troops by April 1990.

a month. Among those assassinated during 1989 was Appapillai Amirthalingam, the leader of the TULF, and Rohana Wijeweera, who had led the JVP since its formation in 1967.

Sri Lanka remains a member of the ◊Commonwealth and ◊non-aligned movement and joined the ◊South Asian Association for Regional Cooperation 1985. Its relations with India deteriorated during the early 1980s over the Tamil issue, but in the 1987 agreement Rajiv Gandhi pledged to enforce the peace with Indian troops if necessary and to stop Tamil militants from using S India as a base.

Srinagar /srɪ'nʌgə/ summer capital of the state of ◊Jammu and Kashmir, India; population (1981) 520,000. It is a beautiful resort, intersected by waterways, and has carpet, papier mâché, and leather industries. The university of Jammu and Kashmir was established 1948.

SS Nazi elite corps (German *Schutz-Staffel* 'protective squadron') established 1925. Under ◊Himmler its 500,000 membership included the full-time *Waffen-SS* (armed SS), which fought in World War II, and spare-time members. The SS performed state police duties and was brutal in its treatment of the Jews and others in the concentration camps and occupied territories. It was condemned at the Nuremberg Trials of war criminals.

SSR abbreviation for *Soviet Socialist Republic*.

stability in physics, how difficult it is to move an object from a position of ◊equilibrium. A stable object returns to its rest position after being shifted slightly. An unstable object topples or falls when shifted slightly.

stabilizer one of a pair of fins fitted to the sides of a ship and governed automatically by ◊gyroscope mechanism, designed to reduce side-to-side rolling of the ship in rough weather.

stack in computing, a method of storing data in which the most recent item stored will be the next to be retrieved. The technique is commonly called 'last in, first out'. Stacks are used to solve problems involving nested structures; for example, to analyse an arithmetical expression containing subexpressions in parentheses, or to work out a route between two points where there are many different paths.

Stade Roland Garros French lawn-tennis centre at Auteil, Paris, built in the 1920s for the French team to play their matches in defence of the Davis Cup. It became the home of the French Championships 1928.

stadholder or *stadtholder* the leader of the United Provinces of the Netherlands from the 15th to the 18th century.

Staël /staːl/ Anne Louise Germaine Necker, Madame de Staël 1766–1817. French author, daughter of the financier ◊Necker. She wrote semi-autobiographical novels such as *Delphine* 1802 and *Corinne* 1807, and the critical work *De l'Allemagne* 1810, on German literature.

Staffa /'stæfə/ uninhabited island in the Inner Hebrides, west of Mull. It has a rugged coastline and many caves, including ◊Fingal's Cave.

Staffordshire /'stæfədʃə/ county in W central England

area 2,720 sq km/1,050 sq mi

towns administrative headquarters Stafford; Stoke-on-Trent

features largely flat, comprising the Vale of Trent and its tributaries; Cannock Chase; Keele University 1962; Staffordshire bull terriers

products coal in north; china and earthenware

population (1987) 1,028,000

famous people Peter de Wint.

Staffordshire porcelain pottery from Staffordshire, England, one of the largest pottery-producing regions in the world, built up around an area rich in clay. Different companies, the first of which was Longton, have produced stoneware and earthenware from the 17th century onwards. Chinaware is produced in the ◊Potteries, Stoke-on-Trent, and china and earthenware in the upper Trent basin. See also ◊pottery and porcelain.

Staffs abbreviation for ◊*Staffordshire*.

stagflation economic condition (experienced in Europe in the 1970s) in which rapid inflation is accompanied by stagnating, even declining, output and by increasing unemployment. Its cause is often sharp increases in costs of raw materials and/or labour.

Stahl /ʃtaːl/ George 1660–1734. German chemist who produced a fallacious theory of combustion. He was professor of medicine at Halle, and as physician to the king of Prussia. He argued that objects burn in so far as they contain a combustible substance, phlogiston. Substances rich in phlogiston, like wood, burn almost completely away. Metals, which are low in phlogiston, burn less well. Chemists spent much of the century evaluating Stahl's theories before they were finally overthrown by ◊Lavoisier.

Stahlhelm German paramilitary and ex-servicemen's organization prominent in the 1920s and 1930s and associated with the German National People's Party (DNVP) and German People's Party (DVP).

stain in chemistry, a coloured compound that will bind to other substances. Stains are used extensively in microbiology to colour microorganisms and in histochemistry to detect the presence and whereabouts in plant and animal tissue of substances such as fats, cellulose, and proteins.

stained glass coloured pieces of glass that are joined by lead strips to form a pictorial window design.

The art is said to have originated in the Middle East. At first it was usual for only one monumental figure to be represented on each window, but by the middle of the 12th century incidents in the life of Jesus or of one of the saints were commonly depicted. Some of the most beautiful examples of medieval stained glass are to be found in the cathedrals of Canterbury, Lincoln, Chartres, Cologne, and Rouen. More recent designers include ◊Morris, ◊Burne-Jones, and ◊Chagall. Since World War II the use of thick, faceted glass joined by cement (common in the 6th century) has been revived.

Stainer /'steɪnə/ John 1840–1901. English organist and composer who became organist of St Paul's in 1872. His religious choral works are *The Crucifixion* 1887, an oratorio, and *The Daughter of Jairus* 1878, a cantata.

stainless steel a widely used ◊alloy of iron, chromium and nickel that resists rusting. Its chromium content also gives it a high tensile strength. It is used for cutlery and kitchen fittings.

Stakhanov /stə'kaːnɒf/ Aleksei 1906–1977. Soviet miner who exceeded production norms, and

Staffordshire

stalactite and stalagmite *Large stalagmites with stalactites above in Ogof Ffynnon Dhu (Cave of the Black Spring), South Wales.*

who gave his name to the **Stakhanovite** movement of the 1930s, when workers were encouraged to simplify and reorganize work processes in order to increase production.

stalactite and stalagmite cave structures formed by the deposition of calcite dissolved in groundwater. *Stalactites* grow downwards from the roofs or walls and can be icicle-shaped, straw-shaped, curtain-shaped, or formed as terraces. *Stalagmites* grow upwards from the cave floor and can be conical, fir-cone-shaped, or resemble a stack of saucers. Growing stalactites and stalagmites may meet to form a continuous column from floor to ceiling.

Stalactites are formed when groundwater, hanging as a drip, loses a proportion of its carbon dioxide into the air of the cave. This reduces the amount of calcite that can be held in solution, and a small trace of calcite is deposited. Successive drips build up the stalactite over many years. In stalagmite formation the calcite comes out of the solution because of agitation—the shock of a drop of water hitting the floor is sufficient to remove some calcite from the drop. The different shapes result from the splashing of the falling water.

Stalin /'stɑːlɪn/ former name 1949–56 of the port of ◊Varna, Bulgaria.

Stalin /'stɑːlɪn/ Joseph. Adopted name (Russian 'steel') of Joseph Vissarionovich Djugashvili 1879–1953. Soviet politician. A member of the October Revolution Committee 1917, Stalin became General Secretary of the Communist party 1922. After ◊Lenin's death 1924, Stalin sought to create 'socialism in one country' and clashed with ◊Trotsky, who denied the possibility of socialism inside Russia until revolution had occurred in W Europe. Stalin won this ideological struggle by 1927, and a series of five-year plans was launched to collectivize industry and agriculture from 1928. All opposition was eliminated by the Great Purge 1936–38 by which Stalin disposed of all real and fancied enemies. During World War II, Stalin intervened in the military direction of the campaigns against Nazi Germany. His role was denounced after his death by Khrushchev and other members of the Soviet regime.

Born in Georgia, the son of a shoemaker, he was educated for the priesthood, but was expelled from his seminary for Marxist propaganda. He became a member of the Social Democratic Party 1898, and joined Lenin and the Bolsheviks 1903. He was repeatedly exiled to Siberia 1903–13. He then became a member of the Communist Party's ◊Politburo, and sat on the October Revolution committee. Stalin rapidly consolidated a powerful following (including Molotov); in 1921 he became commissar for nationalities in the Soviet government, responsible for the decree granting equal rights to all peoples of the Russian Empire, and was appointed general secretary of the Communist party 1922. He met Churchill and Roosevelt at Tehran 1943 and at Yalta 1945, and took part in the Potsdam conference. After the war, Stalin maintained an autocratic rule.

Stalingrad /'stɑːlɪŋɡræd/ former name (1925–1961) of the Soviet city of ◊Volgograd.

Stalin *Soviet leader Stalin taking the salute during a march past of workers in Red Square, Moscow, in May 1932.*

Stalinsk /'stɑːlɪnsk/ former name (1932–61) of ◊Novokuznetsk, city in USSR.

Stalker affair an inquiry begun 1984 by John Stalker, deputy chief constable in Manchester, England, into the killing of six unarmed men in 1982 by Royal Ulster Constabulary (RUC) special units in Northern Ireland. The inquiry was halted and Stalker suspended from duty in 1986. Although he was later reinstated, the inquiry did not reopen, and no reason for his suspension was given.

Stallone Sylvester 1946– . US film actor. He played bit parts and occasional leads in exploitation films before starring in *Rocky* 1976, which he also wrote. His later films have mostly been based around violence, and include *F.I.S.T.* 1978, *First Blood* 1982, and *Rambo* 1985.

Stamboul /ˌstæmˈbuːl/ the old part of the Turkish city of ◊Istanbul, the area formerly occupied by ◊Byzantium.

stamen the male reproductive organ of a flower. The stamens are collectively referred to as the ◊androecium. A typical stamen consists of a stalk, or *filament* with an *anther*, the pollen-bearing organ, at its apex, but in some primitive plants, such as *Magnolia*, the stamen may not be markedly differentiated.

The number and position of the stamens are important characters in the classification of flowering plants. Generally the more advanced plant

Stallone *US actor Sylvester Stallone specializes in portraying virile and violent men, such as Rambo 1985.*

stamen

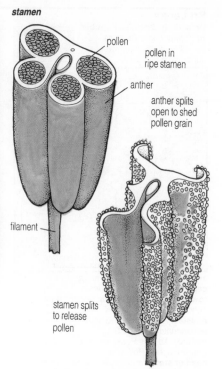

pollen

pollen in ripe stamen

anther

anther splits open to shed pollen grain

filament

stamen splits to release pollen

families have fewer stamens, but they are often positioned more effectively so that the likelihood of successful pollination is not reduced.

Stamp Act an act of Parliament in 1765 which taxed (by requiring an official stamp) all publications and legal documents published in British colonies. A blockade of British merchant shipping proved so effective that the act was repealed the following year. It was a precursor of the War of ◊American Independence.

The act provoked vandalism and looting in America, and the *Stamp Act Congress* in Oct of that year (the first intercolonial congress) declared the act unconstitutional, with the slogan 'No taxation without representation', because the colonies were not represented in the British Parliament.

standard atmosphere unit of pressure, approximately equal to the the average pressure of the Earth's ◊atmosphere (760 mmHg, 1013.25 millibars, or 1.01325×10^5 newtons per square metre).

standard deviation in statistics, a measure of the spread of data. The deviation (difference) of each of the data items from the mean is found, and their values squared. The mean value of these squares is then calculated. The standard deviation is the square root of this mean.

For example, to find the standard deviation of the ages of a group of eight people in a room, the mean is first found (in this case by adding all the ages together and dividing the total by 8), and the deviations between all the individual ages and the mean calculated. Thus, if the ages of the eight people are 14, 14$\frac{1}{2}$, 15, 15$\frac{1}{2}$, 16, 17, 19, and 21, the mean age is 132 ÷ 8 = 16.5. The deviations between the individual ages and this mean age are −2.5, −2, −1.5, −1, −0.5, +0.5, +2.5 and + 4.5. These values are then squared to give 6.25, 4, 2.25, 1, 0.25, 6.25 and 20.25, with a mean value of 40.5 ÷ 8 = 5.0625. The square root of this figure is 2.25, which is the standard deviation in years.

standard form a method of writing numbers often used by scientists, particularly for very large or very small numbers. The numbers are written with one digit before the decimal point and multiplied by a power of 10. The number of digits given after the decimal point depends on the accuracy required. For example, the ◊speed of light is 2.9979×10^8 metres per second.

standard gravity the acceleration due to gravity, generally taken as 9.81274 metres per second per second. See ◊G scale.

standard illuminants three standard light intensities, A, B, and C, used for illumination when phenomena involving colour are measured. A is the light from a filament at 2,848 K (2,575°C), B is noon sunlight, and C is normal daylight. B and C are defined with respect to A. Standardization is necessary because colours appear different when viewed in different lights.

standard of living in economics, the measure of consumption and welfare of a country, community, class, or person. Individual standard-of-living expectations are heavily influenced by the income and consumption of other people in similar jobs.

Universal measures of standards of living cannot be applied to individuals. National income and gross national product, which measure a country's wealth, do not take into account unpaid work (housework and family labour) or quality of life, and do not show the distribution of wealth, or reflect the particular national or individual aspirations, which differ widely from person to person, class to class, and country to country.

standard temperature and pressure (STP) in chemistry, a standard set of conditions for experimental measurements, to enable comparisons to be made between sets of results. Standard temperature is 0°C and standard pressure 1 atmosphere (101,325 Pa).

standard volume in physics, the volume occupied by 1 kilogram molecule (the molecular mass in kilograms) of any gas at standard temperature and pressure. Its value is approximately 22.414 cubic metres.

standing committee a committee of the UK House of Commons that examines parliamentary bills (proposed acts of Parliament) for detailed correction and amendment. The committee comprises members of Parliament from the main political parties, with a majority usually held by the government. Several standing committees may be in existence at any time, each usually created for a particular bill.

standing crop in ecology, the total number of individuals of a given species alive in a particular area at any moment. It is sometimes measured as the weight (or ◊biomass) of a given species in a sample section.

standing order in banking, an instruction (banker's order) by a depositor with the bank to pay a certain sum of money at regular intervals. In some cases, the bank may be billed by a third party such as a supplier of gas or electricity, who is authorized to invoice the bank directly, which in turn will pay out the sum demanded (known as **direct debit**).

standing wave a wave in which the positions of ◊nodes (positions of zero vibration) and antinodes (positions of maximum vibration) do not move. Standing waves result when two similar waves travel in opposite directions through the same space.

For example, when a sound wave is reflected back along its own path, as when a stretched string is plucked, a standing wave is formed. In this case the antinode remains fixed at the centre and the nodes are at the two ends. Water and ◊electromagnetic waves can form standing waves in the same way.

St Andrews /sənt 'ændru:z/ a town at the E tip of Fife, Scotland, 19 km/12 mi SE of Dundee; population (1981) 11,400. Its university (1411) is the oldest in Scotland, and the Royal and Ancient Club (1754) is the ruling body in the sporting world of golf.

St Andrews /sənt 'ændru:z/ Scottish golf course near the town of St Andrews in Fife. It is regarded as the home of British golf and the Royal and Ancient Club, the game's ruling body, has its headquarters there. There are four courses, all municipal; the Old Course dates from the 16th century. One of the earliest patrons was Mary

Queen of Scots. The best-known hole is the 17th, the 'Road Hole'. St Andrews has been used to stage the British Open 24 times between 1873 and 1984.

Stanford /'stænfəd/ Charles Villiers 1852–1924. British composer and teacher, born in Ireland. A leading figure in the 19th-century renaissance of British music, his many works include operas such as *Shamus O'Brien* 1896, seven symphonies, chamber music, and church music. Among his pupils were Vaughan Williams, Holst, and Bridge.

Stanhope /'stænəp/ Hester Lucy 1776–1839. English traveller who left England in 1810 to tour the Levant with Bedouins and eventually settled there. She adopted local dress and became involved in Eastern politics.

Stanislavsky /ˌstænɪ'slævski/ Konstantin Sergeivich 1863–1938. Russian actor, director, and teacher. He founded the Moscow Art Theatre 1898 and directed productions of Chekhov and Gorky. He was the originator of ◊Method acting, described in *My Life in Art* 1924 and other works.

The Method had considerable influence on acting techniques in Europe and the USA (resulting in the founding of the ◊Actors Studio). He rejected the declamatory style of acting in favour of a more realistic approach, concentrating on the psychological basis for the development of character.

Stanley /'stænli/ family name of earls of ◊Derby.

Stanley /'stænli/ town on E Falkland, capital of the ◊Falkland Islands; population (1986) 1,200. After changing its name only once between 1843 and 1982, it was renamed five times in the space of six weeks during the Falklands War in Apr–June 1982.

Stanley /'stænli/ Henry Morton 1841–1904. Welsh-born US explorer and journalist who made four expeditions in Africa. He and ◊Livingstone met at Ujiji 1871 and explored Lake Tanganyika. He traced the course of the river Zaïre (Congo) to the sea 1874–77, established the Congo Free State (Zaïre) 1879–84, and charted much of the interior 1887–89.

Stanley fought in the Confederate army in the US Civil War. He worked for the *New York Herald* from 1867, and in 1871 he was sent by the editor James Gordon Bennett to find Livingstone, which he did on 10th Nov. From Africa he returned to the UK and was elected to Parliament 1895.

Stanley /'stænli/ Wendell 1904–1971. US biochemist. Working at the Rockefeller Institute, Princeton, Stanley succeeded, in 1935, in crystallizing a virus: the tobacco mosaic virus (TMV). He went on to demonstrate that, despite its crystalline state, TMV remained infectious. Along with John Northrop and James Sumner, Stanley received the 1946 Nobel Chemistry Prize.

Stanley Cup North American ◊ice-hockey tournament played at the end of the regular season in the National Hockey League (NHL). It was inaugurated in 1917 and named after Lord Stanley of Preston, former governor-general of Canada.

Stanley Falls /'stænli/ former name (until 1972) of ◊Boyoma Falls, on the Zaïre river.

Stanley Pool /'stænli/ former name (until 1972) of ◊Pool Malebo, on the Zaïre river.

Stanleyville /'stænlɪvɪl/ former name (until 1966) of the Zaïrean port of ◊Kisangani.

Stansted /'stænsted/ site of London's third airport, in ◊Essex, England.

Stanton /'stæntən/ Elizabeth Cady 1815–1902. US feminist who, with Susan B ◊Anthony, founded the National Woman Suffrage Association 1869, the first women's movement in the USA. She and Anthony wrote and compiled the *History of Women's Suffrage* 1881–86. Stanton also worked for the abolition of slavery.

She organized the International Council of Women in Washington DC. She was the first president of the National Woman Suffrage Association. Her publications include *Degradation of Disenfranchisement* and *Solitude of Self* 1892, and

in 1885 and 1898 she published (in two parts) a feminist critique of the Bible, *The Woman's Bible*.

Stanwyck /'stænwɪk/ Barbara. Stage name of Ruby Stevens 1907–1990. US film actress of the 1930s to 1950s. Often cast as an independently minded woman of the world, she also excelled in villainous roles, as in *Double Indemnity* 1944. Her other films include *Stella Dallas* 1937, *Ball of Fire* 1942, and *Executive Suite* 1954.

stanza (Italian 'resting or stopping place') a group of lines in a poem. Each stanza has a set, repeatable pattern of metre and rhyme and is normally divided from the following stanza by a blank line.

staple in medieval Europe, a riverside town where merchants had to offer their wares for sale before proceeding to their destination, a practice which constituted a form of toll; such towns were particularly common on the Rhine.

In English usage, it referred to a town either in England or abroad, appointed as the exclusive market for a particular commodity, especially wool. The wool staple was established by the English crown in Calais in 1353. This form of monopoly trading was finally abandoned in 1617.

star a luminous globe of gas, producing its own heat and light by nuclear reactions. They are born from ◊nebulae, and consist mostly of hydrogen and helium gas. Surface temperatures range from 2,000°C to above 30,000°C, and the corresponding colours from blue-white to red. The brightest stars have masses 100 times that of the Sun, and emit as much light as millions of suns. They live for less than a million years before exploding as ◊supernovae. The faintest stars are the ◊red dwarfs, less than one-thousandth the brightness of the Sun.

The smallest mass possible for a star is about 8% that of the Sun (80 times the mass of the planet Jupiter), otherwise nuclear reactions do not take place. Objects with less than this critical mass shine only dimly, and are termed **brown dwarfs**. There is no firm distinction between a small brown dwarf and a large planet. Towards the end of its life, a star like the Sun swells up into a ◊red giant, before losing its outer layers as a ◊planetary nebula, and finally shrinking to become a ◊white dwarf. See also ◊supergiant, ◊binary star, ◊Hertzsprung-Russell diagram, ◊variable star.

starch a widely distributed, high-molecular-mass ◊carbohydrate, produced by plants as a food store; main dietary sources are cereals, pulses, and tubers, including potatoes. It consists of both straight-chain ◊polysaccharide chains (amylose) and branched polysaccharide molecules (amylopectin).

Purified starch is a white powder used to stiffen textiles and paper and as a raw material for making various chemicals. It is used in the food industry as a thickening agent. Chemical treatment of starch gives rise to a range of 'modified starches' with varying properties. Hydrolysis (splitting) of starch by acid or enzymes generates a variety of 'glucose syrups' or 'liquid glucose' for use in the food industry. Complete hydrolysis of starch with acid generates the ◊monosaccharide glucose only. Incomplete hydrolysis or enzymic hydrolysis yields a mixture of glucose, maltose and non-hydrolysed fractions called 'dextrins'.

Star Chamber in English history, a civil and criminal court, so named because of the star-shaped ceiling decoration of the room in the Palace of Westminster, London, where its first meetings were held. Created in 1487 by Henry VII, the Star Chamber comprised some 20 or 30 judges. It was abolished 1641 by the ◊Long Parliament.

The Star Chamber became notorious under Charles I for judgements favourable to the king and to Archbishop ◊Laud (for example, the branding on both cheeks of William Prynne in 1637 for seditious libel). Under the Thatcher government the term was revived for private ministerial meetings at which disputes between the Treasury and high-spending departments are resolved.

starfish

crown of thorns
starfish

star cluster a group of related stars, usually held together by gravity. Members of a star cluster are thought to form together from one large cloud of gas in space. *Open clusters* such as the Pleiades contain from a dozen to many hundreds of young stars, loosely scattered over several light years. ◊*Globular clusters* are larger and much more densely packed, containing perhaps 100,000 old stars.

starfish an echinoderm with arms radiating from a central body. Usually there are five arms, but some species have more. They are covered with spines and small pincer-like organs. There are also a number of small tubular processes on the skin surface which assist in respiration. Starfish are predators, and vary in size from 1.2 cm/0.5 in to 90 cm/3 ft.

Some species use their suckered tube-feet to pull open the shells of bivalve molluscs, then evert the stomach to surround and digest the animal inside. The poisonous and predatory crown-of-thorns of the Pacific is very destructive to coral, and severely damaged Australia's Great Barrier Reef when it multiplied prolifically in the 1960s–70s.

Stark /stɑːk/ Freya 1893– . English traveller, mountaineer, and writer. She described her explorations in the Middle East in many books, including *The Valley of the Assassins* 1934, *The Southern Gates of Arabia* 1936, and *A Winter in Arabia* 1940.

starling bird *Sturnus vulgaris* common in N Eurasia and naturalized in North America from the late 19th century. The black, speckled plumage is glossed with green and purple. Its own call is a bright whistle, but it is a mimic of the songs of other birds. It is about 20 cm/8 in long.

Strikingly gregarious in feeding, flight, and roosting, it often becomes a pest in large cities, where it becomes attached to certain buildings as 'dormitories', returning each night from omnivorous foraging in the countryside. If disturbed, starlings have been known to lay eggs in the nests of other birds before starting a new nest with their mate elsewhere. More than 100 species of starling, family Sturnidae, are found in the Old World.

Starling /ˈstɑːlɪŋ/ Ernest Henry 1866–1927. English physiologist who discovered ◊secretin, and coined the word 'hormone' to describe chemicals of this sort. He formulated *Starling's law*, which states that the force of the heart's contraction is a function of the length of the muscle fibres.

Starling was Jodrell professor of physiology at University College, London. His textbook on physiology was a standard in its day. He is regarded, with ◊Bayliss and ◊Sharpey-Schäfer, as a founder of endocrinology.

Star of David or *Magen David* (Hebrew 'shield of David') six-pointed star, a symbol of Judaism and used on the flag of Israel.

START abbreviation for ◊Strategic Arms Reduction Talks.

Star Wars popular term for the ◊Strategic Defense Initiative (SDI) announced by US president Reagan in 1983.

state a territory that forms its own domestic and foreign policy, acting through laws which are typically decided by a government and carried out, by force

if necessary, by agents of that government. It can be argued that growth of regional international bodies such as the European Community means that states no longer enjoy absolute sovereignty.

Although most states are members of the United Nations, this is not a completely reliable criterion: some are not members by choice, like Switzerland; some have been deliberately excluded, like Taiwan; and some are members but do not enjoy complete national sovereignty, like Byelorussia and Ukraine, which both form part of the USSR. The classic definition of a state is given by R M MacIver (*The Modern State* 1926): 'An association which, acting through law as promulgated by a government endowed to this end with coercive power, maintains within a community territorially demarcated the universal external conditions of social order.' There are four essential elements in this definition: that people have formed an association to create and preserve social order; that the community comprising the state is clearly defined in territorial terms; that the government representing the people acts according to promulgated laws; and that it has power to enforce these laws. Today, the state is seen as the nation state so that any community that has absolute sovereignty over a specific area is a state. Thus the so-called states of the USA, which are to some degree subject to the will of the federal government, are not states in international terms, nor are colonial or similar possessions which, too, are subject to an overriding authority.

state change in science, a change in the physical state of a material. For instance, melting, boiling, evaporation, and their opposites (solidification and condensing) are state changes. These changes require heat, called ◊latent heat, even though the temperature of the material does not change during the transition between states.

State Department (Department of State) US government department responsible for ◊foreign relations.

Staten Island /ˈstætn/ island in New York harbour, part of New York city, USA, constituting the borough of Richmond; area 155 sq km/60 sq mi; population (1980) 352,500.

States General the former French parliament which consisted of three estates—nobility, clergy, and commons. First summoned in 1302, it declined in importance as the power of the crown grew. It was not called at all between 1614 and 1789 when the crown needed to institute fiscal reforms to avoid financial collapse. Once called, the demands made by the States General formed the first phase in the ◊French Revolution. The term States General is also the name of the Dutch parliament.

states of matter the forms (solid, liquid, or gas) in which material can exist. Whether a material is solid, liquid, or gas depends on its temperature and the pressure on it. The transition between states takes place at definite temperatures, called melting point and boiling point.

◊Kinetic theory describes how the state of a material depends on the movement and arrangement of its atoms or molecules. A hot ionized gas or ◊plasma is often called the fourth state of matter, but ◊liquid crystals, ◊colloids, and glass also have a claim to this title.

static electricity ◊electric charge acquired by a body by means of electrostatic induction or friction. Rubbing different materials can produce static electricity, seen in the sparks produced on combing one's hair or removing a nylon shirt. In some processes, static electricity is useful, as in paint spraying where the parts to be sprayed are charged with electricity of opposite polarity to that on the paint droplets, and in ◊xerography.

statics branch of mechanics concerned with the behaviour of bodies at rest and forces in equilibrium, and distinguished from ◊dynamics.

Stationery Office, His/Her Majesty's (HMSO) office established in 1786 to supply books and stationery to British government departments, and to superintend the printing of government

reports and other papers, and books and pamphlets on subjects ranging from national works of art to industrial and agricultural processes. The corresponding establishment in the USA is the Government Printing Office.

Stations of the Cross in the Christian church, a series of 14 crosses, usually each with a picture or image, depicting the 14 stages in Jesus Christ's journey to the crucifixion.

statistical mechanics branch of physics in which the properties of large collections of ◊particles are predicted by considering the motions of the constituent particles.

statistics the branch of mathematics concerned with the meaningful collection and interpretation of data. For example, to determine the ◊mean age of the children in a school, a statistically acceptable answer might be obtained by calculating an average based on the ages of a representative sample, consisting, for example, of a random tenth of the pupils from each class. ◊Probability is the branch of statistics dealing with predictions of events.

status in the social sciences, an individual's social position, or the esteem in which he or she is held by others in society. Both within and between most occupations or social positions there is a status hierarchy. *Status symbols*, such as insignia of office or an expensive car, often accompany high status.

The two forms of social prestige may be separate or interlinked. Formal social status is attached to a particular social position, occupation, role, or office. Informal social status is based on an individual's own personal talents, skills, or personality. Sociologists distinguish between *ascribed status*, which is bestowed by birth, and *achieved status*, the result of one's own efforts.

The German sociologist Max Weber analysed social stratification in terms of three separate but interlinked dimensions: class, status, and power. Status is seen as a key influence on human behaviour, on the way people evaluate themselves and others.

status quo (Latin 'the state in which') the current situation, without change.

Staudinger /ˈʃtaʊdɪŋə/ Hermann 1881–1965. German organic chemist, founder of macro-molecular chemistry, who carried out pioneering research into the structure of albumen and cellulose. Nobel prize 1953.

Stauffenberg /ˈʃtaʊfənbeək/ Claus von 1907–1944. German colonel in World War II, who planted a bomb in Hitler's headquarters conference room in the Wolf's Lair at Rastenburg, East Prussia, 20 July 1944. Hitler was injured, and Stauffenberg and 200 others were later executed.

Stavanger /stəˈvæŋə/ seaport and capital of Rogaland county, SW Norway, population (1988) 96,000. It has fish-canning, oil, and shipbuilding industries.

Stavropol /ˈstævrəpɒl/ a territory of the Russian Soviet Federal Socialist Republic, lying N of the Caucasus mountains; area 80,600 km²/31,128 sq mi; population(1985) 2,715,000. Capital is Stavropol. Irrigated land produces grain but sheep are also reared. There are natural gas deposits.

Stavropol /ˈstævrəpɒl/ formerly (1935–43) *Voroshilovsk* town SE of Rostov, in the N Caucasus, USSR; population (1987) 306,000. Founded 1777 as a fortress town, it is now a market centre for an agricultural area, and makes agricultural machinery, textiles, and food products.

STDs abbreviation for *sexually transmitted diseases*, a term encompassing not only traditional ◊venereal disease, but also a growing list of conditions, such as ◊AIDS and scabies, which are known to be spread primarily by sexual contact.

One effect of the global preoccupation with AIDS has been to divert attention away from the non-notifiable STDs: conditions such as genital herpes which, though not fatal, may harm health and relationships. There are some non-sexual diseases that are nevertheless sexual in ori-

Steele *As founder of* The Tatler *in 1709, Richard Steele aimed to raise moral and Christian standards as well as to amuse.*

gin, such as viral ◊hepatitis and cancer of the cervix.

Stead /sted/ Christina (Ellen) 1902–1983. Australian writer, who lived in Europe and the US 1928–68. Her novels include *The Man Who Loved Children* 1940, *Dark Places of the Heart* 1966 (published as *Cotter's England* in London), and *I'm Dying Laughing* 1986.

steady-state theory theory that the universe is in a steady state: it appears the same wherever (and whenever) viewed. The theory seems to be refuted by the existence of cosmic background radiation. Held by ◊Lyell, among others, it was revived 1948 by Hermann Bondi, Thomas Gold, and Fred ◊Hoyle.

steam in chemistry, a dry, invisible gas formed by vaporizing water. The visible cloud which normally forms in the air when water is vaporized is due to minute suspended water particles. Steam is widely used in chemical and other industrial processes, and for the generation of power.

steam engine engine that uses the power of steam to produce useful work. It was the principal power source during the British Industrial Revolution in the 18th century. The first successful steam engine was built 1712 by Thomas Newcomen: steam was admitted to a cylinder as a piston moved up, and was then condensed by a spray of water, allowing air pressure to force the piston downwards. James Watt improved Newcomen's engine in 1769 by condensing the steam outside the cylinder (thus saving energy formerly used to reheat the cylinder) and by using steam to force the piston upwards. Watt also introduced the *double-acting engine*, in which steam is alternately sent to each end of the cylinder. The *compound engine* (1781) uses the exhaust from one cylinder to drive the piston of another. The *high-pressure steam engine* was developed 1802 by Richard Trevithick, and led to the development of the steam locomotive. A later development was the steam ◊turbine, still used today to power ships and generators in power stations. See ◊internal combustion engine.

stearic acid $CH_3(CH_2)_{16}CO_2H$ a saturated long-chain fatty acid, soluble in alcohol and ether but not in water. It is found in many fats and oils, and used to make soap and candles, and as a lubricant. The salts of stearic acid are called stearates.

stearin a mixture of stearic and palmitic acids, used to make soap.

Stębark /'stembɑːk/ Polish name (since 1945) for the village of ◊Tannenberg, formerly in East Prussia, now part of Poland.

Steed /stiːd/ Henry Wickham 1871–1956. British journalist. Foreign correspondent for *The Times*

in Vienna 1902–13, he was then foreign editor 1914–19 and editor 1919–22.

steel an alloy or mixture of iron and up to 1.7% carbon, sometimes with other elements such as manganese, phosphorus, sulphur, and silicon. The USA, the USSR, and Japan are the main steel producers. Steel has innumerable uses, including ship and automobile manufacture, skyscraper frames, and machinery of all kinds.

Steels with only small amounts of other metals are called *carbon steels*. These steels are far stronger than pure iron, with properties varying with the composition. *Alloy steels* contain greater amounts of other metals. Low-alloy steels have less than 5% of the alloying material; high-alloy steels have more. Low-alloy steels containing up to 5% silicon with relatively little carbon have a high electrical resistance and are used in power transformers and motor or generator cores, for example. *Stainless steel* is a high-alloy steel containing at least 11% chromium. Steels with up to 20% tungsten are very hard and are used in high-speed cutting tools.

Steel is produced by removing impurities, such as carbon, from raw or pig iron, produced by a ◊blast furnace. The main industrial process is the ◊basic-oxygen process, in which molten pig iron and scrap steel is placed in a container lined with heat-resistant, alkaline (basic) bricks. A pipe or lance is lowered near to the surface of the molten metal and pure oxygen blown through it at high pressure. The surface of the metal is disturbed by the blast and the impurities are oxidized (burnt out). The *open-hearth process* is an older steelmaking method in which molten iron and limestone are placed in a shallow bowl or hearth (see ◊open-hearth furnace). Burning oil or gas is blown over the surface of the metal, and the impurities are oxidized. High-quality steel is made in an *electric furnace*. A large electric current flows through electrodes in the furnace, melting a charge of scrap steel and iron. The quality of the steel produced can be controlled precisely because the temperature of the furnace can be maintained exactly and there are no combustion by-products to contaminate the steel. Electric furnaces are also used to refine steel, producing the extra-pure steels used, for example, in the petrochemical industry.

The steel produced is cast into ingots, which can be worked when hot by hammering (forging) or pressing between rollers to produce sheet steel. Alternatively, the *continuous-cast process*, in which the molten metal is fed into an open-ended mould cooled by water, produces an unbroken slab of steel.

Steel /stiːl/ David 1938– . British politician, leader of the Liberal Party 1976–88. He entered into a compact with the Labour government 1977–78, and into an alliance with the Social Democratic Party (SDP) 1983. Having supported the Liberal–SDP merger (◊Social and Liberal Democrats), he resigned the leadership 1988.

steel band type of musical ensemble common in the West Indies, especially Trinidad, consisting mostly of percussion instruments made from oil drums.

Steele /stiːl/ Richard 1672–1729. Irish essayist, who founded the journal *The Tatler* 1709–11, in which ◊Addison collaborated. They continued their joint work in *The Spectator*, also founded by Steele, 1711–12, and *The Guardian* 1713. He also wrote plays, such as *The Conscious Lovers* 1722.

Steen /steɪn/ Jan 1626–1679. Dutch painter. Born in Leiden, he was also active in The Hague, Delft, and Haarlem. He painted humorous genre scenes, mainly set in taverns or bourgeois households, as well as portraits and landscapes.

Steep Point /stiːp/ the most westerly extremity of Australia, in Western Australia, NW of the Murchison River.

Steer /stɪə/ Philip Wilson 1860–1942. British painter, influenced by the French Impressionists, known for seaside scenes such as *The Beach at Walberswick* (Tate Gallery, London).

Steen The Harpsichord Lesson *Wallace Collection, London.*

Steer, born in Birkenhead on Merseyside, studied in Paris. He became a leader (with ◊Sickert) of the English movement and founder member of the ◊New English Art Club.

Stefan /'ʃtefæn/ Joseph 1835–1893. Austrian physicist who established one of the basic laws of heat radiation in 1874, since known as the ◊Stefan–Boltzmann law. This stated that the heat radiated by a hot body is proportional to the fourth power of its absolute temperature.

Stefan–Boltzmann constant in physics, a constant relating the energy emitted by a black body (a hypothetical body that absorbs or emits all the energy falling on it) to its temperature. Its value is 5.6697×10^{-8} W m^{-2} K^{-4}.

Stefan–Boltzmann law in physics, a law that relates the energy, E, radiated away from a perfect emitter (a ◊black body), to the temperature, T, of the body. It has the form $M = \sigma T^4$, where M is the energy radiated per unit area per second, T is the temperature, and σ is the Stefan–Boltzmann constant.

Steichen /'staɪkən/ Edward 1897–1973. US photographer in both world wars, and also an innovative fashion and portrait photographer.

Steiermark /'ʃtaɪəmɑːk/ German name for ◊Styria, province of Austria.

Steiger /'staɪgə/ Rod(ney Stephen) 1925– . US character actor, often in leading film roles. His work includes *On the Waterfront* 1954, *In the Heat of the Night* 1967, and the title role in *W C Fields and Me* 1976.

Stein /ʃtaɪn/ Aurel 1862–1943. Hungarian archaeologist and explorer who carried out studies for the Indian government in Chinese Turkestan and Tibet 1900–15.

Stein /staɪn/ Gertrude 1874–1946. US writer. She influenced writers such as ◊Hemingway and Scott ◊Fitzgerald by her cinematic technique, use of repetition and absence of punctuation; devices to convey immediacy and realism. Her works include the self-portrait *The Autobiography of Alice B Toklas* 1933.

Steinbeck /'staɪnbek/ John (Ernst) 1902–1968. US novelist. His work includes *Of Mice and Men* 1937, and *The Grapes of Wrath* 1939, *Cannery Row* 1945, and *East of Eden* 1952. Nobel prize 1962.

He first achieved success with *Tortilla Flat* 1935, a humorous study of the *paisanos* (farmers) in Monterey, California; most of his books deal with the lives of working people. *East of Eden* was filmed with James Dean. His later work, less highly thought of, includes *Winter of our Discontent* 1961.

Steinem /'staɪnəm/ Gloria 1934– . US journalist and liberal feminist who emerged as a leading figure in the US women's movement in the late 1960s. She was also involved in radical protest campaigns against racism and the Vietnam War. She co-founded the Women's Action Alliance 1970 and *Ms* magazine. In 1983 a collection of her best-known articles was published as *Outrageous Acts and Everyday Rebellions*.

Steiner /'ʃtaɪnə/ Max(imilian Raoul) 1888–1971. Austrian composer of film music who lived in the USA from 1914. He composed his first film score in 1929 and produced some of the cinema's finest music, including the scores to *King Kong* 1933, *Gone with the Wind* 1939, and *Casablanca* 1942.

Steiner /'ʃtaɪnə/ Rudolf 1861–1925. Austrian philosopher, originally a ◊theosophist, who developed his own mystic and spiritual teaching, anthroposophy, designed to develop the whole human being. His method of teaching is followed by a number of schools named after him, but the schools also include the possibilities for pupils to take state exams.

Steinmetz /'staɪnmets/ Charles 1865–1923. US engineer who formulated the *Steinmetz hysteresis law* in 1891, which describes the dissipation of energy that occurs when a system is subject to an alternating electrical force. He worked on the design of alternating current transmission and 1894–1923 served as consulting engineer to General Electric.

Stella /'stelə/ Frank 1936– . US painter, a pioneer of the hard-edged geometric trend in abstract art that succeeded Abstract Expressionism. From around 1960 he also experimented with the shape of his canvases.

Stellenbosch /,stelən'bɒs/ town in Cape Province, South Africa; population (1985) 43,000. It is the centre of a wine-producing district. It was founded 1679, and is the oldest European settlement in South Africa after Cape Town.

stem the main supporting axis of a plant that bears the leaves, buds, and reproductive structures; it may be simple or branched. The plant stem usually grows above ground, although some grow underground, including ◊rhizomes, ◊corms, ◊rootstocks, and ◊tubers. Stems contain a continuous ◊vascular system that conducts water and food to and from all parts of the plant.

The point on a stem from which a leaf or leaves arise is called a node, and the space between two successive nodes is the internode. In some plants, the stem is highly modified; for example, it may form a leaflike ◊cladode or it may be twining, as in many climbing plants, or fleshy and swollen to store water, as in cacti and other succulents. In plants exhibiting ◊secondary growth the stem may become woody, forming a main trunk, as in trees, or a number of branches from ground level, as in shrubs.

Stendhal /stæn'dæl/ Pen name of Marie Henri Beyle 1783–1842. French novelist. His two major novels ◊*Le Rouge et le Noir*/*The Red and the Black* 1830 and *La Chartreuse de Parme*/*The Charterhouse of Parme* 1839 were pioneering works in their treatment of disguise and hypocrisy; a review of the latter by ◊Balzac in 1840 furthered his reputation.

Born in Grenoble, he served in Napoleon's armies, taking part in the ill-fated Russian campaign, and, failing in his hopes of becoming a prefect, lived in Italy from 1814 until suspicion of espionage drove him back to Paris in 1821, where he lived by literary hackwork. From 1830 he was a member of the consular service, spending his leaves in Paris.

Stenmark Ingemar 1956– . Swedish skiier who won a record 85 World Cup races 1974–87, including a record 13 in 1979. He won a total of 18 titles, including the overall title three times.

CAREER HIGHLIGHTS

Olympic Games
giant slalom: 1980
slalom: 1980
World Cup
overall: 1976–78
giant slalom: 1975–76, 1978–81, 1984
slalom: 1975–81, 1983
World Championships
giant slalom: 1978
slalom: 1978, 1982

stenosis narrowing of a body vessel, duct, or opening, usually due to disease.

Stephen /'sti:vən/ *c.* 1097–1154. King of England from 1135. A grandson of William I, he was elected

king 1135, although he had previously recognized Henry I's daughter ◊Matilda as heiress to the throne. Matilda landed in England 1139, and civil war disrupted the country until 1153, when Stephen acknowledged Matilda's son, Henry II, as his own heir.

Stephen /'sti:vən/ Leslie 1832–1904. English critic, first editor of the *Dictionary of National Biography* and father of novelist Virginia ◊Woolf.

Stephen I, St /'sti:vən/ 975–1038. King of Hungary from 997, when he succeeded his father. He completed the conversion of Hungary to Christianity, and was canonized in 1803. His crown, symbol of Hungarian nationhood, was removed to the USA in 1945, but returned 1978.

Stephens /'sti:vənz/ John Lloyd 1805–1852. US explorer in Central America, with Frederick Catherwood. He recorded his findings of ruined Mayan cities in his two volumes *Incidents of Travel in Central America, Chiapas and Yucatan* 1841–43.

Stephen, St died *c.* AD 35. The first Christian martyr; he was stoned to death. Feast day 26 Dec.

Stephenson /'sti:vənsən/ George 1781–1848. English engineer who built the first successful steam locomotive, and who also invented a safety lamp in 1815. He was appointed engineer of the Stockton and Darlington Railway, the world's first public railway, in 1821, and of the Liverpool and Manchester Railway in 1826. In 1829 he won a £500 prize with his locomotive, *Rocket*.

Stephenson /'sti:vənsən/ Robert 1803–1859. English civil engineer, who constructed railway bridges such as the high-level bridge at Newcastle upon Tyne, England, and the Menai and Conway tubular bridges in North Wales. He was the son of George Stephenson.

Stepney /'stepni/ district of London, now part of the borough of ◊Tower Hamlets, north of the Thames, and east of the City of London.

steppe the temperate grasslands of Europe and Asia. Sometimes the term refers to other temperate grasslands and semi-arid desert edges.

Steppenwolf a novel by Hermann Hesse, published 1927. Henry Haller ('Steppenwolf') is contemplating suicide, but comes to terms with the world around him following a visit to the surreal Magic Theatre.

step rocket or *multi-stage rocket* a rocket launch vehicle made up of several rocket stages (often three) joined end to end. The bottom stage fires first, boosting the vehicle to high speed, then it falls away. The next stage fires, thrusting the now lighter vehicle even faster. The remaining stages fire and fall away in turn, boosting the vehicle's payload (cargo) to an orbital speed that can reach 28,000 kph/17,500 mph.

Steptoe /'steptəʊ/ Patrick Christopher 1913–1988. English obstetrician who pioneered *in vitro* or 'test-tube' fertilization. Steptoe, together with biologist Robert Edwards, was the first to succeed in implanting in the womb an egg fertilized outside the body. This procedure, known as *in vitro* fertilization, was the result of a ten-year cooperation between the two men. Success came only after some 500 failures. The first 'test-tube baby' was Louise Brown, born by Caesarean section in 1978.

steradian unit of solid (three-dimensional) angle, the three-dimensional equivalent of the ◊radian. One steradian is the angle at the centre of a sphere when an area on the surface of the sphere equal to the square of the sphere's radius is joined to the centre.

Sterea Ellas-Evvoia /'steriə 'elæs 'eviə/ the region of central Greece and Euboea, occupying the southern part of the Greek mainland between the Ionian and Aegean seas and including the island of Euboea; population (1981) 1,099,800; area 24,391 km2/9,421 sq mi. Chief city is Athens.

stereophonic sound a system of sound reproduction using two loudspeakers, which give a more natural 'depth' to the sound. See ◊hi-fi.

stereotype (Greek 'fixed impression') a one-sided, exaggerated, and preconceived idea about a particular group or society. It is based on prejudice rather than fact, but by repetition stereotypes become fixed in people's minds, resistant to change or factual evidence to the contrary.

The term, originally used for a method of duplicate printing, was adopted in a social sense by the US journalist Walter Lippman in 1922. Stereotypes can prove dangerous when used to justify persecution and discrimination. Some sociologists believe that stereotyping reflects a power structure in which one group in society uses labelling to keep another group 'in its place'.

sterilization an operation to terminate the power of reproduction. In women, this is normally achieved by sealing or tying off the ◊Fallopian tubes (tubal ligation) so that fertilization can no longer take place. In men, the transmission of sperm is blocked by ◊vasectomy. Compulsory sterilization may form part of a eugenic policy (see ◊eugenics).

sterilization the killing or removal of living organisms such as bacteria and fungi. A sterile environment is necessary in medicine, food processing, and some scientific experiments. Methods include heat treatment (such as boiling), the use of chemicals (such as disinfectants), irradiation with gamma rays, and filtration.

sterling silver an ◊alloy containing 925 parts of silver and 75 parts of copper. The copper hardens the metal, making it more useful for jewellery.

Stern /ʃtɜ:n/ Otto 1888–1969. German physicist. Stern studied with Einstein in Prague and Zürich, where he became a lecturer in 1914. After World War I he demonstrated by means of the *Stern–Gerlach apparatus* that elementary particles have wave-like properties as well as the properties of matter that had been demonstrated. He left Germany for the USA in 1933. Nobel prize 1943.

Sternberg /'ʃteənbeək/ Josef von 1894–1969. Austrian film director who lived in the USA from childhood. He worked with Marlene Dietrich on *The Blue Angel*/*Der blaue Engel* 1930 and other films. He favoured striking imagery over narrative in his work, which includes *Underworld* 1927 and *Blonde Venus* 1932.

Sterne /stɜ:n/ Laurence 1713–1768. Irish writer, creator of the comic anti-hero Tristram Shandy. *The Life and Opinions of Tristram Shandy, Gent* 1760–67, an eccentrically whimsical and bawdy novel, foreshadowed many of the techniques and devices of 20th-century novelists, including James Joyce. His other works include *A Sentimental Journey from France and Italy* 1768.

Sterne, born in Clonmel, Ireland, took orders in 1737 and became vicar of Sutton-in-the-Forest, Yorkshire, in the next year. In 1741 he married Elizabeth Lumley, an unhappy union largely because of his infidelity. He had a sentimental love affair with Eliza Draper, of which the *Letters of Yorick to Eliza* 1775 is a record.

Stern Gang formal name *Fighters for the Freedom of Israel* a Zionist guerrilla group founded 1940 by Abraham Stern (1907–42). The group carried out anti-British attacks during the UK mandate rule in Palestine, both on individuals and on strategic targets. Stern was killed by British forces, but the group survived until 1948, when it was outlawed with the creation of the independent state of Israel.

steroid in biology, a type of lipid (fat), derived from sterols, with a complex molecular structure consisting of four carbon rings. Steroids include the sex hormones, such as ◊testosterone, the corticosteroid hormones produced by the ◊adrenal gland, and ◊cholesterol. The term is commonly used to refer to ◊anabolic steroid.

sterol one of a group of organic alcohols, with a complex structure, consisting of four carbon rings. Steroids are derived from sterols, and have the same ring structure, but with various other chemical groups attached. They are physiologically very active.

stethoscope instrument used to ascertain the condition of the heart and lungs by listening to their action. It consists of two earpieces connected by flexible tubes to a small plate which is placed against the body. It was invented in 1819 by René Théophile Hyacinthe Laënnec (1781–1826).

Stettin /ʃteˈtiːn/ German name for the Polish city of ◊Szczecin.

Stevenage /ˈstiːvənɪdʒ/ town in Hertfordshire, England, 45 km/28 mi north of London; population (1981) 74,000. Dating from medieval times, in 1946 Stevenage was the first place chosen for development as a ◊new town.

Stevens /ˈstiːvənz/ Alfred 1817–1875. British sculptor, painter, and designer. He created the *Wellington monument* begun 1858 (St Paul's, London). He was devoted to High Renaissance art, especially to Raphael, and studied in Italy in 1833.

Stevens /ˈstiːvənz/ George 1904–1975. US film director who began as a director of photography. He made films such as *Swing Time* 1936 and *Gunga Din* 1939, and his reputation grew steadily, as did the length of his films. His later work included *A Place in the Sun* 1951, *Shane* 1953, and *Giant* 1956.

Stevens /ˈstiːvənz/ Siaka Probin 1905–1988. Sierra Leone politician, president 1971–85. He was the leader of the moderate left-wing All People's Congress (APC), from 1978 the country's only legal political party.

Stevens was a policeman, industrial worker, and trade unionist before founding the APC. He became prime minister in 1968 and in 1971, under a revised constitution, became Sierra Leone's first president. He created a one-party state based on the APC, and remained in power until his retirement at the age of 80.

Stevens /ˈstiːvənz/ Wallace 1879–1955. US poet. His volumes of poems include *Harmonium* 1923, *The Man with the Blue Guitar* 1937, and *Transport to Summer* 1947. *The Necessary Angel* 1951 is a collection of essays. An elegant and philosophical poet, he won a Pulitzer prize 1954 for his *Collected Poems*.

Stevenson /ˈstiːvənsən/ Adlai 1900–1965. US Democrat politician. As governor of Illinois 1949–53 he campaigned vigorously against corruption in public life, and as Democratic candidate for the presidency 1952 and 1956 was twice defeated by Eisenhower. In 1945 he was chief US delegate at the founding conference of the United Nations.

Stevenson /ˈstiːvənsən/ Robert 1772–1850. Scottish engineer, born in Glasgow, who built many lighthouses, including the Bell Rock lighthouse, 1807–11.

Stevenson /ˈstiːvənsən/ Robert Louis 1850–1894. Scottish novelist and poet. Early works included *An Island Voyage* 1878 and *Travels with a Donkey* 1879, but he achieved fame with his adventure novel *Treasure Island* 1883. Later works included the novels *Kidnapped* 1886, *The Master of Ballantrae* 1889, *Dr Jekyll and Mr Hyde* 1886, and the anthology *A Child's Garden of Verses* 1885. In 1890 he settled at Vailima, in Samoa, where he sought a cure for the tuberculosis of which he died.

Stevenson was born in Edinburgh. He studied at the university and qualified as an advocate, but never practised. He travelled in Europe to improve his health. In 1879 he went to the USA, married Fanny Osbourne, and, returning to Britain in 1880, published a volume of stories, *The New Arabian Nights* 1882, and essays, for example *Virginibus Puerisque* 1881, and *Familiar Studies of Men and Books* 1882. The humorous *The Wrong Box* 1889 and the novels *The Wrecker* 1892 and *The Ebb-tide* 1894 were written in collaboration with his stepson, Lloyd Osbourne (1868–1920).

Stewart /ˈstjuːət/ 'Jackie' (John Young) 1939– . Scottish motor-racing driver. Until surpassed by

Stewart Famous for his roles as the stubbornly honest, upright American, actor James Stewart is seen here portraying a dedicated investigator in the film The FBI Story.

Alain ◊Prost (France) 1987, Stewart held the record for the most Formula One Grand Prix wins (27).

His first win was in 1965 and he started in 99 races. With manufacturer Ken Tyrrell, Stewart built up one of the sport's great partnerships. His last race was the 1973 Canadian Grand Prix. He pulled out of the next race (which would have been his 100th) because of the death of his teammate Francois Cevert. He became a motor-racing commentator.

CAREER HIGHLIGHTS

world champion
1969: Matra
1971: Tyrrell
1973: Tyrrell
Formula One Grand Prix
races: 99
wins: 27
first: 1965 (South African Grand Prix; BRM)
last: 1973 (Canadian Grand Prix; Tyrrell)

Stewart /ˈstjuːət/ James 1908– . US film actor. Gangling and speaking with a soft drawl, he specialized in the role of the stubbornly honest, ordinary American in such films as *You Can't Take It With You* 1938, *The Philadelphia Story* 1940, *Harvey* 1950, *The Man from Laramie* 1955, and *The FBI Story* 1959.

Stewart Island /ˈstjuːət/ volcanic island divided from South Island, New Zealand, by the Foveaux Strait; area 1,750 sq km/676 sq mi; population (1981) 600. Industries include farming, fishing, and granite quarrying. Oban is the main settlement.

stick insect insect of the order Phasmida, closely resembling a stick or twig. Many species are wingless. The longest reach a length of 30 cm/1 ft.

stickleback fish of the family Gasterosteidae, found in the N hemisphere. It has a long body which can grow to 18 cm/7 in. It has spines along the back which take the place of the first dorsal fin, and which can be raised to make the fish difficult to eat for predators. The common three-spined stickleback, *Gasterosteus aculeatus*, up to 10 cm/4 in long, is found in most freshwater habitats and also on coasts.

Stieglitz /ˈstaɪɡlɪts/ Alfred 1864–1946. US photographer. After forming the Photo Secession group in 1903, he began the magazine *Camera Work*. Through exhibitions at his gallery '291' in New York he helped to establish photography as an

art form. His works include 'Winter, Fifth Avenue' 1893 and 'Steerage' 1907. In 1924 he married the painter Georgia O'Keeffe, who was the model in many of his photographs.

stigma in a flower, the receptive surface at the tip of a ◊carpel which receives the ◊pollen. It often has short outgrowths, flaps, or hairs to trap pollen, and may produce a sticky secretion to which the grains adhere.

stigmata impressions or marks corresponding to the five wounds Jesus received at his crucifixion, which are said to have appeared spontaneously on St Francis and other saints.

Stijl, de (Dutch 'the style') a group of 20th-century Dutch artists and architects led by ◊Mondrian from 1917. They believed in the concept of the 'designer'; that all life, work, and leisure should be surrounded by art; and that everything functional should also be aesthetic. The group had a strong influence on the ◊Bauhaus school. The name came from a magazine, *De Stijl*, founded 1917 by Mondrian and Theo van Doesburg (1883–1931).

Stilicho /ˈstɪlɪkəʊ/ Flavius 359–408 AD. Roman general, of ◊Vandal origin, who campaigned successfully against the Visigoths and Ostrogoths. He virtually ruled the western empire as guardian of Honorius (son of ◊Theodosius I) but was executed on the orders of Honorius when he was suspected of wanting to make his own son successor to another son of Theodosius in the eastern empire.

Stilton /ˈstɪltən/ village in Cambridgeshire, England, 10 km/6 mi SW of Peterborough. It gives its name to a cheese brought here in coaching days for transport to London, and still made at and around ◊Melton Mowbray.

Stilwell /ˈstɪlwel/ Joseph Warren 1883–1946. US general, nicknamed 'Vinegar Joe'. In 1942 he became US military representative in China, when he commanded the Chinese forces cooperating with the British (with whom he quarrelled) in Burma; he later commanded all US forces in the Chinese, Burmese, and Indian theatres until recalled to the USA 1944 after differences over nationalist policy with the ◊Guomindang leader Chiang Kai-shek. Subsequently he commanded the US 10th Army on the Japanese island of Okinawa.

Stimson /ˈstɪmsən/ Henry Lewis 1867–1950. US politician. He was war secretary in Taft's cabinet 1911–13, Hoover's secretary of state 1929–33, and war secretary 1940–45.

stimulant a drug which acts on the brain to increase alertness and activity. When given to children, it may have a paradoxical, calming effect. Stimulants have limited therapeutic value and are now given only to treat ◊narcolepsy.

stinkhorn species of fungus *Phallus impudicus*; it first appears as a white ball.

stinkwood various trees with unpleasant-smelling wood. The S African tree *Ocotea bullata*, family Lauraceae, has offensive-smelling wood when newly felled, but fine, durable timber used for furniture. Another stinkwood is *Gustavia augusta* from tropical America.

stipule an outgrowth arising from the base of a leaf or leaf stalk in certain plants. Stipules usually occur in pairs, or fused into a single semicircular structure. They may have a leaf-like appearance, as in goosegrass *Galium aparine*, be spiny, as in false acacia *Robina*, or look like small scales. In some species they are large, and contribute significantly to the photosynthetic area, as in the garden pea *Pisum sativum*.

Stirling /ˈstɜːlɪŋ/ administrative headquarters of Central region, Scotland, on the river Forth; population (1981) 39,000. Industries include the manufacture of agricultural machinery, textiles, and carpets. The castle, which guarded a key crossing of the river, predates the 12th century, and was long a Scottish royal residence. Wallace won a victory at Stirling bridge 1297. Edward II of England (in raising a Scottish siege of the town) went into battle at Bannockburn 1314, and was defeated by Robert I (the Bruce).

Stirling British architect James Stirling emphasizes the three-dimensional character of building elements, as shown here in a detail from the Clore Gallery at the Tate Gallery, London.

Stirling /'stɜːlɪŋ/ James 1926– . British architect associated with collegiate and museum architecture. His works include the engineering building at Leicester University, and the Clore Gallery (the extension to house the Tate's ◊Turner collection) at the Tate Gallery, London, opened 1987.

Stirling engine a hot-air engine invented by Scottish priest Robert Stirling in 1876. It is a piston engine that uses hot air as a working fluid.

Stirlingshire /'stɜːlɪŋʃə/ former county of Scotland. In 1975 most of it was merged with Central region, but a SW section, including Kilsyth, went to Strathclyde. The area lay between the Firth of Forth and Loch Lomond, and included the Lennox hills and the fringe of the Highlands. The county town was Stirling.

stoat carnivorous mammal *Mustela erminea* of the weasel family, about 37 cm/15 in long including black-tipped tail. It has a long body and a flattened head. The upper parts and tail are red-brown, and the underparts are white. Stoats live in Europe, Asia, and North America. In the colder regions, the coat turns white (ermine) in winter.

stock UK term for the fully paid-up capital of a company. It is bought and sold by subscribers not in units or shares, but in terms of its current cash value. In US usage the term stock generally means an ordinary share.

stock in botany, herbaceous plants of the genus *Matthiola*, commonly grown as garden ornamentals. Many cultivated varieties, including **simple-stemmed**, **queen's** and **ten-week**, have been derived from the wild stock *Matthiola incana*; **night-scented stock** is *Matthiola bicornis*.

stock-car racing sport popular in the UK and USA, but in two different forms. In the UK the cars are 'old bangers', which attempt to force the other cars off the track or to come to a standstill. In the USA the cars are high-powered sports cars which race on purpose-built tracks, normally over 400–500 miles.

stock exchange institution for the buying and selling of stocks and shares (securities). The world's largest stock exchanges are London, New York (Wall Street), and Tokyo. London's is the oldest stock exchange in the world, opened 1801. The former division on the London Stock Exchange between brokers (who bought shares from jobbers to sell to the public) and jobbers (who sold them only to brokers on commission, the 'jobbers' turn') was abolished 1986.

Stock Exchange Automation System (SEAQ) a computerized system of share price monitoring. From Oct 1987, SEAQ began displaying market maker's quotations for UK stocks, having

only been operational previously for overseas equities.

Stockhausen /'ʃtɒk,haʊzən/ Karlheinz 1928– . German composer of avant-garde music, who has continued to explore new musical sounds and compositional techniques since the 1950s. His major works include *Gesang der Jünglinge* 1956 and *Kontakte* 1960 (electronic music); *Klavierstücke* 1952–85; *Momente* 1961–64, revised 1972, *Mikrophonie I* 1964, and *Sirius* 1977. Since 1977 all his works have been part of *Licht*, a cycle of seven musical ceremonies, intended for performance on the evenings of a week. He has completed *Donnerstag* 1980, *Samstag* 1984, and *Montag* 1988.

Stockholm /'stɒkhəʊm/ capital and industrial port of Sweden; population (1988) 667,000. It is built on a number of islands. Industries include engineering, brewing, electrical goods, paper, textiles, and pottery.

A network of bridges links the islands and the mainland; an underground railway was completed 1957. The 18th-century royal palace stands on the site of the 13th-century fortress which defended the trading settlements of Lake Mälar, around which the town first developed. The old town is well preserved and has a church 1264. The town hall was designed by Ragnar Östberg 1923. Most of Sweden's educational institutions are in Stockholm (including the ◊Nobel Institute). The warship *Wasa* (built for King Gustavus Adolphus) sank in the harbour 1628, was raised 1961, and is preserved in a museum.

Stockport /'stɒkpɔːt/ town in Greater Manchester, England; population (1981) 137,000. The Tame and Goyt rivers join here to form the Mersey. Industries include electronics, chemicals, engineering, and still some cotton textiles.

stocks wooden frame with holes used until the 19th century to confine the legs and sometimes the arms of minor offenders, and expose them to public humiliation. The ◊pillory had a similar purpose.

stocks and shares investment holdings (securities) in private or public undertakings. Although distinctions have become blurred, in the UK stock usually means fixed-interest securities, for example, those issued by central and local government, while shares represent a stake in the ownership of a trading company which, if they are ordinary shares, yield to the owner dividends reflecting the success of the company. In the USA the term stock generally signifies what in the UK are ordinary shares.

Stockton /'stɒktən/ industrial river port (agricultural machinery, food processing) on the San Joaquin in California, USA; population (1980) 149,779.

Stockton-on-Tees /'stɒktən ɒn 'tiːz/ town and port on the river Tees, Cleveland, NE England; population (1981) 155,000. There are shipbuilding, steel, and chemical industries, and it was the starting point for the world's first passenger railway 1825. It has the oldest railway-station building in the world, and there are many Georgian buildings.

Stockwood /'stɒkwʊd/ Arthur Mervyn 1913– . British Anglican cleric. As bishop of Southwark 1959–80, he expressed unorthodox views on homosexuality and in favour of the ordination of women.

stoicism (Greek *stoa* 'porch') a Greek school of philosophy, founded about 300 BC by Zeno of Citium. The stoics were pantheistic materialists who believed that happiness lies in accepting the law of the universe. They emphasized human brotherhood, denounced slavery, and were internationalist. The name is derived from the porch on which Zeno taught.

In the 3rd and 2nd centuries BC, stoics took a prominent part in Greek and Roman revolutionary movements. After the 1st century BC stoicism became the philosophy of the Roman ruling class and lost its revolutionary significance; outstanding

stoics of this period were Seneca, Epictetus, and Marcus Aurelius Antoninus.

Stoke-on-Trent /'stəʊk ɒn 'trent/ city in Staffordshire, England, on the river Trent; population (1981) 253,000. It is the heart of the ◊Potteries, and a major ceramic centre. Other industries include steel, chemicals, engineering machinery, paper, rubber, and coal.

Stoke was formed 1910 from Burslem, Hanley, Longton, Stoke-upon-Trent, Fenton, and Tunstall. The ceramics factories of ◊Minton and ◊Wedgwood are here; the Gladstone Pottery Museum is the only working pottery museum.

Stoke Poges /'stəʊk 'pəʊdʒɪz/ village in Berkshire, England, 3 km/2 mi N of Slough, which inspired Thomas ◊Gray to write his 'Elegy in a Country Churchyard'; the poet is buried here.

Stoker /'stəʊkə/ Bram (Abraham) 1847–1912. Irish novelist, actor, theatre manager, and author. His novel ◊*Dracula* 1897 crystallized most aspects of the traditional vampire legend and became the source for all subsequent popular fiction and films on the subject.

A civil servant 1866–78, he then became business manager to the theatre producer Henry Irving. Stoker wrote a number of stories and novels of fantasy and horror, such as *The Lady of the Shroud* 1909.

stokes c. g. s. unit (symbol St) of kinematic viscosity (rate of flow of a liquid). Liquids with higher kinematic viscosity have higher turbulence than those with low kinematic viscosity. It is found by dividing the dynamic viscosity in ◊poise by the density of the liquid.

Stokes /'stəʊks/ George Gabriel 1819–1903. Irish physicist. During the late 1840s, he studied the ◊viscosity (resistance to relative motions) of fluids. This culminated in *Stokes' law*, which applies to a sphere falling under gravity through a liquid. It states that if a sphere of radius r falls with a velocity v through a liquid of viscosity gE, the force acting on it $F = 6\pi gErv$.

Stokowski /stə'kɒfski/ Leopold 1882–1977. US conductor, born in London. An outstanding experimentalist, he introduced modern music (for example, Mahler's Eighth Symphony) to the US; appeared in several films; and conducted the music for Walt Disney's animated film *Fantasia* 1940.

STOL *s*hort *t*ake *o*ff and *l*anding. A type of aircraft, STOL craft are fitted with special devices on the wings (such as sucking flaps), which increase aerodynamic lift at low speeds. Small passenger and freight STOL craft are likely to become common with the demand for city-centre airports.

stolon a type of ◊runner.

stoma (plural *stomata*) in botany, a pore in the epidermis of a plant. Each stoma is surrounded by a pair of guard cells that are crescent-shaped

stoma

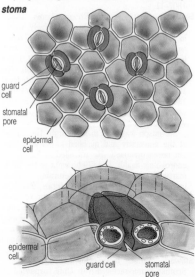

guard cell

stomatal pore

epidermal cell

epidermal cell

guard cell

stomatal pore

when the stoma is open, but can collapse to an oval shape, thus closing off the opening between them. Stomata allow the exchange of carbon dioxide and oxygen (needed for ◊photosynthesis and ◊respiration) between the internal tissues of the plant and the outside atmosphere. They are also the main route by which water is lost from the plant, and they can be closed to conserve water, the movements being controlled by changes in turgidity of the guard cells.

Stomata occur in large numbers on the aerial parts of a plant, and on the undersurface of leaves, where there may be as many as 45,000 per square centimetre.

stomach the first cavity in the digestive system of animals. In mammals, it is a bag of muscle situated just below the diaphragm. Food enters it from the oesophagus, is digested by the acid and ◊enzymes secreted by the stomach lining, and then passes into the duodenum. Some plant-eating (herbivorous) mammals have multi-chambered stomachs, which harbour bacteria in one of the chambers to assist in the digestion of ◊cellulose. The gizzard is part of the stomach in birds.

Stone /stəʊn/ John Richard 1932– . British economist, a statistics expert, whose system of 'national income accounting' has been adopted in many countries. Nobel prize 1984.

Stone /stəʊn/ Lucy 1818–1893. US feminist orator and editor. Married to the radical Henry Blackwell 1855 after a mutual declaration rejecting the legal superiority of the man in marriage, she gained wide publicity when she chose to retain her own surname despite her marriage. The epithet 'Lucy Stoner' was coined to mean a woman who advocated doing the same.

In the 1860s she helped to establish the American Woman Suffrage Association and founded and edited the Boston *Woman's Journal*, a suffragist paper which was later edited by her daughter, Alice Stone Blackwell (1857–1950).

stone (plural *stone*) imperial unit (symbol st) of weight. One stone is 14 lb (6.35 kg).

Stone /stəʊn/ Robert 1937– . US novelist and journalist. His *Dog Soldiers* 1974 is a classic novel about the moral destructiveness of the Vietnam War. *A Flag for Sunrise* 1982 similarly explores the political and moral consequences of US intervention in a corrupt South American republic.

Stone Age the period in ◊prehistory before the use of metals, when tools and weapons were made chiefly of flint. The Stone Age is subdivided into the Old or Palaeolithic, the Middle or Mesolithic and the New or Neolithic. The people of the Old Stone Age were hunters, whereas the Neolithic people progressed to making the first steps in agriculture, domestication of animals, weaving, and pottery making.

stonechat bird *Saxicola torquata* of the thrush family (Turdidae) frequently found in Eurasia and Africa on open land with bushes. The male has a black head and throat, tawny breast, and dark back; the female is browner. They are about 12 cm/5 in long.

stonecrop different species of the genus *Sedum*, family Crassulaceae, a succulent herb with fleshy leaves and clusters of star-like flowers. They are characteristic of dry rocky places and some grow on walls.

Biting stonecrop Sedum acre is a low-growing evergreen with bright yellow flowers in early summer. It lives on dry grassland, shingle, and on walls in Europe, N Asia and N Africa. It gets its name from its peppery taste.

stonefish fish *Synanceia verrucosa* that lives in shallow waters of the Indian and Pacific Oceans. It is about 35 cm/14 in long, and camouflaged to resemble encrusted rock. It has poisonous spines that can inflict painful venom.

stonefly insect of the order Plecoptera, with long tails and antennae and two pairs of membranous wings. They live near fresh water. There are over 1300 species.

stomach

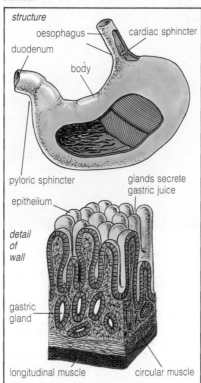

structure
oesophagus — cardiac sphincter
duodenum
body
pyloric sphincter
glands secrete gastric juice
epithelium
detail of wall
gastric gland
longitudinal muscle   circular muscle

Stonehenge /ˌstəʊnˈhendʒ/ megalithic monument dating from about 2000 BC on Salisbury Plain, Wiltshire, England. It consisted originally of a circle of 30 upright stones, their tops linked by lintelstones to form a continuous circle about 30 m/100 ft across. Within the circle was a horseshoe arrangement of five trilithons (two uprights plus a lintel, set as five separate entities), and a so-called 'altar stone'—an upright pillar—on the axis of the horseshoe at the open, NE end, which faces in the direction of the rising sun. It has been suggested that it served as an observatory.

The local sandstone, or sarsen, was used for the uprights, which measure 5.5 by 2 m/18 by 7 ft and weigh some 26 tonnes each. To give true perspective, they were made slightly convex. A secondary

Stone The phrase 'Lucy Stoner' was coined for women who followed Lucy Stone's example and kept their maiden name after marriage; she even refused to open letters addressed to her under her husband's surname.

Stonehenge The standing stones of Stonehenge are Europe's most important neolithic temple. Constructed in three main stages, it served not only as a burial complex but also as a permanent stone calendar.

circle and horseshoe were built of bluestones, originally brought from Pembrokeshire, Wales.

Stonehenge is one of a number of prehistoric structures on Salisbury Plain, including about 400 round ◊barrows, Durrington Walls (once a structure similar to that in Avebury), Woodhenge (a henge, or enclosure, once consisting of great wooden posts), and the Cursus (a pair of banked ditches, about 100 m/300 ft apart, which run straight for some 3 km/2 mi; dated 4th millennium BC). The purpose of none of these is known, but it may have been ritual.

Although Stonehenge is far older than ◊Druidism, an annual Druid ceremony is held there at the summer solstice. At that time it is also a spiritual focus for many people with a nomadic way of life, who on several consecutive midsummers in the 1980s were forcibly kept from access to Stonehenge by police.

Stonehouse /'stəʊnhaʊs/ John (Thompson) 1925– 1988. British Labour Party politician. An active member of the Co-operative Movement, he entered Parliament in 1957 and held junior posts under Harold Wilson before joining his cabinet in 1967. In 1974 he disappeared in Florida in mysterious circumstances, surfacing in Australia, amid suspicions of fraudulent dealings. Extradited to Britain, he was tried and imprisoned for embezzlement. He won an early release in 1979, but was unable to resume a political career.

stoneware a very hard opaque pottery made of non-porous clay with a high silica content, fired at high temperature.

stoolball an ancient game, considered the ancestor of cricket, the main differences being that in stoolball bowling is underarm, and the ball is soft, the bat is wooden, and shaped like a tennis racket.

Stopes /stəʊps/ Marie (Carmichael) 1880–1958. Scottish birth-control campaigner. With her husband H V Roe (1878–1949), an aircraft manufacturer, she founded a London birth-control clinic

Stopes Scottish birth-control campaigner Marie Stopes.

Stowe *US novelist Harriet Beecher Stowe wrote frequently on religious themes.*

1921. The Well Woman Centre in Marie Stopes House, London, commemorates her work. She wrote plays and verse as well as the best-selling manual *Married Love* 1918.

Stoppard /'stɒpɑːd/ Tom 1937– . Czechoslovak-born British playwright, whose works use wit and wordplay to explore logical and philosophical ideas. He achieved fame with *Rosencrantz and Guildenstern are Dead* 1967. This was followed by comedies including *The Real Inspector Hound* 1968, *Jumpers* 1972, *Travesties* 1974, *Dirty Linen* 1976, and *The Real Thing* 1982. He has also written radio, television, and screenplays.

Storey /'stɔːri/ David Malcolm 1933– . English dramatist and novelist. His plays include *In Celebration* 1969, *Home* 1970, and *Early Days* 1980. Novels include *This Sporting Life* 1960.

stork carnivorous wading bird of the mainly tropical order Ciconiiformes, with a long beak, slender body, long, powerful wings, and long thin neck and legs. Some species grow up to 150 cm/5 ft tall.

Species include the *white stork Ciconia ciconia*, which is encouraged to build on rooftops in Europe as a luck and fertility symbol; and the *jabiru Jabiru mycteria* of the Americas. Up to 1.5 m/5 ft high, it is white plumaged, but with a black and red head.

Stornoway /'stɔːnəweɪ/ port on the island of Lewis in the Outer ◊Hebrides; population (1981) 8,660. It is the administrative centre for the Western Isles. The economy is based on fishing, tourism, tweeds, and offshore oil. Stornoway was founded by James VI of Scotland (James I of England).

Storting the Norwegian parliament, which consists of 150 representatives, elected every four years.

Stoss /ʃtəʊs/ Veit. Also known as **Wit Stwosz** c. 1450–1533. German sculptor and painter, active in Nuremberg and 1477–96 in Poland. He carved a wooden altarpiece with high relief panels in St Mary's, Kraków, a complicated design with numerous figures which centres on the *Death of the Virgin*.

Stoss was born in Nuremberg and returned there from Poland. The figure of St Roch in Sta Annunziata, Florence, shows his characteristic figure style and sculpted drapery.

Stourbridge /'staʊəbrɪdʒ/ market town in the West Midlands, England, on the Stour river, SW of Birmingham; population (1981) 55,000. Industries include the manufacture of glass and bricks.

Stowe /stəʊ/ Harriet Beecher 1811–1896. US suffragist, abolitionist, and author of of the anti-slavery novel ◊*Uncle Tom's Cabin*, first published as a serial 1851–52.

She was a daughter of Lyman ◊Beecher, and in 1836 married C E Stowe, a professor of theology.

Strafford *Thomas Wentworth, the Earl of Strafford, aimed to make Charles I 'the most absolute prince in Christendom', but after his failure to quell rebellion in Scotland, he was impeached by Parliament and the king was forced to assent to his execution.*

Her book was radical in its time and did much to spread anti-slavery sentiment, but has later been criticized for sentimentality and racism.

STP abbreviation for ◊*standard temperature and pressure*.

Strabo /'streɪbəʊ/ c. 63 BC–AD 24. Greek geographer and historian, who travelled widely to collect first-hand material for his *Geography*.

Strachey /'streɪtʃi/ (Giles) Lytton 1880–1932. English critic and biographer, a member of the ◊Bloomsbury Group of writers and artists. He wrote *Landmarks in French Literature* 1912. The mocking and witty treatment of Cardinal Manning, Florence Nightingale, Thomas Arnold, and General Gordon in *Eminent Victorians* 1918 won him recognition. His biography of *Queen Victoria* 1921 was more affectionate.

Stradivari /ˌstrædɪ'vɑːri/ Antonio. In Latin form *Stradivarius* 1644–1737. Italian stringed instrument maker, generally considered the greatest of all violin makers. He was born in Cremona and studied there with Nicolo ◊Amati. He produced more than 1,100 instruments from his family workshops.

Strafford /'stræfəd/ Thomas Wentworth, 1st Earl of Strafford 1593–1641. English politician, originally an opponent of Charles I, but from 1628 on the Royalist side. He ruled despotically as Lord Deputy of Ireland 1632–39, when he returned to England as Charles's chief adviser and received an earldom. He was impeached in 1640 by Parliament, abandoned by Charles as a scapegoat, and beheaded.

straits question international and diplomatic debate in the 19th and 20th centuries over Russian naval access to the Mediterranean from the Black Sea via the Bosporus.

Straits Settlements /'streɪts 'setlmənts/ former province of the ◊East India Company 1826–58, and British Crown colony 1867–1946: it comprised Singapore, Malacca, Penang, Cocos Islands, Christmas Island, and Labuan.

Stralsund, Peace of in 1369, the peace between Waldemar IV of Denmark and the Hanseatic League (association of N German trading towns) which concluded the Hanse war 1362–69.

Denmark had unsuccessfully attempted to reduce the power of the Hanseatic League in Scandinavia, and by this peace, Waldemar had to recognize the League's trading rights in his territories, and assent to an enlargement of its privileges.

Strand /strænd/ Paul 1890–1976. US photographer who used large-format cameras for his strong, clear, close-up photographs of natural objects.

Strange /streɪndʒ/ Curtis Northrup 1955– . US golfer, professional from 1976. In 1989 he became the fifth person to win $5 million in a golfing career.

Strange was born in Virginia. He won his first tournament 1979 (Pensacola Open). He became the first person to win $1 million in a season in 1988. He has won over 20 tournaments, including two 'majors', the 1988 and 1989 US Opens.

CAREER HIGHLIGHTS

US Open: 1988, 1989
Canadian Open: 1985
US Ryder Cup team: 1983, 1985, 1987, 1989

Stranraer /ˌstræn'rɑː/ port in Dumfries and Galloway region, Scotland; population (1981) 10,800. There is a ferry service to Larne in Northern Ireland.

Strasberg /'stræzbɜːg/ Lee 1902–1982. US actor and artistic director of the ◊Actors Studio from 1948, who developed Method acting from ◊Stanislavsky's system; pupils have included Jane Fonda, John Garfield, Sidney Poitier, and Paul Newman.

Strasbourg /'stræzbʊəg/ city on the river Ill, in Bas-Rhin *département*, capital of Alsace, France; population (1982) 373,000. Industries include car manufacture, tobacco, printing and publishing, and preserves. The ◊Council of Europe meets here, and sessions of the European Parliament alternate between Strasbourg and Luxembourg. Seized by France 1681, it was surrendered to Germany 1870–1919 and 1940–44. It has a 13th-century cathedral.

Strassburg /'strɑːsbʊəg/ Gottfried von lived c. 1210. German poet, author of the unfinished epic *Tristan und Isolde*, which inspired ◊Wagner.

strata (singular **stratum**) layers or ◊beds of ◊sedimentary rock.

Strategic Arms Limitation Talks (SALT) a series of US-Soviet discussions aimed at reducing the rate of nuclear-arms build-up. The talks began 1969 between the US president Johnson and the Soviet leader Brezhnev. Neither the SALT I accord (effective 1972–77) nor SALT II called for reductions in nuclear weaponry, merely a limit on the expansion of these forces. SALT II was mainly negotiated by US president Ford before 1976 and signed by Brezhnev and Carter 1979, but was never ratified because of the the Soviet occupation of Afghanistan.

Strategic Arms Reduction Talks (START) a phase in US-Soviet peace discussions. START began with talks in Geneva 1983, leading to the signing of the ◊Intermediate Nuclear Forces (INF) treaty 1987. In 1989 proposals for reductions in conventional weapons were added to the agenda.

Strategic Defense Initiative (SDI) also called *Star Wars* an attempt by the USA to develop a defence system against incoming nuclear missiles, based in part outside the Earth's atmosphere. It was announced by President Reagan Mar 1983, and the research had by 1990 cost over $16.5 billion. In 1988, the joint chiefs of staff announced that they expected to be able to intercept no more than 30% of incoming missiles.

The essence of the SDI is to attack enemy missiles at several different stages of their trajectory,

US-Soviet summits

1969 SALT talks began in Helsinki
1972 Nixon and Brezhnev signed SALT I accord
1973 Brezhnev met Nixon in Washington DC
1974 (June) Nixon met Brezhnev in Moscow
1974 (Nov) Ford met Brezhnev in Vladivostok
1975 Ford and Brezhnev at 35-nation meeting in Helsinki
1979 Carter and Brezhnev signed SALT II accord in Vienna
1983 Strategic Arms Reduction Talks (START) in Geneva
1986 Reagan and Gorbachev met in Reykjavik
1987 Intermediate Nuclear Forces treaty signed in Washington DC
1989 Cuts on short-range missiles in Europe proposed conditional on reduction of conventional forces.

using advanced laser and particle-beam technology, thus increasing the chances of disabling them. Israel, Japan, and the UK are among the nations assisting in SDI research and development. In 1987 Gorbachev acknowledged that the USSR was developing a similar defence system.

strategic islands islands (Azores, Canary Islands, Cyprus, Iceland, Madeira, and Malta) of great political and military significance likely to affect their stability; they held their first international conference in 1979.

Stratford /'strætfəd/ port and industrial town in SW Ontario, Canada; population (1981) 26,000. It is the site of a Shakespeare festival.

Stratford-upon-Avon /'strætfəd əpɒn 'eɪvən/ market town on the river Avon, in Warwickshire, England; population (1981) 21,000. It is the birthplace of William ◊Shakespeare.

The Royal Shakespeare Theatre 1932 replaced an earlier building 1877–79 which burned down 1926. Shakespeare's birthplace contains relics of his life and times. His grave is in the parish church. Anne ◊Hathaway's cottage is nearby.

Strathclyde /,stræθ'klaɪd/ region of Scotland
area 13,900 sq km/5,367 sq mi
towns administrative headquarters Glasgow; Paisley, Greenock, Kilmarnock, Clydebank, Hamilton, Coatbridge, Prestwick
features includes some of Inner ◊Hebrides; river Clyde; part of Loch Lomond; Glencoe, site of the massacre of the Macdonald clan; Breadalbane; the islands of Arran, Bute, and Mull
products dairy, pig, and poultry products, shipbuilding, engineering, coal from Ayr and Lanark, oil-related services
population (1987) 2,333,000, half the population of Scotland
famous people David Livingstone, William Burrell.

stratigraphy branch of geology that deals with the sequence of formation of ◊sedimentary rock layers and the conditions under which they were formed. Its basis was developed by William ◊Smith, a British canal engineer.

Stratigraphy involves both the investigation of sedimentary structures to determine ancient geographies and environments, and the study of fossils for identifying and dating particular beds of rock.

stratosphere that part of the atmosphere 10–40 km/6–25 mi from Earth, where the temperature slowly rises from a low of –55°C/–67°F to around 0°C/32°F. The air is rarefied and at around 25 km/15 mi much ◊ozone is concentrated.

Straus /straʊs/ Oscar 1870–1954. Austrian composer, born in Vienna. He is remembered for the operetta *The Chocolate Soldier* 1909.

Strauss /straʊs/ Franz-Josef 1915–1988. West German conservative politician, leader of the

---

Strathclyde

Bavarian Christian Social Union (CSU) party 1961–88, premier of Bavaria 1978–88.

Born and educated in Munich, Strauss, after military service 1939–45, joined the CSU and was elected to the *Bundestag* (parliament) in 1949. He held ministerial posts during the 1950s and 1960s and became leader of the CSU 1961. In 1962 he lost his post as minister of defence when he illegally shut down the offices of *Der Spiegel* for a month, after the magazine revealed details of a failed NATO exercise. In the 1970s, Strauss opposed ◊Ostpolitik. He left the *Bundestag* to become premier of Bavaria in 1978, and was heavily defeated in 1980 as chancellor candidate. From 1982 Strauss sought to force changes in economic and foreign policy of the coalition under Chancellor Kohl.

Strauss /straʊs/ Johann (Baptist) 1825–1899. Austrian conductor and composer, the son of Johann Strauss (1804–49). In 1872 he gave up conducting and wrote operettas, such as *Die Fledermaus* 1874, and numerous waltzes, such as *The Blue Danube* and *Tales from the Vienna Woods*, which gained him the title 'The Waltz King'.

Strauss /straʊs/ Richard (Georg) 1864–1949. German composer and conductor. He followed the German Romantic tradition but had a strongly personal style, characterized by his bold, colourful orchestration. He first wrote tone poems such as *Don Juan* 1889, *Till Eulenspiegel's Merry Pranks* 1895, and *Also sprach Zarathustra* 1896. He then moved on to opera with *Salome* 1905, and *Elektra* 1909, both of which have elements of polytonality. He reverted to a more traditional style with *Der Rosenkavalier* 1911.

Stravinsky /strə'vɪnski/ Igor 1882–1971. Russian composer, later of French (1934) and US (1945) nationality. He studied under ◊Rimsky-Korsakov and wrote the music for the Diaghilev ballets *The Firebird* 1910, *Petrushka* 1911, and *The Rite of Spring* 1913 (controversial at the time for their unorthodox rhythms and harmonies). His versatile work ranges from his Neo-Classical ballet *Pulcinella* 1920, to the choral-orchestral *Symphony of Psalms* 1930. He later made use of serial techniques in works such as the *Canticum Sacrum* 1955 and the ballet *Agon* 1953–57.

strawberry low-growing perennial plant of the genus *Fragaria*, family Rosaceae, widely cultivated for its red fruit which is rich in vitamin C. Commercial cultivated forms bear one crop of fruit in summer and multiply by runners. Alpine garden varieties are derived from the wild strawberry *Fragaria vesca* which has small aromatic fruit.

streaming in education, the practice of dividing pupils for all classes according to an estimate of their overall ability, with arrangements for 'promotion' and 'demotion' at the end of each academic year.

In the UK, rigid streaming was unusual in secondary education in the 1980s, and had disappeared from primary education.

streamlining shaping a body so that it offers the least resistance when travelling through an element, usually air or water. Aircraft, for example, must be carefully streamlined to reduce air resistance, or ◊drag. High-speed aircraft must have swept-back wings, supersonic craft a sharp nose and narrow body.

stream of consciousness narrative technique in which a writer presents directly the uninterrupted flow of a character's thoughts, impressions, and feelings, without the conventional devices of dialogue and description. It first came to be widely used in the early 20th century. Leading exponents have included the novelists Virginia Woolf and James Joyce.

Molly Bloom's soliloquy in Joyce's *Ulysses* is a major example of the genre. The English writer Dorothy Richardson (1873–1957) is said to have originated the technique in her novel sequence *Pilgrimage*, the first volume of which was published 1915 and the last posthumously. The term 'stream of consciousness' was introduced by the philosopher William James in 1890.

Streep US actress Meryl Streep is known for her portrayal of strong, independent women, such as Karen Blixen in Out of Africa *1985.*

Streep /striːp/ Meryl 1949– . US actress noted for her strong character roles. Her films include *The Deer Hunter* 1978, *Kramer vs Kramer* 1979, *Out of Africa* 1985, *Ironweed* 1988, and *A Cry in the Dark* 1989.

Street J(abez) C(urry) 1906–1989. US physicist who, with E C Stevenson, discovered the muon (an ◊elementary particle) in 1937.

street hockey form of hockey played on roller skates. At one time played mostly on streets, notably in the USA, it is now played in indoor arenas. It rapidly increased in popularity in the UK in the late 1980s.

Streeton /'striːtn/ Arthur 1867–1943. Australian artist, who pioneered Impressionistic renderings of Australia's landscape.

Streisand /'straɪsænd/ 'Barbra' (Barbara Joan) 1942– . US singer and actress, who became a film star in *Funny Girl* 1968. Her subsequent films include *What's Up Doc?* 1972, *A Star is Born* 1979, and *Yentl* 1983, which she also directed.

strength of acids and bases in chemistry, the ability of ◊acids and ◊bases to dissociate in solution with water, and hence to produce a high or low ◊pH.

A strong acid is fully dissociated in aqueous solution, whereas a weak acid is only partly dissociated. Since the ◊dissociation of acids generates hydrogen ions, a solution of a strong acid will have a low pH. Similarly, a strong base will have a high pH, whereas a weaker base will not dissociate completely and will have a pH of nearer 7.

streptomycin ◊antibiotic discovered 1944, used to treat tuberculosis, influenzal meningitis, and other infections, some of which are unaffected by ◊penicillin.

stress in psychology, any event or situation that makes demands on a person's mental or emotional resources. Stress can be caused by overwork, anxiety about exams, money, or job security, unemployment, bereavement, poor relationships, marriage breakdown, sexual difficulties, poor living or working conditions, and constant exposure to loud noise.

Many changes that are apparently 'for the better', such as being promoted at work, going to a new school, moving house, and getting married, are also a source of stress. Stress can cause, or aggravate, physical illnesses, among them psoriasis, eczema, asthma, stomach and mouth ulcers. Apart from removing the source of stress, acquiring some control over it and learning to relax when possible are the best treatments.

stress and strain in the science of materials, measures of the deforming force applied to a body and of the resulting change in its shape. For a perfectly elastic material, stress is proportional to strain (◊Hooke's law).

Stretford /'stretfəd/ town in Greater ◊Manchester, England; population (1981) 48,000. It includes the Old Trafford cricket ground. There are engineering, chemical, and textile industries.

stridulatory organs in insects, organs that produce sound when rubbed together. Crickets rub their wings together, but grasshoppers rub the hind leg

Streisand US singer, actress, and entertainer Barbra Streisand. Her comic appeal ensured her success in films such as Funny Girl 1968.

against the wing. Stridulation is thought to be used for attracting mates, but may also be used to mark territory.

strike and lockout a *strike* is a stoppage of work by employees, often as members of a trade union, to obtain or resist change in wages, hours, or conditions. *Lockout* is a weapon of an employer to enforce such change by preventing employees working. Another measure is *work to rule*, when production is virtually brought to a halt by strict observance of union rules.

Strikes may be 'official' (union-authorized) or 'wildcat' (undertaken spontaneously), and may be accompanied by a *sit-in* or *work-in*, the one being worker occupation of a factory and the other continuation of work in a plant the employer wishes to close. In a 'sympathetic' strike, action is in support of other workers on strike elsewhere, possibly in a different industry.

In the UK, under the Thatcher government, various measures to curb trade-union power to strike were introduced, for example, the act of 1984 that provided for loss of immunity from legal action if a secret ballot of members is not held before a strike. See also ◊industrial relations.

Strindberg /ˈstrɪndbɜːg/ August 1849–1912. Swedish playwright and novelist. His plays, influential in the development of dramatic technique, are in a variety of styles including historical plays, symbolic dramas (the two-part *Dödsdansen/The Dance of Death* 1901) and 'chamber plays' such as *Spöksonaten/The Ghost (or Spook) Sonata* 1907. *Fadren/The Father* 1887 and *Fröken Julie/Miss Julie* 1888 are among his best-known works.

Born in Stockholm, he lived mainly abroad after 1883, having been unsuccessfully prosecuted for blasphemy in 1884 following publication of his short stories *Giftas/Marrying*. His life was stormy and controversial. His work has been criticized for its hostile attitude to women, but he is regarded as one of Sweden's greatest writers.

stringed instrument musical instrument that produces a sound by making a stretched string vibrate. Types include: *bowed* violin family, viol family; *plucked* guitar, ukelele, lute, sitar, harp, banjo, lyre; *plucked mechanically* harpsichord; *struck mechanically* piano, clavichord; *hammered* dulcimer.

string theory mathematical theory developed in the 1980s; see ◊superstring theory.

strobilus in botany, a reproductive structure found in most ◊gymnosperms and some pteridophytes, notably the club mosses. In conifers the strobilus is commonly known as a ◊cone.

stroboscope instrument for studying continuous periodic motion by using light flashing at the same frequency as that of the motion; for example, rotating machinery can be 'stopped' by illuminating it with a stroboscope flashing at the exact rate of rotation.

Strindberg Drawing of Swedish dramatist August Strindberg by his friend Carl Larsson.

Stroessner /ˈstresnə/ Alfredo 1912– . Military leader and president of Paraguay 1954–89. As head of the armed forces from 1951, he seized power in a coup in 1954 sponsored by the right-wing ruling Colorado Party. Accused by his opponents of harsh repression, his regime spent heavily on the military to preserve his authority. He was overthrown by a military coup and gained asylum in Brazil.

Stroheim /ˈʃtrəʊhaɪm/ Erich von. Assumed name of Erich Oswald Stroheim 1885–1957. Austrian actor and director, who worked in Hollywood from 1914. Successful as an actor in villainous roles, his career as a director was wrecked by his extravagance and he returned to acting in international films such as *Grand Illusion/La Grande Illusion* 1937 and *Sunset Boulevard* 1950. His films as director include *Greed* 1923 and *Queen Kelly* 1928 (unfinished).

stroke a sudden episode involving the blood supply to the brain. It may also be termed a cerebrovascular accident (CVA) or apoplexy. Strokes are caused by a sudden bleed in the brain (cerebral haemhorrhage), or to interruption of the blood supply to part of the brain due to ◊embolism or ◊thrombosis. They vary in severity from producing almost no symptoms to proving rapidly fatal. In between are those leaving a wide range of impaired function, depending on the size and location of the event.

Transient ischaemic attacks (TIAs), or 'mini-strokes', with effects lasting only briefly, require investigation to try to forestall the possibility of a subsequent full-blown stroke.

The disease of the arteries that predisposes to stroke is ◊atherosclerosis. High blood pressure (◊hypertension) is also a precipitating factor. Strokes can sometimes be prevented by surgery, or by use of ◊anticoagulant drugs and daily aspirin to minimize the risk of stroke due to obstructed blood vessels.

Stromboli /ˈstrɒmbəli/ Italian island in the Tyrrhenian Sea, one of the ◊Lipari Islands; area 12 sq km/5 sq mi. It has an active volcano, 926 m/3,039 ft high. The island produces Malmsey wine and capers.

strontium metallic element, symbol Sr, atomic number 38, relative atomic mass 87.63. Isolated electrolytically by ◊Davy in 1808, it is widely distributed in small quantities as sulphate and carbonate. The silver-white ductile metal, which is used in electronics, resembles calcium. Its salts give a brilliant red colour to a flame and are used for fireworks.

Strophanthus genus of tropical plants of Afro-Asia, family Apocynaceae. Seeds of the handsome climber *Strophanthus gratus* yield a poison, used on arrows in hunting, and in medicine as a heart stimulant.

structuralism a 20th-century philosophical movement that has been influential in such areas as linguistics, anthropology, and literary criticism. Inspired by the work of the Swiss linguist Ferdinand de Saussure (1857–1913), structuralists believe that objects should be analysed as systems of relations, rather than as positive entities.

Saussure proposed that language is a system of arbitrary signs, meaning that there is no intrinsic link between the 'signifier' (the sound or mark) and the 'signified' (the concept it represents). Hence any linguistic term can only be defined by its differences from other terms. His ideas were taken further by Roman Jakobson (1896–) and the Prague school of linguistics, and were extended into a general method for the social sciences by the French anthropologist Claude Lévi-Strauss. The French writer Roland Barthes took the lead in applying the ideas of structuralism to literary criticism, arguing that the critic should identify the structures within a text that determine its possible meanings, independently of any reference to the real. This approach is radicalized in Barthes' later work, and in the practice of 'deconstruction', pioneered by the French philosopher Jacques Derrida (1930–). Here the text comes to be viewed as a 'decentred' play of structures, lacking any ultimately determinable meaning.

structured programming the process of writing a computer program in small, independent parts. This allows a more easily controlled program development and the individual design and testing of the component parts. Structured programs are built up from units called *modules*, which normally correspond to single procedures or functions. Some programming languages, such as PASCAL and Modula-2, are more suited to structural programming than others.

Struwwelpeter a collection of cautionary tales written and illustrated by German author Heinrich Hoffman (1809–94), published in German 1845 (English translation 1848). The tales, in verse form, feature characters such as 'Shock-head Peter' (*Struwwelpeter*), 'Johnny Head-in-Air', and 'Augustus who would not have any Soup'.

strychnine $C_{21}H_{22}O_2N_2$ a bitter-tasting poisonous alkaloid. It is a violent poison, causing muscular spasms. It is usually obtained by powdering the seeds of plants of the genus *Strychnos*, for example *Strychnos nux vomica*. Curare is a related drug.

Stuart /ˈstjuːət/ John McDouall 1815–1866. Scottish-born Australian explorer. He went with ◊Sturt on his 1844 expedition, and in 1860, after two unsuccessful attempts, crossed the centre of Australia from Adelaide in the SE to the coast of Arnhem Land. He almost lost his life on the return journey.

Stuart, house of /ˈstjuːət/ or *Stewart* royal family who inherited the Scottish throne in 1371 and the English throne in 1603.

Stuart Highway first Australian all-weather route north to south across the continent (Darwin–Alice Springs 1943, extended to Adelaide 1985); it was named after the explorer John Stuart, as was Mount Stuart on the same route.

Stubbs /stʌbz/ George 1724–1806. British artist, known for paintings of horses. After the publication of his book of engravings *The Anatomy of the Horse* 1766, he was widely commissioned as an animal painter and group portraitist.

Stubbs began as a portrait painter and medical illustrator in Liverpool. In 1754 he went to Rome, continuing to study nature and anatomy. Before settling in London in the 1760s he rented a farm and carried out a long series of dissections of horses which resulted in his book. The dramatic *Lion Attacking a Horse* 1770 (Yale University Art

Stubbs John Gascoigne with Bay Horse *(1791) Royal Collection, Windsor.*

Stuttgart Staatsgalerie, Stuttgart, by Stirling and Wilford. British architect James Stirling has long been associated with collegiate and museum architecture.

Gallery, New Haven, Connecticut) and the peaceful *Reapers* 1786 (Tate Gallery, London) show the variety of mood in his painting.

Stud, National British establishment founded 1915, and since 1964 located at Newmarket, where stallions are kept for visiting mares in order to breed racehorses. It is now maintained by the Horserace Betting Levy Board.

Students for a Democratic Society (SDS) US student movement, founded 1962, which steered a middle line between Marxism and orthodox left-wing politics; its members opposed racism and imperialism. At its peak it had some 100,000 members. In 1968 they were split by the hardline Weatherman faction, which aimed for violent revolution and control from above.

sturgeon fish of subclass Chondrostei. Sturgeons are large, with five rows of bony plates, small mouths, and four barbels. They are voracious feeders.

The *beluga Huso huso* of the Caspian can reach a length of 8 m/25 ft and weigh 1,500 kg/3,300 lb. The *common sturgeon* (*Acipenser sturio*) of the Atlantic and Mediterranean reaches a length of 3.5 m/12 ft.

Sturges /'stɜːdʒɪz/ Preston. Adopted name of Edmond Biden 1898–1959. US film director and writer who enjoyed great success with a series of comedies in the early 1940s, including *Sullivan's Travels* 1941, *The Palm Beach Story*, and *The Miracle of Morgan's Creek* 1943.

Sturluson /'stuələsɒn/ Snorri 1179–1241. Icelandic author of the Old Norse poems called ◊Eddas, and the *Heimskringla*, a saga chronicle of Norwegian kings until 1177.

Sturm Abteilung (German 'storm section') (SA) terrorist militia, also known as *Brownshirts*, of the ◊Nazi Party, established 1921 under the leadership of ◊Röhm, in charge of physical training and political indoctrination.

Sturm und Drang (German 'storm and stress') German early Romantic movement in literature and music, from about 1775, concerned with depiction of extravagant passions. Writers associated include Herder, Goethe, and Schiller. The name is taken from a play by Friedrich von Klinger 1776.

Sturt /stɜːt/ Charles 1795–1869. British explorer and soldier. In 1828 he sailed down the Murrumbidgee River in SE Australia to the estuary of the Murray in circumstances of great hardship, charting the entire river system of the region.

Born in India, he served in the army, and in 1827 discovered with the Australian explorer Hamilton Hume the river ◊Darling. Drawn by his concept of a great inland sea, he set out for the interior 1844, crossing the Sturt Desert, but failing to penetrate the Simpson Desert.

Stuttgart /'ʃtʊtgɑːt/ capital of Baden-Württemberg, West Germany; population (1988) 565,000. Industries include publishing and the manufacture of vehicles and electrical goods. It is the headquarters of US European Command (Eucom). ◊Hegel was born here.

style in flowers, the part of the ◊carpel bearing the ◊stigma at its tip. In some flowers it is very short or completely lacking, while in others it may be long and slender, positioning the stigma in the most effective place to receive the pollen. Usually the style withers after fertilization but in certain species, such as traveller's joy *Clematis vitalba*, it develops into a long feathery plume which aids dispersal of the fruit.

Style, Old and New forms of dating; see ◊calendar.

Styria /'stɪriə/ (German *Steiermark*) alpine province of SE Austria; area 16,400 sq km/6,330 sq mi; population (1987) 1,181,000. Its capital is Graz, and its industries include iron, steel, lignite, vehicles, electrical goods, and engineering. An independent state from 1056 until it passed to the ◊Habsburgs in the 13th century, it was annexed by Germany 1938.

Styx /stɪks/ in Greek mythology, the river surrounding the underworld.

Suárez González /'swɑːreθ gɒn'θɑːleθ/ Adolfo 1933– . Spanish politician, prime minister 1976–81. A friend of King Juan Carlos, he worked in the National Movement for 18 years, but in 1975 became president of the newly established Unión del Pueblo Español (UPE). He took office as prime minister at the request of the king, to speed the reform programme. He suddenly resigned 1981.

subatomic particle see ◊particle, subatomic, and ◊elementary particle.

sub judice (Latin 'under a judge') not yet decided by a court of law.

sublimation in chemistry, the conversion of a solid to vapour without passing through the liquid phase. Some substances that do not sublime at atmospheric pressure can be made to do so at low pressures. This is the principle of freeze-drying, during which ice sublimes at low pressure.

subliminal message a message delivered beneath the human conscious threshold or perception. It may be visual (words or images flashed between the frames of a cinema or TV film), or aural (a radio message broadcast constantly at very low volume). The aim may be commercial (to sell a product) or psychological (to wean a patient from alcohol or smoking). Subliminal advertising is illegal in many countries, including Britain.

submarine an underwater ship, especially a warship. The first underwater boat was constructed for James I of England by the Dutch scientist Cornelius van Drebbel (1572–1633) 1620. A naval submarine, or submersible torpedo boat, the *Gymnote*, was launched by France 1888. The conventional submarine of World War I was driven by diesel engine on the surface and by battery-powered electric motors underwater. The diesel engine also drove a generator that produced electricity to charge the batteries.

In 1954 the USA launched the first nuclear-powered submarine, the *Nautilus*. The nuclear submarine *Ohio*, USA, in service from 1981, is 170 m/560 ft long, weighs about 18,700 tonnes, and carries 24 Trident missiles, each with 12 independently targetable nuclear warheads. Operating depth is usually up to 300 m/1,000 ft, and nuclear-powered speeds of 30 knots (55 kph/34 mph) are reached. As in all nuclear submarines, propulsion is by steam turbine driving a propeller. The steam is raised using the heat given off by the nuclear reactor (see ◊nuclear energy).

In the 1760s, the American David Bushness designed a submarine called *Turtle* for attacking British ships, and in 1800, Robert Fulton designed a submarine called *Nautilus* for Napoleon for the same purpose. John P Holland, an Irish emigrant to the USA, designed a submarine about 1875, which was used by both the US and the British navies at the turn of the century. In both world wars submarines, from the ocean-going to the midget type, played a vital role. In World War I, the German U-boats were feared.

In oceanography, salvage, and pipe-laying, smaller submarines called submersibles are used. The Royal Navy's surface diving ship *Challenger* (1980) not only supports divers operating at 300 m/1,000 ft, but acts as mother ship for deep-diving submersibles which are hauled up a stern ramp. It also has a 'moon' pool, or cylindrical vertical internal shaft, down which a three-person ◊diving bell can be lowered. Depths of 6,000 m/20,000 ft are reached.

submersible a small submarine used by engineers and research scientists, and as a ferry craft to support diving operations. The most advanced submersibles are the so-called lock-out type, which have two compartments: one for the pilot, the other to carry divers. The diving compartment is pressurized and provides access to the sea.

They are used to ferry 'saturation' divers between compression chambers on a support ship and their place of work on the sea bed. The divers remain under compression for days at a time, avoiding the long decompression periods needed after every deep dive.

Subotica /'suːbətɪtsa/ largest town in Vojvodina, NW Serbia, Yugoslavia; population (1981) 155,000. Industries include chemicals and electrical machinery.

subpoena (Latin 'under penalty') in law, a writ requiring someone who might not otherwise come forward of his or her own volition to give evidence before a court or judicial official at a specific time and place.

subroutine in computing, a small section of a program that is executed ('called') from another part of the program. Subroutines provide a method of performing the same task at more than one point in the program, and also of separating the details of a program from its main logic. In some computer languages, subroutines are similar to ◊functions or ◊procedures.

subsidiary a company that is legally controlled by another company having 50% or more of its shares. A parent company may believe that having a subsidiary is preferable to full integration for taxation purposes, or may allow local participation if the subsidiary is in another country.

subsidy government payment or concession granted to a state or private company, or an individual. A subsidy may be provided to keep prices down, to stimulate the market for a particular product, or because it is perceived to be in the public interest.

The payment of subsidies may distort the market, create shortages, reduce efficiency, or waste resources that could be used more beneficially elsewhere. Export subsidies are usually condemned because they represent unfair competition.

Many countries provide subsidies for transport systems and public utilities such as water, gas, and electricity supplies. Subsidies are also given for art, science, and religion when they cannot be self-supporting to the standards perceived desirable.

subsistence farming term used for farming when the produce is enough to feed only the farmer and family.

substitution reaction in chemistry, the replacement of one atom or ◊functional group in an organic molecule by another.

substrate in biochemistry, a compound or mixture of compounds acted on by an enzyme. The term is also used to refer to a substance such as ◊agar that provides the nutrients for the metabolism of microorganisms. Since the enzyme systems of microorganisms regulate their metabolism, the essential meaning is the same.

subway North American term for ◊underground railway.

succession in ecology, series of changes that occur in the structure and composition of the vegetation in a given area from the time it is first colonized by plants (*primary succession*), or after it has been disturbed by fire, flood, or clearing (*secondary succession*).

If allowed to proceed undisturbed, succession leads naturally to a stable ◊climax community (for example, oak and hickory forest or savannah grassland) that is determined by the climate and soil characteristics of the area.

Succot or *Sukkoth* Jewish festival celebrated in Oct, also known as the *Feast of Booths*, which commemorates the time when the Israelites lived in the wilderness during the ◊Exodus from Egypt. As a reminder of the shelters used in the wilderness, huts are built and used for eating and sleeping in during the seven days of the festival.

succubus a female spirit; see ◊incubus.

succulent plant a thick, fleshy plant that stores water in its tissues, for example cacti and stonecrops (*Sedum*). Succulents live either in areas where water is very scarce, such as deserts, or in places where it is not easily obtainable because of the high concentrations of salts in the soil, as in salt marshes. See also ◊xerophyte.

Suceava /ˌsuːtʃiˈɑːvə/ capital of Suceava county, N Romania; population (1985) 93,000. Industries include textiles and lumber. It was a former centre of pilgrimage and capital of Moldavia 32 1388–1564.

sucker fish another name for ◊remora.

suckering in plants, reproduction by new shoots arising from an existing root system rather than from seed. Examples include elm, dandelion, and expand to explain how this non-sexual reproduction results in widely differing forms.

Suckling /ˈsʌklɪŋ/ John 1609–1642. English poet and dramatist. He was an ardent Royalist who tried to effect ◊Strafford's escape from the Tower of London. On his failure, he fled to France and may have committed suicide. His chief lyrics appeared in *Fragmenta Aurea* and include 'Why so pale and wan, fond lover?'

Sucre /ˈsuːkreɪ/ legal capital and judicial seat of Bolivia; population (1985) 87,000. It stands on the central plateau at an altitude of 2,840 m/ 9,320 ft.

Founded 1538, its cathedral dates from 1553, and the University of San Francisco Xavier 1624 is probably the oldest in South America. The first revolt against Spanish rule in South America began here 25 May 1809.

Sucre /ˈsuːkreɪ/ Antonio José de 1795–1830. South American revolutionary leader. As chief lieutenant of Simón ◊Bolívar, he won several battles in freeing the colonies of Ecuador and Bolivia from Spanish rule, and in 1826 became president of Bolivia. After a mutiny by the army and invasion by Peru, he resigned 1828 and was assassinated 1830 on his way to join Bolívar.

sucrose (chemical formula $C_{12}H_{22}O_{10}$) chemical name for the ◊disaccharide known commonly as ◊sugar, cane sugar or beet sugar.

A single molecule of sucrose consists of a ◊glucose molecule and a ◊fructose molecule bonded together. Sucrose does not have the reducing properties associated with most simple carbohydrates.

Sudan /suːˈdɑːn/ country in NE Africa, S of Egypt, with a Red Sea coast; it is the largest country in Africa.

government After a military coup Apr 1985 a transitional constitution was introduced, providing for a 264-member legislative assembly, a supreme council under a president, and a council of ministers led by a prime minister. The assembly is charged with the task of producing a new constitution and, after a further transitional period, of declaring itself a parliament, subject to election every four years.

history The region was once known as ◊Nubia and settled by Egypt. The people were converted to Coptic Christianity in the 6th century and to Islam in the 15th century when Arabs invaded. Sudan was again ruled by Egypt from 1820. A revolt began 1881, led by a sheik who took the title of ◊Mahdi and captured ◊Khartoum 1885. It was subdued by an Anglo-Egyptian army under ◊Kitchener 1896–98 and administered as an Anglo-Egyptian condominium from 1899.

The Sudan, as it was then called, achieved independence as a republic 1956. Two years later a coup ousted the civil administration and a military government was set up, which in 1964 was itself overthrown and civilian rule was reinstated, but five years later the army returned in a coup led by Col Gaafar Mohammed Nimeri. All political bodies were abolished, the Revolutionary Command Council (RCC) set up, and the country's name changed to the Democratic Republic of Sudan. Close links were soon established with Egypt and in 1970 an agreement in principle was reached for eventual union. In 1972 this should have become, with the addition of Syria, the Federation of Arab Republics, but internal opposition blocked both

succession

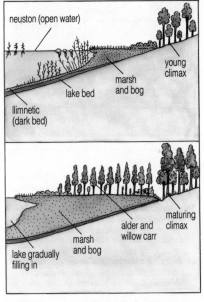

developments. In 1971 a new constitution was adopted, Nimeri confirmed as president and the Sudanese Socialist Union (SSU) declared to be the only party.

The most serious problem confronting Nimeri was open aggression between the Muslim north and the chiefly Christian south, which had started as long ago as 1955. At a conference in Addis Ababa 1972 he granted the three southern provinces a considerable degree of autonomy, but fighting continued. Nimeri had come to power in a left-wing revolution but soon turned to the West, and particularly the USA, for support. By 1974 he had established a national assembly, but his position still relied on army backing. In 1983 he was re-elected for a third term but his regional problems persisted. By sending more troops south against the Sudan People's Liberation Army he alienated the north and then caused considerable resentment in the south by replacing the penal code with strict Islamic law. His economic policies contributed to the widespread unrest.

In Mar 1985 a general strike was provoked by a sharp devaluation of the Sudanese pound and an increase in bread prices. Nimeri was in the USA when army mutiny threatened. One of his supporters, Gen Swar al-Dahab, took over in a bloodless coup. He set up a transitional military council, and held elections for a legislative assembly Apr 1986, contested by more than 40 parties, the three most significant being the New National Umma Party (NNUP), which won 99 seats, the Democratic Unionist Party (DUP), 63 seats, and the National Islamic Front, 51 seats. A coalition government was formed, with Ahmed Ali El-Mirghani (DUP) as president of the Supreme Council and Oxford-educated Sadiq al-Mahdi (NNUP) as prime minister. Strikes and shortages persisted, with inflation running at about 100% and the highest national debt in Africa, and in July 1987 a state of emergency was declared. In Oct 1987 the prime minister announced the break-up of the government of national unity and the formation of a new coalition. In Dec 1988 the signing of a peace agreement with the Sudan People's Liberation Movement (SPLM), led by John Garang, threatened to split the coalition government and eventually led to a military takeover, by Gen Ahmed el-Bashir, in July 1989. El-Bashir established a National Salvation Revolutionary Council and said that he intended to end the civil war.

Sudbury /ˈsʌdbəri/ city in Ontario, Canada; population (1986) 149,000. A buried meteorite there yields 90% of the world's nickel.

submersible

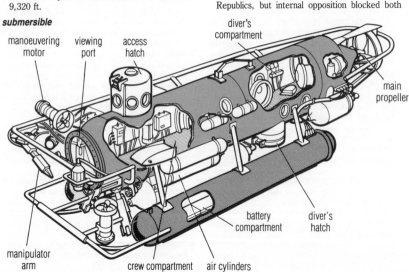

manoeuvering motor · viewing port · access hatch · diver's compartment · main propeller · manipulator arm · crew compartment · air cylinders · battery compartment · diver's hatch

Sudan
Democratic Republic of
(Jamhuryat es-Sudan)

area 2,505,800 sq km/967,489 sq mi
capital Khartoum
towns Omdurman, Juba, Wadi Medani, al-Obeid, Kassala, Atbara, al-Qadarif, Kosti; chief port Port Sudan
physical fertile valley of the river Nile separates Libyan Desert in west from high rocky Nubian Desert in east
features Sudd swamp; largest country in Africa
head of state and government Gen Omar Hasan Ahmed el-Bashir from 1989
government military republic
political parties New National Umma Party (NNUP), Islamic, nationalist; Democratic Unionist Party (DUP), moderate, nationalist; National Islamic Front, Islamic nationalist
exports cotton, gum arabic, sesame, groundnuts, durra
currency Sudanese pound (19.49 = £1 Feb 1990)
population (1989) 25,008,000 (70% of whom are Muslim, Arab-speaking, and in the N; speakers of African languages in the S); annual growth rate 2.9%
life expectancy men 47, women 49
language 51% Arabic (official); 6% Darfurian; 18% Nilotic (Dinka and Nuer); 5% Nilo-Hamitic; 5% Sudanic

religion Sunni Muslim in the north, animist in the south, with a Christian minority
literacy 38% male/14% female (1981 est)
GNP $27.3 bn (1983); $361 per head of population
chronology
1955 Civil war between the Muslim N and non-Muslim S.
1956 Sudan achieved independence as a republic.
1958 Military coup replaced the civilian government with a Supreme Council of the Armed Forces.
1964 Civilian rule reinstated.
1969 Coup led by Col Gaafar Mohammed Nimeri established a Revolutionary Command Council (RCC) and the country's name changed to the Democratic Republic of Sudan.
1970 Agreement in principle on union with Egypt.
1971 New constitution adopted, Nimeri confirmed as president, and the Sudanese Socialist Union (SSU) declared to be the only legal party.
1972 Proposed Federation of Arab Republics, comprising Sudan, Egypt, and Syria, abandoned. Addis Ababa conference proposed autonomy for southern provinces.
1974 National assembly established.
1983 Nimeri re-elected amid growing opposition to his social, economic, and religious policies. *Sharia* (Islamic law) introduced.
1985 Nimeri deposed in a bloodless coup led by Gen Swar al-Dahab, who set up a transitional military council. State of emergency declared.
1986 More than 40 political parties fought the general election and a coalition government was formed.
1987 Virtual civil war with Sudan People's Liberation Movement (SPLM).
1988 Al-Mahdi formed a new coalition. Another flare-up of civil war between N and S created tens of thousands of refugees. Floods made 1.5 million people homeless. Peace pact signed with Sudan People's Liberation Movement.
1989 Sadiq Al-Mahdi overthrown in coup led by Gen Omar Hasan Ahmed el-Bashir.

sudden infant death syndrome (SIDS) formal term for ◊cot death, or crib death.
Sudetenland /suːˈdeɪtnlænd/ mountainous region of N Czechoslovakia, annexed by Germany under the ◊Munich Agreement 1938; returned to Czechoslovakia 1945.
Suetonius /suːˈɪtəʊnɪəs/ (Gaius Suetonius Tranquillius) *c.*AD 69–140. Roman historian, author of *Lives of the Caesars* (Julius Caesar to Domitian).
Suez /ˈsuːɪz/ (Arabic *El Suweis*) port at the Red Sea terminus of the ◊Suez Canal; population (1985) 254,000. Industries include oil refining and the manufacture of fertilizers. It was reconstructed after the ◊Arab-Israeli Wars.
Suez Canal /ˈsuːɪz/ artificial waterway, 160 km/100 mi long, from Port Said to Suez, linking the Mediterranean and Red seas, separating Africa from Asia, and providing the shortest sea route from Europe eastwards. It was opened 1869, nationalized 1956, blocked by Egypt during the Arab-Israeli war 1967, and not re-opened until 1975.

The French Suez Canal Company was formed 1858 to execute the scheme of Ferdinand de Lesseps. The canal was opened 1869, and in 1875 British prime minister ◊Disraeli acquired a major shareholding for Britain from the khedive of Egypt. The 1888 Convention of Constantinople opened it to all nations. The Suez Canal was admininstered by a company with offices in Paris controlled by a council of 33 (ten of them British) until 1956 when it was forcibly nationalized by President ◊Nasser of Egypt. The new Damietta port complex on

the Mediterranean at the mouth of the canal was inaugurated July 1986. The port is designed to handle 16 million tons of cargo.
Suez Crisis incident Oct–Dec 1956 following the nationalization of the ◊Suez Canal by President Nasser of Egypt. In an attempt to reassert international control of the canal, Israel launched an attack towards the canal, after which British and French troops landed. Widespread international censure (Soviet protest, US non-support, and considerable opposition within Britain) soon led to withdrawal of the troops and the resignation of British prime minister Eden.
suff. in grammar, abbreviation for *suffix*.
suffix a letter or group of letters added to the end of a word in order to form a new word. For example, the suffix 'ist' can be added to 'sex' to form the word 'sexist'.
Suffolk /ˈsʌfək/ county of E England
area 3,800 sq km/1,467 sq mi
towns administrative headquarters Ipswich; Bury St Edmunds, Lowestoft, Felixstowe
physical low undulating surface and flat coastline; rivers Waveney, Alde, Deben, Orwell, Stour; part of the Norfolk Broads
features Minsmere marshland bird reserve, near Aldeburgh; site of ◊Sutton Hoo (7th-century ship-burial); site of 'Sizewell B', planned as the first of Britain's pressurized-water reactor (PWR) plants (approved 1987).
products cereals, sugar beet, working horses (Suffolk punches), fertilizers, agricultural machinery
population (1987) 635,000

famous people Constable, Gainsborough, Elizabeth Garrett Anderson, Benjamin Britten, George Crabbe.
suffragan (Latin *suffragor* 'vote for, support') in the Christian church, an assistant bishop, appointed to work in a part of the diocese.
suffragette a woman fighting for the right to vote; in the USA, the preferred term was *suffragist*. In the UK, women's suffrage bills were repeatedly introduced and defeated in Parliament between 1886 and 1911, and a militant campaign was launched 1906 by Emmeline ◊Pankhurst and her daughters. In 1918 women were granted limited franchise; in 1928 it was extended to all women over 21. In the USA the 19th amendment to the constitution 1920 gave women the vote in federal and state elections.

Suffragettes (the term was coined by a *Daily Mail* reporter) chained themselves to railings, heckled political meetings, refused to pay taxes, and in 1913 bombed the home

Suffolk

of Lloyd George, then chancellor of the Exchequer. One woman, Emily ◊Davison, threw herself under the king's horse at the Derby 1913 and was killed. Many suffragettes were imprisoned and were force-fed when they went on hunger strike; under the notorious 'Cat and Mouse Act' of 1913 they could be repeatedly released to regain their health and then re-arrested. The struggle was called off on the outbreak of World War I.

suffragist US term for ◊suffragette.

Sufism a mystical movement of ◊Islam which originated in the 8th century. Sufis believe that deep intuition is the only real guide to knowledge. The movement has a strong strain of asceticism. The name derives from the *suf*, a rough woollen robe worn as an indication of their disregard for material things. There are a number of groups or brotherhoods within Sufism, each with its own method of meditative practice, one of which is the whirling dance of the ◊dervishes.

sugar sweet, soluble carbohydrate, either a monosaccharide or disaccharide. The major sources are tropical cane sugar, which accounts for about two-thirds of production, and temperate sugar beet.

Cane, which is a grass, usually yields over 20 tonnes of sugar per hectare per year, while sugar beet rarely exceeds 7 tonnes per hectare per year. Beet sugar is more expensive to produce, and is often subsidized by governments that wish to support the agricultural sector and avoid over-dependence on the volatile world sugar market. Minor quantities of sugar are produced from the sap of maple trees, and from sorghum and date palms. Sugar is a major source of energy, but can also contribute to tooth decay.

Monosaccharides are the simplest of sugars; examples include fructose and glucose, both obtained from fruit and honey.

Disaccharides are sugars that, when hydrolysed by dilute acids, give two of either the same or different simple sugars (monosaccharides). An example is sucrose from sugar cane.

Polysaccharides, for example, starch and cellulose, hydrolyse to many simple sugars.

Commercially, sugar sucrose is produced from *sugar cane*, one of the grasses, by crushing the stem. *Molasses* is the uncrystallized syrup drained from the sugar (fermented, it forms rum), and is then refined by stages to 'pure' whiteness. Demerara, or coffee sugar, is a stage along the way. *Treacle* and *golden syrup* are successive liquid stages in the refining of molasses. Highly refined forms of sugar include cube, granulated, caster, and icing. Sugar is also produced from *sugar beet*, of which remaining pulp is used as cattle feed. Bagasse, the fibrous residue of sugar cane, is used for paper-making, cattle feed, and fuel, and new types of cane are being bred for low sugar and high fuel production.

Introduced to Europe in the 8th century, sugar became known in England around 1100 when the Crusaders brought some from the Middle East. Sugar was first imported to England in 1319, but was taxed from 1685 to 1874, and only became widespread after then. In 1985 the average Briton consumed 0.8 kg of sugar per week. In the same year world production of sugar was 37% from sugar beet and 63% from cane sugar. The production and trade in each is controlled by a monopoly in Britain.

Sugar /'ʃʊgə/ Alan 1947– . British entrepreneur, founder of the Amstrad electronics company 1968 which holds a major position in the European personal-computer market. In 1985 he introduced a complete word processing system at the price of £399. Subsequent models consolidated his success internationally.

sugar maple North American ◊maple tree *Acer saccharum.*

sugar production manufacturing process involving the refinement of either harvested sugar cane or sugar beet for human consumption. Approximately 9 million hectares/22.25 million acres of

Sugar British entrepreneur Alan Sugar.

beet grown mostly in Europe and the USSR, and 13 million hectares/32 million acres of cane, grown in tropical and subtropical countries, together produce 100 million tonnes of raw sugar each year.

Of the 100 sugar cane-producing countries, India and Brazil are the largest, with 3 million and 2.5 million hectares/7.5 million acres and 6 million acres respectively. In many smaller countries, such as Barbados and Mauritius, sugar production is a vital component of the national economy.

Suger /su:'ʒeɪ/ *c.* 1081–1151. French historian and politician, regent of France during the Second Crusade. In 1122 he was elected of St Denis, Paris, and was counsellor to, and biographer of, Louis VI and Louis VII. He began the reconstruction of St Denis as the first large-scale Gothic building.

Suharto /su:'ha:təʊ/ Raden 1921– . Indonesian politician and general. He ousted Sukarno to become president 1967. He ended confrontation with Malaysia, invaded East Timor 1975, and reached a cooperation agreement with Papua New Guinea 1979. His authoritarian rule has met domestic opposition from the left. He was re-elected 1973, 1978, 1983, and 1988.

Suhl /su:l/ county in East Germany; area 3,860 sq km/1,490 sq mi; population (1986) 549,000. Its capital is Suhl. It is dominated by the Thuringian forest.

suicide self-murder. Until 1961 it was a criminal offence in English law, if committed while of sound mind. In earlier times it was punished by the confiscation of the suicide's possessions. Even until 1823 burial was at night, without burial service, and with a stake through the heart. To aid and abet another's suicide is an offence, and euthanasia, or mercy killing, may amount to aiding in this context. In 1988, there were 4,193 suicides in England and Wales. Four times as many young men kill themselves as women in the UK.

Where there is a suicide pact and one survives, he or she may be charged with ◊manslaughter. In Japan ◊hara-kiri is considered honourable. There are 140,000 suicides a year in China, 70% of whom are women.

suite in music, formerly a grouping of old dance forms; later the term came to be used to describe a set of instrumental pieces, sometimes assembled from a stage work, such as Tchaikovsky's *Nutcracker Suite* 1891–2.

Sukarno /su:'ka:nəʊ/ Achmed 1901–1970. Indonesian nationalist, president 1945–67. During World War II he cooperated in the local administration set up by the Japanese, replacing Dutch rule. After the war he became the first president of the new Indonesian republic, becoming president-for-life 1966; he was ousted by ◊Suharto.

Sukkur /su'kʊə/ or *Sakhar* port in Sind province, Pakistan, on the Indus; population (1981) 191,000. The Sukkur-Lloyd Barrage 1928–32 lies to the west.

Sulawesi /su:lə'weɪsi/ (formerly *Celebes*) island in E Indonesia, one of the Sunda Islands; area (with dependent islands) 190,000 sq km/73,000 sq mi; population (1980) 10,410,000. It is mountainous and forested, and produces copra and nickel.

Suharto General Suharto, president of Indonesia.

Suleiman /su:li'ma:n/ or *Solyman* 1494–1566. Ottoman sultan from 1520, known as *the Magnificent* and *the Lawgiver*. Under his rule the Ottoman Empire flourished and reached its largest extent. He made conquests in the Balkans, the Mediterranean, Persia, and N Africa, but was defeated at Vienna 1529 and Valletta 1565. He was a patron of the arts, a poet, and an administrator.

Suleiman captured Belgrade 1521, the Mediterranean island of Rhodes 1522, defeated the Hungarians at Mohács 1526, and was halted in his advance into Europe only by his failure to take Vienna, capital of the Austro-Hungarian Empire, after a siege Sept–Oct 1529. In 1534 he turned more successfully against Persia, and then in campaigns against the Arab world took almost all N Africa and the Red Sea port of Aden. Only the Knights of Malta inflicted severe defeat on both his army and fleet when he tried to take Valletta 1565.

Sulla /'sʌlə/ Lucius Cornelius 138–78 BC. Roman general and politician, a leader of the senatorial party. Forcibly suppressing the democrats in 88 BC, he departed for a successful campaign against ◊Mithridates VI of Pontus. The democrats seized power in his absence, but on his return Sulla captured Rome and massacred all opponents. As dictator, his reforms, which strengthened the Senate, were backward-looking and short-lived. He retired 79 BC.

Sullivan /'sʌlɪvən/ Arthur (Seymour) 1842–1900. English composer who wrote operettas in collaboration with William Gilbert, including *HMS Pinafore* 1878, *The Pirates of Penzance* 1879, and *The Mikado* 1885. Their partnership broke down 1896. Sullivan also composed serious instrumental, choral, and operatic works—for example, the opera *Ivanhoe* 1890—which he valued more highly than the operettas. Other Gilbert and Sullivan operettas include *Patience* (which ridiculed the Aesthetic movement) 1881, *The Yeomen of the Guard* 1888, and *The Gondoliers* 1889.

Sullivan /'sʌlɪvən/ Jim 1903–1977. Welsh-born rugby player. A great goal-kicker, he kicked a record 2,867 points in a 25-year Rugby League career covering 928 matches.

He played Rugby Union for Cardiff before joining Wigan RLFC in 1921. He kicked 193 goals in 1933–34 (a record at the time) and against Flimby and Fothergill in 1925 he kicked 22 goals, still a record.

CAREER HIGHLIGHTS

for Wigan 1921–46
Appearances: 774; tries: 66; goals: 2,317; points: 4,883
for Great Britain 1924–34
tries: 0; goals: 64; Appearances: 25

Sullivan /'sʌlɪvən/ Louis Henry 1856–1924. US architect, who worked in Chicago and designed early skyscrapers such as the Wainwright Building, St Louis, 1890 and the Guaranty Building,

Buffalo, 1894. He was influential in the anti-ornament movement. Frank Lloyd ◊Wright was his pupil.

Sully /sjuːˈliː/ Maximilien de Béthune, Duc de Sully 1560–1641. French politician, who served with the Protestant ◊Huguenots in the wars of religion, and, as Henry IV's superintendent of finances 1598–1611, aided French recovery.

Sully-Prudhomme /sjuːˈliː pruːˈdɒm/ Armand 1839–1907. French poet, who wrote philosophical verse including *Les Solitudes/Solitude* 1869, *La Justice/Justice* 1878, and *Le Bonheur/Happiness* 1888. Nobel prize 1901.

sulphate a salt or ester derived from sulphuric acid. It is characterized by the SO_4^{2-} ion (salt) or SO_4 group (ester).

If only one of the hydrogen atoms from the sulphuric acid reacts with a base or alcohol, the resulting product is a hydrogen sulphate (bisulphate), which still has acidic properties.

sulphide a compound of sulphur and another element, in which sulphur is the more ◊electronegative element. Sulphides occur in a number of minerals. Some of the more volatile sulphides have extremely unpleasant odours (hydrogen sulphide smells of bad eggs).

sulphite a salt or ester derived from sulphurous acid. It is characterized by the SO_3^{2-} anion (salt) or SO_3 group (ester).

sulphonamide drug any of a group of compounds containing the chemical group sulphonamide SO_2NH_2, or its derivatives, which were, and still are in places, used to treat bacterial diseases.

Sulphonamide was the first commercially available antibacterial drug. The identification of sulphonilamide, a bacteriostatic (halting growth) compound in the textile dye prontosil red, led to the development of Prontosil, the forerunner of a large group of sulphonamides. Toxicity and increasing resistance have limited their use chiefly to the treatment of urinary-tract infection.

sulphur a non-metallic element, symbol S, atomic number 16, relative atomic mass 32.066. It is a pale yellow, odourless, brittle solid. Insoluble in water, but soluble in carbon disulphide, it is a good electrical insulator. It is widely used in the manufacture of sulphuric acid and in chemicals, explosives, matches, fireworks, dyes, fungicides, drugs, and in vulcanizing rubber, particularly for tyres.

There are two crystalline forms and an allotropic plastic form. It resembles oxygen chemically, and can replace this element to form innumerable organic and inorganic compounds. It was known in ancient times.

sulphur dioxide SO_2 a pungent gas, produced by burning sulphur in air or oxygen. It is used widely for disinfecting food vessels and equipment, and as a preservative in some food products. It occurs in industrial flue gases and is a major cause of ◊acid rain.

sulphuric acid H_2SO_4 (also called *oil of vitriol*) a dense, oily, colourless liquid which gives out heat when added to water. It is used extensively in the chemical industry, petrol refining, and in manufacturing fertilizers, detergents, explosives, and dyes.

sulphurous acid (chemical formula H_2SO_3) a solution of sulphur dioxide (SO_2) in water. It is a weak acid.

Sulu Archipelago /ˈsuːluː ˌɑːkɪˈpeləgəʊ/ group of about 870 islands off SW Mindanao in the Philippines, between the Sulawesi and Sulu seas; area 2,700 sq km/1,042 sq mi; population (1980) 361,000. The capital is Jolo, on the island (the largest) of the same name. Until 1940 the islands were an autonomous sultanate.

Sumatra /suːˈmɑːtrə/ or **Sumatera** second largest island of Indonesia, one of the Sunda Islands; area 473,600 sq km/182,800 sq mi; population (1980) 28,016,000. East of a longitudinal volcanic mountain range is a wide plain; both are heavily forested. Products include

rubber, rice, tobacco, tea, timber, tin, and petroleum.

Northern Sumatra is rapidly being industrialized, and the Asakan river (rising in Lake Toba) was dammed for power 1974. The main towns are Palembang, Padang, and Benkuelen.

history A Hindu empire was found in the 8th century, but Islam was introduced by Arab traders from the 13th century, and by the 16th century was adopted throughout the island.

Sumer /ˈsuːmə/ area of S Iraq where the Sumerian civilization was established; part of Babylonia (see ◊Babylon).

Sumerian civilization the world's earliest civilization, which arose about 3400 BC in lower Mesopotamia (modern Iraq); it is known to have had a city-state, with priests as secular rulers, and a common culture. Cities included ◊Lagash, ◊Eridu, and ◊Ur.

summer camp in the USA, a place in the country where children are sent without their parents during summer vacation; they offer outdoor recreation (such as hiking, swimming, and canoeing) as well as nature studies and crafts. Summer camps developed in the 1900s. Similar camps exist in France (*colonies de vacances*).

summer time practice (introduced in the UK 1916) whereby legal time from spring to autumn is an hour in advance of Greenwich mean time. Continental Europe 'puts the clock back' a month earlier than the UK in autumn. British summer time was permanently in force Feb 1940–Oct 1945 and Feb 1968–Oct 1971. Double summer time (2 hours in advance) was in force in summer 1941–45 and 1947. In North America the practice is known as *daylight saving time*.

summons in law, a court order officially delivered, requiring someone to appear in court on a certain date. It is used for appearances at ◊magistrates courts and county courts, and for procedural matters in higher courts.

Sumner /ˈsʌmnə/ James 1887–1955. US biochemist. In 1926 he succeeded in crystallizing the enzyme urease and demonstrating its protein nature. For this work Sumner shared the 1946 Nobel Prize for Chemistry with John Northrop and Wendell Stanley. Despite the loss of an arm as a youth, Sumner spent his entire career as an experimental chemist at Cornell University, New York.

sumo wrestling national sport of Japan. Fighters of larger than average size (rarely less than 130 kg/21 st) try to push, pull, or throw each other out of a circular ring. Fighters follow a traditional diet and eat a great deal to build up body

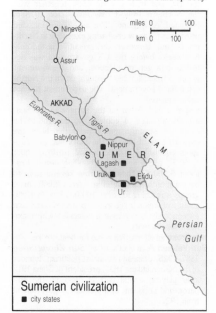

Sumerian civilization
■ city states

sumo wrestling *A sumo wrestling exhibition match in Paris, France, 1986.*

weight. In the ring, they try to get their centre of gravity as low to the ground as possible. Championships, lasting up to 15 days each, are held six times a year in Japan, and thousands of fans watch the contests live and on television. Sumo wrestling originated as a religious ritual performed at Shinto shrines. In the 17th and 18th centuries it evolved into a popular spectator sport.

sumptuary law a law restraining excessive individual consumption, such as expenditure on dress, or attempting to control religious or moral conduct. The Romans had several sumptuary laws; for example the *lex Orchia* in 181 BC limited the number of dishes at a feast. In England sumptuary laws were introduced by Edward III and Henry VII.

Sun the ◊star at the centre of the solar system. Its diameter is 1,392,000 km/865,000 mi, its temperature at the surface about 6,000K, and at the centre 15,000,000K. It is composed of about 70% hydrogen and 30% helium, with other elements making up less than 1%. The Sun generates energy by nuclear fusion reactions that turn hydrogen into helium at its centre. It is about 4,700 million years old, with a predicted lifetime of 10,000 million years. At the end of its life, it will expand to become a ◊red giant the size of Mars' orbit, and then shrink to become a ◊white dwarf.

The Sun spins on its axis every 25 days near its equator, but more slowly towards the poles. Its rotation can be followed by watching the passage of dark ◊sunspots across its disc. Sometimes bright eruptions called ◊flares occur near sunspots. Above the Sun's ◊photosphere lies a layer of thinner gas called the ◊chromosphere, visible only in special instruments or at eclipses. Tongues of gas called ◊prominences extend from the chromosphere into the corona, a halo of hot, tenuous gas surrounding the Sun. Gas boiling from the corona streams outwards through the solar system, forming the ◊solar wind. Activity on the Sun, including sunspots, flares, and prominences, waxes and wanes during the *solar cycle*, which peaks every 11 years or so.

Sunbelt popular name given to a region of the USA, south of Washington DC, between the Pacific and Atlantic coasts, because of its climate.

Sunbury-on-Thames /ˈsʌnbəri ɒn ˈtemz/ market town and boating centre in Surrey, NE England, on the river Thames; population (1981) 39,000.

Sun City /ˈsʌn ˈsɪti/ alternative name for ◊Mmabatho, resort in Bophuthatswana, South Africa.

Sunda Islands /ˈsʌndə/ islands west of the Moluccas, in the Malay Archipelago, the greater number belonging to Indonesia. They are so named because they lie largely on the Indonesian extension of the Sunda continental shelf. The *Greater Sundas* include Borneo, Java (including

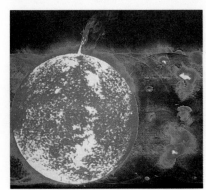

Sun *Ultraviolet image of the solar disc and solar prominence, recorded by the Skylab space station in 1973.*

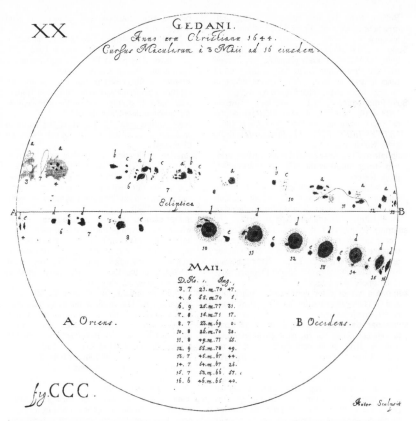

sunspot A line drawing by Hevelius of sunspots observed as long ago as May 1644. Usually occurring in groups, sunspots may influence the Earth's climate.

the small island of Madura), Sumatra, Sulawesi, and Belitung. The **Lesser Sundas** (Indonesian *Nusa Tenggara*) are all Indonesian, and include Bali, Lombok, Flores, Sumba, Sumbawa, and Timor.

sun dance a North American Indian ceremony, performed by ◊Plains Indians.

Sunday seventh day of the week, when banks and offices are generally closed. In the Christian religion Sunday is set aside for worship in commemoration of Christ's resurrection (replacing the Jewish ◊Sabbath). In the UK activities such as shopping and the drinking of alcohol have been restricted since medieval times on this day; in 1969 curbs on sports, theatres, and dancing were lifted. A bill to enable widespread Sunday trading was defeated Apr 1986. Similar legislation in the USA has long been very laxly enforced, and in some cases repealed.

Sunderland /'sʌndələnd/ port in Tyne and Wear, England; population (1981) 196,150. Industries were formerly only coalmining and shipbuilding, but have now diversified to electronics, glass, and furniture. There is a polytechnic and a civic theatre, the Sunderland Empire.

Sunderland /'sʌndələnd/ Robert Spencer, 2nd Earl of Sunderland 1640–1702. English politician, a sceptical intriguer who converted to Roman Catholicism to secure his place under James II, and then reverted with the political tide. In 1688 he fled to Holland (disguised as a woman), where he made himself invaluable to the future William III. Now a Whig, he advised the new king to adopt the system, which still prevails, of choosing the government from the dominant party in the Commons.

sundew insectivorous plant, genus *Drosera*, with viscid hairs on the leaves for catching prey.

sundial instrument measuring time by means of a shadow cast by the Sun. Almost completely superseded by the invention of clocks, it survives ornamentally in gardens. The dial is marked with the hours at graduated distances, and a style or gnomon (parallel to Earth's axis and pointing to the north) casts the shadow.

Sundsvall /'sundsvæl/ port in E Sweden; population (1986) 93,000. It has oil, timber, and wood-pulp industries.

sunfish marine fish *Mola mola* with disc-shaped body 3 m/10 ft long, found in all temperate and tropical oceans. The term also applies to fish of the North American freshwater Centrarchidae family, which have compressed, almost circular bodies, up to 80 cm/2.6 ft long, and are nestbuilders and avid predators.

sunflower plant of the genus *Helianthus*, family Compositae. The **common sunflower** *Helianthus annuus*, probably native to Mexico, grows to 4.5 m/15 ft in favourable conditions. It is commercially cultivated in central Europe and the USSR for the oil-bearing seeds that follow the yellow-petalled flowers.

Sungari /'suŋgəri/ river in Manchuria, NE China, which joins the Amur on the Siberian frontier; length 1,300 km/800 mi.

Sunni a member of the larger of the two main sects of ◊Islam, with about 680 million adherents. Sunni Muslims believe that the first four caliphs were all legitimate successors of the prophet Muhammad, and that guidance on belief and life should come from the Koran and the Hadith, and from the Shari'a, not from a human authority or spiritual leader. Imams in Sunni Islam are educated lay teachers of the faith and prayer leaders.

Sunningdale Agreement an agreement reached by the UK and Irish governments, together with the Northern Ireland executive, Dec 1973 in Sunningdale, England. The agreement included provisions for a power-sharing executive in Northern Ireland. However, the executive lasted only five weeks before the UK government was defeated in a general election, and a subsequent general strike May 1974 brought down the Northern Ireland government. The experiment has not been repeated.

sunspot a dark patch on the surface of the Sun, actually an area of cooler gas, thought to be caused by strong magnetic fields that block the outward flow of heat to the Sun's surface. Sunspots consist of a dark central **umbra**, about 4,000 K, and a lighter surrounding **penumbra**, about 5,500 K. They last from several days to over a month, ranging in size from 2,000 km to groups stretching for over 100,000 km. In 1989, a study of weather records in Britain showed that exceptionally heavy rainfall coincides with maximum solar activity.

sunstroke an alternative name for heat stroke.

Sun Yat-sen /'sʌn ˌjæt'sen/ or **Sun Zhong Shan** 1867–1925. Chinese nationalist politician, founder of the ◊Guomindang 1894, president of China 1912 after playing a vital part in deposing the emperor, and president of a breakaway government from 1921.

Sun Yat-sen was the son of a Christian farmer. After many years in exile he returned to China during the 1911 revolution that overthrew the Manchu dynasty and was provisional president of the republic 1912. The reactionaries, however, soon gained the ascendant, and he broke away to try to establish an independent republic in S China based on Canton. He was criticized for lack of organizational ability, but his 'three people's principles' of nationalism, democracy, and social reform are accepted by both the Guomindang and the Chinese communists.

Sun Zhong Shan /'sʌn ˌdzʌŋ'ʃɑːn/ Pinyin transliteration of ◊Sun Yat-sen.

Super Bowl US football contest, inaugurated 1966. It is the annual end-of-season match between the American Football Conference (AFC) and National Football Conference (NFC) champions. See ◊football, American.

supercomputer the fastest, most powerful type of computer, capable of performing its basic operations in picoseconds (thousand-billionths of a

Sun Yat-sen *The founder of the nationalist Guomindang party, and the guiding force behind the Chinese revolution in 1911.*

second), rather than nanoseconds (billionths of a second) as most other computers do.

Supercomputers use several processors working together and other techniques (such as cooling processors down to nearly ◊absolute zero temperature so that their components conduct electricity many times faster than normal) to achieve this enormous increase in speed.

superconductivity in physics, increase in electrical conductivity at low temperatures. The resistance of some metals and metallic compounds decreases uniformly with decreasing temperature until at a critical temperature (the superconducting point), within a few degrees of absolute zero (0 K/–273°C), the resistance suddenly falls to zero.

In this superconducting state, an electric current will continue indefinitely after the magnetic field has been removed, provided that the material remains below the superconducting point. In 1986 IBM researchers achieved superconductivity with some ceramics at –243°C; Paul Chu at the University of Houston, Texas, achieved superconductivity at –179°C, a temperature that can be sustained using liquid nitrogen.

Some metals, for example platinum and copper, do not become superconductive; as the temperature decreases, their resistance decreases to a certain point, but then rises again. Superconductivity can be nullified by the application of a large magnetic field. Superconductivity has been produced in a synthetic organic conductor which would operate at much higher temperatures, thus cutting costs.

The phenomenon was discovered by the Dutch scientist Kamerlingh Onnes (1853–1926) in 1911. A high-temperature superconductivity research centre was opened in Cambridge, England, 1988.

supercooling in physics, the lowering in temperature of a ◊saturated solution without crystallization taking place, forming a supersaturated solution. Usually crystallization rapidly follows the introduction of a small (seed) crystal or agitation of the supercooled solution.

superego in Freudian psychology, the element of the human mind concerned with the ideal, responsible for ethics and self-imposed standards of behaviour. It is characterized as a form of conscience, restraining the ◊ego, and responsible for feelings of guilt when the moral code is broken.

supergiant the largest and most luminous type of star known, with a diameter of up to 1,000 times that of the Sun and absolute magnitudes of between –5 and –9.

Superior, Lake /suːˈpɪərɪə/ largest of the ◊Great Lakes, and the second largest lake in the world; area 83,300 sq km/32,200 sq mi.

superior planet a planet that is farther away from the Sun than the Earth.

Superman comic-strip hero created 1938 in the USA by writer Jerome Siegel and artist Joseph Shuster, later featured in television, films, and other media.

Superman was the first comic-book superhero. Born on the planet Krypton, he has extraordinary powers and can fly; he is vulnerable only to kryptonite. Between feats of crime-fighting or rescuing accident victims, he leads an ordinary life as a bespectacled journalist, Clark Kent.

In the writings of German philosopher ◊Nietzsche, his ideal future human being was the ◊*Übermensch*, or Superman.

supermarket a large self-service shop selling food and household goods. The first was introduced by US retailer Clarence Saunders in Memphis, Tennessee, 1919.

supernova the explosive death of a star, which temporarily attains a brightness of 100 million Suns or more, so that it can shine as brilliantly as a small galaxy for a few days or weeks.

Type I supernovae are thought to occur in ◊binary star systems in which gas from one star falls on to a white dwarf, causing it to explode.

Type II supernovae occur in stars ten times

or more as massive as the Sun, which suffer runaway internal nuclear reactions at the ends of their lives, leading to an explosion. These are thought to leave behind ◊neutron stars and ◊black holes. Gas ejected by the explosion causes an expanding radio source, such as the ◊Crab Nebula. Supernovae are thought to be the main source of elements heavier than hydrogen and helium.

The last supernova occurring in our Galaxy was in 1604, but they occur in other galaxies. In 1987 a supernova visible to the unaided eye occurred in the Large ◊Magellanic Cloud, a small neighbouring galaxy. Eta Carinae, visible in the southern hemisphere, may become a supernova in a few hundred years.

superpower term used to describe the USA and the USSR from the end of World War II 1945, when they emerged as significantly stronger than all other countries.

supersaturation in chemistry, the state of a solution that has a higher concentration of ◊solute than would normally be obtained in a ◊saturated solution.

Many solutes have a higher ◊solubility at high temperatures. If a hot saturated solution is cooled slowly, sometimes the excess solute does not come out of solution. This is an unstable situation and the introduction of a small solid particle will encourage the release of excess solute.

supersonic speed speed greater than that at which sound travels, measured in ◊Mach numbers. In dry air at 0°C, it is about 1,170 kph/727 mph, but decreases with altitude until, at 12,000 m/ 39,000 ft, it is only 1,060 kph, remaining constant above that height.

When an aircraft passes the ◊sound barrier, shock waves are built up which give rise to ◊sonic boom, often heard at ground level. Squadron Leader John Derry (UK) was the first to achieve supersonic flight, in a De Havilland 108 research aircraft, 6 Sept 1948.

superstring theory mathematical theory developed in the 1980s to explain the properties of the ◊fundamental particles and the forces between them (in particular, gravity and the nuclear forces) in a way that combines ◊relativity and ◊quantum theory. In string theory, the fundamental objects in the universe are not pointlike particles but extremely small stringlike objects. These objects exist in a universe of ten dimensions, although, for reasons not yet understood, only three space dimensions and one dimension of time are discernable. There are many unresolved difficulties with superstring theory, but some physicists think it may be the ultimate 'theory of everything' that explains all aspects of the universe within one framework.

supplementary benefit in Britain, former name (1966–88) for *income support*, weekly ◊social security payments by the state to those with low incomes.

The payments were called national assistance 1948–66 in Britain and consisted of a weekly payment made by the government to individuals whose income was considered to be lower than a legally determined minimum and who did not qualify for contributory benefits such as unemployment benefit or earnings-related pensions. Until 1983 it included housing subsidies. The theory of such a system, to catch those falling through the benefits 'act', formed part of the ◊Beveridge Report.

supply in economics, the production of goods or services for a market in anticipation of an expected ◊demand. There is no guarantee that supply will match actual demand.

supply and demand one of the fundamental approaches to economics, which examines and compares the supply of a good with its demand (usually in the form of a graph of supply and demand curves plotted against price). For a typical good, the supply curve is upward sloping (the higher the price, the more the manufacturer is willing to sell), while the demand curve is downward-sloping (the

cheaper the good, the more demand there is for it). The point where the curves intersect is the equilibrium at which supply equals demand.

support environment in computing, a collection of programs (◊software) used to help people to design and write other programs. At its simplest, this includes a ◊text editor (word-processing software) and a ◊compiler for translating programs into executable form; but can also include interactive debuggers for helping to locate faults, data dictionaries for keeping track of the data used, and rapid prototyping tools for producing quick, experimental mock-ups of programs.

suprarenal gland another name for the ◊adrenal gland.

Supremacy, Acts of two acts of the English Parliament 1534 and 1559, which established Henry VIII and Elizabeth I respectively as head of the English church in place of the pope.

Suprematism Russian abstract-art movement developed about 1913 by ◊Malevich. The Suprematist paintings gradually became more severe, until in 1918 they reached a climax with the *White on White* series showing white geometrical shapes on a white ground.

Suprematism was inspired in part by Futurist and Cubist ideas. Early paintings such as *Black Square* 1915 (Russian Museum, Leningrad) used purely geometrical shapes in bold dynamic compositions. The aims of the movement were expressed by Malevich as 'the supremacy of pure feeling or perception in the pictorial arts—the expression of non-objectivity'.

Supreme Court highest US judicial tribunal, composed of a chief justice (William Rehnquist from 1986) and eight associate justices. Appointments are made by the president, and members can be removed only by impeachment. In Britain, the Supreme Court of Judicature is made up of the Court of Appeal and the High Court.

Supremes, the US vocal group, pioneers of the Motown sound, formed 1959 in Detroit, from 1962 a trio comprising, initially, Diana Ross (1944–), Mary Wilson (1944–), and Florence Ballard (1943–76). The most successful female group of the 1960s, they had a string of pop hits beginning with 'Where Did Our Love Go?' 1964 and 'Baby Love' 1964. Diana Ross left for a solo career 1969.

Sur /suːə/ or *Soûr* Arabic name for the Lebanese port of ◊Tyre.

Surabaya /ˌsuərəˈbaɪə/ port on the island of Java, Indonesia; population (1980) 2,028,000. It has oil refineries and shipyards, and is a naval base.

Suraj-ud-Dowlah /suːˈrɑːdʒ ud daʊlə/ 1728–1757. Nawab of Bengal, India. He captured Calcutta from the British 1756 and imprisoned some of the British in the ◊Black Hole of Calcutta, but was defeated 1757 by Robert ◊Clive, and lost Bengal to the British at the Battle of ◊Plassey. He was killed in his capital, Murshidabad.

Surat /suːˈrɑːt/ city in Gujarat, W India, at the mouth of the Tapti; population (1981) 932 32,000. The chief industry is textiles. The first East India Company trading post in India was established here 1612.

surd term for the mathematical root of a quantity that can never be exactly expressed because it is an ◊irrational number, for example, $\sqrt{3} = 1.73205\ldots$.

Sûreté the criminal investigation department of the French police.

surface area to volume ratio the ratio of an animal's surface area (the area covered by its skin) to its total volume. This is high for small animals, but low for large animals such as elephants.

The ratio is important for endothermic (warm-blooded) animals because the amount of heat lost by the body is proportional to its surface area, whereas the amount generated is proportional to its volume. Very small birds and mammals, such as hummingbirds and shrews, lose a lot of heat and need a high intake of food to maintain their body temperature. Elephants, on the other hand, are in danger of overheating, which is why they have no fur.

surface tension in physics, the property that causes the surface of a liquid to behave as if it were covered with a weak elastic skin; this is why a needle can float on water. It is caused by cohesive forces between water ◊molecules. Allied phenomena include the formation of droplets and the ◊capillary action by which water soaks into a sponge.

surfing sport of riding on the crest of large waves while standing on a narrow, keeled surfboard, usually of light synthetic material, about 1.8 m/5 ft long, as first developed in Hawaii and Australia. ◊Windsurfing is a recent development.

surgeon fish fish of the tropical marine family Acanthuridae. It has a flat body up to 50 cm/1.7 ft long, is brightly coloured, and has a moveable spine on each side of the tail which can be used as a weapon.

surgery in medicine, originally the removal of diseased parts or foreign substances from the body. The surgeon now uses not only the scalpel and electric cautery, but beamed high-energy ultrasonic waves, binocular magnifiers for microsurgery, and the intense light energy of the laser.

There are many specialized fields, including cardiac (heart), orthopaedic (bones and joints), ophthalmic (eye), neuro (brain and nerves), thoracic (chest), and renal (kidney) surgery. Modern extensions of the field of surgery include:

microsurgery for which the surgeon uses a binocular microscope, magnifying 25 times, for example in rejoining a severed limb. Sewing of the nerves and blood vessels is done with a nylon thread so fine that it is only just visible to the naked eye. Restoration of movement and sensation may be comparatively limited;

plastic surgery repair of damaged tissue (for example skin grafts for burns) and restructuring of damaged or deformed parts of the body; also *cosmetic surgery* for serious aesthetic reasons, when the patient is psychologically damaged by injury or deformity, and for reasons of vanity, as in removal of bags under the eyes or a double chin;

transplant surgery the transfer of an embryo, genetic material, an organ, tissue, and so on, from one part of the body to another, or to another body. Under the UK transplant code of 1979 covering the use of material from a donor, two doctors (being both independent of the tranplant team and clinically independent of each other) must certify the brain death of the donor.

surgical spirit ◊ethanol to which has been added a small amount of methanol to render it unfit to drink. It is used to sterilize surfaces and to cleanse skin abrasions and sores.

Suriname /ˌsuərɪˈnæm/ country on the northern coast of South America, on the Atlantic coast, between Guyana and French Guiana.

government The constitution was suspended in 1980 and in 1982 an interim president took office as head of state, with ultimate power held by the army through its commander-in-chief who is also chair of the Supreme Council, the country's controlling group. A nominated 31-member national assembly was established in Jan 1985, consisting of 14 military, 11 trade union, and six business nominees. It was given 27 months in which to prepare a new constitution.

history For early history, see ◊American Indian, ◊South America. Founded as a colony by the English 1650, Suriname became Dutch in 1667. In 1954, as Dutch Guiana, it was made an equal member of the Kingdom of the Netherlands, with internal self-government. Full independence was achieved in 1975, with Dr Johan Ferrier as president and Henck Arron, leader of the mainly Creole Suriname National Party (NPS), as prime minister. In 1980 Arron's government was overthrown in an army coup but President Ferrier refused to recognize the military regime and appointed

Suriname
Republic of

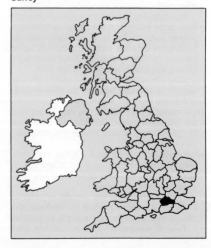

area 163,800 sq km/63,243 sq mi
capital Paramaribo
physical hilly and forested, with flat coast
features river Surinam
head of state and government Ramsewak Shankar from 1988
government democratic republic
political parties Party for National Unity and Solidarity (KTPI)*, Indonesian, left-of-centre; Suriname National Party (NPS)*, Creole, left-of-centre; Progressive Reform Party (VHP)*, Indian, left-of-centre; National Democratic Party (NDP), nationalist, left-of-centre

*members of Front for Democracy and Development (FDD)
exports bauxite, rice, citrus, timber
currency Suriname guilder (3.30 = £1 Feb 1990)
population (1989) 400,000 (Creole, Chinese, Hindu, and Indonesian peoples); annual growth rate 1.1%
life expectancy men 66, women 71
language Dutch, English (both official)
religion Christian 35%, Hindu 25%, Muslim 17%
literacy 90% male/90% female (1985)
GNP $1.2 bn (1983); $2,600 per head of population
chronology
1954 Granted internal self-government as Dutch Guiana.
1975 Achieved full independence with Dr Johan Ferrier as president and Henck Arron as prime minister. About 40% of the population, especially those of East Indian origin, emigrated to the Netherlands.
1980 Arron's government overthrown in an army coup but Ferrier refused to recognize the military regime and appointed Dr Henk Chin A Sen to lead a civilian administration. Army replaced Ferrier with Dr Chin A Sen.
1982 Army, led by Lt-Col Desi Bouterse, seized power, setting up a Revolutionary People's Front.
1985 Ban on political activities lifted.
1987 New constitution approved.
1988 Ramsewak Shankar elected president.

Dr Henk Chin A Sen, of the Nationalist Republican Party, to head a civilian administration. Five months later the army staged another coup and President Ferrier was replaced by Dr Chin A Sen. The new president announced details of a draft constitution which would reduce the army's role in government, whereupon the army, led by Lt-Col Desi Bouterse, dismissed Dr Chin A Sen and set up the Revolutionary People's Front.

There followed months of confusion in which a state of siege and then martial law were imposed. In the period Feb 1980–Jan 1983 there were no fewer than six attempted coups by different army groups. Because of the chaos, Netherlands and US aid was stopped and Bouterse turned to Libya and Cuba for assistance. The partnership between the army, the trade unions, and business, which had operated since 1981, broke up in 1985 and Bouterse turned to the traditional parties that had operated before the 1980 coup: the NPS, the left-wing Indian VHP and the Indonesian KTPI. The ban on political activity was lifted and leaders of the three main parties were invited to take seats on the Supreme Council, with Wym Udenhout as prime minister. The Nov 1987 election was won by the three-party FDD and Rameswak Shankar was elected president of the National Assembly. In Mar 1989 a new constitution was approved prior to an election in Nov.

Surrealism movement in art, literature, and film, which developed out of ◊Dada around 1922. Led by André ◊Breton, who produced the *Surrealist Manifesto* 1924, the Surrealists were inspired by the thoughts and visions of the subconscious mind. They explored highly varied styles and techniques, and the movement was a dominant force in Western art between World Wars I and II.

Surrealism followed the Freudian theory of the unconscious. In art it encompassed ◊Masson's automatic drawings, paintings based on emotive semi-abstract forms (Ernst, Miró, Tanguy), and dreamlike images painted in a realistic style (Dali, Magritte). The poets Aragon and Eluard and the film-maker Buñuel were also part of the movement.

Surrey /ˈsʌri/ county in S England
  area 1,660 sq km/641 sq mi

towns administrative headquarters Kingston upon Thames; Guildford, Woking
features rivers Thames, Mole, and Wey; Box and Leith Hills; North Downs; Runnymede, Thameside site of the signing of ◊Magna Carta; Yehudi ◊Menuhin School; Kew Palace and Royal Botanic Gardens
products market garden vegetables, agricultural products, service industries
population (1987) 1,000,000
famous people John Galsworthy.

Surrey /ˈsʌri/ Henry Howard, Earl of Surrey *c.*1517–1547. English courtier and poet, executed on a poorly based charge of high treason. With ◊Wyatt, he introduced the sonnet to England, and was a pioneer of blank verse.

surrogacy the practice whereby a woman becomes pregnant with the intention of handing over the resultant child to a couple (of whom the man may be the natural father, usually by artificial insemination), usually in return for payment. It is illegal (since 1985) in the UK. Such commercial surrogacy is practised in some European

Surrey

Sutherland Study for Origins of the Land *(1950) Courtauld Collection, London.*

countries and in the USA. See also ◊embryo research.

Surtees /'sɜːtiːz/ John 1934– . British racing driver and motorcyclist, the only person to win world titles on two and four wheels.

After winning seven world motorcycling titles 1956–60, he turned to motor racing and won the world title in 1964. He later produced his own racing cars, but with little success.

CAREER HIGHLIGHTS

motorcycling
world titles:
350cc: 1958–60 (all MV Agusta)
500cc: 1956, 1958–60 (all MV Agusta)
Isle of Man TT titles:
Senior TT: 1956, 1958–60 (all MV Agusta)
Junior TT: 1958–59 (all MV Agusta)
motor racing
world champion: 1964 (Ferrari)
Formula One Grand Prix:
races: 111; wins: 6
first: 1960 (Monaco Grand Prix; Lotus)
last: 1972 (Italian Grand Prix; Surtees)

Surtsey /'sɜːtsi/ a volcanic island 20 km/12 mi SW of Heimaey in the Westman islands of Iceland. The island was created following an underwater volcanic eruption Nov 1963.

surveying the accurate measurements of the Earth's crust, or of land features or buildings. It is used to establish boundaries, and to evaluate the topography for engineering work. The measurements used are both linear and angular, and geometry and trigonometry are applied in the calculations.

Sūrya /'suəriə/ in Hindu mythology, the Sun god, son of the sky god Indra. His daughter, also named Surya, is a female personification of the Sun.

Susa /'suːzə/ (French *Sousse*) port and commercial centre in NE Tunisia; population (1984) 83,500. It was founded by the Phoenicians, and has Roman ruins.

suslik type of ground ◊squirrel.

suspension in physics, a colloidal state consisting of small solid particles dispersed in a liquid or gas (see ◊colloid).

Susquehanna /ˌsʌskwɪˈhænə/ river rising in central New York state, USA, and flowing 715 km/444 mi to Chesapeake Bay. It is used for hydroelectric power. On the strength of its

musical name, Samuel ◊Coleridge planned to establish a Pantisocratic (communal) settlement here with his fellow poet Robert Southey.

Sussex /'sʌsɪks/ former county of England, on the south coast, now divided into ◊East Sussex and ◊West Sussex. According to tradition, the Saxon Ella landed here 477, defeated the inhabitants, and founded the kingdom of the South Saxons which was absorbed by Wessex 825.

sustained-yield cropping in ecology, the removal of surplus individuals from a ◊population of organisms so that the population maintains a constant size. This usually requires selective removal of animals of all ages and both sexes to ensure a balanced population structure. Excessive cropping of young females, for example, may lead to fewer births in following years, and a fall in population size. Appropriate cropping frequencies can be determined from an analysis of a ◊life table.

Sutcliff /'sʌtklɪf/ Rosemary 1920– . British historical novelist, who writes for both adults and children. Her books include *The Eagle of the Ninth* 1954, *Tristan and Iseult* 1971, and *The Road to Camlann* 1981.

Sutherland /'sʌðələnd/ Donald 1934– . Canadian film actor, usually in offbeat roles. He starred in *M.A.S.H.* 1970, and his subsequent films include *Klute* 1971, *Don't Look Now* 1973, and *Revolution* 1986.

Sutherland /'sʌðələnd/ Earl Wilbur 1915–1974. US physiologist, discoverer of a chemical 'messenger' made by a special enzyme in the wall of living cells. Many hormones operate by means of this messenger. Nobel prize 1971.

Sutherland /'sʌðələnd/ Graham (Vivian) 1903–1980. English painter, graphic artist, and designer, active mainly in France from the late 1940s. He painted portraits, landscapes, and religious subjects.

In the late 1940s Sutherland turned increasingly to characterful portraiture, for example *Somerset Maugham* 1949 (Tate Gallery, London). His portrait of *Winston Churchill* 1954 was disliked by its subject and eventually burned on the instructions of Lady Churchill (studies survive). His *Christ in Glory* tapestry 1962 is in Coventry Cathedral. Other work includes ceramics and designs for posters, stage costumes and sets.

Sutherland /'sʌðələnd/ Joan 1926– . Australian soprano. She went to England in 1951, where she

made her debut the next year in *The Magic Flute*; later roles included *Lucia di Lammermoor*, Donna Anna in *Don Giovanni*, and Desdemona in *Otello*.

Sutherlandshire /'sʌðələndʃə/ former county of Scotland. In 1975 it was merged with Highland Region. Dornoch was the administrative headquarters.

Sutlej /'sʌtlɪdʒ/ river in Pakistan, a tributary of the river ◊Indus; length 1,370 km/851 mi.

sūtra in Buddhism, discourse attributed to the historical Buddha. In Hinduism, the term generally describes any sayings that contain moral instruction.

suttee Hindu custom whereby a widow committed suicide on her husband's funeral pyre, often under public and family pressure. Banned in the 17th century by the Mogul emperors, it was made illegal under British rule 1829. There have been sporadic revivals; in 1988 a public ceremony took place in Rajasthan and a temple was erected on the site.

Sutton /'sʌtn/ borough of S Greater London; population (1981) 168,000. It was the site of Nonsuch Palace built by Henry VIII, which was demolished in the 17th century.

Sutton Coldfield /'sʌtn 'kəʊldfiːld/ a residential part of the West Midlands conurbation around ◊Birmingham, England; population (1981) 103,000.

Sutton Hoo /'sʌtn 'huː/ village near Woodbridge, Suffolk, England, where in 1939 a Saxon ship burial was excavated. It is the funeral monument of Raedwald, king of the East Angles, who died about 624 or 625. The jewellery, armour, and weapons discovered were placed in the British Museum, London.

Sutton-in-Ashfield /'sʌtn ɪn 'æʃfiːld/ town in Nottinghamshire, England; population (1981) 41,000. It has coal, hosiery, and plastics industries.

suture a surgical stitch used to draw together the edges of a wound.

Suva /'suːvə/ capital and industrial port of Fiji, on Viti Levu; population (1981) 68,000. It produces soap and coconut oil.

Suvorov /su'vɔːrɒv/ Aleksandr Vasilyevich 1729–1800. Russian field marshal, victorious against the Turks 1787–91, the Poles 1794, and the French army in Italy 1798–99 in the Revolutionary Wars.

Suzhou /ˌsuːˈdʒəʊ/ formerly ***Soochow*** and ***Wuhsien*** 1912–49 city on the ◊Grand Canal, in Jiangsu province, China; population (1983) 670,000. It has embroidery and jade-carving traditions, and Shizilin and Zhuozheng gardens.

Suzhou The Tiger Hill Pagoda near Suzhou, China. *Built in 961, it is five degrees out of perpendicular, making the top 2 m out from the vertical.*

The city dates from about 1000 BC, and the name Suzhou from the 7th century AD; it was reputedly visited by Marco ◊Polo.

Suzman /'suzmən/ Helen 1917– . South African politician and human-rights activist. A university lecturer concerned about the inhumanity of the apartheid system, she joined the white opposition to the ruling National Party and became a strong advocate of racial equality, respected by black communities inside and outside South Africa. In 1978 she received the UN Human Rights Award. She retired from active politics in 1989.

Suzuki /su'zu:ki/ Zenko 1911– . Japanese politician. Originally a socialist member of the Diet in 1947, he became a conservative (Liberal Democrat) in 1949, and was prime minister 1980–82.

Svalbard /'sva:lbɑ:/ Norwegian archipelago in the Arctic Ocean. The main island is Spitsbergen; other islands include North East Land, Edge Island, Barents Island, and Prince Charles Foreland
area 62,000 sq km/23,938 sq mi
towns Long Year City on Spitsbergen
features weather and research stations. Wildlife includes walrus and polar bear; fossil palms show that it was in the tropics 40 million years ago
products coal, phosphates, asbestos, iron ore, and galena are mined by the USSR and Norway
population (1982) 4,000, including 1,450 Norwegians and 2,500 Russians
history under the *Svalbard Treaty* 1925, Norway has sovereignty, but allows free scientific and economic access to others.

Svedberg /'sved,beri/ Theodor 1884–1971. Swedish chemist. In 1924 he constructed the first ultracentrifuge, a machine that allowed the rapid separation of particles by mass. Nobel Prize for Chemistry 1926.

Svengali a person who moulds another into a performer and masterminds their career. The original Svengali was a character in the novel *Trilby* 1894 by George ◊Du Maurier.

Sverdlovsk /svɪəd'lovsk/ formerly *Ekaterinburg* (until 1924) industrial town in W USSR, in the E foothills of the Urals; population (1987) 1,331,000. Industries include copper, iron, platinum, engineering, and chemicals. ◊Nicholas II and his family were murdered here 1918.

Svetambara ('white-clad') member of a sect of Jain monks (see ◊Jainism), who wear a white loincloth.

Svevo /'sveɪvəʊ/ Italo. Pen name of Ettore Schmitz 1861–1928. Italian novelist, whose books include *As a Man Grows Older* 1898 and *Confessions of Zeno* 1923.

Swabia /'sweɪbiə/ (German *Schwaben*) historic region of SW Germany, an independent duchy in the Middle Ages. It includes Augsburg and Ulm, and forms part of the *Länder* (states) of Baden-Württemberg, Bavaria, and Hessen.

Swahili people living along the coast of Kenya and Tanzania. The Swahili are not an isolated group, but are part of a mixed coastal society engaged in fishing and trading.

Swahili language a language of Bantu origin and strongly influenced by Arabic, a widespread ◊lingua franca of E Africa and the national language of Tanzania (1967) and Kenya (1973).

swallow insect-eating bird of the family Hirundinidae, found worldwide. It has a dark-blue back, brown head and throat, and pinkish breast. Its tail feathers are forked, and its wings are long and narrow.

The *common swallow Hirundo rustica* winters in Africa and visits Europe Apr–Sept. It feeds in flight. Two broods a year are reared in nests of mud and straw shaped like a half-saucer and built on ledges.

Swallows and Amazons the first of a series of novels by British author Arthur ◊Ransome, published in the UK 1930–47, describing the adventures of children on holiday, set in the English Lake District and East Anglia, and always involving boats.

Swallows and Amazons 1930 introduces the two families featuring in most of the series, the Walk-

Swaziland
Kingdom of

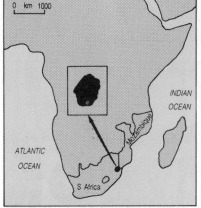

area 17,400 sq km/6,716 sq mi
capital Mbabane
physical central valley; mountains in W
features landlocked enclave between South Africa and Mozambique
head of state and government King Mswati III from 1986
government near-absolute monarchy
political parties Imbokodvo National Movement (INM), nationalistic monarchist
exports sugar, citrus, timber, asbestos, iron ore
currency lilangeni (4.33 = £1 Feb 1990)
population (1989) 757,000; annual growth rate 3%
life expectancy men 47, women 50
language Swazi 90%, English (both official)
religion Christian, both Protestant and Catholic; animist
literacy 70% male/66% female (1985 est)
GNP $610 million (1983); $790 per head of population
chronology
1967 Achieved internal self-government.
1968 Achieved full independence from Britain, within the Commonwealth, as the Kingdom of Swaziland, with King Sobhuza II as head of state.
1973 The king suspended the constitution and assumed absolute powers.
1978 New constitution adopted.
1982 King Sobhuza died and his place was taken by one of his wives, Dzeliewe, until his son, Prince Makhosetive, reached the age of 21.
1983 Queen Dzeliewe ousted by another wife, Ntombi.
1984 After a royal power struggle, it was announced that the crown prince would become king at the age of 18.
1986 Crown prince formally invested as King Mswati III.
1987 A power struggle developed between the advisory council Liqoqo and Queen Ntombi over the accession of the king. Mswati dissolved parliament and a new government was elected with Sotsha Dlamini as prime minister.

ers and the Blacketts, and their sailing dinghies, *Swallow* and *Amazon* respectively. Later books in the series include *Peter Duck* 1932, *Pigeon Post* 1936, and *We Didn't Mean to Go to Sea* 1937.

swami title of respect for a Hindu teacher.

swamp low-lying, permanently waterlogged tract of land, often overgrown with plant growth.

swamp cypress species of tree of the genus ◊*Taxodium*.

swan large long-necked bird of the duck family. The *mute swan Cygnus olor* is up to 150 cm/5 ft long, has white plumage, an orange bill with a black knob surmounting it, and black legs; the voice is a harsh hiss. Pairing is generally for life, and the young (cygnets) are at first grey, later brownish. It is wild in eastern Europe, and semi-domesticated in the west.

Other species include the *whooper Cygnus cygnus* of N Europe and Asia, and *Bewick's swan Cygnus bewicki*, both rare in Britain; the *black swan* of Australia, *Cygnus atratus*; and the North American *trumpeter swan Cygnus buccinator*. In England the swan is a royal bird, since it was once highly valued as food. On the Thames, at the annual 'swan-upping', the cygnets are still marked on the beak as either the property of the crown or of the two privileged City of London companies, the Dyers and Vintners.

Swan /swɒn/ Joseph Wilson 1828–1914. English inventor of the incandescent filament electric lamp, and of bromide paper for use in photography.

Swanage /'swɒnɪdʒ/ town on the Isle of Purbeck, ◊Dorset, England.

Swansea /'swɒnzi/ (Welsh *Abertawe*) port and administrative headquarters of West Glamorgan, S Wales, at the mouth of the river Tawe where it meets the Bristol Channel; population (1981) 168,000. It has oil refineries and metallurgical industries, and is the vehicle licensing centre of the UK.

Swanson /'swɒnsən/ Gloria. Stage name of Gloria Josephine Mae Svenson 1897–1983. US actress, a star of silent films who retired in 1932 but made several comebacks. Her work includes *Sadie

Thompson 1928, *Queen Kelly* 1928 (unfinished), and *Sunset Boulevard* 1950.

SWAPO *South West African People's Organization* organization formed 1959 in South West Africa (now ◊Namibia) to oppose South African rule. SWAPO guerrillas, led by Sam Nujoma, began attacking with support from Angola. In 1966 SWAPO was recognized by the United Nations as the legitimate government of Namibia, and won the first independent election 1989.

swastika cross in which the bars are extended at right angles in the same clockwise or anticlockwise direction. An ancient good-luck symbol in both the New and the Old World and an Aryan and Buddhist mystic sign, it was adopted by Hitler as the emblem of the Nazi Party and incorporated into the German national flag 1935–45.

Swatow /,swɑ:'taʊ/ another name for the Chinese port of ◊Shantou.

Swazi inhabitant of Swaziland. The Swazi are primarily engaged in cultivating and raising livestock, but many work in industries in South Africa. The Swazi language belongs to the Bantu branch of the Niger-Congo family.

Swazi kingdom Southern African kingdom, established by Sobhuza (died about 1840) as a result of the ◊Mfecane disturbances, and named after his successor Mswati (ruled 1840–75).

Swaziland /'swɑ:zɪlænd/ country in SE Africa, bounded by Mozambique and the Transvaal province of South Africa.

government Swaziland is a monarchy within the Commonwealth. Under the 1978 constitution the monarch is head of both state and of government, and chooses the prime minister and cabinet. There is a two-chamber legislature, the *Libandla*, consisting of a 20-member senate and a 50-member house of assembly. Ten senators are appointed by the sovereign and ten elected by and from an 80-member electoral college, made up of two representatives from each of the country's 40 chieftancies (*Tinkhundla*). Forty of the House of Assembly deputies are also elected by the electoral college, with the remaining ten appointed by the monarch.

The constitution makes the Imbokodvo National Movement (INM) the only legal political party, although there are at least three opposition groups based outside Swaziland.

history for early history, see ◊African history, ◊South Africa. Its original autonomy guaranteed by Britain and the Transvaal, Swaziland became a special High Commission territory in 1903. The South African government repeatedly asked for Swaziland to be placed under its jurisdiction but this call was resisted by the British government as well as the people of Swaziland. In 1967 the country was granted internal self-government and 1968 full independence within the Commonwealth, with King Sobhuza II as head of state. In 1973 the king suspended the constitution and assumed absolute powers. In 1978 the new constitution was announced.

King Sobhuza died in 1982 and the role of head of state passed to the queen mother, Dzeliwe, until the king's heir, Prince Makhosetive, should reach the age of 21 in 1989, but a power struggle developed within the royal family. Queen Dzeliwe was ousted by another of King Sobhuza's wives, Ntombi, who became queen regent in Oct 1983, and in Apr 1986 the crown prince was finally invested as King Mswati III. He has a supreme advisory body, the *Liqoqo*, all of whose 11 members are appointed by him.

Swaziland needs to maintain good relations with South Africa as well as with other African states, and this has often been difficult, since the formerly banned African National Congress (ANC) tried to use it as a base.

sweat gland a ◊gland within the skin of mammals which produces surface perspiration. Primatial sweat glands are distributed over the whole body, but in most mammals are more localized; in cats and dogs they are normally restricted to the feet and around the face.

sweatshop a workshop or factory where employees work long hours for poor wages. Conditions are generally poor and employees may be under the legal working age. Sweatshops exist either because (a) factory and employment legislation exists but is not complied with (as with many factories in the East End of London employing illegal immigrants who are unable to complain), or (b) legislation does not exist or does not apply (as with homeworkers, numbering about 1 million in the UK in 1990, and very small companies). In less-developed countries children are often employed.

In Britain, under the Trade Boards Act 1909, four sweated trades (lacemaking, tailoring, chain making, and cardboard-box making) were given a minimum wage. Others were added 1913.

swede annual or biennial plant *Brassica napus*, widely cultivated for its edible root, which is purple, white, or yellow. It is similar in taste to the turnip *Brassica rapa* but is of greater food value, firmer fleshed, and longer keeping. The yellow variety is commonly known as *rutabaga*.

Sweden /'swi:dn/ country in N Europe on the Baltic Sea, bounded to the W by Norway and to the NE by Finland.

government Sweden has a hereditary monarch as formal head of state and a popularly elected government. The constitution from 1809, several times amended, is based on four fundamental laws: the Instrument of Government Act, the Act of Succession, the Freedom of the Press Act, and the Riksdag Act. The *Riksdag* is a single-chamber parliament of 349 members, elected by universal suffrage, through a system of proportional representation, for a three-year term.

The prime minister is nominated by the Speaker of the *Riksdag* and confirmed by a vote of the whole house. The prime minister chooses a cabinet and all are then responsible to the *Riksdag*. The king or queen now has a purely formal role; the normal duties of a constitutional monarch, such as dissolving parliament and deciding who should be asked to form an administration, are undertaken by the Speaker.

history S Sweden has been inhabited since about 6000 BC. The Swedish Vikings in 800–1060 AD sailed mainly E and founded the principality of ◊Novgorod. In the mid-12th century the Swedes in the N were united with the Goths in the S and accepted Christianity. A series of crusades in the 12th–14th centuries brought Finland under Swedish rule. Sweden, Norway, and Denmark were united under a Danish dynasty 1397–1520. ◊Gustavus Vasa was subsequently elected king of Sweden; he established Lutheranism as the state religion 1527. The Vasa line ruled until 1818, when the French marshal Bernadotte established the present dynasty.

Sweden's territorial ambitions led to warfare in Europe in the 16th–18th centuries (see ◊Gustavus Adolphus, ◊Thirty Years' War, ◊Charles X, ◊Charles XII) which left the country impoverished. Science and culture flourished under Gustavus III 1771–91. Sweden lost Finland to Russia 1809 but seized Norway 1814, a union dissolved 1905.

Sweden has a long tradition of neutrality and political stability, and a highly developed social welfare system. The office of ombudsman is a Swedish invention and Sweden was one of the first countries to adopt a system of open government.

The Social Democratic Labour Party (SAP) was continuously in power 1951–76, usually in coalition. In 1969 the leadership of the party changed hands and Olof Palme became prime minister. He carried out two major reforms of the constitution, reducing the chambers in parliament from two to one 1971, and 1975 removing the last of the monarch's constitutional powers. In 1976 the general election was fought on the issue of the level of taxation needed to fund the welfare system and Palme was defeated. Thorbjorn Fälldin, leader of the Centre Party, formed a centre-right coalition

government. The Fälldin administration fell 1978 over its wish to follow a non-nuclear energy policy and it was replaced by a minority Liberal government led by Ola Ullsten. Fälldin returned 1979, heading another coalition, and in a referendum the following year there was a narrow majority in favour of continuing with a limited nuclear-energy programme. Fälldin remained in power until 1982, when the Social Democrats, with Olof Palme, returned with a minority government. Palme was soon faced with deteriorating relations with the USSR, arising from suspected violation of Swedish territorial waters. The situation had improved substantially by 1985. After the general election in that year, Palme's party had 159 *Riksdag* seats and he was able to continue with Communist support. In Feb 1986 Olof Palme was murdered by an unknown assailant in the centre of Stockholm. His deputy, Ingvar Carlsson, took over as prime minister and leader of the SAP. In the Sept 1988 general election Carlsson and the SAP were re-elected with a reduced majority and in Feb 1990, with mounting opposition to its economic policies, the government resigned, leaving Carlsson as a caretaker prime minister.

Swedenborg /'swi:dnbɔ:g/ Emanuel 1688–1772. Swedish theologian and philosopher. He trained as a scientist, but from 1747 concentrated on scriptural study, and in *Divine Love and Wisdom* 1763 concluded that the Last Judgment had taken place 1757, and that the **New Church**, of which he was the prophet, had now been inaugurated. His writings are the scriptures of the sect popularly known as Swedenborgians, and his works are kept in circulation by the Swedenborg Society, London.

Swedish architecture the architecture of Sweden. *medieval* The Romanesque cathedrals of Uppsala (brick) and Lund (stone) are from the 11th century. Gothic churches include Riddarholms church in Stockholm and the cathedral in Linköping. The

---

Sweden
Kingdom of
(Konungariket Sverige)

area 450,000 sq km/173,745 sq mi
capital Stockholm
towns Göteborg, Malmö, Uppsala, Norrköping, Västera
physical mountains in the NW; plains in the south; much of the land is forested
features many lakes, for example Väner, Vätter, Mälar, Hjälmar; islands of Öland and Gotland; large herds of wild elk
head of state Carl XVI Gustaf from 1973
head of government Ingvar Carlsson from 1986
government constitutional monarchy
political parties Social Democratic Labour party (SAP), moderate, left-of-centre; Moderate Party, right-of-centre; Liberal Party, centre-left; Centre Party, centrist; Christian Democratic Party, Christian, centrist; Left (Communist) Party, European, Marxist
exports aircraft, cars, domestic equipment,

ballbearings, drills, missiles, electronics, petrochemicals, textiles, furnishings, ornamental glass
currency krona (10.44 = £1 Feb 1990)
population (1989) 8,371,000 (including 1,200,000 postwar immigrants from Finland, Turkey, Yugoslavia, Greece); annual growth rate 0.1%
life expectancy men 73, women 79
language Swedish, one of the Scandinavian division of Germanic languages
religion Christian (Evangelical Lutheran)
literacy 99% (1984)
GNP $88 bn (1983); $14,821 per head of population
chronology
12th century United as an independent nation.
1397–1520 Under Danish rule.
1914–45 Neutral in both World Wars.
1951–76 Social Democratic Labour Party (SAP) in power.
1969 Olof Palme became SAP leader and prime minister.
1971 Constitution amended, creating a single-chamber parliament.
1975 Monarch's constitutional powers reduced.
1976 Thorbjörn Fälldin, leader of the Centre Party, became prime minister, heading centre-right coalition.
1982 SAP, led by Palme, returned to power.
1985 SAP won the largest number of seats in parliament and formed a minority government, with communist support.
1986 Olof Palme murdered in Stockholm. Ingvar Carlsson became prime minister and SAP party leader.
1988 SAP re-elected with reduced majority; Green Party increased its vote dramatically.
1990 SAP government resigned.

former Hanseatic city of Visby, Gotland, has three Gothic churches and the ruins of 12 more; some medieval domestic buildings have also survived there within the old city wall.

16th century This was a time for building and rebuilding castles under German Renaissance influence. Examples are Gripsholm, Vadstena, and Kalmar.

17th century Three architects emerged who had studied Baroque in Rome: Jean de la Vallée (1620–96), Nicodemus Tessin the Elder (1615–81), and his son Nicodemus Tessin the Younger (1654–1728). Together or separately they created several important buildings in Stockholm and elsewhere, for example Drottningholm Palace, begun 1662.

18th century Rococo prevailed in midcentury and left its traces mostly in interiors, for example the Royal Palace in Stockholm.

early 19th century Neo-Classical architecture includes what is now the State Historical Museum, Stockholm.

late 19th–early 20th century Jugend style, exemplified by the Royal Dramatic Theatre, Stockholm, gave way to a domestic nationalist style with simple lines, built in brick and granite, used in many public and residential buildings.

mid–late 20th century Modernism took off in Sweden in the 1930s.

Swedish art painting and sculpture of Sweden. A geometrically stylized dragon ornament characterized Swedish art and crafts before and during the Viking period. Bright and cheerful folk art flourished in church and secular decorations from the Middle Ages into the 19th century. Although the main movements in European art have successively taken hold in Sweden, artists have repeatedly returned to a national tradition.

5000–500 BC Animal pictures carved in or painted on rock can be found in central Sweden.

500 BC–11th century AD Bronze and gold jewellery; memorial stones carved with runes and ornaments.

12th–16th centuries Woven tapestries show the geometrically stylized animals that also occur in jewellery and carvings. Churches were decorated with lively, richly ornamented frescoes. Wooden sculptures were initially stiff and solemn, later more realistic and expressive.

17th century Sculptors and portrait painters who had studied Italian Baroque were patronized by Sweden's rulers.

18th century Swedish Rococo was more restrained than its French models; chinoiserie was popular because of Swedish trade with the orient. Alexander Roslin (1718–93) was one of several portrait painters who continued their career in France. Rococo was supplanted towards the end of the century by a light Neo-Classical style known as Gustavian. The sculptor J T Sergel based his strong, sensual work on studies of ancient art in Rome.

19th century Academic history painting was superseded by the work of artists influenced by the French Impressionists and by the nationalist spirit current in many countries. The watercolour interiors by Carl Larsson (1853–1919) of his home were hugely popular. Anders Zorn (1860–1920) loved colour and nudes. Bruno Liljefors (1860–1939) specialized in paintings of animals.

early 20th century The Romantic nationalist Jugend style can be seen in the monumental sculptures of Carl Milles (1875–1955) throughout Sweden and in the USA. Albert Engström (1869–1940) was a prolific illustrator and cartoonist. Nils von Dardel (1888–1943) was an early Surrealist painter.

late 20th century Figurative art predominated, ranging from the dreamlike, symbolic paintings of Lena Cronqvist, Åosa Moberg, and others to the realistic still-life graphics of Philip von Schantz (1928–).

Swift *Nearly all Jonathan Swift's works were published anonymously, and with the exception of* Gulliver's Travels, *he received no payment for his work.*

Swedish language a member of the Germanic branch of the Indo-European language family, spoken in Sweden and Finland and closely related to Danish and Norwegian.

Sweet /swiːt/ Henry 1845–1912. British philologist, author of works on Old and Middle English, who took to England German scientific techniques of language study. He was said to be the original of Professor Higgins in Shaw's play *Pygmalion*.

sweet cicely plant *Myrrhis odorata*, family Umbelliferae, native to S Europe; the root is eaten as a vegetable and the aniseed-flavoured leaves are used in salads.

sweet pea see ◊pea.

sweet potato tropical American plant *Ipomoea batatas*, family Convolvulaceae; the white/orange tuberous root is used as a source of starch and alcohol, and eaten as a vegetable.

sweet william biennial to perennial plant *Dianthus barbatus*, family Caryophyllaceae, native to S Europe and also known as *the bearded pink*. It is grown for its fragrant red, white, and pink flowers.

Sweyn I /sweɪn/ died 1014. King of Denmark from *c.* 986, nicknamed 'Forkbeard'. He raided England, finally conquered it in 1013, and styled himself king, but his early death led to the return of ◊Ethelred II.

swift fast-flying, short-legged bird of the family Apodidae, of which there are about 75 species, found largely in the tropics. They are 9–23 cm/4–11 in long, with brown or grey plumage, and a forked tail. They are capable of flying 110 kph/70 mph.

The *swift Apus apus*, about 16.5 cm/6.5 in long, dark brown with long swept-back wings, migrates to Europe in summer from Africa. It catches insects on the wing, and rarely perches except at the nest, even sleeping on the wing high in the air. Swifts often make colonies of nests on buildings, sticking the nest material together with saliva. The nests of the *grey-rumped swiftlet Collocalia francica* of Borneo are almost entirely solidified saliva, and are harvested for birds'-nest soup.

Swift /swɪft/ Jonathan 1667–1745. Irish satirist and Anglican cleric, author of *Gulliver's Travels* 1726, an allegory describing travel to lands inhabited by giants, miniature people, and intelligent horses. Other works include *The Tale of a Tub* 1704, attacking corruption in religion and learning; contributions to the Tory paper *The Examiner* of which he was editor 1710–11; *A Modest Proposal* 1729, which suggested that children of the poor should be eaten; and many essays and pamphlets.

Swift, born in Dublin, became secretary to the diplomat William Temple (1628–1699) at Moor Park, Surrey, where his friendship with the child 'Stella' (Hester Johnson 1681–1728) began in 1689. Returning to Ireland, he was ordained in the Church of England 1694, and in 1699 was made a prebendary of St Patrick's, Dublin. In 1710 he became a Tory pamphleteer, and obtained the deanery of St Patrick in 1713. His *Journal to Stella* is a series of letters, 1710–13, in which he described his life in London. 'Stella' remained the love of his life, but 'Vanessa' (Esther Vanhomrigh 1690–1723), a Dublin woman who had fallen in love with him, jealously wrote to her rival in 1723 and so shattered his relationship with both women. From about 1738 his mind began to fail.

swim bladder a thin-walled air-filled sac found in bony fishes, between the gut and the spine. Air enters the bladder from the gut or from surrounding ◊capillaries, and changes of air pressure within the bladder maintain buoyancy whatever the water depth.

swimming self-propulsion of the body through water. As a competitive sport there are four strokes: freestyle, breaststroke, backstroke, and butterfly. Distances of races vary between 50 and 1,500 m. Olympic-size pools are 50 m/55 yd long and have eight lanes.

Swimming has been known since ancient times, in the training of Greek and Roman warriors. Competitive swimming is known to have taken place in Japan 36 BC, and became compulsory in schools there 1603. Fear of infection prevented Europeans from swimming during the Middle Ages.

The *freestyle* stroke (also known as front crawl) is the fastest stroke. It was developed by Australians from a South Sea island technique in the early 20th century. The *breaststroke* is the slowest of the four strokes and was developed in the 16th century. The *backstroke* was developed in the 1920s and, because the swimmer's head is out of the water, makes breathing easier. The newest and second fastest of the strokes is the *butterfly*, developed in the USA in the 1930s from the breaststroke. In races the swimmers enter the water with a 'racing plunge' (a form of dive) with the exception of the backstroke, when competitors start in the water. *Synchronized swimming* is a form of 'ballet' performed in and under water. *Underwater swimming* developed with the invention of such equipment as flippers, snorkel, and self-contained underwater breathing apparatus (scuba). See also ◊diving.

swimming, synchronized a swimming discipline that demands artistry as opposed to speed. Competitors, either individual (solo) or in pairs, perform rhythmic routines to music. Points are awarded for interpretation and style. It was introduced into the Olympic swimming programme 1984.

Swinburne /'swɪnbɜːn/ Algernon Charles 1837–1909. English poet. He attracted attention with the choruses of his Greek-style tragedy *Atalanta in Calydon* 1865, but he and ◊Rossetti were attacked 1871 as leaders of 'the fleshly school of poetry', and the revolutionary politics of *Songs before Sunrise* 1871 alienated others.

Swindon /'swɪndən/ town in Wiltshire, 124 km/77 mi west of London, England; population (1981) 91,000. Since 1841 the site of the British Rail Engineering Works, it has diversified since 1950 into heavy engineering, electronics, and electrical manufacture.

swine fever virus disease (hog cholera) of pigs, almost eradicated in the UK from 1963 by a slaughter policy. *Swine flu* is a virulent form of influenza, closely resembling that in humans.

Swine vesicular disease is a virus disease (porcine enterovirus) closely resembling foot and mouth, and communicable to humans. Known in Italy and Hong Kong, it first occurred in Britain in 1972, and a slaughter policy was pursued. It may have originated in the infection of

swing-wing

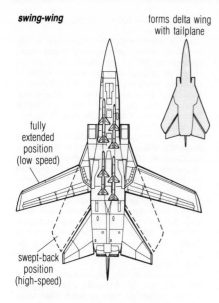

forms delta wing
with tailplane

fully
extended
position
(low speed)

swept-back
position
(high-speed)

pigs by a virus causing flu-like symptoms in humans.

Swineshead Richard active about 1350. British scientist and leading member of a group of natural scientists associated with Merton College, Oxford, who attempted to analyse and quantify the various forms of motion. Swineshead was known as the Calculator.

swing music jazz style popular in the 1930s–40s, with a simple harmonic base of varying tempo from the rhythm section (percussion, guitar, piano), and superimposed solo melodic line, for example from trumpet, clarinet, or saxophone. Exponents included Benny Goodman, Duke Ellington, and Glenn Miller.

swing-wing correctly *variable-geometry wing* an aircraft wing that can be moved during flight to provide a suitable configuration for both low-speed and high-speed flight. The British engineer Barnes ◊Wallis developed the idea of the swing-wing, now used in several aircraft, including the European Tornado and the US F-111. These craft have their wings projecting nearly at right angles for takeoff and landing and low-speed flight, but swing them back for high-speed flight.

Swinton /'swɪntən/ Ernest 1868–1951. British soldier and historian. He served in South Africa and World War I, and was the inventor of the tank in 1916.

Swiss cheese plant common name for ◊*Monstera*, plant of the Arum family.

Swiss Family Robinson, The a children's adventure story by Swiss author Johann ◊Wyss, published in German 1812–13 and greatly expanded by subsequent editors and translators. Modelled on Defoe's *Robinson Crusoe*, it tells of a Swiss family shipwrecked on a desert island and the lessons that the children of the family are taught by their adventures there.

Swithun, St /'swɪθən/ died 862. English priest, chancellor of King Ethelwolf and bishop of Winchester from 852. According to legend, the weather on his feast day (15 Jul) is said to continue as either wet or fine for 40 days.

Switzerland /'swɪtzələnd/ landlocked country in W Europe, bounded to the N by West Germany, to the E by Austria, to the S by Italy, and to the W by France.

government Switzerland is a federation of 20 cantons and six half-cantons (canton is the name for a political division, derived from Old French). The constitution dates from 1874 and provides for a two-chamber federal assembly, consisting of the National Council and the Council of States. The National Council has 200 members, elected by

Switzerland
Swiss Confederation (German *Schweiz*, French *Suisse*, Italian, *Svizzera*)

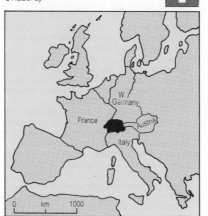

area 41,300 sq km/15,946 sq mi
capital Bern
towns Zürich, Geneva, Lausanne; river port Basel
physical most mountainous country in Europe (Alps and Jura Mountains)
features winter sports area of the upper valley of the river Inn (Engadine); lakes Maggiore, Lucerne, Geneva, Constance
head of state and government Arnold Koller

from 1990
government federal democratic republic
political parties Radical Democratic Party (FDP), radical, centre-left; Social Democratic party (SPS), moderate, left-of-centre; Christian Democratic Party (PDC), Christian, moderate, centrist; People's Party (SVP), centre-left; Liberal Party (PLS), federalist, centre-left; Green Party, ecological
exports electrical goods, chemicals, pharmaceuticals, watches, precision instruments, confectionery, banking, insurance; tourism is important
currency Swiss franc (2.53 = £1 Feb 1990)
population (1989) 6,485,000; annual growth rate 0.2%
life expectancy men 73, women 80
language German 65%, French 18%, Italian 10%, Romansch 1%
religion Roman Catholic 50%, Protestant 48%
literacy 99% (1985)
GNP $93.7 bn (1984); $14,408 per head of population
chronology
1648 Became independent of the Holy Roman Empire.
1798–1815 Helvetic Republic established by French Revolutionary armies.
1847 Civil war resulted in greater centralization.
1971 Women given the vote in federal elections.
1984 First female cabinet minister appointed.
1986 Referendum rejected a proposal for membership of United Nations.

universal suffrage, through a system of proportional representation, for a four-year term. The Council of States has 46 members, each canton electing two representatives and each half-canton one. Members of the Council of States are elected for three or four years, depending on the constitutions of the individual cantons.

The federal government is in the hands of the Federal Council, consisting of seven members elected for a four-year term by the assembly, each heading a particular federal department. The federal assembly also appoints one member to act as federal head of state and head of government for a year, the term of office beginning on 1 Jan. The federal government is allocated specific powers by the constitution and the residue is left with the cantons, each having its own constitution, assembly, and government. At a level below the cantons are more than 3,000 communes, whose populations range from fewer than 20 to 350,000. Direct democracy is encouraged through communal assemblies and referenda.

history In 1291 the cantons of Schwyz, Uri, and Lower Unterwalden formed the Everlasting League to defend their liberties against their ◊Habsburg overlords. More towns and districts joined them, and there were 13 cantons by 1513. The Reformation was accepted during 1523–29 by Zürich, Berne, and Basel, but the rural cantons remained Catholic. Switzerland gradually won more freedom from Habsburg control until its complete independence was recognized by the Treaty of Westphalia 1648.

A peasant uprising 1653 was suppressed. A French invasion 1798 established the Helvetic Republic with a centralized government; this was modified by Napoleon's Act of Mediation 1803, which made Switzerland a democratic federation. The Congress of Vienna 1815 guaranteed Swiss neutrality, and Switzerland received Geneva and other territories, increasing the number of cantons to 22. After a civil war between the *Sonderbund* (a union of the Catholic cantons Lucerne, Zug, Freiburg, and Valais) and the Liberals, a revised federal constitution, giving the central government wide powers, was introduced 1848; a further revision 1874 increased its

powers and introduced the principle of the referendum.

Switzerland, for centuries a neutral country, has been the base for many international organizations and the host of many international peace conferences. A referendum 1986 rejected the advice of the government and came out overwhelmingly against membership of the United Nations. Its domestic politics have been characterized by coalition governments and a stability that has enabled it to become one of the world's richest countries (per person).

Of several political parties, the most significant are the Radical Democratic Party, the Social Democratic Party, the Christian Democratic Party, the People's Party, and the Liberal Party. Women were not allowed to vote in federal elections until 1971. The first female cabinet minister was appointed 1984. After the Oct 1987 election, the four-party coalition continued in power, although there was a significant increase in the number of seats held by the Green Party.

swordfish fish of the family Xiphiidae, characterized by the long sword-like beak protruding from the upper jaw. They may reach 4.5 m/15 ft in length and weigh 450 kg/1,000 lbs.

sycamore tree *Acer pseudoplatanus*, native to Europe. The leaves are five-lobed, and the hanging racemes of flowers are followed by winged fruits. The timber is used for furniture making.

The sycamore was introduced to Britain by the 16th century. It is a rapidly growing and tenacious tree that displaces other trees in woodland.

Sydenham /'sɪdənəm/ Thomas 1624–1689. English physician, the first to describe measles and to recommend the use of quinine for relieving symptoms of malaria. His original reputation as 'the English Hippocrates' rested upon his belief that careful observation is more useful than speculation. *Observationes medicae* was published in 1676.

Sydney /'sɪdni/ capital and port of New South Wales, Australia; population (1986) 3,431,000. Industries include engineering, oil refining, electronics, scientific equipment, chemicals,

sycamore

clothing, and furniture. It is a financial centre, and has three universities.

history Originally a British penal colony 1788, Sydney developed rapidly following the discovery of gold in the surrounding area. The main streets still follow the lines of the original wagon tracks, and the Regency Bligh House survives. Modern landmarks are the harbour bridge (single span 503.5 m/1,652 ft) 1923–32; Opera House 1959–73; Centre Point Tower 1980.

Sydow /'si:dəʊ/ 'Max' von (Carl Adolf) 1929– . Swedish actor associated with the director Ingmar Bergman. He made his US debut as Christ in *The Greatest Story Ever Told* 1965. His other films include *The Seventh Seal* 1957, *The Exorcist* 1973, and *Hannah and her Sisters* 1985.

syenite a grey, crystalline, plutonic (intrusive) ◊igneous rock, consisting of feldspar and hornblende; other minerals may also be present, including small amounts of quartz.

Sykes /saɪks/ Percy Molesworth 1867–1945. English explorer, soldier, and administrator who surveyed much of the territory in SW Asia between Baghdad, the Caspian Sea, and the Hindu Kush during World War I (1914–18).

In 1894 he was the first British consul to Kerman (now in Iran) and Persian Baluchistan. Later he raised and commanded the South Persian Rifles. His histories of Persia and Afghanistan were published in 1915 and 1940.

Syktyvkar /,sɪktɪf'kɑː/ capital of Komi Republic, USSR; population (1987) 224,000. Industries include timber, paper, and tanning. It was founded 1740 as a Russian colony.

Sylhet /sɪl'het/ capital of Sylhet region, NE Bangladesh; population (1981) 168,000. It is a tea-growing centre, and also produces rice, jute, and sugar. There is natural gas nearby. It is the former capital of a Hindu kingdom, and was conquered by Muslims in the 14th century. In the 1971 civil war, which led to the establishment of Bangladesh, it was the scene of heavy fighting.

syllogism a set of philosophical statements devised by Aristotle in his work on logic. It establishes the conditions under which a valid conclusion follows or does not follow by deduction from given premises. The following is an example of a valid syllogism: 'All men are mortal, Socrates is a man, therefore Socrates is mortal'.

Sylvanus in Roman mythology, another name for ◊Silvanus.

Sydney *The Opera House in Sydney, Australia.*

symbiosis any close relationship between two organisms of different species, and one where both partners benefit from the association. A well-known example is the pollination relationship between insects and flowers, where the insects feed on nectar and carry pollen from one flower to another. This is sometimes known as ◊mutualism. Symbiosis in a broader sense includes ◊commensalism and ◊parasitism.

symbol in general, something that stands for something else. A symbol may be an aesthetic device, or a sign used to convey information visually, thus saving time, eliminating language barriers, or overcoming illiteracy.

Symbols are used in art and literature; for practical use in science and medicine; for road signs; and as warnings—for example a skull and crossbones to indicate dangerous contents.

symbolic interactionism sociological method, founded by the US pragmatist G H ◊Mead, that studies the behaviour of individuals and small groups through observation and description, viewing people's appearance, gestures, and language as symbols they use to interact with others in social situations. In contrast to theories such as Marxism or functionalism that attempt to analyse society as a whole, through economic or political systems, it takes a perspective of society from within, as created by people themselves.

symbolic processor a computer purpose-built to run so-called symbol-manipulation programs rather than programs involving a great deal of numerical computation. Mostly, they exist for the ◊artificial intelligence language ◊Lisp, although some have also been built to run ◊Prolog.

symbolism in the arts, the use of symbols as a device for concentrating or intensifying meaning. In particular, the term is used for a late 19th-century movement in French poetry, associated with Verlaine, Mallarmé, and Rimbaud, who used words for their symbolic rather than concrete meaning.

Symbolism a movement in late 19th-century painting that emerged in France, inspired by the trend in poetry. The subjects were often mythological, mystical, or fantastic. Gustave Moreau was a leading Symbolist painter; others included Puvis de Chavannes and Redon in France, Böcklin in Switzerland, and Burne-Jones in the UK. Statuesque female figures were often used to embody qualities or emotions.

Symington /'sɪmɪŋtən/ William 1763–1831. Scottish engineer who built the first successful steamboat. He invented the steam road locomotive 1787 and a steamboat engine 1788. His steamboat, the *Charlotte Dundas*, was completed in 1802.

symmetry the property of having similar parts arranged around a line, point, or plane. A circle is symmetrical about its centre, for example. In a wider sense, symmetry is present if a change in the system leaves the essential features of the system unchanged; for example, reversing the sign of electric charges does not change the electrical behaviour of an arrangement of charges.

Symonds /'sɪməndz/ John Addington 1840–1893. British critic, who spent much of his life in Italy and Switzerland, and campaigned for homosexual rights. He was author of *The Renaissance in Italy* 1875–86. His frank memoirs were finally published in 1984.

Symons /'sɪmənz/ Arthur 1865–1945. Welsh critic, follower of ◊Pater, and friend of Toulouse-Lautrec, Mallarmé, Beardsley, Yeats, and Conrad. He introduced Eliot to the work of Laforgue and wrote *The Symbolist Movement in Literature* 1900.

symphonic poem in music, a term originated by Liszt for his 13 one-movement orchestral works that interpret a story from literature or history, also used by many other composers. Richard Strauss preferred the title *tone poem*.

symphony a musical composition for orchestra, traditionally in four separate but closely related movements. It developed from the smaller ◊sonata form, the Italian overture, and the dance suite of the 18th century.

Haydn established the mature form of the symphony, written in slow, minuet, and allegro movements. Mozart and Beethoven (who replaced the ◊minuet with the scherzo) expanded the form, which has been developed further by successive composers: Brahms, Tchaikovsky, Bruckner, Dvořák, Mahler, Sibelius, Vaughan Williams, Piston, Prokofiev, Nielsen, Shostakovich, Stravinsky, and Copland.

symptom any change or manifestation in the body suggestive of disease as perceived by the sufferer. Symptoms are subjective phenomena. In strict usage, *symptoms* are events or changes reported by the patient; *signs* are noted by the doctor during the patient's examination.

synagogue a Jewish place of worship, also (in the USA) called a temple. As an institution it dates from the destruction of the temple in Jerusalem AD 70, though it had been in course of development from the time of the Exile in the gathering of exiles for prayer and worship. See under ◊Judaism.

In addition to the ark, the ornamental cupboard that holds the Torah scrolls, the synagogue contains a raised platform, or bimah, from which the service is conducted. There are usually two tablets above the ark inscribed with the Ten Commandments. In Orthodox synagogues women do not sit with men, but in a gallery above the main body of the synagogue.

synapse the junction between two ◊nerve cells of an animal, or between a nerve cell and a muscle. The two cells involved are not in direct contact but separated by a narrow gap called the synaptic cleft. Across this gap flow chemical ◊neurotransmitters, which have a specific effect on the receiving cell when they bind to special receptors on its surface. The response may be a nervous impulse in a nerve cell, for example contraction in a muscle cell.

Synapsida mammal-like reptiles living 315–195 million years ago, whose fossil record is largely complete, and who were for a long time the dominant land animals.

syncline geological term for a fold in the rocks of the Earth's crust in which the layers or ◊beds dip inwards, thus forming a trough-like structure with a sag in the middle. The opposite, with the beds arching upwards, is an ◊anticline.

syncopation in music, the deliberate upsetting of rhythm by shifting the accent to a beat that is normally unaccented.

syncope medical term for a temporary loss of consciousness, as in ◊fainting.

syndicalism (French *syndicat* 'trade union') political movement that rejected parliamentary activity in favour of direct action, culminating in a revolutionary general strike to secure worker ownership and control of industry. The idea originated under Robert ◊Owen's influence in the 1830s, acquired its name and its more violent aspects in France from the philosopher ◊Sorel, and also reached the USA (see ◊Industrial Workers of the World). After 1918 syndicalism was absorbed in communism, although it continued to have an independent existence in Spain until the late 1930s.

syndrome in medicine, a collection of signs and symptoms that always occur together, thus characterizing a particular condition or disorder.

synecdoche (Greek 'accepted together') a ◊figure of speech that either uses the part to represent the whole ('There were some new faces at the meeting', rather than *new people*), or the whole to stand for the part ('The West Indies beat England at cricket', rather than naming the national teams in question).

synergy (Greek 'combined action') in medicine, the 'cooperative' action of two or more drugs, muscles, or organs; in architecture, the augmented strength of systems, where the strength of a wall is greater than the added total of its individual units. An example is the stone walls of early South American civilizations, not held together by cement or mortar.

Synge /sɪŋ/ J(ohn) M(illington) 1871–1909. Irish playwright, a leading figure in the Irish dramatic revival of the early 20th century. His six plays reflect the speech patterns of the Aran Islands and W Ireland. They include *In the Shadow of the Glen* 1903, *Riders to the Sea* 1904, and *The Playboy of the Western World* 1907, which caused riots at the Abbey Theatre, Dublin, when first performed.

Synge /sɪŋ/ Richard 1914– . British biochemist who investigated paper ◊chromatography. By 1940 techniques of chromatography for separating proteins had been devised. Still lacking were comparable techniques for distinguishing the amino acids that constituted the proteins. By 1944, Synge and his colleague Archer Martin had worked out a procedure, known as ascending chromatography, which filled this gap and won them the 1952 Nobel Prize for Chemistry.

synodic period the interval between successive ◊oppositions of a superior planet (those from Mars outwards) or inferior ◊conjunctions of an inferior planet (Venus or Mercury).

synonymy near or identical meaning between or among words. There are very few strict synonyms in any language, although there may be many near-synonyms, depending upon the contexts in which the words are used. Thus 'brotherly' and 'fraternal' are synonyms in English, but a 'brotherhood' is not exactly the same as a 'fraternity'.

synovial fluid a viscous yellow fluid that bathes movable joints between the bones of vertebrates. It nourishes and lubricates the ◊cartilage at the end of each bone.

synovitis inflammation of the lining of a joint, caused by injury or infection.

Syntax, Doctor a fictional cleric invented by William Combe (1741–1823), who appeared in a series of verse satires, with drawings by Thomas ◊Rowlandson. The first was *Doctor Syntax in Search of the Picturesque* 1809.

synthesizer device that uses electrical components to produce sounds, such as conventional musical instruments, or in free creativity. In *pre-set synthesizers*, the sound of various instruments is produced by a built-in computer-type memory. In *programmable synthesizers* any number of new instrumental or other sounds may be produced at the will of the performer. *Speech synthesizers* can break down speech into 128 basic elements (allophones), which are then combined into words and sentences, as in the voices of electronic teaching aids; see ◊speech synthesis.

In pre-set synthesizers the memory triggers all the control settings required to produce the sound of a trumpet or violin. For example, the 'sawtooth' sound wave produced by a violin is artificially produced by an electrical tone generator, or oscillator, and then fed into an electrical filter set to have the resonances characteristic of a violin body.

synthetic an artificial material made from chemicals. Many of the materials used in everyday life are artificial, including plastics (polythene, polystyrene), ◊synthetic fibres (nylon, acrylics, polyesters), synthetic resins, and synthetic rubber. Plastics are made mainly from petroleum chemicals by ◊polymerization, in which small molecules are joined to make very large ones.

synthetic in philosophy, a term employed by ◊Kant to describe a judgment in which the predicate is not contained within the subject; for example, 'The flower is blue' is synthetic, since every flower is not blue. It is the converse of ◊analytic.

synthetic fibre an artificial fibre, unknown in nature. There are two kinds of artificial fibres. One is made from natural materials that have been chemically processed in some way; ◊rayon, for example, is made by processing the cellulose in woodpulp. The other type is the true synthetic

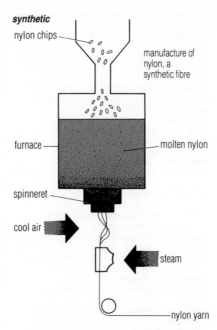

synthetic

nylon chips

manufacture of nylon, a synthetic fibre

furnace

molten nylon

spinneret

cool air

steam

nylon yarn

fibre, made entirely from chemicals. ◊Nylon was the original synthetic fibre, made from chemicals obtained from petroleum (crude oil).

Fibres are drawn out into long threads or filaments, usually by so-called 'spinning' methods, melting or dissolving the parent material and then forcing it through the holes of a perforated plate, or spinneret.

syphilis a venereal disease caused by the spiral-shaped bacterium (spirochete) *Treponema pallidum*. Untreated, it runs its course over many years, starting with a hard sore, or chancre, developing on the genitals within a month of infection, and leading to blindness, insanity, and death.

With widespread availability of antibiotics, syphilis is now increasingly rare in the developed world. Certainly the final stage of the disease (paralysis and dementia) is hardly ever seen. However, there remain the risks that the disease may go undiagnosed, or that it may affect a baby in the womb.

Syracuse /'sɪrəkjuːz/ industrial city on Lake Onondaga, in New York State, USA; population (1980) 170,000. Industries include the manufacture of electrical and other machinery, paper, and food processing. There are canal links with the ◊Great Lakes, and the Hudson and St Lawrence rivers. Syracuse was founded 1805 on the site of an ◊Iroquois Indian capital.

Syracuse /'saɪrəkjuːz/ (Italian *Siracusa*) industrial port (chemicals, salt) in E Sicily; population (1988) 124,000. It has a cathedral and remains of temples, aqueducts, catacombs, and an amphitheatre. Founded 734 BC by the Corinthians, it became a centre of Greek culture, especially under the elder and younger ◊Dionysius. After a three-year siege it was taken by Rome 212 BC. In 878 it was destroyed by the Arabs, and the rebuilt town came under Norman rule in the 11th century.

Syria /'sɪrɪə/ country in W Asia, on the Mediterranean, bounded to the N by Turkey, to the E by Iraq, to the S by Jordan, and to the SW by Israel and Lebanon.

government The 1973 constitution provides for a president elected by universal adult suffrage for a seven-year term, who appoints and governs with the help of a prime minister and a council of ministers. There is a single-chamber legislature, the 195-member *Majlis al-Sha'ab*, also elected by universal adult suffrage.

history Syria was originally divided between various small kingdoms that fought against

Israel and were subdued by the Assyrians. It was subsequently occupied by Babylonia, Persia, and Macedonia, but gained prominence under Seleucus Nicator, founder of ◊Antioch 300 BC, and ◊Antiochus the Great. After forming part of the Roman and Byzantine empires, it was conquered by the Saracens 636. During the Middle Ages Syria was the scene of many of the Crusaders' exploits.

Syria was part of the ◊Ottoman Empire 1516–1918. It was occupied by British and French troops 1918–19 and in 1920 placed under French mandate. Syria became independent 1946 and three years later came under military rule.

In 1958 Syria merged with Egypt, to become the United Arab Republic (UAR), but after an army coup 1961 Syria seceded and the independent Syrian Arab Republic was established. In 1963 a government was formed, mainly from members of the Arab Socialist Renaissance (Ba'ath) Party, but three years later the army removed it. In 1970 the moderate wing of the Ba'ath Party, led by Lt-Gen Hafez al-Assad, secured power in a bloodless coup and in the following year Assad was elected president.

Since then President Assad has remained in office without any serious challenges to his leadership. He is head of state, head of government, secretary-general of the Ba'ath Arab Socialist Party, and president of the National Progressive Front (NPF), an umbrella organization for the five main socialist parties. Syria is therefore in reality, if not in a strictly legal sense, a one-party state. Since 1983 Assad's health has suffered but no obvious successor has emerged. In the 1986 elections the NPF won 151 of the 195 seats.

Externally Syria has, under President Assad, played a leading role in Middle East affairs. In the Six-Day War 1967 it lost territory to Israel and after the Yom Kippur War 1973 Israel formally annexed the Golan Heights, which had previously been part of Syria. During 1976 Assad progressively intervened in the civil war in Lebanon, eventually committing some 50,000 troops to the operations. Relations between Syria and Egypt cooled after President Sadat's Israel peace initiative 1977 and the subsequent Camp David agreement. Assad has consistently opposed US-sponsored peace moves in Lebanon, arguing that they infringed Lebanese sovereignty. He has also questioned Yasser Arafat's leadership of the Palestine Liberation Organization (PLO) and supported opposition to him.

In 1984 President Assad and the Lebanese president Amin Gemayel approved plans for a government of national unity in Lebanon, which would give equal representation to Muslims and Christians, and secured the reluctant agreement of Nabih Berri of the Shi'ite Amal Militia and Walid Joumblatt, leader of the ◊Druze. Fighting still continued, and Assad's credibility suffered, but in 1985 his authority proved sufficient to secure the release of 39 US hostages from an aircraft hijacked by the extremist Shi'ite group Hezbollah (Party of God). In Nov 1986 Britain broke off diplomatic relations after claiming to have proof of Syrian involvement in international terrorism, when a Syrian citizen attempted to blow up an Israeli plane at Heathrow, London. In July 1987 Syria instigated a crackdown on the pro-Iranian Hezbollah party. Syria has been leaning to the west, its policies in Lebanon in direct conflict with Iran's dream of an Islamic republic, and its crumbling economy has been promised Arab aid if Damascus switches allegiance. In June 1987, following a private visit by former US president Jimmy ◊Carter, Syria's relations with the US began to improve, and efforts were made to arrange the release of Western hostages in Lebanon.

Syriac language an ancient Semitic language, originally the Aramaic dialect spoken in and around Edessa (now in Turkey) and widely used in W Asia from about 700 BC to AD 700. From the

Syria
Syrian Arab Republic
(al-Jamhuriya al-Arabya as-Suriya)

area 185,200 sq km/71,506 sq mi
capital Damascus
towns Aleppo, Homs, Hama; chief port Latakia
physical mountains alternate with fertile plains and desert areas; river Euphrates
features Mount Hermon, Golan Heights; crusader castles (Krak des Chevaliers); Phoenician city sites (Ugarit)
head of state and government Hafez al-Assad from 1971
government socialist republic
political parties National Progressive Front (NPF), pro-Arab, socialist; Communist Action Party, socialist
exports cotton, cereals, oil, phosphates
currency Syrian pound (official rate 35.75 = £1 Feb 1990)
population (1989) 12,210,000; annual growth rate 3.5%

life expectancy men 61, women 64
language Arabic (official) 89%, Kurdish 6%, Armenian 3%
religion Sunni Muslim, but the ruling minority is Alawite, an Islamic sect; also Druse, again an Islamic sect
literacy 76% male/43% female (1985 est)
GNP $16.5 bn (1983); $702 per head of population
chronology
1946 Achieved full independence from France.
1958 Merged with Egypt to form the United Arab Republic (UAR).
1961 UAR disintegrated.
1967 Six-Day War resulted in the loss of territory to Israel.
1970–71 Syria supported Palestinian guerrillas against Jordanian troops.
1971 Following a bloodless coup, Hafez al-Assad became president.
1973 Israel consolidated its control of the Golan Heights after the Yom Kippur War.
1976 Substantial numbers of troops committed to the civil war in Lebanon.
1978 Assad re-elected.
1981–82 Further military engagements in Lebanon.
1982 Islamic militant uprising suppressed; 5,000 dead.
1984 Presidents Assad and Gemayel approved a plan for government of national unity in Lebanon.
1985 Assad secured the release of US hostages held in an aircraft hijacked by an extremist Shi'ite group. Assad re-elected.
1987 Improved relations with US and attempts to secure the release of western hostages in Lebanon.
1989 Diplomatic relations with Morocco restored. Continued fighting in Lebanon.

3rd to 7th centuries it was an important Christian liturgical and literary language.

syringa common, but incorrect, name for the ◊mock orange *Philadelphus*. The genus *Syringa* includes ◊lilac *Syringa vulgaris*, and is not related to mock orange.

Système International d'Unités see ◊SI units.

systemic in medicine, relating to or affecting the body as a whole. A systemic disease is one whose effects are present throughout the body, as opposed to local disease, such as ◊conjunctivitis, which is confined to one part.

systems analysis in computing, the investigation of a business activity or clerical procedure, with a view to deciding if and how it can be computerized. The analyst discusses the existing procedures with the people involved, observes the flow of data through the business, and draws up an outline specification of the required computer system (see also ◊systems design).

systems design in computing, the detailed design of an ◊application. The designer breaks the system down into component programs and designs the required input forms, screen layouts and printouts. Systems design forms a link between systems analysis and ◊programming.

System X in communications, a modular, computer-controlled, digital switching system used in telephone exchanges. System X was originally developed by the UK companies GEC, Plessey, and STC at the request of the Post Office, beginning 1969. A prototype exchange was finally commissioned 1978, and the system launched 1980. STC left the consortium in 1982.

Szczecin /ˈʃtʃetʃiːn/ (German *Stettin*) industrial (shipbuilding, fish processing, synthetic fibres, tools, iron) port on the river Oder, in NW Poland; population (1989) 391,000. A ◊Hanseatic port from 1278, it was Swedish 1648–1720, when it was taken by Prussia. It was Germany's chief Baltic port until captured by the Russians 1945, and came under Polish administration. ◊Catherine the Great was born here.

Szechwan /ˌseɪˈtʃwɑːn/ alternative spelling for the central Chinese province of ◊Sichuan.

Szeged /ˈseged/ port on river Tisza, and capital of Csongrad county, S Hungary; population (1988) 188,000. The chief industry is textiles, and the port trades in timber and salt.

Székesfehérvár /ˈseɪkeʃˌfeheəvɑː/ industrial city in W central Hungary; population (1988) 13232,000. It is a market centre for wine, tobacco, and fruit, and manufactures metal products.

Szent-Gyorgi /sentˈdʒɜːdʒi/ Albert 1893–1986. Hungarian-born US biochemist who isolated vitamin C and studied the chemistry of musclar activity. In 1928 Szent-Gyorgi isolated a substance from the adrenal glands that he named hexuronic acid; when he found the same substance in cabbages and oranges, he suspected that he had finally isolated vitamin C. Nobel Prize for Medicine 1937. In 1947 he moved to the USA.

Szilard /ˈsɪlɑːd/ Leo 1898–1964. Hungarian-born US physicist who, in 1934, was one of the first scientists to realize that nuclear fission, or atom splitting, could lead to a chain reaction releasing enormous amounts of instantaneous energy. He emigrated to the US in 1938 and there influenced ◊Einstein to advise President Roosevelt to begin the nuclear arms programme. In post-war years he turned his attention to the newly emerging field of molecular biology.

Szymanowski /ˌʃɪməˈnɒfski/ Karol (Maliej) 1882–1937. Polish composer of orchestral works, operas, piano music, and violin concertos. He was director of the Conservatoire in Warsaw from 1926.

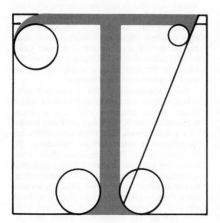

T the 20th letter of the alphabet, whose sound is usually a voiceless alveolar plosive. The earliest form was X, which the Phoenicians called *tau*, a cross or sign, but in the Greek alphabet its form was T.

t abbreviation for ◊*tonne*.

Tabah /ˈtɑːbə/ or **Taba** small area of disputed territory, 1 km long, between Eilat (Israel) to the E and the Sinai Desert (Egypt) to the W on the Red Sea. Under an Anglo-Egyptian-Turkish agreement 1906, the border ran through Tabah; under a British survey of 1915 headed by T E ◊Lawrence (who made 'adjustments' allegedly under British government orders) it runs to the east. Taken by Israel 1967, it was returned to Egypt 1989.

Table Bay /ˈteɪbəl ˈbeɪ/ inlet on the SW coast of the Cape of Good Hope, South Africa, on which Cape Town stands. It is overlooked by Table Mountain (highest point Maclear's Beacon 1,087 m/3,568 ft), the cloud often above it being known as the 'tablecloth'.

table tennis or *ping pong* indoor ball game played on a rectangular table by two or four players. It was developed in Britain about 1880 and derived from lawn tennis.

Play takes place on a table measuring 2.74 m/9 ft long by 1.52 m/5 ft wide. Across the middle is a 15.25 cm/6 in high net over which the ball must be hit. The players use a wooden bat covered in sponge or rubber. A feature of the game is the amount of spin put on the small plastic ball. Points are scored by forcing the opponent(s) into an error. The first to score 21 wins the game. Volleying is not allowed. A match may consist of three or five games. In doubles play, the players must hit the ball in strict rotation.

Tabligh (Arabic 'revival') missionary movement in Islam, which developed after 1945 and feeds the militant organizations for the 'true Islamic state'; there is an annual gathering at Tongi, near Dhaka.

Table tennis: World Champions

Swaythling Cup (men's team)	
1971	China
1973	Sweden
1975	China
1977	China
1979	Hungary
1981	China
1983	China
1985	China
1987	China
1989	Sweden
Corbillon Cup (women's team)	
1971	Japan
1973	South Korea
1975	China
1977	China
1979	China
1981	China
1983	China
1985	China
1987	China
1989	China
men's singles	
1971	Stellan Bengtsson *(Sweden)*
1973	Hsi En-Ting *(China)*
1975	Istvan Jonyer *(Hungary)*
1977	Mitsuru Kohno *(Japan)*
1979	Seiji Ono *(Japan)*
1981	Guo Yue-Hua *(China)*
1983	Guo Yue-Hua *(China)*
1985	Jiang Jialiang *(China)*
1987	Jiang Jialiang *(China)*
1989	Jan-Ove Waldner *(Sweden)*
women's singles	
1971	Lin Hui-Ching *(China)*
1973	Hu Yu-Lan *(China)*
1975	Pak Yung-Sun *(North Korea)*
1977	Pak Yung-Sun *(North Korea)*
1979	Ke Hsin-Ai *(China)*
1981	Ting Ling *(China)*
1983	Cao Yan-Hua *(China)*
1985	Cao Yan-Hua *(China)*
1987	He Zhili *(China)*
1989	Qiuo Hong *(China)*

taboo (Polynesian *tabu* 'forbidden') prohibition applied to magical and religious objects. In psychology and the social sciences the term is used for practices which are generally prohibited because of religious or social pressures; for example, incest is forbidden in most societies.

Tabora /təˈbɔːrə/ trading centre in W Tanzania; population (1978) 67,400. It was founded about 1820 by Arab traders of slaves and ivory.

Tabriz /tæˈbriːz/ city in NW Iran; population (1986) 972,000. Industries include metal casting, carpets, cotton, and silk textiles.

tabula rasa (Latin 'scraped tablet', from the Romans' use of wax-covered tablets which could be written on with a pointed stick and cleared by smoothing over the surface) a mind without any preconceived ideas.

tacet (Latin 'it is silent') in music, score indication used when an instrument is to be silent for a complete movement or section of a movement.

tachograph combined speedometer and clock which records a vehicle's speed (on a small card disc, magnetic disc, or tape) and the length of time the vehicle is moving or stationary. It is used to monitor a lorry-driver's working practice.

Tacitus /ˈtæsɪtəs/ Publius Cornelius AD *c.* 55–*c.* 120. Roman historian. A public orator in Rome, he was consul under Nerva 97–98 and proconsul of Asia 112–113. He wrote histories of the Roman Empire, *Annales* and *Historiae*, covering the years AD 14–68 and 69–97 respectively. He also wrote *Life of Agricola* 97 (he married Agricola's daughter in 77) and a description of the German tribes, *Germania* 98.

Tacna /ˈtækna/ city in S Peru; population (1988) 138,000. It is undergoing industrial development.

In 1880 Chile defeated a combined Peruvian-Bolivian army nearby, and occupied Tacna until 1929.

Tacoma /təˈkəʊmə/ port in Washington state, USA, on Puget Sound, 40 km/25 mi S of Seattle; population (1980) 483,000. Founded 1868, it developed after being chosen as the terminus of the North Pacific Railroad 1873.

Tadmur /ˈtædmʊə/ Arabic name for the ancient city of Palmyra in Syria.

Tadzhik or *Tajik* speaker of any of the Tadzhik dialects, which belong to the Iranian branch of the Indo-European family. The Tadzhiks have long been associated with neighbouring Turkic peoples and their language contains Altaic loan words. The Tadzhiks inhabit Tadzhikistan (part of the USSR) and Afghanistan.

Tadzhikistan /tæˌdʒiːkɪˈstɑːn/ constituent republic of the S central USSR from 1929, part of Soviet Central Asia
area 143,100 sq km/55,251 sq mi
capital Dushanbe
features few areas are below 3,500 m/11,000 ft; includes ◊Communism Peak; health resorts and mineral springs
products fruit, cereals, cotton, cattle, sheep, silks, carpets, coal, lead, zinc, chemicals, oil, gas
population (1987) 4,807,000; 59% Tadzhik, 23% Uzbek, 11% Russian or Ukrainian
language Tadzhik, similar to Farsi (Persian)
religion Sunni Muslim
recent history formed 1924 from the Tadzhik areas of Bokhara and Turkestan. It experienced a devastating earthquake Jan 1989 and ethnic conflict 1989–90.

Taegu /ˌteɪˈguː/ largest inland city of South Korea after Seoul; population (1985) 2,031,000.

Taejon /ˌteɪˈdʒɒn/ (Korean 'large rice paddy') capital of South Chungchong province, central South Korea; population (1985) 866,000. Korea's tallest standing Buddha and oldest wooden building are found NE of the city at Popchusa in the Mount Songnisan National Park.

tae kwon do Korean ◊martial art similar to ◊karate which includes punching and kicking. It was included in the 1988 Olympic Games as a demonstration sport.

Tafawa Balewa /təˈfɑːwə bəˈleɪwə/ Alhaji Abubakar 1912–1966. Nigerian politician, prime minister from 1957. He entered the House of Representatives 1952, was minister of works 1952–54, and minister of transport 1954–57. He was assassinated in the coup d'état Jan 1966.

taffeta (Persian 'spun') light, plainly woven silk fabric with a high lustre.

Taff Vale judgement a decision by the British law lords 1902 that trade unions were liable for their members' actions, and could hence be sued for damages in the event of a strike picketing or boycotting an employer. It resulted in a rapid growth of union membership, and was repealed by the Trades Disputes Act 1906.

Tadzhikistan

Dushanbe

Taft /tæft/ Robert Alphonso 1889–1953. US Republican senator from 1939, and a candidate for the presidential nomination 1940, 1944, 1948, and 1952. He sponsored the Taft–Hartley Labor Act 1947, restricting union power. He was the son of President William Taft.

Taft /tæft/ William Howard 1857–1930. 27th president of the USA 1909–13, a Republican. He was secretary of war 1904–08 in Theodore Roosevelt's administration, but as president his conservatism provoked Roosevelt to stand against him in the 1912 election. Taft served as chief justice of the Supreme Court 1921–30.

Taganrog /ˌtægənˈrɒg/ port in the NE corner of the Sea of Azov, S USSR, W of Rostov; population (1987) 295,000. Industries include iron, steel, metal goods, aircraft, machinery, and shoes. A museum commemorates the playwright Chekhov, who was born here.

tagging, electronic the monitoring of the movement of criminals, thus enabling them to be detained in their homes rather than in prison. In the UK, the system was being tested in Nottingham from Aug 1989. The system is already in use in the USA.

Tagliacozzi /ˌtæljəˈkɒtsi/ Gaspare 1546–1599. Italian surgeon who pioneered plastic surgery. He was the first to repair noses lost in duels or through ◊syphilis. He also carried out repair of ears. His method involved taking flaps of skin from the arm and grafting them into place.

Taglioni /tælˈjəuni/ Marie 1804–1884. Italian dancer. The most important ballerina of the Romantic era, acclaimed for her ethereal style and exceptional lightness, she was the first to use ◊pointe work, or dancing on the toes, as an expressive part of ballet rather than as sheer technique. She created many roles, including the title role in *La Sylphide* 1832, first performed at the Paris Opéra, and choreographed by her father Filippo (1771–1871). Marie's brother Paolo (1808–1884) was a choreographer and ballet master at Berlin Court Opera 1856–83, and his daughter Marie (1833–1891) danced in Berlin and London, creating many roles in her father's ballets.

Tagore /təˈgɔː/ Rabindranath 1861–1941. Bengali Indian writer, born in Calcutta. One of the most influential Indian authors of the 20th century, he translated his own verse *Gitanjali* ('song offerings') 1912 and his verse play *Chitra* 1896 into English. Nobel prize 1913.

Tagus /ˈteɪgəs/ (Spanish *Tajo*, Portuguese *Tejo*) river rising in Aragon, Spain, and reaching the Atlantic at Lisbon, Portugal; length

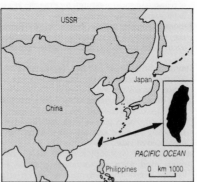

Tagore Indian writer Rabindranath Tagore photographed in 1920. He was an ardent nationalist and urged social reform. He resigned his knighthood as a gesture of protest against British repression.

1,007 km/626 mi. At Lisbon it is crossed by the April 25 (formerly Salazar) Bridge, so named in honour of the 1974 revolution. The *Tagus-Segura* irrigation scheme serves the rainless Murcia/Alicante region for early fruit and vegetable growing.

Tahiti /təˈhiːti/ largest of the Society Islands, in ◊French Polynesia; area 1,042 sq km/402 sq mi; population (1983) 116,000. Its capital is Papeete. Tahiti was visited by Capt James ◊Cook 1769 and by ◊Bligh of the *Bounty* 1788. It came under French control 1843 and became a colony 1880. It has attracted artists such as Gauguin, and modern tourists.

Tai speakers of Tai languages, all of which belong to the Sino-Tibetan family. There are over 60 million speakers of Tai languages, the majority of whom live in Thailand. Tai peoples are also found in SW China, NW Myanmar (Burma), Laos, and N Vietnam.

Tai Chi series of 108 complex, slow-motion movements, each named (for example, The White Crane Spreads its Wings) and designed to ensure effective circulation of the *chi* or intrinsic energy of the universe through the mind and body. It derives partly from the Shaolin ◊martial arts of China and partly from ◊Taoism.

taiga /ˈtaɪgə/ Russian name for heavily forested territory, some of it in the ◊permafrost zone, in Siberia. There is varied fauna and flora, in delicate balance because the conditions of life are so precarious; this ecology is threatened by railway construction, mining, and forestry. The name is also applied to similar regions elsewhere.

Taine /teɪn/ Hippolyte Adolphe 1828–1893. French critic and historian. He analysed literary works as products of period and environment, for example in *Histoire de la littérature anglaise/History of English Literature* 1863 and *Philosophie de l'art/Philosophy of Art* 1865–69.

taipan type of small-headed cobra *Oxyuranus scutellatus* found in NE Australia and New Guinea. It is about 3 m/10 ft long, and has a brown back and yellow belly. Its venom is fatal within minutes.

Taipei /ˌtaɪˈpeɪ/ (*Taibei*) capital and commercial centre of Taiwan; population (1987) 2,640,000. Industries include electronics, plastics, textiles, and machinery. The National Palace Museum 1965 houses the world's greatest collection of Chinese art, taken there from the mainland 1948.

Taiwan /ˌtaɪˈwɑːn/ country in SE Asia, officially the Republic of China, occupying the island of Taiwan between the E China Sea and the S China Sea.

government The c. 900-member National Assembly (Kuo-Min Ta-Hui) elects the president and vice-president and has power to amend the constitution of 1947. Its members, originally elected from mainland China, have retained their seats ever since their constituencies fell under Communist Chinese control 1949, and are termed 'life members'. Fresh elections have only been held for seats vacated by deceased deputies.

Taiwan's president, elected for a six-year term, is head of state, commander-in-chief of the armed forces, and promulgates laws. The president works with a cabinet, the Executive *Yuan*, headed by a prime minister (Lee Huan from 1989), responsible to a single-chamber legislature, the Legislative *Yuan*. The Legislative *Yuan* comprises 260 members, some of them presidential appointees but the majority 'life members' from former mainland seats. Since 1972, 70 vacated seats have, on average, been subject to fresh elections at three-yearly intervals. Three Control, Judicial, and Examination *Yuans* also exist, with the tasks of investigating the work of the executive, interpreting the constitution, and overseeing entrance examinations for public offices.

The dominant political force is the Nationalist Party of China (Kuomintang: KMT), which is still primarily staffed at its senior levels by pre-1949 mainlanders though their numbers are being rapidly reduced through 'natural attrition'. It is anticommunist and Chinese nationalist. The principal opposition party is the Democratic Progressive Party (DPP), which is heir to an earlier, informal, non-party 'tangwai' opposition grouping.

Taiwan
Republic of China
(Chung Hua Min Kuo)

area 36,179 sq km/13,965 sq mi
capital Taipei
towns ports Keelung, Kaohsiung
physical island (formerly Formosa) off the coast of the People's Republic of China; mountainous, with lowlands in the W
features Penghu (Pescadores), Jinmen (Quemoy), and Mazu (Matsu) islands
head of state Lee Teng-hui from 1988
head of government Lee Huan from 1989
government system emergent democracy
political parties Nationalist Party of China (Kuomintang: KMT), anti-communist, Chinese nationalist; Democratic Progressive Party (DPP), centrist-pluralist, though internally highly-factionalized, pro-self determination grouping; Workers party (Kungtang), left-of-centre.
exports with US aid, Taiwan is highly industrialized: textiles, petrochemicals, steel, plastics, electronics
currency Taiwan dollar (44.50 = £1 Mar 1990)
population (1989) 20,283,000 (89% Taiwanese, 11% mainlanders whose dominance causes resentment); annual growth rate 1.4%
language Mandarin Chinese
religion officially atheist, but traditional religions are Taoist, Confucian, and Buddhist
literacy 89% (1983)
GNP $56.6 bn (1984); $3,000 per head of population
chronology
1683 Taiwan (Formosa) annexed by China.
1895 Ceded to Japan.
1945 Recovered by China.
1949 Flight of Nationalist government to Taiwan after Chinese revolution.
1954 US-Taiwanese mutual defence treaty.
1971 Expulsion from United Nations.
1972 Commencement of legislature elections.
1975 President Chiang Kai-shek died and was replaced as Kuomintang leader by his son, Chiang Ching-kuo.
1979 US severed diplomatic relations and annulled security pact.
1986 Formation of first opposition party to the Nationalist Kuomintang.
1987 Martial law lifted.
1988 President Chiang Ching-kuo died and was replaced by Taiwanese-born Lee Teng-hui.
1989 Kuomintang win in first free assembly elections.

history Taiwan, then known as Formosa ('The Beautiful'), was settled by ◊China from the 15th century, briefly occupied by the Dutch during the mid-17th century, and annexed by the Manchu dynasty 1683. It was ceded to Japan under the terms of the Treaty of Shimonoseki after the 1895 Sino-Japanese war and not regained by China until the Japanese surrender Aug 1945.

In Dec 1949 Taiwan became the refuge for the Chinese Nationalist government forces of ◊Chiang Kai-shek which were compelled to evacuate the mainland after their defeat by the Communist troops of ◊Mao Zedong. Chiang and his Nationalist followers, though only a 15% minority, dominated the island and maintained an army of 600,000 in the hope of reconquering the mainland, over which they still claimed sovereignty. They continued to be recognized by the USA as the legitimate government of China, and occupied China's United Nations and Security Council seats until Oct 1971 when they were expelled and replaced by the People's Republic.

Taiwan was protected by US naval forces during the Korean War 1950–53 and signed a mutual defence treaty with the USA 1954. Benefiting from such security, the country enjoyed a period of rapid economic growth during the 1950s and 1960s, emerging as an export-oriented, newly industrialized country. Political power during these years was concentrated in the hands of the Kuomintang and the armed forces led by President Chiang Kai-shek, with martial law imposed and opposition activity outlawed. During the 1970s the Taiwanese government was forced to adjust to rapid external changes as the USA adopted a new policy of détente towards Communist China. In Jan 1979 this culminated in the full normalization of Sino-US relations, the severing of Taiwanese-US diplomatic contacts, and the annulment of the USA's 1954 security pact. Other Western nations followed suit in ending diplomatic relations with Taiwan during the 1970s and early 1980s.

These developments, coupled with generational change within the Kuomintang, have prompted a slow review of Taiwanese policies, both domestic and external. Chiang Kai-shek died Apr 1975 and his son Chiang Ching-kuo (1910–88) became party chair and, from 1978, state president. Under his stewardship, a new programme of gradual democratization and 'Taiwanization' was adopted, with elections being held for 'vacated seats' within the National Assembly and Legislative Yuan and native Taiwanese being more rapidly inducted into the Kuomintang. In the Dec 1986 elections a formal opposition party, the Democratic Progressive Party (DPP), led by Chiang Peng-chien, was tolerated and captured 22% of the vote to the Kuomintang's 69%. After the election, in July 1987, martial law was lifted and replaced with a new national security law under which demonstrations and the formation of opposition parties were legalized, so long as they forswore communism and supported Taiwanese independence, and press restrictions were lifted.

President Chiang was succeeded on his death, in Jan 1988, by ◊Lee Teng-hui, a Taiwan-born Christian who had been vice president since 1984. The new president, who headed the party's modernizing technocrat wing, accelerated the pace of reform. Many 'old guard' figures were retired during 1988–89 and a plan for phasing out by 1992, through voluntary retirement, up to 200 mainland constituencies and replacing them with Taiwanese deputies was approved. In the Dec 1989 Legislative Yuan elections, the first to be freely held on the island, the Kuomintang's vote share fell to 59% and the DPP increased its number of seats from 12 to 21.

Taiyuan /ˌtaɪjuˈɑːn/ capital of Shanxi province, NE China; population (1986) 1,880,000. Industries include iron, steel, agricultural machinery, and textiles. It is a walled city, founded in the 5th century AD, on the river Fen He, and is the seat of Shanxi university.

Ta'iz /taːˈɪz/ third largest city of North Yemen; situated in the south of the country at the centre of a coffee-growing region. Cotton, leather and jewellery are also produced.

Taizé /teɪˈzeɪ/ ecumenical Christian community based in the village of that name in SE France. Founded in 1940 by Swiss theologian Roger Schutz (1915–), it has been since the 1960s a centre for people interested in the 'struggle and contemplation' of contemporary Christianity.

Taj Mahal /ˈtɑːdʒ məˈhɑːl/ a white marble mausoleum built on the river Jumna near Agra, India. Built by Shah Jehan to the memory of his favourite wife, it is a celebrated example of Indo-Islamic architecture, the fusion of Muslim and Hindu styles.

20,000 labourers worked from 1634 to 1656 to build the Taj Mahal, which has a central dome, and minarets on each corner. Every facade is inlaid with semi-precious stones. Ransacked in the 18th century, it was restored in the early 20th century and is a symbol of India to the world.

Tajo /ˈtɑːxəʊ/ Spanish name for the river ◊Tagus.

takahe bird *Notornis mantelli* of the rail family and native to New Zealand. A heavy flightless species, about 60 cm/2 ft tall, with blue and green plumage and a red beak, the takahe was thought to have become extinct at the end of the 19th century, but in 1948 small numbers were rediscovered in the tussock grass of a mountain valley on South Island.

Takao /tæˈkaʊ/ Japanese name for ◊Kaohsiung, a city on the W coast of Taiwan.

take-home pay a worker's actual wage or salary, after deductions have been made for such things as taxation, national insurance schemes, and employers' pension funds. *Disposable income* is take-home pay minus mortgage payments, rent, rates, bills, and so on.

takeover in business, the acquisition by one company of a sufficient number of shares in another company to have effective control of that company — usually 51%, although a controlling stake may be as little as 30%. Takeovers may be agreed or contested; methods employed include the ◊*dawn raid*, and methods of avoiding an unwelcome takeover include ◊*reverse takeover* or inviting a ◊*white knight* to make a takeover bid.

Takeshita /tæˈkeʃtə/ Noboru 1924– . Japanese right-wing politician. Elected to parliament as a Liberal Democratic Party (LDP) deputy 1958, he became president of the LDP and prime minister Oct 1987. His administration was undermined by the ◊Recruit insider-trading scandal and in Apr 1989 he resigned because of his involvement.

Takeshita, the son of a *sake* brewer, trained as a kamikaze pilot during World War II. He was a schoolteacher before beginning his political career in the House of Representatives, rising to chief cabinet secretary to Prime Minister Satō 1971–72 and finance minister under Nakasone.

As prime minister he introduced a *furusato* (hometown) project of giving 3,200 towns and villages a grant of 100 million yen (£500,000) each. This benefited construction companies, who are among the main backers of Takeshita's LDP

Taj Mahal *Over 20,000 labourers were employed in the construction of the Taj Mahal (1634–56), in Agra, N India.*

faction. The Recruit scandal and the introduction of a consumption tax, however, caused popular approval of Takeshita's government to drop dramatically.

Takoradi /ˌtɑːkəˈrɑːdi/ port in Ghana, administered with ◊Sekondi.

Talavera de la Reina /ˌtæləˈveərə de lə reɪnə/ town in Castilla-León, central Spain, on the ◊Tagus, 120 km/75 mi SW of Madrid; population (1970) 46,000. It produces soap, pharmaceuticals, and textiles. Spanish and British forces defeated the French here in the ◊Peninsular War 1809.

Talbot /ˈtɔːlbət/ William Henry Fox 1800–1877. English pioneer of photography. He invented the ◊calotype process and the first ◊negative/positive method. *The Pencil of Nature* 1844–46 by Talbot was the first book of photographs published. In 1851 he made instantaneous photographs and in 1852 photo engravings. Talbot made ◊photograms several years before Daguerre's invention was announced.

talc a mineral, hydrous magnesium silicate, $Mg_3Si_4O_{10}(OH)_2$. It occurs in tabular crystals, but the massive impure form, known as *steatite* or *soapstone*, is more common. It is formed by the alteration of magnesium compounds, and usually found in metamorphic rocks. Talc is very soft, ranked 1 on the Mohs' scale of hardness. It is used in powdered form in cosmetics, lubricants, and as an additive in paper manufacture.

French chalk and potstone are varieties of talc. Soapstone has a greasy feel to it, and is used for carvings such as Inuit sculptures.

Talcahuano /ˌtælkəˈwɑːnəʊ/ port and chief naval base in Biobio region, Chile; population (1987) 231,000. Industries include oil refining and timber.

Talien /ˈtælien/ part of the port of ◊Lüda, China.

Taliesin /tælˈjesɪn/ lived *c.* 550. Legendary Welsh poet, a bard at the court of the king of Rheged in S Scotland. Taliesin allegedly died at Taliesin (named after him) in Dyfed.

Talking Heads US new-wave rock group formed 1975 in New York. Their nervy minimalist music was inspired by African rhythms; albums include *More Songs About Buildings and Food* 1978, *Little Creatures* 1985, and *Naked* 1988.

All band members have recorded separately. The vocalist, David Byrne (1952–), has composed avant-garde and ballet music, and made the film *True Stories* 1986. The bass player, Tina Weymouth (1950–), and drummer, Chris Frantz (1951–), have had hits as the Tom Tom Club.

tallage English tax paid by cities, boroughs, and royal ◊demesnes, first levied under Henry II as a replacement for ◊danegeld. It was abolished 1340

Talbot *Daguerreotype of William Henry Fox Talbot, who invented new techniques in photography, including the photographic negative from which copies could be made on paper.*

after it had been superseded by grants of taxation voted by Parliament.

Tallahassee /ˌtæləˈhæsi/ (Cree Indian 'old town') capital of Florida, USA; population (1980) 82,000. It is an agricultural and lumbering centre. The explorer ◊De Soto found an Indian settlement here 1539. It has many pre-Civil War mansions.

Talleyrand /ˈtælɪrænd/ Charles Maurice de Talleyrand-Périgord 1754–1838. French politician. As bishop of Autun 1789–91 he supported moderate reform in the ◊French Revolution, and fled to the USA during the Reign of Terror (persecution of anti-revolutionaries). He became foreign minister under the Directory 1797–99 and under Napoleon 1799–1807. He represented France at the Congress of ◊Vienna 1814–15.

Tallinn /ˈtælɪn/ (German **Reval**) naval port and capital of Estonian Republic, NW USSR; population (1987) 478,000. Industries include electrical and oil drilling machinery, textiles, and paper. Founded 1219, it was a member of the ◊Hanseatic League, passed to Sweden 1561, and to Russia 1750. Vyshgorod castle (13th century) and other medieval buildings remain. It is a yachting centre.

Tallis /ˈtælɪs/ Thomas c. 1505–1585. English composer in the polyphonic style. He wrote masses, anthems, and other church music. Among his works are the setting for five voices of the *Lamentations of Jeremiah*, and for 40 of *Spem in alium*.

tallith four-cornered, fringed shawl worn by Jewish men during morning prayers.

Talmud chief work of Jewish post-Biblical literature, providing a compilation of ancient Jewish law and tradition, based on the ◊Mishna. To this was added the *Gemara*, discussions centring on its texts, during the 3rd and 4th centuries AD.

tal. qual. abbreviation for *talis qualis* (Latin 'just as they come').

Tamale /təˈmɑːli/ town in NE Ghana; population (1982) 227,000. It is a commercial centre, dealing in rice, cotton, and peanuts.

tamandua tree-living toothless anteater *Tamandua tetradactyla* found in tropical forests and tree savannah from S Mexico to Brazil. About 56 cm/1.8 ft long with a prehensile tail of equal length, it has strong foreclaws with which it can break into nests of tree ants and termites, which it licks up with its narrow tongue.

Tamar /ˈteɪmɑː/ in the Old Testament, the sister of ◊Absalom. She was raped by her half-brother Amnon, who was then killed by Absalom.

Tamar /ˈteɪmə/ river rising in N Cornwall, England, and flowing to Plymouth Sound; for most of its

Talleyrand *French politician Talleyrand, whose astute diplomatic skills enabled him to remain in office both in the Revolutionary period and under Napoleon.*

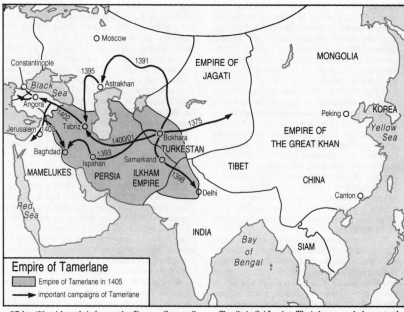

Empire of Tamerlane

▨ Empire of Tamerlane in 1405
→ important campaigns of Tamerlane

97 km/60 mi length it forms the Devon–Cornwall border.

Tamar /ˈteɪmɑː/ river flowing into Bass Strait, Tasmania, formed by the union of the N and S Esk; length 65 km/40 mi.

tamarack coniferous tree *Larix laricina*; a type of larch native to North America where it is used for timber.

tamarind evergreen tropical tree *Tamarindus indica*, family Leguminosae, with pinnate leaves, and reddish-yellow flowers, followed by pods. The pulp surrounding the seeds is used as a flavouring and medicinally.

tamarisk shrub of the genus *Tamarix*, flourishing in warm, salty, desert regions where no other vegetation is found. The common tamarisk *Tamarix gallica* has scale-like leaves and spikes of very small, pink flowers.

Tamatave /ˌtæməˈtɑːv/ former name (until 1979) for ◊Toamasina, the chief port of Madagascar.

Tambo /ˈtæmbəʊ/ Oliver 1917– . South African nationalist politician, in exile from 1960, president of the African National Congress (ANC) from 1977.

Tambo was expelled from teacher training for organizing a student protest, and joined the ANC 1944. He set up a law practice with Nelson ◊Mandela in Johannesburg in 1952. In 1956 Tambo, with other ANC members, was arrested on charges of treason; he was released the following year. When the ANC was banned in 1960, he left South Africa to set up an external wing. He became acting ANC president in 1967 and president in 1977, during Mandela's imprisonment.

tambourine musical percussion instrument of ancient origin, almost unchanged since Roman times, consisting of a shallow drum with a single skin and loosely set jingles in the rim that increase its effect.

Tambov /tæmˈbɒv/ city in W central USSR; population (1987) 305,000. Industries include engineering, flour milling, and the manufacture of rubber and synthetic chemicals.

Tamerlane /ˈtæməleɪn/ or **Tamburlaine** or **Timur i Leng** 1336–1405. Mongol ruler of ◊Samarkand from 1369, who conquered Persia, Azerbaijan, Armenia, and Georgia. He defeated the ◊Golden Horde 1395, sacked Delhi 1398, invaded Syria and Anatolia, and captured the Ottoman sultan in Ankara 1402. He died invading China.

Tamil person of Tamil culture. The majority of Tamils live in the Indian state of Tamil Nadu (formerly Madras), though there are approximately 3 million

Tamils in Sri Lanka. Their language belongs to the Dravidian family.

Tamil language a Dravidian language of SE India, spoken principally in the state of Tamil Nadu and also in N Sri Lanka. It is written in its own distinctive script.

Tamil Nadu /ˈtæmɪl nɑːˈduː/ state of SE India; former name (to 1968) **Madras State**
area 130,100 sq km/50,219 sq mi
capital Madras
products mainly industrial (cotton, textiles, silk, electrical machinery, tractors, rubber, sugar refining)
population (1981) 48,297,000
language Tamil
history the present state was formed 1956. Tamil Nadu comprises part of the former British Madras presidency (later province) formed from areas taken from France and Tipu Sahib, the sultan of Mysore, in the 18th century, which became a state of the Republic of India 1950. The NE was detached to form Andhra Pradesh 1953; other areas went to Kerala and Mysore (now Karnataka) 1956, and the Laccadive Islands (now Lakshadweep) became a separate Union Territory.

Taming of the Shrew, The a comedy by William Shakespeare, first performed 1593–94. Bianca, who has many suitors, must not marry until her sister Katherina (the shrew) has done so. Petruchio agrees to woo Katherina so that his friend Hortensio may marry Bianca. Petruchio succeeds in 'taming' Katherina but Bianca marries another.

Tamil Nadu

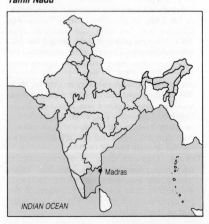

Tammany Hall Democratic Party organization in New York. It originated 1789 as the Society of St Tammany, named after an American Indian chief. It was dominant from 1800 until the 1930s and gained a reputation for gangsterism; its domination was broken by Mayor ◊La Guardia.

Tammuz /'tæmu:z/ in Sumerian legend, a vegetation god, who died at midsummer and was brought back from the underworld in spring by his lover Ishtar. His cult spread over Babylonia, Syria, Phoenicia, and Palestine. In Greek mythology Tammuz appears as ◊Adonis.

Tampa /'tæmpə/ port and resort in W Florida, USA; population (1986) 279,000. Industries include fruit and vegetable canning, shipbuilding, and the manufacture of fertilizers, clothing, and cigars.

Tampere /'tæmpəreɪ/ (Swedish **Tammerfors**) city in SW Finland; population (1988) 171,000, metropolitan area 258,000. It is the second largest city in Finland. Industries include textiles, paper, footwear, and turbines.

Tampico /tæm'pi:kəʊ/ port on the Rio Pánuco, 10 km/6 mi from the Gulf of Mexico, in Tamaulipas state, Mexico; population (1980) 268,000. Industries include oil refining and fishing.

Tamworth /'tæmwɜ:θ/ town in Staffordshire, England, on the Tame, NE of Birmingham; population (1981) 64,000. Industries include engineering, paper, and clothing.

Tamworth /'tæmwɜ:θ/ dairying centre with furniture industry in New South Wales, Australia, on the river Peel; population (1984) 34,000.

Tana /'tɑ:nə/ lake in Ethiopia, 1,800 m/5,900 ft above sea level; area 3,600 sq km/1,390 sq mi. It is the source of the Blue Nile.

Tanabata Japanese 'star festival' celebrated annually on 7 July, introduced from China in the 8th century. It is dedicated to Altair and Vega, two stars in the constellation Aquila, which are united once yearly in the Milky Way. According to legend they represent two star-crossed lovers allowed by the gods to meet on that night.

tanager bird of the family Emberizidae, related to buntings. There are about 230 species in forests of Central and South America, all brilliantly coloured. They are 10–20 cm/4–8 in long, with plump bodies and conical beaks.

Tanagra /'tænəgrə/ ancient city in ◊Boeotia, central Greece. Sparta defeated Athens there 457 BC. Terracotta statuettes called **tanagra** were excavated in 1874.

Tanaka /tə'nɑ:kə/ Kakuei 1918– . Japanese right-wing politician, leader of the dominant Liberal Democratic Party (LDP) and prime minister 1972–74. In 1976 he was charged with corruption and resigned from the LDP but remained a powerful faction leader.

Tanaka was minister of finance 1962–65 and of international trade and industry 1971–72, before becoming LDP leader. In 1976 he was arrested for accepting bribes from the Lockheed Corporation when premier and found guilty in 1983, being fined and sentenced to four years' imprisonment. His appeal against the 1983 Tokyo district court ruling was rejected by the High Court in 1987, but a further appeal was made to the Supreme Court. In the meantime Tanaka remained in parliament as an independent deputy. He was also implicated in the 1988–89 Recruit insider-trading scandal.

Tananarive /tə,nænə'ri:v/ former name for ◊Antananarivo, the capital of Madagascar.

Tanga /'tæŋgə/ seaport and capital of Tanga region, NE Tanzania, on the Indian Ocean; population (1978) 103,000. The port trades in sisal, fruit, cocoa, tea, and fish.

Tanganyika /,tæŋgən'ji:kə/ former British colony in E Africa, which now forms the mainland of ◊Tanzania.

Tanganyika, Lake /,tæŋgən'ji:kə/ lake 772 m/2,534 ft above sea level in the Great Rift Valley, E Africa, with Zaïre to the west and Tanzania and Burundi to the east. It is about 645 km/400 mi long, with an area of about 31,000

TANGENT OF AN ANGLE

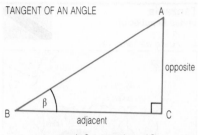

$$\tan(\text{gent}) \beta = \frac{\sin \beta}{\cos \beta} = \frac{\text{opposite}}{\text{adjacent}} = \frac{AC}{BC}$$

sq km/12,000 sq mi, and is the deepest lake in Africa (1,435 m/4,710 ft). The mountains around its shores rise to about 2,700 m/8,860 ft. The chief ports are Bujumbura (Burundi), Kigoma (Tanzania), and Kalé mié (Zaïre).

Tange /'tæŋgeɪ/ Kenzo 1913– . Japanese architect. His works include the National Gymnasium, Tokyo, for the 1964 Olympics, and the city-plan of Abuja, the capital of Nigeria.

tangent in trigonometry, a function of an angle in a right-angled triangle, defined as the ratio of the length of the side opposite the angle (not the right angle) to the length of the side adjacent to it; a way of expressing the slope of a line. In geometry, a tangent is a straight line that touches a curve and has the same slope as the curve at the point of contact. At a ◊maximum or minimum, the tangent to a curve has zero slope.

tangerine type of small ◊orange *Citrus reticulata*.

Tangier /tæn'dʒɪə/ or **Tangiers** or **Tanger** port in N Morocco, on the Strait of Gibraltar; population (1982) 436,227. It was an important Phoenician trading centre in the 15th century BC. It was captured by the Portuguese 1471 and passed to England 1662 as part of the dowry of ◊Catherine of Braganza, but was abandoned 1684 and later became a lair of ◊Barbary pirates. From 1923, Tangier and a small surrounding enclave became an international zone, which was administered by Spain 1940–45. In 1956 it was transferred to independent Morocco, and became a free port 1962.

tango slow dance in two-four time of partly African origin which came to Europe via South America, where it had blended with Spanish elements (such as the ◊habanera).

Tangshan /,tæŋ'ʃæn/ industrial city in Hebei province, China; population (1986) 1,390,000. Almost destroyed by an earthquake 1976, with 200,000 killed, it was rebuilt on a new site, coal seams being opened up under the old city.

Tanguy /toŋ'gi:/ Yves 1900–1955. French Surrealist painter, who lived in the USA from 1939. His inventive canvases feature semi-abstract creatures in a barren landscape.

Tanguy was first inspired to paint by de ◊Chirico's work and in 1925 he joined the Surrealist movement. He soon developed his characteristic style with bizarre, slender forms in a typically Surrealist wasteland.

Tanizaki /,tæni'zɑ:ki/ Jun-ichirō 1886–1965. Japanese novelist. His works include a modern version of ◊Murasaki's *The Tale of Genji* 1939–41, *The Makioka Sisters* in three volumes 1943–48, and *The Key* 1956. His work matured when he moved to Tokyo after the earthquake of 1923 to the Kyoto-Osaka region, where ancient tradition is stronger.

tank an armoured fighting vehicle that runs on tracks and is fitted with weaponry capable of destroying life and property and defeating other tanks. The term was originally a code name given to the first effective tracked and armoured fighting vehicle, invented by the British soldier and scholar Ernest Swinton, and used in the battle of the Somme 1916.

A tank consists of a body or hull of thick steel, on which are mounted machine guns and a larger gun. The hull contains the crew (usually consisting of a commander, driver, and one or two soldiers),

engine, radio, fuel tanks, and ammunition. The tank travels on caterpillar tracks that enable it to cross rough ground and debris.

tanker ship with tanks for carrying mineral oil, liquefied gas, and molasses in bulk. Currently the biggest oil tanker is the *Seawise Giant*, 458.5 m/1,504 ft long and nearly 565,000 tonnes deadweight.

Tannenberg, Battle of /'tænənbɜ:g/ two battles, named after a village now in N Poland:
1410 the Poles and Lithuanians defeated the Teutonic Knights, establishing Poland as a major power;
1914 during World War I, when Tannenberg was part of East Prussia, ◊Hindenburg defeated the Russians.

Tanner /'tænə/ Beatrice Stella. Unmarried name of actress Mrs Patrick ◊Campbell.

tannic acid or **tannin** a stringent substance, composed of several ◊phenol rings, occurring in the bark, wood, roots, fruits, and galls (growths) of certain trees, such as the oak. It precipitates gelatin to give an insoluble compound, used in the manufacture of leather from hides (tanning).

tanning treating animal skins to preserve them and make them into leather. This may be done by vegetable tanning: soaking the prepared skins in tannic acid. Chrome tanning, which is much quicker, uses solutions of chromium salts.

Tannu-Tuva /'tænu: 'tu:və/ former independent republic in NE Asia; see ◊Tuva.

tansy perennial herb *Tanacetum vulgare*, family Compositae, native to Europe. The yellow flowerheads grow in clusters and the aromatic leaves are used in cookery.

tantalum a metallic element, symbol Ta, atomic number 73, relative atomic mass 180.95. Tantalum can be drawn into wire with a very high melting point and great tenacity (useful for filament lamps subject to vibration). It is also used in alloys, for corrosion-resistant laboratory apparatus and chemical equipment, as a catalyst in the manufacture of synthetic rubber, in tools and instruments, and in rectifiers and capacitors. It resembles platinum when polished. It is a bluish-white metal, ductile and malleable.

It was discovered in 1802 by Swedish chemist Anders Ekeberg (1767–1813), and occurs chiefly in the mineral tantalite. Tantalum carbide is an important abrasive.

Tantalus /'tæntələs/ in Greek mythology, a king whose crimes were punished in ◊Tartarus by food and drink he could not reach, hence the name *tantalus* for a lockable container for wine bottles, which leaves the drink still visible.

tant mieux (French) so much the better.

tant pis (French) so much the worse.

Tantrism forms of Hinduism and Buddhism that emphasize the division of the universe into male and female forces that maintain its unity by their interaction; this gives women equal status. Tantric Hinduism is associated with magical and sexual yoga practices that imitate the union of Siva and Sakti, as described in religious books known as the *Tantras*. In Buddhism, the *Tantras* are texts attributed to the Buddha, describing methods of attaining enlightenment.

Tantric Buddhism, practised in medieval India, depended on the tuition of teachers and the use of yoga, mantras, and meditation to enable its followers to master themselves and gain oneness with the universe.

Tanzania /,tænzə'ni:ə/ country in E Africa, on the Indian Ocean, bounded to the N by Uganda and Kenya, to the S by Mozambique, Malawi, and Zambia, and to the W by Zaïre, Burundi, and Rwanda.

government The 1977 constitution made Tanzania a one-party socialist republic with the Revolutionary Party of Tanzania (CCM). The president is chosen by the party to serve a maximum of two five-year terms. The president appoints two vice presidents from members of the National Assembly and if the president comes from the mainland, the first vice president must come from Zanzibar. The second vice president is termed prime minister. The president also appoints and presides over a cabinet.

The single-chamber National Assembly has 243 members: 118 directly elected by universal suffrage for the mainland, 50 for the islands of Zanzibar and Pemba, 25 'ex officio' regional commissioners, 15 nominated by the president and 35 indirectly elected, to represent specific sections, including women and party organizations.

history For early history, see ◊Africa. Zanzibar was under Portuguese control during the 16th–17th centuries. In 1822 it was united with the nearby island of Pemba. It was a British protectorate 1890–1963, when it became an independent sultanate; an uprising followed and the sultan was overthrown 1964.

Tanganyika was a German colony 1884–1914, until conquered by Britain during World War I; it was a British League of Nations mandate 1920–46 and came under United Nations (UN) trusteeship 1946–62. It achieved full independence, within the Commonwealth, in 1961, with Julius ◊Nyerere as prime minister. He gave up the post some six weeks after independence to devote himself to the development of the Tanganyika African National Union (TANU) but in Dec 1962, when Tanganyika became a republic, he returned to become the nation's first president.

Tanzania was founded by the union of Tanganyika and Zanzibar in Apr 1964. Nyerere became president of the new United Republic of Tanzania and dominated the nation's politics for the next 20 years, being re-elected in 1965, 1970, 1975, and 1980. Known throughout Tanzania as Mwalimu (teacher), he established himself as a genuine Christian socialist who attempted to put into practice a philosophy that he fervently believed would secure his country's future. He committed himself in the Arusha Declaration of 1967 (the name comes from the N Tanzanian town where he made his historic statement) to building a socialist state for the millions of poor peasants through a series of village co-operatives (*Ujamas*). Nyerere became one of Africa's most respected politicians. In the final years of his presidency economic pressures, domestic and international, forced him to compromise his ideals and accept a more capitalistic society than he would have wished, but his achievements have included the best public health service on the African continent, according to UN officials, and a universal primary school system.

Relations between Tanzania and its neighbours have been variable. The East African Community (EAC) of Tanzania, Kenya, and Uganda, formed in 1967, broke up in 1977, and relations between Tanzania and the more capitalistic Kenya became uneasy. In 1979 Nyerere sent troops to support the Uganda National Liberation Front in its bid to overthrow President Idi Amin. This enhanced Nyerere's reputation but damaged his country's economy. Tanzania also supported the liberation movements in Mozambique and Rhodesia.

In 1977 TANU and the Afro-Shirazi Party of Zanzibar merged to become the Revolutionary Party of Tanzania (CCM) and this was made the only legal political organization. In Mar 1984 Nyerere announced his impending retirement and it was widely expected that he would be succeeded by the prime minister, Edward Sokoine, but Sokoine was killed in a road accident in the same year. The president of Zanzibar, Ali Hassan Mwinyi, was adopted as the sole presidential candidate by the CCM congress in Dec 1985. Until the retirement of Julius Nyerere in 1985, the offices of state president and chair of CCM were held by the same person. Now, although Nyerere has given up the presidency, he is still party chair, and in Oct 1987 was renominated for another term.

Taoiseach /'tiːʃəx/ Gaelic name for the prime minister of the Irish Republic.

Tanzania
United Republic of
(Jamhuri ya Muungano wa Tanzania)

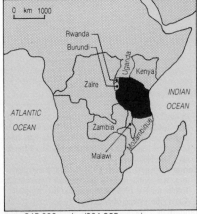

area 945,000 sq km/364,865 sq mi
capital Dodoma
towns chief port Dar es Salaam
physical a central plateau with lakes in the west and coastal plains
features comprises the islands of Zanzibar and nearby Pemba; Mount Kilimanjaro, called 'shining mountain', because of snow and glaciers which crown it (Kibo, an extinct volcano and its highest peak, is the highest mountain in Africa 5,895 m/19,347 ft); parts of Lakes Victoria and Tanganyika; Serengeti National Park, and the Olduvai Gorge; Ngorongoro Crater 14.5 km/9 mi across and 762 m/2,500 ft deep
head of state and government Ali Hassan

Mwinyi from 1985
government system one-party socialist republic
political parties Revolutionary Party of Tanzania (CCM), African, socialist.
exports coffee, cotton, sisal, cloves from Zanzibar, tea, tobacco
currency Tanzanian shilling (327.80 = £1 Mar 1990)
population (1989) 24,746,000; annual growth rate 3.5%
life expectancy men 49, women 53
language Kiswahili, English (both official)
religion Muslim 35%, Christian 35%, traditional 30%
literacy 78% male/70% female (1978)
GNP $4.9 bn (1983); $225 per head of population
chronology
1961 Tanganyika achieved full independence, within the Commonwealth, with Julius Nyerere as prime minister.
1962 Tanganyika became a republic with Nyerere as president.
1964 Tanganyika and Zanzibar became the United Republic of Tanzania with Nyerere as president.
1967 East African Community (EAC) formed. Arusha Declaration.
1977 Revolutionary Party of Tanzania (CCM) proclaimed the only legal party. EAC dissolved.
1979 Tanzanian troops sent to Uganda to help overthrow the president, Idi Amin.
1984 Nyerere announced his retirement but stayed on as CCM leader. Prime Minister Edward Sokoine killed in a road accident.
1985 Ali Hassan Mwinyi elected president.

Taoism Chinese philosophical system, traditionally founded by the Chinese philosopher Lao Zi 6th century BC, though the scriptures, *Tao Te Ching*, were apparently compiled 3rd century BC. The 'tao' or 'way' denotes the hidden principle of the universe, and less stress is laid on good deeds than on harmonious interaction with the environment, which automatically ensures right behaviour. The second important work is that of Zhuangzi (*c.* 389–286 BC), *The Way of Zhuangzi*. The magical side of Taoism is illustrated by the *I Ching* or *Book of Changes*, a book of divination.

This magic, ritualistic aspect of Taoism developed from the 2nd century AD and was largely responsible for its popular growth; it stresses physical immortality, and this was attempted by means ranging from dietary regulation and fasting to alchemy. By the 3rd century, worship of gods had begun to appear, including that of the stove god Tsao Chun. From the 4th century, rivalry between Taoists and Mahayana Buddhists was strong in China, leading to persecution of one religion by the other; this was resolved by mutual assimilation, and Taoism developed monastic communities similar to those of the Buddhists.

Taormina /ˌtɑːɔː'miːnə/ coastal resort in E Sicily, at the foot of Mount Etna; population (1985) 9,000. It has an ancient Greek theatre.

tap dancing a rapid step dance, derived from clog dancing. Its main characteristic is the tapping of toes and heels accentuated by steel taps affixed to the shoes. It was popularized in ◊vaudeville and in 1930s films by dancers such as Fred Astaire and Bill 'Bojangles' Robinson (1878–1949).

tape recording, magnetic method of recording electric signals on a layer of iron oxide, or other magnetic material, coating a thin plastic tape. The electrical impulses are fed to the electromagnetic recording head, which magnetizes the tape in accordance with the frequency and amplitude of the original signal, and may be audio (for sound recording), video (for television), or data (for computer). For playback, the tape is passed over the same or another head to convert magnetic into electrical impulses, which are then amplified for reproduction. Tapes are easily demagnetized (erased) for re-use, and come in cassette, cartridge, or reel form.

tapestry ornamental woven textile used for wall-hangings, furniture, and curtains. The tapestry design is threaded into the warp with various shades of wool.

Tapestries have been woven for centuries in many countries, and during the Middle Ages the art was practised in monasteries. European tapestries of the 13th century frequently featured oriental designs brought back by the Crusaders. The great European centres of tapestry weaving were at Arras, Brussels, Aubusson, Beauvais, and Mortlake. The ◊Gobelins tapestry factory of Paris was made a royal establishment in the 17th century. In England, William ◊Morris established the Merton Abbey looms in the late 19th century. Many fine tapestries are still made in France, for example, the tapestry designed by Graham Sutherland for Coventry cathedral, which was made at Felletin, where tapestries have been woven since the 15th century. Other designers have included ◊Raphael, ◊Rubens, and ◊Burne-Jones. The ◊Bayeux Tapestry is in fact an embroidery rather than a true tapestry.

tapeworm flat parasitic worm in the class Cestoda, of the phylum Platyhelminthes (flatworms), with no digestive or sense organs. It can reach a length of 15 m/50 ft, and attaches itself to its host's intestines by means of hooks and suckers. Tapeworms usually reach humans in imperfectly cooked meat or fish, causing anaemia and intestinal disorders.

tapioca a starch used in cooking, produced from the ◊cassava root.

tapir mammal of the ancient family Tapiridae, which grows to a maximum of 1 m/3 ft at the shoulder, and weighs 350 kg/770 lb. Tapirs have thick, hairy, black skin, short tails and trunks, and no horns. They are vegetarian, harmless, shy inhabitants of the forests of Central and South America, and also Malaysia. Their survival is

tapeworm *Electron microscope picture of the head of a tapeworm showing the hooks which are used to cling on to the host's tissues.*

in danger because of destruction of the forests.

They are related to the ◊rhinoceros, and slightly more distantly to the horse. The Malaysian tapir *Tapirus indicus* is black with a large white patch on the back and hindquarters. The South American species is brown.

taproot in botany, a single, robust, main ◊root which is derived from the embryonic root, or ◊radicle, and grows vertically downwards, often for some considerable depth. Taproots are often modified for food storage and are common in biennial plants such as the carrot *Daucus carota*, where they act as ◊perennating organs.

tar a dark brown or black viscous liquid, obtained by the destructive distillation of coal, shale, and wood. Tars consist of a mixture of hydrocarbons, acids, and bases. Creosote and paraffin are produced from wood tar. See also ◊coaltar.

Tara Hill /'tɑːrə/ ancient religious and political centre in County Meath, S Ireland. It is the site of a palace and coronation place of many Irish kings, abandoned in the 6th century. St ◊Patrick preached here.

Taranaki /ˌtærəˈnæki/ peninsula in North Island, New Zealand, dominated by Mount ◊Egmont; volcanic soil makes it a rich dairy farming area, noted for cheese.

tarantella a peasant dance of southern Italy; also a piece of music composed for, or in the rhythm of, this dance in fast six-eight time.

Taranto /təˈræntəu/ naval base and port in Puglia region, SE Italy; population (1988) 245,000. An important commercial centre, its steelworks are part of the new industrial complex of S Italy. It was the site of the ancient Greek *Tarentum*, founded in the 8th century BC by ◊Sparta, and was captured by the Romans 272 BC.

tarantula poisonous spider *Lycosa tarantula* with a 2.5 cm/1 in body. It spins no web, relying on its speed in hunting to catch its prey.

In the Middle Ages, its bite was thought to cause hysterical ailments for which dancing was the cure, hence the dance named tarantella. The name is also used for the large bird-eating spiders of the tropics. It is named after the town of Taranto in Puglia, Italy.

Tarawa /təˈrɑːwə/ port and capital of Kiribati; population (1985) 21,000.

Tarbes /tɑːb/ capital of Hautes-Pyrénées *département*, SW France, a tourist centre for the Pyrenees; population (1983) 55,000. It belonged to England 1360–1406.

tare alternative common name for ◊vetch.

Taree /ˌtɑːˈriː/ town in a dairying area of NE

New South Wales, Australia; population (1981) 16,000.

tariff a tax on imports or exports from a country. Tariffs have generally been used by governments to protect home industries from lower-priced foreign goods, and have been opposed by supporters of free trade. For a tariff to be successful, it must not provoke retaliatory tariffs from other countries. Organizations such as the European Community, EFTA, and the General Agreement on Tariffs and Trade (GATT) 1948, have worked towards mutual lowering of tariffs between countries.

Tariff Reform League an organization set up in 1903 as a vehicle for the ideas of Joseph ◊Chamberlain on protective tariffs. It aimed to unify the British Empire by promoting imperial preference in trade. This policy was unacceptable to dominion governments as it would constrict their economic policies and put taxation on to foodstuffs imported into Britain. Consequently, the League's objective became the introduction of protection for British goods, against competition from Germany and the USA.

Tarim Basin /ˌtɑːˈriːm/ (Chinese *Tarim Pendi*) internal drainage area in Xinjiang Uygur province, NW China, between the Tien Shan and Kunlun Mountains; area about 900,000 sq km/350,000 sq mi. It is crossed by the Tarim He river, and includes the lake of Lop Nur. The Taklimakan desert lies to the south of the Tarim He.

Tarkington /'tɑːkɪŋtən/ Booth 1869–1946. US novelist, born in Indiana, author of *Monsieur Beaucaire* 1900 and novels of the Middle West, for example *The Magnificent Ambersons* 1918.

Tarkovsky /tɑːˈkɒfski/ Andrei 1932–1986. Soviet film director, whose work is characterized by unorthodox cinematic techniques and visual beauty. His films include the science-fiction epic *Solaris* 1972, *Mirror* 1975, and *The Sacrifice* 1986.

Tarn /tɑːn/ river in SW France, rising in the Cévennes and flowing 350 km/217 mi to the Garonne. It cuts the limestone plateaux in picturesque gorges.

taro or *cocco* or *eddo* plant *Colocasia esculenta* of the family Araceae, native to tropical Asia; the tubers are edible.

tarot cards fortune-telling aid of unknown, probably medieval origin, consisting of 78 cards: the *minor arcana* in four suits (resembling modern playing cards) and the *major arcana*, 22 cards with densely symbolic illustrations that have links with astrology and Kabbala.

history The earliest known reference to tarot cards is from 1392. The pack may have been designed in Europe in the early 14th century as a repository of Gnostic ideas then being suppressed by the Christian church. Since the 18th century the tarot has interested occult scholars.

tarpon marine herring-like fish *Tarpon atlanticus*. It reaches 2 m/6 ft, and may weigh 135 kg/300 lb. It lives in warm Atlantic waters.

Tarquinius Superbus /tɑːˈkwɪnɪəs suːˈpɜːbəs/

tarragon

flower

lived 5th century BC. Last king of Rome 534–510 BC. He abolished certain rights of Romans, and made the city powerful. He was deposed when his son Sextus raped ◊Lucretia.

tarragon perennial bushy herb *Artemisia dracunculus* of the daisy family, growing to 1.5 m/5 ft, with narrow leaves and small green-white flowerheads arranged in groups. Tarragon contains an aromatic oil; its leaves are used to flavour salads, pickles, and sauce tartare.

Tarragona /ˌtærəˈgəunə/ port in Catalonia, Spain; population (1986) 110,000. Industries include petrochemicals, pharmaceuticals, and electrical goods. It has a cathedral and Roman remains, including an aqueduct and amphitheatre.

Tarrasa /təˈrɑːsə/ town in Catalonia, NE Spain; industries include textiles and fertilizers; population (1986) 160,000.

Tarshish /'tɑːʃɪʃ/ a city mentioned in the Old Testament, probably the Phoenician settlement of Tartessus in Spain.

tarsier Malaysian primate *Tarsius spectrum*, about the size of a rat. It has thick, light brown fur, very large eyes, and long feet and hands. It is nocturnal, arboreal, and eats insects and lizards. Tarsiers are intermediate on the evolutionary scale between lemurs and anthropoids.

Tarsus /'tɑːsəs/ city in İçel province, SE Turkey, on the river Pamuk; population (1980) 121,000. It was formerly the capital of the Roman province of Cilicia, and the birthplace of St ◊Paul.

tartan woollen cloth woven in specific chequered patterns individual to Scottish clans, with stripes and squares of different widths and colours criss-crossing, and used in making plaids, kilts, and trousers. Developed in the 17th century, tartan was banned after the 1745 ◊Jacobite rebellion, and not legalized again until 1782.

Tartar a variant spelling of ◊Tatar, member of a Turkic people now living mainly in the USSR.

tartaric acid $CO_2H(CHOH)_2CO_2H$ an organic acid. Present in fruit juices in the form of salts of potassium, calcium, and magnesium, it is used in fizzy drinks and baking powders.

Tartarus /'tɑːtərəs/ in Greek mythology, a part of ◊Hades, the underworld, where the wicked were punished.

Tartini /tɑːˈtiːni/ Giuseppe 1692–1770. Italian composer and violinist. In 1728 he founded a school of violin playing in Padua. A leading exponent of violin technique, he composed the *Devil's Trill* sonata.

Tartu /'tɑːtuː/ city in Estonian Republic, USSR; industries include engineering and food processing; population (1981) 107,000. Once a stronghold of the ◊Teutonic Knights, it was taken by Russia 1558, and then held by Sweden and Poland, but has been under Russian control since 1704.

Tarzan fictitious hero inhabiting the African rainforest, created by the US writer Edgar Rice ◊Burroughs in *Tarzan of the Apes* 1914, with numerous sequels. He and his partner Jane have featured in films, comic strips, and televison serials.

Tarzan, raised by apes from infancy, is in fact a British peer, Lord Greystoke. He has enormous physical strength, and the ability to communicate with animals. Jane Porter, an American, falls in love with him while on safari and elects to stay.

Tas. abbreviation for ◊*Tasmania*.

Tasaday a people of the rainforests of Mindanao in the ◊Philippines.

Tashkent /ˌtæʃˈkent/ capital of Uzbek Republic, S central USSR; population (1987) 2,124,000. Industries include the manufacture of mining machinery, chemicals, textiles, and leather goods. Founded in the 7th century, it was taken by the Turks in the 12th century, and captured by Tamerlane 1361. In 1865 it was taken by the Russians. It was severely damaged by an earthquake 1966.

A temporary truce between Pakistan and India over ◊Kashmir was established at the *Declaration of Tashkent* 1966.

Tasman /'tæzmən/ Abel Janszoon 1603–1659. Dutch navigator. In 1642, he was the first European to see

Tasmania

Tasmania. He also made the first European sightings of New Zealand, Tonga, and Fiji.

He called Tasmania Van Diemen's Land in honour of the governor general of the Netherlands Indies; it was subsequently renamed Tasmania in his honour in 1856.

Tasmania /tæz'meɪnɪə/ island off the S coast of Australia, a state of the Commonwealth of Australia

area 67,800 sq km/26,171 sq mi

capital Hobart

towns chief port Launceston

features an island state (including small islands in the Bass Strait, and Macquarie Island); Franklin river, a wilderness area saved from a hydroelectric scheme 1983, which also has a prehistoric site; unique fauna include Tasmanian devil, Tasmanian 'tiger'

products wool, dairy products, apples and other fruit, timber, iron, tin, coal, copper, silver

population (1987) 448,000

history the first European to visit Tasmania was Abel Tasman 1642; it joined the Australian Commonwealth as a state 1901. The last of the Tasmanian Aboriginals died 1876.

Tasmanian devil bear-like marsupial *Sarcophilus harrisii*, about 65 cm/2.1 ft long with a 25 cm/10 in bushy tail. It has a large head, strong teeth, and is blackish with white patches on the chest and hind parts. It is nocturnal, carnivorous, and can be ferocious, especially when cornered. It has recently become extinct in Australia, and survives only in remote parts of Tasmania.

Tasmanian tiger/wolf or *thylacine* carnivorous marsupial *Thylacinus cynocephalus*; it is dog-like in appearance and can be nearly 2 m/6 ft from nose to tail tip. It was hunted to probable extinction in the 1930s, but there are still occasional but unconfirmed reports of sightings in Tasmania. The dingo exterminated the thylacine on the Australian mainland.

Tasman Sea /'tæzmən/ the part of the ◊Pacific Ocean between SE Australia and NW New Zealand. It is named after the Dutch explorer Abel Tasman.

Tass /tæs/ Soviet news agency: *Telegrafnoye Agentstvo Sovyetskovo Soyuza.*

Tasso /'tæsəʊ/ Torquato 1544–1595. Italian poet, author of the romantic epic poem of the First Crusade *La Gerusalemme Liberata/Jerusalem Delivered* 1574, followed by the *Gerusalemme Conquistata/Jerusalem Conquered*, written during the period from 1576 when he was mentally unstable.

Tasmanian devil

At first a law student at Padua, he overcame his father's opposition to a literary career by the success of his romantic poem *Rinaldo* 1562, dedicated to Cardinal Luigi d'Este, who took him to Paris, where he met the members of the ◊Pléiade. Under the patronage of Duke Alfonso d'Este of Ferrara, he wrote his pastoral play *Aminta* in 1573.

taste a sense that detects some of the chemical constituents of food. The human ◊tongue can distinguish only four basic tastes (sweet, sour, bitter, and salty) but it is supplemented by the nose's sense of smell. What we refer to as taste is really a composite sense made up of both taste and smell.

Tatar /'tɑːtə/ member of a Turkic, mainly Muslim people, the descendants of the followers of ◊Genghis Khan, called the Golden Horde because of the wealth they gained by plunder. They now live mainly in Tatar and Uzbekistan (where they were deported from the Crimea 1944) and SW Siberia, USSR. Their language belongs to the Altaic family.

Following Tatar demonstrations in Moscow July 1987 demanding the restoration of the Crimea as an autonomous republic to which they could return, a special commission was established under Andrei ◊Gromyko to look into the community's grievances. It reported, however, that such a move was not feasible as the Crimea had been repopulated by Russians and Ukrainians since 1944.

Tatar Autonomous Republic /'tɑːtə/ administrative region of W central USSR

capital Kazan

area 68,000 sq km/26,250 sq mi

population (1986) 3,537,000

products oil, chemicals, textiles, timber

history from 10th–13th centuries, territory of Volga-Kama Bulgar state; conquered by Mongols until 15th century; conquered by Russia 1552; became an autonomous republic 1920.

Tate /teɪt/ Jeffrey 1943– . British conductor. He was appointed principal conductor of the English Chamber Orchestra in 1985 and principal conductor of the Royal Opera House, Covent Garden, London, in 1986. He has conducted opera in Paris, in Geneva, and at the Metropolitan Opera, New York. He qualified as a doctor before turning to a career in music.

Tate /teɪt/ Nahum 1652–1715. Irish poet, born in Dublin. He wrote an adaptation of Shakespeare's *King Lear* with a happy ending. He also produced a version of the psalms, and hymns; among his poems is 'While shepherds watched'. He became British Poet Laureate 1692.

Tate /teɪt/ Phyllis (Margaret) 1911–1987. British

Tate *English conductor Jeffrey Tate.*

composer. Her works include *Concerto for Saxophone and Strings* 1944, the opera *The Lodger* 1960, based on the story of Jack the Ripper, and *Serenade to Christmas* for soprano, chorus and orchestra 1972.

Tate Gallery art gallery (British art from late 16th century, and international from 1810) at Millbank, London. Endowed by the sugar-merchant Henry Tate (1819–99), it was opened 1897; enlarged by Sir J Duveen and his son Lord Duveen of Millbank; later extensions include the Clore Gallery for Turner paintings, opened in 1987. A Liverpool branch of the Tate Gallery opened in 1988.

Tati /'tæ'tiː/ Jacques. Stage name of Jacques Tatischeff 1908–1982. French comic actor, director, and writer. He portrayed Monsieur Hulot, a character embodying polite opposition to modern mechanization in a series of films including *Les Vacances de M Hulot/Monsieur Hulot's Holiday* 1953.

Tatlin /'tætlɪn/ Vladimir 1885–1953. Russian artist, co-founder of ◊**Constructivism**. After encountering Cubism in Paris 1913 he evolved his first Constructivist works, using raw materials such as tin, glass, plaster, and wood to create abstract sculptures which he suspended in the air.

As a *Monument to the Third International* 1919 he designed a large diagonal spiral of glass and painted steel; this was never built, but drawings survive.

Tatra Mountains /'tɑːtrə/ range in central Europe, extending for about 65 km/40 mi along the Polish-Czechoslovakian border; the highest part of the central ◊Carpathians.

Tattersall's /'tætəsɔːlz/ British auctioneers of race-horses established at Knightsbridge Green, SW London, since 1864. The firm is named after Richard Tattersall (1724–95), who founded Tattersall's at Hyde Park Corner in 1766.

tatting lacework in cotton, made from medieval times by knotting, with the aid of a small shuttle.

Tatum /'teɪtəm/ Art(hur) 1910–1956. US jazz pianist, who worked mainly as a soloist. His technique and chromatic harmonies influenced many musicians. He played improvisations with the guitarist Tiny Grimes (1916–) in a trio from 1943.

Tatum /'teɪtəm/ Edward Lawrie 1909–1975. US microbiologist. For his work on biochemical genetics, he shared the Nobel prize with G W Beadle 1958.

Taube /'tɔːbi/ Henry 1915– . US chemist, who established the basis of modern inorganic chemistry by his study of the loss or gain of electrons by atoms during chemical reactions. He was awarded a Nobel prize in 1983.

Tau Ceti one of the nearest stars visible to the naked eye, 11.9 light years away. It has a diameter slightly less than that of the Sun, and an actual luminosity of about 45% of the Sun's. Its similarity to the Sun is sufficient to suggest that Tau Ceti may possess a planetary system, although observations have yet to reveal definite evidence of this.

Taunton /'tɔːntən/ market town and administrative headquarters of Somerset, England; population (1985) 56,000. The Elizabethan hall survives, in which Judge ◊Jeffreys held the Bloody Assizes 1685 after the Duke of Monmouth's rebellion.

Taunus Mountains /'taʊnəs/ mountain range in Hessen, West Germany, noted for its mineral spas.

Taupo /'taʊpəʊ/ largest lake in New Zealand, in a volcanic area of hot springs; area 620 sq km/239 sq mi. It is the source of the Waikato river.

Tauranga /taʊ'ræŋə/ port in North Island, New Zealand; exports (citrus fruit, dairy produce, timber); population (1986) 59,000.

Taurus /'tɔːrəs/ zodiac constellation in the northern hemisphere near Orion, represented as a bull. The Sun passes through Taurus from mid-May to late June. Its brightest star is Aldebaran, seen as the bull's red eye. Taurus contains the Hyades and Pleiades open ◊star clusters, and the Crab Nebula.

In astrology, the dates for Taurus are between about 20 Apr and 20 May (see ◊precession).

Taurus Mountains /ˈtɔːrəs/ (Turkish *Toros Dağlari*) mountain range in S ◊Turkey, forming the southern edge of the Anatolian plateau, and rising to over 3,656 m/12,000 ft.

Taussig /ˈausɪg/ Helen Brooke 1898–1986. US cardiologist who developed surgery for 'blue' babies. Such babies are born with one or more congenital deformities, which cause the blood to circulate in the body without first passing through the lungs. The babies are chronically short of oxygen and may not survive.

tautology repetition of the same thing in different words; or the ungrammatical use of unnecessary words; for example, it is tautologous to say something is *most unique* as something unique cannot, by definition, be comparative.

Tavener /ˈtævənə/ John (Kenneth) 1944– . English composer, whose individual and sometimes abrasive works include the dramatic cantata *The Whale* 1968 and the opera *Thérèse* 1979. He has also composed music for the Eastern Orthodox Church.

Taverner /ˈtævənə/ John 1495–1545. English organist and composer. He wrote masses and motets in polyphonic style, showing great contrapuntal skill, but as a Protestant renounced his art. He was imprisoned 1528 for heresy, and, as an agent of Thomas Cromwell, assisted in the dissolution of the monasteries.

Tavistock /ˈtævɪstɒk/ market town 24 km/15 mi N of Plymouth, Devon, England; population (1981) 9,000.

taxation the raising of money from individuals and organizations by the state in order to pay for the goods and services it provides. Taxation can be *direct* (a deduction from income) or *indirect* (added to the purchase price of goods or services, that is, a tax on consumption). The standard form of indirect taxation in Europe is *value-added tax* (VAT). *Income tax* is the most common form of direct taxation.

The proportions of direct and indirect taxation in the total tax revenue vary widely from country to country. By varying the effect of a tax on the richer and poorer members of society, a government can attempt to redistribute wealth from the richer to the poorer, both by taxing the rich more severely and by returning some of the collected wealth in the form of *benefits*. A *progressive* tax is one that falls proportionally more on the rich; most income taxes, for example, have higher rates for those with higher incomes. A *regressive* tax, on the other hand, affects the poor proportionally more than the rich.

In Britain, income tax is collected by the Inland Revenue, as are the other direct taxes, namely *corporation tax* on company profits; *capital gains tax*, introduced to prevent the use of capital as untaxed income in 1961; and *inheritance tax* (which replaced capital transfer tax). The USA has a high proportion of indirect taxation, while the UK has a higher proportion of direct taxation.

VAT is based on the French TVA (*Taxe sur la Valeur Ajoutée*), and was introduced in the UK 1973. It is paid on the value added to any goods or services at each particular stage of the process of production or distribution, and although collected from traders at each stage, it is in effect a tax on consumer expenditure. In some states of the USA a similar result is achieved by a *sales tax* deducted by the retailer at the point of sale.

In the UK, a *poll tax*, or community charge, levied on each person of voting age is the form of taxation that pays for local government (in other countries, including the USA, the equivalents are local property taxes or a local income tax). In Britain taxes are also levied on tobacco, wine, beer, and petrol, in the form of *excise duties*.

The UK tax system has been criticized in many respects; alternatives include an *expenditure tax*, which would be imposed only on income spent, and the *tax-credit system* under which all

are guaranteed an income bolstered as necessary by social security benefits, taxation beginning only above that level, hence eliminating the 'poverty trap', by which the unemployed receiving state benefits may have a net loss in income if they take employment at a low wage.

tax avoidance the conducting of financial affairs in such a way as to keep tax liability to a minimum within the law.

tax deductible an item that may be offset against tax liability, such as the cost of a car where it is required as an integral part of a job.

tax evasion failure to meet tax liabilities by illegal action, such as non-declaration of income. Tax evasion is a criminal offence.

tax haven a country or state where taxes are much less than elsewhere. It is often used by companies of another country which register in the tax haven to avoid tax. Any business transacted is treated as completely confidential. Tax havens include the Channel Islands, Switzerland, Bermuda, the Bahamas, and Liberia.

taxis (plural *taxes*) or *tactic movement* in biology, the movement of a single cell, such as a bacterium, protozoan, single-celled alga, or gamete, in response to an external stimulus. A movement directed towards the stimulus is described as positive taxis, and away from it as negative taxis. The alga *Chlamydomonas*, for example, demonstrates positive *phototaxis* by swimming towards a light source to increase the rate of photosynthesis. *Chemotaxis* is a response to a chemical stimulus, as seen in many bacteria that move towards higher concentrations of nutrients.

tax loophole a gap in the law that can be exploited to gain a tax advantage, not intended by the government when the law was made.

Taxodium genus of tree of the family Taxodiaceae. The deciduous swamp cypress *Taxodium distichum* grows in or near water in SE USA and Mexico, and is a valuable timber tree.

taxonomy another name for the ◊classification of living organisms.

tax shelter an investment opportunity designed to

reduce the tax burden on an individual or group of individuals, but at the same time to stimulate finance in the direction of a particular location or activity. Such shelters might be tax exempt or lightly taxed securities in government or a local authority, or forestry or energy projects.

Tay /teɪ/ the longest river in Scotland; length 189 km/118 mi. Rising in NW Central region, it flows NE through Loch Tay, then E and SE past Perth to the Firth of Tay, crossed at Dundee by the Tay Bridge, before joining the North Sea. The Tay has important salmon fisheries; its main tributaries are the Tummel, Isla, and Earn.

Taylor /ˈteɪlə/ A(lan) J(ohn) P(ercivale) 1906– . British historian and television lecturer. International history lecturer at Oxford 1953–63, and author of *The Struggle for Mastery in Europe* 1954, *The Origins of World War II* 1961, and *English History 1914–1945* 1965.

Taylor /ˈteɪlə/ Elizabeth 1932– . US actress, born in England, whose films include *National Velvet* 1944, *Cat on a Hot Tin Roof* 1958, *Butterfield 8* 1960 (Academy Award), *Cleopatra* 1963, and *Who's Afraid of Virginia Woolf?* 1966. Her seven husbands have included the actors Michael Wilding (1912–1979) and Richard ◊Burton (twice).

Taylor /ˈteɪlə/ Elizabeth (born Coles) 1912–1975. British novelist. Her books include *At Mrs Lippincote's* 1946 and *Angel* 1957.

Taylor /ˈteɪlə/ Frederick Winslow 1856–1915. US engineer and management consultant, the founder of scientific management. His ideas, published in *Principles of Scientific Management* 1911, were based on the breakdown of work to the simplest tasks, the separation of planning from execution of tasks, and the introduction of time and motion studies. His methods were most clearly expressed in assembly-line factories, but have been criticized for degrading and alienating workers and producing managerial dictatorship.

Tay-Sachs disease an inherited disorder, caused by a defective gene, leading to blindness, retardation, and death in childhood. It is most common in people of Jewish descent.

Taylor *English-born actress Elizabeth Taylor with co-star Montgomery Clift in a scene from* Raintree County *1957.*

Tayside /'teɪsaɪd/ region of Scotland
area 7,700 sq km/2,973 sq mi
towns administrative headquarters Dundee; Perth, Arbroath, Forfar
features river Tay; ◊Grampian Mountains; Lochs Tay and Rannoch; Ochil and Sidlaw Hills; vales of the North and South Esk
products beef and dairy products, soft fruit from the fertile Carse of Gowrie (SW of Dundee)
population (1987) 394,000
famous people James Barrie.

TB abbreviation for the infectious disease ◊*tuberculosis*.

Tbilisi /dbɪ'liːsi/ formerly *Tiflis* capital of the Georgian Republic, SW USSR; population (1987) 1,194,000. Industries include textiles, machinery, ceramics, and tobacco. Dating from the 5th century AD, it is a centre of Georgian culture, with fine medieval churches. Public demonstrations, following rejected demands for autonomy from Abkhazia enclave, were quashed here by troops 1989, resulting in 19 deaths from poison gas (containing chloroacetophenone) and 100 injured.

T cell or *T lymphocyte* a type of immune cell (see ◊immunity; ◊lymphocyte) that plays several important roles in the body's defences. T cells are so called because they mature in the ◊thymus.

There are three main types of T cells: T helper cells (Th cells), which allow other immune cells to go into action; T suppressor cells (Ts cells), which stop specific immune reactions from occurring; and T cytotoxic cells (Tc cells), which kill cells that are cancerous or infected with viruses. Like ◊B cells, to which they are related, T cells have surface receptors that make them specific for particular antigens.

Tchaikovsky /tʃaɪ'kɒfski/ Pyotr Il'yich 1840–1893. Russian composer. His strong sense of melody, personal expression, and brilliant orchestration are clear throughout his many Romantic works, which include six symphonies; three piano concertos and a violin concerto; operas (for example, *Eugene Onegin* 1879); ballets (for example, *The Nutcracker* 1892); orchestral fantasies (for example, *Romeo and Juliet* 1870); and chamber and vocal music.

Professor of harmony at Moscow in 1865, he later met ◊Balakirev, becoming involved with the nationalist movement in music. He was the first Russian composer to establish a reputation with Western audiences.

TD abbreviation for *Teachta Dála* (Irish 'a member of the Irish Parliament').

tea evergreen shrub *Camellia sinensis*, of which the fermented, dried leaves are infused to make a beverage of the same name. Known in China as early as 2737 BC, tea was first brought to Europe AD 1610 where it rapidly became a fashionable drink. In 1823 it was found growing wild in N India and plantations were later established in Assam and Sri Lanka; modern producers include Africa, South America, the USSR, Indonesia, and Iran.

Growing naturally to 12 m/40 ft, the tea plant is restricted in cultivation to bushes 1.5 m/4 ft high. The young shoots and leaves are picked every five years. After 24 hours spread on shelves in withering lofts, they are broken up by rolling machines to release the essential oils, and then left to ferment. This process is halted by passing the leaves through ovens where moisture is removed and the blackish-brown *black* tea emerges ready for sifting into various grades. *Green* tea is steamed and quickly dried before fermentation, remaining partly green in colour.

Tea was not in use in England until 1657. It rapidly became a fashionable drink but remained expensive because cargoes had to be brought from China in the fast tea clippers. Methods of consumption vary; in Japan special tea houses and an elaborate tea ceremony have evolved; in England afternoon tea has its own ritual; and in Tibet hard slabs of compressed tea are used as money before being finally brewed.

teacher training in the UK, teachers are trained by means of the four-year Bachelor of Education degree, which integrates professional training and the study of academic subjects, or by means of the post-graduate Certificate of Education, which offers one year of professional training to follow a degree course in a specialist subject.

teak tropical Asian timber tree *Tectona grandis*, family Verbenaceae, used in furniture and shipbuilding.

teal small freshwater duck *Anas crecca* of the N hemisphere, about 35 cm/14 in long. The drake has a reddish-brown head with green and buff markings on either side, and a black and white line on the wing. The female is buff and brown.

Teapot Dome Scandal US political scandal which revealed the corruption of the Harding administration. It centred on the leasing of naval oil reserves 1921 at Teapot Dome, Wyoming, without competitive bidding as a result of bribing the secretary of the interior, Albert B Fall (1861–1944). Fall was tried and imprisoned 1929.

tear gas lacrimatory and irritant vapour used as a riot-control agent. The gas is delivered in pressurized, liquid-filled canisters or grenades, thrown by hand or launched from a specially adapted rifle. Gases such as Mace cause violent coughing and blinding tears, which pass when the victim breathes fresh air, and there are no lasting effects. Blister gases (such as mustard gas) and nerve gases are more harmful and may cause permanent injury or death.

teasel erect, prickly, biennial herb *Dipsacus fullonum*, family Dipsacaceae, native to Eurasia. The dry seed heads were once used industrially to tease, or raise the nap of, cloth.

Tebaldi /te'bældi/ Renata 1922– . Italian dramatic soprano, renowned for the controlled purity of her voice and for her roles in ◊Puccini operas.

Tebbit /'tebɪt/ Norman 1931– . British Conservative politician. His first career was as an airline pilot, when he held various trade-union posts. He was minister for employment 1981–83, for trade and industry 1983–85, chancellor of the Duchy of Lancaster 1985–87, and chair of the party 1985–87. He was injured in a bomb blast during the 1985 Conservative Party conference in Brighton.

technetium (Greek *technetos* 'artificial') the first artificially made element, symbol Tc, atomic number 43. Originally produced by Perrier and Segré 1937 by bombarding molybdenum with deuterons or neutrons, it was later isolated in large amounts from the fission products of uranium. It is used as a hardener in steel alloys.

Technicolor trade name for a film colour process using three separate negatives. It was invented by Daniel F Comstock and Herbert T Kalmus in the USA 1922. Originally, Technicolor was a two-colour process in which superimposed red and green images were thrown on to the screen by a special projector. This proved expensive and imperfect, but when the three-colour process was introduced 1932 (producing separate negatives of blue, green, and red images) the system was widely adopted, culminating in its use in *Gone with the Wind* 1939. Despite increasing competition, Technicolor remains the most commonly used colour process for cinematography.

technocracy a society controlled by technical experts such as scientists and engineers. The term was invented by Californian engineer W H Smyth 1919 to describe his proposed 'rule by technicians', and was popularized by James Burham (1903–) in *Managerial Revolution* 1941.

technology the practical application of science in everyday life. The growth of technology began with the ◊Industrial Revolution in the second half of the 18th century with the introduction of the steam engine. The introduction of electricity as a power source and of the internal combustion engine (leading to the motor car and aircraft) in the early 20th century transformed everyday life in the industrialized countries. The pace of technological development has escalated in the middle and late 20th century with the introduction of ◊electronics, ◊nuclear power, ◊computers, ◊robots, and space ◊satellites. Areas of current development include information technology (the use of computers to store, retrieve, and manipulate information by using systems such as ◊teletext and ◊videotext), medical technology (organ ◊transplants and ◊tomography), military technology (such as the US ◊Strategic Defense Initiative), energy (◊solar energy and tidal power stations), communications (the ◊cellphone and ◊optical fibres), and entertainment (◊television and ◊video). See also ◊engineering.

technology education the practical application of science in industry and commerce. Britain's industrial revolution preceded that of Europe by half a century and its prosperity stimulated countries to encourage technological education. France established the Ecole Polytechnique, the first technological university, in 1794, and Germany founded the Technische Hochschulen in Berlin 1799. Britain founded the mechanics institutes for education in technology, notably the University of Manchester Institute of Science and Technology (founded 1824) which, together with the Imperial College of Science and Technology (established 1907), still forms a focus of technological research in the UK.

tectonics in geology, the study of the movements of rocks. On a small scale tectonics involves the formation of ◊folds and ◊faults, but on a large scale ◊plate tectonics deals with the movement of the Earth's surface as a whole.

Tecumseh /tɪ'kʌmsə/ 1768–1813. North American Indian chief of the Shawnee. He attempted to unite the Indian peoples from Canada to Florida against the encroachment of white settlers, but the defeat of his brother Tenskwatawa, 'The Prophet', at the battle of Tippecanoe Nov 1811 by Governor W H Harrison, largely destroyed the confederacy

Tayside

Tchaikovsky Russian composer Pyotr Il'yich Tchaikovsky.

built up by Tecumseh. He was commissioned a brigadier general in the British army during the War of 1812, and died in battle.

Tedder /ˈtedə/ Arthur William, 1st Baron Tedder 1890–1967. UK marshal of the Royal Air Force in World War II. As deputy supreme commander under US general Eisenhower 1943–45, he was largely responsible for the initial success of the 1944 Normandy landings.

He was air officer commanding RAF Middle East 1941–43, where his method of pattern bombing became known as 'Tedder's carpet'.

Teddington /ˈtedɪŋtən/ part of Twickenham, in the Greater London borough of ◊Richmond upon Thames; site of the National Physical Laboratory, established 1900.

Tees /tiːz/ river flowing from the Pennines in Cumbria, England, to the North Sea via Tees Bay in ◊Cleveland; length 130 km/80 mi.

Teesside /ˈtiːzsaɪd/ industrial area at the mouth of the river Tees, Cleveland, NE England; population (1981) 382,700. Industries include high-technology, capital-intensive steelmaking, chemicals, an oil fuel terminal, and the main North Sea natural-gas terminal. Middlesbrough is a major port.

tefillin or **phylacteries** two leather boxes worn by Jewish men during weekday prayer. They contain small scrolls from the Torah and are strapped to the left arm and the forehead.

Teflon a trade name for the plastic ◊PTFE.

Tegucigalpa /teɪˌɡusɪˈɡælpə/ capital of Honduras, population (1986) 605,000. It has textile and food processing industries. It was founded 1524 as a gold and silver mining centre.

Tehran /ˌteəˈrɑːn/ capital of Iran; population (1986) 6,043,000. Industries include textiles, chemicals, engineering, and tobacco. It was founded in the 12th century, and made the capital 1788 by Muhammad Shah. Much of the city was rebuilt in the 1920s and 1930s. Tehran is the site of the Gulistan Palace (the former royal residence).

Tehran Conference conference held 1943 in Tehran, Iran, the first meeting of World War II Allied leaders Churchill, Roosevelt, and Stalin.

Teignmouth /ˈtɪnməθ/ port and resort in S Devon, England, at the mouth of the Teign; population (1985) 14,000.

Teilhard de Chardin /teɪˈɑː də ʃɑːˈdæŋ/ Pierre 1881–1955. French Jesuit mystic. Born in the Puy-de-Dôme, he entered the Society of Jesus in 1899, was ordained in 1911, and during World War I was a stretcher bearer, taking his final vows in 1918. Publication of his *Le Phénomène humain/ The Phenomenon of Man* 1955 was delayed until after his death by the embargo of his superiors. He envisaged humanity as eventually in charge of its own evolution, and developed the concept of the *noosphere*, the unconscious union of thought among human beings.

Tej Bahadur 1621–1675. Indian religious leader, ninth guru (teacher) of Sikhism 1664– 75, executed for refusing to renounce his faith.

Tejo /ˈtaʒuː/ Portuguese name for the river ◊Tagus.

Te Kanawa /teɪ ˈkɑːnəwə/ Kiri 1944– . New Zealand opera singer. Her first major role was the Countess in Mozart's *The Marriage of Figaro* at Covent Garden, London, 1971.

tektite (from Greek *tektos* 'molten') small, rounded glassy stone, found in certain regions of Earth, such as Australasia. They are probably the scattered drops of molten rock thrown out by the impact of a large ◊meteorite.

Tel Aviv /ˈtel əˈviːv ˈdʒæfə/ officially **Tel Aviv-Jaffa** city in Israel, on the Mediterranean Sea; population (1987) 320,000. Industries include textiles, chemicals, sugar, printing, and publishing. Tel Aviv was founded 1909 as a Jewish residential area in the Arab town of Jaffa, with which it was combined 1949; their ports were superseded 1965 by Ashdod to the south.

telecommunications communications over a distance. Long-distance voice communication was

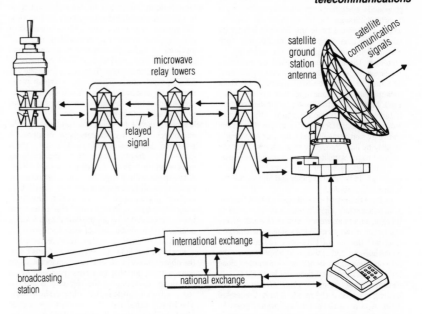

telecommunications

pioneered 1876 by Alexander Graham Bell, when he invented the telephone as a result of Faraday's discovery of electromagnetism. Today it is possible to communicate with most countries by telephone cable, or by satellite or microwave link, with over 100,000 simultaneous conversations and several television channels being carried by the latest satellites. Integrated service digital network (ISDN) is a system that transmits voice and image data on a single transmission line by changing them into digital signals, making videophones and high-quality fax possible; the world's first large-scale centre of ISDN began operating in Japan 1988. The chief method of relaying long-distance calls on land is microwave radio transmission.

The first mechanical telecommunications systems were the ◊semaphore and heliograph (using flashes of sunlight), invented in the mid 19th century, but the forerunner of the modern telecommunications age was the electric telegraph. The earliest practicable telegraph instrument was invented by Cooke and ◊Wheatstone in Britain 1837, and used by railway companies, the first public line being laid between Paddington and Slough 1843. In the USA Morse invented a signalling code, ◊Morse code, which is still used, and a recording telegraph, first used commercially between England and France 1851. As a result of ◊Hertz's discoveries using electromagnetic waves, ◊Marconi pioneered a 'wireless' telegraph, ancestor of the radio. He established wireless communication between England and France 1899 and across the Atlantic 1901. The modern telegraph uses teleprinters to send coded messages along telecommunications lines. They are keyboard-operated machines which transmit a five-unit Baudot code (see ◊baud). The receiving teleprinter automatically prints the received message.

The drawback to long-distance voice communication via microwave radio transmission is that the transmissions follow a straight line from tower to tower, so that over the sea the system becomes

telecommunications chronology

1794	Claude Chappe in France built a long-distance signalling system using semaphore.
1839	Charles Wheatstone and William Cooke devised an electric telegraph in England.
1843	Samuel Morse transmitted the first message along a telegraph line in the USA, using his Morse code of signals—short (dots) and long (dashes).
1858	The first transatlantic telegraph cable was laid.
1876	Alexander Graham Bell invented the telephone.
1877	Thomas Edison invented the carbon transmitter for the telephone.
1894	Marconi pioneered wireless telegraphy in Italy, later moving to England.
1900	Fessenden in the USA first broadcast voice by radio.
1901	Marconi transmitted the first radio signals across the Atlantic.
1904	Fleming invented the thermionic valve.
1907	Charles Krumm introduced the forerunner of the teleprinter.
1920	Stations in Detroit and Pittsburgh began regular radio broadcasts.
1922	The BBC began its first radio transmissions, for the London station 2LO.
1932	The Post Office introduced the Telex in Britain.
1956	The first transatlantic telephone cable was laid.
1962	Telstar pioneers transatlantic satellite communications, transmitting live TV pictures.
1966	Charles Kao in England advanced the idea of using optical fibres for telecommunications transmissions.
1969	Live TV pictures were sent from astronauts on the moon back to Earth.
1975	The Post Office announced Prestel, the world's first viewdata system, using the telephone lines to link a computer data bank with the TV screen.
1977	The first optical fibre cable was installed in California.
1986	Voyager 2 transmitted images of the planet Uranus over a distance of 3 billion km/2 billion mi, the signals taking 2 hours 45 minutes to make the journey back to Earth.
1989	Voyager 2 transmitted images of the planet Neptune; the first trans-oceanic optical fibre cable, capable of carrying 40,000 simultaneous telephone conversations, was laid between Europe and the USA.

impracticable. A solution was put forward 1945 by Arthur C Clarke in *Wireless World*, when he proposed a system of communications satellites in an orbit 35,900 km/22,300 mi above the Equator, where they would circle the Earth in exactly 24 hours, and thus appear fixed in the sky. Such a system is now in operation internationally, by ◊Intelsat. The satellites are called geostationary satellites, or synchronous satellites (syncoms). The first to be successfully launched, by Delta rocket from Cape Canaveral, was *Syncom 2* July 1963. Many such satellites are now in use, concentrated over heavy traffic areas such as the Atlantic, Indian, and Pacific Oceans. Telegraphy, telephony, and television transmissions are carried simultaneously by high-frequency radio waves. They are beamed to the satellites from large dish antennae or Earth stations, which connect with international networks. In Britain Goonhilly and Madley are the main Earth stations.

In 1980 the Post Office opened its first System X (all-electronic, digital) telephone exchange in London, a method already adopted in North America. Other advances include facsimile transmission (fax) and the use of fibre-optic cables for telephone lines instead of the usual copper cables; the telecommunications signals are transmitted along the fine glass fibres on pulses of laser light.

Telecom Tower formerly *Post Office Tower* building in London, 189 m/620 ft high. Completed 1966, it is a microwave relay tower capable of handling up to 150,000 simultaneous telephone conversations and over 40 television channels.

telegraphy the transmission of coded messages along wires by means of electrical signals. The first modern form of telecommunication, it now uses printers for the transmission and receipt of messages. Telex is an international telegraphy network.

Telemann /'teɪləmæn/ Georg Philipp 1681–1767. German Baroque composer, organist, and conductor at the Johanneum, Hamburg, from 1721. He was one of the most prolific composers ever, producing 25 operas, 1,800 church cantatas, hundreds of other vocal works, and 600 instrumental works.

telemetry measurement at a distance. It refers particularly to the systems by which information is obtained and sent back by instruments on board a spacecraft. See ◊remote sensing.

telepathy 'the communication of impressions of any kind from one mind to another, independently of the recognized channels of sense', as defined by F W H Myers who coined the term.

telephone an instrument for communicating by voice over long distances, invented by Alexander Graham ◊Bell 1876. The transmitter (mouthpiece) consists of a carbon microphone, with a diaphragm that vibrates when a person speaks into it. The diaphragm vibrations compress grains of carbon to a greater or lesser extent, altering their resistance to an electric current passing through them. This sets up variable electrical signals, which travel along the telephone lines to the receiver of the person being called. There they cause the magnetism of an electromagnet to vary, making a diaphragm above the electromagnet vibrate and give out sound waves, which mirror those that entered the mouthpiece originally.

The standard instrument has a handset, which houses the transmitter (mouthpiece) and receiver (earpiece) resting on a base, which has a dial or push-button mechanism for dialling a telephone number. Many kinds of mouthpiece are now in use. Some combine a push-button mechanism and mouthpiece and earpiece in one unit. A cordless telephone uses a unit of this kind, which is connected to a base unit not by wires but by radio. It can be used at distances up to about 100 m/330 ft from the base unit.

telephone tapping method of listening in on a telephone conversation; in the UK a criminal offence if done without a warrant or the consent of the person concerned. According to a 1988 estimate,

30,000 telephone taps a year were carried out in the UK at a cost of some £10 million.

telephoto lens a photographic lens of longer focal length than normal that takes a very narrow view and gives a large image through a combination of telescopic and ordinary photographic lenses.

teleprinter or *teletypewriter* a transmitting and receiving device used in telecommunications to handle coded messages. Teleprinters are like automatic typewriters. They convert typed words into electrical signals (using a 5-unit Baudot code, see ◊baud) at the transmitting end, and signals into typed words at the receiving end.

telescope a device for collecting and focusing light and other forms of electromagnetic radiation. A telescope produces a magnified image, which makes the object seem nearer, and it shows objects fainter than can be seen by the eye alone. A telescope with a large *aperture*, or opening, can distinguish finer detail and fainter objects than one with a small aperture. The *refracting telescope* uses lenses, and the *reflecting telescope* uses mirrors. A third type, the *catadioptric telescope*, with a combination of lenses and mirrors, is used increasingly. See also ◊radio telescope.

In a refractor, light is collected by a ◊lens called the *object glass* or *objective* which focuses light down a tube, forming an image magnified by an *eyepiece*. Invention of the refractor is attributed to a Dutch optician, Hans ◊Lippershey, 1608. The largest refracting telescope in the world, at ◊Yerkes Observatory, Wisconsin, USA has an aperture of 102 cm/40 in.

In a reflector, light is collected and focused by a concave mirror. The first reflector was built about 1670 by Isaac ◊Newton. Large mirrors are cheaper to make and easier to mount than large lenses, so all the largest telescopes are reflectors. The largest reflector, with a 6 m/236 in mirror, is at Zelenchukskaya, USSR. Telescopes with larger apertures are planned, some of which will be composed of numerous smaller mirrors. The first such *multiple-mirror telescope* was installed on Mount Hopkins, Arizona, 1979. It consists of six mirrors of 1.8 m/72 in aperture, which perform like a single 4.5 m/176 in mirror. *Schmidt telescopes* are used for taking wide-field photographs of the sky. They have a main mirror, plus a thin

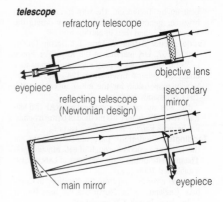

telescope

refractory telescope

objective lens

eyepiece

reflecting telescope (Newtonian design)

secondary mirror

main mirror

eyepiece

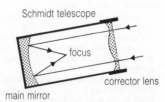

Schmidt telescope

focus

corrector lens

main mirror

lens at the front of the tube to increase the field of view.

Large telescopes can now be placed in orbit, above the distorting effects of the Earth's atmosphere. Telescopes in space have been used to study ◊infrared, ◊ultraviolet and X-rays that do not penetrate the atmosphere, but which carry much information about the births, lives and deaths of stars and galaxies. The 2.4 m/95 in Hubble Space Telescope, launched in April 1990, can see the sky more clearly than any telescope on Earth.

teletext broadcast system of displaying information on television screens (entertainment, sport, finance) which is constantly updated. It is a form of ◊videotext, pioneered in Britain by the British Broadcasting Corporation with ◊Ceefax and by Independent Television with ◊Oracle.

televangelist in North America, a fundamentalist Christian minister, especially of the Pentecostal

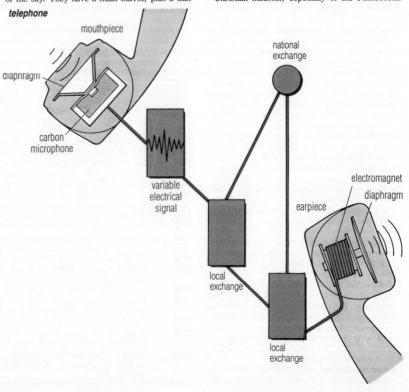

telephone

mouthpiece

diaphragm

carbon microphone

variable electrical signal

national exchange

local exchange

local exchange

earpiece

electromagnet

diaphragm

television

television transmitter (essentials)

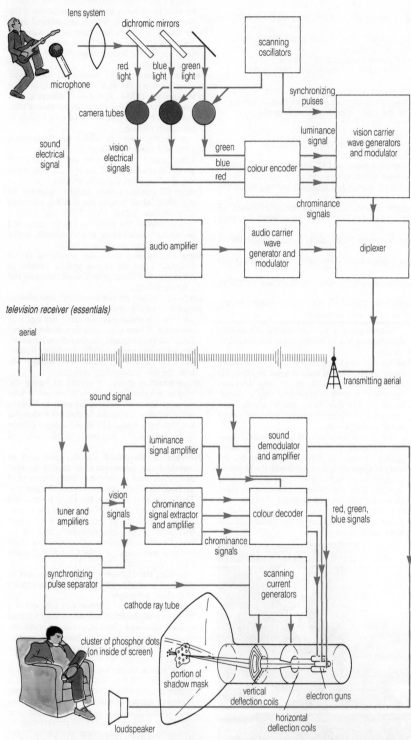

television receiver (essentials)

church, who hosts a television show and solicits donations from viewers. Well-known televangelists include Jim Bakker, convicted in 1989 of fraudulent misuse of donations, and Jimmy Swaggart.

television the reproduction at a distance by radio waves of visual images. For transmission, a television camera converts the pattern of light it takes in into a pattern of electrical charges. This is scanned line-by-line by a beam of electrons from an electron gun, resulting in variable electrical signals that represent the visual picture. These vision signals

are combined with a radio carrier wave and broadcast. The TV aerial picks up the wave and feeds it to the receiver (TV set). This separates out the vision signals, which pass to a cathode-ray tube. The vision signals control the strength of a beam of electrons from an electron gun, aimed at the screen and making it glow more or less brightly. At the same time the beam is made to scan across the screen line-by-line, mirroring the action of the gun in the TV camera. The result is a recreation, spot-by-spot, line-by-line, of the pattern of light

that entered the camera. Twenty-five pictures are built up each second with interlaced scanning (30 in North America), with a total of 625 lines in Europe, or 525 lines in North America and Japan.

television channels In addition to transmissions received by all viewers, the 1970s and 1980s saw the growth of *pay television*, which is received only by special subscribers, and of devices, such as those used in the Qube system (USA), which allow the viewers' opinion to be transmitted instantaneously to the studio via a response button, so that, for example, unpopular performers can be taken off the television at once. The number of programme channels continues to increase, following the introduction of satellite television. Further use of the television set has been brought about by ◊videotext and the use of video recorders to record programmes for playback later or to play pre-recorded videocassettes. In the UK, the average viewing time per person is 25.5 hours each week.

The world's first public television service was started from the BBC station at the Alexandra Palace, in N London, 2 Nov 1936.

history In 1873 it was realized that, since the electrical properties of the non-metallic element selenium vary according to the amount of light to which it is exposed, light could be converted into electrical impulses, making it possible to transmit such impulses over a distance and then re-convert them into light. The chief difficulty was seen to be the 'splitting of the picture' so that the infinite variety of light and shade values might be transmitted and reproduced.

In 1908 Campbell-Swinton pointed out that cathode-ray tubes would best effect transmission and reception. Mechanical devices were used at the first practical demonstration of actual television, given by J L Baird in London 27 Jan 1926, and cathode-ray tubes were used experimentally by the BBC from 1934.

colour television Baird gave a demonstration of colour television in London 1928, but it was not until Dec 1953 that the first successful system was adopted for broadcasting, in the USA. This is called the NTSC system, since it was developed by the National Television System Committee, and variations of it have been developed in Europe, for example SECAM (sequential and memory) system in France and the PAL (phase alternation by line) in West Germany. The three differ only in the way colour signals are prepared for transmission. When there was no agreement on a universal European system 1964, in 1967 the UK adopted PAL (as did West Germany, The Netherlands, and Switzerland) while France and the USSR adopted SECAM.

The method of colour reproduction in television is related to that used in colour photography and printing. It uses the principle that any colour can be made by mixing the primary colours red, green, and blue in appropriate proportions. In colour television the receiver reproduces only three basic colours: red, green, and blue. The effect of yellow, for example, is reproduced by combining equal amounts of red and green light, while white is formed by a mixture of all three basic colours. It is thus possible to specify the colour which it is required to transmit by sending signals which indicate the amounts of red, green, and blue light which are to be generated at the receiver.

To transmit each of these three signals in the same way as the single brightness signal in black and white television would need three times the normal bandwidth, and reduce the number of possible stations and programmes to one-third of that possible with monochrome television. The three signals are therefore coded into one complex signal which is transmitted as a more or less normal black and white signal, and which produces a satisfactory—or compatible—picture on black and white receivers. A fraction of each primary red, green, and blue signal is added together to

television chronology

1878	William Crookes in England invented the Crookes tube, which produced cathode rays.
1884	Paul Nipkow in Germany built a mechanical scanning device, the Nipkow disc, a rotating disc with a spiral pattern of holes in it.
1897	Karl Ferdinand Braun, also in Germany, modified the Crookes tube to produce the ancestor of the modern TV receiver picture tube.
1906	Boris Rosing in Russia began experimenting with the Nipkow disc and cathode-ray tube, eventually succeeding in transmitting some crud e TV pictures.
1923	Zworykin in the USA invented the first electronic camera tube, the iconoscope.
1926	Baird demonstrated a workable TV system, using mechanical scanning by Nipkow disc.
1928	Baird demonstrated colour TV.
1929	The BBC began broadcasting experimental TV programmes using Baird's system.
1936	The BBC began regular broadcasting using Baird's system from Alexandra Palace, London.
1940	Experimental colour TV transmission began in the USA, using the modern system of colour reproduction.
1953	Successful colour TV transmissions began in the USA.
1956	The first videotape recorder was produced in California by the Ampex Corporation.
1962	TV signals were transmitted across the Atlantic via the Telstar satellite.
1970	The first videodisc system was announced by Decca in Britain and AEG-Telefunken in Germany, but it was not perfected until the 1980s, when laser scanning was used for playback.
1973	The BBC and Independent Television introduced the world's first teletext systems, Ceefax and Oracle, respectively.
1975	Sony introduced their videocassette tape recorder system, Betamax, for domestic viewers, six years after their professional U-Matic system. The British Post Office (now British Telecom) announced their Prestel viewdata system.
1979	Matsushita in Japan developed a pocket-sized flat-screen TV set, using a liquid-crystal display (LCD).
1986	Data broadcasting using digital techniques was developed; an enhancement of teletext was produced.
1989	The Japanese began broadcasting high-definition television; satellite television was introduced in the UK.
1990	The BBC introduced a digital stereo sound system (NICAM); MAC, a European system allowing greater picture definition, more data, and sound tracks, was introduced.

produce the normal brightness, or luminance signal. The minimum of extra colouring information is then sent by a special subcarrier signal, which is superimposed on the brightness signal. This extra colouring information corresponds to the hue and saturation of the transmitted colour, but without any of the fine detail of the picture. The impression of sharpness is conveyed only by the brightness signal, the colouring being added as a broad colour wash. The various colour systems differ only in the way in which the colouring signals are sent on the subcarrier signal.

The colour receiver has to amplify the complex signal and decode it back to the basic red, green, and blue signals; these primary signals are then applied to a colour cathode-ray tube. The colour display tube is the heart of any colour receiver. Many designs of colour picture tube have been invented and the most successful of these is known as the 'shadow mask tube'. It operates on similar electronic principles to the black and white television picture tube, but the screen is composed of a fine mosaic of over one million dots arranged in an orderly fashion. One-third of the dots glow red when bombarded by electrons, one-third glow green, and one-third blue. There are three sources of electrons, respectively modulated by the red, green, and blue signals. The tube is arranged so that the shadow mask allows only the red signals to hit red dots, the green signals to hit green dots, and the blue signals to hit blue dots. The glowing dots are so small that from a normal viewing distance the colours merge into one another and a picture with a full range of colours is seen.

telex *tele*typewriter *ex*change service, an international telecommunications network that handles telegraph messages in the form of coded signals. It uses ◊teleprinters for transmitting and receiving, and makes use of land lines (cables), radio and satellite links to make connections between subscribers.

Telford /'telfəd/ Thomas 1757–1834. Scottish civil engineer who opened up N Scotland by building roads and waterways. He constructed many aqueducts and canals, including the Caledonian 1802–23, and erected the Menai road suspension bridge 1819–26, a structure scarcely tried previously in England. In Scotland he constructed over 1,600 km/1,000 mi of road, and 1,200 bridges, churches, and harbours.

In 1963 the new town of Telford, Shropshire, 32 km/20 mi NW of Birmingham, was named after him.

Tell /tel/ Wilhelm (William) legendary 14th century Swiss archer, said to have refused to salute the Habsburg badge at Altdorf on Lake Lucerne. Sentenced to shoot an apple from his son's head, he did so, then shot the tyrannical Austrian ruler Gessler, symbolizing his people's refusal to submit to external authority.

The first written account of the legend dates from 1474, the period of the wars of the Swiss against Charles the Bold of Burgundy; but the story of a man showing his skill with the crossbow in such a way is much earlier. The legend has been used for plays (by Schiller, 1804) and an opera (Rossini, 1829), as well as filmed versions.

Tell el Amarna /'tel el ə'ma:nə/ site of the ancient Egyptian capital ◊Akhetaton. The ◊Amarna tablets were found there.

Telford *Portrait of the Scottish engineer Thomas Telford by W Raddon, 1831. Telford constructed bridges over the river Severn and the Ellesmere Canal (1773–1805).*

Teller /'telə/ Edward 1908– . US physicist known as the 'father' of the H-bomb, which he worked on at Los Alamos in World War II. He was born in Hungary and emigrated to the US in 1935. In 1954, he was a key witness against ◊Oppenheimer at the security hearings. He was widely believed to be the model for the leading character in ◊Kubrick's 1964 film *Dr Strangelove*. More recently he has been one of the leading supporters of the Star Wars programme.

tellurium a semi-metallic element of the sulphur group, symbol Te, atomic number 52, relative atomic mass 127.61. It is used in colouring glass (blue to brown), in the electrolytic refining of zinc, and in electronics. It is also used as a catalyst in petroleum refining.

It was discovered by Müller von Richtenstein 1782, and named by Klaproth 1798 (from Latin *tellus*, earth). Its strength and hardness are greatly increased by addition of 0.1% lead, when it is used for pipes and cable sheaths.

Telstar US communications satellite, launched 10 July 1962, which relayed the first live television transmissions between the USA and Europe. Telstar orbited the Earth in 158 minutes, and so had to be tracked by ground stations, unlike the geostationary satellites of today.

Tema /'ti:mə/ port in Ghana; population (1982) 324,000. It has the largest artificial harbour in Africa, opened 1962, as well as oil refineries and a fishing industry.

temp. abbreviation for *temperature; temporary*.

tempera a painting medium in which powdered pigments are bound together, usually with egg yolk and water. A form of tempera was used in ancient Egypt, and egg tempera was the foremost medium for panel painting in late medieval and early Renaissance Europe. It was gradually superseded by oils from the late 15th century onwards.

temperament in music, a system of tuning the pitches of a mode or scale; in folk music to preserve its emotional or ritual meaning, in Western music to allow maximum flexibility for changing key. J S Bach wrote *The Well-Tempered Clavier* to demonstrate the superiority of this system of tuning.

Temperance Movement societies dedicated to curtailing the consumption of alcohol by total prohibition, local restriction or encouragement of declarations of personal abstinence ('the pledge'). They were first set up in the USA, Ireland, and Scotland, then in the N of England in the 1830s.

The proponents of temperance were drawn from evangelicals, nonconformists, trade unionists, Chartists, members of co-operatives, the self-help movement, and the Church of England temperance society. After 1871 the movement supported the ◊Liberal Party in its attempts to use the licensing laws to restrict the consumption of alcoholic beverages.

temperature the state of hotness or coldness of a body, and the condition that determines whether or not it will transfer heat to, or receive heat from, another body according to the laws of ◊thermodynamics. It is measured in degrees Celsius (before 1948 called centigrade), Kelvin, or Fahrenheit.

The normal temperature of the human body is about 36.9°C/98.4°F. Variation by more than a degree or so indicates ill-health, a rise signifying excessive activity (usually due to infection), and a decrease signifying deficient heat production (usually due to lessened vitality). To convert degrees Celsius to degrees Fahrenheit, multiply by 9/5 and add 32; Fahrenheit to Celsius, subtract 32, then multiply by 5/9. A useful quick approximation for converting Celsius to Fahrenheit is to double the Celsius and add 30, for example 12°C = 24 + 30 = 54°F.

tempering heat treatment used for improving the properties of metals, particularly steel alloys. It involves heating the metal to a certain temperature and then cooling it suddenly in a water or oil bath.

Tempest, The a romantic drama by William Shakespeare, first performed 1611–12. Prospero, usurped as duke of Milan by his brother Antonio, lives on a remote island with his daughter Miranda and Caliban, a deformed creature. Prospero uses magic to shipwreck Antonio and his party on the island and with the help of the spirit Ariel regains his dukedom.

Templar /ˈtemplə/ member of a Christian military order, founded in Jerusalem 1119, the **Knights of the Temple of Solomon**. The knights took vows of poverty, chastity, and obedience and devoted themselves to the recovery of Palestine from the Muslims.

They played a distinguished part in the Crusades of the 12th and 13th centuries. The enormous wealth of the order aroused the envy of Philip IV of France, who arranged for charges of heresy to be brought against its members 1307, and the order was suppressed 1308–1312.

temple a place of religious worship. In US usage, temple is another name for ◊synagogue.

Temple the centre of Jewish national worship in Jerusalem. The Western Wall, or **Wailing Wall**, is the surviving part of the western wall of the platform of the enclosure of the Temple of Herod. Since the destruction of the Temple AD 70, Jews have gone there to pray and to mourn their dispersion and the loss of their homeland.

Three temples have occupied the site: **Solomon's Temple**, which was destroyed by the Babylonian king Nebuchadnezzar in the 6th century BC; **Zerubbabel's Temple**, built after the return of the Jews from the Babylonian captivity 536 BC; and **Herod's Temple**, which was destroyed by the Romans. The Mosque of Omar now stands on the site. Under Jordanian rule Jews had no access to the place, but the Israelis took this part of the city in the 1967 war.

Temple /ˈtempl/ Shirley 1928– . US actress, who became the most successful child star of the 1930s. Her films include *Bright Eyes* 1934, in which she sang 'On the Good Ship Lollipop'. As Shirley Temple Black, she was active in the Republican Party, and was US Chief of Protocol 1976–77. She was appointed US ambassador to Czechoslovakia in 1989.

Temple Bar former western gateway of the City of London, between Fleet Street and the Strand (site marked by griffin); the heads of traitors were formerly displayed above it on spikes. Rebuilt by Wren 1672, it was at Theobald's Park, Hertfordshire from 1878 until 1985, when it was placed near St Paul's Cathedral.

Temple *Child actress Shirley Temple salutes and wins the hearts of cinema-goers and critics in Bright Eyes 1934, for which she received an Oscar. From being the most successful child star of the 1930s, she went on to become prominent in US politics in the 1970s.*

tempo (Italian 'time') in music, the speed at which a piece is played.

tempus fugit (Latin) time flies.

Temuco /teˈmuːkəʊ/ market town and capital of Araucanía region, Chile; population (1987) 218,000.

tenant farming system whereby farmers rent their holdings from a landowner in return for the use of agricultural land.

In 19th-century Britain, most farmland was organized into landed estates containing tenanted farms. A marked change began after World War I when, owing to the agricultural depression, many landowners sold off all or part of their estates, often to the sitting tenant farmers. Although in 1950 50% of the country's farms were still rented, the current figure is less than 25%.

tench European freshwater fish *Tinca tinca*. A member of the carp family, it is about 45 cm/18 in long, weighing 2 kg/4.5 lbs, coloured olive-green above and grey beneath. The scales are small and there is a barbel at each side of the mouth.

tennis

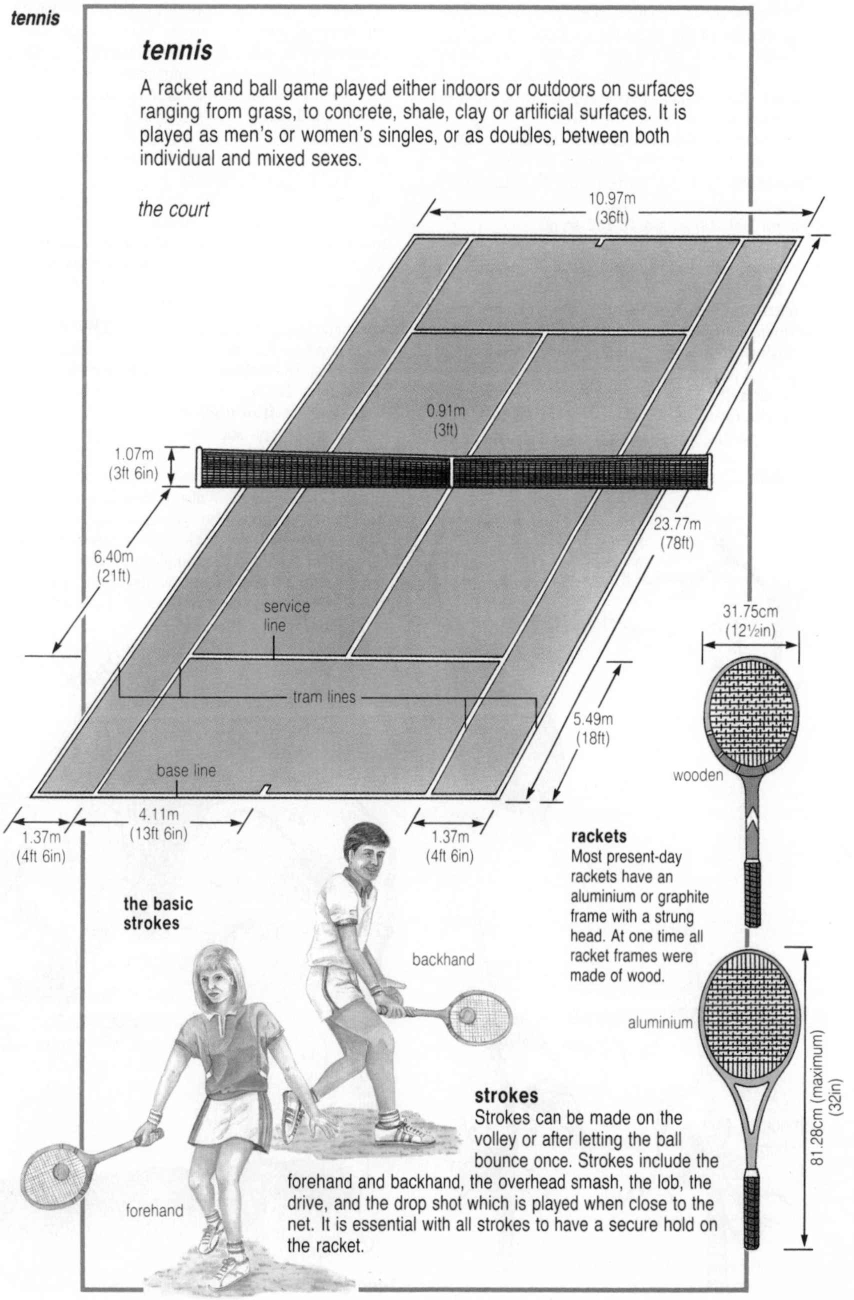

tennis

A racket and ball game played either indoors or outdoors on surfaces ranging from grass, to concrete, shale, clay or artificial surfaces. It is played as men's or women's singles, or as doubles, between both individual and mixed sexes.

the court

10.97m (36ft)

0.91m (3ft)

1.07m (3ft 6in)

23.77m (78ft)

6.40m (21ft)

service line

tram lines

5.49m (18ft)

base line

4.11m (13ft 6in)

1.37m (4ft 6in)

1.37m (4ft 6in)

the basic strokes

backhand

forehand

31.75cm (12½in)

wooden

rackets
Most present-day rackets have an aluminium or graphite frame with a strung head. At one time all racket frames were made of wood.

aluminium

81.28cm (maximum) (32in)

strokes
Strokes can be made on the volley or after letting the ball bounce once. Strokes include the forehand and backhand, the overhead smash, the lob, the drive, and the drop shot which is played when close to the net. It is essential with all strokes to have a secure hold on the racket.

Ten Commandments in the Old Testament or Hebrew Bible, the laws given by God to the Israelite leader Moses on Mount Sinai, engraved on two tablets of stone. They are: to have no other gods besides Jehovah; to make no idols; not to misuse the name of God; to keep the sabbath holy; to honour one's parents; not to commit murder, adultery, or theft; not to give false evidence; not to be covetous. They form the basis of Jewish and Christian moral codes; the 'tablets of the Law' given to Moses are also mentioned in the Koran.

tendon a type of connective tissue that joins muscle to bone in vertebrates. Tendons are largely composed of the protein collagen, and because of their inelasticity are very efficient at transforming muscle power into movement.

tendril in botany, a slender, threadlike structure that supports a climbing plant by coiling around suitable supports, such as the stems and branches of other plants. It may be a modified stem, leaf, leaflet, flower, leaf stalk, or stipule (a small appendage on either side of the leaf stalk), and may be simple or branched. The tendrils of Virginia creeper *Parthenocissus quinquefolia* are modified flower-heads with suckerlike pads at the end that stick to walls, while those of the grapevine *Vitis* grow away from the light and thus enter dark crevices where they expand to anchor the plant firmly.

Tenerife /ˌtenəˈriːf/ largest of the ◊Canary Islands, Spain; area 2,060 sq km/795 sq mi; population (1981) 557,000. *Santa Cruz* is the main town, and *Pico de Teide* is an active volcano.

Teng Hsiao-ping /ˈteŋ ˌʃaʊˈpɪŋ/ alternative spelling of ◊Deng Xiaoping, Chinese politician.

Ten Hours Act 1847 British act of Parliament that restricted the working day of all workers except adult males. It was prompted by the public campaign (the 'Ten Hours Movement') set up in 1831. Women and young people were restricted to a 10½ hour day, with 1½ hours for meals, between 6 am and 6 pm.

Teniers /ˈteniəz/ family of Flemish painters, active in Antwerp. *David Teniers the Younger* (David II, 1610–90) became court painter to Archduke Leopold William, governor of the Netherlands, in Brussels. He painted scenes of peasant life. As curator of the archduke's art collection, David Teniers made many copies of the pictures, and a collection of engravings, *Theatrum Pictorium* 1660. His peasant scenes are humorous and full of vitality, inspired by ◊Brouwer.

His father, *David Teniers the Elder* (David I, 1582–1649), painted religious pictures.

Tennessee /ˌtenəˈsiː/ state of the E central USA; nickname Volunteer State

area 109,200 sq km/42,151 sq mi

capital Nashville

towns Memphis, Knoxville, Chattanooga, Clarksville

features Tennessee Valley Authority; Great Smoky Mountains National Park; Grand Old Opry, Nashville; research centres include Oak Ridge and the Arnold Engineering Development Centre for aircraft

products cereals, cotton, tobacco, timber, coal, zinc, pyrites, phosphates, iron, steel, chemicals

tendrils

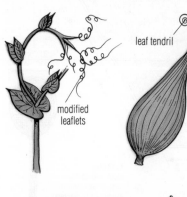

leaf tendril

modified leaflets

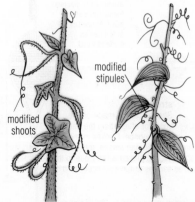

modified stipules

modified shoots

population (1987) 4,855,000

famous people Davy Crockett, David Farragut, W C Handy, Bessie Smith

history first settled 1757, it became a state 1796.

Tennessee Valley Authority (TVA) US government corporation founded 1933 to develop the Tennessee River basin (an area of some 104,000 sq km/40,000 sq mi) by building hydroelectric power stations, producing and distributing fertilizers, and similar activities. The TVA was one of President F D Roosevelt's ◊New Deal measures, promoting economic growth by government investment.

Tenniel /ˈtenjəl/ John 1820–1914. British illustrator and cartoonist, known for his illustrations for Lewis Carroll's *Alice's Adventures in Wonderland* 1865 and *Through the Looking-Glass* 1872. He joined the satirical magazine *Punch* in 1850, and for over 50 years he was one of its leading cartoonists.

tennis, lawn a racket and ball game invented in England towards the end of the 19th century. It derived from ◊real tennis. Although played on different surfaces (grass, wood, shale, clay, concrete) it is still called 'lawn tennis'.

The aim of the two or four players is to strike the ball into the prescribed area of the court, with oval-headed rackets (strung with gut or nylon), in such a way that it cannot be returned. The game is won by those first winning four points (called 15, 30, 40, game), unless both sides reach 40 (deuce) when two consecutive points are needed to win. A set is won by winning six games with a margin of two over opponents, though a tie-break system operates, that is at six games to each side (or in some cases eight) except in the final set. Major events include the ◊*Davis Cup* 1900 for international men's competition, and ◊*Wightman Cup* 1923 for US and UK women's teams, and the annual All England Tennis Club championships (originating 1877), an open event for players of both sexes at **Wimbledon.**

Winner of six successive women's titles at Wimbledon is Martina ◊Navratilova 1982–87; of the men Björn ◊Borg has won five successive titles 1976–80 and William Renshaw won six between 1881–86; the youngest male winner was 17-year-old West German Boris ◊Becker, 1985. The Wimbledon championship is one of the sport's four *Grand Slam* events; the others are the US Open (first held 1881 as the United States

Nashville

Championship), French Championships, and Australian Championships.

tennis: recent winners

Wimbledon Championships
men's singles
1980 Björn Borg *(Sweden)*
1981 John McEnroe *(USA)*
1982 Jimmy Connors *(USA)*
1983 John McEnroe *(USA)*
1984 John McEnroe *(USA)*
1985 Boris Becker *(West Germany)*
1986 Boris Becker *(West Germany)*
1987 Pat Cash *(Australia)*
1988 Stefan Edberg *(Sweden)*
1989 Boris Becker *(West Germany)*
women's singles
1980 Evonne Goolagong-Cawley *(Australia)*
1981 Chris Evert-Lloyd *(USA)*
1982 Martina Navratilova *(USA)*
1983 Martina Navratilova *(USA)*
1984 Martina Navratilova *(USA)*
1985 Martina Navratilova *(USA)*
1986 Martina Navratilova *(USA)*
1987 Martina Navratilova *(USA)*
1988 Steffi Graf *(West Germany)*
1989 Steffi Graf *(West Germany)*
United States Open
men's singles
1980 John McEnroe *(USA)*
1981 John McEnroe *(USA)*
1982 Jimmy Connors *(USA)*
1983 Jimmy Connors *(USA)*
1984 John McEnroe *(USA)*
1985 Ivan Lendl *(Czechoslovakia)*
1986 Ivan Lendl *(Czechoslovakia)*
1987 Ivan Lendl *(Czechoslovakia)*
1988 Mats Wilander *(Sweden)*

Tenniel *The Mad Hatter's tea party, from Lewis Carroll's* Alice in Wonderland, *illustrated by John Tenniel.*

tennis, lawn (Above) Boris Becker (West Germany) playing the Stella Artois tournament, 1987. (Right) Gabriela Sabatini (Argentina) playing the US Open tournament, 1988.

1989 Boris Becker *(West Germany)*
   women's singles
1980 Chris Evert-Lloyd *(USA)*
1981 Tracy Austin *(USA)*
1982 Chris Evert-Lloyd *(USA)*
1983 Martina Navratilova *(USA)*
1984 Martina Navratilova *(USA)*
1985 Hana Mandlikova *(Czechoslovakia)*
1986 Martina Navratilova *(USA)*
1987 Martina Navratilova *(USA)*
1988 Steffi Graf *(West Germany)*
1989 Steffi Graf *(West Germany)*
Davis Cup
1980 Czechoslovakia
1981 USA
1982 USA
1983 Australia
1984 Sweden
1985 Sweden
1986 Australia
1987 Sweden
1988 West Germany
1989 West Germany

Tennstedt /'tenʃtet/ Klaus 1926– . East German conductor, musical director of the London Philharmonic Orchestra 1983–87. He is renowned for his interpretations of works by Mozart, Beethoven, Bruckner, and Mahler.

Tennyson /'tenɪsən/ Alfred, 1st Baron Tennyson 1809–1892. English poet, poet laureate 1850–96, noted for the majestic musical language of his verse. His works include 'The Lady of Shalott', 'The Lotus Eaters', 'Ulysses', 'Break, Break, Break', 'The Charge of the Light Brigade'; the longer narratives *Locksley Hall* 1832, and *Maud* 1855; the elegy *In Memoriam* 1850; and a long series of poems on the Arthurian legends *The Idylls of the King* 1857–85.

Tennyson was born at Somersby, Lincolnshire. The death of A H Hallam (a close friend during his years at Trinity College, Cambridge) 1833 prompted the elegiac *In Memoriam*, unpublished until 1850, the year in which he succeeded Wordsworth as poet laureate and married Emily Sellwood.

tenor in music, the highest range of adult male voice when not using ◊falsetto.

tenpin bowling indoor sport popular in North America. As in skittles, the object is to bowl a ball down an alley at pins (ten as opposed to nine). The game is usually between two players or teams. A game of ten pins is made up of ten 'frames'. The frame is the bowler's turn to play and in each frame he or she may bowl twice. One point is scored for each pin knocked down, with bonus points for knocking all ten pins down in either one ball or two. The player or team making the greater score wins.

The game of ninepins was introduced to America by Dutch immigrants in the 17th century. By the end of the 19th century it was very popular as a gambling game on the streets of New York. Consequently it was outlawed; to get round the law the extra pin was added.

Modern bowling lanes measure 18.3 m/60 ft to the nearest pin and have an extra 4.57 m/15 ft approach area; they are 1 m/3 ft 6 in wide. Balls weighing up to 7.25 kg/16 lb are made of rubber composition and drilled with holes for thumb and two fingers. Pins made of maple are 38.1 cm/ 1 ft 3 in high. The US National Bowling Association was formed 1875, and since the 1960s the game has become popular in Britain.

tenure employment terms and conditions. Security of tenure is often granted to the judiciary, civil servants, and others in public office, particularly where impartiality and freedom from political control are considered important. The length of tenure depends on the particular service involved and termination of it would only occur in exceptional cases, such as serious misconduct.

Tenzing Norgay /'tensɪŋ/ known as *Sherpa Tenzing* 1914–1986. Nepalese mountaineer. In 1953 he was the first, with Edmund Hillary, to reach the summit of Mount Everest.

He had previously made 19 Himalayan expeditions as a porter. He subsequently became a director of the Himalayan Mountaineering Institute, Darjeeling.

Teotihuacán /ˌteɪəʊˌtiːwəˈkaːn/ ancient city in central Mexico, the religious centre of the ◊Toltec civilization.

Teplice /'teplɪtseɪ/ industrial (peat- and lignite-mining, glass, porcelain, cement, paper) city and spa in Czechoslovakia; population (1984) 54,000.

tequila Mexican alcoholic drink made from the ◊agave plant and named from the place, near Guadalajara, where the conquistadors first developed it from Aztec *pulque*, which would keep for only a day.

teratogen a chemical that can induce deformities in unborn children if absorbed by the mother during pregnancy. Teratogens known to cause human malformations include some drugs (notably ◊thalidomide), and other chemicals, certain disease organisms, and high-level radiation.

terbium a metallic element, symbol Tb, atomic number 65, relative atomic mass 158.93. One of the lanthanide series, it is used in lasers, semiconductors, and television tubes.

Terborch /təˈbɔːx/ Gerard 1617–1681. Dutch painter of small-scale portraits and genre scenes, mainly of soldiers at rest or wealthy families in their homes. He travelled widely in Europe. *The Peace of Münster* 1648 (National Gallery, London) is an official group portrait.

Terbrugghen /təˈbruːxən/ Hendrik 1588–1629. Dutch painter, a leader of the *Utrecht school* with Honthorst. He visited Rome around 1604 and was inspired by Caravaggio's work. He painted religious subjects and genre scenes.

Terence /'terəns/ (Publius Terentius Afer) 190–159 BC. Roman dramatist, born in Carthage and brought as a slave to Rome, where he was freed and came under ◊Scipio's patronage. His surviving six comedies (including *The Eunuch*

161 BC) are subtly characterized and based on Greek models.

Terengganu alternative spelling of ◊Trengganu, state in Peninsular Malaysia.

Teresa, St /təˈriːzə/ 1515–1582. Spanish mystic, born in Avila. She became a Carmelite nun, and in 1562 founded a new and stricter order. She was subject to fainting fits, during which she saw visions. She wrote *The Way to Perfection* 1583, and an autobiography, *Life of the Mother Theresa of Jesus* 1611. In 1622 she was canonized, and became the first woman Doctor of the Church 1970.

Tereshkova /ˌterɪʃˈkəʊvə/ Valentina Vladimirovna 1937– . Soviet cosmonaut, the first woman to fly in space. In June 1963 she made a three-day flight in Vostok 6, orbiting the Earth 48 times.

term in architecture, a pillar in the form of a pedestal supporting the bust of a human or animal figure. Such objects derive from Roman boundary-marks sacred to *Terminus*, the god of boundaries, whose feast day was Feb 23.

terminal in computing, a device consisting of a keyboard and screen (or, in older systems, a teleprinter) to enable the operator to communicate with the computer. The terminal might be physically attached to the computer or linked to it over a telephone line.

termite soft-bodied social insect, of the tropical order Isoptera, living in large colonies that comprise one or more queens (of relatively enormous size and producing an egg every two seconds), much smaller kings, and still smaller soldiers, workers, and immature forms. Termites build galleried nests of soil particles that may be 6 m/20 ft high.

The Macrotermitinae construct fungus gardens from their own faeces, which are then infected with a special fungus that digests the faeces and renders them once more edible. Termites may dispose of a quarter of the vegetation litter of an area, and their fondness for wood (as in houses and other buildings) brings them into conflict with humans. The wood is broken down in their stomachs by numerous microorganisms living in ◊symbiosis with their hosts.

tern lightly built gull-like seabird, 20–50 cm/8–20 in long, characterized by long pointed wings and a forked tail. Terns are white, black, or a combination of the two.

The *common tern Sterna hirundo* has white underparts, grey upper wings, and a black crown on its head. The *Arctic tern Sterna paradisea* migrates from northern parts of Greenland, North America, and Europe to the Antarctic.

Terni /'teəni/ industrial city in the valley of the Nera river, Umbria region, central Italy; population (1987) 111,000. The nearby Marmore Falls, the highest in Italy, were created by the Romans in order to drain the Rieti marshes.

Terpsichore in Greek mythology, the muse of dance and choral song.

terracotta (Italian 'baked earth') brownish-red baked clay used in building, sculpture, and pottery. It was used in ancient times in countries where no stone was available. The term is specifically applied to small figures or figurines, such as those found at ◊Tanagra. Recent excavations at Xian, China, have revealed life-size terracotta figures of the army of the Emperor Qin dating from the 3rd century.

terra firma (Latin) dry land; solid earth.

terra incognita (Latin) an unknown region.

terrapin member of some species of the order Chelonia (◊turtles and ◊tortoises). Terrapins are small to medium-sized, aquatic or semi-aquatic, and found widely in temperate zones. They are omnivorous, but generally eat aquatic animals. Species include the *diamondback terrapin Malaclemys terrapin* of the eastern USA, the *yellow-bellied terrapin*, and the *red-eared terrapin Pseudemys scripta elegans*. Some species are in danger of extinction owing to collection for the pet trade; most of the animals collected die in transit.

termite

termite – a typical termite mound

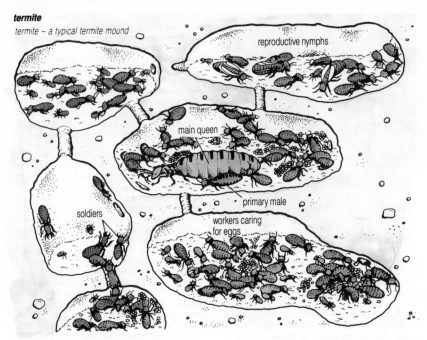

reproductive nymphs

main queen

primary male

soldiers

workers caring
for eggs

Terre Adélie /'teər ædeı'li/ French name for
◊Adélie Land.

Terre Haute /'terə 'həʊt/ city in W Indiana, USA,
on the Wabash; industries (plastics, chemicals,
glass); population (1980) 61,000.

terrier highly intelligent, active dog. They are usually small. Types include the bull, cairn, fox,
Irish, Scottish, Sealyham, Skye, and Yorkshire
terriers. They were originally bred for hunting
rabbits and following quarry such as foxes down
into burrows.

Territorial Army British force of volunteer soldiers,
created from volunteer regiments (incorporated
1872) as the *Territorial Force* 1908. It was
raised and administered by county associations,
and intended primarily for home defence. It was
renamed Territorial Army 1922. Merged with the
Regular Army in World War II, it was revived
1947, and replaced by a smaller, more highly
trained Territorial and Army Volunteer Reserve,
again renamed Territorial Army 1979.

territorial behaviour in biology, the active defence
of a ◊territory. It may involve aggressively driving
out intruders, marking the boundary (with dung
piles or deposits from special scent glands), conspicuous visual displays, characteristic songs, or
loud calls. In general, the territory owner repels
only individuals of its own species.

territorial waters an area of sea over which the
adjoining coastal state claims territorial rights.
This is most commonly a distance of 12 nautical mi/22.2 km from the coast, but, increasingly, states claim fishing and other rights up to
200 mi/370 km.

territory in animal behaviour, an area that is actively
defended by an individual or group. Animals may
hold territories for many different reasons, for
example, to provide a constant food supply, to
monopolize potential mates, or to ensure access
to refuges or nest sites. The size of a territory
depends in part on its function: some nesting and
mating territories may be only a few square metres, whereas feeding territories may be as large
as hundreds of square kilometres.

terrorism systematic violence in the furtherance
of political aims, especially by small ◊guerrilla
groups such as the Fatah Revolutionary Council
(FRC) led by Abu Nidal, a splinter group that
split from the Palestine Liberation Organization
in 1973.

Terror, Reign of the period of the ◊French Revolution when the Jacobins were in power (Oct
1793–July 1794) under Maximilien ◊Robespierre

and instituted mass persecution of their opponents. About 1,400 were executed, until public
indignation rose and Robespierre was overthrown
in July 1794.

Terry /'teri/ (John) Quinlan 1937– . British Neo-
Classical architect. His work includes country
houses, for example Merks Hall, Great Dunmow,
Essex, 1982, and the larger-scale Richmond, London, riverside project, commissioned 1984.

Terry /'teri/ Ellen 1847–1928. British actress, leading lady to Henry ◊Irving from 1878. She excelled
in Shakespearean roles, such as Ophelia in *Hamlet*.
She had a correspondence with the playwright G
B Shaw.

tertiary in the Roman Catholic church, a member of
a 'third order' (see under ◊Holy Orders); a lay
person who, while marrying and following a normal
employment, attempts to live in accordance with a
modified version of the rule of one of the religious
orders. The first such order was founded by St
◊Francis 1221.

Tertiary period of geological time 65–1.8 million years ago, divided into into five epochs:
Palaeocene, Eocene, Oligocene, Miocene, and
Pliocene. During the Tertiary mammals became
the prevalent land animals and grasslands expanded.

tertiary college in the UK, a college for students
over 16 that combines the work of a ◊sixth form
and a ◊further education college.

Tertullian /tɜ:'tʌliən/ Quintus Septimius Florens
AD 155–222. Carthaginian Father of the Church,
the first important Christian writer in Latin; he
became involved with ◊Montanism 213.

Terylene trade name for a polyester synthetic fibre
produced by the chemicals company ICI. It is made
by polymerizing ethylene glycol and terephthalic
acid. Cloth made from Terylene keeps its shape
after washing and is hard-wearing.

terza rima a poetical metre used in Dante's *Divine
Comedy*, consisting of three-line stanzas in which
the second line rhymes with the first and third of
the following stanza. Shelley's 'Ode to the West
Wind' is another example.

tesla metric unit (symbol T) of ◊magnetic flux
density. One tesla represents a flux density of
1 ◊weber per square metre, or 10 ◊gauss. It is
named after the Croatian engineer Nikola Tesla.

Tesla /'teslə/ Nikola 1856–1943. Croatian electrical engineer, who emigrated to the USA 1884. He
invented fluorescent lighting, the Tesla induction
motor, and the Tesla coil, and developed the ◊al-
ternating current (AC) electrical supply system.

Test Act act of Parliament passed in England in
1673, more than 100 years after similar legislation
in Scotland, requiring holders of public office to
renounce the doctrine of ◊transubstantiation and
take the sacrament in an Anglican church, thus
excluding Catholics, Nonconformists, and non-
Christians from office. Its clauses were repealed
in 1828–29. Scottish tests were abolished in 1889.
In Ireland the Test Act was introduced in 1704 and
English legislation on oaths of allegiance and religious declarations were made valid there in 1782.
All these provisions were abolished in 1871. The
University Test Act 1871 abolished the theological
test required for the MA degree and for Oxford
University and College offices.

Test Ban Treaty a treaty signed by the USA, the
USSR, and the UK 5 Aug 1963 which agreed
to test nuclear weapons only underground. In
the following two years 90 other nations signed
the treaty, the only major non-signatories being
France and China, who continued underwater and
ground-level tests.

testis (plural *testes*) the organ that produces
◊sperm in male (and hermaphrodite) animals. In
most animals it is internal, but in mammals (other
than marine mammals), the paired testes descend
from the body cavity during development, to hang
outside the abdomen in a scrotal sac.

testosterone a hormone secreted chiefly by the testes of vertebrates. It promotes the development of
secondary sexual characteristics in males. In animals with a breeding season, the onset of breeding
behaviour is accompanied by a rise in the level of
testosterone in the blood.

Synthetic or animal testosterone is used to treat
inadequate development of male characteristics
or (illegally) to aid athletes' muscular development. Like other sex hormones, testosterone is
a ◊steroid.

tetanus or *lockjaw* an acute disease caused by the
bacillus *Clostridium tetani* entering a wound. The
bacterium is chiefly found in richly manured soil.
Untreated, tetanus produces muscular spasm,
convulsions, and death. There is a vaccine.

tête-à-tête (French 'head-to-head') a private meeting between two people.

Tethys /'ti:θɪs/ in Greek mythology, one of the
◊Titans, the wife of the god ◊Oceanus.

Tethys Sea /'ti:θɪs/ sea which once separated
◊Laurasia from ◊Gondwanaland; roughly corresponding to the present-day Mediterranean.

Tet Offensive in the Vietnam War, a prolonged
attack mounted by the Vietcong against Saigon
Jan–Feb 1968. Although the Vietcong were forced
to withdraw, the attack on the South Vietnamese
capital brought into question the ability of the
South Vietnamese and their US allies to win
the war.

tetra a brightly coloured tropical fish of the family
Characidae.

tetrahedron (plural *tetrahedra*) in geometry, a
solid figure (◊polyhedron) with four triangular
faces; that is, a ◊pyramid on a triangular base.
A regular tetrahedron has equilateral triangles as
its faces.

Tetrahedra are important in chemistry and
crystallography in describing the shapes of molecules and crystals; for example, the carbon atoms
in a crystal of diamond are arranged in space as a
set of interconnected regular tetrahedra.

tetrapod (Latin 'four-legged') a type of ◊vertebrate.
The group includes mammals, birds, reptiles,
and amphibians. Birds are included because they

tetra

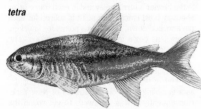

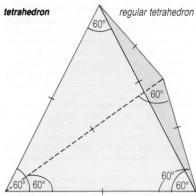

tetrahedron — regular tetrahedron

evolved from four-legged ancestors, the forelimbs having become modified to form wings.

Tetuán /te'twɑːn/ or **Tétouan** town in NE Morocco, near the Mediterranean coast, 64 km/40 mi SE of Tangier; population (1982) 372,000. Products include textiles, leather, and soap. It was settled by Moorish exiles from Spain in the 16th century.

Teutonic Knight member of a German Christian military order, the *Knights of the Teutonic Order*, founded 1190 by Hermann of Salza in Palestine. They crusaded against the pagan Prussians and Lithuanians from 1228, and controlled Prussia until the 16th century. Their capital was Marienburg (now Malbork, Poland).

The Teutonic Knights were originally members of the German aristocracy, who founded an order of hospitallers in Acre 1190, and became a military order 1198. They wore white robes with black crosses. They were based in the Holy Land until 1268 when they were expelled by the Mameluks, after which they concentrated on taking Roman Catholicism into E Europe under the control of the pope. They were prevented from expanding into Russia by ◊Alexander Nevsky at the battle of Lake Peipus 1243, but they ruthlessly colonized Prussia 1226–1283. By the 15th century, pressure from neighbouring powers and the decline of the crusader ideal led to their containment within East Prussia. Their influence ended 1525 when their grand master Albert of Brandenburg was converted to Lutheranism and declared Prussia to be a secular duchy.

Texas /'teksəs/ state of the SW USA; nickname Lone Star State
area 691,200 sq km/266,803 sq mi
capital Austin
towns Houston, Dallas-Fort Worth, San Antonio, El Paso, Corpus Christi, Lubbock
features Rio Grande del Norte and Red rivers; arid Staked Plains, reclaimed by irrigation; the Great Plains
products rice, cotton, sorghum, peanuts, pecans, vegetables, fruit, meat products, oil (one third of the needs of the USA), natural gas, asphalt, graphite, sulphur, salt, helium, chemicals, oil products, processed food, machinery, transport equipment
population (1985) 16,370,000
famous people James Bowie, Buddy Holly, Sam Houston, Howard Hughes, Lyndon Johnson, Janis Joplin, Katherine Anne Porter
history settled by the Spanish 1682; part of Mexico 1821–36; Santa Anna massacred the Alamo garrison

Texas

Austin

1836, but was defeated by Sam Houston at San Jacinto the same year; Texas became an independent republic 1836–45, with Houston as president; in 1845 it became a state of the USA. Texas is the only state in the USA to have previously been an independent republic.

Texel /'tesəl/ or **Tessel** largest and most westerly of the ◊Frisian Islands, in North Holland province, the Netherlands; area 190 sq km/73 sq mi. Den Burg is the chief settlement.

text editor in computing, a program that allows the user to edit text on the screen and to store it in a file. Text editors are similar to ◊word processors, except that they lack the ability to format text into paragraphs and pages and to apply different typefaces and styles.

texte intégral (French 'the complete text') unabridged.

textile (Latin *texere* 'to weave') formerly a material woven from natural spun thread, now loosely extended to machine knits and spun-bonded fabrics (in which a web of fibre is created and then fusebonded by passing it through controlled heat).
natural Textiles made from natural fibres include cotton, linen, silk, and wool (including angora, llama, and many others). For particular qualities, such as flame resistance or water and stain repellence, these may be combined with synthetic fibres or treated with various chemicals.
synthetic The first commercial synthetic thread was 'artificial silk' or rayon (see ◊Chardonnet), with filaments made from modified cellulose (wood pulp) and known according to later methods of manufacture as *viscose* (using caustic soda and carbon disulphide) or *acetate* (using acetic acid). The first fully synthetic textile fibre was ◊nylon 1937; these, with *acrylics*, such as Orlon, used in knitwear, *polyesters*, such as Terylene, and *spandex* or *elastomeric fibres*, for example Lycra, form the basis of most of today's industry.
geotextiles Textiles made from plastic and synthetic fibres, and either felted for use as filters or stabilizing grids, or woven for strength. They form part of drainage systems, road foundations, and barriers to sea and river defences against erosion.

textured vegetable protein a manufactured foodstuff; see ◊TVP.

Teyte /teɪt/ Maggie 1888–1976. British lyric soprano. She is remembered for her Mozartian roles, such as Cherubino in *The Marriage of Figaro*, and was coached as Mélisande in *Pelléas et Mélisande* by the opera's composer Debussy.

TGV *train à grande vitesse* (French 'high speed train') French electrically powered train that provides the world's fastest rail service. Introduced in 1981, it holds the world speed record for a train of 482.4 kmh/301.5 mph (about half the speed of a passenger jet aircraft), reached at a stretch near Tours in 1989. In its regular service, the TGV covers the 425 km/264 mi distance between Paris and Lyons in two hours.

Thackeray /'θækərɪ/ William Makepeace 1811–1863. English novelist and essayist, born in Calcutta, India. He was a regular contributor to *Fraser's Magazine* and *Punch*. *Vanity Fair* 1847–48 was his first novel, followed by *Pendennis* 1848, *Henry Esmond* 1852 (and its sequel *The Virginians* 1857–59), and *The Newcomes* 1853–55, in which Thackeray's tendency to sentimentality is most marked.

Son of an East India Company official, he was educated at Charterhouse and Trinity College, Cambridge. He studied law in the Middle Temple, and then art in Paris, before ultimately settling to journalism in London. Other works include *The Book of Snobs* 1848 and the fairy tale *The Rose and the Ring* 1855.

Thailand /'taɪlænd/ country in SE Asia on the Gulf of Siam, bounded to the E by Laos and Cambodia, to the S by Malaysia, and to the W by Myanmar (Burma).
government Under the constitution of 1978, Thailand is ruled by a hereditary monarch working with a two-chamber legislature, the National

Assembly. The monarch is head of state and head of the armed forces and appoints a prime minister on the advice of the National Assembly. The prime minister and a selected cabinet formulate policy and are in charge of day-to-day government administration. These ministers may speak but not vote at National Assembly meetings; they must not be serving military officers.

The upper house of the National Assembly, the Senate (Wuthisapha) comprises 268 members who are appointed for six-year terms by the monarch on the recommendation of the prime minister. Senators must not be members of any political party. The lower house, the House of Representatives (Saphaphutan) comprises 357 members who are elected from single-member constituencies by universal suffrage for four-year terms.

Far-left parties, such as the Communist Party, are outlawed, as are parties that field candidates in fewer than half the nation's constituencies. Effective political power in Thailand remains ultimately with the army leadership.

history Thailand has an ancient civilization, with Bronze Age artefacts from as early as 4000 BC. Siam, as it was called until 1939 (and 1945–49), has been united as a kingdom since 1350; the present dynasty dates from 1782. It was reached by Portuguese traders in 1511, followed by the British East India Company and the Dutch in the 17th century. Treaties of friendship and trade 1826 and 1855 established Britain as the paramount power in the region and opened Siam to foreign commerce. Anglo-French diplomatic agreements of 1896 and 1904 established Siam as a neutral buffer kingdom between British Burma and French Indochina.

After World War I, a movement for national renaissance developed, which culminated in a coup against the absolute monarch King Prajadhipok and the establishment instead of a constitutional monarchy and an elected, representative system of government 1932. The name of Muang Thai (Land of the Free) was adopted 1939. Thailand was occupied by Japan 1941–44. The government collaborated, but there was a guerrilla resistance movement. A period of instability followed the Japanese withdrawal, King Ananda Mahidol was assassinated 1946, and the army seized power in a coup 1947 led by Field Marshal Pibul Songgram.

The army retained control during the next two decades, with the leader of the military junta periodically changed by a series of bloodless coups: Field Marshal Pibul Songgram 1947–57, Field Marshal Sarit Thanarat 1958–63, and Gen Thanom Kittikachorn 1964–73. The monarch, King ◊Bhumibol Adulyadej, was only a figurehead, and experiments with elected assemblies were undertaken 1957–58 and 1968–71. During this era of junta rule, Thailand allied itself with the USA and encountered serious Communist guerrilla insurgency along its borders with ◊Laos, ◊Kampuchea and ◊Malaysia. Despite achievements in the economic sphere, the junta was overthrown by violent student riots in Oct 1973. A democratic constitution was adopted a year later, and free elections were held in 1975 and 1976. A series of coalition governments lacked stability and the military assumed power again 1976–77, annulling the 1974 constitution.

The army supreme commander, Gen Kriangsak Chomanan, held power 1977–80 and promulgated a new constitution in Dec 1978. This established a mixed civilian and military form of government under the monarch's direction. Having deposed Gen Kriangsak in Oct 1980, Gen Prem Tinsulanonda (1920–) formally relinquished his army office and headed the civilian coalition governments that were formed after the parliamentary elections of Apr 1983 and July 1986.

Attempted coups in Apr 1983 and Sept 1985 (the latter involving Gen Kriangsak) were easily crushed by Prime Minister Prem, who has ruled in a cautious apolitical manner and has retained

Thailand
Kingdom of
(Prathet Thai or Muang-Thai)

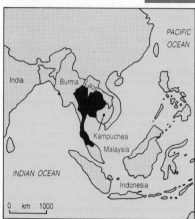

area 513,100 sq km/198,108 sq mi
capital and chief port Bangkok
towns Chiangmai
physical central valley flanked by highlands;
tropical rainforest
features rivers Chao Phraya, Mekong,
Salween; tools and weapons from the Bronze
Age
head of state King Bhumibol Adulyadej
from 1946
head of government Chatichai Choonhavan
from 1988
government system emergent democracy
political parties Thai Ntion (Chart Thai)
conservative, pro-business; Democratic Party
(Prachipat) right-of-centre, pro-monarchist; Social
Action Party (Kij Sangkhom) right-of-centre; Citizen's Party (Rassadorn) conservative; Solidarity
Party (Ekkaparb), right-of-centre opposition force
formed through mergers in 1989; Thai Citizens'
party (Prachakorn Thai) far-right, monarchist;
the Righteous Force (Palang Dharma), a
Bangkok-based anti-corruption, Buddhist
grouping
exports rice, sugar, rubber, teak, tin (fifth
largest producer), rubies, sapphires
currency baht (43.20 = £1 Mar 1990)
population (1989) 55,017,000 (Thai 75%,
Chinese 14%); annual growth rate 2%
life expectancy men 61, women 65
language Thai and Chinese (both official)
religion Buddhist
literacy 94% male/88% female (1985 est)
GNP $42 bn (1985); $828 per head of
population
chronology
1782 Siam absolutist dynasty commenced.
1896 Anglo-French agreement recognized Siam
as independent buffer state.
1932 Constitutional monarchy established.
1939 Name of Thailand adopted.
1941–44 Japanese occupation.
1947 Military seized power in coup.
1972 Withdrawal of Thai troops from South
Vietnam.
1973 Military government overthrown.
1976 Military reassumed control.
1980 Gen Prem Tinsulanonda assumed power.
1983 Civilian government formed but martial
law maintained.
1988 Prime Minister Prem resigned and
was replaced by the conservative Chatichai
Choonhavan.
1989 Thai pirates continued to murder, pillage,
and kidnap Vietnamese 'boat people' on the
high seas.

the confidence of the army leadership and the public. Under his stewardship, the country achieved
a rapid rate of economic growth, 9–10% per
year, emerging as an export-oriented newly
industrializing country (NIC). However, during
the spring of 1988 divisions began to emerge
within the ruling coalition and parliament was
dissolved in Apr 1988. Following the general election of July 1988, a six-party coalition, consisting
of the Thai Nation, Democratic, Social Action,
Rassadorn, United Democratic, and Muan Chon
parties, was formed, which asked Prem to come
into parliament and assume its leadership. Prem
declined this offer for 'personal' reasons and the
Thai Nation's leader took over as premier. He
proceeded to pursue a similar, growth-oriented,
policy course to his predecessor.

The continuing civil war in Cambodia and Laos,
which has resulted in the flight of more than
500,000 refugees to Thailand since 1975, has
provided justification for continued quasi-military
rule and the maintenance of martial law. Thailand
has drawn closer to its ◊ASEAN allies, who jointly
support the Cambodian guerrilla movement, and
its relations with Communist China have seen
a thaw.

Thaïs /'θeɪɪs/ 4th century BC. Greek courtesan,
mistress of ◊Alexander the Great and later wife of
◊Ptolemy I, king of Egypt. She allegedly instigated
the burning of ◊Persepolis.

thalassaemia or *Cooley's anaemia* hereditary
blood disorder that is widespread in the Mediterranean countries, also in Africa and Asia. It is
characterized by an abnormality in the red blood
cells and bone marrow, with enlargement of the
spleen.

Thalberg /'θɔːlbɜːg/ Irving 1899–1936. US film
producer. At the age of 20 he was head of
production at Universal Pictures, and in 1924
he became production supervisor of the newly
formed Metro-Goldwyn-Mayer (MGM). He was
responsible for such prestige films as *Ben-Hur*
1926 and *Mutiny on the Bounty* 1935. With Louis
B Mayer he built up MGM into one of the biggest
Hollywood studios of the 1930s.

Thales /'θeɪliːz/ 640–546 BC. Greek philosopher
and scientist. He made advances in geometry,
predicted the Sun's eclipse 585 BC, and, as a philosophical materialist, theorized that water was the
first principle of all things, that the Earth floated
on water, and so proposed an explanation for
earthquakes. He lived at Miletus in Asia Minor.

Thalia /θə'laɪə/ in Greek mythology, the Muse of
comedy and pastoral poetry.

thalidomide ◊hypnotic drug developed in the 1950s
for use as a sedative. When taken in early pregnancy, it caused malformation of the fetus in
over 5,000 recognized cases, and the drug was
withdrawn. It has limited use in the treatment of
leprosy.

thallium a metallic element, symbol Tl, atomic
number 81, relative atomic mass 204.39. It is
a soft, bluish-grey metal which tarnishes in air,
and is malleable but of low tenacity. It is a poor
conductor of electricity and its compounds are
poisonous, being used as rat poison and insecticide. Other compounds are used in optical and
infrared glass making, and in photoelectric cells. It
was discovered spectroscopically (see ◊spectros-
copy) and isolated by Crookes 1861, and by
Lamy 1862.

thallus any plant body that is not divided into
true leaves, stems, and roots. It is often thin
and flattened, as in the body of a seaweed, lichen, liverwort, and the gametophyte generation
(◊prothallus) of a fern.

Some flowering plants (◊angiosperms) that are
adapted to an aquatic way of life may have a very
simple plant body which is described as a thallus
(for example duckweed *Lemna*).

Thames /temz/ river in SE England; length
338 km/210 mi. It rises in the Cotswolds above
Cirencester, and is tidal as far as Teddington. Below London there is protection from flooding by
means of the Thames barrier. The headstreams
unite at Lechlade. Tributaries from the north
are the Windrush, Evenlode, Cherwell, Thame,
Colne, Lea, and Roding; and from the south,
Kennet, Loddon, Wey, Mole, Darent, and Medway. Above Oxford it is sometimes poetically
called *Isis*.

Thames barrier a moveable barrier built across the
river Thames at Woolwich, London, as part of
the city's flood defences. Completed 1982, the
barrier comprises curved flood gates which are
rotated 90° into position from beneath the water
to form a barrier when exceptionally high tides are
expected.

Thames, Firth of /temz/ inlet between Auckland
and the Coromandel Peninsula, New Zealand.

thane or *thegn* an Anglo-Saxon hereditary nobleman rewarded by the granting of land for service
to the king or a lord.

Thanet, Isle of /'θænɪt/ NE corner of Kent, SE
England, bounded by the North Sea and the river
Stour. It was an island until the 16th century,
and includes the coastal resorts of Broadstairs,
Margate, and Ramsgate.

Thanksgiving (Day) national holiday in the USA
(fourth Thursday in Nov) and Canada (second
Monday in Oct), first celebrated by the Pilgrim settlers in Massachusetts on their first
harvest 1621.

Thar Desert /tɑː/ or *Indian Desert* desert on the
borders of ◊Rajasthan and Pakistan; area about
250,000 sq km/96,500 sq mi.

Thatcher /'θætʃə/ Margaret Hilda (born Roberts)
1925– . British Conservative politician, in Parliament from 1959, party leader from 1975, and
prime minister from 1979. Landmarks of the
Thatcher government include the ◊Falklands conflict 1982; the 1984–85 miners' strike; large-scale
privatization, combined with attempted control of
the money supply and reduction of state borrowing; the attempt to suppress the publication of
◊*Spycatcher*; the ◊Anglo-Irish Agreement 1985;
the introduction of the community charge, or ◊poll
tax; and increases in home and share ownership,
unemployment, interest rates, trade deficit, and
homelessness.

Her father, a grocer, was later mayor of Grantham.
She was educated at Oxford and qualified as a
research chemist and barrister. As minister of
education 1970–74, she caused controversy when
she abolished free milk for schoolchildren. She
defeated Heath for the Conservative leadership
1975, and became prime minister 1979. She was
re-elected 1983 and 1987, the first British prime
minister to be elected for a third term since Lord
Liverpool.

thaumatrope in photography, a disc with two different pictures at opposite ends of its surface. The
images combine into one when rapidly rotated
because of the persistence of visual impressions.

theatre broad term applied to a performance by actors for an audience, which may include ◊drama,
dancing, music, ◊mime, and ◊puppets. The term is
also used for the place or building in which dramatic

Thatcher Conservative politician and prime minister
Margaret Thatcher.

performances take place. Theatre history can be traced to Egyptian religious ritualistic drama as long ago as 3200 BC. The first known European theatres were in Greece from about 600 BC.

history The earliest Greek theatres were open spaces around the altar of Dionysus. The great stone theatre at Athens was built about 500 BC, and its semicircular plan provided for an audience of 20,000–30,000 people sitting in tiers on the surrounding slopes; it served as a model for the theatres that were erected in all the important cities of the Graeco-Roman world. After the collapse of the Roman Empire the theatres were deserted. Examples of Roman theatres still exist at Orange, France, near St Albans, England, and elsewhere.

In medieval times, temporary stages of wood and canvas, one for every scene, were set up side by side in fairgrounds and market squares for the performance of mimes and ◊miracle plays.

Small enclosed theatres were built in the 16th century, for example in Vicenza, Italy (by the architect Palladio). The first London theatre was built in Shoreditch 1576 by James ◊Burbage, who also opened the first covered theatre in London, the Blackfriars 1596. His son was responsible for building the ◊Globe Theatre, the venue for Shakespeare's plays.

In the USA the modern centre of commercial theatre is New York City, with numerous theatres on or near ◊Broadway, although Williamsburg, Virginia (1716), and Philadelphia (1766) had the first known American theatres. The 'little theatres', off-Broadway, developed to present less commercial productions, often presenting a dramatist's first production, and of these the first was the Theater Guild (1919); off-off-Broadway then developed as ◊fringe or alternative theatre.

In Britain repertory theatres (theatres running a different play every few weeks) proliferated until World War II, for example, the ◊Old Vic; and in Ireland the ◊Abbey became the first state-subsidized theatre 1924. Although the repertory movement declined from the 1950s with the spread of cinema and television, a number of regional community theatres developed. Recently established theatres are often associated with a university or are part of a larger cultural centre.

The ◊Comédie Française in Paris (founded by Louis XIV 1690 and given a permanent home 1792) was the first national theatre. In Britain the ◊National Theatre company was established 1963; other national theatres exist in Stockholm, Moscow, Athens, Copenhagen, Vienna, Warsaw, and elsewhere.

Historic London theatres include the Haymarket (1720, rebuilt 1821), Drury Lane (1663), and Her Majesty's (1705), both rebuilt several times. The English Stage company was established at the Royal Court Theatre 1956 to provide a platform for new works.

Theatre Museum museum housing memorabilia from the worlds of the theatre, opera, ballet, dance, circus, puppetry, pop, and rock and roll. It opened in Covent Garden, London, 1987.

thebaine highly poisonous extract of ◊opium.

Thebes /'θiːbz/ capital of Boeotia in ancient Greece. In the Peloponnesian War it was allied with Sparta against Athens. For a short time after 371 BC when Thebes defeated Sparta at Leuctra, it was the most powerful state in Greece. Alexander the Great destroyed it 336 BC and although it was restored, it never regained its former power.

Thebes /'θiːbz/ Greek name of an ancient city (Niut-Ammon) in Upper Egypt, on the Nile. Probably founded under the first dynasty, it was the centre of the worship of Ammon, and the Egyptian capital under the New Kingdom about 1600 BC. Temple ruins survive near the villages of Karnak and Luxor, and in the nearby **Valley of the Kings** the 18th–20th dynasty kings, including Tutankhamen and Amenhotep III, are buried.

theatre chronology

c.600 BC	Choral performances (dithyrambs) in honour of Dionysus formed beginnings of Greek tragedy, according to Aristotle.
500–300 BC	Great age of Greek drama which included tragedy, comedy, and satyr plays (grotesque farce).
468 BC	Sophocles' first victory at Athens festival. His use of a third actor altered the course of the tragic form.
458 BC–	Aeschylus' *Oresteia* first performed.
c.425–	
388 BC	Comedies of Aristophanes including *The Birds* 414, *Lysistrata* 411, and *The Frogs* 405. In tragedy the importance of the chorus diminished under Euripedes, author of *The Bacchae* 405.
c.350 BC	Menander's 'New Comedy' of social manners developed.
c.240 BC–	
AD 500	Emergence of Roman drama, adapted from Greek originals. Plautus, Terence, and Seneca were the main playwrights.
c.AD 375	Kālidāsa's *Sakuntalā* marked the height of Sanskrit drama in India.
c.1250–1500	European mystery (or miracle) plays flourished, first in the churches, later in marketplaces, and were performed in England by town guilds.
c.1375	Nō (or Noh) drama developed in Japan.
c.1495	*Everyman*, the best known of all the morality plays, first performed.
1500–1600	Italian *commedia dell'arte* troupes performed popular, improvised comedies; they were to have a large influence on Molière and on English harlequinade and pantomime.
c.1551	Nicholas Udall wrote *Ralph Roister Doister*, the first English comedy.
c.1576	First English playhouse, 'The Theatre', built by James Burbage in London.
1587	Marlowe's play *Tamburlaine the Great* marked the beginning of the great age of Elizabethan and Jacobean drama in England.
c.1589	Kyd's play *The Spanish Tragedy* was the first of the 'revenge' tragedies.
c.1590–1612	Shakespeare's greatest plays, including *Hamlet* and *King Lear*, were written.
1604	Inigo Jones designed *The Masque of Blackness* for James I, written by Ben Jonson.
1614	Lope de Vega's *Fuenteovejuna* marked Spanish renaissance in drama.
1637	Corneille's *Le Cid* established classical tragedy in France.
1642	Act of Parliament closed all English theatres.
1660	With the restoration of Charles II to the English throne, dramatic performances recommenced.
1664	Molière's *Tartuffe* was banned for three years by religious factions.
1667	Racine's first success, *Andromaque*.
1680	Comédie Française formed by Louis XIV.
1700	Congreve, the greatest exponent of Restoration comedy, wrote *The Way of the World*.
1716	First known American theatre built in Williamsburg, Virginia.
1728	Gay's *The Beggar's Opera* first performed.
1737	Stage Licensing Act in England required all plays to be approved by the Lord Chamberlain before performance.
1747	The actor Garrick became manager of the Drury Lane Theatre, London.
1773	In England, Goldsmith's *She Stoops to Conquer* and Sheridan's *The Rivals* 1775 established the 'comedy of manners'. Goethe's *Götz von Berlichingen* was the first *Sturm und Drang* play (literally, storm and stress).
1781	Schiller's *Die Räuber/The Robbers*.
1784	Beaumarchais' *Le Mariage de Figaro/The Marriage of Figaro* (written 1778).
1830	Hugo's *Hernani* caused riots in Paris. His work marked the beginning of a new Romantic drama, changing the course of French theatre.
1878	Henry Irving became actor-manager of the Lyceum with Ellen Terry as leading lady.
1879	Ibsen's *A Doll's House*, an early example of realism in European theatre.
1893	Shaw wrote *Mrs Warren's Profession* (banned until 1902 because it deals with prostitution).
1895	Wilde's comedy *The Importance of Being Earnest*. Alfred Jarry's *Ubu Roi*, a forerunner of Surrealism.
1896	The first performance of Chekhov's *The Seagull* failed.
1899	Abbey Theatre, Dublin, founded by W B Yeats and Lady Gregory, marked the beginning of an Irish dramatic revival.
1904	Chekhov's *The Cherry Orchard*.
1919	Theater Guild founded in USA to perform less commercial new plays.
1920	*Beyond the Horizon*, O'Neill's first play, marked the beginning of serious theatre in the USA.
1928	Brecht's *Die Dreigroschenoper/The Threepenny Opera* with score by Kurt Weill; other political satires by Čapek and E Rice. In the USA Jerome Kern's *Show Boat* with Paul Robeson, and other musical comedies by Cole Porter, Irving Berlin, and George Gershwin, became popular.
1930s	US social-protest plays of Odets, Hellman, Wilder, and Saroyan.
1938	Publication of Artaud's *Theatre and Its Double*.
post-1945	Resurgence of German-language theatre, including, Frisch, Dürrenmatt, and Weiss.
1947	Tennessee Williams's *A Streetcar Named Desire*. First Edinburgh Festival, Scotland, with fringe theatre events.
1953	Arthur Miller's *The Crucible* opened in the USA; *En attendant Godot/Waiting for Godot* by Beckett exemplified the Theatre of the Absurd.
1956	English Stage Company formed at the Royal Court Theatre to provide a platform for new dramatists. Osborne's *Look Back in Anger* included in its first season.
1957	Bernstein's *West Side Story* opened in New York.
1960	Pinter's *The Caretaker* produced in London.
1960s	Off-off-Broadway theatre, a more daring and experimental type of drama, began to develop in New York.
1961	Royal Shakespeare Company formed in the UK under directorship of Peter Hall.
1963–64	UK National Theatre Company formed at the Old Vic under the directorship of Laurence Olivier.
1967	Success in USA of *Hair*, first of the 'rock' musicals
1968	Abolition of theatre censorship in the UK.
1975	*A Chorus Line*, to become the longest-running musical, opened in New York.
1989	Discovery of the remains of the 16th-century Rose and Globe Theatres, London.

permanently. In Britain, under the Theft Act 1968, the maximum penalty is ten years' imprisonment. The act placed under a single heading forms of theft which had formerly been dealt with individually, for example burglary and larceny.

thegn alternative spelling of ◊thane.

theism belief in the existence of gods, but more especially in that of a single personal God, made known to the world in a special revelation.

theme in music, a basic melody or musical figure, which often occurs with variations.

Themis /ˈθemɪs/ in Greek mythology, one of the ◊Titans, the daughter of Uranus and Gaia. She was the personification of law and order.

Themistocles /θəˈmɪstəkliːz/ c. 525–c. 460 BC. Athenian soldier and politician. Largely through his policies in Athens (creating its navy and strengthening its walls) Greece was saved from Persian conquest. He fought with distinction in the Battle of ◊Salamis 480 BC during the Persian War. About 470 BC he was accused of embezzlement and conspiracy against Athens, and banished by Spartan influence. He fled to Asia, where Artaxerxes, the Persian king, received him with favour. Themistocles died in Magnesia, Thessaly.

Theocritus /θiˈɒkrɪtəs/ c. 310–c. 250 BC. Greek poet. Probably born at Syracuse, he spent much of his life at Alexandria. His *Idylls* became models for later pastoral poetry.

theodolite instrument for the measurement of horizontal and vertical angles, used in surveying. It consists of a small telescope mounted so as to move on two graduate circles, one horizontal and the other vertical, while its axes pass through the centre of the circles. See also ◊triangulation.

Theodora /ˌθiːəˈdɔːrə/ 508–548. Byzantine empress from 527, originally the mistress of Emperor Justinian, and his consort from about 523. She earned a reputation for charity and courage.

Theodorakis /ˌθɪədəˈrɑːkɪs/ Mikis 1925– . Greek composer. He was imprisoned 1967–70 for attempting to overthrow the military regime of Greece.

Theodoric of Freiburg /θiˈɒdərɪk, ˈfraɪbɜːg/ c. 1250–1310. German friar and scientist. He studied in Paris 1275–77. In his work *De Iride/On the Rainbow* he describes how he used a water-filled sphere to simulate a raindrop, and determined that colours are formed in the raindrops and that light is reflected within the drop and can be reflected again, which explains secondary rainbows.

Theodoric the Great /θiˈɒdərɪk/ c. 455–526. King of the Ostrogoths from 474 in succession to his father. He invaded Italy 488, overthrew King Odoacer (whom he murdered) and established his own Ostrogothic kingdom there, with its capital in Ravenna. He had no strong successor, and his kingdom eventually became part of the Byzantine Empire of Justinian.

Theodosius II /ˌθiːəˈdəʊsiəs/ 401–450. Byzantine emperor from 408, who defeated the Persians 421 and 441, and from 441 bought off ◊Attila's Huns with tribute.

theology the study of God or gods, either by reasoned deduction from the natural world, or through revelation, as in the scriptures of Christianity, Islam, or other religions.

Theophanes the Greek 14th century. Byzantine painter active in Russia. He influenced painting in Novgorod, where his frescoes in Our Saviour of the Transfiguration are dated to 1378. He also worked in Moscow with Andrei ◊Rublev.

theorbo a long-necked ◊lute that has additional strings.

theory in science, a set of ideas, concepts, principles, or methods used to explain a wide set of observed facts. Among the major theories of modern science are ◊relativity, ◊quantum theory, ◊evolution, and ◊plate tectonics.

theosophy any religious or philosophical system based on intuitive insight into the nature of the divine, but especially that of the Theosophical Society, founded in New York 1875 by Madame Blavatsky and Colonel H S Olcott. It was based on Hindu ideas of ◊karma and ◊reincarnation, with ◊nirvana as the eventual aim.

Theravāda one of the two major forms of ◊Buddhism, common in S Asia (Sri Lanka, Thailand, Cambodia, and Burma); the other is the later Mahāyāna.

Theresa /təˈreɪzə/ Mother. Born Agnes Bojaxhiu 1910– . Roman Catholic nun. She was born in Skopje, Albania, and at 18 entered a Calcutta convent and became a teacher. In 1948 she became an Indian citizen and founded the Missionaries of Charity, an order for men and women based in Calcutta that helps abandoned children and the dying. Nobel Peace Prize 1979.

Thérèse of Lisieux /təˈreɪz liːˈsjɜː/ 1873–1897. French saint. She was born at Alençon, and entered a Carmelite convent at Lisieux at 15, where her holy life induced her superior to ask her to write her spiritual autobiography. She advocated the 'Little Way of Goodness' in small things in everyday life, and became known as the 'Little Flower of Jesus'. She died of tuberculosis and was canonized 1925.

therm unit of energy defined as 10^5 British thermal units; equivalent to 1.055×10^8 joules. It is no longer in scientific use.

thermal capacity the heat energy, C, required to increase the temperature of an object by one degree. It is measured in joules per degree, J/°C or J/K. If an object has mass m and is made of a substance with ◊specific heat capacity c, then $C = mc$.

thermal conductivity in physics, the ability of a substance to conduct heat. Good thermal conductors, like good electrical conductors, are generally materials with many free electrons (such as metals).

Thermal conductivity is expressed in units of joules per second per metre per Kelvin (J s⁻¹ m⁻¹ K⁻¹) For a block of material of cross-sectional area a and length l, with temperatures T_1 and T_2 at its end faces, the thermal conductivity α equals $Hl/at(T_2 - T_1)$, where H is the amount of heat transferred in time t.

thermal expansion or *expansivity* in physics, expansion that is due to a rise in temperature. It can be expressed in terms of linear, area, or volume expansion.

The coefficient of linear expansion α is the increase in unit length per degree temperature rise; area, or superficial, expansion β is the increase in unit area per degree; and volume, or cubic, expansion γ is the increase in unit volume per degree. To a good approximation, $\beta = 2\alpha$ and $\gamma = 3\alpha$.

thermic lance cutting tool consisting of a tube of mild steel, enclosing tightly packed small steel rods and fed with oxygen. On ignition temperatures above 3000°C are produced and the thermic lance becomes its own sustaining fuel. It rapidly penetrates walls and a 23 cm/9 in steel door can be cut through in less than 30 seconds.

Thermidor 11th month of the French Revolutionary calendar, which gave its name to the period after the fall of the Jacobins and the proscription of Robespierre by the National Convention 9 Thermidor 1794.

thermionics branch of electronics dealing with the emission of electrons from matter under the influence of heat.

A thermionic valve, used in telegraphy and telephony and in radio and radar, is a device using space conduction by thermionically emitted electrons. Classification is into diode, triode, and multi-electrode valves, but in most applications valves have been replaced by ◊transistors. Thermionics was named by O W ◊Richardson.

thermistor a device whose electrical ◊resistance falls as temperature rises. The current passing through a thermistor increases rapidly as its temperature rises, and so they are used in electrical thermometers.

thermite process a process used in incendiary devices and welding operations. It uses a powdered mixture of aluminium and (usually) iron oxide, which, when ignited, gives out enormous heat. The oxide is reduced to iron, which is molten at the high temperatures produced. This can be used to make a weld. The process was discovered by German chemist Hans Goldschmidt (1861–1923) 1895.

thermocouple electric temperature-measuring device consisting of a circuit having two wires made of different metals welded together at their ends. A current flows in the circuit when the two junctions are maintained at different temperatures (◊Seebeck effect). The electromotive force generated—measured by a millivoltmeter—is proportional to the temperature difference.

thermodynamics branch of physics dealing with the transformation of heat into other forms of energy, on which is based the study of the efficient working of engines, such as the steam and internal combustion engines. The three laws of thermodynamics are: (1) energy can be neither created nor destroyed, heat and mechanical work being mutually convertible; (2) it is impossible for an unaided self-acting machine to convey heat from one body to another at a higher temperature; (3) it is impossible by any procedure, no matter how idealized, to reduce any system to the ◊absolute zero of temperature (0 K/–273°C) in a finite number of operations. Put into mathematical form, these have widespread applications in physics and chemistry.

thermography the photographic recording of heat patterns. It is used medically as an imaging technique to identify 'hot spots' in the body, for example tumours, where cells are more active than usual.

It was developed in the 1970s and 1980s by the military to assist night vision, by detecting the body heat of an enemy, or the hot engine of a tank. It uses a photographic method called the Aga system.

thermoluminescence light released by a material that is heated after it is exposed to ◊irradiation. It occurs with most crystalline substances to some extent. It is used in archaeology to date pottery, and by geologists in studying terrestrial rocks and meteorites.

thermometer Instrument for measuring temperature. There are many types, designed to measure different temperature ranges to varying degrees of accuracy. Each makes use of a different physical effect of temperature.

Expansion of a liquid is employed in common *liquid-in-glass thermometers*, such as those

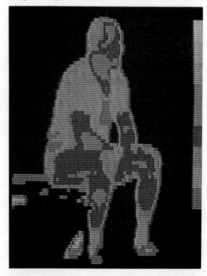

thermography *Thermogram, or heat image, of a man. The warmest parts of his body show as spots of red; the cooler areas are blue, green and purple.*

containing mercury or alcohol. The more accurate *gas thermometer* uses the effect of temperature on the pressure of a gas held at constant volume. A *resistance thermometer* takes advantage of the change in resistance of a conductor (such as a platinum wire) with variation in temperature. Another electrical thermometer is the ◊thermocouple. Mechanically, temperature change can be indicated by the change in curvature of a *bimetallic strip* (as commonly used in a ◊thermostat).

thermoplastic a type of ◊plastic.

Thermopylae, Battle of /θɜːˈmɒpɪliː/ battle during the ◊Persian wars 480 BC when Leonidas, king of Sparta, and 1,000 men defended the pass of Thermopylae to the death against a much greater force of Persians. The pass led from Thessaly to Locris in central Greece.

Thermos trade name for a type of ◊vacuum flask.

thermoset a type of ◊plastic.

thermosphere the layer in the Earth's ◊atmosphere above the mesosphere and below the exosphere. Its lower level is about 80 km/50 mi above the ground but its upper level is undefined. The ionosphere is located in the thermosphere. In the thermosphere the temperature rises with increasing height, to several thousand degrees Celsius. However, because of the thinness of the air, very little heat is present.

thermostat a temperature-controlling device that makes use of feedback. It employs a temperature sensor (often a bimetallic strip) to operate a switch or valve to control electricity or fuel supply. Thermostats are used in central heating, ovens, and car engines.

At the required pre-set temperature (for example of a room or gas oven), the movement of the sensor switches off the supply of electricity to the room heater or gas to the oven. As the room or oven cools down, the sensor turns back on the supply of electricity or gas.

Theroux /θəˈruː/ Paul (Edward) 1941– . US novelist and travel writer whose works include *Saint Jack* 1973, *Picture Palace* 1978, *The Mosquito Coast* 1981, *Doctor Slaughter* 1984, and *The Great Railway Bazaar* 1975.

thesaurus (Greek 'treasure') a collection of synonyms or words with related meaning. Early thesaurus compilers include ◊Pliny, Francis ◊Bacon, and Comenius (1592–1670), but the best-known is Peter Mark ◊Roget, whose work was published 1852.

Theseus legendary hero of ◊Attica, supposed to have united the states of the area under a constitutional government at Athens. Ariadne, whom he later abandoned on Naxos, helped him find his

thermometer

capillary tube

graduation

mercury in bore of tube

sliding maximum marker

bulb

way through the labyrinth to kill the ◊Minotaur. He also fought the Amazons and was one of the Argonauts.

Thesiger /ˈθesɪdʒə/ Wilfred Patrick 1912– . English explorer and writer. His travels and military adventures in Abyssinia, North Africa, and Arabia are recounted in a number of books including *Arabian Sands* 1959, *The Marsh Arabs* 1964, *Desert Marsh and Mountain* 1979, *Visions of a Nomad* 1987, and the autobiographical *The Life of My Choice* 1987.

Thespis 6th century BC. Greek poet, born in Attica, said to have introduced the first actor into plays (previously presented by choruses only), hence the word 'thespian' for an actor. He was also said to have invented tragedy and to have introduced the wearing of linen masks.

Thessaloniki /ˌθesəlɒˈniːkiː/ (English **Salonika**) port in Macedonia, NE Greece, at the head of the Gulf of Thessaloniki, the second largest city of Greece; population (1981) 706,200. Industries include textiles, shipbuilding, chemicals, brewing, and tanning. It was founded from Corinth by the Romans 315 BC as **Thessalonica** (to whose inhabitants St Paul addressed two epistles), captured by the Saracens AD 904, by the Turks 1430, and restored to Greece 1912.

Thessaly /ˈθesəli/ (Greek **Thessalia**) region of E central Greece, on the Aegean; area 13,904 sq km/5,367 sq mi; population (1981) 695,650. It is a major area of cereal production. It was an independent state in ancient Greece, and later formed part of the Roman province of ◊Macedonia. It was Turkish from the 14th century until incorporated in Greece 1881.

Thetford /ˈθetfəd/ market town in Norfolk, England; population (1982) 19,000. It is the birthplace of Thomas Paine.

Thetford Mines /ˈθetfəd/ site of the world's largest asbestos deposits, 80 km/50 mi S of Québec, Canada; discovered 1876.

thiamine a ◊vitamin of the B complex (B₁). Its absence from the diet causes the disease beri-beri.

Thibault /tiːˈbəʊ/ Anatole-François. Real name of French writer Anatole ◊France.

Thiers /tiˈeə/ Louis Adolphe 1797–1877. French politician and historian. He held cabinet posts under Louis Philippe, led the parliamentary opposition to Napoleon III from 1863, and as head of the provisional government 1871 negotiated peace with Prussia and suppressed the ◊Paris Commune. He was first president of the Third Republic 1871–73. His books include *Histoire de la Révolution française/History of the French Revolution* 1823–27.

Thimbu /ˈθɪmbuː/ or **Thimphu** capital since 1962 of the Himalayan state of ◊Bhutan; population (1982) 15,000.

thing an assembly of freemen in the Norse lands (Scandinavia) during the medieval period. It could encompass a meeting of the whole nation (*Althing*) or of a small town or community (*Husthing*).

thing-in-itself (German *Ding-an-sich*) a technical term in the philosophy of ◊Kant, employed to denote the unknowable source of the sensory component of our experience. Later thinkers, including ◊Fichte and ◊Hegel, denied the coherence of this concept.

Think Tank popular name for *Central Policy Review Staff* consultative body to the UK government 1970–83, set up to provide Cabinet ministers with informed background advice on major policy decisions.

Created by Conservative Prime Minister Edward Heath, the Think Tank was intended to provide the Cabinet and individual ministers with advice on government strategy, decision-making, and public expenditure. It was headed by Lord Rothschild 1970–74; its 15 members had backgrounds ranging from industry to higher education. It was abolished by Margaret Thatcher 1983, but partly replaced by a policy body reporting directly to her under Ferdinand Mount.

Thin Man, The 1934 novel by the US writer Dashiell Hammett, introducing the tough-guy style of detective fiction. It was made into a film 1936 starring William Powell (1892–1984) and Myrna Loy (1905–).

Third Reich (Third Empire) a term coined by the German writer Moeller van den Bruck (1876–1925) in the 1920s and used by the Nazis to describe the years of Hitler's dictatorship after 1933.

The idea of the Third Reich was based on the existence of two previous German empires, the medieval Holy Roman Empire and the second empire 1871–1918.

Third World those countries defined by the World Bank as the world's hundred poorest, measured by their income per person; they are concentrated in Asia, Africa, and Central America. They are divided into low-income countries, including China and India, and middle-income countries such as Nigeria, Indonesia, and Brazil.

Problems associated with these countries include high population growth and mortality rates, poor educational and health facilities, heavy dependence on agriculture and commodities for which prices and demand fluctuates, high levels of underemployment and, in some cases, political instability. Third World countries account for over 75% of all arms imports. Their economic performance in recent years has been mixed, with sub-Saharan Africa remaining in serious difficulties and others, in Asia, making significant progress. Failure by many poor countries to meet their enormous debt obligations has led to more stringent terms being imposed on loans by industrialized countries, as well as rescheduling (deferring payment).

Thirteen Colonies the 13 colonies of the USA that signed the ◊Declaration of Independence from Britain 1776. Led by George Washington, they defeated the British army in the War of American Independence 1776–81 to become the original 13 United States of America. They were: Connecticut, Delaware, Georgia, Maryland, Massachusetts, New Hampshire, New Jersey, New York, North Carolina, Pennsylvania, Rhode Island, South Carolina, and Virginia.

Thirty Years' War

miles 0   50
km 0   50

Groningen

Amsterdam

Utrecht

Arnhem

The Hague

Rotterdam

Cleves

Breda

Sluys

Antwerp

Cologne

Ghent

Aachen

Calais

Brussels

Namur

Mons

Thirty Years' War
The Netherlands after the Peace of Westphalia 1648

United Provinces

The Generality, i.e. areas seized from the Spanish Netherlands by the United Provinces

Spanish Netherlands

thistle

38th parallel the demarcation line between North and South Korea, agreed at the Yalta Conference 1945 and largely unaltered by the Korean War 1950–53.

35 mm a width of photographic film, the most popular format for the modern camera. The 35 mm camera falls into two categories, the ◊SLR and the ◊rangefinder.

Thirty-Nine Articles a set of articles of faith defining the doctrine of the Anglican Church; see under ◊Anglican Communion.

Thirty Years' War major war in central Europe 1618–48. Beginning as a German conflict between Protestants and Catholics, it gradually became transformed into a struggle to determine whether the ruling Austrian Habsburg family would gain control of all Germany.

1618–20 A Bohemian revolt against Austrian rule was defeated. Some Protestant princes continued the struggle against Austria.

1625–27 Denmark entered the war on the Protestant side.

1630 Gustavus Adolphus of Sweden intervened on the Protestant side, overrunning N Germany.

1631 The Catholic commander Tilly stormed Magdeburg.

1632 Tilly was defeated at Breitenfeld and the Lech, and died. The German general Wallenstein defeated at Battle of Lützen; Gustavus Adolphus killed.

1634 When the Swedes were defeated at Nördlingen, ◊Richelieu brought France into the war to inflict several defeats on Austria's Spanish allies. Wallenstein was assassinated.

1648 The *Treaty of Westphalia* gave France S Alsace, and Sweden got certain Baltic provinces, the emperor's authority in Germany becoming only nominal. The mercenary armies of Wallenstein, Tilly, and Mansfeld devastated Germany.

thistle species of prickly plant of several genera, such as *Carduus* and *Cirsium*, in the family Compositae, found in the N hemisphere. The stems are spiny, the flowerheads purple and cottony, and the leaves deeply indented. The thistle is the Scottish national emblem.

Thistle, Order of the a Scottish order of ◊knighthood.

Thistlewood /'θɪsəlwʊd/ Arthur 1770–1820. English Radical. A follower of the pamphleteer Thomas Spence (1750–1814), he was active in the Radical movement and was executed as the chief leader of the ◊Cato Street Conspiracy to murder government minister.

Thomas /'tɒməs/ Dylan (Marlais) 1914–1953. Welsh poet. His poems include the celebration of his 30th birthday 'Poem in October' and the evocation of his youth 'Fern Hill' 1946. His radio play *Under Milk Wood* 1954 and the short stories of *Portrait of the Artist as a Young Dog* 1940 are autobiographical.

Born in Swansea, son of the English teacher at the local grammar school where he was educated, he worked as a reporter on the *South Wales Evening Post*, then settled as a journalist in London and published his first volume *Eighteen Poems* in 1934.

Thomas /'tɒməs/ Edward (Philip) 1878–1917. English poet, born in London of Welsh parents.

He met the US poet Robert Frost and began writing poetry under his influence. Twenty-seven of his poems were published early in 1917 under the pseudonym Edward Eastaway in *An Anthology of New Verse*. *Poems* was published Oct 1917 after his death in World War I, followed by *Last Poems* 1918.

Thomas /'tɒməs/ Ronald Stuart 1913– . Welsh poet, vicar of St Hywyn, Aberdaron, 1967–78. His verse, as in *Song at the Year's Turning* 1955, contrasts traditional Welsh values with encroaching 'English' sterility.

Thomas /'tɒməs/ Terry-. Stage name of Thomas Terry Hoar Stevens 1911–1990. British film comedy actor, who portrayed upper-class English fools in such films as *I'm All Right Jack* 1959, *It's a Mad, Mad, Mad, Mad World* 1963, and *How to Murder Your Wife* 1965.

Thomas à Kempis /'tɒməs ə 'kempɪs/ 1380–1471. German Augustinian monk who lived at the monastery of Zwolle. He took his name from his birthplace Kempen; his real surname was Hammerken. His *De Imitatione Christi/Imitation of Christ* is probably the most widely known devotional work ever written.

Thomas, St /'tɒməs/ in the New Testament, one of the 12 Apostles, said to have preached in S India, hence the ancient churches there were referred to as the 'Christians of St Thomas'. He is not the author of the Gospel of St Thomas, the Gnostic collection of Jesus' sayings.

Thomism in philosophy, the method and approach of Thomas ◊Aquinas. Neo-Thomists apply this philosophical method to contemporary problems.

Thompson /'tɒmpsən/ 'Daley' (Francis Morgan) 1958– . English decathlete, who has broken the world decathlon record four times since winning the Commonwealth Games decathlon title in 1978. He has won two more Commonwealth titles, two Olympic gold medals (1980, 1984), three European titles, and a world title.

Thompson /'tɒmpsən/ David 1770–1857. Canadian explorer and surveyor who mapped extensive areas of western Canada including the Columbia River for the Hudson's Bay Company 1789–1811.

Thompson /'tɒmpsən/ Flora 1877–1948. English novelist, whose trilogy *Lark Rise to Candleford* 1945 describes late Victorian rural life.

Thompson /'tɒmpsən/ Francis 1859–1907. British poet. Born in Preston, he settled in London, where he fell into poverty and ill health. In *Sister Songs 1895* and *New Poems* 1897 Thompson, who was a Roman Catholic, expressed a mystic view of life.

Thompson /'tɒmpsən/ John Taliaferro 1860–1940. US colonel, inventor of the Thompson submachine-gun (see ◊machine gun).

Thomsen /'tɒmsən/ Christian (Jürgensen) 1788–1865. Danish archaeologist. He devised the classification of prehistoric cultures into Stone Age, Bronze Age, and Iron Age.

Thomson /'tɒmsən/ Elihu 1853–1937. US inventor. He founded, with E J Houston, the Thomson-Houston Electric Company 1882, later merging with the Edison Company to form the General Electric Company. He made important advances into the nature of the ◊electric arc,

Thompson Daley Thompson broke the decathlon world record four times and has won two Olympic titles, one world title, three European titles, and three Commonwealth titles.

and invented the first high-frequency ◊dynamo and ◊transformer.

Thomson /'tɒmsən/ George Paget 1892–1975. English physicist, son of J J ◊Thomson. His work on ◊interference phenomena in the scattering of electrons by crystals helped to confirm the wave-like nature of particles. He shared a Nobel prize with C J ◊Davisson 1937.

Thomson /'tɒmsən/ James 1700–1748. Scottish poet, whose descriptive blank verse poem *The Seasons* 1726–30 was a forerunner of the Romantic movement. He also wrote the words of 'Rule, Britannia'.

Thomson /'tɒmsən/ James 1834–1882. Scottish poet, remembered for his despairing poem 'The City of Dreadful Night' 1880.

Thomson /'tɒmsən/ Joseph John 1856–1940. English physicist, who discovered the ◊electron. He was responsible for organizing the Cavendish atomic research laboratory. His work inaugurated the electrical theory of the atom, and his elucidation of positive rays and their application to an analysis of neon led to ◊Aston's discovery of ◊isotopes. Nobel prize 1906.

Thomson /'tɒmsən/ Virgil 1896–1989. US composer and critic. His large body of work, characterized by a clarity and simplicity of style, includes operas such as *Four Saints in Three Acts* (libretto by Gertrude Stein) 1934; orchestral, choral, and chamber music; and film scores.

Thor /θɔː/ in Norse mythology, god of thunder (his hammer), and represented as a man of enormous strength defending humanity against demons. He was the son of Odin and Freya, and Thursday is named after him.

thorax in vertebrates, the part of the body containing the heart and lungs, and protected by the rib cage; in arthropods, the middle part of the body, between the head and abdomen.

In mammals, the thorax is separated from the abdomen by the muscular diaphragm. In insects, the thorax bears the legs and wings. The thorax of spiders and crustaceans is fused with the head, to form the cephalothorax.

Thoreau /'θɔːrəʊ/ Henry David 1817–1862. US author and naturalist. His work *Walden, or Life in the Woods* 1854 stimulated the back-to-nature movement, and he completed some 30 volumes based on his daily nature walks. His essay 'Civil Disobedience' 1849, advocating peaceful resistance to unjust laws, had a wide impact.

thorium a dark grey, naturally radioactive metal, widely distributed throughout the world in minerals, particularly monazite beach sands; symbol Th, atomic number 90, atomic weight 232.05. Discovered by Berzelius 1828, it has a half-life of 1.39×10^{10} years, and its greatest potential use is breeding uranium-233, a fuel for nuclear power reactors.

thorn apple or *jimsonweed* annual plant *Datura stramonium*, growing to 2 m/6 ft in northern temperate and subtropical areas. It bears white or violet trumpet-shaped flowers and capsule-like fruit that split to release black seeds. All parts of the plant are poisonous.

Thorndike /'θɔːndaɪk/ Sybil 1882–1976. British actress for whom Shaw wrote *St Joan*. The Thorndike Theatre (1969), Leatherhead, Surrey, is named after her.

thoroughbred horse specially bred for racing purposes. All racehorses are thoroughbreds, and all male thoroughbreds are direct descendants of one of three stallions imported into Britain during the 17th and 18th centuries: the Darley Arabian, Byerley Turk, and Godolphin Barb.

Thorpe /θɔːp/ Jeremy 1929– . British Liberal politician, leader of the Liberal Party 1967–76.

Thorwaldsen /'tɔːvælsən/ Bertel 1770–1844. Danish Neo-Classical sculptor. He went to Italy on a scholarship in 1796 and stayed in Rome for most of his life, producing portraits, monuments, religious and mythological works. Much of his work is housed in the Thorvaldsen Museum, Copenhagen.

Thoth /təʊt/ in Egyptian mythology, god of wisdom and learning. He was represented as a scribe with the head of an ◊ibis, the bird sacred to him.

Thothmes /'təʊtmes/ four Egyptian kings of the 18th dynasty, including:

Thothmes I King of Egypt 1540–1501 BC. He founded the Egyptian empire in Syria.

Thothmes III King of Egypt about 1500–1446 BC. He extended the empire to the Euphrates, and conquered Nubia. He was a grandson of Thothmes I.

Thousand and One Nights a collection of Oriental tales, also known as the ◊*Arabian Nights*.

thousand days the period of office of US president John F Kennedy from 20 Jan 1961 to his assassination on 22 Nov 1963.

Thousand Islands group of about 1,500 islands on the border between Canada and the USA in the upper St Lawrence river.

Thrace /θreɪs/ (Greek *Thráki*) ancient empire (6000 BC–AD 300) in the Balkans, SE Europe, formed by parts of Greece and Bulgaria. It was held successively by the Greeks, Persians, Macedonians, and Romans.

The area was divided 1923 into western Thrace (the Greek province of Thráki) and eastern Thrace (European Turkey). However, the heart of the ancient Thracian Empire was Bulgaria, where since 1945 there have been tomb finds of gold and silver dishes, drinking vessels, and jewellery with animal designs. The legend of ◊Orpheus and the cult of ◊Dionysus were both derived by the Greeks from Thrace. The area was conquered by Persia 6th–5th centuries BC and by Macedon 4th–2nd centuries BC. From AD 46 it was a Roman province, then part of the Byzantine Empire, and Turkish from the 15th century until 1878; it was then subject to constant dispute until after World War I.

threadworm a type of ◊nematode.

three-day week in the UK, the policy adopted by prime minister Edward Heath Jan 1974 to combat an economic crisis and coal miners' strike. A shortage of electrical power led to the allocation of energy to industry for only three days each week. A general election was called Feb 1974, which the government lost.

Three Mile Island an island in the Shenandoah River near Harrisburg, Pennsylvania, the site of a nuclear power station which was put out of action following a major accident in Mar 1979. Opposition

Thoreau *Author and naturalist Henry Thoreau, whose views on peaceful resistance to unjust laws were widely supported in the USA.*

to nuclear power in the USA was reinforced after this accident and safety standards reassessed.

Three Musketeers, The a romance by Dumas *père*, published 1844–45. D'Artagnan, a poor gentleman, joins forces with three of King Louis XIII's musketeers, Athos, Porthos, and Aramis, in a series of adventures.

Three Rivers English name for the Canadian port of ◊Trois-Rivières.

Three Sisters, The a play by Anton Chekhov, first produced 1901. A family, bored and frustrated by life in the provinces, dream that if they move to Moscow their problems will disappear. However, apathy prevents the dream becoming reality.

threshing agricultural process of separating cereal grains from the plant. Traditionally, the work was carried out by hand in winter months using the flail, a jointed beating stick. Today, threshing is done automatically inside the combine harvester at the time of cutting.

From the late 18th century, through the work of Andrew ◊Meikle and others, machine threshing slowly overtook the flail and made rapid progress after 1850.

thrift plant of the genus *Armeria*, family Plumbaginaceae. **Thrift** or **sea pink** *Armeria maritima* occurs on seashores and cliffs in Europe. The leaves are small and linear; the dense round heads of pink flowers rise on straight stems.

thrips tiny insect with feathery wings, of the order Thysanoptera. Many of the 3,000 species live in flowers, and suck their juices, causing damage and spreading disease. Others eat fungi, decaying matter, or smaller insects.

throat in human anatomy, the passage that leads from the back of the nose and mouth to the ◊trachea and ◊oesophagus. It includes the ◊pharynx and the ◊larynx, the latter being at the top of the trachea. The word 'throat' is also used to mean the front part of the neck, both in humans and other vertebrates, for example, in describing the plumage of birds. In engineering, it is any narrowing entry, such as the throat of a carburettor.

thrombosis a condition in which the blood clots in a vein or artery, causing loss of circulation to the area served by the vessel.

Thrombosis in veins is often seen in association with ◊phlebitis, and in arteries with ◊atheroma. Thrombosis increases the risk of heart attack (myocardial ◊infarct) and ◊stroke. It is treated by surgery and/or ◊anticoagulant drugs.

throwing event field athletic contest. There are four at most major international track and field meetings: ◊discus, ◊hammer, ◊javelin, and ◊shot put. ◊Caber tossing is also a throwing event but found only at ◊Highland Games.

thrush bird of the family Turdidae, found worldwide, noted for its song. Thrushes are usually brown with speckles of other colours. They are 12–30 cm/5–12 in long.

The **song thrush** *Turdus philomelos* is 23 cm/9 in long, brown above and with a paler throat and breast speckled with dark brown. Slightly larger is the **mistle thrush** *Turdus viscivorus*, nicknamed the stormcock because it often sings before and during wild, wet weather. North American species include the **hermit thrush** *Catharus guttatus* and the **wood thrush** *Hylocichla mustelina*.

thrush infection usually of the mouth, but also sometimes of the vagina, caused by a yeastlike fungus. It is seen as white patches on the mucous membrane.

Thrush, also known as *candidiasis* after the causative organism, may be caused by antibiotics. It is treated with a further antibiotic.

Thrust 2 jet-propelled car in which British driver Richard Noble set a new world land speed record in the Black Rock Desert of Nevada, USA, Oct 1983. The record speed was 1,019.4 kph/633.468 mph.

Thucydides /θjuː'sɪdɪdiːz/ 460–400 BC. Athenian historian, who exercised command in the ◊Peloponnesian War 424 with so little success that he was banished until 404. In his *History of* *the Peloponnesian War*, he attempted a scientific impartiality.

thug originally a member of a Hindu sect who strangled travellers as sacrifices to ◊Kali the goddess of destruction. They were suppressed about 1830.

Thule /'θjuːli/ Greek and Roman name for the most northerly land known. It was applied to the Shetlands, the Orkneys, and Iceland, and by later writers to Scandinavia.

thulium a metallic element, symbol Tm, atomic number 69, relative atomic mass 168.94. One of the lanthanide series of elements, it is used in arc lighting. The isotope Tm-170 is used as an X-ray source.

Thunder Bay /'θʌndə 'beɪ/ city and port on Lake Superior, Ontario, Canada, formed by the union of Port Arthur and its twin city of Fort William to the S; industries include shipbuilding, timber, paper, wood pulp, and export of wheat; population (1986) 122,000.

Thunderbird a legendary bird of the North American Plains Indians, the creator of the storms of the great plains.

Thünen /'tjuːnən/ Johann von 1785–1850. German economist and geographer, who believed that the success of a state depends on the well-being of its farmers. His book *The Isolated State* 1820, a pioneering study of land use, includes the earliest example of ◊*marginal productivity theory*, a theory which Thunen developed to calculate the natural wage for a farmworker. He has been described as the first modern economist.

Thurber /'θɜːbə/ James (Grover) 1894–1961. US humorist. His short stories, written mainly for the *New Yorker* magazine, include 'The Secret Life of Walter Mitty' 1932, and his doodle drawings include fanciful impressions of dogs. Partially blind from childhood, he became totally blind in the last ten years of his life but continued to work.

Thuringia /θjuˈrɪndʒɪə/ former state of central Germany 1919–46; capital Weimar. The area includes the *Thuringian Forest*. Thuringia was a *Land* until 1952, when it became the East German counties of Erfurt, Gera, and Suhl.

Thursday Island /'θɜːzdeɪ/ island in Torres Strait, Queensland, Australia; area 4 sq km/1.5 sq mi; chief centre Port Kennedy. It is a centre of the pearl fishing industry.

Thurso /'θɜːsəʊ/ port in Highland region, Scotland. It is the mainland terminus of the steamer service to the Orkneys, and the experimental atomic station of Dounreay lies to the west.

thylacine another name for the ◊Tasmanian tiger/wolf.

thyme herb, genus *Thymus*, of the family Labiatae. Garden thyme *Thymus vulgaris*, a native of the Mediterranean, grows to 30 cm/1 ft high, and has aromatic leaves used for seasoning, and pinkish flowers.

thymus an organ in vertebrates, situated in the upper chest cavity in humans. The thymus processes the ◊lymphocyte cells to produce T-lymphocytes (T denotes 'thymus-derived'), which are responsible for binding to specific invading organisms and killing them, or rendering them harmless.

The thymus reaches full size at puberty, and shrinks thereafter; the stock of T-lymphocytes is built up early in life, so this function diminishes in adults, but the thymus continues to function as an ◊endocrine gland, producing the hormone thymosin, which stimulates the activity of the T-lymphocytes.

thyristor a type of ◊rectifier, an electronic device that conducts electricity in one direction only. The thyristor is composed of layers of ◊semiconductor material sandwiched between two electrodes called the anode and cathode. The current can be switched on by using a third electrode called the gate. Thyristors are used to control mains-driven motors and in lighting dimmer controls.

thyroid an ◊endocrine gland of vertebrates, situated in the neck. It secretes thyroxin, a hormone containing iodine. This stimulates growth, metabolism, and other functions of the body. Abnormal action produces Graves' disease, with bulging eyeballs, while deficient action produces ◊myxoedema in adults and dwarfism in juveniles.

thyrotoxicosis a synonym for ◊hyperthyroidism.

Thyssen /'tɪsən/ Fritz 1873–1951. German industrialist who based his business on the Ruhr iron and steel industry. Fearful of the communist threat, Thyssen became an early supporter of Hitler and contributed large amounts of money to his early political campaigns. By 1839 he had broken with the Nazis and fled first to Switzerland and later to Italy, where in 1941 he was sent to a concentration camp. Released in 1945, he was ordered to surrender 15% of his property.

Tianamen Square (Square of the Gate of heavenly Peace) central square in Beijing (Peking), China, the largest in public square in the world (area 0.4 sq km/0.14 sq mi). On 3–4 June 1989 at least 2,000 unarmed protesters were killed by government troops, in a massacre that crashed ◊China's emerging pro-democracy movement.

Hundreds of thousands of demonstrators had occupied the square from early May, calling for political reform and the resignation of the Communist leadership. The were led by students, 3,000 of whom staged a hunger strike in the square.

Tianjin /,tjenˈdʒɪn/ formerly *Tientsin* port and industrial and commercial city in Hubei province, central China; population (1986) 5,380,000. The special municipality of Tianjin has an area of 4,000 sq km/1,544 sq mi, and a population of 8,190,000. Its handmade silk and wool carpets are renowned. Dagan oilfield is nearby. Tianjin was opened to foreign trade 1860, and occupied by the Japanese 1937.

Tian Shan /tiˈæn ˈʃɑːn/ (Chinese *Tien Shan*) mountain system on the Soviet-Chinese border. *Pik Pobedy* on the Xinjiang–Kirghizia border is the highest peak at 7,439 m/24,415 ft. The British climber Chris Bonington led the expedition that first reached the summit of Kongur Shan 1981.

tiara the triple crown worn by the pope, or a semi-circular headdress worn by women for formal occasions. The term was originally applied to a headdress worn by the ancient Persians.

Tiber /'taɪbə/ (Italian *Tevere*) river in Italy on which Rome stands; length from the Apennines to the Tyrrhenian Sea 400 km/250 mi.

Tiberias, Lake /taɪˈbɪəriæs/ or *Sea of Galilee* lake in N Israel, 210 m/689 ft below sea level, into which the ◊Jordan flows; area 170 sq km/66 sq mi. The first Israeli ◊kibbutz area was founded nearby 1909.

Tiberius /taɪˈbɪəriəs/ Claudius Nero 42 BC–AD 37. Roman emperor, the stepson, adopted son, and successor of Augustus from AD 14. A distinguished soldier, he was a conscientious ruler under whom the empire prospered.

Tibesti Mountains /tɪˈbesti/ range in the central Sahara, N Chad; highest peak *Emi Koussi* 3,415 m/11,208 ft.

Tibet /tɪˈbet/ autonomous region of SW China (Pinyin form *Xizang*)
area 1,221,600 sq km/471,538 sq mi
capital Lhasa
features Tibet occupies a barren plateau bounded S and SW by the Himalayas and N by the Kunlun Mountains, traversed W–E by the Bukamagna, Karakoram, and other ranges, and having an average elevation of 4,000–4,500 m/13,000–15,000 ft. The Sutlej, Brahmaputra, and Indus rivers rise in Tibet, which has numerous lakes, many of which are salty. The ◊yak is the most important domestic animal
products wool, borax, salt, horn, musk, herbs, furs, gold, iron pyrites, lapis lazuli, mercury, textiles, chemicals, agricultural machinery
population (1986) 2,030,000; many Chinese have settled in Tibet
government Tibet is an autonomous region of China, with its own People's Government and People's Congress. The controlling force in Tibet is the Communist Party of China, represented locally by First Secretary Wu Jinghua from 1985

history Tibet was an independent kingdom from the 5th century AD. It came under nominal Chinese suzerainty about 1700. Independence was regained after a revolt 1912. China regained control 1951 when the historic ruler, the ◊Dalai Lama, was driven from the country and the monks (who formed 25% of the population) were forced out of the monasteries. Between 1951 and 1959 the Chinese People's Liberation Army (PLA) controlled Tibet, although the Dalai Lama returned as nominal spiritual and temporal head of state. In 1959 a Tibetan uprising spread from bordering regions to Lhasa and was supported by the Tibet local government. The rebellion was suppressed by the PLA, prompting the Dalai Lama and 9,000 Tibetans to flee to India. The Chinese proceeded to dissolve the Tibet local government, abolish serfdom, collectivize agriculture, and suppress ◊Lamaism. In 1965 Tibet became an autonomous region of China. Chinese rule continued to be resented, however, and the economy languished.

From 1979, the leadership in Beijing adopted a more liberal and pragmatic policy towards Tibet. Traditional agriculture, livestock, and trading practices have been restored (under the 1980 slogan 'relax, relax, and relax again'), a number of older political leaders and rebels have been rehabilitated or pardoned, and the promotion of local Tibetan cadres has been encouraged. In addition, a more tolerant attitude towards Lamaism was adopted (temples damaged during the 1965–68 Cultural Revolution were repaired) and attempts, thus far unsuccessful, have were to persuade the Dalai Lama to return from exile.

The pro-independence demonstrations by Buddhist monks, which erupted in Lhasa in Sept–Oct 1987, in Mar and Dec 1988 and in Mar 1989 and were forcibly suppressed by Chinese troops, exhibit the continuing strength of nationalist feeling. The country is of immense strategic importance to China, being the site of 50,000–100,000 troops and a major nuclear missile base at Nagchuka.

Tibetan person of Tibetan culture. The majority of Tibetans live in Tibet, though there are refugee communities in India and Nepál. The Tibetan language belongs to the Sino-Tibetan language family.

tick arachnid allied to the ◊mites; ticks are bloodsucking, disease-carrying parasites on humans, animals, and birds.

tidal power station a kind of ◊hydroelectric power plant that uses the 'head' of water created by the

Tiberius A bust of the Roman emperor Tiberius.

rise and fall of the ocean tides to spin the water turbines. An example is located on the estuary of the river Rance in the Gulf of St Malo, Brittany, France, which has been in use since 1966.

tidal wave a misleading name for a ◊tsunami.

tide rise and fall of sea level due to the gravitational forces of the Moon and Sun. High water occurs at an average interval of 12 hr 24 min 30 sec. The highest or *spring tides* are at or near new and full Moon; the lowest or *neap tides* when the Moon is in its first or third quarter. Some seas, such as the Mediterranean, have very small tides.

Other factors affecting sea level are (1) a combination of naturally high tides with storm surge, as sometimes happens along the low-lying coasts of Germany and the Netherlands; (2) the water walls created by typhoons and hurricanes, such as often hit Bangladesh; (3) underwater upheavals in the Earth's crust which may cause a ◊tsunami; and (4) global temperature change melting the polar ice caps.

Gravitational tides—the pull of nearby groups of stars—have been observed to affect the galaxies.

Tieck /tiːk/ Johann Ludwig 1773–1853. German Romantic poet and collector of folk-tales, some of which he dramatized, for example *Puss in Boots*.

Tien-Shan /ˈtjen ˈʃɑːn/ Chinese form of ◊Tian-Shan, a mountain system of central Asia.

Tientsin /ˌtjenˈtsɪn/ alternative name for ◊Tianjin, an industrial city in NE China.

Tiepolo /tiˈepələu/ Giovanni Battista 1696–1770. Italian painter, born in Venice. He created monumental Rococo decorative schemes in palaces and churches in NE Italy, SW Germany, and in Madrid (1762–70). The style is light-hearted, the palette light and warm, and he made great play with illusion.

Tiepolo painted religious and, above all, historical or allegorical pictures, for example scenes from the life of Cleopatra 1745 (Palazzo Labia, Venice) and from the life of Frederick Barbarossa 1757 (Kaisersaal, Würzburg Palace). His sons were among his many assistants.

Tierra del Fuego /tiˈeərə del ˈfweɪgəu/ island group divided between Chile and Argentina. It is separated from the mainland of South America by the Strait of Magellan, and Cape Horn is at the southernmost point. Ushuaia, Argentina, is the chief town and the world's most southerly town. Industries include oil and sheep farming.

tide

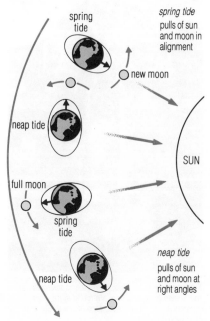

spring tide
spring tide pulls of sun and moon in alignment

new moon

neap tide

SUN

full moon

spring tide

neap tide

neap tide
neap tide pulls of sun and moon at right angles

Tiepolo The Immaculate Conception *(commissioned 1767) Courtauld Collection, London.*

To the south of the main island is *Beagle Channel* (named after the ship of Charles ◊Darwin's voyage) with three islands at the east end, finally awarded 1985 to Chile rather than Argentina.

Tiffany /ˈtɪfəni/ Louis Comfort 1848–1933. US artist and glassmaker, son of Charles Louis Tiffany who founded the New York jewellers. He produced stained glass windows, iridescent Favrile (Latin *faber* 'craftsman') glass, and lampshades.

Tiflis /ˈtɪflɪs/ former name (until 1936) of the city of ◊Tbilisi in the USSR.

tiger largest of the great cats *Panthera tigris*, formerly found in much of central and S Asia but nearing extinction due to hunting and the destruction of their natural habitat. The tiger can grow to 3.6 m/12 ft long, and weigh 300 kg/660 lbs; it has a yellow-orange coat with black stripes. It is solitary, and feeds on deer and cattle. It is a good swimmer.

Tigers will usually only eat humans as the result of weakened powers or shortage of game. The striped markings—black on reddish fawn—are present from birth, though rare cream or black specimens have been known.

In Sumatra there are about 800 tigers left, and 200 are killed each year by poachers. They are continually losing their jungle habitat; companies plunder the forest for timber and minerals, and then farmers, often transplanted from other parts of Indonesia, move in and take over the land, often ruining it after a few years owing to poor farming practices.

Tigray /ˈtiːgreɪ/ or *Tigré* region in the northern highlands of Ethiopia; area 65,900 sq km/25,444 sq mi. Chief town is Mekele. The region had an estimated population of 2.4 million in 1984, at a time when drought and famine were driving large numbers of people to fertile land in the south or into neighbouring Sudan. Since 1978 a guerrilla group known as the Tigray People's Liberation Front has been fighting for regional autonomy.

Tigris /ˈtaɪgrɪs/ (Arabic *Shatt Dijla*) river flowing through Turkey and Iraq (see also ◊Mesopotamia), joining the ◊Euphrates above Basra, where it forms the ◊Shatt-al-Arab; length 1,600 km/1,000 mi.

Tihuanaco /ˌtiːwəˈnɑːkəu/ site of a Peruvian city, S of Lake Titicaca in the Andes, which gave its name to the 8th–14th-century civilization that preceded the Inca.

Tijuana /tɪˈwɑːnə/ city and resort in NW Mexico; population (1980) 461,257; noted for horse races and casinos. ◊San Diego adjoins it across the US border.

Tikhonov /ˈtiːxɒnɒf/ Nikolai 1905– . Soviet politician. He was a close associate of President Brezhnev, joining the Politburo 1979, and was prime minister (chair of the Council of Ministers) 1980–85. In Apr 1989 he was removed from the central committee.

Tilbury /ˈtɪlbəri/ port in Essex, on the N bank of the Thames; population (1981) 12,000. Greatly extended 1976, it became London's largest container port. It dates from Roman times.

till a deposit of clay, mud, gravel, and boulders left by a glacier. Till is unsorted, all sizes of fragments mixed up together, and it shows no stratification; that is, it does not form clear layers or ◊beds.

Tilly /ˈtɪli/ Jan Tserklaes, Count Tilly 1559–1632. Flemish commander of the army of the Catholic League and imperial forces in the ◊Thirty Years' War. Notorious for his storming of Magdeburg, E Germany, 1631, he was defeated by the Swedish king Gustavus Adolphus at Breitenfeld, and at the river Lech in SW Germany, where he was mortally wounded.

Tilsit /ˈtɪlzɪt/ former name (until 1945) of the Soviet town of ◊Sovetsk.

tilt-rotor aircraft type of vertical take-off aircraft, also called a ◊convertiplane.

Timaru /ˈtɪməru/ (Maori 'place of shelter') industrial port and resort in South Island, New Zealand; industries include flour milling, deep freezing, pottery, and brewing; population (1983) 29,000.

timber wood used in construction, furniture and paper pulp. *Hardwoods* include tropical mahogany, teak, ebony, rosewood, temperate oak, elm, beech, and eucalyptus. All are slow-growing and world supplies are near exhaustion. *Softwoods* comprise the ◊conifers (pine, fir, spruce, and larch) which are quick to grow and easy to work, but inferior in quality of grain. *White woods* include ash, birch, and sycamore; all have light-coloured timber, are fast-growing, and can be used as veneers on cheaper timber.

timbre in music, the tone colour of an instrument.

Timbuktu /ˌtɪmbʌkˈtuː/ or *Tombouctou* town in Mali; population (1976) 20,500. A camel caravan centre from the 11th century on the fringe of the Sahara, since 1960 it has been surrounded by the southward movement of the desert, and the former canal link with the Niger is dry. Products include salt.

time the continuous passage of existence, recorded by division into hours, minutes, and seconds. Formerly measurement of time was based on the Earth's rotation on its axis, but this was found to be irregular. The second, the standard ◊SI unit of time, was therefore redefined 1956 in terms of the Earth's annual orbit of the Sun, and 1967 in terms of a radiation pattern of the element caesium.

Universal Time (UT), based on the Earth's actual rotation, was replaced by Coordinated Universal Time (UTC) 1972, the difference between the two involving the addition (or subtraction) of leap seconds on the last day of June or Dec. National observatories (in the UK the Royal Greenwich Observatory) make standard time available, and the BBC broadcasts six pips at certain hours (five short, from second 55 to second 59, and one long, the start of which indicates the precise minute). From 1986 the term Greenwich Mean Time was replaced by UTC. However, the Greenwich meridian, adopted 1884, remains that from which all longitudes are measured, and the world's standard time zones are calculated from it.

time and motion study process of analysis applied to a job or number of jobs to check the efficiency of the work method, equipment used, and the worker. Its findings are used to improve performance.

Time and motion studies were introduced in the USA by Frederick Taylor (1856–1915) at the beginning of the 20th century. Since then, the practice has spread throughout the world.

Times Beach town in Missouri, USA, which accidentally became contaminated with ◊dioxin, and was bought in 1983 by the Environmental Protection Agency for cleansing.

time-sharing in computing, a method of enabling several users to access the same computer at the same time. The computer rapidly switches between programs, giving each user the impression that he or she has sole use of the system.

Timişoara /ˌtɪmɪˈʃwɑːrə/ capital of Timiş county, W Romania; population (1985) 319,000. Demonstrations there Dec 1989 sparked off the Romanian revolution (see ◊Romania).

Timor /ˈtiːmɔː/ largest and most easterly of the Sunda Islands, part of Indonesia; area 33,610 sq km/12,973 sq mi. West Timor (capital Kupang) was formerly Dutch and was included in Indonesian independence. East Timor (capital Dili) was an overseas province of Portugal until it was annexed by Indonesia 1975. Guerrilla warfare by local people seeking independence continues. Since 1975 over 500,000 have been killed or have resettled in West Timor, according to Amnesty International. Products include coffee, maize, rice, and coconuts.

Timothy /ˈtɪməθi/ in the New Testament, companion to St ◊Paul, both on his missionary journeys and in prison. Two of the Pauline epistles are addressed to him.

tin a silver-white, crystalline metal, malleable and somewhat ductile, which crumbles to a greyish powder at low temperatures; symbol Sn (Latin *stannum*), atomic number 50, atomic weight 118.70. It is used in alloys and containers. Tin is found chiefly in the mineral cassiterite, SnO_2, in Malaysia, Indonesia, and Bolivia.

It is used as a protective coating to resist corrosion of iron and steel, for example the tin-can food container. Its use was known in the ancient world, and the mines in Cornwall, England, where working was renewed between the 1960s and 1980s, were being worked in the Bronze Age. Other important alloys, besides bronze, include solder, type metal, pewter, and metals for bearings.

tinamou South American bird of the order Tinamiformes, of which there are some 45 species. Tinamous are up to 40 cm/16 in long, and their drab colour provides good camouflage. They may be related to the flightless birds, and

are themselves poor flyers. They are mainly vegetarian, but sometimes eat insects. They escape predators by remaining still, or by burrowing through dense cover.

Tinbergen /ˈtɪnbɜːɡən/ Jan 1903–1988. Dutch economist. He shared a Nobel prize 1969 with Ragnar Frisch for his work on ◊econometrics (the mathematical-statistical expression of economic theory).

Tinbergen /ˈtɪnbɜːɡən/ Nikolaas 1907– . Dutch zoologist. He was one of the founders of ◊ethology, the scientific study of animal behaviour in natural surroundings. Specializing in the study of instinctive behaviour, he shared a Nobel prize with Konrad Lorenz and Karl von ◊Frisch 1973. He is the brother of Jan Tinbergen.

Tindouf /tɪnˈduːf/ a Saharan oasis in the Aïn-Sefra region of Algeria, crossed by the Agadir–Dakar desert route. There are large iron deposits in the area; the oasis is a base for exiled Polisario guerrillas of the Western Sahara.

Ting /tɪŋ/ Samuel 1936– . US high-energy physicist. In 1974 he detected a new particle, known as the J particle, similar to the ◄ (psi) particle of Burton ◊Richter, with whom he shared the 1976 Nobel Physics Prize.

tinnitus internal sounds, inaudible to others, which are heard by sufferers of malfunctions of hearing, often from infection of the middle or inner ear.

In some cases there is a hum at a frequency of about 40 Hz, which resembles that heard by people troubled by environmental ◊hum but may include whistles and other noises resembling a machine workshop. Being in a place where external noises drown the internal ones gives some relief, and devices may be worn which create pleasant, soothing sounds to override the internal noise.

tinplate the metal used for most 'tin' cans, which is mild steel coated with tin. The steel provides the strength and the tin provides the corrosion resistance, ensuring that the food inside is not contaminated. Tinplate may be made by ◊electroplating, or by dipping in a bath of molten tin.

Tintagel /tɪnˈtædʒəl/ village resort on the coast of N Cornwall, England. There are castle ruins, and legend has it that King ◊Arthur was born and held court here.

Tintoretto /ˌtɪntəˈretəʊ/ Real name Jacopo Robusti 1518–1594. Italian painter, active in Venice. His dramatic religious paintings are spectacularly lit and full of movement, such as his canvases of the lives of Christ and the Virgin in the Scuola di San Rocco, Venice, 1564–88.

He was a student of ◊Titian and admirer of Michelangelo. *Miracle of St Mark Rescuing a*

Slave 1548 (Accademia, Venice) marked the start of his successful career. In the Scuola di Sta Rocco he created a sequence of heroic scenes with bold gesture and foreshortening, and effects of supernatural light. He also painted canvases for the Doge's Palace.

Tiomkin /ˈtjɒmkɪn/ Dimitri 1899–1979. Russian composer who lived in the USA from 1925. From 1930 he wrote Hollywood film scores including music for *Duel in the Sun* 1946, *The Thing* 1951, and *Rio Bravo* 1959. His score for *High Noon* 1952 won him an Academy Award.

Tipperary /ˌtɪpəˈreəri/ county in the Republic of Ireland, province of Munster, divided into north and south regions. **North Tipperary** administrative headquarters Nenagh; area 2,000 sq km/772 sq mi; population (1986) 59,000. **South Tipperary** administrative headquarters Clonmel; area 2,260 sq km/872 sq mi; population (1986) 77,000. It includes part of the Golden Vale, a dairy-farming region.

Tippett /ˈtɪpɪt/ Michael (Kemp) 1905– . English composer whose works include the operas *The Midsummer Marriage* 1952 and *The Knot Garden* 1970; four symphonies; *Songs for Ariel* 1962; and choral music including *The Mask of Time* 1982.

Tippu Sultan /ˈtɪpuː/ *c.* 1750–1799. Sultan of Mysore (now Karnataka) from the death of his father, ◊Hyder Ali, in 1782. He died of wounds when his capital, Seringapatam, was captured by the British. His rocket brigade led Sir William Congreve (1772–1828) to develop the weapon for use in the Napoleonic Wars.

TIR abbreviation for *Transports Internationaux Routiers* (French 'International Road Transport').

Tirana /tɪˈrɑːnə/ or *Tiranë* capital (since 1920) of Albania; population (1983) 206,000. Industries include metallurgy, cotton textiles, soap, and cigarettes. It was founded in the early 17th century by Turks when part of the Ottoman Empire. Although the city is now mainly modern, some older districts and mosques have been preserved.

Tiresias or *Teiresias* in Greek mythology, a man blinded by the gods and given the ability to predict the future.

Tipperary *Celtic crosses, with their characteristic intertwined ornamentation, are found in the Irish countryside. This is the east face of South Cross at Ahenny in Tipperary.*

Tintagel *The ruins of King Arthur's castle at Tintagel, Cornwall, England.*

According to the poet Ovid, Tiresias once saw two snakes mating, struck at them, and was changed into a woman. Seven years later, in a repetition of the same scene, he reverted back to manhood. Later, he was called upon to settle a dispute between the two gods Zeus and Hera on whether men or women enjoy sex more. He declared for women, and as a result Hera blinded him, but Zeus gave him the gift of foresight.

Tirol /tɪˈrəʊl/ federal province of Austria; area 12,600 sq km/4,864 sq mi; population (1987) 610,000. Its capital is Innsbruck, and it produces diesel engines, optical instruments, and hydroelectric power. Tirol was formerly a province (from 1363) of the Austrian Empire, divided 1919 between Austria and Italy (see ◊Trentino-Alto Adige).

Tirpitz /ˈtɜːpɪts/ Alfred von 1849–1930. German admiral. As secretary for the navy 1897–1916, he created the modern German navy and planned the World War I U-boat campaign.

Tirso de Molina /ˈtɪəsəʊ deɪ məˈliːnə/ Pen name of Gabriel Telléz 1571–1648. Spanish dramatist and monk, who wrote more than 400 plays, of which eight are extant, including comedies, historical and biblical dramas, and a series based on the legend of Don Juan.

Tiruchirapalli /ˌtɪrətʃɪˈrɑːpəli/ formerly **Trichinopoly** ('three-headed demon') city in Tamil Nadu, India; chief industries (cotton textiles, cigars, and gold and silver filigree); population (1981) 362,000. It is a place of pilgrimage, and was the capital of Tamil kingdoms during the 10th–17th centuries.

Tiryns /ˈtɪrɪns/ ancient Greek city in the Peloponnese on the plain of Argos, with remains of the ◊Mycenaean culture.

Tiselius /tɪˈseɪlɪəs/ Arne 1902–1971. Swedish chemist who developed a powerful method of chemical analysis known as ◊electrophoresis. Tiselius applied his new techniques to the analysis of animal proteins and received the Nobel Chemistry Prize 1948.

Tissot /tiːˈsəʊ/ James (Joseph Jacques) 1836–1902. French painter who produced detailed portraits of fashionable Victorian society during a ten-year stay in England. In the 1880s Tissot visited Palestine. His religious works were much admired.

tissue in biology, a general term for any kind of cellular fabric that occurs in an organism's body. Several kinds of tissue can usually be distinguished, each consisting of cells of a particular kind bound together by cell walls (in plants) or extracellular matrix (in animals). Thus nerve and muscle are different kinds of tissue in animals, as are ◊parenchyma and ◊sclerenchyma in plants.

tissue culture a process in which cells from a plant or animal are removed from the organism, and grown under carefully controlled conditions in a sterile medium containing all the necessary nutrients. Tissue culture can provide information on cell growth and differentiation, and is also used in plant propagation and drug production. See also ◊meristem.

tissue plasminogen activator (TPA) a naturally occurring substance in the body tissues that activates the enzyme plasmin, which is able to dissolve blood clots. Human TPA, produced in bacteria by genetic engineering, has been used to try to dissolve blood clots in the coronary arteries of heart attack victims.

Tisza /ˈtiːsə/ tributary of the river ◊Danube, rising in the USSR and flowing through Hungary to Yugoslavia; length 967 km/601 mi.

tit or **titmouse** insectivorous, acrobatic bird of the family Paridae, of which there are 65 species. They are 8–20 cm/3–8 in long, have grey or black plumage, often with blue or yellow markings. They are found in Eurasia and Africa, and also in North America, where they are called **chickadees**.

Species in Britain include the bluetit *Parus caeruleus*, the great tit *Parus major*, and the coal, willow, marsh, and long-tailed tits. The crested tit is found only in Scotland.

Titan /ˈtaɪtn/ in astronomy, largest moon of the planet Saturn, with a diameter of 5,150 km/3,200 mi, and a mean distance from Saturn of 1,222,000 km/759,000 mi. It was discovered 1655 by Christiaan Huygens.

Titan is the only moon in the solar system with a substantial atmosphere (mostly nitrogen), topped with smoggy orange clouds that obscure the surface, which may be covered with liquid ethane lakes. Its surface atmospheric pressure is greater than Earth's. Radar signals suggest that Titan has dry land as well as oceans (only Earth has both in the solar system).

Titan /ˈtaɪtn/ in Greek mythology, any of the giant children of Uranus and Gaia, who included Kronos, Rhea, Themis (mother of Prometheus and personification of law and order) and Oceanus. Kronos and Rhea were in turn the parents of Zeus, who ousted Kronos as the ruler of the world.

Titanic /taɪˈtænɪk/ British passenger liner, supposedly unsinkable, that struck an iceberg and sank off the Grand Banks of Newfoundland on its maiden voyage 14–15 Apr 1912; 1,513 lives were lost. In 1985 it was located by robot submarine 4 km/2.5 mi down in an ocean canyon, preserved by the cold environment. In 1987 salvage operations began.

titanium a lustrous, steel-like white metal resembling iron, burning in air, and the only metal to burn in nitrogen; symbol Ti, atomic weight 47.90, atomic number 22. It is very strong and resistant to corrosion, and is used in many high-speed aeroplanes and spacecraft.

Discovered by the British mineralogist William Gregor 1791, titanium was named by the German chemist Klaproth 1795 and obtained pure by Hunter 1910. Its compounds occur in practically all igneous rocks and their sedimentary deposits. The oxide is used in high-grade white pigments, and some barium compounds are used in high-value capacitors. It was found on the Moon in the Sea of Tranquillity.

Titan rocket a family of US space rockets, developed from the Titan intercontinental missile. Two-stage Titan rockets launched the ◊Gemini manned missions. More powerful Titans, with additional stages and strap-on boosters, were used to launch spy satellites and space probes, including ◊Viking and ◊Voyager.

tithe formerly, a payment exacted from the inhabitants of a parish for the maintenance of the church and its incumbent; some religious groups continue the practice by giving 10% of members' incomes to charity.

It was originally the grant of a tenth of all agricultural produce made to priests in Hebrew society. In the Middle Ages the tithe was adopted as a tax in kind paid to the local parish church, usually for the support of the incumbent, and as such, it survived into modern times. In Protestant countries, these payments were often appropriated by lay landlords. In the 19th century a rent charge was substituted. By the Tithe Commutation Act 1836, tithes were abolished and replaced by 'redemption annuities' payable to the Crown, government stock being issued to tithe-owners.

Titian /ˈtɪʃən/ Anglicized form of the name of Tiziano Vecellio c. 1487–1576. Italian painter, active in Venice, one of the greatest artists of the High Renaissance. In 1533 he became court painter to Charles V, Holy Roman emperor, whose son Philip II of Spain later became his patron. Titian's work is richly coloured, with inventive composition. He produced a vast number of portraits, religious paintings, and mythological scenes, including *Bacchus and Ariadne* 1520–23, *Venus and Adonis* 1554, and the *Entombment of Christ* 1559.

Titian probably studied with Giovanni ◊Bellini but also learned much from ◊Giorgione and seems to have completed some of Giorgione's unfinished works, such as *Noli Me Tangere* (National Gallery, London). His first great painting is the *Assumption of the Virgin* 1518 (Church of the Frari, Venice), typically sublime in mood, with upward-thrusting layers of figures. Three large mythologies painted in the next few years for the d'Estes of Ferrara show yet more brilliant use of colour, and numerous statuesque figures suggest the influence of classical art. By the 1530s Titian's reputation was widespread.

In the 1540s Titian visited Rome to paint the pope; in Augsburg, Germany, 1548–49 and 1550–51 he painted members of the imperial court. In his later years he produced a series of mythologies for Philip II, notably *The Rape of Europa* 1562 (Isabella Stewart Gardner Museum, Boston, Massachusetts). His handling became increasingly free and his palette sombre, but his work remained full of drama. He made an impact not just on Venetian painting but on art throughout Europe.

Titicaca /ˌtɪtɪˈkɑːkə/ lake in the Andes, 3,810 m/ 12,500 ft above sea level; area 8,300 sq km/ 3,200 sq mi, the largest lake in South America. It is divided between Bolivia (port at Guaqui) and Peru (ports at Puno and Huancane). It has huge edible frogs.

Tito /ˈtiːtəʊ/ Adopted name of Josip Broz 1892–1980. Yugoslav soldier and communist politician. In World War II he organized the National Liberation Army to carry on guerrilla warfare against the German invasion 1941, and was created marshal 1943. As prime minister 1946–53 and president from 1953, he followed a foreign policy of 'positive neutralism'.

Born in Croatia, Tito served in the Austrian army during World War I, was captured by the Russians, and fought in the Red Army during the Civil Wars. Returning to Yugoslavia 1923, he became prominent as a Communist and during World War II as ◊partisan leader against the Nazis. In 1943 he established a provisional government, and with Soviet help proclaimed the federal republic 1945. As prime minister, he settled the Yugoslav minorities question on a federal basis, and in 1953

Titian *A portrait of the Holy Roman Emperor Charles V, by Titian.*

took the newly created post of president (for life from 1974). He was attacked by the ◊Cominform, particularly the USSR, 1948 for his successful system of decentralized profit-sharing workers' councils, and became the leader of the ◊nonaligned movement.

Tito *Marshal Tito, the former president of Yugoslavia.*

Titograd /'tiːtəʊgræd/ formerly ***Podgorica*** capital of Montenegro, Yugoslavia; population (1981) 132,300. Industries include metal working, furniture making, and tobacco. It was damaged in World War II, and after rebuilding was renamed 1948 in honour of Tito. It was the birthplace of the Roman emperor Diocletian.

titration in analytical chemistry, a technique to find the concentration of one compound in a solution by determining how much of it will react with a known amount of another compound in solution.

One of the solutions is measured by ◊pipette into the reaction vessel. The other is added a little at a time from a ◊burette. The end-point of the reaction is determined with an ◊indicator or an electrochemical device.

Titus /'taɪtəs/ Flavius Sabinus Vespasianus AD 39–81. Roman emperor from AD 79. Eldest son of ◊Vespasian, he stormed Jerusalem 70 to end the Jewish revolt in Roman Palestine. He completed the Colosseum, and enjoyed a peaceful reign, except for ◊Agricola's campaigns in Britain.

Tivoli /'tɪvəli/ town NE of Rome, Italy; population (1981) 52,000. It has remains of Hadrian's villa, with gardens; and the Villa d'Este with Renaissance gardens laid out 1549 for Cardinal Ippolito d'Este.

Tlatelolco, Treaty of international agreement signed 1967 in Tlatelolco, Mexico, prohibiting nuclear weapons in Latin America.

Tlemcen /tlem'sen/ (Roman ***Pomaria***) town in NW Algeria; population (1983) 146,000. Carpets and leather goods are made, and there is a 12th-century Great Mosque.

Tlingit /'tlɪŋgɪt/ North American Indian people, living on the SE coast and nearby islands. They carved wooden totem poles bearing animals: the mythical 'thunderbird', raven, whale, octopus, beaver, bear, and wolf.

TLR camera a twin-lens reflex camera that has a viewing lens of the same angle of view and focal length mounted above and parallel to the taking lens.

TM abbreviation for ◊*transcendental meditation*.

TN abbreviation for ◊*Tennessee*.

TNT abbreviation for trinitrotoluene, $CH_3C_6H_2(NO_3)_3$, a powerful high explosive. It is a yellow solid, prepared from toluene by using sulphuric and nitric acids.

toad general name for over 2,500 species of tailless amphibians, which are slow-moving, stout, and have dry warty skins. They live in cool, moist places, lay their eggs in water, and grow up to 25 cm/10 in long.

The ***common toad*** *Bufo bufo* of Europe and Asia has a rough, usually dark brown skin in which

there are glands secreting a poisonous fluid which makes it unattractive as food for other animals; it needs this protection as its usual progress is a slow, ungainly crawl. The eggs are laid, not in a mass as with frogs, but in long strings.

toadflax small plant, species of the genus *Linaria*, family Scrophulariaceae, with spurred two-lipped flowers.

toadstool inedible or poisonous type of ◊fungus with a fleshy gilled fruiting body on a stalk.

tobacco large-leaved plant *Nicotiana tabacum*, family Solanaceae; native to tropical parts of the Americas, it is widely cultivated as an annual in warm, dry climates for use in cigars and cigarettes, and in powdered form as snuff. The worldwide profits of the tobacco industry are estimated to be over £4 billion annually.

The leaves are cured, or dried, and matured in storage for two to three years before use. Introduced to Europe as a medicine in the 16th century, tobacco was recognized from the 1950s as a major health hazard; see ◊cancer. The leaves also yield the alkaloid **nicotine**, a colourless oil, one of the most powerful poisons known, and addictive in humans. It is used in insecticides.

Tobago /tə'beɪgəʊ/ island in the West Indies; part of ◊Trinidad and Tobago.

Tobin /'təʊbɪn/ James 1918– . US Keynesian economist. He was awarded a Nobel prize 1981 for his 'general equilibrium' theory, which states that other criteria than monetary considerations are applied by households and firms when making decisions on consumption and investment.

toboggan flat-bottomed sledge, curved upward at the front, used on snow or ice slopes or banked artificial courses, such as the Cresta run in Switzerland.

Olympic toboggans are either ***luge type*** seating 1/2, without brakes or steering; or ***bobsleighs*** seating 2/4, with streamlined 'cowls' at the front, steering and brakes. A ***skibob*** is like a bicycle with skis replacing the wheels, and the rider wears miniature foot skis up to 50 cm/20 in long.

Tobolsk /tə'bɒlsk/ river port and lumber centre at the confluence of the Tobol and Irtysh rivers in N Tyumen, W Siberia, USSR; population (1985) 75,000. It was founded by ◊Cossacks 1587; Tsar Nicholas II was exiled here 1917.

Tobruk /tə'brʊk/ Libyan port; population (1984) 94,000. Occupied by Italy 1911, it was taken by Britain 1941, and unsuccessfully besieged by Axis forces Apr–Dec 1941. It was captured by Germany June 1942 after the retreat of the main British force to Egypt, and this precipitated the replacement of Auchinleck by Montgomery as British commander.

toccata in music, a display piece for keyboard instruments, particularly the organ.

Toc H /'tɒk 'eɪtʃ/ interdenominational organization for Christian fellowship, founded 1915 in Belgium as a welfare society with a Christian basis for troops in World War I, by Neville Talbot and P T B Clayton (1885–1972).

Tocqueville /tɒk'viːl/ Alexis de 1805–1859. French politician and political scientist, author of the first analytical study of the US constitution *De la Démocratie en Amérique*/*Democracy in America* 1835, and of a penetrating description of France before the Revolution, *L'Ancien Régime et la Révolution*/*The Old Regime and the Revolution* 1856.

Todd /tɒd/ Ron(ald) 1927– . British trade-union leader. The son of a London market trader, he

rose from shop steward to general secretary of Britain's largest trade union, the Transport and General Workers' (TGWU). Although backing the Labour Party leadership, he has openly criticized its attitude towards nuclear disarmament.

Todd /tɒd/ Alexander, Baron Todd 1907– . British organic chemist, who won a Nobel prize 1957 for his work on the role of nucleic acids in genetics. He also synthesized vitamins B_1, B_{12}, and E.

Born in Glasgow, Todd began his work on the synthesis of organic molecules in 1934. He was professor at Manchester 1983–44 and Cambridge 1944–71.

Todt /təʊt/ Fritz 1891–1942. German engineer, who was responsible for the construction of the autobahns (German motorways) and, in World War II, the Siegfried Line and the Atlantic Wall.

tofu ◊soya bean curd derived from soya milk. It is a good source of protein and naturally low in fat.

Tofu comes in two varieties: firm, in small white blocks, used for stir-frying or steaming, and as a junket-like solid used in making dips, salad dressing or ice cream. Although bland in flavour, it can readily be combined with other ingredients.

tog measure of thermal insulation used in the textile trade; a light summer suit provides 1.0 tog.

The tog-value of an object is equal to ten times the temperature difference (in °C) between its two surfaces when the flow of heat is equal to one watt per square metre. One tog = 0.645 ◊clo.

Togare /tə'gɑːri/ Stage name of Georg Kulovits 1900–1988. Austrian wild-animal tamer and circus performer. Togare invented the character of the exotic Oriental lion tamer after watching Douglas Fairbanks in *The Thief of Baghdad*. In his circus appearances he displayed a nonchalant disregard for danger.

Togliatti /tɒl'jæti/ or ***Tolyatti*** formerly ***Stavropol*** port on the river Volga, W central USSR; industries include engineering and food processing; population (1987) 627,000. The city was relocated in the 1950s after a flood and renamed after the Italian Communist Palmiro Togliatti.

Togliatti /tɒl'jæti/ Palmiro 1893–1964. Founding member of the Italian Communist Party in 1921, and effectively leader for almost 40 years from 1926 until his death. In exile from 1926 until 1944, he returned to become a member of Badoglio's government and held office until 1946.

Togliatti trained as a lawyer, but served in the army and was wounded during World War I. He was associated with the revolutionary wing of the Italian socialist party which left to form the Communist party in 1921. From 1922 to 1924 he edited the newspaper *Il Communista* and became a member of the party's central committee. In Moscow when Mussolini outlawed the party, he stayed there to become a leading member of the ◊Comintern joining the Secretariat in 1935. Returning to Italy after Mussolini's downfall, he advocated coalition politics with other leftist and democratic parties, a policy which came to fruition in the elections of 1948 where the communists won 135 seats.

Togo /'təʊgəʊ/ country in W Africa, bounded to the W by Ghana, to the E by Benin, and to the N by Burkina Faso.

government The 1979 constitution created a one-party, socialist republic based on the Assembly of the Togolese People (RPT). The president is elected by universal suffrage for a seven-year term and is eligible for re-election. The president is head of state and head of government, appointing and presiding over a council of ministers, and is also president of RPT.

There is a single-chamber legislature, the National Assembly, of 77 members, elected by universal suffrage from a list of RPT nominees and serving for five years. There is an illegal opposition party, the Togolese Movement for Democracy, which is based in Paris.

history For early history, see ◊Africa. Called Togoland, the country was a German protectorate

toad

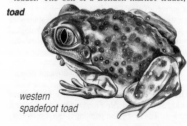

western spadefoot toad

1885–1914, when it was captured by Anglo-French forces. It was divided between Britain and France in 1922 under a League of Nations mandate and continued under United Nations trusteeship from 1946. In 1956 British Togoland voted for integration with Ghana, where it became Volta region 1957.

French Togoland voted to become an autonomous republic within the French union. The new Togolese republic achieved internal self-government in 1956 and full independence in 1960. Sylvanus Olympio, leader of the United Togolese (UT) party, became president in an unopposed election in Apr 1961. In 1963 Olympio was killed in a military coup and his brother-in-law Nicolas Grunitzky, who had gone into exile, was recalled to become president.

In 1967 Grunitzky was, in turn, deposed in a bloodless military coup, led by Lt-Gen Etienne Gnassingbe Eyadema. The new constitution was suspended, Eyadema assumed the presidency and banned all political activity. Six years later he founded a new party, the socialist, nationalist Assembly of the Togolese People, and declared it the only legal political organization. Between 1967 and 1977 there were several attempts to overthrow him but by 1979 Eyadema felt sufficiently secure to propose a new coalition and embark on a policy of gradual democratization. An attempt to overthrow him in Oct 1986, by mercenaries from Burkina Faso and Ghana, was easily thwarted.

Togo /ˈtəʊgəʊ/ Heihachiro 1846–1934. Japanese admiral who commanded the fleet at the battle of Tsushima Strait 27 May 1905 when Japan decisively defeated the Russians and effectively ended the Russo-Japanese war of 1904–05.

Tohoku /təʊˈhəʊkuː/ mountainous region of N Honshu island, Japan; population (1986) 9,737,000; area 66,971sq km/25,867 sq mi. Timber, fruit, fish, and livestock are produced. Chief city is Sendai. It is linked to the island of Hokkaido by the Seikan tunnel, the world's longest underwater tunnel.

toilet a place where waste products from the body are excreted. Simple latrines, with sewers to carry away waste, have been found in the Indus Valley and ancient Babylon; the medieval ◊garderobe is essentially the same, even though flushing lavatories had been known to the Romans, for example at Housesteads Fort on Hadrian's Wall. The valve cistern, with a base that could be opened

or closed, was invented by John Harington, godson of Queen Elizabeth I; it was described by him in 1596, although, following the introduction of the ball valve in 1748, it was independently reinvented and patented by Alexander Cummings in 1775. Cumming's design included a U-bend to keep smells out. This design was then improved by Joseph ◊Bramah in 1778, establishing the basic action that has largely continued to the present day. The present style of toilet dates from about 1889.

Tojo /ˈtəʊdʒəʊ/ Hideki 1884–1948. Japanese general and prime minister 1941–44. Promoted to chief of staff of the Guangdong army 1937, he served as minister for war 1938–39 and 1940–41. He was held responsible for defeats in the Pacific 1944 and forced to resign. He was hanged as a war criminal.

tokamak an experimental machine designed to investigate nuclear fusion. It consists of a chamber surrounded by electromagnets capable of exerting very powerful magnetic fields. The fields are generated to confine very hot (millions of degrees) ◊plasma, keeping it away from the chamber walls. See also ◊JET.

Tokay /təʊˈkeɪ/ sweet white wine made near the Hungarian town of Tokaj; also the grape from which it is made.

Tokelau /ˈtəʊkəlaʊ/ formerly **Union Islands** overseas territory of New Zealand, 480 km/300 mi north of Western Samoa, comprising three coral atolls: Atafu, Fakaofo, and Nukunonu; area 10 sq km/4 sq mi; population (19860) 1,700. The islands belong to the Polynesian group. Their resources are small and until 1975 many of the inhabitants settled in New Zealand, which has administered them since 1926 when they were separated from the British Gilbert and Ellice Islands colony.

Tokugawa the military family that controlled Japan 1603–1867. **Iyeyasu** or **Ieyasu Tokugawa** (1542–1616) was the Japanese general and politician who established the Tokugawa shogunate. They were feudal lords who ruled about one quarter of Japan.

Tokyo /ˈtəʊkiəʊ/ capital of Japan, on ◊Honshu Island; population (1987) 8,209,000, the metropolitan area of Tokyo-to over 12,000,000. The Sumida river delta separates the city from its suburb of Honjo. It is Japan's main cultural and industrial centre (engineering, chemicals, textiles,

electrical goods). Founded in the 16th century as Yedo, it was renamed when the emperor moved his court there from Kyoto 1868. An earthquake 1923 killed 58,000 people. The city was severely damaged by Allied bombing in World War II. The subsequent rebuilding has made it into one of the world's most modern cities.

Features include the Imperial Palace, National Diet (parliament), National Theatre, Tokyo University 1877, and the National Athletic Stadium.

Toland /ˈtəʊlənd/ Gregory 1904–1948. US director of film photography, who used deep focus to good effect in such films as *Wuthering Heights* 1939, *Citizen Kane* 1941, *The Grapes of Wrath* 1940, and *The Best Years of our Lives* 1946.

Toledo /tɒˈleɪdəʊ/ city on the river Tagus, Castilla–La Mancha, central Spain; population (1982) 62,000. It was the capital of the Visigoth kingdom 534–711 (see ◊Goths), then became a Moorish city, and was the Castilian capital 1085–1560.

In the 12th century, Toledo had a flourishing steel industry, and a school of translators, run by Archbishop Raymond (1125–1151), writing Latin versions of Arabic philosophical works. The painter El Greco worked here from about 1575 (his house and garden are preserved), and the local landscape is the setting of Cervantes' novel *Don Quixote*.

Toledo /təˈliːdəʊ/ port on Lake Erie, Ohio, USA, at the mouth of the Maumee river; industries include food processing and the manufacture of vehicles, electrical goods, and glass; population (1980) 355,000.

Tolkien /ˈtɒlkiːn/ J(ohn) R(onald) R(euel) 1892–1973. English writer, who created the fictional world of Middle Earth in *The Hobbit* 1937 and the trilogy *The Lord of the Rings* 1954–55, fantasy novels peopled with hobbits, dwarves, and strange magical creatures. His work became a cult in the 1960s and had many imitations.

He was professor of Anglo-Saxon 1925–45, and Merton professor of English at Oxford, 1945–59.

Tolpuddle Martyrs /ˈtɒlpʌdl/ six farm labourers of Tolpuddle, near Dorchester, England, who were transported to Australia in 1834 for forming a trade union. After nationwide agitation they were pardoned two years later.

Tolstoy /ˈtɒlstɔɪ/ Leo Nikolaievich 1828–1910. Russian novelist, who wrote *Tales from Sebastopol* 1856, ◊*War and Peace* 1863–69, and ◊*Anna Karenina* 1873–77. From 1880 Tolstoy underwent a profound spiritual crisis and took up moral positions including passive resistance to evil, rejection of authority (religious or civil) and of private ownership, and a return to basic mystical Christianity. He was excommunicated by the Orthodox Church, and his later works were banned.

Tolstoy was born of noble family at Yasnaya Polyana, near Tula, and fought in the Crimean War. His first published work was *Childhood* 1852, the first part of the trilogy that was completed with *Boyhood* 1854 and *Youth* 1857; later books include *What I Believe* 1883 and *The Kreutzer Sonata* 1889, and the novel *Resurrection* 1900. His home became a place of pilgrimage. His desire to give up his property and live as a peasant disrupted his family life, and he finally fled his home and died of pneumonia at the railway station at Astapovo.

Toltec member of an American Indian people who ruled much of Mayan central Mexico in the 10th–12th centuries, with their capital at Tula. Their religious centre was at Teotihuacán, where there are temples of the Sun and Moon, and to their serpent god Quetzalcoatl.

toluene or **methyl benzene** ($C_6H_5CH_3$) a colourless, inflammable liquid, insoluble in water, derived from petroleum. It is used as a solvent, in aircraft fuels, in preparing phenol (carbolic acid, used in making resins for adhesives, pharmaceuticals, and as a disinfectant), and the powerful high explosive TNT (trinitrotoluene).

Tomasi /təʊˈmɑːsi/ Giuseppe, Prince of Lampedusa. Italian writer; see ◊Lampedusa.

Togo
Republic of
(République Togolaise)

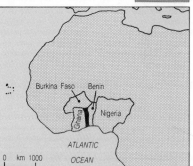

area 56,800 sq km/21,930 sq mi
capital Lomé
physical two savanna plains, divided by a range of hills NE–SW
features rich mineral deposits (phosphates, bauxite, marble, iron ore, limestone); dry plains, forest, and arable land
head of state and of government Etienne Gnassingbe Eyadema from 1967
government system one-party socialist republic
political parties Assembly of the Tongolese People (RPT), nationalist, socialist
exports cocoa, coffee, coconuts, copra, phosphate, bauxite
currency CFA franc (485.00 = £1 Mar 1990)
population (1986) 3,423,000; annual growth rate 3%
life expectancy men 49, women 52
language French (official), many local languages
religion traditional 60%, Muslim 20%, Christian 20%
literacy 53% male/28% female (1985 est)
GNP $790 million (1983); $348 per head of population
chronology
1960 Achieved full independence as the Republic of Togo with Sylvanus Olympio as head of state.
1963 Olympio killed in a military coup. Nicolas Grunitzky became president.
1967 Grunitzky replaced by Lt-Gen Etienne Gnassingbe Eyadema in a bloodless coup.
1973 The Assembly of Togolese People (RPT) formed as the only legal political party.
1979 Eyadema returned in election.
1986 Attempted coup failed.

tomato annual plant *Lycopersicon esculentum*, family Solanaceae; native to South America, it is widely cultivated for the many-seeded red fruit, used in salads and cooking.

Tombaugh /'tɒmbɔː/ Clyde (William) 1906– . US astronomer, who discovered the planet ◊Pluto 1930.

Born in Streator, Illinois, Tombaugh became an assistant at the Lowell Observatory in Flagstaff, Arizona, in 1929, and photographed the sky in search of an undiscovered remote planet as predicted by the observatory's founder, Percival ◊Lowell. Tombaugh found Pluto 18 Feb 1930, from plates taken three weeks earlier. He continued his search for new planets across the entire sky; his failure to find any placed strict limits on the possible existence of planets beyond Pluto.

Tombstone /'tuːmstəun/ former silver-mining town in the desert of SE Arizona, USA. The *gunfight at the OK Corral*, deputy marshal Wyatt Earp, his brothers, and 'Doc' Holliday against the Clanton gang, took place here 26 Oct 1881.

Tom Jones, The History of novel by Henry Fielding, published 1749. It describes the complicated, and not always reputable, early life of Tom Jones, an orphan, who is good-natured but hot-headed.

Tommy gun popular name for Thompson submachine-gun; see ◊machine gun.

tomography the obtaining of plane section photographs, which show a 'slice' through any object. Crystal detectors and amplifiers can be used that have a sensitivity a hundred times greater than X-ray film, and, in conjunction with a computer system, can detect, for example, the difference between a brain tumour and healthy brain tissue.

Godfrey Hounsfield was a leading pioneer in the development of this technique. In modern medical imaging there are several types, such as ◊CAT (computerized axial tomography) scan.

Tom Sawyer, The Adventures of novel by US author Mark Twain, published 1876. It describes the childhood escapades of Tom Sawyer and his friends Huckleberry Finn and Joe Harper in a small Mississippi community before the American Civil War. It and its sequel *The Adventures of Huckleberry Finn* 1885 are notable for their rejection of the high moral tone prevalent in 19th-century children's literature.

Tomsk /tɒmsk/ city on the river Tom, W central Siberia; industries (synthetic fibres, timber, distilling, plastics, electrical motors); population (1987) 489,000. It was formerly a gold-mining town and the administrative centre of much of Siberia.

Tom Thumb a tiny hero of English folk tale, whose name has often been given to those of small stature, including *Charles Sherwood Stratton* 1838–83, nicknamed General Tom Thumb. In the fairy tale, collected by the Grimm brothers but referred to in English as early as 1597, an old, childless couple wish for a son and are granted a thumb-sized boy. After many adventures he ends as a brave, miniature knight at the court of King Arthur.

ton imperial unit of mass. The *long ton*, used in the UK, is 2,240 lb/1,016 kg; the *short ton*, used in the USA, is 2,000 lb/907 kg. The *metric ton* or *tonne* is 1,000 kg/2,204.6 lb.

ton in shipping, a unit of volume equal to 2.83 cu m/100 cu ft. *Gross tonnage* is the total internal volume of a ship in tons; *net register tonnage* is the volume used for carrying cargo or passengers. *Displacement tonnage* is the weight of the vessel, in terms of the number of imperial tons of seawater displaced when the ship is loaded to its load line; it is used to describe warships.

tonality in music, the observance of a key structure, that is, the recognition of the importance of a tonic or key note and of the diatonic scale built upon it. See also ◊atonality and ◊polytonality.

Tone /təun/ (Theobald) Wolfe 1763–1798. Irish nationalist, called to the Bar 1789, and prominent in the revolutionary society of the United

Tonga
Kingdom of
(Pule'anga Fakatu'i 'o Tonga)
or **Friendly Islands**

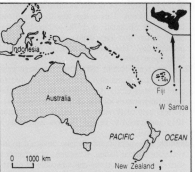

area 750 sq km/290 sq mi
capital Nuku'alofa on Tongatapu
physical comprises three groups of islands in the SW Pacific, mostly coral formations, but the western are actively volcanic
features fewer than one-third of the islands are inhabited
head of state and of government King Taufa'ahau Tupou IV from 1965
political system absolute monarchy
political parties none
currency Tongan dollar or pa'anga (2.08 = £1 Mar 1989)
population (1988) 95,000; annual growth rate 2.4%
language Tongan and English
religion Wesleyan 47%, Roman Catholic 14%, Free Church of Tonga 14%, Mormon 9%, Church of Tonga 9%
literacy 93% (1985)
GNP $80 million (1983); $430 per head of population
chronology
1831 Tongan dynasty founded by Prince Taufa'ahau Tupou
1900 Became a British protectorate
1965 Death of Queen Salote. She was succeeded by her son, Prince Tupout'a, who took the title King Tupou IV.
1970 Achieved full independence within the Commonwealth.

Irishmen. In 1798 he accompanied the French invasion of Ireland, was captured and condemned to death, but slit his own throat in prison.

tone poem in music, another name for ◊symphonic poem, as used, for example, by Richard Strauss.

Tonga /'tɒŋə/ country in the SW Pacific, in ◊Polynesia.

government Tonga is an independent hereditary monarchy within the Commonwealth. Its constitution dates from 1875 and provides for a monarch who is both head of state and head of government. The monarch chooses and presides over the Privy Council, a cabinet of nine ministers appointed for life.

There is a single-chamber legislature, the Legislative Assembly, of 29 members, which include the monarch, the Privy Council, nine hereditary nobles, and nine representatives of the people, elected by universal adult suffrage. The assembly has a life of three years. There are no political parties in Tonga.

history The first European visitors to the islands were Dutch, 1616 and 1643 (Abel Tasman). Captain Cook dubbed them the Friendly Islands 1773. The contemporary Tongan dynasty was founded in 1831 by Prince Taufa'ahau Tupou, who assumed the designation King George Tupou I

Tom Thumb *Midget performer General Tom Thumb (Charles Stratton), who joined P T Barnum's circus at the age of five, with his wife Lavinia Warren. He stood 3ft 4 in/1 m tall as an adult.*

when he ascended the throne. He consolidated the kingdom by conquest, encouraged the spread of Christianity and granted a constitution. Tonga became a British protectorate from 1900, but under the terms of revised treaties of 1958 and 1967 recovered increased control over its internal affairs.

Queen Salote Tupou III died 1965 and was succeeded by her son Prince Tupouto'a Tungi, who as King Tupou IV led his nation to full independence, within the Commonwealth, 1970. He is still the country's ruler.

Tongariro /,tɒŋə'rɪərəu/ volcanic peak at the centre of North Island, New Zealand. Sacred to the Maori, the mountain was presented to the government by chief Te Heuheu Tukino IV 1887. It was New Zealand's first national park and the fourth to be designated in the world.

tongue in tetrapod (four-limbed) vertebrates, a muscular organ usually attached to the floor of the mouth. It has a thick root attached to a U-shaped bone (hyoid) behind, and is covered with a ◊mucous membrane containing nerves and 'taste buds'. It directs food and drink to the teeth and into the throat for chewing and swallowing. In humans, it is important for speech; in other animals, for lapping up water and for grooming, among others.

tonic in music, the first degree or key note of a scale (for example, the note C in the scale of C major).

tonka South American tree *Dipteryx odorata*, family Leguminosae; the fruit, a dry fibrous pod, encloses a black aromatic seed used in flavouring, perfumery, and the manufacture of snuff and tobacco.

Tonkin /,tɒn'kɪn/ or *Tongking* former region of Vietnam, on the China Sea; area 103,500 sq km/39,951 sq mi. Under Chinese rule from 111 BC, Tonkin became independent AD 939, and remained self-governing until the 19th century. A part of French Indochina 1885–1946, capital Hanoi, it was part of North Vietnam from 1954, and was merged with Vietnam after the Vietnam War.

Tonkin Gulf Incident clash that triggered US entry into the Vietnam War in Aug 1964. Two US destroyers (USS *C Turner Joy* and USS *Maddox*) reported that they were fired on by North Vietnamese torpedo boats. It is unclear whether hostile shots were actually fired, but the reported attack was taken as a pretext for retaliatory air raids against North Vietnam. On 7 Aug the US Congress passed the *Tonkin Resolution*, which allowed President Johnson 'to take all necessary steps, including the use of armed forces' to help SEATO (South-East Asia Treaty Organization) members 'defend their freedom'. This resolution formed the basis for the considerable increase in US military involvement in the Vietnam War; it was repealed 1970.

Tonkin, Gulf of /ˌtɒnˈkɪn/ part of the South China Sea, with oil resources. China and Vietnam disagree over their territorial boundaries in the area.

Tonle Sap /ˈtɒnli ˈsæp/ or **Great Lake** lake on a tributary of the ◊Mekong river, W Cambodia; area 2,600 sq km/1,000 sq mi to 6,500 sq km/2,500 sq mi at the height of the monsoon. During the June–Nov wet season it acts as a natural flood reservoir.

tonnage and poundage duties granted in England 1371–1787 by Parliament to the crown on imports and exports of wine and other goods. They were controversially levied by Charles I in 1626 without parliamentary consent.

tonne the metric ton of 1,000 kg/2,204.6 lb, equivalent to 0.9842 of an imperial ton.

Tönnies /ˈtʌnɪəs/ Ferdinand 1855–1936. German social theorist and philosopher, one of the founders of the sociological tradition of community studies and urban sociology through his key work, ◊*Gemeinschaft–Gesellschaft* 1887.

Tönnies contrasted the nature of social relationships in traditional societies and small organizations (*Gemeinschaft*, 'community') with those in modern industrial societies and large organizations (*Gesellschaft*, 'association'). He was pessimistic about the effect of industrialization and urbanization on the social and moral order, seeing them as a threat to traditional society's sense of community.

tonsil a lump of lymphatic tissue situated at the back of the mouth and throat in higher vertebrates. The tonsils contain many ◊lymphocytes and are part of the body's defence system against infection.

tonsillectomy surgical removal of the tonsils.

tonsillitis an inflammation of the ◊tonsils.

tonsure the shaving of the hair of the head as a symbol of being a priest. Until 1973 in the Roman Catholic Church, the crown was shaved (leaving a surrounding fringe to resemble Jesus's crown of thorns); in the Eastern Orthodox Church the hair is merely shorn close.

Tonton Macoute member of a private army of death squads on Haiti. The Tontons Macoutes were initially organized by François ◊Duvalier, president of Haiti 1957–71.

Tony award annual award by the League of New York Theaters to playwrights, performers, and technicians in ◊Broadway plays. It is named after the US actress and producer Antoinette Perry (1888–1946).

Tooke /tʊk/ John Horne 1736–1812. British politician, who established a Constitutional Society for parliamentary reform 1771. He was elected a member of Parliament 1801.

tool an implement that gives the user a ◊mechanical advantage, such as a hammer or a saw; a *machine tool* is a tool operated by power. Tools are the basis of industrial production; the chief machine tool is the ◊lathe. The industrial potential of a country is often calculated by the number of machine tools available. Automatic control of machine tools, an important development, is known as ◊automation.

tooth in vertebrates, a hard structure in the mouth, used for biting and chewing food, and in defence and aggression. In humans, the first set (20 milk teeth) appear from age six months to two-and-a-half years. The permanent dentition replaces these from the sixth year onwards; the wisdom teeth (third molars) sometimes not appearing until the age of 25 or 30. Adults have 32 teeth: two incisors, one canine (eye tooth), two premolars, and three molars on each side of each jaw. The tooth is hollow, and filled with a highly sensitive pulp made of nerves and blood vessels. It has a root or roots set in a socket of fine bone, a neck covered by the ◊gum, covered with a crown of a bony substance (dentine) and hard white enamel.

The chief diseases of teeth are misplacements resulting from defect or disturbance of the tooth-germs before birth, eruption out of the proper places, and caries (decay).

Toowoomba /təˈwʊmbə/ town and commercial and industrial (coal-mining, iron-working, engineering, clothing) centre in the Darling Downs, SE Queensland, Australia; population (1987) 79,000.

topaz a mineral, aluminium fluosilicate, Al_2SiO_4 $(F,OH)_2$. It is usually yellow, but pink if it has been heated, and is used as a gemstone when transparent. It ranks 8 on the Mohs' scale of hardness.

tope slender shark *Galeorhinus galeus* ranging through temperate and tropical seas. Dark grey above and white beneath, it reaches 2 m/6 ft in lenght. The young are born well-formed, sometimes 40 at a time.

tope type of tumulus found in India and SE Asia; a Buddhist monument usually built over a relic of Buddha or his disciples. They date from 400–300 BC, including ones at Sanchi, near Bhilsa, central India.

Topeka /təˈpiːkə/ capital of Kansas, USA; population (1980) 119,000. It is a major centre for psychiatric research and agricultural trade, with engineering and textile industries.

topi or *korrigum* antelope *Damaliscus korrigum* of equatorial Africa, head and body about 1.7 m/5.5 ft long, 1.1 m/3.5 ft high at the shoulder, with a chocolate-brown coat.

topiary the clipping of trees and shrubs into ornamental shapes, originated by the Romans in the 1st century and revived in the 16th–17th centuries in formal gardens.

Toplady /ˈtɒpleɪdi/ Augustus Montague 1740–1778. British Anglican priest, the author of the hymn 'Rock of Ages' 1775.

topography the surface shape and aspect of the land, and its study. Topography deals with relief and contours, the distribution of mountains and valleys, the patterns of rivers, and all other features, natural and artificial, that produce the landscape.

topology the branch of geometry that deals with those properties of a figure that remain unchanged even when the figure is transformed (bent or stretched), for example when a square painted

tooth

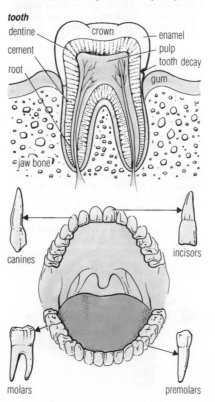

tooth

on a rubber sheet is deformed by distorting the sheet. Topology has scientific applications, as in the study of turbulence in fluids. The map of the London Underground system is an example of the topological representation of the rail network. Connectivity (the way the lines join together) is preserved, but shape and size are not. A topological problem (studied extensively by the Norwegian mathematician Oystein Ore) is to provide a proof that only four colours are needed in producing a map to give all adjoining areas different colours.

topsoil the upper, cultivated layer of soil, which may vary in depth from 8 to 45 cm/3 to 18 in. It contains organic matter, the decayed remains of vegetation, which plants need for active growth.

tor isolated mass of rock, usually granite, left upstanding on a moor after the surrounding rock has been worn away. Erosion takes place along the joints in the rock, wearing the outcrop into a mass of rounded lumps.

Torah in ◊Judaism, the first five books of the Hebrew Bible (Christian Old Testament), which are ascribed to Moses. It contains a traditional history of the world from the Creation to the death of Moses; and rules and guidelines for religious observance and social conduct, including the Ten Commandments.

Scrolls on which the Torah is hand-written in the original Hebrew are housed in a special cupboard, the ark, in every synagogue, and are treated with great respect. Jews believe that by observing the guidelines laid down in the Torah, they fulfil their part of their covenant with God.

Torbay /ˌtɔːˈbeɪ/ district in S Devon, England; population (1981) 116,000. It was created 1968 by the union of the seaside resorts of Paignton, Torquay, and Brixham.

Torgau /ˈtɔːgaʊ/ town in Leipzig county, East Germany; population 20,000. In 1760, during the Seven Years' War Frederick II of Prussia defeated the Austrians nearby, and in World War II the US and Soviet forces first met here.

Torino /tɒˈriːnəʊ/ Italian name for the city of ◊Turin.

tornado extremely violent revolving storm with swirling, funnel-shaped clouds, caused by a rising column of warm air propelled by strong wind. A tornado can rise to a great height, but with a diameter of only a few hundred yards or metres or less. Tornadoes move with wind speeds of 160–480 kph/100–300 mph, destroying everything in their path. They are common in the central USA and Australia.

Torness /ˌtɔːˈnes/ site of an advanced gas-cooled nuclear reactor 7 km/4.5 mi SW of Dunbar, East

topology

this figure is topologically equivalent to this one

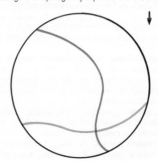

Lothian, Scotland. It started to generate power 1987.

torong musical instrument of the aboriginal Tay people of central Vietnam (Nguyen) and now common throughout Vietnam. It consists of differing lengths of hanging bamboo that are struck with a stick.

Toronto /təˈrɒntəʊ/ port on Lake Ontario, capital of Ontario, Canada; metropolitan population (1985) 3,427,000. It is Canada's main industrial and commercial centre (banking, shipbuilding, cars, farm machinery, food processing, publishing), and also a cultural centre, with theatres and a film industry. A French fort was established 1749, and the site became the provincial capital (then named York) 1793; it was renamed Toronto (North American Indian 'place of meeting') 1834, when incorporated as a city.

torpedo type of ray (fish) whose electric organs between the pectoral fin and the head can give a powerful shock. They can grow to 180 cm/6 ft in length. The electric ray *Torpedo nobiliana* is found off Britain.

torpedo self-propelled underwater missile, invented 1866 by British engineer Robert ◊Whitehead. Modern torpedoes are homing missiles; some resemble mines in that they lie on the seabed until activated by the acoustic signal of a passing ship. A television camera enables them to be remotely controlled, and in the final stage of attack they lock on to the radar or sonar signals of the target ship.

Torquay /ˌtɔːˈkiː/ resort in S Devon, England, part of the district of ◊Torbay.

torque the turning effect of force on an object. A turbine produces a torque that turns an electricity generator in a power station. Torque is measured by multiplying the force by its perpendicular distance from the turning point.

torque converter a device similar to a turbine, filled with oil, used in automatic transmission systems in cars, locomotives, and other vehicles to transmit power between the engine and the gearbox.

Torquemada /ˌtɔːkɪˈmɑːdə/ Tomás de 1420–1498. Spanish Dominican friar, confessor to Queen Isabella I. In 1483 he revived the ◊Inquisition on her behalf, and at least 2,000 'heretics' were burned; Torquemada also expelled the Jews from Spain, with a resultant decline of the economy.

torr unit of pressure equal to 1/760 of an ◊atmosphere, used mainly in high-vacuum technology. One torr is equivalent to 133.322 pascals, and for practical purposes is the same as the millimetre of mercury. It is named after the Italian physicist Evangelista Torricelli.

Torrens /ˈtɒrənz/ salt lake 8 m/25 ft below sea level in E South Australia; area 5,800 sq km/2,239 sq mi. It is reduced to a marsh in dry weather.

Torreón /ˌtɒriˈɒn/ industrial and agricultural city in Coahuila state, N Mexico, on the river Nazas at an altitude of 1,127 m/3,700 ft; population (1986) 730,000. Before the arrival of the railway 1907 Torreón was the largest of the Laguna cotton district tri-cities (with Gómez Palacio and Ciudad Lerdo). Since then it has developed as a major thoroughfare and commercial centre.

Torres-García /ˈtɒrɪs ɡɑːˈθiːə/ Joaquim 1874–1949. Uruguayan artist, born in Montevideo. In Paris from 1926, he was influenced by ◊Mondrian and others and, after going to Madrid in 1932, by Inca and Nazca pottery. His mature style is based on a grid pattern derived from the ◊golden section.

Torres Strait /ˈtɒrɪs/ channel separating New Guinea from Australia, with scattered reefs; width 130 km/80 mi. The first European to sail through it was the Spanish navigator Luis Vaez de Torres 1606.

Torricelli /ˌtɒrɪˈtʃeli/ Evangelista 1608–1647. Italian physicist and pupil of ◊Galileo, who devised the mercury ◊barometer.

torsion in physics, the state of strain set up in a twisted material; for example, when a thread, wire, or rod is twisted, the torsion set up in the material tends to return the material to its original state. The ***torsion balance***, a sensitive device for measuring small gravitational or magnetic forces, or electric charges, balances these against the restoring force set up by them in a torsion suspension.

tort in law, a wrongful act for which someone can be sued for damages in a civil court. It includes such acts as libel, trespass, injury done to someone (whether intentionally or by negligence), and inducement to break a contract (although breach of contract itself is not a tort).

In general a tort is distinguished from a crime in that it affects the interests of an individual rather than of society at large, but some crimes can also be torts (for example ◊assault).

tortoise reptile of the order Chelonia, family Testudinidae, with the body enclosed in a hard shell. Tortoises are related to the ◊terrapins and ◊turtles, and range in length from 10 cm/4 in to 150 cm/5 ft. The shell consists of a curved upper carapace and flattened lower plastron joined at the sides. The head and limbs may be withdrawn into it when the tortoise is in danger. Most land tortoises are herbivorous and have no teeth. The mouth forms a sharp-edged 'beak'. Eggs are laid in warm earth in great numbers, and are not incubated by the mother. Some tortoises are known to live for 150 years.

The small ***spur-thighed tortoise*** *Testudo graeca* is found in Asia Minor, the Balkans, and N Africa. The ***giant tortoises*** of the Galapagos and Seychelles may reach a length of 150 cm/5 ft and weigh over 225 kg/500 lbs, and yield about 90 kg/200 lbs of meat; hence their almost complete extermination by sailors in passing ships. The spur-thighed tortoise was extensively exported, often in appalling conditions, until the 1980s, when strict regulations were introduced to prevent its probable extinction.

Tortoiseshell is the semi-transparent shell of the hawksbill turtle.

Tortuga /tɔːˈtuːgə/ (French *La Tortue* 'turtle') island off the N coast of ◊Haiti; area 180 sq km/69 sq mi. It was a pirate lair during the 17th century.

torture infliction of bodily pain, to extort evidence or confession. Legally abolished in England about 1640, torture was allowed in Scotland until 1708 and until 1789 in France. In the 20th century torture is widely used, though in most countries unofficially, used.

Physical torture in the Middle Ages employed devices such as the rack (to stretch the victim's joints to breaking point), the thumbscrew, the boot (which crushed the foot), heavy weights that crushed the whole body, the iron maiden (cage shaped like a human being with interior spikes to spear the occupant), and so on. While similar methods survive today, electric shocks and sexual assault are also common.

Brainwashing was developed in both the communist and the Western bloc in the 1950s, often using drugs. From the early 1960s a method used in the West replaced isolation by severe sensory deprivation; for example, IRA guerrillas were prevented from seeing by a hood, from feeling by being swathed in a loose-fitting garment, and

from hearing by a continuous loud noise at about 85 decibels, while being forced to maintain themselves in a 'search' position against a wall by their fingertips. The European Commission on Human Rights found Britain guilty of torture, although the European Court of Human Rights classed it only as 'inhuman and degrading treatment'.

The human-rights organization ◊Amnesty International investigates and publicizes the use of torture on prisoners of conscience, and there is now a centre in Copenhagen, Denmark, where torture victims are rehabilitated and studies are carried out into the effects of torture.

Toruń /ˈtɒrʊn/ (German *Thorn*) industrial (electronics, fertilizers, synthetic fibres) river port in N Poland, on the Vistula; population (1982) 183,000. It was founded by the ◊Teutonic Knights 1230, and is the birthplace of the astronomer Copernicus.

Torvill and Dean Jayne Torvill (1957–) and Christopher Dean (1959–) British ice-dance champions, both from Nottingham. They won the world title four times and were the 1984 Olympic champions.

Tory democracy a concept attributed to the 19th-century British Conservative Party, and to the campaign of Lord Randolph ◊Churchill against Stafford Northcote in the early 1880s. The slogan was not backed up by any specific policy proposals. 'Tory democracy' was revived in the 1980s as a rallying cry for conservatives with a social conscience.

Tory Party the forerunner of the British ◊Conservative Party 1680–1830. It was the party of the squire and parson, as opposed to the Whigs (supported by the trading classes and Nonconformists). The name is still applied colloquially to the Conservative Party. In the USA a Tory was an opponent of the break with Britain in the War of American Independence 1775–83.

The original Tories were Irish guerrillas who attacked the English, and the name was applied (at first insultingly) to royalists who opposed the Exclusion Bill (see under Duke of ◊Monmouth). Although largely supporting the 1688 revolution, the Tories were suspected of ◊Jacobite sympathies, and were kept from power 1714–60, but then held office almost continuously until 1830.

Toscana /tɒˈskɑːnə/ Italian name for the region of ◊Tuscany.

Toscanini /ˌtɒskəˈniːni/ Arturo 1867–1957. Italian conductor. He made La Scala, Milan (where he conducted 1898–1903, 1906–08, and 1921–29), the world's leading opera house. However, he was opposed to the Fascist regime and in 1936 returned to the USA, where he had conducted at the Metropolitan Opera 1908–15. The NBC Symphony Orchestra was formed for him in 1937. He retired in 1954.

total internal reflection the complete reflection of a beam of light from the surface of an optically 'less dense' material. For example, a beam from an underwater light source can be reflected from the surface of the water, rather than escaping through the surface. This can only happen if the light beam hits the surface at an angle greater than the ◊critical angle.

Total internal reflection is used in some optical instruments that use prisms instead of mirrors.

totalitarianism government control of all activities within a country, overtly political or otherwise, as in fascist or communist dictatorships.

totalizator or *Tote* a system of betting on racehorses or greyhounds. All money received is divided in equal shares amongst winning ticket owners, less expenses. It was first introduced 1928; see under ◊betting.

totemism (Algonquin Indian 'my guardian spirit') belief in individual or clan kinship with an animal, plant, or object. This totem is sacred to those concerned, and they are forbidden to eat or desecrate it; marriage within the clan is usually forbidden. Totemism occurs among Pacific Islanders and Australian Aborigines, and was formerly prevalent throughout Europe, Africa, and Asia.

tortoise

toucan

Most North and South American Indian societies had totems as well.

Totem poles are carved by Native Americans of the NW coast of North America and incorporate totem objects (carved and painted) as a symbol of the people or to commemorate the dead.

Totenkopfverbände the 'death's head' units of the Nazi ◊SS organization. Originally used to guard concentration camps after 1935, they later became an elite fighting division attached to the Waffen-SS during World War II.

Totila /'tɒtɪlə/ died 522. King of the Ostrogoths, who warred with the Byzantine emperor Justinian for Italy, and was killed by Gen Narses at the battle of Taginae in the Apennines.

Totò /'təʊtəʊ/ Stage name of Antonio Furst de Curtis Gagliardi Ducas Comneno di Bisanzio 1898–1967. Italian comedian who moved to films from the music hall. Something of a national institution, his films, such as *Totò le Moko* 1949 and *L'Oro di Napoli/Gold of Naples* 1954, made him the most famous comic actor of his generation in Italy.

Tottenham /'tɒtənəm/ district of the Greater London borough of ◊Haringey.

toucan South and Central American forest-dwelling bird of the family Ramphastidae. Toucans have very large, brilliantly coloured beaks, and often have handsome plumage. They live in small flocks, eat fruits, seeds, and insects, and lay their eggs in holes in trees. They grow to 64 cm/2 ft in length. There are 37 species.

touch a sensation produced by specialized nerve endings in the skin. Some respond to light pressure, others to heavy pressure. Temperature detection may also contribute to the overall sensation of touch. Many animals, especially nocturnal ones, rely on touch more than humans do. Some have specialized organs of touch that project from the body, such as whiskers or antennae.

touch screen in computing, an input device allowing the user to communicate with the computer by touching a display screen with a finger. In this way, the user can point to a required ◊menu option or item of data. Touch screens are used less widely than other pointing devices such as the ◊joystick or ◊mouse.

Typically, the screen detects the finger either through a sensitive membrane or when the finger interrupts a grid of light beams crossing the screen surface.

touch sensor in a computer-controlled ◊robot, a device used to give the robot a sense of touch, allowing it to manipulate delicate objects or move automatically about a room. Touch sensors provide the feedback necessary for the robot to adjust the force of its movements and the pressure of its grip. The main types include the strain gauge and microswitch.

Toulon /tuːˈlɒn/ port and capital of Var *département*, SE France, on the Mediterranean Sea, 48 km/30 mi SE of Marseille; population (1983) 410,000. It is the chief Mediterranean naval station of France. Industries include oil refining, chemicals, furniture, and clothing. Toulon was the

Roman *Telo Martius*, and was made a port by Henry IV. It was occupied by the British 1793, and Napoleon first distinguished himself in driving them out. In World War II the French fleet was scuttled here to avoid its passing to German control.

Toulouse /tuːˈluːz/ capital of Haute-Garonne *département*, S France, on the river Garonne SE of Bordeaux; population (1982) 541,000. The chief industries are textiles and aircraft construction (Concorde was built here). Toulouse was the capital of the Visigoths (see ◊Goth), and later of Aquitaine 781–843. The university was founded 1229 to combat heresy.

Toulouse has a 12th–13th century cathedral. The Duke of Wellington repulsed the French marshal Soult at Toulouse 1814 in the ◊Peninsular War.

Toulouse-Lautrec /tuːˈluːz ləʊˈtrek/ Henri Marie Raymond de 1864–1901. French artist, associated with the Impressionists. He was active in Paris, where he painted entertainers and prostitutes. From. 1891 his lithograph posters were a great success.

Toulouse-Lautrec showed an early gift for drawing and in 1882 began to study art in Paris. He admired Goya's etchings and Degas's work, and in the 1880s he met Gauguin and was inspired by Japanese prints. Lautrec became a familiar figure drawing and painting in the dance halls, theatres, cafés, circuses, and brothels. Many of his finished works have the spontaneous character of sketches. He often painted with thinned-out oils on cardboard.

touraco fruit-eating African bird of the family Musophagidae. They have short, rounded wings, long tails, and erectile crests. The largest are 70 cm/28 in long. The **white-cheeked touraco** *Touraco leucotis* resembles a multi-coloured magpie.

Touraine /tuəˈreɪn/ former province of W central France, now part of the *départements* of Indre-et-Loire and Vienne; capital Tours.

Tourcoing /tuəˈkwæŋ/ town in Nord *département*, France, part of metropolitan Lille; population (1983) 102,000. It is situated near the Belgian border, and has been a textile centre since the 12th century.

tour de force (French 'feat of strength') a remarkable accomplishment.

Tour de France French road race for professional cyclists held annually over approximately 4,800 km/3,000 mi of French roads. The race takes about three weeks to complete and the route varies each year, often taking in adjoining

Toulouse-Lautrec The Two Friends *(1894) Tate Gallery, London.*

countries, but always ending in Paris. A separate stage is held every day, and the overall leader at the end of each stage wears the coveted leader's 'yellow jersey' (French *maillot jaune*).

First held in 1903, it is now the most watched sporting event in the world, with more than 10 million live spectators. Although it is a race for individuals, sponsored teams of 12 riders take part, each with its own 'star' rider whom team members support. Winners include Fausto Coppi (Italy), Louison Bobet (France), Jacques Anquetil (France), Eddie Merckx (Belgium) and Bernard Hinault (France). The **Milk Race** is the English equivalent of the Tour de France but on a smaller scale, and involving amateur and professional teams.

tourmaline a hard, brittle mineral, a complex of various metal silicates, but mainly sodium aluminium borosilicate. Small tourmalines are found in granites and gneisses. The common varieties range from black (schorl) to pink, and the transparent gemstones may be colourless (achroite), rose pink (rubellite), green (Brazilian emerald), blue (indicolite, verdelite, Brazilian sapphire), or brown (dravite).

Tournai /tuəˈneɪ/ (Flemish **Doornik**) town in Hainaut province, Belgium, on the Scheldt; population (1983) 67,000. Industries include carpets, cement, and leather. It stands on the site of a Roman relay post, and has an 11th-century Romanesque cathedral.

Tourneur /'tɜːnə/ Cyril 1575–1626. English dramatist. Little is known about his life but *The Atheist's Tragedy* 1611 and *The Revenger's Tragedy* 1607 (thought by some scholars to be by ◊Middleton) are among the most powerful of Jacobean dramas.

Tours /tuə/ industrial (chemicals, textiles, machinery) city and capital of the Indre-et-Loire *département*, W central France, on the Loire; population (1982) 263,000. It has a 13th–15th century cathedral. An ancient city, and former capital of ◊Touraine, it was the site of the French defeat of the Arabs 732 under ◊Charles Martel. Tours became the French capital for four days during World War II.

Toussaint L'Ouverture /tuːˈsæŋ ˌluːvəˈtjuə/ Pierre Dominique *c.* 1743–1803. Haitian revolutionary leader, born a slave. He joined the insurrection of 1791 against the French colonizers and was made governor by the revolutionary French government. He expelled the Spanish and British, but when the French emperor Napoleon reimposed slavery he revolted, was captured, and died in prison in France. In 1983 his remains were returned to Haiti.

tout de suite (French) immediately.

tout ensemble (French 'all together') the overall effect.

Tower /'taʊə/ John 1925– . US Republican politician, a Texas senator 1961–83. Despite having been a paid arms-industry consultant, he was selected in 1989 by President Bush to serve as defence secretary, but the Senate refused to approve the appointment because of Tower's alleged heavy drinking.

Tower, born in Houston, became the first Republican to be elected senator for Texas in 1961, after Lyndon Johnson left to become vice president. Tower emerged as a military expert in the Senate, becoming chair of the Armed Services Committee in 1981. After his retirement from the Senate in 1983, he hired out as a consultant to arms manufacturers and chaired the 1986–87 Tower Commission, which investigated aspects of the Irangate arms-for-hostages scandal.

Tower Hamlets /'taʊə 'hæmləts/ borough of E Greater London; population (1984) 146,000. It includes the Tower of London, and the World Trade Centre in former St Katharine's Dock; **Isle of Dogs** bounded on three sides by the Thames, including the former India and Millwall Docks; redevelopment includes Billingsgate fish market, removed here 1982, and the Docklands

Toussaint L'Ouverture *An 1805 print showing the Haitian revolutionary leader Pierre Toussaint L'Ouverture. Born a slave, he became governor of Haiti during the French Revolution.*

railway, linking the isle with the City; *Limehouse district*; *Spitalfields district*; *Bethnal Green* has a Museum of Childhood; *Wapping* has replaced Fleet Street as the centre of the newspaper industry.

Tower of London fortress on the Thames bank to the E of the City. The keep, or White Tower, was built about 1078 by Bishop Gundulf on the site of British and Roman fortifications. It is surrounded by two strong walls and a moat (now dry), and was for centuries a royal residence and the principal state prison. Today it is a barracks, an armoury, and a museum.

Among prisoners executed there were Thomas More, Anne Boleyn, Katherine Howard, Lady Jane Grey, Essex, Strafford, Laud, and Monmouth.

Townes /taʊnz/ Charles 1915– . US physicist who, while working at Columbia, New York, succeeded in 1953, against much competition, in designing and constructing the first ◊maser. For this work, he shared the 1964 Nobel Prize for Physics with Soviet physicists Basov and ◊Prokhorov.

town planning the design of buildings or groups of buildings in a physical and social context, concentrating on the relationship between various buildings and their environment, as well

as on their uses. See also ◊garden city; ◊new town.

Townsend /taʊnzend/ Sue 1946– . English humorous novelist, author of *The Secret Diary of Adrian Mole, aged 13³/4* 1982 and later sequels.

Townshend /taʊnzend/ Charles 1725–1767. British politician, chancellor of the Exchequer 1766–67. The *Townshend Acts* taxed imports (such as tea, glass, and paper) into Britain's North American colonies, and precipitated the War of American Independence.

Townshend /taʊnzend/ Charles, 2nd Viscount Townshend (known as 'Turnip' Townshend) 1674–1738. English politician and agriculturalist. He was secretary of state under George I 1714–17, when dismissed for opposing the king's foreign policy, and 1721–30, after which he retired to his farm and did valuable work in developing crop rotation and cultivating winter feeds for cattle (hence his nickname).

Townshend did not, in fact, originate the new techniques with which his name has become associated. Turnips, for example, were already being grown in E Anglia, England, as a fodder crop from at least the 1660s, and it is unlikely that he ever adopted the four-course turnips–barley–clover–wheat rotation. This was not taken up until many

years after his death. Through the successful development of his agricultural estate at Rainham in W Norfolk, however, Townshend brought a range of improved cultivation practices to wider public notice.

Townshend /taʊnzend/ Pete 1945– . UK rock musician, founder member of the ◊Who.

Townsville /taʊnzvɪl/ port on Cleveland Bay, N Queensland, Australia; population (1987) 108,000. It is the centre of a mining and agricultural area, and exports meat, wool, sugar, and minerals, including gold and silver.

Townswomen's Guilds, National Union of in the UK, an urban version of the ◊Women's Institute. It was founded 1929.

toxaemia blood poisoning, the presence of toxins in the blood derived from a bacterial infection in some part of the body. *Toxaemia of pregnancy* is a potentially serious condition marked by high blood pressure, ◊oedema, and sometimes convulsions. Arising from unknown causes, it disappears as soon as pregnancy is over.

toxicity tests tests carried out on new drugs, cosmetics, food additives, pesticides, and other synthetic chemicals to see whether they are safe for humans to use. They aim to identify potential toxins, carcinogens, teratogens, and mutagens.

Traditionally such tests use live animals such as rats, rabbits and mice. Such tests have become a target for criticism by ◊anti-vivisection groups, and alternatives have been sought. These include tests on human cells cultured in a test tube and on bacteria.

toxic syndrome fatal disease caused by adulterated industrial oil, illegally imported from France into Spain, re-refined, and sold for human consumption from 1981. More than 20,000 people became ill, and 600–700 died.

toxin any chemical molecule that can damage the living body. In vertebrates, toxins are broken down by ◊enzyme action, mainly in the liver.

toxocariasis infection of humans by a canine intestinal worm, which results in a swollen liver and sometimes eye damage.

Toynbee /tɔɪnbi/ Arnold 1852–1883. English economic historian, who coined the term 'industrial revolution' in his *Lectures on the Industrial Revolution*, published 1884. Toynbee Hall, an education settlement in the east end of London, was named after him.

Toynbee /tɔɪnbi/ Arnold Joseph 1889–1975. English historian, whose *A Study of History* 1934–61 was an attempt to discover the laws governing the rise and fall of civilizations. He was the nephew of the economic historian Arnold Toynbee.

Trabzon /træbzɒn/ formerly *Trebizond* port on the Black Sea, NE Turkey, 355 km/220 mi SW of Batum; population (1985) 156,000. Its exports include fruit, tobacco, and hides.

trace element a chemical element necessary in minute quantities for the health of a plant or animal. For example, magnesium, which occurs in chlorophyll, is essential to photosynthesis, and iodine is needed by the thyroid gland of mammals for making hormones that control growth and body chemistry.

tracer in science, a small quantity of a radioactive ◊isotope (form of an element) used to follow the path of a chemical reaction or a physical or biological process. The location (and possibly concentration) of the tracer is usually detected by using a Geiger–Muller counter.

For example, the activity of the thyroid gland can be followed by giving the patient an injection containing a small dose of a radioactive isotope of iodine, which is selectively absorbed from the bloodstream by the gland.

trachea tube that forms an airway in air-breathing animals. In land-living ◊vertebrates, including humans, it is known as the *windpipe* and is the largest airway, running from the larynx to the upper part of the chest. Its diameter is about 1.5 cm/0.6 in and its length 10 cm/4 in. It is strong and flexible, and reinforced by rings of ◊cartilage.

In the upper chest, the trachea branches into two tubes, the left and right bronchi, which enter the lungs. Insects have a branching network of tubes, the tracheae, which conduct air from holes in the body surface (◊spiracles) to all the body tissues. The finest branches of the tracheae are called tracheoles.

Some spiders also have tracheae but, unlike insects, rely on their circulatory system to transport gases throughout the body.

tracheid a type of cell found in the water-conducting tissue (◊xylem) of many plants, particularly gymnosperms (conifers) and pteridophytes (ferns). It is long and thin with pointed ends. The cell walls are thickened by ◊lignin except for numerous small rounded areas, or pits, through which water and dissolved minerals pass from one cell to another. Once mature, the cell itself dies and only its walls remain.

tracheostomy the creation of an opening in the windpipe (trachea) into which a tube is inserted to enable the patient to breathe. It is done either to bypass the airway impaired by disease or injury, or to safeguard it during surgery or a prolonged period of mechanical ventilation.

trachoma a chronic eye infection, resembling severe ◊conjunctivitis. The conjunctiva becomes inflamed, with scarring and formation of pus, and there may be damage to the cornea, the delicate front 'window' of the eye. It is caused by a virus-like organism, and is a disease of dry tropical regions. Although it responds well to antibiotics, numerically it remains the biggest single cause of blindness worldwide.

tracked vehicle a vehicle, such as a tank or bulldozer, that runs on its own tracks (known as ◊caterpillar tracks).

tracking agent a chemical compound (most usually NPPD, nitrophenyl pentadiene) used in espionage. It is applied to people, clothes, and cars to trace their movements and contacts.

Tractarianism another name for the ◊Oxford Movement, 19th-century movement for Catholic revival within the Church of England.

tractor in agriculture, a four-wheeled motor vehicle commonly having two large rear wheels, used for pulling farm machinery and loads.

It is usually powered by a diesel engine and has a power-take-off (PTO) mechanism for driving machinery, and a hydraulic lift for raising and lowering implements. In military usage, a **combat tractor**

trachea

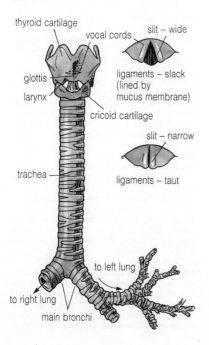

usually has two drivers (one forwards, one backwards), and can excavate 2 tonnes in a single action, so as, for example, to hide a Chieftain tank in 11 minutes. It can also cross rivers, operate in nuclear radiation, and clear minefields.

Tracy /ˈtreɪsi/ Spencer 1900–1967. US actor, noted for his understated, seemingly effortless natural performances. His films include *Captains Courageous* 1937 and *Boys' Town* 1938 (for both of which he won Academy Awards), and he starred with Katharine Hepburn in nine films, including *Adam's Rib* 1949 and *Guess Who's Coming to Dinner* 1967. His other films include *Bad Day at Black Rock* 1955.

trade cycle or *business cycle* period of time that includes a peak and trough of economic activity, as measured by a country's national income. In Keynesian economics, one of the main roles of the government is to smooth out the peaks and troughs of the trade cycle by intervening in the economy, thus minimizing 'overheating' and 'stagnation'.

trade description the description of the characteristics of goods, including their quality, quantity, and fitness for the purpose for which they are required. Under the Trade Descriptions Acts 1968 and 1972, making a false trade description is a criminal offence in English law. The offence may be committed by applying a false trade description directly, such as on a label attached to goods; indirectly, such as by deliberately concealing faults in goods; or in an advertisement. Misleading statements are also illegal.

trademark a name or symbol distinctive of a marketed product. The owner may register the mark to prevent its unauthorized use.

Tradescant /trəˈdeskənt/ John 1570–1638. English gardener and botanist, who travelled widely in Europe and may have introduced the cos lettuce to England, from the Greek island bearing the same name. He was appointed as gardener to Charles I and was succeeded by his son, John Tradescant the Younger (1608–1662), after his death. The younger Tradescant undertook three plant-collecting trips to Virginia, USA, and Linnaeus named the genus *Tradescantia* in his honour.

The Tradescants introduced many new plants to Britain, including the acacia, lilac and occidental plane. Their collection of plants formed the nucleus of the Ashmolean Museum in Oxford.

Tradescantia genus of plants of the family Commelinaceae, native to North and Central America. The **spiderwort** *Tradescantia virginiana* is a cultivated garden plant; the **wandering jew** *Tradescantia albiflora* is a common houseplant, with green oval leaves tinged with pink or purple or silver-striped.

Trades Union Congress (TUC) voluntary organization of trade unions, founded in the UK 1868, in which delegates of affiliated unions meet annually to consider matters affecting their members. In 1988 there were some 100 affiliated unions, with an aggregate membership of about 11 million.

trade union organization of employed workers formed to undertake collective bargaining with employers and to try to achieve improved working conditions for its members. Attitudes of government to unions and of unions to management vary greatly from country to country. Probably the most effective trade-union system is that of Sweden, and the best-known union is the Polish ◊Solidarity.

history Trade unions of a kind existed in the Middle Ages as artisans' guilds, and combinations of wage earners were formed in the 18th century, but modern trade unionism is a product of the Industrial Revolution.

history, UK Five centuries of repressive legislation in Britain culminated in the passing of the ◊Combination Laws 1799 and 1800 which made unions illegal. On the repeal of these 1824–25, organizations of workers were permitted to engage in collective bargaining, although still subject to legal restrictions and with no legal protection for their funds until the enactment of a series of Trade Union Acts 1871–76. Successive acts of Parliament broadened the unions' field of action, such as the 1913 Act which allowed the unions to engage in political activities.

The ◊Trades Union Congress was for many years representative mainly of unions of skilled workers, but in the 1890s the organization of unskilled labour spread rapidly. Industrial Unionism (the organization of all workers in one industry or trade) began about this time, but characteristic of the so-called New Unionism at the time of the 1889 dock strike was the rise of general labour unions (for example, the Dock Workers and General Labourers in the gas industry). The restrictive Trade Disputes and Trade Union Act 1927, which was passed in the wake of the 1926 general strike, was repealed under the Attlee government 1946.

The postwar period was marked by increased unionism among white-collar workers. The Wilson government 1964–70 attempted to introduce legislative reform of the unions, but their unwillingness to accept it led to its abandonment 1969. The Heath government's Industrial Relations Act 1971 (including registration of trade unions, legal enforcement of collective agreements, compulsory 'cooling-off' periods, and strike ballots) was repealed by the succeeding Wilson government 1974, and voluntary wage restraint attempted under a ◊social contract. An Advisory Conciliation and Arbitration Service (ACAS) was set up 1975.

The Thatcher government, in the Employment Acts of 1980 and 1982, restricted the closed shop, picketing, secondary action against anyone other than the employer in dispute, immunity of trade unions in respect of unlawful activity by their officials, and the definition of a trade dispute, which must be between workers and employers, not between workers. The Trade Union Act 1984 made it compulsory to have secret ballots for elections and before strikes. The Employment Act 1988 contains further provisions regulating union affairs, including: further requirements for ballots; rights for members not to be unfairly undisciplined (for example, for failing to support a strike); and prohibiting the use of union funds to indemnify union officers fined for ◊contempt of court or other offences.

history, US The great growth of US trade unionism, apart from the abortive Knights of Labor 1869–86 (see also ◊American Federation of Labor) came in the post-Depression years. Employers and the US government have historically been more opposed to trade unionism than in Britain, often using police and armed guards to harass pickets and protect strike breakers, which has led to episodes of violence and bitter confrontation. US legislation includes the Taft–Hartley Act 1947, which among other measures outlaws the closed shop. In the present day US unions have the reputation of being open to the acceptance of new techniques, taking a broad view of these as conducive to greater eventual prosperity.

international In Sweden conflicts of unions within an industry (demarcation disputes) are largely eliminated, and unions and employers cooperate freely. In 1973 a European Trade Union Confederation (ETUC) was established, membership 29 million, and there is an International Labour Organization, established 1919 and affiliated to the United Nations from 1945, which formulates standards for labour and social conditions.

trade unionism, international worldwide cooperation between unions. Modern organizations are the International Confederation of Free Trade Unions (ICFTU 1949), including the American Federation of Labor and Congress of Industrial Organizations and the UK Trades Union Congress, and the World Federation of Trade Unions (WFTU 1945).

trade wind prevailing wind that blows towards the equator from the NE and SE. Trade winds are caused by hot air rising at the equator and the

Figure labels (trachea diagram):
thyroid cartilage
vocal cords
slit – wide
glottis
ligaments – slack (lined by mucus membrane)
larynx
cricoid cartilage
slit – narrow
trachea
ligaments – taut
to left lung
to right lung
main bronchi

consequent movement of air from N and S to take its place. The winds are deflected towards the W because of the Earth's W-to-E rotation. The unpredictable calms known as the ◊doldrums lie at their convergence.

The trade-wind belts move N and S about 5° with the seasons. The name is derived from the obsolete expression 'to blow *trade*' meaning consistently in a constant direction, which indicates the trade winds' importance to navigation in the days of cargo-carrying sailing ships.

trading stamp a stamp given by retailers to customers according to the value of goods purchased; when a sufficient number has been collected, the stamps can be redeemed for goods or money.

They originated in Britain about 1851, were subsequently introduced in the USA, and reimported to the UK 1958 (Green Shield stamps). They were reintroduced 1986. Trading stamps companies profit from their stamp sales to retailers (at greater than cost) and from the fact that many stamps are not redeemed.

Trafalgar, Battle of /trə'fælgə/ battle 21 Oct 1805 in the ◊Napoleonic Wars. The British fleet under Nelson defeated a Franco-Spanish fleet; Nelson was mortally wounded. It is named after Cape Trafalgar, a low headland in SW Spain, near the western entrance to the Straits of Gibraltar.

traffic vehicles using public roads. In 1988 there were 4,470 deaths from motor vehicle traffic accidents in England and Wales. In 1989 UK road traffic forecasts predicted traffic demand would rise between 83% and 142% by the year 2025.

tragedy in the theatre, a play dealing with a serious theme, traditionally one in which a character meets disaster either as a result of personal failings or circumstances beyond his or her control. Historically the Greek view of tragedy, as defined by Aristotle and expressed by the great tragedians Aeschylus, Euripides, and Sophocles, has been the most influential. In the 20th century tragedies in the narrow Greek sense of dealing with exalted personages in an elevated manner have virtually died out. Tragedy has been replaced by dramas with 'tragic' implications or overtones, as in the work of Ibsen, O'Neill, Tennessee Williams, Pinter, and Osborne, for example, or by the hybrid tragicomedy.

The Greek view of tragedy provided the subject matter for later tragic dramas, but it was the Roman Seneca (whose works were intended to be read rather than acted) that influenced the Elizabethan tragedies of Marlowe and Shakespeare. French classical tragedy developed under the influence of both Seneca and an interpretation of Aristotle which gave rise to the theory of unities of time, place, and action, as observed by Racine, one of its greatest exponents. In Germany the tragedies of Goethe and Schiller led to the exaggerated ◊melodrama, which replaced pure tragedy. In the 18th century unsuccessful attempts were made to 'domesticate' tragedy. In the 20th century 'tragedy' has come to refer to dramas with 'tragic' implications for individuals or society.

tragicomedy a drama which contains elements of tragedy and comedy; for example, Shakespeare's 'reconciliation' plays, such as *The Winter's Tale*, which reach a tragic climax but then lighten to a happy conclusion. A tragicomedy is the usual form for plays in the tradition of the Theatre of the ◊Absurd, such as ◊Beckett's *En attendant Godot/Waiting for Godot* 1953 and ◊Stoppard's *Rosencrantz and Guildenstern are Dead* 1967.

tragopan type of short-tailed pheasant (bird) of which there are several species living in wet forests along the S Himalayas. Tragopans are brilliantly coloured, with arrays of spots. They have long crown feathers and two blue erectile crests. Males inflate coloured wattles and throat pouches in their spring courtship displays. All tragopans have been reduced in numbers by destruction of their habitat. The western tragopan is the rarest, as a result of extensive deforestation.

Traherne /trə'hɜːn/ Thomas 1637–1674. English mystic, vicar of Teddington 1667–74. His moving lyric poetry and his prose *Centuries of Meditations* were unpublished until 1903.

trahison des clercs (French 'the treason of the intellectuals') the involvement of intellectuals in active politics.

Trail /treɪl/ mining centre in British Columbia, Canada, on the Columbia river; population (1981) 10,000. It has lead, zinc, and copper industries.

train vehicle which moves on a ◊railway.

trainbands in English history, a civil militia first formed in 1573 by Elizabeth I to meet the possibility of invasion. Although used by Charles I against the Scots in 1639, their lack of training meant they were of dubious military value.

Training Agency UK government-sponsored organization responsible for retraining of unemployed workers. Founded as the *Manpower Services Commission* 1974, the organization operated such schemes as the Training Opportunities Scheme (TOPS), the Youth Opportunities Programme (YOP) 1978, the Youth Training Scheme (YTS) 1983, and the Technical and Vocational Initiative (TVEI).

Trajan /'treɪdʒən/ Marcus Ulpius (Trajanus) AD 52–117. Roman emperor and soldier, born in Seville. He was adopted as heir by ◊Nerva, whom he succeeded AD 98.

He was a just and conscientious ruler, corresponded with Pliny about the Christians, and conquered Dacia (Romania) 101–07 and much of ◊Parthia. *Trajan's Column*, Rome, commemorates his victories.

trampolining gymnastics performed on a sprung canvas sheet which allows the performer to reach great heights before landing again. Marks are gained for carrying out difficult manoeuvres. Synchronized trampolining and tumbling are also popular forms of the sport.

Originally used as a circus or show business act, trampolining dates to the early part of the 20th century. It developed as a sport 1936 when George Nissen of the USA developed a prototype model 'T' trampoline.

trampolining: world champions

men
1970 Wayne Miller *(USA)*
1972 Paul Luxon *(Great Britain)*
1974 Richard Tisson *(France)*
1976 Richard Tisson *(France)* and Evgeni Janes *(USSR)*
1978 Evgeni Janes *(USSR)*
1980 Stewart Matthews *(Great Britain)*
1982 Carl Furrer *(Great Britain)*
1984 Lionel Pioline *(France)*
1986 Lionel Pioline *(France)*
1988 Vadim Krasonchapka *(USSR)*
women
1970 Renee Ransom *(USA)*
1972 Alexandra Nicholson *(USA)*
1974 Alexandra Nicholson *(USA)*
1976 Svetlana Levina *(USSR)*
1978 Tatyana Anisimova *(USSR)*
1980 Ruth Keller *(Switzerland)*
1982 Ruth Keller *(Switzerland)*
1984 Sue Shotton *(Great Britain)*
1986 Tatyana Lushina *(USSR)*
1988 Khoperla Rusudum *(USSR)*

tragopan

western

tramway a transport system, widespread in Europe from the late 19th to mid 20th century, where wheeled vehicles run along parallel rails. Trams are powered either by electric conductor rails below ground or conductor arms connected to overhead wires, but their use on public roads is limited because of their lack of manoeuvrability. Greater flexibility can be achieved with the *trolleybus*, similarly powered by conductor arms overhead, but without tracks. In the 1980s both trams and trolleybuses were being revived in some areas. Both vehicles have the advantage of being non-polluting.

trance mental state in which the subject loses the ordinary perceptions of time and space, and even of his or her own body.

In this highly aroused state, often induced by rhythmic music, 'speaking in tongues' may occur (see ◊Pentecostal Movement), which usually consists of the rhythmic repetition of apparently meaningless syllables, with a euphoric return to consciousness. It is also practised by Bush healers, Afro-Brazilian spirit mediums, and Siberian shamans.

tranquillizer common name for a drug for reducing anxiety or tension (◊anxiolytic). Antipsychotic drugs are not tranquillizers.

Trans-Alaskan Pipeline Scheme one of the world's greatest civil engineering projects, the construction of a 1,285 km/800 mi long pipeline to carry petroleum (crude oil) from N Alaska to the icefree port of Valdez. It was completed 1977 after three years' work.

The engineers had to elevate nearly half of the pipeline on supports above ground level to avoid thawing the permanently frozen ground which would have caused much environmental damage. They also had to cross 600 rivers and streams, two mountain ranges, and allow for earthquakes.

Trans-Amazonian Highway or *Transamazonica* road linking Recife in the east with the provinces of Rondonia, Amazonas and Acre in the west of Brazil. Initiated as part of the Brazilian National Integration Programme (PIN) in 1970, the Trans-Amazonian Highway was designed to enhance national security, aid the development of the north of Brazil and act as a safety valve for the overpopulated coastal regions.

Transcaucasia /ˌtrænzkɔː'keɪzɪə/ region of the USSR south of the Caucasus. It includes Armenia, Azerbaijan, and ◊Georgia, which formed the *Transcaucasian Republic* 1922, broken up 1936 when each became a separate republic of the USSR.

transcendentalism a form of philosophy inaugurated by Kant. As opposed to ◊metaphysics in the traditional sense, transcendental philosophy is concerned with the conditions of possibility of experience, rather than the nature of being. It seeks to show the necessary structure of our 'point of view' on the world. Introduced to England, it influenced Coleridge and Carlyle. It developed in New England, USA, about 1840–60, influenced by European Romanticism, into a mystical doctrine (Thoreau, Emerson, Margaret Fuller, Orestes Brownson) which saw God as immanent in nature and the human soul. It had religious, philosophical, and political implications, shaping American ideals of self-reliance, attitudes to reform and slavery-abolition, feminism, and various forms of Utopian idealism displayed in its experimental community at Brook Farm. Emphasizing the role of the poet and the need for an original US literature, it also had literary consequences, and out of it came Emerson's essays and poems, Jones Very's poetry, Thoreau's *Walden* 1854, and, less directly, the novels and stories of Hawthorne, and Walt Whitman's *Leaves of Grass* 1855.

transcendental meditation (TM) a technique for relieving stress, based in part on Hindu meditation. Meditators are given a mantra (a special word or phrase) to repeat over and over in the mind. The mantra is never written down or divulged to anyone else. It was introduced to the West by

Maharishi Mahesh Yogi and popularized by the Beatles in the late 1960s. Practitioners claim that if even as few as 1% of the population meditated in this way, society would see much less stress.

transcription in living cells, the process by which the information for the synthesis of a protein is transferred from the ◊DNA strand on which it is carried to the messenger ◊RNA strand involved in the actual synthesis. It occurs by the formation of ◊base pairs between the DNA molecule and the nucleotides that make up the new RNA strand.

transducer power-transforming device that enables ◊energy in any form (electrical, acoustical, mechanical) to flow from one transmission system to another.

The energy flowing to and from a transducer may be of the same or of different forms, for example, an electric motor receives electrical energy and delivers it to a mechanical system; a gramophone pick-up crystal receives mechanical energy from the stylus and delivers it as electrical energy; and a loudspeaker receives an electrical input and delivers an acoustical output.

transfer orbit the elliptical path followed by a spacecraft moving from one orbit to another, designed to save fuel by moving for most of the journey in free fall.

Space probes travel to the planets on transfer orbits. A probe aimed at Venus has to be 'slowed down' relative to the Earth, so that it enters an elliptical transfer orbit with its perigee (point of closest approach to the Sun) at the same distance as the orbit of Venus; with Mars, the vehicle has to be 'speeded up' relative to the Earth, so that it reaches its apogee (furthest point from the Sun) at the same distance as the orbit of Mars. *Geostationary transfer orbit* is the path followed by satellites to be placed in ◊geostationary orbit around the Earth (an orbit coincident with Earth's rotation). A small rocket is fired at the transfer orbit's apogee to place the satellite in geostationary orbit.

transformational grammar a theory of language structure initiated by Noam ◊Chomsky, which proposes that below the actual phrases and sentences of a language (its *surface structure*) there lies a more basic layer (its *deep structure*), which is processed by various transformational rules when we speak and write.

Below the surface structure 'the girl opened the door' would lie the deep structure 'the girl open + *past tense* the door'. Note that there is usually more than one way in which a deep structure can be realized; in this case 'the door was opened by the girl'.

transformer device in which, by electromagnetic induction, an alternating or intermittent current of one voltage is transformed to another voltage, without change of ◊frequency. Transformers are widely used in electrical apparatus of all kinds, and in particular in power transmission where high voltages and low currents are utilized.

A transformer has two coils, a primary for the input, and a secondary for the output, wound on a common iron core. The ratio of the primary to the secondary voltages (and currents) is directly (and inversely) proportional to the number of turns in the primary and secondary coils.

transfer orbit

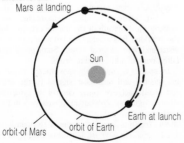

transfusion the delivery of blood or blood products (plasma, red cells) into a patient's circulation to make good deficiencies due to disease, injury, or surgical intervention.

Blood transfusion, first successfully pioneered in human beings 1818, remained highly risky until the discovery of blood groups, by ◊Landsteiner 1900, indicated the need for compatibility of donated blood. Today, crossmatching is carried out to ensure the patient receives the same type of blood.

transgenic organism a plant, animal, bacterium or other living organism which has had a foreign gene added to it by means of ◊genetic engineering.

transistor electronic component, made of ◊semiconductor material, with three or more ◊electrodes, that can regulate a current passing through it. A transistor can act as an amplifier, ◊oscillator, ◊photocell, or switch, and usually operates on a very small amount of power. Transistors commonly consist of a tiny sandwich of ◊germanium or ◊silicon, alternate layers having different electrical properties. A crystal of pure germanium or silicon would act as an insulator (non-conductor).

By introducing impurities in the form of atoms of other materials (for example, boron, arsenic, or indium) in minute amounts, the layers may be made either *n-type*, having an excess of electrons, or *p-type*, having a deficiency of electrons. This enables electrons to flow from one layer to another in one direction only.

Transistors have had a great impact on the electronics industry, and are now made in thousands of millions each year. They perform many of the same functions as the thermionic valve, but have the advantages of greater reliability, long life, compactness and instantaneous action, no warming-up period being necessary. They are widely used in most electronic equipment, including portable radios and televisions, computers, satellites and space research, and are the basis of the ◊integrated circuit (silicon chip). They were invented at Bell Telephone Laboratories in the USA in 1948 by John ◊Bardeen and Walter ◊Brittain, developing the work of William ◊Shockley.

transit in astronomy, the passage of a smaller object across the visible disc of a larger one. Transits of the inferior planets occur when they pass directly between the Earth and Sun, and are seen as tiny dark spots against the Sun's disc.

There are other forms of transit, including the passage of a Jovian satellite across the disc of the planet and the passage of planetary surface features across the central ◊meridian of that planet as seen from Earth. The passage of an object in the sky across the observer's meridian is also known as a transit.

transition metal one of a group of metals with variable valency, for example cobalt, copper, iron, and molybdenum. They are excellent conductors of electricity, and generally form highly coloured compounds.

Transjordan /trænzˈdʒɔːdn/ former name (1923–49) of the Hashemite kingdom of ◊Jordan.

Transkei /ˌtrænsˈkaɪ/ largest of South Africa's Bantu Homelands, extending NE from the Great Kei River, on the coast of Cape Province, to the border of Natal; area 43,808 sq km/16,910 sq mi; population (1985) 3,000,000, including small white and Asian minorities. It became self-governing 1963, and achieved full 'independence' 1976. Its capital is Umtata, and it has a port at Mnganzana. It is one of the two homelands of the Xhosa people (see ◊Ciskei), and products include livestock, coffee, tea, sugar, maize, and sorghum. Its government consists of a president (paramount chief Tutor Nyangelizwe Vulinolela Ndamase from 1986) and single-chamber national assembly.

translation in literature, the rendering of words from one language to another. The first recorded named translator was Livius Andronicus, who translated the *Odyssey* from Greek to Latin in 240 BC.

translation in living cells, the process by which proteins are synthesized. During translation, the information coded as a sequence of nucleotides in messenger ◊RNA is transformed into a sequence of amino acids in a peptide chain. The process involves the 'translation' of the ◊genetic code. See also ◊transcription.

transmigration of souls another name for ◊reincarnation.

transpiration the loss of water from a plant by evaporation. Most water is lost from the leaves through pores known as ◊stomata, whose primary function is to allow gas exchange between the internal plant tissues and the atmosphere. Transpiration from the leaf surfaces causes a continuous upward flow of water from the roots via the ◊xylem, which is known as the transpiration stream.

A single maize plant has been estimated to transpire 245 litres (54 gallons) of water in one growing season.

transplantation in medicine, the transfer of a tissue or organ from one human being to another. In most organ transplants, the operation is life-saving (although kidney patients have the alternative of ◊dialysis).

Corneal grafting, which may restore sight to a diseased or damaged eye, was pioneered 1905, and is the oldest successful human transplant procedure. Of the internal organs, kidneys were first transplanted successfully in the early 1950s. Modern transplantation also encompasses hearts, lungs, livers, and pancreatic tissue. Most transplant material is taken from cadaver donors, usually those suffering death of the ◊brainstem. In rare cases, kidneys and corneas may be obtained

translation: chronology

3rd century BC–1st century AD	
	Septuagint: Greek translation of Old Testament and Apocrypha.
4th century	Vulgate Latin translation of Bible by St Jerome and the first complete translation direct from Hebrew.
8th–9th centuries	Arabic scholars, mostly based in Baghdad, translate many of the Greek classics into Arabic.
12th century	Translations from Arabic to Latin, centred in Toledo, Spain (school of translators founded by Archbishop Raymund I 1126–51); translations of Aristotle and Avicenna by, for example, Gerard of Cremona, John of Seville, Adelard of Bath.
1382	Wycliffe first translation of the Bible into English.
1522	Luther's translation of the New Testament into German.
1525	Tyndale's English translation of the New Testament.
1537	Coverdale's translation of the Bible into English.
1579	North's translation of Plutarch (actually from French).
1598–1616	Chapman's translations of the *Iliad* and *Odyssey* of Homer.
1603	Florio's translation of Montaigne's Essays.
1603–11	Authorized Version of the Bible.
1693	Dryden's version of Juvenal.
1697	Dryden's translation of Virgil's *Aeneid*.
1715–26	Pope: *Iliad* and *Odyssey*.
1859	Edward Fitzgerald: *Rubaiyat of Omar Khayyam*.
1966	The Jerusalem Bible (from the original languages).

from living donors. Besides the notorious shortage of donated material, the main problem facing transplant surgeons is rejection of the donated organ by the new body.

Transport and General Workers Union (TGWU) UK trade union founded 1921 by the amalgamation of a number of dockers' and road-transport workers' unions, previously associated in the Transport Workers' Federation. It is the largest trade union in Britain.

transportation in the UK, a former punishment which involved sending convicted persons to overseas British territories either for life or for shorter periods. It was introduced in England towards the end of the 17th century and was abolished 1857 after many thousands had been transported, especially to Australia. It was also used for punishment of criminals by France until 1938.

transputer an electronic device introduced in computers to increase computing power. In the circuits of a standard computer the processing of data takes place in sequence. In a transputer's circuits

processing takes place in parallel, greatly reducing computing time for programs written specifically for the transputer.

transsexual a person who identifies himself/herself completely with the opposite sex, believing that the wrong sex was assigned at birth. Unlike *transvestism*, which is the desire to dress in clothes traditionally worn by the opposite sex, transsexuals think and feel emotionally in a way typically considered appropriate to members of the opposite sex, and may undergo surgery to modify external sexual characteristics.

Trans-Siberian Railway /,trænsaɪ'bɪərɪən/ railway line connecting the cities of European Russia with Omsk, Novosibirsk, Irkutsk, and Khabarovsk, and terminating at Vladivostok on the Pacific. It was built 1891–1905; from Leningrad to Vladivostok is about 8,700 km/5,400 mi. A 3,102 km/1,928 mi northern line was completed 1984 after ten years' work.

transubstantiation in Christian theology, the doctrine that the whole substance of the bread and wine changes into the substance of the body

and blood of Jesus when consecrated in the ◊Eucharist.

transuranic element or *transuranium element* a chemical element with an atomic number of 93 or more, that is, with a greater number of protons in the nucleus than uranium. Apart from neptunium and plutonium, none of these has been found in nature, but they have been created in nuclear reactions.

Transvaal /'trænzvɑːl/ province of NE South Africa, bordering Zimbabwe in the N; area 262,499 sq km/101,325 sq mi; population (1985) 7,532,000. Its capital is Pretoria, and towns include Johannesburg, Germiston, Brakpan, Springs, Benoni, Krugersdorp, and Roodepoort. Products include diamonds, coal, iron ore, copper, lead, tin, manganese, meat, maize, tobacco, and fruit. The main rivers are the Vaal and Limpopo with their tributaries. Swaziland forms an enclave on the Natal border. It was settled by *Voortrekkers* who left Cape Colony in the Great Trek from 1831. Independence was recognized by Britain 1852, until the settlers' difficulties with the conquered Zulus led to British annexation 1877. It was made a British colony after the South African War 1899–1902, and in 1910 became a province of the Union of South Africa.

Transylvania /,trænsɪl'veɪnɪə/ mountainous area of central and NW Romania, bounded to the S by the Transylvanian Alps (an extension of the ◊Carpathians), formerly a province, with its capital at Cluj. It was part of Hungary from about 1000 until its people voted to unite with Romania 1918. It is the home of the vampire legends.

Trapani /'trɑːpəni/ port and naval base in NW Sicily, about 48 km/30 mi north of Marsala; population (1981) 72,000. It trades in wine, salt, and fish.

trapezium (North American *trapezoid*) in geometry, a four-sided plane figure (quadrilateral) with two of its sides parallel. If the parallel sides have lengths a and b and the perpendicular distance between them is h (the height of the trapezium), its area $A = \frac{1}{2}h(a + b)$.

An isosceles trapezium has its sloping sides equal, and is symmetrical about a line drawn through the mid-points of its parallel sides.

Trappist member of a Roman Catholic order of monks and nuns, renowned for the strictness of their rules, which includes the maintenance of silence. It originated 1664 at La Trappe, in Normandy, as a reformed version of the ◊Cistercian order under which it is now governed once more.

trasformismo (Italian 'transformation') the practice of government by coalition, using tactics of reforming new cabinets and political alliances, often between conflicting interest groups, in order to retain power. The term has been applied cynically to describe changing the appearance while the essence remains the same. It was first used to describe the way the Italian nationalist leader Cavour held on to power.

trauma a powerful shock which may have a long-term effect; also any physical damage or injury.

travelator a moving walkway, rather like a flat ◊escalator.

traveller an itinerant wanderer; the term is applied to the ◊Romany people and other gypsies and tinkers.

travel sickness nausea and vomiting caused by travel. Constant vibration and movement may stimulate changes in the semicircular canals forming the labyrinth of the middle ear, to which the individual fails to adapt, and to which are added visual and psychological factors. Some proprietary cures contain antihistamine drugs.

In space, normal body movements result in unexpected and unfamiliar signals to the brain. Astronauts achieve some control of symptoms when weightless by wedging themselves in their bunks.

Traven /'trɑːvən/ Ben. Pen name of Herman Feige 1882–1969. US novelist, born in Germany, whose

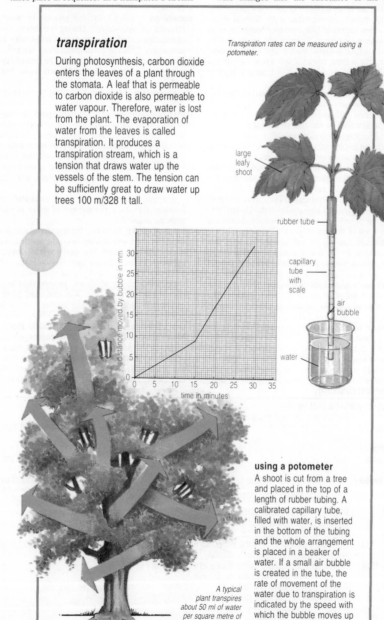

transpiration

During photosynthesis, carbon dioxide enters the leaves of a plant through the stomata. A leaf that is permeable to carbon dioxide is also permeable to water vapour. Therefore, water is lost from the plant. The evaporation of water from the leaves is called transpiration. It produces a transpiration stream, which is a tension that draws water up the vessels of the stem. The tension can be sufficiently great to draw water up trees 100 m/328 ft tall.

Transpiration rates can be measured using a potometer.

large leafy shoot

rubber tube

capillary tube with scale

air bubble

water

A typical plant transpires about 50 ml of water per square metre of leaf surface every hour.

using a potometer

A shoot is cut from a tree and placed in the top of a length of rubber tubing. A calibrated capillary tube, filled with water, is inserted in the bottom of the tubing and the whole arrangement is placed in a beaker of water. If a small air bubble is created in the tube, the rate of movement of the water due to transpiration is indicated by the speed with which the bubble moves up the tube.

transuranium elements

Atomic Number	Name	Symbol	Year discovered	Source of first preparation	Isotope identified	Half life of first isotope identified
Actinide series						
93	neptunium	Np	1940	Irradiation of uranium-238 with neutrons	Np^{239}	2.35 days
94	plutonium	Pu	1941	Bombardment of uranium-238 with deutrons	Pu^{238}	86.4 years
95	americium	Am	1944	Irradiation of plutonium-239 with neutrons	Am^{241}	458 years
96	curium	Cm	1944	Bombardment of plutonium-239 with helium ions	Cm^{242}	162.5 days
97	berkelium	Bk	1949	Bombardment of americium-241 with helium ions	Bk^{243}	4.5 hours
98	californium	Cf	1950	Bombardment of curium-242 with helium ions	Cf^{245}	44 minutes
99	einsteinium	Es	1952	Irradiation of uranium-238 with neutrons in first thermonuclear explosion	Es^{253}	20 days
100	fermium	Fm	1953	Irradiation of uranium-238 with neutrons in first thermonuclear explosion	Fm^{255}	16 hours
101	mendelevium	Md	1955	Bombardment of einsteinium-253 with helium ions	Md^{256}	1.5 hours
102	nobelium	No	1958	Bombardment of curium-246 with carbon ions	No^{255}	3 seconds
103	lawrencium	Lr	1961	Bombardment of californium-252 with boron ions	Lr^{257}	8 seconds
Super-heavy elements						
104	unnilquadium* (old name rutherfordium)	Rf	1969	Bombardment of californium-249 with ions of carbon-12	Ru^{257}	4 seconds
105	unnilpentium* (old name hahnium)	Ha	1970	Bombardment of californium-249 with nuclei of nitrogen-15 ions	Ha^{260}	1.6 seconds
106	unnilsexium*		1974	Bombardment of californium-249 with oxygen-18 ions	U6^{263}	0.9 seconds
107	unnilseptium*	Uns	1977	Bombardment of bismuth-209 with nuclei of chromium-54	U7	2 milliseconds
108	unniloctium*	Uno	1984	Bombardment of lead-208	U8^{265}	a few milliseconds
109	unnilnonium*		1982	Bombardment of bismuth-209	U9	5 milliseconds

*Names for elements 104–109 are as proposed by the International Union for Pure and Applied Chemistry in 1980.

true identity was unrevealed until 1979. His books include the bestseller *The Death Ship* 1926, and *The Treasure of Sierra Madre* 1934, filmed 1948 starring Humphrey Bogart.

Born in the part of Germany now in Poland, he was in turn known as the anarchist Maret Rut, Traven Torsvan, and Hollywood scriptwriter Hal Croves. Between the two world wars he lived in obscurity in Mexico and avoided recognition.

Travers /'trævəz/ Ben(jamin) 1886–1980. British dramatist. He wrote (for actors Tom Walls, Ralph Lynn, and Robertson Hare) the 'Aldwych farces' of the 1920s, so named from the London theatre in which they were played. They include *A Cuckoo in the Nest* 1925 and *Rookery Nook* 1926.

Travers /'trævəz/ Morris William 1872–1961. English chemist who, with William Ramsay, first identified the inert gases krypton, xenon, and radon (1894–1908).

treadmill wheel turned by foot power (often by a domesticated animal) and used, for instance, to raise water from a well.

In 1818, William Cubitt (1785–1861), on the principle of this ancient device, introduced in Britain a large cylinder to be operated by convicts treading on steps on its periphery. Such treadmills went out of use early in the 20th century.

treason an act of betrayal, generally used of acts against the sovereign or the state to which the offender owes allegiance. It is punishable in Britain by death.

In Britain, treason includes: plotting the wounding or death of the sovereign, or his or her spouse or heir; levying war against the sovereign in his or her realm; and giving aid or comfort to the sovereign's enemies in wartime. During World War II, treachery (aiding enemy forces or impeding the Crown) was punishable by death, whether or not the offender owed allegiance to the Crown. Sixteen spies (not normally capable of treason, though liable to be shot in the field) were convicted under these provisions. William Joyce (Lord Haw-Haw), although a US citizen, was executed for treason because he carried a British passport when he went to Germany in 1939.

In the USA, treason consists of levying war against the United States, or adhering to their enemies, giving them aid and comfort. Congress has the power to declare the punishment for treason.

Treasure Island an adventure story for children by R L ◊Stevenson, published in 1883. Jim Hawkins, the story's narrator, sets sail with Squire Trelawney in the *Hispaniola*, armed with a map showing the location of buried treasure. Attempts by the ship's crew of pirates, including Long John Silver, to seize the map are foiled after much fighting and the Squire finds the treasure.

treasure trove in England, any gold or silver, plate or bullion found concealed in a house or the ground, the owner being unknown. Normally, treasure originally hidden, and not abandoned, belongs to the Crown, but if the treasure was casually lost or intentionally abandoned, the first finder is entitled to it against all but the true owner. Objects buried with no intention of recovering

them, for example in a burial mound, do not rank as treasure trove, and belong to the owner of the ground.

Treasury the UK government department established 1612 to collect and manage the public revenue and coordinate national economic policy. Technically, the prime minister is the first lord of the Treasury, but the chancellor of the Exchequer is the acting financial head.

Treasury bill in Britain, borrowing by the government in the form of a promissory note to repay the bearer 91 days from the date of issue; such bills represent a flexible and relatively cheap way for the government to borrow money for immediate needs.

treaty a written agreement between two or more states. Treaties take effect either immediately on signature or, more often, on ratification. Ratification involves a further exchange of documents and usually takes place after the internal governments have approved the terms of the treaty. Treaties are binding in international law, the rules being

Transylvania

laid down in the Vienna Convention on the Law of Treaties 1969.

Trebizond /'trebizɒnd/ former English name of ◊Trabzon, a city in Turkey.

tree a perennial plant with a woody stem, usually a single stem or 'trunk'; this is made up of ◊wood, and protected by an outer layer of ◊bark. It absorbs water through a ◊root system. There is no clear dividing line between ◊shrubs and trees, but sometimes a minimum height of six metres is used to define a tree.

A tree-like form has evolved independently many times in different groups of plants. Among the ◊angiosperms or flowering plants, most trees are ◊dicotyledons. This group includes trees such as oak, beech, ash, chestnut, lime, and maple, and they are often referred to as ◊broad-leaved trees, because their leaves are broader than those of conifers, such as pine and spruce. In temperate regions angiosperm trees are mostly ◊deciduous, that is they lose their leaves in winter, but in the tropics most angiosperm trees are evergreen. There are fewer trees among the ◊monocotyledons, but the palms and bamboos (some of which are tree-like) belong to this group. The ◊gymnosperms include many trees and they are classified into four orders: Cycadales, including cycads and sago palms; Coniferales, the conifers; Ginkgoales, including only one living species, the ginkgo or maidenhair tree; and Taxales, including yews. Apart from the ginkgo and the larches (conifers) most gymnosperm trees are evergreen. There are also a few living trees in the ◊pteridophyte group, known as tree-ferns. In the swamp-forests of the Carboniferous era, 300 million years ago, there were also giant tree-like horsetails and clubmosses.

The great storm Oct 1987 destroyed some 15 million trees in Britain, and showed that large roots are less significant than those of 10 cm/4 in diameter or less. If enough of these are cut, the tree dies or falls.

Tree /tri:/ Herbert Beerbohm 1853–1917. British actor and theatre manager, half-brother of Max ◊Beerbohm. Noted for his Shakespeare productions, he was founder of the ◊Royal Academy of Dramatic Art (RADA).

tree creeper small, short-legged bird of the family Certhiidae, that spirals with a mouse-like movement up tree trunks searching for food with its thin downcurved beak. The **common treecreeper** *Certhia familiaris* is 12 cm/5 in long, brown above, white below, and is found across Europe, N Asia and North America.

trefoil several plants of the genus *Trifolium*, family Leguminosae, the leaves of which appear to be divided into three leaflets. **Birdsfoot trefoil** *Lotus corniculatus* is a low-growing perennial found in grassy places through Europe, N Asia, and parts of Africa. Its has five leaflets to each leaf, but the first two are bent back so it appears to have only three. The yellow flowers, often tinged orange or red, are borne in heads with only a few blooms. **Hop trefoil** *Trifolium campestre* has leaves with only three leaflets and tight-packed round heads of yellow flowers about 1.5 cm/0.6 in across. It also grows in grassy places through Europe, W Asia N Africa, and North America.

Trefusis /trɪ'fju:sɪs/ Violet 1894–1972. British hostess and writer. Daughter of Mrs Keppel, who was later the mistress of Edward VII, she had a disastrous marriage to cavalry officer Denys Trefusis and a passionate elopement with Vita ◊Sackville-West.

Treitschke /'traɪtʃkə/ Heinrich von 1834–1896. German historian. At first a Liberal, he later adopted a Pan-German standpoint. He is known for the *Deutsche Geschichte im 19 Jahrhundert/History of Germany in the 19th Century* 1879–94.

trematode a parasitic flatworm with an oval non-segmented body, of the class Trematoda, including the ◊fluke.

tremor minor ◊earthquake.

Trenchard /'trentʃəd/ Hugh Montague, 1st Viscount Trenchard 1873–1956. British aviator and police commissioner. He commanded the Royal Flying Corps in World War I 1915–17, and 1918–29 organized the Royal Air Force, becoming first marshal of the Royal Air Force 1927. As commissioner of the Metropolitan Police, he established the Police College at Hendon and carried out the Trenchard Reforms, which introduced more scientific methods of detection.

Trengganu /treŋ'ga:nu/ or **Terengganu** state of E Peninsular Malaysia; capital Kuala Trengganu; area 13,000 sq km/5,018 sq mi; population (1980) 541,000. Its exports include copra, black pepper, tin, and tungsten; there are also fishing and offshore oil industries.

Trent /trent/ third longest river of England; length 275 km/170 mi. Rising in the S Pennines, it flows first south and then NE through the Midlands to the Humber. It is navigable by barge for nearly 160 km/100 mi.

Trent, Council of 1545–1563. Council held by the Roman Catholic Church at Trento, N Italy; initiating the ◊Counter-Reformation; see also ◊Reformation.

Trent Bridge test cricket ground situated in Nottingham and home of the Nottinghamshire county side. One of the oldest cricket grounds in Britain, it was opened 1838.

The ground covers approximately 2.5 hectares and the present-day capacity is around 30,000. A total crowd of 101,886 watched the England–Australia test match in 1948. It has staged test cricket since 1899.

Trentino–Alto Adige /tren'ti:nəu 'æltəu 'ædɪdʒeɪ/ autonomous region of N Italy, comprising the provinces of Bolzano and Trento; capital Trento; chief towns Trento in the Italian-speaking southern area, and Bolzano-Bozen in the northern German-speaking area of South ◊Tirol (the region was Austrian until ceded to Italy 1919); area 13,600 sq km/5,250 sq mi; population (1988) 882,000.

Trento /'trentəu/ capital of Trentino–Alto Adige region, Italy, on the Adige River; population (1988) 101,000. Industries include the manufacture of electrical goods and chemicals. The Council of ◊Trent was held here 1545–63.

Trenton /'trentən/ capital of New Jersey, USA, on the Delaware river; population (1980) 92,000. It has metalworking and ceramics industries. It was first settled by Quakers 1679; George Washington defeated the British here 1776.

trepang name for ◊sea cucumbers used as food.

trespass going on to the land of another without authority. In English law, a landowner has the right to eject a trespasser by the use of reasonable force, and can sue for any damage caused. A trespasser who refuses to leave when requested may, in certain circumstances, be committing a criminal offence under the Public Order Act 1986 (designed to combat convoys of caravans trespassing on farm land). A trespasser injured on another's land cannot usually recover damages from the landowner unless the latter did him or her some positive injury.

Tressell /'tresəl/ Robert. Pseudonym of Robert Noonan 1868–1911. British author, whose *The Ragged Trousered Philanthropists*, published in an abridged form 1914, gave a detailed account of working people's lives.

Treurnicht /'trɜ:nɪxt/ Andries Petrus 1921– . South African Conservative Party politician. A former minister of the Dutch Reformed Church, he was elected to the South African parliament as a National Party (NP) member but left it to form a new right-wing Conservative Party, opposed to any dilution of the ◊apartheid system.

Trevelyan /trɪ'vɪljən/ George Macaulay 1876–1962. British historian. Regius professor of history at Cambridge 1927–40, he pioneered the study of social history, as in his *English Social History* 1942.

Trèves /trev/ the French name for ◊Trier, a city in West Germany.

Treviso /tre'vi:zəu/ city in Veneto, NE Italy; population (1981) 88,000. Its industries include the manufacture of machinery and ceramics. The 11th-century cathedral has an altarpiece by Titian.

Trevithick /'trɪ'vɪθɪk/ Richard 1771–1833. British engineer, constructor of a steam road locomotive 1801 and the first steam engine to run on rails 1804.

Triad secret society, founded in China as a Buddhist cult AD 36. It became known as the Triad because the triangle played an important part in the initiation ceremony. Later it became political, aiming at the overthrow of the Manchu dynasty, and backed the Taiping Rebellion 1851 and Sun Yat-sen's establishment of a republic 1912. Today it has a reputation for organized crime (drugs, gambling, prostitution) among overseas Chinese. Its headquarters are alleged to be in Hong Kong.

trial by ordeal in the Middle Ages, a test of guilt or innocence by which God's judgment of the case was supposedly revealed through the accused's exposure to fire, water, or blessed bread. The practice originated with the Franks in the 8th century, and survived until the 13th century. In the ordeal by cold water, the accused would be bound and thrown into the water. If he or she sank, it would prove innocence, but if they remained alive, it would show guilt. If the accused ate blessed bread, the theory was that the guilty would not be able to swallow it.

Trial, The (German *Der Prozess*) novel by Franz Kafka, published 1925. It deals with the sinister circumstances in which a man is arrested for no apparent reason, and with his consequent feelings of guilt and alienation, culminating in his 'execution'.

triangle in geometry, a three-sided plane figure. A **scalene triangle** has no sides of equal length; an **isosceles triangle** has two equal sides (and two equal angles); an **equilateral triangle** has three equal sides (and three equal angles of 60°). A right-angled triangle has one angle of 90°. If the length of one side of a triangle is l and the perpendicular distance from that side to the opposite corner is h (the height or altitude of the triangle), its area $A = 1/2\,l \times h$.

triangle of forces a method of calculating the force produced by two other forces (the resultant). It is based on the fact that if three forces acting at a point can be represented by the sides of a triangle, the forces are in equilibrium. See ◊parallelogram of forces.

triangulation a technique used in surveying to determine distances, using the properties of the triangle. In triangulation, surveyors measure a certain length exactly to provide a base line. From each end of this line they then measure the angle to a distant point, using a ◊theodolite. They now have a triangle in which they know the length of one side and the two adjacent angles. By simple trigonometry they can work out the lengths of the other two sides. To make a complete survey of the region, they repeat the process, building on the first triangle.

Trianon /'tri:ənɒn/ two palaces in the park at ◊Versailles, France: Le Grand Trianon built for Louis XIV, and Le Petit Trianon for Louis XV.

Triassic period of geological time 248–213 million years ago, the first period of the Mesozoic era. The continents were fused together to form the world continent ◊Pangaea. Triassic sediments contain remains of early dinosaurs and other reptiles now extinct. By late Triassic times, the first mammals had evolved. The climate was generally dry; desert sandstones are typical Triassic rocks.

triathlon a test of stamina involving three sports: swimming 3.8 km/2.4 mi, cycling 180 km/112 mi, and running a marathon, each one immediately following the last. It was first established as a sport in the USA 1974. The most famous event is the Hawaii Ironman.

Tribal Areas, Federally administered area of Pakistan; area 27,200 sq km/10,499 sq mi; population (1985) 2,467,000.

triangle

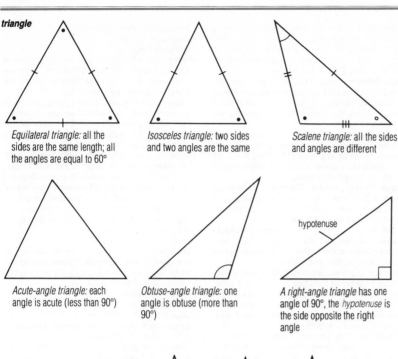

Equilateral triangle: all the sides are the same length; all the angles are equal to 60°

Isosceles triangle: two sides and two angles are the same

Scalene triangle: all the sides and angles are different

Acute-angle triangle: each angle is acute (less than 90°)

Obtuse-angle triangle: one angle is obtuse (more than 90°)

A right-angle triangle has one angle of 90°, the *hypotenuse* is the side opposite the right angle

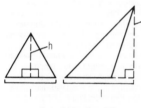

Area of triangle = ½lh

Triangles are *congruent* if corresponding sides and corresponding angles are equal

Similar triangles have corresponding angles that are equal; they therefore have the same shape

tribal society a way of life in which people govern their own affairs as independent local communities without central government organizations or states, in parts of SE Asia, New Guinea, South America, and Africa. People in tribal societies share in the production of food and other necessities, and learn basic skills rather than specializing in certain tasks and developing elaborate technologies.

As the world economy continues to expand, the natural resources belonging to tribal peoples are increasingly in demand for farming or industrial development and the people themselves are frequently dispossessed. Pressure groups such as Survival International and Cultural Survival have been established in some Western countries to support the struggle of tribal people for civil rights.

tribunal strictly, a court of justice, but used in English law for a body appointed by the government to arbitrate in disputes, or investigate certain matters. They usually consist of a lawyer as chair, sitting with two lay assessors.

In English law, there are various kinds of tribunal. *Administrative tribunals* deal with claims and disputes about rights and duties under statutory schemes; for example industrial tribunals (dealing with employment rights, such as unfair dismissal claims) and rent tribunals (fixing fair rents for protected tenants). *Domestic tribunals* are the internal disciplinary bodies of organizations such as professional bodies and trade unions. *Tribunals of inquiry* are set up by the government to investigate matters of public concern, for example the King's Cross Fire Disaster Inquiry and the Cleveland Child Abuse Inquiry, both 1988.

tribune Roman magistrate of ◊plebeian family, elected annually to defend the interests of the common people; only two were originally provided

for in 494 BC, but there were later ten. They could veto the decisions of any other magistrate.

triceratops rhinoceros-like dinosaur with three horns and a neck frill. Up to 8 m/25 ft long, it lived in the Cretaceous period.

Trichinopoly /ˌtrɪkɪˈnɒpəli/ former name for ◊Tiruchirapalli, a city in India.

trichloromethane modern name for ◊chloroform.

tricolour the French national flag of three vertical bands of red, white, and blue. The red and blue were the colours of Paris and the white represented the royal house of Bourbon. The flag was first adopted during the French Revolution, three days after the storming of the Bastille, on 17 July 1789.

tricoteuse in the French Revolution, one of the women who sat knitting in the National Convention and beneath the guillotine.

Trier /trɪə/ (French *Trèves*) city in Rhineland-Palatinate, West Germany; population (1984) 95,000. Once the capital of the Treveri, a Celto-Germanic tribe, it became known as *Augusta Treverorum* under the Roman emperor Augustus about 15 BC, and was the capital of an ecclesiastical principality during the 14th–18th centuries. Karl Marx was born here.

Trieste /triːˈest/ port on the Adriatic, opposite Venice, in Friuli-Venezia-Giulia, Italy; population (1988) 237,000, including a large Slovene minority. It is the site of the International Centre for Theoretical Physics, established 1964.

Trieste was under Austrian rule from 1382 (apart from Napoleonic occupation 1809–14) until transferred to Italy 1918. It was claimed after World War II by Yugoslavia, and the city and surrounding territory were divided 1954 between Italy and Yugoslavia.

trigger-fish marine fish of the family Balistidae, with a laterally compressed body, up to 60 cm/2 ft long, and deep belly. They have small mouths but strong

jaws and teeth. The first spine on the dorsal fin locks into an erect position, which can enable them to lock themselves into crevices for protection, and can only be moved by depressing the smaller third ('trigger') spine. There are many species, especially in warm waters, and some are very colourful.

Triglav /ˈtriːɡlaʊ/ mountain in the Julian Alps, rising to 2,863 m/9,393 ft. It is the highest peak in Yugoslavia.

trigonometry branch of mathematics that solves problems relating to plane and spherical triangles. Its principles are based on the fixed proportions of sides for a particular angle in a right-angled triangle, the simplest of which are known as the ◊sine, ◊cosine, and ◊tangent (so-called trigonometrical ratios). It is of practical importance in navigation, surveying, and simple harmonic motion in physics.

Invented by ◊Hipparchus, trigonometry was developed by ◊Ptolemy of Alexandria and was known to early Hindu and Arab mathematicians.

triiodomethane modern name for ◊iodoform.

trilobite extinct, marine, invertebrate arthropod of the Palaeozoic era, with a flattened, oval, segmented body, 1–65 cm/0.4–26 in long, covered with a shell.

Some were burrowing, others floating. Their worldwide distribution, many species, and the immense quantities of their remains make them useful in dating remains of other creatures.

Trimurti /trɪˈmʊəti/ the Hindu triad of gods, representing the Absolute Spirit in its three aspects: Brahma, personifying creation; Vishnu, preservation; and Siva, destruction.

Trincomalee /ˌtrɪŋkəməˈliː/ port in NE Sri Lanka; population (1981) 45,000. It was an early Tamil settlement, and a British naval base until 1957.

Trinidad /ˌtrɪnɪˈdæd/ town in Beni region, N Bolivia, near the river Mamoré, 400 km/250 mi NE of La Paz; population (1980) 36,000. It is built on an artificial earth mound, above flood-level, the work of a little-known early American Indian people.

Trinidad and Tobago /ˈtrɪnɪdæd, təˈbeɪɡəʊ/ country in the West Indies, off the coast of Venezuela.

government Trinidad and Tobago is an independent republic within the Commonwealth. The 1976 constitution provides for a president as head of state, and a two-chamber parliament, consisting of a senate of 31 members and a house of representatives of 36. The president appoints the prime minister and cabinet, who are collectively responsible to Parliament. The president also appoints the senators, 16 on the advice of the prime minister, six on the advice of the leader of the opposition, and nine after wider consultation. The 36 members of the House of Representatives are elected by universal adult suffrage. Parliament has a life of five years.

Tobago was given its own House of Assembly 1980. It has 15 members, 12 popularly elected and three chosen by the majority party.

history For early history, see ◊American Indian. Trinidad and Tobago were discovered by Columbus 1498. Trinidad was colonized by Spain from 1532 and ceded to Britain 1802, having been captured 1797. Tobago was settled by the Netherlands in the 1630s and subsequently occupied by various countries before being ceded to Britain by France 1814. Trinidad and Tobago were amalgamated 1888 as a British colony.

trigger-fish

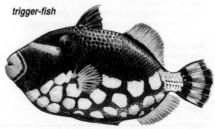

Trinidad and Tobago's first political party, the People's National Movement (PNM), was formed 1956 by Dr Eric Williams and when the colony achieved granted internal self-government 1959 he became the first chief minister. Between 1958 and 1961 it was a member of the Federation of the West Indies but withdrew and achieved full independence, within the Commonwealth, 1967, Dr Williams becoming the first prime minister.

A new constitution was adopted 1976 which made Trinidad and Tobago a republic. The former governor-general, Ellis Clarke, became the first president and Dr Williams continued as prime minister. He died Mar 1981 without having nominated a successor and the president appointed George Chambers; the PNM formally adopted him as leader May 1981. The opposition, a moderate left-wing party grouping led by the deputy prime minister, Arthur Robinson, was during the next few years reorganized as the National Alliance for Reconstruction (NAR), until in the 1986 general election it swept the PNM from power and Arthur Robinson became prime minister.

Trinitarianism a belief in the Christian Trinity.

Trinity in the Christian religion, the threefold union of three persons in one godhead, namely Father, Son, and Holy Ghost/Spirit. The precise meaning of the doctrine has been the cause of unending dispute, and was the chief cause of the split between the Orthodox and Roman Catholic churches. *Trinity Sunday* occurs on the Sunday after Whit Sunday.

triode a three-electrode thermionic valve containing an anode and a cathode (as does a ◊diode) with an additional negatively biased control grid. Small variations in voltage on the grid bias result in large variations in the current. The triode was commonly used in amplifiers until largely superseded by the ◊transistor.

Tripitaka (Pāli 'three baskets') the canonical texts of Theravāda Buddhism, divided into three parts.

Triple Alliance an alliance from 1882 between Germany, Austria-Hungary, and Italy to offset the power of Russia and France. It was last renewed 1912 but during World War I, Italy's initial neutrality gradually changed, and it denounced

the alliance 1915. The term also refers to other alliances: 1668 England, Holland, and Sweden; 1717 Britain, Holland, and France (joined 1718 by Austria); 1788 Britain, Prussia, and Holland; 1795 Britain, Russia, and Austria.

Triple Entente alliance of Britain, France, and Russia 1907–17. In 1911 this became a military alliance and formed the basis of the Allied powers in World War I against the Central Powers, Germany and Austria-Hungary.

The failure of the alliance system to create a stable balance of power, coupled with universal horror of the carnage created by World War I, led to attempts to create a new international order with the League of Nations.

Tripoli /'trɪpəli/ (Arabic **Tarabolus esh-sham**) port in N Lebanon, 65 km/40 mi NE of Beirut; population (1980) 175,000. It stands on the site of the Phoenician city of Oea.

Tripoli /'trɪpəli/ (Arabic **Tarabolus al-Gharb**) capital and chief port of Libya, on the Mediterranean; population (1980) 980,000. Products include olive oil, fruit, fish, and textiles.

history Tripoli was founded about the 7th century BC by Phoenicians from Oea (now Tripoli in Lebanon). It was an important base for Axis powers during World War II. In 1986 it was bombed by the US Air Force in response to perceived international guerrilla activity.

Tripolitania /,trɪpəli'teɪniə/ former province of Libya, stretching from Cyrenaica in the east to Tunisia in the west. Italy captured it from Turkey 1912, and the British captured it from Italy 1942, and controlled it until the formation of the newly independent United Kingdom of Libya 1951. In 1963 Tripolitania was subdivided into administrative divisions.

Tripura /'trɪpurə/ state of NE India since 1972, formerly a princely state, between Bangladesh and Assam

area 10,500 sq km/4,053 sq mi

capital Agartala

products rice, cotton, tea, sugar cane; steel, jute

features agriculture on a shifting system in the jungle, now being superseded by modern methods

population (1981) 2,060,000

language Bengali

religion Hindu.

trireme ancient Greek warship with three banks of oars as well as sails, 38 m/115 ft long. Triremes were used at the battle of ◊Salamis and by the Romans until the 4th century AD.

Tristan /'trɪstən/ hero of Celtic legend, who fell in love with Iseult, the bride he was sent to win for his uncle King Mark of Cornwall; the story became part of the Arthurian cycle, and is the subject of Wagner's opera *Tristan and Isolde*.

Tristan /'trɪstən/ Flora 1803–1844. French socialist writer and activist, author of *Promenades dans Londres/The London Journal* 1840, a vivid record of social conditions, and *L'Union ouvrière/Workers' Union* 1843, an outline of a worker's utopia.

Tristan da Cunha /'trɪstən də 'kuːnjə/ group of islands in the S Atlantic, part of the British dependency of St Helena

area 110 sq km/42 sq mi

features comprises four islands: Tristan, Gough, Inaccessible, and Nightingale. Tristan consists of a single volcano 2,060 m/6,761 ft; it is an important meteorological and radio station

exports crawfish

currency pound sterling

population (1982) 325

government administrator, plus island council, as a dependency of ◊St Helena

history the first European to visit the islands was the Portuguese admiral after whom they are named, in 1506; they were annexed by Britain 1816. Believed to be extinct, the Tristan volcano erupted 1961 and the population were evacuated, but in 1963 they chose to return.

Tristano /trɪ'staːnəu/ 'Lennie' (Lennard Joseph) 1919–1978. US jazz pianist and composer. An austere musician, he gave an academic foundation to the 'cool' school of jazz in the 1940s and 1950s, at odds with the bebop tradition, and was active as a teacher.

Tristram Shandy a novel by Laurence Sterne, published 1759–67. The work, a forerunner of the 20th-century stream-of-consciousness novel, has no coherent plot and uses typographical devices to emphasize the author's disdain for the structured novels of his contemporaries.

triticale cereal crop of recent origin that is a cross between wheat (genus *Triticum*) and rye (genus *Secale*). It can produce heavy yields of high-protein grain principally for use as an animal feed.

tritium unstable isotope of hydrogen, with two neutrons as well as one proton in its nucleus.

Triton /'traɪtn/ in Greek mythology, a merman sea-god, the son of ◊Poseidon and the sea-goddess Amphitrite. He is shown blowing on a conch shell.

Triton /'traɪtn/ in astronomy, one of the moons of Neptune. It has a diameter of 2,720 km/1,690 mi, and orbits Neptune every 5.88 days in a retrograde (east to west) direction. Its surface has many fault

Trinidad and Tobago
Republic of

area Trinidad 4,800 sq km/1,853 sq mi and Tobago 300 sq km/116 sq mi

capital Port of Spain

towns San Fernando

physical comprises the two main islands, and some smaller ones; Trinidad has coastal swamps, and hills E–W

features Pitch Lake is a self-renewing source of asphalt and was used by the 16th-century explorer Walter Raleigh when repairing his ships

head of state Noor Hassanali from 1987

head of government Arthur Robinson from 1986

government system democratic republic

political parties National Alliance for Reconstruction (NAR), nationalistic, left-of-centre; People's National Movement (PNM), nationalistic, moderate, centrist.

exports angostura bitters, asphalt, natural gas, oil

currency Trinidad and Tobago dollar (7.23 = £1 Mar 1990)

population (1988) 1,261,000 (equally divided between those of African and E Indian descent), 1.2 million on Trinidad; annual growth rate 1.6%

life expectancy men 66, women 71

language English (official), Hindi, French, Spanish

religion Roman Catholic 33%, Protestant 14%, Hindu 25%, Muslim 6%

literacy 97% male/95% female (1985 est)

GNP $6.8 bn (1983); $6,800 per head of population

chronology

1956 The People's National Movement (PNM) founded.

1959 Granted internal self-government, with PNM leader Eric Williams as chief minister.

1967 Achieved full independence, within the Commonwealth, with Williams as prime minister.

1976 Became a republic, with Ellis Clarke as president and Williams as prime minister.

1981 Williams died and was succeeded by George Chambers, with Arthur Robinson as leader of the opposition.

1986 Arthur Robinson became prime minister.

1987 Noor Hassanali became president.

Tripura

lines and a bright polar region which reflects 90% of the sunlight it receives. Its atmosphere is composed of methane and nitrogen, and has a pressure only 0.00001 that of the Earth at sea level. Triton was discovered 1846.

Other surface features include what appear to be frozen lakes, perhaps formed when material ejected from Triton's interior froze in low-lying areas of the surface. Chemical reaction between the material on Triton's surface and solar radiation are probably responsible for the pinkish colouring across the southern hemisphere. The low number of craters suggests that the surface may be fairly young on the geological time scale, perhaps less than 500 million years. It is possible that Triton may still be volcanically active. Dark streaks near the south pole may be formed from liquid nitrogen thrown up into the atmosphere to heights of several tens of kilometres, becoming frozen and then being blown by gentle winds and deposited across the surface. The features resemble streaks seen elsewhere in the solar system.

triumvir one of a group of three administrators sharing power in ancient Rome, as in the *First Triumvirate* 60 BC: Caesar, Pompey, Crassus; and *Second Triumvirate* 43 BC: Augustus, Antony, and Lepidus.

Trivandrum /trɪˈvændrəm/ capital of Kerala, SW India; population (1981) 483,000. It has chemical, textile, and rubber industries. Formerly the capital of the princely state of Travancore, it has many palaces, an old fort, and a shrine.

trivium in medieval education, the three lower liberal arts (grammar, rhetoric, and logic) studied before the ◊quadrivium.

troglodyte Greek term for a cave-dweller, designating certain peoples in the ancient world. The troglodytes of S Egypt and Ethiopia were a pastoral people.

trogon tropical bird, up to 50 cm/1.7 ft long, with resplendent plumage, living in the Americas and Afro-Asia, order Trogoniformes. Most striking is the ◊quetzal.

Trois-Rivières /ˈtrwɑː rɪvˈjeə/ port on the St Lawrence River, Québec, Canada; population (1986) 129,000. The chief industry is the production of newsprint.

Trojan horse a seemingly innocuous but treacherous gift from an enemy. In Greek legend, during the siege of Troy, the Greek army left a huge wooden horse outside the gate of the city and retreated. When the Trojans had brought it in, Greek soldiers emerged from within the hollow horse, and opened the city gates to enable it to be captured.

Trojan horse a computer program that appears to function normally but which, undetected by the normal user, at the same time causes damage to other files or which circumvents security procedures. The earliest appeared in the UK in about 1988.

trolleybus type of bus driven by electric power collected from overhead wires. It has greater manoeuvrability than a tram (see ◊tramway), but its obstructiveness in modern traffic conditions led to its withdrawal.

Germany has developed new types which operate, by means of three tonnes of batteries, for 10 km/6 mi without drawing current from an overhead wire.

Trollope /ˈtrɒləp/ Anthony 1815–1882. English novelist, who delineated provincial English middle-class society in his Barchester series of novels. *The Warden* 1855 began the series, which includes *Barchester Towers* 1857, *Doctor Thorne* 1858, and *The Last Chronicle of Barset* 1867.

trombone a ◊brass wind musical instrument developed from the sackbut. It consists of a tube bent double, varied notes being obtained by an inner sliding tube. Usual sizes of trombone are alto, tenor, bass, and contra-bass.

Tromp /trɒmp/ Maarten Harpertszoon 1597–1653. Dutch admiral. He twice defeated the occupying Spaniards 1639. He was defeated by the British

admiral Blake May 1652, but in Nov triumphed over Blake in the Strait of Dover. In Feb–June 1653 he was defeated by Blake and Monk, and was killed off the Dutch coast. His son, *Cornelius Tromp* (1629–91), also an admiral, fought a battle against the English and French fleets in 1673.

trompe l'oeil (French 'deceives the eye') painting that gives a convincing illusion of three-dimensional reality. It has been common in most periods in the West, from classical Greece through the Renaissance and later.

Tromsø /ˈtrɒmsɜː/ fishing port and the largest town in NW Norway, on Tromsø island; population (1988) 49,000.

Trondheim /ˈtrɒndhaɪm/ fishing port in Norway; population (1988) 136,000. It has canning, textile, margarine, and soap industries. It was the medieval capital of Norway, and Norwegian kings are crowned in the cathedral.

trophic level in ecology, the position occupied by a species (or group of species) in a ◊food chain. The main levels are *primary producers* (photosynthetic plants), *primary consumers* (herbivores), *secondary consumers* (carnivores), and *decomposers* (bacteria and fungi).

tropics the area between the tropics of Cancer and Capricorn, defined by the parallels of latitude approximately 23° 30 ′ N and S of the equator. They are the limits of the area of Earth's surface in which the Sun can be directly overhead.

tropine a white crystalline solid formed by the hydrolysis of alkaloid atropine.

tropism or *tropic movement* the directional growth of a plant, or part of a plant, in response to an external stimulus. If the movement is directed towards the stimulus it is described as positive, if away from it, as negative. *Geotropism*, the response of plants to gravity, causes the root (positively geotropic) to grow downwards, and the stem (negatively geotropic) to grow upwards. *Phototropism* occurs in response to light, *hydrotropism* to water, *chemotropism* to a chemical stimulus, and *thigmotropism*, or *haptotropism*, to physical contact, as in the tendrils of climbing plants when they touch a support and then grow around it.

Tropic movements are the result of a greater rate of growth on one side of the plant organ than the other. Tropism differs from a ◊nastic movement in being influenced by the direction of the stimulus.

troposphere lower part of the Earth's ◊atmosphere extending about 10.5 km/6.5 mi from the Earth's surface, in which temperature decreases with height to about −60°C/−76°F except in local layers of temperature inversion. The *tropopause* is the upper boundary of the troposphere above which the temperature increases slowly with height within the ◊atmosphere.

Trossachs /ˈtrɒsəks/ woodland glen between Lochs Katrine and Achray in Central Region, Scotland, 3 km/2 mi long. Featured in the novels of Walter Scott, it has become a favoured tourist spot.

Trotsky /ˈtrɒtski/ Leon. Adopted name of Lev Davidovitch Bronstein 1879–1940. Russian revolutionary. He joined the Bolshevik party and took a leading part in the seizure of power and raising the Red Army which fought the Civil War 1918–20. In the struggle for power that followed ◊Lenin's death 1924, ◊Stalin defeated him, and this and other differences with the Communist Party led to his exile 1929. Trotsky settled in Mexico, where he was assassinated with an ice pick, possibly at Stalin's instigation. Trotsky believed in world revolution and in permanent revolution, and was an uncompromising, if liberal, idealist.

Although as a young man Trotsky admired Lenin, when he worked with him organizing the revolution of 1917 he objected to Lenin's dictatorial ways. Trotsky's later works are critical of the Soviet regime, for example *The Revolution Betrayed* 1937. His greatest work is his

magisterial *History of the Russian Revolution* 1932–33.

Trotskyism the form of Marxism advocated by Leon Trotsky. Its central concept is that of *permanent revolution*. In his view a proletarian revolution, leading to a socialist society, could not be achieved in isolation, so it would be necessary to spark off further revolutions throughout Europe and ultimately worldwide. This was in direct opposition to the Stalinist view that socialism should be built and consolidated within individual countries.

Trotskyism was developed in an attempt to reconcile Marxist theory with actual conditions in Russia in the early 20th century, but it was never officially accepted within the USSR. Instead it has found much support worldwide, especially in Third World countries, and the Fourth ◊International, which Trotsky founded in 1937, has sections in over 60 countries.

troubadour one of a group of poet-musicians in Provence and S France, in the 12th–13th centuries, that included both nobles and wandering minstrels. The troubadours originated a type of lyric poetry devoted to themes of courtly love and the idealization of women and to glorifying the deeds of their patrons, reflecting the chivalric ideals of the period. Little is known of the music, which was passed down orally.

Among the troubadours were Bertran de Born (1140–*c.*1215), who was mentioned by Dante, Arnaut Daniel, and Bernard de Ventadour. The troubadour tradition spread to other parts of Europe, including northern France (the *trouvères*) and Germany (the *Minnesingers*).

trout fish closely related to the salmon. It has a thick body and a blunt head, and varies in colour. It is native to the northern hemisphere, usually in fresh waters.

The common trout *Salmo trutta* is widely distributed in Europe, occurring in British fresh and coastal waters. Sea trout are generally silvery and river trout olive-brown, both having spotted fins and sides. In the USA, the name 'trout' is given to various species, notably to the rainbow trout *Salmo gairdneri*, which has been naturalized in many other countries.

Trowbridge /ˈtrəʊbrɪdʒ/ market town in Wiltshire, England; population (1981) 23,000. Its industries include dairy produce, bacon, ham, and wool.

Troy /trɔɪ/ (Latin *Ilium*) ancient city of Asia Minor. In the *Iliad*, the poet Homer described Troy as besieged in the ten-year Trojan War (mid-13th century BC), and falling to the Greeks by the stratagem of the ◊Trojan horse.

Nine cities buried one beneath another on the site at Hissarlik, near the Dardanelles, were originally excavated by ◊Schliemann. Recent research suggests that the seventh, sacked and burned about 1250 BC, is probably the Homeric Troy, which was succeeded by a shanty town, sacked

Trotsky Leon Trotsky in 1917, the year of the Russian Revolution.

by the ◊Sea Peoples about 780 BC. It has been suggested that the Homeric war might have a basis in fact, for example a conflict arising from trade rivalry (Troy was on a tin trade route), which could have been triggered by such an incident as Paris running off with ◊Helen. The wooden horse could have been a votive offering left behind by the Greeks after ◊Poseidon (whose emblem was a horse) had opened breaches in the city walls for them by an earthquake.

Troyes /trwɑ:/ industrial (textiles and food processing) town in Champagne-Ardenne, NE France; population (1982) 65,000. The **Treaty of Troyes** 1420 granted the French crown to Henry V of England.

troy system system of units used for precious metals and gems. The troy pound (0.37 kg) consists of 12 ounces (each of 120 carats) or 5,760 grains (each equal to 65 mg).

Trucial States /'tru:ʃəl 'steɪts/ former name (until 1971) of the ◊United Arab Emirates. It derives from the agreements made with Britain 1820 to ensure a truce in the area, and to suppress piracy and slavery.

Truck Acts UK acts of Parliament introduced 1831, 1887, 1896, and 1940 to prevent employers misusing wage payment systems to the detriment of their workers. The legislation made it illegal to pay wages with goods in kind or with tokens for use in shops owned by the employers. The 1940 act prevented employers giving canteen meals in lieu of wages.

The 1831 act had no means of enforcement, and even after the 1887 act, responsibility and costs of bringing prosecutions lay with the aggrieved worker.

Trudeau /tru:'dəʊ/ Pierre (Elliott) 1919– . Canadian Liberal politician. He was prime minister 1968–79 and won again by a landslide Feb 1980. In 1980 his work helped to defeat the Québec independence movement in a referendum. He repatriated the constitution from Britain 1982, but by 1984 had so lost support that he resigned.

True Cross the instrument of Jesus's crucifixion, supposedly found by St Helena, the mother of the emperor Constantine, at ◊Calvary 326. She is reputed to have placed most of it in a church built on the site, and to have taken the rest to Constantinople. During the Middle Ages, there appeared a large number of relics claimed as fragments of the True Cross.

Truffaut /tru'fəʊ/ François 1932–1984. French film director, whose gently comic films include *Jules et Jim* 1961, and *La Nuit américaine/Day for Night* 1973 (for which he won an Academy Award). His work was influenced by Hitchcock, and also draws on Surrealist and comic traditions.

truffle subterranean fungus of the order Tuberales. Certain species are valued as edible delicacies, in particular *Tuber melanosporum*, native to to the Perigord region of France and generally found growing under oak trees; it is rounded, blackish brown, covered with warts externally, and with blackish flesh.

Trujillo /tru:'xi:əʊ/ city in NW Peru, with its port at Salaverry; population (1988) 491,000. Industries include engineering, copper, sugar milling, and vehicle assembly.

Trujillo Molina /məʊ'li:nə/ Rafael (Leónidas) 1891–1961. Dictator of the Dominican Republic from 1930. As commander of the Dominican Guard, he seized power and established a ruthless dictatorship. He was assassinated.

Truman /'tru:mən/ Harry S 1884–1972. 33rd president of the USA 1945–53, a Democrat. In Jan 1945 he became vice president to F D Roosevelt, and president when Roosevelt died in Apr that year. He used the atom bombs against Japan, launched the ◊Marshall Plan to restore W Europe's economy, and nurtured the European Community and NATO (including the rearmament of West Germany).

Born in Lamar, Missouri, he ran a clothing store that was bankrupted by the Great Depression.

He became a senator 1934, was selected as Roosevelt's last vice president, and in 1948 was elected for a second term in a surprise victory over Thomas Dewey (1902–1971), the governor of New York. At home, he had difficulty converting the economy back to peacetime conditions, and failed to prevent the witch-hunts on suspected communists (see ◊Hiss, ◊McCarthy). In Korea, he intervened when the South was invaded, but sacked Gen ◊MacArthur when the general's policy threatened to start World War III. Truman's decision not to enter Chinese territory, betrayed by the double agent Kim Philby, led to China's entry into the war. Truman had a sign on his desk that said: 'The buck stops here.'

Truman Doctrine US president Harry Truman's 1947 doctrine that the USA would 'support free peoples who are resisting attempted subjugation by armed minorities or by outside pressures'. It was used to justify sending US troops abroad, for example to Korea.

trumpet a small high-register ◊brass wind instrument; a doubled tube with valves.

trumpeter South American bird, up to 50 cm/20 in tall, genus *Psophia*, related to the cranes. It has long legs, a short bill, and dark plumage. It is also a type of ◊swan.

Truong Sa /,tru:ɒŋ' sɑ:/ one of the ◊Spratly Islands, in the South China Sea.

Truro /'truərəʊ/ city in Cornwall, England, and administrative headquarters of the county; population (1982) 16,000. Truro was the traditional meeting place of the *Stannary* (see ◊Cornwall); the nearby tin mines flourished briefly in the early 1980s.

trust an arrangement whereby a person or group of people holds property for the benefit of others entitled to the beneficial interest.

A trust can be a **legal arrangement** under which A is empowered to administer property belonging to B for the benefit of C. A and B may be the same person; B and C may not. A ◊**unit trust** holds and manages a number of marketable securities; by buying a 'unit' in such a trust, the purchaser has a proportionate interest in each of the securities so that his or her risk is spread. An **investment trust** is not in modern times a trust, but a public company investing in marketable securities money subscribed by its shareholders who receive dividends from the income earned. A **charitable trust** such as the ◊National Trust, or the Ford Foundation, administers funds for charitable purposes. A **business trust** is formed by linking several companies by transferring shares in them to trustees; or by the creation of a holding

Truman *US politician and president Harry Truman presided over the Allied victory in World War II and US involvement in the Korean War.*

company, whose shares are exchanged for those of the separate companies. Competition is thus eliminated, and in the USA both types were outlawed by the Sherman Anti-Trust Act 1890 (first fully enforced by 'trust buster' Theodore ◊Roosevelt, as in the break-up of the Standard Oil Company of New Jersey by the Supreme Court 1911).

Trustee, Public in England, an official empowered to act as executor and trustee, either alone or with others, of the estate of anyone who appoints him or her. In 1986 powers were extended to cover (among other things) the affairs of mental patients.

trust territory territory formerly held under the United Nations trusteeship system to be prepared for independence, either former ◊mandates, territories taken over by the Allies in World War II, or those voluntarily placed under the UN by the administering state.

Truth /tru:θ/ Sojourner. Adopted name of Isabella Baumfree, subsequently Isabella Van Wagener 1797–1883. US anti-slavery campaigner. Born a slave, she obtained her freedom and that of her son, and became involved with religious groups. In 1843 she was 'commanded in a vision' to adopt the name Sojourner Truth. She published an autobiography, *The Narrative of Sojourner Truth* 1850.

truth table in computing, a diagram showing the effect of a particular ◊logic gate on every combination of inputs.

trypanosomiasis collection of debilitating long-term diseases caused by infestation with the microscopic single-celled *Trypanosoma*. They include sleeping sickness (nagana) in Africa, transmitted by the bites of ◊tsetse flies, and Chagas' disease in the Americas, spread by assassin-bugs. Millions of people are affected in warmer regions of the world; the diseases also affect cattle, which form a reservoir of infection.

Ts'ao Chan former name for the Chinese novelist ◊Cao Chan.

Tsar the Russian imperial title, derived from Latin *Caesar*.

Tsaritsyn /tsɑ:'rɪtsɪn/ a former name (until 1925) of ◊Volgograd, a city in the USSR.

Tsavo /'tsɑ:vəʊ/ one of the world's largest national parks, established 1948, comprising East and West Tsavo. It occupies 20,821 sq km/8,036 sq mi of SE Kenya.

Tschiffley /'tʃɪfli/ Aimé Felix 1895–1954. Swiss writer and traveller whose 16,000 km/10,000 mi journey on horseback from Buenos Aires to New York was known as 'Tschiffley's Ride' from his account of that journey, *Southern Cross to Pole Star* 1933.

tsetse African fly of the genus *Glossina*, related to the house fly, which transmits the disease nagana to cattle and sleeping sickness to human beings. It grows up to 1.5 cm/0.6 in long.

Tsinan /,tsi:'næn/ another name for ◊Jinan, capital of Shandong province, E China.

Tsingtao /,tsɪŋ'taʊ/ another name for ◊Qingdao, a port in E China.

Tsiolkovsky /tsɪəl'kɒfski/ Konstantin 1857–1935. Russian scientist. He published the first practical paper on astronautics 1903, covering rocket space travel using liquid propellants, such as liquid oxygen.

Tsumeb /'tsu:meb/ the principal mining centre (diamonds, copper, lead, zinc) of N Namibia, NW of Grootfontein; population 13,500.

tsunami (Japanese 'harbour wave') giant wave generated by an undersea ◊earthquake or other disturbance. In the open ocean it may take the form of several successive waves, travelling at tens of kilometres or miles per hour but with an amplitude (height) of approximately a yard or metre. In the coastal shallows, however, ' . · slow down and build up, producing towerin wa es that can sweep inland and cause great loss of life and property.

Before each wave there may be a sudden, unexpected withdrawal of water from the beach.

Used synonymously with tsunami, the popular term 'tidal wave' is misleading.

Tsung Dao Lee /'tsʊŋ ˌdaʊ 'li:/ 1926– . US physicist of Chinese origin. His research centred on the physics of weak interactions between particles. In 1956 Lee proposed that such interactions might disobey certain key assumptions, for instance the conservation of parity. He shared the 1957 Nobel Prize for Physics with his colleague Chen Ning Yang (1922–).

Tsung Li Yamen an advisory body created in China after 1861 to deal with foreign affairs and other state modernization projects. It consisted of national and provincial state officials but was limited by a lack of power and the creation of an admiralty in 1885 and a formal foreign office after 1901.

Tsushima /'tsu:ʃiːmɑ:/ Japanese island between Korea and Japan in Tsushima Strait; area 702 sq km/ 271 sq mi. The Russian fleet was destroyed by the Japanese here 1905 (see ◊Russo–Japanese War). The chief settlement is Izuhara.

Tsvetaeva /svɪ'taɪəvə/ Marina 1892–1941. Russian poet, born in Moscow. She wrote mythic, romantic, frenetic verse, including *The Demesne of the Swans*.

TT abbreviation for *Tourist Trophy*; *teetotal*; tuberculin tested.

Tuamotu Archipelago /ˌtuːəˈməʊtuː/ two parallel ranges of 78 atolls, part of ◊French Polynesia; area 690 sq km/266 sq mi; population (1983) 11,800, including ◊Gambier Islands to the east. The atolls stretch 2,100 km/1,300 mi north and east of the Society Islands. The administrative headquarters is Apataki. The largest atoll is Rangiroa, and the most important Hao; they produce pearl shell and copra. Mururoa and Fangataufa atolls to the southeast have been a French nuclear test site since 1966. Spanish explorers landed 1606, and the islands were annexed by France 1881.

Tuareg nomadic ◊Hamite people of the Sahara.

tuatara lizard-like reptile *Sphenodon punctatus*, found only on a few islands off New Zealand. It grows up to 70 cm/2.3 ft long, is greenish or black, and has a spiny crest down its back. On the top of its head is the pineal organ, or so-called 'third eye', linked to the brain, which probably acts as a kind of light meter.

It is the sole survivor of the reptilian order Rhynchocephalia. It lays eggs in burrows which it shares with seabirds, and has the longest incubation period of all reptiles (up to 15 months).

tuba a large bass ◊brass wind musical instrument.

tuber a swollen region of an underground stem or root which is usually modified for storing food. The potato is a **stem tuber**, as shown by the presence of terminal and lateral buds, the 'eyes' of the potato. *Root tubers*, developed from adventitious roots, lack these. Both types of tuber can give rise to new individuals and so provide a means of ◊vegetative reproduction.

Unlike a bulb, a tuber persists for one season only; new tubers developing on a plant in the following year are formed in different places. See also ◊rhizome.

tuberculosis (TB) formerly known as *consumption* or *phthisis* an infectious disease caused by the bacillus *Mycobacterium tuberculosis*. It takes several forms, of which pulmonary tuberculosis is by far the most common.

In pulmonary TB, a patch of inflammation develops in the lung, with formation of an abscess. Often, this heals spontaneously, leaving only scar tissue. The dangers are of rapid spread through both lungs (what used to be called 'galloping consumption') or the development of miliary tuberculosis (spreading in the bloodstream to other sites) or tuberculous meningitis. The first antituberculosis drug, streptomycin, was developed in 1944.

In practice, most people who are infected do not become ill, and, with public health measures such as screening of individuals and the pasteurization of milk, active tuberculosis is fairly rare in the developed world. It still threatens, however, where

there is malnutrition and overcrowding. Vulnerable populations may be protected by means of the ◊BCG vaccine.

tuberose Mexican flowering plant *Polianthes tuberosa*, related to the ◊agave, grown as a sweet-smelling greenhouse plant.

Tübingen /'tjuː bɪŋən/ town in Baden-Württemberg, West Germany, on the Neckar river, 30 km/19 m S of Stuttgart; population (1985) 75,000. Industries include paper, textiles, and surgical instruments. It was capital of the French zone of occupation after World War II.

Tubman /'tʌbmən/ Harriet Ross 1821–1913. US abolitionist. Born a slave in Maryland, she escaped to Philadelphia (where slavery was outlawed) 1849. She set up the **Underground Railroad** to help slaves escape to the northern states and Canada. During the Civil War she served as a spy for the Union army. She spoke against slavery and for women's rights, and founded schools for freed slaves after the Civil War.

Tubman /'tʌbmən/ William V S 1895–1971. Liberian politician. The descendant of US slaves, he was a lawyer in the USA. After his election to the presidency of Liberia 1944 he concentrated on uniting the various ethnic groups. Re-elected several times, he died naturally in office despite frequent assassination attempts.

Tubuai Islands /ˌtuːbuːˈaɪ/ or *Austral Islands* chain of volcanic islands and reefs 1,300 km/ 800 mi long, in ◊French Polynesia, south of the Society Islands; area 148 sq km/57 sq mi; population (1983) 6,300. The main settlement is Mataura on Tubuai. They were visited by Capt Cook 1777, and annexed by France 1880.

TUC abbreviation for ◊*Trades Union Congress*.

Tucana constellation of the southern hemisphere, represented as a toucan. It contains the second most prominent ◊globular cluster in the sky, called 47 Tucanae, and the Small ◊Magellanic Cloud.

Tucson /'tuːsɒn/ town and resort in the Sonora Desert in SE Arizona, USA; population (1986) 384,000. It stands 760 m/2,500 ft above sea level, and the Santa Catalina Mountains to the NE rise to about 2,750 m/9,000 ft. Industries include aircraft, electronics, and copper smelting.

Tucumán /ˌtuːkuːˈmɑːn/ or *San Miguel de Tucumán* capital of Tucumán province, NW Argentina, on the Rio Sali, in the foothills of the Andes; population (1980) 497,000. Industries include sugar mills and distilleries. Founded 1565, Tucumán was the site of the signing of the Argentine declaration of independence from Spain 1816.

tucu-tuco South American burrowing rodent, genus *Ctenomys*, about 20 cm/8 in long with a 7 cm/3 in tail. It has a large head, sensitive ears, and huge incisor teeth.

It spends most of its time below ground in a burrow system, one animal to a burrow. The

name tucu-tuco is an attempt to imitate the bubbling call.

Tudor /'tjuːdə/ English dynasty descended from the Welsh Owen Tudor (c.1400–1461), the second husband of Catherine of Valois (the widow of Henry V of England). Their son Edmund married Margaret Beaufort (1443–1509), the great-granddaughter of ◊John of Gaunt, and was the father of Henry VII, who ascended the throne 1485.

The dynasty, which ended with the death of Elizabeth I 1603, was portrayed in a favourable light in Shakespeare's history plays.

tufa or *travertine* a soft, porous, ◊limestone rock, white in colour, deposited from solution from carbonate-saturated ground water around hot springs and in caves.

Tu Fu /'tuː 'fuː/ 712–770. Chinese poet, who wrote about the social injustices of his time, peasant suffering, and war, as in 'The Army Carts'.

Tukano indigenous people of the Vaupés Region on the Colombian-Brazilian border, numbering approximately 2,000.

Tula /'tuːlə/ city in W central USSR, on the river Upa, 193 km/ 121 mi south of Moscow; population (1987) 538,000. Industries include engineering and metallurgy. Site of the government ordnance factory, founded 1712 by Peter the Great.

Tula de Allende /'tuːlə deɪ aɪˈendɪ/ town in Mexico, near the site of the ancient ◊Toltec capital.

tulip plant of the genus *Tulipa*, family Liliaceae, with usually single goblet-shaped flowers on the end of an upright stem and leaves of a narrow oval shape with pointed ends. It is widely cultivated as a garden flower.

Tulipa gesnerana, from which most of the garden cultivars have been derived, probably originated in the Middle East. Quickly adopted in Europe during the 16th century, it became a craze in 17th-century Holland when extravagant prices were paid for bulbs of rare colours. Today it is commercially cultivated on a large scale in the Netherlands and East Anglia.

The *tulip tree Liriodendron tulipifera* is a member of the magnolia family, with large tulip-shaped blooms.

Tull /tʌl/ Jethro 1674–1741. English agriculturist who developed a drill about 1701, which enabled seeds to be sown mechanically and spaced so that cultivation between rows was possible in the growth period. His major work, *Horse-Hoeing Husbandry*, was published 1731.

tumour an overproduction of cells in a specific area of the body, often leading to a swelling or lump. Tumours are classified as **benign** or **malignant** (see ◊cancer).

Benign tumours are less serious because they grow more slowly, do not invade surrounding tissues, do not spread to other parts of the body, and do not usually recur after removal. However, some benign tumours can be more serious, especially in the brain. The most familiar types of benign tumour are warts on the skin. In some cases, there is no sharp dividing line between benign and malignant tumours.

tuna fish of the mackerel family *Thunnus thynnus*, up to 2.5 m/8 ft long and 200 kg/440 lbs. It is also known as **tunny**.

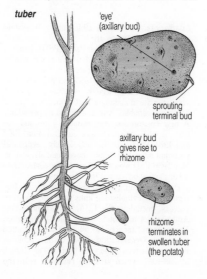

tuber

'eye' (axillary bud)

sprouting terminal bud

axillary bud gives rise to rhizome

rhizome terminates in swollen tuber (the potato)

tulip

Tunbridge Wells, Royal /'tʌnbrɪdʒ 'welz/ spa town in Kent, SE England, with iron-rich springs discovered 1606; population (1985) 98,500. There is an expanding light industrial estate. The shopping parade, or *Pantiles* (paved with tiles in the reign of Queen Anne), was a fashionable resort; 'Royal' since 1909.

Tunbs, the /tʊnbz/ two islands in the Strait of Hormuz, formerly held by Ras al Khaimah, and annexed from other Gulf states by Iran 1971; their return to their former owners was an Iraqi aim in the Iran–Iraq War.

tundra /'tʌndrə/ region of high latitude almost devoid of trees, resulting from the presence of ◊permafrost. The vegetation consists mostly of grasses, sedges, heather, mosses, and lichens. Tundra stretches in a continous belt across N North America, and Eurasia. The term, formerly applied to part of N Russia, is now used for all such regions.

tung oil oil used in paints and varnishes, obtained from trees of the genus *Aleurites*, family Euphorbiaceae, native to China.

tungsten or *wolfram* a metallic element, symbol W, atomic number 74, relative atomic mass 183.86. A grey hard metal, insoluble except in a mixture of nitric and hydrofluoric acids, it has the highest melting point (3,370°C) of any metal. Tungsten is used in alloy steels for armour plate, projectiles, high-speed cutting tools, lamp filaments, and thermionic valves. Its salts are used in the paint and tanning industries.

It was recognized and named by Scheele in 1781, and discovered by the d'Elhujar brothers in 1783. It occurs as wolframite ($FeWO_4$), scheelite ($CaWO_4$), and huberite ($MnWO_4$).

Tunguska Event an explosion at Tunguska, central Siberia, in June 1908 which devastated around 6,500 sq km/2,500 sq mi of forest. It is thought to have been caused by either a cometary nucleus or a fragment of ◊Encke's comet. The magnitude of the explosion was equivalent to an atom bomb and produced a colossal shock wave; a bright falling object was seen 600 km /375 mi away and was heard up to 1,000 km/ 625 mi away.

An expedition to the site was made in 1927. The central area of devastation was occupied by trees which were erect but stripped of their branches. Farther out, to a radius of 20 km/12 mi, trees were flattened and laid out radially.

tunicate any ◊chordate of the sub-phylum Tunicata (Urochordata), for example the ◊sea-squirt. Tunicates have transparent or translucent tunics made of cellulose. They vary in size from a few millimetres to 30 cm/1 ft in length, and are cylindrical, circular, or irregular in shape.

tuning-fork in music, a device for providing a reference pitch. It is made from hardened metal and consists of parallel bars 7.5–10 cm/3–4 in long joined at one end and terminating in a blunt point. When struck and the point placed on a wooden surface, a pure tone is heard.

Tunis /'tjuːnɪs/ capital and chief port of Tunisia; population (1984) 597,000. Industries include chemicals and textiles. Founded by the Arabs, it was occupied by the French 1881, and by the Axis powers 1942–43. The ruins of ancient ◊Carthage are to the NE.

Tunisia /tjuːˈnɪzɪə/ country in N Africa, on the Mediterranean, bounded to the SE by Libya and to the W by Algeria.

government A new constitution was adopted 1959, providing for a president who is both head of state and head of government, elected by universal suffrage for a five-year term and eligible for re-election. The president governs through an appointed council of ministers. There is a single-chamber national assembly of 141 members, elected in the same way and for the same term as the president.

history Founded as ◊Carthage by the Phoenicians in the 8th century BC, Tunisia was under Arab rule from the 7th century AD until it became part of the ◊Ottoman Empire 1574. It harboured the

tundra habitat

The landscape around the ice caps at the North and South Poles consists of an open treeless plain called tundra, or muskeg in North America. Winters last for about eight or nine months and the temperature can fall to −30°C (−86°F). The ground is frozen for most of the year, and in the summer there is only time for the topmost layer of soil to thaw. The meltwater cannot drain away and this gives rise to a waterlogged landscape where only low stunted plants grow. Insects flourish during the short summer, and birds migrate into the area to feed on them. Other animals winter in the forests in warmer latitudes and migrate into the region in the summer.

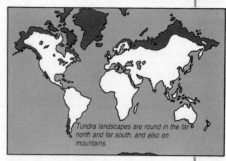

Tundra landscapes are round in the far north and far south, and also on mountains.

Herds of reindeer migrate into the area in the summer to feed on vegetation. Clouds of insects emerge from the ponds and lakes to take advantage of the brief period of sunlight.

reindeer

Water from a spring may freeze underground and eventually force up a dome-shaped hill of ice known as a a pingo.

Arctic hare

Arctic foxes

insects

Expansion and contraction of freezing soil produces wedges of ice that split the ground into polygonal shapes. The outlines of the polygons are marked by channels of rocks or by distinctive vegetation.

Some animals, such as Arctic foxes, develop a white coat in winter.

In the summer only the top few metres of soil can thaw. Below this the ground remains permanently frozen – a condition known as permafrost.

ducks

Canada geese

In winter, the low ground-hugging plants are blanketed and insulated by snow.

◊Barbary pirates until the 19th century. It became a French protectorate 1881.

The Socialist Destourien Party (PSD), founded 1934 by Habib Bourguiba, led Tunisia's campaign for independence from France. It was granted internal self-government 1955 and full independence 1956, with Bourguiba as prime minister. A year later the monarchy was abolished and Tunisia became a republic, with Bourguiba as president. A new constitution was adopted 1959 and the first national assembly elected. Between 1963 and 1981 PSD was the only legally recognized party but since then others have been allowed. In Nov 1986 PSD won all the assembly seats, while other parties boycotted the elections.

President Bourguiba followed a distinctive foreign policy, establishing links with the Western powers, including the USA, but joining other Arab states in condemning the US-inspired Egypt–Israel treaty. He allowed the Palestine Liberation Organization (PLO) to use Tunis as its headquarters, and this led to an Israeli attack 1985 which strained relations with the USA. Diplomatic links with Libya were severed 1985.

Bourguiba's firm and paternalistic rule, and his long period in Tunisian politics, made him a national legend, evidenced by the elaborate mausoleum which was built in anticipation of his death. However, in Nov 1987 he was deposed and replaced by Zine al-Abidine Ben Ali. In July 1988, a number of significant constitutional changes were announced, presaging a move to more pluralist politics, but in the April 1989 elections the RDC won all 141 assembly seats.

tunnel an underground passageway. Tunnelling is an increasingly important branch of civil engineering in mining and transport. In the 19th century there were two major advances: the use of compressed air within the tunnel to balance the external pressure of water, and of the tunnel shield to support the face and assist excavation. In recent years there have been notable developments in linings, for example concrete segments and steel liner plates; in the use of rotary diggers and cutters; and of explosives.

Major tunnels include:

Orange-Fish River (South Africa) 1975, longest irrigation tunnel 82 km/51 mi;

Chesapeake Bay Bridge-Tunnel (USA) 1963, combined bridge and tunnel structure, 28 km/17.5 mi;

St Gotthard (Switzerland–Italy) 1980, longest road tunnel 16.3 km/10.1 mi;

Seikan (Japan) 1964–85, longest rail tunnel, Honshu–Hokkaido, under Tsugaru Strait, 53.9 km/33.5 mi, 23.3 km/14.5 mi undersea (it is a white elephant because a bullet train service can no longer be afforded);

Simplon (Switzerland–Italy) 1906, longest rail tunnel on land 19.8 km/12.3 mi;

Rogers Pass (Canada) 1989, longest tunnel in the western hemisphere, 35 km/22 mi long, through the Selkirk Mountains, British Columbia.

A ◊Channel tunnel, or Chunnel, beneath the English Channel was planned as a military measure by Napoleon 1802. Excavations were made from both shores in the 1880s, but work was halted by Parliament for security reasons. In 1986 a scheme for twin rail tunnels was approved by the French and British governments, and work is underway with a schedule to complete in the early 1990s.

Tunnicliffe /'tʌnɪklɪf/ C(harles) F(rederick) 1901–1979. English painter of birds, born in Macclesfield, who worked in Anglesey.

tunny another name for ◊tuna.

Túpac Amarú /'tuːpæk ə'maːruː/ Adopted name of José Gabriel Condorcanqui *c.* 1742–1781. Peruvian Indian revolutionary leader, executed for his revolt against Spanish rule 1780; he claimed to be descended from the last chieftain of the Incas.

Tupamaros urban guerrilla movement operating in Uruguay, largely active in the 1960s–70s, named after the 18th-century revolutionary Túpac Amarú.

turbine an engine in which steam, water, or gas is made to spin a rotating shaft by pushing on angled blades, like a fan. Turbines are among the most powerful machines. Steam turbines are used to drive generators in power stations and ships' propellers; water turbines spin the generators in hydroelectric power plants; and gas turbines, in the guise of jet engines, power most aircraft, and drive machines in industry.

The high-temperature, high-pressure steam for steam turbines is raised in boilers heated by furnaces burning coal, oil, or gas, or by nuclear energy. A steam turbine consists of a shaft, or rotor, which rotates inside a fixed casing (stator). The rotor carries 'wheels' consisting of blades, or vanes. The stator has vanes set between the vanes of the rotor, which direct the steam through

Tunisia *The fortified mosque or ribat in Sousse, Tunisia.*

Tunisia
Republic of
(al-Jumhuriya at-Tunisiya)

area 154,500 sq km/59,652 sq mi
capital and chief port Tunis
towns ports Sfax, Sousse, Bizerta
physical arable and forested land in the N changes to desert in the S
features fertile island of Jerba, linked to the mainland by a causeway, and identified with the island of the lotus-eaters; Shott el Jerid salt lakes; holy city of Kairouan, ruins of Carthage
head of state and of government Zine el Abdin Ben Ali from 1987

the rotor vanes at the optimum angle. When steam expands through the turbine, it spins the rotor by ◊reaction. The steam engine of Hero of Alexandria (130 BC), called the *aeolipile*, was the prototype of this type of turbine, called a *reaction turbine*. Modern development of the reaction turbine is largely due to Charles ◊Parsons. Less widely used is the *impulse turbine*, patented by Carl Gustaf Patrick de Laval (1845–1913) 1882. It works by directing a jet of steam at blades on a rotor. Similarly there are reaction and impulse water turbines: impulse turbines work on the same principle as the waterwheel, and consist of sets of buckets arranged around the edge of a wheel; reaction turbines look much like propellers and are fully immersed in the water. In a *gas turbine* a compressed mixture of air and gas, or vaporized fuel, is ignited, and the hot gases produced expand through the turbine blades, spinning the rotor. In the industrial gas turbine, the rotor shaft drives machines. In the jet engine, the turbine drives the compressor, which supplies the compressed air to the engine, but most of the power developed comes from the jet exhaust in the form of propulsive thrust.

turbocharger a turbine-driven device fitted to engines to force more air into the cylinders, producing extra power. The turbocharger consists of a 'blower' or ◊compressor, driven by a turbine, which in most units is driven by the exhaust gases leaving the engine.

turbofan an alternative name for the ◊fan jet, or by-pass ◊turbojet.

turbojet a type of jet engine, which derives its thrust from a jet of hot exhaust gases. Pure turbojets can be very powerful but use a lot of fuel.

A single-shaft turbojet consists of a shaft (rotor) rotating in a casing. At the front is a multiblade ◊compressor, which takes in and compresses air and delivers it to one or more combustion chambers. Fuel (kerosene) is then sprayed in and ignited. The hot gases expand through a nozzle at the rear of the engine after spinning a ◊turbine. The turbine drives the compressor. Reaction to the backward stream of gases produces a forward propulsive thrust.

turboprop a jet engine that derives its thrust partly from a jet of exhaust gases, but mainly from a propeller powered by a turbine in the jet exhaust.

political system emergent democratic republic
political parties Constitutional Democratic Rally (RDC), nationalistic, moderate, socialist
exports oil, phosphates, iron ore
currency dinar (1.53 = £1 Mar 1990)
population (1989) 7,930,000; annual growth rate 2%
life expectancy men 60, women 61
language Arabic (official), French
religion Sunni Muslim, with a politically active fundamentalist opposition to the government; Jewish and Christian minorities
literacy 68% male/41% female (1985 est)
GNP $8.8 bn (1983); $844 per head of population
chronology
1955 Granted internal self-government.
1956 Achieved full independence as a monarchy, with Habib Bourguiba as prime minister.
1957 Became a republic with Bourguiba as president.
1975 Bourguiba made president for life.
1985 Diplomatic relations with Libya severed.
1987 In Oct Bourguiba removed Prime Minister Rashed Sfar and appointed Zine el Abdin Ben Ali. In Nov Ben Ali had Bourguiba declared incompetent and seized power.
1988 Constitutional changes towards democracy announced. Diplomatic relations with Libya restored.
1989 Government party, RCD, won all assembly seats in general election.

Turboprops are more economical than turbojets, but can only be used at relatively low speeds.

A turboprop has typically a twin-shaft rotor. One shaft carries the compressor and is spun by one turbine, while the other shaft carries a propeller and is spun by a second turbine.

turbot carnivorous flat-fish *Scophthalmus maximus* found in European waters. It grows up to 1 m/3 ft long and weighs up to 14 kg/30 lb. It is brownish above and whitish underneath.

Turenne /tjʊ'ren/ Henry de la Tour d'Auvergne, Vicomte de Turenne 1611–1675. French marshal under Louis XIV, known for his siege technique.

Turgenev /tʊə'geɪnjef/ Ivan Sergeievich 1818–1883. Russian writer, noted for poetic realism, pessimism, and skill at characterization. His works include the play *A Month in the Country* 1849, and the novels *A Nest of Gentlefolk* 1858, *Fathers and Sons* 1862, and *Virgin Soil* 1877. His series of *A Sportsman's Sketches* 1852 criticized serfdom.

Turgot /tjʊə'gəʊ/ Anne Robert Jacques 1727–1781. French finance minister 1774–76, whose reforming economies led to his dismissal.

Turin /tjʊ'rɪn/ (Italian *Torino*) capital of Piedmont, NW Italy, on the river Po; population (1988)

turbocharger

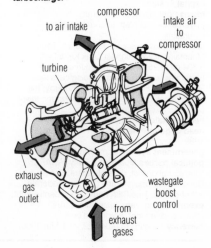

1,025,000. Industries include iron, steel, cars, silk and other textiles, fashion goods, chocolate, and wine. It was the first capital of united Italy 1861–64.

Turing /'tjʊərɪŋ/ Alan Mathison 1912–1954. British mathematician and logician. In 1936 he described a 'universal computing machine' that could theoretically be programmed to solve any problem capable of solution by a specially designed machine. This concept, now called the *Turing machine*, foreshadowed the digital computer.

He is also believed to have been the first to suggest the possibility of machine learning and artificial intelligence. His test for distinguishing between real (human) and simulated (computer) thought is known as the *Turing test*: a human being is placed in one room, the machine in another, and an interrogator in yet another room asks any questions in order to distinguish between the two. When the interrogator cannot distinguish between them, the machine will have reached a state of human-like intelligence.

During World War II Turing worked on the Ultra project in the team that cracked the German Enigma code. Turing studied at King's College, Cambridge, and became a fellow there in 1935. He studied at Princeton 1936–38.

Turin shroud ancient piece of linen bearing the image of a body, claimed to be that of Jesus. Independent tests carried out 1988 by scientists in Switzerland, the USA, and the UK showed that the cloth of the shroud dated from between 1260 and 1390. The shroud, property of the pope, is kept in Turin Cathedral, Italy.

Turkana, Lake /tɜː'kɑːnə/ formerly *Lake Rudolf* lake in the Great Rift Valley, 375 m/1,230 ft above sea level, with its northernmost end in Ethiopia and

the rest in Kenya; area 9,000 sq km/3,475 sq mi. It is saline, and shrinking by evaporation. Its shores were an early human hunting ground, and valuable remains have been found which are accurately datable because of undisturbed stratification.

Turkestan /,tɜːkɪ'stɑːn/ the area of central Asia divided among USSR (Kazakh, Kirghiz, Tadzhik, Turkmen and Uzbek republics), Afghanistan, and China (part of Xinjiang Uygur).

turkey bird related to the pheasants. The wild turkey reaches a length of 1.3 m/4.3 ft, and is native to North and Central American woodlands. The domesticated turkey *Meleagris gallopavo* derives from the American wild species. The ocellated turkey is found in Central America.

The common turkey was introduced to Europe in the 16th century. Since World War II, it has been intensively bred, in the same way as chicken. It is gregarious, except at breeding time.

Turkey /'tɜːki/ country between the Black Sea and the Mediterranean, bounded to the E by the USSR and Iran, to the S by Iraq and Syria.

government The constitution of 1982 provides for a single-chamber legislature of 450 members, the National Assembly, and a president who is both head of state and head of government. The president is elected by the assembly for a seven-year term. The assembly is elected by universal suffrage for a five-year term.

history The Turks originally came from Mongolia and spread into Turkestan in the 6th century AD. During the 7th century they adopted Islam. In 1055 the ◊Seljuk Turks secured political control of the caliphate, and established an empire in Asia Minor. The ◊Ottoman Turks, driven from central Asia by the Mongols, entered the service of the Seljuks, and Osman I founded a kingdom

turkey

of his own 1299. Having overrun Asia Minor, the Ottomans began their European conquests by seizing Gallipoli 1354, captured Constantinople 1453, and by 1480 were masters of the Balkans. By 1550 they had conquered Egypt, Syria, Arabia, Mesopotamia, Tripoli, and most of Hungary; thereafter the empire ceased to expand, although Cyprus was taken 1571 and Crete 1669.

The Christian counter-offensive opened 1683 with the defeat of the Turks before Vienna; in 1699 the Turks lost Hungary, and in 1774 Russia ousted them from Moldavia, Wallachia, and the Crimea. In the Balkans there was an unsuccessful revolt in Serbia 1804, but in 1821–29 Greece threw off Turkish rule. Russia's attempts to exploit this situation were resisted by Britain and France, which in the Crimean War (1854–56) fought on the Turkish side. The Bulgarian rising of 1876 led to a new war between Turkey and Russia, and by the Treaty of Berlin 1878 Turkey lost Bulgaria, Bosnia, and Herzegovina. A militant nationalist group, the Young Turks, secured the grant of a constitution 1908; Italy took advantage of the ensuing crisis to seize Tripoli in 1911–12, while the Balkan states in 1912–13 expelled the Turks from Albania and Macedonia. Turkey entered World War I on the German side 1914, only to lose Syria, Arabia, Mesopotamia, and its nominal suzerainty in Egypt.

The Greek occupation of Izmir 1919 provoked the establishment of a nationalist congress with Mustafa Kemal (◊Atatürk) as president. Having defeated Italian and French forces, he expelled the Greeks 1922. Peace was concluded 1923 with the Treaty of ◊Lausanne and Turkey was proclaimed an independent republic with Kemal as its first president. He introduced a policy of westernization and a new legal code. He died 1938 but his People's Party remained in power.

Turkey's first free elections were held 1950 and won by the Democratic Party (DP), led by Celal Bayar and Adnan Menderes. Bayar became president and Menderes prime minister. In 1960, after a military coup, President Bayar was imprisoned and Menderes executed. A new constitution was adopted 1961 and civilian rule restored, but with the leader of the coup, Gen Cemal Gursel, as president. There followed a series of civilian governments, led mainly by the veteran politician Ismet Inonu until 1965, when the Justice Party (JP), led by Suleyman Demirel, came to power. Prompted by strikes and student unrest, the army forced Demirel to resign 1971 and for the next two years the country came under military rule again.

A civilian government was restored 1973, a coalition led by Bulent Ecevit. The following year Turkey sent troops to Cyprus to protect the Turkish-Cypriot community, resulting in the effective partition of the island. Ecevit's government fell when he refused to annexe N Cyprus and in 1975 Suleyman Demirel returned at the head of a right-wing coalition. Elections held 1977 were inconclusive and Demirel precariously held on to power until 1978 when Ecevit returned, leading another coalition. He was faced with a

Turkey
Republic of
(Türkiye Cumhuriyeti)

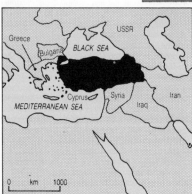

area 779,500 sq km/300,965 sq mi
capital Ankara
towns ports Istanbul and Izmir
physical central plateau surrounded by mountains
features Bosporus and Dardanelles; Taurus Mountains in SW (highest peak Kaldi Daĝ, 3,734 m/12,255 ft); in E the sources of the Euphrates and Tigris. Archaeological sites include Catal Hüyük, Ephesus, and Troy; the rock villages of Cappadocia, and historic towns (Antioch, Iskenderun, Tarsus)
head of state Turgut Ozal from 1989
head of government Vildirim Akbulut from 1989
government system democratic republic
political parties Motherland Party (ANAP), Islamic, nationalist, right-of-centre; Social Democratic Populist Party (SDPP), moderate, left-of-centre; True Path Party (TPP), centre-right
exports cotton, yarn, hazelnuts, citrus, tobacco, dried fruit, chromium ores
currency Turkish lira (4040.52 = £1 Mar 1990)

population (1989) 55,377,000 (85% Turkish, 12% Kurdish); annual growth rate 2.1%
life expectancy men 60, women 63
language Turkish (official; related to Mongolian, but written in the Western Latin script), Kurdish Arabic
religion Sunni Muslim
literacy 86% male/62% female (1985)
GNP $58 bn (1983); $1,000 per head of population
chronology
1919–22 Turkish War of Independence provoked by Greek occupation of Izmir. Mustafa Kemal (Atatürk), leader of nationalist congress, defeated Italian, French, and Greek forces.
1923 Treaty of Lausanne established Turkey as independent republic under Kemal. Westernization began.
1950 First free elections; Adnan Menderes became prime minister.
1960 Menderes executed after military coup by Gen Cemal Gürsel.
1965 Suleyman Demirel became prime minister.
1971 Army forced Demirel to resign.
1973 Civilian rule returned under Bulent Ecevit.
1974 Turkish troops sent to protect the Turkish community in Cyprus.
1975 Demirel returned at the head of a right-wing coalition.
1978 Ecevit returned, in the face of economic difficulties and factional violence.
1979 Demeril returned. Violence grew.
1980 Army took over and Bulent Ulusu became prime minister. Harsh repression of political activists attracted international criticism.
1982 New constitution adopted.
1983 Ban on political activity lifted. Turgut Ozal became prime minister.
1987 Ozal maintained his majority in general election.
1988 Improved relations and talks with Greece.
1989 Turgot Ozal elected president; Turkey's application for EC membership refused

deteriorating economy and outbreaks of sectional violence and by 1979 had lost his working majority and resigned.

Demirel returned in Nov but the violence continued and in Sept l980 the army stepped in and set up a national security council (NSC), with Bulent Ulusu as prime minister. Martial law was imposed, political activity suspended and a harsh regime established. Strong international pressure was put on Turkey to return to a more democratic system of government and work was begun on a new constitution. In May 1983 political parties were allowed to operate again. The old parties reformed under new names and in Nov three of them fought the assembly elections: the conservative Motherland Party (ANAP), the Nationalist Democracy Party (MDP), and the Populist Party (SDHP). ANAP won 212 assembly seats, SDHP 117, and MDP 71, and ANAP's leader, Turgut Ozal, became prime minister. Since 1984 there has been guerrilla fighting in ◊Kurdistan and a separatist Kurdish Workers' Party (PKK) is active.

After World War II Turkey felt itself threatened by the USSR and joined a number of collective defence organizations, including NATO 1952 and the Baghdad Pact 1955, which became the Central Treaty Organization (CENTO) 1959 and was dissolved 1979. Turkey strengthened Western links and by 1987 was making overtures to the European Community. Turkey has long been criticized for the harshness of its penal system and its violation of human rights. Its future role will depend on its willingness and ability to create a more humane and fully democratic system of government, but, despite significant advances since 1983, at the end of 1989 it learned that its application for membership of the European Community had been refused and would not be considered until at least the mid-1990s.

Turkish language a language of central and W Asia, the national language of Turkey. Originally written in Arabic script, the Turkish of Turkey has been written in a variant of the Roman alphabet since 1928. Varieties of Turkish are spoken in NW Iran and several of the Asian republics of the USSR, and all have been influenced by Arabic and Persian.

Turkish literature for centuries Turkish literature was based on Persian models, but under ◊Suleiman the Great (1494–1566) the Golden Age began of which the poet Fuzuli (died 1563) is the great exemplar, and which continued in the following century with the great poet satirist Nef'i of Erzerum (died 1635) and others. During the 19th century westernization overtook Turkish literature, for example the following of French models by Ibrahim Shinasi Effendi (1826–71), poet and prose writer, who was co-founder of the New School with Mehmed Namik Kemal (1840–80), poet and author of the revolutionary play *Vatan/The Fatherland*, which led to his exile by the sultan. Unlike these the poet Tevfik Fikret (1867–1915) turned rather to Persian and Arabic than to native sources for his vocabulary. The poet Mehmed Akif (1873–1936) was the author of the words of the Turkish national anthem; and the best-known contemporary poet and novelist is Yashar Kemal (1923–), whose novels describe the hard life of the peasant (*Memed, My Hawk* 1955 and *The Wind from the Plain* 1961).

Turkmenistan /ˌtɜːkmenɪˈstɑːn/ constituent republic of the USSR from 1924, part of Soviet Central Asia
area 488,100 sq km/188,455 sq mi
capital Ashkhabad
features Kara Kum 'Black Sands' desert, which occupies most of the republic, area about 310,800 sq km/120,000 sq mi (on its edge is *Altyn Depe*, 'golden hill', site of a ruined city with a ◊ziggurat excavated from 1967); river Amu Darya
products silk, sheep, astrakhan fur, carpets, oil, chemicals
population (1987) 3,361,000; 69% Turkmenian, 13% Russian, 9% Uzbek, 3% Kazakh

Turner The 'Fighting Téméraire' *(1838) Tate Gallery, London.*

language West Turkic, closely related to ◊Turkish
religion Sunni Muslim.

Turkoman person of Turkoman culture. They live around the Kara Kum desert, to the E of the Caspian Sea, and straddle the borders of Afghanistan, Iran, and the USSR. Their language belongs to the Turkic branch of the Altaic family.

Turks and Caicos Islands /tɜːks, ˈkeɪkɒs/ a British crown colony in the West Indies, the SE archipelago of the Bahamas
area 430 sq km/166 sq mi
capital Cockburn Town on Grand Turk
features a group of 30 islands, of which six are inhabited. The largest is the uninhabited *Grand Caicos*; others include *Grand Turk* (population 3,100), *South Caicos* (1,400), *Middle Caicos* (400), *North Caicos* (1,300), *Providenciales* (1,000), and *Salt Cay* (300); since 1982 the Turks and Caicos have developed as a tax haven
exports crayfish and conch (flesh and shell)
currency US dollar
population (1980) 7,500, 90% of African descent
language English, French Creole
religion Christian
government governor, with executive and legislative councils (chief minister from 1985 Nathaniel Francis, Progressive National Party)
history secured by Britain 1766 against French and Spanish claims, the islands were a Jamaican dependency 1873–1962, and in 1976 attained internal self-government. The chief minister, Norman Saunders, resigned 1985 after his arrest in Miami on drugs charges, of which he was convicted.

Turku /ˈtʊəkuː/ (Swedish *Åbo*) port in SW Finland, near the mouth of the river Aura, on the Gulf of Bothnia; population (1988) 262,000. Industries include shipbuilding, engineering, textiles, and food processing. It was the capital of Finland until 1812.

turmeric perennial plant *Curcuma longa* of the ginger family, native to India; also the ground powder from its tuberous rhizomes, used in curries to give a yellow colour, and as a dyestuff.

Turner /ˈtɜːnə/ Eva 1892– . English soprano. She was prima donna of the Carl Rosa Opera Company 1916–24.

Turner /ˈtɜːnə/ Frederick Jackson 1861–1932. US historian, professor at Harvard 1910–1924. He was the author of a thesis (first presented to the American Historical Association 1893) concerning the significance of the frontier in US historical development. It attributed the distinctive character of US society to the influence of changing frontiers over three centuries of westward expansion.

Turner /ˈtɜːnə/ John Napier 1929– . Canadian Liberal politician, prime minister 1984. He was elected to the House of Commons 1962 and served in the cabinet of Pierre Trudeau, until resigning 1975. He succeeded Trudeau as party leader and prime minister 1984, but lost the 1984 and 1988 elections. Turner resigned as leader 1989, and returned to his law practice. He was replaced as Liberal Party chief by Herbert Gray in Feb 1990.

Turner /ˈtɜːnə/ Joseph Mallord William 1775–1851. English landscape painter. He travelled widely in Europe, and his landscapes became increasingly Romantic, with the subject often transformed in scale and flooded with brilliant, hazy light. Many later works appear to anticipate Impressionism, for example *Rain, Steam and Speed* 1844 (National Gallery, London).

A precocious talent, Turner went to the Royal Academy schools in 1789. In 1792 he made the first of several European tours, from which numerous watercolour sketches survive. His early oil paintings show Dutch influence, but by the 1800s he had begun to paint landscapes in the grand manner, reflecting the styles of ◊Claude Lorrain and Richard ◊Wilson. His use of colour was enhanced by trips to Italy (1819, 1828, 1835, 1840), and

Turkmenistan

Ashkhabad

his brushwork became increasingly free. Early in his career he was encouraged by the portraitist Thomas Lawrence and others, but he failed to achieve much recognition and became a reclusive figure. Much later he was championed by the critic John Ruskin in his book *Modern Painters* 1843.

Many of Turner's most dramatic works are set in Europe or at sea, for example *Snowstorm: Hannibal Crossing the Alps* 1812 (Tate Gallery, London), *The Slave Ship* 1839 (Museum of Fine Arts, Boston, Massachusetts), and *Shipwreck* 1805 (Tate Gallery). He was also devoted to literary themes and mythologies, for example *Ulysses Deriding Polyphemus* (Tate Gallery). In 1987 the Clore Gallery extension to the Tate Gallery, London, was opened to display the collection of his works he left to the nation.

Turner /'tɜ:nə/ Lana (Julia Jean Mildred Frances) 1920– . US actress who appeared in melodramatic films of the 1940s and 1950s such as *Peyton Place* 1957. Her other films include *The Postman Always Rings Twice* 1946, *The Three Musketeers* 1948, and *Imitation of Life* 1959.

Turner /'tɜ:nə/ Nat 1800–1831. US slave and Baptist preacher, who led 60 slaves in the most important US slave revolt—the **Southampton Insurrection** of 1831—in Southampton County, Virginia. Before he and 16 of the others were hanged, at least 55 people had been killed.

Turner /'tɜ:nə/ Tina. Adopted name of Annie Mae Bullock 1938– . US rhythm-and-blues singer who recorded 1960–76 with her husband, Ike Turner (1931–), notably *River Deep, Mountain High* 1966, produced by Phil Spector. Tina Turner had success in the 1980s as a solo performer, for example *Private Dancer* 1984.

turnip biennial plant *Brassica rapa* cultivated in temperate regions for its edible white- or yellow-fleshed root and the young leaves, which are used as a green vegetable. Closely allied to it is the ◊swede *Brassica napus*.

turnstone wading bird *Arenaria interpres*, which breeds in the Arctic and migrates to the S hemisphere. It is seen on rocky beaches, turning over stones for small crustaceans and insects. It is about 23 cm/9 in long, has a summer plumage of black and chestnut above, white below, and is duller in winter.

turpentine solution of resins distilled from the sap of conifers, used in varnish and as a paint solvent, but now largely replaced by ◊white spirit.

Turpin /'tɜ:pɪn/ Ben 1940–1974. US comedian, a star of silent films. His trademark was being cross-eyed, and he parodied screen stars and their films. His work includes *The Shriek of Araby* 1923, *A Harem Knight* 1926, and *Broke in China* 1927.

Turpin /'tɜ:pɪn/ Dick 1706–1739. English highwayman. The son of an innkeeper, he turned to highway robbery, cattle-thieving, and smuggling, and was hanged.

turquoise a mineral, hydrous basic copper aluminium phosphate. Blue-green, blue, or green, it is a gemstone. Turquoise is found in Iran, Turkestan, Mexico, and southwestern USA.

turtle freshwater and marine reptiles, whose bodies are protected by shells. They are related to tortoises, and some species can grow to a length of up to 2.5 m/8 ft. They are excellent swimmers, having legs which are modified to oar-like flippers, but which make them awkward on land. The shell is more streamlined and lighter than that of the tortoise. They often travel long distances to lay their eggs on the beaches where they were born.

Species include the green turtle *Chelonia mydas*; the loggerhead *Caretta caretta*; the giant leathery *Dermochelys coriacea* which can weigh half a tonne; and the hawksbill *Eretmochelys imbricata*. Like many species of turtle, the hawksbill is now endangered, mainly through being hunted for its shell, which provides 'tortoise-shell'. Other turtles have suffered through destruction of their breeding sites (often for tourist developments) and egg-collecting.

Turner *US singer Tina Turner in London, 1986.*

Tuscan in classical architecture, one of the five types of ◊column. See ◊order.

Tuscany /'tʌskəni/ (Italian **Toscana**) region of central Italy; area 23,000 sq km/8,878 sq mi; population (1988) 3,568,000. Its capital is Florence, and towns include Pisa, Livorno, and Siena. The area is mainly agricultural, with many vineyards, especially in the Chianti hills; it also has lignite and iron mines, and marble quarries. The Tuscan dialect has been adopted as the standard form of Italian. Tuscany was formerly the Roman *Etruria* (see ◊Etruscan). In medieval times the area was divided into small states, united under Florentine rule during the 15th–16th centuries. It became part of united Italy 1861.

Tussaud /'tu:səu/ Madame (Anne Marie Grosholtz) 1761–1850. French wax-modeller. In 1802 she established an exhibition of wax models of famous people in London. It was destroyed by fire 1925, but reopened 1928.

Born in Strasbourg, she went to Paris 1766 to live with her wax-modeller uncle, Philippe Curtius, whom she soon surpassed in technique. During the French Revolution they were forced to take death masks of many victims and leaders (some still exist in the Chamber of Horrors).

Originally housed in the Strand, the exhibition was transferred to Baker Street in 1883 and to its present site in Marylebone Road in 1884.

Tutankhamen /,tu:tən'kɑ:men/ c. 1360–1350 BC. King of Egypt of the 18th dynasty. A son of Ikhnaton or of Amenhotep III, he was probably about 11 at his accession. In 1922 his tomb was discovered by the British archaeologists Lord Carnarvon and Howard Carter in the Valley of the Kings at Luxor, almost untouched by tomb robbers. The contents included many works of art and his solid-gold coffin, which are now displayed in Cairo museum.

Tutin /'tju:tɪn/ Dorothy 1930– . British actress, whose roles include most of Shakespeare's leading heroines (including Portia, Viola, and Juliet) for the Royal Shakespeare Company and Lady Macbeth for the National Theatre Company.

Tutu /'tu:tu:/ Desmond (Mpilo) 1931– . South African priest, Anglican archbishop of Cape Town and general secretary of the South African Council of Churches. He is one of the leading figures in the struggle against apartheid in the

Republic of South Africa. Nobel Peace Prize 1984.

Tuva /'tu:və/ (Russian **Tuvinskaya**) autonomous republic (administrative unit) of the USSR, NW of Mongolia, **capital** Kyzyl

area 170,500 sq km/65,813 sq mi

population (1986) 284,000

features good pasture; gold, asbestos, cobalt

history part of Mongolia until 1911 and declared a Russian protectorate 1914, after the 1917 revolution it became the independent Tannu-Tuva republic 1920, until incorporated in the USSR as an autonomous region 1944. It was made the Tuva Autonomous Republic 1961.

Tuvalu /,tu:və'lu:/ country in the SW Pacific, on the former Ellice Islands; part of ◊Polynesia.

government The constitution dates from 1978 when Tuvalu became an independent state within the Commonwealth, accepting the British monarch as head of state represented by a resident governor-general, who must be a Tuvaluan citizen and is appointed on the recommendation of the prime minister.

There is a single-chamber parliament of 12 members and a prime minister and cabinet elected by and responsible to it. Members of Parliament are elected by universal suffrage for a four-year term. There are no political parties. Each of the inhabited atolls of the Tuvalu group has its own elected island council, responsible for local affairs.

history The islands were invaded and occupied by Samoans during the 16th century and were later first reached by Europeans in 1765. During the mid-19th century European slave traders captured the indigenous Melanesians for forced labour on plantations in South America. As a result of this, and the importation of European diseases, the population declined from an estimated 20,000 to barely 3,000. Originally known as the Ellice Islands, they were a British protectorate 1892–1915 and part of the Gilbert and Ellice Islands colony 1915–75, when they became a separate British colony.

In 1978 the Ellice Islands became fully independent within the Commonwealth, reverting to their old name of Tuvalu, meaning 'eight standing together'. Because of its small size, Tuvalu is a 'special member' of the Commonwealth and does not have direct representation at meetings of heads of government. Its first prime minister was Toaripi Lauti, replaced 1981 as a result of his involvement in an alleged investment scandal, by Dr Tomasi Pupaua who was re-elected 1985. In 1986

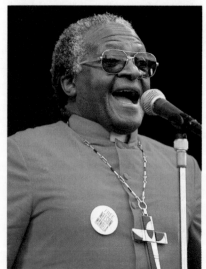

Tutu *South African Anglican archbishop Desmond Tutu. A prominent civil-rights campaigner, he is pictured speaking at Nelson Mandela's 70th-birthday concert in 1988.*

turtle *common mud turtle*

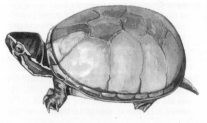

Tuvalu
South West Pacific State of

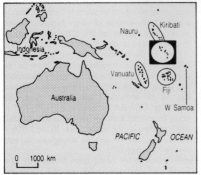

area 25 sq km/9.5 sq mi
capital Funafuti
physical low coral atolls in Polynesia
features the name means 'cluster of eight' islands (there are actually nine, but one is very small)

head of state Elizabeth II from 1978 represented by Tupua Leupena from 1986
head of government Bikenibeu Paeniu from 1989
government system liberal democracy
political parties none, members are elected to parliament as independents.
exports phosphates, copra, handicrafts, stamps
currency Australian dollar (2.23 = £1 Mar 1990)
population (1989) 9,000 (mainly Polynesian); annual growth rate 3.4%
language Tuvaluan and English
religion Christian, chiefly Protestant
literacy 96% (1979)
GDP (1983) $711 per head of population
chronology
1978 Achieved full independence within the Commonwealth with Toaripi Lauti as prime minister.
1981 Dr Tomasi Puapua replaced Lauti as premier
1986 Islanders rejected proposal for republican status.
1989 Bikenibeu Paeniu elected new prime minister

a poll was taken to decide whether Tuvalu should remain a constitutional monarchy or become a republic. Only one atoll favoured republican status. Following new elections in Sept 1989, Puapua was replaced as prime minister by Bikenibeu Paeniu, whose new administration pledged to reduce the country's dependence on foreign aid, which contributes more than a quarter of Gross Domestic Product.

TVEI (Technical and Vocational Education Initiative) in the UK, scheme funded by the Training Commission, and intended to provide secondary schools with equipment and teaching expertise to allow them to expand their vocational and technical courses for 14–18-year-olds.

Tver /tveə/ former name (until 1932) of ◊Kalinin, a city in the USSR.

TVP abbreviation for *Texturized Vegetable Protein*, a meat substitute made usually from soya beans. In manufacture, the soya-bean solids (what remains after oil has been removed) are ground finely and mixed with a binder to form a sticky mixture. This is forced through a spinneret and extruded into fibres, which are treated with salts and flavourings, wound into hanks, and then chopped up to resemble meat chunks.

Twain /tweɪn/ Mark. Pen name of Samuel Langhorne Clemens 1835–1910. US humorous writer. He established his reputation with the comic *The Innocents Abroad* 1869, and two children's books, *The Adventures of Tom Sawyer* 1876 and *The Adventures of Huckleberry Finn* 1885. He also wrote satire, as in *A Connecticut Yankee at King Arthur's Court* 1889.

Tweed /twiːd/ river rising in SW Borders region, Scotland, and entering the North Sea at Berwick-upon-Tweed, Northumberland; length 156 km/97 mi.

tweed cloth made of woollen yarn, usually of several shades, but in its original form without regular pattern and woven on a hand loom in the remoter parts of Ireland, Wales, and Scotland.

Harris Tweed is made on the island of Harris in the Outer Hebrides; it is highly durable and largely weatherproof. Nowadays it is often machine-woven, patterned, and processed.

Twelfth Day the 12th and final day of the Christmas celebrations, 6 Jan; the feast of the ◊Epiphany.

Twelfth Night a comedy by William Shakespeare, performed 1601–02. The plot builds on misunderstandings and mistaken identity, leading to the successful romantic unions of Sebastian and his twin sister Viola with Olivia and Duke Orsino respectively, and the downfall of Olivia's steward Malvolio.

Twelver member of a Shi'ite Muslim sect who believes that the 12th imam (Islamic leader) did not die, but is waiting to return towards the end of the world as the Mahdi, the 'rightly guided one', to establish a reign of peace and justice on Earth.

twelve-tone system or ***twelve-note system*** a system of musical composition in which the 12 notes of the chromatic scale are arranged in a particular order, called a 'series' or 'tone-row'. A work using the system consists of restatements of the series in any of its formations. ◊Schoenberg and ◊Webern were exponents of this technique.

Twentieth Century Fox US film production company, formed 1935 when the Fox Company merged with Twentieth Century. Its president was Joseph Schenck (1878–1961), and Darryl Zanuck (1902–1979) was vice-president in charge of production. The company made high-quality films and, despite a financial crisis in the early 1960s, is still a major studio. Recent successes include the *Star Wars* trilogy (1977–1983).

Twickenham /'twɪkənəm/ district in the Greater London borough of ◊Richmond-upon-Thames.

Twickenham England international rugby ground, laid out on 4.2 hectares of land in SW London at the suggestion of local athlete Billy Williams. The first international was held there in 1910. The Rugby Football Union have their headquarters at Twickenham and the Harlequins club play some of their home matches there.

The ground was originally an allotment and was known affectionately as 'Billy Williams' Cabbage Patch'.

Twain *US novelist Mark Twain.*

twin one of two young produced from a single pregnancy. Human twins may be genetically identical, having been formed from one fertilized egg which split into two cells, both of which became implanted. Non-identical twins are formed when two eggs are fertilized at the same time.

twitch alternative common name for ◊couch grass.

two-stroke cycle an operating cycle for internal combustion piston engines. The engine cycle is completed after just two strokes (movement up or down) of the piston unlike the more common ◊four-stroke cycle. All lightweight motorbikes use two-stroke petrol engines, which are cheaper and simpler than four-strokes.

Most marine diesel engines are also two-strokes. In a typical two-stroke motorbike engine, fuel mixture is drawn into the crankcase as the piston moves up on its first stroke to compress the mixture above it. Then the compressed mixture is ignited and hot gases are produced, which drive the piston down on its second stroke. As it moves down, it uncovers an opening (port) that allows the fresh fuel mixture in the crankcase to flow into the combustion space above the piston. At the same time the exhaust gases leave through another port.

TX abbreviation for ◊*Texas*.

Tyburn /'taɪbən/ stream in London, England (now underground) near which (at the junction of Oxford Street and Edgware Road) Tyburn gallows stood from the 12th century until 1783.

tycoon a person who has acquired great wealth through business achievements. Examples include J Pierpont ◊Morgan (1837–1913) and J D ◊Rockefeller (1839–1937).

Tyler /'taɪlə/ John 1790–1862. 10th president of the USA 1841–45, succeeding Benjamin ◊Harrison, who died after only a month in office. His government annexed Texas 1845.

Tyler /'taɪlə/ Wat. English leader of the ◊Peasants' Revolt of 1381. He was probably born in Kent or Essex, and may have served in the French wars. After taking Canterbury he led the peasant army to Blackheath and occupied London. At Mile End King Richard II met the rebels and promised to redress their grievances, which included the imposition of a poll tax. At a further conference at Smithfield, Tyler was murdered.

Tynan /'taɪnən/ Kenneth 1927–1980. British author and theatre critic, a leading cultural figure of the radical 1960s. He devised the nude revue *Oh Calcutta!* 1969, first staged in New York.

Tyndale /'tɪndl/ William 1492–1536. English translator of the Bible. The printing of his New Testament (basis of the Authorized Version) was begun in Cologne 1525, and, after he had been forced to flee, completed in Worms. He was strangled and burned as a heretic at Vilvorde in Belgium.

Tyndall /'tɪndl/ John 1820–1893. Irish physicist, who in 1869 studied the scattering of light by invisibly small suspended particles. Known as the ***Tyndall effect***, it was first observed with ◊colloidal solutions, in which a beam of light is made visible when it is scattered by minute colloidal particles (whereas a pure solvent does not scatter light). Similar scattering of blue wavelengths of sunlight by particles in the atmosphere makes the sky look blue (beyond the atmosphere, the sky is black).

Tyne /taɪn/ river of NE England formed by the union of the N Tyne (rising in the Cheviot Hills) and S Tyne (rising in Cumbria) near Hexham, Northumberland, and reaching the North Sea at Tynemouth; length 72 km/45 mi. Kielder Water (1980) in the N Tyne Valley is Europe's largest artificial lake, 12 km/7.5 mi long and 0.8 km/0.5 mi wide, and supplies the industries of Tyneside, Wearside, and Teesside.

Tyne and Wear /taɪn, wɪə/ metropolitan county in NE England, created 1974, originally administered by an elected metropolitan council; its powers reverted to district councils 1986
area 540 sq km/208 sq mi

towns administrative headquarters Newcastle-upon-Tyne; South Shields, Gateshead, Sunderland

features bisected by the rivers Tyne and Wear; includes part of ◊Hadrian's Wall; Newcastle and Gateshead are linked with each other and with the coast on both sides by the Tyne and Wear Metro (a light railway using existing suburban lines, extending 54 km/34 mi beneath both cities)

products once a centre of heavy industry, it is now being redeveloped and diversified

population (1987) 1,136,000

famous people Thomas Bewick, Robert Stephenson, Harry Patterson/'Jack Higgins'.

Tynemouth /ˈtaɪnmaʊθ, ˈtɪnməθ/ port and resort in Tyne and Wear, England; population (1985) 9,442.

Tynwald /ˈtɪnwəld/ the parliament of the ◊Isle of Man.

typeface a style of printed lettering. Books, newspapers, and other printed matter are produced in different styles of lettering; examples include Times and Baskerville. These different 'families' of alphabets have been designed over the centuries since printing was invented and each has distinguishing characteristics.

Famous typeface designers include John ◊Baskerville and Edward Johnston, who designed the lettering used by London Transport. See also ◊typography.

type metal an ◊alloy of tin, lead, and antimony, used for making the metal type printers use.

typesetting the means by which text is prepared for ◊printing, now usually carried out by computer. Text is keyed on a typesetting machine in a similar way to typing. Laser or light impulses are projected onto light-sensitive film which when developed can be used to make plates for printing.

typewriter a hand-operated machine for producing characters on paper. The first practicable typewriter was built 1867 at Milwaukee, Wisconsin, USA, by C L Sholes, C Glidden, and S W Soulé. By 1874 E Remington and Sons, the gun makers whose name was soon given to the typewriters, produced under contract the first machines for sale.

The QWERTY keyboard was designed 1873 by Christopher Sholes in order to slow down typists who were too fast for their mechanical keyboards. Later developments include tabulators from about 1898, portable machines about 1907, gradual introduction of electrical operation (allowing increased speed, since the keys are touched not depressed), proportional spacing 1940, and rotating typehead with stationary plates 1962. More recent typewriters work electronically. They can be equipped with a memory, and be given an interface which enables them to be connected to a computer.

typhoid fever infectious disease caused by the bacterium *Salmonella typhi*, and usually contracted through contaminated food or fluids. It is characterized by fever, and damage to internal organs, mainly the spleen and intestine. Treatment is with antibiotics.

The combined TAB vaccine protects both against this and the milder, related condition known as **paratyphoid fever**.

typhoon violently revolving storm, a type of ◊cyclone.

typhus an infectious disease, often fatal, caused by a microbe carried in the excreta of lice. It enters the body usually by abrasions in the feet, and is epidemic among human beings in overcrowded conditions. Treatment is by antibiotics.

typography the design and layout of the printed word. Typography began with the invention of writing and developed as printing spread throughout Europe following the invention of metal moveable type by Johann ◊Gutenberg about 1440. Hundreds of variations have followed since, but the basic design of the Frenchman Nicholas Jensen (*c.*1420–80), with a few modifications, is still in use today as the ordinary ('roman') type used in printing.

In Britain, type sizes are measured in points (there are approximately 2.8 points to the millimetre); the length of a typeset line, called the measure, is measured in pica ems (1 pica em has a width of a little over 4 mm/0.15 in). The space between lines (known as leading) is also measured in points, although new photosetting and computer-assisted setting systems also work in metric sizes.

Tyr /tɪə/ in Norse mythology, the god of battles, whom the Anglo-Saxons called Týw, hence 'Tuesday'.

tyrannosaurus largest known meat-eating dinosaur, which lived in North America about 70 million years ago. It had two feet, was up to 15 m/50 ft long, 6.5 m/20 ft tall, weighed 10 tonnes, and had teeth 15 cm/6 in long.

tyre (North American *tire*) the rubber hoop fitted round the rims of bicycle, car, and other road-vehicle wheels. The first pneumatic rubber tyre was patented by R W Thompson 1845, but it was John Boyd Dunlop of Belfast who independently re-invented pneumatic tyres for use with bicycles 1888–89.

Tyre /ˈtaɪə/ (Arabic *Sur* or *Soûr*) town in SW Lebanon, about 80 km/50 mi south of Beirut, formerly a port until its harbour silted up; population about 14,000. It stands on the site of the ancient city of the same name, a seaport of ◊Phoenicia.

Built on the mainland and two small islands, the city was a commercial centre, known for its purple dye. Besieged and captured by Alexander the Great 333–332 BC, it came under Roman rule 64 BC and was taken by the Arabs AD 638. The Crusaders captured it 1124, and it never recovered from the destruction it suffered when retaken by the Arabs 1291. In the 1970s it became a Palestinian guerrilla stronghold, and was shelled by Israel 1979.

Tyrell British motor racing team founded by Ken Tyrell 1970 although he had run the Matra and March teams in the two previous seasons. He formed a partnership with Jackie Stewart and the famous driver won all three of his world titles in Tyrell-run teams. Tyrell's only Constructor's title was in 1971.

When turbo-charged cars took over Grand Prix racing in the late 1970s, Tyrell continued with his normally aspirated engines which were not competitive enough. He changed to turbo power too late and his cars have struggled to compete with ◊Williams's and ◊McLaren's in recent years. They were banned 1984 following a dispute over the octane rating of the cars, but subsequently cleared.

Tyrol a variant spelling of ◊Tirol, state of Austria.

Tyrone /tɪˈrəʊn/ county of Northern Ireland
area 3,160 sq km/1,220 sq mi
towns county town Omagh; Dungannon, Strabane, Cookstown
features rivers Derg, Blackwater, and Foyle; Lough Neagh
products mainly agricultural
population (1981) 144,000

Tyne and Wear

typewriter *Today's streamlined electronic models are a far cry from this Waverley typewriter of 1895, but the principle of a hand-operated machine for producing printed characters on paper remains the same. Contemporary versions are often linked to a computer.*

Tyson *US boxer and former heavyweight champion of the world, Mike Tyson.*

Tyson /ˈtaɪsən/ Mike 1966– . US heavyweight champion boxer. He won the WBC heavyweight title 1986 when he beat Trevor Berbick to become the youngest world heavyweight champion. He beat James 'Bonecrusher' Smith for the WBA title 1987 and later that year he became the first undisputed champion since 1978 when he beat Tony Tucker for the IBF title. He was undefeated until 1990 when he was lost the championship to a relative outsider, James 'Buster' Douglas.

He turned professional 1985. Fifteen of his first 25 opponents were knocked out in the first round.

Tyumen /tjuːˈmen/ oldest town in Siberia, central USSR (founded 1586), on the river Nitsa; population (1987) 456,000. Industries include oil refining, machine tools, and chemicals.

Tyuratam /ˌtjuərəˈtaːm/ site of the ◊Baikonur Cosmodrome.

Tywi /ˈtaʊi/ or *Towy* river in Dyfed, SW Wales; length 108 km/68 mi. It rises in the Cambrian Mountains of central Wales, flowing SW to enter Camarthen Bay.

Tzu-Hsi /ˌtsuːˈʃiː/ former spelling of ◊Zi Xi, dowager empress of China.

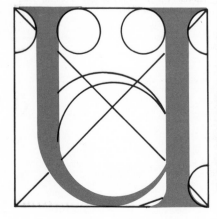

U2 *Irish rock band U2, who became international stars in the 1980s.*

Uccello *St George and the Dragon (c.1460) National Gallery, London.*

U the 21st letter of the English alphabet, and the 20th in the ancient Roman, in which it was identical with V. U and V were not definitely separated in English dictionaries until the 19th century. U has various sounds, as in the pronunciation of the English words *truth, bull, duke, busy, bury*.

U-2 a US military reconnaissance aeroplane, used in clandestine flights over the USSR from 1956 to photograph military installations. In 1960 a U-2 was shot down over the USSR and the pilot, Gary Powers, was captured and imprisoned. He was exchanged for a Soviet agent two years later.

The U-2 affair led to greatly increased Soviet arms spending in the 1960s and 1970s. U-2 flights in 1962 revealed the construction of Soviet missile bases in Cuba. Designed by Richard Bissell, the U-2 flew higher (21,000 m/70,000 ft) and further (3,500 km/2,200 mi) than any previous plane.

U2 Irish rock group formed 1977 by singer Bono Vox (Paul Hewson, 1960–), guitarist Dave 'The Edge' Evans (1961–), bassist Adam Clayton (1960–), and drummer Larry Mullen (1961–). Committed Christians, they play socially concerned stadium rock, and their albums include *The Unforgettable Fire* 1984, *The Joshua Tree* 1987, and the soundtrack from their documentary film *Rattle and Hum* 1988.

uakari rare South American monkey, genus *Cacajao*, of which there are three species. They have bald faces and long fur. About 55 cm/1.8 ft long in head and body, and with a comparatively short 15 cm/6 in tail, they rarely leap, but are good climbers, remaining in the tops of the trees in swampy forests and feeding largely on fruit. The black uakari is in danger of extinction because it is found in such small numbers already, and the forests where it lives are fast being destroyed.

Ubangi-Shari /uːˈbæŋɡi ˈʃɑːri/ former name for the ◊Central African Republic.

Übermensel (German 'Superman') in the writings of Nietszche the ideal to which humans should aspire,

set out in *Thus Spake Zarathustra* 1883–85. The term was popularised in George Bernard Shaw's play *Man and Superman* 1903.

U-boat (German *Unterseeboot* 'underwater boat') German submarine. In both world wars they were designated U followed by a number.

Uccello /uːˈtʃeləu/ Paolo. Adopted name of Paolo di Dono 1397–1475. Italian painter, active in Florence, celebrated for his early use of perspective. His surviving paintings date from the 1430s onwards. Decorative colour and detail dominate his later pictures. His works include *St George and the Dragon* about 1460 (National Gallery, London).

Uccello is recorded as an apprentice in Ghiberti's workshop in 1407. His fresco *The Deluge* about 1431 (Sta Maria Novella, Florence) shows his concern for pictorial perspective, but in later works this aspect becomes superficial. His three battle scenes painted in the 1450s for the Palazzo Medici, Florence, are now in the Ashmolean Museum, Oxford; National Gallery, London; Louvre, Paris.

Udaipur /uːˈdaɪpʊə/ or *Mecvar* industrial city (cotton, grain) in Rajasthan, India, capital of the former princely state of Udaipur; population (1981) 232,588. It was founded 1568, has several palaces (two on islands in a lake) and the Jagannath Hindu temple 1640.

Udall /ˈjuːdl/ Nicholas 1504–1556. English schoolmaster and playwright. He was the author of *Ralph Roister Doister* about 1553, the first known English comedy.

UDC abbreviation for *urban district council*.

uakari

UDI abbreviation for *unilateral declaration of independence*, usually applied to the declaration of Ian Smith's Rhodesian Front government on 11 Nov 1965, announcing the independence of Rhodesia (now Zimbabwe) from the British crown.

Udine /ˈuːdɪneɪ/ industrial city (chemicals, textiles), NE of Venice, Italy; population (1984) 101,000. Udine was the capital of Friuli in the 13th century, and passed to Venice 1420.

Udmurt /ˈʊdmʊət/ (Russian *Udmurtskaya*) autonomous republic in the W Ural foothills, central USSR
area 42,100 sq km/16,200 sq mi
capital Izhevsk
products timber, flax, potatoes, peat, quartz
population (1985) 1,559,000; Udmurt 33%, Tatar 7%, Russian 58%
history conquered in the 15th–16th centuries; constituted the Votyak Autonomous Region 1920; name changed to Udmurt 1932; Autonomous Republic 1934.

Uelsmann /ˈjuːlzmən/ Jerry 1934– . US photographer noted for his dreamlike images, created by synthesizing many elements into one with great technical skill.

Ufa /uːˈfɑː/ industrial city (engineering, oil refining, petrochemicals, distilling, timber) and capital of the Republic of Bashkir, central USSR, on the river Bielaia, in the W Urals; population (1987) 1,092,000. It was founded by Russia 1574 as a fortress.

Uffizi an art gallery in Florence, Italy. Its collection is one of the finest in Europe, based on that of the Medici family.

Uganda /juːˈɡændə/ landlocked country in E Africa, bounded to the N by Sudan, to the E by Kenya, to the S by Tanzania and Rwanda, and to the W by Zaïre.
government The 1969 constitution provides for a single-chamber national assembly of 126 elected members and a president who is both head of state and head of government. In 1985 a military coup suspended the constitution and dissolved the National Assembly. The National Resistance Council (NRC) is an interim legislative body.
history For early history, see ◊Africa. Uganda was a British protectorate 1894–1962.

Uganda became an independent member of the Commonwealth in 1962, with Dr Milton Obote, leader of the Uganda People's Congress (UPC), as prime minister. In 1963 it was proclaimed a federal republic; King Mutesa II became president, ruling through a cabinet. King Mutesa was deposed in a coup 1966 and Obote became executive president. One of his first acts was to end the federal status. After an attempt to assassinate him in 1969, Obote banned all opposition and established what was effectively a one-party state.

In 1971 Obote was overthrown in an army coup led by Maj-Gen Idi Amin Dada, who suspended the constitution and all political activity and took legislative and executive powers into his own hands. Obote fled to Tanzania. Amin proceeded to wage what he called an 'economic war' against foreign domination, resulting in the mass expulsion of Asians, many of whom settled in Britain. In 1976 Amin claimed that large tracts

Uganda
Republic of

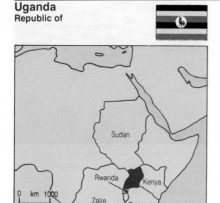

area 236,600 sq km/91,350 sq mi
capital Kampala
towns Jingar, M'Bale, Entebbe
physical plateau with mountains in W; forest
and grassland; arid in N
features Ruwenzori Range; national parks with
wildlife (chimpanzees, some of Africa's largest
crocodiles, and Nile perch to 70 kg/160 lb);
Owen Falls on the White Nile where it leaves
Lake Victoria
head of state and government Yoweri
Museveni from 1986
government emergent democratic republic
political parties National Resistance Movement
(NRM), left-of-centre; Democratic Party (DP),
centre-left; Conservative Party (CP), centre-right;
Uganda People's Congress (UPC), left-of-centre;
Uganda Freedom Movement (UFM),
left-of-centre
exports coffee, cotton, tea, copper
currency Uganda new shilling (648.98 = £1
Mar 1990)
population (1987) 15,500,000 (the largest

ethnic group is the Baganda, from whom the
name of the country comes; others include the
Langi and Acholi, and there are a few surviving
Pygmies); annual growth rate 3.3%
life expectancy men 47, women 51
language English (official); Swahili is a lingua
franca
religion Christian 50%, animist 45%, Muslim
5%
literacy 70% male/45% female (1985 est)
GNP $6.2 bn (1984); $400 per head of
population
chronology
1962 Achieved independence within the
Commonwealth, with Milton Obote as prime
minister.
1963 Proclaimed a federal republic with King
Mutesa II as president.
1966 King Mutesa ousted in a coup led by
Obote, who ended the federal status and
became executive president.
1969 All opposition parties banned after an
assassination attempt on Obote.
1971 Obote overthrown in an army coup led by
Maj-Gen Idi Amin, who established a ruthlessly
dictatorial regime, expelling nearly 49,000
Ugandan Asians. Up to 300,000 opponents of
the regime are said to have been killed.
1978 After heavy fighting, Amin was forced to
leave the country. A provisional government
was set up with Yusuf Lule as president. Lule
was replaced by Godfrey Binaisa.
1978–79 Fighting with Tanzanian troops.
1980 Binaisa overthrown by the army. Elections
held and Milton Obote returned to power.
1985 After years of opposition, mainly by
the National Resistance Army (NRA), and
uncontrolled indiscipline in the regular army,
Obote was ousted by Brig Basilio Okello, who
entered a power-sharing agreement with the
NRA leader, Yoweri Museveni.
1986 Agreement ended and Museveni became
president, heading a broad-based coalition
government.

of Kenya historically belonged to Uganda and
accused Kenya of cooperating with the Israeli
government in a raid on Entebbe airport to
free hostages held in a hijacked aircraft. Relations with Kenya became strained and diplomatic links with Britain were severed. During
the next two years the Amin regime carried
out a widespread campaign against any likely
opposition, resulting in thousands of deaths and
imprisonments.

In 1978, when Amin annexed the Kagera area of
Tanzania, near the Uganda border, the Tanzanian
president, Julius Nyerere, sent troops to support
the Uganda National Liberation Army (UNLA),
which had been formed to fight Amin. Within
five months Tanzanian troops had entered the
Uganda capital, Kampala, forcing Amin to flee,
first to Libya and then to Saudi Arabia. A provisional government, drawn from a cross-section
of exiled groups, was set up, with Dr Yusuf Lule
as president. Two months later Lule was replaced
by Godfrey Binaisa who, in turn, was overthrown
by the army. A military commission made arrangements for national elections, which were won by
the UPC, and Milton Obote came back to power.

Obote's government was soon under pressure
from a range of exiled groups operating outside
the country and guerrilla forces inside and he
was only kept in office by the presence of
Tanzanian troops. When they were withdrawn
in June 1982 a major offensive was launched
against the Obote government by the National
Resistance Movement (NRM) and the National
Resistance Army (NRA) led by Dr Lule and
Yoweri Museveni. By 1985 Obote was unable
to control the army, which had been involved
in indiscriminate killings, and he was ousted in
July in a coup led by Brig Tito Okello. Obote fled

to Kenya and then Zambia, where he was given
political aslyum.

Okello had little more success in controlling the
army and, after a brief period of power-sharing
with the NRA, fled to Sudan in Jan 1986. Museveni
was sworn in as president and announced a policy
of national reconciliation, promising a return to
normal parliamentary government within three to
five years. He formed a cabinet in which most
of Uganda's political parties were represented,
including the NRM, which is the political wing of
the NRA, the Democratic Party, the Conservative
Party, the Uganda People's Congress, and the
Uganda Freedom Movement.
Uganda Martyrs 22 Africans, of whom 12 were boy
pages, put to death 1885–87 by King Mwanga of
Uganda for refusing to renounce Christianity. They
were canonized as the first African saints of the
Roman Catholic Church in 1964.
Ugarit /'uːgərɪt/ ancient trading city kingdom (modern **Ras Shamra**) on the Syrian coast. It was
excavated by the French archaeologist Claude
Schaeffer (1898–1982) from 1929, finds ranging
from about 7000 to 15–13th centuries BC, including the earliest known alphabet.
ugli fruit citrus fruit, a cross between a grapefruit
and a tangerine. Sweeter than a grapefruit but
sharper than a tangerine, with rough skin, it is
native to the East Indies. It is used in jams and
preserves for a sweet-sour flavour.
UHF abbreviation for **ultra high frequency**, referring to radio waves of very short wavelength,
used, for example, for television broadcasting.
Uhland /'uːlænt/ Johann Ludwig 1787–1862. German poet, author of ballads and lyrics in the Romantic tradition.
UHT abbreviation for **ultra heat treated**; see ◊food
processing.

Uist /'juːɪst/ two small islands in the Outer
◊Hebrides, Scotland: North Uist and South Uist.
uitlander (Dutch 'foreigner') in South African history, term applied by the Boer inhabitants of
the Transvaal to immigrants of non-Dutch origin (mostly British) in the late 19th century.
The uitlanders' inferior political position in the
Transvaal led to the Second ◊South African War
1899–1902.
Ujiji /uː'dʒiːdʒi/ port on Lake Tanganyika, Tanzania, where ◊Stanley found Livingstone 1871;
population (1970) 17,000. It was originally an Arab
trading post for slaves and ivory.
Ujung Pandang /'uːdʒʊŋ pæn'dæn/ **Macassar**
or **Makassar** until 1973 chief port (trading in
coffee, rubber, copra, and spices) on Sulawesi,
Indonesia, with fishing and food-processing industries; population (1980) 709,000. Established by
the Dutch 1607.
UK abbreviation for ◊**United Kingdom**.
UKAEA abbreviation for **United Kingdom Atomic
Energy Authority**.
Ukraine /juː'kreɪn/ constituent republic of the SE
USSR from 1923
area 603,700 sq km/233,089 sq mi
capital Kiev
towns Kharkov, Donetsk, Odessa, Dnieropet-
rovsk, Lvov, Zaporozhe, Krivoi Rog
physical Russian plain, Carpathian and Crimean
Mountains; rivers Dnieper (with the Dnieper dam
1932), Donetz, and Bug
products grain; 60% of Soviet coal reserves; oil
and other minerals
population (1987) 51,201,000; Ukrainian 74%,
Russian 21%, Russian-speaking Jews 2%. Some
1.5 million émigrés live in the USA, 750,000 in
Canada
language Ukrainian (Slavonic), with a literature
that goes back to the Middle Ages; noted writers are Ivan Kotlyarevsky (1769–1838) and Taras
Shevchenko (1814–1861)
religion traditionally Ukrainian Orthodox
recent history a state by the 9th century; under Polish rule from the 14th; Russia absorbed
E Ukraine 1667, the rest 1793, from Austrian
rule; proclaimed itself a people's republic 1918;
from 1920, one of the republics of the USSR;
overrun by Germans in World War II. In the
famine of 1932–33 more than 7.5 million people died. Since the ◊Chernobyl incident in 1986
there has been a growing popular environmentalist movement in the Ukraine. Nationalist and
pro-reform demonstrations have also increased,
led by the People's Movement of the Ukraine
(*Rukh*), established June 1989. There have been
demonstrations calling for the legalization of the
Ukrainian Uniate Catholic Church, which was proscribed by Stalin in 1946 and forcibly merged with
the Russian Orthodox Church, and strikes by miners during 1989 in the Donbas coalfield. In Jan 1990
millions of Ukrainians formed a 300-mile-long human chain linking Liev and Lvov to commemorate
the territory's unification, 1918, as an independent
republic.
Ukrainian language a member of the Slavonic
branch of the Indo-European language family,

Ukraine

Ulbricht *East German politician Walter Ulbricht (front row, third from right).*

spoken in Ukraine. It is closely related to Russian and is sometimes referred to by Russians as 'Little Russian', although this is a description that Ukrainians generally do not find appropriate. Ukrainian communities are also found in Canada and the USA.

ukulele a type of small four-stringed ◊guitar.

Ulaanbaatar /'uːlɑːn 'bɑːtɔː/ or *Ulan Bator*; until 1924 *Urga* capital of the Mongolian Republic, a trading centre producing carpets, textiles, vodka; population (1988) 500,000.

Ulan Bator /'uːlɑːn 'bɑːtɔː/ alternative name of Ulaanbaatar, capital of Mongolia.

Ulanova /uːˈlɑːnəvə/ Galina 1910– . Soviet dancer. Prima ballerina of the Bolshoi Theatre Ballet 1944–61, she excelled as Juliet and Giselle and created the principal role of Katerina in Prokofiev's *The Stone Flower.*

Ulan-Ude /ʊˈlɑːn ʊˈdeɪ/ formerly (until 1934) *Verkhne-Udinsk* industrial city (sawmills, cars, glass) and capital of the Republic of Buryat in SE USSR, on the river Ibla and the Trans-Siberian railway; population (1987) 351,000. It was founded as a Cossack settlement in the 1660s.

Ulbricht /'ʊlbrɪkt/ Walter 1893–1973. East German politician. After exile in the USSR during Hitler's rule, he became first secretary of the Socialist Unity Party in East Germany 1950 and (as chair of the Council of State from 1960) was instrumental in the building of the Berlin Wall 1961. He established East Germany's economy and recognition outside the East European bloc.

ulcer a persistent breach in a body surface (skin or mucous membrane). It may be caused by infection, irritation, or tumour.

Bleeding stomach ulcers can be repaired without an operation by the use of endoscopy. A flexible, fibre-optic tube is passed into the stomach and under direct vision a remote-controlled stitching machine sews up the ulcer.

Uleåborg /'uːliɔːˌbɔrj/ Swedish name for the Finnish port of ◊Oulu.

Ullman /'ʊlmən/ Liv 1939– . Norwegian actress who was critically acclaimed for her roles in first Swedish and then international films. Her work includes *Persona* 1966, the title role in *Pope Joan* 1972, and *Autumn Sonata* 1978.

Ulm /ʊlm/ industrial city (vehicles, agricultural machinery, precision instruments, textiles) in Baden-Württemberg, West Germany, on the river Danube; population (1988) 101,000. Its Gothic cathedral with the highest stone spire ever built (161 m/528 ft) escaped damage in World War II when two-thirds of Ulm was destroyed. It was a free imperial city from the 14th century to 1802. Albert Einstein was born here.

Ulsan /ˌʊlˈsæn/ industrial city (vehicles, shipbuilding, oil refining, petrochemicals) in South Kyongsang province, SE South Korea; population (1985) 551,000.

Ulster /'ʌlstə/ former kingdom in Northern Ireland, annexed by England 1461, from Jacobean times a centre of English, and later Scottish, settlement on land confiscated from its owners; divided 1921 into Northern Ireland (counties Antrim, Armagh, Down, Fermanagh, Londonderry, and Tyrone) and Cavan, Donegal, and Monaghan in the Republic of Ireland.

Ultra abbreviation of *Ultra Secret*, term used by the British from spring 1940 in World War II to denote intelligence gained by deciphering German signals.

Ultra decoding took place at the interception centre in Bletchley Park, Buckinghamshire. Failure to use such information in the Battle of ◊Anzio meant that Allied troops were stranded for a time.

ultra (Latin) extreme.

ultrabasic in geology, an igneous rock with a lower silica content than basic rocks (less than 45% silica).

Ultramontanism (Latin 'beyond the mountains'; that is, the Alps) in the Roman Catholic Church, the tenets of the Italian party that stresses papal authority rather than nationalism in the church.

ultrasonics the study and application of the sound and vibrations produced by ultrasonic pressure waves (see ◊ultrasound).

The earliest practical application was to detect submarines during World War I, but recently the field of ultrasonics has greatly expanded. Frequencies above 80,000 Hz have been used to produce echoes as a means of measuring the depth of the sea, to detect flaws in metal, and, in medicine, high-frequency pressure waves are used to investigate various body organs. Ultrasonic pressure waves transmitted through the body are absorbed and reflected to different degrees by different body tissues. By recording the 'echoes', a picture of the different structures being scanned can be built up. Ultrasound scanning is valued as a safe, noninvasive technique which often eliminates the need for exploratory surgery. Free of the risks of ionizing radiation (unlike X-rays and ◊CAT scan), it is especially valuable in obstetrics, where it has revolutionized fetal evaluation and diagnosis. High-power ultrasound has been used with focusing arrangements to destroy tissue at a depth in the body, and extremely high frequencies of 1,000 MHz (megahertz) or more are used in ultrasonic microscopes.

ultrasound pressure waves similar in nature to sound waves but occurring at frequencies above 20,000 hertz (cycles per second), the approximate upper limit of human hearing. Ultrasonics is concerned with the study and practical application of these phenomena.

ultraviolet astronomy the study of cosmic ultraviolet emissions using artificial satellites. The USA has launched a series of satellites for this purpose, receiving the first useful data in 1968. Only a tiny percentage of solar ultraviolet radiation penetrates the atmosphere, this being the less dangerous longer-wavelength ultraviolet. The dangerous shorter-wavelength radiation is absorbed by gases in the ozone layer high in the Earth's upper atmosphere.

The US Orbiting Astronomical Observatory (OAO) satellites provided scientists with a great deal of information regarding cosmic ultraviolet emissions. OAO-1, launched 1966, failed after only three days, but OAO-2, put into orbit 1968, operated for four years instead of the intended one year, and carried out the first ultraviolet observations of a supernova and also of Uranus. OAO-B failed to achieve orbit 1970, but OAO-3 (*Copernicus*), launched 1972, continued transmissions into the 1980s. OAO-3 discovered many new ultraviolet sources. The International Ultraviolet Explorer (IUE), launched Jan 1978 and still operating in the early 1990s, observed all the main objects in the solar system (including Halley's comet), stars, galaxies, and the interstellar medium.

unconformity The Great Unconformity, between the Hakatai shales and the overlying Tapeats sandstone, in the Grand Canyon, Colorado, USA.

ultraviolet radiation light rays invisible to the human eye, of wavelengths from about 4×10 to 5×10 metres (where the ◊X-ray range begins). Physiologically, they are extremely powerful, producing sunburn and causing the formation of vitamin D in the skin.

Ultraviolet rays are strongly germicidal and may be produced artificially by mercury vapour and arc lamps for therapeutic use. The radiation may be detected with ordinary photographic plates or films down to 2×10 metres. It can also be studied by its fluorescent effect on certain materials. The desert iguana *disposaurus dorsalis* uses it to locate the boundaries of its territory and to find food.

Ulundi /ʊˈlʊndi/ capital of KwaZulu in South Africa.

Ulysses /juːˈlɪsiːz/ Roman name for ◊Odysseus, Greek mythological hero.

Ulysses a novel by James Joyce, published 1922. It employs stream of consciousness, linguistic experiment, and parody to describe in enormous detail a single day (16 June 1904) in the life of its characters in Dublin. It was first published in Paris but, because of obscenity prosecutions, not until 1936 in the UK.

Umar died AD 644. 2nd caliph (head) of Islam, noted as a strong disciplinarian. Under his rule Islam spread to Egypt and Persia. He was assassinated in Medina.

Umayyad alternative spelling for ◊Omayyad dynasty.

Umberto /ʊmˈbeətəʊ/ two kings of Italy:

Umberto I 1844–1900. King of Italy from 1878, who joined the Triple Alliance 1882 with Germany and Austria-Hungary; his colonial ventures included the defeat at Aduwa, Abyssinia, 1896. He was assassinated by an anarchist.

Umberto II 1904–1983. Last king of Italy 1946. On the abdication of his father, Victor Emmanuel III, he ruled 9 May–13 June 1946, when he also abdicated and left the country.

umbilical cord the connection between the ◊embryo and the ◊placenta of placental mammals. It has one vein and two arteries, transporting oxygen and nutrients to the developing young, and removing waste products. At birth, the connection between the young and the umbilical cord is severed, leaving a scar called the navel.

umbrella portable protection against the rain (when used in the sun usually called a parasol or sunshade). In use in China for more than a thousand years, umbrellas were also held over the rulers of ancient Egypt and Assyria as symbols of power and had a similar significance for Aztec and African rulers and dignitaries of the Roman Catholic Church.

Revived in clerical use in 16th century Italy, umbrellas were used by women in England from the 17th century, but Jonas Hanway (1712–86) was the first to make it part of the Englishman's everyday 'City uniform'.

Umbria /'ʌmbriə/ mountainous region of Italy in the central Apennines; including the provinces of Perugia and Terni; area 8,500 sq km/3,281 sq mi; population (1988) 818,000. Its capital is Perugia, and it includes the river Tiber. Industry includes

underground *The inaugural trip of the Metropolitan Line undergound train at Edgware Road station, London, 1863. Among the passengers, seated third and fourth from the right, are Prime Minister Gladstone and his wife.*

wine, grain, olives, tobacco, textiles, chemicals, and metalworking. This is the home of the Umbrian school of artists, including Raphael.

Umm al Qaiwain /'ʊm æl kaɪ'waɪŋ/ one of the ◊United Arab Emirates.

Umtali /ʊm'tɑːli/ former name (until 1982) for the town of ◊Mutare in Zimbabwe.

Umtata /ʊm'tɑːtə/ capital of the South African Bantu homeland of ◊Transkei; population (1976) 25,000.

UN abbreviation for ◊*United Nations*.

Unamuno /ˌuːnə'muːnəʊ/ Miguel de 1864–1936. Spanish writer of Basque origin, exiled 1924–30 for criticism of the military directorate of Primo de ◊Rivera. His works include mystic poems and the study *Del sentimiento trágico de la vida/ The Tragic Sense of Life* 1913, about the conflict of reason and belief in religion.

uncertainty principle or *indeterminacy principle* in quantum mechanics, the principle that it is meaningless to speak of a particle's position, momentum, or other parameters, except as results of measurements; measuring, however, involves an interaction (such as a ◊photon of light bouncing off the particle under scrutiny), which must disturb the particle, though the disturbance is noticeable only at an atomic scale. The principle implies that one cannot, even in theory, predict the moment-to-moment behaviour of such a system.

It was established by ◊Heisenberg, and gave a theoretical limit to the precision with which a particle's momentum and position can be measured simultaneously: the more accurately the one is determined the more uncertainty there is in the other.

Uncle Remus US folk tales of Brer Rabbit, Brer Fox, and others, taken from black plantation legends by Joel Chandler Harris in the 1870s and 1880s, and important in the tradition of US Southern humour.

Uncle Sam /'ʌŋkəl 'sæm/ nickname for the US government. It originated during the War of 1812, probably from the initials U S placed on government property.

Uncle Tom's Cabin best-selling US novel by Harriet Beecher Stowe, written 1851–52, a sentimental but powerful portrayal of the cruelties of slave life on Southern plantations which promoted the call for Abolition. The heroically loyal slave Uncle Tom has in the 20th century become a byword for black subservience.

Abraham Lincoln acknowledged that it had stirred Northern sentiments and helped precipitate the American Civil War.

Uncle Vanya a play by Anton Chekhov, first produced 1897. Serebryakov, a retired professor, realizes the futility of his intellectual ideals when faced with the practical demands of life.

unconformity in geology, a break in the sequence of ◊sedimentary rocks. It is usually seen as an eroded surface, with the ◊beds above and below lying at different angles. An unconformity represents an ancient land surface, where exposed rocks were worn down by erosion and later covered in a renewed cycle of deposition.

unconscious in psychoanalysis, part of the personality of which the individual is unaware, and which contains impulses or urges that are held back, or repressed, from conscious awareness.

UNCTAD abbreviation for *United Nations Commission on Trade and Development*.

underground (North American *subway*) a rail service that runs underground. The first underground line in the world was in London, opened 1863; it was essentially a roofed-in trench. The London Underground is still the longest, with over 400 km/250 mi of routes. Many major cities throughout the world have similar systems, and Moscow's underground, the Metro, handles up to 6.5 million passengers a day.

Underground Railroad in US history, a network established in the Northern states before the Civil War to provide sanctuary and assistance for black slaves on the run from their owners. Safe houses, transport facilities, and conductors existed to lead the slaves to safety in the North.

Underwood /'ʌndəwʊd/ Leon 1890–1975. British artist and sculptor. He travelled to Iceland, the USA, Mexico, and West Africa, devoting several books to masks, wood carvings, and bronzes. His rhythmic figures are powerful symbols of human myth.

Undset /'ʊnset/ Sigrid 1882–1949. Norwegian novelist, author of *Kristin Lavransdatter* 1920–22, a strongly Catholic novel set in the 14th century. Nobel prize 1928.

unemployment an involuntary lack of paid employment. Unemployment is generally subdivided into *frictional unemployment*, the inevitable temporary unemployment of those moving from one job to another; *cyclical unemployment*, caused by a downswing in the ◊trade cycle; *seasonal unemployment*, in an area where there is high demand only during holiday periods, for example; and *structural unemployment*, where changing technology or other long-term change in the economy results in large numbers without work. Periods of widespread unemployment in Europe and the USA this century include 1929–1930s, and the years since the mid-1970s.

Many Third World countries suffer from severe unemployment and underemployment; the problem is exacerbated by rapid growth of population and lack of skills. In industrialized countries unemployment has been a phenomenon since the mid-1970s, when the rise in world oil prices caused a downturn in economic activity, and greater use of high technology has improved output without the need for more jobs. The average unemployment rate in industrialized countries (the members of the Organization for Economic Cooperation and Development) rose to 11% in 1987 compared with only 3% in 1970, with some countries, such as Spain and Ireland, suffering around 20%. There continues to be a great deal of youth unemployment despite government training and job creation schemes. In the USA the unemployment rate was 5.3% in 1989. In China, nearly a quarter of the urban labour force is unemployed.

In Britain, for at least 150 years before 1939, the supply of labour always exceeded demand except in wartime, and economic crises accompanied by mass unemployment were recurrent from 1785. The percentage of unemployed in

unemployment

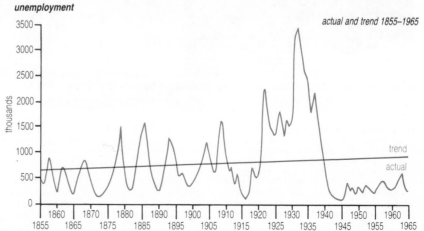

actual and trend 1855–1965

unemployment *In 1936, at the height of the Great Depression in Britain, the closure of Palmer's shipyard in Jarrow prompted the 'Jarrow Crusaders' to carry a petition to London and hand it to Stanley Baldwin, the prime minister. A similar People's March for Jobs walked from Liverpool to deliver a petition to Margaret Thatcher in 1981.*

trade unions averaged 6% during 1883–1913 and 14.2% (of those covered by the old Unemployment Insurance Acts) 1921–38. World War II and the rebuilding and expansion which followed meant shortage of labour rather than unemployment in the Western world, and in Britain in the 1950s the unemployment rate fell to 1.5%. Fluctuation

in employment returned in the 1960s, and in the recession of the mid-1970s to 1980s was a world-wide problem. In Britain deflationary economic measures tended to exacerbate the trend, and in the mid-1980s the rate had risen to 14% (although the basis on which it is calculated has in recent years been changed several times and

many commentators argue that the real rate is higher).

Most modern governments attempt to prevent some or all of the various forms of unemployment. The ideas of Keynes influenced British government unemployment policies during the 1950s and 1960s. The existence of a clear link

between unemployment and inflation (that high unemployment can be dealt with by governments only at the cost of higher inflation) is now disputed.

UNEP abbreviation for *United Nations Environmental Programme*.

UNESCO abbreviation for *United Nations Educational, Scientific, and Cultural Organization*, an agency of the UN, established 1946, with its headquarters in Paris. The USA, contributor of 25% of its budget, withdrew 1984 on grounds of its over-politicization, and Britain followed 1985.

Ungaretti /ˌʊŋɡəˈreti/ Giuseppe 1888–1970. Italian poet who lived in France and Brazil. His lyrics show a cosmopolitan independence of Italian poetic tradition. His poems, such as the *Allegria di naufragi/Joy of Shipwrecks* 1919, are noted for their simplicity.

Ungava /ʌŋˈɡɑːvə/ district in N Québec and Labrador, Canada, E of Hudson Bay; area 351,780 sq mi/911,110 sq km. It has large deposits of iron-ore.

ungulate general name for any hoofed mammal.

UNHCR abbreviation for *United Nations High Commission for Refugees*.

Uniate Church any of the ◊Orthodox churches that accept the Catholic faith and the supremacy of the pope, and are in full communion with the Roman Catholic Church, but retain their own liturgy and separate organization.

In the Ukraine, USSR, despite being proscribed 1946–89, the Uniate Church claimed some 4.5 million adherents when it was once more officially recognized.

UNICEF abbreviation for *United Nations International Children's Emergency Fund*.

unicellular organism an animal or plant consisting of a single cell. Most are invisible without a microscope but a few, such as the giant ◊amoeba, may be visible to the naked eye. The main groups of unicellular organisms are ◊bacteria, ◊protozoa, unicellular ◊algae, and unicellular fungi or ◊yeasts.

unicorn mythical animal referred to by Classical writers, said to live in India and to be like a horse but with one spiralled horn growing from the forehead.

unidentified flying object (UFO) any light or object seen in the sky whose immediate identity is not apparent. The term *flying saucer* was coined 1947.

On investigation, the vast majority of UFOs turn out to be natural or identifiable objects, notably bright stars and planets, meteors, aircraft, and satellites. There is no evidence that UFOs are alien spacecraft.

Unification Church or *Moonies* church founded in Korea 1954 by the Reverend Sun Myung ◊Moon. World membership is about 200,000. The theology unites Christian and Taoist ideas, and is based on Moon's book *Divine Principle* which teaches that the original purpose of creation was to set up a perfect family, in a perfect relationship with God.

The Unification Church believes that marriage is essential for spiritual fulfilment, and marriage partners are chosen for members by S M Moon, though individuals are free to reject a chosen partner. Marriage, which takes the form of mass blessings by Reverend and Mrs Moon, is the most important ritual of the church; it is preceded by the wine or engagement ceremony. In the 1970s, the Unification Church was criticized for its methods of recruitment and alleged 'brainwashing'.

unified field theory in physics, the theory which attempts to explain the four natural forces (strong nuclear, weak nuclear, electromagnetic, and gravitational) in terms of a single unified force.

Research was begun by Einstein and, by 1971, a theory developed by Weinberg, Glashow, Salam, and others, had demonstrated the link between the weak and electromagnetic forces. The next stage is to develop a theory (called the ◊Grand Unified Theory, or GUT) that combines the strong nuclear force with the electroweak force. The final stage will be to incorporate gravity into the scheme. Work on ◊superstring theory indicates that this may be the ultimate 'theory of everything'.

uniformitarianism in geology, the principle that processes that can be seen to occur on the Earth's surface today are the same as those that have occurred throughout geological time. For example, desert sandstones containing sand-dune structures must have been formed under conditions similar to those present in deserts today. The principle was formulated by James ◊Hutton and expounded by Charles ◊Lyell.

Uniformity, Acts of two acts of Parliament in England. The first in 1559 imposed the Prayer Book on the whole English kingdom; the second in 1662 required the Prayer Book to be used in all

churches, and some 2,000 ministers who refused to comply were ejected.

unilateralism in politics, support for *unilateral nuclear disarmament*: scrapping a country's nuclear weapons without waiting for other countries to agree to do so at the same time. In the UK this principle was Labour Party policy in the 1980s but was abandoned 1989.

Union, Act of act of 1707 that brought about the union of England and Scotland; that of 1801 united England and Ireland. The latter was revoked when the Irish Free State was constituted in 1922.

union flag the British national ◊flag. It is popularly called the *Union Jack*, although, strictly speaking, this name applies only when it is flown on the jackstaff of a warship.

Union Movement British political group. Founded as the New Party by Sir Oswald ◊Mosley and a number of Labour Members of Parliament 1931, it developed into the British Union of Fascists 1932. In 1940 the organization was declared illegal and its leaders interned, but at the end of World War II it was revived as the Union Movement, characterized by racist doctrines including anti-Semitism.

An attempt by the 'blackshirts' to march through the East End of London in 1936 led to prohibition of the wearing of such political uniforms.

Union of Soviet Socialist Republics (USSR) country in N Asia and E Europe, stretching from the Baltic Sea and the Black Sea to the Arctic and Pacific oceans.

government Under the 1977 constitution, as amended in 1989, the USSR is a federal state comprising 15 constituent union republics (see table). Each union republic enjoys, in theory, the right of secession and has its own constitution, legislature, and government (Council of Ministers) which is responsible for local administration. A number of union republics in turn include autonomous republics and regions in which special regard is paid to local culture, customs, and languages. The central (federal) government is solely responsible for armed forces, foreign policy, foreign trade, communications, and heavy industries. In other spheres the scope for initiative by union and autonomous republic governments is restricted by the centrally planned nature of the Soviet economy and the constant scrutiny of the Communist Party.

The highest organ of the Moscow-based central government is the Congress of the USSR People's Deputies (CUPD), which comprises 2,250 members. 750 of these are elected every five years by universal suffrage, and in competitive contests, from demographically equal-sized single-member constituencies from across the USSR. 750 are elected to national-territorial constituencies on the basis of 32 deputies per union republic, 11 from each of the 20 autonomous republics, five from each of the eight autonomous regions and one from each of the ten national districts within the Russian Soviet Federal Socialist Republic (RSFSR). The remaining 750 seats in the CUPD are allocated among 32 officially recognized 'social organizations', with the Communist Party and trade unions each being accorded 100 seats and the Communist Youth League (Komsomol) 75.

The CUPD, which was created in 1989 by adding the 750 'social organization' seats to the existing 1,500 members of the former Supreme Soviet (although the former 'reserved seats' are set to be abolished when the CUPD is next elected), functions as an 'overarching' constitutional assembly rather than as a legislature. It convenes for several days each year to decide key constitutional, political and socio-economic questions and elects, at its outset, a state president, vice-president, prime minister, who is chair of the 60–70 member council of ministers (the body which has charge of the USSR's day-to-day executive administration), and the chair of the Supreme Court. The state president has responsiblity for directing military and foreign policy and for guiding the drafting of legislation.

From its ranks, the CUPD also elects, by secret ballot, 542 members to serve in a Supreme Soviet which, meeting in spring and summer sessions for eight months a year, functions as the country's effective legislature. Its members are elected in accordance with regional quotas, with a proportion being annually rotated. Like its predecessor, it is divided into two chambers, the 271-member Soviet of Nationalities, whose task it is to concentrate on legislation which specifically affects the territorial subdivisions of the USSR, and the 271-member Soviet of the Union, which concentrates on civil rights, socio-economic, military, and international matters. The state president chairs the Supreme Soviet's presidium and there is a structure of committees. Approval from the Supreme Soviet and its committees is required for the prime minister's nominated ministerial team, nine nominees actually being rejected in July 1989.

Lower-level elected soviets operate at the village, town, regional, and republic levels. However, the dominating force in the country is the Communist Party of the Soviet Union (CPSU). The CPSU, with 18,000,000 members, is the only currently permitted political party in the USSR and forms a second and parallel form of government which dominates the state tier. It is set up like a pyramid with at its base over 400,000 primary party branches in factories and villages. The party, being organized on 'democratic centralist' lines, is controlled from above, with candidates for election being vetted and selected by their superiors. The CPSU's highest authority is its Party Congress, which meets every five years and includes 5,000 selected members. Congress ratifies party programmes and elects a Central Committee of currently 251 full members to assume authority over the party between congresses.

The Central Committee meets twice a year and elects the Politburo of normally eleven full members and seven candidates and the specialist twelve-member administrative Secretariat. The Politburo is the most important political body in the USSR. It meets fortnightly as an executive cabinet, controls and determines the policy of the CPSU, and sets out the medium and long-term goals for the nation. Its members select from their ranks the party leader, or general secretary (since

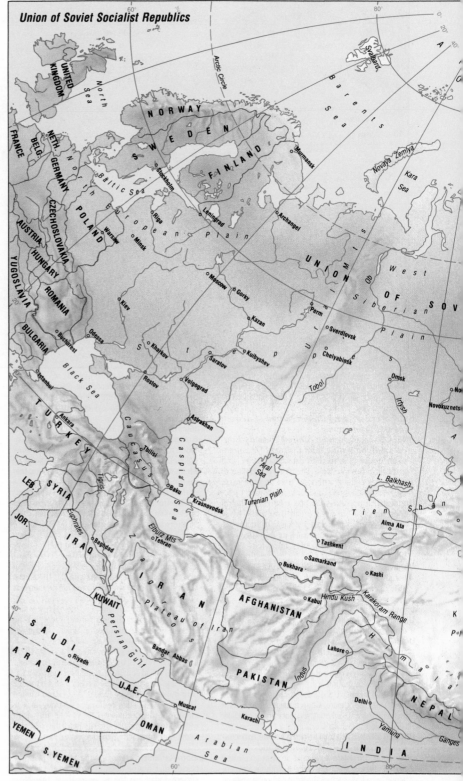

Union of Soviet Socialist Republics

Mar 1985 Mikhail Gorbachev), who presides over the Secretariat and serves in practice as the leader of the Soviet Union.

The CPSU dominates the state system of government through the control it exercises over appointments and candidatures in elections. More than 85% of CUPD delegates are members of the CPSU, while the state's policy-making and executive organs, the Presidium and Council of Ministers, are tightly controlled by leading members of the CPSU Central Committee and Politburo. This inner circle of CPSU leaders determines state and party policy. However, growing factional divisions within the party elite, combined with the administrative reforms of 1988–89, have meant that there is growing debate within the CUPD, Supreme Soviet and the CPSU's Central Committee and Congress. A gradual power shift away from party towards state executive organs is becoming increasingly evident.

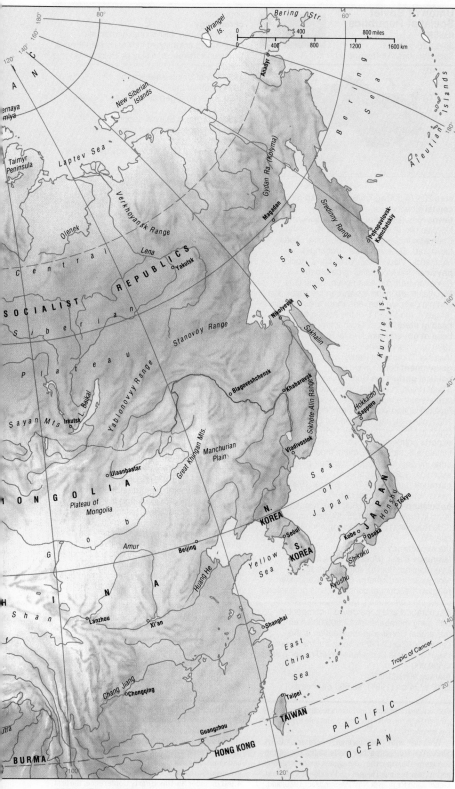

millions dying in the Ukraine and Kazakhstan famine of 1932–34, as well as in the political purges and liquidations launched during the 1920s and 1930s. Leading party figures, including Bukharin, Kamenev, and Zinoviev, were victims of these 'show trial' purges. In the process, the Soviet political system was deformed, as inner-party democracy gave way to autocracy based around a Stalinist personality cult.

From 1933 the USSR put forward a policy of collective resistance to aggression. In 1939 it concluded a nonaggression pact with Germany, and Poland was invaded and divided between them. The USSR invaded ◊Finland 1939 but signed a brief peace 1940. For events 1941–45, see ◊World War II. 25 million Russians perished during this 'Great Patriotic War'.

During the immediate postwar years the USSR concentrated on consolidating its new empire in Eastern Europe and on providing indirect support to anti-colonial movements in the Far East. Relations with the West, particularly the USA, sharply deteriorated. On the death of Stalin in Mar 1953 a collective leadership, including Nikita Khrushchev (CPSU first or general secretary 1953–64), Georgi Malenkov (prime minister 1953–55), Nikolai Bulganin (prime minister 1955–58), Vyacheslav Molotov (foreign minister 1953–56), and Lazar Kaganovich, assumed power. They combined to remove the secret-police chief Lavrenti Beria in Dec 1953 and introduced a new legal code which regularized the political system. Strong differences emerged within the collective leadership over future political and economic reform and a fierce succession struggle developed.

Khrushchev emerged dominant from this contest, ousting Malenkov, Molotov, and Kaganovich (the 'anti-party' group) June 1957 and Bulganin June 1958 to combine the posts of prime minister and party first secretary. At the 1961 Party Congress, Khrushchev introduced a new party programme for rapid agricultural, industrial, and technological development to enable the USSR to move ahead of the USA in economic terms by 1980 and attain full Communism. He launched a 'virgin lands' cultivation campaign in Kazakhstan, increased rural incentives and decentralized industrial management through the creation of new regional economic councils (*sovnarkhozy*). In addition, Khrushchev introduced radical new party rule changes, sanctioned a cultural thaw and enunciated the principle of 'peaceful coexistence' with the West to divert resources from the military sector. These reforms enjoyed initial success; having exploded its first hydrogen bomb 1953 and launched a space satellite (Sputnik I) 1957, the USSR emerged as a serious technological rival to the USA. But Khrushchev's liberalization policy and his denunciation of the errors and crimes of the Stalin era at the Feb 1956 Party Congress had serious repercussions among the USSR's satellites—a nationalist revolt in Hungary and a breach in relations with Yugoslavia and China—while his administrative reforms were fiercely opposed by senior party and state officials. After a series of poor harvests in overcropped Kazakhstan and the ◊Cuban missile crisis 1962, these opponents succeeded in ousting Khrushchev at the Central Committee meeting Oct 1964.

A new and conservative collective leadership, based around the figures of Leonid Brezhnev (CPSU general secretary 1964–82), Alexei Kosygin (prime minister 1964–80), Nikolai Podgorny (state president 1965–77), and Mikhail Suslov (ideology secretary 1964–82), assumed power and immediately abandoned Khrushchev's *sovnarkhozy* and party reforms and reimposed strict censorship in the cultural sphere. Priority was now given to the expansion and modernization of the Soviet armed forces, including the creation of a naval force with global reach. This, coupled with the Soviet invasion of Czechoslovakia 1968, resulted in a renewal of the ◊cold war 1964–70.

history For early history, see ◊Russian history; also Armenia, Azerbaijan, Byelorussia, Estonia, Georgia, Kirghizia, Latvia, Lithuania, Moldavia, Russia, Tadzhikistan, Turkmenistan, Ukraine, and Uzbekistan.

The Union of Soviet Socialist Republics was formed 1922 and a constitution adopted 1923. Lenin, who had led the new regime, died 1924 and an internal party controversy broke out between Stalin and Trotsky over the future of socialism and the necessity of world revolution. Trotsky was expelled 1927 and Stalin's policy of socialism in one country adopted. During the first two five-year plans 1928–39 heavy and light industries were developed and agriculture collectivized.

The country was transformed as industry grew at an annual (official) rate of 16% with, as a consequence, the size of the manual workforce quadrupling and the urban population doubling. However, the social cost was enormous, with

USSR: political leaders since 1945

*State President**

Nikolai Shvernik	1946–1953
Klimentiy Voroshilov	1953–1960
Leonid Brezhnev	1960–1964
Anastas Mikoyan	1964–1965
Nikolai Podgorny	1965–1977
Leonid Brezhnev	1977–1982
Vasily Kuznetsov**	1982–1983
Yuri Andropov	1983–1984
Vasily Kuznetsov**	1984–1984
Konstantin Chernenko	1984–1985
Vasily Kuznetsov**	1985–1985
Andrei Gromyko	1985–1989
Mikhail Gorbachev	1989-

*Chairman of the Presidium of the Supreme Soviet.

**Kuznetsov, who was First Deputy Chairman of the Presidium (Vice-President), served as a temporary acting President.

During the later 1960s, Leonid Brezhnev, through inducting his supporters into the CPSU Politburo and Secretariat, slowly emerged as the dominant figure. He governed in a cautious and consensual manner and brought into the Politburo leaders from all the significant centres of power, including the ◊KGB (Yuri Andropov), the army (Marshal Andrei Grechko), and the diplomatic service (Andrei Gromyko). Working with Prime Minister Kosygin, Brezhnev introduced a series of minor economic reforms and gave new priority to agricultural and consumer-goods production. In 1977 he oversaw the framing of a new constitution where the limits for dissent were clearly set out.

Brezhnev, who became the new state president May 1977, emerged as an international figure during the 1970s, frequently meeting Western leaders during a new era of détente. The landmarks of this period were the Salt-1 and Salt-2 Soviet-US arms-limitation agreements of 1972 and 1979 (see ◊strategic arms limitation) and the Helsinki Accord 1975, which brought Western recognition of the postwar division of E Europe. Another cultural thaw resulted in the emergence of a vocal dissident movement. The political and military influence of the USSR was extended into Africa with the establishment of new Communist governments in Mozambique 1974, Angola and Ethiopia 1975, and South Yemen 1978. The détente era was brought to an end by the Soviet invasion of Afghanistan Dec 1979 and the ◊Polish crisis 1980–81. The final years of the Brezhnev administration were ones of hardening policy, mounting corruption, and economic stagnation.

Yuri Andropov, the former KGB chief, was elected CPSU leader on Brezhnev's death Nov 1982 and began energetically to introduce a series of radical economic reforms aimed at streamlining and decentralizing the planning system and inculcating greater labour discipline. Andropov also launched a major campaign directed against corrupt and complacent party and state bureaucrats. These measures had a perceptible impact on the Soviet economy during 1983, but when Andropov died Feb 1984 he was succeeded by the cautious and elderly Brezhnev supporter, Konstantin Chernenko. Chernenko held power as a stop-gap leader for 13 months, his sole initiative being a renewed search for détente with the USA, which was rejected by the hardline Reagan administration.

On Chernenko's death Mar 1985, power was transferred to a new generation led by Mikhail Gorbachev, the protégé of Andropov, at 54 the CPSU's youngest leader since Stalin. Gorbachev introduced a number of reforms. He began to free farmers and factory managers from bureaucratic interference and to increase material incentives in a 'market socialist' manner. Working with Ideology Secretary Yegor Ligachev and Prime Minister Nikolai Ryzhkov, he restructured the party and state bureaucracies and replaced cautious Brezhnevites with ambitious new technocrats. Under the slogan *glasnost* (openness), he

Union of Soviet Socialist Republics (USSR);

Soyuz Sovyetskikh Sotsialisticheskikh Respublik)

area 22,274,500 sq km/8,600,184 sq mi
capital Moscow
towns Kiev, Tashkent, Kharkov, Gorky, Novosibirsk, Minsk, Sverdlovsk, Kuibyshev, Chelyabinsk, Dnepropetrovsk, Tbilisi; ports Leningrad, Odessa, Baku, Archangel, Murmansk, Vladivostok, Vostochny, Rostov
physical Ural Mountains separate the European from the Asian plain; Caucasus Mountains are in the S between the Black Sea and the Caspian Sea, and there are mountain ranges in the S and E of the Asiatic part
head of state Mikhail Gorbachev from 1988
head of government Nikolai Ryzhkov from 1985 (premier); Mikhail Gorbachev from 1985 (head of Communist Party)
government communism
political parties the Communist Party of the Soviet Union; nationalist 'Popular Fronts' now operate at the republic level; a conservative Russian United Workers' Front established 1989; pluralist, intelligentsia-led Democratic Union in Moscow from May 1988
exports cotton, timber, iron, steel, non-ferrous metals, electrical equipment, machinery, arms, oil and natural gas and their products, asbestos, gold, manganese
currency rouble (1.0176 = £1 Mar 1990, but this is not a commercial rate)
population (1988) 284,500,000 (two-thirds living in towns, and of 125 different nationalities; 52% Russian, 17% Ukrainian); annual growth rate 1%
life expectancy men 67, women 75
language Slavic (Russian, Ukrainian, Byelorussian, Polish), Altaic (Turkish, Mongolian, and others), Uralian, Caucasian
religion 'freedom of conscience' is guaranteed under the constitution, but religious belief is discouraged and considered incompatible with party membership (17,500,000 members); the largest Christian denomination is the Orthodox Church (30 million), but the largest religious sect is Sunni Muslim (40 million), Jews 2,500,000
literacy 99% (1985)
GNP $734 bn (1984); $2,600 per head of

population
chronology
1917 Revolution: provisional democratic government established in Mar by Mensheviks. Communist takeover in Nov by Bolsheviks under Lenin.
1922 Soviet Union established.
1924 Death of Lenin.
1928 Stalin emerged as absolute ruler after ousting Trotsky.
1930s Purges of Stalin's opponents.
1939 Nonaggression pact signed with Germany.
1941–45 Great Patriotic War against Germany.
1949 Creation of Comecon.
1953 Death of Stalin. Removal of Beria. 'Collective leadership' in power.
1955 Creation of Warsaw Pact.
1956 Khrushchev's February 'secret speech'.
1957–58 Ousting of 'anti-party' group and Bulganin.
1960 Sino-Soviet rift.
1962 Cuban missile crisis.
1964 Khrushchev ousted by new 'collective leadership'.
1968 Invasion of Czechoslovakia.
1969 Sino-Soviet border war.
1972 Salt I arms-limitation agreement with USA.
1977 Brezhnev elected president.
1979 Salt II. Soviet invasion of Afghanistan.
1982 Deaths of Suslov and Brezhnev. Andropov new Communist Party leader.
1984 Chernenko succeeded Andropov.
1985 Gorbachev succeeded Chernenko and introduced wide-ranging reforms. Gromyko appointed president.
1986 Gorbachev's power consolidated at 27th Party Congress. Chernobyl nuclear disaster.
1987 USSR and USA agreed to scrap intermediate-range nuclear missiles. Boris Yeltsin, Moscow party chief, dismissed for criticizing the slow pace of reform.
1988 Nationalist challenges in Kazakhstan, Baltic republics, Armenia, and Azerbaijan. Earthquake killed 100,000 in Armenia. Radical constitutional overhaul and encouragement of the private sector approved at Party Conference. Gorbachev replaced Gromyko as head of state.
1989 Troop withdrawal from Afghanistan completed.General election held, with candidate choice for new congress of People's Deputies. 20 killed in nationalist riots in Georgia. 74 members of CPSU Central Committee (mostly conservatives) removed, a quarter of the total. Gorbachev elected by CUPD as state president. Abandoning 'Brezhnev Doctrine' Gorbachev allowed overthrow of conservative communist regimes in Eastern Europe. Relations with China normalized (first time since 1960s).
1990 Troops sent to Azerbaijan during civil war with Armenia. CPSU Central Committee agrees end to one-party rule.

encouraged criticism of inefficiencies and made party officials (*apparatchiks*) more accountable to rank-and-file members.

Working with the foreign secretary, E A Shevardnadze, Gorbachev made skilful use of the foreign media to put the case against space weapons and nuclear testing. He met US President Reagan at Geneva and Reykjavik Nov 1985 and Oct 1986, and, at the Washington summit in Dec 1987, he concluded a treaty designed to eliminate medium-range Intermediate Nuclear Forces (INF) from European soil. This treaty was formally ratified at the Moscow summit of May–June 1988. As part of the new détente initiative, the USSR also effected a full withdrawal of its troops from Afghanistan in Feb 1989 and made broad cutbacks in the size of its conventional forces during 1989–90.

Gorbachev pressed for an acceleration (*uskoreniye*) of his domestic, economic, and political programme

of restructuring (*perestroika*) from 1987, but faced growing opposition both from conservatives grouped around Egor Ligachev and radicals led by Boris Yeltsin. His glasnost policy helped fan growing nationalist demands for secession among the republics of the Baltic and Transcaucasia. To add momentum to the reform process, Gorbachev convened, in June 1988, a special 4,991 member All-Union Party Conference, the first since 1941. At this meeting a radical constitutional overhaul was approved. A new 'super-legislature', the CUPD, was created from which a full-time working parliament was subsequently to be elected, headed by a state president with increased powers. The members of this CUPD were to be chosen in competition with one another. The authority of the local soviets was enhanced and their structures made more democratic, while, in the economic sphere, it was agreed to re-introduce private leasehold farming, reform the

USSR: Constituent Republics

Republic	Capital	Area in sq km	Date of joining USSR
Armenia	Yerevan	29,800	**1936
Azerbaijan	Baku	86,600	**1936
Byelorussia	Minsk	207,600	1922
Estonia	Tallinn	45,100	1940
Georgia	Tbilisi	69,700	**1936
Kazakhstan	Alma-Ata	2,717,300	*1936
Kirghizia	Frunze	198,500	*1936
Latvia	Riga	63,700	1940
Lithuania	Vilnius	65,200	1940
Moldavia	Kishinev	33,700	1940
Russian Soviet Federal Socialist Republic (RSFSR)	Moscow	17,075,000	1922
Tadzhikistan	Dushanbe	143,100	*1929
Turkmenistan	Ashkhabad	488,100	*1924
Ukraine	Kiev	603,700	1922
Uzbekistan	Tashkent	447,400	*1924
USSR	Moscow	22,274,500	1922

* formerly Autonomous Republics with the USSR
** formerly part of the Trans-Caucasian Soviet Socialist Republic, which joined the USSR 1922.

price system and allow part-time private enterprise in the service and small-scale industry sectors.

The June 1988 reforms constituted the most fundamental re-ordering of the Soviet policy since the 'Stalinist departure' of 1928, entailing the creation of a new type of 'socialist democracy', as well as a new mixed, private-public economic system. In the CUPD elections of Mar–Apr 1989, public opposition to conservative apparatchiks was made apparent. In May 1989, the CUPD elected Gorbachev as its chair, and thus as state president. During 1989 this movement towards 'socialist pluralism' was furthered by Gorbachev's abandonment of the ◊Brezhnev doctrine and his sanctioning of the establishment of non-communist and 'reform communist' governments elsewhere in Eastern Europe. This led to the ruling regimes of Poland, Czechoslovakia and Romania being overthrown in a wave of 'people's power'. Responding to these developments in Feb 1990, the CPSU Central Committee agreed to create a new, directly elected state executive presidency on the US and French models.

The Gorbachev reform programme showed signs of running out of control during 1989–90 as a result both of growing nationalist tensions—which in Apr 1989 and Jan 1990 had prompted the dispatch of troops to the Caucasus region, first to break up demonstrations in Tbilisi, Georgia, and then to attempt to quell a civil war that had broken out between Armenia and Azerbaijan over the disputed enclave of ◊Nagorno-Karabakh—and mounting popular discontent over the failure of perestroika to improve living standards.

UNITA abbreviation for *National Union for the Total Independence of Angola*, an Angolan nationalist movement backed by South Africa, which continued to wage guerrilla warfare against the ruling MPLA regime after the latter gained control of the country in 1976.

Unitarianism a Christian denomination that rejects the orthodox doctrine of the Trinity, asserts the fatherhood of God and the brotherhood of man, and gives a pre-eminent position to Jesus as a religious teacher, while denying his deity.

Unitarians believe in individual conscience and reason as a guide to right action, rejecting the doctrines of original sin, the atonement, and eternal punishment. It is widespread in England and North America. See also ◊Arianism and ◊Socinianism.

United Arab Emirates federation in SW Asia, on the Arabian Gulf, bounded to the SW by Saudi Arabia and to the SE by Oman.

government A provisional constitution for the United Arab Emirates (UAE) has been in effect since Dec 1971 and provides a federal structure for a union of seven sheikdoms. The highest authority is the Supreme Council of Rulers, which includes all seven sheiks. Each is a hereditary emir and an absolute monarch in his own country. The council elects two of its members to be president and vice president of the federal state for a five-year term. The president then appoints a prime minister and council of ministers.

There is a federal National Council of 40 members appointed by the emirates for a two-year term and this operates as a consultative assembly. There are no political parties.

history For early history, see ◊Arabia. In 1952 the seven sheikdoms of Abu Dhabi, Ajman, Dubai, Fujairah, Ras al Khaimah, Sharjah, and Umm al Qaiwain set up, on British advice, the Trucial Council, consisting of all seven rulers, with a view to eventually establishing a federation. In the 1960s the Trucial States, as they were known, became very wealthy through the exploitation of oil deposits.

The whole area was under British protection but in 1968 the British government announced that it was withdrawing its forces within three years. The seven Trucial States, with Bahrain and Qatar, formed the Federation of Arab Emirates, which was intended to become a federal state, but in 1971 Bahrain and Qatar seceded to become independent nations. Six of the Trucial States then combined to form the United Arab Emirates. The remaining sheikdom, Ras al Khaimah, joined Feb 1972. Sheik Zayed Bin al-Nahayan, the ruler of Abu Dhabi, became the first president.

In 1976 Sheik Zayed, disappointed with the slow progress towards centralization, was persuaded to accept another term as president only with assurances that the federal government would be given more control over such activities as defence and internal security. In recent years the United Arab Emirates has played an increasingly important role in Middle East affairs and in 1985 it established diplomatic and economic links with the USSR and China.

The Supreme Council of Rulers comprises:
Abu Dhabi Sheikh Zayed Bin Sultan al-Nahayan (1966)
Dubai Sheikh Rashid Bin Said al-Maktoum (1958)
Sharjah Sheikh Sultan Bin Muhammad al-Quasimi (1972)
Ras al Khaimah Sheikh Saqr Bin Muhammad al-Quasimi (1948)
Umm al Qaiwain Sheikh Rashid Bin Ahmad al-Mu'alla (1981)
Ajman Sheikh Humaid Bin Rashid al-Nuami (1981)
Fujairah Sheikh Hamad Bin Muhammad al-Sharqi (1974).

United Arab Republic union formed 1958, broken 1961, between ◊Egypt and ◊Syria. Egypt continued to use the name after the breach until 1971.

United Artists (UA) Hollywood film studio formed 1919 by silent-screen stars Charles Chaplin, Mary Pickford, and Douglas Fairbanks, and director D W Griffiths, in order to take control of their artistic and financial affairs. Smaller than the other major studios, UA concentrated on producing adaptations of literary works in the 1930s and 1940s, including *Wuthering Heights* 1939, *Rebecca* 1940, and *Major Barbara* 1941. The company nearly collapsed after the box-office disaster of Michael Cimino's *Heaven's Gate* 1980, and UA was subsequently bought by MGM.

United Australia Party Australian political party formed by J A ◊Lyons 1931 from the right-wing Nationalist Party. It was led by Robert Menzies after the death of Lyons. Considered to have become too dominated by financial interests, it lost heavily to the Labor Party 1943, and was reorganized as the ◊Liberal Party 1944.

United Democratic Front moderate political organization in South Africa, formed in the 1980s. It was the main focus of anti-apartheid action within South Africa until 1989, while the African National Congress and Pan-Africanist Congress were illegal.

United Irishmen a society formed 1791 by Wolfe ◊Tone to campaign for parliamentary reform in Ireland. It later became a secret revolutionary group.

Inspired by the Republican ideals of the French Revolution, the United Irishmen was initially a debating society, calling for reforms such as the right of Catholics to vote in Irish elections, but after an attempt to suppress it in 1793 the organization became secret, looking to France for military aid. An attempted insurrection in 1798 was quickly defeated and the leaders captured.

United Kingdom country in NW Europe off the coast of France, consisting of England, Scotland, Wales, and Northern Ireland.

government The UK is a constitutional monarchy with parliamentary government. There is no written constitution. Cabinet government, which is at the heart of the system, is founded on rigid convention, and the relationship between the monarch as head of state and the prime minister as

Soviet Union

The Soviet Republics

United Arab Emirates

(UAE) federation of the emirates of **Abu Dhabi, Ajman, Dubai, Fujairah, Sharjah, Umm al Qaiwain, Ras al Khaimah**

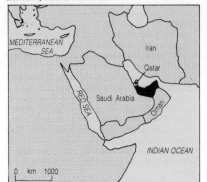

total area 83,657 sq km/32,292 sq mi
capital Abu Dhabi
towns chief port Dubai
physical mainly desert; mountains in E
features linked by their dependence on oil revenues
head of state and of government Zayed Bin

Sultan al-Nahayan from 1971
government absolutism
political parties no recognisable political parties
exports oil, natural gas
currency UAE dirham (1.00 = £1 Mar 1990)
population (1986) 1,770,000 (10% are nomadic); annual growth rate 6.1%
life expectancy men 65, women 70
language Arabic (official); Farsi, Hindi and Urdu are spoken by immigrant oilfield workers from Iran, India, and Pakistan
religion Muslim 90%, Christian, Hindu
literacy 56% (1985)
GNP $25 bn (1983); $23,000 per head of population
chronology
1952 Trucial Council established.
1971 Federation of Arab Emirates came into being but was later dissolved. Six of the Trucial States formed the United Arab Emirates, with the ruler of Abu Dhabi, Sheik Zayed, as president.
1972 The seventh state joined.
1976 Sheik Zayed threatened to relinquish presidency unless progress towards centralization became more rapid.
1985 Diplomatic and economic links with the USSR and China established.
1987 Diplomatic relations with Egypt restored.

head of government is similarly based. Parliament is sovereign, in that it is free to make and unmake any laws that it chooses, and the government is subject to the laws that Parliament makes, as interpreted by the courts.

Parliament has two legislative and debating chambers, the House of Lords and the House of Commons. The House of Lords has three main kinds of members: those who are there by accident of birth, the hereditary peers; those who are there because of some office they hold; and those who are appointed to serve for life, the life peers. There are nearly 800 hereditary peers. Among those sitting by virtue of their position are 2 archbishops and 24 bishops of the Church of England and 9 senior judges, known as the law lords. The appointed life peers now include about 65 women, or peeresses. The House of Commons has 650 members, elected by universal adult suffrage from single-member geographical constituencies, each constituency containing, on average, about 65,000 electors.

Although the House of Lords is termed the upper house, its powers, in relation to those of the Commons, have been steadily reduced so that now it has no control over financial legislation and merely a delaying power, of a year, over other bills. Before an act of Parliament becomes law it must pass through a five-stage process in each chamber, first reading, second reading, committee stage, report stage, and third reading, and then receive the formal royal assent. Bills, other than financial ones, can be introduced in either house, but most begin in the Commons.

The monarch appoints as prime minister the leader of the party with most support in the House of Commons and he or she, in turn, chooses and presides over a cabinet. The voting system, which does not include any form of proportional representation, favours two-party politics, and both chambers of Parliament are physically designed to accommodate two parties, the ruling party sitting on one side of the presiding Speaker and the opposition on the other. The party with the second largest number of seats in the Commons is recognized as the official opposition, and its leader is paid a salary out of public funds and provided with an office within the Palace of Westminster, as the Houses of Parliament are called.

history For early history, see ◊Britain, ancient; ◊England, history; ◊Scotland, history; ◊Wales,

history; ◊Ireland, history. The term 'United Kingdom' became official 1801, but was in use from 1707, when the Act of Union combined Scotland and England into the United Kingdom of Great Britain. Cabinet government developed under Robert Walpole, in practice the first prime minister (1721–42). Two ◊Jacobite rebellions sought to restore the Stuarts to the throne until the Battle of ◊Culloden 1746, after which the Scottish Highlanders were brutally suppressed. The American colonies were lost in the War of ◊American Independence.

The Act of Ireland 1801 united Britain and Ireland. This was the time of the ◊Industrial Revolution, the mechanization of production that shifted the balance of political power from the landowner to the industrial capitalist and created an exploited urban working class. In protest, the ◊Luddites destroyed machinery. Agricultural ◊enclosures were driving the small farmers off the land. The alliance of the industrialists with the ◊Whigs produced a new party, the Liberals, with an ideology of ◊free trade and nonintervention in economic affairs. In 1832 they carried a Reform Bill transferring political power from the aristocracy to the middle classes and for the next 40 years the Liberal Party was a major force. The working classes, who had no vote, created their own organizations in the trade unions and ◊Chartism; their attempts to seek parliamentary reform were brutally suppressed (◊Peterloo Massacre 1819). The Conservative minister Robert Peel introduced a number of domestic reforms, including the repeal of the Corn Laws 1846.

After 1875 the UK's industrial monopoly was challenged by Germany and the USA. To seek new markets and sources of raw materials, the Conservatives under Disraeli launched the UK on a career of imperialist expansion in Egypt, South Africa, and elsewhere. Canada, Australia, and New Zealand became self-governing dominions.

The domestic issues after 1900 were social reform and home rule for Ireland; the Labour Party emerged from an alliance of trade unions and small socialist bodies 1900; the ◊suffragettes were active until ◊World War I. After the war a wave of strikes culminated in the general strike 1926; three years later a world economic crisis precipitated the Depression that marked the 1930s and brought to power a coalition government 1931.

In 1945 the UK was still nominally at the head of an empire that covered a quarter of

the world's surface and included a quarter of its population and, although two world wars had gravely weakened it, many of its citizens and some of its politicians still saw it as a world power. The reality of its position soon became apparent when the newly elected Labour government, led by Clement Attlee, confronted the problems of rebuilding the damaged economy. This renewal was greatly helped, as in other West European countries, by support from the USA through the Marshall Plan. Between 1945 and 1951 the Labour government carried out an ambitious programme of public ownership and investment, and laid the foundations of a national health service and welfare state. During the same period the dismemberment of the British Empire, restyled the British ◊Commonwealth, was begun, a process that was to continue into the 1980s.

When in 1951 the Conservative Party was returned to power, under Winston Churchill, the essential features of the welfare state and the public sector were retained. In 1955 Churchill, in his 81st year, handed over to the foreign secretary, Anthony Eden. In 1956 Eden found himself confronted by the takeover of the Suez Canal by the president of Egypt, Gamal Nasser. Eden's perception of the threat posed by Nasser was not shared by everyone, even within the Conservative Party. The British invasion of Egypt, in conjunction with France and Israel, brought widespread criticism and was abandoned in the face of pressure from the USA and the United Nations. Eden resigned, on the grounds of ill health, and the Conservatives chose Harold Macmillan as their new leader and prime minister.

By the early 1960s, the economy had improved, living standards had risen, and Macmillan was known as 'Supermac'. Internationally, he established working relationships with the US presidents Eisenhower and Kennedy. He also did much for the Commonwealth, but he was sufficiently realistic to see that the UK's long-term economic and political future lay in Europe. By the mid-1950s the framework for the European Community (EC) had been created, with the UK an onlooker rather than a participant. The Conservatives won the 1959 general election with an increased majority and in 1961 the first serious attempt was made to join the EC, only to have it blocked by the French president, Charles de Gaulle.

Despite rising living standards, the UK's economic performance was not as successful as that of many of its competitors, particularly West Germany and Japan. There was a growing awareness that there was insufficient investment in industry, that the best young talent was going into the professions or financial institutions rather than manufacturing, and that training was poorly planned and inadequately funded. It was against this background that Macmillan unexpectedly resigned 1963, on the grounds of ill health, and was succeeded by the foreign secretary, Lord Home, who immediately renounced his title to become Alec Douglas-Home.

In the general election 1964 the Labour Party won a slender majority and its leader, Harold Wilson, became prime minister. The election had been fought on the issue of the economy. Wilson created the Department of Economic Affairs (DEA) to challenge the short-term conservatism of the Treasury, and brought in a leading trade unionist to head a new Department of Technology. In an early general election 1966 Wilson increased his Commons majority but his promises of fundamental changes in economic planning, industrial investment, and improved work practices were not fulfilled. The DEA was disbanded 1969 and an ambitious plan for the reform of industrial relations was dropped in the face of trade-union opposition.

In 1970 the Conservatives returned to power under Edward Heath. He, too, saw institutional change as one way of achieving industrial reform and created two new central departments (Trade and Industry, Environment) and a 'think tank' to advise the government on long-term strategy, the Central Policy Review Staff (CPRS). He attempted to change the climate of industrial relations through a long and complicated Industrial Relations Bill. He saw entry into the EC as the 'cold shower of competition' that industry needed, and membership was negotiated 1972.

Heath's 'counterrevolution', as he saw it, was frustrated by the trade unions, and the sharp rise in oil prices 1973 forced a U-turn in economic policy. Instead of abandoning 'lame ducks' to their fate, he found it necessary to take ailing industrial companies, such as Rolls-Royce, into public ownership. The introduction of a statutory incomes policy precipitated a national miners' strike in the winter of 1973–74 and Heath decided to challenge the unions by holding an early general election 1974. The result was a hung Parliament, with Labour winning the biggest number of seats but no single party having an overall majority. Heath tried briefly to form a coalition with the Liberals and, when this failed, resigned.

Harold Wilson returned to the premiership, heading a minority government, but in another general election later the same year won enough additional seats to give him a working majority. He had taken over a damaged economy and a nation puzzled and divided by the events of the previous years. He turned to Labour's natural ally and founder, the trade-union movement, for support and jointly they agreed a 'social contract': the government pledged itself to redress the imbalance between management and unions created by the Heath industrial-relations legislation, and the unions promised to cooperate in a voluntary industrial and incomes policy. Wilson met criticism from a growing left-wing movement within his party, impatient for radical change. In Mar 1976 Wilson, apparently tired and disillusioned, retired in mid-term.

Wilson was succeeded by James Callaghan, his senior by some four years. In the other two parties, Heath had unexpectedly been ousted by Margaret Thatcher, and the Liberal Party leader, Jeremy Thorpe, had resigned after a personal scandal and been succeeded by the young Scottish MP David Steel. Callaghan was now leading a divided party and a government with a dwindling parliamentary majority. Later in 1976 an unexpected financial crisis arose from a drop in confidence in the overseas exchange markets, a rapidly falling pound, and a drain on the country's foreign reserves. After considerable debate within the cabinet both before and afterwards, it was decided to seek help from the IMF and submit to its stringent economic policies. Within weeks the crisis was over and within months the economy was showing clear signs of improvement.

In 1977, to shore up his slender parliamentary majority, Callaghan entered into an agreement with the new leader of the Liberal Party, David Steel. Under the 'Lib-Lab Pact' Labour pursued moderate, nonconfrontational policies in consultation with the Liberals, who, in turn, voted with the government, and the economy improved dramatically. The Lib-Lab Pact had effectively finished by the autumn of 1978 and soon the social contract with the unions began to disintegrate. Widespread and damaging strikes in the public sector badly affected essential services during what became known as the 'winter of discontent'. At the end of Mar 1979 Callaghan lost a vote of confidence in the House of Commons and was forced into a general election.

The Conservatives returned to power under the UK's first female prime minister, Margaret Thatcher. She inherited a number of inflationary public-sector pay awards which, together with a budget that doubled the rate of value added tax, resulted in a sharp rise in prices and interest rates. The Conservatives were pledged to reduce inflation, and did so by mainly monetarist

policies, which caused the number of unemployed to rise from 1.3 million to 2 million in the first year. Thatcher had experience in only one government department, and it was nearly two years before she made any major changes to the cabinet she inherited from Heath. In foreign affairs Zimbabwe became independent 1980 after many years, and without the bloodshed many had feared.

Meanwhile, important changes were taking place in the other parties. Callaghan resigned the leadership of the Labour Party 1980 and was replaced by the left-winger Michael Foot, and early in 1981 three Labour shadow cabinet members, David Owen, Shirley Williams, and William Rodgers, with the former deputy leader Roy Jenkins (collectively dubbed the 'Gang of Four'), broke away to form a new centrist group,

United Kingdom

© Century Hutchinson Limited

United Kingdom

United Kingdom

The districts of Northern Ireland
1 Londonderry
2 Limavady
3 Coleraine
4 Ballymoney
5 Moyle
6 Larne
7 Ballymena
8 Magherafelt
9 Cookstown
10 Strabane
11 Omagh
12 Fernanagh
13 Dungannon
14 Craigavon
15 Armagh
16 Newry and Mourne
17 Banbridge
18 Down
19 Lisburn
20 Antrim
21 Newtownabbey
22 Carrickfergus
23 North Down
24 Arda
25 Castlereagh
26 Belfast

party since 1945, although with appreciably less than half the popular vote. Thatcher was now able to establish her position firmly, replacing most of her original cabinet.

The next three years were marked by rising unemployment and growing dissent: a dispute at the government's main intelligence-gathering station, GCHQ; a bitter and protracted miners' strike; increasing violence in Northern Ireland; an attempted assassination of leading members of the Conservative Party during their annual conference; riots in inner-city areas of London, Bristol, and Liverpool. The government was further embarrassed by its own prosecutions under the Official Secrets Act and the resignations of two prominent cabinet ministers. With the short-term profits from North Sea oil and an ambitious privatization programme, the inflation rate continued to fall and by the winter of 1986–87 the economy was buoyant enough to allow the Chancellor of the Exchequer to arrange a pre-election spending and credit boom.

There had been leadership changes in two of the other parties. Michael Foot was replaced by his Welsh protégé, Neil Kinnock; Roy Jenkins was replaced by David Owen as SDP leader, to be succeeded in turn by Robert Maclennan Sept 1987, when the SDP and Liberal parties voted to initiate talks with a view to an eventual merger. Despite the unemployment figures and Thatcher's increasingly authoritarian style of government, the Conservatives were re-elected June 1987, although with virtually no popular support in Scotland and Wales.

The merger of the Liberal and Social Democratic parties was an acrimonious affair, with the SDP, led by David Owen, refusing to join the merged party and operating as a rival group. Paddy Ashdown emerged as the leader of the new party. The long-drawn legal battle of the government to prevent publication of Peter Wright's *Spycatcher* memoirs was finally lost in 1989.

In a major cabinet reshuffle in July 1989, Geoffrey Howe was replaced as foreign secretary by John Major. In Oct 1989 chancellor of the Exchequer Nigel Lawson resigned because of disagreements with the prime minister, and Major replaced him. Douglas Hurd took over the foreign office. In Nov 1989 live television transmissions of House of Commons proceedings began for a trial period, and in Dec 1989 Mrs Thatcher won the first election for the leadership of her party since 1975. The government was criticized for its decision to forcibly repatriate Vietnamese 'boat people' and for its decision to give UK right of abode to the families of 50,000 'key' Hong Kong citizens, after the transfer of the colony to China in 1997.

United Kingdom Atomic Energy Authority UK national authority, established 1954, responsible for research and development of all nonmilitary aspects of nuclear energy. The authority also provides private industry with contract research and development, and specialized technical and advanced engineering services.

The main areas of research are: thermal reactors, fast reactors, fusion, decommissioning of plants and radioactive waste management, nuclear fuels, and environmental and energy technology. The principal establishments are at the Atomic Energy Research Establishment, Harwell, Oxfordshire; the Culham Laboratory, Oxfordshire; Dounreay, Scotland; Risley, Cheshire; and Winfrith, Dorset.

United Nations (UN) association of states (successor to the ◊League of Nations) for international peace, security, and cooperation, with its headquarters in New York. Its charter was drawn up at the San Francisco Conference 1945, based on proposals drafted at the Dumbarton Oaks conference. The original intention was that the UN's Security Council would preserve the wartime alliance of the USA, USSR, and Britain (with France and China also permanent members) in order to maintain the peace. This never happened

the ◊Social Democratic Party (SDP). The new party made an early impression, winning a series of by-elections within months of its creation. From 1983 to 1988 the Liberals and the SDP were linked in an electoral pact, the Alliance. They advocated the introduction of a system of ◊proportional representation, which would ensure a fairer parity between votes and seats won.

Unemployment continued to rise, passing the 3-million mark in Jan 1982, and the Conservatives,

and their leader in particular, were receiving low ratings in the public-opinion polls. An unforeseen event rescued them, the Argentine invasion of the Falkland Islands. Thatcher's decision to send a battle fleet to recover them paid off. The general election 1983 was fought with the euphoria of the Falklands victory still in the air and the Labour Party, under its new leader, divided and unconvincing. The Conservatives had a landslide victory, winning more Commons seats than any

United Kingdom
of Great Britain and Northern Ireland (UK)

area 243,363 sq km/93,938 sq mi
capital London
towns Birmingham, Glasgow, Leeds, Sheffield. Liverpool, Manchester, Edinburgh, Bradford, Bristol, Belfast, Newcastle-upon-Tyne, Cardiff
physical rolling landscape, becoming increasingly mountainous towards the north, with the Grampian Mountains in Scotland and Snowdon in Wales; rivers Thames and Severn
head of state Elizabeth II from 1952
head of government Margaret Thatcher from 1979
government liberal democracy
political parties Conservative and Unionist Party, right-of centre; Labour Party, moderate, left-of-centre; Social and Liberal Democrats, centre-left; Social Democratic Party (SDP) centrist; Scottish National Party (SNP), Scottish nationalist; Plaid Cymru (Welsh Nationalist Party), Welsh nationalist; Official Ulster Unionist Party (OUP), Northern Ireland moderate right-of-centre; Democratic Unionist Party (DUP), Northern Ireland, right-of-centre; Social Democratic Labour Party (SDLP), Northern Ireland, moderate, left-of-centre; Ulster People's Unionist Party (UPUP), Northern Ireland, militant right-of-centre; Sinn Fein, Northern Ireland, pro-united Ireland; Green Party, ecological
exports cereals, rape, sugar beet, potatoes, meat and meat products, poultry, dairy products, electronic and telecommunications equipment, engineering equipment and scientific instruments, North Sea oil and gas, chemicals, film and television programmes; tourism
currency pound sterling
population (1985) 56,620,000; annual growth rate 0.1%
religion mainly Christian (Church of England and other Protestant sects with Roman Catholic minority); Jewish, Muslim, Hindu minorities
language English, Welsh, Gaelic

literacy 99% (1984)
GNP $505 bn (1983); $7,216 per head of population
chronology
1707 Act of Union between England and Scotland under Queen Anne.
1783 Loss of the American colonies.
1801 Act of Ireland united Britain and Ireland.
1832 Great Reform Bill became law, shifting political power from upper to middle class.
1848 Chartist working-class movement formed.
1867 Second Reform Bill extended franchise.
1906 Liberal victory; programme of social reform.
1911 Powers of House of Lords curbed.
1914 Irish Home Rule Bill introduced.
1916 Lloyd George became prime minister.
1920 Home Rule Act incorporated the NE of Ireland (Ulster) into the United Kingdom of Great Britain and Northern Ireland.
1921 Ireland, except for Ulster, became a dominion (Irish Free State, later Eire, 1937).
1924 First Labour government led by Ramsay MacDonald.
1926 General Strike.
1931 National government; unemployment reached 3 million.
1940 Winston Churchill became head of coalition government.
1945 Labour government under Clement Attlee; birth of welfare state.
1951 Conservatives defeated Labour.
1956 Suez crisis.
1964 Labour victory under Harold Wilson.
1970 Conservatives under Edward Heath defeated Labour.
1972 Parliament prorogued in Northern Ireland; direct rule from Westminster began.
1973 UK joined European Community.
1974 Three-day week, coal strike; Wilson replaced Heath.
1976 James Callaghan replaced Wilson as prime minister.
1977 Liberal-Labour pact.
1979 Victory for Conservatives under Margaret Thatcher.
1981 Formation of Social Democratic Party (SDP). Riots in inner cities.
1982 Unemployment over 3 million. Falklands War.
1983 Thatcher re-elected.
1984–85 Coal strike, the longest in British history.
1986 Abolition of metropolitan counties.
1987 Thatcher re-elected for third term.
1988 Liberals and most of SDP merged into the Social and Liberal Democrats.
1989 The Green Party polled 2 million votes in the European election and finished third behind Labour and the Conservatives. Margaret Thatcher re-elected as Conservative Party leader.
1990 Riots as Poll Tax introduced in England.

of South African and Cuban troops from Angola, paving the way for the independence of Namibia. He has also initiated talks between Greek and Turkish leaders in Cyprus.

The UN comprises:

General Assembly one member from each of 159 member states who meet annually; decisions on important questions require a two-thirds majority, while on minor ones, a simple majority suffices;

Security Council five permanent members (UK, USA, USSR, France, China, who exercise a veto in that their support is requisite for all decisions), plus ten others who hold office on a rotating basis. It may undertake investigations into disputes and make recommendations to the parties concerned, and may call on all members to take economic or military measures to enforce its decisions;

Economic and Social Council 18 members elected for three years. It initiates studies of international economic, social, cultural, educational, health, and related matters, and may make recommendations to the General Assembly. It operates largely through specialized commissions of international experts on economics, transport and communications, human rights, status of women, and so on. It coordinates the activities of the ◊*Food and Agriculture Organization* (FAO);

General Agreement on Tariffs and Trade (GATT) established 1948, headquarters in Geneva; reduction of trade barriers, anti-dumping code, assistance to trade of Third World countries;

◊*International Atomic Energy Agency* (IAEA);

International Bank for Reconstruction and Development (IBRD) popularly known as the ◊World Bank;

International Civil Aviation Organization (ICAO) established 1947, headquarters in Montreal; safety and efficiency, international facilities and air law;

International Development Association (IDA) administered by the World Bank;

International Finance Corporation (IFC) established 1956; affiliated to the World Bank, it encourages private enterprise in less industrialized countries;

International Fund for Agricultural Development (IFAD) established 1977, headquarters in Rome; additional funds for benefiting the poorest in Third World countries;

◊*International Labour Organization* (ILO);

International Maritime Organization (IMO) established 1958, headquarters in London; safety at sea, pollution control, abolition of restrictive practices;

◊*International Monetary Fund* (IMF);

International Telecommunication Union (ITU) established 1934, headquarters in Geneva; allocation of radio frequencies; promotes low tariffs and life-saving measures for, for example, disasters at sea;

United Nations Educational, Scientific, and Cultural Organization (◊UNESCO);

◊*Universal Postal Union* (UPU);

◊*World Health Organization* (WHO);

World Intellectual Property Organization (WIPO) established 1974, headquarters in Geneva; protection of copyright in the arts, science, and industry;

World Meteorological Organization (WMO) established 1951, headquarters in Geneva;

Trusteeship Council consisting of members administering ◊trust territories, other permanent members of the Security Council, plus sufficient other elected members to balance the administering powers;

International Court of Justice at The Hague, with 15 judges elected by the General Assembly and Security Council;

Secretariat headed by a secretary general who is elected for five years by the General Assembly.

United Provinces of Agra and Oudh /ˈɑːɡrə, aʊd/ former province of British India which

because of the outbreak of the Cold War, but the UN has played a role in many other areas such as refugees, development assistance, disaster relief, and cultural cooperation.

Members contribute financially according to their resources, an apportionment being made by the General Assembly, with the addition of voluntary contributions from some governments to the funds of the UN. These finance the programme of assistance carried out by the UN intergovernmental agencies, the *United Nations Children's Fund* (UNICEF), the UN refugee organizations, and the *United Nations Special Fund* for developing countries. There are six official working languages: English, French, Russian, Spanish, Chinese, and Arabic.

The influence in the UN, originally with the Allied states of World War II, is now more widely

spread. Although part of the value of the UN lies in recognition of member states as sovereign and equal, the rapid increase in membership of minor—in some cases minute—states was causing concern by 1980 (154 members) as lessening the weight of voting decisions. Taiwan, formerly a permanent member of the Security Council, was expelled 1971 on the admission of China. The UN also suffers from the lack of adequate and independent funds and forces, the latter having been employed with varying success, for example, in Korea, Cyprus, and Sinai, and the intrusion of the Cold War which divided members into adherents of the East or West and the uncommitted. However, since becoming UN secretary-general in 1982, Javier Pérez de Cuellar has been responsible for several successful peace initiatives, including the ending of the Iran–Iraq war and the withdrawal

United Nations peacekeeping forces

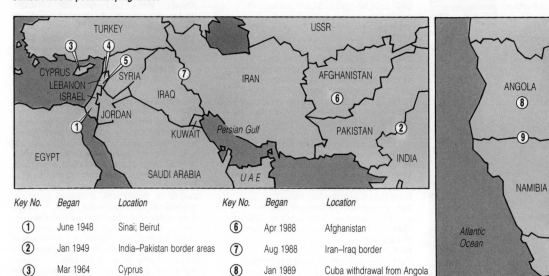

Key No.	Began	Location
①	June 1948	Sinai; Beirut
②	Jan 1949	India–Pakistan border areas
③	Mar 1964	Cyprus
④	June 1974	Golan Heights
⑤	Mar 1978	Southern Lebanon

Key No.	Began	Location
⑥	Apr 1988	Afghanistan
⑦	Aug 1988	Iran–Iraq border
⑧	Jan 1989	Cuba withdrawal from Angola
⑨	Apr 1989	Namibia

300 miles

formed the major part of the state of ◊Uttar Pradesh; see also ◊Agra, ◊Oudh.

United Provinces of Central America political union 1823–38 between the the the Central American states of Costa Rica, El Salvador, Guatemala, Honduras, and Nicaragua. The union followed the break-up of the Spanish empire and was initially dominated by Guatemala. Its unity was more apparent than real, and the federation fell apart in 1838. Subsequent attempts at reunification foundered.

United States architecture native American architecture survives largely in the southwest along with Spanish influence from early colonizers, but on the east coast from the 17th century English immigrants had the main influence. The USA has constantly adopted traditions from elsewhere: 17th-century English, 18th-century English Neo-Classical, French influences in the 19th century, followed by the Queen Anne style, then another Neo-Classical phase. The ◊skyscraper is most characteristic of contemporary US architecture.

history:

17th century: English influence—early buildings at Harvard University in Massachusetts and at William and Mary College in Virginia resemble Oxford and Cambridge. Georgian houses proliferate in Virginia, Philadelphia, and Boston.

18th century: Neo-Classical phase introduced by Thomas Jefferson (Jefferson's house at Monticello, the Federal Capitol at Washington by William Thornton, the ◊White House by James Hoban).

19th century: Post–Civil War generation of French-trained architects such as H H Richardson, and development of a modified Romanesque style. Late 19th century saw a revival of the Queen Anne style followed by a second Classical revival (Columbia University, New York).

20th century: Some of the best early skyscrapers were designed by L H ◊Sullivan. Frank Lloyd Wright was a great innovator. Walter Gropius and Ludwig Mies van der Rohe, successive directors of the ◊Bauhaus, and the Saarinens were all European exiles. Recent architects include Philip Johnson, Robert Venturi, and Chinese-born Ieoh Ming Pei.

United States art painting and sculpture in the USA from colonial times to the present. The unspoiled landscapes romantically depicted in the 18th and 19th centuries gave way to realistic city scenes in the 20th. Modern movements have flourished in the USA, among them Abstract Expressionism and Pop art.

colonial The first American-born artist in the European tradition was the portraitist Robert Feke (1705–50). The historical painter Benjamin West, working mainly in England, encouraged the portraitist John Singleton Copley. Charles Willson Peale painted the founders of the new nation.

19th century The dramatic landscapes of Washington Allston, the nature pictures of Audubon, the seascapes of Winslow Homer, the realism of Thomas Eakins, and the Romantic landscapes of the Hudson River school represent the vitality of US art in this period. The Impressionist-influenced James Whistler and Mary Cassatt and the society painter John Singer Sargent were active mainly in Europe.

early 20th century The Ashcan school depicted slum squalor. The Armory Show introduced Europe's most avant-garde styles, Cubism and Futurism; Dada arrived soon after. In the 1930s and 1940s several major European artists emigrated to the USA, notably Max Ernst, Max Beckmann, Piet Mondrian, Hans Hoffmann, and Lyonel Feininger. The giant heads of presidents carved out of Mount Rushmore are by G Borglum.

mid-20th century Abstract Expressionism was exemplified by the inventor of action painting, Jackson Pollock, and the spiritual Mark Rothko. More politically concerned, Ben Shahn created influential graphics. The sculptor Alexander Calder invented mobiles.

late 20th century The Pop-art movement dominated the 1960s and led to multimedia works and performance art in the following decades.

United States literature US literature falls into two distinct periods: colonial writing 1620–1776, largely dominated by the Puritans, and post-Revolutionary literature after 1787, when the ideal of US literature developed, and poetry, fiction, and drama began to evolve on national principles. Between 1840 and the Civil War a new literature grew under the influence of Transcendentalism, including the work of R W Emerson and H D Thoreau in prose, Hawthorne and Melville in fiction, and Walt Whitman in poetry. The period after the Civil War saw a rise of realism and regional writing, dominated by Twain, James, Howells, and Stephen Crane, with Whitman and Emily Dickinson in poetry. After 1900 the impact of the modern movement grew through expatriates like Stein, Pound, and T S Eliot. The dominant figures of the first

half of the 20th century—Pound, Eliot, Stevens, Hemingway, Faulkner, Dos Passos, Fitzgerald, O'Neill—show this influence. After World War II, US writers became internationally known. Faulkner, Hemingway, Steinbeck, Bellow, and I B Singer won Nobel prizes, the plays of Arthur Miller and Tennessee Williams were internationally performed, and acknowledgement of the past achievement of US literature increased. US literature stands as a major contributor to the 19th- and 20th-century arts, influencing the direction of literature everywhere.

American literature of the *colonial period* 1607–1765 includes travel books and religious verse, but is mainly theological: Roger Williams, Cotton Mather, and Jonathan Edwards were typical Puritan writers. Benjamin Franklin's *Autobiography* is the first work of more than historical interest.

The *post-Revolutionary period* 1785–1820 produced much political writing, by Paine, Jefferson, and Hamilton, and one noteworthy poet, Philip Freneau.

In the *early 19th century* the influence of English Romantics became evident, notably on the poems of William Cullen Bryant (1794–1878), Washington Irving's tales, Charles Brockden Brown's Gothic fiction, and James Fenimore Cooper's novels of frontier life. During 1830–60 intellectual life centred on New England, which produced the essayists Emerson, Thoreau, and Holmes; the poets Longfellow, J R Lowell, and Whittier; the historians Parkman, W H Prescott (1796–1859), and J L Motley (1814–77); and the novelist Hawthorne. Outside the New England circle stood Poe and Melville.

The disillusionment of the *post–Civil War period* 1865–1900 found expression in the realistic or psychological novel. Ambrose Bierce and Stephen Crane wrote realistic war stories; Mark Twain and Bret Harte dealt with western life; the growth of industrialism led to the novel of social realism, notably in the work of W D Howells and Frank Norris; while Henry James and his disciple Edith Wharton developed the novel of psychological analysis. The dominant poets were Walt Whitman and Emily Dickinson.

Since 1900 the main trend of *fiction* has been realistic, as in the work of Jack London, Upton Sinclair, and Theodore Dreiser, or has been influenced by modernist experiment. After World War I Sherwood Anderson, Sinclair Lewis,

United States of America (USA)

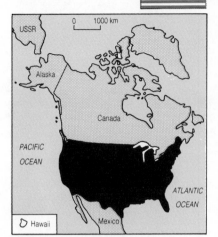

area 9,391,900 sq km/3,626,213 sq mi
capital Washington DC
towns New York, Los Angeles, Chicago, Philadelphia, Detroit, San Francisco, Washington,
Dallas, San Diego, San Antonio, Houston,
Boston, Baltimore, Phoenix, Indianapolis,
Memphis: all metropolitan areas over 2 million
population
physical includes almost every kind of topography and vegetation; mountain ranges parallel
with E and W coasts, and the Rocky Mountains
separate rivers emptying into the Pacific from
those flowing into the Gulf of Mexico; Great
Lakes in N; rivers Hudson, Mississippi, Missouri,
Colorado, Columbia
head of state and of government George
Bush from 1989
government liberal-democracy
political parties Democratic Party, liberal,
centre; Republican Party, centre-right
currency US dollar (1.70 = £1 Mar 1990)
population (1985) 238,740,000 (ethnic
minorities include 26,500,000 black, about
20,000,000 Hispanic, and 1,000,000 American
Indians, of whom 50% concentrated in
Arizona, California, New Mexico, North Carolina,
Oklahoma); annual growth rate 0.9%
life expectancy men 71, women 78
language English; largest minority language
Spanish
religion 73 million Protestant, 50 million Roman
Catholic, 6 million Jewish, 4 million Eastern
Orthodox
literacy 99% (1985)
GNP $3,855 bn (1983); $13,451 per head of
population
chronology
1776 Declaration of Independence.
1787 US constitution drawn up.
1789 Washington elected as first president.
1803 Louisiana Purchase.
1812–14 War of 1812 with England,
1819 Florida purchased from Spain.
1836 The battle of the Alamo, won by Mexico.
1841 First wagon train left Missouri with
emigrants for California.
1846–48 Mexican War resulted in cession to US
of Arizona, California, Colorado (part), Nevada,
New Mexico, Texas, and Utah.
1848 California gold rush.
1860 Lincoln elected president.
1861–65 Civil War between North and South.
1865 Slavery abolished. Lincoln assassinated.
1867 Alaska bought from Russia.
1890 Battle of Wounded Knee, last major battle
between American Indians and US troops.
1898 War with Spain ended with the Spanish
cession of Philippines, Puerto Rico, and Guam;
it was agreed that Cuba be independent.
1898 Hawaii annexed.
1917–18 USA entered World War I.
1929 Wall Street stock-market crash.
1933 F D Roosevelt's New Deal to alleviate the
Depression put into force.
1941 The Japanese attack on Pearl Harbor
precipitated US entry into World War II.
1950–53 US involvement in Korean war.
McCarthy anti-communist investigations.
1952 Gen Eisenhower elected president.
1960 J F Kennedy elected president.
1961 Bay of Pigs abortive CIA-backed invasion
of Cuba.
1963 Assassination of Kennedy. Johnson
assumed the presidency.
1964–68 'Great Society' civil-rights and welfare
measures.
1964–73 US involvement in Vietnam War.
1968 Nixon elected president.
1973–74 Watergate scandal.
1974 Nixon resigned as president; replaced by
Gerald Ford.
1975 Final US withdrawal from Vietnam.
1976 Carter elected president.
1979 US-Chinese diplomatic relations
normalized.
1979–80 Iranian hostage crisis.
1980 Reagan elected president. Republicans
gained Senate majority.
1983 US invasion of Grenada.
1986 Republicans lost Senate majority. Scandal
over secret US arms sales to Iran and subsidies
to Contra guerrillas in Nicaragua.
1987 INF treaty with USSR. Wall Street
stock-market crash.
1988 Vice president Bush elected president.
Democrats retained control over both houses of
Congress. US becomes world's largest debtor
nation, owing $532 billion.
1989 US troops overthrow Noriega regime in
Panama.
1990 Widespread cuts in defence expenditure
proposed.

United States of America

State	Capital	Area sq km	Date of joining the Union
Alabama	Montgomery	134,700	1819
Alaska	Juneau	1,531,100	1959
Arizona	Phoenix	294,100	1912
Arkansas	Little Rock	137,800	1836
California	Sacramento	411,100	1850
Colorado	Denver	269,700	1876
Connecticut	Hartford	13,000	1788
Delaware	Dover	5,300	1787
Florida	Tallahassee	152,000	1845
Georgia	Atlanta	152,600	1788
Hawaii	Honolulu	16,800	1959
Idaho	Boise	216,500	1890
Illinois	Springfield	146,100	1818
Indiana	Indianapolis	93,700	1816
Iowa	Des Moines	145,800	1846
Kansas	Topeka	213,200	1861
Kentucky	Frankfort	104,700	1792
Louisiana	Baton Rouge	135,900	1812
Maine	Augusta	86,200	1820
Maryland	Annapolis	31,600	1788
Massachusetts	Boston	21,500	1788
Michigan	Lansing	151,600	1837
Minnesota	St Paul	218,700	1858
Mississippi	Jackson	123,600	1817
Missouri	Jefferson City	180,600	1821
Montana	Helena	381,200	1889
Nebraska	Lincoln	200,400	1867
Nevada	Carson City	286,400	1864
New Hampshire	Concord	24,000	1788
New Jersey	Trenton	20,200	1787
New Mexico	Santa Fé	315,000	1912
New York	Albany	127,200	1788
North Carolina	Raleigh	136,400	1789
North Dakota	Bismarck	183,100	1889
Ohio	Columbus	107,100	1803
Oklahoma	Oklahoma City	181,100	1907
Oregon	Salem	251,500	1859
Pennsylvania	Harrisburg	117,400	1787
Rhode Island	Providence	3,100	1790
South Carolina	Columbia	80,600	1788
South Dakota	Pierre	199,800	1889
Tennessee	Nashville	109,200	1796
Texas	Austin	691,200	1845
Utah	Salt Lake City	219,900	1896
Vermont	Montpelier	24,900	1791
Virginia	Richmond	105,600	1788
Washington	Olympia	176,700	1889
West Virginia	Charleston	62,900	1863
Wisconsin	Madison	145,500	1848
Wyoming	Cheyenne	253,400	1890
District of Columbia	Washington	180	
Total		9,391,880	

In *literary criticism* Irving Babbitt (1865–
1933), George Santayana, H L Mencken, and
Edmund Wilson were dominant figures, followed
by Lionel Trilling (1905–75), Cleanth Brooks, Yvor
Winters (1900–68), and John Crowe Ransom,
author of *The New Criticism* 1941, which stressed
structural and linguistic factors; more recently US
criticism has been influenced by French literary
theory.

Recent US literature increasingly expresses
the cultural pluralism, regional variety, and ethnic range of US life, and the strong impact of
feminism. Black women writers like Alice Walker
and Toni Morrison typify its continuing imaginative
variety.

United States of America (USA) country in North
America, extending from the Atlantic to the Pacific, bounded by Canada to the N and Mexico to
the S, and including the outlying states of Alaska
and Hawaii.

government The USA is a federal republic comprising 50 states and the District of ◊Columbia.
Under its 1787 constitution, which has had 26
amendments, the constituent states are reserved
considerable powers of self-government. The

Ernest Hemingway, William Faulkner, F Scott
Fitzgerald, John Dos Passos, Henry Miller, and
Richard Wright established main directions in US
fiction. Among the internationally known novelists
since World War II have been Truman Capote,
J D Salinger, Saul Bellow, John Updike, Norman
Mailer, Vladimir Nabokov, Bernard Malamud,
Philip Roth, Ralph Ellison, and James Baldwin.

The **short story** has attracted many of the major novelists from James onward, and was popularized as a form by O Henry; writers specializing in
it included Ring Lardner, Katharine Anne Porter,
William Saroyan, Eudora Welty, Grace Paley, and
Raymond Carver.

In *drama* the USA produced between the wars
a powerful group of dramatists, including Eugene
O'Neill, Maxwell Anderson, Lillian Hellman, Elmer
Rice, Thornton Wilder, and Clifford Odets. This
led towards the work of Arthur Miller and Tennessee Williams, and of a later generation which
includes Edward Albee, Neil Simon, David Mamet,
and Sam Shepard.

Poets like E A Robinson, Carl Sandburg, Vachel
Lindsay, Robert Frost, and Edna St Vincent Millay
extended the older poetic tradition, but after the
◊Imagist movement of 1912–14 an experimental
modern tradition arose with Ezra Pound, T S Eliot,
William Carlos Williams, Marianne Moore, 'HD'
(Hilda Doolittle), and Wallace Stevens. Attempts at
writing the modern US epic include Pound's *Can-
tos*, Hart Crane's *The Bridge*, and W C Williams's
Paterson. Among the most striking post–World
War II poets are Karl Shapiro, Theodore
Roethke, Robert Lowell, Charles Olson, Sylvia
Plath, Gwendolyn Brooks, Denise Levertov, John
Ashbery, and A R Ammons.

federal government concentrated originally on military and foreign affairs, and the coordination of interstate concerns, leaving legislation in other spheres to the states, each with its own constitution, elected legislature, governor, supreme court, and local taxation powers. Since the 1930s, however, the federal government has increasingly impinged upon state affairs and has become the principal revenue-raising and spending agency.

The executive branch of US federal government is deliberately separate from the legislature and judiciary. At the head of the executive branch of government is a president elected every four years in a national contest by universal adult suffrage. Votes are counted at the state level on a first-past-the-post basis, with each state being assigned seats (equivalent to the number of its congressional representatives) in a national electoral college which formally elects the president. The president serves as head of state, of the armed forces and the civil service. He or she is restricted to a maximum of two terms and, once elected, cannot be removed except through impeachment and subsequent conviction by Congress. The president works with a personally selected cabinet team, subject to the Senate's approval, whose members are debarred from serving in the legislature.

The second branch of government, Congress, the federal legislature, comprises two equally powerful houses, the 100-member Senate and the 435-member House of Representatives. Senators serve six-year terms, and there are two from each state regardless of size and population. Every two years a third of the seats come up for election. Representatives are elected from single-member constituencies of roughly equal demographic size to serve for two-year terms.

Congress operates through a system of specialized standing committees. The Senate is the most powerful chamber of Congress, its approval being required for key federal appointments and for the ratification of foreign treaties. The president's policy programme needs the approval of Congress, and the president addresses Congress in Jan for an annual 'State of the Union' speech and sends periodic 'messages' and 'recommendations'. The success of a president depends on party support in Congress, bargaining skills, and public support.

Proposed legislation, to become law (an Act of Congress), requires the approval of both chambers of Congress. If differences exist, 'conference committees' are convened to effect compromise agreements. The president can impose a veto, which can be overridden only by two-thirds majorities in both congressional houses. Constitutional amendments require two-thirds majorities from both chambers of Congress and the support of three-quarters of the nation's 50 state legislatures.

The third branch of government, the judiciary, headed by the Supreme Court, interprets the written US constitution to ensure that a correct balance is maintained between federal and state institutions and the executive and legislature and to uphold the civil rights enshrined in the first ten amendments (the ◊Bill of Rights). The Supreme Court comprises nine judges appointed by the president with the Senate's approval, who serve life terms and can only be removed by impeachment. It is an unusually influential body.

Two broad catch-all party coalitions, divided regionally and ideologically, dominate US politics: the Democrats and the Republicans. Since the 1930s the Democrats have been pre-eminent both at local and at congressional level. The party is dominated by its northeast liberal wing, which supports social reform and government intervention, but the conservative southern wing is also powerful. The Republicans have been most successful during recent decades in presidential contests. They are strongest in the central and western states and adhere, in general, to a conservative 'small government' philosophy.

Both parties have only a rudimentary national organization and seldom vote as a block in Congress. Party organization is centred instead at the state and local level.

The USA administers a number of Pacific island territories, including American Samoa and the US Virgin Islands, which have local legislatures and a governor. These territories, as well as the 'self-governing territories' of Puerto Rico and Guam, each send a nonvoting delegate to the US House of Representatives.

The District of Columbia, centred around Washington DC, is the site of the federal legislature and executive. Since 1971 it has sent one nonvoting delegate to the House and since 1961 its citizens have been able to vote in presidential elections (the District having three votes in the national electoral college).

history For early history, see ◊American Indian. Spaniards first settled in Florida 1565. The first permanent English settlement was at Jamestown, Virginia, 1607. In 1620 the ◊Pilgrim Fathers landed in New England and founded Massachusetts. English Catholics founded Maryland 1634; English Quakers founded Pennsylvania 1682. A Dutch settlement (1611) on Manhattan Island, named New Amsterdam 1626, was renamed New York after it was taken by England 1664. In the 18th century the English colonies were threatened by French expansion from the Great Lakes in Canada to Louisiana until the Seven Years' War 1756–63.

In 1775 the 13 colonies (New Hampshire, Massachusetts, Rhode Island, Connecticut, New York, New Jersey, Pennsylvania, Delaware, Virginia, North Carolina, South Carolina, Maryland, and Georgia) rose against the government in Britain, declaring themselves in 1776 to be 'free and independent states'. Led by George Washington, they defeated George III's armies in the War of ◊American Independence. By the Treaty of Paris 1783 Britain recognized the independence of the 13 colonies. The constitution came into force 1789. Washington was chosen as the first president.

Louisiana was bought from Napoleon 1803 and Florida from Spain 1819. Napoleon's trade blockade of British ships led indirectly to the Anglo-American war 1812–14, and British troops captured and burned Washington. Later expansion to the west reached the Pacific, and the war with Mexico 1846–48 secured the areas of California, Utah, New Mexico, and Texas. Alaska was purchased from Russia 1867. Hawaii ceded itself to the USA 1898.

The ◊Civil War 1861–65 put an end to slavery but left ill feeling between north and south. It stimulated the industrial development of the north, and the construction of roads and railways continued until the end of the century. The USA entered ◊World War I 1917; it was not a party to the Treaty of Versailles but made peace by separate treaties 1921. A period of isolationism followed. The country's economic, industrial, and agricultural expansion was brought to a halt by the stock-market crash 1929 which marked the start of the ◊Depression. President Roosevelt's ◊New Deal 1933 tackled but did not solve the problem and only ◊World War II brought full employment. The USA stayed out of the war until Japan attacked ◊Pearl Harbor on Honolulu Dec 1941.

The USA, having emerged as a superpower, remained internationalist during the postwar era. Under the presidency of Harry S Truman (Democrat) a doctrine of intervention in support of endangered 'free peoples' and of containing the spread of communism was devised by Secretary of State Dean Acheson. This led to the USA's safeguarding of Nationalist Taiwan 1949 and its participation in the ◊Korean War 1950–53. The USA, in addition, created new global and regional bodies designed to maintain the peace—the United Nations (UN, 1945), the Organization of American States (OAS, 1948), the North Atlantic Treaty Organization (NATO, 1949), the South-East Asia

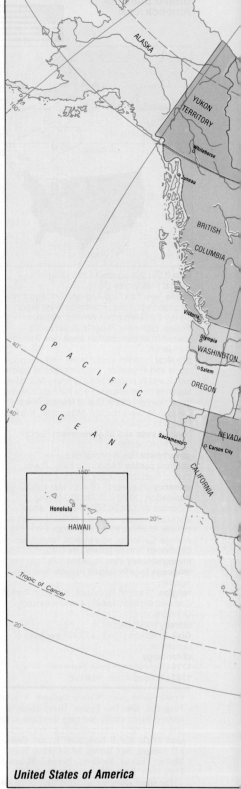

United States of America

Treaty Organization (SEATO, 1954)—and launched the Marshall Plan to strengthen the economies of its allies. Domestically, President Truman sought to introduce liberal reforms designed at extending civil and welfare rights under the slogan 'a fair deal'. These measures were blocked by a combination of southern Democrats and Republicans in Congress. Truman's foreign policy was criticized as being 'soft on Communism' between 1950 and 1952, as a wave

leadership of Dr Martin Luther King. Promising a 'New Frontier' programme of social reform, John F Kennedy (Democrat) won the presidential election Nov 1960. The new president emerged as an active opponent of Communism abroad (see ◊Bay of Pigs). He was assassinated Nov 1963.

It was left to his deputy and successor, the Texan Lyndon B Johnson, to oversee the passage of Kennedy's 'Great Society' reforms. These measures, which included the Equal Opportunities, Voting Rights, Housing, and Medicare acts, guaranteed blacks civil rights and significantly extended the reach of the federal government. They were buttressed by the judicial rulings of the Supreme Court chaired by Chief Justice Earl Warren. Abroad, President Johnson became embroiled in the ◊Vietnam War (1964–73), which polarized US public opinion and deeply divided the Democratic Party.

Johnson declined to run for re-election Nov 1968 and his former vice president Hubert Humphrey was defeated by the experienced Republican Richard Nixon. Nixon, a conservative, sent the National Guard against student demonstrators at home. Abroad, working with National Security Adviser Henry Kissinger, he began a gradual disengagement from Vietnam and launched a policy of ◊détente which brought an improvement in relations with the Soviet Union (see ◊Strategic Arms Limitation Talks) and Communist China. Nixon, faced with a divided opposition led by the liberal George McGovern, gained re-election by an overwhelming margin Nov 1972. During the campaign, Nixon's staff broke into the Democratic Party's ◊Watergate headquarters. When this and the attempts at cover-up came to light, the scandal forced the resignation of the president Aug 1974.

Watergate shook the US public's confidence in the Washington establishment. Gerald Ford, who had been vice president only since Dec 1973, kept the services of Kissinger and the policy of détente when he succeeded Nixon. He faced, however, a hostile, Democrat-dominated Congress which introduced legislation curbing the powers of the presidency and forcing isolationism abroad. He also had to deal with an economic recession and increased oil prices.

Ford contested the presidential election Nov 1976, but was defeated by the 'born again' Christian and outsider in Washington Jimmy Carter, who promised open and honest government. Carter was a fiscal conservative but social liberal, who sought to extend welfare provision through greater administrative efficiency. He substantially ended the fuel crisis through enforced conservation in the energy bills 1978 and 1980. In foreign relations President Carter emphasized human rights. In the Middle East, he moved close to a peace settlement 1978–79 (see ◊Camp David Agreements) and in Jan 1979 the USA's diplomatic relations with Communist China were fully normalized.

The Carter presidency was brought down by two foreign-policy crises 1979–80: the fall of the shah of Iran and the Soviet invasion of Afghanistan. The president's vacillating leadership style, military expenditure economies, and moralistic foreign policy were blamed for weakening US influence abroad. There was a swell of anti-Communist feeling and mounting support for a new policy of rearmament and selective interventionism. President Carter responded to this new mood by enunciating the hawkish ◊Carter Doctrine 1980 and supporting a new arms-development programme, but his popularity plunged during 1980 as economic recession gripped the country and US embassy staff were held hostage by Shi'ite fundamentalists in Tehran.

The Republican Ronald Reagan benefited from Carter's difficulties and was elected Nov 1980, when the Democrats also lost control of the Senate. The new president had risen to prominence as an effective, television-skilled campaigner. He purported to believe in a return to traditional Christian and family values and promoted a domestic policy of decentralization and deregulation. The early years of the Reagan presidency witnessed substantial reductions in taxation and cutbacks in federal welfare

of anti-Soviet hysteria, spearheaded by Senator Joseph McCarthy, swept the nation.

This rightward shift in the public mood brought Republican victory in the congressional and presidential elections 1952. The popular military commander General Dwight D Eisenhower became president and was re-elected by an increased margin Nov 1956. Working with Secretary of State John Foster Dulles, Eisenhower adhered to the Truman-Acheson doctrine of 'containment', while at home he pursued a policy of 'progressive conservatism' designed to encourage business enterprise. The Eisenhower era was one of growth, involving the migration of southern blacks to the northern industrial cities and a rapid expansion in the educational sector. In the southern states, where racial discrimination was openly practised, a new black-rights movement developed under the

programmes that created serious hardship as economic recession gripped the nation.

Reagan rejected détente and spoke of the USSR as an 'evil empire' which needed to be checked by a military build-up and a readiness to employ force. This led to a sharp deterioration in Soviet-US relations, ushering in a new cold war during the Polish crisis 1981. Reagan's popularity was restored by Oct 1983 with the successful invasion of ◊Grenada and the recovery of the economy. He was re-elected on a wave of optimistic patriotism Nov 1984, defeating the Democrat ticket of Walter Mondale and Geraldine Ferraro by a record margin. A radical tax-cutting bill was passed through Congress, and in 1986 a huge budget and trade deficit developed. At home and overseas the president faced mounting public opposition to his intervention in Central America. The new Soviet leader Mikhail Gorbachev pressed unsuccessfully for arms reduction during superpower summits at Geneva (Nov 1985) and Reykjavik (Oct 1986), but a further summit Dec 1987, with an agreement to scrap intermediate-range nuclear missiles, appeared to promise a new détente.

In Nov 1986 the Republican party lost control of the Senate in the midterm elections, just before the disclosure of a scandal concerning US arms sales to Iran in return for hostages held in Beirut, with the profits illegally diverted to help the Nicaraguan Contra (anti-government) guerrillas.

The ◊Irangate scandal briefly dented public confidence in the administration and forced the dismissal and resignation of key cabinet members, including national security adviser John Poindexter, in Nov 1986, and chief of staff Donald Regan, in Feb 1987. During the last two years of his presidency, a more consensual Reagan was on view and, helped by his Dec 1987 arms reduction deal, he left office with much of his popular affection restored.

Reagan's popularity transferred itself to vice president George Bush who, despite selecting the inexperienced Dan Quayle as his running-mate and despite evidence that he had been indirectly involved in the Irangate proceedings, defeated the Democrat's candidate Michael Dukakis in the presidential election of Nov 1988, after conducting one of the most scurrilous campaigns on record.

Bush came to power, after six years of growth, at a time of economic uncertainty. Reagan's tax-cutting policy had led to mounting federal trade and budget deficits which had served to turn the USA into a debtor nation for the first time in its history and had precipitated a ◊Wall Street share crash in Oct 1987. Retrenchment was thus needed and this became concentrated, during 1989–90, in the military sphere, being helped by continuing Soviet moves towards both conventional and nuclear forces reduction. Domestically, Bush used as a slogan the goal of a 'kinder, gentler nation', and unveiled initiatives in the areas of education, drugs-control and the environment designed to deal with problems that had surfaced during the Reagan years.The start of his presidency was marred by the Senate's rejection of his nominee to be defence secretary, John Tower, as a result of criticisms of Tower's lifestyle and his links to military contracting companies. With his overthrowing of his former ally, the corrupt Panamanian leader Gen Manuel Noriega, in Dec 1989, the Bush presidency had established itself.

United World Colleges six colleges worldwide with admission by scholarship for students aged 16–18. Their curriculum demands both academic achievement and service to the community. They were the inspiration of German educationalist Kurt ◊Hahn.

units standard quantities in relation to which other quantities are measured. There have been many systems of units. Some ancient units, such as the day, the foot, and the pound, are still in use. ◊SI units, the latest version of the metric system, are widely used in science.

unit trust a company that invests its clients' funds in other companies. The units it issues represent holdings of shares, which means unit shareholders

United States: presidents and elections

Year	President	Party	Losing candidate(s)	Party
1789	1. George Washington	Federalist	no opponent	
1792	re-elected		no opponent	
1796	2. John Adams	Federalist	Thomas Jefferson	Democrat-Republican
1800	3. Thomas Jefferson	Democrat-Republican	Aaron Burr	Democrat-Republican
1804	re-elected		Charles Pinckney	Federalist
1808	4. James Madison	Democrat-Republican	Charles Pinckney	Federalist
1812	re-elected		DeWitt Clinton	Federalist
1816	5. James Monroe	Democrat-Republican	Rufus King	Federalist
1820	re-elected		John Quincy Adams	Democrat-Republican
1824	6. John Quincy Adams	Democrat-Republican	Andrew Jackson	Democrat-Republican
			Henry Clay	Democrat-Republican
			William H Crawford	Democrat-Republican
1828	7. Andrew Jackson	Democrat	John Quincy Adams	National Republican
1832	re-elected		Henry Clay	National Republican
1836	8. Martin Van Buren	Democrat	William Henry Harrison	Whig
1840	9. William Henry Harrison	Whig	Martin Van Buren	Democrat
	10. John Tyler[1]	Whig		
1844	11. James K Polk	Democrat	Henry Clay	Whig
1848	12. Zachary Taylor	Whig	Lewis Cass	Democrat
	13. Millard Fillmore[2]	Whig		
1852	14. Franklin Pierce	Democrat	Winfield Scott	Whig
1856	15. James Buchanan	Democrat	John C Fremont	Republican
1860	16. Abraham Lincoln	Republican	Stephen Douglas	Democrat
			John Breckinridge	Democrat
			John Bell	Constitutional Union
1864	re-elected		George McClellan	Democrat
	17. Andrew Johnson[3]	Democrat		
1868	18. Ulysses S Grant	Republican	Horatio Seymour	Democrat
1872	re-elected		Horace Greeley	Democrat-Liberal Republican
1876	19. Rutherford B Hayes	Republican	Samuel Tilden	Democrat
1880	20. James A Garfield	Republican	Winfield Hancock	Democrat
	21. Chester A Arthur[4]	Republican		
1884	22. Grover Cleveland	Democrat	James Blaine	Republican
1888	23. Benjamin Harrison	Republican	Grover Cleveland	Democrat
1892	24. Grover Cleveland	Democrat	Benjamin Harrison	Republican
			James Weaver	People's
1896	25. William McKinley	Republican	William J Bryan	Democrat-People's
1900	re-elected		William J Bryan	Democrat
	26. Theodore Roosevelt[5]	Republican		
1904	re-elected		Alton B Parker	Democrat
1908	27. William H Taft	Republican	William J Bryan	Democrat
1912	28. Woodrow Wilson	Democrat	Theodore Roosevelt	Progressive
			William H Taft	Republican
1916	re-elected		Charles E Hughes	Republican
1920	29. Warren G Harding	Republican	James M Cox	Democrat
1924	30. Calvin Coolidge	Republican	John W Davis	Democrat
			Robert M LaFollette	Progressive
1928	31. Herbert Hoover	Republican	Alfred E Smith	Democrat
1932	32. Franklin D Roosevelt	Democrat	Herbert Hoover	Republican
			Norman Thomas	Socialist
1936	re-elected		Alfred Landon	Republican
1940	re-elected		Wendell Willkie	Republican
1944	re-elected		Thomas E Dewey	Republican
	33. Harry S Truman[6]	Democrat		
1948	re-elected		Thomas E Dewey	Republican
			J Strom Thurmond	States' Rights
			Henry A Wallace	Progressive
1952	34. Dwight D Eisenhower	Republican	Adlai E Stevenson	Democrat
1956	re-elected		Adlai E Stevenson	Democrat
1960	35. John F Kennedy	Democrat	Richard M Nixon	Republican
	36. Lyndon B Johnson[7]	Democrat		
1964	re-elected		Barry M Goldwater	Republican
1968	37. Richard M Nixon	Republican	Hubert H Humphrey	Democrat
			George C Wallace	
1972	re-elected		George S McGovern	Democrat
	38. Gerald R Ford[8]	Republican		
1976	39. Jimmy Carter	Democrat	Gerald R Ford	Republican
1980	40. Ronald Reagan	Republican	Jimmy Carter	Democrat
			John B Anderson	independent
1984	re-elected		Walter Mondale	Democrat
1988	41. George Bush	Republican	Michael Dukakis	Democrat

[1] became president 1841 on death of Harrison.
[2] became president 1850 on death of Taylor.
[3] became president 1865 on assassination of Lincoln.
[4] became president 1881 on assassination of Garfield.
[5] became president 1901 on assassination of McKinley.
[6] became president 1945 on death of F D Roosevelt.
[7] became president 1963 on assassination of Kennedy.
[8] became president 1974 on resignation of Nixon.

universities in the United Kingdom

Name	Date founded	No of students
Aberdeen	1945	5,700
Aston	1966	3,900
Bath	1966	3,700
Belfast	1908	7,200
Birmingham	1900	9,000
Bradford	1966	4,200
Bristol	1966	7,200
Brunel	1966	2,900
Buckingham	1983	700
Cambridge	13th cent.	9,800
City	1966	3,200
Dundee	1967	3,800
Durham	1832	5,100
East Anglia	1963	4,400
Edinburgh	1583	10,100
Essex	1964	3,000
Exeter	1955	5,000
Glasgow	1451	10,500
Heriot-Watt	1966	3,800
Hull	1954	4,800
Keele	1962	2,400
Kent	1965	4,200
Lancaster	1964	4,600
Leeds	1904	10,300
Leicester	1957	4,900
Liverpool	1903	7,600
London	1836	50,200
Loughborough	1966	5,800
Manchester	1851	11,100
Newcastle upon Tyne	1852	7,800
Nottingham	1948	7,000
Open University	1969	149,500
Oxford	12th cent.	9,700
Reading	1926	5,900
Salford	1967	3,800
Sheffield	1905	8,000
Southampton	1952	6,400
St Andrews	1411	3,800
Stirling	1967	2,900
Strathclyde	1964	7,500
Surrey	1966	3,400
Sussex	1961	4,600
Ulster	1984	7,600
Wales	1893	21,300
Warwick	1965	5,900
York	1963	3,400

have a wider spread of capital than if they bought shares on the stock market.

Unit trusts appeal to the small investor, and in recent years, business generated by them has increased rapidly. Many unit trusts specialize in a geographical region or particular type of industry, using their expertise more effectively than if they were to make random investments.

universal in philosophy, a property which is instantiated by all the individual things of a specific class: for example, all red things instantiate 'redness'. Many philosophical debates have centred on the status of universals, including the medieval debate between ◊nominalism and ◊realism.

Universal Hollywood film studio founded 1915 by Carl Laemmle. Despite *All Quiet on the Western Front* 1930 being its most highly regarded film, the changeover to sound caused a decline in the studio's fortunes. In the 1970s–80s Universal emerged as one of the industry's leaders with box-office hits from the producer and director Steven Spielberg such as *ET the Extra-Terrestrial* 1982 and *Back to the Future* 1985.

Universal also made a cycle of classic horror movies such as *Dracula* 1931, *Frankenstein* 1931, and *The Mummy* 1932.

universal indicator in chemistry, a mixture of ◊pH ◊indicators, each of which changes colour at a different pH value. The indicator is a different colour at different values of pH, ranging from red (at pH1) to purple (at pH13).

universal joint a flexible coupling used to join rotating shafts, for example, the propeller shaft in a car. In a typical universal joint the ends of the shafts to be joined end in U-shaped yokes. They dovetail into each other and pivot flexibly about an X-shaped spider. This construction allows side-to-side and up-and-down movement, while still transmitting rotary motion.

Universal Postal Union an agency of the United Nations responsible for collaboration of postal services. It was first established in 1875, with headquarters in Berne, Switzerland.

universal time (UT) another name for ◊Greenwich Mean Time. It is based on the rotation of the Earth, which is not quite constant. Since 1972, UT has been replaced by ***coordinated universal time*** (UTC), which is based on uniform atomic time; see ◊time.

universe all of space and its contents, the study of which is called cosmology. The universe is thought to be between 10,000 million and 20,000 million years old, and is mostly empty space, dotted with ◊galaxies for as far as telescopes can see. The most distant detected galaxies and ◊quasars lie 10,000 million light years away and are moving farther from us as the universe expands. Several theories attempt to explain how the universe came into being and evolved, for example, the ◊oscillating universe theory and the contradictory ◊steady state theory.

Apart from those galaxies within the ◊Local Group, all the galaxies we see display ◊red shifts in their spectra; the farther we look into space, the greater are the observed red shifts. That means they are moving away at ever greater speed. This is known as ◊Hubble's constant, and increases in proportion with the distance apart of the galaxies (Hubble's law).

university an institution of higher learning for those who have completed primary and secondary education. There are now 45 universities in the UK which are funded by the government through the University Funding Committee. The USA has both state universities (funded by the individual states) and private universities. The oldest universities in the USA are all private: Harvard 1636, William and Mary 1693, Yale 1701, Pennsylvania 1741, and Princeton 1746. Recent innovations include universities serving international areas, for example, the Middle East Technical University 1961 in Ankara, Turkey, supported by the United Nations; the United Nations university in Tokyo 1974; and the British ◊Open University 1969.

The first European university was Salerno, established in the 9th century, followed by Bologna, Paris, Oxford, and Cambridge in the 12th century. St Andrew's, the first Scottish university, was founded in 1411, and Trinity College, Dublin, in 1591. In the UK, a number of universities were founded in the 19th and earlier 20th centuries (London 1836, Manchester 1851, Wales 1893, Liverpool 1903, Bristol 1909, and Reading 1926). These became known as the 'red brick' universities, as opposed to the ancient stone of Oxford and Cambridge. After World War II, many more universities were founding, among them Nottingham 1948, Exeter 1955, and Sussex 1961, and were nicknamed, from their ultra-modern buildings, the 'plate-glass' universities.

Unix an ◊operating system designed for minicomputers but becoming increasingly popular on large microcomputers, workstations, and supercomputers. It was developed by Bell Laboratories in the late 1960s, and is closely related to the programming language C. Its wide range of functions and flexibility have made it widely used by universities and in commercial software.

Unknown Soldier unidentified dead soldier, for whom a tomb is erected as a memorial to other unidentified soldiers killed in war.

In Britain, the practice began in World War I; the British Unknown Soldier was buried in Westminster Abbey in 1920. France, Belgium, the USA, and other countries also have Unknown Soldier tombs.

unnilennium a synthetically made element, symbol Une, atomic number 109. It was first synthesized in 1974.

unnilhexium a synthetically made element, symbol Unh, atomic number 106. It was first synthesized in 1974.

unniloctium a synthetically made element, symbol Uno, atomic number 108. It was first synthesized in 1981.

unnilpentium a synthetically made element, symbol Unp, atomic number 105. Credit for its discovery is disputed between the USA (who named it ***hahnium***) and the USSR (who named it ***nielsbohrium***).

unnilquadium a synthetically made element, symbol Unq, atomic number 104. It is also named ***kurchitovium*** and ***rutherfordium*** by teams in the USSR and the USA respectively.

unnilseptium a synthetically made element, symbol Uns, atomic number 107. It was first synthesized in 1976.

Uno /ˈuno/ Sosuke 1922– . Japanese Liberal Democrat politician. Having held various cabinet posts since 1976, he was designated prime minister June 1989 in an attempt to restore the image of the Liberal Democrats after several scandals. He resigned after only a month in office when his affairs with geishas and prostitutes became public knowledge. The Liberal Democrats were re-elected, but with reduced majority, in Feb 1990, paving the way for Uno's return to power.

unsaturated compound a chemical compound in which two adjacent atoms are bonded by two or more bonds.

Examples are ◊alkenes and ◊alkynes, where the two adjacent atoms are both carbon, and ◊ketones, where the unsaturation exists between atoms of different elements.

untouchable or *harijan* the lowest Indian ◊caste, whom members of the other castes were forbidden to touch.

Unwin /ˈʌnwɪn/ Raymond 1863–1940. English town planner. He put the Garden City ideals of Sir Ebenezer Howard into practice, overseeing Letchworth (begun 1903), Hampstead Garden Suburb (begun 1907), and Wythenshawe, Manchester (begun 1927).

uomo universale (Italian) universal man, someone who is at home in all spheres of knowledge; one of the ideals of the ◊Renaissance.

Upanishad one of a collection of Hindu sacred treatises, written in Sanskrit, connected with the ◊Vedas but composed later, about 800–200 BC. Metaphysical and ethical, their doctrine equated the atman (self) with the Brahman (supreme spirit): '*Tat tvam asi (Thou art that)*', and developed the theory of the transmigration of souls.

upas tree SE Asian tree *Antiaris toxicaria*, family Moraceae, with a poisonous latex used for arrows, and traditionally reputed to kill all who fell asleep under it.

Updike /ˈʌpdaɪk/ John (Hoyer) 1932– . US writer. Associated with the *New Yorker* magazine from 1955, he soon established a reputation for polished prose, poetry, and criticism. His novels include *Couples* 1968 and *Roger's Version* 1986 and deal with contemporary US middle-class life.

Two characters recur in his work: the basketball player 'Rabbit' Angstrom (introduced in *Rabbit, Run* 1960) and the novelist Henry Bech.

Upington /ˈʌpɪŋtən/ town in Transvaal, South Africa 800 km/500 mi W of Pretoria. In Nov 1985 it was the scene of a demonstration against high rents that resulted in the death of a police officer and the subsequent arrest of 25 people. The 'Upington 25', as they came to be known, were later found guilty of murder under the law of common purpose.

Upper Austria (German ***Oberösterreich***) mountainous federal province of Austria, drained by the Danube; area 12,000 sq km/4,632 sq mi; population (1987) 1,294,000. Its capital is Linz. In addition to wine, sugar-beet, and grain, there are

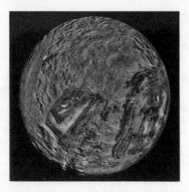

Uranus *A mosaic of photographs of the battered face of Miranda, the fourth largest moon of Uranus, seen from Voyager 2.*

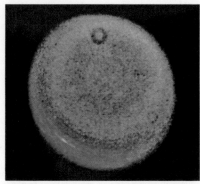

Uranus *False colour image of clouds in the upper atmosphere of Uranus, seen from Voyager 2.*

reserves of oil. Manufactured products include textiles, chemicals, and metal goods.

Upper Volta /ˈvɒltə/ former name (until 1984) of ◊Burkina Faso.

Uppsala /ʊpˈsɑːlə/ city in Sweden, NW of Stockholm; population (1988) 160,000. Industries include engineering and pharmaceuticals. The botanist Linnaeus lived here.

Ur an ancient city of the Sumerian civilization, now in S Iraq. Excavations by the British archaeologist Leonard Woolley show that it was inhabited 3500 BC. He discovered evidence of a flood that may have inspired the biblical account, and remains of ziggurats, or step pyramids, as well as social and cultural relics.

uraemia an excess of the waste product known as urea in the blood due to kidney damage.

Ural Mountains /ˈjʊərəl/ (Russian *Ural'skiy Khrebet*) mountain system running from the Arctic to the Caspian Sea, traditionally separating Europe from Asia. The highest peak is Naradnaya 1,894 m/6,214 ft. It has vast mineral wealth.

The middle Urals is one of the most important industrial regions of the USSR. Perm, Chelyabinsk, Sverdlovsk, Magnitogorsk, and Zlatoust are industrial centres.

Urania in Greek mythology, the ◊muse of astronomy.

uranium a metallic element, symbol U, atomic number 92, relative atomic mass 338.07. It is a lustrous white metal, malleable and ductile, tarnishing in air. The chief ore is uranite (pitchblende, U_3O_8), and recent technological advances have made possible its extraction from low-grade ores. Its chief use is in the form of the radioactive isotope uranium-235, used as a source of nuclear energy. Small amounts of its compounds are used in the ceramics industry to give yellow glazes, and as a mordant in dyeing.

It was discovered by Klaproth in 1789 in pitchblende, and first prepared by Peligot in 1842. Many countries mine uranium; large deposits are found in Canada, the USA, Australia, and South Africa.

Uranus /jʊˈreɪnəs/ in Greek mythology, the primeval sky god. He was responsible for both the sun and the rain, and was the son and husband of ◊Gaia the goddess of the Earth, by whom he fathered ◊Kronos and the ◊Titans.

Uranus /jʊˈreɪnəs/ the seventh planet from the Sun, discovered by William ◊Herschel 1781. Uranus has a diameter of 50,800 km/31,600 mi and a mass 14.5 times that of Earth. It orbits the Sun in 84 years at an average distance of 2,870 million km/1,783 million mi. Uranus is thought to have a large rocky core overlain by ice, with a deep atmosphere mostly of hydrogen and helium, plus traces of methane which give the planet a greenish tinge. The spin axis of Uranus is tilted at 98°, so that at times its poles point towards the Sun, giving extreme seasons. It has 15 moons, and in 1977 astronomers discovered that Uranus has thin rings around its equator.

In 1986 the second of the ◊Voyager probes reached Uranus, detecting 11 rings in all, and finding ten small moons in addition to the five visible from Earth. The largest moon, Titania, has a diameter of 1,610 km/1,000 mi. The rings are charcoal black, and are probably debris of former 'moonlets' that have broken up. Uranus has a peculiar magnetic field, whose axis is tilted at 60° to its axis of spin, and is displaced about one-third of the way from the planet's centre to its surface. Observations of the magnetic field show that the solid body of the planet rotates every 17.2 hours. Uranus spins from east to west, the opposite of the other planets, with the exception of Venus and possibly Pluto. The rotation rate of the atmosphere varies with latitude, from about 16 hours in mid-southern latitudes to longer than 17 hours at the equator.

Urban II /ˈɜːbən/ c. 1042–1099. Pope 1088–99. He launched the First Crusade at the Council of Clermont in France 1095.

urbanization the process by which the proportion of a population living in or around towns and cities increases through migration. The growth of urban concentrations is a relatively recent phenomenon, dating back only about 150 years, although the world's first cities were built more than 5,000 years ago.

Urbanization has had a major effect on the social structures of industrial societies, affecting not only where people live but how they live, and urban sociology has emerged as a distinct area of study.

urban legend a largely new mode of folklore thriving in big cities, mainly in the USA, in the mid-20th century, and passed along, usually orally, and always at second or later hand. Some of the material—hitchhikers that turn out to be ghosts, spiders breeding in elaborate hairstyles—is preindustrial in origin, but transformed to fit new circumstances; others, notably the pet in the microwave oven, are of their essence entirely new.

urban renewal the adaptation of existing buildings in towns and cities to meet changes in economic, social, and environmental requirements, rather than demolishing them.

Urban renewal has become an increasingly important element of urban policy since the early 1970s. A major objective is to preserve the historical and cultural character of a locality, but at the same time to improve the environment and meet new demands, such as rapidly increasing motor traffic.

urbi et orbi (Latin 'to the city and to the world') a papal proclamation.

Urdu language a member of the Indo-Iranian branch of the Indo-European language family, related to Hindi and written not in Devanagari but in Arabic script. Urdu is strongly influenced by Persian and Arabic. It is the official language of Pakistan and a language used by Muslims in India.

urea $CO(NH2)_2$ waste product formed when nitrogen compounds are broken down by mammals. It is excreted in urine. In industry it is used in pharmaceuticals and fertilizers.

Urey /ˈjʊəri/ Harold Clayton 1893–1981. US chemist. In 1932 he isolated ◊heavy water and discovered deuterium; Nobel prize 1934.

He was director of the War Research Atomic Bomb Project, Columbia, 1940–45. His books include studies of nuclear and atomic structure, and the origin of the planet and of life.

Urga /ˈɜːgə/ former name (until 1924) of ◊Ulaanbaatar, the capital of Mongolia.

uric acid $C_5H_4N_4O_3$ a nitrogen-containing waste substance, formed from the breakdown of food and body protein. It is a normal constituent of urine in reptiles and birds, but not in most mammals.

Humans and other primates produce some uric acid, in place of urea, the normal nitrogen-waste product. If formed in excess and not excreted, it

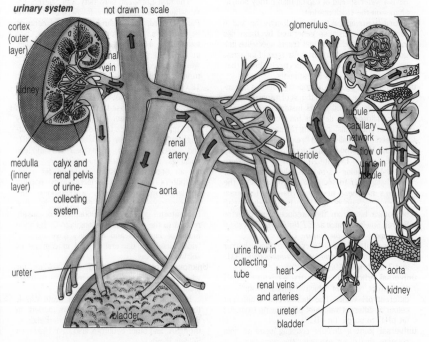

urinary system   not drawn to scale

cortex (outer layer)
renal vein
kidney
medulla (inner layer)
calyx and renal pelvis of urine-collecting system
renal artery
aorta
ureter
bladder

glomerulus
tubule capillary network
arteriole
flow of urine in tubule
urine flow in collecting tube
heart
renal veins and arteries
ureter
bladder
aorta
kidney

urine

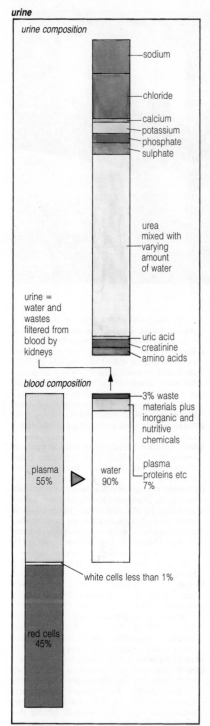

urine composition

— sodium
— chloride
— calcium
— potassium
— phosphate
— sulphate

urea
mixed with
varying
amount
of water

urine =
water and
wastes
filtered from
blood by
kidneys

— uric acid
— creatinine
— amino acids

blood composition

— 3% waste
materials plus
inorganic and
nutritive
chemicals

plasma
55%

water
90%

plasma
proteins etc
7%

white cells less than 1%

red cells
45%

---

may be deposited in sharp crystals in the joints and other tissues, causing gout; or it may form stones in the kidneys or bladder (calculi).

urinary system the system of organs that removes nitrogeneous excretory products and excess water from the bodies of animals. In mammals, it consists of a pair of kidneys, ureters, which drain the kidneys, and a bladder, which stores urine before its discharge through the urethra.

urine an amber-coloured fluid made by the kidneys from the blood. It contains excess water, salts, protein, waste products, a pigment, and some acid.

urology branch of medicine concerned with diseases of the urinary tract.

Uruguay
Oriental Republic of
(República
Oriental del Uruguay)

Brazil

PACIFIC
OCEAN

ATLANTIC
OCEAN

Argentina

0 1000 km

area 176,200 sq km/68,031 sq mi
capital Montevideo
physical grassy plains (pampas)
features smallest of the South American republics; rivers Negro and Uruguay
head of state and of government Luis Lacalle Herrera from 1989
government democratic republic
political parties Colorado Party (PC), progressive, centre-left; National (Blanco) Party (PN), traditionalist, right-of-centre; Amplio Front (FA), moderate, left-wing

Ursa Major (Latin 'Great Bear') the third largest constellation in the sky, in the north polar region. Its seven brightest stars make up the familiar shape of the *Big Dipper* or *Plough*. The second star of the 'handle' of the dipper, called Mizar, has a companion star, Alcor. Two stars in the 'bowl' act as pointers to the north pole star, Polaris.

Ursa Minor (Latin 'Little Bear') constellation in the northern sky. It is shaped like a little dipper, with the north pole star Polaris at the end of the handle. It contains the orange subgiant Kochab.

Ursula, St /'ɜːsjʊlə/ English legendary saint, supposed to have been martyred with 11 virgins (misread as 11,000 in the Middle Ages), by the Huns in the Rhineland, in the 4th century.

Ursuline a Roman Catholic religious order, founded in Brescia, Italy, by St Angela Merici 1537; it is renowned for its educational work among girls.

urticaria or *nettle rash* an irritant skin condition characterized by the spontaneous appearance of weals. Treatment is usually by soothing lotions and, in severe cases, by antihistamines or steroids. Its causes are varied, and may include allergy and stress.

Uruguay /'juərəgwaɪ/ country in South America, on the Atlantic, bounded N by Brazil and W by Argentina.

government The 1966 constitution provides for a president who is head of state and head of government, elected by universal suffrage for a five-year term, and a two-chamber legislature, comprising a senate and a federal chamber of deputies. The president is assisted by a vice president and presides over a council of ministers.

The Senate has up to 30 members and the Chamber of Deputies 99, all elected for a five-year term by universal suffrage through system of proportional representation. The voting system ensures that there are at least two deputies representing each of the republic's 19 departments.

history For early history, see ◊American Indian. The area that is now Uruguay was settled by both Spain 1624 and Portugal 1680, but Spain secured the whole in the 18th century. In 1814 Spanish

---

exports meat and meat products, leather, wool, textiles
currency nuevo peso (1487.75 = £1 Mar 1990)
population (1988) 3,080,000 (mainly of Spanish and Italian descent, also mestizo, mulatto, and black); annual growth rate 0.7%
life expectancy men 67, women 74
language Spanish
religion Roman Catholic 60%
literacy 95% male/95% female (1980 est)
GNP $7.3 bn (1983); $1,665 per head of population
chronology
1958 Blanco Party in power.
1966 Colorado Party elected. President Jorge Pacheco Areco outlawed left-wing parties. Tupamaro guerrilla activity began.
1971 The Colorado Party returned, with Juan Maria Bordaberry Arocena as president.
1973 Having crushed the Tupamaros, the military seized effective control, leaving Bordaberry as a figurehead.
1976 Bordaberry deposed by the army and Dr Méndez Manfredini became president.
1980 World's highest proportion of political prisoners (1 in 50 citizens). Some 350,000 political exiles.
1984 Violent anti-government protests after ten years of repressive rule.
1985 Agreement reached between the army and political leaders for a return to constitutional government. Colorado Party narrowly won the general election and Dr Julio Maria Sanguinetti became president.
1986 A government of national accord established under President Sanguinetti's leadership.
1989 Luis Lacalle elected president.

rule was overthrown under the leadership of José Artigas, dictator until driven out by Brazil 1820. Disputed between Argentina and Brazil 1825–28, Uruguay was declared independent 1828, although not recognized by its neighbours until 1853.

The names of Uruguay's two main political parties, the liberal Colorado (the Reds) and the conservative Blanco (the Whites), are derived from the colours of the flags carried in the civil war 1836. During 1951–66 there was a collective leadership called 'collegiate government' and then a new constitution was adopted and a single president elected, the Blanco candidate, Jorge Pacheco Areco. His presidency was marked by high inflation, labour unrest, and growing guerrilla activity by left-wing sugar workers, the ◊Tupamaros.

In 1972 Pacheco was replaced by the Colorado candidate, Juan Maria Bordaberry Arocena. Within a year the Tupamaros had been crushed and all other left-wing groups banned. Bordaberry now headed a repressive regime, under which the normal democratic institutions had been dissolved. In 1976, he refused any movement towards constitutional government, was deposed by the army, and Dr Aparicio Méndez Manfredini made president. Despite promises to return to democratic government, the severe repression continued and political opponents were imprisoned.

In 1981 the deteriorating economy made the army anxious to return to constitutional government and a retired general, Gregorio Alvarez Armellino, was appointed president for an interim period. Discussions between the army and the main political parties failed to agree on the form of constitution to be adopted and civil unrest, in the shape of strikes and demonstrations, grew. By 1984 anti-government activity had reached a crisis point and eventually all the main political leaders signed an agreement for a 'Programme of National Accord'. The 1966 constitution, with some modifications, was restored and in 1985 a general election was held. The Colorado Party won a narrow majority and its leader, Dr Julio Maria Sanguinetti, became president. The army stepped down and

Utah

by 1986 President Sanguinetti was presiding over a government of national accord in which all the main parties—Colorado, Blanco, and the left-wing Broad Front—were represented. In the Nov 1989 elections Luis Lacalle Herrera (PN), was narrowly elected president, with 37% of the vote compared with 30% for his PC opponent.

Urumchi former name for the city of ◊Urumqi, China.

Urumqi /ʊˈruːmtʃiː/ formerly *Urumchi* industrial city and capital of Xinjiang Uygur autonomous region, China, at the N foot of the Tyan Shan mountains; population (1986) 1,147,000. It produces cotton textiles, cement, chemicals, iron, and steel.

USA abbreviation for the ◊*United States of America*.

user interface in computing, procedures and methods through which the user operates a program. These might include ◊menus, input forms, error messages, and keyboard procedures. A graphical user interface is one that uses icons and allows the user to make menu selections with a mouse (see also ◊WIMP).

The study of human–computer interaction to achieve easier and more effective use of the machine and greater human satisfaction is the subject of a sub-branch of ergonomics, which has become a focus for many national and international research programmes.

Ushant /ˈʌʃənt/ French *Ouessant* French island 18 km/11 mi W of Brittany, off which the British admiral R ◊Howe defeated the French navy 1794 on 'the Glorious First of June'.

Usher /ˈʌʃə/ James 1581–1656. Irish priest, archbishop of Armagh from 1625. He was responsible for the dating of creation as the year 4004 BC, a figure that was inserted in the margin of the Authorized Version of the Bible until the 19th century.

Ushuaia /uːˈswaɪə/ southernmost town in the world, at the tip of Tierra del Fuego, Argentina, less than 1,000 km/620 mi from Antarctica; population (1980) 11,000. It is a free port and naval base.

Usküb /ˈʊskuːb/ Turkish name of ◊Skopje, a city in Yugoslavia.

Usküdar /ˌʊskuːˈdɑː/ suburb of Istanbul, Turkey; formerly a separate town, which under the name *Scutari* was the site of the hospital set up by Florence Nightingale during the Crimean War.

Ussher alternative spelling of James ◊Usher.

USSR abbreviation for the ◊*Union of Soviet Socialist Republics*.

Ussuri /ʊˈsʊəri/ river in E Asia, tributary of the Amur. Rising north of Vladivostok and joining the Amur south of Khabarovsk, it forms part of the border between the Chinese province of Heilongjiang and the USSR. There were military clashes 1968–69 over the sovereignty of Damansky Island (Chenpao).

Ustinov /ˈjuːstɪnɒf/ Peter 1921– . English stage and film actor, writer, and director. He won an Oscar for Best Supporting Actor in *Spartacus* 1960. Other films he appeared in are *Topkapi* 1964, *Death on the Nile* 1978, and *Evil under the Sun* 1981.

Ust-Kamenogorsk /ˈuːst kkəˌmenəˈɡɔːsk/ river port and chief centre of the nuclear industry in

Utrillo Street at Sannois *(1913) Courtauld Collection, London.*

the USSR, situated in the Altai mountains, on the river Irtysh; population (1987) 321,000.

usury former term for charging interest on a loan of money. In medieval times, usury was held to be a sin, and Christians were forbidden to lend (although not to borrow).

Under English law, usury remained forbidden until the 13th century, when trade and the need for credit was increased; for example, Jews were absolved from the ban on usury by the Fourth Lateran Council of 1215. The practice of charging interest is still regarded as usury in some Muslim countries.

Utagawa /ˌuːtəˈɡɑːwə/ Kuniyoshi Japanese printmaker; see ◊Kuniyoshi Utagawa.

Utah /ˈjuːtɑː/ state of the W USA; nickname Beehive State

area 219,900 sq km/84,881 sq mi

capital Salt Lake City

towns Provo, Ogden

physical Colorado Plateau to the east; mountains in centre; Great Basin to the west; Great Salt Lake

features Great American Desert; Colorado rivers system; Dinosaur National Monument; Rainbow Bridge

products wool, gold, silver, uranium, coal, salt, steel

population (1985) 1,645,000

famous people Brigham Young

history part of the area ceded by Mexico 1848; developed by Mormons, still the largest religious sect in the state; territory 1850, but not admitted to statehood until 1896 because of Mormon reluctance to relinquish plural marriage.

Utamaro /ˌuːtəˈmɑːrəʊ/ Kitagawa 1753–1806. Japanese artist of the *ukiyo-e* ('floating world') school, who created muted colour prints of beautiful women, including informal studies of prostitutes.

His style was distinctive: his subject is often seen close up, sometimes from unusual angles or viewpoints, and he made use of bold curvaceous lines and highly decorative textiles.

UTC abbreviation for Coordinated Universal Time, the standard measurement of ◊time.

uterus a hollow muscular organ of female mammals, lying between the bladder and rectum, and connected to the Fallopian tubes and vagina. The embryo develops within it, and is attached via the ◊placenta and umbilical cord after implantation. The lining of the uterus changes during the ◊menstrual cycle. In humans and other higher primates, it is a single structure, but in other mammals it is paired.

The outer wall of the uterus is composed of smooth muscle, capable of powerful contractions (induced by hormones) during childbirth.

U Thant /ˈuː ˈθænt/ 1909–1974. Burmese diplomat, secretary-general of the United Nations 1962–71. He helped to resolve the US-Soviet crisis over the Soviet installation of missiles in Cuba, and he made the controversial decision to withdraw the UN peacekeeping force from the Egypt–Israel border 1967 (◊Arab-Israeli Wars).

Uthman another name for ◊Othman, third caliph of Islam.

Utica /ˈjuːtɪkə/ industrial city (textiles, firearms) in central New York State, USA; population (1980) 75,500. The first Woolworth store was opened here 1879.

utilitarianism a philosophical theory of ethics outlined by the philosopher Jeremy Bentham, and developed by J S Mill. According to utilitarianism, an action is morally right if it has consequences which lead to happiness, and wrong if it brings about the reverse of happiness. Thus, society should aim for the greatest happiness of the greatest number.

Its chief opponents were F H Bradley and T H Green.

Utopia (Greek 'no place') any ideal state in literature, named after philosopher Thomas More's ideal commonwealth in his book *Utopia* 1516.

Others include Plato's *Republic*, Bacon's *New Atlantis* 1626, and *City of the Sun* by the Italian Tommaso Campanella (1568–1639). Utopias are a common subject in ◊science fiction.

ut pictura poesis (Latin) a poem is as a picture.

Utrecht /ˈjuːtrekt/ a province of the Netherlands lying SE of Amsterdam on the Kromme Rijn (crooked Rhine); area 1,330 sq km/513 sq mi; population (1988) 965,000. In rural areas livestock farming predominates. Manufactured products include textiles, chemicals, fertilizers, and electrical goods. The capital is Utrecht, which forms the NE corner of the Randstad conurbation; population (1988) 522,000. It has a Gothic cathedral, and a university 1636.

Utrecht, Treaty of treaty signed 1713 that ended the War of the ◊Spanish Succession. Philip V was recognized as the legitimate king of Spain, thus founding the Spanish branch of the Bourbon dynasty; the Netherlands, Milan, and Naples were ceded to Austria; Britain gained Gibraltar; the duchy of Savoy was granted Sicily.

Utrecht, Union of in 1579, the union of seven provinces of the N Netherlands: Holland, Zeeland, Friesland, Groningen, Utrecht, Gelderland, and Overijssel, which became the basis of opposition

Uttar Pradesh

Uzbekistan

to the Spanish crown and the foundation of the modern Dutch state.

Utrillo /juːˈtrɪləʊ/ Maurice 1883–1955. French artist. He painted townscapes of his native Paris, especially Montmartre, often from postcard photographs.

Uttar Pradesh /ˈʊtə prəˈdeʃ/ state of N India
area 294,400 sq km/113,638 sq mi
capital Lucknow
towns Kanpur, Varanasi, Agra, Allahabad, Meerut

features most populous state; Himalayan peak Nanda Devi 7,817 m/25,655 ft
population (1981) 110,858,000
famous people Indira Gandhi, Ravi Shankar
language Hindi
religion Hindu 80%, Muslim 15%
history formerly the heart of the Mogul Empire, and generating point of the ◊Indian Mutiny 1857 and subsequent opposition to British rule; see also the ◊United Provinces of ◊Agra and ◊Oudh.

UV in physics, the abbreviation for *ultraviolet*.

uvula fleshy flap that hangs at the back of the throat in humans.

Uzbek person of Uzbek culture. They comprise approximately 70% of the population of Uzbekistan in the USSR. The Uzbek language belongs to the Turkic branch of the Altaic family.

Uzbekistan /ʊzˌbekɪˈstɑːn/ constituent republic of the SE USSR, part of Soviet Central Asia
area 447,400 sq km/172,741 sq mi
capital Tashkent
towns Samarkand
physical oases in the deserts; rivers Amu Darya and Syr Darya; Fergana Valley
products rice, dried fruit, vines (all grown by irrigation), cotton, silk
population (1987) 19,026,000; 69% Uzbek, 11% Russian, 4% Tadzhik, 4% Tatar
language Uzbek
religion Sunni Muslim
history part of Turkestan, it was conquered by Russia 1865–76. The Tashkent soviet gradually extended its power 1917–24 and Uzbekistan became a constituent republic of the USSR 1925. Some 160,000 Mesketian Turks were forcibly transported from their native Georgia to Uzbekistan by Stalin 1944. In June 1989 Tashlak, Yaipan, and Fergana were the scenes of riots in which Mesketian Turks were attacked. 70 were killed and 850 wounded. In Sept 1989 an Uzbek nationalist organization, the Birlik ('Unity') People's Movement, was formed.

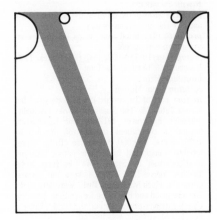

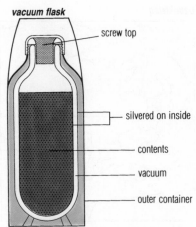

vacuum flask

- screw top
- silvered on inside
- contents
- vacuum
- outer container

V 22nd letter of the alphabet. It was not differentiated from U until about the 16th century. In sound it is the voiced labiodental fricative.

V abbreviation for *five* (Roman); in physics, abbreviation for *volt*.

v abbreviation for *velocity*.

V1, V2 (German *Vergeltungswaffe* 'revenge weapons') German flying bombs of World War II, launched against Britain in 1944 and 1945. The V1, also called the doodle-bug and buzz bomb, was a flying bomb powered by a simple kind of jet engine called a pulse jet. The V2, a rocket bomb, was the first long-range ballistic missile. It was 14 m/47 ft long, carried a 1-tonne warhead, and hit its target at a speed of 5,000 kph/3,000 mph.

Vaal /vɑːl/ river in South Africa, the chief tributary of the Orange. It rises in the Drakensberg and for much of its course of 1,200 km/750 mi it separates Transvaal from Orange Free State.

vaccination the use of specially prepared microbes (bacteria and viruses) to confer immunity to the diseases with which they are associated. When injected or taken by mouth, a vaccine stimulates the production of antibodies to protect against that particular disease. Vaccination is the oldest form of ◊immunization.

vaccine modified preparation of viruses or bacteria that is introduced into the body either orally or by a hypodermic syringe to induce the general reaction that produces ◊immunity.

In 1796, Edward ◊Jenner was the first to inoculate a child successfully with cowpox virus to produce immunity to smallpox.

vacuole in biology, a fluid-filled, membrane-bound cavity inside a cell. It may be a reservoir for fluids that the cell will secrete to the outside, or filled with excretory products or essential nutrients that the cell needs to store. In amoebae (single-cell animals) vacuoles are formed around food particles. Plant cells usually have a large central vacuole for storage.

vacuum in general, a region completely empty of matter; in physics, any enclosure in which the gas pressure is considerably less than atmospheric pressure (101,325 pascals).

vacuum cleaner cleaning device invented 1901 by the Scot Hubert Cecil Booth 1871–1955. Having seen an ineffective dust-blowing machine, he reversed the process so that his machine (originally on wheels, and operated from the street by means of tubes running into the house) operated by suction.

vacuum flask or *Dewar flask* or *Thermos flask* a container for keeping things either hot or cold. It consists of a glass double-walled vessel containing a vacuum, and the insides of the walls are silvered. This design reduces the three forms of heat transfer: radiation (prevented by the silvering), conduction, and convection (prevented by the vacuum and insulation). A vacuum flask is therefore equally efficient at keeping cold liquids cold, or hot liquids hot. It was invented by James Dewar (1842–1923) about 1872 to store liquefied gases.

vade mecum (Latin 'go with me') a useful handbook carried about for reference.

Vadodara /wə'dəudərə/ formerly *Baroda*, until 1976 industrial city (metal goods, chemicals, textiles) and rail junction in Gujarat, India; population (1981) 744,881.

Vaduz /fæ'duts/ capital of the European principality of Liechtenstein; population (1984) 5,000. Industries include engineering and agricultural trade.

vagina the front passage in a woman linking the womb to the exterior. It admits the penis during sexual intercourse, and is the birth canal down which the fetus passes during delivery.

vaginismus spasmodic contraction of the entrance to the vagina during attempted intercourse, thus preventing the entrance of the penis. It is usually of psychological origin, although it may rarely be due to inflammation of the vagina, causing a reflex contraction.

Vairochana the cosmic Buddha, *Dainichi* in Japan; central to esoteric Buddhism.

Valdai Hills /væl'daɪ/ small forested plateau between Leningrad and Moscow, where the Volga and W Dvina rivers rise. The Viking founders of the Russian state used it as a river route centre to reach the Baltic, Black, Caspian, and White seas. From the 15th century it was dominated by Moscow.

Valdemar alternative spelling of ◊Waldemar, name of four kings of Denmark.

Valdivia /væl'diːvɪə/ industrial port (shipbuilding, leather, beer, soap) and resort in Chile; population (1983) 115,500. It was founded 1552 by the Spanish conquistador Pedro de Valdivia (c.1500–54), conqueror of Chile.

Valdívia /væl'diːvɪə/ Pedro de c.1497–1554. Spanish explorer who travelled to Venezuela around 1530 and accompanied Francisco ◊Pizarro on his second expedition to Peru. He then went south into Chile, where he founded the cities of Santiago

1541 and Valdívia 1544. In 1552 he crossed the Andes to explore the Negro River. He was killed by Araucanian Indians.

Valence /væ'lɒns/ market town and capital of Drôme *département*; SE France, on the Rhône; population (1982) 68,100. Industries include electrical goods and components for aerospace. It is of pre-Roman origin, and has a Romanesque cathedral consecrated 1095.

Valencia /və'lensɪə/ industrial city (textiles, leather, sugar) and agricultural centre in Carabobo state, N Venezuela, on the Cabriales River; population (1981) 624,000. It is 478 m/1,569 ft above sea level, and was founded 1555.

Valencia /və'lensɪə/ industrial city (wine, fruit, chemicals, textiles, ship repair) in Valencia region, E Spain; population (1986) 739,000. The Valencian Community, consisting of Alicante, Castellón, and Valencia, has an area of 23,300 sq km/8,994 sq mi, and a population of 3,772,000.

Valencia was ruled by El ◊Cid 1094–99, after he recaptured it from the Moors. There is a cathedral of the 13th–15th centuries, and a university 1500.

Valenciennes /ˌvælɒnsi'en/ industrial town in Nord *département*, NE France, near the Belgian border, once known for its lace; population (1982) 349,500. It became French in 1678.

valency the measure of an element's ability to combine with other elements, expressed as the number of atoms of hydrogen (or any other standard univalent element) capable of uniting with (or replacing) its atoms.

The elements are described as uni-, di-, tri-, and tetravalent when they unite with 1, 2, 3, and 4 univalent atoms respectively. Some elements have *variable valency*, for example nitrogen and phosphorus, both 3 and 5. The valency of oxygen is two; hence the formula for water is H_2O (hydrogen being univalent).

Valentine, St /'væləntaɪn/ died 270. According to tradition a bishop of Terni martyred at Rome, now omitted from the calendar of saints' days as probably nonexistent. His festival was 14 Feb, but the custom of sending 'valentines' to a loved one on that day seems to have arisen because the day accidentally coincided with the Roman mid-Feb festival of ◊Lupercalia.

Valentino /ˌvælən'tiːnəu/ Rudolf 1895–1926. Italian film actor, the archetypal romantic lover of the Hollywood silent movies. His films include *The Sheik* 1921 and *Blood and Sand* 1922.

Valera Éamon de. Irish politician; see ◊de Valera.

valerian perennial plant of either of two genera, *Valeriana* or *Centranthus*, native to the N hemisphere, with clustered heads of fragrant tubular flowers in red, white, or pink. The root of the common valerian *Valeriana officinalis* is used medicinally to relieve flatulence and as a sedative.

Valéry /ˌvælea'riː/ Paul 1871–1945. French poet and mathematician. His poems include *La Jeune Parque/The Young Fate* 1917 and *Charmes/Enchantments* 1922.

Valhalla /væl'hælə/ in Norse mythology, the hall in ◊Odin's palace where he feasts with the souls of heroes killed in battles.

Valkyrie in Norse mythology, any of the female attendants of ◊Odin. They select those who are to die in battle and escort them to Valhalla.

Valladolid /ˌvæljədəu'liːð/ industrial town (food processing, vehicles, textiles, engineering), capital of Valladolid province, Spain; population (1986) 341,000.

It was the capital of Castile and Leon in the 14th–15th centuries, then of Spain until 1560. Ferdinand and Isabella were married at Valladolid 1469. The home of the writer Cervantes is preserved, and Columbus died here. It has a university 1346 and a cathedral 1595.

Valle d'Aosta /'væleɪ dɑː'ɒstə/ autonomous region of NW Italy; area 3,300 sq km/1,274 sq mi; population (1988) 114,000, many of whom are French-speaking. It produces wine and live-stock. Its capital is Aosta.

Valle-Inclán /'væljeɪ iːn'klɑːn/ Ramón Maria de 1866–1936. Spanish author of erotic and symbolist works including *Sonatas* 1902–05 and, set in South America, the novel *Tirano Banderas/The Tyrant* 1926.

Valletta /vəˈletə/ capital and port of Malta; population (1987) 9,000, but the urban harbour area is 101,000.

It was founded 1566 by the Knights of ◊St John of Jerusalem, and named after their grand master Jean de la Valette (1494–1568), who fended off a Turkish siege May–Sept 1565. The 16th-century palace of the grand masters survives. Malta was formerly a British naval base, and was under heavy attack in World War II.

Valley Forge /'væli 'fɔːdʒ/ site in Pennsylvania 32 km/20 mi NW of Philadelphia, USA, where Washington's army spent the winter of 1777–78 in great hardship during the War of ◊American Independence.

Valley of Ten Thousand Smokes valley in SW Alaska, on the Alaska Peninsula, where in 1912 Mount Katmai erupted in one of the largest volcanic explosions ever known, though without loss of human life since the area was uninhabited. It was dedicated in 1918 as the Katmai National Monument. Thousands of fissures on the valley floor continue to emit steam and gases.

Valley of the Kings burial place of ancient kings opposite ◊Thebes, Egypt, on the left bank of the Nile.

Valmy, Battle of /væl'miː/ battle in 1792 in which the army of the French Revolution under Gen ◊Dumouriez defeated the Prussians at a French village in the Marne *département*. See ◊Revolutionary Wars.

Valois /væl'wɑː/ branch of the Capetian dynasty (see Hugh ◊Capet) in France, members of which occupied the French throne from Philip VI 1328 to Henry III 1589.

Valona /vəˈləʊnə/ Italian form of ◊Vlorë, port in Albania.

Valparaiso /ˌvælpəˈraɪzəʊ/ industrial port in Chile, capital of Valparaiso province, on the Pacific; population (1987) 279,000. Industries include sugar refining, textiles, and chemicals. Founded 1536, it was occupied by ◊Drake 1578, by ◊Hawkins 1595, pillaged by the Dutch 1600, and bombarded by Spain 1866; it has also suffered from earthquakes.

value-added tax a type of consumption tax; see ◊VAT.

valve in control engineering, a device that controls the flow of a fluid or along a pipeline. Inside a valve, a plug moves to widen or close the opening through which the fluid passes.

Common valves include the cone or needle valve, the globe valve, and butterfly valve, all named after the shape of the plug. Specialized valves include the one-way valve, which permits fluid flow in one direction only, and the safety valve, which cuts off flow under certain conditions.

valve or *electron tube* in electronics, a glass tube containing gas at low pressure, which is used to control the flow of electricity in a circuit. Three or more metal electrodes are inset into the tube. By varying the voltage on one of them, called the **grid electrode**, the current through the valve can be controlled, and the valve can act as an amplifier. They have been replaced for most applications by ◊transistors. However, they are still used in high-power transmitters and amplifiers, and in some hi-fi systems.

Vámbéry /'vɑːmbeəri/ Arminius 1832–1913. Hungarian traveller and writer who crossed the deserts of Central Asia to Khiva and Samarkand dressed as a ◊dervish, a classic journey described in his *Travels and Adventures in Central Asia* 1864.

vampire in Slav demonology, an 'undead' corpse that returns to 'life' by sucking the blood of the living.

vampire bat

◊Dracula is the best-known vampire in popular fiction.

vampire bat South and Central American bat of the family Desmodontidae, of which there are three species. The **common vampire** *Desmodus rotundus* is found from N Mexico to central Argentina. Its head and body grow to 9 cm/3.5 in. Vampires feed on the blood of mammals; they slice a piece of skin from a victim with their sharp incisor teeth and lap up the flowing blood.

Vampires feed on all kinds of mammals including horses, cattle, and occasionally people. They fly low, and settle on the ground before running to a victim. The bite is painless and the loss of blood is small; the victim seldom comes to any harm. Vampire bats are intelligent and among the few mammals to manifest altruistic behaviour (they adopt orphans and help other bats in need).

Van /vɑːn/ city in Turkey on a site on **Lake Van** that has been inhabited for more than 3,000 years; population (1985) 121,000. It is a commercial centre for a fruit and grain producing area.

vanadium a silver-white hard metal, symbol V, atomic number 23, atomic weight 50.94. It occurs in the rare minerals vanadinite and patronite; its chief use is in alloying steel to which it imparts toughness, elasticity, and tensile strength. It was discovered by Spanish mineralogist Andrés del Rio (1764–1849) 1801, and isolated by Henry Rosco 1869. Vanadium compounds (vanadates) are used in the preparation of aniline black for colouring glass.

Van Allen /væn 'ælən/ James Alfred 1914– . US physicist, whose instruments aboard the first US satellite Explorer 1 in 1958 led to the discovery of the Van Allen belts, two zones of intense radiation around the Earth. He pioneered high-altitude research with rockets after World War II, and became professor of physics at the University of Iowa 1951.

Van Allen belts two doughnut-shaped zones of atomic particles around Earth, discovered 1958 by James Van Allen. The atomic particles come from the Earth's upper atmosphere and the ◊solar wind, and are trapped by the Earth's magnetic field. The inner belt lies 1,000–5,000 km/620–3,100 mi above the Earth, and contains ◊protons and ◊electrons. The outer belt lies 15,000–25,000 km/9,300–15,500 mi above the equator, but is lower around the magnetic poles. It contains mostly electrons from the solar wind. The Van Allen belts are hazardous to astronauts, and interfere with electronic equipment on satellites.

Van Allen belts

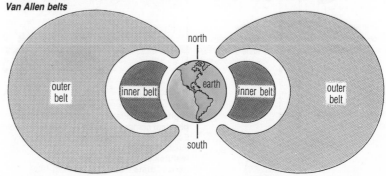

Van Basten /væn 'bæstən/ Marco 1964– . Dutch international footballer, noted as a striker. He helped the Netherlands to win the European Championship in 1988 and scored two goals for AC Milan in the European Cup final in 1989.

He started his career with top Dutch side Ajax and won many domestic honours. In 1987 he transferred to AC Milan for £3.3 million.

CAREER HIGHLIGHTS

Dutch League 1982–83, 1985
Dutch Cup 1981, 1986–87
European Cup-winners' Cup 1987
European Championship 1988
European Cup 1989
European Super Cup 1989

Vanbrugh /'vænbrə/ John 1664–1726. English Baroque architect and dramatist. He designed Blenheim Palace, Oxfordshire, and Castle Howard, Yorkshire, and wrote the comedy plays *The Relapse* 1696 and *The Provok'd Wife* 1697. He was imprisoned in France 1688–93 as a political hostage by the French authorities.

Van Buren /væn 'bjʊərən/ Martin 1782–1862. 8th president of the USA, a Democrat, born in Kinderhook, New York, of Dutch ancestry. He was a senator 1821–28, governor of New York State 1828–29, secretary of state 1829–31, minister to Britain 1831–33, vice president 1833–37, and president 1837–41. He initiated the independent treasury system, but his refusal to spend land revenues cost him the 1840 election. He lost the 1844 Democratic nomination to Polk, and in 1848 ran unsuccessfully for president as the Free Soil candidate.

Vance /væns/ Cyrus 1917– . US Democrat politician, secretary of state 1977–80. He resigned because he did not support President Carter's abortive mission to rescue the US hostages in Iran.

Vancouver /vænˈkuːvə/ industrial city (oil refining, engineering, shipbuilding, aircraft, timber, pulp and paper, textiles, fisheries) in Canada, its chief Pacific seaport, on the mainland of British Columbia; population (1986) 1,381,000.

It is situated on Burrard Inlet, at the mouth of the Fraser River. The site was taken possession of by George Vancouver for Britain 1792. It was settled by 1875, under the name of Granville, and was renamed when it became a city 1886, having been reached by the Canadian Pacific Railroad.

Vancouver /vænˈkuːvə/ George c. 1758–1798. British navigator who made extensive exploration of the W coast of North America. He accompanied James ◊Cook on two voyages, and served in the West Indies. He also surveyed parts of Australia, New Zealand, Tahiti, and Hawaii.

Vancouver Island /vænˈkuːvə/ island off the W coast of Canada, part of British Columbia
area 32,136 sq km/12,404 sq mi
towns Victoria, Nanaimo, naval base Esquimalt
products coal, timber, fish
history Vancouver Island was visited by the British explorer Cook 1778, and was surveyed 1792 by Capt George Vancouver.

Vandal /ˈvændl/ member of a Germanic people related to the ◊Goths. In the 5th century AD the Vandals moved from N Germany to invade Roman ◊Gaul and Spain, many settling in Andalusia (formerly Vandalitia) and others reaching N Africa 429. They sacked Rome 455 but accepted Roman suzerainty in the 6th century.

van de Graaff /ˌvæn də ˈgræf/ Robert Jemison 1901–1967. US physicist who from 1929 developed a high-voltage generator, which in its modern form can produce more than a million volts. It consists of an endless vertical conveyor belt that carries electrostatic charges (resulting from friction) up to a large hollow sphere supported on an insulated stand. The lower end of the belt is earthed, so that charge accumulates on the sphere. The size of the voltage built up in air depends on the radius of the sphere, but can be increased by enclosing the generator in an inert atmosphere, such as nitrogen.

Vanderbilt /ˈvændəbɪlt/ Cornelius 1794–1877. US industrialist, who made a fortune in steamships and (from the age of 70) by financing railways.

Van der Post /ˌvæn də ˈpəʊst/ Laurens (Jan) 1906– . South African writer, whose books, many of them autobiographical, are concerned with the duality of human existence. They include the novels *Flamingo Feather* 1955, *The Seed and the Sower* 1963 (set in Java, Japan, Britain, and Africa) and *A Story like the Wind* 1972. His travel books include *Venture to the Interior* 1952.

Van der Waals /ˌvæn də ˈvɑːls/ Johannes Diderik 1837–1923. Dutch physicist who was awarded a Nobel prize in 1910 for his theoretical study of gases. He emphasized the forces of attraction and repulsion between atoms and molecules in describing the behaviour of real gases, as opposed to the ideal gases dealt with in ◊Boyle's law and ◊Charles's law.

van Diemen Anthony, Dutch admiral, see ◊Diemen, Anthony van.

van Dyck Anthony. Flemish painter, see ◊Dyck, Anthony van.

Vane /veɪn/ Henry 1613–1662. English politician. In 1640 elected a member of the ◊Long Parliament, he was prominent in the impeachment of Archbishop ◊Laud, and 1643–53 was in effect the civilian head of the Parliamentary government. At the Restoration he was executed.

Vane /veɪn/ John 1923– . British pharmacologist who discovered the wide role of prostaglandins in the human body, produced in response to illness and stress. He shared a Nobel prize 1982.

Vänern, Lake /ˈvenən/ largest lake in Sweden, area 5,550 sq km/2,140 sq mi.

Vanderbilt American tycoon Cornelius Vanderbilt, who made his fortune developing steamships and railways in the USA.

van Eyck Jan. Flemish painter, see ◊Eyck, Jan van.

van Gogh Vincent. Dutch painter, see ◊Gogh, Vincent van.

Vanguard an early series of US Earth-orbiting satellites and their associated rocket launcher. Vanguard 1 was the second US satellite, launched 17 Mar 1958 by the three-stage Vanguard rocket. Tracking of its orbit revealed that Earth is slightly pear-shaped. The series ended Sept 1959 with Vanguard 3.

vanilla group of climbing orchids, native to Mexico but cultivated elsewhere, with large white or yellow flowers. The dried and fermented fruit, or pods, of *Vanilla planifolia* are the original source of the vanilla flavouring used in cookery; vanilla flavouring can now be produced artificially.

Vanity Fair a novel by William Makepeace Thackeray, published in the UK 1847–48. It deals with the contrasting fortunes of the tough orphan Becky Sharp and the soft-hearted, privileged Amelia Sedley, who first meet at Miss Pinkerton's Academy for young ladies.

van Meegeren Hans. Dutch forger, see ◊Meegeren, Hans van.

Vannin, Ellan /ˈelən ˈvænɪn/ Gaelic name for ◊Isle of Man.

Vansittart /vænˈsɪtət/ Robert Gilbert, 1st Baron Vansittart 1881–1957. British diplomat, noted for his anti-German polemic. He was permanent undersecretary of state for foreign affairs 1930–38 and chief diplomatic adviser to the foreign secretary 1938–41.

van t'Hoff /væn tˈhɒf/ Jacobus Henricus 1852–1911. Dutch physical chemist. He explained the 'asymmetric' carbon atom occurring in optically active compounds. His greatest work—the concept of chemical affinity as the maximum work obtainable from a reaction—was shown with measurements of osmotic and gas pressures, and reversible electric batteries. He was the first recipient of the Nobel prize in 1901.

Vanuatu /ˌvænuːˈɑːtuː/ group of islands in the S Pacific, part of ◊Melanesia.

government Vanuatu is an independent republic within the ◊Commonwealth. The constitution dates from independence in 1980. It provides for a president, who is formal head of state, elected for a five-year term by an electoral college consisting of Parliament and the presidents of the country's regional councils. Parliament consists of a single chamber of 46 members, elected by universal suffrage, through a system of proportional representation, for a four-year term. From among their members they elect a prime minister who then appoints and presides over a council of ministers.

history The islands were first reached from Europe 1606 by the Portuguese navigator Pedro Fernandez de Queiras. Called the New Hebrides, they were jointly administered by France and Britain from 1906.

Vanuatu escaped Japanese occupation during World War II. In the 1970s two political parties were formed, the New Hebrides National Party, supported by British interests, and the Union of New Hebrides Communities, supported by France. Discussions began in London about eventual independence and they resulted in the election of a representative assembly in Nov 1975. Independence was delayed because of objections by the National Party, which had changed its name to the Vanuaaku Party (VP). A government of national unity was formed in Dec 1978 with Father Gerard Leymang as chief minister and the VP leader, Father Walter Lini, as his deputy. In 1980 a revolt by French settlers and plantation workers in the island of Espiritu Santo was put down by British, French and Papua New Guinean troops.

Later in 1980 the New Hebrides became independent, within the Commonwealth, as the Republic of Vanuatu. The first president was George

---

van de Graaff

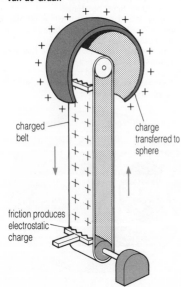

charged belt

friction produces electrostatic charge

charge transferred to sphere

Vanuatu
Republic of

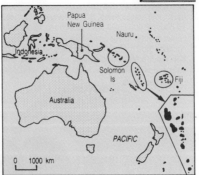

Papua New Guinea

Nauru

Indonesia

Solomon Is

Fiji

Australia

PACIFIC

0   1000 km

area 14,800 sq km/5,714 sq mi
capital Vila on Efate
physical comprises about 70 islands, including Espiritu Santo, Malekala, and Efate; densely forested
features three active volcanoes
head of state Fred Timakata from 1989
head of government Walter Lini from 1980

government democratic republic
political parties Vanuaaki Pati (VP: 'Party of Our Land'), Melanesian socialist; Union of Moderate Parties (UMP), Francophone opposition grouping
exports copra, fish, coffee; tourism is important
currency vatu (192.50 = £1 Mar 1990)
population (1988) 149,400 (90% Melanesian); annual growth rate 23.6%
language Bislama 82%, English, French, all official
religion Presbyterian 40%, Roman Catholic 16%, Anglican 14%, animist 15%
chronology
1975 Representative assembly established.
1978 Government of national unity formed, with Father Gerard Leymang as chief minister.
1980 Revolt on the island of Espiritu Santo delayed independence but it was achieved, within the Commonwealth, with George Sokomanu as president and Father Walter Lini as prime minister.
1988 An attempt by Sokomanu to unseat Lini led to Sokomanou's arrest for treason.
1989 Sokomanu sentenced to six years' imprisonment and succeeded as president by Fred Timakata.

Varèse *An experimental composer, Edgard Varèse rejected the classical tradition. He shocked audiences of his day by introducing dissonant brass and percussion effects into the orchestra; he was also a pioneer of electronic music.*

Kalkoa, who adopted the name *Sokomanu* ('leader of thousands'), and the first prime minister was Father Lini. In the 1983 general election the VP won 24 seats and Father Lini continued as prime minister. The Union of Moderate Parties won 12 seats.

Lini proceeded to pursue a left-of-centre, non-aligned foreign policy, which included support for the Kanak separatist movement in New Caledonia. This soured relations with France and provoked mounting opposition within Parliament. Despite the VP retaining its majority after the Nov 1987 general election, this opposition continued, prompting Lini, in July 1988, to expel from Parliament his rival Barak Sope. Lini was then dismissed as prime minister and Parliament dissolved by president Sokomanu, who appointed his nephew Sope head of an interim government. However, the Supreme Court ruled these actions unconstitutional and security forces loyal to Lini arrested the president, Sope and opposition leader Maxime Carlot (who were each later sentenced to 5–6 years' imprisonment) and reinstated the former prime minister.

Externally, since independence, Vanuatu has sought to promote greater cooperation among the states of the Pacific region. As part of this strategy, along with Papua New Guinea and the Solomon Islands, it formed, in Mar 1988, the 'Spearhead Group', whose aim is to preserve Melanesian cultural tradition and campaign for New Caledonia's independence.

Vanwall British motor-racing team, the first winners of the Constructor's Championship 1958. The company was stared by Tony Vandervell and they launched their first car 1954. It was designed around a Ferrari chassis with a Norton engine. Stirling Moss drove for Vanwall and won the 1956 International Trophy.

In 1957 Moss and Tony Brooks shared the driving to win the British Grand Prix at Aintree, the first win for a British car in over 30 years. They went on to win six Grand Prix 1958. Ill health forced Vandervell to retire and at the same time the team quit Formula One racing.

vapour density density of a gas, expressed as the ◊mass of a given volume of the gas divided by the mass of an equal volume of a reference gas (such as hydrogen or air) at the same temperature and pressure. It is equal to half the relative molecular weight (mass) of the gas.

vapour pressure pressure of a vapour given off by (evaporated from) a liquid or solid, caused by vibrating atoms or molecules continuously

escaping from its surface. In an enclosed space, a maximum value is reached when the number of particles leaving the surface is in equilibrium with those returning to it; this is known as the *saturated vapour pressure*.

Var /vɑ:/ river in S France, rising in the Maritime Alps and flowing generally SSE for 134 km/84 mi into the Mediterranean near Nice. It gives its name to a *département* in the Provence-Alpes-Côte d'Azur region.

Varanasi /vəˈrɑːnəsi/ or **Benares** holy city of the Hindus in Uttar Pradesh, India, on the Ganges; population (1981) 794,000. There are 1,500 golden shrines, and a 5 km/3 mi frontage to the Ganges with sacred stairways (ghats) for purification by bathing. At the burning ghats, the ashes of the dead are scattered on the river to ensure a favourable reincarnation. There are two universities 1916 and 1957.

Varangian member of a widespread Swedish Viking people in E Europe and the Balkans, and more particularly a member of the Byzantine imperial guard founded 988 by Vladimir of Kiev (955–1015), which lasted until the fall of Constantinople 1453.

From the late 11th century, the Byzantine guard included English and Norman mercenaries, as well as Scandinavians. It was feared and respected as an elite military force, but also occasionally dabbled in politics.

Vardon /ˈvɑːdn/ Harry 1870–1937. British golfer, born in Jersey. He won the British Open a record six times 1896–1914. He formed a partnership with James Braid and John Henry Taylor, which became known as 'the Great Triumvirate', and dominated British golf in the years up to World War I. Vardon was the first UK golfer to win the US Open 1900.

Varèse /vaˈrez/ Edgard 1885–1965. French composer, who settled in New York 1916 where he founded the New Symphony Orchestra 1919 to advance the cause of modern music. His work is experimental and often dissonant, combining electronic sounds with orchestral instruments, and includes *Hyperprism* 1923, *Intégrales* 1931, and *Poème Electronique* 1958.

Vargas /ˈvɑːgəs/ Getúlio 1883–1954. President of Brazil 1930–45 and 1951–54. He overthrew the republic 1930 and in 1937 he set up a totalitarian, pro-fascist state known as the *Estado Novo*. Ousted by a military coup 1945, he returned as president 1951 but, amid mounting opposition and political scandal, committed suicide 1954.

Vargas Llosa /ˈvɑːgəs ˈjəʊsə/ Mario 1937– . Peruvian novelist and conservative politician, unsuccessful presidential candidate 1990. His novels include *La ciudad y los perros/The Time of the Hero* 1963 and *La guerra del fin del mundo/The War at the End of the World* 1982.

Vargas Llosa began as a communist and turned to the political right. He has been criticized for being out of touch with Peru's large Quechua Indian community. As a writer he belongs to the magic realist school. *La tía Julia y el escribidor/Aunt Julia and the Scriptwriter* 1977 is a humorously autobiographical novel.

variable in mathematics, a changing quantity (one that can take various values), as opposed to a ◊constant. For example, in the algebraic expression $y = 4x + 2$, the variables are x and y, whereas 4 and 2 are constants.

A variable may be dependent or independent. Thus if y is a ◊function of x, written $y = f(x)$, such that $y = 4x + 2$, the domain of the function includes all values of the independent variable x while the range (or codomain) of the function is defined by the values of the dependent variable y.

variable-geometry wing technical term for what is popularly called a ◊swing-wing, a type of moveable aircraft wing.

variable star a star whose brightness changes, either regularly or irregularly, over a period ranging from a few hours to months or even years. The ◊Cepheid variables regularly expand and contract in size every few days or weeks.

Stars that change in size and brightness at less precise intervals include *long-period variables* such as the red giant Mira (period about 330 days), and *irregular variables* such as some red supergiants. *Eruptive variables* emit sudden outbursts of light. Some suffer flares on their surfaces, while others, such as a ◊nova, result from transfer of gas between a close pair of stars. A ◊supernova is the explosive death of a star. In an ◊eclipsing binary, the variation is due not to any change in the star itself, but to the periodical eclipse of a star by a close companion; see ◊Epsilon Aurigae, ◊Algol.

variations in music, a form based on constant repetition of a simple theme, each new version being elaborated or treated in a different manner. The theme is easily recognizable, either as a popular tune or—as a gesture of respect—as the work of a fellow composer, for example, Brahms honours Bach in the *Variations on the St Antony Chorale*.

varicose veins a condition where the veins become swollen and twisted. The veins of the leg are most often affected, although other vulnerable sites include the rectum (◊haemorrhoids) and testes. Some people have an inherited tendency to varicose veins, but obstructed blood flow is the direct cause. Surgery may be needed.

variegation a description of plant leaves or stems that exhibit patches of different colours. The term is usually applied to plants that show white, cream, or yellow on their leaves, caused by areas of tissue that lack the green pigment ◊chlorophyll. Variegated plants are bred for their decorative value, but they are often considerably weaker than the normal all-green plant. Many will not breed true and require ◊vegetative reproduction.

The term is sometimes applied to abnormal patchy colouring of petals, as in the variegated petals of certain tulips, caused by a virus infection. A mineral deficiency in the soil may also be the cause of variegation.

Varley /ˈvɑːli/ John 1778–1842. English water-colour painter of landscapes, and friend of the poet and artist ◊Blake.

Varna /ˈvɑːnə/ port in Bulgaria, on an inlet of the Black Sea; population (1987) 306,000. Industries include shipbuilding and the manufacture of chemicals. It was a Greek colony in the 6th century BC, and part of the Ottoman Empire 1391–1878; renamed Stalin 1949–56.

varnish a solution of resins or resinous gums in linseed oil, turpentine, and other solvents; also synthetic equivalents. It is used to give a shiny, sealed surface to furniture and interior fittings.

Varuna in early Hindu mythology, sky god and king of the universe.

Vasarély /ˌvæzəreɪˈliː/ Victor 1908– . French artist, born in Hungary. In the 1940s he developed his precise geometric compositions, full of visual puzzles and effects of movement, which he created with complex arrangements of hard-edged geometric shapes and subtle variations in colours.

He was active in Paris from 1930, then in the south of France from 1960. He initially worked as a graphic artist, concentrating on black and white.

Vasari /vəˈsɑːri/ Giorgio 1511–1574. Italian art historian, architect, and painter, author of *Lives of the Most Excellent Architects, Painters and Sculptors* 1550 (enlarged and revised 1568), in which he proposed the theory of a Renaissance of the arts beginning with Giotto and culminating with Michelangelo. He designed the Uffizi Palace, Florence.

Vasari was a prolific Mannerist painter. His basic view of art history has remained unchallenged, despite his prejudices and his delight in often ill-founded, libellous anecdotes.

Vasco da Gama Portuguese navigator; see ◊Gama.

vascular bundle a strand of primary conducting tissue (a 'vein') in vascular plants, consisting mainly of water-conducting tissues, metaxylem and protoxylem, which together make up the

Vatican City State
(Stato della Città del Vaticano)

area 0.4 sq km/109 acres
physical forms an enclave in the heart of

Rome, Italy
features Vatican Palace, official residence of the pope; the basilica and square of St Peter's; also includes a number of churches in and near Rome, and the pope's summer villa at Castel Gandolfo
head of state and government John Paul II from 1978
government absolute Catholic
currency issues its own coinage, which circulates together with that of Italy
population (1985) 1,000
language Italian
religion Roman Catholic
chronology
1947 New Italian constitution confirmed the sovereignty of the Vatican City State.
1978 John Paul II became the first non-Italian pope for more than 400 years.
1985 New concordat signed under which Roman Catholicism ceased to be the state religion.

primary ◊xylem, and nutrient-conducting tissue, ◊phloem. It extends from the roots to the stems and leaves. Typically the phloem is situated nearest to the epidermis and the xylem towards the centre of the bundle. In plants exhibiting ◊secondary growth, the xylem and phloem are separated by a thin layer of vascular ◊cambium, which gives rise to new conducting tissues.

vascular plant a plant containing vascular bundles. Pteridophytes (ferns, horsetails, and clubmosses), gymnosperms (conifers and cycads), and angiosperms (flowering plants) are all vascular plants.

vasectomy (sometimes known as male sterilization) an operation to cut and tie the vessels that carry sperm from the testes to the penis. Vasectomy does not affect sexual performance, but the semen produced at ejaculation no longer contains sperm.

vassal in medieval Europe, one who paid feudal homage to a superior lord (see ◊feudalism), and who promised to give him military service and advice in return for a grant of land. The term was used from the 9th century.

The relationship of vassalage was the mainstay of the feudal system, and declined along with it during the transition to bastard feudalism.

Vassilou /væˈsiːluː/ Georgios Vassos 1931– Greek-Cypriot politician and entrepreneur, president from 1988. A self-made millionaire, he entered politics as an independent and in 1988 won the presidency, with Communist Party support. He has since, with United Nations help, tried unsuccessfully to heal the rift between the Greek and Turkish communities.

VAT abbreviation for *value-added tax* a tax on goods and services. VAT is imposed by the

vascular bundle

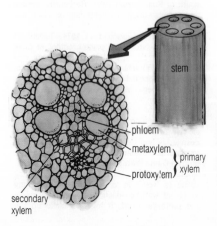

European Community on member states. The tax varies from state to state (in the UK it is 15% of the value of most goods and services). An agreed proportion of the tax money is used to fund the EC.

VAT is applied at each stage of the production of a commodity and it is charged only on the value added at that stage. It is not levied, unlike purchase tax, on the sale of the commodity itself, but at this stage the VAT paid at earlier stages of the good's manufacture cannot be reclaimed. In the UK food, newspapers, and books are exempt from VAT.

A form of VAT was introduced in Japan 1989, its unpopularity contributing to the downfall of Prime Minister Takeshita. Canada announced in 1989 an intention to impose VAT (termed GST) from 1991.

Vatican City State /ˈvætɪkən/ sovereign area in central Rome, Italy.

government The pope, elected for life by the Sacred College of ◊Cardinals, is absolute head of state. He appoints a pontifical commission to administer the state's affairs on his behalf and under his direction.

history The pope has traditionally been based in Rome, where the Vatican has been a papal residence since 1377. The Vatican Palace is one of the largest in the world and contains a valuable collection of works of art.

The Vatican City State came into being through the Lateran Treaty of 1929, under which Italy recognized the sovereignty of the pope over the city of the Vatican. The 1947 Italian constitution reaffirmed the Lateran Treaty, and under its terms, Roman Catholicism became the state religion in Italy, enjoying special privileges. This remained so until under a new 1984 Concordat (ratified 1985) Catholicism ceased to be the state religion. Karol Wojtyla, formerly archbishop of Krakow in Poland, has been pope since 1978 under the title of ◊John Paul II.

Vatican City State *St Peter's Square in the Vatican City State, central Rome, Italy.*

vector

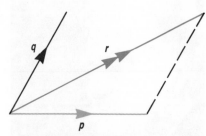

In 1982 Roberto Calvi, known as 'God's banker' because of his ties with the Vatican, was found hanged under a London bridge shortly before the collapse of the Italian bank of which he was chair, Banco Ambrosiano, and warrants were issued in Italy against three Vatican Bank executives held responsible for the crash. The warrants were annulled 1987 because the affairs of the Vatican Bank, officially known as the Institute for Religious Works (IOR), are outside Italian jurisdiction.

Vatican Councils Roman Catholic ecumenical councils called by Pope Pius IX 1869 (which met 1870) and by Pope John XXIII 1959 (which met 1962). These councils considered major elements of church policy.

Vauban /vəʊˈbɒn/ Sébastien le Prestre de 1633–1707. French marshal and military engineer. In Louis XIV's wars he conducted many sieges and rebuilt many of the fortresses on France's eastern frontier.

Vaucluse /vəʊˈkluːz/ mountain range in SE France, part of the Provence Alps, E of Avignon, rising to 1,242 m/4,075 ft. It gives its name to a *département*. The Italian poet Petrarch lived in the Vale of Vaucluse 1337–53.

vaudeville variety entertainment popular in the USA from the 1890s to the 1920s; in the same tradition as ◊music hall in Britain.

Vaughan /vɔːn/ Henry 1622–1695. Welsh poet and physician. He published several volumes of metaphysical religious verse and prose devotions. His mystical outlook on nature influenced later poets, including Wordsworth.

Vaughan Williams /ˈvɔːn ˈwɪljəmz/ Ralph 1872– 1958. English composer. His style was tonal and often evocative of the English countryside through the use of folk themes. Among his works are the orchestral *Fantasia on a Theme by Thomas Tallis* 1910; the opera *Sir John in Love* 1929, featuring the Elizabethan song 'Greensleeves'; and nine symphonies 1909–57.

He studied at Cambridge, the Royal College of Music, and with Max ◊Bruch in Berlin and Maurice ◊Ravel in Paris. His choral poems include *Toward the Unknown Region* (Whitman) 1907 and *On Wenlock Edge* (Housman) 1909, *A Sea Symphony* 1910, and *A London Symphony* 1914. Later works include *Sinfonia Antartica* 1953, developed from his film score for *Scott of the Antarctic* 1948, and a Ninth Symphony 1958. He also wrote *A Pastoral Symphony* 1922, sacred music for unaccompanied choir, the ballad opera *Hugh the Drover* 1924, and the operatic morality play *The Pilgrim's Progress* 1951.

vb in grammar, abbreviation for ◊verb.

VDU abbreviation for *visual display unit* an electronic output device for displaying the data processed by a computer on a screen. The oldest and the most popular type is the ◊cathode-ray tube (CRT), which uses essentially the same technology as a television screen. Other types use plasma display technology and ◊liquid crystal displays.

vector any physical quantity that has both magnitude and direction, such as the velocity or acceleration of an object, as distinct from a scalar quantity which has magnitude but no direction, such as speed, density, or mass. A vector is represented geometrically by an arrow whose length corresponds to its magnitude, and in an appropriate direction. Vectors can be added graphically by constructing a triangle of vectors (such as the triangle of forces commonly employed in physics and engineering).

If two forces *p* and *q* are acting on a body at *A*, then the parallelogram of forces is drawn to determine the resultant force and direction *r*. The forces *p*, *q*, and *r* are vectors. In technical writing, vectors are denoted by bold (clarendon) type, or underlined *AB* or overlined *AB*.

Veda /'veɪdə/ (Sanskrit 'divine knowledge') the most sacred of the Hindu scriptures, hymns written in an old form of Sanskrit; the oldest may date from 1500 or 2000 BC. The four main collections are: the *Rigveda* (hymns and praises); *Yajurveda* (prayers and sacrificial formulae); *Sâmaveda* (tunes and chants); and *Atharvaveda*, or Veda of the Atharvans, the officiating priests at the sacrifices.

Vedānta school of Hindu philosophy that developed the teachings of the *Upanishads*. One of its teachers was Śamkara, who lived in S India in the 8th century AD and is generally regarded as a manifestation of Siva. He taught that there is only one reality, Brahman, and that knowledge of Brahman leads finally to *moksha*, or liberation from reincarnation.

Vedda person of Vedda culture, a distinct group who are thought to be descendants of the people who inhabited Sri Lanka before the arrival of the Aryans around 550 BC. They live mainly in the central highlands of Sri Lanka, and many practise shifting cultivation.

Vega /'veɪgə/ the fifth brightest star in the sky, and the brightest in the constellation Lyra. It is a blue-white star, 27 light years away, with a luminosity of 50 Suns.

In 1983 the Infrared Astronomy Satellite (IRAS) discovered a ring of dust around Vega, possibly a disc from which a planetary system is forming.

vegan a person who eats no foods of animal origin, including eggs, milk, and honey.

Theoretically vegans are at risk of a deficiency of vitamin B12, which is needed by the body for blood-cell and nerve formation (see ◊vitamin), but it can be absorbed from fortified soya products and yeast extracts. Vegans must ensure an adequate supply of calcium from nuts and soya products, and vitamin D from sunshine and margarine, as these are normally obtained from dairy products in the diet.

vegetarianism the practice of restricting diet to foods obtained without slaughter, for humanitarian, aesthetic, or health reasons. Vegans abstain from all food that comes from animals.

vegetative reproduction a type of ◊asexual reproduction in plants that relies not on spores, but on multicellular structures formed by the parent plant. Some of the main types are ◊stolons and runners, ◊gemmae, ◊bulbils, sucker shoots produced from the roots of some species, such as creeping thistle (*Cirsium arvense*), ◊tubers, ◊bulbs, ◊corms, and ◊rhizomes. Vegetative reproduction has long been exploited in horticulture and agriculture, with various methods employed to multiply stocks of plants.

Veidt /faɪt/ Conrad 1893–1943. German film actor, memorable as the sleepwalker in *Das Kabinett des Dr Caligari/The Cabinet of Dr Caligari* 1919 and as the evil caliph in *The Thief of Bagdad* 1940. In international films from the 1920s, he moved to Hollywood in the 1940s.

Veil /veɪ/ Simone 1927– . French politician. A survivor of Hitler's concentration camps, she was minister of health 1974–79, and framed the French abortion bill. In 1979–81 she was president of the European Parliament.

vein in animals with a circulatory system, a vessel that carries blood from the body to the heart. Veins contain valves that prevent the blood from

running back when moving against gravity. They always carry deoxygenated blood, with the exception of the veins leading from the lungs to the heart in birds and mammals, which carry newly oxygenated blood.

The term is also used more loosely for any system of channels that strengthens living tissues and supplies them with nutrients for example, leaf veins (see ◊vascular bundle), and the veins in insects' wings.

Vela /'vilə/ constellation of the southern hemisphere, represented as the sails of a ship. It contains large wisps of gas (called the Gum Nebula after its discoverer), believed to be the remains of one or more ◊supernovae. Vela also contains the second optical ◊pulsar (a pulsar that flashes at a visible wavelength) to be discovered.

Velázquez /vɪ'læskwɪz/ Diego Rodriguez de Silva y 1599–1660. Spanish painter, born in Seville, the outstanding Spanish artist of the 17th century. In 1623 he became court painter to Philip IV in Madrid, where he produced many portraits of the royal family, as well as occasional religious paintings, genre scenes, and other subjects. *Las Meninas/The Ladies-in-Waiting* 1655 (Prado, Madrid) is a complex group portrait which includes a self-portrait, but nevertheless focuses clearly on the doll-like figure of the Infanta Margareta Teresa.

His early work in Seville shows exceptional realism and dignity, delight in capturing a variety of textures, rich use of colour and contrasts of light and shade. In Madrid he was inspired by works by Titian in the royal collection, and by Rubens, whom he met in 1628. He was in Italy 1629–31 and 1648–51; on his second visit he painted *Pope Innocent X* (Doria Gallery, Rome).

Velázquez's work includes an outstanding formal history painting, *The Surrender of Breda* 1634–35 (Prado), studies of the male nude, and a reclining female nude, *The Rokeby Venus* about 1648 (National Gallery, London).

Velcro (from 'velvet' and 'crochet') a system of hooks and eyes for fastening clothing, developed by Swiss inventor Georges de Mestral (1902–90) after studying why burrs stuck to his trousers and noting that they were made of thousands of tiny hooks.

Velde, van de /,væn də 'feldə/ family of Dutch artists. Both *Willem van de Velde* the Elder 1611–93 and his son *Willem van de Velde* the Younger 1633–1707 painted sea battles for Charles II and James II (having settled in London 1672). Another son *Adriaen van de Velde* 1636–72 painted landscapes.

Willem the Younger achieved an atmosphere of harmony and dignity in highly detailed views of fighting ships at sea. The National Maritime Museum in Greenwich, London, has a fine collection of his works.

veldt subtropical grassland in South Africa, equivalent to the ◊Pampas of South America.

vellum a type of parchment made from the skin of a calf, kid, or lamb. It was used during the Middle Ages, and occasionally later, for exceptionally important documents and the finest manuscripts. It is now used to describe thick, high-quality paper that resembles fine parchment.

velocity the speed of an object in a given direction. Velocity is a ◊vector quantity, since its direction is important as well as its magnitude (or speed).

The velocity at any instant of a particle travelling in a curved path is in the direction of the tangent to the path at the instant considered.

velvet a fabric of silk, cotton, nylon, or other textile, with a short, thick pile. Utrecht, Netherlands, and Genoa, Italy, are traditional centres of manufacture.

Venda /'vendə/ ◊Black National State from 1979, near the Zimbabwe border, in South Africa
area 6,500 sq km/2,510 sq mi
capital Thohoyandou
towns MaKearela
features homeland of the Vhavenda people

government executive president (paramount chief P R Mphephu in office from Sept 1979) and national assembly
products coal, copper, graphite, construction stone
population (1980) 343,500
language Luvenda, English.

Vendée /vɒn'deɪ/ river in W France that rises near the village of La Châtaigneraie and flows 72 km/45 mi to join the Sèvre Niortaise 11 km/7 mi E of the Bay of Biscay.

Vendée, Wars of the /vɒn'deɪ/ in the French Revolution, a series of peasant risings against the Revolutionary government that began in the Vendée *département*, W France 1793, and spread to other areas of France, lasting until 1795.

vendetta any prolonged feud, in particular the practice that existed until recently in Corsica, Sardinia, and Sicily of exacting revenge for the murder of a relative by killing a member of the murderer's family.

Vendôme /vɒn'dəʊm/ Louis Joseph, Duc de Vendôme 1654–1712. Marshal of France, who lost his command after defeat by the British commander Marlborough at Oudenaarde, Belgium, 1708, but achieved successes in the 1710 Spanish campaign during the War of the ◊Spanish Succession.

venereal disease (VD) any disease mainly transmitted by sexual contact, although commonly the term is used specifically for gonorrhea and syphilis, both occurring worldwide, and chancroid ('soft sore') and lymphogranuloma venerum, seen mostly in the tropics. The term *sexually transmitted diseases* (◊STDs) is more often used to encompass a growing list of conditions passed on primarily, but not exclusively, in this way.

Venetia /vɪ'niːʃə/ Roman name of that part of NE Italy which later became the republic of Venice, including the ◊Veneto region.

Veneto /'venətəʊ/ region of NE Italy, comprising the provinces of Belluno, Padova (Padua), Treviso, Rovigo, Venezia (Venice), and Vicenza; area 18,400 sq km/7,102 sq mi; population (1988) 4,375,000. Its capital is Venice, and towns include Padua, Verona, and Vicenza. Veneto forms part of the N Italian plain, with the delta of the Po; it includes part of the Alps and Dolomites, and Lake Garda. Products include cereals, fruit, vegetables, wine, chemicals, shipbuilding, and textiles.

Venezia /ve'netsiə/ Italian form of ◊Venice, city, port, and naval base on the Adriatic.

Venezuela /,venɪ'zweɪlə/ country in northern South America, on the Caribbean Sea, bounded E by Guyana, S by Brazil, and W by Colombia.
government Venezuela is a federal republic of 20 states, two federal territories, and a federal district based on the capital, Caracas. The 1961 constitution provides for a president, who is head of state and head of government, and a two-chamber national congress, consisting of a senate and a chamber of deputies. The president is elected by universal suffrage for a five-year term and may not serve two consecutive terms. The president appoints and presides over a council of ministers.

The Senate has 44 members elected by universal suffrage, on the basis of two representatives for each state and two for the federal district, plus any living ex-presidents. The Chamber has 196 deputies, also elected by universal suffrage. Both chambers serve five-year terms.
history For early history, see ◊American Indian, ◊South America. Columbus visited Venezuela 1498 and there was a Spanish settlement from 1520. In 1811 a rebellion against Spain began, led by Simón Bolívar, and Venezuela became independent 1830.

After a long history of dictatorial rule, Venezuela adopted a new constitution 1961 and three years later Rómulo Betancourt became the first president to have served a full term of office. He was succeeded by Dr Raúl Leoni 1964 and by Dr Rafael

Venezuela
Republic of
(República de Venezuela)

area 912,100 sq km/352,162 sq mi
capital Caracas
towns Barquisimeto, Valencia; port Maracaibo
physical valleys and delta of river Orinoco flanked by mountains
features Lake Maracaibo, Angel Falls; unique flora and fauna; annual rainfall over 7,600 mm/300 in
head of state and of government Carlos Andrés Pérez from 1988
government federal democratic republic
political parties Democratic Action Party (AD), moderate, left-of-centre; Christian Social Party (COPEI), Christian centre-right ; Movement towards Socialism (MAS), left-of-centre
exports coffee, cocoa, timber, oil, aluminium,

iron ore, petrochemicals
currency bolívar (74.16 = £1 Mar 1990)
population (1988) 18,770,000 (70% mestizos, 32,000 American Indians); annual growth rate 2.8%
life expectancy men 66, women 72
religion Roman Catholic
language Spanish (official), Indian languages 2%
literacy 84% male/78% female (1980 est)
GNP $70.8 bn (1983); $4,716 per head of population
chronology
1961 New constitution adopted, with Rómulo Betancourt as president.
1964 Dr Raúl Leoni became president.
1969 Dr Rafael Caldera became president.
1974 Carlos Andrés Pérez Rodríguez became president.
1979 Dr Luis Herrera became president.
1984 Dr Jaime Lusinchi became president. He tried to solve the nation's economic problems through a social pact between the government, trade unions, and business, and by rescheduling the national debt.
1987 Widespread social unrest triggered by inflation; student demonstrators shot by police.
1988 Andrés Pérez elected president. Venezuela suspends payments on foreign debts, which had increased due to the drop in oil prices since the 1970s.
1989 Economic austerity programme enforced by $4.3 billion loan from International Monetary Fund. Price rises triggered riots in which 300 people were killed; martial law declared in Feb. General strike in May.

Caldera Rodríguez 1969. The latter did much to bring economic and political stability, although underground abductions and assassinations still occurred. In 1974 Carlos Andres Rodríguez, of the Democratic Action Party (AD), became president and stability increased. In 1979 Dr Luis Herrera, leader of the Social Christian Party (COPEI), was elected.

Against a background of growing economic problems, the 1983 general election was contested by 20 parties and 13 presidential candidates. It was a bitterly fought campaign and resulted in the election of Dr Jaime Lusinchi as president and a win for the Democratic Action Party (AD) in Congress, with 109 Chamber and 27 Senate seats. COPEI won 60 Chamber and 16 Senate seats, and the Socialist Movement (MAS) ten Chamber and two Senate seats. President Lusinchi's austere economic policies were unpopular and he tried to conclude a social pact between the government, trade unions, and business. He reached an agreement with the government's creditor bankers for a rescheduling of Venezuela's large public debt.

In 1988 Venezuela suspended payment on their foreign debt, which had grown due to a drop in oil prices since the 1970s. The Dec 1988 presidential election was won decisively by the AD candidate, Andres Perez. In Feb 1989 there were riots in which 300 people were killed, following price increases to satisfy the loan terms of the International Monetary Fund. Martial law was declared. In May 1989 there was a general strike in protest at government austerity measures.

Venice /'venɪs/ (Italian **Venezia**) city, port, and naval base, capital of Veneto, Italy, on the Adriatic; population (1988) 328,000. The old city is built on piles on low-lying islands. Apart from tourism, industries include glass, jewellery, textiles, and lace. Venice was an independent trading republic from the 10th century, ruled by a doge, or chief magistrate, and was one of the centres of the Italian Renaissance.

It is now connected with the mainland and its industrial suburb, Mestre, by road and rail viaduct. The Grand Canal divides the city and is crossed by the Rialto bridge; transport is by traditional gondola or *vaporetto* (water bus).

St Mark's Square has the 11th-century Byzantine cathedral of San Marco, the 9th–16th century campanile (rebuilt 1902), and the 14th–15th century Gothic Doge's Palace (linked to the former state prison by the 17th-century Bridge of Sighs). The nearby Lido is a bathing resort. The **Venetian School** of artists includes the Bellinis, Carpaccio, Giorgione, Titian, Tintoretto, and Veronese.

Venice was founded in the 5th century by refugees from mainland cities sacked by the Huns, and became a wealthy independent trading republic in the 10th century, stretching by the mid-15th century to the Alps and including Crete. It was governed by an aristocratic oligarchy, the Council of Ten, and a senate, which appointed the doge, or chief magistrate, 697–1797. Venice helped defeat the Ottoman Empire in the naval battle of Lepanto 1571, but was overthrown by Napoleon 1797. It passed to Austria 1815, but finally became part of the kingdom of Italy 1866.

veni, vidi, vici (Latin 'I came, I saw, I conquered') Julius ◊Caesar's description of his victory over King Pharnaces II (63–47 BC) at Zela in 47 BC.

Venizelos /ˌvenɪˈzelɒs/ Eleutherios 1864–1936. Greek politician born in Crete, leader of the Cretan movement against Turkish rule until the union of the island with Greece in 1905. He later became prime minister of the Greek state on five occasions, 1910–15, 1917–20, 1924, 1928–32 and 1933, before being exiled to France in 1935.

Having led the fight against Turkish rule in Crete, Venizelos became president of the Cretan assembly and declared the union of the island with Greece in 1905. As prime minister of Greece from 1910, he instituted financial, military, and constitutional reforms and took Greece into the Balkan Wars. As a result, Greece annexed Macedonia, but attempts by Venizelos to join the war on the allied side led to his dismissal by King

Venus The Venus de Milo *in the Louvre, Paris.*

Constantine. Leading a rebel government in Crete and later in Salonika, he declared war on Bulgaria and Germany and secured the abdication of King Constantine.

As prime minister from 1917 he attended the Paris Peace Conference in 1919. By provoking a war with Turkey over Anatolia in 1920 he suffered an electoral defeat. On his last return to office in 1933, he was implicated in an uprising by his supporters and fled to France, where he died.

Venn diagram in mathematics, a diagram representing a ◊set or sets and the logical relationships between them. Sets are drawn as circles. An area of overlap between two circles (sets) contains elements that are common to both sets, and thus represents a third set. Circles that do not overlap represent sets with no elements in common (disjoint sets). The method is named after the British logician John Venn (1834–1923).

Vent, Iles du /'iːl djuː 'vɒn/ French name for the Windward Islands, part of the ◊Society Islands in ◊French Polynesia. The Leeward Islands are known as the ***Iles sous le Vent***.

Ventris /'ventrɪs/ Michael (George Francis) 1922–1956. English archaeologist. Deciphering Minoan Linear B, the language of the tablets found at Knossos and Pylos, he showed that it was a very early form of Greek, thus revising existing views on early Greek history. *Documents in Mycenaean Greek*, written with John Chadwick, was published shortly after he died in a road accident.

venture capital or ***risk capital*** money put up by investors such as merchant banks to fund a new company or expansion of an established company. The organization providing the money receives a share of the company's equity and seeks to make a profit by rapid growth in the value of its stake, as a result of expansion by the start-up company or 'venture'. Any money invested in a company is, of course, at risk in that the money may be lost if the company goes bankrupt.

Venus *Venus photographed from a Pioneer probe. The planet has a cloud cover that permanently obscures the surface.*

Venturi /ven'tjʊəri/ Robert 1925– . US architect. He pioneered Post-Modernism through his books, *Complexity and Contradiction in Architecture* 1967 and *Learning from Las Vegas* 1972. In 1986 he was commissioned to design the extension to the National Gallery, London.

Venus /'viːnəs/ the second planet in order of distance from the Sun. It orbits the Sun every 225 days at an average distance of 108.2 million km/67.2 mi and can approach the Earth to within 38 million km/24 million mi, closer than any other planet. Its diameter is 12,100 km/7,500 mi and its mass is 0.82 that of Earth. Venus rotates on its axis more slowly than any other planet, once every 243 days and from east to west, the opposite direction to the other planets (except Uranus). Venus is shrouded by clouds of sulphuric acid droplets, which sweep across the planet from east to west every four days. The atmosphere is almost entirely carbon dioxide, which traps the Sun's heat by the ◊greenhouse effect to raise the planet's surface temperature to 480°C, with an atmospheric pressure 90 times that at Earth's surface.

The surface of Venus consists mainly of plains dotted with eroded craters, presumably formed by meteorite impacts. The largest highland area is Aphrodite Terra near the equator, half the size of Africa. The highest mountains are on the northern highland region of Ishtar Terra, where the massif of Maxwell Montes rises to 10,600 m/35,000 ft above the average surface level. The highland areas on Venus were formed by volcanoes, which may still be active.

The first artificial object to hit another planet was the Soviet probe Venera 3, which crashed on Venus 1 Mar 1966. Later Venera probes parachuted down through the atmosphere and landed successfully on its surface, analysing surface material, and sending back information and pictures. In Dec 1978 a US Pioneer-Venus probe (see ◊Pioneer) went into orbit around the planet

Venus flytrap

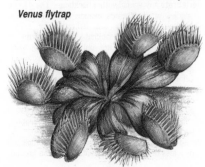

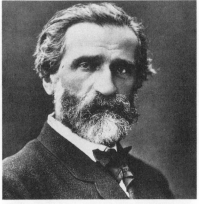

Verdi *Giuseppe Verdi, the Italian opera composer.*

and mapped most of its surface by radar, which penetrates clouds.

Venus /'viːnəs/ in Roman mythology, the goddess of love (Greek **Aphrodite**).

Venus flytrap North American insectivorous plant *Dionaea muscipula*, the leaf of which folds together to trap insects.

Veracruz /ˌverə'kruːz/ port (trading in coffee, tobacco, and vanilla) in E Mexico, on the Gulf of Mexico; population (1980) 305,456. Products include chemicals, sisal, and textiles. It was founded by Cortez as Villa Nueva de la Vera Cruz (new town of the true cross) on a nearby site 1519, and transferred to its present site 1599.

verb the grammatical part of speech for what someone or something does (*to go*), experiences (*to live*), or is (*to be*). Verbs involve the grammatical categories known as number (singular or plural: 'He *runs*; they *run*'), voice (active or passive: 'She *writes* books; it *is written*'), mood (statements, questions, orders, emphasis, necessity, condition), aspect (completed or continuing action: 'She *danced*; she *was dancing*'), and tense (variation according to time: simple present tense, present continuous/progressive tense, simple past tense, and so on).

Verbs are formed from nouns and adjectives by adding affixes (prison: *imprison*; light: *enlighten*; fresh: *freshen up*; pure: *purify*). Some words function as both nouns and verbs (*crack*, *run*), both adjectives and verbs (*clean*; *ready*), and as nouns, adjectives, and verbs (*fancy*).

Types of verb are as follows:

A **transitive** verb takes a direct object ('he *saw* the house').

An **intransitive** verb has no object ('She *laughed*').

An **auxiliary or helping** verb is used to express tense and/or mood ('He *was* seen'; 'They *may* come').

A **modal** verb or **modal auxiliary** generally shows only mood; common modals are *may/might, will/would, can/could, shall/should, must*.

The **infinitive** of the verb usually includes 'to' (*to go, to run* and so on), but may be a bare infinitive (for example, after modals, as in 'She *may go*').

A **regular** verb forms tenses in the normal way (*I walk: I walked: I have walked*); irregular verbs do not (*swim: swam: swum; put: put: put*, and so on). Because of their conventional nature, regular verbs are also known as weak verbs, while some irregular verbs are strong verbs with special vowel changes across tenses, as in *swim: swam: swum* and *ride: rode: ridden*.

A **phrasal verb** is a construction in which a particle attaches to a usually single-syllable verb (for example, *put* becoming *put up*, as in 'He put up some money for the project', and *put up with*, as in 'I can't put up with this nonsense any longer').

verbena genus of plants *Verbena*, family Verbenaceae, of about 100 species, mostly found in the American tropics. The leaves are fragrant and the

Vermeer *A Young Woman standing at a Virginal (c.1670) National Gallery, London.*

tubular flowers arranged in close spikes in colours ranging from white to rose, violet, and purple. The garden verbena is a hybrid annual.

Vercingetorix /ˌvɜːsɪn'dʒetərɪks/ Gallic chieftain. Leader of a revolt against the Romans 52 BC, he was displayed in Caesar's triumph 46 BC, and later executed.

Verdi /'veədi/ Giuseppe (Fortunino Francesco) 1813–1901. Italian opera composer of the Romantic period, who took his native operatic style to new heights of dramatic expression. In 1842 he wrote the opera *Nabucco*, followed by *Ernani* 1844 and *Rigoletto* 1851. Other works include *Il Trovatore* and *La Traviata* both 1853, *Aïda* 1871, and the masterpieces of his old age, *Otello* 1887 and *Falstaff* 1893. His *Requiem* 1874 commemorates Alessandro ◊Manzoni.

verdict in law, a jury's decision, usually a finding of 'guilty' or 'not guilty'. In Scotland a third option is 'not proven' where the jury is not convinced either way. In Britain majority verdicts are acceptable if a unanimous verdict cannot be reached.

verdigris a basic copper acetate and irritant formerly used in wood preservatives, anti-fouling compositions, and green paints.

Verdun /vɜː'dʌn/ fortress town in NE France on the Meuse. During World War I it became the symbol of French resistance, withstanding a German onslaught in 1916.

Vergil alternative spelling for ◊Virgil, Roman poet.

vérité (French) realism, as in the phrase cinéma vérité, used to describe a realistic or documentary style.

Verlaine /veə'leɪn/ Paul 1844–1896. French lyrical poet who was influenced by the poets Baudelaire and ◊Rimbaud. His volumes of verse include *Poèmes saturniens/Saturnine Poems* 1866, *Fêtes galantes/Amorous Entertainments* 1869 and *Romances sans paroles/Songs without Words* 1874. In 1873 he was imprisoned for attempting to shoot Rimbaud. His later works reflect his attempts to lead a reformed life and he was acknowledged as leader of the Symbolist poets.

Vermeer /veə'mɪə/ Jan 1632–1675. Dutch painter, active in Delft. Most of his pictures are ◊genre scenes, with a limpid clarity and distinct air of stillness, and a harmonious palette often focusing on yellow and blue. He frequently depicted single women in domestic settings, as in *The Lacemaker* (Louvre, Paris).

Vermeer is thought to have spent his whole life in Delft. Around 40 paintings are ascribed to him. His work fell into obscurity until the mid- to late 19th century, but he is now ranked as one of the greatest Dutch artists.

In addition to genre scenes, his work comprises one religious painting, a few portraits, and two townscapes, of which the fresh and naturalistic

Vermont

View of Delft about 1660 (Mauritshuis, The Hague) triggered the revival of interest in Vermeer. *The Artist's Studio* about 1665–70 (Kunsthistorisches Museum, Vienna) is one of his most elaborate compositions; the subject appears to be allegorical, but the exact meaning remains a mystery.

Vermont /vɜːˈmɒnt/ state of the USA in New England; nickname Green Mountain State
area 24,900 sq km/9,611 sq mi
capital Montpelier
towns Burlington, Rutland
features noted for brilliant foliage in the autumn, and winter sports; Green Mountains; Lake Champlain
products apples, maple syrup, dairy products, china clay, asbestos, granite, marble, slate, business machines, furniture, paper
population (1986) 541,000
history explored by Champlain from 1609; settled 1724; state 1791. The **Green Mountain Boys** were irregulars who fought to keep Vermont from New York interference.

vermouth a white wine flavoured with bitter herbs and fortified by alcohol. It is made in France and Italy.

vernal equinox see ◊equinox.

vernalization the stimulation of flowering by exposure to cold. Certain plants will not flower unless subjected to low temperatures during their development. For example, winter wheat will flower in summer only if planted in the previous autumn. However, by placing partially germinated seeds in low temperatures for several days, the cold requirement can be supplied artificially, allowing the wheat to be sown in the spring.

Verne /vɜːn/ Jules 1828–1905. French author of tales of adventure that anticipated future scientific developments: *Five Weeks in a Balloon*

1862, *Journey to the Centre of the Earth* 1864, *Twenty Thousand Leagues under the Sea* 1870, and *Around the World in Eighty Days* 1873.

Verney /ˈvɜːni/ Edmund 1590–1642. English courtier, knight-marshal to Charles I from 1626. He sat as a member of both the Short and Long parliaments and, though sympathizing with the parliamentary position, remained true to his allegiance: he died at his post as royal standard bearer at the Battle of ◊Edgehill.

His son Ralph (1613–96) supported the Parliamentarians. The **Verney papers** are a valuable record of this and later periods.

vernier device for taking readings on a graduated scale to a fraction of a division. It consists of a short divided scale which carries an index or pointer and is slid along a main scale. It was invented by Pierre Vernier.

Vernier /ˈvɜːnɪeɪ/ Pierre 1580–1637. French mathematician who invented very precise measurements by the operation of what has since been called the vernier scale. He was a French government official and in 1631 published a book explaining his method called 'a new mathematical quadrant'.

Vernon /ˈvɜːnən/ Edward 1684–1757. English admiral who captured Portobello from the Spanish in the Caribbean in 1739, with a loss of only seven men.

Verona /vəˈrəʊnə/ industrial city (printing, paper, plastics, furniture, pasta) in Veneto, Italy, on the Adige; population (1988) 259,000.

It trades in fruit and vegetables. It has Roman ruins, including an amphitheatre, and a 12th-century cathedral.

Veronese /ˌverəʊˈneɪzi/ Paolo *c.*1528–1588. Italian painter, born in Verona, active mainly in Venice (from about 1553). He specialized in grand decorative schemes, such as his ceilings in the Doge's Palace in Venice, with *trompe l'oeil* effects and inventive detail. The subjects are religious, mythological, historical, and allegorical.

Titian was an important influence, but Veronese also knew the work of Giulio Romano and Michelangelo. His decorations in the Villa Barbera at Maser near Vicenza show his skill at illusionism and a typically Venetian rich use of colour; they are also characteristically full of inventive fantasy. He took the same approach to religious works, and as a result his *Last Supper* 1573 (Accademia, Venice, renamed *The Feast in the House of Levi*) was the subject of a trial by the Inquisition, since the holy event seems to be almost subordinated by profane details: figures of drunkards, soldiers conversing, dogs, and so forth.

Veronica, St /vəˈrɒnɪkə/ a woman of Jerusalem who, according to tradition, lent her veil to Jesus to wipe the sweat from his brow on the road to Calvary, whereupon the image of his face was printed upon it. What is alleged to be the actual veil is preserved in St Peter's, Rome.

Verrocchio /veˈrɒkɪəʊ/ Andrea del 1435–1488. Italian painter, sculptor, and goldsmith, born in Florence, where he ran a large workshop and received commissions from the Medici family. The vigorous equestrian statue of *Bartolommeo Colleoni*, begun 1481 (Campo SS Giovanni e Paolo, Venice), was his last work.

Verrocchio was a pupil of ◊Donatello and himself the early teacher of Leonardo da Vinci. In his *Baptism* about 1472 (Uffizi, Florence) Leonardo is said to have painted the kneeling angel shown in profile. Verrocchio's sculptures include a bronze *Christ and St Thomas* 1465 (Or S Michele, Florence) and *David* 1476 (Bargello, Florence).

verruca growth on the skin; see ◊wart.

Versailles /veəˈsaɪ/ city in N France, capital of Les Yvelines *département*, on the outskirts of Paris; population (1982) 95,240. It grew up around the palace of Louis XV. Within the palace park are two small châteaux, Le Grand and Le Petit ◊Trianon, built for Louis XIV (by J-H ◊Mansart) and Louis XV (by J A Gabriel 1698–1782) respectively.

Versailles, Treaty of /veəˈsaɪ/ peace treaty after World War I between the Allies and Germany, signed 28 June 1919. It established the League of Nations. Germany surrendered Alsace-Lorraine to France, large areas in the east to Poland, and made smaller cessions to Czechoslovakia, Lithuania, Belgium, and Denmark. The Rhineland was demilitarized, German rearmament was restricted, and Germany agreed to pay reparations for war damage. The treaty was never ratified by the USA, which made a separate peace with Germany and Austria 1921.

verse arrangement of words in rhythmic pattern, which may depend on the length of syllables (as in Greek or Latin verse), or on stress, as in English.

Classical Greek verse depended upon quantity, a long syllable being regarded as occupying twice the time taken up by a short syllable. Long and short syllables were combined in *feet*, such as:
dactyl (long, short, short)
spondee (long, long)
anapaest (short, short, long)
iamb (short, long)
trochee (long, short).
Rhyme (identity of sound in the endings of words) was introduced to Western European verse in late Latin poetry, and *alliteration* (repetition of the same initial letter in successive words) was the dominant feature of Anglo-Saxon poetry. Both these elements helped to make verse easily remembered in the days when it was spoken rather than written.

form The Spenserian stanza (in which ◊Spenser wrote *The Faerie Queene*) has nine iambic lines rhyming ababbcbcc. The ◊sonnet has 14 lines, in English generally of ten syllables; it has several rhyme schemes.

Blank verse, consisting of unrhymed five-stress lines, as used by Marlowe, Shakespeare, and Milton, develops an inner cohesion that replaces the props provided by rhyme and stanza. It became the standard metre for English dramatic and epic poetry. ◊Free verse or *vers libre* avoids rhyme, stanza form, and any obvious rhythmical basis.

versus (abbreviation v. or vs; Latin) against.

vertebrate any animal with a backbone. The 41,000 species of vertebrates include mammals, birds, reptiles, amphibians, and fishes. They include most of the larger animals, but in terms of numbers of species are only a tiny proportion of the world's animals. The zoological taxonomic group Vertebrata is a subgroup of the ◊phylum Chordata.

vertical takeoff aircraft an aircraft that can take off and land vertically (VTOL). The helicopter, airship, and balloon can do this, as can a few fixed-wing aeroplanes like the Harrier. See ◊helicopter, ◊convertiplane.

vertigo dizziness; a whirling sensation accompanied by a loss of any feeling of contact with the ground.

Verne French adventure and science-fiction novelist Jules Verne.

Veronese Allegory of Love, III *(1570s)*, National Gallery, London.

It may be due to temporary disturbance of the sense of balance (as in spinning for too long on one spot), disease, or intoxication.

Verulamium /ˌveruˈleɪmiəm/ Roman-British town whose remains have been excavated close to St Albans, Hertfordshire.

Verwoerd /fəˈvʊət/ Hendrik (Frensch) 1901–1966. South African right-wing Nationalist Party politician, prime minister from 1958. As minister of native affairs 1950–58, he was the chief promoter of apartheid legislation. He made the country a republic 1961. He was assassinated in the House of Assembly by a parliamentary messenger, Dimitri Tsafendas.

Very Large Array (VLA) the largest and most complex single-site radio telescope in the world. It is located on the Plains of San Augustine, 80 km/50 mi west of Socorro, New Mexico, USA. It consists of 27 dish antennae, each 25 m/82 ft in diameter, arranged along three equally spaced arms forming a Y-shaped array. Two of the arms are 21 km/13 mi long, and the third, to the north, is 19 km/11.8 mi long. The dishes are mounted on railway tracks enabling the configuration and size of the array to be altered as required.

There are four standard configurations of antennae ranging from A (the most extended) through B and C to D. In the A configuration the antennae are spread out along the full extent of the arms and the VLA can map small, intense radio sources with high resolution. The smallest configuration, D, uses arms that are just 0.6 km/0.4 mi long for mapping larger sources. Here the resolution is lower although there is greater sensitivity to fainter, extended fields of radio emission. Pairs of dishes can also be used as separate interferometers (see ◊radio telescope), each dish having its own individual receivers which are remotely controlled, enabling many different frequencies to be studied.

Vesalius /vɪˈseɪliəs/ Andreas 1514–1564. Belgian physician who revolutionized anatomy. His great innovations were to perform postmortem dissections, and to make use of illustrations in teaching anatomy.

This enabled him to discover that ◊Galen's system of medicine was based on fundamental anatomical errors. Vesalius' book *De Humani Corporis Fabrica/On the Structure of the Human Body* 1543, published in the same year as Copernicus' *De revolutionibus*, marked the dawn of the modern scientific era.

Vespasian /veˈspeɪʒən/ (Titus Flavius Vespasianus) AD 9–79. Roman emperor from AD 69. He was the son of a moneylender, and had a distinguished military career. He was proclaimed emperor by his soldiers while he was campaigning in Palestine. He reorganized the eastern provinces, and was a capable administrator.

vespers the seventh of the eight canonical hours in the Catholic Church.

The phrase *Sicilian Vespers* refers to the massacre of the French rulers in Sicily in 1282, signalled by vesper bells on Easter Monday.

Vespucci /vesˈpuːtʃi/ Amerigo 1454–1512. Florentine merchant. The Americas were named after him as a result of the widespread circulation of his accounts of his explorations, but his accounts of the voyage 1499–1501 indicate that he had been to places he could not possibly have reached (the Pacific Ocean, British Columbia, Antarctica).

Vesta /ˈvestə/ in Roman mythology, the goddess of the hearth (Greek *Hestia*). In Rome, the sacred flame in her shrine in the Forum was kept constantly lit by the six *Vestal Virgins*.

vestigial organ in biology, an organ that remains in diminished form after it has ceased to have any significant function in the adult organism. In humans, the appendix is vestigial, having once had a digestive function in our ancestors.

Vesuvius /vɪˈsuːviəs/ (Italian *Vesuvio*) active volcano SE of Naples, Italy; height 1,277 m/4,190 ft. In 79 BC it destroyed the cities of Pompeii, ◊Herculaneum, and Oplonti.

vetch trailing or climbing plants of several genera, family Leguminosae, with pinnate leaves and purple, yellow, or white flowers, including the fodder crop alfalfa *Medicago sativa*.

Veterans Day in the USA, the name adopted 1954 for ◊Armistice Day and from 1971 observed by most states on the fourth Monday in Oct. The equivalent in the UK and Canada is ◊Remembrance Sunday.

veterinary science the prevention and cure of disease in animals. More generally, it covers their anatomy, breeding, and relations to humans. Professional bodies include the Royal College of Veterinary Surgeons 1844 in the UK, and the American Veterinary Medical Association 1883 in the USA.

veto (Latin 'I forbid') exercise by a sovereign, branch of legislature, or other political power, of the right to prevent the enactment or operation of a law, or the taking of some course of action.

In the UK the sovereign has a right to refuse assent to any measure passed by Parliament, but this has not been exercised since the 18th century; the House of Lords also has a suspensory veto on all legislation except finance measures, but this is comparatively seldom exercised. In the USA, the president may veto legislation, but this can be overruled by a two-thirds majority in Congress. At the United Nations, members of the Security Council can exercise a veto on resolutions.

Veuster /vɜːˈsteə/ Joseph de 1840–1889. Belgian missionary, known as Father Damien. He entered the order of the Fathers of the Sacred Heart at Louvain, went to Hawaii, and from 1873 was resident priest in the leper settlement at Molokai. He eventually became infected and died there.

VHF very *h*igh *f*requency, referring to radio waves. VHF waves, which have very short wavelengths, are used for interference-free ◊FM (frequency-modulated) transmissions. VHF transmitters have relatively short range because the waves cannot be reflected over the horizon like longer radio waves.

v.i. abbreviation for *verb intransitive*.

VI abbreviation for *Virgin Islands*; *Vancouver Island*.

Vian /ˈvaɪən/ Philip 1894–1968. British admiral of the fleet in World War II. In 1940 he was the hero of the ◊Altmark incident, and in 1941 commanded the destroyers that chased the *Bismarck*.

Viborg /ˈviːbɔː/ industrial town (brewing, engineering, textiles, tobacco) in Jutland, Denmark; population (1981) 28,700. It is also the Swedish name for ◊Vyborg, port and naval base in the USSR.

vibraphone an electrically amplified musical percussion instrument resembling a ◊xylophone but with metal keys. Spinning discs within the resonating tubes give the instrument a vibrato sound that can be controlled in speed and worked with a foot pedal.

vibrato in music, a slight but rapid fluctuation of pitch in voice or instrument.

viburnum genus of temperate and subtropical trees and shrubs, family Caprifoliaceae, including the ◊*wayfaring tree*, the *laurustinus*, and the *guelder rose*.

vicar a Church of England priest, originally one who acted as deputy to a ◊rector, but now also a parish priest.

Vicenza /vɪˈtʃentsə/ city in Veneto region, NE Italy, capital of Veneto province, manufacturing textiles and musical instruments; population (1988) 110,000. It has a 13th-century cathedral and many buildings by ◊Palladio, including the Teatro Olimpico 1583.

viceroy the chief officer of the crown in many Spanish and Portuguese American colonies who had ultimate responsibility for administration and military matters. The office of viceroy was also used by the British crown to rule India.

vice versa (Latin) the other way around.

Vichy /ˈviːʃi/ health resort with thermal springs, known to the Romans, on the river Allier in Allier

département, central France. During World War II it was the seat of the Vichy government), which collaborated with the Nazis.

Vichy government in World War II, the government of unoccupied France after the defeat by the Germans in June 1940, named after the town where the cabinet under Prime Minister Pétain was based until the liberation 1944. *Vichy France* was that part of France not occupied by German troops until Nov 1942. Authoritarian and collaborationist, the Vichy regime cooperated with the Germans even after they had moved to the unoccupied zone in November 1942.

Vico /ˈviːkəʊ/ Giambattista 1668–1744. Italian philosopher, considered the founder of the modern philosophy of history. He rejected Descartes' emphasis on the mathematical and natural sciences, and argued that we can understand history more adequately than nature, since it is we who have made it. He believed that the study of language, ritual, and myth was a way of understanding earlier societies. His cyclical theory of history (the birth, development, and decline of human societies) was put forward in *New Science* 1725.

He postulated that society passes through a cycle of four phases: the divine, or theocratic, when people are governed by their awe of the supernatural; the aristocratic, or 'heroic' (Homer, *Beowulf*); the democratic and individualistic; and chaos, a fall into confusion that startles people back into supernatural reverence. This is expressed in his dictum *verum et factum convertuntur* ('the true and the made are convertible'). His belief that the study of language and rituals was a better way of understanding early societies was a departure from the traditional ways of writing history as either biographies, or as pre-ordained God's will. He was born in Naples, and was professor of rhetoric there 1698. He became historiographer to the King of Naples 1735.

Victor Emmanuel /ˈvɪktər ɪˈmænjuəl/ three kings of Italy, including:

Victor Emmanuel II 1820–1878. First king of united Italy from 1861. He became king of Sardinia on the abdication of his father Charles Albert 1849. In 1855 he allied Sardinia with France and the UK in the Crimean War. In 1859 in alliance with the French he defeated the Austrians and annexed Lombardy. By 1860 most of Italy had come under his rule, and in 1861 he was proclaimed king of Italy. In 1870 he made Rome his capital.

Victor Emmanuel III 1869–1947. King of Italy from the assassination of his father Umberto I 1900. He acquiesced in the Fascist regime of Mussolini but cooperated with the Allies; he abdicated 1946.

Victoria /vɪkˈtɔːriə/ state of SE Australia
area 227,600 sq km/87,854 sq mi
capital Melbourne
towns Geelong, Ballarat, Bendigo
physical part of the Great Dividing Range runs E–W and includes the larger part of the Australian Alps; Gippsland lakes, shallow lagoons on the coast; the ◊mallee shrub region
products sheep, beef cattle, dairy products, tobacco, wheat; vines for wine and dried fruit, orchard fruits, vegetables, gold, brown coal

Victoria

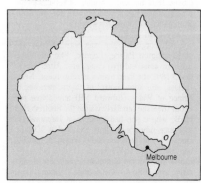
Melbourne

Victoria *Queen Victoria reading official dispatches at Frogmore, England, with an Indian servant in attendance, 1893.*

(Latrobe Valley), oil and natural gas in Bass Strait

population (1987) 4,184,000; 70% live in the Melbourne area

history annexed for Britain by Cook 1770; settled in the 1830s; after being part of New South Wales, it became a separate colony 1851, named after Queen Victoria; became a state 1901.

Victoria /vɪkˈtɔːrɪə/ industrial port (shipbuilding, chemicals, clothing, furniture) on Vancouver Island, capital of British Columbia, Canada; population (1986) 256,000.

It was founded as Fort Victoria 1843 by the Hudson's Bay Company. Its university was founded 1964.

Victoria /vɪkˈtɔːrɪə/ port and capital of the Seychelles, on Mahé island; population (1985) 23,000.

Victoria /vɪkˈtɔːrɪə/ district of ◊Hong Kong, rising to 554 m/1,800 ft at Victoria Park.

Victoria /vɪkˈtɔːrɪə/ 1819–1901. Queen of the UK from 1837, when she suceeded her uncle William IV, and empress of India from 1876. In 1840 she married Prince ◊Albert of Saxe-Coburg and Gotha. Her relations with her prime ministers ranged from the affectionate (Melbourne and Disraeli) to the stormy (Peel, Palmerston, and Gladstone). Her golden jubilee 1887 and diamond jubilee 1897 marked a waning of republican sentiment, which had developed with her withdrawal from public life on Albert's death.

Only child of Edward, duke of Kent, fourth son of George III, she was born 24 May 1819 at Kensington Palace, London. She and Albert had four sons and five daughters. After Albert's death 1861 she lived mainly in retirement. Nevertheless, she kept control of affairs, refusing the Prince of Wales (Edward VII) any active role. From 1848 she regularly visited the Scottish Highlands, where she had a house at Balmoral built to Prince Albert's designs. She died at ◊Osborne House, her home in the Isle of Wight, 22 Jan 1901, and was buried at Windsor.

Victoria and Albert Museum a museum of decorative arts in South Kensington, London, opened 1909, inspired by Henry Cole (1808–82) and Prince ◊Albert.

Originally called the Museum of Ornamental Art, it had developed from the Museum of Manufacturers at Marlborough House, which had been founded in the aftermath of the Great Exhibition of 1851. The musuem houses prints, paintings, and temporary exhibitions, as well as one of the largest collections of decorative arts in the world.

Victoria Cross British decoration for conspicuous bravery in wartime, instituted by Queen Victoria 1856.

It is bronze, with a 4 cm/1.5 in diameter, and has a crimson ribbon. Until the supply was exhausted 1942 all Victoria Crosses were struck from the metal of cannon captured from the Russians at Sevastopol; they are now made from gunmetal supplied by the Royal Mint.

Victoria Falls /vɪkˈtɔːrɪə/ or ***Mosi-oa-tunya*** waterfall on the river Zambezi, on the Zambia–Zimbabwe border. The river is 1,700 m/5,580 ft wide, and drops 120 m/400 ft to flow through a 30 m/100 ft wide gorge. It was named after Queen

vicuna

Victoria by the Scottish explorer Livingstone in 1855.

Victoria, Lake /vɪkˈtɔːrɪə/ or ***Victoria Nyanza*** largest lake in Africa, over 69,400 sq km /26,800 sq mi (410 km/255 mi long) on the equator at an altitude of 1,136 m/3,728 ft. It lies between Uganda, Kenya, and Tanzania, and is a source of the Nile. The British explorer Speke named it after Queen Victoria 1858.

Victorian of the mid- and late 19th century in England, covering the reign of Queen Victoria. Victorian style was often very ornate, markedly so in architecture, and Victorian Gothic harked back to the original Gothic architecture of medieval times. It was also an era when increasing machine mass-production threatened the existence of crafts and craft skills.

Despite the popularity of extravagant decoration, Renaissance styles were also favoured and many people, such as John ◊Ruskin, believed in the importance of objects and architecture being designed primarily according to their function and not for the sake of appearances.

Victorian Order, Royal one of the fraternities carrying with it the rank of knight; see ◊knighthood.

Victory British battleship, 2,198 tonnes/2,164 tons, launched in 1765, and now in dry dock in Portsmouth harbour. It was the flagship of Admiral Nelson at Trafalgar.

vicuna ruminant mammal *Lama vicugna* of the camel family which lives in herds on the Andean plateau. They can run at speeds of 50 kph/30 mph. They have good eyesight, fair hearing, and a poor sense of smell. They were hunted close to extinction for their meat and soft brown fur, which was used in textile manufacture, but the vicuna is now a protected species. Populations are increasing thanks to strict conservation measures.

Vidal /viːˈdæl/ Gore 1925– . US writer and critic. Much of his work deals satirically with history and politics and includes the novels *Myra Breckinridge* 1968, *Burr* 1973, and *Empire* 1987, plays and screenplays, including *Suddenly Last Summer* 1958, and essays, such as *Armageddon?* 1987.

video camera a portable television camera that takes 'movie' pictures electronically. It produces an electrical output signal corresponding to rapid line-by-line scanning of the field of view. The output is recorded on videotape and is played back on a television screen via a videotape recorder.

video disc a disc with pictures and sounds recorded on it, played back by laser. The video disc works in the same way as a ◊compact disc.

The video disc (originated by Baird 1928; commercially available from 1978) is chiefly used to provide commercial films for private viewing. The Philips ***Laservision*** system uses a 30 cm/12 in rotating vinyl disc coated with a reflective material. Laser scanning recovers picture and sound signals from the surface where they are recorded as a spiral of microscopic pits.

video game or ***telegame*** electronic game played on a visual-display screen or, by means of special additional or built-in components, on the screen of a television set. The first commercially sold was a simple bat-and-ball game developed in the USA in 1972, but complex variants are now available in colour and with special sound effects.

In television 'tennis' a quartz crystal oscillator supplies a clock pulse input to the microprocessor in the component, so that the speed of the 'ball' across the screen can be controlled, and the player uses a simple potentiometer to control the movement of the 'racket'.

videotape recorder (VTR) a device for recording television programmes, or pictures for replaying on a TV set, on magnetic tape. The recorder may be connected to a TV set or a ◊video camera. A ***camcorder*** is a portable videotape recorder with a built-in camera.

Video recording works in the same way as audio ◊tape recording: the picture information is stored as a line of varying magnetism, or track, on a plastic tape covered with magnetic material. The main

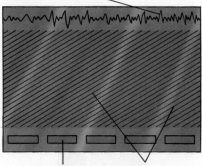

video tape   sound track

control track   video tracks

difficulty—the huge amount of information needed to reproduce a picture—is overcome by arranging the video track diagonally across the tape. During recording, the tape is wrapped around a drum in a spiral fashion. The recording head rotates inside the drum. The combination of the forward motion of the tape and the rotation of the head produces a diagonal track. The audio signal accompanying the video signal is recorded as a separate track along the edge of the tape.

Home video recorders use tape cassettes. Systems include Sony Betamax and JVC Video Home System (VHS). The Betamax system uses a slightly larger cassette to give a greater playing time, up to four hours.

videotext a system in which information (text) is displayed on a television (video) screen. There are two basic systems, known as ◊teletext and ◊viewdata. In the teletext system information is broadcast with the ordinary television signals, while in viewdata information is relayed to the screen from a central data bank via the telephone network. Both systems require the use of a television receiver with special decoder.

Vidocq /viːˈdɒk/ François Eugène 1775–1857. French criminal who, in 1809, became a spy for the Paris police, and rose to become chief of the detective department.

Vidor /ˈviːdɔː/ King 1894–1982. US film director, who made epics including *The Big Parade* 1925 and *Duel in the Sun* 1946. He has been praised as a cinematic innovator, and received an honorary Academy Award in 1979. His other films include *The Crowd* 1928 and *Guerra e Pace/War and Peace* 1956.

Vienna /viˈenə/, /viːn/ (German *Wien*) capital of Austria, on the river Danube at the foot of the Wiener Wald (Vienna Woods); population (1986) 1,481,000. Industries include engineering and the production of electrical goods and precision instruments.

The United Nations city 1979 houses the United Nations Industrial Development Organization (UNIDO) and the International Atomic Energy Agency (IAEA).

features Renaissance and baroque architecture; the Hofburg (former imperial palace), the 18th-century royal palaces of Schönbrunn and Belvedere, with formal gardens; the Steiner house 1910 by Adolf Loos; several notable collections of paintings; Vienna is known for its theatre and opera; the psychoanalyst Freud's home is a museum; university 1365.

history Vienna was the capital of the Austro-Hungarian Empire 1278–1918 and the commercial centre of E Europe. The old city walls were replaced by a wide street, the Ringstrasse, 1860. After much destruction in World War II the city was divided into US, British, French, and Soviet occupation zones 1945–55. Vienna is associated with Haydn, Mozart, Beethoven, Schubert, Strauss waltzes, and the development of atonal music; with the Vienna Sezession group of painters; the philosophical Vienna Circle; and psychoanalysis originated here.

Vienna, Congress of /viˈenə/ the international conference held 1814–15, which agreed the settlement of Europe after the Napoleonic Wars. National representatives included the Austrian foreign minister Metternich, Alexander I of Russia, the British foreign secretary Castlereagh and military commander Wellington, and the French politician Talleyrand.

Vientiane /viˌentiˈɑːn/ capital and chief port of Laos on the Mekong river; population (1985) 377,000.

Vietcong (Vietnamese 'Vietnamese Communists') in the Vietnam War, the members of the National Front for the Liberation of South Vietnam, founded 1960, who fought the South Vietnamese and US forces. The name was coined by the South Vietnamese government to differentiate these communist guerrillas from the ◊Vietminh.

Viète /viˈet/ François 1540–1603. French mathematician who developed algebra and its notation. He was the first mathematician to use letters of the alphabet to denote both known and unknown quantities.

Vietminh the Vietnam Independence League, founded 1941 to oppose the Japanese occupation of Indo-China and later directed against the French colonial power. The Vietminh were instrumental in achieving Vietnamese independence through military victory at Dien Bien Phu 1954.

Vietnam /viˌetˈnæm/ country in SE Asia, on the South China Sea, bounded N by China and W by Cambodia and Laos.

government Under the constitution 1980, the highest state authority and sole legislative chamber in Vietnam is the National Assembly, composed of 496 members directly elected every five years by universal suffrage. The assembly meets twice a year and elects from its ranks a permanent, 15-member council of state, whose chair acts as state president, to function in its absence. The executive government is the council of ministers, headed by the prime minister, which is responsible to the National Assembly.

The dominating force in Vietnam is the Communist Party (Dang Cong san Viet-Nam), headed since 1986 by Nguyen Van Linh (1914–). It is controlled by a politburo and is prescribed a 'leading role' by the constitution.

history Vietnam was founded 208 BC in the Red River delta in the north, under Chinese overlordship. Under direct Chinese rule 111 BC–AD 939, it was thereafter at times nominally subject to China. It annexed land to the south and defeated the forces of Kublai Khan 1288. European traders arrived in the 16th century. The country was united under one dynasty 1802.

France conquered Vietnam between 1858–1884, and it joined Cambodia, Laos, and Annam as the French colonial possessions of IndoChina. French IndoChina was occupied by Japan 1940–45.

Ho Chi Minh, who had built up the Vietminh (Independence) League, overthrew the Japanese-supported regime of Bao Dai, the former emperor of Annam, Sept 1945. French attempts to regain control and restore Bao Dai led to bitter fighting 1946–54, and final defeat at Dien Bien Phu. At the 1954 Geneva Conference the country was divided along the 17th parallel of latitude into communist North Vietnam, led by Ho Chi Minh and with its capital at Hanoi, and pro-Western South Vietnam, led by Ngo Dinh Diem (the former premier to Bao Dai) and with its capital at Saigon.

Within South Vietnam, the communist guerrilla National Liberation Front, or Vietcong, gained strength, being supplied with military aid by North Vietnam and China. The USA gave strong backing to the incumbent government in South Vietnam and became, following the Aug 1964 ◊Tonkin Gulf incident, actively embroiled in the ◊Vietnam War. The years 1964–68 witnessed an escalation in US military involvement. From 1969, however, as a result of mounting casualties and domestic opposition, the USA gradually began to withdraw its forces and sue for peace. A ceasefire agreement was negotiated Jan 1973, but was breached by the North Vietnamese who proceeded to move south, surrounding and capturing Saigon (which was renamed Ho Chi Minh City) Apr 1975.

The Socialist Republic of Vietnam was proclaimed July 1976 and a programme to integrate the south was launched. The new

---

Vietnam
Socialist Republic of
(Công Hòa Xã Hôi Chu Nghĩa Viêt Nam)

area 329,600 sq km/127,260 sq mi
capital Hanoi
towns ports Ho Chi Minh City (formerly Saigon), Da Nang, and Haiphong
physical Red River and Mekong deltas, where cultivation and population are concentrated; some tropical rainforest; the rest is barren and mountainous
head of state Vo Chi Cong from 1987
head of government Do Muoi from 1988
government communism
exports rice, rubber, coal, iron, apatite
currency dong (7661.25 = £1 Mar 1990)

population (1989) 64,000,000 (750,000 refugees, the majority ethnic Chinese, left the country 1975–79, some settling in SW China, others fleeing by sea – the 'boat people' – to Hong Kong and elsewhere); annual growth rate 2%
life expectancy men 57, women 61
language Vietnamese, of uncertain origin but tonal like Chinese and Thai
religion traditionally Buddhist and Taoist
literacy 78% (1978)
GNP $9.8 bn (1983); $189 per head of population
chronology
1945 Japanese removed from Vietnam.
1946 Commencement of Vietminh war against French.
1954 France defeated at Dien Bien Phu. Vietnam divided along 17th parallel.
1964 USA entered Vietnam War.
1973 Paris ceasefire agreement.
1975 Saigon captured by North Vietnam.
1976 Socialist Republic of Vietnam proclaimed.
1978 Admission into Comecon. Invasion of Kampuchea (Cambodia).
1979 Sino-Vietnamese border war.
1986 Retirement of old-guard leaders.
1987–88 Over 10,000 political prisoners released.
1988–89 Troop withdrawals from Cambodia continued.
1989 'Boat people' leaving Vietnam continuing to be murdered and robbed on the high seas by Thai pirates. Troop withdrawal from Cambodia completed.
1990 Inflation reduced to 25%, but unemployment over 20%.

Vietnam War *US troops of the 1st Cavalry Division, Vietnam 1967.*

republic encountered considerable problems. The economy was in ruins: two decades of war having claimed the lives of more than 2 million, maimed 4 million, left more than half the population homeless and resulted in the destruction of 70% of the country's industrial capacity. In addition, the new communist administration faced opposition from the intelligentsia (many of whom were imprisoned) and from rural groups, who refused to cooperate in the drive to collectivize southern agriculture. In Dec 1978 Vietnam was at war again, toppling the pro-Chinese Khmer Rouge government in Kampuchea (Cambodia) led by Pol Pot and installing a puppet administration led by Heng Samrin. A year later, in response to accusations of maltreatment of ethnic Chinese living in Vietnam, China mounted a brief, but largely unsuccessful, punitive invasion of North Vietnam 17 Feb–16 Mar 1979. These actions, coupled with the contemporary campaigns against private businesses in the south, induced the flight of about 700,000 Chinese and middle-class Vietnamese from the country 1978–79, often by sea (the 'boat people'). Economic and diplomatic relations with China were severed as Vietnam became closer to the Soviet Union, being admitted into Comecon June 1978.

Despite considerable economic aid from the Eastern bloc, Vietnam did not reach its planned growth targets 1976–85. This forced policy adjustments, extending incentives and decentralizing decision-taking, 1979 and 1985. Further economic liberalization followed the death of Le Duan (1907–86), effective leader since 1969, and the retirement at the Dec 1986 Communist Party Congress of other prominent 'old guard' leaders, including Prime Minister Pham Van Dong and President Truong Chinh. Under the pragmatic lead of Nguyen Van Linh, a 'renovation' programme was launched. The private marketing of agriculture produce and formation of private businesses were now permitted, agricultural cooperatives partially dismantled (farmers were given 15-year land leases instead), foreign 'joint venture' inward-investment encouraged and more than 10,000 political prisoners were released. Economic reform proved most successful in the south. In general, however, the country faced a severe economic crisis from 1988, with inflation, famine conditions in rural areas, and rising urban unemployment inducing a further flight of 'boat people' refugees during 1989–90, predominantly to Hong Kong. Vietnam ranks as the third-largest communist power in the world, exerting control over Laos and Cambodia (where Vietnamese

troops were still based 1988). Border disputes with China and guerrilla resistance in Cambodia accounts for continue, and military spending a third of gross national product.

Vietnamese inhabitant of Vietnam. The Annamese comprise approximately 90% of the population. Although Annamese is an independent language, it has been influenced by Chinese and there are Khmer loan words. The majority of Vienamese live in the fertile valleys of the Red and Mekong rivers.

Vietnam War 1954–75. War between communist North Vietnam and US-backed South Vietnam. 200,000 South Vietnamese soldiers, 1 million North Vietnamese soldiers, and 500,000 civilians were killed. 56,555 US soldiers were killed 1961–75, a fifth of whom were killed by their own troops. Cambodia, a neutral neighbour, was bombed by the USA 1969–75, with 1 million killed or wounded.

1954 Under the Geneva Convention the former French colony of Indo-China was divided into the separate states of North Vietnam and South Vietnam. Within South Vietnam the communist

Vietcong, supported by North Vietnam and China, attempted to seize power. The USA provided military aid to the South Vietnamese government.

1964 The Tonkin Gulf Incident.

1967 Several large-scale invasion attempts by North Vietnam were defeated by local and US forces.

1968 My Lai massacre.

1969 US bombing incursions into Cambodia began, without endorsement from Congress for this widening of the war.

1973 The unpopularity of the war within the USA led to the start of US withdrawal. A peace treaty was signed between North Vietnam and South Vietnam.

1975 South Vietnam was invaded by North Vietnam in Mar.

1976 South Vietnam was annexed by North Vietnam and the two countries were renamed the Socialist Republic of Vietnam.

viewdata a system of displaying information on a television screen in which the information is extracted from a computer data bank and

---

Viking

In their narrow, shallow-draughted and highly manoeuvrable longships, the Vikings spread from their Scandinavian homelands to fight, trade and settle through most of the coastal regions of 8th to 11th-century Europe. They established kingdoms in the British Isles, Normandy, and Russia. As Normans they founded a kingdom in Sicily and in 1066 achieved a second conquest of England. They are believed to have sailed to North America and as far south as the Byzantine Empire where Swedish Vikings (Varangians) formed the imperial guard.

A stone cross (below) from Middleton, Yorkshire, depicting a well-armed Viking warrior. His weapons include a spear, sword, axe and dagger.

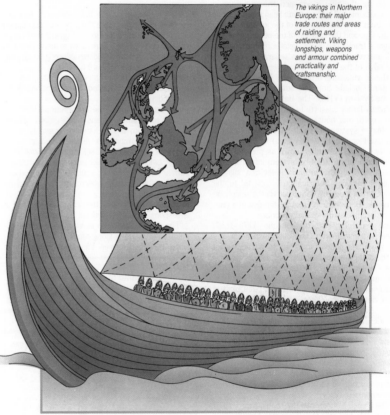

The vikings in Northern Europe: their major trade routes and areas of raiding and settlement. Viking longships, weapons and armour combined practicality and craftsmanship.

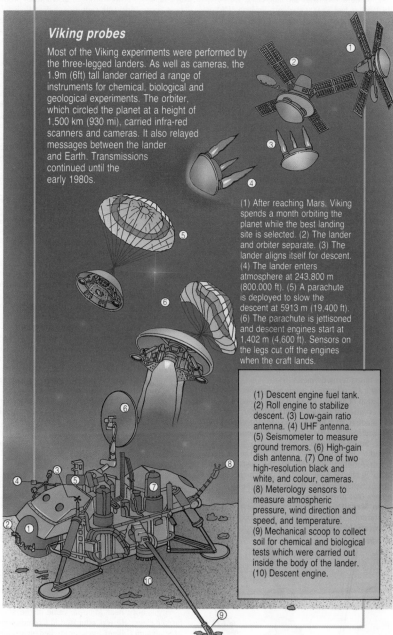

Viking probes

Most of the Viking experiments were performed by the three-legged landers. As well as cameras, the 1.9m (6ft) tall lander carried a range of instruments for chemical, biological and geological experiments. The orbiter, which circled the planet at a height of 1,500 km (930 mi), carried infra-red scanners and cameras. It also relayed messages between the lander and Earth. Transmissions continued until the early 1980s.

(1) After reaching Mars, Viking spends a month orbiting the planet while the best landing site is selected. (2) The lander and orbiter separate. (3) The lander aligns itself for descent. (4) The lander enters atmosphere at 243,800 m (800,000 ft). (5) A parachute is deployed to slow the descent at 5913 m (19,400 ft). (6) The parachute is jettisoned and descent engines start at 1,402 m (4,600 ft). Sensors on the legs cut off the engines when the craft lands.

(1) Descent engine fuel tank. (2) Roll engine to stabilize descent. (3) Low-gain ratio antenna. (4) UHF antenna. (5) Seismometer to measure ground tremors. (6) High-gain dish antenna. (7) One of two high-resolution black and white, and colour, cameras. (8) Meterology sensors to measure atmospheric pressure, wind direction and speed, and temperature. (9) Mechanical scoop to collect soil for chemical and biological tests which were carried out inside the body of the lander. (10) Descent engine.

transmitted via the telephone lines. It is one form of ◊videotext. The British Post Office (now British Telecom) developed the world's first viewdata system, ◊Prestel, in 1975, and similar systems are now in widespread use in other countries. Viewdata users have access to an almost unlimited store of information, presented on the screen in the form of 'pages'.

Prestel has hundreds of thousands of pages available presenting all kinds of information, from local weather and restaurant menus to share prices and airport timetables. Since viewdata uses telephone lines, it can become a two-way information system, making possible, for example, home banking and shopping.

Vigée-Lebrun /ˌviːʒeɪ ləˈbrɜːn/ Elisabeth 1755–1842. French portrait painter, trained by her father (a painter in pastels) and ◊Greuze. She became painter to Queen Marie Antoinette in the 1780s (many royal portraits survive).

At the outbreak of the Revolution 1789 she left France and travelled in Europe, staying in St Petersburg, Russia, 1795–1802. She resettled in Paris 1809. She published her *Souvenirs* 1835–37, written in the form of letters.

Vigeland /ˈviːgələn/ Gustav 1869–1943. Norwegian sculptor. He studied in Oslo and Copenhagen and with ◊Rodin in Paris 1892. His programme of sculpture in Frogner Park, Oslo, conceived in 1900, was never finished. The style is heavy and monumental; the sculpted figures and animals enigmatic.

vigilante in US history, originally a member of a 'vigilance committee', a self-appointed group to maintain public order in the absence of organized authority. The vigilante tradition continues with present-day urban groups patrolling subways to deter muggers and rapists, for example the Guardian Angels in New York and the Community Volunteers in London.

Early vigilante groups included the 'Regulators' in South Carolina in the 1760s, and in Pennsylvania 1794 during the Whiskey Rebellion. Many more appeared in the 19th century in frontier towns. Once authorized police forces existed, vigilante groups like the ◊Ku Klux Klan operated outside the law, often as perpetrators of mob violence such as lynching.

Vigny /viːnˈjiː/ Alfred, Comte de 1797–1863. French romantic writer, whose works include the historical novel *Cinq-Mars* 1826, the play *Chatterton* 1835, and poetry, for example, *Les Destinées/Destinies* 1864.

Vigo /ˈviːgəʊ/ industrial port (oil refining, leather, paper, distilling) and naval station on Vigo bay, Galicia, NW Spain; population (1986) 264,000.

Vigo /ˈviːgəʊ/ Jean. Adopted name of Jean Almereyda 1905–1934. French director of bizarre experimental films. He made only three feature films: *A Propos de Nice* 1930, *Zéro de conduite/Nothing for Conduct* 1933, and *L'Atalante* 1934.

Viipuri /ˈviːpʊri/ Finnish name of ◊Vyborg, port and naval base in the USSR.

Viking or *Norseman* Scandinavian sea warrior. The Vikings raided Europe in the 8th–11th centuries, and often settled. In France they were given ◊Normandy. They conquered England 1013 under Sweyn I, and his son Canute was king of England as well as Denmark and Norway. In the east they established the first Russian state and founded ◊Novgorod. They reached the Byzantine Empire in the south and, in the west, Ireland, Iceland, Greenland, and North America; see ◊Eric the Red, Leif ◊Ericsson.

In their narrow, shallow-draught, highly manoeuvrable longships, the Vikings penetrated far inland along rivers. They plundered for gold and land, and the need for organized resistance accelerated the growth of the feudal system. In England and Ireland they were known as 'Danes'. They created settlements, for example in York, and greatly influenced the development of the English language, and as 'Normans' they achieved a second conquest of the country 1066. The Vikings had a sophisticated literary culture (◊sagas), and an organized system of government with an assembly (◊thing). The Swedish *Varangians* were invited to settle differences among the Slav chieftains in Russia 862. The Varangians also formed the imperial guard in Constantinople.

Viking art sculpture and design of the Vikings. Viking artists are known for woodcarving and metalwork, and for an intricate interlacing ornament similar to that found in Celtic art.

The burial ship from Oseberg (University Museum, Oslo) is an early example. The dragon is a recurring motif. After the conversion to Christianity in the 10th century, the traditional Viking ornament continued, for example carvings on the wooden stave churches of Norway, in Borgund and Urnes. Viking art was gradually absorbed into the Romanesque style.

Viking probes two US space probes to Mars, each one consisting of an orbiter and a lander. They were launched 20 Aug and 9 Sept 1975. They transmitted colour pictures, and analysed the soil.

The Viking 1 lander touched down in the Chryse lowland area 20 July 1976; Viking 2 landed in Utopia 3 Sept 1976.

Vila /ˈviːlə/ or *Port-Vila* port and capital of Vanuatu, on the SW of Efate island; population (1988) 15,000.

village college a type of ◊community school. They were first established in Cambridgeshire, England, by Henry ◊Morris.

Villa-Lobos /ˈvɪlə ˈləʊbɒs/ Heitor 1887–1959. Brazilian composer. His style was based on folk tunes collected on travels in his country; for example, in the *Bachianas Brasileiras* 1930–44, he treats them in the manner of Bach. His works range from guitar solos to film scores to opera; he produced 2,000 works, including 12 symphonies.

Villehardouin /ˌviːlɑːˈdwæn/ Geoffroy de *c.* 1160–1213. French historian, the first to write in the French language. He was born near Troyes, and was a leader of the Fourth ◊Crusade, of which

violet

his *Conquest of Constantinople*, about 1209, is an account.

villeinage the system of serfdom that prevailed in Europe in the Middle Ages. A villein was a peasant who gave dues and services to his lord in exchange for land.

In France until the 13th century, 'villeins' could refer to rural or urban non-nobles, but after this, it came to mean exclusively rural non-noble freemen. In Norman England, it referred to free peasants of relatively high status. At the time of the Domesday Book, the villeins were the most numerous element in the English population, providing the labour force for the manors. Their social position declined until, by the early 14th century, their personal and juridicial status was close to that of serfs. After the mid-14th century, as the effects of the Black Death led to a severe labour shortage, their status improved. By the 15th century villeinage had been supplanted by a system of free tenure and labour, but it continued in France until 1789.

Villiers de l'Isle Adam /viːlˈjeɪ də ˈliːl ævˈdɒm/ Philippe Auguste Mathias, comte de Villiers de l'Isle Adam 1838–1889. French poet, the inaugurator of the Symbolist movement. He wrote the drama *Axel* 1890; *Isis* 1862, a romance of the supernatural; verse, and short stories.

Villon /viːˈɒn/ François 1431–*c*.1465. French poet, noted for his satiric humour, pathos, and lyric power in works which used the *argot* (slang) of the time. Very little of his work survives, but it includes the *Ballade des dames du temps jadis/Ballad of the ladies of former times*, *Petit Testament* 1456, and *Grand Testament* 1461.

Born in Paris, he dropped his surname (Montcorbier or de Logos) to assume that of a canon—a relative who sent him to study at the Sorbonne, where he graduated 1449 and took his MA 1452. In 1455 he stabbed a priest in a street fight and had to flee the city. Pardoned the next year, he returned to Paris, but was soon in flight again after robbing the College of Navarre, and was briefly at rest at the court of the duke of Orléans until sentenced to death for an unknown offence from which he was saved by the amnesty of a public holiday. Theft and public brawling continued to occupy his time, in addition to the production of the *Grand Testament* 1461, but in 1463 a sentence of death in Paris, commuted to ten-year banishment, is the last that is known of his life.

Vilnius /ˈvɪlnɪʊs/ capital of Lithuanian Republic, USSR; population (1987) 566,000. Industries include engineering, and the manufacture of textiles, chemicals, and foodstuffs.

From a 10th-century settlement, Vilnius became the Lithuanian capital 1323 and a centre of Polish and Jewish culture. It was then Polish from 1386 until the Russian annexation 1795. Claimed by both Poland and Lithuania after World War I, it was given to Poland 1921, occupied by the USSR 1939, and immediately transferred to Lithuania. Its university was founded 1578.

Vimy Ridge /ˈviːmɪ/ hill in N France, taken in World War I by Canadian troops during the battle of Arras, Apr 1917, at the cost of 11,285 lives. It is a spur of the ridge of Nôtre Dame de Lorette, 8 km/5 mi NE of Arras.

Vincennes /væn'sen/ the University of Paris VIII, usually known as Vincennes from the suburb of E Paris where it was founded in 1970 (following the

1968 student rebellion) for blue-collar workers. By 1980, it had 32,000 students. In June 1980, it was moved to the industrial suburb of St-Denis.

Vincent de Paul, St /ˈvɪnsənt də ˈpɔːl/ *c*.1580–1660. French Roman Catholic priest and founder of the two charitable orders of Dazarists 1625 and Sisters of Charity 1634. Born in Gascony, he was ordained 1600, then captured by Barbary pirates and was a slave in Tunis until he escaped 1607. He was canonized 1737; feast day 19 July.

Vincent of Beauvais /ˈvɪnsənt/, /boʊˈveɪ/ *c*.1190–1264. French scholar, encyclopedist, and Dominican priest. A chaplain to the court of Louis IX, he is mainly remembered for his *Speculum majus/Great Mirror* 1220–44, a reference work summarizing contemporary knowledge on virtually every subject, including science, natural history, literature, and law. It also contained a history of the world from the creation. It is noteworthy for its positive attitude towards classical literature, whose reputation had undergone a period of eclipse in the preceding centuries.

vincristine an ◊alkaloid extracted from the blue periwinkle plant. Developed as an anticancer agent, it has revolutionized the treatment of childhood acute leukaemias; it is also included in ◊chemotherapy regimens for some lymphomas (cancers arising in the lymph tissues), lung and breast cancers. Side effects, such as nerve damage and loss of hair, are severe but usually reversible.

vine climbing plant *Vitis vinifera* of the family Vitaceae. It is native to Asia Minor and cultivated from antiquity for its fruit, which is eaten or made into wine or other fermented drinks; dried fruits of certain varieties are known as raisins and currants. Other species of climbing plant are sometimes termed vines.

vinegar a 4% solution of acetic acid produced by the oxidation of alcohol, used to flavour food and as a preservative in pickles. *Malt vinegar* is brown and made from malted cereals; *white vinegar* is distilled from it. Other sources of vinegar include cider, inferior wine, and honey.

Vinland /ˈvɪnlənd/ Norse name for the area of North America, probably on the east coast of Nova Scotia or New England, which the Viking Leif ◊Ericsson visited. It was named after the wild grapes that grew there.

Vinson Massif /ˈvɪnsən mæ'siːf/ highest point in ◊Antarctica, rising to 5,140 m/16,863 ft in the Ellsworth Mountains.

violin

bow

viola

violin

double bass

cello

viol a family of bowed stringed instruments prominent in the 16th–18th centuries, before their role was taken by the violins. Developed for close-harmony chamber music, they have a pure and restrained tone. Viols normally have six strings, a flat back, and narrow shoulders.

Members of the family include treble, alto, tenor, bass (or *viola da gamba*), and double bass (or *violone*). The smaller instruments are rested on the knee, not held under the chin. They are tuned in fourths, like a guitar. The only viol to survive in use in the symphony orchestra is the double bass.

viola a bowed, stringed musical instrument of the ◊violin family.

violet plant of the genus *Viola*, family Violaceae, with toothed leaves and mauve, blue, or white flowers, such as the **heath dog violet** *Viola canina* and **sweet violet** *Viola odorata*. **Pansies** are very close relatives.

violin a family of bowed stringed instruments developed in Italy during the 17th century, which eventually superseded the viols and formed the basis of the modern orchestra. There are three instruments: violin, viola, and cello (the double bass is descended from the viol).

Viollet-le-Duc /ˌviːəˈleɪ lə ˈdjuːk/ Eugène Emmanuel 1814–1849. French architect. Leader of the Gothic revival in France, he also restored medieval buildings.

violoncello or *cello* a bowed, stringed musical instrument of the ◊violin family.

VIP abbreviation for *very important person*.

viper front-fanged venomous snake of the family Viperidae. They range in size from 30 cm/1 ft to 3 m/9.8 ft, and often have diamond or jagged markings. Most give birth to live young.

There are 150 species of viper. The true vipers, sub family *Viperinae*, abundant in Africa and SW Asia, include the adder *Vipera berus*, Britain's only poisonous snake; the African puff adder *Bitis arietans* and the horned viper of North Africa *Cerastes cornutus*. The second subfamily *Crotalinae* includes the pit vipers and rattlesnakes of the Americas, which have heat-sensitive pits between the eye and nostril.

Virchow /ˈfɪəkəʊ/ Rudolf Ludwig Carl 1821–1902. German pathologist and founder of cellular pathology. Virchow was the first to describe leukaemia (cancer of the blood). In his book *Die Cellulare Pathologie/Cellular Pathology* 1858, he proposed that disease is not due to sudden invasions or changes, but to slow processes in which normal cells give rise to abnormal ones.

Virgil /ˈvɜːdʒəl/ Publius Vergilius Maro 70–19 BC. Roman poet who wrote the *Eclogues* 37 BC, a series of pastoral poems, the *Georgics* 30 BC, four books on the art of farming and his masterpiece, the ◊Aeneid.

Virgil, born near Mantua, came of the small farmer class. He was educated in Cremona and Mediolanum (Milan) and later studied philosophy and rhetoric in Rome before returning to his farm, where he began the *Eclogues* 43 BC. He wrote the *Georgics* at the suggestion of his patron, Maecenas, to whom he introduced Horace. Virgil devoted the last 11 years of his life to the composition of the *Aeneid*, considered to be the most important poem in Latin literature and a great influence on later European literature.

virginal in music, a small type of ◊harpsichord.

Virginia /vəˈdʒɪnɪə/ state of the S USA; nickname Old Dominion

viper

common viper

Virginia

area 105,600 sq km/40,762 sq mi
capital Richmond
towns Norfolk, Virginia Beach, Newport News, Hampton, Chesapeake, Portsmouth
features Blue Ridge mountains, which include the Shenandoah National Park; Arlington National Cemetery; Mount Vernon, the village where George Washington lived 1752–99; Monticello (Thomas Jefferson's home at Charlottesville); Stratford Hall (Robert E Lee's birthplace at Lexington)
products sweet potatoes, corn, tobacco, apples, peanuts, coal, furniture, paper, chemicals, processed food, textiles
population (1986) 5,787,000
famous people Richard E Byrd, Patrick Henry, Meriwether Lewis and William Clark, Edgar Allan Poe, Booker T Washington
history named in honour of Elizabeth I; Jamestown first permanent English settlement in the New World 1607; took a leading part in the American Revolution, and was one of the original Thirteen States; joined the Confederacy in the Civil War.

Virgin Islands /'vɜːdʒɪn/ group of about 100 small islands, northernmost of the Leeward Islands in the Antilles, West Indies. Tourism is the main industry.

They comprise the **US Virgin Islands** St Thomas (with the capital, Charlotte Amalie), St Croix, St John, and about 50 small islets; area 350 sq km/135 sq mi; population (1985) 111,000; and the **British Virgin Islands** Tortola (with the capital, Road Town), Virgin Gorda, Anegada, Jost van Dykes, and about 40 islets; area 150 sq km/58 sq mi; population (1987) 13,250. The US Virgin Islands were purchased from Denmark 1917, and form an 'unincorporated territory'. The British Virgin Islands were taken over from the Dutch by British settlers 1666, and have partial internal self-government.

Virgo /'vɜːgə/ constellation of the zodiac, and the second largest in the sky, representing a maiden holding an ear of wheat. The Sun passes through Virgo from late Sept to the end of Oct. Virgo's brightest star is the first-magnitude Spica, a blue-white star about 250 light years away. Virgo contains the nearest large cluster of galaxies to us, 50 million light years away, consisting of about 3,000 galaxies centred on the giant elliptical galaxy M87. Also in Virgo is the nearest ◊quasar, 3 273, an estimated 3 billion light years distant. In **astrology**, the dates for Virgo are between about 23 Aug and 22 Sept (see ◊precession).

Virgin Islands

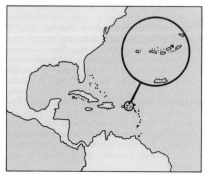

virion a single mature ◊virus particle.

Virtanen /'vɪətənen/ Artturi Ilmari 1895–1973. Finnish chemist who from 1920 made discoveries in agricultural chemistry. Because green fodder tends to ferment and produce a variety of harmful acids, it cannot be preserved for long. Virtanen prevented the process from starting by acidifying the fodder. In this form it lasted longer and remained nutritious. Nobel prize 1945.

virtual memory in computing, a technique whereby a portion of external ◊memory is used as an extension of internal memory. The contents of an area of ◊RAM are stored on, say, a hard disc while they are not needed, and brought back into main memory when required. The process, which is called either paging or segmentation, is hidden from the programmer, to whom the computer appears to have a much larger amount of internal memory than actually exists.

virus an infectious particle consisting of a core of nucleic acids (DNA or RNA) enclosed in a protein shell. Viruses are acellular, able to function and reproduce only if they can force their way into a living cell to use the cell's system to replicate themselves. In doing so, they may disrupt or alter the host cell's own DNA. The healthy human body reacts by producing an antiviral protein, ◊interferon, which prevents the infection spreading to adjacent cells.

Among diseases caused by viruses are canine distemper, chickenpox, common cold, herpes, influenza, rabies, smallpox, yellow fever, AIDS, and many plant diseases. Recent evidence implicates viruses in the development of some forms of cancer (see ◊oncogenes). **Bacteriophages** are viruses that infect bacterial cells. **Retroviruses** are of special interest because they have an RNA genome, and can produce DNA from this RNA. **Viroids**, discovered in 1971, are even smaller than viruses, a single strand of nucleic acid with no protein coat. They may cause stunting in plants and some rare diseases in animals, including humans. It is debatable whether viruses and viroids are truly living organisms, since they are incapable of an independent existence. Outside the cell of another organism they remain completely inert. The origin of viruses is also unclear, but it is believed that they are degenerate forms of life, derived from cellular organisms, or pieces of nucleic acid that have broken away from the genome of some higher organism and taken up a parasitic existence. **Antiviral drugs** are difficult to develop because viruses replicate by using the genetic machinery of host cells, so that drugs tend to affect the host cell as well as the virus. Acyclovir (used against the herpes group of diseases) is one of the few drugs so far developed that is successfully selective in its action. It is converted to its active form by an enzyme that is specific to the virus, and it then specifically inhibits viral replication. Some viruses have shown developing resistance to the few antiviral drugs available.

Viruses have recently been found to be very abundant in seas and lakes with between 5 and 10 million per millilitre of water at most sites tested, but up to 250 million per millilitre in one polluted lake. These viruses infect bacteria and possibly single-celled algae. They may play a crucial role in controlling the survival of bacteria and algae in the plankton.

virus in computing, a piece of ◊software that can replicate itself and transfer itself from one computer to another, without the user being aware of it. Some viruses are relatively harmless, but others can damage or destroy data. There are written by anonymous programmers, often maliciously, and are spread along telephone lines or on ◊floppy discs. Most are very difficult to eradicate.

vis-à-vis (French 'face-to-face') with regard to.

Visby /'vɪsbɪ/ historic town and bishopric on the Swedish island of Gotland in the Baltic.

It was founded as a Viking trading post on the route from Novgorod to the west. During the 12th and 13th centuries, the Scandinavian population became outnumbered by German colonists, and Visby became the nucleus of the German ◊Hanseatic League. In 1361, it was conquered by Waldemar IV. It possesses impressive fortifications, dated from the time of the Hanse, and many Gothic churches.

viscacha Argentinian pampas and scrubland-dwelling rodent *Lagostomus maximus* of the chinchilla family. It is up to 66 cm/2.2 ft long with a 20 cm/8 in tail, and weighs 7 kg/15 lbs. It is grey and black, and has a large head and small ears. Viscachas live in warrens of up to 30 individuals. They are nocturnal, and feed on grasses, roots, and seeds.

Mountain viscachas, genus *Lagidium*, are smaller and have long ears and tails, and are found in rocky places feeding by day on sparse vegetation.

viscera a general term for the organs contained in the chest and abdominal cavities.

Visconti Luchino 1906–1976. Italian film and theatre director. The film *Ossessione* 1942 pioneers his work with Neo-Realist theories; later works include *The Leopard* 1963 and *Death in Venice* 1971. His powerful social comment in documentaries led to clashes with the Italian government and Roman Catholic Church.

Visconti, dukes of Milan /vɪ'skɒntɪ/ rulers of Milan 1277–1447. They originated as N Italian feudal lords who attained dominance over the city as a result of their alliance with the Holy Roman emperors. By the mid-14th century, they ruled 15 other major towns in N Italy.

They had no formal title until Gian Galeazzo (died 1402) bought the title of duke from Emperor Wenceslas IV (1361–1419). On the death of the last male Visconti, Filippo Maria, 1447, the duchy was inherited by his son-in-law, Francesco Sforza.

viscose the most common type of ◊rayon, made by dissolving the cellulose in ◊woodpulp in an acid bath and regenerating it in the form of continuous filament or fibres.

viscosity in physics, the resistance of a fluid to flow. It applies to the motion of an object moving through a fluid as well as the motion of a fluid passing by an object.

Fluids such as pitch, treacle, and heavy oils are highly viscous; for the purposes of calculation, many fluids in physics are considered to be perfect, or nonviscous.

viscount in the UK peerage, the fourth degree of nobility, between earl and baron.

Vishnu /'vɪʃnuː/ in Hinduism, the second in the triad of gods (with Brahma and Siva) representing three aspects of the supreme spirit. He is the **Preserver**, and is believed to have assumed human appearance in nine *avatāra*s, or incarnations, in such forms as Rama and Krishna. His worshippers are the Vaishnavas.

Visigoths branch of ◊Goths, an East Germanic people.

vision defects abnormalities of the eye that cause less than perfect sight. In a **short-sighted** eye, the lens is fatter than normal, causing light from distant objects to be focused in front and not on the retina. A person with this complaint, called ◊myopia, cannot see clearly for distances over a few metres, and needs spectacles with diverging lenses. **Long sight**, also called hypermetropia or presbyopia, is caused by an eye lens thinner than normal that focuses light from distant objects behind the retina. The sufferer cannot see close objects clearly, and needs converging-lens spectacles. There are other vision defects, such as ◊colour blindness.

vision system a computer-based device for interpreting visual signals from a video camera. Computer vision is important in robotics where sensory abilities would considerably increase the flexibility and usefulness of a robot. Although some vision systems exist for recognizing simple shapes, the technology is still in its infancy.

visitation in the Christian church, a formal visit by a bishop or church official to examine the churches or abbeys within his jurisdiction. In medieval visitations, records were kept of the *detecta*, matters disclosed to the visitor, and *comperta*, what the visitor found for himself.

Vistula /'vɪstjʊlə/, Polish **Wisla** /'viːswɑː/ river in Poland, which rises in the Carpathians and runs SE to the Baltic at Gdańsk; length 1,090 km/677 mi. It is heavily polluted, carrying into the Baltic every year large quantities of industrial and agricultural waste, including phosphorus, oil, nitrogen, mercury, cadmium, and zinc.

vitalism the idea that living organisms derive their characteristic properties from a universal life force. The view is associated in the present century with the philosopher Henri ◊Bergson.

vitamin one of a number of chemically unrelated organic compounds that are necessary in small quantities for the normal functioning of the body. Many act as coenzymes, small molecules that enable ◊enzymes to function effectively. They are normally present in adequate amounts in a 'balanced diet'. Deficiency of a vitamin will normally lead to a metabolic disorder ('deficiency disease'), which can be remedied by sufficient intake of the vitamin. They are generally classified as **water-soluble** (B and C) or **fat-soluble** (A, D, E, and K).

Scurvy (the result of vitamin C deficiency) was observed at least 3,500 years ago, and sailors from the 1600s were given fresh sprouting cereals or citrus fruit juice to prevent or cure it. The concept of scurvy as a deficiency disease, however, caused by the absence of a specific substance, only emerged later. In the 1890s, a Dutch doctor, Christiaan ◊Eijkman, discovered that he could cure hens suffering from a condition like beriberi by feeding them on wholegrain, rather than polished, rice. In 1912, Casimir Funk, a Polish-born biochemist, had proposed the existence of what he called 'vitamines', but it was not fully established until about 1915 that several deficiency diseases were preventable and curable by extracts from certain foods. By then it was known that two groups of factors were involved, one being water-soluble and present, for example, in yeast, rice-polishings, and wheat germ, and the other being fat-soluble and present in egg yolk, butter, and fish-liver oils. The water-soluble substance, known to be effective against beri-beri, was named vitamin B. The fat-soluble vitamin complex was at first called vitamin A. With improving analytical techniques these have been subsequently separated into their various components, and others have been discovered. Current trends in 'megavitamin therapy' have yielded at best unproven effects; some vitamins (A, for example) are extremely toxic in high doses.

Other animals may also need vitamins, but not necessarily the same ones. For example, choline, which humans can synthesize, is essential to rats and some birds, which cannot produce sufficient for themselves.

vitamin C another name for ◊ascorbic acid.

Vitebsk /'viːtebsk/ industrial city (glass, textiles, machine tools, shoes) in NE Byelorussia, USSR, on the Dvina River; population (1987) 347,000. Vitebsk dates from the 10th century and has been Lithuanian, Russian, and Polish.

Vitoria /vɪ'tɔːriə/ capital of Alava province, in the Basque country, N Spain; population (1986) 208,000. Products include motor vehicles, agricultural machinery, and furniture.

vitriol any of a number of sulphate salts. Blue, green, and white vitriols are copper, ferrous, and zinc sulphate respectively. Oil of vitriol is sulphuric acid.

Vitruvius /vɪ'truːviəs/ (Marcus Vitruvius Pollio) 1st century BC. Roman architect, whose ten-volume interpretation of Roman architecture *De architectura* influenced Alberti and Palladio.

Vittorio Veneto /vɪ'tɔːriəʊ 'venɪtəʊ/ industrial town (motorcycles, agricultural machinery, furniture, paper, textiles) in Veneto, NE Italy, which gives its name to the final victory of Italy and Britain over Austria Oct 1918; population (1981) 30,000.

Vitus, St /'vaɪtəs/ Christian saint, probably Sicilian, who was martyred at Rome early in the 4th century.

Vivaldi /vɪ'vældi/ Antonio (Lucio) 1678–1741. Italian Baroque composer, violinist, and conductor. He wrote 23 symphonies, 75 sonatas, over 400 concertos, including the *Four Seasons* (about 1725) for violin and orchestra, over 40 operas, and much sacred music. His work was largely neglected until the 1930s.

viva voce (Latin 'with living voice') an oral examination.

vivipary in animals, a method of reproduction in which the embryo develops inside the body of the female from which it gains nourishment (in contrast to ◊ovipary and ◊ovovivipary). Vivipary is best developed in mammals, but also occurs in some arthropods, fish, amphibians, and reptiles. In plants, it is the formation of young plantlets or bulbils instead of flowers. The term also describes seeds that germinate prematurely, before falling from the parent plant.

Premature germination is common in mangrove trees, where the seedlings develop sizeable spearlike roots before dropping into the swamp below; this prevents then being washed away by the tide.

vivisection literally, cutting into a living animal. Used originally to mean experimental surgery or dissection practised on a live subject, it is now often used by ◊anti-vivisection campaigners to include any experiment on animals, surgical or otherwise.

viz abbreviation for *videlicet* (Latin 'that is to say', 'namely').

Vizcaya /vɪ'skaɪə/ Basque form of ◊Biscay, a bay in the Atlantic off France and Spain. Also the name of one of the three Spanish Basque provinces.

Vladimir I /'vlædɪmɪə/ St 956–1015. Russian saint and prince of Kiev. Converted to Christianity 988, he married Anna, Christian sister of the Byzantine emperor ◊Basil II, and established Orthodox Christianity as the Russian national faith. Feast day 15 July.

Vladivostok /,vlædɪ'vɒstɒk/ port (naval and commercial) in E USSR at the Amur Bay on the Pacific coast; population (1987) 615,000. It is kept open by icebreakers during winter. Industries include shipbuilding, and the manufacture of precision instruments.

It was established 1860 as a military port. It is the administrative centre of the Far East Science Centre 1969, with subsidiaries at Petropavlovsk, Khabarovsk, and Magadan.

Vlaminck /vlæ'mæŋk/ Maurice de 1876–1958. French painter, who began using brilliant colour as an early member of the ◊Fauves, mainly painting landscapes. Later he abandoned Fauve colour. He also wrote poetry, novels, and essays.

Initially he was inspired by van ◊Gogh but by 1908 ◊Cézanne had become the chief influence. Vlaminck was a multitalented eccentric: his careers included cycling, playing the violin, and farming.

VLF in physics, the abbreviation for *very low ◊frequency*.

Vlissingen /'flɪsɪŋə/ Dutch form of ◊Flushing, a port in SW Netherlands.

Vlorë /'vlɔːrə/ port and capital of Vlorë province, SW Albania, population (1980) 58,000. A Turkish possession from 1464, it was the site of the declaration of independence by Albania 1912.

VLSI *very large-scale integration* the current level of advanced technology in the microminiaturization of ◊integrated circuits, and an order of magnitude smaller than ◊LSI.

voc. in grammar, abbreviation for *vocative*.

vocal cords folds of tissue within a mammal's larynx, and a bird's syrinx. Air passing over them makes them vibrate, producing sounds. Muscles in the larynx change the pitch of the sound by adjusting the tension of the vocal cords.

vocational education education relevant to a specific job or career and referring to medical and legal education in the universities as well as further education courses in craft skills.

In the UK, the ◊TVEI (Technical and Vocational Education Initiative) funded by the Training Commission intends to allow the expansion of vocational education in schools.

vocative in the grammar of certain inflected languages, for example, Latin, the form of a word, especially a name, that is used to indicate that a person or thing is being addressed.

vodka a strong colourless alcoholic liquor distilled from rye, potatoes, maize, or barley.

Vogel /'fəʊgəl/ Hans-Jochen 1926– . West German socialist politician, chair of the Social Democratic Party (SPD) from 1987. A former leader of the SPD in Bavaria and mayor of Munich, he served in the Brandt and Schmidt governments in the 1970s as housing and then justice minister and then, briefly, as mayor of West Berlin.

A centrist, compromise figure, Vogel unsuccessfully contested the 1983 federal election as chancellor candidate for the SPD and in 1987 replaced Brandt as party chair.

voice sound produced by the passage of air between the ◊vocal cords. In humans the sound is much amplified by the hollow sinuses of the face, and is modified by the movements of the lips, tongue, and cheeks.

voiceprint an individual pattern of lines made by the human voice when visually recorded. First used as evidence in criminal trials in USA in 1966, voiceprints were banned in 1974 by the US Court of Appeal as 'not yet sufficiently accepted by scientists'.

Voight /vɔɪt/ Jon 1938– . US actor who starred with Dustin Hoffman in *Midnight Cowboy* 1969. His subsequent films include *Deliverance* 1972, *Coming Home* 1978, and *Runaway Train* 1985.

Vojvodina /,vɔɪvə'diːnə/ autonomous area in N Serbia, Yugoslavia; area 21,500 sq km/8,299 sq mi; population (1986) 2,050,000, including 1,110,000 Serbs and 390,000 Hungarians. Its capital is Novi Sad.

vol abbreviation for *volume*.

volatile in chemistry, a term describing a substance that readily passes from the liquid to the vapour phase. Volatile substances have a high ◊vapour pressure.

volcanic rock ◊igneous rock formed at the surface of the Earth. It is usually fine-grained, unlike the more coarse-grained intrusive (under the surface) types of igneous rocks. Volcanic rock can be either *lava* (solidified magma) or a *pyroclastic deposit* (fragmentary lava or ash) such as tuff (volcanic ash that has fused to form rock). Basalt and andesite are the main types of lava. Rhyolite often occurs as a pyroclastic deposit.

volcano vent in the Earth's ◊crust from which molten rock, lava, ashes, and gases are ejected. Usually it is cone-shaped with a pitlike opening at the top called the crater. Some volcanoes, for example Stromboli and Vesuvius in Italy, eject the material with explosive violence; others are quiet and the lava simply rises into the crater and flows over the rim. Some volcanoes may be inactive for long periods.

Volcanoes are closely associated with the movements of lithospheric plates (the top layer of the Earth's structure), particularly around plate boundaries; see ◊plate tectonics. Many volcanoes are submarine and occur along mid-ocean ridges. The chief terrestrial volcanic regions are around the Pacific rim (Cape Horn to Alaska); the central Andes of Chile (with the world's highest volcano, Guallatiri, 6,060 m/19,900 ft); North Island, New Zealand; Hawaii; Japan; and Antarctica. There are about 600 active volcanoes on Earth. Volcanism has helped shape other members of the solar system, including the Moon, Mars, Venus, and Jupiter's moon Io. some volcanoes may be inactive for long periods.

volcano

volcanoes

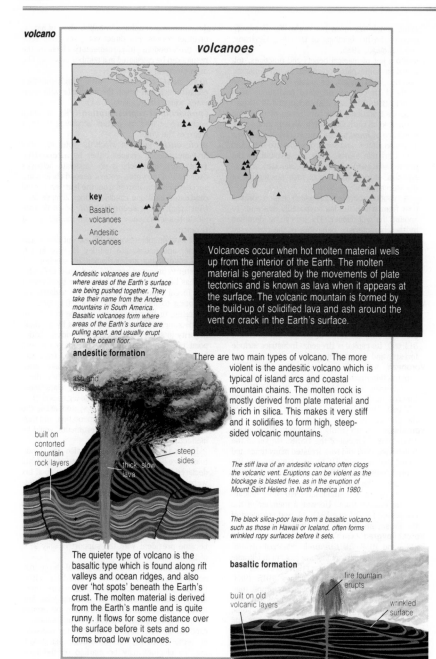

key

▲ Basaltic volcanoes

▲ Andesitic volcanoes

Andesitic volcanoes are found where areas of the Earth's surface are being pushed together. They take their name from the Andes mountains in South America. Basaltic volcanoes form where areas of the Earth's surface are pulling apart. and usually erupt from the ocean floor.

Volcanoes occur when hot molten material wells up from the interior of the Earth. The molten material is generated by the movements of plate tectonics and is known as lava when it appears at the surface. The volcanic mountain is formed by the build-up of solidified lava and ash around the vent or crack in the Earth's surface.

andesitic formation

ash and dust

built on contorted mountain rock layers

thick. slow lava

steep sides

There are two main types of volcano. The more violent is the andesitic volcano which is typical of island arcs and coastal mountain chains. The molten rock is mostly derived from plate material and is rich in silica. This makes it very stiff and it solidifies to form high, steep-sided volcanic mountains.

The stiff lava of an andesitic volcano often clogs the volcanic vent. Eruptions can be violent as the blockage is blasted free. as in the eruption of Mount Saint Helens in North America in 1980.

The black silica-poor lava from a basaltic volcano. such as those in Hawaii or Iceland. often forms wrinkled ropy surfaces before it sets.

The quieter type of volcano is the basaltic type which is found along rift valleys and ocean ridges, and also over 'hot spots' beneath the Earth's crust. The molten material is derived from the Earth's mantle and is quite runny. It flows for some distance over the surface before it sets and so forms broad low volcanoes.

basaltic formation

fire fountain erupts

built on old volcanic layers

wrinkled surface

Volcker /ˈvɔʊlkə/ Paul 1927– . US economist. As chair of the board of governors of the Federal Reserve System 1979–87, he controlled the amount of money in circulation in the USA. He was succeeded by Alan Greenspan.

vole rodent of the family Cricetidae, distributed over Europe, Asia, and North America, and related to hamsters and lemmings. They have brown or grey fur, blunt noses, and some species reach a length of 30 cm/2 ft. They feed on grasses, seeds, aquatic plants, and insects.

British species include the water vole or water 'rat' *Arvicola terrestris*, brownish above and grey-white below; and the field vole *Microtus agrestis*.

Volga /ˈvɒlgə/ longest river in Europe; 3,685 km/ 2,290 mi, 3,540 km/2,200 mi of which are navigable. It drains most of the central and eastern parts of European USSR, rises in the Valdai plateau and flows into the Caspian Sea 88 km/55 mi below Astrakhan.

The Soviet Union is going ahead with controversial schemes for diverting water from north-flowing rivers, east and west of the Urals,

to irrigate the croplands of central Asia. Diversion of water into the south-flowing Volga from the Sukhona river and surrounding lakes is due for completion 1990. A canal stretching 2,400 km/1,500 miles from the river Ob to Amu Darya is still in the planning stage.

Volgograd /ˈvɒlgəgræd/ industrial city (metal goods, machinery, sawmills, oil refining) in SW USSR, on the river Volga; population (1987) 988,000. It was called Tsaritsyn until 1925, and Stalingrad 1925–61. Its successful defence 1942–43 against Germany was a turning point in World War II.

Völkerwanderung (German 'nations wandering') the migration of peoples, usually with reference to the Slavic and Germanic movement in Europe 2nd–11th centuries AD.

Volkswagen (German 'the people's car') German car manufacturer. The original VW, with its distinctive beetle shape, was produced in Germany 1938, a design by Ferdinand ◊Porsche. It was still in production in Latin America in the late 1980s, by which time it had exceeded 20 million sales.

---

volleyball an indoor team game played on a court between two teams of six players each. A net is placed across the centre of the court, and players hit the ball with their hands over it, the aim being to ground it in the opponents' court.

Originally called Mintonette, the game was invented 1895 by William G Morgan in Massachusetts, USA, as a rival to the newly developed basketball. The playing area measures 18 m/59 ft by 9 m/29 ft 6 in. The ball, slightly smaller than a basketball, may not be hit more than three times on one team's side of the net.

Volleyball: recent winners

World Championships first held 1949 for men, 1952 for women

men
1970 East Germany
1972 Japan
1974 Poland
1976 Poland
1978 USSR
1980 USSR
1982 USSR
1984 USA
1986 USA
1988 USA
women
1970 USSR
1972 USSR
1974 Japan
1976 Japan
1978 Cuba
1980 USSR
1982 China
1984 China
1986 USA
1988 USSR

volt SI unit (symbol V) of electromotive force or electric potential. A small battery has a potential of 1½ volts; the domestic electricity supply in the UK is 240 volts (110 volts in the USA); and a high-tension transmission line may carry up to 765,000 volts.

The absolute volt is defined as the potential difference necessary to produce a current of 1 amp through an electric circuit with resistance 1 ohm. It is named after the Italian scientist Alessandro Volta.

Volta /ˈvɒltə/ main river in Ghana, about 1,600 km/1,000 mi long, with two main upper branches, the Black and White Volta. It has been dammed to provide power.

Volta, Upper /ˈvɒltə/ name until 1984 of ◊Burkina Faso.

Volta /ˈvɒltə/ Alessandro 1745–1827. Italian physicist. He invented the voltaic pile (the first battery), the electrophorus (an early electrostatic generator), and an ◊electroscope. Born in Como, he was a professor there and at Pavia. The ◊volt is named after him.

Voltaire /vɒlˈteə/ Pen name of François-Marie Arouet 1694–1778. French writer, who believed in ◊deism, and devoted himself to tolerance, justice, and humanity. He was threatened with arrest for *Lettres philosophiques sur les anglais/Philosophical Letters on the English* 1733, essays in favour of English ways, thought, and political practice, and had to take refuge. Other writings include *Le Siècle de Louis XIV/The Age of Louis XIV* 1751; *Candide* 1759, a parody on ◊Leibniz's 'best of all possible worlds'; and *Dictionnaire Philosophique* 1764.

Born in Paris, son of a notary, he adopted his pen name 1718. He was twice imprisoned in the Bastille and exiled from Paris between 1716 and 1726 for libellous political verse. *Oedipe/Oedipus*, his first essay in tragedy, was staged 1718. While in England 1726–29 he dedicated an epic poem on Henry IV, *La Henriade/The Henriade*, to Queen Caroline, and on returning to France published the successful *Histoire de Charles XII/History of Charles XII* 1731, and produced the play *Zaïre* 1732. He took refuge with his mistress,

Voltaire *French writer and philosopher Voltaire.*

the Marquise de ◊Châtelet, at Cirey in Champagne, where he wrote the play *Mérope* 1743 and much of *Le Siècle de Louis XIV*. Among his other works are histories of Peter the Great, Louis XV, and India, *La Pucelle/The Maid*, on Joan of Arc; the satirical tale *Zadig* 1748; and the tragedy *Irène* 1778. In 1751–53 he stayed at the court of Frederick II (the Great) of Prussia, who had long been an admirer, but the association ended in deep enmity. From 1754 he established himself near Geneva, and after 1758 at Ferney, just across the French border. His remains were transferred in 1791 to the Panthéon in Paris.

voltmeter instrument for measuring potential difference (voltage). It has a high internal resistance (so that it passes only a small current), such as a sensitive moving-coil ◊galvanometer in series with a high-value resistor. To measure an alternating voltage, the circuit also includes a rectifier. A moving-iron instrument can be used to measure AC (◊alternating current) voltages without the need for a rectifier.

volume in geometry, the space occupied by a three-dimensional solid object. A cube, cuboid, other prismatic figure, or cylinder has a volume equal to the area of the base multiplied by the height. For a pyramid or cone, the volume is equal to one-third of the area of the base multiplied by the perpendicular height. The volume of a sphere is equal to $4/3\pi r$. Volumes of irregular solids may be calculated by the technique of ◊integration.

vomiting the expulsion of the contents of the stomach through the mouth. It may have very many causes, including direct irritation of the stomach, severe pain, dizziness, and emotion. Sustained or repeated vomiting is always a serious symptom, both because it may indicate serious disease, and because dangerous loss of water, salt, and acid may result.

von Braun /fɒn ˈbraʊn/ Wernher 1912–1977. German rocket engineer who developed German military rockets (V1 and V2) during World War II, and later worked for ◊NASA in the USA.

During the 1940s his research team at Peenemünde on the Baltic coast produced the V1 (flying bomb) and supersonic V2 rockets. In the 1950s von Braun was part of the team that produced rockets for US satellites (the first, *Explorer I*, was launched early 1958) and early space flights by astronauts.

von Gesner /fɒn ˈgesnə/ Konrad 1516–1565. Swiss naturalist who produced an encyclopedia of the animal world, the *Historia animalium* 1551–58.

Gesner was a victim of the Black Death and could not complete a similar project on the plants. He is considered a founder of the science of zoology, but was also an expert in languages and an authority on the Classical writers.

von Karajan Herbert. Austrian conductor, see ◊Karajan, Herbert von.

Vonnegut /ˈvɒnɪgʌt/ Kurt, Jr 1922– . US writer whose work generally has a science-fiction or fantasy element; his novels include *The Sirens of Titan* 1958, *Cat's Cradle* 1963, *Slaughterhouse-Five*

1969, which draws on his World War II experience of the fire-bombing of Dresden, Germany, and *Galapagos* 1985.

voodoo a set of magical beliefs and practices, followed in some parts of Africa, South America, and the West Indies, especially Haiti. It arose in the 17th century on slave plantations as a combination of Roman Catholicism and W African religious traditions; believers retain membership in the Roman Catholic Church. Beliefs include the existence of ***loas***, spirits who involve themselves in human affairs, and some of whom are identified with Christian saints. They are invoked by the priest (*houngan*) or priestess (*mambo*) at ceremonies, during which loas take possession of the worshippers.

A voodoo temple (*houmfort*) has a central post from which the loa supposedly descends to 'mount' the worshipper. The loa can be identified by the characteristic behaviour of the possessed person. Loas include Baron Samedi, who watches over the land of the dead; Erzulie, the black Virgin or Earth goddess; Ogu, a warrior, corresponding to St James the Great; and Legba, the lord of the road and interpreter between humans and spirits, who corresponds to St Anthony the hermit.

Vorarlberg /ˈfɔːrˌɑːlbɜːg/ ('in front of the Arlberg') alpine federal province of W Austria draining into the Rhine and Lake Constance; area 2,600 sq km/1,004 sq mi; population (1987) 314,000. Its capital is Bregenz. Industries include forestry and dairy farming.

Voronezh /vəˈrɒneʃ/ industrial city (chemicals, construction machinery, electrical equipment) and capital of the Voronezh region of the USSR, S of Moscow on the Voronezh river; population (1987) 872,000. There has been a town on the site since the 11th century.

Voroshilov /ˌvɒrəˈʃiːlɒf/ Klement Efremovich 1881–1969. Marshal of the USSR. He joined the Bolsheviks 1903 and was arrested many times and exiled, but escaped. He became a member of the central committee 1921, commissar for war 1925, member of the Politburo 1926, marshal 1935. He was removed as commissar 1940 after defeats on the Finland front. He was a member of the committee for defence 1941–44, and president of the Presidium of the USSR 1953–60.

Voroshilovgrad /ˌvɒrəˈʃiːlɒfgræd/ formerly (until 1935 and 1958–70) *Lugansk* industrial city (locomotives, textiles, mining machinery) in Ukraine Republic, USSR; population (1987) 509,000.

Vorster /ˈfɔːstə/ Balthazar Johannes 1915–1983. South African Nationalist politician, prime minister 1966–78, in succession to Verwoerd, and president 1978–79. During his premiership some elements of apartheid were allowed to lapse, and attempts were made to improve relations with the outside world. He resigned when it was discovered that the Department of Information had made unauthorized use of public funds during his premiership.

Vorticism a short-lived movement in British painting, begun 1913 by Wyndham ◊Lewis. Influenced by Cubism and Futurism, he believed that painting should reflect the complexity and changefulness of the modern world. He had a harsh, angular, semi-abstract style.

Vosges /vəʊʒ/ mountain range in E France, rising in the Ballon de Guebwiller to 1,422 m/4,667 ft and forming the W edge of the Rhine rift valley.

Voskhod (Russian 'ascent') Soviet spacecraft used in the mid-1960s, modified from the single-seat Vostok, and the first spacecraft capable of carrying two or three cosmonauts. During the second Voskhod flight 1965, Alexei Leonov made the first space walk.

Vostok (Russian 'east') the first Soviet spacecraft, capable of carrying one cosmonaut, used 1961–63, which made flights lasting up to five days. Vostok was a metal sphere 2.3 m/7.5 ft in diameter. Vostok 1 carried the first person into space, Yuri ◊Gagarin.

vote expression of opinion by ballot, show of hands, or other means. For direct vote, see ◊plebiscite and ◊referendum. In parliamentary elections the results can be calculated in a number of ways. The main electoral systems are:

first past the post, with single-member constituencies in which the candidate with most votes wins (UK, Canada, USA);

◊***proportional representation*** (PR), in which seats are shared by parties according to their share of the vote;

preferential vote, in which the voter indicates first and second choices either by ***alternative vote*** (AV), in which, if no candidate achieves over 50% of the votes, voters' second choices are successively transferred from the least successful candidates until one candidate does achieve 50% (Australia); or by ***second ballot***, when no candidate has an absolute majority on the first count (France).

All British subjects over 18, except peers, the insane, and felons, are entitled to vote in UK local government and parliamentary elections. A register is prepared annually, and since 1872 voting has been by secret ballot. Under the Corrupt and Illegal Practices Act 1883 any candidate attempting to influence voters by gifts, loans or promises, or by intimidation, is liable to a fine or imprisonment. The voting system is by a simple majority in single-member constituencies. Critics point out that under this system many electors have no say, since votes for a defeated candidate are wasted, and governments may take office with a minority of the total vote. When there are two main parties, divided along class lines, the one in power often undoes the legislation of its predecessor. Supporters of the system argue the danger of increasing party fragmentation, and they believe continual coalition governments would be ineffective.

In the USA the voting age is also 18. Conditions of residence vary from state to state. Until declared illegal 1965, literacy tests or a ◊poll tax were often used to prevent black people from voting in the South. Voter registration and turnout in the USA remains the lowest in the industrialized world. In 1988, 37% of potential voters failed to register and barely 50% bothered to vote in the presidential election, so that George Bush became president with the support of only 27% of the people.

In one-party states some degree of choice may occur by voting for particular candidates within the party list. In some countries where there are problems of literacy or differing local languages, pictorial party emblems may be printed on the ballot paper instead of the names of candidates. The absence of accurate registers in some countries can encourage plural voting, so electors may be marked on the hand with temporarily indelible ink after they have voted.

Voyager probes two US space probes, originally ◊Mariners. Voyager 1, launched 5 Sept 1977, passed Jupiter Mar 1979, and reached Saturn Nov 1980. Voyager 2 was launched earlier, 20 Aug 1977, on a slower trajectory that took it past Jupiter July 1979, Saturn Aug 1981, Uranus Jan 1986, and Neptune Aug 1989. Like the ◊Pioneer probes, the Voyagers are on their way out of the solar system. Their tasks now include helping scientists to locate the position of the heliopause, the boundary at which the influence of the Sun gives way to the forces exerted by other stars. Both Voyagers carry long-playing records called 'Sounds of Earth' for the enlightenment of any other civilizations that might find them.

Voyager 2 was not intended to visit Uranus and Neptune, but the scientists were able to reprogram its computer to take it to those planets. Voyager 2 passed by Neptune at an altitude of 4,800 km/3,000 mi. The radio signals took 4 hr 6 min to reach Earth.

Voysey English architect Charles Voysey, whose small country houses are increasingly admired. This typical example is 'The Hill', Northamptonshire.

vulture

Voysey /ˈvɔɪzi/ Charles Francis Annesley 1857–1941. English architect and designer. He designed country houses which were characteristically asymmetrical with massive buttresses, long sloping roofs, and rough-cast walls. He also designed textiles and wallpaper.

Vranitzky /vræˈnɪtski/ Franz 1937– . Austrian socialist politician, federal chancellor from 1986. Vranitzky first went into banking and in 1970 became adviser on economic and financial policy to the minister of finance. After a return to the banking world he entered the political arena through the Socialist Party of Austria, and became minister of finance in 1984. He succeeded Fred Sinowatz as federal chancellor in 1986, heading an SPÖ-ÖVP (Austrian People's Party) coalition.

Vries /friːs/ Hugo de 1848–1935. Dutch botanist, who conducted important research on osmosis in plant cells and was a pioneer in the study of plant evolution. His work led to the rediscovery of ◊Mendel's laws and the formulation of the theory of mutation.

v.t. in grammar, the abbreviation for **verb transitive**.

VT abbreviation for ◊Vermont.

Vuillard /vwiːˈɑː/ (Jean) Edouard 1886–1940. French painter and printmaker, a founder member of **les ◊Nabis**. His work is mainly decorative, with an emphasis on surface pattern reflecting the influence of Japanese prints. With ◊Bonnard he produced numerous lithographs and paintings of simple domestic interiors, works that are generally categorized as *intimiste*.

Vulcan /ˈvʌlkən/ in Roman mythology, the god of fire and destruction, later identified with the Greek god ◊Hephaestus.

vulcanization technique for hardening rubber by heating it with, and chemically combining it with, sulphur. The process also makes the rubber stronger and more elastic. If the sulphur content is increased to as much as 30%, the product is the inelastic solid known as ebonite. More expensive alternatives to sulphur, such as selenium and telurium, are used to vulcanize rubber for specialized products such as vehicle tyres. The process was discovered accidentally by US inventor Charles ◊Goodyear 1839.

Accelerators can be added to speed the vulcanization process, which takes from a few minutes for small objects to an hour or more for vehicle tyres. Moulded objects are often shaped and vulcanized simultaneously in heated moulds; other objects may be vulcanized in hot water, hot air, or steam.

vulcanology study of ◊volcanoes and the geological phenomena that cause them.

Vulgate the Latin translation of the Bible, mostly by St Jerome 4th century, so called because of its vulgar (common) use in the Roman Catholic Church.

Vulpecula /vʌlˈpɛkjʊlə/ small constellation in the northern hemisphere of the sky, in the shape of a fox. It contains a major planetary ◊nebula (interstellar gas and dust), the Dumb-bell, and the first ◊pulsar (pulsating radio source) to be discovered.

vulture a carrion-eating bird up to 1 m/3.3 ft long, with a wingspan of up to 3.5 m/11.5 ft. It has a bare head and neck, shaggy black or brown plumage, and hooked beak and claws. True vultures occur only in the Old World; the New World forms include the ◊condor and turkey buzzard.

The vulture has keen senses of sight and smell. Its eyes are adapted to give an overall view with a magnifying area in the centre, enabling it to locate possible food sources and see the exact site in detail.

Vyborg /ˈviːbɔːg/ (Finnish *Viipuri*) port (trading in timber and wood products) and naval base in E Karelia, USSR, on the Gulf of Finland, 112 km/70 mi NW of Leningrad; population (1973) 51,000. Products include electrical equipment and agricultural machinery. Founded by the Swedes 1293, it was Finnish 1918–40.

Vyshinsky /vɪˈʃɪnski/ Andrei 1883–1954. Soviet politician. As commissar for justice he acted as prosecutor at the treason trials 1936–38. He was foreign minister 1949–53, and often represented the USSR at the United Nations.

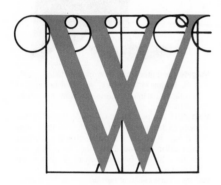

W the 23rd letter of the English alphabet, representing a labial-velar semi-vowel: a *u* in consonantal function. It is called double *u* because it was written *uu* or *vv*, which in ligature resulted in *w*. It is not pronounced before *r* (*write*, *wren*) and in cases such as *two* and *sword*.

W abbreviation for *west; watt*.

WA abbreviation for ◊*Washington* (state); ◊*Western Australia*.

Wace /weɪs/ Robert *c.* 1100–*c.* 1175. Anglo-Norman poet and chronicler of early chivalry. His major works, both written in Norman French, were *Roman de Brut* (also known as *Geste des Bretons*) 1155, and *Roman de Rou* (or *Geste des Normanz*) 1160–62.

He was born in Jersey to a noble family, educated at Paris and Caen in Normandy, and made prebend of Bayeaux by the gift of Henry II. *Roman de Brut* was adapted from Geoffrey of Monmouth's *Historia Regum Britanniae*; *Roman de Rou* was a chronicle of the dukes of Normandy.

Waddenzee /'wɒdnzeɪ/ European estuarine area (tidal flats, salt marshes, islands, and inlets) N of the Netherlands and West Germany, and W of Denmark; area 10,000 sq km/4,000 sq mi. It is the nursery for the North Sea fisheries, but the ecology is threatened by tourism and other development.

Waddington /'wɒdɪŋtən/ David Charles 1929– . British Conservative politician, home secretary from 1989. A barrister, he became an MP in 1978. A Conservative whip from 1979, Waddington was a junior minister in the Department of Employment and in the Home Office before becoming chief whip in 1987.

wadi in arid regions of the Middle East, a steep-sided valley containing an intermittent stream that flows in the wet season.

Wadi Halfa /'wɒdi 'haɪfə/ frontier town in Sudan, NE Africa, on Lake Nuba (the Sudanese section of Lake Nasser, formed by the Nile dam at Aswan,

Egypt, which partly flooded the archaeological sites here).

Wafd (Arabic 'deputation') the main Egyptian nationalist party between World Wars I and II. Under Nahas Pasha it formed a number of governments in the 1920s and 1930s. Dismissed by King Farouk in 1938, it was reinstated by the British in 1941. The party's pro-British stance weakened its claim to lead the nationalist movement and the party was again dismissed by Farouk in 1952, shortly before his own deposition. Wafd was banned in Jan 1953.

wafer in microelectronics, a 'super-chip' some 8–10 cm/3–4 in in diameter, for which wafer-scale integration (WSI) is used to link the equivalent of many individual ◊silicon chips, improving reliability, speed, and cooling.

Wagga Wagga /'wɒgə 'wɒgə/ agricultural town in SE New South Wales, Australia; population (1985) 49,500.

Wagner /'vɑːgnə/ Otto 1841–1918. Viennese architect. Initially designing in the Art Nouveau style, for example Vienna Stadtbahn 1894–97, he later rejected ornament for rationalism, as in the Post Office Savings Bank, Vienna, 1904–06. He influenced Viennese architects such as Josef Hoffmann, Adolf Loos, and Joseph Olbrich.

Wagner /'vɑːgnə/ Richard 1813–1883. German opera composer. He revolutionized the 19th-century conception of opera, envisaging it as a wholly new art form in which musical, poetic, and scenic elements should be unified through such devices as the ◊leitmotif. His operas include *Tannhäuser* 1845, *Lohengrin* 1850, and *Tristan und Isolde* 1865. In 1872 he founded the Festival Theatre in Bayreuth; his masterpiece *Der Ring des Nibelungen/The Ring of the Nibelung*, a sequence of four operas, was first performed there in 1876. His last work, *Parsifal*, was produced in 1882.

Wagner's early career was as director of the Magdeburg Theatre, where he unsuccessfully produced his first opera *Das Liebesverbot/Forbidden Love* in 1836. He lived in Paris 1839–42 and conducted the Dresden Opera House 1842–48. He fled Germany to escape arrest for his part in the 1848 revolution, but in 1861 he was allowed to return. He won the favour of Ludwig II of Bavaria in 1864 and was thus able to set up the Festival Theatre in Bayreuth. The Bayreuth tradition was continued by his wife Cosima, ◊Liszt's daughter, whom he married after her divorce from Hans von ◊Bülow; by his son *Siegfried Wagner* (1869–1930), a composer of operas such as *Der Bärenhäuter*; and by later descendants.

Wagner-Jauregg /'vɑːgnə jaʊrek/ Julius 1857–1940. Austrian neurologist. He received a Nobel prize in 1927 for his work on the use of induced fevers in treating mental illness.

Wagram, Battle of /'vɑːgrəm/ battle in July 1809 when the French emperor Napoleon defeated the Austrians under Archduke Charles near the village of Wagram, NE of Vienna, Austria.

Wagner German composer Richard Wagner.

wagtail slim narrow-billed bird *Motacilla*, about 18 cm/7 in long, with a characteristic flicking movement of the tail. There are about 30 species, mostly in Eurasia and Africa. British species include the *pied wagtail Motacilla alba* with black, grey, and white plumage, the *grey wagtail Motacilla cinerae*, and the summer visitor *yellow wagtail Motacilla flava*.

Wahabi the purist Saudi Islamic sect founded by Muhammad ibn-Abd-al-Wahab (1703–92), which regards all other sects as heresies whose followers are liable to the death penalty.

Waikato /waɪ'kætəʊ/ river on North Island, New Zealand, 355 km/220 m long; Waikato is also the name of the dairy area the river traverses, chief town Hamilton.

Wailing Wall or (in Judaism) *Western Wall* in Jerusalem, the remaining part of the ◊Temple, a site of pilgrimage. There Jews offer prayers either aloud ('wailing') or on pieces of paper placed between the stones of the wall.

Wain /weɪn/ John (Barrington) 1925– . British author. His best-known work is his first novel, *Hurry on Down* 1953. He was professor of poetry at Oxford 1973–80.

Wairarapa /waɪrə'ræpə/ area of North Island, New Zealand, round Lake Wairarapa, specializing in lamb and dairy farming; population (1986) 39,600. The chief market centre is Masterton.

Wairau /'waɪrau/ river in N South Island, New Zealand, flowing 170 km/105 m NE to Cook Strait.

Waitaki /waɪ'tæki/ river in SE South Island, New Zealand, which flows 215 km/135 mi to the Pacific. The Benmore hydroelectric installation has created an artificial lake.

Waitangi Day the national day of New Zealand: 6 Feb.

Waite /weɪt/ 'Terry' (Terence Hardy) 1939– . British religious adviser from 1980 to the archbishop of Canterbury, Dr Robert ◊Runcie. Waite undertook many overseas assignments, and disappeared in 1987 while making enquiries in Beirut, Lebanon, about European hostages. Worldwide efforts to secure his release, and that of his fellow hostages, have proved unsuccessful.

Waits /weɪts/ Tom 1949– . US singer and songwriter, with a characteristic gravelly voice. His songs typically deal with urban street life, and have jazz-influenced arrangements. He has written music for and acted in several films, including Jim Jarmusch's *Down by Law* 1986.

Waite Envoy to the archbishop of Canterbury, Terry Waite has been held hostage in Lebanon since 1987. He was seized while seeking to negotiate the release of others.

Wajda /ˈvaɪdə/ Andrzej 1926– . Polish film director, one of the major figures in postwar European cinema. His films typically deal with the predicament and disillusion of individuals caught up in political events. His works include *Ashes and Diamonds* 1958, *Man of Marble* 1977, *Man of Iron* 1981, and *Danton* 1982.

wake a watch kept over the body of a dead person during the night before their funeral; it originated in Anglo-Saxon times as the eve before a festival.

In the north of England, *wakes week* is the week when a whole town or city traditionally has its annual holiday, and during that period factories and shops are closed.

Wakefield /ˈweɪkfiːld/ industrial city (chemicals, machine tools), administrative headquarters of West Yorkshire, England, on the river Calder, S of Leeds; population (1981) 310,200. The Lancastrians defeated the Yorkists here 1460, during the Wars of the Roses.

Wakefield /ˈweɪkfiːld/ Edward Gibbon 1796–1862. British colonial administrator. He was imprisoned 1826–29 for abducting an heiress, and became manager of the South Australian Association which founded a colony in 1836. He was an agent for the New Zealand Land Company 1839–46, and emigrated there in 1853. His son *Edward Jerningham Wakefield* (1820–79) wrote *Adventure in New Zealand* 1845.

Wake Islands /weɪk/ a small Pacific atoll comprising three islands 3,700 km/2,300 mi west of Hawaii, under US Air Force administration since 1972; area 8 sq km/3 sq mi; population (1980) 300. It was discovered by Captain William Wake 1841, annexed by the USA 1898, and uninhabited until 1935 when it was made an air staging point, with a garrison. It was occupied by Japan 1941–45.

Wakhan Salient /wəˈkɑːn/ narrow strip of territory in Afghanistan bordered by the USSR, China, and Pakistan. It was effectively annexed by the USSR in 1980 to halt alleged arms supplies to Afghan guerrillas from China and Pakistan.

Waksman /ˈwæksmən/ Selman Abraham 1888–1973. US biochemist, born in Ukraine. He coined the word 'antibiotic' for bacteria-killing chemicals derived from microorganisms, and won Nobel prize 1952 for the discovery of streptomycin, an antibiotic used against tuberculosis.

Walachia /wɒˈleɪkiə/ alternative spelling of ◊Wallachia, part of Romania.

Walcheren /ˈvɑːlkərən/ island in Zeeland province, Netherlands, in the estuary of the Scheldt
area 200 sq km/80 sq mi
capital Middelburg
towns Flushing (Vlissingen)
features flat and for the most part below sea level
products dairy, sugar-beet, and root vegetables
history a British force seized Walcheren in 1809; after 7,000 of the garrison of 15,000 had died of malaria, the remainder were withdrawn. It was flooded by deliberate breaching of the dykes to drive out the Germans 1944–45, and in 1953 by abnormally high tides.

Wald /wɔːld/ George 1906– . US biochemist who explored the chemistry of vision. He found that a crucial role was played by the retinal pigment rhodopsin, derived in part from vitamin A. For this he shared the 1967 Nobel Physiology or Medicine Prize with Ragnar Granit (1900–) and Haldan Hartline (1903–).

Waldemar /ˈvældəmɑː/ or *Valdemar* four kings of Denmark, including:

Waldemar I *the Great* 1131–1182. King of Denmark from 1157, who defeated rival claimants to the throne, and overcame the Wends on the Baltic island of Rügen in 1169.

Waldemar II *the Conqueror* 1170–1241. King of Denmark from 1202. He was the second son of Waldemar I, and succeeded his brother Canute VI. He gained control of land N of the river Elbe (which he later lost), as well as much of

Estonia, and he completed the codification of Danish law.

Waldemar IV 1320–1375. King of Denmark from 1340, responsible for reuniting his country by capturing Skåne (S Sweden) and the island of Gotland in 1361. However, the resulting conflict with the Hanseatic League led to defeat by them, and in 1370 he was forced to submit to the Peace of Stralsund.

Walden or *Life in the Woods* 1854, classic literary work of US Transcendentalism, the record kept by Henry David Thoreau of his attempt to 'front the essential facts of life' by building a simple cabin at Walden Pond, near Concord, Massachusetts, and observing nature there.

Walden /ˈwɔːldən/ Brian (Alistair) 1932– . British journalist and, from 1977, television presenter. He was a Labour member of Parliament 1964–77.

Walden was a university lecturer before entering Parliament. Disillusioned with party politics, he cut short his parliamentary career in 1977 and became presenter of the current-affairs TV programme *Weekend World*, with a direct and uninhibited style of interviewing public figures. He also contributes to the *Sunday Times* and *Evening Standard* newspapers.

Waldenses also known as *Waldensians or Vaudois* Protestant religious sect, founded about 1170 by Peter Waldo, a merchant of Lyons. They were allied to the ◊Albigenses. They lived in voluntary poverty, refused to take oaths or take part in war, and later rejected the doctrines of transubstantiation, purgatory, and the invocation of saints. Although subjected to persecution until the 17th century, they spread in France, Germany, and Italy, and still survive in Piedmont.

Waldheim /ˈvældhaɪm/ Kurt 1918– . Austrian politician and diplomat. He was secretary general of the United Nations 1972–81, having been Austria's representative there 1964–68 and 1970–71. In 1986 he was elected president of Austria, but his tenure of office was clouded by revelations that during World War II he had been an intelligence officer in an army unit responsible for transporting Jews to death camps.

Wales /weɪlz/ (Welsh *Cymru*) Principality of
area 20,780 sq km/8,021 sq mi
capital Cardiff
towns Swansea
features Snowdonia mountains (Snowdon 1,085 m/3,561 ft, the highest point in England and Wales) in the NW and in the SE the Black Mountain, Brecon Beacons, and Black Forest ranges; rivers Severn, Wye, Usk, and Dee

Waldheim *Austrian chancellor Kurt Waldheim, elected in 1986 despite his wartime service with the German army in Yugoslavia. He was secretary-general of the United Nations 1972–81.*

exports traditional industries (coal and steel) have declined, but varied modern and high-technology ventures are being developed; Wales has the largest concentration of Japanese-owned plants in the UK. It also has the highest density of sheep in the world and a dairy industry; tourism is important
currency pound sterling
population (1987) 2,836,000
language Welsh 19% (1981), English
religion Nonconformist Protestant denominations; Roman Catholic minority
government returns 38 members to the UK Parliament.

Wales: counties

County	Administrative Headquarters	Area sq km
Clwyd	Mold	2,420
Dyfed	Carmarthen	5,770
Gwent	Cwmbran	1,380
Gwynedd	Caernarvon	3,870
Mid Glamorgan	Cardiff	1,020
Powys	Llandrindod Wells	5,080
South Glamorgan	Cardiff	420
West Glamorgan	Swansea	820
		20,780

Walesa /væˈwensə/ Lech 1947– . Polish trade-union leader, founder of ◊Solidarity 1980 (*Solidarność*), an organization, independent of the Communist Party, which forced substantial political and economic concessions from the Polish government 1980–81 until being outlawed. Walesa, as an electrician at the Lenin shipyard at Gdańsk, became a trade-union organizer. A series of strikes led by Walesa, a devout Catholic, drew wide public support. In Dec 1981 Solidarity was outlawed and Walesa arrested, following the imposition of martial law by the Polish leader Gen Jaruzelski. Walesa was released 1982.

After leading a further series of strikes during 1988, he negotiated an agreement with the Jaruzelski government in Apr 1989 under the terms of which Solidarity once more became legal and a new, semi-pluralist 'socialist democracy' was established. The coalition government elected in Sept 1989 was dominated by Solidarity.

Wales, Church in the Welsh Anglican Church, independent from the ◊Church of England.

The Welsh church became strongly Protestant in the 16th century, but in the 17th–18th centuries declined from being led by a succession of English-appointed bishops. Disestablished by an act of Parliament in 1920, with its endowments appropriated, the Church in Wales today comprises six dioceses (with bishops elected by an

Walesa *Polish trade unionist and leader of Solidarity Lech Walesa.*

electoral college of clergy and lay people) with an archbishop elected from among the six bishops.

Wales: history for ancient history, see also ◊Britain, ancient.

c.400 BC Wales occupied by Celts from central Europe.

AD 50–60 Wales became part of the Roman Empire.

c.200 Christianity adopted.

c.450–600 Wales became the chief Celtic stronghold in the west as a result of the Saxon invasions of S Britain. Celtic tribes united against England.

8th century Frontier pushed back to ◊Offa's Dyke.

9th–11th centuries Vikings raided the coasts. At this time Wales was divided into small states organized on a clan basis, although princes such as Rhodri (844–878), Howel the Good (*c.* 904–949), and Griffith ap Llewelyn (1039–1063) temporarily united the country.

11th–12th centuries Continual pressure on Wales from across the English border resisted notably by ◊Llewelyn I and II.

1277 Edward I of England accepted as overlord by the Welsh.

1284 Edward I completed the conquest of Wales which had been begun by the Normans.

1294 Revolt against English rule put down by Edward I.

1350–1500 Welsh nationalist uprisings against the English, the most notable of which was that led by Owen Glendower (1359–1415).

1485 Henry Tudor, a Welshman, became Henry VII of England.

1536–43 Acts of Union united England and Wales after conquest under Henry VIII. Wales sent representatives to the English Parliament; English law established in Wales; English became the official language.

18th century Evangelical revival made Nonconformity a powerful factor in Welsh life. A strong coal and iron industry developed in the south.

19th century The miners and ironworkers were militant supporters of Chartism, and Wales became a stronghold of trade unionism and socialism.

1893 University of Wales founded.

1920s–30s Wales suffered greatly from industrial depression; unemployment reached 21% 1937, and a considerable exodus of population took place.

post-1945 Growing nationalist movement and a revival of the language, earlier suppressed or discouraged (there is a Welsh television channel).

1966 ◊Plaid Cymru, the Welsh National Party, returned its first member to Westminster.

1979 Referendum rejected a proposal for limited home rule.

1988 Bombing campaign against estate agents selling Welsh properties to English buyers.

For other history, see ◊England, history; ◊United Kingdom.

Wales, Prince of /weɪlz/ title conferred on the eldest son of the United Kingdom's sovereign. Prince ◊Charles was invested as 21st Prince of Wales at Caernarvon 1969 by his mother, Elizabeth II.

Waley /'weɪlɪ/ Arthur 1889–1966. English orientalist, who translated from both Japanese and Chinese, including such works as the Japanese classics *The Tale of Genji* 1925–33 and *The Pillowbook of Sei Shōnagon* 1928, and the 16th-century Chinese novel *Monkey* 1942. He never visited the Far East.

walkabout Australian Aboriginal English for a nomadic ritual excursion into the bush. The term was adopted in 1970, during tours of Australia and New Zealand by Elizabeth II, for informal public-relations walks by politicians and royalty.

Walker /'wɔːkə/ Alice 1944– . US poet, novelist, critic, and essay writer. She was active in the civil-rights movement in the USA in the 1960s, and as a black woman has written about the double burden for women of racist and sexist oppression.

Her novel *The Color Purple* 1983 won the Pulitzer Prize.

Walker /'wɔːkə/ Peter (Edward) 1932– . British Conservative politician, energy secretary 1983–87, secretary of state for Wales from 1987.

As energy secretary from 1983, he managed the government's response to the national miners' strike 1984–85 that resulted in the capitulation of the National Union of Miners.

Walker /'wɔːkə/ William 1824–1860. US adventurer who for a short time established himself as president of a republic in NW Mexico, and was briefly president of Nicaragua 1856–57. He was eventually executed and is now regarded as a symbol of US imperialism in Central America.

wallaby any of several small members of the ◊kangaroo family.

Wallace /'wɒlɪs/ Alfred Russel 1823–1913. English naturalist who collected animal and plant specimens in South America and the Far East, and independently arrived at a theory of evolution by ◊natural selection similar to that of Charles Darwin.

Wallace /'wɒlɪs/ Edgar 1875–1932. English writer of thrillers. His prolific output includes *The Four Just Men* 1905; a series set in Africa and including *Sanders of the River* 1911; crime novels such as *A King by Night* 1926; and melodramas such as *The Ringer* 1926.

Wallace /'wɒlɪs/ George 1919– . US right-wing politician, governor of Alabama 1962–66. He contested the presidency in 1968 as an independent, and in 1972 campaigned for the Democratic nomination, but was shot at a rally and became partly paralysed.

Wallace /'wɒlɪs/ Lewis 1827–1905. US general and novelist. He served in the Mexican and Civil wars, and subsequently became governor of New Mexico and minister to Turkey. He wrote the historical novels *The Fair God* 1873 and *Ben Hur* 1880.

Wallace /'wɒlɪs/ Richard 1818–1890. British art collector. He inherited a valuable art collection from his father, the Marquess of Hertford, which was given by his widow to the UK as the *Wallace Collection*, containing many 18th-century French paintings. It is now at Hertford House, London.

Wallace /'wɒlɪs/ William 1272–1305. Scottish nationalist who led a revolt against English rule in 1297, won a victory at Stirling, and assumed the title 'governor of Scotland'. Edward I defeated him at Falkirk in 1298, and Wallace was captured and executed.

Wallace line an imaginary line running down the Lombok Strait in SE Asia, between the island of Bali and the islands of Lombok and Sulawesi. It

Wallace Alfred Russel Wallace was an English naturalist who independently evolved a theory of evolution similar to that of Charles Darwin. He had a special interest in the geographical distribution of animal species.

was identified by the naturalist A R Wallace as separating the Asian and Australian biogeographical regions, each of which has its own distinctive animals.

Subsequently, others have placed the boundary between these two regions at different points in the Malay archipelago, owing to overlapping migration patterns.

Wallachia /wɒˈleɪkɪə/ independent medieval principality, under Turkish rule 1387–1861, when it was united with Moldavia to form Romania.

Wallenberg /'wɒlənbɜːg/ Raoul 1912–1947. Swedish businessman who attempted to rescue several thousand Jews from German-occupied Budapest in 1944 in World War II.

There he tried to rescue and support Jews in safe houses, and provided them with false papers to save them from deportation to extermination camps. After the arrival of Soviet troops in Budapest, he reported to the Russian commander in Jan 1945 and then disappeared. The Soviet gvernment later claimed that he died of a heart attack in July 1947. However, rumours persist that he is still alive and held in a Soviet prison camp.

Wallenstein /'vælənʃtaɪn/ Albrecht Eusebius Wenzel von 1583–1634. German general who, until his defeat at Lützen in 1632, led the Habsburg armies in the Thirty Years' War. He was assassinated.

Waller /'wɒlə/ Edmund 1606–1687. English poet who managed to eulogize both Cromwell and Charles II; now mainly remembered for lyrics such as 'Go, lovely rose'.

wallflower perennial plant *Cheiranthus cheiri*, family Cruciferae, with fragrant red or yellow flowers in spring.

Wallis /'wɒlɪs/ Barnes (Neville) 1887–1979. British aeronautical engineer who designed the airship R-100 and during World War II perfected the 'bouncing bombs' used against the German Möhne and Eder dams in 1943 by the Royal Air Force Dambusters Squadron. He also assisted the development of the Concorde supersonic airliner, and developed the swing-wing aircraft.

Wallis and Futuna /'wɒlɪs, fuːˈtjuːnə/ two island groups in the SW Pacific, an overseas territory of France; area 367 sq km/143 sq mi; population (1983) 12,400. Discovered by European sailors in the 18th century, it became a French protectorate 1842, and an overseas territory 1961. Products include copra, yams, and bananas.

Walloon /wɒˈluːnz/ member of a French-speaking people of SE Belgium and adjacent areas of France.

Wallsend /'wɔːlzend/ town in Tyne and Wear, NE England, on the River Tyne at the E end of Hadrian's Wall; population (1981) 45,000. Industries include shipbuilding, engineering, and coalmining.

Wall Street /wɔːl/ street in Manhattan, New York, on which the stock exchange is situated, and a synonym for stock dealing in the USA. It is so called from a stockade erected 1653.

walnut tree *Juglans regia*, probably originating in SE Europe. It can reach 30 m/100 ft, and produces a

walnut

full crop of nuts about a dozen years from planting; the timber is used in furniture and the oil in
cooking.

Walpole /'wɔ:lpəʊl/ Horace, 4th Earl of Orford
1717–1797. English novelist and politician, the
son of Robert Walpole. He was a Whig member
of Parliament 1741–67. He converted his house
at Strawberry Hill, Twickenham, into a Gothic
castle; his *The Castle of Otranto* 1764 established
the genre of the ◊Gothic novel.

Walpole /'wɔ:lpəʊl/ Robert, 1st Earl of Orford
1676–1745. British Whig politician, the first 'prime
minister' as 1st Lord of the Treasury and chancellor of the Exchequer 1715–17 and 1721–42. He
encouraged trade by his peaceful foreign policy
(until forced into the War of Jenkins's Ear with
Spain in 1739), and received an earldom when he
eventually retired in 1742.

Walpurga, St /væl'pʊəgə/ English nun who
preached Christianity in Germany. **Walpurgis
Night** the night before 1 May, one of her
feast days, was formerly associated with
witches' sabbaths. Her main feast day is
25 Feb.

Walras /væl'rɑ:/ Léon 1834–1910. French economist. In his *Éléments d'économie politique pure*
1874–77 he developed a unified model for general equilibrium theory (a hypothetical situation in
which demand equals supply in all markets). He
also originated the theory of diminishing marginal
utility of a good (the increased value to a person
of consuming more of a product).

walrus seal-like marine mammal *Odobenus rosmarus*
found in the far N Atlantic and the Arctic. It can
reach 4 m/13 ft in length, and weigh up to 1,400
kg/3,000 lb. It has webbed flippers, a bristly
moustache, and large tusks. It is gregarious
except at breeding time, and feeds mainly on
shellfish. It has been hunted close to extinction
for its ivory tusks, hide, and blubber. The Alaskan
walrus is rarer than the African elephant, and is
close to extinction.

Walsall /'wɔ:lsəl/ industrial town (castings, tubes,
electrical equipment, leather goods) in West Midlands, England, 13 km/8 mi NW of Birmingham;
population (1981) 179,000.

Walsh /wɔ:lʃ/ Raoul 1887–1981. US film director,
originally an actor. He directed his first film 1914
and went on to become one of Hollywood's most
prolific directors. He made a number of outstanding films, including *The Thief of Baghdad* 1924, *The
Roaring Twenties* 1939, and *White Heat* 1949. He
retired 1964.

Walsingham /'wɔ:lsɪŋəm/ Francis *c.* 1530–1590.
English politician who, as secretary of state from
1573, both advocated a strong anti-Spanish policy
and ran the efficient government spy system that
made it work.

Walter /'wɔ:ltə/ Hubert died 1205. Archbishop of
Canterbury 1193–1205. As justiciar (chief political
and legal officer) 1193–98, he ruled England during
Richard I's absence and introduced the offices of
coroner and justice of the peace.

Walter /'wɔ:ltə/ John 1739–1812. British newspaper editor, founder of *The Times* (originally
the *Daily Universal Register* 1785, but renamed
in 1788).

Walter /'wɔ:ltə/ Lucy *c.*1630–1658. Mistress of
◊Charles II, whom she met while a Royalist

walrus

refugee in The Hague, Netherlands, in 1648; the
Duke of ◊Monmouth was their son.

Walters /'wɔ:ltəz/ Alan (Arthur) 1927– . British
economist and government adviser 1981–89. A
believer in ◊monetarism, he became economics
adviser to Prime Minister Thatcher, but his publicly stated differences with the policies of her
chancellor Nigel ◊Lawson precipitated, in 1989,
Lawson's resignation from the government as well
as Walters's own departure.

Walther von der Vogelweide /'væltə fɒn deə
'fəʊgəlvaɪdə/ *c.*1170–*c.*1230. German poet,
greatest of the ◊Minnesingers. Of noble birth,
he lived in his youth at the Austrian ducal court
in Vienna, adopting a wandering life after the death
of his patron in 1198. His lyrics deal mostly with
love, but also with religion and politics.

Walton /'wɔ:ltən/ Ernest 1903– . Irish physicist
who, as a young doctoral student at the Cavendish laboratory in Cambridge, collaborated with
◊Cockcroft on the structure of the atom. In 1932
they succeeded in splitting the atom and for this
experiment, they shared the Nobel prize, 1951.

Walton /'wɔ:ltən/ Izaak 1593–1683. English author
of the classic *Compleat Angler* 1653. He was born
in Stafford, and settled in London as an iron-
monger. He also wrote short biographies of the
poets George Herbert and John Donne, and the
theologian Richard Hooker.

Walton /'wɔ:ltən/ William (Turner) 1902–1983.
English composer. Among his works are *Façade*
1923, a series of instrumental pieces designed
to be played in conjunction with the recitation of poems by Edith Sitwell; the oratorio
Belshazzar's Feast 1931; and *Variations on a
Theme by Hindemith* 1963. He also composed
a viola concerto 1929; two symphonies 1935; a
violin concerto 1939; and a sonata for violin and
pianoforte 1950.

waltz a ballroom dance in three-four time evolved
from the Austrian *Ländler* (traditional peasants'
country dance) and later made popular by the
◊Strauss family in Vienna.

Walvis Bay /'wɔ:lvɪs 'beɪ/ chief port of Namibia,
SW Africa; population (1980) 26,000. It has
a fishing industry with allied trades. It has
been a detached part of Cape Province, area
1,100 sq km/425 sq mi, from 1884, but administered by South Africa from 1922.

wampum cylindrical beads ground from sea shells
and formerly used as currency and in decoration by
North American Indians of the NE woodlands.

Wandering Jew in medieval legend, a Jew named
Ahasuerus, said to have insulted Jesus on his way
to Calvary and been condemned to wander the
world until the Second Coming.

Wanganui /ˌwɒŋə'nu:i/ port (textiles, clothing) in
SW North Island, New Zealand, at the mouth of
the Wanganui river; population (1986) 41,000.

Wankel engine a rotary petrol engine developed
by the German engineer Felix Wankel (1902–)
in the 1950s. It operates according to the same
stages as the ◊four-stroke petrol engine cycle,
but these stages take place in different sectors
of a figure-of-eight chamber in the space between
the chamber walls and a triangular rotor. Power
is produced once on every turn on the rotor. The
Wankel engine is simpler in construction than the
normal piston petrol engine, and produces rotary
power directly (instead of via a crankshaft). Problems with rotor seals have prevented its widespread use.

Wankie /'wæŋki/ name until 1982 of ◊Hwange, a
town and national park in Zimbabwe.

wapiti or *elk* species of deer *Cervus canadensis*,
native to North America, Europe, and Asia. It
is reddish-brown in colour, about 1.5 m/5 ft at
the shoulder, weighs up to 450 kg/1,000 lb, and
has antlers up to 1.2 m/4 ft long. It is becoming
increasingly rare.

Wapping /'wɒpɪŋ/ district of the Greater London
borough of Tower Hamlets; situated between the
Thames and the former London Docks. In the
1980s it replaced Fleet Street as the centre of
the UK newspaper industry.

war an act of force, usually on behalf of the state,
intended to compel a declared enemy to obey the
will of the other. The aim is to render the opponent
incapable of further resistance by destroying its
capability and will to bear arms in pursuit of its own
aims. War is therefore a continuation of politics
carried on with violent and destructive means, as
an instrument of policy.

The estimated figure for loss of life in Third
World wars since 1945 is 17 million. War is generally divided into **strategy**, the planning and
conduct of a war, and **tactics**, the deployment
of forces in battle.

Types of war include:

guerrilla war the waging of low-level conflict
by irregular forces against an occupying army or
against the rear of an enemy force. Examples
include Mao Zedong's campaign against the Nationalist Chinese and T E Lawrence's Arab revolt
against the Turks;

low-intensity conflict US term for its interventions in the Third World (stepped up in the 1980s),
ranging from drug-running to funding and training
guerrillas, and fought with political, economic, and
cultural weapons as well as specially designed military technology;

civil war the waging of war by opposing parties,
or members of different regions, within a state.
The American Civil War 1861–65, the English Civil
War of the 17th century, and the Spanish Civil War
1936–39 are notable examples;

limited war the concept that a war may be limited in both geographical extent and levels of force
exerted and have aims that stop short of achieving
the destruction of the enemy. The Korean War
1950–53 falls within this category;

total war the waging of war against both combatants and noncombatants, taking the view that
no distinction should be made between them. The
Spanish Civil War marked the beginning of this
type of warfare, in which bombing from the air
included both civilian and military targets;

absolute war the view that there should be no
limitations, such as law, compassion, or prudence,
in the application of force, the sole aim being to
achieve the complete annihilation of one's opponent. Such a concept contradicts the notion, formulated by ◊Clausewitz, of war as an instrument of
political dialogue since it implies that no dialogue is
actually intended. It has been claimed that ◊nuclear
warfare would assume such proportions and would

Walpole Horace Walpole, Earl of Orford, English
writer and member of Parliament. He converted his
house in Twickenham, near London, into a small
Gothic castle called Strawberry Hill, and wrote a
Gothic novel which was a forerunner of the modern
terror-mystery genre.

be in accordance with the doctrine of mutually assured destruction.

War and Peace a novel by Leo Tolstoy, published 1863–69. It chronicles the lives of three noble families during the Napoleonic Wars and is notable for its complex characters and optimistic tone.

waratah Australian shrub or tree, of the family Proteaceae, especially the crimson-flowered *Telopea speciosissima*, emblem of New South Wales.

Warbeck /'wɔ:bek/ Perkin *c.*1474–1499. Flemish pretender to the English throne. Claiming to be Richard, brother of Edward V, he led a rising against Henry VII in 1497, and was hanged after attempting to escape from the Tower of London.

War Between the States another (usually Southern) name for the ◊American Civil War (now seldom used in standard histories).

warbler family of songbirds, order Passeriformes. The Old World birds are drab-coloured, and the New World birds are brightly plumed in the spring. They grow up to 25 cm/10 in long, and feed on berries and insects.

Old World species include the ◊*chiffchaff*, **blackcap**, **goldcrest**, **willow warbler**, and the tropical long-tailed *tailorbird Orthotomus sutorius*, which builds a nest inside two large leaves it sews together. The New World warblers, family Parulidae, are brighter and related to the ◊tanagers.

The *Dartford warbler Sylvia undata* is one of Britain's rarest birds.

Warburg /'vɑ:bʊək/ Otto 1878–1976. German biochemist, who in 1923 devised a manometer sensitive enough to measure oxygen uptake of respiring tissue. By measuring the rate that cells absorb oxygen under differing conditions, Warburg was able to show that enzymes called **cytochromes** enable cells to process oxygen. Nobel Prize for Medicine 1931. Warburg also demonstrated that cancerous cells absorb less oxygen than normal cells.

war crime act (such as murder of a civilian or a prisoner of war) that contravenes the internationally accepted laws governing the conduct of, and wars, particularly the Hague Convention 1907 and the Geneva Convention 1949. Nazi war criminals were tried after World War II at the ◊Nuremberg Trials. A key principle of the law relating to such crimes is that obedience to the orders of a superior is no defence.

In practice, prosecutions are generally brought by the victorious side. Spies in wartime are not war criminals; technically they are 'unprivileged belligerents', can be killed, and have no right to be treated as prisoners of war.

War crimes became a major issue in the aftermath of World War II. The United Nations War Crimes Commission was set up in 1943 to investigate German atrocities against Allied nationals. Leading Nazis were tried in Nuremberg 1945–46. High-ranking Japanese defendants were tried in Tokyo before the International Military Tribunal, and others by the legal section of the Allied supreme command.

In subsequent years the hunt for Nazis who escaped justice has continued, led notably by Simon Wiesenthal (1909–), who tracked down Adolf ◊Eichmann in 1960. Perhaps the last major Nazi war criminal to be brought to justice was Klaus Barbie, tried in France 1987 for crimes committed while he was commandant at Lyons.

Subsequent wars have had their full measure of crimes, a notable example being the ◊My Lai massacre 1968, during the Vietnam War, when US troops murdered 200 unarmed civilians.

Ward /wɔ:d/ Artemus. Pen name of Charles Farrar Browne 1834–1867. US humorist who achieved great popularity with comic writings such as *Artemus Ward: His Book* 1862 and *Artemus Ward: His Travels* 1865.

Ward /wɔ:d/ Barbara 1914–1981. British economist. She became president of the Institute for Environment and Development in 1973. In 1976 she received a life peerage as Baroness Jackson of Wadsworth. Her books include *Policy for the West* 1951 and *The Widening Gap* 1971.

Ward /wɔ:d/ Leslie 1851–1922. British caricaturist, known under the pseudonym 'Spy' for his caricatures in *Vanity Fair*.

Ward /wɔ:d/ Mrs Humphry (born Mary Augusta Arnold) 1851–1920. English novelist who wrote serious didactic books, such as *Robert Elsmere* 1888, a study of religious doubt. She was an opponent of women's emancipation.

warfarin an anticoagulant (prevents blood clotting) which works by inhibiting the action of vitamin K. It can be taken by mouth and begins to act several days after the initial dose.

◊Heparin may be given at the same time and discontinued when warfarin takes effect. It is often given as a preventive measure, to reduce the risk of ◊thrombosis or ◊embolism after major surgery. In large doses, it is used in rat poison.

Warhol /'wɔ:həʊl/ Andy 1928–1987. US Pop artist and filmmaker. He made his name in 1962 with paintings of Campbell's soup tins, Coca-Cola bottles, and film stars. In his notorious New York studio, the Factory, he produced series of garish silk-screen prints. His films include the semi-documentary *Chelsea Girls* 1966 and *Trash* 1970.

Warhol was born in Pittsburgh, where he studied art. In the 1950s he became a leading commercial artist in New York. With the breakthrough of Pop art, his bizarre personality and flair for self-publicity made him a household name. He was a pioneer of multimedia events with the Exploding Plastic Inevitable touring show in 1966 featuring the Velvet Underground (see Lou ◊Reed). In 1968 he was shot and nearly killed by a radical feminist, Valerie Solanas.

In the 1970s and 1980s Warhol was primarily a society portraitist, although his activities included a magazine (*Interview*) and a cable TV show.

Successful early silk-screen series dealt with car crashes and suicides, Marilyn Monroe, Elvis Presley and flowers. His films, beginning with *Sleep* 1963 and ending with *Bad* 1977, had a strong documentary or improvisational element. His books include *The Philosophy of Andy Warhol (From A to B and Back Again)* 1975 and *Popism* 1980.

Warlock /'wɔ:lɒk/ Peter. Pen name of British composer Philip ◊Heseltine.

warlord in China, any of the provincial leaders who, between 1916 and 1928, took advantage of central government weakness to organize their own private armies and fiefdoms.

Warner /'wɔ:nə/ Deborah 1959– . British theatre director. Discarding period costume and furnished sets, she adopted an uncluttered approach to the classics, including productions of many Shakespeare plays and Sophocles' *Electra*.

Warner Brothers US film production company, founded 1923 by Harry, Albert, Sam, and Jack Warner. It became one of the major Hollywood studios after releasing the first talking film, *The Jazz Singer* 1927. In the 1930s–50s, the company's stars included Humphrey Bogart, Erroll Flynn, and Bette Davis. It suffered in the 1960s through competition with television and was taken over by Seven Art Productions. In 1969 there was another takeover by Kinney National Service, and the whole company became known as *Warner Communications*.

Warner Brothers Records (now WEA) was formed in the late 1950s, releasing mostly middle-of-the-road pop music; an early signing was the Everly Brothers. It became one of the six major record companies in the 1970s, with artists like Joni Mitchell, Randy Newman, and Prince. Warner Communications subsidiaries include Sire, which in 1983 signed Madonna.

warning coloration in biology, an alternative term for ◊aposematic coloration.

War of 1812 a war between the USA and Britain caused by British interference with US trade as part of the economic warfare against Napoleonic France. Tensions with the British in Canada led to plans for a US invasion but these were never realized and success was limited to the capture of Detroit and a few notable naval victories. In 1814, British forces occupied Washington DC and burned many public buildings. A treaty signed in Ghent, Belgium, Dec 1814 ended the conflict.

War Office former British government department controlling military affairs. The Board of Ordnance, which existed in the 14th century, was absorbed into the War Department after the Crimean War and the whole named the War Office. In 1964 its core became a subordinate branch of the newly established *Ministry of ◊Defence*.

War Powers Act legislation passed 1973 enabling the US president to deploy US forces abroad for combat without prior Congressional approval. The president is nevertheless required to report to both Houses of Congress within 48 hours of having taken such action. Congress may restrict the continuation of troop deployment despite any presidential veto.

warrant officer rank between commissioned and senior noncommissioned officer (SNCO) in the British army, and the highest noncommissioned rank in ground trades of the Royal Air Force and the RAF regiment.

Warren /'wɒrən/ Earl 1891–1974. US jurist and politician. As Chief Justice of the US Supreme Court 1953–69 he took a stand against racial discrimination, ruling that segregation in schools was unconstitutional. He headed the commission that investigated President Kennedy's assassination 1964, which made the controversial finding that Lee Harvey Oswald acted alone.

Warren /'wɒrən/ Frank 1952– . British boxing promoter who helped bring world title-fight boxing to commercial television. He set up the London Arena in the Docklands. In 1989 he was seriously wounded in a shotgun attack.

Warren /'wɒrən/ Robert Penn 1905–1989. US poet and novelist, the only author to receive a Pulitzer prize for both prose and poetry. In 1986 he became the USA's first Poet Laureate.

His novel *All the King's Men* 1946 was modelled on the career of Huey Long, and he won the Pulitzer prize for *Promises* 1968 and *Now and Then: Poems* 1976–78.

Warrington /'wɒrɪŋtən/ industrial town (metal goods, chemicals, brewing) in Cheshire, NW England, on the river Mersey; population (1985) 178,000. An important trading centre since Roman times, it was designated a 'new town' 1968.

Warrnambool /'wɔ:nəmbu:l/ port near the mouth of Hopkins river, SW Victoria, Australia; population (1981) 22,000. A tourist centre, it also manufactures textiles and dairy products.

Warrumbungle Range /ˌwɒrəm'bʌŋgəl/ mountain range of volcanic origin in New South Wales, Australia. ◊Siding Spring Mountain 859 m/2,819 ft is the site of an observatory; the Breadknife is a 90 m/300 ft high rock only 150 cm/5 ft wide; the highest point is Mount Exmouth 1,228 m/4,030 ft. The name is Aboriginal and means 'broken-up small mountains'.

Warsaw /'wɔ:sɔ:/ (Polish *Warszawa*) capital of Poland, on the river Vistula; population (1985) 1,649,000. Industries include engineering, food processing, printing, clothing, and pharmaceuticals.

Founded in the 13th century, it replaced Kraków as capital 1595. Its university was founded 1818. It was taken by the Germans 27 Sept 1939 and 250,000 Poles were killed during two months of street fighting that started 1 Aug 1944. It was finally liberated 17 Jan 1945. The old city was virtually destroyed in World War II but has been reconstructed. Marie Curie was born here.

Warsaw Pact military alliance established 1955 between the USSR and E European communist states as a response to the admission of West Germany into NATO.

warship a fighting ship armed and crewed for war. The supremacy of the battleship at the beginning of the 20th century was superseded during World War I by the development of ◊submarine attack, and was rendered obsolete in World War II with the growth of long-range air attack. The largest surface warships are ◊aircraft carriers, which together with submarines are now considered the most important warships.

aircraft carriers The large-scale aircraft carrier was temporarily out of favour, as too vulnerable, until the resumption of building, especially by the USSR, in the late 1970s and 1980s. The *Carl Vinson* USA 1982 weighs 81,600 tonnes.

Some countries, particularly the UK, have opted for **mini-carriers** with vertical takeoff aircraft and long-range helicopters. Mini-carriers evolved in the early 1970s and have been advocated by US military reformers. The USSR has ships of this kind carrying as many as 30 helicopters.

sensor system The modern warship carries three types: (1) radar for surface-search and tracking, navigation, air surveillance, and indication of targets to weapon-control systems; (2) sonar for detection of surface and subsurface targets; and (3) liod (*l*ightweight *o*ptronic *d*etector) for processing the optical contrast of a target against its background, as viewed by a television or infrared camera. The information thus collected is then processed by computer and presented to senior officers through the combat information centre, which at the same time collects information from other fleet units and distributes its own data to them. Finally, weapon-control systems guide the selected weapons most efficiently to the targets.

Smaller auxiliary warships include **mine-hunters** for countering blockade of home ports, especially the base ports of submarines. In the 1980s these were made of glass-reinforced plastic.

submarines The first nuclear-powered submarine was the US *Nautilus* 1955; the first Polaris was the *George Washington* 1960. Submarines fall into two classes: the specially designed, almost silent **attack submarine**, intended to release its fast torpedoes and missiles at comparatively close range, and the **ballistic-missile submarine** with guided missiles of such long range that the submarine itself is virtually undetectable to the enemy. For the USA these submarines form one leg of the strategic 'triad' of land-based missiles, crewed bombers, and submarine-launched missiles.

The first British nuclear-powered submarine was the *Dreadnought* 1963. Nuclear power for surface warships still presents safety problems. Surface ships are increasingly driven by gas turbines, steam turbines being phased out, and include guided-missile **destroyers** and multipurpose **frigates**. The latter carry such varied equipment as guns, depth-charge mortars, mine-laying rails, torpedoes, air-defence missiles, and surface-to-surface missiles.

wart protuberance composed of a local overgrowth of skin. The common wart (*verruca vulgaris*) is due to a virus infection, and usually disappears spontaneously within two years, but can be treated with peeling applications, burning away (cautery), or freezing (cryosurgery).

wart hog species of African wild pig *Phacochoerus aethiopicus*, which has a large head with a bristly mane, fleshy pads beneath the eyes, and four large tusks. It has short legs, and can grow to 75 cm/2.5 ft at the shoulder.

Warton /'wɔ:tn/ Joseph 1722–1800. English poet, headmaster of Winchester 1766–93, whose verse and *Essay on the Writings and Genius of Pope* 1756–82 marked an 'anti-classical' reaction.

Warton /'wɔ:tn/ Thomas Wain 1728–1790. English critic. He was professor of poetry at Oxford 1757–67 and published the first *History of English Poetry* 1774–81. Poet Laureate from 1785.

Warwick /'wɒrɪk/ market town, administrative headquarters of Warwickshire, England; population (1981) 22,000. Industries include carpets

wart hog

and engineering. Founded 914, it has many fine medieval buildings including a 14th-century castle.

Warwick /'wɒrɪk/ Richard Neville, Earl of Warwick 1428–1471. English politician, called the Kingmaker. During the Wars of the ◊Roses he fought at first on the Yorkist side, and was largely responsible for placing Edward IV on the throne. Having quarrelled with him, he restored Henry VI in 1470, but was defeated and killed by Edward at Barnet, Hertfordshire.

Warwickshire /'wɒrɪkʃə/ county in central England
area 1,980 sq km/764 sq mi
towns administrative headquarters Warwick; Leamington, Nuneaton, Rugby, Stratford-upon-Avon
features Kenilworth and Warwick castles; remains of the 'Forest of Arden' (portrayed by Shakespeare in *As You Like It*); site of the Battle of Edgehill
products mainly agricultural, engineering, textiles
population (1987) 484,000
famous people George Eliot, William Shakespeare.

washing soda common name of sodium carbonate decahydrate ($Na_2CO_3.10H_2O$). The name is derived from the practice of adding it to washing water to 'soften' it (see ◊water, hardness of).

Washington /'wɒʃɪŋtən/ state of the NW USA; nickname Evergreen State
area 176,700 sq km/68,206 sq mi
capital Olympia
towns Seattle, Spokane, Tacoma
features Columbia river; Olympic (Olympic Mountains) National Park, and Mount Rainier (Cascade Range) National Park
products apples, cereals, livestock, processed food, timber, chemicals, cement, zinc, uranium, lead, gold, silver, aircraft, ships, road transport vehicles
population (1987) 4,481,000, including 61,000 Indians, mainly of the Yakima people
famous people Bing Crosby, Jimi Hendrix, Frances Farmer
history settled from 1811, it became a state 1889. Labour disputes occurred here in the 1910s, brutally suppressed by the authorities.

Warwickshire

Washington *US teacher and reformer Booker T Washington.*

Washington /'wɒʃɪŋtən/ town on the River Wear, Tyne and Wear, NE England, designated a 'new town' 1964; population (1985) 56,000. Industries include textiles, electronics, and car assembly.

Washington /'wɒʃɪŋtən/ Booker T(aliaferro) 1856–1915. US educationist, pioneer in higher education for black people in the southern USA. He was the founder and first principal of Tuskegee Institute, Alabama, in 1881, originally a training college for blacks, which became a respected academic institution. He maintained that economic independence was the way for blacks to achieve social equality.

Washington /'wɒʃɪŋtən/ George 1732–1799. First president of the USA 1789–97. As a strong opponent of the British government's policy, he sat in the ◊Continental Congresses of 1774 and 1775, and on the outbreak of the War of ◊American Independence was chosen commander in chief. After the war he retired to his Virginia estate, Mount Vernon, but in 1787 he re-entered politics as president of the Constitutional Convention. Although he attempted to draw his ministers from all factions, his aristocratic outlook alienated his secretary of state, Thomas Jefferson, who resigned 1793, thus creating the two-party system.

Washington took part in campaigns against the French and American Indians 1753–57, and was elected to the Virginia House of Burgesses. He

Washington *The first president of the USA, George Washington. He served as commander in chief of the American forces during the War of Independence.*

Washington

was elected president of the USA in 1789 and re-elected in 1793, but refused to serve a third term, setting a precedent that was followed until 1940. He scrupulously avoided overstepping the constitutional boundaries of presidential power. In his farewell address 1796, he maintained that the USA should avoid European quarrels and entangling alliances. He is buried at Mount Vernon.

Washington Convention an alternative name for ◊*CITES*, the international agreement that regulates trade in endangered species.

Washington DC /'wɒʃɪŋtən/ (District of Columbia) national capital of the USA, on the Potomac river.
area 180 sq km/69 sq mi
capital the District of Columbia covers only the area of the city of Washington
features it was designed by a French engineer, Pierre L'Enfant (1754–1825). Among buildings of architectural note are the Capitol, the Pentagon, the White House, and the Lincoln Memorial. The National Gallery has a good collection of paintings; libraries include the Library of Congress, the National Archives, and the Folger Shakespeare Library. The Smithsonian Institute is here
population (1983) 623,000 (metropolitan area, extending outside the District of Columbia, 3 million)
history the District of Columbia, initially land ceded from Maryland and Virginia, was established by Act of Congress 1790–91, and was first used as the seat of Congress 1800. The right to vote in national elections was not granted to residents until 1961.

Wash, the /wɒʃ/ bay of the North Sea between Norfolk and Lincolnshire, England. King John lost his baggage and treasure in crossing it 1216.

wasp stinging insect of the order Hymenoptera, characterized by a thin join between the thorax and the abdomen. Wasps can be social or solitary. Among social wasps, the queens devote themselves to egg-laying, the fertilized eggs producing female workers; the males come from unfertilized eggs, and have no sting. The larvae are fed on

Washington DC *The Capitol, Washington DC, national capital of the USA.*

insects, but the mature wasps feed mainly on fruit and sugar. In winter, the fertilized queens hibernate, but the other wasps die.

Of the 290 British species, only a few are true wasps, Vespidae; the rest are digger wasps. There are seven British species of social wasps in the genus *Vespa*, some nesting below ground, others in trees or bushes, the largest being the hornet; all the others are solitary.

Wassermann /'væsəmæn/ August von 1866–1925. German professor of medicine. In 1907 he discovered a sero-diagnosis of syphilis, known as the *Wassermann reaction*.

waste materials that are no longer needed and are discarded. Examples are household waste, industrial waste (which usually contains toxic chemicals), medical waste (which may contain organisms that cause disease), and nuclear waste (which is radioactive). By ◊recycling, some materials in waste can be reclaimed for further use. In the USA, 40 tonnes of solid waste is generated annually per person.

In Britain, the average person throws away about ten times their own body weight in household refuse each year. In Britain in 1986, nearly 4.5 billion drink cans were thrown away and 2.5 million tonnes of plastic were used.

waste disposal depositing waste. Methods of waste disposal vary according to the materials in the waste and include incineration, burial at designated sites, and dumping at sea. Organic waste can be treated and reused as fertilizer (see ◊sewage disposal). Nuclear and toxic waste is usually buried or dumped at sea, although this does not negate the danger.

Waste disposal is an increasing problem in the late 20th century. Environmental groups, such as Greenpeace and Friends of the Earth, are campaigning for more recycling, a change in

wasp *Head of a hornet showing the biting mouthparts, large compound eyes, and branched antennae.*

lifestyle so that less waste (from packaging and containers to nuclear materials) is produced, and safer methods of disposal.

The industrial waste dumped every year by the UK in the North Sea includes 550,000 tons of fly ash from coal-fired power stations. The British government agreed in 1989 to stop North Sea dumping from 1993, but dumping in the heavily polluted Irish Sea will continue. It receives 80 tonnes of uranium a year from phosphate rock processing, and 300 million gallons of sewage every day, 80% of it untreated or merely screened.

'Waste Land, The' a poem by T S Eliot, first published 1922. It expressed the prevalent mood of depression after World War I, and is a key work of Modernism in literature.

watch a personal portable timepiece. In the 20th century increasing miniaturization, mass production, and the need for accurate timekeeping in World War I led to the watch moving from the pocket to the wrist. Watches were given further refinements, such as being made antimagnetic, self-winding, or shock-resistant. In 1957 the electric watch was developed, and in the 1970s came the digital watch, in which all moving parts are dispensed with.

Miniature sundials were the earliest form, the first true watches being developed in the 15th century when they were miniature clocks attached to the girdle. By the 18th century the watch mechanism had been perfected by inventors such as Thomas Tompion (1639–1713) and Thomas Earnshaw (1749–1829), but throughout the 19th century watches remained articles of value.

An electric watch has no mainspring, the mechanism being kept in motion by the mutual attraction of a permanent magnet and an electromagnet, which pushes the balance wheel. In a digital watch the time measurement is done by a quartz crystal ◊oscillator linked to digital counting and display circuits. The time is usually indicated by ◊liquid crystal display.

water (H_2O) a liquid without colour, taste, or odour. It is an oxide of hydrogen. Water begins to freeze solid at 0°C or 32°F, and to boil at 100°C or 212°F. When liquid, it is virtually incompressible; frozen, it expands by $1/11$ of its volume. 1 cubic cm weighs 1 gram at 4°C, its maximum density, forming the unit of specific gravity. It has the highest known specific heat, and acts as an efficient solvent, particularly when hot. Most of the

wasp

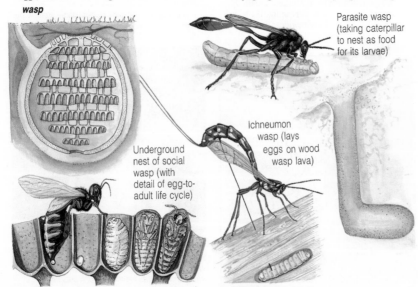

Parasite wasp (taking caterpillar to nest as food for its larvae)

Underground nest of social wasp (with detail of egg-to-adult life cycle)

Ichneumon wasp (lays eggs on wood wasp lava)

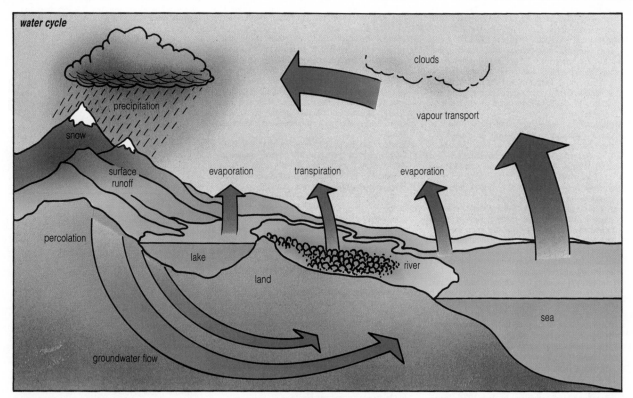

water cycle

world's water is in the sea; less than 0.01% is fresh water.

Water takes the form of sea, rain, and vapour, and supports all forms of land and marine life. As distinct from heavy water, which contains deuterium, ordinary water is sometimes referred to as 'light water'.

Water covers 70% of the Earth's surface. Water supply in sparsely populated regions usually comes from underground water rising to the surface in natural springs, supplemented by pumps and wells. Urban sources are deep artesian wells, rivers, and reservoirs, usually formed from enlarged lakes or dammed and flooded valleys, from which water is conveyed by pipes, conduits, and aqueducts to filter beds. As water seeps through layers of shingle, gravel, and sand, harmful organisms are removed and the water is then distributed by pumping or gravitation through mains and pipes. Often other substances are added to the water, such as chlorine and fluorine; ◊aluminium sulphate is the most widely used chemical in water treatment. In towns, besides industrial demands, domestic and municipal (road washing, sewage) needs account for about 135 litres/30 gallons per head each day. In coastal desert areas, such as the Arabian peninsula, desalination plants remove salt from sea water.

The British water industry was privatized 1989, and the European Commission announced its intention to take the UK to court for failing to meet EC drinking water standards. Pesticides and fertilizers used in agriculture and weedkillers from road verges are washed into ground water used for public water supplies; industrial chemicals get into drinking water from rivers; see ◊National Rivers Authority.

Water Babies, The a fantasy by British author Charles ◊Kingsley, published in England 1863. Tom, an orphan child, is employed to climb up chimneys and clear out the soot. While engaged in this task, he inadvertently frightens a girl, Ellie, and runs away. He drowns and is immortalized as an amphibious 'water baby'. After redeeming his moral character by the instruction of Mrs Bedonebyasyoudid and Mrs

Doasyouwouldbedoneby, Tom is reunited with Ellie, who drowns while trying to reach him.

water boatman water bug of the family Corixidae that feeds on plant debris and algae. It has a flattened body 1.5 cm/0.6 in long, with oarlike legs. The name also applies to the backswimmers, genus *Notecta*, which are superficially similar.

waterbuck African antelope *Kobus ellipsiprymnus* with characteristic white ring marking on the rump. It is about 2 m/6 ft long and 1.4 m/4.5 ft at the shoulder, and has long, coarse, brown fur. The males have big horns with corrugated surfaces.

In spite of the name, waterbuck are not confined to wet areas. The *defassa waterbuck Kobus defassa* is similar but with a large white rump patch.

Major waterfalls

Name	location	Total drop	
		m	ft
Angel Falls	Venezuela	979	3,212
Yosemite	USA	739	2,425
Mardalsfossen–South	Norway	655	2,149
Tugela Falls	South Africa	614	2,014
Cuquenan	Venezuela	610	2,000
Sutherland	New Zealand	580	1,903
Takkakaw Falls	Canada	503	1,650
Ribbon Fall, Yosemite	USA	491	1,612
Great Karamang River Falls	Guyana	488	1,600
Mardalsfossen–North	Norway	468	1,535
Della Falls	Canada	440	1,443
Gavarnie	France	422	1,385
Skjeggedal	Norway	420	1,378
Glass Falls	Brazil	404	1,325
Krimml	Austria	400	1,312
Trummelbach Falls	Switzerland	400	1,312
Silver Strand Falls, Yosemite	USA	357	1,170
Wallaman, Stony Creek	Australia	346	1,137
Wollomombi	Australia	335	1,100
Cusiana River Falls	Colombia	300	984
Giessbach	Switzerland	300	984
Skykkjedalsfossen	Norway	300	984
Staubbach	Switzerland	300	984

Waterbury /'wɔːtəbəri/ city in W Connecticut, USA, on the Naugatuck river; population (1980) 103,000. Poducts include clocks, watches, brass and copper ware, and plastics. It was founded 1674.

water closet (WC) flushing lavatory that works by siphon action. The first widely used WC was produced in the 1770s by Alexander Cummings in London. The modern type dates from Davis Bostel's invention of 1889, which featured a ballcock valve system to refill the flushing cistern.

watercolour painting method of painting with pigments mixed with water, known in China as early as the 3rd century. The art as practised today began in England with the work of Paul Sandby (1725–1809). Other excellent European watercolourists were Turner and Cézanne. The Royal Society of Painters in Water Colours was founded 1804.

The technique of watercolour painting requires great skill since its transparency rules out overpainting, and many artists prefer acrylic paint which, as well as drying rapidly, is easier to handle.

watercress perennial aquatic plant *Nasturtium officinale*, found in Europe and Asia, and cultivated as a salad crop. It requires 4.5 million litres/1 million gallons of running water daily per hectare/2.5 acres in cultivation.

water cycle in ecology, the natural circulation of water through the ◊biosphere. Water is lost from the Earth's surface to the atmosphere either by evaporation from the surface of lakes, rivers, and oceans or through the transpiration of plants. This atmospheric water forms clouds that condense to deposit moisture on the land and sea as rain or snow.

waterfall a cascade of water in a stream or river, which occurs when an area of underlying soft rock has been eroded to form a steep, vertical drop. As the river ages, continuing erosion causes the waterfall to move upstream and lose height until it becomes a series of rapids, and eventually disappears.

waterflea any aquatic crustacean in the order Cladocera, of which there are over 400 species. The commonest species is *Daphnia pulex*.

Waterford /'wɔːtəfəd/ county in Munster province, Republic of Ireland; area 1,840 sq km/710 sq mi; population (1986) 91,000. The county town is Waterford. The county includes the rivers Suir and Blackwater, and the Comeragh and Monavallagh mountain ranges in the north and centre. Products include cattle, beer, whiskey, and glassware.

Waterford /'wɔːtəfəd/ port and county town of County Waterford, SE Republic of Ireland, on the Suir; population (1986) 41,000. Handmade Waterford crystal glass (34% lead content instead of the normal 24%) was made here until 1851 and again from 1951.

waterfowl order of birds, Anseriformes, which includes ducks, geese, and swans.

water gas fuel gas consisting of a mixture of carbon monoxide and hydrogen, made by passing steam over red-hot coke. The gas was once the chief source of hydrogen for chemical syntheses such as the Haber process for making ammonia, but has been largely superseded in this and other reactions by hydrogen obtained from natural gas.

Watergate /'wɔːtəgeɪt/ US political scandal, named after the building in Washington DC that housed the Democrats' campaign headquarters in the 1972 presidential election. Five men, hired by the Republican Committee to Re-elect the President (CREEP), were caught inside the Watergate with electronic surveillance equipment. Over the next two years, investigation by the media and a Senate committee revealed that the White House was implicated in the break-in, and that there was a 'slush fund', used to finance unethical activities. In Aug 1974, President ◊Nixon was forced to surrender to Congress tape recordings of conversations he had held with administration officials, and these indicated his complicity in a cover-up. Nixon resigned, the only president to have left office through resignation.

water glass common name for the colourless, jellylike substance sodium metasilicate (Na_2SiO_3). It dissolves readily in water to give a solution that is used for preserving eggs and fireproofing porous materials such as cloth, paper, and wood. It is also used as an adhesive for paper and card, and in the manufacture of soap and silica gel, a substance that absorbs moisture.

water, hardness of a term used to describe the inability of some water to form a lather with soap, and the production of 'fur' or 'scale' in kettles. It is caused by the presence of certain salts of calcium and magnesium.

Temporary hardness is due to hydrogen carbonates which, on boiling, are converted to insoluble carbonates to give scale in kettles. *Permanent hardness* is due to sulphates and silicates, which are not affected by boiling, but can be removed by using a water softener.

Waterhouse /'wɔːtəhaʊs/ Alfred 1830–1905. English architect. He was a leading exponent of Victorian Neo-Gothic using, typically, multicoloured tiles and bricks. His works include the Natural History Museum in London 1868.

water hyacinth tropical aquatic plant *Eichhornia crassipes* of the family Pontederiaceae. In one growing season 25 plants can produce 2 million plants. It is liable to choke waterways, depleting the water of nutrients and blocking the sunlight, but is valued as a purifier of sewage-polluted water, and is used in making methane gas, compost, concentrated protein, paper, and baskets. Originating in South America, it now grows in more than 50 countries.

water lily aquatic plant of the family Nymphaeaceae. The fleshy roots are embedded in mud and the large round leaves float on the water. The cup-shaped flowers may be white, pink, yellow, or blue. The white *Nymphaea alba* and yellow *Nuphar lutea* are common in Europe, and *Victoria regia*, with leaves about 2 m/6 ft in diameter, occurs in the Amazon, South America.

Waterloo, Battle of /ˌwɔːtəˈluː/ battle on 18 June 1815 in which the British commander Wellington defeated the French emperor Napoleon near the village of Waterloo, 13 km/8 mi S of Brussels, Belgium. Wellington had 68,000 men, of whom 24,000 were British, the remainder being German, Dutch, and Belgian, and Napoleon had 72,000. During the last stage of the battle Wellington was supported by the Prussians under Gen Blücher.

Waterloo Cup the principal greyhound race in England, known as the 'courser's Derby'. Staged at Altcar, near Formby, Merseyside, each year, it is named after the nearby Waterloo Hotel whose proprietor originated the race in 1936.

It is also the name of the trophy given to the winner of the *Waterloo Handicap*, a crown green bowls competition held at the Waterloo Hotel, Blackpool, every year.

water meadow an irrigated meadow. By flooding the land for part of each year, increased yields of hay are obtained. Water meadows were common in Italy, Switzerland, and England (from 1523).

watermelon large, pink-fleshed ◊melon with a green rind, native to tropical Africa and widely cultivated.

water mill a machine that harnesses the energy in flowing water to produce mechanical power, typically for milling (grinding) grain. Water from a stream is directed against the paddles of a water wheel and makes it turn. Simple gearing transfers this motion to the millstones. The modern equivalent of the water wheel is the water turbine, used in ◊hydroelectric power plants.

The familiar vertical water wheel came into widespread use in Roman times. There were two types: **undershot**, in which the wheel simply dipped into the stream; and the more powerful **overshot**, in which the water was directed at the top of the wheel. The Domesday Book records over 7,000 water mills in Britain. Water wheels remained the prime source of mechanical power until the development of a reliable steam engine in the 1700s, not only for milling, but also for metalworking, crushing and grinding operations, and driving machines in the early factories.

water pollution see ◊pollution, ◊water, ◊leaching, and ◊sewage disposal.

water polo a water sport developed in England 1869, originally called 'soccer-in-water'. The aim is to score goals, as in soccer, at each end of a swimming pool.

An inflated ball is passed among the players, who must swim around the pool without touching the bottom. A goal is scored when the ball is thrown past the goalkeeper and into the net. The Swimming Association of Great Britain recognized the game 1885. World championships were first held 1973; they are held during the world swimming championships.

water polo

World Champions

1973	Hungary
1975	USSR
1978	Italy
1982	USSR
1986	Yugoslavia

water skiing a watersport in which a person is towed across water on a ski or skis, wider than those used for skiing on snow, by means of a rope (23 m/75 ft long) attached to a speedboat. Competitions are held for overall performances, slalom, tricks, and jumping.

The first person known to have 'danced on water' on a wooden plank was Eliseo of Tarentum in the 14th century. Ralph Samuelson (USA) pioneered the sport as it is known today in 1922. The governing body, the Union Internationale de Ski Nautique, was founded in 1946.

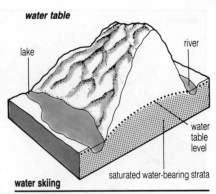

water table

lake　　　　　　　　river

water table level

saturated water-bearing strata

water skiing

World Champions
men–overall

1971	George Athans *(Canada)*
1973	George Athans *(Canada)*
1975	Carlos Suarez *(Venezuela)*
1977	Mike Hazelwood *(Great Britain)*
1979	Joel McClintock *(Canada)*
1981	Sammy Duvall *(USA)*
1983	Sammy Duvall *(USA)*
1985	Sammy Duvall *(USA)*
1987	Sammy Duvall *(USA)*
1989	Patrice Martin *(France)*

women–overall

1971	Christy Weir *(USA)*
1973	Lisa St John *(USA)*
1975	Liz Allan-Shetter *(USA)*
1977	Cindy Todd *(USA)*
1979	Cindy Todd *(USA)*
1981	Karin Roberge *(USA)*
1983	Ana-Maria Carrasco *(Venezuela)*
1985	Karen Neville *(Australia)*
1987	Deena Brush *(USA)*
1989	Deena Mapple (née Brush) *(USA)*

water softener a substance or unit that removes the hardness from water. Hardness is caused by the presence of calcium and magnesium ions, which combine with soap to form an insoluble scum and prevent lathering, and cause pipes and kettles to fur up. A water softener replaces these ions by sodium ions, which are fully soluble and cause no scum.

water table level of ground below which the rocks are saturated with water. Thus above the water table water will drain downwards, and where the water table cuts the surface of the ground a spring results. The water table usually follows surface contours, and it varies with rainfall.

Waterton /'wɔːtətən/ Charles 1783–1865. British naturalist who travelled extensively in South and North America 1804–24. In the UK, he was the first person to protest against pollution from industry, and created a nature reservation around his home in Yorkshire.

Watford /'wɒtfəd/ industrial town (printing, engineering, and electronics) in Hertfordshire, SE England; dormitory town for London; population (1986) 77,000.

Watkins /'wɒtkɪnz/ Henry George (Gino) 1907–1932. English polar explorer whose expeditions in Labrador and Greenland helped to open up an Arctic air route during the 1930s. He was drowned in a kayak accident while leading an expedition in Greenland.

Watling Street a Roman road running from London to Wroxeter (*Viroconium*) near Chester, NW England. Its name derives from *Waetlingacaester*, the Anglo-Saxon name for St Albans, through which it passed.

Watson /'wɒtsən/ James Dewey 1928– . US biologist whose researches on the molecular structure of DNA (the genetic code), in collaboration with Francis ◊Crick, earned him a shared Nobel prize 1962.

Watson /'wɒtsən/ John B(roadus) 1878–1958. US psychologist, founder of behaviourism. He rejected introspection (observation by an individual

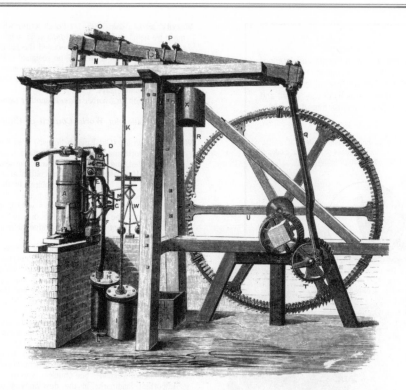

Watt *Drawing published 1865 in Samuel Smiles's* Lives of Boulton and Watt *of James Watt's prototype steam engine, Old Bess. In this engine, reciprocating motion was turned to rotary motion by a sun-and-planet gear train.*

of his or her own mental processes) and regarded psychology as the study of observable behaviour, within the scientific tradition.

Watson /'wɒtsən/ 'Tom' (Thomas Sturgess) 1949– . US golfer. In 1988 he succeeded Jack ◊Nicklaus as the game's biggest money winner, but was overtaken by Tom Kite in 1989.

Watson, born in Kansas City, turned professional in 1971 and has won more than 30 tournaments on the US Tour, including the Masters and US Open, and the British Open a record five times.

CAREER HIGHLIGHTS

US Open: 1982
British Open: 1975, 1977, 1980, 1982–83
US Masters: 1977, 1981
US Ryder Cup team: 1977, 1981, 1983, 1989

Watson-Watt /'wɒtsən 'wɒt/ Robert Alexander 1892–1973. Scottish physicist who developed a forerunner of ◊radar. During a long career in government service (1915–1952) he proposed in 1935 a method of radiolocation of aircraft—a key factor in Britain's victory in World War II.

watt SI unit (symbol W) of power (the rate of expenditure or consumption of energy). A lightbulb may use 40, 100, or 150 watts of power; an electric heater will use several kilowatts (thousands of watts).

The absolute watt is defined as the power used when 1 joule of work is done in 1 second. In electrical terms, the flow of 1 amp of current through a conductor whose ends are at a potential difference of 1 volt uses 1 watt of power (watts = volts × amps). It is named after the British scientist James Watt.

Watt /wɒt/ James 1736–1819. Scottish engineer who developed the steam engine. He made ◊Newcomen's steam engine vastly more efficient by cooling the used steam in a condenser separate from the main cylinder.

Steam engines incorporating governors, sun-and-planet gears, and other devices of his invention were successfully built by him in partnership with Matthew Boulton, and were vital to the ◊Industrial Revolution.

Watteau /'wɒtəʊ/ Jean-Antoine 1684–1721. French Rococo painter. He developed a new category of genre painting known as the *fête galante*, scenes of a kind of aristocratic pastoral fantasy world. One of these pictures, *The Embarkation for Cythera* 1717 (Louvre, Paris), won him membership of the French Academy.

Watteau was born in Valenciennes. At first inspired by Flemish genre painters, he produced tavern and military scenes. His early years in Paris, from 1702, introduced him to fashionable French paintings and in particular to decorative styles and theatrical design. He was also influenced by ◊Giorgione and ◊Rubens.

wattle certain species of acacia in Australia, where its fluffy golden flowers are the national emblem. Adapted to drought conditions, the tough leaves further avoid loss of water through transpiration by turning their edges to the direct rays of

Watteau Gilles and his family *(c. 1717), Wallace Collection, London.*

the sun. Wattles are used for tanning and in fencing.

wattle and daub a method of constructing walls consisting of upright stakes bound together with withes (strong flexible shoots or twigs, usually of willow), and covered in mud or plaster. It was the usual way of building houses in the Middle Ages.

Watts /wɒts/ George Frederick 1817–1904. English painter and sculptor. He painted allegorical, biblical, and classical subjects, investing his work with a solemn morality. Many of his portraits are in the National Portrait Gallery, London.

Born in London, he studied in the Royal Academy schools. In 1864 he married actress Ellen Terry; later the marriage was dissolved. As a sculptor he executed *Physical Energy* for Rhodes's memorial in South Africa; a replica is in Kensington Gardens, London.

Watts /wɒts/ Isaac 1674–1748. English Nonconformist writer of hymns, including 'O God, our help in ages past'.

Waugh /wɔː/ Evelyn (Arthur St John) 1903–1966. English novelist. He made his name with social satire, for example *Decline and Fall* 1928, *Vile Bodies* 1930, and *The Loved One* 1948. A Roman Catholic convert from 1930, he developed a serious concern with such issues in *Brideshead Revisited* 1945. *The Ordeal of Gilbert Pinfold* 1957 is largely autobiographical.

wave in physics, a disturbance travelling through a medium (or space). There are two types: in a *longitudinal wave* (such as a ◊sound wave) the disturbance is parallel to the wave's direction of travel; in a *transverse wave* (such as an ◊electromagnetic wave) it is perpendicular. The medium (for example the Earth, for seismic waves) is not permanently displaced by the passage of a wave.

wave in the oceans, the formation of a ridge or swell by wind or other causes. Freak or 'episodic' waves form under particular weather conditions at certain times of the year, travelling long distances in the Atlantic, Indian, and Pacific oceans. They are considered responsible for the sudden disappearance, without distress calls, of many ships. A ◊tsunami is a type of freak wave.

Freak waves become extremely dangerous when they reach the shallow waters of the continental shelves at 100 fathoms (180 m/600 ft), especially when they meet currents, for example, the Agulhas Current to the E of South Africa, and the Gulf Stream in the N Atlantic. A wave height of 34 m/112 ft has been recorded.

wavelength the distance between successive crests of a ◊wave. The wavelength of a light wave determines its colour; red light has a wavelength of about 700 nanometres, for example. The complete range of wavelengths of electromagnetic waves is called the electromagnetic ◊spectrum.

Wavell /'weɪvəl/ Archibald, 1st Earl Wavell 1883–1950. British field marshal in World War II, appointed commander in chief Middle East July 1939. He conducted the North African war against Italy 1940–41, and achieved successes there as well as in Ethiopia. He was transferred as commander in chief in India July 1941, and was viceroy 1943–47.

wave power power obtained by harnessing the energy of water waves. Various schemes have been advanced since 1973, when oil prices rose dramatically and an energy shortage threatened. In 1974 the British engineer Stephen Salter developed the duck, a floating boom whose segments nod up and down with the waves. The nodding motion can be used to drive pumps and spin generators. Another device, developed in Japan, uses an oscillating water column to harness wave power.

Waverley /'weɪvəli/ John Anderson, 1st Viscount Waverley 1882–1958. British administrator. He organized civil defence for World War II, becoming home secretary and minister for home security in 1939 (the nationally distributed *Anderson shelters*, home outdoor air-raid shelters, were named

weathering

Frost, wind, rain and sunshine all have a part to play in the gradual wearing away of the landscape. As soon as an area of rock is exposed on the surface of the Earth, it is attacked over time by the weather, which reduces it to sand and rubble. This material is carried downwards by gravity, rivers and glaciers and redeposited in low areas. Eventually it may be turned back into solid rock.

Frost shattering produces spiky peaks.

In mountainous areas the water that collects in rock cracks freezes regularly. As it does so. it expands, forcing the rocks apart.

A combination of temperature, moisture and chemical effects can wear away the outer skin of a rock. As a result it may peel off, layer by layer. This process is known as onion-skin weathering.

The debris broken off the peaks by the frost piles up as slopes of scree.

Soft soil may be washed away by the rain. Where a boulder provides protection only the surrounding soil may be washed away, leaving the boulder on a soil pedestal.

The debris produced by weathering forms the basis of soil. It can work its way downhill in a process known as soil creep, causing trees to bend and posts to lean.

The carbon dioxide in rainwater produces weak carbonic acid. This reacts with some minerals, and causes spheroidal weathering of dolerite, the opening up of cracks called grykes in limestone, and the decay of granite into china clay.

Soil creep may give rise to a stepped appearance – terracettes – on a hillside.

after him). He was chancellor of the Exchequer 1943–45.

wax solid fatty substance of animal, vegetable, or mineral origin. The most important modern waxes are mineral waxes obtained from petroleum. They vary in hardness from the soft petroleum jelly (or petrolatum) used in ointments to the hard paraffin wax employed for making candles and waxed paper for drinks cartons.

Animal waxes include beeswax, the wool wax lanolin, and spermaceti from sperm whale oil; they are used mainly in cosmetics, ointments, and polishes. Another important animal wax is tallow, a form of suet once widely used to make candles and soap.

Vegetable waxes, which usually occur as a water-proof coating on plants that grow in hot, arid regions, include carnauba wax (from the leaves of the carnauba palm) and candelilla wax, both of which are components of hard polishes such as car wax. Sealing wax is made from lac or shellac, a resinous substance also obtained from plants.

waxbill small African seed-eating bird, genus *Estrilda*. Waxbills grow to 15 cm/6 in long, are brown and grey with yellow, red or brown markings, and have waxy-looking red or pink beaks. They sometimes raise the young of ◊whydahs, who lay their eggs in the waxbill's nest.

waxwing bird *Bombycilla garrulus* found in the northern hemisphere. It is about 18 cm/7 in long, and is greyish brown above with a reddish-chestnut crest, black streak at the eye, and variegated wings. It undertakes mass migrations in some years.

wayfaring tree shrub *Viburnum lantana*, with clusters of fragrant white flowers, found on limy soils.

Wayne /weɪn/ Anthony 1745–1796. American general who founded ◊Fort Wayne, USA.

Wayne /weɪn/ John ('Duke'). Stage name of Marion Morrison 1907–1979. US film actor who was the archetypal western star. His films include *Stagecoach* 1939 and *True Grit* 1969.

Waziristan /wəˈzɪərɪˈstɑːn/ mountainous territory in Pakistan, on the border with Afghanistan, inhabited by Waziris and Mahsuds.

Wazyk /'væzɪk/ Adam 1905– . Polish writer who made his name with *Poem for Adults* 1955, a protest against the regime that preceded the fall of the Stalinists in 1956. In 1957 he resigned with others from the Communist Party, disappointed by First Secretary Gomulka's illiberalism. He also wrote novels and plays.

w.c. abbreviation for ◊*water closet*, another name for a toilet.

WCC abbreviation for *World Council of Churches*.

Weald, the /wiːld/ (Old English 'forest') area between the North and South Downs, England, once thickly wooded, and forming part of Kent, Sussex, Surrey, and Hampshire. Now an agricultural area, it produces fruit, hops, and vegetables. In the Middle Ages, its timber and iron ore made it the industrial heart of England, and its oaks were used in shipbuilding. The name often refers only to the area of Kent SW of the greensand ridge running from Hythe to Westerham.

weapon an implement used for attack and defence, from simple clubs and bows and arrows in prehistoric times to machine guns and nuclear bombs in modern times. The first revolution in warfare came with the invention of ◊gunpowder and the development of handguns and cannons. Many other weapons now exist, such as grenades, shells, torpedoes, rockets, and guided missiles. The ultimate in explosive weapons are the atomic (fission) and hydrogen (fusion) bombs. They release the enormous energy produced when atoms split or fuse together. There are also chemical and bacteriological weapons. See ◊nuclear warfare.

Important landmarks in the development of weapons include:

11th century gunpowder in use by the Chinese;
13th century gunpowder known in the West (described in 1242 by Roger Bacon);
c.1300 guns invented by the Arabs, with bamboo muzzles reinforced with iron;
1346 Battle of Crécy, in which gunpowder was probably used in battle for the first time;
1376 Venice used explosive shells;
17th century widespread use of guns and cannon in the Thirty Years' War and English Civil War;
1800 Henry Shrapnel invented shrapnel for the British army;
1863 TNT discovered by German chemist J Wilbrand;
1867 dynamite patented by Alfred Nobel;
1915 poison gas (chlorine) used for the first time by the Germans in World War I;
1916 tanks used for the first time by the British at Cambrai;
1945 first test explosion of atom bomb;
1954–73 Vietnam War, use of chemical warfare (defoliants and other substances) by the USA;
1973 rapid Egyptian initial advance made possible in the Fourth Arab-Israeli War by electronically operated targeting devices;
1982 Falklands conflict: Argentinians sank British destroyer with French Exocet missile fired from an aircraft;

Wayne US film actor John Wayne in The Man Who Shot Liberty Valance, Dec 1961.

weathering

Physical weathering

temperature changes	weakening rocks by expansion and contraction
frost	wedging rocks apart by the expansion of water on freezing
rain	making loose slopes unstable
wind	wearing away rocks by sandblasting, and moving sand dunes along
unloading	the loosening of rock layers by release of pressure after the erosion and removal of those layers above

Chemical weathering

carbonation	the breakdown of calcite by reaction with carbonic acid in rainwater
hydrolysis	the breakdown of feldspar into china clay by reaction with carbonic acid in rainwater
oxidation	the breakdown of iron-rich minerals due to rusting
hydration	the expansion of certain minerals due to the uptake of water

Gravity

soil creep	the slow downslope movement of surface material
landslide	the rapid downward movement of solid material
avalanche	scouring by ice, snow, and accumulated debris

Rivers

| abrasion | wearing away stream beds and banks by trundling boulders along |
| corrasion | the wear on the boulders themselves as they are carried along |

Glaciers

| deepening | of valleys by the weight of ice |
| scouring | of rock surfaces by embedded rocky debris |

Sea

hydraulic effect	expansion of air pockets in rocks and cliffs by constant hammering by waves
abrasion	see *Rivers* above
corrasion	see *Rivers* above

1983 Star Wars or Strategic Defence Initiative to develop space laser and particle-beam weapons, supposedly as a defence umbrella against ballistic missiles, announced by USA.

Wear /wɪə/ river in NE England; length 107 km/ 67 mi. From its source in the Pennines it flows E past Durham to meet the North Sea at Sunderland.

weasel mammal of the family Mustelidae, which feeds mainly on mice, voles, and rats. It has a long body (20 cm/8 in, with 5 cm/2 in tail) and neck, short ears and legs, and dense fur, brownish above and white below. It is found in Eurasia, N Africa, and the Americas.

The weasel *Mustela nivalis* of Europe and Asia becomes white in winter in cold climates as camouflage against snow.

weather the day-to-day variations of meteorological and climatic conditions at a particular place. See ◊meteorology and ◊climate.

weather areas divisions of the sea around the British Isles for the purpose of weather forecasting for shipping. They are used to indicate where strong and gale-force winds are expected.

weathering process by which exposed rocks are broken down by the action of rain, frost, wind, and other elements of the weather. Two types of weathering are recognized: physical and chemical. They usually occur together.

Physical weathering involves such effects as: frost wedging, in which water trapped in a crack in a rock expands on freezing and splits the rock; sand blasting, in which exposed rock faces are worn away by sand particles blown by

weaver

the wind; and ◊soil creep, in which soil particles gradually move downhill under the influence of gravity.

Chemical weathering is a process by which carbon dioxide in the atmosphere combines with rainwater to produce weak carbonic acid, which may then react with certain minerals in the rocks and break them down. Examples are the solution of caverns in limestone terrains, and the breakdown of feldspars in granite to form china clay or kaolin, thus loosening the other minerals present—quartz and mica—which are washed away as sand.

Although physical and chemical weathering normally occur together, in some instances it is difficult to determine which type is involved. For example, onion-skin weathering, which produces rounded ◊inselbergs in arid regions, such as Ayers Rock in central Australia, may be caused by the daily physical expansion and contraction of the surface layers of the rock in the heat of the Sun, or by the chemical reaction of the minerals just

beneath the surface during the infrequent rains of these areas.

weaver any small bird of the family Ploceidae, mostly about 15 cm/6 in long; the group includes the house sparrow. The majority of weavers are African, a few Asian. The males use grasses to weave elaborate globular nests in bushes and trees. Males are often more brightly coloured than females.

Many kinds are polygamous, so build several nests, and some species build large communal nests with many chambers. One species, the **quelea** *Quelea quelea*, lives and breeds in huge flocks that migrate to follow food sources. Their destructive power can equal that of locusts.

weaving the production of ◊textile fabric by means of a loom. The basic process is the interlacing at right angles of longitudinal threads (the warp) and crosswise threads (the weft), the latter being carried across from one side of the loom to the other by a type of bobbin called the shuttle.

The technique of weaving has been used all over the world since ancient times and more recently been mechanized. Hand looms are still used, for example in the manufacture of tweeds in the British Isles. They may be horizontal or vertical; industrial looms are generally vertical. Of great importance in the hand-loom era was the ◊Jacquard machine, the last in a series of inventions for producing complicated designs, which was perfected in the early 19th century. The power loom 1786 was essentially the invention of an English clergyman, Edmund ◊Cartwright. The speed limitations caused by the slow passage of the shuttle have been partly overcome by the use of water- and air-jet insertion methods, and by the development in the 1970s of 'multiphase' looms in which weft is inserted in continuous waves across the machine, rather than one weft at a time.

Webb /web/ Aston 1849–1930. British architect. His work in London includes the front of Buckingham Palace, Admiralty Arch, and the chief section of the Victoria and Albert Museum.

Webb /web/ (Martha) Beatrice (born Potter) 1858–1943 and Sidney (James), Baron Passfield 1859–1947. English social reformers, writers, and founders of the London School of Economics 1895. They argued for social insurance in their minority report (1909) of the Poor Law Commission, and wrote many influential books, including *The History of Trade Unionism* 1894, *English Local Government* 1906, and *Soviet Communism* 1935. Sidney Webb was professor of public administration at the LSE 1912–27. He was a member of the Labour Party executive 1915–25, entered Parliament

weaving loom

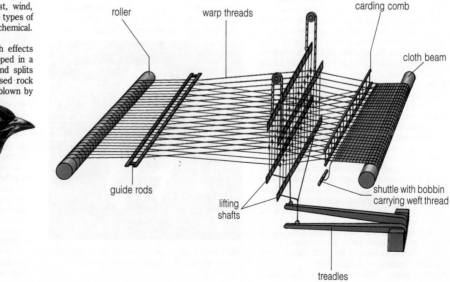

roller · warp threads · carding comb · cloth beam · guide rods · lifting shafts · shuttle with bobbin carrying weft thread · treadles

Webb *English socialist Beatrice Webb.*

1922, and was president of the Board of Trade 1924, dominions secretary 1929–30, and colonial secretary 1929–31. He received a peerage 1929. Beatrice also wrote *The Co-operative Movement in Great Britain* 1891, *My Apprenticeship* 1926, and *Our Partnership* 1948. They were early members of the ◊Fabian Society, and were married 1892.

Webb /web/ Mary 1882–1927. English novelist. Born in Shropshire, she wrote of country life and characters, for example in *Precious Bane* 1924, which became known through a recommendation by Stanley Baldwin.

Webb /web/ Philip (Speakman) 1831–1915. English architect. He mostly designed private houses, including the Red House, Bexley Heath, Sussex, for William ◊Morris, and was one of the leading figures, with Richard Norman ◊Shaw and C F A ◊Voysey, in the revival of domestic English architecture in the late 19th century.

Webber /'webə/ Andrew Lloyd. British composer of musicals; see ◊Lloyd Webber.

weber SI unit (symbol Wb) of ◊magnetic flux (the magnetic field strength multiplied by the area through which the field passes). One weber = 10 ◊maxwells.

A change of flux at a uniform rate of 1 weber per second in an electrical coil with 1 turn produces an electromotive force of 1 volt in the coil.

Weber /'veɪbə/ Carl Maria Friedrich Ernst von 1786–1826. German composer who established the Romantic school of opera with *Der Freischütz* 1821 and *Euryanthe* 1823. He was *Kapellmeister* at Breslau 1804–06, Prague 1813–16, and Dresden 1816. He died during a visit to London where he produced his opera *Oberon* 1826, written for the Covent Garden theatre.

Weber /'veɪbə/ Ernst 1795–1878. German physicist whose work formed the basis of the Weber-Fechner law.

Weber /'veɪbə/ Max 1864–1920. German sociologist, one of the founders of modern sociology. He emphasized cultural and political factors as key influences on economic development and individual behaviour.

Weber argued for a scientific and value-free approach to research, yet highlighted the importance of meaning and consciousness in understanding social action. His ideas continue to stimulate modern thought on social stratification, power, organizations, law, and religion.

Key works include *The Protestant Ethic and the Spirit of Capitalism* 1902, *Economy and Society* 1922, *The Methodology of the Social Sciences* 1949, and *The Sociology of Religion* 1920.

Weber /'veɪbə/ Wilhelm Eduard 1804–1891.

German physicist, who studied magnetism and electricity. Working with Karl Gauss, he made sensitive magnetometers to measure magnetic fields, and instruments to measure direct and alternating currents. He also built an electric telegraph. The SI unit of magnetic flux, the weber, is named after him.

Webern /'veɪbən/ Anton (Friedrich Wilhelm von) 1883–1945. Austrian composer. A pupil of ◊Schoenberg, whose 12-tone technique he adopted. He wrote works of extreme brevity; for example, the oratorio *Das Augenlicht* 1935, and songs to words by Stefan George and poems of Rilke.

Webster /'webstə/ Daniel 1782–1852. US politician and orator, born in New Hampshire. He sat in the House of Representatives from 1813 and in the Senate from 1827, at first as a Federalist and later as a Whig. He was secretary of state 1841–43 and 1850–52, and negotiated the Ashburton Treaty 1842, which fixed the Maine–Canada boundary. His celebrated 'seventh of March' speech in the Senate in 1850 helped secure a compromise on the slavery issue.

Webster /'webstə/ John *c.*1580–1634. English dramatist, who ranks after Shakespeare as the greatest tragedian of his time and is the Jacobean whose plays are most frequently performed today. His two great plays *The White Devil* 1608 and *The Duchess of Malfi* 1614 are dark, violent tragedies obsessed with death and decay and infused with poetic brilliance.

Webster /'webstə/ Noah 1758–1843. US lexicographer, whose books on grammar and spelling and *American Dictionary of the English Language* 1828 standardized US English.

Weddell /wedl/ James 1787–1834. British Antarctic explorer. In 1823, he reached 75° S latitude and 35° W longitude. The Weddell Sea is named after him.

Weddell Sea /wedl/ an arm of the S Atlantic Ocean that cuts into the Antarctic continent SE of Cape Horn; area 8,000,000 sq km/3,000,000 sq mi. Much of it is covered with thick pack ice for most of the year. It is named after the British explorer James Weddell.

Wedekind /'veɪdəkɪnt/ Frank 1864–1918. German dramatist. He was a forerunner of Expressionism with *Frühlings Erwachen/The Awakening of Spring* 1891, and *Der Erdgeist/The Earth Spirit* 1895 and its sequel *Der Marquis von Keith*. *Die Büchse der Pandora/Pandora's Box* 1904 was the source for Berg's opera *Lulu*.

wedge a block of triangular cross-section which can be used as a simple machine. An axe is a wedge; it splits wood by redirecting the energy of the downward blow sideways, where it exerts the force needed to split the wood.

Wedgwood /'wedʒwʊd/ C(icely) V(eronica) 1910– . British historian. An authority on the 17th century, she has published studies of

Webb *Sidney Webb, who, in partnership with his wife Beatrice, influenced the early socialist movement in Britain.*

weevil *Electron microscope picture of a grain weevil emerging from a wheat grain.*

Cromwell 1939 and *The Trial of Charles I* 1964. Created Dame of the British Empire 1968, she was awarded the Order of Merit 1969.

Wedgwood /'wedʒwʊd/ Josiah 1730–1795. English pottery manufacturer. He set up business in Burslem, Staffordshire, in the early 1760s, to produce his unglazed blue or green stoneware decorated with white Neo-Classical designs, using pigments of his own invention.

weedkiller or ***herbicide*** chemical that kills some or all plants. Selective herbicides are effective with cereal crops, as they kill all broad-leaved plants without affecting the grasslike leaves. Those that kill all plants include sodium chlorate and ◊paraquat; see also ◊Agent Orange. The widespread use of weedkillers in agriculture has led to a dramatic increase in crop yield but also to pollution of ◊water supplies.

weever fish European fish, genus *Trachinus*, with poison glands on dorsal fin and gill cover that can give a painful sting. It grows up to 5 cm/2 in long, has eyes near the top of its head, and lives on sandy seabeds.

weevil superfamily of beetles, Curculionoidea, in the order Coleoptera. Weevils are usually less than 6 mm/0.25 in long. The head has a prolonged rostrum, which is used for boring into plant stems and trees for feeding, and in the female's case for depositing eggs.

The larvae are white; the adult beetles of *Phyllobius* and *Polydrusus*, the common British genera, are bright green. They feed on vegetable matter. The grain weevil *Sitophilus granarius* is a serious pest and the cotton-boll weevil *Anthonomus grandis* damages cotton crops.

Wegener /'veɪgənə/ Alfred Lothar 1880–1930. German meteorologist and geophysicist, whose theory of ◊continental drift, expounded in *Origin of Continents and Oceans* 1915, was originally known as Wegener's hypothesis. His ideas can now be explained in terms of ◊plate tectonics.

weight the force exerted on an object by ◊gravity. The weight of an object depends on its mass—the amount of material in it—and the strength of the Earth's gravitational pull, which decreases with height. Consequently, an object weighs less at the top of a mountain than at sea level. On the Moon, an object weighs only one-sixth of its weight on Earth, because the pull of the Moon's gravity is one-sixth that of the Earth.

weightlessness condition in which there is no gravitational force acting on a body, either because gravitational force is cancelled out by equal and opposite acceleration, or because the body is so far outside a planet's gravitational field that it exerts no force upon it.

weightlifting the sport of lifting the heaviest possible weight above one's head to the satisfaction of judges. In international competitions there are two standard lifts: **snatch** and **jerk**.

In the *snatch*, the bar and weights are lifted from the floor to a position with the arms outstretched and above the head in one continuous movement. The arms must be locked for two seconds for the lift to be good. The *jerk* is a two-movement lift: from the floor to the chest, and from the chest to the outstretched position. The aggregate weight of the two lifts counts. The International Weightlifting Federation was formed 1920, although a world championship was first held 1891.

weightlifting: recent winners

weight	1987 world champions
52 kg	Sevdalin Marinov (Bulgaria)
56 kg	Nerno Terziiski (Bulgaria)
60 kg	Stefan Topurov (Bulgaria)
67.5 kg	Michail Petrov (Bulgaria)
75 kg	Borislav Guidikov (Bulgaria)
82.5 kg	L Barsi (Hungary)
90 kg	Anatoliy Khrapati (USSR)
100 kg	Pavel Kouznetsov (USSR)
110 kg	Yuriy Zacharovich (USSR)
110+ kg	Alexandre Kurlovich (USSR)
	1988 Olympic champions
52 kg	Sevdalin Marinov (Bulgaria)
56 kg	Oxen Mirzoian (USSR)
60 kg	Naim Suleymanoglu (Turkey)
67.5 kg	Joachim Kunz (East Germany)
75 kg	Borislav Guidikov (Bulgaria)
82.5 kg	Israil Arsanmakov (USSR)
90 kg	Anatoliy Khrapati (USSR)
100 kg	Pavel Kouznetsov (USSR)
110 kg	Yuriy Zacharovich (USSR)
110 kg	Alexandre Kurlovich (USSR).

weights and measures see under ◊c.g.s. system, ◊f.p.s. system, ◊MKS system, ◊SI units.

Weihai /ˈweɪˈhaɪ/ commercial port (textiles, rubber articles, matches, soap, vegetable oils) in Shandong, China; population about 220,000. It was leased to Britain 1898–1930, during which time it was a naval and coaling station; occupied by Japan 1938–45.

Weil /veɪ/ Simone 1909–1943. French writer, who became a practising Catholic after a mystical experience in 1938. Apart from essays, her works (advocating political passivity) were posthumously published, including *Waiting for God* 1951, *The Need for Roots* 1952, and *Notebooks* 1956.

Weill /vaɪl/ Kurt (Julian) 1900–1950. German composer, US citizen from 1943. He wrote chamber and orchestral music and collaborated with ◊Brecht on operas such as *Die Dreigroschenoper/The Threepenny Opera* 1928 and *Aufsteig und Fall der Stadt Mahagonny/The Rise and Fall of the City of Mahagonny* 1930, all attacking social corruption (*Mahagonny* caused a riot at its premiere in Leipzig). He tried to evolve a new form of ◊music theatre, using subjects with a contemporary relevance and the simplest musical means. In 1935 he left Germany for the USA, where he wrote a number of successful scores for Broadway, among them the antiwar musical *Johnny Johnson* 1936 (including the often covered 'September Song') and *Street Scene* 1947 based on an Elmer Rice play of the Depression.

Weil's disease an infectious disease of animals (also known as leptospirosis) which is occasionally transmitted to human beings, usually by contact with water contaminated by rat urine. It is characterized by acute fever, and infection may spread to the liver, kidneys, and heart.

The usual form occurring in humans is caused by a spiral-shaped bacterium that is a common parasite of rats. The condition responds poorly to antibiotics, and death may result.

Weimar /ˈvaɪmɑː/ town in SW East Germany, on the river Elm; population (1980) 64,000. Products include farm machinery and textiles. It was the capital of the grand duchy of Saxe-Weimar 1815–1918; in 1919 the German National Assembly drew up the constitution of the new ◊Weimar Republic here. The writers Goethe, Schiller, and

Weizmann *Chaim Weizmann, Russian-born chemist and Zionist leader. He did scientific work for the UK in both world wars, was head of the Hebrew University in Jerusalem, and in 1948 became the first president of Israel.*

Herder, and the composer Liszt lived in the town; the former concentration camp of Buchenwald is nearby.

Weimar Republic the constitutional republic in Germany 1919–33, which was crippled by the election of antidemocratic parties to the ◊Reichstag, and then subverted by the Nazi leader Hitler after his appointment as Chancellor in 1933. It took its name from the city where in Feb 1919 a constituent assembly met to draw up a democratic constitution.

Weinberg /ˈwaɪnbɜːg/ Steven 1933– . US physicist, who in 1967 demonstrated, together with Abdus ◊Salam, that the weak nuclear force and the electromagnetic force are variations of a single underlying force, now called the electroweak force. Weinberg and Salam shared a Nobel prize with Sheldon ◊Glashow in 1979.

Weinberger /ˈwaɪnbɜːgə/ Caspar (Willard) 1917– . US Republican politician. He served under presidents Nixon and Ford, and was Reagan's defense secretary 1981–87.

weir a low wall built across a river to raise the water level. The oldest surviving weir in England is at Chester, across the river Dee, dating from around 1100.

Weir /wɪə/ Peter 1938– . Australian film director. His films have an atmospheric quality and often contain a strong spiritual element. They include *Picnic at Hanging Rock* 1975, *Witness* 1985, and *Mosquito Coast* 1986.

Weismann /ˈvaɪsmən/ August 1834–1914. German biologist. His failing eyesight forced him to turn from microscopy to theoretic work. In 1892 he proposed that changes to the body do not in turn cause an alteration of the genetic material.

This 'central dogma' of biology remains of vital importance to biologists supporting the Darwinian theory of evolution. If the genetic material can only be altered by chance mutation and recombination, then the Lamarckian view that acquired bodily changes can subsequently be inherited becomes obsolete.

Weismuller /ˈwaɪsmʊlə/ 'Johnny' (Peter John) 1904–1984. US film actor, formerly an Olympic swimmer, who played Tarzan in a long-running series of films for MGM and RKO including *Tarzan the Ape Man* 1932, *Tarzan and His Mate* 1934, and *Tarzan and the Leopard Woman* 1946.

Weizmann /ˈvaɪtsmæn/ Chaim 1874–1952. Zionist leader (president of Israel 1948–52) and chemist,

born in Russia. He became a naturalized British subject, and as director of the Admiralty laboratories 1916–19 discovered a process for manufacturing acetone, a solvent. He conducted the negotiations leading up to the ◊Balfour Declaration. He was head of the Hebrew University in Jerusalem, and in 1948 became the first president of the new republic of Israel.

Weizsäcker /ˈvaɪtsˌzekə/ Richard Freiherr Baron von 1920– . West German Christian Democrat politician, president from 1984. He began his career as a lawyer and was also active in the German Protestant church and in Christian Democratic Union (CDU) party politics. He was elected to the Bundestag in 1969 and served as mayor of West Berlin from 1981, before being elected federal president in 1984.

Welch /welʃ/ (Maurice) Denton 1915–1948. English writer and artist. His works include the novel *In Youth is Pleasure* 1944 and the autobiographical *A Voice Through a Cloud* 1950.

Welch /welʃ/ Raquel. Stage name of Raquel Tejada 1940– . US actress, a sex symbol of the 1960s in such films as *One Million Years BC* 1966, *Myra Breckinridge* 1970, and *The Three Musketeers* 1973.

welding joining pieces of metal (or non-metal) at faces rendered plastic or liquid by heat or pressure (or both). Forge, or hammer welding, employed by blacksmiths since early times, was the only method available until near the end of the 19th century. The principal modern processes are gas and electric-arc welding, in which the heat from a gas flame or an electric arc melts the faces to be joined. Additional 'filler metal' is usually added to the joint.

Resistance welding is another electric method in which the weld is formed by a combination of resistance heating from an electric current, and pressure. Recent developments include electric-slag, electron-beam, high-energy laser, and the still experimental radio-wave energy-beam welding processes.

Weldon /ˈweldən/ Fay 1931– . British novelist and dramatist, whose work deals with feminist themes, often in an ironic or comic manner. Novels include *The Fat Woman's Joke* 1967, *Female Friends* 1975, *Remember Me* 1976, *Puffball* 1980, and *The Life and Loves of a She-Devil* 1984. She has also written plays for the stage, radio, and television.

Welensky /wəˈlenski/ Roy 1907– . Rhodesian right-wing politician. He was instrumental in the creation of a federation of N and S Rhodesia and Nyasaland in 1953 and was prime minister 1956–63. His Federal Party was defeated by Ian Smith's Rhodesian Front in 1964.

Welhaven /ˈvelhɑːvən/ Johan Sebastian Cammermeyer 1807–1873. Norwegian poet, professor of philosophy at Christiania (now Oslo) 1839–68. A supporter of the Dano-Norwegian culture, he is

Welles *US actor and director Orson Welles.*

Wellington *Arthur Wellesley, 1st Duke of Wellington, known as the Iron Duke .*

considered one of the greatest Norwegian masters of poetic form. His works include the satiric *Norges Daemring* 1834.

Welland Ship Canal /'welənd/ Canadian waterway, part of the ◊St Lawrence Seaway, linking Lake Erie to Lake Ontario.

Welles /welz/ (George) Orson 1915–1985. US actor and director. He produced a radio version of H G Wells's novel *The War of the Worlds* 1938, and then produced, directed, and starred in *Citizen Kane* 1941, a landmark in the history of cinema, yet he directed very few films subsequently in Hollywood. Later films as an actor include *The Lady from Shanghai* 1948 and *The Third Man* 1949.

In 1937 he founded the Mercury Theater, New York, with John Houseman, where their repertory productions included a modern-dress version of *Julius Caesar*. The realistic radio broadcast of H G Wells's *The War of the Worlds* in 1938 caused panic and fear of Martian invasion in the USA. He directed the films *Touch of Evil* 1958 and *Chimes at Midnight* 1967, a Shakespeare adaptation.

Wellesley family name of dukes of Wellington; seated at Stratfield Saye, Berkshire, England.

Wellesley /'welzli/ Richard Colley, Marquess Wellesley 1760–1842. British administrator. He was governor general of India 1798–1805, and by his victories over the ◊Mahrattas greatly extended the territory under British rule. He was foreign secretary 1809–12, and lord lieutenant of Ireland 1821–28 and 1833–34. He was a brother of the Duke of Wellington.

Wellesz /'velis/ Egon (Joseph) 1885–1974. Austrian composer and musicologist. He specialized in the history of Byzantine, Renaissance, and modern music. He moved to England in 1938 and lectured at Oxford from 1943. His compositions include operas such as *Alkestis* 1924; symphonies, notably the Fifth 1957; ballet music; and a series of string quartets.

Wellington /'weliŋtən/ capital and industrial port (woollen textiles, chemicals, soap, footwear, bricks) of New Zealand in North Island on Cook Strait; population (1987) 351,000. The harbour was first sighted by Captain Cook in 1773.

Founded 1840 by Edward Gibbon Wakefield as the first settlement of the New Zealand Company, it has been the seat of government since 1865, when it replaced Auckland. Victoria University was founded 1897. A new assembly hall (designed by the British architect Basil Spence and popularly called 'the beehive' because of its shape) was opened 1977 alongside the original parliament building.

Wellington /'weliŋtən/ Arthur Wellesley, 1st Duke of Wellington 1769–1852. British soldier and Tory politician. As commander in the ◊Peninsular War, he expelled the French from Spain in 1814. He defeated Napoleon Bonaparte at Quatre-Bras and Waterloo in 1815, and was a member of the Congress of Vienna. As prime minister 1828–30, he

was forced to concede Roman Catholic emancipation.

Wellington was born in Ireland, son of an Irish peer, and sat for a time in the Irish parliament. He was knighted for his army service in India and became a national hero with his victories 1808–14 in the Peninsular War and as general of the allies against Napoleon. At the Congress of Vienna he opposed the dismemberment of France and supported restoration of the Bourbons. As prime minister he modified the Corn Laws but became unpopular for his opposition to parliamentary reform and his lack of opposition to Catholic emancipation. He was foreign secretary 1834–35 and a member of the cabinet 1841–46. He held the office of commander in chief of the forces at various times from 1827 and for life from 1842. His home was Apsley House in London.

Wells /welz/ market town in Somerset, SW England; population (1981) 8,500. Industries include printing and the manufacture of animal foodstuffs. The 12th–13th century cathedral, built near the site of a Saxon church, has a west front with 386 carved figures. Wells was made the seat of a bishopric about 900 (Bath and Wells from 1244) and has a bishop's palace.

Wells /welz/ H(erbert) G(eorge) 1866–1946. English writer. He first made his name with 'scientific romances' such as *The Time Machine* 1895 and *The War of the Worlds* 1898. Later novels had an anti-establishment, anti-conventional humour remarkable in its day, for example *Kipps* 1905 and *Tono-Bungay* 1909. His many other books include *Outline of History* 1920 and *The Shape of Things to Come* 1933, from which a number of his prophecies have since been fulfilled. He also wrote many short stories.

Welsh /welʃ/ people of ◊Wales; see also ◊Celts. The word Welsh is thought to be derived from an old Germanic term for 'foreigner', and so linked to Walloon (Belgium) and Wallachian (Romania). It is possible that it is also derived from the Latin Volcae, the name of a Celtic people.

Welsh corgi breed of dog with a foxlike head and pricked ears. The coat is dense, with several varieties of colouring. Corgis are about 30 cm/1 ft at the shoulder, and weigh up to 12 kg/27 lbs.

There are two types, the Pembrokeshire and the heavier Cardiganshire. Corgis were originally bred for cattle herding. Their size was an advantage because cattle were unable to bend low enough to gore them.

Welsh language (Welsh *Cymraeg*) a member of the Celtic branch of the Indo-European language family, spoken chiefly in the rural north and west of Wales; it is the strongest of the surviving Celtic languages, and in 1981 was spoken by 18.9% of the Welsh population.

Welsh has been in retreat in the face of English expansion since the accession of the Welsh Henry Tudor (as Henry VII) to the throne of England. Modern Welsh, like English, is not a highly inflected language, but British, the Celtic ancestor of Welsh, was, like Latin and Anglo-Saxon, a highly inflected form. The continuous literature of

Wells *English journalist and novelist H G Wells.*

Welsh, from the 6th century onwards, contains the whole range of change from British to present-day Welsh. Nowadays, few Welsh people speak only Welsh; they are either bilingual or speak only English.

Welsh literature the chief remains of early Welsh literature are contained in the Four Ancient Books of Wales—the Black Book of Carmarthen, the Book of Taliesin, the Book of Aneirin, and the Red Book of Hergest—anthologies of prose and verse of the 6th–14th centuries. Characteristic of Welsh poetry is the bardic system which ensured the continuance of traditional conventions; most celebrated of the 12th-century bards was Cynddelw.

The English conquest of 1282 involved the fall of the princes who supported these bards, but after a period of decline a new school arose in South Wales with a new freedom in form and sentiment, the most famous poet being the 14th-century Dafydd ap Gwilym, and in the next century the classical metrist Dafydd ap Edmwnd. With the Reformation biblical translations were undertaken, and Morgan Llwyd and Ellis Wynn o Lasynys wrote religious prose. Popular metres resembling those of England developed, for example the poems of Huw Morys.

In the 18th century the classical poetic forms revived with Goronwy Owen, and the Eisteddfod (song festival) movement began: popular measures were used by the hymn-writer William Williams. The 19th century saw few notable figures save the novelist Daniel Owen, but the foundation of a Welsh university and the work there of Sir John Morris Jones (1864–1929) produced a 20th-century revival, including Thomas Gwynn Jones (1871–1949), W J Gruffydd (1881–1954), and Robert Williams Parry (1884–1956). Later poets included J Kitchener Davies (1902–52), Saunders Lewis (1893–), and in the period after World War II Waldo Williams (1904–71), Euros Bowen (1904–), and Bobi Jones (1929–). Still best known outside Wales are those who have expressed the Welsh spirit in English, such as Henry Vaughan, Edward Thomas, Vernon Watkins (1906–67), Dylan Thomas, and Ronald Thomas.

Weltanschauung (German 'worldview') a philosophy of life.

Weltpolitik (German 'world politics') term applied to German foreign policy after about 1890, which represented Emperor Wilhelm II's attempt to make Germany into a world power through a more aggressive foreign policy on colonies and naval building combined with an increase in nationalism at home.

Welty /'welti/ Eudora 1909– . US novelist and short-story writer, born in Jackson, Mississippi. Her works reflect life in the US South and are notable for their creation of character and accurate rendition of local dialect. Her novels include *Delta Wedding* 1946, *Losing Battles* 1970, and *The Optimist's Daughter* 1972.

welwitschia woody plant *Welwitschia mirabilis* of the Gnetales order, found in the deserts of SW Africa. It has a long, water-absorbent taproot, and may live a hundred years.

Welwyn Garden City /'welin/ industrial town (chemicals, electrical engineering, clothing, food) in Hertfordshire, England, 32 km/20 mi north of London; population (1981) 41,000. It was founded as a ◊garden city 1919–20 by Ebenezer Howard, and designated a 'new town' 1948.

Wembley /'wembli/ district of the Greater London borough of Brent. Wembley Stadium, opened 1924, has been the scene of the British Empire Exhibition, the annual Football Association Cup final, the 1948 Olympic Games, the Live Aid concert 1985, and many other concerts. A conference centre was opened 1977.

Wembley Stadium sports ground in north London, completed 1923 for the British Empire Exhibition. The FA Cup final has been played there since that year. It is also used for concerts. Adjacent to the main stadium are the Wembley indoor arena and conference centre. Wembley Stadium holds 78,000 people.

The largest recorded crowd at Wembley is 129,000 for the first FA Cup final; the capacity has been reduced by additional seating. England play most of their home soccer matches at Wembley. Other sports events over the years have included show jumping, American football, Rugby League, hockey, Gaelic football, hurling, and baseball. The opening and closing ceremonies and the athletics events of the 1948 Olympic Games were held at the stadium.

Wenceslas, St /ˈwensəslæs/ 907–929. Duke of Bohemia who attempted to Christianize his people and was murdered by his brother. He is patron saint of Czechoslovakia and the 'good King Wenceslas' of the carol. Feast day 28 Sept.

Wenchow /ˌwenˈtʃaʊ/ former name of Chinese town ◊Wenzhou.

Wends the NW Slavonic peoples who settled the area east of the rivers Elbe and Saale in the 6th–8th centuries. By the 12th century most had been forcibly Christianized and absorbed by invading Germans; a few preserved their identity and survive as the Sorbs of Lusatia (East Germany/Poland).

Wentworth /ˈwentwəθ/ William Charles 1790–1872. Australian politician, the son of D'Arcy Wentworth (c.1762–1827), surgeon of the penal settlement at Norfolk Island. In 1855 he was in Britain to steer the New South Wales constitution through Parliament, and campaigned for Australian federalism and self-government.

Wenzhou /ˌwenˈdʒəʊ/ industrial port (textiles, medicine) in Zhejiang, SE China; population (1984) 519,000. It was opened to foreign trade 1877 and is now a special economic zone.

werewolf in folk belief, a human being either turned by spell into a wolf or having the ability to assume a wolf form. The symptoms of ◊porphyria may have fostered the legends.

Werfel /ˈveəfəl/ Franz 1890–1945. Austrian poet, dramatist, and novelist, a leading Expressionist. His works include the poems 'Der Weltfreund der Gerichtstag'/'The Day of Judgment' 1919; the plays *Juarez und Maximilian* 1924, and *Das Reich Gottes in Böhmen/The Kingdom of God in Bohemia* 1930; and the novels *Verdi* 1924 and *Das Lied von Bernadette/The Song of Bernadette* 1941.

Born in Prague, he lived in Germany, Austria, and France, and in 1940 escaped from a French concentration camp to the USA, where he died. In 1929 he married Alma Mahler, daughter of the composer.

Wergeland /ˈveəɡəlæn/ Henrik 1808–1845. Norwegian lyric poet. He was the greatest leader of the Norwegian revival, and is known for his epic *Skabelsen, Mennesket, og Messias/Creation, Humanity, and Messiah* 1830.

wergild or *wergeld* in Anglo-Saxon and Germanic law during the Middle Ages, the compensation paid by a murderer to the relatives of the victim, its value dependent on the social rank of the deceased. It originated in tribal society as a substitute for the blood feud (essentially a form of ◊vendetta), and was replaced by punishments imposed by courts of law during the 10th and 11th centuries.

Werner /ˈveənə/ Abraham Gottlob 1750–1815. German geologist, one of the first to classify minerals systematically. He also developed the later discarded theory of neptunianism—that the Earth was initially covered by water, with every mineral in suspension; as the water receded, layers of rocks 'crystallized'.

Werner /ˈveənə/ Alfred 1866–1919. Swiss chemist. He was awarded a Nobel prize in 1913 for his work on valency theory.

Wesermünde /ˌveɪzəˈmʊndə/ name until 1947 of ◊Bremerhaven, a port in West Germany.

Wesker /ˈweskə/ Arnold 1932– . British playwright. His socialist beliefs were reflected in the successful trilogy *Chicken Soup with Barley, Roots, I'm Talking About Jerusalem* 1958–60. He

established a catchphrase with *Chips with Everything* 1962.

In 1962, Wesker tried unsuccessfully to establish a working-class theatre with trade union backing. Later plays include *The Merchant* 1978.

Wesley /ˈwesli/ Charles 1707–1788. Brother of John Wesley and one of the original Methodists at Oxford. He became a principal preacher and theologian of the Wesleyan Methodists. He wrote some 6,500 hymns, including 'Jesu, lover of my soul'.

Wesley /ˈwesli/ John 1703–1791. English founder of ◊Methodism. When the pulpits of the established church were closed to him and his followers, he took the gospel to the people. For 50 years he rode about the country on horseback, preaching daily, largely in the open air. His sermons became the doctrinal standard of the Wesleyan Methodist Church.

He was born at Epworth, Lincolnshire, where his father was the rector, and went to Oxford University together with his brother Charles, where their circle was nicknamed Methodists because of their religious observances. He was ordained in the Church of England in 1728 and returned to his Oxford college in 1729 as a tutor. In 1735 he went to Georgia, USA, as a missionary. On his return he experienced 'conversion' in 1738, and from being rigidly High Church developed into an ardent Evangelical. His *Journal* gives an intimate picture of the man and his work.

Wesley /ˈwesli/ Samuel 1776–1837. Son of Charles Wesley. He was an organist and composer of oratorios, church and chamber music.

Wessex /ˈwesɪks/ the kingdom of the West Saxons in Britain, said to have been founded by Cerdic about AD 500, covering present-day Hampshire, Dorset, Wiltshire, Berkshire, Somerset, and Devon. In 829 Egbert established West Saxon supremacy over all England. Thomas ◊Hardy used the term Wessex in his novels for the SW counties of England.

West /west/ Benjamin 1738–1820. American painter, active in London from 1763. He enjoyed the patronage of George III for many years and painted historical pictures.

West was born in Pennsylvania. He became president of the Royal Academy in 1792. *The Death of Wolfe* 1770 (National Gallery, Ottawa) began a vogue for painting recent historical events in contemporary costume. Many early American artists studied with him.

West /west/ Mae 1892–1980. US vaudeville and film actress. She wrote her own dialogue, sending herself up as a sex symbol. Her films include *She Done Him Wrong* 1933.

West *The journalist and novelist Rebecca West took her pen name from a character in Ibsen's play* Rosmersholm. *She continued writing until her death at almost 90.*

West /west/ Nathanael. Pen name of Nathan Weinstein 1904–1940. US black-humour novelist, born in New York. West's surrealist influenced novels capture the absurdity and extremity of modern American life and the dark side of the American dream. *The Day of the Locust* 1939 explores the violent fantasies induced by Hollywood, where West was a screenwriter.

Miss Lonelyhearts 1933 is about an agonized agony aunt on a newspaper who feels the misfortunes of his correspondents; *A Cool Million* 1934 satirizes the Horatio Alger rags-to-riches dream of success.

West /west/ Rebecca. Pen name of Cicily Isabel Fairfield 1892–1983. British journalist and novelist, an active feminist from 1911. *The Meaning of Treason* 1959 deals with the spies Burgess and Maclean. Her novels include *The Fountain Overflows* 1956.

West African Economic Community international organization established 1975 to end barriers in trade and cooperation in development; members in 1988 include Burkina Faso, Ivory Coast, Mali, Mauritania, Niger, and Senegal; Benin and Togo have observer status.

West, American the Great Plains region of the USA to the E of the Rocky Mountains from Canada to Texas.

1250 Unidentified epidemic weakened American Indian civilization.

1650 Horses introduced by the Spanish.

1775 Wilderness Road opened by Daniel ◊Boone.

1805 Zebulon Pike (see ◊Pikes Peak) explored the Mississippi.

1819 Maj Stephen Long, a US government topographical engineer, explored the Great Plains.

1822 ◊Santa Fe Trail established.

1824 Great Salt Lake discovered by Jim Bridger, 'mountain man', trapper and guide.

1836 Defeat of Davy Crockett and other Texans by Mexicans at Alamo.

1840–60 ◊Oregon Trail in use.

1846 Mormon trek to Utah under Brigham ◊Young.

1846–48 ◊Mexican War.

1849–56 California gold rush.

1860 Pony Express (St Joseph, Missouri–San Francisco, California) 3 Apr–22 Oct; superseded by the telegraph.

1863 On 1 Jan the first homestead was filed; followed by the settlement of the Western Prairies and Great Plains.

1865–90 Period of the Indian Wars, accompanied by rapid extermination of the buffalo, upon which much of Indian life depended.

1867–80s Period of the 'cattle kingdom', and cowboy trails such as the Chisholm Trail from Texas to the railheads at Abilene, Wichita, Dodge City.

1869 First transcontinental railroad completed by Central Pacific company, building eastward from Sacramento, California, and Union Pacific company, building westward from Omaha, Nebraska.

West Bengal

1876 Battle of Little Bighorn; see Gen ◊Custer and ◊Plains Indians.

1890 Battle of ◊Wounded Knee; official census declaration that the West no longer had a frontier line.

West Bank the area (5,879 sq km/2,270 sq mi) on the west bank of the river Jordan; population (1988) 866,000. The West Bank was taken by the Jordanian army 1948 at the end of the Arab-Israeli war which resulted in the creation of Israel, and was captured by Israel during the Six-Day War 5–10 June 1967. The continuing Israeli occupation has created tensions with the Arab population, especially as a result of Jewish Israeli settlements in the area.

West Bengal /ben'gɔːl/ state of NE India
area 87,900 sq km/33,929 sq mi
capital Calcutta
towns Asansol, Durgarpur
physical occupies the W part of the vast alluvial plain created by the Ganges and Brahmaputra, with the Hooghly river; annual rainfall in excess of 250 cm/100 in
products rice, jute, tea, coal, iron, steel, cars, locomotives, aluminium, fertilizers
population (1981) 54,486,000
history created 1947 from the former British province of Bengal, with later territories added: Cooch Behar 1950, Chandernagore 1954, and part of Bihar 1956.

West Bromwich /'brɒmɪdʒ/ industrial town (metalworking, springs, tubes) in West Midlands, England, NW of Birmingham; population (1981) 155,000.

Westerlies prevailing winds from the W that occur in both hemispheres between latitudes of about 35° and 60°. Unlike the ◊trade winds, they are very variable and produce stormy weather.

The Westerlies blow mainly from the SW in the N hemisphere and the NW in the S hemisphere, bringing moist weather to the W coast of the landmasses in these latitudes.

western genre of popular fiction based on the landscape and settlement of the western USA. It developed in US ◊dime novels and ◊frontier literature. The western became established in written form with novels such as *The Virginian* 1902 by Owen Wister (1860–1938) and *Riders of the Purple Sage* 1912 by Zane Grey. See also ◊western film.

Westerns go back to J F Cooper's *Leatherstocking Tales* and the hunter stories of the German Karl May. In stylized form, they became frontier stories of cowboy rangers and Indian villains, set vaguely in the post-Civil War era. Most westerns are nostalgic, written after the frontier officially closed 1890. *The Virginian* is the 'serious' version of the form, but prolific writers like Zane Grey and Frederick Faust developed its pulp possibilities and its place in universal fantasy.

Western Australia /ɒ'streɪlɪə/ state of Australia
area 2,525,500 sq km/974,843 sq mi
capital Perth
towns main port Fremantle, Bunbury, Geraldton, Kalgoorlie-Boulder, Albany
features largest state in Australia; Monte Bello

Western Australia

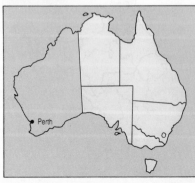

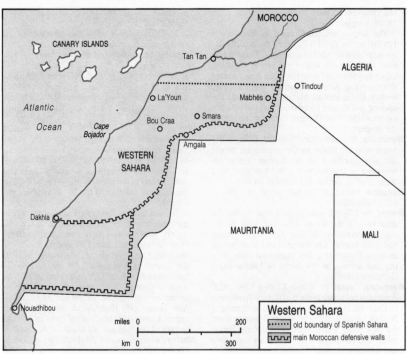

Western Sahara
······· old boundary of Spanish Sahara
ᴜᴜᴜ main Moroccan defensive walls

Islands; rivers Fitzroy, Fortescue, Gascoyne, Murchison, and Swan; NW coast subject to hurricanes ('willy-willies'); ◊Lasseter's Reef
products wheat, fresh and dried fruit, meat and dairy products; natural gas (NW Shelf) and oil (Canning Basin), iron (the Pilbara), copper, nickel, uranium, gold, diamonds
population (1987) 1,478,000
history a short-lived convict settlement at King George Sound 1826; Captain James Stirling (1791–1865) founded the modern state at Perth 1829; self-government 1890; state 1901.

Western European Union (WEU) organization established 1955 as a consultative forum for military issues among the W European governments: Belgium, France, Holland, Italy, Luxembourg, the UK, West Germany, and (from 1988) Spain and Portugal.

Policy is agreed during meetings of the foreign ministers of the member nations, with administrative work carried out by a permanent secretariat and specialist committees. The WEU is charged under its charter with ensuring close cooperation with NATO. During its early years the WEU supervised the gradual rearmament of West Germany and the transfer of the Saarland back to West German rule 1957. More recently attempts have been made, particularly by France, to transform the WEU into a coordinating body for W European military policy and to frame a 'charter of security principles'.

western film genre of films based loosely on the history of the American ◊West and evolved from the written ◊western. As a genre, the western is virtually as old as the cinema. Italian 'spaghetti westerns' and Japanese westerns established it as an international form. In the 1980s only *Pale Rider* 1985 and *Young Guns* 1988 were commercially successful.

A memorable early example is *The Great Train Robbery* 1903. The silent era produced such epics as *The Iron Horse* 1924, and the genre remained popular into the coming of sound. The 1930s saw many epics, such as *Union Pacific* 1939, whereas the 1940s often dwelt on specific historical events (including Custer's last stand in *They Died With Their Boots On* 1941). The 1950s brought more realism and serious issues, such as the treatment of the Indians. 1960s westerns contained an increased amount of violence, partly owing to the influence of the Italian 'spaghetti westerns' (often

directed by Sergio ◊Leone), a development carried further into the 1970s with films such as *The Wild Bunch* 1969. The artistic and commercial disaster of *Heaven's Gate* 1980 signalled the virtual death of the genre.

Western Isles island area of Scotland, comprising the Outer Hebrides (Lewis, Harris, North and South Uist, and Barra); unofficially the Inner and Outer Hebrides generally
area 2,900 sq km/1,120 sq mi
towns administrative headquarters Stornoway on Lewis
features divided from the mainland by the Minch; Callanish monolithic circles of the Stone Age on Lewis
products Harris tweed, sheep, fish, cattle
population (1987) 31,000.

Western Provinces in Canada, the provinces of ◊Alberta, ◊British Columbia, ◊Manitoba, and ◊Saskatchewan.

Western Sahara /sə'hɑːrə/ formerly *Spanish Sahara* disputed territory in NW Africa bounded to the N by Morocco, to the W and S by Mauritania, and to the E by the Atlantic Ocean.
area 266,800 sq km/103,011 sq mi
capital La'Youn (Arabic *al-Aaiún*)
towns phosphate mining town of Bou Craa

Western Isles

features defensive electrically monitored fortified wall enclosing the phosphate area
exports phosphates
currency dirham
population (1988) 181,400; another estimated 165,000 live in refugee camps near Tindouf, SW Algeria. Ethnic composition: Sawrawis (traditionally nomadic herdsmen)
language Arabic
religion Sunni Muslim
government administered by Morocco
history this 1,000-km-long Saharan coastal region, which during the 19th century separated French-dominated Morocco and Mauritania, was designated a Spanish 'sphere of influence' in 1884 because it lies opposite the Spanish-ruled Canary Islands. On securing its independence in 1956, Morocco laid claim to and invaded this 'Spanish Sahara' territory, but was repulsed. Moroccan interest was rekindled from 1965, following the discovery of rich phosphate resources at Bou-Craa, and within Spanish Sahara a pro-independence nationalist movement developed, spearheaded by the Popular Front for the Liberation of Saguia al Hamra and Rio de Oro (Polisario), which was established in 1973. After the death of the Spanish ruler Gen Franco, Spain withdrew and the territory was partitioned between Morocco and Mauritania. Polisario rejected this partition, declared their own independent Saharan Arab Democratic Republic (SADR), and proceeded to wage a guerrilla war, securing indirect support from Algeria and, later, Libya. By 1979 they had succeeded in their struggle against Mauritania, who withdrew from their southern sector and concluded a peace agreement with Polisario, and in 1982 the SADR was accepted as a full member of the ◊Organization of African Unity. By the end of 1989, 70 countries had granted diplomatic recognition to the SADR.

Morocco, who occupied the Mauritanian-evacuated zone, still retained control over the bulk of the territory, including the key towns and phosphate mines, which they protected with an 2,500-km-long 'electronic defensive wall'. From the mid-1980s this wall was gradually extended outwards as Libya and Algeria reduced their support for Polisario and drew closer to Morocco. In 1988, Morocco and the Polisario Front agreed to United Nations-sponsored plans for a cease-fire and a referendum in Western Sahara, based on 1974 voting rolls, to decide the territory's future. However, divisions persisted during 1989–90 over the terms of the referendum and sporadic fighting continued.

Western Samoa see ◊Samoa, Western.
West Germany see ◊Germany, West.
West Glamorgan /glə'mɔːgən/ county in SW Wales
area 820 sq km/317 sq mi
towns administrative headquarters Swansea; Port Talbot, Neath
features Gower Peninsula
products tinplate, copper, steel, chemicals
population (1987) 363,000
language 16% Welsh, English.

West Indian inhabitant of the West Indies or person of West Indian descent. The West Indies are culturally heterogenous; in addition to the indigenous Caribs, there are peoples of African, European, and Asian descent.

West Indies /'ɪndiz/ archipelago of about 1,200 islands, dividing the Atlantic from the Gulf of Mexico and the Caribbean. The islands are divided into:
Bahamas
Greater Antilles Cuba, Hispaniola (Haiti, Dominican Republic), Jamaica, Puerto Rico
Lesser Antilles Aruba, Netherlands Antilles, Trinidad and Tobago, the Windward Islands (Grenada, Barbados, St Vincent, St Lucia, Martinique, Dominica, Guadeloupe), the Leeward Islands (Montserrat, Antigua, St Christopher (St Kitts)-Nevis, Barbuda, Anguilla, St Martin, British and US Virgin Islands), and many smaller islands.

West Indies, Federation of the federal union 1958–62 comprising Antigua, Barbados, Dominica, Grenada, Jamaica, Montserrat, St Christopher (St Kitts)–Nevis and Anguilla, St Lucia, St Vincent, and Trinidad and Tobago. This federation came to an end when first Jamaica and then Trinidad and Tobago withdrew.

Westinghouse /'westɪŋhaʊs/ George 1846–1914. US inventor and founder of the Westinghouse Corporation in 1886. After service in the Civil War he patented a powerful air brake for trains in 1869. His invention allowed trains to run more safely with greater loads at greater speeds. In the 1880s, he turned his attention to the generation of electricity. Unlike Thomas ◊Edison, Westinghouse introduced alternating current into his power stations.

West Irian /'ɪriən/ former name for ◊Irian Jaya.
Westland affair in UK politics, the events surrounding the takeover of the British Westland helicopter company in 1985–86. There was much political acrimony in the cabinet and allegations of malpractice. The affair led to the resignation of two cabinet ministers: Michael Heseltine, minister of defence, and the secretary for trade and industry, Leon Brittan.

West Lothian /'west 'ləʊðiən/ former county of central Scotland, bordering the S shore of the Firth of Forth; from 1975 included (except for the Bo'ness area, which went to Central region) in Lothian region. Linlithgow was the administrative headquarters.

Westmacott /'westməkɒt/ Richard 1775–1856. British sculptor. He studied under ◊Canova in Rome, was elected to the Royal Academy 1811 and became a professor there. He executed monuments in Westminster Abbey and in St Paul's Cathedral, and the *Achilles* in Hyde Park, all in London.

Westman Islands small group of islands off the south coast of Iceland. In 1973 volcanic eruption caused the population of 5,200 to be temporarily evacuated, and added 2.5 sq km/1 sq mi to the islands' area. Heimaey is one of Iceland's chief fishing ports.

Westmeath /ˌwest'miːð/ inland county of Leinster province, Republic of Ireland
area 1,760 sq km/679 sq mi
town county town Mullingar
physical rivers Shannon, Inny, and Brosna; lakes Ree, Sheelin, and Ennell
products agricultural and dairy products, limestone, textiles
population (1986) 63,000.

West Midlands /'west 'mɪdləndz/ metropolitan county in central England, created 1974, originally administered by an elected council; its powers reverted to district councils from 1986
area 900 sq km/347 sq mi
towns administrative headquarters Birmingham
features created 1974 from the area around and including Birmingham, and comprising Wolverhampton, Walsall, Dudley, West Bromwich, Smethwick, Coventry
products manufacturing industrial goods
population (1987) 2,624,000
famous people Philip Larkin.

Westminster, City of /'west·mɪnstə/ borough of central Greater London, on the north bank of the Thames between Kensington and the City of London; population (1986) 176,000. It encompasses Bayswater, Belgravia, Mayfair, Paddington, Pimlico, Soho, St John's Wood, and Westminster.
Bayswater is a residential and hotel area north of Kensington Gardens.
Belgravia, bounded to the north by Knightsbridge, has squares laid out 1825–30 by Thomas ◊Cubitt.
Mayfair, between Oxford Street and Piccadilly, includes Park Lane and Grosvenor Square (with the US embassy).
Paddington contains Little Venice on the Grand Union Canal.
Pimlico has the Tate Gallery (Turner collection, British and modern art).
Soho has many restaurants and a Chinese community around Gerrard Street; it was formerly known for strip clubs and sex shops.
St John's Wood has Lord's cricket ground and the studios at 11 Abbey Road where the Beatles recorded their music.
Westminster encompasses Buckingham Palace (royal residence), Green Park, St James's Park and St James's Palace (16th century), Marlborough House, Westminster Abbey, Westminster Hall (1097–1401), the Houses of Parliament with Big Ben, Whitehall (government offices), Downing

West Glamorgan

West Midlands

West Sussex

Street (homes of the prime minister at number 10 and the chancellor of the Exchequer at number 11), Hyde Park with the Albert Memorial opposite the Royal Albert Hall, Trafalgar Square with the National Gallery and National Portrait Gallery.

Westminster Abbey Gothic church in central London, officially the Collegiate Church of St Peter. It was built 1050–1745 and consecrated under Edward the Confessor in 1065. The west towers are by ◊Hawksmoor 1740. Since William I nearly all English monarchs have been crowned in the abbey, and several are buried there; many poets are buried or commemorated there, at Poets' Corner.

The Coronation Chair includes the Stone of Scone, on which Scottish kings were crowned, brought here by Edward I in 1296; Poets' Corner was begun with the burial of ◊Spenser 1599. Westminster School, a public school with ancient and modern buildings nearby, was once the Abbey School.

Westmorland /ˈwestmələnd/ former county in the Lake District, England, part of Cumbria from 1974.

Weston /ˈwestən/ Edward 1886–1958. US photographer. A founder member of the F64 group, a school of photography advocating sharp definition, he is noted for the technical mastery in his Californian landscapes and nude studies.

Weston-super-Mare /ˈwestən ˌsuːpə ˈmeə/ seaside resort and town in Avon, SW England, on the Bristol Channel; population (1984) 170,000. Industries include plastics, and engineering.

Westphalia /westˈfeɪlɪə/ an independent medieval duchy, incorporated in Prussia by the Congress of Vienna 1815, and made a province 1816 with Münster as its capital. Since 1946 it has been part of the West German *Land* (region) of ◊North Rhine–Westphalia.

Westphalia included the Ruhr, the chief industrial area of Germany, and was the scene of violent fighting during the last stages of World War II. The kingdom of Westphalia, created by the French emperor Napoleon 1807–13, did not include the duchy, but was made up of Prussian lands W of the Elbe, Hessen, Brunswick, and Hanover.

Westphalia, Treaty of agreement 1648 ending the ◊Thirty Years' War.

West Point /ˈwest ˈpɔɪnt/ former fort in New York State, on the Hudson River, 80 km/50 mi N of New York City, site of the US Military Academy (commonly referred to as West Point), established in 1802. Women were admitted 1976. West Point has been a military post since 1778.

West Sussex /ˈwest ˈsʌsɪks/ county on the S coast of England
area 2,020 sq km/780 sq mi
towns administrative headquarters Chichester; Crawley, Horsham, Haywards Heath; resorts Worthing, Littlehampton, Bognor Regis; port Shoreham
physical the Weald, South Downs; rivers Arun, West Rother, Adur
features Arundel and Bramber castles; Goodwood, Petworth House (17th century), and Wakehurst Place, where the Royal Botanic Gardens, Kew, has additional grounds
population (1987) 700,000.

West Virginia /ˈwest vəˈdʒɪnɪə/ state of the E USA; nickname Mountain State
area 62,900 sq km/24,279 sq mi
capital Charleston
towns Huntington, Wheeling
physical Allegheny Mountains; Ohio river
features port of Harper's Ferry, restored as when John Brown seized the US armoury 1859
products fruit, poultry, dairy and meat products, timber, coal, natural gas, oil, chemicals, synthetic fibres, plastics, steel, glass, pottery
population (1986) 1,919,000
famous people Pearl Buck, Thomas 'Stonewall' Jackson
history mound builders 6th century; explorers and fur traders 1670s; German settlements 1730s;

West Virginia

industrial development early 19th century; on the secession of Virginia from the Union 1862, West Virginians dissented, and formed a new state 1863; industrial expansion accompanied by labor strife early 20th century.

West Yorkshire /ˈwest ˈjɔːksə/ metropolitan county in NE England, created 1976, originally administered by an elected metropolitan council; its powers reverted to district councils from 1986
area 2,040 sq km/787 sq mi
towns administrative headquarters Wakefield; Leeds, Bradford, Halifax, Huddersfield
features Ilkley Moor, Haworth Moor, Haworth Parsonage; part of the Peak District National Park
products coal, woollen textiles
population (1987) 2,052,000
famous people the Brontës, David Hockney, Henry Moore, J B Priestley.

wet in UK politics, a derogatory term used to describe a moderate or left-wing supporter of the Conservative Party who opposes the monetary or other hard-line policies of its leader Margaret Thatcher.

weta flightless insect *Deinacrida rugosa*, resembling a large grasshopper (8.5 cm/3.5 in long), found on offshore islands of New Zealand.

wetback derogatory term for an illegal immigrant from Mexico who lives and works in the USA. The name derives from the traditional mode of entry—by swimming across the Rio Grande.

Wexford /ˈweksfəd/ seaport and county town of Wexford, Republic of Ireland; population (1981) 15,000. Products include textiles, cheese, and agricultural machinery. It was founded by the Danes in the 9th century, and devastated by Cromwell 1649.

Wexford /ˈweksfəd/ county in the Republic of Ireland, province of Leinster

West Yorkshire

area 2,350 sq km/907 sq mi
towns county town Wexford; Rosslare
products fish, livestock, oats, barley, potatoes
population (1986) 102,000.

Weyden /ˈwaɪdə/ Rogier van der *c.*1399–1464. Netherlandish painter, official painter to the city of Brussels from 1436. He painted portraits and religious subjects, such as *The Last Judgement* about 1450 (Hôtel-Dieu, Beaune). His refined style had considerable impact on Netherlandish painting.

Little is known of his life and none of his works have been dated, but he was widely admired in his day and was known in Italy. His *Deposition* before 1443 (Prado, Madrid) shows the influence of Robert ◊Campin.

Weygand /veɪˈɡɒn/ Maxime 1867–1965. French general. In 1940, as French commander in chief, he advised surrender to Germany, and was subsequently high commissioner of N Africa 1940–41. He was a prisoner in Germany 1942–45, and was arrested after his return to France; he was released in 1946, and in 1949 the sentence of national infamy was quashed.

Weymouth /ˈweɪməθ/ seaport and resort in Dorset, S England; population (1981) 46,000. It is linked by ferry to France and the Channel Islands. Weymouth, dating from the 10th century,

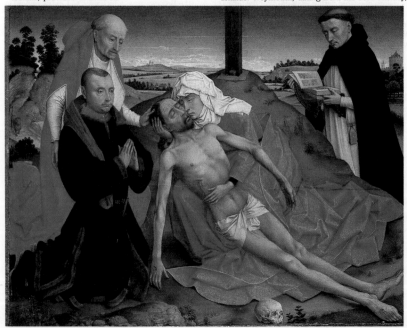

Weyden Pietà, National Gallery, London.

whale

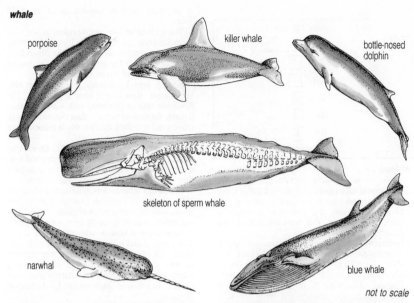

porpoise

killer whale

bottle-nosed dolphin

skeleton of sperm whale

narwhal

blue whale

not to scale

was the first place in England to suffer from the Black Death 1348, and was popularized as a bathing resort by George III.

whale large marine mammal of the order Cetacea, with internal vestiges of hind limbs. When whales surface to breathe, they eject air in a spout through the blowhole in the top of the head. There were hundreds of thousands of whales at the beginning of the 20th century, but they have been hunted close to extinction; see ◊whaling.

Whales are extremely intelligent and have a complex communication system, known as 'songs'. Mass strandings where whales swim onto a beach occur occasionally for unknown reasons; it may have something to do with pollution. Group loyalty is strong, and whales may follow a confused leader to disaster.

The ***blue whale***, 31 m/100 ft long, and weighing over 100 tonnes, is the largest animal ever to inhabit the planet. It feeds on plankton, strained through its whalebone 'plates'. The common ***rorqual** Balaenoptera physalas* is slate-coloured, and not quite so large. Largest of the ***toothed whales***, suborder Odontoceti, which feed on fish and larger animals, is the ***sperm whale** Physeter catodon* (see ◊spermaceti). The ***killer whale*** is a member of the ◊dolphin family and is often exhibited in oceanaria. Killer whales in the wild have 8–15 special calls, and each family group, or 'pod', has its own particular dialect: they are the first mammals known to have dialects in the same way as human language. See also ◊bowhead whale.

Whale /weɪl/ James 1886–1957. British film director. He initially went to Hollywood to film his stage success, *Journey's End* 1930, and went

wheat

on to direct four horror films: *Frankenstein* 1931, *The Old Dark House* 1932, *The Invisible Man* 1933, and *Bride of Frankenstein* 1935. He also directed *Showboat* 1936.

whaling the hunting of whales. Whales are hunted for whale oil (made from the thick layer of fat under the skin called 'blubber'), which is used for food and cosmetics; for the large reserve of oil in the head of the sperm whale, which is used in the leather industry; and for ◊*ambergris*, a waxlike substance from the intestines, used in making perfumes. There are synthetic substitutes for all these products. Whales are also killed for their meat, sold as pet food in the USA and Europe, and eaten by humans in Japan.

The International Whaling Commission, established 1946, failed to enforce quotas on whale killing until world concern about their possible extinction mounted in the 1970s. By the end of the following decade, 90% of blue, fin, humpback, and sperm whales had been wiped out. Low reproduction rates mean that protected species are slow to recover. After 1986 only Iceland, Japan, Norway, and the USSR continued with limited whaling for 'scientific purposes', but pirates also operate.

Wharton /ˈwɔːtn/ Edith (born Jones) 1862–1937. US novelist. Her work was influenced by her friend Henry James, and mostly set in New York society. It includes *The House of Mirth* 1905, the rural *Ethan Frome* 1911, *The Custom of the Country* 1913, and *The Age of Innocence* 1920.

wheat cereal plant derived from the wild *Triticum*, a grass native to the Middle East. It is the chief cereal used in breadmaking and is widely cultivated in temperate climates suited to its growth. Wheat

is killed by frost, and damp renders the grain soft, so warm, dry regions produce the most valuable grain.

The main wheat-producing areas of the world are Ukraine in the USSR, the prairie states of the USA, the Punjab in India, the prairie provinces of Canada, parts of France, Poland, S Germany, Italy, Argentina, and SE Australia. Flour is milled from the ◊endosperm; the coatings of the grain produce bran. Semolina is also prepared from wheat; it is a meal byproduct from the manufacture of fine flour.

wheatear small (15 cm/6 in long) migratory bird *Oenanthe oenanthe* found throughout the Old World and also in parts of North America. The plumage is light grey above and white below, with a white patch on the back, a black face-patch, and black and white wings and tail.

Wheatley /ˈwiːtli/ Dennis (Yates) 1897–1977. British thriller and adventure novelist. He is known for his series dealing with black magic and occultism, but also wrote crime novels in which the reader was invited to play the detective, as in *Murder off Miami* 1936, with real clues such as ticket stubs.

Wheatstone /ˈwiːtstən/ Charles 1802–1875. English physicist and inventor. With William Cooke, he patented a railway telegraph in 1837, and, developing an idea of Samuel Christie's, devised the ***Wheatstone bridge***, an electrical network for measuring resistance. Originally a musical-instrument maker, he invented the harmonica and the concertina.

wheel and axle a simple machine with a rope wound round an axle connected to a larger wheel with another rope attached to its rim. Pulling on the wheel rope (applying an effort) lifts a load attached to the axle rope. The velocity ratio of the machine (load divided by distance moved by effort) is equal to the ratio of the wheel radius to the axle radius.

Wheeler /ˈwiːlə/ Mortimer 1890–1976. English archaeologist. While he was keeper of the London Museum 1926–44, his digs included Caerleon in Wales 1926–27 and Maiden Castle in Dorset 1934–37. As director-general of archaeology in India 1944–48 he revealed the Indus Valley civilization. He helped to popularize archaeology by his television appearances.

whelk type of marine gastropod with a thick spiral shell. Whelks are scavengers, and will eat other shellfish. The largest grow to 40 cm/16 in long. Tropical species are very colourful. The common whelk *Buccinum undatum* is widely distributed round the North Sea and Atlantic.

Whewell /ˈhjuːəl/ William 1794–1866. British physicist and philosopher who coined the term 'scientist' along with such words as Eocene and Miocene, electrode, cathode, and anode. Most of his career was connected with Cambridge, where he became the Master of Trinity College. His most enduring influence rests on two works of great scholarship and acuteness, *The History of the Inductive Sciences* 1837 and *The Philosophy of*

wheat

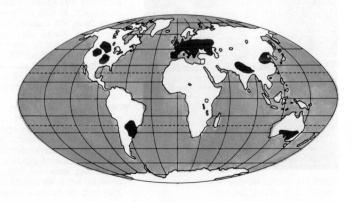

■ major areas

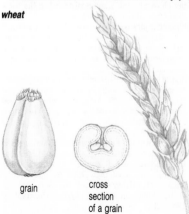

grain

cross
section
of a grain

wheat

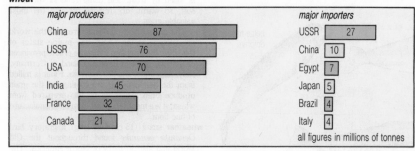

major producers		major importers	
China	87	USSR	27
USSR	76	China	10
USA	70	Egypt	7
India	45	Japan	5
France	32	Brazil	4
Canada	21	Italy	4
		all figures in millions of tonnes	

the Inductive Sciences 1840, both still in print and widely read.

whey watery by-product of the cheesemaking process, which is drained off after the milk has been heated and ◊rennet (a curdling agent) added to induce its coagulation.

Whig Party /wɪg/ the UK predecessor of the Liberal Party. The name was first used of rebel ◊Covenanters and then of those who wished to exclude James II from the English succession (as a Roman Catholic). They were in power continuously 1714–60 and pressed for industrial and commercial development, a vigorous foreign policy, and religious toleration. During the French Revolution, the Whigs demanded parliamentary reform in Britain, and from the passing of the Reform Bill in 1832 became known as Liberals.

Whig Party /wɪg/ in the USA, political party opposed to the autocratic presidency of Andrew Jackson from 1834. They elected the presidents W H Harrison, Taylor, and Fillmore. The party diverged over the issue of slavery 1852; the Northern Whigs joined the Republican party; the Southern or 'Cotton' Whigs joined the Democrats. The title was taken from the British Whig Party which supported Parliament against the king. During the War of American Independence, American patriots described themselves as Whigs, while those remaining loyal to Britain were known as Tories.

whimbrel wading bird *Numenius phaeopus* related to the curlew but with a shorter down-curved bill, streaked brown plumage, and head stripes. About 40 cm/1.3 ft long, it breeds in the Arctic, and winters in Africa, South America, and S Asia.

whip (the whipper-in of hounds at a foxhunt) in UK politics, the member of Parliament who ensures the presence of colleagues in the party when there is to be a vote in Parliament at the end of a debate. The written appeal sent by the whips to MPs is also called a whip; this letter is underlined once, twice, or three times to indicate its importance. A **three-line whip** is the most urgent, and every MP is expected to attend and vote with their party.

The government chief whip and the three junior whips are salaried officials; some opposition whips also receive a salary. Conservative whips are chosen by the leader of the party; Labour whips are chosen by the prime minister when the party is in office, otherwise by election.

whiplash injury damage to the neck vertebrae and their attachments caused by a sudden backward jerk of the head and neck. It is most often seen in vehicle occupants as a result of the rapid deceleration experienced in a crash.

whippet breed of dog resembling a small greyhound. It grows to 56 cm/22 in at the shoulder, and 9 kg/20 lb in weight. Whippets were developed by northern English colliers for racing. They were probably produced by crossing a terrier and a greyhound.

Whipple /'wɪpəl/ Fred Lawrence 1906– . US astronomer, whose hypothesis in 1949 that the nucleus of a comet is like a dirty snowball was confirmed 1986 by space-probe studies of ◊Halley's comet. He was director of the Smithsonian Astrophysical Observatory 1955–73.

Whipple /'wɪpəl/ George 1878–1976. US physiologist whose research interest concerned the formation of haemoglobin. He showed that anaemic dogs, kept under restricted diets, responded well to a liver regime, and that their haemoglobin quickly regenerated. This work led to a cure for pernicious anaemia.

whippoorwill North American insectivorous nightjar *Caprimulgus vociferus*, so called from its cry. It is about 25 cm/10 in long, and is mottled brown.

Whipsnade /'wɪpsneɪd/ a zoo in Bedfordshire, England, 5 km/3 mi S of Dunstable, opened 1931, where wild animals and birds are bred and exhibited in conditions resembling their natural state.

whip snake several species of slender-bodied tree-dwelling snakes. The European **western whip snake** *Coluber viridiflavus* is nonvenomous and lives in France and Italy. It grows to a maximum 2 m/6 ft, is fast-moving, climbing as well as sliding along the ground, and feeds on lizards, mammals, and some other snakes. Various whip snakes (*Coluber* species) live in North America, especially the dry southwest, and others in tropical Asia and Australasia.

whisky or **whiskey** a distilled spirit made from cereals: Scotch and Irish whisky usually from barley, and North American whiskey or bourbon from maize or rye. Scotch is usually blended; pure malt whisky is more expensive. Whisky

Whistler Miss Cicely Alexander, harmony in grey and green *(1872)* Tate Gallery, London.

is generally aged in wooden casks for 4–12 years.

The spelling 'whisky' usually refers to Scotch or Canadian drink and 'whiskey' to Irish or American. The earliest written record of whisky comes from Scotland 1494 but the art of distillation is thought to have been used before this time.

Scotch whisky is made primarily from barley, malted, then heated over a peat fire. The flavoured malt is combined with water to make a mash, fermented to beer, then distilled twice to make whisky at 70% alcohol; this is reduced with water to 43% of volume.

Irish whiskey is made as Scotch, except that the malt is not exposed to the peat fire and thus does not have a smoky quality, and it is distilled three times. Irish whisky is usually blended.

Canadian whisky was introduced early in the 19th century and is a blend of flavoured and neutral whiskies made from mashes of maize, rye, wheat, and barley malt. It is usually aged for six years.

American whiskey was introduced in the 18th century and is made from barley malt with maize and rye, made into a beer, then distilled to 80% alcohol and reduced to 50–52% with water, and is aged in unused, charred white-oak barrels. Bourbon is characterized by the flavour of maize.

Japanese whisky is made by the Scotch process and blended.

Straight whisky is unmixed or mixed with whisky from the same distillery or period; *blended whisky* is a mixture of neutral products with straight whiskies or may contain small quantities of sherry, fruit juice, and other flavours; *grain whisky* is made from unmalted grain mixed with malt.

whist a card game for four, predecessor of ◊bridge, in which the partners try to win a majority of the 13 tricks (the highest card played being the winner).

Whistler 'wɪslə/ James Abbott McNeill 1834–1903. US painter and etcher, active in London from 1859. His riverscapes and portraits show subtle composition and colour harmonies, for example *Arrangement in Grey and Black: Portrait of the Painter's Mother* 1871 (Louvre, Paris).

Whistler was born in Massachusetts. He abandoned a military career and in 1855 went to Paris where he was associated with the Impressionists. He then settled in Chelsea, London, and his views of the Thames include *Old Battersea Bridge* (Tate Gallery, London). Some of his *Nocturnes* 1877 were adversely criticized by ◊Ruskin and led to a libel trial in which Whistler was awarded a farthing damages. Whistler retaliated in 1890 with *The Gentle Art of Making Enemies*.

Whistler /wɪslə/ Rex John 1905–1944. English artist. He painted fanciful murals, for example *In Pursuit of Rare Meats* in the Tate Gallery restaurant, London.

Whitby /wɪtbi/ port and resort in N Yorkshire, England, on the North Sea coast; population (1981) 14,000. Industries include boatbuilding, fishing, and plastics. Remains of a Benedictine abbey built 1078 survive on the site of the original foundation by St Hilda 657, which was destroyed by the Danes 867. Captain Cook's ship *Resolution* was built in Whitby, where he had served his apprenticeship, and he sailed from here on his voyage to the Pacific in 1768.

Whitby, Synod of council summoned by King Oswy of Northumbria in 664, which decided to adopt the Roman rather than the Celtic form of Christianity for Britain.

White a counter-revolutionary, especially during the Russian civil wars 1917–21. Originally the term described the party opposing the French Revolution, when the royalists used the white lily of the French monarchy as their badge.

White /waɪt/ E(lwyn) B(rooks) 1899–1985. US writer, long associated with the *New Yorker*, noted for satire, for example *Is Sex Necessary?* 1929 (with the humorist James Thurber). White

Whitby A view of Whitby about 1900. Now a fishing port and resort, Whitby was an important ecclesiastical centre in the Middle Ages.

also wrote two children's classics, *Stuart Little* 1945 and *Charlotte's Web* 1952.

White /waɪt/ Gilbert 1720–1793. English cleric and naturalist, born at Selborne, Hampshire, and author of *Natural History and Antiquities of Selborne* 1789.

White /waɪt/ Patrick 1912– . Australian novelist. Born in London, he settled in Australia in the 1940s. His novels (with allegorical overtones) include *The Aunt's Story* 1948, *Voss* (based on the 19th-century explorer Leichhardt) 1957, and *The Twyborn Affair* 1979. Nobel Prize 1973.

White /waɪt/ T(erence) H(anbury) 1906–1964. English writer, who retold the Arthurian legend in four volumes of *The Once and Future King* 1938–58.

whitebait the young of the ◊herring.

whitebeam tree *Sorbus aria*, native to S Europe, usually found growing on chalk or limestone. It can reach 20 m/60 ft. It takes its name from the leaves, which have a dense coat of short white hairs on the underside.

white blood cell another name for ◊leucocyte. There are at least ten different types of white blood cell, and they are not just found in the blood. They also occur in the ◊lymph and throughout the body, where they play an important role in ◊immunity.

white dwarf a small, hot star, the last stage in the life of a star such as the Sun. White dwarfs have a mass similar to that of the Sun, but only 1% of the Sun's diameter, similar in size to the Earth.

White House The official residence of the president of the USA, in Washington DC.

Most have surface temperatures of 8,000°C or more, hotter than the Sun. Yet, being so small, their overall luminosities are 1% that of the Sun or less.

White dwarfs consist of degenerate matter in which gravity has packed the protons and electrons together as tightly as is physically possible, so that a spoonful of it weighs several tonnes. White dwarfs are thought to be the shrunken remains of stars that have exhausted their internal energy supplies. They slowly cool and fade over billions of years.

white elephant any useless and cumbersome gift. In Thailand the monarch would formerly present a white elephant to a person out of favour: being the country's sacred animal, it could not be used for work, and its upkeep was ruinously expensive.

Whitefield George 1714–1770. British Methodist evangelist. He was a student at Oxford and took orders 1738, but was suspended for his unorthodox doctrines and methods. For many years he travelled through Britain and America, and by his preaching contributed greatly to the religious revival. Whitefield's Tabernacle was built for him in Tottenham Court Road, London (1756; bombed 1945 but rebuilt).

whitefish any freshwater fish of the salmon family, belonging to the genus *Coregonus*. They live in deep lakes and rivers of North America, Europe, and Asia. Three species are found in Britain.

Whitehall /waɪtˈhɔːl/ street in central London, between Trafalgar Square and the Houses of Parliament, with many government offices and the Cenotaph war memorial.

Whitehaven /waɪt·heɪvən/ town and port in Cumbria, NW England, on the Irish sea coast; population (1981) 27,000. Indstries include chemicals and printing. Britain's first nuclear power station was sited at Calder Hall to the SE, where there is also a plant for reprocessing spent nuclear fuel at *Sellafield* (formerly Windscale).

Whitehead /waɪthed/ Alfred North 1861–1947. English philosopher and mathematician. In his 'theory of organism', he attempted a synthesis of metaphysics and science. His works include *Principia Mathematica* 1910–13 (with Bertrand Russell), *The Concept of Nature* 1920, and *Adventures of Ideas* 1933.

He was professor of applied mathematics at London University 1914–24, professor of philosophy at Harvard University, USA, 1924–37,

and received the Order of Merit 1945. Other works include *Principles of Natural Knowledge* 1919, *Science and the Modern World* 1925, and *Process and Reality* 1929.

Whitehead /waɪthed/ Robert 1823–1905. English engineer who invented the self-propelled torpedo 1866.

He developed the torpedo in Austria in 1866, and within two years was manufacturing 4 m/13 ft torpedoes which could carry a 9 kg/20 lb dynamite warhead at a speed of 7 knots, subsequently improved to 29 knots. They were powered by compressed air and had a balancing mechanism and, later, gyroscopic controls.

Whitehorse /waɪthɔːs/ capital of Yukon Territory, Canada; population (1986) 20,000. Whitehorse is on the NW Highway. It replaced Dawson as capital in 1953.

White Horse any of several hill figures in England, including the one on Bratton Hill, Wiltshire, said to commemorate Alfred the Great's victory over the Danes at Ethandun 878; and the one at Uffington, Berkshire, 110 m/360 ft long, and probably a tribal totem of the Early Iron Age, 1st century BC.

White House /waɪthaʊs/ official residence of the president of the USA, in Washington DC. It is a plain edifice of sandstone, built in the Italian renaissance style 1792–99 to the designs of James Hoban, who also restored it after it was burned by the British 1814; it was then painted white to hide the scars.

The interior was completely rebuilt 1948–52. The president's study is known from its shape as the **Oval Office**. The name White House, first recorded in 1811, is often adapted to refer to other residences of the president, for example Little White House, at Warm Springs, Georgia, where F D Roosevelt died; Western White House, at San Clemente, California, where Nixon had a home.

Whitehouse /waɪthaʊs/ Mary 1910– . British media activist; as founder of the National Viewers' and Listeners' Association, she has campaigned to censor radio and television in their treatment of sex and violence.

white knight in business, a company invited by the target of a takeover bid to make a rival bid. The company invited to bid is usually one which is already on good terms with the target company.

Whitelaw /waɪtlɔː/ William, Viscount Whitelaw 1918– . British Conservative politician. As secretary of state for Northern Ireland he introduced the concept of power sharing. He was Chief Conservative whip 1964–70, and leader of the House of Commons 1970–72. He became secretary of state for employment 1973–74, but failed to conciliate the unions. He was chair of the Conservative Party 1974, and home secretary 1979–83, when he was made a peer. He resigned 1988.

Whiteman /waɪtmən/ Paul 1890–1967. US dance-band leader specializing in symphonic jazz. He commissioned Gershwin's *Rhapsody in Blue*, conducting its premiere in 1924.

whiteout 'fog' of grains of dry snow caused by strong winds in temperatures of between –18°C/0°F and –1°C/30°F. The uniform whiteness of the ground and air causes disorientation in humans.

White Paper in the UK and some other countries, an official document that expresses government policy on an issue. It is usually preparatory to the introduction of a parliamentary bill (a proposed act of Parliament). Its name derives from its having fewer pages than a government 'blue book', and therefore needing no blue paper cover.

White Russia English translation of ◊Byelorussia, republic of the USSR.

White Sea (Russian *Beloye More*) gulf of the Arctic Ocean, on which the port of Archangel stands. There is a Soviet warship construction base, including nuclear submarines, at Severodvinsk. The North Dvina and Onega rivers flow into it, and there are canal links with the Baltic, Black, and Caspian seas.

white spirit a colourless liquid derived from petrol; it is used as a solvent and in paints and varnishes.

White terror general term used by socialists and Marxists to describe a right-wing counter-revolution, for example, the attempts by the Chinese Guomindang to massacre the communists 1927–1931; see ◊White.

whitethroat bird *Sylvia communis* of the warbler group, found in scrub, hedges, and wood clearings of Eurasia in summer, migrating to Africa in winter. It is about 14 cm/5.5 in long. The female is dull brown, but the male is reddish-brown, with a grey head and white throat, and performs an acrobatic aerial display during courtship. The *lesser whitethroat Sylvia curruca* is a little smaller, and a shyer bird.

whiting predatory fish *Merlangius merlangus* common in shallow sandy N European waters. It grows to 70 cm/2.3 ft.

Whitlam /'wɪtləm/ (Edward) Gough 1916– . Australian politician, leader of the Labor Party 1967–78 and prime minister 1972–75. He cultivated closer relations with Asia, attempted redistribution of wealth, and raised loans to increase national ownership of industry and resources.

When the opposition blocked finance bills in the Senate, following a crisis of confidence, Whitlam refused to call a general election, and was dismissed by the governor general (John Kerr). He was defeated in the general election eventually called by Malcolm ◊Fraser.

Whitman /'wɪtmən/ Walt(er) 1819–1892. US poet who published *Leaves of Grass* 1855, which contains the symbolic 'Song of Myself'. It used unconventional ◊free verse and scandalized the public by its frank celebration of sexuality.

Born in West Hill, New York, as a young man Whitman worked as a printer, teacher, and journalist. In 1865 he published *Drum-Taps*, a volume inspired by his work as an army nurse during the Civil War. He also wrote an elegy on Abraham Lincoln, 'When Lilacs Last in the Dooryard Bloom'd'. He preached a US vision of individual freedom and human brotherhood.

Whitney /'wɪtni/ Eli 1765–1825. US inventor who in 1793 patented the *cotton gin*, a device for separating cotton fibre from its seeds.

Whitstable /'wɪtstəbəl/ resort in Kent, SE England, at the mouth of the river Swale, noted for its oysters; population (1985) 27,000.

Whit Sunday Christian church festival held seven weeks after Easter, corresponding to the Jewish Pentecost and commemorating the descent of

Whitman US poet Walt Whitman, whose breaking away from conventional form made him one of the most influential writers of his generation.

the Holy Spirit on the Apostles. The name is probably derived from the white garments worn by candidates for baptism at the festival.

Whitten-Brown /'wɪtn'braʊn/ Arthur 1886–1948. British aviator. After serving in World War I, he took part in the first nonstop flight across the Atlantic as navigator to Captain John ◊Alcock in 1919.

Whittier /'wɪtɪə/ John Greenleaf 1807–1892. US poet who was a powerful opponent of slavery, as shown in the verse *Voices of Freedom* 1846. Among his other works are *Legends of New England in Prose and Verse, Songs of Labor* 1850, and the New England nature poem *Snow-Bound* 1866.

Whittington /'wɪtɪŋtən/ Dick (Richard) lived 13th–14th centuries. English cloth merchant who was mayor of London 1397–98, 1406–07, and 1419–20. According to legend, he came to London as a poor boy with his cat when he heard that the streets were paved with gold and silver. His cat first appears in a play from 1605.

Whittle /'wɪtl/ Frank 1907– . British engineer who invented the jet engine in 1930. In the Royal Air Force he worked on jet propulsion 1937–46. In May 1941 the Gloster E 28/39 aircraft first flew with the Whittle jet engine.

WHO abbreviation for ◊*World Health Organization*.

Who, the English rock group, formed 1964, with a hard, aggressive sound, high harmonies, and a stage show that often included destroying their instruments. Their albums include *Tommy* 1969, *Who's Next* 1971, and *Quadrophenia* 1973. Originally a mod band, the Who comprised Pete Townshend (1945–), guitar and songwriter; Roger Daltrey (1944–), vocals; John Entwistle (1944–), bass; Keith Moon (1947–78), drums.

wholesale the business of selling merchandise to anyone other than the final customer. Most manufacturers or producers sell in bulk to a wholesale organization which distributes the smaller quantities required by retail outlets.

The wholesaling business grew rapidly in the 19th century in line with increasing mass production of goods, which created the need for an intermediary to handle the relatively small orders required by retailers.

whooping cough or *pertussis* an infectious disease, mainly seen in children, caused by colonization of the air passages by the bacterium *Haemophilus pertussis*. There may be catarrh, mild fever, and loss of appetite, but the main symptom is paroxysmal coughing, associated with the sharp intake of breath which is the characteristic 'whoop', and often followed by vomiting and severe nose bleeds. The cough may persist for weeks.

Although debilitating, the disease is seldom serious in older children, but infants are at risk both from the illness itself and from susceptibility to other conditions such as ◊pneumonia and ◊tuberculosis. Immunization lessens the incidence and severity of whooping cough.

whortleberry a form of ◊bilberry.

Whyalla /waɪ'ælə/ port and industrial city (iron and steel) in South Australia; population (1985) 30,000.

whydah African bird, genus *Vidua*, of the weaver family. It lays its eggs in the nest of a waxbill, which rears the young. The young bird resembles the young waxbill, but the adult does not. Males have long tail feathers used in courtship displays.

Whymper /'wɪmpə/ Edward 1840–1911. English mountaineer. He made the first ascent of many Alpine peaks, including the Matterhorn 1865, and in the Andes scaled Chimborazo and other mountains. He wrote *Scrambles amongst the Alps* 1871 and *Zermatt and the Matterhorn* 1897.

WI abbreviation for ◊*West Indies*; ◊*Wisconsin*.

Wichita /'wɪtʃɪtɔ:/ industrial city (oil refining, aircraft, motor vehicles) in S Kansas, USA; population (1980) 280,000. It was settled 1864 and named after an Indian tribe.

Wick /wɪk/ fishing port and industrial town (shipping, distilleries, North Sea oil) in NE Scotland, in the Highland region; population about 8,000. Air services to the Orkneys and Shetlands operate from here.

Wickham /'wɪkəm/ Henry 1846–1928. British planter who founded the rubber plantations of Sri Lanka and Malaysia, and broke the monopoly in rubber production then held by Brazil. He collected rubber seeds from Brazil, where they grew naturally, cultivated them at Kew Gardens, and re-exported them to the Far East.

Wicklow /'wɪkləʊ/ county in the Republic of Ireland, province of Leinster
area 2,030 sq km/784 sq mi
towns county town Wicklow
physical Wicklow Mountains; rivers Slane and Liffey
features the village of Shillelagh gave its name to rough cudgels of oak or blackthorn made there
population (1986) 94,000.

Wicklow /'wɪkləʊ/ port and county town of County Wicklow, Republic of Ireland; population (1981) 5,000.

wide-angle lens a photographic lens of shorter focal length than normal, taking in a wider angle of view.

Widmark /'wɪdmɑːk/ Richard 1914–. US actor who made his film debut in *Kiss of Death* 1947 as a psychopath. He subsequently appeared in a great variety of roles in films including *The Alamo* 1960, *Madigan* 1968, and *Coma* 1978.

Wieland /'viːlænt/ Christoph Martin 1733–1813. German poet and novelist. After attempts at religious poetry, he came under the influence of Voltaire and Rousseau, and wrote novels such as *Agathon* and the satirical *Abderiten*, and tales in verse such as *Oberon, Musarion*, and others. He translated Shakespeare into German 1762–66.

Wien /viːn/ German name for ◊Vienna, capital of Austria.

Wien /viːn/ Wilhelm 1864–1928. German physicist who worked with radiation and established the principle, since known as ◊Wien's law, that the wavelength carrying the maximum energy is inversely proportional to the body's absolute temperature (that is, the hotter the body, the shorter the wavelength). For this, and other work on radiation, he was awarded the 1911 Nobel physics prize.

Wiene /'viːnə/ Robert 1880–1938. German film director of the bizarre Expressionist film *Das Kabinett des Dr Caligari/The Cabinet of Dr Caligari* 1919. He also directed *Orlacs Hände/The Hands of Orlac* 1924, *Der Rosenkavalier* 1926, and *Ultimatum* 1938.

Wiener /'wiːnə/ Norbert 1984–1964. US mathematician, credited with the establishment of the science of cybernetics in his book *Cybernetics* 1948. In mathematics, he laid the foundation of the study of stochastic processes (those dependent on random events), particularly ◊Brownian movement.

Wiener Werkstätte (German *Vienna Workshops*) group of Vienna artisans and artists, founded in 1903 by Josef ◊Hoffmann and Kolo Moser, who were both members of the Vienna ◊Sezession. They designed objects ranging from furniture and jewellery to metal and books, in a rectilinear Art Nouveau style influenced by Charles Rennie ◊Mackintosh. The workshop, financed by Fritz Wärndorfer, closed in 1932.

Wien's law in physics, a law of radiation stating that the wavelength carrying the maximum energy is inversely proportional to the body's absolute temperature: the hotter a body is, the shorter the wavelength. It has the form $\lambda_{max}T = $ constant, where λ_{max} is the wavelength of maximum intensity and T is the temperature. The law is named after the German physicist Wilhelm Wien.

Wiesbaden /'viːsbɑːdn/ spa town and capital of Hessen, West Germany, on the Rhine 20 km/12 mi west of Frankfurt; population (1988) 267,000. Products include cement, plastics, wines and spirits; most of the German sparkling wine cellars are in this area. Wiesbaden was the capital of the former duchy of Nassau 12th century–1866.

Wiesel /'vi:zəl/ Elie 1928– . US academic and human-rights campaigner, born in Romania. He was held in Buchenwald concentration camp during World War II, and has assiduously documented wartime atrocities against the Jews in an effort to alert the world to the dangers of racism and violence. Nobel Peace Prize 1986.

Wigan /'wɪgən/ industrial town (food processing, engineering, paper) in Greater Manchester, NW England; population (1981) 80,000. The *Wigan Alps* are a recreation area with ski slopes and water sports created from industrial dereliction including colliery spoil heaps.

wigeon wild duck *Anas penelope* about 45 cm/18 in long. The male has a red-brown head with cream crown, greyish-pink breast and white beneath. The bill is blue-grey. The female is brown with a white belly and shoulders. It breeds in N Eurasia, and winters in Africa or S Asia.

Wiggin /'wɪgɪn/ Kate Douglas 1856–1923. US writer, born in Philadelphia. She was a pioneer in the running of kindergartens in the USA, and wrote the children's classic *Rebecca of Sunnybrook Farm* 1903 and its sequels.

Isle of Wight

Wight, Isle of /waɪt/ island and county in S England
area 380 sq km/147 sq mi
tows administrative headquarters Newport; Ryde, Sandown, Shanklin, Ventnor
features the *Needles* a group of pointed chalk rocks up to 30 m/100 ft high in the sea to the west; the *Solent* the sea channel between Hampshire and the island (including the anchorage of *Spithead* opposite Portsmouth, used for naval reviews); *Cowes*, venue of Regatta Week and headquarters of the Royal Yacht Squadron; *Osborne House*, near Cowes, a home of Queen Victoria, for whom it was built 1845; *Farringford*, home of Tennyson, near Freshwater
economy agriculture, tourism
population (1987) 127,000
history called *Vectis* ('separate division') by the Romans, who conquered it AD 43. Charles I was imprisoned 1647–48 in Carisbrooke Castle, now ruined.

Wightman Cup annual lawn-tennis competition between international women's teams from the USA and the UK. The trophy, first contested in 1923, was donated by Hazel Wightman (born Hotchkiss; 1886–1974), a former US lawn-tennis player who won singles, doubles, and mixed doubles titles at the US Championships 1909–1911.

Wigner /'wɪgnə/ Eugene 1902– . US physicist, born in Hungary, who introduced the notion of parity into nuclear physics with the consequence that all nuclear processes should

be indistinguishable from their mirror images. For this, and other work on nuclear structure, he shared the 1963 Nobel Prize for Physics with ◊Goeppert-Mayer and Jensen.

Wigtown /'wɪgtaʊn/ former county of SW Scotland extending to the Irish Sea, merged 1975 in Dumfries and Galloway. The administrative headquarters was Wigtown.

Wilander /vɪ'lændə/ Mats 1964– . Swedish lawn-tennis player. He won his first Grand Slam event 1982 when he beat Guillermo Vilas to win the French Open, and had won eight Grand Slam titles by 1990. He played a prominent role in Sweden's rise to the forefront of men's tennis in the 1980s, including Davis Cup successes.

Wilberforce /'wɪlbəfɔ:s/ William 1759–1833. English reformer who was instrumental in abolishing slavery in the British Empire. He began his attacks on slavery while at school, and from 1788 devoted himself to its abolition. He entered Parliament in 1780; in 1807 his bill for the abolition of the slave trade was passed, and in 1833, largely through his efforts, slavery was abolished throughout the empire.

Wilbur /'wɪlbə/ Richard 1921– . US poet, whose witty verse is found in several volumes including *Poems 1943–56* 1957 and *The Mind Reader* 1971.

Wild /waɪld/ Jonathan c. 1682–1725. English criminal who organized the thieves of London and ran an office which, for a payment, returned stolen goods to their owners. He was hanged at Tyburn.

Wilde /waɪld/ Cornel(ius Louis) 1915–1989. US actor and film director, born in Austro-Hungary. He starred in *A Song to Remember* 1945, and directed *The Naked Prey* 1966 (in which he also acted) and *No Blade of Grass* 1970.

Wilde /waɪld/ Oscar (Fingal O'Flahertie Wills) 1854–1900. Irish writer. With his flamboyant style and quotable conversation, he dazzled London society and, on his lecture tour in 1882, the USA. He published his only novel *The Picture of Dorian Gray* 1891, followed by witty plays including *A Woman of No Importance* 1893 and *The Importance of Being Earnest* 1895. In 1895 he was imprisoned for two years for homosexual offences; he died in exile.

Wilde was born in Dublin and studied at Dublin and Oxford, where he became known as a supporter of the ◊Aesthetic movement. He published *Poems* 1881, and also wrote fairy tales and other stories, criticism, and a long, anarchic political essay, 'The Soul of Man Under Socialism' 1891. His elegant social comedies include *Lady Windermere's Fan* 1892 and *An Ideal Husband* 1895. The drama *Salome* 1893, based on the biblical character, was written in French; considered scandalous by the British censor, it was first performed in Paris 1896 with the actress Sarah Bernhardt in the title role.

Among his lovers was Lord Alfred ◊Douglas, whose father provoked Wilde into a lawsuit that led to his social and financial ruin and imprisonment. The long poem *Ballad of Reading Gaol* 1898 and

Wilde Irish writer and poet Oscar Wilde was a leading figure of the Aesthetic movement.

a letter published as *De Profundis* 1905 were written in jail to explain his side of the relationship. After his release from prison in 1897, he lived in France and is buried in Paris.

wildebeest another name for ◊gnu.

Wilder /'waɪldə/ Billy 1906– . US film director, born in Austria. He directed and collaborated on the script of *Double Indemnity* 1944, *The Lost Weekend* 1945, *Sunset Boulevard* 1950, and *Some Like it Hot* 1959.

Born in Vienna, he was in Hollywood from 1934, and worked with Charles Brackett on film scripts such as *Ninotchka* 1939. His films as director include *The Apartment* 1960.

Wilder /'waɪldə/ Thornton (Niven) 1897–1975. US playwright and novelist. He won the Pulitzer Prize for the novel *The Bridge of San Luis Rey* 1927, and for the plays *Our Town* 1938 and *The Skin of Our Teeth* 1942. His play *The Matchmaker* appeared at the Edinburgh Festival in 1954, and as the hit musical entitled *Hello Dolly!* in New York in 1964, and in London the following year.

wilderness area of uncultivated and uninhabited land, which is usually located some distance from towns and cities. In the USA wilderness areas are specially designated by Congress and protected by federal agencies.

wild type in genetics, the naturally occurring gene for a particular character that is typical of most individuals of a given species, as distinct from new genes that arise by mutation.

Wilfrid, St /'wɪlfrɪd/ 634–709. Northumbrian-born bishop of York from 665. He defended the cause of the Roman Church at the Synod of ◊Whitby in 664 against that of Celtic Christianity. Feast day 12 Oct.

Wilhelm /'vɪlhelm/ (English *William*) two emperors of Germany:

Wilhelm I 1797–1888. King of Prussia from 1861 and emperor of Germany from 1871; the son of Friedrich Wilhelm III. He served in the Napoleonic Wars 1814–15 and helped to crush the 1848 revolution. After he succeeded his brother Friedrich Wilhelm IV to the throne of Prussia, his policy was largely dictated by his chancellor ◊Bismarck, who secured his proclamation as emperor.

Wilhelm II 1859–1941. Emperor of Germany from 1888, the son of Frederick III and Victoria, daughter of Queen Victoria. In 1890 he forced Chancellor Bismarck to resign and began to direct foreign policy himself, which proved disastrous. In 1914 he first approved Austria's ultimatum to Serbia and then, when he realized war was inevitable, tried in vain to prevent it. In 1918 he fled to Holland.

Wilhelmshaven /ˌvɪlhelms'hɑ:fən/ North Sea industrial port, resort, and naval base in Lower Saxony, West Germany, on Jade Bay; population (1983) 99,000. Products include chemicals, textiles, and machinery.

Wilkes /wɪlks/ John 1727–1797. British Radical politician, imprisoned for his political views; member of Parliament 1757–64 and from 1774. He championed parliamentary reform, religious toleration, and US independence.

Wilkes, born in Clerkenwell, London, entered Parliament as a Whig 1757. His attacks on the Tory prime minister Bute in his paper *The North Briton* led to his outlawry 1764; he fled to France, and on his return 1768 was imprisoned. He was four times elected MP for Middlesex, but the Commons refused to admit him and finally declared his opponent elected. This secured him strong working- and middle-class support, and in 1774 he was allowed to take his seat in Parliament.

Wilkie /'wɪlki/ David 1785–1841. Scottish genre and portrait painter, active in London from 1805. His paintings are in the 17th-century Dutch tradition.

Wilkins /'wɪlkɪnz/ George Hubert 1888–1958. Australian polar explorer, a pioneer in the use of surveys by both aircraft and submarines. He studied engineering, learned to fly in 1910, and visited both polar regions. In 1928 he flew from Barrow (Alaska) to Green Harbour (Spitsbergen), and in 1928–29 made an Antarctic flight that proved that Graham Land is an island. He also planned to reach the North Pole by submarine.

Wilkins /'wɪlkɪnz/ Maurice Hugh Frederick 1916– . New Zealand scientist. In 1962 he shared the Nobel Prize for Medicine or Physiology with Francis ◊Crick and James ◊Watson for his work on the molecular structure of nucleic acids, particularly ◊DNA, using X-ray diffraction.

Wilkins began his career as a physicist working on luminescence and phosphorescence, radar, and the separation of uranium isotopes, and worked in the USA during World War II on the development of the atomic bomb. After the war, he turned his attention from nuclear physics to biophysics, and studied the genetic effects of ultrasonic waves, nucleic acids, and viruses by using ultraviolet light.

Wilkins /'wɪlkɪnz/ William 1778–1839. English architect. He pioneered the Greek revival in England with his design for Downing College, Cambridge. Other works include the main block of University College London 1827–28, and the National Gallery, London, 1834–38.

will in law, declaration of how a person wishes his or her property to be disposed of after death. It also appoints administrators of the estate (◊executors), and may contain wishes on other matters, such as place of burial or use of organs for transplant. Wills must comply with formal legal requirements.

In English law wills must be in writing or print, and signed by the testator (the person making the will) in the presence of two witnesses who must also sign, and who may not be beneficiaries under the will. Wills cannot be made by minors, or by the mentally incapable. There are exceptions in formalities for active servicemen, who can make a will in any clear form, and when under 18. In the USA, the practice is based on similar lines.

Willem Dutch form of ◊William.

William /'wɪljəm/ 1143–1214. King of Scotland from 1165, known as **William the Lion**. He was captured by Henry II while invading England 1174, and forced to do homage, but Richard I abandoned the English claim to suzerainty for a money payment 1189. In 1209 William was forced by John I to renounce his claim to Northumberland.

William /'wɪljəm/ 1533–1584. Prince of Orange from 1544, known as **William the Silent** because of his absolute discretion. He was appointed governor of Holland by Philip II of Spain in 1559, but joined the revolt of 1572 against Spain's oppressive rule, and, as a Protestant from 1573, became the national leader. He briefly succeeded in uniting the Catholic south and Protestant northern provinces, but the former provinces submitted to Spain while the latter formed a federation in 1579 which repudiated Spanish suzerainty in 1581. He was assassinated by a Spanish agent.

William the badly behaved schoolboy hero of a series of children's books by British author Richmal ◊Crompton, published 1922–70. William rebels against conventional English family life and, with his fellow 'Outlaws', Henry, Douglas, and Ginger, has many mishaps from which there is no honourable escape. Violet Elizabeth Bott, a 'soppy' girl, is an unwelcome addition to the Outlaws.

William /'wɪljəm/ four kings of England:

William I *the Conqueror* c. 1027–1087. King of England from 1066. He was the illegitimate son of Duke Robert the Devil, and succeeded his father as duke of Normandy 1035. Claiming that his relative Edward the Confessor had bequeathed him the English throne, William invaded the country 1066, defeating ◊Harold II at Hastings, Sussex, and was crowned king of England (as depicted in the Bayeux Tapestry).

He was crowned in Westminster Abbey on Christmas Day 1066. He completed the establishment of feudalism in England (see ◊Domesday Book) and kept the barons firmly under control. He died in Rouen after a fall from

his horse and is buried in Caen, France. He was succeeded by his son William II.

William II *Rufus, 'the Red'* c.1056–1100. King of England from 1087, the third son of William I. He spent most of his reign attempting to capture Normandy from his brother ◊Robert II, duke of Normandy. His extortion of money led his barons to revolt and caused confrontation with Bishop Anselm. He was killed while hunting in the New Forest, and was succeeded by his brother Henry I.

William III (William of Orange) 1650–1702. King of Great Britain and Ireland from 1688, the son of William II of Orange and Mary, daughter of Charles I. He was offered the English crown by the parliamentary opposition to James II. He invaded England 1688 and in 1689 became joint sovereign with his wife Mary. He spent much of his reign campaigning, first in Ireland, where he defeated James II at the ◊Boyne 1690, and later against the French in Flanders. He was succeeded by Anne.

Born in the Netherlands, he was made *stadtholder* 1672 to resist the French invasion. He forced Louis XIV to make peace 1678 and then concentrated on building up a European alliance against France. In 1677 he married his cousin Mary, daughter of the future James II. When invited by both Whig and Tory leaders to take the crown from James, he landed with a large force at Torbay, Devon. James fled to France, and his Scottish and Irish supporters were defeated at the battles of Dunkeld 1689 and the Boyne 1690.

William IV 1765–1837. King of the United Kingdom from 1830, when he succeeded his brother George IV, and third son of George III. He was created duke of Clarence 1789, and married Adelaide of Saxe-Meiningen (1792–1849) 1818. During the Reform Bill crisis he secured its passage by agreeing to create new peers to overcome the hostile majority in the House of Lords. He was succeeded by Victoria.

William /'wɪljəm/ (full name William Arthur Philip Louis) 1982– . Prince of the United Kingdom, first child of the Prince and Princess of Wales.

William I /'wɪljəm/ three kings of the Netherlands:

William I 1772–1844. King of the Netherlands 1815–40. He lived in exile during the French occupation 1795–1813, and fought against the emperor Napoleon at Jena and Wagram. The Austrian Netherlands were added to his kingdom by the Allies 1815, but secured independence (recognized by the major European states 1839) by the revolution of 1830. William's unpopularity led to his abdication 1840.

William II 1792–1849. King of the Netherlands 1840–49, son of William I. He served with the British army in the Peninsular War and at Waterloo. In 1848 he averted revolution by conceding a liberal constitution.

William III 1817–1890. King of the Netherlands 1849–90, the son of William II. In 1862 he abolished slavery in the Dutch East Indies.

William of Malmesbury /'wɪljəm 'mɑːmzbri/ c.1080–c.1143. English historian and monk. He compiled the *Gesta regum/Deeds of the Kings* about 1120–40 and *Historia novella*, which together formed a history of England to 1142.

William of Wykeham /'wɪkəm/ c.1323–1404. English politician, bishop of Winchester from 1367, Lord Chancellor 1367–72 and 1389–91, and founder of Winchester College (public school) in 1378 and New College, Oxford, in 1379.

Williams British racing-car manufacturing company started by Frank Williams in 1969 when he modified a Brabham BT26A. The first Williams Grand Prix car was designed by Patrick Head in 1978 and since then the team has been one of the most successful in Grand Prix racing.

Alan Jones captured the world title in a Williams in 1979 and other champions have been Keke Rosberg 1981 and Nelson Piquet 1987. The team captured the Constructor's title in 1980–81 and 1986–87.

Williams US playwright Tennessee Williams. All his most influential works are set in the Deep South where he grew up.

Williams /'wɪljəmz/ (George) Emlyn 1905–1987. Welsh actor and playwright. His plays, in which he appeared, include *Night Must Fall* 1935 and *The Corn Is Green* 1938. His play *How Green Was My Valley* was filmed (Academy Award 1941). He gave early encouragement to the actor Richard Burton.

Williams /'wɪljəmz/ George 1821–1905. Founder of the ◊Young Men's Christian Association (YMCA).

Williams /'wɪljəmz/ John (Christopher) 1942– . Australian guitarist, whose extensive repertoire includes contemporary music and jazz.

Williams /'wɪljəmz/ Roger c.1604–1684. British founder of Rhode Island colony in North America 1636, on a basis of democracy and complete religious freedom.

Williams /'wɪljəmz/ Shirley 1930– . British Social Democrat Party politician. She was Labour minister for prices and consumer protection 1974–76, and education and science 1976–79. She became a founder member of the SDP 1981 and its president 1982. In 1983 she lost her parliamentary seat. She is the daughter of the socialist writer Vera ◊Brittain.

Williams /'wɪljəmz/ Tennessee (Thomas Lanier) 1911–1983. US playwright, born in Mississippi. His work is characterized by fluent dialogue and searching analysis of the psychological deficiencies of his characters. His plays, usually set in the Deep South against a background of decadence and degradation, include *The Glass Menagerie* 1945 and *A Streetcar Named Desire* 1947.

Williams /'wɪljəmz/ William Carlos 1883–1963. US poet. His spare images and language reflect everyday speech. His epic poem *Paterson* 1946–58 celebrates his home town in New Jersey. *Pictures from Brueghel* 1963 won a Pulitzer prize. His work had great impact on younger US poets.

Williamsburg /'wɪljəmzbɜːg/ historic city in Virginia, USA; population (1980) 10,000. Founded in 1632, capital of the colony of Virginia 1699–1779, much of it has been restored to its 18th-century appearance. The College of William and Mary 1693 is one of the oldest in the USA.

Williams-Ellis /'wɪljəmz elɪs/ Clough 1883–1978. British architect, designer of the fantasy resort of Portmeirion, N Wales.

Williamson /'wɪljəmsən/ Henry 1895–1977. English author, known for stories of animal life such as *Tarka the Otter* 1927.

willow

Williamson /'wɪljəmsən/ Malcolm (Benjamin Graham Christopher) 1931– . Australian composer, pianist, and organist, who settled in Britain in 1953. His works include operas (*Our Man in Havana* 1963), symphonies, and chamber music. He became Master of the Queen's Music 1975.

William the Marshall /'mɑːʃəl/ 1st Earl of Pembroke c. 1146–1219. English knight, regent of England from 1216. After supporting the dying Henry II against Richard (later Richard I), he went on a crusade to Palestine, was pardoned by Richard, and was granted an earldom in 1189. On King John's death he was appointed guardian of the future Henry III, and defeated the French under Louis VIII to enable Henry to gain the throne.

William's life was a model of chivalric loyalty, serving four successive kings of England. He grew up as a squire in Normandy, and became tutor in 1170 to Henry, son of Henry II of England.

Willis /'wɪlɪs/ Norman David 1933– . British trade-union leader. A trade union official since leaving school, he succeeded Len Murray as the general secretary of the Trades Union Congress (TUC) in 1984.

He has presided over the TUC at a time of falling union membership, hostile legislation from the Conservative government, and a major review of the role and policies of the Labour Party.

will-o'-the-wisp light sometimes seen over marshy ground, believed to be burning gas containing methane from decaying organic matter.

willow tree or shrub of the genus *Salix*, family Salicaceae, which flourishes in damp places. The leaves are often lance-shaped, and the male and female catkins are found on separate trees. Species include the crack willow *Salix fragilis*, the white willow *Salix alba*, the goat willow *Salix caprea*, the weeping willow *Salix babylonica*, a native of China, and the common osier *Salix viminalis*.

willowherb plant of either of two genera, *Epilobium* or *Chamaenerion*; it is a perennial weed. The rosebay willowherb or fireweed *Chamaenerion angustifolium* is common in woods and waste places. It grows to 1.2 m/4 ft with long terminal racemes of red or purplish flowers.

willow warbler bird *Phylloscopus trochilus* that migrates from N Eurasia to Africa. It is about 11 cm/4 in long, similar in appearance to the chiffchaff, but with a distinctive song, and found in woods and shrubberies.

willy-willy Australian Aboriginal term for a cyclonic whirlwind.

Wilmington /'wɪlmɪŋtən/ industrial port and city (chemicals, textiles, shipbuilding, iron and steel goods, headquarters of Du Pont enterprises) in Delaware, USA; population (1980) 70,000. Founded by Swedish settlers as Fort Christina 1638; taken and renamed by the British in the 1730s.

Wilms' tumour or *nephroblastoma* one of the rare cancers of infancy, arising in the kidneys. Often the only symptom is abdominal swelling. Treatment is by removal of the affected kidney (nephrectomy), followed by radiotherapy and ◊cytotoxic drugs.

Wilson /'wɪlsən/ Brian 1942– . US pop musician, founder member of the ◊Beach Boys.

Wilson /'wɪlsən/ Angus (Frank Johnstone) 1913– . British novelist, whose acidly humorous books include *Anglo-Saxon Attitudes* 1956 and *The Old Men at the Zoo* 1961.

Wilson /'wɪlsən/ Charles Thomson Rees 1869–1959. British physicist, who in 1911 invented the Wilson ◊cloud chamber, an apparatus for studying subatomic particles. He shared a Nobel prize in 1927.

Wilson /'wɪlsən/ Colin 1931– . British author of *The Outsider* 1956, and of thrillers, including *Necessary Doubt* 1964. Later works such as *Mysteries* 1978 are about the occult.

Wilson /'wɪlsən/ Edmund 1895–1972. US critic and writer, born in New Jersey. *Axel's Castle* 1931 is a survey of symbolism and *The Wound and the Bow* 1941 a study of art and neurosis. He also produced the satirical sketches in *Memoirs of Hecate County* 1946.

Wilson /'wɪlsən/ Edward O 1929– . US zoologist, whose books have stimulated interest in ◊biogeography and the evolution of behaviour, or ◊sociobiology. His works include *Sociobiology* 1975 and *On Human Nature* 1978.

Wilson /'wɪlsən/ (James) Harold, Baron Wilson of Rievaulx 1916– . British Labour politician, party leader from 1963, prime minister 1964–70 and 1974–76. His premiership was dominated by the issue of UK admission to EEC membership, the social contract (unofficial agreement with the trade unions), and economic difficulties.

Wilson, born in Huddersfield, West Yorkshire, was president of the Board of Trade 1947–51 (when he resigned because of social service cuts). In 1963 he succeeded Gaitskell as Labour leader and became prime minister the following year, increasing his majority 1966. He formed a minority government Feb 1974 and achieved a majority of three Oct 1974. He resigned 1976, and was succeeded by James Callaghan. He was knighted 1976, and became a peer 1983.

Wilson /'wɪlsən/ ('Jumbo') Henry Maitland, 1st Baron Wilson 1881–1964. British field marshal in World War II. He was commander in chief in Egypt in 1939, led the unsuccessful Greek campaign of 1941, was commander in chief in the Middle East in 1943, and in 1944 was supreme Allied commander in the Mediterranean.

Wilson /'wɪlsən/ Richard 1714–1782. British painter, whose English and Welsh landscapes are infused with an Italianate atmosphere and recomposed in a Classical manner. They influenced the development of an English landscape-painting tradition.

Wilson *US president Woodrow Wilson, who took the USA into World War I. He created the basis for a peace settlement and the League of Nations.*

Wilson /'wɪlsən/ (Thomas) Woodrow 1856–1924. 28th president of the USA 1913–21, a Democrat. He kept the USA out of World War I until 1917, and in Jan 1918 issued his ◊Fourteen Points as a basis for a just peace settlement. At the peace conference in Paris he secured the inclusion of the ◊League of Nations in individual peace treaties, but these were not ratified by Congress, so the USA did not join the League. Nobel Peace prize 1919.

Wilson, born in Virginia, became president of Princeton University 1902. In 1910 he became governor of New Jersey. Elected president 1912 against Theodore Roosevelt and Taft, he initiated anti-trust legislation and secured valuable social reforms in his progressive 'New Freedom' programme. He strove to keep the USA neutral during World War I but the German U-boat campaign forced him to declare war 1917. In 1919 he suffered a stroke from which he never fully recovered.

Wilton /'wɪltən/ market town in Wiltshire, S England, outside Salisbury; population (1981) 4,000. It has manufactured carpets since the 16th century. *Wilton House*, the seat of the earls of Pembroke, was built from designs by Holbein and Inigo Jones, and is associated with Sir Philip Sidney and Shakespeare.

Wilts abbreviation for ◊*Wiltshire*.

Wiltshire /'wɪltʃə/ county in SW England
area 3,480 sq km/1,343 sq mi
towns administrative headquarters Trowbridge; Salisbury, Swindon, Wilton
physical Marlborough Downs, Savernake Forest; rivers Kennet, and Salisbury and Bristol Avons; Salisbury Plain, including Stonehenge
features Salisbury Plain has been used as a military training area since Napoleonic times; Longleat House (Marquess of Bath), Wilton House (Earl of Pembroke), and Stourhead with 18th-century gardens
products wheat, cattle, carpets, rubber, engineering
population (1987) 551,000.

Wimbledon /'wɪmbəldən/ district of the Greater London borough of Merton, headquarters of the All-England Lawn Tennis and Croquet Club where international matches have been held since 1877.

Wimbledon English lawn-tennis centre used for world tennis matches, situated in south London. There are currently 18 courts.

The first centre was at Worple Road when it was the home of the All England Croquet Club. Tennis was first played there in 1875, and in 1877 the club was renamed the All England Lawn Tennis and Croquet Club. The first all England championship was held in the same year. The club and championship moved to their present home in Church Road in 1922.

WIMP *windows, icons, menus, pointing device* in computing, a type of ◊user interface, in which

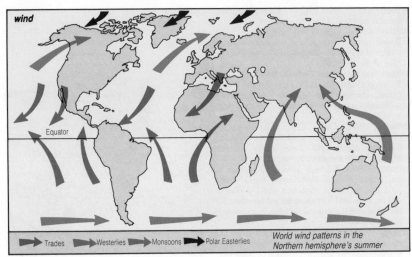

wind

Trades   Westerlies   Monsoons   Polar Easterlies   *World wind patterns in the Northern hemisphere's summer*

programs and files appear as ◊icons, menus drop down from a bar along the top of the screen, and data are displayed in rectangular areas, called windows, which the operator can manipulate in various ways. The operator uses a pointing device, typically a ◊mouse, to make selections and initiate actions.

Winchell /'wɪntʃəl/ Walter 1897–1972. US journalist, born in New York. He was a columnist on the *New York Mirror* 1929–69, and his bitingly satiric writings were syndicated throughout the USA.

Winchester /'wɪntʃɪstə/ cathedral city and administrative headquarters of Hampshire, on the river Itchen; population (1984) 93,000. Tourism is important and there is also light industry. Originally a Roman town, Winchester was the capital of Wessex. Winchester Cathedral is the longest medieval church in Europe and was remodelled from Norman-Romanesque to Perpendicular Gothic under the patronage of William of Wykeham (founder of Winchester College 1382), who is buried there, as are Saxon kings, St ◊Swithun, and the writers Izaac Walton and Jane Austen. A medieval 'reconstruction' of Arthur's Round Table is preserved in the 13th-century hall (all that survives) of the castle.

Winchester disc an alternative name for ◊hard disc.

wind lateral movement of the Earth's atmosphere from high- to low-pressure areas. Although modified by features such as land and water, there is a basic worldwide system of ◊trade winds, ◊Westerlies, ◊monsoons, and others.

A belt of low pressure (the ◊doldrums) lies along the equator. The trade winds blow towards this from the horse latitudes (areas of high pressure at about 30° N and 30° S of the equator), blowing from the NE in the northern hemisphere, and from the SE in the southern. The Westerlies (also from the horse latitudes) blow north of the equator from the SW and south of the equator from the NW.

Cold winds blow outwards from high-pressure areas at the poles. More local effects result from landmasses heating and cooling faster than the adjacent sea, producing onshore winds in the daytime and offshore winds at night.

The ◊monsoon is a seasonal wind of S Asia, blowing from the SW in summer and bringing the rain on which crops depend. It blows from the NE in winter.

Famous or notorious warm winds include the *chinook* of the eastern Rocky Mountains, North

America; the *föhn* of Europe's Alpine valleys; the *sirocco* (Italy)/*khamsin* (Egypt)/*sharav* (Israel), spring winds that bring warm air from the Sahara and Arabian deserts across the Mediterranean; and the *Santa Ana*, a periodic warm wind from the inland deserts that strikes the California coast.

The dry northerly *bise* (Switzerland) and the *mistral*, which strikes the Mediterranean area of France, are unpleasantly cold winds.

wind-chill factor an estimate of how much colder it feels when a wind is blowing. It is the sum of the temperature (in °F below zero) and the wind speed (in miles per hour). So for a wind of 15 mph at an air temperature of –5°F, the wind-chill factor is 20; the equivalent temperature is –38°F.

Windermere /'wɪndəmɪə/ largest lake in England, in Cumbria, 17 km/10.5 mi long and 1.6 km/1 mi wide.

Windhoek /'wɪndhʊk/ capital of Namibia; population (1988) 115,000. It is just north of the Tropic of Capricorn, 290 km/180 mi from the W coast.

wind instrument a musical instrument that uses the performer's breath to make a column of air vibrate. The pitch of the note is controlled by the length of the column. The main types are ◊woodwind instruments and ◊brass instruments.

Wind in the Willows, The a fantasy for children by British author Kenneth ◊Grahame, published in the UK 1908. The story relates the adventures of a group of humanlike animals—Rat, Mole, Badger, and Toad. It was dramatized by A A ◊Milne as *Toad of Toad Hall* 1930.

windmill a mill with sails or vanes which by the action of wind upon them drive machinery for grinding corn or pumping water, for example. Modern wind turbines, designed to use wind power on a large scale, usually have a propeller-type rotor mounted on a tall shell tower. The turbine drives a generator for producing electricity.

Windmills were used in the East in ancient times, and in Europe they were first used in Germany and the Netherlands in the 12th century. The main types of traditional windmill are the *post mill*, which is turned round a post when the direction of the wind changes, and the *tower mill*, which has a revolving turret on top. It usually has a device (fantail) that keeps the sails pointing into the wind. In the USA a light type of windmill with steel sails supported on a long steel girder shaft was introduced for use on farms.

Windscale /'wɪndskeɪl/ former name of Sellafield in Cumbria.

Windsor /'wɪnzə/ industrial lake port (car engines, pharmaceuticals, iron and steel goods, paint, and bricks) in Ontario, SE Canada, opposite Detroit, USA; population (1986) 254,000. It was founded as a Hudson Bay Company post 1853.

Windsor, House of official name of the British royal family since 1917, adopted in place of Saxe-Coburg-Gotha. Since 1960 those descendants of Elizabeth II not entitled to the prefix HRH have borne the surname Mountbatten-Windsor.

Windsor /'wɪnzə/ town in Berkshire, S England, on the river Thames; population (1981) 28,000. It is the site of Windsor Castle, Eton College (public school) 1540, and has a 17th-century guildhall designed by Christopher Wren.

Windsor Duchess of. Title of Wallis Warfield ◊Simpson.

Windsor Duke of. Title of ◊Edward VIII.

Windsor Castle British royal residence in Windsor, Berkshire, founded by William the Conqueror on the site of an earlier fortress. It includes the Perpendicular Gothic St George's Chapel and the Albert Memorial Chapel, beneath which George III, George IV, and William IV are buried. In the Home Park adjoining the castle is the Royal Mausoleum where Queen Victoria and Prince Albert are buried.

St George's is the chapel of the Order of the Garter. Other members of the royal family are buried under the Albert Memorial Chapel. Beyond the Round Tower or Keep are the state apartments

windmill

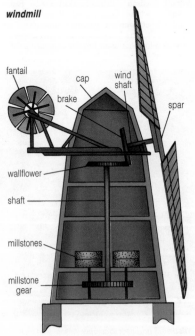

fantail
cap
wind shaft
brake
spar
wallflower
shaft
millstones
millstone gear

windsurfing French windsurfing champion Pascal Maka.

and the sovereign's private apartments. Windsor Great Park lies to the south.

windsurfing a water sport combining elements of surfing and sailing. The windsurfer stands on a board 2.5–4 m/8–13 ft long, which is propelled and steered by means of a sail attached to a mast that is articulated at the foot. The sport was first developed in the US in 1968, and is sometimes called **boardsailing** or **sailboarding**.

wind tunnel a test tunnel in which air is blown over a stationary model aircraft, car, truck, or locomotive to simulate the effects of movement. Lift, drag, and air-flow patterns are observed by the use of special cameras and sensitive instruments. Wind-tunnel testing assesses the aerodynamic design, preparatory to full-scale construction.

wind turbine a modern type of ◊windmill of advanced aerodynamic design used in modern wind-power installations. Some consist of large propellers mounted on tall towers, such as that at Tvind in Denmark. It has an output of some 2 megawatts. Other machines use novel rotors, such as the 'egg-beater' design developed at Sandia Laboratories in New Mexico, USA.

Windward Islands /'wɪndwəd/ islands in the path of the prevailing wind, notably:
West Indies see under ◊Antilles;
◊*Cape Verde Islands*;
◊*French Polynesia* (Tahiti, Moorea, and Makatea).

wine liquor of fermented grape pulp. **Red wine** is the product of the grape with the skin; **white wine** of the inner pulp only. The sugar content is converted to ethyl alcohol by the yeast *Saccharomyces ellipsoideus*, which lives on the skin of the grape. For **dry wine** the fermentation is allowed to go on longer than for **sweet** or **medium**; ◊champagne is bottled while still fermenting, but other sparkling wines are artificially carbonated. The world's largest producers are Italy, France, the USSR, and Spain; others include Germany, Australia, South Africa, California, and Chile; a small quantity of wine is produced in the UK.

A *vintage wine* is that from a good year (as regards quality of wine, produced by favourable weather conditions) in recognized vineyards of a particular area; France has a guarantee of origin (*appellation controlée*), as do Italy (*Denominazione di Origine Controllata*), Spain (*Denominacion Controllata*), and Germany (a series of graded qualities running from *Qualitätswein* to *Beerenauslese*).

wing in biology, the modified forelimb of birds and bats, or the membranous outgrowths of the ◊exoskeleton of insects, which give the power of flight. Birds and bats have two wings. Bird wings have feathers, while bat wings consist of skin stretched between the digits ('fingers') of the limb. Most insects have four wings, which are strengthened by wing veins. The wings of butterflies and moths are covered with wing scales. The hind pair of a fly's wings are modified to form two balancing organs which provide no lift.

Wingate /'wɪŋgeɪt/ Orde Charles 1903–1944. British soldier. In 1936 he established a reputation for unorthodox tactics in Palestine. In World War II he served in the Middle East, and later led the ◊Chindits in guerrilla operations against the Japanese army in Burma.

Winnie-the-Pooh collection of children's stories by British author A A ◊Milne, published in 1926, illustrated by E H Shepard. The stories featured the author's son Christopher Robin, his teddy

wine

bear Winnie-the-Pooh, and a group of toy animals, including Piglet, Eeyore, Rabbit, Owl, Kanga and Roo, and Tigger. Further stories appeared in *The House at Pooh Corner* 1928.

Winnipeg /'wɪnɪpeg/ capital and industrial city (sawmills, textiles, meat packing) in Manitoba, Canada, on the Red River, south of Lake Winnipeg; population (1986) 623,000. Established as Winnipeg 1873 on the site of earlier forts, the city expanded with the arrival of the Canadian Pacific Railroad 1881.

Winnipeg, Lake /'wɪnɪpeg/ lake in S Manitoba, Canada, draining much of the Canadian prairies; area 24,500 sq km/9,460 sq mi.

wintergreen plant of the genus *Pyrola*, family Pyrolaceae. *Pyrola minor*, with rounded white flowers, is a woodland plant. Oil of wintergreen, used in treating rheumatism, is extracted from the leaves of the North American *Gaultheria procumbens*.

Winterhalter /'vɪntə·hæltə/ Franz Xavier 1805–1873. German portraitist. He became court painter to Grand Duke Leopold at Karlsruhe, then, in 1834, moved to Paris and enjoyed the patronage of European royalty.

winter of discontent the winter of 1978–79 in Britain, which was marked by a series of strikes

wing *comparison of wing shapes*

beetle

butterfly

bat

bird of prey

eagle

wine *The upper valley of the river Douro is the centre of northern Portugal's port-wine region. Terraced vineyards, olive groves, and fields of corn surround a typical quinta (estate) near Peso de Regua.*

that contributed to the defeat of the Labour government in the general election of spring 1979. The phrase is from Shakespeare's *Richard III*: 'Now is the winter of our discontent/Made glorious summer by this sun of York.'

The strikes included Ford Motor Company workers Sept–Nov 1978, bakery workers Nov–Dec 1978, lorry drivers Jan–Feb 1979, train drivers Jan 1979, local-authority workers and health-service ancillaries and ambulance crews Jan–Mar 1979 (which led to the much publicized failure to bury dead bodies and to the partial breakdown of some hospital services), water and sewerage workers Feb 1979, and civil servants Feb and Apr 1979.

Winterthur /'vɪntətʊə/ Swiss town and spa NE of Zürich; population (1987) 108,000. Manufacturing includes engines and textiles.

Winter War the USSR's invasion of Finland 30 Nov 1939–12 Mar 1940.

wire a thread of metal, made by drawing a rod through progressively smaller-diameter dies. Fine-gauge wire is used for electrical power transmission; heavier-gauge wire is used to make load-bearing cables.

Gold, silver, and bronze wire has been found in the ruins of Troy and in ancient Egyptian tombs. From early times to the 14th century, wire was made by hammering metal into sheets, cutting thin strips, and making the strips round by hammering them. The Romans made wire by hammering heated metal rods.

Wire drawing was introduced in Germany in the 14th century. In this process, a metal rod is pulled (drawn) through a small hole in a mould (die). Until the 19th century this was done by hand; now all wire is drawn by machine. Metal rods are pulled through a series of progressively smaller tungsten carbide dies to produce large-diameter wire, and through diamond dies for very fine wire. The die is funnel-shaped, with the smaller opening smaller than the diameter of the rod. The rod, which is pointed at one end, is coated with a lubricant to allow it to slip through the die. Pincers pull the rod through until it can be wound round a drum. The drum then rotates, drawing the wire through the die and winding it into a coil.

There are many kinds of wire for different uses: galvanized wire (coated with zinc), which does not rust; ◊barbed wire and wire mesh for fencing; and wire cable, made by weaving thin wires into ropes. Needles, pins, nails, and rivets are made from wire.

Wisconsin

wireless original name for a radio receiver. In early experiments with transmission by radio waves, notably by ◊Marconi in Britain, signals were sent in Morse code, as in telegraphy. Radio, unlike the telegraph, used no wires for transmission, and the means of communication was termed 'wireless telegraphy'.

wireworm the larva of the ◊click beetle.

Wisconsin /wɪˈskɒnsɪn/ state of the north central USA; nickname Badger State
area 145,500 sq km/56,163 sq mi
capital Madison
towns Milwaukee, Green Bay, Racine
features Great Lakes
products premier dairying state, cereals, coal, iron, zinc, lead, agricultural machinery, precision instruments, plumbing equipment
population (1988) 4,816,000
famous people Edna Ferber, Harry Houdini, Joseph McCarthy, Spencer Tracy, Orson Welles, Thornton Wilder, Frank Lloyd Wright
history originally settled by the French; passed to Britain 1763; became American 1783; state 1848.

Wise /waɪz/ Robert 1914– . US film director who began as a film editor. His debut was a horror film, *Curse of the Cat People* 1944; he progressed to such large-scale projects as *The Sound of Music* 1965 and *Star* 1968. His other films include *The Body Snatcher* 1945 and *Star Trek: The Motion Picture* 1979.

Wise /waɪz/ Thomas James 1859–1937. British bibliographer. He collected the Ashley Library of first editions, chiefly English poets and dramatists 1890–1930, acquired by the British Museum at his death, and made many forgeries of supposed privately printed first editions of Browning, Tennyson, and Swinburne.

Wiseman /ˈwaɪzmən/ Nicholas Patrick Stephen 1802–1865. British Catholic priest who became the first archbishop of Westminster 1850.

wisent another name for the European ◊bison.

Wishart /ˈwɪʃət/ George c.1513–1546. Scottish Protestant reformer burned for heresy, who probably converted John ◊Knox.

Wister /ˈwɪstə/ Owen 1860–1938. US novelist who created the genre of the ◊western. He was born in Philadelphia, a grandson of the British actress Fanny Kemble, but became known for stories of cowboys in the American West; for example *The Virginian* 1902.

wisteria climbing shrub *Wistaria sinensis* of the family Leguminosae, native to China. It has racemes of pale mauve flowers, and pinnate leaves.

Witan /ˈwɪtn/ or *Witenagemot* council of the Anglo-Saxon kings, the forerunner of Parliament, but including only royal household officials, great landowners, and top churchmen.

witchcraft the alleged possession and exercise of magical powers (**black magic** if used with evil intent, and **white magic** if benign). Its origins lie in traditional beliefs and religions. Practitioners of witchcraft have often had considerable skill in, for example, herbal medicine and traditional remedies; in 1976 the World Health Organization therefore recommended the integration of traditional healers into the health teams of African states.

The Christian church persecuted witches in Europe during the 15th–17th centuries and in North America (see ◊Salem). The last official execution of a witch in Europe was in 1782 of Anna Goddi, hanged in Switzerland. *Obi* is the witchcraft of black Africa imported to the West Indies, and including Christian elements; ◊voodoo is a similar cult.

witch hazel flowering shrub *Hamamelis virginiana*, native to E Asia and North America. An astringent extract prepared from the bark or leaves is used in medicine.

witch-hunt the persecution of minority political-opposition or socially nonconformist groups without any regard for their guilt or innocence. Witch-hunts are often accompanied by a degree of public hysteria, for example the ◊McCarthy anticommunist hearings during the 1950s in the USA.

withholding tax personal income tax on wages, salaries, dividends, or other income that is taxed at source or by a bank to ensure that it reaches the tax authority. Those not liable to the tax have to reclaim it. In the UK, the withholding of taxes on wages and salaries is known as PAYE (Pay As You Earn).

witness in law, a person who was present at some event (such as an accident, a crime, or the signing of a document) or has relevant special knowledge (such as a medical expert), and can be called on to give evidence in a court of law.

Witt /wɪt/ Johann de 1625–1672. Dutch politician, Grand Pensionary of Holland and virtual prime minister from 1653. His skilful diplomacy ended the Dutch Wars of 1652–54 and 1665–67, and in 1668 he formed a triple alliance with England and Sweden against Louis XIV of France. He was murdered by a rioting mob.

Witt /vɪt/ Katerina 1965– . East German ice skater. She was 1984 Olympic champion and had by 1990 won four world titles and six consecutive European titles.

Wittelsbach /ˈvɪtlzbæx/ Bavarian dynasty, who ruled Bavaria as dukes from 1180, electors from 1623, and kings 1806–1918.

Witten /ˈvɪtn/ city in North Rhine-Westphalia, West Germany; population (1988) 102,000.

Wittenberg /ˈvɪtnbeək/ town in East Germany, on the river Elbe, SW of Berlin, long known for its university (1502, but transferred to Halle 1815); population (1981) 54,000. Luther preached in the Stadtkirche (in which he is buried), nailed his 95 theses to the door of the Schlosskirche 1517, and taught philosophy at the university. The artists Lucas Cranach, father and son, lived here.

Wittgenstein /ˈvɪtɡənʃtaɪn/ Ludwig 1889–1951. Austrian philosopher. *Tractatus Logico-Philosophicus* 1922 postulated the 'picture theory' of language: that words represent things according to social agreement. He subsequently rejected this idea, and developed the idea that usage was more important than convention.

The picture theory said that it must be possible to break down a sentence into 'atomic propositions' whose elements stand for elements of the real world. After he rejected this idea, his later philosophy developed a quite different, anthropological view of language: words are used according to different rules in a variety of human activities—different 'language games' are played with them. The traditional philosophical problems arise through the assumption that words (like 'exist' in the sentence 'Physical objects do not really exist') carry a fixed meaning with them, independent of context.

He taught at Cambridge University, England, in the 1930s and 1940s. *Philosophical Investigations* 1954 and *On Certainty* 1969 were published posthumously.

Witwatersrand /wɪtˈwɔːtəzrænd/ or **the Rand** the economic heartland of S Transvaal, South Africa. Its gold-bearing reef, which streches nearly 100 km/62 mi, produces over half the world's gold. The chief city of the region is Johannesburg.

Wizard of Oz, The Wonderful classic US children's tale of Dorothy's journey by the yellow brick road to an imaginary kingdom, written by L Frank Baum 1900, with many sequels, and made into a musical film 1939 with Judy Garland.

woad biennial plant *Isatis tinctoria*, family Cruciferae, with arrow-shaped leaves and clusters of yellow flowers. Ancient Britons used the blue dye from its leaves as a body paint in battle.

Wodehouse /ˈwʊdhaʊs/ P(elham) G(renville) 1881–1975. English novelist, a US citizen from 1955, whose humorous novels portray the accident-prone world of such characters as the socialite Bertie Wooster and his invaluable and impeccable manservant Jeeves, and Lord Emsworth of Blandings Castle with his prize pig, the Empress of Blandings.

From 1906, Wodehouse also collaborated on the lyrics of Broadway musicals by Jerome Kern, Gershwin, and others. He spent most of his life in the USA. Staying in France in 1941, during World War II, he was interned by the Germans; he made some humorous broadcasts from Berlin, which were taken amiss in Britain at the time, but he was later exonerated, and was knighted 1975. His work is admired for its style and geniality, and includes *Indiscretions of Archie* 1921, *Uncle Fred in the Springtime* 1939, and *Aunts Aren't Gentlemen* 1974.

Woden /ˈwəʊdn/ or *Wodan* the foremost Anglo-Saxon god, whose Norse counterpart is ◊Odin.

Woffington /ˈwɒfɪŋtən/ 'Peg' (Margaret) c. 1714–1760. Irish actress, who played in Dublin as a child and made her debut at Covent Garden, London, in 1740. She acted in many Restoration comedies, often taking male roles, such as Lothario in Rowe's *The Fair Penitent*.

Wöhler /ˈvəʊlə/ Friedrich 1800–1882. German chemist who synthesized the first organic compound (urea) from an inorganic compound (ammonium cyanate). He also isolated the elements aluminium, beryllium, yttrium, and titanium.

wolf /vʊlf/ largest wild member *Canis lupus* of the dog family, found in Eurasia and North America. It is gregarious, grows to 90 cm/3 ft at the shoulder, and can weigh 45 kg/100 lb.

In North America, it is also known as the *timber* or *grey wolf*, to distinguish it from the rare *red wolf* of E Texas and the 'prairie wolf' or ◊coyote. It is now restricted by urban expansion to deep forest country or remote regions.

Wolves disappeared from England at the end of the 13th century, and from Scotland by the 17th century.

Wolf /vʊlf/ Hugo (Filipp Jakob) 1860–1903. Austrian composer, whose songs are in the German *Lieder* tradition. He also composed the opera *Der Corregidor* 1895 and orchestral works, such as *Italian Serenade* 1892.

Wolfe /wʊlf/ Gene 1931– . US writer known for the science-fiction series *The Book of the New Sun* 1980–83, with a Surrealist treatment of stock themes, and for the urban fantasy *Free, Live Free* 1985.

Wolfe /wʊlf/ James 1727–1759. British soldier. He fought at the battles of ◊Dettingen, Falkirk, and ◊Culloden. In 1758 he served in Canada, and played a conspicuous part in the siege of the French stronghold of Louisburg. He was promoted to major-general 1759 and commanded a victorious expedition against Québec, in which he was killed.

Wolfe /wʊlf/ Thomas 1900–1938. US novelist. He wrote four long and powerful autobiographical novels: *Look Homeward, Angel* 1929, *Of Time and the River* 1935, and the posthumous *The Web and the Rock* 1939 and *You Can't Go Home Again* 1940.

Wolfe /wʊlf/ Tom 1931– . US journalist and novelist. In the 1960s a founder of the 'New Journalism', which brought fiction's methods to reportage, Wolfe recorded US mores and fashions in Pop style in *The Kandy-Kolored Tangerine-Flake Streamline Baby* 1965. His sharp social eye is applied to the New York of the 1980s in his novel *The Bonfire of the Vanities* 1988.

Wolfe coined the term 'radical chic' in the late 1960s, reporting on a party held by New York socialites for the Black Panthers. His book *The Right Stuff*, describing the US space programme, was later filmed.

Wolfenden Report /ˈwʊlfəndən/ a report published 1957 of a British royal commission on homosexuality and prostitution. The report recommended legalizing homosexual acts between consenting adults of 21 and over, in private. This became law in 1967.

Wolf-Ferrari /ˈvɒlf feˈrɑːri/ Ermanno 1876–1948. Italian composer whose operas include *Il segreto di Susanna*/*Susanna's Secret* 1909 and the realistic tragedy *I gioielli di Madonna*/*The Jewels of the Madonna* 1911.

Wolfit /ˈwʊlfɪt/ Donald 1902–1968. British actor and manager. He formed his own theatre company in 1937, and excelled in the Shakespearean roles of Shylock and Lear, and Volpone (in Ben Jonson's play).

wolfram another name for ◊tungsten.

Wolfsburg /ˈvɒlfsbʊək/ town NE of Brunswick in West Germany, chosen 1938 as the Volkswagen (Hitler's 'People's Car') factory site; population (1988) 122,000.

Wolfson /ˈwʊlfsən/ Isaac 1897– . British store magnate and philanthropist, chair of Great Universal Stores from 1946. He established the *Wolfson Foundation* 1955 to promote health, education, and youth activities, founded Wolfson College, Cambridge, 1965, and (with the Ford Foundation) endowed Wolfson College, Oxford, 1966.

Wollaston /ˈwʊləstən/ William 1766–1828. British chemist and physicist. Wollaston amassed a large fortune through his discovery in 1804 of how to make malleable platinum. He went on to discover the new elements palladium in 1804 and rhodium in 1805. He also contributed to optics through the invention of a number of ingenious and still useful measuring instruments.

Wollongong /ˈwʊləŋgɒŋ/ industrial city (iron, steel) in New South Wales, Australia, 65 km/40 mi south of Sydney; population (1985, with Port Kembla) 238,000.

Wollstonecraft /ˈwʊlstənkrɑːft/ Mary 1759–1797. British feminist, member of a group of radical intellectuals called the English Jacobins, whose book *Vindication of the Rights of Women* 1792 demanded equal educational opportunities for women. She married William Godwin and died in giving birth to a daughter, Mary (see Mary ◊Shelley).

Wolseley /ˈwʊlzli/ Garnet Joseph, 1st Viscount Wolseley 1833–1913. British field marshal who, as commander in chief 1895–1900, began modernizing the army.

Wolsey /ˈwʊlzi/ Thomas *c.*1475–1530. English cardinal and politician. Under Henry VIII he became both cardinal and lord chancellor 1515, and began the dissolution of the monasteries. His reluctance to further Henry's divorce from Catherine of Aragon, partly because of his ambitions to be pope, led to his downfall 1529. He was charged with high treason 1530 but died before being tried.

Wolverhampton /ˌwʊlvəˈhæmptən/ industrial city (metalworking, chemicals, tyres, aircraft, commercial vehicles) in West Midlands, England, 20 km/12 mi NW of Birmingham; population (1984) 254,000.

Women's Institute (WI) local organization in country districts in the UK for the development of community welfare and the practice of rural crafts.

The first such institute was founded 1897 at Stoney Creek, Ontario, Canada, under the presidency of Adelaide Hoodless; the National Federation of Women's Institutes in the UK was founded 1915. The *National Union of Townswomen's Guilds*, founded 1929, is the urban equivalent. The WI is not associated with any religious faith or political party.

Wolsey English cardinal Thomas Wolsey.

Women's Land Army organization founded 1916 for the recruitment of women to work on farms during World War I. At its peak in Sept 1918 it had 16,000 members. It re-formed June 1939, before the outbreak of World War II. Many 'Land Girls'

wombat

joined up to help the war effort and by Aug 1943, 87,000 were employed in farm work.

women's movement the campaign for the rights of women, including social, political, and economic equality with men. Early campaigners fought for women's right to own property, to have access to higher education, and to vote (see ◊suffragette). Once women's suffrage was achieved, the emphasis of the movement shifted to the goals of equal social and economic opportunities for women, including employment. A current area of concern in industrialized countries is the contradiction between the now generally accepted principle of equality and the demonstrable inequalities between the sexes that remain, both in state policies and in everyday life.

Pioneer 19th-century feminists, considered radical for their belief in the equality of the sexes, include Mary ◊Wollstonecraft and Emmeline ◊Pankhurst in the UK, and Susan

Wolsey *A letter from Henry VIII to Cardinal Wolsey in July 1518, in which the king plays the role of anxious husband. He is hopeful that the queen (Catherine of Aragon) is pregnant, and is 'loath to repair to London', since he wishes to move her 'as little as I may now'.*

B ◊Anthony and Elizabeth Cady ◊Stanton in the USA.

The women's movement gained worldwide impetus after World War II with such theorists as Simone de ◊Beauvoir, Betty ◊Friedan, Kate ◊Millett, Gloria ◊Steinem, and Germaine ◊Greer, and the founding of the National Organization of Women (NOW) in New York 1966. From the late 1960s the radical and militant wing of the movement, as represented by *Women's Liberation* in the USA, argued that women were oppressed by the male-dominated social structure as a whole, which they saw as pervaded by ◊sexism, despite legal concessions towards equality of the sexes.

In the UK since 1975 discrimination against women in employment, education, housing, and provision of goods, facilities, and services to the public has been illegal under the Sex Discrimination and Equal Pay Acts; in the USA the Equal Employment Opportunity Commission, a government agency, was formed 1964 to end discrimination (including sex discrimination) in hiring, but the Equal Rights Amendment (ERA), a proposed constitutional amendment prohibiting sex discrimination passed by Congress in 1972, failed to be ratified by the necessary majority of 38 states.

The economic value of women's unpaid work has been estimated at £2 trillion annually.

women's services the organized military use of women on a large scale, a 20th-century development. First, women replaced men in factories, on farms, and in noncombat tasks during wartime; they are now found in combat units in many countries, including the USA, Cuba, the UK, the USSR, and Israel.

The USA has a separate Women's Army Corps (WAC), established 1948, which developed from the Women's Army Auxiliary Corps (WAAC); but in the navy and air force women are integrated into the general structure. There are separate nurse corps for the three services.

In Britain there are separate corps for all three services: *Women's Royal Army Corps* (WRAC) created 1949 to take over the functions of the Auxiliary Territorial Service, established 1938 – its World War I equivalent was the Women's Army Auxiliary Corps (WAAC); *Women's Royal Naval Service* (WRNS) 1917–19 and 1939 onwards, allowed in combat roles on surface ships from 1990; and the *Women's Royal Air Force* (WRAF) established 1918 but known 1939–48 as the Women's Auxiliary Air Force (WAAF). There are also nursing services: Queen Alexandra's Royal Army Nursing Corps (QARANC) and Naval Nursing Service, and for the RAF Princess Mary's Nursing Service.

Women's Social and Political Union, The (WSPU) British political movement founded 1903 by Emmeline ◊Pankhurst to organize a militant crusade for female suffrage.

In 1909, faced with government indifference, the WSPU embarked on a campaign of window smashing, painting slashing, telephone wire cutting, and arson of public buildings. This civil disobedience had little result and was overtaken by the outbreak of World War I. In Nov 1917, the WSPU became the *Women's Party* led by Christabel Pankhurst.

Wonder /'wʌndə/ Stevie. Stage name of Steveland Judkins Morris 1950– . US pop musician, singer, and songwriter, associated with Motown Records. His hits include 'My Cherie Amour' 1973, 'Master Blaster (Jammin')' 1980, and the album *Innervisions* 1973.

wood the hard tissue beneath the bark of many perennial plants; it is composed of water-conducting cells, or secondary ◊xylem, and gains its hardness and strength from deposits of ◊lignin. It has commercial value as a structural material and for furniture (*hardwoods* such as oak, *softwoods* such as pine).

Wood /wʊd/ Grant 1892–1942. US painter based mainly in his native Iowa. Though his work is highly stylized, he struck a note of hard realism in his studies of farmers, such as *American Gothic* 1930 (Art Institute, Chicago).

Wood /wʊd/ Haydn 1882–1959. British composer. A violinist, he wrote a violin concerto among other works, and is known for his songs, which include 'Roses of Picardy', associated with World War I.

Wood /wʊd/ Henry (Joseph) 1869–1944. English conductor, from 1895 until his death, of the London Promenade Concerts, now named after him. He promoted a national interest in music and encouraged many young composers.

He studied at the Royal Academy of Music and

Women's movement: UK chronology

1562	Statute of Artificers made it illegal to employ men or women in a trade before they had served seven years apprenticeship. (It was never strictly enforced for women, as many guilds still allowed members to employ their wives and daughters in workshops).
1753	Lord Hardwick's Marriage Act brought marriage under state control and created a firmer distinction between the married and unmarried.
1803	Abortion was made illegal.
1836	Marriage Act reform permitted civil weddings and enforced the official registration of births, deaths and marriages.
1839	Custody of Infants Act allowed mothers to have custody of their children under seven years old.
1840s	A series of factory acts limited the working day and occupations of women and children. Bastardy amendment put all the responsibility for the maintenance of an illegitimate child onto its mother.
1857	Marriage and Divorce Act enabled a man to obtain divorce if his wife had committed adultery. (Women were only eligible for divorce if their husband's adultery was combined with incest, sodomy, cruelty, etc.)
1857–82	Married Women's Property Acts allowed them to own possessions of various kinds for the first time.
1861	Abortion became a criminal offence even if performed as a life-saving act or done by the woman herself.
1862–70	Contagious Diseases Acts introduced compulsory examination of prostitutes for venereal disease.
1860s	Fathers could be named and required to pay maintenance for illegitimate children.
1864	Schools Enquiry Commission recommendations led to the establishment of high schools for girls.
1867	Second Reform Act enfranchised the majority of male householders. First women's suffrage committee was formed in Manchester.
1869	Women ratepayers were allowed to vote in municipal (local) elections.
1871	Newham College, Cambridge, was founded for women.
1872	Elizabeth Garrett Anderson Hospital for women opened in London.
1874	London School of Medicine for women was founded.
1878	Judicial separation of married couple became possible. Maintenance orders could be enforced in court.
1880	TUC adopted principle of equal pay for women.
1882	Married Women's Property Act meant that wives were given legal control over their own earned income.
1883	Contagious Diseases Acts were repealed.
1885	Age of consent was raised to 16.
1887	National Union of Women's Suffrage Societies became a nationwide group under Millicent Fawcett.
1903	Women's Social and Political Union was founded by Emmeline and Christabel Pankhurst.
1905–10	Militant campaigns split WSPU. Sylvia Pankhurst formed East London Women's Federation.
1918	Parliament (Qualification of Women) Act gave the vote to women householders over 30.
1923	Wives were given equal rights to sue for divorce on the grounds of adultery.
1925	Guardianship of Infants Act gave women equal rights to the guardianship of their children.
1928	The 'Flapper' Vote: all women over 21 were given the vote.
1937	Matrimonial Causes Act gave new grounds for divorce including desertion for three years and cruelty.
1946	Royal commission on equal pay was formed.
1944	Butler Education Act introduced free secondary education for all.
1948	Cambridge University allowed women candidates to be awarded degrees.
1960	Legal aid became available for divorce cases.
1967	Abortion Law Reform Act made abortion legal under medical supervision and within certain criteria.
1969	Divorce reform was introduced which reduced the time a petitioner needed to wait before applying for a divorce.
1973	Matrimonial Causes Act provided legislation to enable financial provision to be granted on divorce.
1975	Sex Discrimination and Equal Pay Acts. National and Scottish Women's Aid Federations were formed.
1976	Domestic Violence and Matrimonial Proceedings Act. Sexual Offences (Amendment) Act attempted to limit a man's defence of consent in rape cases.
1977	Phasing out of employed married women's option to stay partially out of the National Insurance system. Women qualified for their own pensions.
1980	Social Security Act allowed a married woman to claim Supplementary Benefit and Family Income Supplement if she was the main breadwinner.
1983	Government forced to amend the 1975 Equal Pay Act to conform to EEC directives.
1984	Matrimonial and Family Proceedings Act made it less likely for a woman to be granted maintenance on divorce. It also reduced the number of years a petitioner must wait before applying for a divorce to one year.
1986	Granting of invalid care allowance was successfully challenged in European Court of Justice. Sex Discrimination Act (Amendment) allowed women to retire at the same age as men, and lifted legal restrictions preventing women from working night shifts in manufacturing industries. Firms with less than five employees were no longer exempt from the act.
1990	Legal limit for abortion reduced to 24 weeks.

woodpecker

green woodpecker

became an organist and operatic conductor. As a composer he is remembered for the *Fantasia on British Sea Songs* 1905, which ends each Promenade season.

Wood /wʊd/ John *c.* 1705–1754. British architect, known as 'Wood of Bath' because of his many works in that city. Like many of his designs, Royal Crescent was executed by his son, also *John Wood* (1728–81).

Wood /wʊd/ Mrs Henry (born Ellen Price) 1814–1887. British novelist, a pioneer of crime fiction such as the melodramatic *East Lynne* 1861.

Wood /wʊd/ Natalie. Stage name of Natasha Gurdin 1938–1981. US film actress who began as a child star. Her films include *Miracle on 34th Street* 1947, *The Searchers* 1956, and *Bob and Carol and Ted and Alice* 1969.

wood carving an art form practised since prehistoric times, including W Africa where there is a long tradition, notably in Nigeria, but surviving less often than sculpture in stone or metal because of the comparative fragility of the material. European exponents include Veit ◊Stoss and Grinling ◊Gibbons.

woodcock Eurasian wading bird *Scolopax rusticola*, about 35 cm/14 in long, with mottled plumage, a long bill, short legs, and a short tail.

Woodcraft Folk British name for the youth organization founded in the USA as the Woodcraft League by Ernest Thompson Seton 1902, with branches in many countries. Inspired by the ◊Scouts, it differs in that it is for mixed groups and is socialist in aim.

woodcut print made by a woodblock in which a picture or design has been cut in relief. The woodcut is the oldest type of print, invented in China in the 5th century AD. In the Middle Ages woodcuts became popular in Europe, illustrating early printed books and broadsides.

The German artist Dürer was an early adept of the technique. Multicoloured woodblock prints were developed in Japan in the mid-18th century.

Woodforde /'wʊdfəd/ James 1740–1803. British

cleric whose diaries 1758–1802 form a record of rural England.

woodland area in which trees grow more or less thickly; generally smaller than a forest. Temperate climates, with four distinct seasons per year, tend to support a mixed woodland habitat, with some conifers but mostly broad-leaved and deciduous trees, shedding their leaves in autumn and regrowing them in spring. In the Mediterranean region and parts of the southern hemisphere, the trees are mostly evergreen.

Temperate woodlands grow in the zone between the cold coniferous forest and the tropical forests of the hotter climates near the equator. They develop in areas where the closeness of the sea keeps the climate mild and moist.

woodlouse crustacean of the order Isopoda. woodlice have segmented bodies and flattened undersides. The eggs are carried by the female in a pouch beneath the thorax. Most common in Britain are the genera *Oniscus* and *Porcellio*.

woodmouse rodent *Apodemus sylvaticus* that lives in woodlands, hedgerows, and sometimes open fields in Britain and Europe. About 9 cm/3.5 in long, with a similar length of tail, it is yellow brown above, white below, and has long oval ears. It is nocturnal and feeds largely on seeds, but eats a range of foods, including some insects.

woodpecker bird of the family Picidae, which drills holes in trees to obtain insects. There are about 200 species worldwide. The largest of these, the imperial woodpecker of Mexico, is very rare and may already be extinct.

The European green woodpecker or yaffle *Picus viridis* is green with red crown and yellow rump, and about the size of a jay. The greater and lesser spotted woodpeckers *Dendrocopos major* and *Dendrocopos minor*, also British species, have black, red, and white plumage.

wood pitch a by-product of charcoal manufacture, made from *wood tar*, the condensed liquid produced from burning charcoal gases. The wood

---

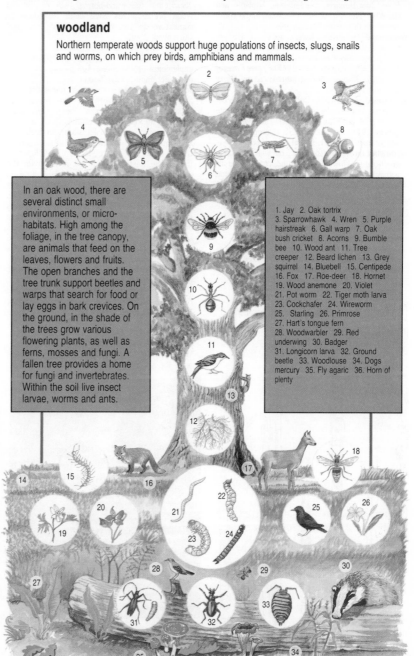

woodland

Northern temperate woods support huge populations of insects, slugs, snails and worms, on which prey birds, amphibians and mammals.

In an oak wood, there are several distinct small environments, or micro-habitats. High among the foliage, in the tree canopy, are animals that feed on the leaves, flowers and fruits. The open branches and the tree trunk support beetles and warps that search for food or lay eggs in bark crevices. On the ground, in the shade of the trees grow various flowering plants, as well as ferns, mosses and fungi. A fallen tree provides a home for fungi and invertebrates. Within the soil live insect larvae, worms and ants.

1. Jay 2. Oak tortrix 3. Sparrowhawk 4. Wren 5. Purple hairstreak 6. Gall warp 7. Oak bush cricket 8. Acorns 9. Bumble bee 10. Wood ant 11. Tree creeper 12. Beard lichen 13. Grey squirrel 14. Bluebell 15. Centipede 16. Fox 17. Roe-deer 18. Hornet 19. Wood anemone 20. Violet 21. Pot worm 22. Tiger moth larva 23. Cockchafer 24. Wireworm 25. Starling 26. Primrose 27. Hart's tongue fern 28. Woodwarbler 29. Red underwing 30. Badger 31. Longicorn larva 32. Ground beetle 33. Woodlouse 34. Dogs mercury 35. Fly agaric 36. Horn of plenty

---

Wonder *US multi-instrumentalist and singer Stevie Wonder began his career with Motown Records at the age of ten.*

tar is boiled to produce the correct consistency. It has been used since ancient times for caulking wooden ships (filling in the spaces between the hull planks to make them watertight).

woodpulp wood that has been processed into a pulpy mass of fibres. Its main use is for making paper, but it is also used in making ◊rayon and other cellulose fibres and plastics.

There are two methods of making woodpulp—mechanical and chemical. In the former, debarked logs are ground with water (to prevent charring) by rotating grindstones. The wood fibres are physically torn apart. In the latter, log chips are digested with chemicals (such as sodium sulphite). The chemicals dissolve the material holding the fibres together.

Woodstock /'wʊdstɒk/ the first free rock festival, held near Bethel, New York State, USA, over three days in Aug 1969. It was attended by 400,000 people, and performers included the Band, Country Joe and the Fish, the Grateful Dead, Jimi Hendrix, the Jefferson Airplane, and the Who. The festival was a landmark in the youth culture of the 1960s (see ◊hippie).

Woodward /'wʊdwəd/ Joanne 1930– . US actress, active in film, television, and theatre. She was directed by Paul Newman in the film *Rachel Rachel* 1968, and also starred in *The Three Faces of Eve* 1957, *They Might Be Giants* 1971, and *Harry and Son* 1984.

Woodward /'wʊdwəd/ Robert 1917–1979. US chemist who worked on synthesizing a large number of complex molecules. These included quinine 1944, cholesterol 1951, chlorophyll 1960, and vitamin B_{12} 1971. Nobel prize 1965.

woodwind musical instrument from which sound is produced by blowing into a tube, causing the air within to vibrate. Woodwind instruments include those, like the flute, originally made of wood but now more commonly of metal. The saxophone, made of metal, is an honorary woodwind because it is related to the clarinet. The oboe, bassoon, flute, and clarinet make up the normal woodwind section of an orchestra.

Woodwind instruments fall into two categories: **reed instruments**, in which air vibrates a reed (a thin piece of wood attached to the mouthpiece

woodwind

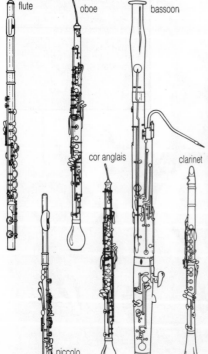

flute oboe bassoon
cor anglais clarinet
piccolo

through which air is blown); and those **without a reed** in which air is simply blown into or across a tube. In both cases, different notes are obtained by changing the length of the tube by covering holes along it. Reed instruments include clarinet, oboe (evolved from the medieval shawm and hautboy), cor anglais, saxophone, and bassoon. Woodwind instruments without a reed include recorder, flute, and piccolo.

There is an enormous variety of woodwind instruments throughout the world.

woodworm the larval stage of certain wood-boring beetles. Dead or injured trees are their natural target, but they also attack structural timber and furniture.

Most common in Britain are the **furniture beetle** *Anobium punctatum*, which attacks older timber, and is estimated to be present in half the country's buildings; the **powder-post beetle** *Lyctus*, which attacks newer timber; the ◊**death-watch** beetle, whose presence always coincides with fungal decay; and the wood-boring ◊weevils. Special wood preservatives have been developed to combat woodworm, which has markedly increased since about 1950.

Wookey Hole /'wʊki 'həʊl/ natural cave near Wells, Somerset, England, in which flint implements of Old Stone Age people and bones of extinct animals have been found.

wool the natural hair covering of the sheep, and also of the llama, angora goat, and some other ◊mammals. The domestic sheep *Ovis aries* provides the great bulk of the fibres used in (textile) commerce. Lanolin is a by-product.

Sheep have been bred for their wool since ancient times. Hundreds of breeds were developed in the Middle East, Europe, and Britain over the centuries, several dozen of which are still raised for their wool today. Most of the world's finest wool comes from the merino sheep, originally from Spain. In 1797 it was introduced into Australia, which has become the world's largest producer of merino wool; South Africa and South America are also large producers. Wools from crossbred sheep (usually a cross of one of the British breeds class with a merino) are produced in New Zealand. Since the 1940s, blendings of wool with synthetic fibres have been developed for textiles.

In Britain there are some 40 breeds of sheep, and the wool is classified as lustre (including Lincoln, Leicester, S Devon, Cotswold, Dartmoor), demi-lustre (Cheviot, Exmoor Horn, Romney Marsh), down (Dorset, Oxford, Suffolk, Hampshire, Southdown), and mountain (Blackface, Swaledale, Welsh White, Welsh Black). Lustre wools are used for making worsted dress fabrics, linings,

Wordsworth One of the greatest English poets, Wordsworth turned to nature for his inspiration, in particular to his native Lake District. This portrait is by Benjamin Haydon.

and braids. Demi-lustre wools are rather finer in quality, and are used for suitings, overcoats, and costumes, and worsted serge fabrics. Finest of English-grown wools are the down; they are used for hosiery yarns, and some for woollen cloths. Mountain wools are coarse and poor in quality, often comprising wool and hair mixed; they are useful for making carpets, homespun tweeds, and low-quality woollen suits and socks.

Woolf /wʊlf/ Virginia (born Virginia Stephen) 1882–1941. English novelist and critic. Her first novel, *The Voyage Out* 1915, explored the tensions experienced by women who want marriage and a career. In *Mrs Dalloway* 1925 she perfected her 'stream of consciousness' technique. Among her later books are *To the Lighthouse* 1927, *Orlando* 1928, and *The Years* 1937, which considers the importance of economic independence for women.

Woollett /'wʊlɪt/ William 1735–1785. British engraver. In 1775 he was appointed engraver to George III.

Woolley /'wʊli/ (Charles) Leonard 1880–1960. British archaeologist. He excavated at Carchemish in Syria, Tell el Amarna in Egypt, Atchana (the ancient Alalakh) on the Turkish-Syrian border, and Ur in Iraq.

Woolman /'wʊlmən/ John 1720–1772. American Quaker, born in New Jersey; he was one of the first antislavery agitators, and left an important *Journal*.

woolsack in the UK, the seat of the Lord High Chancellor in the House of Lords: it is a large square bag of wool and is a reminder of the principal source of English wealth in the Middle Ages.

Woolwich /'wʊlɪdʒ/ London district cut through by the Thames, the northern section being in the borough of Newham and the southern in Greenwich. There is a ferry here and a flood barrier 1984. The Royal Arsenal, an ordnance depot from 1518, was closed down 1967.

Woolworth /'wʊlwəθ/ Frank Winfield 1852–1919. US entrepreneur. He opened his first successful 'five and ten cent' store in Lancaster, Pennsylvania, 1879, and, together with his brother C S Woolworth (1856–1947), built up a chain of similar shops throughout the USA, Canada, the UK, and Europe.

Woomera /'wʊmərə/ (Aboriginal 'weapon-thrower') town in South Australia, site of a rocket range from 1946; population (1984) 1,800.

Wootton /'wʊtn/ Barbara Frances Wootton, Baroness Wootton of Abinger 1897–1988. British educationist and economist. She taught at London University, and worked in the fields of politics, media, social welfare, and penal reform. Her books include *Freedom under Planning* 1945 and *Social Science and Social Pathology* 1959. She was given a life peerage 1965.

Worcester /'wʊstə/ cathedral city with industries (gloves, shoes, Worcester sauce; Royal Worcester porcelain from 1751) in Hereford and Worcester, W central England, administrative headquarters of the county, on the river Severn; population (1985) 76,000. The cathedral dates from the 13th–14th centuries. The birthplace of the composer Elgar at nearby Broadheath is a museum. At the **Battle of Worcester** 1651 Cromwell defeated Charles I.

Worcester /'wʊstə/ industrial port (textiles, engineering, printing) in central Massachusetts, USA, on the Blackstone river; population (1980) 373,000. It was founded 1713.

Worcester Porcelain Factory English porcelain factory, since 1862 the Royal Worcester Porcelain Factory. The factory was founded 1751, and produced a hard-wearing type of softpaste porcelain, mainly as tableware and decorative china.

Worcester became associated with advanced transfer printing techniques used on a variety of shapes often based on Chinese porcelain.

Worcestershire /'wʊstəʃə/ former Midland county of England, merged 1974 with Herefordshire in the

World War I *George V touches his cap to infantrymen in Fouquerueil, Aug 1916 .*

new county of Hereford and Worcester, except for a small projection in the north, which went to West Midlands. Worcester was the county town.

Worcs abbreviation for ◊*Worcestershire*.

word in computing, a unit of storage. The size of a word varies from one computer to another. In a popular microcomputer, it is 16 ◊bits or two ◊bytes; on many mainframes it is 32 bits.

word processor in computing, a program that allows the input, amendment, manipulation, storage, and retrieval of text; or a computer system that runs such software. Since word-processing programs became available to microcomputers, the method is gradually replacing the typewriter for producing letters or other text.

Wordsworth /ˈwɜːdzwəθ/ Dorothy 1771–1855. English writer. She lived with her brother William ◊Wordsworth as a companion and support from 1795 until his death, and her many journals describing their life at Grasmere in the Lake District and their travels provided inspiration and material for his poetry.

Wordsworth /ˈwɜːdzwəθ/ William 1770–1850.

English Romantic poet. In 1797 he moved with his sister Dorothy to Somerset to be near ◊Coleridge, collaborating with him on *Lyrical Ballads* 1798 (which included 'Tintern Abbey'). From 1799 he lived in the Lake District, and later works include *Poems* 1807 (including 'Intimations of Immortality') and *The Prelude* (written by 1805, published 1850). He was appointed poet laureate 1843.

Born in Cockermouth, Cumbria, he was educated at Cambridge University. In 1791 he returned from a visit to France, having fallen in love with Marie-Anne Vallon, who bore him an illegitimate daughter. In 1802 he married Mary Hutchinson. *The Prelude* was written to form part of the autobigraphical work *The Recluse*, never completed.

work in physics, a measure of the result of transferring energy from one system to another to cause an object to move. Work should not be confused with ◊energy (the capacity to do work, which is also measured in ◊joules) or ◊power (the rate of doing work, measured in joules per second).

Work W is equal to the product of the force F used and the distance d moved by the object ($W = F \times d$). For example, the work done when a force of 10 newtons moves an object 5 metres against some sort of resistance is 50 newton-metres (= 50 joules).

Workers' Educational Association (WEA) British organization founded 1913 to provide adult education. It had its origins in classes on cooperation organized by Albert Mansbridge, a clerk at a cooperative store near Toynbee Hall, where meetings were held.

Funding was obtained from the Co-operative Union, trade unions, local education authorities, the Board of Education, and universities. The WEA used a tutorial system that drew on lecturers in higher education and mroe recently its activities have depended upon the extramural departments of universities.

Workmen's Compensation Act 1897 British legislation that conferred on workers a right to compensation for the loss of earnings resulting from an injury at work.

Worksop /ˈwɜːksɒp/ market and industrial town (coal, glass, chemicals, engineering) in Nottinghamshire, central England, on the river Ryton; population (1981) 37,000. Mary Queen of Scots was imprisoned at Worksop Manor (burned 1761).

World Bank popular name for the *International Bank for Reconstruction and Development*, established 1945 under the 1944 Bretton Woods agreement, which also created the International Monetary Fund. The World Bank is a specialized agency of the United Nations that borrows in the commercial market and lends on commercial terms. The *International Development Association* is an arm of the World Bank.

The World Bank now earns almost as much money from interest and loan repayments as it hands out in new loans every year. Over 60% of the bank's loans goes to suppliers outside the borrower countries for such things as consultancy services, oil, and machinery. Control of the bank is vested in a board of executives representing national governments, whose votes are apportioned according to the

World War I *Men of the Middlesex regiment wheeling wounded comrades from the trenches of the Somme to their quarters, Nov 1916.*

World War I (left) Soldiers struggling to move a field gun in muddy conditions. (right) Prisoners from Guilemont pass by troops, Sept 1916.

amount they have funded the bank. Thus the USA has nearly 20% of the vote and always appoints the board's president.

World Cup competitions in football, cricket, rugby union, and other sports, held every four years. The 1986 World Cup of football was won by Argentina, the 1987 cricket World Cup by Australia, and the 1987 rugby World Cup by New Zealand.

The 1994 football World Cup will be hosted by the USA.

World Health Organization (WHO) an agency of the United Nations established 1946 to prevent the spread of diseases, and to eradicate them. Its headquarters are in Geneva, Switzerland.

World Intellectual Property Organization (WIPO) specialist agency of the United Nations established 1974 to coordinate the international protection (initiated by the Paris convention 1883) of inventions, trademarks, and industrial designs, and also literary and artistic works (as initiated by the Berne convention 1886).

World Meteorological Organization agency, part of the United Nations since 1950, that promotes the international exchange of weather information

through the establishment of a worldwide network of meteorological stations. It was founded as the International Meteorological Organization 1873, and its headquarters are now in Geneva, Switzerland.

World Series baseball competition between the winners of the National League (NL) and American League (AL) in the USA. It is a best-of-seven series played each October, and was inaugurated 1903 by the newspaper *New York World*. See also ◊baseball.

World War I 1914–1918. War between the Central Powers (Germany, Austria-Hungary, and allies) on one side and the Triple Entente (Britain and the British Empire, France, and Russia) and their allies, including the USA (which entered 1917), on the other side. An estimated 10 million lives were lost and twice that number were wounded.

outbreak On 28 June the heir to the Austrian throne was assassinated in Sarajevo, Serbia; on 28 July Austria declared war on Serbia; as Russia mobilized, Germany declared war on Russia and France, taking a short cut in the west by invading Belgium; on 4 Aug Britain declared war on Germany.

1914 Western Front The German advance reached within a few miles of Paris, but an Allied counterattack at Marne drove them back to the Aisne River; the opposing lines then settled into trench warfare.

Eastern Front The German commander Hindenburg halted the Russian advance through the Ukraine and across Austria-Hungary at the Battle of Tannenberg in E Prussia.

Africa On 16 Sept all Germany's African colonies were in Allied hands.

Middle East On 1 Nov Turkey entered the war on the side of the Central Powers and soon attacked Russia in the Caucasus Mountains.

1915 Western Front Several offensives on both sides resulted in insignificant gains. At Ypres, Belgium, the Germans used poison gas for the first time.

Eastern Front The German field marshals Mackensen and Hindenburg drove back the Russians and took Poland.

Middle East British attacks against Turkey in Mesopotamia (Iraq), the Dardanelles, and at Gallipoli were all unsuccessful.

World War II Lille Sédin, 1940. Pilots at a Royal Air Force fighter aerodrome in France race to their Hurricane aircraft.

Italy declared war on Austria; Bulgaria joined the Central Powers.

war at sea Germany declared all-out U-boat war, but the sinking of the British ocean liner *Lusitania* (with Americans among the 1,198 lost) led to demands that the USA enter the war.

1916 Western Front German attack at Verdun was countered by the Allies on the Somme, where tanks were used for the first time.

Eastern Front Romania joined the Allies but was soon overrun by Germany.

Middle East Kut-al-Imara, Iraq, was taken from the British by the Turks.

war at sea The Battle of Jutland between England and Germany which, although indecisive, put a stop to further German naval participation in the war.

1917 The USA entered the war. The UK launched the third battle at Ypres and by Nov had taken Passchendaele.

1918 Eastern Front On 3 Mar Soviet Russia signed the Treaty of Brest-Litovsk with Germany, ending Russian participation in the war (the Russian Revolution 1917 led into their civil war 1918–21).

Western Front Germany began a final offensive. In Apr the Allies appointed the French marshal Foch supreme commander, but by June (when the first US troops went into battle) the Allies had lost all gains since 1915, and the Germans were on the Marne. The battle at Amiens marked the launch of the victorious Allied offensive.

Italy At Vittorio Veneto the British and Italians finally defeated the Austrians.

German capitulation began with naval mutinies at Kiel, followed by uprisings in the major cities. Kaiser Wilhelm II abdicated, and on 11 Nov the armistice was signed.

1919 18 June, peace treaty of Versailles. (The USA signed a separate peace accord with Germany and Austria 1921.)

World War II 1939–1945. War between Germany, Italy, and Japan (the Axis powers) on one side, and Britain, the Commonwealth, France, the USA, the USSR, and China (the Allied powers) on the other.

World War II *The liberation of Paris by the Allies in June 1944; General de Gaulle leads jubilant Parisians down the Champs-Elysées.*

An estimated 55 million lives were lost, 20 million of them citizens of the USSR.

1939 Sept German invasion of Poland; Britain and France declared war on Germany; USSR invaded Poland; fall of Warsaw (Poland divided between Germany and USSR).

Nov USSR invaded Finland.

1940 Mar Soviet peace treaty with Finland.

Apr Germany occupied Denmark, Norway, the Netherlands, Belgium, and Luxembourg. In Britain, a coalition government was formed under Churchill.

May Germany outflanked the defensive French Maginot Line.

May–June Evacuation of 337,131 Allied troops from Dunkirk, France, across the Channel to England.

June Italy declared war on Britain and France; Germans entered Paris; the French prime minister Pétain signed an armistice with Germany and moved the seat of government to Vichy.

July–Oct Battle of Britain between British and German air forces.

Sept Japanese invasion of French Indo-China.

Oct Abortive Italian invasion of Greece.

1941 Apr Germany occupied Greece and Yugoslavia.

June Germany invaded the USSR; Finland declared war on the USSR.

July Germans entered Smolensk, USSR.

Dec Germans within 40 km/25 mi of Moscow, with Leningrad under siege. First Soviet counteroffensive. Japan bombed Pearl Harbor, Hawaii, and declared war on the USA and Britain. Germany and Italy declared war on the USA.

1942 Jan Japanese conquest of the Philippines.

June Naval battle of Midway, the turning point of the Pacific War.

Aug German attack on Stalingrad, USSR.

Oct–Nov Battle of El Alamein in N Africa, turn of the tide for the Western Allies.

Nov Soviet counteroffensive on Stalingrad.

1943 Jan Casablanca Conference issued Allied demand of unconditional surrender; Germans retreated from Stalingrad.

Mar USSR drove Germans back to the river Donetz.

May End of Axis resistance in N Africa.

Aug Beginning of campaign against Japanese in Burma; US Marines landed on Guadalcanal, Solomon Islands.

Sept Italy surrendered to Allies; Allied landings at Salerno; the USSR retook Smolensk.

Oct Italy declared war on Germany.

Nov US Navy defeated the Japanese in Battle of Guadalcanal.

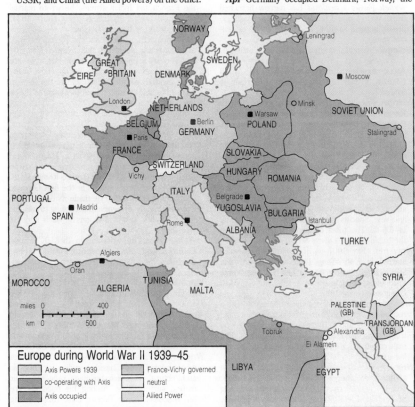

Europe during World War II 1939–45

Axis Powers 1939
co-operating with Axis
Axis occupied
France-Vichy governed
neutral
Allied Power

Nov-Dec Allied leaders met at Tehran Conference.
1944 Jan Allied landing in Nazi-occupied Italy: Battle of Anzio.
Mar End of German U-boat campaign in the Atlantic.
May Fall of Monte Cassino, S Italy.
6 June D-day: Allied landings in Nazi-occupied and heavily defended Normandy.
July Bomb plot of German generals against Hitler failed.
Aug Romania joined Allies.
Sept Battle of Arnhem on the Rhine; Soviet armistice with Finland.
Oct The Yugoslav guerrilla leader Tito and Soviets entered Belgrade.
Dec German counteroffensive, Battle of the Bulge.
1945 Feb Soviets reached German border; Yalta conference; Allied bombing campaign over Germany (Dresden destroyed); US reconquest of the Philippines completed; Americans landed on Iwo Jima, S of Japan.
Apr Hitler committed suicide.
May German surrender to the Allies.
June US troops completed the conquest of Okinawa (one of the Japanese Ryukyu Islands).
July Potsdam Conference issued Allied ultimatum to Japan.
Aug Atom bombs dropped by the USA on Hiroshima and Nagasaki; Japan surrendered.

World Wide Fund for Nature (WWF, formerly the *World Wildlife Fund*) an international organization established 1961 to raise funds for conservation by public appeal. Its headquarters are in Gland, Switzerland. Projects include conservation of particular species (for example, the tiger and giant panda) and special areas (such as the Simen Mountains, Ethiopia).

worm any of various elongated limbless creatures. Worms include the flatworms, such as ◊flukes and ◊tapeworms; the roundworms or ◊nematodes, such as the potato eelworm and the hookworm, an animal parasite; the marine ribbon worms or nemerteans; and the segmented worms or ◊annelids.

In 1979, giant sea worms about 3 m/10 ft long, living within tubes created by their own excretions, were discovered 2,450 m/8,000 ft beneath the Pacific NE of the Galápagos Islands. The New Zealand flatworm *Artioposthia triangulata*, 15 cm/6 in long and weighing 2 g/0.07 oz, had by 1990 colonized every county of Northern Ireland and parts of Scotland. It can eat an ◊earthworm in 30 minutes and so destroys soil fertility.

WORM *write once, read many times* in computing, a storage device, similar to ◊CD-ROM. The computer can write to the disc directly, but cannot subsequently erase or overwrite the same area. WORMs are mainly used for archiving and backup copies.

Worms /wɜːmz, German vɔːms/ industrial town in Rhineland-Palatinate, West Germany, on the Rhine; population (1984) 73,000. Liebfraumilch wine is produced here. The Protestant reformer Luther appeared before the *Diet* (Assembly) *of Worms* 1521, and was declared an outlaw by the Roman Catholic church.

wormwood aromatic herb *Artemisia absinthium*, family Compositae; the leaves are used in ◊absinthe.

Worner /'vɔːnə/ Manfred 1934– . West German politician, NATO Secretary-General from 1988. He was elected for the conservative Christian Democratic Union (CDU) to the Bundestag (parliament) in 1965 and, as a specialist in strategic affairs, served as defence minister under Chancellor Kohl 1982–88. A proponent of closer European military collaboration, he succeeded Peter Carrington as secretary general of NATO in July 1988.

Worrall /'worəl/ Denis John 1935– . South African politician, member of the white opposition to apartheid.

A former academic and journalist, he joined the National Party (NP) and was made ambassador in London 1984–87. On his return to South Africa he resigned from the NP and in 1988 established the Independent Party (IP), which later merged with other white opposition parties to form the reformist Democratic Party (DP), advocating dismantlement of the ◊apartheid system and universal adult suffrage. A co-leader of the DP, he was elected to parliament in 1989.

worsted (from Worstead, Norfolk, where it was first made) a stiff, smooth woollen fabric.

Worthing /'wɜːðɪŋ/ seaside resort in West Sussex, England, at the foot of the South Downs; population (1984) 94,000. Industries include electronics, engineering, plastics, and furniture. There are traces of prehistoric and Roman occupation in the vicinity.

Wotton /'wʊtn/ Henry 1568–1639. English poet and diplomat under James I, provost of Eton public school from 1624. He defined an ambassador as 'an honest man sent to lie abroad for the good of his country'. *Reliquiae Wottonianae* 1651 includes the lyric 'You meaner beauties of the night'.

Wounded Knee /'wuːndɪd 'niː/ site on the Oglala Sioux Reservation, South Dakota, USA, of a confrontation between the US Army and American Indians. Sitting Bull was killed, supposedly resisting arrest, on 15 Dec 1890, and on 29 Dec a group of Indians involved with him in the Ghost Dance Movement (aimed at resumption of Indian control of North America with the aid of the spirits of dead braves) were surrounded and 153 killed.

In 1973 the militant American Indian Movement, in the siege of Wounded Knee 27 Feb–8 May, held hostages and demanded a government investigation of the Indian treaties.

Wouvermans /'waʊvəmæn/ family of Dutch painters, based in Haarlem. The brothers *Philips Wouvermans* (1619–68), *Pieter Wouvermans* (1623–82), and *Jan Wouvermans* (1629–66) specialized in landscapes with horses and riders, and military scenes.

W particle type of ◊elementary particle.

wpm abbreviation for *words per minute*.

wrack any of the large brown seaweeds characteristic of rocky shores. The *bladder wrack Fucus vesiculosus* has narrow branched fronds up to 1 m/3.3 ft long, with oval air bladders, usually in pairs on either side of the midrib or central vein.

Wrangel /'ræŋgəl, 'vræŋgɪl/ Ferdinand Petrovich, Baron von 1794–1870. Russian vice admiral and Arctic explorer, after whom Wrangel Island (Ostrov Vrangelya) in the Soviet Arctic is named.

Wrangel /'ræŋgəl, 'vræŋgɪl/ Peter Nicolaievich, Baron von 1878–1928. Russian general, born in St Petersburg. He commanded a division of Cossacks in World War I, and in 1920 became commander in chief of the White army in the Crimea fighting against the Bolsheviks.

wrasse fish of the family Labridae, found in temperate and tropical seas. They are slender, and often brightly coloured, with a single long dorsal fin. They have elaborate courtship rituals, and some species can change their colouring and sex. Species vary in size from 5–200 cm/2 in–6.5 ft. The most common British species is the ballan wrasse *Labrus bergylta*.

Wray /reɪ/ Fay 1907– . US film actress who starred in *King Kong* 1933 after playing the lead in Erich von Stroheim's *The Wedding March* 1928 and starring in *Doctor X* 1932 and *The Most Dangerous Game* 1932.

wren small brown bird *Troglodytes troglodytes* with a cocked tail, found in North America, Europe, and N Asia. It is about 10 cm/4 in long, has a loud trilling song, and feeds on insects and spiders. The male constructs a domed nest of moss, grass, and leaves.

Wren /ren/ Christopher 1632–1723. English architect, designer of St Paul's Cathedral, London, built 1675–1710; many London churches including St Bride's, Fleet Street, and St Mary-le-Bow,

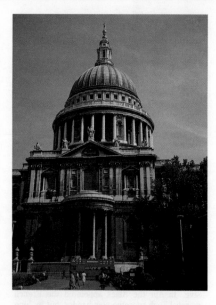

Wren The largest of London's churches and symbol of Christopher Wren's architectural achievement, St Paul's Cathedral, built 1675–1710.

Cheapside; the Royal Exchange; Marlborough House; and the Sheldonian Theatre, Oxford.

Wren studied mathematics, and in 1660 became a professor of astronomy at Oxford. His opportunity as an architect came after the Great Fire of London 1666. He prepared a plan for rebuilding the city, but it was not adopted. Instead, Wren was commissioned to rebuild 51 City churches and St Paul's Cathedral. The west towers of Westminster Abbey, often attributed to him, were the design of his pupil ◊Hawksmoor.

Wren /ren/ P(ercival) C(hristopher) 1885–1941. British novelist. Drawing on his experiences in the French and Indian armies, he wrote martial adventure novels including *Beau Geste* 1924, dealing with the Foreign Legion.

wrestling sport popular in ancient Egypt, Greece, and Rome, and included in the Olympics from 704 BC. The two main modern international styles are *Graeco-Roman*, concentrating on above-waist holds, and *freestyle*, which allows the legs to be used to hold or trip; in both the aim is to throw the opponent to the ground.

Many countries have their own forms of wrestling. *Glima* is unique to Iceland; *Kushti* is the national style practised in Iran; *Schwingen* has been practised in Switzerland for hundreds of years; and ◊sumo is the national sport in Japan. World championships for freestyle wrestling have existed since 1951 and since 1921 for Graeco-Roman style. Graeco-Roman was included in the first Olympic programme 1896; freestyle made its debut 1904. Competitors are categorized according to weight: there are ten weight divisions in each style of wrestling.

Other forms of wrestling in the UK include *Cumberland and Westmoreland, West Country*, and *Lancashire*. Each has its own rules, peculiar to the style of wrestling.

Wrexham /'reksəm/ town in Clwyd, NE Wales, 19 km/12 mi SW of Chester; population (1983) 40,000. Industries include coal, electronics, and pharmaceuticals. It is the seat of the Roman Catholic bishopric of Menevia (Wales). Elihu Yale, benefactor of Yale university, died in Wrexham and is buried in the 15th-century church of St Giles.

Wright /raɪt/ Frank Lloyd 1869–1959. US architect who rejected Neo-Classicist styles for 'organic architecture', in which buildings reflected their natural surroundings. Among his buildings are his Wisconsin home Taliesin East 1925; Falling

Wright *US architect Frank Lloyd Wright at 87. The originality of his work stands out in city buildings like the Guggenheim Museum in New York 1959. He condemned the growing congestion of cities and encouraged closeness to nature.*

Water, Pittsburgh, Pennsylvania, 1936; and the Guggenheim Museum, New York, 1959.

Wright /raɪt/ Joseph 1855–1930. English philologist. He was professor of comparative philology at Oxford 1901–25, and recorded English local speech in his six-volume *English Dialect Dictionary* 1896–1905.

Wright /raɪt/ Joseph 1734–1797. British painter, known as *Wright of Derby* from his birthplace. He painted portraits, landscapes, and scientific experiments. His work is often dramatically lit, by fire, candlelight, or even volcanic explosion.

Several of his subjects are highly original, for example *The Experiment on a Bird in the Air Pump* 1768 (National Gallery, London). His portraits include the reclining figure of *Sir Brooke Boothby* 1781 (Tate Gallery, London).

Wright /raɪt/ Judith 1915– . Australian poet, author of *The Moving Image* 1946 and *Alive* 1972.

Wright /raɪt/ Orville 1871–1948 and Wilbur 1867–1912. US brothers who pioneered powered flight. Inspired by ◊Lilienthal's gliding, they perfected their piloted glider 1902. In 1903 they built a powered machine and became the first to make a successful powered flight, near Kitty Hawk, North Carolina.

Wright /raɪt/ Peter 1917– . British intelligence agent. His book *Spycatcher* 1987, written after his retirement, caused an international stir when the British government tried unsuccessfully to block its publication anywhere in the world because of its damaging revelations about the secret service.

Wright /raɪt/ Richard 1908–1960. US novelist. He was one of the first to depict the condition of black people in 20th-century US society with *Native Son* 1940 and the autobiography *Black Boy* 1945.

Wright /raɪt/ Sewall 1889–1988. US geneticist and statistician. During the 1920s he helped modernize ◊Darwin's theory of evolution, using statistics to model the behaviour of populations of genes.

Wright's work on genetic drift centred on a phenomenon occurring in small isolated colonies where the chance disappearance of some types of gene leads to evolution without the influence of natural selection.

writ in English law, a document issued in the name of an executive officer of the crown, such as the Lord Chancellor or a judge, commanding some act

from a subject. A writ of summons is the first step in legal proceedings in the High Court.

The writ originated in the Carolingian bureaucracy but reached its fullest development in post-Conquest England. By the High Middle Ages, the royal writ took three main forms: *letters close*, addressed to a specified individual or group; *letters patent*, addressed to all who should see them, and usually conferring licences or commissions; and *charters*, which recorded grants of land or privileges.

Writers to the Signet a society of Scottish ◊solicitors. Their predecessors were originally clerks in the secretary of state's office entrusted with the preparation of documents requiring the signet, or seal. Scottish solicitors may be members of other societies, such as the Royal Faculty of Procurators in Glasgow.

writing a written form of communication using a set of symbols: see ◊alphabet, ◊cuneiform, ◊hieroglyphic. The last two used ideographs (picture writing) and phonetic word symbols side by side, as does modern Chinese. Syllabic writing, as in Japanese, develops from the continued use of a symbol to represent the sound of a short word. 8,000-year-old inscriptions, thought to be pictographs, were found on animal bones and tortoise shells in Henan province, China, at a Neolithic site at Jiahu. They are thought to predate the oldest known writing (Mesopotamian) by 2,500 years.

Wrocław /ˈvrɒtswɑːf/ industrial river port in Poland, on the river Oder; population (1985) 636,000. Under the German name of Breslau, it was the capital of former German Silesia. Industries include shipbuilding, engineering, textiles, and electronics.

wrought iron fairly pure iron containing beads of slag, widely used for construction work before the days of cheap steel. It is strong, tough, and easy to machine. It is made in a puddling furnace invented by Henry Colt in England 1784. Pig iron is remelted and heated strongly in air with iron ore, burning out the carbon in the metal, leaving quite pure iron and a slag containing impurities. The pasty metal resulting is then hammered to remove as much of the remaining slag as possible.

wt abbreviation for *weight*.

Wuchang /ˌwuːˈtʃæŋ/ former city in China; amalgamated with ◊Wuhan.

Wuhan /ˌwuːˈhæn/ river port and capital of Hubei province, China, at the confluence of the Han and Chang Jiang, formed 1950 as one of China's greatest industrial areas by the amalgamation of Hankou, Hanyang, and Wuchang; population (1986) 3,400,000. It produces iron, steel, machine tools, textiles, and fertilizer.

A centre of revolt in both the Taiping Rebellion 1851–65 and the 1911 revolution, it had an anti-Mao revolt 1967 during the Cultural Revolution.

Wuhsien /ˌwuːˈʃiˈen/ another name for ◊Suzhou, a city in China.

Wundt /vʊnt/ Wilhelm Max 1832–1920. German physiologist, who regarded psychology as the study of internal experience or consciousness. His main psychological method was introspection; he also studied sensation, perception of space and time, and reaction times.

Wuppertal /ˈvʊpətɑːl/ industrial town in North Rhine-Westphalia, West Germany, 32 km/20 mi east of Düsseldorf; population (1988) 374,000. Industries include textiles, plastics, brewing, and electronics. It was formed 1929 (named 1931) by uniting Elberfeld (13th century) and Barmen (11th century).

Württemberg /ˈvɜːtəmbɜːg/ former kingdom in SW Germany, 1805–1918, which joined the German Reich in 1870. Its capital was Stuttgart. Divided in 1946 between the administrative West German *Länder* of Württemberg-Baden and Württemberg-Hohenzollern, from 1952 it was part of the *Land* of ◊Baden-Württemberg.

Würzburg /ˈvɜːtsbɜːg/ industrial town (engineering, printing, wine, brewing) in NW Bavaria, West Germany; population (1988) 127,000. The bishop's palace was decorated by Tiepolo.

Wyoming

Wuthering Heights a novel by Emily Brontë, published in the UK 1847, which chronicles the tumultuous relationship of Heathcliff and Catherine.

Heathcliff is taken in as a child by the Earnshaw family and forms an intense relationship with Catherine Earnshaw but is cruelly treated by her brother Hindley. Heathcliff flees, believing Catherine has rejected him, but returns after a few years to wreak his revenge. He marries Isabella, sister of Catherine's husband, and when Catherine dies in childbirth Heathcliff forces her daughter Cathy to marry his son Linton. When Linton dies, Cathy turns to Hindley's son Hareton.

WV abbreviation for ◊*West Virginia*.

WY abbreviation for ◊*Wyoming*.

Wyatt /ˈwaɪət/ James 1747–1813. English architect, contemporary of the Adam brothers, who designed in the Neo-Gothic style. His over enthusiastic 'restorations' of medieval cathedrals earned him the nickname 'Wyatt the Destroyer'.

Wyatt /ˈwaɪət/ Thomas *c.* 1503–1542. English poet. He was employed on diplomatic missions by Henry VIII, and in 1536 was imprisoned for a time in the Tower of London, since he was thought to have been the lover of Henry VIII's second wife, Anne Boleyn. In 1541 Wyatt was again imprisoned on charges of treason. With the Earl of Surrey, he pioneered the use of the sonnet in England.

Wyatville /ˈwaɪətvɪl/ Jeffrey. Adopted name of Jeffrey Wyatt 1766–1840. English architect who remodelled Windsor Castle, Berkshire. He was a nephew of the architect James Wyatt.

Wycherley /ˈwɪtʃəli/ William 1640–1710. English Restoration playwright. His first comedy *Love in a Wood* won him court favour 1671, and later bawdy works include *The Country Wife* 1675 and *The Plain Dealer* 1676.

Wycliffe /ˈwɪklɪf/ John *c.* 1320–1384. English religious reformer. Allying himself with the party of John of Gaunt, which was opposed to ecclesiastical influence at court, he attacked abuses in the church, maintaining that the Bible rather than the church was the supreme authority. About 1378 he criticized such fundamental doctrines as priestly absolution, confession, and indulgences. He set disciples to work on translating the Bible into English.

Having studied at Oxford University, he became master of Balliol College, and sent out bands of travelling preachers. He was denounced as a heretic.

Wye /waɪ/ river in Wales and England; length 208 km/130 mi. It rises on Plynlimmon, NE Dyfed, flowing SE and E through Powys, and Hereford and Worcester, then follows the Gwent/Gloucestershire border before joining the river Severn S of Chepstow. Other rivers of the same name in the UK are found in Buckinghamshire (15 km/9 mi) and Derbyshire (32 km/20 mi).

Wyeth /ˈwaɪəθ/ Andrew (Newell) 1917– . US painter, based in Maine. His portraits and landscapes, usually in watercolour or tempera, are naturalistic and minutely detailed and often have a strong sense of the isolation of the countryside, for example *Christina's World* 1948.

Wyler /ˈwaɪlə/ William 1902–1981. German-born film director who lived in the USA from 1922. He directed *Wuthering Heights* 1939, *Mrs Miniver*

1942, *Ben-Hur* 1959 and *Funny Girl* 1968, among others.

Wyndham /ˈwaɪlə/ John. Pen name of John Wyndham Parkes Lucas Beynon Harris 1903–1969. English science-fiction writer who wrote *The Day of the Triffids* 1951, *The Chrysalids* 1955, and *The Midwich Cuckoos* 1957. A recurrent theme in his work is people's response to disaster, whether caused by nature, aliens, or human error.

Wynne-Edwards /ˈwɪn ˈedwədz/ Vera 1906– . English zoologist who argued that animal behaviour is often altruistic and that animals will behave for the good of the group, even if this entails individual sacrifice. Her study *Animal Dispersal in Relation to Social Behaviour* was published in 1962.

The theory that animals are genetically programmed to behave for the good of the species has since fallen into disrepute. From this dispute grew a new interpretation of animal behaviour, seen in the work of biologist E O ◊Wilson.

Wyoming /waɪˈəʊmɪŋ/ state of W USA; nickname Equality State
area 253,400 sq km/97,812 sq mi
capital Cheyenne
towns Casper, Laramie
features Rocky Mountains; Yellowstone (including the geyser Old Faithful) and Grand Teton national parks
products oil, natural gas, tin, sodium salts, coal, phosphates, sulphur, uranium, sheep, beef
population (1988) 477,000

famous people Buffalo Bill Cody
history part of the ◊Louisiana Purchase; first settled by whites 1834; granted women the vote 1869; state 1890.

WYSIWYG *what you see is what you get* in computing, a program that attempts to display on the screen a faithful representation of the final printed output. For example, a WYSIWYG ◊word processor would show actual line widths, page breaks, and the sizes and styles of type.

Wyss /viːs/ Johann David 1743–1818. Swiss author of the children's classic *Swiss Family Robinson* 1813.

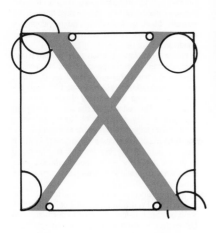

xerophyte

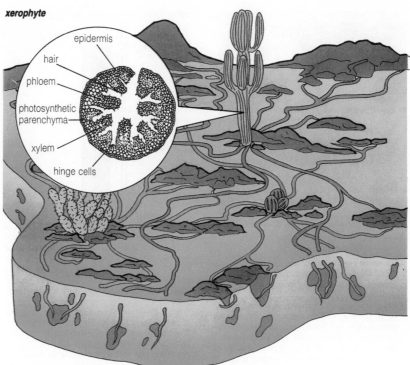

epidermis
hair
phloem
photosynthetic parenchyma
xylem
hinge cells

X the 24th letter of the English alphabet, with a sound that can be well represented medially by ks and initially by z. It is derived through Latin from the alphabet of W Greece, and was the last letter in the earlier Latin alphabet.

X abbreviation for *ten* (Roman).

Xavier, St Francis /ˈzeɪvɪə/ 1506–1552. Spanish Jesuit missionary. He went as a Catholic missionary to the Portuguese colonies in the Indies, arriving at Goa in 1542. He was in Japan 1549–51, establishing a Christian mission which lasted for 100 years. He returned to Goa in 1552, and sailed for China, but died of fever there. He was canonized in 1622.

X-chromosome the larger of the two sex chromosomes, the smaller being the ◊Y-chromosome. These two chromosomes are involved in ◊sex determination. Genes carried on the X-chromosome produce the phenomenon of ◊sex linkage.

xenon gaseous element, symbol Xe, atomic number 54, relative atomic mass 131.30. It is a heavy, inert gas, used in lasers, incandescent lamps, and electronic flash lamps. It was discovered in 1898 by Ramsay and Travers in the residue from liquid air. It occurs in the atmosphere about one part in 20 million, and is a fission product of uranium nuclear reactors.

Radioactive xenon has been used to measure the blood flow to the brain when testing the effects of supersonic speeds on humans.

Xenophon /ˈzenəfən/ c.430–354 BC. Greek historian, philosopher, and soldier. He was a disciple of ◊Socrates (described in Xenophon's *Symposium*). In 401 BC he joined a Greek mercenary army aiding the Persian prince Cyrus, and on Cyrus' death took command. His *Anabasis* describes how he led 10,000 Greeks in a 1,000-mile march home across enemy territory. His other works include *Memorabilia* and *Apology*.

xerography a dry, non-chemical method of producing images without the use of negatives or sensitized paper, invented in the USA by Chester Carlson in 1938 and applied in the Xerox ◊photocopier.

xerophyte a plant that is adapted to live in dry conditions. Common adaptations to reduce the rate of ◊transpiration include a reduction of leaf size, sometimes to spines or scales; a dense covering of hairs over the leaf to trap a layer of moist air (as in edelweiss); and permanently rolled leaves or leaves that roll up in dry weather (as in marram grass). Many desert cacti are xerophytes.

Xerxes /ˈzɜːksiːz/ c. 519–465 BC. King of Persia from 485 BC, when he succeeded his father Darius and continued the Persian invasion of Greece. In 480 BC, at the head of an army of some 400,000 men and supported by a fleet of 800 ships, he crossed the ◊Hellespont strait over a bridge of boats. He defeated the Greek fleet at Artemisium and captured and burned Athens, but Themistocles annihilated the Persian fleet at Salamis and Xerxes was forced to retreat. He spent his later years working on a grandiose extension of the capital Persepolis and was eventually murdered in a court intrigue.

Xhosa /ˈkɔːsə/ people of South Africa, living mainly in the Black National State of ◊Transkei. Their Bantu language belongs to the Niger-Congo family.

Xiamen /ʃiˌɑːˈmʌn/ formerly *Amoy* port on Ku Lang island in Fujian province, SE China; population (1984) 533,000. Industries include textiles, food products, and electronics. It was one of the original five treaty ports used for trade under foreign control 1842–1943 and a special export-trade zone from 1979.

Xian /ʃiːˈæn/ industrial city and capital of Shaanxi province, China; population (1986) 2,330,000. It produces chemicals, electrical equipment, and fertilizers. It was the capital of China under the Zhou dynasty (1126–255 BC); under the Han dynasty (206 BC–AD 220), when it was called Changan ('long peace'); under the Tang dynasty 618–906, as Siking ('western capital'); the Manchus called it Sian ('western peace'), now spelled Xian; it reverted to Changan 1913–32; was Siking 1932–43; and again Sian from 1943. It was here that the imperial court retired after the Boxer rising 1900. Its treasures include the 600-year-old Ming wall; the pottery soldiers buried to protect the tomb of the first Qin emperor (see ◊Shi Huangdi); Big Wild Goose Pagoda, one of the oldest in China; and the Great Mosque 742.

Xian Incident kidnapping of the Chinese generalissimo and politician ◊Chiang Kai-shek 12 Dec 1936, by one of his own generals, to force his cooperation with the communists against the Japanese invaders.

Xi Jiang /ˈʃiː dʒiˈæŋ/ or *Si-Kiang* river in China, which rises in Yunnan and flows into the South China Sea; length 1,900 km/1,200 mi. Guangzhou lies on the N arm of its delta, and Hong Kong island at its mouth. The name means West River.

Xingú /ʃɪŋˈguː/ river rising in the Mato Grosso, Brazil, and flowing 1,932 km/1,200 mi to the Amazon delta.

Xingú river (Amazon tributary) and region in Pará, Brazil. In 1989 Xingú Indians protested at the creation of a huge, intrusive lake for the Babaquara and Kararao dams of the Altamira complex.

Xinhua /ˌʃɪnˈhwɑː/ official Chinese news agency.

Xining /ˌʃiːˈnɪŋ/ or *Sining* industrial city, capital of Qinghai province, China; population (1982) 873,000.

Xinjiang Uygur /ˌʃɪndʒiˈæŋ ˈwiːguə/ or *Sinkiang Uighur* autonomous region of NW China
area 1,646,800 sq km/635,665 sq mi
capital Urumqi
features largest of Chinese administrative areas; Junggar Pendi (Dzungarian Basin) and Tarim Pendi (Tarim Basin, which includes ◊Lop Nur, China's nuclear testing ground, though the research centres were moved to the central province of Sichuan 1972) separated by the Tian Shan mountains
products cereals, cotton, fruit in valleys and oases; uranium, coal, iron, copper, tin, oil
population (1986) 13,840,000
religion 50% Muslim
history under Manchu rule from the 18th century; large sections ceded to Russia 1864 and 1881; China has raised the question of their return and regards the 480 km/300 mi frontier between Xinjiang Uygur and Soviet Tadzikistan as undemarcated.

Xizang /ˌʃiːˈzæŋ/ Chinese name for ◊Tibet, an autonomous region of SW China from 1965.

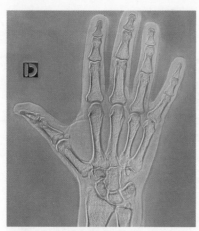

X-ray X-ray of a normal human hand and wrist, obtained by using xerography.

Xochimilco /ˌsɒtʃɪˈmɪlkəʊ/ lake about 11 km/7 mi SE of Mexico City, Mexico, noted for its floating gardens, all that remains of an ancient water-based agricultural system.

X-ray electromagnetic radiation in the wavelength range 10^{-11} to 10^{-9} m (shorter wavelengths are gamma rays; see ◊electromagnetic waves). Applications of X-rays make use of their short wavelength (such as X-ray crystallography) or their penetrating power (as in medical X-rays of internal body tissues). High doses of X-rays are dangerous, and can cause cancer.

X-rays are produced when high-energy electrons from a heated filament cathode strike the surface of a target (usually made of tungsten) on the face of a massive heat-conducting anode, between which a high alternative voltage (about 100 kV) is applied.

X-ray

radiation shielding

X-ray beam

tungsten target

specimen

photographic plate or imager

electron source

an X-ray imager

X-ray astronomy detection of X-rays from intensely hot gas in the universe. Such X-rays are prevented from reaching the Earth's surface by the atmosphere, so detectors must be placed in rockets and satellites. The first celestial X-ray source, Scorpius X-1, was discovered by a rocket flight in 1962.

Since 1970, special satellites have been orbited to study X-rays from the Sun, stars and galaxies. Many X-ray sources are believed to be gas falling onto ◊neutron stars and ◊black holes.

X-ray diffraction method of studying the atomic and molecular structure of crystalline substances by using ◊X-rays. X-rays directed at such substances spread out as they pass through the crystals owing to ◊diffraction (the slight spreading of waves around the edge of an opaque object) of the rays around the atoms. By using measurements of the position and intensity of the diffracted waves, it is possible to calculate the shape and size of the atoms in the crystal. The method has been used to study substances such as DNA that are found in living material.

xylem a tissue found in ◊vascular plants, whose main function is to conduct water and dissolved mineral nutrients from the roots to other parts of the plant. Xylem is composed of a number of different types of cell, and may include long, thin, usually dead cells known as ◊tracheids, fibres, thin-walled ◊parenchyma cells, and conducting vessels. In most flowering plants water is translocated through the vessels. Most gymnosperms and pteridophytes lack vessels and depend on tracheids for water conduction.

Non-woody plants contain only ***primary xylem,*** derived from the procambium, whereas in trees and shrubs this is replaced for the most part by ***secondary xylem,*** formed by ◊secondary growth from the actively dividing vascular ◊cambium. The cell walls of the secondary xylem are thickened by a deposit of ◊lignin, providing mechanical support to the plant; see ◊wood.

xylophone musical ◊percussion instrument in which wooden bars of varying lengths are arranged in graded pitch, or as a piano keyboard, over resonators to produce sounds when struck with hammers.

XYZ affair in American history, an incident 1797–98 in which the French were accused of demanding a $250,000 bribe before agreeing to negotiate with US envoys in Paris in an attempt to resolve a crisis in Franco-US relations caused by the war in Europe. Three French agents (referred to by President John Adams 1797 as X, Y, and Z) held secret talks with the envoys over the money. Publicity fuelled anti-French feelings in the USA and led to increased military spending.

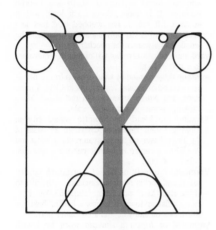

Y the 25th letter in the English alphabet, derived through the later Latin alphabet from the Greek letter *upsilon*. In modern English it represents the same vowel sounds as *i* when used as a vowel, and as a consonant, in words such as *yoke, yacht*, a palatal approximant.

yachting pleasure cruising or racing a small and light vessel, whether sailing or power-driven. At the Olympic Games, seven categories exist: Soling, Flying Dutchman, Star, Finn, Tornado, 470, and Sailboard (◊windsurfing), which was introduced at the 1984 Los Angeles games. The Finn and Sailboard are solo events, the Soling class is for three-person crews, while all other classes are for crews of two.

Most prominent of English yacht clubs is the Royal Yacht Squadron, established at Cowes in 1812, and the Yacht Racing Association was founded in 1875 to regulate the sport. The Observer Single-handed Transatlantic Race (1960) is held every four years: the record, set 1984 by Yvon Fauconnier (France), is 16 days 6 hrs 25 mins.

Yachting: recent winners

America's Cup first contested 1870. All winners have been US boats except *Australia II* 1983 and *New Zealand* 1989, who won the trophy after a lengthy legal battle.

1962 *Weatherly*
1964 *Constellation*
1967 *Intrepid*
1970 *Intrepid*
1974 *Courageous*
1977 *Courageous*
1980 *Freedom*
1983 *Australia II*
1987 *Stars and Stripes*
1989 *New Zealand* (despite losing to *Stars and Stripes* in a special challenge).

Admiral's Cup first organized 1957; a team event of six races in which each country is represented by three boats.
1969 USA
1971 Great Britain
1973 West Germany
1975 Great Britain
1977 Great Britain
1979 Australia
1981 Great Britain
1983 West Germany
1985 West Germany
1987 New Zealand
1989 Great Britain

Yahya Khan /ˈjɑːjəˈkɑːn/ Agha Muhammad 1917–1980. Former Pakistani leader, president 1969–71. His mishandling of the Bangladesh separatist issue led to civil war, and he was forced to resign. Yahya Khan fought with the British army in the Middle East during World War II, escaping German capture in Italy. Later, as Pakistan's chief of army general staff, he supported Gen Ayub Khan's 1958 coup and in 1969 became military ruler. Following defeat by India in 1971, he resigned and was under house arrest 1972–75.

yak wild ox *Bos grunniens* which lives in herds at high altitudes in Tibet. It stands about 2 m/6 ft at the shoulder, and has long shaggy hair on the underparts. It has large, upward-curving horns and humped shoulders. The yak is in danger of becoming extinct.

In the wild, yaks are brown or black, but the domesticated variety may be white. It is used for milk, meat, leather, and as a beast of burden.

Yakut /jæˈkut/ (Russian *Yakutskaya*) Autonomous Soviet Socialist Republic in NE USSR
area 3,103,000 sq km/1,197,760 sq mi
capital Yakutsk
features Yakut is one of world's coldest inhabited places; river Lena
products furs; gold, natural gas, some agriculture in the south
population (1986) 1,009,000; Yakuts 37%, Russians 50%
history the nomadic Yakuts were conquered by Russia 17th century; Yakut became a Soviet republic 1922.

Yakutsk /jæˈkutsk/ capital of Yakut Republic, USSR, on the river Lena; population (1987) 184,000. Industries include timber, tanning, and brick-making. It is the coldest point of the Arctic in NE Siberia, and has an institute for studying the permanently frozen soil area (permafrost).

yakuza (Japanese 'good for nothing') Japanese gangster. Organized crime in Japan is highly structured, and the various syndicates between them employed some 110,000 people in 1989, with a turnover of an estimated 1.5 trillion yen. The *yakuza* are unofficially tolerated and very powerful.

Their main areas of activity are prostitution, pornography, sports, entertainment, and moneylending; they have close links with the construction industry and with some politicians. There is considerable rivalry between gangs. Many *yakuza* have one or more missing fingertips, a self-inflicted ritual injury in atonement for an error.

Yale lock a pin-tumbler ◊lock invented by Linus Yale Jr (1821–68) in 1865 and still widely used. It consists of a cylinder which can rotate inside a housing to turn the bolt. In the cylinder is a row of holes, which match another row in the housing.

yak

When the lock is locked, two pins, held in each of the holes by a spring, prevent the cylinder turning. When the correct key is inserted, the lower pins are raised so that they reach the edge of the cylinder and allow it to turn.

Yale University /jeɪl/ US university, founded 1701 in New Haven, Connecticut. It was named after Elihu Yale (1648–1721), born in Boston, Massachusetts, one-time governor of Fort St George, Madras, India.

Yalow /ˈjæləu/ Rosalind 1921– . US physicist who developed radioimmunoassay (RIA), a technique for detecting minute quantities of ◊hormones present in the blood. It can be used to discover a range of hormones produced in the hypothalamic region of the brain.

Yalta Conference /ˈjæltə/ in 1945, a conference at which the Allied leaders Churchill, Roosevelt, and Stalin completed plans for the defeat of Germany in World War II and the foundation of the United Nations. It took place in Yalta, a Soviet holiday resort in the Crimea.

Yalu /ˈjɑːluː/ river forming the N boundary between North Korea and Jilin and Liaoning provinces (Manchuria) in China; length 790 km/491 mi. It is only navigable near the mouth and is frozen from Nov to Mar.

yam tuber of tropical plant, genus *Dioscorea*, of the family Dioscoreaceae, cultivated in wet regions and eaten as a vegetable. The *Mexican yam Dioscorea composita* contains a chemical used in the manufacture of the contraceptive pill.

Yamagata /ˌjæməˈgɑːtə/ Aritomo 1838–1922. Japanese soldier and politician, prime minister 1890–91 and 1898–1900. As chief of the imperial general staff in the 1870s and 1880s he was largely responsible for the modernization of the military system. He returned as chief of staff during the Russo-Japanese war 1904–05 and remained an influential political figure until he was disgraced 1921 for having meddled in the marriage arrangements of the crown prince.

Yamal Peninsula /jəˈmɑːl/ peninsula in NW Siberia, USSR, with gas reserves estimated at 6 trillion cubic metres; supplies are piped to W Europe.

Yamamoto /jæməˈməutəu/ Gombei 1852–1933. Japanese admiral and politician. As prime minister 1913–14, he began Japanese expansion on the Chinese mainland and initiated reforms in the political system. He was briefly again premier in the aftermath of the Tokyo earthquake 1923.

Yamoussoukro /ˌjæmuːˈsuːkrəu/ capital designate of ◊Ivory Coast (Côte d'Ivoire); population (1986) 120,000. The economy is based on tourism and agricultural trade.

Yamuna /ˈjæmunə/ alternative name for the ◊Jumna River in India.

Yanamamo indigenous American people, numbering approximately 15,000, who live in S Venezuela and N Brazil. The Yanamamo language is divided into several dialects, though there is a common ritual language.

Yan'an /ˌjænˈæn/ formerly *Yenan* industrial city in Shaanxi province, central China; population (1984)

Yalta Conference The Allied leaders Churchill, Roosevelt, and Stalin at the Yalta Conference, 1945.

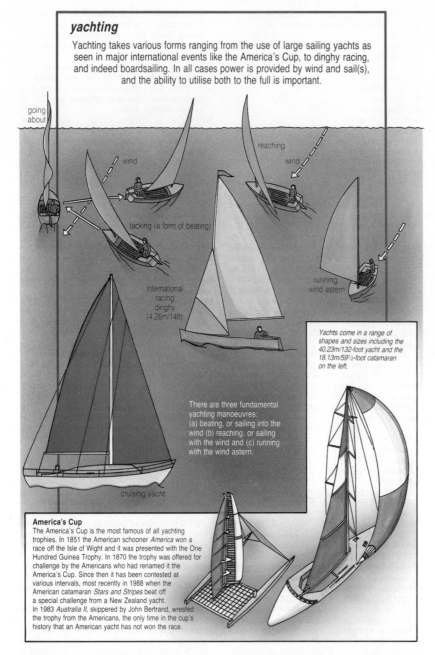

yachting

Yachting takes various forms ranging from the use of large sailing yachts as seen in major international events like the America's Cup, to dinghy racing, and indeed boardsailing. In all cases power is provided by wind and sail(s), and the ability to utilise both to the full is important.

going about

reaching

wind

wind

tacking (a form of beating)

international racing dinghy (4.26m/14ft)

running wind astern

Yachts come in a range of shapes and sizes including the 40.23m/132-foot yacht and the 18.13m/59½-foot catamaran on the left.

There are three fundamental yachting manoeuvres: (a) beating, or sailing into the wind (b) reaching, or sailing with the wind and (c) running with the wind astern.

cruising yacht

America's Cup
The America's Cup is the most famous of all yachting trophies. In 1851 the American schooner *America* won a race off the Isle of Wight and it was presented with the One Hundred Guinea Trophy. In 1870 the trophy was offered for challenge by the Americans who had renamed it the America's Cup. Since then it has been contested at various intervals, most recently in 1988 when the American catamaran *Stars and Stripes* beat off a special challenge from a New Zealand yacht.
In 1983 *Australia II*, skippered by John Bertrand, wrested the trophy from the Americans, the only time in the cup's history that an American yacht has not won the race.

254,000. The ◊Long March ended here Jan 1937, and it was the communist headquarters 1936–47 (the caves in which Mao lived are preserved).

Yangon /ˌjæŋ'gɒn/ former name until 1989 *Rangoon* capital and chief port of Myanmar, on the Rangoon River, 32 km/20 mi from the Indian Ocean; population (1983) 2,459,000. Products include timber, oil, and rice. The city Dagon was founded on the site AD 746; it was given the name Rangoon (meaning 'end of conflict') by King Alaungpaya 1755.

Yang Shangkun /'jæŋ ˌʃæŋ'kʊn/ 1907– . Chinese communist politician. He held a senior position in the party 1956–66, but was demoted during the Cultural Revolution. He was rehabilitated 1978, elected to the Politburo 1982, and to the position of state president 1988.

The son of a wealthy Sichuan landlord and a veteran of the Long March 1934–35 and the war against Japan 1937–45, Yang rose in the ranks of the Chinese Communist Party (CCP) before being purged for alleged revisionism in the Cultural Revolution. He is viewed as a trusted supporter of Deng Xiaoping.

Yangtze-Kiang /'jæŋktsi ki'æŋ/ former name for ◊Chang Jiang, greatest Chinese river.

Yangzhou /ˌjæŋ'dʒəʊ/ formerly *Yangchow* canal port in Jiangsu province, E China, on the Yangtze river; population (1984) 382,000. It is noted for its gardens and pavilions and is an artistic centre for crafts, jade carving, and printing.

Yankee /'jæŋki/ colloquial (often disparaging) term for an American. Outside the USA the term is applied to any American. During the American Civil War, the term was applied by Southerners to any Northerner or member of the Union Army and is still used today to refer to Northerners. In the North, a 'real yankee' is a person from the New England states, especially someone descended from a colonial founding family. The word has come to connote craftiness and business acumen, as in 'yankee ingenuity'.

Yantai /ˌjæn'taɪ/ formerly *Chefoo* ice-free port in Shandong province, E China; population (1984) 700,000. A special economic zone; industries include tourism, wine, and fishing.

Yaoundé /jaʊnde/ capital of Cameroon, 210 km/130 mi E of the port of Douala; population (1984) 552,000. Industry includes tourism, oil refining, and cigarette manufacturing. Established by the Germans as a military port 1899, it became capital of French Cameroon 1921.

yapok nocturnal fish-eating marsupial *Chironectes minimus* found in tropical South and Central America. It is about 33 cm/1.1 ft long, with a 40 cm/1.3 ft tail. It has webbed hind feet and thick fur, and is the only aquatic marsupial. The female has a watertight pouch.

yard imperial unit (symbol yd) of length, equivalent to 3 ft/0.9144 m.

yardang ridge formed by wind erosion from a dried-up riverbed or similar feature, as in Chad, China, Peru, and North America. On the planet Mars yardangs occur on a massive scale.

Yarkand /ˌjɑː'kænd/ or *Shache* walled city in Xinjiang Uygur region of China, in an oasis on the Tarim basin, on the caravan route to India and W USSR; a centre of Islamic culture; population (1985) 100,000.

Yarmouth /'jɑːməθ/ or *Great Yarmouth* holiday resort and port in Norfolk, England, at the mouth of the river Yare; population (1981) 55,000. Formerly a fishing town, it is now a leading base for North Sea oil and gas, and a container port.

yarmulke or *kippa* a skullcap worn by Jewish men.

Yaroslavl /ˌjærə'slɑːvəl/ industrial city (textiles, rubber, paints, commercial vehicles) in the USSR, capital of Yaroslavl region, on the Volga 250 km/155 mi NE of Moscow; population (1987) 634,000.

yarrow or *milfoil* perennial herb *Achillea millefolium* of the family Compositae, with feathery scented leaves and flat-topped clusters of white or pink flowers.

yashmak traditional Muslim headscarf, worn by devout Muslim women in the presence of men.

yaws contagious tropical disease common in the West Indies, characterized by red, raspberrylike eruptions on the face, toes, and other parts of the body. A very similar disease is found in W Africa. Treatment is by antibiotics.

Yazd /jɑːzd/ or *Yezd* silk-weaving town in central Iran, in an oasis on a trade route; population (1986) 231,000.

Y-chromosome the smaller of the two sex chromosomes. It only ever occurs paired with the other type of sex chromosome (X), which carries far more genes. Thus individuals are either XY (male) or XX (female); see ◊sex determination. The Y-chromosome is the smallest of all the mammalian chromosomes and is considered to be inert (without direct effect on the physical body).

In humans, about one in 300 males inherits two Y-chromosomes at conception: this gives added height, greater emotional instability, and great aggressiveness. The gene determining that a human being is male was in 1989 found to occur on the X as well as on the Y chromosome, but is not activated in the female.

yd abbreviation for *yard*.

year a unit of time measurement, based on the orbital period of the Earth around the Sun. The *tropical year*, from one spring ◊equinox to the next, lasts 365.2422 days. It governs the occurrence of the seasons, and is the period on which the ◊calendar year is based. The *sidereal year* is the time taken for the Earth to complete one orbit relative to the fixed stars, and lasts 365.2564 days (about 20 minutes longer than a tropical year). The difference is due to the effect of ◊precession, which slowly moves the position of the equinoxes. The calendar year consists of 365 days, with an extra day added at the end of Feb each leap year. *Leap years* occur in every year that is divisible by 4, except that a century year is not a leap year unless it is divisible by 400. Hence 1900 was not a leap year, but 2000 will be. A historical year

yeast

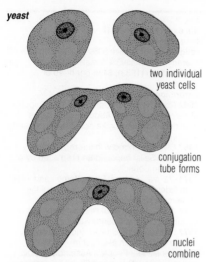

two individual
yeast cells

conjugation
tube forms

nuclei
combine

begins on 1 Jan but up to 1752 in England the civil or legal year began on 25 Mar. The English **fiscal/financial year** still ends on 5 Apr, which is 25 Mar plus 11 days added under the reform of the calendar in 1752. The **regnal year** begins on the anniversary of the sovereign's accession; it is used in the dating of acts of Parliament.

yeast mass of minute circular or oval fungal cells, each of which is a complete fungus capable of reproducing new cells by budding. When placed in a sugar solution they multiply and convert the sugar into alcohol and carbon dioxide. Yeasts are used as fermenting agents in baking, brewing, and the making of wine and spirits. **Brewer's yeast** *Saccharomyces cerevisiae* is a rich source of vitamin B.

Yeats /jeɪts/ Jack Butler 1871–1957. Irish painter and illustrator. His vivid scenes of Irish life, for example *Back from the Races* 1925 (Tate Gallery, London), and Celtic mythology reflected a new consciousness of Irish nationalism. He was the brother of the poet W B Yeats.

Yeats /jeɪts/ W(illiam) B(utler) 1865–1939. Irish poet. He was a leader of the Celtic revival and a founder of the Abbey Theatre in Dublin. His early work was romantic and lyrical, as in the poem 'The Lake Isle of Innisfree' and plays *The Countess Cathleen* 1892 and *The Land of Heart's Desire* 1894. His later books of poetry include *The Wild Swans at Coole* 1917 and *The Winding Stair* 1929. He was a senator of the Irish Free State 1922–28. Nobel prize 1923.

Yeats was born in Dublin. His early poetry, such as *The Wind Among the Reeds* 1899, is romantically and exotically lyrical, and he drew on Irish legend for his poetic plays, including *Deirdre* 1907, but broke through to a new sharply resilient style with *Responsibilities* 1914. In his personal life there was also a break: the beautiful Maude Gonne, to whom many of his poems had been

Yeats *Irish poet and dramatist W B Yeats.*

addressed, refused to marry him, and in 1917 he married Georgie Hyde-Lees, whose work as a medium reinforced his leanings towards mystic symbolism, as in the prose work *A Vision* 1925 and 1937. His later volumes of verse include *The Tower* 1928 and *Last Poems and Two Plays* 1939. His other prose works include *Autobiographies* 1926, *Dramatis Personae* 1936, *Letters* 1954, and *My Theologies* 1959.

Yedo /'jedəʊ/ or **Edo** former name of ◊Tokyo, Japan, until 1868.

yellow archangel flowering plant *Lamiastrum galeobdolon* of the family Labiatae, found over much of Europe. It grows up to 60 cm/2 ft tall and has nettlelike leaves and whorls of yellow flowers, the lower lips streaked with red, in early summer.

Yellow Book 1894–1897. Illustrated literary and artistic quarterly in the UK to which the artists Aubrey Beardsley and Walter Sickert and the writers Max Beerbohm and Henry James contributed.

yellow fever tropical viral fever, sometimes called yellow jack, prevalent in the Caribbean area, Brazil, and the W coast of Africa. Its symptoms are a high fever and yellowish skin (jaundice, possibly leading to liver failure); the heart and kidneys may also be affected.

Before the arrival of Europans, yellow fever was not a problem because indigenous people had built up an immunity. The disease was brought under control after the discovery that it is carried by the Aëdes mosquito. The first effective vaccines were produced by Max Theiler of New York (winner of the Nobel prize 1951).

yellowhammer bird *Emberiza citrinella* of the bunting family, found in open country across Eurasia. About 16.5 cm/6.5 in long, the male has a yellow head and underside, a chestnut rump, and a brown-streaked back. The female is duller. The song is sometimes supposed to sound like 'a little bit of bread and no cheese'.

Yellowknife /'jeləʊnaɪf/ capital of Northwest Territories, Canada, on the north shore of Great Slave Lake; population (1984) 11,000. It was founded 1935 when gold was discovered in the area, and became the capital 1967.

Yellow River English name for the ◊Huang He river, China.

Yellow Sea /'jeləʊ/ gulf of the Pacific Ocean between China and Korea; area 466,200 sq km/180,000 sq mi. It receives the Huang He (Yellow River) and Chang Jiang.

Yellowstone National Park /'jeləʊstəʊn/ largest US nature reserve, established 1872, on a broad plateau in the Rocky Mountains, Wyoming. 1 million of its 2.2 million acres have been destroyed by fire since July 1988.

Yeltsin /'jeltsɪn/ Boris Nikolayevich 1931– . Soviet communist politician, Moscow party chief 1985–87, when he was dismissed after criticizing the slow pace of political and economic reform. He was re-elected in Mar 1989 with a 89% share of the vote, defeating an 'official Communist Party' candidate, and was elected to the Supreme Soviet in May 1989. In 1990 he was elected president of the Russian Republic, the largest republic of the USSR.

yellowhammer

Born in Sverdlovsk, in the W central USSR, and educated at the same Urals Polytechnic Institute as Nikolai Ryzhkov, Yeltsin began his career in the construction industry. He joined the Communist Party of the Soviet Union (CPSU) in 1961 and became district party leader in Sverdlovsk 1976. He was brought to Moscow by Mikhail Gorbachev and Ryzhkov in 1985, appointed secretary for construction and then, in Dec 1985, Moscow party chief.

A blunt-talking, hands-on reformer, Yeltsin was demoted to the post of first deputy chair of the State Construction Committee in Nov 1987. This was seen as a blow to Gorbachev's ◊perestroika initiative and a victory for the conservatives grouped around Yegor Ligachev.

Yemen /'jemən/ two countries (North Yemen and South Yemen) between which union took place in May 1990 to form the Yemen Republic

Yemen, North country in SW Asia, on the Red Sea, bounded to the N by Saudi Arabia and to the S by South Yemen.

government The system of government is based on a provisional constitution published June 1974 by the Military Command Council, which seized power some six days before. In Feb 1978 the Command Council appointed the Constituent People's Assembly to draw up proposals for a permanent constitution and in April the Command Council was dissolved. In 1979 the Assembly was increased to 159 members and a 15-member consultative council was set up. In 1980 a meeting was held of the General People's Congress, consisting of 700 elected and 300 appointed members. It agreed on a national charter and elected a permanent 52-member committee for national consultation.

The General People's Congress now meets every two years and is re-elected every four, whereas the Constituent People's Assembly continues as the nation's parliament. The president of the republic is both head of state and head of government, and is elected for a five-year term by the Assembly. He governs with an appointed prime minister and council of ministers. There are no political parties as such.

history North Yemen was a kingdom in the 2nd millennium BC before it came under, successively, Egyptian, Roman, and Ethiopian rule. It adopted Islam 628, formed part of the ◊Ottoman Empire 1538–1630, and was occupied by Turkey in the 19th century.

The last king of North Yemen, Imam Muhammad, was killed in a military coup 1962. The declaration of the new Yemen Arab Republic (YAR) provoked a civil war between royalist forces, assisted by Saudi Arabia, and republicans, helped by Egypt. By 1967 the republicans, under Marshal Abdullah al-Sallal, had won. Later that year Sallal was deposed while on a foreign visit and a Republican Council took over.

Meanwhile, Britain had withdrawn from South Yemen and, with the installation of a repressive regime there, hundreds of thousands of South Yemenis fled to the YAR, many of them forming guerrilla groups with the aim of overthrowing the communist regime in South Yemen. This resulted in a war between the two Yemens 1971–72, when, under the auspices of the Arab League, a cease-fire was arranged. Both sides agreed to a union of the two countries but this was never implemented. In 1974 the pro-Saudi Col Ibrahim al-Hamadi seized power and by 1975 there were rumours of an attempt to restore the monarchy.

In 1977 Hamadi was assassinated and another member of the Military Command Council, which Hamdadi had set up 1974, Col Ahmed ibn Hussein al-Ghashmi, took over. In 1978 a gradual move towards a more constitutional form of government was started, with the appointment of the Constituent People's Assembly, the dissolution of the Military Command Council, and the installation of Ghashmi as president. In 1978 Ghashmi was killed when a bomb exploded in a suitcase carried by an envoy from South Yemen. Col Ali Abdullah Saleh became president and war broke out again between the two Yemens.

A cease-fire was again arranged by the Arab League and, for the second time, the two countries agreed to unite. This time more progress was made; there have been regular meetings of a joint council and in Mar 1984 a joint committee on foreign policy sat for the first time in Aden. In 1983 President Saleh was re-elected for a further five years.

Yemen, South country in SW Asia, on the Arabian Sea, bounded to the N by Saudi Arabia, to the E by Oman, and to the NW by North Yemen.

government The 1970 constitution provides for a one-party state based on the Yemen Socialist Party (YSP), with a single-chamber legislature, the Supreme People's Council (SPC), and a president who is both head of state and head of government. The SPC has 111 elected members, 71 representing the YSP and 40 independents. It appoints a presidium and a council of ministers. The president is secretary general of the party, chair of the presidium, and governs through the council of ministers. The YSP is, therefore, the ultimate source of political power through the SPC and the political bureau.

history For early history, see ◊Arabia. The People's Republic of Southern Yemen was founded 1967 by the union of ◊Aden and the Federation of South Arabia, both of which had been under British rule or protection. Before Britain withdrew, two rival factions fought for power, the Marxist National Liberation Front (NLF) and the Front for the Liberation of Occupied South Yemen (FLOSY). The NLF eventually won and assumed power as the National Front (NF). On the anniversary of three years of independence, 1 Nov 1970, the country was renamed the People's Democratic Republic of Yemen, and a provisional Supreme People's Council (SPC) was set up 1971 as the nation's parliament. The accession of the left-wing NF government caused hundreds of thousands of people to flee to North Yemen, where a more moderate regime was in power. This resulted in clashes between the South Yemen government and mercenaries operating from North Yemen, and war broke out 1971. The Arab League arranged a cease-fire 1972 and the two countries signed an agreement to merge, but the agreement was never honoured.

In 1978 the president of North Yemen was killed by a bomb carried by an envoy from South Yemen. In the aftermath of the killing the South Yemen president, Rubayi Ali, was deposed and executed. Two days later the three political parties agreed to merge to form a 'Marxist-Leninist vanguard party', the Yemen Socialist Party (YSP), and Abdul Fattah Ismail became its secretary general. In Dec 1978 Ismail was appointed head of state but four months later resigned and went into exile in the USSR. He was succeeded by Ali Nasser Muhammad. In 1979 South Yemen's neighbours became concerned when a 20-year Treaty of Friendship and Cooperation was signed, allowing the USSR to station troops in the country, and three years later an aid agreement between the two countries was concluded. A subsequent aid agreement with Kuwait did something to reduce anxieties.

War broke out again after the assassination of the president of North Yemen. The Arab League again intervened to arrange a cease-fire 1979 and for the second time the two countries agreed to unite. This time definite progress was made so that by 1983 a joint Yemen council was meeting at six-monthly intervals. In 1985 Ali Nasser Muhammad was re-elected secretary general of the YSP and its political bureau for another five years. He soon began taking steps to remove his opponents, his personal guard shooting and killing

Yemen, North
Yemen Arab Republic (*al Jamhuriya al Arabiya al Yamaniya*)

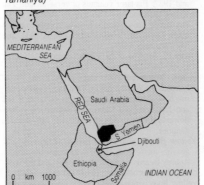

area 195,000 sq km/75,290 sq mi
capital San'a
towns Ta'iz, and chief port Hodeida
physical hot moist coastal plain, rising to plateau
features known in classical times as *Arabia felix* because of its fertility
head of state and of government Ali Abdullah Saleh from 1978
goverment system authoritarian republic
political parties no recognizable parties
exports cotton, coffee, grapes
currency rial (16.59 = £1 Mar 1990)
population (1989) 6,937,000; annual growth rate 2.7%
life expectancy men 47, women 50
language Arabic
religion Sunni Muslim 50%, Shi'ite Muslim 50%
literacy 27% male/3% female (1985 est)
GNP $3.9 bn (1983); $475 per head of population
chronology
1962 North Yemen declared the Arab Republic of Yemen (YAR), with Abdullah al-Sallal as president. Civil war broke out between royalists and republicans.
1967 Civil war ended with the republicans victorious. Sallal deposed and replaced by a Republican Council.
1971–72 War between South Yemen and YAR. Both sides finally agreed to a union but the agreement was not kept.
1974 Ibrahim al-Hamadi seized power and a Military Command Council was set up.
1977 Hamadi assassinated and replaced by Ahmed ibn Hussein al-Ghashmi.
1978 Constituent People's Assembly appointed and the Military Command Council dissolved. Ghashmi killed by an envoy from South Yemen and succeeded by Ali Abdullah Saleh. War broke out again between the two Yemens.
1979 Ceasefire agreed with, again, a commitment to a future union.
1983 Saleh elected president for a further five-year term.
1984 Joint committee on foreign policy for the two Yemens met in Aden.
1988 President Saleh re-elected.
1989 Draft constitution for single Yemen state published.
1990 Border with South Yemen opened.

three bureau members. This led to a short civil war and the dismissal of Ali Nasser from all his posts in the party and the government. A new administration was formed, headed by Haydar Abu Bakr al-Attas, which immediately committed itself to eventual union with North Yemen. A draft constitution for the unified state of Yemen was published in Dec 1989 and in Jan 1990 the border between the two countries was opened to allow free movement for all citizens.

yen the standard currency of Japan.

Yenan /ˌjʌn'æn/ former name for city of ◊Yan'an in Chinese province of Shaanxi.

Yemen, South
People's Democratic Republic of Yemen
(*Jumhuriyah al-Yemen al Dimuqratiyah al Sha'abiyah*)

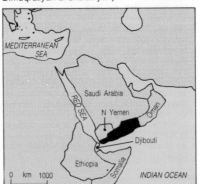

area 336,900 sq km/130,077 sq mi
capital Aden
physical desert and mountains; very hot and dry
features it includes the islands of Perim (in the strait of Bab-el-Mandeb, at the southern entrance to the Red Sea), Socotra, and Kamaran; Aden is used by the USSR as a naval base
head of state and government Haydar Abu Bakr al-Attas from 1986
government system one-party socialist republic
political parties Yemen Socialist Party (YSP), Marxist-Leninist
exports cotton goods, coffee
currency Yemeni dinar (0.58=£1 Mar 1990)
population (1989) 2,488,000; annual growth rate 2.8%
life expectancy men 47, women 50
language Arabic
religion Sunni Muslim 91%
literacy 39% (1980)
GNP $1 bn (1983); $310 per head of population
chronology
1967 People's Republic of Southern Yemen founded.
1970 Country renamed the People's Democratic Republic of Yemen (PDRY), led by the Marxist National Front Party (NF).
1971–72 War with North Yemen.
1978 North Yemen president killed by a bomb carried by a PDRY envoy. Yemen Socialist Party (YSP) formed as a 'Marxist-Leninist vanguard party'. War between North and South Yemen.
1979 Ceasefire agreed and the two Yemens agreed to move towards eventual union.
1983 Joint Yemen council established.
1985 Ali Nasser Muhammad elected president but was deposed after his personal guards killed three of his party opponents.
1986 Hayder Abu Bakr al-Attas became president and secretary general of the YPS Politburo.
1987 Discussions with North Yemen about possible merger.
1989 Draft constitution for unified state published.
1990 Border with North Yemen opened.

Yenisei /ˌjenɪˈseɪ/ river in Asiatic USSR, rising in Tuva region and flowing across the Siberian plain into the Arctic Ocean; length 4,100 km/2,550 mi.

yeoman small English landowner who farmed his own fields between the break-up of the feudal system and the agricultural revolution of the 18th–19th centuries.

Yeomanry English volunteer cavalry organized 1794, and incorporated into volunteer regiments which became first the Territorial Force 1908 and then the ◊Territorial Army 1922.

Yeomen of the Guard English military corps, popularly known as *Beefeaters*, the sovereign's bodyguard since the corps was founded by Henry VII in 1485. Its duties are now purely ceremonial.

There are Yeomen warders at the Tower of London, and the uniform and weapons are much as they were in Tudor times. The nickname Beefeaters is supposed to have originated in 1669 when the Grand Duke of Tuscany ascribed their fine appearance to beef.

Yerevan /ˌjerɪˈvæn/ industrial city (tractor parts, machine tools, chemicals, bricks, bicycles, wine, fruit canning), capital of Armenian Republic, USSR, a few miles north of the Turkish border; population (1987) 1,168,000. It was founded 7th century, and was alternately Turkish and Persian from the 15th century until ceded to Russia 1828. Its university was founded 1921. The city has been the scene of mounting inter-ethnic violence and huge Armenian nationalist demonstrations since 1988, fanned by the Nagorno-Karabakh dispute. In Dec 1988 it was virtually destroyed by an earthquake.

Yerkes Observatory astronomical centre in Wisconsin, USA, founded by George Hale in 1897. It houses the world's largest refracting optical ◊telescope, with a lens of diameter 102 cm/40 in.

Yersin /jeəˈsæŋ/ Alexandre Emile Jean 1863–1943. Swiss bacteriologist, who discovered the bubonic plague bacillus in Hong Kong in 1894 and prepared a serum against it.

Yesenin /jɪˈseɪnɪn/ Sergei. Alternative form of ◊Esenin, Russian poet.

yeti Tibetan for the ◊abominable snowman.

Yevele Henry (died 1400). English architect, mason of the naves of Westminster Abbey (begun 1375), Canterbury Cathedral, and Westminster Hall (1394), with its majestic hammerbeam roof.

Yevtushenko /ˌjevtʊˈʃeŋkəʊ/ Yevgeny Aleksandrovich 1933– . Soviet poet, born in Siberia. He aroused controversy by his anti-Stalinist 'Stalin's Heirs' 1956, published with Khrushchev's support,

Yevtushenko *A master of the conversational, confessional style, the Soviet poet Yevtushenko has walked a thin line between Communist idealism and raising sensitive issues.*

yew

and 'Babi Yar' 1961. His *Autobiography* was published in 1963.

yew evergreen coniferous tree *Taxus baccata* of the family Taxaceae, native to the N hemisphere. The leaves and bright red berrylike seeds are poisonous; the wood is hard and close-grained.

Yezd /jezd/ another name for the Iranian town of ◊Yazd.

Yezidi Islamic group originating as disciples of the Sufi saint Sheikh Adi ibn Musafir (12th century). Their beliefs, which mingle folk traditions with Islam, also incorporate features of Judaism and Christianity: they practise circumcision and baptism, and have a cult of the Fallen Angel who has been reconciled with God.

Yezo /ˈjezəʊ/ another name for ◊Hokkaido, most northerly of the four main islands of Japan.

Yggdrasil in Scandinavian mythology, the world tree, a sacred ash that spans heaven and hell. It is is evergreen and tended by the Norns, goddesses of past, present, and future.

Yggdrasil has three roots with a spring under each one. One root covers Nifelheim, the realm of the dead; another runs under Jotunheim, where the giants live; the third under Asgard, home of the gods. By the Norns' well at the third root the gods regularly gather to confer. Various animals inhabit and eat of the tree.

YHA abbreviation for ◊*Youth Hostels Association*.

Yichang /jiːˈtʃæŋ/ port at the head of navigation of the Chang Jiang, Hubei province, China; population (1982) 175,000.

Yiddish language a member of the Germanic branch of the Indo-European language family, deriving from Rhineland German and spoken by Polish and Russian Jews, who have carried it to Israel, the USA, and many other parts of the world.

In the USA, Yiddish has had a powerful impact on English, especially in the city of New York and in the national media. Such words as *bagel, chutzpah, kibbitz, mensh, nosh, schlemiel, schmaltz,* and *schmuck* have entered the American language, but are less used in Britain. Isaac Bashevis ◊Singer writes in Yiddish.

yin and yang (Chinese 'dark' and 'bright') respectively, the interdependent passive (thought of as feminine, negative, intuitive) and active (thought of as masculine, positive, intellectual) principles of nature. In Taoism and Confucianism they are represented by two interlocked curved shapes within a circle, one white, one black, with a spot of the contrasting colour within the head of each.

Yinchuan /ˌjɪnˈtʃwaːn/ capital of Ningxia autonomous region, NW China; population (1984) 383,000.

Yippie member of the *Youth International Party* (YIP), led by Abbie ◊Hoffmann and Jerry Rubin, known for their antics during the 1960s as they mocked the US political process.

Ymir in Scandinavian mythology, the first living being, a giant who grew from melting frost. Among his descendants, the god Odin with two brothers killed Ymir and created heaven and earth from parts of his body.

yoga (Sanskrit 'union') Hindu philosophic system attributed to Patanjali, who lived about 150 BC at Gonda, Uttar Pradesh, India. He preached mystical union with a personal deity by the practice of self-hypnosis and a rising above the senses by abstract meditation, adoption of special postures, and ascetic practices. As practised in the West, yoga is more a system of induced relaxation and mental and physical exercise.

yoghurt or *yogurt* or *yoghourt* food made from milk fermented with bacteria, often with fruit or other flavourings added.

Heat-treated, homogenized milk is inoculated with a culture of *Streptococcus thermophilus* and *Lactobacillus bulgaricus* in equal amounts, which change the lactose in the milk to lactic acid. Acetaldehyde gives yoghurt its characteristic flavour. Commercially, fruit, flavourings, and colouring and thickening agents are added to the fermented yoghurt.

Yogyakarta /ˌjɒgjəˈkaːtə/ city in Java, Indonesia, capital 1945–49; population (1980) 399,000. The Buddhist pyramid shrine to the NW at Borobudur (122 m/400 ft square) was built AD 750–850.

Yokohama /ˌjəʊkəʊˈhaːmə/ Japanese port on Tokyo Bay; population (1987) 3,072,000. Industries include shipbuilding, oil refining, engineering, textiles, glass, and clothing.

In 1859, it was the first Japanese port opened to foreign trade. From then it grew rapidly from a small fishing village to the chief centre of trade with Europe and the USA. Almost destroyed in an earthquake 1923, it was again rebuilt after World War II.

Yokosuka /ˌjəʊkəʊˈsuːkə/ Japanese seaport and naval base (1884) on Tokyo Bay, south of Yokohama; population (1984) 428,000.

yolk a store of food, mostly in the form of fats and proteins, found in the ◊eggs of many animals; it provides nourishment for the growing embryo.

yolk sac the sac containing the yolk in the egg of most vertebrates. The term is also used for the membrane surrounding the developing mammalian embryo.

Yom Kippur the Jewish Day of ◊Atonement.

Yom Kippur War the 1973 *October War* between the Arabs and Israelis; see ◊Arab-Israeli Wars. It is named after the Jewish holiday on which it began.

Yonge /jʌŋ/ Charlotte M(ary) 1823–1901. English novelist. Her books deal mainly with family life, and are strongly influenced by the High Church philosophy of the ◊Oxford Movement. Her best-known work is *The Heir of Redclyffe* 1853.

yoni in Hinduism, an image of the female genitals as an object of worship, a manifestation of ◊Sakti; the male equivalent is the lingam.

Yonkers /ˈjɒŋkəz/ city in Westchester county, New York, USA, on the Hudson; population (1980) 204,000. It was a Dutch settlement from about 1650.

Yonne /jɒn/ French river, 290 km/180 mi long, rising in central France and flowing north into the Seine; it gives its name to a *département* in Burgundy region.

York /jɔːk/ cathedral and industrial city (railway rolling stock, scientific instruments, sugar, chocolate, and glass) in North Yorkshire, N England; population (1985) 102,000.

features The Gothic York Minster contains medieval stained glass. Much of the 14th-century city wall survives, with four gates or 'bars', as well as the medieval shambles (slaughterhouse). Jorvik Viking Centre opened 1984 after excavation of site at Coppergate, containing wooden remains of Viking houses. Also notable are 17th–18th-century domestic architecture; the Theatre Royal, site of a theatre since 1765; Castle Museum; National Railway Museum and the 19th-century railway station; university 1963.

history York was a British city, traditionally the capital of the north of England, before becoming from AD 71 the Roman fortress of Eboracum, and the first bishop of York (Paulinus) was consecrated

yoga

lotus

headstand

triangle

backward bend

627 in the wooden church which first preceded York Minster. Paulinus baptized King Edwin there 627 and York was created an archbishopric 732. In the 10th century it was a Viking settlement. Its commercial prosperity depended on the wool trade in the Middle Ages. An active Quaker element in the 18th and 19th centuries included the Rowntree family that founded the chocolate factory.

York /jɔːk/ English dynasty founded by Richard, duke of York (1411–60). He claimed the throne through his descent from Lionel, duke of Clarence (1338–68), third son of Edward III, whereas the reigning monarch, Henry VI of the rival house of Lancaster, was descended from the fourth son. The argument was fought out in the Wars of the ◊Roses. York was killed at the Battle of Wakefield 1460, but next year his son became king as Edward IV, in turn succeeded by his son Edward V and then by his brother Richard III, with whose death at Bosworth the line ended. The Lancastrian victor in that battle became king as Henry VII, and consolidated his claim by marrying Edward IV's eldest daughter, Elizabeth.

York, archbishop of /jɔːk/ metropolitan of the northern province of the Anglican Church in England, hence Primate of England.

York, duke of /jɔːk/ title often borne by younger sons of British sovereigns, for example George V, George VI, and Prince ◊Andrew from 1986.

York, Duke of second son of Queen Elizabeth II of the UK; see ◊Andrew.

York /jɔːk/ Frederick Augustus, Duke of York 1763–1827. Second son of George III. He was an unsuccessful commander in the Netherlands 1793–99, and British commander in chief 1798–1809. The nursery rhyme about the 'grand old duke of York' who marched his troops up the hill and down again commemorates him, as does the Duke of York's column in Waterloo Place, London.

Yorks. abbreviation for ◊*Yorkshire*.

Yorkshire /ˈjɔːkʃə/ county in NE England on the North Sea, formerly divided into north, east, and west ridings (thirds), but in 1974 reorganized to form a number of new counties: the major part of *Cleveland* and *Humberside*; *North Yorkshire*, *South Yorkshire*, and *West Yorkshire*. Small outlying areas also went to Durham, Cumbria, Lancashire, and Greater Manchester. South and West Yorkshire are both former metropolitan counties.

Yoruba person of Yoruba culture from SW Nigeria and E Benin. They number approximately 12 million, and their language belongs to the Kwa branch of the Niger-Congo family.

Yosemite /jəʊˈsemɪti/ area in the Sierra Nevada, E California, USA, a national park from 1890. It includes Yosemite Gorge, Yosemite Falls, 762 m/2,500 ft in three leaps, and many others, and groves of giant sequoias.

Yoshida /jɒˈʃiːdə/ Shigeru 1878–1967. Japanese politician and prime minister. He held various diplomatic posts in the 1920s and 1930s before becoming leader of the Liberal party and serving as prime minister for most of the 1946–54 period.

Young /jʌŋ/ Arthur 1741–1820. English writer and publicizer of the new farm practices associated with the ◊agricultural revolution. When the Board of Agriculture was established 1792, Young was appointed secretary, and was the guiding force behind the production of a county-by-county survey of British agriculture.

Yosemite *The entrance to the Yosemite Valley, California, where the first of its massive falls descends in a triple cascade.*

Young Mormon leader Brigham Young in 1846.
He led the church to its present home in Salt Lake
City, Utah.

His early works, such as *Farmer's Tour through
the East of England* and *A Six Months' Tour
through the North of England*, contained extensive
comment and observations gathered during the
course of a series of journeys around the country.
In 1771 he published the *Farmers' Calendar*, and
in 1784 began the *Annals of Agriculture*, which ran
for 45 volumes, and contained contributions from
many eminent farmers of the day.

Young /jʌŋ/ Brigham 1801–1877. US ◊Mormon
religious leader, born in Vermont. He joined the
Mormon Church 1832, and three years later was
appointed an apostle. After a successful recruiting
mission in Liverpool, he returned to the USA,
and as successor of Joseph Smith, who had been
murdered, led the Mormon migration to the Great
Salt Lake in Utah 1846, founded Salt Lake City,
and ruled the colony until his death.

Young /jʌŋ/ David Ivor (Baron Young of Graffham)
1932– . British Conservative politician, chair
of the Manpower Services Commission (MSC)
1982–84, secretary for employment from 1985,
trade and industry secretary 1987–89.

Young /jʌŋ/ Edward 1683–1765. British poet,
author of *Night Thoughts on Life, Death and
Immortality* 1742–45.

Young /jʌŋ/ John Watts 1930– . US astronaut.
His first flight was on Gemini 3 in 1965. He landed
on the Moon with Apollo 16 in 1972, and was
commander of the first flight of the space shuttle
in 1981.

Young /jʌŋ/ Lester (Willis) 'Pres' 1909–1959. US
tenor saxophonist and jazz composer. He was a
major figure in the development of his instrument
for jazz music from the 1930s, and was an accompanist to the singer Billie Holiday.

Young /jʌŋ/ Thomas 1773–1829. British physicist
who revived the wave theory of light and in 1801
identified the phenomenon of ◊interference. A
child prodigy and man of universal genius, he had
mastered most European languages and many of
the Eastern tongues by the age of 20. He had also
absorbed the physics of Newton and the chemistry
of Lavoisier. He further displayed his versatility by
publishing an account of the Rosetta stone which
played a crucial role in its eventual decipherment
by ◊Champollion.

Young England group of Cambridge-educated English aristocrats, newly elected to Parliament in
1841, who shared a distaste for the growth of democracy and manufacturing industry in contemporary England, and who promoted instead a revived
traditional church and aristocracy to preserve society. The movement faded within five years, but its
spirit was captured by Benjamin ◊Disraeli, the future prime minister, in his novel *Coningsby* 1844.

Younghusband /'jʌŋ,hʌzbənd/ Francis 1863–
1942. British soldier and explorer, born in India.
He entered the army in 1882 and 20 years later
accompanied the mission that opened up Tibet. He
wrote travel books on India and Central Asia and
works on comparative religion.

Young Ireland Irish nationalist organization, founded
1840 by William Smith O'Brien (1803–64), who
rejected the nonviolent policies of Daniel
◊O'Connell's Repeal Association. It attempted
an abortive insurrection of the peasants against
the British at Tipperary in 1848. O'Brien was
sentenced to death, but later pardoned.

Young Italy Italian nationalist organization, founded
1831 by Giuseppe ◊Mazzini while in exile in Marseille. The movement, which was immediately
popular, was followed the next year by Young
Germany, Young Poland, and similar organizations. All the groups were linked by Mazzini in
his Young Europe movement, but none achieved
much practical success; attempted uprisings by
Young Italy in 1834 and 1844 failed miserably.

Young Men's Christian Association (YMCA) international organization founded 1844 by George
Williams (1821–1905) in London. It aims at self-
improvement—spiritual, intellectual, and physical.
From 1971 women were accepted as members.

Young Plan plan devised by US entrepreneur
Owen D Young to reschedule German payments
of war reparations in 1929.

Young Pretender nickname of ◊Charles Edward
Stuart, claimant to the Scottish and English
thrones.

Youngstown /'jʌŋztaʊn/ industrial city (iron and
steel) in E Ohio, USA, on the river Mahoning;
population (1980) 116,000.

Young Turk member of a reformist movement
of young army officers in the Ottoman Empire
founded 1889. The movement was instrumental
in the constitutional changes of 1908 and gained
prestige during the Balkan Wars 1912–13; it also
encouraged Turkish links with the German empire. Its influence diminished after 1918. The
term is now used for a member of any radical or
rebellious faction within a party or organization.

Young Women's Christian Association (YWCA)
organization for women and girls, formed in 1887
when two organizations, both founded in 1855—
the one by Emma Robarts and the other by Lady
Kinnaird—combined their work.

Yourcenar /ˌjʊəsəˈnɑː/ Marguerite. Pen name of
Marguerite de Crayencour 1903–1987. French
writer, born in Belgium. She achieved a reputation
as a novelist in France in the 1930s (for example with *La Nouvelle Euridyce/The New Euridyce*
1931), but after World War II she settled in the
USA. Novels such as *Les Mémoires d'Hadrien/The
Memoirs of Hadrian* 1951 won her acclaim as a
historical novelist. In 1980 she became the first
woman to be elected to the French Academy.

Youth Hostels Association (YHA) a registered
charity founded in Britain 1930 to promote knowledge and care of the countryside by providing
cheap overnight accommodation for young people
on active holidays (such as walking or cycling).
Types of accommodation range from castles to log
cabins. YHA is a member of the *International
Youth Hostel Federation*, with over 3 million
members and 5,000 youth hostels in 58 countries.

YHA membership is open to individuals of 14
or over (or 5 if accompanied by an adult). There
are 260 hostels in England and Wales. In addition
to basic accommodation, YHA provides sporting
activities including climbing, windsurfing, hang
gliding, and horse riding.

Ypres /'iːprə/ (Flemish *Ieper*) Belgian town in W
Flanders, 40 km/25 mi S of Ostend, a centre of
fighting in World War I. The Menin Gate 1927
is a memorial to British soldiers lost in the great
battles fought around the town 1914–18.

Ypres, 1st Earl of title of Sir John ◊French, British
field marshal.

Ysselmeer alternative spelling of ◊IJsselmeer, lake
in the Netherlands.

YTS *Youth Training Scheme* in the UK, a mandatory one- or two-year course of training and work
experience for unemployed school leavers aged 16
and 17. Opponents argue that it is a form of extremely cheap forced labour for employers, does
not provide young people with the high-technology
skills that will be needed in the future, and does not
pay well enough.

The one-year student has 13 weeks of training,
and the rest of the time is on-the-job experience;
the two-year student has 20 weeks of training.
They are paid £28.50 per week rising to £35 per
week.

ytterbium metallic element, symbol Yb, atomic
number 70; a member of the ◊lanthanide series.
It occurs in monazite and is used in steelmaking.

yttrium silvery metallic element, symbol Yt, atomic
number 39. A member of the ◊lanthanide series,
it occurs in monazite and is used to reduce steel
corrosion.

Yucatán /ˌjuːkəˈtɑːn/ peninsula in Central Amer-
ica, divided between Mexico, Belize, and
Guatemala; area 180,000 sq km/70,000 sq mi.
Tropical crops are grown. It is inhabited by
◊Maya Indians and contains the remains of
their civilization, with ruins at Chichén Itzá and
Uxmal.

The Mexican state of Yucatán has an area
of 38,402 sq km/14,823 sq mi, and a population
(1980) of 1,035,000. Its capital is Mérida.

yucca plant of the genus *Yucca*, family Liliaceae,
with some 40 species found in Mexico and SW
USA. The leaves are stiff and sword-shaped and
the flowers white and campanulate (bell-shaped).

Yugoslavia /ˌjuːgəʊˈslɑːviə/ country in SE
Europe, on the Adriatic Sea, bounded W by
Italy, N by Austria and Hungary, E by Romania
and Bulgaria, and S by Greece and Albania.

government Under the 1974 constitution, amended
1981, Yugoslavia is a federal republic consisting
of six socialist republics and two socialist autonomous provinces (Kosovo and Vojvodina, which
lie within Serbia), each with its own assembly. The federal republic itself has a two-chamber
legislative assembly comprising the 220-member
Federal Chamber and the 88-member Chamber
of Republics and Provinces, whose members are
indirectly elected every four years, with fixed
quotas assigned to the constituent republics and
autonomous provinces.

The legislature elects the executive branch of
government, since May 1980 a nine-member collective presidency, consisting of the head of the
Communist Party together with a representative
from each republic and province. The presidency's
members are appointed for five-year terms, with
titular leadership of the body rotating annually.
Day-to-day government administration is carried
out by the Federal Executive Council (headed by a
president or prime minister), whose members are
elected by the legislature for four-year terms.

The only political party permitted is the Communist Party (League of Communists of Yugoslavia), which is controlled by a 23-member presidium (with a rotating presidency) and directs the
broader Socialist Alliance of the Working People
of Yugoslavia. The dominating practice is that of
self-management, with elected workers' assemblies at all levels.

history Formerly under Roman rule, during the
early medieval period the present day republics
of Yugoslavia existed as substantially independent
bodies, the most important being the kingdom
of Serbia. During the 14th and 15th centuries
much of the country was conquered by the Turks
and incorporated into the Ottoman Empire. The
exceptions were mountainous Montenegro, which
survived as a sovereign principality, and Croatia
and Slovenia in the NW, which formed part of
the Austro-Hungarian Hapsburg empire. Anti-
Ottoman uprisings secured Serbia a measure of
autonomy from the early 19th century and full
independence from 1878, and the new kingdom
proceeded to enlarge its territory, at Turkey and

Yugoslavia
Socialist Federal Republic of
(Socijalistička Federativna Republika Jugoslavija)

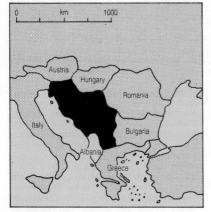

area 255,800 sq km/98,739 sq mi
capital Belgrade
towns Zagreb, Skopje, Ljubljana; ports Split, Rijeka
physical mountainous; river Danube plains in north and east
features constituent republics of Bosnia and Herzegovina, Croatia, Macedonia, Montenegro, Serbia (including the autonomous provinces of Kosovo and Vojvodina), and Slovenia; scenic Dalmatian coast and Dinaric Alps; Lake Shkodër
head of state Janez Drovsek from 1988
head of government Ante Markovic from 1989
government system communism
political parties League of Communists of Yugoslavia (SKJ), Marxist-Leninist-Titoist; new competing parties are beginning to emerge in Croatia and Slovenia
exports machinery, electrical goods, chemicals

currency dinar (19.91=£1 Mar 1989)
population (1989) 23,753,000 (Serbs 36%, Croats 20%, Muslims 9%, Slovenes 8%, Albanians 8%, Macedonians 6%, Montenegrins 3%, Hungarians 2%, 5.5% declared themselves to be 'Yugoslavs'); annual growth rate 0.8%
life expectancy men 68, women 74
language individual national languages have equality, but Serbo-Croat is the most widespread
religion Orthodox (Serbs), Roman Catholic (Croats), Muslim (50% in Bosnia)
literacy 97% male/86% female (1985 est)
GNP $46.3 bn (1984); $3,109 per head of population
chronology
1917–18 Creation of Kingdom of the Serbs, Croats, and Slovenes.
1929 Name of Yugoslavia adopted.
1941 Invasion by Germany.
1945 Communist federal republic formed under leadership of Tito.
1948 Split with USSR.
1953 Self-management principle enshrined in constitution.
1961 Formation of Nonaligned Movement under Yugoslavia's leadership.
1974 New constitution adopted.
1980 Death of Tito. Collective leadership assumed power.
1987 Threat to use the army to curb unrest.
1988 Economic difficulties: 1,800 strikes, inflation over 250%, almost 20% unemployment. Ethnic unrest in Montenegro and Vojvodina led to party reshuffles and the resignation of the government.
1989 A reformist Croatian, Ante Markovic, became prime minister. 29 died in ethnic riots in Kosovo province and state of emergency imposed. Inflation rate over 1,000%
1990 Communist Party voted to end monopoly of power (Jan). Multi-party systems established in Slovenia and Croatia.

Yugoslavia: Constituent Republics

Republic	Capital	Area sq km
Bosnia and Herzegovina	Sarajevo	51,100
Croatia	Zagreb	56,500
Macedonia	Skopje	25,700
Montenegro	Titograd	13,800
Serbia	Belgrade	88,400
Kosovo	Pristina	10,900
Vojvodina	Novi Sad	21,500
Slovenia	Ljubljana	20,300
		255,800

of strikes and mounting internal disorder, Mikulic was replaced as prime minister in Jan 1989 by Ante Markovic, a reformist Croatian. The unity of the ruling Communist party began to crumble between 1988 and 1990 as both personal and ideologically based feuds developed between the leaders of its republican branches. In particular, Slobodan Milosevic, the hardline Serbian party chief, began to wage a populist campaign designed to terminate Kosovo and Vojvodina's autonomous province status and secure their reintegration within Serbia. This led to a violent ethnic Albanian backlash in Kosovo during 1989–90 and to growing pressure in more liberal, pro-pluralist Croatia and Slovenia for their republics to break away from the federation. The schism within the Communist Party was confirmed in Jan 1990 when its Congress had to be abandoned following a walk-out by the Slovene delegation.

Yugoslav literature the Yugoslav or Serbo-Croat language belongs to the southern branch of the Slavonic languages. Yugoslavian literature begins in the 9th century with the translation into Slavonic of the church service books. Its great glory is folk poetry, particularly the song cycles dealing with the battle of Kosovo and the hero Marko Kraljeviác. After centuries of national repression a revival came, notably under Dositej Obradović (1739–1811). Poets of the earlier 19th century include bishop Petar Njegoš (1813–51), France Prešern (1800–49), and Ivan Mažuranić (1814–90). Later, Russian influence predominated. 20th-century writers include the novelists Ivan Cankar (1876–1918), Ivo Andrić (1892–1974), and Miroslav Krleža (1893–), whose collected works cover 36 volumes, and the poet Oton Župančič (1878–1949)

Yukawa /juːˈkɑːwə/ Hideki 1907–1981. Japanese physicist who predicted the existence of the ◊meson 1935. Nobel prize 1949.

Yukon /ˈjuːkɒn/ territory of NW Canada
area 483,500 sq km/186,631 sq mi
towns capital Whitehorse; Dawson City
features named after its chief river, the Yukon; includes the highest point in Canada, Mount Logan 6,050 m/19,850 ft
products oil, natural gas, gold, silver, coal
population (1986) 24,000
history settlement dates from the gold rush 1896–1910, when 30,000 people moved to the ◊Klondike river valley (silver is now worked there); became separate from Northwest

Yukon Territory

Whitehorse

Bulgaria's expense, during the Balkan Wars of 1912–13. However, not until the collapse of the Austro-Hungarian empire at the end of World War I were Croatia and Slovenia liberated from foreign control. A new 'Kingdom of the Serbs, Croats and Slovenes' was formed in Dec 1918, with the Serbian Peter Karageorgevic at its helm, to which Montenegro acceded following its people's deposition of its own ruler, King Nicholas.

Peter I died 1921 and was succeeded by his son Alexander, who renamed the country Yugoslavia ('nation of the South Slavs') and who, faced with opposition from the Croatians at home and from the Italians abroad, established a military dictatorship 1929. He was assassinated Oct 1934 in Marseille, France, by a Macedonian with Croatian dissident links. Alexander's young son ◊Peter II succeeded and a regency under the latter's uncle Paul (1893–1976) was set up which came under increasing influence from Germany and Italy. The regency was briefly overthrown by pro-Allied groups Mar 1941, precipitating a successful invasion by German troops. King Peter II fled, while two guerrilla groups—the pro-royalist, Serbian-based Chetniks, led by General Draza ◊Mihailovič, and the Communist Partisans, led by Josip Broz (Marshal ◊Tito)—engaged in resistance activities.

Tito established a provisional government at liberated Jajce in Bosnia Nov 1943 and proclaimed the Yugoslav Federal Republic Nov 1945 after the expulsion, with Soviet help, of the remaining German forces. Elections were held, a communist constitution on the Soviet model was introduced and remaining royalist opposition crushed. Tito broke with Stalin 1948 and, with the constitutional law of 1953, adopted a more liberal and decentralized form of communism

centred around workers' self-management and the support of private farming. Tito became the dominating force in Yugoslavia and held the newly created post of president from 1953 until his death May 1980.

In foreign affairs, the country sought to stand intermediate between East and West and played a leading role in the creation of the ◊nonaligned movement 1961. Domestically, the nation experienced continuing regional discontent, particularly in ◊Croatia where a violent separatist movement gained ground in the 1970s. To deal with these problems, Tito encouraged further decentralization and devolution of power to the constituent republics. A system of collective leadership and the regular rotation of office posts was introduced to prevent the creation of regional cliques. This collective leadership has held power since Tito's death. However, the problems of regionalist unrest have grown worse since 1980, especially in Kosovo (see ◊Serbia) and ◊Bosnia, where Albanian and Islamic nationalism respectively are strong.

This regionalist discontent has been fanned by a general decline in living standards since 1980, caused by a mounting level of foreign debt, whose servicing absorbs more than 10% of GNP, and a spiralling inflation rate, which reached 200% in 1988 and 700% in 1989. During 1987–88 the federal government under the leadership of prime minister Branko Mikulic, a Bosnian, instituted a 'market socialist' programme of prices and wages decontrol and the greater encouragement of the private sector and foreign 'inward investment'. However, the short-term consequence of this restructuring programme was a period of increased economic austerity and a rise in the unemployment rate to 15%. Following a wave

Territories 1898, with Dawson City as the original capital.

Yukon River /ˈjuːkɒn/ a river rising in the Yukon Territory of NW Canada. It flows 3,680 km/2,300 mi from Lake Tagish into Alaska where it empties into the Bering Sea in a great delta.

Yungning /ˌjʊŋˈnɪŋ/ former name 1913–45 for Chinese port of ◊Nanning.

Yunnan /ˌjuːˈnæn/ province of SW China, adjoining Burma, Laos, and Vietnam

area 436,200 sq km/168,373 sq mi

capital Kunming

physical Chang Jiang, Salween, and Mekong rivers; crossed by the Burma Road; mountainous and well forested

products rice, tea, timber, wheat, cotton, rubber, tin, copper, lead, zinc, coal, salt

population (1986) 34,560,000.

Yuzovka /ˈjuːzəvkə/ former name (1872–1924) for the town of ◊Dometsk, Ukraine, USSR, named after the Welshman John Hughes who established a metallurgical factory there in the 1870s.

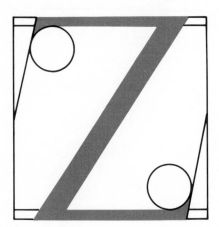

Z the 26th and last letter in the English and other modern alphabets. It was the 6th in the classical Greek alphabet. It is used initially and medially in many words of Greek or Oriental origin, and the modern tendency is to employ it in preference to *s* in such words as *baptize, organize*, when the suffix is derived ultimately from the Greek.

Z in physics, the symbol for *impedance* (electricity and magnetism).

Zaandam /ˌzɑːnˈdæm/ industrial port (timber, paper) in North Holland province, Netherlands, on the Zaan, NW of Amsterdam, since 1974 included in the municipality of ◊Zaanstad.

Zaanstad /ˈzɑːnstæd/ industrial town in W Netherlands which includes the port of ◊Zaandam; population (1988) 129,000.

Zabrze /ˈzæbʒeɪ/ industrial city (coalmining, iron, chemicals) in Silesia, S Poland, formerly the German town of Hindenburg; population (1985) 198,000.

Zadar /ˈzædɑː/ (Italian *Zara*) port and resort in Croatia, W Yugoslavia; population (1981) 116,000. It was alternately held and lost by the Venetian republic from the 12th century until its seizure by Austria 1813. It was the capital of Dalmatia 1815–1918, and part of Italy 1920–47, when it became part of Yugoslavia. The city was sacked by the army of the Fourth Crusade 1202, which led to the Crusade being excommunicated by Pope Innocent III.

Zadkine /ˈzædkiːn/ Ossip 1890–1967. French Cubist sculptor, born in Russia, active in Paris from 1909. He represented the human form in dramatic, semi-abstract terms, as in the monument *To a Destroyed City* 1953 (Rotterdam).

Zagorsk /zəˈgɔːsk/ town 70 km/45 mi NE of Moscow, USSR; population (1983) 111,000. The Trinity Monastery of St Sergius 1337, surrounded by a fortified wall, has a large collection of medieval Russian architecture and art.

Zagreb /ˈzɑːgreb/ industrial city (leather, linen, carpets, paper, and electrical goods), capital of Croatia, Yugoslavia, on the Sava river; population (1981) 1,174,512. Zagreb was a Roman city (Aemona) and has a Gothic cathedral. Its university was founded 1874.

Zahir /zəˈhɪə/ ud-din Mohammed 1483–1530. First Great Mogul of India from 1526, called Baber (Arabic 'lion'). He was the great-grandson of the Mongol conqueror Tamerlane and, at the age of 12, succeeded his father, Omar Sheikh Mirza, as ruler of Ferghana (Turkestan). In 1526 he defeated the emperor of Delhi at Panipat in the Punjab, captured Delhi and ◊Agra, and established a dynasty which lasted until 1858.

Zahir Shah /zəˈhɪəˈʃɑː/ Mohammed 1914– . King of Afghanistan 1933–73. Zahir, educated in Kabul and Paris, served in the government 1932–33 before being crowned king. He was overthrown in 1973 by a republican coup and went into exile. He has been a symbol of national unity for the ◊mujaheddin resistance groups.

zaibatsu (Japanese 'financial clique') industrial conglomerate, especially in Japan; see ◊cartel.

The old, family-owned Japanese *zaibatsu* had been involved in the military buildup preceding World War II, and were in 1945, after the country's defeat, broken up by the authorities of the US occupation. Similar conglomerates soon formed in the course of Japan's industrial revival. By the late 1980s there were six *zaibatsu* with 650 member companies between them, employing 6% of the country's workforce and controlling more than 2% of the world economy.

za'im in Lebanon, a political leader, originally the holder of a feudal office. The office is largely hereditary; an example is the Jumblatt family, traditional leaders of the Druse party. The pattern of Lebanese politics has been that individual *za'ims*, rather than parties or even government ministers, wield effective power.

Zaïre /zɑːˈɪə/ country in central Africa.

government Zaïre is a one-party state, based on the Popular Movement of the Revolution (MPR). Under the 1978 constitution, the leader of the MPR is automatically elected president for a nonrenewable seven-year term. The president,

head of state and head of government, appoints and presides over the National Executive Council. There is a single-chamber legislature, the National Legislative Council, whose 210 members are elected by universal suffrage for a five-year term. Ultimate power lies with the MPR, whose highest policy-making body is the 80-member Central Committee, which elects the 14-member Political Bureau.

history The name Zaïre (from *Zadi* 'big water') was given by Portuguese explorers who arrived on the country's Atlantic coast in the 15th century. The great medieval kingdom of Kongo, centred on the banks of the Zaïre River, was then in decline, and the subsequent slave trade weakened it further. The interior was not explored by Europeans until the arrival of ◊Stanley and ◊Livingstone in the 1870s, partly financed by Leopold II of Belgium, who established the Congo Free State under his personal rule 1885. Local resistance was suppressed and the inhabitants were oppressively exploited. When the atrocious treatment of local labour was made public, Belgium annexed the country as a colony, the Belgian Congo, 1908, and conditions were somewhat improved.

Zaïre was given full independence in June 1960 as the Republic of the Congo. Many thought the Belgian government's decision too precipitate in that it produced a number of immediate problems that could have been anticipated. The new state was intended to be governed centrally from Leopoldville by President Joseph Kasavubu and Prime Minister Patrice Lumumba, but Moise Tshombe immediately declared the rich mining province of Katanga independent under his leadership. Fighting broke out, which was not properly quelled by Belgian troops, and the United Nations (UN) Security Council agreed to send a force to restore order and protect lives. Meanwhile, disagreements between Kasavubu and Lumumba on how the crisis should be tackled prompted the Congolese army commander, Col Joseph-Désiré ◊Mobutu, to step in and temporarily take over the government. Lumumba was imprisoned and later released and five months later power was handed back to Kasavubu. Soon afterwards it was announced that Lumumba had been murdered and the white

---

Zaïre
Republic of
(République du Zaïre)

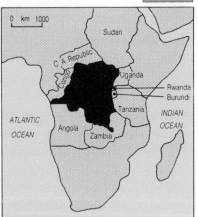

area 2,344,900 sq km/905,366 sq mi
capital Kinshasa
towns Lubumbashi, Kananga, Kisangani; ports Matadi, Boma
physical Zaïre river basin has tropical rainforest and savanna; mountains in east and west
features lakes Tanganyika, Mobutu Sésé Séko, and Edward; Ruwenzori mountains
head of state and of government Mobuto Sésé Séko Kuku Ngbendu wa Zabanga

from 1965
government system one-party socialist republic
political parties Popular Movement of the Revolution (MPR), African socialist.
exports palm oil, coffee, tea, rubber, timber, copper, cobalt (80% of world output), zinc, cadmium, industrial diamonds
currency zaïre (804.05 = £1 Mar 1989)
population (1988) 33,991,000; annual growth rate 2.9%
life expectancy men 48, women 52
language French (official), Swahili, Lingala
religion 70% Christian, 10% Muslim
literacy 79% male/45% female (1985 est)
GNP $5 bn (1983); $127 per head of population
chronology
1960 Achieved full independence as the Republic of the Congo. Civil war roke out between the central government and Katanga province.
1963 Katanga war ended.
1967 New constitution adopted.
1970 Col Mobutu elected president.
1971 Country became the Republic of Zaïre, with the Popular Movement of the Revolution (MPR) the only legal political party.
1974 Foreign-owned businesses and plantations seized by Mobutu and given in political patronage.
1977 Original owners of confiscated properties invited back. Mobutu re-elected.
1984 Mobutu re-elected.
1988 Potential rift with Belgium avoided.

mercenaries employed by Tshombe were thought to be responsible. The outcry that followed resulted in a new government being formed, with Cyrille Adoula as prime minister.

During the fighting between Tshombe's mercenaries and UN forces the UN secretary general, Dag Hammarskjöld, flew to Katanga province to mediate and was killed in an air crash on the border with Northern Rhodesia. The attempted secession of Katanga was finally stopped in 1963 when Tshombe went into exile, taking many of his followers with him to form the Congolese National Liberation Front (FNLC). In July 1964 Tshombe returned from exile and President Kasavubu appointed him interim prime minister until elections for a new government could be held. In Aug the country was renamed the Democratic Republic of the Congo.

A power struggle soon developed between Kasavubu and Tshombe and again the army, under Mobutu, intervened, establishing a 'second republic' in Nov 1965. A new constitution was adopted 1967 and 1970 Mobutu was elected president for a seven-year term. The following year the country became the Republic of Zaïre and in 1972 the Popular Movement of the Revolution (MPR) was declared the only legal political party. In the same year the president became known as Mobutu Sese Seko.

Mobutu, re-elected 1977, carried out a large number of political and constitutional reforms. He gradually improved the structure of public administration and brought stability to what had once seemed an ungovernable country. However, the harshness of some of his policies brought international criticism and 1983 he offered amnesty to all political exiles. Despite some demonstrations of opposition, Marshal Mobutu, as he now was, was re-elected 1984 for a third term. Towards the end of 1988 a potentially dangerous, and not fully explained, rift with Belgium was narrowly averted.

Zaïre /zɑː'ɪə/ formerly (until 1971) *Congo* second longest river in Africa, rising near the Zambia–Zaïre border (and known as the Lualaba river in the upper reaches) and flowing 4,500 km/2,800 mi to the Atlantic, running in a great curve which crosses the Equator twice, and discharging a volume of water second only to the Amazon. The chief tributaries are the Ubangi, Sangha, and Kasai.

Navigation is interrupted by dangerous rapids up to 160 km/100 mi long, notably from the Zambian border to Bukama; below Kongolo, where the gorge known as the Gates of Hell is located; above Kisangani, where the Stanley Falls are situated; and between Kinshasa and Matadi.

Boma is a large port on the estuary; Matadi is a port 80 km/50 mi from the Atlantic, for ocean-going ships; and at Pool Malebo (formerly Stanley Pool), a widening of the river 560 km/350 mi from its mouth which encloses the marshy island of Bamu, are Brazzaville on the western shore and

River Zaïre

Kinshasa on the southwestern. The Inga dam supplies Matadi and Kinshasa with electricity.

history The mouth of the Zaïre was seen by the Portuguese navigator Diogo Cão 1482, but the vast extent of its system became known to Europeans only with the explorations of Livingstone and Stanley. Its navigation from source to mouth was completed by the expedition 1974 led by the English explorer John Blashford-Snell, supported by President Mobutu.

Zákinthos /'zækɪnθɒs/ or *Zante* most southerly of the ◊Ionian Islands, Greece; area 410 sq km/158 sq mi; population (1981) 30,000. Products include olives, currants, grapes, and carpets.

Zama, Battle of /'zɑːmə/ battle fought in 202 BC in Numidia (now Algeria), in which the Carthaginians under Hannibal were defeated by the Romans under Scipio, so ending the Second Punic War.

Zambezi /zæm'biːzi/ river in central and SE Africa; length 2,650 km/1,650 mi from NW Zambia through Mozambique to the Indian Ocean, with a wide delta near Chinde. Major tributaries include the Kafue in Zambia.

It is interrupted by rapids, and includes on the Zimbabwe–Zambia border the Victoria Falls (Mosi-oa-tunya) and Kariba Dam, which forms the reservoir of Lake Kariba with large fisheries.

Zambia /'zæmbiə/ landlocked country in central Africa.

government Zambia is an independent republic within the Commonwealth. It was proclaimed a one-party state in 1972 and the constitution was adopted 1973. The party is the United National Independence Party (UNIP), and its president is the state president, elected by universal suffrage for a five-year term, and who may be re-elected. The president governs with an appointed cabinet and is advised by the House of Chiefs, consisting of chiefs from the country's nine provinces. There is a single-chamber national assembly of 135 members, 125 elected by universal suffrage and 10 nominated by the president. The assembly has a life of five years. Ultimate power lies with UNIP, whose Central Committee is chaired by the president.

history For early history, see ◊Africa. The country was visited by Portuguese in the late 18th century and by ◊Livingstone 1851. As Northern

Rhodesia it became a British protectorate 1924, together with the former kingdom of Barotseland (now Western province), taken under British protection at the request of its ruler 1890.

From 1953 the country, with Southern Rhodesia (now Zimbabwe) and Nyasaland (now Malawi), was part of the Federation of Rhodesia and Nyasaland, dissolved 1963. Northern Rhodesia became an independent republic 1964, within the Commonwealth, with Dr Kenneth ◊Kaunda, leader of the United Independence Party (UNIP), as its first president. Between 1964 and 1972, when it was declared a one-party state, Zambia was troubled with frequent outbreaks of violence because of disputes within the governing party and conflicts between the country's more than 70 tribes.

Zambia was economically dependent on neighbouring white-ruled Rhodesia but tolerated liberation groups operating on the border, and relations between the two countries deteriorated. The border was closed 1973 and 1976 Kaunda declared his support for the Patriotic Front, led by Robert Mugabe and Joshua Nkomo, which was fighting the white regime in Rhodesia. In 1980 there was an unsuccessful coup against the president, allegedly promoted by South Africa. Despite his imposition of strict economic policies, Kaunda was convincingly re-elected 1983. He has played an important role in African politics and 1985 was appointed to succeed President Nyerere of Tanzania as chair of the black African Front Line States. In Oct 1988 he was re-elected, unopposed, for a sixth consecutive term.

Zamenhof /'zæmənhɒf/ Lazarus Ludovik 1859–1917. Polish inventor of the international language ◊Esperanto in 1887.

Zampieri /ˌzæmpi'eəri/ Domenico. Italian Baroque painter, known as ◊Domenichino.

Zante /'zænti/ Italian name for the Ionian island of ◊Zákinthos, Greece.

ZANU *Zimbabwe African National Union* political organization founded in Aug 1963 by Ndabaningi Sithole with Robert Mugabe as secretary general. It was banned 1964 by Ian Smith's Rhodesian Front government, against which it conducted a guerrilla war from Zambia until the free elections of 1980, when the ZANU (PF) party, led by Mugabe,

Zambia
Republic of

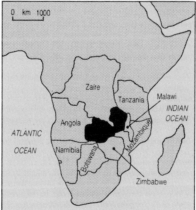

area 752,600 sq km/290,579 sq mi
capital Lusaka
towns Kitwe, Ndola, Kabwe, Chipata, Livingstone
physical a forested plateau cut through by rivers
features Zambezi River, Kariba Dam; Luangwa Valley national park has one of the greatest concentrations of animal life in Africa
head of state and government Kenneth Kaunda from 1964
government system one-party socialist republic
political parties United National Independence Party (UNIP), African socialist
exports copper, emeralds, tobacco
currency kwacha (40.50 = £1 Mar 1989)
population (1989) 7,770,000; annual growth rate 3.3%
life expectancy men 50, women 53
language English (official); the majority speak Bantu languages
religion mainly animist, 21% Roman Catholic, also Protestant, Hindu, and Muslim minorities
literacy 84% male/67% female (1985 est)
GNP $2.6 bn (1984); $570 per head of population
chronology
1964 Achieved full independence, within the Commonwealth, as the Republic of Zambia, with Kenneth Kaunda as president.
1972 United Independence Party (UNIP) declared the only legal party.
1976 Support for the Patriotic Front in Rhodesia declared.
1980 Unsuccessful coup against President Kaunda.
1985 Kaunda elected chair of the Front Line States.
1987 Kaunda elected chair of the Organization of African Unity (OAU).
1988 Kaunda re-elected unopposed for sixth term.

won 63% of the vote. In 1987 it merged with ◊ZAPU in preparation for making Zimbabwe a one-party state.

Zanzibar /ˌzænzɪˈbɑː/ island region of Tanzania
area 1,658 sq km/640 sq mi (80 km/50 mi long)
towns Zanzibar
products cloves, copra
population (1985) 571,000
history Arab traders settled in the 7th century, and Zanzibar became a sultanate; under British protection 1890–1963; together with the island of Pemba, some nearby islets, and a strip of mainland territory, it became a republic; merged with Tanganyika as Tanzania 1964.

Zanzotto /zænˈzɒtəʊ/ Andrea 1921– . Italian poet. A teacher from the Veneto, he has published much verse, including the collection *La beltà/Beauty* 1968, with a strong metaphysical element.

Zapata /səˈpɑːtə/ Emiliano 1879–1919. Mexican Indian revolutionary leader. He led a revolt against dictator Porfirio Díaz (1830–1915) from 1911 under the slogan 'Land and Liberty', to repossess for the indigenous Mexicans the land taken by the Spanish. He was driven into retreat by 1915, and was assassinated.

Zaporozhye /ˌzæpəˈrɒʒi/ formerly (until 1921) *Aleksandrovsk* industrial city (steel, chemicals, aluminium goods, pig iron, magnesium) in Ukraine, USSR, on the Dnieper, capital of Zaporozhye region and site of the Dnieper Dam; population (1987) 875,000. It was occupied by Germany 1941–43.

Zapotec indigenous American people of S Mexico, numbering approximately 250,000, living mainly in Oaxaca. The Zapotec language, which belongs to the Oto-Mangean family, has nine dialects. The ancestors of the Zapotec built the city of Monte Albán 1000–500 BC.

ZAPU *Zimbabwe African People's Union* political organization founded by Joshua Nkomo in 1961 and banned 1962 by the Rhodesian government. It engaged in a guerrilla war in alliance with ◊ZANU against the Rhodesian regime until late 1979. In the 1980 elections ZAPU was defeated and was then persecuted by the ruling ZANU (PF) party. In 1987 the two parties merged.

Zara /ˈzɑːrə/ Italian name for ◊Zadar, port on the Adriatic coast of Yugoslavia.

Zaragoza /ˌsærəˈɡɒsə/ (English **Saragossa**) industrial city in Aragon, Spain; population (1986) 596,000. It produces iron, steel, chemicals, plastics, canned food, and electrical goods. The medieval city walls and bridges over the Ebro survive, and there is a 15th-century cathedral.
history Founded as Salduba in pre-Roman days, it took its present name from Roman conqueror Caesar Augustus; later it was captured by Visigoths and Moors, and was taken in 1118 by Alfonso the Warrior, King of Navarre and Aragon, after a nine-month siege. It remained capital of Aragon until the end of the 15th century. From June 1808 to Feb 1809, in the Peninsular War, it resisted a French siege. Maria Augustin, known as the 'Maid of Zaragoza' who died 1859, became a national hero for her part in the defence; her story is told in Byron's *Childe Harold* 1812–18.

zarzuela (from La Zarzuela, royal country house where it was first developed) Spanish musical theatre form combining song, dance, and speech. It originated as amusement for royalty in the 17th century, and the playwright Calderón was an early zarzuela writer. It is often satirical, and gained renewed popularity in the 20th century with the works of Frederico Moreno Tórroba (1891–1982).

His *La Chulapona*, staged at the 1989 Edinburgh Festival was claimed to be the first zarzuela to be seen in Britain.

zazen formal seated meditation in Zen Buddhism. Correct posture and breathing are important.

zB abbreviation for *zum Beispiel* (German 'for example').

zebra

Zealand /ˈziːlənd/ another name for ◊Sjælland, main island of Denmark, and for ◊Zeeland, SW province of the Netherlands.

zebra black and white striped members of the horse family found in Africa; the stripes serve as camouflage or dazzle and confuse predators. They are about 1.5 m/5 ft high at the shoulder, with a stout body, and a short, thick mane. They live in herds on mountains and plains, and can run at up to 60 kph/40 mph.

The *mountain zebra Equus zebra* was once common in Cape Colony and Natal and still survives in parts of South Africa and Angola. It has long ears and is silvery-white with black or dark brown markings. *Grevy's zebra Equus grevyi* is much larger, with finer and clearer markings; it inhabits Ethiopia and Somalia; *Burchell's* or the *common zebra Equus burchelli*, which is intermediate in size, has white ears, a long mane, and full tail; it roams the plains north of the Orange River, South Africa.

zebu ox *Bos indicus* found in E Asia, India, and Africa. It is usually light-coloured, with large horns and a large fatty hump near the shoulders. It is used for pulling loads, and is held by some Hindus to be sacred.

Zebus have been cross-bred with other species of cattle in hot countries to pass on their qualities of heat tolerance and insect resistance. In the USA, they are called Brahman cattle. They are larger and leaner than western cattle.

Zedekiah /ˌzedɪˈkaɪə/ in the Old Testament, last king of Judah 597–586 BC. Placed on the throne by Nebuchadnezzar, he died a blinded captive in Babylon.

Zeebrugge /ˈziːbrʊɡə/ small Belgian ferry port on the North Sea, linked to Bruges by 14 km/9 mi canal (built 1896–1907). In Mar 1987 it was the scene of a disaster in which over 180 passengers lost their lives when the car ferry *Herald of Free Enterprise* put to sea from Zeebrugge with its car-loading doors not properly closed.

Zeeland /ˈziːlənd/ province of the SW Netherlands; capital Middelburg; area 1,790 sq km/691 sq mi; population (1988) 356,000. It includes the estuary of the Scheldt and the island of Walcheren and North and South Beveland. Most of Zeeland is below sea level.

Zeeman /ˈzeɪmən/ Pieter 1865–1943. Dutch physicist who discovered in 1896 that when light from certain elements, such as sodium or lithium flame, was passed through a spectroscope in the presence of a strong magnetic field, the spectrum split into a number of distinct lines. This is known as the *Zeeman effect* and won him a share of the 1902 Nobel physics prize.

Zeffirelli /ˌzefɪˈreli/ Franco 1923– . Italian theatre and film director and designer, noted for his stylish designs and lavish productions. His films include *Jesus of Nazareth* 1977 and *La Traviata* 1983.

Other work includes a production of the opera *Tosca* 1964, and films of the Shakespeare plays *The Taming of the Shrew* 1967 and *Romeo and Juliet* 1968.

Zeiss /zaɪs/ Carl 1816–1888. German optician. He opened his first workshop in Jena in 1846, and in 1866 joined forces with Ernst Abbe (1840–1905) producing cameras, microscopes, and binoculars.

Zeitgeist (German 'time spirit') spirit of the age.

Zelenka /zeˈlɪŋkə/ Jan Dismas 1679–1745. Bohemian composer who worked at the court of Dresden and became director of church music in 1729. His compositions were rediscovered in the 1970s.

Zelenograd /ˌzelɪnəˈɡræd/ city 145 km/90 mi NE of Moscow, USSR, where much of the Soviet microelectronics industry is concentrated.

zemstvo Russian provincial or district councils established by Tsar Alexander II in 1864. They were responsible for local administration until the revolution of 1917.

Zen abbreviation of Japanese *zenna*, 'quiet mind concentration', a form of ◊Buddhism introduced from India to Japan via China in the 12th century.

zenana (Hindi) the part of a house used by the female members of the household.

Zendavesta the sacred scriptures of ◊Zoroastrianism, today practised by the Parsees. They comprise the *Avesta* (liturgical books for the priests); the *Gathas* (the discourses and revelations of Zoroaster); and the *Zend* (commentary upon them).

zenith the upper pole of the celestial horizon, the point immediately above the observer; the ◊nadir is below, diametrically opposite. See ◊celestial sphere.

Zenobia /zɪˈnəʊbɪə/ queen of Palmyra AD 266–272. She assumed the crown in the Syrian desert as regent for her sons, after the death of her husband Odaenathus, and in 272 was defeated at Homs by Aurelian and taken as a captive to Rome.

Zeno of Citium /ˈziːnəʊˌsɪtɪəm/ *c.*335–262 BC. Greek founder of the ◊stoic school of philosophy in Athens, about 300 BC.

Zeno of Elea /ˈziːnəʊˌeliə/ *c.*490–430 BC. Greek philosopher, whose paradoxes raised 'modern' problems of space and time. For example, motion is an illusion, since an arrow in flight must occupy a determinate space at each instant, and therefore must be at rest.

Zentrumspartei German name for the ◊Centre Party 1871–1933.

zeolite any of the hydrous aluminium silicates, also containing sodium, calcium, barium, strontium, and potassium, chiefly found in igneous rocks and characterized by a ready loss or gain of water. Zeolites are used as 'molecular sieves' to separate mixtures because they are capable of selective absorption. They have a high ion-exchange capacity and can be used to make petrol, benzene, and toluene from low-grade raw materials, such as coal and methanol. Permutit is a synthetic zeolite used to soften hard water.

Zeppelin /ˈzepəlɪn/ Ferdinand, Count von Zeppelin 1838–1917. German ◊airship pioneer. On retiring from the army in 1891, he devoted himself to the study of aeronautics, and his first airship was built and tested in 1900. During World War I a number of Zeppelin airships bombed England. They were also used for luxury passenger transport but the construction of hydrogen-filled airships with rigid keels was abandoned after several disasters in the 1920s and 1930s. Zeppelin also helped to pioneer large multi-engine bomber planes.

Zermatt /ˈzɜːmæt/ tourist centre in the Valais canton, Switzerland, at the foot of the Matterhorn; population (1985) 3,700.

Zernicke /zˈeɒnɪkə/ Frits 1888–1966. Dutch physicist who developed the phase-contrast microscope 1935. Earlier microscopes allowed many specimens to be examined only after they had been transformed by heavy staining and other treatment. The phase-contrast microscope allowed living cells to be directly observed by depending on the difference in refractive indices between specimens and medium. Nobel physics prize 1953.

Zeppelin The Hindenburg disaster, 6 May 1937, when all those on board were killed.

Zetland /ˈzetlənd/ official form until 1974 of ◊Shetland, islands of N Scotland.

Zeus /zju:s/ in Greek mythology, chief of the gods (Roman Jupiter). He was the son of Kronos, whom he overthrew; his brothers included Hades and Poseidon, his sisters Demeter and Hera. As the supreme god he dispensed good and evil and was the father and ruler of all humankind. His emblems are the thunderbolt and aegis (shield), representing the thunder cloud.

He ate his pregnant first wife Metis (goddess of wisdom), fearing their child (Athena) would be greater than himself. His second wife was Hera, but he also fathered children by other women and goddesses. The offspring, either gods and goddesses or godlike humans, included Apollo, Artemis, Castor and Polydeuces/Pollux, Dionysus, Hebe, Heracles, Hermes, Minos, Perseus, and Persephone.

Zhangjiakou /ˌdʒæŋdʒiəˈkəʊ/ (or *Changchiakow*) historic town and trade centre in Hebei province, China, 160 km/100 mi NW of Beijing, on the Great Wall; population (1980) 1,100,000. Zhangjiakou is on the border of Inner Mongolia (its Mongolian name is Kalgan, 'gate') and on the road and railway to Ulaanbaatar in Mongolia. It developed under the Manchu dynasty, and was the centre of the tea trade from China to Russia.

Zhao Ziyang /ˈdʒaʊ ˌdziːˈjæŋ/ 1918– . Chinese politician, prime minister from 1980, and secretary of the Chinese Communist Party (CCP) 1987–89. His reforms included self-management and incentives for workers and factories. He lost his secretaryship and other posts after the Tiananmen Square massacre in Beijing June 1989.

Zhao, son of a wealthy landlord from Henan province, joined the Communist Youth League 1932 and worked underground as a CCP official during the liberation war 1937–49. He rose to prominence in the party in Guangdong from 1951. As a supporter of the reforms of Liu Shaoqi, he was dismissed during the 1966–69 Cultural Revolution, paraded through Canton in a dunce's cap and sent to Inner Mongolia.

He was rehabilitated by Zhou Enlai 1973 and sent to China's largest province, Sichuan, as first party secretary 1975. Here he introduced radical and successful market-oriented rural reforms. Deng Xiaoping had him inducted into the Politburo 1977. After six months as a vice premier, Zhao was appointed prime minister 1980 and assumed, in addition, the post of CCP general secretary Jan 1987. His economic reforms were criticized for causing inflation, and his liberal views of the pro-democracy demonstrations that culminated in the student occupation of Tiananmen Square led to his downfall.

Zhdanov /ˈʒdɑːnɒv/ industrial port (iron, steel) in Ukraine, USSR, on the Sea of Azov; population (1987) 529,000. Formerly Mariupol, it was renamed 1948 in honour of Andrei Zhdanov (1896–1948), politician and defender of Leningrad, who was born at Mariupol. In 1989, following the communist party's condemnation of Zhdanov as having been one of the chief organizers of the Stalinist mass repressions of the 1930s and 1940s, it was decided that the city should revert to its former designation, Mariupol.

Zhejiang /ˌdʒɜːdʒiˈæŋ/ or *Chekiang* province of SE China
area 101,800 sq km/39,295 sq mi
capital Hangzhou
features smallest of the Chinese provinces, it was the base of the Song dynasty 12th–13th centuries; it is densely populated
products rice, cotton, sugar, jute, maize; timber on the uplands
population (1986) 40,700,000.

Zhengzhou /ˌdʒʌŋˈdʒəʊ/ or *Chengchow* industrial city (light engineering, cotton textiles, foods), capital of Henan province (from 1954), China, on the Huang Ho; population (1986) 1,590,000.

In the 1970s the earliest city yet found in China, from 1500 BC, was excavated near the walls of Zhengzhou. The Shaolin temple, where the martial art of kung fu originated, is nearby.

Zhitomir /ʒɪˈtəʊmɪə/ capital of Zhitomir region in Ukraine, USSR, west of Kiev; population (1987) 287,000. It is a timber and grain centre, and has furniture factories. Zhitomir dates from the 13th century.

Zhivkov /ˈʒɪvkɒf/ Todor 1911– . Bulgarian Communist Party leader from 1954, prime minister 1962–71, president 1971–89. His period in office was one of caution and conservatism.

Zhivkov, a printing worker, joined the BCP in 1932 and was active in the resistance 1941–44. After the war, he was elected to the National Assembly and soon promoted into the BCP secretariat and Politburo. As BCP first secretary, Zhivkov became the dominant political figure in Bulgaria after the death of Vulko Chervenkov 1956. Zhivkov was elected to the new post of state president in 1971 and lasted until the East bloc upheavals of 1989.

Zhonghua Renmin Gonghe Guo /ˌdʒɒŋˈhwɑː ˌrenˈmɪn ˌɡɒŋhɜːˈgwəʊ/ Chinese for People's Republic of ◊China.

Zhou Enlai /ˈdʒəʊ ˌenˈlaɪ/ or *Chou En-lai* 1898–1976. Chinese politician. Zhou, a member of the Chinese Communist Party from the 1920s, was prime minister 1949–76 and foreign minister 1949–58. He was a moderate Maoist, and weathered the Cultural Revolution. He played a key role in foreign affairs.

Born into a declining mandarin gentry family near Shanghai, Zhou studied in Japan and Paris, where he became a founder member of the overseas branch of the CCP. He adhered to the Moscow line of urban-based revolution in China, organizing communist cells in Shanghai and an abortive uprising in Nanchang 1927. In 1935 Zhou supported the election of Mao Zedong as CCP leader and remained a loyal ally during the next 40 years. He served as liaison officer 1937–46 between the CCP and Chiang Kai-shek's nationalist Guomindang government. In 1949 he became prime minister, an office he held until his death Jan 1976.

Zhou, a moderator between the opposing camps of Liu Shaoqi and Mao Zedong, restored orderly progress after the Great Leap Forward (1958–60) and the Cultural Revolution (1966–69), and was the architect of the Four Modernizations programme in 1975. Abroad, Zhou sought to foster Third World unity at the Bandung Conference 1955, averted an outright border confrontation with the USSR by negotiation with Prime Minister Kosygin 1969, and was the principal advocate of détente with the USA during the early 1970s.

Zhubov scale scale for measuring ice coverage, used in the USSR. The unit is the *ball*; 1 ball is 10% coverage, 2 balls 20%, and so on.

Zhao Ziyang An economic expert with a pragmatic outlook, Zhao Ziyang.

Zhou Enlai Chinese politician and prime minister Zhou Enlai, 1971

Zhu De /'dʒu:'deɪ/ or **Chu Teh** 1886–1976. Chinese Red Army leader from 1931. He devised the tactic of mobile guerrilla warfare and organized the Long March to Shaanxi 1934–36. He was made a marshal 1955.

The son of a wealthy Sichuan landlord, Zhu served in the Chinese Imperial Army before supporting Sun Yat-sen in the 1911 revolution. He studied communism in Germany and Paris 1922–25 and joined the Chinese Communist Party (CCP) on his return, becoming commander in chief of the Red Army. Working closely with Mao Zedong, Zhu organized the Red Army's Jiangxi break-out 1931 and led the 18th Route Army during the liberation war 1937–49. He served as head of state (chair of the Standing Committee of the National People's Congress) 1975–76.

Zhukov /'ʒu:kɒv/ Grigory Konstantinovich 1896–1974. Marshal of the USSR in World War II and minister of defence 1955–57. As chief of staff from 1941, he defended Moscow 1941, counterattacked at Stalingrad, organized the relief of Leningrad 1943, and led the offensive from Ukraine Mar 1944 which ended in the fall of Berlin. He subsequently commanded the Soviet occupation forces in Germany.

Zian another spelling of ◊Xian, city in China.

Zia ul-Haq /'zɪə ʊl'hæk/ Mohammad 1924–1988. Pakistani general, in power from 1977 until his assassination. He was a career soldier from a middle-class Punjabi Muslim family, and became army chief of staff 1976. He led the military coup against Zulfiqar Ali ◊Bhutto 1977 and became president 1978. Zia introduced a fundamentalist Islamic regime and restricted political activity.

Zia's opposition to the Soviet invasion of Afghanistan 1979 drew support from the USA, but his refusal to commute the death sentence imposed on Zulfiqar Ali Bhutto was widely condemned. He lifted martial law 1985. The US Central Intelligence Agency is widely rumoured to have engineered his death.

zidovudine (formerly known as AZT) the only drug licensed for treatment of AIDS. It causes severe side effects, including anaemia.

It can significantly slow the onset of AIDS in people with preliminary symptoms before the full-blown disease has developed. Developed under successive code names Compound S and AZT 509, it was first approved by the US Food and Drug Administration as azidothymidine before acquiring its current name.

Ziegler /'tsi:glə/ Karl 1898–1973. German organic chemist. In 1963 he was awarded a Nobel prize for his work on the chemistry and technology of high polymers. He combined molecules of the gas ethylene (now called ethene) into the plastic polyethylene (polythene).

ZIFT abbreviation for *zygote inter-fallopian transfer* a modified form of ◊in vitro fertilization in which the fertilized ovum is reintroduced

Zia ul-Haq *Pakistani president General Mohammad Zia ul-Haq.*

Zimbabwe
Republic of

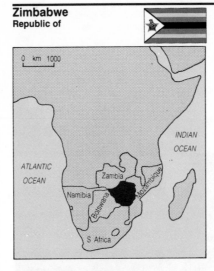

area 390,300 sq km/150,695 sq mi
capital Harare
towns Bulawayo, Gweru, Kwekwe, Mutare, Hwange
physical a high plateau with mountains in the east
features Hwange National Park, part of Kalahari Desert
head of state and government Robert Mugabe from 1987
government system effectively one party socialist republic
political parties Zimbabwe African National Union-Patriotic Front (ZANU-PF), African socialist.
exports tobacco, citrus, tea, coffee, gold, silver
currency Zimbabwe dollar (3.92 = £1 Mar 1989)
population (1989) 9,987,000 (Shona 80%, Ndbele, of Zulu descent, 19%; before independence there were some 275,000 whites, in 1985 about 100,000); annual growth rate 3.5%
life expectancy men 54, women 58
language English (official); Shona, Ndbele,

Nyanja
religion Christian
literacy 81% male/67% female (1985 est)
GDP $5 bn (1983); $640 per head of population
chronology
1961 Zimbabwe African People's Union (ZAPU) formed, with Joshua Nkomo as leader.
1962 ZAPU declared illegal.
1963 Zimbabawe African National Union (ZANU) formed, with Robert Mugabe as secretary general.
1964 Ian Smith became prime minister. Nkomo and Mugabe imprisoned.
1965 ZANU banned. Smith declared unilateral independence.
1966–68 Abortive talks between Smith and UK prime minister Harold Wilson.
1974 Nkomo and Mugabe released.
1975 Geneva conference agreed a date for constitutional independence.
1979 Smith produced a new constitution and established a government with Bishop Abel Muzorewa as prime minister. New government denounced by Nkomo and Mugabe. Conference in London agreed independence arrangements (Lancaster House Agreement).
1980 Full independence achieved, with Robert Mugabe as prime minister.
1981 Rift between Mugabe and Nkomo.
1982 Nkomo dismissed from the cabinet and left the country temporarily.
1984 ZANU-People's Front (PF) Party Congress agreed to create a one-party state at some time in the future.
1985 Relations between Mugabe and Nkomo improved.
1986 Joint ZANU-PF rally held amid plans for merger.
1987 White-roll seats in the assembly were abolished. President Banana retired and Mugabe combined the posts of head of state and prime minister with the title executive president.
1988 Nkomo returned to the cabinet and appointed vice-president.
1989 Opposition party, the Zimbabwe Unity Movement, formed by Edgar Tekere. ZANU and ZAPU formally merged.
1990 Mugabe and ZANU-PF re-elected.

into the mother's ◊fallopian tube before it has undergone its first cell division. This mimics the natural processes of fertilization (which normally occurs in the fallopian tube) and implantation more effectively than older techniques do.

ziggurat in ancient Babylonia and Assyria, a step pyramid of sun-baked brick faced with glazed bricks or tiles on which stood a shrine. The Tower of Babel described in the Bible may have been a ziggurat.

Zimbabwe /zɪm'bɑ:bwɪ/ extensive ruins near Victoria in Mashonaland, Zimbabwe. They were probably the work of a highly advanced Bantu-speaking people from Zaïre or Ethiopia, smelters of iron, who were in the area before AD 300. The new state of Zimbabwe took its name from these ruins, and the national emblem is a bird derived from soapstone sculptures of fish eagles found in them.

Zimbabwe /zɪm'bɑ:bwɪ/ landlocked country in central Africa.

government Zimbabwe is an independent republic within the Commonwealth. Its constitution dates from 1980 and provides for a president who is a formal head of state, a two-chamber parliament consisting of the Senate and the House of Assembly, and a prime minister and cabinet drawn from and responsible to Parliament.

In recognition of the rights of the white minority, there were two sets of constituencies for parlimentary elections, a 'common roll' which included all voters, and a 'white roll' for white voters. The white roll was abolished in 1987. The Senate has 40 members, 24 indirectly elected

through an electoral college, 5 elected by Mashona chiefs, 5 chiefs sitting 'ex officio', and 6 appointed by the president. The House of Assembly has 100 members elected by universal suffrage, through a party list system of proportional representation. Both chambers serve a five-year term and are subject to dissolution within that period. The president is elected by Parliament for a six-year term and in turn appoints the prime minister and cabinet on the basis of parliamentary support.

The two main political parties are the Zimbabwe African National Union–Patriotic Front (ZANU–PF) and the Patriotic Front (PF, formerly the Zimbabwe African People's Union, ZAPU).

history For early history, see ◊Africa. There was a Bantu-speaking civilization in the area before AD 300. By 1200 ◊Mashonaland, now E Zimbabwe, was an important settlement of the Shona people, who had moved in from the N and erected stone buildings. The name Zimbabwe means 'stone house' in Bantu. In the 15th century the Shona empire, under Mutota, expanded across Zimbabwe before it fell to the Rozwi, who ruled until the 19th century. Portuguese explorers reached the area in the early 16th century. In 1837 the Matabele, a Bantu people, in retreat after unsuccessful battles with the ◊Boers, settled in W Zimbabwe. Mashonaland and ◊Matabeleland, together with what is now Zambia, were granted to the British South Africa Company 1889, and the whole was named ◊Rhodesia 1895 in honour of Cecil ◊Rhodes. King ◊Lobengula of Matabeleland accepted British protection 1888 but rebelled 1893; he was defeated, but 1896 after the ◊Jameson Raid the Matabele once more unsuccessfully tried to regain their independence. The portion of the area S of the Zambezi River, then known as Southern Rhodesia, became self-governing 1923 and a member of the Federation of Rhodesia and Nyasaland 1953.

African nationalists were campaigning for full democracy and the African National Congress (ANC), which had been present since 1934, was reconvened 1957 under the leadership of Joshua Nkomo. It was banned 1959 and Nkomo went into exile to become leader of the National Democratic Party (NDP), which had been formed by some ANC members. When the NDP was banned, 1961, Nkomo created the Zimbabwe African People's Union (ZAPU); this was banned 1962. In 1963 a splinter group developed from ZAPU, the Zimbabwe African National Union (ZANU), led by the Rev Ndabaningi Sithole, with Robert ◊Mugabe as its secretary general.

After the dissolution of the Federation of Rhodesia and Nyasaland 1963 the leader of the Rhodesian Front party (RF), Winston Field, became the first prime minister of Rhodesia. The RF was a grouping of white politicians committed to maintaining racial segregation. In Apr 1964 Field resigned and was replaced by Ian ◊Smith, who rejected terms for independence proposed by Britain, which required clear progress towards majority rule. Four months later ZANU was banned and Nkomo and Mugabe imprisoned. In Nov 1965, after further British attempts to negotiate a formula for independence, Smith annulled the 1961 constitution and unilaterally announced Rhodesia's independence. Britain broke off diplomatic and trading links and the United Nations initiated economic sanctions, but these were bypassed by many multinational companies. The British prime minister, Harold Wilson, had abortive talks with Smith 1966 and 1968.

In 1969 Rhodesia declared itself a republic and adopted a new constitution, with white majority representation in a two-chamber legislature. Armed South African police at times supported the Smith regime against ZAPU and ZANU guerrillas. In 1972 another draft agreement for independence was rejected by the British government as not acceptable to the Rhodesian people 'as a whole'. A conference in Geneva 1975 was attended by deputations from the British government, the Smith regime, and the African nationalists, represented by Bishop Abel Muzorewa, president of the African National Council, which had been formed 1971 to oppose the earlier independence arrangements, and Robert Mugabe and Joshua Nkomo, who had been released from detention and had jointly formed the Patriotic Front.

At the beginning of 1979 Smith produced a new 'majority rule' constitution, which contained an inbuilt protection for the white minority but which he had managed to get Muzorewa to accept. In June 1979 Bishop Muzorewa was pronounced prime minister of what was to be called Zimbabwe Rhodesia. The new constitution was denounced by Mugabe and Nkomo as another attempt by Smith to perpetuate the white domination, and they continued to lead the Zimbabwe African National Liberation Army from bases in neighbouring Mozambique.

In Aug 1979 the new British prime minister, Margaret Thatcher, under the influence of her foreign secretary, Lord Carrington, and President Kaunda of Zambia, agreed to the holding of a constitutional conference in London at which all shades of political opinion in Rhodesia would be represented. The conference, in Sept 1979, resulted in what became known as the Lancaster House Agreement and paved the way for full independence. A member of the British cabinet, Lord Soames, was sent to Rhodesia as governor-general to arrange a timetable for independence. Economic and trade sanctions were lifted. A small Commonwealth Monitoring Force supervised the disarming of the thousands of guerrilla fighters who brought their weapons and ammunition from all parts of the country.

A new constitution was adopted and elections were held, under independent supervision, in Feb 1980. They resulted in a decisive win for Robert Mugabe's ZANU-PF party. The new state of Zimbabe became fully independent in Apr 1980, with the Rev Canaan Banana as president and Robert Mugabe as prime minister. During the next few years a rift developed between Mugabe and Nkomo and between ZANU-PF and ZAPU supporters. Nkomo was accused of trying to undermine Mugabe's administration and was dismissed from the cabinet. Fearing for his safety, he spent some months in the UK. ZAPU was opposed to the 1984 proposal by ZANU-PF for the eventual creation of a one-party state.

Mugabe's party increased its majority in the 1985 elections with 63 seats against 15 and early in 1986 he announced that the separate seats for the whites in the Assembly would be abolished within a year. Relations between the two parties and the two leaders eventually improved and by 1986 discussions of a merger were under way. The merger was concluded in Dec 1989.

zinc a bluish-white metallic element, symbol Zn, atomic number 30, relative atomic mass 65.38. The principal source is the USA. Zinc's chief uses are in the production of galvanized iron and in alloys, especially brass. Its compounds include zinc oxide, used in ointments and cosmetics, paint, glass, and printing ink. Zinc sulphide is used in television screens and X-ray apparatus.

Ores occur in many parts of the world. From very early times zinc has been used as a component of brass, but it was not recognized as a separate metal until 1746 by Andreas Sigismund Marggraf (1709–82).

Zinneman /'tsɪnəmæn/ Fred(erick) 1907– . Austrian film director, in the USA from 1921. His films include *High Noon* 1952, *The Nun's Story* 1959, *The Day of the Jackal* 1973, and *Five Days One Summer* 1982.

zinnia annual plants of the family Compositae, native to Mexico, especially the cultivated hybrids of *Zinnia elegans*, with brightly coloured daisylike flowers.

Zinoviev /zɪ'nɒvief/ Alexander 1922– . Soviet philosopher, noted for his satire on the USSR *The Yawning Heights* 1976, which led to his exile 1978, and *The Reality of Communism* 1984, where he argued that communism is the natural consequence of masses of people living under deprived conditions, and thus bound to expand.

Zinoviev /zɪ'nɒvief/ Grigory 1883–1936. Russian politician. A prominent Bolshevik, he returned to Russia in 1917 with Lenin and played a leading part in the Revolution. As head of the Communist ◊International 1919, his name was attached to a forgery, the ***Zinoviev letter***, inciting Britain's communists to rise, which helped to topple the Labour government in 1924. As one of the 'Old Bolsheviks', he was seen by Stalin as a threat. He was accused of complicity in the murder of the Bolshevik leader Kirov, and shot.

zinnia

Zion /'zaɪən/ Jebusite (Amorites of Canaan) stronghold in Jerusalem on which King David built the Temple, symbol of Jerusalem and of Israel as a homeland for the Jews.

Zionism a Jewish movement for the establishment in Palestine of a Jewish homeland, the 'promised land' of the Bible, with its capital Jerusalem, the 'city of Zion'.

1896 As a response to European ◊anti-Semitism, Theodor Herzl published his *Jewish State*, outlining a scheme for setting up an autonomous Jewish commonwealth under Turkish suzerainty.

1897 The World Zionist Congress was established in Basel, Switzerland, with Herzl as its first president.

1917 The ◊Balfour Declaration was secured by Chaim Weizmann. It promised the Jews a homeland in Palestine.

1940–48 Jewish settlement in the British mandate of Palestine led to armed conflict between militant Zionists (see ◊Irgun, ◊Stern Gang) and both Palestinian Arabs and the British.

1947 In Nov 1947 the United Nations divided Palestine into Jewish and Arab states.

1948 The Jews in Palestine proclaimed the state of Israel, but the Arab states rejected both the partition of Palestine and the existence of Israel.

1975 The General Assembly of the UN condemned Zionism as 'a form of racism and racial discrimination'; among those voting against the resolution were the USA and the members of the European Community.

zip fastener a fastening device used in clothing, invented in the USA by Whitcomb Judson in 1891, originally for doing up shoes. It has two sets of interlocking teeth, meshed by means of a slide.

Zircon the codename for a British signals-intelligence satellite originally intended to be launched in 1988. The revelation of the existence of the Zircon project (which had been concealed by the government) and the government's subsequent efforts to suppress a programme about it on BBC television, caused much controversy in 1987.

Its function would be to intercept radio and other signals from the USSR, Europe, and the Middle East and transmit them to the Government Communications Headquarters in Cheltenham, England.

zirconium a metallic element, symbol Zr, atomic number 40, relative atomic mass 91.22. It is used in highly corrosion-resistant ceramic oxide coatings in, for example, chemical plant, and also in nuclear plant where its low neutron absorption is advantageous. In steelmaking it is used as a deoxidizer. It was isolated by Jöns Jakob Berzelius in 1824.

zither an Austrian Alpine folk instrument, consisting of up to 45 strings, stretched across a flat wooden soundbox about 60 cm/24 in long. Five strings are plucked with a plectrum for melody, and pass over frets, while the rest are plucked with the fingers for harmonic accompaniment.

Zi Xi /'zi: 'tʃi:/ (or Tzu-Hsi) 1836–1908. Dowager empress of China. She was presented as a concubine to the emperor Hsien-Feng. On his death 1861 she became regent for her son T'ung Chih, and, when he died in 1875, for her nephew Guang Xu (1871–1908).

Zlatoust /ˌzlætəʊ'uːst/ industrial city (metallurgy) in Chelyabinsk region, USSR, in the S Urals; population (1987) 206,000. It was founded 1754 as an iron and copper-working settlement, destroyed 1774 by a peasant rising, but developed as an armaments centre from the time of Napoleon's invasion of Russia.

zodiac the zone of the heavens containing the paths of the Sun, Moon, and planets. When this was devised by the ancient Greeks, only five planets were known, making the zodiac about 16° wide. The stars in it are grouped into 12 signs, each 30° in extent: Aries, Taurus, Gemini, Cancer, Leo, Virgo, Libra, Scorpius, Sagittarius, Capricornus,

Aquarius, and Pisces. Because of the ◊precession of the equinoxes, the modern constellations do not cover the same areas of sky as the zodiacal signs of the same name.

zodiacal light a cone-shaped light sometimes seen extending from the Sun along the ecliptic, visible after sunset or before sunrise. It is due to thinly spread dust particles in the central plane of the solar system. It is very faint, and requires a dark, clear sky to be seen.

zoetrope an optical toy with a series of pictures on the inner surface of a cylinder. When the pictures are rotated and viewed through a slit, it gives the impression of continuous motion.

Zoffany /ˈzɒfəni/ Johann 1733–1810. British portrait painter, born in Germany, based in London from about 1761. Under the patronage of George III he painted many portraits of the royal family. He spent several years in Florence (1770s) and India (1780s).

Zog /zɒg/ Ahmed Beg Zogu 1895–1961. King of Albania 1928–39. He became prime minister of Albania in 1922, president of the republic in 1925, and proclaimed himself king in 1928. He was driven out by the Italians in 1939, and settled in England.

Zola /ˈzəʊlə/ Emile Edouard Charles Antoine 1840–1902. French novelist and social reformer. With *La Fortune des Rougon/The Fortune of the Rougons* 1867 he began a series of some 20 naturalistic novels, portraying the fortunes of a French family under the Second Empire. They include *Le Ventre de Paris/The Underbelly of Paris* 1873, *Nana* 1880, and *La Débâcle/The Debacle* 1892. In 1898 he published *J'accuse/I Accuse*, a pamphlet indicting the persecutors of ◊Dreyfus, for which he was prosecuted but later pardoned.

Born in Paris, Zola was a journalist and clerk in Paris until his *Contes à Ninon/Stories for Ninon* 1864 enabled him to devote himself to literature. Some of the titles in *La Fortune des Rougon/The Fortune of the Rougons* series are *La Faute de l'Abbé Mouret/The Simple Priest* 1875, *L'Assommoir/Drunkard* 1878, *Germinal* 1885 and *La Terre/Earth* 1888. Among later novels is the trilogy *Trois Villes/Three Cities* 1894–98, and *Fécondité/Fecundity* 1899.

Zollverein a 19th-century German customs union, begun under Prussian auspices in 1828; the union included most German-speaking states except Austria by 1834.

Although designed to remove tariff barriers and facilitate trade within the German confederation, the Zollverein also had a political effect in isolating Austria. The Austrians were committed to trade tariffs to protect their agriculture and industry; thus their inability to join the Zollverein served to increase Prussian power in the confederation.

Zomba /ˈzɒmbə/ former capital of Malawi, 32 km/20 mi W of Lake Shirwa: population (1985) 53,000. It was replaced by Lilongwe as capital 1975, but remains the university town.

zombie a corpse believed (especially in Haiti) to be reanimated by a spirit and enslaved. The idea possibly arose from voodoo priests using the nerve poison tetrodotoxin (from the puffer fish) to produce a semblance of death from which the victim afterwards physically recovers. Those eating incorrectly prepared puffer fish in Japan have been similarly affected.

zone system in photography, a system of exposure estimation invented by Ansel ◊Adams that groups infinite tonal gradations into ten zones, zone 0 being black and zone 10 white. An ◊f-stop change in exposure is required from zone to zone.

zoo short for ***zoological gardens***, a place where animals are kept in captivity, either as a spectacle or in pursuit of scientific knowledge.

Henry I started a royal menagerie at Woodstock, Oxfordshire, later transferred to the Tower of London, and in 1831 the king presented the collection to the Zoological Society in Regent's Park, London. Other notable zoos are those in

zodiac Celestial planisphere showing the signs of the zodiac from Harmonia Macro Cosima (1708) British Library, London.

New York (Bronx Zoo), Toronto, Chicago, Paris, and Berlin.

zoology the branch of biology concerned with the study of animals. It includes description of present-day animals, the study of evolution of animal forms, anatomy, physiology, embryology, and geographical distribution.

zoom lens a photographic lens that, by variation of focal length, allows speedy transition from long shots to close-ups.

zoonosis any infectious disease that can afflict both human beings and animals. Probably the most feared example is ◊rabies.

Some disease-producing organisms are adapted to a single host species. Some, such as the yellow-fever virus or the trypanosome of sleeping sickness, can live harmlessly in or on animals, but cause illness in humans. Control of such diseases is often achieved by eradicating the host, as in the case of the *Anopheles* mosquito, responsible for the spread of malaria.

Zoroaster /ˌzɒrəʊˈæstə/ or ***Zarathustra*** *c.* 628–*c.* 551 BC. Persian prophet and religious teacher, founder of Zoroastrianism.

Zoroastrianism pre-Islamic Persian religion founded

Zola French novelist and reformer Emile Zola.

by Zoroaster, and still practised by the ◊Parsees in India. The ◊*Zendavesta* are the sacred scriptures of the faith. The theology is dualistic, **Ahura Mazda** or **Ormuzd** (the good God) being in conflict with **Ahriman** (the evil God), but the former is assured of eventual victory.

The return of Zoroaster will presage the resurrection of the dead and creation of a paradise on Earth by Ahura Mazda. The free choice of good or evil renders believers responsible for their fate after death in heaven or hell. Procreation and life are valued, but death defiles—hence the custom of exposing corpses to be devoured by vultures. Worship is at altars on which the sacred fire burns.

Zorrilla y Moral /θɒˈriːljə/ José 1817–1893. Spanish poet and playwright. Born in Valladolid, he based his plays chiefly on national legends, such as the *Don Juan Tenorio* 1844.

Zouave /zuːˈɑːv/ member of a corps of French infantry soldiers, first raised in Algeria in 1831 from the Berber Kabyle people of Zouaves. The term came to be used for soldiers in other corps modelled on the French Zouaves.

Z particle type of ◊elementary particle.

Zsigmondy /ˈʃɪgmɒndi/ Richard 1865–1929. Austrian chemist who devised and built an ultramicroscope in 1903. The microscope's illumination was placed at right angles to the axis. (In a conventional microscope the light source is placed parallel to the instrument's axis.) Zsigmondy's arrangement made it possible to observe gold particles with a diameter of 10-millionth of a millimetre. Nobel prize 1925.

ZST abbreviation for ***Zone Standard Time***.

zucchini alternative common name for the courgette, a type of ◊marrow.

Zugzwang (German) a position in chess from which it is impossible to move without worsening one's situation.

Zuider Zee /ˈzaɪdə ˈziː/ former sea inlet in Holland, cut off from the North Sea by the closing of a dyke in 1932, much of which has been reclaimed as land. The remaining lake is called the ◊IJsselmeer.

Zulu person of Zulu culture from Natal, South Africa. The modern homeland, Kwazulu, represents the nucleus of the old Zulu kingdom.

Zwingli *Swiss religious reformer Ulrich Zwingli, whose insistence on the authority of the Bible was later incorporated into Calvinist doctrine.*

The Zulu language belongs to the Bantu branch of the Niger-Congo family.

Zululand /'zu:lu:lænd/ region in Natal, South Africa, largely corresponding to the Black National State, Kwazulu. It was formerly a province, annexed to Natal 1897.

Zurbarán /ˌθuəbə'ræn/ Francisco de 1598–1664. Spanish painter, based in Seville. He painted religious subjects in a powerful, austere style, often focusing on a single figure in prayer.

Zurbarán used deep contrasts of light and shade to create an intense spirituality in his works, and received many commissions from religious orders in Spain and South America. During the 1640s the softer, sweeter style of Murillo displaced Zurbarán's art in public favour in Seville, and in 1658 he moved to Madrid.

Zürich /'zjuərɪk/ financial centre and industrial city (machinery, electrical goods, textiles) on Lake Zürich, capital of Zürich canton, the largest city in Switzerland; population (1987) 840,000. The university was refounded 1833.

Zutphen /'zʌtfən/ town in Gelderland province, Netherlands; population (1987) 31,000.

Zweig /tsvaɪk/ Arnold 1887–1968. German novelist, playwright, and poet. He is remembered for his realistic novel of a Russian peasant in the German army *Der Streit um den Sergeanten Grischa/The Case of Sergeant Grischa* 1927.

Zweig /tsvaɪk/ Stefan 1881–1942. Austrian writer, author of plays, poems, and many biographies of writers (Balzac, Dickens) and historical figures (Marie Antoinette, Mary Stuart). He and his wife, exiles from the Nazis from 1934, despairing at what they saw as the end of civilization and culture, committed suicide in Brazil.

Zwickau /'tsvɪkaʊ/ coalmining and industrial town in Karl-Marx-Stadt county, East Germany, on the Mulde; population (1986) 121,000. It is the birthplace of the composer Robert Schumann.

Zwingli /'zwɪŋgli/ Ulrich 1484–1531. Swiss Protestant, born in St Gallen. He was ordained a Roman Catholic priest 1506, but by 1519 was a Reformer, and led the Reformation in Switzerland with his insistence on the sole authority of the Scriptures. In a war against the cantons that had not accepted the Reformation he was killed in a skirmish at Kappel.

Zwolle /'zwɒlə/ capital of Overijssel province, Netherlands, a market town with brewing, distilling, butter making and other industries; population (1988) 91,000.

Zworykin /'zwɔːrɪkɪn/ Vladimir Kosma 1889–1982. Russian electronics engineer, in the USA from 1919. He invented a television camera tube and the ◊electron microscope.

zydeco style of dance music originating in Louisiana, USA, similar to ◊Cajun but more heavily influenced by blues and West Indian music.

Zydeco is fast and bouncy, using instruments like accordion, saxophone, and washboard. It was widely popularized by the singer and accordion player Clifton Chenier (1925–87).

zygote an ◊ovum (egg) after ◊fertilization but before it undergoes cleavage at the start of its development.

Acknowledgements

For permission to reproduce illustrations and copyright material we are grateful to the following:

Ace Photo Library
Alinari-Giraudon
All Souls'College, Oxford
Allsport Photographic
Heather Angel
Arcaid
Ardea
G Ronald Austing
Australian Information Service
Austrian State Tourist Department
Baltimore Museum of Art
Clive Barda
Barnaby's Picture Library
BBC Hulton Picture Library
Belgian National Tourist Office
Boehm
Bridgeman Art Library
British Antarctic Survey
British Museum, London
British Nuclear Fuels
British Petroleum Company
British Tourist Authority
Bubbles Photo Library
Syndics of Cambridge University
Camera Press
Canadian National Railways
J Allan Cash
Cavendish Laboratory, University of Cambridge
Central Electricity Generating Board
Central Office of Information
Central Press Photos Ltd
Christie's, London
Michael Clark
Bruce Coleman
Commissioners of Public Works in Ireland
Commonwealth Secretariat
Courtauld Institute Galleries
Crown Copyright
Daily Telegraph
Danish Tourist Board
Douglas Dickens
Duckworth & Co Ltd
Dulwich Picture Gallery
Esso Petroleum Company
Thomas Fall Ltd
Feature-Pix
Financial Times
Fox Photos
Foxboro Co.
Peter Fraenkel
Frank Spooner Pictures
French Railways
Friends of the Earth
Galerie otto Stangli, Munich
GeoScience Features Picture Library

Geoslides Photo Library
Gernsheim Collection
Sally and Richard Greenhill
Susan Griggs Agency
Hale Observatories
Hewlett Packard
John Hillelson Agency Ltd
Historical Museum, Vienna
Michael Holford
Eric Hosking
Paul Howard
Humber Bridge Board
Hutchinson Picture Library
Ikon
Image Bank
Imperial Chemical Industries
Imperial War Museum, London
Indian Tourist Office
Information Service of the European Communities
Italian State Tourist Office
Japan National Tourist Organization
Japan Information and Cultural Centre
John Soane Museum, London
Keystone Photos
Lacock Abbey Collection
Anthony Lambert
Lambeth Palace Library
Lauros-Giraudon
Lebanese National Tourist Council
Lefevre Gallery (Alex Reid & Lefevre Ltd)
Gary C Lewis
Lewis Walpole Library, Yale University
London Corporation
London Transport Executive
Lufthansa
Mansell Collection
Marconi Communication Systems
Marineland, Florida
Marlborough Fine Art (London) Ltd
Mary Evans Picture Library
Maxim
Godfrey MacDominic
Angus McBean
McCill University
Merseyside County Art Galleries
Meteorological Office
Michael Nicholson
Military Archive and Research Services
David Munro
John Murray
Musée du Louvre
Museum of London
Museum of Modern Art, New York
NASA
National Army Museum
National Film Archive, London
National Galleries of Scotland
National Gallery, London

National Library of Australia
National Portrait Gallery, London
National Travel Association of Denmark
National Trust
Peter Newark's Western Americana
Norwegian Embassy
Novosty Press Agency
Philadelphia Museum of Art
Photo Source
Photographers Photo Library
Axel Poignant
Popperfoto
Beatrix Potter Trust
Punch Publications
QA Photos Ltd
RAF Museum
The Registrar General
REX Features
Fulvio Roiter
Romanian National Tourist Office
Ann Ronan Picture Library
Royal Astronomical Society
Royal Collection, Windsor
Royal College of Music
Royal Danish Ministry of Foreign Affairs
Royal Doulton
Royal Greenwich Observatory
Royal Observatory, Edinburgh
Royal Norwegian Agency
RTHPL
Sachem Publishing Associates
Science Museum, London
Science Photo Library
Society for Anglo-Chinese Understanding
Sotheby Parke Bernet & Co
Spanish National Tourist Authority
Christian Steiner
Sugar Bureau
Survival Anglia
Sutcliffe Gallery
Swiss National Tourist Office
Tate Gallery, London
Thai National Tourist Office
Thames Water
The Times
John Topham Picture Library
US Department of the Interior
USIS
Michael Upshall
Mireille Vautier
Vautier-De Nanxe
Victoria and Albert Museum, London
Virago Press
Virgin Group
Walker Art Gallery, Liverpool
Penelope Wallace
Wallace Collection
Western American Picture Library
Witt Library
Prof. H Wright Baker
Yerkes Regional Primate Center
Zoological Society of London

Pronunciation key

Pronunciations are transcribed using the International Phonetic Alphabet (IPA). In general, only one pronunciation is given for each word. The pronunciation given for foreign names is the generally agreed English form, if there is one; otherwise an approximation using English sounds is given.

ɑː	father /'fɑːðə/, start /stɑːt/		ɬ	Llanelli /ɬæ'neɬi/
aɪ	price /praɪs/, high /haɪ/		m	minimum /'mɪnɪməm/
aʊ	mouth /maʊθ/, how /haʊ/		n	nine /naɪn/
æ	trap /træp/, man /mæn/		ŋ	sing /sɪŋ/, uncle /'ʌŋkl/
b	baby /'beɪbɪ/		ɒ	lot /lɒt/, watch /wɒtʃ/
d	dead /ded/		ɔː	thought /θɔːt/, north /nɔːθ/
dʒ	judge /dʒʌdʒ/		ɔɪ	choice /tʃɔɪs/, boy /bɔɪ/
ð	this /ðɪs/, other /'ʌðə/		p	paper /'peɪpə/
e	dress /dres/, men /men/		r	red /red/, carry /'kærɪ/
eɪ	face /feɪs/, wait /weɪt/		s	space /speɪs/
eə	square /skweə/, fair /feə/		ʃ	ship /ʃɪp/, motion /'məʊʃən/
ɜː	nurse /nɜːs/, pearl /pɜːl/		t	totter /'tɒtə/
ə	another /ə'nʌðə/		tʃ	church /tʃɜːtʃ/
əʊ	goat /gəʊt/, snow /snəʊ/		θ	thick /θɪk/, author /'ɔːθə/
f	fifty /'fɪftɪ/		uː	goose /'guːs/, soup /suːp/
g	giggle /'gɪgl/		u	influence /'ɪnfluəns/
h	hot /hɒt/		ʊ	foot /fʊt/, push /pʊʃ/
iː	fleece /fliːs/, sea /siː/		ʊə	poor /pʊə/, cure /kjʊə/
i	happy /'hæpi/, glorious /'glɔːriəs/		v	vivid /'vɪvɪd/
ɪ	kit /kɪt/, tin /tɪn/		ʌ	strut /strʌt/, love /lʌv/
ɪə	near /nɪə/, idea /aɪ'dɪə/		w	west /west/
j	yellow /'jeləʊ/, few /fjuː/		x	loch /lɒx/
k	kick /kɪk/		z	zones /zəʊnz/
l	little /'lɪtl/		ʒ	pleasure /'pleʒə/

Consonants

p b t d k g tʃ dʒ f v θ ð s z ʃ ʒ m n ŋ r l w j ɬ x

Vowels and Diphthongs

iː ɪ e æ ɑː ɒ ɔ ɔː ʊ uː ʌ ɜː ə eɪ əʊ aɪ aʊ ɔɪ ɪə eə ʊə

Stress marks

' (primary word stress)　　　　, (secondary word stress)